DOMI MINA
NVS TIO
ILLV MEA

THE OXFORD ENGLISH DICTIONARY

SECOND EDITION

THE OXFORD ENGLISH DICTIONARY

First Edited by

JAMES A. H. MURRAY, HENRY BRADLEY, W. A. CRAIGIE
and C. T. ONIONS

COMBINED WITH

A SUPPLEMENT TO THE OXFORD ENGLISH DICTIONARY

Edited by

R. W. BURCHFIELD

AND RESET WITH CORRECTIONS, REVISIONS
AND ADDITIONAL VOCABULARY

THE OXFORD ENGLISH DICTIONARY

SECOND EDITION

Prepared by
J. A. SIMPSON *and* E. S. C. WEINER

VOLUME X
Moul–Ovum

CLARENDON PRESS · OXFORD

Oxford University Press, Great Clarendon Street, Oxford OX2 6DP
Oxford New York
Athens Auckland Bangkok Bogotá Buenos Aires Calcutta
Cape Town Chennai Dar es Salaam Delhi Florence Hong Kong Istanbul
Karachi Kuala Lumpur Madrid Melbourne Mexico City Mumbai
Nairobi Paris São Paulo Singapore Taipei Tokyo Toronto Warsaw
and associated companies in
Berlin Ibadan

Oxford is a registered trade mark of Oxford University Press

First published 1989
Reprinted 1991 (with corrections), 1998

British Library Cataloguing in Publication Data
Oxford English dictionary.—2nd ed.
1. English language—Dictionaries
I. Simpson, J. A. (John Andrew), 1953-
II. Weiner, Edmund S. C., 1950-
423
ISBN 0-19-861222-2 (vol. X)
ISBN 0-19-861186-2 (set)

Library of Congress Cataloging-in-Publication Data
The Oxford English dictionary.—2nd ed.
prepared by J. A. Simpson and E. S. C. Weiner
Bibliography: p.
ISBN 0-19-861222-2 (vol. X)
ISBN 0-19-861186-2 (set)
1. English language—Dictionaries. I. Simpson, J. A.
II. Weiner, E. S. C. III. Oxford University Press.
PE1625.087 1989
423—dc19 88-5330

Data capture by ICC, Fort Washington, Pa.
Text-processing by Oxford University Press
Typesetting by Pindar Graphics Origination, Scarborough, N. Yorks.
Manufactured in the United States of America by
World Color Book Services, Taunton, Mass.

KEY TO THE PRONUNCIATION

THE pronunciations given are those in use in the educated speech of southern England (the so-called 'Received Standard'), and the keywords given are to be understood as pronounced in such speech.

I. *Consonants*

b, d, f, k, l, m, n, p, t, v, z *have their usual English values*

g as in *go* (gəʊ)
h ... *ho!* (həʊ)
r ... *run* (rʌn), *terrier* ('tɛrɪə(r))
(r) ... *her* (hɜː(r))
s ... *see* (siː), *success* (sək'sɛs)
w ... *wear* (wɛə(r))
hw ... *when* (hwɛn)
j ... *yes* (jɛs)

θ as in *th*in (θɪn), ba*th* (bɑːθ)
ð ... *then* (ðɛn), ba*the* (beɪð)
ʃ ... *shop* (ʃɒp), di*sh* (dɪʃ)
tʃ ... *chop* (tʃɒp), di*tch* (dɪtʃ)
ʒ ... vi*si*on ('vɪʒən), dé*j*euner (deʒøne)
dʒ ... *judge* (dʒʌdʒ)
ŋ ... si*ng*ing ('sɪŋɪŋ), thi*n*k (θiŋk)
ŋg ... fi*ng*er ('fɪŋgə(r))

(FOREIGN AND NON-SOUTHERN)
ʎ as in It. serra*gli*o (ser'raʎo)
ɲ ... Fr. co*gn*ac (kɔɲak)
x ... Ger. a*ch* (ax), Sc. lo*ch* (lɒx), Sp. fri*j*oles (fri'xoles)
ç ... Ger. i*ch* (ɪç), Sc. ni*ch*t (nɪçt)
ɣ ... North Ger. sa*g*en ('zaːɣən)
c ... Afrikaans baardmanne*tj*ie ('baːrtmanəci)
ɥ ... Fr. c*u*isine (kɥizin)

Symbols in parentheses are used to denote elements that may be omitted either by individual speakers or in particular phonetic contexts: e.g. *bottle* ('bɒt(ə)l), *Mercian* ('mɜːʃ(ɪ)ən), *suit* (s(j)uːt), *impromptu* (ɪm'prɒm(p)tjuː), *father* ('fɑːðə(r)).

II. *Vowels and Diphthongs*

SHORT
ɪ as in p*i*t (pɪt), -n*e*ss, (-nɪs)
ɛ ... p*e*t (pɛt), Fr. *sept* (sɛt)
æ ... p*a*t (pæt)
ʌ ... p*u*tt (pʌt)
ɒ ... p*o*t (pɒt)
ʊ ... p*u*t (pʊt)
ə ... *a*nother (ə'nʌðə(r))
(ə) ... beat*e*n ('biːt(ə)n)
i ... Fr. s*i* (si)
e ... Fr. b*é*b*é* (bebe)
a ... Fr. m*a*ri (mari)
ɑ ... Fr. b*â*timent (bɑtimɑ̃)
ɔ ... Fr. h*o*mme (ɔm)
o ... Fr. *eau* (o)
ø ... Fr. p*eu* (pø)
œ ... Fr. b*oeu*f (bœf) c*oeu*r (kœr)
u ... Fr. d*ou*ce (dus)
ʏ ... Ger. M*ü*ller ('mʏlər)
y ... Fr. d*u* (dy)

LONG
iː as in b*ea*n (biːn)
ɑː ... b*ar*n (bɑːn)
ɔː ... b*or*n (bɔːn)
uː ... b*oo*n (buːn)
ɜː ... b*ur*n (bɜːn)
eː ... Ger. Schn*ee* (ʃneː)
ɛː ... Ger. F*äh*re ('fɛːrə)
aː ... Ger. T*a*g (taːk)
oː ... Ger. S*oh*n (zoːn)
øː ... Ger. G*oe*the ('gøːtə)
yː ... Ger. gr*ü*n (gryːn)

NASAL
ɛ̃, æ̃ as in Fr. f*in* (fɛ̃, fæ̃)
ɑ̃ ... Fr. fr*an*c (frɑ̃)
ɔ̃ ... Fr. b*on* (bɔ̃)
œ̃ ... Fr. *un* (œ̃)

DIPHTHONGS, etc.
eɪ as in b*ay* (beɪ)
aɪ ... b*uy* (baɪ)
ɔɪ ... b*oy* (bɔɪ)
əʊ ... n*o* (nəʊ)
aʊ ... n*ow* (naʊ)
ɪə ... p*eer* (pɪə(r))
ɛə ... p*air* (pɛə(r))
ʊə ... t*our* (tʊə(r))
ɔə ... b*oar* (bɔə(r))

aɪə as in f*ier*y ('faɪərɪ)
aʊə ... s*our* (saʊə(r))

The incidence of main stress is shown by a superior stress mark (') preceding the stressed syllable, and a secondary stress by an inferior stress mark (ˌ), e.g. *pronunciation* (prəˌnʌnsɪ'eɪʃ(ə)n).

For further explanation of the transcription used, see *General Explanations*, Volume I.

LIST OF ABBREVIATIONS, SIGNS, ETC.

Some abbreviations listed here in italics are also in certain cases printed in roman type, and vice versa.

a. (in Etym.)	adoption of, adopted from
a (as *a* 1850)	*ante*, 'before', 'not later than'
a.	adjective
abbrev.	abbreviation (of)
abl.	ablative
absol.	absolute, -ly
Abstr.	(in titles) *Abstract, -s*
acc.	accusative
Acct.	(in titles) *Account*
A.D.	*Anno Domini*
ad. (in Etym.)	adaptation of
Add.	Addenda
adj.	adjective
Adv.	(in titles) *Advance, -d, -s*
adv.	adverb
advb.	adverbial, -ly
Advt.	advertisement
Aeronaut.	(as label) in Aeronautics; (in titles) *Aeronautic, -al, -s*
AF., AFr.	Anglo-French
Afr.	Africa, -n
Agric.	(as label) in Agriculture; (in titles) *Agriculture, -al*
Alb.	Albanian
Amer.	American
Amer. Ind.	American Indian
Anat.	(as label) in Anatomy; (in titles) *Anatomy, -ical*
Anc.	(in titles) *Ancient*
Anglo-Ind.	Anglo-Indian
Anglo-Ir.	Anglo-Irish
Ann.	Annals
Anthrop., Anthropol.	(as label) in Anthropology; (in titles) *Anthropology, -ical*
Antiq.	(as label) in Antiquities; (in titles) *Antiquity*
aphet.	aphetic, aphetized
app.	apparently
Appl.	(in titles) *Applied*
Applic.	(in titles) *Application, -s*
appos.	appositive, -ly
Arab.	Arabic
Aram.	Aramaic
Arch.	in Architecture
arch.	archaic
Archæol.	in Archæology
Archit.	(as label) in Architecture; (in titles) *Architecture, -al*
Arm.	Armenian
assoc.	association
Astr.	in Astronomy
Astrol.	in Astrology
Astron.	(in titles) *Astronomy, -ical*
Astronaut.	(in titles) *Astronautic, -s*
attrib.	attributive, -ly
Austral.	Australian
Autobiogr.	(in titles) *Autobiography, -ical*
A.V.	Authorized Version
B.C.	Before Christ
B.C.	(in titles) British Columbia
bef.	before
Bibliogr.	(as label) in Bibliography; (in titles) *Bibliography, -ical*
Biochem.	(as label) in Biochemistry; (in titles) *Biochemistry, -ical*
Biol.	(as label) in Biology; (in titles) *Biology, -ical*
Bk.	*Book*
Bot.	(as label) in Botany; (in titles) *Botany, -ical*
Bp.	Bishop
Brit.	(in titles) *Britain, British*
Bulg.	Bulgarian
Bull.	(in titles) *Bulletin*
c (as *c* 1700)	*circa*, 'about'
c. (as 19th c.)	century
Cal.	(in titles) *Calendar*
Cambr.	(in titles) *Cambridge*
Canad.	Canadian
Cat.	Catalan
catachr.	catachrestically
Catal.	(in titles) *Catalogue*
Celt.	Celtic
Cent.	(in titles) *Century, Central*
Cent. Dict.	*Century Dictionary*
Cf., cf.	*confer*, 'compare'
Ch.	Church
Chem.	(as label) in Chemistry; (in titles) *Chemistry, -ical*
Chr.	(in titles) *Christian*
Chron.	(in titles) *Chronicle*
Chronol.	(in titles) *Chronology, -ical*
Cinemat., Cinematogr.	in Cinematography
Clin.	(in titles) *Clinical*
cl. L.	classical Latin
cogn. w.	cognate with
Col.	(in titles) *Colonel, Colony*
Coll.	(in titles) *Collection*
collect.	collective, -ly
colloq.	colloquial, -ly
comb.	combined, -ing
Comb.	Combinations
Comm.	in Commercial usage
Communic.	in Communications
comp.	compound, composition
Compan.	(in titles) *Companion*
compar.	comparative
compl.	complement
Compl.	(in titles) *Complete*
Conc.	(in titles) *Concise*
Conch.	in Conchology
concr.	concrete, -ly
Conf.	(in titles) *Conference*
Congr.	(in titles) *Congress*
conj.	conjunction
cons.	consonant
const.	construction, construed with
contr.	contrast (with)
Contrib.	(in titles) *Contribution*
Corr.	(in titles) *Correspondence*
corresp.	corresponding (to)
Cotgr.	R. Cotgrave, *Dictionarie of the French and English Tongues*
cpd.	compound
Crit.	(in titles) *Criticism, Critical*
Cryst.	in Crystallography
Cycl.	(in titles) *Cyclopædia, -ic*
Cytol.	(in titles) *Cytology, -ical*
Da.	Danish
D.A.	*Dictionary of Americanisms*
D.A.E.	*Dictionary of American English*
dat.	dative
D.C.	District of Columbia
Deb.	(in titles) *Debate, -s*
def.	definite, -ition
dem.	demonstrative
deriv.	derivative, -ation
derog.	derogatory
Descr.	(in titles) *Description, -tive*
Devel.	(in titles) *Development, -al*
Diagn.	(in titles) *Diagnosis, Diagnostic*
dial.	dialect, -al
Dict.	Dictionary; *spec.*, the *Oxford English Dictionary*
dim.	diminutive
Dis.	(in titles) *Disease*
Diss.	(in titles) *Dissertation*
D.O.S.T.	*Dictionary of the Older Scottish Tongue*
Du.	Dutch
E.	East
Eccl.	(as label) in Ecclesiastical usage; (in titles) *Ecclesiastical*
Ecol.	in Ecology
Econ.	(as label) in Economics; (in titles) *Economy, -ics*
ed.	edition
E.D.D.	*English Dialect Dictionary*
Edin.	(in titles) *Edinburgh*
Educ.	(as label) in Education; (in titles) *Education, -al*
EE.	Early English
e.g.	*exempli gratia*, 'for example'
Electr.	(as label) in Electricity; (in titles) *Electricity, -ical*
Electron.	(in titles) *Electronic, -s*
Elem.	(in titles) *Element, -ary*
ellipt.	elliptical, -ly
Embryol.	in Embryology
e.midl.	east midland (dialect)
Encycl.	(in titles) *Encyclopædia, -ic*
Eng.	England, English
Engin.	in Engineering
Ent.	in Entomology
Entomol.	(in titles) *Entomology, -logical*
erron.	erroneous, -ly
esp.	especially
Ess.	(in titles) *Essay, -s*
et al.	*et alii*, 'and others'
etc.	et cetera
Ethnol.	in Ethnology
etym.	etymology
euphem.	euphemistically
Exam.	(in titles) *Examination*
exc.	except
Exerc.	(in titles) *Exercise, -s*
Exper.	(in titles) *Experiment, -al*
Explor.	(in titles) *Exploration, -s*
f.	feminine
f. (in Etym.)	formed on
f. (in subordinate entries)	form of
F.	French
fem. (*rarely* f.)	feminine
fig.	figurative, -ly
Finn.	Finnish
fl.	*floruit*, 'flourished'
Found.	(in titles) *Foundation, -s*
Fr.	French
freq.	frequent, -ly
Fris.	Frisian
Fund.	(in titles) *Fundamental, -s*
Funk or *Funk's Stand. Dict.*	*Funk and Wagnalls Standard Dictionary*
G.	German
Gael.	Gaelic
Gaz.	(in titles) *Gazette*
gen.	genitive
gen.	general, -ly
Geogr.	(as label) in Geography; (in titles) *Geography, -ical*

Geol.	(as label) in Geology; (in titles) *Geology, -ical*
Geom.	in Geometry
Geomorphol.	in Geomorphology
Ger.	German
Gloss.	Glossary
Gmc.	Germanic
Godef.	F. Godefroy, *Dictionnaire de l'ancienne langue française*
Goth.	Gothic
Govt.	(in titles) *Government*
Gr.	Greek
Gram.	(as label) in Grammar; (in titles) *Grammar, -tical*
Gt.	Great
Heb.	Hebrew
Her.	in Heraldry
Herb.	among herbalists
Hind.	Hindustani
Hist.	(as label) in History; (in titles) *History, -ical*
hist.	historical
Histol.	(in titles) *Histology, -ical*
Hort.	in Horticulture
Househ.	(in titles) *Household*
Housek.	(in titles) *Housekeeping*
Ibid.	*Ibidem*, 'in the same book or passage'
Icel.	Icelandic
Ichthyol.	in Ichthyology
id.	*idem*, 'the same'
i.e.	*id est*, 'that is'
IE.	Indo-European
Illustr.	(in titles) *Illustration, -ted*
imit.	imitative
Immunol.	in Immunology
imp.	imperative
impers.	impersonal
impf.	imperfect
ind.	indicative
indef.	indefinite
Industr.	(in titles) *Industry, -ial*
inf.	infinitive
infl.	influenced
Inorg.	(in titles) *Inorganic*
Ins.	(in titles) *Insurance*
Inst.	(in titles) *Institute, -tion*
int.	interjection
intr.	intransitive
Introd.	(in titles) *Introduction*
Ir.	Irish
irreg.	irregular, -ly
It.	Italian
J., (J.)	(quoted from) Johnson's *Dictionary*
(Jam.)	Jamieson, *Scottish Dict.*
Jap.	Japanese
joc.	jocular, -ly
Jrnl.	(in titles) *Journal*
Jun.	(in titles) *Junior*
Knowl.	(in titles) *Knowledge*
l.	line
L.	Latin
lang.	language
Lect.	(in titles) *Lecture, -s*
Less.	(in titles) *Lesson, -s*
Let., Lett.	letter, letters
LG.	Low German
lit.	literal, -ly
Lit.	Literary
Lith.	Lithuanian
LXX	Septuagint
m.	masculine
Mag.	(in titles) *Magazine*
Magn.	(in titles) *Magnetic, -ism*
Mal.	Malay, Malayan
Man.	(in titles) *Manual*
Managem.	(in titles) *Management*
Manch.	(in titles) *Manchester*
Manuf.	in Manufacture, -ing
Mar.	(in titles) *Marine*
masc. (*rarely* m.)	masculine
Math.	(as label) in Mathematics; (in titles) *Mathematics, -al*
MDu.	Middle Dutch
ME.	Middle English
Mech.	(as label) in Mechanics; (in titles) *Mechanics, -al*
Med.	(as label) in Medicine; (in titles) *Medicine, -ical*
med.L.	medieval Latin
Mem.	(in titles) *Memoir, -s*
Metaph.	in Metaphysics
Meteorol.	(as label) in Meteorology; (in titles) *Meteorology, -ical*
MHG.	Middle High German
midl.	midland (dialect)
Mil.	in military usage
Min.	(as label) in Mineralogy; (in titles) *Ministry*
Mineral.	(in titles) *Mineralogy, -ical*
MLG.	Middle Low German
Misc.	(in titles) *Miscellany, -eous*
mod.	modern
mod.L.	modern Latin
(Morris),	(quoted from) E. E. Morris's *Austral English*
Mus.	(as label) in Music; (in titles) *Music, -al; Museum*
Myst.	(in titles) *Mystery*
Mythol.	in Mythology
N.	North
n.	neuter
N. Amer.	North America, -n
N. & Q.	*Notes and Queries*
Narr.	(in titles) *Narrative*
Nat.	(in titles) *Natural*
Nat. Hist.	in Natural History
Naut.	in nautical language
N.E.	North East
N.E.D.	*New English Dictionary*, original title of the *Oxford English Dictionary* (first edition)
Neurol.	in Neurology
neut. (*rarely* n.)	neuter
NF., NFr.	Northern French
No.	Number
nom.	nominative
north.	northern (dialect)
Norw.	Norwegian
n.q.	no quotations
N.T.	New Testament
Nucl.	Nuclear
Numism.	in Numismatics
N.W.	North West
N.Z.	New Zealand
obj.	object
obl.	oblique
Obs., obs.	obsolete
Obstetr.	(in titles) *Obstetrics*
occas.	occasionally
OE.	Old English (= Anglo-Saxon)
OF., OFr.	Old French
OFris.	Old Frisian
OHG.	Old High German
OIr.	Old Irish
ON.	Old Norse
ONF.	Old Northern French
Ophthalm.	in Ophthalmology
opp.	opposed (to), the opposite (of)
Opt.	in Optics
Org.	(in titles) *Organic*
orig.	origin, -al, -ally
Ornith.	(as label) in Ornithology; (in titles) *Ornithology, -ical*
OS.	Old Saxon
OSl.	Old (Church) Slavonic
O.T.	Old Testament
Outl.	(in titles) *Outline*
Oxf.	(in titles) *Oxford*
p.	page
Palæogr.	in Palæography
Palæont.	(as label) in Palæontology; (in titles) *Palæontology, -ical*
pa. pple.	passive participle, past participle
(Partridge),	(quoted from) E. Partridge's *Dictionary of Slang and Unconventional English*
pass.	passive, -ly
pa.t.	past tense
Path.	(as label) in Pathology; (in titles) *Pathology, -ical*
perh.	perhaps
Pers.	Persian
pers.	person, -al
Petrogr.	in Petrography
Petrol.	(as label) in Petrology; (in titles) *Petrology, -ical*
(Pettman),	(quoted from) C. Pettman's *Africanderisms*
pf.	perfect
Pg.	Portuguese
Pharm.	in Pharmacology
Philol.	(as label) in Philology; (in titles) *Philology, -ical*
Philos.	(as label) in Philosophy; (in titles) *Philosophy, -ic*
phonet.	phonetic, -ally
Photogr.	(as label) in Photography; (in titles) *Photography, -ical*
phr.	phrase
Phys.	physical; (*rarely*) in Physiology
Physiol.	(as label) in Physiology; (in titles) *Physiology, -ical*
Pict.	(in titles) *Picture, Pictorial*
pl., plur.	plural
poet.	poetic, -al
Pol.	Polish
Pol.	(as label) in Politics; (in titles) *Politics, -al*
Pol. Econ.	in Political Economy
Polit.	(in titles) *Politics, -al*
pop.	popular, -ly
Porc.	(in titles) *Porcelain*
poss.	possessive
Pott.	(in titles) *Pottery*
ppl. a., pple. adj.	participial adjective
pple.	participle
Pr.	Provençal
pr.	present
Pract.	(in titles) *Practice, -al*
prec.	preceding (word or article)
pred.	predicative
pref.	prefix
pref., Pref.	preface
prep.	preposition
pres.	present
Princ.	(in titles) *Principle, -s*
priv.	privative
prob.	probably
Probl.	(in titles) *Problem*
Proc.	(in titles) *Proceedings*
pron.	pronoun
pronunc.	pronunciation
prop.	properly
Pros.	in Prosody
Prov.	Provençal
pr. pple.	present participle
Psych.	in Psychology
Psychol.	(as label) in Psychology; (in titles) *Psychology, -ical*
Publ.	(in titles) *Publications*
Q.	(in titles) *Quarterly*
quot(s).	quotation(s)
q.v.	*quod vide*, 'which see'
R.	(in titles) *Royal*
Radiol.	in Radiology
R.C.Ch.	Roman Catholic Church
Rec.	(in titles) *Record*
redupl.	reduplicating
Ref.	(in titles) *Reference*
refash.	refashioned, -ing
refl.	reflexive
Reg.	(in titles) *Register*

reg.	regular
rel.	related to
Reminisc.	(in titles) *Reminiscence, -s*
Rep.	(in titles) *Report, -s*
repr.	representative, representing
Res.	(in titles) *Research*
Rev.	(in titles) *Review*
rev.	revised
Rhet.	in Rhetoric
Rom.	Roman, -ce, -ic
Rum.	Rumanian
Russ.	Russian
S.	South
S.Afr.	South Africa, -n
sb.	substantive
sc.	*scilicet*, 'understand' or 'supply'
Sc., Scot.	Scottish
Scand.	(in titles) *Scandinavia, -n*
Sch.	(in titles) *School*
Sc. Nat. Dict.	*Scottish National Dictionary*
Scotl.	(in titles) *Scotland*
Sel.	(in titles) *Selection, -s*
Ser.	Series
sing.	singular
Sk.	(in titles) *Sketch*
Skr.	Sanskrit
Slav.	Slavonic
S.N.D.	*Scottish National Dictionary*
Soc.	(in titles) *Society*
Sociol.	(as label) in Sociology; (in titles) *Sociology, -ical*
Sp.	Spanish
Sp.	(in titles) *Speech, -es*
sp.	spelling
spec.	specifically
Spec.	(in titles) *Specimen*
St.	Saint
Stand.	(in titles) *Standard*
Stanf.	(quoted from) *Stanford Dictionary of Anglicised Words & Phrases*
str.	strong
Struct.	(in titles) *Structure, -al*
Stud.	(in titles) *Studies*
subj.	subject
subord. cl.	subordinate clause
subseq.	subsequent, -ly
subst.	substantively
suff.	suffix
superl.	superlative
Suppl.	Supplement
Surg.	(as label) in Surgery; (in titles) *Surgery, Surgical*
s.v.	*sub voce*, 'under the word'
Sw.	Swedish
s.w.	south-western (dialect)
Syd. Soc. Lex.	Sydenham Society, *Lexicon of Medicine & Allied Sciences*
syll.	syllable
Syr.	Syrian
Syst.	(in titles) *System, -atic*
Taxon.	(in titles) *Taxonomy, -ical*
techn.	technical, -ly
Technol.	(in titles) *Technology, -ical*
Telegr.	in Telegraphy
Teleph.	in Telephony
(Th.),	(quoted from) Thornton's *American Glossary*
Theatr.	in the Theatre, theatrical
Theol.	(as label) in Theology; (in titles) *Theology, -ical*
Theoret.	(in titles) *Theoretical*
Tokh.	Tokharian
tr., transl.	translated, translation
Trans.	(in titles) *Transactions*
trans.	transitive
transf.	transferred sense
Trav.	(in titles) *Travel(s)*
Treas.	(in titles) *Treasury*
Treat.	(in titles) *Treatise*
Treatm.	(in titles) *Treatment*
Trig.	in Trigonometry
Trop.	(in titles) *Tropical*
Turk.	Turkish
Typog., Typogr.	in Typography
ult.	ultimately
Univ.	(in titles) *University*
unkn.	unknown
U.S.	United States
U.S.S.R.	Union of Soviet Socialist Republics
usu.	usually
v., vb.	verb
var(r)., vars.	variant(s) of
vbl. sb.	verbal substantive
Vertebr.	(in titles) *Vertebrate, -s*
Vet.	(as label) in Veterinary Science; (in titles) *Veterinary*
Vet. Sci.	in Veterinary Science
viz.	*videlicet*, 'namely'
Voy.	(in titles) *Voyage, -s*
v.str.	strong verb
vulg.	vulgar
v.w.	weak verb
W.	Welsh; West
wd.	word
Webster	*Webster's (New International) Dictionary*
Westm.	(in titles) *Westminster*
WGmc.	West Germanic
Wks.	(in titles) *Works*
w.midl.	west midland (dialect)
WS.	West Saxon
(Y.),	(quoted from) Yule & Burnell's *Hobson-Jobson*
Yrs.	(in titles) *Years*
Zoogeogr.	in Zoogeography
Zool.	(as label) in Zoology; (in titles) *Zoology, -ical*

Signs and Other Conventions

Before a word or sense

† = obsolete
‖ = not naturalized, alien
¶ = catachrestic and erroneous uses

In the listing of Forms

1 = before 1100
2 = 12th c. (1100 to 1200)
3 = 13th c. (1200 to 1300), etc.
5–7 = 15th to 17th century
20 = 20th century

In the etymologies

* indicates a word or form not actually found, but of which the existence is inferred
:— = normal development of

The printing of a word in SMALL CAPITALS indicates that further information will be found under the word so referred to.

.. indicates an omitted part of a quotation.

- (in a quotation) indicates a hyphen doubtfully present in the original; (in other text) indicates a hyphen inserted only for the sake of a line-break.

PROPRIETARY NAMES

THIS Dictionary includes some words which are or are asserted to be proprietary names or trade marks. Their inclusion does not imply that they have acquired for legal purposes a non-proprietary or general significance nor any other judgement concerning their legal status. In cases where the editorial staff have established in the records of the Patent Offices of the United Kingdom and of the United States that a word is registered as a proprietary name or trade mark this is indicated, but no judgement concerning the legal status of such words is made or implied thereby.

† **moul**, *sb.*[1] *Obs. rare.* In 5 mowle. [Related to MOUL *v.*[1]; cf. ON. *mygla* fem., Sw. *mögel* neut.] = MOULD *sb.*[4]

c **1440** *Promp. Parv.* 346/2 Mowlynge, of mowle (*S.* or mowle), *mucor*, C.F. *mucidus*.

† **moul**, *sb.*[2] *Obs.* Also 6 moule, mowle, 7 *Sc.* mule. [var. of MOULD *sb.*[3], perh. in part an intentional alteration after mod.F. *moule*.] = MOULD *sb.*[3]

1565–6 *Trin. Coll. Acc.* in Willis & Clark *Cambridge* (1886) II. 570 Paper to make mowles for the pillers. **1593** *Tell-Troth's N.Y. Gift* (1876) 45 Your selues being of the purest mettall, and hauing your hartes framed of the kindest moule. **1606** WARNER *Albions Eng.* xv. xcvii. 387 Kist with a kisse of Iudas moule. **1647** H. MORE *Song of Soul* III. App. xxiv, How the præexistent soul..enters bodies here below, And then entire, unhurt, can leave this moul. **1655** R. BAILLIE *Lett. & Jrnls.* (1841) III. 289 [The Parliament]..flew so high, as to mind nothing but a Fifth Monarchie on earth..and put all in a new mule of their owne.

moul, *v.*[1] *Obs.* or *dial.* Forms: 3 muwlen, 4–6 moule, mowle, 6 mowl, 8–9 moul. [Early ME. *muwle*:—older **muȝle*, a. or cogn. w. ON. **mugla* (OIcel. with umlaut *mygla*, MSw. *moghla-s*, *möghla*, mod.Sw. *mögla*, Norw. *mugla*, *mygla*, Da. dial. *mugle*), f. Teut. root **mug-*, whence Da. *muggen* mouldy, *mugne* to grow mouldy.]

1. *intr.* To grow mouldy, to mould. Also *fig.*

a **1225** *Ancr. R.* 344 Leten þinges muwlen oðer rusten, oðer uorrotien. **13..** *Metr. Hom.* in *Archiv Stud. neu. Spr.* LVII. 288 Fleschlich lust Makeþ Monnes soule Rote and Rust..and Moule. *c* **1386** CHAUCER *Man of Law's Prol.* 32 Lat us nat moulen thus in ydelnesse. *c* **1412** HOCCLEVE *De Reg. Princ.* 1420 Ententifly he kepiþ his seruise In courte; his labour þere schal not moule. **1550** CRANMER *Defence* 21 The wyne..wylle..tourne to vyneiger, and the breadde wylle mowle. **1789** D. SILLAR *Poems* 120 Your pickle cash Will ly an' moul, like ither useless trash. **1818** HOGG *Brownie of Bodsbeck*, etc. II. 164 They'll..leave the good substantial ait-meal bannocks to stand till they moul. **1828** *Craven Gloss.*, *Moul*, to grow mouldy.

2. *trans.* To make mouldy.

c **1380** WYCLIF *Wks.* (1880) 153 A loof, þat trespasid not, was mowlid & fordon. *a* **1535** *Communycacyon* (W. de W.) Bj, Thy drynke soureth and mouleth thy mete Wherwith the poore man myght wele fare.

† **moul**, *v.*[2] *Obs. rare.* Also 6 mowle, 7 moule. [var. of MOULD *v.*[2], perh. after F. *moule-r*. Cf. MOUL *sb.*[2]] *trans.* = MOULD *v.*[2]

1530 PALSGR. 641/2 This stone is nat carved with the hande, but mowled. *a* **1660** *Contemp. Hist. Irel.* (Ir. Archæol. Soc.) II. 121 The Pharoes of Dublin..to whom wee did not onely moule theire breeke at our owne proper charges, but [etc.]. *c* **1710** *Mack Gregory's Advt.* 2 Reliefs Moul'd in Boss and in Solid.

moul: see MOLE *sb.*[2], MOOL, MULE.

moula(h, obs. forms of MULLAH.

moulage (ˈmuːlɑːʒ). [F. *moulage* action of moulding, moulded reproduction, f. *mouler* to mould.] An impression of a (part of a) person or of an object, the material used, or the process of taking an impression. Also *attrib.*

1902 *Encycl. Brit.* XXX. 788/2 In anatomy and physiology, models are specially employed as aids in teaching and study, and the method of *moulage* or chromoplastic yields excellent impressions of living organisms, and enables anatomical and medical preparations to be copied both in form and colour. **1940** R. MORRISH *Police and Crime Detection* xii. 120 In these days an attempt is made to create a complete image of the murdered person by casts. This is called the 'Moulage' system. The results are almost as lifelike as the dummies in Madame Tussaud's. **1947** C. BROOKS *Well Wrought Urn* iv. 69 A detective making a moulage of a footprint in wet clay. **1947** J. C. RICH *Materials & Methods Sculpture* v. 96 The late Dr. Alphons Poller was among the first to utilize agar as a negative mold material in fashioning molds from flesh. He developed a moulage system and subsequently wrote a book on the subject. Poller's moulage compounds were patented and the trade names of his negative mold compositions..were registered. **1957** V. J. KEHOE *Technique Film & Television Make-Up* iii. 35 Moulage is a general name for impression materials some of which can be remelted and re-used (regular hydrocolloids)..and others (known as non-reversible hydrocolloids),..which are alginate non-reusable materials. **1969** R. MAYER *Dict. Art Terms & Techniques* 254/1 A specially prepared moulage plaster..may be used on delicate or valuable materials. **1973** R. C. DENNIS *Sweat of Fear* xi. 81 The detection of murder no longer need depend on fingerprints, blood types and moulages.

moulavee, -vie, variant forms of MOOLVEE.

moulbery, obs. form of MULBERRY.

mould (məʊld), *sb.*[1] Forms: 1–6 molde, 3– (now *U.S.*) mold, 5 moold, 5–6 mulde, 6 moulde, *Sc.* muild, 6– mould. [OE. *molde* wk. fem = OFris. *molde*, MDu. *moude*, *mouwe* (Du. *moude*, LG. *mold*), OHG. *molta* fem., also *molt* masc. (MHG. *molte*, *molde*, mod.Ger. dial. *molt*, *molten* masc.), ON. *mold* (Sw. *mull*, Da. *muld*), Goth. *mulda* str. fem.:—OTeut. **moldā*, *muldā*, root **mul-* (:*mel-*:*mal-*) to pulverize, grind: see MEAL *sb.*[1], and cf. MULL *sb.*[1]]

1. Loose, broken, or friable earth; hence, the surface soil, which may be readily broken up. Also *pl.* (now only *dial.*) lumps or clods of earth; in mod. dial. use commonly equivalent to the sing.

c **725** *Corpus Gloss.* (Hessels) S 10, *Sablo*, molde. *c* **900** tr. *Bæda's Hist.* III. ii. (1890) 154 Mid moldan [*puluere terræ*]. *a* **1300** *Cursor M.* 898 Mold sal be þi mete for nede. *c* **1400** *Destr. Troy* 4320 Maumettes to make of moldes & clay. **1577–87** HARRISON *England* II. xxii. (1877) I. 346 Wood, which being felled..in processe of time became to be quite ouergrowne with earth and moulds. **1668** H. MORE *Div. Dial.* II. vi. (1713) 103 It is as unskilfully alledged against Nature that all the Earth is not soft moulds. **1703** MAUNDRELL *Journ. Jerus.* (1732) 3 Vast naked Rocks without the least sign of Mould. **1767** A. YOUNG *Farmer's Lett.* 133 This would by no means do for ploughed lands, as we always throw the moulds of such drains one way. **1792** M. RIDDELL *Voy. Madeira* 43 The rains continually washing down the mold, &c. into the bottom, have formed a thick rich soil there. **1827** J. CLARE *Sheph. Cal.* 34 In fresh-turn'd moulds which first beheld the sun.

† **b.** Used disparagingly for land (as a possession); = DIRT *sb.* 2 e. *Obs.*

c **1570** *Pride & Lowl.* (1841) 77 His hart encreaseth not thereby ne lesseth Ase doon these fooles for they have gotten molde.

2. The earth of the grave. Also *pl.* ***to bring to mould***: to bury. (***laid, lapped, wrapped) in the moulds***: buried. (Cf. MOOL *sb.* 2.) Now only *poet.* or *dial.*

c **1000** *Creed* 34 (Gr.) þæs þy ðriddan dæȝe þeoda wealdend aras..of moldan. *c* **1330** *Arth. & Merl.* 2734 (Kölbing) His moder starf..& richeliche was brouȝt in mold. **13..** *E.E. Allit. P.* C. 494, I wolde I were of þis worlde wrapped in moldez. **1535** STEWART *Cron. Scot.* II. 524 Syne suddantlie the deid corpis in tha flang; And syne kest on the muldis on the clay, The grene erd syne. **1560** PILKINGTON *Expos. Aggeus* (1562) 110 Those which then were buried in no halowed churche nor churchyarde, nor christen moldes, as they be called. **1602** MARSTON *Antonio's Rev.* III. ii. Wks. 1856 I. 107 The mould that presseth downe My deade fathers sculle. *a* **1656** USSHER *Ann.* (1658) 103 That they should wrap his body neither in gold nor silver, but in plain moulds. **1746** COLLINS *Ode written in* 1746, When Spring with dewy fingers cold Returns to deck their hallowed mold. **1800** WORDSW. *Michael* 370 They were not loth To give their bodies to the family mould. **1824** SCOTT *Redgauntlet* let. xi, After Sir John and her ain gudeman were baith in the moulds. **1896** A. E. HOUSMAN *Shropshire Lad* xxx, The bed of mould Where there's neither heat nor cold.

3. The upper soil of cultivated land; garden-soil; *spec.* soil rich in organic matter and suitable for cultivation of plants. Also with qualifying word, e.g. ***leaf-mould, vegetable mould*** (see these words).

1340 *Ayenb.* 95 þyse þri þinges byeþ nyeduolle to alle þe þinges þet in þe erþe wexeþ. Guod molde [etc.]. *c* **1420** *Pallad. on Husb.* I. 293 A gret labour is to correcte A moold in this maner that is enfecte. **1601** R. JOHNSON *Kingd. & Commw.* (1603) 113 Being broken with the plough it is founde to be excellent good mould. **1731** MILLER *Gard. Dict.* s.v., The Moulds that are of a bright Chesnut or Hazelly Colour. **1771** N. NICHOLLS *Lett.* in *Corr. w. Gray* (1843) 131 The loose and fermenting mould of the garden and fields. **1796** KIRWAN *Elem. Min.* (ed. 2) I. 373 Moulds are loams mixed with animal and vegetable remains, particularly from putrefaction. **1881** G. ROMANES in *Nature* No. 624. 555 Many quantitative results are given of the amount of mould which worms are able to cast up. **1885** *Manch. Exam.* 13 June 5/3 So covetable does the rich, fat mould appear to the South African farmers.

fig. *c* **1200** *Vices & Virtues* 69 For ði ne mai wexen non god sad of godes wordes on ȝeure herte molde. **1651** N. BACON *Disc. Govt. Eng.* II. xxxvii. (1739) 166 Bared of the old Soil of the Papacy, yet transplanted into the new Mould of Royalty. **1828** CARLYLE *Misc.* (1857) I. 219 Our literature no longer grows in water but in mould.

4. Earth regarded as the material of the human body. (In ME. also *erþe molde.*) *Obs.* or *poet.*

c **1250** *Hymn to God* 10 in *Trin. Coll. Hom.* App. 258þu sscope eld & wind & water þe molde is þet feorþe Of wham we alle imaked beoð þat is þe holi eorþe. *c* **1275** *O.E. Misc.* 142 For he scop vs and alle þing of þar eorþe molde. **1535** COVERDALE *Tobit* viii. 6 Thou maydest Adam of the moulde of the earth. **1590** MARLOWE *2nd Pt. Tamburl.* IV. i, Made of the mould whereof thy selfe consists. **1629** MILTON *Hymn Nativ.* xiv, And leprous sin will melt from earthly mould.

b. ***man of mould***: a mortal man. By mod. writers, through misunderstanding of Shaks. *Hen. V*, III. ii. 23 (cf. MOULD *sb.*[3]), sometimes used for 'a man of parts or distinction'.

c **1320** *Sir Tristr.* 639 þe pouer man of mold Tok forþ anoþer ring. *c* **1330** R. BRUNNE *Chron. Wace* (Rolls) 446 þat neuere man of erthe molde Mighte hit wynne byfore wiþ fyght. *c* **1400** *Sowdone Bab.* 136 Of Babiloyne the riche Sowdon, Moost myghty man he was of moolde. **1599** SHAKS. *Hen. V*, III. ii. 23 Be mercifull great Duke to men of mould. **1843** CARLYLE *Past & Pr.* II. xvii, She begins to be uncertain as to what they were, whether spirits or men of mould. **1847** EMERSON *Poems, Monadnoc* Wks. (Bohn) I. 435 When he would prepare For the next ages, men of mould Well embodied, well ensouled. **1887** SAINTSBURY *Hist. Elizab. Lit.* i. 26 Though one at least of his contributors, W. Hunnis, was a man of mould.

† **c.** The 'dust' to which a human body 'returns' after death; the ashes of the dead. *Obs.*

a **1425** *Cursor M.* 22800 (Trin.) Miȝt he not penne wiþ his mayn þat ilke molde [*earlier texts* erþ] make flesshe aȝayn? **1562** WINȜET *Cert. Tractates* Wks. (S.T.S.) II. 27 The muildis of thame now laid on sleip. **1638** G. SANDYS *Paraphr. Job* xix. (1648) 29 Though wormes devoure mee, though I turne to mold.

† **5.** The ground regarded as a surface or as a solid stratum. ***under mould***: under the ground; buried. In ME. sometimes *pl.* *Obs.*

a **1000** *Elene* 55 (Gr.) Mearh moldan træd. *a* **1272** *O.E. Misc.* 93 Vnder molde hi liggeþ colde. *a* **1330** *Otuel* 1530 þo was garsie wel nyȝ wood, For wraþþe on molde þere he stood. *c* **1400** *Destr. Troy* 4774 Mynours then mightely the moldes did serche. *c* **1470** HENRY *Wallace* II. 213 Hyr most desyr was to be wndyr mold. **1596** DRAYTON *Legends* iv. 375 Where now it lyes even levell'd with the mold. **1596** GOSSON *Pleas. Quippes* 184 These corked shooes to beare them hie makes them to trip it on the molde. **1624** WOTTON *Archit.* I. 23 Aduising vs, not to rest vpon any appearing Soliditie, vnlesse the whole Mould through which wee cut, haue likewise beene solid.

6. The world on which we dwell; the earth. Chiefly in phr. ***on (the) mould***: in the world. Also, the land of a particular region. *Obs.* or *poet.*

a **1000** *Guthlac* 1203 (Gr.) þæs þe ic..anȝum ne wolde monna ofer moldan melda weorðan. *a* **1310** in Wright *Lyric P.* viii. 33 On molde y holde the murgest mon. *c* **1315** SHOREHAM VII. 68 þe wolkne by-clepþ al þe molde. **1362** LANGL. *P. Pl.* A. I. 64 The moste mischeef on molde mounteth vp faste. *a* **1400–50** *Alexander* 25 For þai þe mesure & þe mett of all þe mulde couthe. *c* **1435** *Torr. Portugal* 425 A better than yt know I nowght With in crystyn mold. **1549–62** STERNHOLD & H. *Ps.* xc. 10 Our time is three score yeare and ten, that we do liue on mould. **1575** GASCOIGNE *Posies, Hearbes* 159 Which framed mee so lucklesse on the molde. **1614** J. DAVIES *Eclog. Willy & Wernocke* 187, I ne wot, on mould what feater skill Can bee yhugg'd in Lordings pectorall. **1810** SCOTT *Lady of L.* IV. xv, The fairest knight on Scottish mold.

† **7.** *Her.* The 'field' of an escutcheon. *Obs.*

c **1435** *Torr. Portugal* 1123 Sir Torrent ordenyth hym a sheld,..On azure a squier off gold, Richely bett on mold. *c* **1450** HOLLAND *Howlat* 413 Syne in asure the mold, A lyoun crovnit with gold.

8. *attrib.* and *Comb.*, as ***mould-earth***, †***-rake***, ***-side***; † **mould-ale**, a funeral banquet; **mould-furrow** *sb.* (see quot. 1851); **mould-furrow** *v.*, to plough with a mould-furrow; **mould iron**, an iron mould-board; † **mould-meat** *Sc.*, (*a*) a funeral banquet; (*b*) the last food a person eats before death (see Jam.); **mould-plate**, the plate of a mould-board. Also ***mould-basket, -screen, -scuttle, -sieve*** (see Loudon *Encycl. Gard.* 1829, §§ 1392–4–6, 1401).

c **1440** *Promp. Parv.* 341/2 *Moldale (*MS.S.* 1498 molde ale), *potacio funerosa, vel funeralis*. **1844** H. STEPHENS *Bk. Farm* I. 507 Whilst the principal workman is rutting off the second side of the top of the drain..the other two begin to dig and shovel out the *mould-earth. **1851** *Ibid.* (ed. 2) I. 171/2 The divisions between the ridges [are called] the open furrows,..and the last furrows ploughed in the open furrows are named the *mould or hint-end furrows. *Ibid.* 185/2 The headridges should be cloven down with a gore-furrow along the ends of the ridges, and *mould-furrowed in the crowns. **1807** A. YOUNG *Agric. Essex* (1813) I. 127 The *mould-iron [of the plough], or plat, as it is called in Norfolk. **1513** DOUGLAS *Æneis* v. ii. 118 To roist in threit The raw spaldis ordanit for the *muld meit. **1805** R. W. DICKSON *Pract. Agric.* I. Plate v, The *mould plates. **1574** *Richmond Wills* (Surtees) 254 Spaydes, axes, *mold-raiks. **1805** R. W. DICKSON *Pract. Agric.* I. 123 In some cases the plants are placed in an horizontal direction upon sods turned *mould-side upwards.

mould (məʊld), *sb.*[2] Forms: 1 molda (or -e), 4–6 molde, moolde, 6–7 moulde, 7 mold, 6– mould. [OE. *molda* or *molde* = MDu. *moude* 'fonticulus'. Brugmann connects Skr. *mūrdhán* height, highest point, head, Gr. βλωθρό-ς tall:—Indo-Germanic **mḷdh-*.] The top or dome of the head; also the fontanelle in an infant's head. (See also HEAD-MOULD[1].)

c **1000** *Sax. Leechd.* III. 42 Ærest on þæt wynstre eare, þænne on þæt swiðre eare, þænne ufan þæs mannes moldan. *c* **1380** *Sir Ferumb.* 4939 þe ymage of Mahoun..Wiþ þe axe smot he oppon þe molde, þat al þat heued to-flente. **1398** TREVISA *Barth. De P.R.* IX. xxxi. (1495) 367 With Crysma chyldern ben cremyd and enoynted of a symple preeste on the molde. *a* **1425** *Cursor M.* 9098 (Trin.) His riche crowne of stone & golde he dud hit..take of his molde [*Cott. MS.* heued]. **1519** HORMAN *Vulg.* 25 The moolde of yonge babys quauereth. **1601** HOLLAND *Pliny* I. 152 What a while continueth the mould and crowne of our heads to beate and pant, before our braine is well settled. **1612** PAULE *Life Whitgift* 89 He complained..of a great colde, which he had then taken in the mould of his head. **1687** A. LOVELL tr. *Thevenot's Trav.* II. 6 Betwixt the two eyes, it [the porpess] hath a hole like the mould in the head of a man. **1706** PHILLIPS (ed. Kersey), *Mould*,..the Dent in the upper Part of the Head. **1854** BAKER *Northamp. Gloss.*, *Mould*, the opening of the suture of an infant's skull. **1886** W. BARNES *Dorset Gloss.*, *Mould*, the top of the head or skull.

b. *attrib.* **mould-shot** = HEAD-MOULD-SHOT.

1754–64 SMELLIE *Midwifery* I. 430 If the ossa parietalia rise over the os Frontis the case is called the mould-shot.

mould (məʊld), *sb.*[3] Forms: 3– (now *U.S.*) mold, 4–5, 6 *Sc.* muld(e, 4–6 molde, 5 mowlld(e, 5–6 moold(e, mowld(e, moulde, 6 moald(e, 6– mould. See also MOUL *sb.*[2] [ME. *mold(e*, app. metathetic alteration (either in OF. or in ME.) of OF. *modle* (later *molle*, *mole*, mod.F. *moule*) = Pr. *molle*, Sp., Pg. *molde*:—L. *modulum* (see MODULE).]

I. A pattern by which something is shaped.

1. a. A pattern, commonly a thin plate of wood or metal, used by masons, bricklayers, and plasterers as a guide in shaping mouldings, etc.; a templet.

(For *face mould*, *falling mould*, see those words.)

1323 *Ely Sacrist Roll* in R. Willis *Arch. Nomencl. Mid. Ages* (1844) 22 Bordis empt' pro moldis cementariorum faciendum. **1377** LANGL. *P. Pl.* B. XI. 341 If any masoun made a molde þer-to moche wonder it were. **1458** in Parker *Dom. Archit.* (1859) III. 42 Then must they have moolds to make on the bowys. **1513** in Willis & Clark *Cambridge* (1886) I. 613 Lyme, sand,.. mooldes, ordinaunces, and euery other thyng concernyng the..seid vawtes. **1663** GERBIER *Counsel* 28 As for the workmen, they must observe exactly their Surveyours Molds. **1793** SMEATON *Edystone L.* §107 A gang of masons..who were, according to moulds and drawings, to hew the stones. **1825** J. NICHOLSON *Operat. Mechanic* 541 To find the moulds necessary for the construction of a semicircular arch, cutting a straight wall obliquely. **1876** *Encycl. Brit.* IV. 507/1 The mouldings and cornices are run with moulds.

b. *Shipbuilding.* See quot. *c* 1850.

1769 FALCONER *Dict. Marine* (1780) s.v., There are two sorts of these, namely, the bend-mould and hollow-mould: the former..determines the convexity of the timbers, and the latter, their concavity on the outside. *c* **1850** *Rudim. Navig.* (Weale) 134 *Moulds*, pieces of deal or board made to the shape of the lines on the mould-loft floor, as the timbers, harpins, ribands, &c., for the purpose of cutting out the different pieces of timber, &c., for the ship. Also the thin flexible pieces of pear-tree or box used in constructing the.. plans of ships. **1893** *Westm. Gaz.* 22 Mar. 2/1 The moulds in their place, the cedar skin is stretched over them.

c. A glass-cutter's pattern.

1688 R. HOLME *Armoury* III. ix. 384 A Quarry Mould..is a Blew Slate, whereon are drawn the several sorts or sizes of Quarries of Glass.

2. a. A hollow form or matrix into which fluid or plastic material is cast or pressed and allowed to cool or harden so as to form an object of a particular shape or pattern. Also with qualifying word, as ***brick-mould, bullet-mould.***

1389 in Riley *Mem. London* (1868) 513 [He shall set no new] molde [to finish, after Noon rung]. **1428** *E.E. Wills* (1882) 82 All my mooldes & instrumentis to my craft [*sc.* of wax-chandler] longyng. *c* **1440** *Promp. Parv.* 342/1 Moold for a belle, or a potte, *effigies.* **1485** *Cely Papers* (1900) 177 A mowllde of stone to caste leyd in. **1549** *Privy Council Acts* (1890) II. 350 Mowldes for fawcon,..moulds for saker,.. mowldes for demyculverin. **1667** MILTON *P.L.* XI. 567 The liquid Ore he dreined Into fit moulds prepar'd. **1687** A. LOVELL tr. *Thevenot's Trav.* III. 43 Moulds for casting of Bullets, or Small-shot. **1762** H. WALPOLE *Vertue's Anecd. Paint.* (1765) I. ii. 32 B. and Godfrey of Woodstreet, goldsmiths, made the moulds, and cast the images of the king and queen. **1825** J. NICHOLSON *Operat. Mechanic* 616 The casts are made of..plaster of Paris,..and the wax mould is oiled previously to its being put in. **1884** W. H. GREENWOOD *Steel & Iron* §809 The moulds in which Bessemer steel ingots are cast are usually of cast iron.

†**b.** ***of a*** (or *o*) ***mould***: cast in the same mould, of the same shape. *Obs.*

c **1320** *Sir Tristr.* 942 Of mone of amold þre hundred pounde of latoun Schuld he. *a* **1450** *Sir Degrev.* 1435 Arcangelus of rede golde, ffyfty mad of o molde.

c. ***to break the mould***: *fig.* to render impossible the repetition of a certain type of creation.

1566 PAINTER *Pal. Pleas.* I. 141 b, I thinke dame Nature her selfe hath broken the mould. **1605** SHAKS. *Lear* III. ii. 8 And thou all-shaking Thunder,..Cracke Natures moulds. **1661** WRIGHT in Spurgeon *Treas. Dav.* lix. 8 There is a counsel in heaven, that will dash the mould of all contrary counsels upon the earth. **1847** EMERSON *Poems, Monadnoc* Wks. (Bohn) I. 434 But if the brave old mould is broke, And end in churls the mountain folk. **1869** MOZLEY *Univ. Serm.* i. 24 The mould in which they were made is broken.

d. *gen.* A modelled surface from which an impression can be taken.

1530 PALSGR. 157 A moulde, to moulde or print a thyng in. **1626** BACON *Sylva* §502 It is a Curiosity to haue Fruits of Diuers Shapes... This is..performed by Moulding them, when the Fruit is young, with Moulds of Earth, or Wood. **1687** A. LOVELL tr. *Thevenot's Trav.* I. 201 They fill it [a wooden mould] with Coal-dust, and apply it to your Arm, so that they leave upon the same, the Mark of what is cut in the Mould.

e. An arrangement of two or more boards forming a cavity in which concrete or earth is placed in order to be moulded into the desired shape.

c **1870** R. S. BURN *Guide to Masonry* 161 Care must be taken to prevent rain saturating the earth with water, as in this state it will form more mud in the mould. *Ibid.*, The difficulty of adjusting the moulds necessary to contain the concrete.

3. *spec.* in *Cookery.* A hollow utensil of metal or earthenware used to give a shape to puddings, jelly, etc. Also, a pudding, etc., shaped in a mould.

1573 in Cunningham *Revels at Crt.* (1842) 37 Mony by him payde for Mowldes to cast the frutes and ffishes in. **1608** WILLET *Hexapla Exod.* 590 Iron moulds and dishes which they baked the bread in. **1747–96** MRS. GLASSE *Cookery* xiv. 231 Make it into cakes, or just what shape you please with moulds. **1769** MRS. RAFFALD *Eng. Housekpr.* (1778) 193 Be careful you keep stirring it till cold, or it will run in lumps when you turn it out of the mould. **18..** *Novels & Tales fr. Househ. Words* VI. 34 (Hoppe) We had preserved plums to the mould of rice. **1904** *Daily Chron.* 21 Apr. 8/5 Turn the mixture into a well-buttered border-mould and bake for twenty-five minutes in a moderate oven.

4. *transf.* and *fig.* **a.** Said of things serving as a matrix or model; esp. in phr. ***to be cast in a*** (certain) ***mould***: to have a certain form or character.

1557 CHEKE *Let. to Hoby* in *Courtier* (1561) Zz v, If..the mould of our own tung could serue vs to fascion a woord of our own. *a* **1569** KINGESMYLL *Man's Est.* x. (1580) 64 The Sonne of God was well-pleased to be cast in the moulde and simple shape of man. **1607** SHAKS. *Cor.* v. iii. 22 My wife comes formost, then the honour'd mould Wherein this Trunke was fram'd. **1612** HIERON (*title*) A Helpe vnto Deuotion: Containing Certain Moulds or Forms of Prayer, fitted to seueral occasions. **1689** SWIFT *Ode to Sir W. Temple* xi, Shall I believe a Spirit so divine Was cast in the same Mold with mine? **1738** WESLEY *Ps.* LI. vi, Cast in the Mould of Sin I am. **1825** COLERIDGE *Aids Refl.* (1836) App. xxix. 24 The shapes of the recent and nearer become a mould for the objects in the distance. **1839–52** BAILEY *Festus* 328 Maid-mother! mould of God. **1878** BOSW. SMITH *Carthage* 369 A father and son, each cast in so truly heroic a mould.

†**b.** Said of the body with reference to its clothes.

In quot. 1639 after F. *le moule du pourpoint.*

1605 SHAKS. *Macb.* I. iii. 145 New Honors come vpon him Like our strange Garments cleaue not to their mould, But with the aid of vse. **1639** DU VERGER tr. *Camus' Admir. Events* 221 Tygris playing at false company saved the mold of his doublet, and left his brother ingaged in a fray.

†**5.** An object of imitation; a model, a pattern.

a **1547** SURREY in *Tottel's Misc.* (Arb.) 20 The whole effect of natures plaint, When she had lost the perfit mold, The like to whom she could not paint. **1570–6** LAMBARDE *Peramb. Kent* (1826) p. vi, Having neither good arte..nor yet approved patterne or Moald to imitate and follow. **1602** SHAKS. *Ham.* III. i. 161 The glasse of Fashion, and the mould of Forme. **1618** E. ELTON *Expos. Rom. vii.* (1622) 249 The man or woman that suffer themselues to bee changed into the mould and patterne of the good word of God.

6. A frame or body on or round which a manufactured article is made.

†**a.** The shaped piece of wood, etc. over which silk or other material is drawn to make a button. †**b.** The body of an artificial bait. **c.** The frame on which a sheet of paper, a basket, a hurdle (etc.) is made. †**d.** In pin-making, a length of wire of the thickness of the pin-stems, round which finer wire was coiled to form the heads.

1655 WALTON *Angler* I. v. (1661) 96 The mould or body of the minnow was cloth, and wrought upon, or over it thus with a needle. **1682** GREW *Anat. Plants* 86 The Shape of a Button dependeth on the Mould; the Silk and other Materials wrought upon it, being always conformable thereunto. **1727–52** CHAMBERS *Cycl.* s.v., Moulds used in basket-making are very simple, consisting ordinarily of a willow or osier turned or bent into an oval, circle, square, or other figure. *Ibid.*, Moulds in the manufacture of paper are little frames composed of several brass or iron wires fastened together by another wire still finer. **1747** *Gentl. Mag.* XVII. 311 The wooden molds of 8 buttons. **1766** LEADBETTER *Roy. Gauger* II. xiv. (ed. 6) 370 There are Moulds to answer each Size of Paper designed to be made and the Bottom of each Mould is of Brass-Wire. **1840** *Penny Cycl.* XVIII. 161/2 The next step is to form the head, which is effected by a piece of wire called the mould, the same size as that used for the stems. **1875** KNIGHT *Dict. Mech.* 1464/2 Hand made paper is made by a mold and deckle.

7. A package of leaves of gold-beaters' skin between which gold-leaf is placed for beating.

1727–52 CHAMBERS *Cycl.*, *Mould*, among gold-beaters, a certain number of leaves of velom..between which they put the leaves of gold and silver which they beat on the marble with the hammer. **1879** *Encycl. Brit.* X. 753/1 A 'mould', composed of about 950 of the finest gold-beaters' skins.

8. *Photo-engraving.* The gelatine which receives the impression from the negative and from which the copper plate is taken; also, the metal plate itself.

1875 *Ure's Dict. Arts* III. 564 This process does not in the least injure the gelatine mould. *Ibid.*, The process of printing from the metal mould is conducted in the following manner. **1883** HARDWICK *Photo-Chem.* 358. **1885** *Encycl. Brit.* XVIII. 833/1 By means of very heavy pressure..the mould was squeezed into soft metal.

II. Imparted form or make; result of moulding.

9. Distinctive nature as indicative of origin; esp. of persons, native constitution or character.

This, the earliest sense in Eng., is perh. orig. derived directly from the primary abstract sense of the OF. word = L. *modulus* prescribed measure; but in later use there is a reference to sense 2 and to MOULD *v.*[2] In expressions like 'of base mould', 'of the purest mould', there may be association with MOULD *sb.*[1]

a **1225** *Ancr. R.* 84 (MS. Cott. Nero lf. 20 b) þet ȝe þe bet icnowen ham ȝif eni cumeð touward ou, lo her hore molden. Uikelares beoð þreo kunnes. **1390** GOWER *Conf.* II. 39 Mi Sone, if thou of such a molde Art mad, now tell me plein thi schrifte. **1447** BOKENHAM *Seyntys* (Roxb.) 282 Of men and wummen also The molde these dayis ys so sore alayde Wyth froward wyl. **1589** *Late Voy. Sp. & Port.* (1881) 81 They bee of so base a mould, as they can verie well subiect themselves to any government. *c* **1592** MARLOWE *Jew of Malta* I, ad init., Giue me the Merchants of the Indian mynes, That trade in mettall of the purest mould. **1596** SHAKS. *Tam. Shr.* I. i. 60 No mates for you, Vnlesse you were of gentler milder mould. **1613** PURCHAS *Pilgrimage* (1614) 526 Other gods of a lesse mould they call *Camis.* **1647** CLARENDON *Hist. Reb.* I. §120 William Earl of Pembroke.. a man of another mould and making. **1707** PRIOR *Hans Carvel* 2 Hans Carvel..Married a lass of London mould. **1805** SCOTT *Last Minstr.* I. xix, Their hearts of rugged mould. **1827** LYTTON *Pelham* v, Her mind was wholly of a different mould from my own. **1875** JOWETT *Plato* (ed. 2) II. 158 He has a character of a finer mould.

10. a. The form or shape of an animal body, or (less usually) of something inanimate. Now *technical* (among cattle- or stud-breeders); otherwise only *rhetorical.*

15.. *Tye the mare* 13 in Ritson *Anc. Songs* (1792) 131 A mare of good mold. **1590** SPENSER *F.Q.* I. ii. 39 She now is turnd to treen mould. **1598** YONG *Diana* 226 They iudged our beautious features, and gentle inclinations to differ farre from Shepherdes mouldes and dispositions. **1607** TOPSELL *Four-f. Beasts* 228 About the mold or bigness of a young Fox of six months old. **1711** STEELE *Spect.* No. 17 ¶1, I am a little unhappy in the Mold of my Face, which is not quite so long as it is broad. **1725** POPE *Odyss.* I. 124 The sandals of cælestial mold. **1813** SCOTT *Rokeby* I. vi, The buff-coat.. Mantles his form's gigantic mould. **1816** BYRON *Prisoner of Chillon* ii, There are seven pillars of Gothic mould. **1844** H. STEPHENS *Bk. Farm* III. 1259 He should select 1 or 2 of the best mares in his possession to breed from, and if he has none possessing youth and beauty of mould [etc.]. **1873** HOLLAND *A. Bonnic.* vii. 122 Manly in size, mould and bearing.

b. *concr.* Bodily form, body. Chiefly *poet.*

1579 LYLY *Euphues* (Arb.) 458 This Beautifull moulde when I behelde to be endued with chastitie..and all other good giftes. **1590** SPENSER *F.Q.* II. vii. 42 For nothing might abash the villein bold, Ne mortall steele emperce his miscreated mould. **1712–14** POPE *Rape Lock* I. 48 As now your own, our beings were of old, And once inclos'd in Woman's beauteous mould. **1815** WORDSW. *Laodamia* 16 Whom doth she behold?..His vital presence? his corporeal mould? **1865** SWINBURNE *Atalanta* 60 [The boar] trampled, springing sideways from the tusk, Too tardy a moving mould of heavy strength, Ancæus.

†**11.** The form or structural type or model of a building or a ship. *Obs.*

1570 DEE *Math. Pref.* 32 Now, may you, of any Mould, or Modell of a Ship, make one, of the same Mould..bigger or lesser. **1577–87** HARRISON *England* II. ii. 141/1 in *Holinshed*, Howbeit the moold of the quire [of the cathedrall church] was not statelie inough. **1570–6** LAMBARDE *Peramb. Kent* (1826) 315 All these ships Q. Eliz[th] hath either wholy built upon the stockes or newly reedified upon the olde moaldes. **1666** DRYDEN *Ann. Mirab.* lxxii, Of ships which by their mould bring new supplies And in their colours Belgian lions bear. **1774** M. MACKENZIE *Maritime Surv.* 106 A Vessel..of such a Mould as to draw little Water.

†**12.** Style, fashion, mode. *Obs.*

1603 FLORIO *Montaigne* III. xiii. 664 The best..lives..are ..those which..are ranged to the common mould and humane model. **1624** WOTTON *Archit.* I. 14 All Nations doe start at Novelties, and are indeede married to their owne Moulds. **1650** R. HOLLINGWORTH *Exerc. Usurped Powers* 5 A party..shall rise up..and set up a new mould of government. **1656** HEYLIN *Surv. France* 70 The houses of the new mould in London, are just after their fashion.

13. a. That which is moulded or fashioned. *rare.*

1667 MILTON *P.L.* VI. 576 A triple-mounted row of Pillars laid On Wheels..Brass, Iron, Stonie mould. **1814** CARY *Dante, Paradise* IV. 53 When nature gave it [*sc.* the soul] to inform her mold. **1833** TENNYSON *Two Voices* 28 Think you this mould of hopes and fears Could find no statelier than his peers In yonder hundred million spheres?

†**b.** Plastic material. *Obs. rare.*

1547 J. HARRISON *Exhort. Scottes* 210 All mennes expectacion is, that hauyng so apte a moulde to worke vpon, you shall..frame his youthe with verteous preceptes. **1667** MILTON *P.L.* III. 708 When at his Word the formless Mass, This worlds material mould, came to a heap.

14. *Arch.* A moulding or group of mouldings belonging to a particular member of a building. (See also HOOD-MOULD.)

1480 BOTONER *Itin.* 268 The west dore frettyd yn the hede with grete gentese and small and fylled wyth entayle wyth a double moolde costely don and wrought. **1501** [see BROACH *sb.*[1] 6]. **1850** *Parker's Gloss. Archit.* I. 134 A *mould* is also the entire group or set of *mouldings* with which any architectural member is furnished, as *arch-mould, jamb-mould*, &c.

15. *Geol.* An impression made in earth by the convex side of a fossil shell; sometimes misused for CAST *sb.* 30 b.

'Mould' and 'cast' are termed in Fr. respectively *moule externe* and *moule interne.*

1839 *Civil Eng. & Arch. Jrnl.* II. 375/2 They [*sc.* the roach beds] are full of cavities formed by the moulds of shells. **1854** WOODWARD *Mollusca* 286 Specimens frequently occur in which the outer shell layer is preserved, whilst the inner is wanting, and the mould ('birostrites') remains loose in the centre. **1862** *Chamb. Encycl.* IV. 448/2 Sometimes the whole organism is dissolved and carried off by water percolating the rock, and its former presence is indicated by the mould of its outer surface and the cast of its inner in the rocky matrix.

16. Short for *mould-candle* (see 17).

1812 BYRON *Waltz* vi. *note*, Best moulds (four to the pound). **1831** T. L. PEACOCK *Crotchet Castle* ii, She is a greasy subject, and would have burned like a short mould. **1856** *Orr's Circ. Sci., Pract. Chem.* 449 Two sorts of candles are commonly met with in commerce, namely, dips and moulds.

III. 17. *attrib.* and *Comb.*, as ***mould-carver, -maker, -making, -turner***; often = made or cast in a mould, as ***mould cigar, shot, ware, work***; ***mould-cutting, -resisting*** adjs. and sbs.; **mould-blowing** *Glass-making*, the blowing of glass inside a mould to give it the required shape; so **mould-blown** *a.*; **mould candle**, a candle made in a mould (as distinguished from a dip-candle); **mould cavity** (see quots.); **mould-loft** *Shipbuilding* and *Aeronaut.*, a room on the floor of which the plans of the ship are drawn at full size; **mould-made** *a.*, of paper, made on a type of machine which produces sheets having characteristics imitating those of hand-made paper, esp. the so-called deckle edge; †**mould-man**, a moulder; **mould oil** *Building*, an oil applied to formwork to prevent concrete adhering to it; **mould-room** = *mould-loft*; **mould-runner**, an operative in a pottery responsible for transferring a completed article, still attached to its mould, to the drying-oven; hence **mould-running** *vbl. sb.*; †**mould-stone**, stone used for moulded work.

1948 E. B. HAYNES *Glass through Ages* 307 *Mould-blowing. **1949** P. DAVIS *Devel. Amer. Glass Industry* iv. 48

Glass for purposes other than glazing..was made by two different processes known technically as 'off-hand blowing' and 'mold-blowing'. **1972** E. Fletcher *Bottle Collecting* iii. 48 Most of the early examples of case bottles to survive have sides which sagged badly after removal from the mould; but the techniques of mould-blowing were soon to improve. **1925** Hodkin & Cousen *Text-bk. Glass Technol.* xxxii. 412 Much of the preliminary work in shaping parisons for *mould-blown bottles might be mechanically performed. **1970** *Ashmolean Mus. Rep. Visitors 1969* 15 A clear green glass flask with hexagonal mould blown body decorated with panels of lattice and chevron pattern. **1711** *Act 10 Anne* c. 19 §109 If such Making or Course is intended to be of *Mould Candles. **1876** Miss Braddon *J. Haggard's Dau.* I. 59 Sally came in presently with a pair of mould candles. **1873** Spon *Workshop Rec.* Ser. I. 431/1 The *mould carver makes his mould look..directly the reverse of what he wishes the ornament to appear. **1951** *Gloss. Terms Plastics Industry (B.S.I.)* 37 **Mould cavity* (cavity), the female portion of a mould impression. **1971** W. K. V. Gale *Iron & Steel Industry: Dict. Terms* 136 *Mould cavity*, the impression left in a foundry mould after the pattern has been removed. **1896** *Daily News* 15 Oct. 8/5 To make *mould cigars. **1947** J. C. Rich *Materials & Methods Sculpture* v. 114 The author has employed dental floss, which is waxed silk thread, for *mold-cutting purposes, with good results. **1711** W. Sutherland *Shipbuild. Assist.* 77 The Platform fitted for such a Design is call'd a *Mould-loft. **1866** *Chamb. Encycl.* VIII. 683/1 The first process is to develop, or 'lay off', on the mould-loft floor, certain full-size working sections of the required ship. **1947** *Jrnl. R. Aeronaut. Soc.* LI. 307/2 The mold loft consisted of a building with a large floor area, the floor being painted a mat black. **1916** H. A. Maddox *Paper* viii. 120 *Mould-made imitations of hand-made paper are produced..by several types of apparatus. **1923** —— *Dict. Stationery* 53 *Mould-made paper*, a class of high-grade paper which closely embodies the characteristic features of handmade. The sheets are made on a special machine which forms them singly and imparts four deckled edges... In selling mould-made note paper the stationer is legally compelled to describe it as such. **1938** *Times Lit. Suppl.* 15 Jan. 40/4 The text of the poem [*sc.* the Nonesuch edition of *Comus*] is printed in Fell types..on Pannekoek mould-made paper, at the Oxford University Press. **1955** S. C. Gilmour *Paper* vii. 64 Nowadays the relatively few mould-made papers that are produced rank as a close second in character and quality to hand-mades, though not altogether comparable. **1973** S. Jennett *Making of Bks.* (ed. 5) xi. 182 Mould-made Papers are a paradox. They are in effect hand-made papers made by machine. **1780** in Hone *Everyday Bk.* II. 1477 If any engraver, paper-maker, *mould-maker or printer, can give information of the.. making any mould or paper. **1825** J. Nicholson *Operat. Mechanic* 465 The mould-maker receives the model, and forms from it the requisite moulds. **1849** Noad *Electricity* (ed. 3) 230 *Mould-making, soldering, and gilding. **1576** in Cunningham *Revels at Crt.* (1842) 110 The *Mowldeman for a houndes head mowlded for a Cenofall ij[s]. **1939** W. H. Glanville *Mod. Concrete Construction* I. vi. 166 *Mould oils of a variety of types are used in the various fields of concrete products manufacture. **1948** L. J. Murdock *Concrete Materials & Pract.* xvi. 240 The requirements of a good mould oil are that it shall prevent sticking, it shall reduce to a minimum adsorption of water by the formwork, and it shall not harm the concrete either by staining or by softening of the surface. **1962** D. F. Orchard *Concrete Technol.* II. xi. 321 Care must be taken to see that the plywood or hardboard does not buckle through expansion due to atmospheric influences or the absorption of water from the concrete; several coats of mould oil or a brush on plastic are a great help in this respect. **1962** *Mould-resisting [see *damp-proofing* vbl. sb.]. **1791** Smeaton *Edystone Lightho.* §157 The work-yard, *mould-room, &c. **1863** *1st Rep. Children's Employment Comm.* p. ix, in *Parl. Papers* XVIII. 9 As the potter forms the plate or saucer in the mould, the *mould runner runs off with it into the 'store'. **1910** A. Bennett *Clayhanger* I. iv. 29 He was 'mould-runner' to a 'muffin-maker', a muffin being..a small plate, fashioned by its maker on a mould. **1961** M. Jones *Potbank* viii. 34 In the older workshops..the mould-runner really does plenty of running. **1910** A. Bennett *Clayhanger* I. iv. 31 The labour was much lighter than that of *mould-running and clay-wedging. **1675** Worlidge *Syst. Agric.* 241, I shall..here set down the true Process of making of it [*sc.* shot], of what size you please under *Mould-shot. **1832** Col. Hawker *Diary* (1893) II. 34, I.. blew both barrels into them with mould shot. **1353** *Ely Roll* in R. Willis *Arch. Nomencl. Mid. Ages* (1844) 50, 17 de *muldestones pro fenestris ecclesiæ parochialis. **1777** *Birmingham Directory* 8 Brooks, William, *Mould-turner. **1612** Sturtevant *Metallica* 91 Presse-ware or *Mould-ware, is any thing that can bee made, wrought, or formed of clay and earth..by presse and mould. **1626** Bacon *Sylva* §502 The Fruit..would..fill the Concaue, and so be turned into the Shape desired; As it is in *Mould-workes of Liquid Things.

mould (məʊld), *sb.*[4] Also 5 mowlde, 8- (now *U.S.*) mold. [Perh. developed from mould *a.* used in contexts in which it was not clear whether it was a sb. or an adj.; or perh. an altered form of moul *sb.*[1], due to association with mould *sb.*[1]] **a.** A woolly or furry growth (consisting of minute fungi) which forms on vegetable and animal substances that lie for some time in moist warm air. As a disease of the hop plant = fen *sb.*[2]

Also *Bot.*, any one of the species of fungi (constituting the order *Mucorini*) of which this growth consists.

c **1425** *Voc.* in Wr.-Wülcker 658/6 *Hic mucor*, mowlde. **1626** Bacon *Nat. Hist.* §339 All Moulds are Inceptions of Putrefaction; As the Moulds of Pyes and Flesh. **1714** Mandeville *Fab. Bees* (1725) I. 361 A man that hates cheese must call me fool for loving blue mold. **1731**, etc. [see fen *sb.*[2]]. **1794** J. Clark *Agric. Heref.* 51 *note*, Too much moisture subjects the [hop-] plants to the mould. **1848** Dickens *Dombey* xxiii, Mildew and mould began to lurk in closets. **1864** *Chamb. Encycl.* VI. 592/2 Mildews and Moulds are very nearly allied. **1874** H. V. Carter *Mycetoma* 10 The red mould (*Chionyphe*). **1877** Huxley & Martin *Elem. Biol.* 31 One of the commonest Moulds, the *Penicillium glaucum*, which is familiar to every one from its forming sage-green crusts upon bread, jam, old boots, &c.

b. *fig.*

1741 Watts *Improv. Mind* I. ii. Wks. 1753 V. 200 A hermit who has been shut up in his cell in a college, has contracted a sort of mould and rust upon his soul. **1771** P. Parsons *Newmarket* I. 32 Their researches into the mould of libraries. **1829** D'Israeli *Let.* 28 Jan. in *Croker Papers* (1884) II. 40 Letters..having..escaped the fury of cooks,.. the mould of time [etc.]. **1853** C. Bronte *Villette* ix, I was getting on, not lying the stagnant prey of mould and rust.

c. *attrib.* and *Comb.*

1699 Pepys *Let.* 19 Oct. (1926) I. 200, I have found time ..to looke over all my heads; 'tis only mould-spotts some of them are touched with, by being putt together before they were dry. **1800** Coleridge *Piccolom.* I. iv, Mould-rotted papers. **1874** H. V. Carter *Mycetoma* 35 *note*, The infecting Filaria and Mould-spore. **1876** tr. *Wagner's Gen. Pathol.* 95 The mould-diseases are conditional upon the above-mentioned mould-fungi. **1879** *Encycl. Brit.* IX. 98/2 A certain species of mould-plant which he calls *Mycoderma aceti*. **1944** J. S. Huxley *On Living in Revolution* v. 64 Some [butterfly wings like dead leaves] even go so far as to be marked with imitation mould-spots and holes.

mould, *sb.*[5] In 6 mold. A corrupted form of mole *sb.*[1] Cf. iron-mould.

1596 Spenser *F.Q.* vi. xii. 7 Upon the litle brest, like christall bright, She mote perceive a litle purple mold.

mould (məʊld), *sb.*[6] = mould-board[1].

1858 *Trans. Illinois Agric. Soc.* III. 367 In fall-plowing we run the share and mould of the plow under the soil and invert it. **1868** *Rep. Iowa Agric. Soc. 1867* 266 There is no clogging, and the mould and lay are so hardened that they scour readily.

mould (məʊld), *a.* (orig. *ppl.*) *Obs.* exc. *dial.* (see E.D.D.) Forms: 4 **moweld**, 4-6 **mouled, mowled,** (5 -id, -yd, *Sc.* -it), 6 **moulde,** 6- **mould.** [f. moul *v.*[1] + -ed[1].] Mouldy. Also *fig.*

13.. *Metr. Hom.* in *Archiv Stud. neu. Spr.* LVII. 288 For stunch þe hermite his neose held þat of þat mouled flesch he feled. **1340** Hampole *Pr. Consc.* 5570 þe ruste of þat moweld mone. *c* **1386** Chaucer *Reeve's Prol.* 16 Myn herte is al-so mowled as myne heres. *c* **1430** in *Pol. Rel. & L. Poems* (1903) 213 þi drinkis þat sowren, & þi mowlid mete. **1535** Coverdale *Josh.* ix. 12 This oure bred..was new..but now lo, it is harde & moulde. **1583** Stubbes *Anat. Abus.* II. (1882) 49 They keepe their butter and cheese till it be mustie and mould.

mould (məʊld), *v.*[1] Also mold. [f. mould *sb.*[1]]

†**1.** *trans.* To bury. *Obs.*

1530 *Test Ebor.* (Surtees) V. 294, I bequeith..my bonys to be moldid w[t]in the sanctwary of Swyne. **1570** Levins *Manip.* 218/47 To Mould, *inhumare.*

2. To cover (plants) with mould; to earth *up.*

1601 Holland *Pliny* I. 429 The Oliue trees..need neither the hooke to be pruned, nor the rake and harrow to be moulded. **1649** Blithe *Eng. Improv. Impr.* (1653) 126 In setting of it be carefull of Moulding it plentifully with the best Mould you can get. **1778** [W. Marshall] *Minutes Agric.* 9 Mar. an. 1775 Digging the trench, putting in the plants, and moulding them with finely tilled soil. **1837** *Flemish Husb.* 38 in *Lib. Usef. Knowl., Husb.* III, If..the potato-plants have been well hoed and moulded up.

†**3.** *to mould away*: to moulder, crumble away.

1545 Brinklow *Lament.* (1874) 100 It [*sc.* this Sacrament] hathe a begynnynge, and maye perishe and moulde away. **1607** Tourneur *Rev. Trag.* II. i. C 3 b, For his white father do's but moulde away. **1633** J. Clarke *Two-fold Praxis* 28 It is a strange sight to see the haire of the heads..mold away, and the gristle of the nose consume.

mould (məʊld), *v.*[2] Forms: see mould *sb.*[3] [f. mould *sb.*[3]]

1. *trans.* To mix or knead (dough, bread); now used technically in the baking trade for: To shape into loaves (see quot. 1841).

14.. *Voc.* in Wr.-Wülcker 603/14 *Pistrio*, to moolde or bake. *c* **1430** *Pilgr. Lyf Manhode* I. lxxiv. (1869) 44 She wolde it [*sc.* bread] were so wysliche moolded,..that [etc.]. **1530** Palsgr. 641/1 He can better eate a lofe than mowlde it. **1542** Boorde *Dyetary* xi. (1870) 262 Breade..must be well muldyd; it must be thorowe bake. **1577** B. Googe *Heresbach's Husb.* I. (1586) 10 b. Here are..troughes to lay leauen in, and there is a fayre table to mould vpon. **1688** R. Holme *Armoury* III. 85/2 Mould it [*sc.* the dough] into Loaves or Roulls. **1841** *Guide to Trade, Baker* 38 The operation of moulding the dough..consists in cutting the masses of weighed dough, each into two equal parts. They are then kneaded either round or long, and one placed in a hollow made in the other; and the union is completed by a turn of the knuckles on the centre of the upper piece.

fig. **1692** Dryden *Cleomenes* II. ii. 21 When the Gods moulded up the Paste of Man, Some of their Dough was left upon their hands, For want of Souls.

†**2.** To mix (ingredients) to form a paste. *Obs.*

c **1430** *Two Cookery-bks.* I. 35 Take pouder of Gyngere & Canelle, & wryng it, & molde it to-gederys in þin hondys. **1587** Fleming *Contn. Holinshed* III. 1003/1 [They] caused bran and meale to be moulded vp in cloth, for otherwise it would not sticke togither. **1604** E. G[rimstone] *D'Acosta's Hist. Indies* v. xxiv. 393 They did mould it with honie, making an idoll of that paste. **1645–52** Boate *Irel. Nat. Hist.* (1860) 125 Certain women..who mold the mud using nothing else to it but their hands.

†**b.** *fig.* To mix *up* or blend (*with*). *Obs.*

1701 Swift *Contests Nobles & Comm.* v. Wks. 1751 IV. 53 A Faction..which, under the name of Puritan, began to grow popular, by molding up their new Schemes of Religion with republican principles in Government. **1855** Milman *Lat. Chr.* VII. i. (1864) IV. 25 In Dunstan were moulded together the asceticism almost of an Eastern anchorite.. with some of the industry and accomplishment of a Benedictine. *Ibid.* VIII. viii. V. 32 Henry in whose character impetuosity was strangely moulded up with irresolution.

3. To produce or create (a material object) in a certain form; to shape as a sculptor or modeller; to fashion, form, model. Chiefly *poet.*

c **1475** *Cath. Angl.* 246/2 (MS. Addit.) To mowlde (**1483** mulde), *conformare.* **1590** Shaks. *Mids. N.* III. ii. 211 Two louely berries molded on one stem. **1608** —— *Per.* III. (Gower) 11 Hymen hath brought the Bride to bed, Where by the losse of maydenhead, A Babe is moulded. **1667** Milton *P.L.* x. 744 Did I request thee, Maker, from my Clay To mould me Man. **1725** Pope *Odyss.* IV. 773 From the bleak pole no winds inclement blow, Mold the round hail, or flake the fleecy snow. **1766** Goldsm. *Vic. W.* xxviii, The change which I saw in her countenance struck me... The hand of death seemed to have moulded every feature to alarm me. *a* **1822** Shelley *Triumph Life* 532 Obscure clouds, moulded by the casual air. **1865** Swinburne *Atalanta* 406 Seeing you so fair, and moulded like a god.

†**b.** *absol.* To make a model. *Obs.*

1644 Evelyn *Diary* 8 Feb., Monsieur Saracin, who was moulding for an image of a Madona to be cast in gold.

4. To shape (fluid or plastic matter) in or as in a mould; to press or cast *into* a particular form.

1573–4 in Cunningham *Revels at Crt.* (1842) 55 For the Mowldes and for Mowlding the frutes made of the stuf aforesaide. *a* **1676** Hale *Prim. Orig. Man.* I. ii. 65 He forgeth and mouldeth Metals. **1695** Woodward *Nat. Hist. Earth* IV. 184 No Metall, when..cast in a Mould, can ever..represent the Concavity of that Mould with greater Exactness than these Flints and other Minerals do the Concavities of the Shells wherein they were thus moulded. **1716** Gay *Trivia* II. 329 In harden'd orbs the school-boy moulds the snow. **1857** Miller *Elem. Chem.* (1862) III. 272 The fat..finally is melted and moulded into candles. **1865** Lubbock *Preh. Times* 414 The extraordinary practice of moulding the form of the head was also common to several of the Indian tribes. **1879** J. Wrightson in *Cassell's Techn. Educ.* IV. 246/2 The butter is then salted..moulded and printed.

5. *transf.* and *fig.* To create, produce, or form *out of* certain elements or material, or *upon* a certain pattern; also, to plan, design. Also with *up.*

1603 Shaks. *Meas. for M.* v. i. 444 They say best men are moulded out of faults. **1641** J. Jackson *True Evang. T.* III. 199 A..plot, moulded in the depths of satanicall contrivances. *a* **1667** Cowley *Miscell.*, *Wit* ix, But Love that moulds One Man up out of Two, Makes me forget and injure you. **1710** Addison *Whig Examiner* No. 5 ⁋3 There is great art in moulding a question. **1818** Cruise *Digest* (ed. 2) II. 333 Judges in such cases must mould and frame such estates as are agreeable to the plain intention of the legislature. **1863** Geo. Eliot *Romola* I. xi, On that fuller knowledge he hoped to mould a statement. **1893** *Fam. Herald* 167/2 A lovely brilliant girl, moulded on Di Vernon.

†**b.** *to mould up*: to go to form. *Obs.*

1602 Marston *Ant. & Mel.* III. Wks. 1856 I. 31 Earthly durt makes all things, makes the man, Moulds me up honour. **1613** Shaks. *Hen. VIII*, v. v. 27 All Princely Graces That mould vp such a mighty Piece as this is.

6. To bring into or reduce to a particular shape or form; to shape or model the character or style of. Const. *into, to.* †Also with *up.*

1605 Bacon *Adv. Learn.* II. xxii. §15 It will follow that hee shall Moulde himselfe into al vertue at once. **1622** Callis *Stat. Sewers* (1647) 47 The Estate..shall be melted and newly molded by this Condition. **1642** Fuller *Holy & Prof. St.* II. xvi. 109 God mouldeth some for a School-masters life. **1695** Ld. Preston *Boeth.* III. 142 They are the perfect Good when they are molded up into one Form. **1741** Watts *Improv. Mind* I. xvii. Wks. 1753 V. 282 Fabellus would never learn any moral lessons till they were moulded into the form of some..fable. **1818** Cruise *Digest* (ed. 2) VI. 428 In which case the Court assumed greater latitude of moulding the will according to the intention of the testator. **1859** Max Müller *Chips* (1880) III. iv. 87 His character was chiefly moulded by his intercourse with men. **1857** Willmott *Pleas. Lit.* xi. 50 Buffon has told us how patiently he moulded his loose sentences into symmetry. **1868** Huxley *Lay Serm.* iii. (1870) 35 If we could mould the fates to our own will. **1875** Jowett *Plato* (ed. 2) I. 419 Logic was beginning to mould human thought.

7. *intr.* and *refl.* (now *rare*). To assume a certain form; to become shaped; to shape itself (*into*).

1612 Dekker *If it be not Good* B 4, Blest raigne! The Golden worlde is molding new againe. **1768** Tucker *Lt. Nat.* II. 291 When growing and moulding in the womb, what were we better than a worm? **1842** Tennyson *Daydream* 86 The silk star-broider'd coverlid Unto her limbs itself doth mould Languidly ever. **1858** *Ecclesiologist* XIX. 315 When the Norman man-at-arms had begun to mould into the English country gentleman. **1871** L. Stephen *Playgr. Eur.* vi. (1894) 140 The Jungfrau seems gradually to mould itself out of darkness.

8. *trans. Shipbuilding.* To give a particular mould to (a vessel) (? *obs.*); to shape (timbers) with moulds. (See mould *sb.*[3] 11 and 1 b.)

1570–6 Lambarde *Peramb. Kent* (1826) 311 No shipping any where els..to be founde either more artificially moalded under the water or more gorgeously decked above. **1797** *Encycl. Brit.* (ed 3) XVII. 407/1 The moulds being thus prepared, we shall apply them to mould timber 7. **1830** Hedderwick *Marine Archit.* 265 You then mark the number of the frame to which the floor belongs, and proceed to mould the two first futtocks.

9. To take a cast of. ? *Obs.*

1698 Fryer *Acc. E. India & P.* 213 You must never mould any Diamond in Sand or Cuttle-bone. **1735** *Dict. Polygraph.* II. K k 6 b, How to mould the Face without much trouble to a person. *Ibid.*, To mould off the Face of a person in Wax.

10. Of clothes: To fit close to (the figure).

[After F. *mouler.*]

1896 *Godey's Mag.* Feb. 214/1 The cut and fit are perfection, the jersey molding the figure like a glove.

mould (məʊld), *v.*^{3} Also **mold**. [f. MOULD *sb.*^{4}; or f. MOUL *v.* by addition of excrescent *d.*]

1. *trans.* †**a.** To allow to become mouldy. *Obs.* **b.** To cause to contract mould: see also MOULDED^{2}.

c **1460–70** in *Pol. Rel. & L. Poems* (1903) 212 þou lettest poore men go bare, thy drynkis soweren, þou mouledest metis [*v.r.* þi mowlid mete] where-with the febull myght wele fare. **1613–16** W. BROWNE *Brit. Past.* I. ii. 29 Like hoording huswiues that doe mold their food, And keepe from others, what doth them no good. **1634** RAINBOW *Labour* (1635) 37 Sloth moulding some, anxiety consuming others. **1764** *Museum Rust.* III. ii. 4 This manure..is also much less inclined to mould and burn the seed.

2. *intr.* To become mouldy or covered with mould.

1530 PALSGR. 641/2 It is tyme to eate this breed, for it begynneth to mowlde. **1626** BACON *Sylva* §809 There be some Houses wherein..Baked Meats will mould, more than in others. **1707** MORTIMER *Husb.* (1721) I. 155 Unless the Seed be kept dry, 'tis apt to mould. **1885** A. WATT *Leather Manuf.* 152 If the drying be too slow, especially in damp weather, the leather is apt to mould.

b. *transf.* and *fig.* of things that lie unused.

a **1547** SURREY *Eccles.* ii. 79 And wretched herts have they that let their tressures mold. **1590** SPENSER *F.Q.* II. iii. 41 The man that moulds in ydle cell. **1611** BIBLE *Transl. Pref.* ¶6 The Grecians..were not wont to suffer bookes of worth to lye moulding in Kings Libraries. **1776** JOHNSON *Let. to Mrs. Thrale* 18 May, He carries with him two or three good resolutions; I hope they will not mould upon the road.

mould, obs. form of MOLE *sb.*^{2} and *sb.*^{3}

mouldable ('məʊldəb(ə)l), *a.* Also (now *U.S.*) **moldable**. [f. MOULD *v.*^{2} + -ABLE.] Capable of being moulded (*into*).

1626 BACON *Sylva* §846 The Differences of Impressible and Not Impressible,..Mouldable, and Not Mouldable, Scissible, and Not Scissible. **1753** tr. *Genard's School of Man* 15 The heart of a child is like soft wax, Mouldable into every form. **1883** *Chr. Commw.* 22 Nov. 137/3 These very women..are the most mouldable creatures possible. **1884** *Century Mag.* XXVIII. 124 When the mind of the parent was in a pliant and moldable condition.

Hence '**mouldableness**, **moulda'bility**, the quality or condition of being mouldable.

1883 H. DRUMMOND *Nat. Law in Spir. W.* ix. (1884) 300 The other quality we are to look for in the soul is mouldableness, plasticity. **1890** *Century Dict.*, *Moldability, mouldability*, capability of being moulded. **1938** H. I. LEWENZ tr. *Brandenburger's Processes & Machinery Plastics Industry* vi. 97 (*heading*) The effect of fillers on the mouldability of compounds. **1956** J. N. ANDERSON *Appl. Dental Materials* xix. 228 The water also improves mouldability by acting as a plasticizer. **1970** *Cabinet Maker & Retail Furnisher* 23 Oct. 174/3 Melded fabrics..have a sufficient degree of stretch and 'mouldability' to aid the upholstering of curved areas.

mould-board^{1} ('məʊldbɔəd). Forms: α. 6 **moldbo(o)rde**, 7 **mould bord**, 8– **mold-**, **mould-board**; β. 4 **molebrod**, 6 **moulebord**, 7 **moleboord**. [f. MOULD *sb.*^{1} + BOARD *sb.* Cf. Du. *molbord*, and next word.] The board or metal plate in a plough, which turns over the furrow-slice. Also *attrib.*, as ***mould-board clout***, ***plough***.

α. **1508** *Test. Ebor.* (Surtees) VI. 62 Item..Willelmo Farechild xij le moldboordes. **1688** R. HOLME *Armoury* III. 333/1 The parts of a Plow..The Mould Board. **1765** A. DICKSON *Treat. Agric.* (ed. 2) 209 The curved mold-board, by turning the earth of the furrow suddenly by the fore part of it, meets with more resistance than the common mold board. **1805** R. W. DICKSON *Pract. Agric.* (1807) I. 5 Giving ..to the mould-board that kind of hollowed-out and twisted form which..tends to lessen friction. *Ibid.* Plate ix, The mould-board hooks. **1808** W. H. MARSHALL *Rev. Rep. to Board Agric. from N. Eng.* I. 79 The seed is covered in by going once over with a light harrow, or..by a double-mould-board-plough. **1858** *Trans. Illinois Agric. Soc.* III. 366 A bull-tongue or shovel plow put to the same depth, will raise better corn than a mouldboard plow. **1902** LUBBOCK (LD. AVEBURY) *Scenery Eng.* 475 The ridge of soil raised by the mould-board of the plough. **1971** *Power Farming* Mar. 31/1 There is a definite place for machines of this type to replace the mouldboard plough under certain circumstances.

β. **1395** *Cartular. Abb. de Whiteby* (Surtees) 618 It. pro ix molebrodclowtys, iiis. xd. **1583** *Wills & Inv. N.C.* (Surtees) II. 80 A hundreth heads and shares, moulebords [*printed* moutebords], spades. **1610** HEALEY *St. Aug. Citie of God* (1620) 542 The plough may not lack other instruments, e.g. the culter,..the mole-boord [etc.].

'**mould-board**^{2}. [MOULD *sb.*^{3} or MOULD *v.*^{2}]

1. *Founding.* = MOULDING-BOARD 3.

1875 KNIGHT *Dict. Mech.*

2. One of the boards forming a 'mould' for concrete: see MOULD *sb.*^{3} 2 e.

1881 F. YOUNG *Every Man his own Mech.* §1251 These mould-boards should be of good pine wood, not less than 1 in. in thickness.

†'**mouldbred.** *Obs.* Forms: 4 **mold(e)-**, **mulde-**, 5 **mule-**, 9 **mool-**. [f. MOULD *sb.*^{1} + BRED. Cf. OHG. *moldbret*, Du. *molberd.*] = MOULD-BOARD^{1}. ***mouldbred clout***: see CLOUT *sb.*^{1} 2.

1343 *Durham Acc. Rolls* (Surtees) 205, i clitta pro molde-bredd. **1348** *Jarrow Rolls* (Surtees) 53, j mold-bredeclouthe. *c* **1375** *Sc. Leg. Saints* xxv. (*Julian*) 131 þe patyl his hand clewyt to, þe muldebred quhen he suld mvk. **1465** in *Finchale Priory Charters*, etc. (Surtees) p. ccxcix, iij plowys, iij plowbands, ij mulebred clowtis. **1824** MACTAGGART *Gallovid. Encycl.* 460 Another article belonging to the ploughman's business, such as the mool-bred.

moulded ('məʊldɪd), *ppl. a.*^{1} Also (now *U.S.*) **molded**. [f. MOULD *v.*^{2} + -ED^{1}.]

1. Shaped or cast in a mould; made according to a mould; cut or shaped to a mould.

1727–51 CHAMBERS *Cycl.* s.v. *Column*, Moulded Column is that made by impastation, of gravel and flints of divers colours, which are bound together with a cement, which grows perfectly hard, and receives a polish like marble. **1766** W. GORDON *Gen. Counting-ho.* 385, 10 boxes, containing moulded candles. **1853** URE *Dict. Arts* II. 386 The preparation or marking of the paper..is done by means of a moulded piece of wood. **1854** RONALDS & RICHARDSON *Chem. Technol.* (ed. 2) I. 97 The moulded charcoal being more dense than that made by the old plan. **1874** GOUFFÉ *Roy. Bk. Pastry*, etc. 193 Moulded cakes for entremets.

b. *Shipbuilding* (see MOULD *sb.*^{3} 1 b and *v.*^{2} 8). ***moulded breadth, width***: the greatest breadth of a vessel.

1773 *Life N. Frowde* 99 She..was as complete a molded Vessel as ever came out of a Dock. **1797** *Encycl. Brit.* (ed. 3) XVII. 405/1 The length of the keel being 29 feet, and breadth moulded nine feet. *c* **1850** *Rudim. Navig.* (Weale) 134 *Moulded*, cut to the mould. Also the size or bigness of the timbers that way the mould is laid. **1867** SMYTH *Sailor's Word-bk.*, *Moulded breadth.* **1887** *Pall Mall G.* 19 Aug. 8/2 The vessel..was 44 ft. in moulded width of beam.

2. *Arch.* Consisting of a moulding or mouldings; ornamented with mouldings.

1688 R. HOLME *Armoury* III. xiii. 473 A Foure Square Stee[p]le, each corner Supported with a Buttrice, the Top set off with Moulded Battlements. **1823** P. NICHOLSON *Pract. Build.* 316 Moulded-work is that which is formed into various forms on the edges, as cornices architraves, &c. **1843** C. BARRY in *2nd Rep. Comm. Fine Arts* 7 That such of the ceilings as are flat should be formed into compartments by moulded ribs. **1878** SIR G. G. SCOTT *Lect. Archit.* I. 157 Another great characteristic of English architecture is the moulded (unfoliated) capital.

moulded ('məʊldɪd), *ppl. a.*^{2} [f. MOULD *v.*^{3} or *sb.*^{4} + -ED.] Mouldy.

a **1552** LELAND *Itin.* (1769) VII. 57 Mony hid yn Pottes so hold and muldid that when y^{t} was strongly towchid yt went almost to mowlder. **1603** KNOLLES *Hist. Turks* (1621) 624 Verie course, hoarie, moulded [1638 mouldy] bread. **1795** *Trans. Soc. Arts* XIII. 181 Not having had one rotten or moulded piece this year.

†'**moulden**, *ppl. a.* *Obs.* [str. pa. pple. of MOULD *v.*^{3}] Mouldy.

1533 MORE *Debell. Salem* Pref., Wks. 930/1 He spake but of moulden breade.

moulder ('məʊldə(r)), *sb.*^{1} Also (now *U.S.*) **molder**. [f. MOULD *v.*^{2} + -ER^{1}.]

1. a. One who 'moulds' dough or bread.

c **1440** *Promp. Parv.* 342/1 Mooldare of paste (*K.*, *P.* moldare of bred),..*pistrio*. *c* **1475** *Voc.* in Wr.-Wülcker 809/11 *Hic panificator*, a mouldere. **1837** SIR R. PHILIPS in Whittock, etc. *Bk. Trades* (1842) 19 The dough..is.. handed over to a second workman, who slices it with a large knife for the bakers, of whom there are five. The first, or the moulder, forms the biscuits two at a time; the second [etc.]. **1880** *Daily Tel.* 24 Feb., To Bakers.—Wanted, a respectable young man. Good moulder.

b. (See quot.)

1894 *Gloss. Terms Evidence R. Comm. Labour* 58/1 in *Parl. Papers 1893–4* (C. 7063) XXXVIII. 411 *Moulders*, men in the seed-crushing industry who draw the rolled seed from the fixture wherein it is made hot, and..subject it to a slight pressure.

2. a. One who is employed in making moulds for casting. **b.** One who moulds clay into bricks.

1535 COVERDALE *Isa.* xli. 7 The Smyth comforted the moulder, & the Ironsmyth the hammerman. **1599** T. M[OUFET] *Silkwormes* 24 Eu'n as a lumpe of rude and shapeless clay Into the mould a Moulder cunning brings. **1684** E. CHAMBERLAYNE *Present St. Eng.* II. (ed. 15) 225 There belong also to the Mint many officers and others, as melters, smiths..blanchers, moulders. **1847** SMEATON *Builder's Man.* 23 Between five in the morning and eight at night, a good moulder will produce five thousand bricks. **1883** T. D. WEST *Amer. Foundry Pract.* 27 Moulders frequently entertain the idea that the heavier the casting, the harder should be the surface of the mould.

3. *transf.* and *fig.*

1736 BERKELEY *Disc.* Wks. 1871 III. 424 Reformers, and new moulders of the constitution. **1846** GROTE *Greece* I. iii. I. 102 In the primitive..legend Prometheus is not the Creator or Moulder of man. **1892** W. PIKE *North. Canada* 142 Wonderful moulders of geography they [beavers] are.

4. An instrument for moulding; a mould. ? *Obs.*

1612 STURTEVANT *Metallica* xiii. 96 A Mould or Moulder is an artificiall instrument which mouldeth..the tempered earth. **1633** D. ROGERS *Treat. Sacraments* II. 60 Better and holier ones than my selfe, such as stand with their moulders ready to catch any good speech! **1823** *New Monthly Mag.* VIII. 503 The hill-side shall still ring with my song—the metal be fashioned in my moulder.

†'**moulder**, *sb.*^{2} *Obs.* [? f. MOULD *sb.*^{1} by association with MOULDER *v.*] Mould; clay; dust.

a **1552** [see MOULDED *ppl. a.*^{2}]. **1592** NASHE *P. Penilesse* (ed. 2) 37 b, Men,..that are chained to such heauie earthlie moulder.

moulder ('məʊldə(r)), *sb.*^{3} *rare.* [? f. MOULD *sb.*^{4} by association with MOULDER *v.*] Mould.

1817 I. BLACKBURN *Sci. Ship-building* 145 Without almost constant fires, furniture, linen, silks, &c. &c. will be continually damaging, from moulder, rust, and mildew.

moulder ('məʊldə(r)), *v.* Also 6 (9 *dial.*) **mulder**, (7 **moudre**, 8 **muller**, 9 *dial.* **mooler**), 6– (now *U.S.*) **molder**. [? f. MOULD *sb.*^{1} + -ER^{5}; but cf. Norw. dial. *muldra* to crumble (trans. and refl.), G. *multern* to rot, grow mouldy. See also MOULTER *v.*^{2}]

1. a. *intr.* To turn to dust by natural decay; to waste away; to crumble. Also with *away*, *down*.

1531 ELYOT *Governour* III. xix. (1880) II. 316 It aught to be well considered that the cement..be firme... For if it be brokle, and will mouldre a way with euery showre of raine, the buyldynge may nat contynewe. **1565** JEWEL *Repl. Harding* (1611) 445 God..caused the Sacrament to mulder into ashes in his hands. **1579** TOMSON *Calvin's Serm. Tim.* 414/1 A thing moldred for verie age. **1616** W. FORDE *Serm.* 22 Thy house will shortly fall and moudre. *a* **1674** CLARENDON *Surv. Leviath.* (1676) 171 Sand, that, assoon as you come to rest upon it, molders away to nothing. **1700** PRIOR *Carmen Seculare* 459 When statues moulder, and when arches fall. **1776** GIBSON *Decl. & F.* x. I. 268 The ancient walls were suffered to moulder away. **1807** HEADRICK *Arran* 40 Exposure to the air causes this limestone to moulder down. **1810** SOUTHEY *Kehama* XVI. xi, The robes of royalty which once they wore Long since had moulder'd off and left them bare. **1851** BORROW *Lavengro* xciv, Both gouty George and his devoted servant will be mouldering in their tombs. **1877** RUSKIN *Arrows of Chace* (1880) I. 236 Those traceries should be..left in reverence until they moulder away.

b. *fig.*

1649 MILTON *Eikon.* xxvii. Wks. 1851 III. 511 As to those offerd condescensions..they moulder into nothing. **1679** C. NESSE *Antichrist* 162 This Western empire was forsaken, which after molder'd into an ignoble exarchate. *a* **1688** SIR J. LAUDER (Fountainhall) *Hist. Notices Sc. Aff.* (1848) 161 The use of Weapon-shawings is very ancient with us, and ware founded [etc.]..and then they mouldred away. **1758** J. RUTTY *Spir. Diary* (ed. 2) 110 O, how my friendships have mouldered! **1847** TENNYSON *Princess* Prol. 180 Never man, I think, So moulder'd in a sinecure as he.

2. *transf.* To be diminished in number; to dwindle. Said chiefly of armies. Also with *away*. Now *rare* or *Obs.*

a **1674** CLARENDON *Hist. Reb.* VIII. §73 If he had sat still the other great army would have mouldered to nothing. **1711** ADDISON *Spect.* No. 221 ¶5 The other [preacher] finding his Congregation mouldering every Sunday. **1769** *Junius Lett.* i. (1770) 13 A gallant army..mouldering away for want of the direction of a man of common abilities. **1823** LINGARD *Hist. Eng.* (1827) III. ii. 127 (Funk) The Christian army..was mouldering away with disease on the sultry coast of Mauritania.

3. a. *trans.* To cause to crumble, fall to pieces, or decay. Also with *away*, *down*. Now *rare* or *dial.*

1649 BLITHE *Eng. Improv. Impr.* vi. 34 And so cut the Turfe, that the Soard may have all the Winters frost to wroxe, and moulder it. **1672** SIR T. BROWNE *Let. Friend* §12 Sharp and corroding Rheums had so early mouldred those Rocks and hardest parts of his Fabrick [viz. his teeth]. **1752** *Scotland's Glory* III. (1786) 55 Those who once built Zion's walls are mouldering them to rubbish. **1807** WORDSW. *Let. to Lady Beaumont* 21 May, Long after we..are mouldered in our graves. **1844** H. STEPHENS *Bk. Farm* I. 596 A sudden frost..moulders down still more of the earth from both sides. **1892** *Northumbld. Gloss.* s.v. *Mooler*.

b. *transf.* and *fig.*

1603 FLORIO *Montaigne* II. iii. 210 To be mouldred and crushed to death, vnder the Chariots wheeles. *a* **1631** DONNE *Serm.* ix. (1640) 88 How many men have we seene Molder and crumble away great Estates. **1759** SARAH FIELDING *C'tess of Dellwyn* II. 101 A Man who moulders away his Understanding. **1826** E. IRVING *Spir. Econ. Scotl.* Writ. 1865 III. 475 The causes which have..mouldered the excellency of our spiritual and moral institutions.

4. *intr.* To move *off* in an aimless or lifeless manner. *rare.*

1945 E. BOWEN *Demon Lover* 48, I mouldered off by myself..to watch the old clock.

mouldered ('məʊldəd), *ppl. a.* [f. prec. + -ED^{1}.] Turned to dust; crumbled; decayed.

1615 BRATHWAIT *Strappado* (1878) 15 All the misers-Mammons mouldred-pelfe. **1728** P. WALKER *Life Peden* Pref. (1827) 27 That the Souls of our Worthies were come from Heaven, and the Dust of their mullered Bodies from their Graves. **1794** COLERIDGE *Melancholy* I. Stretch'd on a moulder'd Abbey's broadest wall. **1807** WORDSW. *White Doe* VII. 79 A mouldered tree, A self-surviving leafless oak. **1855** BROWNING *How it Strikes a Contemp.* 19 Some house Intact yet with its mouldered Moorish work. **1857** MILLER *Elem. Chem.* (1862) III. 122 Mouldered wood from the trunk of a decaying tree.

'**mouldering**, *vbl. sb.* Also 6 **muldring**, 7–8 **mouldring**. [-ING^{1}.] The action of MOULDER *v.*

1562 TURNER *Herbal* II. 28 b, The Larche tre..is not hurted w^{t} rottyng or muldring. **1626** BACON *Sylva* §337 The Mouldring of Earth in Frosts and Sunne. **1748** *Anson's Voy.* I. i. 3 Their cannon..useless by the mouldring of their carriages. **1850** TENNYSON *In Mem.* lxxvi, Thy deepest lays are dumb Before the mouldering of a yew.

'**mouldering**, *ppl. a.* [-ING^{2}.] That moulders.

1661 J. CHILDREY *Brit. Baconica* 133 Under this upper Clay lyes a mouldring washy Clay. **1709** STEELE *Tatler* No. 104 ¶5 A few crumbling Bones, and a little mouldring Heap of Earth. **1715** POPE *Ep. Addison* 11 Some felt the silent stroke of mould'ring age. **1842** J. AITON *Domest. Econ.* (1857) 166 The mouldering earth falling from this second spade is cleared out by a corresponding shovel. **1847** DISRAELI *Tancred* VI. iv, We shall..sweep away the mouldering remnants of the Tataric system.

mouldery ('məʊldərɪ), *a.* *rare* or *dial.* [f. MOULDER *v.* + -Y.] Crumbly, friable.

1600 SURFLET *Country Farm* III. xxxiii. 492 The walnut tree..especially delighteth in a fat mouldrie, light..ground. **1632** J. HAYWARD tr. *Biondi's Eromena* 184 A hollow vault of a soft mouldrie stone. **1846** WORCESTER (cites Loudon). **1895** *E. Anglian Gloss.*, *Muldry*, said of earth greatly affected by the frost, finely pulverized.

mouldily ('məʊldɪlɪ), *adv. rare.* [f. MOULDY *a.* + -LY[2].] In a mouldy condition.

1869 DICKENS *Lett.* (1880) II. 413 This mouldy old roosting-place comes out mouldily as to let of course.

mouldiness ('məʊldɪnɪs). [f. MOULDY *a.* + -NESS.] The condition of being mouldy; often *concr.* mouldy growth, mould. Also *fig.*, esp. a state of boredom or discontent. Cf. MOULDY *a.*[2] 2 b.

1577 HARRISON *England* II. xxiv. (1877) I. 359 A few ancient rolles of parchment..defaced with mouldinesse, and rotten for age. **1685** *Gracian's Courtier's Orac.* 14 Circumstances make things grow young again, they cure them of the musty scent, and the mouldiness of *Too often.* **1742** H. BAKER *Microsc.* II. lii. 305 Those exceedingly small Plants, invisible to the naked Eye, which compose what we call Mouldiness. **1880** MISS BRADDON *Just as I am* x, A kind of pallid mouldiness pervaded everything. **1916** 'TAFFRAIL' *Stand By!* 23 Our mouldiness in the morning is merely temporary.

'moulding, *vbl. sb.*[1] [f. MOULD *v.*[1] + -ING[1].] The application of soil to the stems and roots of plants; earthing-*up*.

1699 EVELYN *Kal. Hort., Jan.* (ed. 9) 13 Dress your Sweet-herb Beds..with a new Moulding every second Year. **1805** R. W. DICKSON *Pract. Agric.* II. 751 The moulding should take place in the early part of August. **1899** *19th Cent.* June 876 The potatoes want moulding up.

'moulding, *vbl. sb.*[2] [f. MOULD *v.*[2] + -ING[1].]

1. a. The action of MOULD *v.*[2]; in various senses.

1327 [see MOULDING-BOARD 1]. **1389** in Riley *Mem. London* (1868) 513 [That no one in the said trade shall make any manner of] moldyng, turnyng, ffilyng, garnesshyng [by night]. *c* **1440** *Promp. Parv.* 342/1 Mooldynge of paste, *pistura, ducamen. c* **1575** J. HOOKER *Life Sir P. Carew* (1857) 116 Whether it were for the building of a house, the moulding of a ship..or [etc.]. **1594** PLAT *Jewel Ho.* 49 The Art of molding and casting. **1608** WILLET *Hexapla Exod.* 590 In the moulding, kneading and baking. *a* **1625** FLETCHER *Woman's Prize* III. iii, For there was never man without our molding, Without our stampe upon him. **1876** *Encycl. Brit.* IV. 283/2 (Brick), The temporary product ..[is] then passed through the pug-mill, after which it is generally ready for moulding. **1891** C. T. C. JAMES *Rom. Rigmarole* 82 The moulding I have given to your character.

b. Bodily form; = MOULD *sb.*[3] 10 b. *rare.*

1814 SCOTT *Ld. of Isles* I. xxx, Wanderers of a moulding stark, And bearing martial mien.

2. *concr.* A moulded object.

1727–41 CHAMBERS *Cycl., Moulding,* any thing cast in a mould, or that seems to have been so, though in reality it were cut with a chissel, or the ax. **1844** *Civil Eng. & Arch. Jrnl.* VII. 60/2 In this state the piece of iron is technically called a 'moulding,' and is completed in a tin-plate mill. **1857** MILLER *Elem. Chem.* (1862) III. 593 Below 212° it [*sc.* gutta percha] becomes so soft that it may be moulded like wax..it will copy the finest lines with fidelity; beautiful mouldings..are thus made with great facility.

3. *spec.* **a.** *Archit.* An ornamental variety of contour given to members or subordinate parts of a building, such as cornices, capitals, jambs. †Also *occas.*, moulded work or ornamentation.

1643 EVELYN *Diary* 24 Dec., A stately pedestal.. compos'd of various sorts of polish'd marble and rich mouldings. **1688** R. HOLME *Armoury* III. ix. 394 An O.G. moulding for the Cornice. **1756** BURKE *Subl. & B.* III. vii, A much worse-proportioned room with elegant mouldings and fine festoons. **1849** JAMES *Woodman* ii, The doorways and the two windows were richly decorated with innumerable mouldings.

b. *Carpentry,* etc. A similar variety of outline in ornamental woodwork, effected either by means of carving or by the application of raised pieces following a definite outline or pattern; hence, woodwork shaped and prepared for application in this way. Also applied to the ornamental parts of a gun, or other metal-work.

1679 MOXON *Mech. Exerc.* ix. 169 Moldings are stuck upon the edges of stuff to Ornament it. **1769** FALCONER *Dict. Marine* (1780) s.v. *Cannon,* If a cannon was without cascabel, trunnion, and mouldings, it would exactly resemble the frustrum of a cone. *Ibid., Midship frame,* The string, with the moulding under the gun-wale. **1802** C. JAMES *Milit. Dict., Mouldings,* of a gun or mortar, are all the eminent parts, as squares or rounds, which serve for ornaments. **1839** URE *Dict. Arts* 611 The finished leaves of gold..are then cut to one size, by a sharp-edge square moulding of cane, glued on a flat board. **1845** P. BARLOW in *Encycl. Metrop.* VIII. 677/1 The ornamental beadings and mouldings, seen in many plated articles. **1874** MICKLETHWAITE *Mod. Par. Churches* 220 A plain rectangular [notice-] board is the best; a simple moulding round the edge will do no harm. **1876** *Encycl. Brit.* V. 170/1 Fashion in picture frames..fluctuates greatly. Mouldings of the prevailing sizes and patterns are..manufactured in special factories. **1902** *How to make Things* 48/1 The edges of sides and bottom are concealed by the gluing on of strips of moulding.

4. *attrib.*, as ***moulding basket, -box, dimension, -edge, -loft*** (= mould-loft), ***machine, -mill, -plan, -plane, powder, -sand, -table, -trough, -wire, -work.***

(For various others see Knight *Dict. Mech.* (1875) and Lockwood *Gloss. Mech. Engin.* 1888.)

1857 MILLER *Elem. Chem.* (1862) III. 142 The dough is then drawn off into pans or *moulding baskets, and baked in the usual way. **1837** *Lond. Jrnl. of Arts* IX. 269 The clay is introduced into the *moulding boxes from the hopper. **1867** SMYTH *Sailor's Word-bk.*, **Moulding dimension,* in ship-building, implies the depth or thickness of any piece of timber. **1830** HEDDERWICK *Marine Archit.* 265 The sirmarks are sawn in on the *moulding-edge. *Ibid.* 245 The platform or *moulding-loft being prepared, make a proper set of battens for describing the curve-lines on the floor. **1890** *Cent. Dict.*, *Molding-machine. **1921** *Daily Colonist* (Victoria, B.C.) 25 Mar. 8/4 To meet the needs of the small foundry with a varied demand, a British firm has, however, introduced an adaptable molding machine which can be quickly and easily adjusted to take molding boxes and pattern plates of any size within a comparatively wide range. **1858** SIMMONDS *Dict. Trade,* **Moulding-mill,* a saw-mill or shaping mill for timber. **1830** HEDDERWICK *Marine Archit.* 176 Directions for drawing the *moulding plans..of merchant vessels. **1678** MOXON *Mech. Exerc.* iv. 70 There are several other Plains in use among Joyners, called *Molding-plains; as, the Round, the Hollow, the Ogee, ..&c. **1964** W. L. GOODMAN *Hist. Woodworking Tools* 52 The remainder include moulding plane irons,..rebate- and shoulder-plane irons, and plough irons. **1940** *Chambers's Techn. Dict.* 560/1 **Moulding powder,* the finely ground mixture of binder, accelerator, colouring matter, filler, and lubricant which is converted under pressure into the final moulding. **1957** *Which?* Autumn 9/1 Plastic frames should be made of optical sheet. The reason for this is that frames made from moulding powder are not so practical. **1840** *Civil Eng. & Arch. Jrnl.* III. 33/1 Where the operations are conducted with a black material, namely, the *moulding sand. **1930** *Engineering* 21 Feb. 247/1 Simple tests have been devised for regular daily foundry control of moulding sands. **1969** BENNISON & WRIGHT *Geol. Hist. Brit. Isles* xii. 274 The Pebble Beds are followed by the Upper Mottled Sandstone ≡ Moulding Sand... The term moulding sand refers to their widespread use. **1688** R. HOLME *Armoury* III. 315/2 Sable, a Molding Board or *Moulding Table, Argent; in chief a Dough knife, proper. **1485** *Naval Acc. Hen. VII* (1896) 51 *Moldyng trowghes. **1688** R. HOLME *Armoury* III. xxii. (Roxb.) 271/2 Tobacco Pipe makers Tooles... A *Moulding Wyer: it is to make an hole all though the length of the shank. **1613–39** I. JONES in Leoni *Palladio's Archit.* (1742) II. 48 This Cornice seems to be big..; but it is the *Molding-work that makes it appear larger.

'moulding, *vbl. sb.*[3] [f. MOULD *v.*[3] + -ING[1].]

1. The process of becoming mouldy.

1530 PALSGR. 640/1, I keep breed from moldyng and drinke from sowryng. **1617** MORYSON *Itin.* III. 82 This juyce..may long be preserved from moulding. **1707** MORTIMER *Husb.* (1721) II. 56 The staking and binding it up to a pyramidical Form..heats the inward Branches..and occasions their Moulding. **1883** R. HALDANE *Workshop Receipts* Ser. II. 98/1 Where paste is to be kept for a long time, various ingredients may be added, to prevent souring and moulding.

†**2.** *concr.* Mould, mouldy growth. *Obs.*

c **1610** BODLEY in *Reliq. B.* (1703) 111 He should..with clean Cloths strike away the Dust and moulding of the Books. **1663** GERBIER *Counsel* 55 Green molding, which breaks through the whited walls. **1670** in *Cosin's Corr.* (Surtees) II. 257 The bookes..will contract moulding.

3. (See quot.)

1885 *Cassell's Encycl. Dict., Moulding,* the ore found on the top of veins near the surface of the ground.

'moulding, *ppl. a.*[1] [f. MOULD *v.*[1] + -ING[2].] Mouldering.

1826 P. POUNDEN *France & Italy* 64 The stately pile..was then beginning to suffer from the moulding touch of time. **1907** *Academy* 23 Mar. 283/2 The moulding corpses.

'moulding, *ppl. a.*[2] [f. MOULD *v.*[2] + -ING[2].] Forming, shaping.

1848 R. I. WILBERFORCE *Doctr. Incarnation* v. (1852) 103 Under the moulding power of the Holy Ghost. **1885** *Athenæum* 25 July 105/2 The environment has more moulding force in early life.

'moulding-board. [MOULDING *vbl. sb.*[2]]

1. *Baking.* A board on which dough or paste is kneaded and shaped.

1327 *Munim. Gildh. Lond.* (Rolls) III. 416 Quamdam tabulam suam, quæ vocatur 'moldingborde'. **1450** *Test. Ebor.* (Surtees) II. 144 Item in brasina..unum moldyng bord. **1534** *Eng. Ch. Furniture* (Peacock 1866) 189 Item a mele seve, a moldynge boorde. **1612** in *Antiquary* Jan. (1906) 29 In the Kytchin..a mouldinge boorde. **1688** [see *moulding-table,* MOULDING *vbl. sb.*[2] 4]. **1841** *Guide to Trade, Baker* 44 After the dough is well broken..it is put on the moulding board, which is placed near the mouth of the oven. **1852** MRS. STOWE *Uncle Tom's C.* xiii, Rachel now took down a snowy moulding-board, and..proceeded quietly to make up some biscuits.

2. A board on which bricks are moulded.

1688 R. HOLME *Armoury* III. ix. 395 A Brickmakers Moulding Board, with the Tub by the side of it.

3. *Founding.* The board on which the pattern for a mould is laid.

1882 OGILVIE. **1888** LOCKWOOD *Gloss. Mech. Engin.*

'mouldish, *a.*[1] *rare*$^{-1}$. [MOULD *sb.*[1]] Like mould, or fine soil.

1866 G. STEPHENS *Runic Mon.* I. 76 Sandy earth, finer and more mouldish than that with which the mound was made.

'mouldish, *a.*[2] *rare*$^{-0}$. [MOULD *sb.*[4]] Mouldy.

1648–60 HEXHAM, *Kaemachtigh,* Hoarish or Mouldish.

†**'mouldness.** *Obs. rare*$^{-0}$. In 5–6 mowldnes. [f. MOULD *a.* + -NESS.] Mouldiness, mould.

1483 *Cath. Angl.* 244/2 A mowldnes,..*mucor.* **1595** DUNCAN *App. Etym.* (E.D.S.) 71 *Mucor,* hery mowldnes.

'mouldress. *rare*$^{-1}$. [f. MOULDER *sb.*[1] + -ESS.] A female moulder or former.

1599 T. M[OUFET] *Silkwormes* 47 Dedalian mouldresse both of great and small.

mouldrie, obs. form of MOULDERY.

†**'mouldry.** *Sc. Obs.* Also 6 muldry, -ie, 7 muildry. [f. MOULD *sb.*[3] + -RY.]

1. Moulded work; moulding.

1501 DOUGLAS *Pal. Hon.* III. xvii, Subtile muldrie wrocht mony day agone. **1536** BELLENDENE *Cron. Scot.* (1821) II. 227 Maist subtil muldry of sindry flouris and imageris. **1616** *Aberdeen Reg.* (1848) II. 339 Gangand round about with hewen muildries the foirsyid of the pendis.

2. The making of mason's moulds.

1629 in *Archit. Publ. Soc. Dict.* III. 135/1 Ten cliftis of seasoned wanscot for the mouldrie.

†**mouldure.** *Obs.* [f. MOULD *v.*[2] + -URE, after F. *moulure.*] = MOULDING *vbl. sb.*[2] 3 b.

1628 R. NORTON *Gunner* 72 All which Mouldures, Rings, Armes, Deuices..may be at pleasure added therevnto.

mouldwarp ('məʊldwɔːp). Now chiefly *north. dial.* (see E.D.D.). Forms: *α.* 4–7 **moldewarp(e, 5–6 moldwarppe, 5–7 -warpe,** (4 **mold(e)werp, mald(e)worp, -werp, 7 mowld-, mould(e)warp, 9 moldwark, mould-warper,** etc.,) 4– **moldwarp,** 6– **mouldwarp.** *β.* 4 **molwarp(pe, -worp,** 6 **moul(e)warp(e, 7 molewarp, mowlewarp(e.** *γ.* 7 **mouldwart, moulwatt,** 9 **moulderd, motherd, mowthad,** etc. *δ.* 4–6 **moldywarp,** 6 **moudy warpe, mowldiwarp,** 7 **moldiwarpe,** 8–9 **mowde-, mowdywarp,** 9 **mou(l)di-, mou(l)dy-, modi-, moudi-, mowdi(e)-, mouly-warp, (-warf, -wark); moudy-, mouley-rat.** *ε.* (chiefly *Sc.*) 5–7 **mowdewart,** 6 **mode-, modi-, mody-, moodiewart, modeuart,** 6, 9 **moudie-wart,** 7 **moudewort,** 8–9 **moudiewort,** 9 **mowdie-, mo(u)di-, muddywort.** [ME. *mold-warp, molwarp, -werp,* repr. OE. **moldweorp* = MLG. *moldewerp, molwerp,* early mod.Du. *mol-, mulworp,* OHG. *multwurf* (MHG. *moltworf, -werf(e)*; also Norw. *moldvarp,* MSw. *mold-, mol-, mulvarper, -värpil,* etc., Sw. dial. *mullvarp,* Da. *muldvarp,* Icel. *moldvarpa*:—OTeut. **moldo-worpo(n)-, -werpo(n)-,* literally 'earth-thrower', f. **moldā* MOULD *sb.*[1] + *-*wurp-, werp-* to throw. See also MOLE *sb.*[2]

In English, as in other Germanic languages (cf. OHG. *mûwurf, mûwerfo, mûwerft,* MHG. *mûwerfe, mûlwurf,* G. *maulwurf,* LG. *mol(t)worm,* Sw. *mullvad*), the word has undergone various etymologizing perversions.]

1. = MOLE *sb.*[2] Also *fig.* (cf. MOLE *sb.*[2] 1 b, 2) and *poet.*

α. c **1325** *Gloss. W. de Bibbesw.* in Wright *Voc.* 166 *Taupes,* moldewarpes. *c* **1380** WYCLIF *Sel. Wks.* III. 315 þes blynde moldewerpis, evere wrotyng in þe erþe aboute erþely muk. **1480** CAXTON *Chron. Eng.* lxxv. 60 After this lambe shal come a mold warpe. **1595** SPENSER *Col. Clout* 763 They.. drownded lie in pleasures wastefull well, In which like Moldwarps nousling still they lurke. **1596** SHAKS. *1 Hen. IV,* III. i. 149. **1655** WALTON *Angler* i. (1661) 15 The Feret, the Pole-cat, the Mouldwarp, [etc.]. **1691** RAY *N.C. Words* 135 A *Mould Warp,* a Mole. **1813** HOGG *Queen's Wake* 103 The moldwarp digs his mossy grave. **1829** J. L. KNAPP *Jrnl. Nat.* 142 The mole, want, mouldwarper, or mould-turner. **1916** BLUNDEN *Harbingers* 59 Mouldwarps working late. **1928** A. D. MACKIE *Poems in Two Tongues* 51 Alang his pad the mowdie-worps Like sma' Assyrians lie.

β. c **1380** WYCLIF *Serm.* Sel. Wks. I. 402 Many men have molworpis ȝen. **1483** *Cath. Angl.* 242/2 A Molwarppe, *talpa.* **1580** LYLY *Euphues* (Arb.) 350 A Moulwarpes skinne. **1596** LODGE *Wits Miserie* (1879) 37, I will make the old moule-warpe hang himselfe in his owne garters to see his villanies opened. **1605** *Tryall Chev.* III. i. in Bullen *O. Pl.* III. 307, I took you for a spy. Yet saw me not no more then a Mole-warp. **1607** J. KING *Serm.* 5 Nov. 29 They begin their worke with a mine vnder ground (Romish pioners, Anti-christian molewarps..). **1636** JAMES *Iter Lanc.* (Chetham Soc.) 370 The leadsmen..who lives of molewarps have.

γ. **1604** BROUGHTON *Corrupt. Handl. Relig.* (1605) 88 They..may well holde vs as Battes and Moulwattes that cannot see that. **1688** R. HOLME *Armoury* II. 204/2 He beareth Argent, a Mole (or Mouldwart), Sable.

δ. c **1380** WYCLIF *Sel. Wks.* III. 478 How þen durne þese erthly moldy-warpis take so grete burthen of worldly dritte upon hem? *c* **1420** *Pallad. on Husb.* I. 924 The moldywarp the Grekis thus pursue. **1577** *Nottingham Rec.* IV. 168 Payd Bakyn..for takyng of mowdy warpes. **1621** BURTON *Anat. Mel.* II. iii. I. i. (1624) 256 As the moldiwarpe in Æsope told the Fox. *c* **1746** J. COLLIER (Tim Bobbin) *View Lanc. Dial.* Wks. (1862) 57 Hoos..os smoot os o Mowde-warp. **1829** BROCKETT *N.C. Words, Moudy-rat, Moudy-warp, Mouley-rat.* **1886** *S.W. Linc. Gloss.* s.v., Our cat brings in a moulywarp nows and thens.

ε. c **1470** HENRYSON *Mor. Fab.* v. (*Parl. Beasts*) xviii, The marmisset the mowdewart couth leid, Becaus that nature had denyit hir sicht. **1589** R. BRUCE *Serm.* (Wodrow Soc.) 107 Blinde as a modewart. **1598** FLORIO, *Talpa,*..a moodie-wart. *a* **1600** MONTGOMERIE *Misc. Poems* xviii. 57 Hir meit of modeuarts and myce. **1786** BURNS *Twa Dogs* 40 Whyles mice an' moudieworts they howkit. **1825** J. WILSON *Noct. Ambr.* Wks. 1855 I. 18 Mowdiewarts, they might as weel look at the newharled gable end of a barn. **1828** FLEMING *Hist. Brit. Anim.* 9 *Talpa europæa*... English, Moldwark; Scottish, Muddywort. **1859** RAMSAY *Remin.* 189, I was married to a moudiwart last, but now I am getting a husband who can see me.

2. *attrib.* and *Comb.*, as ***mouldwarp foot, hand, hill; mouldwarp-like*** adv.; †**mouldwarp hat,** a moleskin hat; †**mouldwarp-staff,** a stick for killing moles.

1591 in Ritchie *Ch. St. Baldred* (1880) 106 Having *moudie-wart feet on a purse given him by Satan. **1647** H. MORE *Cupid's Confl.* lx, What their *mole-warp hands can feel and trie By groping touch. **1570** *Richmond Wills*

(Surtees) 229 One *mold warppe hatt. **1483** *Cath. Angl.* 242/2 A *Molwarpphylle. **1523** FITZHERB. *Husb.* §23 Take hede..that the moldywarpe hilles be spredde. **1597** H. LOK *Eccles.* v. 9 But *mouldwarp like, these blindfold grope in vaine. **1584** *MS. Inv. J. Forcet of Wawne* (E. Rid. Yorks.), A *moldwarp stafe.

mouldy ('məʊldɪ), *a.*[1] [f. MOULD *sb.*[1] + -Y.] Of the nature of mould or fine soil.

1615 W. LAWSON *Country Housew. Gard.* (1626) 20 That the earth be mouldy..that it may run among the small tangles without straining or bruising. **1825** LOUDON *Encycl. Agric.* §2070. 312 Species [of soils]. Loamy, Peaty, Mouldy.

mouldy ('məʊldɪ), *a.*[2] [f. MOULD *sb.*[4] + -Y.]

1. a. Overgrown or covered with mould; hence, decaying or decayed, mouldering or mouldered.

1398 TREVISA *Barth. De P.R.* XIX. xciii. (1495) 916 In an hote place and mouldy. **1570** LEVINS *Manip.* 97/15 Mouldie, *mucidus.* **1597** SHAKS. *2 Hen. IV*, II. iv. 158 Hee liues vpon mouldie stew'd Pruines. **1649** JER. TAYLOR *Gt. Exemp.* III. Ad Sect. xv. 104 Searching his scrip in expectation to have found in it mouldy bread. **1681** DRYDEN *Abs. & Achit.* I. 302 A successive title long and dark, Drawn from the mouldy rolls of Noah's ark. **1784** COWPER *Task* v. 418 To read engraven on the mouldy walls..his predecessor's tale. **1830** LINDLEY *Nat. Syst. Bot.* 338 Books will not become mouldy in the neighbourhood of Russia leather. **1848** DICKENS *Dombey* iv, His nephew standing on the mouldy staircase. **1888** F. HUME *Mme. Midas* I. Prol., A bag of mouldy biscuits.

b. Of, consisting of, or resembling mould. *rare.*

1579 SPENSER *Sheph. Cal.* Feb. 135 The mouldie mosse, which thee accloieth. *a* **1719** ADDISON *Milton's Style Imit.* 68 The walls On all sides furr'd with mouldy damps. **1878** tr. *von Ziemssen's Cycl. Med.* XVII. 942 The formation of mouldy fungi. **1891** *Century Mag.* Nov. 60 The moldy blue bloom of the hemlock.

2. a. *transf.* and *fig.* (See also MOULDY-CHAPS.)

1576 FLEMING *Panopl. Epist.* 399 Very many obseruations out of rustie and mouldie antiquaries. **1597** SHAKS. *2 Hen. IV*, II. iv. 139 Away you mouldie Rogue, away. **1605** B. JONSON *Volpone* II. ii, With their mouldy tales out of Boccacio. **1673** [R. LEIGH] *Transp. Reh.* 43 Turning over the moth-eaten criticks, or the mouldy councils. **1780** COWPER *Lett.* 6 Aug., Wks. (1876) 55 It is to be hoped that the present century has nothing to do with the mouldy opinions of the last. **1889** *Spectator* 2 Nov., The ancient joke about smelling the paper-knife is one of the mouldiest of witticisms.

b. Wretched, boring, depressing, gloomy, sick. *colloq.* or *slang.*

1876 STEVENSON *Lett.* (1903) I. iii. 117, I have had to fight against pretty mouldy health. **1896** FARMER & HENLEY *Slang* IV. 362/1 *Mouldy*,..worthless: *e.g.*, a *mouldy* offer. **1912** F. M. HUEFFER *Parnel* I. iii. 93, I slogged like that for Nancy... We could have got along on a major's pay, out there. Just got along! And then the blasted girl goes and gets rotten titles and mouldy houses to her back on the day the bottom drops out of me. **1916** E. V. LUCAS *Vermilion Box* 220, I should be mouldy company for you, I fear, because I can't talk. **1916** 'TAFFRAIL' *Pincher Martin* x. 174 Since you're all so mouldy, I suppose I must..turn in. **1924** M. KENNEDY *Constant Nymph* IV. xxiii. 322 She looked more wan and frail than ever and he exclaimed: 'You look very mouldy.' **1936** —— *Together & Apart* I. 95 Do please come home soon, for it's mouldy without you. **1956** A. HUXLEY *Let.* 25 Dec. (1969) 814 One feels a bit low and mouldy after those bouts of flu. **1962** *Guardian* 20 Jan. 3/6 Local support for the event had deteriorated, but it did not deserve to be called 'mouldy'. **1972** *Sat. Rev.* (U.S.) 9 Sept. 92/1 The average cabby is a moldy old fascist.

c. ***mouldy fig***: a supporter (occas., a performer) of traditional jazz. Also *attrib.* or as quasi-*adj.*

1945 *Esquire* Mar. 10/2 Why do aforementioned connoisseurs insist upon maintaining that the Chicago and New York (white) styles are the real Jazz, when it's perfectly obvious that New Orleans was—and is—the birthplace of the true 'stuff'?.. Sincerely, Moldy Fig, France. **1945** S. PLATT in *Ibid.* June 10/3, I wish to protest against the 'Moldy Fig' genre of music lovers. There seems to be some perverse streak in critics such as Avakian or 'Moldy Fig' which prevents them from liking anything but the very oldest available. **1958** G. LEA *Somewhere there's Music* x. 83 Dixie Cats and the rest of the Moldy Figs, okay for them, they don't need to think. **1959** *Hi Fi Rev.* Apr. 79/2 Lines of seething fury were drawn between the [jazz] traditionalists and the boppers who viewed each other as 'moldy figs', on the one hand, and players of 'all them wrong notes', on the other. **1968** *Listener* 4 Apr. 450/3 Readers over 30 will remember the term 'Mouldy Figge' as contemporaneous with Little Jackie Dennis and Suez. **1968** *Blues Unlimited* Nov. 7 Many collectors are mouldy-fig enough to believe that virtually every worthwhile blues singer was recorded at least once in the '20s and '30s. **1973** *National Observer* (U.S.) 6 Oct. 23/1 Charles Keil satirizes the 'moldy-fig' aspirations of earlier blues scholars.

3. *Comb.*, as ***mouldy-minded*** adj.

1906 HARDY *Dynasts* II. VI. vii. 320 The rawest Dynast.. Will..Down-topple to the dust like soldier Saul, And Europe's mouldy-minded oligarchs Be propped anew.

†**mouldy**, *a.*[3] *Obs.* [f. MULED + -Y.] = MULED *a.*[1]

1578 LYTE *Dodoens* V. lxxviii. 646 The inner part of Squilla..is applyed with great profite to..kibed or moldyeheeles.

mouldy ('məʊldɪ), *a.*[4] [f. MOULD *sb.*[3] + -Y.] Of sheep: Well-shaped. (Cf. MOULD *sb.*[3] 10.)

1863 *Jrnl. R. Agric. Soc.* XXIV. II. 475 Mr. F.'s first pen [of ewes] were very 'mouldy', but hardly big enough.

mouldy ('məʊldɪ), *sb. Navy* and *R.A.F. slang.* [Origin unknown.] **1.** A torpedo.

1916 M. T. HAINSSELIN *In Northern Mists* xvi. 62 A German submarine..kept one of the bug-traps bailed up.. for a week by waiting..ready to squirt a mouldy at her directly she showed her nose outside... To fire a torpedo at her, of course! **1918** *Yachting Monthly* XXIV. 297/1 When H.M.S. Carraco was torpedoed she received the mouldy right forward. **1928** *Observer* 11 Mar. 17/4 The King of Afghanistan will be given a lesson in torpedo firing and himself discharge a 'mouldy' from one of L22's tubes. **1932** *Flight* 19 Aug. 777/1 At the same time, no doubt, the A.A. gunners on board are gleefully telling all and sundry how they simply riddled the 'Horsleys' with shells before ever a mouldy was dropped. **1943** C. H. WARD-JACKSON *Piece of Cake* 43 *Mouldy*, a torpedo..was brought into air force use by the Royal Naval Air Service.

2. A confection sold at naval colleges.

1916 G. FRANKLIN *Naval Digression* xii. 105 The various cadets engaged in stuffing themselves with 'pinkmen', 'mouldies'..and suchlike *vinos y comida*. **1962** GRANVILLE *Dict. Sailors' Slang* 78/2 *Mouldy*,..confection popular at Dartmouth.

†'**mouldy-chaps, -chops.** *Obs.* [f. MOULDY *a.* + CHAP *sb.*[2], CHOP *sb.*[2]] A term of abuse.

[**1597** SHAKS. *2 Hen. IV*, II. iv. 139 Ile thrust my Knife in your mouldie Chappes. **1667** DRYDEN *Sir M. Mar-All* II. i, Pox of her old mouldy chops.]

1595 WARNER tr. *Plautus' Menæcmi* II. i, Where's mouldichappes that must dine with ye? A murrain on his manners. **1611** COTGR., *Rocard*,..a hoarse mouldichaps. **1634** MASSINGER *Very Woman* III. i, Sirrah, You mouldy chops, know your crib, I would wish you.

mouldy-grubs, obs. form of MULLIGRUBS.

‖**moule** (mul). [Fr.] A mussel, *spec.* in **moules (à la) marinière**, mussels served in their shells and cooked in a wine and onion sauce.

1890 E. LEBOUR-FAWSSETT *French Cookery for Ladies* 161 *Moules à la Marinière*... After you have taken your mussels out of the saucepan.., put in three onions,..two sliced carrots, [etc.]. **1928** D. L. SAYERS *Unpleasantness at Bellona Club* ix. 106, I was just wondering whether to have *moules marinières* or not. **1950** D. AMES *Corpse Diplomatique* iv. 33 She was almost up to her elbows in a dish of *moules à la marinière*. **1959** *Good Food Guide* 36 The cooking is something above 'plain English' and even includes moules marinières quite frequently. *Ibid.* 162 Take moules Mendip (2/6), pâté (2/6), various vol-au-vent (3/–). **1971** COOMBES & WAKELIN *Good Housek. Advanced Cooking is Fun* 117 *Mussels* (Moules Marinière): These are best eaten from a bowl or soup plate, with a fork to get the mussel from the shell..and a spoon for the liquor.

moule, var. MOUL; also of MULE, chilblain.

moulet, variant of MULET *Obs.*, young mule.

moulewy, obs. form of MOOLVEE.

Mouli ('muːlɪ). Also **mouli.** A proprietary name, shortened from MOULINETTE. Also *attrib.*

1937 *Trade Marks Jrnl.* 21 July 862/2 Mouli... All goods included in Class 6. [Machinery of all kinds, and parts of machinery, except agricultural and horticultural machines and their parts.] Mouliware Limited,..London,..; manufacturers and merchants. **1969** O. JOHN *Dead on Time* I. 11 Homus bathini is made from chick peas.., put.. through a mouli. **1972** C. FREMLIN *Appointment with Yesterday* vii. 51 The burnt chip-pan. And all that white, sticky stuff in the Mouli-Mixer. **1972** *Times* 12 Aug. 11/1 Pass the soup through a 'mouli' soup mill, this..keeps back all the stalky bits.

‖**moulin** (mulɛ̃). [F. *moulin*, lit. a mill.

The term is suggested in sense 1 by the swirling motion of the water as it falls down the shaft.]

1. A nearly vertical circular well or shaft in a glacier, formed by the surface water falling through a crack in the ice, and gradually scooping out a deep chasm.

1860 TYNDALL *Glac.* II. xxv. 363 These moulins occur only at those parts of the glacier which are not much rent by fissures. **1889** G. F. WRIGHT *Ice Age N. Amer.* 19 Neither moulins nor regular dirt-bands are present.

2. A kitchen utensil used for grinding food or reducing it to pulp. (See MILL *sb.*[1] 2 a.)

1959 *Listener* 17 Dec. 1095/1 Put it through a sieve, or a *moulin à legumes*. **1962** *Harper's Bazaar* Aug. 37 Black pepper freshly ground from the *moulin*. **1966** 'K. NICHOLSON' *Hook, Line & Sinker* viii. 92 In the kitchen Mrs. Chilperic..was urging the apple sauce through the moulin.

moulin, var. MOOLIN *Sc.*

Moulin-à-Vent (mulɛ̃avɑ̃). Also **Moulin à Vent.** [Fr. place-name.] The name of a Beaujolais wine produced in the commune of Moulin-à-Vent.

1833 C. REDDING *Hist. Mod. Wines* v. 112 The first class of Burgundies in the Saone and Loire, are Moulin à Vent, Torins, and Chenas. **1927** A. E. HOUSMAN *Let.* 17 Oct. (1971) 254 We had two bottles of white wine (the first probably Pouilly-Fuissé) and then half a bottle of *Moulin-à-Vent*. **1961** 'J. WELCOME' *Beware of Midnight* vi. 79, I ordered..a bottle of Moulin à Vent. **1967** A. LICHINE *Encycl. Wines* 121 Such a quintessential Beaujolais as Fleurie will be more characteristic than the bigger wines —the Morgon and Moulin-à-Vent. **1968** 'G. BAGBY' *Corpse Candle* vi. 67 There was even a respectable wine, a Moulin-à-Vent.

moulinet (muːlɪ'nɛt). [a. F. *moulinet*, dim. of *moulin* mill: see -ET[1]. Cf. MOLINET.]

1. a. *Antiq.* A portable apparatus carried by crossbow-men for winding up their bows.

1846 FAIRHOLT *Costume in Eng.* 222 One..carries his bow over his shoulder, and has suspended from his waist a moulinet, and pulley for winding up his bow.

b. A wheel or winch used to turn the drum of a hoisting machine or the like. ? *Obs.*

1662 EVELYN *Sculptura* II. (1906) 7 The Moulinet, or wheele..is made to turne the upper Roller. **1706** in PHILLIPS (ed. Kersey). **1784–5** *Ann. Reg.* 324, I was obliged to unscrew and cast away our moulinet. **1855** OGILVIE *Suppl.*

†**2.** A kind of turnstile. *Obs.*

1706 in PHILLIPS (ed. Kersey). In mod. Dicts.

3. *Fencing.* A circular swing of a sword or sabre.

1875 KINGLAKE *Crimea* (1877) V. i. 126 The swift circling 'moulinet',..his sabre whirling round and round overhead. **1887** GILLIAT *Forest Outlaws* 235 Lucky for me I could play a pretty game at moulinet.

Moulinette (muːlɪ'nɛt). Also **moulinette.** The proprietary name of a type of food mill.

1936 *Trade Marks Jrnl.* 23 Dec. 1585/2 The Moulinette. .. Food strainers and sieves all of ordinary metal. Mantelet & Boucher.., Bagnolet (Seine), France; manufacturers and merchants. **1951** *Ibid.* 7 Mar. 229/1 Moulinette... Hand operated mincing machines for food. Mouliware Limited, ..London,..; manufacturers and merchants. **1951** E. DAVID *French Country Cooking* 19 A purée-maker or food mill, usually called a *moulinette* in France. For soups, fruit and vegetable purées this is absolutely invaluable. **1961** *Listener* 24 Aug. 295/1 If you enjoy sieved greens, fruits, and other purées, a *moulinette*, or rotary sieve..will pay its way.

†'**mouling,** *vbl. sb. Obs.* [f. MOUL *v.*[1] + -ING[1].] = MOULDING *vbl. sb.*[3]

13.. *St. Erkenwolde* 86 in Horstm. *Altengl. Leg.* (1881) 268 Wemles were his wedes with-outen any teiche Oþer of moulynge oþer of motes. *c* **1440** *Promp. Parv.* 346/2 Mowlynge, of mowle..*mucor.* **1550** BALE *Eng. Votaries* II. Oj, For feare of worme eatyng, mowlynge, or stynking.

moulled, variant of MULED *ppl. a.*

‖**moulleen** (muː'liːn). *Anglo-Ir.* [Irish *maolín*, dim. of *maol* bald, hornless.] A cow without horns.

1830–3 W. CARLETON *Traits Irish Peas.* (1843) I. 54 The two moulleens that her uncle Jack left her.

moully, variant of MULEY *a.*

‖**moulrush** ('muːlrʌʃ). [Irish *mulrus* (Dinneen).] The coal-fish, *Gadus virens.*

1863 COUCH *Brit. Fishes* III. 84.

moult (məʊlt), *sb.* Also 9– molt. [f. MOULT *v.*] The action of moulting: **a.** In birds. ***in the moult***, in a condition of moulting.

1819 *Sporting Mag.* IV. 247 Those we have just seen are at present in the moult, and on account of their passage are in poor condition. **1874** COUES *Birds N.-W.* 44 Before the Larks leave Northern Dakota..they go into moult. **1894** R. B. SHARPE *Handbk. Birds Gt. Brit.* I. 5 The young birds retain their feathered face after their first moult.

b. *transf.* in reptiles, crustacea, etc.

1815 KIRBY & SP. *Entomol.* vi. (1818) I. 197 This larva is ..shagreened..with minute black tubercles, which it loses at its last moult. **1837** *Penny Cycl.* VIII. 190/1 Eight moults in the short space of seventeen days have been observed in a young *Daphia*. **1871** DARWIN *Desc. Man* II. xi. (1890) 328 The..organs of certain male Orthoptera are not fully developed until the last moult.

moult (məʊlt), *v.* Forms: 4–7 mout, 5–7 mowt(e, 6–7 mute, 6–8 (9– *U.S.*) molt, 7 moote, 7– moult. [ME. *mouten*:—OE. **mútian* (implied in *bimútian* to exchange, *mútung* exchange, incorrectly glossing L. *mutuum*), a Com. WGer. adoption of L. *mūtāre* to change; cf. OLow Frankish *gemûtôn* to change, MDu., MLG. *mûten* to change, moult (mod.Du. *muiten* to moult), OHG. *mûzôn*, *gimûzôn* to change, MHG. *mûzen* to change, moult, mod.Ger. *mausen* (hence the frequentative *mausern*) to moult. The *l* was introduced late in the 16th c., on the analogy of words like *fault*, which had an etymological (orig. silent) *l* before *t*; the modern pronunciation is based on the spelling.]

†**1.** *intr.* Of feathers; To be shed in the process of change of plumage. *Obs.* Also with *off.* Hence loosely of hair: To fall off.

1340 HAMPOLE *Pr. Consc.* 781 His haire moutes, his eghen rynnes. *c* **1430** LYDG. *Hors, Shepe & G.* 180 Fetheres of goos whan thei falle or mout [**1479** mowte] To gadre hem vp heerdis hem delite. **1515** BARCLAY *Egloges* iv. (1570) C iij b/1 What time the Cuckowes fethers mout and fall From sight she lurketh. **1591** LYLY *Endym.* v. iii. 190 Mee thinkes I feele my ioyntes stronge, and these mouldy haires to molt. **1647** H. MORE *Philos. Poems* 368 Souls that have their feathers moult off of them and so are fain to flag among the dirty desires of the world.

transf. **1760–72** H. BROOKE *Fool of Qual.* (1809) I. 82 His teeth, that then happened to be moulting.

2. Of birds: To shed or cast feathers as part of the process of a change of plumage.

c **1440** *Promp. Parv.* 347/2 Mowtyn, as fowlys, *plumeo.* **1611** [see MOULTER *sb.*]. **1616** SURFL. & MARKH. *Country Farm* 70 When they are casting off their feathers, otherwise called of the common people moulting. **1780** HUNTER in *Phil. Trans.* LXX. 534 In the following year, she moulted again, and produced the same feathers. **1831** CARLYLE *Sart. Res.* II. vii, The Eagle when he moults is sickly. **1867** BAKER *Nile Tribut.* viii. (1872) 122 The birds in this country moult twice a year.

b. *transf.* and *fig.*

1612 STURTEVANT *Metallica* xiii. 94 Freestone..in continuance of time..moulteth, or crometh away. **1792** W. ROBERTS *Looker-on* No. 52 (1795) III. 23 The said dutchesses and countesses were visibly moulting very fast, and baring their necks and shoulders. **1843** LYTTON *Last Bar.* I. iii, Birds of a feather must keep shy of those that moult other colours. **1884** GOLDW. SMITH in *Fortn. Rev.* Jan. 37 England is moulting. Opinions..are..in a state of flux.

c. In extended sense, of reptiles, crustaceans, and occas. of other animals: To shed or cast some integument or other part, the place of which is supplied by a new growth.

1399 [see MOULTING *vbl. sb.*] **1868** *Rep. U.S. Commissioner Agric.* (1869) 298 On the sixth day they [*sc.* young worms] begin to molt, or change their skin. **1898** P. MANSON *Trop. Diseases* xxxv. 540 During this time it [ankylostomum] moults twice. **1902** CORNISH *Naturalist Thames* 54 The youthful crayfish 'moult', or shed their shells 8 times in their first twelvemonth of life.

3. *trans.* Of birds: To shed or cast (feathers) in the process of renewal of plumage. Hence of other animals (cf. 2c): To shed (renewable integuments or other parts). †Also with *away*, *off*.

1530 PALSGR. 643/1 This hauke begynneth to mute her fethers. **1545** ASCHAM *Toxoph.* (Arb.) 26 Some hauinge their fethers mowted awaye..sanke downe into earthlie things. **1760** *Phil. Trans.* LI. 834 It [has] not, as he thinks, molted off all its first, or chicken feathers. **1774** GOLDSM. *Nat. Hist.* (1824) II. ii. 37 One of these [ermines]..he..kept, in order to observe the manner of moulting its hair. **1875** C. C. BLAKE *Zool.* 140 Many reptiles cast or moult their skin. **1894** W. B. TEGETMEIER in *Field* 9 June 850/1, I frequently come across birds that have moulted every chicken feather in May, and the cockerels sometimes furnish the additional..peculiarity of having moulted their spurs also.

b. *fig.* and in figurative context.

1602 SHAKS. *Ham.* II. ii. 306 So shall..your secricie to the King and Queene moult no feather. *a* **1641** SUCKLING *Last Rem.* (1659) 2 Time shall moult away his wings, Ere he shall discover..Such a constant Lover. **1768** H. WALPOLE *Let. to G. Montagu* 10 Nov., I moulted my stick to-day. **1835** SOUTHEY *Doctor* lxxx. III. 62 We all moult our names in the natural course of life. **1871** TYNDALL *Fragm. Sci.* (1879) II. 221 The errors of ignorance are continually moulted, and ruth is organised. **1880** MCCARTHY *Own Times* IV. xlviii. 12 His self-confidence moulted no feather.

refl. **1839** LONGF. *Celest. Pilot* 24 The eternal pinions, That do not moult themselves [It. *si mutan*] like mortal hair!

c. *nonce-use.* To cause (feathers) to be shed.

1634 SANDERSON *Serm.* II. 291 Some write of the ostriches feather, that it will in time moult and consume all the feathers in the tub wherein it is put.

moult, obs. f. MELT *v.*; obs. pa. pple. of MELT *v.*

†**'moultard.** *Obs. rare.* In 5 mowtard, 7 (*erron.*) moultered. [f. MOULT *v.* + -ARD.] A moulter; a bird that is shedding its plumage.

c **1440** *Promp. Parv.* 347/2 Mowtare, or mowtard, byrde, *plutor.* **1650** GENTILIS *Considerations* 58 Whereas the other moultered..runnes and flyes without stay or guide.

'moulted, *ppl. a.* [f. MOULT *v.* + -ED[1].]

1. Deprived of feathers by or as by moulting. Also *transf.* and *fig.*

c **1440** *Promp. Parv.* 347/2 Mowtyd, *deplumatus.* **1533–4** *Act 25 Hen. VIII*, c. 11 §1 At suche time as the saide olde fowle be mouted and not replenished with fethers to flie. **1666** DRYDEN *Ann. Mirab.* cxliii, With cord and canvas from rich Hamburg sent His Navy's moulted wings he imps once more. **1689** *Lond. Gaz.* No. 2494/4 His Mane and Tail of a black Grey, but something shed or moulted. **1748** THOMSON *Cast. Indol.* I. xxxi, Ah! how shall I for this uprear my moulted wing? **1813** HOGG *Queen's Wake, Kilmeny* XXI, With ane mootit wing, and wefu mene, The egil sochte her eiry agene.

2. Shed during moulting. Also *fig.*

1833 LAMB *Elia* Ser. II, *Barrenness Imag. Faculty*, Imagine..the Georges and garters, jewels, bracelets, moulted upon the occasion! **1855** BROWNING *Memorab.* iv, I put inside my breast A moulted feather, an eagle-feather.

†**'moulten,** *ppl. a. Obs.* [irreg. strong pa. pple. of MOULT *v.*] Having moulted.

1596 SHAKS. *1 Hen. IV*, III. i. 152 A clip-wing'd Griffin, and a moulten Rauen.

moulten, obs. form of MOLTEN.

moulter ('məʊltə(r)), *sb. rare.* Also 5 **mowtare**, 7 **mooter.** [f. MOULT *v.* + -ER[1].] A bird that is moulting.

c **1440** [see MOULTARD]. **1611** COTGR., *Albrent*, a young wild Ducke; also, (a mooter, or moulter,) the old one when she mootes, or hath cast her feathers. **1820** J. H. REYNOLDS *Fancy* (1906) 26 Have you not seen a pigeon, wheeling, fly Above a pigeon-house..; Lure one and all—the full-plumed and the moulter, The tumbler, and the carrier, and the poulter—Take them to other dove-cotes, there to die?

'moulter, *v.*[1] *Obs.* exc. *dial.* Also 6–7 **molter**, 7 **moulter, -tre**, 9 *dial.* **multer, mouter, mowter.** [Perh. an altered form of MOULDER *v.*, influenced by *molten.*] *trans.* and *intr.* = MOULDER *v.* Hence **'moultering** *ppl. a.*

1568 T. HOWELL *Arb. Amitie* (1879) 71 But passe not those for moltring muck, the pestlent poole of woe. **1603** OWEN *Pembrokeshire* (1892) 70 The next showre of rayne maketh it [the lime] to Molter and fall into dust. **1631** R. BYFIELD *Doctr. Sabb.* 52 Till..he may correct the fading and moultring discipline. **1632** *Florio's Montaigne* III. viii. 523 It [*sc.* religion] would have escaped and moultred [1603 mouldred] away betweene their fingers, if [etc.]. **1636** FEATLY *Clavis Myst.* lxvii. 864 The Sea-mew..is forced daily to repaire it [*sc.* her nest], because every day the violent assault of the sea waves moulter away some part thereof. **1659** in *Glover's Hist. Derby* (1829) I. App. 85 Afterwards they drew into a town, and moultered away, so that this morning there was not one left to appear. *a* **1668** LASSELS *Voy. Italy* ii. (1698) 83 It's only time..that hath battered this Triumphal arch, and moultered even marble. **1808–80** JAMIESON, *To Mouter*, to fret, to fall off in consequence of friction or some similar cause... It is applied to friable stones, rotten wood, &c. **1881** *Leicester Gloss.*, *Moulter*..to moulder; applied particularly to fallow soil. **1890** *Gloucester. Gloss.* s.v., Bricks..are said to moulter with the frost.

†**'moulter,** *v.*[2] *Obs.* [? f. MOULTER *sb.*] *intr.* and *trans.* To moult. Hence **'mouItering** *vbl. sb.*

1632 MARMION *Holland's Leaguer* II. iii, Summer birds..that once a year..moulter. **1648** MAYNE *Amorous War* v. iii, Flying Like Owles by Twilight, and moultring these our feathers. **1681** GREW *Musæum* I. IV. i. 55 On the top of his Head, hath a horny Crown, which falls off when he moulters. **1696** *Phil. Trans.* XIX. 343 About Midsummer (when Moultering time is) several Persons,..with long Poles knock them [*sc.* Ducks] down. **1706** PHILLIPS (ed. Kersey), To *Moult* or *Moulter*, to cast, or shed the Feathers, as Birds do.

moulter, obs. and dial. form of MULTURE *sb.*

†**'mouItering,** *a. Obs.* [f. *moult*, MELT *v.*, ? after *sweltering.*] 'Melting', sweltering.

1606 J. RAYNOLDS *Dolarney's Prim.* (1880) 107 The day and battaile, were so moultring hot.

'moulting, *vbl. sb.* [f. MOULT *v.* + -ING[1].]

1. The action of the verb MOULT, *lit.* and *fig.*

1399 LANGL. *Rich. Redeles* II. 12 þe seson was paste ffor hertis..To make ony myrthe ffor mowtynge þat nyghed. *c* **1440** *Promp. Parv.* 347/2 Mowtynge, *deplumacio, plutura.* **1626** BACON *Sylva* §851 Some Birds there be, that vpon their Moulting doe turne Colour. *a* **1661** FULLER *Worthies* xxiv. (1662) I. 69 Yet have our wars..been a main cause of the moulting of many Eminent and Worthy persons of this Profession. **1756** FOOTE *Eng. fr. Paris* I. Wks. 1799 I. 101, I suppose..your parrot died in moulting. **1860** PUSEY *Min. Proph.* 303 The moulting of the eagle involves some degree of weakness. **1897** *Allbutt's Syst. Med.* II. 1040 After the second moulting it passes into a sort of larval state.

b. Applied to the change of voice at puberty. [So Du. *muiten.*]

1835–6 *Todd's Cycl. Anat.* I. 70/2 At this epoch [*i.e.* puberty] occurs the moulting of the voice.

†**2.** *concr.* What is shed in the process of moulting.

1610 BARROUGH *Meth. Physick* IV. v. (1639) 228 A bath..bringeth forth excrements or moltings, if any sticke within the skinne.

3. *attrib.* in ***moulting season, sickness, time.***

1457 *Sc. Acts Jas. II*, c. 94 (1566) 44 That na man..slay wylde foulis in mouting tyme. **1622** DRAYTON *Poly-olb.* xxv. 120 The multitudes of Fowle in Mooting time they draw. **1687** [see BENTING *vbl. sb.*]. **1710** *Act 9 Anne* c. 27 §5 In any of the Fens..or other Places of resort for Wild Fowl in the molting Season. **1835** URE *Philos. Manuf.* 238 On the fourth day they [*sc.* silkworms] labour under the moulting sickness.

'moulting, *ppl. a.* [f. MOULT *v.* + -ING[2].] That moults.

1635 QUARLES *Embl.* III. xv. 34 Or be thy moulting wings vnapt to flie? **1694** MOTTEUX *Rabelais* v. vii. (1737) 25 Crest-fallen, and drooping, like a Mooting Duck. **1778** BP. LOWTH *Transl. Isaiah* xl. 31 (ed. 12) 75 They shall put forth fresh feathers like the moulting eagle. **1869** 'MARK TWAIN' *Innoc. Abr.* ii, Looking as droopy..as..molting chickens. **1887** BESANT *The World went* xxiv, Sitting mum, like a moulting canary-bird.

moultiplye, obs. form of MULTIPLY.

moulture, obs. form of MULTURE.

moultytude, obs. form of MULTITUDE.

‖**moulure.** *Obs.* [Fr., f. *mouler* to mould.] ? A moulding.

c **1710** *Mack Gregory's Advt.* 2 Sculptures, Chizzelures, Moulures, Founts, Earth-Works [etc.].

moulvee, -vi(e, variant forms of MOOLVEE.

moulwarpe, obs. form of MOLDWARP.

'mouly, *a. Obs.* exc. *dial.* (see E.D.D.) Also 5–6 **mowly**, 6, 9 **moulie**, 9 **mooly.** [f. MOUL *v.* + -Y.] = MOULDY *a.*[2]

1483 CAXTON *Gold. Leg.* 107 b/2 As the kyng sate atte mete all the brede..waxed anon mowly..that noman myght ete of it. **1550** CRANMER *Defence* 21 Sowre wyne and mowled bread, whiche could not waxe sowre nor mowly, yf there were no breade nor wyne there at all. **1597** *Pilgr. Parnass.* v. 573 Everye one of them a fustie, moulie worde in his mouthe that's able to breede a plague in a pure aire.

moun, obs. form of MAY *v.*[1], MOUNT *sb.*[2]

†**mouncel.** *Obs. rare*[−1]. [a. OF. *moncel* lit. heap (mod.F. *monceau*):—late L. *monticellum* (*-us*), dim. of *mont-*, *mons*: see MOUNT.] An assemblage (of animals), a division of a herd.

c **1450** *Merlin* xxiii. 413 The crowned lyon that hadde his bestes departed in to xviij mouncels, and in eche mouncell was a lyonsewe that hadde lordshippe ouer hem.

mounch, -che, obs. forms of MUNCH *v.*, MONK.

mounck(e, -ery, obs. Sc. ff. MONK, -ERY.

mound (maʊnd), *sb.*[1] Also 3–6 **mounde**, 7–8 **mond(e**, 7, 9 **mund.** [a. F. *monde* (It. *mondo*, Sp., Pg. *mundo*):—L. *mundus* the world (see MUNDANE): cf. MAPPEMONDE.]

†**1.** The world; the earth as man's abode. *Obs.*

a **1290** in Horstm. *Altengl. Leg.* (1881) 221/2 þe wounde þat god for al þe mounde On rode heuede I-sprad. **13..** *Seuyn Sag.* (W.) 1928 Hold the to thine husbounde,..thou schalt haue al the mounde. *c* **1320** R. BRUNNE *Medit.* 942 For synneles y bare þe yn to þys mounde.

2. An orb or ball of gold or other precious material, intended to represent the globe of the earth; often surmounting a crown, or otherwise forming part of the insignia of royalty. Also *Her.* a figure of this, as a bearing; often used as including the cross which commonly surmounts the 'mound' properly so called.

1562 LEIGH *Armorie* 63 He beareth Azure, a Mounde Argent, enuironed and a crosse botone Or. **1586** FERNE *Blaz. Gentrie* I. 144 Other insignes..as, a Mond, or ball of gold, with the crosse vpon it. **1599** B. JONSON *Cynthia's Rev.* v. ii, She wilde them to present this Christall Mound, a note of Monarchy, and Symbole of Perfection, to thy more worthy Deity. **1660** F. BROOKE tr. *Le Blanc's Trav.* 310 On the top stands a golden Mund, and on that a Cressant. *Ibid.* 361 They set the Image of Pachacamac with a Monde under his Feet. **1754** A. DRUMMOND *Trav.* i. 8 Jesus Christ is represented..with..a gold crown much larger than the head, and a monde in his hand. **1793** *Encycl. Brit.* (ed. 3) VIII. 462/2 From the middle of this cap rises an arched fillet..surmounted of a mound, whereon is a cross. **1849** ROCK *Ch. of Fathers* I. iii. 258 Another angel, nimbed, supporting in his muffled hand a mund or ball. **1872** [see ORB II]. **1882** CUSSANS *Her.* (ed. 3) 178 The Ball on the top [of the crown] which supports the Cross is termed a Mound.

†**mound,** *sb.*[2] *poet. Obs.* Also 3 **mund, mond.** [Of obscure origin: perh. due to misapprehension of some poetic use of MUND hand, guardianship.] Power, strength; value, importance, dignity.

Very common in *Arthur and Merlin.*

a **1300** *St. Gregory* 747 in *Archiv Stud. neu. Spr.* LVII. 67 Gregori was knyȝt of muche mond [*v.r.* michel of mounde] ac he was wonderliche pore. *c* **1325** *Song of Passion* 12 in *O.E. Misc.* 197 þat child þat is so milde and wlong, and eke of grete munde [*rimes* ibunde, wunde]. **13..** *K. Alis.* 2207 Gef ye lustneth me to, Ye schole here geste of mounde. *Ibid.* 2655 To hyghe stretis, Al so noble of riche mounde, So is Chepe in this londe [*MS. Laud* þat is in londe (= London)]. **13..** *Guy Warw.* (A.) 3 Michel he couþe of hauk & hounde Of estriche faucouns of gret mounde. *a* **1330** *Roland & V.* 853 Mahoun & Iubiter..þat beþ so michel of mounde. *c* **1330** *Arth. & Merl.* (Kölb.) 3091 A swiþe miȝti man of mounde & kniȝt of þe tabel rounde. *Ibid.* 3354 Doun fel Yder, bi godes mounde. *a* **1400** *Launfal* 597 A knyght of mochel mounde.

¶ In the following quot. it is doubtful whether *mounde* is this word in the concrete sense 'force', or whether, as the Fr. phrase in the context suggests, it is the F. *monde* (MOUND *sb.*[1]) in the sense 'number of people'.

c **1305** *Pol. Songs* (Camden) 189 He wende toward Bruges *pas pur pas*, with swithe gret mounde.

mound (maʊnd), *sb.*[3] Also 6 **mownde**, 7 **mounde.** [Of obscure origin; the related MOUND *v.* occurs earlier in our quots., and may possibly be the source of the sb.

The sb. has commonly been supposed to represent the OE. *mund* (cf. MOUND *sb.*[2]); but that word means not 'defence', but 'guardianship, tutelage' (of persons). The OE. *mundbeorȝ as* (rendering L. *montes* in Ps. cxxiv. 3), which has been appealed to to show that *mund* might have the sense of material defence or protection, is prob. a mistake for a tautological **muntbeorȝas*.

Sense 2 appears to have arisen from the modification of the original sense 'fence' by association with MOUNT *sb.*[1]; the same influence afterwards produced the now prevailing sense 'tumulus', which first occurs in the 18th c.]

1. a. A hedge or other fence bounding a field or garden. Now only *dial.*

Now current only in Oxfordshire and the counties near its border. The early examples of the sb. and the related verb are all from writers belonging to these localities.

1551 CROWLEY *Pleas. & Payne* 110 Your greedye gutte could neuer stynt, Tyll all the good and fruitfull grounde Were hedged in whythin your mownde. **1563** *Stanford Churchw. Acc.* in *Antiquary* Apr. (1888) 169 For mendyng a paue [*read* pane] of the churche mownde ij[d]. **1565** COOPER *Thesaurus*, *Sepes*, an hedge, a mownde. **1590** SPENSER *F.Q.* II. vii. 56 This great gardin, compast with a mound. **1697** DRYDEN *Virg. Past.* x. 83 Nor Cold shall hinder me, with Horns and Hounds, To thrid the Thickets, or to leap the Mounds. **1724** *MS. Indenture, Estate at Mappleton, co. Derby*, Together with all mounds, fences, hedges, hadlands. **1726** —— *Estate at Syersham, co. Northampt.*, With all mounds, hedgerows, freeboards, &c. **1789** W. MARSHALL *Glouc.* I. 330 *Mounds*, field fences of every kind. **1893** *Wiltshire Gloss.*, *Mound*,..A hedge.

†**b.** *fig.* A boundary. *Obs.*

1591 SYLVESTER *Du Bartas* I. vi. 939 New Stars, whose whirling courses..Mark the true mounds of Years, and Months, and Daies. **1660** JER. TAYLOR *Duct. Dubit.* II. ii.

Rule ii. (1676) 214 Which precept was the mounds of cruelty, God so restraining them from cruelty even to beasts. *a* **1716** SOUTH *Serm.* (1823) V. 184 All those mounds and hinderances that God hath laid between them and the gratification of their vice. **1742** YOUNG *Nt. Th.* IV. 94, I see the circling hunt, of noisy men, Burst law's inclosure, leap the mounds of right.

2. *Mil.* = MOUNT *sb.*[1] 2a. Hence *gen.* an embankment, a dam. Also *fig.* Now *rare.*

1558 J. HIGHFIELD in Ld. Hardwicke *St. Papers* (1778) I. 116 The enemy..consumed some of the gunners, which stood very open for lack of mounds and good fortification. [Cf. *supra* 115 Thereupon there were two mounts repaired for the better defence.] **1615** CROOKE *Body of Man* (1631) 62 As a Mound of Earth within a Citie, serues to make vp the breaches of the Wall, so [etc.]. **1669** WORLIDGE *Syst. Agric.* (1681) 329 *Mounds*, Banks or Bounds. **1701** NORRIS *Ideal World* I. ii. 59 Geometry..in all ages has stood an invincible mound and bank against the overflowing tides of scepticism. **1718** ROWE tr. *Lucan* I. 193 But if the mound gives way, strait roaring loud In at the breach the rushing torrents croud. **1728** THOMSON *Spring* 839 The circly Mound That runs around the Hill; the Rampart once Of Iron War. **1755** JOHNSON, *Mound*, anything raised to fortify or defend; usually a bank of earth and stone. **1796** BURKE *Let. Noble Ld.* Wks. VIII. 49 The mounds and dykes of the low fat Bedford level. **1808** SCOTT *Marmion* v. xxxiii, The fourth [side] did battled walls enclose, And double mound and fosse. **1832** LONGF. *Coplas de Manrique* xlvii, Bastion, and moated wall, and mound.

3. a. An artificial elevation of earth or stones, a tumulus; esp. the earth heaped up upon a grave.

1726 POPE *Odyss.* XXIV. 102 Now all the sons of warlike Greece surround Thy destin'd tomb, and cast a mighty mound. **1821** CLARE *Vill. Minstr.* I. 8 He..scarce could pass A church-yard's dreary mounds at silent night, But.. ghosts 'hind grave-stones stood. **1830** M. DONOVAN *Dom. Econ.* I. 301 Crabs [grow] on any mound or bank that may be raised on a heath. **1844** N. PATERSON *Manse Garden* II. (1860) 130 The intervening mounds will serve for earthing up..the leeks. **1871** PALGRAVE *Lyr. Poems* 18 To the small churchyard and the mound of green She look'd.

transf. **1863** MISS BRADDON *Eleanor's Vict.* i, Small mounds or barrows of luggage. **1886** *Manch. Exam.* 8 Jan. 6/1 Brushing the snow and slush into little mounds.

b. A natural elevation of inconsiderable size, resembling a heap or pile of earth; a hillock, 'mount'.

1810 SCOTT *Lady of L.* I. xiii, The shaggy mounds no longer stood, Emerging from entangled wood. **1871** FREEMAN *Norm. Conq.* (1876) IV. xviii. 161 The mound which..received the name of Rougemont, overlooked the city. **1878** HUXLEY *Physiogr.* 190 The volcanic beds which make up the mass of the mound.

transf. **1839** J. STERLING *Poems* 193 Finer and finer the watery mound Softens and melts to a thin-spun veil.

c. In *Baseball*, 'the slightly elevated ground from which the pitcher pitches' (D.A.).

1914 *Collier's* 7 Feb. 7/2 There's a pitcher who never has to be urged to go to the mound. **1957** [see BULL-PEN 1 b]. **1974** *Evening Herald* (Rock Hill, S. Carolina) 18 Apr. 6/3 Mussman went the entire nine inning stint on the mound for Rock Hill and was credited with the win.

4. *spec.* **a.** A pile of fuel specially constructed for the 'roasting' of metallic ores. **b.** The heap of earth, dead leaves and other refuse in which certain megapodes ('mound-builders') place their eggs. **c.** *Archæol.* An elevation produced upon a land surface by the natural burial of a ruined or abandoned city. **d.** (See quot. 1875). **e.** A kind of earthwork formerly constructed by the natives of parts of North America. **f.** = KITCHEN-MIDDEN.

1839 URE *Dict. Arts* 820 The roasting [of metallic ore] in mounds, as practised near Goslar. *Ibid.* 996 A simple coking *meiler* or *mound.* **1847** SQUIER & DAVIS *Monum. Mississ. Valley* (1848) 140 The mounds are for the most part composed of earth, though stone mounds are by no means rare. *Ibid.* 143 Altar or sacrificial mounds. *Ibid.* 161 Mounds of sepulture. *Ibid.* 172 Earthworks—Temple mounds. **1855** W. S. DALLAS in *Syst. Nat. Hist.* II. 219 Each of these mounds is produced by the united efforts of several pairs of birds. **1861** BATEMAN *19 Years' Diggings* 271 Remains of two individuals from the destroyed Mound at Crake Low. **1862** RAWLINSON *Anc. Mon.* I. i. 247 Mounds, probably Assyrian, are known to exist along the course of the Khabour's great western affluent. **1875** KNIGHT *Dict. Mech.*, *Mound* (Civil Engineering), a lump of original ground left at intervals to show the depth of ground excavated. **1883** L. CARR *Mounds Mississ. Valley* 3 Not only has there not, as yet, been anything taken from the mounds indicating a higher stage of development than the red Indian ..is known to have reached, but [etc.]. **1902** *Encycl. Brit.* XXXI. 666/1 The 'mound-builder'..buries its large eggs.. under great mounds of earth and dead leaves.

5. *attrib.* and *Comb.*, as ***mound-like***, ***-making***, ***-raising*** adjs.; **mound ant** *Austral.* = *meat-ant* (MEAT *sb.* 6); **mound-bird** = MOUND-BUILDER 2; **mound-burial** *Archæol.*, the practice of burying beneath a mound or cairn; **Mound City** *U.S.*, a name for St. Louis, Missouri; **mound-dweller**, a primitive man who dwelt in a rudely erected mound; **mound-dwelling**, a mound erected as a dwelling by primitive man; **mound-kiln**, a lime-kiln in the form of a mound; **mound-maker** = MOUND-BUILDER 1 (*Cent. Dict.* 1890); **mound-man** = *mound-dweller*; **Mound of Venus** = *Mons Veneris* (s.v. MONS a, b); **mound region**, a region in which there are many mounds; **mound-work**, an ornamental bank of stone and earth.

1907 *Mound Ant [see *meat-ant* s.v. MEAT *sb.* 6]. **1926** *Austral. Encycl.* I. 68/2 Amongst the objectionable species the Mound Ant (*Iridomyrmex detectus*) is prominent; its huge nests are particularly destructive to garden paths. **1935** K. C. MCKEOWN *Insect Wonders Austral.* 5 The Mound Ants form their great gravel nests in the grassy plains, scouring in search of food..to the dead body of some horse or sheep which has perished in time of drought, the marauders issuing from holes in the carcass in long streams, each ant bearing a fragment of flesh in its jaw. **1855** W. S. DALLAS in *Syst. Nat. Hist.* II. 219 The *Megapodinæ*, or *Mound birds. **1896** SPENCER *Through Larapinta Land* 83 We passed a mound-bird's nest. **1865** LUBBOCK *Preh. Times* 86 '*Mound-burial' was prevalent in the earliest times of which we have any historical record. **1855** MAYNE REID *Hunters' Feast* i. 5 On the western bank of the Mississippi.. stands the large town of St. Louis, poetically known as the '*Mound City'. **1860** BARTLETT *Dict. Amer.* (ed. 3) 282 *Mound-City*, the city of St. Louis, so-called from the number of artificial mounds that occupied the site on which the city is built. **1899** SPENCE *Shetland Folk-Lore* 55 The *mound-dwellers, or *Pechts*, became associated in the public mind with the brochs. **1897** *Antiquary* May 135 An Aberdeenshire *mound-dwelling. **1839** URE *Dict. Arts* 869 In England the stones [for hydraulic mortar] are calcined in shaft-kilns, or sometimes in *mound-kilns. **1843** R. J. GRAVES *Syst. Clin. Med.* xxviii. 355 The large *mound-like indurations are best treated by poultices. **1876** *Beneden's Anim. Parasites* 8 The *mound-making Megapode. **1899** MUNRO *Preh. Scot.* iii. 82 The *mound-men had feasted probably during 'hard times' on their own species. **1865** R. BEAMISH *Psychonomy Hand* 35 The *mound of Venus, devoid of lines, is the index of chastity, coldness, tranquility in love. **1963** C. R. MUELLER tr. *Büchner's Danton's Death* I. v, in *Compl. Plays & Prose* 20 A woman's thighs will be your guillotine, and her mound of Venus your Tarpeian rock. **1848** GOULD *Birds Austral.* V. pl. 79 Megapodius tumulus, Gould. *Mound-raising Megapode. **1873** J. H. BEADLE *Undevel. West* i. 38 This is the centre of the '*Mound Region' of Wisconsin—so called from the many Indian mounds scattered about the valley. **1705** ADDISON *Italy* 42 The State of Milan is like a vast Garden, surrounded by a Noble *Mound-Work of Rocks and Mountains.

mound (maʊnd), *v.* [See MOUND *sb.*[3]]

1. *trans.* To enclose or bound with a fence. Also *absol.* or *intr.*, to make fences. *Obs.* exc. *dial.*

1515 in W. H. Turner *Select. Rec. Oxford* (1880) 12 Ye same ground [they] have mounded and inclosed. **1565** COOPER *Thesaurus* s.v. *Aruum, Ab aruis arua reuellere*, to mounde one from an other. **1589** —— *Admon.* 249 The Lorde hath chosen this lande, as his..vineyard, he hath mounded it with his gratious fauour and diuine protection. **1608** DOD & CLEAVER *Expos. Prov.* xi–xii. 57 Their pastures are mounded, banked, and trenched. **1731–3** TULL *Horse-Hoeing Husb.* xviii. 258 To mound over the Hill would require double the Rails, or double the Hedge-wood..as to mound the Base. **1759** in *Q. Jrnl. Economics* (1907) Nov. 79 It is order'd by the Jury that the gaps in Ayls hedge be mounded by the Owners on or before Lady day next. **1789** *Coniston Incl. Act* 9 The allotments..shall be respectively mounded round.

transf. and *fig.* **1591** SYLVESTER *Du Bartas* I. vii. 539 Honor is like Cinnamon, Which Nature mounds with many a million Of thorny pricks. **1652** W. HARTLEY *Inf. Bapt.* Ded. 1 Your discourse was so well mounded with exceptions, as not a sheep-gap open for argument to try your doctrine.

2. To enclose, bound, or fortify with an embankment.

1600 HOLLAND *Livy* 1350 Whereas before it was mounded about with rubbish,..Tarquin..was the first that enclosed it with a wall. **1612** DRAYTON *Poly-olb.* vii. 95 For, from the rising banks, that stronglie mound them in The Valley (as betwixt) her name did first begin. **1755** JOHNSON, *To Mound*,..to fortify with a mound. **1800** COLERIDGE *Wallenstein* II. viii. 54 At once Revolt is mounded, and the high-swoln current Shrinks back into the old bed of obedience. **1807** J. BARLOW *Columb.* I. 433 Columbus traced, with swift exploring eye,..The realms that mound the unmeasured magazine. **1830** TENNYSON *Ode to Memory* 98 A sand-built ridge Of heaped hills that mound the sea.

3. To heap up in a mound or hillock.

1859 G. MEREDITH *R. Feverel* ii, Banks of moveless cloud hung about the horizon, mounded to the west, where slept the wind. **1874** SYMONDS *Sk. Italy & Greece* (1898) I. i. 22 Snow lies mounded on the roads and fields. **1905** L. BINYON in *Academy* 7 Oct. 1029/2 As we rounded Old hills greenly mounded.

4. *intr.* (*Path.*) See MOUNDING *vbl. sb.* 2.

†**mound**, *a.* *Obs. rare*⁻¹. [ad. F. *monde* pure, ad. L. *mundus* clean.] Pure.

c **1560** A. SCOTT *Poems* (S.T.S.) xxxvi. 42 Creat wᵗin me and infound Ane hart immaculat and mound.

'mound-ˌbuilder.

1. One of a prehistoric race of Indians, formerly inhabiting the Mississippi valley and other parts of North America, by whom were erected earthworks of immense extent as well as numerous smaller tumuli or mounds.

1841 BRYANT *Poems, Prairies* 11 And the mound-builders vanish'd from the earth. **1847** SQUIER & DAVIS *Monum. Mississ. Valley* (1848) 188 Among the mound-builders the art of pottery attained to a considerable degree of perfection. **1893** *Critic* 25 Mar. 177/1 It is now generally held that the Ohio Moundbuilders..fled southward.

2. Any one of the megapode birds which deposit their eggs in a 'mound' (see MOUND *sb.*[3] 4 b).

1880 A. R. WALLACE *Isl. Life* iii. 46 The strange brush-turkeys and mound-builders, the only birds that never sit upon their eggs. **1895** C. DIXON in *Fortn. Rev.* Apr. 643 The Megapodidæ or mound-builders.

So **'mound-ˌbuilding** *sb.* and *a.*

1853 LAPHAM *Antiq. Wisconsin* (1855) 89 These later tribes continued the practice of mound-building so far as to erect a circular or conical tumulus over their dead. **1855** W. S. DALLAS in *Syst. Nat. Hist.* II. 219 The most remarkable of the mound-building birds is the Australian Brush-Turkey. **1902** HULBERT *Hist. Highways Amer.* I. (*title*) Paths of the Mound-Building Indians [etc.].

mounde, obs. variant of MUND.

mounded ('maʊndɪd), *a.* [f. MOUND *v.* + -ED[1].]

1. † **a.** Enclosed or bounded with a fence. *Obs.* **b.** Confined or fortified with an embankment.

1565 COOPER *Thesaurus* s.v. *Ager, Discretus ager*.. seperated: bounded: mounded. **1694** WOOD *Life* July (O.H.S.) III. 461 Rainsborow—a campe double-mounded: the inner mound neare half a mile in compass, the outer more. **1708** J. PHILIPS *Cyder* I. 12 A spacious City stood, with firmest Walls Sure mounded. **1807** J. BARLOW *Columb.* I. 211 The lakes, high mounded, point the streams their way. **1819** SHELLEY *Prometh. Unb.* III. i. 75 Let hell unlock Its mounded oceans of tempestuous fire.

2. Consisting of mounds or hillocks; having the form of a mound; heaped up into a mound.

1843 RUSKIN *Mod. Paint.* I. II. II. v. §8. 193 A gentle, mounded, melting undulation. **1863** WOOLNER *My Beautiful Lady* 151 The mounded harvest wains. **1890** *Gentl. Mag.* Feb. 166 Mounded dykes crowned with dwarf oak hedges.

moundiness ('maʊndɪnɪs). [f. MOUNDY *a.* + -NESS.] The quality of being moundy.

1863 A. C. RAMSAY *Phys. Geogr.* xxvi. (1878) 429 The original moundiness has..been nearly obliterated.

'mounding, *vbl. sb.* [f. MOUND *v.* + -ING[1].]

1. The process of piling earth in mounds.

1827 STEUART *Planter's G.* (1828) 343 It will save the labour of mounding, or bringing extra earth from a distance. **1844** N. PATERSON *Manse Garden* II. 211 Every pair of drills must have greater distance for the convenience of mounding.

2. (See quot.)

1891 *Syd. Soc. Lex.* s.v., *Mounding*, the rising of muscle into a low lump when struck by a light, sharp blow, as in some forms of locomotor ataxia, and in the weak and thin.

†**'moundless**, *a.* *nonce-wd.* [f. MOUND *sb.*[1] + -LESS.] That is no (true) world.

1591 SYLVESTER *Du Bartas* I. ii. 59 That great moundlesse Mound [orig. *ce grande monde, sans monde*], I meane that Chaos

moundlet ('maʊndlɪt). [f. MOUND *sb.*[3] + -LET.] A hillock, small mound.

1885 MCCOOK *Tenants Old Farm* 166 The conical moundlet thus formed was composed of fine fibres of the excavated rootlets.

moundy ('maʊndɪ), *a.* [f. MOUND *sb.*[3] + -Y.] Covered with mounds.

1851 W. KELLY *Excursion Calif.* I. vi. 97 Revealing a range of elevated hills stretching north and south, moundy on the surface and where they were broken showing a fine light rabbit sand. *a* **1861** D. GRAY *Poet. Wks.* (1874) 113 The moundy sward. **1871** *Daily News* 15 Aug., A vast moundy space. **1955** D. D. C. P. MOULD *Irish Pilgrimage* iv. 44 Mirage may lift them out of the water, so that they float above the sea, dark moundy masses.

mounger, obs. form of MONGER *sb.*

moungrel(l, -ill, obs. forms of MONGREL.

mounk(e, obs. Sc. forms of MONK.

† **mouns.** *Obs. rare.* Also 3 mons. [a. OF. *monz*, pl. of *mont*: see MOUNT *sb.*[1]] The 'mountains', i.e. the Alps.

1297 R. GLOUC. (Rolls) 4496 Þo adde king arþure ywonne fram þe west moste se Anon to þe mouns [*v.r.* mons] al þat lond. *Ibid.* 8071 Þer of he sende prechors þoru al cristendom, & him sulf a þes half þe mouns [*v.r.* mons] & to france com.

mounseer (maʊn'sɪə(r)). *arch.* An antiquated anglicized pronunciation of MONSIEUR, which survived as a vulgarism down to the 19th c., and occasionally appears either in representations of illiterate speech or in derisive allusion to English prejudice against foreigners. (Cf. MOSSOO.)

a **1641** SUCKLING *Poems* (1648) 10 But the Mounsier was modest, and silence confest. **1755** *Gentl. Mag.* XXV. 229 Shall I again to sea—and bang Mounseer? **1815** *Sporting Mag.* XLV. 164 These Mounseers do not trust 'em. **1851** THACKERAY *Eng. Humourists* v. (1853) 236 A hearty, plain-spoken man,..having a proper *bourgeois* scorn for French frogs, for mounseers, and wooden shoes in general.

mounsoon, obs. form of MONSOON.

mount (maʊnt), *sb.*[1] Forms: 1–5 munt, 3 (*Ormin*) munnt, 4 munte, 2–7 mont, 4 monte, mownte, 4–6 mounte, 5 montt, mownt, 6 monnte, 3– mount. [OE. *munt* masc., ad. L. *mont-em*, *mons*. The word was in the 12th c. taken up afresh from the F. *mont*, which the mod. form represents with normal phonetic development. Cf. Sp., Pg., It. *monte*.

The form *munnt* in Ormin *c* 1200 descends from the OE. *munt*; the later ME spelling *munt* may represent the word as adopted from Fr.]

I. A mountain, hill.

1. In early use, a mountain, lofty hill; from the 17th c. in prose use chiefly a more or less conical hill of moderate height rising from a plain; a hillock. Now chiefly *poet.* exc. in proper names of mountains or hills, as *Mount Vesuvius, Mount Everest, the Mount of Olives, St. Michael's Mount*, and in *the Sermon on the Mount*, the usual name for the discourse of Christ in Matt. v–vii.

When prefixed commonly abbreviated *Mt.*

c **893** K. ÆLFRED *Oros.* IV. viii. §2, & siþþan he ȝefor ofer þa moneȝan þeoda, oþ he com to Alpis þæm muntum. *c* **1000** *Ags. Gosp.* Matt. v. 1 Þa se hælend ȝe-seh þa meniȝu he astah on þone munt. *c* **1175** *Lamb. Hom.* 87 Uppon ane dune þat is þe mont of synai. *c* **1200** ORMIN 2862 Þatt ure laffdiȝ Marȝe wass þreo moneþþ i þe munntess Wiþþ hire meȝhe Elysabæþ. *c* **1250** *Gen. & Ex.* 2853 To mount synai forð he nam. **1297** R. GLOUC. (Rolls) 4161 Þe mount of sein michel. *c* **1380** WYCLIF *Wks.* (1880) 457 Ȝif þe pope speke bi þe contrarie, as a mount haþ his name of mouyng [etc.]. *a* **1400–50** *Alexander* 5117 Quat suld we moue in-to þe montts? *a* **1490** BOTONER *Itin.* (1778) 127 Mount Mygell ultra Excestre 100 miliaria. **1526** *Pilgr. Perf.* (W. de W. 1531) 1 b, The sermon that he made in the mount. **1741** *Corr. betw. C'tess Hartford & C'tess Pomfret* (1805) III. 265 A lake; and in the midst of it a green mount, on which stood a small castle. **1807** P. GASS *Jrnl.* 225 We ascended a high mount with a good deal of difficulty, as the path was very slippery. **1820** BYRON *Morg. Mag.* xiv, I shall repass the mounts. **1878** BROWNING *La Saisiaz* 75 Ye mounts Where I climb to 'scape my fellow.

b. *transf.* and *fig.*

c **1200** *Vices & Virtues* 79 Oðer hwa mai him resten upe ðin haliȝe munte of heueneriche. **1576** FLEMING *Panopl. Epist.* 267 It is thought to aduaunce the poore patients to the mount of felicitie. **1602** MARSTON *Antonio's Rev.* IV. iii, I have a mount of mischiefe clogs my soule, As waightie as the high-nol'd Appenine. **1742** YOUNG *Nt. Th.* VIII. 1082 Behold him seated on a mount serene, Above the fogs of sense. **1894** MAX PEMBERTON *Sea Wolves* vii, A low mount of black cloud upon the horizon.

c. *Her.* A representation of a hillock.

It is usually coloured vert (as turf) and borne in the base of the escutcheon, but it may be charged upon an ordinary or form part of a crest.

1611 GUILLIM *Her.* III. xiv. 129 He beareth Argent on a Mount Proper, a Stagge Couchant, Gules. **1688** R. HOLME *Armory* III. 479/2 The second [figure] is a Mountain, or Mount Trebble mounted, or a Hill of three ascents. **1828–40** BERRY *Encycl. Herald.* I, *Mount grieced* or *in degrees*, mounts cut in form of steps. *Mount mounted*, also called a *shapournet shapourned, mounted*, or *crested*, and a *mount with a hill upon it.* **1871** *Burke's Peerage*, etc. 867/1 A fess, arg., charged with a mount. **1882** CUSSANS *Her.* (ed. 3) 107 Or; on a Mount vert, a Tree proper.

†**d.** ? A representation of a mountain belonging to a pageant. *Obs.*

1580 in Cunningham *Revels at Crt.* (1842) 157 Hoopes to make a Mounte iij[s]. *Ibid.* 162 The payntinge of vij Cities, one villadge,..and a mount for Christmas iij Holidaies.

2. *Mil.* **a.** A substantial defensive or protective work of earth or other material, thrown up to resist an attack or to advance an assault. *Obs.* exc. *Hist.*

1558 J. HIGHFIELD in Ld. Hardwicke *St. Papers* (1778) I. 115 Thereupon there were two mounts repaired for the better defence. **1568** GRAFTON *Chron.* II. 465 As sone as the king was come he cast a depe trench with a high mount to prohibite them within the towne to haue any egresse. **1600** HOLLAND *Livy* XXVI. xlv. 620 As for fabricks and mounts to be raised and planted against it [*i.e.* the City], they..would aske some long time. **1611** BIBLE *Isa.* xxix. 3, I..will lay siege against thee with a mount, and I will raise forts against thee. **1697** POTTER *Antiq. Greece* III. x. (1715) 97 Their Mounts they let fall to the Ground by Undermining the Foundations. **1770** LANGHORNE *Plutarch* (1879) II. 726/2 He besieged that city seven months, during which time he erected vast mounts of earth..and invested it. **1860** PUSEY *Min. Proph.* 410 The mount, or heaped-up earth, by which the besiegers fought on a level with the besieged.

†**b.** = CAVALIER *sb.* 4. Also *fig. Obs.*

1590 SIR J. SMYTH *Disc. Weapons* Ded. *** iij, The Caueleeres (by vs called Mounts). **1630** *R. Johnson's Kingd. & Commw.* 348 It standeth well also for the conquest of Greece, bordering upon it, as it were a strong mount or Cavallier. **1701** BOYER *Draughts Fortified Towns* 2 A Cavalier or Mount, is a great Body of Earth, rais'd on the Terraplain. **1721** DE FOE *Mem. Cavalier* (1840) 98 A battery of six pieces of cannon..besides three small mounts,.. which had each of them two pieces upon them.

†**c.** *U.S.* (See quot.) *Obs.*

1724 in Temple & Sheldon *Hist. Northfield, Mass.* (1875) 202 Self and team to cart mount timber 1 day; and self one day's work at the mount..0 7 0. [*Note*, The mounts were square towers, from 14 to 20 feet high..; were made of heavy timbers..with the upper story..fitted up for a sentry.]

†**3.** An artificial mound of earth, stones, or the like; esp. a raised piece of ground, or walk, in a garden. *Obs.*

1591 SPENSER *Virg. Gnat* 660 A little mount, of greene turffs edifide. *Ibid.* 686 He..reard a mount of earth. **1615** W. LAWSON *Country Housew. Gard.* (1626) 55 In diuers corners of your Orchard Mounts of stone, or wood curiously wrought. **1625** BACON *Ess., Gardens* (Arb.) 563 At the End of both the Side Grounds, I would haue a Mount of some Pretty Height..to looke abroad into the Fields. **1653** H. COGAN tr. *Pinto's Trav.* xxxv. 140 Behind their houses.. were two great Mounts of dead mens bones. **1759** JOHNSON *Idler* No. 73 ¶9 Another [of his friends] has been for three years digging canals and raising mounts. **1791** W. BARTRAM *Carolina* 517 The nearest kindred or friends..lastly, cover all over with earth, which raises a conical hill or mount. **1800** BENTHAM *Mem. & Corr.* Wks. 1843 X. 347 It will form a mount in my garden. **1813** HOBHOUSE *Journey* (ed. 2) 716 Barrows—Short Account of those ancient Mounts.

b. *transf.*

1638 SIR T. HERBERT *Trav.* (ed. 2) 302 Their beloved Priapus is imperiously inthroniz'd upon a brazen Mount. **1685** DRYDEN tr. *Horace, Odes* I. ix. 2 Behold yon mountain's hoary height, Made higher with new mounts of snow.

II. In various transferred senses.

†**4.** The quantity of 30 cwt. of plaster of Paris.

[So OF. *mont* (15th c. in Godefr.); a specific application of the common transferred sense 'heap'.]

1532 *Lett. & Pap. Hen. VIII*, V. 446 [Plaster of Paris..a] mount [containing 30 cwt.]. **1706** in PHILLIPS (ed. Kersey).

†**5.** [After It. *monte.*] A bank. *Obs.*

1622 BACON *Let. to Bp. Andrews* Misc. Wks. (1629) 85 To put forth that poore Talent..that God hath giuen me..to Banks or Mounts of Perpetuity, which will not breake. **1765** BLACKSTONE *Comm.* I. 326 A system which seems to have had it's original in the state of Florence, *A.D.* 1344: which government then owed about 60,000 *l.* sterling: and, being unable to pay it, formed the principal into an aggregate sum, called metaphorically a mount or bank, the shares whereof were transferrable like our stocks, with interest at 5 per cent.

†**b. mount of piety, mount piety**, a rendering of It. *monte di pietà*, Fr. *mont-de-piété*, in Italy and France a pawnbroking establishment instituted and carried on by the state for the purpose of affording loans to the poor at low interest.

c **1618** MORYSON *Itin.* IV. viii. (1903) 160 For vsury five in the hundreth is allowed in the mounts of piety, which are bankes of mony to be lent to the poore. **1661** (*title*) Observations Manifesting the Conveniency and Commodity of Mount-Pietyes, or Publick Bancks for Relief of the Poor and others in distress upon Pawns. **1765** *Ann. Reg.* 153 He has left..500,000 crowns in the Mount of Piety.

6. *Palmistry.* One of the fleshy prominences on the palm of the hand by the development of which palmists profess to ascertain the degree of influence exercised by a particular planet. (Cf. MONS a.)

1644 BULWER *Chiron.* 101 With the Thumbe bended in, and reaching to the mount of Mercurie. **1653** R. SANDERS *Physiogn.* 63 At the root of each finger there is a little rising, the which we call the mounts of the Planets. **1695** CONGREVE *Love for L.* II. iii, She has..a moist Palm, and an open Liberality on the Mount of Venus.

III. 7. *attrib.* and *Comb.*, as ***mount-moving*** adj.; †**mount-egg** (see quot.).

1647 H. MORE *Char. & Hum.* 3 Deep-searching wit, mount-moving might Are nought compar'd to that good spright. **1710** J. HARRIS *Lex. Techn.* II. s.v., After Tin from the burnt Ore is melted down and remelted, there will sometimes remain a different Slugg in the bottom of the Float, this they call Mount-Egg.

mount (maʊnt), *sb.*[2] [f. MOUNT *v.* Cf. F. *monte* fem. (which may be the source of some of the senses), Sp., It. *monta*, a Com. Rom. vbl. sb.]

†**1.** = AMOUNT *sb. Obs.*

13.. *Gaw. & Gr. Knt.* 718 So mony meruayl bi mount þer þe mon fyndez, Hit were to tore for to telle of þe tenþe dole. **14..** in *Hist. Coll. Citizen Lond.* (Camden) 15 There wolde be schot..A hundryd gounnys..With[in] the mount of ij halfe hourys. **1651** *Raleigh's Ghost* 218 They again enjoying a long peace and increasing the mount of their former sins, ..they were once more cast into the hands of Philistins.

2. a. An act of mounting (*rare*); †*spec.* (of a bird) a rising from the ground; a manner of mounting; †(of a gun) elevation.

1486 *Bk. St. Albans* D j b, She toke it at the mounte or at the souce. **1571** DIGGES *Pantom.* I. xxx. I iv b, Making seueral angles proportionally to the seueral mounts of the peece. **1596** HARINGTON *Metam. Ajax* 31 Doe you not sometime..talke..of putting a heron to the mount? **1602** MARSTON *Ant. & Mel.* v. Wks. 1856 I. 58 Now, capring wits, Rise to your highest mount. **1660** F. BROOKE tr. *Le Blanc's Trav.* 224 The first..at two or three mounts and active leaps spear-high, fetches down the piece of meat. **1872** JENKINSON *Guide Eng. Lakes* (1879) 51 After another slight descent, and then a gradual mount, the top of Thornthwaite Crag is gained. **1891** *Cycling* (Badm. Libr.) viii. (ed. 3) 254 This mount, when once perfectly acquired, is deliberate and graceful.

†**b.** Mil. *to sound a mount*: to give a trumpet signal for mounting. *Obs.*

1659 HOWELL *Vocab.* v.

c. An act of copulation.

1896 FARMER & HENLEY *Slang* IV. 362/1 *Mount*, an act of coition. **1937** PARTRIDGE *Dict. Slang* 226/2 *Do a grind, a mount*, to have sexual intercourse (of men). **1970** *Nature* 12 Dec. 1107/1 In mounts from behind, the mounting cat often had its pelvic region well forward on the back of the mounted cat.

3. a. That in or on which anything is mounted, fitted, supported, or placed; a 'mounting', 'fitting', or ' setting' [cf. F. *monture*]; *spec.* (*a*) the margin surrounding a picture, or the cardboard upon which a drawing is mounted; (*b*) *pl.* the metal ornaments serving as borders, edges, or guards to the angles and prominent parts of *e.g.* the decorative furniture of the 18th c.; (*c*) the glass slip with its adjuncts used to preserve objects for examination under the microscope.

1739 *Act 12 Geo. II*, c. 26 §6 Mounts, Screws, or Stoppers to Stone or Glass Bottles or Phials. **1854** FAIRHOLT *Dict. Terms Arts, Mount*,..the paper or card-board upon which a drawing is placed. **1859** GULLICK & TIMBS *Paint.* 315 The mount or margin intervening between the water-colour painting and its frame is almost invariably white. **1883** A. H. CHURCH *Prec. Stones* 101 Diamond..½ in. diam.; claw setting on swing mount... Diamond..bordered with 12 brilliants set in silver, on gold mount. **1884** *Cyclist* 13 Feb. 243/1 Salad bowls and servers, with silver mounts. **1888** *Century Mag.* Oct. 889/1 The carriages and mounts of the guns are made entirely of bronze and steel.

b. Of a fan: (*a*) The pieces of wood, ivory, etc., forming the frame or support (see also *fan-mount* under FAN *sb.*). (*b*) The silk, paper, or similar material forming the surface of the fan.

1811 *Self Instructor* 121, 2 fans, French mounts. **1869** *Art Jrnl.* Mar. 90/3 Perforated cedar, sandal-wood, nacre, ivory —such is the proper mount of an elegant fan. **1878** *Ibid.* Aug. 173/2 Coryat..mentions some [fans]..consisting of a paper mount pasted on a wooden handle. [Coryat does not use the word.] **1889** *Harper's Mag.* Aug. 404/2 In these [Cabriolet fans] the mount is in two parts, the lower and narrower mount being half-way up the stick, the second mount in the usual place at the top of the stick.

4. a. *colloq.* A horse (or other animal, occas. a bicycle, etc.) on which one is mounted; a horse, etc., provided for a person's riding.

1856 'STONEHENGE' *Brit. Rural Sports* 363/1 The jockey .. receiving information from the trainer as to the peculiarities of his mount. **1883** E. PENNELL-ELMHIRST *Cream Leicestersh.* 235 Others merely give their mounts a kick in the ribs and gallop onwards. **1885** *Century Mag.* Mar. 653/1 A good high-bred dromedary is as comfortable a mount as can be desired. **1885** *Cyclist* 19 Aug. 1088/1 This is easily accounted for by the number of strange [cycle] riders and the changing of mounts from roadsters to racers. **1889** *Standard* 17 Mar., There is every reason to believe that, in mounts as in ordnance, Great Britain will be self-sufficing.

b. *collect.* A supply of riding- or draft-horses.

1907 S. E. WHITE *Arizona Nights* I. iii. 53 He kept his own mount of horses, took care of them. **1933** *Amer. Speech* VIII. I. 30/1 *Mount*, a string of horses, usually eight or ten, assigned by the boss to one man.

5. An opportunity or occasion of 'getting into the saddle'; hence, an undertaking to ride or an act of riding (a horse) in a race.

1856 'STONEHENGE' *Brit. Rural Sports* 361/1 The jockey ..is now expected to ride to orders in most cases, though there are still some who would refuse such a mount. **1882** B. D. W. RAMSAY *Recoll. Mil. Serv.* I. i. 15 [He] had been kind to me..giving me a mount occasionally on one of his numerous stud. **1884** *Illustr. Lond. News* 1 Nov. 410/2 The custom is to pay at least twenty-five pounds for a mount in the Derby and St. Leger. *Ibid.* 410/3 The leader of his profession, whose mounts for this year are not yet finished. **1888** SIR C. RUSSELL in *Times* 26 June 4/4 The regular fees for his [a jockey's] ridings or 'mounts'.

6. A stuffed and mounted bird-skin.

1935 *Auk* LII. 281 Since the mounts were similarly posed, it seemed that the male Northern Yellow-throat was discriminating between the sexes primarily on a basis of color pattern. **1938** *Brit. Birds* XXXII. 30 The female mount..had a half-spread tail. **1957** J. W. MOYER *Pract. Taxidermy* v. 34 Tie down the feathers with soft, fine thread or string to hold them in place until the mount is dry.

7. *attrib.* (in sense 3: see quots.).

1881 *Instr. Census Clerks* (1885) 83 Mount, Passe partout —Cutter, Binder, Gilder, Maker (for Photographs, Drawings, &c.). **1896** *Daily News* 14 Sept. 2/7 A mount cutter was charged with having stolen..a quantity of cardboard patterns, mounts, &c.

†**mount**, *sb.*[3] *Obs. rare*$^{-1}$. [Perh. transf. use of MOUNT *sb.*[1]; but cf. MOUND *sb.*[1]] A spherical box.

1562 *New Yr.'s Gifts* in Nichols *Progr. Eliz.* (1823) I. 108 A little rounde mounte of golde to conteyne a pomaunder in it.

mount (maʊnt), *v.* Also 4–5 **munt(e, monte,** 4–6 **mont.** [ME. *munte, monte*, a. OF. *munter, monter* (mod.F. *monter*) = Pr., Sp., Pg. *montar*, It. *montare*:—popular L. **montāre*, f. *mont-*, *mons* MOUNT *sb.*[1] With regard to the sense cf. F. *amont* uphill, up the stream (:— L. *ad montem* lit. 'to the hill').

The principal senses, intransitive and transitive, were adopted from Fr. The sense 'to ride', prominent in the Rom. langs., never passed into Eng.; cf. senses 3 and 9.]

I. *intr.*

1. To go upwards, ascend. Also with *up*.

a. To fly upwards, to soar. †Of a missile: To rise in its flight.

c **1384** CHAUCER *H. Fame* II. 445 He..lat the reynes gon Of his hors and they anoon Gonne vp to mounten and doun descende Til both the eyre and erthe brende. *a* **1425** *Cursor M.* 23894 (Trin.) He ȝyue vs grace so to acounte þat we may to heuen mounte. *c* **1450** HOLLAND *Howlat* 638 Than rerit thir Merlȝeonis that mountis so hie. **1535** COVERDALE *Job* xxxix. 27 Doth the Aegle mounte vp..at thy commaundement? **1590** SIR J. SMYTH *Disc. Weapons* 15 By reason that the bullets being so much lower than the heigth of their peeces..doo naturallie mount and flie vncertainlie. **1602** MARSTON *Ant. & Mel.* v. Wks. 1856 I. 65 O that my spirit in a sigh could mount Into the spheare, where thy sweet soule doth rest! **1742** YOUNG *Nt. Th.* II. 604 Like birds, whose beauties languish, half conceal'd, Till mounted on the wing, their glossy plumes Expanded shine. **1799** G. SMITH *Laboratory* I. 9 If it [a rocket] mounts even and high. **1854** ALLINGHAM *Day & Nt. Songs, Lover & Birds* v, The Lark hurried, mounting from the lea.

b. To travel or proceed in an upward direction. Now usually implying a somewhat steep ascent, e.g. that of a flight of steps.

1471 CAXTON *Recuyell* (Sommer) II. 422 Hercules.. began to mounte and goo vpon the degrees or steyres. *c* **1489** —— *Blanchardyn* lii. 198 The prouoste..cam in to the towne and syth mounted to the paleys. *a* **1533** LD. BERNERS *Huon* lix. 204 They causyd the mynstrell to mount vp on y[e] ladder. **1552** HULOET, Mount ouer, *trascendo.* **1604** E.

G[RIMSTONE] *D' Acosta's Hist. Indies* III. xv. 164 They [*sc.* certain fish] mount from the sea into the rivers. **1678** DRYDEN *All for Love* v. i, Antony Is mounted up the Pharos; from whose turret, He stands surveying our Egyptian galleys, Engaged with Cæsar's fleet. **1726** SHELVOCKE *Voy. round World* 105 They have abundance of very handsome middle-sized horses, which are said to mount with great dexterity. **1774** GOLDSM. *Nat. Hist.* (1776) III. 66 [The chamois] always mount or descend in an oblique direction. **1853** KINGSLEY *Hypatia* xxii, A body of gladiators.. planting their scaling-ladders.. mounted to the attack. **1872** JENKINSON *Guide Eng. Lakes* (1879) 293 On arriving at a streamlet, cross it near its source, and then mount by the side of the Pillar.

†**c.** To move towards culmination. *Obs.*

1594 BLUNDEVIL *Exerc.* IV. xxxii. (1636) 488 In a right Spheare the star called Cor Leonis,.. riseth, mounteth, and setteth with the 145 degree 30' of the Equinoctiall. **1604** E. G[RIMSTONE] *D' Acosta's Hist. Indies* II. x. 104 Where the sphere is straight, and the signes mount directly, there the dayes and nights are equall.

d. To tower (*obs.*); also, to extend in an upward direction. *rare.*

1561 DAUS tr. *Bullinger on Apoc.* (1573) 22 b, The temple of Dian of Ephesus.. mounted up in the middes of the Citie. **1679** T. KIRKE *Mod. Acc. Scot.* 6 The Houses mount seven or eight stories high, with many Families on one Floor. **1839** MURCHISON *Silur. Syst.* I. xxxii. 439 The overlying strata, mounting into the hills above Llanfihangel.

e. Of inanimate things: To rise, move *upwards* as if spontaneously. ? *Obs.*

1594 HOOKER *Eccl. Pol.* I. iii. §5 When things naturall in that regard forget their ordinary naturall woont, that which is heauie mounting sometime vpwardes of its owne accord. **1657** BAXTER *Call to Unconverted* Wks. (1846) 83 As fire doth mount upward.. so the converted soul is inclined to God. **1705** ADDISON *Italy* 370 At the same time are seen little Flakes of Scurfe rising up, that are probably the Parts which compose the Islands, for they often mount of themselves, tho' the Water is not troubled. **1711** —— *Spect.* No. 62 ¶5 His ambitious Love is a Fire that naturally mounts upwards.

f. To grow in an upward direction. ? *Obs.*

1638 SIR T. HERBERT *Trav.* (ed. 2) 322 They grow till fifteen, in that time mounting to foure and twenty foot. **1671** GREW *Anat. Plants* iii. App. §4 The use of these Parts may be observed as the Trunk Mounts, or as it Trails. **1693** EVELYN *De la Quint. Compl. Gard.* II. 155 We replant none of those [Cabbages] that begin to mount, that is, to run up their stalks, as if they were going to Seed.

g. Of the blood: To rise into the cheeks. Also, of the effects of wine: To 'go' to the head.

1625 MIDDLETON *Game at Chess* III. i, Ha! all my body's blood mounts to my face To look upon this letter. **1867** TROLLOPE *Chron. Barset* I. xxiv. 206 The blood mounted all over his face. **1884** TENNYSON *Becket* Prol., When the Gascon wine mounts to my head.

h. Of silkworms (see quots.).

1796 *Encycl. Brit.* (ed. 3) XVII. 485/1 When the worms are ready to mount, in order to spin, if [etc.]. **1876** B. F. COBB *Silk* (Brit. Manuf. Industries) 149 At the end of the last stage the worm 'mounts', that is to say, ceases to feed, climbs up from the feeding tray to the 'bush',.. or whatever may have been prepared for it, and spins its cocoon.

2. *fig.* **a.** To ascend to a higher level in rank, estimation, power, excellence, completeness, etc.

1390 GOWER *Conf.* I. 145 Thogh it [Pride] mounte for a throwe, It schal doun falle and overthrowe. **1484** CAXTON *Fables of Auian* ii, Who so mounteth hyher than he shold he falleth lower than he wold. **1567** *Satir. Poems Reform.* vii. 226 Thair laude and fame sall mont abone the skyis. *a* **1613** BACON *Case Post-nati Scot.* Wks. 1826 V. 116 Naturalization is best discerned in the degrees whereby the law doth mount and ascend thereunto. **1622** *Interpreter* 4 Knowing.. that Simplicitie hath onely mounted by vertue. **1647** N. BACON *Disc. Govt. Eng.* I. xiv. (1739) 26 The Prelacy beginning to mount, nibbled at it in the second Century. **1882** *Athenæum* 22 Apr. 501 [Mr. Spencer] shows how.. men mount from the lowly estate of chiefless Eskimo.. to despotisms, republics, [etc.].

b. To become elevated in spirit.

1481 CAXTON *Godeffroy* ccxii 309 Of this auenture mounted the turke in grete pryde. **1802** WORDSW. *Resolution & Independ.* 4 As high as we have mounted in delight In our dejection do we sink as low.

c. To ascend or go back in time.

1796 MORSE *Amer. Geog.* II. 467 [They] seem to fix their foundation to a period before the Christian era, but without mounting to the ancient times of the Jews or the Phoenicians. **1803** *Med. Jrnl.* IX. 369 For the antiquity of which [method] we must mount up to Celsus. **1859** JEPHSON *Brittany* vii. 83 An antiquity which mounts up to the eighth century of our era.

3. To get upon the back of a horse or other animal (occas. upon a person's shoulders) for the purpose of riding. Const. *on*, *upon*, †*to*.

1509 HAWES *Past. Pleas.* xxvii. (Percy Soc.) 131 My fayre barbed stede, On whome I mounted. **1565** STAPLETON tr. *Bede's Hist. Ch. Eng.* v. vi. 159, I was able to mounte to my horse. **1582** STANYHURST *Æneis* II. (Arb.) 66 Wel father in Gods name, mount on my shoulder, I pray you. **1596** SPENSER *F.Q.* v. x. 16 He was readie to his steede to mount. **1660** F. BROOKE tr. *Le Blanc's Trav.* 225 After this.. appears ..one.. mounted on an Elephant. **1662** J. DAVIES tr. *Olearius' Voy. Ambass.* 18 We mounted at the same place where we alighted, and return'd to our Lodgings. **1788** GIBBON *Decl. & F.* xlvi. IV. 505 Six thousand guards successively mounted before the palace gate. *c* **1850** *Arab. Nts.* (Rtldg.) 631 Each man then returned to his horse, put on its bridle,.. and then mounted.

4. a. To get up *on* something that serves to raise one above the ground.

1642 MILTON *Apol. Smect.* 10 The idlest and the paltriest Mime that ever mounted upon banke. **1726** SWIFT *Gulliver* II. viii, I mounted on the Chair. **1753** *Lond. Mag.* Sept. 396 But mount on French heels when you go to a ball, 'Tis the fashion to totter and shew you can fall. **1852** THACKERAY *Esmond* v, The window was too high to reach from the ground; but, mounting on a buffet which stood beneath it, Father Holt showed me how [etc.].

†**b.** *simply.* To ascend the stage, platform, rostrum, etc.; to make an appearance as a performer, orator, etc. *Obs.*

1745 *Daily Advertiser* 28 Sept. 3/3 [Advt. of a Prize-fight] The Doors will be open'd at Ten, and the Champions mount at Twelve. **1760** FOOTE *Minor* II. Wks. 1799 I. 259 It being impossible he should mount [as an auctioneer], I have consented to sell. **1764** —— *Patron* I. ibid. 335, I never got salt to my porridge till I mounted [*sc.* on the pillory] at the Royal Exchange.

5. To rise in amount; to increase by addition. Chiefly with *up*. Also, †to be amassed.

1362 LANGL. *P. Pl.* A. Prol. 64 But holychirche bi-ginne holde bet to-gedere, þe moste Mischeef on molde mounteþ vp faste. **1601** ? MARSTON *Pasquil & Kath.* I. 92 So great a masse of coyne might mount from wholsome thrift. **1622** FLETCHER *Beggar's Bush* IV. i, Sir, you know not To what a masse, the little we get dayly, Mounts in seven yeares. **1695** J. EDWARDS *Perfect. Script.* 220 It is by the fault of the transcribers that the arithmetick mounts so high. **1798** COLERIDGE *To Lesbia* 13 To the store Add hundreds—then a thousand more! And when they to a million mount, Let confusion take the account. **1874** GREEN *Short Hist.* iii. §5. 141 The debts of the Crown mounted to four times its annual income. *Mod.* The debt will mount up fearfully at such a rate of interest.

†**6.** To amount or be equal *to* a certain sum, number, or quantity. *Obs.*

13.. *E.E. Allit. P.* C. 332 þose vnwyse ledes þat affyen hym in vanyte & in vayne þynges, For þink þat mountes to noȝt, her mercy forsaken. **1521** TUNSTAL in Ellis *Orig. Lett.* Ser. III. I. 273, I have.. lent M. Spinel money which monteth in al to thyrty[li] sterlinge. **1534** *Act. 26 Hen. VIII*, c. 3 §22 The incumbent.. shall not.. pay.. more.. than the value of the thirde parte of his.. benefice.. shall mounte vnto. **1560** BIBLE (Geneva) *Acts.* xix. 19 *marg., Fiftie thousand pieces of siluer.* This mounteth to of our money about 2000 markes. **1734** POPE *Ess. Man* IV. 270 Bring then these blessings to a strict account; Make fair deductions; see to what they mount. **1738** SWIFT *Pol. Conversat.* Introd. 40 The old Stock-Oaths.. do not mount to above forty five, or fifty at most.

7. *slang.* [? An application of 4 b.] (See quots.)

1789 G. PARKER *Life's Painter* (1800) 145 These kind of men attend the courts of law..; their price is five shillings for what they call mounting; they have been known to mount two or three times in one day. **1812** J. H. VAUX *Flash Dict., Mount*, to swear, or give evidence falsely for the sake of a gratuity. To *mount for* a person is also synonymous with *bonnetting for* him. **1902** *Daily Chron.* 6 Mar. 8/2 He subpœnaed Roseblade as a witness for him at his trial, but, said Williams, dejectedly, 'he mounted and come it on me'. Mr. P.: What do you mean? Williams: He gave evidence against me.

II. *trans.* equivalent to intr. uses with prep.

8. a. To ascend or climb up (a mountain, hill, rock, tree); to ascend (a river, a stair).

c **1500** *Melusine* 324 Geffray.. mounted the mountayne. **1615** G. SANDYS *Trav.* 289 We mounted a paire of high staires. **1769** E. BANCROFT *Guiana* 15 He mounted the river of Essequebo. **1796** MORSE *Amer. Geog.* II. 17 The birdmen ..are amazingly dexterous in mounting the steepest rocks. **1843** LEVER *J. Hinton* iii, We mounted an old-fashioned and rickety stair. **1866** ROGERS *Agric. & Prices* I. xxiv. 611 While the fish were mounting the river. **1886** ASHBY-STERRY *Lazy Minstrel* 196 You Should mount the Hill and see the view.

b. Said of a rising road, stair, etc.

1611 SHAKS. *Cymb.* I. vi. 106 Lippes as common as the stayres That mount the Capitoll. **1872** JENKINSON *Guide Eng. Lakes* (1879) 13 The road.. mounts a steep rising ground.

c. *to mount a breach*: to ascend it for the purpose of assault or attack.

1704 SWIFT *T. Tub* Ded., Your Lordships.. undaunted Courage in mounting a Breach or scaling a Wall. **1814** SCOTT *Wav.* xiii, Being the first to mount the breach. **1841** ELPHINSTONE *Hist. Ind.* II. 301 The breach had been built up to such a height as to render it impossible to mount it.

†**d.** To rise or soar into. *Obs.*

1675 DRYDEN & MULGRAVE *Ess. Sat.* 117 So men in rapture think they mount the sky, While on the ground th'entranced wretches lie. **1707** *Curios. in Husb. & Gard.* 24 He sees the Sun rise every Morning and mount the Horizon. **1746–7** HERVEY *Medit.* (1818) 190 Did He.. not only mount the lower firmament, but ascend the heaven of heavens.

†**e.** *fig.* To rise to the level of, to rival. *Obs.*

1628 EARLE *Microcosm, Detractor* (Arb.) 43 He is.. ambitious to match others, not by mounting their worth, but bringing them downe with his Tongue to his owne poorenesse.

f. To rise on to an obstruction, etc.

1930 *Morning Post* 19 July 12/6 He just managed to avoid a crash by cutting out to his right and in doing so he mounted the footpath.

9. To get upon the back of (a horse or other animal, a bicycle) for the purpose of riding.

1599 SHAKS. *Hen. V*, III. vii. 25 The dull Elements.. neuer appeare in him, but only in patient stillnesse while his rider mounts him: hee is indeede a Horse. **1693** *Humours Town* 19 I'll mount your Horse, and ride down. **1789** ANBUREY *Trav.* II. 397, I went to his house just as he had mounted horse. **1819** BYRON *Juan* I. ix, A better cavalier ne'er mounted horse. **1843** BORROW *Bible in Spain* vi. 41, I now.. having mounted my mule, set forward. *c* **1884** 'MARK TWAIN' *Speeches* (1923) 109, I renewed my youth, to outward appearance, by mounting a bicycle. **1907** *Academy* 12 Jan. 36/2 One of the majors was accustomed to mount his horse from a chair. **1912** W. OWEN *Let.* 1 Feb. (1967) 113, I had arranged to go to the Cyclists.. the machine is only £5.19.6!.. It *will* be a *joy-ride* when I am mounted on one of these!

transf. **1808** SCOTT *Marmion* II. Introd., And mark the wild-swans mount the gale.

10. To get upon, for the purpose of copulation.

[**1592** SHAKS. *Ven. & Ad.* 596 Now is she in the verie lists of loue, Her champion mounted for the hot incounter: All is imaginarie she doth proue, He will not mannage her, although he mount her. **1630** B. JONSON *New Inn* I. iii, Instead of backing the braue Steed, o' mornings, To mount the Chambermaid.] **1697** DRYDEN *Virg. Georg.* III. 328 Whether the Bull or Courser be thy Care, Let him not leap the Cow, or mount the Mare. **1963** A. HERON *Towards Quaker View of Sex* 54 The young bachelor males of herds where the overlord male jealously protects his harem will mount each other. **1970** *Nature* 12 Dec. 1107/2 A mounting female was frequently immediately mounted by the cat she was mounting, or by another oestrous female. **1970** MASTERS & JOHNSON *Human Sexual Inadequacy* 307 The wife once mounted is instructed to hold herself quite still. **1971** 'V. X. SCOTT' *Surrogate Wife* 19, I was a man, mounting a beautiful and passionate woman. **1973** J. ELSOM *Erotic Theatre* ix. 174 Men no longer want to mount women simply because, like Everest, they are there.

11. To ascend and take a place in or on; to get upon or into, from below.

1698 FRYER *Acc. E. India & P.* 83 We were forced to mount the Indian Hackery. **1711** ADDISON *Spect.* No. 46 ¶2 The Boy accordingly mounted the Pulpit. *a* **1758** RAMSAY *The Mill-O* ii, My lass, like a fool, had mounted the stool. **1839** THIRLWALL *Greece* VI. 191 Since he himself had mounted the throne. **1888** *Spectator* 30 June 883/2 Racing notabilities, and betting men, and blacklegs, all mounting the stand and giving their evidence. **1891** 'MARK TWAIN' in *Illustr. Lond. News* 26 Dec. 834/1 Everybody else had ..'mounted the train', as they say in those regions [e.g. Geneva].

III. *trans.* in causative uses.

†**12. a.** To cause to ascend or rise; to elevate, lift, draw or drive up. Also with *up*. *Obs.*

1538 ELYOT *Dict., Exalto*, to mounte or lyfte up. *c* **1590** MARLOWE *Faust* vi. (*Chorus*), Learned Faustus, To know the secrets of Astronomy.. Did mount himselfe to scale Olympus top, Being seated in a chariot burning bright. **1604** E. G[RIMSTONE] *D' Acosta's Hist. Indies* V. xxiv. 395 They did mount it [*sc.* the idol] in this manner, for that the staires of the Temple were very steepe.., while they mounted vp the idoll, all the people stoode in the Court. **1610** W. FOLKINGHAM *Art. of Survey* I. ix. 20 Some Enginarie aide must bee assistant to mount the water by Screwes, Pullies, Poizes. **1613** SHAKS. *Hen. VIII*, I. i. 144 The fire that mounts the liquor til't run ore, In seeming to augment it, wasts it. **1614** RALEIGH *Hist. World* I. iii. §7. 45 A bird, hauing therein no feeling of her wings, or any sensible resistance of aire to mount her selfe by. **1640** tr. *Verdere's Rom. Rom.* III. 68 O from what an abisme am I mounted, said Florimond. **1647** N. BACON *Disc. Govt. Eng.* I. lvii. (1739) 104 Like a Vapour mounted up by the Clergy. **1705** tr. *Bosman's Guinea* 282 Mounting their Heads and half their Bodies above the surface of the Water. **1766** *Compl. Farmer* s.v. *Mulberry*, When they were quite divested of the side shoots, the sap is mounted to the top.

b. To erect. *Obs. rare.*

1610 SHAKS. *Temp.* II. ii. 11 Then like Hedg-hogs, which Lye tumbling in my bare-foote way, and mount Their pricks at my foot-fall. **1821** CLARE *Vill. Minstr.* II. 100 Water-lilies mount their snowy buds.

c. To direct to a higher point. *Obs.*

1582 STANYHURST *Æneis* II. (Arb.) 65 But father Anchises, mounting his sight to the skyward,.. hertly thus his orison vttred. **1675** tr. *Machiavelli's Prince* vi. (Rtldg.) 36 By mounting their arrow to a certain proportion, they may come nearer to the mark.

†**13.** In various *fig.* or non-material senses:

a. To raise in honour, estimation, power, or wealth. Rarely with *up*. *Obs.*

1581 *Satir. Poems Reform.* xliii. 103 So Fortoun montit neuer man on hicht, Bot sho can law him within a litill quhyle. *c* **1586** C'TESS PEMBROKE *Ps.* LXIX. xi, My God, me poore and low, High shall mount from need and woe. **1621** QUARLES *Esther* vi. Medit., Who mounts the meeke, and beates the lofty downe. **1647** N. BACON *Disc. Govt. Eng.* I. xvii. (1739) 34 This hath mounted up Kings to the top more than their own ambition. *a* **1661** FULLER *Worthies, Surrey* (1662) III. 83 Abbot.. was mounted from a Lecturer to a Dignitary. *a* **1711** KEN *Hymnotheo* Poet Wks. 1721 III. 29 Damning themselves, to mount him to his crown. **1728** YOUNG *Love Fame* I. 283 Is there whom his tenth epic mounts to fame?

b. To elevate spiritually; to raise to higher objects of contemplation; to excite to a higher degree of activity or emotion. *Obs.*

a **1546** G. WISHART tr. *Conf. Faith Sweuerland* in *Wodrow Soc. Misc.* (1844) 13 Except we be elluminat, styred up and mounted, by the grace of Chryst. **1591** SYLVESTER *Du Bartas* I. vii. 409 That we, down-treading earthly cogitations, May mount our thoughts to heav'nly meditations. **1601** SIR W. CORNWALLIS *Disc. Seneca* (1631) 80 There is no circumstance but is a steppe, mounting the understanding to the truth. **1601** SHAKS. *All's Well* I. i. 235 What power is it, which mounts my loue so hye. **1602** MARSTON *Ant. & Mel.* IV. Wks. 1856 I. 52 Young Prince, mount up your spirits, and prepare To solemnise your nuptials eve with pompe. **1636** HEYWOOD *Challenge Beautie* V. I 3, What prostrates them Mounts me to expectations. *a* **1644** QUARLES *Sol. Recant.* Sol. viii. 30 This mounts thy soule with more heroick fires. **1647** FULLER *Good Th. in Worse T.* v. viii. 214 May not man, by custome and improvement of Piety, mount himselfe neere to an Angelicall nature. **1742** YOUNG *Nt. Th.* IV. 262 Such contemplations.. should mount The mind still higher. **1796** BURKE *Regic. Peace* i. Wks. VIII. 157 They [William III's ministers] were not yet mounted to the elevation of the king.

c. To exalt, magnify. *Obs.*

1651 DAVENANT *Gondibert* III. v. 27 Love seeks no honor, but does honor bring, Mounts others value, and her own lets fall! **1673** MARVEL *Reh. Transp.* II. 244 If you would mount what is said to mean Conscience, the Clause does not.. exclude it.

d. To raise the value or price of. *Obs.*

1708 J. CHAMBERLAYNE *St. Gt. Brit.* II. III. ii. (1737) 402 James the IId.. mounted the Ounce of Silver to 12s. **1772** FOOTE *Nabob* II. (1778) 39 Suppose they have mounted the beef and mutton a trifle; ar'n't we obliged to them too for raising the value of boroughs?

e. To 'lift up' (the voice). *Obs.*

1601 ? MARSTON *Pasquil & Kath.* II. 13 Boy cleere thy throte, and mount thy sweetest notes. **1602** —— *Antonio's Rev.* v. iv, Why then Io to Hymen, mount a loftie note.

f. To represent as amounting *to* a certain sum or number. *Obs.*

1639 FULLER *Holy War* v. xxx. (1640) 284 Some have mounted his ordinarie yearly in-come to eight millions of gold. **1655** —— *Hist Camb.* 27 The Oxford Antiquary insulteth on the paucity of ancient Hostles in Cambridge.. much boasting of the numerousness of the Halls in Oxford, which he mounteth to above two hundred.

14. To set or place upon an elevation. Now only with const. *on, upon.*

1567 *Satir. Poems Reform.* vii. 43 To se ane monstuire, full of fylthynes, Abone the rest heich mountit vp in gloir. **1577** B. GOOGE *Heresbach's Husb.* I. (1586) 9. I haue set my house in this place without the bankes, and mounted it as hie as I could. **1590** GREENE *Orl. Fur.* (1599) A 3 b, From thence, mounted vpon a Spanish Barke Such as transported Iason to the fleece:..I furrowed Neptunes Seas. **1607** MARSTON *What you Will* II. ii, *Ped.* Sance delaies,..mount him, mount him! [i.e. 'horse' him for a flogging.] **1615** G. SANDYS *Trav.* 186 Mounted a good height on the side of the mountain is Aceldama. *c* **1662** *Roxb. Ball.* (1887) VI. 359 O the Pinacle of Shrowsbury shews itself still, For it's mounted gallantly on a high Hill. **1678** BUTLER *Hud.* III. ii. 972 For Chiarlatans can do no good, Until th' are mounted in a Crowd. **1683** *Condemn. & Exec. A. Sydney* 2 They.. Conveyed him to the Scaffold..on which being Mounted, he Bowed. *a* **1700** DRYDEN *Iliad* I. 239 We bear thee on our Backs and mount thee on the Throne. **1742** POPE *Dunc.* IV. 564 Gone ev'ry blush, and silent all reproach, Contending Princes mount them in their Coach. **1870** J. H. NEWMAN *Gram. Assent* II. vii. 222 No wonder we see more than the ancients, because we are mounted upon their shoulders. **1897** MARY KINGSLEY *W. Africa* 386 A cluster of outbuildings..each mounted on poles.

15. a. To set on horseback; to help into the saddle; also, to furnish with a saddle horse. In *passive*, to be seated on horseback.

1603 KNOLLES *Hist. Turks* (1638) 52 Isaac..royally mounted vpon one of the Emperors horses..was..brought ..to the court. *c* **1618** MORYSON *Itin.* IV. v. i. (1903) 438 Next rode some 400. gentlemen of Rome brauely mounted. **1647** W. BROWNE *Polex.* I. 199 He was..mounted on a Black Barbary. **1662** J. DAVIES tr. *Olearius' Voy. Ambass.* 202 He was..excellently well mounted, on a very gallant horse. **1678** BUTLER *Hud.* III. ii. 1547 He's mounted on a hazel bavin. **1697** DRYDEN *Æneid* VII. 381 Of these [horses] he chose the fairest and the best, To mount the Trojan troup. **1701** GREW *Cosm. Sacra* II. vii. 73 Phancy without Reason; is like a Horse without a Rider; and Reason without Phancy is not well Mounted. **1728** MORGAN *Algiers* II. iv. 283 He hastily mounted his own Wife and Daughter. **1774** GOLDSM. *Nat. Hist.* (1776) IV. 299 High enough to admit a man mounted upon a middle-sized horse. **1838** PRESCOTT *Ferd. & Isa.* II. xii. III. 131 He commanded that each trooper should take one of the infantry on his crupper, setting the example himself by mounting a German ensign behind him on his own horse. **1848** THACKERAY *Bk. Snobs* xxix, He.. rides when somebody mounts him. **1853** J. H. NEWMAN *Hist. Sk.* (1873) II. I. i. 11 These populations have in all ages been shepherds, mounted on horseback. **1877** 'RITA' *Vivienne* I. ii, Now mount me, please. It is time we were off. **1883** S. C. HALL *Retrospect* II. 305 He had horses more than enough to mount a regiment of cavalry.

b. Of a horse: To carry (its rider).

1737 BRACKEN *Farriery Impr.* (1757) II. 27 The hollowback Horse generally puts out a good Neck, and mounts the Rider handsomely.

16. *Mil.* **a.** To raise (guns) into position; to place in a position ready for use.

1539 in *Archæologia* XI. 437 A saker of brasse..mountyd uppon shod whelys. **1565** *Reg. Privy Council Scot.* I. 402 Propositioun wes maid of befoir..how all the artailyearie.. mycht be perfytlie montit, ordourit, and put in dowbill equippage. **1595** SHAKS. *John* II. i. 381 By East and West let France and England mount Their battering Canon charged to the mouthes. **1653** H. COGAN tr. *Pinto's Trav.* x. 33 The General..caused his forces to land, and mounting twelve great pieces he renewed the battery. *c* **1710** CELIA FIENNES *Diary* (1888) 215 The plattform for the Gunns w[ch] are well mounted and very well kept. **1838** PRESCOTT *Ferd. & Is.* II. xii. III. 131 On this rampart he mounted his little train of artillery.

b. Of a fort, a ship: To have (cannon) in position.

1748 *Anson's Voy.* III. v. 338 One is..an insignificant fortress, mounting only five guns eight pounders; the other ..fort mounts the same number of guns. **1831** SIR J. SINCLAIR *Corr.* II. 277 He met only four ships, three of which escaped, but one, mounting 64 guns, struck on a rock. **1841** ELPHINSTONE *Hist. Ind.* II. 207 He..sent out vessels mounting guns from Cambay.

c. *passive.* To be provided *with* cannon.

1662 J. DAVIES tr. *Olearius' Voy. Ambass.* 57 The Great Duke's Palace..is..very well mounted with Cannon. **1743** tr. *Mem. M. Du Gué-Trouin* (ed. 2) 14 The commadore, bored for 40 guns, and mounted by 28, was boarded and carried. **1748** *Anson's Voy.* III. x. 415 Four..junks,.. mounted only with eight or ten guns. **1867** H. LATHAM *Black & White* 104 Earthworks mounted with cannon.

d. To raise the muzzle of (a gun); to place at a particular angle of elevation. Cf. 12 c.

1545 *St. Papers Hen. VIII* (1834) III. 543 Item, in Crabbez, to mounte or level thOrdnaunce. **1669** STURMY *Mariner's Mag.* v. xii. 72 Find what deg. you shall need Mount the Gun to for any other shot. **1688** R. HOLME *Armoury* III. xviii. (Roxb.) 142/1 Mount the Morter, is to turne it in the carriage with the mouth vpwards. *Ibid.* xix. 153/1 Granadeers on Horseback... Vnsling your musket. Mount your musket. **1692** *Capt. Smith's Seaman's Gram.* II. xxxi. 146 To so many degrees of Mounture must the Morter be mounted. **1706** PHILLIPS (ed. Kersey), *To Mount a Piece*, ..to lay its Mouth higher.

e. To set up or post for the purpose of defence or observation. Hence, ***to mount (†the) guard***: to go on duty as a guard.

1706 PHILLIPS (ed. Kersey), *To Mount the Guard*,..is to go on that Duty. **1737** *Gentl. Mag.* VII. 538/2 The Nature of that Watch and Ward was, that each Burgher, for perhaps 5 or 6 Days in a Month, should mount Guard. **1764** *Mem. G. Psalmanazar* 161, I have seen many of them go up to the gallows..as if they were mounting the guard. **1781** GIBBON *Decl. & F.* xvii. (1787) II. 57 They mounted guard in the interior apartments. **1783** B. G. JACKSON *Orders* in *Harper's Mag.* Nov. (1883) 921/1 *note*, Each Battalion will mount a Piquett. **1826** SCOTT *Woodst.* iii, The yeomen of the guard, who mounted their watch there. **1872** *Punch* 21 Sept. 116/1 Let an intelligent policeman be told off to mount guard. **1894** *Outing* XXIV. 313/2 At this camp, guard was mounted twice a day.

absol. **1844** *Regul. & Ord. Army* 31 The Royal Standard.. is never to be carried by any Guard, except that which mounts on the Person of the Sovereign.

f. *transf.*

1843 DICKENS *Chr. Carol* iii, The two young Cratchits set chairs for everybody,..and mounting guard upon their posts [etc.]. **1884** RIDER HAGGARD *Dawn* xliii, Miss Terry mounted guard over the plates and dishes.

g. ***to mount an attack, offensive***, etc. Also *fig.*

1952 *N.Y. Times* 3 May 2/4 Striking at Communist targets in excellent flying weather (Thursday) warplanes of the Far East Air Forces mounted 1,283 sorties. **1957** *Times Lit. Suppl.* 20 Dec. 771/1 A British private-army leader would have mounted, or at least planned, an incessant series of operations. **1965** *Listener* 2 Sept. 334/1 Governments mount big campaigns to secure an 'incomes policy'. **1966** *Ibid.* 20 Oct. 579/2, I am mounting a devastating attack on the seriousness of the book. **1972** *Daily Mirror* 12 Oct. 1 An all-out attack is to be mounted against the porn-pushers in Britain's High Streets.

17. To set up or prepare for use. **a.** To fix in position for the accomplishment of a particular purpose; to put in working order. ***to mount a loom*** (see quot. 1831).

1712 J. JAMES tr. *Le Blond's Gardening* 81 The Semi-circle is mounted upon a Knee-Joint. **1763** *Museum Rust.* I. 160 When the scythe is mounted, from the point of the blade to the end of the long handle measures an angle of seven feet. **1831** G. R. PORTER *Silk Manuf.* 220 In mounting the loom —that is in fixing the warp preparatory to the commencement of actual weaving. **1839** URE *Dict. Arts* 817 A set of stamping and washing works..as mounted at Bockwiese. **1857** MILLER *Elem. Chem.* (1862) III. 898 The apparatus having been mounted, was caused to rotate. **1873** E. SPON *Workshop Receipts* Ser. I. 387/2 Marble workers mount and fasten their works upon plaster. **1895** *Outing* XXVI. 370/1 He mounted his rod, and tried casting in shallow water.

b. To set or place in or upon a mount or support; *spec.*, to fit a picture on or in a mount. Also, to fit with decorative appendages, as metal plates, ferrules, or the like.

1806 PIKE *Sources Mississ.* (1810) 84 A bear skin (the most beautiful I ever saw, which I wanted to mount a saddle). **1841** C. V. WALKER *Electrotype Manip.* I. 36 A method of mounting the medals obtained from the fusible moulds, which..enhances their value in the cabinet. **1859** GULLICK & TIMBS *Paint.* 302 The paste used for 'mounting' water-colour paintings. **1867** F. FRANCIS *Angling* x. (1880) 352 Most of the Findhorn flies are mounted in this way.

c. *Microscopy.* To fix (objects) upon a slide or in a cell for examination under a microscope. Also, to fit up (a microscope-slide) in this way.

1839 *Penny Cycl.* XV. 188/2 The objects should be mounted between spherical glasses. **1884** G. ALLEN *Philistia* I. 198 Looking up from the microscope slides she had begun to mount. **1885** HINDE in *Phil. Trans.* CLXXVI. 426 The spicules..when mounted in Canada balsam are nearly transparent.

d. To put (a play) on the stage; to adapt for exhibition by the provision of suitable accessories. Also, to put on or produce (a radio or television programme).

1870 *N.Y. Times* 11 Oct. 5/5 'The Two Roses' is..prettily mounted, and nicely, if not greatly acted. **1874** *Slang Dict.*, *Mount*, in theatrical parlance, to prepare for production on the stage. 'The piece was excellently mounted.' **1884** MALMESBURY in *Pall Mall G.* 11 Nov. 5/1 They 'mount' the events presented and the persons introduced very happily. **1962** *Listener* 10 May 808/1 It is the first town that approached us and asked us to mount a the festival. *Ibid.* 30 Aug. 328/1 His staff..mounted several brisk little propaganda numbers about social evils in Britain. *Ibid.* 20 Sept. 437/1 The Arts Council has mounted..an exhibition which has certain flaws. **1963** *Times* 8 Feb. 14/2 The production is mounted in the later Brechtian manner. **1971** *Daily Tel.* 2 Dec. 12 The BBC is scrapping normal programme schedules..during Christmas to enable it to mount special productions.

e. *slang.* To provide, 'set up'. ? *Obs.*

1775 D. GRAHAM *Lothian Tom* v. Writ. (1883) II. 79 The old woman bestowed a vast of presents on Tom, and mounted him like a gentleman.

18. a. To put on, assume, display oneself as wearing (some special article of costume).

1812 *Sporting Mag.* XXXIX. 239 A dashing buck having just mounted a fashionable great coat. **1815** W. IRVING in *Life & Lett.* (1864) I. 340, I expect he has mounted a pair of leather breeches, and is playing off the knowing one on the turf. **1842** S. LOVER *Handy Andy* xxi, It was time to..mount fresh linen and cambric. **1889** DOYLE *Micah Clarke* 138 Our friend was permitted to wear his gay trappings..without being suspected of having mounted the livery of Satan.

b. *transf.* ? Chiefly *U.S.*

1842 W. IRVING in *Life & Lett.* (1866) III. 211 My desire has been not to mount the Minister..until my arrival in Spain. **1884** *Harper's Mag.* Nov. 889/2 When rumor of bacteria..reached the vulgar ear, [she] had mounted the germ theory. **1894** G. MEREDITH *Ld. Ormont* iii, The reason why I mount red a little—if I do it—is, you mention Lord Ormont.

mountable ('maʊntəb(ə)l), *a.* [f. MOUNT *v.* + -ABLE.] Capable of being mounted or ascended.

a **1608** SIR F. VERE *Comm.* (1657) 38 [The rampier] was very mountable, and lay close to the old wall of the town. **1611** COTGR., *Montable*, mountable, ascendable, climable.

mountain ('maʊntɪn). Forms: 3 **monetain**, 3–5 **-a(i)n**, 3–6 **-ayn, mo(u)ntayne**, 4 **monteyne, -eine, muntayne**, 4–6 **mo(u)ntaigne, mounteyn, -ayn**, *Sc.* **montane**, 4–7 **mountaine**, 5 **-eyne, mowntan, -eyne, -ane**, (*pl.* **-aunce**), **montagne**, 5–6 *Sc.* **mountane, -ene**, 6 **-eine**, 8 *Sc. dial.* **muntain**, 4– **mountain.** [a. OF. *montaigne* (mod.F. *montagne*) = Pr., Pg. *montanha*, Sp. *montaña*, It. *montagna*:—popular L. **montānia*, **montānea* fem., mountain region; a use either of the fem. sing. (with ellipsis of *regio, terra*), or perh. orig. of the neut. pl. used absol., of **montāneus* pertaining to mountains (class. Latin has the parallel derivative *montānus*), f. *mont-em, mons* MOUNT *sb.*[1]]

I. The simple word.

1. a. A natural elevation of the earth's surface rising more or less abruptly from the surrounding level, and attaining an altitude which, relatively to adjacent elevations, is impressive or notable.

With regard to the modern limitation of use see also HILL *sb.*[1] Down to the 18th c. often applied to elevations of moderate altitude (cf. e.g. quots. 1766, 1773).

c **1205** LAY. 1282 Bi Ruscikadan heo nomen þa sæ & bi þe montaine of Azare. *a* **1300** *Cursor M.* 1776 Þe water wex oute ouer þe plains, þe bestes ran þan to monetains. *c* **1350** *Will. Palerne* 2619 Þe werwolf hem ladde ouer mures & muntaynes. *c* **1430** LYDG. *Min. Poems* (Percy Soc.) 24 Mistis blake..At whos uprist mounteyns be maade so feyre. **1523** LD. BERNERS *Froiss.* I. clxii. 198 They sawe a rowt of Englysshmen commynge downe a lytell mountayne a horse-backe. **1602** SHAKS. *Ham.* IV. i. 29 The Sun no sooner shall the Mountaines touch, But we will ship him hence. **1685** DRYDEN *Hor.* I. ix. 1 Behold yon mountain's hoary height Made higher with new mounts of snow. **1765** P. THICKNESSE *Observ. Customs Fr. Nation* 39 St. Germain [near Paris] is situated upon a very high mountain. **1773** G. WHITE *Selborne, Let. to Barrington* 9 Dec., That chain of majestic mountains [*sc.* the Sussex Downs]. **1799** KIRWAN *Geol. Ess.* v. 156 In common language, mountains are distinguished from hills only by annexing to them the idea of a superior height... Geologists have aimed at greater precision; Pini and Mitterpachter call any earthy elevation a mountain whose declivity makes with the horizon an angle of at least 13°, and whose perpendicular height is not less than ⅛ of the declivity. **1859** TENNYSON *Merlin & Vivien* 525 Writ in a language that has long gone by. So long, that mountains have arisen since With cities on their flanks. **1879** GEIKIE in *Encycl. Brit.* X. 258 Mountains formed in the volcanic way are almost always conical.

b. ***cat of the mountain***: see CATAMOUNTAIN.

1432–50 tr. *Higden* (Rolls) III. 123 A catte of þe mowntaunce.

c. In allusions to a well-known story of Muhammad told by Bacon *Ess.* xii. (*Boldness*): see MAHOMET 1 (quot. 1625).

1642 OWEN *Display Armin.* viii. (1643) 85 If the mountaine will not come to Mahomet, Mahomet will goe to the mountaine. [The allusion is still proverbially current.]

d. *poet.* Used in *pl.* as the type of a region remote from civilization.

1601 SHAKS. *Twel. N.* IV. i. 52 Fit for the Mountaines, and the barbarous Caues, Where manners nere were preach'd. *a* **1645** WALLER *Palamede to Zelinde* 19 Great Iulius, on the Mountaines bred, A flock perhaps or herd had led.

e. *Anglo-Irish.* (See quot.)

1834 *Brit. Husb.* I. 30 (*Ireland*) Large tracts are in what is there called 'mountain'; but the term is applied to all waste land on which young cattle and sheep are fed until they are fit to be sent into the richer pastures.

f. ***mountains high***: said hyperbolically of waves. Cf. *mountain-high* (7 c below).

1719 DE FOE *Crusoe* (Globe) 9 The Sea went Mountains high. **1726** SHELVOCKE *Voy. round World* (1757) 187 Where the sea breaks mountains-high, if I may use that sea phrase. **1878** HUXLEY *Physiogr.* 172 It is not uncommon to hear of the sea running 'mountains high'; yet..the height of a wave ..rarely exceeds 40 ft.

†g. Applied to an artificial hill or tumulus of great size. *Obs.*

1568 GRAFTON *Chron.* II. 584 The Lorde Talbot.. enuironed the towne of Depe, with depe trenches, and great mountaynes. **1590** WEBBE *Trav.* (Arb.) 32 There [within sixe miles of the Gran Caer] are seauen Mountaines builded on the out side, like vnto ye point of a Diamond, which Mountaines were builded in King Pharoes time for to keepe Corne in, and they are Mountaines of great strength. **1636** E. DACRES tr. *Machiavel's Disc. Livy* 423 They made towres of wood, or cast up mountaines of earth, which leaned upon the wall on the outside.

†h. *Her.* = MOUNT *sb.*[1] 1 b. *Obs.*

1610 GUILLIM *Heraldry* III. iv. (1611) 96 The Field is Or, a Mountaine Azure, inflamed proper.

2. *transf.* **a.** A huge heap or pile; a towering mass. †***mountain of ice*** = ICEBERG.

c **1450** *Merlin* 333 The mounteins of bodyes were a-boute hem so grete that noon myght come to hem but launchinge. **1590** SHAKS. *Com. Err.* IV. iv. 158 But for the Mountaine of mad flesh that claimes mariage of me, I could finde in my heart to stay heere still. **1613** PURCHAS *Pilgrimage* (1614) 740 The entrance..was barred with Mountaines of Ice. **1698** FRYER *Acc. E. India & P.* 157 Mountains of Fish salted on the Beach. **1830** MACAULAY in *Life & Lett.* (1880) I. 157 We have oceans of beer, and mountains of potatoes, for dinner. **1855** ORR *Geol.* 3 In the cold seas,..blue mountains of ice..are every day broken off.

b. (transl. of Norw. *berg*.) A 'swarm' (of fish).

1880 *Daily News* 30 Sept. 5/3 The mountain consists of banks of fish escorted and driven in by whales. **1883** HUXLEY in *Standard* 19 June 3/2 The codfish formed what was called a cod's mountain of from 120 ft. to 180 ft. deep.

c. A stockpile, a surplus.

1969 *Times* 10 Sept. 11/4 In Germany..they are beginning to resent it [*sc.* the price for protection], as the sardonic remarks in the supermarkets about the 'Butter Mountain' reveal. **1974** *Daily Tel.* 5 Feb. 2/4 It is intervention buying that leads to the creation of the Common Market's notorious commodity 'mountains'. **1974** *Times* 1 May 4/7 Measures designed to disperse the Community's growing beef surpluses. The beef mountain now stands at more than 70,000 tons. **1975** *Times* 7 Feb. 4/8 The prospect of a 'cheese mountain' in the EEC.

3. *fig.* **a.** A quantity or amount impressive by its vast proportions.

1592 *Conspir. Pretended Ref.* 94 Entertayning the said twelue persons with mountaines of large promises. **1623** BINGHAM *Xenophon* 111 They heard, that all that followed Cyrus gathered mountaines of wealth. **1771** *Junius Lett.* xlix. (1820) 253 The favour of a king can remove mountains of infamy. **1894** PARRY *Stud. Gt. Composers, Beethoven* 171 The word 'memory' carries a mountain of meaning.

b. ***to make a mountain (out) of a molehill***: see MOLEHILL 2.

4. ***mountain of piety*** = ***mount of piety*** (see MOUNT *sb.*[1] 5 b.). Now *jocular*, in allusion to the Fr. or Italian term.

1617 MORYSON *Itin.* I. 93 A house called the mountaine of piety, where poore men may borrow money freely, bringing pawnes. **1797** W. JOHNSTON tr. *Beckmann's Invent.* III. 18 The Pope declared the holy mountains of piety..to be legal. **1891** *Daily News* 15 Apr. 7/1 You had to resort to what is called 'climbing the mountain of piety'?..Yes, I had to pledge nearly all my jewellery.

5. (In full ***mountain wine***.) A variety of Malaga wine, made from grapes grown on the mountains.

1710 *Lond. Gaz.* No. 4782/3 There is also good Mountain ..to be Retaled at 6*s.* 6*d.* per Gallon. **1730** FIELDING *Rape upon Rape* IV. vi, Women love white best.—Boy, bring half a pint of mountain. **1744** BERKELEY *Siris* §115 A spoonful of mountain-wine in each glass. **1833** REDDING *Mod. Wines* (1851) 201 Very little old Mountain or Malaga sweet wine is grown at present.

6. ***the Mountain*** [Fr. *la Montagne*]: an extreme party led by Robespierre and Danton in the first French Revolution, from the fact that it occupied the most elevated position in the chamber of assembly.

The term was also applied in England to an extreme party in parliament at the close of the 18th and beginning of the 19th c., and was revived in France *c* 1848 to describe the extreme republican party of that epoch. In England also applied to a group of Conservatives at the beginning of the 20th c.

[**1792** *Pref. Explan. New Terms* in *Ann. Reg.* p. xii, The *Mountain*. The higher or most elevated seats in the hall of the Assembly; occupied by the violent revolutionists, or democrats.] **1827** SCOTT *Napoleon* Introd., Wks. 1870 IX. 295 They were..deputies of the Mountain gang. **1829** H. HARDINGE *Let.* 19 June in C. Arbuthnot *Corr.* (1941) 116 It would, if true, keep the high Whigs disunited from the Mountain, & assist our union with our old Tory party. **1839** ALISON *Hist. Europe* (1847) XIII. 35 The Jacobins [occupied] the seats on the summit of the left; whence their designation of 'The Mountain' was derived. **1848** BP. S. WILBERFORCE in R. G. Wilberforce *Life* (1881) II. 11 The high 'Mountain' party attended in force [a meeting of the National Society] on a summons sent round by Mr. G. Denison. **1880** DISRAELI *Endym.* lxxvi, There is this difference between the English Mountain and the French. The English Mountain has its government prepared. **1965** E. FELLOWES in *Political Q.* XXXVI. 257 Among the Supporters of the Government [in the Parliament of 1918] was the National Party led by Sir Henry Page-Croft, and a group of Conservative backbenchers (the 'Mountain'), not so formally organised, but working in concert... This..group in fact often proved a more successful opposition than the Labour and Liberal parties, who shared the Opposition front bench.

II. *attrib.* and *Comb.* (and quasi-*adj.*).

7. a. Simple *attrib.*, as ***mountain breast, brow, -echo, foot, head, pass, peak, slope, top, -wreath***. Also appositive, as ***mountain-barrier, -island, -wall***.

1742 YOUNG *Nt. Th.* IV. 726 Death's terror is the mountain faith removes; That *mountain barrier between man and peace. **1876** G. W. COX *Gen. Hist. Greece* II. i. 102 The chain of Tauros..extends its huge mountain-barrier to the north of the Kilikian country. **1810** SCOTT *Lady of L.* VI. xxvii, As wreath of snow on *mountain-breast, Slides from the rock that gave it rest. **1728–46** THOMSON *Spring* 829 The *mountain-brow, Where sits the shepherd. **1805–6** WORDSWORTH *Prelude* (1959) I. 390 Not without the voice Of *mountain-echoes did my Boat move on. **1591** SHAKS. *Two Gent.* V. ii. 46 The rising of the *Mountaine foote That leads toward Mantua. **1844** MRS. BROWNING *Brown Rosary* II. Poems 1850 II. 28, I saw his steed on *mountain-head, I heard it on the plain. **1871** MORRIS in Mackail *Life* (1899) I. 247 A hog-backed steep *mountain-island. **1830** SCOTT *Macduff's Cross* Prel. 5 The summit of this *mountain pass. **1834** *Penny Cycl.* II. 470/1 The highest *mountain peak in this country. **1841** THOREAU *Jrnl.* 4 Mar. in *Writings* (1906) VII. 228 Their way is a *mountain slope, a river valley's course. **1930** A. CLARKE *Coll. Plays* (1963) 63 To look across Kildare in sun and know The far flocks move along the mountain slope. **1593** SHAKS. *2 Hen. VI*, III. ii. 336 Well could I curse away a Winters night, Though standing naked on a *Mountaine top. **1816** WORDSW. *2nd Ode Battle of Waterloo*, Like mountain-tops whose mists have rolled away. **1849** J. FORBES *Physic. Holiday* xv. (1850) 134 The *mountain-walls of it [*sc.* the valley] are very precipitous. **1871** MORRIS in Mackail *Life* (1899) I. 256 The great mountain-wall closes up the valley. **1928** BLUNDEN *Retreat* 70 Warm furze-perfume, stern *mountain-wreath Of pines.

b. objective, as ***mountain-climbing, -making; mountain-cresting, -loving, -walking*** adjs.; ***mountain-climber***.

1880 'MARK TWAIN' *Tramp Abroad* xxxvi. 375 We were in the..home of the *mountain-climbers. **1872** JENKINSON *Guide Eng. Lakes* (1879) Introd., The lover of natural scenery and of *mountain-climbing. **1951** S. SPENDER *World within World* iii. 179 Then we came to that extraordinary river-encircled, *mountain-cresting city of Toledo. **1621** SANDYS *Ovid's Met.* I. (1632) 7 Where *Mountaine-louing Goats did lately graze. **1810** SCOTT *Lady of L.* VI. iii, The mountain-loving Switzer. **1886** A. WINCHELL *Walks Geol. Field* 117 *Mountain-making may be another incident of the earth's contraction. **1821** SHELLEY *Let.* 22 Oct. (1964) II. 361, I..raised a small turf altar to the *mountain-walking Pan.

c. similative, as ***mountain-clear, -cool, -high, -like***, adjs. and advs.; parasynthetic, as ***mountain-bellied, -headed, -sized*** adjs.

1654 GATAKER *Disc. Apol.* 67 That more eminent *mountain-bellied..Proteus. **1955** P. LARKIN *Less Deceived* 36 Their visions *mountain-clear. **1919** A. HUXLEY *Leda* (1920) 1 Brown and bright as an agate, *mountain-cool. **1925** BLUNDEN *Eng. Poems* 104 O firmament, O *mountain-headed march Of clouds through that blue arch. **1693** T. POWER in *Dryden's Juvenal* XII. (1697) 313 High, *Mountain-high, be pil'd the shining Ore. **1815** MRS. PILKINGTON *Celebrity* III. 114 At one moment the vessel was elevated mountain high. **1851** THORPE *North. Mythol.* I. 68 He struck its [the Midgard serpent's] mountain-high head with his hammer. **1719** DE FOE *Crusoe* I. 50 A raging Wave, *Mountain-like, came rowling a-stern of us. **1868** BROWNING *Ring & Bk.* I. III. 1322 Oh mouse-birth of that mountain-like revenge! **1839** BAILEY *Festus* ix. (1852) 111 In form and stature they are *mountain-sized.

d. locative, as ***mountain battle, -journey*** sbs.; ***mountain-built, dwelling*** adjs.

a **1835** MRS. HEMANS *Spells of Home* 28 The *mountain battles of his land. **1819** KEATS *Ode Grecian Urn* 35 What little town..*mountain-built with peaceful citadel. **1603** FLORIO *Montaigne* III. xiii. 646 Will any beleeve..that milke or whit-meates are hurtfull vnto a *mountaine-dwelling people? **1837** W. IRVING *Capt. Bonneville* I. 158 In the course of this *mountain-journey.

e. instrumental, as ***mountain-bound, -circled, -cradled, -echoed, -girdled, -guarded, -roofed, -sheltered, -walled*** adjs.

1860 G. M. HOPKINS *Poems* (1967) 3 There is a massy pile above the waste Amongst Castilian barrens mountain-bound. **1858** O. W. HOLMES *Aut. Breakf.-t.* x. (1895) 248 The mountain-circled green of Grafton. **1954** W. FAULKNER *Fable* 158 That thirty-mile-long mountain-cradled saucer. **1860** G. M. HOPKINS *Poems* (1967) 6 Then pass'd the wind, and sobb'd with mountain-echo'd woe. **1859** HAWTHORNE *Fr. & It. Note-Bks.* II. 261 A vast mountain-girdled plain. **1939** BELLOC *Decameron* in *Tablet* 11 Feb. 166/2 Mountain-guarded gardens. **1937** BLUNDEN *Elegy* 90 The rough walls back to Chaucer reach, Near windowless, mountain-roofed, wry-angled. **1924** W. J. LOCKE *Coming of Amos* xiii. 169 A coast of romantic mountain-sheltered creeks. **1897** MARY KINGSLEY *W. Africa* 180 We seem to be in a mountain-walled lake.

8. *attrib.* passing into adj., with the senses:

a. Of, or belonging to mountains; situated in or on mountains; consisting of mountains.

1807 SOUTHEY *Lett. from Eng.* II. xli. 201 The *mountain air had made us almost ravenous. **1810** E. WEETON *Let.* 11–15 Nov. (1969) I. 314 The keen mountain air had sharpened our appetites. **1865** ALLINGHAM *Among the Heather* ii, Your mountain air is sweet. **1965** *Listener* 30 Dec. 1063/1 The notes of *Colonel Bogey*, played by a military band.., sounding so clearly in the crystalline mountain air. **1808** ELEANOR SLEATH *Bristol Heiress* V. 207 A *mountain-beck, or brook. **1801** SCOTT *Eve St. John* xv, The *mountain-blast was still. **1730–46** THOMSON *Autumn* 409 The mazes of the *mountain brook. **1817** BYRON *Manfred* III. i. 109 The *mountain-cataract. *c* **1380** WYCLIF *Serm.* Sel. Wks. II. 9 Marie..wente into *monteyne contre wiþ haste. **1577–87** HOLINSHED *Chron.* I. 170/2 The pleasant mountaine-countrie of Belsham. **1726** POPE *Odyss.* XIX. 621 The bird of Jove Fierce from his *mountain-eyrie downward drove. **1837** YOUATT *Sheep* vii. 294 The time for shearing, in a *mountain-farm, is of considerable importance. **1860** PUSEY *Min. Proph.* 181 A *mountain fastness in a rich valley. **1776** G. SEMPLE *Building in Water* 59 Sudden *Mountain Floods. **1813** SCOTT *Rokeby* IV. vi, [He] bore them to his *mountain-hold. **1827** G. DARLEY *Sylvia* 25 Cyclops' *mountain-home. **1833** *Penny Cycl.* I. 433/1 The *mountain-masses in North America. **1812** BYRON *Ch. Har.* II. xxxvi, We have many a *mountain-path to tread. **1821** tr. *Decandolle & Sprengel's Elem. Philos. Plants* IV. v. 281 From the high *mountain plains of central Asia. **1833** *Penny Cycl.* I. 182/1 The *mountain regions of the Atlas. **1895** R. HORSLEY in *Yng. England* XVI. 18/1 Up the steep *mountain road they went. **1922** W. G. KENDREW *Climates of Continents* xxvii. 188 There are almost constant north-west winds, strongest where there is no *mountain shelter. **1611** SHAKS. *Cymb.* III. iii. 10 Now for our *Mountaine sport. **1816** H. G. KNIGHT *Ilderim* 275 Where ..*mountain stream and mountain turf was found. **1802** COLERIDGE *Dejection* 100 Bare crag, or *mountain-tairn, or blasted tree. **1814** SCOTT *Ld. of Isles* VI. xxiv, They come like *mountain-torrent red. **1610** SHAKS. *Temp.* I. ii. 499 As free As *mountaine windes.

b. Born in or inhabiting mountains; having (one's) abode in mountains; coming from the mountains; native of a mountain region.

1812 BYRON *Ch. Har.* II. xlvii, Yet here and there some daring *mountain-band Disdain his power. **1725** POPE *Odyss.* IX. 347 He..devours it like a *mountain beast. **1591** FRAUNCE *C'tess Pembr. Yvychurch* I. II. i, This *Mountaine-byrd, Montanus daughter. *c* **1700** CONGREVE *Homer's Hymn Venus* 10 She [Diana] loves..To wound the *Mountain Boar. **1808** SCOTT *Marm.* II. Introd., The mountain-boar on battle set. **1777** HAMILTON *Wks.* (1886) VII. 522 Nixon's brigades, and Colonel Warner's *mountain boys. *c* **1614** MURE *Dido & Æneas* II. 300 *Montaine Faryes did bewaile the chance. **1599** SHAKS. *Hen. V*, IV. iv. 20 Thou damned and luxurious *Mountaine Goat. **1604** E. G[RIMSTONE] *D'Acosta's Hist. Indies* IV. xlii. 324 The mountaine goates, which are nourished and fed vpon poison. **1831** *Sutherland Farm Rep.* 80 in *Libr. Usef. Knowl., Husb.* III, The sweetest of the *mountain-grass. **1720** GAY *Rur. Sports* 355 Nor shall the *mountain lark the muse detain. **1601** R. JOHNSON *Kingd. & Commw.* (1603) 7 The *mountaine men cannot live any long time without..trafficke with the men of the plaine countrey. **1755** SMOLLETT *Quix.* (1803) I. 238 The leaves of these *mountain-oaks. **1881** *Harper's Mag.* Nov. 868/2 They are poor *mountain people. **1596** SHAKS. *Merch. V.* IV. i. 75 You may as well forbid the *Mountaine Pines To wagge their high tops. **1814** WORDSW. *Excurs.* VII. 181 Long enduring *mountain-plants. **1697** DRYDEN *Virg. Georg.* III. 621 Thy faithful Dogs..who..hold at Bay The *Mountain Robbers. **1809** BYRON *Bards & Rev.* 155 While *mountain spirits prate to river sprites. **1599** SHAKS. *Hen. V*, V. i. 37 You call'd me yesterday *Mountaine-Squier. **1693** CONGREVE *Old Bach.* IV. xxii, Thou hast the heart of a *mountain-tiger. **1845** KITTO *Cycl. Bibl. Lit.* (1849) I. 247/1 The Kenites, a *mountain tribe on the east side of Jordan. **1617** DRUMM. OF HAWTH. *Forth Feasting* A 4, To pearce the *mountaine Wolf with feathred Dart.

c. Used in the mountains.

1848 tr. *Hoffmeister's Trav. Ceylon*, etc. iii. 153 In the most extraordinary costumes,..hats of basket-work plait, 'leechstockings,'..and over these a sort of mountain shoes. **1849** F. PARKMAN *Calif. & Oregon Trail* 145 Though aided by the high-bowed 'mountain-saddle' I could scarcely keep my seat on horseback. **1867** W. H. DIXON *New Amer.* (ed. 6) I. 170, I had the honour of riding in the mountain wagon with an old road-agent. **1897** *Outing* XXX. 135/2 The mountain-chaises and the stage-coaches. **1900** CROCKETT *Fitting of Peats* vi. Love Idylls (1901) 38 Behind a red-bodied mountain cart. **1906** *Macm. Mag.* Apr. 457 A courteous constable, who kindly procured me a mountain-chair.

d. Resembling a mountain; huge, enormous. With ***mountain-mass*** cf. quot. 1833 in sense 8 a.

1693 DRYDEN *Juvenal* x. (1697) 269 Sporus..nor crooked was, nor lame With *mountain Back. **1887** STEVENSON *Misadv. J. Nicholson* ii, The *mountain bulk of his misfortunes. **1798** COLERIDGE *Fears in Solitude* 184 Thy lakes and *mountain hills. **1816** BYRON *Ch. Har.* III. lxvii, The high, the *mountain-majesty of worth. **1918** A. HUXLEY *Defeat of Youth* 21 Soon will they lift towards the summer sky Their *mountain-mass of clotted greenery. **1795** FAWCETT *Art of War* 47 Smite *Mountain-mischief, Evil's mightier fiend. **1656** COWLEY *Pindar. Odes, Life & Fame* ii, Some build enormous *Mountain-Palaces. **1696** TATE & BRADY *Ps.* lxxxviii. 7 Me all thy *Mountain Waves have press'd.

9. a. Special comb.: **mountain artillery**, light ordnance for use in mountainous countries; **mountain barometer**, a barometer adapted for measuring the heights of mountains (Ogilvie *Suppl.* 1855); **mountain battery**, a battery of light guns capable of being transported in hilly country on the backs of mules; **mountain-building**, the formation of mountains, esp. as a result of folding and thrusting of the earth's crust; **mountain chain**, a connected series of mountains, esp. an aggregate of ranges of mountains having a common geographical relation; **mountain cross** *Her.*, a plain cross humetty (Berry *Encycl. Her.* I. 1828–40); **mountain cure**, the cure of disease (esp. of a tuberculous character) by residence in the rarefied atmosphere of high elevations; **mountain Damara**: see DAMARA; **mountain dew**, Scotch whisky; also used for other, esp. home-made or illicit, whiskies; **mountain fever**, a name loosely applied to malarial or typhoid fevers contracted in mountain regions; **mountain-folding**, the formation of mountains as a result of folding of the earth's crust; †**mountain folks**, a designation of the Scottish Cameronians; **mountain guide**, one whose local knowledge enables him to act as a guide amongst mountains; *spec.* a person specially trained to act as guide in dangerous mountain ascents; **mountain-gun, -howitzer**, a gun or howitzer specially adapted for use in a mountainous country; **mountain land**, in Ireland and New England, wild unenclosed pasture, frequently on the slopes of hills; **mountain man**, (*a*) *pl.* = *mountain folk*; (*b*) *U.S.* a trapper; (*c*) *fig.* = PIONEER *sb.* 3; **mountain oyster** = *lamb's fry* (LAMB *sb.* 7); **mountain railway**, (*a*) a light railway for transport in mountain regions; (*b*) a miniature ascending railway designed for amusement; a scenic railway; a funiculaire; **mountain range**, a series of mountains ranged in a line, and connected by elevated ground; **mountain-schooner**, a wagon used in mountainous country; **mountain-sick** *a.*, suffering from mountain sickness; **mountain sickness**, a malady caused by breathing the rarefied air of mountain heights; **mountain slide**, a landslip occurring on a mountain side;

mountain spectre, a reflection (of persons or things) seen under certain conditions on a mountain (cf. BROCKEN); **mountain (standard) time** *N. Amer.*, 'the time of the seventh time zone west of Greenwich based on the 105th meridian and used in west central Canada and the U.S.' (Webster 1961); **mountain system**, a group of mountain ranges showing similarity in form, orientation, etc., and assumed to be due to the same general causes; **mountain wine** (see 5 above).

1860 *Chamb. Encycl.* I. 455/1 There are several kinds of equipments of Light Artillery, under the names of horse, field, rocket, *mountain, and reserve. **1875** *Encycl. Brit.* III. 443/1 In *mountain and position batteries both gunners and drivers usually walk. **1871** J. D. Whitney in *N. Amer. Rev.* CXIII. 238 We cannot separate the phenomena of volcanoes and earthquakes from those of *mountain-building and continental growth. **1919** *Jrnl. Geol.* XXVII. 250 Only moderate igneous activity was associated with the mountain building. **1944** J. S. Huxley *On Living in Revolution* p. vii, Periods of mountain-building accompanied by the emergence of more land from the sea. **1971** I. G. Gass et al. *Understanding Earth* i. 26/2 Andesites are typical of the world's greatest volcanoes lying in zones of active mountain building. **1821** tr. *Decandolle & Sprengel's Elem. Philos. Plants* IV. v. 281 When a particular *mountain chain stretches into the level country beneath it, its peculiar plants will also appear in the low land. **1876** Tollemache in *Fortn. Rev.* Mar. 340 Very many invalids seek the *mountain-cure. **1816** Scott *Old Mort.* Introd., A pleasing..liquor, which was vended..under the name of **mountain dew.* **1855** [Burn] *Autobiog. of Beggar Boy* x. (1859) 153 The exhilarating fumes of mountain dew, vulgarly called whisky toddy. **1899** R. L. Taylor in B. A. Botkin *Treas. Amer. Folklore* (1944) III. 411 They gathered there on rainy days to talk politics and religion, and to drink 'mountain' dew and fight. **1945** Baker *Austral. Lang.* ix. 168 Illicit whisky, as made in stills in bush areas, is known as *mountain dew.* This is a variation of the Standard English use of the term for genuine Scotch whisky. It is also used in America. **1970** *Times* 15 Oct. 30/3 The distilled spirits industry..wages an expensive propaganda campaign against..mountain dew. **1849** O. W. Lipe *Let.* 15 Aug. in R. P. Bieber *Southern Trails to Calif. in 1849* (1937) 346 There has been much sickness in our company; the disease is *mountain fever. **1875** tr. *von Ziemmsen's Cycl. Med.* II. 567 Whether similar conditions will be found to exist, explaining the origin of 'mountain fever'..is not yet determined. *a* **1918** G. Stuart *40 Yrs. on Frontier* (1925) I. 51 A severe attack of mountain fever..laid me on my back in the wagon. **1970** *Islander* (Victoria, B.C.) 10 May 7/1 An epidemic of mountain fever struck the Kootenays in 1884. **1925** J. Joly *Surface-Hist. Earth* 170 The effects of these conditions on *mountain-folding would probably be principally experienced where the geosynclines had forced the continental materials deep into the magma. **1971** *Geogr. Abstr.* A. 445 (*heading*) Fundamental principles of the development of collapses and slips in mountain-folding regions. **1713** Wodrow *Corr.* (1843) I. 520 The *mountain folks, as they were called, who did not join in hearing till they gave in a written testimony against the indulgence, hearing conformists [etc.]. **1810** Scott *Lady of L.* II. vi, With a trusty *mountain-guide. **1881** *Instr. Census Clerks* (1885) 31 Mountain Guide. **1904** *Blackw. Mag.* Feb. 183/1 In still denser dust swing by the *mountain-guns. **1812** Byron *Ch. Har.* I. li, The *mountain-howitzer, the broken road,..Portend the deeds to come. **1667** in *10th Rep. Hist. MSS. Comm.* App. v. 39 Barren *mountaine lands, not worth six pence an acre yearely. **1797** J. A. Graham *Pres. St. Vermont* 166 There is much Mountain land in these districts. **1691** J. Howie in *Collect. Dying Test.* (1806) 19, I testify against those that were called '*Mountain-men'. **1781** *Calendar Virginia State Papers* (1875) I. 494 A late pressing application of General Greene for the aid of the Mountain Men. **1851** Mayne Reid *Scalp Hunt.* xx, These were the trappers, the prairie hunters, the mountain men. **1973** R. D. Symons *Where Wagon Led* I. vii. 117 In the United States the 'Mountain Men',—beaver trappers mostly—penetrated the western wilderness at an early date, before and during the middle years of the last century. **1973** *Sci. Amer.* Aug. 113/1 Professor Luria is an authentic pioneer of molecular biology. Even before the first wagon train set out he ventured as a mountain man among bacterial viruses. **1890** *Cent. Dict.* s.v. *Oyster*, **Mountain-oyster*, a lamb's testicle. **1951** E. Paul *Springtime in Paris* xi. 189, I have consumed mountain oysters and prairie dancers that are actually poetic. **1962** *Alberta Hist. Rev.* Autumn 15/2 In the commissariat department [are] 'dope' (butter)... 'Mountain oysters' (calves fries). **1880** 'Mark Twain' *Tramp Abroad* xxviii. 256, I..in the distance detected a long worm of black smoke crawling lazily up the steep mountain. Of course that was the locomotive...we had never seen a *mountain railway yet. **1898** *Daily News* 22 Nov. 5/1 The mountain railway reaches an elevation of nearly five thousand feet. **1910** *Penny Guide Japan-Brit. Exhib.* 23 Mountain Railway. The visitor enters the cars which travel slowly round and upward until the top of the mountain range is reached. **1925** A. Huxley *Those Barren Leaves* II. iii. 106 The switchback, the water-shoot and the mountain railway. **1831** M. Russell *Egypt* xi. §1 (1832) 470 The alluvial soil of valleys near a *mountain-range. **1869** C. L. Brace *New West* xiv. 188 It is more than a hundred miles away from the first link with civilization, and yet coaches, wagons, and the stream of '*mountain-schooners' pour into it unceasingly. **1937** *Discovery* June 171/1 People have been very *mountain-sick at this hut. **1848** tr. *Hoffmeister's Trav. Ceylon*, etc. x. 351 The feelings of indisposition caused by the **mountain sickness.* **1897** *Allbutt's Syst. Med.* III. 456 The supposition,..of heart failure as a cause of mountain-sickness. **1830** *Mass. Spy* 25 Aug. (Th.), *Mountain slides. **1886** A. Winchell *Walks Geol. Field* 106 Mountain-slides ..sometimes occasion genuine earthquake tremours. **1880** *Encycl. Brit.* XI. 399/2 *Mountain spectres are caused by reflexion, and often appear accompanied by chromatic halos. **1935** *World Almanac* (ed. 50) 115/2 *Mountain Standard Time is the local time of the 105th meridian. **1968** *Globe & Mail* (Toronto) 5 Feb. 22/8 Sealed tenders..will be received up to 2 o'clock P.M. Mountain Standard Time. **1882** A. Geikie *Text-bk. Geol.* 918 The Alps offer an instructive example of a great *mountain system formed by repeated movements during a long succession of geological periods. **1931** C. M. Nevin *Princ. Struct. Geol.* xi. 289 A mountain system is characterized by folding, faulting, and igneous activities that vary in their complexity and relative importance throughout the zone of deformation. **1953** *Q. Jrnl. Geol. Soc.* CVIII. 2 The great mountain systems, or orogens, are zones of extreme compression of the earth's crust weaving a complex pattern of majestic sweeps around the world. **1968** R. A. Lyttleton *Mysteries Solar Syst.* iii. 91 It can be expected that mountain-systems will have formed on Venus comparable with those on Earth. **1891** *Cent. Dict.* s.v. *Time*[1] 19, The time of the 105th meridian (called **mountain time*). **1952** B. Malamud *Natural* 12 It looked around half-past five, but he couldn't be sure because somewhere near they left Mountain Time.

b. In the names of minerals and mineral substances, etc. [chiefly after G. compounds of *berg-*]: †**mountain blue** [after G. *bergblau*], a native carbonate of copper; **mountain butter** (tr. G. *bergbutter*, A. G. Werner 1789) = ALUNOGEN; **mountain cork, flesh, leather, paper, wood** (also MOUNTAIN FLAX 2), descriptive names for varieties of asbestos; **mountain crystal** = ROCK-CRYSTAL; **mountain flour, meal** (tr. G. *bergmehl*), (*a*) a recent freshwater deposit consisting of the siliceous frustules of diatoms; (*b*) a white cotton-like variety of calcite occurring as an efflorescence on rocks; **mountain limestone** *Geol.*, a thick massive limestone belonging to the Carboniferous series; **mountain milk** (see quot.); †**mountain mine**, epithet applied to the group of rocks forming the lower coal measures; †**mountain pitch**, a kind of native bitumen; **mountain soap** (G. *bergseife*, A. G. Werner 1780), a kind of bole of a blackish colour; **mountain tallow** = HATCHETTITE (Crabb *Tech. Dict.* 1823); †**mountain tar** = PISSASPHALT; †**mountain yellow** [after G. *berggelb*], yellow ochre; hence as the name of a colour.

1801 *Encycl. Brit.* Suppl. II. 237/1 Earthy blue carbonat. **Mountain blue.* **1796** Kirwan *Elem. Min.* (ed. 2) I. 163 *Mountain cork. **1753** Chambers *Cycl. Supp.* s.v. *Milk*, The internal use..of calcin'd *mountain crystals, in powder. **1796** Kirwan *Elem. Min.* (ed. 2) I. 241 Mountain or Rock Crystal. **1883** *Encycl. Brit.* XVI. 418/1 Structure [of Pilolite] varies considerably, and has given rise to trivial names, as ..*mountain flesh..&c. **1861** *Chamb. Encycl.* II. 49/1 *Bergmehl*, or **mountain-flour*, is a recent deposit of a white or cream-coloured powder. **1796** Kirwan *Elem. Min.* (ed. 2) I. 163 It is found..in thin flat pieces, then called *mountain leather, or paper. **1819** Brande *Man. Chem.* 517 The banks of the Avon too, in the vicinity of Chepstow, are of *mountain limestone. **1865** Lyell *Elem. Geol.* 513 Crinoidea are also common in the Mountain Lime-stone. **1823** W. Phillips *Introd. Min.* (ed. 3) 54 *Mountain-meal. Bergmehl. **1876** Goode *Anim. Resources U.S.* 66 'Mountain meal', a kind of infusorial earth, mixed with flour, and used as food in Lapland and China. **1842** Brande *Dict. Sci.* etc., **Mountain milk*, a very soft spongy variety of carbonate of lime. **1855** J. Phillips *Man. Geol.* 184 The lower coal measures or '*mountain mine' group. **1796** *Mountain paper [see *mountain-leather*]. **1883** *Encycl. Brit.* XVI. 418/1 Mountain Paper occurs in thin sheets at Boyne Castle near Banff. **1797** Hatchett in *Nicholson's Jrnl.* (1799) II. 203 Mineral Tar, Bitumen Petroleum tarde fluens..*Mountain or Mineral pitch—Bitumen Maltha. **1796** Kirwan *Elem. Min.* (ed. 2) I. 189 The earth called *mountain soap. **1797** Hatchett in *Nicholson's Jrnl.* (1799) II. 203 *Mountain or Mineral Tar. **1816** Jameson *Syst. Min.* (ed. 2) III. 577 *Mountain or rock wood. **1801** *Encycl. Brit.* Suppl. II. 218/2 Colour..olive or mountain green, pale flesh red, and *mountain yellow.

c. Prefixed to the names of many animals found in upland districts. **mountain antelope** = GORAL (Webster 1897); **mountain-barbel**, a cyprinoid fish of the genus *Schizothorax*, or of certain other allied genera; **mountain bat**, a very small social bat, *Emballonura monticola*, native of Borneo, Java, Sumatra and the Philippine Islands; **mountain beauty** *U.S.*, the black spotted trout, *Salmo purpuratus* (*Cent. Dict.* 1890); **mountain beaver** *U.S.*, a small haplodont, *Haplodon rufus*, native of Washington, Oregon and parts of California; **mountain blackbird**, the ring ouzel, *Turdus torquatus* (Swainson 1885); **mountain bluebird** *N. Amer.*, a bluebird of western North America, *Sialia currucoides*, distinguished by a blue breast instead of a red one; **mountain boomer** *U.S.*, (*a*) the sewellel or mountain beaver, *Aplodontia rufa*; (*b*) the red squirrel, *Sciurus hudsonicus*; also *transf.*; **mountain buffalo** *U.S.*, (*a*) = MOUNTAIN SHEEP 2; (*b*) a mountain variety of the American buffalo, *Bison bison*; **mountain bunting**, the snow bunting, *Plectrophanes nivalis*; **mountain burnet**, a species of burnet moth, *Zygæna Exulans*; **mountain cat**, a catamount or catamountain; **mountain cock**, (*a*) = CAPERCAILYE; (*b*) *U.S.* = PRAIRIE-CHICKEN, *cock of the plains* (COCK *sb.*[1] 10); †**mountain cow**, the tapir; **mountain crab**, a land crab (*Cent. Dict.*); **mountain devil** = MOLOCH 2; **mountain duck** (see quot.); **mountain eagle**, the golden eagle, *Aquila chrysaëtus*; **mountain finch** = BRAMBLING; also any bird of the genus *Montifringilla*; **mountain goat** = MAZAME 2; see also sense 8 b; **mountain hare**, (*a*) the Cape jerboa, *Pedetes capensis*, native of South Africa; (*b*) the alpine hare, *Lepus variabilis*, native of the northern parts of both hemispheres; (*c*) a tailless hare, *Lagomys Roylii*, native of Ceylon; **mountain hawk**, a kind of buzzard, *Regerhinus uncinatus*, native of Grenada in the West Indies; **mountain herring** *U.S.*, a salmonoid fish, *Coregonus Williamsoni*; **mountain jay** *U.S.*, Steller's jay, *Cyanocitta stelleri*; **mountain linnet**, a kind of finch, *Linota montium*, native of Europe; **mountain lion** = PUMA; **mountain magpie**, the green woodpecker, *Picus viridis*; **mountain mocking-bird**, *Oreoscoptes montanus*, native of the interior table-land of North America; †**mountain mouse**, the MARMOT; **mountain nymph** (see quot.); **mountain ouzel** (see OUZEL 1 b); **mountain panther**, (*a*) = OUNCE *sb.*[2] 2; (*b*) = PUMA (Webster *Suppl.* 1902); **mountain parrot** = KEA; **mountain partridge** (see PARTRIDGE 2); **mountain pheasant**, the lyre-bird; **mountain plover** *U.S.*, a small plover, *Eupoda montana*; **mountain quail** = *plumed partridge* (see PARTRIDGE 2); **mountain ram** = *mountain sheep*; **mountain rat** = MARMOT; **mountain ringlet**, an alpine satyrid butterfly, *Erebia epiphron*, found in limited parts of the Lake District, Scotland, and western Ireland; cf. RINGLET 4; **mountain sheep**, the Rocky Mountain sheep, *Ovis montana*; **mountain sparrow**, the tree sparrow, *Passer montanus*; **mountain thrush**, (*a*) an Australian thrush, *Oreocincla lunulata*; (*b*) the ring ouzel (Swainson 1885); **mountain tortoise**, a large African tortoise, *Geochelone pardalis*, also known as the leopard-tortoise (LEOPARD 6 b); **mountain trout**, (*a*) a name for two Californian species of trout, *Salmo irideus* and *S. purpureus*; (*b*) any one of the acanthopterygian fishes of the genus *Galaxias*, native of Australia, etc.; **mountain white butterfly**, a European 'white', *Pieris Callidice*; **mountain witch**, a ground dove, *Geotrygon sylvatica* or *cristata*, native of Jamaica.

1880 Günther *Fishes* xvii. 242 The alpine freshwater fishes..are principally Salmonoids; and in Asia, besides, *mountain-barbels and Loaches. **187.** *Cassell's Nat. Hist.* I. 314 The *Mountain Bat. **1885** *Riverside Nat. Hist.* (1888) V. 121 This is the..'Sewellel' of the aborigines..known to.. trappers as the 'Boomer' and '*Mountain Beaver'. **1860** S. F. Baird *Birds N. Amer.* I. 224 *Sialia arctica*, Swainson. Rocky *Mountain Blue Bird. **1904** I. G. Wheelock *Birds Calif.* 506 The exquisite coloring of the Mountain Bluebird renders him easily the most beautiful of all Californian birds. **1971** *Islander* (Victoria, B.C.) 13 June 13/1 We were fortunate to see such birds as..a sky-blue mountain bluebird. **1858** D. K. Bennett *Chronol. N. Carolina* 94 The only inhabitants we saw on these high points were pheasants, cross bills,..and *mountain boomers, a sort of squirrel. **1859** H. E. Taliaferro *Fisher's River* 33 A mountain 'Boomer' dressed in a linsey hunting-shirt down to his knees. **1922** H. Kephart *Our Southern Highlanders* (new ed.) 87 Out of a tree overhead hopped a mountain 'boomer'. *Ibid.* 280 They call themselves mountain people, or citizens; sometimes humorously 'mountain boomers'. **1940** *Mt. Hood Guide* 21 The sewellel or mountain beaver, sometimes colloquially called 'mountain boomer'.. resembles the porcupine and marmot rather than the beaver. **1958** *Amer. Speech* XXXIII. 265 (*table*) Pejorative designations of rural dwellers in the Upper Midwest.. mountain boomer. **1868** *Amer. Naturalist* II. 538 '*Mountain Buffalo'... The Bighorn is sometimes called so. *Ibid.*, I saw no difference in the skulls, indicating a different species, or 'Mountain Buffalo' of the hunters. **1884** *Encycl. Brit.* Amer. Suppl. I. 540/2 Buffaloes long inhabiting other localities than the open plains, their natural homes, acquire distinguishable varietal characters. They are known as 'wood-buffalo' and 'mountain-buffalo'. **1892** *Scribner's Mag.* Sept. 277/1 There are, besides the ordinary animal of the plains, the 'mountain buffalo',..the 'wood buffalo',.. and the 'beaver buffalo'. **1768** Pennant *Brit. Zool.* (1776) I. 281 *Mountain Bunting. **1882** W. F. Kirby *Europ. Butterfl. & M.* (1903) Plate xxii, Zygæna Exulans—*Mountain Burnet. **1709** J. Lawn *New Voy. Carolina* 118 Cat-a-Mount. The *Mountain-Cat, so call'd, because he lives in the Mountainous Parts of America. **1780** Edmondson *Heraldry* II. Alphabet, *Keate*,..ar. three mountain-cats passant in pale sa. **1810** Scott *Lady of L.* v. xvi, Like mountain-cat who guards her young, Full at Fitz-James's throat he sprung. **1802** Montagu *Ornith. Dict.* (1831), **Mountain cock*, a name for the Capercalzie. **1805** M. Lewis in Lewis & Clark *Orig. Jrnls. Lewis & Clark Expedition* (1905) II. 124 Saw (near the hills) a flock of the mountain cock, or a large species of heath hen with a long pointed tail which the Indians informed us were common to the Rocky Mountains. **1943** H. Drake-Brockman in *Coast to Coast 1942* 158 There were little barking lizards and mountain-devils and eagle-hawks and white owls in the blow-holes. **1966** *Times* 11 Nov. (W. Austral. Suppl.) p. iv/4 The hideous little mountain devil (*Moloch horridus*)..trades on its frightening aspect while sustaining a perfectly blameless existence on a diet of ants. **1699** Dampier *Voy.* II. II. iv. 102 Horses, and other Animals, amongst which the *Mountain Cow..is most remarkable. **1827** Roberts *Voy. Centr. Amer.* 45 The tapir, or mountain cow. **1853** *Proc. Roy. Soc. Van Diemen's Land* II. 515 (Morris) *Mountain-devil. **1894** Newton *Dict. Birds* 600 *Mountain-Duck, several species of *Anatidæ*—and in New Zealand apparently applied colloquially to *Tadorna tadornoides* (Sheld-drake). **1877** —— in *Encycl. Brit.* VII. 590/1 The Golden or *Mountain-Eagle..is the second British species. **1678** Ray *Willughby's Ornith.* 255 The great pied *Mountain-Finch or Bramlin. **1800** Coleridge *Keepsake* 6 The foxglove..bends beneath the up-springing lark Or mountain-finch alighting. **1867** A. L. Adams *Wand. Naturalist India* 283 The black-headed mountain-finch *Montifringilla hæmatopygia* is often seen around the lake. **1841** G. Catlin *Lett. on N. Amer. Indians* II. 196 His leggings and shirt were of the *mountain goat skin. **1859** S. Baird *Mammals N. Amer.* 671 *Aplocerus montanus*..Mountain Goat, Mountain Sheep, White Goat, &c. **1936** D. McCowan *Animals Canad. Rockies* xiv. 119 A herd of mountain goats on an immense buttress of rock. **1966** *Globe & Mail* (Toronto) 7 May 41/2 Mountain goat also abound in the mountainous region..in..south-eastern British Columbia. **1785** G. Forster tr. *Sparrman's Voy. Cape G. Hope* II. 195 By the colonists it is called *berg-haas*, ..(the *mountain..hare). **1848** tr. *Hoffmeister's Trav. Ceylon*, etc. xii. 446 Tall bushes of furze, the home of a multitude of..small mountain-hares. **187.** *Cassell's Nat. Hist.* III. 149 The Mountain Hare (*Lepus variabilis*) or Northern Hare. **1877** C. Hallock *Sportsman's Gazetteer* 350 Williamson's Whitefish; *Mountain Herring.—*Coregonus williamsoni*. **1888** Goode *Amer. Fishes* 490 This species is usually known..in Utah as the 'Mountain Herring'. **1872** *Amer. Naturalist* VI. 398 The great-crested, Woodhouse's and the Canada jays were of frequent occurrence in the mountains, the former being familiarly known as the '*mountain jay'. **1917** T. G. Pearson *Birds Amer.* II. 219 Steller's Jay...[also called] Mountain Jay; Pine Jay; Conifer Jay. **1678** Ray *Willughby's Ornith.* 261 The *Mountain Linnet: *Linaria Montana*. **1859** G. A. Jackson *Diary* 1 Jan. in *Colorado Mag.* (1935) XII. 204 Killed a *mountain lion today. **1874** G. Kingsley *Notes Sport & Trav.* (1900) 172 *note*, It was not a bear we were after; it was a *mountain lion... Our lion is the puma. **1936** D. McCowan *Animals Canad. Rockies* ix. 77 The cougar or mountain lion is a large tawny brown cat with a small head, rather slender body and long round tail. **1972** *Radio Times* 1 June 30/1 Wild life to be found in different parts of Canada including a mountain lion and a wapiti. **1802** Montagu *Ornith. Dict.* (1831), **Mountain magpie*, a name for the Popinjay. **1883** Newton in *Encycl. Brit.* XVI. 541/1 The so-called *Mountain Mocking-bird..is a form not very distant from *Mimus*. **1607** Topsell *Four-f. Beasts* 687 A Dormouse, a *Mountain-mouse, and such like. **1869–73** T. R. Jones *Cassell's Bk. Birds* III. 52 The *Mountain Nymphs (*Oreotrochilus*). **1678** Ray *Willughby's Ornith.* 195 The Rock Ouzel, or *Mountain Ouzel of Gesner. **1894** Newton *Dict. Birds* 600 *Mountain-Parrot. **1884** *Cassell's Fam. Mag.* Apr. 272/1 The 'lyre-bird', or *mountain pheasant. **1858** S. F. Baird in *Rep. Explor. Route to Pacific* (U.S. War Dept.) IX. 693 *Mountain Plover..is only known to inhabit the western countries of North America. **1917** T. G. Pearson *Birds Amer.* I. 267 Mountain Plover... Nest: On the open prairies; a depression in the ground, lined with leaves and grass. **1807** P. Gass *Jrnl.* 74 Horns of the *Mountain ram. **1753** Chambers *Cycl. Supp., App.* s.v. *Rat*, *Mountain-rat, the English name of a creature, otherwise called the Marmotte. **1859** Farrar *J. Home* xvi. 208 With all the ardour of a young entomologist in full chase of a little *mountain-ringlet. **1870** F. O. Morris *Hist. Brit. Butterflies* (ed. 5) 53 (*heading*) Small Ringlet. Mountain Ringlet. **1945** E. B. Ford *Butterflies* xiii. 288 The Mountain Ringlet, *Erebia epiphron*, cannot live in England at an altitude of less than 1800 feet, but in Scotland it is able to descend to about 1500 feet. **1975** *Times* 12 Nov. 14/6 The Mountain Ringlet is an extremely rare butterfly that may still exist in the wild, high mountains of Western Ireland. **1807** P. Gass *Jrnl.* 82 We saw some *Mountain sheep. **1738** Albin *Nat. Hist. Birds* III. 62 The *Mountain Sparrow. **1848** J. Gould *Birds Australia* IV. pl. 7 *Oreocincla lunulata*, *Mountain Thrush, ..Colonists of Van Diemen's Land. **1958** L. van der Post *Lost World of Kalahari* i. 26 For the equivalent of cello and bass violin he used the shell of our big dark *mountain tortoises. **1966** E. Palmer *Plains of Camdeboo* xiii. 228 Mountain tortoises are said to have a great homing instinct. **1971** D. J. Potgieter et al. *Animal Life S. Afr.* 303/2 Mountain or leopard tortoise..is a widely distributed species, extending from the Sudan and Ethiopia in the north to the Cape in the south. **1886** J. T. Cunningham in *Encycl. Brit.* XXI. 223/1 The Californian *Mountain, or Rainbow Trout. **1898** Morris *Austral Eng.* 304/2 *Mountain-Trout*, species of *Galaxias*. **1882** W. F. Kirby *Europ. Butterfl. & M.* (1903) Plate iii, Pieris Callidice..*Mountain White Butterfly. **1847** Gosse *Birds Jamaica* 318 These moans, heard..while the bird is rarely seen, have..given it the name of *Mountain Witch.

d. In the names of plants, their fruits, etc., growing in elevated situations. **mountain arnica** = *mountain tobacco*; **mountain avens**, a subalpine plant, *Dryas octopetala*; **mountain balm** *U.S.*, (*a*) = *bastard balm*; (*b*) a trade name for Oswego tea (*Cent. Dict.* 1890); (*c*) an evergreen plant, *Eriodictyon glutinosum*, also prob. *E. didyma* (*Ibid.*); **mountain balsam** *U.S.*, a coniferous tree, *Abies subalpina*; **mountain bay**, a small ornamental tree, *Gordonia pubescens*, native of Georgia and Florida (Funk's *Stand. Dict.* 1895); **mountain beech**, †(*a*) ? = *Dutch beech*, the white poplar, *Populus alba*; (*b*) *Austral.*, the proteaceous tree *Lomatia longifolia* (Morris 1898); (*c*) *N.Z.*, the evergreen tree, *Nothofagus cliffortioides*; **mountain-bell**, an alpine species of *Campanula*; **mountain bindweed**, a plant of the primulaceous genus *Soldanella*; **mountain bramble** = cloudberry; **mountain cabbage (tree)**, a West Indian palm tree of the genus *Oreodoxa*; †**mountain calamint**, calamint (cf. *mountain mint*); **mountain cherry** *U.S.*, one of several wild cherries; **mountain chestnut oak** *U.S.*, an American oak, *Quercus montana*, with leaves resembling those of the chestnut; **mountain chickweed** (see quot.); **mountain clover**, a papilionaceous subalpine plant, *Trifolium montanum*; **mountain coralline** = reindeer-moss; **mountain cowslip**, a herbaceous plant, *Primula Auricula*, native of the Swiss Alps; **mountain cranberry** *U.S.* = cowberry (*Cent. Dict.*); **mountain daisy** *N.Z.*, a perennial herb of the genus *Celmisia*, belonging to the family Compositæ; **mountain damson**, a simarubaceous tree, native of the West Indies and Guyana, esp. *Simaruba glauca*, native of Jamaica; †**mountain dock**, Welsh sorrel, *Oxyria reniformis* (Withering *Brit. Plants*, ed. 3, 1796); **mountain ebony**, a leguminous tree of the genus *Bauhinia* having dark-coloured and hard wood; also the wood itself; **mountain fern**, *Thelypteris limbosperma*; **mountain flower**, a kind of crane's bill, *Geranium sylvaticum*; **mountain fringe** *U.S.*, a climbing biennial fumariaceous plant, *Adlumia cirrhosa*; **mountain grape (tree)** (see quots.); **mountain groundsel**, the *Senecio sylvaticus*; **mountain guava** (see guava 1); **mountain heath**, a handsome ericaceous shrub, *Menziesia taxifolia*, native of North America; **mountain hemlock**, a large coniferous tree, *Tsuga mertensiana*, of the family Pinaceæ, native to western North America; **mountain hemp**, a species of henbane, *Hyoscyamus insanus*, native of Baluchistan; **mountain holly**, an aquifoliaceous tree, *Nemopanthes Canadensis*, native of North America; **mountain ironwort**, a labiate plant, *Sideritis montana*; **mountain larch**, a kind of fir, *Larix lyalli*, native of the Rocky Mountains; **mountain laver** (see quot.); **mountain lily** = martagon; **mountain liquorice**, a kind of trefoil, *Trifolium alpinum*, native of Europe; **mountain magnolia**, *Magnolia acuminata*; **mountain mahogany** *U.S.*, (*a*) = *mahogany birch* (mahogany 7); (*b*) a shrub or small tree of the genus *Cercocarpus*, esp. *C. ledifolius*, belonging to the family Rosaceæ and native to western North America; **mountain manchineel**, a West Indian sumac, *Rhus Metopium*; **mountain mango**, the fruit of certain species of *Clusia*, grown in the West Indies; **mountain maple** *U.S.*, one of several maples found in upland areas, esp. *Acer spicatum*; **mountain mint**, †(*a*) calamint; (*b*) the U.S. genus *Pycnanthemum*; **mountain moss**, the lycopodiaceous plant *Selaginella selaginoides* (Britton & Brown *Amer. Flora* 1897–8); **mountain parsley** (see parsley 2); **mountain pine**, (*a*) a dwarf alpine pine, *Pinus Pumilio*, native of Europe; (*b*) *N.Z.*, a small evergreen tree, *Dacrydium bidwillii*, found in boggy or subalpine regions; **mountain pink**, an alpine species of *Dianthus*; **mountain plum**, an olæaceous tree, *Ximenia americana*, native of tropical America; **mountain poly** (see poly[1] c); **mountain pride** = mountain green 2; **mountain puliol** (see puliol); **mountain rice**, (*a*) a variety of rice grown in upland districts where irrigation is impossible (in Dicts.); (*b*) any grass of the genus *Oryzopsis*; **mountain rose**, the rhododendron; †**mountain rose bay**, the kalmia (Miller *Gard. Dict.* ed. 1759, Index); **mountain saffron**, a liliaceous plant, *Anthericum serotinum*; **mountain sandwort**, a caryophyllaceous plant, *Arenaria groenlandica* (in recent Dicts.); †**mountain siler**, a kind of willow; **mountain sorrel**, *Oxyria reniformis*; **mountain spiderwort** = *mountain saffron*; **mountain spinach** = orach; **mountain stone parsley**, ? = *mountain parsley* (a); **mountain sweet** (see quot.); **mountain tea**, *Gaultheria procumbens*; also its leaves used for infusion; *N. Amer.*, the wintergreen, *Gaultheria procumbens*, or the beverage made from its leaves; **mountain tea-tree**, *Kunzea pedunculata* (Morris *Austral Eng.*); **mountain tobacco**, *Arnica montana*.

1861 Bentley *Man. Bot.* 580 *Mountain Arnica,..or Leopard's bane, is an acrid stimulant. **1796** Withering *Brit. Plants* (ed. 3) II. 478 *Dryas octopetala*... *Mountain Avens. **1856** Mayne *Expos. Lex.*, **Mountain Balm*, common name for the *Melittis melissophylum*. **1902** *Encycl. Brit.* XXXI. 263/2 The principal trees of the Rocky Mountains are aspen and..*mountain balsam. **1707** Mortimer *Husb.* (1721) II. 26 The *Mountain-Beech is the whitest and most sought after by the Turner. **1884** A. Nilson *Timber Trees New South Wales* 92 *L[omatia] longifolia*.—Mountain Beech.—An erect small tree. **1928** Cockayne & Turner *Trees N.Z.* 154 *Nothofagus cliffortioides* (mountain-beech) is of little value as a timber, for it decays rapidly. **1959** A. McLintock *Descr. Atlas N.Z.* p. xv, The forest is of silver and mountain beech, with traces of red beech and podocarps at low altitude. **1965** *Austral. Encycl.* V. 360/2 *L[omatia] longifolia* (sometimes called mountain beech), has a hard light-coloured ornamental wood, used for turnery. **1923** D. H. Lawrence *Ladybird* 227 Sometimes the hairy *mountain-bell, pale-blue and bristling, stood alone. **1597** Gerarde *Herbal* II. ccxciii. 690 *Soldanella* or *mountaine Bindweed, hath many round leaues spred vpon the ground. **1818** Withering *Brit. Plants* (ed. 6) III. 625 *Rubus Chamæmorus*... Cloud-berry, *Mountain Bramble, Knot-berries. **1681** Grew *Musæum* II. i. §1. 181 Part of the Trunk of a young *Mountain Cabbige. **1796** Stedman *Surinam* II. xvi. 23 A tree called the mountain-cabbage-tree, which is one of the palm species. *c* **1450** J. Metham *Wks.* (E.E.T.S.) 49 Modyrwort, rwe, red malwys, and *calamynt mowateyn [*read* mownteyn]. **1813** H. Muhlenberg *Catal. Plantarum Americæ Septentrionalis* 48 *Prunus montana*,..*mountain cherry. **1847** Darlington *Amer. Weeds*, etc. (1860) 117 *Chicasa Prunus*...Mountain Cherry. **1871** *Harper's Mag.* Oct. 707 We must..gather mountain cherries (*Prunus cerasus*). **1801** A. Michaux *Hist. Chênes de l'Amérique* sig. 6₁v *Mountain Chesnut Oak. **1821** T. Nuttall *Jrnl. Trav. Arkansa* i. 42 Much of the *Quercus Prima monticola* (or mountain chestnut oak) presents itself on the mountain. **1778** Pennant *Tour in Wales* (1883) I. 27 The *Arenaria Verna*, or *Mountain chickweed. **1882** W. F. Kirby *Europ. Butterfl. & M.* (1903) Plate xxii, Plants... *Mountain Clover. **1598** Florio, *Corallina*..also Corall or *mountain coralline. **1753** Chambers *Cycl. Supp.* s.v. *Heath-moss*, The alpine coralline-like *Coralloides*. This is called, by some, mountain Coralline. **1597** Gerarde *Herbal* II. cclxii. 640 There be diuers sorts of *Mountaine Cowslips, or Beares eares. **1863** Prior *Plant-n.* 156 Mountain Cowslip, *Primula auricula*. **1857** J. T. Thomson in N. M. Taylor *Early Travellers N.Z.* (1959) 335 Half-way up the mountains some pretty flowers were gathered, amongst which the *mountain daisy deserves notice. **1900** A. Dendy in *Canterbury Old & New* 188 Only rivalled in beauty by the marguerite-like flowers of 'cotton plant' or mountain daisy (species of *Celmisia*). **1959** A. McLintock *Descr. Atlas N.Z.* p. xv, The upper mountain limits were covered with alpine vegetation —mountain daisies (Celmisia), [etc.]. **1814** Lunan *Hortus Jamaic.* I. 521 Mountain Damson, *Quassia*..*Simaruba*.. This tree is known in Jamaica by the name of *mountain damson, bitter damson, or stavewood. **1864** Grisebach *Flora W. Ind. Isl.* 785 Mountain-damson, *Simaruba amara*. **1725** Sloane *Jamaica* II. 51 *Mountain Ebony. This tree rises to about fifteen foot high. **1756** P. Browne *Jamaica* (1789) 287 *Bauhinia*... Mountain Ebeny. **1814** Lunan *Hortus Jamaic.* I. 278 Mountain Ebony. *Bauhinia*.. *Porrecta*. Stretched. **1864** Grisebach *Flora W. Ind. Isl.* 785 Mountain-ebony, *Casparea porrecta*, and *Bauhinia megalandra*. **1898** Morris *Austral Eng.* 134/1 Both [*Bauhinia Carronii* and *B. Hookeri*] are called Queensland or Mountain Ebony. **1840** E. Newman *Hist. Brit. Ferns* 47 (*heading*) *Mountain fern. **1863** Prior *Plant-n.* 156 Mountain fern, *Aspidium Oreopteris*. **1879–81** J. Britten *European Ferns* 151 The Mountain Fern, as *L[astrea] Oreopteris* is sometimes called,..is well worthy of cultivation. **1960** P. Taylor *Brit. Ferns & Mosses* 155 The Mountain Fern is widely distributed throughout the northern hemisphere. **1853** G. Johnston *Bot. E. Bord.* 48 *Geranium sylvaticum*. The King's-Hood: *Mountain-Flower. **1846–50** A. Wood *Class-bk. Bot.* 158 *Adlumia cirrhosa*... *Mountain Fringe. **1756** P. Browne *Jamaica* (1789) 210 *Coccolobis* 4... The *Mountain Grape-Tree. **1864** Grisebach *Flora W. Ind. Isl.* 785 Mountain-grape, black, *Guettarda longiflora*. Mountain-grape, common, *Coccoloba tenuifolia*. Mountain-grape, large-leaved, *Coccoloba Plumieri*. **1880** *Encycl. Brit.* XI. 221/2 *Senecio sylvaticus* and *S. viscosus* are known respectively as *mountain groundsel and stinking groundsel. **1846–50** A. Wood *Class-bk. Bot.* 373 *Mountain Heath. **1884** C. S. Sargent *Rep. Forests N. Amer.* 572 The timber on these ridges [in Idaho] was often small and scattered..with larch and red fir, balsam, hemlock, and sometimes *mountain hemlock. **1969** T. H. Everett *Living Trees of World* 64/2 Another western American, the usually bluish-leaved mountain hemlock.., occurs at high altitudes from Alaska to California. **1974** *Daily Colonist* (Victoria, B.C.) 24 Dec. 32/2 The major reason for establishing the reserve..is to allow biologists to study mountain hemlock. **1887** Bentley *Man. Bot.* (ed. 5) 632 *Hyoscyamus insanus*..is called *Mountain Hemp. **1807** P. Gass *Jrnl.* 130 There is also a small bush..about 6 inches high, which bears a small bunch of small purple berries. Some call it *mountain holly; the fruit is of an acid taste. **1822** *Hortus Anglicus* II. 75 *Sideritis Montana*. *Mountain Iron Wort. Herbaceous, decumbent, hairy. **1891** in *Syd. Soc. Lex.* **1902** *Encycl. Brit.* XXXI. 263/2 *Mountain larch (*Larix lyallii*). **1866** *Treas. Bot.*, **Mountain laver*, a reddish gelatinous *Alga*, belonging to the genus *Palmella*,..growing on the sides of mountains. **1664** Evelyn *Kal. Hort.*, *June* (1679) 19 Campions or Sultans, *Mountain Lillies white, red. **1728** J. Gardiner tr. *Rapin's Of Gardens* Index, Martagon, or Mountain Lilly. **1829** Loudon *Encycl. Plants* 1153 *Mountain liquorice. **1884** Sargent *Rep. Forests N. Amer.* (10th Census IX) 20 Magnolia acuminata..*Mountain magnolia. **1810** F. A. Michaux *Hist. Arbres Forestiers de l'Amérique Septentrionale* I. 26 Sweet birch, [ou] *Mountain Mahogany dans Virginia. **1832** D. J. Browne *Sylva Amer.* 118 Wherever it grows in the United States, it is known by the name of Black Birch: its secondary denominations are Mountain Mahogany in Virginia, [etc.]. **1875** *Amer. Naturalist* IX. 201 Much more attractive with its glossy foliage and long feathery seeds, is the mountain mahogany *Cercocarpus ledifolius* Nutt. **1951** *Dict. Gardening* (R. Hort. Soc.) I. 440/1 *C[ercocarpus] ledifolius*. Mountain mahogany. Erect slender tree up to 40 ft. **1884** Sargent *Rep. Forests N. Amer.* (10th Census IX) 54 Rhus Metopium..*Mountain Manchineel. **1861** Bentley *Man. Bot.* 478 In Nevis and St. Kitt's the three species [of *Clusia*] are known indifferently under the names of Fat Pork, Monkey Apple, and *Mountain or Wild Mango. **1785** H. Marshall *Arbustrum Amer.* 2 *Acer pennsylvanicum*, Pennsylvanian Dwarf *Mountain Maple,..grows naturally upon the mountains in the back parts of Pennsylvania. **1832** D. J. Browne *Sylva Amer.* 102 The mountain maple seldom rises above 20 feet in height. **1969** T. H. Everett *Living Trees of World* 222/2 Similar in size [to the moosewood] and also favoring shaded locations through much of eastern and central North America is the mountain maple (*A. spicatum*). **1671** Salmon *Syn. Med.* III. xxii. 393 Calamintha..*Mountain-Mint. **1866** *Treas. Bot.*, *Pycnanthemum*, the generic name of the Mountain Mints of the United States. **1777** Robson *Brit. Flora* 264 *Lycopodium Selaginoides*... Prickly Wolfsclaw.

Seeding *Mountain-moss. **1856** MAYNE *Expos. Lex.*, **Mountain Pine*, common name for the *Pinus pumilio*. **1933** L. G. D. ACLAND in *Press* (Christchurch, N.Z.) 4 Nov. 15/7 Mountain... Often used..of a species found in the back country, mostly smaller than their down-country relatives, e.g. mountain pine. **1963** POOLE & ADAMS *Trees & Shrubs N.Z.* 26 *D[acrydium] bidwillii*... Bog pine, mountain pine. Reaching 4 m. Leaves: juvenile linear, sessile, passing abruptly into adult foliage with scale-like, imbricate leaves. **1850** L. SAWYER *Diary* 12 June in *Way Sk.* (1926) 53 We found some grass and some beautiful specimens of what we called *mountain pink. It is much smaller than our garden pink, but resembles it somewhat in form, but more in its sweet perfume. **1936** *Discovery* Feb. 46/2 There [*sc.* on a mountain in Yugoslavia] I found tall mountain pinks of deep crimson, single-flowering. **1864** GRISEBACH *Flora W. Ind. Isl.* 786 *Mountain-plum, *Ximenia americana*. **1814** LUNAN *Hortus Jamaic.* I. 524 *Mountain Pride. *Spathelia*.. *Simplex*. **1845–50** MRS. LINCOLN *Lect. Bot.* App. 134/2 *Oryzopsis asperifolia* (*mountain rice..). **1739** MILLER *Gard. Dict.* II., *Chamærhododendron*, Sweet *Mountain Rose. **1826** P. POUNDEN *France & Italy* 197 The rhododendron, or mountain-rose. **1838** MARY HOWITT *Birds & Flowers, Mill-stream* ii, Into the mad Mill-stream The mountain-roses fall. **1796** WITHERING *Brit. Plants* (ed. 3) II. 339 *Anthericum serotinum*... *Mountain Saffron. [**1765** in D. Campbell *Hist. Prince Edward Island* (1875) 6 The *Mountain Shrub and Maiden Hair are also pretty common, of whose leaves and berries the Acadian settlers frequently make a kind of tea.] **1785** H. MARSHALL *Arbustrum Amer.* 53 *Gaultheria procumbens*. Canadian Gaultheria, or Mountain Tea... The leaves have been used as a substitute for Bohea Tea, whence the name of Mountain Tea. **1804** [see *grouse-berry*]. **1830** *Trans. Lit. & Hist. Soc. Quebec* (1837) III. 96 Mountain tea [is] a very small evergreen half-shrubby plant, with strong, shining, leathery leaves. **1832** W. D. WILLIAMSON *Hist. State Maine* I. 121 This 'mountain tea' promotes mammillary secretions. **1858** [see TEA *sb.* 6]. **1886** *Harper's Mag.* June 62/1 Another beverage is 'mountain tea' which is made from the sweet scented golden-rod and from winter-green. **1891** M. E. RYAN *Pagan of Alleghanies* 65 They reached the level above the cliff, the level carpeted with mountain-tea and rabbit-berries. **1941** J. STUART *Men of Mountains* 187, I would love to get out with you and get mountain tea from the knolls. **1964** H. D. WILSON *Tales from Barrett's Landing* 44 To supplement our meals..we ate berries, mountain teas (a leaf that tastes like wintergreen), and seaweed. *c* **1550** LLOYD *Treas. Health* Lvb, Syler, *montayne and Comin sod in wyne. **1863** PRIOR *Plant-n.* 156 *Mountain sorrel, *Oxyria reniformis*. **1849** CRAIG, *Mountain-spiderwort, the plant *Anthericum serotinum*. **1829** LOUDON *Encycl. Plants* 863 *Atriplex hortensis*, sometimes called *mountain spinach, was formerly cultivated as a culinary herb. **1719** QUINCY *Lex. Physico-Med.* (1722) 348/1 *Mountain-Stone-Parsley. **1866** *Treas. Bot.*, **Mountain-sweet*, a Canadian name for *Ceanothus americanus*. **1861** BENTLEY *Man. Bot.* 585 An infusion of the leaves [of the Partridge Berry] is employed in certain parts of North America, as a substitute for China tea, under the name of *Mountain or Salvador Tea. **1846** LINDLEY *Veg. Kingd.* 707 *Arnica montana*, a Swiss herb, called in our gardens *Mountain Tobacco.

mountain ash.

1. The tree *Pyrus* (formerly *Sorbus*) *Aucuparia*, characterized by its delicate pinnate leaves and masses of bright scarlet berries. In North America applied to the native species, *Pyrus americana* and *P. sambucifolia*. Also ***bastard mountain ash***: see quot. 1812.

1597 GERARDE *Herbal* III. civ. 1290 The..*Ornus* which also is named ὀρεινὴ μελία, or *Montana Fraxinus*, mountaine Ash. **1697** DRYDEN *Æneid* x. 1087 Like a mountain ash [L. *ornum*], whose roots are spread, Deep fix'd in earth. **1745** P. THOMAS *Jrnl. Anson's Voy.* 36 Besides those Myrtle Trees, there are the Mountain-Ash..the Pepper Tree [etc.]. **1812** *Sowerby's Eng. Bot.* XXXIII. 2331 *Pyrus pinnatifida*. Bastard Mountain Ash. **1845–50** MRS. LINCOLN *Lect. Bot.* App. 172 *Sorbus americana* (mountain ash..). **1875** *Encycl. Brit.* II. 680/2 Pear trees are sometimes grafted on the mountain ash.

2. a. *dial.*; **b.** *Austral.* (see quots. 1884–1957).

1871 *Scott. Naturalist* I. 54 In Inverness-shire, the Aspen (*Populus tremula*) is known as the Mountain, or Quaking, Ash. **1884** A. NILSON *Timber Trees New South Wales* 74 *E[ucalyptus] virgata*.—Mountain ash; White-top.—A tree of considerable size. *Ibid.*, *E. micrococca*.—Mountain Ash... Habitat, brush forests, from Illawarra to the Richmond River and New England; also Blue Mountains. **1898** MORRIS *Austral Eng.* 304/1 *Mountain-Ash*, a name applied to various Eucalypts, and to the tree *Alphitonia excelsa*, Reiss. **1934** [see BLACKBUTT]. **1957** *N.Z. Timber Jrnl.* Dec. 59/1 Mountain ash. *Eucalyptus regnans* F. Muell. and *E. delegatensis* R.T.B... Victoria and Tasmania. Also called Tasmanian oak and Australian oak. Moderately hard, heavy, durable, strong, elastic and resilient.

mountained ('maʊntɪnd), *ppl. a. poet. rare.* [f. **mountain* vb. (f. MOUNTAIN *sb.*) + -ED[1].]

1. Stationed upon a mountain; elevated, lofty.

1628 FELTHAM *Resolves* I. ii. 5 In high and mountain'd Fortunes resolution is necessary, to insafe vs from the.. wyles of prosperity... In the wane of Fortune, Resolution is likewise necessary, to [etc.]. **1818** KEATS *Endym.* II. 197 Like old Deucalion mountain'd o'er the flood.

†**2.** Heaped 'mountain high'. *Obs.*

1655 H. VAUGHAN *Silex Scint.* I. *Storm* i, Yet have I.. boyling stremes that rave With the same curling force, and hisse, As doth the mountain'd wave. **1748** J. BROWN *Ess. Satire* 302 When Giant-Vice and Irreligion rise On mountain'd falsehoods to invade the skies. **1762–9** FALCONER *Shipwr.* III. 491 Now no more a-lee Her trembling side could bear the mountain'd sea.

3. †**a.** Obstructed by mountains (*obs.*). **b.** Containing mountains.

1655 H. VAUGHAN *Silex Scint.* I. *Regeneration* ii, My walke a monstrous, mountain'd thing, Rough-cast with rocks and snow. **1820** KEATS *Hyperion* II. 123 Such noise is like the roar of bleak-grown pines: Which, when it ceases in this mountain'd world, No other sound succeeds; but ceasing here, among these fallen [etc.].

mountaineer (maʊntɪ'nɪə(r)). Also 7 **-ier, -tanier, -taneer, -tineer.** [f. MOUNTAIN + -EER[1]. Cf. MOUNTAINER and OF. *montagnier, montainier* adj., mountain-dwelling.]

1. A native of or dweller amongst mountains. Also *attrib.* as adj.

1610 SHAKS. *Temp.* III. iii. 44 When wee were Boyes Who would beleeue that there were Mountayneeres, Dew-lapt [etc.]. **1625** TUKE *Conc. Holy Eucharist* 6 That Mountineer, Michah of Ephraim. **1630** DRAYTON *Muses' Elysium* Nymphal ii. 10 This Cleon was a Mountaineer. **1678** R. L'ESTRANGE *Seneca's Mor., Happy Life* xvii. (1696) 268 The Mountanier makes the best Soldier. **1725** DE FOE *Voy. round World* (1840) 277 We saw several huts of the mountaineer inhabitants. **1821** BYRON *Two Foscari* III. i, The longing sorrow Of the sad mountaineer when far away. **1879** CHR. G. ROSSETTI *Seek & F.* 91 The Mountaineer is characteristically hardy,..a lover of freedom, a patriot.

2. A member of the 'Mountain' (see MOUNTAIN 6).

1802 *Sketch of Paris* II. liii. 197 The *montagnards* or mountaineers, that is, those monsters who were always thirsting for blood. **1827** SCOTT *Napoleon* Introd., Wks. 1870 IX. 263 The Mountaineers, his former associates.

3. One skilled or occupied in mountain climbing.

1860 TYNDALL *Glac.* I. xvi. 116, I had improved as a mountaineer since my ascent of Mont Blanc. **1872** JENKINSON *Guide Eng. Lakes* (1879) 221 The experienced mountaineer may have a rough and romantic walk by descending along the side of the Comb Gill ravine.

Hence **mountai'neer** *v. intr.*, to be a mountain climber; usually in *vbl. sb.* and *ppl. a.*

1803 SOUTHEY *Lett.* (1856) I. 247 My mountaineering recollections are to come in the next book. **1862** TYNDALL (*title*), Mountaineering in 1861. **1890** *Dickens' Dict. Lond.* 23/2 The mountaineering qualification of the club is a severe one. **1892** C. T. DENT *Mountaineering* ii. 61 Those who mountaineer in regions where the heights are undetermined must not depend on aneroids alone. **1897** MARY KINGSLEY *W. Africa* 582, I wish I had got the mountaineering spirit.

†**mountainer.** *Obs.* [f. MOUNTAIN + -ER[1]: cf. MOUNTAINEER.] = MOUNTAINEER 1.

1598 LE ROY *Aristotle's Polit.* v. 267 For the Mountainers were Democraticall; those of the champion countrey, Oligarchical. **1692** BENTLEY *Boyle Lect.* iii. 96 Being illiterate Rustics, as Mountainers always are.

mountainet, -ette (maʊntɪ'nɛt). [a. F. *montagnette*, dim. of *montagne* mountain.] A small mountain; a hillock, mound. Also *fig.*

a **1586** SIDNEY *Arcadia* I. (1590) 60 b, Her breasts (which sweetly rase vp like two faire Mountainets in the pleasaunt vale of Tempe). *c* **1586** C'TESS PEMBROKE *Ps.* LXVIII. vi, This mountainett..doth God desire. *a* **1603** T. CARTWRIGHT *Confut. Rhem. N.T.* (1618) 86 He hath cast down many.. mountaines and mountainets. **1859** SINGLETON *Virgil* II. 218 And work with Share Rutulian mountainets [*Æn.* VII. 798 *collis*]. **1892** S. R. HOLE *Mem.* 238 The most perfect of rock-gardens, a natural conjunction of mountainettes and streamlets.

mountain flax.

1. A name for various plants. **a.** = MILL-MOUNTAIN. **b.** The centaury, *Erythræa Centaurium* (Cumberland Gloss. 1878). **c.** Quaking-grass, *Briza media*. **d.** The corn spurry, *Spergula arvensis* (Miss Jackson *Shropshire Word-book*, 1879). **e.** U.S. *Polygala Senega*. **f.** *N.Z. Phormium colensoi*, a smaller and hardier form of the New Zealand flax, *P. tenax*.

1718 QUINCY *Comp. Disp.* 186 Mountain Flax.—This is own'd in Medicine only by the common People. **1788** W. MARSHALL *Yorks.* II. 119 Mountain flax—*linum catharticum* —purging flax. **1845–50** MRS. LINCOLN *Lect. Bot.* App. 144/2 *Polygala senega* (seneca snake-root, mountainflax). **1867** E. SAUTER tr. *F. von Hochstetter's New Zealand* vii. 152 We may distinguish about three principal varieties ..*Wharariki*, mountain flax, with coarse fibres; little used. **1871** *Scott. Naturalist* I. 54 In Kirkcudbrightshire, the Quaking Grass (*Briza*) is called Mountain Flax. **1949** P. BUCK *Coming of Maori* (1950) II. v. 167 Relief in decoration was obtained by spacing tags of the mountain flax (*Phormium colensoi*) which turn a distinct yellow in colour.

2. A kind of asbestos; = AMIANTHUS 1.

1807 AIKIN *Dict. Chem. & Min.* I. 107 Amianth or Mountain Flax. **1856** A. FAULKNER *Dict. Comm. Terms* 6.

mountain-green. [After G. *berggrün*.]

1. *Min.* †**a.** = MALACHITE. *Obs.*

1727–52 CHAMBERS *Cycl.* s.v. *Green*, Mountain Green..is a sort of greenish powder found..among the mountains of Kernausent, Hungary. **1836–41** BRANDE *Chem.* (ed. 5) 825 The pulverulent variety [of malachite] has been termed *chrysocolla* and *mountain-green*.

b. Glauconite or green earth.

1822 CLEAVELAND *Min. & Geol.* I. 445 Green Earth..is employed as a pigment, and sometimes called *mountain green*.

2. As the name of a colour. Also *adj.*

1796 KIRWAN *Elem. Min.* (ed. 2) I. 389 Mountain green hornstone is often debased, apparently by green earth. **1807** AIKIN *Dict. Chem. & Min.* I. 541 Green Earth... The colour of this mineral is celandine green..passing into mountain and blackish-green. **1835** *Penny Cycl.* IV. 336/2 Various shades of sky-blue or mountain-green.

3. A handsome simarubaceous plant, *Spathelia simplex*, native of the West Indies.

1864 GRISEBACH *Flora W. Ind. Isl.* 786.

mountainier, obs. form of MOUNTAINEER.

†**mountainist.** *Obs. rare.* [f. MOUNTAIN + -IST.] = MOUNTAINEER 1.

1625 N. CARPENTER *Geog. Del.* II. x. (1635) 174 Bodin seemes to make a Harmony and Concent betwixt the Northerne man and the Mountainist.

mountain laurel. = KALMIA.

1759 MILLER *Gard. Dict.* (ed. 7) s.v. *Kalmia* Ever-green Rose Laurel..commonly called in America Mountain Laurel. **1810** F. A. MICHAUX *Hist. Arbres Forestiers de l'Amérique Septentrionale* I. 35 Mountain laurel,.. dénomination la plus générale. **1832** D. J. BROWNE *Sylva Amer.* 191 The Mountain Laurel is a large shrub, which indifferently bears the name Mountain Laurel, Laurel, Ivy, and Calico Tree. **1845** S. JUDD *Margaret* I. ii. 8 She got running mosses..and mountain laurel blossoms. **1880** *Harper's Mag.* June 80 The mountain laurel, with its deep green foliage and showy clusters peers above that rocky crag. **1887** BENTLEY *Man. Bot.* (ed. 5) 605 The leaves, under the name of 'Mountain Laurel', are said to be a valuable remedy in obstinate diarrhœa. **1906** J. A. HARRISON *George Washington* 91 The bluish-pink masses of the mountain-laurel. **1955** [see KALMIA]. **1973** ROBICHAUD & BUELL *Vegetation of New Jersey* 329 Kalmia..latifolia. Mountain laurel.

†**'mountainly**, *a. Obs.* [f. MOUNTAIN + -LY[1].] Mountainous, hilly.

1603 OWEN *Pembrokeshire* (1892) 61 The Causes whie these mountenlie partes doe vse this tillinge of oates..are diverse.

mountainous ('maʊntɪnəs), *a.* Also 4–5 **mounteynous,** 7 **-aynous, -aignous, montanous,** 7–8 **mountanous.** [a. F. *montagneux* (= Sp. *montañoso*, Pg. *montanhoso*, It. *montagnoso*) :—popular L. **montāniōsus* mountainous, f. **montānia*, **montānea* MOUNTAIN: see -OUS.]

†**1.** Situated in the mountains. *Obs. rare.*

a **1430** mounteynous [in several MSS. of *Wyclif's Bible*, Jer. xvii. 26, xxxiii. 13, where the MSS. followed by the editors have *mountuous, mountewous*]. *a* **1649** DRUMM. OF HAWTH. *Irene* Wks. (1711) 171 The eccho's, so often redoubled and multiplied amongst mountanous concavities.

2. Characterized by mountains; abounding in mountains; of the nature of a mountain.

1601 R. JOHNSON *Kingd. & Commw.* (1603) 4 Those countries, whereof one part is plaine and fruitefull, and the other mountaynous and barren. **1687** A. LOVELL tr. *Thevenot's Trav.* I. 11 This little Isle..is..almost all cultivated, though it be mountanous. **1737** WHISTON *Josephus, Antiq.* V. i. §18 (1834) 131/2 The mountainous parts of Canaan. **1846** MCCulloch *Acc. Brit. Empire* (1854) I. 275 The greater part of the surface is mountainous.

3. Resembling a mountain or mountains; huge, enormous. Now *rare*.

1607 SHAKS. *Cor.* II. iii. 127 The Dust on antique Time would lye vnswept, And mountainous Error be too highly heapt, For Truth to o're-peere. **1641** MILTON *Animadv.* Wks. 1851 III. 215 Hee may perhaps delight the eyes of some with his huge and mountainous Bulk. **1678** J. PHILLIPS *Tavernier's Trav., India* II. II. iv. 114 The Raja..made him mountainous promises to no effect. **1749** FIELDING *Tom Jones* v. viii, The two mountainous cheek-bones of the house-keeper. **1768** J. BYRON *Narr. Patagonia* (ed. 2) 10 However, a mountainous sea hove her off. **1822** SCOTT *Pirate* xi, Mordaunt..placed her upon the summit of her mountainous saddle. **1889** RUSKIN *Præterita* III. 182 The white edges of the mountainous clouds.

†**4.** Inhabiting mountains; dwelling in inaccessible mountain regions; hence, barbarous. *Obs.*

1613 PURCHAS *Pilgrimage* (1614) 789 This wilde Mountainous people. **1625** BACON *Ess., Viciss. Things* (Arb.) 569 The Remnant of People, which hap to be reserued, are commonly Ignorant and Mountanous People, that can giue no Account, of the Time past. **1703** SAVAGE *Lett. Antients* cxiv. 283 The Mountainous People no sooner saw me,.. than they cry'd out.

†**5.** Derived from or owing characteristics to mountains. *Obs.*

1683 PETTUS *Fleta Min.* I. 287 Others say, That the Goslarish Calaminaris brings more increase than the mountanous Calaminaris. **1799** R. WARNER *Walk* (1800) 45 The yew, the ash, and other mountainous trees. **1801** ANNA SEWARD *Lett.* (1811) V. 387 The pure gales, mountainous and maritime, which blow around your delightful retreat.

Hence **'mountainously** *adv.*, **'mountainousness.**

1612 DRAYTON *Poly-olb.* xv. 31 Chiltern..mountainously hie. **1716** BREREWOOD *Disc. Learning* (J.), Armenia is so called from the mountainousness of it. **1845** JANE ROBINSON *Whitehall* I. 354 The waves mountainously rolling. **1854** *Chamb. Jrnl.* II. 161 Even in the quality of mountainousness ..some parts are strikingly unlike others.

mountain rescue. Used *attrib.* and *absol.* to designate an organization for rescuing mountaineers (sense 3) in distress.

1956 F. T. K. BULLMORE *Dark Haven* xxiv. 182, I think the best thing I can do is to have all leaders of Mountain Rescue Units up to London for a round-table talk. *Ibid.*, I couldn't help thinking of the many..difficulties that these Mountain Rescue Squads would have to face. *Ibid.* xxvi. 189 Roxborough had been making great progress with the Mountain Rescue Organization. To help him with the technical difficulties of mountaineering he had unearthed.. an Austrian mountain guide. **1957** R. G. COLLOMB *Dict. Mountaineering* 108 Mountain districts in Britain and the Alps have their own mountain rescue posts... Mountain rescue teams are local organizations made up of people working in the district. **1959** 'G. CARR' *Swing Away, Climber* iv. 74 Telephone Higgs at the Pen-y-gwryd for the mountain rescue stretcher. **1971** O. NORTON *Corpse-Bird Cries* v. 85 There was a mountain rescue van there. **1973** C. BONINGTON *Next Horizon* i. 26 He..had spent some years with the Royal Air Force in Mountain Rescue, and was a good steady goer.

mountain sheep. **1.** [MOUNTAIN 8 b.] Sheep kept in mountainous regions. Cf. SHEEP *sb.* 1 b.

1829 T. L. PEACOCK *Misfortunes Elphin* xi. 141 The mountain sheep are sweeter, But the valley sheep are fatter. **1910** W. DE LA MARE *Three Mulla-Mulgars* 17 The little coat of mountain-sheep's wool. **1961** J. GUNSTON *Profit from Sheep* i. 11 Great experience of local conditions and practice is the only real guide to the proper management of mountain sheep. **1975** *Country Life* 9 Oct. 942/1 The Castlemartin range..is..a custom-built wintering ground for mountain sheep.

2. *U.S.* [MOUNTAIN 9 c.] Either of two species of North American wild sheep, the bighorn, *Ovis canadensis*, or the Dall sheep, *Ovis dalli*.

1802 in *Med. Repository 1803* 240 The mountain ram, or sheep, though not very often seen, is to be met with, in considerable numbers, in some parts of the mountains. **1807** P. GASS *Jrnl.* vii. 82 On the top of the highest [bluff] we saw some Mountain sheep, which the natives say are common about the Rocky mountains. **1837** W. IRVING *Capt. Bonneville* I. iii. 69 This animal is commonly called the mountain sheep, and is often confounded with another animal, the 'woolly sheep' found more to the northward. **1841** G. CATLIN *Lett. on N. Amer. Indians* II. 188 Dressed in a beautiful costume of the mountain-sheep skin. **1846** R. B. SAGE *Scenes Rocky Mts.* xiv. 121 In size the mountain sheep is larger than the domestic animal of that name, and its general appearance is in every respect dissimilar—excepting the head and horns. **1918** T. ROOSEVELT in *Maine my State* (Maine Writers Research Club) (1919) 21 We had a couple of antelope and a yearling mountain sheep. **1947** *Trail & Timberline* Feb. 15/2 We saw moose, bear, caribou, mountain (Dall) sheep, and wolves almost every trip.

mountain side. Also with hyphen or as one word. The sloping surface of a mountain below the summit. Also *fig.*

c **1350** *St. John* 533 in Horstm. *Altengl. Leg.* (1881) 41 By a mountayne syide þai dweld. *c* **1460** *Towneley Myst.* viii. 98 Now am I sett to kepe, vnder thys montayn syde, Byshope lettyr shepe. **1697** DRYDEN *Æneid* I. 120 He..hurld against the Mountain side His quiv'ring Spear. **1860** TYNDALL *Glac.* I. xviii. 123 We went along the mountain-side for a time. **1910** W. DE LA MARE *Three Mulla-Mulgars* xiii. 175 The bare, snow-flecked mountain-side. **1913** J. HULBERT in *Granta* 7 Mar. 255/1 No man is helped up the mountain side of toil by undue ragging. **1960** *Farmer & Stockbreeder* 23 Feb. Suppl. 2/1, I was late and began to run, panting up the mountainside with my hand under my heart. *a* **1963** L. MACNEICE *Astrol.* (1964) ix. 286 (*caption*) A recent 'end-of-world' forecast was the catastrophe predicted by Indian astrologists in 1962. In Britain, a mountain-side prayer meeting was held to avert this disaster.

mountain snow.

1. Snow lying white on the mountains.

1592 SHAKS. *Ven. & Ad.* 750 As mountain snow melts with the midday sonne. **1602** —— *Ham.* IV. v. 35 White his Shrow'd as the Mountaine Snow. **1845** G. MURRAY *Islaford* 16 Her brow was like a wreath of mountain-snow.

2. (See quot.)

1878 ABNEY *Photogr.* (1881) 154 Barium sulphate, known as 'Mountain snow'.

3. *U.S.* The plant *Euphorbia marginata*.

1889 'C. E. CRADDOCK' *Despot of Broomsedge Cove* ix. 159 He mechanically noted..how the blooming 'Mountain snow' brushed his mare's fine coat. **1897–8** BRITTON & BROWN *Amer. Flora.* **1913** BRITTON & BROWN *Illustr. Flora Northern U.S.* (ed. 2) II. 469 *Euphorbia marginata*... In dry soil, Minnesota to Colorado, south to Texas. Introduced into waste places in the Central and Atlantic States. Snow-on-the-mountain... Mountain-snow.

mountainward ('maʊntɪnwəd), *a.* and *adv.* [f. MOUNTAIN + -WARD.] **a.** *adj.* Directed towards mountains. **b.** *adv.* In the direction of mountains. Also **mountainwards**.

1834 MUDIE *Brit. Birds* (1841) II. 80 Mountainward they approach. **1885** *Century Mag.* XXIX. 839 Tenanted by the most advanced settler mountainwards in the Yakima Valley. **1898** *Pop. Sci. Monthly* LIII. 792 Mountainward tourists need their water boots.

mountainy ('maʊntɪnɪ), *a.* ? Now *Anglo-Irish.* Also 7 **-any.** [f. MOUNTAIN + -Y.] **a.** Having mountains or hills. **b.** Belonging to or dwelling in the mountains.

1613 PURCHAS *Pilgrimage* (1614) 379 To be conueied to Zalga, a strong mountainy place. **1637** T. MORTON *New Eng. Canaan* (1883) 122 The Massachusetts..is a very beautifull Land, not mountany nor inclininge to mountany. **1744** A. DOBBS *Hudson's Bay* 140 In Lat. 44° 30' it was mountainy, and full of Silver Mines. **1780** A. YOUNG *Tour Irel.* (1887) 65 Crossed an immense mountainy bog. **1825** T. C. CROKER *Fairy Leg.* (new ed.) 357 He rented a small mountainy farm. **1881** MISS LAFFAN in *Macm. Mag.* XLIV. 386 The mountainy people brought down but little [butter].

mountan, obs. form of MUNTIN.

† '**mountance.** *Obs.* Forms: 3–4 **mountaunce**, 4 **-touns**, 4–5 **mo(u)ntance**, 5 **mountans(e)**, **mowntans**, **-ance**, **-aunse**. [a. OF. *montance*, f. *monter* to rise: see MOUNT *v.* and -ANCE.] Amount, value.

c **1290** *S. Eng. Leg.* I. 384/280 þe sike Men alle..leiȝen þare..þe mountaunce of half a tide. **1303** R. BRUNNE *Handl. Synne* 5768 And withholde þerof no þyng, þe mountouns of a ferþyng. *c* **1386** CHAUCER *Manciple's T.* 151 Noght worth to thee in comparison The montance of a gnat. *c* **1485** *E.E. Misc.* (Warton Club) 85 Salle-peter the mowntance of the 3olke of an egge.

mountaneer, -ier, obs. var. ff. MOUNTAINEER.

mountanous, obs. variant of MOUNTAINOUS.

† **mountant**, *a.* and *sb.*[1] *Obs.* [a. F. *montant*, pr. pple. of *monter* MOUNT *v.*]

A. *sb.* *Astrol.* Ascendant.

c **1400** tr. *Secreta Secret., Gov. Lordsh.* 112 þe mountant, or þe vpspryngand.

B. *adj.* Mounting, rising.

1525 LD. BERNERS *Froiss.* II. 658 They caused him to have, in ready money, mountante to the somme of thyrty thousande pounds. **1607** SHAKS. *Timon* IV. iii. 135 Hold vp you Sluts Your Aprons mountant; you're not Oathable, Although I know you'l sweare. **1625** C. BROOKE *On Sir A. Chichester* Poems (1872) 222 That fyre shall make hym mountant, and aspire A radiant light. **1812** W. TENNANT *Anster F.* II. lxiv, Tumblers..mountant from the scaffolds planks, Kick with their whirling heels the clouds on high.

mountant ('maʊntənt), *sb.*[2] [f. MOUNT *sb.*[2] + -ANT[1], after F. *montant*: see prec.] An adhesive substance with which to mount photographs, etc.

1886 *Queen* LXXX. 538 Several mountants are daily employed, such as common glue, gum, and clear starch paste. **1892** *Photogr. Ann.* II. 956 Any gelatine mountant.

mountany, obs. form of MOUNTAINY.

mountayne, obs. form of MUNTIN.

mountbanke, obs. form of MOUNTEBANK.

† **mount cent.** *Obs.* Also 6–7 **mount sant**, 7 **mount saint**, **mounte cent.** [Of obscure origin. The evidence of the first quot. suggests connexion with CENT[2], Sp. *ciento* hundred; the first element may be connected with MOUNT *v.* in the sense 'to amount'.] A card game resembling piquet.

1599 MINSHEU *Sp. Dict., Dialogues* 25, *L.* Let vs play at Loadam. *M.* It is a play of much patience... *L.* At mount sant [Sp. *a los cientos*]. *M.* It makes my head to be in a swoune to be alwaies counting. **1607** T. COCKS *Diary* 17 Apr. (1901) 4 Wonne at mounte cent 4d and vyed ruffe. **1610** *Ibid.* 21 June 100 Lost at mountcent xij d. **1608** MACHIN *Dumb Knt.* IV. H 3 b, *Que.* Come.., here are cards. .. *Phi*... At what game will your Maiesty play? *Que.* At mount saint. **1609** MARKHAM *Famous Whore* (1868) 34 Were it Mount cent, Primero, or at chesse. *a* **1621** SIR F. MOORE *Reports* (1688) 776 Action sur le case..p[our] luy disceaver al cards, al un game le mountsant.

mountebank ('maʊntɪbæŋk), *sb.* Forms: 6 **mounterbanck**, **mountbanke**, **mountebancke**, 6–7 **mountebanke**, **-iban(c)k(e**, 7 **mountabanke**, **-ebanque**, **-ebanc(k**, **montabanke**, **-eban(c)ke**, **-ebank**, *Sc.* **muntibank**, **(montibanchi** *pl.*), **monte-banke**, **mowntibanck**, 8 **mountabanck**, 7–**mountebank.** [ad. It. *montambanco*, *montimbanco*, contracted form of the older *monta in banco* (Florio), lit. 'mount-on-bench' (*monta* imperative of *montare* MOUNT *v.*, *banco* bench). Cf. SALTIMBANCO.

Florio 1598 gives *montar' in banco* (lit. 'to mount on a bench') 'to plaie the mountibanke'. Godefr. has one instance of OF. *montenbancque*, and Sherwood 1632 gives F. *monte-banc* as the rendering of MOUNTEBANK.]

1. An itinerant quack who from an elevated platform appealed to his audience by means of stories, tricks, juggling, and the like, in which he was often assisted by a professional clown or fool.

1577 [see 6 below]. *a* **1586** SIDNEY *Apol. Poetry* (Arb.) 61 Poets..are almost in as good reputation, as the Mountibancks at Venice. **1605** BACON *Adv. Learn.* II. x. §2. 39 Men..will often preferre a Mountabanke or Witch, before a learned Phisitian. **1672** [H. STUBBE] *Rosemary & Bayes* 2 If you will now examine this new book, it will appear like a mountebank's ball. **1714** GAY *Sheph. Week* Sat. 83 The mountebank now treads the stage, and sells His pills, his balsams, and his ague-spells. **1871** ROSSETTI *Last Confession* 502 A poor painted mountebank was playing tricks and shouting in a crowd.

attrib. **1713** SWIFT *Frenzy of J. Dennis* Wks. 1755 III. I. 147 He hath told others..that he had seen me upon a mountebank stage in Moorfields.

2. *fig.* An impudent pretender to skill or knowledge, a charlatan; one who resorts to degrading means to obtain notoriety. So ***to play the mountebank.***

1589 NASHE *Pasquill's Counter-C.* A iij b, To discredite the Phisitions of their soules vnto them, and to suffer euerie Martin and Mounte-bancke to practise on them. **1610** BOYS *Expos. Dom. Epist. & Gosp.* Wks. (1622) 111 He that will not be a mountaine in Christs way, must not bee a mount-banke of his owne vertue. **1624** WOTTON in *Reliq.* (1672) 545 Upon the Design you must play the Mountebank. And tell the Duke, that [etc.]. *a* **1704** T. BROWN *Two Oxford Schol.* Wks. 1730 I. 2 Nature has fitted me pretty well to be one of these godly Mountebanks. **1817** COLERIDGE *'Blessed are ye'* 24 The Mountebanks and Zanies of Patriotism. **1877** MRS. FORRESTER *Mignon* I. 33 One can hardly wonder at the women when the men make such asses and mountebanks of themselves.

† **3.** = MOUNTEBANKERY. *Obs.*

1638 *Penit. Conf.* vii. (1657) 154 O Devillish Mountebanke! by which Spiritual kind of Cosenage many are perswaded. **1722** DE FOE *Plague* (1756) 277 As for Quackery and Mountebank, of which the Town was so full [etc.].

4. The short-tailed African kite, *Helotarsus ecaudatus* (*Cent. Dict.* 1890).

5. *appositive.* (quasi-*adj.*) That is a mountebank; characteristic of a mountebank.

1603 HOLLAND *Plutarch's Mor.* III. These Mount-bank Chirurgians. **1614** LATHAM *Falconry* To Rdr., I could haue vsed a more mountebanque preface. **1852** GLADSTONE *Glean.* IV. ii. 141 Theatrical, not to say charlatan and mountebank, politics.

6. *Comb.*

1577 STANYHURST *Descr. Irel.* ii. 8/2 in *Holinshed*, He shoulde haue gone shotfree with his complices, and haue made in Mounterbanckwyse the most he coulde of his wares. **1654** WHITLOCK *Zootomia* 46 How easily might I here digresse in Satyre against Mountebanck-making Patients. **1727** DE FOE *Syst. Magic* I. iii. (1840) 68 They were counted the best and wisest men, who, mountebank like, could show most tricks.

Hence '**mountebankish** *a.*, worthy of a mountebank. '**mountebankism**, the practice or method of a mountebank. † '**mountebankly** *adv.*, after the manner of a mountebank.

1619 PURCHAS *Microcosmus* lviii. 562 Nature, by some Naturalists hath beene too Mounte-bankly magnified. **1653** R. SANDERS *Physiogn.* 50 An inclination to all sorts of Cheateries and Mountebankism. **1660** HOWELL *Parly Beasts* 87 A Saturnian Merchant..whom..for som Hocos-pocos and Mountebank tricks I transformed to a Fox. **1882** *Society* 7 Oct. 14/2 If he is..able to stem the tide of musical mountebankism rampant at another series of.. concerts.

'**mountebank**, *v.* [f. MOUNTEBANK *sb.*]

† **1.** *trans.* To prevail over (a person) by 'mountebank' persuasion. *Obs.*

1607 SHAKS. *Cor.* III. ii. 132 Ile Mountebanke their Loues, Cogge their Hearts from them, and come home belou'd Of all the Trades in Rome. **1702** DE FOE *Reform. Manners* I. 124 With Eloquence endu'd To Mountebank the listning Multitude.

† **2.** To introduce by mountebank persuasions; to transform by mountebank trickery. *Obs.*

1647 WARD *Simp. Cobler* 2 Men of Paracelsian parts..are fittest to Mountebanke his [Satan's] Chimistry into sicke Churches and weake Iudgements. **1702** DE FOE *Reform. Manners* I. 316 The wondring Bubbles stand amaz'd to see Their Money Mountebank'd to Mercury.

3. *intr.* To play the mountebank. Usually with *it.*

1814 BYRON *Let. to Moore* 9 Apr., I..will mountebank it no longer. **1848** KINGSLEY *Saint's Trag.* II. v, Say if 'tis wise to..mountebank it in the public ways Till she becomes a jest? **1882** STEVENSON *New Arab. Nts.* (1884) 302, I find you mountebanking in a public café.

Hence '**mountebanking** *vbl. sb.* and *ppl. a.*

1602 MARSTON *Ant. & Mel.* Induct., Wks. 1856 I. 2, I play Balurdo, a wealthie mountbanking burgomasco's heire of Venice. **1705** *Dyet of Poland* 17 The Quacking, Mountebanking Tool of State. **1860** THACKERAY *Round. Papers, De Juventute* 77 Do not suppose I am going..to indulge in moralities about buffoons..and mountebanking.

mountebankery ('maʊntɪbæŋkərɪ). [f. as prec. + -ERY.] Action, or an act, which bespeaks or characterizes a mountebank.

1618 SIR R. NAUNTON in *Fortescue Papers* (Camden) 71 For giving no easier way to theyr mountebanqueries. **1677** GILPIN *Demonol.* (1867) 421 When I have sometime observed a mountebank..giving excessive commendations of a trivial medicine..it hath put me in mind of this spiritual mountebankery of the devil. **1845** *Medico-Chirurg. Rev.* Apr. 370 Our author is too acute to believe in any of the mountebankeries..of this 'forlorn thing'[*i.e.* mesmerism]. **1887** *Sat. Rev.* 16 July 71/1 The kind of mountebankery which has carried many a man into power in France.

mounte cent, variant of MOUNT CENT.

mounted ('maʊntɪd), *a.* [f. MOUNT *v.* + -ED[1].]

1. Of material things: Elevated or piled up like a mountain. Now *rare.*

1582 STANYHURST *Æneis* II. (Arb.) 69 Lucifer owtpeaking in tips of mounted hil Ida On draws thee dawning. **1614** SIR A. GORGES tr. *Lucan* I. 26 The stilled maine Reclaimes her mounted waues againe. **1859** G. MEREDITH *R. Feverel* xix, At the farthest bourne of mounted eastern cloud, the heralds of the sun lay rosy fingers.

† **2. a.** Elevated in situation. Also *fig.* *Obs.*

1601 ? MARSTON *Pasquil & Kath.* I. 115 What's wealth without respect and mounted place? *a* **1645** HABINGTON *Surv. Worc.* in *Worc. Hist. Soc. Proc.* II. 271 Descendinge from the mounted Prioryes of Maluerne..I come to Hanly Castele.

b. Elevated on a platform or stage. *Obs.*

1683 in Kennett tr. *Erasm. on Folly* (e) 3 b, While mounted Andrews, bawdy, bold, and loud, Like Cocks, alarum all the drowsie Crowd.

3. a. Seated on the back of a horse or other animal. Also, of soldiers: Appointed to serve on horseback. *attrib.*, as ***mounted branch***, ***infantry***, ***police***, ***rifles*** (see quots.).

In more recent use said also of the rider of a bicycle or tricycle.

1598 BARRET *Theor. Warres* 141 These mounted people ought to haue some skill in diseases of horses. **1792** *Deb. Congress U.S.* (1849) 18 Sept. 1134 General Harman.. detached..the mounted infantry. **1799** *Instr. & Reg. Cavalry* (1813) 279 In passing on foot, all mounted officers are in front of the regiment, except the adjutant. **1834** R. M. MARTIN *Hist. Brit. Colonies* I. iii. 147 There is a mounted police officered by [Indian] natives. **1858** E. H. D. DOMENECH *Missionary Adventures Texas & Mexico* 177 The Indians were once nearly taking prisoners a whole company of mounted infantry. **1859** J. BLACKWOOD *Let.* 24 July in Geo. Eliot *Lett.* (1954) III. 121 The animal is..under charge of..the veterinary of the Mounted Police. **1878** *Saskatchewan Herald* (Battleford) 25 Aug. 1/2 Shoal Lake has been created the headquarters of the Mounted Police for that district. **1882** *Army & Navy Mag.* May 19 The ideal Mounted Infantry is, what the name implies, infantry soldiers mounted on horseback for the purpose of enabling them to get with celerity from one position to another. **1901** *Empire Rev.* I 375 While Mounted Infantry are footmen trained for purposes of mobility to ride a horse or bicycle, Mounted Rifles are horsemen trained to fight on foot. **1935** N. MITCHISON *We have been Warned* IV. 452 Six mounted police went by at the trot, scattering the crowd. **1963** *Calgary Herald Mag.* 4 Oct. 48/4 An old Mounted Police stable may..be seen. **1970** P. LAURIE *Scotland Yard* ii. 50 A specialist job: the CID..Mounted Branch.

b. Of evolutions, etc.: Performed on horseback.

1883 *Daily News* 31 Aug. 6/6 A series of mounted contests promoted for the entertainment of the garrison.

4. Set up or adjusted for use; placed on a stand or support; fitted.

1692 SIR W. HOPE *Fencing-Master* (ed. 2) 161 A well mounted sword, which is light before the Hand... If the Hilt contrepoise the Blade, it is well mounted, otherwise not. **1854** FAIRHOLT *Dict. Terms Art, Mounted*, secured to a *mount*. A term applied to a print or drawing fastened upon mounting-paper or card-board. **1855** HOPKINS *Organ* 122 The Mounted Cornet is a Compound-stop, consisting usually of 5 ranks of pipes, made to a very large scale. **1879** *Cassell's Techn. Educ.* IV. 123/1 The stuffed animals and mounted skeletons. **1900** *Daily News* 1 June 2/7 A fine five-inch equatorially mounted astronomical telescope.

5. *Mil.* Of cannon: Set up for use. Of a fort, a ship, etc.: Furnished (*with* cannon).

1639 BAILLIE in Boyd *Zion's Flowers* (1855) Introd. 45 Our Hill was garnished..with our mounted canon. **1769** FALCONER *Dict. Marine* (1780), *Mounted*, the state of being armed..with a certain number of cannon; expressed of a vessel of war. **1829** MARRYAT *F. Mildmay* iv, The quarter-deck guns all adrift, and not even mounted.

6. *Her.* **a.** Of a horse: Bearing a rider. **b.** Of a cross or the like: Set upon greces or degrees.

1828–40 BERRY *Encycl. Herald.* I.

7. Of a project, exhibition, or radio or television programme: produced, directed, arranged. Cf. MOUNT *v.* 17 d.

1895 in *Funk's Stand. Dict.* **1966** *Listener* 30 June 945/2 The carefully mounted [broadcast] series for mentally handicapped children. **1971** *Nature* 9 July 74/1 The medical problems of many developing countries,..should be amenable to all kinds of internationally mounted projects.

†**mountee.** *Mil. Obs.* In 5 mowntee. [a. F. *montée*: see MOUNTY.] (See quot.)

1415 *Stat. Hen. V* in Upton *De Studio Milit.* IV. (1654) 137 Volumus..quod nullus..clamores vel turbationes facere audeat, quibus nos vel excercitum nostrum turbari contingat quovismodo. Et specialiter illum clamorem, quem Mowntee appellamus. **1701** in *Cowel's Interpr.* (ed. Kennett), *Mowntee*, an Out-cry or Alarm to mount, and make some speedy Expedition. **1706** PHILLIPS (ed. Kersey), *Mountee*, or *Mowntee*.

mountee, -teer, obs. ff. MOUNTY, MONTERO.

mountein(e, -elet, obs. ff. MOUNTAIN, -LET.

mounten, obs. form of MOUNTAIN.

†**mountenance.** *Obs.* Forms: 3–4 **montenance,** 4–6 **mountenaunce,** 5 **mowntenawnce, -awns,** 5–7 **mountenance.** [App. a corruption of MOUNTANCE, assimilated to *maintenance.*] Amount in extent, quantity, or value.

a **1300** *Cursor M.* 29166 Þai sal eiþer for þair foly bren in þe fier of purgatori, to þe montenance o þat plight, agh for þat sin was here to right. **1387–8** T. USK *Test. Love* I. ix. (Skeat) 49 As farre in a moment, as in mountenaunce of ten Winter. *c* **1420** *Liber Cocorum* (1862) 26 Take powder þo mountenaunce of a pownde. **1579** BAKER *Guydon's Quest. Chirurg.* 30 The gaule..conteyneth peradventure a glasse ful, or the mountenance of a Viole. **1674** JOSSELYN *Voy. New Eng.* 130 They satisfie themselves with a small quantity of meal,..which taken to the mountenance of a Bean would satisfie both thirst and hunger.

b. Total quantity, mass.

1615 CROOKE *Body of Man* 35 The third Region comprehendeth the Muscles, Membranes, Bones, and in a word, all the *Moles* or mountenance of the body.

†**mountenesse.** *Obs. rare.* [? Corruption of MOUNTANCE, as if f. MOUNT *v.* + -NESS.] = prec.

c **1420** *Chron. Vilod.* 2278 Þis twaylle y-bordryd abouȝt was Wᵗ palle þe mountenesse ofe han hondbrede. *c* **1420** *St. Etheldred* 8 in Horstm. *Altengl. Leg.* (1881) 283 Þe mountenesse of two and thretty full ȝere.

mountenous, obs. form of MOUNTAINOUS.

†**'mounter**[1]. *Obs. rare.* Also 6 mownter. [? var. of MOUNTURE. (Cf. provincial F. *monture* cattle on a farm (Godefr.).] ? A portion of the chattels of a deceased tenant which was due by feudal custom to the lord; cf. HERIOT.

c **1500** in I. S. Leadam *Star Chamber Cases* (1903) 101 The seid Erle owght to haue by deth of his tenaunt a mownter and a heryott. *Ibid.* 104 For part of the seid heriottes or mownters the seid Erle toke vj Oxen and a hors.

mounter[2] ('maʊntə(r)). [f. MOUNT *v.* + -ER[1].] In various senses of the verb.

1. *gen.* One who ascends.

1609 BIBLE (Douay) *Deut.* xxxiii. 26 The mownter of heaven is thy helper. **1627** DRAYTON *Agincourt*, etc. 131 And though they to the earth were throwne, Yet quickly they regain'd their owne,..They were two Gallant Mounters. **1827** HOOD *Monkey Martyr* vii, He went above—a solitary mounter Up gloomy stairs.

2. One whose business it is to mount, fit, or set (anything) in place or order.

1747 *Gentl. Mag.* 101 Stick-maker, flint-maker, and mounter or screwer together. **1863** *Reader* 24 Jan. 101 Nothing but practice..will make any one a good mounter [of microscope slides]. **1881** *Instr. Census Clerks* (1885) 50 Scabbard Making (Leather):..Gilder, Mounter. **1884** C. G. W. LOCK *Workshop Receipts* Ser. III. 19/2 After the chaser has finished his work, the piece returns to the mounter, who definitively secures the elements of the pieces in their places.

3. (See quot.)

1812 J. H. VAUX *Flash Dict.*, *Mounter*, a man who lives by mounting, or perjury, who is always ready for a guinea or two to swear whatever is proposed to him.

mountera, -re, -ro, obs. forms of MONTERO.

mounteyn, obs. form of MOUNTAIN.

‖**mountflascon.** *Obs.* [ad. It. *Monte Fiascone* (Englished *mounth Flask* by Bokenham 1447).] A wine produced at Monte Fiascone in Italy.

1566 DRANT *Horace, Sat.* II. iv. Hj, If thou wilte purge mounteflascon wynes..Set them abrode in open ayre.

mountiban(c)k(e, obs. forms of MOUNTEBANK.

Mountie ('maʊntɪ). *colloq.* Also **Mounty.** [f. MOUNT(ED *a.* + -IE, -Y[6].] **1.** A member of the Royal Canadian (formerly North West) Mounted Police.

1914 *Eye Opener* (Calgary) 12 Dec. 3/4 Ketchen, the Mountie,..was easily placated. **1924** A. J. SMALL *Frozen Gold* vi. 139 A sentence that is at once the badge and boast of the Mounted—'the Mounties never come in without their man'. **1927** *Sunday at Home* 106/2 The Eskimo borrowed the Mounty's gun and shot him. **1971** D. HEFFRON *Nice Fire & Some Moonpennies* i. 12 We all looked all around us as though there might be a Mountie skulking behind every tree. **1973** *Saturday Night* (Toronto) Feb. 22/1 All I could see was the Mounties' legs.

2. A member of a similar police force outside Canada.

1931 *Skipper* 25 Apr. 112 A detachment of the Camel Corps on the march outside Cairo. These desert 'mounties' keep law and order in Egypt. **1953** R. CAMPBELL *Mamba's Precipice* 125, I wonder why such a smart man with a castle in England has to come out here [*sc.* S. Africa] and work as an ordinary Mountie.

mountie, variant of MOUNTY *Obs.*

mountineer, obs. form of MOUNTAINEER.

mounting ('maʊntɪŋ), *vbl. sb.* [f. MOUNT *v.* + -ING[1].]

1. a. The action of the verb MOUNT in various senses.

c **1440** *Promp. Parv.* 347/1 Mowntynge, or steynynge (*sic*, *S.* styynge), *ascensus*. **1515** *Acc. Ld. Treas. Scotl.* V. 17 To pas..to Glasgw, for the stokking, monting, drawing, and making of crane and wyndais for fourtene pecis of artalȝary. **1624** WOTTON *Archit.* II. 109 From this [terrace] the Beholder descending many steps, was afterwards conueyed againe, by seuerall mountings and valings, to various entertainements of his sent, and sight. **1805** WORDSW. *Prelude* I. 19 Trances of thought and mountings of the mind Come fast upon me. **1816** BYRON *Ch. Har.* III. xxv, And there was mounting in hot haste. **1828** J. EBERS *Seven Yrs. King's Theatre* xii. 331 The mounting of this, the first performance of the season, afforded me an illustration of the obliging disposition of Madame Biagioli. **1846** *Swell's Night Guide* 43 She undertakes the art of mounting, which she teaches with considerable success. **1880** *Athenæum* 6 Mar. 322 As regards mounting and general decorations the revival is superior to any previous performance of *As You Like It*. **1892** MONIER-WILLIAMS, etc. *Figure-Skating* 8 The mounting of the blade and its attachment to the boot are important. **1959** *Times Lit. Suppl.* 16 Jan. 27/2 Twenty per cent. of the current United States military budget is to be allocated to economic aid and industrial development of the underdeveloped countries, including the mounting of a crash programme for the development of compact and readily transportable atomic power plants. **1962** *Listener* 14 June 1016/2 Ministers of Defence connived at the mounting of an abusive legal action which again jeopardized the journal's financial stability. **1974** H. WAUGH *Parrish for Defence* (1975) xliii. 200 It aroused him, and his second mounting was in the nature of an unbridled emotion.

b. *attrib.*, as **mounting-block,** a block of stone from which to mount on horseback. Similarly ***mounting-place, -stone.*** Also ***mounting board, bracket, point, ring, test.***

c **1489** CAXTON *Blanchardyn* xix. 61 Theire coursers.. were brought anone to the mountyng place before the halle. **1659** HOWELL *Vocab.* ii, A mounting block. **1854** FAIRHOLT *Dict. Terms Art, Mount* (*Mounting-board, Mounting-paper*), the paper or cardboard upon which a drawing is placed. **1869** TOZER *Highl. Turkey* I. 334 To cross [this bridge] on foot..appears to be the custom among the natives, from the mounting stones which are placed at either end. **1899** SOMERVILLE & ROSS *Irish R. M.* 297, I smoked in the yard, seated on the old mounting-block by the gate. **1926** *Paper Terminol.* (Spalding & Hodge) 18 *Mounting boards* are made up of a wood pulp centre lined on one or both sides with paper. **1937** E. J. LABARRE *Dict. Paper* 177/1 *Mounting test*, a method of testing the absorbing power of blotting paper by allowing the ink or water to 'mount' up a strip of blotting, the 'weight test' determining the weight of liquid absorbed. **1944** *R.A.F. Jrnl.* Aug. 292 Strange is the conversation to the uninitiated ear—Mounting rings..—Double engine changes—these are the phrases heard. **1962** *Which? Car Suppl.* Oct. 131/1 The mounting points for the sun visors.. were metal and unguarded. *Ibid.* 138/2 The mounting bracket for the accelerator linkage. *Ibid.* 143/1 Safety belt mounting points..are now fitted as standard equipment.

c. The angle at which the iron of a plane is set.

1678 MOXON *Mech. Exerc.* iv. 70.

2. *concr.* **a.** Something that serves as a mount, support, or setting to anything.

c **1618** MORYSON *Itin.* IV. (1903) 422 The Italians..excell in the Art of setting Jewells, and making Cabinetts, tables and mountings, of Christall, corall, Jasper, and other precious stones. **1716** ADDISON *Freeholder* No. 15 ¶5 Another..has filled her Fan with the Figure of a huge taudry Woman... The following Designs are already executed on several Mountings. **1727–41** CHAMBERS *Cycl.*, *Mounting of a fan*, the sticks which serve to open and shut it. **1763** *Museum Rust.* I. 160, Fig. 7. is the handle, or mounting of the largest scythe. **1767** FERGUSSON *Dict. Terms Small Sword* 12 *Hilt*, the head or mounting of a sword. **1793** W. & S. JONES *Catal. Optical*, etc. *Instr.* 1. Reading and burning glasses, in various mountings. **1899** R. MUNRO *Prehist. Scotl.* vi. 196 Sheaths of bronze or wood with bronze mounting were used to protect the blades. **1914** C. F. TWENEY *Dict. Naval & Mil. Terms* 157 *Mountings*, a term applied to the platforms on which heavy naval guns and guns of position for fortresses are mounted. **1962** *Which? Car Suppl.* Oct. 138/2 Flexible gear box rear mounting made gear lever vibrate considerably on rough ground. *Ibid.* 139/2 Fuel pump mounting [was] slightly insecure. *Ibid.*, Central mounting of exhaust system failed.

†**b.** *sing.* and *pl. Mil.* A soldier's outfit or 'kit'; also, in narrower sense, 'The shirt, shoes, stock, and hose, or stockings, formerly furnished by the colonel or commandant of the corps every year' (Crabb). Also, ***half*** or ***small mounting*** in the same sense (C. James *Milit. Dict.* 1802). *Obs.*

a **1700** B. E. *Dict. Cant. Crew, Mountings*, a Soldier's Arms and Cloths. **1702** *Lond. Gaz.* No. 3860/4 Deserted.. John Hellier,..and John Brown,..with their whole Mounting, being Red lined with Yellow. **1722** DE FOE *Col. Jack* (1840) 115 They stood upon their defence, having the regiment sword on,..but none of the mounting or clothing.

c. 'That which is or may be mounted for use or ornament' (*Cent. Dict.*).

3. = HARNESS *sb.* 6 (Knight *Dict. Mech.* 1875).

4. Used for MUNTIN.

1823 P. NICHOLSON *Pract. Build.* 160 Vertical pieces, that separate the panels [are denominated] mountings. **1879** *Cassell's Techn. Educ.* I. 184 The extreme parts of the frame ..are called the stiles, and the intermediate ones.. mountings.

'mounting, *ppl. a.* [f. MOUNT *v.* + -ING[2].]

1. Rising, ascending, soaring. *lit.* and *fig.*

1563 B. GOOGE *Cupido* 230 in *Eglogs*, etc. (Arb.) 113 We flewe, my Guyde and I, with mowntyng flyght apace. **1577** WHETSTONE *Gascoigne* (Arb.) 18 The mounting minde had rather sterue in need. [Cf. SHAKS. *L.L.L.* IV. i. 4.] **1590** SPENSER *F.Q.* I. xi. 51 With mery note her lowd salutes the mounting larke. **1664** DRYDEN *Rival Ladies* I. ii, I am no more afraid of flying Censures, Than Heav'n of being fir'd with mounting Sparkles. **1720** GAY *Rur. Sports* 45 While with the mounting sun the meadow glows. **1859** GEO. ELIOT *A. Bede* vii, Straining your eyes after the mounting lark.

†**b.** *Her.* (see quot. 1731). *Obs. rare.*

1688 R. HOLME *Armoury* II. 175/2 He beareth Sable, a demy Ram mounting, Argent. **1731** BAILEY (vol. II.), *Mounting* signifies the same spoken of beasts of chase, as rampant does of beasts of prey.

†**2.** Amounting, resulting. *Obs.*

1571 DIGGES *Pantom.* II. xxiv. Piij b, If ye square the perpendicular, the mounting summe will be [etc.].

Hence **'mountingly** *adv.*, so as to rise high.

a **1640** MASSINGER, etc., *Old Law* II. i, I..leapt for joy So mountingly I touchd the stars me thought.

mountire, obs. form of MONTERO.

mountjack, obs. form of MANJAK.

†**'mountlet.** *Obs.* Also 7 mountelet. [f. MOUNT *sb.*[1] + -LET.] A little mount.

1610 G. FLETCHER *Christ's Vict.* I. l, Those snowie mountelets, through which do creep The milkie rivers, that are inly bred. [Echoed by later 17th c. poets.]

Mountmellick (maʊnt'mɛlɪk). The name of a town in the Irish Republic used *attrib.* to designate a type of white-work embroidery made there.

1893 E. T. MASTERS *Gentlewoman's Bk. Art Needlework* iii. 77 The material upon which the original Mountmellick embroidery was executed was a stout make of white satin jean, white knitting-cotton of various sizes being used to form the stitches. The designs are usually somewhat naturalistic in style. **1920** A. K. ARTHUR *Embroidery Bk.* viii. 85 Bullion knots are used very frequently in Mountmellick work. **1936** M. THOMAS *Embroidery Bk.* 187 Contrary to most other forms of white work, there are no open or drawn spaces in Mountmellick Embroidery. The stitches are planned to lie on the surface of the material with as little thread as possible beneath, and to provide the sense of 'stitchery in relief'. *Ibid.* 194 The following is a list of stitches, suitable for Mountmellick Embroidery. **1959** *Chambers's Encycl.* V. 156/1 Mountmellick embroidery is an Irish form of white work, using a variety of stitches but no open spaces. **1960** H. HAYWARD *Antique Coll.* 191/2 *Mount Mellick embroidery*, a type of white-work, first introduced about 1830 at Mountmellick in Queen's County, Ireland, and revived as a local industry in the 1880s. **1962** B. MORRIS *Victorian Embroidery* ii. 40 An entirely different type of whitework known as 'Mountmellick embroidery' was popular throughout the Victorian period. **1967** E. SHORT *Embroidery & Fabric Collage* i. 19 *Mountmellick embroidery.* This embroidery relies on padded stitches, knots, etc., giving a raised surface to the embroidery.

†**mountredinctido.** ? = MOUNTEBANK.
1651 C. WALKER *Hist. Independ.* III. 25 William Pemoier Esquire was heretofore an ape-carrier, Cherry-lickom or Mountredinctido.

†**Moun'trose.** *Obs.* Some kind of wine.
?*c* **1475** *Sqr. Lowe Degre* 755 Both ypocrasse, and vernage wyne, Mountrose and wyne of Greke.

†'**mountuous,** *a.* *Obs.* Also **montuous, mountewous.** [ad. L. *montuōs-us* (also *montōsus*), f. *mont-*, *mons* mountain: see MOUNT *sb.*[1] and -OUS. Cf. OF. *montueux.*] Mountainous, hilly. Also, situated among mountains.
1382 WYCLIF *Jer.* xvii. 26 Fro the mountuous places [Vulg. *de montuosis*]. *Ibid.* xxxiii. 13 In the mountewous [*v.r.* mountuous] cities. **1387** TREVISA *Higden* (Rolls) I. 157 Ethiopia haþ þre parties, þe firste is hilly and montuous.

†'**mounture.** *Obs.* [a. OF. *monteure* (mod.F. *monture*), f. *monte-r* to MOUNT.]
1. A horse (or other animal) for riding.
13.. *Gaw. & Gr. Knt.* 1691 Miry was þe mornyng, his mounture he askes. *c* **1420** *Anturs of Arth.* 555 (Douce MS.), I mourne for no monture, for I may gete mare. **1481** CAXTON *Godeffroy* xc. 141 More hurte in theyr mounture than alle the other of thoost. **1579–80** NORTH *Plutarch, Alexander* (1657) 584 Porus..being upon an Elephants backe he wanted nothing in height and bignesse to be proportionable for his mounture. **1600** FAIRFAX *Tasso* XVII. xxviii, An Elephant this furious Giant bore, He fierce as fire, his mounture swift as winde.
2. a. An erection to mount upon. **b.** A mound or hillock.
c **1400** MAUNDEV. (1839) xx. 217 In the myddes of this Palays is the Mountour [L. *ascensorium*, F. *mountaynette*] for the grete Cane, that is alle wrought of Gold and of precyous Stones and grete Perles. **1614** RALEIGH *Hist. World* I. (1634) 89 There were removed divers old heapes and mountures of ground.
3. = MOUNTING *vbl. sb.* 2.
1489 CAXTON *Faytes of A.* I. 17 Be he habylled and arrayed rychely in harnoys and mountures. **1575** GASCOIGNE *Posies, Weeds* 183 The brauest peece for breech and bore, that euer yet was bought: The mounture so well made.
4. = ELEVATION 10.
1613 T. MILLES tr. *Mexia's Treas. Anc. & Mod. T.* 56 The Barbacanes or Subburbes, which were of as high mounture and strength, as the walles of the City.
5. *Mil.* The angle at which a gun is elevated.
1628 R. NORTON *Gunner* 60 The proportion of powder, fitting each sort of Shot and Mounture. **1644** NYE *Gunnery* II. (1647) 8 The next Shot was at five Degrees Randon, at which mounture shee conveyed 416 paces. **1692** *Capt. Smith's Seaman's Gram.* II. xxvi. 138 If a Piece carries her Shot, at 16 deg. of Mounture 1074 Paces, the Horizontal Rainge of that Peece will be found to be 374 Paces.
6. ? = HARNESS *sb.* 6.
1799 G. SMITH *Laboratory* II. 50 These are called the tail of the mounture; and from each of these packthreads, just by the side of the loom, are fastened other packthreads.

†'**mounty.** *Falconry. Obs.* Also 6–7 **mountie,** 7 **mountee.** [a. F. *montée*, n. of action f. *monter* to MOUNT. Cf. MOUNTEE.] The action, or an act, of rising in pursuit of the quarry.
a **1586** SIDNEY *Arcadia* II. (1590) 114 But the sporte which for that daie Basilius would principallie shewe to Zelmane, was the mountie at a Hearne. **1615** LATHAM *Falconry* (1633) 73 Then ought you to be most carefull of the yong Ger-Faulcon, whom you intend to make to the high mounty, and stately flight of the Hearne. **1650** WELDON *Crt. Jas. I* 105 To see that flight..for the high mountee;..the flight was shewed, but the Kite went to such a mountee, as all the field lost sight of Kite and Hawke and all. **1657** R. LIGON *Barbadoes* 105 No mountie at a Hieron, to cause the lustie Jerfaulcon to raise her to a losse of her selfe.

Mounty, var. MOUNTIE.

mountycle, obs. form of MONTICULE.

moup, moop (muːp), *v. Sc.* [Of obscure origin; possibly two different words.]
1. *trans.* (See quot. 1721.) Also *intr.* or *absol.*
1513 DOUGLAS *Æneis* VII. iii. 22 The paringis of thair breid to movp wp sone. **1721** RAMSAY *Keitha* 3 My sheep and kye neglect to moup their food. **1721** —— *Poems* Gloss., *Moup*, to eat, generally used of children, or of old people, who have but few teeth, and make their lips move fast tho' they eat but slow.
2. To associate *with*. Phr. ***to moup and mell.***
1783 BURNS *Death Poor Mailie* 55 But ay keep mind to moop an' mell Wi' sheep o' credit like thysel! *a* **1796** —— *Gude Ale* ii, Guid ale hauds me bare and busy, Gars me moop wi' the servant hizzie.
Hence '**mouping** *ppl. a.*, mumbling, toothless.
1718 RAMSAY *Christ's Kirk Gr.* III. v, A moupin runkled granny.

mour(e, variant forms of MAUR and MORE *sb.*[2]

mourdant, mourdre, obs. ff. MORDANT, MURDER.

Moure, mourish, obs. ff. MOOR *sb.*[2], MORRIS *sb.*[1]

†'**mourken,** *v. Obs. rare*$^{-1}$. [a. ON. *morkna.*] *intr.* To rot.
13.. *E.E. Allit. P.* B. 407 Þenne mourkne in þe mudde most ful nede Alle þat spyrakle in-spranc.

mourkenen, obs. variant of MURKEN *v.*

mourkenes, obs. form of MURKNESS.

mourn, *sb. Obs.* exc. *dial.* [f. MOURN *v.*] Sorrow, lamentation, grief, mourning; also *dial.* a murmur, a murmuring sound.
a **1300** *Cursor M.* 10478 Son quen sco was comun þar, Sco gaf hir al to murn and care. *Ibid.* 24229 He þat sa reufulli was dight, If he þe said oght for to light þi mode þat was in murn. **1470–85** MALORY *Arthur* II. xii. 89 Sire ryght now cam rydynge this way a knyght makynge grete moorne for what cause I can not telle. **1594** LODGE & GREENE *Looking-gl.* (1598) C 3, Is she not faire?..A pretie peate to driue your mourne away. **1824** MRS. CAMERON *Marten & his Schol.* vii, I helped to carry him to the grave, poor lad! His parents made great mourn over him.

†**mourn,** *a. Obs.* Forms: 3 **mourne,** 3–4 **murne,** 4 **morne.** [Perh. a. F. *morne*, believed to be of Teut. origin cogn. w. MOURN *v.* Cf. however OE. *unmurn* untroubled.] Sad, mournful.
c **1205** LAY. 16159 Þa weoren Bruttes mid blisse auulled ..þæ ær weoren murne. *a* **1300** *K. Horn* 748 (Camb. MS.) Alymar aȝen gan turne, Wel Modi and wel Murne [*MS. Laud* Mourne]. *c* **1315** SHOREHAM *Poems* ii. 40 O swete leuedy, wat þey was wo, Þo ihesus by-come morne. *c* **1330** *Arth. & Merl.* 8213 (Kölbing) His hert was sore, his cher murne.

mourn (mɔən), *v.*[1] Forms: 1 **murnan,** 3 **morȝne(n,** 3–4 **morun,** 3–6 **morn(e,** 3–7 **mourne, murn(e,** 4 **morene, mourene,** 4–6 **moorn(e,** 5 **mowrn(e,** 6– **mourn,** (9 *dial.* **moorn, murn).** [Com. Teut.: OE. *murnan* wk. vb. (commonly str., pret. *mearn*, pl. *murnon*) + OS. *mornon* (also *mornian*), OHG. *mornên* to be anxious or careful, ON. *morna* to pine away (so Norw. *morna*, Ross), Goth. *maurnan* to be anxious; the Teut. root **mur-* is commonly referred to the Indogermanic **smer-* to remember, whence Gr. μέριμνα care, sorrow; some scholars, however, taking the ON. sense as primary, suggest the root **mer-* to die, wither.]
I. *intr.*
1. To feel sorrow, grief, or regret (often with added notion of expressing one's grief); to sorrow, grieve, lament. (†In OE. also to be anxious or careful.)
In early use often said of the heart, soul, etc. Also †***to mourn in** (one's) **mood, mind, heart, thought***, etc.
c **888** K. ÆLFRED *Boeth.* vii. §2 Ȝif þu þonne heora þeȝen beon wilt & þe heora þeawas liciað, to hwon myrnst þu swa swiðe? *a* **1000** *Andreas* 99 (Gr.) Ne beo ðu on sefan to forht ne on mode ne murn! *c* **1205** LAY. 3116 In hire bure heo [Cordoille] abed & þolede þene mod-kare & mornede swþe. *c* **1250** *Gen. & Ex.* 2053 He [Joseph] herde hem [the butler and baker] murnen, he hem freinde for-quat. *c* **1375** *Sc. Leg. Saints* xxx. (*Theodora*) 346 Þane scho cane murne, gretand sare. **1382** WYCLIF *Matt.* v. 5 Blessid be thei that mournen [*c* **1400** *Apol. Loll.* 7 mornun], for thei shuln be comfortid. *c* **1386** CHAUCER *Wife's Prol.* 848, I shal make thyn herte for to morne ffor wel I woot thy pacience is gon. *c* **1440** *Promp. Parv.* 344/1 Moornyn, and sorowyn, *mereo, gemo.* *c* **1470** *Gol. & Gaw.* 1128 The king precious in pane Sair murnand in mude. **1508** DUNBAR *Tua Mariit Wemen* 212 Apone sic materis I muse, at mydnyght, full oft, And murnys so in my mynd, I murdris my selfin. **1526** *Pilgr. Perf.* (W. de W. 1531) 86 b, In all euyll thou mayst fynde cause to mourne and sorowe. *a* **1533** LD. BERNERS *Huon* liv. 181 When Huon sawe howe he had not wherewith to arme him his hert mourned ryght sore. **1590** SHAKS. *Com. Err.* I. i. 74 The prettie babes That mourn'd for fashion, ignorant what to feare. **1697** CONGREVE *Mourn. Bride* I. iv, Some Here are, who seem to mourn at our Success! **1784** BURNS *Man was Made to Mourn* viii, Unmindful, tho' a weeping wife, And helpless offspring mourn. **1860** PUSEY *Min. Proph.* 299 It is as we would say, 'Let me mourn on', a mourning inexhaustible, because the woe too and the cause of grief was unceasing.
b. Const. *for*, *over*, also †*of*, †*on*, †*upon*.
a **1000** *Waldere* i. 43 Ne murn ðu for ði mece ðe wearð maðma cyst. *a* **1300** *Cursor M.* 19014 For þair misdedes morun. **1530** PALSGR. 640/2 He morneth sore for the losse of his father. **1535** COVERDALE *Hos.* x. 5 Therfore shall the people mourne ouer them. **1602** SHAKS. *Ham.* II. ii. 151 (1604 Qo.) He..Fell..by this declension, Into the madnes wherein now he raues, And all we mourne for. **1611** BIBLE *1 Esdras* viii. 72, I mourned for the iniquitie. **1715** DE FOE *Fam. Instruct.* I. v. (1841) I. 106 What we laughed at and made a jest of in our children before, we must now mourn over, and correct them for. **1789** WITHERSPOON *Regeneration* iii. §4 They never mourned for sin in a manner corresponding to the strong scripture declarations of its odious and hateful nature. **1829** LYTTON *Disowned* x, Let us not waste them in mourning over blighted hopes and severed hearts. **1875** J. P. HOPPS *Princ. Relig.* iii. (1878) 12 We have, then, not a past to mourn for, but a future to win.
c. To utter lamentations *to* some one. *rare.*
1533 GAU *Richt Vay* (S.T.S.) 5 Bot ane chrissine prayer is quhen ane man prais and murnis inuertlie in his hart to god efter his help. **1704** POPE *Pastorals, Autumn* 21 Far from Delia, to the winds I mourn. **1742** GRAY *Sonnet Death R. West* 13, I fruitless mourn to him that cannot hear.
†**d.** Of animals: To pine. *Obs.*
1577 B. GOOGE *Heresbach's Husb.* IV. (1586) 169 b, The Pigion..mourneth, if she be restrained of her liberty. **1613** PURCHAS *Pilgrimage* (1614) 631 The cattell mourned for want of milkers. **1725** BRADLEY *Fam. Dict.* s.v. *Rabbit*, [The female rabbits] will otherwise mourn, and hardly bring up their Young. **1784** COWPER *Task* v. 27 The cattle mourn in corners where the fence Screens them [from the cold].
e. *fig.* Of a plant or flower. †Also, in gardening language, to droop, hang down.
1626 BACON *Sylva* §493 Mary-golds..and indeed most Flowers, doe open or spread their Leaues abroad, when the Sunne shineth serene and faire;..They reioyce at the presence of the Sunne; and mourne at the absence thereof. **1798** *Trans. Soc. Arts* XVI. 164 And by being dryer, the plants did not mourn so much as the others when the weather was wet. *a* **1832** 'B. CORNWALL' *Eng. Songs* 3 The weed mourns on the castle wall.
2. *esp.* To lament the death of some one. Const. *for*.
a **1300** *Cursor M.* 23984 Clething wil i me tak o care..And murn wit hir þat him [*sc.* Christ] bar. *c* **1330** R. BRUNNE *Chron.* (1810) 20 Of his body was no force, non for him wild murne. *c* **1470** *Gol. & Gaw.* 796 Than schir Spynagros.. Murnyt for schir Gawyne. **1535** COVERDALE *2 Chron.* xxxv. 24 All Iuda and Ierusalem mourned for Iosias. **1559** *Mirr. Mag., Dk. York* i, Nor yet to mourne, for this my sonne is dead. **1601** SHAKS. *All's Well* IV. iii. 102, I haue..buried a wife, mourn'd for her [etc.]. *c* **1611** CHAPMAN *Iliad* VII. 357 Priam commanded none should mourne, but in still silence yeeld Their honord carkasses to fire, and onely grieue in heart. **1695** PRIOR *Ode Queen's Death* iii, For Her the Wise and Great shall mourn. **1756** C. SMART tr. *Horace, Art P.* (1826) II. 351 Those who mourn at funerals for pay, do and say more than those that are afflicted from their hearts. **1822** SHELLEY *Chas. I*, v. 10 A widow bird sate mourning for her love Upon a wintry bough. **1849** TENNYSON *In Mem.* ix. 5 So draw him home to those that mourn In vain. **1881** BESANT & RICE *Chapl. Fleet* I. 3 The people listen, now, to the solemn words of a service which seems spoken by the dead man himself to those who mourn.
b. To exhibit the conventional signs of grief for a period following the death of a person; *esp.* to wear mourning garments. †***to mourn up***: to complete the period of mourning.
1530 PALSGR. 640/2, I morne for a deed man, I weare blacke garmentes, *je porte le dueil.* Yonder gentylman morneth, by lykelyhodde his father is deed. **1546** LANGLEY *Pol. Verg. De Invent.* VI. vii. (1663) 239 Wherefore Numa ordained that such as mourned up before the day limited should offer a Cow..for an expiation. **1591** SHAKS. *1 Hen VI*, I. i. 17 We mourne in black, why mourn we not in blood? Henry is dead, and neuer shall reuiue. **1661** HEYLIN *Hist. Ref.* II. iii. §3. 69 A Levite that mourned might not serve or sing. **1717** POPE *Elegy Unfort. Lady* 56 What tho' no friends in sable weeds appear, Grieve for an hour, perhaps, then mourn a year. **1727–41** CHAMBERS *Cycl.* s.v. *Mourning*, The antient Spartan and Roman ladies mourned in white;.. Kings and cardinals mourn in purple. **1737** WHISTON *Josephus, Antiq.* IV. v. §1 The people mourned for Aaron thirty days. **1849** MACAULAY *Hist. Eng.* ii. I. 250 When foreign princes died, he [Dk. of Monmouth] had mourned for them in the long purple cloak, which [etc.]. **1885** H. CONWAY *Family Affair* xxvi, He knew that for all that had befallen she was mourning in mental sackcloth and ashes.
†**3.** To have a painful longing. Const. *after*; also *to* with *inf.* In OE. also to care *for*. *Obs.*
a **1000** *Andreas* 37 (Gr.) Hyȝe wæs oncyrred, þæt hie ne murndan æfter mandreame. *c* **1205** LAY. 14369 He murnede ful swiðe to habben þat mæiden to wiue. *a* **1225** *Ancr. R.* 366 His deore spuse murnede so swuðe efter him þet heo wiðuten him nefde no delit i none þinge. *c* **1386** CHAUCER *Miller's T.* 518, I moorne as dooth a lamb after the tete.
4. To make a low inarticulate sound indicative of pain or grief. In literary use only of a dove (with mixture of sense 1); *dial.* = MOAN *v.*
1535 COVERDALE *Isa.* lix. 11 We roare all like Beeres, & mourne stil like doues. **1632** SHERWOOD, To mourne or croo like a Doue, *roucouler.* **1822** SHELLEY *Fragm. Unfinished Drama* 68 The dove mourned in the pine, Sad prophetess of sorrows not her own. **1881** *Oxfordsh. Gloss.* Suppl., s.v., That poor baby do moorn.
II. *trans.*
5. To grieve or sorrow for (something); to lament, deplore, bewail, bemoan.
a **1000** *Bi Manna Wyrdum* 20 (Gr.) Sumne sceal.. murnan meotudȝesceaft mode ȝebysȝad. **1586** ? C'TESS PEMBROKE *Clorinda* 96 Thus do we weep and waile,.. Mourning, in others, our own miseries. **1596** DALRYMPLE tr. *Leslie's Hist. Scot.* v. 298 To murne and Lament thair sinis. **1604** SHAKS. *Oth.* I. iii. 204 To mourne a Mischeefe that is past and gon, Is the next way to draw new mischiefe on. **1697** CONGREVE *Mourn. Bride* III. viii, All those Ills which thou so long hast mourn'd. **1713** ADDISON *Cato* I. vi, Portius himself oft falls in tears before me, As if he mourn'd his rival's ill success. **1817** SHELLEY *Rev. Islam* x. xliii, As near one lover's tomb Two gentle sisters mourn their desolation. **1900** H. LAWSON *Over Shiprails* 108 Finally he was left, the last of his tribe, to mourn his lot in solitude.
b. With *clause* as obj.
c **1400** *Destr. Troy* 6591 Then Menestaus mournyt, & mykell sorow hade, That Troilus, þe triet, was takyn of his hond. **1567** *Gude & Godlie Ball.* (S.T.S.) 95 Thow sall not follow wickit mennis wayis, Nor zit murne that sinfull haif gude dayis. **1588** SHAKS. *L.L.L.* IV. iii. 259 O if in blacke my Ladies browes be deckt, It mournes, that painting vsurping haire Should rauish doters with a false aspect. **1817** SHELLEY *Rev. Islam* II. xxxvi, She mourned that grace and power were thrown as food To the hyaena lust.
6. To lament, grieve, or sorrow for, to express grief for (someone dead, or someone's death).
1526 *Pilgr. Perf.* (W. de W. 1531) 306 Mournynge thy deth, after y[e] custome of y[e] iewes. *c* **1586** ? BRYSKETT *Past. Aegl. Death Sidney* 18 Now hath the pore turtle gon to school..To learne to mourne her lost make! **1601** SHAKS. *Jul. C.* III. ii. 45 Here comes his Body, mourn'd by Marke Antony. **1667** MILTON *P.L.* XI. 760 As when a Father mourns His Children. **1685** DRYDEN *Thren. August.* 372 The Muse that mourns him now his happy triumph sung. **1742** YOUNG *Nt. Th.* II. 22 Dost thou mourn Philander's fate? **1805** SCOTT *Last Minstr.* VI. xxiii, Soft is the note, and sad the lay, That mourns the lovely Rosabelle. **1863** WOOLNER *My Beautiful Lady* 105 Thou mourn'd'st not most the vanished soul Which was my Lord's through thine. **1880** MISS BRADDON *Just as I am* vi, She loved him dearly, and mourned him more deeply than any of us.
7. 'To utter in a sorrowful manner' (J.).
1607 TOPSELL *Four-f. Beasts* (1658) 361 The Lion sighed deeply, and mourned forth a lamentable roaring. **1634** MILTON *Comus* 235 Where the love-lorn Nightingale Nightly to thee her sad Song mourneth well. **1819** KEATS

Isabella xli, The Spirit mourn'd 'Adieu!' **1889** W. S. GILBERT *Gondoliers* I. 14 Bury love that all condemn, And let the whirlwind mourn its requiem!

† **mourn**, *v.*[2] *Obs. rare.* [A perversion of the Fr. name for glanders (see MORTECHIEN), due to association with prec.] *intr.* Only in ***to mourn of the chine***: to suffer from glanders. Cf. MOSE *v.*

1590 GREENE *Never too late* (1600) 55 Well, this Louer.. began.. to mourne of the chine, and to hang the lip.

mourn(e, obs. forms of MORNE *sb.*[1], MOURN.

mournaval, obs. form of MOURNIVAL.

mourned, variant of MORNED *a. Her.*

1847 *Gloss. Heraldry, Mourned*, blunted.

mourner[1] ('mɔənə(r)). Also 4-5 morener, 6 moerner, 7 mournour, morner. [f. MOURN *v.*[1] + -ER[1].]

1. a. One who mourns, laments, or grieves; *spec.* one who mourns the death of a friend or relation; one who attends a funeral out of respect or affection for the deceased.

chief (or †***principal***) ***mourner***: the nearest relative who is present at a funeral. † ***close mourner***: a near relative of the deceased.

1388 WYCLIF *Isa.* lvii. 18, Y 3af coumfortyngis to hym, and to the moreneris of hym. *c* **1525** *Elegy Hen. VIII's Fool* in Halliw. *Nugæ Poet.* 45 Ye as chefe moerner yn your own folys hode. **1535** COVERDALE *Eccl.* xii. 2 When.. the mourners go aboute the stretes. **1594** SHAKS. *Rich. III*, III. ii. 51, I am no mourner for that newes. *c* **1618** MORYSON *Itin.* IV. (1903) 334 The men that are cheefe Mournours haue their faces Covered with blacke Sipres. *a* **1662** HEYLIN *Laud* (1668) 133 The Funeral he attended in his own Person, as the principal Mourner. **1688** R. HOLME *Armoury* III. 20/1 These kind of hoods.. are to this day worn by close Mourners at the Solemnities of great Funerals. **1762** GOLDSM. *Nash* 177 The masters of the assembly-room followed as chief mourners. **1820** SHELLEY *Sensit. Pl.* III. 8 The sobs of the mourners. **1870** DICKENS *E. Drood* iv, I have been since a solitary mourner.

fig. *c* **1600** SHAKS. *Sonn.* cxxxii, Thine eies.. Haue put on black, and louing mourners bee.

b. One employed or hired to attend funerals in a habit of mourning, or to utter wailing cries or songs of lamentation for the dead.

1692 R. L'ESTRANGE *Fables* cxcviii. 168 A Woman that had Two Daughters, Bury'd one of them, and Mourners were Provided to Attend the Funeral. **1741** tr. *D' Argen's Chinese Lett.* xl. 313 The Muscovites pay Mourners to shed Tears at the Interment of their Kindred.

¶ **c.** quasi-*adj.* (cf. Chaucer *Parl. Foules* 180).

1700 DRYDEN *Pal. & Arc.* III. 961 The Mourner Eugh, and Builder Oak were there.

d. *U.S.* (See quot. 1859.)

1834 F. LIEBER *Lett. to Gent. in Germany* xvi. 312 These tents.. are divided lengthwise by a bench about a foot high, and called the mourners' bench. **1845** J. J. HOOPER *Some Adventures Simon Suggs* x. 121 Having thus deposited his charge among the mourners, he started out, summarily to convert another soul! *Ibid.* 126 'And then,' continued Simon, 'I had to go yonder'—pointing to the mourner's seat. **1857** P. CARTWRIGHT *Autobiogr.* xxvi. 403 You must go to the Methodist's despised mourner's bench. **1859** BARTLETT *Dict. Amer., Mourners.* Persons on the 'anxious seat'.. at 'revival' meetings are technically termed 'mourners'; that is persons mourning for their sins. **1885** 'MARK TWAIN' in *Century Mag.* Feb. 549/2 Folks got up.. and worked their way.. to the mourners' bench, with the tears running down their faces. **1888** [see ANXIOUS *a.* 2]. **1891** *Harper's Mag.* Jan. 214/2 Everybody else war either convicted o' sin, an' at the mourner's bench [etc.]. **1904** *Charlotte* (N. Carolina) *Observer* 27 July 4 In the city police court a motley crowd of prisoners filled the mourners' benches. **1972** *News & Observer* (Raleigh, N. Carolina) 30 Dec. 4/3 The August meeting, the mourner's bench and the amen corner have gone out with stewards who yelled out 'amen' during the sermon.

2. ***Indian mourner***: the SAD-TREE.

1890 in *Century Dict.*

† **'mourner**[2]. *Obs. rare*[−1]. [f. MOURN *v.*[2] + -ER[1].] One who has the 'mourning of the chine'. In quot. *transf.*

a **1625** FLETCHER & MASS. *Cust. Country* III. iii, Hee's chin'd, he's chin'd good man; he is a mourner.

† **'mourneress.** *Obs. rare*[−1]. [f. MOURNER[1] + -ESS[1].] A female mourner.

1596 SMYTH *Lives Berkeleys* (1883) II. 389 The seaven principall mourneresses and estates of the funeralls.

mourneval, obs. form of MOURNIVAL.

mournful ('mɔənfʊl), *a.* (and *sb.*) [f. MOURN *v.*[1] + -FUL.]

1. Expressing or betokening mourning or sorrow; doleful, sad, dismal.

Now only of expressions, looks, sounds, scenery; formerly also of costume, etc.

1542 UDALL *Erasm. Apoph.* 14 Nor maketh any mournefull chere when he hath lost a frende. **1588** SHAKS. *Tit. A.* v. iii. 196-7 No Funerall Rite, nor man in mournfull Weeds: No mournfull Bell shall ring her Buriall. **1667** MILTON *P.L.* I. 244 Is.. this the seat That we must change for Heav'n, this mournful gloom For that celestial light? **1697** DRYDEN *Virg. Georg.* IV. 494 A mournful Sound agen the Mother hears. **1747** CARTE *Hist. Eng.* I. 113 The women running about, like furies, in a mournful habit. **1784** COWPER *Task* IV. 756 Much consoled That here and there some sprigs of mournful mint, Of nightshade, or valerian, grace the well He cultivates. **1850** DICKENS *Lett.* (1880) I. 231 He shook his head with an intensely mournful air. **1883** 'OUIDA' *Wanda* I. 2 The scene was bleak and mournful.

2. Full of, or oppressed with, sorrow or grief; sad, sorrowful, grieving; †making display of sorrow.

1579 SPENSER *Sheph. Cal.* Nov. 53 Vp then *Melpomene* thou mournefulst Muse of nyne. **1593** SHAKS. *2 Hen. VI*, III. i. 226 Glosters shew Beguiles him, as the mournefull Crocodile With sorrow snares relenting passengers. **1697** DRYDEN *Virg. Georg.* IV. 671 His mournful Mind, with Musick to restore. **1738** WESLEY *Ps.* LI. ix, Thou wilt the mournful Spirit chear. **1880** A. B. TODD *Circling Year* Poet. Wks. (1906) 203 The sweet lambs Call mournful for their mothers.

Comb. *a* **1835** MRS. HEMANS *Sicilian Captive* Poems (1875) 413 The mournful-sounding seas?

3. Causing sorrow or grief; deplorable.

1591 SHAKS. *1 Hen. VI*, II. ii. 16 His mournefull death.

†**4.** *sb.* ***the mournfuls***: low spirits, 'the blues'.

c **1800** R. CUMBERLAND *John De Lancaster* (1809) I. 136 You have cured me of the mournfuls.

5. Mournful Maria (? *obs.*) = *Mournful Mary* (*b*); **Mournful Mary** *Forces' slang* (? *obs.*), (*a*) a siren; (*b*) *spec.* the siren used at Dunkirk during the 1914–18 war; **Mournful Monday**, 30 Oct. 1899, the day of the British defeat at Nicholson's Nek; **mournful widow** (? *obs.*) = *mourning-bride.*

1866 *Treas. Bot.* 1027/2 *Scabiosa atropurpurea*, called Mournful Widow in cottage gardens. **1902** *Times Hist. War S. Africa* II. vi. 256 It is not difficult to point out specific reasons for the failure of 'Mournful Monday'. **1918** K. MACLEISH *Let.* 6 May in R. D. Paine *First Yale Unit* (1925) II. 162 The French have installed about six new, loud 'Mournful Marys'. **1918** in J. McG. Grider *War Birds* (1926) 185 Everybody knows when to take shelter and Mournful Mary, the siren, goes off automatically ten minutes before. **1920** G. S. MAXWELL *Motor Launch Patrol* ix. 151 Above all the voice of the siren—the famous Mournful Mary—kept up a moaning obbligato. **1925** FRASER & GIBBONS *Soldier & Sailor Words* 160 *Mournful Maria*, a nickname given to the Dunkirk syren, employed to give warning of enemy air attacks and long range shelling. **1927** E. W. SPRINGS *Nocturne Militaire* 77 Soon Mournful Mary, the siren in Dunkirk, sounded the All Clear.

mournfully ('mɔənfʊlɪ), *adv.* [f. MOURNFUL *a.* + -LY[2].] In a mournful or sorrowful manner.

1607 SHAKS. *Cor.* v. vi. 151 Beate thou the Drumme that it speake mournfully. **1611** BIBLE *Mal.* iii. 14 Wee haue walked mournfully before the Lord of hosts. **1791** MRS. RADCLIFFE *Rom. Forest* iv, Having mournfully bade each other good-night, they lay down and implored rest. **1838** DICKENS *Nich. Nick.* xx, 'No', said Smike, shaking his head mournfully, 'I must talk of something else to-day'. **1882** 'OUIDA' *In Maremma* I. ii. 34 The old mule.. only had long journeys twice a year, and resented them mournfully.

mournfulness ('mɔənfʊlnɪs). [-NESS.] The condition or quality of being mournful.

1633 P. FLETCHER *Piscat. Eclogs*, etc. 62 Then would I.. Sing of Eliza's fixed mournfulness, And much bewail such wofull heaviness. **1755** JOHNSON, *Mournfulness*,.. 1. Sorrow; grief. 2. Show of grief; appearance of sorrow. *a* **1835** MRS. HEMANS *Sound of Sea* ii, And hush'd is many a lovely [voice] Of mournfulness or mirth. **1870** MORRIS *Earthly Par.* III. IV. 177 Just so the mournfulness Of the tale told out did their hearts oppress.

mournifal, obs. form of MOURNIVAL.

mourning ('mɔənɪŋ), *vbl. sb.*[1] [f. MOURN *v.*[1] + -ING[1].]

1. The action of MOURN *v.*[1]; feeling or expression of sorrow; sorrowing, lamentation. Also with *a* or in *pl.*

a **1225** *Ancr. R.* 342 Heui murnunge. *c* **1250** *Gen. & Ex.* 3205 For swinc and murning hem was on. *a* **1310** in Wright *Lyric P.* xvi. 54 For hire love mournyng y make more then eny mon. *c* **1380** *Sir Ferumb.* 3797 Whar-for was mad þat gret mornyng Amonges þe Sarazyns olde & ȝyng, As hy þar herden alle. *c* **1386** CHAUCER *Miller's T.* 520 Ywis lemman I haue swich loue longynge That lik a turtel trewe is my moornynge. *c* **1440** *Jacob's Well* xviii. 125 In þis mournyng, an aungyl com to hym. **1535** COVERDALE *Ps.* ci[i]. 20 He maye heare the mournynges of soch as be in captiuyte. *a* **1631** DONNE *Lam. Jeremy* iii. 19 But when my mourning I do thinke upon My wormwood, hemlocke and affliction; My Soule is humbled in remembring this. *a* **1716** SOUTH *Serm.* (1744) VII. vi. 129 Neither mourning for sin, or confession of it, avail any thing but a new creature. **1868** MORRIS *Earthly Par.* I. II. 545 With mourning sore Toward the king's palace did they take their way.

2. *spec.* The feeling or the expression of sorrow for the death of a person; also, an expression of grief, a lament. Phrase, † ***to make mourning***.

c **1290** *S. Eng. Leg.* I. 51/172 Heo bi-lefte, þo it was non oþur in gret deol and mournyng. *a* **1300** *Cursor M.* 14239 At þat castel his frendes bade, And for þair frend gret murning made. *c* **1420** *Sir Amadace* (Camden) xxxvii, Sir Amadace wasse in mournyng broȝte. **1509** FISHER *Funeral Serm. C'tess Richmond* Wks. (1876) 301 Thes sorrowfull cryes of her thy seruaunte with the other lamentable mornynges of her frendes & seruauntes. **1589** PUTTENHAM *Eng. Poesie* I. xxiv. (Arb.) 63 Poeticall mournings in verse. *a* **1644** QUARLES *Sol. Recant.* ch. VII. iv, The wise mans sober heart is always turning His wary footsteps to the house of mourning. **1828** SCOTT *F.M. Perth* xxviii, The Highlanders .. are wont to mingle a degree of solemn mirth with their mourning. **1852** TENNYSON *Ode Death Dk. Wellington* 4 Let us bury the Great Duke To the noise of the mourning of a mighty nation.

3. a. The conventional or ceremonial manifestation of sorrow for the death of a person; esp. the wearing of black garments. Also, the period during which such garments are worn.

c **1532** DU WES *Introd. Fr.* in *Palsgr.* 920/1 Mournyng, deul. *a* **1548** HALL *Chron., Hen. VIII* 228 The kynge ware whyte for mournyng. **1641** SHIRLEY *Cardinal* I. (1652) 1 How does her Grace since she left her mourning For the young Duke Mendoza, whose timeless death At Sea, left her a Virgin and a Widow? **1683** PENN *Lett. conc. Pennsylv.* 6 Their Mourning is blacking of their faces, which they continue for a year. *a* **1854** H. REED *Lect. Brit. Poets* viii. (1857) 281 Those who, after a long mourning, resume their ordinary dresses. **1868** MARRIOTT *Vest. Chr.* p. xvii, Thus, where the hair is ordinarily worn short it is a sign of mourning to let it grow long.

b. An instance of this; a ceremonial manifestation of grief for the death of a person. Now *rare.*

1611 BIBLE *Gen.* l. 10 And he made a mourning for his father seuen dayes. **1753** CHAMBERS *Cycl. Supp.* s.v., In public Mournings at Rome the shops were shut up, the women laid aside all their ornaments [etc.]. **1776** ADAM SMITH *W.N.* I. x. II. (1869) I. 149 Except in the case of a general mourning. **1803–6** WORDSW. *Ode Intim. Immort.* 95 A wedding or a festival, A mourning or a funeral.

4. a. The dress or customary garment (now usually black) worn by mourners. Also occas. applied to the black draperies placed on furniture or the walls of buildings, etc., on occasions of mourning.

deep, half, second mourning: see those words. † ***close mourning***: mourning such as is worn by the nearest relatives; = deep mourning.

1654–66 EARL ORRERY *Parthen.* (1676) 606 All.. should for the revolution of twelve Moons wear close Mourning. **1661** PEPYS *Diary* 23 July, Put on my mourning. **1663** WOOD *Life* July (O.H.S.) I. 479 Three tressels theron, covered with mourning. **1700** DRYDEN *Pal. & Arc.* III. 942 They.. through the Master-Street the Corps convey'd. The Houses to their Tops with Black were spread, And ev'n the Pavements were with Mourning hid. **1708** SWIFT *Bickerstaff Detected* Wks. 1751 IV. 207 The Stair-case, I believe, and these two apartments hung in close Mourning will be sufficient. **1752** JOHNSON *Let. to Taylor* 18 Mar. in *Boswell*, Pray desire Mrs. Taylor to inform me what mourning I should buy for my mother and Miss Porter. **1833** HT. MARTINEAU *Loom & Lugger* II. iii. 43 They had at first offered to make up her mourning for her.

b. *pl.* in the same sense. Now *Sc.* and *north.*

1634 W. TIRWHYT tr. *Balzac's Lett.* (vol. I) 97 If we hold all the men in the world to be of our affinity, let us make account to weare mournings all our life. **1650** R. STAPYLTON *Strada's Low C. Wars* I. 9 Putting on mournings, [he] commanded an adjournment of the Courts of Justice. **1822** GALT *Sir A. Wylie* ii, To the total wreck and destruction of all the unfinished bravery of mournings which lay scattered around. **1838** W. BELL *Dict. Law Scot.* 662 A widow has a legal claim to mournings for her husband. *a* **1842** A. CUNNINGHAM *Burns & Byron*, They came into the street in their mournings.

c. Phr. ***in mourning*** (as adjectival phrase): wearing the garments indicative of grief. Also *Naut.* (see quot. 1867). So ***to go*** or ***put into mourning; to be out of mourning***, etc.

a **1656** HALES *Gold. Rem.* III. *Serm.*, etc. (1673) 21 Demades the Oratour was wont to say of the Athenians, that they never came to consult of peace, *nisi atrati*, but in blacks and mourning. **1683** WOOD *Life* 23 Aug. (O.H.S.) III. 66 An hears.. followed by 5 coaches in morning. **1711** SWIFT *Jrnl. to Stella* 25 Dec., Her brother would fain have her death a secret, to save the charge of bringing her up here to bury her, or going into mourning. **1778** MISS BURNEY *Evelina* xiv, She was already out of mourning. **1821** BYRON *Juan* III. vii, Sad thought! to lose the spouse that was adorning Our days, and put one's servants into mourning. **1860** MISS YONGE *Stokesley Secret* iii, There were two ladies, one in stately handsome slight mourning. **1867** SMYTH *Sailor's Word-bk.* s.v., A ship is in mourning with her ensign and pennant half-mast, her yards topped awry, or apeek, or alternately topped an-end. If the sides are painted blue instead of white, it denotes deep mourning. **1869** TOZER *Highl. Turkey* II. 310 Seeing the wife of the priest.. in mourning.

d. *slang* or *jocular.* ***to be in mourning***: said of the eyes when blackened by fighting. Also of the finger-nails when allowed to become dirty.

1814 *Sporting Mag.* XLIII. 70 Bolter.. had his eyes in mourning. **1867** O. W. HOLMES *Guardian Angel* x, His eyes were 'in mourning', as the gentlemen of the ring say. **1890** BARRÈRE & LELAND *Dict. Slang* (1897), *Mourning* (common), a full suit of mourning, two black eyes; half-mourning, one black eye.

5. *attrib.* and *Comb.*, as ***mourning apparel, armlet, attire, badge, bonnet, card, clothes, coat, colour, -dress, duty, garment, gown, habit, handkerchief, hat,*** † ***head,*** † ***hood, house, livery, millinery, note-paper, picture, song, tie, time, veil, weeds***, etc.; also **mourning-band**, (*a*) see quot. *c* 1618; (*b*) a strip of black cloth or crape worn round the sleeve of a coat or round a hat in token of bereavement; (*c*) *slang*, a dirty or black edge to a finger-nail; **mourning border**, a black border on note-paper, envelopes, etc., used by persons who are 'in mourning'; hence ***mourning-bordered*** adj.; **mourning-brooch**, a brooch of jet or other black material, worn by women when mourning; † **mourning carriage**, in quot. a carriage for conveying a corpse; † **mourning chariot** = *mourning coach*; **mourning cloak**, † (*a*) a cloak formerly worn by persons following a funeral, usually hired from the undertaker; (*b*) a butterfly, the Camberwell beauty, *Vanessa antiopa*; **mourning coach**, (*a*) a coach of black colour formerly used by a person during the whole period of his mourning; (*b*) a closed carriage, usually black, used to convey mourners on the occasion of a funeral; †**mourning coffin, hearse** (app. = 'coffin', 'hearse', simply; possibly, however, one of a black colour or with black draperies); **mourning envelope**, a mourning-bordered envelope; †**mourning horse**, the horse belonging to a deceased person, led riderless and draped with black in the funeral procession; **mourning iris**, *Iris susiana* (see quots.); **mourning jewellery**, jewellery decorated with miniature funereal ornaments or pictures; **mourning-paper**, note-paper with a black edge; **mourning-piece** *U.S.*, a pictorial representation of a tomb, etc., intended as a memorial of the dead; **mourning-pin**, a black pin for use with mourning-attire (Worcester 1860); **mourning-ring**, a ring worn as a memorial of a deceased person; **mourning shirt**, (*a*) see quot. 1650; (*b*) *slang*, a flannel shirt, as it does not require washing so often as others; †**mourning-staff**, a black pole carried in a funeral procession; **mourning-stuff**, 'a lusterless black textile material, such as crape, cashmere, or merino, regarded as especially fitted for mourning-garments' (*Cent. Dict.*); **mourning-vein**, a vein of mourning granite; **mourning warehouse**, a warehouse selling mourning clothes, etc. (cf. WAREHOUSE *sb.* 1 e).

1565 COOPER *Thesaurus* s.v. *Lugeo, Lugubris ornatus.* Cic[ero] *Mournyng apparell. **1611** BIBLE *2 Sam.* xiv. 2. **1966** *Olney Amsden & Sons Ltd. Price List* 29 *Mourning armlets. **1503–4** *Act 19 Hen. VII*, c. 14 §11 Any lyvere.. giffyn by any executoures at the interement of any person for any *mornyng array. **1611** COTGR., *Dueil*, dole, griefe,.. also, mourning weeds, or *mourning attire; as, *Il porte le dueil.* **1968** MRS. L. B. JOHNSON *White House Diary* 8 Oct. (1970) 718 A *mourning badge worn after Lincoln's assassination. *c* **1618** MORYSON *Itin.* IV. (1903) 334 The other men that followe the Herse haue.. hattbandes of black Sipres hanging downe behynde, Called Trawerbandes that is *mourning bandes. *c* **1874** D. BOUCICAULT in M. R. Booth *Eng. Plays of 19th Cent.* (1969) II. 211, I was wrong to come here at all. I feel like a mourning band on a white hat. **1884** *St. James's Gaz.* 5 Dec. 6/1 The 'mourning-bands' on the finger-nails are faithfully recorded. **1966** J. POTTS *Footsteps on Stairs* (1967) ii. 19 Enid kept her loneliness hidden, while Martin's was there for all the world to see; he wore it like a mourning band. **1897** *Sears, Roebuck Catal.* 302/2 Ladies' *Mourning Bonnet.. a very handsome Bonnet and Mourning Veil. **1899** *Westm. Gaz.* 16 Nov. 2/3 *Mourning-bordered envelopes. **1804** M. WILMOT *Let.* 2 Jan. in *Russ. Jrnls.* (1934) 72 A *Mourning Card was presented to the Princess. **1939–40** *Army & Navy Stores Catal.* 301 Mourning note papers, cards,.. and envelopes. **1710** M. HENRY *Life Lieut. Illidge* Wks. 1853 II. 585/1 His corpse was carried on a *mourning carriage to Witembury. **1703** *Lond. Gaz.* No. 3945/4 At Mr. Harrison's, Coach-Maker,.. is a Mourning Coach and Harness,.. also a *Mourning Charriot. **1610–11** in Halliwell *Anc. Invent.* (1854) 66 Item, one *mourning cloak. **1898** W. J. HOLLAND *Butterfly Bk.* (1902) 169 *Vanessa antiopa*... (The Mourning-cloak; The Camberwell Beauty.) **1535** COVERDALE *Baruch* v. 1 Put of thy *mournynge clothes (o Ierusalem). **1690** LUTTRELL *Brief Rel.* (1857) II. 148 The 23rd, sir John Johnston, condemned for stealing Mrs. Wharton, went up in a *mourning coach to Tyburn, and was executed for the same. **1714** A. SMITH *Lives Highwaymen* II. 18 He was.. carry'd into a mourning Coach, and so convey'd to the Tangier-Tavern. **1840** DICKENS *Barn. Rudge* ix, I wish I may.. never be buried decent with a mourning-coach and feathers. **1586** T. BRYSKETT *Past. Aegl. Death Sidney* 28 Hath not the aire put on his *mourning coat, And testified his grief with flowing teares? **1683** *Condemn. & Exec. A. Sydney* 2 They put it [the body] into a *Mourning-Coffin.. and conveyed it thence, in order to its Interment. **1564** BULLEYN *Dial. agst. Pest.* Ded. (1888) 1 My Chamber.. hanged al in one *mournyng darcke colour. **1885** DILLON *Fairholt's Costume in Eng.* II. Gloss. 290 Black appears to have been the mourning colour generally worn in England. **1840** *Knickerbocker* XVI. 70 A conclusive proof that the *mourning-dress is an empty ordinance of Fashion. **1843** DICKENS *Christmas Carol* ii. 65 A fair young girl in a mourning-dress. *a* **1922** L. LUCK in J. Burnett *Useful Toil* (1974) I. 72, I had my new mourning dress torn from my back, through trying to part them when fighting. **1602** SHAKS. *Ham.* I. ii. 88 'Tis sweet and commendable In your Nature Hamlet, To giue these *mourning duties to your Father. **1862** *Mourning envelope [see NOTE-PAPER]. **1907** *Yesterday's Shopping* (1969) 332/1 Mourning envelopes. **1939–40** Mourning envelope [see *mourning card* above]. **1530** PALSGR. 246/2 *Mournyng garment, *habit de dveil.* **1535** COVERDALE *2 Sam.* xiv. 2. **1593** SHAKS. *3 Hen. VI*, II. i. 161 Wrap our bodies in blacke *mourning Gownes. *c* **1380** WYCLIF *Wks.* (1880) 4 þei maken hem self in siȝte of peple more holi þan oþere men and bosten þereof in outward signes or wordes, as *mornynge abite, lettris of fraternite. **1897** *Sears, Roebuck Catal.* 226/3 *Mourning Handkerchiefs ..with neat fast black hem-stitched borders. **1907** *Yesterday's Shopping* (1969) 819/2 Mourning Handkerchiefs. With black border. **1896** *T. Eaton & Co. Catal.* Spring & Summer 46/3 Telegraph orders for *Mourning Hats continue to be received. **1899** in A. Adburgham *Shops & Shopping* (1964) xxii. 261 Mourning hat bands. **1736** AINSWORTH *Lat. Dict.*, A *mourning hat-band, *Torulus atratus.* **1530** PALSGR. 253/1 Peake of a ladyes *mournyng heed, *biquoquet.* **1641** EVELYN *Diary* 2 Jan., We at night followed the *mourning hearse to the Church at Wotton. *c* **1495** *Epitaffe*, etc. in *Skelton's Wks.* (1843) II. 391 Of with your rich caperons, put on your *mourning hodes. **1736** AINSWORTH *Lat. Dict.*, A mourning hood, *Epomis atrata.* **1695** *Lond. Gaz.* No. 3059/1 Then followed the *Mourning Horse, led by the Lord Viscount Villers, Master of the Horse to Her late Majesty, attended by two Equerries. **1402** *Repl. Friar Daw Topias* in *Pol. Poems* (Rolls) II. 76 To make sich housynge to men that ben deede, to whiche longith but graves and *mornynge housis. **1588** SHAKS. *L.L.L.* v. ii. 818, I will.. shut My wofull selfe vp in a mourning house, Raining the teares of lamentation, For the remembrance of my Fathers death. **1883** W. ROBINSON *Eng. Flower Garden* 158/1 *I[ris] susiana* (*Mourning I[ris]). .. The flowers, which are produced in early summer, are very large and densely spotted and striped with dark purple on a grey ground. **1966** M. PRICE *Iris Bk.* vii. 78 The celebrated silver and black mourning iris.. is easiest. **1895** *Montgomery Ward Catal.* 179 Real onyx and jet *mourning jewelry. **1960** H. HAYWARD *Antique Coll.* 192/1 *Mourning jewellery* became particularly fashionable in the second half of the 18th cent... Earlier mourning jewellery of the 16th and 17th cent.. was of a more gloomy kind. **1760–72** H. BROOKE *Fool of Qual.* (1809) IV. 26 Two footmen in *mourning-liveries. **1896** *T. Eaton & Co. Catal.* Spring & Summer 46/3 *Mourning Millinery. **1862** *Mourning note-paper [see NOTE-PAPER]. **1907** *Yesterday's Shopping* (1969) 332/1 Mourning note paper. **1800** MAR. EDGEWORTH *Belinda* (1832) II. xxv. 155 The letter was copied upon a sheet of *mourning paper. **1947** T. H. WHITE *Elephant & Kangaroo* (1948) xxi. 170 Two *mourning pictures of her father and mother. **1972** *Village Voice* (N.Y.) 1 June 3/4 Crewel work and other kinds of embroidery, mourning pictures, theorems, and stencil work. **1843** *Knickerbocker* XXII. 189 The parlor.. was ornamented.. among the rest, [with] the indispensable family *mourning-piece. **1889** M. C. LEE *Quaker Girl of Nantucket* iii. 48 There ain't a house on the island, I expect, but what's got a mourning piece hangin' up in the front room. **1967** MRS. L. B. JOHNSON *White House Diary* 12 Nov. (1970) 588 On the walls are samplers and 'mourning pieces' and quaint American primitive portraits. **1970** *New Yorker* 28 Nov. 158/2 The picture is one of the earliest examples of the mourning piece —a folk genre that originated at the time of Wash.'s death. **1840** *Penny Cycl.* XVIII. 162/2 *Mourning pins may be made of brass,.. varnishing being substituted for tinning. **1703** *Lond. Gaz.* No. 3897/4, 3 other *Mourning Rings, with W.C. ob. 18 Dec. 1702. **1852** MISS MULOCK *Agatha's Husb.* xii. (1875) 306 The large diamond mourning ring which the widower always wore, 'In memory of Catherine Harper'. **1634** W. TIRWHYT tr. *Balzac's Lett.* (vol. I) 105 Your *Mourning-robes. **1650** FULLER *Pisgah* IV. vi. 98 As we say *mourning shirts, it being customary for men in sadness, to spare the pains of their laundresses. **1736** AINSWORTH *Lat. Dict.*, A *mourning song, *Nenia, carmen lugubre, threnodia.* *c* **1730** SAVAGE *Author to be let* Publ. Pref., Had it not been more laudable in Mr. Roome, the son of an undertaker, to have borne a link and a *mourning-staff in the long procession of a funeral, than [etc.]. **1881** M. ARNOLD *Westminster Abbey* x, The *mourning-stole no more Mantled her form. **1703** *Burgh Rec. Stirling* (1889) 99 Four *mourning strings.. which they are to wear above their belts that day upon account of the funerals of the deceast John Stivensone, provost. **1662** GURNALL *Chr. in Arm.* verse 18. I. xlv. §1 (1669) 402/2 Gaudy rich cloaths on a fast-day do no better, than a light trimming on a *mourning suit. **1819** BYRON *Juan* II. cxxxix, And night is flung off like a mourning suit Worn for a husband,—or some other brute. **1970** B. KNOX *Children of Mist* vii. 155 A black *mourning tie knotted neatly at his shirt collar. *c* **1407** LYDG. *Reson & Sens.* 6926 Ther ys.. woman noon so stedefast That, whan *Mowrenyng tyme is past, she may of mercy and pite save and kepe hir honeste, And forsake hir clothes blake And chesen hir a nywe make. **1821** SHELLEY *Adonais* xli, Thou Air, Which like a *mourning veil thy scarf hadst thrown O'er the abandoned Earth. **1897** Mourning veil [see *mourning bonnet* above]. **1872** *Rep. Vermont Board Agric.* I. 662 The other layers most desirable and most valuable are the dark and light *mourning veins. *c* **1860** in A. Adburgham *Shops & Shopping* (1964) vi. 65 The London General *Mourning Ware-house. **1885** *List of Subscribers, Classified* (United Telephone Co.) (ed. 6) 157 Mourning Warehouses. **1572** *Lament. Lady Scot.* 6 in *Satir. Poems Reform.* xxxiii, With ȝour *murning weid absconse my face. **1588** SHAKS. *Tit. A.* I. i. 70 Haile Rome: Victorious in thy Mourning Weedes.

†'**mourning**, *vbl. sb.*[2] *Obs.* [f. MOURN *v.*[2] + -ING[1].] ***mourning of the chine***: The disease of glanders. Cf. MORTECHIEN.

1523 FITZHERB. *Husb.* §87 Mournynge on the chyne.. appereth at his nosethryll lyke oke-water. *Ibid.* §119 The frenche-man saythe, *Mort de langue et de eschine Sount maladyes saunce medicine.* The mournynge of the tongue, and of the chyne, are diseases without remedy or medicyne. **1598** FLORIO, *Ciamorro*, a disease in horses called the mourning of the chine, issuing at the nosthrils. **1607** TOPSELL *Four-f. Beasts* 371 This word mourning of the Chine, is a corrupt name borrowed of the French toong, wherein it is cald *mote* [1658 *Morte*] *deschien*, that is to say the death of the backe. Because many do hold this opinion that this disease doth consume the marrow of the backe. **1611** COTGR., *Mourne*, the Mumpes; and (in a horse, &c.) the mourning of the Chyne. **1735** BURDON *Pocket Farriery* 74 The Mourning of the Chine is downright Poverty of Flesh and Blood.

'**mourning**, *ppl. a.* [f. MOURN *v.*[1] + -ING[2].]

1. That mourns; sorrowing, lamenting; characterized by or expressive of grief.

Beowulf 50 Him wæs ȝeomor sefa, murnende mod. *a* **1300** *Cursor M.* 4963 He mened him þus, wit murnand cher. **1382** WYCLIF *Ezek.* xxiv. 17 Nether thou shalt ete meet of mournynge men. *c* **1550** *Knt. Curtesy* 59 in Hazl. *E.P.P.* II. 69 Alas! he sayd, with murnynge eyen, Now is my herte in wo and payne. **1590** SPENSER *F.Q.* I. iii. 36 When mourning altars, purg'd with enemies life, The black infernall furies doen aslake. **1622** MABBE tr. *Aleman's Guzman D'Alf.* I. 134, I put on a mourning-face, looke sad [etc.]. **1797** *Encycl. Brit.* (ed. 3) XII. 436/1 *Præficæ*, or mourning women,.. went about the streets. **1815** SHELLEY *Alastor* 55 No mourning maiden decked With weeping flowers.

2. *transf.* Bruised. Cf. MOURNING *vbl. sb.*[1] 4 d.

1708 MRS. CENTLIVRE *Busy Body* I. i, On condition you'll give us a true account how you came by that mourning nose.

3. mourning bride, a popular name for the sweet scabious, *Scabiosa atropurpurea*; **mourning dove**, *N. Amer.*, a blue-grey pigeon, *Zenaidura macroura carolinensis*, distinguished by its plaintive call; **mourning warbler**, an American warbler, *Geothlypis philadelphia*; **mourning widow**, (*a*) a European geranium with petals of a dusky colour, *Geranium phæum*; (*b*) = *mourning bride* (*Cent. Dict.* 1890); **mourning willow**, the weeping willow.

1846–50 A. WOOD *Class-bk. Bot.* 310 *Scabiosa atropurpurea*, *Mourning Bride. **1839** PEABODY in *Boston Jrnl. Nat. Hist.* (1841) III. 192 The Carolina Turtle Dove.. is called [in western Massachusetts] the *Mourning Dove. **1841** G. CATLIN *Lett. on N. Amer. Indians* I. 158 The mourning or turtle-dove.. is not to be destroyed or harmed by anyone. **1880** J. M. FARRAR *Five Yrs. Minnesota* 166 Mourning-doves fill every wood with their plaintive notes. **1929** M. DE LA ROCHE *Whiteoaks* xvi. 203 High in the pines she heard the plaintive notes of a mourning dove. **1968** *Globe & Mail* (Toronto) 13 Jan. 41/2 Once again Ontario gunners are asking for an open season on mourning doves and once again considerations of sentimentality.. will almost certainly defeat them. **1975** A. DILLARD *Pilgrim at Tinker Creek* ii. 33, I saw the backyard cedar where the mourning doves roost. **1808–13** A. WILSON *Amer. Ornith.* (1831) II. 140 *Sylvia Philadelphia*, Wilson.—*Mourning warbler. **1866** *Treas. Bot.*, *Mourning widow. *Geranium phæum.* **1813** H. MUHLENBERG *Catal. Plantarum Americæ Septentrionalis* 91 *Mourning Willow.

mourningly ('mɔənɪŋlɪ), *adv.* [f. MOURNING *ppl. a.* + -LY[2].] In a mourning manner.

1519 in *Fabric Rolls York Minster* (Surtees) 268 Item we thynke it were convenient that whene we fetche a corse to the Churche that we shulde be in our blak abbettes mornyngly. **1601** SHAKS. *All's Well* I. i. 34 The King very latelie spoke of him.. mourningly. **1831** LYTTON *Godolphin* lxvii, The wind.. swept mourningly over the.. leaves.

mournival ('mɔənɪvəl). *Cards.* Now only *Hist.* Forms: 6 **mornyfle**, 7 **mournaval, mornevall, mournivall, murnivall, mornivall, mournifal,** (*erron.* **murrinall**), 8 **mourneval**, 7– **mournival, murnival.** [a. F. *mornifle*, of obscure origin. The word also means 'a slap in the face', which is perh. the primary sense.]

1. A set of four aces, kings, queens, or knaves, in one hand. Also in figurative context.

1530 PALSGR. 246/1 Mornyfle a maner of play, *mornifle.* **1614, 1615** [see GLEEK *sb.*[1] 2]. **1674** COTTON *Gamester* (1680) 68 A Mournival is either all the Aces, the four Kings, Queens, or Knaves. **1719** D'URFEY *Pills* I. 331 I'se ne'er win by Mournival or blaze, Or conquering Knave. **1822** SCOTT *Nigel* xvi, Concerning a certain game at gleek, and a certain mournival of aces held by his lordship.

†**2.** *transf.* A set of four (things or persons). *Obs.*

1625 B. JONSON *Staple of N.* IV. Interm. 81 *Cen.* Let a protest goe out against him. *Mir.* A mourniuall of protests; or a gleeke at least! *c* **1650** J. POOLE *Eng. Parnassus* (1657) 272 Elements.. Natures first mournival. *a* **1711** KEN *Hymnotheo* Poet. Wks. 1721 III. 390 With his double mourneval of Eyes, Tarantula a poor Apulian spies.

†'**mournless**, *a. nonce-wd.* [f. MOURN *sb.* + -LESS.] That mourns not, failing to mourn.

1633 D. ROGERS *Treat. Sacraments* II. 139, I hope you mourne, that you are so mournelesse.

mournour, obs. form of MOURNER.

'**mournsome**, *a. nonce-wd.* [irreg. f. MOURN *v.*[1] + -SOME.] Mournful.

1869 BLACKMORE *Lorna D.* iii, Then there came a mellow noise, very low and mournsome.

mourron, mourther: see MORION, MURDER.

mous, obs. pl. form of MOW *sb.*[2]

mousaique, obs. form of MOSAIC *a.*[1] and *sb.*

mouse (maʊs), *sb.* Pl. mice (maɪs). Forms: *sing.* 1 mús, muus, 2, 5 mus, 4–5 mows, 4–7 mous, 5 mows(s)e, 6 mowss, mousse, 4– mouse. *pl.* 1 mýs, 4–5 mys, 4 myys, musz, myis, 4–5, (9 *dial.*) mees, muys, myes, 4–6 myse, 4–7 myce, 5 muyse, mysz, myesse, 6 myss, miese, mise, 7, (9 *dial.*) meece, 6– mice; also 4 musus, 8 (in sense 4 a) mouses. [Com. Teut. and Indo-Germanic: OE. *mús* fem. = OFris., OS. *mûs* (Du. *muis*), OHG. *mûs* (MHG. *mûs*, mod.G. *maus*), ON. *mús* (Sw., Da. *mus*), L. *mūs*, Gr. μῦς, Skr. *mūš*:—Indo-Germanic **mūs-* (cons.-stem).]

I. 1. a. An animal of any of the smaller species of the genus *Mus* of rodents.

Most commonly applied to the house mouse, *M. musculus*. Other species are the field or wood mouse, *M. sylvaticus*, the harvest mouse, *M. minutus*, and the Barbary mouse of North Africa, *M. barbarus*.

c **888** K. ÆLFRED *Boeth.* xvi. §2 ȝif ȝe nu ȝesawan hwelce mus þæt wære hlaford ofer oðre mys, & sette him domas.. hu wunderlic wolde eow ðæt þincan. *c* **1175** *Lamb. Hom.* 53 þurh þe sweote smel of þe chese he bicherreð monie mus to þe stoke. **1303** R. BRUNNE *Handl. Synne* 5383 For þou ȝyuest myys [*v.r.* mys] to ȝete þ at was ordeyned to mannys mete. *c* **1374** CHAUCER *Boeth.* II. Pr. vi. 41 (Camb. MS.) Now yif thow saye a mous amonges oother musus [*v.r.* myse] þat chalengede to hym self ward ryht and power ouer alle oother mysus [*v.r.* myse] how gret scorn woldisthow han of hit. **1387** TREVISA *Higden* (Rolls) VII. 297 While a myȝti man sat at þe feste muys [MS. β. muyse, *Caxton* myes] bysette hym sodenliche al aboute. *c* **1450** *Merlin* xxxiii. 665 He seide that he hadde nede ther-of in his house for rattes and mees. **1535** STEWART *Cron. Scot.* (Rolls) III. 388 Ouir Albione aboundit so the myss, Ouir all the feild in mony hoill and dyke, And in the houssis.. That [etc.]. **1562** TURNER *Herbal* II. 160 It [Hellebore] kylleth miese knodden wyth mele and honye. **1605** SHAKS. *Lear* IV. vi. 18 The Fishermen, that walk'd vpon the beach Appeare like Mice. **1822** SHELLEY tr. *Goethe's Faust* i. 84 For I am like a cat—I like to play A little with the mouse before I eat it. **1864** TENNYSON *Aylmer's F.* 853 The thin weasel there Follows the mouse, and all is open field. **1894** *Spectator* 30 June 901 There are those who have tried the bat, and found it taste like a house-mouse, only mousier.

fig. *c* **1374** CHAUCER *Troylus* III. 687 (736) Quod Pandarus thow wrecched mouses herte. Art þow a-garst so þat she wole þe byte. **1633** *Costlie Whore* I. ii. in Bullen *O. Pl.* IV, Oh wherefore should we fawne upon such curres, The mice of mankind, and the scorne of earth?

b. Popularly applied to animals of other genera having some resemblance to mice, esp. the shrews (*Sorex*) and the voles (*Arvicola*). Also in booknames (chiefly translations from mod.Latin) of various exotic animals, e.g. †*Alpine mouse*, †*mouse of the mountain*, the Marmot; †*Indian mouse*, †*Pharaoh's mouse*, the ichneumon; †*Pontic mouse*, an animal described by Pliny, commonly identified with the ermine.

a **700** *Epinal Gloss.* 977 *Sorix (-ex), id. est*: mus. *a* **1593** HESTER 114 *Exper. Paracelsus* (1596) 12 Anointing the outward parts with the oyle of the mouse of the mountaine. **1607** TOPSELL *Four-f. Beasts* 448 Marcellus and Solinus, doe make question of this beast (Ichneumon) to be a kind of Otter... There be some that call it an Indian Mouse. *Ibid.* 532 The Movse Pontiqve. **1617** MORYSON *Itin.* I. 151 An Indian Mouse. **1864** *Chamb. Encycl.* VI. 597/2 The name Mouse is often popularly given to animals considerably different from the true mice, as the Voles. **1868** GRAY in *Proc. Zool. Soc.* 199 The species of *Saccomyinæ*, or Pouched Mice. **1889** [see POUCHED *a.* 1].

2. Phrases. **a.** In various similes: *drunk as a mouse*, earlier †*drunk as a dreynt* (= drowned) *mouse*; *mum, mute, quiet, still*, etc., *as a mouse* (†*in a cheese*). Also, †(*to speak*) *like a mouse in a cheese*, i.e. with a muffled voice, inaudibly; *like a drowned mouse*, i.e. in a miserable plight.

a **1310** in Wright *Lyric P.* xxxix. 111 When that he is dronke ase a dreynt mous, thenne we shule borewe the wed ate bayly. *c* **1386** CHAUCER *Wife's Prol.* 246 Thou comest hoom as dronken as a Mous. **1536** in *Lett. Suppress. Monast.* (Camden) 133 Monckes drynk an bowll after collacyon tell ten or xii. of the clock, and cum to mattens as dronck as myss. **1591** SHAKS. *1 Hen. VI*, I. ii. 12 Or pitteous they will looke, like drowned Mice. **1599** PORTER *Angry Wom. Abingt.* (1841) 71 Mum, mouse in cheese, cat is neare. **1686** E. VERNEY 24 June in *Verney Mem.* (1899) IV. x. 381 Child, —I pray when you speak in the Theatre [Oxf.] doe not speak like a mouse in a chees.., but speak out your words boldly and distinctly. **1736** AINSWORTH *Lat. Dict.* s.v., He speaketh like a mouse in a cheese, *mussat, mussitat; occulte & depressa voce loquitur.* **1856** MISS YONGE *Daisy Chain* II. xxv. 636 If I only begin to say 'Miss May told me—' they are all like mice. **1859** GEO. ELIOT *A. Bede* v, She looks as quiet as a mouse. There's something rather striking about her, though. **1883** STEVENSON *Treasure Isl.* xiv, I squatted there, hearkening, as silent as a mouse.

b. In alliterative association with *man.* (*a*) See MAN *sb.*[1] 7; (*b*) *neither man nor mouse*, not a creature; *mouse and man*, every living thing.

1627 W. HAWKINS *Apollo Shroving* I. v. 14 Looke Præco, canst thou see no audience? *Præco.* Nor man, nor mouse. **1785** R. BURNS *To a Mouse* in *Poems & Songs* (1968) I. 128 The best laid schemes o' Mice an' Men, Gang aft agley. **1845** CARLYLE *Cromwell* v. lxxix. I. 483 Poor Prince Maurice, sea-roving.. sank, in the West Indies, mouse and man. **1937** J. STEINBECK (*title*) Of mice and men. **1938** *Time* 30 May 48/3 Are we mice or men? **1961** *Times* 24 Nov. 15/1 There is a particularly good comic performance by Mr. Denys Graham as the mouse who for one glorious moment believes he is a man. **1975** L. DEIGHTON *Yesterday's Spy* xxii. 169 She gave a mocking laugh. 'What are you?.. A man or a mouse?'

c. As a type of something small or insignificant. Chiefly after Horace (see quot. *a* 1637).

1584 LYLY *Campaspe* Prol. at Bl. Fryers, So we hope, if the shower of our swelling mountaine seeme to bring foorth some Eliphant, perfourme but a mouse, you will gently say, this is a beast. **1596** LODGE *Wits Miserie* 4 At euery word he speaketh, hee makes a mouse of an elephant, he telleth them of wonders done in Spaine by his ancestors. **1598** F. ROUS *Thule* B j, Nor let your harts great hils bring foorth a mouse. *a* **1637** B. JONSON tr. *Horace, Art P.* 199 The mountains travail'd, and brought forth A scorned mouse! **1887** *Times* (weekly ed.) 14 Oct. 14/4 It is curious that such a grave contingency should spring from such a trivial cause. This time it is the mouse that brings forth the mountain.

d. Proverbs, and proverbial sayings.

c **1386** CHAUCER *Wife's Prol.* 572, I holde a Mouses herte nat worth a leek, That hath but oon hole for to sterte to And if þat faille, thanne is al ydo. *c* **1430** LYDG. *Min. Poems* (Percy Soc.) 167 An hardy mowse, that is bold to breede In cattis eeris. *c* **1530** R. HILLES *Common-Pl. Bk.* (1858) 140 It ys a sotyll mouse that slepyth in the cattys ear. *a* **1700** B. E. *Dict. Cant. Crew* s.v. *Mouse-trap, A sorry Mouse, that has but one Hole*, or a poor Creature that has but one Shift. *Ibid.*, *A Mouse in the Pot is better than no Flesh*, or something has some savour.

†**3. a.** As a playful term of endearment, chiefly addressed to a woman. *Obs.*

c **1520** [see PRIM *sb.*[1]]. **1567** *Triall Treas.* E j, My dere lady. My mouse my nobs and cony swete. **1586** WARNER *Alb. Eng.* II. x. (1592) 42 God blesse thee Mouse the Bridegroome sayd, and smakt her on the lips. **1588** SHAKS. *L.L.L.* v. ii. 19. **1602** —— *Ham.* III. iv. 183. **1607** DEKKER & WEBSTER *Westw. Hoe* II. i, *Iud.* [to her husband] I am so troubled with the rheume too: Mouse whats good fort? **1655** MENNIS & SMITH *Mus. Delic.* (1656) 14 Mopsa, even Mopsa, prety Mouse. **1798** JOANNA BAILLIE *Tryal* IV. ii. *Plays on Passions* (1821) I. 263 *Agnes.* You are an idler! *Harwood.* You are a little mouse!

b. *slang.* (See quot.) *Obs.*

1781 R. KING *Mod. Lond. Spy* 38 The harlots or women taken up for assault or night-brawls were there [in Wood Street Compter] called Mice.

4. *Technical uses.* Applied to various things resembling a mouse in shape or appearance.

a. *Naut.* (See quots.)

1750 BLANCKLEY *Naval Expos.*, *Mouse* is a large Knot artificially made by the Riggers on the Ship's Stays. **1769** FALCONER *Dict. Marine* (1780), *Mouse*, a sort of knob, usually in the shape of a pear, wrought on the outside of a rope, by means of spun yarn, parceling, &c... It is used to confine some other [rope] securely to the former, and prevent it from sliding along its surface. These mouses are particularly used on the stays of the lower-mast, to prevent the *eye* from slipping up to the mast. **1833** MARRYAT *P. Simple* vi, And then he asked the first lieutenant whether something should not be fitted with a *mouse* or only a *turk's-head.* **1867** SMYTH *Sailor's Word-bk.*, *Mouse*, a kind of ball or knob, wrought on the collars of stays by means of spun-yarn,..&c. The mouse prevents the running eye from slipping... Also, a mark made upon braces and other ropes, to show their squaring or tallying home. **1875** KNIGHT *Dict. Mech.*, *Mouse*,..*b.* a turn or two of spun-yarn uniting the point of a hook to the shank to prevent its unhooking.

b. A match used in firing a mine or a gun.

1867 SMYTH *Sailor's Word-bk.*, *Mouse*,..a match used in firing a mine. **1875** KNIGHT *Dict. Mech.*, *Mouse*,..2. (*Blasting*) A match used in firing guns or mines.

c. *U.S.* A small round cushion-shaped hair-pad.

1888 [see RAT *sb.*[1] 5 a]. **1895** in *Funk's Stand. Dict.*

d. (See quot.)

187. *Archit. Publ. Soc. Dict.*, *Mouse*, a small weight to which a cord is attached, used by plumbers for clearing a stoppage in a closet pipe. The carpenters also use a similar weight for passing a sash line over the pulley.

e. (See quot.)

1905 *Jrnl. Franklin Inst.* Mar. 185 A fine wire is sometimes drawn through a duct by a conical piece of wood with a thin leather washer filling the duct, and forced ahead by the air pressure at the rear... This piece of wood is termed the 'mouse'.

f. *Computing.* A small hand-held device which is moved over a flat surface to produce a corresponding movement of a cursor or arrow on a VDU, and which usu. has fingertip controls for selecting a function or entering a command.

1965 ENGLISH & ENGELHARDT *Computer Aided-Display Control* 6 Within comfortable reach of the user's right hand is a device called the 'mouse' which we developed for evaluation..as a means for selecting those displayed text entities upon which the commands are to operate. **1977** *Sci. Amer.* Sept. 234/2 The user makes his primary input through a typewriterlike keyboard and a pointing device called a mouse, which controls the position of an arrow on the screen as it is pushed about on the table beside the display. **1982** *N.Y. Times* 26 Nov. D1 Instead of typing commands or code words to request information, users can point to words or symbols on the screen..through manipulation of a hand-held device known as a mouse. **1983** *Mini-Micro Systems* Feb. 19/3 Using the mouse to point and select, a user can bring a 'page' to the top of the screen and shrink or expand the size of the window. **1984** PHILLIPS & SCELLATO *Apple IIc User Guide* xvi. 272 There are two main types of 'mice', mechanical and optical. **1986** *Which Computer?* Oct. 42/2 The mouse used for controlling much of the new picture-based software to be offered for this machine plugs into the keyboard, not at the back of the machine.

5. A species of cowry.

1815 S. BROOKES *Introd. Conch.* 156 Mouse, *Cypræa Mus.*

6. *slang.* A lump or discoloured bruise, *esp.* one on or near the eye, caused by a blow; a black eye.

1854 'C. BEDE' *Verdant Green* II. iv, That'll raise a tidy mouse on your ogle, my lad! **1886** SIR F. H. DOYLE *Remin. & Opin.* iv. 81 He acquired a severe black eye, of that peculiar kind known to professional pugilists as a 'mouse'.

7. Short for *mouse-moth* (see 10 f).

1829 J. F. STEPHENS *Catal. Brit. Insects* II. 77 *Pyrophila.. Tragopogonis.* Mouse. **1832** RENNIE *Conspect. Butterfl. & M.* 63 The Mouse..appears in June... First pair [of wings] mouse-brown. **1882** W. F. KIRBY *Europ. Butterfl. & M.* (1903) 192/1 When disturbed in the day time it falls down and shuffles about in such a manner that it has acquired the name of 'the Mouse'.

II. 8. A muscle. *Obs.* in general sense (see 9).

[Cf. the similar use of OHG. *mûs*, mod.G. *maus*, Du. *muis*, ON. *mús*; also Gr. μῦς.]

c **1000** ÆLFRIC *Gloss.* in Wr.-Wülcker 158/6 *Torus, uel musculus, uel lacertus*, mus ðæs earmes. **1561** HOLLYBUSH *Hom. Apoth.* 12 b, Binde the garlike vpon the wrest of the arme..so that it do not touche the mousse of the hande.

9. *spec.* Applied variously to certain muscular parts of meat (see quots.). Now only *dial.*

[Cf. **1530** *mouse-piece.*] **1584** LYLY *Sappho* I. iii. 11 *Criti.* ..but come among vs, and you shall see vs once in a morning haue a mouse at a bay. *Molus.* A mouse? vnproperly spoken. *Criti.* Aptly vnderstoode, a mouse of beafe. *Molus.* I thinke indeed a peece of beafe as bigge as a mouse, serues a great companie of such cattes. **1808** JAMIESON, *Mouse*, the outermost fleshy part of a leg of mutton, when dressed; the bulb of flesh on the extremity of the shank, S. pron. *moose.* When roasted, it formerly used to be prepared with salt and pepper. **1854** MISS BAKER *Northamptonsh. Gloss.* II. 36 *Mouse*, the strongest muscle in the shoulder of a pig; which, when drawn out quickly from the flitch, makes a squeaking noise; and children often say to the butcher, 'Come, let's hear the mouse squeak.' **1881** *Oxfordsh. Gloss.* Suppl., *Mouse*, a small piece of meat under the spare-rib of a pig, about the size of a mouse.

III. 10. *attrib.* and *Comb.* (the pl. form *mice-* has occas. been used instead of *mouse-*).

a. simple attributive, as *mouse-birth*, *-cage*, *dung*, *-skin*, etc.; (in sense 4 f) *mouse button.*

1868 BROWNING *Ring & Bk.* III. 1322 Oh *mouse-birth of that mountain-like revenge! **1983** *Austral. Personal Computer* Aug. 38/1 By selecting View from the menu while holding the *mouse button down, [etc.]. **1855** DICKENS *Dorrit* I. xviii, Here Young John turned the great hat round and round upon his left-hand, like a slowly twirling *mouse-cage. **1538** ELYOT *Dict.*, *Muscerda*, *mouse dunge. **1581** W. FULKE in *Confer.* III. (1584) Xj, He should keepe the Pix diligently from mise dung. **1609** HOLLAND *Amm. Marcell.* 400 They are clad all over in garments made of linnen, or else patched up of wild *mice skinnes. **1483** *Cath. Angl.* 245/1 A *Mowsse turde, *musterda.*

b. objective, and obj. genitive, as *mouse-catcher*, *-killer*, *-killing* (adj.), *-slayer*, *-taker.*

1483 *Cath. Angl.* 244/2 A Mowse slaer, *muricida. Ibid.*, A Mowsse taker, *muscipulator.* **1538** ELYOT *Dict.*, *Muricidus*, a mouse killer. **1611** COTGR., *Souricier*, a Mouser, or Mouse-catcher. **1647** TRAPP *Comm. Epist.* 153 Those Popish Muscipulatores or Mice-catchers, as the story calleth them, that raked together their Peter-pence, and other moneys here in England by most detestable arts. **1772** FOOTE *Nabob* III. Wks. 1799 II. 317 The..mouse-killing cat.

c. adverbial, as *mouse-proof.*

1895 *Outing* (U.S.) XXVI. 365/2 A mouse-proof locker.

d. instrumental, as *mouse-crope* (dial.), *-eaten*, *-gnawn* adjs.; (in sense 4 f) *mouse-controlled*, *-driven.*

1983 *Austral. Personal Computer* Aug. 60/3 *Mouse-controlled movements can be made highly accurate. **1721** BAILEY, **Mouse-crope*, a Beast that is run over the Back by a Shrew Mouse is said to be so. *C*[*ountry word.*] **1866** *Treas. Bot.* s.v. *Rubus*, We have heard of cows that were said to be mouse-crope, or to have been walked over by a shrew-mouse (an ancient way of accounting for paralysis), being [etc.]. **1983** *Austral. Personal Computer* Apr. 10/3 *Mouse-driven software has caught the imagination of American hardware designers. **1985** *Pract. Computing* May 20 (Advt.), The latest members of the Apple family will be running the latest mouse-driven software. *a* **1586** SIDNEY *Apol. Poetrie* (Arb.) 31 The Historian..loden with old *Mouse-eaten records. **1921** W. DE LA MARE *Veil* 1 From crock of bone-dry crusts and *mouse-gnawn cheese.

e. similative, as *mouse-brown*, *-grey* (also *sb.*), †*-haired*, *-like*, *-poor*, *-quiet*, *-still* adjs. Also *mouse-like* adv. See also MOUSE-COLOURED, MOUSE-DUN.

1796 WITHERING *Brit. Plants* (ed. 3) IV. 247 Pileus *mouse brown. **1834** *Encycl. Metrop.* (1845) XXII. 249/1 The fur..of a uniform *mouse-grey above. **1839** URE *Dict. Arts* 619 Mouse-gray is obtained, when with the same proportions as for ash-gray. *c* **1420** *Pallad. on Husb.* IV. 913 A staloun asse..al blaak Or *moushered or reed is to been hadde. **1838** DICKENS *Nich. Nick.* xxviii, Inserting her *mouse-like feet in the blue satin slippers. **1874** LISLE CARR *Jud. Gwynne* I. vi. 172 She crept mouse-like to the bedside. **1921** R. GRAVES *Pier-glass* 50 Baffled, aghast with hate, *mouse-poor. **1946** —— *Poems 1938–45* 13 And we remain *mouse-quiet when they begin Suddenly in their unpredictable way To weave an allegory of their lives. **1871** LONGF. *Wayside Inn* II. *Cobbler of Hagenau* 70 His quiet little dame..Eager, excited, but *mouse-still.

f. Special comb.: †**mouse ballock**, some plant; **mouse-bane**, *Aconitum myoctonum* (Treas. Bot. 1866); **mouse barley**, *Hordeum murinum*; **mouse-bird**, (*a*) any bird of the African genus *Colius*; one of the colies; (*b*) 'a whidah-bird (genus *Vidua*)' (*Funk's Stand. Dict.* 1895); **mouse-bur**, the seeds of *Martynia proboscidea*; **mouse buttock** 'the fleshy piece which is cut from a round of beef' (*Eng. Dial. Dict.*); †**mouse catch**, a mousetrap; **mouse chop**, *Mesembryanthemum murinum*, (Treas. Bot.); **mouse-fish**, *Pterophryne* (or *Antennarius*) *histrio*, a fish which builds a sort of nest in the Sargasso Sea; †**mouse-foot**, (*a*) in *by the mouse-foot*, an old oath; (*b*) a plant; **mouse-galago**, a small West African galago, *Galago murinus* (*Funk's Stand. Dict.*); **mouse-grass**, †(*a*) a species of stonecrop; (*b*) a dial. name for the silvery hair grass, *Aira caryophyllea*; (*c*) an Australian name for *Dichelachne crinita*; **mouse-hare**, a rodent of the genus *Lagomys*, esp. *L. roylei*; **mouse-hawk**, (*a*) a hawk that devours mice; (*b*) the short-eared owl or hawk-owl, *Asio brachyotus*; (*c*) *U.S.* 'the rough-legged buzzard' (*Cent. Dict.* 1890), *Archibuteo lagopus*; **mouse-hood**, a fungus (see quot.); **mouse lemur**, any small Madagascan lemur of the genus *Chirogaleus*; **mouse-mark**, a birth-mark resembling a mouse; **mouse-mill** (see quot.); **mouse-moth**, the moth *Amphipyra tragopogonis* (see 7); **mouse-piece** = *mouse-buttock*; **mouse-powder**, a poison for mice; **mouse pox** = ECTROMELIA 2; **mouse-roller** *Printing* (see quot.); **mouse-sight**, a pseudo-etymological rendering of *Myopia*; †**mouse-stock**, a mousetrap; **mouse-thorn** (see quot.); †**mouse-wort**, another name for mugwort. See also MOUSE-COLOUR, MOUSE-DUN, MOUSE-EAR, MOUSE-FALL, MOUSE-HOLE, MOUSE-HUNT, etc.

c **1450** *Alphita* (Anecd. Oxon.) 184/2 Testiculus muris folia habet ualde parua. ang. *museballok. **1840** W. BAXTER *Brit. Phænog. Bot.* V. 344 *Hordeum murinum*, Wall Barley. Way-side Barley. *Mouse Barley. **1822** J. LATHAM *Gen. Hist. Birds* V. 196 These birds [*sc.* Colies] are called at the Cape *Mouse Birds. **1893** SELOUS *Trav. S.E. Africa* 64 A flock of parroquets, or mouse birds, of a species unknown to me. They were of a pale green colour, with rose-coloured heads and long tails. **1877** LADY BRASSEY *Voy. Sunbeam* vi. (1878) 84 The seeds of the Martynia proboscidea, *mouse-burrs, as they call them. **1818** *Min. Evid. Comm. Prisons Metrop., Lond.* 38 That [meat] which I bought for them is called the *mouse buttock. **1382** WYCLIF *Wisd.* xiv. 11 Into a *mousecacche [Vulg. *in muscipulam*]. **1876** G. B. GOODE *Anim. Recources U.S.* 13 *Pediculati.* (Sea-bats or devil-fish, goose-fish or angler, *mouse-fish, &c.) c **1560** *Misogonus* III. i. 255 Bith *mouse foote, do so, Mr. **1605** *Lond. Prodigal* II. ii, I'll come and visit you; by the mouse-foot I will. **1607** TOPSELL *Four-f. Beasts* 504 Plants..receiued names from this little beast, as..Mouse-foot, and such like. **1611** COTGR., *Ioubarbe sauvage*, *Mouse-grasse, wild Prickmadame. **1888–91** BLANFORD *Mammalia India* 456 *Lagomys roylei*. The Himalayan *Mouse-Hare. c **725** *Corpus Gloss.* 1890 *Soricarius*: *mushabuc. c **1050** *Voc.* in Wr.-Wülcker 259/10 *Suricaricis*, mushafuc. **1772** FORSTER in *Phil. Trans.* LXII. 384, *Strix*..Brachyotos. The short-eared Owl. .. Mouse Hawk at Hudson's Bay. **1840** MACGILLIVRAY *Man. Brit. Birds* (1846) 67 *Asio Brachyotus*... *Mouse-hawk.* **1887** HAY *Brit. Fungi* 175 *Hygrophorus murinaceus*, the *Mouse Hood. **1893–4** *Lydekker's Roy. Nat. Hist.* I. 219 The tiny creatures known as the *mouse-lemurs. **1725** RAMSAY *Gentle Sheph.* III. ii, I'll wager there's a *mouse-mark on your side. **1876** *Jrnl. Soc. Telegr. Engineers* V. 186 The electrification of the ink is effected by means of an electrostatic induction machine called the *mouse mill, which is driven either by clockwork or by an electro-magnetic arrangement. **1819** G. SAMOUELLE *Entomol. Compend.* 251 *Mouse moth (*Noctua Tragopogonus*). **1530** PALSGR. 246/2 *Mouspece of an oxe, *moufle*. **1696** AUBREY *Misc.* 109 There is a certain piece in the Beef, called the Mouse-piece, which given to the Child, or Party so affected, to Eat, doth certainly Cure the Thrush. **1886** *York Herald* 10 Aug. 5/6 After the death of Mrs. Dixon, Mrs. Britland..suggested that they might have been poisoned with *mouse powder. **1947** F. FENNER in *Austral. Jrnl. Exper. Biol. & Med. Sci.* XXV. 334 Marchal originally proposed the name 'infectious ectromelia' on account of the frequency with which amputation of the extremities occurred. Few subsequent observers have found this at all common... In view of this and of the newly found close relationship of the disease to the mammalian pox diseases, Professor F. M. Burnet has suggested that '*mouse pox' should be used as a synonym for 'infectious ectromelia'. **1948** *Brit. Jrnl. Exper. Path.* XXIX. 77 Mice dying of acute mouse-pox do not shed much virus into the environment. **1955** F. M. BURNET *Princ. Animal Virology* vii. 157 The content of elementary bodies was very clearly shown in ultraviolet micrographs of the..mouse-pox inclusion body. **1970** S. M. BROOKS *World of Viruses* v. 47 The so-called variola-like poxviruses cause smallpox,..mousepox,..and turkey-pox. **1888** JACOBI *Printer's Vocab.*, **Mouse roller*, a small additional roller for the better distribution of ink on a machine. **1822–34** *Good's Study Med.* (ed. 4) III. 152 Mice are said to have this kind of vision naturally, and hence one of the technical names for it is myopia or myopiasis, literally '*mouse-sight'. c **1175** *Lamb. Hom.* 53 þeos wimmen..beoð þes deofles *musestoch iclepede, for þenne þe mon wule tilden his musestoch he binde𝑝 uppon þa swike chese and bret hine for þon þet he scolde swote smelle. **1866** *Treas. Bot.*, *Mouse-thorn. *Centaurea myacantha.* **1607** TOPSELL *Four-f. Beasts* 512 Mug-wort, otherwise cald *mouse-wort.

mouse (maʊz), *v.* Also 3 muse, 5–7 mowse, mouze, 7 mowze, 9 *dial.* moose. [f. MOUSE *sb.* Cf. G. *mausen*, Du. *muizen*.]

1. *intr.* To hunt for or catch mice; said esp. of a cat or an owl.

a **1250** *Prov. Ælfred* 296 in *O.E. Misc.* 120 For ofte Museþ þe kat after hire moder. c **1440** *Promp. Parv.* 347/1 Mowsyn, or take myse, *muricapio*. **1692** R. L'ESTRANGE *Fables* lxxxi. 79 An Old Weazle that was now almost past Mousing. **1791** HUDDESFORD *Salmag., Monody Death of Dick* 133 Thee, generous Dick, the Cat-controlling Powers Ordained to mouse in Academic Bowers. **1856** MISS YONGE *Daisy Chain* I. xxi, The large white owl floating over the fields as it moused in the long grass. **1871** BLACKIE *Four Phases* i. 42 You expect..your cat to mouse well.

2. *transf.* and *fig.* To hunt or search industriously or captiously; to go or move *about* softly in search of something, to prowl. Also with *around*, *along*.

1575 TURBERV. *Venerie* 153 When he [*sc.* the Bore]..doth but a little turne vp the grounde with his nose, he seeketh for wormes. So may you say that he hath been mowsing. **1673** MARVELL *Reh. Transp.* II. 254 You fall a mousing about the definition of a Quibble. **1778** WOLCOT (P. Pindar) *Epist. to Reviewers* xxviii, There, Wisdom,..I've seen o'er pamphlets,..Mousing for faults, or, if you'll have it, Owling. **1842** J. FOSTER in *Life & Corr.* (1846) II. 421 This has been the consequence of mousing for them [engravings] during a good many years. **1849** W. IRVING *Goldsmith* xiii. 143 He..wrote in a more free and fluent style than if he had been mousing at the time among authorities. **1856** R. A. VAUGHAN *Mystics* IX. iii. (1860) II. 135 He..mouses for flaws of regulation. **1874** G. H. KINGSLEY *Sport & Trav.* vi. (1900) 161, I was mousing around by myself the other day. **1885** H. C. MCCOOK *Tenants of Old Farm* 365 Maybe they peep and mouse into the tunnels and caves of worms.

b. ***to mouse over*** (a book): to study eagerly. *U.S.*

1807–8 W. IRVING *Salmag.* (1824) 385 With..a table full of books before me, to mouse over them alternately. **1864** B. TAYLOR in *Life & Lett.* (1884) II. xvii. 422, I have Little and Brown's 'British Poets' complete now, so you'll have wherewithal to mouse over. **1889** GRETTON *Memory's Harkb.* 137 He was..always 'mousing' over books.

c. *trans.* To hunt for by patient and careful search. Also with *out*. *U.S.*

1864 *N.Y. Evangelist* 20 Oct. (Cent.), He..usually returned laden with boxes and bundles of literary odds and ends, moused from rural attics and bought or begged for his collection. **1870** H. STEVENS *Bibl. Histor.* Introd. 11 They are driven..to mouse out in foreign countries..what ought to be at home..in the public libraries.

†**3.** *trans.* To handle as a cat does a mouse; to tear, bite. *Obs.*

1530 TINDALE *Answ. More* III. xiii. Wks. (1573) 311/1 In the xiii. [chapter]..he biteth, sucketh, gnaweth, towseth, and mowseth Tyndall. **1573** TUSSER *Husb.* (1878) 91 Keepe sheepe from dog, keepe lambes from hog. If foxes mowse them, then watch or howse them. **1595** SHAKS. *John* II. i. 354 *Bast.* Oh, now doth Death line his dead chaps with steele;.. And now he feasts, mousing the flesh of men, In vndetermin'd differences of kings! **1603** DEKKER *Wonderful Year* C 2 b, Whilst Troy was swilling sack and sugar, and mowsing fat venison, the mad Greekes made bonefires of their houses. **1647** FANSHAWE *Il Pastor Fido* IV. 124 But 't had been worse t' have been prisoner To such a beast; Who though he doth not bear A mouses heart, might have mouz'd me.

†**b.** To pull about good-naturedly, but roughly; chiefly *touse and mouse*; cf. MOUSLE *v.* *Obs.*

1607 MIDDLETON *Fam. of Love* V. iii. 334 Yet if you did but see how like a cock sparrow he mouses and touses my little Bess already. a **1627** H. SHIRLEY *Mart. Souldier* IV. iii. in Bullen *O. Pl.* I. 235 Is't the kings pleasure that I should mouse her, and before all these people? **1675** WYCHERLY *Country Wife* II. i, He would not let me come near the gentry, who sat under us [at the play]... He told me, none but naughty women sat there, whom they toused and moused. **1691** SHADWELL *Scourers* IV. i, My dear chicken, I'll mouse thee.

absol. **1681** OTWAY *Soldier's Fort.* I. i, To see a pretty Wench and a young Fellow touze and rouze and frouze and mouze.

†**4.** To ransack, rummage, pillage. *Obs.*

c **1580** JEFFERIE *Bugbears* II. i. in *Archiv Stud. neu. Spr.* (1897), They have rifeled and mowsed the cofer by a false key thei made.

5. *Naut.* To put a mouse (see MOUSE *sb.* 4 a) on (a stay); to secure (a hook) with a mouse.

1769 FALCONER *Dict. Marine* (1780), *Mousing a hook*, the operation of fastening a small cord..across the upper-part, from the point to the back.., in order to prevent it from unhooking. **1837** MARRYAT *Dog-fiend* ix, I can bring my tarry trousers to an anchor—mousing the mainstay, or puddening the anchor. **1867** SMYTH *Sailor's Word-bk*, s.v. *Mouse, To mouse a hook.*

Hence **moused** *ppl. a.*, supplied with mousing.

1883 *Fisheries Exhib. Catal.* 9 These Patent Slip-Hooks.. form an automatically 'Moused' hook when in use.

mouse: see MOOSE² and MUSA¹ (banana).

mouseare, obs. form of MOUSE-EAR.

mousebunker: see MOSSBUNKER.

ˈ**mouse-colour**, *sb.* (*a.*)

1. A colour resembling that of the common mouse; a dark grey with a yellowish tinge.

1606 *Jrnls. Ho. Comm.* I. 309/1 A strange Spanyell, of Mouse-colour, came into the House. **1797** *Encycl. Brit.* (ed. 3) XVIII. 648/1 The fur is of a mouse-colour, tinged with reddish. **1903** 'MARJORIBANKS' *Fluff-Hunters* 65 Her hair was of that subtle half-shade known as mouse-colour.

2. *attrib.* passing into *adj.* Mouse-coloured.

1716 *Lond. Gaz.* No. 5481/4 Lost.., a Mouse-Colour Mare. **1728–9** MRS. DELANY in *Life & Corr.* (1861) I. 193 The Prince of Wales was in mouse-colour velvet. **1828** STARK *Elem. Nat. Hist.* I. 120 Fur mouse-colour.

So **mouse-coloured** *a.*

1687 *Lond. Gaz.* No. 2307/4 Lost..a little Greyhound,.. her Ears Mouse-coloured,..and several Mouse-coloured spots on her Body. **1861** F. METCALFE *Oxonian in Icel.* ix. (1867) 129 The mouse-coloured horse which I am riding is crossed..with black streaks. **1900** *Daily News* 10 Feb. 6/3 The rest of the dress was mouse-coloured cloth.

ˈ**mouse-deer.** Also 9 moose-. [*Moose-deer* and *mouse-deer* seem to be corruptions of *musk-deer*, a name which was early misapplied to this animal; the former due to association with the known *moose-deer* = MOOSE, the latter perh. suggested by the animal's small size and the colour of its hair.] A chevrotain, a small deer-like mammal of the genus *Tragulus*, found in southern Asia, Sumatra, Borneo, and Java.

1836 *Penny Cycl.* VI. 454/1 (*Ceylon*) There is also another of very diminutive size, called the moose deer. **1874** JERDON *Mammals of India* 269 *Memimna indica*... The Mouse-deer. **1914** *Oxf. Survey Brit. Empire* II. xii. 383 The Indian pig, the mouse-deer..are found throughout the territories. **1965** R. MCKIE *Company of Animals* x. 153 Joe's mouse-deer are about nine inches high. **1969** LD. MEDWAY *Wild Mammals Malaya* 106/1 Mouse-deer are true forest mammals.

mouse-dun, *a.* and *sb.* **a.** *adj.* Mouse-coloured. **b.** *sb.* The dun colour of a mouse; mouse-colour.

c **1420** *Pallad. on Husb.* IV. 832 Black bay, & permixt gray, mousdon [L. *murinus*]..and many mo [colours]. **1577** B. GOOGE *Heresbach's Husb.* III. 116 b, Touching the colours.. the mousedun, and the grisel weare most esteemed. **1611** COTGR. s.v. *Poil*, *Couleur de poil de souris*, a Mouse-colour, or Mouse-dunne. **1639** T. DE GRAY *Compl. Horsem.* 58 Your mouse-dunne and such like rusty and sut colours. **1686** *Lond. Gaz.* No. 2146/4 Stray'd or stolen.., a dark mouse dun long made Gelding. **1859** DARWIN *Orig. Spec.* v. (1873) 129 These stripes occur far oftenest in duns and mouse-duns. **1907** *Q. Rev.* Apr. 554 The mouse-dun Tarpan of the Russian steppes.

ˈ**mouse-ear.** Also 3 musere, 4 mouser, 4–5 mous(h)ere, 5 mowseer, mushere, mousher. [transl. of med.L. *auricula muris*, Gr. μυὸς ὠτίς: see MYOSOTIS. Cf. OHG. *mûsôra* 'pilosa', G. *mäuse-*, *mauseohr*.

In senses 1–3 the name seems to refer to the hairy leaves of the plants.]

1. A species of hawkweed, *Hieracium Pilosella*. Also ***mouse-ear hawkweed***.

Bastard Mouse-ear *Hieracium Pseudo-Pilosella* (Treas. Bot. 1866). Golden Mouse-ear, *Hieracium aurantiacum*.

c **1265** *Voc. Plants* in Wr.-Wülcker 558/18 *Pilosella*, peluselle, musere. a **1387** *Sinon. Barthol.* (Anecd. Oxon.) 33/2 *Pelvette*, mouser. c **1440** *Pol. Rel. & L. Poems* Add. (1903) 311 Tak an handful of Bugyl..an oþer of Pympurnele, an oþer of mousere. **1578** LYTE *Dodoens* I. xxxvi. 53 Mouse eare..hath many small and slender stemmes somewhat redde bylow. *Ibid.* 54 *Auricula muris Matthioli.* Mouse eare. **1597** GERARDE *Herbal* II. xxxvi. (1633) 305 Golden mouse-eare or Grimme the Colliar. **1612** DRAYTON *Poly-olb.* xiii. 224 To him that hath a flux, of Sheepheards purse he giues, And Mous-eare vnto him whom some sharpe rupture grieues. **1682** WHELER *Journ. Greece* I. 25 This Plant is very like to the Great Mouse-Ear. **1760** J. LEE *Introd. Bot.* App. 319 Mouse-ear, Creeping, *Hieracium*. **1789** W. AITON *Hortus Kewensis* III. 121 *Hieracium Pilosella*... Mouse-ear Hawkweed. **1806** GALPINE *Brit. Bot.* §346 Hieracium... Pilosella... Mouse-ear. **1855** MISS PRATT *Flower. Pl.* (1861) III. 213 Orange Hawkweed... The plant is sometimes called by gardeners Golden Mouse-ear.

2. (More fully ***mouse ear chickweed***.) A plant of the genus *Cerastium*, somewhat resembling chickweed, esp. *C. vulgatum*, *C. triviale*, and *C. viscosum*; also applied to *Holosteum umbellatum*, a plant with flowers like chickweed.

1578 LYTE *Dodoens* I. xxxvi. 53 There is yet an other herbe, which some holde for Mouse eare:..set about with a fine and softe heare, the rest is very like the second Chickeweede. **1585** HIGINS tr. *Junius' Nomencl.* 115/1 *Alsine.* Chickweede or mouseare. **1731** P. MILLER *Gard. Dict.*, *Myosotis*, *Mouse-ear Chickweed... The Species are; 1. *Myosotis*; *Hispanica, segetum. Tourn.* Spanish Corn Mouse-ear Chickweed. 2. *Myosotis*; *Alpina, latifolia. Tourn.* Broad-leav'd Mouse-ear Chickweed of the Alps. **1799** J. HULL *Brit. Flora* 30 *Holosteum umbellatum*... Umbelliferous Mouse-ear. *Ibid.* 101 *Cerastium viscosum*... Clammy Mouse-ear... *C. vulgatum*... Narrow-leaved Mouse-ear [and others]. **1840–8** MAUNDER *Sci. & Lit. Treas.* (ed. 5), *Mouse-ear*, in botany, a plant of the genus *Cerastium*, very similar to chickweed. **1866** *Treas. Bot.*, *Cerastium*, a rather extensive genus of *Caryophyllaceæ*, containing small white-flowered plants, generally called Mouse-ear Chickweeds.

3. A plant of the genus *Myosotis*, esp. the forget-me-not, *M. palustris* and *M. arvensis*. Also ***mouse-ear scorpion grass***.

1597 GERARDE *Herbal* II. cxciv. 514 *Pilosella flore cæruleo.* Blewe Mouseare. **1690** RAY *Synopsis Meth. Stirpium* (1724) 229 Mouse-ear Scorpion-Grass. **1776–96** WITHERING *Brit. Plants* (ed. 3) II. 225 *Myosotis arvensis*... Field Mouse-ear. Scorpion-grass. **1845–50** MRS. LINCOLN *Lect. Bot.* xxv. 146 The Mouse-ear (*Myosotis*) is valued for its medicinal properties; a species, the *arvensis*, or Forget-me-not, is an interesting little blue flower. **1883** 'OUIDA' *Wanda* I. 157 The swollen brooks were blue with mouse-ear.

4. The name of various other plants. **a.** The cruciferous plant *Sisymbrium Thaliana*; more fully ***mouse-ear cress***, †***mouse-ear molewort***, ***codded*** (or ***podded***) ***mouse-ear***. **b.** *dial.* Various species of woundwort, esp. *Stachys germanica* and *S. lanata*. **c.** *U.S.* A species of everlasting flower, *Antennaria plantaginifolia*, having small grey soft leaves resembling a mouse's ear; also called ***mouse-ear everlasting*** (Cent. Dict.), †***mouse-ear plantain***.

1578 LYTE *Dodoens* I. xxxvi. 53 Bysides these two there is yet a kinde of Mouse-eare whiche..standeth vpright, growing amongst other herbes, lyke to the others in stemme and leaues, but it is greater and of colour white, couered ouer with a clammy Downe or Cotton, in handling as though it were bedewed or moystened with Honie, and cleaueth to the fingers. **1696** PLUKENET *Opera Bot.* (1769) II. 298 Plantago Virginiana Pilosellæ foliis angustis radice turbinata.. *Mouse-ear Plantain.* **1732** J. MARTYN *Tournefort's Hist. Pl.* II. 318 *Turritis vulgaris*... Codded Mouse-ear. **1770** J. HILL *Herb. Brit.* II. 269, 1. *Arabis Thaliana.* Mouse-ear Molewort. *Folia integerrima.* Podded Mouse-ear. **1874** GRAY *Less. Bot.* 70 *Sisymbrium Thaliana*,..(Mouse-ear Cress). **1879** MISS JACKSON *Shropsh. Word-bk.*, Mouse-ear, *Stachys Germanica*, downy Woundwort (garden plant). **1882** FRIEND *Devonsh. Plant-n.*, Mouse's Ear, *Stachys lanata*, L. the white-leaved garden variety.

So ˈ**mouse-eared** *a.*, having an appendage resembling a mouse's ear; *spec.* †(*a*) of willows, having catkins; (*b*) in ***mouse-eared chickweed***, ***hawkweed*** = MOUSE-EAR 1, 2; (*c*) ***mouse-eared bat***, a brown bat, *Myotis myotis*, with greyish-white underside, found in Europe, parts of western Asia, and, rarely, in Britain.

1641 BEST *Farm. Bks.* (Surtees) 15 The best wood for barres is the willow; but such as have had experience advise not to fell them till such time as they beginne to budde and bee mouse-ear'd. **1789** J. PILKINGTON *View Derbysh.* I. 344 *Myosotis scorpioides.* Mouse-eared Scorpiongrass. *Ibid.* 397 *Cerastium vulgatum.* Common mouse-eared Chickweed. *Ibid.* 449 *Hieracium pilosella.* Creeping Mouse-Ear or Mouse-eared Hawkweed. **1910** G. E. H. BARRETT-HAMILTON *Hist. Brit. Mammals* I. 191 The Mouse-eared bat, should it occur again in Britain, can hardly be mistaken for any other. **1956** *Proc. Zool. Soc.* CXXVII. 201 The animal was indentified as a Mouse-eared Bat *Myotis myotis* .. and then photographed *in situ* before being touched. **1975** *Observer* 26 Jan. 1/8 Mr Peter Hardy..said mouse-eared bats survived in Britain in only a single colony.

'mouse-fall. *Obs.* exc. *dial.* [f. MOUSE *sb.* + FALL *sb.*[2] Cf. OHG. *mûsfalla* (mod.G. *mausfalle*, *mäuse-*, *mausefalle*), Du. *muizenval*, Da. *musefælde*.] A mousetrap.

*c*725 *Corpus Gloss.* 1340 *Muscipula*: muusfalle. *c* **1050** *Voc.* in Wr.-Wülcker 477/17 *Pelx*, musfealle. *c* **1440** *Promp. Parv.* 347/1 Mowsfalle, *muscipula*. **1866** EDMONDSTON *Shetl. & Orkney Dial.* 74 *Moosfa*, a trap for catching mice.

'mouse-hole. A hole used by a mouse for passage or abode; a hole only big enough to admit a mouse. Also *transf.* and *fig.* Hence **'mousehole** *v. trans.* and *intr.*, to make a narrow passage or tunnel (through); **'mouseholed** *ppl. a.*

c **1420** LYDG. *Assembly of Gods* 1953 For feere I lookyd as blak as a coole, I wold haue cropyn in a mouse hole. **1483** *Cath. Angl.* 244/2 A Mosse (MS. A. mowse) hole, *amfractus*. **1603** DEKKER *Wonderfull Yeare* Ej, Not a creuis but was stopt, not a mouse-hole left open. **1679** T. KIRKE *Mod. Acc. Scot.* 10 Men, Women, and Children pigg altogether in a poor Mouse-hole of Mud. **1708** MRS. CENTLIVRE *Busie Body* III. iii, Have you let a Man into my House?.. I'll not leave a Mouse-hole unsearch'd. **1888** EGGLESTON *Graysons* xx. 216 Bob..liked this lurking for prey as a cat likes the watching at a mouse-hole. **1950** O. NASH *Family Reunion* (1951) 40 Little mouse Blink strategically mouseholed. **1967** L. DEIGHTON *Expensive Place* xx. 137 It was another half-hour before they had broken into the cellars..and then it took twenty minutes more to mousehole through into Datt's house. *Ibid.* 138 Loiscau's men were moving up from the mouse-holed cellars.

'mouse-hunt[1]. *Obs.* exc. *dial.* Also 5 **muse-hont.** [a. MDu. *muushont* weasel (mod.Du. *muishond*), f. *muus* mouse + *hont* dog (see HOUND *sb.*); there may also have been a native word, f. MOUSE *sb.* + HUNT *sb.*[1]] **a.** A weasel. **b.** *gen.* An animal that hunts mice.

Halliwell (1847) gives '*Mouse-hound*, a weasel, *East*'. In S. African Du. *muishond* is a synonym of MEERKAT, whence the use in quot. 1850.

1481 CAXTON *Reynard* (Arb.) 79 The squyrel, the musehont [*printed* -hout], the fychews. **1592** SHAKS. *Rom. & Jul.* IV. iv. 11, I haue watcht ere now All night for lesse[r] cause, and nere beene sicke. *La.* I you haue bin a Mouse-hunt in your time. **1611** COTGR. s.v. *Geline*, *Qui naist de geline il aime a grater*: Prov. Cat after kind good Mouse-hunt. **1641** MILTON *Reform.* I. Wks. 1851 III. 31 Many of those that pretend to be great Rabbies in these studies.. have bin but the Ferrets and Moushunts of an Index. [**1850** R. G. CUMMING *Hunter's Life S. Afr.* (ed. 2) I. 102 The whole ground was undermined with the holes of colonies of meercat or mouse-hunts.]

mouse-hunt[2]. [HUNT *sb.*[2]] A hunt for mice.

1828–32 in WEBSTER. **1975** *Country Life* 27 Mar. 761/1 Our adopted cat..no longer seems to want to be off on a nocturnal mousehunt.

'mousekin. *rare.* [-KIN.] = MOUSELING.

1859 THACKERAY *Virgin.* xxxviii, 'Frisk about, pretty little mousekin,' says grey Grimalkin.

mousel, obs. form of MUZZLE.

mouselet ('maʊslɪt). *rare.* [f. MOUSE *sb.* + -LET.] = MOUSELING. Also a species of moth.

1832 RENNIE *Conspect. Butterfl. & M.* 89 *Simyra*... The Mouselet appears near marshes. **1873** T. W. HIGGINSON *Oldport Days* iii. 78 This [nest] contained, moreover, a small family of mouselets. **1906** *Athenæum* 30 June 796/2 Though mountains heave in all directions, the outcome is likely to be some ridiculous mouselet.

mouseling ('maʊslɪŋ). *rare.* [f. MOUSE *sb.* + -LING.] A small or young mouse.

1832 J. BREE *St. Herbert's Isl.*, etc. 149 So in the silly mouseling went..Here, eat this silly mouseling up! **1860** GOSSE *Rom. Nat. Hist.* Ser. I. 148 The tiny harvest mouse, ..which brings up its large little family of eight hopeful mouselings in a nest no bigger than a cricket-ball.

mousell, obs. form of MUZZLE.

'mouse-pea. *Obs.* exc. *dial.* Forms: 1 músepise, 4 **muspese, mous pese,** 5 **mousepese,** 6 **mowsepease,** 9 *dial.* **moose's, mouse's peas,** 9– **mouse-pea.** The Heath-pea (*Lathyrus macrorrhizus*); also the Meadow Vetchling (*L. pratensis*).

c **1000** ÆLFRIC *Gloss.* in Wr.-Wülcker 148/35 *Uicia*, musepise. *a* **1387** *Sinon. Barthol.* (Anecd. Oxon.) 32/2 *Orobus* sive *orobum* est pisa agrestis, s. muspese. *Ibid.* 43/1 *Vesces*, i. fecches vel mous pese, orobus idem. *a* **1400–50** *Stockh. Med. MS.* in *Archæologia* XXX. 410/2 Monsope [*read* mousepe]: *erobus*. *c* **1450** *Alphita* (Anecd. Oxon.) 131/1 *Orobus*,..anglice thare uel mousepese. **1597** GERARDE *Herbal* App., Mowsepease is *Orobus*. **1665** LOVELL *Herbal* (ed. 2) 292 Mouse-pease, see Bitter-vetch. **1894** *Northumbld. Gloss.*, *Moose's peas*, *mouse's peas*, the tufted vetch, *Vicia cracca*.

mouser ('maʊzə(r)). Forms: 5 **mowsare,** 6– **mouser.** [f. MOUSE *v.* + -ER[1].]

1. An animal that catches mice; *esp.* applied to a cat, or an owl.

c **1400** *Promp. Parv.* 347/1 Mowsare, as a catte, *musceps*. **1573** TUSSER *Husb.* (1878) 172 Though cat (a good mouser) doth dwell in a house, yet euer in dairie haue trap for a mouse. **1692** R. L'ESTRANGE *Fables* lxi. 61 For Puss, even when she's a Madam, will be a Mouser still. **1771** FOOTE *Maid of B.* II. Wks. 1799 II. 222 Owls..are counted very good mousers. **1839–40** W. IRVING *Wolfert's R.* (1855) 9 Watching for hours together any ship or galley at anchor or becalmed—as a valorous mouser will watch a rat hole. **1921** T. S. ELIOT *Let.* c 11 Oct. in *Waste Land Drafts* (1971) p. xxi, Would you be able to house a small cat which we are very fond of?.. It is a very good mouser. **1939** —— *Old Possum's Pract. Cats* 38 No commonplace mousers have such well-cut trousers. **1966** A. CHRISTIE *Third Girl* xvii. 178 You're so exactly like a good mouser. A cat sitting over a hole waiting for the mouse to come out.

fig. **1608** DAY *Law-Tricks* III. E 2, Bring the Lady a Diamond,..for I can tel you these same paultrie stones are in high request amongst Ladies, especially such old mowsers as I haue beene in my time. **1848** LOWELL *Lett.* (1894) I. 147 He [Shakspeare] invented a new order of poetry; for, let the mousers trace all the resemblances they will, it is entirely new in its idea.

2. *slang.* **a.** (see quot. 1802); **b.** a detective.

1802 C. JAMES *Milit. Dict.*, *Mouser*, an ironical term, which is sometimes used in the British militia to distinguish battalion men from the flank companies. It is indeed generally applied to them by the grenadiers and light bobs, meaning, that while the latter are detached, the former remain in quarters, like cats, to watch the mice, &c. **1863** *Confess. Ticket of Leave Man* 266 Two shrewd 'mousers', were sent off at once with Mr. Gee to York Street.

mouser(e, obs. forms of MOUSE-EAR.

mouseroll, obs. form of MUSROLL.

mousery ('maʊsərɪ). [f. MOUS(E *sb.* + -ERY.]

a. A place where mice abound; a colony of mice.

1888 F. A. LUCAS in *Auk* V. 280 The occasional disturbance of this populous mousery by the visits of Owls. **1925** W. DE LA MARE *Broomsticks* 109 He never paid the smallest attention to mouse or mouse-hole or mousery.

b. A place where mice are bred or kept.

1935 A. CARROL *Man the Unknown* vi. 207 The mice belonging to one of the strains kept in the mousery of the Rockefeller Institute died of pneumonia in the proportion of fifty-two per cent while subjected to the standard diet. **1946** *All Pets Mag.* Sept. 64/3, I will try and give you a picture of my mousery. I use twelve..breeding units [etc.]. **1949** *Amer. Small Stock Farmer* Sept. 10 Weltytown Mousery. Breeders of white mice for laboratory and research.

'mouseship. *nonce-wd.* [-SHIP.] The condition of being a mouse; a mock title for a mouse.

1702 *Mouse grown a Rat* 15 My Mouseship had not a Hole to creep into. **1802–12** BENTHAM *Ration. Judic. Evid.* (1827) V. 65 Debates..concerning the comparative value..of a possible Angelship and a present Mouseship.

'mousetail. [f. MOUSE *sb.* + TAIL *sb.*[1]]

†**1.** The stonecrop, *Sedum acre*. *Obs.*

1548 TURNER *Names of Herbes*, *Sedum*, The thyrd kinde is called in Englishe Mouse tayle or little stoncroppe. **1597** GERARDE *Herbal* II. cxxxvii. 415 Stonecrop..Mousetaile. **1611** COTGR. *Pain d'oiseau*, Stonecrop,..Mousetaile.

2. A plant of the genus *Myosurus*, esp. *M. minimus*, from the shape of its seed receptacle.

1578 LYTE *Dodoens* I. lxv. 96 Of Bloud strange or Mouse tayle. Mouse tayle is a small low herbe, with small leaues and very narrow [etc.]. **1597** GERARDE *Herbal* II. xcv. 345 Mousetaile or *Cauda muris*, resembleth the last kind of wild Coronopus or sea Plantain. **1789** J. PILKINGTON *View Derbysh.* I. 376 *Myosurus minimus.* Little Mousetail. **1866** *Treas. Bot.* 769/2 *Myosurus minimus*, or Mouse-tail,..rarely attains more than three or four inches in height.

3. Applied to other plants, as (*a*) *Alopecurus agrestis* (cf. 5); (*b*) the genus *Mygalurus*; (*c*) the orchid *Dendrobium Myosurus*.

1866 *Treas. Bot.*, Mousetail, *Mygalurus*; also *Myosurus minimus*, and *Dendrobium Myosurus*. **1893** *Wiltsh. Gloss.*, *Mousetails*, a kind of grass, perhaps Cats'-tail, but not *Myosurus*.

4. *pl.* Moustaches. *jocular.*

1855 SMEDLEY *H. Coverdale* iv, 'Why the brute actually wears moustaches.' 'He..sports the mouse-tails on the strength of his military pretensions.'

5. *attrib.*: **mousetail grass**, (*a*) one of the foxtail grasses, *Alopecurus agrestis*; (*b*) a fescue grass, *Festuca Myurus* (*Cent. Dict.* 1890).

1696 RAY *Synopsis Meth. Stirp.* (1724) 397 *Gramen myosuroides majus*... The greater Mouse-tail-Grass... *Gramen myosuroides minus*... The lesser Mouse-tail-Grass. **1766** *Museum Rust.* VI. 442 Field Fox-tail..or Mouse-tail Grass. **1792–4** MARTYN *Flora Rustica* 22 *Alopecurus agrestis*. Field Fox-tail Grass, or Mouse-tail Grass.

mousetrap ('maʊstræp), *sb.* Pl. **mousetraps,** also 7 **mice-traps.** [f. MOUSE *sb.* + TRAP.]

1. a. A trap for catching mice. (Cf. the older MOUSEFALL and *mouse-stock*.)

In England usually a small cage inside which the bait (a piece of toasted cheese) is so suspended that when the mouse seizes it a spring is released which closes the door. In Scotland a wholly different contrivance is used, which is baited with meal, and is constructed to catch *and kill* two or three mice without being re-set. (*N.E.D.*)

c **1475** *Cath. Angl.* 245/1 (MS. Addit.) A Mowse trape, *muscipula*. **1526** *Pilgr. Perf.* (W. de W. 1531) 127 b, And he sayth that in contrary wyse, they be as mouse trappes to them that be vnwyse. **1607** TOPSELL *Four-f. Beasts* 510 There are many kinds of mice-traps where mice do perish by the waight thereof. **1623** MIDDLETON *More Dissemblers* IV. i. 220 Like a mouse-trap baited with bacon. **1772** WESLEY *Jrnl.* 14 Jan., He could invent the best mouse-trap. **1842** LOUDON *Encycl. Gardening* § 1478 The garden mouse-trap is generally composed of a slate and a brick, supported by.. three slips of wood.

b. *fig.* A device for enticing a person to his destruction or defeat.

1577 *F. de L'isle's Legendarie* F vij, They..called the kings letters patents the mousetrappes to catch fooles. **1613** HAYWARD *Norm. Kings* 12 Others demanded if he had any more mouse-traps to lead them into. **1674** *Essex Papers* (Camden) 256 A moustrap laid by Orrery & that gang. *a* **1700** B. E. *Dict. Cant. Crew*, The Parson's *Mouse-trap*, Marriage. **1887** H. R. HAWEIS *Lt. of Ages* v. 139 He [the Greek] did not look upon the senses as so many mouse-traps. **1945** R. HARGREAVES *Enemy at Gate* 84 Wounded at the 'mouse-trap' of Dettingen, he was present at Fontenoy. **1966** M. R. D. FOOT *SOE in France* viii. 203 All the agents taken in the Villa des Bois mousetrap at Marseilles..were in the noisome Béleyme prison at Périgueux.

appositive. **1678** BUTLER *Hud.* III. iii. 751 Ply her with love-letters and billets, And bait 'em well,..And if she miss the mouse-trap lines, They'll serve for other by-designs.

c. *transf.* Applied humorously to a tiny house.

1839 TENNYSON in Ld. Tennyson *Mem.* (1897) I. 171 The house at Tunbridge is too small, a mere mouse-trap. **1885** *Harper's Mag.* Mar. 545/2 They have hunted up a..house ..—the most dingy..little mouse-trap you ever saw.

d. In various *transf.* and *fig.* uses.

1903 *Dialect Notes* II. 342 *Mouse-trap*, an implement 'for cutting and fishing out rope when matted in the well. It will also take out small pieces of iron or steel, or any small object'. **1929** *Papers Mich. Acad. Sci., Arts & Lett.* X. 309 *Mouse-trap*, a plant at Willoughby, near Cleveland, built for the manufacture of Lewisite. It was so called by the workmen because every one who entered it did so under an agreement not to leave until the end of the war. **1941** *Reader's Digest* Feb. 54 The boys of Britain's R.A.F. have developed a language all their own...'roller skates' are tanks, and 'mousetraps' submarines. **1953** ROWLAND & BOYD *U.S. Navy Bureau of Ordnance in World War II* 137 The NDRC project thus became an attempt to combine the respective virtues of the Hedgehog and rockets. By the spring of 1942 the solution was at hand in the Mousetrap, an antisubmarine projector that launched a salvo of sixteen 7".2 rockets ahead of the attacking ship. **1957** *Amer. Speech* XXXII. 194 *Mouse trap*, any device of an unorthodox nature attached to a handgun for the purpose of making it more accurate or, less frequently, of making it function more smoothly.

2. The cheese with which a mousetrap is baited. Now used *joc.* to denote inferior or unpalatable cheese. Also ***mousetrap cheese***.

1650 B. *Discolliminium* 17 Their Braines are made of grated Mouse-traps, steep'd in the spirits of Projects. **1936** R. LEHMANN *Weather in Streets* III. iii. 299 A portion of mousetrap cheese, extra charge threepence. **1947** F. SMYTHE *Again Switzerland* iii. 53 The tasty local cheese—what a change from the eternal 'mousetrap'! **1958** *Times Rev. Industry* Sept. 104/3 Statistics are silent as to whether the cheese is 'mousetrap'..a processed type or..has a character of its own. **1960** *News Chron.* 18 Feb. 3/6, I don't even know what kind of cheese they will be serving. But.. mousetrap would be the most suitable. **1972** *Times* 2 Sept. 15/7 Salty butter, red 'mousetrap' cheese. **1975** *Observer* (Colour Suppl.) 27 Apr. 10/1 Although sometimes dismissed as 'mousetrap', Cheddar is much the most popular cheese in Britian.

3. *attrib.* and *Comb.*, as ***mousetrap-gun***, ***-maker***, ***-man***, ***mechanism***; **mousetrap cheese** (see sense 2); **mousetrap-switch** *Electr.*, an automatic switch moved by a spring which is released when the current through a controlling magnet falls below a certain limit.

1964 H. L. PETERSON *Encycl. Firearms* 325/1 Some collectors called Cochran rifles '*mousetrap guns'. *a* **1695** WOOD in Hearne *Liber Niger Scaccarii* (1728) II. 594 Mr. Selden said, they had as good inquire, whether they had best admitt Inigo Jones, the Kings Architect, to the Company of *Mous-trapmakers, &c. **1894** *Daily News* 30 Nov. 5/5 Among the curious occupations taken up by boys is that of bird dealer, crossing sweeper,..mousetrap maker [etc.]. **1631** B. JONSON *Barth. Fair* Dram. Pers., Costard-monger. *Movsetrap-man. Clothier [etc.]. **1708** SWIFT *Hist. Vanbrug's Ho.* 48 We might expect to see next year, A Mouse-trap Man, Chief Engineer. **1969** *Guardian* 25 July 4/4 Watson gave him a smoke grenade which had a '*mousetrap' mechanism.

Hence **mouse-trapped** *ppl. a.*, caught like a mouse in a trap.

1607 DEKKER & WEBSTER *Westw. Hoe* v. iv, You shall heare the poore mouse-trapt-guilty-gentlemen call for mercy.

mousetrap ('maʊstræp), *v.* [f. the sb.] *trans.* To entrap, deceive, fool (a person, etc.).

1890 *Cent. Dict.*, *Mouse-trap*, to catch, as a mouse, in a trap; entrap. **1960** WENTWORTH & FLEXNER *Dict. Amer. Slang* 346/1 *Mousetrap, v.t.* 1. In sports, to feint an opponent out of position. 2. To fool or mislead by false promises; to entice; to cajole. **1961** *Guardian* 13 Feb. 16/7 The whole system..is close to insane. It is this system which has mouse-trapped Secretary McNamara. **1964** MRS. L. B. JOHNSON *White House Diary* 24 July (1970) 183 Bryson Rash used the expression that Lyndon had 'mouse-trapped' Goldwater by leaving him nothing to say about his appointment.

'mouse-web. *Sc.* and *north.* Also 6 **mous-, muswob.** [app. f. MOUSE *sb.* + WEB *sb.*, though the reason for the application is not clear.

Possibly so called because dusty cobwebs suggest the colour of mice, or because cobwebs and mice are both associated with neglected buildings.]

A spider's web, cobweb.

1567 *Gude & Godlie Ball.* (S.T.S.) 110 Thir Imagis..ar ouergane with mouswobis [*v.r.* musewobs] & moitis. **1819** W. TENNANT *Papistry Storm'd* (1827) 197 The..wind.. Blew down the mouse-webs black and mirk.

transf. **1773** FERGUSSON *Wks.* (1807) 272 Ye benders a',.. You'll tak your liquor clean cap out; Synd your mouse-wabs wi' reamin stout, While ye hae cash.

mousey, variant of MOUSY *a.*

mousher(e, obs. forms of MOUSE-EAR.

mousherom, moushrimpe, obs. ff. MUSHROOM.

mousick, -ike, obs. ff. MOUJIK.

mousie, variant of MOUSY *sb.*

mousil, obs. form of MUZZLE *sb.*

mousiness ('maʊsɪnɪs). [f. MOUSY *a.* + -NESS.] The condition of being mousy.
1882 M. A. PAULL *Thistledown Lodge* III. 88 A musty odour joined to the greasiness and mousiness of the apartment.

mousing ('maʊzɪŋ), *vbl. sb.* [f. MOUSE *v.* + -ING[1].]
1. The action of catching or hunting for mice.
1856 F. E. PAGET *Owlet of Owlst.* 10 Ever since her accident, my mother finds mousing much more difficult. *Ibid.* 41 For the present I must cease, and go a mousing. **1863** GEO. ELIOT *Romola* i, A handsome..'Tom', with the highest character for mousing.
b. Searching, rummaging. *U.S.*
1870 H. STEVENS *Bibl. Histor.* 223 It has been the good fortune of the writer, in his bibliographical mousings up and down the world, to light upon the original paintings. **1875** STEDMAN *Victorian Poets* 179 This may be..a result of his mousing among Pre-Chaucerian ballads.
2. *Naut.* **a.** The action of fastening spun yarn or rope, etc., round the point and shank of a hook; *concr.* the rope or yarn so fastened, or a 'latch connecting the bill with the shank of a hook' (Knight *Dict. Mech.* 1875); **b.** The action of making a 'mouse' on a rope; *concr.* the 'mouse' so made.
1832 MARRYAT *N. Forster* xlv, The mousing of a stay or the strapping of a block. **1844** *Civil Eng. & Arch. Jrnl.* VII. 35/1 The two parts of the hook thus formed, when affixed to the rigging, are secured by a cord or 'mousing'.
3. In a loom: A movement similar to that of a ratchet-wheel.
1875 KNIGHT *Dict. Mech.*
4. *attrib.* (sense 1) as ***mousing-place***; (sense 2) as ***mousing-arm, -block, -hook, -link*** (see KNIGHT *Dict. Mech.* 1875 and Suppl. 1884).
1856 F. E. PAGET *Owlet of Owlst.* 11 Fold-yards, and other good mousing-places. **1883** *Fisheries Exhib. Catal.* 45 Samples of Patent Mousing Hook, for all kinds of hooks.

mousing ('maʊzɪŋ), *ppl. a.* [f. MOUSE *v.* + -ING[2].] That hunts or catches mice; given to hunting or catching mice.
1605 SHAKS. *Macb.* II. iv. 13 A Faulcon towring in her pride of place, Was by a Mowsing Owle hawkt at, and kill'd. **1904** W. H. HUDSON in *Speaker* 9 Jan. 359/2 The gentle mousing wind-hover has a nobler spirit than any crow of them all.
b. *transf.* Prying, prowling, rapacious, inquisitive; hunting as a cat does.
1692 R. L'ESTRANGE *Fables* cccxviii. 279 The Mouse that took this Cat for a Saint, has very Good Company... For we have seen a whole Assembly of these Mousing Saints, that under the Masque of Zeal, Conscience, and Good Nature, have made a Shift to lay I know not how many Kingdoms in Bloud and Ashes. **1866** FELTON *Anc. & Mod. Greece* II. xii. 521 The dialects..will have become..obsolete curiosities for the researches of the mousing antiquarian. **1883** H. C. LODGE *D. Webster* iii. (1885) 107 One Parker Noyes, a mousing, learned New Hampshire lawyer.

mousle ('maʊz(ə)l), *v. arch.* Also 7 mouzle, mowsle, 9 mowzle. [frequentative of MOUSE *v.* 2 c: cf. TOUSLE *v.*] *trans.* To pull about roughly.
1662 J. WILSON *Cheats* II. iv, Away Captain:—You do so mousle one. **1675** WYCHERLEY *Country Wife* IV. ii, He put the tip of his tongue between my lips, and so mousled me. **1695** CONGREVE *Love for L.* III. ix, He has got her into a Corner,..he'll touzle her, and mouzle her.
transf. **1672** MARVELL *Reh. Transp.* I. 214 The poor word is sure to be mumbled and mowsled to purpose.
Hence '**mousled** *ppl. a.*, pulled about roughly.
1691 J. WILSON *Belphegor* III. iii, I see a mousled Hood, rumpled Tippet, or tumbled Petty-coat wou'd not down with you! **1878** H. S. WILSON *Alp. Ascents* iv. 121 But there were the mowzled blobs.

‖**mousmee** ('musme). Also musume(e, -më, -mé, musmé, -me, moosme, mousmé. [Japanese *musume.*] An unmarried Japanese girl; *esp.* applied to a Japanese tea-girl or waitress.
1880 H. C. ST. JOHN *Wild Coast Nipon* 217 The gentle kindness and pretty ways of the musumees. **1905** *Longm. Mag.* July 228 A weeping mousmee brought the news to O Takke San as she lay in her room.

‖**mousquetaire** (muskətɛr). Also *erron.* mus-. [Fr.: see MUSKETEER.]
1. *Fr. Hist.* Originally, a foot-soldier armed with a musket; in the 17th and 18th c. a member of either of two bodies (called respectively the Grey or White and the Black Mousquetaires, from the colour of their horses) which formed part of the king's household troops. They were all of noble birth, and were famous as dandies.
1706 PHILLIPS (ed. Kersey), *Mousquetaire* (*Fr.*), a Foot-Soldier, armed with a Musket; a Musketeer. *Mousquetaires* are also certain Troops of Horse that belong to the French King's House-hold. *a***1715** BURNET *Own Time* (1734) II. 451 Both the French *Mousquetaires* and the *Cuirassiers* were there [*sc.* at 'Ramellies']. **1775** *Ann. Reg.* 188 The French King having thought proper..to suppress the Mousquetaires, that well-known body, as being entirely composed of young gentlemen of the best families in France. **1842** BARHAM *Ingol. Leg.* Ser. II. *Black Mousquetaire*, François Xavier Auguste was a gay Mousquetaire, The Pride of the Camp, the delight of the Fair.
2. Applied *attrib.* to certain styles of articles of female attire that have been in fashion at various times from the middle of the 19th c., as ***mousquetaire cloak, cuff, glove, hat, sleeve*** (transl. of Fr. *manchette, manteau,* etc., *mousquetaire* or *à la mousquetaire*). Also short for *mousquetaire glove.*
[**1850** *Ladies' Gaz. Fashion* Oct. 270/2 The sleeves..with wide and deep open cuffs of the old-fashioned military form, called *à la mousquetaire*. **1852** *Lond. & Paris Ladies' Mag. Fashion* Mar. 11/3 The sleeves mousquetaire to correspond. **1857** *Ibid.* Jan. 3/2 The Parisian name is *chapeau mousquetaire*.] **1860** M. A. & R. H. M. WALLACE-DUNLOP *How we spent the Autumn; or, Wanderings in Brittany* 223, I was often struck by the number of fashions we seem to have borrowed from Brittany; for instance, mousquetaire sleeves have their origin there. **1872** *Young Englishwoman* Dec. 651/2 Sleeves with a mousquetaire cuff. **1873** *Ibid.* Oct. 493/2 A mousquetaire hat is of grey felt, turned up with maroon velvet. *Ibid.* 494/1 The redingote tunic of grey poplin, with mousquetaire revers. **1881** C. C. HARRISON *Woman's Handiwork* III. 203 Sachets vary in size..to the..very long ones, meant to contain sixteen-buttoned or mousquetaire gloves. **1883** MISS BRADDON *Gold. Calf* I. iv. 91 Hat and feather, pongee sunshade, mousquetaire gloves, **1888** *Lady* 25 Oct. 378/1 The three-cornered 'Mousquetaire' hat is again to be worn. **1890** *Daily News* 8 Jan. 7/7. 10-button length Suede Mousquetaires, 23d. per pair. **1896** *Boston* (Mass.) *Jrnl.* 3 Dec. 5/2 Showing the long mousquetaire sleeves of the gown. **1897** *Daily News* 2 Oct. 6/4 The sleeves are furnished with pointed mousquetaire cuffs [of red velvet].

‖**moussaka** (mu:'sɑ:kə, mu:sə'kɑ:). Also mousaka. [ult. ad. Egyptian Arab. *musakk'a* through Turk.: cf. mod. Gr. *μουσακᾶς*, Rum. *musaca*, Alb., Bulg. *musaka*, etc.] A Balkan and eastern Mediterranean dish of minced beef or lamb, aubergines or potatoes, and onions.
1941 H. D. HARRISON *Soul of Yugoslavia* 284 Moussaka is another dish which savours of the east. An earthenware dish is filled with alternative layers of minced mutton and slices of potato or egg plant which have been dipped in batter and lightly fried. Over this is poured a batter of eggs and sour cream and the whole is baked slowly for some hours. **1950** E. DAVID *Bk. Mediterranean Food* 33 (*heading*) Moussaka. Mince 1 lb. of beef or lamb very fine... Stir the yolk of an egg into..cream or milk and pour it on top of the Moussaka. .. The egg and the cream form a kind of custard on the top of the Moussaka. **1957** L. DURRELL *Bitter Lemons* 215 We lunched..on a deserted beach to the west of Kyrenia,.. eating a *moussaka*. **1960** *Sunday Express* 25 Dec. 8/7 Exotic dishes: stuffed *dolmas, mousaka*. **1962** *Listener* 2 Aug. 191/2 Ask six people for a recipe for the Balkan dish *mousaka* and you will get six different answers, but they are all variations on the theme of minced meat (generally lamb) layered with vegetables. **1966** *Punch* 3 Aug. 189/3 We were suspicious when she started us automatically with ouzo, and brought three bottles of retzina with the moussaka. **1972** J. AIKEN *Butterfly Picnic* i. 19 Moussaka..is a sort of super-shepherds-pie with a cheese omelette on top.

mousse (mu:s), *sb.* [a. Fr.; app. identical with *mousse* MOSS *sb.*[1] 3.] **1.** *Cookery.* A frothy dish made with a savoury or sweet purée or other base, stiffened with cream, gelatine, or egg whites, and freq. served chilled.
1892 *Encycl. Cookery* (ed. Garrett) I. 366/2 Chestnut Mousse.—Mix [etc.]... To serve, dip the mould in hot water, wipe it, and turn the Mousse out on a folded napkin. *Ibid.* 949/2 Mousse.—Fr. for froth or foam, and applied to some forms of culinary preparations, such as Chestnut Mousse, Chocolate Mousse, Coffee Mousse, Strawberry Mousse, &c. **1899** *Daily News* 15 July 7/5 While strawberries are still with us, the following Mousse should be tried. *Ibid.*, A peach or apricot Mousse would be made very similarly. *Ibid.*, These Mousses should turn out quite solid, but will never be hard on account of the cream. **1906** *Mrs. Beeton's Bk. Househ. Managem.* xxxiii. 989 Parfaits, mousses, and soufflés differ from ordinary ices, inasmuch as the cream preparation is at once moulded and placed on ice. **1908** *Daily Chron.* 22 July 7/4 A mousse is nothing more than the addition of whipped cream instead of plain cream when making ices. **1948** *Good Housek. Cookery Bk.* 490 (*heading*) A mousse or soufflé. A very light frozen mixture, usually containing stiffly beaten egg whites. **1960** E. DAVID *French Provincial Cooking* 445 Nearly everyone knows and appreciates the old and reliable formula for a chocolate mousse—4 yolks beaten into 4 oz. of melted bitter chocolate, and the 4 whipped whites folded in. **1965** L. DEIGHTON *Action Cook Bk.* 119 In France a mousse is part of an ice cream. **1970** SIMON & HOWE *Dict. Gastron.* 269/2 As entrées, main dishes for lunch, or a fine addition to a buffet, savoury mousses of puréed meat or fish, poultry, game or vegetables can be served hot or cold. **1972** K. STEWART *Times Cookery Bk.* ii. 22 (*heading*) Cucumber and cream cheese mousse. *Ibid.*, Allow several hours for mousse to chill. **1975** *Times* 16 Apr. 12 The fruit I can use..for hot crumble or cobbler or cold in a mousse.
2. *Hairdressing.* A substance for setting or colouring the hair, sold as a foam or froth in a pressurized container.
[**1966** J. S. COX *Illustr. Dict. Hairdressing* 100/1 *Mousse*, froth, foam, lather.] **1982** *Financial Times* 15 May I. 11/3 Anybody with soft, limp hair..might like to know about a new mousse created by Michaeljohn. **1985** *N.Y. Times* 12 May III. 25/1 In March 1983, mousse was offered to consumers in Britain. **1985** *Company* Dec. 60/3 (Advt.), Make a quick change from your natural 9 to 5 colour with new Shaders & Toners colour styling mousse. **1986** *Blactress* July 10/2 Mousse will provide extra volume and glamour.

mousse, *v. Hairdressing.* [f. MOUSSE *sb.* 2.] *trans.* To apply mousse to (hair); to set or colour (hair) using mousse. Hence **moussed** *ppl. a.*
1984 *New York* 11 June 19/1 If all of America is soon to be moussed, what will the hair-care industry think of next? **1984** *People Weekly* 10 Sept. 79/3 'People will try to mousse everything,' predicts stylist Louis Licari. **1985** *Hair* Summer 20/1 Revamp a day style simply by hair-spraying or moussing a part of your hair. **1985** *Washington Post* 14 Oct. B2/3 He rushes up to a mirror and surveys his mucho moussed hair, most of which is now sticking straight up in the air. **1986** *Blactress* July 10/2 Mousse each section before winding on rollers.

mousse, obs. form of MOUSE *sb.*

‖**mousseline** (muslin). Also 9 *erron.* **mouseline, mousselaine.** [Fr.: see MUSLIN.]
1. French muslin; also, a dress of this material. (Often short for *mousseline-de-laine*: see b.)
1696 PHILLIPS (ed. 5), *Mousseline*, a sort of Linen, made of Cotton, very clear, very fine, but not very close woven, nor very smooth, but full of Puffs, like Moss. **1847** MRS. HAWTHORNE in *N. Hawthorne & Wife* (1885) I. 311 The dark purple mousseline which I wore in Boston I had to give up. **1884** KNIGHT *Dict. Mech.*, Suppl., *Mousseline*, a fine wool French goods, taffeta woven.
attrib. **1901** *Westm. Gaz.* 25 Feb. 3/2 The insertion lace.. is enriched by little mousseline roses.
b. mousseline-de-laine ('muslin of wool'), a dress-material originally composed wholly of wool, but afterwards of wool and cotton, printed with varied patterns. Also *attrib.*
1835 *Court Mag.* VI. p. xviii/2 The *mousslines de laine* ..are printed in very small patterns. **1840** THACKERAY *Shabby Genteel Story* iii, Dressed in a sweet yellow *mousseline de laine*. **1851** *Official Catal. Gt. Exhib.* III. 1373 A variety of French merinos,..mousseline de laines and satin de laines, of different colours. **1861** MRS. H. WOOD *East Lynne* (1888) 99 All three of my damsels decked out in fine mousseline-de-laine gowns.
c. mousseline de soie [= 'muslin of silk'], a thin silk fabric with a texture like that of muslin.
1850 *Ladies' Gaz. Fashion* Aug. 255/1 Plain *mousseline de soie*..begins to be a good deal seen in half-dress. *Ibid.* 256/2 Pink *mousseline de soie* robe. **1900** *Westm. Gaz.* 3 May 3/2 A lining of chiffon—or, as we now call it, mousseline de soie.
2. A very thin blown glass-ware with ornamentation resembling muslin or lace; in full ***mousseline-glass***. Also, a wine-glass made of this.
1862 THACKERAY *Philip* xxxii, These *mousseline* glasses are not only enormous, but they break by dozens. **1867** 'OUIDA' *Idalia* vii, Deep claret glasses, broad champagne goblets, and tiny spiral mousselines for liqueurs.

moussell, obs. form of MUZZLE.

‖**mousseron** (musrõ). Forms: 7 **muceron**, 8 (*erron.* in Ash) **mousgeron, 7- mousseron.** [Fr.: see MUSHROOM.] A white mushroom, common in woods, pastures, etc., *Agaricus prunulus.*
*a***1655** T. MAYERNE *Archimag. Anglo-Gall.* xx. (1658) 19 You may also adde thereunto [*sc.* the pasty] Mucerons. **1706** PHILLIPS (ed. Kersey), *Mousseron*, a kind of white Mushroom. **1736** BAILEY *Househ. Dict.* 463 Mix all well together with parsly, chibbols, mousserons, common mushrooms [etc.]. **1887** HAY *Brit. Fungi* 66 *Agaricus prunulus*; *Clitopilus prunulus*: The Mousseron.

‖**mousseux** (musø), *a.* [Fr.] = SPARKLING *ppl. a.*[1] 3 c (often placed after the sb.). Also *fig.* Also as *sb.*, a sparkling wine.
[**1789** A. YOUNG *Jrnl.* 7 July in *Travels* (1792) I. 132, I solaced myself with a bottle of excellent *vin mousseux* for 40*s*.] **1819** H. BUSK *Dessert* 25 The sillery champagne, champagne mousseux, Clear as their taper vase escape the view. **1861** MRS. BEETON *Bk. Househ. Managem.* 889 There are the sparkling wines (*mousseux*), and the still wines (*non-mousseux*). **1906** W. DE MORGAN *Joseph Vance* xl. 400, I feel like the contents of a bottle, and am very curious to know what will happen when the bottle is uncorked. Perhaps I shall be *mousseux*—who knows? **1951** R. POSTGATE *Plain Man's Guide to Wine* v. 92 Not one of the 'mousseux', 'méthode champenoise' or 'gazifiés' possesses the clean, hard flinty taste of champagne. **1968** L. DEIGHTON *Continental Dossier* 29 At St. Péray they make mousseux wine—and say they have made it as long as they have in Champagne. **1973** P. AUDEMARS *Delicate Dust of Death* vii. 95 This is a local *mousseux*... *Mousseux* is drunk after the grapes are gathered—in October and November.

Mussiliman, obs. form of MUSSULMAN.

moust: see MUST *sb.*, MUST *v.* (powder).

‖**moustac.** *Obs.* Also moustoc, mustac. [Fr.] The moustached guenon, *Cercopithecus cephus.*
1774 GOLDSM. *Nat. Hist.* IV. 234 The seventh [monkey] is the Moustoc, or White Nose. **1828-32** WEBSTER, *Mustac.*

moustache, mustache (mʊ'stɑ:ʃ, -æ-, məs-), *sb.* Forms: 7 **mostache, mustage, mustachis** (*Sc. pl.*), 8 **mustachus** (*pl.*), 6- **mustache**, 6, 9- **moustache.** [a. F. *moustache* fem., ad. It. *mostaccio, mostacchio*: see MUSTACHIO.
In present British use the unaltered Fr. spelling *moustache* greatly predominates, but the earlier British Dicts. (Johnson, Walker, Smart) and all the American Dicts. prefer the semi-Anglicized form *mustache*. With regard to the pronunciation, British usage is divided between (ʊ) and (ə) in the first syllable; in the U.S. (ə) appears to be general.]

1. The hair which grows upon the upper lip of men. **a.** The hair on both sides of the upper lip taken to form a single moustache.

1585 T. WASHINGTON tr. *Nicholay's Voy.* III. iii. 73 b, [They] let their mustaches grow very long. *Ibid.* IV. xii. 125 [They] suffered no haire to grow, but only the moustaches betwixt the nose & the mouth. **1637** ADAMSON *Muses Threnodie* (1774) 30 Their horrid beardes, thrown browes, brustled mustages. **1653** R. SANDERS *Physiogn.* 170 Those that have but a little Mustache, are of an ill nature. **1720** DE FOE *Capt. Singleton* v. (1840) 84 They saw..men with beards, that is to say, mustaches. **1823** SCOTT *Peveril* xxiv, Men wiped their mouths and mustaches. **1860** C. A. COLLINS *Eye-witness* ii. 16 He was a little, middle-aged gentleman,..with..a dyed moustache.

b. The hair covering either side of the upper lip; one half of a 'pair of moustaches'.

1603 HOLLAND *Plutarch's Mor.* 541 The..*Ephori*.. cause proclamation to be published..that no man should weare mustaches, or nourish the haire on their upper lips. *a* **1680** BUTLER *Rem.* (1759) I. 194 Two fair, And large, well-grown Mustaches. **1828** tr. *Manzoni's Betrothed Lovers* I. i. 8 Two long mustaches were curled at the extremities. **1842** BARHAM *Ingol. Leg.* Ser. II. *Black Mousquetaire*, And he twirl'd his moustache with so charming an air,—His moustaches I should say, because he'd a pair. **1902** A. E. W. MASON *Four Feathers* xiv, He twirled first one moustache and then the other before he spoke again.

c. Applied to hair on the upper lip of a woman.

1893 SLOANE-STANLEY *Remin. Midshipm. Life* xxx. 402 A woman with a black and bristly moustache.

2. a. *Zool.* Hairs or bristles, resembling a moustache, round the mouth of certain animals.

a **1605** MONTGOMERIE *Cherrie & Slae* (revision) iii, The con, the cuning, and the cat, Quhais dainty downs with dew were wat, With stiff mustachis strange. **1622** R. HAWKINS *Voy. S. Sea* xxxi. 75 Seales..are beneficiall to man in their skinnes for many purposes; In their mostaches for Pick-tooths. **1677** J. PHILLIPS tr. *Tavernier's Trav.* I. III. iv. 107 The Fish had a great Head, and a large Mustache. **1828** STARK *Elem. Nat. Hist.* I. 161 Mustaches [of the manatee] composed of a bundle of very strong hairs directed downwards, and forming on each side a kind of corneous tusk.

b. *Ornith.* A stripe of colour on the side of the head of a bird beneath the eye. (In recent Dicts.)

†**3.** A lock of hair worn at the temples. *Obs.*

1662 J. DAVIES tr. *Olearius' Voy. Ambass.* 9 Children..so dress'd as that we could not distinguish the Boies from the Girles, for both had their hair cut all off, excepting only two mustaches, which were suffered to grow at their Temples.

4. Short for *moustache monkey.*

1797 *Encycl. Brit.* (ed. 3) XVII. 498/1 The mustache, or cercopithecus cephus, has a beard on the cheeks. **1823** CRABB *Technol. Dict., Moustache (Zool.).* **1895** *Funk's Stand. Dict., Mustache.*

5. ***old moustache*** [tr. F. *vieille moustache*]: an old soldier.

1828 [MARQ. NORMANBY] *Engl. in France* II. 67 These old *moustaches* are so modest, that they never allude to their exploits. **1859** LONGF. *Children's Hour* viii, Do you think, O blue-eyed banditti Because you have scaled the wall, Such an old mustache as I am Is not a match for you all!

6. *attrib.* and *Comb.*: **moustache-cup**, a cup with a partial cover to protect the moustache when drinking; **moustache-lifter**, a device for lifting one's moustache when drinking, sleeping, etc.; **moustache monkey**, a West African monkey, *Cercopithecus cephus*; **moustache tern**, *Sterna* (*Viralva*) *leucopareia.*

1886 *N. Zealand Herald* 1 June 1/6 *Moustache Cups. **1906** *Macm. Mag.* Apr. 407 It's the only moustache-cup we have. **1906** *Trans. Asiatic Soc. Japan* XXXIV. II. 122 (*caption*) Ainu *moustache lifters. *a* **1930** D. H. LAWRENCE *Phoenix II* (1968) 261 Before the war, in Germany I used to see advertised in the newspapers a moustache-lifter, which you tied on at night and it would make your moustache stay turned up. **1966** J. S. COX *Illustr. Dict. Hairdressing* 100/2 *Moustache lifter*, an implement shaped like a paper knife and used by the male hairy ainu of Japan when drinking, to lift his moustache away from the liquid. **1771** PENNANT *Syn. Quadrup.* 114. [*Mustache monkey]. **1840** tr. *Cuvier's Anim. Kingd.* 57 The Moustache Monkey (*Simia cephus*, Lin.). **1871** DARWIN *Desc. Man* II. xviii. (1890) 552 The moustache-monkey. **1837** GOULD *Birds Europe* V. pl. 424 *Moustache Tern.

Hence **mou'stacheless** *a.*, having no moustache.

1873 MISS BROUGHTON *Nancy* I. 210 With a rather triumphant smile on his handsome moustacheless lips.

moustached (mʊ'stɑːʃt, -æ-, məs-), *a.* [f. MOUSTACHE *sb.* + -ED².] Furnished with a moustache.

1843 BORROW *Bible in Spain* xl, His..moustached lips. *transf.* **1881** BLACKMORE *Christowell* xiii, The trees, moustached with moss and fungus.

b. *spec.* in names of animals, as ***moustached guenon, honey-eater, monkey, tamarin, warbler.***

1837 GOULD *Birds Europe* II. pl. 111 Moustached Warbler. **1848** —— *Birds Australia* IV. pl. 26 *Meliphaga mystacalis*, Gould. Moustached Honey-eater. **1866** H. O. FORBES *Hand-bk. Primates* I. 142 The so-called Moustached Tamarin (*Midas mystax*, Spix). **1897** *Ibid.* II. 53 The Moustached Guenon. *Cercopithecus cephus. Ibid.* 54 The Moustached Monkey.

moustachial (mʊ'stɑːʃɪəl, -æ-, məs-), *a. Nat. Hist.* [f. MOUSTACHE *sb.* + -IAL.] Resembling a moustache.

a **1873** E. BLYTH *Catal. Mammals & Birds Burma* 57 The red of the breast [of the parrot] is continued past the black moustachial streak and the ear-coverts. **1888** NEWTON in *Encycl. Brit.* XXIV. 652/1 *note*, A patch of conspicuous colour, generally red, on this part [*sc.* the base of the lower mandible] is characteristic of very many Woodpeckers, and careless writers often call it 'mystacial', or some more barbarously 'moustachial'. **1894** R. B. SHARPE *Handbk. Birds Gt. Brit.* I. 72 Cheeks..separated from the throat by a distinct moustachial streak of dusky greenish-olive.

moustachio(e: see MUSTACHIO.

moustaffa, obs. form of MUSTAPHA.

moustang, -guer, var. ff. MUSTANG, -GUER.

mousted, variant of MUSTED *ppl. a.*

mouster, obs. form of MUSTER.

Mousterian, Moustierian (muː'stɪərɪən), *a.* and *sb.* [ad. F. *moustiérien* (G. de Mortillet *a* 1873, in *Classification des diverses périodes de l'âge de la Pierre* 4), f. *Moustier* (see below) + -IAN.] **A.** *adj.* Of or pertaining to the people, culture, and tools, esp. the flint industries, typified by remains found in the Moustier cave in the Dordogne region of France, and properly attributed to the Neanderthal peoples living in Europe and round the Mediterranean; of the Middle Palæolithic period (*c* 70,000–30,000 B.C.) during which these tools were made. Also *absol.*, this culture. **B.** *sb.* A Mousterian man or woman.

1890 T. WILSON in *Rep. U.S. Nat. Museum 1888* 614 The Mousterian implements have been found in the river gravels of Europe. **1896** A. H. KEANE *Ethnol.* 86 Moustierian or First Cave Age. *Ibid.* 90 K. Moustierian bed, with typical pointed flint. **1907** *Ann. Rep. Board of Regents Smithsonian Inst. 1906* 374 Glacial period: Mousterian culture. **1912** *Edin. Rev.* Apr. 366 The first discovery of Mousterian man to excite interest was made in 1856 near Düsseldorf. **1912** R. R. MARETT *Anthropol.* ii. 45 Those were the days of the Mousterians who dined off woolly rhinoceros in Jersey. **1927** PEAKE & FLEURE *Hunters & Artists* iv. 39 Breuil thinks that the Neanderthal men of Mousterian culture lived in western Europe from the time of the Riss on through the Würm glaciation. **1927** H. G. WELLS *Short Stories* 679 These Mousterians are also called Neandertalers. **1928**, etc. [see ATERIAN *a.*]. **1947** J. & C. HAWKES *Prehist. Brit.* (rev. ed.) i. 14 One of the products of the stimulating interaction between the older traditions was a new flake culture, the Mousterian, which enjoyed its heyday during the final glaciation of the Ice Age. **1949** M. E. BOYLE tr. *Breuil's Beyond Bounds of Hist.* 47 A party of courageous hunters is attacking a group of Mammoth with lances and axes of the type known as Mousterian. **1970** J. D. CLARK *Prehist. Afr.* iv. 116 Some forty-five feet of stratified occupation waste and cave earth, showing a long sequence of developing Mousterian overlying an industry made on long blades and blade-like flakes. **1974** *Sci. Amer.* June 101/1 The artifacts..have been assigned to two successive cultural units. The earlier of the two is known as the Mousterian. *Ibid.* 101/2 The Mousterian stone tools from various Ukrainian sites. *Ibid.* 104/3 Like the Mousterians, Upper Paleolithic peoples often buried their dead.

Hence **Mou'sterioid, 'Mousteroid** *adjs.*, resembling the Mousterian culture or tools.

1946 F. E. ZEUNER *Dating Past* ix. 287 Quite probably, many 'mousterioid' industries mentioned in literature are of the same type. **1950** *Proc. Prehist. Soc.* XVI. 176 Among a handful of mousteroid specimens from the cave of Bacho Kiro in Bulgaria a typical specimen of a miniature plano-convex point may be noted. **1969** C. S. CHARD *Man in Prehistory* xi. 114 Since it seems desirable to have a broad term..to designate the flake industries of the neanderthaloid phase in the stretch of contiguous territory from western Europe to Mongolia and south to the Near East and North Africa, which all share certain common features..while retaining their individuality, the label 'Mousteroid' would probably be acceptable.

†**moustick, -ique.** *Obs. rare.* Also 7 moustico. [a. F. *moustique.*] = MOSQUITO.

1666 J. DAVIES *Hist. Caribby Isles* 146 A sort of very small Flies, by some called Mousticoes, which are felt commonly before they are seen. **1698** FROGER *Voy.* 152 The Inhabitants..are much incommoded with Ants, Mousticks [etc.]. **1801** C. GRANT *Hist. Mauritius* 68 The gnat called moustique or maringouin is very troublesome.

‖**Moustiers** (mustje). The name of a small French town, *Moustiers*-Sainte-Marie, in the Basses Alpes, used *attrib.* or *absol.* to designate a type of faience made there.

1863 W. CHAFFERS *Marks Pott. & Porc.* 96 *Moustiers*... This beautiful ware much resembles porcelain and the early pieces are generally painted in monochrome, in blue, brown, or green; the later specimens are usually in more than one colour. **1870** C. SCHREIBER *Jrnl.* (1911) I. 99 A very fine Moustier Ware dish. **1872** *Ibid.* 162 The specimens were.. not equal to fine Moustiers or Marseilles. **1900** F. LITCHFIELD *Pott. & Porc.* vii. 214 Barber's dish of Moustiers faience. **1962** *House & Garden* Dec. 58/2 We've bought..a French Moustiers blue and white dish. **1970** G. SAVAGE *Dict. Antiques* 281/2 (*caption*) *Moustiers.* Dish painted in high-temperature colours with a pastoral scene within rococo scroll borders. Moustiers faience..*c* 1740.

moustoc: see MOUSTAC.

moustre, obs. form of MUSTER.

mousum, variant of MOWSOME *a. Obs.*

mousy ('maʊsɪ), *sb.* Also **mousie.** [f. MOUSE *sb.* + -Y⁴.] A playful diminutive of *mouse.*

1693 *Scotch Presbyt. Eloquence* (1738) 138 Thou'rt like a Mousie peeping out at the Hole in the Wall. **1785** BURNS *To Mouse* vii, But Mousie, thou art no thy lane, In proving foresight may be vain. **1845** *Zoologist* III. 1030 On my return [I] found poor mousy in convulsions.

mousy ('maʊsɪ), *a.* Also **mousey.** [f. MOUSE *sb.* + -Y¹.]

1. Resembling a mouse, its colour, smell, etc.

1853 MRS. GASKELL *Cranford* ix. 164, I was..most particularly anxious to prevent her from disfiguring her small gentle mousey face with a great Saracen's-head turban. **1859** F. E. PAGET *Curate of Cumberworth* 348 A taste ..which I can only describe as mousy. **1865** LIVINGSTONE *Zambesi* xxviii. 575 Where we inhaled so much of the heavy mousey smell that it was distinguishable in the odour of our shirts and flannels. **1888** G. MACDONALD *Elect Lady* 10 He would..pass a white left hand through his short-cut mousey hair. **1888** 'R. BOLDREWOOD' *Robbery under Arms* (1890) 355 The doctor's short-tailed, mousy mare. **1897** *Star* 4 Jan. 1/7 A curious shade of mousy grey. **1936** K. A. PORTER *Flowering Judas* 107 He could not bear hearing Miriam called a mousy little nit-wit. **1959** W. GOLDING *Free Fall* iv. 82 Fair heads and mousy ones. **1959** 'O. MILLS' *Stairway to Murder* vi. 61 Her skin was sallow, her hair was 'mousey', and her forehead was the lowest Charles had ever seen. **1975** *Times* 15 Feb. 14/2 Hair which is 'light brown' sounds more becoming than hair which is 'mousy'.

2. As quiet as a mouse.

1812 *Sporting Mag.* XXXIX. 210 A man ought not to remain mousy [*note*, idle]. **1863** HOLME LEE *A. Warleigh* II. 309 To marry that most tiresome and disagreeable of mousy men. **1887** FLO. MARRYAT *Dau. of Tropics* I. xiii. 209, I always suspect those very quiet, mousey, saint-like creatures.

3. Abounding in, or infested with mice.

1871 STORMONTH *Dict.* **1876** MISS BRADDON *Dead Men's Shoes* I. i. 11 She has tea-things and tea-kettle to her hand in the roomy and mousey old closet beside the fire place.

4. *Comb.*, as ***mousy-eyed, -faced, -quiet*** adjs.

1909 M. B. SAUNDERS *Litany Lane* I. ii. 13 Only a fold of dark chestnut hair and a hint of red in the lip gave colour —otherwise a little mousy-eyed *gamin* of a thing. **1880** MRS. LYNN LINTON *Rebel of Family* iii, A pale, light-haired, mousey-faced little woman. **1958** *Observer* 3 Aug. 10/6 Young married business man, cleared by mousey quiet private detective. **1902** KIPLING *Just So Stories* 146 Taffy took a marrow-bone and sat mousy quiet for ten whole minutes.

mout, obs. f. MOULT; obs. pa. t. of MAY *v.*¹

moutan ('muːtən). [Chinese.] The tree peony, *Pæonia suffruticosa*, of the family Ranunculaceæ, a large shrub bearing pale pink flowers, native to China and Tibet, the parent of many garden varieties producing single or double flowers of many colours.

1808 *Curtis's Bot. Mag.* XXIX. 1154 The Moutan, though cultivated in China about fourteen hundred years, is considered in that ancient empire..as rather of modern introduction. **1880** *Encycl. Brit.* XII. 258/1 The Moutans or Tree Pæonies are remarkable for their sub-shrubby habit, forming vigorous plants sometimes attaining a height of 6 to 8 feet. **1963** M. HAWORTH-BOOTH *Moutan* i. 11 In Chinese art each month is represented by a flower, and Moutan is specifically the flower for March.

mouter, obs. form of MULTURE.

mouth (maʊθ), *sb.* Forms: 1 **múþ**, 3–4 **muth**, (**mudh, moth**), 3–5 **mouþ(e**, (3 **mouthþ**, 4 **mouht**, 6 **mothe**, *Sc.* **mwtht**), 4–7 **mowth(e**, 6 **mougth, mought**, 9 *Sc.* **muthe**, 3– **mouth**. [Com. Teut.: OE. *múþ* masc. = OFris. *mûth* masc. (in later texts *mund, mond*; mod.NFris. *müth, müt, müs*), OS. *mûth* masc., MDu. *mont, mond, munt* masc. and fem. (Du. *mond* masc.), OHG., MHG., mod.G. *mund* masc., ON. *munn-r, muð-r* masc. (Sw. *mun* masc., Da. *mund*), Goth. *munþ-s* masc.:—OTeut. **munþo-z*:—pre-Teut. **mn̥to-s*, corresponding formally to L. *mentum* chin.]

I. 1. a. The external orifice in an animal body which serves for the ingestion of food, together with the cavity to which this leads, containing the apparatus of mastication and (in man and other lungbreathing animals) the organs of vocal utterance.

c **1000** *Ags. Gosp.* Matt. xv. 17 Ne onȝyte ȝe þæt eall þæt on þone muþ gæþ on þa wambe. *c* **1250** *Gen. & Ex.* 2655 An in hise muth so depe he is [*sc.* burning coals] dede Hise tunges ende is brent ðor-mide. *a* **1300** *Cursor M.* 1904 Son sco [*sc.* the dove] com and duelld noght, An oliue branche in moth sco broght. **1486** *Bk. St. Albans* C vj b, For blaynis in haukes mouthes cald frounches. **1593** SHAKS. *2 Hen. VI*, IV. vii. 10 He was thrust in the mouth with a Speare. **1661** J. D. *Civ. Warres* 164 Every man might march away..Matches Lighted, Bullet in Mouth, &c. **1789** W. BUCHAN *Dom. Med.* (1790) 185 When it happens to burst within the lungs, the matter may be discharged by the mouth. **1875** *Encycl. Brit.* I. 837/1 The cavity of the mouth forms the commencement of the alimentary canal.

b. In invertebrate animals.

1753 CHAMBERS *Cycl. Supp.* s.v., The mouth [of the garden-snail] is like a hare's. **1826** KIRBY & SP. *Entomol.* III. 416 The Mouth, or rather the orifice in which the trophi or organs of manducation are inserted. **1881** E. R. LANKESTER in *Encycl. Brit.* XII. 556/2 *Hydrozoa.* The mouth is either a simple opening at the termination of a rudimentary manubrium.., or it is provided with four or eight arm-like processes.

c. In references to an open or gaping mouth as expressive of wonderment or vacancy of mind.

1693 DRYDEN *Persius* i. (1726) 239 The nauseous Nobles ..With gaping Mouths to these Rehearsals come. **1859**

Tennyson *Lancelot* 1242 Mouths that gaped, and eyes that ask'd 'What is it?'

†**d.** ***to draw one's mouth***: to extract a tooth.

1669 Pepys *Diary* 18 May, She being much troubled with the tooth-ake..I staid till a surgeon of hers come,..who hath formerly drawn her mouth, and he advised her to draw it.

e. In expressions like ***a good, bad, hard,*** etc., ***mouth,*** used with reference to a horse's readiness or the contrary to feel and obey the pressure of the bit. Hence *abstr.* of a horse: Capability of being guided by the bit.

1727–51 Chambers *Cycl.* s.v. *Amble,* Others attempt it by sudden stoping..but this is apt to spoil a good mouth and rein. **1731** Bailey vol. II. s.v., A fine mouth [*Horsemanship*]. *A fix'd mouth, a certain mouth. A false mouth. A mouth of a full Appui.* **1791** 'G. Gambado' *Ann. Horsem.* xvi. (1809) 133 One of my neighbours..tells me he has a horse that has no mouth. **1856** 'Stonehenge' *Brit. Rural Sports* 346/1 The ..delicacy of mouth which is so essential to the action of the racehorse. *Ibid.* 347/1 To obtain the desired result of its [*sc.* the bit's] presence in the mouth, which is called 'getting a mouth', and which is merely the giving to the sense of touch in the lips an extra degree of delicacy. **1863** Le Fanu *Ho. by Churchyard* (ed. 2) III. 310 In the end his 'mouth was made'.

2. a. Considered as the receptacle of food or with reference to swallowing, devouring, the function of taste, etc.

c **897** K. Ælfred *Gregory's Past. C.* xvi. 104 Ne forbinde ȝe no ðæm ðerscendum oxum ðone muð. **1297** R. Glouc. (Rolls) 7028 þe mossel he dude in to is mouþ. *c* **1320** *Sir Tristr.* 1519 His mouþe opened þai And pelt treacle in þat man. *c* **1475** *Babees Bk.* 149 Withe the fulle mouthe drynke in no wyse. **1526** *Pilgr. Perf.* (W. de W. 1531) 5 b, Whiche had the taste in theyr mouthes of all thynges pleasaunt and delectable. **1530** Palsgr. 468/2 This axes hath brought my mouthe quyte out of taste. **1719** De Foe *Crusoe* (Globe) 216 And putting a little into his own Mouth, he seem'd to nauseate it. **1859** Tennyson *Lancelot* 771 This fruit is hung too high For any mouth to gape for save a queen's.

b. *transf.* and *fig.*

1596 Bp. W. Barlow *Three Serm.* i. 129 They fal into ye mouths and teeth of biting and deuouring vsurers. **1601** Shaks. *Twel. N.* v. i. 81 That..boy..From the rude seas enrag'd and foamy mouth Did I redeeme. **1660** Jer. Taylor *Worthy Communic.* I. ii. 43 Christians are spiritual men; faith is their mouth, and wisdome is their food. **1857** Miller *Elem. Chem.* (1862) III. 823 The root of a plant may be considered as its mouth.

c. Phrases. ***the mouth waters*** (***after, at*** something), (it) ***makes*** (one's) ***mouth water***, referring to the flow of saliva caused by the anticipation of appetizing food; also *fig.* ***to have one's mouth made up*** (U.S.), to have an expectant desire *for* (a particular kind of food); also *fig.* †***to make up one's mouth,*** to finish one's meal with something specially delicious; also *fig.* †***to meet..in the mouth,*** †***to run into*** (another's) ***mouth,*** to meet face to face or full face. ***to open one's mouth wide,*** to ask a high price. See also Hand to mouth.

1555 Eden *Decades* 143 These craftie foxes [*sc.* cannibals] ..espying their enemies a farre of, beganne to swalowe theyr spettle as their mouthes watered for greedines of theyr pray. **1657** *North's Plutarch, Add. Lives* (1676) 76 The Mountains of Gold also..made his [Cortez's] mouth water. **1762** Sterne *Tr. Shandy* VI. xxviii, Never did my uncle Toby's mouth water so much for a pipe in his life. **1860** Gosse *Rom. Nat. Hist.* 274 He has drawn a picture..such as makes a brother naturalist's mouth water.

1890 *Century Dict.* s.v. *Mouth,* His mouth was made up for a chicken salad. **1890** *Harper's Mag.* Oct. 715/2 No one who has his mouth made up for a laugh is prepared to relish a dose of reason.

1546 Heywood *Prov.* (1867) 36 His wife to make vp my mouthe, Not onely hir husbandes tauntyng tale auouthe, But therto deuiseth to cast in my teeth, Checks and chokyng oysters. **1549** Latimer *1st Serm. bef. Edw. VI* D vij, Surueiers there be, y^t gredily gorge vp their couitouse guttes,..honest men I touch not, but al such as so suruai thei make vp their mouthes, but the commens be vtterlye vndone by them. **1584** Cogan *Haven Health* (1636) 170 Commonly at great feasts..they use to serve vp sturgeon last, as it were to make up the mouth. **1640** Bp. Hall *Chr. Moder.* II. x. 75 He to make up his mouth, shall goe away with an opinion of an hundred severall foule errors in Iohn Calvin. **1720** C'tess Cowper *Diary* (1864) 153 Walpole [is] to make up his Mouth by a Bubble, because he did not get enough in South Sea.

1599 Shaks. *Hen. V,* III. vii. 154 Foolish Curres, that runne winking into the mouth of a Russian Beare. **1605** —— *Lear* III. iv. 11 Thou'dst shun a Beare, But if thy flight lay toward the roaring Sea, Thou'dst meete the Beare i' th' mouth. **1671** Milton *Samson* 1521 Best keep together here, lest running thither We unawares run into dangers mouth. **1737** Whiston *Josephus, Wars* III. x. (1834) 672/1 So Titus pressed upon the hindmost, and slew them;..and some he prevented, and met them in the mouth, and run them through. **1762** Foote *Lyar* II. Wks. 1799 I. 291 Gad, I had like to have run into the old gentleman's mouth.

1891 C. Roberts *Adrift Amer.* 251 To use a vulgarism, he did not open his mouth so wide as the other, but at once offered me a through ticket to Liverpool for $72. **1898** *Daily News* 28 Oct. 3/1 Directly the word England is mentioned, the mouths of the Continental artists are opened so unconscionably wide.

†**d.** ***the king's mouth***: what pertains to the providing and preparing of food for the king. Cf. Bouche *sb.*[1] *Obs.*

1433 *Rolls of Parlt.* V. 433/2 Suche [servants] as serve aboute the Kyngs persone, and for his mouthe. **1450** *Ibid.* 194/1 Yoman of oure Larder for oure Mouth. **1567** Edwards *Damon & Pithias* (1571) F j, Was it you sir, who cryed so lowde, I trow And bid us take in Coles for the Kinges mouth euen now? **1578** *Reg. Privy Council Scot.* II. 689 The cair of the attendance upoun his Hienes mowth and dyet.

e. A person viewed only as a consumer of food. ***useless mouth,*** one who does no work but yet has to be fed. Cf. F. *bouche inutile.*

c **1550** *Decay of Eng. by Shepe* (E.E.T.S.) 97 So many mouthes goith to motton, whiche causeth motton to be deare. **1609** B. Jonson *Sil. Wom.* III. v, Where are all my eaters? my mouthes now? barre vp my dores, you varlets. **1637** Milton *Lycidas* 119 Of other care they little reck'ning make, Then how to scramble at the shearers feast,..Blind mouthes! **1722** De Foe *Plague* (1884) 253 Those who in Case of a Siege, are call'd the useless Mouths. **1875** *Encycl. Brit.* III. 496/1 Having thus got rid of the useless mouths [*sc.* the drones] which consumed, without any advantage to the public, a large portion of their provisions [etc.].

3. a. Considered as the instrument of speech or voice.

Much less frequent in ordinary use than *tongue.* All the Eng. versions of the Bible have many examples in passages literally rendered from Hebrew or Hebraistic Greek.

c **1000** Ælfric *Hom.* I. 366 Hi habbað dumne muð and blinde eaȝan. *c* **1205** Lay. 5726 Mid muðen heo seiden mid aðen heo hit sworen. **1297** R. Glouc. (Rolls) 1030 þe toun me clupeþ ludestoun þat is wide coup & now me clupeþ it londone þat is liȝtore in þe mouþ. **1362** Langl. *P. Pl.* A. iv. 105 Rede me not..Reuþe to haue, Til Clerkes and knihtes ben Corteis of heore Mouþes. **1382** Wyclif *Prov.* xiii. 3 Who kepeth his mouth [Vulg. *Qui custodit os suum*], kepeth his soule. *a* **1450** Myrc 27 Of honde & mowþe þou moste be trewe. **1513** More in Grafton *Chron.* (1568) II. 778 Neyther can there be any thing..amisse..but it shoulde be in mine eares or it were well out of their mouthes. *c* **1550** Cheke *Matt.* xv. 18 Thoos thinges y^t commeth forth of ye mougth commeth forth of ye hart, aud y^{ei} defile a man. **1600** Shaks. *A. Y. L.* III. ii. 239 You must borrow me Gargantuas mouth first: 'tis a Word too great for any mouth of this Ages size. **1611** —— *Cymb.* IV. ii. 79 Thy words I grant are bigger: for I weare not My Dagger in my mouth. **1638** R. Baker tr. *Balzac's Lett.* (vol. II) 77, I will come and learne from your own Mouth, all the particulars. **1724** De Foe *Mem. Cavalier* (1840) 38, I had the relation from his own mouth. **1845** M. Pattison *Ess.* (1889) I. 16 The Frank..learned..his faith from the mouth of the Roman priest.

transf. and *fig.* **1595** Shaks. *John* III. iii. 38 The mid-night bell Did with his yron tongue, and brazen mouth Sound on. *a* **1628** Preston *New Covt.* (1634) 440 Where the Scripture hath a mouth to speake, Faith hath an eare to heare. **1667** Milton *P.L.* II. 967 And Discord with a thousand various mouths.

b. Used as the subject of a verb of speaking. Hence *rhetorically* put for the person speaking.

c **1250** *Kent. Serm.* in *O.E. Misc.* 30 Ase godes oghe mudh hit seid. *a* **1400–50** *Alexander* 904 As Alexander awyn mouth had þam all enfourmed. **1474** Caxton *Chesse* III. iii. 104 Saynt Bernard..sayth that the mouthe that lyeth destroyeth the sowle. **1508** Dunbar *Gold. Targe* 265 O morall Gower, and Ludgate laureate,..Your angel mouthis most mellifluate Our rude langage has clere illumynate. **1662** Stillingfl. *Orig. Sacr.* II. vi. §1 His own mouth told him he was a lying Prophet. **1713** Addison *Cato* II. ii, You don't now thunder in the capitol, With all the mouths of Rome to second you. **1864** Tennyson *Sea Dreams* 14 He cursed..that one unctuous mouth which lured him, rogue, To buy strange shares in some Peruvian mine.

c. †***by mouth*** (obs.), ***by word of mouth***: by spoken words, orally; often opposed to 'by writing'.

c **1330** R. Brunne *Chron.* (1810) 299 Bi letter & bi mouth he praied þam of socoure. *c* **1420** Lydg. *Assembly of Gods* 2060, I had left hit vntolde—Nowthyr by mowthe nor in remembraunce Put hit in wrytyng. **1560** Daus tr. *Sleidane's Comm.* 29 Commaunding thee..to declare what thou wilte do herein, by mouthe, and not by writynge. **1601** Shaks. *Twel. N.* III. iv. 209, I will deliuer his Challenge by word of mouth. **1720** Gordon *Independent Whig* No. 6. 41 Not content to abuse each other by Word of Mouth, they sometimes scolded in Writing. **1849** Macaulay *Hist. Eng.* vi. II. 96 'This', he said, 'is not a court in which written charges are exhibited. Our proceedings are summary, and by word of mouth.'

d. ***by*** (formerly †***through***) ***the mouth of***: through (some one) as spokesman. (Cf. *Luke* i. 70.)

c **1400** *Rule St. Benet* (E.E.T.S.) 2 We aske þe, lauerd, þurȝ þe muȝ [*read* muþ] of þe profete. **1560** Daus tr. *Sleidane's Comm.* 24 b, They rode forthe to mete the Emperour, whom..they receiued honorably by the mouthe of my Lorde of Mentz. **1870** *Eng. Gilds* (E.E.T.S.) Gloss., *Assoyne,*..excuse sent by the mouth of another for non-appearance.

e. ***from the mouth of*** (a person): from him as the speaker. ***in the mouth of*** (a person): when spoken or spoken of by (him); †also *transf.* So ***in*** or ***with a French, an English,*** etc. ***mouth*** (sometimes with reference to pronunciation). ***it does not lie in his mouth to*** (say something): it is not befitting for him. (***to condemn a person***) out of his ***own mouth*** (Luke xix. 22): by his own evidence.

1596 Shaks. *1 Hen. IV,* I. iii. 153 And for whose death, we in the worlds wide mouth Liue scandaliz'd. **1614** Bradshaw *Unreasonableness Separ.* (1640) 56 Why may not preaching [etc.]..be sufficient to argue our ministers to be true pastors and teachers, notwithstanding that in the mouth of the Law, they are sometimes called Priests and Deacons. **1644** Milton *Educ.* 4 To smatter Latin with an english mouth, is as ill a hearing as law French. **1781** Cowper *Table-T.* 500 Hence, in a Roman mouth, the graceful name Of prophet and of poet was the same. **1828** Scott *F.M. Perth* xiii, My princely nephew entertains with so much suspicion any admonition coming from my mouth. **1859** Tennyson *Merlin & Vivien* 644 How, in the mouths of base interpreters..Is thy white blamelessness accounted blame! **1861** Hughes *Tom Brown at Oxf.* xxxv, It did not lie in his mouth to be curious on the subject. **1874** L. Stephen *Hours in Library* (1892) II. vii. 221 In other mouths Rousseau's sentiment..became unequivocally misanthropical. **1885** Ld. R. Churchill *Sp.* (1889) I. 245 Does it lie in the mouth of members of that Government to taunt the Tory party with having no policy?

f. ***from mouth to mouth***: from one speaker to another; also, speaking in turn or in succession.

1838 Dickens *Nich. Nick.* xxx, The stories they invent.. and bandy from mouth to mouth! **1847** Tennyson *Princess* Prol. 189 We..often told a tale from mouth to mouth As here at Christmas.

g. † (***to have..***) ***in mouth*** (obs.), (***to be***) ***in the mouth*** or ***mouths of*** = in one's speech or conversation, on one's lips.

a **1300** *Cursor M.* 4136 And fra þis dede be made couþe alle men sal ȝou haue in mouþ. **1513** More in Grafton *Chron.* (1568) II. 767 It redowneth greatly to the dishonour..of the kinges highnesse..to haue it runne in euery mans mouth.. that the kings brother should be faine to kepe sanctuarie. **1555** Eden *Decades* 242 Which sayinge was afterwarde in euery mans mouth. **1562** Winȝet *Cert. Tractates* i. (S.T.S.) I. 13 All man hes this word reformatioun in mothe. **1595** Shaks. *John* IV. ii. 187 Yong Arthurs death is common in their mouths. **1712** Addison *Spect.* No. 447 ¶1 A Common Saying..we often hear in the Mouths of the Vulgar. **1855** Macaulay *Hist. Eng.* xv. III. 505 The names of..the.. chiefs of the conquering army, were in many mouths.

†**h.** ***with full mouth*** [= L. *pleno ore*], ***with open mouth***: loudly, aloud. ***to open full mouth***: to rail furiously. Also (***to come, laugh***) ***full mouth,*** = 'with full mouth'. *Obs.*

c **1290** *S. Eng. Leg.* I. 86/93 Loude he gradde with folle Mouth: 'Ich am cristine Man.' **1303** R. Brunne *Handl. Synne* 4442 þey..bad me þat y shuld hyt rede..; And y þat neuer on boke couþe, Alle y hit red with opun mouthe. **1539** Taverner *Erasm. Prov.* (1545) 39 The fryer..ragynge oute with open mouthe lyke a madde man agaynste the lyfe of princes. **1599** Shaks. *Hen. V,* I. ii. 230 Either our History shall with full mouth Speake freely of our Acts, or else our graue, Like Turkish mute, shall haue a tonguelesse mouth. **1652** J. Wright tr. *Camus' Nat. Paradox* IX. 215 Then Belinda, who being a Married Wife had somewhat more confidence, laughing full mouth, said [etc.]. **1677** *Govt. Venice* 117 The Embassador coming to the Colledg full mouth with the news of his Master's Victory. **1687** A. Lovell tr. *Thevenot's Trav.* I. xxix. 52 He opened full mouth against the Christians. **1702** Farquhar *Inconstant* II. 16 She was coming full mouth upon me with her Contract.

i. ***with one mouth,*** with one voice or one consent; unanimously. (A Hebraism, as in 2 Chron. xviii. 12, *margin.*) Now *rare.*

c **1290** *Beket* 915 in *S. Eng. Leg.* I. 132 We habbez ore red þarof i-nome: and mid one mouþe ech-on to queme þe kinge we redez þe. *a* **1300** *Cursor M.* 15039 All þai sang als wit a muth. **1738** Wesley *Jrnl.* 12 May, They added with one mouth that this faith was the gift..of God.

j. ***mouth to mouth,*** also, more rarely †***mouth with mouth,*** = in close and intimate conference; face to face. (Now *rare*; a Hebraism, as in Num. xii. 8, where the Vulgate has *ore ad os.*) Hence ***mouth-to-mouth*** vb. (burlesque *nonce-wd.*) to speak face to face.

c **1200** *Trin. Coll. Hom.* 105 And bigan to turnen þe iuele to gode mid his wise wordes, þe he wið hem spec muð wið muðe. **1529** More *Dyaloge* I. Wks. 174/2 But he [God] tolde it you not mouth to mouth. **1607** Tourneur *Rev. Trag.* II. i, Madona, there is one..that would very desireously mouth to mouth with you. **1895** Salmond *Chr. Doctr. Immort.* II. iv. 241 A fellowship in which Jehovah speaks mouth to mouth with his servant.

k. †***to hold one's mouth*** [cf. G. *den mund halten*] = to 'hold one's tongue', be silent. ***to open one's mouth***: to begin speaking. ***to open the mouth of***: to give the power of speech to. (See also Open *v.* IV.) ***to close, shut one's mouth***: to refrain from speaking. †***to make up one's mouth***: to finish speaking. ***to stop*** (a person's) ***mouth*** = to keep (him) from talking.

c **1290** *Beket* 2035 in *S. Eng. Leg.* I. 165 Beo stille,..hold þinne mouthþ. *a* **1300** *Cursor M.* 19941 Petre opend þan his muth..he said [etc.]. **1390** Gower *Conf.* I. 85 Sche Commandeth me my mowth to close. *c* **1520** Nisbet *New Test. in Scots* (S.T.S.) I. 11 And how Christ stoppit the mowthis of the Saduceis. **1549** Latimer *3rd Serm. bef. Edw. VI,* E viij *margin,* A preacher offyce is to be a mouth stopper. But not to haue hys one mouthe stopped wyth a benefice or byshoprike. **1605** Shaks. *Lear* V. iii. 154 Shut your mouth Dame, Or with this paper shall I stop it. **1606** Dekker *Sev. Sins* I. 2 The poore Orator hauing made vp his mouth, Bankruptisme gaue him very good words. **1720** De Foe *Capt. Singleton* xiii. (1840) 219 We stopped his mouth with his share of two hundred thousand pieces of eight. **1847** Marryat *Childr. N. Forest* xiii, I stopped his mouth by telling him that [etc.]. **1895** Pocock *Rules of Game* I (Farmer) 'Shut your mouth', he said, 'or I'll knife you!'

l. ***to put words into another's mouth*** = to tell him what to say. ***to put*** (a speech) ***into a person's mouth***: to represent him as having uttered it. ***to take the words out of*** another's ***mouth***: to anticipate what another was about to say.

1382 Wyclif *2 Sam.* xiv. 3 Forsothe Joab putte the wordis in hire mouth. **1530** Palsgr. 751/1 It is no good maner to take the worde out of my mouthe, or I have made an ende of my tale. **1568** Grafton *Chron.* II. 100 The Pope..takyng their wordes out of their mouthes, sayd [etc.]. **1599** Shaks. *Hen. V,* IV. vii. 45 It is not well done (marke you now) to take the tales out of my mouth, ere it is made and finished. **1725** Pope *Wks. of Shaks.* Pref. 19 Many speeches also were put into the mouths of wrong persons, where the Author now seems chargeable with making them speak out of character.

1867 FREEMAN *Norm. Conq.* (1877) I. App. 627 The strong legitimist harangue which is put into his mouth by Richer.

m. ***to make a poor mouth, to put on*** (or ***up***) ***a poor mouth***, to plead poverty.

1822 *Blackw. Mag.* Sept. 307/1 I'm sure ye may weel spare twa three pounds... It's no right o' you to be aye making a puir mouth. 1885 HOWELLS *Silas Lapham* xxv, You wanted to.. make a poor mouth to Mrs. Lapham. 1892 'MARK TWAIN' *Amer. Claimant* iii. 37 Any selfish tramp.. can come and put up a poor mouth. 1949 F. URQUHART *Ferret was Abraham's Daughter* I. vii. 26 'Charity!' Bert shouted. 'Aye puttin' on a poor mouth.'

†**n.** Used for: (A person's) utterance. *Obs.*

a 1400 *Pistill of Susan* 253 (Vernon MS.) For I am dampned, I ne dar disparage þi mouþ. 1583 GOLDING *Calvin on Deut.* vi. 33 Wherby we see that they flatly resist Gods mouth. 1702 *Lex Vera* 1 They unanimously barricado'd their Ears against the Mouth of the Prophet.

o. ***give it mouth*** imp. = express it with vehemence. ***to give mouth to*** = to express in words.

1840 DICKENS *Barn. Rudge* lxv, What I say in respect to the speeches always is, Give it mouth. 1865 —— *Mut. Fr.* II. vii, I have an opinion of you, sir, to which it is not easy to give mouth. 1880 MISS BRADDON *Just as I am* xxi, Give it mouth, boys.

p. With reference to the barking or baying of a hound. ***to spend their mouths, to give mouth***: to bark or bay vehemently, to give tongue, also *transf.* of a person.

1590 COKAINE *Treat. Hunting* D ij b, At which time the houndes will spend their mouthes verie lustely. *Ibid.*, They will so double their mouthes and teare them together, that you would thinke there were more houndes in companie than your owne. 1590 SHAKS. *Mids. N.* IV. i. 128 My hounds are.. match'd in mouth like bels. 1591 —— *1 Hen. VI*, II. iv. 12. 1599 —— *Hen. V*, II. iv. 70. 1648 HEYLIN *Relat. & Observ.* I. 134 The Beagles of the faction spent their mouths freely against the said Commissioners again. 1700 DRYDEN *Meleager & Atalanta* 108 The boar Deals glancing wounds; the fearful dogs divide: All spend their mouth aloft, but none abide. 1854 CARDL. WISEMAN *Fabiola* I. vi, Calpurnius, thus challenged,.. solemnly gave mouth: 'The Christians', said he, 'are a foreign sect' [etc.]. 1859 TENNYSON *Marr. Geraint* 186 They listen'd.. for the baying of Cavall, King Arthur's hound of deepest mouth. *a* 1872 B. HARTE *Goddess* 28 The watch-dog on the distant shore Gives mouth.

q. ***plum-in-the-mouth*** adj. phr.: see PLUM *sb.*

4. a. The exterior opening or orifice of the mouth considered as part of the face.

a 900 tr. *Bæda's Hist.* III. ii. (1890) 156 Swa þæt he for þy sare ne meahte furðon his hond to muðe ȝedon. *a* 1225 *Ancr. R.* 102 *Osculetur me osculo oris sui*; þæt is cus me, mi leofmon, mid cosse of þine muðe, muðene swetest. *a* 1300 *Cursor M.* 8081 Þair muthes wide, þair eien brade, Vn-freli was þair face made! *c* 1386 CHAUCER *Prol.* 153 Hir mouth ful smal, and ther-to softe and reed. 1457–8 *Anc. Cal. Rec. Dublin* (1889) I. 298 Men with bardys above the mowth. 1599 SHAKS. *Hen. V*, II. iii. 61 *Pist.* Touch her soft mouth, and march. *Bard.* Farwell Hostesse. 1690 LOCKE *Hum. Und.* III. vi. §26 There can be no reason given,.. why, a visage somewhat longer,.. or a wider mouth, could not have consisted.. with such a soul. 1719 DE FOE *Crusoe* (Globe) 209 A very good Mouth, thin Lips, and his fine Teeth well set. 1797 *Encycl. Brit.* (ed. 3) VI. 112/1 Of Drawing Faces. .. The middle of the mouth must always be placed upon the perpendicular line. 1820 KEATS *Lamia* I. 60 She had a woman's mouth with all its pearls complete. 1847 TENNYSON *Princess* VI. 252 And on her mouth A doubtful smile dwelt like a clouded moon In a still water. 1875 *Encycl. Brit.* I. 837/1 The corners of the mouth can be drawn to one side or the other, by the action of various muscles.

b. Phrases. ***down in*** (rarely ***of***) ***the mouth***, having the corners of the mouth turned downwards, as a sign of dissatisfaction; dejected, dispirited; so also ***down-at-mouth***. ***to flap in the mouth*** (***with a lie***): see FLAP *v.* 1 c. ***to laugh*** (***on***) ***the wrong side of one's mouth***, in early use to laugh in an evidently forced manner; now, to lament instead of laughing (see LAUGH *v.* 1 b); so, ***to sing on the wrong side of one's mouth***. ***to make a*** (***wry, ugly, hard***, etc.) ***mouth***, or ***mouths***: to express disapproval, derision, etc., by distorting or putting awry one's mouth, to grimace; of an animal, to menace with the mouth; also *fig.* to refuse to believe or accept. Const. *at, upon*. ***to shoot off one's mouth***: see SHOOT *v.* 23 g.

1649 BP. HALL *Cases Consc.* I. vi. (1650) 43 The Roman Orator was downe in the mouth; finding himselfe thus cheated by the money-changer. 1694 MOTTEUX *Rabelais* v. (1737) 224 You are damnably down o' the Mouth. 1764 FOOTE *Patron* III. Wks. 1799 I. 356 Poor lad! he will be most horribly down in the mouth: a little comfort won't come amiss. *a* 1850 ROSSETTI *Dante & Circle* I. (1874) 224 He'll never more be down-at-mouth, but fill His beak at his own beck. 1891 FREEMAN in *Life & Lett.* (1895) II. 426, I got down-in-the-mouth yesterday.

1714 T. LUCAS *Mem. Gamesters* (ed. 2) 65 But tho' he laugh'd; 'twas on the wrong side of his Mouth. 1761 *Brit. Mag.* II. 498 They'll quick make you sing the wrong side of your mouth. 1884 W. E. NORRIS *Thirlby Hall* xxxiii, We shall be laughing on the wrong side of our mouths before the day is over, unless I'm mistaken.

1551 ROBINSON tr. *More's Utop.* I. (1895) 71 And as he was thus saying, he shaked his heade, and made a wrie mouth. 1579 G. HARVEY *Letter-bk.* (Camden) 69 Me thinkes I see the make a mowthe At certayne Tuscane brave conceites. 1590 SHAKS. *Mids. N.* III. ii. 238 Counterfeit sad lookes, Make mouthes vpon me when I turne my backe, Winke each at other. 1681 OTWAY *Soldier's Fort.* II. i, I desire you to.. make ugly Mouths, laugh aloud, and look back at me. 1712 ADDISON *Spect.* No. 481 ¶3 They say he's a warm Man, and does not care to be made Mouths at. 1868 BROWNING *Ring & Bk.* IV. 127 How long, now, would the roughest marketman.. Harass a mutton ere she made a mouth Or menaced biting?

II. Transferred applications to persons.

5. One who speaks on behalf of another or of others; a spokesman. Cf. MOUTHPIECE. *Obs.* exc. in renderings of foreign modes of speech.

1563 J. DAVIDSON in *Wodrow Soc. Misc.* (1844) I. 253 The Spirit of God, quha spake be his prophetis,.. (as his mouth). 1591 R. BRUCE *Serm.* iii. E 7 For seing the Lord hath appoynted vs to be his mouth, we man not speak what we please. 1666 PEPYS *Diary* 20 Oct., I was but the mouth of the rest, and spoke what they have dictated to me. 1712 ADDISON *Spect.* No. 403 ¶2 Every Coffee-house has some particular Statesman belonging to it, who is the Mouth of the Street where he lives. 1892 RIDER HAGGARD *Nada* 188 You are a little man to be the mouth of so big a chief.

6. *slang.* **a.** A silly person; a dupe.

1680 COTTON *Compl. Gamester* (ed. 2) 7 The whole Gang will be ever and anon watching an opportunity to make a Mouth of you. 1753 *Discov. J. Poulter* (ed. 2) 31 One shall lead a Horse about, and another shall look out for a Mouth [*note*, an ignorant Person] that has a Horse to sell or change. 1823 'JON BEE' *Dict. Turf*, s.v., 'I've a mouth at the Mint, as brings me out plenty o' gold blanks'.

b. A noisy person.

a 1700 B. E. *Dict. Cant. Crew Mouth*, a noisy Fellow. 1725 in *New Cant. Dict.* 1811 in *Lex. Balatr.*

III. Applied to things resembling a mouth.

7. a. The opening of anything having a containing capacity, by which it is filled or emptied.

c 1250 *Gen. & Ex.* 2216 Ðo breðere seckes hauen he filt.. And bunden ðe muðes ðor bi-foren. *c* 1400 *Lanfranc's Cirurg.* 21 Þe maris.. closiþ hir mouþ, þat þer myȝte not entre the poynt of a nedle. *c* 1440 *Promp. Parv.* 347/2 Mowthe of a bottelle, *lura*. 1583 STUBBES *Anat. Abus.* II. (1882) 47 They will put good corne in the top or mouth of the bag. 1664 POWER *Exp. Philos.* 97 Stop the mouth of your Syringe close with your finger. *a* 1745 SWIFT *Direct. Serv.* i. Wks. 1751 XIV. 18 And lastly, wipe the Mouth of the Bottle with the Palm of your Hand. 1822–34 *Good's Study Med.* (ed. 4) IV. 139 In natural labour which, consists in a gradual enlargement of the mouth of the womb, &c.

b. The aperture for charging or filling (an oven, a furnace, or the like).

1574 R. SCOT *Hoppe Garden* 41 At one ende belowe, besides the mouth of the furnace, you must make a little doore into the roume beneath the bedde [or upper floor of the 'Oste']. 1608 SHAKS. *Per.* III. Gower 7 And Cricket sing at the Ouens mouth. 1667 MILTON *P.L.* II. 888 They.. like a Furnace mouth Cast forth redounding smoak and ruddy flame. 1797 *Encycl. Brit.* (ed. 3) XV. 389/1 He then discontinues the fire, and entirely closes up the mouth of the [porcelain] furnace. 1875 KNIGHT *Dict. Mech.*, *Mouth*, the hole in a furnace out of which melted metal flows.

8. The 'door' of a beehive, entrance-hole to a nest, etc.

1523 FITZHERB. *Husb.* §122 It is conuenyent that the hyue be set in a garden.. and the mouth of the hyue towarde the sonne. 1607 TOPSELL *Four-f. Beasts* 657 The mouth of their [*sc.* Squirrels'] nest is variable, sometimes at the sides, and sometimes at the top. 1697 DRYDEN *Virg. Georg.* IV. 49 Whether thou build the Palace of thy Bees With twisted Osiers, or with Barks of Trees; make but a narrow Mouth.

9. a. The surface opening of a pit, cave, well, ditch, and *fig.* of the pit of Hell.

c 1200 *Trin. Coll. Hom.* 43 Þe pit tineð his muð ouer þe man, þe lið on fule synnen. *c* 1375 *Sc. Leg. Saints* xxiii. (*VII Sleperis*) 159 Þane til his mene cane he byd, þat þai suld.. þe cawe mowth stope. 1551 RECORDE *Pathw. Knowl.* Pref., In dichyng, if he kepe not a proportion of bredth in the mouthe, to the bredthe of the bottome.. the diche shall be faultie. 1590 SPENSER *F.Q.* I. xi. 12 His deepe devouring jawes Wyde gaped, like the griesly mouth of hell. 1610 SHAKS. *Temp.* IV. i. 216 This is the mouth o'th Cell. 1702 SAVERY *Miner's Friend* 35 The Coals commonly burned on the Mouths of the Coal-Pits. 1876 FAWCETT *Pol. Econ.* III. iii. (ed. 5) 334 The rise in price at the pit's mouth was.. not less than 10s. a ton.

b. The crater of a volcano.

1604 E. G[RIMSTONE] *D'Acosta's Hist. Indies* III. ii. 119 Those which are in the Vulcans and mouths of fire at the Indies. 1613 PURCHAS *Pilgrimage* (1614) 59 A mouth continually throwing forth boiling pitch. 1813 BAKEWELL *Introd. Geol.* (1815) 230 The ancient mouth or crater of Teneriffe. 1830 LYELL *Princ. Geol.* I. 340 The great crater of Vesuvius had been gradually filled by lava.. and by scoriæ falling from the explosions of minor mouths.

10. The muzzle (of a gun).

1587 FLEMING *Contn. Holinshed* III. 1410/1 The earle.. laid the mouth of the dag vpon his left pap.. and.. discharged the same. 1595 SHAKS. *John* II. i. 381 Their battering Canon charged to the mouthes. 1669 STURMY *Mariner's Mag.* V. xii. 72 You put the Brass into the Mouth of the Piece. 1802 GOUV. MORRIS in Sparks *Life & Writ.* (1832) III. 396 Are our arguments to fly from the mouths of our cannon?

11. The outfall of a river; the entrance to a haven, valley, etc.

In this sense OE. had the derivative *múða* str. masc. (= OFris. *mûtha*, ON. *munne*:—OTeut. **munþon*-); but this did not survive into ME. Cf. F. *bouche*.

a 1122 *O.E. Chron.* an. 792 (Laud MS.), & his lic ligð æt Tinan muþe. 1297 R. GLOUC. (Rolls) 474 A lute bi norþe cornewaile as in an hauene mouþ. 1398 TREVISA *Barth. De P.R.* XV. cix. (1495) 528 Hollond is a prouynce by the mouth of the Ryne. 1585 T. WASHINGTON tr. *Nicholay's Voy.* IV. ix. 121 [Arabia] ioyneth there with the firme land of Egypt.. at the mouth of the red sea. 1613 PURCHAS *Pilgrimage* (1614) 422 The riuer Volga.. hath threescore and ten mouthes or falls into the Caspian Sea. 1725 DE FOE *Voy. round World* (1840) 15 We stood south again past the mouth of the Straits of Magellan. 1796 MARSHALL *W. Eng.* II. 178 The narrowed mouth of the Vale of Taunton. 1849 MACAULAY *Hist. Eng.* v. I. 556 The castle of Ealan Ghierig, situated at the mouth of Loch Riddan.

12. The opening out of a tube, passage, drain, burrow, and the like; *spec.* in *Physiol.* of a vessel.

1582 N. LICHEFIELD tr. *Castanheda's Conq. E. Ind.* I. 79 b, There were twentie Trumpets.. the mouthes whereof, were .. set with stone. 1634 T. JOHNSON *Parey's Chirurg.* IX. i. (1678) 216 That solution of Continuity, which happens in the vessels, their mouths being open, is termed Anastomosis. 1839 LONGF. *Hyperion* I. vi, The valley.. opens upon the broad plain of the Rhine, like the mouth of a trumpet. 1839–47 TODD *Cycl. Anat.* III. 228/2 The lacteals commence.. not by open mouths, but by a delicate network of vessels. 1844 H. STEPHENS *Bk. Farm* I. 563 The mouth of the main drain at its outlet should be protected with masonry. 1899 *Allbutt's Syst. Med.* VIII. 865 The mouth of the burrow.. is usually marked by a vesicle.

13. a. The hole in the stock of a plane through which the shavings pass.

1694 MOXON *Mech. Exerc.* ii. 68 Nor doth it [*sc.* the Rabbet-Plane] deliver its shaving at a Mouth on the top of the Stock as the other Planes do: But it hath its mouth on the sides. 1846 HOLTZAPFFEL *Turning*, etc. II. 478 In all the bench planes.. the mouth is a wedge-formed cavity.

b. The aperture in a musical pipe by means of which the sound is produced.

1727–52 [see LIP *sb.* 5 f]. 1855 HOPKINS *Organ* xviii. 83 The mouth.. is the horizontal cutting or opening that occurs at the junction of the body and foot of the pipe. 1875 KNIGHT *Dict. Mech.*, *Mouth*, in a flute,—the edge of the opening against which the air from the mouth of the performer is cut.

14. *Conch.* The aperture of a univalve shell.

1774 GOLDSM. *Nat. Hist.* (1824) III. 104 As the body of the snail can be extended no where but to the aperture, the mouth of the shell only can.. receive augmentation. 1776 DA COSTA *Elem. Conchol.* 97 The mouth is oblong-oval. 1838 *Penny Cycl.* XII. 107/1 [Helix.] 4th Group... Mouth rounded.

15. *Bot.* **a.** The orifice of the tube of a corolla. **b.** The opening which is produced by the dehiscence of the sporangium of mosses (*Syd. Soc. Lex.* 1891).

a. 1759 MILLER *Gard. Dict.* (ed. 7) *Rosmarinus*.. The Flower has.. the Mouth erect, and divided into two Lips. 1785 MARTYN *Rousseau's Bot.* xxii. (1794) 314 Snapdragon. .. The colours of these are red with white or yellow mouths. 1857 MISS PRATT *Flower. Pl.* (1861) IV. 32 (Hound's Tongue.)... Its mouth closed by prominent blunt scales. **b.** 1857 HENFREY *Bot.* 161 When the lid falls off, the border of the mouth of the capsule [of moss] is found either naked or furnished with.. teeth. 1861 BENTLEY *Man. Bot.* 377 The stoma or mouth is entire.

16. The fork between the open jaws of scissors, pincers, or a vice.

1576 R. SCOT *Hoppe Garden* 23 They [*sc.* pincers] must be one yarde in length, whereof sixe or seauen ynches maye be allowed for the mouth or lower end of them, which serueth to claspe.. the Poale,.. the mouth [should be] somewhat hollowe in the middest. 1611 COTGR., *Forpie*, the mouth, or middle of an opened paire of sheeres. 1875 KNIGHT *Dict. Mech.*, *Mouth*, the opening of a vice between its chops, chaps, cheeks, or jaws.

17. The cutting or working edge (of a tool).

1615, etc. [implied in *broad-mouthed*: see MOUTHED]. 1851 H. STEPHENS *Bk. Farm* (ed. 2) §5812 The.. earth is removed .. with the narrow spade.. having a mouth 6 inches wide.

18. *Fortif.* (See quots.)

1839 F. A. GRIFFITHS *Artill. Man.* xi. 223 The mouth of the embrazure is the outward or widest part of it. 1876 VOYLE & STEVENSON *Milit. Dict.* 126 The opening of the embrasure is termed the neck,.. that towards the country, the mouth.

19. Short for *mouth-piece*: **a.** of a bridle bit; **b.** of a pipe. ? *Obs.*

1607 MARKHAM *Caval.* II. (1617) 53 This mouth giueth all possible libertie to the tongue. 1727–51 CHAMBERS *Cycl.* s.v. *Bit*, The cannon with a fast mouth all of a piece. 1821 BYRON *Juan* V. liii, Pipes decorated With amber mouths.

IV. Attributive uses and Combinations.

20. a. simple attrib., as ***mouth-aperture, -articulation, -cavity, -gesture, -gymnastics, -heat, -opening, -part, -passage, -rim, -sound***; (surgical instruments for the mouth), as ***mouth-gag, -glass, -syringe***, etc.; (pertaining to or composing the oral cavity in echinodermata), as ***mouth-papillæ, parts, -plate, -shield***; with the meaning 'coming from the mouth only and not from the heart', as ***mouth-charity, -friend, -honour, -love, -mercy***; **b.** objective as ***mouth-stopper***; ***mouth-embracing, -opening, -stopping*** adjs.; **c.** appositive, as ***mouth-hole***; **d.** locative, as ***mouth-deep, -high*** advs.; ***mouth-shrivelled*** adj.; **e.** instrumental, as ***mouth-breathing***; ***mouth-blown, -formed, -made*** adjs.

1953 K. JACKSON *Lang. & Hist. Early Brit.* 573 The degree of *mouth-aperture. 1934 J. J. HOGAN *Outl. Eng. Philol.* 6 The nasal consonants *n* and *m* are stops in their *mouth-articulation, opens in their nasality. 1930 R. PAGET *Human Speech* 231 A separate *mouth-blown vowel or consonant resonator. 1897 *Allbutt's Syst. Med.* IV. 673 The difficulty in breathing through the nose leads to *mouth-breathing. 1924 R. M. OGDEN tr. *Koffka's Growth of Mind* iii. 132 The most primitive phenomena are figural; as examples.. the too cold or too warm milk in contrast with the temperature level of the *mouth-cavity. 1964 C. BARBER *Ling. Change Present-Day Eng.* iii. 38 A vowel is a voiced sound.. in which there is a free flow of air out of the mouth, without any audible friction or any obstruction of the mouth-cavity. 1692 SOUTH *Serm.* (1697) I. 463 Why, then answers the Man of *Mouth-Charity again, and tells you, That.. he can give nothing, but he will be sure to pray for the poor Gentleman. 1906 *Daily Chron.* 28 June 5/3 Two had to wade *mouth-deep in water. **1883** E. R. Lankester in *Encycl. Brit.* XVI. 674/1 The *mouth-embracing foot [of a Nautilus]. **1930** R. Paget *Human Speech* 111 A *mouth-formed whistle. **1607** Shaks. *Timon* III. vi. 99 May you a better Feast neuer behold You knot of *Mouth-Friends. **1895** *Arnold & Sons' Catal. Surg. Instruments* 217 Harelip, mouth and cleft palate instruments. *Mouth Gag. Mouth Prop. Mouth Dilator. Mouth Retractor. Mouth Speculum. **1930** R. Paget *Babel* 60 Making the same *mouth-gesture. **1858** Simmonds *Dict. Trade*, **Mouth glass*, a small hand-mirror for inspecting the teeth and gums, &c. **1921** H. E. Palmer *Princ. Lang.-Stud.* 89 We must go through a course of *mouth-gymnastics. **1942** W. Faulkner *Go Down, Moses* 103 Not even warmed from *mouth-heat. **1790** J. Fisher *Poems* 66, I did awake—my heart yet loups *Mouth high for fear. **1683** Pettus *Fleta Min.* I. iii. 10 Leave in the sides [of the assay-oven] Wind-holes, and in the fore-part leave also a *Mouth-hole. **1605** Shaks. *Macb.* v. iii. 27 Honor, Loue, Obedience..I must not looke to haue: but in their steed, Curses,..*Mouth-honor. **1907** G. B. Shaw *Major Barbara* Pref. 157 The mouth-honor paid to poverty and obedience by rich and insubordinate do-nothings. *a* **1586** Sidney *Arcadia* I. (1622) 64 Vowing..that neither heart nor *mouth-loue should euer anie more intangle him. **1606** Shaks. *Ant. & Cl.* I. iii. 30 Those *mouth-made vowes, Which breake themselues in swearing. **1647** Trapp *Comm. 1 John* iii. 18 There is a great deal of *mouth-mercy abroad. **1875** Huxley & Martin *Elem. Biol.* (1883) 208 Enlarge the *mouth-opening. **1960** *Guardian* 3 May 7/7 A truly mouth-opening recording of Handel's 'Messiah'. **1876** J. H. Kidder *Nat. Hist. Kerguelen Isl.* II. 74 This species..[of Echinoderm] differs widely..in the characters of the *mouth-papillæ and mouth-shields. **1799** G. Smith *Laboratory* I. 119 Let the *mouth part of the muffle be placed fronting the mouth of the furnace. **1964** C. Barber *Ling. Change Present-Day Eng.* iii. 47 This [l] is a *lateral* consonant: to produce it, you press the tip of the tongue against the teeth-ridge, thus blocking the centre of the *mouth-passage. **1882** Sladen in *Jrnl. Linn. Soc., Zool.* XVI. 194 *Mouth-plates short. **1933** *Burlington Mag.* June 265/1 It was customary to bind the *mouth-rims of bowls and dishes with metal. **1876** *Mouth shield [see *mouth-papillæ*]. **1925** Blunden *Eng. Poems* 89 That old man, face like parchment tanned, Wrinkled, *mouth-shrivelled. **1929** W. Faulkner *Sartoris* II. i. 74 All the other *mouth-sounds that stood for repose. **1549** A *mouthe stopper [see 3 k]. **1641** 'Smectymnuus' *Vind. Answ.* §6. 85 Good reader, consider this mighty *mouth-stopping argument. **1688** R. Holme *Armoury* III. 427/1 A *Mouth or Ear Syringe; so called, because used chiefly about those parts.

21. Special comb.: **mouth-arm**, each of the several tentacles or prolongations from the mouth of a jelly-fish, with which it catches its prey; **mouth-bearing** *a.*, (of a protozoan) having a definite oral cavity or cell-mouth; **mouth-blower** (*Cent. Dict.* 1889), **blowpipe**, a blowpipe operated by the mouth; **mouth-board**, a wooden instrument to which the mouth is applied, in order to secure a constant position of the head for observation or experiments; **mouth-breather**, a person who breathes through the mouth; **mouth-breeder**, a fish of the families Cichlidæ or Ariidæ which protects its eggs, and sometimes its newly-hatched offspring, by carrying them in its mouth; so **mouth-breeding** *ppl. a.*; **mouth canker** *Path.*, gangrenous stomatitis or *Noma* (*Syd. Soc. Lex.* 1891); **mouth-case**, that part of the integument of a pupa that covers the mouth (*Cent. Dict.*); **mouth-filling** *a. fig.*, (of an oath, compliment, etc.) that fills the mouth, bombastic, inflated; **mouth-flying** *a.*, that evades the mouth; **mouth-foot** = *foot-jaw* (see foot *sb.* 35); so **mouth-footed** *a.* (see quot.); **mouth-funnel**, the funnel-shaped mouth of a rotifer; **mouth-gauge** (see quot.); †**mouth-grenado** [after *hand grenade*], a violent or 'explosive' speech; **mouth guard**, a protector for the mouth of an operative in needle-manufacture; **mouth-harness** *jocular*, provisions of food; **mouth-harp** = mouth-organ 1; **mouth hoop**, the hoop forming the entrance to a decoy; **mouth infection**, communication of disease by the medium of the mouth; **mouth music**, (*a*) = *mouth-harp*; (*b*) singing without distinct utterance of words; **mouthparts** *Ent.*, the organs surrounding the mouth of an insect or other arthropod, specially adapted to the particular method of feeding of the animal concerned; **mouth pipe** *Organ-building* (see quot.); **mouth plate**, a plate fitted into the mouth in the surgical treatment of the palate; **mouth-pore** *Physiol. Bot.*, a stoma or breathing-pore in leaf-structure; **mouth provision**, provisions of food (for an expedition); **mouth ring**, (*a*) the ring forming the mouth of a bottle; (*b*) = *nerve ring* (see nerve *sb.* 12); **mouth root** *U.S.*, the plant *Coptis trifolia* (see quot.); **mouth rot**, an oral canker sometimes affecting snakes in captivity; **mouth-to-mouth** *a.*, involving the contact of one individual's mouth with another's; *spec.* applied to a method of artificial respiration in which a person places his mouth tightly over the patient's and blows into him every few seconds so as to inflate his lungs; also *absol.*; (for *fig.* sense see 3 j); similarly **mouth-to-nose** *a.*; **mouth wash, -water**, (*a*) a therapeutic wash for the mouth; also *transf.*; (*b*) nonsense, twaddle; **mouth-watering** *sb.*, the flowing of saliva in the mouth (cf. 2 c above); **mouth-watering** *a.*, (of a person) that experiences mouth-watering; (of a thing) that causes the mouth to water; **mouth-way**, entrance; **mouth-wise** *adv.* (*nonce-wd.*), by means of the mouth, by speech.

1884 R. von Lendenfeld in *Ann. & Mag. Nat. Hist.* Dec. 411 The Melbourne specimens [of this medusa] possess *mouth-arms which are deep purple throughout. **1885** E. R. Lankester in *Encycl. Brit.* XIX. 835/1 The *mouth-bearing corticate Protozoa. **1827** Faraday *Chem. Manip.* iv. 109 The *mouth blow-pipe. **1901** E. B. Titchener *Exper. Psychol.* I. II. 245 Materials.—Head-rest, with *mouth-board and sighting mark. **1910** *Practitioner* Jan. 69 The child was a *mouth-breather and showed signs of adenoids. **1927** *Sunday at Home* June 239/1 The *mouth-breeder protects her eggs by carrying them about in her mouth. **1962** K. F. Lagler et al. *Ichthyol.* x. 298 (*caption*) Mouthbreeding catfish. *Ibid.* 301 Some African fishes, *Tilapia*, are called 'mouth-breeders' because the young when they are hatched escape at time of danger into the oral cavity of the female. **1596** Shaks. *1 Hen. IV*, III. i. 259 Sweare me..A good *mouth-filling Oath. **1873** L. Stephen *Ess. Freethinking* 286 The flattery..was..reciprocal; and perhaps the great man pours out more mouth-filling compliments than his satellite. **1625** K. Long tr. *Barclay's Argenis* v. i. 330 Condemn'd, like Tantalus, with vaine pursuit To gape at water, and *mouth-flying fruit. **1841–71** T. R. Jones *Anim. Kingd.* (ed. 4) 448 The Stomapoda (*Mouth-footed Crustaceans) are so called on account of the size and preponderant development of the jaw-feet. **1877** *Encycl. Brit.* VI. 662/1 The sub-class Gnathopoda, 'mouth-footed'. **1862** Gosse *Rotifera* in *Pop. Sci. Rev.* I. 40 The *mouth-funnel was well marked. **1875** Knight *Dict. Mech.*, **Mouth-gage* (Saddlery), a device for measuring a horse's mouth. **1651** Cleveland *Poems* 34 Yet to expresse a Scot, to play that prize, Not all those *mouth-Granadoes can suffice. **1693** *Humours Town* 27 The roaring Mouth-Granado's of Oaths. **1852** M. T. Morrall *Needle-Making* (1862) 25 A *mouth guard, which was approved of and found to answer when used by the needle pointers. **1653** Urquhart *Rabelais* I. xxxii. 147 We are here but badly victualled, and furnished with *mouth-harnasse very slenderly. **1903** Ade *In Babel* 40 I'd walked from Loueyville over to Terry Hut with a nigger that played the *mouth-harp. **1968** *Publ. Amer. Dial. Soc.* XLIX. 15 The lack of familiarity with the musical instrument probably accounts for the decline of *juice harp* and *jew's harp* and the student's use of *mouth harp*. **1972** *Village Voice* (N.Y.) 1 June 76/5 She takes out a mouth harp, fills her cheeks with wind, and blows 'the ballad of the shadows'. **1895** Suffling *Land of Broads* 28 The *mouthhoop would be perhaps 5 yds. across. **1903** *Brit. Med. Jrnl.* 14 Mar. 43 A paper on *mouth infection. **1887** *Lantern* (New Orleans) 3 Sept. 3/2 The music was furnished by a kid with a *mouth music. **1936** C. Day Lewis *Hope for Poetry* (Postscript) 93 A new language of purely emotive sounds (e.g. the 'mouth-music' of the Hebridean islanders). **1938** L. MacNeice *I crossed Minch* I. iv. 45 An example of the old 'mouth-music'—Port a Beul—to which the islanders used to dance before they had musical instruments. **1973** Boyd & Parkes *Dark Number* ix. 96 He gave way to a brief rendering of the mouth music of his youth. **1869** A. S. Packard *Guide to Study of Insects* 34 We have already treated of the external appendages (*mouth-parts) which prepare the food for digestion. **1905** V. L. Kellogg *Amer. Insects* i. 6 Attached to the thorax are three pairs of legs, which are jointed appendages, homologous in origin and fundamental structure with the mouth-parts and antennæ. **1932** *Times Lit. Suppl.* 17 Mar. 206/2 There are, too, such enigmas as *trophia*, for which we guess mouthparts. **1972** L. E. Chadwick tr. *Linsenmaier's Insects of World* 24/1 The variations of the insect mouth and mouthparts are nearly limitless. Here we find an assemblage of instruments such as only a surgeon, an artisan, or a burglar might wish for—from a harmless sucking proboscis, through implements for boring, sawing, pinching, and cutting, to such devilish contraptions as poison syringes or stilettos that snap out to pierce the prey. **1974** *Sci. Amer.* Apr. 103/1 When feeding, adult beetles busily squeeze pellets of moist dung between their mouthparts and suck in the expressed juice. **1855** Hopkins *Organ* xviii. 83 Lip, *mouth, or flue pipes..are such as have an oblong opening, called the *mouth*, at the junction of the body with the foot. **1876** *Trans. Clinical Soc.* IX. 126 That part which connected the *mouth-plate with the nasal rim. **1888** Clodd *Story Creation* (1894) 72 The carbonic acid which the plant absorbs through the numberless stomata or *mouth-pores in its leaves or integuments. **1746** *Rep. Cond. Sir J. Cope* 184 We..have no other Way of carrying '*Mouth Provision' with us but by the East Coast. **1839** Ure *Dict. Arts* 578 The finisher..cracks off the bottle smoothly at its *mouth-ring. **1903** *Contemp. Rev.* Sept. 384 The anterior knots of the mouth-ring [of the cray-fish] have swelled into a still larger brain. **1784** Cutler in *Mem. Amer. Acad. Arts & Sci.* (1785) I. 457 Goldenthread. *Mouth Root...The roots are astringent, and of a bitterish taste. Chewed in the mouth they cure apthas and cankerous sores. **1847** W. Darlington *Amer. Weeds* (1860) 31 *Coptis trifolia*... A domestic remedy for the sore mouths of children; whence the name 'Mouth-root'. **1931** W. N. Clute *Common Names of Plants* 123 The canker-root (*Coptis trifolia*) or mouth-root, as it is called,..continues to hold its place among medicines for the cure of sore mouth. **1961** C. H. Pope *Giant Snakes* (1962) 195 Another threat to captive snakes..is *mouth rot, which is also called canker mouth and osteomyelitis. **1965** R. & D. Morris *Men & Snakes* vii. 145 Snakes are very liable to mouth-rot when their jaws are damaged. **1969** A. Bellairs *Life of Reptiles* II. xii. 516 Among the more important bacterial diseases are the oral canker or 'mouth rot' seen in captive snakes and apparently caused by species of *Pseudomonas* and *Pasteurella*. **1909** *Lancet* 13 Mar. 747/2 By 1782 the Royal Humane Society recommended inflation by bellows in preference to the *mouth-to-mouth method. **1932** E. Step *Bees, Wasps, Ants* 32 The first eggs hatch, and the legless little [bee] larvae have to be fed, which is a direct mouth-to-mouth exchange between mother and larva. **1941** *Jrnl. Amer. Med. Assoc.* 6 Dec. 1942/2 Mouth to mouth insufflation has many adherents. It permits an exchange of gases under proper conditions as to temperature, content of moisture and carbon dioxide. **1961** *Sunday Times* 17 Sept. 4/5 Mouth-to-mouth resuscitation, by which a life-saver inflates a victim's lungs with his own breath, was approved officially by the British Red Cross Society last week. **1968** K. Weatherley *Roo Shooter* 113 The bush nurse gave him mouth to mouth and got his heart going again. **1970** S. J. Perelman *Baby, it's Cold Inside* 203 Luckily, before Wemyss had to apply mouth-to-mouth breathing, the three of us recovered. **1954** *New Eng. Jrnl. Med.* 6 May 754 Without the mask a *mouth-to-nose technic with a handkerchief 'filter' is effective. **1961** *Times* 6 Dec. 9/4 A life-size inflatable doll for demonstrating mouth-to-mouth and mouth-to-nose artificial respiration. **1962** S. Miles *Underwater Med.* xiv. 224 Those who advocate 'mouth to mouth' claim that better inflation is possible, it is more natural and nasal obstruction may be an obstacle if 'mouth to nose' is used. **1840** Pereira *Mat. Med.* 1260 An astringent *mouth-wash. **1920** Ade *Hand-Made Fables* 5 The Cleaners left nothing behind them in Glass Receptacles except Bluing and Mouth-Wash. **1951** M. McLuhan *Mech. Bride* (1967) 60/2 Mouth washes, gargles..are backed by long-standing national advertising campaigns. **1957** C. S. Lewis *Let.* 2 Sept. (1966) 279 Give your imagination a good mouth-wash by a reading..of the *Odyssey*. **1971** *Mod. Law Rev.* XXXIV. 630 Any suggestion that the principle was also applied can be dismissed as so much mouth-wash. **1597** A. M. tr. *Guillemeau's Fr. Chirurg.* 24 b/2, A *mouth-water, or gargrise, made of barley-water. **1706** S. Sewall *Diary* 28 Dec., He call'd for Mouth-Water..and then for his little pot to void it into. **1822–34** *Good's Study Med.* (ed. 4) I. 71 *Mouth-watering:—Produced by the sight, smell or thought of agreeable food. **1845** Ford *Handbk. Spain* I. 67 The mouth watering bystanders sigh as they see and smell the rich freight steaming away from them. **1900** *Speakers* 3 Jan. 338/2 The White Star shareholders have made a most mouth-watering bargain. **1960** *Guardian* 7 Oct. 12/5 A mouth-watering bowl of fruit. **1973** *Country Life* 29 Nov. 1796/2 Mouthwatering grills—fish, meat, vegetables. **1920** A. E. W. Mason *Summons* xii. 121 Crossed the road and disappeared into the *mouth-way of an alley. **1876** Browning *Pacchiarotto* 403 So grind away, *mouth-wise and pen-wise, Do all that we can to make men wise!

mouth (maʊð), *v.* [f. mouth *sb.*]

1. a. *trans.* To pronounce, speak; to give utterance to. *Obs.* exc. *arch.*

a **1300** *Cursor M.* 18941 Was na langage man for to muth, at þai [*sc.* the apostles] ne all kindli it cuth. **1377** Langl. *P. Pl.* B. IV. 115 Til lordes and ladies louien alle treuthe, And haten al harlotrye to heren it, or to mouthen it. *c* **1450** J. Metham *Wks.* (E.E.T.S.) 33 And Amoryus this mowthyd to plese Cleopes. **1621** Quarles *Argalus & P.* (1678) 47 He that knows not how to mouth a curse. **1744** Akenside *Ep. to Curio*, From year to year the stubborn herd to sway Mouth all their wrongs. **1822** Byron *Werner* II. ii, Who Taught you to mouth that name of 'villain'? **1871** Rossetti *Dante at Verona* xlviii, Lords mouthed approval.

†**b.** *intr.* To speak, talk. *Obs.*

a **1375** *Cursor M.* 21419 (Fairf.) Quat þing þat ho him of wald mouþ atte hir deuise make he couþe. *c* **1400** *Destr. Troy* 686 Þere Medea the mylde met hym hir one, And with myrthe at þere metyng mowthet togethir.

2. a. *trans.* To utter in a pompously oratorical style, or with great distinctness of articulation; to declaim. Also with *out.*

1602 *2nd Pt. Return fr. Parnass.* v. i, With mouthing words that better wits haue framed, They [*sc.* actors] purchase lands. **1602** Shaks. *Ham.* III. ii. 3. **1603** Florio *Montaigne* I. li. (1632) 167 When I heare our Architects mouth-out those big, and ratling words of Pilasters, Architraves [etc.]. **1761** Churchill *Rosciad* Poems 1763 I. 16 He..mouths a sentence, as curs mouth a bone. **1842** Tennyson *Epic* 50 And the poet..Read, mouthing out his hollow oes and aes. **1892** A. Birrell *Res Judicatæ* v. 144 The pompous high-placed imbecile mouthing his platitudes.

b. *intr.* To admit of being 'mouthed'.

1762 Wilkes *N. Briton* No. 11 It [the word 'glorification'] found favour among their long-winded divines, only because it was so long, and mouthed so well.

c. *trans.* To declaim against. *rare*$^{-1}$.

1742 R. Blair *Grave* 386 Then might the debauchee Untrembling mouth the heavens.

3. *intr.* To mouth one's words; to use a pompous or affected style of utterance; to declaim. Also *to mouth it.*

1602 Shaks. *Ham.* v. i. 306 Nay, and thoul't mouth, Ile rant as well as thou. **1682** Dryden & Lee *Dk. Guise* II. ii, You have Mouth'd it bravely. **1713** Addison *Cato* I. iii, I'll ..mouth at Cæsar 'till I shake the Senate. **1891** E. W. Gosse *Gossip in Library* xx. 256 The poet tramped the grassy heights..mouthing and murmuring as he went.

4. a. *trans.* To put or take (something, esp. as food) in the mouth; to seize with the mouth; to press (a thing) with the mouth or lips.

a **1400–50** *Alexander* 748* (Dubl. MS.) For other mete þan manysflesche mouthed he neuer. **1573** Tusser *Husb.* (1878) 132 Corne carried, let such as be poore go and gleane, and after, thy cattle to mowth it vp cleane. **1602** Shaks. *Ham.* IV. ii. 20 He keepes them like an Ape in the corner of his iaw, first mouth'd to be last swallowed. **1621** G. Sandys *Ovid's Met.* VII. (1626) 146 The Beast..Appeares to catch th'vncaught; and mouthes the aire. **1693** Dryden *Persius* (1697) 417 He mouth'd 'em, and betwixt his Grinders caught. **1717** Eusden *Ovid's Met.* IV. 162 She found the veil, and mouthing it all o'er, With bloody jaws the lifeless prey she tore. **1847** Tennyson *Princess* VI. 196 [She] in her hunger mouth'd and mumbled it [*sc.* her restored babe], And hid her bosom with it. **1855** Bain *Senses & Int.* 406 *note*, The satisfaction first of mouthing the object [the lamb's mother's teat]. **1867** F. Francis *Angling* iv. (1880) 119 If the fish mouths it.

b. *spec.* Of a hound: To mangle (dead game) with the mouth.

[**1693**: see 6.] **1884** Speedy *Sport* ix. 158 It [*sc.* the dog] showed a very slight disposition to mouth its game when shot.

c. *Cock-fighting. to mouth it*: to fight with the mouth or beak.

a **1700** B. E. *Dict. Cant. Crew, Sparring-blows*,.. those in a Battel before the Cocks come to Mouth it.

5. To train the mouth of (a horse); to accustom to the use of the bit.

a **1533** LD. BERNERS *Gold. Bk. M. Aurel.* (1546) E vij b, Gyue hym..a sharpe bytte to thentente that he be well mouthed. **1618** M. BARET *Horsemanship* I. 14 For he is accompted a good Horse-man in other parts thereof if he can but mouth a Horse. **1690** *Lond. Gaz.* No. 2590/4 Stolen.., a bay Colt.., newly mouth'd and pac'd. **1860** *Luck of Ladysmede* (1862) I. 339 There is the new palfrey which you have been mouthing for me. **1890** 'R. BOLDREWOOD' *Col. Reformer* (1891) 94 Why, he cannot be nearly mouthed.

†6. *intr.* (*contemptuously*.) To join lips (*with*); to kiss. (In quot. 1693 app. with allusion to 4 b.)

1603 SHAKS. *Meas. for M.* III. ii. 194 The Duke..would mouth with a beggar, though she smelt browne-bread and Garlicke. **1693** CONGREVE *Old Bach.* I. iv, *Heart.* And it should be mine to let 'em [*sc.* partridges] go again. *Sharp.* Not till you had mouthed a little, George.

7. To 'make mouths'; to grimace; to make derisive grimaces and noises with the mouth.

1827 DISRAELI *Viv. Grey* VI. i, He drew the cork from his bottle..and mouthed at his companions even while he bowed to them. **1883** LD. R. GOWER *My Remin.* I. viii. 148 The unfortunate queen..retaining her calm demeanour as the mob shouted and mouthed around her.

8. Of a river: To disembogue (*in, into*).

1598 FLORIO, *Sboccare*, to mouth, or fall into the sea, as a river doth. **1831** MRS. F. TROLLOPE *Dom. Manners Amer.* (1894) II. 16 The Ohio and Chesapeake canal..there mouths into the Potomac. **1881** R. F. BURTON in *Academy* 21 May 366/1 He had originally intended to explore this great stream, which mouths as the 'Nourse River.'

9. *trans.* To point the mouth of (a pistol). *nonce-use.*

1612 DEKKER *If it be not good* K i b, Fetch me deare friend, An armed Pistoll, and mouth it at my breast.

10. *trans.* To estimate the age of (a sheep) by examining the teeth. *Austral.* and *N.Z.*

1933 *Bulletin* (Sydney) 6 Sept. 24/1 Graziers buy old ewes without troubling to 'mouth' them. *a* **1948** L. G. D. ACLAND *Early Canterbury Runs* (1951) 404 A competent shepherd should be able to do anything necessary with sheep—draft, shear, mouth, [etc.]. **1972** P. NEWTON *Sheep Thief* ix. 74, I found the opportunity to mouth several of those double fork sheep—and one was only a four tooth.

mouth, obs. pa. t. of MAY *v.*[1]

mouthable ('maʊðəb(ə)l), *a.* [f. MOUTH *v.* + -ABLE.] That may be uttered with good effect; suitable for oratory or recitation.

1825 J. WILSON in *Blackw. Mag.* XVII. 127 Fine mouthable apophthegms. **1887** O. W. HOLMES in *Atlantic Monthly* LIX. 640 Good mouthable lines.

mouthacho, -chato: see MUSTACHIO.

mouthe, form of MOTH; obs. pa. t. of MAY *v.*[1]

mouthed (maʊðd), *a.* [f. MOUTH *sb.* + -ED[2].]

1. Having a mouth, or a mouth of a certain kind (in various senses of the sb.).

13.. *K. Alis.* 6125 Rowgh they weore so a beore, They weore mowthed so a mare. **1590** SPENSER *F.Q.* II. xi. 12 A grysie rablement; Some mouth'd like greedy Oystriges; some faste Like loathly Toades. **1637** T. MORTON *New Eng. Canaan* (1883) 204 The Beaver..[is] mouthed like a cunny. **1741** *Compl. Fam. Piece* II. i. 296 Which this Sort will do, having Courage and a thick Skin, as participating of the Cur, and mouthed from the Beagle. **1820** KEATS *Hyperion* II. 270, I..sat me down, and took a mouthed shell.

†2. Gaping, open-mouthed. *Obs.*

1599 B. JONSON *Cynthia's Rev.* v. iv, Reflect: what meanes hee by that mouthed waue. *c* **1600** SHAKS. *Sonn.* lxxvii, The wrinckles..Of mouthed graues will giue thee memorie. **1649** G. DANIEL *Trinarch.* To Rdr. 81 As mouthéd Peasants (throng to see the state,..And Gape vpon the Gowne,..) magnifie Merit. *Ibid.*, *Hen. IV*, cclxviii.

3. In parasynthetic derivatives.

1390 GOWER *Conf.* II. 144 A janglere, an evel mouthed oon. **1393** LANGL. *P. Pl.* C. x. 126 For hit aren murye-mouthede men mynstrales of heuene. **1551** BIBLE *Exod.* iv. 10 But I am slowe mouthed and slowe tongued. **1590** SPENSER *F.Q.* I. viii. 6 And every head was..bloody mouthed with late cruell feast. **1593** MARKHAM *Horsmanship* ii. F j, But if he [your Horse] be..gentle mouthed, then shall the cheeke of your Bytte be made but vppon one degree. **1634** SIR T. HERBERT *Trav.* 95 Seuentie mouthed Volga. *a* **1680** BUTLER *Rem.* (1759) II. 316 He prefers a Cry of Lawyers at the Bar before any Pack of the best mouthed Dogs in all the North. **1853** MARKHAM *Skoda's Auscult.* 139 A single-mouthed fistulous opening. **1899** F. T. BULLEN *Way Navy* 68 An occasional blast from our bull-mouthed siren is also inimical to slumber. **1905** HOLMAN HUNT *Pre-Raphælitism* II. 295 A many-mouthed chorus began.

mouther[1] ('maʊðə(r)). [f. MOUTH *v.* + -ER[1].] One who mouths; one given to vain, boastful, or declamatory speech.

1822 SCOTT *Nigel* xiii, Courtiers..whose only merit to their masters is to repeat their own words after them—a pack of mouthers, and flatterers, and ear-wigs. **1886** *American* XII. 175 Were there less loafing about bars by windy mouthers and less frothy talk.

mouther[2] ('maʊθə(r)). *Pugilistic slang.* [f. MOUTH *sb.* + -ER[1].] A blow on the mouth.

1814 *Sporting Mag.* XLIII. 68, B. gave a mouther which told.

mouthful ('maʊθfʊl). [f. MOUTH *sb.* + -FUL.]

a. A quantity that fills the mouth; as much as a mouth can hold or take in at one time; hence, a small quantity (*of* something).

1530 PALSGR. 247/1 Mouthfull, *baufre.* *c* **1532** DU WES *Introd. Fr.* in *Palsgr.* 1017 In their mouthfull takyng refection. **1608** SHAKS. *Per.* II. i. 35 A [*sc.* a whale] playes and tumbles, Dryuing the poore Fry before him, And at last, deuowre them all at a mouthfull. **1692** R. L'ESTRANGE *Fables* xxviii. 28 A Goat that was going out one Morning for a Mouthful of Fresh Grass, Charg'd her Kid..not to Open the Door. **1693** DRYDEN *Juvenal* iii. *ad fin.*, When..You to your own Aquinum shall repair, To take a mouthful of sweet Country air. **1827** FARADAY *Chem. Manip.* iv. 113 Acquire the power of using the air of one inspiration by mouthfuls. **1837** W. IRVING *Capt. Bonneville* I. 176 They were three entire days without a mouthful of food. **1899** *Allbutt's Syst. Med.* VI. 71 He was continually bringing up mouthfuls of dark-coloured mucus.

b. *transf.* Phr. *to say a mouthful*, to make a striking or important statement; to say something noteworthy. *colloq.* (orig. *U.S.*).

1748 SMOLLETT *Rod. Rand.* lvi, I can't have a mouthful of English for love or money. [**1790** *Sessions Papers* Sept. 781/1, I never said a *mouth full of ill against her* in my life.] **1884** F. M. CRAWFORD *Rom. Singer* ii. 31 'He taught me to pronounce the name Königgratz, so—Conigherazzo', said the maestro... 'Capperi! What a mouthful', said I. **1922** C. SANDBURG *Slabs of Sunburnt West* 7 You said a mouthful. **1924** A. J. SMALL *Frozen Gold* i. 14 A fight, he says—and he don't know what a mouthful he's said. **1929** A. CONAN DOYLE *Maracot Deep* vi. 165 He said a mouthful when he asked her to marry him. **1947** L. HASTINGS *Dragons are Extra* vii. 143 And that says a mouthful. **1973** WODEHOUSE *Bachelors Anonymous* xii. 153 'Nice nurse?' 'Ah, there you have said a mouthful, Pickering. I have a Grade A nurse.'

mouth glue.

1. Glue to be used by moistening with the tongue (see GLUE *sb.* 2); originally, a preparation of isinglass. †Hence used for isinglass itself.

1573-80 BARET *Alv.* G 288 Glue made of fish skinnes, mouthglue. *Icthyocolla.* **1661** LOVELL *Hist. Anim. & Min.* 238 *Ichthiocolla...* It's used in gellies: boiled with white Sugar it becommeth white, and is called mouth glew. **1727** BRADLEY *Fam. Dict.* s.v. *Glass*, Put some Mouth-glue into a Porringer upon the Fire, with some Spirit of Wine, and when the Glue is become liquid enough, rub the Pieces of Glass therewith, and they will re-unite. **1766** *Compl. Farmer* s.v. *Surveying*, These sheets may be pieced together with mouth-glew. **1889** in *Century Dict.* s.v. *Glue.*

†2. *fig.* (*allusive.*) 'Glue' made of words.

1615 J. STEPHENS *Ess. & Char., Gossip* (2nd impr.) 368 By the vertue of a speciall mouth-glew, she cleaues readily to all acquaintance. **1700** CONGREVE *Way of World* v. ix, My contract went no further than a little Mouth-Glew, and that's hardly dry.

mouthing ('maʊθɪŋ), *sb. Mining.* [f. MOUTH *sb.* + -ING[1].] The entrance to a mine.

1883 GRESLEY *Gloss. Coal Mining.* **1902** *Daily Chron.* 4 Apr. 6/4 It is only a new mine, and there was only three yards in the mouthing.

mouthing ('maʊðɪŋ), *vbl. sb.* [f. MOUTH *v.* + -ING[1].] a. The action of the verb MOUTH.

1598 FLORIO, *Sbarléffo*..a mouthinge, or looking staringlie. **1646** SIR T. BROWNE *Pseud. Ep.* III. vi. 117 The beholder at first sight, conceives it [*sc.* the cub] a rude and informous lumpe of flesh, and imputes the ensuing shape unto the mouthing of the Dam. **1728** POPE *Dunc.* II. 237 The monkey-mimics rush discordant in; Twas chatt'ring, grinning, mouthing, jabbring all. **1874** L. STEPHEN *Hours in Library* (1892) II. i. 14 Thomson..too often falls into mere pompous mouthing. **1884** YATES *Recoll.* v. 205 A fine old-crusted actor, full of mouthings and conventionalisms. *a* **1948** L. ACLAND *Early Canterbury Runs* (1951) 391 s.v. *Race.* Narrow passage in a sheepyard, for drafting, mouthing, branding, etc. **1950** *N.Z. Jrnl. Agric.* Feb. 122 (*caption*) The photograph shows part of the preparation of a breeding flock for the season, which entails mouthing, drafting for wool, age, and other factors.

b. Comb.: **mouthing bit**, a bit used in 'mouthing' a horse; **mouthing machine** (see quot. 1884).

1856 'STONEHENGE' *Brit. Sports* II. I. viii. §5. 346/1 The Mouthing-Bit may now be put on. **1884** KNIGHT *Dict. Mech.* Suppl., *Mouthing Machine* (Sheet-metal Working), a machine for crimping bottoms and swaging or mouthing the tops of open-top cans, to receive the covers.

mouthing ('maʊðɪŋ), *ppl. a.* [f. MOUTH *v.* + -ING[2].] That mouths, in the senses of the verb.

1681 W. ROBERTSON *Phraseol. Gen.* (1693) 898 A mouthing fellow, *Clamosus.* **1693** DRYDEN *Persius* v. (1697) 471 When Progne's or Thyestes' Feast they write; And, for the mouthing Actor, Verse indite. **1865** CARLYLE *Fredk. Gt.* XXI. iv. (1872) X. 23 A solemn, arrogant, mouthing..kind of man. **1904** EDITH RICKERT *Reaper* 62 One might see in her withered mouthing face the wreckage of a great beauty.

b. Of speech, etc.: Characterized by grandiloquence or pomposity.

1814 L. HUNT *Feast of Poets*, etc. (1815) 50 A translation ..which..is at least..much above the mouthing nonentities which have been palmed upon us of late years for that wonderful poet. **1877** MRS. OLIPHANT *Makers Flor.* v. 128 That fine mouthing speech of his, magniloquent and generous.

Hence **'mouthingly** *adv.*, in a mouthing manner.

1903 *Blackw. Mag.* Aug. 277/2 What the philosophical Radicals..mouthingly extolled as 'individual initiative'.

'mouthishly, *adv.* [f. MOUTH *sb.* + -ISH + -LY[2].] In a mouthy manner.

1798 COLERIDGE *Lett.* (1895) 251 *note*, Flat lines forced into poetry by italics (signifying how well and mouthishly the author would read them).

mouthless ('maʊθlɪs), *a.* [f. MOUTH *sb.* + -LESS.] Having no mouth.

a **1000** *Riddles* lxi. 9 (Gr.) Lyt ic wende, þæt ic..æfre sceolde..muðleas sprecan, wordum wrixlan. **1552** HULOET Mouthles beastes, *inora.* **1856** MAYNE *Expos. Lex.*, *Mouthless, Bot., Zoöl.* **1877** HUXLEY *Anat. Inv. Anim.* iii. 131 The gonophores are developed upon special stalks, each of which has essentially the structure of a mouthless hydranth.

†**'mouthly**, *a.* and *adv. Obs. rare.* [f. MOUTH *sb.* + -LY[1] and [2].]

a. *adj.* Done with the mouth. b. *adv.* By or with the mouth.

c **1400** *Destr. Troy* 3538 Vnto Menelay, the mene tyme, mowthly was told Of the rape vnrightwis of his Riche qwene. **1537** COVERDALE *Exp. Ps. xxii.* C viij b, By the mouthly preachynge of the worde which goeth in at the eares. **1653** [? HALES] *Brevis Disquisitio* ix. 29 The mouthly eating and consubstantiation of the Lutherans.

mouth-organ.

1. A musical instrument operated by the mouth. a. = PAN-PIPE; b. = HARMONICA, -ON; c. *dial.* = JEWS' HARP.

a **1668** LASSELS *Voy. Italy* (1698) II. 199 Pan also plays on his mouth-organ tuneably. **1836-9** DICKENS *Sk. Boz, First of May*, The instrumental accompaniments rarely extended beyond the shovels and a set of Pan-pipes, better known to many, as a 'mouth-organ'. **1887** *Sci. Amer.* 19 Feb. 120/3 The mouth organ, or harmonica, is a familiar example of a simple reed instrument.

2. *Zool.* One of the parts or appendages forming the mouth (of an insect, crustacean, etc.).

1863 DANA in *Amer. Jrnl. Sci.* Ser. II. XXXVI. 4 Insects, ..have three pairs of mouth-organs, and three pairs of legs. **1866** H. WOODWARD *Brit. Fossil Crustacea* I. 37. **1878** BELL *Gegenbaur's Comp. Anat.* 239 Such of these more anterior ventral appendages as lie near the mouth are converted into mouth-organs.

'mouthpiece, 'mouth-piece.

1. a. A piece placed at or forming the mouth (of a receptacle, organ-pipe, tool, and the like).

1683 MOXON *Mech. Exerc., Printing* xv. ¶6 Letter-Founders call this altogether a Mouth-Piece. **1832** G. R. PORTER *Porcelain & Gl.* I. v. 59 These openings [for fuel] are provided with mouth pieces of plate iron. **1855** HOPKINS *Organ* xviii. 83 Reed or tongue pipes are..those which are made to sound through the medium of a mouth-piece. **1893** *Labour Commission* Gloss., *Mouth-pieces*, castings fixed on the open ends of 'retorts' [in gas-making]... The term is also applied to the pipes conveying the gas from the retorts.

b. The part of a telephone into which one speaks.

1888 *Encycl. Brit.* XXIII. 131/1 The [Reis telephone] receiver consists of an electromagnet made up of a magnetized coil.., with a stout knitting needle for a core. When in use these two instruments are joined in circuit with a battery.., so that under ordinary circumstances a continuous current is flowing through the line. Suppose a sound is then produced in front of the mouthpiece.., the successive variations in the pressure of the air are communicated to the inside of the box, and cause the membrane to vibrate in unison with the sound. **1907** *Sears, Roebuck Catal.* 204/2 Telephone mouthpieces. Male or female thread. **1926** T. E. LAWRENCE *Seven Pillars* (1935) I. viii. 71 Abdulla went to the telephone..and transferred the mouthpiece to Storrs. **1941** [see INTERCOM]. **1955** W. GADDIS *Recognitions* II. v. 509 He turned quickly into the other telephone booth, dialed and stood bent rigid before the mouthpiece.

2. a. *joc.* Used for *mouth* (cf. *headpiece*). b. The part (of a model) representing the mouth.

1738 SWIFT *Pol. Conversat.* 41 You have made a fine speech, Colonel. Pray, what will you take for your Mouthpiece? **1831** BREWSTER *Nat. Magic* viii. (1833) 209 To the mouth-piece was added a nose made of two tin tubes.

3. Something to put in the mouth. a. That part of a musical instrument, a pipe, etc., which is placed between the lips, usually adjustable and of a material agreeable to the mouth, as silver, amber, etc. Also, a tube by which a cigar or cigarette is held in the mouth.

1776 BURNEY *Hist. Mus.* I. 279 This contrivance..left only a small aperture between the lips, just sufficient to receive the mouth-piece of the flute. **1857** W. COLLINS *Dead Secret* III. i, His lips began to work round the mouth-piece of the pipe. **1876** *Smoker's Guide* v. 61 For our part, to smoke a cigar through a mouthpiece is equivalent to kissing a lady through a respirator. **1896** *Allbutt's Syst. Med.* I. 414 To..allow the child to suck the mixture from the sterilising bottle fitted with a mouth-piece.

b. That part of a bit which crosses the horse's mouth.

1727-51 CHAMBERS *Cycl.* s.v. *Bit*, The several parts of a snaffle or curb-bit are—the mouth-piece, the cheeks [etc.]. **1833** *Regul. Instr. Cavalry* I. 83 Each regiment should have a few bits with different and easy mouth-pieces and curbs. **1897** J. L. ALLEN *Choir Invisible* xiii. 197 Her face concealed by a black velvet riding-mask kept in place by a silver mouth-piece held between her teeth.

4. a. One who voices the sentiments, opinions, etc., of (a party); one who speaks on behalf of (another or others); one who gives official or

public expression to (common opinion or sentiment); a spokesman.

1805 SOUTHEY *Madoc in W.* viii, They look'd Toward their chief and mouth-piece, the High Priest Tezozomoc. **1818** COBBETT *Pol. Reg.* XXXIII. 64 The thing called the Cabinet is nothing more than the mouth-piece of the Boroughmongers. **1874** GREEN *Short Hist.* viii. §9. 557 The popular discontent at once found a mouthpiece in John Lilburne.

b. *slang.* A solicitor.

1857 'DUCANGE ANGLICUS' *Vulgar Tongue* 13 *Mouthpiece*, ..counsel. **1883** GREENWOOD *Odd People* (1888) 18 It was for the benefit of a man..who was 'in trouble'..to 'procure him a mouthpiece',—which..is another word for a defending counsel among those sort of characters. **1914** [see FIXER 1]. **1926** E. WALLACE *More Educated Evans* iv. 91 Mouthpiece!.. Why, all these so-and-so lawyers hang together. **1931** [see BOTTLE *sb.*[2] 1 g (*a*)]. **1960** L. COOPER *Accomplices* III. iii. 164 I'm an Australian citizen and I know my rights and I want to see my mouthpiece before I say any more. **1974** 'P. B. YUILL' *Hazell plays Solomon* xii. 144 The Abreys would get legal aid. The state would fix them up with a good mouthpiece.

5. A protector for the mouth; a respirator.

1884 *Health Exhib. Catal.* 129/1 Mouthpiece for unhealthy and poisonous trades.

mouthy ('maʊðɪ), *a.* [f. MOUTH *sb.* + -Y.] Characterized by railing, ranting, or the use of bombastic language: **a.** of persons.

1589 PUTTENHAM *Eng. Poesie* III. xvii. (Arb.) 189 As another said to a mouthy Aduocate, why barkest thou at me so sore? **1617** COLLINS *Def. Bp. Ely* To Rdr. 15 Bestow these thy qualicums (thou mouthy Sophister) vpon some younger eares. **1819** BYRON *Juan* I. ccv, Thou shalt not set up Wordsworth, Coleridge, Southey; Because the first is crazed ..the third so quaint and mouthy. **1850** W. IRVING *Goldsmith* 137 He..was prone to be mouthy and magniloquent. **1957** M. SPARK *Comforters* v. 102 Before they said good night, Eleanor, slurred and mouthy, declared, 'Now, Laurence, take care of Caroline.' **1963** W. H. BOORE *Valley & Shadow* ix. 43 Too free you have been ..with your talk... Too mouthy all of you. **1968** *Sun Mag.* (Baltimore) 13 Oct. 19/2, I was kind of a big mouth. I wasn't a bully, just mouthy. **1972** *News & Observer* (Raleigh, N. Carolina) 30 Dec. 4/2 Whatever else they are, kids aren't biggity, mouthy [any more].

b. of language.

1827 *Blackw. Mag.* XXI. 737 Much more to the same purpose, mouthy and magnificent. **1887** *Athenæum* 3 Sept. 302/3 Although somewhat 'mouthy', it [the poem] possesses considerable power and impressiveness.

c. Of a hound: (see quots.).

1946 M. C. SELF *Horseman's Encycl.* 457 A hound that is noisy and a babbler is said to be 'mouthy'. **1968** J. GORDON *Beagle Guide* 173 A hound which babbles or is unnecessarily noisy is said to be mouthy.

Hence '**mouthily** *adv.*, '**mouthiness**.

1830 *Blackw. Mag.* XXVII. 142 Playing the Mocking Bird to the Muse, with a monotonous mouthiness..that cannot deceive a schoolboy.

moutne, obs. form of MUTTON.

mouton ('muːtɒn). Forms: 4–6 **moto(u)n**, 5 **moutoun**, 6 **motton**, 7, 9 **mutton**, 6–9 **mouton**. [a. OF. *mouton*, lit. 'sheep' (see MUTTON).]

1. *Hist.* A French gold coin, bearing the figure of the Lamb of God (whence the name), current in the 14th and 15th centuries.

The 'mouton' issued by Edw. III and Hen. V for use in the English possessions in France, is said to have had the value of five shillings sterling.

1377 LANGL. *P. Pl.* B. III. 24 Mildeliche Mede..gaf.. The leste man of here meyne a motoun of golde. **1494** FABYAN *Chron.* (1533) 104 b/1, A moton is a coyne vsed in Fraunce and Brytayne, and is of value after the rate of sterlynge money vppon v. s. or there aboute. **1523** LD. BERNERS *Froiss.* I. clxxi. 208 These thre estates [France, 1356] made newe money to be forged of fyne gold, called moutons. **1562** LEIGH *Armorie* 229 Certeyne skinnes, of this beast [the Panther], whiche were valued, at 5000 mottons of gold. **1828** SCOTT *F.M. Perth* vi, My father..will pay you gallantly—a French mutton for every hide I have spoiled. **1894** LANE-POOLE *Coins & Medals* 111 The gold coins of Edw. III. were the *guiennois*..and *mouton* (Paschal Lamb). *Ibid.* 112 Henry V. struck in gold moutons and demi-moutons.

2. *Hist.* (See quot.) Cf. *ram.*

1523 LD. BERNERS *Froiss.* I. ccccxiii. 701 They..made..a marueylus gret engyn, xx. fote large and xl. foote longe; they called this engyn a moton; it was to cast gret stones into the towne to beate downe houses.

‖**3.** (Pronounced (mutɔ̃).) A spy quartered with an accused person with a view to obtaining incriminating evidence.

1804 *Edin. Rev.* III. 442 A *mouton*, or jail-spy [was] quartered in his chamber. **1902** LANG *Hist. Scotl.* II. ix. 239 A mouton or prison-spy had extracted much of the truth from Bailey.

4. (See quot. 1950.)

1950 WEBSTER Add., *Mouton*, the skin of sheep, usually of Merino Sheep, processed, sheared, and dyed to resemble beaver or a certain type of seal. **1963** *Retail Trading-Standards Assoc. Bull.* Aug./Sept. 3/1 The following names [for furs] may be used notwithstanding the general rule:—*Animal*: Sheep (skin). *Accepted Trade Name*: Lamb or Mouton.

mouton, obs. form of MUTTON.

‖**mouton enragé** (mutɔ̃ ɑ̃raʒe). [Fr., lit. angry sheep.] A normally calm person who has become suddenly enraged or violent.

1932 *Times Lit. Suppl.* 27 Oct. 784/4 Her *mouton enragé* of a discarded adorer. **1955** J. THOMAS *No Banners* xii. 101 Many of them were peace-loving idealists who, like *moutons enragés*, had been literally goaded into ridding the earth of the Nazi pestilence. **1965** *Economist* 23 Jan. 307/1 The most unenviable reputation as the *moutons enragés* of this Parliament.

‖**moutonnée** (mutɔne), *a.* *Geol.* Also in adapted form **moutonnéed**. [Fr. (in *roche moutonnée*), fem. pa. pple. of *moutonner*, f. *mouton* sheep: see MUTTON.] Rounded like a sheep's back: said of rocks that have been subjected to glacial action.

1872 W. S. SYMONDS *Rec. Rocks* ii. 23 At a point close to the road..is a roche moutonnée..and on the opposite side of the lake is a hill moutonnéed and rounded like a barrow. **1876** A. H. GREEN *Phys. Geol.* (1877) 456 If the moutonnéed surfaces are preserved, we learn from them in what direction to look for the source of the ice. **1893** H. H. HOWORTH *Glacial Nightmare* II. 428 We ought to have the proper marks of ice action..polished, moutonnée surfaces.

Mouton Rothschild ('mutɔ̃ 'rɒθstʃaɪld). A type of Médoc produced in the Château Mouton-Rothschild, formerly the Château Mouton d'Armailhacq until purchased by the Rothschild family in 1853. Also *ellipt.* as *Mouton*.

[**1860** C. REDDING *French Wines & Vineyards* ix. 82 Messrs. Scott,..and d'Armailhac, at Mouton,..are the largest producers... The famous Bran-Mouton is from this district.] **1877** TROLLOPE *Amer. Senator* II. xv. 156, I think you will find that claret what you like... It's a '57 Mouton. **1888** *Encycl. Brit.* XXIV. 605/1 Second Growths. Château Mouton-Rothschild, Pauillac. **1935** M. MORPHY *Recipes of all Nations* 102 (*heading*) Growths: Among the best are Château Mouton-Rothschild. **1958** A. L. SIMON *Dict. Wines* 115/2 *Mouton-Rothschild, Château*, the first of the second *Crus Classés* of the Médoc (Pauillac). **1974** L. DEIGHTON *Spy Story* xi. 111 What's he going to do..? Put Mouton Rothschild labels on the Algerian? **1974** *Listener* 18 Apr. 487/1 In July 1973 the French Government saw the light and elevated Chateau Mouton Rothschild to one of the top five wines of the Médoc.

‖**mouvementé** (muvmɑ̃te), *a.* [Fr.] Animated, agitated, bustling, full of variety; *spec.* of music: lively.

1918 L. STRACHEY *Eminent Victorians* 238 The next three years were the most *mouvementés* of his life. **1929** *Theatre Arts Monthly* Mar. 231/2 The chief figure of her time led a life exceedingly *mouvementé*. **1938** *Oxf. Compan. Mus.* 597/1 *Mouvementé*, 'bustling', animated. **1950** A. L. ROWSE *England of Elizabeth* vi. 222 We may say that Tudor society was..more flexible and *mouvementé* than is altogether realised. **1961** B. FERGUSSON *Watery Maze* viii. 201 He had so far had a highly *mouvementé* war, beginning in a Q-ship in Norwegian waters before being appointed navigating officer to the force assembled early in 1941 for the assault on Rhodes. **1963** G. BATTISCOMBE *John Keble* i. 4 Even today.. the district round Oxford can hardly be described as *mouvementé*. **1965** *Guardian* 8 Dec. 8/5 Her life has been unusually mouvementé—and erratic.

mouwe, mouwen, obs. ff. MOW, MAY *v.*[1]

mouzhik, var. MOUJIK, MUZHIK.

mouzle, mouzy, var. ff. MOUSLE *v.*, MOSY *a.*

movability (muːvə'bɪlɪtɪ). Forms: 3–4 **moeuablite**, 9 **mov(e)ability**. [f. MOVABLE *a.*: see -ITY. (Chaucer's form is a. OF. *movableté*.)] The quality or condition of being movable; mobility.

c **1374** CHAUCER *Boeth.* IV. Pr. vi. 106 (Camb. MS.) They sormownten the ordre of destynal moeuablete. **1824** LOUDON *Encycl. Gardening* §926 Primitive surfaces affect vegetables mechanically according to their different degrees of moveability or tenacity. **1846** BRITTAN tr. *Malgaigne's Man. Oper. Surg.* 295 The eye had resumed its moveability on the inside but not on the outside. **1894** *Thinker Mag.* V. 153 Without beginning, without any movability of change, and without end.

movable, moveable ('muːvəb(ə)l), *a.* and *sb.* Forms: 4 **moeveable, movabele**, 4–5 **moevable**, 5 **me(o)veable, mov(ey)abylle, mofabil**, 5–6 **mevable**, 6 **movabul**, (*Sc.*) **movabil(l**, 7 **mooveable**, *Sc.* **movabell**, 5– **movable, moveable**. [a. OF. *movable*, f. *mov-oir* (mod.F. *mouvoir*) to MOVE: see -ABLE. Cf. MOBLE, MOBILE.]

A. *adj.*

†**1.** Apt or disposed to movement; quick or ready in movement; having a tendency to move. *Obs.*

1398 TREVISA *Barth. De P.R.* XI. i. (1495) 381 By cause of his substancyall lyghtnesse ayre is kyndly meuable and also chaungable. *c* **1400** MAUNDEV. (1839) xv. 162 Therfore is ther gret multitude of peple: but thei ben not sterynge ne mevable, be cause that thei ben in the firste Clymat, that is of Saturne. **1426** LYDG. *De Guil. Pilgr.* 12332 And thyderward they [the planets] be meveable, To thylke poynt to kome ageyn, Fro wych they meuede ffyrst certeyn. **1526** *Pilgr. Perf.* (W. de W. 1531) 234 Of all the membres of the body, nature hath made the eye moost mouable. **1592** R. D. *Hypnerotomachia* 83 b, And somtimes her fine and moveable legges..discovered themselves. **1607** TOPSELL *Four-f. Beasts* (1658) 188 Goats are nimble, moveable, and inconstant, and therefore apt to depart away, except they be restrained by the herd and his Dog. **1705** ADDISON *Italy* 370 Any one that sees the Teverone must..conclude it to be one of the most moveable Rivers in the World, that has its Stream broken by such a Multitude of Cascades, and is so often shifted out of one Channel into other.

†**2.** *fig.* Changeable, fickle, inconstant; capable of being influenced or prevailed upon. *Obs.*

c **1374** CHAUCER *Boeth.* IV. Met. v. 103 (Camb. MS.) The moeuable poeple [orig. *mobile vulgus*]. **1477** EARL RIVERS (Caxton) *Dictes* 75 Trust not in eny thingis of this moeuaeble world. **1582** N. LICHEFIELD tr. *Castanheda's Conq. E. Ind.* I. xxi. 55 The King was moueable, and therefore it was possible that the Moores would alter his minde. **1611** BIBLE *Prov.* v. 6 Her wayes are moueable, that thou canst not know them. **1682** BUNYAN *Holy War* 129 O full of deceit, how movable are thy ways! how often hast thou changed and rechanged.

3. Capable of being moved; not fixed in one place or posture. Sometimes used *Phys.* and *Path.* as a synonym of FLOATING *ppl. a.*, as in ***movable kidney, rib.***

a **1400** in Halliwell *Rara Mathem.* (1841) 65 þe side of þe quadrat bitwene A and B mote be persede reulefully, in whilk persyng put a chippe like þe oþer thre, bot it sale be moveable fro A to B. **1539** in *Archæologia* XI. 440, 4 payer of geests of woode dormint, two payer of geests movable. **1553** EDEN *Decades* 360 The degrees of the Equinoctiall distaunte..from the moueable meridian. **1597** HOOKER *Eccl. Pol.* v. xi. §1 In the vast wildernes when the people of God had themselues no settled habitation, yet a moueable tabernacle they were commanded of God to make. **1656** *Hobbes's Elem. Philos.* (1839) 141 We must also have in our mind an imagination of some moveable thing passing over that line. **1707** MORTIMER *Husb.* (1721) II. 282 He was proposing to me to have a moveable Sty, and about it to make a Yard with Hurdles, to remove from one Tree to another. **1788** COWPER *Gratitude* 25 This moveable structure of shelves. **1802** C. JAMES *Milit. Dict.* s.v., When the pivot flank of any body of men describe in the wheel a smaller circle than the wheeling flank, the wheel is said to be made on a moveable pivot. **1849** MACAULAY *Hist. Eng.* iii. I. 346 Some of these cabins were moveable, and were carried on sledges from one part of the common to another. **1835–6** OWEN in *Todd's Cycl. Anat.* I. 280/2 If the moveable ribs had commenced as in Mammalia, by extending to the sternum. **1878** tr. *von Ziemssen's Cycl. Med.* XV. 763 The clinical history of the movable kidney dates from the time of Rayer. **1879** HARLAN *Eyesight* ii. 23 The upper lid..is very movable, while the lower one is almost stationary.

4. Of property: Admitting of being removed or displaced; applied to 'personal' as opposed to 'real' property. In *Sc. Law*, the distinctive appellation of such property as does not pass by inheritance: opposed to HERITABLE *a.*

1418 *E.E. Wills* (1882) 32 Alle othere meuable Godes ther-in beyng. **1482** *Charters Edinb.* (1871) 156 Gudis mofabil and vnmofabill. **1538** in *Lett. Suppress. Monasteries* (Camden) 175 Certen other catell and movable goodes that dyd belong to the howse. **1549** *Compl. Scot.* xvii. 150 Ane person may succeid to heretage and to mouabil gudis of his predecessours. **1618** NAUNTON in *Fortescue Papers* (Camden) 63 Who committed her and her porcion and all her moveable estate unto me at his death. **1754** ERSKINE *Princ. Sc. Law* (1809) 71 The right of the husband to the wife's moveable estate, is burdened with the moveable debts contracted by her before marriage. **1818** HALLAM *Mid. Ages* vii. (1868) 376 The first eminent instance of a general tax required from the clergy was the famous Saladine tithe; a tenth of all movable estate, imposed by the kings of France and England upon all their subjects..to defray the expense of their intended crusade. **1838** W. BELL *Dict. Law Scotl.* s.v. *Heritable and moveable*, Things, in their nature heritable, may become moveable by being made part of a moveable *universitas*. Thus, a share of heritable subjects, forming part of the stock of a trading company is moveable. **1871** FREEMAN *Norm. Conq.* xvii. (1876) IV. 60 Besides these seizures of landed property William also possessed himself of great moveable wealth from various sources.

5. Changing from one date to another every year.

movable feast: one which, though always on the same day of the week, varies its date in the calendar.

1430 in Halliwell *Rara Mathem.* (1841) 92 þe table of þe 5 festes moveyabylle. *c* **1440** *Astron. Cal.* (MS. Ashm. 391), Than foloweþ a noþer table of all mouable feestes. **1694** HOLDER *Disc. Time* i. 20 The Lunar Month..by which the Moveable Festivals of the Christian Church are regulated. **1825** HONE *Every-Day Bk.* I. 189 Shrove Tuesday regulates most of the moveable feasts.

transf. (*Mod. colloq.*) Breakfast is a movable feast with us.

†**6.** *Astron.* (See quot. 1696.) *Obs. rare.*

1647 LILLY *Chr. Astrol.* vii. 52 If she [i.e. the moon] be posited therein, especially in a moodable [*sic*] Signe, it's an argument of much travell, trotting and trudging. **1696** PHILLIPS (ed. 5), *Moveable Signs*, the same that are named Cardinal, as *Aries*, *Cancer*, *Libra*, and *Capricorn*, as from which the Changes of the Seasons are made in Spring, Summer, Autumn, and Winter.

7. a. *Semitic Grammar.* Of certain letters, etc.: Pronounced; not 'quiescent'.

1837 G. PHILLIPS *Syriac Gram.* 33 In the plural Yud quiescent is changed into Yud moveable. **1839** CONANT tr. *Gesenius' Hebr. Gram.* 15 Where they [*sc.* א, ה, ו, י] serve as vowels they are called quiescents (*quiescentes*); where they are consonants, moveable (*mobiles*). **1847** M^c CAUL *Introd. Hebr. Gram.* 9 The Gutturals, when a moveable Sh'va is required, take the compound Sh'va.

b. *Philol.* Designating a consonant or other element affixed to a word, usu. under determined phonetic conditions.

1933 C. D. BUCK *Compar. Gram. Greek & Latin* 160 The ν movable in forms like λέγουσι(ν), εἶπε(ν), etc., is an added element which, except for a few examples of dat. pl. -σιν in other dialects, is peculiar to Attic-Ionic. **1951** STURTEVANT & HAHN *Compar. Gram. Hittite Lang.* (ed. 2) 66, *s* Movable. **1958** PRIEBSCH & COLLINSON *German Lang.* (rev. ed.) 70 'Movable' *s* is prefixed in Indo-European to many roots. **1973** A. H. SOMMERSTEIN *Sound Pattern Anc. Greek* ii. 40 *Moveable Nu.* This is the name given in traditional studies of Greek to a dental nasal which is inserted at the end of certain words that would otherwise end in a vowel, if the following word begins with a vowel or [h] (that is, with a non-consonantal segment), or if a major pause follows.

8. ***movable type***: pieces of metal type, individually cast, usu. with reference to early printing.

[**1732** S. PALMER *Gen. Hist. Printing* 5 With the great space so many Pages of Wood must take up, we shall perceive the necessity of inventing moveable Metal Types.] **1770** P. LUCKOMBE *Conc. Hist. Printing* 2 Those who have asserted that Faust was the first inventor of printing, have given for a reason, that they have never seen any book with Guttemberg's name to it; without considering, that their first essays in printing, both by blocks and moveable types, ..were anonymous. **1816** W. Y. OTTLEY *Inquiry Orig. & Early Hist. Engraving* I. 6 The prodigious number of these characters..renders it impracticable for them [*sc.* the Chinese] to print their books with moveable types. **1859** *Abridgements of Specifications relating to Printing* (Patent Office) 15 Where, when, and by whom printing with moveable types was first practised, it seems impossible to determine with any certainty. **1933** T. S. BARBER in W. Atkins *Art & Pract. Printing* IV. xx. 239 One of the difficulties encountered in actual printing with movable types was the fact that at times they moved and became displaced when the printer had no desire they should. **1955** S. H. STEINBERG *500 Yrs. Printing* i. 22 The available evidence about the invention of printing with movable types cast from matrices is unfortunately less conclusive than might be wished. **1965** J. MORAN *Composition of Reading Matter* i. 11 The basis of making pieces of movable type was the punch, matrix and mould. **1974** *Bertram Rota Ltd. Catal.* No. 192. 2 Now the steady advance of film-setting may be heralding the beginning of the end of printing from moveable type.

B. *sb.*

†**1.** In the Ptolemaic astronomy: Any of the nine concentric revolving spheres of the heavens. Chiefly in ***first*** or ***highest movable*** = PRIMUM MOBILE. *Obs.*

c **1391** CHAUCER *Astrol.* I. §17 And *nota*, that firste Moeuyng is cleped 'Moeuyng' of the firste Moeuable of the 8 spere. *a* **1649** DRUMM. OF HAWTH. *Irene* Wks. (1711) 171 The planets have a motion contrary to the first moveable. **1669** STURMY *Mariner's Mag.* I. i. 2 The Figure, Number, and Motion made in the Heavens by the highest Moveable called Primum Mobile. **1690** LEYBOURN *Curs. Math.* 760, I now enter upon their Hypotheses, that suppose it [the Earth] to be mov'd about the Sun. But before the Phaenomena of the secondary Moveables can be explained by this supposition, we must first understand [etc.].

2. *pl.* Personal property; property that is capable of being moved; any species of property not fixed, as distinguished from real or fixed property (as land, houses, etc.). In *Sc.* and *Civil Law*, 'movable' as distinguished from 'heritable' property (see A.4).

c **1440** *Gesta Rom.* xiv. 180 (Add. MS.) My sone, I have none mevables that I may yeve to the, But I have iij. Iewelx, that I bequethe to the. **1537** *Bury Wills* (Camden) 133, I wyll that Margary my wyff haue all my mouables, as corne and catall. **1594** SHAKS. *Rich. III*, III. i. 195 When I am King, clayme thou of me The Earledome of Hereford, and all the moueables Whereof the King, my Brother, was possest. *a* **1655** VINES *Lord's Supp.* (1677) 113 These I say are moveables and not of the free-hold. **1766** W. GORDON *Gen. Counting-ho.* 486 Moveables..is the stock that receives the addition, diminution, or variation. **1884** *Law Times Rep.* LI. 119/1 The property..as regards movables..is governed by the law of Spain, the country of her domicile.

3. An article of furniture that may be removed from the building in which it is placed: opposed to *fixture*. Now chiefly in *pl.* †Also, a portable object belonging to a person, as an article of clothing, a jewel, a tool, etc. (*obs.*).

1523 LD. BERNERS *Froiss.* I. clv. 187 They shall pay nothyng for that they may spende aboue v.M.li. nor for their mouables. **1596** SHAKS. *Tam. Shr.* II. i. 198 You were a mouable. *Pet.* Why, what's a mouable? *Kat.* A ioyn'd stoole. **1605** B. JONSON *Volpone* IV. i, I..tooke me a house, Dealt with my Iewes, to furnish it with moueables. **1645** EVELYN *Diary* 5 May, It has in the middle a hall furnish'd with excellent marbles and rare pictures..the moveables are princely and rich. **1685** SIR E. VERNEY *MS. Let. to Son at Oxford* June, I will supply you with [money] very shortly but not to lay out in vain moveables. *a* **1700** B. E. *Dict. Cant. Crew, Moveables*, Rings, Watches, Swords, and such Toies of value. As we bit all the Cull's Cole and Moveables, we Won all the Man's Money, Rings, Watches, &c. **1709** STEELE *Tatler* No. 49 ¶7 As capable of being dispos'd of elsewhere, as any other Moveable. **1727–41** CHAMBERS *Cycl., Parasol*, a little moveable, in manner of a canopy, bore in the hand to screen the head from the sun, rain, &c. **1820** BYRON *Let. to Hoppner* 20 Jan., I wrote to you..for my movables. **1878** SIR G. G. SCOTT *Lect. Archit.* I. 328 The movables..are the richest inheritance of the German churches... Besides the more ordinary objects, such as chancel fittings, reredoses, bronze gates [etc.].

fig. **1841** EMERSON *Misc.* (1855) 222 So that a man may say, his religion is now no more within himself, but is become a dividual movable.

†**4. a.** Something capable of being moved or set in motion. *Obs.*

1629 H. BURTON *Truths Triumph* 348 He would remoue this whole terrestriall Globe, if he had but a Ground or Base to fasten his Engine vpon (although the Base must needes be farre bigger than the Moueable). **1656** [? J. SERGEANT] tr. *T. White's Peripat. Inst.* 73 If a Moveable be violently struck against a hard resister. **1682** CREECH tr. *Lucretius* I. (1683) 13 This could not be, were there no empty space, Thro which these Moveables might freely pass.

†**b.** *spec.* Any part of the 'works' of a watch. *Obs.*

1709 *Lond. Gaz.* No. 4599/4 Lost.., a small Gold Watch with a plain Gold Case, the Moveables pretty old. **1779** *Phil. Trans.* LXVIII. 979 What is meant by a pinion in watch-making is that moveable which is set in action by another of a greater number of teeth.

†**5.** A person given to movement or change.

1621–2 LAUD. *Serm.* 24 Mar. 35 And this is a great Successe. To haue to doe with the greatest mooueables in the world, the people, and not miscarry. **1632** MARMION *Holland's Leaguer* I. i, His business Is only to be busy, and his tongue's still walking Though himself be one of the worst moveables. **1658** E. PHILLIPS *Myst. Love* 175 What is a Tinker? He is a moveable, for he hath no certain abiding.

†**'movabled,** *a. Obs. rare*$^{-1}$. [f. MOVABLE *sb.* + -ED[2].] Furnished with 'movables'; furnished.

a **1693** *Urquhart's Rabelais* III. xvii. 137 That straw-thatch'd Cottage, scurvily built, naughtily movabled.

movableness ('mu:vəb(ə)lnɪs). [-NESS.] The attribute of being movable; mobility.

1398 TREVISA *Barth. De P.R.* V. xxix. (1495) 140 The meuablenes of the fingres is conuenyent to take and to holde. **1530** PALSGR. 246/2 Movableness, *mobilité*. **1643** LIGHTFOOT *Glean. Ex.* (1648) 22 This mooveablenesse of this Feast. **1878** SPURGEON *Treas. Dav.* Ps. cxiv. 4 The movableness of things which appear to be fixed and settled.

movably ('mu:vəblɪ), *adv. rare.* [-LY[2].] In a movable manner; so as to be movable.

1681 GREW *Musæum* I. i. §2. 20 His [the Armadillo's] Back-piece..is composed of several Plates, in number eighteen, moveably joyned together by as many intermediate Skins. **1835–6** OWEN in *Todd's Cycl. Anat.* I. 281/1 The true ribs are not joined to the sternum by elastic cartilages, but by straight osseous portions, called sternal ribs, which are moveably connected at both their extremities. **1899** CAGNEY tr. *Jaksch's Clin. Diagn.* x. (ed. 4) 431 An Abbe's or other condenser adjusted movably to the microscope-stand is needed.

†**'moval.** *Obs. rare.* [f. MOVE *v.* + -AL[1], after *removal*.] The fact of being moved.

1632 VICARS *Virgil* VIII. 315 Whereat he by and by Put forth his strength, and rous'd it from the root, And it remov'd: whose movall with loud shout Did fill the echoing aire. **1769** R. GRIFFITH *Gordian Knot* I. 44 (F. H.).

movant ('mu:vənt). *U.S. Law.* [f. MOVE *v.* + -ANT[1]: cf. MOVENT *a.* b.] One who applies to or petitions a court of law or a judge with the intention of obtaining a ruling in his favour. Also *attrib.* or as *adj.*

1927 *Corpus Juris* XLII. 517/1 A 'renewal' of the motion, so-called, is the remedy usually available to the dissatisfied movant whose motion has been denied. **1949** *Corpus Juris Secundum* LX. 38/1 Relief to Movant... In the absence of a prayer for general relief, the moving party usually is confined to the relief asked for in his motion. **1961** *Words & Phrases State & Federal Courts* XXVII. A. 353/1 Intention was that such statute should be remedial in operation, to permit court to correct errors..into which it has been led.. by the party opposing movant. **1972** *N.Y. Law Jrnl.* 22 Aug. 2/3 Motion is granted and the requested subpoena shall issue. Movant shall furnish a copy of the records produced to the other parties. **1973** *Ibid.* 19 July 11/1 The movant fails to establish either defective service of the notice of petition and petition, upon which the default was granted, or a meritorious defense thereto, since nothing is asserted beyond an expression of dissatisfaction with the award. *Ibid.* 1 Aug. 14/2 It is ordered that this motion by defendant..is denied without prejudice to the right of movant defendant to oppose the application of a general preference made by plaintiffs.

move (mu:v), *sb.* Also 5 **meeve**. [f. MOVE *v.*]

†**1.** A proposal: motion. *Obs. rare*$^{-1}$.

1439 *Rolls of Parlt.* V. 17/2 Ye seide John, many tymes hath made diverse meeves and tretice, for to have pees with ye seide Phelip.

2. a. *Chess, Draughts*, etc. The moving or changing of position of a piece in the regular course of the game; the manner or mode in which a piece is allowed to be moved; (a player's) turn to move. (Cf. REMOVE *sb.* 3 c.)

the move: the right to make the first move in the game (similarly in ***pawn and move*** in chess, with reference to odds); also the superiority of position (at any stage of the game) which depends on having the turn to move at the right moment.

1656 COWLEY *Pindar. Odes, Destiny* ii, I saw two Angels play'd the Mate. With Man, alas, no otherwise it proves; An unseen Hand makes all their Moves. **1761** HOYLE (*title*) An Essay towards making the Game of Chess easily learned, by those who know the moves only. **1797** *Encycl. Brit.* (ed. 3) IV. 640/2 When the game is near finished, each party having only three or four pawns,..the kings must endeavour to gain the move. **1800** J. STURGES *Draughts* 2 The first move of each Game to be taken by both players alternately. **1808** SARRATT *Chess* (1822) 3 The player who gives odds has always the advantage of the move; except, of course, in those games where the move is also given to the inferior player. **1850** *Bohn's Handbk. Games* 381 (Backgammon) The moves of the men are determined by the throws of the dice. **1870** HARDY & WARE *Mod. Hoyle, Draughts* 107 White may.. capture the whole of the three black men in one move. **1876** W. N. POTTER in *Encycl. Brit.* V. 592/1 Those to whom the masters of the game can only concede the small odds of 'pawn and move'. *Ibid.* 593/2 *Castling*.—This is a peculiar move permitted to the king once in the game. **1884** TENNYSON *Becket* Prol. 8 *Becket.* It is your move. *Henry.* Well—there.

b. *fig.* A device, trick; an action calculated to secure some end. ***a (good, bad,*** etc.) ***move***: a (prudent or imprudent) step or proceeding. ***to be up to every move on the board, to be up to*** (or ***know) a move or two***: to be cunning, smart, wide-awake, experienced.

1812 J. H. VAUX *Flash Dict.* s.v., To be flash to every move upon the board, is to have a general knowledge of the world, and all its numerous deceptions. **1840** HALIBURTON *Clockm.* Ser. III. viii. 105 And a-travellin' about, and a-livin' on the best, and sleepin' in the spare bed always, ain't a bad move nother. **1844** DICKENS *Christmas Carol* iii, Gentlemen of the free-and-easy sort, who plume themselves on being acquainted with a move or two. **1861** HUGHES *Tom Brown at Oxf.* vi. A cunning old beggar,..up to every move on the board. **1868** E. YATES *Rock Ahead* III. ii, He has sent for his own housekeeper, which is a good move. **1884** *Gd. Words* June 400/1 The practical details of prison discipline, and the moves by which its rigours may be softened or evaded by the old birds.

3. ***on the move***: in process of moving from one place to another, travelling, moving about.

1796 *Instr. & Reg. Cavalry* (1813) 165 Column of half squadrons is then formed, either from the halt, or on the move. **1811** L. M. HAWKINS *C'tess. & Gertr.* II. 357 (K.O.) On the move [said of people]. **1849** THACKERAY *Pendennis* xxxi, Everybody seemed to be busy, humming, and on the move. **1889** JESSOPP *Coming of Friars* ii. 104 The Bishop.. was always on the move when he was in his diocese.

fig. **1881** TYLOR *Anthrop.* i. 18 It does not follow from such arguments as these that civilization is always on the move, or that its movement is always progress.

4. An act of moving from a stationary position; a beginning of movement or departure; a 'rise' from the (dinner) table (to go to the drawing-room), etc.; esp. in phrase ***to make a move***.

1827 DISRAELI *Viv. Grey* v. vi, The Grand Duke, bowing to his circle, made a move. **1855** HALIBURTON *Nat. & Hum. Nat.* I. xii. 381 So in due time we parted... Cutler made the first move by ascending the companion-ladder. **1856** WHYTE MELVILLE *Kate Cov.* xx, Lady Scapegrace..'made the move', at which we all sailed away to tea and coffee in the drawing-room. *Ibid.* xxi, Directly there was a move, the ladies went to bed. **1858** GREENER *Gunnery* 76 The great principle in a propellant force is so to arrange it that you do not obtain too great a velocity at the first move of the projectile. **1883** *Daily Tel.* 10 Nov. 5/1 Without such decided moves forward on his part, many other friends of progress would have hesitated to move at all.

5. A change of habitation or place of sojourn.

1853 LYNCH *Self-Improv.* 47 Christianity is just now moving to a larger house, and everybody knows how confusing and laborious a move is. **1857** MRS. CARLYLE *Lett.* (1883) II. 325 Making no further move that is not a move homeward. **1885** *Manch. Exam.* 29 June 5/3 The first holiday-seekers are making a move to the seaside.

6. *colloq.* (orig. *U.S.*) ***to get a move on one***: to hasten one's steps, to hurry up. Now usu. ***to get a move on.***

1888 *Troy* (Alabama) *Enquirer* 28 July, Get a move on you. **1893** *Columbus* (Ohio) *Dispatch* 7 July, Now is the time for the mover of dead animals 'to get a move on himself'. **1899** A. H. QUINN *Pennsylvania Stories* 138 Come, get a move on. **1906** E. DYSON *Fact'ry 'Ands* xiv. 183 Get er move on, 'r you'll get ther shoot. **1911** C. E. MULFORD *Bar-20 Days* x. 107 Come on! Come on!.. Get a move on! Will you hurry up! *Ibid.* xx. 198 But why in Jericho don't you fellers get a move on you? **1914** W. G. LAWRENCE *Let.* 13 Aug. in T. E. Lawrence *Home Lett.* (1954) 569 In ten days time we should get a move on, but we won't go far. **1920** [see GAS *sb.*[1]]. **1937** D. L. SAYERS *Busman's Honeymoon* vii. 149, I only hope they're getting a move on out there. **1973** 'D. MARINER' *Beaufort Dossier* vii. 138 What about getting a move on, then! Get out on the flaming roof an' grab them!

7. *Glass-making.* (See quot.)

1849 PELLATT *Curios. Glass Making* 90 The mode of reckoning the piece-work of Glass-makers is peculiar. The 'move', as it is technically called, is a nominal period of six hours; and the payment is proportionate to the number of articles supposed, by fair exertion, capable of being made in that time by a set of ordinary workmen.

8. *Comb.* **move-man** (see quots.).

1923 J. M. SCOTT-MAXWELL *Costing & Price-fixing* 94 Move-men are the men who move the raw material and manufactured parts from the store to the shop, and move all jobs from one machine to another or one department to another. **1955** *Amer. Speech* XXX. 226 *Move man*, the dispatcher in the [aircraft production] shop who moves parts from one operation to the next.

move (mu:v), *v.* Inflected moving, moved. Forms: *α.* 3–5 **meove**, 3–6 **moeve, meve**, 4–5 **mew(e, meuve, mefe, meefe, meffe**, 4–6 **meeve**, 6 **mieve**. *β.* 3– **move**, (4 **mwe**), 4–6 *north.* **mow(e**, 4–7 **moove**. Also *north.* and *Sc.* 4–6 **mofe**, 5 **moffe, moyfe, moyff, mowff, muff, mwff**, 5–6 **muve, mufe**, 6 **muif, moif(f, mwve**. [ME. *move*, a. AF. *mov-er*, OF. *mov-oir*, *mouvoir* (mod.F. *mouvoir*), = Pr., Sp., Pg. *mover*, It. *movere*, *muovere*:—L. *movēre* (derivation-stem *mō-* for **movi-*: see MOBILE *a.*, MOMENT, MOTILE *a.*, MOTION, MOTIVE, MOTOR). The intransitive use (developed from refl.), almost non-existent in Latin and in mod.Fr., was extensively current in OFr., and came into Eng. at least as early as the transitive use.

The *α* forms, *moeve, meove, mēve* represent the OF. flexional forms with root-stress, e.g. 3 plur. pres. ind. *muevent, moevent* (mod. F. *meuvent*). Cf. the parallel forms of PROVE *v.*, and the ME. *poeple, people, pēple* repr. OF. *pueple, poeple* (mod.F. *peuple*), PEOPLE *sb.*]

I. Transitive senses.

1. a. To change the place or position of; to take from one place or situation to another; to shift, remove; *occas.* to dislodge or displace (something fixed). Also, ***to move away, along***, etc.

1382 WYCLIF *Acts* v. 6 ȝonge men rysinge mouedyn hym awey. *c* **1420** *Chron. Vilod.* 2498 þe vrthe þat my body lyȝt on, is mevyd, also, Y-mevyd alle from þe grounde an hyȝe. c 1440 *Promp. Parv.* 336/2 Mevyn, or remevyn,..*amoveo*. 1470–85 MALORY *Arthur* I. iii. 40 But none myght stere the swerd nor meue hit. 1535 COVERDALE *Job* xxxvii. 1 At this my hert is astonnied, and moued out of his place. [Also 1611.] 1697 DRYDEN *Virg. Georg.* III. 366 He moves his Camp, to meet his careless Foe. 1791 M. CUTLER in *Life*, etc. (1888) I. 466 My barn was moved from the Hubbard house round the north end of the Meeting House to my other barn. 1832 TENNYSON *Miller's Daughter* 125 At last you rose and moved the light. 1897 'SARAH GRAND' *Beth Bk.* xx, She.. moved the tray, and put the table back in its place.

fig. 1538 ELYOT *Dict.*, *Deduco*..sometime to moue from his purpose. 1601 BP. W. BARLOW *Serm. Paules Crosse* 30 Neither did it moue my affection from him. 1697 DRYDEN *Æneid* VII. 523 When she saw her Reasons idly spent, And cou'd not move him from his fix'd Intent; She flew to rage.

b. *Chess*, *Draughts*, etc. To change the position of (a piece) in the course of play; to transfer from one position to another. (Cf. REMOVE *v.* 2c.) †Also *refl.* of the piece (= sense 16e).

1474 CAXTON *Chesse* IV. ii. 163 We ought to knowe..how the kynge meueth hym and yssueth oute of his place. 1761 HOYLE *Ess. Chess* Pref., When you castle your King, do not move the Pawns before him till forced to it. 1800 J. STURGES *Draughts* 2 If..you move your Man..over the Angle which divides the Squares..you must finish your move so begun. 1884 TENNYSON *Becket* Prol., My liege, I move my bishop.

†c. To bring or apply (something) *to*; to administer (a remedy). *Obs.*

c 1374 CHAUCER *Boeth.* II. pr. iii. 25 (Camb. MS.) For wan þat tyme is, I shal moeue [L. *admovebo*] swych thinges þat percen hem self depe. 1538 ELYOT *Dict.*, *Admoueo*, to moue to, or put to. 1607 TOPSELL *Four-f. Beasts* (1658) 509 They use their forefeet in stead of hands,..and move their meat to their mouth with them. 1611 BIBLE *Deut.* xxiii. 25 But thou shalt not mooue a sickle vnto thy neighbours standing corne.

†d. To promote or advance *to* an office. (Cf. MOTION *sb.* 1f.) *Obs. rare.*

1556 LAUDER *Tractate* 335 And, geue thay haue the floke abusit, ȝe, Kyngs, sall be for that accusit.. Because ȝe mouit thame to sic curis Quhilk nother techis ryche nor puris.

e. To take off or lift (a hat, cap) from one's head, as a gesture of salutation.

1573 G. HARVEY *Letter-bk.* (Camden) 5, I passing bi him, and mouing mi cap. 1647 CLARENDON *Hist. Reb.* VII. §232 That every member might, as a testimony of his particular acknowledgment, stir or move his hat towards him; the which..when very many did, the lord Falkland,..instead of moving his hat,..held it close down to his head. 1825 T. COSNETT *Footman's Direct.* 175 Always show your respect to the family by moving your hat when you meet any of them.

f. *Comm.* in *passive*, of merchandise: To 'go off', find purchasers. Also *trans.*, to sell; to cause to be sold. Cf. 16j.

1900 *Daily News* 20 June 9/1 There has been a rather better demand for leather during the week, and some fair parcels have been moved. 1938 *Sun* (Baltimore) 20 Sept. 10/1 A drastic tax on chain stores has been defeated in a referendum in California, where the function of the chains in 'moving' citrus-fruit surpluses is now more fully appreciated. 1962 *Guardian* 5 Nov. 3/6 Our displays are moving about 25,000 cans a week. 1971 *Ibid.* 24 Dec. 2/5 The boys..are causing the sales lady a good deal of worry. ..She simply cannot move Indians this season, even with a wigwam. 1975 *Publishers Weekly* 6 Jan. 54/1 Booksellers should easily be able to move this slender 'autobiography' of Lincoln.

g. *Cricket.* To cause (the ball) to swerve.

1956 N. CARDUS *Close of Play* 37 We are supposed to be enlightened by news that Lindwall is 'moving' the ball. 1962 *Times* 24 May 4/2 Platt, however, kept plugging away around the good length mark, moving the ball a little either way and generally looking a thoroughly useful practitioner.

2. a. To put or keep in motion; to shake, stir, or disturb (an object which would otherwise be at rest).

to move heaven and earth: to make unheard-of efforts (*to* effect or obtain something).

1377 LANGL. *P. Pl.* B. XVI. 77 And þanne comsed it to crye, And wagged wydwehode and it wepte after. And whan it meued Matrimoigne it made a foule noyse. c 1384 CHAUCER *H. Fame* II. 305 Euery worde..That lowde or pryvee y-spoken ys, Moveth first an ayre a-boute, And of thys movynge, out of doute, Another ayre anoon ys meved. 1471 RIPLEY *Comp. Alch.* II. xv. in Ashm. *Theat. Chem. Brit.* (1652) 138 Beware thy Glasse thou never opyn ne meve. 1539 BIBLE (Great) *Ps.* lxviii. 8 Euen as Sinai also was moued at yᵉ presence of God. 1585 T. WASHINGTON tr. *Nicholay's Voy.* II. xv. 50 The chanell..was so moued that by great surges, it cast the water ouer the walles. 1792 A. YOUNG *Trav. France* 225 Englishmen..would move heaven and earth to establish a better conveyance, at a higher price. 1846 KEIGHTLEY *Notes Virg.*, *Bucol.* v. 5 The shadows..are unsteady, in consequence of the western breezes moving the trees. 1885 'F. ANSTEY' *Tinted Venus* 49 There's the police moving heaven and earth to get you back again.

b. To put or keep in motion which is of a continuous, regular, or recurrent kind, or which effects some result; to impel or agitate (an implement, etc.) in the proper way; to actuate (a machine). In early use chiefly of God as the mover of the universe. Also with advs. as *to and fro*, etc.

c 1375 *Sc. Leg. Saints* l. (*Katerine*) 475 ȝe suld kene þat bot a god sulde be, þat mad & mowis alkine thing. 1566 PAINTER *Pal. Pleas.* II. 308 The courteous Gods that gives me lyfe now mooves the planets all. 1651 HOBBES *Leviath.* Introd. 1 *Automata* (Engines that move themselves by springs and wheeles as doth a watch). 1709 *Tatler* No. 100 ¶1 As she moved it [a mirror] in her Hand, it brightened the Heavens, the Air, or the Earth. 1797 G. JEE in *Trans. Soc. Arts* XVI. 303 The handle is required to be turned one way only, which moves the machine more steadily. 1857 MILLER *Elem. Chem.* (1862) III. 193 If a glass rod be..moved quickly through the air.

3. a. Of a living being or its powers: To change the position or posture of (its body or any member).

1382 WYCLIF *Isa.* xxxvii. 22 Aftir thee the hed he mouede, thou maide doȝter of Jerusalem. 1398 TREVISA *Barth. De P.R.* III. xii. (1495) 55 The vertue that hyghte animalis motiua..moeuyth all the lymmes. 1533 GAU *Richt Vay* (S.T.S.) 83 Quhen men mwuis the mwtht and the lippis and the tunge wtuertlie without ye hart and mind. 1588 SHAKS. *L.L.L.* v. ii. 146 But shall we dance, if they desire vs too't? *Quee.* No, to the death we will not moue a foot. 1611 BIBLE *Exod.* xi. 7 But against any of the children of Israel, shal not a dog moue his tongue. 1807–26 COOPER *First Lines Surg.* (ed. 5) 274 Inability to move or use the limb. 1878 T. HARDY *Ret. Native* IV. vii, She moved her lips..but could not speak. 1907 J. H. PATTERSON *Man-Eaters of Tsavo* xviii. 201 Had either of us moved hand or foot just then, it would, I am convinced, have at once brought on another and probably a fatal charge.

†b. *refl.* To set oneself in motion, change place or posture, stir. Also, to go, proceed. = senses 16, 17.

c 1290 *St. Brendan* 674 in *S. Eng. Leg.* 238 þe fisch bi-gan to meouen him..And bar þis Monekes forth with him. c 1400 *Destr. Troy* 9740 Meue you with manhode to mar of your fos. c 1440 *Alphabet of Tales* 120 When a man is deadlie syn, all his membres is bon, & he may not mofe hym. c 1500 *Melusine* 8 He lept & mevyd hym as a man wakynge from slep. 1530 PALSGR. 641/1 He is so sycke that he can nat move hime in his bedde.

†4. To put forth, utter (sound). *Obs.*

1607 TOPSELL *Four-f. Beasts* (1658) 125 There is no creature that will more stir, bark, and move noise, then one of these against thief or wilde beast. 1667 MILTON *P.L.* III. 37 Then feed on thoughts, that voluntarie move Harmonious numbers. 1674 PLAYFORD *Skill Mus.* I. 58 A full Chorus of four or five Parts, which moveth a kind of Heavenly Harmony.

5. *Med.* **a.** To provoke (an excretion or discharge). ? *Obs.*

1597 GERARDE *Herbal* I. xxix. §2. 40 Camels haie.. mooueth the tearmes. 1605 TIMME *Quersit.* I. vii. 31 Salt.. hath vertue..to move sweates.

b. To cause (the bowels) to act; also *absol.* Also *intr.* of the bowels = to be moved, to act.

a 1700 B. E. *Dict. Cant. Crew*, s.v. *Pass*, *Do the Waters Pass well?* much in use at the Wells, do they Move as they ought? 1808 *Med. Jrnl.* XIX. 308 The very large doses of medicine that were necessary to move her bowels. 1889 J. M. DUNCAN *Clin. Lect. Dis. Wom.* xiv. (ed. 4) 101 Even when the bowels were truly described as moving regularly. 1897 *Allbutt's Syst. Med.* III. 414 The bowels being moved immediately after each meal.

6. ***to move*** (a person's) ***blood***: to make it flow more rapidly; hence, to excite or stir a passion in one. In early use said of the person himself = to become excited, angry, etc.; similarly † ***to move one's mood*** = to wax wroth.

a 1330 *Otuel* 355 King charle gan to meuen his blod. 1377 LANGL. *P. Pl.* B. x. 263 Why meuestow þi mode for a mote in þi brotheres eye. c 1400 *Laud Troy Bk.* 16791 That bold mayden meved hir blod, When sche tho tydandes vndirstode. c 1460 *Towneley Myst.* xvi. 472 For to se this flode..Mefys nothing my mode. 1471 CAXTON *Recuyell* (Sommer) I. 257 In this chaungyng of colour there was not a vayne but he was meuyd. 1697 DRYDEN *Virg. Georg.* III. 155 When his Blood no Youthful Spirits move.

7. a. To stir up or excite (an emotion, appetite, etc.) in a person; to provoke (laughter, contradiction).

1377 LANGL. *P. Pl.* B. XII. 126 And medle we nauȝt muche with hem to meuen any wrathe. 1474 CAXTON *Chesse* III. vi. 132 Anon as he is chauffed lecherye is meuyd in hym. 1588 SHAKS. *L.L.L.* v. ii. 865 To moue wilde laughter in the throate of death? 1605 BACON *Adv. Learn.* II. viii. §4 Wherein if I haue differed from the ancient, and receiued doctrines, and thereby shall moue contradiction. 1676 DRYDEN *State Innoc.* v. i, Your Penitence does my Compassion move. 1711 FELTON *Dissert. Classicks* (1753) 83 Images are very sparingly to be introduced;..their Use is to move Pity or Terror, Admiration [etc.]. 1849 MACAULAY *Hist. Eng.* ii. I. 243 All the prejudices, all the exaggerations of both the great parties in the state, moved his scorn. 1878 BOSW. SMITH *Carthage* 26 Such delicious fruits as those with which Cato moved the astonishment and the envy of the senators.

†b. *occas.* To excite, evoke (a state, activity, etc., in a person); to affect (a sense). *Obs.*

1528 LYNDESAY *Dreme* 811 Quhate dois mufe our Misere? Or quhareof dois proceid our pouertie? 1551 T. WILSON *Logike* (1580) 1 All soundes and noises that be made moue the hearyng, as coughyng. 1626 BACON *Sylva* §978 It is said to moue Dreames also. 1633 BP. HALL *Hard Texts N.T.* 116 His proper worke is both to lie, and to move lies in others.

8. To stir up, commence (strife, war, and the like). Now *rare* or *Obs.*

[Cf. L. *arma*, *bellum*, *tragœdias movere*.]

c 1330 R. BRUNNE *Chron.* (1725) 206 Bot Jon was þe enchesonne, & moued per a strif. c 1386 CHAUCER *Melib.* ¶683, I se wel, that..ye wole moeue werre and bataille. c 1425 WYNTOUN *Cron.* II. i. 17 Opir nacionys..þat latthe was bargan for to moyff. 1570–6 LAMBARDE *Peramb. Kent* (1826) 200 Odo..mooved many Tragedies within this Realme, and was in the end throwen from the Stage. 1585 *Act 27 Eliz.* c. 2 §1 Seminarie Priestes..stire up and move Sedition, Rebellion and open Hostilitie within her Highnesse Realmes. 1612 DAVIES *Why Ireland*, etc. (1747) 79 His foure sonnes..rose in armes and mooued warre against him. 1680 COTTON *Compl. Gamester* xxxvii. (ed. 2) 169 Turn him [*sc.* the cock] into the Pit to move his fortune.

9. a. To affect with emotion; to rouse or excite feeling in (a person); to stir (the feelings, etc.); to trouble, disquiet, perturb in one's mind; to excite *to* (laughter, pity, tears, etc.). Often *spec.* to affect with tender or compassionate emotion.

a 1300 *Cursor M.* 9738 Merci me mous wit her praier. c 1375 *Sc. Leg. Saints* vii. (*Jacobus*) 118 þe folk with a sowdane cry þai mewit þan sa sodanly, þat þai war in wil for to stane þe apostollis. c 1440 *York Myst.* v. 2 For woo my witte es in a were, That moffes me mykill in my mynde. 1483 CAXTON *G. de la Tour* c ij b, Yf the knyght hadde be sore meuyd and sorrowful at the deth of his first wyf. 1549 LATIMER *3rd Serm. bef. Edw. VI* (Arb.) 84 They were so moued wyth his preachynge, that they returned home agayne. 1596 SPENSER *F.Q.* IV. xii. 26 To disclose Which of the Nymphes his heart so sore did mieve. 1611 BIBLE *Mark* i. 41 And Iesus mooued with compassion, put foorth his hand, and touched him. 1667 MILTON *P.L.* IX. 1143 To whom soon mov'd with touch of blame thus Eve. a 1715 BURNET *Own Time* (1897) I. 476 He commonly gives all he has about him, when he meets an object that moves him. 1807 WORDSW. *Sonn.*, '*The world is too much with us*', For this, for everything, we are out of tune; It moves us not. 1835 MARRYAT *Jac. Faithf.* xxxiii, I was moved with the kindness of the old couple. 1849 MACAULAY *Hist. Eng.* i. I. 66 They were an ardent and impetuous race, easily moved to tears or to laughter, to fury or to love. 1896 T. F. TOUT *Edw. I*, iii. 50 All Christendom was terribly moved by the assassination.

b. To provoke to anger; to make angry. *Obs.* exc. in the full phr. ***to move to anger***, ***wrath***, etc.

a 1400–50 *Alexander* 1217 þan was ser Meliager moued & maynly debatis. 1470–85 MALORY *Arthur* XIX. v. 779 Syre Launcelot why be ye soo moeued... Me semeth said sir launcelot ye ouȝte to be more wrothe than I am. 1526 *Pilgr. Perf.* (W. de W. 1531) 234 Therfore let it moue no body, yf in the entreatynge of these matters, somtyme we [etc.]. 1548–9 (Mar.) *Bk. Com. Prayer*, *Burial*, O Lorde, whiche for our synnes iustly art moued. c 1592 MARLOWE *Jew of Malta* IV. v, 'Tis not 500 Crownes that I esteeme; I am not mou'd at that: this angers me, That he [etc.]. 1624 CAPT. SMITH *Virginia* 144 But Jack so moued their patience, they shot him. 1737 WHISTON *Josephus, Antiq.* III. xv. §1 God was moved at their abuse of him, and would inflict punishment upon them.

†c. *refl.* To be perturbed; to become excited or angry. *Obs.*

c 1290 *Beket* 485 in *S. Eng. Leg.* I. 120 Sire, quath þis holi man, ne meue ȝe ov riȝt nouȝt! c 1460 *Towneley Myst.* xx. 150 Sir pylate, mefe you now no mare, bot mese youre hart and mend youre mode. 1567 *Gude & Godlie Ball.* (S.T.S.) 96 Mufe the not at thair prosperitie.

10. a. To operate as a motive or influence of the volition or belief of (a person); to prompt, actuate, or impel *to* (an action) or *to do* (something).

1297 R. GLOUC. (Rolls) 9304 Ac an oþer reson wel ver meueþ more me þer to. a 1533 LD. BERNERS *Huon* lii. 177 What hathe moued the thus to do? c 1560 A. SCOTT *Poems* (S.T.S.) xxxiv. 97 Quhair money may ȝow moif, I hald it awerryce. 1603 KNOLLES *Hist. Turks* (1638) 634 Their furious minds more desirous of reuenge than mony, were not to be moued with any gold. 1651 HOBBES *Leviath.* III. xxxiii. 205 Some are moved to beleeve for one, and others for other reasons. 1693 DRYDEN *Juvenal* vi. (1726) 74 What reason shou'd thy Mind to Marriage move? 1732 BERKELEY *Alciphr.* II. §4 What moves men to build and plant but vanity. 1821 BYRON *Two Foscari* IV. i, I have prepared such arguments as will not Fail to move them. 1857 BUCKLE *Civiliz.* I. xi. 630 The two great principles which move the world are the love of wealth and the love of knowledge.

b. *absol.*

1573 *Satir. Poems Reform.* xl. 90 Becaus exempills fetchit far Mufis not so muche as thay thingis quhilk we se. 1588 SHAKS. *L.L.L.* IV. iii. 55, I feare these stubborn lines lack power to moue. 1611 TOURNEUR *Ath. Trag.* IV. v, To make th'example moue more forceably To vertue.

11. a. Of God, good or evil spirits, one's own heart, etc.: To prompt, impel *to* some action; in *passive*, to have an inward prompting, to feel inclined.

the spirit moves me: a phrase orig. in Quaker use, of promptings attributed to the Holy Spirit; now often used (without any irreverent intention) for 'I feel impelled or in the humour (*to do* something)'.

c 1380 WYCLIF *Sel. Wks.* III. 412 What profit were hit Crist to begge þus, siþ he myght mefe men to gif hym when hym nedid, wiþouten any bisynes of askyng of hom? 1426 LYDG. *De Guil. Pilgr.* 11215 Wolde god yt stoode so That ye wer mevyd, & that a-noon, To passe the way that I shal gon. c 1450 *Cov. Myst.* xi. (Shaks. Soc.) 106 The aungel..Whos synne hath mad hym a devyl in helle, He mevyd man to be so contraryous. 1530 PALSGR. 318/2 Meved or inclyned to do a thynge, *enclin*. 1552 *Bk. Com. Prayer*, *Ordering Deacons*, Doe you trust that you are inwardlye moued by the holye Ghoste to take vpon you thys office and ministracion..? 1656 G. FOX *Jrnl.* (1852) I. 271 The power of the Lord God arose in me, and I was moved in it 'to bid him lay down his crown at the feet of Jesus'. 1835 J. H. NEWMAN *Par. Serm.* (1837) I. viii. 128 God moves us in order to make the beginning of duty easy. 1850 MRS. CARLYLE *Lett.* (1883) II. 105 The spirit moves me to write you a letter.

†b. *passive.* To be inclined to think. *Obs.*

1586 MARLOWE *1st Pt. Tamburl.* II. v, I am strongly mou'd, That if I should desire the Persian crown, I could attain it with a wondrous ease.

†12. a. To urge (a person) *to* (an action) or *to do* (something); to exhort, incite; to apply or appeal to; to make a proposal or request to. *Obs.*

1377 LANGL. *P. Pl.* B. XII. 4 Many tymes [I] haue moeued þe to þinke on þine ende. c 1440 *Alphabet of Tales* 527 A preste movid ane vsurar when he was seke to dispose hym for þe heale of his sawle. 1476 *Paston Lett.* III. 157 Wherto I promysed hym my poore helpe, as ferforthe as I durst meve your good lordshepp for hym. 1552 *Bk. Com. Prayer*, *Morn. Prayer*, The scripture moueth vs in sondrie places to acknowledge and confess our manifold synnes and wickedness. 1617 MORYSON *Itin.* II. 84 He had earnestly moved her Majesty to give him leave to come over for a short time. 1662 *Bk. Com. Prayer*, *Visit. Sick* (rubric), Here shall the sick person be moved to make a special confession of his sins. **1726** SWIFT *Gulliver* III. i, I..begged him..that he would move the Captains to take some Pity on us.

b. To apply to or solicit (a person) *for* something, or *in* or *of* a matter. *Obs.*

1399 LANGL. *Rich. Redeles* Prol. 32 To meuve him of mysserewle, his mynde to reffresshe. *Ibid.* III. 2 For mater þat my mynde is meued in now. *c* **1440** *Generydes* 1760 The Sowdon..ganne his councell to meve Of that mater that towchid hym soo nere, And Askid ther avise in this mater. **1582** N. LICHFIELD tr. *Castanheda's Conq. E. Ind.* I. xxi. 55 Did therfore moue yᵉ King of Calicut by a messenger for license to send the same. *a* **1674** CLARENDON *Hist. Reb.* XIII. §28 If he desired any thing..he would move the King in it. **1768** FOOTE *Devil on 2 Sticks* I. Wks. 1799 II. 243 If you want money..you move me for further supplies.

13. a. To make a formal application, suit, or request to (the sovereign, a court, Parliament, etc.). Const. *for*. Cf. MOTION *sb.* 8 a, b.

1683 TEMPLE *Mem.* Wks. 1731 I. 464 He would move the Parliament to have my Statue set up. **1796** J. ANSTEY *Pleader's G.* (1803) 41 Down to the hall of Erebus I'll go, And move some Dæmon in the Courts below. **1816** *Ann. Reg.* 20 The Earl of Liverpool moved the House..on the subject of an address upon the treaties. **1885** *Standard* 20 Mar. 6/1 The Bank now moved the Court..for..a reversal of the verdict.

b. const. *that* (something be done). Cf. 15 c.

1660 INGELO *Bentiv. & Ur.* I. (1682) 103 He moved the Company that the arrogant fool might be put out of the Room. **1739** *Wks. Learned* I. 48 Dr. Reynolds..moved his Majesty, on the second Day of the Dispute, that there might be a New Translation of the Bible.

†**14. a.** To propose or suggest (something to be done); to prefer (a request); to lodge (a complaint); to bring forward, propound (a question, etc.), mention (a matter). Const. *to* (a person).

1362 LANGL. *P.Pl.* A. IX. 113, I durste meue no mateere to make him to Iangle. *c* **1385** CHAUCER *L.G.W.* Prol. 344 ȝe motyn herkenyn If he can replye A-geyns these poyntys that ȝe han to hym mevid. *c* **1440** *Alphabet of Tales* 304 On a tyme when Saynt Petur prechid, þer was som þat wolde mofe vnto hym vnprofitable questions. **1524** J. ALEN in *Carew MSS.* (1867) I. 25 The doubts that I moved to your Grace. **1540** HEYWOOD *Four PP.* 1034 (Manly), I could ryght well ten tymes souner all that haue beleued Then the tenth parte of that he hath meued. **1625** BACON *Ess., Cunning* (Arb.) 437 The like Surprize, may be made, by Mouing things, when the Party is in haste, and cannot stay, to consider aduisedly, of that is moued. **1676** DRYDEN *Aurengz.* IV. 55 To Indamora you my Suit must move. **1710** PRIDEAUX *Orig. Tithes* iv. 193 The third Difficulty moved concerning this matter is whether the Grant was made for all the Lands of the Kingdom. *a* **1715** BURNET *Own Time* (1900) II. 383 No man ever had the impudence to move to him any thing with relation to the king's life. **1759** ROBERTSON *Hist. Scot.* v. Wks. 1813 I. 370 Elizabeth..did not expect that he would have moved any such difficulty.

b. *to move in one's mind*: to revolve, turn over (a question). In quots. with clause as object. *Obs.*

c **1450** *St. Cuthbert* (Surtees) 5763 He moued [*printed* moned] and moysid in his mynde, þat þe se passid his kynde. *a* **1578** LINDESAY (Pitscottie) *Chron. Scot.* (S.T.S.) I. 166 Conjectering and moving in his mynd quhome this sould be.

15. *spec.* †**a.** To plead (a cause or suit) in a court; to bring (an action at law). *Obs.*

c **1420** LYDG. *Assembly of Gods* 145 Loke thow fayle nought Thy sentence to yeue without favour so, Lyke as thou hast herde the causys meuyd the to. *c* **1450** *Godstow Reg.* 507 A plee I-meved by a breef of the kyngis I-called Cessauit bitwene the abbesse and Andrew Culuarde. **1571–2** *Reg. Privy Council Scot.* II. 129 The awnaris thairof wald move actioun aganis him thairfoir. **1641** W. SHEPPARD *Court-Keepers Guide* (1654) 48 *Barretor*, one that moves suits and that commonly for small matters and taking the worst side.

b. To propose (a question, resolution, etc.) formally in a deliberative assembly.

1452 in Gross *Gild Merch.* (1890) II. 68 That all brethirn may be sworne to kepe all cownsayll of all matters that bene mewit in the sembles. **1789** PITT in *G. Rose's Diaries* (1860) I. 93 Your Lordship would undertake to move the Address. **1828** *Hansard's Parl. Debates* 25 Apr. XIX. 141 Mr. C. Grant moved the order of the day. **1838–42** ARNOLD *Hist. Rome* (1846) III. xliv. 147 The resolutions which he moved were..unanimously adopted. **1849** MACAULAY *Hist. Eng.* vi. II. 24 The opposition moved the previous question.

c. with clause: To propose (now only, in a formal manner) *that* something be done, or *to do* something. †Formerly also with clause expressing a fact: To put in a plea or suggestion *that*...

1605 BACON *Adv. Learn.* II. xxiii. §41 The two frogs, which consulted when their plash was drie, whether they should go: and the one mooued to go down into a pit because it was not likely the water would dry there. **1621** ELSING *Debates Ho. Lords* (Camden) 20, I moved first that the L. Chancellor be brought to the barre. **1720** POPE *Iliad* XVIII. 300 In free Debate, my Friends, your Sentence speak; For me, I move, before the Morning break To raise our Camp. **1817** JAS. MILL *Brit. India* II. v. viii. 661 It was moved by Mr. Stables..that the inquiry should be instituted. **1886** *Law Rep., Weekly Notes* 196/1 The plaintiff now moved that the foreclosure be made absolute. **1897** FLANDRAU *Harvard Episodes* 151, I move we adjourn.

II. Intransitive senses.

16. a. Of persons and things: To go, advance, proceed, pass from one place to another. Usu. implying deliberate or measured or laborious progress. Also with advs., as *about*, *away*, etc.

c **1250** *Kent. Serm.* in *O.E. Misc.* 29 Þo seide ure lord to þo serganz. Moveth to-gidere and bereth to Architriclin. *c* **1350** *Will. Palerne* 4285 With here menskful meyne sche meued on gate. *c* **1400** *Destr. Troy* 1601 Thurgh myddis þe mekill toune meuyt a water, And disseuert þe Cite. *c* **1450** HOLLAND *Howlat* 677 All thus thai mufe to the meit. **1508** DUNBAR *Tua Mariit Wemen* 2 Apon the Midsumer ewin.. I muvit furth allane. **1605** SHAKS. *Macb.* v. v. 35 Me thought The Wood began to moue. *a* **1691** BOYLE *Hist. Air* (1692) 194 As if a shining fish were moving to and fro very swiftly in a somewhat troubled water. **1725** POPE *Odyss.* VIII. 395 To the soft Cyprian shores the Goddess moves. **1747** RICHARDSON *Clarissa* (1768) I. xxi. 147 Not a door opens; not a soul stirs. Hannah, as she moves up and down, is shunned as a person infected. *a* **1774** GOLDSM. *Surv. Exp. Philos.* (1776) I. 299 A globe moving through a fluid, such as air, that closes behind the body as it moves. **1831** CARLYLE *Sart. Res.* II. iii, The aproned or disaproned Burghers moving-in to breakfast. **1853** M. ARNOLD *Scholar Gypsy* xi, And marked thee..Through the long dewy grass move slow away. **1855** TENNYSON *Brook* 87 Katie never ran: she moved To meet me, winding under woodbine flowers. **1861** ANDERSSON *Okavango River* 94 They [*sc.* elephants] would then as suddenly move off at full speed. **1871** R. ELLIS *Catullus* lxiv. 249 She, as his onward keel still moved, still mournfully follow'd.

fig. **1681** FLAVEL *Meth. Grace* xxxi. 533 Were there a principle of spiritual life in their souls, they would move Christ-ward. **1876** L. STEPHEN *Eng. Th. 18th Cent.* I. 3 Thought moves in a spiral curve, not in a straight line.

b. of the heavenly bodies in their regular course.

c **1391** CHAUCER *Astrol.* ii. §35 The Moone Moeuyth the contrarie from othere planetes as in hire Episicle. *c* **1400** MAUNDEV. (1839) xvii. 181 And tho ij. sterres ne meeven neuere. **1667** MILTON *P.L.* VIII. 70 Whether Heav'n move or Earth Imports not, if thou reck'n right. **1842** TENNYSON *Move Eastward* 1 Move eastward, happy earth.

c. Of an army or body of men (or their leader): To go forward, march. Also, to quit one's position.

c **1330** R. BRUNNE *Chron. Wace* (Rolls) 13460 Þey meoued fro Langres toward Ostum Wyþ mikel folk & grete route. ?*a* **1400** *Morte Arth.* 2001 Sir Lott and sir Launcelote.. Salle lenge on his lefte hande, wyth legyones ynewe, To meue in þe morne-while, ȝif þe myste happynne. **1667** MILTON *P.L.* I. 549 Anon they move In perfect Phalanx to the Dorian mood. **1779** J. MOORE *View Soc. Fr.* II. liv. 46 Observing that the King had moved at a greater distance than usual from the town. **1844** H. H. WILSON *Brit. India* II. 254 He again moved in pursuit. **1847** L. HUNT *Jar Honey* x. (1848) 132 Religious processions move through the streets.

d. *transf.* Of time, a narrative, a piece of work, etc.: To advance, make progress. Also in *Music*, of a voice or part: To proceed from note to note.

c **1400** *Destr. Troy* 7167 By two monethes were myldly mouit to end. **1694** PRIOR *Hymn to Sun* ii, From the Blessings They bestow, Our Times are dated, and our Æra's move. **1712** HEARNE *Collect.* (O.H.S.) III. 426 The 9ᵗʰ Vol. (which will be the last) moves apace. **1771** *Encycl. Brit.* III. 333/2 The part for the organ should move in long notes, and by the least intervals. **1819** KEATS *Isabella* xx, Then the tale Shall move on soberly. **1842** TENNYSON *Locksley Hall* 134 Science moves, but slowly slowly, creeping on from point to point. **1877** STAINER *Harmony* vi. §73 Oblique [motion is] when one part is stationary and another moves. **1890** *Spectator* 31 May 765 The story moves far too slowly, and the long conversations..are tiresome. **1902** T. M. LINDSAY *Ch. & Min. in Early Cent.* iv. 149 Things move fast in young communities organising themselves for the first time.

e. *Chess*, *Draughts*, etc. (*a*) Of a piece: To be transferred, pass, from one position to another in the course of the game (= 1 b *refl.*); (*b*) Of a player: To make a move (= 1 b *absol.*).

1474 CAXTON *Chesse* IV. ii. 165 Therefore may the kynge meue on the lifte side of his propre poynt. **1734** R. SEYMOUR *Compl. Gamester* (ed. 5) I. 128 The Gamesters must move by Turns, as they do at Draughts. **1800** J. STURGES *Draughts* 2 You are allowed five minutes more to move, and in default of moving in that time you lose the Game. **1876** W. N. POTTER in *Encycl. Brit.* V. 593/1 They [*sc.* knights] move from one corner of any rectangle of three squares by two to the opposite corner. **1884** TENNYSON *Becket* Prol., Check —you move so wildly.

f. To depart, start off; = to move off or away. Now *colloq.*

c **1450** *Merlin* 130 Than they graunted to the Messagers that thei sholde meve the thirde day. *c* **1470** HENRY *Wallace* IV. 698 Thar twa dayis our thar lugyng still thai maid; On the thrid nycht thai mowit but mar abaid. **1756** TOLDERVY *Hist. 2 Orphans* II. 116 As I shall lay with a friend two miles off, 'tis high time to be moving. **1855** HALIBURTON *Nat. & Hum. Nat.* I. xii. 376 As soon as the ceremony was over, 'Now,' sais I, 'we must be a movin'.

g. To change one's abode; to go from one house or residence to another. Also *to move about*, etc., to keep changing one's abode. *to move in*, to take possession of a new domicile. So, *to move house*. Also, *to move in on*: to take up residence with (someone), esp. so as to inconvenience or annoy; to attach oneself to, put pressure on, or take control of (a person, project, etc.).

a **1707** BP. PATRICK *Autobiog.* (1839) 244 He was afterwards the occasion of his leaving the College, and moving towards London. **1751** EARL CHATHAM *Lett. Nephew* ii. 5, I have been moving about from place to place. **1796** LAMB *Let. to Coleridge* 2 Dec., Write to me when you move, lest I should direct wrong. **1887** A. BIRRELL *Obiter Dicta* Ser. II. 63 In 1715 Pope moved with his parents to Chiswick. **1891** N. GOULD *Double Event* 18 You shall have the place Thurton had..and you can move into his cottage as soon as you please. **1898** G. B. SHAW *You never can Tell* I. 216, I spent my last sovereign on moving in; and I havnt paid a shilling of rent yet. **1924** R. MACAULAY *Orphan Island* ii. 22 Your aunt and Martha and myself have recently moved house. **1941** N. COWARD *Australia Visited* VII. 47 God help us when the scenery and properties move in on us, when we have to adapt ourselves to new settings and different furniture. **1945** E. BOWEN *Demon Lover* 91 Mona moved out..and moved in on Isobel. **1966** *Listener* 6 Jan. 14/2 The society was formed about four years ago... We still have not moved in. **1967** J. REDGATE *Killing Season* (1968) II. xviii. 147 We'll give him a few months to get entrenched in England... Then we'll move in on him. **1968** M. WOODHOUSE *Rock Baby* xviii. 180 That was the idea, if somebody hadn't moved in on the operation. **1973** 'D. HALLIDAY' *Dolly & Starry Bird* xiv. 205 Sophia deciding to move in on somebody was a sight worth selling tickets for. **1974** R. RENDELL *Face of Trespass* 10 If you ever feel like moving house to live among your constituents I'll be happy to oblige.

h. *to move off*: to die. *colloq.* (Cf. *go off*.)

1764 FOOTE *Mayor of G.* I. (1783) 11 Whether from the fall or the fright, the Major mov'd off in a month.

i. *move on*: the order given by a policeman to a pedestrian who is standing too long in one place so as to cause obstruction. Hence occas. *trans.* = to order to 'move on'. Also (with hyphen) as *attrib. phr.*

1831 *Blackw. Mag.* Jan. 83/2 He possesses the power..of ordering them to 'move on'. **1855** THACKERAY *Newcomes* lviii, In vain policemen told them to move on; fresh groups gathered after the seceders. **1894** *Times* (weekly ed.) 19 Jan. 56/2 The proceedings were..abruptly closed by the intervention of the police, who 'moved on' the preacher. **1908** E. J. BANFIELD *Confessions of Beachcomber* II. i. 246 He was almost knocked down by a move-on sort of shove. **1971** *Ceylon Daily News* 17 Sept. 1/5 The vagrancy laws and the move-on by-law of the Municipality.

j. Of merchandise: To change hands, circulate, find buyers. Also, of a stock of goods, an edition or impression of a book, *to move off*: to be in course of being sold off (more or less rapidly).

1759 GOLDSM. *Pres. St. Polite Learn.* vi. Wks. (Globe) 432/2 To borrow a bookseller's phrase, the whole impression moves off. **1876** BREWER *Eng. Studies* ii. (1881) 50 A second or third edition moves off languidly enough. **1888** *Jrnl. R. Agric. Soc.* Apr. 52 The new crop does not begin to move to any considerable extent before the middle of that month. **1893** E. W. GOSSE *Questions at Issue* 60 Both of them achieved fame..long before their books began to 'move', as publishers call it.

k. To go quickly. *colloq.*

1954 *Amer. Speech* XXIX. 100 It can really move. **1959** M. GILBERT *Blood & Judgement* xvi. 164 'What price the law's delays.' 'They can move when they have to.' **1967** 'G. NORTH' *Sgt. Cluff & Day of Reckoning* ii. 23 You'll have to run to catch him:..when he's in that frame of mind, he can move. **1969** J. FREDMAN *Fourth Agency* vii. 53 The car was rocketing along... We were moving all right. **1973** W. MCCARTHY *Detail* ii. 77 Immediately the large man..was out of the apartment and through the fire door. It took him little more than two seconds. God, he can move, Ben thought.

l. To dance or play music energetically or with a strong rhythm; to be exciting or dynamic. *colloq.*

1955 *Down Beat* 6 Apr. 15 The only time it does start to move is in the second chorus, with Charlie Shavers. **1958** G. V. KENNARD in R. J. Gleason *Jam Session* 176 'It's got to move,' jazzmen say. If it doesn't 'swing', it's not jazz. **1959** [see DRIVE *v.* 25 *c*]. **1968** [see GROOVE *v.* 5]. **1969** N. COHN *AWopBopaLooBop* (1970) ix. 85 Go to a club one week, go back the next and everyone is moving differently.

17. a. Of living beings: To change position or posture, to exhibit motion or physical activity (in respect of the whole body or of a member). Freq. with negative = to remain still, not to stir.

c **1330** R. BRUNNE *Chron. Wace* (Rolls) 13330 Meue nought, for oughte þat may bytide, Til þat y come, when y se nede. *a* **1400** *Prymer* (1891) 25 (*Benedicite*) Alle that mevith in wateres. **1470–85** MALORY *Arthur* VIII. xxxii. 321 But at that tyme there was not one wold meue for his wordes. **1513** DOUGLAS *Æneis* v. viii. 32 Entellus standis stif and grave of cors, Nocht moiffand fra his first stand in a fors. **1592** SHAKS. *Rom. & Jul.* II. i. 15 He heareth not, he stirreth not, he moueth not. **1774** GOLDSM. *Nat. Hist.* (1776) VIII. 191 The animal..has been cut in every division, yet still it continued to move. **1865** TENNYSON *Princess* VI. (*Song*), Yet she neither spoke nor moved. **1898** G. B. SHAW *Plays* II. *You never can tell* 297 He moves as if to go.

b. of a part of the body.

1535 COVERDALE 1 *Sam.* i. 13 Hir lippes onely moued, but hir voyce was not herde. **1596** SHAKS. *Merch. V.* III. ii. 116 Moue these eies? **1717** PRIOR *Alma* I. 312 Both Legs and Arms spontaneous move. **1898** HENLEY *Lond. Types*, *Guardsman*, Nor would his lips Move, though his gorge with throttled oaths were charred!

c. To dance. Also with cognate object. Now *rare.*

1594 MARLOWE & NASHE *Dido* III. D 4 b, What more then delian musicke doe I heare, That calles my soule.. To moue vnto the measures of delight. **1667** MILTON *P.L.* III. 579 As they move Thir Starry dance in numbers that compute Days, months, and years. **1785** G. A. BELLAMY *Apology*, etc. VI. 23, I beheld a lady moving a minuet with infinite grace.

d. To bow in salutation.

1594 *1st Pt. Contention* (1843) 33 He will neither move nor speak to us. **1852** DICKENS *Bleak Ho.* xxix, I have the pleasure of being acquainted with Mr. Tulkinghorn—at least we move when we meet one another.

†**e.** Of speech: To be uttered. *Obs.*

c **1470** *Gol. & Gaw.* 1166 Thair wes na word muuand, Sa war thai all stil.

18. a. Of inanimate objects: To suffer change of position or posture (as a whole or in respect of the parts); to be stirred.

c **1400** MAUNDEV. (1839) iv. 22 Men may see þere the erthe of the tombe apertly many tymes steren and meuen, as þere weren quykke thinges vnder. *c* **1420** *Chron. Vilod.* 3108

Hurre thouȝt he say þe clothe þat honged vpone hurre tombe þere þo Meue ofte and store wondere fast. **1535** COVERDALE *Jer.* x. 4 They hewe downe a tre..: they fasten it with nales and hammers, that it moue not. **1676** J. BEAUMONT in *Phil. Trans.* XI. 731 The Stones, I have given you an account of, generally move in Vinegar. **1842** TENNYSON *Sir Galahad* 77 Then move the trees, the copses nod. **1890** CLARK RUSSELL *Marriage at Sea* ii, I believe there's a little air of wind a-moving.

b. Of a piece of machinery: To turn, work, revolve. Also *fig.*

a **1400–50** *Alexander* 5292 Þis selere was be sorsry selcuthely foundid, Made for a mervall to meeue with engine. **1669** STURMY *Mariner's Mag.* II. vi. 67 This Instrument contains two Parts..moving one upon the other. **1726** SWIFT *Gulliver* II. viii, The Door did not move on Hinges, but up and down like a Sash. **1798** JOANNA BAILLIE *Tryal* II. ii, I thought I heard a door move.

19. a. Of animate beings: To exist, live; 'to have vital action' (J.). Also, to live *in* a particular sphere; to comport oneself in a specified way.

13.. *E.E. Allit. P.* B. 303 Alle-kynez flesch þat on vrthe meuez. *c* **1430** LYDG. *Min. Poems* (Percy Soc.) 243 For rihte as Ver ay moveth in grennesse, So doth childhood in amerows lustynesse. *a* **1713** ELLWOOD *Autobiog.* (1765) 1 My Station not being so eminent..as others who have moved in higher Orbs. **1837** DISRAELI *Venetia* II. ii, With no aspirations beyond the little world in which she moved. **1847** TENNYSON *Princess* I. 75, I have a sister at the foreign court, Who moves about the Princess. **1886** RUSKIN *Præterita* I. v. 170 A man of great power..moving in the first Circles of Edinburgh.

b. *transf.* or *fig.* of things.

13.. *E.E. Allit. P.* A. 64 My goste is gon in godez grace, In auenture þer meruaylez meuen. **1865** GLADSTONE in Morley *Life* (1903) II. v. ix. 148 In a cold and lukewarm period, and such is this in public affairs, everything which moves and lives is called extreme. **1874** H. R. REYNOLDS *John Bapt.* i. §3. 20 If the narrative..moved completely in the region of the natural.

c. ***to move with the times***, to be up to date in one's way of living.

1936 ROBINSON & BROWNE *How to live in a Flat* 90 We have no hesitation in offering the following hints to those who—wishing to move with the times..—desire to construct a service-flat for their own use. **1960** L. P. HARTLEY *Facial Justice* xvii. 144 You must try to move with the times. **1973** *Times* 28 Nov. 22/6 If you change anything, you are accused of eroding history. If you change nothing, you are accused of failing to move with the times.

20. To take action, act, proceed (*in* an affair). Also with cognate obj. (fig.) ***to move a step***. †***to move against***, to oppose (cf. OF. *mouvoir contre*).

c **1380** WYCLIF *Sel. Wks.* III. 407 Bot ȝitte ageyns þis sentence meefes Anticrist. *a* **1400–50** *Alexander* 2382 (Ashm. MS.) And for Strasagirs þe strang he of his strenth priued, ȝe meue al þus malicoly his maieste a-gayne. **1709** STEELE *Tatler* No. 67 ¶5 Sacred Persons move upon greater Motives than that of Fame. **1720** OZELL *Vertot's Rom. Rep.* I. v. 300 Valerius and Horatius, declared they wou'd not move a Step, so long as [etc.]. **1791** COWPER *Retired Cat* 114 That all around, in all that's done, Must move and act for him alone. **1879** LUBBOCK *Addr. Pol. & Educ.* iii. 69, I would urge parents to move in the matter.

†**21.** Of a war, strife, etc.: To break out, be stirred up. (Cf. sense 8.) *Obs.*

c **1470** HENRY *Wallace* VIII. 551 We sall do nocht, less than it mowe in yow. **1485** CAXTON *Paris & V.* 10 There moeved a strife betwyxte the barons and knyghtes. **1523** LD. BERNERS *Froiss.* I. iv. *heading*, The occasion wherby the warre moued bitwene the kyngis of Fraunce and Ingland. **1562** A. SCOTT *Poems* (S.T.S.) i. 44 Be bissie now to banisch all debatis Betuix kirkmen and temporall men dois mufe.

†**22.** ***to move to mind*** = to come to mind (in quot. *impers.*). ***to move of*** or ***out of mind***, to be forgotten. *Obs.*

c **1400** *Destr. Troy* Prol. 30 Þof fele yeres ben faren syn þe fight endid, And it meuyt out of mynd, myn hit I thinke. *Ibid.* 1691 Then meuyt to his mynde, as yt most nede, þat his Cite was sure of hym selfe wroght. *Ibid.* 2340 Hit is not meuyt of mynde ne mony day past. *c* **1460** *Play Sacram.* 453 Now by Machomyth so myghty yᵗ meuyth in my mode thys ys masterly ment.

†**23.** To proceed, emanate, originate *from*. *Obs.*

1390 GOWER *Conf.* I. 322 The will which of my bodi moeveth, Whos werkes that the god reproeveth, I have restreigned everemore. **1615** SIR R. COTTON in *Buccleuch MSS.* (Hist. MSS. Comm.) I. 163 The King..could not with his greatness answer the proposition, moving only but from Count de Somerset and Cavillero Cotton. **1676** DRYDEN *State Innoc.* IV. i, Smiles, not allow'd to Beasts, from Reason move.

†**24.** ***to move of, by***: Of property: To be held by, to belong or pertain to. *Obs.*

Cf. OF. *movoir (de)* 'relever, dépendre, en terme de féodalité' (Godefroy).

1438 *E.E. Wills* (1882) 111 That the saide Iohn Russell haue & reioyce for euer more all the lyuelode that meueth of his moder after her deces. **1587** HARRISON *England* II. ix. (1877) I. 203 The husband that marieth an heire to haue such lands as moue by hir during his naturall life.

†**25.** To incline, tend *to* or *to do* (something); to incline *toward* (a proposal). *Obs.*

c **1384** CHAUCER *H. Fame* II. 227 Vnto whiche place euery thynge Thorgh his kyndely enclynynge Moveth for to come to Whan that hyt is awey therfro. *c* **1450** HOLLAND *Howlat* 396 Furth on my matir to muse I mufe as I may. **1573** TUSSER *Husb.* (1878) 184 Ill huswiferie mooueth with gossep to spend. **1677** MARVELL *Corr.* cccviii. Wks. (Grosart) II. 551 Some of the House seemed to move toward the 600,000*l.*

†**26.** Of the passions, etc.: To be stirred or excited (*to*). *Obs.*

1483 CAXTON *Gold. Leg.* 37 b, Their flesshe began to meue and stire to concupiscence. *c* **1586** C'TESS PEMBROKE *Ps.* LXXVIII. ix, The raked sparkes in flame began t' appeare, And staied choller fresh again to move.

†**27.** To speak, treat, or argue *of* (a matter). (Cf. 12 b and OF. *movoir de.*) Also in indirect passive.

c **1320** *Cast. Love* 401 (Halliw.) This thralle of whom my sustren mevyn Hath dome deserved, as ȝe ȝevyn. **1387–8** T. USK *Test. Love* III. v. (*ad fin.*), And this, me thinketh, shulde be the wexing tree, of which ye first meved. *c* **1400** *Destr. Troy* 7206 Of þat mater was meuit no more at þat tyme. **1423** JAS. I *Kingis Q.* clxxvii, Moving within my spirit of this sight. **1509** HAWES *Past. Pleas.* xxix. (Percy Soc.) 138, I durst never of the matter meve Unto your person, lest it should you greve. *Ibid.* 139 It should be meved To her of love.

28. ***to move for***: to make a request, proposal, or application for (something). (*absol.* from 12 b, 13.)

1638 H. SPELMAN in *Lett. Lit. Men* (Camden) 154, I gave my Lord of Eely thanks in your behalfe, and moved also for the continuance of his favour about the Lyving you ayme at. **1700** S. L. tr. *Fryke's Voy. E. Ind.* 111 My business now was to have leave my self, which indeed I had moved for at a distance before. *a* **1707** BP. PATRICK *Autobiog.* (1839) 44 All my acquaintance..advised me to move for a mandamus in the King's bench. *Ibid.* 76, I moved for a physician to be sent to her from Oxford. **1800** *Proc. E. Ind. Ho.* in *Asiat. Ann. Reg.* 64/1 The Chairman said it was customary, when papers were moved for, that the sense of the court should be taken on the motion before they were produced. **1828** *Hansard's Parl. Debates* 5 May XIX. 345 The Duke of Richmond said, that in rising to move for a Committee to inquire into the state of the Wool-trade, he [etc.]. **1868** HELPS *Realmah* ix. (1876) 244 Cranmer was prepared to move for the destruction of all fables.

moveable: see MOVABLE.

†**'move-all.** *Obs.* [f. MOVE *v.* + ALL.] Some indoor game.

1782 MISS BURNEY *Cecilia* I. ii, Come, Morrice, you that love Christmas sports, what say you to the game of move-all?

moved (muːvd), *ppl. a.* [f. MOVE *v.* + -ED¹.] In senses of the verb. In attributive use now rare exc. with prefixed adv., as ***easily-moved***.

1592 SHAKS. *Rom. & Jul.* I. i. 95 Hear the Sentence of your moouued Prince. **1610** —— *Temp.* IV. i. 146 You doe looke (my son) in a mou'd sort, As if you were dismaid. **1644** DIGBY *Nat. Bodies* ix. §7. 69 More then these three, we can not expect to find in a moued body. **1704** HEARNE *Duct. Hist.* (1714) I. 129 Thucydides is the best Representer of mov'd affections, Herodotus of Calm. **1838** tr. *Strauss's Lutheran Clergyman* i. 23 Many a sigh follows you from the moved breast. **1900** *Daily News* 12 May 3/1 Loud cries..from the more easily-moved members of the audience.

†**2.** quasi-*sb.* Something moved. *Obs. rare*⁻¹.

1722 WOLLASTON *Relig. Nat.* v. 65 Z, Y, X are *moveds*, or rather Z more Y more X, taken together, are *one moved*:.. without W there would be a *moved* without a *mover*.

moveless ('muːvlıs), *a.* [f. MOVE *v.* + -LESS.] Having no movement or motion, not moving, motionless; immovable, fixed.

1578 T. PROCTOR *Gorg. Gallery* H ij b, Whose mooueles loue and trust, doth reason far surmount. **1598** SYLVESTER *Du Bartas* II. ii. I. *Ark* 169, I conceiue aright Th' Almighty-most to be most infinite:..That moueless, all he moues. **1665** BOYLE *Occas. Refl.* IV. i. (1848) 167 My Body as yet lay moveless in the Bed. **1718** POPE *Iliad* XV. 744 The Grecian Phalanx moveless as a Tow'r, On all sides batter'd, yet resists his Pow'r. **1836–7** SIR W. HAMILTON *Metaph.* xviii. (1870) 353 The intermediate balls which remain moveless, but communicate the impulse. **1860** S. BROOKS *Gordian Knot* xiii. 95 The policeman inspected all parties with a moveless countenance. **1885** HOWELLS *Silas Lapham* II. 93 The reins lay loose in his moveless hand.

Hence **'movelessly** *adv.*, **'movelessness**.

1667 HOOK in *Phil. Trans.* II. 540 It was not the subsiding or movelesness of the Lungs, that was the immediate cause of Death. **1813** SHELLEY *Q. Mab* VII. 262 Yet peacefully and movelessly it [an oak] braves The midnight conflict of the wintry storm. **1865** RUSKIN *Sesame* 121 A king's majesty or 'state', then, and the right of his kingdom to be called a state, depends on the movelessness of both. **1866** ALEX. SMITH *A. Hagart's Househ.* I. 7 He would be touched by the silence and movelessness of the mighty landscape.

movement ('muːvmənt), *sb.* Forms: 4 **moevement, 5 mouvement, 5– movement.** [a. OF. *movement, moevement* (mod.F. *mouvement*), ad. med.L. *movimentum*, f. L. *movēre*: see MOVE *v.* and -MENT. Cf. Pr. *movemen-s*, Catalan *moviment*, Sp. *movimiento*, Pg., It. *movimento*.

Somewhat rare between the 14th and the 18th c.; not found, e.g., in Shaks., Milton's poetry, or the Bible of 1611.]

1. a. The action or process of moving (in the intransitive senses of the verb); change of position; passage from place to place, or from one situation to another. Also, an instance or kind of this; a particular act or manner of moving.

c **1374** CHAUCER *Boeth.* IV. Pr. ii. 89 (Camb. MS.) Thow nylt nat thanne denoye quod she þat the Moeuement [*v.r.* moeuementz] of goynge nis in Men by kynde. **1390** GOWER *Conf.* III. 107 Astronomie is the science..Which makth a man have knowlechinge Of Sterres in the firmament, Figure, cercle and moevement Of ech of hem in sondri place. **1456** SIR G. HAYE *Law Arms* (S.T.S.) 75 The hevin ..moves fra the orient to the occident..Bot the things that ar corporale in this erde..movis nocht with the moving of it, ..bot ȝit have thai othir naturale movementis. **1698** NORRIS *Pract. Disc.* (1707) IV. 238 All the Movement of the Soul here is only to will the Movement of the Body towards these things. **1706** PHILLIPS (ed. Kersey), *Movement*, Motion, Moving, particularly in Dancing, &c. **1732** POPE *Ess. Man* I. 54 In human works, tho' labour'd on with pain, A thousand movements scarce one purpose gain. **1832** TENNYSON *Pal. Art* 246 A spot of dull stagnation, without light Or power of movement, seem'd my soul. **1849** BALFOUR *Man. Bot.* §657 These spores, from their movements, have received the name of Zoospores. **1858** O. W. HOLMES *Aut. Breakf.-t.* xi, The schoolmistress stepped back with a sudden movement. **1855** BAIN *Senses & Intell.* I. i. 75 In wakening from sleep movement precedes sensation. If light were essential to the movements concerned in vision, it would be impossible to open the eyes. **1868** —— *Ment. & Mor. Sci.* III. xiii. 303 The movements, as well as attitudes, of a graceful form, can hardly be other than graceful. **1878** HUXLEY *Physiogr.* 205 Such movements of the land..must have been brought about by the comparatively sudden action of subterranean forces. **1894** S. FISKE *Holiday Stories* (1900) 30 There was a general movement toward the door. **1903** *Mission. Rec. U.F. Ch. Scot.* Sept. 394/1 There have been considerable movements of population from the Continent to Canada.

b. *Mil.* A change of position which a body undergoes in tactical or strategical evolutions. Also 'the regular and orderly motion of an army for some particular purpose' (Voyle & Stevenson *Milit. Dict.* ed. 3, 1876).

1784 W. CARTER (*title*) Genuine Detail of the several Engagements, Positions and Movements of the Royal and American Armies during the years 1775 and 1776. **1802** C. JAMES *Milit. Dict.* s.v., Hurry and delay, in military movements, are two extremes which should be equally avoided. **1827** SOUTHEY *Hist. Penins. War* II. 401 But the march of Mortier with some 15,000 men from Aragon to their assistance had been ascertained, and it was certain therefore that a movement might be apprehended from that quarter. **1889** *Infantry Drill* III. 89 The double march is not applied to the movements of large bodies of troops for a longer distance than is required in a charge, or [etc.].

†**c.** *Chess.* A move. *Obs.*

1734 R. SEYMOUR *Compl. Gamester* (ed. 5) I. 128 The Queen..may pass from one end of the Board to the other at one Movement. *Ibid.* 131 After some Movements, you will find it impossible to proceed without exposing your Men or Officers.

d. Chiefly *pl.*: Actions, activities, 'doings' of a person or body of persons.

1833 CHALMERS in Hanna *Mem.* (1851) III. 388 He was one of the five who called the night before, and arranged for us then part of the movements of this day. **1861** M. PATTISON *Ess.* (1889) I. 34 The close attention which was paid in England to every step and movement of the new emperor. *Mod.* They eyed his movements with keen interest. The police watched the movements of the mob.

e. The conveying of cattle from one district to another, often prohibited or restricted during an epidemic of cattle disease.

1869 *Act 32 & 33 Vict.* c. 70 §48 Every local authority and the police of every county..shall..do or cause to be done all things..necessary..for securing, as far as may be, the effectual isolation of infected places in respect of the movement of animals and things. **1878** *Act 41 & 42 Vict.* c. 74 §32 Prohibiting or regulating the movement of animals and persons into, in, or out of an infected place or area. **1954** W. R. WOOLDRIDGE *Farm Animals* iv. 74 The Contagious Diseases (Animals) Act..gave adequate powers for the control of all movement of cattle. *Ibid.* vi. 173 Much has been written for and against the policy of suppressing the disease [*sc.* foot-and-mouth] by..rigid control of movement within a wide area.

f. The departure or arrival of an aircraft.

1961 P. W. BROOKS *Mod. Airliner* vi. 144, 130 aircraft movements (arrivals and departures) on a peak Summer day. **1969** *Sunday Times* (Colour Suppl.) 17 Aug. 19/1 Many of the major airports are suffering from aerial traffic jams, and the 747 will mean only one movement where there might have been two or more. **1971** *Physics Bull.* Nov. 660/2 Night flying also assumes a significant percentage of the total number of movements.

†**2.** Used for *moment*. *Obs.*

1490 CAXTON *Eneydos* xxi. 76 That man..that..hath vttered his secretes vnto the entierly, so that thou knowest.. the places, the houres & mouementes, and the oportunyte of the tyme moost propyce for to speke wyth hym.

3. *concr.* **a.** A cause of movement. *Obs. rare*⁻¹.

1725 N. ROBINSON *Th. Physick* 25, I shall take it as a Postulatum granted, *viz.* That the Heart is the principal Movement in human Bodies.

b. *Mech.* (*a*) *sing.* and *pl.* The moving (as distinguished from the stationary) parts of a mechanism, e.g. of a watch or clock; (*b*) a particular part or group of parts in a mechanism serving some special purpose.

1678 *Lond. Gaz.* No. 1296/4 A Watch, with two silver Cases belonging to it, the Moodment [*sic*] being ungilt. **1684** WHEELER in *Phil. Trans.* XIV. 648 This hoop and the 2 Plates form the Case of the Movement. **1704** J. HARRIS *Lex. Techn.* I, *Movement*..signifies all those Parts of a Watch, Clock, or any such curious Engine which are in motion. **1710** BERKELEY *Princ. Hum. Knowl.* I. §60 The spring and wheels, and every movement of a watch. **1776** ADAM SMITH *W.N.* I. xi, A better movement of a watch, than about the middle of the last century could have been bought for twenty pounds, may now perhaps be had for twenty shillings. **1825** J. CROSSE *York Festival* 137 There are movements likewise for enabling the performer to play two or three sets of keys at once [on the organ]. **1860** EMERSON *Cond. Life* v. Wks. (Bohn) II. 383 Men are like Geneva watches with crystal faces which expose the whole movement. **1880** E. J. HOPKINS in Grove *Dict. Mus.* II. 607/2 A second substitute for the long tracker movements, etc., in large or separated organs, is the 'pneumatic tubular transmission system'. **1884** F. J. BRITTEN *Watch & Clockm.* 179 The plates and train of a watch without the escapement are also spoken of as the movement.

4. In certain figurative and immaterial applications. **a.** A 'moving' (of the mind) towards or from some object; an impulse of desire or aversion, an act of volition. Now *rare*. †*of* (one's) *proper movement* = of one's own motion.

1456 SIR G. HAYE *Law Arms* (S.T.S.) 26 He came nocht to his presence of his proper mouvement. *Ibid.* 141 To be renouned a worthy man of armes..was his principale movement. **1732** POPE *Ess. Man* II. 36 Could he, whose rules the rapid Comet bind, Describe or fix one movement of his Mind? **1752** HUME *Ess. & Treat.* (1777) I. 88 He has forgotten the movements of his heart. **1768** STERNE *Sent. Journ., Snuff-box* I. 57, I blush'd in my turn; but from what movements I leave to the few who feel to analyse. **1813** SHELLEY *Q. Mab* II. 50 The light and crimson mists.. Yielded to every movement of the will. **1852** THACKERAY *Shabby Genteel Story* ix, Brandon had some good movements in him. **1868** BAIN *Ment. & Mor. Sci.* I. iv. 80 The movements of the will are select and pointed to an end.

b. *Philos.* The regular process or course of thought in reasoning.

1869 *Jrnl. Specul. Philos.* III. 363 *note*, The movement (or dialectic) of the syllogism consists in mediating each term so that in the higher forms each (term) becomes a complete realization of the Comprehension (or Totality).

c. In a poem or narrative: Progress of incidents, development of plot; the quality of having abundance of incident, or of carrying on the interest of the reader.

1838 PRESCOTT *Ferd. & Is.* I. xx. II. 324 The dialogue is written with much vivacity and grace, and with as much dramatic movement as is compatible with only two interlocutors. **1878-83** VILLARI *Life & Times Machiavelli* (1898) I. ix. 410 He wrote Latin verses full of movement and fervour.

d. *Fine Art.* In a work of painting or sculpture, the quality of suggesting that the figures represented are moving. Also, in *Arch.*, harmonious variety in the lines and ornamentation of a building; freedom alike from monotony and incongruity.

1773-8 R. & J. ADAM *Wks. in Archit.* Pref. 3 *note*, 'Movement'; meant to express, the rise and fall, the advance and recess with other diversity of form, in the different parts of a building, so as to add greatly to the picturesque of the composition. *c* **1782** *Exhibition, or second Anticipation* 35 They are nobly negligent of the constituent parts, and trust for the effect to the movement. **1867** A. BARRY *Sir C. Barry* iv. 126 Repose, rather than what artists call 'movement', was the characteristic of his designs.

5. a. *Music.* (*a*) The manner in which a piece or a passage 'moves': variously applied to manner of melodic progression, 'tempo' or relative speed of performance, and rhythm or accentual character. (*b*) quasi-*concr.* A principal division of a musical work, having a distinctive melodic and rhythmical structure of its own.

1771 *Encycl. Brit.* III. 326/1 The most common movement of jiggs, which is by six or twelve quavers in a bar, have their bass, for the smoothness of the movement, often written in plain crotchets. **1776** BURNEY *Hist. Mus.* (1789) I. iv. 56 The beginning or first movement of the piece he mentions was in *A*. **1818** BUSBY *Gram. Mus.* 476 If the piece be intended for an overture to a three-act opera..or a grand sonata, it ought not to consist of fewer than three movements. **1823** CRABB *Technol. Dict., Movement* (*Mus.*), the progress or course of sounds from grave to acute, or from acute to grave. **1846** KEBLE *Lyra Innoc.* (1873) 204 Some heart-thrilling chime, Some Dorian movement, bold or grave.

transf. **1822** *Blackw. Mag.* XII. 28 She is led up from hall to hall of the high-piled edifice, in one continued movement, may we call it, of the poem.

b. *Prosody.* Rhythmical or accentual character; in classical prosody often applied to the manner in which what is theoretically the same metre may be differentiated by variety of treatment.

1871 B. TAYLOR *Faust* I. 274 The movement of the original is as important as its meaning. Shelley's translation of the stanza's, however, is preferable to Hayward's. **1871** *Public Sch. Lat. Gram.* 468 Propertius..in his later [poems] ..approaches much nearer to the Ovidian movement. **1887** BOWEN *Virg.* Pref. (1889) 9 The orderly and majestic movement of the Roman hexameter.

c. *Dancing.* (See quot. 1967.)

1949 SHURR & YOCOM *Mod. Dance* v. 135 When the count is finally speeded-up, do *not* omit any of the suspended movements. **1949** *Ballet Ann.* III. 40 Movement after movement was ruined by the broken line. **1967** CHUJOY & MANCHESTER *Dance Encycl.* (rev. ed.) 647/2 *Movement*, the fundamental language of dance; a purposeful change of weight or position, as contrasted with motion, which in dance is considered as purely kinetic, i.e. physical, while movement is metakinetic.

6. a. A course or series of actions and endeavours on the part of a body of persons, moving or tending more or less continuously towards some special end. Often with defining word prefixed, as in ***the Oxford movement*** (see OXFORD).

1828 D'ISRAELI *Chas. I*, I. viii. 250 A long line of secret communication made him the centre of every political movement. **1856** FROUDE *Hist. Eng.* (1858) II. vii. 137 The Reformation was essentially a Teutonic movement. **1885** *Pall Mall G.* 1 Dec. 4/1 Oxford is the home they say of movements, and Cambridge of men. **1903** C. E. OSBORNE *Fr. Dolling* xxii, The main aims and principles of the Catholic Movement in the Anglican Church.

b. ***in the movement***: 'in the swim', (moving or taking part) in the direction or tendency of things which is prevalent at a particular period or in a particular field.

1894 *World* 5 Sept. 11/2 We have in *The New Woman* a live play, a play which is distinctly in the movement. **1907** *Q. Rev.* July 160 To make life vivid: to be 'in the movement', this was his [*sc.* Disraeli's] desire. **1926** C. SIDGWICK *Sack & Sugar* xxvi. 299 She..had quite antiquated Victorian ideas of what English people had nowadays if they were in the movement. She had not got beyond shiny chintzes and overmantels.

c. The way in which 'things' are moving at a particular time or in a particular sphere.

1846 J. D. MORELL *View Specul. Philos.* I. 152 By so doing, he [*sc.* Descartes] has unquestionably merited the reputation of standing at the head of the whole modern movement of metaphysical philosophy. **1861** BUCKLE *Civiliz.* II. vi. 587 Read by..thousands..who accept its conclusions because they like them; which is merely saying, because the movement of the age tends that way. **1874** GREEN *Short Hist.* viii. §1. 449 It was long before the religious movement..came into conflict with general culture.

d. (With capital initial.) A group of English poets in the nineteen-fifties, their characteristics, or their influence. Also *attrib.*

[**1954** *Spectator* 27 Aug. 261/1 Poets of the Fifties... For better or for worse, we are now in the presence of the only considerable movement in English poetry since the Thirties.] *Ibid.* 1 Oct. 399/1 (*heading*) In the Movement. *Ibid.* 399/2 In these columns some weeks ago Mr. Anthony Hartley remarked upon some of the characteristics of this new Movement of the Fifties—its metaphysical wit, its glittering intellectuality, its rich Empsonian ambiguities. *Ibid.* 400/2 Genuflections towards Dr. Leavis and Professor Empson, admiration for people whom the Thirties by-passed, Orwell above all..are indeed signs by which you may recognise the Movement... The Movement, as well as being anti-phoney, is anti-wet. **1958** A. ALVAREZ in *Internat. Literary Ann.* I. 99, I have been using the past tense because the Movement has now ended and its poets have gone off on their separate ways... The Movement, for all its limitations and negatives, was immensely valuable. **1958** *Times Lit. Suppl.* 17 Jan. 30/4 The poetry-fanciers say that there are two better Movement poets than either Mr Wain or Mr Amis. *Ibid.* 7 Mar. 127/1 The outstanding performer, or even the 'real poet' of the original Movement is Mr. Philip Larkin. **1959** *Ibid.* 27 Feb. 114/2 Around 1953, Mr. Larkin, Mr. Amis, Mr. Wain and the rest of them burst on a startled world—and 'the Movement' restored to English poetry self-control, precision, and clarity. **1961** *Listener* 24 Aug. 268/1 The decade just ended, a decade dominated by a group of university poets usually referred to as the Movement. **1972** *Times Lit. Suppl.* 14 Apr. 411/3 One need only look at the standard Movement and post-Movement poetry of that period. **1972** D. TIMMS *Philip Larkin* i. 15, I am reminded here of John Wain's description of the Movement as an *avant garde* that was a rear guard.

7. [After F. *le parti du mouvement.*] Applied, in the first half of the 19th c., to designate the aims of the 'liberal' or innovating parties in European politics. Chiefly *attrib.*, as in ***movement party***.

1835 DE QUINCEY *Wks.* (1863) XV. 213 The new doctrines of Radical Reformers, and of that section amongst political men denominated the Movement party. **1835** *Court Mag.* VI. 116/2 If the movement party retains its ascendency. **1838** MILL *A. de Vigny* Diss. & Disc. (1859) I. 291 The sympathies of the Radical or Movement poet will take the opposite direction. **1842** T. ARNOLD *Lect. Mod. Hist.* v. 246 The popular side in the great questions of English history, the side, in later language, of the movement.

8. *Comm.* Activity in the market for some commodity. Also, a rise or fall in price.

1886 *Rep. Sec. Treas.* I. 58 (Cent.) The total movement of bonds held for national banks was $87,967,300. **1890** *Century Dict.* s.v., The movement in coffee is insignificant. **1895** *Funk's Stand. Dict.* s.v., An upward movement in stocks.

9. = MOTION *sb.* 11.

1891 *Syd. Soc. Lex., Movement,*..the act of evacuating the bowels; as well as the matter resulting therefrom.

10. *attrib.* and *Comb.*, as ***movement area***, ***-complex***, ***control***, ***-habit***, ***-illusion***, ***-impulse***, ***-melody***, ***order***, ***-response***, ***-sensation***, ***-study***, ***time***; (sense 3 b) ***movement-maker***; (sense 6) ***movement party***; **movement cure** = *kinesipathy*: see KINESI-; **movement permit**, permission to move cattle from a particular district; **movement restriction**, a ban on the movement of cattle from a district, esp. when cattle disease is present.

1958 *Chambers's Techn. Dict.* 995/2 **Movement area*, that part of an aerodrome reserved for the take-off, landing and movement of aircraft. **1924** R. M. OGDEN tr. *Koffka's Growth of Mind* v. 251 *Movement-complexes of grasping and touching..are learnt even earlier than walking. **1956** W. A. HEFLIN *U.S. Air Force Dict.* 334/2 *Movement control. **1969** *Times* 6 Jan. 7/7 Secondary effects of movement control and closed markets left a trail of expense and inconvenience. **1972** L. LAMB *Picture Frame* ii. 21 He arranged with movement control to go a different way. **1856** M. ROTH (*title*) The *Movement Cure. **1920** T. P. NUNN *Education* xiii. 169 Recognition-habits of increasing complexity corresponding to the increasingly complex *movement-habits of writing. **1894** CREIGHTON & TITCHENER tr. *Wundt's Human & Animal Psychol.* ix. 137 It has sometimes been thought that the act of will suffices of itself to explain these subjective *movement-illusions. **1924** R. M. OGDEN tr. *Koffka's Growth of Mind* iv. 156 The sensory impressions and the *movement-impulse of the animal under investigation. **1736** AINSWORTH *Lat. Dict.*, A *movement maker, *Internarum horologii portatilis partium faber.* **1884** F. J. BRITTEN *Watch & Clockm.* 82 What movement-makers call a bay-leaf pinion. **1924** R. M. OGDEN tr. *Koffka's Growth of Mind* v. 259 In this unification a '*movement-melody' composes itself. **1956** W. A. HEFLIN *U.S. Air Force Dict.* 334/2 *Movement order. **1957** P. KEMP *Mine were of Trouble* iii. 51 Your Movement Order will be sent to your Squadron in a few days. **1973** *Radio Times* 8 Nov. 19/2 It's really like the movement order for an operation. You move up to your start line. **1969** *Times* 27 Jan. 10/8 Brucellosis accredited cattle only will be shown at the Surrey county show... Cattle entered there will require only a *movement permit. **1954** L. B. AMES et al. *Rorschach Responses in Old Age* xii. 141 Human *movement responses become more passive with increasing deterioration of subjects. **1969** *Times* 6 Jan. 7/7 Hogs kept at home, and sometimes in one field because of *movement restrictions, fared less well. **1898** G. F. STOUT *Man. Psychol.* I. II. vi. 192 The distinction between position-sensations and *movement-sensations is important. **1951** J. M. FRASER *Psychol.* xv. 187 It is fatally easy to make *movement-study sound difficult. **1952** *New Biol.* XIII. 58 The time between the beginning of his movement and the moment at which he starts to return back again is called 'The *Movement Time'. **1968** R. N. SINGER *Motor Learning & Human Performance* iii. 67 Movement time may include reflex or reaction time, or, as it is usually viewed in research literature, the time a particular act takes to be completed after it has been initiated.

†**'moven**, *a. Obs.* [irreg. pa. pple. of MOVE *v.*; cf. *proven.*] Motioned; proposed; brought forward.

1641 PRYNNE *Antip.* 78 They..agreed to offer the King a great summe of mony, to stay this new moven Demand.

†**'movent**, *a.* and *sb. Obs.* [ad. L. *movent-em*, pres. pple. of *movēre* to MOVE.] **A.** *adj.* That moves or is moved; moving.

1644 DIGBY *Nat. Bodies* ix. §11. 73 The force of the velocity is equall to a reciprocall force of weight in the vertue mouent. **1665** HOOKE *Microgr.* 197 The smooth wing'd Insects have the strongest muscles or movent parts of their wings. *a* **1734** NORTH *Life Ld. Kpr. Guilford* (1742) 292 Whoever observes them, even in their most quiet State, shall discern their Fins more or less movent and employ'd.

b. *Law.* (See quot.)

1837 T. D. HARDY *Rot. Chart.* Pref. 23 Comprised in the premisses of a charter, and generally following the salutation, occurs the Movent Clause, which is here so called because it states the reasons moving the king to make the grant.

B. *sb.* Something that moves or is moved.

1656 tr. *Hobbes' Elem. Philos.* (1839) 212, I define force to be the impetus or quickness of motion multiplied either into itself, or into the magnitude of the movent, by means whereof the said movent works more or less upon the body that resists it. **1665** G. HARVEY *Advice agst. Plague* 1 Physicians can never discharge their Duty with greater Applause than by contributing their aid to popular Diseases, which at this season is the prime movent of these Meditations. **1706** in PHILLIPS (ed. Kersey).

mover[1] ('muːvə(r)). Also 4 **moevere**, 4-5 **mever**, 6 **meever**, *Sc.* **movar**, 6-7 **moover**. [f. MOVE *v.* + -ER[1]; cf. OF. *mo(u)veor*, *mo(u)veur.*]

1. One who moves or sets in motion. Applied *esp.* to God, as moving the universe; also ***First Mover*** (cf. 2 a).

c **1384** CHAUCER *H. Fame* I. 81 He that mouer ys of alle. *c* **1386** —— *Knt.'s T.* 2129 The firste moeuere of the cause aboue. **1593** SHAKS. *2 Hen. VI*, III. iii. 19 Oh thou eternall mouer of the heauens. **1667** MILTON *P.L.* VII. 500 Now Heav'n..rowld Her motions, as the great first-Movers hand First wheeld thir course. **1772** PRIESTLEY *Inst. Relig.* (1782) I. 10 How could these atoms move without a mover. **1817** J. SCOTT *Paris Revisit.* (ed. 4) 120 The whole dreadful machine [*sc.* the army] was now in motion,—..the eye of the mover superintending and understanding all. **1879** DORA L. SHEPHERD *Liturg. Year* I. iii. 11 The soul yields herself up ..to the impulse of the divine Mover.

2. Something which sets in motion or actuates. **a.** ***first mover***, in mediæval astronomy = *first motor*, PRIMUM MOBILE. Also *fig.*

1586 T. B. *La Primaud. Fr. Acad.* I. (1594) 72 From the tower of the highest heaven, called the first moover, unto the center of the earth. **1617** BACON *Sp. in Star-Chamber* Resusc. (1657) 87 Do therefore, as they [*sc.* the planets] do; Move alwayes and be carried, with the Motion of your first Mover, which is your Soveraign. **1676** DRYDEN *State Innoc.* IV. i, So Orbs, from the first Mover, Motion take.

b. A machine or mechanical agency which imparts motion. ***first mover***: an initial source, natural or mechanical, of motive power; *spec.* a machine which receives and modifies motive power supplied by some natural source. See also PRIME MOVER.

1654 J. OWEN *Doctr. Saints Persev.* v. §5. 113 In your Automata, there is one originall spring or wheele, that giveth motion to sundry lesser and subordinate movers. **1711** W. SUTHERLAND *Shipbuild. Assist.* 108 The Main-mast is the first Mover. **1815** J. SMITH *Panorama Sci. & Art* I. 402 When a fly is used merely as a regulator, it should be near the first mover. **1845** *Encycl. Metrop.* VIII. 88/1 Of water as a first mover.

fig. **1788** JEFFERSON *Writ.* 1859 II. 471 The treasury became literally moneyless and all purposes depending on this mover, came to a stand.

†**c.** A cause (*of*). *Obs.*

1611 SHAKS. *Cymb.* I. v. 9 These most poysonous compounds, Which are the moouers of a languishing death.

3. a. One who incites or instigates to action; one who promotes or originates (an action, etc.). Sometimes ***first mover*** (cf. 2 a, b) and PRIME MOVER.

1497 BP. ALCOCK *Mons Perfect.* A iij, The pryncipal & fyrst meuer to vertue in our soules. **1513** MORE in Grafton *Chron.* (1568) II. 776 The Duke was the first moouer of the Protector to thys matter. **1578** *Reg. Privy Council Scotl.* III.

20 The movaris of his majestie to attempt the same governament..hes sensyne..dissobeyit his majesteis chairgis. **1704** DE FOE in *15th Rep. Hist. MSS. Comm.* App. IV. 83 Providence, which I humbly recognize as the first mover of your thoughts in my favour. **1711** SWIFT *Jrnl. to Stella* 22 Apr., They will want him prodigiously in the House of Commons, of which he is the great mover. **1838** THIRLWALL *Greece* IV. xxvii. 17 The chief movers of the rebellion made their escape. **1826** DISRAELI *Viv. Grey* III. i, Who is the mover of the party?

b. *spec.* One who moves a proposition or proposal in a deliberative assembly.

1737 *Gentl. Mag.* VII. 525/1 Therefore we must suppose, that without any Regard to the Mover, the Parliament approved of the Motion. **1795** WINDHAM *Speeches Parl.* 27 May (1812) I. 268 The house had now heard the reasons urged by the Honourable Mover and Seconder, in support of a motion so extraordinary. **1876** BANCROFT *Hist. U.S.* V. lxix. 317 In the absence of the mover of the resolution, the eyes of everyone turned towards its seconder, John Adams.

4. A person or thing that moves or is in motion. Now chiefly of an animal, with prefixed adj. indicating the manner or speed of his motion or 'going'.

1592 SHAKS. *Ven. & Ad.* 368 O fairest mouer on this mortall round. **1597** J. S. *Guistard & Sismond* II. C 3, O slow malicious meeuer, thou cursed Saturne. **1736** BUTLER *Anal.* I. i. 22 Nor is there any Ground to think..that his Eyes are the Seers or his Feet the Movers. **1895** J. G. MILLAIS *Breath fr. Veldt* (1899) 157 Though elegant in form, this buck is but a poor mover.

5. *U.S.* One who is 'on the move' or flitting from one place to another; *spec.* a person migrating westwards; a tenant farmer who moves on after exhausting the fertility of a piece of land.

1810 M. DWIGHT *Journey to Ohio* (1912) 47 We are..near a tavern which is fill'd with movers & waggoners. **1822** J. FLINT *Lett. Amer.* 53 The other tavern was so completely thronged with movers, that [etc.]. **1849** LYELL *2nd Visit U.S.* (1850) II. 109 On board were many 'movers' going to Texas with their slaves. **1878** J. H. BEADLE *Western Wilds* xx. 327 Reluctantly the 'movers' consented to his remaining for the night. **1913** J. LONDON *Valley of Moon* 434 The 'movers'..lease, clean out and gut a place in several years, and then move on. **1944** W. BLAIR *Tall Tale America* 100 Instead of selling the seedlings from these nurseries..he'd ..give them to the movers—free. **1945** J. L. MARSHALL *Santa Fe* 230 'Boomers' and 'movers' tried again and again to take up land, filtering down from Kansas and up from Texas along the Santa Fe track.

6. A remover; one whose business it is to move furniture and other household goods, from one residence to another. *N. Amer.*

1838, etc. [see *house-mover* s.v. HOUSE *sb.*[1] 24]. **1894** *Boston Directory* 1944 J. W. Cook & Son,..movers of pianofortes, furniture, etc. *Ibid.* 1947 T. G. Buckley, piano and furniture mover. **1956** W. H. WHYTE *Organization Man* (1957) 286 It's a hell of a day—the kids are crying..and the movers won't be finished till late. **1968** *Globe & Mail* (Toronto) 3 Feb. 3/9 'The honorable gentleman will be glad to know that I will be getting out as soon as I can get a mover,' the Prime Minister replied.

7. *Chess.* With prefixed numeral, denoting a problem in which the king is to be mated in a specified number of moves.

[*Two-, three-mover*, etc., are properly distinct words, f. numeral + MOVE *sb.* + -ER[1].]

1900 *Westm. Gaz.* 14 Apr. 3/3 A three-mover by Loyd which we consider a remarkable composition.

†**mover**[2]. *Obs.* In ***office of mover*** = AMOBRESHIP, MOBARSHIP.

1473 *Rolls of Parlt.* VI. 86/1 Th' office of mover within Dynbiegh Land in Wales.

[ˈ**moveress.** A female mover.

Introduced by modern editors into the text of Chaucer *Rom. Rose* 149, where Thynne and the MS. have *mynoresse*. Although Méon's edition of the French original has *moverresse*, other texts have *meneresse*, which is doubtless the reading that Chaucer had before him. There is therefore no ground for altering Thynne's text.]

†ˈ**movership.** *nonce-wd. Obs.* [f. MOVER[1] + -SHIP.] ***first movership***: the office of a 'first mover'.

1658 BRAMHALL *Schism guarded* I. xii. Wks. (1677) 351 He urgeth that I ascribe no more to St. Peter and the Pope for their first Movership, but onely authority to sit first in Council or some such things.

movie (ˈmuːvɪ). orig. *U.S.* Also †**movy.** [Abbrev. of MOVING PICTURE: see -IE, -Y[6].]

a. = MOVING PICTURE; also, a moving-picture show; a cinema; *pl.* (freq. ***the movies***), motion pictures as an industry, an art-form, or a form of entertainment; a cinema or a cinema-show.

1912 *Survey* (N.Y.) 20 Jan. 1628 (*heading*) 'Movies' and the law. **1912** J. SANDILANDS *Western Canad. Dict.* 30 *Movie*, a moving picture show. **1913** F. A. TALBOT *Pract. Cinematogr.* iii. 22 Taking the 'movies' is quite as simple as snap-shot photography with a Kodak. **1913** *N.Y. Even. Post* 10 July 5/7 Guiding the wheel-chair through the entrance gate of the outdoor 'movie'. **1913** *Home Chat* 27 Sept. 578/1 The comparatively small towns [in America] have installed 'movies'—as they call them over there—in their schools. **1914** M. CARRINGTON *Memories* I. 69 A night at the 'movies'. **1916** 'B. M. BOWER' *Phantom Herd* xi. 193 Say, do I get it right that you're in the movies. **1918** C. SANDBURG *Cornhusker* 51 There is drama in that point... Griffith would make a movie of it to fetch sobs. **1918** G. B. SHAW *Pen Portraits* (1932) 36 Is an evening with Ibsen as popular as an evening with Mary Pickford at the movies? **1919** —— *Heartbreak House* I. 26 You frequent picture palaces... Talk like a man, not like a movy. **1925** F. SCOTT FITZGERALD *Great Gatsby* (1926) vii. 150 Those big movies around Fiftieth Street are cool. **1929** H. G. WELLS *King who was King* i. 15 It was possible for some of us to forget the crude, shallow trade 'movies' we had seen. **1938** E. BOWEN *Death of Heart* II. v. 268 Some of the party wished to go to a movie. *Ibid.* vi. 281 He wanted me to cut off with him somewhere last night, after the movies. **1942** *Short Guide Gt. Brit.* (U.S. War Dept.) 13 The British have theaters and movies (which they call 'cinemas') as we do. **1950** T. S. ELIOT *Cocktail Party* III. 148 You must have been living a quiet life! Don't you go to the movies? **1971** *Mod. Law Rev.* XXXIV. 705 There is so much happening in the field of human rights that there is a great temptation to postpone publication until we see how the movie is going to end.

b. *attrib.* and *Comb.*, as ***movie actor, actress, ad, advertisement, buff, business, camera, cowboy, fan, film, hero, industry, king, -land, magazine, -maker, -making, -man, medium, picture, play, projector, queen, scenario, script, show, star, studio, test, theatre***; **moviegoer**, one who goes to the cinema; one who frequently attends film-shows; hence **moviegoing** *vbl. sb.* and *ppl. a.*; **movie house**, a cinema; **movie palace**, a (palatial) cinema.

1913 *Writer's Mag.* Dec. 264/2 If you want a chance to pay tribute to some 'movie' actor get a copy of the *Ladies World*, and 'full particulars'. **1935** WODEHOUSE *Luck of Bodkins* xv. 178 The kid points and says: 'Look, mamma. Movie actors!' And the mother says: 'Hush, dear—you don't know what *you* may come to some day.' **1924** 'J. SUTHERLAND' *Circle of Stars* xi. 114 Mountrose is going to marry an American movie-actress. **1949** M. LOWRY *Let.* 1 July (1967) 180 My.. brother-in-law, who entertains himself..by listening to the chests of movie actresses. **1951** M. MCLUHAN *Mech. Bride.* (1967) 82/1 In one movie ad the woman says: 'I killed a man for this kiss.' **1918** N. ANGELL *Political Conditions Allied Success* p. vii, As the movie advertisement of the war play says: 'You can't put up a good fight until your blood boils.' **1973** *Guardian* 30 Mar. 12/6 Imagine the feelings of a movie-buff if he were told he'd have to get along without Bunuel, Bergman, Chabrol, [etc.]. **1916** 'B. M. BOWER' *Phantom Herd* v. 71 There's no art for art's sake in the movie business. **1925** H. L. FOSTER *Trop. Tramp with Tourists* 118 The company's cinema operator had his movie camera set up in one corner. **1934** *Punch* 14 Nov. 536/2 He and another journalist..bought..a couple of small movie-cameras and all the film there was in Australia. **1961** T. HENROT *Belgium* 185 You may bring in..a small movie-camera with fifteen meters of film. **1926** A. HUXLEY *Let.* 13 May (1969) 269 One mounts a mule and goes off with a movie cowboy down into the gulf. **1941** AUDEN *New Year Let.* III. 68 Some Texas where real cowboys seem Lost in a movie-cowboy's dream. **1913** *Outlook* 5 Apr. 784/1 The 'movie' fan lays himself open to overtired eye nerves. **1952** S. KAUFFMANN *Philanderer* (1953) iv. 59 There were seven pulps, ten comic magazines, three movie-fan magazines, three confession magazines. **1922** *Atlantic Monthly* June 775 Half the movie films seem almost to have been made for the flapper. **1959** HALAS & MANVELL *Technique Film Animation* 11 A movie film exposed at normal speed can..be said to analyse every second of live action in terms of a given number of successive phases of movement. **1923** T. LANE *What's Wrong with Movies* 49 The author's name..means absolutely nothing to the bulk of movie-goers. **1953** *Time* 27 July 76/1 There is..a danger that some impressionable movie-goers, unable to make up their minds which of the stars they prefer, may go quietly hysterical. **1973** *Sat. Rev. Society* (U.S.) Mar. 80/1 *Deep Throat* has grossed nearly a million dollars from moviegoers. **1938** I. BARRY tr. *Burdèche & Brasillach's Hist. Motion Pict.* 68 Further *Nick Carter* series..taught the public the habit of regular moviegoing. **1946** A. WARREN in W. S. Knickerbocker *20th Cent. English* III. 312 His conclusions..reassure the parents of movie-going children. **1951** 'J. WYNDHAM' *Day of Triffids* ii. 43 The great movie-going public. **1958** J. BALDWIN in W. King *Black Short Story Anthol.* (1972) 284 A lifetime of moviegoing behind her. **1928** *Manch. Guardian Weekly* 5 Oct. 266/4 The movie hero's knack Of dangling from a trembling wire Across a railway track. **1914** *Automobile Topics* XXXIV. 190/1 Selected bits of the picture..are being shown in the local 'movie houses'. **1932** *Times Lit. Suppl.* 22 Dec. 976/1 Sam, ticket-chopper in a movie-house. **1967** 'LA MERI' *Spanish Dancing* (ed. 2) 9 Maria Montero in whose group I danced in vaudeville and the movie houses. **1974** *Times* 19 Jan. 10/1 Local movie houses offering major releases. **1928** H. CRANE *Let.* 27 Apr. (1965) 325 'Crashing the gate'..seems to be exclusively applied to the movie industry. **1917** *Vanity Fair* (N.Y.) Dec. 68 Here we are privileged to behold the interior of a movie king's office. **1914** C. L. HAGEN in R. Grau *Theatre of Science* p. xxiv, Is it to be wondered at..that authors, actors, and science await the call to 'movie' land? **1928** *Daily Express* 16 Mar. 4/2 There are few people..better qualified to explain the mysteries of movie-land and of the technical side of films. **1929** E. WILSON *I thought of Daisy* ii. 90 It was a movie magazine called *Photo-Life*. **1955** W. GADDIS *Recognitions* I. v. 180 Movie magazines, simply all sex. **1957** N. FRYE *Anat. Crit.* 164 The moviemakers find some difficulty in getting anyone over the age of seventeen into their audiences. **1975** *Listener* 20 Mar. 387 Ingmar Bergman is not everyone's favourite movie maker. **1939** F. SCOTT FITZGERALD *Lett.* (1964) 415 To be plunged immediately into movie-making. **1973** *Listener* 22 Nov. 716/3 Movie-making depends on movie distributors. **1915** *Pearson's Mag.* Jan. 80 My first action..was to ask a movie-man going home with films, to bring me back a blue serge suit. **1916** 'B. M. BOWER' *Phantom Herd* xix. 309 The movie-man that runs this show for the Convention. **1948** *Sun* (Baltimore) 1 Dec. 17/4 Because the most hotly disputed of the series came unexpectedly the movie men did not have their cameras directed at second base. **1951** M. MCLUHAN *Mech. Bride* (1967) p. vi/1 A film expert, speaking of the value of the movie medium. **1917** *Chicago Defender* 22 Dec., Watch for our new movie palace. **1936** A. HUXLEY *Olive Tree* 40 When I was last at Margate a gigantic new movie palace had just been opened. **1955** W. GADDIS *Recognitions* I. vi. 220 The woman with me led me down a long street, and we came to a movie palace. **1966** L. COHEN *Beautiful Losers* (1970) I. 22 Let..no naked flashing breasts lure the dirty laundry of our daily lives into the movie palace. **1916** E. V. LUCAS *Vermilion Box* ccxiii. 250 I wish a movie picture could be taken of him. **1917** 'W. WYNNING' *Princes St. & Other Otago Rhymes* 11 A girl one sees in 'movie' plays. **1936** CHESTERTON *As I was Saying* xxxi. 191 The fiction on the film, the partisan version in the movie-play. **1959** *Sears, Roebuck Catal.* Spring & Summer 1396/7 Movie Projectors. **1962** M. MCLUHAN *Gutenberg Galaxy* 124 The reading of print puts the reader in the role of the movie projector. **1927** U. SINCLAIR *Oil!* xiii. 314 It's cost me eight million dollars to make a movie queen out of this baby. **1917** H. CRANE *Let.* 8 Oct. (1965) 10 Mrs. Walton and I are working out movie scenarios. **1964** M. MCLUHAN *Understanding Media* (1967) I. v. 65 When the movie scenario or picture story was applied to the *idea* article. **1950** M. LOWRY *Lett.* (1967) 2/9 Have written..a detailed movie script. **1973** L. HELLMAN *Pentimento* (1974) 268 The money I got from the movie script of *The Little Foxes*. **1913** *Technical World* Mar. 17/1 This novel feeling of amused satisfaction over a 'movie' show deepened. **1925** A. P. HERBERT *Laughing Ann* 33, I.. wish That life was a little like a movie-show. **1974** M. Z. LEWIN *Enemies Within* xxv. 107 I'll..tell Janie about the movie shows at the frat. **1919** H. L. WILSON *Ma Pettengill* ii. 39 [They saw] how much they were paying their president ..quoted beside some movie star's salary. **1937** H. G. WELLS *Brynhild* vi. 78 Two other of the applicants had 'done publicity' for movie stars. **1973** D. RAMSAY *Deadly Discretion* 129 Why do you conceal your beautiful eyes..? You are practising to be a movie star? **1914** *Munsey's Mag.* Jan. 735/2 Then he closed the door and advanced into the 'movie' studio. **1926** A. HUXLEY *Jesting Pilate* 261 Within the movie studio there shone no sun, only the lamps. **1952** M. MCCARTHY *Groves of Academe* (1953) x. 197 One of Furness's long-tressed Ritas was promised a movie-test. **1915** *Film Flashes* 13 Nov. 1 It's a long lane that has no movie theatre. **1968** *Michelin Guide N.Y. City* 9 Movie Theaters.—Like the theaters, many first-run movie houses are clustered in the Broadway area.

moviedom (ˈmuːvɪdəm). orig. *U.S.* Also **Moviedom.** [f. MOVIE + -DOM.] = *filmdom* (s.v. FILM *sb.*).

1916 in *Dialect Notes* (1918) V. 7 Methra Morrell, Moviedom's Greatest Actress. **1927** *Daily Express* 28 Nov. 13 Adolphe Zukor, from whose weakening hand the sceptre of Moviedom has been wrested by Joseph M. Schenck. **1947** *N.Y. Times* 27 July II. 4/3 Even in its depiction of moviedom, Hollywood has seen fit to glamourize itself. **1973** *Lebende Sprachen* XVIII. 38/2 US moviedom—BE/US film industry, BE cinema industry—Filmindustrie.

Movieola, var. MOVIOLA.

Movietone (ˈmuːvɪtəʊn). Also **movietone.** [f. MOVIE + TONE *sb.*] The proprietary name of a system employed in the making of sound films; a film made by this system; also used allusively of the style of presentation of newsreels formerly produced by the Movietone Company. Also *attrib.*

1927 *Daily Express* 27 Aug. 1/3 The 'movietone' is an invention with the same technical basis as the 'phonofilm'. **1927** *Glasgow Herald* 12 Oct. 11/1 The movietone..is a vast improvement on previous talking films. **1927** G. B. SHAW *Platform & Pulpit* (1962) 178, I am an actual real animal; I am not the latest movietone illusion. **1928** *Trade Marks Jrnl* 4 Apr. 534/1 Movietone... Cinematograph transparencies for exhibition. Fox Case Corporation..City..of New York, United States of America; manufacturers. **1928** *Liberty* 11 Aug. 25/2 George Bernard Shaw as he appears in a strip of Movietone film. Note the sound track on the left margin. **1930** *Nature* 19 July 93/1 With such a sound standard at a known distance from the movietone microphone, a record of pitch and intensity of pure notes covering a wide range of frequencies and intensities may be recorded on the film. *Ibid.*, Fig. 1 is a reproduction of a movietone film of an orchestra and the micro-photometric record of the music recorded. **1939** *Motion Pict. Herald* 28 Oct. 30/1 Movietone News has devoted two complete issues to the war. **1953** L. J. WHEELER *Princ. Cinematogr.* vii. 213 An invention by Theodore W. Case made possible the Fox-Case Movietone news, photographed by cameras fitted with a device capable of recording sound alongside the picture and on the same negative film. The Movietone camera was made possible by the ability of certain gas-filled lamps to vary in brightness in true relationship to the current which is passing through them. **1969** *Listener* 23 Jan. 123/2 A reading from the Old Testament about the death of Moses delivered in a hushed movietone voice.

moving (ˈmuːvɪŋ), *vbl. sb.* Forms: see MOVE *v.*; also 6 *Sc.* muyn. [f. MOVE *v.* + -ING[1].]

1. a. The action of the verb MOVE (in trans. and intr. uses); changing of place or position; stirring, motion, movement.

c **1380** WYCLIF *Sel. Wks.* II. 406 þes foure wyndis þat Crist spekiþ of moun be foure mevyngis of þe eir. **1398** TREVISA *Barth. De P.R.* IX. i. (1495) 345 There ben syxe manere meuynges, that ben callyd generacion, corrupcion, alteracion, augmentacyon, dimynucion and chaungynge of place. **1427** *Rec. St. Mary at Hill* (1905) 67 Payd for certeyne pavynge & mevynge of pewes in the cherche..vij s. ix d. **1570** BILLINGSLEY *Euclid.* I. def. ii. 2 A lyne is the mouyng of a pointe. **1610** BARROUGH *Meth. Physick* I. xxix. (1639) 48 Tremor..is a disease which is accompanied with two sundry movings. **1726** LEONI *Alberti's Archit.* II. 12/2 These forces..are of great power for the moving of any weight. **1850** TENNYSON *In Mem.* cxxi, Thou hear'st the village hammer clink, And see'st the moving of the team.

b. *spec.* The motion of the heavenly bodies. *Obs.*

1340 HAMPOLE *Pr. Consc.* 7609 Of þair moveyng þan have yhe no wonder. *c* **1391** CHAUCER *Astrol.* Prol., The .4. partie shal ben a theorik to declare the Moeuynge of the celestial bodies. **1426** LYDG. *De Guil. Pilgr.* 12323 The planetys..in ther mevynges. **1535** STEWART *Cron. Scot.* (Rolls) I. 87 [He knew the sun's] proper muyn and his mot raptyne. **1591** SHAKS. *1 Hen. VI*, I. ii. 1 Mars his true mouing. **1594**

BLUNDEVIL *Exerc.* III. I. viii. (1636) 285 The ninth heauen is . . without starres, hauing two mouings, the one from East to West upon the Poles of the world . ., and the other from West to East upon his owne Poles.

†c. Bodily movement or gesture. *Obs.*

1577 NORTHBROOKE *Dicing* (1843) 92 Those filthie and vnhonest gestures and mouings of enterlude players. **1602** SHAKS. *Ham.* II. ii. 317 What a piece of worke is a man! . . in forme and mouing how expresse and admirable? **1607** MARKHAM *Caval.* II. (1617) 123 Let him goe and come continuall with easie, soft, and vndisturbing mouings.

†d. Power or faculty of motion. *Obs.*

1499 CAXTON *Eneydos* iv. 29 Lyke a corps . . wythoute partycypacion of sensityf moeuynge. **1580** BLUNDEVIL *Order Curing Horses Dis.* xvi. 8 Those conduits through which the spirites animall do giue feeling, and mouing to the bodie.

†e. *Chess.* A move. *Obs.*

1474 CAXTON *Chesse* IV. vii. (1883) 179 One yssue and one mouynge apperteyneth vnto alle the peple [= pawns]. For they may goo fro the poynt they stande in at the first meuynge vnto the thirde poynt right forth to fore them [etc.].

f. ***moving of the waters***: used after John v. 3 for: A stir or excitement, a change or disturbance in the course of events.

[**1388** WYCLIF *John* v. 3 In these lay a greet multitude . . abidynge the mouyng of the watir. (So in all later versions.)] **1900** J. A. H. MURRAY *Evol. Eng. Lexicogr.* 27 But by the end of the sixteenth century, as by the end of the nineteenth, there was a moving of the waters.

†**2.** *fig.* A disturbance or commotion. *Obs.*

c **1450** *Godstow Reg.* 367 They considered . . that ther shold come therof, by the occasion of such maner of discencion, not all-only dyuerse mevyngis, but also . . harmes and expensis.

3. The action of prompting, instigating, etc.; †an inward prompting or impulse (= MOTION *sb.* 9).

c **1386** CHAUCER *Melib.* ¶273 Youre conseil . . ne sholde nat . . be called a conseillyng, but a mocion or a moeuyng of folye. *c* **1450** *Mirour Saluacioun* 4265 Oure wille and oure movinges knawes he wele evry whitte. **1502** ATKYNSON tr. *De Imitatione* III. lix. 249 Se thou gyue hede dylygentlye vnto the mouynges of nature & grace. *a* **1716** SOUTH *Serm.* (1744) XI. viii. 190 He also suffers by the movings and yearnings of his own compassion.

4. *Fencing*, etc. (see quot.). ? *Obs.*

1747 J. GODFREY *Sci. Defence* 31 The going down to the Leg . . is done after receiving or moving. . . Receiving is the stopping our Adversary's Blow first, and then going to his Leg: Moving is going down without receiving, but taking care before you go down, to move his Sword out of the Line. *Ibid.* 32 It is a difficult Matter for him to . . guard against your little or no notice-giving Movings and going down.

5. *attrib.*: ***moving business, -van***; †**moving-bell** (see quot.); **Moving Day**, (*a*) *U.S.* the first of May, being the usual day in New York for household removals (Schele de Vere *Americanisms*, 1872, p. 92); also (with lower-case initials), any other day on which people move to new premises; (*b*) *Mil.* a day on which a regiment or troops are on the march; **moving-man** *N. Amer.* = MOVER[1] 6.

?*c* **1760** NOLLEKENS in J. T. Smith *Life* (1828) I. 54 The Moving-bell . . goes when they move a body out of one parish to the next. **1973** *Times* 23 Oct. (Pickfords Suppl.) 1 Three hundred years experience in the moving business has helped keep Pickfords the biggest name in household removals. **1832** J. F. WATSON *Hist. Tales N.-Y.* 123 'Moving day' was, as now, the first of May. **1855** *Knickerbocker* XLV. 585 In the southern part of New-Jersey, one who rents or purchases a house or farm usually takes possession of the same on the twenty-fifth day of the present month [*sc.* March], which is therefore denominated 'moving-day'. **1897** *Cavalry Tactics* ii. 7 It is better to lengthen the marches on the moving days than to omit the rest day. **1947** *Pasadena* (Calif.) *Star-News* 9 Sept. 16/6 Moving days are ahead for several county departments in the Hall of Records and Hall of Justice, Los Angeles. **1973** Moving day [see *moving-man* below]. **1922** H. L. FOSTER *Adventures Trop. Tramp* xii. 179 While he shipped the furniture from the old place, I was to go down to the new one to see that the moving-men stole none of it en route. **1965** M. MCINTYRE *Place of Quiet Waters* ii. 29 'How right you are, Miss,' said the moving-man. **1973** *National Observer* (U.S.) 3 Feb., When our moving men finally showed up ('removals' in their business, whether you are coming or going, and on moving day we hardly knew which we were) we received another language lesson. **1898** *Kansas City* (Missouri) *Star* 21 Dec. 9/2 The moving vans and pie-wagons of New York are changing their pictures. **1925** T. DREISER *Amer. Trag.* (1926) II. III. xxvii. 334 A venal moving-van company had revealed her address. **1963** *PMLA* Dec. p. vii/2 U.K. removals lorry: U.S. moving van.

moving (ˈmuːvɪŋ), *ppl. a.* [f. MOVE *v.* + -ING[2].] **1. a.** That moves (in intransitive senses); that passes from one place to another; capable of moving, or of being moved; not fixed or stationary.

In quot. *c* 1386 *firste moevyng* may be *absol.* = PRIMUM MOBILE, in apposition with *firmament*.

c **1386** CHAUCER *Man of Law's T.* 197 O firste moeuyng crueel firmament. *c* **1400** MAUNDEV. (1839) xxviii. 282 Dreadfulle Eyen, that ben evere more mevynge and sparklynge, as Fuyr. **1605** SHAKS. *Macb.* v. v. 38 Within this three Mile you may see it comming, I say, a mouing Groue. **1683** MOXON *Mech. Exerc., Printing* xii. ¶6 Extend the moving Foot of your Compasses where it will fall in the Circle, and make there a Mark. **1798** COLERIDGE *Anc. Mar.* IV. x, The moving Moon went up the sky, And nowhere did abide. **1859** FITZGERALD tr. *Omar* li, The Moving Finger writes; and, having writ, Moves on. **1882** MINCHIN *Unipl. Kinemat.* 32 Path of a moving point relatively to a moving plane.

absol. *c* **1391** CHAUCER *Astrol.* I. §17 This equinoxial is cleped the girdel of the firste moeving. **1594** R. ASHLEY tr. *Loys le Roy* 125 b, They which in times past beheld the heauens, found but few mouings, and could scarce perceiue ten.

b. ***moving plant***: the Indian plant *Desmodium gyrans*, in which the leaflets are constantly moving.

1787 tr. *Linnæus' Fam. Plants* I. p. xix, The Moving plant (*Hedysarum movens*). **1866** *Treas. Bot.* 395/1.

c. *fig.* Unstable, changeful.

1560 ROLLAND *Crt. Venus* Prol. 61 For he that hes of the Air the nature, Is oft muifand, licht, merie, with plesure. **1599** *Pass. Pilgr.* xv, The morning rise Doth scite each mouing scence from Idle rest. **1712–14** POPE *Rape Lock* I. 100 The moving Toyshop of their heart.

d. That progresses, or moves forward.

1903 MORLEY *Gladstone* II. v. i. 4 Austria, in turn, was far too slow for a moving age.

2. That moves (in transitive senses).

a. That causes or produces motion.

1659 LEAK *Waterwks.* 8 The more the moving force is distant from the center of motion, so much the more force it shall have. **1822** IMISON *Sci. & Art* I. 52 The motion of machines must be excited and kept up by some cause which is called the moving power. **1838** KEBLE *Serm.* ix. (1848) 245 Which, had she been free and erect she might have achieved by her own moving force applied to her own machinery.

b. *transf.* That originates, causes, instigates, or actuates.

c **1489** CAXTON *Blanchardyn* xx. 65 Concedere you not that ye be occasion, and the cause mouyng of thassemble of the ostis that are for your towne, and of the shedyng of bloode that procedeth therof. **1682** *Eng. Elect. Sheriffs* 38 Nor may it be amiss briefly here to unfold both the first occasion of, and the moving Reason unto it. **1724** DE FOE *Mem. Cavalier* (1840) 172 The great moving men began to go out of town. **1833** J. H. NEWMAN *Arians* v. i. (1876) 353 The error . . of mistaking whatever shows itself on the surface of the Apostolic Community . . for the real moving principle and life of the system. **1902** R. LOVETT *Jas. Chalmers* ii. 46 He was a moving spirit in fun and mischief.

c. That touches, or has power to touch, the feelings; that affects or influences the mind.

1591 SHAKS. *Two Gent.* v. iv. 55 If the gentle spirit of mouing words Can no way change you to a milder forme; Ile wooe you like a Souldier. **1599** NASHE *Lenten Stuffe* 5 The delectablest lustie sight and mouingest obiect, me thought it was that our Ile sets forth. **1658** SLINGSBY *Diary* (1836) 220 Sure I am that the dying words of an affectionate Father cannot but fasten deeper, and retain a Memory longer then the speech of the movingst Orator. **1726** SWIFT *Gulliver* II. viii, I . . begged, by all that was moving, to be delivered out of the Dungeon I was in. **1837** MRS. CARLYLE *Lett.* (1883) I. 67 Mrs. Marsh, the moving authoress of the 'Old Man's Tales'. **1875** JOWETT *Plato* (ed. 2) I. 367 How he produced his children in court, which was a moving spectacle.

d. Of a question: Exciting public interest.

1907 *Outlook* 23 Mar. 390/1 His subject . . is one of the moving questions of our time.

3. Special collocations: **moving average**, an average derived from a series of values in which the interval contributing to it is of constant size but is moved progressively along the series (usually one value at a time) to give a succession of averages; **moving-coil** *attrib.*, denoting electrical instruments and apparatus in which a coil of wire is situated in a magnetic field, so that either the coil moves when a current flows through it or else a current is generated when it is caused to move; similarly **moving-conductor**; **moving-iron** *attrib.*, denoting electrical instruments and apparatus in which the passage of a current through a fixed coil of wire causes the movement of a piece of iron inside it; **moving map**, a map carried in a ship, aircraft, etc., which is displayed so that as the craft moves its position always corresponds to a fixed point in the middle of the map; **moving pavement**, a section of pavement arranged as a conveyer belt for the carrying of passengers; **moving stair(case)**, an escalator; also *fig.*; **moving-target** *attrib.*, applied to radar apparatus or techniques which give an indication only of targets moving relative to the transmitter, signals from stationary targets being eliminated.

1912 W. I. KING *Elem. Statistical Method* xv. 168 In determining on the size of groups to be used in calculating a moving average, one should use a period of time approximately equal to the length of the cycle which it is desired to eliminate. **1969** J. ARGENTI *Managem. Techniques* 174 If demand for a product over the past four weeks has been for 20, 23, 19, 19 units respectively, the average demand has been for 20 units. Now suppose another week passes in which the demand is 22 units, the new moving average is 20·5. This is calculated by dropping the earliest figure (20), adding the latest (22) and averaging again. **1896** W. E. AYRTON *Pract. Electr.* (new ed.) I. ii. 144 A very convenient, portable and accurate moving coil ammeter has been perfected by Mr. Weston, of Newark, America. **1903** G. D. A. PARR *Electr. Engin. Measuring Instruments* iii. 106 The ammeters belonging to the class of moving coil instrument measure current indirectly by indicating the fall of potential down a low-resistance 'shunt'. **1930** *Manch. Guardian* 20 Sept. 15/7 Moving-coil loud speakers are, of course, strongly in evidence. **1933** L. E. C. HUGHES *Elem. Engin. Acoustics* v. 77 The three forms of diaphragm action are incorporated respectively in the condenser (Wente) microphone, the moving-coil (Sykes) microphone, and the ribbon (Olson) microphone. **1968** *Radio Communication Handbk.* (ed. 4) ix. 12/2 A miniature moving-coil loudspeaker can sometimes be made to serve as a fairly satisfactory microphone. **1933** K. HENNEY *Radio Engin. Handbk.* xvi. 421 These have practically been superseded by the moving conductor drive (principally electrodynamic) and the larger portion of all loud-speakers in use today are of this type. **1966** *McGraw-Hill Encycl. Sci. & Technol.* VIII. 360/2 A moving conductor microphone consists of a straight-line conductor located in a magnetic field and coupled to a V-shaped diaphragm acted upon by sound waves. **1908** K. EDGCUMBE *Industr. Electr. Measuring Instruments* 27 One of the simplest windings to calculate is that of an ammeter coil such as would be used for a moving-iron instrument. **1940** A. WOOD *Acoustics* xviii. 529 The large diaphragm required in lieu of a horn may also be driven by an arrangement of the 'moving iron' type. **1966** *McGraw-Hill Encycl. Sci. & Technol.* XIV. 372/2 The moving-iron instrument, like the electrodynamic voltmeter, when properly calibrated indicates true rms volts. **1969** *Daily Tel.* 6 Mar. 18 The former Ministry of Aviation applied for Patent No. 926448 in 1960 to cover the moving map developed by that Ministry. **1969** *Sunday Tel.* 30 Mar. 1/4 Throughout the world more than 13,500 ships, 2,000 aircraft and some 1,000 helicopters use Decca navigation equipment including many 'moving map' displays. **1970** *New Scientist* 12 Mar. 508/2 The aircraft's position at any instant is shown by a spot of light at the centre of a six-inch moving-map display, showing the area over which the aircraft is flying. **1960** *Times Rev. Industry* Apr. 28/1 Passenger-carrying conveyor belt . . known as moving pavements. **1971** *Guardian* 22 June 6/6 Passenger conveyor systems, popularly known as moving pavements, could become a major form of city transport. **1922** Moving stair [see ESCALATE *v.* 1]. **1940** L. MACNEICE *Last Ditch* 12 And two people with the one pulse (Somebody stopped the moving stairs): Time was away and somewhere else. **1910** Moving staircase [see ESCALATOR 1]. **1927** HALDANE & HUXLEY *Animal Biol.* xiii. 309 The gill cilia are so arranged that all food-particles strained off by the gills are driven up to the dorsal groove. Here they become entangled and stuck in the slime, and are passed on by this sort of moving staircase to be digested in the intestine. **1959** *Chambers's Encycl.* V. 389/1 The escalator or moving staircase was originally developed in America; it was exhibited at the Paris Exposition in 1900, and the first to be installed in Britain (in 1911) was at Earl's Court station, London. **1953** PENROSE & BOULDING *Princ. & Pract. Radar* (ed. 4) xxiv. 645 The principles on which moving target indication and permanent echo cancellation work. **1966** E. LARSEN *Radar works like This* (rev. ed.) 39 An important advance in airport radar is the 'moving target indicator' . ., a type of radar equipment which shows only moving aircraft on the PPI. **1972** A. SUNDARABABU *Fund. Radar* xviii. 485 (*heading*) Moving target indication.

movingly (ˈmuːvɪŋlɪ), *adv.* [f. prec. + -LY[2].] In a moving, touching, or affecting manner.

1591 SHAKS. *Two Gent.* II. i. 134, I would haue had them writ more mouingly. *c* **1611** CHAPMAN *Iliad* III. 412 So fresh, and mouingly attir'd. **1711** STEELE *Spect.* No. 147 ¶2 The Art of Reading movingly and fervently. **1893** STEVENSON *Catriona* xix, 'And she pled for me?' says I. 'She did that, and very movingly'.

ˈmovingness. [f. MOVING *ppl. a.* + -NESS.] The quality of being moving or affecting.

1661 BOYLE *Style of Script.* 242 There is a strange Movingnesse . . to be found in some Passages of the Scripture, which is to be found no where else. **1669** GALE *Crt. Gentiles* I. III. x. 107 Plato commends . . the use of Repetitions as that which carries in it a great . . movingness of Affection [in oratory]. **1927** BEERBOHM *Lett. to R. Turner* (1964) 268, I do so agree about the movingness of the Jews at the Süss funeral. **1930** G. GREENE *Two Witnesses* 99 He was touched almost to speechlessness by the movingness of Christ.

moving picture. [f. MOVING *ppl. a.* + PICTURE *sb.*] †**1.** A picture in which objects move, or appear to move, in imitation of their natural motion. *Obs.*

1709 *Daily Courant* 9 May, The most Famous, Artificial and Wonderful Moving Picture that came from Germany. **1709–10** *Tatler* No. 129 ¶1 The moving Picture in Fleet-Street. **1713** SWIFT *Jrnl. to Stella* 27 Mar. (1948) II. 647, I went afterwards to see a famous moving Picture, & I never saw any thing so pretty. **1715** *Boston News-Let.* 14 Mar. 2/2 The Italian Matchean, or Moving Picture, wherein are to be seen, Wind-Mills and Water-Mills moving round. **1727** M. W. MONTAGU *Let.* Mar. (1966) II. 73, I now and then peep upon these things with the same coldness I would do on a moving Picture. **1782** *Town & Country Mag.* Apr. 208/2 With moving pictures Loutherburg displays His graphic skill. . . He derives new pow'rs, To drive fatigue from exhibition hours. **1822** *Hive* I. 66/1 The illustrations consisted of a series of finely painted scenes, which were made to change their effect and constructions, and accompany, in a rapid and beautiful manner, the progress of the story, embodying, as it were, in a moving picture, almost as vivid as the tablet of a camera obscura, every circumstance as it fell from the speaker's lips. **1899** *Science Siftings* XV. 242/1 A second edition has reached us of the 'Motograph Moving Picture Book' . . . These moving pictures should prove interesting to children.

2. A cinematographic picture or film. Also *attrib.*

1896 QUEEN VICTORIA *Jrnl.* 3 Oct. in *Lett.* (1932) 3rd Ser. III. 87 We were all photographed . . by the new cinematograph process, which makes moving pictures by winding off a reel of films. **1897** *Sketch* 13 Oct. 480/2 One guinea and half-a-guinea are being asked for stalls to see the moving pictures of the Corbett-Fitzsimmons fight at the Empress Theatre. **1898** *N.Y. Tribune* 30 Oct. 8/3 The always interesting moving pictures in the biograph . . will include . . four new scenes. **1906** 'O. HENRY' *Four Million* 3 He cursed the moving pictures. **1907** *Pearson's Mag.* Jan. (Advt.), Moving Picture Machines. **1912** F. A. TALBOT (*title*) Moving pictures: how they are made and worked. **1913** *Punch* 2 Apr. 253/3 It [*sc.* Mexico] contains a town of 10,000 inhabitants where there is no moving picture palace. **1921** G. B. SHAW *Back to Methuselah* III. 103 What earthly interest is there in looking at a moving picture of a lot of people merely because they were drowned? *Ibid.* 105 Weve had moving pictures of all four put on the screen today for this American. **1934** W. SAROYAN *Daring Young Man* 184 This sense of being out of time has driven thousands of people from their homes into moving-picture theatres where new universes appear before them. **1950** T. S. ELIOT *Cocktail Party* I. i. 34 A common interest in the moving pictures Frequently brings young people together. **1959** *Observer* 22 Feb. 19/6 The film is interesting, as a moving-picture record of a movement of our times.

Moviola (mu:vɪ'əʊlə). *Cinemat.* orig. *U.S.* Also **Movieola**, and with small initial. [f. MOVIE + *-ola*, after PIANOLA.] The proprietary name of a device whereby the picture and sound of a cinematographic film are reproduced on a small scale so that the film may be edited or checked.

1929 *Photoplay* (Chicago) Apr. 31/2 *Movieola*, miniature projection machine with earphones used in the cutting room of a talking picture studio for rapid viewing of pieces of film. **1931** B. BROWN *Talking Pict.* xi. 276 Lately, a device known as the 'Movieola' has been adopted,.. a miniature peep show projector with a loud speaker. **1933** C. WINCHESTER *World Film Encycl.* 483/1 *Moviola*, a little machine used by the film editors to see and hear the picture. **1944** *Trade Marks Jrnl.* 20 Sept. 455/1 Moviola... Projectors, synchronizing apparatus, film measuring machines, sound reading apparatus, sound amplifiers and re-winding apparatus; all for use in editing cinematographic films. Iwan Serrurier, trading as Moviola Company,.. Hollywood. **1959** HALAS & MANVELL *Technique Film Animation* xxv. 302 Music track run on a movieola and each note, phrase and sentence marked with grease pencil. **1970** *Daily Tel.* (Colour Suppl.) 6 Feb. 22/3 For ten weeks, three weeks longer than it took to shoot the movie, he works with the editor at the movieola. **1970** *Times* 5 Dec. 19/6 There was no movieola in those days... You just ran the film through your fingers and cut with a pair of scissors.

mow (maʊ), *sb.*[1] Forms: 1 **múȝa, múha, múwa**, 3 **moue, muȝe**, 3–7 **mowe**, 4 **mou**, 4, 7, 8 **mough**, 5 **moghe, mughe**, 6 **moowe, mowgh(e**, 8 **maw**, 9 *dial.* **mew, moo, mow**, 5– **mow**. [OE. *múȝa, múwa, múha* wk. masc., corresponding to ON. *múge* swath, also crowd of people (in the latter sense also *múg-r* str. masc.; cf. MSw. *moghe* masc., multitude, Sw. dial. *muga, muva* fem., heap, Norw. *muga, mua, mue* fem., heap, *muge* masc., heap, crowd). The word also exists in the compound ON. *almúge, almúg-r* (MSw. *almoghe, -mogher*, Sw. *allmoge*, Da. *almue*), common people.

Evidence that the word existed in some other Teut. lang. may possibly be afforded by Sp. *muga* landmark, pile (so app. med.L. *muga* from Spain), which, however, some scholars assert to be from Basque; and med.L. *mugium* haystack (one example from Italy dated 1334). The conjecture that the first element in OHG., MHG. *mûwerf* MOULDWARP represents this word is very doubtful.]

In England now mainly dialectal; in the U.S. it seems to be general.

1. A stack of hay, corn, beans, peas, etc.; also, a heap of grain or hay in a barn. Cf. HAY-MOW.

c **725** *Corpus Gloss.* (Hessels) A 108 *Acervus*, muha. *c* **1000** ÆLFRIC *Exod.* xxii. 6 ȝif fyr bærne muȝan oððe standende æceras. *c* **1050** *Voc.* in Wr.-Wülcker 348/6 *Aceruum*, muwan. *c* **1205** LAY. 29280, I þan euesen he [*sc.* þa sparwen] grupen swa heo duden in þen muȝen. *a* **1300** *Cursor M.* 6760 If fire be kyndeld and ouertak Thoru feld, or corn, or mou, or stak. **1375** BARBOUR *Bruce* IV. 117 He tuk a culter hat glowand, That het wes in a fyre byrnand... And heych vpon a mow [it] did. **1398** TREVISA *Barth. De P.R.* IV. i. (1495) 77 As it faryth in a were mough of whete. *a* **1400–50** *Alexander* 4434 þan as a Mare at a moghe ȝoure mawis ȝe fill. *c* **1470** HENRY *Wallace* XI. 339 A mow off corn he biggit thaim about. **1483** *Cath. Angl.* 245/2 A Mughe, *archonicus*. **1523** FITZHERB. *Husb.* 25 For and it sweate not in the heycockes it wyll sweate in the mowe. **1539** *Knaresborough Wills* (Surtees) I. 58 The value of a mowghe of hay. **1573** TUSSER *Husb.* (1878) 131 In gouing at haruest, learne skilfully how ech graine for to laie by it selfe on a mow. **1609** HOLLAND *Amm. Marcell.* 220 The whole mow or stacke being shaken was borne downe. **1718** RAMSAY *Christ's Kirk Gr.* III. xxi, But Lawrie he took out his nap Upon a mow o' pease. **1794** BILLINGSLEY *Agric. Surv. Somerset* (1797) 310 It is very difficult to keep the mows on stadles free from them [*sc.* rats and mice]. **1844** STEPHENS *Bk. Farm* II. 264 To pile up the sheaves as they are brought in into what are called *mows*, that is, the sheaves are placed in rows. **1862** LONGF. *Wayside Inn, Prel.* 28 The barns display.. their mows of hay. **1896** *Daily News* 19 Sept. 2/5 The stooks, locally called mows, present a mass of green shoots.

2. A place in a barn where hay or corn is heaped up.

1755 JOHNSON, *Mow*, a loft or chamber where hay or corn is laid up. **1856** G. HENDERSON *Pop. Rhymes Berwick* 91 They were engaged in carrying his corn from the stack in the barn-yard to the mow in the barn. **1884** *W. Sussex Gaz.* 25 Sept., Good spacious barn, asphalte floor, and mow.

†**3.** A heap or pile; also, a heap of earth, a mound, hillock. *Obs.*

1424 in Picton *L'pool Munic. Rec.* (1883) I. 23 On a mow within the said town we saw the said Sir Richard. **1513** DOUGLAS *Æneis* IV. ix. 69 Abufe the mowe the foirsaid bed was maid. **1681** W. ROBERTSON *Phraseol. Gen.* (1693) 899 A mow or heap, *strues*.

4. *attrib.* and *Comb.*: ***mow-breast, -maker, -side, -stack, -yard***; **mow-barton**, a stackyard; †**mow-floor**, the floor of a barn in which hay or corn is stored; **mow-heat**, a disease of hay or corn caused by overheating and fermenting in the mow; **mow-staddle**, 'the framework or stone upon which a stack is built' (*Eng. Dial. Dict.*); **mowstead**, (*a*) the place where the rick stands; the stand or supports which raise the rick from the ground; (*b*) a bay or division between the threshing-floor and the end of the barn; (*c*) a mass of hay or corn filling such a bay.

1789 *Trans. Soc. Arts*, etc. VII. 12 For [the] Fence of a *Maw-Barton on the same Farm. **1895** W. RAYMOND *Tryphena in Love* i. 8 He looked upon.. the cow-stalls and mow-barton full of yellow stacks. **1641** BEST *Farm. Bks.* (Surtees) 75 Putte them into the hey-house, and lette them lye att the *mowe-brest all night. **1868** *Rep. U.S. Commissioner Agric.* (1869) 424 Making chimneys, so to speak, in the mow, by putting barrels on the *mow floor and drawing them up as the hay was stowed about them. **1896** P. A. BRUCE *Econ. Hist. Virginia* I. 453 Spontaneous combustion, *mowheat, and the depreciation resulting from the entrance of sea water. **1766** *Chron.* in *Ann. Reg.* IX. 117/2 Let the *mow-maker be provided with a quantity of salt. **1865** MRS. WHITNEY *Gayworthys* I. 240 Wealthy tossed down great trusses of hay to them from the *mowside. **1894** BLACKMORE *Perlycross* 368 *Mowstack and oak-wood, farm-house and abbey. **1235–53** *Rentalia Glaston.* (Som. Rec. Soc.) 140 Et debet habere *mugstathel et unum sedlep plenum de frumente. **1530** *Will T. Tubbe of E. Challow, Berks*, So that shoe have my parlor & the over-chambre unto hir use wth a *mowsted in the north ende of my barne. **1629** *Inventory* in *Best's Farm. Bks.* (Surtees) 110 A piece of a mewstead of wheate and maslin unthresht 6 l. **1833** LOUDON *Encycl. Archit.* §889 Along the sides of the threshing-floor are what are called mowsteads. **1869** BLACKMORE *Lorna D.* xxxix, And here was our own *mowyard better filled than we could remember.

mow (maʊ, məʊ), *sb.*[2] Forms: 4 **mouwe**, 4–6 **mowe**, 5 **mawe**, 6 **mew**, 6–7 **moe**. *Pl.* 6 **moues, -is, mowis**, 6–8 **mows**, 6–7 **mowes**, 6, 9 **mous, mowse**. [a. OF. *moe, moue* mouth, lip, pout (mod.F. *moue* pouting grimace), of obscure origin; or perh. a. MDu. *mouwe* of the same meaning.

The MDu. word is prob. from OFr.; some, however, think that it was the source, regarding it as a special use of *mouwe* thick flesh (MOW *sb.*[4]), from which sense the senses 'thick lip', 'pout' are assumed to have been developed.

In England the word has little colloquial currency, and the pronunciation is uncertain. The British Dicts. give (maʊ), the recent U.S. Dicts. (moʊ). In Scotland, where the word is still in use, the sound is (mʌu).]

1. A grimace; esp., a derisive grimace.

c **1325** *Poems Times Edw. II* 348 in *Pol. Songs* (Camden) 339 He makketh the a mouwe. *c* **1374** CHAUCER *Troylus* IV. Prol. 7 And when a wight is from hire whiel Ithrowe, Than laugheth she and maketh hym þe mowe. **1390** GOWER *Conf.* II. 32 Wherof bejaped with a mowe He goth. *a* **1400–50** *Alexander* 4728 þan stode þai glorand on his gome with grisely mawis. *c* **1440** *Promp. Parv.* 346/1 Mowe, or skorne, *vangia, vel valgia*. **1484** CAXTON *Curiall* 4 The man that hath grete corage & vertuous mespriseth her lawhynges and mowes. **1535** COVERDALE *Ps.* xxxiv. 15 Yee ye very lame come together agaynst me vnawarres, makynge mowes at me, & cease not. **1581** PETTIE tr. *Guazzo's Civ. Conv.* III. (1586) 170 [They] will not stick to make moes at their maister behinde his back. **1611** SHAKS. *Cymb.* I. vi. 41 Apes, and Monkeys 'Twixt two such she's would chatter this way, and Contemne with mowes the other. **1660** F. BROOKE tr. *Le Blanc's Trav.* 333 One that we preserved alive was quite amazed, and made us good laughing, with his mows and monkey faces. **1794** GODWIN *Cal. Williams* 80 By that devil that.. made mows and mocking at his insufferable tortures. **1808** LAMB *Let. to Manning* 26 Feb., A sort of a frantic yell, ..with roaring sometimes, like bears, mows and mops like apes. **1847** LYTTON *Lucretia* II. vii, Bob grinned, made a mow at Mr. Grabman, and scampered up the stairs.

b. In phrases ***mops and mows*** (see MOP *sb.*[3]), ***mocks and mows, mows and mocks***.

1508 KENNEDIE *Flyting w. Dunbar* 353 In to thy mowis and mokis, It may be verifeit that thy wit is thin. **1602** FULBECKE *1st Pt. Parall.* 71 Things must be recompenced with things... And wordes with wordes, and taunts with mockes, and mowes. **1681** W. ROBERTSON *Phraseol. Gen.* (1693) 898 Mocks and mows with the mouth, *sannæ*.

2. *Sc.* †**a.** A jest. *Obs.*

c **1450** HOLLAND *Howlat* 831 The fulis fonde in the flet, And mony mowis at mete On the flure maid. **1501** DOUGLAS *Pal. Hon.* III. xlix, And Benytas of ane mussill maid ane aip, With mony vther subtill mow and jaip. **1535** STEWART *Cron. Scot.* (Rolls) II. 375 Mony mow & knak. *a* **1578** LINDESAY (Pitscottie) *Chron. Scot.* (S.T.S.) I. 198 Everie word was ane mow that he spak.

b. The plural form is used (latterly without consciousness of its grammatical character) with the sense 'jest' (as opposed to earnest). Often *predicatively* (quasi-*adj.*), esp. in negative contexts, = '(no) laughing matter', '(not) to be trifled with'.

1530 LYNDESAY *Test. Papyngo* 71, I maid it bot in mowis. *a* **1550** *Christis Kirke Gr.* 155 The millar wes of manly mak, To meit him wes na mowis. *a* **1578** LINDESAY (Pitscottie) *Chron. Scot.* (S.T.S.) I. 175 My lordis, is it mowse or earnest? **1728** RAMSAY *Archers diverting themselves* 156 Or in earnest, or in mows, Be still successful. **1877** G. MACDONALD *Mrq. Lossie* lvii, Juist tak tent the morn what ye say whan Jean's i' the room.. for she's no mowse. **1888** BARRIE *Auld Licht Idylls* xii, Its not mous to be out at such a time.

mow, *sb.*[3] *dial.* East Anglian var. of MAW *sb.*[3], a gull.

c **1440** *Promp. Parv.* 346/1 Mowe, byrd, or semewe. *a* **1490** BOTONER *Itin.* (1778) 111 Et ibi nidificant aves vocatæ ganettys, gullys, see mowys, et cæteræ aves marinæ. **1893** *Broad Norfolk* (ed. Cozens-Hardy) 49 Mow, Gull (in general).

†**mow**, *sb.*[4] *Sc. Obs.* [App. a var. of *moll*, MULL *sb.*[1]] Dust, mould.

c **1470** HENRYSON *Mor. Fab.* VIII. (*Preach. Swallow*) xliii, Like to the mow before the face of wind Quhiskis away, and makis wratchis blind. **1535** STEWART *Cron. Scot.* (Rolls) II. 79 For-quhy that wall wes nocht biggit with lyme, Bot with dry mow that wes of lytill effect.

†**mow**, *sb.*[5] *Obs. rare*$^{-1}$. [a. MDu. *mouwe* = mod.G. *maue*.] Fleshy part, muscle.

c **1489** CAXTON *Sonnes of Aymon* vii. 173 Mawgys.. cam to bayarde, and bounde hym the mowes of the feete there wyth all well streyghte.

mow (məʊ), *sb.*[6] [f. MOW *v.*[1] 3 d.] In *Cricket*, a sweeping stroke to leg.

1925 D. J. KNIGHT in *Country Life* 15 Aug. 244/1 Leg-side shots. They are the glides,.. the mow and the pull. **1926** J. B. HOBBS *Test Match Surprise* xvi. 171 What he intended for a leg glance was nothing more than a 'mow' between square leg and mid-on.

mow (məʊ), *v.*[1] Forms: 1–2 **máwan**, 2–4 **mowen**, 3 **meowen, mewen, mouin**, 3–8 **mowe**, 5–9 *dial.* **maw(e**, 7 **mough**, 6– **mow**. *Pa. t.* 5, 8 (9 *dial.*) **mew(e**, 8– **mowed**. *Pa. pple.* 1 **máwen**, 5 **mowe**, 5–7 **mowen**, 6 **mowne**, 8 *Sc.* **mawn**, 6– **mowed**, 7– **mown**. [A Com. WGer. (orig. reduplicating) verb: OE. *máwan* (pa. t. **méow*, pa. pple. *máwen*); in the other langs. conjugated weak: OFris. *mêa*, MLG. *meien*, MDu. *maeien* (Du. *maaien*), OHG. *mâen* (MHG. *mæjen*, mod.G. *mähen*); from LG. are Sw. *meja*, Da. *meie*. The root, OTeut. **mǣ-*, pre-Teut. **mē-*, occurs in MEAD, MEADOW, and in Gr. ἀμᾶν to reap; an extended form is found in L. *mēt-ĕre* to reap.

The pa. t. is now always *mowed*; in the pa. pple. the str. and wk. forms are both current.]

1. a. *trans.* To cut down (grass, corn, etc.) with a scythe, or (in recent use) with a machine that operates like a scythe. Also with *away, down*.

a **900** tr. *Bæda's Hist.* I. i. (1890) 28 þær nænig mann for wintres cyle on sumera heȝ ne maweþ. **1297** R. GLOUC. (Rolls) 5253 þe gode kniȝtes leye adoun as gras þat me doþ mowe. **14..** *Child. Jesus* 26 in Horstm. *Altengl. Leg.* (1878) 111 þen men hyre corne repyd & mew. *c* **1462–3** *Pol. Poems* (Rolls) II. 269 Withe wedys, whiche must be mowen doune playne. *c* **1482** in *Cal. Proc. Chanc. Q. Eliz.* (1830) II. Pref. 69 Alianore.. mewe down his corn growyng grene on the felde. **1530** PALSGR. 641/1, I mowe with a sythe, *je fauche*. Wyll you mowe this corne or shere it? **1607** SHAKS. *Cor.* I. iii. 39 Like to a Harvest man, that task'd to mowe Or all, or loose his hyre. **1660** F. BROOKE tr. *Le Blanc's Trav.* 371 They mowed green corn, to give the blades to horses. **1668** DRYDEN *Even. Love* I. ii, Our love here is like our grass, if it be not mowed quickly 'tis burnt up. **1711** SWIFT *Jrnl. to Stella* 13 May, The hay of our town is almost fit to be mowed. **1847** MARRYAT *Childr. N. Forest* v, It was time to mow down grass to make into hay for the winter. **1875** *Encycl. Brit.* I. 323/1 It can.. be kept going sixteen hours a day, and will easily mow from 16 to 18 acres of seeds or meadow in that time.

b. In figurative context. Now *rare*.

†Formerly used (instead of *reap*) antithetically with *sow*.

c **1250** *Prov. Ælfred* 83 in *O.E. Misc.* 106 Hwych so þe mon soweþ Al swuch he schal mowe. **1390** GOWER *Conf.* I. 239 For Supplant with his slyhe cast Fulofte happneth for-to mowe Thing which an other man hath sowe. **1549** COVERDALE, etc. *Erasm. Par. Gal.* 20 Suche seede as euery man soweth, suche shal he mowe. **1628** WITHER *Brit. Rememb.* III. 67 And I mow Oft times with mirth, what I in teares did sow. **1690** W. WALKER *Idiomat. Anglo-Lat.* 305 What you sow so that you must mow.

c. *transf.* and *fig.* To cut (*off, down*, etc.) with a sweeping stroke like that of a scythe; to destroy or kill indiscriminately or in great numbers. Now *rare* exc. with *down*, in reference to slaughter in battle by cannon-shot or fusillade.

c **1430** *Pilgr. Lyf Manhode* II. cl. (1869) 135 It is thilke that moweth the lyfe and the gost out of the bodi. **1513** DOUGLAS *Æneis* X. ix. 10 Than, as wod lyoun, ruschyt he in the fycht, And all quham he arekis nerrest hand Without reskew dovn mawis with his brand. **1593** SHAKS. *3 Hen. VI*, V. vii. 4 What valiant Foe-men, like to Autumnes Corne, Haue we mow'd downe in tops of all their pride? **1609** B. JONSON *Sil. Wom.* IV. v, Hee has got some-bodies old two-hand-sword, to mow you off at the knees. **1625** BACON *Ess., Seditions* (Arb.) 405 The Population of a Kingdome (especially if it be not mowen downe by warrs). **1697** DRYDEN *Æneid* X. 775 He.. Mows off his Head. **1720** POPE *Iliad* XX. 406 'Tis not in me, tho' favour'd by the Sky, To mow whole Troops, and make whole Armies fly. **1836** ALISON *Hist. Europe* (1849–50) VII. xliii. §38. 120 The Imperial had seen 500 of its bravest sailors mowed down by the irresistible fire of the English vessels. **1884** *Manch. Exam.* 21 Mar. 5/1 The rifle mowed them down as they approached till not more than a score lived to reach the lines.

2. a. To cut down the produce of (a field, etc.) with a scythe or (in recent use) with a mowing machine.

In early use always with the etymologically related *mead, meadow*, as cognate object.

c **893** K. ÆLFRED *Oros.* II. viii. §2 Ðelice & mon mæd mawe. *c* **1205** LAY. 1942 Cornes heo seowen medewen heo meowen. *c* **1425** [see MASTERY 3 b]. **1523** FITZHERB. *Husb.* §25 Whan thy medowes be mowed, they [etc.]. *a* **1550** *Treat. Galaunt* 145 in Hazl. *E.P.P.* III. 157 The florysshynge mede of our welth we haue begon to mawe. **1604** DEKKER *Honest Wh.* Wks. 1873 II. 103 Are not the fields mowen and cut downe? **1664** EVELYN *Kal. Hort.* Apr. 65 Mow Carpet-walks. **1788** BURNS *Bonie Moor-Hen* i, The heather was blooming, the meadows were mawn. **1871** R. ELLIS *Catullus* lxiv. 354 As some labourer.. Under a flaming sun, mows fields ripe-yellow in harvest. **1900** MRS. GLYN *Visits Eliz.*

(1906) 65 He looks as quiet and respectable as the pony that mows the lawn.

†*fig.* **1711** in *10th Rep. Hist. MSS. Comm.* App. v. 153 The Irish foot.. were moweing the field of honour.

b. *transf.* in jocular use: To shave.

1650 BULWER *Anthropomet.* Pref., Here the luxuriant Chin quite down is mown. **1719** D'URFEY *Pills* I. 229 My Holiday Cloaths on, and face newly Mow'd. **1833** J. HOLLAND *Manuf. Metal* II. 27 'So', said one of the metropolitan journalists, 'we may one day mow our beards with a relic of old London Bridge'. *a* **1839** PRAED *Poems* (1864) II. 99 He.. mows his beard *en militaire*.

3. *absol.* **a.** To cut down grass, corn, etc., with a scythe, or (in recent use) with a mowing machine.

a **1100** *Gerefa* in *Anglia* (1886) IX. 261 In Agusto and Septembri and Octobri mawan. **1340** *Ayenb.* 214 Huo þanne ssolde erye and zawe ripe and mawe. **1523** FITZHERB. *Husb.* §22 In the later ende of Iune is tyme to begyn to mowe. **1605** BACON *Adv. Learn.* I. viii. §2 Like an ill Mower, that mowes on still, and neuer whets his Syth. **1711** SWIFT *Jrnl. to Stella* 19 May, About our town we are mowing already and making hay. **1772** C. ROBINSON *Let. to J. Grimston* 19 July in *Grimston Papers*, My mowers the other day mew over a partridge nest with sixteen eggs. **1785** BURNS *Death & Dr. Hornbook* viii, Friend! hae ye been mawin, When ither folk are busy sawin? **1863** A. H. CHARTERIS *Jas. Robertson* iii. 48 Saying, he was going to mow.

b. in figurative context. (Cf. 1 b.)

c **1175** *Lamb. Hom.* 131 þe ðe saweð on blescunge he scal mawen of blescunge. *c* **1200** *Trin. Coll. Hom.* 147 Hie hiden wepende and sewende, and shule cumen mid blisse and mowen. **1633** BP. HALL *Occas. Medit.* (1851) 144 He, therefore, that spends his whole time in recreation, is ever whetting, never mowing. **1655** WALLER *Panegyric to Ld. Protector* 63 Ours is the Harvest where the Indians mowe.

c. *transf.* To sweep down men in battle. Hence *trans.* with cognate obj., to make (one's way, a passage) by 'mowing'.

c **1300** *Havelok* 1852 But thanne bigan he for to mowe With the barre, and let hem shewe, Hw he cowthe sore smite. **1678** DRYDEN *All for Love* I. i, Mow 'em out a Passage, And, entring where the foremost Squadrons yield, Begin the noble Harvest of the Field. **1757** GRAY *Bard* 86 Long years of havock.. thro' the kindred squadrons mow their way.

d. *Cricket.* To make a sweeping stroke to leg as if mowing the grass with a scythe. Also *trans.*

1844 *Bradford Observer* 8 Aug., Holmes cleverly mowed the ball from the off stump to the leg side. **1868** J. LILLYWHITE *Cricketers' Compan.* 81 H. M. Mills.. might score well if he did not think it necessary to mow at straight long-hops. **1925** D. J. KNIGHT in *Country Life* 15 Aug. 245/1 Supposing there is a deep square-leg, it is better.. to kneel down on your right knee and mow or drag the ball round in the direction of long-leg.

4. Combs. containing the verb stem, as **mow-land** *U.S.*, land where grass is grown for mowing; **mow-lot**, a plot of this land.

1845 S. JUDD *Margaret* II. i. 214 She saw.. women.. raking and turning hay among alders and willows that yet flourished in their best mow-lands. **1874** *Rep. Vermont Board Agric.* II. 411 The breeding of wrinkled sheep is like a farmer who ridges up his level mow-land and seeds the ridges with an inferior grass. **1845** S. JUDD *Margaret* II. viii. 325, I kept him here in the mow-lot.

mow (maʊ), *v.*[2] Now *dial.* (see E.D.D.). Also 4, 7 mowe, 5 moweye, mughe, 7 mough, moow. [f. MOW *sb.*[1]] *trans.* To put in mows. Also with *up*.

1393 LANGL. *P. Pl.* C. VI. 14 (MS. Vespasian B. xvi.) Canst þow.. Mowe oþer mouwen [*MS. Phillipps* 8231 mowen, *MS. Camb. Univ. Libr.* muwe] oþer make bond for sheues. **14..** *Voc.* in Wr.-Wülcker 565/17 *Archonizo*, to moweye. **1483** *Cath. Angl.* 245/2 To mughe hay, *archoniare, archonizere*. **1609** HOLLAND *Amm. Marcell.* XXIII. ii. 220 In this maner in those countries such kinds of farage are mowed up. **1620** MARKHAM *Farew. Husb.* xii. 80 How to Stacke or Moow your Corne without the dores. **1764** *Museum Rust.* II. xxxiii. 107 Let them be thrown promiscuously into the bay of the barn, and not regularly mowed.

mow (maʊ, məʊ), *v.*[3] Also 5–6, 9 mowe, 6 moo, mowgh, 7, 9 moe. [f. MOW *sb.*[2]]

1. *intr.* To make mouths or grimaces.

c **1430** LYDG. *Min. Poems* (Percy Soc.) 255 To skoffe and mowe lyk a wantoun ape. **1522** *World & Child* (Roxb.) A iij, I can mowe on a man And make a lesynge well I can. **1589** R. HARVEY *Pl. Perc.* (1590) 11 He spide a Iacke an apes, in a gaie cote, sit mooing on a Marchants bulke. **1610** SHAKS. *Temp.* II. ii. 9 Sometime like Apes, that moe and chatter at me, And after bite me. **1647** TRAPP *Comm. Heb.* xi. 36 So they mowed at David. mocked at Isaiah.. jeared our Saviour. **1748** SMOLLETT *Rod. Rand.* lviii, A noise like that of a baboon when he mows and chatters. **1819** SHELLEY *Peter Bell 3rd* VI. xx, With Flibbertigibbet, imp of pride, Mocking and mowing by his side. **1855** J. H. NEWMAN *Callista* (1890) 264 An animal of some wonderful species.. proceeded to creep and crawl, moeing and twisting as it went. **1884** W. C. SMITH *Kildrostan* 45 Every streak of mist.. Pointed and mowed and mocked and laughed at him.

†**2.** *Sc.* **a.** *intr.* To jest. **b.** *trans.* To deride, mock. *Obs.*

1456 SIR G. HAYE *Law Arms* (S.T.S.) 208 He did bot scornyt the merchand, and mowit the lettres of the kingis. **1529** LYNDESAY *Compl.* 246 Quod the third man; thow dois bot mow. **1596** DALRYMPLE tr. *Leslie's Hist. Scot.* (S.T.S.) v. 268 The king mowit verie oft with him.

†**mow**, *v.*[4] Also 7 mowe. [Echoic.] = MOO *v.*

1603 HOLLAND *Plutarch's Mor.* 4 Brute and wilde beasts, which hardly are parted from their companie,.. but still they lowe and mowe after them. **1641** J. JACKSON *True Evang. T.* II. 112 S. Luke.. an Oxe indeed,.. that he did mow and low the Gospel abroad over all the world.

Hence '**mowing** *vbl. sb.* Also '**mower**, a cow.

1556 WITHALS *Dict.* (1568) 16 a/1 The mowynge or lowynge of beastes, *mugitus*. **1578** BEST in *Hakluyt's Voy.* (1600) III. 63 Making great noise, with cries like the mowing of Buls. *a* **1700** B. E. *Dict. Cant. Crew*, *Mower*, a Cow.

mow, obs. form of MAY *v.*[1]

mow, var. MOU.

mowable ('məʊəb(ə)l), *a.* Also 7 moable. [f. MOW *v.*[1] + -ABLE.] That can be mown; capable of growing grass for hay.

1607 NORDEN *Surv. Dial.* v. 196 Because we speake of upland meddowes, we will accept all mowable grounds in that sence. **1793** WASHINGTON *Let.* 12 Dec., Writ. 1891 XII. 364 For every acre of ploughable and mowable ground.

mowah, mowar(e: see MAHWA, MOWER.

mowburn ('məʊbɜːn), *v.* [Back-formation from MOWBURNT.] *intr.* Of hay, corn, etc.: To heat and ferment through being stacked too green.

1707 MORTIMER *Husb.* (1721) I. 134 Be careful not to house it green, lest it mow-burn. **1876** *Encycl. Brit.* IV. 266/2 The buyer has also to judge if it has been heated or 'mow-burnt', while lying in the field after being cut, or in the stack.

Hence '**mowburn** *sb.*, the process of becoming mowburnt; = *mowheat* (MOW *sb.*[1] 4).

1764 *Museum Rust.* II. lxxv. 251 Your correspondent's method seems to threaten that dreadful malady, mow-burn.

mowburnt ('məʊbɜːnt), *a.* [f. MOW *sb.*[1] + BURNT *ppl. a.*] Of hay, corn, etc.: Spoilt by becoming overheated in the mow.

1548 *Act 2 & 3 Edw. VI*, c. 10 §2 Any Malte.. beinge made of mowburnte or spired Barley. **1641** BEST *Farm. Bks.* (Surtees) 54 To lye such barley aside for seede as is.. moweburnt. **1764** *Museum Rust.* II. lxxi. 234 The hay stacked in this damp state is always mow-burnt. **1900** *Daily News* 23 May 9/1 The greater part was good, but there was a mixture of bad mowburnt (overheated in the rick).

mowchatowe, obs. form of MUSTACHIO.

mowche, obs. form of MOOCH *v.*

mowcht, mowcte, obs. pa. t. of MAY *v.*[1]

mowdie, -y, var. forms of MOUDIE.

mowd(i)ewart, -wort, etc.: see MOULDWARP.

†**mowe.** *Obs.* Forms: 1 máȝe, 2–3 maȝe, 3 mawe, mohe, mouie, moȝe, mowe, 4 mau, 4–5 mow. [OE. *máȝe* (also *mǽȝe*):—OTeut. type **mǣgōn-*; the corresponding fem. to *mǽȝ* MAY *sb.*[2]] A female relative, kinswoman; esp. by marriage, as an aunt, niece, sister-in-law.

Beowulf 1391 Grendles maȝan gang. *c* **1200** *Trin. Coll. Hom.* 125 Seinte marie.. com to hire moȝe Seinte elizabet. *c* **1250** *Gen. & Ex.* 1651 He was hire mouies sune. **1297** R. GLOUC. (Rolls) 6458 Suþþe he made þe oþer þat het edward spousi þe emperours mowe. *a* **1300** *Cursor M.* 2807 'Has þou her', þai said, 'ani man, Sun or doghter, mik or mau'. *c* **1440** *Promp. Parv.* 345/2 Mow, husbondys syster, or wyfys systyr, or syster in lawe.

mowe, obs. f. MAY *v.*[1], MEW *sb.*[2], MOVE *v.*, MOW.

moweare, obs. form of MOWER[1].

mowed (məʊd), *ppl. a. rare.* [f. MOW *v.*[1] + -ED[1].] = MOWN *ppl. a.*

1659 HAMMOND *On Ps.* lxxii. 6 Like rain upon the mowed grass. **1859** P. BEATON *Jews in the East* II. vii. 261 Fields of mowed corn.

†'**mowel.** *Obs.* [? repr. OE. **múȝel*, a. L. *mūgil*.] The mullet.

c **1475** *Pict. Voc.* in Wr.-Wülcker 765/1 *Hic mugilus*, a mowel.

mowen, obs. f. MAY *v.*[1]; obs. pa. pple. of MOW *v.*[1]

mowence, variant of MUANCE.

mower[1] ('məʊə(r)). Also 5 moware, -eare, -eer, -ere, 6 mowyer. [f. MOW *v.*[1] + -ER[1].

With regard to the form *mowyer*, see -IER.]

1. One who cuts grass, etc., with a scythe.

c **1440** *Promp. Parv.* 345/2 Moware wythe a sythe, *falcator, metellus*. **1573** TUSSER *Husb.* (1878) 120 Set mowers a mowing, where meadow is growne. **1632** MILTON *L'Allegro* 66 The Mower whets his sithe. **1727** in *6th Rep. Dep. Kpr.* App. II. 118 The Office of Keeper of Bushy Park.. and of Paler and Mower of the Brakes thereof. **1866** M. ARNOLD *Thyrsis* xiii, Where are the mowers, who.. Stood with suspended scythe to see us pass?

b. Prov. phrase. *no meat for mowers*: unsuitable to, or unobtainable by, people of low degree.

1542 UDALL *Erasm. Apoph.* 342 Lais an harlot of Corinthe of excellent beautie, but so dere & costely that she was no morsell for mowyers. **1552** LATIMER *Serm., Septuag.* (1584) 322 b, Therefore it [*sc.* this parable] may well be called hard meate, not meate for mowers nor ignorant people. **1581** MULCASTER *Positions* xxxviii. (1887) 179 To hope for hie mariages, is good meat, but not for mowers.

c. mower's mite, the *Leptus autumnalis*.

1891 in *Syd. Soc. Lex.*

2. A mowing machine.

1852 in *Encycl. Brit.* (1853) II. 279/1 Mowers and reapers must become as indispensable.. as horse-rakes, ploughs and thrashing machines. **1903** *Motor. Ann.* 245 This machine is designed to draw mowers and reapers in the field.

†'**mower**[2]. *Obs.* Also 5 moware, 6 mowar. [f. MOW *v.*[3] + -ER[1].] One who makes mouths; a jester, a mocker.

c **1440** *Promp. Parv.* 345/2 Moware, or makere of a mowe, ..*valgiator*. **1500–20** DUNBAR *Poems* lxxxii. 34 Think ȝe nocht schame, To hold sic moweris on the moune. **1501** DOUGLAS *Pal. Hon.* II. li, Juuenall like ane mowar him allone, Stude scornand euerie man as thay ȝeid by. **1530** PALSGR. 246/2 Mower skorner, *mocquevr*.

mower[3]: see MOW *v.*[4]

mowest, moweye, obs. ff. MOIST *a.*, MOW *v.*[2]

mowgh, obs. form of MOW *sb.*[1], MOW *v.*[3]

mowghe, obs. form of MAY *v.*[1], MOW *sb.*[1]

mowght(e, mowhair, obs. ff. MOTH, MOHAIR.

Mowhake, -hawke, obs. forms of MOHAWK.

mowhay ('məʊheɪ, 'məʊɪ). *dial.* [f. MOW *sb.*[1] + HAY *sb.*[2] 2.] A stack-yard, a rick-yard.

Given as Devon and Cornwall in *E.D.D.*

1862 R. S. HAWKER *Let.* 14 Sept. in C. E. Byles *Life & Lett. R. S. Hawker* (1905) xvi. 362 Now I trust to be able to pay my Farm Wages in Wheat as the custom is, while for the last two years I have had to find money instead. To small Farmers and Vicars the Mowhay is the Farm Bank. **1880** M. A. COURTNEY in Courtney & Couch *Gloss. Words Cornwall* 38/2 *Mowhay*, an enclosure of ricks of corn or hay. **1959** *Listener* 22 Jan. 174/2 The granite shafts in the old mowhay.

mowing ('məʊɪŋ), *vbl. sb.*[1] [f. MOW *v.*[1] + -ING[1].]

1. a. The action of MOW *v.*[1]

1494 *Nottingham Rec.* III. 278 Paid for mowyng and teddyng. **1575** *Stanford Churchw. Acc.* in *Antiquary* XVII. 171 It. for moyng and kockyng of an acre of pulsse. **1858** GLENNY *Gard. Every-day Bk.* Dec. 283/2 Mowing must not be neglected where you have to keep the grass in good order.

b. *concr.* The quantity of grass cut at one time; also *pl.* grass removed by mowing.

1764 *Ann. Reg.* 48, I sold the first, second, third, and fourth mowings at a shilling per rod. **1802** W. FORSYTH *Fruit Trees* xxv. (1824) 349 You must lay some short grass mowings.. at the bottoms of the large baskets.

2. *U.S.* Land on which grass is grown for hay.

1786 *Mem. Amer. Acad. Sci.* (1793) II. 120 This extent contains.. as fine ploughland and luxuriant pasture and mowing, as I had before seen. **1788** [see ORCHARDING 2]. **1869** MRS. STOWE *Old Town Folks* iv. (1870) 33 And be off lying in the mowing, like a partridge, when they come after ye.

3. *attrib.* and *Comb.*, as *mowing crook, -crop, ground, land, -machine, meadow*; **mowing grass**, grass reserved for mowing; **mowing-machine bird**, the grasshopper warbler, *Locustella nævia*.

1943 *Antiquity* XVII. 203 To use a *mowing-crook such as one still sees used in connection with the swap-hook in this country. **1766** *Museum Rust.* VI. 30 Burnet will rarely make a *mowing-crop the first year. **1773** *Ann. Reg.* 112 A horse had got into his *mowing-grass. **1884** JEFFERIES *Life of Fields* 50 Only a few [bees] go down to the mowing grass. **1636** in *1st Cent. Hist. Springfield, Mass.* (1898) I. 158 Less than three acres of *mowinge ground. **1654** *Rec. Early Hist. Boston* (1880) VI. 17 Twenty acres more or lesse of mowing ground upon the marsh. **1722** in *Essex Inst. Hist. Coll.* (1906) XLII. 90 [To pay damages for] digging in any Corne field,.. mowing ground. **1770** in *Ibid.* (1872) XI. 31 My little mare had provided for herself, by leaping out of a bare pasture into a lot of mowing ground. **1787** G. WASHINGTON *Diaries* (1925) III. 222 The same difference was equally obvious on a piece of mowing grd. not far distant from it. **1640** in *Connecticut Hist. Soc. Coll.* (1912) XIV. 357 One parsell called Swamp, now *mowing land. **1704** *Proprietors' Rec. Waterbury, Connecticut* (1911) 60 No man shal stak horses in the moing land in said feild. **1816** *North Amer. Rev.* III. 428 At the distance of five or six miles it begins to wind gently through large tracts of fine rich mowing land. **1858** C. L. FLINT *Milch Cows* 169 The grasses differ widely; and their value as feed for cows will depend.. on the management of pastures and mowing-lands. **1884** ROE *Nat. Ser. Story* viii, The mowing machine would be used in the timothy fields. **1823** *H. R. Doc. 17th U.S. Congress 2 Sess.* No. 36. 6 Improvement in the *mowing machine, Feb. 13, [1822], Jeremiah Baily. **1838** H. W. ELLSWORTH *Valley Upper Wabash* v. 47, I have a plan in view.. and that is, to introduce the mowing and grain-cutting machine into this state. **1887** A. C. SMITH *Birds Wiltsh.* 154 [The Grasshopper Warbler] is.. known as the '*mowing-machine bird', in allusion to its remarkable note. **1799** WASHINGTON *Writ.* (1893) XIV. 231, I am not sanguine enough to expect that it will make good *mowing meadow.

mowing ('maʊɪŋ), *vbl. sb.*[2] [f. MOW *v.*[2] + -ING[1].] The process of placing in a mow.

1572 HULOET (ed. Higins), Mowghing or heaping, *aceruatio*. **1828–32** in WEBSTER; and in later Dicts.

mowing (maʊ-, 'məʊɪŋ), *vbl. sb.*[3] [f. MOW *v.*[3] + -ING[1].] The action of making grimaces; an instance of this; also, derision.

1382 WYCLIF *Hosea* vii. 16 This the mowyng, or scornynge, of hem in the lond of Egypt. *c* **1430** *Stans Puer ad Mensam* 29 in *Babees Bk.* 278 Grennynge & mowynge at þi table eschewe. *a* **1568** ASCHAM *Scholem.* I. (Arb.) 54 If som Smithfeild Ruffian take up.. som new mowing with the mouth. **1607** TOPSELL *Four-f. Beasts* 7 Because of their marueilous and diuers mowings, mouings, voices, and gestures. **1833** M. SCOTT *Tom Cringle* xi. (1842) 248 He skipped up to us.. with sundry moppings and mowings. **1881** [see MOPPING *vbl. sb.*[1]].

†'**mowing**, *vbl. sb.*[4] *Obs.* [f. *mowe* (see MAY *v.*[1]) + -ING[1].] Ability.

c **1374** CHAUCER *Boeth.* IV. pr. iv. 99 (Camb. MS.) The Mowynge of shrewes [orig. *malorum potestas*] which Mowynge the semyth to ben vnworthy nis no mowynge.

mowing, *vbl. sb.*[5]: see MOW *v.*[4]

mowing ('maʊɪŋ, 'məʊɪŋ), *ppl. a.* [f. MOW *v.*[3] + -ING[2].] Grimacing; mocking, derisive.

a **1518** SKELTON *Magnyf.* 2124 To mockynge, to mowynge, to lyke a iackenapes. **1532** MORE *Confut. Tindale* Wks. 358/1 And then should stande vp and preache vppon a stoole and make a mowyng sermon. **1858** S. WILBERFORCE *Let.* in R. G. Wilberforce *Life* (1881) II. xi. 394 To get rid of the nauseous Romanizing peculiarities of these mowing apes.

mowkisin, obs. form of MOCCASIN.

mowl, *v. rare*[−1]. In phr. ***mope and mowl***, substituted by Carlyle for 'mop and mow': see MOW *v.*[3]

1837 CARLYLE *Fr. Rev.* I. I. iv, With these it is a hollow phantasmagory, where like mimes they mope and mowl.

mowl(e, variant forms of MOOL *sb. dial.*

mowla, mowld, obs. ff. MULLAH, MOULD.

mowlewarp(e, obs. forms of MOULDWARP.

mowl(l)e, variant forms of MULE, chilblain.

mown (məʊn), *ppl. a.* [pa. pple. of MOW *v.*[1]] Cut down with a scythe or mowing-machine. See also NEW-MOWN.

c **1000** *Ags. Ps.* (Th.) cii. 14 Beoð mannes daȝas mawenum heȝe æȝhwær anlice. **1611** BIBLE *Ps.* lxxii. 6 He shall come down like rain upon the mown grass. **1844** STEPHENS *Bk. Farm* III. 1068 A mown stook does not look so well as a reaped one. **1906** *Edin. Rev.* Apr. 386 Untrodden stretches of mown grass.

mown(e, obs. forms of MAY *v.*[1]

mowntan, obs. form of MOUNTAIN.

mowntance, -ans, obs. ff. MOUNTANCE.

mowr, variant form of MAUR *Obs.*, ant.

mowra(h), var. MAHWA.

mowre, var. MAUR *Obs.*; obs. form of MOOR *sb.*[2]

mows, obs. f. MEUSE, MOUSE; obs. pl. MOW *sb.*[2]

mowsare, obs. form of MOUSER.

mowse, obs. f. MEWS, MOUSE; obs. pl. MOW *sb.*[2]

mowseale, obs. form of MUZZLE *v.*

mowsle, variant of MOUSLE *v.*

†'**mowsome**, *a. Sc. Obs.* In 6 **mowsum**, mousum. [f. MOW *sb.*[2] + -SOME.] Jocular.

1596 DALRYMPLE tr. *Leslie's Hist. Scot.* v. (S.T.S.) 268 This Jhone, quha naturalie was iocund, Jellie, and mowsum. *Ibid.*, His honest, wittie, mousum, and mirrie conceitis.

mowss(e, mowster, obs. ff. MOUSE, MUSTER.

mowster de vylers: see MUSTER-DEVILLERS.

mowstre, obs. form of MUSTER *sb.*

†'**mowsy**, *a. Obs.* [Cf. *mosey* (*moisy*, *mouzy*, etc.) 'mouldy, rotten, over-ripe' in E.D.D., and F. *moisi* mouldy.] ? Mouldy (in quot. *fig.*).

1581 J. BELL *Haddon's Answ. Osor.* 211 b, This mowsy and drossy chaffe long sithence bloune abroad in yͤ eyes of Augustine by the Pelagianes.

mowsyn, mowt(e, obs. ff. MUSE *v.*, MOULT *v.*

mowte, mowter, obs. ff. MOTE *v.*[1], MULTURE.

mowth (məʊθ). [app. a refashioning of MATH after MOW *v.*] A mowing, MATH.

1711 J. GREENWOOD *Eng. Gram.* 175 Later-mow'th, the after-mowth, now call'd Math. **1817** V. THOMAS *Papers* (Bodl. MS. Top. Oxon b. 19) lf. 174 A man's Mowth is reckoned at a Statute Acre. **1886** *Schedule to Conveyance* Oct., The first mowth of an allotment in Burcott Revel Mead.

mowth, obs. pa. t. of MAY *v.*[1]

mowthad, variant of MOULDWARP.

mowthe, mowȝhe, obs. forms of MOTH.

†'**mowyer**[1]. *Obs.* Also 5 **mugher, muwyer**. [f. MOW *v.*[2]: see -IER.] One who puts hay in mows.

14.. *Voc.* in Wr.-Wülcker 565/18 *Archonistus*, a mowyer. *Ibid.* 577/2 *Cumularius*, a muwyer. **1483** *Cath. Angl.* 245/2 A Mugher of hay, *archonizator*.

mowyer[2] ('məʊjə(r)). *U.S.* The long-billed or sickle-billed curlew, *Numenius longirostris*.

1888 in TRUMBULL *Names Birds* 198.

mowyer, obs. form of MOWER[1].

moxa ('mɒksə). [a. Jap. *mokusa* (phonetically 'moksa), contracted from *moe kusa* burning herb.]

1. The downy covering of the dried leaves of *Artemisia moxa*; esp. as prepared in the form of a cone or cylinder for burning on the skin as a counter-irritant for gout, etc. Also, the plant itself.

1677 *Phil. Trans.* XII. 904 He did me the favour to shew me some of that Moxa, which by burning it upon any gouty part removeth the Gout. **1693** tr. *Blancard's Phys. Dict.* (ed. 2), *Moxa*, a certain Down growing upon the lower part of the Leaves of Mugwort; it comes from Japan and China. **1707** FLOYER *Physic. Pulse-Watch* 214 The Artery will shrink by any sort of Burning such as is made with Moxa, or hot Irons. **1822–34** *Good's Study Med.* (ed. 4) I. 51 The burning of a little cone of moxa behind the ear.

2. Any substance used like moxa for burning on the skin.

1833 *Cycl. Pract. Med.* I. 492/1 The material generally employed in Europe for moxas is cotton, rendered downy by carding, and made into a roll an inch long, and from half an inch to two inches in diameter. **1846** BRITTAN tr. *Malgaignes' Man. Oper. Surg.* 63 A small pad was made with spider's web, and placed on the corn; it was then lighted, and left to burn as a moxa. **1877** tr. *von Ziemssen's Cycl. Med.* VII. 227 Mustard plasters, blisters, the actual cautery, the moxa &c. to the epigastrium, have sometimes given relief.

Hence **moxi'bustion** [irreg. after COMBUSTION; cf. F. *moxibustion* (Littré 1885)], cauterization by means of a moxa (Dunglison 1833–55); ‖**moxo'causis** [mod.L., f. Gr. καῦσις burning] = prec. (*Syd. Soc. Lex.* 1891).

1910 E. PLAYFAIR tr. *Neuburger's Hist. Med.* I. 71 Moxibustion..also serves as a prophylactic. *Ibid.* 78 Moxibustion and acupuncture were also in Japan the favourite methods of treatment. **1958** *Manch. Guardian* 6 Dec. 4/3 This has a history of three thousand years, and works in various ways: by acupuncture..; by moxibustion ..; and by medicaments prepared from herbs and parts of animals. **1965** *New Scientist* 15 July 129/1 Chinese surgery has clearly advanced at a pretty phenomenal rate. Presumably this is why traditional methods like acupuncture, moxibustion (the burning of a herbal mixture on part of the body to transfer the site of irritation from one place to another)..are still respected. **1974** *Sci. Amer.* Apr. 25/1 The years since 1949 have seen the general adoption of certain traditional techniques: the use of herbal preparations, of gymnastics and respiratory exercises, and of two related treatments, moxibustion and acupuncture.

moxie ('mɒksɪ). *U.S. slang.* [f. the name of an American soft drink.] Courage, 'guts', 'nerve'; energy, pep.

1930 D. RUNYON in *Collier's* 20 Dec. 32/3 Personally, I always figure Louie a petty-larceny kind of guy, with no more moxie than a canary bird. **1943** M. SHULMAN *Barefoot Boy with Cheek* xv. 158 We knew you had the old moxie, the old get out and get. **1947** S. J. PERELMAN *Westward Ha!* (1949) x. 122 Before I could summon up enough moxie to bolt after them,..the attendants herded us into Indian file. **1955** *Publ. Amer. Dial. Soc.* xxiv. 94 If he admits his own limitations, he loses his nerve (blows his moxie). **1959** C. WILLIAMS *Man in motion* iv. 47 She's a real Latin type, dark brown eyes with a lot of moxie in 'em. **1967** *Telegraph* (Brisbane) 6 Mar. 7/2 A girl with all the moxie (outstanding intelligence). **1969** *Maclean's Mag.* Aug. 1/3 The qualities that make business click—qualities such as moxie and timing and stealth. And wealth. **1970** *New Yorker* 29 Aug. 19/1 It takes moxie, skill, and self-reliance. **1975** *Daily Colonist* (Victoria, B.C.) 16 Mar. 17/3, I was very impressed with his all-round moxie. He could snap back at any of them, news reporters, police, and me.

†**moy**, *sb.*[1] *Obs.* Also 6 **moye**. [Assumed sing. form of MOYSE, taken as pl.] Only in ***apple moy*** = APPLE-MOSE.

c **1390** *Form of Cury* in Warner *Antiq. Culin.* (1790) 42 Appulmoy. **1594** *Gd. Huswife's Handmaid to Kitchin* 43 b, To make an Apple Moye. **1802** J. WILSON *MS. Let. to J. Boucher* 17 Apr., Apple moy, or Apple de moy, the Pulp of boiled Apples sweetened and put by ready for Use.

†**moy**, *sb.*[2] *Sc. Obs.* [app. a. F. *muid* (OF. *mui*) 'bushel':—L. *modium* (-*us*). Cf. MUID.] A measure used for salt; ? a bushel.

1535 *Aberdeen Reg.* XVI. 693 (Jam.) Twenty twa moys of gryt salt. **1538** *Ibid.*, Ane moy of salt.

[**moy**, *sb.*[3] An imaginary name of a coin, evolved by 'Ancient Pistol' from a misunderstanding of the Fr. *moy* (me) in his prisoner's speech.

It seems unnecessary to suppose that there is an allusion to any genuine name of a coin. MOIDORE, if the word existed so early, may have furnished Shaks. with the suggestion; but our oldest instance is of the 18th c. That the Pg. *moeda* was familiar to Shaks. is unlikely. Still less plausible is Douce's suggestion, that the word is the F. *muid* (MOY *sb.*[2]).

1599 SHAKS. *Hen. V*, IV. iv. 15 *French. O prennes miserecordio aye pitez de moy. Pist.* Moy shall not serue, I will haue fortie Moyes... *French. O perdonne moy. Pist.* Say'st thou me so? is that a Tonne of Moyes?]

moy (mɔɪ), *a. Sc.* and *north.* Mild, gentle; demure. Also, affected in manners, prim.

14.. *How Gd. Wife taught Dau.* 20 Suet and hamly, sempill and coy, Vith fenȝeit fair nocht mak our moy. **1500–20** DUNBAR *Poems* xliii. 11 Richt myld and moy. **1721** KELLY *Scot. Prov.* 31 A bit butt, and bit bend, make a moy Maiden at the board end. **1855** ROBINSON *Whitby Gloss.*, *Moy*, demure, close or unsocial.

Hence '**moyly** *adv.*, gently, demurely.

1529 LYNDESAY *Compl.* 333 Geue thay can..mollet moylie on ane Mule. a **1585** MONTGOMERIE *Cherrie & Slae* 111 So moylie and coylie He lukit like ane sant.

‖**moya** ('moja). *Geol.* [? S. American Sp.] A name for volcanic mud.

1830 LYELL *Princ. Geol.* I. 410 Streams of water and fetid mud, called 'moya', poured out, overflowing and wasting everything. **1884** *Leisure Hour* Apr. 246/2 A substance called moya, composed of augite, carbon, and infusoria.

moya (mɔɪ'ɑː), *int. Ireland.* Also **maureeyah, mauryah, mor-yah, moyah, moy-yah.** [ad. Ir. *mar dh'eadh*, as if it were so.] Used as an ironic interjection (see quots.).

The spelling in the head-word, which is that of James Joyce, is not otherwise authenticated.

1910 P. W. JOYCE *Eng. as we speak it in Ireland* 296 Moryah; a derisive expression of dissent to drive home the untruthfulness of some assertion or supposition or pretence, something like the English 'forsooth', but infinitely stronger. **1911** *Jrnl. Co. Kildare Archæol. Soc.* VI. 535 *Maureeyah*, this expression denotes a strong doubt as to the truthfulness of a statement. 'That notorious poacher, Loughlin Murphy, tould the magistrates he didn't know how to set a snare, Maureeyah.' *Ibid.*, *Moy-yah*, this is much the same expression as *Maureeyah*... It conveys the same sense as the English saying, 'You may tell that to the Horse Marines'. **1914** JOYCE *Dubliners* 151 And the men used to go in on Sunday morning before the houses were open to buy a waistcoat or a trousers—moya! **1922** —— *Ulysses* 327 Beggar my neighbour is his motto. Love, Moya! **1925** *Blackw. Mag.* Dec. 784/2 'Tis a bad pair to beat we are, moyah! **1939** JOYCE *Finnegans Wake* 375 The wonder of the women of the world together, moya! **1944** *Béaloideas* XIV. 176 Mauryah. A word implying doubt and irony.

moyan(n(e, variant forms of MOYEN.

†**moyce.** *Eccl. Obs.* Also 6 **moseye, moyse.** [? Corrupt var. of MORSE *sb.*[1] (Cf. *moose* in quot. 1489–90 s.v.)] ? = MORSE *sb.*[1]

c **1550** *Fabric Rolls York Minster* (Surtees) 311 Moyses. A riche Moseye of goulde with ruby in the middest. Another with the image of our Ladye... Two ould Moyses. **1889** J. RAINE *Hist. Hemingborough* 77 Gisburgh's will is dated.. 1479... He gave to the minister a green cope of tissue with an eagle standing upon a book on the moyce.

moyd, obs. f. MOOD *sb.*[1]

moye: see MOY *sb.*[1]

moyen ('mɔɪən), *sb.*[1] After 15th c. only *Sc.* Forms: 5 **moene**, 5–6 **moyane, -ene, moyne**, 5, 7 **moien**, 5–9 **moyan**, 6 **moyanne, myane**, *pl.* **moyance**, 7 **moyand**, 8 **moyean**, 5– **moyen**. [a. OF. *moien* (mod.F. *moyen*), subst. use of *moien* (*moyen*), later form of *meien* adj., middle: see MEAN *a.*[2] Cf. MEAN *sb.*[2]]

†**1.** A middle condition or quality; = MEAN *sb.*[2] 1.

1484 CAXTON *Chivalry* 86 Yf there were no vertue bytwene the ouer grete and ouer lytyl there shold be no moyen.

†**2.** Something interposed or intervening; = MEAN *sb.*[2] 6. *Obs.*

1483 CAXTON *Gold. Leg.* 24 b/1 Syth the pryncypal angellis ben nyghe to god, and ben without moyen enlumyned of god.

†**3.** A mediator. = MEAN *sb.*[2] 9, 9 c. *Obs.*

1455 *Rolls of Parlt.* V. 286/1 Request made unto you..to be moyen unto the Kynges Highnesse to ordeyne and name a persone. **1458** *Paston Lett.* I. 421 To bee my good and tendre moyen..unto the Kinges goode grace, for th' excuse of my nown comyng. **1483** CAXTON *Gold. Leg.* 279 b/1 Thenne late us praye unto this hooly Saynt Saynt Iohan baptist to be a moyen bytwene god and us.

†**4.** A means, agency. = MEAN *sb.*[2] 10. *Obs.*

to make moyen(s: to take steps, use efforts. ***to find (the) moyen(s***: to find out a way, contrive. Cf. MEAN *sb.*[2] 10 d.

1440 in *Wars Eng. in France* (1864) II. 444 Youre partie aduerse and the saide due might not godely haue founden the moyens and the weyes to haue communed to geder. a **1470** TIPTOFT *Tulle on Friendsh.* (Caxton 1481) b j, That the said feblenesse sholde be the moyen to attain to that which they desire in friendship. **1502** in *Lett. Rich. III & Hen. VII* (Rolls) II. 112 We have made suche secrete moynes as we can to knowe howe the exchaunge of the said. l. M. crownes myght be made. **1572** *Satir. Poems Reform.* xxxi. 117 The moyane for till find, How that yai micht eschew ye quene. **1581** HAMILTON *Cath. Traictise* 20 Thir sort of men not onlie be sic moyens drauis sindrie to thair faction, but also [etc.].

†**b.** Means, resources. = MEAN *sb.*[2] 12. Also *pl.*

1580 *Reg. Privy Council Scot.* III. 316 Personis..that hes the moyen to leif on thair awin. **1591** ABP. ADAMSON *Recant.* (1598) B j b, I..beseekis zou to make intercessionne..to the King, that I may haif sum moyance to liue. **1593** *Aberdeen Reg.* (1848) II. 84 To have sufficient rent of thair awin, or some honest moyen, industrie, craft or occupatioun, to leive on. **1609** HUME *Admonit.* in *Wodrow Soc. Misc.* (1844) 587 Thei who have best moyen to remane, perhappis werie first. **1617** J. CHAMBERLAIN in *Crt. & Times Jas. I* (1848) II. 7 The greatest part of the prime Scots..make no great haste homeward, which perhaps may be for want of *moyens*, as they call it, to carry them along.

5. Mediation, intercession; exercise of influence to bring about something, instigation; influence used on behalf of another, interest. †***moyen of*** (or ***at***) ***court***: court influence. ***to make moyen(s***, to intercede, make interest, negotiate (*with*), make overtures. = MEAN *sb.*[2] 13 a.

1454 *Paston Lett.* I. 309 And that ye lyke seke a moyen of such frendys as ye can best avyse and may verrayly trust uppon to gyde thys mater. **15..** in Cochran-Patrick *Rec. Coinage Scotl.* (1876) I. 98 Ane Inglischmane..vpon fair promisis be moyen of cowrte was appointed maister

Coinyeour. **1581** *Aberdeen Reg.* (1848) II. 42 Thair be moyanne of court, sinister and wrang informatioun, hes purchest ane gift and preuilege of our said Souerane Lord. **1583** *Leg. Bp. St. Androis* 800 With Monsier then he moyen maid. *c* **1610** SIR J. MELVIL *Mem.* (1735) 347 The Master of Gray had made moyen for Mr. Archibald. **1636** RUTHERFORD *Lett.* (1862) I. lix. 160 We are using our weak moyen and credit for you up at our own court. **1649** BP. GUTHRY *Mem.* (1702) 14 King Charles.. preferr'd Men by Moyen at Court. *a* **1651** CALDERWOOD *Hist. Kirk* (1678) 243 By moyen he [Bothwell] got presence of the King in the garden. **1706** A. SHIELDS *Ch. Commun.* (1747) 62 The Priesthood was acquired and kept by Moyen. **1717** *Wodrow Corr.* (1843) II. 221, I hear he has been at London making moyen and friends to be made Principal of the Old Town College. **1721** KELLY *Scot. Prov.* 243 Moyen does mickle but Money does more. **1777** J. LOVE in *Mem.* (1857) I. 330 Little improving of the *moyen* which I have through Christ in heaven. *c* **1820** G. BEATTIE *John o' Arnha* (1826) 17 When Charlie Stuart, the vile Pretender, Made moyen to be our Faith's Defender. **1871** W. ALEXANDER *Johnny Gibb* xxxix. (1873) 218 His purpose being, as his father phrased it, 'to lay moyen for a placie come time'.

b. *pl.* in the same sense.

1471 *Arriv. Edw. IV* (Camden) 9 Dayly came certayne personns on the sayd Erlls behalve to the Kinge, and made great moynes, and desired him to treat withe hym. *a* **1578** LINDESAY (Pitscottie) *Chron. Scot.* (S.T.S.) I. 165 Thinkand na thing better nor they wald mak thair moyenis witht him. **1873** *Leg. North, Guidman o' Inglismill* 30, I mith hae moyens laid to win wi' you.

†**6.** Instrumentality. Chiefly in phrases *by* or *through* (*the*) *moyen of*: (*a*) by the instrumentality of (a person or thing); (*b*) in consequence of, by reason of, owing to. ***by this or that moyen***, by means of this or that; in this or that way; thus. Cf. MEAN *sb.*[2] 14. *Obs.*

14.. *Lett. Marg. Anjou & Bp. Beckington* (Camden) 160 The socour and trust of oure moene that she putteth in us. **1456** SIR G. HAYE *Law Arms* (S.T.S.) 268 The witnes.., be the moyen of the quhilkis ilk ane.. thinkis to prove his ententioun. *a* **1578** LINDESAY (Pitscottie) *Chron. Scot.* (S.T.S.) I. 108 Be quhat moyane sall I red me of this mischeif. *a* **1651** CALDERWOOD *Hist. Kirk* (1843) II. 198 By my moyen muche innocent blood hath beene spilt. **1703** D. WILLIAMSON *Serm. bef. Gen. Assemb.* 58 Connived at by the Moyen of the.. Noble Lord.

†**b.** *pl.* with *sing.* sense. *Obs.*

a **1578** LINDESAY (Pitscottie) *Chron. Scot.* (S.T.S.) I. 284 Convenit ane consall be his moyance of the maist pairt of the nobilitie at Edinburgh. *Ibid.* 331 Quhither the castell was so strong or the gouneris corrupit be the Earle of Angus moyans, I can nocht tell.

†**'moyen**, *sb.*[2] *Obs.* Forms: 6 **mayan, moyan(e, myan(d, myone, 6–9 moyen, 7 moyenne, 9** *Hist.* **moienne.** [a. OF. *moyenne*, subst. use of *moyenne* fem. of *moyen* adj., middle(-sized): see MOYEN *a.*] A kind of cannon; = *culverin moyen* (see MOYEN *a.* c.).

1509 in Tytler *Hist. Scot.* (1864) II. 279 *note*, Three hundred small artillery, under the names of myand, culverins, and double-dogs. **1569** *Reg. Privy Council Scot.* II. 25 That thair be ane moyen and ane falconer convoyit towart Dunbartane. **1577** *Ibid.* 655 Twa myonis. **1797** *Encycl. Brit.* (ed. 3) VIII. 194/2 Moyens, which carried a ball of 10 or 12 ounces. **1802** C. JAMES *Milit. Dict.*, *Moienne*, Fr. A piece of ordnance, which is now called a four pounder, and which is ten feet long, was formerly so called.

†**'moyen**, *a. Obs.* [a. F. *moyen* middle: see MEAN *a.*[2]] Middle.

1481 CAXTON *Myrr.* II. iii. 68 Thise two flodes [Tigris and Euphrates] trauerse many grete contrees so longe tyl they mete in the see moyen. **1550** J. COKE *Eng. & Fr. Heralds* §26 (1877) 63 As well of tyme past, moyene as present.

b. Of middle rank. (In quot. 1483 *absol.* with plural ending).

1481 CAXTON *Godefroy* xxvi. 59 Here ye maye here how so moche peple was loste by the folye of the moyen peple. **1483** —— *Gold. Leg.* 308/1 Alle spirites ben sent for us. The superyors ben sente to the moyens, the moyens [*printed* moyest] ben sente to the lowest. **1485** —— *Chas. Gt.* 82 And in thys batayle was slayn.. many other of the moyen people.

c. Of middle size.

1513 *Acc. Ld. Treas. Scot.* (1902) IV. 510 For xxvj chargeouris to the culvering moyaine. *Ibid.* 517 Item, the first culvering moiyane, drawin with viij oxin. **1515** *Ibid.* (1903) V. 27 Chargit with twa culvering myance.

moyen ('mɔɪən), *v. Sc.* [f. MOYEN *sb.*[1], or a. F. *moyenner* of equivalent formation.]

1. *trans.* To accomplish by the use of means; 'to manage or bring about' (E.D.D.).

1589 R. BRUCE *Serm. Sacram.* ii. (1590) H3b, This conjunction is moyaned, be twa speciall moyans.

†**2.** To compromise. *Obs.*

1598 J. MELVILL *Autobiog. & Diary* (Wodrow Soc.) 441 The best part thought it meittest to tak tyme to mollefie and moyen maters.

Moyen Age (mwajɛnaʒ). Also **moyen âge**, etc. [Fr.] The Middle Ages, the medieval period. Also, a representation of medieval life. Also as quasi-*adj.*: of the Middle Ages, medieval.

1849 THACKERAY *Pendennis* I. xxiii. 213 We'll.. furnish the oak room with the Moyen-age cabinet and armour. **1852** E. RUSKIN *Let.* 10 Jan. in M. Lutyens *Effie in Venice* (1965) II. 245 The traditions of their families moved with Moyen-age sentiments of Chivalry. *Ibid.* 26 Jan. A coiffure I have made for myself which John says is decidedly Moyen-age. **1864** G. A. SALA *Quite Alone* I. ii. 37 'If a man wants to get on in life, he can't do better than study the History of the Middle Ages'. To which Moyen Age culture Mr. Blunt owed much of his success. **1870** C. SCHREIBER *Jrnl.* (1911) I. 78, I cannot describe the collection. It was entirely Moyen Age. **1923** R. FRY *Let.* 21 May (1972) II. 535 Spain.. this big rich and on the whole up-to-date civilisation which is yet definitely *moyen age*. **1927** R. H. WILENSKI *Mod. Movement in Art* 66 Moyen-âge elements in their art. **1961** M. LEVY *Studio Dict. Art Terms* 77 *Moyenage*, paintings depicting reconstructed scenes, etc. from the Medieval period. **1962** R. G. HAGGAR *Dict. Art Terms* 219/2 *Moyenage*, pictorial reconstruction of the Middle Ages.

†**'moyenant**, *prep. Obs.* Also 5 **moiena(u)nt, moyenaunt,** 6 **moynant.** [a. F. *moyennant*, orig. pr. pple. of *moyenner*: see MOYEN *v.*] By means of. ***moyenant that***: on condition that.

1471 *Arriv. Edw. IV* (Camden) 21 Moyenaunt he false faynyd fables and disclandars, that.. were wont to be seditiously sowne & blowne abowt. **1471** CAXTON *Recuyell* (Sommer) I. 206, I geue the thy lif and gyue the plain absolucion of all, moienant that neuer after thou replicque ne reherce this trespaas. **1483** —— *Gold. Leg.* 417/b/2, Thy fader the deuyl ouer whome I haue hope to haue vyctorye moyenaunt on hym the name of Jhesu cryst. *a* **1500** in *Three 15th Cent. Chron.* (Camden) 81 At the whiche daye, moynant the grace of Almyghty Jesu, the saide towne and castell were delivered unto the saide good Kynge Edward.

moyenau, moyeneaw, var. ff. MOINEAU.

†**'moyener.** *Sc. Obs.* In 6–7 **moyan(n)er.** [f. MOYEN *v.* + -ER[1].] A mediator, a 'go-between'.

1589 R. BRUCE *Serm. Sacram.* ii. (1590) Hj, Quhilk ar the moyaners of this conjunction, vpon the part of God; and quhilk are the moyaners vpon the part of man? **1609** HUME *Admonit.* in *Wodrow Soc. Misc.* (1894) 570 Yow hold.. that Bishops should be.. moyanners and mediatoris between the Kirk and the Prince.

†**'moyening**, *prep. Obs.* In 6 **moiening.** [f. MOYEN *v.* + -ING[2].] = MOYENANT.

?*c* **1520** R. COPLAND *Prol. to Helyas* in Thoms *Prose Rom.* (1828) III. 2, I Robert Copland have me applied moiening the helpe of god to reduce.. it into our.. english tonge.

†**'moyenless**, *a. Obs.* [f. MOYEN *sb.*[1] + -LESS.] Having no means or resources.

1587 HUME *Ep. G. Montcrief* 203 Simple sauls, unskilfull, moyenles.

moyenne, variant of MOYEN *sb.*[2]

Moygashel ('mɔɪgæʃəl). Also **moygashel.** [Name of a village in Co. Tyrone, N. Ireland.] The proprietary name of a type of Irish linen.

1931 *Trade Marks Jrnl.* 11 Nov. 1506/1 Moygashel... Linen piece goods. Stevenson & Son, Limited, Moygashel Mills, Dungannon, County Tyrone, Ireland. **1958** *Woman* 1 Mar. 4/2 (Advt.), Unlined suit, trimmed white pique in a moygashel pebble line tweed. **1966** *Punch* 7 Sept. 363/2, I placed the card in the pocket of my moygashel jacket.

moyhair, moyitie, obs. ff. MOHAIR, MOIETY.

moyl(e: see MOIL *sbs.* and *v.*, MULE *sbs.*

moyle. *Mining.* Also **moil.** [? f. the surname *Moyle.*] (See quots.)

1874 J. H. COLLINS *Metal Mining* 64 The larger kinds of wedges known in Cornwall as 'moyles' are used more especially in quarry work. **1881** RAYMOND *Mining Gloss.*, *Moil* or *Moyle* (Cornw.). A drill pointed like a gad.

moylere, moylet, obs. ff. MULIER, MULET.

moyleteer, obs. form of MULETEER.

moylie, variant of MOILEY *dial.*

moyn, obs. form of MOAN.

moynant, variant of MOYENANT *Obs.*

moynd, moyne, obs. forms of MINE *sb.*

1542 *Invent. R. Wardr.* (1815) 63 Item, ane uthir peice of gold of the moynd unmoltin. *a* **1548** HALL *Chron., Hen. VI* 113 So thei cast trenches and made moynes.

moyne, variant of MOYEN.

moynel(l, -iele, obs. forms of MONIAL *sb.*[2]

moynȝeoun, obs. Sc. form of MINION.

moyodore, obs. form of MOIDORE.

moyre, obs. f. MIRE, MOIRE; var. MURE *a. Obs.*

Moysaicall, obs. form of MOSAICAL *a.*[2]

†**moyse.** *Obs.* Also 5 **moys**; and see MOY *sb.*[1] [The last element in *apple-moyse*, APPLE-MOSE, used as a word by itself.] (See quot. 1611.) Cf. also MOOSE[2].

[*c* **1430** *Two Cookery-bks.* 113 (Laud MS. 553) Apple moys. **1597** *Bk. Cookerie* F v b, To make an apple moyse.] **1611** FLORIO, *Mosa*... Also a moyse, or phroise made of egges, milke, butter and spice and so fride in a pan.

moyse, obs. var. MOIS, MOYCE, MUSE *v.*

moysin, moyso(u)n: see MOISTEN, MOISON.

moyster, obs. form of MOISTURE, MUSTER *sb.*

moyte(e, -ie, obs. forms of MOIETY.

moy-yah, var. MOYA *int.*

Mozambican (məʊzæm'biːkən), *a.* and *sb.* Also †**Mosambican.** [f. MOZAMBIQUE + -AN.]

A. *adj.* Of or pertaining to Mozambique.

1875 *Encycl. Brit.* III. 758/2 The Libyan Subregion.. is then succeeded by the 'Mosambican' Subregion, which continues perhaps to Sofala. **1893** A. NEWTON *Dict. Birds* II. 352 The 'Mosambican' Province next follows. **1970** *Guardian* 1 Aug. 9/1 A Mozambican consciousness, an awareness of African history. **1971** *Standard* (Tanzania) 7 Apr. 4/1 Mozambican freedom fighters. **1974** *Daily News* (Tanzania) 13 Sept. 4/1 This bunch of bandits.. is desperately trying to oppose the Mozambican People's and the Portuguese People's wish for peace.

B. *sb.* A native or inhabitant of Mozambique.

1971 *Standard* (Tanzania) 7 Apr. 4/1 This news was joyfully received by other Mozambicans. **1973** *Times* 17 Feb. (Mozambique Suppl.) p. ii/2 The identity card carried by any Mozambican is exactly the same document as that carried by anyone in Lisbon.

Mozambique (məʊzæm'biːk). [The name of an independent state (formerly a Portuguese territory) on the East coast of Africa.] A name given to various kinds of dress material.

1875 KNIGHT *Dict. Mech.*, *Mozambique* (Fabric), an open dress-goods having a chain in which the cotton threads are associated in pairs, and the woolen filling is soft and fleecy. **1896** *Godey's Mag.* Apr. 436/1 A new material of mohair and silk is known as Mozambique.

Also **Mozam'biquer**, a native or inhabitant of Mozambique.

1803 R. SEMPLE *Walks & Sk. Cape Good Hope* iii. 40 Without the inactivity or dulness of the Mozambiquer or the penetrative genius of the Malay, he [*sc.* the Malabar slave] forms an excellent medium between the two. **1876** F. BOYLE *Savage Life* 271 Besides this, we had.. two cooks, a Malay and a Mozambiquer.

mozan, obs. Sc. form of MIZEN.

Mozarab (məʊ'zærəb). *Hist.* Also **Mozarabe, Muzarab.** [a. Sp. *Mozárabe* (med.L. *Mosarabes* pl., and with etymologizing perversion *Mixtarabes*), corrupt form of Arab. *mustaɛrib*, 'would-be Arab', active pple. of a verb of the 10th (desiderative) conjugation f. *ɛarab* ARAB.] In Spain under Moorish rule: One of those Christians who, on condition of owning allegiance to the Moorish king, and conforming to certain Moorish customs, were allowed the exercise of their own religion.

1788 GIBBON *Decl. & F.* li. V. 387 The name of Mozarabes (adoptive Arabs) was applied to their civil or religious conformity. **1840** *Penny Cycl.* XVI. 35/2 *Muzarab*, *i.e.* a Christian living under the sway of the Arabs.

Mozarabic (məʊ'zærəbɪk), *a.* Also **Mos-, Mus-, Muzarabic.** [f. MOZARAB + -IC.] Of or pertaining to the Mozarabs.

Mozarabic liturgy (***rite, use, office***, etc.): the ancient ritual of the Spanish Church, so called prob. as having been retained by the Mozarabs after it was disused by other Spanish Christians. A modified form of it is still used in some few chapels in Spain.

1706 tr. *Dupin's Eccl. Hist. 16th C.* II. III. 251 Then he mentioned the Musarabic Use, according to which Mass was still celebrated every Sunday. **1791** J. TOWNSEND *Journ. Spain* (1792) I. 311 In one of the chapels, where they use only the Mozarabic Missal. **1863** J. M. NEALE *Ess. Liturgiology* 125 The Mozarabic Liturgy. *Ibid.* 126 The Mozarabic Office. *Ibid.* 134 Three Priests of Mozarabic churches. *Ibid.* 135 The present state of the Mozarabic Rite. *Ibid.*, The question of mixed marriages between Roman and Mozarabic Christians.

Mozartian (məʊ'zɑːtɪən), *a.* and *sb.* Also **-ean.** [f. the name of the musician W. A. *Mozart* (1756–91) + -IAN.] Characteristic of the music of Mozart. Also as *sb.*, an admirer or adherent of Mozart; an interpreter of his works.

1845 E. HOLMES *Mozart* 272 The combination of playfulness and grace.. imparts to 'Figaro'.. a more decided Mozartean character than any other of his works. **1881** *Athenæum* 19 Feb. 273/1 The composer welds his themes together with absolute Mozartian ease and grace. **1898** G. B. SHAW *Perfect Wagnerite* 114 The Mozartian method. **1947** [see CHROMATICISM]. **1947** A. EINSTEIN *Mus. Romantic Era* v. 44 Even in the 19th century there were still many.. who demanded no more than that of music: they were the 'Mozartians', the opponents particularly of Wagner and Liszt. **1955** *Times* 14 May 4/5 It was a curious whim that brought a Mozartian body all the way from Germany in order to play Beethoven's Eighth Symphony. **1958** *Spectator* 10 Jan. 50/2 Despite one or two very lovely movements, this is only for the insatiable Mozartian. **1959** *Listener* 15 Jan. 131/3 The Mozartian aristocracy has long disappeared [in Prague]. **1960** *20th Cent.* Aug. 141 A mood of carnival that one might call Mozartian. **1975** *Daily Tel.* 1 May 13/8 Once again the young Jamaican Nerine Barrett proved last night a natural-born Mozartian.

Also **Mozarti'ana** *sb. pl.* (ANA *suff.*), minor works by Mozart; **Mo'zartianly** *adv.*, in the manner or style of Mozart's music; **Mo'zartish** *a.*, somewhat resembling the music of Mozart; **Mo'zartism**, partisanship of Mozart as against other composers; **Mozart-lover**; **Mozart-like, -size** *adjs.*

1825 LAMB *Lett.* (1888) II. 132 My sister's cold is as obstinate as an old Handelian, whom a modern amateur is trying to convert to Mozart-ism. **1845** E. HOLMES *Mozart* 318 Why my productions take from my hand that particular form and style that makes them Mozartish.. is probably owing to [etc.]. **1925** W. DE LA MARE *Two Tales* 55 The

Mozart-like light and sweetness. **1928** *Observer* 24 June 23 The other three..give the elegant (and in the last movement Mozartianly deep) music an air of special distinction. **1955** H. van Thal *Fanfare for E. Newman* x. 147 But he also thought the Finale of Beethoven's *Eroica*, with its 'gentle Mozartisms', unworthy of the rest. **1958** *Spectator* 10 Jan. 50/2 A rarer contribution to recorded Mozartiana is the fifteen one-movement Church Sonatas for chamber orchestra and organ. **1959** D. Cooke *Lang. Mus.* v. 236 True Mozart-lovers of the nineteenth and twentieth centuries. *Ibid.* 245 Only those who have heard the work played in a small hall, by a Mozart-size orchestra with a handful of strings, can be said to have experienced the truly violent impact of the symphony. **1963** *Punch* 3 Apr. 496/3 *Così fan Tutte* is..brightly and strongly though not always Mozartianly sung.

moze (məʊz), *v.* In 6 moise, 7 mose. [Perh. a derivative of moss *sb.*[1] (in the sense of 'nap': cf. moss *sb.*[1] 5).] *trans.* To gig (cloth); to subject to the operation of a gig-mill. Hence **'mozing** *vbl. sb.*

1505–6 *Corporation Minutes York* IX. 32 (MS.) To crop and moise every suche clothe. **1633** *Proclam.* in Rymer *Foedera* XIX. 446/1 Whereas..the use of Gigmills is forbidden..yet of late time the same Mills are used under the name of mosing Mills. *Ibid.*, All mosing Mills shall be taken down before Midsomer next. **1842** *Encycl. Brit.* (ed. 7) XXI. 934/2 After being sheared, it is subject to the gig-mill in one direction only, which is called *mozing*. **1875** Knight *Dict. Mech.*, *Mozing*, gigging of cloth.

mozel(l, mozki, obs. ff. muzzle, mosque.

‖**mozo** ('moθo). *Latin America.* [Sp.] **1.** A male servant or attendant; a groom; a labourer.

1836 C. J. Latrobe *Rambler in Mexico* 49 The remainder were sent in advance under his domestics or mozos. **1847** G. A. F. Ruxton *Adventures Mexico & Rocky Mts.* vii. 48, I at length hired a *mozo* to proceed with me as far as Durango. **1904** Conrad *Nostromo* I. viii. 107 But Captain Mitchell's right-hand man..after looking down critically at the ragged mozo, shook his head. **1923** *Blackw. Mag.* July 46/2 The mozo, the ostler lad,..was a son of the house. **1936** A. Huxley *Eyeless in Gaza* xli. 495 The *mozos* had loaded their baggage on to the pack-mules. **1955** W. Gaddis *Recognitions* III. iii. 819 It turned out that the Señorito had asked the same question, and fled directly he got this same answer, leaving this mozo behind, to chat with her.

2. A bull-fighter's attendant.

1926 [see espada]. **1934** H. Baerlein *Belmonte the Matador* iii. 37 Every matador has got a valet, his *mozo de estoques*, whose important days are those on which there is a fight, not only in the dressing of his master but the duties of attendance..at the ring-side, preparing the muletas and handing to his master the swords as he requires them. *Ibid.* 38 Antonio Conde..undertook the part of mozo which he kept throughout the years. **1963** *Parade* (Austral.) Dec. 47/1 Meijas had to start at the bottom of the ladder as a 'mozo', the attendant who waits on a matador. **1967** McCormick & Mascareñas *Compl. Aficionado* iv. 146 *Mozo(s)*, the badly paid and often brave ring-attendants who clean up the mess, accompany the picador on foot, [etc.].

mozy, variant of mosy *a. dial.*, mossy.

mozza, var. matzah.

mozzarella (mɒtsə'rɛlə). Also **mozarella**; *pl.* **moz(z)arelle**. [It.] In full, ***mozzarella cheese***. An Italian cheese originally made in the Naples area from buffalo milk.

1911 C. Besana in *Bull. Bureau Agric. Intelligence & Plant-Dis.* (Internat. Inst. Agric., Rome) Nos. 8–10. 2231 With Buffalo milk..'pasta filata' cheeses are made, which are eaten fresh and much esteemed. These are 'Provature', 'Mozarelle', etc. **1912** *Experiment Station Rec.* (USDA) Oct. 475 Provature, or Provole, and Mozzarelle cheeses are made from buffalo milk. **1935** M. Morphy *Recipes of all Nations* 160 Slices of Mozzarella cheese. **1962** *Spectator* 16 Feb. 219/2 Was the mozzarella cheese dripping, positively dripping, fresh? **1962** L. Deighton *Ipcress File* ii. 19 The girl in the delicatessen was small,..and rather delicious. We had been flirting across the mozzarella for years. **1969** *Daily Tel.* (Colour Suppl.) 5 Sept. 33/3 Limpid responsive eyes, and a chin that slopes back from a face as pale and bland as mozzarella. **1974** *Times* 2 Nov. 11/4 Fresh mozarella..for making pizza.

mozzetta, mozetta (məʊ'zɛtə, ‖mot'tsetta). *Eccl.* Also 8 **mozet**, 9 *pl.* **mozzette**. [It. *mozzetta*, dim. of *mozza*: see amice[2].] (See quot. 1885.)

1774 T. West *Antiq. Furness* 51 Their choir dress was a white or grey Cassock,..over that a mozet, or hood. **1849** Rock *Ch. of Fathers* II. 417 The old hood was close all round, whereas the mozetta is cut in front. **1866** F. G. Lee *Direct. Angl.* (ed. 3) 356 Mozetta, a cape with a small hood worn by canons and others in the Latin Communion. **1885** *Catholic Dict.* (ed. 3) 654 *Mozetta*,..a short vestment, quite open in front, which can, however, be buttoned over the breast, covering the shoulders and with a little hood behind. It is worn by the Pope, by cardinals, bishops, abbots, and others who do so by custom or Papal privilege. *Ibid.*, The Pope wears five different mozzette.

mozzle ('mɒz(ə)l). *Austral. slang.* Also moz, mozz. [ad. Heb. *mazzāl* luck; cf. shemozzle.] Luck; *spec.* in phr. ***to put the moz on***, to inconvenience; to jinx. Also as *v. trans.*, to hinder, interrupt.

1898 *Bulletin* (Sydney) 17 Dec. (Red Page), *Mozzle* is luck... *Good mozzle* = good luck; *Kronk mozzle* = bad luck. **1903** 'T. Collins' *Such is Life* vi. 225 'And how much do you stand to lose, if your mozzle is out?' I asked. **1919** E. Dyson *Hello Soldier!* 32 'Twas rotten mozzle, Neddo. We had blown out every clip. **1941** Baker *Dict. Austral. Slang* 47 *Moz*, to interrupt, to hinder. 'Put the moz on someone', to inconvenience a person. *Mozzle, to*, as for 'moz'. **1956** A. Marshall *How's Andy Going?* 200 'Looking ahead like that never does any bloody good to any man,' observed Pat. 'It puts the moz on him.' **1963** H. Porter *Watcher on Cast-Iron Balcony* 81 Mother is wishing Miss Brewer some female ill, is putting the mozz on her. **1965** F. Hardy *Yarns Billy Borker* xx. 107 'Don't mozz a man,' I tells him. 'You're well named, I'll say that for you, Calamity.' **1974** J. Powers *Last of Knucklemen* 49 Don't let him mozz you, Monk. **1974** K. Stackpole *Not just for Openers* ii. 32 She felt she put the moz on him... She couldn't bear to go in case she was a jinx.

M.P. The usual abbreviation for 'Member of Parliament'. Often treated (*colloq.* or in informal writing) as a word, with the pronunciation (ɛm piː); the plural is written *M.P.'s*, sometimes *M.P.s*.

1809 Byron *Bards & Rev.* 273 All hail, M.P.! from whose infernal brain Thin-sheeted phantoms glide. **1868** Holme Lee *B. Godfrey* xxviii, M.P. to their name is a handsome advertisement. **1870** Disraeli *Lothair* viii, There were no less than four M.P.s, one of whom was even in office. **1886** Kipling *Departm. Ditties*, etc. (1888) 53 'Skittles!' says Pagett, M.P. **1889** E. Parry *Gay Umbrella* iii, I shall represent the City And be known as the gay M.P.

Hence **M.P.-ship**, the office of an M.P.

1832 Miss Mitford *Village* Ser. v. 83 The son's M.P.-ship had probably tended to make his mamma epistolary. **1886** Tupper *My Life as Author* 67 As to M.P.ship I may have had other chances.

mpalla, var. impala.

mph ((ə)mh), *int.* Also **mphm**. [Imit.] Used to express an inarticulate sound of disapproval, doubt, or qualified approval. Cf. umph *int.*

1876 'Mark Twain' *Tom Sawyer* 272 What would people say? 'Mph! Tom Sawyer's gang! pretty low characters in it.' **1949** 'N. Blake' *Head of Traveller* vii. 105 To conceal the way he was killed? Mphm. Don't see how it helps us.

Mpret (brɛt). Also **Mbret, M'pret**. [ad. Alb. *mbret*, f. L. *imperator* emperor.] The title given to William of Wied, elected ruler of Albania after the declaration of Albanian independence in 1913.

1914 *Conc. Oxf. Dict.* Add., *Mpret*, Albanian ruler [L. *imperator*, emperor]. **1915** *Truth* 27 Jan. 133/2 He and not the Prince of Wied ought to be M'pret. **1921** C. Torr *Small Talk at Wreyland* 2nd Ser. 83 When I first went to Greece, they still spelled Byron's name phonetically Mpairon. They pronounce *b* like our *v*, but *mp* like our *b*—a fact unknown to many of the people who talk about the Mpret of Albania. **1954** M. Hasluck *Unwritten Law in Albania* xv. 154 Esad Pashë Toptani revolted against Prince William of Wied, then *Mbret* (king) of Albania. **1959** *Chambers's Encycl.* I. 221/2 The European ruler selected to be 'mpret' of Albania —the German prince William of Wied.

Mr. [Orig. an abbreviation of master.]

†**1.** In the 16th and 17th c. used for master in any of the applications of the word. *Obs.*

1538 Cromwell in Merriman *Life & Lett.* (1902) II. 139 My Lordes Letteres Syngnyfing to my Mr. he hath apoyncted the Abbot of Kenelworth for his yerlie pencion c. li. **1575** *Gamm. Gurton* (title-p.) Made by Mr. S. Mr. of Art. **1597** *1st Pt. Return fr. Parnass.* iv. i. 1324 But tell mee, art thou put away nowe for whippinge thy yonge M^r? **1617** *Court-bk. Merch.-Taylors' Comp.* VI. 633 in *Webster's Wks.* (Rtldg.) p. ix. *note*, John Webster made free by Henry Clinckard his M^r. **1631** W. Foster *Hoplocrismaspongus* 2, I am a M^r. of Arts in both Vniversities. **1657** Austen *Fruit Trees* 1. 133 Bare the Roots and cut off a Mr Root or two from the Tree. **1669** Sturmy *Mariner's Mag.* v. xii. 71 All Mr Gunners should be able to draw. **1674** R. Godfrey *Inj. & Ab. Physic* 141, I refused the Title of Mr. of Arts.

2. a. As a prefixed title. Now pronounced ('mɪstə(r)), or with entire absence of stress (mɪstə(r), mstə(r)). The want of a plural form is supplied by *Messrs.*, messieurs 2.

Until the latter half of the 17th c. the title was often written in the full form *master*; but there is reason for believing that from the 16th c. it was, at least in rapid or careless speech, treated proclitically, with consequent alteration of the vowel of the first syllable. (See mister *sb.*[2] 1, quot. 1551.) Eventually the word came to have the weakened pronunciation whenever it was used as a prefixed title, and it became customary to employ the abbreviated spelling always for this use, and for this only. Hence at the beginning of the 18th c. *master* and *Mr.* were already regarded as distinct words. Cf. mister *sb.*[2], which is merely an occasional (chiefly jocular) rendering of the pronunciation of the word of which 'Mr.' is the accepted spelling.

The early history of the application of *Mr.* is identical with that of the use of its fuller form: see master *sb.* 21. From the 17th c. it has been the customary ceremonious prefix to the name of any man below the rank of knight and above some humble but undefined level of social status, except where usage requires the substitution of some honorific title, such, for instance, as those denoting military and naval rank. As with other titles of courtesy, the inferior limit for its application has been continually lowered; at the present day any man however low in station would be styled 'Mr.' on certain occasions, e.g. in the address of a letter. Modern custom forbids the use of the prefix when *Esquire* is appended to the name, and it is now omitted after 'The Hon.' and 'The Rev.' (though some still write 'the Rev. Mr. A.' when the Christian name happens to be unknown); but in other than ceremonious use 'Mr.' is substituted for these titles.

The use of *Mr.* before a *prefixed* title of office is nearly obsolete. The Judges of the Supreme Court are still styled 'Mr. Justice A.'; the designations 'Mr. Baron A.', 'Mr. Serjeant B.', belonged to dignities now abolished. In municipal use we still occasionally read of 'Mr. Alderman A.', 'Mr. Deputy B.', 'Mr. Councillor C.'.

Before an official title *not* followed by the name, the prefix *Mr.* is still common, as in 'Mr. Chairman', 'Mr. Editor', 'Mr. President', 'Mr. Mayor'. These are now used only vocatively; 'Mr. Speaker' is used also in the 3rd person.

1447–8 Shillingford *Lett.* (Camden) 89 Maister John Waryn Mr William Filham. *c* **1524** More in Ellis *Orig. Lett.* Ser. II. I. 294 All the lettres of M^r. Secretary sent unto your Grace. **1553** *Respublica* I. iii. 61 (Brandl) Nowe, Mr Insolence, to your ghostelye purpose. **1557** in *Shropsh. Parish Documents* (1903) 58 Item Re'd of Mr. Vicar for olde shingle vi^d. **1597** *1st Pt. Return fr. Parnass.* iv. i. 1211 Let mee heare Mr. Shakspear's veyne. **1600** Shaks. *A.Y.L.* III. iii. 74 Good euen good M^r what ye cal't. **1662** *Tryal Sir H. Vane* 84 He further told Mr. Sheriff, he was ready: but the Sheriff said, he was not. **1680** Ld. Russell in *Parl. Debates* 1 Mr. Speaker, Sir, seeing by Gods Providence [etc.]. **1706** Hearne *Collect.* 13 Mar. (O.H.S.) I. 203 Mr. Poley, Esqr., Member of Parliament. **1841** R. H. Dana *Seaman's Man.* 154 Both the chief and second mates are always addressed by their surnames, with *Mr.* prefixed. **1844** Owen in *Hunterian Lect.* (1846) II. 1 Mr. President and Gentlemen. **1865** *Even. Standard* 10 Mar., At the meeting to-day Mr. Vice Chancellor, the rev. the Master of St. Peter's, presided. **1886** Tupper *Autobiog.* 58 'What have I done, Mr. Dean?..' 'Why, sir, the porter states that this is the fifth time you have not come into college until past twelve o'clock.'

b. *jocularly.*

1655 Walton *Angler* x. (1661) 176 If Mr. Pike be there, then the little Fish will skip out of the water. **1757** W. Thompson *R.N. Advoc.* 45 With a handsome Salary for Mr. Operator. **1895** J. G. Millais *Breath fr. Veldt* (1899) 161 There..stood Mr. and Mrs. Pig and the entire Pig family.

c. Prefixed to a foreign name. Now *rare*, the usual practice being to employ *Monsieur* (*M.*), *Herr*, *Signor*, or the like.

In French *Mr.* is used (beside *M.*) as an abbreviation of *Monsieur*. It may possibly be so intended in the Shaks. quot. below, where modern editors print *Monsieur*.

1601 Shaks. *All's Well* v. ii. 1 Good Mr Lauetch giue my Lord Lafew this letter. **1746** Francis tr. *Horace, Ep.* II. i. 158 *note*, Mr. Sanadon thinks [etc.]. **1778** Fletcher *Lett.* Wks. 1795 VII. 223 Mr. Tronchin the physician of the Duke of Orleans was sent for to attend Voltaire. **1817** Coleridge *Satyrane's Lett.* iii, W—— and myself accompanied Mr. Klopstock to the house of his brother, the poet.

d. One who is entitled to be addressed as 'Mr.'; the word 'Mr.' as a title (in correspondence).

a **1817** Jane Austen *Persuasion* (1818) III. iii. 55 'I have let my house to Admiral Croft,' would sound extremely well; very much better than to any mere *Mr.*——; a *Mr.* (save, perhaps, some half dozen in the nation,) always needs a note of explanation. **1857** Geo. Eliot *Let.* 2 June (1954) II. 337 Mr. Eliot..may be a relation of Mr. Liggins's or some other 'Mr.' who knows Coton stories. **1882** W. Pater *Let.* 4 Nov. (1970) 43 My dear Sharp, (I think we have known each other long enough to drop the 'Mr.'). **1915** R. Fry *Let.* 26 Aug. (1972) II. 389 Dear Waley (May we drop the Mr).

e. Used with following adj. or sb. to denote an exemplar, a type, or a victor in a contest; esp. **Mr. Big**, the head of an organization of criminals; also, any important man; **Mr. Charley, Charlie** (see Charley, Charlie 7); **Mr. Clean**, an honourable or incorruptible politician; **Mr. Fix** (see quot. 1950); **Mr. Fixit**, one who does repairs or odd jobs; one skilled at managing difficult problems or situations; a 'trouble-shooter'; **Mr. Right**, a man who would make the ideal husband; a 'Prince Charming'.

See 1958 *Amer. Speech* XXXIII. II. ii. 84–87.

1814 H. Brougham *Let.* June in T. Creevey *Creevey Papers* (1903) I. ix. 194, I was finally decided in favour of publishing to-day by the apprehension of Alexr., &c., coming in a day or two, and taking off the attention of Mr. and Mrs. Bull. **1913** C. Mackenzie *Sinister St.* I. I. ii. 28 Because he had been slow in choosing..he had been called Mr. Particular. **1922** Joyce *Ulysses* 362 Till Mr Right comes along then meet once in a blue moon. **1925** R. Lardner in *Liberty* 9 May 5 (*title*) Mr. and Mrs. Fix-It. **1937** E. H. Sutherland *Professional Thief* v. 129 Since most of the cases of professional thieves in the stores are taken care of by Mr. Fix, it is evident that the store detectives must get an end. **1940** G. Marx *Let.* 10 Oct. (1967) 26, I may motor east ..to see your 'Mr. Big'. **1950** H. E. Goldin *Dict. Amer. Underworld Lingo* 139/1 *Mister fix*, a go-between, especially one who shuttles between the underworld and the overworld, handling bribes, ransom payments, etc. **1951** J. Cannan *And All I Learned* vi. 76 Stevens offered her the last cake on a plate... Mildred laughed and replied, 'What about Mr Manners?' but took the cake. **1952** M. Laski *Village* i. 24 In the ordinary way you'd expect someone like Miss Margaret to stay at home and go to tennis-parties and things until Mr. Right came along and she could make a home of her own. **1953** R. Chandler *Long Good-Bye* xxxii. 200 He was Mr. Big, the winner. **1959** A. W. Sherring *Tip Off* iii. 28 Hardly the kind of district one would expect to find Mr. Big of London's underworld. **1962** E. Cleaver in A. Dundes *Mother Wit* (1973) 18/1 To..crown him..Mister ..Universe. **1967** P. E. H. Durston *Mortissimo* (1968) xii. 100 He's got very little decent for sale. More of what the Americans call a 'Mr. Fixit'. Mends things. **1968** 'J. Le Carré' *Small Town in Germany* v. 71 Do you a girl as well, would he? Mister Fixit, is that it? **1969** C. Booker *Neophiliacs* vii. 179 Hints of the existence of a powerful 'Mr. Big'. **1970** G. Greer *Female Eunuch* 88 The whole point of a woman's existence is to be exploited by Mr Right. **1970** *Sunday Times* (Colour Suppl.) 20 Dec. 35/3 Still an entrepreneur and a Mr Fix-it, Levis..died from cirrhosis of the liver. **1972** *Village Voice* (N.Y.) 1 June 15/1 Peter M. Flanigan..became an assistant to the President and acquired a reputation as 'Richard Nixon's "Mr. Fixit" when it comes to powerful business interests'. **1973** J. Mann *Only Security* x. 132 Sylvester..could have modelled as a Mr Average. **1973** *Times* 21 Nov. 8/4 Mr Elliot Richardson, who resigned as Attorney General..is Mr Clean to many Republicans. **1974** E. McGirr *Murderous Journey* 59, I.. asked if I could go through Siskin's papers... He'd been a methodical man... It was more or less the picture of Mr. America. **1974** *Guardian* 28 Jan. 2/5 Mr Shultz himself had never been touched by Watergate... His reputation as a 'Mr

Clean'..has led him..to voice a growing sense of unease. **1974** *Observer* 17 Feb. 5/5 Smalls said he had not seen a 'Police 5' TV programme about the Wembley raid, but agreed that Turner's photograph was 'splashed in the papers', accompanied by the title of 'Mr Big'.

Hence **Mr.** *v.*, *trans.* to address as 'Mr.'; **Mr.-ship**, the position of being styled 'Mr.'

1747 H. WALPOLE *Let. to Mann* 26 June, Archer and Rolle have only changed their Mr.-ships for Lordships. **1850** SMEDLEY *Frank Fairleigh* vi, I tell you what it is, Oaklands (we don't Mr. each other here), you are a right good fellow.

mrad: see M 5 d.

mridangam ((ə)mrɪ'daŋam). Also **m'ridang(a)**. [a. Sanskrit *mṛidaṃga* a kind of drum.] A double-headed, barrel-shaped drum, once made of clay, now usually of wood, with one head larger than the other, used in southern Indian music. Also *attrib.*

1888 A. J. HIPKINS *Mus. Instruments* 87 The Drum with the striped body and leather braces is a kind of M'ridang. The genuine Drum bearing this name is longer in proportion to its diameter, and has one head larger than the other. *Ibid.*, A good Tabla or M'ridang player will earn from 100 to 150 rupees, per month... The M'ridang is considered to be the most ancient of Indian Drums; its origin is popularly ascribed to the god Mahadeo (S'iva). **1891** C. R. DAY *Mus. & Mus. Instruments S. India* vi. 138 (*caption*) The Mridang is beaten by the hands, finger-tips, and wrists... The smaller head of the Mridang is struck by the right hand, the larger head by the left. **1921** H. A. POPLEY *Mus. India* vii. 120 The *Mṛidaṅga* or *Mardala* is the most common and probably the most ancient of Indian drums... The word *mṛidaṅga* or *mardala* means 'made of clay', and probably therefore its body was originally of mud. **1968** *N.Y. Times* 12 Sept. 56 Palghat Raghu on the mridanga and Alla Rakha on the tabla. **1968** *Daily Tel.* 28 Sept. 13/3 Among them was a drum dialogue between Alla Rakha (tabla) and Palghat Raghu (mridangam), a tour de force of fantastic subtlety and eloquence. **1970** *Ibid.* 6 July 12/6 A musical interlude in which Nagarajan on the mridangam drum had a friendly battle..with the dance director. **1971** *Shankar's Weekly* (Delhi) 4 Apr. 24/1 The infinite variety of the mridangam includes some of the elemental sequences that jazz makes capital out of.

Mris., obs. abbreviation of *mistris*, MISTRESS.

Mrs. [Orig. an abbreviation of MISTRESS.]

†**1.** In the 17th c. often written for MISTRESS in all uses. *Obs.*

a **1612** SIR J. HARINGTON *Brief View* (1653) 4 [Q. Eliz. to Abp. Parker's wife] And you (saith she), Madam, I may not call you, and Mrs. I am ashamed to call you, so as I know not what to call you, but yet I do thank you. **1615** SIR G. HELWYS in *Buccleuch MSS.* (Hist. MSS. Comm.) I. 161 A man of Mrs. Turner's was sent..to meet his Mrs. at Ware. **1632** B. JONSON *Magn. Lady* I. (1640) 19 [If he could] beget him a reputation, and marry an Emperours Daughter for his Mrs. **1637** —— *Sad Sheph.* II. ii, I give 'hem yee; As presents Mrs. **1677** W. HUBBARD *Narrative* (1865) II. 158 Knowing enough before of their Villanys, how well soever her Mrs...might think of them. **1679** *Trials of White, & Other Jesuits* 80 Pray Mrs. what did that Minister say to you ..concerning Mr. Oates?

2. As a prefixed title of courtesy. Now pronounced ('mɪsɪs, 'mɪsɪz).

In the latter half of the 17th c. there was a general tendency to confine the use of written abbreviations to words of inferior syntactical importance, such as prefixed titles. The form *Mrs.* for *mistress* therefore fell into disuse exc. when prefixed to a name; and in this position the writing of the full form gradually became unusual. The contracted pronunciation, which in other applications of the word has never been more than a vulgarism (see MISSIS), became, for the prefixed title, first a permitted colloquial licence, and ultimately the only allowable pronunciation. When this stage was reached, *Mrs.* (with the contracted pronunciation) became a distinct word from *mistress*. As to the chronology of these changes evidence is wanting; but it may be noted that Walker 1828 says that *mistress* as a title of civility is pronounced *missis*, and that 'to pronounce the word as it is written would, in these cases, appear quaint and pedantick'.

a. Prefixed to the surname of a married woman (sometimes with her Christian name or that of her husband intervening). Also prefixed to the Christian name of the husband (without a following surname).

'Originally distinctive of gentlewomen, the use of the prefix has gradually extended downwards; at the present time, every married woman who has no superior title is styled 'Mrs.' even though her husband is of so humble a position as not ordinarily to be referred to as 'Mr.'. In British use the insertion of a woman's Christian name after *Mrs.* (as 'Mrs. Mary Smith') is rare exc. in legal documents, cheques, or the like, the normal practice when distinction is needed being to insert the husband's name (as 'Mrs. John Smith'). In the U.S. both these modes of designation are in general use' (*N.E.D.*, *1908*).

1615 [see 1]. **1647** *Moder. Intell.* No. 129. 1 Sept., Mrs. Car being a second wife of the said Mr. Car. **1745** H. WALPOLE *Let. to Mann* 11 May, Just as a woman is not called Mrs. till she is married. **1794** C. PIGOT *Female Jockey Club* 54 Yet Mrs Bull is still tenacious of the honour of her master. *a* **1817** JANE AUSTEN *Persuasion* (1818) III. vi. 103, I shall tell *you*, Miss Anne..that I have no very good opinion of Mrs. Charles's nursery-maid. **1819** SHELLEY *Peter Bell 3rd* VI. ix. 2 And who *Is* Mrs. Foy? **1842** GEO. ELIOT *Let.* 18 Feb. (1954) I. 126, I imagine, from a message my sister Mrs. Isaac told me of, that you had the idea that I was at Griff. **1857** C. M. YONGE *Dynevor Terr.* II. vi. 81 Is it in the nature of things that she should live in such society as Mrs. Walby's and Mrs. Richardson's? People who call her Mrs. James! **1870** MISS BRIDGMAN *R. Lynne* II. iii. 66 Mrs. This and Mrs. That..approved of the..friends of their respective husbands. **1910** E. M. FORSTER *Howard's End* xxxiii. 335 Mrs. Charles is expecting her fourth. **1953** A. CHRISTIE *Pocket Full of Rye* iv. 28 'Who was at breakfast?' 'Mrs. Fortescue, Miss Fortescue, Mrs. Val Fortescue... Mrs. Val and Miss Fortescue always eat a hearty breakfast.' **1971** E. LEMARCHAND *Death on Doomsday* vi. 97 We know Mrs Giles has got a key into the public rooms.

†**b.** In the 17th and 18th c. prefixed to the name of an unmarried lady or girl; equivalent to the mod. use of MISS *sb.*² *Obs.*

Late in the 18th c. the title (usually, but not always, followed by the Christian name) was applied occasionally to elderly maiden ladies (as 'Mrs. Elizabeth Carter', 'Mrs. Hannah More') after this use had ceased to be general.

c **1645** HOWELL *Lett.* (1655) I. v. 235 An ill-favoured quarrell..about Mrs. Baker, the Maid of honor. **1707** HEARNE *Collect.* (O.H.S.) II. 17 M^rs. Molly Levins..Which M^rs. Levins is a Beautifull young Brisk Lady of about 16 or 17 Years of Age. **1722** DE FOE *Col. Jack*, etc. (1840) 342 Mrs. Veal was a maiden gentlewoman. **1751** SMOLLETT *Per. Pic.* i, His only sister Mrs. Grizzle..was now in the thirtieth year of her maidenhood. **1791** BOSWELL *Johnson* an. 1781, The company was..Mrs. Elizabeth Carter, Sir Joshua Reynolds [etc.]. *Ibid.*, Mrs. Carter said [etc.].

c. A wife (with ellipsis of the name of her husband). *colloq.*

1913 R. BROOKE *Let.* 22 Nov. (1968) 535 He passed through Fiji lately... Mrs, I gather, is not with him. **1938** M. ALLINGHAM *Fashion in Shrouds* vi. 82 Paul Taretan is taking 'three girls from totally different environments', and 'Mrs.' has selected one rather beastly little boy. **1950** J. CANNAN *Murder Included* i. 9 Mr and Mrs Scampnell... Mrs has a daughter by her first husband. **1970** A. MORICE *Death in Grand Manor* iv. 35 Mr Cornford wasn't so bad.. but Mrs was awful. **1974** J. MONTGOMERIE *Implosion* x. 67 Another picture of Mrs., side-view.

d. ***the Mrs.***: one's wife. *colloq.*

The examples happen to be U.S. but the use is widespread: cf. MISSIS 1.

1920 [see *monkey suit* s.v. MONKEY *sb.* 18 a]. **1937** *Amer. Speech* XII. 103 The farmer will often refer to his wife as the Mrs. and he commonly addresses her as Wife. **1944** *Publ. Amer. Dial. Soc.* II. 58 *The Mrs.*, the wife. **1967** E. BULLINS *Theme is Blackness* (1973) 96 I'll have the Mrs. call the doctor as soon as I get home. **1973** *Philadelphia Inquirer* (Today Suppl.) 7 Oct. 42/3 You know, when I go home, the Mrs. says to me: 'Well, what happened tonight, night clerk?'

e. Prefixed to the surname of (the husband of) an actual or a fictional married woman, or to a generic sb., indicating esp. a woman of a certain occupation or temperament, as **Mrs. Beeton** (abbr. **Mrs. B.**) [the name of Isabella Mary *Beeton* (1836–65), nominal author of a Book on Household Management], an authority on cooking and domestic subjects; also *transf.*; **Mrs. Dale** [the name of the wife of a doctor in a former radio serial], a conventional, middle-class woman; so **Mrs. Dale-ish** *a.*, middle-class; **Mrs. Grundy** (see GRUNDY³); **Mrs. Mop(p** [the name of a charwoman in a radio series], (a nickname for) a charwoman; the typical charwoman; also *attrib.*; **Mrs. next-door** (see NEXT DOOR 1 b); **Mrs. Thing** [THING *sb.*¹ 10], used in place of a married woman's name of which the speaker is uncertain.

1970 *Times* 9 Feb. 8/6 Explains Ita Jones, Light's switched-on *Mrs B.: 'Though serving up this food may blow some minds, remember that you eat the animal because you love it.' **1960** *Listener* 7 Jan. 18/2 The modern trick, I am told by Dr. Spock and the other *Mrs. Beetons of child care, is not to show anxiety to children. **1954** A. MELVILLE *Simon & Laura* in *Plays of Year* XI. 36 You probably get the idea it's to be a sort of TV '*Mrs Dale'. It's not: we want interesting people who meet other interesting people: people..with a bit of—..glamour, colour, excitement in their lives. **1961** *Times Lit. Suppl.* 24 Nov. 851/1 The setting is suburban, even *Mrs. Dale-ish. **1948** J. F. WOLFENDEN *Public Schools To-day* v. 99 A great deal of the welfare..of a boarding school depends upon the unsung 'warrant officers and N.C.O.s', from the school messenger to *Mrs. Mop. **1950** A. CHRISTIE *Murder is Announced* vii. 60 Our Mrs Mopp says he came from one of the big hotels. **1956** 'A. GILBERT' *Riddle of Lady* x. 145 A machine in a Mrs Mopp apron. **1972** *Listener* 27 July 105/1 Today's generation monotonously describe char-women as Mrs Mops. **1939** N. MARSH *Overture to Death* iii. 41 The other one—*Mrs. Thing or whoever she is! **1960** 'R. EAST' *Kingston Black* xiv. 136 Old Mrs. Thing at the exchange may listen in.

MS.¹, abbreviation of MANUSCRIPT (L. *manu scriptum*). Formerly also **MS^t**, *erron.* **MSS^t**. The form **MSS.** is used for the pl. *manuscripts*; by some writers also (after the custom in mod.Latin) for *manuscript* adj. when agreeing with a plural sb.

1670 BLOUNT *Glossogr.* (ed. 3), *M.S.* stands for *manuscriptum*, a Manuscript. **1699** BENTLEY *Phal.* Introd. 22 To shew that it was not taken out of some ancient MS. *Ibid.* 32 Though some of the MSS Copies of Eusebius date it VI Years before. **1709** MS^t [see MATTER *sb.*¹ 19 d]. **1716** HEARNE *Collect.* (O.H.S.) V. 334 A little MSS^t. containing MSS. Additions to Guil. Neubr. **1780** C. BURNEY in Louisa Twining *Recreat. & Stud.* (1882) 82 A coachfull of the MSS. I had collected for my 'History'. **1798** *Brit. Crit.* XI. 111 A selection of all the most important readings from MSS. editions, and versions. **1883** *A. Barratt's Phys. Metempiric* Pref. 21 He generally kept his MSS. at his chambers in Lincoln's Inn.

¶**b.** Treated jocularly as a word (ɛm ɛs).

1818 BYRON *Occas. Pieces, To Mr. Murray* ii, To thee.. The unfledged MS. authors come. **1821** —— *Vis. Judgm.* cii, He..drew forth an MS.

Ms² (mɪz). Also **Ms.** (with full stop). [A 'compromise' between MRS. and MISS *sb.*²] A title prefixed to the surname of a woman, regardless of her marital status. Hence as *sb.*, a woman so designated. Cf. MIZ 2.

An increasingly common, but not universally accepted, use.

1952 *The Simplified Letter* (Nat. Office Managem. Assoc., Philadelphia) Jan. 4 Use abbreviation Ms. for *all women* addressees. This modern style solves an age-old problem. **1952** *Ibid.* (rev. ed.) June 4 Use abbreviation Ms. if not sure whether to use Mrs. or Miss. **1970** *Daily Tel.* 28 Aug. 14 The American feminists..object to being addressed as Mrs or Miss but admit that Ms, which the New York Commission on Human Rights has adopted for correspondence, [etc.]. **1970** *New Yorker* 5 Sept. 27 'How come no woman heads a super-agency?' demanded Ms. Komisar. **1971** *Publishers' Weekly* 1 Nov. 22 A crowded New York press conference heard this morning that a new magazine, called *Ms.* (pronounced 'Miz'), will begin publication in January. **1972** *Guardian* 29 Mar. 11 Mrs Chisholm (and it is definitely Mrs not Ms). **1973** *Lancet* 24 Mar. 633/2 We thank Ms Payge Hodapp for technical assistance. **1974** *Daily Tel.* 21 May 1/6 The Passport Office yesterday conceded the right to women to call themselves Ms (pronounced Miz) on their passports instead of Mrs or Miss. This followed a month's campaign by Women's Lib. **1975** *Publishers Weekly* 27 Jan. 232/1 *Sanditon* by Jane Austen and Another Lady..Ms. Austen's seventh and unfinished novel. *Ibid.* 19 May 170/1 Samantha Lay, a comely Ms. who devises gimmicks like a 'flying bullpen'. **1975** *Times* 17 Sept. 16/2 A circular..states grandly: 'Female staff in this department may..use the Ms title (usually pronounced Miz) as an alternative to the Miss or Mrs.' *Ibid.* 16/3 The Civil Service Department..has a fair sprinkling of Mss among its own staff.

msasa ((ə)m'sasa). Also **m'sassa**, **musaasa**. [Mashona.] A Central African tree, *Brachystegia spiciformis*, of the family Leguminosæ, distinguished by compound leaves, racemes of small, fragrant, white flowers, and a spreading crown of branches. Also *attrib.*

1923 *Kew Bull.* 133 'Musaasa'..is by far the most common of the bark trees and is found all over Southern Rhodesia at an altitude of from 3,000 to 6,000 feet. It grows to 30 or 40 feet in height, has a rough outer bark in the large trees but almost smooth in the young trees... The trunks of the 'Musaasa' vary in diameter from 8 to 24 inches. **1949** K. L. SIMMS *Sun-Drenched Veld* iii. 33 On these islets you can ..amuse yourself by trying to pick out the various trees. There is..the crimson-leaved m'sasa..and the scarlet-flowering kaffirboom. **1951** D. LESSING *This was Old Chief's Country* i. 8 This child could not see a msasa tree, or the thorn, for what they were. **1964** *Listener* 6 Aug. 191/1 The black shadow of the African msasa Squats among the lawn's colonial company. **1973** PALMER & PITMAN *Trees S. Afr.* II. 847 The msasa is one of the few trees, growing beyond the borders of the Republic, that is well-known to South Africans. It is the dominant tree in most of the savannah forest of Rhodesia, reaching northwards to Zambia and Malawi, and is famous for the gorgeous pink, wine red, copper and bronze colours of its spring foliage.

Mt., abbreviation of MOUNT *sb.*¹

mtepe ((ə)m'teɪpeɪ). [Swahili.] A sailing craft characterized by a square matting sail, used on the East coast of Africa.

1872 R. F. BURTON *Zanzibar* I. iv. 73 Various native craft ..anchor close in shore... The quaintest and freshest local build is to us the Mtepe, which the Arabs call Muntafiyah. **1938** *Jrnl. R. Anthrop. Inst.* LXVIII. 343 It is only when the Swahili coast is reached that the oculus is again encountered. In this region the only sea-going craft that can be classed as indigenous is the *mtepe*. **1942** *E. African Ann.* *1941–2* 27/1 His 'M'tepe' squatted, with many others, on the deep waters beyond the jetty. The tapering mast, raking forwards, was now devoid of its lateen sail.

m'tutor: see M' = my.

mu (mjuː). [a. Gr. $\mu\tilde{\upsilon}$, name of the letter *M*, μ (see M).] **1.** One micrometre (micron). Usu. denoted by μ.

[**1880**: see MICRON.] **1888** *Nature* 8 Mar. 438/1 *Micron* is currently used here to express 1/1000 of a millimetre. French botanists call it μ, and seldom use its first decimal because they cannot see such a small space. **1900** DORLAND *Med. Dict.* 398/2 *Mu*, in micrometry, a micron or micro-millimeter. **1957** *Jrnl. Anat.* XCI. 2 The mean nuclear volume in six [vole] oocytes was found to be 5200 μ^3. **1958** *Times Rev. Industry* June 53/2 It [*sc.* the Mercast process] yields castings to extremely close dimensional limits, one example quoted being..a surface finish of 60μ an inch or better. **1959** *Listener* 31 Dec. 1161/1 Cell sizes range from a few mu to a few dozens of mu. **1970** AMBROSE & EASTY *Cell Biol.* i. 7 Bacteria..vary greatly in size from a diameter of 5,000 Å for the cocci up to about 20 μ in length for some of the filamentous bacteria.

2. *Electronics.* The amplification factor of a valve.

1918 H. J. VAN DER BIJL in *Physical Rev.* XII. 184 The factor μ_0, which plays a very important part in the theory of operation of the thermionic amplifier, can be more easily and accurately determined with the help of equation (19), which gives the relation between the anode and grid potentials necessary to maintain the current at some convenient constant value. *Ibid.* 192 The voltage amplification μ is given by $\mu = \mu_0 R/(R + R_0)$. **1927** B. F. DASHIELL *Pop. Guide Radio* vi. 98 The amplification constant of a tube, usually designated as mu, is a measure of the relative effect of changing the grid bias compared to changes in the plate voltage. **1931** *Electronics* Apr. 609/1 Mutual conductance meter... The compensator dial is set for the value most nearly corresponding to the 'Mu' of the tube under test. **1962** *Newnes Conc. Encycl. Electr. Engin.* 860/1 A coarse-pitch grid gives a low magnification and requires greater bias to cutoff. In the variable-mu valve the grid is graded, and this gives a valve whose gain can be altered by changing the bias applied to it.

mu, var. MOU.

†**muable**, *a. Obs.* Also 4 muuable. [a. OF. *muable*:—L. *mūtābilem*: see MUTABLE *a.*] Mutable, changeable, variable.

c **1374** CHAUCER *Boeth.* IV. Pr. vi. 104 (Camb. MS.) Alle the progression of Muable nature..taketh his causes..of the stablenesse of the dyuine thowght. **1390** GOWER *Conf.* III. 295 Fortune hath evere be muable And mai no while stonde stable. **1481** CAXTON *Myrr.* I. xiii. 42 Thus ben not the sciences muable but alleway ben estable and trewe.

‖**Muʿallaqat** (muala'kɑːt), *sb. pl.* Also **Moallakat, Muallakat.** [a. Arab. *muʿallaḳāt*, lit. suspended odes, pl. of *muʿallaqa*.] An anthology of seven pre-Islamic Arabian poems made by the rawi Hammad al Rawija (d. 772). Also in shortened form **Moal.**

1782 (*title*) The Moallakát, or seven Arabian poems.. with a translation..by William Jones. **1834** *Penny Cycl.* II. 219/1 The poems called Moallakat. **1875** *Encycl. Brit.* II. 263/1 Seven of these, known in Arab literature by the title of the *Müallakat* or 'Suspended',..all of them belonging to the 6th century, have become..the..classical standards of Arab poetical composition. **1905** G. BELL *Let.* 12 Feb. (1927) I. 186 At dinner I produced the Muallakat (pre-Muhammadan poems). **1930** R. A. NICHOLSON *Lit. Hist. Arabs* iii. 101, I will now turn directly to those celebrated odes which are well known by the title of *Muʿallaqât*, or 'Suspended Poems', to all who take the slightest interest in Arabic literature. **1959** *N. & Q.* June 216/2 'The Poem of Amriolkais', the *moâl* upon which Tennyson relied for the framework of 'Locksley Hall'. **1964** *Listener* 25 June 1036/1 Behind the *qasidas* of Andalusia lay..the *Muʿallaqat*, the 'hanging odes' of the pre-Islamic oral verse of the Arabian desert.

†**muance.** *Obs.* Also 4 *Sc.* mowence. [a. OF. *muance* = Sp. *mudanza*, It. *mutanza*:—popular L. **mūtantia*, f. *mūtant-em*, pr. pple. of *mūtāre* to change.] Change, mutation.

1375 BARBOUR *Bruce* I. 134 God..Reserwyt till his maieste For to knaw..Off alkyn tyme the mowence. **1480** CAXTON *Ovid's Met.* XIV. xii, Lytil avaylled hym thise changes & muances.

†**muant**, *a. Obs.* In 5 muaunt. [a. OF. *muant*:—L. *mūtant-em*: see prec.] Changing.

? *a* **1412** LYDG. *Two Merchants* 574 My fulle is derkyd into wane, With wynd forwhirlyd as is a mvaunt fane.

muasin, obs. form of MUEZZIN.

†**mubble-fubbles**, *sb. pl. slang. Obs.* Also 6–7 muble-fubles, 7 mumble-. Depression of spirits, 'blue devils'.

1589 *Pappe w. Hatchet* in *Lyly's Wks.* (1902) III. 410 Ile make him pull his powting croscloath ouer his beetle browes for melancholie, and then my next booke shall be Martin in his mubble fubbles. **1592** LYLY *Midas* v. ii, Melancholy is the creast of Courtiers armes, and now euerie base companion, beeing in his muble fubles, sayes he is melancholy. **1607** *Acc. Christmas Prince* 55 in *Misc. Antiq. Angl.* (1816) I, And when your brayne, feels any payne, With cares of state & troubles, We'el come in kindnesse to put your highnesse Out of yʳ mumble fubbles. **1654** GAYTON *Pleas. Notes* III. xi. 145 When shee was in the Mubble-fubles.

mubulle, muc, variant forms of MOBLE, MUCK.

†**mucage.** *Med. Obs.* [a. med.L. *mūcāgo* (*mūcāgin-*), f. *mūcus*: see MUCUS.] = MUCILAGE.

1657 TOMLINSON *Renou's Disp.* 194 If the Mucage should be more crass, then the quantity of roots..must be augmented.

†**mu'caginous**, *a. Obs.* [f. med.L. *mūcāgin-*: see prec. and -OUS.] = MUCILAGINOUS.

1657 TOMLINSON *Renou's Disp.* 133 External Unguents, mucaginous Salves, and Pultises. **1806** ABERNETHY *Surg. Obs.* II. 87 The soapy or mucaginous feel of bile.

'**mucate.** *Chem.* [see -ATE.] A salt of mucic acid.

1838 T. THOMSON *Chem. Org. Bodies* 78 They found the mucate of silver composed of Mucic acid [and] Oxide of silver.

mucche, mucchel, obs. ff. MOUCH *v.*, MICKLE.

muccilaginous, obs. form of MUCILAGINOUS.

muccinigo, variant of MOCCENIGO.

muccomucco, obs. form of MOCO-MOCO.

muccuck, var. MOCOCK.

muccudum, variant of MOKADDAM.

mucculent, muccus: see MUCULENT, MUCUS.

muce, variant of MEUSE.

mucedin (mjuː'siːdɪn). *Chem.* [f. L. *mūcēdo* (see MUCEDINOUS) + -IN.] A nitrogenous substance, one of the constituents of gluten.

1871 WATTS tr. *Gmelin's Handbk. Chem.* XVIII. 443 Wheat-mucedin... Properties. Mucedin, which is gummy when separated, forms, after drying in a vacuum, slightly coherent lumps [etc.]. *Ibid.* 444 Rye-mucedin. **1879** *Encycl. Brit.* X. 696 It [*sc.* gluten]..according to Ritthausen consists of *glutencasein*.., *glutenfibrin, gliadin*.., *glutin*, and *mucedin*.

mucedinous (mjuː'siːdɪnəs), *a. Bot.* [f. L. *mūcēdin-*, *mūcēdo* mucus (in mod.L. used for 'mould', after L. *mūcēre* to be mouldy) + -OUS.] Having the character of mould; resembling mould.

1857 BERKELEY *Cryptog. Bot.* §224 A mucedinous mass of threads or cells from which the plant grows. **1867** J. HOGG *Microsc.* II. i. 332 Another more closely connected growth of mucedinous fungi, commonly called mushroom spawn.

muceron, obs. form of MOUSSERON.

much (mʌtʃ), *a.*, quasi-*sb.*, and *adv.* Forms: 3–6 **muche, miche, moche,** 4–6 **meche, mouche, mych(e,** 5–6 **moch, mich,** 5 **mech,** 6 **mutch, mitch, mytch, mushe,** 3– **much.** [Early ME. *muche, moche, meche, miche*, shortened from *muchel, mochel, mechel, michel*: see MICKLE.

The shortening may have been suggested by the relation of *lut* to the longer form *lutel* (see LITE and LITTLE *adjs.*, *advs.*, and *sbs.*). The cause, however, may have been phonetic; another instance of the loss of *l* after *ch* seems to exist in *wench*, 14th c. *wenche*, app. from early ME. *wenchel.*]

A. *adj.*

1. = GREAT *a.*, in various applications.

†**a.** with reference to size, bulk, stature. Of persons, occas.: Adult, grown up. *Obs.*

Surviving in certain names of English villages, as Much Burstead, Much Leighes (now Great Leighs), Much Wenlock (in 17th c. also More Wenlock). Cf. GREAT *a.* 6 e.

c **1205** LAY. 28036 Al þere muche halle rof mid hire honden heo to-droh. **1303** R. BRUNNE *Handl. Synne* 4467 A stounde sate þey by me styl And drogh furþ a moche boke. **1362** LANGL. *P. Pl.* A. IX. 61 A Muche Mon, me þouhte lyk to my-seluen. *c* **1400** *Lanfranc's Cirurg.* 323 In þis maner þou schalt bringe in þe boon of a child wel ynow. If it be a miche man, lete him ligge adoun streiȝt. *c* **1450** *Merlin* I. 97 Antor, that hadde this childe norisshed till he was a moche man of xv yere of age, he hadde hym trewly norisshed, so that he was faire and moche. **1460** CAPGRAVE *Chron.* (Rolls) 132 This William mad Westminster Halle: and whan he sei it first, he seide it was not half mech inow. **1509** BARCLAY *Shyp of Folys* (1874) I. 112 Whiche in a nother's iye can spye a lytell mote And in his owne can nat fele nor espye A moche stycke. **1573** TUSSER *Husb.* (1878) 38 A sheepe marke, a tar kettle, little or mitch, two pottles of tar to a pottle of pitch.

†**b.** with reference to power, rank, importance, or eminence. *Obs.*

c **1205** LAY. 11537 Hercne Maximian þu ært of much cunne. *c* **1325** *Chron. Eng.* (Ritson) 11 A muche mon com from Troye, y wis, Wes icleped Bruyt Sylvius. *a* **1400** *Pistill of Susan* 315 Bi þe muche god, þat most is of miht. *a* **1450** MYRC 1268 Any mon myche or luyte.

†**c.** with reference to amount or degree. *Obs.*

c **1200** *Trin. Coll. Hom.* 203 þe me ledeð fram miche wowe to michele wele. **13..** *Guy Warw.* (A.) 164 Al þai wonderd strongliche, For his feirhed was so miche. **1697** J. BLAIR in W. S. Perry *Hist. Coll. Amer. Col. Ch.* I. 15 Those Gentlemen sold themselves so much bargains of the Kings tobacco that [etc.].

†**d.** said of a numerical aggregate, proportion, etc. ***much deal***: a great part; also *advb.* in great part, largely. *Obs.*

c **1205** LAY. 14224 A-buten he bilæde muche [*c* **1275** moche] del of londe. *c* **1275** *Ibid.* 3689 ȝeo sal fare mid þee mid mochere [*c* **1205** mochelere] ferde. **1297** R. GLOUC. (Rolls) 4920 + 32 He lay muchedel of þe nyȝt in wo & in sorwe. *Ibid.* 7719 Monye heyemen of þe lond in prison he huld strong, So þat muchedel engelond þoȝte is lif to long. **1413** *Pilgr. Sowle* (Caxton 1483) IV. xxvi. 72 What so euer the body hath done, he hath hit done by the, be it good or bad, and moch dele by thyn excitacion. **1509** BARCLAY *Shyp of Folys* (1874) I. 76 Of other folys yet is a moche nomber. **1531** *Dial. on Laws Eng.* II. xxv. 54 b, Moche parte of the lawe is in suche speche that fewe men haue knowlege of it. **1566** DRANT *Horace, Sat.* vi. D vj, My many muche, my traine of men. **1609** BIBLE (Douay) *Exod.* i. 9 Behold the people of Israel is much, and stronger than we.

†**e.** qualifying the designation of a person with the sense: Entitled to the designation in a high degree. *Obs.*

c **1325** *Spec. Gy de Warewyke* 102 Nu i wole nempne þe wicke þewes, þat beþ noht gode, ac muche shrewes. *a* **1400** HYLTON *Scala Perf.* (W. de W. 1494) II. xviii, Sothly he were a moche foole. *c* **1400** *Gamelyn* 230 Whyl thou were a yong boy a moche schrewe thou were.

†**f.** const. *in*, *of* (some quality). *Obs.*

1303 R. BRUNNE *Handl. Synne* 4011 Florens was nat so moche yn lore, Yn preyours he was euermore. *c* **1460** *Play Sacram.* 194 In eraclea ys noon so moche of myght.

2. a. A great quantity or amount of, existing or present in great quantity.

In ***as much, so much, thus much, how much, that much, this much***, the adj., like others of similar meaning, often loses its distinctive sense and expresses merely relative quantity (whether great or small). For idiomatic uses of these collocations, see the first words. ***too much***: see TOO.

c **1205** LAY. 136 Muche lond he him ȝef. *a* **1300** *K. Horn* 1211 (Camb. MS.) Wyn nelle ihc, Muche ne lite, Bute of cuppe white. *c* **1380** WYCLIF *Sel. Wks.* III. 305 For aquitaunce [þei] taken moche gold. *c* **1425** *Hampole's Psalter* Metr. Pref. 15 Mych vertu he may him wynne. *c* **1435** *Torr. Portugal* 1399 She toke the ryngis with moche care. **1458** in Parker *Dom. Archit.* III. 41 In labor & lavyng moche money was lore. **1523** [COVERDALE] *Old God & New* (1534) H iv b, The tree hath miche worke to growe. **1535** —— *Deut.* xxviii. 38 Thou shalt cary out moch sede in to yᵉ felde, and shalt gather but litle in. **1601** SHAKS. *Jul. C.* I. ii. 177, I am glad that my weake words Haue strucke but thus much shew of fire from Brutus. **1710** SWIFT *Jrnl. to Stella* 10 Oct., Mr. Harley..presented me to the Attorney-General, Sir Simon Harcourt, with much compliment on all sides, etc. **1831** COLERIDGE *Table-t.* 1 Aug., There is much beast and some devil in man. **1875** JOWETT *Plato* (ed. 2) I. 81 There is much truth in that remark of yours. **1903** *Mission Field* May 17 Over as much space as possible.

ellipt. **1766** GOLDSM. *Vic. W.* viii, An amour, which promises little good fortune, yet may be productive of much.

†**b.** Qualifying *people*, etc.: A great number of.

c **1205** LAY. 23204 Muche moncum [*c* **1275** moche folk] he þer of-sloh. **1470–85** MALORY *Arthur* I. i. 36 There was.. moche peple slayne. **1538** LONDON in *Lett. Suppress. Monast.* (Camden) 225 Thys ys a towne of moch power people. **1606** SHAKS. *Ant. & Cl.* II. vi. 7 Let vs know, If 'twill..carry back to Cicelie much tall youth That else must perish heere. **1611** BIBLE *Num.* xx. 20 And Edom came out against him with much people.

†**c.** ***much thing***: many a thing, many things.

1390 GOWER *Conf.* I. 49 So schal I moche thing foryete. *c* **1450** *Merlin* I. 17 The Iuges seiden he moste be counynge of moche thynge yef he shulde saue his moder.

d. Used (where *many* would now be substituted) with a plural sb. taken collectively. Now chiefly *U.S. dial.* and in echoes of quot. 1602.

1565 STAPLETON tr. *Bede's Hist. Ch. Eng.* Ded., The same Emperour after much disputations and conferences had with the Arrians,..commaunded [etc.]. **1591** SPARRY tr. *Cattan's Geomancie* 165 This figure..sheweth that the seruantes of the saide Lords shall get much friends. **1602** SHAKS. *Ham.* I. i. 8 For this releefe much thankes. **1660** GAUDEN *Brownrig* 238 All these died..in the foresight and fear of much future miseries impending over us. **1664** PEPYS *Diary* 17 July, After dinner walked to my Lord's, and there found him and much other guests at table at dinner. **1719** D'URFEY *Pills* III. 315 Much Pagan Pates, he made to tumble in Dust. **1889** *Kansas City* (Missouri) *Times & Star* 13 Dec., For the latter's fall-down, much thanks. **1890** S. HALE *Lett.* (1919) 253, I have much funny things to tell you. **1928** J. PETERKIN *Scarlet Sister Mary* (1929) xxii. 217 How much chillen you had? **1952** E. O'NEILL *Moon for Misbegotten* I. 17 You didn't get much thanks from Mike, I'll wager, for your help.

e. Forming with its sb. a kind of combination, with the abstract sense 'abundance of' (what the sb. denotes).

1609 BIBLE (Douay) 2 *Kings* i. Comm., Elias was knowen by his much hayre. **1630** WINTHROP *New Eng.* (1825) I. 377 My much business hath made me too oft forget Mondays and Fridays. **1650** W. BROUGH *Manual* (1659) 214 Keep me from the much evill of an Idle life! **1872** TENNYSON *Last Tournament* 724 Now mocking at the much ungainliness.. of Mark. **1891** KIPLING *Light that Failed* (1900) 39 A pale yellow sun..showed the much dirt of the place.

f. *ironically*, where *no* would be used in serious language. Also in the derisive wish ***much good may it do you*** (formerly in many corrupt forms: see DICH = do it).

1542 UDALL *Erasm. Apoph.* 84 In the wayе of mockage, biddyng muche good dooe it hym. **1598** B. JONSON *Ev. Man in Hum.* IV. iv, Much wench, or much sonne! **1600** SHAKS. *A.Y.L.* IV. iii. 2 Is it not past two a clock? And heere much Orlando. **1622** MABBE tr. *Aleman's Guzman d'Alf.* I. 109 So many Ryals (Gentlemen) and so many Maravedis miche yee God diche you, and you are hartily welcome. **1630** *R. Johnson's Kingd. & Commw.* 87 So mich God dich you with your sustenancelesse sauce. **1783** [see GOOD C. 5 a]. **1843** DICKENS *Christmas Carol* i, 'Let me leave it [Christmas] alone, then,' said Scrooge. 'Much good may it do you. Much good it has ever done you!' *Mod.* Much right he has to interfere with me!

3. With agent-noun: that is much in the habit of performing the action. *rare.* [From the *adv.*]

1711 SWIFT *Jrnl. to Stella* 28 Apr., I have heard them say, 'Much talkers, little walkers'. **1833** LAMB *Elia* Ser. II. Pref. (1865) 236 Your long and much talkers hated him.

B. *absol.* and quasi-*sb.*

The word never completely assumes the character of a sb.; in sense 2 it admits of being qualified by advs. like *very*, *rather*. Unlike *little*, it never takes the indefinite article.

†**1.** Used *absol.* in the sense 'great'. Only in the phrases ***much and lite, much and little*** = persons high and low; all (people) without exception. *Obs.*

13.. *Seuyn Sag.* (W.) 1137 He let of-sende moche and lite, Hise neyebours to visite. *a* **1375** *Cursor M.* 23154 (Fairf.) Wite ȝe for-soþ al þat is suche sal be dampned litel & muche. *c* **1386** CHAUCER *Prol.* 494 He ne lafte nat..to visite The ferreste in his parisshe, muche and lite.

2. a. A great deal, a great quantity. Proverb ***much will have more.***

13.. *Minor Poems fr. Vernon MS.* xlix. 53 ȝif þou haue muchel, muche ȝiue also; ȝif þou haue nouȝt, muche þou schalt ȝiue. *c* **1350** *Old Usages Winchester* in *Eng. Gilds* (1870) 355 To þe clerk a peny. ȝif he selleþ meche by ȝere; and ȝif he sulleþ lasse, vp-on þe quantite. *a* **1450** *Knt. de la Tour* (1906) 74, I wylle not say moche nor al. **1610** SHAKS. *Temp.* II. i. 55 He misses not much. **1615** W. LAWSON *Country Housew. Gard.* (1626) 5 Much will haue more: and once poore, seldome or neuer rich. **1710** *Tatler* No. 241 ¶ 1 He who drinks much is a Slave to himself. **1814** BYRON *Lara* I. xvii, In him inexplicably appear'd Much to be loved and hated, sought and fear'd. **1849** MACAULAY *Hist. Eng.* ii. I. 169 He bestowed much; yet he neither enjoyed the pleasure nor acquired the fame of beneficence. **1885** *Times* 25 May 10 Much is due to the prejudices of well-meaning but uncultured people.

b. followed by *of* partitive.

c **1380** WYCLIF *Sel. Wks.* III. 438 Siche apostataes marren meche of Cristis ordre. **1568** GRAFTON *Chron.* II. 38 The French king..lost much of his people. **1655** tr. *Com. Hist. Francion* XII. 29 There must be much of Malice in his accusation. *a* **1761** CAWTHORN *Antiquarians* 85 Pythagoras ..With much of thought, and pains, and care, Found [etc.]. **1817** JAS. MILL *Brit. India* III. VI. i. 10 That friendship.. which Mr. Hastings claimed so much of merit for maintaining. **1871** FREEMAN *Norm. Conq.* (ed. 2) IV. xvii. 84 There was room for much of thoughtful consultation.

c. with *the* (or other defining word).

1568 GRAFTON *Chron.* II. 631 Therefore the French aucthors make of a litle, much, and yet their much (all things consydered) is in effect nothing at all. **1594** CAREW *Huarte's Exam. Wits* (1616) 11 Our vnderstanding is not filled by the much which wee read in little time. **1646** H. P. *Medit. Seige* 69 How apt are they to boast the little they have done, whilst they utterly forget the much that is behinde? **1700** DRYDEN *Iliad* I. 250 Nor grudge I thee, the much the Grecians give; Nor murm'ring take the little I receive. **1778** BURKE *Corr.* (1844) II. 247 If I, or mine, can contribute our mite, or our much,.. we shall not omit to serve you. **1804** EUGENIA DE ACTON *Tale without Title* III. 190 Every one endeavoured to say something of the much with which his heart was filled. **1866** G. MEREDITH *Vittoria* xxxi, The much which hangs on little was then set in motion.

d. ***by much***: by a great deal. †Formerly often (with comparative or superlative, or *too*) = *much* adv.

c **1450** MYRC (1902) 1517 A-bregge hys penaunce þen by myche. **1536** CROMWELL in Merriman *Life & Lett.* (1902) II. 16 Whiche his grace will neyther by moche seke ne yet refuse if it be put unto him. **1622** GATAKER *Spirituall Watch* (ed. 2) 87 [Death] is neerer by much many times then we are aware of. **1628** DIGBY *Voy. Medit.* (Camden) 46 Now my shippe outsayled all my fleete by much. *a* **1634** RANDOLPH *Muses' Looking-Gl.* IV. i, She hath made this cheek By much too pale. **1793** *Minstrel* III. 185 The third, by much the least hardened,.. was struck with remorse.

e. In negative or interrogative context: Any great amount, anything important.

1847 A. BRONTË *Agnes Grey* xvii. 251, I paid more attention to dress than ever I had done before... This is not saying much, for hitherto I had been a little neglectful in that particular. **1871** G. MEREDITH *H. Richmond* xl, It was comical and not likely to lead to much. *Mod.* I do not think the evidence amounts to very much. Does all this come to much? No!

f. ***to think much of***: see THINK *v.* ***to make much of***: see MAKE *v.* 18 d, 21, OF 20.

g. Used predicatively. ***to be much***: to be a great thing, an important point, matter, etc. ***to think (it) much*** (with *inf.*): to regard as important or onerous; to be 'shy of' (doing something). ***not to be much to look at***: to be of insignificant or unattractive appearance. ***a bit much***: see BIT *sb.*[2] 5. Also in similar phrases with the same sense, as ***a trifle much, rather much***.

c **1325** *Spec. Gy de Warewyke* 150 Sinful men þat þinkeþ it were muche for hem To haue gret worldes honour. **1568** GRAFTON *Chron.* II. 301 They thought it much if they coulde bring the French King.. in safetie to Burdeaux. **1610** SHAKS. *Temp.* I. ii. 252 Thou.. thinkst it much to tread ye Ooze Of the salt deepe. **1618** W. LAWSON *New Orchard* (1623) 24 For men not knowing.. this secret of needfull distance,.. thinke much to pull vp any [trees], though they pine one another. **1622** BACON *Hen. VII.* 234 It was also much, that one that was so great a Louer of Peace should bee so happy in Warre. **1667** MILTON *P.L.* x. 219 He.. thought not much to cloath his Enemies. **1671** TILLOTSON *Serm.* i. 30 It is much, if Men were from eternity, that they should not find out the way of Writing in all that long long duration which had past before that Time. **1700** DRYDEN *Wife of Bath* 78 The ladies.. thought it much a man should die for love, And with their mistress join'd in close debate. **1861** DICKENS *Gt. Expect.* v, You are not much to look at. **1875** *Encycl. Brit.* II. 252/1 All men allow their beards, whiskers, and moustaches full growth, though none of these are much to speak of. **1911** O. ONIONS *Widdershins* 265, I too smiled... 'It *was* rather much, wasn't it?' I said. **1930** R. LEHMANN *Note in Music* v. 200 After all, perhaps it would have been a trifle much, applied to mother. **1964** J. SYMONS *End of Solomon Grundy* I. i. 27 It's enough to break up any party. I must say I thought it was rather much.

h. ***much of a...*** (colloq.): in negative contexts = 'a great...', 'a... of any noteworthy quality', 'a... in any great degree'.

1843 DICKENS *Christmas Carol* iii, What's the consequence? He don't lose much of a dinner. **1889** J. K. JEROME *Three Men in Boat* 114 You don't look for much of a voice in a comic song. *Mod.* He is not much of a scholar.

i. *ironically* (cf. A 2 e above).

Mod. Much you know about the matter!

3. a. With modified sense, in absolute uses of the adj. as qualified by *as, so, thus, how, that, this, too*: see those words and A 2 above.

†b. ***like*** or ***a like much***: a similar quantity. *Obs.*

1544 PHAER *Regim. Lyfe* (1560) B iv b, Take lytarge of Sylver, and Brymstone, of eche lyke muche, and seethe them. *Ibid.* D iij, Of eche a lyke muche. *c* **1550** LLOYD *Treas. Health* H iij, Take of Castoreum, of Pellytory, of Pyonye rootes, of eche lyke muche make pylles wyth Triakell.

4. *Comb.*, objective with pr. pples., as ***much-containing, -devouring, -enduring, -suffering*** adjs.

c **1611** CHAPMAN *Iliad* XXIII. 631 The much-suffering man. **1725** POPE *Odyss.* VIII. 172 A.. much-enduring man. **1828** PUSEY *Hist. Enq.* I. 156 In his concise but deep and much-containing essay. **1873** LONGF. *Wayside Inn* III. *Interlude* iii. 32 Wood, To feed the much-devouring fire.

C. *adv.*

1. In a great degree; to a great extent; greatly.

a. qualifying a verb or the whole predication.

a **1225** *Leg. Kath.* 229 Ne ne mei na þing wiðstonden his wille, þah he muche þolie. **1382** WYCLIF *Luke* vii. 47 Manye synnes ben forȝouun to hire, for sche hath loued myche. *a* **1425** *Cursor M.* 10941 (Trin.) Muche þerfore þei mournyng were. **1526** *Pilgr. Perf.* (W. de W. 1531) 2 Some in religyon be ryght holy & moche exercysed in goostly conuersacyon. **1573** BARET *Alv.* M. 496 Saie that I am here much against my will. **1603** SHAKS. *Meas. for M.* IV. iii. 9 Ginger was not much in request, for the olde Women were all dead. **1662** J. DAVIES tr. *Olearius' Voy. Ambass.* 422 The Ambassadors.. made him some other Presents, which.. made him very much our friend. **1766** GOLDSM. *Vic. W.* vii, For my part, I don't much like it. **1785** COWPER *Let. to Newton* 27 Aug., The publisher of it is neither much a friend to the cause of religion nor to the author's memory. **1854** H. MILLER *Sch. & Schm.* ii. (1857) 37, I was much a favourite with Uncle James. **1863** W. C. BALDWIN *Afr. Hunting* viii. 350 He complained much of his poverty. **1891** E. PEACOCK *N. Brendon* I. 208 'Thank you very much,' she said. **1902** ELIZ. L. BANKS *Newspaper Girl* 211 I'm much obliged to you.

b. qualifying comparatives or words implying comparison; occasionally with the intervention of *the* (pron.) before a comparative.

In the 17th c., when *a* or *an* preceded the comparative, *much* was sometimes interposed instead of being placed first. (Strictly, this construction belongs rather to 1 a.)

c **1275** LAY. 3201 He moche þe wodlokere wilnede þat mayde. *Ibid.* 9911 Wel riche was Aruiragus and moche richere was Maurus. *c* **1380** WYCLIF *Sel. Wks.* III. 334 And ȝif it fare þus wiþ hiere penytaunceris.. it is moche þe werse on alle ordris. *c* **1450** *Merlin* 4 He dought that yef he dide hym gretter damage, that he wolde be moche wrother. **1505** in *Mem. Hen. VII* (Rolls) 231 Much the less we could come by the very knowledge of that cause for that the queen weared black kerchowes. **1590** SPENSER *F.Q.* III. ix. 33 Troy, thou art now nought but an idle name,.. Though whilome far much greater then thy fame. **1654–66** EARL ORRERY *Parthen.* (1676) 370 She manifested by the esteem she plac'd upon the performance, how much a higher one she had for him for whom 'twas performed. **1668–9** MARVELL *Corr.* Wks. (Grosart) II. 267 It will be some expense, but much otherwise husbanded then formerly. **167.** PRIDEAUX *Lett.* (Camden) 64 The translation of Æmilius Porta is much the best. *a* **1674** CLARENDON *Surv. Leviath.* (1676) 255 Euripides.. is much a graver writer. **1688** COLLIER *Sev. Disc.* xii. (1725) 385 A grateful.. Receiver is much a greater Man than such a pretended Benefactor. **1711** in *10th Rep. Hist. MSS. Comm.* App. v. 170 The much major part of the souldiery. **1711–12** SWIFT *Jrnl. to Stella* 23 Feb., The Secretary is much the greatest commoner in England. **1766** GOLDSM. *Vic. W.* xviii, Our modern dialect is much more natural. **1838** MOORE *Mem.* (1856) VII. 218 Nothing much different to add in the subject. **1875** *Encycl. Brit.* II. 707/1 Much the largest river of the peninsula is the Halys.

c. qualifying positive or uncompared adjs. and advs.; = VERY. *Obs.* exc. with *like* (now only as quasi-prep.) and in *U.S. dial.*

c **1449** PECOCKE *Repr.* I. x. 53 Y wolde not make me miche bisi forto seie ther aȝens. *c* **1483** CAXTON *Dialogues* 32 Yet is he moche dangerous. **1490** —— *Eneydos* x. 40 Dydo toke grete playsir in his conuersacyon and deuysed wyth him moche gladely. **1539** CROMWELL in Merriman *Life & Lett.* (1902) II. 214 She confesseth in substance, the moche like wordes to have ben told her. **1550** CRANMER *Defence* 65 b, And *contra Adamantium* he writeth much like, saying [etc.]. **1551** ROBINSON tr. *More's Utop.* Ep. P. Giles (1895) 11 Beynge muche lyke vncourteis, vnthankefull, and chourlishe guestes. **1612** BACON *Ess., Parents & Child.* (Arb.) 276/1 In nature it is much a like matter. **1650** EARL MONM. tr. *Senault's Man bec. Guilty* 212 Health so dearly bought, cannot be much delightfull. **1796** MRS. J. WEST *Gossip's Story* I. 156 'Twas much unkind to go. **1916** *Dialect Notes* IV. 347, I don't guess she's much old. **1929** W. FAULKNER *Sound & Fury* 268, I.. went up front. 'Been much busy?' Earl says. 'Not much,' I says.

d. Used ironically for 'not at all'. Also (now only *U.S.*) *ellipt.* as a derisive exclamation indicating incredulity. ***not much***: certainly not, far from it, 'not likely'; also occas. (ironically), certainly, 'not half' (*colloq.*).

c **1590** MARLOWE *Faustus* (2nd vers.) (1631) E 2, *Vint.*.. Come giue it to me againe. *Rob.* I much, when can you tell? **1597** SHAKS. *2 Hen. IV*, II. iv. 143 Since when, I pray you, Sir? what, with two Points on your shoulder? much. **1598–9** B. JONSON *Case is Altered* III. i, And to solicite his remembrance still In his enforced absence, much, I faith. **1599** —— *Ev. Man out of Hum.* I. iii, To charge me bring my Graine into the markets: I, much, when I haue neither Barne nor Garner. **1873** 'SUSAN COOLIDGE' *What Katy did at Sch.* ix, 'Much you don't like oranges?' he said... 'Much! I've seen you eat two at a time, without stopping.' **1879** BESANT & RICE *Seamy Side* 114 'Oh! yes,' he says, 'you think it's yours, do you? Much. I'm the owner, I am.' **1886** *Harper's Mag.* Dec. 148/1 'Go home?—explain?' he began, more calmly. 'Not much.' **1888** 'R. BOLDREWOOD' *Robbery under Arms* I. xviii. 248 Starlight and I wasn't likely to break down—not much—whatever the jury did. **1904** E. NESBIT *Phoenix & Carpet* xi. 212 'He didn't mean stay and be roasted,' said Robert. 'No boys on burning decks for me, thank you.' 'Not much,' said Cyril. *a* **1908** *Mod.* Much *you* care about my feelings! **1911** A. BENNETT *Card* x. 255 Do you suppose I was going to let you go by that steamer? Not much. **1928** D. L. SAYERS *Unpleasantness at Bellona Club* xvi. 188 'They can get it from Robert or George Fentiman,' warned Wimsey. 'Not much, they won't,' said Salcombe Hardy feelingly. **1970** A. ROSS *Manchester Thing* 81 'Got a going over, did you?' 'Not much, I got a going over. Want to see the bruises?' **1973** J. PORTER *It's Murder with Dover* i. 1 'I am not asking for any preferential treatment,' said Lord Crouch... Not bloody much! thought the Chief Constable.. and tried to work out what His Nibs was up to.

e. ***not to be*** (or ***go***) ***much on*** (or ***for***): (*a*) not to be enthusiastic about (something); not to like or care for; (*b*) not to be useful or effective for (a purpose); to be no good at (something). *colloq.*

1896 *Dialect Notes* I. 417 'I don't go much on that', I don't care much for that. **1908** A. BENNETT *Buried Alive* v. 111 'I'm not much for these restaurants,' she said, over grilled kidneys. 'No?' he responded tentatively. 'I'm sorry.' **1928** R. BRADFORD in B. A. Botkin *Treas. S. Folklore* (1949) III. ii. 485 Angels is all right for singin' and playin' and flyin' round, but they ain't much on workin' de crops and buildin' de levees. **1968** A. MUNRO in R. Weaver *Canad. Short Stories* 2nd Ser. 262 They may not be much on intellectual conversation but their hearts are in the right place.

2. In modified sense, qualified by *as, how, so, too* (cf. A 2, B 3 above): see those advs.

3. Pretty nearly, approximately. Chiefly qualifying expressions denoting similarity, as in ***much as, much of an age, of a muchness, of a size, of a piece***; † ***much at one***. Also prefixed to *about* prep., to emphasize the notion of indefiniteness.

1560 DAUS tr. *Sleidane's Comm.* 203 Moche aboute thys same tyme. *a* **1568** ASCHAM *Scholem.* Pref. (Arb.) 20, I heare saie, you haue a sonne, moch of his age. **1662** J. DAVIES tr. *Mandelslo's Trav.* 112 The death of Derma, and that of the King of Candy.. happened much about a time. **1686** J. S[ERGEANT] *Hist. Monast. Convent.* 100 The word Allon, which is much at one with Allons in French. *a* **1699** TEMPLE *Misc.* III. i. Wks. 1720 I. 257 All of them left the World much as they found it. **1704** N. N. tr. *Boccalini's Advts. fr. Parnass.* III. 340 It was much about that time. **1739** 'R. BULL' tr. *Dedekindus' Grobianus* 136 Old Men are much at one. **1741** *Corr. betw. C'tess Hartford & C'tess Pomfret* (1805) II. 256 The siege and the soldiers are much of a piece with the fire. **1763** SCRAFTON *Indostan* (1770) 56 He marched against his relation.. who was much such a giddy abandoned youth as himself. **1859** W. COLLINS '*Blow up with the Brig!*', I.. lose myself in my memory now, much as I lost myself in my own feelings at the time. **1884** J. G. BOURKE *Snake Dance of Moquis* xv, He sprinkled water upon the ground, very much as a Catholic priest would asperse his congregation.

4. 'Often or long' (J.); for a large part of one's time.

1798 JOANNA BAILLIE *Tryal* v. ii, I have been pretty much with him these two days past, and I don't believe he gives me great thanks for my company. **1839** DARWIN in *Life & Lett.* (1887) I. 300 Read little, was much unwell, and scandalously idle. *Mod.* I have not been much away from home of late.

5. Comb.: (*a*) with pa. pples., as in ***much-abused, -admired, -branched, -criticized, -debated, -discussed, -dreaded, -loved, -needed, -quoted, -travelled, -used, valued, -vaunted***; (*b*) with pples. of indirect passive, as in ***much talked of***; (*c*) with adjectival phrases composed of *to be* and pa. pple., as in ***much-to-be-admired, -to-be-pitied***.

1879 W. JAMES *Coll. Ess. & Rev.* (1920) 95 The *much-abused subject of mental physiology. **1936** *Discovery* Dec. 382/1 The much abused engine.. gave out utterly. **1960** *Farmer & Stockbreeder* 23 Feb. 75/1 The next big price was 3,000gs paid by exporter Mr. James Schofield for Westdrums Winson, Messrs. Boots' *much-admired reserve best two-year-old. **1612** DRAYTON *Poly-olb.* xvi. 311 To *much beloued Lee, this scarcely Sturt had spoke. **1927** HALDANE & HUXLEY *Animal Biol.* i. 35 Most glands.. are many-celled tubes or pockets of epithelium, either unbranched or slightly branched.. or *much-branched like the liver or salivary gland. **1970** T. J. ROSS *Film & Liberal Arts* 148 The *much-criticized woodenness of her playing is of small matter. **1843** MILL *Logic* I. 9 To this science [*sc.* metaphysics] appertain the great and *much debated questions of the existence of matter. **1956** *Nature* 11 Feb. 262/2 The whole of the much-debated line up Borrowdale. **1946** *Ibid.* 23 Nov. 759/2 The *much-discussed hypothesis that galactic noise is analogous to the noise associated with solar flares. **1865** G. M. HOPKINS *Poems* (1967) 150 You may trust Your footing now to the *much-dreaded dust. **1879** HUXLEY *Hume* i. 56 This full-crammed and *much-examined generation. **1873** HOWELLS *Chance Acquaintance* i. (1883) 23 A *much-galleried hotel. **1785** BURNS *Cotter's Sat. Night* xx, A virtuous populace may rise the while, And stand a wall of fire around their *much-lov'd Isle. **1886** E. G. WHITE *Notes of Trav.* in *Hist. Sk. Foreign Missions Seventh Day Adventists* 236/1 We might obtain a little *much-needed rest. **1936** *Burlington Mag.* Apr. 202/2 It is a pity not to have given the *Birth of Venus*.. a much-needed rest. **1964** *Ann. Reg. 1963* 229 The United States and Canada traditionally supplied much-needed grain. **1927** *Mod. Philology* Nov. 224 The *much-quoted example.. does not illustrate sound change. **1645** R. BAILLIE *Lett. & Jrnls.* (Bannatyne Club) II. 267 The *much-talked of weakness of our army. **1912** 'SAKI' *Chron. Clovis* 196 The County.. mustered in full strength to witness the *much-talked-of production. **1634–5** BRERETON *Trav.* (Chetham Soc.) 175 Although there be many grafts of the old thorn engrafted, yet all (save this) degenerate from this *much-to-be-admired budding and blossoming at this time. **1820** SOUTHEY *Wesley* I. 180 This so much-to-be-admired eternal Providence. **1928** C. SINGER *From Magic to Sci.* I. 12 This erudite and *much travelled man exhibits great industry. **1595** SHAKS. *John* IV. ii. 73 A *much troubled brest. **1890** W. JAMES *Princ. Psychol.* II. xviii. 58 In one it [*sc.* cerebral injury] will throw a *much-used brain-tract out of gear; in the other it may affect an unimportant region. **1791** BOSWELL *Johnson* (1831) I. 310 His *much-valued friend. **1939** W. S. CHURCHILL *Into Battle* (1941) 150 The magnetic mine.. may perhaps be Herr Hitler's *much vaunted secret weapon. **1974** *Times* 9 Dec. 12/2 Mr Tanaka rashly published his much vaunted plan for decentralizing industry.

much (mʌtʃ), *v. dial.* [f. MUCH quasi-*sb.*] *trans.* To make much of; to pet, fondle, caress.

1736 PEGGE *Kenticisms* (E.D.S.) 38 To much a child, to fondle it when it is peevish. **1848** LOWELL *Fable for Critics* Poet. Wks. (1879) 154 As soon as she's touched it And (to borrow a phrase from the nursery) *muched* it.

muchache, -ate, -ato(e, obs. ff. MUSTACHIO.

muchacho (mə'tʃɑːtʃəʊ). [Sp.] A boy, young man; a male servant. Also *attrib.* So **mu'chacha**, a girl.

1591 GARRARD & HITCHCOCK *Arte of Warre* III. 212 The followers of the campe, pages and muchachos, who must be chosen able to fight in a day of seruice, for the defence of themselues and their masters baggage. **1852** *San Diego Herald* 10 Apr. 2/2 Gay, dashing muchachos in boots and spurs. **1877** B. HARTE *Story of a Mine* 412 Father Pedro had taken a muchacho foundling for adoption. **1888** 'R. BOLDREWOOD' *Robbery under Arms* II. xi. 190 So the muchacha went back on yer. **1904** CONRAD *Nostromo* I. viii. 119 Would not the muchachos of Hernandez like to get hold of this insignificant object..? **1963** *Punch* 23 Oct. 589/3 What we're going on with now, muchachos..is how to catch squid.

muchalka, -are, var. ff. MUCHULKA, MICHER.

muchán, mucharn, varr. MACHAN.

muche, obs. form of MOUCH *v.*

muchel(e -ell, -head, -ness: see MICKLE, etc.

mucherus, variant of MOCHRAS.

†**muchet.** *Obs.* [a. F. *mouchet.*] A tuft.

1601 HOLLAND *Pliny* II. 4 A fourth kind of linnen.. commeth from a certaine fennie reed..I meane the tender muchets or chats thereof.

†'**muchfold,** *a. Obs.* [f. MUCH *a.* + -FOLD.] = MANIFOLD *a.*

1382 WYCLIF *Eph.* iii. 10 The mochefold wysdom of God. **1387-8** T. USK *Test. Love* I. viii. (Skeat) l. 43 Thou were ensample of moche folde errour.

†**much good.** *Obs. rare.* Mountain parsley.

1597 GERARDE *Herbal* II. ccclxxxii. 863, 864. **1665** LOVELL *Herbal* (ed. 2) 292 Much good, see Mountain parsly.

†**muchhead.** *Obs. rare*$^{-1}$. [f. MUCH *a.* + -HEAD, -HOOD.] = MICKLEHEAD.

13.. *K. Alis.* 7352 Pors afyed in his streynthe, In his muchehed, and in his leynthe.

muchi, var. MOOCHA.

muchil, -in, variant forms of MICKLE, MUCIN.

muchi-ras, variant of MOCHRAS.

†**muchity.** *Obs. rare.* [f. MUCH *a.* + -ITY.]

a. A thing of importance. **b.** Great bulk or size.

1621 BP. MOUNTAGU *Diatribæ* 72 For those especially obserued mutchities, in the eyght last Chapters, I haue reason to think..they were also scored vnto your hand. *Ibid.* 221 Liberality is discouered two wayes: by the Quality, and goodnesse of the gift: by the quantity and muchity of what is presented.

muchly ('mʌtʃlɪ), *adv.* Now *jocular.* [f. MUCH *a.* + -LY[2].] Much, exceedingly.

1621 *MS. Bibl. Reg.* 17 B. xv. (Halliwell), The Ladie Cantabrigia..Went gravelie dight to entertaine the dame, They muchlie lov'd, and honor'd in her name. **1647** J. BIRKENHEAD *Assembly-Man* (1662-3) 14 Commonly 'tis larded with fine new words, as Savingable, Muchly, Christ-Jesusness [etc.]. **1881** MISS BRADDON *Asph.* I. 33 Thank you muchly. And now my box? **1882** MORRIS in Mackail *Life* (1899) II. 70, I took this place muchly for the sake of its water-power.

†**much-making,** *vbl. sb. Obs. rare.* [f. MUCH quasi-*sb.* + MAKING *vbl. sb.* Cf. *to make much of*: see MAKE *v.* 18 d., 21.] The action of making much (of a person or thing).

a **1656** HALES *Serm. Eton* i. (1673) 4 Sick persons must not look for smoothing, and much-making, but for that which fits their malady. **1828** E. IRVING *Last Days* 6 The admiration and much making either of the love of Christ or the work of the Spirit.

muchness ('mʌtʃnɪs). Also 4 mochenesse, 5 -nes. [f. MUCH *a.* + -NESS: cf. MICKLENESS.]

†**1.** Large size or bulk; bigness; also, size, magnitude (large or small). *Obs.*

1398 TREVISA *Barth. De P.R.* v. xli. (1495) 158 Yf the mylte is somdeale more drawynge to litylnesse thanne to mochenesse it is a sygne and token of good complexyon. **1496** *Fysshynge w. Angle* (1883) 30 The gogen is a good fisshe of the mocheness. **1572** J. JONES *Bathes of Bath* II. 17 By reason of the smalnesse or muchnesse of the same. **1631** R. BOLTON *Comf. Affl. Consc.* (1635) 296 It is not so much the muchnesse and measure of our sorrow, as the truth and heartinesse which fits us for the promises and comforts of mercy.

2. Greatness in quantity, number, or degree.

a **1400** HYLTON *Scala Perf.* (W. de W. 1494) II. xxxiv, The endles mochenes of the loue of god. **1559** *Mirr. Mag., Jas. I*, xviii, Attaste no poyson..beware eke of to much, All kil through muchnes, sum with only touche. **1669** PEPYS *Diary* 27 Mar., To bed, my head a little troubled with the muchness of the business I have upon me at present. **1744** T. EAYRE in *Mem. W. Stukeley* (Surtees) I. 368 [I] do fear the muchness of the worke will prevent it. **1863** HAWTHORNE *Our Old Home* (1883) I. 66 She imposes awe and respect by the muchness of her personality. **1887** JAMES in *Mind* No. 45. 15 We have relations of muchness and littleness between times,..as well as spaces.

b. An instance of this.

1674 N. FAIRFAX *Bulk & Selv.* 21 After the nice brattling out of reality, into muchnesses and littlenesses, there falls to the share of this, as little as may be. *a* **1680** CHARNOCK *Attrib. God* (1834) II. 677 He will have a muchness of mercy for those that are prepared..by faith and repentance. **1893** J. MOYES in *Dublin Rev.* Apr. 246 A muchness of going and coming between Rome and this country.

3. ***much of a muchness***: much of the same importance or value; very much the same or alike. *colloq.*

1728 VANBR. & CIB. *Prov. Husb.* I. i, *Man.* I hope..you and your good woman agree still? *I. Moody.* Ay, ay; much of a muchness. **1845** DE QUINCEY *Goldsmith* Wks. 1857 VI. 217 Compare Addison's age..with Goldsmith's..the two ages will be found to offer 'much of a muchness'. **1893** KATH. SIMPSON *Yorks. Stories* 255 Gifts seem to me much of a muchness. They are apt to create a sense of obligation.

muchocho, var. MOHOOHOO.

mucht, obs. pa. t. of MAY *v.*[1]

‖**muchulka** (muː'tʃʌlkə). Also 9 muchelka, muchalka, moochulka. [Hindī *mučalkā.*] A written bond.

1803 WELLINGTON in Gurw. *Desp.* (1844) I. 323 The soubahdar insisting upon the man giving a muckelka [*sic*] to produce the stolen goods was an assumption of authority, highly unwarrantable. **1818** SIR. T. MUNRO in Gleig *Life* (1849) 265 Lord B—— told me that I should have ten thousand pagodas per annum, and all my expenses paid;.. I never thought of taking a Muchalka from Lord B——, because [etc.]. **1886** YULE & BURNELL *Anglo-Ind. Gloss.*, *Moochulka.*

†'**muchwhat,** *sb.* and *adv. Obs.* [f. MUCH *adv.* + WHAT *pron.*] **a.** *sb.* Many matters. **b.** *adv.* Greatly; nearly, almost; just; 'pretty much', 'pretty well'. (Very common in the 17th c.)

a. 13.. *Gaw. & Gr. Knt.* 1280 Þus þay meled of muchquat, til myd-morn paste.

b. 1494 FABYAN *Chron.* v. cxxiii 100 He was by theyr counceyll moch what aduyzed and gyded. **1548** GEST *Pr. Masse* L vj, Notwithstanding..I hertofor haue moch what vehemently gaynsayd the preuie masse. **1619** W. SCLATER *Exp. 1 Thess.* (1630) 450 They think of this second Adam, much what as Pelagians of the first. **1631** WEEVER *Anc. Funeral Mon.* 138 Their first comming into England was much what about the yeare 1414. **1662** GLANVILL *Lux Orient.* xiv. 148 All things proceed much-what in like manner as before. **1701** COLLIER *M. Aurel.* (1726) 201 The world in a dream, and the world out on't, will appear much what the same thing. **1796** 'TIM BOBBIN THE 2ND' *Plebeian Politics* (1801) 29, I think eawer kese is mitchwhot th' same. **1899** B. W. GREEN *Word-bk. Virginia Folk-Speech* 246 *Much-what*, nearly; almost. For the most part. 'They are all *much-what.*' **1922** JOYCE *Ulysses* 388 It was muchwhat indifferent.

mucic ('mjuːsɪk), *a. Chem.* [a. F. *mucique*, f. L. *mūc-us*: see MUCUS and -IC.] ***mucic acid***: an acid formed by the action of dilute nitric acid upon various kinds of gum. ***mucic ether***, an ether obtained from mucic acid.

1809 YOUNG in *Phil. Trans.* XCIX. 158 Sulfuric acid 1000 ..Mucic 900. **1838** T. THOMSON *Chem. Org. Bodies* 337 Of mucic ether... One part of mucic acid was mixed with parts of sulphuric acid. *c* **1865** J. WYLDE in *Circ. Sci.* I 412/2 Mucic acid is obtained by the action of nitric acid on gum, and the sugar of milk.

mucid ('mjuːsɪd), *a. rare.* [ad. L. *mūcid-us*, f. *mūcēre*, to be mouldy.] Mouldy, musty.

1656 BLOUNT *Glossogr.*, *Mucid*, finued, hoary, mouldy, filthy. **1694** WESTMACOTT *Script. Herb.* (1695) 6 A few mucid and decayed Anise-Seeds. **1710** T. FULLER *Pharm. Extemp.* 213 And where they..find it degenerated into Mucid, Salt or Sharp, they..reduce it to Freshness. **1837** *Civil Eng. & Arch. Jrnl.* I. 57/1 A lazy old water wheel, which lifts into elevated reservoirs the mucid quantum of supply.

Hence **mu'cidity, 'mucidness,** *rare*$^{-0}$.

1658 PHILLIPS, *Mucidity*, or *Mucour*, mouldinesse, hoarinesse, filthinesse. **1731** BAILEY vol. II, Mucidness.

mucidine, erroneous form of MUCEDINE.

mucidous ('mjuːsɪdəs), *a. rare*$^{-0}$. [f. L. *mūcid-us* MUCID + -OUS.] = MUCID.

1866 *Treas. Bot.*, *Mucidous*, musty; smelling of mouldiness.

†'**muciduct.** *Obs. rare*$^{-1}$. [f. L. *mūc-us* MUCUS + *duct-us* DUCT *sb.* Cf. MUCODUCT.] A canal (in the root of a plant) by which mucilage is conveyed.

1672-3 GREW *Anat. Roots* I. iii. §18 The proper Liquor of these Muciducts.

muciferous (mjuː'sɪfərəs), *a.* [f. mod.L. type **mūcifer* (f. *mūc-us* MUCUS + *-fer* bearing) + -OUS: see -FEROUS.] Secreting or conveying mucus.

1842 *Proc. Berw. Nat. Club* II. No. 10. 36 These hollow places..are excavated..by long maceration of the soft muciferous foot upon the rock. **1881** GÜNTHER in *Encycl. Brit.* XII. 689/2 Bones of the head with wide muciferous channels. **1882** TENISON-WOODS *Fish & Fisheries N.S. Wales* 8 This perforated line is provided with abundant nerves, and is called the *muciferous* system.

mucific (mjuː'sɪfɪk), *a. Phys.* and *Path.* [f. L. *mūc-us* + -FIC.] Producing mucus.

1833-55 in DUNGLISON *Med. Lex.*

mucification (mjuːsɪfɪ'keɪʃən). *Physiol.* [f. MUC(US + -IFICATION.] Transformation (of epithelial cells) into mucus-secreting cells.

1930 *Proc. R. Soc. Edin.* L. 88 Mucification..is typical of the second phase of the genital cycle; it always accompanies true or pseudo-pregnancy. **1957** *Brit. Jrnl. Radiol.* XXX. 243/1 The intermediate cells did not cornify but instead differentiated into mucus-secreting cells, the mucification being most marked on the third and fourth days after the end of treatment. **1973** *Nature* 9 Feb. 398/1 Progesterone administered for 9 weeks..to..3-month-old mice induced a strong intracellular reaction of mucification along the vaginal mucosa.

So '**mucify** *v. intr.*, to undergo mucification; '**mucified** *ppl. a.*; '**mucifying** *ppl. a.*

1930 *Proc. R. Soc. Edin.* L. 95 On sectioning, the wall was found to be thickened and lined with a mucified epithelium. **1941** *Endocrinology* XXVIII. 314, 72 to 96 hours are required for the mucified vagina to become fully cornified after the influence of the corpus luteum hormone has been removed. **1962** *Brit. Jrnl. Cancer* XVI. 648 Castration and progestational hormones have a mucifying effect on the cervico-vaginal epithelium of mice. **1973** *Nature* 9 Feb. 398/1 It is well known that ambivalent cells of the vaginal squamous epithelium..mucify when progesterone acts synergically with oestrogen.

muciform ('mjuːsɪfɔːm), *a. Phys.* [f. L. *mūc-us* + -FORM.] Resembling mucus.

1833-55 in DUNGLISON *Med. Lex.*

mucigen ('mjuːsɪdʒən). *Chem.* [f. L. *mūcus*: see MUCUS and -GEN 1.] The substance of the granules forming a mucous cell.

1876 in DUNGLISON *Med. Lex.* **1882** *Quain's Anat.* (ed. 9) II. 225 The clear substance which accumulates within the cells is not mucin, but a precursor of mucin, which is termed 'mucigen'.

mucigenous (mjuː'sɪdʒənəs), *a.* [f. L. *mūcus* + -GEN + -OUS.] **a.** Producing mucus. **b.** Of the nature of mucigen.

1886 *Buck's Handbk. Med. Sci.* II. 448/2 The transparent mucigenous..substance has almost wholly disappeared. **1888** *Nature* 13 Dec. 168/1 Out of the breeding season none of these mucigenous cells are to be found in the kidneys.

mucilage ('mjuːsɪlɪdʒ). Forms: 5 muscillage, 5-7 muscilage, 6 muscellage, musilage, mus(se)lege, mucculage, 6-7 mucillage, 7 mussilage, mus(i)lidge, mucilege, 8 mucillage, 9 musilage, 7- mucilage. [a. F. *mucilage* (14th c.), ad. late L. *mūcilāgo* (*c* 400) musty juice (whence Sp. *mucilago*, Pg. *mucilagem*, It. *mucillaggine*, *mucellaggine*), f. L. *mūcus* MUCUS.]

1. a. A viscous substance obtained from the roots, seeds, and other parts of plants by maceration in water. Also *pl.* in the same sense.

c **1400** *Lanfranc's Cirurg.* 245 Tempere hem wiþ muscilage of fenigrec. **15..** in *Vicary's Anat.* (1888) App. ix. 221 Put in x vnces of the saide muscellage. **1575** TURBERV. *Falconrie* 222 A mucillage of Psillium. **1681** tr. *Willis' Rem. Med. Wks.* Vocab., *Mucilage*, thick boiling up of a thing to a gelly, or thick consistency. **1746** H. PEMBERTON *Dispens.* 349 Oil of Mucilages. **1747** WESLEY *Prim. Physic* (1762) 118 Boil Comfrey Roots to a thick Mucilage. **1842** PARNELL *Chem. Anal.* (1845) 37 The mucilage may be prepared by rubbing common starch with cold water. **1887** MOLONEY *Forestry W. Afr.* 282 *Urena lobata*, L.—A common Tropical weed, used medicinally as a mucilage.

b. *transf.* A viscous mass, a pulp.

1657-83 EVELYN *Hist. Relig.* (1850) I. 196 The hardest seeds corrupt and are turned to mucilage and rottenness. **1692** BENTLEY *Boyle Lect.* v. 124 A mucilage of bruised spiders. **1766** *Museum Rust.* VI. 318 To pound their bodies and eggs together into one common mucilage. **1812** J. J. HENRY *Camp. agst. Quebec* 96 The meat required no cutting, as it was reduced to a musilage, or at least to shreds.

fig. **1825** *Examiner* 271/2 Their dramatic dialogue is..a mucilage of sentiment without natural bones or substance.

c. *spec.* Chiefly *U.S.* An aqueous solution of gum or of substances allied to it, used as an adhesive (Webster 1897).

In England commonly called 'gum'.

1859 *La Crosse* (Wisconsin) *Daily Union* 15 Oct. 3/3 Mucilage, sealing wax, playing cards. **1880** W. NEWTON *Serm. for Boys & G.* (1881) 413 She [a spider] makes mucilage in her body and fastens the two pieces down.

2. A viscous lubricating fluid (e.g. mucus, synovia) in animal bodies.

1600 SURFLET *Country Farm* I. xii. 58 The mucilage of shell snailes. **1689** HAVERS *Osteol. Nova* (1691) 201 The Liquor separated by them [*i.e.* the mucilaginous glands] is a Mucilage, which is almost like the white of an Egg. **1717** J. KEILL *Anim. Oecon.* (1738) 120 The most viscid Secretions, such as the Mucilage of the Joints, are separated at the greatest Distance from the Heart. **1718** J. CHAMBERLAYNE *Relig. Philos.* (1730) I. iv. §8 The Mucilage or Slime of the Stomach. **1802** PALEY *Nat. Theol.* vii. (1819) 76 The slippery mucilage which lubricates the joints. **1831** R. KNOX *Cloquet's Anat.* 566 M. Vauquelin thinks that three substances form the base of the cerumen: a fat oil, an albuminous animal mucilage, and a colouring matter.

3. a. *Bot.* A gummy secretion present in various parts of vegetable organisms.

1677 GREW *Anat. Fruits* i. §14 Out of all these sap-vessels, issues a transparent and viscous Mucilage. **1807** J. E. SMITH *Phys. Bot.* 70 The most distinct secretions of vegetables require to be enumerated..Gum or mucilage, a viscid substance..is very general. **1884** BOWER & SCOTT *De Bary's Phaner.* 510 In other woods..a transformation into disorganised masses of mucilage and gum takes place.

b. *Chem.* 'Vegetable gelatine belonging to the amylose group of carbohydrates' (B. D. Jackson *Gloss. Bot. Terms* 1900).

1807 T. THOMSON *Chem.* (ed. 3) II. 293 He concluded that mucilage had been present; for mucilage is composed of carbon, hydrogen, and oxygen. **1857** MILLER *Elem. Chem.* (1862) III. 109 Mucilage or bassorin ($C_{12}H_{10}O_{10}$) is a modification of gum which is insoluble in water.

4. *Comb.*, as ***mucilage-containing*** adj.; also †**mucilage mallow,** *Althæa officinalis*; **mucilage-passage** *Bot.*, a vessel or duct by which mucilage is conveyed.

1578 LYTE *Dodoens* v. xxvii. 586 The Mucculage Mallowe. **1884** BOWER & SCOTT *De Bary's Phaner.* 137 This plant has mucilage-containing sacs and cavities. *Ibid.* 202 Mucilage- and gum-passages in the Marattiaceæ [etc.].

mucilaginous (mju:sɪ'lædʒɪnəs), *a.* Also 7 muccilaginous. [ad. F. *mucilagineux*, ad. mod.L. type **mūcilāginōsus*, f. late L. *mūcilāgin-*, (*-āgo*) MUCILAGE: see -OUS.]

1. Having the nature or properties of mucilage; of a soft, moist, and viscous quality or appearance. Also, pertaining to or characteristic of mucilage.

1646 SIR T. BROWNE *Pseud. Ep.* III. xxiii. 168 A jelly, or muccilaginous concretion. **1651** FRENCH *Distill.* v. 109 Stones are produced out of water that hath a mucilaginous Mercury, which the Salt..fixeth into stones. **1710** T. FULLER *Pharm. Extemp.* 71 A Pectoral Decoction..is endow'd with a mucilaginous..Sweetness. **1845** DARWIN *Voy. Nat.* xi. (1879) 236 It has a mucilaginous, slightly sweet taste. **1884** M. MACKENZIE *Dis. Throat & Nose* II. 49 Occasionally warm mucilaginous drinks are more soothing. **1884** BOWER & SCOTT *De Bary's Phaner.* 534 In many species..the mucilaginous disorganisation begins early.

2. Containing or secreting mucilage. ***mucilaginous glands***: the fringed vascular folds of the synovial membrane.

1689 HAVERS *Osteol. Nova* (1691) 189, I shall give them a more comprehensive name, such as *Glandulæ Mucilaginosæ*, or the mucilaginous Glands. **1796** MORSE *Amer. Geog.* I. 195 In summer they feed on wild grasses, and the leaves of the most mucilaginous shrubs.

Hence **muci'laginously** *adv.*, †**muci'laginousness**.

1651 FRENCH *Distill.* v. 112 It attracts to it selfe the mucilaginousnesse of the water. **1859** SALA *Tw. round Clock* (1861) 79, I have..known them [*i.e.* eggs] by bits of straw and flecks of dirt mucilaginously adhering to their shells.

mucin ('mju:sɪn). *Phys.* Also 9 -ine. [a. F. *mucine*, f. L. *mūc-us* MUCUS: see -IN 1.]

a. Mucus. **b.** Any of the glycoproteins found in the mucus of various animals.

1833–55 DUNGLISON *Med. Lex.*, *Mucin*, mucus. **1846** CARPENTER *Princ. Hum. Phys.* (ed. 3) 131 The chief organic constituent [of bronchial and nasal mucus] is a substance termed *Mucin.* **1871** WATTS tr. *Gmelin's Handbk. Chem.* XVIII. 340 Mucin... To be distinguished from the mucin of wheat-gluten. **1872** THUDICHUM *Chem. Phys.* 48 Mucine has never been found in pus. **1905** *Chambers's Jrnl.* Jan. 84/2 The mucine which issues from the body of the garden snail. **1938** *Cold Spring Harbor Symp. Quant. Biol.* VI. 91/2 The term 'mucin' is entirely avoided. It should be used only in a physiological sense to denote a viscous fluid of secretory origin. **1966** SCHULTZE & HEREMANS *Molecular Biol. Human Proteins* I. IV. iv. 769 Salivary mucins are most abundant in sublingual saliva. *Ibid.*, The main sublingual mucin, at least in cattle, differs in composition from submaxillary mucin, as it contains less sialic acid and much more hexose and fucose than the latter product.

c. *attrib.* and *Comb.*

1878 FOSTER *Phys.* (ed. 2) 221 The greater part of the protoplasm of the cells has become converted into a mucin-bearing substance. **1882** *Quain's Anat.* (ed. 9) II. 580 The mucin-cells become gradually smaller and less clear. **1897** *Allbutt's Syst. Med.* IV. 476 A mucin-yielding modification ..of the connective tissue.

mucinogen (mju:'sɪnədʒɪn). *Phys.* [f. MUCIN + -(O)GEN.] = MUCIGEN.

1886 *Buck's Handbk. Med. Sci.* II. 448/2 The sequence, then, is protoplasm, mucinogen, mucin, over and over again.

mucinoid ('mju:sɪnɔɪd), *a.* and *sb.* [f. MUCIN + -OID.] **a.** *adj.* Resembling mucin. **b.** *sb.* = MUCOID (Webster *Suppl.* 1902).

1900 *Lancet* 28 July 249/1 Mucin and mucinoid bodies.

mucinous ('mju:sɪnəs), *a.* [f. MUCIN + -OUS.] Pertaining to or resembling mucin.

1863 AITKEN *Pract. Med.* (1866) II. 59 Such [fluids] as contain albuminous, fibrinous, mucinous, or caseinous substances. **1876** DUNGLISON *Med. Lex.*, *Mucinous Cysts*... *Mucinous exudations.* **1897** *Allbutt's Syst. Med.* IV. 467 Mucinous degeneration of the connective tissue.

muciparous (mju:'sɪpərəs), *a.* [f. L. *mūc-us* + *-par-us* producing (f. *parĕre* to bring forth) + -OUS.] Producing or secreting mucus.

1835–6 *Todd's Cycl. Anat.* I. 310/1 The pituitary membrane..displays numerous pores of muciparous glands. **1878** FOSTER *Text Bk. Physiol.* (ed. 2) 221 In addition to these 'muciparous cells' are seen a number of smaller..cells.

mucivore ('mju:sɪvɔə(r)). *Ent.* [ad. mod.L. *Mucivora* neut. pl., f. *mūc-us* + *-vor-us* devouring.] A dipterous insect of the family *Mucivora* (Webster 1864). Hence **mu'civorous** *a.*, 'feeding upon the juices of plants' (*Cent. Dict.* 1890).

muck (mʌk), *sb.*[1] Forms: 3–4 muc, 3 mokke, 3–5 mukke, 3–6 muk, 3–4, 6 *Sc.* mok, 4 moke, 4–7 mucke, 5–6 muke, 6 mouk(e, *Sc.* mwk, 5– muck. [Early ME. *muk*, prob. of Scandinavian origin: cf. ON. *myki* fem., dung (Da. *møg*, in 16th c. *mwgh* neut., *mug*, *mog*, *møk*, Norw. *myk*) :—**mukîn-* wk. fem., prob. f. OTeut. **muk-* wk. grade of **meuk-* soft (see MEEK *a.*). ON. has the cognate verb *moka* to shovel (manure): see MUCK *v.*]

1. a. The dung of cattle (usually mixed with decomposing vegetable refuse) used for manure; farm-yard manure. Now chiefly *dial.* and *vulgar*.

c **1250** *Gen. & Ex.* 2557 Summe he deden..Muc and fen ut of burȝes beren ðus bitterlike he gun hem deren. **1303** R. BRUNNE *Handl. Synne* 2301 Þe muk ys þe more stynkyngge þere þe sunne ys more shynyngge. *c* **1325** *Knowe þi self* 80 in *E.E.P.* (1862) 132 Eueri mok most in-to myre. **1377** LANGL. *P. Pl.* B. VI. 144 Ac ȝe myȝte trauaille..Diken or deluen..or bere mukke a-felde. **1538** in *Lett. Suppress. Monast.* (Camden) 176 Our lond is not tylde, muke is not led, our corne lyth in the barn [etc.]. **1615** W. LAWSON *Country Housew. Gard.* (1626) 3 Digge a trench halfe a yard deepe,..and fill the same with good short, hot, and tender mucke. **1725** RAMSAY *Gentle Sheph.* II. iii, Is there nae muck to lead? **1813** SIR H. DAVY *Agric. Chem.* (1814) 303 The violent fermentation which is necessary for reducing farm-yard manure to the state in which it is called short muck. **1857** HUGHES *Tom Brown* I. ii, The shaky surface of the great muck reservoir. **1890** *Farmer's Gaz.* 4 Jan. 7/3 Want of 'muck' causes want of apples.

†**b.** Applied to other fertilizers. *Obs.*

1669 *Phil. Trans.* IV. 1079 All the ground, where Salt or Brine is spilt, is, when dugg up, excellent Muck for Grazing Ground. **1772** *Projects* in *Ann. Reg.* 108/1 The ashes, which are called pot-ash muck, make excellent manure... The principal inducement to make pot-ash is, for the muck.

c. Phr. ***wet as muck*** (cf. *muck-wet*).

1782 MISS BURNEY *Cecilia* II. ix, 'But how did you find yourself when you got home, sir?' 'How? why wet as muck.' **1787** WOLCOT (P. Pindar) *Apol. Post. to Ode upon Ode* Wks. 1812 I. 458 Wet as muck.

d. *U.S.* Soil material consisting of decayed plant remains, similar to peat; in mod. use distinguished from peat by being more thoroughly decomposed (and usu. darker in colour) and having a higher mineral content.

1832 H. L. BARNUM *Farmer's Own Bk.* 35 On tearing up some handfuls of the ground, this is well blackened of course, and little is thought of looking for the sub-soil, as those invariably do, who have once been deceived by black muck, and these soft beds of leaves. **1839** J. BUEL *Farmer's Compan.* ix. 73 Peat earth, or swamp muck, is vegetable food, in an insoluble state, and requires only such a chemical change as shall render it soluable, to convert it into an active manure. **1849** E. CHAMBERLAIN *Indiana Gazetteer* (ed. 3) II. 305 The soil is a black muck, based on clay. **1859** S. W. JOHNSON *Ess. Peat, Muck, & Commercial Manures* 63 Some intelligent farmers call the surface layers of their swamps, which are loose and light in texture, swamp muck, and to the bottom layers, which are more compact and often serviceable as fuel, they apply the term peat. **1862** DANA *Man. Geol.* 614 Muck is another name for peat,..especially when the material is employed as a manure. **1889** *Century Mag.* Dec. 217/2 The soil proved to be a wet muck, overlaying sand with boulders. **1897** G. P. MERRILL *Treat. Rocks* II. ii. 149 An impure variety [of peat] containing a considerable quantity of siliceous sand, and locally known as 'muck', is used as a fertilizer for 'multching' throughout New England. **1928** *Bull. Amer. Soil Survey Assoc.* IX. 44 Peat has been defined as containing over 65% of organic matter and Muck as containing from 25% to 65%. It does not appear desirable to place such definite limits of composition but rather to base the distinction mainly on the degree of decomposition and secondarily on the content of mineral material. **1930** C. E. THORNE *Maintenance Soil Fertility* ii. 15 Beds of muck and peat..are found on the watershed and in some of the river valleys. *Ibid.*, The distinction between peat and muck is that in these bogs the lower strata, being continually covered with water, may still consist of only partially decomposed fibrous matter, brownish in color, while the surface that has been exposed to the air has more completely decayed, losing its fibrous texture and becoming darker in color. Muck and peat, therefore, may be compared to soil and subsoil. **1943** MILLAR & TURK *Fund. Soil Sci.* ii. 63 When these organic deposits are yet in the crude, fibrous state, they are frequently designated as peat, but when decay has broken down the plant tissues until the material has something of a loamy consistency, it is called muck. **1971** *Gloss. Soil Sci. Terms* (Soil Sci. Soc. Amer.) 11/2 *Muck*, highly decomposed organic material in which the original plant parts are not recognizable.

†**2.** *fig.* Contemptuously applied to money. *Obs.*

a **1300** *Sarmun* xx. in *E.E.P.* (1862) 3 Þe wrecchis wringit þe mok so fast up ham silf hi nul noȝt spened. *c* **1380** WYCLIF *Wks.* (1880) 147 Ʒif þei ben pore..þei ben cursed for þei han not moche muk. *c* **1412** HOCCLEVE *De Reg. Princ.* 1632 But þey þat marien hem for muk & good Only, & noght for loue [etc.]. **1526** *Pilgr. Perf.* (W. de W. 1531) 17 The drosse and mucke of this worldly Egypte. **1633** ROWLEY *Match at Midnt.* I. i. Bjb, I tell 'em I haue given over Brokering, moyling for mucke and trash. **1710** LADY M. W. MONTAGU *Lett.*, *To Mrs. Wortley* 113 For those that do not regard worldly muck, there is extraordinary good choice indeed.

3. a. Unclean matter such as soils that upon which it is deposited or to which it adheres; dirt, filth. Also *fig.* Now *vulgar*.

13.. *Minor Poems fr. Vernon MS.* xxxv. 63 Þou proude mon, þou art nouȝt elles But of Muk bretful a sekke. **1439** *Coventry Leet Bk.* (E.E.T.S.) 191 They ordeyne that from thys tyme forward that any muk or ffilth be Cast ther by eny person, but ȝif the Comyn seriant do execucion he schall lese his office. *c* **1440** *Promp. Parv.* 348/1 Muk, or duste.., *pulvis.* **1505** *Burgh Rec. Edin.* (1869) I. 105 For purgeing and clengeing of the hie streitt..of all maner of mwk, filth of fische and flesche, and fulzie weit and dry. **1533** *Presentm. of Juries* in *Surtees Misc.* (1888) 34 That no man cast eny..mouk uppon the chanell. **1596** DALRYMPLE *Leslie's Hist. Scot.* x. (S.T.S.) 462 Now thair conschiences ar compellit be force of the Edictes of the Catholikis, in thair muk to clag and fyle thame selfe. **1607** SHAKS. *Cor.* II. ii. 130. **1661** GLANVILL *Van. Dogm.* xxiv. *Apol. Philos.* 247 The Swine may see the Pearl, which yet he values but with the ordinary muck. **1668** BP. HOPKINS *Serm.*, *Vanity* (1685) 10 Whence is it, that we..lie here groveling in the thick clay and muck of this world? **1682** DRYDEN & LEE *Duke of Guise* III. i, You moving Dirt, you rank stark Muck o' th' World. **1849** DICKENS *Dav. Copp.* iii, Mr. Peggotty went out to wash himself in a kettleful of hot water, remarking that 'cold would never get *his* muck off'. **1861** CALVERLEY *Verses* (1862) 20 Who fled like an arrow, nor turned a hair, Through all the mire and muck.

b. *colloq.* Anything disgusting.

1882 'F. ANSTEY' *Vice Versâ* xvi. 282 'If you think the tea worth racing like that for, I don't,' said Coggs viciously; 'it's muck.' **1899** E. PHILLPOTTS *Human Boy* 108 There were bottles of stuff to rub bruises with..and some muck for his eye. *Ibid.* 174 The muck doctors give you. **1928** W. PONDER *Clara Butt* 138 All I can say is..sing 'em muck! It's all they can understand. **1943** K. TENNANT *Ride on Stranger* iv. 34 He had a habit of greeting any new dish with a loud: 'What's this muck?' **1959** I. & P. OPIE *Lore & Lang. Schoolch.* ix. 162 School dinners are 'muck', 'pig swill', 'poison', 'slops',..and Y.M.C.A. (Yesterday's Muck Cooked Again). **1967** *Listener* 20 Apr. 524/3 Is this the kind of muck which the National Film Theatre is going to bring to Norwich?

c. (Commercial slang.) ***muck and truck***: miscellaneous articles of trade.

1898 *Daily News* 22 July 4/7 'Sufficient attention is not paid to muck and truck'. So says the British Consul at Shanghai.

d. Waste material that is removed during mining or civil engineering operations; *spec.* (*U.S.*), surface material that overlies a placer deposit.

1883 W. S. GRESLEY *Gloss. Terms Coal Mining* 171 *Muck* (Y[orkshire]), see *Dirt* [= 'clay, bind, or other useless rubbish produced in mining, and which accidentally is sent out of the pit mixed with the coal']. **1897** J. W. LEONARD *Gold Fields Klondike* 180 The top 'muck', as it is called by the miners, is, when thawed out, about two-thirds water and one-third sediment. **1908** J. M. MACLAREN *Gold* II. 484 The low-level gravels..lie on decomposed schist bed-rock, and are covered by black frozen 'muck' (silt, vegetable matter, and ice, the last forming 75 per cent. of the mass) of a thickness of 2 to 30 feet. **1914** G. ATHERTON *Perch of Devil* I. 148 His..hands were white with 'muck', a mixture of rock-dust and water. **1959** *Times* 16 Nov. 8/5 About 400,000 tons of spoil (or muck as the mining engineer calls it) will be brought to the surface. **1960** *Vancouver Sun* 4 June 2/4, 150 vertical feet of muck in the stope above had settled gently down over the mule, the string of cars—and our only way out.

e. Phrases. ***as muck***: used emphatically following adj.; ***like muck***: used negatively with a statement.

1935 J. C. MASTERMAN *Fate cannot harm Me* viii. 154 He would be out any ball and poor old George would be as sick as muck. **1952** [see DRUNK *sb.*[2] 1].

f. *R.A.F. slang.* (*a*) Hostile anti-aircraft fire; (*b*) (see quot. 1943).

1940 MICHIE & GRAEBNER *Their Finest Hour* iv. 65, I climbed to 12,000 feet, circling along the outside of the searchlights and all the muck [gunfire] that was coming up. **1943** HUNT & PRINGLE *Service Slang* 46 *Muck*, dirty weather.

g. ***Lord Muck***: see LORD *sb.* 14c. So ***Lady Muck.***

1957 I. CROSS *God Boy* (1958) xxii. 190 She sat there, sipping away at her tea like Lady Muck. **1966** 'L. LANE' *ABZ of Scouse* 61 Lady Muck of Muck Hall: A woman who puts on airs, has a condescending manner and is regarded as excessively conceited.

4. *colloq.* or *vulgar.* **a.** An uncleanly or untidy condition. ***to be in, all of a muck***, to be 'smothered' in dirt. Also *fig.*

1766 GOLDSM. *Vic. W.* ix, She observed, that 'by the living jingo, she was all of a muck of sweat'. **1800** *Sporting Mag.* XVI. 284 'I'm all in such a muck', she cried, 'with so much dust and jolting'. **1876** 'MARK TWAIN' *Tom Sawyer* xxiii, When a body's in such a muck of trouble.

b. ***to make a muck of***, to do (something) badly; to spoil or bungle.

1906 D. F. T. COKE *Bending of Twig* xiv. 222 There'll be nobody much there, so it doesn't matter if you *do* make a muck of it. **1936** R. LEHMANN *Weather in Streets* III. i. 265, I would like to paint her, but..would make a muck of it. **1947** 'N. SHUTE' *Chequer Board* iv. 94 He's made a bloody muck o' things, the way I knew he would. **1970** Y. CARTER *Mr. Campion's Falcon* xxi. 159 I've made a muck of it. What the hell can I do now?

5. *attrib.* and *Comb.*, as ***muck-headed***, †***-hearted***, †***-sprung*** adjs.; (sense 1 d) ***muck-bed***, ***-land***, ***-swamp***; **muck-bar** (see quot. 1875); **muck-cart**, a cart in which 'muck' is carried; **muck-crome**, **-crome**, **-croom** [CROME, CROMB *sb.*], a dung-fork; †**muck crook** = ? *muck-hack*; †**muck-hack**, an implement for raising and dragging manure from the dunghill; †**muck-heaping**, *fig.* amassing of wealth; †**muck-hook** = *muck-hack*; **muck-iron** (see quot.); **muck-man** = SCAVENGER; †**muck-midden**, a dung-hill; †**muck-monger**, a miser; **muck-pit**, a cesspool; **muck-pot** ? *nonce-wd.* = *muck-spout*; **muck-roll** (see quot.); †**muckscrap**, a miser; **muck-shifter**, a man who or a machine which removes earth; **muck-shoveller**, (*a*) a farmhand employed in collecting or distributing dung; (*b*) *Austral. slang* (see quot. 1945); so ***muck-shovelling*** vbl. sb.; †**mucksled**, a manure cart; **muck-snipe** *slang* (see quot.); **muck soil**, a soil composed of muck (sense 1 d) (see quot. 1928[1]); **muck-spout** *dial.* and *slang*, one who uses obscene language or who displays a salacious mentality; **muck-spreader**, a machine for spreading dung; **muck-spreading** *vbl. sb.*, the action of distributing dung over a field; **muck-sweat**, profuse sweat; **muck-thrift** = MUCKWORM; † **muckwain**, a manure cart; **muck water**, liquid manure drained from a dunghill; **muckweed** (see quots.); † **muck-wet** *a.*, 'wet as muck' (see 1 c), thoroughly wet.

1875 KNIGHT *Dict. Mech.*, *Muck-bar, bar-iron which has passed once through the *rolls.* **1872** A. DE MORGAN *Budget of Paradoxes* 163, I certainly think the words would never have come together except in this way:—I, quart pyx, who fling *muck beds. **14..** *Tournament of Tottenham* 287 in Hazl. *E.P.P.* III. 95 The nedur lippe of a larke Was broght in a *muk cart And set befor the lorde. **1519** in *Archæologia* XXV. 421 For ij dayes worke, fyllyng of the mucke carts. **1823** E. MOOR *Suffolk Words & Phr.* 239 A crooked fork for pulling the article out of carts on to heaps we call *muck-crome. **1846** Muck-croom [see CROME, CROMB *sb.*]. **1969** G. E. EVANS *Farm & Village* x. 111, I got an old *muck-crone* (a fork with curved tines), and I used to put this muck-crone under the door and draw a slab of linseed cake through. **1971** *Country Life* 11 Mar. 533/1, I got out o' me punt and stuck a muck-crome, a muck-rake in it [*sc.* a stranded sturgeon]. **1573** *Lanc. Wills* (Chetham Soc.) III. 61 One *muckecrooke and thre wymble bitts. **1411** in *Finchale Priory Charters*, etc. (Surtees) p. clviii, Item, j *mokhak. **1465** *Ibid.* p. ccxcix, j mukhak. **1570** *Wills & Inv. N.C.* (Surtees) I. 342 One muck hacke, a grape, and iij forkes viij[d]. **1909** H. G. WELLS *Ann Veronica* xiii. 272 'Ass!' he went on, still warming. '*Muck-headed moral ass! I ought to have done anything.' *c* **1425** HOCCLEVE *Min. Poems* 200/587 Eerthely loue and to greet greedynesse In *muk-hepynge blynden many an herte. **1820** J. SCOTT in *Lond. Mag.* Jan. 14/2 An incurably wretched, grovelling, *muck-hearted creature. **1577** *Wills & Inv. N.C.* (Surtees) I. 420, ij *mocke hoockes one old sleade, and twoo olde ropes. **1766** *Compl. Farmer* s.v. *Fallow-Cleansing*, A man must be ready with a muck-hook to clear them backward. **1884** KNIGHT *Dict. Mech.* Suppl., **Muck Iron*, crude puddled iron ready for the squeezer or rollers. **1847** W. BACON *Let.* 24 Nov. in *Rep. Comm. Patents 1847* (U.S.) (1848) 358 They have been planted the present year, on deep *muck lands. **1936** *Sun* (Baltimore) 17 Jan. 3/4 Shattered remnants of the transcontinental airliner which plunged seventeen persons to death in a nearby muckland. **1950** *Daily Progress* (Charlottesville, Virginia) 24 July 1/2 It plunged into the pine-spotted muckland. **1680** SIR J. FOULIS *Acc. Bk.* 10 Jan. (S.H.S.) 19 To y[e] *muckman that dights y[e] close. **1689** *Depos. Cast. York* (Surtees) 291 Josias Swallow and one John Walker.. buried him in the *muck-midding. *a* **1859** DENHAM *Tracts* (1895) II. 97 There is an old proverb which says, 'The muck-midden is the mother of the meal-ark'. **1566** DRANT *Horace, Sat.* I. vi. Dv, If gainegroper or *muckmunger, I can not proue it be. **1598** MARSTON *Sco. Villanie* III. xi, Brothell rime, That stinks like Aiax froth, or *muck-pit slime. **1938** DYLAN THOMAS *Let.* 6 July (1966) 205 It's a crack at young Georgians,.. intellectual *muckpots leaning on a theory, post-surrealists and orgasmists. **1875** KNIGHT *Dict. Mech.*, **Muck-roll*, the *roughing* or first roll of a rolling-mill train. **1589** R. ROBINSON *Gold. Mirr.* (Chetham Soc.) 36 The worldly *Muckscraps for their goods did daily loose their life. **1880** D. W. BARRETT *Life & Work among Navvies* II. ii. 43 Navvies themselves speak of one another as *muck-shifters, or thick-legs. **1961** *Engineering* 9 June 797 Designed to work under rugged off-highway conditions as a muck-shifter. **1967** G. F. FIENNES *I tried to run a Railway* vi. 63 *Muck shifting is easy nowadays. **1970** *Daily Tel.* 5 Nov. 13/6 The whole 'muck-shifting' industry changing the shape of the landscape is experimenting all the time with bigger, and sometimes better, machines. **1945** BAKER *Austral. Lang.* v. 98 **Muck-shoveller*, a tin miner. **1960** *Farmer & Stockbreeder* 23 Feb. 105/3 Of these 32 [farmers], 21 simply wanted a muck-shoveller. **1560** *Burgh Rec. Stirling* (1887) 72 Ane *mwksled, ane hand towall [etc.]. **1851** MAYHEW *Lond. Labour* I. 259 A *muck-snipe, Sir, is a man regularly done up, coopered, and humped altogether. **1928** *Bull. Amer. Soil Survey Assoc.* IX. 44 **Muck soil*, soil composed of thoroughly decomposed organic material, with a considerable amount of mineral soil material, finely divided and with few fibrous remains. **1928** F. E. BEAR *Theory & Pract. in Use of Fertilizers* xvii. 280 If.. more potash can be used to advantage.. the.. analysis might well be changed in that direction. This may be the case with muck soils. **1970** *Jrnl. Econ. Entomol.* LXIII. 1283/1 Studies were made to determine the fate of ^{14}C-labeled aldicarb in sand, loam, clay, and muck soils maintained at different moisture levels. *a* **1825** R. FORBY *Vocab. E. Anglia* (1830) II. 223 **Muck-spout*, one who is at once very loquacious and very foul-mouthed. **1916** D. H. LAWRENCE *Let. c* 15 Dec. (1962) 492 And Murry.. is a little muck-spout. **1961** *Guardian* 30 May 5/1 In the more developed countries everything from washing machines to *muck-spreaders has been mechanised. **1975** *Listener* 29 May 702/2 Gardeners going berserk with mechanical diggers and muck-spreaders. **1903** *Eng. Dial. Dict.* IV. 187/1 [Nottinghamshire] A farmer on being asked in Court when the event occurred, said, 'It wor abaout three weeks afore *muck spreading.' **1948** *Brit. Birds* XLI. 358 This is paralleled by the Faeroe farmers' belief that muck-spreading should be completed before the coming of the White Wagtail. **1960** *Farmer & Stockbreeder* 8 Mar. 74/1 An interesting attachment designed for fitting to conventional tipping trailers was this p.t.o.-driven *muck-spreading device. **1647** H. MORE *Cupid's Confl.* lvi, The *muck-sprung learning cannot long endure. **1870** *Rep. Comm. Agric. 1869* (U.S. Dept. Agric.) 270 The soil was.. black mud or muck swamp, five feet deep, containing a mixture of sand. **1699** L. WAFER *Voy.* (1729) 291 They came out.. all in a *muck-sweat. **1765** BICKERSTAFFE *Maid of Mill* II. vii. 35 You have put yourself into a muck-sweat already. **1879** BROWNING *Dramatic Idyls* 115 Publican Black Ned Bratts and Tabby his big wife too: Both in a muck-sweat. **1922** JOYCE *Ulysses* 515 I'm all of a mucksweat. **1953** R. LEHMANN *Echoing Grove* 48 Must have a shower. I've been in a muck sweat all day. **1972** J. PORTER *Meddler & her Murder* i. 10 There's nothing for you to get into a muck sweat about. **1852** D. JERROLD *Wks.* (1864) II. 239 The old *muckthrift.. was wont to familiarise his thoughts with the angel of death. **1523** FITZHERB. *Husb.* §146 It is a wyues occupacyon.. to helpe her husbande to fyll the *mucke wayne or donge cart. **1626** BACON *Sylva* §405 To water it with *Muck water.. is not practised. **1787** W. MARSHALL *Norfolk* (1795) II. 384 Gloss. *Muckweed, or Fat-hen, *Chenopodium album*, common goose-foot. **1854** MISS BAKER *Northampt. Gloss.*, *Muck-weed*, pond-weed. *Potamogeton crispum*? **1567** DRANT *Horace, Epist.* I. xi. Ej, *Mucke weete with myer. **1676** *Phil. Trans.* XI. 712 They rose up, finding their Horses muck-wet all over.

muck (mʌk), *sb.*[2] Also 7 moqua, mocca. [The second syll. of *amuck* (see AMOK), erroneously regarded as a sb. preceded by an indefinite article.] In the phrase ***to run a muck*** (sometimes with adj.) = 'to run AMOK'. Hence, an act of running amok.

[**1678** J. PHILLIPS tr. *Tavernier's Voy.* II. 199 Behind the Pales a Rascally Bantamois had hid himself; one of those that was newly come from Mecca, and was upon the design of Moqua. *Ibid.* 202 Which the Java Lords seeing, call'd the English Traytors, and drawing their poyson'd Daggers, cry'd *a Mocca* upon the English.] **1687** DRYDEN *Hind & P.* III. 1188 Frontless, and Satyr-proof he scow'rs the streets, And runs an Indian muck at all he meets. **1783** MARSDEN *Sumatra* 241 Those desperate acts of indiscriminate murder, called by us, *mucks* and by the natives *mongamo*. **1848** LOWELL *Biglow P.* Poems 1890 II. 131 The late muck which the country has been running has materially changed my views. **1880** MRS. RIDDELL *Myst. Palace Gard.* xxiv, She would run the pecuniary muck on which she had evidently started.

muck (mʌk), *v.* [f. MUCK *sb.*[1] Cf. ON. *moka* to shovel (manure), Da. *muge*, dial. *moge* to remove dung, clear out a stable.]

1. *trans.* To free from muck. Freq. with *out*, and occas. with *off*, and *absol.* Also *fig.*

c **1375** *Sc. Leg. Saints* xxv. (*Julian*) 131 þe patyl his hand clewyt to, þe muldebred quhen he suld mvk. **1500–20** DUNBAR *Poems* lx. 52 Sa far abowe him sett at tabell That wont was for to muk the stabell. *a* **1578** LINDESAY (Pitscottie) *Chron. Scot.* (S.T.S.) I. 181 He.. wssit all thingis at.. thair consall quho.. was not worthie to be in that rowme to haue gevin ane prince counsall bot rather to haue haldin the pleugh.. or, witht ȝour reverence, had mokit clossitis. **1641** BEST *Farm. Bks.* (Surtees) 102 When they come backe, they fall to muckinge of the stables. **1657** THORNLEY tr. *Longus' Daphnis & Chloe* 170 He muckt the Cottage, lest the dung should offend him with the smell. **1851** *Beck's Florist* 157 He would not half muck his stables out, for he said he wanted his horses to lay warm. **1914** KIPLING *Divers. Creatures* (1917) 52, I was obligin' Jim that evenin' muckin' out his pig-pen. **1921** [see CLEANER a]. **1950** *Landfall* XIII. 16 They always want one [*sc.* a cup of tea] after they've finished mucking out. **1952** R. S. SUMMERHAYS *Elem. Riding* (ed. 3) iii. 23 The deep bedding has now been 'mucked out'. **1958** J. BETJEMAN *Coll. Poems* 252 She can muck out the stables and clean Her snaffle and saddle and bridle. **1966** M. TORRIE *Heavy as Lead* xiv. 169 Sir G. had told me special to muck out the pigs. **1967** C. WATSON *Lonelyheart 4122* ix. 91 He would have to be strong, energetic, used to stud work and willing to muck out. **1973** J. BURROWS *Like an Evening Gone* ii. 30 I've mucked out the henhouses.

2. To dress with muck, to manure. Also *absol.* Now *rare* exc. *dial.*

c **1440** *Promp. Parv.* 341/2 Moke vynys, *pastino. Ibid.*, Mokke londe wythe donge, *fimo, infimo.* **1530** PALSGR. 641/2 If this land be well mucked, it wyll beare corne ynough the nexte yere. **1693** EVELYN *De La Quint. Compl. Gard.* II. 172 We transport our rotten Dung to those places we design to muck. **1763** MILLS *Pract. Husb.* I. 102 Ground mucked with horse-dung is always the most infected of any. **1855** *Jrnl. R. Agric. Soc.* XVI. I. 135 If you clay heavily.. you must muck heavily. **1890** *Farmer's Gaz.* 4 Jan. 7/2 You always muck your orchard, do you not?

†*fig. a* **1555** BRADFORD in Coverdale *Lett. Mart.* (1564) 462 Yf god.. beginne to mucke and marle you: to pour hys showers vpon you [etc.]. **1598** MARSTON *Sco. Villanie* II. vii, O Canaans dread curse To liue in peoples sinnes. Nay far more worse To muke ranke hate.

3. *refl.* To 'sweat', fag. *rare.*

1817–18 COBBETT *Resid. U.S.* (1822) 181 They.. toil and muck themselves half to death to dig as much ground in a day as a Surrey man would dig in about an hour of hard work.

4. a. *trans.* To make dirty; to soil. ***to muck up***, to litter (now *vulgar*). Also, to mix *up*.

1832 LAMB *Let. to Moxon* in *Final Mem.* viii. 272 'Tis like a dirty pocket-handkerchief, mucked with tears. **1883** STEVENSON *Treas. Isl.* x, You can't touch pitch and not be mucked. **1896** MRS. CAFFYN *Quaker Grandmother* 77, I like them well enough in their places, which isn't mucking up my rooms. **1909** H. G. WELLS *Tono-Bungay* III. i. 279 It's a festering mass of earths and heavy metals... There they are, mucked up together in a sort of rotting sand. **1916** 'BOYD CABLE' *Action Front* 109 If it [*sc.* a shell] had fell in the trench, now, and mucked up half a dozen men, there'd have been something to squeal about. **1949** 'J. TEY' *Brat Farrar* xi. 85 You don't want that dazzling outfit of yours to be mucked up.

b. *fig.* To make a 'mess' of. Freq with *up* or *about. slang.*

1886 in H. BAUMANN *Londinismen.* **1899** KIPLING *Stalky* 190, I shall muck it. I know I shall. **1922** 'R. CROMPTON' *Just—William* viii. 161 You seem to have pretty well mucked it up. **1935** 'N. BLAKE' *Question of Proof* i. 17 Old Simmie will probably muck up the stop-watch like he did last year. **1946** K. TENNANT *Lost Haven* (1947) xi. 180 This is a real good stove... She isn't mucked about and cleaned, and that's what makes her a good stove. **1959** 'M. CRONIN' *Dead & Done With* vi. 99 'Lena could muck it all up.' 'I don't think she will, so long as she's scared about herself.' **1959** ANON. *Streetwalker* iii. 58 Muck me about and you're out. **1966** *Listener* 17 Nov. 719/2, I was delighted to see Mr Bernard Levin.. heading a review..'*Much Ado About Nothing*, by William Shakespeare, the text mucked about by Robert Graves'. **1971** *Nature* 7 May 65/3 Let us not muck up our language, lest we also muddle our minds. **1973** *Nation Rev.* (Melbourne) 31 Aug. 1446/6 But she went and mucked it all up with her television debut.

5. a. *intr.* ***to muck about***, to go aimlessly about; to 'mess around'. Freq. with *with*, and also with *around. slang.*

1856 H. PHILLIPS *Jrnl.* 26 Sept. (typescript) 41 Cutting firewood and mucking about the house. **1896** KIPLING *Seven Seas, Cholera Camp* (1897) 188 Our Colonel.. mucks about in 'orspital. **1918** H. G. WELLS *Joan & Peter* xi. 391 They had long bicycle rides together... They 'mucked about' with Baker's boat. *Ibid.* xiii. 659 He would be climbing trees with Joan, 'mucking about' in the boats with Joan. **1928** D. L. SAYERS *Lord Peter views Body* 276 His art.. [is] the one thing a genuine artist won't muck about with. **1935** N. MARSH *Enter Murderer* vii. 90 'E was a-mucking arahnd Trixie. **1946** K. TENNANT *Lost Haven* (1947) x. 152 We been mucking about and mucking about, and got nowhere. **1957** P. MANSFIELD *Final Exposure* ix. 121 Why don't you haul him in instead of mucking around asking me bloody silly questions? **1959** 'M. NEVILLE' *Sweet Night for Murder* xiii. 128 They get fed up with their own wives and have to go mucking about with someone new. **1959** *Engineering* 13 Mar. 343/3 Those Americans are mucking about with their journal titles again. **1963** *Truth* (Wellington, N.Z.) 9 July (*heading*) Don't muck about, Mac. **1973** *Times* 12 Dec. 2/8 The other girls.. wanted to muck around with boys.

b. ***to muck in with***: to share army rations with; to consort or co-operate with; so ***to muck in***, (*a*) to eat; (*b*) to help, to 'pull one's weight', to participate. Also, *to muck in to.*

1919 *Athenæum* 1 Aug. 695/2 'To muck in' with anyone is to share rations with him. **1929** F. MANNING *Middle Parts of Fortune* I. v. 105 'Martlow and I have mucked in together, since you've been in the orderly-room.' 'Well, the three of us can muck in together now,' said Bourne. *a* **1935** T. E. LAWRENCE *Mint* (1955) I. viii. 30 'Muck in', we did, yet still looked lean. **1936** F. RICHARDS *Old-Soldier Sahib* xiii. 223 For nine months he had been mucking-in with a youngster who had only arrived in the country the previous winter. **1942** G. KERSH *Nine Lives Bill Nelson* v. 26 The Army was hell because I couldn't muck in there. **1942** WODEHOUSE *Money in Bank* (1946) iii. 26 When we came to visit here, I understood that that room was reserved for I and my husband. Nobody ever mentioned that we were supposed to muck in with the butler. **1952** M. LASKI *Village* vi. 112 We all muck in together and the jobs get done in no time. **1958** J. CANNAN *And be a Villain* iv. 89 I'm delighted to muck in, but I'm afraid I'm too conscientious for Mrs Langley. **1959** *Encounter* July 27/1 They want men who will muck in as colleagues. **1966** F. SHAW et al. *Lern Yerself Scouse* 42 *Muck in, yer at yer granny's*! Bon Appetit! **1967** *Guardian* 21 Apr. 7/2 Prince Charles.. will be able to muck in to all the student activities. **1970** *Times* 13 Feb. 10/8 The company.. all muck in, take small or big parts. **1974** J. POPE-HENNESSY *R. L. Stevenson* vi. 128 His readiness to muck in with any of his working-class fellows on boat or train.

c. To search for coal on a coal-tip, a beach, etc.

1935 A. J. CRONIN *Stars look Down* I. ii. 22 'It's my duff,' Softley kept whimpering... 'Aw mucked for it, aw did, for my man to hev a fire.'

6. Euphemistically (chiefly in written work) = FUCK *v.*

1929 R. ALDINGTON *Death of Hero* x. 376 Spree be mukked—one of you * * fired his rifle and muckin' near copped me. **1940** E. HEMINGWAY *For whom Bell Tolls* xxii. 273 He may have just mucked off. *Ibid.* xxxv. 369 You're just mucked.. you're mucked for good. *Ibid.*, Muck my grandfather and muck this whole treacherous muck-faced mucking country. **1941** *Penguin New Writing* II. 90 'I shall report you to the foreman.' 'Muck the foreman!' I said. **1946** D. HAMSON *We fell among Greeks* vii. 85 Another song I used to perpetrate.. was 'I'm a man that's in trouble and sorrow.' .. 'Muck it,.. that's a good song, Denys, let's have it again.' **1949** C. FRY *Lady's not for Burning* 92 Youse only has to say muck off, and I goes, wivout argument. **1950** E. HEMINGWAY *Across River* vii. 58 Now muck off.. try and have some fun. **1974** R. ADAMS *Shardik* xxxvi. 300 Come on, now,.. you'll get nothing here, so just muck off, there's a good lad.

'muck-about. [f. the phrase *to muck about* (MUCK *v.* 5).] **a.** A person who 'mucks about'. **b.** The action of 'mucking about'.

1933 H. G. WELLS *Bulpington of Blup* ix. 353 Rich old women in Paris—middle-aged muck-abouts—art shops. **1968** L. BERG *Risinghill* 122 The boys.. were restless, ready for a 'lark' or a 'muck-about' or a 'giggle'.

muck-a-muck ('mʌkəmʌk). [Chinook jargon.]

1. Used by or with reference to Amerindians of western North America: food.

1847 J. PALMER *Jrnl. Trav. Rocky Mts.* 150 Muck-a-muck, Provisions, eat. **1852** *Oregonian* (Portland) 25 Dec. 2/3 The aborigine.. 'put' for the settlement with a sort of legs-do-your-duty-for-the-body-is-in-danger resolution for his *muckamuck.* **1863** *Norfolk Reformer* (Simcoe, Ontario) 8 Jan. 3/1 On arriving as far back as Lytton or Lilooet, there was employment.. and 'muca muc', as the Indian name implies. **1880** *Forest & Stream* 11 Nov. 285/2 We should have to come ashore and have some 'muck-a-muck'. **1895** H. S. SOMERSET *Land of Muskeg* 167 Yes, all kinds of muck-a-muck at McLeod; jam, cake, biscuits.. plenty plenty muck-a-muck, you see. **1915** R. D. CUMMING *Skookum Chuck Fables* 18 Perhaps he had bought all his luxuries on jaw-bone from one store while he paid cash for his muck-a-muck in another. **1963** R. D. SYMONS *Many Trails* 74 Hi-ya tillicum... You plenty muck-a-muck stop.

2. *fig.* Shortening of HIGH-MUCK-A-MUCK.

1912 KIPLING *Songs from Bks.* (1913) 159 Shaman, Ju-ju or Angekok, Minister, Mukamuk, Bonze. **1914** *Dialect Notes* IV. 113 *Squeegee*, a person of importance; muckamuck:—used derisively. **1966** H. KANE *Conceal & Disguise* iv. 28 Cape Ulrich was for the muckamucks, the coupon-clippers, the expense account lads, the heavy rich.

mucka-mucka ('mʌkəmʌkə). [Native name.] A name used in Guyana for the large perennial herb, *Caladium arborescens*, native to tropical

America and belonging to the family Araceæ. Also *attrib.*

1918 C. W. BEEBE *Jungle Peace* (1919) vi. 123 Mucka-mucka was here and there in the foreground. **1955** *Times* 16 July 7/6 They perched, feeding on the leaves of mucka-mucka, a giant variety of arum. *Ibid.* 23 July 7/6, I sat alone and very still in a primitive dug-out after edging it into the heart of a mucka-mucka plant (*Caladium arborescens*) and tying the boat to one of its thick stems. **1958** J. CAREW *Black Midas* iii. 35 The weeds, the wild cane, the lilies, the mucka-mucka were all still under the burning sun.

ˈmucked, *ppl. a.* [f. MUCK *v.* + -ED¹.]

1. Manured. Now *rare* exc. *dial.*

1574 *Cal. Laing Charters* (1899) 225 Ane strip on the vest syd of the said Mr. Jhonis mwkit land. **1688** R. HOLME *Armoury* III. 73/1 Mucked grounds, is ground spread over with the dung of Beasts. **1890** *Farmer's Gaz.* 4 Jan. 7/2 Every orchard that was last season fruitful was a 'mucked' orchard.

2. With advbs., as **mucked-about**, spoiled, subjected to unnecessary interference; **mucked-up**, bungled, spoiled.

1930 M. ALLINGHAM *Mystery Mile* xxvii. 273, I should be very interested to know how you intend to get away with your reputation all pure and virgie and our Albert's poor little mucked-up corpse lying about. **1930** V. PALMER *Passage* I. iii. 29 It was a mucked-up job. **1966** J. BINGHAM *Double Agent* iv. 52, I don't remember what I ate. Some mucked-about dish of stew.

muckel(le, obs. forms of MUCKHILL.

muckender (ˈmʌkəndə(r)). *Obs.* exc. *dial.* Forms: 5 **mokedore, mokado(u)r, moctour,** 6 **mocke(n)dar, mucketter,** 6–7 **mucketer,** 7 **mucki-, mocketer,** 7–9 **muckinder,** 9 **muckinger,** 7– **muckender.** [In 15th c. *mokedore*, prob. adopted from the equivalent of F. *mouchoir* (see MOUCHOIR) in some Occitanian dialect (see Skeat in *Mod. Lang. Rev.* Oct. 1906, p. 60). Cf. mod.Pr. *moucadour* (Honnorat), Sp. *mocador, -dero*, pocket-handkerchief; also It. *moccadore, moccatore*, 'one who snuffs a candle' (Florio).

The word presumably comes from the language of some district where the article was manufactured. Adoption from Sp. is unlikely for the 15th c., and the Sp. *mocador* is prob. not of native formation, as the vb. corresponding to F. *moucher* seems not to have existed in Sp.]

A handkerchief. †Also, a table-napkin; a bib.

14.. *Voc.* in Wr.-Wülcker 594/29 *Mamphora*, a mokedore. *Ibid.* 614/25 *Sudarium*, a mokedore. *c* **1425** *St. Mary of Oignies* II. x. in *Anglia* VIII. 177/31 A lynnyn moctour, wiþ þe whiche she wipte hir teres. *c* **1450** *Cov. Myst.* xx. (Shaks. Soc.) 190 Goo hom, lytyl babe,.. And put a mokador aforn thi brest. **1530** PALSGR. 246/1 Mockendar for chyldre, *movchover*. *Ibid.* 246/2 Mockedar. **1573–80** BARET *Alv.* B634 A bibbe or mucketter. **1611** COTGR., *Baverette*, a bib, mocket, or mocketer to put before the bosome of a (slauering) child. **1670** COVEL *Diary* (Hakl. Soc.) 261 Into our lap or on our knee was laid a muckender ..to wipe your mouth and beard. *a* **1706** EARL DORSET *To Howard on his Plays* 27 For thy dull fancy a muckinder is fit To wipe the slabberings of thy snotty wit. **1791** H. WALPOLE *Let. to Han. More* 29 Sept., How I laughed at hearing of her throwing a second muckender to a Methusalem! **1815** W. H. IRELAND *Scribbleomania* 262 As for her [Justice's] blinkers, ..They've bound 'em up with muckinger. **1843** F. E. PAGET *Warden of Berk.* 22 Shouldn't I tell mother to take the lace off her caps and stitch it round her muckingers?

ˈmucker, *sb.*¹ [f. MUCK *v.* + -ER¹.]

†**1.** A scavenger. *Obs.*

1483 *Cath. Angl.* 246/1 A Mukker, *eruderista.* **1790** BURNS *Let. to Moore* 14 July, As unsightly a scrawl as Betty Byre-Mucker's answer.

†**2.** A money-grubber. *Obs.*

1567 DRANT *Horace, Epist.* II. ii. H vj, What all wherefore so gredelie the moneie mucker carkes. **1584** T. BASTARD *Chrestoleros* (1880) 91 Fye filthy muckers tis not so, Ye erre, God is not goold I know.

3. Euphemistically (chiefly in written work) = FUCKER. Cf. MUCK *v.* 6.

1929 R. ALDINGTON *Death of Hero* III. i. 263 Does the old mucker think we're going to run away? **1942** *Penguin New Writing* XV. 19 Suddenly old Bob says: 'I lost my kit, Cockney.' Silly mucker! **1952** M. TRIPP *Faith is Windsock* ii. 38, I thought there was twelve hundred muckers in this raid—where's t' other eleven hundred and ninety-nine?

mucker (ˈmʌkə(r)), *sb.*² [f. MUCK *sb.* + -ER¹.]

1. *slang.* A heavy fall, as in the muck; a 'cropper'. Phrase, ***to come, go a mucker***: chiefly *fig.*, to come utterly to grief, to ruin oneself.

1852 KINGSLEY in *Life* (1877) I. 349 The old horse.. earned great honour by leaping in and out of the Loddon; only four more doing it, and one receiving a *mucker*. **1869** BP. M. CREIGHTON in *Life & Lett.* (1904) I. iii. 71 We have both of us gone a mucker in a copy of Mendel's lovely engraving. **1876** J. PAYN *Halves* xiv. II. 17 'I should make a point of.. apologising for our unfortunate mistake'. 'Yes, by Jove, a regular mucker', muttered John. **1904** V. L. WHITECHURCH *Canon in Res.* ii. 36, I came a mucker over the bank on my third run. **1914** GALSWORTHY *Mob* I. 8 You're riding for a fall and a godless mucker it'll be. **1916** 'TAFFRAIL' *Pincher Martin* xiv. 270 'Minefield! I thought the one that got you was a floater.' 'Don't you believe it... You can thank your lucky stars you didn't bump one.'.. 'I'm glad we didn't come a mucker—jolly glad!' **1928** GALSWORTHY *Swan Song* I. vi. 41 But for you, old girl, I might have gone a holy mucker myself. **1943** M. AKLOM *Of Social Significance* in *Best One-Act Plays 1942–43* 166 You know what the Guardianship of Infants Act is. They passed it to prevent legal infants coming matrimonial muckers at the age of indiscretion. **1974** G. MITCHELL *Javelin for Jonah* xii. 154, I like old Jimmy boy and I wouldn't want to see him come a mucker.

2. One who, or a machine which, removes muck (MUCK *sb.*¹ 3 d).

1899 *Harper's Weekly* 20 May 498/1 [The] Company.. paid $3. for miners and $2.50 for 'muckers', or underground laborers. **1908** [see JUMBO 1 c]. **1916** C. SANDBURG *Chicago Poems* 21 Twenty men stand watching the muckers. Stabbing the sides of the ditch.. for the new gas mains. **1923** 'B. M. BOWER' *Parowan Bonanza* viii. 94 Now you've staked yourself to the luxury of a mucker, you can leave him in charge. **1927** *Dialect Notes* V. 456 *Mucker*, a shovel man. **1931** 'D. STIFF' *Milk & Honey Route* ii. 24 The rawjawed teameos and muckers.. who built that railroad got little or no hard cash. **1956** *Fatal Accidents* (Ontario Dept. Mines) Apr. 2 The mucker was hoisted clear of the bottom timber by 10 feet, to where it might normally have been anchored. **1965** S. G. LAWRENCE *40 Yrs. on Yukon Telegraph* iv. 23 A mucker's duties are simply to shovel and wheel out rock, and in those days on a wheelbarrow.

mucker (ˈmʌkə(r)), *sb.*³ *slang* (orig. *U.S.*). [Prob. a. G. *mucker* sulky person, gloomy fanatic or hypocrite.] **1. a.** A fanatic or hypocrite. **b.** 'A person lacking refinement; a coarse, rough person' (*Cent. Dict.* 1890).

1891 in *Cycl. Temp. & Prohib.* (U.S.) 269/2 The saloon-keepers then resolved to make 'the muckers take their own medicine', and insisted that the Mayor should enforce the Sunday law against 'common labor'. **1897** KIPLING *Captains Courageous* x. 242 Don't I know the look on men's faces when they think me a—a 'mucker', as they call it out here? **1900** ADE *Fables in Slang* 108 They were not Muckers; they were Nice Boys. **1905** D. G. PHILLIPS *Plum Tree* 35 He used to class himself and me together as 'us gentlemen', in contrast to 'them muckers', meaning my colleagues. **1920** F. SCOTT FITZGERALD *This Side of Paradise* 175 Why is it that the pick of young Englishmen from Oxford and Cambridge go into politics and in the USA we leave it to the muckers? **1936** A. HUXLEY *Olive Tree* 182 There are the refined and aristocratic Muckers in East Prussia, with their ritual of exhibitionism and long-drawn sexual confessions.

†**c.** A youthful townsman, as distinct from a member of a college; a young 'townee'. *Obs. U.S. University slang.*

1893 W. K. POST *Harvard Stories* 75 On the first corner of Harvard Street were stationed three or four boys (the occasionally useful Cambridge muckers) employed as vedettes. **1899** A. H. QUINN *Pennsylvania Stories* 168 Del went through his pockets to the great joy of a limited assortment of muckers who were following. **1948** [see FÜHRER].

2. [Perh. f. MUCK *v.* 5 b.] A companion, friend, 'mate'. *slang.*

1947 J. BERTRAM *Shadow of War* VII. v. 239 What's the griff, mucker? **1954** 'S. CARNEGIE' *Noble Purpose* 21 McLeod.. was a small dark man of lugubrious appearance. His mucker Reed was fat, fair and cherubic. **1963** 'R. ERSKINE' *Passion Flowers in Italy* v. 56 Well, my father was at Magdalen, but all my muckers seemed to be flocking to the House, so I thought I might as well go there too. **1971** B. W. ALDISS *Soldier Erect* 112 It isn't Taff. It's a mucker of mine down in M/T. Jock McGuffie. He's a real cure. **1972** M. WOODHOUSE *Mama Doll* ix. 120 'Is that my old mucker?' said Bottle. 'None other,' I said.

3. With advbs.: **mucker-in**, one who 'mucks in' (see MUCK *v.* 5 b); **mucker-upper**, a bungler.

1942 A. P. JEPHCOTT *Girls growing Up* iv. 83 When a girl first goes to a factory she may be a 'mucker in' and have to turn her hand to anything. **1972** *Guardian* 18 Feb. 14/1 A raconteur.. good value at a gathering where he knows his audience, a mucker-in, a natural wit. **1942** T. RATTIGAN *Flare Path* I. 9 She's a proper mucker-upper though—she'll go and catch the wrong bus.

mucker (ˈmʌkə(r)), *v.*¹ Also 4 **mokre, mokere.** [? f. MUCK *sb.*¹ + -ER⁵.]

1. *trans.* To hoard (money, goods). Also *absol.* and with *up*. *Obs.* exc. *dial.* (see *E.D.D.*).

[**1303**: implied in MUCKERER.] *c* **1374** CHAUCER *Troylus* III. 1326 (1375) Trowe ye, a coueitous, a wreche.. þat, of þo pans þat he can mokere & crache Was euere 3it I-3eue hym swich delit As is in loue? **1530** WHITFORD *Werke for Householders* Hj, Nygardy.. hurdeth & muckereth up he cannot tell for whom. **1548** FORREST *Pleas. Poesye* 56 In tyme of plentie the riche too vpp mucker Corne, Grayne, or Chafre hopinge vppon dearthe. **1604** BABINGTON *Comf. Notes Exod.* xvi. 16 Note how carefull the Lord is to haue men depend vpon his prouidence,.. and not wretchedly and despairefully to mucker vp what shall never doe them good. **1755** JOHNSON, *To Mucker*, ..to scramble for money; to hoard up; to get or save meanly: a word.. still retained in conversation.

†**2.** *intr.* To 'moil'. *Obs. rare.*

Cf. the dial. sense 'to be dirty' (see *Eng. Dial. Dict.*).

1566 DRANT *Horace, Sat.* I. i. Ajb, And thou that didste disdayne To lyve and leade the Lawyers lyfe Shalt mucker in the grounde.

Hence **ˈmuckering** *vbl. sb.* and *ppl. a.*

a **1400** *Burgh Laws* lxxiii. (*Sc. Stat.* I.), Gif ony suilke of usage hantys to cum on nycht because of mukeryn and tavernys [*causa lucri vel mali ingenii*] his fysche in house by nycht þe quhilk he sulde sell on þe day in þe mercate he sal geyff til his forfalt viij s. **1556** OLDE *Antichrist* 182 For a muckering vile aduantage sake.

mucker (ˈmʌkə(r)), *v.*² *slang.* [f. MUCKER *sb.*²]

a. *intr.* To 'come a mucker'; to come to grief, fail. **b.** *trans.* To ruin (one's chances). Also with *away*: to squander.

1861 H. KINGSLEY *Ravenshoe* xiv, By-the-bye Welter has muckered; you know that by this time. **1869** 'W. BRADWOOD' *The O.V.H.* (1870) 60 It's enough to mucker any chance he has. **1928** H. G. WELLS *Way World is Going* 15 The Western Powers of Europe.. muckered away an enormous amount of war gear and money in supporting crazy 'white hopes' against the nascent new thing in Russia.

muckerdom (ˈmʌkərdəm). [f. MUCKER *sb.*³ + -DOM.] The world of muckers or 'townees'; muckers collectively. So **ˈmuckerish** *a.*, befitting or characteristic of a mucker; **ˈmuckerishly** *adv.*; **ˈmuckerism**, the characteristic conduct of muckers; unsportsmanlike behaviour.

1893 W. K. POST *Harvard Stories* 254 In five minutes all the best talent in muckerdom will be there with tin-cans and stones. **1904** *Public Ledger* (Philadelphia) 4 June 6 If a player on the opponent's side happened to make a muff or misplay, cheering by the side benefited was.., in the elegant language of the campus, 'muckerish'. **1906** *Outing* Jan. 494/1 This year there was caterwauling and shouting by cadets individually and muckerishly that was so unusual and unpleasant as to make one discredit one's ears. *Ibid.* 494/2 We hope it does not mean an entrance of muckerism into our Army and Navy games. **1952** C. STEAD *People with Dogs* 330 It's muckerism, saying we all grunt in monosyllables!

†**ˈmuckerer.** *Obs. rare.* Also 4–5 **mokerer,** 6 *Sc.* **mukerar.** [f. MUCKER *v.*¹ + -ER¹.] One who hoards wealth.

1303 R. BRUNNE *Handl. Synne* 6065 A3ens mokerers wyl y þrepe þat gadren pens vn-to an hepe. *c* **1374** CHAUCER *Boeth.* II. Pr. v. 31 (Camb. MS.) Auarice maketh alwey mokereres to ben hated. *c* **1425** AUDELAY *xi Pains of Hell* 112 in *O.E. Misc.* 214 þese were makers of moné with cursid entent, With wrong mokerers false mesurs and vsere. **1513** DOUGLAS *Æneis* VIII. Prol. 54 The mukerar murnis in his mynd the meyll gaue na price. **1755** JOHNSON *Muckerer*,.. one that muckers.

mucket(t)er, obs. forms of MUCKENDER.

ˈmuck-fork. = DUNG-FORK 1.

c **1340** *Nominale siue Verbale* (Skeat) 519 *Furche, fymere*, mouke-forke. **1453–4** *Durham Acc. Rolls* (Surtees) 150, ij Mukforkez. **1554** in *Midl. Counties Hist. Collector* (1855) I. 234 Itm Spads and mukforks xij^d^. **1846** J. BAXTER *Libr. Pract. Agric.* (ed. 4) II. 118 A common muck-fork.

ˈmuck-heap. A manure-heap, midden. Also *fig.* So **ˈmuck-heapy** *a.*

1303 R. BRUNNE *Handl. Synne* 2300 þogh hyt [*sc.* þe sunne] on þe muk hepe [MS. D. mukhyl] shynes. **1523** FITZHERB. *Husb.* §17 Leue no dounge there-as the mucke-hepe stode. **1556** OLDE *Antichrist* 192 He hathe brought a confused muckeheape and burthen of ceremonies in to the churche. **1619** FAVOUR *Antiq. Triumph* xx. 518 A very midden or muckheap of all the grossest errors and heresies of the Romane Church. **1881** *Punch* 29 Oct. 193/1 We sincerely hope that.. His Grace [of Bedford] drove up Wellington Street, made at once for Mud-Salad Market, and.. examined the streets 'all round and about that quarter', whose greasy, muck-heapy state is still a disgrace to the Metropolis in general. **1889** I. TAYLOR *Orig. Aryans* iii. 182 There were muck-heaps in the palace of Priam. **1938** 'N. SHUTE' *Ruined City* vi. 112 One didn't finance a muck-heap of a country like Laevatia for fun. **1946** *Coast to Coast 1945* 177 Somebody counted fourteen bottles on old Gormie's muck-heap.

†**ˈmuckhill,** *sb. Obs.* Forms: see MUCK *sb.*¹ and HILL *sb.*; also, 5 **muckelle,** 6 **mukylle,** 7 **muckel.** [f. MUCK *sb.* + HILL *sb.*] = MUCK-HEAP. Also *fig.*

1303 [see MUCK-HEAP]. **1427** *Coventry Leet Bk.* (E.E.T.S.) 113 Hit was ordeyned þat noman ley no more muke at þe cross beyonde the Newe-3ate, but vppon þe mukhill besidis þe crosse. *c* **1475** *Pict. Voc.* in Wr.-Wülcker 797/33 *Hoc simarium, Hoc sterculinium*, a muckelle. **1576** FLEMING *Panopl. Epist.* 282 They rake vp clods of clay in a confused heape, as it were a muckhil. **1621** BURTON *Anat. Mel.* I. ii. II. v. 109 Muckels, draughts, sinkes. *ibid.* III. iv. I. i. 712 Why dost thou stand gaping on this drosse, muckhills, filthy excrements? *a* **1781** JAGO *Scavengers* 52 Higher than our house our muck-hill rose!

attrib. **1666** BUNYAN *Grace Ab.* §103 To leap with my head downward into some Muck-hill hole or other.

Hence †**ˈmuckhill** *v. trans.*, to heap *up* with filth.

1596 NASHE *Saffron Walden* T j b, Nor let him muckehill vp so manie pages in saying he lookt for termes of aqua fortis and gunpowder.

†**ˈmuckibus.** *vulgar. Obs.* [A humorous formation from MUCK *sb.*¹, with the ending of a L. ablative pl.] Intoxicated, 'tipsy', 'fuddled'.

1756 H. WALPOLE *Let. to Montagu* 20 Apr., Lady Coventry.. said in a very vulgar accent, if she drank any more, she should be *muckibus*. 'Lord!' said Lady Mary Coke, 'what is that?'—'Oh! it is Irish for *sentimental*'.

muckinder, obs. form of MUCKENDER.

muckiness (ˈmʌkɪnɪs). [f. MUCKY *a.* + -NESS.] The state of being mucky or dirty.

1727 in BAILEY vol. II. **1755** in JOHNSON; and in later Dicts.

ˈmucking, *vbl. sb.* [f. MUCK *v.* + -ING¹.]

†**1.** An application of dung or the like as manure; *concr.* what is applied as manure. *Obs.*

1601 HOLLAND *Pliny* I. 569 The sowing of this Pulse in any ground, is as good as a mucking vnto it. **1611** FLORIO, *Letaminatura*, any kind of mucking. *c* **1707** in *Encycl. Brit.* (1853) II. 262/1 A good stubble is the equalest mucking that is.

2. *colloq.* **a.** *pl.* Rubbish, 'mess'. **b.** An act of 'messing about'. Also ***mucking-about***.

1898 KIPLING in *Morn. Post* 9 Nov. 5/2 She's only burning muckings like the rest of us. She's our 'chummy ship'. **1904** —— *Traffics & Discov.* 68 His photographic muckings. **1937** PARTRIDGE *Dict. Slang* 539/2 *Mucking-*

about,..an intimate fondling: low (mostly costers'). **1969** *Listener* 27 Feb. 264/3 'Knowledge is conceived in the hot womb of Violence,' said Auden in his poem on Oxford: perhaps he knew what he was doing when he omitted the phrase in his last mucking-about with the piece.

3. Also with *out*. The action of removing muck, esp. dung from a stable or waste material from a mine.

1641 [see MUCK *v.* 1]. **1840** *How to buy a Horse* viii. 160 This Augæan labor is termed 'mucking out'. *Ibid.*, In fact, such an operation as 'mucking out' should, in a well-regulated stable, be an impossibility, for there never should be any 'muck' to take away. **1918** H. L. CARR in R. Peele *Mining Engineers' Handbk.* vii. 260 Mucking, or loading broken rock into hoisting conveyance, occupies 50% of shaft-sinking time. **1932** E. WILSON *Devil take Hindmost* xxi. 218 The men, who had been displaced by new mucking machines (mucking is cleaning out the tunnel after the blast), were to be transferred. **1935** *Mining Mag.* LII. 55/2 Two buckets were used in mucking, one of which was being filled while the other was being hoisted. **1957** *Times* 2 July (Agric. Suppl.) p. vi/3 In a modern fattening house we have also to make provision for minimum labour requirements in feeding, mucking out and weighing. **1960** *New Scientist* 7 Jan. 38/1 'Mucking out', as the removal of the rock fragments is termed, is thus simplified and speeded up. **1961** *Encycl. Brit* XV. 543/2 The method of mucking is reflected in the choice and design of the haulage system. **1973** K. GILES *File on Death* v. 147 Old Joe keeps the rain channel free on the duck-pond side... Old Joe does a thorough job at mucking-out.

ˈmucking, *ppl. a.* [f. MUCK *v.* + -ING[2].] Euphemistically (chiefly in written work) = FUCKING *ppl. a.* Cf. MUCK *v.* 6. Also as quasi-*adv.*

1929 R. ALDINGTON *Death of Hero* III. x. 375 What the muckin' hell are you doing, down there? **1933** H. G. WELLS *Bulpington of Blup* vi. 237 Don't be a mucking fool! *Ibid.* 241 Do you think we want to sit round telling ghost stories in this mucking hole? **1935** E. HEMINGWAY *Green Hills Afr.* xiii. 277 And if I ever hit you I'll break your mucking jaw. **1942** *Penguin New Writing* XV. 19 I'll miss the silly mucker... Poor old Bob. Went down with his mucking duffle. **1946** D. HAMSON *We fell among Greeks* v. 61 By Christ, it's that mucking dog. **1974** R. ADAMS *Shardik* xxxvi. 301 You'd better lend him a hand... We'll be 'alf the mucking night else. *Ibid.* xlv. 363 The first man peered in his turn. 'He mucking is, too,' he said. 'Aren't you?'

mucking-togs, perversion of MACKINTOSH.

1842 BARHAM *Ingol. Leg.* Ser. II. *Misadv. Margate*, A little 'gallows-looking chap',..With a 'carpet-swab' and 'muckingtogs', and a hat turn'd up with green.

muckiter, variant form of MUCKENDER.

muckle (ˈmʌk(ə)l). *Fisheries.* [? subst. use of *muckle* MICKLE *a.* (But cf. Du. *moker* heavy hammer.)] A heavy maul used for killing cod.

1897 KIPLING *Captains Courageous* viii. 153 There was no sound except..the flapping of the cod, and the whack of the muckles as the men stunned them.

muckle, dial. variant of MICKLE.

muckluck (ˈmʌklʌk). Also maclock, mucluc, muklek, mukluk. [Eskimo.] A high boot made of sealskin, canvas, etc. Also *attrib.*

1868 F. WHYMPER *Trav. Alaska* 136 Their boots vary in length, and in the material used for the sides, but all have soles of 'maclock', or sealskin, with the hair removed. **1901** *Pall Mall Mag.* Jan. 56 We stop on our way..and buy a pair of mucklucks or Esquimaux seal boots. They are water-tight, clumsy, evil-smelling, [etc.]. **1904** E. ROBINS *Magnetic North* I. 51 Nothing like muck-lucks with a wisp of straw inside for this country. *Ibid.* 176 Stretching out his feet, very comfortable in their straw-lined mucklucks. **1913** R. W. SERVICE *Rhymes of Rolling Stone* 118 Then it's down to chewing muclucs, to the water you can *eat*, To fish you bolt with nose held in your hand. **1924** *Chambers's Jrnl.* Jan. 41/1 He was habited..in anorak and skin breeches and mukluks. **1947** *Chicago Tribune* 11 Dec. 20/3 He was presented with..a pair of mukluk boots made to order for Paul Bunyan. **1962** W. NOYCE *To Unknown Mountain* v. 54 Unable to fit his vast feet into any boots but a pair of canvas mucklucks. **1972** *Daily Tel.* (Colour Suppl.) 8 Dec. 10/4 His legs were now swathed almost to the knee in the white sealskin mukluks that are standard issue in the [Canadian National Parks] Service. **1973** *Observer* 29 Apr. 34/8 His mukleks—the Eskimo moccasins with the hard, sealskin soles.

muckna (ˈmʌknə). *India* and *Sri Lanka.* [Hind., f. Skr. *matkuṇa* (among various senses) an elephant without tusks.] A male elephant without tusks, or one having only rudimentary tusks.

c **1780** R. LINDSAY in A. W. C. Lindsay *Lives of Lindsays* (1849) III. 194 The *muckna*, or elephant born without teeth, is thought the best. **1848** tr. *W. Hoffmeister's Trav. Ceylon & India* vi. 207 Of the herd of elephants,..the largest, whose height does not much exceed nine feet, is a '*Muckua*' [*sic*] *i.e.*, an elephant with short, straight tusks, which never grow. **1878** G. P. SANDERSON *Thirteen Yrs. among Wild Beasts India* vi. 66 Mucknas breed in the herds, and the peculiarity is not hereditary nor transmitted. **1886** G. YULE in Yule & Burnell *Hobson-Jobson* 454/1, I can distinctly call to mind 6 mucknas that I had..out of 30 or 40 elephants that passed through my hands. **1890** S. W. BAKER *Wild Beasts* I. vi. 226 A tiger sprang from the grass, and seized a large muckna (tuskless male) by the trunk.

mucko (ˈmʌkəʊ). *slang.* [? f. MUCK *sb.*[1] 3 + -O[2].] (See quots.)

1937 PARTRIDGE *Dict. Slang* 539/2 *Mucko*, orderly man: military. **1943** BAKER *Dict. Austral. Slang* (ed. 3) 52 *Mucko*, a sailor. (R.A.N. slang.) **1961** PARTRIDGE *Dict. Slang* Suppl. 1191/1 *Mucko*,..esp. a man detailed to serve food to troops aboard ship. **1964** *Punch* 6 May 659/1 No general had..had till then..a mucko-chummo relationship with his men.

ˈmuck-rake, *sb.* A rake for collecting 'muck'. Also *fig.*

The source of the figurative use is Bunyan's description of 'the Man with the Muck-rake', which was intended as an emblem of absorption in the pursuit of worldly gain; but in modern use it is often made to refer generally to a preference for what is comparatively worthless over that which is valuable, or to a depraved interest in what is morally 'unsavoury' or scandalous.

1684 BUNYAN *Pilgr.* II. (1900) 184 The Interpreter..has them first into a Room, where was a man..with a Muckrake in his hand. **1870** SPURGEON *Treas. Dav.* Ps. xxxix. 6 Those all-gathering muckrakes, who in due time are succeeded by all-scattering forks, which scatter riches as profusely as their sires gathered them promiscuously. **1872** SCHELE DE VERE *Americanisms* 618 *Muckrakes*,..persons who 'fish in troubled waters', from the idea of their raking up the muck to see what valuable waifs and strays they may find in it. **1895** *Sat. Rev.* 26 Jan. 125 The 'garbage of mythland' that Wagner gathered together with a 'muck rake'. **1906** *Sun* (N.Y.) 12 Apr. 8/3 On Saturday the President is to pronounce the formal address at the grave of the Man With the Muck Rake... The Muck Rakers worked merrily for a time in their own bright sunshine, and an unthinking populace applauded their performance. **1906** T. ROOSEVELT in *Cincinnati Enquirer* 15 Apr. 4/4 The men with the muck-rakes are often indispensable to the well-being of society; but only if they know when to stop raking the muck. *c* **1926** 'MIXER' *Transport Workers' Song Bk.* 18 Then you start your muckrake scandel [*sic*] And good men you dare defame. **1968** *Listener* 28 Nov. 726/2 Frank Harris deplored the dismal fate of Sophia in a Paris boarding-house,..regretting that Bennett..preferred to give her a muck rake instead of a soul.

ˈmuck-rake, *v.* **1.** [f. the sb.] *intr.* To rake refuse together. Usu. *fig.*

1879 F. HARRISON *Choice Bks.* iv. (1886) 82 Men, forgetful of the perennial poetry of the world, muckraking in a litter of fugitive refuse. **1954** *Amer. Scholar* XXIII. 421 McCarthy would enjoy himself if he could muckrake in our barnyard. **1970** *Guardian* 6 Mar. 8/3 They need no prompting to register complaints, muckrake among the police, petition for redress against indecencies.

2. *trans.* [Back-formation f. MUCK-RAKER.] To subject (powerful persons or institutions) to allegations of corruption or other illegal or scandalous behaviour; to discover and publish (such scandals); to examine (political districts) so as to determine the extent of corruption. *U.S.*

1910 *N.Y. Even. Post* 10 Dec. 8 Their knowledge of how it feels to be a muck-raked millionaire. **1913** J. LONDON *Let.* 26 June (1966) 388, I..muck-rake the powers that be from one end of the world to the other. **1931** *Time & Tide* 22 Aug. 991/2 Steffens was more successful with his experiments when he was muckraking America's big cities. **1943** M. FLAVIN *Journey in Dark* 193 The country has been muckraked from one end to the other. **1973** G. JENKINS *Cleft of Stars* vii. 86, I couldn't bring myself to muck-rake details of the guard's murder.

Hence **ˈmuck-raking, ˈmuck-raked** (*U.S.*), *ppl. adjs.*

1906 *Daily Rec. & Mail* 19 Dec. 5 Few popular institutions in America have escaped violent attacks by muck-racking reformers. **1910** Muck-raked [see MUCK-RAKE *v.*[2]]. **1951** M. MCLUHAN *Mech. Bride* (1967) 7/1 This exciting suspicion about personal plots and dastard motives everywhere led to the popularity of the muckraking press. **1972** J. PHILIPS *Vanishing Senator* (1973) II. i. 48 A muck-raking journalist who's gotten rich on other people's misfortunes.

ˈmuck-raker. [-ER[1].] A person who uses a muck-rake. In literary use only *fig.* † **a.** A miser. *Obs.* (Cf. MUCKWORM 2 a.) **b.** One who seeks out and publishes scandals, allegations of corruption, etc., about prominent people, esp. public officials. orig. *U.S.* **c.** A prurient inquirer into private morals; a writer of pornography.

The source of this figurative use in b is T. Roosevelt's speech (itself reminiscent of Bunyan) cited s.v. MUCK-RAKE *sb.*

1601 A. DENT *Plaine Mans Path-Way to Heaven* 102 We see the world is full of such pinch-pennies, that wil let nothing goe, except it bee wrung from them perforce, as a key out of Hercules hande. These gripple muck-rakers, had as leeue part with their bloud, as their goods. **1906** S. FORD *Shorty McCabe* xi. 233 That's the style you live in when.. you've got to be a top-notch grafter that the muck-rakers ain't jungled yet. **1914** R. BROOKE *Let.* Apr. (1968) 579 Damn it, we're not muck-rakers or German novelists. **1921** G. B. SHAW *Back to Methuselah* IV. I. 159, I leave them to the chumps and noodles, to the blockheads and the muckrakers. **1950** G. BARKER *True Confession* iii. 16 And the muckrakers I have known. **1973** *Guardian* 26 May 1/3 He is a sanctimonious creep..a muck raker. **1974** *Times* 9 May 21/4 In its origins the term 'muckraking' described a tradition of American journalism around the turn of the century which was committed to the exposure of trusts and monopolies and of corruption..; the Muck-rakers..were responsible for progressive reforms.

ˈmuck-raking, *vbl. sb.* [f. MUCK-RAKE *sb.* and *v.* + -ING[1].] The employing of a muck-rake, in fig. senses. Also *concr.*, the results of psychological or social inquiries.

1911 *N.Y. Even. Post* 25 Jan. 14 The same articles brought President Roosevelt to the defence of the Senate, and led him to apply the word 'muck-raking' to the literature of higher exposure. **1919** 'W. N. P. BARBELLION' *Jrnl. Disappointed Man* 211 Any eminently 'right-minded' *Times* or *Spectator* reader will ask: 'Who in Faith's name is interested in your introspective muck-rakings?' **1931** L. STEFFENS *Autobiogr.* I. xiii. 105 My first essay into muck-raking cost me nothing. **1959** [see DEMAGOGUERY]. **1973** 'M. INNES' *Appleby's Answer* xv. 128 Don't imagine I have the slightest wish to be in on your muck-raking.

mucksy (ˈmʌksɪ), *a. dial.* Also 7–8 (New England) muxy. [f. MUCK *sb.* + -SY (cf. *tricksy*, *clumsy*, *tipsy*).] 'Mucky', dirty, slushy.

1666–1715 in *1st Cent. Hist. Springfield* (1899) II. 218, 258, etc., The muxy [muxey, muxie] meddow. **1855** KINGSLEY *Westward Ho!* xiv, Mary runs in,..slips..her best gown over her dirt, and awaits the coming guests, who make a few long faces at the 'mucksy sort of a place'. **1869** BLACKMORE *Lorna D.* xlvi, When the ground appeared through the crust of bubbled snow..it was all so soaked and sodden, and, as we call it, 'mucksy', that [etc.].

ˈmuck-up. *slang.* [f. phr. *to muck up* (MUCK *v.* 4).] A mixing or confusing; a confused situation; a blunder, a fiasco, a mess, a muddle; *Austral.* (see quot. 1945).

1930 *Daily Express* 9 Sept. 8/7 The muck-up of society.. is almost complete. **1934** N. MARSH *Man lay Dead* xii. 217 Only Bathgate's prints on the electric switch and a muck-up of everybody's on the bannister. **1939** N. MONSARRAT *This is Schoolroom* I. i. 33 The muck-up the Labour people had left us in, in 1931. **1942** E. WAUGH *Put out More Flags* iii. 209 You seem to have made a pretty good muck-up. **1945** BAKER *Austral. Lang.* xv. 267 Frigg-up or muck-up, a confusion, a row or argument. **1957** W. CAMP *Prospects of Love* III. iii. 159 Mummy..making me do beastly shorthand in case I make a muck-up of the Latin. **1963** B. JAMES *Austral. Short Stories* 46 The 'muck-up' in 4B died down at this announcement. **1967** K. GILES *Death & Mr Prettyman* iii. 72 Old Jabeez made his usual muck-up. **1972** C. DRUMMOND *Death at Bar* ii. 60 The food was probably fry-ups or nasty little continental muck-ups.

ˈmuckworm. [f. MUCK *sb.*[1] + WORM.]

1. A worm or grub that lives in 'muck'; in U.S. *spec.* (see quot. 1842).

1685 HORNECK *Crucif. Jesus* xxiii. 795 Grovel in the dust like a muckworm. **1842** T. W. HARRIS *Insects Injur. Veget.* (1862) 31 *note*, There is a grub..which is frequently found under old manure-heaps, and is commonly called muckworm. It..is transformed to a dung-beetle called *Scarabæus relictus* by Mr. Say. **1856** BRIMLEY *Ess.* 230 A human soul metamorphosing itself into a muckworm.

2. *fig.* in various applications. **a.** A miserly person, 'money-grubber'.

1598 BP. HALL *Sat.* IV. vi, Each muckworm will be rich with lawless gain. **1681** W. ROBERTSON *Phraseol. Gen.* (1693) 393 He's a covetous fellow, a very muckworm. **1748** THOMSON *Cast. Indol.* I. l, Here you a muckworm of the town might see, At his dull desk. **1873** H. ROGERS *Orig. Bible* vi. 222 A mere muckworm, sordid and rapacious in the extreme.

b. A person of the lowest origin. ? *Obs.*

1695 CONGREVE *Love for L.* II. vii, 'Oons whose Son are you? how were you engendred, Muckworm?

c. One who is mentally or morally degraded. In quots. *appositive* and in *Comb.*

a **1635** RANDOLPH *Hey for Honesty* Wks. (1875) 377 Muckworm-minded men. **1751** SMOLLETT *Per. Pic.* xciii, As light-headed as some muck-worm philosophers.

d. A 'gutter-snipe' or street urchin.

1859 J. R. GREEN *Oxf. Stud.* ii. §4 (O.H.S.) 57 The little Miss..is forbidden to play with the muckworms of the neighborhood. **1891** HALL CAINE *Scapegoat* iii, The veriest muckworm in the market-place spat out at sight of him.

mucky (ˈmʌkɪ), *a.* Somewhat *colloq.* [f. MUCK *sb.*[1] + -Y.]

1. a. Dirty, filthy, muddy.

1538 BP. SHAXTON *Injunct.* A iv, Suche thinges as be set forth..vnder the name of holy relyques... Namely of stynkyng bootes, mucky combes, ragged rochettes [etc.]. **1662** J. CHANDLER tr. *Van Helmont's Oriat.* 151 The residue of the Odour..doth draw a waterish filthiness from the said putrefaction by continuance, and becomes rank, or muckie. **1799** G. SMITH *Laboratory* II. 266 The largest fish lie in the eddies and deep mucky waters. **1894** BLACKMORE *Perlycross* 354 The mucky and murky lane.

b. Of the weather: 'Dirty'; foul; 'thick'. *dial.*

1804 C. B. BROWN tr. *Volney's View Soil U.S.* 143 *note*, A mucky breeze from the south. **1903** *Illustr. Lond. News* 7 Nov. 685/3 Till the mucky weather's done.

† **c.** *fig.* Applied to money, as 'filthy lucre'; also to a miserly person.

1549 LATIMER *2nd Serm. bef. Edw. VI* (Arb.) 54 We be mynded to prefer oure muckye monie..before the ioyse of heauen. **1590** SPENSER *F.Q.* III. ix. 4 His minde is set on mucky pelfe. **1652** BENLOWES *Theoph.* x. lxxxviii, This old muckie wretched elf, Who turns..all that he scrapes, to pelf.

d. More widely: grimy, grubby, horrid.

1872 H. T. DUNN *Let.* 10 Sept. in G. Pedrick *Life with Rossetti* (1964) xiii. 121 'The Beatrice' had been got out of the mucky state in which it was, & now looks a very good copy. **1942** *Tee Emm* (Air Ministry) II. 88 Lack of power through mucky plugs..will immediately be seen on the Rev. counter. **1959** I. & P. OPIE *Lore & Lang. Schoolch.* ix. 161 Juvenile repugnance continues to be expressed by the old standbys..mouldy, mucky, nasty, no fair, no good, orrid (usual spelling).

2. Consisting of or resembling muck.

1570 LEVINS *Manip.* 99/3 Muckye, *fimosus.* **1590** SPENSER *F.Q.* II. vii. 15 But mucky filth his braunching armes annoyes, And with uncomely weedes the gentle wave accloyes. **1840** C. F. HOFFMAN *Greyslaer* I. I. v. 61 He had laid the logs right down on a piece of deep, mucky soil, made up of old roots, rotten leaves, [etc.]. **1861** *Amer. Cycl.* XIII. 75/1 If the peat is of mucky consistence..the practice is to shovel it from its bed. **1874** *Rep. Vermont Board Agric.* II. 548, I have about five acres of mucky meadow that was mostly covered with alders.

mucky ('mʌkɪ), *v. dial.* [f. MUCKY *a.*] *trans.* To make dirty.

1847 C. BRONTË *J. Eyre* xxix, She even brought me a clean towel to spread over my dress, 'lest', as she said, 'I should mucky it'.

'mucky-muck. *N. Amer. slang.* [redupl. MUCKY *a.*, after MUCK-A-MUCK.] = MUCK-A-MUCK 2. Also *attrib.*

1934 H. MILLER *Tropic of Cancer* 194 One of the big mucky-mucks from the other side of the water had decided to make economies. **1941** E. P. O'DONNELL *Great Big Doorstep* iv. 61 The Governor and the big mucky-mucks from New York with the oil company, was passing close to the levee. **1968** 'E. MCBAIN' *Fuzz* iv. 60 That big mucky-muck got shot. *Ibid.* 61 All them big mucky-muck doctors. **1968** *Globe & Mail* (Toronto) 13 Feb. 27/1 Orpen was always let out at the members' enclosure, but he never sat with the mucky-mucks.

mucluc, var. MUCKLUCK.

muco- ('mju:kəʊ), used as a comb. form of MUCUS, employed chiefly *Phys.* and *Path.*, to indicate the presence of mucous matter, and in *Biochem.* (with broader meaning). **muco-'albumen**, a mucous albumen found in bile; hence **muco-al'buminous** *a.*, containing muco-albumen. **muco-'carneous** *a.* composed of mucus and flesh. **muco-'crepitant** *a.*, (of a sound heard in auscultation) partly mucous and partly crepitant. **muco-cu'taneous** *a.*, having relation to the mucous membrane and the external skin. **muco-'dermal** *a.* = prec. **muco-ex'tractive** *a.*, derived from mucus. **muco-ge'latinous** *a.*, containing or resembling mucus and gelatin. **muco'lytic** *a.*, able to disperse or decompose mucus or mucopolysaccharides. **muco-'membranous** *a.*, of or pertaining to the mucous membrane. **muco'peptide** *Biochem.* = MUREIN. **muco-'peptone**, a substance formed by the gastric digestion of mucus associated with certain albuminous bodies. **mucoperi'osteum** *Anat.*, a periosteum closely associated with a mucous membrane. **muco'protein** *Biochem.*, any of a group of compounds (some of which occur in mucus and other body fluids) whose molecules consist of protein or polypeptides in combination with mucopolysaccharides. **muco-'puriform** *a.*, consisting of pus and mucus. **muco-'purulent** *a.*, of the nature of pus and mucus mingled; characterized by the presence of pus and mucus. **'muco-'pus**, pus with which mucus is combined. **muco-'saccharine** *a.*, of a non-crystallizable sugary character. **muco-'salivary** *a.*, resembling or containing mucus and saliva. **muco-san'guineous** *a.*, having blood mixed with mucus. **muco-'serous** *a.*, containing serum mixed with mucus. **,mucovisci'dosis** *Path.* [VISCID *a.* + -OSIS], a congenital metabolic disorder, usually causing early death, in which exocrine glands (such as the pancreas) secrete very viscid mucus, which accumulates and blocks the passageways of the body; also called *cystic fibrosis* (*of the pancreas*), *fibrocystic disease* (*of the pancreas*).

1835–6 *Todd's Cycl. Anat.* I. 376/1 *Muco-albumen [found in gall-stones]. **1857** BULLOCK *Cazeaux' Midwif.* 178 *Muco-albuminous fluid. **1876** DUNGLISON *Med. Lex.*, *Myxosarcoma..Myxomatous* or *Mucocarneous *Sarcoma.* **1853** MARKHAM *Skoda's Auscult.* 286 A peculiar sharp *muco-crepitant râle. **1898** *Allbutt's Syst. Med.* V. 217 The *muco-cutaneous margin of the anus. **1854** OWEN *Skel. & Teeth* in *Orr's Circ. Sci., Org. Nat.* I. 179 The bones of the *muco-dermal system. **1822–34** *Good's Study Med.* (ed. 4) I. 548 Dr. Bostock has since discovered in the serosity..a distinct substance..which Dr. Marcet has called *muco-extractive matter. *Ibid.* 203 Each evacuation consisted merely of two or three table-spoonfuls of *muco-gelatinous matter. **1939** *Nature* 9 Dec. 977/2 (*heading*) A *mucolytic enzyme in testis extracts. **1940** [see HYALURONIDASE]. **1953** *Jrnl. Soc. Leather Trades' Chemists* XXXVII. 80 It should be possible to produce pelt by removing the mucoids with mucolytic enzymes. **1971** *S. Afr. Med. Jrnl.* XLV. 948/1 In patients with acute obstructive airway disease pancreatic dornase and acetyl-L-cysteine (Airbron) showed excellent mucolytic activity. **1870** tr. *Stricker's Man. Histol.* v. 497 (N. Syd. Soc.) Three anatomical different parts can be distinguished in it [*sc.* the mouth], a cutaneous, a transitional and a *muco-membranous portion. **1959** MANDELSTAM & ROGERS in *Biochem. Jrnl.* LXXII. 655/1 This class of substances from cell walls, which will be referred to as *mucopeptides, constitutes a high proportion of the hot trichloroacetic acid-insoluble material from bacteria. **1962** *Jrnl. Exper. Med.* CXV. 60 A rigid mucopeptide structure, composed of *N*-acetylglucosamine, *N*-acetylmuramic acid, and alanine, lysine, glutamic acid, and glycine, has been identified in the cell wall of each of these three groups of streptococci. **1972** Mucopeptide [see MUREIN]. **1875** tr. *von Ziemssen's Cycl. Med.* X. 368 *Muco-peptone. **1903** DORLAND *Med. Dict.* (ed. 3) 419/1 *Mucoperiosteum. **1906** *Practitioner* Nov. 712 Should the carious tooth be in the upper jaw, the pus may travel down alongside of the fang of the tooth, around the free border of the bone, make its way through the muco-periosteum on the outer side, and then point as a gumboil. **1974** W. J. BANKS *Histol.* xix. 205/3 Because of the intimate relationship of the mucosa to the underlying bone, these structures are referred to collectively as a mucoperiosteum. **1925** *Jrnl. Biol. Chem.* LXV. 700 The carbohydrate radicle isolated from the *mucoproteins of the mucus of *Helix aspersa* and *Helix pomatia* belongs to the group of mucoitin sulfuric acid. **1962** D. G. COGAN in A. Pirie *Lens Metabolism Rel. Cataract* 291 The capsule surrounding the lens..stains heavily with periodic acid Schiff (indicating more neutral mucoprotein than most tissues). **1968** Mucoprotein [see *glycoprotein* s.v. GLYCO-]. **1971** *S. Afr. Med. Jrnl.* XLV. 948/1 Normal human bronchial mucus is a semiviscid substance composed almost entirely of mucoprotein and mucopolysaccharide fibres. **1859** SEMPLE *Diphtheria* 68 The *muco-puriform secretion. **1843** R. J. GRAVES *Syst. Clin. Med.* xxi. 251 Copious *muco-purulent expectoration. **1873** RALFE *Phys. Chem.* 168 In ichorous, *muco-, or seropus, the solids are diminished. **1835–6** *Todd's Cycl. Anat.* I. 132/2 Mere water holding..a *muco-saccharine matter. **1884** *Kirke's Handbk. Physiol.* (ed. 11) 282 In the *muco-salivary or mixed glands. **1898** P. MANSON *Trop. Diseases* xviii. 289 The passage of..*muco-sanguineous stools. **1898** *Allbutt's Syst. Med.* V. 351 The *muco-serous (or albuminous) expectoration. **1945** S. FARBER in *Jrnl. Michigan State Med. Soc.* XLIV. 592/2 Until the etiological factors are defined and for the purposes of present convenience only a purely descriptive term suggested by the physical character of the material produced by the mucous glands in this disease may be employed—**muco-viscidosis.* **1949** *New Eng. Jrnl. Med.* 4 Aug. 185 (*heading*) Aureomycin therapy in the pulmonary involvement of pancreatic fibrosis (mucoviscidosis). **1966** WRIGHT & SYMMERS *Systemic Path.* I. xxiii. 692/1 Farber has suggested that the disease [*sc.* fibrocystic disease of the pancreas] is a manifestation of a generalized abnormality of mucus secretion, for which he proposed the term 'mucoviscidosis'. **1973** L. C. CAREY *Pancreas* ix. 181/2 In mucoviscidosis, steatorrhea is usually present.

mucocele ('mju:kəʊsi:l). *Path.* [f. MUCO- + Gr. κήλη tumour.] A mucous dilatation (*a*) of the lachrymal gland; (*b*) of the vermiform appendix.

1819 W. MCKENZIE *Ess. Dis. Excreting Parts of Lachrymal Organs* Pref. 13 The term mucocele, by which the author has ventured to designate an important disease. **1870** *Holmes' Syst. Surg.* (ed. 2) III. 223 The tears passing into the sac will accumulate there, and together with the pent-up mucus, form a swelling termed mucocele. **1897** *Allbutt's Syst. Med.* III. 888 This cystic dilatation [of the appendix vermiformis] has been termed a 'mucocele' by Péré.

mucoduct ('mju:kəʊdʌkt). *Anat.* [f. MUCO- + DUCT *sb.* Cf. MUCIDUCT.] In fishes: A muciferous duct, mucous canal.

1875 C. C. BLAKE *Zool.* 189 In many other fishes the cranial bones emit processes from their surfaces which serve as canals for the mucoducts.

mucoid ('mju:kɔɪd), *sb. Biochem.* [a. G. *mucoid*, f. *mucin* MUCIN + *-oid* -OID.] A mucin-like substance; esp. = *mucoprotein* s.v. MUCO-.

1900 GIES & CUTTER in *Amer. Jrnl. Physiol.* III. p. vi, We believe that continued investigation will show that the differences among the mucins, mucoids, and chondroproteids are not as great as their varying physical properties and behavior have suggested. **1901** *Ibid.* VI. 155 (*heading*) The composition of tendon mucoid. *Ibid.*, Following Cohnheim's suggestion..we use the term 'mucoid', instead of the previously accepted 'mucin', to designate this substance. We agree with Cohnheim that..the term 'mucin' may be best applied to the glucoproteids elaborated by true secretory cells, and the term 'mucoid' to similar substances in the tissues. **1945** *Adv. Protein Chem.* II. 250 As mucoids we define substances which contain a mucopolysaccharide in firm chemical union with a peptide, where the hexosamine content is greater than 4 per cent. **1953** [see *mucolytic* adj. s.v. MUCO-]. **1964** A. WHITE et al. *Princ. Biochem.* (ed. 3) viii. 122 The protein components of mucoids or mucoproteins are combined with large amounts (more than 4 per cent) of carbohydrate, measured as hexosamine. **1967** D. A. L. DAVIES in D. M. Weir *Handbk. Exper. Immunol.* xi. 405 Ovarian cysts are a rich source of mucoids and a classical source of blood-group mucopolysaccharides. **1974** *Nature* 20 Dec. 711/2 Cervical mucus is a heterogeneous secretion, the most important constituent of which is a hydrogel made of glycoproteic mucoids.

mucoid ('mju:kɔɪd), *a.* [f. MUC-US + -OID.] Resembling mucus. ***mucoid degeneration***: see quot. 1866.

1849 *Rep. & Papers Botany* (Ray Soc.) 312 Identity of the Mucoid and Filamentous Confervæ. By Dr. Schaffner. **1866** A. FLINT *Princ. Med.* (1880) 57 Mucoid degeneration consists in the transformation of the albuminous constituents of cells or of intercellular substance into mucin. **1878** TIDY *Handbk. Mod. Chem.* 585 Lævulose (..Mucoid Sugar). **1885** *Lancet* 26 Sept. 562 The cough..was accompanied with frothy mucoid expectoration.

Hence **mu'coidal** *a.* in the same sense.

1849 H. MILLER *Footpr. Creat.* viii. (1874) 147 Those thinner parts of the fin that are traversed by the caudal rays, —wholly mucoidal, as shown by this test.

mucoitin (mju:'kəʊɪtɪn). *Biochem.* [f. MUC(IN + *-oitin*, after CHONDROITIN.] A supposed mucopolysaccharide, now generally considered to be a mixture, occurring in combination with sulphuric acid in the mucin of pigs' stomachs, the cornea, and elsewhere. So ***mucoitinsulphuric acid.***

1916 LEVENE & LÓPEZ-SUÁREZ in *Jrnl. Biol. Chem.* XXV. 513 Further work on mucoitin sulfuric acid (as we propose to name this substance) is now in progress. **1925** P. A. LEVENE *Hexosamines* II. iii. 85 A considerable part of the sulphuric acid radicle had been removed in the process of preparation, so that it was possible to determine the properties of mucoitin and of mucoitin sulphuric acid in the same sample. **1925** [see CHONDROITIN]. **1964** BRIMACOMBE & WEBBER *Mucopolysaccharides* vi. 142 It seems likely that the material originally designated as mucoitin sulphate contained hyaluronic acid admixed with sulphated mucopolysaccharides containing 2-amino-2-deoxy-D-glucose residues. **1967** *Chem. Abstr.* LXVI. 9649/1 The chondroitinsulfuric acid and mucoitinsulfuric acid contents were higher in the umbilical cord and myxoid chondroma.

mucopolysaccharide (,mju:kəʊpɒlɪ'sækəraɪd). *Biochem.* [f. MUCO- + POLYSACCHARIDE.] Any of a group of polysaccharides whose molecules contain amino-sugar residues (*spec.* hexosamine residues) and are often found in complexes with protein molecules, and which include as important examples heparin, hyaluronic acid, keratosulphate, and the blood-group substances.

1938 K. MEYER in *Cold Spring Harbor Symp. Quant. Biol.* VI. 91/1 The mucopolysaccharides of our terminology were formerly included as mucins and as mucoids in the group of conjugated proteins. They occur in nature either as free polysaccharides or as protein salts. **1947** *Physiol. Rev.* XXVII. 335 Hyaluronic acid is a mucopolysaccharide acid which in animal tissues seems to bind water in interstitial spaces. It further holds cells together in a jelly-like matrix and serves as a lubricant and shock-absorber in joints. **1963** R. W. JEANLOZ in Florkin & Stotz *Comprehensive Biochem.* V. vii. 262 Two groups of substances, which in the past had been described under the name of mucopolysaccharide, namely the glycoproteins and the glycolipids, will be discussed in other chapters. **1967** [see MUCOID *sb.*]. **1971** J. Z. YOUNG *Introd. Study Man* xl. 584 There is polymorphic variation in certain mucopolysaccharide constituents of the red cells of the blood.

‖**mucor** ('mju:kɔ:(r)). [L. *mūcor*, f. *mūcēre* to be mouldy.]

†**1.** Mouldiness, mustiness; mould.

1656 BLOUNT *Glossogr.*, *Mucor*, hoariness, filthiness. **1847–54** in WEBSTER; and in later Dicts.

2. *Bot.* The name of a genus of fungi, originally including all the mould-plants, but now somewhat narrowed. Hence, a plant of this genus or of the order *Mucorini*, of which *Mucor* is the type.

[**1769** ELLIS in *Phil. Trans.* LIX. 139 *note*, This species of *Mucor* sends forth a mass of transparent filamentous roots.] **1818** COLEBROOKE *Import. Colonial Corn* 96 Mouldiness is prevented, since the seeds of mucor are shut out. **1836** *Penny Cycl.* V. 244/1 There are plants that are born and die in a day, such as the race of mucors. **1896** *Allbutt's Syst. Med.* III. 505 Some species of mucor are able to act as true alcoholic ferments.

attrib. **1875** HUXLEY & MARTIN *Elem. Biol.* v. (1877) 40 A crop of erect aërial mucor-hyphæ. **1882** VINES tr. *Sachs' Bot.* 266 The so-called *Mucor*-yeast.

Hence **muco'raceous**, **'mucorine**, **-'rinious**, **-'rinous** *adjs.*, belonging to the order *Mucorini* (also called *Mucoraceæ*) of fungi; **mu'corioid** *a.* [see -OID], resembling a mucor.

1862 COOKE *Brit. Fungi* 103 Mucoraceous Fungi. **1865** BERKELEY in *Jrnl. Linn. Soc., Bot.* VIII. 141 Threads which seemed to give rise to the Mucorioid fruit. **1866** *Treas. Bot.* 761/2 *Mucor*, the typical genus of the mucorinous Moulds. **1874** *Q. Jrnl. Microscop. Sci.* XIV. 66 A Mucorinious fungus. **1880** CUNNINGHAM *ibid.* XX. 56 Reproductive bodies occurring in mucorine fungi.

mucormycosis (,mju:kɔ:maɪ'kəʊsɪs). *Path.* Pl. **-mycoses.** [f. MUCOR + MYCOSIS.] = PHYCOMYCOSIS.

1918 STEDMAN *Med. Dict.* (ed. 5) 621/2 *Mucormycosis*, a mycosis caused by a fungus or mould of the family *Mucoraceæ*, one of the slime fungi. **1943** *Bull. Johns Hopkins Hosp.* LXXIII. 405 (*heading*) Mucormycosis of the central nervous system. *Ibid.*, These mucormycoses of animals..may be transferred to humans. **1957** *Jrnl. Amer. Med. Assoc.* 9 Mar. 806/2 Rhizopus, rather than Mucor, appears to be the usual cause of human mucormycosis. **1965** WILSON & PLUNKETT *Fungous Dis. Man* xv. 190 Although the term 'mucormycosis' has long been used synonymously with the newer name 'phycomycosis', species of the genus *Mucor* are not often involved. **1974** PASSMORE & ROBSON *Compan. Med. Stud.* III. I. xii. 94/1 Cerebral mucormycosis presents with drowsiness or stupor.

mucorrhœa (mju:kə'ri:ə). [f. MUCO- + Gr. ῥοία flux, after *gonorrhœa*.] A mucous discharge.

1898 *Allbutt's Syst. Med.* V. 20 The paroxysms of dyspnœa and mucorrhœa may be of isolated occurrence.

‖**mucosa** (mju:'kəʊsə). *Phys.* [mod.L. (*membrāna*) *mūcōsa*, fem. of L. *mūcōsus* MUCOUS *a.*] 'The corium of a mucous membrane' (*Syd. Soc. Lex.*).

1880 M. MACKENZIE *Dis. Throat & Nose* I. 351 Nowhere are there epithelial protrusions into the mucosa. **1897** *Trans. Amer. Pediatric Soc.* IX. 40 The whole of the skin and visible mucosa were of a dark blue color. **1905** H. D. ROLLESTON *Dis. Liver* 272 The mucosa of the intestines.

Hence **mu'cosal** *a.*, pertaining to the mucosa.

1899 *Allbutt's Syst. Med.* VI. 455 These terms [*i.e.* mucoid or dermoid cyst]..might with advantage be replaced by the name mucosal cysts.

mucose ('mju:kəʊs), *a.* [ad. L. *mūcōs-us*: see MUCOUS *a.* and -OSE.] Slimy; covered with mucus.

1731 BAILEY, *Mucose*, full of snot, snotty. **1856–8** W. CLARK *Van der Hoeven's Zool.* II. 90 Body..covered with small scales, mucose. **1866** in *Treas. Bot.* 761/2.

mucosity (mjuːˈkɒsɪtɪ). [ad. F. *mucosité*, ad. mod.L. **mūcōsitāt-em*, f. *mūcōs-us* MUCOUS *a.*]

1. Mucousness, sliminess; a mucous covering.

1684 tr. *Bonet's Merc. Compit.* xvi. 574 This potion.. takes away.. all Mucosities of the Throat. **1752** WATSON in *Phil. Trans.* XLVII. 461 He.. observ'd, that the extremities of the madrepora were soft, and cover'd with a mucosity. **1876** *Beneden's Anim. Parasites* iv. 68 There are mucosities which are incessantly renewed.

2. A fluid containing or resembling mucus.

1833–55 DUNGLISON *Med. Lex.*, *Mucosity*, a fluid, which resembles mucus, or contains a certain quantity of it.

mucoso- (mjuːˈkəʊsəʊ), used [after Fr.] as a comb. form of L. *mūcōsus* mucous in various adjs. with the sense 'partly mucous and partly (something else)'. **muˈcoso-calˈcareous** *a.*, consisting of mucus and lime. **muˈcoso-ˈgranular** *a.*, consisting of granulated mucus. **muˈcoso-ˈpurulent** *a.* = *muco-purulent* (see MUCO-). **muˈcoso-ˈsaccharine** *a.*, having the properties of mucus and sugar.

1840 *Penny Cycl.* XVI. 363/1 Many naturalists appear to be satisfied that these *mucoso-calcareous bodies.. are not of animal origin. **1848** LINDLEY *Introd. Bot.* I. i. §8 (ed. 4) I. 147 [tr. Mohl in *Ann. des Sci.* Ser. II. XIII. 223] The *mucosogranular mass continually increases in the interior wall of these cells. **1856** MAYNE *Expos. Lex.*, *Muco-Purulent*, **Mucoso-Purulent*. **1847–54** WEBSTER, **Mucoso-saccharine*, partaking of the qualities of mucilage and sugar. **1891** *Syd. Soc. Lex.*, *Mucoso-saccharine*.

mucous (ˈmjuːkəs), *a.* [ad. L. *mūcōsus*, f. *mūc-us* MUCUS; see -OUS. Cf. F. *muqueux*, Sp., Pg. *mucoso*, *mocoso*, It. *mucoso*.]

1. Containing, consisting of, or resembling mucus. In early quots. with wider sense: Slimy.

1646 SIR T. BROWNE *Pseud. Ep.* III. xxi. 158 It hath in the tongue a spongy and mucous extremity, whereby.. it inviscates.. insects. **1774** GOLDSM. *Nat. Hist.* (1776) VIII. 194 We shall perceive its whole surface.. covered with a mucous fluid. **1851** WOODWARD *Mollusca* I. 50 The eggs.. of the fresh-water species are soft, mucous, and transparent. **1871** T. R. JONES *Anim. Kingd.* §2290 (ed. 4) 834 The lingual mucous lining seems to be perfectly adapted to gustation. **1878** TIDY *Handbk. Mod. Chem.* 485 The Mucous or Viscous Fermentation, *i.e.* a fermentation characterized by the formation of gummy matters.

2. Characterized by the presence of mucus. Also, in Auscultation, ***mucous râle***, a sound indicating a mucous condition of the lung.

1825 GOOD *Study Med.* (ed. 2) III. 381 Mucous piles. **1834** J. FORBES *Laennec's Dis. Chest* (ed. 4) 91 A chronic mucous catarrh. **1897** *Trans. Amer. Pediatric Soc.* IX. 170 Large number of coarse mucous râles made the first probable.

3. *Bot.* Covered with a viscous secretion or with a coat readily soluble in water.

1839 LINDLEY *Introd. Bot.* III. Gloss. (ed. 3) 471 Mucous or slimy; covered with a slimy secretion. **1870** HOOKER *Stud. Flora* 350 Stratiotes aloides.. Seeds with a mucous coat. **1882–4** COOKE *Brit. Fresh-w. Algæ* I. 179 *Hormiscia zonata* .. More or less bright green, mucous.

4. Special collocations. **mucous canal** *Ichthyology*, one of the canals by which mucus is excreted along the lateral line. **mucous corpuscle**, one of numerous transparent corpuscles, with a cell-wall, a nucleus, and a number of minute moving molecules in the mucous liquid of the mouth. **mucous exudation**, the exudation of mucus mixed with inflammatory matter, from the surface of an inflamed mucous membrane. **mucous gland**, any gland connected with a mucous surface. **mucous layer** = MESOBLAST. **mucous ligament**, a ligament traversing the synovial cavity of the knee. **mucous membrane**, the internal prolongation of the skin, having the surface covered with mucus. **mucous tissue**, gelatinous connective tissue.

1875 HUXLEY in *Encycl. Brit.* I. 762/1 Symmetrically disposed grooves, the so-called '*mucous canals'. **1856** GRIFFITH & HENFREY *Micrgr. Dict.* 443 *Mucous corpuscles. **1876** tr. *Wagner's Gen. Pathol.* 257 *Mucous exudation is sometimes not to be distinguished from normal mucus. **1727–41** CHAMBERS *Cycl.* s.v., The third *mucous gland. **1872** T. BRYANT *Pract. Surg.* (1876) I. 492 The Mucous Glands of the Lip. **1846** CARPENTER *Princ. Hum. Physiol.* (ed. 3) Index, *Mucous layer of germinal membrane. **1891** *Syd. Soc. Lex.* s.v., *Mucous ligament of knee. **1812** J. JACKSON in *Trans. Amer. Pediatric Soc.* (1897) IX. 12 The *mucous membrane of the stomach. **1881** MIVART *Cat* 21 Inside the lips and mouth it becomes soft and moist, and is termed mucous membrane. **1845** *Encycl. Metrop.* VII. 217 The term '*mucous tissue or mucous membrane', commonly applied by anatomists to the internal lining of all the canals and cavities. **1882** *Quain's Anat.* (ed. 9) II. 69 Connective tissue of this nature is known as jellylike or mucous tissue.

Hence †ˈ**mucousness** = MUCOSITY.

1727 BAILEY vol. II, *Mucousness*, snottiness. **1755** JOHNSON, *Mucousness*,.. slime; viscosity.

‖**mucro** (ˈmjuːkrəʊ). *Zool.* and *Bot.* Pl. **mucrones** (mjuːˈkrəʊniːz), **mucros.** [L. *mūcro* point.] A pointed part or organ; esp. **a.** *Ent.* a short, stout, sharp-pointed process; **b.** *Bot.* a sharp terminal point; **c.** *Conch.* the apex of a shell.

1646 SIR T. BROWNE *Pseud. Ep.* IV. ii. 181 The Mucro or point thereof [i.e. of the heart] inclineth unto the left. **1744** J. WILSON *Synopsis of Plants*, *Mucro*, a sharp Point. **1816** KIRBY & SP. *Entomol.* xxiii. (1818) II. 317 The.. elastic beetles.. perform this motion by means of a pectoral process or mucro. **1826** *Ibid.* xxxi. III. 253 The head is armed with two mucros or conical eminences. **1833** HOOKER *Brit. Flora* II. I. 65 *Bryum affine*.. lid conical with a mucro. **1885** MOSELEY in *Q. Jrnl. Microsc. Sci.* XXV. 42 The apices (or mucrones) of the shells.

mucronate (ˈmjuːkrəneɪt), *a.* [ad. L. *mūcrōnāt-us*, f. *mūcrōn-em* MUCRO: see -ATE². Cf. F. *mucroné*.] Terminating in a point; esp. *Bot.* abruptly terminated by a hard short point.

1776 J. LEE *Introd. Bot.* Explan. Terms 384 *Mucronatum*, mucronate, terminating in a small Prickle. **1777** ROBSON *Brit. Flora*, Mucronate leaves. **1826** KIRBY & SP. *Entomol.* xxxvi. III. 708 The podex is sometimes.. mucronate. **1882–4** COOKE *Brit. Freshw. Algæ* I. 32 *Polyedrium enorme*.. sometimes repeatedly bilobed, with the lobes mucronate. *Comb.* **1821** W. P. C. BARTON *Flora N. Amer.* I. 105 Leaves oblong, acuminate; mucronate-serrulate, smooth. **1847** W. E. STEELE *Field Bot.* 57 Leaves.. very large, green on both sides, almost smooth, mucronate-dentate.

mucronated (ˈmjuːkrəʊneɪtɪd), *a.* [formed as prec. + -ED¹.] = prec.

1657 TOMLINSON *Renou's Disp.* 258 Mechoacans leaves are.. mucronated onely on one side. **1695** WOODWARD *Nat. Hist. Earth* (1723) 198 The.. Stones.. [are] mucronated or terminating in a Point. **1819** SAMOUELLE *Entomol. Compend.* 114 Last joint mucronated. **1876** HARLEY *Mat. Med.* (ed. 6) 417 Leaves.. with a few coarse mucronated teeth on each side.

Hence ˈ**mucronately** *adv.*, in a mucronate manner (Worcester 1860.) **mucroˈnation**, the state or quality of being mucronate; also, a mucronate process (*Funk's Stand. Dict.* 1895).

mucroniform (mjuːˈkrɒnɪfɔːm). [f. L. *mūcrōn-em* MUCRO + -(I)FORM.] Shaped like a mucro (Webster *Suppl.* 1902).

mucronulate (mjuːˈkrɒnjʊlət), *a.* [ad. mod.L. *mūcrōnulāt-us*, f. *mūcrōnula* MUCRONULE: see -ATE.] Having a small sharp point.

1829 LOUDON *Encycl. Plants* 87 Leaves whorled.. entire mucronulate. **1845** LINDLEY *Sch. Bot.* iv. (1858) 36.

So **muˈcronulated, mucroˈnulatous** *adjs.*

1806 GALPINE *Brit. Bot.* 6 Leaf eliptic-lanceolate, obtuse, macronulated. **1856** MAYNE *Expos. Lex.*, *Mucronulatus*, having a little point, as the carpels of the *Sida mucronulata*: mucronulatous. **1882** OGILVIE, *Mucronulatous*.

ˈ**mucronule.** [a. mod.L. *mūcrōnula*, f. L. *mūcrōn-* MUCRO.] A small mucro (*Cent. Dict.* 1890).

mucuddum, variant of MOKADDAM.

†ˈ**muculency.** *Obs.* [f. MUCULENT: see -ENCY.] 'Snottiness' (Bailey 1721).

muculent (ˈmjuːkjʊlənt), *a.* Also 7 mucculent. [ad. L. *mūculent-us*, f. *mūcus* MUCUS: see -ULENT.] Slimy; mucous.

1656 BLOUNT *Glossogr.*, *Mucculent* or *Muculent*, full of snot or snivel. **1721** in BAILEY. **1755** in JOHNSON. **1822–34** *Good's Study Med.* (ed. 4) IV. 236 A watery or whey-like sanies, or a muculent pus. **1833–55** DUNGLISON *Med. Lex.*

mucuna (mjuːˈkjuːnə). [a. mod.L. *Mucuna*, the generic name of the plant from which cowage is obtained; orig. a Tupi word.] = COWAGE.

1874 GARROD & BAXTER *Mat. Med.* (1880) 234 The watery or alcoholic solutions of mucuna.

mucus (ˈmjuːkəs). [a. L. *mūcus*, also *muccus*, mucus of the nose, cogn. w. Gr. *μύσσεσθαι* (:—**muky-*) to blow the nose, *μυκτήρ* nose, nostril; the root appears also (with consonant change due to the nasal infix) in L. *ē-mungĕre* to blow the nose.]

1. A viscid or slimy substance not miscible with water, secreted by the mucous membrane of animals.

1661 LOVELL *Hist. Anim. & Min.* 285 Salivous mucus which they vomit out when pricked, is emplastick. **1739** 'R. BULL' tr. *Dedekindus' Grobianus* 209 When to the Mouths of some these Humours rise, Long in their Mouths the plenteous Mucus lies. **1805** BOSTOCK in *Nicholson's Jrnl.* XI. 251 Animal mucus or mucilage enters largely into the constitution of many parts of the body. **1881** MIVART *Cat* 169 A fluid, named mucus, is almost universally present where mucous membrane exists.

2. *Bot.* A gummy or glutinous substance soluble in water, found in all plants.

1839 LINDLEY *Introd. Bot.* I. i. (ed. 3) 2 Meyen admits the fact of the presence of this intercellular mucus [*sc.* in plants]. *Ibid.* ii. 50 External to the epidermis is a thin homogeneous membrane, formed of organic mucus. **1875** DARWIN *Insectiv. Pl.* ix. 209 Some of these leaves secreted much mucus.

3. A viscid substance exuded by certain animals, esp. the slime of fishes.

1835–6 [see *mucus-clad* in 4]. **1855** W. S. DALLAS *Syst. Nat. Hist.* II. 21 *Myxine glutinosa*.. receives its specific name.. from the immense quantity of mucus which it can give off from its skin. **1880** GÜNTHER *Fishes* 49 In many fishes.. the ducts of this muciferous system are.. filled with mucus.

4. *attrib.* and *Comb.*, as ***mucus corpuscle***, ***duct***; ***mucus-clad***, ***-like***, ***-producing*** adjs.

1835–6 *Todd's Cycl. Anat.* I. 529/1 *Mucus-clad fishes. **1846** G. E. DAY tr. *Simon's Anim. Chem.* II. 87 Thin watery pus, rather larger than the *mucus-corpuscles. **1854** OWEN *Skel. & Teeth* in *Orr's Circ. Sci.*, *Org. Nat.* I. 163 In *Mucus-ducts. **1845** *Encycl. Metrop.* VII. 220/2 A greyish-white *mucus-like matter. **1879** FOSTER *Text Bk. Physiol.* (ed. 3) 257 *Mucus-producing cells.

mud (mʌd), *sb.*¹ Forms: 4 mode, 4–6 mudde, 5 moode, 6 moude, mude, mwde, 7 mudd, 5– mud. [ME. *mode*, *mudde*, cogn. w. MLG., LG. *mudde* fem., LG. also *mod*, *mōde*, *mūde* mud, Du. *modden* to dabble in mud (? also with Du. *modde* slut), MHG. *mot* (G. dial. *mott*) bog, bog-earth, peat.

An extended form appears in MLG., Du. *modder* mud, whence G. *moder* masc., mud, state of mouldering or decay; cf. MHG. *moter* (mod.G. dial. *motter*).]

1. a. Wet and soft soil or earthy matter; mire, sludge.

13.. *Coer de L.* 4360 Some.. broughten.. grete schydes, and the wood, And slunge it into the mode. **13..** *E.E. Allit. P.* B. 407 þenne mourkne in þe mudde most ful nede Alle þat spyrakle in-sprang. **14..** *Why I can't be a Nun* 2 in *E.E.P.* (1862) 138 Whan they had resceyvede her charge, They spared nether mud ne myer. **1513** DOUGLAS *Æneis* v. vi. 125 His face he schew besmotterit for a bourd, And all his membris in mude and dung bedoif. **1573** TUSSER *Husb.* (1878) 29 Though.. loftie ships leaue anker in mud [etc.]. **1632** LITHGOW *Trav.* VII. 317 Leauing slime, mood, and Sand behind their breaches. **1697** DRYDEN *Virg. Georg.* IV. 618 The Sun.. darting to the bottom, bak'd the Mud. **1716** GAY *Trivia* I. 200 The spatter'd mud Hides all thy hose behind. **1781** COWPER *Charity* 531 Plung'd in the stream, they lodge upon the mud. **1808** *Med. Jrnl.* XIX. 114 The Ganges has a prodigious quantity of mud at its sides. **1849** JAMES *Woodman* vii, The floor was of mud.

b. *pl.* Tracts of mud on the margin of a tidal river.

1883 G. C. DAVIES *Norfolk Broads* i. 3 At low water, the muds or flats are dry. **1897** *Spectator* 23 Oct. 553/2 Herons —which feed on the muds left by the tide. **1902** CORNISH *Naturalist Thames* 213 There are still no flounders on the famous Bishop's Muds.

c. *Geol.* A mixture of finely comminuted particles of rock with water, having a consistency varying from that of a semi-liquid to that of a soft and plastic solid; usually either deposited from suspension in water, or ejected from volcanos. Also *pl.* kinds of mud.

1878 HUXLEY *Physiogr.* 192 Herculaneum was sealed up by a crust of volcanic mud discharged from Vesuvius. **1885** *Encycl. Brit.* XVIII. 122/1 At some points in the same regions are found green muds and sands, which, as regards their origin.. resemble the blue muds.

d. ***mud and stud*** (dial.): posts and laths filled in with mud, as a material of which walls of cottages, etc., are built (also *stud and mud*: see STUD *sb.*); similarly ***mud and log***, ***mud and reed***, etc.

1839 STONEHOUSE *Axholme* 389 The rectory house was an old fashioned dwelling, with high gables and walls of mud and stud. **1843** MARRYAT *M. Violet* xxxii, The miserable twelve-feet-square mud-and-log cabins. **1900** *Daily News* 18 May 6/2 The mud and reed towns of the negro.

e. *transf.* A 'mud-student' (see sense 5).

1906 C. G. GREY *Sequel to Story Official Life* 9 Some of the men from across Tweed were very kind to us muds.

f. A liquid (commonly a suspension of clay and other substances in water) that is pumped down the inside of the drill pipe and up the outside during the drilling of an oil or gas well, so as to remove the drill cuttings, cool and lubricate the bit, support the sides of the hole against caving, and prevent the leakage into it of gas or water from the formations encountered; also (with *a* and *pl.*), a kind of mud. Orig. called *mud-laden fluid* and later *mud fluid*.

[**1901** J. G. MCINTOSH tr. *Neuberger & Noalhat's Technol. Petroleum* xxix. 379 It is.. by causing a current of water to circulate continually from the surface of the ground to the bottom of the well, and again from the bottom to the surface, that the mud is continually carried away. **1914** *Times Fuel* No. 104/2 Water and heavy mud forced along the column of the pipe.. keep the bit clean and bring the detritus up to the surface.] **1922** D. T. DAY *Handbk. Petroleum Industry* I. 249 A column of pure water exerts a pressure of 43 pounds per square inch for each 100 feet in height but with mud-laden fluid this pressure may be increased to 50 or 55 pounds... This lateral pressure forces the mud into sands and porous structures, stabilizes caving formations and effectively shuts off water, gas or oil. **1926** E. R. LILLEY *Oil Industry* vii. 174 In the rotary system mud is introduced continuously and the control of gas seldom becomes a serious problem. **1938** J. G. CROWTHER *About Petroleum* ix. 73 An artifical mud is preferable, as it is more viscous and does not allow the debris to settle. Drilling-mud serves other important functions. **1957** VAN DER HAVE & VERVER *Petroleum & its Products* ii. 59 Three types of drilling fluid are at present in use: water-base muds, emulsion-type muds and oil-base 'muds'. **1970** W. G. ROBERTS *Quest for Oil* iv. 45 A great deal of research continues into the making of suitable muds. **1970** *Daily Colonist* (Victoria, B.C.) 31 Dec. 3/5 Workers cut off a blazing oil well with heavy 'drilling mud'. **1974** *Daily Mail* 3 Apr. 23/2 The mud men.. supervise the texture of the mud in the giant tanks that are reservoirs for the special lubricant which is pumped into the ocean bed.

2. *fig.* **a.** As a type of what is worthless or polluting.

1563 WINȜET *Wks.* (S.T.S.) II. 78 Lat the cleir fayth and credulitie of our elders be na mixing of glar or mude be tribulit. **1590** GREENWOOD *Answ. Def. Read Prayers* 31 In this your papisticall mudde,.. your reading of mens writings for prayer, is a false worshipp of God. **1707** *Reflex. upon Ridicule* 66 Servile Souls form'd of Mud. **1819** SHELLEY *England in 1819*, Princes, the dregs of their dull race, who flow Through public scorn,—mud from a muddy spring.

†**b.** The lowest or worst part of anything; the lowest stratum; the dregs.

a **1586** SIDNEY *Arcadia* III. (1629) 238 An ordinary person (borne of the mud of the people). **1602** MARSTON *Antonio's Rev.* v. v, Scum of the mud of hell! **1760** FOOTE *Minor* II. Wks. 1799 I. 255 To procure her emersion from the mercantile mud, no consideration wou'd be spar'd. **1856** EMERSON *Eng. Traits, Race* Wks. (Bohn) II. 23 Defoe said in his wrath, 'the Englishman was the mud of all races'.

†**c.** A fool. *slang. Obs.*

1708 *Memoirs Right Villanous John Hall* 22 Mud, a Fool, or Thick skull Fellow. **1886** in H. BAUMANN *Londinismen.*

d. Opium. *U.S. slang.*

1922 *Dialect Notes* V. 182 *Mud*, obviously so-named from the color and consistency of the drug. **1926** *Flynn's* 16 Jan. 638/2 Some stiffs uses mud but coke don't need any jabbin', cookin' or flops. **1935** *Amer. Speech* X. 17/1 *Hop*, opium. Modern mud, O., pen-yen, tar. **1955** *U.S. Senate Hearings* (1956) VIII. 4161 Opium in the underworld is referred to by various names. For instance, 'mud', 'tar', 'black stuff', 'hop', 'pen yan' and 'yen pocks'. **1974** *Publishers Weekly* 11 Feb. 60/1 Western efforts to open up trade with China in the early to mid-19th century were largely unscrupulous, inspired by the immense profits to be made from 'mud' (opium).

e. Coffee. *slang.*

1925 G. H. MULLIN *Adventures Scholar Tramp* iii. 34, I received punk (bread) and a cup of mud (black coffee) or —to use the familiar hobo expression for the combination —duffer. **1931** 'D. STIFF' *Milk & Honey Route* 210 *Mud*, strong coffee mixed with weak milk. **1945** L. SHELLY *Jive Talk Dict.* 15/1 *Mud*, coffee or a homely person. **1957** 'N. CULOTTA' *They're a Weird Mob* (1958) ix. 135 Got another cuppa mud, Joe?

3. Phrases. ***as clear as mud***: said in mock commendation of something that is by no means clear (also used as a burlesque intensive of 'clear'); ***as sure as mud*** (school-slang): absolutely sure; ***to fling*** or ***throw mud***: to make disgraceful imputations; ***to stick in the mud***: see STICK *v.*; ***(as) sick as mud***: depressed, exasperated, furious; ***(here's) mud in your eye***: a toast, 'good health!'; ***one's name is mud***: one is discredited, held in low esteem, ineffective, unlucky [cf. 2c, above]; hence, passing into senses suggested by 2a, b: one is regarded as a pariah, untrustworthy, with the worst reputation; so in allusive phrases; ***up to mud*** (Austral.): see quot. 1945.

1762–71 H. WALPOLE *Vertue's Anecd. Paint.* (1786) IV. 170 Never did two angry men of their abilities throw mud with less dexterity. **1823** 'J. BEE' *Slang* 122 *Mud*—a stupid twaddling fellow. 'And his name is mud!' ejaculated upon the conclusion of a silly oration, or of a *leader* in the Courier. **1842** BARHAM *Ingol. Leg.* Ser. II. *Merch. Venice*, That's clear as mud. **1880** 'MARK TWAIN' *Tramp Abroad* 187 These people fling mud at that elegant Englishman.. and make fun of him. **1884** FL. MARRYAT *Under the Lilies* vii, A woman in my position must expect to have more mud thrown at her than a less important person. **1884** *Nonconf. & Indep.* 24 July 713/3 Using the case to fling mud at Mr. Trevelyan and Earl Spencer. **1887** *Lantern* (New Orleans) 16 Apr. 2/1 Zeller wants to be Recorder.. but his name is mud. **1899** E. PHILLPOTTS *Human Boy* 10, I shall die as sure as mud. **1906** E. DYSON *Fact'ry 'Ands* viii. 92 D'yeh mean to tell me how Hoggy's let you loose agin after you gettin' glorious in his dry-goods, 'n' makin' his name mud all up 'n' down ther town? **1916** C. J. DENNIS *Songs Sentimental Bloke* 13 I'm crook; me name is Mud; I've done me dash. **1927** H. V. MORTON *In Search of England* iii. 60 'Here's mud in your eye!' said one of the modern pilgrims, tossing down his martini. **1929** J. P. MCEVOY *Hollywood Girl* ix. 148 Well, I hope when I'm through I'll have sense enough to know it. Mud in your eye! **1930** K. BRUSH *Young Man of Manhattan* vii. 87 'Well,' somebody said, 'here's mud in your eye.' **1933** *Bulletin* (Sydney) 1 Nov. 42/2 Still, men today are mostly up to mud. **1935** M. DE LA ROCHE *Young Renny* xviii. 152 She hates the thought of his staying on as much as we do. She's as sick as mud about it. **1938** S. V. BENÉT *Thirteen o' Clock* 335 Mud in your eye! **1942** M. DICKENS *One Pair of Feet* vii. 108 Nurse Dickens had no idea of hospital etiquette... Nurse Dickens was too opinionated. Nurse D.'s name, in short, was Mud. **1945** BAKER *Austral. Lang.* vi. 128 *Up to mud, up to tripe*,.. describe things that are bad, disliked or out of order. **1949** WODEHOUSE *Mating Season* xxiii. 198 'Skin off your nose, Jeeves.' 'Mud in your eye, sir, if I may use the expression.' **1954** —— *Jeeves & Feudal Spirit* viii. 72 He's as sick as mud about it. He moons broodingly to and fro, looking like Hamlet. **1956** J. SYMONS *Paper Chase* x. 73 Here's mud in your eye, Eileen. **1957** D. ROBINS *Noble One* xviii. 169 If tha' doan't put ring on finger shortly, my lad, tha' name will be mud in Mountaindale. **1973** W. M. DUNCAN *Big Timer* vii. 51 Riordan his name is and so far as I'm concerned from now on it's Mud.

4. *attrib.* and *Comb.* **a.** simple attrib., as ***mud bigging, cabin, colour, floor, heap, house, hovel, -hut, -land, -puddle, -rush, -scatter, -shoal, -side, -slide, -trap***; **b.** instrumental, as ***mud-bespattered, -built, -caked, -chinked, -choked, -exhausted, -greasy, -layered, -moulded, -shot, -splashed, -splattered, -stained*** adjs.; **c.** parasynthetic, as ***mud-bottomed, -coloured, -floored, -heaped, -roofed*** adjs.; **d.** locative, as ***mud-couched, -lost, -mattressed, -stuck*** adjs.; **e.** objective, as ***mud-feeding*** adj.; **f.** similative, as ***mud-grey*** adj.

1848 DICKENS *Dombey* lv, Rows of *mud-bespattered cows. **1588** *Reg. Privy Council Scot.* IV. 288 The said complenaris foirsaid house.., being laich *mud bigging. **1908** HARDY *Dynasts* III. VII. iii. 492 Where there is a *mud-bottomed stream, the Lasne. **1949** C. LONGFIELD *Dragonflies Brit. Isles* (ed. 2) 132 It inhabits, in England, slow-running, mud-bottomed streams. **1740** THOMSON & MALLET *Alfred* I. ii, That *mud-built cottage is thy sovereign's palace. **1780** A. YOUNG *Tour in Ireland* I. 102 This town appears exceedingly flourishing.. yet 40 years ago.. there were nothing but *mud cabbins in it. **1829** J. MACTAGGART *Three Yrs. Canada* II. 243 It is a singular fact .. with the Irish, that if they can get a *mud-cabin*, they will never think of building one of wood. **1922** JOYCE *Ulysses* 324 Their mudcabins and their shielings by the roadside were laid low by the batteringram. **1912** W. DEEPING *Sincerity* xxxix. 281 Grassless fields, *mud-caked ponds, and empty wells. **1961** *Times* 11 Jan. 16/4 Their mud-caked forwards battled back into the Eastern Counties' 25. **1946** W. FAULKNER *Portable Faulkner* App. 737 Jefferson Mississippi was one long rambling onestorey *mudchinked log building housing the Chickasaw Agent and his tradingpost store. **1922** JOYCE *Ulysses* 98 Past beds of reeds, over slime, *mud-choked bottles, carrion dogs. **1839** HOOD *Hood's Own* I. 32 (*Last Shilling*) A pair of *mud-colour gloves. **1838** MISS PARDOE *River & Desert* I. 110 A sort of *mud-coloured cotton. **1936** W. FAULKNER *Absalom, Absalom!* ii. 44 It was that same Akers who had blundered onto the *mudcouched negro five years ago. **1622** DRAYTON *Poly-olb.* xxvii. 259 The *mud-exhausted Meres. **1926** J. S. HUXLEY *Ess. Pop. Sci.* xvii. 209 The endostyle degenerates together with the rest of the *mud-feeding apparatus. **1843** BORROW *Bible in Spain* ii. 13 A little side-room with a *mud floor. **1960** KOESTLER *Lotus & Robot* I. i. 28 It had brought.. a mud-floor of starved refugees, increased poverty, land hunger, and the threat of civil war. **1951** —— *Age of Longing* I. vi. 108 All men did that who had.. met in *mud-floored rooms before the Great Change. **1921** D. H. LAWRENCE *Sea & Sardinia* ii. 44 Badly paved, *mud-greasy.. road. **1923** —— *Birds, Beasts & Flowers* 169 You meet a huge and *mud-grey elephant. **1871** KINGSLEY *At Last* x, His bare feet plashing from log to log and *mud-heap to mud-heap. **1935** W. EMPSON *Poems* 26 Empty, *mudheaped, through which the alluvial scheme Flows temporary as the modern world. **1548** *Extracts Aberd. Reg.* (1844) I. 260 He has.. distroyit iiij *mwd houissis in my cloise and fald. **1856** LEVER *Martins of Cro' M.* 126 He built a mud-house. **1838** BARHAM *Ingol. Leg.* Ser. I. *Hand of Glory*, Did you see her, in short, that *mud-hovel within. **1803** J. DAVIS *Trav. U.S.* 3, I have entered with equal interest the *mud-hut of the negro, and the log-house of the planter. **1858** T. VIELÉ *Following Drum* 125 Half-a-dozen mud-huts neatly thatched with straw.. presented a study for an artist. **1941** L. HELLMAN *Watch on Rhine* III. 166 In every town.. and every mud hut in the world, there is always a man who.. will fight to make a good world. **1971** *Daily Nation* (Nairobi) 10 Apr. 10 The expression traditional housing is a misnomer... The brick homes in the area will have nothing in common with the traditional mud huts. *a* **1865** SMYTH *Sailor's Word-Bk.* (1867) 487 **Mud-lands*, the extensive marshes left dry by the retiring tide in estuaries and river mouths. **1927** *Daily Tel.* 22 Nov. 14/1 This scheme.. involves the reclamation of over 400 acres of mudland. **1930** BLUNDEN *Poems* 145 *Mud-layered cobble-stones. **1790** COLERIDGE *Devon. Roads* 21 While they their *mud-lost sandals hunt. **1960** S. PLATH *Colossus* (1967) 48 *Mud-mattressed under the sign of the hag In a clench of blood, the sleep-talking virgin Gibbets.. the moon's man. **1901** KIPLING *Kim* iii, A mud-walled, *mud-roofed hamlet. **1906** HARDY *Dynasts* II. v. viii. 288 We are the only phantoms now abroad On this *mud-moulded ball! *a* **1841** W. P. HAWES *Sporting Scenes* (1842) I. 183 The thawing *mud-puddles. **1912** KIPLING *Songs from Books* (1913) 76 As a frog shows in a mud-puddle. **1928** —— *Limits & Renewals* (1932) 3 The advance of education and the standard of living would submerge all mind-marks in one *mudrush of standardised reading-matter. **1919** J. MASEFIELD *Reynard* 78 *Mud-scatters chased him as he scudded. **1842** *Knickerbocker* XX. 309 [He] knew a great deal more about the inconveniences of groping about among *mud-shoals in the dark. **1858** R. S. SURTEES *Ask Mamma* 9 He helped her down the perilous *mud-shot iron steps of the old Independent. **1923** G. B. SHAW *Let.* 5 Apr. in *To a Young Actress* (1960) 42, I am here at the *mudside (the Bristol channel can hardly be called sea) to recuperate. **1921** *Daily Colonist* (Victoria, B.C.) 29 Oct. 1/7 *Mud slides also add to the danger of operating trains until repairs can be effected. **1928** BLUNDEN *Undertones of War* iv. 35 That dugout was a deep one, with a steep mud-slide of an entrance. **1969** *Courier Mail* (Brisbane) 27 Jan. 4/8 Mud-slides buried sleepers alive.. as Southern California was deluged by rain. **1908** *Daily Chron.* 28 Sept. 7/4 He sat his *mud-splashed saddle, motionless under the moon. **1922** JOYCE *Ulysses* 33 The mudsplashed brakes. **1930** J. DOS PASSOS *42nd Parallel* I. 5 *Mudsplattered trouserlegs. *a* **1922** H. LAWSON in *Penguin Bk. Austral. Ballads* (1964) 144 And *mud-stained, wet, and weary, He goes by rock and tree. **1908** HARDY *Dynasts* III. VII. iv. 493 His horse got *mud-stuck in a new-ploughed plot. **1970** *Motoring Which?* July 93/2 Both cars had areas which may well give trouble in a couple of years' time—*mud traps around the headlamp cowls of the 3-litre, [etc.].

5. **a.** Special combinations: **mud balance**, a balance designed for measuring the density of drilling mud; **mud-bar** [BAR *sb.*[1] 15], a bank of mud in a river or off an estuary or a shore; **mud-barge**, a barge transporting dredged mud; **mud-bath**, a medicinal bath of heated mud; also *transf.* and *fig.*; **mud-board**, a flat board fastened under the foot for walking on mud; **mud-boat**, (*a*) a board with sides, used for crossing tidal mud for the purpose of shooting sea-birds; (*b*) a barge for carrying away mud dredged from a river or bar; **mud-boot**, a kind of jack boot worn as a protection from mud; **mud box** *Naut.*, a box containing a coarse filter used to trap sediment in bilge-water; **mud-boy** (see quot.); **mud-brick**, brick that is made with mud; also *attrib.*; **mud-chute**, a chute down which mud is discharged (in quot. *fig.*); **mud-clerk** *U.S.*, an assistant to the purser on a river steamer; **mud-cone**, a cone formed by the accumulation of mud round the vent of a mud-volcano; **mud-crack**, a crack formed in drying mud; **mud-crusher** *slang*, an infantry man; **mud-drum**, a cylindrical chamber attached to a boiler to collect the earthy matter in the water supplied; **mud engineer**, a person responsible for the quality and supply of drilling mud; **mud-fat** *a. Australian*, as fat as possible; **mud fever**, a disease of horses, in which patches of the skin on their feet become inflamed and swollen; **mud flap**, a piece of rubber, metal, etc., hung behind each of the wheels of a vehicle to prevent mud, etc., from splashing; **mud-flat**, (*a*) a stretch of muddy land left uncovered at low tide; (*b*) a mud-bank in a river which is not tidal; (*c*) *N.Z.* (see quot. 1947); **mud-flinger**, a person who hurls abuse [from *to fling mud* (MUD *sb.*[1] 3)]; so **mud-flinging** *vbl. sb.*; **mud-flow**, a (fluid or hardened) stream or avalanche of mud, e.g. one consisting of soil made fluid by excessive water, one produced by a mud volcano, or a lahar; also, the flow or motion of such a stream; **mud fluid** = MUD *sb.*[1] 1 f; **mud flush**, a flush by means of drilling mud; **mudguard**, a piece of metal, leather, celluloid, etc., attached to the wheel of a cycle, etc., to protect the rider from mud; **mudguarded** *a.*, provided with mudguards; **mud-hoe**, a kind of scraper for scraping mud off roads; **mud hog** = *mud pump* below; **mud-honey** (*nonce-wd.*), used *fig.* for degrading pleasures; †**mud-laden fluid** = MUD *sb.*[1] 1 f; **mud-land** (see quot.); **mud-lava**, volcanic mud (= MOYA); **mud-lighter** [LIGHTER *sb.*[1]], a barge for transporting mud; **mud-line**, the line on the sea-bed in front of a coast-line which represents the upper limit at which wave action allows mud to settle permanently on the bottom; **mud logging**, examination of the mud (sense 1 f) coming out of a bore-hole for signs of oil or gas or other indications of the strata being drilled; so **mud logger**, a person responsible for this; **mud-lump** *U.S.* (see quot.); **mud-mask, -pack**, a preparation of fuller's earth applied to the face as a beauty treatment; so **mud-mask** *v. trans.*, to treat with a mud-mask; **mud-patten** = *mud-board*; **mud pie**, mud or wet earth formed by children in the shape of a pie; also *attrib.* and *fig.*; **mud pilot**, a pilot who works in shallow water; also *fig.*; so **mud pilotage**; **mud-plunger** (see quot.); **mud proof** *a.*, impervious to mud; **mud pump**, a pump for circulating mud (sense 1 f) through the drill pipe and up the bore-hole; **mud-quake** *nonce-wd.*, jocularly applied to an earthquake in Holland; **mud room** *N. Amer.*, a cloakroom, *spec.* one in which wet or muddy footwear may be left; **mud runner** *U.S.*, a horse which habitually performs well on a wet racecourse; a MUDDER; **mud-scow**, a flat mud-boat; **mud shine** *nonce-wd.*, the reflexion of light on muddy stones; **mud-shoe** (see quots.); **mud-show** *arch. slang*, an exhibition or performance held in the open air; so **mud showman**; **mud-sill**, (*a*) the lowest sill of a structure, usually embedded in the soil; (*b*) *U.S.* the lowest class of society; also, a person of this class; **mud-slinging, -throwing** *vbl. sbs.* (the employment of) abuse, calumny or slander; malevolent gossip; so **mud-sling** *sb.*, **-slinger**; **mud-splasher** = *mud-board*; **mudstone** *Geol.* (see quot. 1876); **mud-student** *slang*, a student of farming; **mud-valve**, 'a valve by which mud is discharged from a steam boiler' (Knight *Dict. Mech.* 1875); **mud volcano**, (*a*) a mound or cone formed of hardened mud discharged from its centre (usu. of much smaller dimensions than a volcano); also *fig.*; (*b*) *U.S.* = *mud-lump*; **mud wing**, a mudguard, a mud flap.

1960 C. GATLIN *Petroleum Engin.* vi. 70/2 The density of drilling muds is normally measured with a *mud balance. **1899** C. J. C. HYNE *Further Adventures Capt. Kettle* i. 10 There was a *mud-bar with twenty-four feet, but steamers drawing twenty-seven could scrape over, as the bar was soft. **1906** E. DYSON *Fact'ry 'Ands* xviii. 242 Ther toad-stools.. was growin'.. like mussels on er *mudbarge. **1926** W. RUNCIMAN *Collier Brigs* 77 They.. took in chalk ballast from the wharves, and occasionally from mud-barges when they could not get a ready turn at the wharves. **1843** SIR C. SCUDAMORE *Med. Visit Gräfenberg* 64 He next proceeded to Franzens-bad, in Bohemia, and tried the *mud baths for a month. **1851** J. CHAPMAN *Diary* 26 June in G. S. Haight *Geo. Eliot & J. Chapman* (1940) 184 Mrs Hennell.. thinks.. that.. pure monogamy.. will only be reached thro' a previous age of general licence! I don't agree with her that such a mud bath is at all necessary. 1856 D. G. Rossetti Let. 10 Dec. (1965) I. 307 Bath has been a mud-bath ever since I came. 1961 Times 12 May 19/2 Mr. Beckett's anti-metaphysical mudbath. 1971 Sunday Nation (Nairobi) 11 Apr. 5/1 The remaining cars in the Safari braced themselves for a possible mud bath. 1824 Col. Hawker Instr. Yng. Sportsm. 334 plate, Thin oak *Mudboards 16 inches square. 1824 Col. Hawker Instr. Yng. Sportsm. 331 The gunner first lays his piece..into the '*mud-boat', and then [etc.].. Having got pretty near to his birds, he lies down in the 'mud-boat'. 1838 Civil Eng. & Arch. Jrnl. I. 204/2 Petitioning the Admiralty for the loan of a steam-tug or mud-boat. 1831 Carlyle Sart. Res. I. ix, Half-buried under ..overalls and *mudboots. 1883 A. E. Seaton Man. Marine Engin. xii. 231 *Mud boxes. Between the directing box and the pump should be fitted a box with a strainer, which shall intercept such solid matter as would derange the pump valves. 1972 B.S.I. News Oct. 28/2 Mudboxes intended for the coarse filtration of bilge water which accumulates in ships' machinery spaces. 1958 Times 15 May 14/6 The quality of the mud during drilling operations [for oil] is, therefore, very important, and the *mudboy, who is responsible for preparing it, is quite a skilled workman. 1810 Z. M. Pike Acct. Expeditions Sources Mississippi App. II. 7 Houses would be built entirely of *mud-brick (like those in New Spain). 1903 Speaker 5 Sept. 527/2 The old town being built of mud-brick had vanished. 1934 F. Stark Valleys of Assassins I. i. 29 The castle is a mud-brick square with round towers. 1963 M. Laurence Tomorrow-Tamer 227 Then she was gone, shutting quietly behind her the packing-case door of the mudbrick shanty. 1938 H. G. Wells Apropos of Dolores iv. 211 It is the most awful gabble —but it is nothing more than the inevitable end of this *mud-chute called 'history'. 1872 E. Eggleston End of World xxvi. 171 It was natural enough that the '*mud-clerk' on the old steamboat Iatan should have taken a fancy to the 'striker', as the engineer's apprentice was called. 1912 I. S. Cobb Back Home 103 Even her two mud clerks, let alone her captain and her pilots, wore uniforms. 1869 'Mark Twain' Innoc. Abr. lviii. 632 Groups of *mud cones stuck like wasps' nests. 1879 Geikie in Encycl. Brit. X. 251/2 Mud cones or Salses. 1895 Funk's Stand. Dict., *Mud-cracks. 1917 Jrnl. Geol. XXV. 135 (heading) Some factors affecting the development of mud-cracks. 1968 R. W. Fairbridge Encycl. Geomorphol. 761/1 Mud cracks form largely because of solar radiation. 1893 Sir G. Chesney Lesters I. I. xi. 142 'You are too good to be a *mud-crusher, Tommy,' said the Major of the regiment [Hussars] patronisingly. 1890 Century Dict., *Mud drum. 1901 Winston Churchill Crisis II. xxii, The captain knew a mud-drum from a lady's watch. 1970 W. G. Roberts Quest for Oil iv. 46 The *mud engineer and geologist will be examining the mud all the time to find out what sort of rock is being bored. 1975 Petroleum Rev. XXIX. 27/3 The toolpusher was ready,.. the mud engineers, the experts in every field were ready. 1890 'R. Boldrewood' Col. Reformer (1891) 394 Every beast on Rainbar run..will be *mud fat in three months. 1872 W. Williams Princ. & Pract. Vet. Surg. xxxvii. 623 *Mud-fever is occasionally attended with a considerable degree of systemic disturbance. 1901 F. T. Barton Vet. Manual 161 (heading) Erythema and Mud-rash. (Mud fever.)..Sometimes there is a slight degree of fever, hence the term 'mud fever'. 1928 Black's Vet. Dict. 617/2 Mud fever is the popular name for a variety of erythema that attacks the heels and coronets of horses' feet when these parts are subject to long-continued irritation. 1971 G. W. Serth Horse Owner's Guide Common Ailments vi. 63 Mud fever affects the legs and under the belly. 1963 Times 29 Jan. 3/6 Its front wings and front and rear panels are bolted on for easy repair and the car has rubber cushioned over-riders and *mud flaps as standard equipment. 1967 Autocar 28 Dec. 29/2 Rear mud flaps should be made compulsory in the interest of safety. 1972 Guardian 13 Nov. 8/5 The fitting of mud flaps behind the rear wheels should be made compulsory. 1871 Routledge's Ev. Boy's Ann. June 338 The *mudflats of our seaboard. 1885 Froude Oceana xi. (1886) 165 Cranes and other waders stalked about the mud-flats. 1922 H. Footner Huntress 134 The only breaks in the endless panorama of cut-banks, mud-flats, willows, and grass were occasional little inlets. 1943 K. Tennant Ride on Stranger ix. 92 The broken grey rocks sloping down to mud flats. 1947 P. Newton Wayleggo (1949) 154 Mud-flats, a high country man's name for down country flats. Heavy land. 1839 Thackeray Let. 1-2 Dec. in A. T. Ritchie Lett. (1924) i. 8 Very curious the abuse is of that character. Old Southey is one of the chief *mudflingers. 1958 New Statesman 22 Feb. 220/2 This latest torrent of *mud-flinging was, of course, set off by the letter..from Mr A. H. Milward, Chief Executive of British European Airways. 1964 C. S. Lewis Discarded Image iv. 80 This towering vaunt, this philosophic panache which goes beyond mere indifference to mud-flinging and actually courts it, is of Cynic origin. 1901 H. W. Monckton in Q. Jrnl. Geol. Soc. LVII. 295, I have for several years noted details of landslips in the Drift near Scarborough, and, as in other cases, they may be classed as: (1) *Mud-flows. (2) Earth-slips... (3) Falls which, owing to the dryness of the clay, resemble rock-falls. 1902 Bull. Amer. Mus. Nat. Hist. XVI. 347 The largest ejected block that we saw was one on the surface of the mud-flow between the rivers Blanche and Sèche and not more than two hundred yards from the sea coast. 1928 Bull. Geol. Soc. Amer. XXXIX. 465 (heading) Mudflow as a geologic agent in semiarid mountains. 1944 C. A. Cotton Volcanoes xiii. 240 The contents of a large crater lake on St Vincent (Antilles) were ejected so as to generate extensive mudflows which rushed down various radial valleys to the sea. Ibid. 241 Other destructive mudflows..have been ascribed to the melting of snow and glacier ice by volcanic heat. This has occurred in Iceland. 1963 D. W. & E. E. Humphries tr. Termier's Erosion & Sedimentation x. 206 It is probable that earthquake shocks play an important part in initiating submarine mudflows and it is likely that such processes materially assisted in the filling of oceanic basins. 1970 R. J. Small Study of Landforms ii. 30 Mud-flows occur in mountain areas after heavy rainfall, in periglacial areas during the thaw season, on the slopes of erupting volcanoes and even in deserts, when a heavily loaded stream-flood is gradually transformed as it loses its water by evaporation and percolation. 1914 Heggem & Pollard Drilling Wells in Oklahoma by the Mud-Laden Fluid Method (U.S. Bur. of Mines Techn. Paper No. 68) 23 The *mud fluid was then bailed from the inside of the casing and drilling continued. 1921 W. H. Jeffery Deep Well Drilling vii. 240 All this can be prevented by moving the casing as occasion requires, and then the mud fluid will rise uniformly on all sides of the casing and the cuttings will have no chance to pack. 1946 Mod. Petroleum Technol. 88 When drilling through porous sands it is often necessary to prepare a mud fluid..which leaves on the walls of the well a thin and impervious sheath which seals the pores. 1949 Our Industry (Anglo-Iranian Oil Co. Ltd.) (ed. 2) ii. 32 The next essential operation is to remove by a continuous process the debris formed by the action of drilling; this is accomplished by the use of a *mud-flush circulation. 1957 Van der Have & Verver Petroleum & its Products ii. 59 An accumulation of gas in the mud-flush may lower its density to such an extent that the danger of eruption would increase instead of diminishing. 1886 C.T.C. Monthly Gaz. V. 144/1 Hints to tricyclists... Accessories not supplied by the maker. *Mud-guard. 1923 Daily Mail 30 July 6 (Advt.), So well shielded and efficiently *mud-guarded that anyone..can ride it in ordinary costume. 1932 Amer. Speech VII. 268 *Mud-hog. 1939 D. Hager Fund. Petroleum Industry ix. 209 Mud pumps, often called 'mud hogs', are of various sizes. 1844 Stephens Bk. Farm II. 410 A *mud-hole or harle. 1855 Tennyson Maud I. xvi. 5 So that..fulsome Pleasure clog him, and drown His heart in the gross *mud-honey of town. 1914 Pollard & Heggem Mud-laden Fluid Applied to Well Drilling (U.S. Bur. of Mines Techn. Paper No. 66) 7 In this paper the term '*mud-laden fluid' is applied to a mixture of water with any clay which will remain suspended in water for a considerable time. 1914 F. A. Talbot Oil Conquest of World iii. 43 In drilling through sand formations mud-laden fluid is used to seal the sides of the borehole temporarily. 1921 W. H. Jeffery Deep Well Drilling vii. 236 Water impregnated with clay, otherwise known as mud laden fluid, is forced by slush pumps down inside the casing,..returning between the casing and the wall of the hole. 1946 Mod. Petroleum Technol. 88 The circuit of this mud-laden fluid..begins at the slush-pumps. 1867 Smyth Sailor's Word-bk., *Mud-lands, the extensive marshes left dry by the returning tide in estuaries and river mouths. 1899 Daily News 8 Apr. 5/3 Portsmouth Harbour and the mudland in proximity. 1804 Edin. Rev. IV. 28 Showers of rain..were magnified into *mud-lavas. 1879 Encycl. Brit. X. 250/1 Mud-lavas. 1909 Cent. Dict. Suppl., *Mud-lighter. 1915 W. B. Yeats Reveries (1916) 78 He..had nothing to do but work himself into a rage if he saw a mudlighter mismanaged. 1891 Rep. Sci. Results Voy. H.M.S. Challenger: Deep-Sea Deposits iii. 185 The greater the extent and depth of the ocean, the greater the depth to which water-movement extends, and consequently the greater is the depth at which the *mud-line is formed around the coasts, but the average depth of the mud-line may be taken as approximately about 100 fathoms. Ibid. vi. 383 It appears to be most abundant..in the neighbourhood of what we have termed the mud-line surrounding continental shores. 1963 D. W. & E. E. Humphries tr. Termier's Erosion & Sedimentation xi. 226 The maximum amounts of organic matter occur in calm waters, either in estuaries (5-15%) or near the edge of the belt of mud which surrounds the land mass, the 'mud line', where the amount is 6%. 1975 Daily Tel. 9 Jan. 25 (Advt.), NEC Gas have a limited number of vacancies for experienced *Mudloggers and Instrument Technicians with oilfield experience. 1960 C. Gatlin Petroleum Engin. xi. 199/1 Continuous *mud logging is..an excellent exploratory tool. 1868 Putnam's Mag., May 591/2 *Mud-lumps, or more properly Mud-volcanoes, have been known to rise to the height of twenty-five feet. 1872 Schele de Vere Americanisms 508 Mud-lumps, is the technical name of the earliest appearance of soft, spongy land at the mouth of the Mississippi... They are at first conical, not unlike miniature volcanoes, and have little craters at the top, from which flows muddy water. 1928 Daily Express 16 June 3/4, I suggested that I should like a *mud-mask. The assistant appeared to be alarmed. Ibid. 22 Dec. 3/5 Faces have been massaged and mud-masked. 1934 M. Verni Mod. Beauty Culture iv. 28/2 Fuller's earth is a powdered clay with healing properties. Some forms are called 'clay packs', or '*mud packs', and are used as masks. 1938 L. MacNeice Earth Compels 37 Hot towels for the men, mud packs for the women Will smooth the puckered minutes of your lives. 1971 New Scientist 19 Aug. 401/2 The inamorata..wearing a moss-green mud-pack, with hair in rollers. 1791 Gilpin Forest Scenery II. 193 *Mud-pattens are flat pieces of board, which the fowler ties to his feet that he may not sink in the mud. 1788 Ld. Auckland Diary in Spain in Corr. (1861) II. 74 The children amused themselves with making *mud pies. 1885 Mrs. A. Jebb in Contemp. Rev. Oct. 528 Clay-moulding is nothing more than a sort of glorified mud-pie making. 1927 D. H. Lawrence Mornings in Mexico 122 The low, square, mud-pie houses. 1958 Mud-pie [see dribbly a.]. 1856 C. Nordhoff Merchant Vessel viii. 94 A Dungeness or deep-sea pilot as these are called, in contradistinction to the river men, who are known as *mud pilots. 1899 F. T. Bullen Log Sea-waif 342 Somehow the 'mud'-pilot found us, his boat taking away our deep-water man. 1906 Westm. Gaz. 14 Aug. 6/2 'Mud' pilots—i.e., pilots who work above Gravesend. 1934 P. H. Godsell Arctic Trader 265 The captains of the whaling vessels always took care to keep between the ice pack and the shore, and for this reason were often contemptuously referred to as 'Mud-Pilots'. 1946 G. Millar Horned Pigeon xxii. 375 The first guide, a kind of mud-pilot, remained on his bicycle. 1965 R. B. Oram Cargo Handling i. 15 In the port of London, a lesser type of pilot..will take over the ship at the lock from the Trinity House pilot... To indicate his inferior status he is known generally as a mud pilot. 1932 S. G. McNeil In Great Waters viii. 125, I had to do practically all the *mud pilotage myself in the various ports of call. 1892 Labour Commission Gloss., *Mud plungers, men in the chemical industry engaged at bleach plant in stirring up the sediment from manganese and acid to extract the gas. 1897 Sears, Roebuck Catal. 255/1 Extra Superfine, strictly rain and *mud proof French serge. 1926 E. R. Lilley Oil Industry vi. 137 (caption) Duplex slush or *mud pumps. 1973 J. W. Jenner in Hobson & Pohl Mod. Petroleum Technol. (ed. 4) iv. 115 The heart of the fluid circulating system is the mud pumps. 1760 H. Walpole Let. to Mann 3 Feb., The Dutch ..have lately had a *mud-quake, and giving themselves terra-firma airs, call it an earthquake! 1950 A. E. Burke et al. Archit. & Building Trades Dict. 212/1 *Mud room, in building, a small room or entranceway where members of the family remove their muddy overshoes or rubbers before going into any of the other rooms. 1962 F. Williams Amer. Invasion v. 51 The ranch-style houses..with their..sun-rooms, 'bi-level brunch bars', mud rooms [etc.]. 1964 Calgary Herald 13 Feb. 16/5 One of the most common places of theft occurrences in the school is in the mud room. 1970 Globe & Mail (Toronto) 25 Sept. 36/4 (Advt.), Necessary additions as family room with indoor barbecue, ..laundry and mud room..have been architecturally added. 1905 Evening Sun (N.Y.) 17 Aug., All the races.. were won by the product of stallions that in their day were famous *mud runners. 1766 Mass. Gaz. (U.S.) 20 Oct. 1/3 A new *Mud-Scow, 24 Foot long. 1894 Outing (U.S.) XXIV. 325/1 Any kind of a boat from a crack yacht to a mudscow. 1850 L. Hunt Autobiog. I. vi. 247 A roar of hoarse voices round the door, and *mud-shine on the pavement. 1954 Mem. Ghost Pine Homesteaders (Ghost Pine Community Group, Three Hills, Alberta) 119 A chap.. breaking a particularly wet piece of ground, made oval shaped hardwood *mud shoes which he fastened to his horses' shoes to keep the horses from miring. 1959 A. Hardy Fish & Fisheries xvi. 303 The tractors..will..have buoyancy tanks so that they are light enough to skim the bottom on their mud-shoes without sinking in. 1969 E. H. Pinto Treen 93 Elmwood horse mud shoes, with iron staples,..were used to give a horse better bearing in the cranberry swamps of Wisconsin... Similar devices..were known as Fen overshoes. 1909 J. R. Ware Passing Eng. 178/2 *Mud show, an agricultural, or other out-door show. 1931 Amer. Mercury Nov. 353/2 Mud show, the old-time horse-and-wagon circus; now derisive. 1927 K. Nicholson Barker 150 *Mud showman, a carnival man. 1685 Rec. Early Hist. Boston (1881) VII. 178 The middle of the wall to lie even with northerlie or outward side of the said Simkins *Mudsell in the Old Celler. 1741 MS. Estimate of repairs at Northweald Bridge, Essex, 3 mudsells 19 foot long each. 1828-32 Webster, Mud-sill, in bridges, the sill that is laid at the bottom of a river, lake, &c. 1858 Hammond Sp. 4 Mar. (Bartlett), Such a class..constitutes the very mud-sill of society. 1863 O. W. Holmes Inevitable Trial in Old Vol. of Life (1891) 107 What the 'Christian dogs' were to the followers of Mahomet,..the 'Northern mudsills' are to the followers of the Southern Moloch. 1935 S. Lewis It can't happen Here xvii. 177 Talking to the dirtiest and tiredest mudsills as warm friend to friend. 1964 College English Feb. 333/2 The culturally deprived in our great cities—a more massive social mudsill than the most sanguine dream of Calhoun and other slavocrats ever envisaged, the social converse of Madison Avenue's grey-flanneled dream. 1968 Times Lit. Suppl. 4 Apr. 329/3 The mudsill is still Negro, not poor white. 1919 E. Pound Let. 1 Feb. (1971) 146 Stings and *mud-slings of the ungodly and unco-decorous. 1896 Advance (Chicago) 17 Sept. 366 The swarm of caricaturists, libelers and party *mud-slingers. 1930 T. S. Eliot tr. St.-J. Perse's Anabasis 27 Instigator of strife and discord! fed on insults and slanders, mudslinger! 1884 Lisbon (N. Dakota) Star 22 Aug., Campaign lies and *mud slinging fail to carry the day. 1914 National Municipal Rev. (N.Y.) III. 581 This sweeping provision, if constitutional and enforceable, would have the effect of eliminating 'mud-slinging' in political campaigns, perhaps indeed of revolutionizing campaign methods entirely. 1928 Sunday Express 27 May 10/1 The social mud-slinging which gives half society its sole virtuous and intellectual amusement. 1952 R. Knox Hidden Stream xiii. 119 And that something is not affected, really, by all the mud-slinging which starts, among the more embittered kind of Protestants, the moment the sanctity of the Church is mentioned. 1973 J. Thomson Death Cap vii. 98 The accusations..are..not specified, just mud-slinging of a general sort. 1880 Baring-Gould Mehalah xxiii, What do you mean coming to a house of worship in *mud-splashers? 1736 Ainsworth Lat. Dict., A *mud stone, Saxum limosum. 1829 Glover's Hist. Derby I. 50 In some places they are called clunch and mudstone. 1876 A. H. Green Phys. Geol. ii. §6. 72 Mudstone is a convenient name for clayey rocks that have the appearance of partially hardened masses of sandy mud. 1856 N. & Q. 2nd Ser. II. 198/1 With whom a young friend of mine was 'a *mud student', that is, was a farming pupil. 1895 W. H. Chambliss Diary xxii. 276 They were willing to resort to the most detestable methods of '*mud-throwing'. 1931 Times Lit. Suppl. 20 Aug. 633/2 He settles down to protracted mud-throwing with Goodwin Wharton as the target. 1873 'Mark Twain' & Warner Gilded Age 38 The awful thunder of a *mud-valve suddenly burst forth. 1817 Q. Jrnl. Sci. I. 247 The *mud volcanoes of Solo. 1862 G. P. Scrope Volcanos (ed. 2) 401 Mud-volcanos, as they are called, i.e. cones of a ductile unctuous clay,..spurting up waves and lumps of liquid mud. 1868 Mud-volcano [see mud-lump above]. 1902 Ann. Rep. Board of Regents Smithsonian Inst. 1901 71 Within the region [sc. the lower Colorado valley] lie a number of 'mud volcanoes', apparently analogous to the 'mud lumps' of the lower Mississippi. 1914 W. Owen Let. 24 May (1967) 252 My face is certainly satisfactory,..free from whelks and knobs and mud-volcanoes. 1953 Caribbean Q. III. II. 80 The mud volcanoes..are caused..by the seepage of natural hydrocarbon gases from underground. They have been given their name because..they erupt intermittently, they extrude flows of 'Mud lava', and they build up cones. 1955 Bull. Geol. Soc. Amer. LXVI. 1117/1 One mud volcano on an embankment was particularly instructive. Its cone was 7 or 8 feet in diameter. 1967 K. Wilcoxson Volcanoes xv. 158 Mud volcanoes are not true volcanoes at all but have features more in common with hot springs and geysers. 1927 Daily Express 9 Sept. 11/3 All the six 1928 models are of improved appearance, with ..*mudwings which not only look better, but also keep off the mud more efficiently. 1959 Times 27 Apr. (Rubber Industry Suppl.) p. vi/1 On many goods and passenger vehicles rubber mud-wings are used.

b. In names of animals: **mud bass**, an American fish, *Acantharchus pomotis*; **mud-borer**, a crustacean, *Gebia stellata* (A. White *Crustacea Brit. Mus.*, 1850); **mud-burrower**, a crustacean, *Callianassa subterranea* (*Ibid.*); **mud cat** *U.S.*, one of several species of catfish found in the Mississippi valley; also *fig.* and *transf.*, an inhabitant of Mississippi, which was sometimes called the ***Mudcat State***; **mud catfish** *U.S.*, the bullhead, *Ameiurus nebulosus*; **mud coot**, the common American coot, *Fulica americana*

(*Cent. Dict.* 1890); **mud crab**, a crab of the genus *Panopæus*; **mud dab**, the winter flounder, *Pseudopleuronectes americanus*; **mud-dauber**, (*a*) a wasp of the genus *Sceliphron* that builds its nest of mud; (*b*) *U.S.* = *mud swallow*; also *transf.* and *fig.*, a travelling workman; **mud-devil** = HELLBENDER 1; **mud-dipper**, the ruddy duck, *Erismatura rubida* (G. Trumbull *Names of Birds*, 1888, p. 110); **mud duck** *U.S.*, a domestic duck; **mud dweller**, an animal living in a muddy habitat, esp. a water beetle, *Ilybius fuliginosus*; **mud eel**, (*a*) the young of the lamprey; (*b*) = *mud iguana*; **mud-hen**, (*a*) the moor-hen, *Gallinula chloropus*; (*b*) in U.S., *Rallus crepitans*, *R. elegans*, *R. Virginianus*; also the American coot, *Fulica americana*, and the common gallinule, *Gallinula galeata*; (*c*) a bivalve mollusc of the family *Veneridæ* and genus *Tapes* (*Cent. Dict.*); **mud hopper** = *mud-skipper*; **mud iguana**, a name given in S. Carolina to the Siren, *Siren lacertina*; **mud minnow** (see quot.); **mud-poke, -pout** = *mud cat*; **mud-puppy** *U.S.*, a name for the axolotl, also for the hellbender, and other salamanders; **mud shad**, a fish, *Dorosoma cepedianum*; **mud-skipper**, a small Asian, Australasian, or African fish of the family Periophthalmidæ, which is able to scramble over mud and along tree roots, etc.; **mud snail**, either of two species of pond snail, *Lymnæa glabra* or *L. trunculata*; **mud-sucker**, (*a*) an aquatic fowl that obtains its food from mud; (*b*) a catostomoid fish; **mud swallow** *U.S.*, a North American cliff swallow of the genus *Petrochelidon*, which builds jar-shaped nests of mud; also *attrib.* and *fig.*; **mud-terrapin, -tortoise, -turtle** (*dial.* **-turkle**) *U.S.*, a turtle which lives in the mud or muddy water, esp. species of *Trionychidæ* and *Emydidæ*; also *transf.* and *fig.*; so **mud-turtle-shaped** *a.*; **mud trout**, a name used in Newfoundland for the brook trout, *Salvelinus fontinalis*; **mud wasp** *U.S.* = *mud dauber*; **mud-worm**, a worm that lives in the mud, *esp.* one of the *Limicolæ*; also *fig.* applied contemptuously to a person.

1884 GOODE, etc. *Nat. Hist. Aquatic Anim.* 405 The *Mud Bass. **1819** D. THOMAS *Trav. Western Country* 211 The *mud cat is covered with clouded spots, and is a very homely fish. **1872** SCHELE DE VERE *Americanisms* 660 Mississippi is occasionally spoken of humorously as the *Mudcat State*, the inhabitants being quite generally known as Mud-cats. **1882** JORDAN & GILBERT *Synopsis Fishes N. Amer.* 101 *Pilodictis*, ..Mud Cats. **1883** 'MARK TWAIN' *Life on Mississippi* liv. 532 He didn't really catch anything but only just one small useless mud-cat. **1935** in Z. N. Hurston *Mules & Men* (1970) I. vii. 159 Not no great big trouts nor mud-cats but li'l perches and brims. **1945** B. A. BOTKIN *Lay my Burden Down* 27 The next is a mudcat; this kind of a fish likes dark trashy places. **1945** *Chicago Daily News* 16 Aug. 10/7 While we are laying down surrender terms for the Japanese, how about a Declaration on Senator 'Dear Dago' Bilbo, the Mississippi mudcat? **1842** J. E. DEKAY *Zool. N.Y.* IV. 187 The *Mud Catfish..[is] recognized by the scarified and clouded appearance of its skin. **1964** Mud catfish [see GOUJON]. **1713** PETIVER *Aquat. Anim. Amboinæ* 1 Squilla Lutaria *Rum* ...*Mud-Crab. **1884** GOODE, etc. *Nat. Hist. Aquatic Anim.* 772 The Mud Crabs—*Panopeus Herbstii* [etc.]. **1882** JORDAN & GILBERT *Synopsis Fishes N. Amer.* 837 *Pleuronectes americanus*. *Mud dab. **1856** *Zoologist* XIV. 5030 The species of the genus *Pelopæus* are popularly known as *mud-daubers in America. **1866** 'MARK TWAIN' *Sk. New & Old* (1875) 297 The old mud-dobber tackled the piano, and ran his fingers up and down once or twice. **1899** F. BERGEN *Animal & Plant Lore* 34 The building of the mud-daubers, or swallows, on the barn or house is a sign of prosperity to the occupants. **1932** E. STEP *Bees, Wasps, Ants* 71 Mud-daubers (*Sceliphron*) of warmer countries..build great clusters of mud cells for their eggs and prey. **1945** H. S. PEARSON *Country Flavor* 49 There was often a phoebe's home to explore and dozens of mud daubers' nests. **1963** *Amer. Speech* XXXVIII. 271 Mason: *mud dauber*. **1966** C. SWEENEY *Scurrying Bush* v. 76 Mud daubers can be a great nuisance, for they build their nests, stuffed with spiders or caterpillars depending on the species, in any hidden place. **1974** A. DILLARD *Pilgrim at Tinker Creek* xii. 214 My life inside the cottage is mostly Tinker Creek and mud dauber wasps. **1845** *Encycl. Metrop.* XXIV. 269 By the Anglo-Americans it is called Hellbender *Mud Devil [etc.]. **1857** *Spirit of Times* 26 Sept. 54/2 There is duck of every quality, canvas-back, wood, *mud, and various other species. **1903** *Forest & Stream* 27 Feb. 150 They are a cross between the mallard and ordinary mud duck. **1920** E. POUND *Let.* 11 Sept. (1971) 158 If you weren't stupider than a mud-duck you would know that every kick to bad writing is by that much a help for the good. **1952** J. CLEGG *Freshwater Life* xiv. 221 The *Mud Dweller, *Ilybius fuliginosus*, [is] a bronze-coloured beetle with yellow margins to its wing-cases. **1963** *Times* 19 Jan. 10/6 It [*sc.* the Dublin Bay Prawn] feeds, somewhat indiscriminately like all its kind, on its fellow mud-dwellers. **1823** *Charleston* (S. Carolina) *Courier* 7 Mar. 2/4 The British..fairly chased our militiamen across Broad River, to the huge amazement of the *mud eels and cats. **1840** KIRTLAND in *Boston Jrnl. Nat. Hist.* III. 473 *Ammocoetes concolor* Kirtland. The Mud-Eel. **1842** HOLBROOK *N. Amer. Herpetol.* V. 102 *Siren lacertina*... Mud Eel or Siren, *Vulgo*. **1611** FLORIO, *Limósa*, a kind of *Mud or Moore-hen. **1808–13** A. WILSON *Amer. Ornith.* (1831) III. 103 *Rallus crepitans*...Clapper Rail... It is designated..the mud hen. *Ibid.* 108 [The Virginian Rail] is known..along the sea-coast of New Jersey by the name of the fresh-water mud hen. *Ibid.* 124 *Fulica americana*... Cinereous Coot... It is known in Pennsylvania by the name of the mud-hen. **1959** *Listener* 29 Oct. 738/3 The skittering of the *mud hoppers, those extraordinary little fish that can climb trees. **1965** *Sunday Mail Mag.* (Brisbane) 21 Nov. 14/1 The mud-hopper belongs to a special group of goby (or small fish) and is notable for its strange eyes and for the stiff fins which it seems to be able to use like limbs. **1766** J. ELLIS in *Phil. Trans.* LVI. 189 The natives call it *Mud-Inguana [*sic*]. **1882** JORDAN & GILBERT *Synopsis Fishes N. Amer.* 349 *Umbridæ*. (The *Mud Minnows.) **1809** W. IRVING *Knickerb.* IV. ii. (1820) 361 That notable bird ycleped the *Mud-Poke. **1806** FESSENDEN *Orig. Poems* 132 Like an otter that paddles the creek, In quest of a *mud pout or sucker. **1872** SCHELE DE VERE *Americanisms* 382 A species [of Catfish] is known also as *Mudpout*. **1889** *Century Dict.* s.v. *Axolotl*, The various species of *Amblystoma* known in the United States as *mud-puppies, water-dogs [etc.]. **1897** *Outing* (U.S.) XXX. 439/2 The mud-puppy..is a repulsive-looking water-lizard. **1884** GOODE, etc. *Nat. Hist. Aquat. Anim.* 610 The *Mud-shad. **1860** F. MASON *Burmah* 854 *Mud-skipper, *Periophthalmus*. **1957** L. EISELEY *Immense Journey* 58 Of all these fishes the *mud-skipper *Periophthalmus* is perhaps the strangest. **1972** *Islander* (Victoria, B.C.) 16 Apr. 4/2 [Queensland] After exploring the mangroves for the amphibious mudskipper fish [etc.]. **1926** A. E. ELLIS *Brit. Snails* 111 *L*[*imnæa*] *glabra*..*Mud Snail..inhabits ponds and ditches, and frequently lives in places which are left dry in summer. **1972** *Country Life* 2 Mar. 524/3 The damp and muddy slopes where they [*sc.* liver-flukes] can find their next host..the species of snail called the mud-snail, or..*Lymnaea truncutata*. **1688** R. HOLME *Armoury* II. xiii. 313/1 *Mudsuckers, Birds that suck and dabble in muddy waters. **1888** GOODE *Amer. Fishes* 143 *note*, Gaspergou is an Indian word, meaning 'fish', and is applied by Louisianians to anything fishy from the sheepshead to the mudsucker. **1898** M. DELAND *Old Chester Tales* 181 *Mud-swallows had built their nests in the corners. **1917** T. G. PEARSON *Birds Amer.* III. 84 Cliff Swallow... Barn Swallow; Mud Swallow; Republican Swallow. **1873** LELAND *Egypt. Sketch-Bk.* 42 Those curious *mud-swallow nests of little villages. **1859** BARTLETT *Dict. Amer.*, *Mud-Turtle* (*Sternothærus odorata*)...Marsh Tortoise and *Mud Terrapin are other names for the same. **1668** CHARLETON *Onomast.* 28 *Testudo Lutaria*..the *Mud Tortoise. **1841** STORER in *Bost. Jrnl. Nat. Hist.* III. 7 *Sternothaerus odoratus*. The mud Tortoise. **1854** R. OWEN in *Orr's Circ. Sci.*, *Org. Nat.* I. 213 The soft or mud-tortoises (*trionyx* and *sphargis*). **1917** *Dialect Notes* IV. 332 **Mud-trout*, the brook-trout. **1969** H. HORWOOD *Newfoundland* 224 Newfoundland's only native trout..is the speckled brook trout (known locally..as a 'mud trout'). **1884** 'MARK TWAIN' *Huck. Finn* 69 And so you ain't had no meat nor bread to eat all this time? Why didn't you get *mud-turkles? **1909** *Dialect Notes* III. 351 *Mud-turkle*, the mud-turtle: chiefly among the negroes. **1946** *Publ. Amer. Dial. Soc.* VI. 21 *Mud turkle*, a small turtle found in muddy bottoms, in either fresh or salt water. Pamlico. Mainly among Negroes. **1796** *Aurora* (Philadelphia) 17 May (Th.), The crocodile throats of the gentle snappers or *mud tortles in the Jersey market. **1854** R. OWEN in *Orr's Circ. Sci.*, *Org. Nat.* I. 213, The..mud-turtles (*trionyx*). **1873** 'MARK TWAIN' & WARNER *Gilded Age* 48 He's in that pilot-house now, showing those mud-turtles how to hunt for easy water. **1891** C. ROBERTS *Adrift Amer.* 239 In the creeks were plenty of mud turtles. **1896** *Harper's Mag.* Sept. 527 A mud-turtle of a back-settlement lawyer. **1915** CONRAD *Victory* vii. 135 Fancy a mud-turtle like you trying to pass an opinion on a gentleman! **1871** 'MARK TWAIN' *Screamers* 132 A pickininny, *mud-turtle-shaped craft of a schooner. **1824** *Old Colony Memorial* (Plymouth) 6 Mar. (Th.), A sort of would-be dandy; having the bottom of his waist pinched up to the size of a quart pot, and thus resembling in shape what we call a *mud wasp. **1861** *Trans. Illinois Agric. Soc.* IV. 338 The common black and yellow mud wasp (*Pelopæus lunatus*) belongs to this group. **1881** *Amer. Naturalist* XV. 443 Baron Osten Sacken..records the breeding of *A*[*rgyramœba*] *cephus*..from the nest of a Texan mud-wasp. *a* **1814** *Love, Honor & Interest* II. iii. in *New Brit. Theatre* III. 276 The *mud-worm, Vanderclufe! **1865** DICKENS *Mut. Fr.* IV. xiv, When..I saw such a mud-worm as you presume [etc.]. **1870** H. A. NICHOLSON *Man. Zool.* xxix. (1875) 216 The *Limicolæ* or Mud-worms.

c. In names of plants: **mud horsetail**, an *Equisetum*, esp. *E. Telmateia*; **mud knotweed** *U.S.* (see quot.); **mud plantain**, *Heteranthera reniformis* (*Treas. Bot.* 1866); **mud purslane** *U.S.*, *Elatine americana*; **mud-rush, -sedge**, various cyperaceous plants; **mud-weed**, (*a*) *Limosella aquatica*; (*b*) *Helosciadium inundatum* (Treas. Bot. 1866); **mud-wort**, the genus *Limosella*, esp. *L. aquatica*.

1855 MISS PRATT *Flower. Pl.* (1861) VI. 297 Great *Mud Horsetail. **1845–50** MRS. LINCOLN *Lect. Bot.* App. 145/2 *Polygonium amphibium* (*mud knotweed). **1846–50** A. WOOD *Class-bk. Bot.* 195 *Elatine americana*, *Mud Purslane. **1859** MISS PRATT *Flower. Pl.* VI. 11 *Isolepis* (*Mud-rush). **1899** *Edin. Rev.* Apr. 318 The work was done by mud-rushes transporting upwards miscellaneous subterranean *débris*. **1859** MISS PRATT *Flower. Pl.* VI. 37 *Carex limosa* (*Mud Sedge). **1756** J. HILL *Brit. Herbal* 84 *Mudweed. *Plantaginella*. **1796** WITHERING *Brit. Plants* (ed. 3) III. 557 Bastard Plantain, or Plantain Mudweed. **1789** W. AITON *Hortus Kewensis* II. 359 *Limosella aquatica*...Bastard Plantain, or *Mud-wort.

mud (mʌd), *sb.*[2] Also 5 **mudde, mod.** [a. Du. *mudde, mud* = OS. *muddi*, OHG. *mutti* (mod.G. *mütt, mutt*), OE. *mydd*:—WGer. **muddjo*- a. L. *modius*: see MODIUS, MUID.] A Dutch measure of capacity, in Holland now identified with the HECTOLITRE: see MUID.

1477 *Extracts Aberd. Reg.* (1844) I. 408 Item, tuelf mod keling, and threttene mod codlinges. **1483** CAXTON *Golden Leg.* 148b, Two hondred muddes of mele. **1863** W. C. BALDWIN *Afr. Hunting* 30, I..bought a mud of mealies for the horse.

mud (mʌd), *v.*[1] Now *rare*. [f. MUD *sb.*[1]]

1. a. *trans.* To make (water, liquor) turbid by stirring up the mud or sediment at the bottom.

1593 SHAKS. *Lucr.* 577 Mudde not the fountaine that gaue drinke to thee. **1686** GOAD *Celest. Bodies* II. xiv. 341 'Tis a great Stone which upon injection mudds the Water. **1703** MAUNDRELL *Journ. Jerus.* 27 Apr. (1721) 124 The bough is dragg'd all along the Channel, and serves..to mud and fatten the Water for the great benefit of the Gardens. **1876** TENNYSON *Harold* v. i, The wolf Mudded the brook.

†**b.** *transf.* To thicken, to clog. *Obs.*

1669 W. SIMPSON *Hydrol. Chym.* 123 A steam ariseth which..muds the animal spirits.

c. *fig.* (Chiefly with reference to a metaphorical 'stream' or 'fount'.)

1593 NASHE *Christ's T.* 13 The fount of my teares (troubled and mudded with the Toade-like stirring and long-breathed vexation of thy venimous enormities). **1617** HIERON *Wks.* II. 219 Thus had it, I may so speake, mudded his heart, and made his corruption worke more strongly in him. **1697** COLLIER *Immor. Stage* i. (1698) 29 Enough to mud their Fancy, to tarnish their Quality, and make their Passion Scandalous. **1717** *Entertainer* No. 5. 27 When Justice flows in her proper Channels, and is not mudded or soiled with Partiality [etc.]. **1774** *Westm. Mag.* II. 450 The very fountain-head is mudded by these false teachers.

2. a. To cover with mud; to plaster with mud.

1632 SHERWOOD, To mudde, beray or bedash with mudde, sticke in mudde, *embourber, enfanger, embouër*. **1649** BLITHE *Eng. Improv. Impr.* (1653) 125 Lime it well, or Mud it well, and afterward Muck it over with good Cow or Horse Dung. **1769** *Trinculo's Trip* 46 Being so mudded, splash'd and wash'd. **1883** C. J. WILLS *Land of Lion & Sun* 57 A roof some six feet thick, being painted wood mudded over a yard deep.

b. Also with *off* or *up*. (*a*) *trans.* To seal (porous strata) by causing a layer of mud to be deposited on the sides of a bore-hole. (*b*) *intr.* To become coated in this way. Cf. MUD *sb.*[1] 1 f.

1916 JOHNSON & HUNTLEY *Princ. Oil & Gas Production* xii. 123 In drilling by the rotary system, usually there is but one size of hole and but one string of casing used, as the sides of the hole are 'mudded up' as drilling proceeds, and caving beds and minor gas and water sands are shut off in this way. **1916** LEWIS & MCMURRAY *Use of Mud-Laden Fluid in Oil & Gas Wells* (U.S. Bur. of Mines Bull. 134) 23 When a sand is to be 'mudded off', a comparatively thin mixture is first used. **1921** W. H. JEFFERY *Deep Well Drilling* iii. 117 The wire drilling cable now is almost universally used for drilling in deep wet holes and in soft or shale formations that 'mud up'. *Ibid.* xii. 350 The mud fluid under pump pressure has a tendency to 'mud off' an oil or gas producing formation before its paying possibilities may be discovered by the driller. **1924** L. C. UREN *Textbk. Petroleum Production Engin.* ix. 299 It is not always easy to mud an exhausted oil sand, so that it does not continue to absorb fluid. **1926** E. R. LILLEY *Oil Industry* vi. 129 Mud fluid is introduced into the hole. This is primarily for the purpose of mudding up the walls of the hole to prevent caving.

3. a. To bury in mud.

1610 SHAKS. *Temp.* III. iii. 102 I'le seeke him deeper then ere plummet sounded, And with him there lye mudded. *Ibid.* v. i. 151, I wish My selfe were mudded in that oo-zie bed Where my sonne lies.

b. *passive*. To become stuck in the mud.

1854 SIR A. WEST *Recoll.* (1899) I. iv. 146 We were mudded and slipped and slithered about a quarter of a mile. **1873** LELAND *Egypt. Sketch-Bk.* 151 Sometimes they got sanded or mudded.

4. *intr.* Of eels, etc.: To lie dormant in the mud.

1650 *Acad. Complements* 125 Or like a Carp that is lost in mudding. **1895** P. H. EMERSON *Birds, etc. of Norfolk Broadland* II. x. 365 Should a bream catch sight of you, if in a shallow, he will dart off, and 'mud', reappearing later on.

5. *trans.* To supply mud to the bottom of a pond.

1864 *Q. Rev.* CXV. 183 A pond, the owner of which informed us that several years ago he had mudded it, and then put a few eels into it.

6. To throw mud at (a person). *rare*[−1].

1832 *Blackw. Mag.* Jan. 120 Gentlemen dislike being hissed, hooted,..threatened, mudded, maimed, murdered.

Hence **'mudded** *ppl. a.*

1632 SHERWOOD, Mudded, berayed with mud, stucke in Mudde, *embourbé, emboué, enfangé*. **1898** *Daily News* 30 July 5/1 The mudded wastes of the River Crouch.

mud (mʌd), *v.*[2] *dial.* [Of obscure origin.] *trans.* To bring *up* (a child, an animal) by hand; also, to spoil and pamper.

1814 *Monthly Mag.* 1 Sept. 114 (South Wiltshire dialect) Mud the child up, dooke. *a* **1854** CAR. A. SOUTHEY *Poet. Wks.* (1867) 76 Miss will mud it [a lamb] up I know. **1891** 'MAXWELL GRAY' *In Heart of Storm* Prol. iii, Not that she'll ever come to good spoiled and mudded up as she is.

‖**mudalali** ('mʊdəlɑlɪ). *India* and *Sri Lanka*. Also **mutalali**. [Marathi, f. *muddal, mudal* capital, principal, stock; cf. MODELIAR, and Malayalam *mutalali*.] A proprietor, a businessman, a rich trader.

1855 in H. H. WILSON *Gloss. Judicial & Revenue Terms* 359/1 s.v. *Mutalali*. **1913** L. WOOLF *Village in Jungle* ii. 31 The fat Sinhalese Mudalali, Kodikarage Allis Appu, had supplied grain and curry stuffs on the same terms. **1971** *Ceylon Daily News* 18 Sept. 4/1 Beggar auctions where..the beggars themselves have their services bought by bidding beggar mudalalis.

mudar, madar (mə'dɑː(r)). Also **mudhar, mudarrh, muddar, mudir, mador.** [a. Hindī *madār*.] **a.** East Indian name for shrubs of the genus *Calotropis*, esp. *C. gigantea*, the root-bark of which yields a valuable diaphoretic medicine and the inner bark of the stem a strong silky fibre known as yercum. Also *attrib.* **b.** The medicinal product of the root.

1819 ROBINSON in *Med.-Chirurg. Trans.* X. 32 The mudar rapidly recruits the constitution, heals the ulcers [etc.]. *Ibid.* 37 In the first variety I consider Mudarrh.. as the sole effectual remedy. **1823** G. PLAYFAIR in *Trans. Med. & Phys. Soc. Calcutta* (1825) I. 86, I prescribed the Madâr, to the quantity of five grains twice a day. **1826** AINSLIE *Mat. Ind.* I. 487 Mr. Robinson has written a paper..extolling the mudar root (yercum vayr) as most efficacious. **1836** *Penny Cycl.* VI. 168/2 The Mudar, a plant common in sandy places in many parts of India. **1838** LINDLEY *Flora Med.* §1144. 540 Under the names of Mador, Mudar, Akum, and Yercund, the root and bark..are used as..purgatives. **1861** BENTLEY *Man. Bot.* 595 Mudar bark, which has been much employed in India in cutaneous affections. **1873** DRURY *Usef. Plants India* (ed. 2) 101 It yields a kind of manna called Mudar sugar. **1880** *Encycl. Brit.* XI. 339/2 The alstonia.. and the mudar gum..have also been recommended as substitutes for gutta percha.

Hence **'mudarine**, a bitter principle obtained from the root-bark of the mudar.

1829 DUNCAN in *Edin. Med. & Surg. Jrnl.* July 64 It may form a new principle, and, for convenience, I shall provisionally call it Mudarine. **1873** DRURY *Useful Pl. India* (ed. 2) 100 Mudarine.

mud-bank. [f. MUD *sb.*[1] + BANK *sb.*[1]] A bank of mud in the bed of a river or on the bottom of the sea. Also *transf.*

1774 *Virginia Gaz.* (Williamsburg) 17 Mar. 2/2 A Sloop.. ran aground on a Mud Bank, a little Way up the Creek. **1832** W. D. WILLIAMSON *Hist. State Maine* I. 38 From both [islands] a mud bank extends to the main shore. **1908** *Westm. Gaz.* 30 Dec. 8/2 In spite of the employment of many thousands..on..clearing away the muddy remains of the recent snowstorm, the principal roadways..presented an extraordinary spectacle of mud-heaps, mud-rivers, and mud-banks. **1963** W. SOYINKA *Dance of Forests* II. 75 From Limpopo to the Nile coils but one snake On mudbanks, and sandy bed. **1974** P. DICKINSON *Poison Oracle* i. 18 The heated air rose..above reed-bed and mud-bank.

mudd(e, obs. forms of MUD.

mudden ('mʌd(ə)n), *a. rare*[−1]. [f. MUD *sb.*[1] + -EN[4].] Made of mud.

1871 TYERMAN *Wesley* III. 276 Though the windows were unglazed, and the mudden floor was such that his feet often sunk two inches deep during the performance of service.

mudder ('mʌdə(r)). *slang* (chiefly *U.S.*). [f. MUD *sb.*[1] + -ER[1].] A horse which runs well on a wet or muddy racecourse; *transf.*, a sportsman or team similarly proficient.

1903 *Outing* XLIII. 266/2 'He's a mudder,' he growled, 'and the track today will be like lightning.' **1935** *Amer. Speech* X. 315/2 Grand Slam,..winner of the Arlington futurity.., is a good mudder. **1941** *Sun* (Baltimore) 30 Aug. 13/1 Off-Track Seen. Rain today made the prospect for off-going for the first card, thus giving the 'mudders' an opportunity to strut their stuff. **1942** BERREY & VAN DEN BARK *Amer. Thes. Slang* §683/1 Football player...*mudder*, *mudlark*, a player for whom a wet field is no great handicap. **1948** *Time* 1 Nov. 44/3 Halfback Jack Swaner, a superior mudder, had a big day scoring all three touchdowns. **1950** *New Yorker* 11 Nov. 121/2 Cornell's last one [*sc.* fumble] gave Columbia, a remarkably good mudder, the chance to tie the score in the fourth quarter. **1952** *Time* 5 May 71/1 Gehrmann and Druetzler proved no mudders and.. Purdue's Denis Johansson..splashed past the leaders on the last lap. **1960** I. WALLACH *Absence of Cello* (1961) 29 Will-o'-the-Wisp in the fifth at Hialeah... He's a mudder... It rained all last night in Hialeah. **1969** *Courier-Mail* (Brisbane) 1 Jan. 1/9 Chance for 'mudders'..after last night's flash storm in Brisbane. **1975** *New Yorker* 24 Mar. 64/1 In my book, Stardust Mel is the best mudder in California. Early last month Mrs. Marjorie Lindheimer Everett's rangy gray gelding splattered through the rain and murk to win.

muddied ('mʌdɪd), *ppl. a.* [f. MUDDY *v.* + -ED[1].] Covered with mud; made muddy. Of water, turbid. Also *fig.*, esp. in phr. ***muddied oafs*** in allusion to quot. 1902.

1642 H. MORE *Song of Soul* I. II. lx, With muddied arms of trees the earth it strows. **1647** —— *Cupid's Conflict* xvii, How would'st thou then my muddied mind deceive With fading shows. **1656** E. CALAMY in Reyner *Rules Govt. Tongue* A v, The muddied fountain casteth forth foul streams. *a* **1797** MARY WOLLSTONECR. *Posth. Wks.* (1798) IV. 48, I..do not expect muddied water to become clear before it has had time to stand. **1865** W. J. LINTON *Claribel & other P.* 72 Year after year..The muddied Wye still flows. **1902** KIPLING *Islanders* 28 Then ye contented your souls With the flannelled fools at the wicket or the muddied oafs at the goals. **1912** *New Age* 29 Feb. 416/2 The 'flannelled fools' and 'muddied oafs', who come down from Oxford and Cambridge. **1964** C. MACKENZIE *My Life & Times* III. iv. 160 No amount of writing about flannelled fools at the wicket and muddied oafs in the goal by Rudyard Kipling could save the British Empire from ultimate collapse.

muddify ('mʌdɪfaɪ), *v.* [f. MUDDY *a.* + -FY.] *trans.* To make muddy, to muddle.

1789 H. WALPOLE *Let. to Han. More* 4 Nov., Don't muddify your charming simplicity with controversial distinctions. **1889** GRETTON *Memory's Harkb.* 132, I always used to think that if I were on the jury, I should go to consider my verdict muddified rather than enlightened.

muddily ('mʌdɪlɪ), *adv.* [-LY[2].] In a muddy manner (*lit.* and *fig.*).

1648 JENKYN *Blind Guide* iv. 103 You having..gone over my two former quæree s, muddily jumble together my two last. **1693** DRYDEN *Juvenal* Ded. (1697) 43 Lucilius; who writ..loosely, and muddily. [After Hor. *Sat.* I. iv. 11 *Cum flueret lutulentus.*] **1861** *All Year Round* 1 June 235 Warning me not to leap over and be either muddily drowned or beaten to death by the vessel's keel.

muddiness ('mʌdɪnɪs). [-NESS.] The condition of being muddy. Also *fig.*

c **1645** HOWELL *Lett.* (1655) I. 39 If this Letter fail either in point of Orthography or Style, you must impute..the second to the muddinesse of my Brain. **1684–5** BOYLE *Min. Waters* 25 Of the Transparency, the Muddiness, or the Opacity of the Mineral Water. **1784** J. BARRY in *Lect. Paint.* vi. (1848) 217 Warm and cold tints..which by their mixture would produce muddiness and opacity. **1858** HAWTHORNE *Fr. & It. Note-bks.* (1872) I. 32 The horrible muddiness.. of all Paris. **1867** TROLLOPE *Chron. Barset* II. lxi. 187 That muddiness of mind of which he had..accused himself. **1874** GARROD & BAXTER *Mat. Med.* (1880) 120 The solution in distilled water is clear, or has only a slight muddiness. **1915** D. H. LAWRENCE *Let. c* 7 July (1962) I. 352, I am rid of all my Christian religiosity. It was only a muddiness. **1964** S. DUKE-ELDER *Parsons' Dis. Eye* (ed. 14) x. 107 'Muddiness of the iris' is the expression used for indistinctness of the pattern, caused by inflammatory exudates.

mudding ('mʌdɪŋ), *vbl. sb.* [f. MUD *v.*[1] + -ING[1].]

1. a. The action of making muddy.

1632 SHERWOOD, A mudding, beraying with, or sticking in mudde, *embourbement, enfangement.* **1635** A. STAFFORD *Fem. Glory* (1869) 179 The mudding of their purest Fountaine. **1895** H. P. ROBINSON in *Forum* (N.Y.) Jan. 528 The mudding of the stream in Æsop's fable.

b. The filling of cracks in the walls of a house or log-cabin with mud. *Canad.*

1898 F. RUSSELL *Explor. Far North* 2 The autumnal 'mudding' was poorly done. **1965** E. L. MYLES *Emperor of Peace River* II. iii. 209 On the exterior of the logs treatment was a must if the rooms were to be warm in winter. This treatment consisted of an annual 'mudding', the forcing into the chinks between the logs of a mixture of mud and straw.

2. A jocular term for: Plastic work, modelling.

1892 STEVENSON & L. OSBOURNE *Wrecker* 6 'The daubs are mine—and his; the mudding mine.' 'Mudding? What is that?' asked Havens. 'These bronzes,' replied Dodd.

muddir, obs. Sc. form of MOTHER.

muddish ('mʌdɪʃ), *a.* [f. MUD *sb.*[1] + -ISH.] Somewhat muddy.

1658 ROWLAND tr. *Moufet's Theat. Ins.* 940 The back and belly sometimes..of muddish colour. **1829** SCOTT *Diary* 20 Apr. in *Lockhart*, [The wit] of Lord Erskine was moody and muddish.

muddle ('mʌd(ə)l), *sb.* [f. MUDDLE *v.*]

1. A muddled condition; confusion, disorder; mental confusion, bewilderment. Also, a result of muddling, a bungle, 'mess'. Esp. in phr. ***in a muddle. to make a muddle of***: to bungle.

1818 TODD, *Muddle*, a confused or turbid state: a vulgar expression. **1833** J. CONSTABLE *Let.* 14 Jan. in *Corr.* (1965) III. 90, I shall be glad when these great pictures are out of doors—but still it's a good thing to be in a muddle. **1852** DICKENS *Bleak Ho.* v, We both grub on in a muddle. **1857** HUGHES *Tom Brown* Pref. (1871) 18 A pretty muddle we should have been in had he done so. **1871** SMILES *Charac.* ii. (1876) 54 Work can only be got through by method. Muddle flies before it. **1884** *Sat. Rev.* 7 June 732/1 The present Government has made an immortal muddle of the whole business. **1884** A. BAIRD *Egypt. Muddle* 12 The Egyptian muddle—for I can call it nothing else— into which we have been dragged by the Government.

2. A confused assemblage.

1865 DICKENS *Mut. Fr.* I. vii, One dark shop-window with a tallow candle dimly burning in it, and surrounded by a muddle of objects. **1891** KIPLING *Light that Failed* xiii. (1900) 222 A scarred, formless muddle of paint.

3. *U.S.* 'A kind of chowder; a pottle made with crackers' (*Cent. Dict.* 1890).

4. a. *Comb.*, chiefly parasynthetic (after MUDDLE-HEADED *a.*) with the sense 'muddled', as ***muddle-brained, -minded, -thoughted*** adjs.; **muddle-pate** = MUDDLE-HEAD. Also **muddle-room** *rare*[−1], a room set apart for untidy work.

1895 MORRIS in Mackail *Life* (1899) II. 310 Coleridge was a *muddle-brained metaphysician. **1862** H. MARRYAT *Year in Sweden* II. 8 The house keeper—a *muddle-minded woman. *a* **1849** POE *R. H. Horne* Wks. 1864 III. 427 The cant of the *muddlepates who dishonor a profound.. philosophy by styling themselves transcendentalists. **1886** MRS. LYNN LINTON *Paston Carew* v, A..room on the ground-floor, which the Clinton girls had made their '*muddle-room'. **1905** E. PHILLPOTTS *Secret Woman* III. v. 250 What a *muddle-thoughted man you be—all in a maze!

¶ **b.** Taken as adj. = 'muddled'.

1798 JOANNA BAILLIE *Tryal* II. i, Damn your muddle pate!

muddle ('mʌd(ə)l), *v.* Also (? 6,) 7 mudle. [f. MUD *sb.*[1] or *v.*[1]: see -LE. Cf. MDu. *moddelen*, frequentative of *modden* to dabble in mud.]

†**1.** *trans.* ? To throw into the mud, to knock down. *Obs. rare*[−1]. [Possibly some misreading.]

a **1550** *Christis Kirke Gr.* 129 (Bann. MS.), He mudlet thame doun lyk ony myss.

2. a. *intr.* To bathe or wallow in mud or muddy water. Also, 'to rout with the bill, as geese and ducks do' (Phillips, ed. Kersey 1706). *Obs.* exc. *arch.*

1607 TOPSELL *Four-f. Beasts* 714 Paulus Venetus saith, that..Vnicornes muddle in the durt like Swine. **1623** LISLE *Ælfric on O. & N. Test.* To Rdr. 20 As duckes who delight euer to leaue the cleere spring, and muddle in waters of their owne fouling. **1727** BRADLEY *Fam. Dict.* s.v. *Approaching*, They will quit the Middle of the Stream, and muddle along the Sides. *a* **1745** SWIFT *Dick's Variety* 15 He never muddles in the Dirt Nor scowers the Street without a Shirt. **1845** JUDD *Margaret* II. iii, The tree..easier than a duck, muddles for nourishment with its roots.

b. To grub in the soil; to do dirty work; †*fig.* to 'grub' among records. *rare.*

1756 GREVILLE *Maxims* 221 His *summum bonum* is muddling in parchments, in the offals of dulness and tastlessness. **1822** GALT *Sir A. Wylie* xxxv, I'll..muddle about the root o' this affair till I get at it. **1831** CARLYLE *Sart. Res.* III. ix, Dyers, washers and wringers that puddle and muddle in their dark recesses.

3. a. *trans.* To make muddy; to render (liquor) turbid by stirring up the sediment. Now *rare.*

1676 MARVELL *Mr. Smirke* I iv, Where they mudled the Water and Fished after. **1692** R. L'ESTRANGE *Fables* iii. 2 Villain (says he) how dare you lye muddling the Water that I'm a drinking? **1831** BREWSTER *Nat. Magic* xi. (1833) 268 It muddled the water which it drank with its bill. **1885** FAIRBAIRN *Cath. Rom. & Anglican* (1899) II. ii. 61 The churches that do nothing to reach and purify the source only help to muddle the stream.

b. *transf.* To destroy the clearness of (colours). Also † ***to muddle over***: to variegate or mottle.

In quot. 1596, the words seem to be comic perversions of Du. terms of painting; but the passage is obscure.

1596 NASHE *Saffron Walden* F 4, I have..ouzled, gidumbled, muddled, and drizled it [*sc.* the 'picture' of G. Harvey] so finely, that [etc.]. **1647** TRAPP *Comm. Mark* ii. 12 He cares not to gild gold, or muddle over a topaz. **1807** OPIE in *Lect. Paint.* iv. (1848) 320 Colours..little muddled by vehicles, and subsequent attempts to mend the first touches. **1863** E. V. NEALE *Anal. Th. & Nat.* 259 The transparent freshness of water-color drawings, when the washes are not muddled.

c. ? *U.S.* 'To mix; stir: as, to *muddle* chocolate or drinks' (*Cent. Dict.* 1890). Cf. MUDDLER 2.

4. a. To confuse, bewilder, esp. with drink. Also, to render (speech) confused or indistinct.

1687 SEDLEY *Bellamira* v. i. Wks. 1778 II. 178 This drinking does so muddle one's complexion and take off one's mettle. **1692** BENTLEY *Boyle Lect.* ii. 70 Their old Master seems to have had his Brains so muddled. **1718** LADY M. W. MONTAGU *Let. to Mrs. Thistlethwayte* 25 Sept., A head muddled with spleen. **1736** AINSWORTH *Lat. Dict.*, To muddle, or intoxicate with drinking, *Inebrio.* **1819** SHELLEY *Peter Bell 3rd* IV. xvi, A toad-like lump of limb and feature, With mind, and heart, and fancy muddled. **1822–34** *Good's Study Med.* (ed. 4) I. 691 The stupor is increased and the speech muddled. **1873** HOLLAND *A. Bonnic.* xvi, Mullens ran on in this way, muddled by his unexpected good fortune and his greed. **1886** G. ALLEN *Maimie's Sake* xvii, The liquor was muddling her.

b. *intr.* 'To become confused, esp. from drink' (*Cent. Dict.* 1890). † ***to muddle on*** (see quot.).

a **1700** B. E. *Dict. Cant. Crew*, *To Muddle on*, tho' so [*i.e.* 'half drunk'], yet to Drink on.

5. a. *trans.* To mix up blunderingly or sophistically, to confuse *together.* Also with *up.*

1836 S. R. MAITLAND *Remarks*, etc. 57 To muddle the Valdesii..with the Cathari. **1864** J. H. NEWMAN *Apol.* App. 43 My Critic has muddled it together in a most extraordinary manner. **1886** SPURGEON *Treas. Dav.* cxxix. 3 A writer says the metaphor is muddled. **1900** *Westm. Gaz.* 22 Mar. 3/2 It is childish nonsense to muddle good and bad schools together and strike an average. **1944** R. LEHMANN *Ballad & Source* 104 Sometimes she doesn't remember our names and muddles us up.

b. To bungle, mismanage (an affair); also, to render (accounts) unintelligible by want of method.

1885 *Nat. Rev.* July 675 It was only when all services had been muddled, and when the whole Governmental machinery had come to a standstill, that Nubar Pasha put down his foot. **1905** CHESTERTON *Heretics* 18 Now our affairs are hopelessly muddled by strong silent men.

6. a. *intr.* To busy oneself in a confused, unmethodical, and ineffective manner. Also with *at.*

[**1806–7**, **1827**: ? Implied in MUDDLING *ppl. a.*] **1850** W. IRVING *Goldsmith* 87 He meddled or rather muddled with literature. **1882** MISS BRADDON *Mt. Royal* i, We were muddling hopelessly in an endeavour to make good sensible rules. **1895** G. B. SHAW *Let.* 1 Mar. (1965) 491, I should muddle at it until I got it right. **1906** *Outlook* 26 May 710/2 He spends much of his time..in muddling with his flowers and vegetables.

b. With various advs. ***to muddle about***: to 'potter' about, busy oneself with various matters in an unmethodical way. ***to muddle along = to muddle on***: to 'get along' in a haphazard way, to escape absolute failure though trusting to chance and makeshift expedients. ***to muddle through***: to blunder through, to succeed in one's object in spite of one's lack of skill and foresight.

1701 NORRIS *Ideal World* I. viii. 437 Mudling on in the little affairs of a lower and more innocent, perhaps, but not less ingaged life. **1802** H. MARTIN *Helen of Glenross* II. 226 We never could muddle on at Invermay. *c* **1864** BRIGHT in *McCarthy's Remin.* (1899) I. 85 My opinion is that the Northern States will manage somehow to muddle through. **1879** MCCARTHY *Own Times* II. xx. 98 To ask the ministers who had resigned to resume their places and muddle on as they best could. **1888** MRS. H. WARD *R. Elsmere* xviii. 236, I suppose you muddle about among the poor like other people. **1899** J. E. TAYLOR *Let.* 22 Dec. in D. Ayerst *Guardian* (1971) xviii. 245, I suppose we shall muddle along and suffer the natural results. **1901** *Scotsman* 28 Feb. 8/2

They would muddle on in the old slipshod way of trusting to chance. **1910** BELLOC *Verses* 86 A gentleman who cannot jest Remarked that we should muddle through. **1931** *Economist* 21 Mar. 599/1 It reveals us as indolent, complacent, mentally lazy, hide-bound by tradition, content to 'muddle along', neglectful of self-help. **1940** L. MACNEICE *Poems 1925–40* 287 Muddling through and glad to have no answer. **1948** D. B. HAWKINS in R. O'Sullivan *King's Good Servant* viii. 92 You can muddle through only with the aid of sound instincts; without them you make the muddle but you do not get through. **1972** *Village Voice* (N.Y.) 1 June 9/5 In the absence of a national program, America muddles through to produce its energy.

7. *trans.* with *away*. To waste, get rid of (money, time, etc.) without clearly knowing how.

1827 SCOTT *Jrnl.* 10 Dec., I muddled away the evening over my Sheriff-Court processes. **1853** LYTTON *My Novel* II. v, The elder son..had muddled and sotted away much of his share in the Leslie property.

muddled (ˈmʌd(ə)ld), *ppl. a.* [f. prec. + -ED¹.]

†**1.** Made muddy or turbid. *Obs.*

1624 QUARLES *Job* vi. medit. xv, From muddled Springs can Christall Waters come? **1645** G. DANIEL *Poems* Wks. (Grosart) II. 2, I dare not..Soe much derogate from that clear Source, as borrow water from the muddled Cisternes of her Inferiour.

†**b.** Of wine: Thick. *Obs.*

1717 PRIOR *Alma* III. 589 We shall..Drink fine Champaigne, or muddl'd Port. *a* **1748** C. PITT *Dial. betw. Poet & Serv.* 34 Beer at noon, and muddled port at night. **1752** LAW *Spirit of Love* I. (1816) 16 The muddled wine always works right to the utmost of its power.

c. Of colour: Not clear.

1822–34 *Good's Study Med.* (ed. 4) I. 157 A dull muddled white, almost resembling that of tallow, or putty.

2. Confused, dazed, stupefied.

1712 ARBUTHNOT *John Bull* II. viii, I was for five years often drunk, always muddled. **1840** DICKENS *Barn. Rudge* iii, Being at the same time slightly muddled with liquor. **1854** B. TAYLOR in *Life & Letters* (1884) I. xii. 287, I write with a muddled head and a languid pen.

ˈmuddledly, *adv.* [f. MUDDLED *ppl. a.* + -LY².] In a muddled or disorganized manner; with confusion of mind.

1918 E. MARSH in *R. Brooke Coll. Poems* p. cxxv, All these people at the front who are fighting muddledly enough for some idea called England. **1935** F. M. FORD *Let.* 27 Sept. (1965) 243 Though I shall read it..it will probably be rather muddledly.

ˈmuddledom. *jocular.* [f. MUDDLE *sb.* + -DOM.] The condition of muddle; prevalence of muddle.

1891 BARING-GOULD *In Troub. Land* vi. 79, I then learned ..that equations might be complicated to the highest limits of muddledom. **1904** *Tablet* 15 Oct. 632/2 The helpless victim of State muddledom.

ˈmuddle-head. [Formed after next.] A confused or stupid person; a blockhead. Also, a disorganized, vague mind.

1853 READE *Chr. Johnstone* 130 His author, who..belongs to the class muddle-head. **1892** ZANGWILL *Bow Mystery* 16 They are a queer lot of muddle-heads are the police. **1938** H. NICOLSON *Let.* 11 July (1966) 349 About that I think that your dear muddle-head gets confused.

ˈmuddle-ˌheaded, *a.* [f. MUDDLE *sb.* (not found in our quots. before 19th c.) or MUDDLE *v.*] Having a muddled head; characteristic of one with a muddled head; stupid, confused.

1759 STERNE *Tr. Shandy* II. ii, Such a confused, pudding-headed, muddle-headed fellow. **1817–18** COBBETT *Resid. U.S.* (1822) 189 All the materials for making people drunk, or muddle headed, are much cheaper here than in England. **1871** KINGSLEY *At Last* xiii, Muddle-headed craft and elaborate silliness. **1887** A. BIRRELL *C. Brontë* x. 117 The public, muddle-headed at the best of times [etc.].

Hence **muddleˈheadedness.**

1862 *Sat. Rev.* 6 Sept. 274 That sort of utter muddle-headedness which disqualifies a man for reasoning equally with pure ignorance. **1884** SKEAT in *N. & Q.* 12 Jan. 32/2 Such is the muddle-headedness of modern English spelling. **1972** *N.Y. Rev. Bks.* 30 Jan. 38/3, I charge them both with muddle-headedness for their own views on this subject.

muddle-ˈheadedly, *adv.* [f. MUDDLE-HEADED *a.* + -LY².] In a muddle-headed manner, confusedly.

1909 G. B. SHAW *Pen Portraits* (1931) 232 Furtively, hypocritically, and muddle-headedly. **1968** *Trans-Action* V. VIII. 75 The..letters..are simply too muddle-headedly authoritative to let pass. **1973** *Esquire* May 6 Shortsighted obstructionists, muddleheadedly gumming up the wheels of progress.

muddlement (ˈmʌd(ə)lmənt). [f. MUDDLE *v.* + -MENT.] Muddle, confusion, bewilderment.

1857 W. COLLINS *Dead Secret* VI. i, I am lost in my own muddlement. **1910** *Blackw. Mag.* Sept. 422/1 Nor does any amount of sincerity compensate for muddlement. **1948** W. DE LA MARE *Chardin* 22 A picture, which, without risk of muddlement between the arts, may be said to be quiet, sonorous, shrill, strident or harsh. **1968** J. R. ACKERLEY *My Father and Myself* xiii. 146, I had suddenly recollected that my birthday was about to fall and foresaw muddlement.

muddler (ˈmʌd(ə)lə(r)). [f. MUDDLE *v.* + -ER¹.]

1. a. One who muddles.

1885 *L'pool Daily Post* 27 Mar. 4/7 The assumption that those who are not contented to till the narrow barren fields of non-resistance are..inconsistent muddlers. **1903** *Contemp. Rev.* May 610 One Unionist candidate is reduced to the plea that the other side will be 'greater muddlers'.

b. *Comb.*, as ***muddler-through***, one who conducts affairs without system or foresight (see MUDDLE *v.* 6 b).

1930 *New Statesman* 1 Nov. 110/2 That is my complaint against the peace-lovers, the muddlers-through. **1945** G. MILLAR *Maquis* iv. 66, I am a muddler-through if ever there was one.

2. (See quots.)

1880 W. H. PATTERSON *Gloss. Words Antrim & Down* 70 *Mudler*, a small metal stamper, used in public houses to crush the lumps of sugar in punch. **1884** KNIGHT *Dict. Mech.* Suppl., *Muddler*, a churning stick for chocolate. A smaller one for mixing toddies. **1955** M. MCCARTHY *Charmed Life* (1965) 24 She did them [*sc.* Old-Fashioneds] ..in their best glasses..putting in a silver muddler. **1971** *Scope* (S. Afr.) 19 Mar. 77/4 A 'muddler'—for crushing lump sugar and mixing it with bitters or other flavourings in the bottom of a glass.

ˈmuddlesome, *a.* [f. MUDDLE *sb.* or *v.* + -SOME.] Characterized by muddling.

1887 *Gentl. Mag.* Mar. 235 The authorities at Manchester had made extensive but muddlesome preparations.

muddliness (ˈmʌdlɪnɪs). [f. MUDDLY + -NESS.] The condition of being in a muddle.

1891 *Charity Organis. Rev.* May 219, I asked myself if poverty brought muddliness, or muddliness poverty.

muddling (ˈmʌd(ə)lɪŋ), *vbl. sb.* [f. MUDDLE *v.* + -ING¹.] The action of the vb. MUDDLE. Also ***muddling-along, -through*** (see MUDDLE *v.* 6 b).

1829 SCOTT *Jrnl.* 29 Mar., This muddling among old books has the quality of a sedative. **1873** H. SPENCER *Stud. Sociol.* xi. 289 Those muddlings of provisions and confusions of language in Acts of Parliament. **1949** KOESTLER *Promise & Fulfilment* ii. 17 What both Jews and Arabs believed to be a 'diabolic policy' was in fact the traditional muddling-along policy. **1955** *Times* 28 July 3/3 Can it be that..we shall abandon the immemorial practice of muddling through, and discover logic and consistency at last?

muddling (ˈmʌd(ə)lɪŋ), *ppl. a.* [f. MUDDLE *v.* + -ING².] That muddles.

a **1732** GAY *Fables* II. xiii. 17 How muddling 'tis on books to pore! **1806–7** J. BERESFORD *Miseries Hum. Life* (1826) VI. *Stage Coaches* v, Finding..at least one muddling mother with a sick—but not silent— infant. **1827** HONE *Every-day Bk.* II. 388 'Sheelah' is an Irish term,..applied to a slovenly or muddling woman. **1883** *Longm. Mag.* July 256 Copyholders..are as a rule..more muddling in their ways, than the dependent labourer.

Hence **ˈmuddlingly** *adv.*

1830 LAMB *Let. to Dyer* in *Final Mem.* xvii. 167 What a power to intoxicate his crude brains, just muddlingly awake to perceive that something is wrong in the social system.

ˈmuddly, *a.* Also muddley. [f. MUDDLE *sb.* + -Y¹.] Confused, muddled; passing imperceptibly into: confusing, bewildering.

1909 M. B. SAUNDERS *Litany Lane* II. xvii. 227, I gather it from some of the muddly things he said. **1929** D. H. LAWRENCE *Let.* 24 Aug. (1962) II. 1184, I can't make out if I have to pay this muddley bill for the gramophone or not. **1938** N. MARSH *Artists in Crime* ii. 14, I won't have that sort of thing—it's too muddly. **1959** —— *Singing in Shrouds* viii. 161 A long muddly argument. **1970** 'O. JOHN' *Diamond Dress* i. 8 I'm sorry to be so muddly.

†**ˈmuddy,** *sb.*¹ *Obs.* [? Subst. use of MUDDY *a.*: see quot. 1806.] A kind of coach.

1801 in *Spirit Publ. Jrnls.* V. 233 No more the stylish, well-enamell'd fair Lolls in her muddy with affected air. **1806** SURR *Winter in Lond.* II. 210 [She] bespoke..a coach hung so low that it obtained the name of a muddy.

muddy (ˈmʌdɪ), *a.* (and *sb.*²) Also 6 moudy, mudie, 6–7 muddie. [f. MUD *sb.*¹ + -Y.]

1. a. Abounding in mud; turbid or foul with mud; covered or bespattered with mud.

1526 *Pilgr. Perf.* (W. de W. 1531) 114 Take muddy water out of a dyche. **1555** EDEN *Decades* 99 He wandered throughe many..muddy marysshes. **1697** DRYDEN *Virg. Georg.* IV. 687 All these Cocytus bounds with squalid Reeds, With muddy Ditches, and with deadly Weeds. **1756** C. LUCAS *Ess. Waters* I. 36 The stagnant waters of ponds..are always foul, heavy, muddy, and ill-tasted. **1859** KINGSLEY *Misc.* (1860) I. 19 By spreading his cloak over a muddy place for Queen Elizabeth to step on. **1884** *West. Morn. News* 9 Sept. 4/5 The station..was filled by a muddy throng.

b. Of the nature of mud, resembling mud.

1737 WHISTON *Josephus, Wars* VII. viii. §4 Free from the mixture of all terrine and muddy particles of matter. **1864** *Chamb. Encycl.* VI. 162/2 The flesh [of the Lake Loach] is soft and has a muddy flavour. **1880** C. R. MARKHAM *Peruv. Bark* 173 On one morning the surging flood being black,.. and on another a light muddy colour.

c. As *sb.* The Missouri or Mississippi. Esp. *the Big Muddy*, the Missouri River.

1825 in S. F. COOPER *Rural Hours* (1850) 481 Ye plains where sweet Big-Muddy rolls along, and Teapot, one day to be found in song. **1859** *Trans. Illinois Agric. Soc.* III. 352 In the winter of '55–6, when one wide sweep of destruction laid dead most of the orchard trees north of the Big Muddy. **1884** 'MARK TWAIN' *Huck. Finn* lxvi. 130 When it was daylight, here was the clear Ohio water inshore,..and outside was the old regular Muddy. **1948** *Newsweek* 30 Aug. 21/3 We're going clear to the Missouri River and smash this stuff back across the Big Muddy.

2. Living or growing in mud.

1598 Q. ELIZ. *Horace* 6 That face aboue of woman faire, The rest fowle Like the moudy fische. **1611** FLORIO, *Melogna*, a kind of muddy fish. **1818** SHELLEY *Marenghi* xv, And on the other, creeps eternally, Through muddy weeds, the shallow sullen sea. **1883** 'ANNIE THOMAS' *Mod. Housewife* 99 There are plenty of grey mullet to be caught; .. I will dress them in such a way as shall make you fail to recognise our muddy friend.

3. Of a liquid: Not clear, thick, turbid.

1618 LATHAM *2nd Bk. Falconry* (1633) 19 With muddie and bloudie water in it verie often. *a* **1661** FULLER *Worthies, Northampt.* (1662) II. 291 Thus the most generous Wines are the most muddy before they are fine. **1708** J. PHILIPS *Cyder* II. 313 Take care The muddy Bev'rage to serene. **1806** A. HUNTER *Culina* (ed. 3) 148 Nothing is so disagreeable as a muddy gravy soup. **1836** MRS. CARLYLE *Lett.* (1883) I. 61 We breakfasted..on muddy coffee and scorched toast. **1843** BORROW *Bible in Spain* ii. 12 There they..drink the muddy but strong wine of the Alemtejo.

4. *transf.* **a.** Not clear or pure in colour. Of light: Dull, smoky.

1590 SHAKS. *Mids. N.* III. ii. 139 To what, my loue, shall I compare thine eyne! Christall is muddy. **1658** GADBURY *Doctr. Nativities* 83 A muddy-duskish-brown-swarthy Complexion. **1662** BP. HOPKINS *Serm., Funeral* (1685) 91 The dim and muddy light of this world. **1710** *Lond. Gaz.* No. 4737/3 One Timothy Hall, of middle Stature, muddy Complexion. **1784** BARRY in *Lect. Paint.* vi. (1848) 215 When a light colour, though opaque, is thinly spread over a dark one, it is, by the colour underneath, rendered dim and muddy. **1844** DISRAELI *Coningsby* I. i, A muddy mezzotinto of the Duke of Wellington. **1856** KANE *Arct. Expl.* I. xv. 173 We work by muddy tapers of cork and cotton floated in saucers. **1898** P. MANSON *Trop. Diseases* xxii. 350 His friends observed that his face had become muddy and haggard.

b. Of the voice: Thick, esp. through drinking.

1841 J. T. HEWLETT *Parish Clerk* I. 69 The squire..said, with a muddy voice [etc.].

c. Of air: Impure. ? *Obs.*

1726 LEONI *Alberti's Archit.* I. 5/1 The Air for want of Motion will grow thick and muddy.

d. Of a musical sound: blurred, not clearly differentiated.

1962 A. NISBETT *Technique Sound Studio* iii. 55 The balance to seek is one where you get plenty of reverberation, but not so much that the sound becomes muddy or coloured.

5. a. Not clear in mind; confused, muddled.

1611 SHAKS. *Wint. T.* I. ii. 325 Do'st thinke I am so muddy, so vnsetled, To appoint my selfe in this vexation? **1670** BUNYAN *No Way to Heaven but by Christ* Wks. (1845) 122 If the understanding be muddy as to this, it is impossible that such should be sound in the faith. **1682** J. W. *Let. fr. New-Eng.* 7 As to their Drunkenness,..they.. seldom go to bed without muddy brains. **1790** BURKE *Fr. Rev.* Wks. V. 152 Cold hearts and muddy understandings. **1834** HOOD *Lament Toby* x, Day after day my lessons fade, My intellect gets muddy. **1876** GEO. ELIOT *Let.* 25 Feb. (1956) VI. 223, I am rather muddy as to the relation of total sales. **1934** A. HUXLEY *Let.* 28 Apr. (1969) 380 Pareto... doesn't, like these 'deep' and muddy Germans, invent gratuitous metaphysical entities.

b. Partly intoxicated. Now *rare* or *Obs.*

1776 JOHNSON in Boswell *Life* (1831) III. 348 Not that he gets drunk, for he is a very pious man, but he is always muddy. **1843** NICHOLSON *Hist. & Tradit. T.* 414 The fiddler waxed muddy and was often heard scraping behind the fiddle bridge.

6. Of literary style, thought, etc.: Obscure, vague, confused.

1611 BIBLE *Transl. Pref.* ¶7 Therefore the Greeke being not altogether cleare, the Latine deriued from it must needes be muddie. **1643** FEATLEY in *Newman's Concord. Bible* Advt. 4 In this thickest and muddiest passage in which no Lincius [1650 Lynceus] can see any bottome, the Originall is very cleare. **1716** M. DAVIES *Athen. Brit.* III. 31 His own Imitation of Quintilian's muddy Expression. **1741** CHESTERF. *Lett.* (1792) I. lxxvii. 213 Every man..may be clear and perspicuous in his recitals instead of dark and muddy. **1840** THACKERAY *Paris Sk.-bk.* (1872) 173 The present muddy French transcendentalism. *a* **1872** RANKINE *Songs & Fables* (1874) 40 His style is never muddy.

7. Morally impure or 'dirty'. Now *rare*.

1413 *Pilgr. Sowle* (Caxton 1483) IV. ii. 59 Spyrituel men, that ben contemplatyf, hauen sette theyr hertes in heyghte and drawen them oute of this moddy erthe. **1603** H. CROSSE *Vertues Commw.* (1878) 128 She is a muddie queane, a filthy beast. **1653** H. MORE *Conject. Cabbal.* (1713) 25 The muddy and tumultuous suggestions of the Flesh. *a* **1679** W. OUTRAM *Serm.* (1682) 279 On one hand there are stable joys ..on the other muddy and fleeting pleasures. **1793** LD. SPENCER in *Ld. Auckland's Corr.* (1862) III. 114 Renard's is a muddy business. **1882** STEVENSON *New Arab. Nts.* (1884) 142 Your business..is too muddy for such airs.

†**8.** Gloomy; sullen. *Obs.*

1638 BAKER tr. *Balzac's Lett.* (vol. III.) 33 Shee aspires to no glory by sullen humours, she hath nothing muddy, nor clownish in her. **1686** HORNECK *Crucif. Jesus* vii. 124 When a man begins to look with a chearful countenance, and the muddy complexion clears up. **1722** RAMSAY *Three Bonnets* II. 107 Wheel'd round wi' gloomy brows and muddy, And left his brither in a study. **1736** AINSWORTH *Lat. Dict.*, A muddy or cloudy look, *vultus tetricus*.

9. *Comb.*, chiefly parasynthetic: ***muddy-bottomed, -brained, -grey, -headed, -mettled, -minded*** adjs.; ***muddy oaf*** [cf. MUDDIED *ppl. a.*].

1874 J. W. LONG *Amer. Wild-fowl* xiv. 185 They are very partial to small, *muddy-bottomed streams. **1634** FORD *Perk. Warbeck* II. iii, *Muddy brain'd peasants! **1939** 'N. BLAKE' *Smiler with Knife* vi. 96 Her face looked *muddy-grey. **1642** FULLER *Holy & Prof. St.* II. xvi. 110 Many boys are *muddy-headed till they be clarified with age. **1815** R. THORPE *Let. to W. Wilberforce* (ed. 3) 78 *note*, The ignorant and muddy-headed confusion, in which the Institution mixed the two Treaties. **1602** SHAKS. *Ham.* II. ii. 594 A dull and *muddy-metled Rascall. **1601** ? MARSTON *Pasquil & Kath.* II. 145 Let the vnsanctified spirit of ambition Entice the choice of *muddie-minded dames To yoke themselues to swine. **1867** TROLLOPE *Last Chron. Barset* II. lxi. 185 Though he knew himself to be *muddy-minded and addle-pated, he could see that. **1956** W. H. WHYTE *Organization Man* (1957) iv. 33 People who have been the intellectual founders..have not been as muddy-minded. **1934** R. CAMPBELL *Broken Record* ii. 51 Modern international rugby has been going more and more in the *muddy-oaf direction. **1588** FRAUNCE *Lawiers Log.* I. vii. 40 Hee is but a *muddy-pated asse. **1839** *Times* 25 Mar. 4/3 That *muddy-souled economist Joseph Hume. **1872** O. W. HOLMES *Poet Breakf.-t.* i. (1885) 22 If I..were..*muddy-witted.

muddy (ˈmʌdɪ), *v.* [f. MUDDY *a.*]

1. *trans.* To make muddy, in various senses of the adj.; to cover or bespatter with mud; to render (water) turbid with mud; to make confused or obscure. Also with *up*.

1601 SHAKS. *All's Well* v. ii. 4, I am now sir muddied in fortunes mood, and smell somewhat strong of her strong displeasure. *a* **1652** J. SMITH *Sel. Disc.* ix. 461 The Holy Spirit is too pure and gentle a thing to dwell in a mind muddied and disturbed by those impure dregs. **1669** W. SIMPSON *Hydrol. Chym.* 136 Upon which if oyl of vitriol be dropt, it becomes clear again, and by oyl of tartar muddied. **1760** DERRICK *Lett.* (1767) I. 82 The springs and streams being all muddied with the continual rains. **1811** *Self Instructor* 524 The former would be the means of muddying your colours. **1837** *Blackw. Mag.* XLI. 603 He..began to muddy the water. **1893** LELAND *Mem.* II. 122, I only muddied the palms of my gloves, on which I fell. **1905** E. CHANDLER *Unveiling of Lhasa* xi. 206 The..product of restless Western energies, stirring and muddying the shallows of the Eastern mind. **1917** E. POUND *Let.* 10 Nov. (1971) 124 You thank your bloomin gawd you've got enough Spanish blood to muddy up your mind, and prevent the current American ideation from going through it like a blighted collander.

2. *intr.* To become muddy or turbid.

1834 LANDOR *Exam. Shaks.* Wks. 1846 II. 276 Malt before hops, the world over, or the beer muddies.

muddying (ˈmʌdɪɪŋ), *vbl. sb.* [-ING[1].] The action of the vb. MUDDY.

1713 M. HENRY *Meekn. & Quietn. of Spirit* (1822) 115 Those disorderly passions, which tend to the muddying and clouding of the Soul. **1735** *Dict. Polygraph.* s.v. *Ultramarine*, Thus you may get the colour without muddying. **1883** C. FLEET *Our Ancestors in Sussex* Ser. II. 256 The muddying of the clear fancy by all kinds of disturbances.

b. *U.S.* 'A mode of fishing in which attendants stir up the muddy bottom of a lake or stream' (*Cent. Dict.* 1890).

1877 HALLOCK *Sportsman's Gaz.* 371 The season for muddying begins.

muddyish (ˈmʌdɪɪʃ), *a.* [f. MUDDY *a.* + -ISH.] Somewhat muddy.

1853 G. J. CAYLEY *Las Alforjas* II. 148 There are reservoirs of muddyish water, and ducks and geese.

muddywort, variant of MOULDWARP.

mude, obs. form of MOOD *sb.*[1], MUD.

Mudéjar (muːˈdeɪhɑː(r)), *a.* and *sb.* Also **Mudejar**, and with small initial. Pl. **Mudéjares**. [a. Sp. *mudéjar*, f. Arab. *mudajjan* permitted to remain.] **A.** *adj.* Of, pertaining to, or characteristic of the Mudéjares (see below); *spec.* denoting a partly Islamic, partly Gothic style of architecture and decorative art of the 12th to the 15th century. Also *ellipt.* as *sb.*, this style.

1865 H. O'SHEA *Guide to Spain* p. xxix, Moorish architecture may be divided into three periods and styles. 1st. Byzantine-Arabic; 2nd. Mauritane-Almohade; 3rd. Mudejar or Granadine. **1872** M. D. WYATT *Architect's Note-bk. in Spain* p. ix, I have preferred,..in the binding of this volume, to take its ornament in fac-simile from a beautiful little Mudejar casket. **1909** R. TYLER *Spain* ix. 208 The most complete monuments of the Mudejar style are the two synagogues, El Transito and Santa Maria la Blanca. **1927** G. G. KING *Mudéjar* i. 2 Formerly it was customary to define Mudéjar as a hybrid of oriental and Gothic. **1931** J. B. TREND in Arnold & Guillaume *Legacy of Islam* 15 In later years fine and characteristic work was done by Mudéjar bookbinders. **1938** L. MACNEICE *Earth Compels* 31, I was in Spain... Gobbling..the architecture Moorish mudejar churriguerresque. **1946** E. DIEHL *Bookbinding* I. vi. 91 Their [*sc.* the Spaniards'] mudéjar bindings, showing the Arab influence, were characterized by interlaced strapwork patterns. **1961** *Times* 30 Sept. 11/3 The elaborately joined wood ceilings produced by the Mudejar (Moorish) craftsmen in Spain. **1972** F. M. LÓPEZ-MORILLAS in R. Highfield *Spain in 15th Cent.* 197 Aragon, more bound to the Mudéjar tradition of construction in brick, has nevertheless preserved notable examples of Gothic architecture.

B. *sb.* During the reconquest of the Spanish peninsula from the Moors, a subject Muslim who was allowed to retain his laws and religion in return for his loyalty to a Christian king.

1893 H. E. WATTS *Spain* vi. 167 It was the *mudejar* who drew the design, a *mudejar* who laid the stones, a *mudejar* who painted the walls. **1901** H. C. LEA *Moriscos of Spain* i. 4 When, in 1212, Alfonso IX..won the great victory of Las Navas de Tolosa and advanced to Ubeda, where 70,000 Moors had taken refuge, they offered to become Mudéjares and to pay him a ransom. **1938** B. BEVAN *Hist. Spanish Archit.* xii. 107 In Aragon the Mudéjares were not, as they were elsewhere, a servile minority. **1972** F. M. LÓPEZ-MORILLAS in R. Highfield *Spain in 15th Cent.* 152 In Valladolid on November 9, 1408, both regents signed a law concerning the *Mudéjares* who lived in Castile.

'mud-fish. A fish that inhabits mud. Also variously used *spec.* (see below).

a. A kind of loach (Crabb *Technol. Dict.* 1823); **b.** an African dipnoan fish of the family *Lepidosirenidæ*, a lepidosiren; **c.** *U.S.* a fish of the family *Amiidæ*, esp. the bow-fin, *Amia calva*; **d.** a fish of the genus *Umbra* or family *Umbridæ*, a mud minnow; **e.** a name formerly given in New York to the Killifish (*Cent. Dict.*); **f.** a gobiine fish, *Gillichthys mirabilis* (ibid.); **g.** *Melanura pygmæa*; **h.** the Australian barramunda, *Ceratodus forsteri*; **i.** a New Zealand fish, *Neochanna apoda*.

1502 *Maldon, Essex, Court-Rolls* Bundle 61. No. 2 Attachiatus est per M[t]. mudfish, vi[c] stokfishe, x barells samonum. **1558** *Wills & Inv. N.C.* (Surtees) I. 167 viij[bus] of modefyshe. **1699** DAMPIER *Voy.* 128 The Sea also supplys divers sorts of very good Fish, (*viz.*) Snooks, Mullets, Mud-fish. **1756** P. BROWNE *Jamaica* 450 The Mud-fish. The species of this tribe are easily distinguished by the fleshy appendicule at the anus. **1859** BARTLETT *Dict. Amer.*, Mud-Fish (*Melanura pygmæa*), a small fish on the Atlantic coast which burrows in the mud. **1859** DARWIN in *Life & Lett.* II. 174 The mud-fish or lepidosiren. **1880** GÜNTHER *Fishes* 372 The 'Bow-fin' or 'Mud-fish' (*Amia calva*) is not uncommon in many of the fresh waters of the United States. *Ibid.* 619 *Umbra limi*, locally distributed in the United States; called..'Dog fish' or 'Mud-fish' in America. **1882** TENISON-WOODS *Fishes N.S. Wales* 108 *Neochanna* is a remarkable mudfish of New Zealand. **1896** tr. *Boas' Zool.* 386 The Mud-fish or Barramunda (*Ceratodus*) is a large, elongate animal, pointed at both ends.

mudge (mʌdʒ), *v.*[1] *Sc. intr.* and *trans.* = BUDGE *v.*

1802 JAMIESON *Water Kelpie* xv, in Scott *Minstrelsy* (1802) III. 361 Thai dare na mudge for fricht. **1823** GALT *Entail* xxxv, I'll no' mudge the ba' o' my muckle tae in ony sic road. **1835** *Blackw. Mag.* XXXVIII. 161 One never mudged for hours. **1875** ALEX. SMITH *New Hist. Aberdeen.* II. 696 They could'na mudge the brig.

mudge (mʌdʒ), *v.*[2] ? *dial.* [? Related to MUSH *v.* Cf. '*Modge*, to crush or bruise. *Warw.*' (Halliwell).] *trans.* To bruise, crush (hops).

1848 *Jrnl. R. Agric. Soc.* IX. II. 576 Hops may be pressed warmer than they can be trod, without breaking or mudging them.

mudgeon, mudhar: see MURGEON, MUDAR.

'mudhead. [MUD *sb.*[1] 5.] **1.** *U.S. colloq.* A native of Tennessee. *rare.*

1838 HALIBURTON *Clockm.* Ser. II. xix. 289 There's the hoosiers of Indiana,..the mudheads of Tenessee [etc.]. **1949** *Amer. Speech* XX. 27 Buckshine, Mudhead, or Whelp for a Tennessean.

2. *slang.* A fool. So **mud-headed** *a.*, stupid.

1793 in Polwhele *Trad. & Recoll.* (1826) I. 329 There are a parcel of mud-headed fellows down in that country. **1882** W. D. HAY *Brighter Britain!* I. ix. 234 Shut up, you Milesian mudhead, and listen to me. **1886** D. C. MURRAY *First Pers. Singular* xxii, That old mud-head of a Dobroski.

3. The name of a ceremonial clown among the Zuñi people who wears a mud-daubed mask.

1959 E. TUNIS *Indians* 129/1 There were other clowns, too, known as *goyemshi*, or Mudheads.

'mud-hole. Also **mudhole, mud hole.** [f. MUD *sb.*[1] + HOLE *sb.*] **1. a.** A hole containing mud or in which mud collects, esp. as forming a defect or obstacle in a road or highway.

1760 in *Documentary Hist. Amer. Industr. Society* (1910) I. 310 As soon as one Gets out..he Is In a large due or in a mud hole. **1784** A. ELLICOTT in C. V. Mathews *Andrew Ellicott* (1908) 26 The ground [was] covered with Snow which hid the Mud-Holes. **1857** P. CARTWRIGHT *Autobiogr.* xx. 314, I thought of a desperate mudhole about a quarter of a mile ahead;..many wagons had stuck in it. **1911** E. M. CLOWES *On Wallaby* xi. 291 The water-holding frog found in the central deserts, which can blow its body out with a sufficiency of fluid to support it for a year or more in a dried-up mud-hole. **1937** *Discovery* May 148/1 There are many different kinds of baths available, supplying various mineral waters; boiling mud holes innumerable; waterfalls over which hot water flows side by side with cold; [etc.]. **1948** *Coast to Coast 1947* 71 Those tourist people came and looked at his boiling spring and his bubbling mudhole. **1973** *Sci. Amer.* Apr. 88/3 They find themselves in an alley where they sink into a bottomless mudhole.

b. *transf.* and *fig.*

1784 in *Pennsylvania Mag. Hist. & Biogr.* (1877) I. 51 The general curse of the country, disunion, rages in this little mudhole [*sc.* Uniontown, Pa.]. **1890** *Cent. Dict.*, *Mud-hole*, a salt-water lagoon in which whales are captured. [Whalers' slang, California.] **1938** S. V. BENÉT *Thirteen o'Clock* 317 We've all of us been on your back long enough. ..I know of twice you pulled Jerry Pye out of the mudhole. **1958** J. CAREW *Black Midas* x. 231 The thought of returning to the mud-hole where I was born made my shy away.

2. A hole at the base of a boiler, condenser, or other apparatus through which sediment can be removed.

1841 W. TEMPLETON *Locomotive Engine* 16 The mud holes..are for the purpose of removing the sediment and scale that constantly accumulate at the bottom of the water spaces. **1893** LANGMAID & GAISFORD *Elem. Less. Steam Machinery* xiii. 123 To allow access to the inside of the boiler, for examining and cleaning, manholes and mudholes are provided.

mud-hook. *slang.* [MUD *sb.*[1] 5.] **1. a.** An anchor.

1827 J. F. COOPER *Red Rover* I. ii. 44 He would..fasten her to the spot with good hempen cables and iron mud-hooks. **1874** W. M. BAINES *Narr. E. Crewe* vii. 138 Cunningly drop your 'mud-hook' so that you exactly swing with the tide over the right spot. **1884** 'H. COLLINGWOOD' *Under Meteor Flag* 254 We at length found ourselves in port, and the mud-hook down. **1905** J. C. LINCOLN *Partners of Tide* xii. 230 The partners agreed to undertake the job of recovering the lost 'mud-hook'. **1960** M. SHARCOTT *Place of Many Winds* x. 172 Gusts of wind tore their mud-hooks from the bottom of the anchorage.

b. (See quots.)

1918 'TOMMY' *If I goes West!* 25 Forget old Billy Summers with his board at 'crown and anchor'—'The Mud'ook, boys, and now's the time to bet!' **1919** W. H. DOWNING *Digger Dial.* 34 *Mud-hook*..(2) the anchor in the game of 'Crown and Anchor'. **1943** HUNT & PRINGLE *Service Slang* 46 *Mudhook*, Army name for the Crown and Anchor board used surreptitiously by members of the forces.

2. a. A foot. **b.** A hand.

1850 L. H. GARRARD *Wah-to-Yah* xx. 276 This 'mudhook', holding out his foot, hasn't a moccasin on for nothin'. *a* **1897** F. B. LLOYD *Sk. Country Life* (1898) xl. 239 When a farmer goes to foolin with figgers he is puttin his mudhooks on powerful slippery ground. **1915** *Dialect Notes* IV. 244 *Mud hooks*, n. pl. Feet. **1941** BAKER *Dict. Austral. Slang* 47 *Mudhook*, a foot. (2) A hand. **1952** in Wentworth & Flexner *Dict. Amer. Slang* (1960) 347/2 C'mon, lift them mud hooks!

Mudie (ˈmjuːdɪ). The name of Charles Edward *Mudie* (1810-90) used *absol.*, *attrib.*, or in the possessive to designate the lending library opened by him in London in 1842, which continued in business until 1937; or labels, lists, boxes, etc., associated with the library or its contents.

1859 H. C. ROBINSON *Diary* 26 May (1967) 300, I subscribed to Mudie's Library, as I have long intended. *Ibid.* 30 May (1967) 300, I went to Mudie's for the poems of Macdonald. **1864** MRS. GASKELL *French Life* i, in *Fraser's Mag.* Apr. 439/2 They have nothing equivalent to 'Mudie' in Paris. **1879** C. M. YONGE *Magnum Bonum* III. xxxii. 675 'It is the advantage of having no Mudie boxes,' said his mother. 'We are taking up our Southey.' **1885** —— *Nuttie's Father* I. xvi. 191 She could only have recourse to Mudie's box to try to drive dull care away. **1888** *Bks. for Presents & Prizes: Catal. Bks. Best Authors* (Mudie's Select Library) Aug. 1 A few Choice Books in Mudie Calf, Extra Morocco, and other Superior Bindings are also kept in Stock. **1890** S. BUTLER in *Universal Rev.* VIII. 518, I believe I have the smallest library of any literary man in London... I keep my books at the British Museum and at Mudie's. **1908** MRS. H. WARD *Diana Mallory* I. vi. 113 The Book-Club..embraced some ten families who drew up their Mudie lists in common, and sent the books from house to house. **1922** H. S. WALPOLE *Cathedral* I. ii. 28 He looked at them all, with their light yellow Mudie labels, their fresh bindings. **1931** 'G. TREVOR' *Murder at School* ii. 44 He..said you had written a novel... I must get Mudie's to send it down with their next batch. **1966** BERRY & POOLE *Ann. Printing* 230/2 'Mudie's Lending Library'..was to become world famous... As the watch-dog of contemporary literary morals, Mudie soon became a ruthless dictator as to what the public should read. ..'What will Mudie say?' became the proverbial question when new fiction was under consideration in publishers' offices. **1970** G. L. GRIEST (*title*) Mudie's Circulating Library and the Victorian novel.

mudie, obs. form of MUDDY.

‖**mudim** (ˈmuːdɪm). Also 9 **mudin**. [Malay (now *modin*), prob. ad. Arab. *mu'aḏḏin* muezzin.] A junior Muslim official in Malaysia, *spec.* one who performs the operation of circumcision.

1817 T. S. RAFFLES *Hist. Java* I. vi. 284 A *Kabáyan*..with the *Kamitúah* and *Múdin* (priest), formed a court for settling petty village disputes. **1858** *Jrnl. Indian Archipelago* 121 The Mudin or professional circumciser performs the operation in a trice. **1900** W. W. SKEAT *Malay Magic* vi. 360 Among Malays it [*sc.* circumcision] is performed by a functionary called the 'Mudim'. **1966** D. FORBES *Heart of Malaya* xiv. 194 If the traditional *mudim* carries out the operation [*sc.* circumcision] instead of the hospital doctor, he will rub a salve into the wound.

‖**mudir** (muːˈdɪə(r)). Also **moodir, moodeer.** [Turk. use of Arab. *mudīr*, active pple. of *adāra* to administer, govern (Dozy), causative of *dāra* to go round.] In Turkey, the governor of a village or canton; in Egypt, the governor of a province.

1844 A. W. KINGLAKE *Eothen* xxvi. 383 The appointment of a special Commissioner—they called him 'the Modeer'. **1864** *Athenæum* No. 1921. 245/2 The Mudirs or district-governors. **1881** *Blackw. Mag.* June 698 During our stay in the Fayoum we saw a good deal of the mudir or governor. **1885** *Nat. Rev.* July 677 One day the [Egyptian] police was under the Moodeers, the next it was the reverse. **1902** [see MAMUR]. **1958** L. DURRELL *Balthazar* v. 99 Local mudirs and sheiks.

mudir, variant of MUDAR.

mudirate (muːˈdɪərət). Also **mudirat, mudiriate.** [f. MUDIR + -ATE.] = MUDIRIEH.

1881 *Blackw. Mag.* June 699 The exact condition of every village in his mudirate. **1884** GORDON *Jrnls.* (1885) 222 No sentries at the North Fort, or Bourré, or on the Mudirat. **1885** *Pall Mall G.* 16 Feb. 1/1 Because we have taken no steps to set up any Administration in the Mudiriate of Dongola.

‖**mudirieh** (muːˈdɪərɪeɪ). Also **mou-, moodirieh, mudiriet.** [Egyptian Arabic *mudīrīyah*, f. *mudīr* MUDIR.] In Egypt: **a.** The territory of a mudir. **b.** The official head-quarters of a mudir.

1877 McCOAN *Egypt as it is* 114 The following fourteen *mudirìehs* or Prefectures. **1877** E. DE LEON *Khedive's Egypt* 432 Sundry taxes and revenues in the provinces (Moudiriehs). **1898** *Westm. Gaz.* 28 Oct. 7/1 A French traveller is resident at Fashoda, occupies the half-ruined mudirieh or town-hall. **1907** *Blackw. Mag.* July 124/1 At important Mudiriets, where ten years ago British functionaries were in charge.

Mudjur (ˈmʊdʒʊə(r)). Also **Mujur**. The name of a city in central Turkey, used, freq. *attrib.*, to designate rugs made there, usu. with deep borders and prayer arch designs.

1913 W. A. HAWLEY *Oriental Rugs* xvi. 290 Figures of vandykes, which are seen in some Anatolians and Mudjurs, are also a constant feature of Ladiks. **1931** A. U. DILLEY *Oriental Rugs & Carpets* vi. 165 Mujur.. prayer rugs [are distinguished] by central panels covered by 'flight-of-stairs roofs'. **1959** *Chambers's Encycl.* III. 137/2 Mujurs, with long pile and glowing reds and greens, can be sumptuous little rugs. **1967** [see KIR-SHEHR]. **1972** P. L. PHILLIPS tr. *F. Formenton's Oriental Rugs & Carpets* 86 Mudjur carpets are different from Yuruk not only in the fact that they are designed as prayer rugs, but also because of the different colour tones.

mudlark (ˈmʌdlɑːk), *sb.* [f. MUD *sb.*^{1} + LARK *sb.*^{1} (a jocular formation).]

†**1.** *slang.* A hog.

1785 GROSE *Dict. Vulg. Tongue.* **1801** T. CAMPBELL *Mobiade* in W. Beattie *Life & Lett. T. Campbell* (1849) I. 380 Or fry the mud-lark's odoriferous wing... The poetical name for a pig, principally used in.. Kilmainham jail. **1833** J. NEAL *Down-Easters* i. 47, I should like to know.. what upon irth he means by.. mud-larks that's made into Virginny-ham. **1869** *Overland Monthly* III. 129 A hog clandestinely killed outside of camp and smuggled in.. was called a 'slow bear'... 'Mud-lark' signified the same thing. **1923** *Dialect Notes* V. 240 Boiled potatoes an' mud lark.

2. *colloq.* One who dabbles, works, or lives in mud. **a.** (See quots.)

1796–1800 COLQUHOUN *Police Metrop.* (ed. 6) 230 *Mud-Larks*, so called from their being accustomed to prowl about, at low water, under the quarter of West India ships.. under pretence of grubbing in the mud for old ropes, iron.. &c. but whose chief object.. was to receive and conceal small bags of sugar, coffee [etc.].. which they conveyed to such houses as they were directed, and for which services they generally received a share of the booty. **1799** MAR. EDGEWORTH *Lame Jervas* xi, He.. became what is called a mudlark; that is, a plunderer of the ships' cargoes that unload in the Thames. **1801** *Monthly Rev.* XXXV. 243 Miserable beings.. accustomed to grub in the river at low water for old ropes.. known by the appellation of Mud-larks. **1851** MAYHEW *Lond. Labour* II. 155/2 The mud-larks collect whatever they happen to find, such as coals, bits of old-iron [etc.]. **1867** SMYTH *Sailor's Word-bk.*, *Mudlarks*, people who grovel about bays and harbours at low water for anything they can find. **1892** DOBSON *18th Cent. Vignettes* 233 The same crowd of mud-larks and loafers would come rushing into the water to offer.. their services. **1959** *Times* 16 Mar. (Port of London Suppl.) p. xvi/1 'Long apron men' and mudlarks who.. waited to pick up goods thrown to them by accomplices on board merchantmen. **1975** *Times* 17 May 8/4 Jack Dash.. recalling the Mudlarks, river pirates and knife-belted prostitutes.

b. A soldier of the Royal Engineers.

1878 TRIMEN *Regim. Brit. Army* 42 Royal Engineers.. nicknamed 'the Mudlarks'.

c. A man who cleans out common sewers. *rare*$^{-0}$.

1882 in OGILVIE.

d. A gutter child, street urchin. In quot. *transf.*

1865 *Sat. Rev.* 5 July 4 It is Lord Palmerston's misfortune .. to number three or four of these incurable mudlarks among his official offspring. **1890** in *Century Dict.*

3. A name given to various birds: **a.** A kind of Pipit. **b.** The skylark, *Alauda arvensis* (E.D.D.). **c.** A black and white Australian bird, the magpie-lark, *Grallina cyanoleuca*, which builds a nest of mud.

1882 NEWTON in *Encycl. Brit.* XIV. 317/1 The Mud-Lark, Rock-Lark, Titlark, and Tree-Lark are Pipits. **1898** MORRIS *Austral Eng.* 278/1 Magpie-Lark.. an Australian black-and-white bird.. resembling the Magpie in appearance, but smaller; called also Pee-wee, and Mudlark, from its building its nest of mud. **1911** E. M. CLOWES *On Wallaby* xi. 290 The mud larks, rather like our water-wagtails, only much larger, come there with the most wanton flutter of broad black and white tails, to disport themselves upon the patch of green at its verge. **1965** *Austral. Encycl.* V. 460/1 The name 'magpie-lark' was presumably bestowed upon it because it runs on the ground like a lark and has pied plumage;.. 'mud-lark', owing to its preference for the muddy banks of creeks and waterholes.

4. = MUDDER. Cf. *mud runner*.

1909 in *Cent. Dict. Suppl.* **1935** A. J. POLLOCK *Underworld Speaks* 78/2 *Mud lark*, a race horse that excels in mud. **1941** BAKER *Dict. Austral. Slang* 47 *Mudlark*, a racehorse that runs well on a muddy course. Also footballers who play on a sodden field. **1975** *Sunday Tel.* (Sydney) 6 Apr. 48 Born Star a Mudlark. Born Star, a two-year-old, yesterday outclassed the field at Sandown in his first start on a rain-affected track.

5. *attrib.*, as ***mudlark meet*** (see quot.).

1971 *Nat. Geographic* May 719/2 Guernsey invented annual mudlark meets, in which old bangers—near-wrecked automobiles—are raced across the oozing sands at low tide.

mudlark (ˈmʌdlɑːk), *v.* [f. MUDLARK *sb.*] *intr.* To carry on the occupation of a mudlark; also, to 'play about' in the mud. Hence **ˈmudlarking** *vbl. sb.* and *ppl. a.*

1840 MARRYAT *Poor Jack* xi, You mud-larking vagabond. **1851** MAYHEW *Lond. Labour* II. 155/2 This, he says, he liked much better than mud-larking. **1888** *Sat. Rev.* 21 July 66 A series of sunny summers and perfect grounds have not taught us the noble lessons of mudlarking, as it hath often been played in the fens and marshes of rural cricket-grounds. **1894** *Outing* (U.S.) XXIV. 193/2 He mingled with us for some time on the beach, mudlarked with the boys and watched our model yacht matches. **1960** *Life* (Internat. ed.) 1 Feb. 45/1 The back-bruising sport of mudlarking.., one of England's popular recreations, calls for a special-body car.

mudlarker (ˈmʌdlɑːkə(r)). [f. MUDLARK *v.* + -ER^1.] = MUDLARK *sb.* 2 a.

1818 'A. BURTON' *Adventures J. Newcome* I. 26 Slopmen, Mud-larkers and Crimps. **1840** MARRYAT *Poor Jack* viii, I was now what is termed a regular *Mud-larker*, picking up halfpence by running into the water. *Ibid.* xviii, A mudlarker was a man who had an old boat,.. furnished with an iron bar full of hooks, which was lowered down by a rope to catch pieces of cordage, oakum, canvas, or other articles, which might fall overboard from the.. vessels in the river.

mudle, obs. form of MUDDLE *v.*

mudless (ˈmʌdlɪs), *a.* [f. MUD *sb.*^{1} + -LESS.] Free from mud.

1610 HOLLAND *Camden's Brit.* I. 388 The mudlesse Tamis cleere. **1872** *Daily News* 31 July, His life had been as the flowing of a mudless stream. **1884** *Field* 6 Dec. (Cassell), To-day it was clean and mudless.

†**ˈmudly**, *a.* *Obs.*$^{-1}$ [f. MUD *sb.*^{1} + -LY^1.] Muddy.

*a*1340 HAMPOLE *Psalter*, *Cant. Isaye* xii. 4 When ȝe drynke of tha clere wellis & lefis the mudly watirs of erthly lustis.

‖**mudra** (mʌˈdrɑː). *Hinduism.* Also moodra. [Skr. *mudrā* seal, sign, token.] One of a large number of symbolic hand gestures used in Hindu religious ceremonies and (hence) in Indian dance. Also, a movement or pose in Yoga.

1811 W. WARD *Acct. Hindoos* II. 26 The ceremonies called moodra; the names of the different moodras... Certain motions with the hands and fingers. **1832** H. H. WILSON in *Asiatick Researches* XVII. 224 The performance of the *Mudrá*, or gesticulations with the fingers, accompanying the different stages of the ceremony. **1877** M. WILLIAMS *Hinduism* ix. 127 The term *Mudrā* is also used in Tāntrism to denote mystical intertwinings of the fingers so as to form symbolical figures. **1899** MAX MÜLLER *Six Syst. Indian Philos.* vii. 457, I shall abstain from giving descriptions of the Mudrâs (dispositions of upper limbs). **1917** A. COOMARASWAMY in Coomaraswamy & Duggirala tr. *Mirror of Gesture* 8 These poses, chiefly of the hands, are spoken of as *mudrās* (seals), and are more or less familiar to students of Hindū iconography. **1948** G. VENKATACHALAM *Dance in India* xv. 125 There is a regular science of the mudras as there is a science of the mantras. **1952** L. MACNEICE *Ten Burnt Offerings* 84 He was.. A dancer.. a clown, With his gags, his mudras, his entrechats. **1960** KOESTLER *Lotus & Robot* I. iii. 111 The eight siddhis are promised.. in remuneration for the more difficult mudras. **1967** SINGHA & MASSEY *Indian Dances* ix. 93 According to.. a text on Kathakali mudras, there are twenty-four basic hand gestures... The significance of a mudra changes according to the position of the hand. **1970** D. BRAHMACHARI *Yogasana Vijñana: Sci. of Yoga* 3 There is.. no Mudrā (pose) like Khecarī Mudrā (Khechari pose) and nothing that absorbs one's self completely like Nāda (sound). **1972** R. S. MISHRA *Fund. Yoga* ii. 36 *Mudras*,.. movements of limbs and fingers, etc., according to the circulation of *kuṇḍalini* force, magnetic force in the body.

mud wall. A wall built of earth or clay, or of materials laid in clay as a substitute for mortar. †Also, the material forming such a wall.

1395 *Acc. Manor of Savoy* in *Archæologia* XXIV. 313 Pro factura ij perticatarum muri ex parte occidentale gardini vocata mudwall. **1464** *Nottingham Rec.* II. 373 For makyng of the modde walle. **1578** NICHOLAS tr. *Lopez de Gomara's Conq. W. India* 52 The houses are great, made of lime stone & bricke: others there are made of mood wal, and rafters. **1679** T. KIRKE *Mod. Acc. Scot.* 10 The Houses of the Commonalty are very mean, Mud-wall and Thatch the best. **1690** LOCKE *Hum. Und.* IV. xix. (1695) 403 Earthly Minds, like Mud-Walls, resist the strongest Batteries. *a*1771 R. WOOD *Ess. Homer* (1775) 242 The mud walls of a Turkish cottage. **1789** *Trans. Soc. Arts* VII. 34 Two parts old cobb (alias mud-wall). **1833** LOUDON *Encycl. Archit.* §159 Mode of building the Mud Walls of Cottages in Cambridgeshire.

†**b.** *fig.* *Obs.*

1662 BP. HOPKINS *Serm.*, *Funeral* (1685) 78 There stand nothing between us and our eternal state, but this thin mud-wall of our bodies. **1670** *Devout Commun.* (1688) 142 Our mudwall of flesh made spiritual and transparent.

c. *attrib.* and *Comb.*

*c*1470 HENRY *Wallace* XI. 680 Castell was thar nayn, Bot mudwall werk withoutyn lym or stayn. **1543** tr. *Statutes* Table, Mud wall makers. **1785** COWPER *Wks.* 1837 XV. 159 The mud-wall cottages of our poor at Olney.

mudwall: see MODWALL.

mudwalled (ˈmʌdwɔːld), *ppl. a.* [f. MUD *sb.*^{1} + WALL *sb.* + -ED^2.] Having mud walls. Also *fig.*

1607 WALKINGTON *Opt. Glass* 22 This mud-wald cottage. **1630** *Epitaph* in J. R. Leifchild *Cornwall Mines* (1855) 20 O what a bubble, vapour, puffe of breath,.. Is mud-wald man! **1689** PRIOR *Epist. to F. Shephard* 20 As Folks from Mud-wall'd Tenement Bring Landlords Pepper-corn for Rent. **1805** R. W. DICKSON *Pract. Agric.* I. Plate xxviii, A small mud-walled cheap cottage. **1884** J. COLBORNE *Hicks Pasha* 84 Mud-walled streets are unnumbered. **1892** KIPLING *Barrack-Room Ballads* 171 Put them in mud-walled prisons. **1961** L. MUMFORD *City in Hist.* vi. 159 Did the forms of Phidias rise in this barnyard scattering of workshops.. mid these mud-walled huts? **1971** *Inside Kenya Today* Mar. 37/1 The mud-walled and grass-thatched office. **1974** *Nat. Geographic* Aug. 255/1 The traditional mud-walled farmhouse with thatched roof has two bedrooms and a kitchen.

ˈmudwalling, *vbl. sb.* [MUD *sb.*^{1}] (See quots.)

1905 *Tent Catal.* (John Boyle & Co., N.Y.) No. 8. 15 Both grades are provided with sod cloth (mud walling). **1963** *Which?* Apr. 120/2 The outer tent has a strip of heavier, plastic-coated fabric, called mudwalling, round the bottom to protect the tent's walls. **1970** *Ibid.* May 133 The bottom of the walls [of frame tents] is made from plastic (called mudwalling) so that the canvas does not touch the damp ground, and to keep the wind and rain out. **1974** *Camping & Caravanning* Sept. 39/2 (Advt.), 50" PVC Groundsheeting or Mudwalling, 66p. yd.

mue, mued, obs. ff. MEW *sb.*^{2}, *v.*^{1}, ^{2}, MUID.

mueddin, variant of MUEZZIN.

muee, obs. form of MAY *v.*^{1}

muekliche, -nesse: see MEEKLY, MEEKNESS.

‖**muermo** (muːˈɛrməʊ). *Bot.* [Chilean Spanish.] A tall tree native to Chile, *Eucryphia cordifolia*, having a valuable hard wood. Also called ulmo.

1890 in *Century Dict.*; and in later Dicts.

mues, obs. f. MEWS.

muese, var. MEUSE.

muesin, muetden, obs. forms of MUEZZIN.

muesli (ˈmʏslɪ, ˈmuːzlɪ, ˈmjuːzlɪ). Also müesli, musli. [Swiss-Ger.] A dish, originating in Switzerland, consisting of a cereal (usu. oats) and fruit to which milk is added, often eaten as a breakfast dish.

[**1926** BIRCHER-BENNER & BIRCHER *Fruit Dishes & Raw Vegetables* iv. 29 This dish.. is popularly known as 'Birchermüesli'.] **1939** *Ibid.* (ed. 2) iv. 29 The fact that it is cold is never harmful as long as the müesli is well chewed and thus sufficiently warmed in the mouth. **1943** M. Y. BRADY *Health for All: Wartime Recipe Bk.* 58 Müesli is a delicious dish, even when modified to suit wartime shortages. **1965** H. RUBINSTEIN *My Life for Beauty* vi. 76, I lived on a diet of Muesli (a mixture of rolled oats, lemon juice, sweetened condensed milk, grated apples and hazel-nuts). **1971** J. AIKEN *Nightly Deadshade* vii. 71, I find them finishing their breakfast of musli. **1971** M. THOMPSON in C. Bonington *Annapurna South Face* App. D. 274 Ideal High Altitude Rations.. Readi-Brek *or* Muesli, [etc.]. **1973** [see INSTANT *a.* 4 c].

muet, obs. form of MUTE *a.*

‖**muezzin** (muːˈɛzɪn). Forms: α. 6 **maizin**, 7 **meizin, muyezin,** (*pl.* **muyezini**), **muezem, -im,** 7–8 **muezin,** 8 **muasin, mezzin, muesin,** 9 **muezzeem, -im,** 9– **muezzin**; β. 7 **muetden, mouden, -on,** 9 **moo-ed'din, mueddin, mouedhin, mood(d)in.** [Arabic *mu'aððin*, active pple. of *aððana*, 2nd conjug. (frequentative) of *aðana* to proclaim, f. *uðn* ear. The α forms proceed from the widespread dialectal pronunciation with (z) or (dz) for (ð). Some of the forms appear to be meant for Arab. *mu'ðin*, the pple. of the 4th conjug. of the same vb.] In Muslim countries, a public crier who proclaims the regular hours of prayer from the minaret or the roof of a mosque.

α. **1585** T. WASHINGTON tr. *Nicholay's Voy.* III. xxi. 110 b, The Maizins beginne to cry vppon the towres. **1613** PURCHAS *Pilgrimage* (1614) 301 And the Meizin or Muetden (Clarke, Sexten, Priest, Bell-ringer, or Bell rather) standeth up and readeth that Psalme. **1638** SIR T. HERBERT *Trav.* (ed. 2) 267 The Muyezini crie from the tops of Mosques, battologuizing *Llala Hyllula*. **1687** A. LOVELL tr. *Thevenot's Trav.* I. 49 A Muezim goes up to the top of the Minaret and calls to Prayers. *Ibid.* II. 18 The Turks say that the Muesem cannot call to prayers there as at other Mosques. **1702** W. J. *Bruyn's Voy. Levant* xii. 59 These Criers are called *Muasins*. **1704** J. PITTS *Acc. Mohammetans* vi. 38 The Mezzins, or Clerks are ready to observe his motions. **1816** BYRON *Siege Cor.* xi, As rose the Muezzin's voice in air In midnight call to wonted prayer. **1819** T. HOPE *Anastasius* (1820) I. xii. 224 Hark!.. there is the Muezzeem of Sultan Achmet, just calling to prayers. **1820** T. S. HUGHES *Trav. Sicily* II. 25 The sonorous tones of their muzzeins [*sic: misprint.*]

fig. **1907** *Q. Rev.* Apr. 585 His Majesty's Cabinet listened to this call of the muezzin of the revolution from the minaret of the Duma.

β. **1613** PURCHAS *Pilgrimage* (1614) 603 When the Mouden, or Sexten crieth in the steeple. **1615** BEDWELL *Arab. Trudg.*, *Salie*, The Moudon from the top of the steeple cryeth.. *Allah cabir, la allah, illa ilellah.* **1836** LANE *Mod. Egypt.* I. iii. 83 Most of the moo-eddins of Cairo have harmonious and sonorous voices. **1845** FORD *Handbk. Spain* I. 248 The Giralda was the great tower from whence the mueddin summoned the faithful to prayers. **1854** MILMAN *Lat. Chr.* IV. i. (1864) II. 185 The Mouedhin proclaimed from the roof 'There is one God and Mohammed is his prophet'. **1875** W. G. PALGRAVE in *Encycl. Brit.* II. 250/1 In most cases there is no minaret attached [to the mosque], the times of prayer being merely announced by the 'mueddin', or crier, from the roof itself. **1889** HALL CAINE *Scapegoat* xxv, The mooddin was chanting to call to prayers.

†**Muff**, *sb.*^{1} *Obs.* Also 6–7 **muffe.** [a. Du. *mof*, a contemptuous appellation for a Westphalian.] A depreciative term for a German or Swiss; sometimes loosely applied to other foreigners.

1590 MARLOWE *2nd Pt. Tamburl.* I. i, King Sigismond hath brought from Christendome More then his Camp of stout Hungarians, Sclauonians, Almans, Rutters, Muffes, and Danes. **1592** WARNER *Alb. Eng.* VII. xxxv. 151 Those Stiles to him weare strange, but thay Did feofe them on the bace-borne Muffe [*sc.* Warbeck] and him as King obay. **1596** LODGE *Wits Miserie* 35 The Italian ruffe, the French doublet, the Muffes cloak, the Toledo rapier [etc.]. **1598** E.

GUILPIN *Skial.* (1878) 57 Is he not a Sargeant? then say's a muffe For his furr'd sattin cloak. **1598** FLORIO, *Stiticozzi*, swearing or swaggring muffs or dutchmen. *a* **1639** SIR J. RERESBY *Mem. & Trav.* (1904) 135 The Low Dutch call the High, muffes, that is *étourdi*, as the French have it, or blockheads. **1649** W. M. *Wandering Jew* (1857) 61 Shop-keepers..(like a guard of Muffes) every morning wait at their doores to get their money. **1656** FINETT *For. Ambass.* 38 An Ambassador (with his assistant Commissioner Chancellour of Muscovey)..was..received at Tower Wharfe... The Kings Coach, and five or six others tooke them in at Tower Wharfe, but with such disorder..as without my care,..some must of the better sort of Muffes have walked on foote to their Lodgings.

muff (mʌf), *sb.*² Also 6–7 **muffe**. [Prob. a. Du. *mof* (not found earlier than 17th c.), a. F. *moufle* (Walloon *mofe*, *mouffe*): see MUFFLE *sb.*⁵ Cf. G. *muffe*, *muff* (17th c.), Sw. *muff*.]

1. a. A covering (usually of fur and of cylindrical shape) into which both hands may be thrust from opposite ends to keep them warm.

Now used only by women; in 17–18th c. also by men.

1599 B. JONSON *Cynthia's Rev.* II. i, She alwayes weares a Muffe. **1608** H. P. *Epigr.* 32 Should Spruso leaue the wearing of his muffe. **1662** PEPYS *Diary* 30 Nov., This day I first did wear a muffe, being my wife's last year's muffe. **1695** *Lond. Gaz.* No. 3065/4 Lost.., a large Sabble Tip, Mans Muff, with a parting in the middle of it. **1713** GAY *Fan* I. 205 Then in the muff th' unactive fingers lay, Nor taught the fan in various forms to play. **1746** H. WALPOLE *Let. to Mann* 17 Jan., Seeing him [*sc.* a French spy] dangle on a gallows in his muff and boots. **1775** MME. D'ARBLAY *Early Diary* 21 Nov., Another man..carries her muff, in which is her little lap-dog. **1847** ALB. SMITH *Chr. Tadpole* xii, She had also a muff, something like a grenadier's cap. **1902** *Daily Chron.* 20 Dec. 8/3 One of the huge, flat, bag-shaped muffs that are now at the apex of fashion.

b. *transf.* (For *foot-muff*: see FOOT *sb.* 35.)

1797 BAILEY & CULLEY *Agric. Northumb.* 132 The longwoolled sheep..were called Muggs, probably from their faces being covered with a muff of wool. **1802** PALEY *Nat. Theol.* xv. (ed. 2) 292 Such a defence is furnished to the swan in the muff in which its body is wrapped. **1830** M. DONOVAN *Dom. Econ.* I. 223 The bottles may be enveloped in muffs made of thick canvass, to protect them from being broken by striking against each other.

†**c.** = MUFFLE *sb.*⁵ 3, MUFFLER 2 c. *Obs.*

1854 WILKES in *8th Rep. Comm. Lunacy* App. G. 137 The means of restraint employed were the leather muff and wrist-straps, iron hand-cuffs [etc.]. *Ibid.*, One patient..had been for some time wearing the muff and hobbles.

†**2.** = MITTEN *sb.* 2. *Obs.*

Cf. the widespread dialectal use = MITTEN *sb.* 1 (see E.D.D.).

1748 RICHARDSON *Clarissa* (1811) III. iii. 30 On her charming arms a pair of black velvet glove-like muffs of her own invention. **1749** FIELDING *Tom Jones* v. iv, She was playing one of her father's favourite tunes..when the muff fell over her fingers.

3. a. A tuft or crest on the heads of certain birds.

1849 D. J. BROWNE *Amer. Poultry Yd.* (1855) 60 Whether the climate of Northern Europe has any tendency to develop the growth of crests, 'muffs', etc. (as in what are called Siberian fowls or muffed Dorkings), on the heads of fowls.

b. *slang.* The female pudenda. Also *Comb.*, as **muff-diver**, one who practises cunnilingus.

1699 B. E. *New Dict. Cant. Crew*, *Muff*, c. a Woman's Secrets. *To the well-wearing of your Muff Mort*, c. to the happy Consummation of your Marriage Madam, a Health. **1935** J. HARGAN *Gloss. Prison Lang.* 5 *Muff-diver*, performer of cunnilingus. **1961** PARTRIDGE *Dict. Slang* Suppl. 1191/2 *Muff-diver*, a cunilingist [*sic*]. **1972** *Screw* 12 June 5/2 Blowjobs are nice, but blowing into her muff can kill her. **1973** H. MILLER *Open City* xiv. 159 The local bookie's got Polaroids of her flashing her muff.

c. A woman or girl, esp. one of low morals; a prostitute. *slang* (orig. *U.S.*).

1914 [see DRAG *sb.* 3 e]. **1918** *Dialect Notes* V. 26 Muff, a girl. South Idaho and University of Idaho. **1965** H. C. RAE *Skinner* I. i. 10 Flappin' about a muff they found up in the woods.

4. In various technical senses.

a. *Founding.* (See quots.; cf. MUFFLE *sb.*⁴)

1756 *Dict. Arts & Sci.* s.v. *Foundery of Statues*, The furnace consists of a hearth and its muff, a fire-place, an ash-hole, and an earthen bason... The muff is a brick arch made very low to reverberate the flame upon the metal. **1880** *Coach Builders' Art Jrnl.* I. 86 If a silver beading is required a strip of copper and a strip of silver is taken and placed one on the other and put into a furnace (technically termed 'muff') to be annealed, that is, softened.

b. *Glass-manuf.* A cylinder of blown glass for flattening out into a plate.

1875 in KNIGHT *Dict. Mech.*

c. *Plumber's work.* A joining tube driven into the ends of two adjoining pipes.

1875 in KNIGHT *Dict. Mech.*

5. *attrib.* and *Comb.*, as ***muff-chain***, ***-maker***, ***-string***, ***-stuffer***, ***warmer***; ***muff-headed*** adj.; **muff-bag**, a bag, usually of sealskin, on the outside of which is a muff; **muff-box**, (*a*) a box in which a muff is kept, or sold; (*b*) a large hat worn by women at the beginning of the 19th century; **muff-cap** *jocular*, a soldier's bearskin cap; **muff-coated duck** *dial.*, the muscovy duck (Halliwell 1847); **muff coupling**, a cylindrical shaft coupling to fit over the abutting ends of shafts; **muff pistol**, the smallest size of nineteenth-century pocket pistol believed by some to have been designed to be carried in a muff (but see quot. 1969).

1895 *Army & Navy Price List* 15 Sept. 1612/2 A large selection of Real and Imitation Sealskin *Muff Bags in stock. **1816** J. SCOTT *Vis. Paris* (ed. 5) 101 Under the poke and the *muff-box, the face sometimes entirely disappears. **1834** Muff-box [see *bonnet-box* s.v. BONNET *sb.* 10]. **1868** *Mich. Agric. Rep.* VII. 363 Henry Fowler [exhibited]..1 dozen muff and collar boxes, combined in one. **1864** PINEAS *Ergänzungsbl.* 34 *Muff-cap, *Bärenmütze*. **1872** *Daily Tel.* 4 July 5/1 The Americans appear to have a peculiar fondness for the 'busby' and the muff-cap as items of military head-gear. **1902** *Words Eyewitness* 204 The new-fashioned jewelled *muff-chains. **1887** D. A. LOW *Machine Draw.* (1892) 25 **Muff Couplings*. **1768** R. SMITH *Univ. Direct. Rats*, etc. 139 These vermin [Water rats] are something like the Norway Rat, but smaller,..their heads rounder, or what is commonly termed, *muff-headed. **1688** R. HOLME *Armoury* III. 25/1 By this Sign or Cognizance [of two Muffs]..you may easily know where a Furrier or *Muff-maker dwelleth. **1938** J. N. GEORGE *Eng. Pistols & Revolvers* vii. 135 These so-called *muff-pistols were not necessarily intended as ladies' weapons. **1956** W. E. BIRD *Off-Trail in Nova Scotia* vi. 181 Another item is a muff pistol that was fired with a percussion cap and ball. **1969** F. WILKINSON *Antique Firearms* 135 Some very small examples..are often described as muff pistols, although it is not at all clear on what basis this term was chosen. Certainly there is little or no evidence to suggest that they were intended primarily for ladies or indeed were ever carried in the muff, for both men and women of the period used muffs. **1706–7** FARQUHAR *Beaux Strat.* I. i, A contrary sort..contract their spacious acres to the circuit of a *muff-string. **1895** *Army & Navy Price List* 15 Sept. 308 *Muff Warmer, Nickel plated.

muff, *sb.*³ *Obs.* exc. *dial.* [repr. an inarticulate sound; cf. the synonymous G. *muff* int., also HUMPH, BUFF *sb.*⁵, and Eng. dial. *muff* adj. = MUM *a.* (see E.D.D.).] In phr. ***not to say muff***, ***to say neither muff nor mum***: not to utter a sound.

Quot. *c* 1460 s.v. MUFF *v.*¹ may perh. belong to this sb.

1652 C. B. STAPYLTON *Herodian* VI. 45 The drunken guards say not so much as muff. *c* **1681** HICKERINGILL *Trimmer* vi. Wks. 1716 I. 388 The slaves never durst mutter since, nor scarce say muff. **1881** *Leicestersh. Gloss.* s.v. A didn' sey no moor, nayther moof nur moom.

muff (mʌf), *sb.*⁴ *colloq.* [Of doubtful origin.

As the word has not been found earlier than the second quarter of the 19th c. (being unrecorded even in the slang dictionaries), its identity with the long obsolete MUFF *sb.*¹ is unlikely. It may be an application of MUFF *sb.*², conveying the scoffing accusation of keeping one's hands in a muff.]

1. Originally, one who is awkward or stupid in some athletic sport. Hence, in wider sense, one without skill or aptitude for some particular work or pursuit, a 'duffer'; also, one who is generally deficient in practical sense. ***to make a muff of oneself***: to make oneself ridiculous.

1837 DICKENS *Pickw.* vii, Such denunciations as—..'Now butter-fingers'—'Muff'..—and so forth. *a* **1845** HOOD *Pen & Pencil Pict.* (1857) 144 Awful muff! Can't pull two strokes without catching as many crabs. **1857** HUGHES *Tom Brown* II. iv, I didn't think..that you'd have been such a muff as to let him be getting wet through. **1860** W. E. FORSTER *Let.* 5 Dec. in Reid *Life* (1888) I. viii. 324, I find I know absolutely nothing [he was going through a course of instruction in musketry], and am therefore a complete muff. **1866** MANSFIELD *Sch. Life Winchester* (1870) 136, I was..rather a muff at the latter [*sc.* cricket]. **1880** MISS BRADDON *Just as I am* xxi, I know I was a tremendous muff in the hunting-field. **1884** *Nonconf. & Indep.* 25 Sept. 930/3 Both sides have succeeded in making muffs of themselves.

2. [Prob. from the verb.] A failure; anything clumsily or badly done or bungled, as a bad stroke of play in a game of ball; *spec.* in any game at ball, failure to hold a ball that comes into one's hands.

1871 *Punch* 25 Feb. 81/2 *Old Gent.* 'Well, Charlie, what sort of a book is that? interesting?' *Bloodthirsty Young Rascal.* 'Not a bit. It's a great muff. I've read sixty pages and there's only one man killed yet.' **1897** FARMER & HENLEY *Slang*, *Muff*...2. (common).—Anything badly bungled.

muff (mʌf), *sb.*⁵ *dial.* [Perh. a use of MUFF *sb.*², from the ring of outstanding feathers round the neck. But cf. Du. *mof* greenfinch.] The white-throat, *Sylvia cinerea*.

1831 J. RENNIE *Montagu's Ornith. Dict.* 538. **1839** [see MUFFET].

muff (mʌf), *a.* [f. MUFF *v.*⁴] In ***muff glass***: glass which has been 'muffed'.

1865 *Morn. Star* 24 Apr., The subdued light from globes of muff glass... The light was..from globes of muff glass let into the ceiling. **1890** *Century Dict.*, *Muff-glass*.

muff, *v.*¹ *Obs.* exc. *dial.* (see E.D.D.). [Belongs to MUFF *sb.*³] *intr.* With expressed or implied negative: (Not) to say 'muff'; (not) to utter a word.

Quot. *c* 1460 perh. belongs to MUFF *sb.*³

c **1460** *Towneley Myst.* viii. 188 If thou can nother muf nor mom, I shall sheld the from shame. **1645** PAGITT *Heresiogr.* (1647) 74 They dare not so much as whisper, or as much as muffe against it.

†**muff**, *v.*² *Obs. rare.* [f. MUFF *sb.*²] *trans.* To provide with a muff.

1621 BRATHWAIT *Nat. Embassie*, etc. 254 Th' Ladie in her coach..is muff'd when frosts approach. **1688** R. HOLME *Armoury* III. 234/2 The Inhabitants [of France] in cold Weather keep warm, and Muff themselves.

muff, *v.*³ *colloq.* and *slang.* [f. MUFF *sb.*⁴]

1. *trans.* To make a muddle or 'mess' of, to bungle; to perform or play badly or clumsily; to miss (a catch or ball) at cricket or other games. Also *intr.*, to miss catches, to act bunglingly.

[**1827** W. CLARKE *Every Night Bk.* 84 When one of the fancy dies, the survivors say, that he has..'mizzled'—'morrised'—or 'muffed it'!] **1846** W. DENISON *Cricket: Sk. Players* 24 All the best of our players completely muffed their batting. **1857** G. A. LAWRENCE *Guy Liv.* vi. 49, I don't see why you should have muffed that shot. **1860** HUGHES *Tom Brown at Oxf.* xiii, 'Brazen-nose was better steered than Exeter'. 'They muffed it in the Gut, eh?' **1901** *Scotsman* 5 Sept. 7/3 Mr. McDonald muffed his stroke [in golf]. **1950** *Times Lit. Suppl.* 3 Mar. 131/3 It would be impossible for Sir Max Beerbohm to muff a parody. **1968** J. R. ACKERLEY *My Father & Myself* xiii. 145 A few opportunities occurred. He muffed one of them, I another. **1972** *Jazz & Blues* Oct. 30/1 If Mezz is indeed responsible for this exchange then the author muffs his lines badly. **1973** *Tucson* (Arizona) *Daily Citizen* 22 Aug. 57/3 Third baseman Phil Garner muffed a grounder by Bill Ralston.

2. *intr.* To fail (in an examination).

1884 J. STURGIS in *Longm. Mag.* III. 617 Freddy and Tommy and Dicky have all muffed for the army.

Hence **muffed** *ppl. a.*, clumsily missed or bungled; **ˈmuffing** *vbl. sb.* and *ppl. a.*

1841 J. MILLS *Old Eng. Gentlm.* i, You may rest assured that no muffing work would be looked over in any young man. **1876** *World* V. No. 107. 18 A muffed catch raises the first little cloud of chaff. **1905** *Review of Rev.* Feb. 115/2 There must be no more muffing of parliamentary chances.

muff, *v.*⁴ *trans.* = MUFFLE *v.*¹ 5. Hence **muffed** *ppl. a.* = MUFFLED *ppl. a.* 5. (Cf. MUFF *a.*)

1868 *Morn. Star* 7 Jan., A cordon of white-muffed glass burners. **1877** *Eng. Mechanic* 3 Aug. 522/3 Would some correspondent inform me how I am to proceed in muffing glass, leaving ornamental scroll work clear glass on muffed ground?

muffat(t)ee, variant forms of MUFFETEE.

muffe, obs. f. MOVE *v.*, MUFF *sb.*¹ and ².

muffed (mʌft), *a.* [f. MUFF *sb.*² + -ED².]

a. Wearing a muff (in quot. *transf.*). **b.** Of certain birds: Having a crest or tuft on the head.

a. 1813 L. HUNT in *Examiner* 4 Jan. 3/2 The muffed chin was a matter of taste.

b. 1809 T. DONALDSON *Poems* 40 My Hen she was a shining Brown, Wi' Muffi'd head. **1828** MOIR *Mansie Wauch* xx. 290 Finding the head of the muffed hen..lying in a bye corner. **1845** *Zoologist* III. 929, I never met with more than two kinds of woodcocks, the one, the common muffed or muffled cock..and the other a much smaller bird of darker plumage. **1885** *Bazaar* 30 Mar. 1265/1 [Pigeons] warranted good performers, flyers, and breeders, muffed, or clear legged. **1899** *B'ham Weekly Post* 18 Mar. 24/1 The Blondinette [pigeon] is a muffed, crested, and frilled variety.

muffel(le, obs. forms of MUFFLE *v.*

muffet (ˈmʌfɪt), *dial.* Also **muffit**. [f. MUFF *sb.*² + -ET¹.] = MUFF *sb.*⁵

1839 MACGILLIVRAY *Brit. Birds* II. 350 *Sylvia cinerea*. The..White-Throat... Muff. Muffet. Mufty. **1885** SWAINSON *Provinc. Names Birds* 23.

muffetee (mʌfɪˈtiː). Also 8–9 **muffatee**, 9 **muffitee**, (-ies *pl. Sc.*), **muffettee**, **muffattee**, **mufftee**. [App. irreg. f. MUFF *sb.*²]

1. A muffler worn round the neck. *Obs.* exc. *dial.*

c **1706** *Songs Costume* (Percy Soc.) 206 Let 'em [*sc.* the men] mind their ruffles and muffetees. *Ibid.* 207 Scarlet and saxon-green muffetees [worn by men]. **1772** COLMAN *Prose Sev. Occas.* (1787) III. 194 Nay lest Rouleaus themselves should soil their ruffles A muffatee each Pretty Master muffles. **1839** THACKERAY *Leg. St. Sophia of Kioff*, Warm her soldier lad she wrapt in Comforter and muffetee. *a* **1890** E. WAUGH *Tufts of Heather* (1892) I. 25 He'd a thick, red wool muffatee reawnd his neck.

2. A worsted cuff worn on the wrist.

1749 in A. M. Earle *Costume Colonial Times* (1894) 165 Men's fine Worsted Gloves and Muffetees. **1808–18** JAMIESON, *Muffities*,..mittens, either of leather or of knitted worsted, worn by old men. **1842** MRS. STONE *W. Langshawe* I. xii. 180 Her whole pride and delight..were centered in having her husband's hose, gloves, and muffatees—all her own knitted manufacture—in superlative order. **1844** CORNELIA MEE *Comp. Work-Table* 82 New Cross-way Pattern for Gentlemen's Muffatees... For a muffatee, make a chain of 52 stitches [etc.]. **1865** *Cornh. Mag.* XII. 700 She stood..with her red muffetees and her chilblainy hands clasped. **1878** *Yng. Ladies' Jrnl.* Christmas No. 5 Here are a pair of scarlet muffatees for his wrists. **1902** 'MRS. ALEXANDER' *Stronger than Love* xii. 147, I have a little present for Uncle Garth—a pair of rabbit-wool muffatees.

muffin (ˈmʌfɪn). Also 8 **muffin**; *dial.* 8 **moofin**, 9 **mowffin**, **moufin**. [Of obscure origin; but perh. in some way connected with OF. *moufflet* soft (said of bread), also used subst., soft bread.]

1. a. *dial.* (See quots. 1703, 1888.) **b.** A light, flat, circular, spongy cake, eaten toasted and buttered at breakfast or tea.

1703 THORESBY *Let. to Ray* Philos. Lett. (1718) 332 A *Moofin*, a Wheat Cake bak'd upon a Bake-stone over the Fire, as Oat-cakes. **1747** MRS. GLASSE *Cookery* xvii. 151 To make Muffings and Oat-Cakes. **1766** [ANSTEY] *Bath Guide* xiii. 105, I freely will own I the Muffins preferr'd To all the genteel Conversation I heard. **1782** WOLCOT (P. Pindar) *Odes R. Acad.* xiv, A face..That boasts no more expression than a muffin. **1802** LAMB *Let. to Coleridge* 11 Oct., We..can trace the dirt in it to having read it at tea with buttered muffins, or over a pipe. **1886** J. K. JEROME *Idle Thoughts* (1889) 120, I eat a large plateful of hot buttered muffins about an hour beforehand. **1888** JESSIE FOTHERGILL *Lasses of Leverhouse* xix. 179 'Mowffin', a generic name for tea bread in all its varieties.

2. A kind of flat earthenware or china plate.

1864 in WEBSTER. **1885** C. MACKESON in *Brit. Alm. Comp.* 94 In some parts of the country identical titles are very differently applied. Among the double meanings..[are] Muffin Maker for a maker of tea-cakes or the maker of a muffin in China manufacture.

3. *slang* and *colloq.* **a.** = MUFF *sb.*⁴ 1. ? *Obs.* **b.** One who habitually 'muffs' a catch or ball. (*Funk's Stand. Dict.* 1895.)

1830 W. T. MONCRIEFF *Hrt. of Lond.* II. i, A visitor? hurrah! some muffin, I daresay—he must pay his footing.

4. *Canadian slang.* (See quot. 1856.)

1856 MISS BIRD *Englishw. Amer.* 260 Every unmarried gentleman, who chooses to do so, selects a young lady to be his companion in the numerous amusements of the season.. when she acquiesces, [she] is called a 'muffin'. **1904** MAJOR A. GRIFFITHS *50 Yrs. Pub. Serv.* iv. 52 A pleasant *tête-a-tête* drive for many miles..with your 'muffin' by your side.

5. *attrib.* and *Comb.*, as ***muffin-dish, -maker, -plate***; **muffin-bell**, the bell rung by a seller of muffins; **muffin-cap**, a flat woollen cap worn by charity-school boys, etc.; **muffin-countenance, -face** *slang*, an expressionless countenance; so **muffin-faced** *a.* (see also quot. 1823); **muffin-fight** *colloq.* = *muffin-worry*; **muffin-head** *dial.*, a blockhead; **muffin-man**, a man who sells muffins; **muffin-ring, muffin-tin**, 'a ring, usually of tinned iron, in which muffins are cooked' (Worcester 1860); **muffin-worry** *colloq.*, a tea-party.

1840 HOOD *Up Rhine* 89 By and by a bell rang, and that sent him into a fresh tantrum. 'What..has a *muffin-bell to do with religion?' **1840** BARHAM *Ingol. Leg.* Ser. I. *Spectre of Tapp.*, Mr. Peters..had received a liberal education at a charity-school, and was apt to recur to the days of his *muffin-cap and leathers. **1823** *Spirit Publ. Jrnls.* (1825) 53 The *muffin countenance of the renowned Sancho Panza. **1895** *Army & Navy Price List* 15 Sept. 824 *Muffin Dish and Cover. **1777** I. JACKMAN *All World's a Stage* I. ii, Who is that gentleman?.. Has he a *muffin-face? **1823** 'J. BEE' *Dict. Turf*, **Muffin-faced*, one who has large protruding muscles on his phiz, which is pale withal, is 'a muffin-fac'd son of a——. **1837** SYD. SMITH *Let. to Archd. Singleton* Wks. 1859 II. 277/1 His little muffin-faced son. **1887** *Old Man's Favour* I. II. i. 198 A rare dinner, an occasional *muffin-fight. **1892** MRS. H. WARD *D. Grieve* I. v, Yo good-for-nowt, yo *muffin-yed, yo donkey! **1790** *Bystander* 382 The Italian *muffin-maker. **1810** *Splendid Follies* II. 6 A *muffin-man. **1895** *Army & Navy Price List* 15 Sept. 292/2 Hot Water *Muffin-Plate and Cover. **1860** *Hotten's Slang Dict.* (ed. 2), **Muffin-worry*, an old ladies' tea party. **1877** 'OUIDA' *Puck* xvi, Day before yesterday she came to muffin-worry in Fred. Orford's rooms.

muffineer (mʌfɪˈnɪə(r)). [f. MUFFIN + -EER¹.]

1. A small castor with a perforated top for sprinkling salt or sugar on muffins.

1806–7 J. BERESFORD *Miseries Hum. Life* (1826) IX. xli, As you are shaking a muffineer..the cover springing off. **1821** SYD. SMITH *Wks.* (1859) I. 316/2 Is this Mr. Thomas Hope? ..he who meditated on muffineers and planned pokers? **1841** DICKENS *Barn. Rudge* lxx, With regard to the expense ..two or three silver tea or coffee pots, with something additional for drink (such as a muffineer, or toast-rack) would more than cover it. **1897** *Daily News* 17 Sept. 5/2 Silver and turquoise inlaid muffineers.

2. 'A covered dish to keep toasted muffins hot'. The sense perh. never existed, but is the only one recognized in Dicts. before the *Century Dict.* 1890.

1858 in SIMMONDS *Dict. Trade.* **1860** in WORCESTER; and in later Dicts.

3. *nonce-uses.* **a.** A seller of muffins. **b.** A muffin-bell.

1830 *Fraser's Mag.* II. 450 If the thin small voice of the muffineer's ring be justifiable, why is not the baker let loose upon us? **1859** SALA *Tw. round Clock* (1861) 23 A bell to which Great Tom of Lincoln..and our own defunct 'Big Ben', are but as tinkling muffineers.

muffish (ˈmʌfɪʃ), *a. colloq.* [f. MUFF *sb.*⁴ + -ISH.] Of the nature, or characteristic, of a muff.

1858 FARRAR *Eric* II. iii, You don't want to make the whole school such a muffish set as the Rosebuds, do you? **1893** LELAND *Mem.* I. 166 He was always rather mild, quiet, and old-fashioned—in fact, muffish.

Hence **ˈmuffishness**, the quality of being 'muffish.'

1858 FARRAR *Eric* II. vii, He professed to ridicule diligence as an unboyish piece of muffishness. **1868** *Sat. Rev.* 14 Mar. 340/1 The girl of the period has done away with such moral muffishness as..regard for counsel and rebuke.

muffism (ˈmʌfɪz(ə)m). *colloq.* [f. MUFF *sb.*⁴ + -ISM.] The action characteristic of a muff; foolishness.

1854 LADY LYTTON *Behind the Scenes* II. x, The muffism of walking down St. James's Street, on a gusty day in September, in a rough, and somewhat shabby, pilot coat.

muffit, variant of MUFFET *dial.*

muffitee, variant Sc. form of MUFFETEE.

muffity (ˈmʌfɪtɪ). [Origin unknown.] A size of Cotswold stone roofing slate.

1914 [see BACHELOR 4d]. **1929** N. LLOYD *Building Craftsmanship* 93 The names and sizes of Stonefield [*sic*] Quarry slates..are Muffity or movedays 8 in.

mufflar, obs. form of MUFFLER.

muffle (ˈmʌf(ə)l), *sb.*¹ Also 8 (? *erron.*) muftel. [App. f. MUFFLE *v.*¹]

1. Something that muffles or covers the face or neck. = MUFFLER 1 a. *rare.*

1570 LEVINS *Manip.* 184/10 A Muffle, *focale.* *a* **1850** ROSSETTI *Dante & Circ.* I. (1874) 164 Why, with a hood on (if one only thinks) Or muffle of prim veils and scapularies.

†**b.** A muzzle. *Obs.*

1570 LEVINS *Manip.* 184/11 A Muffle for a dog, *fistella* [read *fiscella*].

2. Something that muffles or deadens sound.

1734 in Mackenzie *Newcastle* (1827) I. 314 Muftel's for the bells, 1*s.* **1830** GREVILLE *Mem.* (1874) II. 7 He sent for the officer on guard, and ordered him to take all the muffles off the drums.

3. Muffling effect; muffled sound.

1886 STEVENSON *Dr. Jekyll, Incident of Let.* (ed. 8) 50 The fog still slept on the wing above the drowned city..; and through the muffle and smother of these fallen clouds, the procession of the town's life was still rolling in..with a sound as of a mighty wind. **1902** *Daily Chron.* 11 Oct. 3/4 All one heard was the muffle of many hoofs and the eternal rattle of gun-carriage and baggage wagon.

ˈmuffle, *sb.*² [a. F. *mufle*, of unknown origin.]

1. The thick part of the upper lip and nose of ruminants and rodents. (Cf. quot. 1846.)

1601 HOLLAND *Pliny* I. 331 Some haue but one horne apiece, and that either in the midst of the forehead, as the Oryx; or else in the nose, and muffle, as the Rhinoceros. **1846** G. R. WATERHOUSE *Nat. Hist. Mammalia* I. 50 *note*, The French naturalists use the word 'muffle' for that part at the end of the nose which is naked in the Ox, Dog, &c.; where the same part is covered by hairs, as in the Rabbit, the animal is said to have no muffle. The term will be used to designate the corresponding part of the nose, whether hairy or not, in this work. **1855** LONGF. *Hiaw.* II. 24 Mudjekeewis ..drew the Belt of Wampum..Over the long nose and nostrils, The black muffle of the nostrils [of the Great Bear]. **1891** FLOWER & LYDEKKER *Introd. Mammals* 163 Potorous ...Tarsus short. Muffle naked.

†**b.** A proboscis. *Obs. rare.*

1601 HOLLAND *Pliny* I. 314 Their forefeet..again are charged full by the meanes of their [*sc.* bees'] muffle. *Ibid.* 353 Through that muffle or trunke of his, he [*sc.* the elephant] soundeth (as it were) out of a Trumpet.

2. *Comb.*: **muffle-jaw** *U.S.* = MILLER'S THUMB 2 c.

1882 JORDAN & GILBERT *Synopsis Fishes N. Amer.* 696 *Uranidea richardsonii*...Miller's Thumb;..Muffle-jaw.

†**muffle**, *sb.*³ *Obs. rare*⁻¹. [ad. G. *muffel-(thier)*, a perversion of F. *mouflon.*] = MOUFFLON.

1601 HOLLAND *Pliny* II. 399 A beast [in Sardinia] called Ophion [*marg.*, A Muffle, as Munster taketh it].

muffle (ˈmʌf(ə)l), *sb.*⁴ Also 9 muffel. [a. F. *moufle*, prob. a use of *moufle* mitten (whence MUFFLE *sb.*⁵). Cf. G. *muffel* in the same sense.]

1. A receptacle, placed within a furnace, in which substances may be exposed to heat without coming in contact with the products of combustion.

a. in *Chemistry* and *Metallurgy*, used for cupellation, calcination, annealing, etc.

1644 DIGBY *Nat. Soul* x. §11. 433 It continueth melted, flowing, and in motion vnder the muffle. **1677** tr. *Glaser's Compl. Chem.* 70 Place a good Cupple with its Muffle in a little Furnace made for this purpose. **1791** HAMILTON *Berthollet's Dyeing* II. II. II. i. 54 Indigo exposed to the action of fire..under a muffle fumes and swells. **1825** J. NICHOLSON *Operat. Mechanic* 475 The enamel-kiln is made in the shape of a chemist's muffle. **1868** JOYNSON *Metals* 113 On then heating the metal to bright redness, in a muffle or iron cylinder, a white surface of arsenide of iron is produced. **1884** J. PATON in *Encycl. Brit.* XVII. 314/1 [The needles] are..then re-heated in the muffle. **1897** *Daily News* 2 Oct. 2/5 These odd little furnaces are called 'muffles', and consume the tobacco to get at the ash.

b. *Ceramics*, etc. A chamber in a kiln in which pottery, porcelain, and glass is baked after being painted; also applied to the kiln or furnace containing such a chamber.

1742 *Phil. Trans.* XLII. 188 The Vessels that are painted or cover'd over with this Glazing, must be..put under a Muffle, and as soon as the Glass runs, you must smoak them, and take out the Vessels. **1832** G. R. PORTER *Porcelain & Gl.* II. xiv. 301 The glass is placed during the firing in a close iron box or oven, which is called a muffle. **1881** *Porcelain Works, Worcester* 30 The kilns used for this purpose may properly be called muffles.

2. A receptacle for fuel in a kiln for drying grain.

1797 *Monthly Mag.* III. 49/2 The fuel in these kilns is put into a cast-metal muffle, placed under the centre, and adapted to the size of the kiln. To this muffle are joined pipes of rolled iron, &c. which carry the heat to the extreme parts, and terminate in a chimney.

3. *attrib.*, as ***muffle chamber, furnace, plate.*** **muffle kiln**, a kiln in which the pottery which is being fired is enclosed within a chamber and thus protected from direct contact with the source of heat.

1884 KNIGHT *Dict. Mech., Suppl.* s.v. *Muffle*, The other view has grating *g*, cinder hole *f*, charging hole *d*, *muffle chamber *b*, escape for fumes *l.* **1839** URE *Dict. Arts* 578 Sometimes the cylinders are spread in a large *muffle furnace, in order to protect them from being tarnished by sulphureous and carbonaceous fumes. **1949** *Electronic Engin.* XXI. 412 An apparatus was constructed for holding a bar-shaped specimen in the muffle furnace. **1974** *Nature* 27 Sept. 305/2 Several single crystals were placed on a glass slide and heated in a muffle furnace at 180° C for 24 h. **1897** SPARKES & GANDY *Potters* i. 43 The pigments..are all mixed in vehicles of an oily nature, and a most necessary step is to fire this oil out... This is done in..a *muffle kiln..fired up to red heat only. **1947** W. B. HONEY *German Porcelain* 8 More or less glassy pigments [were] applied over the glaze and fixed by a low-temperature firing in a muffle-kiln. **1971** L. A. BOGER *Dict. World Pott. & Porc.* 260/1 Enamel colors are fired at a comparatively low temperature of 700°C to 900°C in a muffle kiln. **1816** MUSHET in *Encycl. Brit., Suppl.* I. 572/1 Fig. 5 [is] the *muffle plate.

muffle (ˈmʌf(ə)l), *sb.*⁵ [a. F. *moufle* mitten, OF. *mofle, moufle*:—med.L. *muffula* thick glove. Cf. Du. *moffel* muff, mitten.]

1. A boxing-glove; = MUFFLER 2 a. ? *Obs.*

1747 in H. Wilson *Wonderf. Charact.* (1821) III. 448 Muffles are provided, that will effectually secure them [*sc.* pupils] from the inconvenience of black eyes, broken jaws, and bloody noses. **1819** MOORE *Tom Crib* Pref. 19 The Greeks, for mere exercise of sparring, made use of muffles or gloves as we do. **1819** BYRON *Juan* II. xcii, Just like a black eye in a recent scuffle (For sometimes we must box without a muffle). **1858** *Eclectic Rev.* Ser. VI. III. 428 That all boys in a school be taught to box with muffles.

2. = MITTEN *sb.* 1 and 2.

1808 JAMIESON, *Muffles*, s. pl., mittens, gloves that do not cover the fingers, used by women. **18..** D. NICHOLSON *Caithness Words* (E.D.D.), A muffle has only two divisions; one for the thumb, and the other for the four fingers.

3. A sort of leather glove for lunatics who are given to tearing up their clothes, etc. (cf. MUFF *sb.*² 1 b).

1862 MAYHEW & BINNY *Crim. Prisons Lond.* 433 Several handcuffs on pegs, and instruments that appear like leathern bottles, but which, we are informed, are muffles, which were sent from Hanwell some years ago, when some lunatic prisoners were given to tearing up their clothes.

muffle (ˈmʌf(ə)l), *sb.*⁶ [a. F. *moufle.*] 'A pulley-block containing several sheaves' (Knight *Dict. Mech.* 1875).

muffle (ˈmʌf(ə)l), *v.*¹ Forms: 5 **muffelle, moffel**, 5–6 **mufle, muffel, moffle**, 6 **muffyl, -il, moffell**, 6– **muffle.** [Of somewhat obscure origin; app. f. OF. *mofle, moufle* thick glove (see MUFFLE *sb.*⁵, MUFF *sb.*²); but no early instance of the sb. is found in Eng., and of the OF. *mofler* v. Godef. has only one instance in the sense 'to stuff'. Cf. however OF. *enmouflé* 'muffled', from 13th c.]

1. *trans.* To wrap or cover up or enfold *esp.* so as to conceal, also for protection from the weather and for warmth. Freq. with *up*, occas. with *round.*

c **1430** *Syr Gener.* (Roxb.) 7055 She mufled hir face hir to desgyse That noon shuld know hir in noo wise. **1470–85** MALORY *Arthur* VIII. xxv. 311 Thenne came syre Breunor.. wyth his lady in his hand muffeld. ? *a* **1500** *Chester Pl., Antichrist* 390 Moffled in mantells. **1530** PALSGR. 641/2, I muffyl ones visage or his heed, I cover hym with clothes that he shulde nat be knowen, or from colde, *je emmoufle.* **1589** NASHE *Pasquill & Marforius* 12 His face handsomlie muffled with a Diaper-napkin to couer his beard. **1593** SHAKS. *2 Hen. VI*, IV. i. 46 The Duke of Suffolk, muffled vp in rags? **1638** JUNIUS *Paint. Ancients* 131 Michal..muffled up in the bed an image in stead of her husband David. **1657** W. MORICE *Coena quasi Κοινὴ* Deut. iii. 139 To..muffle their left hand when their right dispenseth almes. **1754** RICHARDSON *Grandison* (1811) I. xxxiii. 247 He tied a handkerchief over my face, head, and mouth, having first muffled me up in the cloak. **1815** *Hist. J. Decastro & bro. Bat.* III. 44 A lady is muffled up to the throat. **1847** TENNYSON *Princess* II. 443 But we three Sat muffled like the Fates. **1872** BLACK *Adv. Phaeton* ix, She besought Bell to muffle up her throat. **1876** GEO. ELIOT *Dan. Der.* xxxv, The ladies must muffle themselves: there is only just about time to do it well before sunset.

b. said of a garment, etc.

1754 RICHARDSON *Grandison* (1811) I. xxxiii. 251 The cloak enough muffling me, and the handkerchief being over my mouth. **1828** SCOTT *F.M. Perth* ii, A tall young man wrapped in a cloak, which obscured or muffled a part of his face.

c. *transf.* and *fig.*

1582 STANYHURST *Æneis* III. (Arb.) 86 Thee whilste thee sunbeams are maskt, hyls darcklye be muffled. **1590** SHAKS. *Com. Err.* III. ii. 8 Muffle your false loue with some shew of blindnesse: Let not my sister read it in your eye. **1768** H. WALPOLE *Hist. Doubts* 81 What did Henry ever muffle and disguise but the truth? **1810** SCOTT *Lady of L.* I. Introd., Till envious ivy did around thee cling, Muffling with verdant ringlet every string. **1859** TENNYSON *Vivien* 186 And therefore be as great as ye are named, Not muffled round with selfish reticence. **1871** R. ELLIS *Catullus* lxiv. 260 Mystical emblems, Emblems muffled darkly.

†**2.** To prevent from seeing by covering up the head (or only the eyes); to blindfold; also *fig. Obs.*

1566 GASCOIGNE *Jocasta* III. ii. Hearbes (1587) 99 b, As though our eyes were mufled with a clowde. **1581** J. BELL *Haddon's Answ. Osor.* A v, How long will ye suffer your mouthes to be mooseled, and your eyes muffeled with such blynde errours. **1592** SHAKS. *Rom. & Jul.* I. i. 177 Alas that loue, whose view is muffled still, Should without eyes, see path-wayes to his will. **1658** OSBORN *Jas. I*, Wks. (1673) 499 Muffled with love to the person of that Prince and his own Ambition. **1677** W. HUBBARD *Narrative* 27 Taught by late experience how dangerous it is to sight in such dismal Woods, when their eyes were muffled with the leaves. **1688** SOUTH *Serm.* (1727) I. xii. 490 When the Malefactor comes once to be muffled, and the fatal Cloth drawn over his Eyes. **1700** DRYDEN *Ceyx & Alcyone* 231 And since he was forbid to leave the Skies He muffled with a Cloud his mournful Eyes.

3. To restrain (a person) from speaking by wrapping up his head.

1570 LEVINS *Manip.* 184/13 To Muffle yᵉ mouth, *obturare.* **1601** SHAKS. *All's Well* IV. iii. 134 *Enter Parolles with his Interpreter. Ber.* A plague vpon him, muffeld; he can say nothing of me: hush, hush. **1837** DICKENS *Pickw.* xxvii, 'I vish you could muffle that 'ere Stiggins, and take him with you,' said Mr. Weller. **1846** H. MARSHALL *Milit. Misc.* 373 A practice prevailed at one time in some lunatic asylums, of 'muffling' the more noisy patients, which consisted in binding a cloth tightly over the mouth and nostrils, for the alleged purpose of 'dunning' the noise, and keeping the patients quiet.

4. To envelop or wrap up (oars, a drum, bell, etc.) so as to deaden the sound.

1761 *Brit. Mag.* II. 500 They laid all their oars across, except two in each boat, which they muffled with baize, to prevent their being heard at a distance. **1806** A. DUNCAN *Nelson's Funeral* 28 The drums were muffled with black cloth. *Ibid.*, Ninety-second.. Regiment;.. band playing muffled. **1833** MARRYAT *P. Simple* xliv, Cutting up old blankets to muffle the oars. **1838** DICKENS *Nich. Nick.* xxxvi, Kenwigs proceeded to muffle the knob of the street door knocker therein.

fig. **1901** *Speaker* 20 July 450/1 Academism is all very well, but.. it too often muffles the hammer of criticism, which ought to hit the nails of economic theory hard and on the head.

b. To deaden (a sound). Chiefly in *passive.*

1832 TENNYSON *Œnone* 210 From beneath Whose thick mysterious boughs.. The panther's roar came muffled. **1877** BLACK *Green Past.* i, The call of the cuckoo soft and muffled and remote. **1897** *Allbutt's Syst. Med.* IV. 389 The first [heart] sound is muffled and prolonged.

5. To render (glass) semi-opaque by giving it a crinkled surface. (Cf. MUFF *v.*[4])

1908 *Let. from glass-manufacturer* (Birmingham), We speak of the 'muffling' of the glass being good or bad according as the glass is well or badly 'muffled'. These are the only parts of an imaginary verb 'to muffle' which are used.

†**'muffle,** *v.*[2] *Obs. rare.* [Onomatopœic: cf. MAFFLE *v.* (? Associated with MUFFLE *v.*[1] 3, 4.)] *intr.* To speak indistinctly.

1669 HOLDER *Elem. Speech* 79 On the other side, the closeness and Mufling, and (as I may say) Laziness of speaking.. render the sound of their Speech considerably different.

muffled ('mʌf(ə)ld), *ppl. a.* [f. MUFFLE *v.*[1] + -ED[1].]

1. Wrapped or covered up, *esp.* about the face, for the purpose of concealment or disguise.

1593 SHAKS. *Lucr.* 768 O comfort-killing night!.. Blinde muffled bawd. **1599** B. JONSON *Ev. Man out of Hum.* II. iv, The muffled fates. **1651** CLEVELAND *Poems* 29 His muffled feature speaks him a recluse. **1813** SCOTT *Rokeby* VI. x, A muffled horseman late Had left it at the castle-gate. **1898** J. B. WOLLOCOMBE *From Morn till Eve* iv. 35 Muffled figures, with shawls wrapped over mouth and nose.

b. *transf.* and *fig.*

1599 B. JONSON *Cynthia's Rev.* I. iv, Yet will our muffled thought Choose rather not to see it, then auoide it. **1851** MAYNE REID *Scalp Hunt.* xxvi, The Indians would not fail to notice so many muffled tracks. **1870–74** J. THOMSON *City Dreadf. Nt.* XVI. i, Keen as lightning through a muffled sky.

†c. Blinded. *Obs. rare*$^{-1}$.

1629 T. ADAMS *Medit. Creed* Wks. 1153 Muffled Pagans know there is a God, but not what this God is.

2. Wearing or provided with 'muffles' or boxing-gloves. Also *dial.* wearing 'muffles' or mittens.

1721 KELLY *Sc. Prov.* 50 A mufled Cat was never a good Hunter. **1749** FIELDING *Tom Jones* XIII. v, He was.. a match for one of the first-rate boxers, and could.. have beaten all the muffled graduates of Mr. Broughton's school.

3. Wrapped up so as to deaden sound.

1762 GOLDSM. *Nash* 178 And the muffled bells rung a peal of Bob Major. **1813** BYRON *Giaour* 42 Then stealing with the muffled oar,.. Rush the night-prowlers on the prey. **1839** LONGF. *Psalm of Life* iv, Our hearts.. like muffled drums, are beating Funeral marches to the grave. **1867** SMYTH *Sailor's Word-bk.*, *Muffled drum*, the sound is thus damped at funerals: passing the spare cord, which is made of drummer's plait (to carry the drum over the shoulder), twice through the snares or cords which cross the lower diameter of the drum. **1872** HOLLAND *Marb. Proph.*, etc. 84 But they knock with muffled hammers.

b. *transf.* Of a sound: Deadened as if proceeding from something 'muffled'.

1837 LYTTON *E. Maltrav.* I. ii, His ear.. caught the faint muffled sound of creeping footsteps. **1846** W. BLUNT *Use & Abuse Ch. Bells* 5 Persons.. who ring 'the muffled' or 'the merry peal' for the rich man's sorrow or rejoicing. **1850** TENNYSON *In Mem.* xlix, The sorrow.. Whose muffled motions blindly drown The bases of my life in tears. **1860** TYNDALL *Glac.* I. viii. 57 A low muffled thunder resounding through the valley. **1860** WALSHE *Dis. Lungs* (ed. 3) 77 M. Woillez, correctly distinguishing this tonelessness, from ordinary so-called dulness, invents for it the title *obtusion* of sound—the phrase *muffled tone* will perhaps convey the idea. **1878** H. S. WILSON *Alp. Ascents* i. 16, I heard a muffled stir.

4. *dial.* Of a bird, *esp.* a hen: Having a top-knot or tuft of feathers on its head, or feathers protruding from under the throat; also, covered with feathers. Cf. MUFFED *a.*

1845 [see MUFFED *a.*]. **1888** *Sheffield Gloss.*, *Muffled*, covered with feathers. A fowl is said to be muffled down to its feet.

5. Of glass (see MUFFLE *v.*[1] 5).

Hence **'muffledness** *nonce-wd.*, the state or condition of being muffled (in quot. of sound).

1851 H. MELVILLE *Whale* xxi, He breathed with a sort of muffledness.

muffledly ('mʌf(ə)ldlɪ), *adv.* [-LY[2].] In a muffled manner.

1903 CONRAD & HUEFFER *Romance* I. iii. 21 The church clock began muffledly to chime the quarters. **1946** E. O'NEILL *Iceman Cometh* (1947) III. 178 He hides his face on his arms, sobbing muffledly.

muffler ('mʌflə(r)). Also 6 **mofeler, muffelar,** (? **muffley**), **mufflar,** 6–7 **mufler.** [f. MUFFLE *v.*[1] + -ER[1].]

1. a. A sort of kerchief or scarf worn by women in the 16th and 17th century to cover part of the face and the neck, either for partial concealment when in public, or as a protection against the sun or wind. *Obs.* exc. *Hist.*

1535–6 in Fairholt *Costume* (ed. 3, 1885) II. 292 Muffelars. **1536** in Ellis *Orig. Lett.* Ser. II. II. 80 She hath neither.. handcerchers, nor mofelers, nor begens. **1540** in Strype *Eccl. Mem.* (1721) I. App. cxiv. 311 The Kings Majesty had brought.. a muffley furred, to geve the Quene. **1560** BIBLE (*Geneva*) *Isa.* iii. 21 The rings and the mufflers. **1598** YONG *Diana* 19 Pulling off her muffler, mine eies behelde a face, whose countenance [etc.]. **1651** JER. TAYLOR *Holy Dying* iii. §4 (1686) 75 The image of the Goddess Angerona was with a muffler upon her mouth placed upon the Altar of Volupia, to represent, that those persons who bear their sicknesses and sorrows without murmurs, shall certainly pass from sorrow to pleasure. **1694** MOTTEUX *Rabelais* V. xxvii. (1737) 118 Mufflers.., which they call Masks. **1820** SCOTT *Abbot* xxvii, From some awkwardness in her management of the muffler, she was unable again to adjust it with that dexterity which was a principal accomplishment of the coquettes of the time.

†b. A bandage for blindfolding a person. *Obs.*

1599 SHAKS. *Hen. V*, III. vi. 33. **1609** SIR E. HOBY *Let. to Mr. T. H.* 43 By this you may see, (if the muffler of Superstition hath not cleane hoodwinked your eyes) the weaknes of your first ground. **1621** QUARLES *Esther* xvi, Like as a pris'ner muffl'd at the tree,.. At last (vnlook'd for) comes a slow Reprieue, And makes him (euen as dead) once more aliue: Amaz'd, he rends deaths Muffler from his eyes.

c. A wrap or scarf (usually of wool or silk) worn round the neck or throat, by both men and women, for warmth. Also *gen.* anything used to muffle the head or face or any part of the person.

1594 LYLY *Moth. Bomb.* III. iii, Silena, I praie you looke homeward, it is a colde aire, and you want your mufler. **1698** FRYER *Acc. E. India & P.* 35 Cloath'd with long Breeches to their Toes, and Mufflers on their Hands and Face. **1787** M. CUTLER in *Life*, etc. (1888) I. 200 Very unwell. Went to meeting with my muffler. **1874** SYMONDS *Sk. Italy & Greece* (1898) I. ii. 45 The mufflers in which his father.. has wrapped the child. **1895** *Army & Navy Price List* 15 Sept. 1156/2 Gentlemen's.. Cashmere Mufflers.. Silk Mufflers [etc.].

d. *fig.* Something that muffles or disguises.

1633 D. R[OGERS] *Treat. Sacram.* I. 89 Oh Lord! strip me starke naked, plucke off my mufflers, shame me. **1653** W. HEMINGS *Fatal Contract* II. ii, What man art thou, That hast thy count'nance clouded with thy cloak..? If thy intents deserve a Muffler too, Withdraw, and act them not. **1869** SWINBURNE *Ess. & Stud.* (1875) 236 Passages in which the special experience of the writer is thrust forward under the mask and muffler of allegoric rhapsody.

2. = MUFFLE *sb.*[5] a. A boxing-glove.

1755 DUNCOMBE in *Connoisseur* No. 52 ¶9 He.. is sturdy enough to encounter Broughton without mufflers. **1827** *Sporting Mag.* XX. 72 The mufflers were introduced and some capital first-rate sparring was exhibited. **1891** *Licensed Victualler's Mirror* 30 Jan. 7 (Farmer) There were few, if any, men of about his height and weight who could stand before him with the mufflers.

b. A glove or 'mitten'.

1824 MEYRICK *Anc. Armour* I. 25 Sleeves.. terminating with gloves, manakins, or mufflers, which cover the outsides of the hands and fingers. **1844** DICKENS *Chimes* i. (1845) 11 His chilly hands.. poorly defended from the searching cold by threadbare mufflers of grey worsted, with a private apartment only for the thumb, and a common room or tap for the rest of the fingers. **1883** S. W. BECK *Gloves* 14 The mufflers themselves are very singular.

c. = MUFFLE *sb.*[5] 3.

1846 DICKENS *Cricket on Hearth* ii. 68 Bedlam broke loose!.. We shall arrive at the strait-waistcoat and the mufflers soon.

†3. A jeweller's tool (see quot.). *Obs. rare*$^{-0}$.

1688 R. HOLME *Armoury* III. 382/1 A Mufler.. is a long square piece of Copper Plate turned direct half round, standing like an Arch.

4. Something to deaden sound; *spec.* in a pianoforte, a pad of felt which is inserted between the hammers and the strings by touching a lever; in a steam-engine, a contrivance for rendering noiseless the escape of steam. Also (chiefly *U.S.*) = SILENCER 2.

1856 KANE *Arct. Expl.* II. xxix. 287 Stockings were drawn over the oars as mufflers. **1875** KNIGHT *Dict. Mech.*, *Muffler.* 1. (*Music.*) A soft cushion employed to terminate or soften a note. **1895** in *Funk's Stand. Dict.* **1896** *Cosmopolitan* XX. 420/2 The noise of the exhaust is stifled in a muffler. **1897** [see BACK-FIRING *vbl. sb.* 2]. **1915** [see CHUG *v.*]. **1931** *Economist* 28 Feb. 431/2 There is reason to believe that.. mufflers, chassis springs,.. and accessories are all being manufactured or obtained in France. **1964** M. BANTON *Policeman in Community* iii. 69 An officer had stopped a driver for a faulty muffler (exhaust silencer) and had given him a ticket. **1973** *Houston* (Texas) *Chron.* 21 Oct. 12/1 Congress is being pressured to ease the auto emission standard that would lead to the installation of catalytic mufflers on new cars sold after Jan. 1, 1975. **1973** J. M. WHITE *Garden Game* 136 There was a horrible grinding and clanking under the car.. and I did mental arithmetic about the bill for a new muffler. **1974** *Index-Jrnl.* (Greenwood, S. Carolina) 19 Apr. 5/1 There were also two charges each of muffler violation, disregarding a traffic signal and operating an uninsured vehicle.

5. *dial.* a. = MUFFLIN. b. The great crested grebe.

1868 *Sussex Gloss.* in Hurst *Horsham* (1889), *Muffler*, a long-tail tit. **1889** APLIN *Birds Oxfordsh.* 214 (Local Names) Muffler = Great-crested Grebe.

mufflered ('mʌfləd), *a.* [f. MUFFLER + -ED[2].] Wearing a muffler; characterized by the wearing of mufflers.

1927 *Daily Express* 13 Mar. 5/1 From the bridge the mufflered figures glanced down at the business men moving across the quayside. **1963** *Times* 3 May 16/7 Rain-coated and mufflered, tropical gear a thing of the past, we steamed into cold drizzle and short, steep seas. **1969** *Punch* 26 Mar. 450/2 The hard collar is wilting at last. In a choice between starched indigence and mufflered affluence, proper pride has had it.

muffley, obs. form of MUFFLER.

mufflin ('mʌflɪn). *dial.* [Cf. MUFFLER 5.] The long-tailed titmouse, *Acredula rosea.*

1837 STRICKLAND in *Mag. Nat. Hist.* I. 199 (art.) On the Habits and Peculiarities of the common Bottletit or Mufflin (*Mecistura vagans* Leach). **1839** MACGILLIVRAY *Brit. Birds* II. 421 *Mecistura longicaudata.* Long-tailed Mufflin.

muffling ('mʌflɪŋ), *vbl. sb.* [f. MUFFLE *v.*[1] + -ING[1].] The action of the verb MUFFLE; wrapping up for warmth or for concealment; *concr.* (*sing.* and *pl.*) garments or stuff used for this purpose. Also the deadening of a sound.

1788 MME. D'ARBLAY *Diary* 20 Nov., The face was much hid by the muffling of the high collar to the great coat. **1821** SCOTT *Pirate* xxxvi, Throw back your mufflings from your faces, and don't be afraid, my Lindamiras. **1859** TENNENT *Ceylon* II. VII. vii. 261 European visitors are glad to recall associations of England by producing their winter muffling and surtouts. **1897** *Allbutt's Syst. Med.* III. 45 The area of cardiac dulness increases, and there is muffling of the sound over the mid-cardiac region. **1908** [see MUFFLE *v.*[1] 5].

b. *attrib.* in **muffling-box**, a contrivance for rendering noiseless the escape of steam from a steam-engine; †**muffling-cheat** *slang*, a napkin.

1567 HARMAN *Caveat* (1869) 83 A mofling chete, a napkyn. **1896** *Cosmopolitan* XX. 422/1 The exhaust passing through the muffling box.

muffling ('mʌflɪŋ), *ppl. a.*[1] [f. MUFFLE *v.*[1] + -ING[2].] In senses of the vb.

1638 G. SANDYS *Paraph. Job* xxxiv. (1648) 50 No mufling Clouds, nor Shades Infernall, can From his inquiry hide offending Man. **1839–41** S. WARREN *Ten Thous. a-year* xiii, Next came Mr. Quicksilver, a man of great but wild energy, who received what may be called a *muffling* retainer. **1861** LYTTON *Str. Story* II. 378 Before I could turn, some dark muffling substance fell between my sight and the sun, and I felt a fierce strain at my throat. **1876** GEO. ELIOT *Dan. Der.* lii, Sometimes it occurs to Jacob that Hebrew will be more edifying to him if he stops his ears with his palms, and imitates the venerable sounds as heard through that muffling medium.

†**'muffling,** *ppl. a.*[2] *Obs.* (See MUFFLE *v.*[2])

1616 HOLYDAY *Persius* I. B4, If forsooth one clad in purple cloth's, Snaffle some mustie stuff through's muffling nose.

‖**muffro** ('muffro), **muffrone** (muf'frone). [Corsican: see MOUFLON.] = MOUFLON.

1872 BLACKMORE *Clara Vaughan* (1893) 251 Those islanders [Corsicans].. shoot a man with no more compunction than they shoot a muffro. *Ibid.* 277, I had wondered.. whether he would like to shoot the muffrone.

muffti, -ty, obs. forms of MUFTI.

muffy ('mʌfɪ), *a. nonce-wd.* [f. MUFF *sb.*[2] + -Y.] Resembling a muff.

1831 LYTTON *Godolph.* xlix, A little muffy sort of dog. **1859** *All Year Round* No. 36. 220 A huge, round, high cap, muffy and ridiculous as an English grenadier's, crowned his head.

mufle(r, obs. forms of MUFFLE *v.*, MUFFLER.

‖**mufti**[1] ('mʌftɪ). Forms: 6 **muphtie,** 7 **muftie, muffty, -ti, mophty, -ti, mufiti, mufty, moufti,** 7–8 **muphti,** 7–9 **muftee,** 9 **mooftee, -ti,** 7– **mufti.** [Arab. *muftī*, active pple. of *aftā* (4th conjug. of *fatā*) to give a FETWA or decision on a point of law.] A Muslim priest or expounder of the law; in Turkey restricted to the official head of the religion of the state (formerly often †***grand mufti***) and to deputies appointed by him in some of the larger cities.

1586 T. B. *La Primaud. Fr. Acad.* I. (1594) 631 The muphtie is chiefe of the religion, and looketh unto matters of conscience. **1609** RO. C. *Muley Hamets Rising* I 4 b, The chiefest man for iudgement vnder the King [of Barbary] is the Muftie, to whome the partie greeued may appeale from any other ordinary Iudge. **1624** MASSINGER *Renegado* I. i, One of their Mufties, We call them Priests at Venice, with a Razor Cutts it of. **1690** DRYDEN *Don Sebast.* I. i, I tell thee Mufty, Good feasting is devout: and thou our Head, Hast a Religious ruddy Countenance. **1695** MOTTEUX *St. Olon's Morocco* 115 The Grand Mufti for Affairs of Religion and Justice. **1775** in *Claim of Rada Churn* (1776) 13/2 In the Phousdance Audlaulet [*sic*], the Cauree and Muftee of the district, and two Moulewys, shall sit to expound the Law. **1813** BYRON *Giaour* 491 On her might Muftis gaze, and own That through her eye the Immortal shone. **1852** THACKERAY

Esmond I. xi, Not all the marriage oaths sworn before all the parsons, cardinals,.. muftis and rabbins in the world.

b. *transf.*

1654 GATAKER *Disc. Apol.* 75 A goodlie number of Popelings, and young little Mufties. **1700** W. KING *Transactioneer* 34 He's the very Muffti, the Oracle of our Club. *a* **1716** SOUTH *Serm.* (1717) V. 247 The great Mufti of Geneva. **1835** *Court Mag.* VI. 189/1 'Oh, but', says some she-mufti, in a turban,.. '*if* you have good introductions,.. *then* you are welcome everywhere'. 'Stop, my worthy mufti', I reply; 'do you suppose' [etc.].

Hence **'muftiship**, the office or position of mufti.

1690 DRYDEN *Don Sebast.* IV. ii, The Iniquity of thirty Years Muftiship converted into Diamonds.

mufti[2] ('mʌftɪ). Also **mufty, muftee.** [Perh. a facetious use of prec. It has been suggested that the original application may have been to the costume of dressing-gown, smoking-cap, and slippers, suggesting the attire of the 'mufti' of the stage.]

1. Plain clothes worn by any one who has a right to wear a uniform; esp. in phr. ***in mufti.*** Also *transf.* and *fig.*

1816 'QUIZ' *Grand Master* II. 50 His mufti's off, and now, instead, *Qui hi* per force assumes the red. **1824** in *Spirit Pub. Jrnls.* (1825) 479 A lancer in mufty. **1833** MARRYAT *P. Simple* xiv, Next morning [I] made my appearance in a suit of mufti. **1857** TROLLOPE *Three Clerks* xxxix, He knew that ..he was dogged at the distance of some thirty yards by an amiable policeman in mufti. **1896** N. DAVIS *Three Men & a God* 122 He was made kennel huntsman to the regimental pack, and spent his time, dressed in most disreputable mufti, between the boiling house and kennels. **1930** W. S. MAUGHAM *Cakes & Ale* iv. 52 He looked a little like a dean in mufti on his summer holiday in Switzerland. **1966** *Listener* 13 Oct. 547/1 Students will observe the tears that, Terry-fashion, the actor (in mufti and communing only with the cameras) cannot hold back in the Deposition scene of *Richard II.* **1971** *Illustr. Weekly India* 4 Apr. 23/2 An old man.. was nearly killed by a lathi and was carried away by the police in mufti. **1975** A. CHRISTIE *Curtain* xvii. 182 Nurse Craven I saw for the first time in mufti instead of her nurse's uniform.

attrib. **1854** THACKERAY *Newcomes* viii, He has no mufticoat, except one sent him out.. to India in the year 1821. **1959** *Listener* 16 Apr. 681/3 A time of extravagance already remote from the mufti sobrieties of the Third Republic.

2. A civilian; one who wears, or is in, 'mufti'.

1833 M. SCOTT *Tom Cringle* xx, There was also a sprinkling of civilians, or *muftees*, to use a West India expression.

mufty ('mʌftɪ). *dial.* [Extension of MUFF *sb.*[4]]

a. The whitethroat, *Sylvia cinerea*; **b.** 'A fowl with a tufted or crested head' (E.D.D.).

a. [**1831** J. RENNIE *Montagu's Ornith. Dict.* (ed. 2) 538 Whitethroat... *Provincial.* Nettle-Creeper... Muff. Charlie Muftie. Peggy.] **1839** MACGILLIVRAY *Brit. Birds* II. 354 Even after being shot, you find the feathers of that part [*sc.* the throat] standing out more than is usual in birds: and from this habit is probably derived the familiar names of Muftie or Muffety, or Charlie Muftie, by which it [*sc.* the White-throat] is generally known in Scotland.

b. **1829** J. WILSON *Noct. Ambr.* Wks. 1855 II. 252 What'n a cleckin she's gotten!.. Mufties, too, I declare.

mug (mʌg), *sb.*[1] Also 6 **mugge**, 7–8 **mugg.** [Of unknown origin: cogn. w. LG. *mokke, mukke* mug, Norw. *mugga, mugge* 'an open can or jug, esp. for warm drinks' (Aasen), Sw. *mugg* mug, Norm. dial. *moque* cup, Guernsey *mogue*.]

1. In some northern dialects: Any (large) earthenware vessel or bowl; also, a pot, jug, or ewer. ***pan-mug***: see PAN *sb.* 12 b.

1570 LEVINS *Manip.* 184/24 A Mugge, potte, *ollula.* *a* **1585** POLWART *Flyting w. Montgomerie* 763 Lowsie lugs, leape jugs! toome the mugs on the midding. **1902** MRS. BARNES-GRUNDY *Thames Camp* 176 A large, stone bread-mug.

2. A drinking-vessel, usually cylindrical, with or without a handle.

A silver mug is a common christening gift to a child.

1664 COTTON *Scarron.* I. 107 Dido.. takes a Mug, that held two Quarts,.. And thus begins, Here Sirs, here's to you. **1688** *Lond. Gaz.* No. 2316/4 A Mug,.. a set of Casters, and an Orange-Strainer, all of Silver. **1762–71** H. WALPOLE *Vertue's Anecd. Paint.* (1786) V. 94 Mr. Place discovered.. a method of making porcelaine,.. of which manufacture he gave Thoresby a fine mug. **1844** DICKENS *Chimes* i. (1845) 5 They had had their Godfathers and Godmothers, these Bells.. and had had their silver mugs no doubt, besides. **1846** D. JERROLD *Mrs. Caudle's Curt. Lect.* xiii, Then there's my china mug. **1880** MISS BROUGHTON *Sec. Th.* III. viii, From the time when he held her at the font, and gave her a mug and a rattle, he has always called his betrothed Sophia. **1886** J. K. JEROME *Idle Thoughts* (1889) 142 Life tastes much the same, whether we quaff it from a golden goblet or drink it out of a stone mug.

b. A mug with its contents; the liquid in a mug.

1682 DRYDEN *Mac Fl.* 121 A mighty mug of potent ale. **1739** *Joe Miller's Jests* No. 133, I say, bring this Fellow a Mugg of Strong Beer. **1840** DICKENS *Old C. Shop* i, Kit carried a large slice of bread and meat, and a mug of ale. **1903** *Contemp. Rev.* May 644 Twenty to thirty good sized mugs of malt liquor in an evening is by no means out of the way at academical gatherings.

3. A cooling drink.

1829 *Sporting Mag.* XXIII. 268 The refreshing but dangerous liquor.. known by the appellation of 'mug'. **1865** *Indian Dom. Econ.* (ed. 6) 325 Cool Tankard or Mug.

4. *Comb.*: **mug-hunter** *U.S. colloq.* = POTHUNTER 3; **mugware** *dial.*, earthenware.

1883 *Harper's Mag.* Aug. 443/2 To the.. mug-hunters [at yacht-races] it meant all three. **1900** *Daily News* 9 Oct. 3/1 The old brown mugware settling pans have also passed into the limbo of a now almost forgotten age.

mug (mʌg), *sb.*[2] *dial.* Also **mugg.** In full ***mug sheep***: A breed of sheep having the face completely covered with wool. So ***mug ewe, lamb***, etc.

In some glossaries explained as a 'pollard' or 'hornless' sheep; this may have been the original sense: cf. MUGGED *a.*

1596 in *Archæologia* XLVIII. 152 Item weather mugges xxvij. Item mugge lambes vj[xx]ix. **1621** BRATHWAIT *Nat. Embassie*, etc. (1877) 204 For good mug-sheepe and cattell.. none could come neare thee. **1793** *Statist. Acc. Scot.* VI. 25 The sheep are of the English mugg kind. **1820** SCOTT *Monast.* Introd. Ep., A wig like the curled back of a mug-ewe. **1879** J. LUCAS in *Zoologist* Sept. 356 They are all Scotch ewes for breeding, and first-rate Leicester tups, called in the dale [Nidderdale] 'mugs'.

mug (mʌg), *sb.*[3] *slang.* [Perh. a use of MUG *sb.*[1]; drinking mugs made to represent a grotesque human face were common in the 18th c.]

1. a. The face.

1708 *Brit. Apollo* No. 2. 2/2 My Lawyer has a Desk, nine Law-books without Covers, two with Covers, a Temple-Mug, and the hopes of being a Judge. **1812** J. H. VAUX *Flash Dict.*, *Mug*, the face; a *queer mug* is an ugly face. **1824** EGAN *Boxiana* II. 412 His mug was often disfigured with the claret trickling down. **1850** E. FITZGERALD *Lett.* (1889) I. 200, I found A. Tennyson in chambers at Lincoln's Inn: and recreated myself with a sight of his fine old mug. **1897** G. MEREDITH *Amazing Marr.* I. xvi. 186 Look at old Rufus Abrane. I see the state of the fight on the old fellow's mug. He hasn't a bet left in him!

b. A portrait or photograph of a person, esp. in police records.

1887 *Lantern* (New Orleans) 9 July 2/2 He had his mug taken in fireman's clothes. **1889** CLARKSON & RICHARDSON *Police!* xxiii. 323 Circulating thieves' photos... Pushing the mugs round. **1940** R. CHANDLER *Farewell my Lovely* vi. 43 Nulty turned over a photo.. and handed it to me. It was a police mug, front and profile.

2. The mouth.

1820 J. H. REYNOLDS *Fancy* (1906) 22 Speak, Mrs. Tims; open thy mug, my dear; Mouths here are made to speak, and not to eat. **1835** HALIBURTON *Clockm.* Ser. I. xx. (1837) 202 Hold your mug, you old nigger.

3. The act of throttling or strangling a person; usu. in phr. ***to put the mug on*** (someone).

1862 *Sessions Papers Cent. Criminal Court* 26 Nov. 41 Roberts.. said, 'You want me for putting the *mug* on, do you? I will put the b—y *mug* on you.' *Ibid.*, *Mug* is slang used by thieves; it means garotting. **1940** *Amer. Speech* XV. 121/1 *To put the mug on* (a mark), to put a stranglehold on a mark who grows obstreperous after he has been fleeced. **1955** *Publ. Amer. Dial. Soc.* XXIV. 171 A strangle hold is applied... This hold is called.. a *mug* on the East Coast.

4. *attrib.* and *Comb.*, as **mug book** *U.S.*, (*a*) (see quot. 1935); (*b*) a book kept by the police containing photographs of criminals; **mug-faker**, a street photographer; **mug shot** orig. *U.S.* = sense 1 b above.

1935 A. J. POLLOCK *Underworld Speaks* 78/2 *Mug book*, a book published for prominent business and professional men who are induced by high pressure solicitors to vividly write about themselves with youthful photographs. They pay well for this blue book privilege. **1958** J. & W. HAWKINS *Death Watch* (1959) i. 19, I couldn't find him in the mug books; his picture isn't there. **1933** 'G. ORWELL' *Down & Out* xxxii. 236 A mugfaker—a street photographer. **1952** M. ALLINGHAM *Tiger in Smoke* i. 16 These old photographers —mugfakers we call'em—in the street. **1950** in Wentworth & Flexner *Dict. Amer. Slang* (1960) 349/1 Police passed around a mug shot of Willie. **1962** K. ORVIS *Damned & Destroyed* xxvii. 200 The police record plate number.. indicates that mug-shot was taken in the Receiving Room. **1970** R. JEFFRIES *Dead Man's Bluff* vii. 66 Check through the mug shots and see if you can find him. **1974** *Daily Tel.* 14 Nov 2/2 From the mass of information collected, a picture is built up of the personalities in the IRA's command structure, and this is then used in the 'mugshot' booklets carried by soldiers on the streets.

mug (mʌg), *sb.*[4] *dial.* (E.Angl., Shropsh., etc.) [cogn. w. MUG *v.*[1]; cf. ON. *mugga* mist, drizzle (perh. the source).] 'A fog or mist; a slight rain or drizzle; a damp, dull, gloomy state of the atmosphere' (E.D.D.).

1775 ASH, *Mug* (a cant word), a mist, a fog.

mug (mʌg), *sb.*[5]

1. a. A stupid or incompetent person, a 'muff', 'duffer'; a fool, simpleton; a card-sharper's dupe. *slang.*

1859 MATSELL *Voc.* (Farmer). **1861** MAYHEW *Lond. Labour* III. 193 We sometimes have a greenhorn wants to go out pitching with us—a mug, we calls them. **1894** MASKELYNE *Sharps & Flats* 170 It does not need much persuasion to induce the 'mug' to take the bank. **1900** MRS. GLYN *Visits Elizabeth* (1906) 91 He fished out a scrap of paper from his pocket and pressed it into my hand, and said, 'Don't be a mug this time'.

b. mug's game, a thankless task; a useless, foolish, or unprofitable activity. *colloq.*

1910 BELLOC *Pongo* xv. 233 One cannot arrest millionaires with impunity... Even in a wild democracy to arrest them is Mug's game. **1918** *Flying* 12 June 427/2 Flying's a mug's game, mater, A fact I know full well. **1930** G. B. SHAW *Apple Cart* II. 77, I am going out of politics. Politics is a mug's game. **1959** T. S. ELIOT *Elder Statesman* I. 26 Forgery, I can tell you, is a mug's game. I say that——with conviction. **1973** *Times* 9 Nov. 21/2 Running a reserve currency is a mug's game; and the world is running out of mugs.

c. A person, fellow, chap; *spec.* (*a*) a rough or ugly person; a criminal; (*b*) applied by criminals to someone who is not part of the underworld; (*c*) a policeman. *slang.*

1890 in Barrère & Leland *Dict. Slang* II. 73 'What are *mugs*?' 'Hard characters... Those are thieves from the First Ward, the fellows that rob immigrants, steal cotton from the bales,' [etc.]. **1895** E. W. TOWNSEND *Chimmie Fadden Explains* 15 Dat Mr. Paul is de funniest mug you ever see. *Ibid.* 17 De mug what plays de flute has de music all t'himself when de odder mugs in de orchestra don't do nottin. **1903** H. HAPGOOD *Autobiogr. Thief* (1904) xii. 267 I'm only stealin' for certain mugs (policemen) and fer those 'igher up, so they can buy real estate. **1921** [see GEE *sb.*[4]]. **1930** [see JITTER *sb.* 1]. **1938** F. D. SHARPE *Sharpe of Flying Squad* i. 13 Underworld men and women speak of all outside their world as 'mugs'. **1960** *Observer* 24 Jan. 5/2 There were recognised prop-men or putters up of jobs, what the mugs called master minds.

2. a. *Comb.*: **mug-hunter** (see quot.).

1887 J. W. HORSLEY *Jottings fr. Jail* 95 An old mug-hunter, one, that is to say, of the wretched horde who haunt the street at midnight to rob drunken men.

b. *attrib.*, passing into *adj.*, that is a 'mug' or fool; stupid; easily duped or defeated.

1922 E. WALLACE *Flying Fifty-Five* xxxiii. 197 The mug punter was he who dreamed of long-priced winners and refused to bet on the six to four certainty preferring rather the hopeless proposition that started at twenty to one. **1963** T. TULLETT *Inside Interpol* xvi. 216 There are still thousands of 'mug' criminals.. who invariably make mistakes. **1971** *Sunday Australian* 8 Aug. 5/6 Let's just say I'm a good average mug golfer.

mug (mʌg), *sb.*[6] *slang.* [f. MUG *v.*[5]]

1. An examination.

1853 MAXWELL in L. Campbell *Life* (1882) 191, I was down after the Mug [*note*, Trinity College Examination] with Tayler's uncle in Suffolk.

2. One who 'mugs' or reads hard.

1888 *Berkshire Gloss.*, *Mug*, as a schoolboy's expression to work hard, and one who does so is somewhat contemptuously termed 'a mug' by others who [etc.]. **1901** *Daily News* 6 Feb. 9/5 At the University of Oxford a 'mug' is a person who is not given to sport, or any indulgence, but who reads a great many books which he doesn't understand.

mug (mu:g), *sb.*[7] Also **moog.** Var. of MUNG[2], MOONG.

1840 *Penny Cycl.* XVIII. 57/2 *Phaseolus Mungo*, or Moog, is one of the dry leguminous grains of India. **1876** SIR W. W. HUNTER in *Encycl. Brit.* IV. 23/1 Of the pulses the most important are gram (*Cicer arietinum*), túr.., kulti.., and mug (*Phaseolus Mungo*).

‖**Mug** (mʌg), *sb.*[8] Forms: 8–9 **Mug**, 9 **Mugg, Mugh.** [Bengālī *Magh*, of obscure origin; in 16–17th c. *Mogen, Mog, Mogue* occur as names for Arakan and its people (see Yule s.v.).] The name given in Bengal to natives of Arakan and Chittagong. The Mugs were formerly celebrated as the best native cooks in Calcutta.

1752 in J. Long *Unpubl. Rec. Govt.* (1869) 87 (Yule) The Mugs. **1802** C. JAMES *Milit. Dict.*, *Mugs*, a banditti of plunderers from an Indian nation. **1839** *Court Mag.* VI. 65/2 Two or three stout broad faced Mughs. **1866** TREVELYAN in *Frasers's Mag.* LXXIII. 389 That vegetable curry was excellent. Of course your cook is a Mug?

attrib. **1897** HENTY *On Irrawaddy* 39 This Mug language ..is.. almost the same as Burmese.

mug (mʌg), *v.*[1] *dial.* (see E.D.D.). [Prob. of Scandinavian origin: cf. Norw. *mugga* to drizzle. Cf. MUG *sb.*[4]] *intr.* To drizzle or rain slightly.

13.. *Gaw. & Gr. Knt.* 2080 Þe heuen was vp halt, bot vgly þer vnder, Mist muged on þe mor, malt on þe mountez. **1825–80** JAMIESON, *To Mug, Muggle, v.n.* To drizzle. Aberd.

mug (mʌg), *v.*[2] *slang* and *dial.* Also **mogg.** [? An application of MUG *v.*[1]] *intr.* 'To pout, grow sullen; to mope; to refuse food' (E.D.D.).

c **1730** HAYNES *MS. Dorset. Voc.* in *N. & Q.* 6th Ser. (1883) VIII. 45 To *mogg*, pout or grow sullen. **17..** *Collins' Misc.* (1762) 122 (Halliwell) Wit hung her blob, ev'n Humour seem'd to mourn, And sullenly sat mogging o'er his urn. **1828** *Sporting Mag.* XXIII. 28 Snoozing and mugging over the fire after a hard day's work. **1861** HOLLAND *Less. Life* xx. 283 By 'mugging' over your trouble out of business hours.

mug (mʌg), *v.*[3] [f. MUG *sb.*[3]]

1. *Theatr. slang.* **a.** *intr.* To 'make a face'; to grimace.

b. ***to mug up***: to paint (one's face); to make up. *trans.* and *intr.* for *refl.*

1855 DICKENS *Dorrit* I. xx, The low comedian had 'mugged' at him in his richest manner fifty nights for a wager. **1859** *Hotten's Slang Dict.*, *Mug-up*, to paint one's face. Theat. **1861** MAYHEW *Lond. Labour* III. 193 Then he underwent the operation of mugging him up with oil-colour paint, black, and.. red. **1869** W. S. GILBERT *Bab Ball.*, *Rev. Micah Sowls* 54 He saw a dreary person on the stage, Who mouthed and mugged in simulated rage.

2. orig. *Pugilism. trans.* **a.** To strike in the face; also, to fight, beat up, assault; to strangle; occas. *intr.*, to fight. *slang.* **b.** (Now the prevailing sense). To attack and rob (a person). Now *colloq.* Cf. MUGGING *vbl. sb.* 1.

1818 *Sporting Mag.* II. 279 The latter got away, and in return mugged him. **1846** *Swell's Night Guide* 37 Most of them can.. mug.. alias fight. *Ibid.* 76 She felt inclined to mug her rival, only she thought it would be no bottle. **1859** HOTTEN *Dict. Slang* 65 *Mug*, to fight, or chastise. **1864** *Ibid.* 183 *Mug*,.. to rob by the garrote. **1866** *London Misc.* 5 May

102 Suppose they had mugged you?.. Slogged you, you know. **1904** 'No. 1500' *Life in Sing Sing* 250/2 *Mug*,..to strangle. **1948** *N.Y. Times* 15 Aug. 36 The police said the victims were mugged in the hallways of their homes. **1960** I. WALLACH *Absence of Cello* 23 She's going into Central Park for her constitutional. I hope she gets mugged. **1966** WODEHOUSE *Plum Pie* vii. 166 Somebody mugged Sam last night... Yessir, laid him out cold. **1968** A. DIMENT *Bang Bang Birds* iii. 28 In New York..people conversed about their friends being beaten up and robbed—mugged is the local term. **1971** B. MALAMUD *Tenants* 198 Lesser..daily fears that..the writer will be mugged on the subway stairs and lie there unable to crawl home. **1972** *Daily Tel.* 7 Oct. 2/6 Judge Hines, Q.C., jailed three youths for three years for 'mugging' a middle-aged man and stealing £7 from his wallet.

3. To take a photograph of (a person), esp. for police records. *U.S. slang.*

1899 'J. FLYNT' *Tramping with Tramps* IV. 395 *Mug*,..to photograph. **1912** [see MUGGING *vbl. sb.* 2]. **1929** M. A. GILL *Underworld Slang*, *Mugged*, photographed. **1934** *Sun* (Baltimore) 5 July 13/6 Attempts of Federal authorities to 'mug' him proved futile. When Robert C. Johnson.. prepared to snap a picture of the prisoner, Kent held his hands before his face. **1960** *Wall St. Jrnl.* 3 Nov. 2 More than 15,000 New Jersey securities salesmen are being fingerprinted and 'mugged' at police stations and private detective agencies over the state, under a new state law. **1972** G. V. HIGGINS *Friends of Eddie Coyle* xix. 115 We brought him up to the marshal's office and mugged him and printed him.

4. To kiss, to fondle. *slang* (chiefly *Austral.* and *N.Z.*).

1916 C. J. DENNIS *Songs Sentimental Bloke* 126 *Mug, to*, to kiss. **1932** *Amer. Speech* VII. 334 *Mug*, to kiss. **1957** I. CROSS *God Boy* (1958) x. 80 You think there is something funny about them mugging up each other like that?

mug (mʌg), *v.*[4] *slang* and *dial.* [f. MUG *sb.*[1]] *trans.* To bribe with liquor; to supply with beer or liquor; to buy a drink for (someone). Also *refl.* and *intr.* to get drunk (see E.D.D.).

1830 H. INGELO *Remin.* II. 479 Having..mugged, as we say in England, our pilot. **1854** A. E. BAKER *Gloss. Northamptonshire Words* II. 38 Come! mug the girls, and they'll get on with their work. **1939** *Daily Mirror* 14 Mar., Are you going to 'mug' us... Are you going to stand me a drink? **1966** P. MOLONEY *Plea for Mersey* 23 If ye say to them 'scouse, Mug us dem on de house,' Yerl make Birty and Girty all shirty. **1966** F. SHAW et al. *Lern Yerself Scouse* 42 *Ile mug yer*, allow me to treat you. *Ibid.* 77 Many's the fella dat I use'ter mug.

mug, *v.*[5] *slang.*

1. *intr.* To read or study hard, to 'grind'. Const. *at*; also with *away, on, up*.

1848 MAXWELL in L. Campbell *Life* (1882) 117 Please to write about your Prizes at College, and about coming here to mug. **1860** *Hotten's Slang Dict.* (ed. 2), *Mug-up*... To 'cram' for an examination.—Army. **1878** *About Some Fellows* vii. 45 Stortford, ever since he had settled to work, had..been patiently mugging on at his verses, and had got twelve done. **1893** G. ALLEN *Scallywag* I. 241 That prize essay you were mugging away at.

2. *trans.* To get up (a subject) by hard study. Also with *up*.

1882 BESANT *Revolt of Man* v. 111 When they ought to have been 'mugging bones', or drawing contracts, or reading theology. **1889** G. ALLEN *Tents of Shem* xxiv, I've mugged it all up out of books, that's all. Anybody can mug it all up if he'll only take the pains.

Hence **'mugging** *vbl. sb.*, hard studying, 'swotting'. Usu. with *up*.

1959 I. & P. OPIE *Lore & Lang. Schoolch.* x. 179 'Swotting' or 'mugging up' is only considered good form if a person is on the point of taking an exam. **1959** *Daily Tel.* 10 June 10/2 But no one..after yesterday's inauguration of the new electric services from London to the Kent Coast is going to mind mugging up any number of amended arrival and departure times. **1960** *Guardian* 15 July 6/6 Hasty muggings-up and regurgitations of fact.

mug, *v.*[6] *slang. intr.* 'To crowd, huddle *together* in a confined space' (E.D.D.).

1878 *N. & Q.* 5th Ser. IX. 84/2 They are all, father, mother, and children, mugging together in one room.

mug (mʌg), *v.*[7] *slang* (chiefly *Canad.* and *Naut.*). *intr.* ***to mug up***: to make a plentiful meal. Also, to have a snack, a meal, or a hot drink.

1897 KIPLING *Captain's Courageous* v. 123 No reg'lar meals fer no one then. 'Mug-up when ye're hungry, an' sleep when ye can't keep awake. *Ibid.* ix. 202 Him an' my boy hookin' fried pies an' muggin' up when they ought to ha' been asleep. **1901** *Scribner's Mag.* XXIX. 498/2 Let Martin and me mug up and get over near the fire to dry out, and we'll have it again. **1917** 'BARTIMEUS' *Long Trick* iv. 78 Coats and mufflers were donned and a bottle of sloe-gin uncorked. 'Mug-up!' cried the Sub. 'Mug-up, and let's get 'appy and chatty.' **1927** G. BRADFORD *Gloss. Sea Terms* 117/1 *Mug up*, to have a drink of coffee or tea which is always on the galley stove of a fishing schooner. **1929** F. BOWEN *Sea Slang* 93 *Mug up, to*, to eat, used principally in the Grand Banks schooners. **1936** A. STRINGER *Wife Traders* xv. 214 They fell into the habit of stopping more often to 'mug up' along the trail. **1950** J. HAMBLETON *Abitibi Adventure* 94 René was just 'mugging up' when the shaggy terrier..sent the blackened tea pail flying. **1972** L. HANCOCK *There's a Seal in my Sleeping Bag* v. 84 We..mugged up on boiled eggs, toast, jam, and coffee.

‖**muga** ('mu:gə). Also **mooga, munga, moonga.** [Assamese *mugá.*] A wild silk (of Assam) obtained from the cocoons of the *Saturnia assama*; also the silkworm which produces this silk. Also *attrib.* or *adj.*, as ***muga dhoties*** pl., ***muga silk***, (***silk***) ***worm***.

1833 CAPT. JENKINS in Geoghegan *Parl. Rep. Silk in India* (1874) 113 The fawn-coloured moonga silk. *Ibid.*, The moonga worm. **1850** OGILVIE, *Muggadooties*, in the East Indies, a sort of cloth manufactured from wild silk. **1881** T. WARDLE *Wild Silks of India* 55 The Moonga, Mooga, or Muga Silk. **1887** J. PATON in *Encycl. Brit.* XXII. 60/1 Next in promising qualities is the muga or moonga worm of Assam, *Antheræa assama*, a species to some extent domesticated in its native country.

Muganda (mu:'gændə). Also 9 **Mganda.** Pl. BAGANDA *sb.* and *a.* [Bantu *ganda* + sing. prefix *mu.*] A native or inhabitant of the former kingdom of Buganda, now a province of Uganda; hence, loosely, any native or inhabitant of Uganda. Also *attrib.* and as *adj.*

1862 J. H. SPEKE *Jrnl. Discovery Source of Nile* (1863) xi. 299 Turning round with true Mganda impetuosity, he walked away. *Ibid.* 313 Every Mganda will say the first Uganda year dates from the arrival of the first Mzungû (white) visitor. **1889** R. P. ASHE *Two Kings Uganda* xxiii. 287 A Muganda mother takes no little pride in her child. *Ibid.* 290 Should any person of position suddenly address a Muganda, he should politely reply, 'Kabaka'. **1905** J. F. CUNNINGHAM *Uganda* ix. 185 A Muganda chief looks with loathing on all work in the fields. **1908** *Daily Chron.* 24 Dec. 4/6 Buganda is the country, a Muganda is an individual native, the Baganda are the natives as a whole, and Luganda is the language. **1971** *Sunday Nation* (Nairobi) 11 Apr. 11/7 Possibly he was the greatest Muganda patriot in the four hundred years of the Buganda kingdom's history.

mugearite ('mʌgi:əraɪt). *Petrogr.* [f. *Mugear-y*, the name of a village in the Isle of Skye, Scotland + -ITE[1].] A dark, fine-grained trachyte which has oligoclase as the main feldspar and also contains olivine, orthoclase, and apatite.

1904 A. HARKER *Tertiary Igneous Rocks Skye* xv. 257 The other rock..is, when fresh, a black compact-looking rock without phenocrysts... As this rock..belongs to a peculiar type, we..give it a provisional name..'mugearite', a name adopted from that of Mugeary, the crofter village lying at a short distance north. **1928** *Trans. Geol. Soc. Glasgow* XVIII. 348 A characteristic feature which the mugearites share with the Jedburgh basalts is the presence of close-set parallel somewhat irregular platy joints. **1956** *Trans. R. Soc. Edin.* LXIII. 68 The mugearite lava east of Dunsapie Hill, thought to have been the first of the flows, contains a number of phenocrysts of albitised plagioclase. **1971** *Nature* 23 Apr. 510/2 The lavas [of the Baringo District, Kenya] comprise a succession of alkali-olivine basalts, basanites and mugearites.

Hence **mugea'ritic** *a.*, of or containing mugearite.

1927 *Trans. R. Soc. Edin.* LV. 504 We regard the mugearitic and essexitic intrusions of the Dalmahoy syncline as hypabyssal expressions of the magma which gave rise to the accompanying effusive mugearites and allied basalts. **1973** *Nature* 9 Feb. 375/1 There, the volumes of individual hawaiitic and mugearitic lavas are frequently of the order of 0·1 km³.

mugen, obs. form of MUGGEN *a. dial.*

mugful ('mʌgfʊl). Also †**mug-full.** [f. MUG *sb.*[1] + -FUL.] The contents of a mug; the amount that a mug will hold (in quot. 1867 = bowlful).

1838 DICKENS *Nickleby* (1839) xv. 133 A glass-full of spirits and water for Nicholas, and a cracked mug-full for the joint accommodation of himself and Smike. **1867** J. T. STATON *Rays fro th' Loominary* 110 Aw pusht th' owd woman uv hur bustle in a mugful o dowf [*i.e.* dough]. **1924** J. M. BARRIE *Mary Rose* I. 15, I wonder if you would give me a mug of tea. Not a cup, we drink it by the mugful where I hail from. **1973** J. MANN *Only Security* vi. 59 Roger accepted the plastic mugful of tea.

mugg: see MUG *sb.*[2] (sheep); and obs. f. MUG *sbs.*

muggar, variant of MUGGER *sb.*[1]

†**'muggard**, *a. dial. Obs.* [? f. MUG *v.*[2] + -ARD.] Sullen, displeased.

1746 *Exmoor Scolding* 194 Why, than tha wut be a prilled, or a muggard, a Zennet outreert. *Ibid.* 313. *Ibid.* Vocabulary, *Muggard*, sullen. **1787** GROSE *Provinc. Gloss.*, *Muggard*, sullen. Exm. Hence **1818** in TODD, and in later Dicts.

muggart, dial. form of MUGWORT.

mugged, *a. dial.* [Cf. MUG *sb.*[2] b.] Hornless.

1588 *Wills & Inv. N.C.* (Surtees) II. 33 *note*, To my son Henry Ogle a brass pot, a black tagged cow, a black mugged cow. **1828** *Craven Gloss.* II. 289 Neen gimmer mugg'd hogs.

'muggen, *a. dial.* Also 7 **mugen.** [f. MUG *sb.*[1] I + -EN[4].] Made of earthenware.

1688 R. HOLME *Armoury* III. xiv. (Roxb.) 2/1 Mugen weare. *Ibid.* xxii. 280/1 Made of earth or clay, Muggen weare. **1887** *S. Cheshire Gloss.*, *Muggen, adj.* of earthenware. 'A muggen egg' is the name for a manufactured article used as a nest-egg.

[**muggent**, Gesner's (1555) German rendering (= mod.G. *mückenente*, f. *mücke* fly + *ente* duck) of mod.L. *anas muscaria*, a species of wild duck described by Aldrovandus. Quoted in 1678 in Ray *Willughby's Ornith.* III. iii. 375, and mistaken by some later writers for an Eng. word. Hence in Webster 1828–32, and in later Dicts.]

mugger ('mʌgə(r)), *sb.*[1] *dial.* Also 8 **mogger.** [f. MUG *sb.*[1] + -ER[1].] A hawker of earthenware.

1743 *Heddon-on-the-Wall Par. Reg.*, William, son to Michell the Mogger, bp. 23 March. **1816** SCOTT *Old Mort.* Introd., The ware of Cooper Climent was rejected in horror, much to the benefit of his rivals the muggers, who dealt in earthenware. **1852** R. S. SURTEES *Sponge's Sp. Tour* lix, A nimble-handed mugger or tramp might have carried off whatever he liked with impunity. **1884** *Manch. Exam.* 1 Sept. 5/1 Alnwick is a great resort of..'muggers',..tramps who travel round the district to sell earthenware.

‖**mugger** ('mʌgə(r)), *sb.*[2] Also -ur, -ar. [Hindī *magar.*] The broad-nosed crocodile of India.

1844 J. E. GRAY *Catal. Tortoises*, etc. *Brit. Mus.* 62 The Muggar or Goa. *Crocodilus palustris.* **1854** HOOKER *Himal. Jrnls.* I. ii. 54 Of the short nosed, or mugger kind. **1895** COOK *India, Burma & Ceylon* 68 Muggers or man-eating alligators.

'mugger, *sb.*[3] *slang.* [f. MUG *v.*[4] + -ER[1].] One who 'mugs' or studies diligently.

1883 J. PAYN *Canon's Ward* viii, 'A mugger'—a comprehensive term understood to include all persons with an ambition for University distinction.

mugger ('mʌgə(r)), *sb.*[4] [f. MUG *v.*[3] + -ER[1].]

1. *Theatr. slang.* A comedian who 'mugs' or grimaces.

1892 *Nat. Observ.* 27 Feb. 379/1 None had ever a more expressive viznomy than this prince of 'muggers'.

2. One who 'mugs' people (see MUG *v.*[3] 2); *spec.* one who commits robbery with violence. orig. *U.S.*

1865 J. H. BROWNE *Four Yrs. in Secessia* xlv. 340 The Muggers, like most bullies and ruffians, manifested a fine discrimination respecting the party they attacked, selecting those they thought they could rob with little resistance and entire impunity. **1874** HOTTEN *Slang Dict.* 220 *Maceman*, or *macer*, a welcher, magsman, or general swindler; a 'street-mugger'. **1942** *N.Y. Times* 3 Oct. 17/1 The police were.. tracking down three known..muggers who..had received suspended sentences in a mugging case. **1955** *Sun* (Baltimore) 5 Jan. 2/4 Corporal——..of Cleveland reported to police early today that he had been attacked by two muggers while walking near the Pennsylvania Station. **1965** WODEHOUSE *Galahad at Blandings* i. 11 Muggers, stick-up men and hoodlums in general he disliked. **1970** *Daily Mail* 21 Feb. 9/5 Clarendon Road in London's Notting Hill area..is the haunt of the Muggers—men who clobber you and steal whatever you have of value. **1973** *Sun* 18 Jan. 7 (*headline*) Muggers attacked detective.

mugger ('mʌgə(r)), *sb.*[5] A nail, usually of wrought iron, used for protecting the inner soles of mountaineering boots.

1941 C. F. KIRKUS *Let's go Climbing!* v. 68 For the inner part of the sole muggers, rough wrought iron hobnails, are excellent. **1954** C. D. MILNER *Wedderburn's Alpine Climbing* (ed. 2) ii. 10 The Alpine mugger is a very good nail, but the alternate freezing and thawing of the sole will soon loosen it. **1970** A. BLACKSHAW *Mountaineering* (rev. ed.) iii. 99 Soft iron nails which grip as a result of the rock biting into them (muggers and clinkers).

mugger ('mʌgə(r)), *sb.*[6] and *v.* A slang euphemism for some senses of BUGGER *sb.* and *v.* (see quots.).

1945 'N. SHUTE' *Most Secret* vii. 150 What do you think we stopped to pick the mugger up for? **1948** —— *No Highway* ix. 229 The pilot said, 'I don't give a mugger about that, sir. It's plain bloody nonsense.' **1951** —— *Round the Bend* 69 'Well, I'm muggered,' I said in wonder. **1954** 'G. CARR' *Death under Snowdon* v. 54 Privileges are for the man who works for 'em, not for the mugger who plants his bottom on 'em because his father owned land. **1962** J. P. CARSTAIRS *Pardon my Gun* i. 10 She's muggered off... Hopped it to Italy.

muggert, muggerwarte: see MUGWORT.

mugget[1] ('mʌgɪt). Forms: 6 **muguet**, 6–9 **mugwet**, 9 **mugget.** [a. F. *muguet* (in mod. use lily of the valley and woodruff), semi-popular ad. med.L. *muscātum* 'musk-scented', f. *musc-us* MUSK. Cf. OF. *muguete* nutmeg, ad. (*nux*) *muscāta.*] A name given to several plants: **a.** ***petty mugget*** (***mugwet***), maid's hair, or yellow bedstraw, *Galium verum.* **b.** ***golden mugget***, crosswort, *Galium Cruciata.* **c.** Woodruff, *Asperula odorata.* **d.** The lily of the valley, *Convallaria majalis*, **e.** The guelder rose, *Viburnum Opulus.*

1578 LYTE *Dodoens* IV. lxxv. 539 In French, *Petit Muguet.* .. We may also name it Pety Muguet. *Ibid.* lxxvii. 541 In high Douche, *Golden Walmaister*, that is, Golden Muguet. **1597** GERARDE *Herbal* II. ccccxlviii. 968 In English our Ladies Bedstraw, Cheese renning, Maides Haire, and petie Mugwet. *Ibid.*, Table Eng. Names, Mugwet, that is Woodroofe. **1665** LOVELL *Herbal* (ed. 2) 292 Mug-wet, see Woodroof. Petty mugwet, see Ladies bedstraw. **1871** PULMAN *Rustic Sk.* (ed. 3) 117 'Mugget' is also the local name for the guelder rose.

mugget[2] ('mʌgɪt). *Obs.* exc. *dial.* (see E.D.D.). Forms: 5 *pl.* **mog(g)hettis**, 6 **moget, moquet**, 6–8 **mugwet**, 8–9 **muggut**, 9 **muggat, muggett**, 7– **mugget.** [Of obscure origin; it is difficult to regard it as an application of prec.]

1. The intestines of a calf or sheep, as an article of food. Also = GATHER-BAG.

1481 CAXTON *Reynard* xxxii. (Arb.) 92 The moghettis, Lyuer longes and the Inward [of the calf] shal be for your chyldren. *c* **1550** LACY *Wyl Bucke's Test.* A iij, For the thrid course of the bucke. The potage Mogets and Nowmbleis stued [etc.]. *Ibid.* Bj, For to dight the Moget. **1575** TURBERV. *Venerie* 39 The gatherbagge or Mugwet of a yong harte. **1578** LYTE *Dodoens* v. xviii. 572 Like the Moquet or Chauden of a Calfe. **1605** in *Archæologia* (1800) XIII. 370 Calves-plucke. Calves Mugget. Calves Foote. **1791** WOLCOT (P. Pindar) *Remonstr.* Wks. 1812 II. 452 I'm a poor botching tailor for a court Low bred on liver and what Clowns call mugget. **1864** *E. Cornw. Words* in *Jrnl. R. Inst. Cornw.* Mar. 18, *Muggets*, the small entrails; chitterlings.

†**2.** A dish made from the 'mugget' of a calf or sheep. *Obs. rare.*

1596 *Gd. Huswiues Jewell* C 5, To make muggets. First perboyle them, and take white and chop them both togeather [etc.]. **1597** *Ibid.* II. B iij, You may make a mugget of a Sheepe as these allowes bee, sauing you must put no mutton into it. **1677** LOCKE in Ld. King *Life* (Bohn) 134 At Bristol.. taste.. marrow puddings, cock ale metheglin white and red muggets.

3. *attrib.*: ***mugget-pie*** (also ***muggety pie***).

1696 SALMON *Fam. Dict.* (ed. 2) 212 Mugget Minced-Pye. Boil your Muggets tender, and being cold, mince them small; then put [etc.]. **1800** *Archæologia* XIII. 388 In Cornwall a Muggity Pye is a pye made of Calves intrails.

muggewede, obs. form of MUGWEED.

†**muggill.** *slang. Obs. rare.* A beadle.

1610 ROWLANDS *Martin Mark-all* E 3, The Muggill, the Beadle.

'muggily, *adv. nonce-wd.* [f. MUGGY *a.* + -LY².] In a muggy state or condition.

1867 MISS BROUGHTON *Cometh up as Fl.* xxvii, Winter.. has come in meekly, wetly, muggily.

muggin, variant of MOGGAN *Sc.*

mugginess ('mʌgɪnɪs). [f. MUGGY *a.* + -NESS.] The state, quality, or condition of being muggy.

1856 GEO. ELIOT *Let.* 29 Dec. (1954) II. 284 Don't you enjoy the frost after that long time of mugginess? **1872** —— in Cross *Life* III. 171 We are languishing with headache from two days' damp and mugginess. **1887** MISS BRADDON *Like & Unlike* xix, The mild mugginess of a London autumn.

mugging ('mʌgɪŋ), *vbl. sb.* [f. MUG *v.*³ + -ING¹.]

1. orig. *slang.* The action of MUG *v.*³ 2; *spec.* robbery with violence. Also *attrib.*

1846 *Swell's Night Guide* 75, I knows that 'ere whitehouse warment.. would chaff—and you knows I'm soon shirty, and then we should have a mugging match. **1866** J. E. BROGDEN *Provincial Words Lincolnshire* 131, I gave him a sound mugging, he was so chappy. *a* **1876** E. LEIGH *Gloss. Words Dial. Cheshire* (1877) 139 'To receive a muggin' is to be beaten. **1939** *Fortune* July 168/3 The vicious art of 'mugging' by which a Negro thug grabs the wayfarer around the neck, from behind, while two others with knives clean out his pockets. **1942** [see MUGGER *sb.*⁴ 2]. **1949** *Sat. Even. Post* 8 Oct. 171/2 The only things she reads in our newspapers are the murders and the muggings and the obituaries. **1951** *Manch. Guardian Weekly* 28 June 2/2 The increase in petty thieving, in 'muggings' of night-time strollers, and in prostitution. **1971** B. MALAMUD *Tenants* 64 Bugsy is shot.. in Catshit Alley by two white pigs who had cornered him there after a mugging. **1973** *Guardian* 7 June 9/5 Much of the [crime] increase consists of robberies after sudden attacks in the open, known commonly as mugging.

2. The action of MUG *v.*³ 3; the taking of photographs of persons. Also *attrib. U.S. slang.*

1899 'J. FLYNT' *Tramping with Tramps* IV. 389 In some cities suspicious characters are arrested on general principles and immediately photographed by the police authorities. Such towns are called 'muggin' joints', and the police authorities 'muggin' fiends'. **1912** A. B. REEVE *Poisoned Pen* (1913) ii. 58 An hour later, at headquarters, after the pedigrees had been taken, the 'mugging' done.. O'Connor led the way into his private office. **1912** A. TRAIN *Courts, Criminals & Camorra* 5 'Mugging' was all right, so long as you 'mugged' the right persons.

3. Kissing, love-making, 'necking'. Cf. MUG *v.*³ 4.

1924 P. MARKS *Plastic Age* xxiii. 271, I hate mugging and petting and that sort of thing... Petting is jazzing love; and I hate it. **1926** K. S. PRICHARD *Working Bullocks* xxvii. 242 But Deb had never kissed her mother, as she had seen children in the township kiss and cuddle up to their mothers... Her mother did not encourage 'mugging', as she called it. **1970** C. MAJOR *Dict. Afro-Amer. Slang* 83 *Mugging*,.. making love.

4. Grimacing; making faces (see also quots.). Also *fig.*

1937 *Amer. Speech* XII. 317/2 *Mugging*, motion picture acting. **1961** *Times* 25 Apr. 20/4 Grimaces and gestures straight out of silent films, properly deserving the name 'mugging'. **1968** *Listener* 25 July 124/2 Paul Daneman made a promising start as Higgins, but dwindled into a kind of a verbal mugging.

muggins ('mʌgɪnz), *sb.* [perh. the surname *Muggins*, used arbitrarily with allusion to MUG *sb.*⁵ Cf. the use of the surname in Surtees *Handley Cross* (1843).]

1. *slang.* A fool, simpleton; a 'juggins'. ***to talk muggins***: to say silly, foolish things. Also 'a borough-magnate; a local leader' (Farmer). Freq. used by a speaker to refer to himself.

1855 *Golden Era* 28 Jan. 2/1 You are a veritable 'Muggins' in [choosing] cigars. **1859** C. E. DE LONG in *Calif. Hist. Soc. Q.* (1931) X. 167 Spent the evening until late with Jim in having one of our regular old fashioned long talks about women love &c; and both arrived at the conclusion that we were mugginse's. **1881** *Punch* 10 Sept. 110/2 Well them as talks Muggins like that to our gurls must be milks. **1884** *Ibid.* 11 Oct. 180/1 Must ha' thought me a muggins, old man, To ask sech a question of 'Arry. **1973** *Daily Tel.* 29 Aug. 1/3 The letter bomb was not meant for me personally. I was just the muggins who opened it. **1973** E. LEMARCHAND *Let or Hindrance* 181 'In a nutshell,' Michael said, '.. Muggins [*i.e.* himself] has agreed to be in charge.'

2. a. A children's game of cards.

Each player lays down a card face upwards, forming a pile before him. When the top cards before two players match, the one who first cries 'Muggins' transfers his pile to the other. When all the cards are brought into one pile, the player to whom it belongs is the loser. The word *muggins* is also applied to the player who has to receive cards from another, and to the pool formed by the cards that remain of the pack after an equal division in dealing.

1855 *Pioneer* (San Francisco) Nov. 358 We returned to the hotel, to engage in the intellectual game of Muggins. Ladies and gentlemen were all decided to be Muggins ere the game had closed. **1865** S. JEX-BLAKE *Let.* 18 Aug. in M. Todd *Life S. Jex-Blake* (1918) xiii. 165 After the ices we went back to the Hospital, and played a most ridiculous game of cards called 'Muggins', keeping us in roars of laughter half the time. **1876** HEATHER *Cards & Card Tricks* 199.

b. A game of dominoes in which the players count by fives or multiples of five.

1868 F. B. ZINCKE *Last Winter in U.S.* 268 Consoling herself with a kind of dominoes she called 'muggins'. **1881** *Cassell's Bk. Sports* 390 (Dominoes) The game of All Fives, or Muggins, is very popular in some circles.

'muggish, *a.* ? *Obs.* [f. MUG *sb.*⁴ (though earlier in our quots.) + -ISH.] Damp, musty.

1655 GURNALL *Chr. in Arm.* I. 280 The World we live in is corruptible, and all here is subject to putrifie, as things kept in a rafty muggish Room subject them to mould. **1731** BAILEY vol. II, *Muggish*, inclinable to be musty, or to smell so. **1755** in JOHNSON; and in later Dicts.

†**'muggite.** *Obs.* [f. MUG *sb.*¹ + -ITE¹.] ? A member of a 'mug-house club'.

1718 *Entertainer* No. 30. 205 This would be to take up the Practice of our modern Muggites, to grin like a Dog, and go about the City.

†**'muggle¹.** *Obs. rare.* Also 3 moggle, 4 mughel. [Origin unknown.] An alleged Kentish word for 'tail'. Hence †**'muggling** (also moglynge), a tailed man.

c **1205** LAY. 29588 þa tailes heom comen on; þer uoren heo maȝen iteled beon. Iscend wes þat mon-cun; muggles [*c* **1275** moggles] heo hafden and inne hirede ælches men cleopeð heom muglinges [*c* **1275** moglymges]. *c* **1450** BOWER in *Fordun's Scotichron.* (1759) I. 139 *Vocatur.. cauda ab indigenis, patria lingva*, Mughel.

†**'muggle².** [Origin and meaning obscure.]

1607 MIDDLETON *Your Five Gallants* II. i, Oh the parting of vs twaine, Hath causde me mickle paine, and I shall nere be married Vntill I see my muggle againe. **1617** T. YOUNG *England's Bane* E 4 b, I haue seene a company amongst the very Woods and Forests, drinking for a muggle... Sixe haue determined to trie their strengths who could drinke most glasses for the muggle. The first drinkes a glasse of a pint, the second two, the next three [etc].

muggle³ ('mʌg(ə)l). *slang* (orig. *U.S.*). [Origin unknown.] *pl.* Marijuana; *sing.* or *pl.*, a marijuana cigarette. Also *Comb.*, as **muggle-head, -smoker**, one who smokes marijuana; so **'muggler**, a marijuana addict.

1926 MAINES & GRANT *Wise-Crack Dict.* 11/1 *Muggle-head*, smoker of Mexican loco weed. **1928** L. ARMSTRONG (*title of gramophone record*) Muggles. **1933** C. DE LENOIR *Hundredth Man* i. 10, I found myself on the Mexican border with a bad 'yin', and nothing to relieve me but the native drug marijuana. In New Orleans and other Southern American towns this is known as 'muggles', being sold in the form of cigarettes. **1933** *Fortune* Aug. 90/1 Louis Armstrong, who blew such frenzied tattoos as he has recorded under the titles *Mahogany Hall Stomp*, *Knee Drops*, *Skip the Gutter*, and *Muggles* (named for the Mexican cigarettes drugged with marijuana which have inspired perfectly incredible solos). **1938** *Manch. Guardian Weekly* 2 Sept. 188/3 Many swing players are 'killer-dillers' (first-rate players). Some are 'mugglers' (Marijuana addicts), but very few are 'long-hairs' (people who like classical music). **1946** MEZZROW & WOLFE *Really Blues* (1957) 51 'Ever smoke any muggles?' he asked. **1949** R. CHANDLER *Little Sister* xxxiv. 248 Desk clerk's a muggle-smoker. **1969** A. ARENT *Laying on of Hands* (1971) vi. 50 Offer our guest a muggle. **1972** *Sunday Sun* (Brisbane) 2 July 14 Detectives from the CIB Drug Squad in Brisbane are becoming quite familiar now with words like muggles, griefs, mezz, Mary Jane, jive, tea, rope and loco-weed.

Muggletonian (mʌg(ə)l'təʊnɪən), *a.* and *sb.* Also 7 **Mugultonian.** [f. *Muggleton* (see below) + -IAN.] **a.** *sb.* A member of the sect founded *c* 1651 by Lodowicke Muggleton and John Reeve. **b.** *adj.* Belonging or pertaining to this sect. Hence **Muggle'tonianism.**

The belief of the sect rests on the personal inspiration of its founders, who claimed to be the 'two witnesses' of Rev. xi. 3–6.

a **1670** RUST *Disc. Truth* (1682) 158 The Blasphemies of the present Muggletonians. **1687** T. BROWN in *Dk. Buckhm.'s Wks.* (1705) II. 113 Here started up Presbyterians, there Mugultonians, one making God damn all but themselves; and the other saving him the Labour, and doing it themselves. **1729** FIELDING *Author's Farce* III. Wks. 1882 VIII. 229 A Muggletonian dog stabbed me. **1796** COLQUHOUN *Police Metrop.* 374 [In a list of Meeting houses for Dissenters] 4 for Muggletonians. **1868** *Pall Mall G.* 5 May 8/2 The death is announced of Mr. Joseph Gandar .. and it is added that 'he was a sincere member of the sect called Muggletonians for upwards of sixty years'. There is, it is understood, only one place of worship in London connected with this extraordinary sect of religionists, and not three more in the whole of England. **1881** *N. & Q.* 6th Ser. IV. 431/2 In externals Muggletonianism resembles Quakerism, rejecting as it does all symbolical religion.

Muggur, var. MAGAR².

muggur, variant of MUGGER *sb.*²

muggut, variant of MUGGET² *dial.*

muggy ('mʌgɪ), *sb. dial.* [Alteration of *Moggie*, *Maggie*: cf. PEGGY *sb.*²] (Also ***muggy-cut-throat.***) The white-throat, *Sylvia cinera*; also the lesser white-throat, *Sylvia curruca*.

1829 BROCKETT *N.C. Words* (ed. 2), *Muggy*, the white-throat. **1831** J. RENNIE *Montagu's Ornith. Dict.* 538 *White throat*... Muggy-Cut-Throat. **1894** NEWTON *Dict. Birds* III. 601.

muggy ('mʌgɪ), *a.* [f. MUG *sb.*⁴ or *v.*¹ + -Y.]

1. Mouldy, moist, damp, wet. *Obs.* exc. *dial.*

1731 BAILEY vol. II, *Muggy*, inclinable to be musty, or to smell so. **1902** *Daily Chron.* 25 Oct. 7/6 Was it [the meat] not slimy, and did it not smell?—The Defendant: Oh, it's what we call 'muggy' in the trade. That only has to be wiped off, and then it's all right.

2. Of weather (also of a day, season, place, etc.): Damp, close and warm.

1746 in W. Thompson *R.N. Advoc.* (1757) 24 The Salters complained the Weather was hot and muggy. **1782** MISS BURNEY *Cecilia* v. ix, Weather quite muggy. **1851** D. JERROLD *St. Giles* viii. 72 He heard a far-off voice roar through the muggy air. **1891** T. HARDY *Tess* xxix, The evening, though sunless, had been warm and muggy for the season.

b. Close, stifling.

1820 J. H. REYNOLDS *Fancy* (1906) 51 His two rooms are naked, dun and muggy. **1906** *Pall Mall G.* 19 Mar. 10/1 The 'muggy' smell so generally noticeable in lodging-houses and barrack-rooms.

Mughal, variant of MOGUL.

mughe, obs. f. MAY *v.*¹; MOW *sb.*¹, *v.*²

mughel, mugher: see MUGGLE¹, MOWYER.

'mug-house. [f. MUG *sb.*¹ + HOUSE.]

1. An ale-house, beer-house. ? *Obs.* or *arch.* Also *attrib.* in **mug-house club**, the designation of certain political clubs (of Hanoverian sympathies) which met at 'mug-houses' early in the 18th c.; so ***mug-house chief.***

1685 *Choice Collect.* 180 *Loyal Songs* (ed. 3) 322 The Mug-house. **1710** STEELE *Tatler* No. 180 ¶3 There is a Mug-house near Long-Acre, where [etc.]. **1717** TICKELL *Epist. fr. Lady to Gent. at Avignon* 73 Our sex has dar'd the Mugg-House Chiefs to meet. **1753** H. WALPOLE *Let. to Bentley* Sept., Every ale-house is here [Birmingham] written *mug-house*, a name one has not heard of since the riots in the late King's time. **1827** HONE *Table Bk.* I. 378 At the mug-house club in Long-acre [*temp.* Geo. I]. **1891** BARING-GOULD *Urith* xv, When a young gallant begins to squabble at village mug-houses.

2. *dial.* A pottery.

1841 C. H. HARTSHORNE *Salopia Antiq.* 511.

mught, obs. pa. t. of MAY *v.*¹

mughwarde, obs. form of MUGWORT.

mugient ('mju:dʒɪənt), *a. rare.* [ad. L. *mūgient-em*, pr. pple. of *mūgire* to bellow.] Lowing, bellowing.

1646 SIR T. BROWNE *Pseud. Ep.* III. xxv. 173 A Bittor maketh that mugient noyse, or as we terme it Bumping by putting its bill into a reed [etc.]. **1816** PARR *Let. to Routh* 8 Mar., Wks. 1828 VII. 671 He, like myself, hates the final mugient M in Latin.

Hence †**'mugiency**, a bellowing.

1646 SIR T. BROWNE *Pseud. Ep.* III. xxvii. (1658) 219 This mugiency [*printed* magiency] or boation.

mugike, obs. form of MOUJIK.

‖**mugil** ('mju:dʒɪl). Forms: 4–5 mugill, 6 mugyll, 6– mugil. [L. *mūgil.*] The mullet. In modern use only as the Latin name of the genus.

1398 TREVISA *Barth. De P.R.* XIII. xxvi. (1495) 461 There is a manere fysshe that hyght Mugill whyche is full qwyuer and swyfte. **1526** *Pilgr. Perf.* (W. de W. 1531) 203 In an other kynde of fysshe, called a mugyll, and also in yᵉ ele, neuer man myght discerne ony male or female. **1584** LYLY *Campaspe* II. ii. 51 Mugil, of all fishes the swiftest. **1856** MAYNE *Expos. Lex.*, *Mugil, Silvery Grey. Ichthyol.* Common name for the *Mugil cephalus*.

mugiloid ('mju:dʒɪlɔɪd), *a.* and *sb. Ichthyol.* [ad. mod.L. *Mūgiloīdeī*, f. *mūgil*: see MUGIL and -OID.] **a.** *adj.* Of, pertaining to, or resembling the family *Mugiloidei* (Cuvier) of fishes, of which *Mugil* is the typical genus. **b.** *sb.* A mugiloid fish.

1842 BRANDE *Dict. Sci.*, etc., *Mugiloids*, a family of Acanthopterygian fishes in the system of Cuvier.

†**muglard.** *Obs. rare*⁻⁰. [Cf. Norw. *mugga* to heap up, hoard (money).] A miser.

c **1440** *Promp. Parv.* 347/2 Muglard, or nyggarde, *tenax*.

†**'mugle.** *Obs. rare.* [ad. L. *mūgil*: see MUGIL.] = LUMP *sb.*²

1574 T. N[EWTON] tr. *Gratarolus' Direct. Health* L j b, Those fishes that are called Mugles or Lompes [orig. *qui a Latinis Mugiles, vulgo autem Cephali, quasi capitones dixeris,* *appellantur*]. **1598** FLORIO, *Leucisco*, a kinde of mugle or lamp fish. Some take it for a fresh water mullet.

mugo ('mu:gəʊ). Also **mugho(s)**. [a. Fr. *mugho*, It. *mugo* mountain pine.] In full, ***mugo pine***. The European mountain pine, *Pinus mugo* (or *P. montana*), a large shrub, or one of its many varieties, ranging from dwarf forms to small trees.

c **1756** P. COLLINSON in L. W. Dillwyn *Hortus Collinsonianus* (1843) 40 Mr. P. Miller received seeds of the Cembro and Mugos Pines from the mountains of Valencia in Spain, Sept. 12, 1753. **1822** J. M. GOOD *Study of Med.* I. 315 The Hungarian balsam, or distilled oil of that variety of the *pinus sylvestris* which has been called Mughos. **1861** R. BENTLEY *Man. Bot.* 659 *P[inus] Pumilio*, the Mugho or Mountain Pine, yields by spontaneous exudation an oleo-resin called Hungarian balsam. **1951** H. S. CONARD tr. *Kerner's Background Plant Ecol.* xxiii. 191 The formation of the Rusty Sedge generally occurs in the calcareous Alps as islands in the dark green mugho pine forest. **1966** H. J. WELCH *Dwarf Conifers* v. 266 The Mountain Pine (Mugo is a local name) is a very variable species with a distribution in nature throughout Europe from the Pyrenees to the Balkans. **1967** N. T. MIROU *Genus Pinus* ii. 98 It [*sc. Pinus montana*] grows there [*sc.* in the Carpathians] in a shrub form and is known as variety *mughus*, or Mugo pine. **1969** T. H. EVERETT *Living Trees of World* 52/1 The Swiss mountain pine (*P. mugo*) is best known to many Americans in its dwarf variety, the mugho pine (*P. m. mughus*).

mugster ('mʌgstə(r)). *School slang.* [f. MUG *v.*[5] 4 + -STER.] One who 'mugs' or works hard.

1888 GOSCHEN *Rectorial Addr. to Students of Aberdeen* in *Scotsman* 1 Feb., Schools and colleges.. have invented for this purpose [*viz.* depreciation of hard intellectual work].. phrases.. such as a 'sap', a 'smug',.. a 'mugster'.

muguart, obs. Sc. form of MUGWORT.

‖**muguet** (mygɛ). [Fr.] Lily of the valley; the smell or scent of lily of the valley. Also *attrib.*

[**1873** *Young Englishwoman* May 234/2 Bodice.. edged with muguet fringe of violet silk.] **1919** W. L. DUDLEY *Askinson's Perfumes* (ed. 4) xvi. 208 *Muguet.* Oil of jasmine... Oil of ylang-ylang... Solution of heliotropin. **1928** H. S. REDGROVE *Scent* xi. 66 *Hydroxy-citronellal*.., very useful for making artificial lily of the valley (muguet) perfume. **1957** E. HYAMS *Into Dream* II. iii. 115 She used a little too much scent: Paul identified it as *muguet*. **1970** *Guardian* 12 May 9/2 Coty have recently reformulated their Muguet des Bois fragrance range.

muguet, obs. form of MUGGET[1].

Mugultonian, obs. form of MUGGLETONIAN.

mug-up ('mʌgʌp, mʌg'ʌp). *slang* (chiefly *Canadian* and *Naut.*). [f. MUG *v.*[7]] A snack, a meal, or a drink.

1933 E. MERRICK *True North* 233 Back at the tent we had a mugup, lashed up and said good-bye to the Indians. **1941** *Beaver* Mar. 12 Where the traveller stops long enough to have a 'mug-up', each dog is given about a pound of frozen fish. **1950** R. MOORE *Candlemas Bay* 143 They'd warm up the fishhouse and have a mug-up, before Jeb went to work on his traps for the rest of the daylight. **1961** J. W. ANDERSON *Fur Trader's Story* xxv. 225 The Eskimos too would be entertained, but because of their numbers they would have a picnic 'mug-up' on deck. **1963** J. T. ROWLAND *North to Adventure* ix. 123 We had a mug-up of hot coffee and turned in. **1970** R. PRICE *Howling Arctic* iv. 45 Occasionally they stopped for mug-up.

mugweed ('mʌgwi:d). *dial.* Forms: 4 muggewede, 5 mugwed, muguued, (mogwed), 8- mugweed. [f. *mug-* (in MUGWORT) + WEED; perh. in part an etymologizing perversion of *mugwet* MUGGET[1].] **a.** Mugwort, *Artemisia vulgaris.* **b.** Crosswort, *Galium Cruciata*; also ***golden mugweed*** (Treas. Bot. 1866).

a **1387** *Sinon. Barthol.* (Anecd. Oxon.) 11/2 *Arthemesia*, muggewede. *Ibid.* 20/1. *c* **1450** *Alphita* (ibid.) 13/2 *Archemesia.. angl.* mugwort *uel* mugwed. **1756** WATSON in *Phil. Trans.* XLIX. 853 Crosswort or Mugweed. **1886** *Cheshire Gloss.*, Mugweed, *Artemisia vulgaris.*

mugwet: see MUGGET[1] and [2].

mugwort ('mʌgwɜ:t). Forms: 1 mucgwyrt, (mugcwyrt), mugwyrt, 1-2, 6 mugwurt, 3 mugwet, 4-6 mogwort, mugworte, 5 mugwortt, mughwarde, 6 mogworte, mugwourt, mogworth, *Sc.* muguart, 6-7 mugwoort, 7 muggerwarte, 9 mugworth, *dial.* and *Sc.* muggart, muggert, 5- mugwort. [repr. WGer. *muggiwurti, f. *muggjo- fly, MIDGE + *wurti- plant, WORT; the *i* of the first element seems to have disappeared before the period of umlaut.]

1. The plant *Artemisia vulgaris*, formerly also called *motherwort*. Also applied to other species of *Artemisia*, as wormwood, *A. Absinthium*.

c **1000** *Sax. Leechd.* I. 102 Herba artemesia traganthes þæt is mucgwyrt. *c* **1000** ÆLFRIC *Gloss.* in Wr.-Wülcker 134/15 *Artemisia, uel matrum herba*, mugwyrt. *c* **1265** *Voc. Plants* ibid. 554/3 *Artimesie*, mugwrt, merherbarum. *c* **1450** *ME. Med. Bk.* (Heinrich) 77 Tak mogwort, and stampe hit. **1549** *Compl. Scot.* vi. 67, I sau muguart, that is gude for the suffocatione of ane vomans bayrnis hed. **1641** BEST *Farm. Bks.* (Surtees) 62 Three or fower stalkes of muggerwarte to lye on the bough or place wheare the bees light. **1753** CHAMBERS *Cycl. Supp.*, Mugwort has long been famous as an uterine and antispasmodic. **1799** J. HULL *Brit. Flora* 182 *Artemisia cærulescens*... Bluish Mugwort. **1850** CARLYLE *Latter-d. Pamph.* ii. 71 Fill your thrashing-floor with docks, ragweeds, mugworths, and ply your flail upon them,—that is not the method to obtain sacks of wheat. **1866** *Treas. Bot.*, Mugwort. *Artemisia vulgaris.* ——, Indian. *Artemisia hirsuta.* ——, West Indian. *Parthenium Hysterophorus.*

2. Crosswort, *Galium Cruciata.*

1796 WITHERING *Brit. Plants* (ed. 3) II. 187 *Galium cruciata.* Scop. Crosswort. Mugwort. Mugweed. **1855** MISS PRATT *Flower. Pl.* III. 148.

mugwump ('mʌgwʌmp), *sb.* orig. *U.S.* [a. Natick *mugquomp* great chief (occurring in Eliot's Massachusetts Bible, e.g. in Gen. xxxvi. 15, where it answers to the 'duke' of the Eng. Bible).]

1. A jocular term for: A great man, a 'boss'.

1832 in *Nation* (1891) 21 May 414/3 It has extensively circulated among the Knights of Kadosh and the Most Worshipful Mugwumps of the Cabletow. **1877** J. H. BROMLEY in *N.Y. Tribune* 16 Feb., John A. Logan is the Head Centre, the Hub, the King Pin, the Main Spring, Mogul, and Mugwump of the final plot. **1925** *N.Y. Times* 10 May, The royal red Indian mugwump, the chief, was copiously red-blooded. **1945** [see BIGWIG].

2. One who holds more or less aloof from party-politics, professing disinterested and superior views. In 1884, *spec.* applied to Republicans who refused to support the nominee of their party for president. Also, a person who withdraws his support from any group or organization; one who is aloof, independent, or self-important.

1884 *N.Y. Even. Post* 20 June (Cent.), We have yet to see a Blaine organ which speaks of the Independent Republicans otherwise than as Pharisees, hypocrites, dudes, mugwumps, transcendentalists, or something of that sort. **1884** W. EVERETT *Sp. at Quincy, Mass.* 13 Sept. (Stanf.), I am an independent—a Mugwump. **1884** *Sat. Rev.* 22 Nov. 659/1 It may be that in a few years.. a little group of British Mugwumps.. will arise in their might [etc.]. **1887** J. D. BILLINGS *Hardtack & Coffee* xv. 286 [The mule's] reputation as a kicker is world-wide. He was the Mugwump of the service. **1888** BRYCE *Amer. Commw.* II. III. lvi. 379 The case of these Independents, or Mugwumps, is an illustrative one... Very few.. take an active part in 'politics', however interested they may be in public affairs. **1890** C. L. NORTON *Polit. Americanisms* 74 Mugwump. **1894** P. L. FORD *Hon. Peter Stirling* 302 I'd have believed anything but that you [*sc.* a Democrat] would be a dashed Mugwump! **1898** *Academy* 22 Oct. 109 Halifax is, of course, the typical 'trimmer', which is to say 'mugwump' of Restoration politics. **1903** G. B. SHAW *Man & Superman* III. 116, I told him I did not care whether he got into parliament or not; so he called me Mugwump and went his way. **1923** H. E. BUCHHOLZ *Of what Use are Common People?* vi. 66 Mugwump may be thought of as a fitting term for the man who because of real or imagined superiority separates himself from the group with which he has been associated. *Ibid.* 73 The proposal of the intelligence mugwumps is that the majority of ordinary minds should step out of the picture of the body politic,.. while creatures with better than normal minds should be commissioned to do all the thinking. **1946** *Tuscaloosa* (Alabama) *News* 31 Mar. 4/7 A few moments after Secretary Wallace made his pun, he hastened to add that he himself had been a mugwump. **1975** *Sat. Rev.* 22 Mar. 58/3 Among the delicious names taken by, or given to, minor political parties in the United States (apart from Mugwumps and Bull Moose) are.. Quids, Locofocos, [etc.].

3. *attrib.* or as *adj.* That is a mugwump; of or pertaining to mugwumps.

1887 *Courier-Jrnl.* (Louisville, Kentucky) 8 Jan. 4/5 The Mugwump War Department is a horse-power to the Republican machine. **1923** H. E. BUCHHOLZ *Of what Use are Common People?* viii. 108 The various mugwump groups that propose changing the form of the present government. **1931** H. F. PRINGLE *Theodore Roosevelt* I. ix. 115 Roosevelt's gnawing hatred of the Mugwump independents made it impossible for him to withdraw. **1970** *Times* 9 Dec. 16/2 Even a doubtful and controversial conclusion.. would have been more useful than this irritating mugwump approach.

Hence **'mugwump** *v. intr.*, to play the part of a mugwump; **mug'wumpery**, **'mugwumpism**; **'mugwumpish** *a.*, characteristic of a mugwump; professing disinterestedness; pretentiously superior.

1885 *Boston* (Mass.) *Jrnl.* 13 Apr. 2/2 Will E. Haskell of the Minneapolis Tribune says that 'Previousness is one of the worst characteristics of Mugwumpery'. **1886** *Congress. Rec.* 31 Mar. 2968/1 That maudlin political sentiment which we recognize, for want of a better, under the name of 'Mugwumpism'. **1887** *Nation* 31 Mar. 265/1 It will thus be seen that Mugwumpism is growing both in the East and the West. **1889** *N.Y. Tribune* 10 Mar. (Cent.), They mugwumped in 1884. **1898** G. B. SHAW *Our Theatres in Nineties* (1932) III. 297 It [*sc. Hamlet*] belongs to a detached residence, a select library, an exclusive circle, to no occupation, to fathomless boredom, to impenitent mugwumpism. **1918** F. HACKETT *Ireland* ix. 252 This conviction was accompanied.. with many mugwumpish strictures such as 'in the main', 'within certain limits', [etc.]. **1923** *Spectator* 22 Sept. 390/1 Racial, intellectual or moral tests.. may turn out to be not aristocratic at all, but merely mugwumpish.

muhal, variant of MAHAL.

Muhammad (mə'hæməd). Also 7 **Mahumed**, 7- **Mohammed**, 8 **Muhammed**, 9 **Mahom(m)ed**. The name (repr. Arabic *Muḥammad*) of the founder of the Muslim religion. (See the older European form MAHOMET.)

The older forms with final *t*, which follow the early European tradition, are placed under MAHOMET; those which show recourse to the Arabic form are for convenience collected here, as explaining the diversities of form in the following adj.

1615 BESTWELL (*title*) Mohammedis imposturæ; that is, a discovery of the forgeries, falshoods, and impieties of Mohammed. **1634** SIR. T. HERBERT *Trav.* 36 They [*sc.* the Bannian Priests] hate Mahumed, and acknowledge one God and creatour of all things. **1706** PHILLIPS, *Mahomet* or *Muhammed*, an Arabian Impostor. **1777** J. RICHARDSON *Dict. Persian, Arab.*, etc., Dissert. p. xiii/2 The era of Mohammed. **1814** SOUTHEY *Roderick* xx. 19 The subjected West Should bow in reverence at Mahommed's name. **1891** D. A. CAMERON *Arabic-Eng. Voc.* Introd. (1892) 14 The Moslems reckon from A.D. 622, the date of the Flight.. of Mahomed from Mecca to Medina. **1896** T. P. HUGHES in *Sun* (N.Y.) May, The only correct way of spelling the word under consideration is 'Muhammad'... In writing for the press I very often use the incorrect spelling [Mohammed].

Muhammadan (mə'hæmədən), *a.* and *sb.* Also 7 **Mahumedan**, 8- **Mohammedan**, 9 **Mahomedan**, **Mahommedan**, **Mohummadan**, **Mohammadan**, **Muhammadan**, **Moohummudan**. [f. MUHAMMAD + -AN. Now generally substituted for the older MAHOMETAN. Cf. G. *Mohamedaner*.]

A. *adj.* **a.** Of or pertaining to Muhammad, or to the religion or doctrine of Muhammad.

1681 *Moores Baffled* 23 The Mahumedan Law. **1776** MICKLE tr. *Camoens' Lusiad* VII. 313 *note*, They have long submitted to the oppressions of a few Arabs, their Mohammedan masters. **1832** W. IRVING *Alhambra* I. 145 Mohammedan worship. **1844** H. H. WILSON *Brit. India* I. I. i. 11 The Mohammedan kings of Delhi. **1878** A. BURNELL in *Academy* 28 Dec. 604/1 On medicine eleven Hindu books and one Muhammadan were published last year. **1880** A. RUMSEY (*title*) Moohummudan Law of Inheritance. **1963** *Cambr. Rev.* 20 Apr. 369 (*title*) Oriental Studies at Cambridge: Muhammadan Law and Urdu Literature.

b. ***Mohammedan blue***, a cobalt blue used as an underglaze colour on Chinese porcelain of the Ming dynasty.

1905 MRS. W. HODGSON *How to identify Old Chinese Porc.* 8 The most celebrated colour of the Ming period was 'Mohammedan Blue'. This was brought from Persia, or some neighbouring country, as tribute, and pieces decorated with it were highly valued. **1909** S. W. BUSHELL *Chinese Art* (ed. 2) II. vii. 33 A pale grey-blue of pure tint, called at the time 'Mohammedan blue'. **1954** H. GARNER *Oriental Blue & White* iii. 15 Mohammedan blue by itself tended to run and.. it was mixed with the native ore to give firm outlines. **1964** *Listener* 23 Apr. 683/1 The finished powder was.. a mixture of two crude cobalt ores—one a native ore, the other imported from western Asia and known as Mohammedan blue. **1971** *Country Life* 16 Sept. 666/1 The dish.. is just that, a rare but reasonably familiar type painted in the brilliant so-called Mohammedan blue.

B. *sb.* A follower of Muhammad; a believer in the doctrine of Muhammad.

1777 J. RICHARDSON *Dict. Persian, Arab.*, etc., Dissert. p. xli/1 Many of the Mohammedans having a custom of carrying about them verses or chapters of the Alcoran, by way of preservatives or charms. **1841** LANE *Arab. Nts.* I. 62 A person.. does not.. become free, unless he flies from a foreign infidel master to a Muslim country, and there becomes a Mohammadan. **1878** A. BURNELL in *Academy* 28 Dec. 604/1 The sacred books of the Hindus and Muhammadans. **1888** S. S. ALLNUTT in *Cambr. Rev.* p. lxii, The orthodox Muhammedan in India would disdain [etc.]. **1961** [see *Black Muslim* (BLACK *a.* 19)].

Muhammadanism (mə'hæmɪdənɪz(ə)m). Also 9- **Mohammedanism**, **Muhammedanism**, **Mahommedanism**. [f. prec. + -ISM.] The Muslim religion, Islam.

1815 *Tweddell's Rem.* 329 *note*, Mohammedanism purified from the corruption and degeneracy into which it is pretended, that the genuine faith has lapsed. **1817** C. MILLS (*title*) History of Muhammedanism. **1860** MAX MÜLLER *Chips* (1880) I. xv. 372 Mohammedanism.. is a Semitic religion.

Muhammadanize (mə'hæmədə,naɪz), *v.* [f. MUHAMMADAN + -IZE.] *trans.* To convert to Muhammadanism; to make conformable to the principles and rites of the Muhammadans.

1828–32 in WEBSTER. **1903** *United Free Ch. Mission. Rec.* Apr. 160/1 Aboriginals who were Mohammedanized during the Mohammedan dynasty.

Hence **Mu,hammadani'zation**, **Mu'hammadanizing** *vbl. sb.*, converting to Muhammadanism.

1875 WHITNEY *Life Lang.* xii. 231 After the Mohammedanizing of Persia.

†**Mu'hammadism.** *Obs.* In 7 **Mahumedism(e**, 8- **Mohammedism**. [f. MUHAMMAD + -ISM. Cf. MAHOMETISM.] = MUHAMMADANISM.

1614 SELDEN *Titles Hon.* 105 An African expressly affirms that in Mahumedisme were anciently lxxii. Sects, and now but two. **1788** GLADWIN *Hist. Hindostan* I. 49 Mohammedism first appeared in Cashmeer about the commencement of the eighth century of the Hegira. **1850** F. W. NEWMAN *Phases* 161 Mohammedism.. conquers those Pagan creeds which are morally inferior to it.

Muhammadize (mə'hæmədaɪz), *v.* [f. MUHAMMAD + -IZE.] = MUHAMMADANIZE. Hence **Mu,hammadi'zation.**

1847 in WEBSTER; and in later Dicts. **1906** *Fortn. Rev.* Feb. 366 The Mohammedisation of the Middle East.

†**Mu'hammadry.** *Obs. rare.* [f. MUHAMMAD + -RY. Cf. MAHOMETRY.] = MUHAMMADANISM.

1613 PURCHAS *Pilgrimage* (1614) 378 The Persians are a kinde of.. Puritans in their impure Muhammedrie.

muhar, variant form of MOHUR.

Muharem, -arram, -em: see MOHARRAM.

muhimbi (muːˈhɪmbɪ, muːˈwɪmbɪ). Also muhindi. [Lunyoro.] An evergreen tree, *Cynometra alexandri*, belonging to the family Leguminosæ and native to East Africa, or the timber obtained from it, which is also called Uganda ironwood.

1906 M. T. DAWE *Rep. Bot. Mission through Forest Districts of Buddu* 43 in *Parl. Papers* (Cd. 2904) LXXX. 41 *Cynometra Alexandri*.. Native name, Muhindi: immense and important timber tree. **1939** EGGELING & HARRIS in L. Chalk et al. *Forest Trees & Timbers Brit. Empire* IV. 27 Two pieces of Muhimbi (Ironwood), buried near a termite hill in 1930, were removed after 16 months, in excellent condition. **1951** *Archit. Rev.* CX. 144/3 Muhimbi, an extremely hard wood from Uganda, is here used for the first time in a floor of any appreciable size in this country. **1956** *Handbk. of Hardwoods* (Forest Prod. Res. Lab.) 158 Muhimbi is a heavy, hard timber of equal weight to East African olive. **1971** F. H. TITMUSS *Commercial Timbers of World* (ed. 4) 155 The timber of *Cynometra alexandri*.. is now beginning to be much better known under the title of Muhimbi.

muhooa, variant of MAHWA.

1866 in *Treas. Bot.*

muhr, obs. form of MOHUR.

muhtar, var. MUKHTAR.

muid (mɥi). Forms: 4–7 muy, 5 muye, mue, 6 mui, 5 mewe, 6–8 mew, 7 mued, 7– muid. See also MOY *sb.*[1], MUD *sb.*[2] [a. OF. *mui*, mod.F. *muid*:—L. *modium*: see MODIUS. Cf. Du. *mud(de*, MUD *sb.*[2]]

1. A former French measure of capacity, varying greatly in different localities and as applied to different commodities. *Obs.* exc. *Hist.*

a. A dry measure (for corn, meat, salt, etc.).

In recent times the values assigned to it range from about 52 to about 110 bushels; in early use it was a much smaller measure, often stated as = 4 bushels.

c **1400** *Rom. Rose* 5590 An hundred mauys [*so Thynne*; *read* muys; *Glasgow MS.* mavis; *Fr. orig.* muis] of whete greyn. **1481** CAXTON *Godeffroy* xl. 78 He gaf to hym ten muyes, every muye is four bussehllys. **1549** *Compl. Scot.* xiv. 113 Annibal send to cartage thre muis of gold ryngis. **1692** *Lond. Gaz.* No. 2831/2 The offer.. of furnishing them with 18000 Muids [of Corn] at a reasonable Price. **1703** *Ibid.* No. 3891/4 About 57 Mews of Bay-Salt. **1727** BRADLEY *Fam. Dict.* s.v. *Bushel*, The Half-Minot contains three Bushels, and the Muid of Coals contains thirty Half-Minots. **1771** *Chron.* in *Ann. Reg.* XIV. 100/1 In Swabia the muid of rye sells for 36 florins. **1804** RANKEN *Hist. France* III. v. 318 A modius or muid of seed yielded but a setier. **1859** R. J. MANN *Colony of Natal* 124 One farmer in the Umvoti country reaped 120 muids (of 2$\frac{33}{34}$ bushels each) from 30 acres of land which had been sown with 5 muids of seed. **1873** [see *boermeal* (BOER 2)].

†**b.** A liquid measure; a cask holding this.

The local varieties ranged from 60 to 160 gallons.

1491 CAXTON *Vitas Patr.* (W. de W. 1495) I. xxxvii. 47 There was thenne estemyd fruyte ynough for to gadre an hundred mues, or tonnes of wyne. **1529** RASTELL *Pastyme, Hist. Rom.* (1811) 22 A mew of wyne which is almost iiii galons. *c* **1618** MORYSON *Itin.* IV. (1903) 173 Each Mued of Wyne commonly yeildes the king Eighteene Shillings of our mony. **1655** *Nicholas Papers* (Camden) II. 160 They have established to her her pretentions of soe much upon every muy of wine as amounts unto the best part of a million per annum. **1686** PLOT *Staffordsh.* 62 Accounting 72 Gallons to the Hogshead, the Muid contains scarce ⅘ of a Hogshead. **1727–41** CHAMBERS *Cycl.* s.v., Muid is also one of the nine casks, or regular vessels used in France, to put wine and other liquors in.

2. A French measure of land, representing the area that would require a 'muid' of seed.

1674 JEAKE *Arith.* (1696) 114 A Muid of Land is 12 Septiers or Arpents.

muil, var. MOIL *sb.*[5], MOOL *sb.*, MULE *sb.*[2]

muild, muildry: see MOULD, MOULDRY.

muile, muill(e: see MULE[1] and [2].

muilin, muinde, obs. ff. MOOLIN, MIND.

muir, Sc. variant of MOOR *sb.*[1]

muise, muish, obs. forms of MEUSE.

muishond (ˈmœishɔnt). *S. Afr.* Also 9 mausehund, mousehund. [Afrikaans, f. *muis* MOUSE *sb.* + *hond* dog; cf. MOUSE-HUNT[1].] The Cape polecat, *Ictonyx striatus*, which is black with white stripes, or one of several species of mongoose. Also *fig.*

1796 tr. *F. Le Vaillant's New Trav. Afr.* I. 236 It [*sc.* a stranded whale] was attacked.. by different species of those small quadrupeds.. which, at the Cape, are known under the general name of *muyshond*. *Ibid.* III. 278 My Hottentots of the colony all recognized it as a *muyshond* (mouse-dog), a general name among the inhabitants of the Cape for all the little carnivorous quadrupeds. **1818** C. I. LATROBE *Jrnl. Visit S. Afr.* 36 We observed a tame mongoose or mausehund from Java.. which ran about and suffered itself to be handled. **1835** A. SMITH *Diary* 5 Jan. (1939) I. 204 A hare and a muishond for sale. **1853** *Edin. New Philos. Jrnl.* LV. 210 Two or three different kinds of Mousehund, or weasel.. are commonly seen. **1900** B. MITFORD *Aletta* xii. 111 She went round among her fowl-houses, then strolled along the quince hedges to see if any of the hens had been laying out and in irregular places for the benefit of the egg-loving *muishond*, or similar vermin. **1912** F. W. FITZSIMONS *Snakes S. Afr.* (new ed.) 30 Within two yards of us was a striped Muishond with his paws firmly planted on an adult Black-necked cobra. **1937** H. KLEIN *Stage-Coach Dust* xxiv. 208 A muishond (pole-cat) startled the town-bred horse, and away he galloped. **1946** *Cape Argus* 16 Nov. 6/2 Two varieties of muishond now have prices on their heads. **1952** —— 12 Jan. 4/5 His request for tame 'wild' animals has only produced in Cape Town a muishond and a monkey. **1970** *News/Check* (S. Afr.) 12 June 11 An assumption has grown up over the past year or more that South Africa was well and truly isolated, that it remained the *muishond* of the world with whom nobody wanted anything to do. **1974** *Daily Dispatch* (East London, Cape Province) 21 Nov. 10 A rabid muishond has been killed on Arbrook, farm of Mr. George Michau.

muist, variant of MUST *Obs.*, musk.

muisvoël (ˈmœisfʊəl). *S. Afr.* Also muisvoel, muisvogel (-foːxəl). [Afrikaans, f. as MUISHOND + *voël* bird.] = *mouse-bird* (MOUSE *sb.* 10 f).

1822 W. J. BURCHELL *Trav. S. Afr.* I. xi. 214 Muisvogel (Mouse-bird). *Colius erythropus* of Linnæus. **1849** A. SMITH *Illustr. Zool. S. Afr.: Aves* plate ii, *Chizærhis concolor*.. As soon as it was observed, the Hottentots declared it to be a *muis vogel*, or *Colius*, Lin... which was not surprising, since it evinces considerable similarity to birds of that genus. **1867** E. L. LAYARD *Birds S. Afr.* 221 Of the three species of this genus [sc. *Colius*] found in South Africa, and known by the trivial name of Muisvogel or Mouse-bird, this [sc. *C. erythropus*] is the only one that is found in the neighbourhood of Cape Town. **1920** R. Y. STORMBERG *Mrs. Pieter de Bruyn* 7 It [*sc.* peachblossom] has been vandalised by swarms of 'finks' and wretched little stiff-tailed 'muisvogels' who snip off the blooms most viciously. **1952** *Cape Times* 27 Nov. 2/3 Muisvoëls are destroying whole orchards of early ripening fruit. **1959** *Ibid.* 20 Jan. 7/3 Sparrows and muisvoels are not a pest in areas where our native birds of prey have not been eliminated. **1973** *Eastern Province Herald* (Port Elizabeth) 19 July 17 How many of us city-dwellers.. would know the difference between a mossie and a muisvoël?

muit(e, muitable, obs. ff. MUTE, MUTABLE.

mujahidin (muːdʒɑːhɪˈdiːn), *sb. pl.* Also with capital initial and **mujahed(d)in, mujahideen.** [a. Pers., Arab. *mujāhidīn*, pl. of *mujāhid* one who fights in a JIHAD or holy war: cf. MUJTAHID.] In Islamic countries: freedom fighters; now *spec.* (a body of) fundamentalist Muslims who use guerilla warfare to assert their claims. Also *sing.* as **mujahid.**

1958 O. CAROE *Pathans* xviii. 299 They.. became the patrons of the Mujahidin colony—the so-called Hindustani Fanatics. **1959** *Listener* 14 May 830/2 The Arab *mujahidin* in Oman, Aden and every struggling part of the Arab South. **1978** *Washington Post* 31 Dec. A16/1 The Mujaheddin have a blurry ideology which stems from Shiite Moslem religious fanaticism. **1979** *Summary of World Broadcasts: Middle East* (B.B.C.) 17 Feb. A/9 The mujahid troops, with a hail of machinegun bullets, answered the fire. **1979** *Daily Tel.* 21 Aug. 4/2 The Mujahedin.. played a major role in bringing down the Shah and armed to the teeth. **1979** *Observer* 26 Aug. 12/7 To the east of Kabul.. the rebel *mujahideen*, or 'holy warriors', effectively control all but the provincial capitals and the major towns. **1985** *Listener* 17 Jan. 14/3, I said a Soviet general in Afghanistan would go over to the mujahideen and adopt Islam. **1985** *Times* 27 Dec. 13/3 This factor alone will, of course, not prevent the mujahidin from continuing their spirited assaults.

mujik, variant of MOUJIK.

‖**mujtahid** (muːdʒˈtɑːhɪd). Also **mooshtâhed, mujtehid.** Pl. **mujtahids, mujtahidūn.** [Pers. 'one who strives hard to acquire correct and sound views', 'one who has arrived at the highest degree in knowledge of the law'; Arab. 'one who exerts himself'.] In Islamic countries, the title given to a person accepted as an authority on the interpretation of Islamic law. Now only in Iran.

1815 J. MALCOLM *Hist. Persia* II. xxiii. 428 That power.. is exercised.. by these holy men who are raised, by popular suffrage, to the dignity of Mooshtâhed, or 'high priest'; and who may be deemed at the head of the hierarchy of Persia. **1885** T. P. HUGHES *Dict. Islam* 197/2 *Ijtihād* is the deduction made by a single Mujtahid, whilst *Ijmaʻ* is the collective opinion of a council of Mujtahidūn, or enlightened doctors. **1909** *Daily Chron.* 2 Feb. 1/7 The Shah would be well advised to listen to the petition of the Mujtehids and clergy now being presented,.. begging for the restoration of the Constitution. **1958** A. TOYNBEE *East to West* 161 'The veil between us is very thin,' said the old mujtahid. **1961** *Ann. Reg. 1960* 299 The leading *mujtahid* of the day having declared this law to be contrary to the *shariʻa* and the Constitution, it seemed likely to remain a dead letter.

Mujur, var. MUDJUR.

muk(e, obs. forms of MEEK *a.*, MUCK *sb.*[1]

mukaddim, variant of MOKADDAM, headman.

mukel: see MICKLE.

mukhede, variant of MEEKHEAD *Obs.*

mukhtar (ˈmʊktɑː(r)). Also **muhtar, muktar.** [ad. Arab. *mukhtār* chosen.] The head of the local government of a town or village in Turkey; a minor provincial official. Hence **ˈmukhtarship**, the status or office of a mukhtar.

1911 T. E. LAWRENCE *Let.* 21 May (1938) 104 The Muktar carried off his cousin on his saddle-bow from amid the shrieking women at the spring. **1916** —— *Lett.* (1938) 209 Two Mukhtars and two prominent sheikhs. **1946** [see DUNAM]. **1946** KOESTLER *Thieves in Night* 122 The British rulers had always appointed the most distinguished member of each of the two clans to dual mukhtarship. **1954** F. STARK *Ionia* 65 The mukhtar and the doctor from Pitane.. came to give the city's welcome. **1970** *Guardian* 1 Apr. 4/2 The 'muhtar' (local official) of the village of Kakoy. **1974** *Times* 5 Apr. 16/4 The Mukhtar.. explained: '.. we are Druse and we will never leave our land.'

‖**mukim** (ˈmuːkɪm). Pl. **mukim, mukims.** [Malay, ad. Arab. *muḳīm* remaining, resident.] In Malaysia, a Muslim parish, the smallest administrative district.

1839 T. J. NEWBOLD *Pol. & Statistical Acct. Straits of Malacca* I. v. 247 The immediate religious care of the inhabitants of the Mukim (or parish) to which the mosque belongs, devolves upon the Imam, Khatib, and Bilal. **1907** F. A. SWETTENHAM *Brit. Malaya* x. 228 The districts were again sub-divided into *Mukim*. **1911** *Encycl. Brit.* XVII. 482/2 The state is divided into *mukim* or parishes. **1948** *Malayan Pict. Observer* Dec. 1 In Jimah Mukim of Port Dickson District.. lies the Chuah Indian Settlement. **1958** J. M. GULLICK *Indigenous Political Syst. W. Malaya* ii. 36 A *mukim*, a sub-district which may include several villages... *Mukim* denotes the area served by a mosque and is sometimes translated 'parish'. **1964** K. G. TREGONNING *Hist. Mod. Malaya* vii. 157 By making administration at local *mukim* level the responsibility of people trusted in the kampongs, he created a stable State.

mukke, mukylle, obs. ff. MUCK *sb.*[1], MUCK-HILL.

muklek, mukluk, varr. MUCKLUCK.

muktar, var. MUKHTAR.

mukti (ˈmʌktɪ, ˈmʊktɪ). *Hinduism* and *Jainism*. Also 9 mooktee. [Skr. *mukti* a setting or becoming free, release, f. *muc* to let loose, free, release.] = MOKSHA.

1785 C. WILKINS tr. *Bhăgvăt-Gēētā* 140 The Hindoos believe.. that an eternal release, which they call *Mŏŏktēē*, is only to be attained by a total neglect of all sublunary things. **1801** *Asiatick Researches* VII. 34 Bhooddha after his death ascended to the Hall of Glory, called Mooktzé, otherwise Nirgoowané. **1807** W. JONES *Works* III. 384 The *Mucti*, or *Elysian* happiness of the *Védánta* school is far more sublime. **1811** W. WARD *Acct. Writings, Relig. & Manners Hindoos* IV. x. 315 The shastrŭs teach that there are four kinds of mooktee, or deliverance. **1832** [see BHAKTI]. **1840** [see MOKSHA]. **1875** M. WILLIAMS *Indian Wisdom* iii. 70 The right apprehension of truth.. which, if once acquired by the soul, confers upon it final emancipation, whether called Mukti, Moksha,.. or Nirvana. **1915** *Encycl. Relig. & Ethics* VIII. 773/2 The evolution of *mukti*, or *mokṣa*, in Jainism cannot be adequately dealt with till its early literature is more fully accessible. **1970** T. W. ORGAN *Hindu Quest Perfection of Man* ix. 296 *Mukti* is freedom from the individualistic inlook, and the attainment of the divine outlook.

‖**muktuk** (ˈmʌktʌk). Also **maktuk.** [ad. Eskimo *maktak*.] The skin of any of several species of whales used for food by the Eskimo.

1835 R. HUISH *Last Voy. Sir J. Ross Arctic Regions* 701/2 Skin of a whale.. Maktuk. **1909** A. D. CAMERON *New North* xii. 220 The wedding breakfast consisted of seal-meat, frozen rotten fish, and muktuk (whale meat). **1940** *Beaver* Mar. 25/2 All were chewing *muktuk*—the outer protective skin of the whale—with great enjoyment. **1966** *Star Weekly* (Toronto) 12 Mar. 10/1 The Eskimos love muktuk and eat it raw. It's rather rubbery but doesn't taste bad at all—a bit like hazel nut. **1973** *Nat. Geographic* Mar. 353/1 After the blubber is cut, the Eskimos pare off the tough, rubbery skin and a thin layer of attached blubber—called *muktuk*. A delicacy to the Eskimos, muktuk tastes surprisingly good when boiled and salted. **1974** *N.Y. Times* 30 May 39/2 But the *muktuk*—the skin and outer layer of blubber that is the staple of the Eskimo diet—was fine.

Mukuzani (mʊkʊˈzɑːnɪ). [Russ.] A red wine from Georgia, U.S.S.R.

1961 *Spectator* 7 Apr. 495 The first Soviet wines to be imported into Britain—Mukuzani, Gurdzhaani and Tsinandali, all from Georgia. **1967** A. LICHINE *Encycl. Wines* 470 Some Georgian wines seen abroad are white Myshako Riesling and Ghurdjurni. The Takhetia region is the most successful and the best wines include.. the red Mukuzani. **1968** A. H. GOLD *Wines & Spirits of World* 467 The wines tend to be full and the red ones dark. *Mukuzani* and *Saperavi* are two dark strong red wines of 14° alcoholic strength from the eastern side of Georgia in the Tiflis region.

mulagatoney, obs. form of MULLIGATAWNY.

Mulana, var. MAULANA.

Mulane, obs. form of MILAN[1].

†**ˈmulat.** *Obs.*[−1] Anglicized form of MULATTO.

1678 T. JONES *Heart & Rt. Soveraign* 497 A monstrous equivocal bastard-brood of spiritual-carnal mulats.

mulata, obs. form of MULATTA, MULATTO.

mulateer, -ier, obs. forms of MULETEER.

mulato, mulatow, obs. forms of MULATTO.

mu'latta. Also 7- mulata. [a. Sp. *mulata*, fem. of *mulato* MULATTO.] A female mulatto.

1622 MABBE tr. *Aleman's Guzman d'Alf.* II. 328 *margin*, Mulata, is a maid-childe, that is borne of a Negra, and a fayre man; and so on the contrary. **1668** DRYDEN *Even. Love* IV. (1671) 52 'Tis impossible your love should be so humble, to descend to a Mulatta. **1828** TYERMAN & BENNET *Jrnl. Voy.*, etc. 28 Jan. (1831) II. lii. 491 There is a law here [Mauritius] that no Englishman shall marry a woman of colour, not even a mulatta. **1963** *Times* 12 June 16/6 Of the other painters the pioneers were Di Cavalcanti, famous for his sensuous mulatas, and Portinari. **1965** E. BISHOP *Questions of Travel* 37 Going out, he met a *mulata* Carrying water on her head.

mulatto (mjuːˈlætəʊ), *sb.* and *a.* Forms: 6 mulatow, 7 malato, mallatto, melotto, molata, -o, mol(l)otto, mulata, -o, muletto, mullato, 7–8 molatto, -etto, mullatto, 8 malotto, melatto, moletta, 9 mulattoe, 7- mulatto. [a. Sp. (and Pg.) *mulato* young mule, hence one of mixed race, a mulatto, obscurely derived from *mulo* MULE *sb.*[1]; hence F. *mulâtre* (with assimilation of suffix to *-âtre* = -ASTER), It. *mulatto.*]

A. *sb.*

1. One who is the offspring of a European and a Black; also used loosely for anyone of mixed race resembling a mulatto.

1595 *Drake's Voy.* (Hakl. Soc.) 22 By meanes of a Mulatow and an Indian, we had, this night, forty bundles of dried beife. **1613** PURCHAS *Pilgrimage* VI. xiv. 545 Why then are the Portugalls Children and Generations White, or Mulatos at most. **1657** R. LIGON *Barbadoes* 10 A great fat man,..his face not so black as to be counted a Mollotto. **1697** DAMPIER *Voy.* (1699) 199 The Mulata, because he said he was in the Fireship..was immediately hanged. **1713** C'TESS OF WINCHILSEA *Misc. Poems* 209 Grinning Malottos in true Ermin stare. **1727–41** CHAMBERS *Cycl.*, *Mulatto*, a name given, in the Indies, to those who are begotten by a negro man on an Indian woman; or an Indian man on a negro woman. **1854** THACKERAY *Newcomes* I. 31 Two wooly-headed poor little mulattos. **1885** R. L. & F. STEVENSON *Dynamiter* xi, That hag of a mulatto was no less a person than my wife.

†2. (See quot.) *Obs.*

1664 JER. TAYLOR *Dissuas. Popery* I. i. §3 Purgatory, which is a device to make men be Mulata's as the Spaniard calls half-Christians.

3. *Geol.* The greenstone of Northern Ireland.

1816 CONYBEARE in *Trans. Geol. Soc.* III. 130 Mulattoe, an arenaceous stone, with a calcareous cement of a speckled appearance (whence its name). **1843** PORTLOCK *Geol.* 110 The chalk..rests on..indurated greensand or (as it has been called) mulatto stone.

4. *attrib.* and *Comb.*, as *mulatto-like* adj.; **mulatto-clay** *U.S.*, a dark-coloured clay; **mulatto jack**, a term for *yellow fever* (Syd. Soc. Lex. 1891); **mulatto land, -soil** *U.S.*, a dark coloured fertile kind of soil; **mulatto loam, mould** = *mulatto land*; **mulatto prairie**, a prairie of mulatto-soil; **mulatto tree** (see quot.).

1788 T. JEFFERSON *Tour of Amsterdam* in *Writings* (1854) IX. 386 It has a southern aspect, the soil a barren *mulatto clay, mixed with a good deal of stone, and some slate. **1741** in *Amer. Speech* (1940) XV. 287/2 A Tract of rich *Mulattoe Land, lying in that County. **1794** MORSE *Amer. Geog.* 556 The mulatto lands [of Georgia] are generally strong. **1883** E. A. SMITH *Rep. Geol. Survey Alabama 1881–82* 435 The red or mulatto lands are much the best for cotton. **1719** DE FOE *Crusoe* I. 177 As for my Face, the Colour of it was really not so *Moletta like, as one might expect. **1837** J. L. WILLIAMS *Territory of Florida* 82 The surface is covered with a *mulatto or chocolate colored loam. **1838** *Jeffersonian* (Albany) 28 Apr. 88 (Th.), The *mulatto mould of the Colorado does not surpass in fatness the alluvial soil of Red River. **1869** *Overland Monthly* III. 130 Then there is the 'chocolate' prairie, and the '*mulatto', and the 'mezquite'. **1794** MORSE *Amer. Geog.* 556 The *mulatto soil [of Georgia], consisting of a black mould and red earth. **1819** E. DANA *Geogr. Sk. Western Country* 190 Next to this is very often found a skirt of rich pine land, dark mulatto soil with hickory..characteristic of good land. **1861** *Trans. Illinois Agric. Soc.* IV. 112 He..would not choose the dark prairie mold, but that kind of soil best known in the west as the 'mulatto soil'. **1876** *Encycl. Brit.* IV. 97/1 The *Mulatto tree (*Eukylista Spruceana*), one of the Cinchonaceæ.

B. *adj.*

1. Belonging to the class of mulattos.

1677 *Rec. Court of New Castle on Delaware* (1904) 91 The upholding & detayning of this p[laintiff]'s molatto servant in Maryland. *a* **1704** T. BROWN *Walk round Lond.*, *Tavern* Wks. 1709 III. III. 9, I shall observe your Caution, says my Moletto Comrade [an Indian]. **1837** HT. MARTINEAU *Soc. Amer.* II. 156 She was asked whether she thought of doing anything for her two mulatto children. **1900** DENIKER *Races of Man* xiii. 542 A Mulatto woman, the offspring of a Spaniard and a negress, may give birth to a Morisco by uniting with a Spaniard.

2. Of the colour of a mulatto; tawny.

1622 MABBE tr. *Aleman's Guzman d'Alf.* II. 328, I sweare and vow vnto thee by this my Mulata face, that [etc.]. **1826** PRICHARD *Res. Phys. Hist. Man.* (ed. 2) I. 151 A man, who ..was of a mulatto complexion. **1870** W. M. BAKER *New Timothy* 84 (Cent.) Women of all shades of color, from deepest jet up to light mulatto.

mulattoism (mjuːˈlætəʊɪz(ə)m). [f. MULATTO + -ISM.] The production of mulattos.

1861 VAN EVRIE *Negroes* 147 The fourth generation of mulattoism is as absolutely sterile as muleism.

mulattress (mjuːˈlætrɪs). [ad. F. *mulâtresse*, fem. of *mulâtre* MULATTO.] A female mulatto.

1805 in *Amer. Pioneer* (1843) II. 234 The chief of the audience is formed of mulattresses and negresses. **1845** DARWIN in *Life & Lett.* (1887) I. 344 Our party consisted of two Catholic priests and two Mulattresses. **1887** *Harper's Mag.* Mar. 609/1 A handsome, strong-limbed, and light-footed mulattress. **1932** *Dict. Amer. Biogr.* VIII. 485/1 He lived openly with a mulattress and was only prevented from marrying her by the law against miscegenation.

mulberry (ˈmʌlbərɪ), *sb.* (and *a.*) Forms: α. 4 molberi, moolbery, 4–7 mulberie, -y, 5–6 molbery(e, 6 moulberie, 7 mulburie, 6- mulberry. β. 3 murberie, 5–6 morbery, -berie, 6 more berry. [In 14th c. *mulberie*, prob. ad. MHG. *mûlbere* (mod.G. *maulbeere*):—OHG *mûlberi*, an altered form (cf. *mûlboum* mulberry tree) of *mûr-beri*, *môr-beri* (= Du. *moerbezie*), f. L. *mōr-um* mulberry (see MORE *sb.*[2]) + *beri* BERRY *sb.*

The β forms prob. never had any real currency. In quot. *c* 1265 *mur-* is a. OF. *mure* (mod.F. *mûre*, altered form of *moure*:—L. *mōra* pl.); Caxton's *morberies* is after Du. *moerbezie*; and the 16th c. instances are prob. pedantic corrections of *mulbery* after the Latin.]

1. a. The fruit of any tree of the genus *Morus*, esp. the Black Mulberry, *M. nigra*.

The 'berry', of roundish oval shape, is an aggregate of a multitude of true fruits covered by succulent calyces.

1398 TREVISA *Barth. De P.R.* XVII. i. (Tollem. MS.), In some tren and herbes fruite ripeþ sone, as mulberies [**1535** moulberyes]. *c* **1407** LYDG. *Reson & Sens.* 3954 The Molberye. **1535** COVERDALE *Amos* vii. 14 Now as I was breakynge downe molberies. **1562** TURNER *Herbal* II. 58 The iuice of the rype mulberries is a good mouth medicine. **1592** SHAKS. *Ven. & Ad.* 1103 Some other in their bils Would bring him mulberries & ripe-red cherries. **1718** QUINCY *Compl. Disp.* 100 Mulberries are grateful, cooling, and astringent. **1850** *J. Bell's Syst. Geog.* IV. 314 The white mulberry [*Morus alba*] forms the wealth of the country of the Druses. **1907** *Daily News* 5 Sept. 4 In a good season ripe mulberries may be plucked within fifty yards of Fleet-street.

β. *c* **1265** *Gloss. Plant-n.* in Wr.-Wülcker 557/31 *Celsi*, murer, murberien. *c* **1483** CAXTON *Dialogues* 13 Cheryes, sloes, Morberies, strawberies. *c* **1532** [see *mulberry-tree* in 5]. **1548** TURNER *Names Herbes* (E.D.S.) 9 A litle blacke bery lyke a blacke morbery.

b. = *mulberry-tree*.

1382 WYCLIF *2 Chron.* i. 15 The kyng ȝaue in to Jerusalem ..cedres as long mulberies [Vulg. *cedros quasi sycomoros*]. **1577** B. GOOGE *Heresbach's Husb.* II. (1586) 92 Whensoeuer you see the Mulberie begin to spring, you may bee sure that winter is at an ende. **1617** PURCHAS *Pilgrimage* (ed. 3) 588 Vines, which they plant at the foot of the Mulberrie, the same Tree seeming to beare two Fruits. **1785** MARTYN *Rousseau's Bot.* xxviii. (1794) 436 Black Mulberry has rugged, heart-shaped leaves. **1819** WARDEN *United States* I. 185 Red mulberry, *Morus rubra*. **1882** *Garden* 23 Dec. 545/2 The common Mulberry is a native of Italy, but has been grown in this country for more than 300 years.

2. Applied to plants or trees of other genera; in Eng. dialects often to the Blackberry, *Rubus fruticosus*; in the U.S. to various other species of *Rubus*, otherwise called Raspberry. Also CLOTH-*mulberry*, PAPER-*mulberry*.

1672 JOSSELYN *New Eng. Rarities* 93 Raspberry, here called Mulberry. **1848** *Rural Cycl.* II. 313/1 *Flax-dodder* —botanically *Cuscuta Epilinum*..is popularly known in Somersetshire as 'the mulberry'. **1866** *Treas. Bot.*, Mulberry, Australian, *Hedycarya Pseudo-Morus*. —, Indian, *Morinda citrifolia*. —, New Zealand, *Entelea arborescens*. **1880** BRITTEN & HOLLAND *Eng. Plant-n.* 346 *Mulberry*..(2) *Rubus fruticosus* L.—Norf... (4) *Pyrus Aria*. L.—Aberdeensh. **1897–8** BRITTON & BROWN *Amer. Flora*, Mulberry. *a. Rubus odoratus* (Purple-flowering raspberry). *b. Rubus strigosus* (Wild red raspberry). *c. Rubus Americanus* (Dwarf raspberry). *Ibid.*, Bermuda or French mulberry, *Callicarpa Americana*.

3. The colour of a mulberry. Also as *adj.* = mulberry-coloured.

1837 DICKENS *Pickw.* xxv, If ever there was a wolf in a mulberry suit, that ere Job Trotter's him. **1882** *Garden* 21 Oct. 354/3 Among other seedlings the following struck us as being remarkably fine..Darkness, deep mulberry. **1951** M. KENNEDY *Lucy Carmichael* I. i. 10, I impressed her with my mulberry house-coat. **1971** *Vogue* 15 Oct. 41 Pullover..in Antwerp Brown, French Navy and Mulberry. **1974** R. HARRIS *Double Snare* xii. 83 Sir Jonathan wore a white doublet, and mulberry trunk hose. *Ibid.* xxviii. 226 The colours; dog-rose pink, green, and mulberry.

4. In full, ***Mulberry harbour***. The code name of the prefabricated harbour used in the invasion of the Continent by British and American forces in 1944; also applied to any artificial harbour. Also *attrib.*

1945 *N. & Q.* 15 Dec. 263/2 The word 'Mulberry' was selected as the secret name for the artificial harbour..from its being that which happened to come next in rotation on the Admiralty's List of Ships' Names then available for use. **1946** J. E. TAYLOR *Last Passage* i. 19 Mulberry is the name given to an artificial harbour erected primarily for the landing of stores off the enemy beaches. **1958** *Listener* 5 June 930/2 Further north—in the island of Schouwen-Duiveland —I saw where it had been necessary to float great mulberry harbour caissons in and sink them in the gaps. *Ibid.* 21 Aug. 258/2 The famous Mulberry Project, the creation of vast artificial seaports on the open coast of Normandy. **1965** R. B. ORAM *Cargo Handling* viii. 152 Movable quays of the war time Mulberry pattern. **1972** *Daily Tel.* 11 May 9/3 Vice-Adml Hughes-Hallett told me he..frankly considered the 'embellishments' of the Mulberries quite superfluous.

5. *attrib.* and *Comb.*: ***mulberry-colour***, ***-leaf***, ***-tree***, ***wine***; ***mulberry-coloured***, ***-faced***, ***-leaved***, ***-like***, ***-nosed***, ***-red*** adjs.; **mulberry-bird**, (*a*) *Austral.*, the southern figbird, *Sphecotheres vieilloti*; (*b*) 'the rose-coloured pastor, *Pastor roseus*' (Funk's *Stand. Dict.* 1895); **mulberry blite** (see quot. 1856); **mulberry body** = MORULA 2 (*Syd. Soc. Lex.* 1891); **mulberry bush**, a children's game, with a marching ditty 'Here we go round the mulberry-bush'; **mulberry calculus** *Path.* (see quot. 1872); **mulberry eyelid** = *Trachoma* (Syd. Soc. Lex.); **mulberry germ, mass** = MORULA 2; **mulberry molar** *Med.*, a first molar with a small crown that is nodular and pitted, somewhat like a mulberry, as a result of congenital syphilis; **mulberry rash**, a name given by Sir W. Jenner to the rash of typhus fever; **mulberry shell**, a species of *Dolium* (Chambers *Cycl. Supp.* 1753).

1891 A. J. NORTH in *Rec. Austral. Museum* I. 113 It [*sc.* the Southern Sphecotheres] is fairly common on the Tweed River, where it is locally known as the '*Mulberry-bird', from the decided preference it evinces for that species of fruit. **1966** N. W. CAYLEY *What Bird is That?* (ed. 4) 21 Southern Figbird... Also called Mulberry-bird and Banana-bird... Flocks may be seen feeding in native fruit- and berry-bearing trees, and sometimes in orchards, where they eat mulberries, figs, and other soft fruits. **1760** J. LEE *Introd. Bot.* App. 319 *Mulberry Blite, *Blitum*. **1856** MAYNE *Expos. Lex.*, *Mulberry Blight*, Bot. Common name for the *Chenopodio-morus*, or *Blitum capitatum* of Linn. **1897** FLO. MARRYAT *Blood Vampire* iii, [They] take hands and dance round in a ring as if they were playing at '*Mulberry Bush'. **1822–34** *Good's Study Med.* (ed. 4) IV. 391 **Mulberry calculus*, or oxalate of lime. **1856** DRUITT *Surgeon's Vade Mecum* 572 The Mulberry Calculus is composed of oxalate of lime. It is dark red, rough, and tuberculated. **1822–34** *Good's Study Med.* (ed. 4) IV. 402 A deep reddish-brown or *mulberry colour. **1776–96** WITHERING *Brit. Plants* (ed. 3) II. 415 *Mulberry coloured. **1888** *Encycl. Brit.* XXIII. 677/1 The eruption which..consists of dark red (mulberry coloured) spots or blotches varying in size. **1812** *Sporting Mag.* XL. 23 A *mulberry-faced, bumper-loving blade. **1868** TENNYSON *Lucretius* 54 The mulberry-faced Dictator's orgies. **1879** tr. *Haeckel's Evol. Man* I. 189 We call this mass the *mulberry-germ (*morula*). **1727–41** CHAMBERS *Cycl.* s.v. *Silk*, In this state it feeds on *mulberry-leaves. **1891** *Syd. Soc. Lex.*, *Mulberry-leaved booby bark, the bark of *Cinchona purpurea*. **1883** E. R. LANKESTER in *Encycl. Brit.* XVI. 662/2 At the same time a space—the cleavage cavity or blastocœl—forms in the centre of the *mulberry-like mass. **1851** CARPENTER *Man. Phys.* (ed. 2) 473 A large part of its structure having undergone but little change from the state of the '*mulberry mass'. **1923** *Arch. Dermatol. & Syphilol.* VIII. 794 There is a definite shoulder formation, and the cusps occupy a smaller area..and..are smaller than normal... The grouping or arrangement of these small cusps have suggested the term '*mulberry' molar. **1941** K. H. THOMA *Oral Path.* v. 242 The mulberry molar is covered on the sides with normal, smooth enamel, but the occlusal surface is pinched together, dwarfed, rough, and hypoplastic, often pigmented. *Ibid.*, Often a supernumerary nodule or pseudo-cusp appears which clinicians emphasize as an important feature of the mulberry molar. **1961** R. D. BAKER *Essent. Path.* ix. 199 Stigmata of congenital syphilis may be found in those who survive. These defects are Hutchinson's teeth, mulberry molars, saddle nose, deafness and keratitis. **1924** R. GRAVES *Mock Beggar Hall* 6 A dissolute *Mulberry-nosed philosopher. **1833–55** DUNGLISON *Med. Lex.*, **Mulberry Rash*. **1927** *Mulberry red [see ASH *sb.*[2] 1 d]. **1945** W. DE LA MARE *Scarecrow* 35 His large mulberry-red face and eyes like bits of agate. *a* **1300** *E.E. Psalter* lxxvii. 52 [lxxviii. 47] And þar wine-yherdes in haile he slogh, And þar *molberi-tres in froste inogh. **1480** CAXTON *Ovid's Met.* x. iv. (Roxb. Club), Morbery trees, Okes, Planes [etc.]. *c* **1532** DU WES *Introd. Fr.* in *Palsgr.* 914 More bery tre, *mourier*. **1886** RUSKIN *Præterita* I. 335 Sitting under the mulberry tree in the back garden. **1723** J. NOTT *Cook's & Confectioner's Dict.* sig. T4 To make *mulberry wine. Gather your Mulberries when they are thorough ripe, pick off the Stalks, and press out the Juice. **1971** *Country Life* 23 Dec. 1777/3 There was an abundance of wine, particularly claret, mulberry wine and mead at a peacock feast.

mulce, var. MILCE *sb. Obs.*; obs. f. MULSE.

mulch (mʌlʃ), *sb.* Also 8–9 **mulsh**. [Prob. subst. use of MULCH *a.*] Half-rotten straw; in *Gardening*, a mixture of wet straw, leaves, loose earth, etc., spread on the ground to protect the roots of newly planted trees, etc.

1657 S. PURCHAS *Pol. Flying-Ins.* ix. 114 Then make a smoak of mulch and wet straw. **1674–91** RAY *S. & E.C. Words* 107 *Mulch*; Straw half rotten. **1706** LONDON & WISE *Retir'd Gard.* I. II. ii. 110 We put in a little short Mulsh upon the Root. **1763** MILLS *Pract. Husb.* IV. 367 Laying a little heap of haulm, straw, or any kind of mulch, round the stem of each vine. **1891** T. HARDY *Tess* xvii, His boots were clogged with the mulch of the yard.

†**mulch**, *a. Obs.* In 5 molsh. [ME. *molsh*, prob. related to MELCH; cf. Ger. dial. *molsch* soft, beginning to decay.] Soft.

c **1420** *Pallad. on Husb.* II. 120 Thy vynys soil be not to molsh [L. *resolutum*] or hard, But sumdel molsh.

mulch (mʌlʃ), *v.* Also **mulsh**. [f. MULCH *sb.*] *trans.* To cover with mulch.

1802 W. FORSYTH *Fruit Trees* iii. (1824) 64 Mulch the border with some very rotten leaves, or dung. **1859** R. THOMPSON *Gard. Assist.* 24 Mulch over the roots with stable manure. **1884** *Australasian* 8 Nov. 875/1 The entire surface [was] mulched with straw.

mulching (ˈmʌlʃɪŋ), *vbl. sb.* [f. MULCH *v.* + -ING[1].] The action of covering with mulch.

1817 NEILL in *Edin. Encycl.* XI. 199/1 Mulching.. consists in rendering a portion of the ground thoroughly moist by adding water, and working it like mortar. To increase the retentiveness of moisture, some short stable dung or other litter is added. **1856** DELAMER *Fl. Gard.* (1861) 65 A slight mulching with manure in winter.

b. *concr.* = MULCH *sb.*

1890 *Daily News* 30 May 7/4 In a fortnight's time the rain will have washed the nutriment out of the mulching.

mulciberian (mʌlsɪˈbɪərɪən), *a.* [f. L. *Mulciber* Vulcan + -IAN.] Resembling Vulcan.

1847 THACKERAY *Curates' Walk* i, What powerful Mulciberian fellows they must be, those Goldbeaters?

†ˈmulcible, *a. Obs.* [ad. L. type **mulcibilis*, f. *mulcēre* to soothe.] (See quot.)

1656 BLOUNT *Glossogr.*, Mulcible (*mulcibilis*) which may be appeased.

†ˈmulcify, *v. Obs.* [f. L. *mulcēre* to soothe: see -FY.] *trans.* To allay, to soothe.

1653 R. SANDERS *Physiogn.*, *Moles* 13 If it be red, these sorrows are somewhat mulcified.

mulct (mʌlkt), *sb.* Also 6 multe, 6–8 mult, 7 mulcte, 6– mulct. [ad. L. *mulcta*, *multa*. Cf. obs. F. *mulcte* (earlier *multe*).]

1. A fine imposed for an offence. Also *occas.* in wider sense, a compulsory payment (usually implying unfair or arbitrary exaction).

1591 HORSEY *Trav.* (Hakl. Soc.) 207 This Emperowr reduced..their lawes..into a most..plain forme of a written lawe, for everie man..to..challenge upon a great mult to the crown judgment without delaye. **1598** *Hakluyt's Voy.* I. 266 To set and leuie..penalties and mulcts by fine or imprisonment. **1616** SIR C. MOUNTAGU in *Buccleuch MSS.* (Hist. MSS. Comm.) I. 249 The Low Countries have banished all our dyed cloths, and set such a mult on the white as will mar the trade. **1664** H. MORE *Myst. Iniq.* xix. 71 For multitude and frequency of Transgressours brings in Mulcts and Fees to the Ecclesiastick Officers. **1796** MORSE *Amer. Geog.* II. 86 A rape and adultery is punished with a mulct of nine head of cattle. **1816** T. L. PEACOCK *Headlong Hall* viii, Imposed a heavy mulct on every one of his servants. **1858** CARLYLE *Fredk. Gt.* III. iii. (1872) I. 148 Humiliating peace, with mulct in money, and slightly in territory, attached to it. **1874** STUBBS *Const. Hist.* I. ii. 28 The state received the portion of the mulcts which in the monarchies fell to the king.

attrib. **1610** HEALEY *St. Aug. Citie of God* 174 Which P. Posth. Megellus being Ædile built with the mulct-money hee had gathered.

2. A penalty of any kind.

a **1619** FLETCHER, etc. *Knt. Malta* III. iii, Chastity That lodges in deformity, appeares rather A mulct impos'd by nature, then a blessing. **1657** HAWKE *Killing is M.* 38 He justly paid the mult of his head which forged them, and his hands which pressed them. **1724** R. WELTON *Chr. Faith & Pract.* 113 The losing of the soul..is to have a mulct inflicted upon the soul. **1892** ZANGWILL *Childr. Ghetto* I. 47 Nor was this the only mulct which Providence exacted from the happy father.

¶3. Misused by Massinger for: A blemish.

Cf. quot. 1619 in sense 2, which Massinger has unintelligently imitated.

1632 MASSINGER *Maid of Hon.* I. ii, *Ber.* If so, what diverts Your Favour from me? *Cam.* No mulct in your selfe, Or in your person, mind or fortune. **1639** —— *Unnat. Combat* IV. i, That which all the world Admires and cries up in thee for perfections Are to unhappy me foule blemishes And mulcts in nature.

mulct (mʌlkt), *v.* Also 5–6 multe, 9 *pa. pple.* mulct, mulked. [ad. L. *mulctāre*, *multāre*, f. *mulcta*, *multa* MULCT *sb.* Cf. F. *mulcter* (15th c. *multer*).]

1. *trans.* To punish (a person, †an offence) by a fine. †Also *occas.* to subject to a penalty of any kind. (The penalty or amount is expressed by a second object, or introduced by *in*.)

1483 *Cath. Angl.* 246/2 To Multe, *multare*. **1530** PALSGR. 642/1, I multe. **1611** B. JONSON *Catiline* V. vi, Those townes, then to be mulcted, as enemies to the State. *a* **1619** FOTHERBY *Atheom.* I. x. §4 (1622) 101 They mulcted him with exile. *a* **1626** BACON *New Atl.* (1900) 31 Marriage without consent of Parents they doe not make void, but they mulct it in the Inheritours. **1667** *Causes Decay Chr. Piety* v. 96 He that mulcts the more Indeliberate Oaths, may yet enjoyn a solemn Perjury. **1747** *Gentl. Mag.* 45/1 The master was mulcted all his pay. **1792** BURKE *Let. to Sir H. Langrishe* Wks. VI. 355 Will you punish by deprivation of their privileges, or mulct in any other way, those who have tempted us? **1800** COLQUHOUN *Comm. Thames* 664 On pain of being mulked when such arms are found rusty or unserviceable. **1851** DIXON *W. Penn* xv. (1872) 131 The new sect were..mulcted in heavy fines. **1858** J. B. NORTON *Topics* 81 Mulct the holders of India Stock, the fault is theirs.

2. To deprive or divest *of*.

1748 *Anson's Voy.* III. ix. 397 The Linguist was seized, and..mulcted of all he had gotten in the Commodore's service. **1833** I. TAYLOR *Fanat.* vi. 201 Let any one conceive himself..to be mulct at once of manhood and humanity. **1851** MAYHEW *Lond. Labour* II. 233/1 When..the wages of which the men are mulct go to increase the profits of the capitalist, [etc.]. **1902** *Contemp. Rev.* Dec. 838 Every third year each tree is mulcted of her spreading boughs.

mulctable (ˈmʌlktəb(ə)l), *a.* [f. MULCT *sb.* + -ABLE.] That can be subjected to a mulct; †worthy of being punished.

1658 OSBORN *Q. Eliz.* Wks. (1673) 465 A desire to free the Laity, in all things temporall and mulctable, out of the hands of the Church. **1678** T. JONES *Hrt. & Right Sov.* 436 Which was adjudg'd infamous and mulctable.

†ˈmulctary, *a. Obs.* [f. MULCT *sb.* + -ARY. Cf. MULCTUARY.] Of the nature of a fine.

1695 TEMPLE *Hist. Eng.* (1699) 172 Fines, or some known mulctary Punishments upon other Crimes.

†mulcˈtation. *Obs.* In 5 multation. [ad. L. *mul(c)tātiōn-em*, n. of action f. *mul(c)tāre* to MULCT.] An act of mulcting.

1413 *Pilgr. Sowle* (Caxton 1483) IV. xxxiv. 83 Of suche multacions he muste yeue rekkenynge before the kynges offycers.

†mulctative, *a. Obs.* [f. MULCT *v.* + -ATIVE.] Of or pertaining to punishment by fines.

1610 BP. CARLETON *Jurisd.* 43 Externall Iurisdiction being vnderstood all that is practised in externall Courts or consistories, is either definitiue, or mulctatiue.

ˈmulctuary, *a. rare.* [f. MULCT *sb.*, after *tumultuary*.] **a.** That punishes by a fine. **†b.** Punishable by a fine. *Obs.*

a **1613** OVERBURY *A Wife*, etc. (1638) N4b (*A Reverend Judge*), He wishes fewer Lawes, so they be better observ'd: and for those are mulctuary, he [etc.]. **1689** PALMES *Sp. in Ho. Com.* 16 May, Determine what crimes shall be capital and what mulctuary, before you begin. **1968** *Punch* 25 Sept. 421/2 The taxes used to buy the state industries were collected by savage mulctuary imposts on the rich.

mulcture, variant of MULTURE.

†muld. *Obs. rare*$^{-1}$. Perh. due to some misreading in a MS. of the Latin original; the printed text has *Mercurio mella* (honey).

a **1400–50** *Alexander* 4535 Appollo with a quite swan is paid him to tende; A manere of corne to mercure þat we þi muld call.

muld, muldry: see MULLED, MOULDRY.

mule[1] (mjuːl). Also 1 múl, 4 moul, muile, 4–5 muyle, 5 meule, mewle, (*pl.* moyllez), 5–9 (9 *arch.*) moyle, 6 moole, muill, mull, 6–7 moile, 6–8 moil, moyl. [The OE. *múl* masc., ad. L. *mūlus*, was in early ME. superseded by the adoption of the OF. *mul* masc., *mule* fem. (mod.F. *mule* fem.; for the masc. the dim. *mulet* is used) = Sp., Pg., It. *mulo* masc., *mula* fem.:—L. *mūlus* masc., *mūla* fem.

The L. *mūlus* was adopted at an early period into most of the Teut. langs.: MLG., OHG. (MHG.) *mûl*, MDu. *muul* (mod.Du. *muil*, early mod.G. *maul*), ON. *múll* (Sw. *mula*, Da. *mule*). In the later stages of continental Teut. the simple word largely gave place to combs. with explanatory second element: MHG. *mûltier*, mod.G. *maulthier*, Da. *muldyr* (G. *thier*, Da. *dyr*, animal), G. *maulesel*, Du. *muilezel*, Da. *mulæsel*, Sw. *mulåsna* (G. *esel*, Du. *ezel*, Da. *æsel*, Sw. *åsna* ass), G. *maulpferd* (*pferd*, horse).

A 14th c. survival of the OE. *múl* may perh. be found in the isolated form *moul* in the Göttingen MS. of the *Cursor Mundi*. The obsolete forms *muil*, *moil*, represent an Eng. development of OF. *ü*, which is found also in other words, as *recoil*, *ois* (= USE).]

1. a. The offspring of a he-ass and a mare. Also popularly applied to the offspring of a she-ass and a stallion (technically called a HINNY).

The mule combines the strength of the horse with the endurance and surefootedness of the ass, and is extensively bred for certain employments for which it is more suited than either; it is ordinarily incapable of procreation. With no good grounds, the mule is a proverbial type of obstinacy.

c **1000** *Ags. Ps.* (Th.) xxxi. 10 Ne beo ʒe na swylce hors and mulas. **1297** R. GLOUC. (Rolls) 3913 Mid so gret charge þer to Of mules. **13..** *K. Alis.* 175 A muyle [*MS. Bodl.* mule], al so whit as mylk. **13..** *Cursor M.* 6001 Hors and ass, moul and camayle. **1377** LANGL. *P. Pl.* B. XVII. 48 Þanne seye we a samaritan sittende on a mule. ? *a* **1400** *Morte Arth.* 2287 Moyllez mylke whitte, and meruayllous bestez. *c* **1489** CAXTON *Sonnes of Aymon* viii. 189 A Knyghte mounted vpon a mewle all vnarmed. **1535** COVERDALE *Job* xxxix. 4 Who letteth the wilde asse go fre, or who lowseth the bondes of the Moole? *c* **1560** A. SCOTT *Poems* (S.T.S.) xxxiv. 107 The mull frequentis þe anis, And hir awin kynd abusis. **1653** H. COGAN tr. *Pinto's Trav.* iii. 5 We went by Land mounted upon good Mules. **1679** DRYDEN *Tr. & Cr.* II. ii, I have been labouring in your business like any moyle. **1749** SMOLLETT *Gil Bl.* v. i, A vast barn in which the moyls and the baggage were disposed. **1809–12** MAR. EDGEWORTH *Absentee* xiii, She was as obstinate as a mule on that point. **1822** SCOTT *Nigel* iv, Though he is not just so rich just now as some folks, yet I hope to see him ride upon his moyle. **1875** JOWETT *Plato* (ed. 2) I. 360 You might as well affirm the existence of mules, and deny that of horses and asses.

†b. Phrases. ***one mule doth scrub another***: one fool flatters another. ***to shoe one's mule***: to help oneself out of funds trusted to one's management.

a **1635** RANDOLPH *Muses Looking-Gl.* III. iv, I need not flatter these, they'le doe't themselves, And crosse the Proverb that was wont to say One Mule doth scrub another. **1655** tr. *Com. Hist. Francion* III. 75 He had the keeping..of the Moneyes, and yet shod not his Mule at all.

¶c. Used (= Gr. ἡμίονος) for the Syrian wild ass.

1607 TOPSELL *Four-f. Beasts* 556 There is another kind of mules in Syria, diuers from those which are procreated by the copulation of a mare and an asse... These mules procreate in their owne kinde, and admit no mixture.

2. *transf.* **a.** A person having the characteristics of a mule; *chiefly*, a stupid or obstinate person.

c **1470** ASHBY *Active Pol. Prince* 564 Thaugh he were an asse hede or a dulle mule, He myght not lyve wildly at his pleasance. **1848** DICKENS *Dombey* vi, 'Now don't be a young mule', said Good Mrs. Brown.

†b. ? A strumpet, concubine. *Obs.*

1494 FABYAN *Chron.* VII. ccxxix. 259 Yᵉ Cardynall made sharpe processe agayn prestys, yᵗ noresshed Cristen-moyles, & rebuked them by open publysshement and otherwyse. **1638** FORD *Fancies* I. ii, Trudging between an old moil, and a young calf, my nimble intelligencer? **1746** *Exmoor Courtship* (E.D.S.) 502 A zower-zop'd, yerring, chockling Trash, a buzzom-chuck'd haggaging Moyle, a gurt Fustilug.

c. One who is 'neither one thing nor the other'.

1625 B. JONSON *Staple of N.* II. iv, *Alm.* I wonder what religion hee's of! *Fit.* No certaine species sure, A kinde of mule! That's halfe an Ethnicke, halfe a Christian!

d. *Naut.* A large triangular sail sometimes used on a ketch. So ***mule-rigged*** adj.

1932 *Yachting* Sept. 46 'Tidal wave', winner of the race, at the start, with the mule pulling aloft and motor pushing below. **1954** *Ibid.* Apr. 61 The swell rolls the wind out of her spinnaker, but the 'mule' aloft between her masts is pulling like its long-eared namesake. **1954** *Motor Boating* Dec. 29/1 The mule-rigged yawl Flame at the start in Newport. **1964** M. WEEKS *Compl. Boating Encycl.* 366/2 *Mule*, a large triangular staysail sometimes used on a ketch. It sets on the main backstay and is sheeted to the mizzenmasthead.

e. *U.S. slang.* (See quots.)

1935 A. J. POLLOCK *Underworld Speaks* 78/2 *Mule*, person who carries dope for a drug trafficker and passes drug to buyer after a sale has been made. **1951** *Life* 11 June 126/2 He becomes a 'mule' (delivery boy) for a peddler and earns his own heroin by introducing his friends to dope and making customers of them. **1959** 'E. MCBAIN' *Pusher* viii. 78, I bought from him a coupla times. He was a mule, Dad. That means he pushed to other kids.

3. A hybrid. **a.** Of plants. (See also MOIL *sb.*[2])

1727–41 CHAMBERS *Cycl.*, *Mules*, among gardeners, denote a sort of vegetable monsters produced by putting the *farina fœcundans* of one species of plant into the pistil, or utricle of another. **1731** MILLER *Gard. Dict.* s.v. *Caryophyllus* (*ad fin.*), The Double Rose-colour'd Sweet-John, or Fairchild's Mule. **1857** HENFREY *Elem. Bot.* §948 Gærtner states that in hybrids of *Digitalis* the mules most resembled the female parent, while in *Nicotiana* the reverse appeared.

b. Of animals; also of birds, esp. a mule canary (see 5 c).

1771 FORSTER in *Phil. Trans.* LXI. 319 The mules between carp and tench, partake of the nature of both fish. **1818** *Sporting Mag.* II. 67 As to mules from the fox and dog, they are equally fruitful. **1868** F. SMITH *Canary* xiii. 92 The linnet and the goldfinch..from both of which [with the canary] mules are..obtained. **1884** A. H. BARTLETT in *Proc. Zool. Soc.* 401 The belief, so general, that all hybrids or mules are barren and useless for breeding-purposes is simply a stupid and ignorant prejudice.

c. (See quot.) *rare*$^{-0}$. [So F. *mulet*.]

1856 MAYNE *Expos. Lex.*, *Mule*, applied to insects of which the organs are not properly developed and which are really of neither sex.

4. *techn.* in applications of sense 3.

a. A kind of spinning machine invented by S. Crompton (*died* 1827).

1797 *Encycl. Brit.* (ed. 3) V. 488/2 It is called a *mule*, being a kind of mixture of machinery between the warp-machine of Mr. Arkwright and the woof-machine or hand-jenny of Mr. Hargrave. **1812** *Hansard's Deb.* XXI. 1173 To remedy this defect, the Petitioner [S. Crompton] in the year 1779, completed the discovery of a Machine, now called a Mule, but which, for several years, bore the name of the Hall of the Wood Wheel. **1884** W. S. B. MᶜLAREN *Spinning* (ed. 2) 229 Tatham's woollen mules—which are very different from cotton mules.

b. A boat combining the characteristics of a 'coble' and a fishing boat.

1884 *Whitby Gaz.* 28 June 4/4 Several of the Whitby mules have landed good catches of herrings.

c. *Numism.* (See quots.)

1801 C. PYE *Provincial Coins* 3 The endless varieties (not unaptly termed *mules*) produced by a combination of dies not originally intended for the same coin. **1884** R. S. POOLE in *Encycl. Brit.* XVII. 630/2 A coin which presents two obverse types, or two reverse types, or of which the types of the obverse and reverse do not correspond, is called a mule; it is the result of a mistake or caprice. **1961** G. VAN DER MEER in R. H. M. Dolley *Anglo-Saxon Coins* 183 The variety is an 'Intermediate Small Cross/*Crux*' mule. *Ibid.* 184 The type is a mule of the 'Arm-and-Sceptre' type of 'Cnut' (= Harthacnut) and the '*Pacx*' type of Edward the Confessor.

d. A small tractor or locomotive, usually powered by electricity, used for towing canalboats, moving trailers, etc. (see quots.).

1903 *Electr. World & Engin.* 14 Nov. 795 The 'mule' has two large hooks for the towropes. **1924** *Chambers's Jrnl.* Nov. 731/2 These wire ropes are stretched from the ship to motor-tractors running on rails the length of the docks. Electric 'mules' the tractors are called... These mules both guide and propel the ship. **1928** *Amer. Speech* III. 366 'Mules' are the little gas and electric tractors used in the studios of Hollywood. **1971** M. TAK *Truck Talk* 109 *Mule*, a small tractor used to relocate dollies in a terminal or warehouse.

5. *attrib.* and *Comb.* **a.** Obvious comb., (sense 1) as ***mule-back*** (also *attrib.* and quasi-*adv.*), ***-boy***, ***-bray***, ***-cart***, ***-driver***, ***-hoof***, ***-kick***, ***-load***, ***-man***, ***-meat***, ***-path***, ***-power***, ***-race***, ***-road***, ***-skin***, ***-steak***, ***-team***, ***-track***, ***-trail***, ***-train***, ***-trot***, ***-wagon***, ***-way***; (sense 3 b) as ***mule breeding***; (sense 4 a) as ***mule-carriage***, ***-spinner***, ***-spinning***.

1725 DE FOE *Voy. round World* (1840) 256 His majordomo on horseback, that is to say on *muleback. **1878** *Harper's Mag.* Jan. 283/2 He put it in his broken English, 'On horse-back or mule-back, and many times on foot-back.' **1897** R. M. STUART *In Simpkinsville* 15 Many's the time..he's rode into town, mule-back, with her settin up in front of him.

1904 'O. HENRY' *Cabbages & Kings* I. 16 The mule-back system of transport that prevailed between Coralio and the capital. **1968** D. M. SMITH *Medieval Sicily* xviii. 182 All wheat had to be carried to the ports on muleback. **1973** K. BENTON *Craig & Jaguar* iii. 29 An estate..surrounded by high mountain ranges..and until recently only accessible by mule-back. **1958** J. CAREW *Black Midas* i. 11, I had started work as a *mule boy..trotting beside a mounted overseer. **1960** S. PLATH *Colossus* (1967) 20 *Mule-bray, pig-grunt. **1885** R. L. WALLACE *Canary Bk.* 56 Canaries for *Mule Breeding. **1835** URE *Philos. Manuf.* 301 The *mule-carriage began to recede from the fixed roller beam. **1847** *Knickerbocker* XXX. 228 Our little *mule-cart was but ill-fitted for the passage of so swift a stream. **1929** J. BUCHAN *Courts of Morning* I. 37 Country mule-carts struggled towards the market-place. **1857** P. ST. G. COOKE *Scenes & Adventures* 90 A charge..would have proved disastrous to the *mule-drivers. **1909** 'O. HENRY' *Roads of Destiny* 192 He had been mule-driver..and cattleman. **1880** 'MARK TWAIN' *Tramp Abroad* 486 We found the masonry slightly crumbled, and marked by *mule-hoofs. **1930** BLUNDEN *De Bello Germanico* 5 That sudden backward *mule-kick which gives troop-trains one of their unique charms. **1968** *Globe & Mail* (Toronto) 13 Jan. 24/3 A flying leap known in dancing as a reverse dolphin dive, and in wrestling jargon as a mule kick. **1810** Z. M. PIKE *Acct. Expeditions Sources Mississippi* App. III. 4 There are taken, to be coined, 100 *mule-loads of bullion in silver and gold monthly. **1880** 'MARK TWAIN' *Tramp Abroad* 491 We had plenty of company, in the way of wagon-loads and mule-loads of tourists. **1867** in E. CUSTER *Tenting on Plains* (1887) 537 Teams of luggage, dogs, horsemen, *mulemen, cross and recross at will. **1952** E. F. DAVIES *Illyrian Venture* iii. 60 Hare gave an order to the mulemen to build the fires. **1970** R. LOWELL *Notebk.* 209 The mule-man lost his footing in the clouds. **1846** R. B. SAGE *Scenes Rocky Mts.* xxix. 251 We ended our fast..with a feast of *mule meat. **1891** *Century Mag.* Mar. 774 We made our Christmas and New Year's dinner on mule meat. **1834** A. PIKE *Prose Sk. & Poems* 25 They would find a *mule-path leading from the ford. **1880** 'MARK TWAIN' *Tramp Abroad* 131 Big keel-boats on their way up, using sails, *mule power, and profanity. **1914** *Illustr. London News* 12 Dec. 814/3 The mountain gunners can take their gun, by mule-power or man-power, where the Horse and Field cannot follow. **1937** N. N. PUCKETT in A. Dundes *Mother Wit* (1973) 172/1 On plantations with more abundant mule-power, we find appearing..such..descriptions as Young Beck,..Leader Kit, and even such regular surnames in muledom as Jane Henkel..and Pol Jones. **1883** 'MARK TWAIN' *Life on Mississippi* xlv. 462 The ladies of New Orleans attend so humble an orgy as a *mule-race. **1777** P. THICKNESSE *Year's Journey* I. xxiv. 210 The foot-road..is only one thousand three hundred paces;..the *mule-road is above four times as far. **1880** 'MARK TWAIN' *Tramp Abroad* 445 We followed the mule-road, a zigzag course. **1970** C. KOPAS *Bella Coola* iii. 55 Applied for a contract to build a mule road from Bella Coola to the mouth of the Quesnel. **1897** *Sears, Roebuck Catal.* 228/2 Men's genuine unlined *Mule Skin Gloves. Not very pretty, perhaps, but full of real goodness. **1926** *Daily Colonist* (Victoria, B.C.) 7 Jan. 11/1 Brown Muleskin Gauntlets, warmly lined, cuff has fringe and red star. **1835** URE *Philos. Manuf.* 423 The *mule-spinners..always prefer children who have been educated at an infant school. **1825** J. NICHOLSON *Operat. Mechanic* 379 *Mule-spinning, which is by far the most perfect process, and by which the finest yarn is produced, shall first have our attention. **1854** J. R. BARTLETT *Pers. Narr. Explor. Texas* I. v. 113 We might reach El Paso by..taking an occasional *mule steak. **1846** S. MAGOFFIN *Diary* in *Down Santa Fé Trail* (1926) 25 His *mule team (some eighteen or twenty) were..passing the little wet creek. **1949** L. G. GREEN *In the Land of Afternoon* ix. 131 Every twelve miles along the route a fresh mule team awaited the coach. **1908** A. BENNETT *Old Wives' Tale* I. i. 2 The ineffaceable *mule-tracks that had served centuries before..Watling Street. **1975** P. SOMERVILLE-LARGE *Coach of Earth* x. 181 A traditional mule track that crossed the new road. **1859** *Brit. Colonist* (Victoria, B.C.) 29 Jan. 1/4 A good wagon road to Fort Yale, and a *mule trail thence equal to the best in California. **1932** *World Today* Feb. 217/2 Twenty miles of muletrail were built. **1849** H. PAGE *Let.* 8 May in E. Page *Wagons West* (1930) 116 The Indians..will not trouble us, so much as they will the *mule trains. **1952** E. F. DAVIES *Illyrian Venture* vii. 129 Chesshire and Kadri went back to find Hare and the mule train at dawn. **1871** KINGSLEY *At Last* x, A truck, with chairs on it, as usual here, carried us off at a good *mule-trot. **1846** P. ST. G. COOKE *Jrnl.* 19 Oct. in P. St. G. Cooke et al. *Exploring Southwestern Trails* (1938) 69 There are three *mule wagons to each company. **1863** *Harper's Mag.* June 9/2 With utmost speed, in mule-wagons, they started for the Lower Agency. **1850** J. L. TYSON *Diary of Physician in Calif.* 24 [Down] the only pass ..was a narrow *mule-way. **1930** T. S. ELIOT tr. *St.-J. Perse's Anabasis* 65 The parties for upkeep of muleways.

b. *attrib.* passing into *adj.* in sense 'hybrid'.

1755 *Gentl. Mag.* XXV. 408/1 Other bastard or mule plants. **1800** E. DARWIN *Phytol.* 115 A mule cabbage is described..which is said to fatten a beast six weeks sooner than turneps. *a* **1833** J. T. SMITH *Bk. for Rainy Day* (1861) 163 *note*, Which, by reason of Mr. Bentley's fancy mouldings, interfering so often with parts which are really chaste, must be considered a mule building. **1892** *Berwick Advertiser* 16 Sept. 2/1 Cheviot and mule lambs.

c. Special combinations: **mule armadillo**, *Dasypus septemcinctus* or *hybridus*; **mule-beater**, a stick used for beating mules; **mule-bird, mule canary**, a cross between a canary and another finch, esp. the goldfinch; **mule chest** (see quot. 1911); **mule coble** = sense 4 b; **mule-colt** *U.S.*, a young mule; **mule deer**, *Odocoileus hemionus*, a black-tailed deer native to western North America, and distinguished by its large ears; †**mule-doctor** [= late L. *mūlomedicus*], a veterinary surgeon; **mule doubler** *Cotton manuf.*, a doubling machine resembling the 'mule' (sense 4 a); **mule-ear(ed) rabbit** = JACK-RABBIT; **mule('s) fern**, a name for *Asplenium hemionitis*; **mule-gate**, the space in a spinning-room within which a mule works; **mule-headed** *a.*, stubborn; † **mule herd**, a keeper or driver of mules; **mule jenny** = sense 4 a; **mule-killer** *U.S.*, (*a*) (see quot. 1847); (*b*) (see quots. 1890 and 1899); **mule-litter**, a litter borne by mules; †**mule-medicine** [= late L. *mūlomedicīna*], farriery; hence **mule-medicinal** *a.*; **mule rabbit** *U.S.* (see quot.); = *mule-ear(ed) rabbit*; **mule-skinner** *N. Amer.*, a prairie mule-driver; hence **mule-skinning** *vbl. sb.*; **mule-stair** (? *nonce-wd.*), a mountain ascent practicable for mules; **mule-sweep** = *mule-gate*; **mule twist, yarn**, yarn spun on a mule; **mule-whacker** *U.S.*, a mule-driver.

1840 *Cuvier's Anim. Kingd.* 124 The *Mule Armadillo ..*Dasypus septemcinctus*. **1909** E. BANKS *Mystery F. Farrington* 123 Pedro took up one of the disused *mule-beaters, and laid it on him thick and fast. **1768** PENNANT *Zool.* II. 317 These birds will produce with the goldfinch and linnet, and the offspring is called a *mule-bird, because, like that animal, it proves barren. **1885** *Cassell's Encycl. Dict.*, **Mule canary*. **1911** BLAKE & REVEIRS-HOPKINS *Little Bks. Old Furnit.: Tudor to Stuart* vi. 96 In some cases during the transition from the simple chest to the chest of drawers, we find a chest with drawer or drawers below and false drawer fronts to match on the upper portion. The old chest lid is still retained. This type, being a hybrid, is known amongst collectors as the '*Mule Chest'. **1923** J. C. ROGERS *Eng. Furnit.* ii. 15 The 'mule chest', or dower chest, with its proverbial bottom drawer. **1972** *Country Life* 21 Dec. 1752/1 A well proportioned 18th century mule chest of well coloured mahogany. **1883** *Fisheries Exhib. Catal.* 16 Model of Improved *Mule Coble for Herring Fishery. **1788** G. WASHINGTON *Diaries* (1925) III. 400 Turned..the two yearling *Mule Colts..into the Clover Paddock. **1885** *Rep. Indian Affairs* (U.S.) 11 The increase has been 8 horse and mule colts, 50 calves, and 150 pigs. **1805** M. LEWIS *Jrnl.* 10 May in Lewis & Clark *Orig. Jrnls. Lewis & Clark Expedition* (1904) II. 21 With the *mule deer the horns consist of two beams. **1806** LEWIS & CLARK *Trav. Missouri*, etc. (1893) III. 844 The mule-deer inhabit both the sea-coast and the plains of the Missouri. **1806** W. CLARK *Jrnl.* 11 Mar. in *Ibid.* (1905) IV. 158 The Ears and the tail of this Animale [*sic*] when compared with those of the Common Deer, so well comported with those of the Mule when compared with the Horse, that we have by way of distinction adapted [*sic*] the appellation of the Mule Deer. **1880** *Scribner's Monthly* May 129/1 For meat we have bacon and generally steaks or roasted ribs of elk, mule-deer or mountain sheep. **1936** D. MCCOWAN *Animals Canad. Rockies* xxxi. 265 A full grown Mule deer measures about sixty five inches from nose to tail, stands from forty to forty two inches high at the shoulder and..weighs from two hundred to two hundred and fifty pounds. **1962** E. LUCIA *Klondike Kate* viii. 170 The big handsome mule deer wandered right into the yard. **1972** *Village Voice* (N.Y.) 1 June 75/2 At dusk mule deer venture out to graze under the apple trees. **1706** PHILLIPS (ed. Kersey), *Mulo-medicina*, Medicine for Cattel, the Art and Mystery of a *Mule-Doctor, or Farrier. **1877** I. WATTS in *Encycl. Brit.* VI. 491/1 (*Cotton*), Machines used in cotton-spinning..*mule doublers or twiners. **1855** *Life Illustrated* 10 Nov. 16/3 She will follow the mountain or '*mule-eared' rabbits. **1885** C. A. SIRINGO *Texas Cowboy* 142, I had just eaten a mule-eared rabbit. **1889** H. H. MCCONNELL *Five Yrs. a Cavalryman* 56 The English hare..is not nearly so large as our jack or 'mule-ear' rabbit. **1668** WILKINS *Real Char.* II. iv. §3. 71 *Mule Fearn, *Hemionitis*. **1892** J. NASMITH *Student's Cotton Spinning* 409 The pillars..are so pitched that they fall into the alleys between the mules and not into the mule-gate. **1884** 'MARK TWAIN' *Huck. Finn* xxix. 278 That *mule-headed old fool wouldn't give in then! **1792** in *Patents Abridgm. Specif. Spinning* (1866) 53 Those machines commonly known by the names of roving billies, and slobbing, and common, and *mule jennies. **1847** *Knickerbocker* XXIX. 161 One might have seen a small French cart, of the sort very appropriately called a '*mule-killer'. **1852** J. EVANS *Let.* 30 Apr. in G. N. Jones *Florida Plantation Rec.* (1927) 67, I would Call the New Waggon a nother Mule killer. **1890** *Cent. Dict.*, *Mule-killer*, the whip-tailed scorpion, *Thelyphonus giganteus*. **1899** *Mem. Amer. Folk-Lore Soc.* VII. 63 Mule-killer, devil's war-horse, praying mantis. *Kansas*. **1887** J. D. BILLINGS *Hardtack & Coffee* xvi. 315 Another invention for the transportation of the wounded from the field was the *Cacolet* or **Mule Litter*. **1904** R. J. FARRER *Garden of Asia* 81 Nor does a mule-litter hurry upon the road. **1716** M. DAVIES *Athen. Brit.* III. *Diss. Physick* 46 The old Writers of the Rustick or Country-Physicks are generally the same that writ of *Mule-Medicines. *Ibid.* 44 Those *Mulemedicinal Authors, therein contain'd are Absyrtus, Prusuensis, Æmilius Hispanus [etc.]. **1857** *Spirit of Times* 28 Feb. 414/3 Some of our expedition..went farther out, for the purpose of fetching in some of the deer, bar, and *mule rabbits aforesaid. **1859** BARTLETT *Dict. Amer.*, Jackass Rabbit (*Lepus callotis*)... It is known also by the names of Mule Rabbit, Texan Hare, and Blacktailed Hare. **1877** S. W. COZZENS *Crossing Quicksands* 80 More commonly known as the 'mule' rabbit, so called on account of its enormous ears. **1870** J. H. BEADLE *Life in Utah* 224, I took to the plains..in the capacity of a '*mule-skinner'. **1888** T. ROOSEVELT in *Century Mag.* Feb. 499 The brawny teamsters, known either as 'bull-whackers' or as 'mule-skinners', stalking beside their slow-moving teams. **1889** J. MCLEAN *Indians* v. 198 The men..are called bull-whackers and mule-skinners, applied to freighters who drive oxen or mules. **1962** A. FRY *Ranch on Cariboo* 160 I'd the repertoire of a mule-skinner, developed behind a wide variety of knotheaded horses. **1881** E. W. NYE *Bill Nye & Boomerang* 34 A practical knowledge of..*mule skinning, vocal music, horsemanship. **1945** B. MACDONALD *Egg & I* 50 If only I had studied carpentry or mule skinning instead of ballet. **1971** J. GRAY *Red Lights* vii. 158 Nicholas Sheran gave up mule-skinning for coal mining. **1864** M. J. HIGGINS *Ess.* (1875) 179 The steep and stony *mule-stair between Monaco and Turbia. **1869** *Overland Monthly* III. 9 Here..is a cotton gin..and ponderous wooden wheels, and the *mule-sweep underneath. **1864** TREVELYAN *Compet. Wallah* (1866) 92 *Mule-twist. **1873** J. H. BEADLE *Undevel. West* iv. 88 The streets were thronged with motley crowds of railroad men and *mule-whackers. **1889** H. O'REILLY *50 Yrs. on Trail* 357 The town was full of cow-punchers, mule-whackers, [etc.]. **1825** J. NICHOLSON *Operat. Mechanic* 380 The whole of which are essential in the manufacture of *mule yarn.

mule[2] (mjuːl). Forms: 5 **moule, mowlle**, 5–6 **mowle**, 6–7 **moyle, mull(e**, 6–8 **moile**, 7 **mool(e, muille**, 9 *Sc.* **muil**, 4– **mule**. [a. F. *mule* fem., slipper, *mules* pl., chilblains; corresp. to It. *mula*, Sp. (dim.) *mulilla* slipper; cf. MDu. *mûle* (Du. *muil*) slipper, chilblain (from Fr.).]

†**1.** A chilblain on the heel; also, in later use, a sore on a horse's heel. *Obs.*

a **1400** *Brev. Barth.* in *Sinon. Barthol.* (Anecd. Oxon.) 3 De apostemate et cissuris in calcaneo quæ vulgaliter dicuntur mule. **14..** *Nom.* in Wr.-Wülcker 707/32 *Hec podegra, Hic pernio*, a mowlle. *c* **1500** Mowlis [see MARE[2] 1]. **1607** TOPSELL *Four-f Beasts* (1658) 318 Of Mules or Kibed heels. *c* **1720** W. GIBSON *Farrier's Guide* II. lxxxiii. (1738) 244 Mules or Kib'd Heels..are chinks and sores on the inside of the hind Pasterns, and in the Heels.

2. A kind of slipper or shoe.

Sometimes used to render the like-sounding L. *mulleus*, a coloured shoe worn by Roman magistrates.

1562 J. HEYWOOD *Prov. & Epigr.* (1867) 214 Thou wearst ..Moyles of veluet to saue thy shooes of lether. **1585** HIGINS *Junius' Nomenclator*, *Mulleus*, a shooe with a high sole,..a moyle. *a* **1586** in *Maitland Poems* (1786) 184 Thair mullis glitteran on thair feit. **1603** *Philotus* xix, Lo Maistres heir ȝour Muillis [*v.r.* mooles]. *a* **1670** SPALDING *Troub. Chas. I* (Bannatyne Cl.) II. 249 He had..ane pair of mules on his feit. **1824** SCOTT *Redgauntlet* Let. xi, He seldom wore shoon, unless it were muils when he had the gout. **1894** SIR E. SULLIVAN *Woman* 52 She [Mlle, de Caynon] threw them her velvet mules that the executioner had left her. **1922** S. LEWIS *Babbitt* xx. 254 She wore..torn stockings thrust into streaky pink satin mules. **1944** H. CROOME *You've gone Astray* v. 43 Kitty was gone in a light clatter of pink mules. **1973** 'I. DRUMMOND' *Jaws of Watchdog* xii. 160 The girl.. padded softly across the room in her fluffy mules.

†**mule**[3]. *Obs.*

c **1410** *Master of Game* (MS. Digby 182) xxiv, Whann he hath gret beemes alle aboute, as if it were sette lyke as it were with smale stones, and þe mules nere þe heede. *Ibid.*, Þe aunteleres, þe whiche beth þe first tyndes, beth gret and longe and nere þe mules and wele apperynge.

mule, variant of MEWL *v.* and MOOL *dial.*

†**muled**, *a.*[1] *Obs.* In 6 moulled. [f. MULE[2] + -ED[2].] Having chilblains on the heels.

1551 TURNER *Herbal* I. F iij b, It swageth the paines of the moulled or kibed heles.

muled (mjuːld), *a.*[2] [f. MULE[1] + -ED[2].] Of a coin: that is a mule (sense 4 c).

1914 *Brit. Mus. Return* 115 in *Parl. Papers* LXXI. 193 A muled groat of Henry VIII combining an obverse of the third coinage with a reverse of the second. **1961** DOLLEY & METCALF in R. H. M. Dolley *Anglo-Saxon Coins* 160 *BMC* types III and IV are found muled, though the coins are of the greatest rarity.

muleish, muler: see MULISH, MULLER.

Muler, var. MALER *sb.* and *a.*

mulere(r, mulerie: see MULIER, MULIERY.

Mules (mjuːlz). The name of J. H. W. *Mules* (d. 1946), Australian sheep-farmer, used *attrib.* or in the possessive to designate an operation developed by him to reduce the incidence of blowfly strike in sheep by removing folds of skin from the crutch, the area most likely to be affected. So **mulesed** (mjuːlzd) *ppl. a.*, of a sheep, treated in this way; '**mulesing** *vbl. sb.*, the use of this operation.

1933 *Sci. Bull. Council Sci. & Industr. Res.* (Austral.) No. 40. 9 By the surgical removal of the side folds (e.g., Mules' operation), the breech is opened up, urine soiling reduced, and susceptibility to strike decreased. *Ibid.* 103 By careful surgical procedure on the Mules principle, liability to strike should be reduced considerably, because the folds selected constitute the commonest site of strike. **1946** *Queensland Country Life* 18 Apr. 3 Mulesed sheep are much easier to crutch. *Ibid.*, We don't say that mulesing will stop the fly altogether. **1957** *New Biol.* XXII. 101 This experiment showed clearly that the Mules operation gave good protection against crutch strike in wrinkly breeched sheep. **1965** *Austral. Encycl.* II. 37/1 To effect a permanent improvement in the conformation of the crutch, J. H. W. Mules developed a technique for the surgical removal of the folds of skin occurring in the breech of many ewes. The Mules operation, as it is now called, has been modified and developed to a routine procedure. **1970** *Black's Vet. Dict.* (ed. 9) 558/1 Mules's operation.—This involves the removal of a fold of skin from the crutch of Merino sheep and is carried out by Australian sheepmen for the control of blowfly strike. Mulesing is a synonym.

†'**mulet.** *Obs.* Forms: 5–6 **mulette**, 6 **moulet, moylet, mwlat**, 7 **mulett, mullet**, 4– **mulet**. [a. F. *mulet*, dim. of OF. *mul*: see MULE[1] and -ET[1]. Cf. *Sp. muleto*, It. *muletto*.]

1. A mule, esp. a young or small mule.

13.. *Guy Warw.* (A.) 1330 Now comeþ Gij soft rideing Opon a mulet ambling. **1481** CAXTON *Godeffroy* lxxvi. 122 Horses and mulettis. **1526** *Househ. Ord.* (1790) 200 Moyles 2. Moyletts 23. *Ibid.* 204 Keepers of carriage Moulets. *a* **1548** HALL *Chron., Hen. VIII* 64 One of the Mulettes brake from her keper, and ouerthrewe the chestes. **1563** in *Rental Bk. Cupar Angus* (1879) II. 278 For furnesing of the quenis grace mwlatis. **1686** BURNET *Trav.* iii. (1750) 158 A Mullet's Load of Trunks and Portmanteaus.

2. A muleteer. *rare*⁻¹. (? erron.)

c **1575** J. HOOKER *Life Sir P. Carew* (1857) 7 There as a mulett to attend his master's mule.

3. 'A Portuguese craft, with three lateen sails.'

1867 SMYTH *Sailor's Word-bk.*

mulet, obs. form of MULLET.

‖**muleta** (mə'leɪtə). *Bullfighting.* [Sp.] The red cloth fixed to a stick which is used by a matador during the faena.

1838 *Q. Rev.* LXII. 417 The matador must not let the bull run on the muleta above two or three times. **1846** R. FORD *Gatherings from Spain* xxii. 308 The *matador*.. stands before his victim alone... In his left [hand] he waves the *muleta*, the red flag. **1873** J. W. REVERE *Keel & Saddle* 111 Taking his stand firmly, he slowly unfolded the scarlet *muleta*. **1931** R. CAMPBELL *Georgiad* i. 10 But leave the banderillos in their place Nor shake the red muleta in its face. **1932** E. HEMINGWAY *Death in Afternoon* 304 The muleta is used to defend the man; to tire the bull and regulate the position of his head and feet. **1971** *Guardian* 20 July 8/6 Rita Hayworth .. flaunting her red hair like a muleta.

muleteer (mjuːlɪ'tɪə(r)). Forms: 6 **mulitar, mewlyter, moyleteer, muletour, muletteer, -oure,** 6–7 **muletor, mulet(t)er, muletto(u)r,** 7 **mulateer, -ier, mulet(t)ier, muliter,** 7–8 **muliteer, -ier,** 8– **muleteer.** [a. F. *muletier* (= Sp. *muletero, mulatero*, Pg. *mulateiro*, It. *mulattero*), f. *mulet*: see MULET and -EER¹.] A mule-driver.

1538 *Acc. Ld. Treas. Scotl.* (1905) VI. 404 Mulitaris. **1540–1** ELYOT *Image Gov.* (1556) 51 b, A horse keper and a muletour. **1549** CHALONER *Erasm. on Folly* P j b, Do you judge they coulde easily fynde in theyr hertes that.. so many moyleteers.. shoulde have cause to crie on theim? **1591** SHAKS. *1 Hen. VI*, III. ii. 68 Base Muleters of France. **1645** EVELYN *Diary* 11 Apr., On May-day the greate procession of the Universitie and the Mulatiers at St. Antonie's. **1692** R. L'ESTRANGE *Fables* ccccxvii. (1694) 451 It far'd worse here with the State-Ass than with the Muletiers. **1780** COWPER *Progr. Err.* 541 The creature is so sure to kick and bite A muleteer's the man to set him right. **1845** FORD *Handbk. Spain* I. 16 The muleteers, the 'arrieros' of Spain form a class of themselves.

Hence (irreg.) **'muletress**, a female muleteer.

1867 HOWELLS *Ital. Journ.* 120 The muletresses chosen were a matron of mature years [etc.].

†**mu'letto.** *Obs.* Also **muleto.** [a. It. *muletto*, Sp. *muleto*: see MULET.] (See quots.)

1656 BLOUNT *Glossogr.*, *Muleto*, a Moil or great Mule, a beast much used in France for carrying Sumpters, &c. It may also be taken for a diminutive of (*Mule*) and so signifies a little *Mule*. **1751** R. PALTOCK *P. Wilkins* (1884) I. 59 A muletto very gently put his head into the doorway.

muletto, obs. form of MULATTO.

mulettour(e, obs. forms of MULETEER.

muley, mooley ('mjuːlɪ, 'muːlɪ) *sb.* and *a.*¹ Now chiefly *U.S.* Also 6, 9 **mulley.** [variant of MOILEY.] **A.** *sb.*

1. (Usu. *mooley*). A name for a hornless cow. Also used for any cow.

1573 TUSSER *Husb.* (1878) 135 Leaue milking and drie vp old mulley thy cow. **1838** HALIBURTON *Clockm.* Ser. II. iv, Gives his Old Mooley a chance o' sneakin' into his neighbour's fields o' nights. **1867** 'T. LACKLAND' *Homespun* II. 213 They are all so fond of patient 'mooley' too. **1877** *Rep. Vermont Dairymen's Assoc.* VIII. 50 He should hope that his next beef might come from a polled cow or mooley. **1902** A. D. MCFAUL *Ike Glidden* I. 3, I couldn't help laughing at the sight of your Mooley slinking it for the woods with the cans and milk flying. **1903** A. ADAMS *Log Cowboy* ii. 25 There were a number of muleys among the cattle.

2. *U.S.* A 'muley saw' (see B 2). Also *attrib.*, as ***muley head*** (see quot. 1875 in B 2).

1864 in WEBSTER. **1883** E. INGERSOLL in *Harper's Mag.* Jan. 208/2 The log.. is sent at once against a 'muley', or straight rip-saw.

B. *adj.*

1. Of cattle: Hornless. ***mooley cow***, a hornless cow; a cow.

1840 *Picayune* (New Orleans) 10 Sept. 2/6 Brought to the Pound.. a red and white mooley cow. **1885** HORNADAY *2 Yrs. in Jungle* xv. 169 A stag without its horns.. always reminded me of a mulley cow. **1903** A. ADAMS *Log Cowboy* vi. 83 That muley steer, the white four year old, didn't like to bed down amongst the others. **1946** 'BRAHMS' & 'SIMON' *Trottie True* iv. 55 'Hortense sounds just like an old mooley cow,' she giggled, blissfully unaware that she herself had sounded exactly like a young foghorn.

2. *U.S.* (*Mech.*) In **muley axle**, 'a car axle having no collars at the ends' (*Cent. Dict.* 1890); **muley saw** (see quot. 1875).

[The conjecture that *muley saw* is a perversion of G. *mühlsäge* mill-saw seems to be unfounded: see *Encycl. Brit.* (1886) XXI. 343/2 *note*.]

1872 SCHELE DE VERE *Americanisms* 146 The muley-saw, a saw which is not hung in the gate. **1875** KNIGHT *Dict. Mech.*, *Muley saw*, a mill-saw.. which is not strained in a *gate* or *sash*, but has a more rapid reciprocating motion, and has guide-carriages above and below, called *muley-heads*.

†**'muley,** *a.*² *Obs.* In 7 **moully,** 9 **mooly.** [f. MULE² + -Y.] Having chilblains on the heels.

1610 MARKHAM *Masterp.* II. lxxviii. 351 Scratches, Moully heeles, or any other sciruy scalls whatsoeuer. **1819** W. TENNANT *Papistry Storm'd* (1827) 207 Kickin' the neist to garr him gae On's mooly-heel rapt thorny tae.

muley ('mjuːlɪ), *a.*³ Also **muly.** [f. MULE¹ + -Y¹.] Mulish, stubborn; sulky.

1871 *Yorks. Mag.* I. 28/2 Enah means by and by; *muly*, sulky [etc.]. **1922** J. A. DUNN *Man Trap* v. 68, I got another drink into him, and made a fatal error in doing it, for he turned muley. **1956** *Sat. Even. Post* 21 Apr. 82 With the profits come a steady succession of worries that would discourage any but the most muley.

mulga ('mʌlgə). *Austral.* Also **malga, mulgah, mulgam.** [Native Australian.]

1. a. A small spreading tree, *Acacia aneura*, widespread in dry inland areas of Australia, or one of several related trees found in such regions; also, land covered with vegetation of this kind. Also *attrib.* and used *colloq.* in general sense 'uninhabited or inhospitable region'.

1862 KENDALL *Poems* 79 Look for the malga, and salt-bitten shrubs. **1864** J. M. STUART *Explor. Australia* 190 Our course was through a very thick mulga scrub. *Ibid.* 345, I.. entered a dense forest of tall mulga. **1889** J. H. MAIDEN *Usef. Native Plants Australia* 3 These latter galls are called 'Mulga-apples', and are said to be very welcome to the thirsty traveller. *Ibid.* 82 *Danthonia racemosa*.. 'Mulga Grass'... It derives its vernacular name from being only found where the Mulga-tree (*Acacia aneura* and other species) grows. *Ibid.* 94 *Neurachne Mitchelliana*.. 'Mulga Grass'. **1890** 'R. BOLDREWOOD' *Col. Reformer* (1891) 400 The boundless ocean-plains.. where the saltbush grows, and the myall and the mulgah. **1893** MRS. C. PRAED *Outlaw & Lawmaker* II. 36 She wanted to see if there were any late mulgams.. and.. did find some untimely berries. **1896** H. LAWSON *While Billy Boils* 40 Two or three white-washed galvanized-iron roofs start out of the mulga. **1903** 'T. COLLINS' *Such is Life* 79 When he says 'mulga', he means any tree except pine or currajong. **1909** 'S. RUDD' *From Selection to City* (1910) xiv. 119 We had listened to many lies about the glory of running wild horses and cattle in the mulga. **1911** C. E. W. BEAN '*Dreadnought' of Darling* i. 3 Belts of low mulga scrub. *Ibid.* x. 88 The graceful grey mulga trees.. came right down to the river. **1928** V. PALMER *Man Hamilton* 26 Manager of this isolated place in the mulga, a hundred miles away from anywhere. **1936** F. CLUNE *Roaming round Darling* xxii. 223 A mulgawood causeway was built in front for a distance of thirty yards. **1946** F. D. DAVISON *Dusty* (1947) 1 They live at the bidding of herdsman and drover.., punching stubborn bullocks through the mulga. **1960** *Times* 5 July 11/6 The country was covered with light mulga scrub. **1964** *Punch* 18 Nov. 750/2 To pack a gun around the mulga. **1967** *Sunday Mail Mag.* (Brisbane) 8 Jan. 6/3, I had fancied myself original in conceiving the idea of taking a hot bath at 9 o'clock at night out in the 'mulga' in the middle of winter, and had borrowed a pair of swim trunks for the purpose. **1968** K. WEATHERLY *Roo Shooter* 5 On the stony hills, the mulga trees gave no shade. *Ibid.* 114 In this mental state he couldn't stay out in the mulga. **1969** *Northern Territory News* (Darwin) *Focus '69* 97/1 Contractors take the fuel off the Track to places out in the sticks and the mulga.

b. *Comb.*, as ***mulga-covered, -dotted*** adjs.; **mulga madness** *slang* (see quot. 1943); **mulga parrot**, a brightly coloured parrot, *Psephotus varius*, whose plumage includes patches of red, yellow, blue, and green; **mulga scrubber** *slang* (see quot. 1945); **mulga wire** *slang* = GRAPE-VINE 2 a; a rumour, message, or report; a lie or false report.

1936 I. L. IDRIESS *Cattle King* iv. 27 They rode for thirty miles among the low, mulga-covered ridges that are the foot-hills of the Barrier Range. **1971** *World Archaeol.* III. 170 The mulga-covered flats. **1936** F. CLUNE *Roaming round Darling* xxii. 226 Steep mulga-dotted headland along Bluff Waterhole. **1943** BAKER *Dict. Austral. Slang* (ed. 3) 52 *Mulga madness*, the 'queerness' sometimes developed in lone bushmen or fossickers. **1931** N. W. CAYLEY *What Bird is That?* 144 Mulga Parrot... Also called Many-coloured Parrot and Varied Parrot. **1941** I. L. IDRIESS *Great Boomerang* ii. 12 Mulga parrots and blue-bonnets lent a flash of living colour to the light-grey saltbush. **1968** K. WEATHERLY *Roo Shooter* 115 With the sun would come the parrakeets, mulga parrots, their green wings flashing in the sun. **1945** BAKER *Austral. Lang.* iii. 67 The bullock driver and stockman have invented many terms by which to describe their charges. Here are some of the best:.. *mulga scrubbers*.., stock that have run wild and deteriorated in condition. **1899** Mulga-wire [see sense 3 below]. **1913** H. LAWSON *Triangles of Life* iii, in *Stories* (1964) 3rd Ser. 182 Tom had been out early, or had got what we call a bush telegraphy or mulga wire. **1937** E. HILL *Great Austral. Loneliness* xxiii. 207 Warned by the mulga wires of the approach of a white woman. *Ibid.* 329 *Mulga wires.* Bush telegraph, gossip of the outback. **1940** A. W. UPFIELD *Bushranger of Skies* ix. 101 This morning I found Itcheroo squatted before a little fire and sending or receiving a mulga wire. **1964** *Evening Post* (Wellington, N.Z.) 3 Mar. 17 The grapevine or 'mulga wire' in opera circles was instrumental in the return to Wellington of [a].. mezzo-soprano.

2. Something made of the wood of a mulga tree: **a.** a club; **b.** a shield.

1839 T. L. MITCHELL *Three Exped.* II. 269 The malga is a weapon usually made in the form of fig. 2, but that with which these natives were provided somewhat resembled a pick-axe with one half broken off. **1889** J. H. MAIDEN *Usef. Native Plants Australia* 349 'Mulga' is the name of a long narrow shield of wood, made by the aboriginals out of Acacia wood.

3. *slang.* Short for *mulga wire.*

1899 *Bulletin* (Sydney) 4 Mar. 15/2 A lie or false report is, in N.S.W., a 'Mulga' or 'Mulga-wire'. **1908** E. S. SORENSON *Quinton's Rouseabout* 186 They'll be that delighted to find it was only a mulga that they'd toast you as 'a jolly good fellow'. **1941** BAKER *Dict. Austral. Slang* 47 *Mulga*, a falsehood, a rumour. **1950** K. S. PRICHARD *Winged Seeds* 297 The troops've had it all by mulga. They've heard too.

muliebral (mjuːlɪ'iːbrəl), *a. rare.* [f. L. *muliebr-is* (f. *mulier* woman) + -AL¹.] Of or pertaining to women.

1657 TOMLINSON *Renou's Disp.* 726 The Matrix.. is the very Spring and Continent of most Muliebral Affections.

†**muli'ebrious,** *a. Obs. rare.* [f. L. *muliebri-s* (see prec.) + -OUS.] Effeminate. Hence **muli'ebriousness**, effeminacy.

1652 GAULE *Magastrom.* 185 A little chin signes one envious;.. and a round and smooth chin, muliebrious. *Ibid.* 266 Nor are the French [debarred by nativity] from their muliebriousnesse.

muliebrity (mjuːlɪ'ɛbrɪtɪ). *rare.* [ad. L. *muliebrit-ās*, f. *muliebris*: see MULIEBRAL.] Womanhood: the characteristics or qualities of a woman.

1592 [? KYD] *Soliman & Pers.* IV. ii, The Ladies of Rhodes haue made their petition to Cupid to plague you aboue all.. other, as one preiuditiall to their muliebritie. *a* **1693** *Urquhart's Rabelais* III. xxxii. 270 Individual Womanishness or Muliebrity. **1858** O. W. HOLMES *Aut. Breakf.-t.* ix, The second of the ravishing voices.. had so much woman in it, —muliebrity, as well as femineity. **1888** B. HARTE *Phyllis of Sierras* II. i. 169 This tall.. woman.. possessed a refined muliebrity superior to mere liberality of contour. **1911** H. G. WELLS *New Machiavelli* II. ii. 206 She was one of those women who are wanting in—what is the word?—muliebrity.

†**'mulier,** *sb.*¹ *Obs.*⁻¹ [AF.: see next.] Wife.

a **1375** *Cursor M.* 7849 (Fairf.) Isaac his sone of mulier [*Cotton* o spus] was.

mulier ('mjuːlɪə(r)), *a.* and *sb.*² *Law.* Forms: 4 **moillere, moylere,** 5 **mulire, mulyer,** 6 **melior,** 4– **mulier;** also as variant readings in *Piers Pl.* **moilere, moilre, moilliere, -ller, mul(l)iere, mulere(r.** [repr. AF. *mulieré* (Britton), Law Lat. *mulierātus*, a derivative of AF. *mulier*, OF. *moiller* wife, ad. L. *mulier* woman.

With regard to the dropping of final *é* in Law terms of AF. origin, cf. ASSIGN *sb.*² In the variant MULIERY the *é* is rendered by *y*.]

A. *adj.* Of a child: born in wedlock, legitimate, as opposed to 'bastard'; also in *Eccl. Law*, legitimatized by marriage.

1377 LANGL. *P. Pl.* B. II. 131 Wel ȝe witen.. That fals is faithlees.. And was a bastarde y-bore.. And Mede is moylere a mayden of gode. **1430–1** *Rolls Parlt.* IV. 375/2 To yentent yat she shuld be certified mulire be sum ordinarie. **1527** *Lanc. Wills* (Chetham Soc.) I. 26 Isabelle and Dowce my mulier doughtours.. Kateryn and Anne my bastard doughtours. **1642** tr. *Perkins' Prof. Bk.* i. §49. 22 A bastard eigne who is mulier in the spirituall law.

quasi-*adv.* *c* **1450** LOVELICH *Grail* xxxix. 543 For.. that Mulyer not born he was [*pour chou k'il ne sera pas engenres de mere moillier*]. **1549** *Will of Awbrey* (Somerset Ho.), My base sonne & not melior begotten.

B. *sb.* A legitimate child; a child born in wedlock. ***mulier puisne*** (also anglicized ***mulier youngest***): see BASTARD *sb.* 1.

1377 LANGL. *P. Pl.* B. XVI. 221 Man & his make & moillere her children. **1579** *Expos. Terms Law* 148 And alwayes you shall finde this addicion to them (Basterd eldest, & mulier yongest) when they bee compared together. **1628** COKE *On Litt.* 244 b, If a man hath Issue Bastard eigne and Mulier puisne. *Ibid.* 245 Where the Bastard enter after the death of the father, and the mulier oust him. **1766** BLACKSTONE *Comm.* II. 248.

†**'mulierly,** *adv. Obs.* [f. MULIER *a.* + -LY².; perh. orig. an error for MULIERY.] (Begotten or born) in wedlock; legitimately.

1506 *Pleadings Duchy Lancaster* XXXII. 29 The said Ranlyn had.. iiij Bastardes and never issue mulierly begoten. **1586** J. HOOKER *Hist. Irel.* 113/1 in *Holinshed*, It ought to descend to him, as next heire being mulierlie borne.

mulierose ('mjuːlɪərəʊs), *a. rare*⁻¹. [ad. L. *mulierōs-us*: see MULIEROUS.] Fond of women.

1721 in BAILEY. **1860** [see MULIEROSITY].

mulierosity (ˌmjuːlɪə'rɒsɪtɪ). *rare.* [ad. L. *mulierōsitāt-em*, f. *mulierōs-us* MULIEROUS.] Excessive fondness for women.

1656 in BLOUNT *Glossogr.* **1664** H. MORE *Myst. Iniq.* 393 Both Gaspar Sanctius and he tax Antiochus for his Mulierosity and excess in Luxury. **1860** READE *Cloister & H.* (1861) II. xxxiii. 54 Well then, dame, mulierose—that means wrapped up, body and soul, in women. So prithee tell me; how did you ever detect the noodle's mulierosity?

†**mulierous,** *a. Obs.* [ad. L. *mulierōs-us*, f. *mulier* woman: see -OUS.] Fond of women.

1652 GAULE *Magastrom.* 186 Fat and fleshy hips [of a man] signe mulierous.

†**'mulierty.** *Obs.* [a. AF. *muliertie*: see MULIER *a.* and -TY.] The condition of being a legitimate issue.

1628 COKE *On Litt.* 352 b, Where the Record of the Estoppel doth run to the disabilitie or legitimation of the person, there all strangers shall take benefit of that Record, as Outlawrie.. Bastardie, Muliertie [etc.].

†**muliery,** *a.* and *sb. Obs.* Forms: 4 **moillerie, -ye, mulerie,** 6 **mulyery, malary.** [ad. AF. *mulieré, moilleré*: see MULIER *a.*] **a.** *adj.* = MULIER *a.* (also quasi-*adv.*). **b.** *sb.* Legitimate offspring collectively.

1377 LANGL. *P. Pl.* B. XVI. 219 Ne matrimoigne with-oute moillerye is nouȝt moche to preyse. *c* **1472–3** FORTESCUE

Wks. (1869) 528 Buth not all the heires of Edmonde.. though he hadd be muliery,.. barred for evermore..? **1529** Rastell *Pastyme Hist. Norm.* (1811) 85 The child that was son to Robert and mulyery gotten. **1572** *Schoole Ho. Women* A iij b, Be it malary borne or base.

muling ('mju:lɪŋ), *vbl. sb.* [f. **mule* vb. (f. mule[1]) + -ing[1].] The breeding of mule canaries (see mule[1] 5 c). In quots. *attrib.*

1891 *Bazaar* 20 Feb., Sib bred muling hens [canaries]. **1893** R. L. Wallace *Canary Bk.* (ed. 3) 105 Birds.. to pair with what I may term the regular muling strain. *Ibid.*, When birds are sufficiently 'sib-bred' for muling purposes.

†'**mulion.** *Obs. rare*⁻¹. [ad. L. *mūliōn-em*, f. *mūlus* mule[1].] A keeper of mules.

1422 tr. *Secreta Secret., Priv. Priv.* 178 In a Pasture wythout the Cite was a kepere of Mulis, that Romanes callid a mulion. This Mulion euery day be-helde the hostis [etc.].

mulire, obs. form of mulier.

mulish ('mju:lɪʃ), *a.* [f. mule[1] + -ish.] Characteristic of a mule; resembling a mule; intractable, stubborn. †Also, hybrid (*obs.*).

1751 Smollett *Per. Pic.* x, He was as inflexible and mulish as ever. **1765** Goldsm. *Ess.* xxxiv. Misc. Wks. 1837 I. 372 It will continue a kind of mulish production, with all the defects of its opposite parents. **1880** 'Ouida' *Moths* III. 15 Obstinate is no word for it, for she is mulish.

¶ *nonce-use.* Pertaining to mules.

a **1763** Byrom *Ep. G. Lloyd* iii. x, For Idæus directed the Mulish Machine While Horses drew that in which Priam was seen.

Hence '**mulishly** *adv.*, '**mulishness.**

1763 J. Wilkes *N. Briton* No. 46 A mulishness, which could never be conquered, rendered him the contempt of all. **1835** Booth *Analyt. Dict.* 323 A man of a sullen, obstinate temper is said.. to act Mulishly. **1889** R. S. S. Baden-Powell *Pigsticking* 82 A mulishly obstinate horse.

†'**mulism.** *nonce-wd.* Also muleism. [f. mule[1] + -ism.] **a.** A mulish characteristic; a piece of obstinacy. **b.** Production of mules, hybridism.

1798 Anna Seward *Lett.* (1811) V. 167 It was one of her little mulisms to fancy and assert that she could not understand verse. **1861** [see mulattoism].

mulite(e)r, -ier, obs. forms of muleteer.

mulked, obs. pa. pple. of mulct *v.*

mull (mʌl), *sb.*[1] Forms: α. 4 mol, 5–6 molle, 7 moll; β. 4–6 mul, 4–5 mull(e, 9 *dial.* mull. [ME. *mol, mul*, cogn. w. OE. *myl*, MDu. *mul, mol, mil, mulle* neut. (Du. *mol* neut., *mul* fem.) dust, ON. *mole* crumb, *molna* (intr.) to crumble, *mylja* (pa. t. *mulde*) to shiver, crush; f. Teut. root **mul-* (: *mal-, mel-*): see meal *sb.*[1]] **1. a.** Something reduced to small particles; dust, ashes, mould, rubbish. *Obs.* exc. *dial.*

α. **13..** *E.E. Allit. P.* A. 382, I am bot mol and maneres [*MS.* mareres] misse. *c* **1375** *Sc. Leg. Saints* xxiv. (*Alexis*) 213 In care bed scho lay done, In mol & hayre & woful fude. *c* **1450** *St. Cuthbert* (Surtees) 4682 Molle on þair heueds þai scaterd. **1683** Pettus *Fleta Min.* i. (1686) 304, I conclude it better to melt with Coals, than with Moll, Sod or turf.

β. **1303** R. Brunne *Handl. Synne* 6198 And þere þey fonde þe cofre ful Sperd wyþ þe deuylys mul Of florens [etc.]. **13..** *E.E. Allit. P.* A. 905, I am bot mokke & mul among. **1390** Gower *Conf.* II. 204 That other cofre of straw and mull.. he felde also. **1481** Caxton *Myrr.* i. v. 25 The Cock.. shrapeth so longe in the duste and mulle til he fynde a gemme. **1570** Levins *Manip.* 185/20 Mul, *rudus.* **1729** P. Walkden *Diary* 9 July (1866) 30, I sodded the turf stack top, and dressed the mull from beside it. **1876** *Whitby Gloss., Mull*, dust.

†**b.** *Comb.*: **mull-rain,** fine rain.

c **1440** *Promp. Parv.* 348/1 Mulreyne, *plutina.*

2. A suspension of a finely ground solid in a liquid, esp. one used in recording the infra-red spectrum of the solid.

1956 *Mineral. Mag.* XXXI. 193 Spectra were obtained on the Perkin-Elmer model 21 double-beam instrument, using both the 'Nujol' mull technique and pressed KBr pellets. **1964** H. A. Szymanski *IR: Theory & Pract. Infrared Spectroscopy* iii. 78 Hydrocarbon oils as well as halogenated hydrocarbons have been used as the liquid in mulls. **1971** Skoog & West *Princ. Instrumental Analysis* vi. 152 The resulting mull is then examined as a thin film between flat salt plates.

mull (mʌl), *sb.*[2] *Sc.* Forms: 4 mole, 6–8 mule, 7 mould, 9– mull. [In Gael. *maol*; in Icelandic *múli* (common in place-names; perh. identical with *múli* snout, cogn. w. OHG. *mûl* (G. *maul*).] In Scotland, a promontory or headland.

1375 Barbour *Bruce* iii. 696 Thai raysyt saile, and furth thai far; And by the mole thai passyt ȝar. **1564** *Reg. Privy Council Scot.* I. 306 The boit liand at Garvellane, in the Mule of Galloway. **1632** Lithgow *Trav.* x. 495 Betweene Dungsby head.. and the.. Mould of Galloway. **1795** J. Sinclair *Statist. Acc. Scotl.* XIV. 324 *note*, Such places are quite frequent, both in Shetland, such as the Mule of Unst, and in.. Orkney, called the Mule-head of Deerness. **1846** McCulloch *Acc. Brit. Empire* (1854) I. 242 The coasts of Scotland.. are very much indented, the shores extend into lengthened headlands or mulls.

†**mull,** *sb.*[3] *Sc. Obs.* [Origin and sense uncertain.] ? A lip. Cf. 'Mulls, the lips of a sheep, or, in contempt of a man' (Brockett *N.C. Words*, ed. 3, 1846).

c **1500** Kennedy *Poems* (Schipper) ii. 20 Frely to gife I wald nocht lett, To pleiss þa mullis attour all þingis. *a* **1550** *Freiris Berwik* 142 in *Dunbar's Poems* (S.T.S.) 290 Thir mvllis of ȝouris ar callit to ane feist.

mull (mʌl), *sb.*[4] [a. Du. *mul*, etymologically = mull *sb.*[1]] The lowest of the four qualities of Dutch madder. Also ***mull-madder.***

1640 in Entick *London* (1766) II. 168 Crop madder, and all other bale madder.. Fat madder.. Mull madder. **1834** McCulloch *Dict. Comm.* (ed. 2) 771 Dutch or Zealand madder.. is divided.. into four qualities,.. mull, gamene, ombro, and crops... The first species, or mull, consists of a powder formed by pounding the very small roots.

mull, *sb.*[5] *Obs.* exc. *dial.* [? var. of moil *sb.* Cf. moiley, mully.] A heifer, a cow.

1655 J. Phillips *Sat. agst. Hipocrites* 3 To keep the Sabbath such have been our cares, That Cisly durst not milk the gentle Mulls. *a* **1658** Cleveland *Upon a Miser* Poems (1677) 77 Thou that didst once put on the form of Bull, And turn'd thine Io to a lovely Mull. **1881** *Leicestersh. Gloss., Mull, Mull-cow*, or *Mully-cow*, a child's name for a cow.

mull (mʌl), *sb.*[6] *Sc.* [Sc. form of mill *sb.*[1]] A snuff-box = mill *sb.*[1] 2 c.

1771 Smollett *Humph. Cl.* III. 3 Oct., The lieutenant.. pulled out, instead of his own Scotch mull, a very fine gold snuff-box. **1885** Ross & Stonehewer-Cooper *Highl. Cantabria* 347 A veritable mull of the most approved proportions.

mull (mʌl), *sb.*[7] [Shortened form of mulmull.] **a.** A thin variety of plain muslin, esp. the fine muslin sometimes stuck to the spine of a book before its cover is put on.

1798 Jane Austen *Northang. Abb.* x, The texture of their muslin.. the spotted, the sprigged, the mull or the jackonet. **1880** *Specif. Patent* No. 4765 in *Engineer* L. 76/1 The mulls or butter-cloths in which butter is kept or packed for transmission. **1880** *Boston Sunday Herald* 3 Oct. 10/7 A new fichu comes from Paris. It is made of silk mull. **1880** J. W. Zaehnsdorf *Art of Bookbinding* xix. 85 In 'throw up' backs, or in 'flexible not to show', a piece of thin linen or stuff called mull (muslin) is glued on the back first, and one piece of paper on the top. **1882** Caulfeild & Saward *Dict. Needlework, Mull Muslin*, a very thin and soft variety of Muslin employed for morning dresses, and for trimmings. It is undressed, whereas the Swiss Mull is dressed. **1899** *Allbutt's Syst. Med.* VIII. 520 The plaister muslins (mulls) introduced by Unna. **1951** S. Jennett *Making of Books* xi. 173 A length of mull (the open-weave material that can be seen through the endpapers of most books). **1967** V. Strauss *Printing Industry* x. 673/2 The next preparatory step is lining up. It consists in attaching one or more strips of fabric, known as crash—called mull in Canada—and super, as well as a strip of strong paper to the back of the book.

b. *attrib.*

1873 *Young Englishwoman* Dec. 559/1 This edging may be worked on cambric or mull muslin. **1910** *Encycl. Brit.* VII. 277/2 (*Cotton*) The finer kinds, made from Egyptian yarns, are called mull-dhooties. **1960** Cunnington & Beard *Dict. Eng. Costume* 265/1 *Mull muslin*, 19th c., a soft thin muslin, not silky, finer than nainsook.

mull (mʌl), *sb.*[8] *Anglo-Ind. slang.* [Shortened f. mulligatawny.] Applied as a distinctive sobriquet to members of the service belonging to the Madras Presidency (Yule *Hobson-Jobson*).

1816 'Quiz' *Grand Master* vi. 145 A well-known Mul. popp'd out his head. *Note*, An abbreviation for Mulkatany, a common appellation for Madras officers.

mull (mʌl), *sb.*[9] *colloq.* or *slang.* [Of obscure origin: possibly f. mull *v.*[1]] A muddle, 'mess'. Chiefly in phr. *to make a mull of.*

1821 Egan *Life in Lond.* I. 606 Somebody must make a mull—but Randall's the man. **1840** E. E. Napier *Scenes & Sports For. Lands* II. App. 260 On a subsequent attempt to navigate.. I nearly made a mull of the business. **1870** *Lond. Soc.* Sept. 268 The French are for ever making a mull of our names. **1894** *Rugby U. Football Handbk.* 16 Hanging about off-side on the look-out for a 'mull'.

mull (mʌl), *sb.*[10] *Soil Sci.* [ad. Da. *muld* mould *sb.*[1] (adopted in this specific sense by P. E. Müller 1879, in *Tidsskrift for Skovbrug* III. 7): etymologically = mull *sb.*[1]] Humus which does not form a distinct layer on top of the soil but is admixed with the underlying mineral soil, which is characteristic of grasslands and hardwood forests and is generally weakly acid to weakly alkaline in reaction. Cf. mor.

1928 *Ecology* IX. 9 The soil on this.. was identified by Dr. Hesselman as a true mull profile. *Ibid.* 10 The mull is deepest under ash and sugar maple. **1931** *Ibid.* XII. 570 Müller distinguished two main types of humus layer called *mull*.. and *mor.* **1935** *Forestry* IX. 43 *Mull* or neutral humus .. though usually acid in reaction contains sufficient calcium to allow of a crumb or grain structure with a generally 'loose' or 'porous' constitution. **1952** P. W. Richards *Trop. Rain Forest* ix. 218 The humus of rain-forest soils.. would appear to resemble the 'mull' rather than the 'mor' of temperate forest soils. **1974** *Encycl. Brit. Macropædia* VII. 537/1 In the temperate regions two major types of organic matter predominate, the mull and the mor.

mull (mʌl), *sb.*[11] [f. mull *v.*[3]] Mulled wine.

1925 J. Thomas *Bon Vivant's Compan.* 105 (*heading*) Mulls. **1953** D. A. Embury *Fine Art of Mixing Drinks* xiii. 296 A mull, or mulled wine, is simply a spiced and sweetened wine served piping hot. **1959** *Listener* 24 Dec. 1135/3 The mull must be kept hot. **1962** J. Conil *Epicurean Book* xiii. 209 Do not boil the wine, nor allow the mull to reach boiling point. **1972** *House & Garden* Dec. 103/1 The best mulls have as their base an inexpensive, full-bodied red wine.

mull (mʌl), *v.*[1] [f. mull *sb.*[1] Cf. Du. dial. *mullen.*]

1. a. *trans.* To grind to powder, pulverize; to crumble (cf. Sc. mool *v.* 1). *Obs.* exc. *dial.*

c **1430** *Pilgr. Lyf Manhode* iv. xxxiii. (1869) 194 An oother j sigh that wente bi the cloistre and as me thouhte she bar mete croumed [*MS. St. John's Coll., Camb. fol.* 127*b*, muled, Fr. orig. *enmiellee* (? misread *emiettee*)] up on parchemyn. *c* **1440** *Promp. Parv.* 348/1 Mullyn, or breke to powder, or mulle.., *pulveriso.* **1483** *Cath. Angl.* 246/1 To Mulbrede, *jnterere, micare.* **1620** Middleton & Rowley *World Tost at Tennis* E 2, Herre's one spits fire as he comes, hee will goe nye to mull the world with looking on it, how his eyes sparckle? **1829** Brockett *N.C. Words* (ed. 2) s.v. *Mull*, Oaten bread broken into crumbs, is called mulled bread. **1877** *Holderness Gloss., Moll*, to crumple; to crush... 'Ah can moll it all ti pieces wi mi finger an thumb'.

b. *trans.* To convert (solid material) into a mull (mull *sb.*[1] 2). So **mulled** *ppl. a.*[2]

1941 *Austral. Jrnl. Dentistry* XLV. 163/2 The writer feels justified in urging all dentists to give up the practice of mulling their amalgams in the bare palm of the hand. *Ibid.* 161/2 It should.. be stated that the curves for the mulled specimens are average ones. **1943** *Industr. & Engin. Chem.* (*Analytical Ed.*) XV. 663/2 Samples of insoluble, infusible materials may be prepared for examination by grinding the substance to as fine a powder as possible, then mulling it thoroughly in a straight-chain hydrocarbon, such as Nujol. **1948** *Rev. Sci. Instruments* XIX. 165/1 The present technique is to mull the sample in a mineral oil such as Nujol. **1956** J. N. Anderson *Appl. Dental Materials* xxv. 359 The dentist.. may show symptoms of slight mercurial poisoning if he employs the technique of 'mulling' or 'palming' amalgam in the hand over a period of years. **1964** H. A. Szymanski *IR: Theory & Pract. Infrared Spectroscopy* iii. 78 The name given to this technique [*sc.* dispersing a solid in a liquid] is *mulling* the sample.

†**2.** *intr.* To rain fine rain; to mizzle. *Obs.*⁻⁰

c **1440** *Promp. Parv.* 348/1 Mullyn, or reynyn a mulreyne, *plutinat.*

†**mull,** *v.*[2] *Obs. rare.* [Of obscure origin: perh. a use of mull *v.*[1]] *trans.* To dull, stupefy.

1607 Shaks. *Cor.* iv. v. 239 Let me haue Warre say I... Peace, is a very Apoplexy, Lethargie, mull'd, deafe, sleepe, insensible. *a* **1687** Cotton *Poems* (1689) 96 Till Ale, which crowns all such pretences, Mull'd them again into their senses.

mull (mʌl), *v.*[3] [Of obscure origin.

It is not easy to connect the sense satisfactorily with that of mull *v.*[1] It has been suggested that the vb. is f. mull *sb.*[1] applied to the powdered spices used in mulling; but there is no evidence of such a specific use of the sb. Another unsupported conjecture is that the original sense may have been 'to soften', 'render mild' (cf. Du. *mul* soft) of which mull *v.*[2] might be another application. Quite inadmissible is the notion, which appears in all recent Dicts., that *mulled ale* is a corruption of *moldale* (mould *sb.*[1]) funeral banquet.]

trans. To make (wine, beer, etc.) into a hot drink with the addition of sugar, spices, beaten yolk of egg, etc.

1618 Fletcher *Loyal Subj.* iv. vi, Do not fire the Cellar, There's excellent Wine in't, Captain, and though it be cold weather, I do not love it mull'd. **1636** Davenant *Witts* iv. i. Wks. (1673) 207 The Town affords not Sack enough To mull for a Parsons cold. **1769** Mrs. Raffald *Eng. Housekpr.* (1778) 311 To mull Wine. **1865** Dickens *Mut. Fr.* i. vi, When they mulled your ale.

fig. c **1640** *Capt. Underwit* iv. ii. in Bullen *O. Pl.* II. 376 What shalls doe with him; this Engine burnes like Etna. Throw him into the River. Hee's able to mull the Thames well.

mull (mʌl), *v.*[4] *rare*⁻¹. [App. ad. Hindī *malnā* to rub, anoint.

But possibly associated with an Eng. dialect word (? a developed sense of mull *v.*[1]). Cf. the following:

1881 *Leicestersh. Gloss., Mull*, to.. rub round and round. 'Mulling his knee.' 'That child mulls his tongue.']

trans. To massage.

1825–9 Mrs. Sherwood *Lady of Manor* V. xxix. 74 She.. was rubbed every day with oil, and mulled and kneaded according to the fashion of the country.

mull (mʌl), *v.*[5] [f. mull *sb.*[9]; sense 2 may be a distinct word.]

1. *trans.* (*Athletics.*) To make a failure of.

1862 *Sporting Life* 14 June, Pooley here 'mulled' a catch. **1894–5** *Rugby U. Football Handbk.* 15 Opportunities of scoring are lost in every match by a forward mulling a pass.

2. a. *intr.* (See quots. 1879, 1890.) Chiefly *colloq. U.S.*

1857 J. G. Holland *Bay-Path* xvii. 200 'What do you do with them [troubles]?' 'Let 'em mull.' **1879** Webster Suppl., *Mull*, to work steadily without accomplishing much. (*Colloq. Amer.*) **1890** Webster, *Mull*, v. i. To work (over) mentally; to cogitate; to ruminate; usually with *over*; as, to mull over a thought or a problem. *Colloq. U.S.*

b. ***mull over*** (an idea, etc.), to turn over in one's mind, cogitate upon.

1880 R. Grant *Confess. Friv. Girl* (1881) 155 Not exactly wondering what he was doing, but mulling over the various incidents of our acquaintance. **1889** *Atlantic Monthly* Aug. 188/1 Milborne was not likely to act upon impulse, and there is even reason to believe he took much time mulling over the matter after it developed in his mind. **1910** J. London *Let.* 9 Feb. (1966) 299 If I can get from you a suggestion of a motif.. which, after mulling over, I decide I can do, I could ..join you. **1949** B. Woolfe in A. Dundes *Mother Wit* (1973) 529 The Rabbit mulls the problem over. **1958** *Times* 20 Aug. 10/7 Bill and I discovered a mutual hobby in fishing.

Rods had to be produced for inspection..and experiences mulled over. **1966** *Listener* 3 Nov. 650/2 Of course one mulls over that.

c. *trans.* To consider, ponder upon. *U.S.*

1923 *Dialect Notes* V. 215 *Mull*, v., to ponder over, to cogitate upon. **1949** *Sun* (Baltimore) 27 Dec. 5/1 At last report, the county was mulling a price. **1958** *Wall St. Jrnl.* 29 Oct. 1/5 The idea of a U.S. pledge to facilitate state and local borrowing is mulled by the joint Federal-state committee on swapping services and revenue sources between the U.S. Government and the states. **1972** *Newsweek* 10 Jan. 39/3 Mr. Nixon is mulling two possible tactics. **1972** *Science* 22 Sept. 1081/1 The Germans..were mulling a public recommendation from their safety advisory committee.

mull (mʌl), *v.*^{6} *Lithography.* [Back-formation from MULLER *sb.*^{1}] *trans.* To give a granular surface to (the plate) by means of a muller and sand.

1876 ABNEY *Instr. Photogr.* (ed. 3) 134 The zinc plates.. are mulled in the ordinary manner with a muller and fine sand. *Ibid.* 156 The property that a calcareous stone or mulled zinc plate possesses for absorbing..water.

mull, *v.*^{7} Used (? by mistake) for MILL *v.* 5.

1840 THACKERAY *Paris Sk.-bk.* II. 288 His simple taste found little..to enjoy beyond the mulling of chocolate.

mull (mʌl), *v.*^{8} [Perh. related to other vbl. uses of MULL.] **a.** *trans.* To moisten (leather) during manufacture so as to make it more supple. **b.** *intr.* Of leather: to become soft by moistening. So **mulled** *ppl. a.*^{3}, **ˈmulling** *vbl. sb.*^{3}

1931 F. PLUCKNETT *Boot & Shoe Manuf.* xxvi. 166/2 One of the more recent innovations in the lasting-room is the 'mulling chamber', the idea being that if the upper materials absorb a suitable amount of dampness they will stretch easier. **1953** W. MOORE in J. H. Thornton *Textbk. Footwear Manuf.* xx. 277 A criticism of mulling is that the fibre of the leather is adversely affected... The mulled upper after lasting is rather damp. **1962** *New Scientist* 12 Apr. 33/1 Almost any known leather, it is believed, can be mulled in fewer than four minutes. **1963** *Times* 7 Mar. 20/1 In previous shoemaking methods the uppers of the shoes had to remain on 'lasts' for five or six days in order to get their shape. The new process does the job in half an hour by means of pumping moisture into the leather in a special mulling machine. **1969** T. C. THORSTENSEN *Pract. Leather Technol.* xii. 197 After the oils and greases have been distributed uniformly over the surface, the leather is removed from the drum and allowed to mull, once the initial heat has been removed by air cooling.

mull, obs. form of MULE.

mullah (ˈmʌlə). Forms: 7 **mula, mul(l)ay, mulha, mowla, moolae, moulla, 7–8 molla, 7, 9 mollah, 8 moula, 8–9 moul(l)ah, 7–9 mulla(h, 9 moola(h, moollah.** [a. Pers., Turk., and Urdū *mullā*, corrupt pronunciation of Arab. *maulā* (which some of the earlier forms directly represent).] A title given among Muslims to one learned in theology and sacred law.

1613 PURCHAS *Pilgrimage* (1614) 477 The Mulla's, or Priests of the Mogores. **1662** J. DAVIES tr. *Olearius' Voy. Ambass.* 215 They were all sate against the Wall, excepting only the Molla, or Master of the School. **1687** A. LOVELL tr. *Thevenot's Trav.* II. 102 There are Mulas who have great Salaries..for teaching all comers, Sciences and the Law, and they are properly the Doctors... These Mulas are also in Persia like Clerks or Notaries; they make the deeds of conveyances..and other deeds. **1715** *Lond. Gaz.* No. 5306/2 The Ambassador's Moula, or Doctor of the Mahometan Law. **1849** M. ARNOLD *Sick King in Bokhara*, A certain Moollah, with his robe All rent. **1865** *Q. Jrnl. Sci.* II. 97 He settled..at Constantinople, studying as a Mollah or Divinity Student in the colleges there. **1895** MRS. B. M. CROKER *Village Tales* (1896) 219 This must be the place the preaching moola meant when he spoke of the garden of Paradise.

Mullane, mullat(t)o: see MILAN^1, MULATTO.

mullarkey, var. MALARKEY.

mulle, obs. form of MOLE *sb.*^{2}, MULE^2.

mulled (mʌld), *a. Sc.* [f. MULL *sb.*^{4} + -ED^2.] Hornless, pollard.

1835 *Blackw. Mag.* XXXVII. 434*/2 The worst want of this dilemma is the want of horns. It is like the front of a Galloway stot—mulled.

mulled (mʌld), *ppl. a.*^{1} [f. MULL *v.*^{3} + -ED^1.] Of ale, wine, cider, etc: Made into a sweetened and spiced hot drink and sometimes thickened with beaten yolk of egg. †Of water, vinegar: ? Sweetened and made hot (= MULSED).

1607 G. WILKINS *Mis. Enforced Marr.* F j b, I can drinke Muscadine and Egges, and Muld-sack. **1661** LOVELL *Hist. Anim. & Min.* 13 *Castorium* drunk in mulled water q. drach. 2. looseneth the belly. *Ibid.*, Being given in *unc.* 4. *sem.* of mulled vinegar fasting it helpeth the falling sickness. **1764** ELIZ. MOXON *Eng. Housew.* (ed. 9) 85 Then mix them together as you would do mull'd ale. **1809** W. IRVING *Knickerb.* (1861) 237 The whole community was deluged with cherry-brandy..and mulled cider. **1882** MISS BRADDON *Mt. Royal* II. xi. 265 A tankard of mulled claret.

mulled, *ppl. a.*^{2}, ^{3}: see MULL *v.*^{1}, ^{8}.

mullein (ˈmʌlɪn). Forms: 5–6 **moleyne,** (5 **molyn,** 6 **molin, -en, -ayne**), 6 **mollen, mulleyn(e,** 6–7 **mullin, -eine,** 6– (8–9 *U.S.*) **mullen,** 6– **mullein.** [a. AF. *moleine* (F. *moulaine*, Cotgr.; *molène*, Littré), perh. a derivative of F. *mol* soft. Cf. MULLET^4.

The AF. word occurs in the 13th c. gloss '*Tapsus barbatus*, *i.* moleine, *i.* softe' (*Lat. Fr. Eng. Voc.* in Wr.-Wülcker 556/31), and in *Alphita* (*c*1450) as *molayne*. The OE. *molegn*, explained as 'mullein' in dictionaries, appears to have meant 'curds'.]

1. The common name of various species of the genus *Verbascum*, consisting of herbaceous plants with woolly leaves and an erect woolly raceme of yellow flowers: **a.** esp. *V. Thapsus*, ***common*** or ***great (torch) mullein.***

candlewick mullein: see CANDLE-WICK b.

c **1440** *Promp. Parv.* 342/1 Moleyne, herbe *tapsus*. *c* **1450** *ME. Med. Bk.* (Heinrich) 120 Take molyn, & styue hit in good red wyn, & make a plaster. **1548** TURNER *Names of Herbs* (E.D.S.) 79 Verbascum is called..in englishe Mullen higgis taper or Longe wurt. **1597** GERARDE *Herbal* II. cclvi. 629 The male Mullein..hath broade leaues.., in the midst of which riseth vp a stalke..couered with the like leaues,.. among which, taperwise are set a multitude of yellowe flowers... The female Mullein hath..white flowers. **1782** J. SCOTT *Poet. Wks.* 97 And golden spikes the downy mulleins rear. **1851** MRS. STOWE *Pearl Orr's Isl.* 8 Only savins and mullens with their dark pyramids or white spires of velvet leaves, diversified the sandy wayside. **1866** *Treas. Bot.* s.v., Great Torch Mullein.

b. Applied to other species of the same genus. ***great (white)*** or ***hoary mullein***, *V. Lychnitis*. ***purple mullein*** = MOTH MULLEIN.

1578 LYTE *Dodoens.* I. lxxxi. 118 There be foure sortes of Mulleyne,..whereof yᵉ two first are white Mulleyne..: The third is blacke Mulleyne: The fourth is wilde Mulleyne. *Ibid.* lxxxii. 122 It may be called in English Purple, or Mothe Mulleyn. **1597** GERARDE *Herbal* II. cclvii. 631 Of base Mullein. 1..Base white Mullein. 2..Base black Mullein. **1882** *Garden* 28 Oct. 377/1 The Purple Mullein..is an old garden favourite.

c. Applied to similar plants of other genera.

† ***petty mullein***, *Primula vulgaris* and *P. veris*. † ***wild*** or ***woody mullein***, *Phlomis fruticosa*.

1578 LYTE *Dodoens* I. lxxxiii. 122 Of Petie Mulleyn or the kindes of Primeroses. **1597** GERARDE *Herbal* II. ccliii. 625 *Verbascum Mathioli*. French Sage. Wilde Mullein, woodie Mullein, Mathiolus his Mullein... In English it is generally called French Sage, we may call it Sage Mullein. **1754** *Catal. Seeds* in *Fam. Rose Kilravock* (Spald. Club) 427 Phlomis (Sage-leaf Mullein).

2. Short for *mullein moth* (see 3).

1868 F. O. MORRIS *Brit. Moths* III. 30 *Cucullia Verbasci*. Mullein. **1869** E. NEWMAN *Brit Moths* 430.

3. *attrib.* and *Comb.*: simple attrib., as ***mullein-leaf***; similative, as ***mullein-leaved*** adj.; **mullein foxglove**, a wild plant of the U.S. (see quot.); **mullein moth, shark**, a moth, *Cucullia Verbasci*, whose larva feeds upon the mullein plant; **mullein pink** (see quot.); **mullein tea**, an infusion of mullein leaves; **mullein wave**, the moth *Acidalia promutata*.

1856 GRAY *Man. Bot.* (1860) 292 *Seymeria macrophylla* (*Mullein-Foxglove). **1873** MRS. PHELPS *Trotty's Wedd. Tour* 259 Under a great soft *mullein leaf. **1822** *Hortus Anglicus* II. 75 *Mullein-leaved Iron Wort. **1827** J. F. STEPHENS *Catal. Brit. Insects* II. 102 *Mullein M[oth]. **1846–50** A. WOOD *Class-bk. Bot.* 192 *Lychnis coronaria*... *Mullein Pink. Rose Campion. **1887** J. C. HARRIS *Free Joe*, etc. (1888) 193 She sent me word to make me some *mullein-tea. **1832** J. RENNIE *Conspect. Butterfl. & M.* 140 The *Mullein Wave (*Ptychopoda incanata*, Stephens). **1869** E. NEWMAN *Brit. Moths* 80 The Mullein Wave (*Acidalia promutata*).

ˈmullen. *Obs.* exc. *dial.* Also 9 **mullin.** See also MOLAN. [App. the same word as MOLAN.] A head-stall for a horse. See also E.D.D.

1620 MARKHAM *Farew. Husb.* (1625) 147 He shal make readie his collars, hames, treates, halters, mullens [etc.]. **1879** MISS JACKSON *Shropsh. Word-bk.*, Suppl., *Mullin bridle*, a kind of bridle with blinkers, used for cart-horses.

muller (ˈmʌlə(r)), *sb.*^{1} Forms: 5 **molour, -owre, mulloure,** 6 **mol(l)er, molver,** 7, 9 **mullar,** 8– **muller.** [Perh. a. AF. *moloir (cf. OF. *moloir* adj., serving to pound or grind), f. *mol-*, *moldre* (mod.F. *moudre* to grind.] A stone with a flat base or grinding surface, which is held in the hand and used, in conjunction with a grinding stone or slab, in grinding painters' colours, apothecaries' powders, etc. Also ***muller-stone.***

1404 *Durham Acc. Rolls* (Surtees) 396, j petra cum j molour pro pictoribus. *c* **1440** *Promp. Parv.* 342/1 *Molowre*, gryndynge stone (*K.* for colourys) *mola*. **1612** PEACHAM *Graphice* 69 The choice of your grinding stone and mullar. I like best the porphyrie, white or greene Marble, with a muller or vpper stone of the same. *c* **1790** IMISON *Sch. Art* II. 67 The student must be provided with..a large stone and muller to levigate the colours. **1873** E. SPON *Workshop Receipts* Ser. I. 106/1 The muller is a hard and conical-formed stone, the diameter of the base or rubbing surface of which should be about one-sixth of that of the grindstone.

Comb. **1856** ROYLE & HEADLAND *Mat. Med.* (ed. 3) 687 Tapioca Starch... Grains convex, ovoid, or mullar-shaped.

b. A similar implement used for polishing.

1727–41 CHAMBERS *Cycl.*, *Muller*, is also an instrument used by the glass-grinders; being a piece of wood, to one end whereof is cemented the glass to be ground.

†**c.** Used (? *erron.*) for the slab upon which ingredients are mullered. Also ***muller stone.*** *Obs.*

1559 MORWYNG *Evonym.* 12 Renewing..the destillation, and powering again yᵉ water upon yᵉ dregges grounde vpon a marble moler. **1563** T. GALE *Antidot.* II. 78 Grynde them verye fyne vppon a moller stone.

d. Applied to mechanical contrivances for grinding or crushing.

1858 *Patents Specif., India Rubber* (1875) 133 Disintegrating..india-rubber, and passing it through 'mullers' or rollers heated or not. **1889** C. G. W. LOCK *Pract. Goldmining* 691 The muller runs at 72 revolutions a minute.

†**ˈmuller,** *sb.*^{2} *Sc. Obs.* Also 6 **mullar,** 7 **muler.** [a. F. *moulure*: see MOULURE.] = MOULDING.

1554–5 *Burgh Rec. Edinb.* (1871) II. 354 Item,..mullars to the nether queir dur. **1563** SHUTE *Archit.* 8 The muller or Coronicis, of the antiques. **1635** G. JAMESONE in J. Bulloch *Life* (1885) 92 The pryce [of the picture]..is twentie merkis, ..bot iff I furniss ane double gilt muller, then it is twentie poundis.

Hence †**ˈmullered** *a.*, furnished with a moulding.

1663 in *Kirkcudbr. War-Comm. Min. Bk.* (1855) 188 Ane large keicking glass mulered with eibonie and caice conforme.

Müller (ˈmʏlə(r)), *sb.*^{3} *Min.* Also **Muller.** [f. the surname (supposedly of its discoverer).] ***Müller's glass*** (also † ***Müller glass***, † ***glass of Müller***): = HYALITE.

1794 Müller's Glass [see HYALITE]. **1836** T. THOMSON *Outl. Min., Geol.* I. 73 Hyalite or Muller glass. **1852** Glass of Muller [see HYALITE]. **1940** G. F. H. SMITH *Gemstones* (ed. 9) xxxii. 302 Hyalite, sometimes called Muller's glass after its discoverer, is a remarkable opal which is as clear as glass. **1962** R. WEBSTER *Gems* I. x. 186 Hyalite is a colourless transparent variety of opal that closely resembles melted glass; it is sometimes called Müller's glass.

Müller (ˈmʏlə(r)), *sb.*^{4} *Anat.* The name of Heinrich *Müller* (1820–64), German anatomist, used *attrib.*, in the possessive, and with *of*-adjunct to designate various anatomical structures of the eye which he described, as:

a. Neuroglial cells, having the appearance of fibres, which form the supportive ground tissue of the retina.

1856 G. V. ELLIS *Demonstrations Anat.* (ed. 4) x. 777 Passing vertically through the retina are other fine threads —fibres of Müller. **1886** C. F. POLLOCK *Normal & Path. Histol. Human Eye & Eyelids* 127 The fibres of Müller are the most prominent parts of a supporting matrix, which pervades the retina. **1932** W. PENFIELD *Cytol. & Cellular Path. Nervous Syst.* II. ix. 436 (*heading*) Astrocytes of the retina (Müller's cells). *Ibid.* xvi. 767 In other strata the Müller cells are followed with difficulty. **1961** DUKE-ELDER & WYBAR *Syst. Ophthalm.* II. 256 (*heading*) The fibers of Müller. *Ibid.*, On the vitreal aspect of the retina Müller's fibres terminate in large conical or bulbous expansions. **1971** M. J. HOGAN et al. *Histol. Human Eye* ix. 462 The mature Müller cell is complex in shape.

b. Each of three smooth muscles, of which one is part of the ciliary muscle, one (the orbitalis) is in the orbit, and one (the superior tarsal muscle) is in the upper eyelid.

1875 *Encycl. Brit.* I. 887/2 The inner part of the [ciliary] muscle forms a ring-like arrangement of fasciculi close to the circumference of the iris, and is often called the annular muscle of Müller. **1890** BILLINGS *Med. Dict.* II. 174/1 *Müller's annular muscle*, ciliary muscle. *Ibid.* 174/2 *Müller's muscle*, smooth muscular fibres found in the membrana orbitalis. *Ibid.*, *Müller's palpebral muscle*, a collection of smooth muscle-fibres in the upper eyelid. **1912** A. THOMSON *Anat. Human Eye* i. 13 Corresponding to the bases of the free projecting extremities of the ciliary processes..is a group of fibres..arranged circumferentially; these constitute the circular fibres of Müller. **1921** S. E. WHITNALL *Anat. Human Orbit* 82 This muscle, described by H. Müller in 1858, is known as the 'orbital muscle of Müller', or *musculus orbitalis*. *Ibid.* 296 The palpebral involuntary muscles (of Müller). **1950** *Irish Jrnl. Med. Sci.* 39 (*heading*) Some aspects of Muller's [*sic*] orbital muscle. **1964** [see ENOPHTHALMUS, -MOS]. **1969** BEARD & QUICKERT *Anat. Orbit* 4 Müeller's [*sic*] sympathetic (superior tarsal) muscle can be seen extending from the junction of the muscular levator and the levator aponeurosis to the superior border of the tarsus.

muller (ˈmʌlə(r)), *sb.*^{5} [f. MULL *v.*^{3} + -ER^1.]

1. A vessel in which wine or other liquor is mulled.

1858 SIMMONDS *Dict. Trade*, *Muller*,..a vessel for heating wine over a fire. **1889** A. WATT *Electro-Metall.* 237 Large brass and copper articles, as mullers, for example, must be literally surrounded by anodes, otherwise they will not receive a uniform coating of nickel.

2. One who, or that which, mulls (Webster 1864).

Muller (ˈmʊlə(r)), *sb.*^{6} The name of J. P. *Muller* (b. 1866), Danish physical educationalist, used *attrib.* and in the possessive esp. to designate a set of bodily exercises published and promoted by him.

c **1912** J. P. MULLER *My Syst. for Ladies* 86 In a pamphlet published by the *Ligue des Mères de Famille* (France), the following letter from Mme. A. de Four appeared:—Two years practice of Muller's exercises has given me muscles sufficiently resistive to enable me to leave off wearing the corset. **1921** A. HUXLEY *Crome Yellow* xxiv. 260 He would have to try and do his Muller exercises more regularly. **1952** M. GILBERT *Death in Captivity* xii. 182 We must therefore maintain bodily suppleness and agility by means of Muller's exercises before breakfast and a regular physical training class at least once a day.

müller, *sb.*^{7}: see MÜLLER *v.*^{2}

muller ('mʌlə(r)), *v.*[1] [f. MULLER *sb.*[1]] *trans.* To grind with a muller.

1853 URE *Dict. Arts* II. 127 As long as the phosphorus is being ground or 'mullered', copious fumes are evolved.

müller ('mʏlə(r)), *v.*[2] Also muller ('mʊlə(r)). [f. the name of Franz *Müller*, a murderer, who was convicted in 1864 on circumstantial evidence in which a hat was of considerable significance.] *trans.* To alter (a hat) in the manner alleged to have been done by Franz Müller. Also as *sb.*[7], a type of flat-topped felt hat similar to that associated with Müller.

1864 in Farmer & Henley *Slang* (1896) IV. 384/1 In a small shop not far from Sloane-square, Chelsea, may be seen the following tasteful announcement: Hats muller'd here! **1909** *Daily Chron.* 22 Nov. 4/7 Müller's hat..formed the connecting link in a remarkable chain of circumstantial evidence. Henceforth 'mullers', as they were called, were tabooed. **1934** *Trans. Philol. Soc. 1933* 101 A *Müller hat* is a flat-topped, hard felt.

Müllerian (mʊ'lɪərɪən), *a.*[1] [f. the name of Joh. *Müller* (1801–58), an eminent German physiologist + -IAN.] In ***Müllerian duct***, a duct in a chick, first observed by Müller, which afterwards becomes the oviduct or Fallopian tube in the female.

[**1859** *Todd's Cycl. Anat.* Suppl. 613/1 This is called after its first observer, the duct of Müller.] **1875** *Q. Jrnl. Microscop. Sci.* XV. 91 The Müllerian duct.

Müllerian (mʏ'lɪərɪən), *a.*[2] [f. the name of J. F. T. (Fritz) *Müller* (1821–97), German zoologist, who, in 1878, explained this type of mimicry + -IAN.] In ***Müllerian mimicry, resemblance***, a form of mimicry (see sense 2) in which insects of different species develop similar patterns of coloration, etc., as a protective device. Also ***Müllerian mimic***, an insect exhibiting this type of mimicry.

1899 [see BATESIAN *a.*]. **1934** *Discovery* July 195/1 Two or more, often many, inedible forms assume a similar aspect and thus enjoy a common advantage by virtue of uniting to share the toll levied on them by experimental tasting. This is the kind of assimilation which was explained by Fritz Müller and often goes by the name of Müllerian mimicry. **1951** *New Biol.* X. 73 'Müllerian' resemblance is when two or more distasteful organisms resemble one another, thereby deriving collective advantage in that a predator has only to 'learn' one pattern which will suffice to protect all the species which have it. *Ibid.*, Müllerian and Batesian mimics may be involved together in nature in a complex mimetic association, all the members of which wear the same livery. **1968** R. D. MARTIN tr. *Wickler's Mimicry in Plants & Animals* vii. 78 Most examples of Müllerian mimicry.. involve different species with the same complex patterns. *Ibid.* 79 Müllerian mimicry increases in efficiency the greater the number of species in the system and the better the correspondence in pattern. **1975** *Trans. Roy. Entom. Soc.* CXXVI. 632 *Heliconius* species are frequently highly distasteful, and act as models in many Müllerian systems.

Müller-Lyer (mʏlə 'laɪə(r)). Also erron. Muller-. The name of Franz Carl *Müller-Lyer* (1857–1916), German sociologist and philosopher, used *attrib.* (and *absol.*) to designate an optical illusion he described (*Arch. f. Anat. u. Physiol.* (*Physiol. Abth.*) (1889) Suppl. 263–70), by which a line with a V-shaped arrowhead at each end appears shorter than an adjacent line of equal length but with the V-shaped portions reversed and pointing inwards.

1899 *Psychol. Rev.* VI. 241 Brentano's unsuccessful attempt to explain the Müller-Lyer illusion by the general fact that acute angles are overestimated and obtuse angles are underestimated. **1938** R. S. WOODWORTH *Exper. Psychol.* xxv. 646 One of the two Müller-Lyer figures is kept of constant length and used as a Standard, while the other figure is the Variable. **1958** *New Biol.* XXVII. 27 He chose for his experiment the well-known Muller-Lyer illusion. **1969** F. C. SHONTZ *Perceptual & Cognitive Aspects Body Experience* iii. 41 In certain complex stimuli, like the Müller-Lyer illusion, the organization of a perceptual field may lengthen or shorten the apparent length of a line. **1972** *Jrnl. Social Psychol.* LXXXVII. 144 Samples from Western cultures..are more inclined than Eastern ones to see the Muller-Lyer.

mulleston(e, obs. forms of MILL-STONE.

mullet[1] ('mʌlɪt). Forms: 5 molet, 5–6 molett(e, 5–7 millet, (5 mylet, 7 millett), 6 mullett, 7 mullot, 6– mullet. [ME. *molet, mulet*, a. OF. *mulet*, dim. f. L. *mullus* red mullet.]

1. A name applied, often with an adjective prefixed to it, to any fish of the families Mullidæ, or red mullets, and Mugilidæ, or grey mullets.

c **1440** *Promp. Parv.* 342/1 Molet, fysche, *mullus*. *c* **1450** *Two Cookery-bks.* 104 Take a Millet, and scale him..And boile hem ouer the fire..; or elles..fry him in good oyle. **1513** *Bk. Keruynge* in *Babees Bk.* 166 Base, troute, molette. **1610** B. JONSON *Alch.* IV. i, We will eate our mullets, Sous'd in high-countrey wines. **1732** POPE *Hor. Sat.* II. ii. 21 Of Carps and Mullets why prefer the great? **1802** BINGLEY *Anim. Biog.* (1813) III. 63 The white or common mullet [*Mugil cephalus*]. **1820**, etc. [see KANAE]. **1836** YARRELL *Brit. Fishes* I. 27 The Red Mullets were well known to the ancients. *Ibid.* 28 The Striped Red Mullet is the species which occasionally only attains to so enviable a size in the Mediterranean (*Mullus surmuletus*). **1888** GOODE *Amer. Fishes* 365 On our eastern coast..the most familiar is the Striped Mullet, *Mugil albula*; the other is the so-called 'White Mullet', *Mugil brasiliensis*... On various parts of the coast they have special names... About Cape Hatteras the names 'Jumping Mullet' and 'Sand Mullet' occur; in.. Southeastern Florida 'Silver Mullet' and 'Big-eyed Mullet'. **1895** 'J. BICKERDYKE' *Sea Fishing* xi. 324 The Grey Mullet. .. Of these fish there are two kinds, the great grey mullet (*Mugil capito*) and the lesser grey mullet (*Mugil chelo*). **1925** J. T. JENKINS *Fishes Brit. Isles* 123 There are a large number of species of mullets in the genus *Mugil*. **1951** T. C. ROUGHLEY *Fish Austral.* 31 The mullets contained in the family Mugilidae range through the temperate regions of the world. **1962** K. F. LAGLER et al. *Ichthyol.* ix. 277 Neurosecretory cells in the preoptic nucleus of the hypothalamus lose their secretions rapidly in several marine fishes, including..mullets (Mugilidae) when the fishes are temporarily placed in hypertonic sea water. **1966** *Encycl. N.Z.* II. 600/2 A familiar sight is the gleaming flash as a mullet leaps out of the water and returns to its element. **1969** A. WHEELER *Fishes Brit. Is. & N.-W. Europe* 465/1 Very young mullet are also common in intertidal pools on the Channel coast.

2. Applied to fish of other genera, as **black mullet**, *Menticirrus nebulosus*, the American king-fish; **cucumber m.**, the Australian grayling, *Prototroctes marœna*.

1880 W. SENIOR *Trav. & Trout* I. viii. 93 These must be the long-looked-for cucumber mullet, or fresh-water herring. **1888** GOODE *Amer. Fishes* 123 The King-Fish,.. also known as..the 'Black Mullet' in the Chesapeake.

mullet[2] (mʌlɪt). *Her.* Forms: 5–6 molet, 6 molette, mollet(t, 6– mullet. [a. OF. *molette* rowel, mullet (mod.F. *molette* rowel).]

1. *Her.* A figure of a star, having five straight points (when a larger number is not specified). Given as a mark of cadency for a third son.

Perh. originally pierced to represent a spur-rowel. In modern practice, if the mullet is pierced this is specified in the blazon.

[**1216–72** *Roll temp. Hen. III* in Parker *Gloss. Her.* 1894, Le Conte de Oxford, quartele d'or et de goules [*sic*], ung molet d'argent ent le quarter devant. **1327–77** *Roll, temp. Edw. III* ibid., Monsire Hansted, goules a trois mullets argent.] *c* **1400** *Laud Troy Bk.* 8713 He beres an egle..And he hath rose & he has molettis. **1486** *Bk. St. Albans, Her.* bj b, Fixall in armys is calde the thirde degre..thay may bere there faderis cote armure with a differans molet. **1562** LEIGH *Armorie* 178 A Mullet of v. poyntes sable... This may be also of vii. poyntes, but of no more. **1612** PEACHAM *Gentl. Exerc.* III. (1634) 161 The mullet is often pierced of the field and the Starre never. **1808** SCOTT *Marm.* VI. ii, And in the chief three mullets stood The cognizance of Douglas blood. **1864** BOUTELL *Her. Hist. & Pop.* xv. 184 The St. Johns, in like manner, bear mullets on a chief.

b. *Comb.*, as ***mullet-footed, -shaped*** adjs.

1851 AGNES STRICKLAND *Queens Eng.* I. 236 A mullet-shaped brooch. **1897** *Trans. Glasg. Archæol. Soc.* III. I. 219 This is known as a lobed or mullet-footed chalice.

2. Pseudo-*arch.* The rowel of a spur.

1830 JAMES *Darnley* xxxii. 143/2 The horse's feet were brought on the very brink of the river, and a slight touch of the mullet made him plunge over.

†**'mullet**[3]. *Obs.* [a. F. *molet*.] *pl.* A kind of pincers or tweezers. *Obs.*

1398 *Test. Ebor.* (Surtees) I. 245 [Apothecary's will], j draghyng-dobler, cum les moletts. **1599** B. JONSON *Cynthia's Rev.* v. iv, Here is a haire too much, take it off. Where are thy mullets? **1634** T. JOHNSON *Parey's Chirurg.* XXVII. xvii. (1678) 675 Cutting Mullets. Mullets onely to hold and not to cut. Mullets to take forth splinters of bones. Mullets to draw teeth.

Hence †**'mullet** *v.*, to treat with the 'mullet'.

1649 QUARLES *Virgin Widow* v. i, And then Cis must be call'd, and then her Ladiships haire must be crispt,..and then her Ladiships browes must be mullited.

†**mullet**[4]. *Obs. rare.* = MULLEIN.

1597 GERARDE *Herbal* 390 The first..kind of *Conyza* hath large and broad leaues like *Verbascum nigrum* or black Mullet. *Ibid.* 391, I would gladly haue *Conyza* to be called in English Fleabane Mullet. **1750** E. SMITH *Compl. Housewife* 323 Take of the tops of parsley, of mullet, and of elder buds, of each one handful.

†**'mullet**[5]. Some part of a musket barrel.

1688 R. HOLME *Armoury* III. xviii. (Roxb.) 134/2 The seuerall parts of the Barrell of a Muskett. The Barrell. The squares. The mulletts. **1881** GREENER *Gun* 50 Their [*sc.* the Italian gunsmiths'] early barrels..were beautifully formed on the outside, with many squares and mullers [*sic*].

†**'mullet**[6]. *Obs.* [a. F. *molette*, dim. of *meule* millstone.] = MULLER *sb.*[1]

1755 JOHNSON, *Mullar*... Often called improperly *mullet*.

†**'mullet**[7]. *Obs.* The Puffin, *Fratercula arctica*.

1678 RAY *Willughby's Ornith.* III. v. 325 The Bird called Coulterneb at the Farn Islands,..at Scarburgh Mullet..: Anas Arctica *Clus.* **1852** MACGILLIVRAY *Brit. Birds* V. 365 *Mormon arcticus*. The Arctic Puffin... Mullet.

mullet, variant of MULET *Obs.*

'mulleted, *a. Obs.* [? f. MULLET[2] + -ED[2].] ? Ornamented with mullets.

1610 BODLEY in *Reliq.* (1703) 310 It puts me in a Dump, that my Mason having laid but one only course of Mulleted Work, he should complain so soon of the Badness of the Stone.

mullet-head. [? f. MULLET[1].] **1.** *U.S.* A freshwater fish with a large flat head.

1866 *Harper's Mag.* Sept. 537/1 Dat fish is a mullet-head; it hain't got any brains. **1873** J. H. BEADLE *Undevel. West* v. 102 There is a fish called the mullethead, that cannot be intoxicated by any amount of liquor. **1893** W. FORBES-MITCHELL *Reminisc. Great Mutiny* vi. 110 That fish, my son, is called a mullet-head: it has got no brains.

2. [Cf. *mull-head* a dull, stupid fellow (*E.D.D.*).] A stupid person. So **mullet-headed** *a.*

1857 *Quindaro* (Kansas) *Chindowan* 6 June 1/3 The men, for the most part sleepy, ignorant, mullet-headed looking wretches. **1884** 'MARK TWAIN' *Huck. Finn* xxxix. 370 They're so confiding and mullet-headed they don't take notice of nothing at all. **1916** *Dialect Notes* IV. 278 Look at that *mullet-head* of a Sam Smith. He don't know beans. **1935** Z. N. HURSTON *Mules & Men* (1970) I. i. 30 Hey, you mullet heads! Get out de way. **1942** BERREY & VAN DEN BARK *Amer. Thes. Slang* §150/5 *Stupid*,..mullet-headed. *Ibid.* 433/3 *Stupid person*,..mullet-head.

'mulletry. [f. MULLET[1] + -RY.] A pond or reservoir for breeding mullets (Webster *Suppl.* 1902).

mulley, mulliere: see MULEY, MULIER.

mulligan ('mʌlɪgən). *N. Amer.* [Apparently f. a proper name.] **1.** A stew made from odds and ends of food. Also *attrib.*

1904 *Yukon Midnight Sun* (Dawson, Yukon Territory) 10 Jan. 3/4 All the roadhouses served big Christmas dinners and most of them made a mulligan. **1913** *Collier's* 11 Jan. 16/2, I suppose you never have eaten any 'Mulligan'... The recipe calls for canned Willie, spuds, onions, canned tomatoes, all mixed up together. **1914** *Sat. Even. Post* 4 Apr. 10/1 It was a mulligan. Everything was in that stew—meat, potatoes, onions, bread—an appetizing hodgepodge. **1918** C. SANDBURG *Cornhuskers* 80 Then they go to the bunk cars and eat mulligan and prune sauce. **1926** J. BLACK *You can't Win* vii. 83 There was a grand jungle by a small clean river where they..cooked their mulligans. *Ibid.* xv. 198 He's crazy as a bed bug and the best 'mulligan' maker on the road. **1955** R. P. HOBSON *Nothing too Good for Cowboy* 138 That's what's good for me, a great beeg vegetable mulligan with feesh in it. **1966** H. MARRIOTT *Cariboo Cowboy* ii. 35 Lots of mulligan stew with beef, carrots and onions. **1971** 'R. MACDONALD' *Underground Man* xix. 135 A number of plywood tables had been set up on trestles. A hundred or more men were seated at them, eating mulligan stew.

2. (With capital initial.) *Golf.* An extra stroke awarded after a poor shot, not counted on the score card. *colloq.*

1949 P. CUMMINGS *Dict. Sports* 275 *Mulligan, Golf*, a handicap of a free shot given after a player makes a bad one. **1952** *Golf Digest* May 7 'It's just a friendly match,' he said. 'Wanna take a mulligan?' **1965** H. GRAFFIS *Esquire's World of Golf* xii. 174 Magnanimously, the hustler will allow his prey a Mulligan off the tee now and then. **1971** *Daily Colonist* (Victoria, B.C.) 7 Feb. 1/2 With millions watching on color television, Shepard took another poke—the extra chance golf duffers call a 'Mulligan'—and connected solidly.

mulligatawny (ˌmʌlɪgə'tɔːnɪ). Forms: 8 **mullaghee-tanny, mulagatoney**, 9 **mulkatany, mullikatauny, malaca-tawney, malachatauni, malagatany, mulla-, mulligatawn(e)y**. [a. Tamil *milagu-tannīr* 'pepper-water' (Yule).]

1. An East Indian highly seasoned soup. Also ***mulligatawny soup***.

1784 in Seton-Karr *Select. Calcutta Gaz.* (1864) I. 18 On Mullaghee-tanny we dine. **1798** *Sporting Mag.* XI. 308, I supped..in his house on Mulagatoney or pepper-water. **1829** SOUTHEY *Sir T. More* (1831) II. 286 Curry and malagatany soup from the East Indies. **1863** SALA *Qualk* 61 He..devoured prodigious quantities of curry, pepperpot, chillum, cutlets, capsicum-hash, and mulligatawny soup.

b. ***mulligatawny paste*** (see quot. 1858).

1858 SIMMONDS *Dict. Trade, Mulligatawny-paste*, a curry paste, used for flavouring mulligatawny-soup. **1865** LIVINGSTONE *Zambesi* vi. 130 We had taken a little mulligatawny paste for making soup.

2. *Anglo-Ind.* = MULL *sb.*[8]

1816 'QUIZ' *Grand Master* VI. 147 [He] grew, in fact, a mulkatany.

mulligrubs ('mʌlɪgrʌbz), *pl.* Forms: 6 mulliegrums, (7–8 *Dicts.* mouldy-grubs, 8 malé-grubbles, 9 mulleygrubs), 9 *Sc.* mulligrumphs, 8–9 mullygrubs, 7–9 mulligrubs. [A grotesque arbitrary formation.]

1. A state of depression of spirits; a fit of megrims or spleen; in early use in phr. ***(in) her, his***, etc., ***mulligrubs, sick of the mulligrubs***; hence jocularly, stomach-ache or colic.

1599 NASHE *Lenten Stuffe* 55 The yeoman of the mouth.. rehearsed this second il successe, wherwith Peters successour was so in his mulliegrums that he had thought to haue buffeted him. **1619** FLETCHER *M. Thomas* II. ii, Whither goe all these men-menders, these physitians? Whose dog lyes sicke o' th mulligrubs? **1678** DRYDEN *Limberham* IV. i, She is in her mulligrubs already. **1720** RAMSAY *Rise & Fall of Stocks* 85 It lulls a wee my mullygrubs, To think upon these bitten scrubs. **1736** AINSWORTH *Eng.-Lat. Dict.*, The mouldy grubs, *tormina ventris*. **1789** in *N. Eng. Hist. & Gen. Reg.* (1876) XXX. 47 We had father —— of —— who rolled and bellowed as if he had the *ma-lé-grubbles*, or, as many thought, as if he were in liquor. **1802** G. COLMAN *Br. Grins, Knt. & Friar* II. xxxix, His bowels; Where spasms were..Afflicting him with mulligrubs and colic. **1826** SCOTT *Jrnl.* 14 Mar., I have scarce stirred to take exercise for four or five days, no wonder I had the mulligrubs. **1827** *Ibid.* 19 Sept., Surely these mulligrubs belong to the mind more than the body. **1853** 'C. BEDE' *Verdant Green* I. viii, Peakyish you feel, don't you, now, with a touch of the mulligrubs in your collywobbles?

†2. In sing. form. **a.** Ludicrously applied to a person. **b.** A fit of 'mulligrubs'. *Obs. rare.*

1633 SHIRLEY *Gamester* IV. i, Command my sword, my lungs, my life, Thou art a puffe, a mulligrube, a Metaphysicall Coxcombe, and I honour you with all my hart. **16..** MIDDLETON *Father Hubbard's T.* Wks. (Dyce) V. 597 Some Londoner's son..that must hear twice a-week from his mother, or else he will be sick..of a university-mulligrub.

†**'mulling**, *sb. Obs. rare.* [Cf. MULLY *sb.* and -ING[3].] A term of endearment.

c **1450** *Cov. Myst.* xvi. (Shaks. Soc.) 160 3it fayre mullynge, take it nat at no greve. **1519** HORMAN *Vulg.* 295 This is a feyre and swete mullynge. *Blandus est puerulus insigni festiuitate.* *a* **1529** SKELTON *E. Rummyng* 224 He calleth me his whyting, His mullyng and his mytyng.

mulling ('mʌlɪŋ), *vbl. sb.*[1] Chiefly *U.S.* Bustle, stir, excitement.

1845 S. JUDD *Margaret* 170 (Bartlett) There has been a pretty considerable mullin going on among the doctors. **1866** LOWELL *Biglow P.* II. Introd., We have always heard *mullin* used for *stirring, bustling*, sometimes in an underhand way.

mulling, *vbl. sb.*[2] [f. MULL *v.*[1] + -ING[1].] The process of rubbing or grinding; the conversion of a solid into a mull (MULL *sb.*[1] 2).

1937 *Austral. Jrnl. Dentistry* XLI. 127 Mixing. This consisted of 1, 1½ or 2 minutes trituration in a standard mortar using about 120 revolutions of the pestle per minute, followed by 1 or 1½ minutes mulling in the hand. **1944** E. R. RIEGEL *Chem. Machinery* xi. 249 Mulling is the second way in which solids may be mixed with solids. The mulling action is comparable to the rubbing, kneading, or smearing action of the mortar and pestle; no grinding is involved. The machine for mulling consists of a circular stationary pan in which is mounted a special combination of mullers and plows which revolves. **1964** H. A. SZYMANSKI *IR: Theory & Pract. Infrared Spectroscopy* iii. 79 One of the disadvantages of mulling is that it cannot be used very conveniently on rubber, plastics, or resinous materials. **1971** ROSENBLATT & DAVIS *Laboratory Course Org. Chem.* iii. 71 Another method for preparing a solid sample is to grind 5 mg of the solid to a fine dispersion in a drop of suitable mulling agent. **1971** *Materials & Technol.* II. iii. 140 Mulling improves the final shape of the grain by knocking off its brittle corners, and this is carried out by impact crushing, pan milling, or air blasting.

mulling, *vbl. sb.*[3]: see MULL *v.*[8]

mullion ('mʌljən). *Arch.* Also 6 *Sc.* **mullen.** [Prob. a metathetic alteration of the synonymous *muniall* MONIAL. Cf. MUNNION, which appears somewhat later in our quots.]

1. a. A vertical bar dividing the lights in a window, *esp.* in Gothic architecture; also, a similar bar in screen-work.

1567 HARMAN *Caveat* (1869) 39 The windowes be thicke of mullions, that ther is no kreping in betwene. **1590** in *Compt Bk. D. Wedderburne* (S.H.S.) 64 Item for mending the Mullenis in the sylling xvj[d]. **1793** SMEATON *Edystone L.* Introd. 4 The lantern..was..domed over; the doming being supported upon eight stone pillars or mullions, with openings between them for the passage of the light. *a* **1878** SIR G. G. SCOTT *Lect. Archit.* (1879) I. 163 This is, in fact, the great use of the mullion, to enable you to use wider windows.

b. *attrib.* and *Comb.*: **mullion seat** (see quot.); **mullion window** = mullioned window.

1843 LYTTON *Last Bar.* II. iii, A large mullion window. **1888** C. C. HODGES *Hexham Abbey 30 note*, A reprise or reprisal in the foot of a window mullion or jamb... *Mullionseat* is the term used in some localities.

2. *Geol.* Each of a series of ribs or columns of rock (*spec.* those composed of the local rock) on a rock face, usu. formed by folding. So ***mullion structure***.

1891 E. HULL et al. *Explanatory Mem. Sheets 3-5, 9-11, 15 & 16 Maps Geol. Survey Ireland* iv. 53 To the north of Carnteena, quartzite of the yellowish-white compact variety, forms the bare rocky hills of Crocknaglogh and Croaghnacreggy and in some parts 'mullion structure' was observed—a peculiar fluting due to the shearing of the rocks. **1937** *Q. Jrnl. Geol. Soc.* XCIII. 597 The individual mullions are not always due to the presence of small folds, as is apparently true of the quartz rods of Beinn Thutaig. **1953** *Proc. Geologists' Assoc.* LXIV. 118 Distinction is drawn between mullions which look like ' clustered columns' and are composed of the local country-rock, and rodding. *Ibid.* 124 A remarkable lone mullion resulting from erosion of an abrupt double fold is found at Poll Cròm. **1963** E. S. HILLS *Elem. Struct. Geol.* x. 310 The subdivision of a bed, more particularly a sandstone inter-bedded with slate, into long parallel slabs with smooth rounded surfaces is known as mullion-structure. **1966** E. H. T. WHITTEN *Struct. Geol. Folded Rocks* ix. 313 Excellent mullions developed in these quartzites, and in the granite close to the northwestern contact zone.

mullioned ('mʌljənd), *a.* [f. prec. + -ED[2].] Having mullions; constructed with mullions.

1763 STUKELEY *Palæogr. Sacra* i. 18 The mullion'd lacework of the windows. **1815** J. SMITH *Panorama Sci. & Art* I. 128 The square pannelled mullioned windows..of the great houses of the time of queen Elizabeth. **1853** M. ARNOLD *Church of Brou* II From her mullion'd chamber casement Smiles the Duchess Marguerite.

'mullipuff. *Obs.* exc. *dial.* Forms: 7 **mully-puffe, mullipuff(e,** 8 **mollipuff,** 9 **mully-puff** (E.D.D.). [f. MULLY *a.* + PUFF *sb.*]

1. = FUZZ-BALL; hence, as a term of contempt.

1629 SHIRLEY *Wedding* IV. H 4 b, Thou mully-puffe, were it not iustice to kicke thy guts out. **1674** JOSSELYN *Voy. New Eng.* 81 Fuss-balls, Mullipuffes called by the Fishermen Wolves-farts, are to be found plentifully. **1705** DALE *Pharmacol.* Suppl. 42 *Crepitus Lupi... Lycoperdon vulgare.* .. Puff-Balls, Bull-fists, Mollipuffs.

†**2.** *Surg.* A styptic used instead of fuzz-ball.

1658 A. FOX *Würtz' Surg.* II. viii. 74 The next day..I found the lint mullipuff stick close to the wound.

mullite ('mʌlaɪt). *Min.* [f. *Mull*, the name of an island off the west coast of Scotland + -ITE[1].] A silicate of aluminium, approximately $Al_9Si_3O_{20}$, that occurs as orthorhombic crystals, is formed naturally or artificially by the action of high temperatures on other aluminium silicates, and is used for making refractory porcelains and bricks.

1924 N. L. BOWEN et al. in *Jrnl. Washington Acad. Sci.* XIV. 184 The occurrence in natural rocks necessitates a mineralogical name and for this [*sc.* the compound $3Al_2O_3.2SiO_2$] we propose the term, *mullite*, after the locality whence came the rocks in which it is here first identified, the Island of Mull. **1930** *Engineering* 26 Dec. 813/3 The successful application of refractories prepared from..synthetic mullite emphasised the effect of 'mullite' content in promoting chemical resistance. **1941** *Proc. Prehist. Soc.* VII. 64 Porcellanite..probably representing a pisolitic bauxitic clay from the inter-basaltic horizon..is composed of dark spinel and a light fine-grained aggregate of sillimanite and mullite. **1967** M. CHANDLER *Ceramics in Mod. World* i. 19 Some of these later combine with each other to form new crystalline phases, including needle-like particles of crystalline mullite. **1974** *Nature* 2 Aug. 403/1 Quartz samples..were heated in a vacuum in outgassed mullite or alumina tubes.

Hence **mulliti'zation**, conversion into mullite; **'mullitized** *ppl. a.*

1939 *Ceramic Abstr.* XVIII. 251/1 Mullite is formed rapidly during the firing of clay... The temperature of firing determines the degree of mullitization. **1948** *Jrnl. Amer. Ceramic Soc.* XXXI. 254 (*heading*) Mullitization of kaolinite. *Ibid.* 258 In more completely mullitized instances, e.g., after firing to 1300°C., groups of mullite needles in associated growth simulate hexagonal aggregations.

mullock ('mʌlək), *sb.* Forms: 4 **mulloc, -ok(e,** 6-7 **mullocke,** 7 **mullocke,** 8 **mollock,** 7- **mullock.** [f. MULL *sb.*[1] + -OCK.]

1. a. Rubbish, refuse matter. Now only *dial.*

c **1386** CHAUCER *Reeve's Prol.* 19 That ilke fruyt [*sc.* the medlar] is euer leng the wers Til it be roten in Mullok or in stree. **1555** W. WATREMAN *Fardle Facions* I. vi. F vij, The Ethiopians..gather together..a great deale of rubbeshe and mullocke..apte for firyng. **1570** LEVINS *Manip.* 158/43 Mullocke, *puluis.* **1601** HOLLAND *Pliny* II. 17 It cannot abide rank mucke, but contenteth itselfe with rotten chaffe or pugs, and such like plain mullock. **1624** *Nottingham Rec.* (1889) IV. 389 For layinge his mullocke and ashes short of the place appoynted..vj d. **1735-6** PEGGE *Kenticisms* (E.D.S.) s.v., In Glouc., mould under a faggot-stack is call'd mollock, from its wetness or dampness. **1879** MISS JACKSON *Shropsh. Word-bk.*, *Mullock*, dirt; rubbish, as of the refuse of masons' work, gardeners' sweepings, &c.

2. a. *Austral.* Rock which does not contain gold; also the refuse from which gold has been extracted.

1864 J. ROGERS *New Rush* II. 26 A man each windlass-handle working slow Raises the mullock from his mate below. **1885** MRS. C. PRAED *Head Station* 79 Here and there great heaps of earth and mullock..indicated the whereabouts of a claim. **1895** *Daily News* 19 Feb. 2/1 About 80 ft. and parallel with the main reef is a lode of reef formation divided by bands of mullock, the bands of stone varying from 10 in. to over 2 ft. wide.

b. *transf.* Applied to a person.

1890 'R. BOLDREWOOD' *Miner's Right* iv. 39 Some of the swells here..are the biggest rapscallions out, instead of setting a good example to us poor ignorant lower-class mullocks.

c. *fig.* Worthless information, nonsense. *Austral.* and *N.Z.*

1866 R. BURGESS *Autobiogr.* (typescript) 127 He said, No b....y fear. I should know it was a lot of mullock they were telling for you are not like this Jew. **1911** *Triad* XVIII. 41 We have a lot of trash and maudlin mullock in these days. **1934** *Bulletin* (Sydney) 20 June 47/1 'Cooney,' I said, 'it is madness to present such mullock to an intellectual audience.'

d. ***to poke mullock*** (***at***): to deride, ridicule, make fun of. *Austral.*

1916 C. J. DENNIS *Songs Sentimental Bloke* 126 *Mullock, to poke*—to deride, to tease. **1916** —— *Moods of Ginger Mick* 74, I own me eyes git brighter When I see 'em pokin' mullock at the everlastin' sea. **1931** V. PALMER *Separate Lives* 210 D'you think I'm going to sit in that galley with Curran and the other blokes all poking mullock at me? **1942** G. CASEY *It's Harder for Girls* 153 The chaps poked mullock at me, but it wasn't that that hurt. **1945** BAKER *Austral. Lang.* v. 94 *To poke mullock* (also *muck*) *at*, an extension of *poke borak at*, to make fun of a person. **1957** R. LAWLER *Summer of 17th Doll* 71 Oh, so that's what you got me in for, is it—to poke mullock. **1962** J. MORRISON *Twenty-Three* 86, I heard what you said when you grabbed that rope. Poking mullock at us because we won't go out over an empty hatch.

Hence **'mullocky** *a.*, of the nature of mullock. Also **'mullock** *v. trans.*, to litter (a place), to make slovenly; to do (something) in a slovenly way. Const. with *up*, *over*. (*Sc.*, *dial.*, and *Austral.*)

1862 *Otago Daily Times* 9 July 5 Whether the flat will pay to resluice at present, from its being so much worked and 'mullocked' and also rather deep, is doubtful. **1893** *Age* (Melbourne) 23 Sept. 14/4 No man could shear 321 sheep in eight hours, although I will admit he might do what we shearers call 'mullock over' that number. **1897** *Daily News* 14 Dec. 2/1 In sinking the shaft 'mullocky lode stuff' was passed through. **1945** BAKER *Austral. Lang.* 94 *To mullock over*, to work shoddily. **1965** J. S. GUNN *Terminol. Shearing Industry* II. 5 *Mullock over*, to rush the work quickly and carelessly, thus turning out badly shorn sheep.

†**'mully**, *sb. Obs. rare*[−1]. [Cf. MULLING *sb.*] A term of endearment applied to a woman.

1538 BALE *Thre Lawes* B iiij b, It is myne owne swete bullye, My muskyne and my mullye, My gelouer and my cullye.

'mully, *a. Obs.* exc. *dial.* [f. MULL *sb.*[1] + -Y.] Dusty, powdery.

1570 LEVINS *Manip.* 100/22 Mully, *puluerulentus.* **1855** *Norfolk Wds.* in *Trans. Philol. Soc.* 34 *Mully*, mouldy, powdery.

mully-grub ('mʌlɪgrʌb). *Austral.* [Var. of MULLIGRUBS *pl.*] A witchetty grub (cf. WITCHETTY), the larva of various insects, esp. goat-moths of the family Cossidæ and ghost-moths of the family Hepialidæ, which infest the stems and roots of plants. Mully-grubs are extracted and used as food by Aborigines and as bait by fishermen.

1959 J. WRIGHT *Generations of Men* 28 A gin had gone over to look for mully-grubs in the bush. **1966** *Courier-Mail* (Brisbane) 26 Nov. 8/8 The woman..had told him frequently to 'go and eat his mully grubs', and to 'go back to the bush where you came from'.

mulmull ('mʌlmʌl). Also 7-8 **mulmul,** 8 **mallemolle,** 9 **mull-mull.** [a. Hindī *malmal.*] A thin variety of muslin. Cf. MULL *sb.*[6]

1676 S. MASTER *Diary* 14 Oct. in *Hedges' Diary* (Hakl. Soc.) II. 235 Maulda..is a place where great..Varietyes of Course goods proper for Europe are made and procured, as Cossaes, Hummums, Mulmulls [etc.]. **1721** C. KING *Brit. Merch.* I. 223 Which..I value at 20*s.*, the 10 Yards, from a Long Cloth or Bast to a Mulmul or Dorea. **1862** MRS. SPEID *Last Yrs. India* iv. 86 Our ghost is clad in white. Not in specific white—mull mull or nainsook,..but in white, or whiteness the abstraction.

†**mulo'medic**, *a.* and *sb. Obs.* In 7 **-ick.** [ad. late L. *mūlomedicus*, f. *mūl-us* MULE *sb.*[1] + *medicus* physician.] (See quot.)

1678 PHILLIPS (ed. 4), *Mulomedick*, belonging to the cure of Mules; also substantively taken a *Mulomedick*, is no other then a Farrier, if a Mule-doctor may be so called.

†**mulse.** *Obs.* Also 7 **mulce.** [ad. L. *mulsum*, neut. pa. pple. of *mulcēre* to sweeten.] A liquor made of honey mixed with water or wine; hydromel, mead. Also ***mulse-water***.

1533 ELYOT *Cast. Helth* (1541) 76 b, Paulus Aegineta prayseth moche Mulse, or the water of honye. **1574** HYLL *Ord. Bees* xxix, Of the drinke of Hony which they call the Mulse-water. **1622** MALYNES *Anc. Law-Merch.* 233 Take Mulce, which is eight times so much water as hony, boyled to a quart or three pintes. **1661** LOVELL *Hist. Anim. & Min.* 263 Melicrate hath the same nature as mulse.

†**mulsed**, *a. Obs.* In 6 **mulset.** [f. L. *muls-us* (see prec.) + -ED[1].] Mingled with honey.

1547 RECORDE *Judic. Ur.* 60 The uryne of a wylde Bore with mulset vyneger is good for the fallyng evyll.

mulsh: see MULCH.

mult, multacion: see MULCT, MULCTATION.

†**'multangle.** *Geom. Obs.* [ad. mod.L. *multangulum*, neut. sing. of *multangulus*: see MULTI- and ANGLE *sb.*] A polygon.

1674 JEAKE *Arith.* (1696) 174 If 3 [angles] then called a Triangle, if 4 a Quadrangle, if more a Multangle or Polygone. **1788** T. TAYLOR *Proclus* I. 85 Multangles, and all the figures of many bases, concerning which geometry informs us.

So †**'multangled** *a.* [see ANGLED 4] = next.

1674 JEAKE *Arith.* (1696) 176 Of Triangular, Quadrangular, or Multangled Form at the Base. **1706** PHILLIPS (ed. Kersey), *Multangled* or *Multangular Figure.*

multangular (mʌl'tæŋgjʊlə(r)), *a.* (*sb.*) [ad. mod.L. *multangulāris*: see MULTI- and ANGULAR. Cf. F. *multangulaire.*] **A.** *adj.* Having many angles; many-angled; polygonal.

1679 EVELYN *Sylva* (ed. 3) xxxv. §21 Some [leaves] round; others long, Oval, Multangular, indented. **1683** *Phil. Trans.* XIII. 238 A..Multangular-Tower at York. **1751** R. PALTOCK *P. Wilkins* xxxix, Pikes—some headed with sharp-pointed stone, others with multangular stone. **1831** CARLYLE *Misc.*, *Taylor's Germ. Poetry* (1840) III. 250 Grim boughs dishevelled in multangular complexity. **1875** BLAKE *Zool.* 210 The body covered either with multangular scutes or with spines and rough scales.

B. *sb. rare.* A polygon.

1766 *Complete Farmer* 7 E 2 Regular multangulars take their names from their number of angles.

Hence **mul'tangularly** *adv.*, **mul'tangularness.**

1701 GREW *Cosmol. Sacra* I. iii. 14 Granates are Multangularly Round. **1727** BAILEY vol. II, *Multangularness*, the having many Angles.

†**mul'tangulous**, *a. Obs. rare.* [f. L. *multangul-us* (see MULTANGLE) + -OUS.] Multangular.

1659 STANLEY *Hist. Philos.* XI. ix. (1687) 765/1 He referred Sapours to Figure; the round Atoms..make a sweet Sapor; ..the Multangulous..a harsh. **1680** T. LAWSON *Mite into Treas.* 33 Obtusangulous, Acutangulous, Multangulous.

mul'tanimous, *a. rare*$^{-1}$. [f. L. *mult-us* MULTI- + *anim-us* mind + -OUS: cf. L. *multanimis* courageous.] Having a many-sided mind.

1854 LOWELL *Keats* Prose Wks. 1890 I. 231, I look upon it rather as one of the phenomena of that multanimous nature of the poet, which makes him for the moment that of which he has an intellectual perception.

multar'ticulate, *a. Zool. rare.* [See MULTI-; cf. *multi-articulate*.] Many-jointed.

1681 GREW *Musæum* I. 144 The Multarticulate Oyster with a bended Base. **1778** DA COSTA *Brit. Conchol.* 168 Those [bivalves] that have the hinge set with numerous teeth, or are multarticulate. **1822** *Trans. Geol. Soc.* Ser. II. I. 122 Its small nostrils and multarticulate paddles.

multa'titious, *a. rare*$^{-0}$. [f. L. *multātīci-us*, f. *multāt-*, *multāre* to MULCT.] (See quot.)

1656 BLOUNT *Glossogr.*, *Multatitious*, gotten by fine or forfeit.

multe, obs. form of MELT, MULCT.

multeity (mʌl'tiːɪtɪ). [f. L. *multus* many, perh. after *hæcceity*.] The quality or condition of being many (i.e. more than one); manifoldness.

1814 COLERIDGE *Princ. Genial Crit.* iii, The Philosopher of the later Platonic, or Alexandrine School, named the triangle the first-born of beauty, it being the first and simplest symbol of multëity in unity. **1817** —— *Biog. Lit.* xii. (1847) I. II. 279 The conveniency of the scholastic phrase to..express the kind with the abstraction of degree, as for instance *multeity* instead of multitude. **1881** F. Y. EDGEWORTH *Math. Psychics* 50 That continuity of fluid, that multeity of atoms which constitute the foundations of the uniformities of Physics. **1891** WESTCOTT *Ess.* 170 The central idea of the sacrament is placed in unity realised in multeity.

b. *concr.* or semi-*concr.* A thing consisting of many individual parts or members.

1836 *Fraser's Mag.* XIII. 738 A sonnet consists of fourteen lines. What magic lies within that limitary multeity! **1894** *19th Cent.* Apr. 633 *note*, [History] tells only of the conflict of opposed multeities of men with organisation of each multeity for its hostile purpose.

multen, obs. pa. pple. of MELT $v.^{1}$

† **'multeous**, *a. Obs. rare*$^{-1}$. [f. L. *multus* many + -EOUS. Cf. *multuous*.] Numerous.

1589 WARNER *Alb. Eng.* V. XXV. 112 Yet of more multeous Armies we than Scotland were at cost.

multepli, multer: see MULTIPLY, MULTURE.

multi- ('mʌltɪ), occas. before a vowel **mult-** (e.g. *multangular*, *multarticular*, *multocular*), combining form of L. *multus* much, many. The compounds having this prefix in Latin belong for the most part to non-classical times: they are chiefly of parasynthetic formation, in which *multi-* = 'many', as *multangulus* many-angled, *multicaulis* many-stalked, *multigenerus* of many kinds, but a certain number of objective or adverbial compounds also existed, in which *multi-* = 'much', as *multibibus* much-drinking, *multicupidus* desiring much, *multiscius* knowing much.

In English the compounds of *multi-* were originally either direct adaptations from Latin compounds or were modelled upon them, but in the 19th c. the prefix came into frequent general use with ppl. adjs. and sbs. (Cf. POLY-.) The earliest English borrowings from Latin were *multifary* (Lydgate), *multifarious* (Nashe, 1593), *multiformity* (Puttenham, 1589); they did not become numerous till the middle of the 17th c. The more important compounds (being chiefly those which have a continuous history from the 17th c. onwards) are entered as Main words; the present article comprises a typical selection of modern scientific terms and of compounds of a general character.

1. Forming parasynthetic adjectives, with the sense of 'many'. (From the adjs. are formed advbs. (e.g. *multiserially*) and sbs. (e.g. *multicellularity*).) **a.** In scientific and technical use: *multicelled*, *-molecular*, *-perforated*, *-stranded*; **multi-'angular** = MULTANGULAR. **multi-'areolate**, consisting of many small areas. **multi-ar'ticular**, affecting more than one joint. **multi-ar'ticulate, -ated**, having many articulations, as the legs and antennæ of insects; cf. MULTARTICULATE. **multi'axial**, having many axes or lines of growth. **multi'camerate**, of many chambers. **multi'capsular**, (of a pericarp) having many capsules. **multi-'carinate, -ated** (see quots.). **multi'cellular**, many-celled; hence **ˌmulticellu'larity**, the state or condition of being multicellular. **multi'central**, connected with or dependent upon several centres. **multi'centric**, pertaining to or having many centres or foci; (of a chromosome or chromatid) having many centromeres. **multi'ciliate, -ated**, having many cilia. **multi'capital** [cf. BICIPITAL], many-headed. **multi'coccous** [see COCCUS], having many cocci or cells. **multi'corneal**, having many corneæ. **multi'costate**, having more than one rib; palmately nerved. **multi'cuspid, -'cuspidate**, having more than two cusps. **multi'cyclic** *Geol.*, produced by or having undergone many cycles of erosion and deposition. **multi'dentate**, (*a*) having or armed with many teeth; (*b*) *Chem.* (of a ligand) having more than one point at which it can be attached to a central atom. **multiden'ticulate**, having many denticulations; having a finely-toothed margin. **multi'digitate**, having many fingers or finger-like processes. **multidi'mensional**, of more than three dimensions; hence **ˌmultidimensio'nality**, the property of being multidimensional; **multidi'mensionally** *adv.*, in a manner that involves or requires more than three dimensions. **multifac'torial**, involving or dependent on a number of factors (*spec.* genes) or causes; hence **multifac'torially** *adv.* **multifla'gellate**, having many flagella. **multi'focal**, having or pertaining to several foci, or a range of focal lengths; also as *sb. pl.*, spectacles with multifocal lenses. **multi'foliate, -'foliolate**, having many (more than 7 or 9) leaflets. **multi'ganglionate**, having many ganglia. **multige'neric**, derived from or involving more than one genus. **multi'granulate, -'granulated**, having many granules or grains. **multi'guttulate**, having many drop-like spots. **multijugate** (mʌl'tɪdʒəgət, mʌltɪ'dʒuːgət), **multi-jugous** [L. *jugum* yoke, pair], having many pairs of leaflets. **multila'ciniate**, having many laciniæ. **multila'mellar, -la'mellate, -la'mellous**, having many lamellæ. **multi'laminar, -'laminate, -ated**, having many laminæ or layers. **multi'linear**, having many lines; *Alg.*, applied by MacMahon to an operator invented by him. **multi'literal**, (of an equation) involving several unknowns. **multi-'lobar, -'lobate, 'multilobed**, having many lobes. **multi'lobular, -'lobulate, -ated**, characterized by many lobules. **multi'locular, -'loculate, -ated**, having, consisting of, or characterized by many cells or chambers. **multi'macular**, having many maculæ. **multimammate**, having several pairs of mammæ, esp. used to designate the multimammate rat or mouse, *Mastomys natalensis*, a rodent found in tropical Africa. **multi'nervose**, having many nervures. **multi'nodal, -'nodate, -'nodous**, having many nodes or knots. **multi'nuclear, -ate, -ated**, having more than one nucleus; so **multi'nucleolar, -ate, -ated** (in recent Dicts.). **multi-'ovular, -'ovulate**, containing many ovules. **multipale'aceous**, having numerous paleæ. **multi'perforate**, characterized by many perforations. **multi'pinnate**, many times pinnate. **multi'planar**, consisting of, or related to, a number of planes. **multipo'tential** *Med.*, capable of differentiating into any of several kinds of cell or tissue. **multi'radiate, -ated**, having many rays. **multira'dicular**, having many radicles. **multi'sacculate**, having many sacculi. **multi'segmentate, -'segmented**, having many segments. **multi'septate**, having many septa or partitions; divided into many chambers, as the pith of a walnut. **multi-'serial**, arranged in many series or rows; hence **multi'serially** *adv.*; so **multi'seriate.** **multi'siliquose, -'siliquous**, having or producing many seed-vessels. **multi'spectral**, operating in or involving several of the regions into which the electromagnetic spectrum is conventionally divided. **multi'spermous** [Gr. σπέρμα seed], many-seeded. **multi'spicular** = *multispiculate*. **multi'spiculate**, having many spicules. **multi'spinous**, many-spined. **multi-'spiral**, having many spiral coils or convolutions. **multi'stable**, (of a system) composed of a number of interconnected subsystems each of which can achieve stability independently of the others; so **multista'bility**, the property or state of being multistable. **multi'striate**, marked with numerous striæ or streaks. **multi-'sulcate, -ated**, many-furrowed. **multiten'taculate**, having many tentacles. **multitu'berculated**, having many tubercles. **multi'tubular**, having numerous tubes; applied *esp.* to locomotive boilers having many tubes traversing the flame space. **multi'voltine** [It. *volta* time, turn], (of a silkworm) producing several broods in a year; cf *polyvoltine*.

1842 FRANCIS *Dict. Arts*, **Multiangular*. **1874** H. C. WOOD *Fresh-w. Algæ N. Amer.* 11 Very often triangular, rarely multiangular. **1861** HAGEN *Syn. Neuroptera N. Amer.* (Smithsonian Misc. Collect. IV.) 341 *Multi-areolate. **1879** *St. George's Hosp. Rep.* IX. 232 Two previous attacks had commenced in the typically gouty fashion, but had become subsequently *multi-articular. **1819** SAMOUELLE *Entomol. Compend.* 99 Legs bifid, the last joint of the four anterior pairs..uniarticulate..; of the other pairs of legs *multiarticulate. **1870** ROLLESTON *Anim. Life* 78 The termination of the multi-articulate antennae in a filament, not in a club. **1840** *Cuvier's Anim. Kingd.* 486 A pair of legs terminated by a very long, slender, and *multiarticulated tarsus. **1864** H. SPENCER *Princ. Biol.* I. §50. 137 Of *multiaxial growth that is discontinuous, a familiar instance among plants exists in the common strawberry. **1878** BELL tr. *Gegenbaur's Comp. Anat.* 282 The elongated *multi-camerate hearts found in some Crustacea. **1731** BAILEY vol. II, **Multicapsular*, divided into many partitions, as poppies, flax, &c. **1760** J. LEE *Introd. Bot.* II. xxxiii. (1765) 158 *Reseda*, with a multicapsular Fruit. **1842** BRANDE *Dict. Sci.*, etc., **Multi-carinate*, in Conchology, is applied to a shell which is traversed by many keel-like ridges. **1840** SMART, **Multi-carinated*, having many projections. **1968** *Punch* 31 July 157/2 Some urge..has merged it [*sc.* the public] into one worldwide, *multicelled acerebral organism. **1972** *Sci. Amer.* Apr. 72/2 The globins were evolving to play several different roles during and after this period, as multicelled organisms arose. **1857** HENFREY *Bot.* §626 *Multicellular filaments. **1884** BOWER & SCOTT *De Bary's Phaner.* 95 The celebrated glands of the Hop..are multicellular peltate scales. **1916** W. TROTTER *Instincts of Herd* 18 Looked at in this way, *multicellularity presents itself as an escape from the rigour of natural selection. **1972** *Sci. Amer.* Dec. 95/1 His Mesozoa may yet provide us with valuable evidence on the evolution of multicellularity and on the mechanisms of differentiation and development. **1864** H. SPENCER *Princ. Biol.* I. §50. 137 Central development may be distinguished into *unicentral* and **multicentral*; according as the product of the original germ, develops symmetrically round one centre, or..in subordination to many centres. **1902** *Brit. Med. Jrnl.* 12 Apr. 908 Cancers either started from one centre (unicentral or monocentral) or from many centres (multicentral or plurocentral). **1934** WEBSTER, Multicentric. **1941** *Cold Spring Harbor Symp. Quant. Biol.* IX. 153 Di- and *multicentric chromosomes. **1971** *Brit. Med. Bull.* XXVII. 68/2 Multi-centric hypotheses have not proved as popular as multi-stage hypotheses, or theories which assume that a change from a normal to a malignant cell takes place in stages. **1972** *Year Bk. Dermatol.* 185 The present study examined the ultrastructural characteristics of multicentric reticulohistiocytosis. **1902** *Encycl. Brit.* XXXII. 75/2 The *multiciliate spermatozoids. **1901** *Brit. Med. Jrnl.* 12 Jan. Epitome of Current Lit. 8/3 In *multiciliated species [of Bacteria]. **1857** A. GRAY *First Less. Bot.* Gloss., **Multicipital*, many-headed. **1831** MACGILLIVRAY tr. *Richard's Elem. Bot.* 315 A fruit often raised into ridges, and separating naturally, when ripe, into as many distinct *cocca*, which open longitudinally..; whence the expressions *tricoccous*, **multicoccous*, applied to this kind of fruit. **1883** *Q. Jrnl. Microsc. Sci.* XXIII. 186 The *multi-corneal (polymeniscous) eye of Insects. **1849** BALFOUR *Man. Bot.* §144 Reticulated Venation... I. Unicostate. A single rib or costa in the middle (midrib). II. *Multicostate. More than one rib. **1881** *Linn. Soc. Jrnl.*, *Bot.* XVIII. 271 Achenia multicostate. **1848** *Quain's Anat.* (ed. 5) 971 The molar teeth, true or large molars, or *multicuspid teeth. **1870** H. A. NICHOLSON *Man. Zool.* 58 Minute spherical bodies covered with radiating and multicuspid spines. **1839–47** *Todd's Cycl. Anat.* III. 298/2 The incisors are always very small, the molars generally *multicuspidate. **1952, 1954** *Multicyclic [see MONOCYCLIC *a.* 5]. **1966** G. H. DURY *Ess. Geomorphol.* 128 The degree to which multi-cyclic bevelling is displayed varies widely. **1972** *Science* 3 Nov. 503/1 A large proportion of the grains appears to be multicyclic, having undergone several cycles of erosion and deposition. **1819** SAMOUELLE *Entomol. Compend.* 97 Rostrum descending, *multidentate above. **1959** *Nomencl. Inorg. Chem.* (I.U.P.A.C.) 64 A group containing more than one *potential* co-ordinating atom is termed a multidentate ligand. **1974** *Chem. Rev.* LXXIV. 351/1 This review deals with the synthesis of multidentate macrocyclic compounds. **1873** *Trans. Amer. Philos. Soc.* 287 (Cassell) The species of this group have the anterior tibiæ sometimes *multidenticulate. **1847–9** *Todd's Cycl. Anat.* IV. I. 727/2 In all *multi-digitate mammalia, such as the Quadrumana, Carnivora, Rodentia, and Edentata. **1884** R. A. PROCTOR in *Gentl. Mag.* Jan. 36 Systems of non-Euclidean geometry, or of *multidimensional space. **1956** E. H. HUTTEN *Lang. Mod. Physics* V. 171 The propagation of the wave must be described as taking place, in most instances, in a multi-dimensional hyper-space, and not in ordinary space. **1963** F. G. LOUNSBURY in J. A. Fishman *Readings Social. of Lang.* (1968) 49 Inflection in some languages is carried into several dimensions of variation, resulting in multidimensional paradigms running into hundreds or even thousands of forms. **1970** *Jrnl. Gen. Psychol.* LXXXII. 172 Anxiety is a vague and multidimensional concept. **1967** J. W. JOHNSTON in T. Hayashi *Olfaction & Taste II* 48 This information could be utilized to investigate the relationship between the *multidimensionality of odors and the hypothetical sensor units or sites on the receptor membrane. **1968** W. A. SCOTT in Lindzey & Aronson *Handbk. Social Psychol.* (ed. 2) II. 251 The dilemma of multidimensionality stems from the acceptance of a measurement model which equates dimension, in the geometrical sense, with psychological notions of attribute magnitude. **1970** *Computers & Humanities* IV. 210 Meylan has to be selective in what he chooses for encoding, and is unable to represent the entire 'multidimensionality' of the melody (e.g., its complete context). **1957** C. E. OSGOOD et al. in Saporta & Bastian *Psycholinguistics* (1961) 294/2 We may assume at the outset that meanings vary *multidimensionally. **1920** W. E. CASTLE *Genetics & Eugenics* (ed. 2) xxxi. 275 It would be a mistake to cover up our present ignorance concerning the inheritance of these characters by classifying them either as unifactorial or as *multifactorial. **1937** *Biol. Rev.* XII. 481 The melanism of *Oporinia dilutata* has a multi-factorial basis. **1960** H. J. EYSENCK *Handbk. Abnormal Psychol.* viii. 309/2 Most of the characteristics..are of a quantitatively variable kind, and..regulated by multifactorial and not unifactorial inheritance. **1965** J. POLLITT *Depression & its*

Treatment 96 The use of these terms is not in keeping with the view that the ætiology of depression is multifactorial. **1974** *Nature* 10 May 145/2 It can be assumed that the aetiology of cranioschisis is at least complex and multifactorial involving environmental agents as well as genetic factors. **1954** P. M. Sheppard in J. S. Huxley et al. *Evolution as Process* 212 (*heading*) The evolution of *multifactorially controlled characters. **1973** *Nature* 22 June 433/1 The word genic is extended from its regular use to include multifactorially determined disorders. **1920** T. P. Nunn *Education* 111 The *multi-focal view, to which Thorndike has now transferred his allegiance, holds that our abilities fall into a small number of groups. **1928** S. Duke-Elder *Pract. Refraction* xxiii. 344 In the multifocal lenses, introduced by Gowland of Montreal, in 1922..the reading portion of the lens has a continuous variable curve, there being a gradual accretion of power from the periphery to the reading centre. **1961** *Brit. Jrnl. Surg.* XLIX. 92/1 Low-grade, primary, multifocal osteosarcoma occurring in middle age appears to be a distinct entity. **1962** L. S. Sasieni *Princ. & Pract. Optical Dispensing* v. 125 The accurate fitting of bifocals and multifocals will be considered later. **1971** *Optometry Today* (Amer. Optometric Assoc.) 12 Special optical devices such as multi-focal lenses, contact lenses and other vision aids are used. **1856** Mayne *Expos. Lex.*, *Multifoliatus*, applied to a digitated leaf of which the common petiole terminates by more than nine folioles, as the *Lupinus varius*: *multifoliate. **1884** Bower & Scott *De Bary's Phaner.* 341 One bundle runs out into each of the leaves, which form multifoliate whorls. **1831** Macgillivray tr. *Richard's Elem. Bot.* 138 *Multi-foliolate [leaves], composed of numerous leaflets; as in *Lupinus varius*. **1877** Huxley *Anat. Inv. Anim.* vi. 263 The posterior part of the *multiganglionate cord which surrounds the gullet. **1953** *Internat. Code Nomencl. Cultivated Plants* 25 Such [hybrids] as are trigeneric or *multigeneric. **1971** J. Z. Young *Introd. Study Man* xxxii. 445 It may be that ultimately some or all the forms now called *Australopithecus* will be referred to as various species of the genus *Homo*... We prefer to keep a somewhat more conservative (multi-generic) classification. **1860** Worcester, **Multigranulate*. **1840** Smart, **Multi-granulated*. **1887** W. Phillips *Brit. Discomycetes* 322 Sporidia *multiguttulate. **1831** Macgillivray tr. *Richard's Elem. Bot.* 139 Oppositely pinnate leaves..are said to be ..*Multijugate, when the pairs of leaflets are in indeterminate number. **1828–32** Webster, **Multijugous*. **1871** W. A. Leighton *Lichen-flora* 90 *Evernia furfuracea*.. dichotomously *multi-laciniate. **1878** Bell tr. *Gegenbaur's Comp. Anat.* 398 On one spot of this [visual organ].. is placed a *multi-lamellar refractive apparatus. **1882** Vines tr. *Sachs' Bot.* 95 The multilamellar epidermis. **1846** Dana *Zooph.* (1848) 216 Cells .. infundibuliform, ..*multilamellate. **1839** *Penny Cycl.* XIV. 266/2 Animal.. containing a calcareous *polyparium*..fixed in the lower part, enlarged, flattened, excavated, and *multi-lamellous in the upper part. **1876** tr. *Wagner's Gen. Pathol.* 469 Thickening of the epithelial layer of some mucous membranes with *multilaminar pavement epithelium. **1890** *Century Dict.*, **Multilaminate*. **1877** *Q. Jrnl. Microsc. Sci.* XVII. 182 A *multilaminated coat. **1882** Ogilvie, *Multilineal*, **multilinear*, having many lines. **1886** *Proc. Lond. Math. Soc.* XVIII. 61 The Theory of a Multilinear Partial Differential Operator... By P. A. MacMahon. **1817** H. T. Colebrooke *Algebra*, etc. 227 Analysis by a *Multiliteral equation. **1895** *Funk's Stand. Dict.*, **Multilobar*. **1831** Macgillivray tr. *Richard's Elem. Bot.* 129 [Leaves are] *Multilobate; when the divisions are broader and separated by obtuse sinuses. **1896** *Allbutt's Syst. Med.* I. 81 The cells with multilobate nucleus. **1856** W. Clark *van der Hoeven's Zool.* I. 203 Rotatory organ *multilobed or parted. **1882–4** Cooke *Brit. Freshw. Algæ* I. 202 Cells..bi-, tri-, or multi-lobed. **1874** van Buren *Dis. Genit. Organs* 170 It contains *multilobular mucous glands in its substance. **1905** H. D. Rolleston *Dis. Liver* 176 Multilobular cirrhosis. **1902** *Webster's Dict.* Suppl., **Multilobulate*, *Multilobulated*, having many lobules. **1899** *Allbutt's Syst. Med.* VI. 504 Longitudinal sections show them [*viz.* miliary patches] as *multilobulated masses. **1815** W. Wood *Gen. Conchol.* p. lvii, All chambered shells are *multilocular. **1845** Lindley *Sch. Bot.* i. (ed. 14) 16 If there are more cells than one it [*sc.* the pistil] is either bilocular, trilocular, multilocular, or otherwise. **1854** Badham *Halieut.* 37 He divides and then subdivides it into partitions, almost as multilocular as a painter's box of colors. **1867** J. Hogg *Microsc.* II. ii. 376 The Polythalamia or Multilocular Rhizopods, in their earliest state are unilocular. **1890** *Century Dict.*, **Multiloculate*. **1899** *Allbutt's Syst. Med.* VI. 504 These morbid bodies.. may eventually coalesce with similar bodies..to form large *multiloculated bodies. **1859** *Todd's Cycl. Anat.* V. [134]/2 The germinal vesicle is..*multi-macular in the large-yolked ova. **1902** *Ann. & Mag. Nat. Hist.* IX. 219, I fail to find any point whatever by which *M*[*us*] *Hildegardeæ* can be distinguished externally from the Machakos member of the *multimammate group. **1955** *New Biol.* XIX. 108 House rodents such as the native multimammate mouse..and the black rat, which is replacing it, are the reservoirs [of plague in Central Africa] rather than fully rural species. **1959** *Nature* 12 Sept. 794/2 The multimammate rat is a wild rodent which lives in close contact with man in Africa. **1974** *Ibid.* 13 Sept. 101/3 Lassa virus was isolated from a single murine species, the multimammate rat *Mastomys natalensis*, which is a common commensal rodent in West Africa adapted to life both within houses and in the fields. **1944** S. Brunauer *Adsorption of Gases* I. 6 When the surface can take up only one layer of the adsorbed gas, the adsorption is called uni-molecular; when more than one layer it is called *multi-molecular. **1969** *Science* 12 Dec. 1365/3 Bacteria, viruses, or cells..often called antigens..really are multimolecular mixtures of polydeterminant antigens. **1856** W. Clark *van der Hoeven's Zool.* I. 314 *Hippobosca* Latr. —Wings parallel, incumbent, obtuse, *multinervose. **1839** Lindley *Introd. Bot.* I. ii. (ed. 3) 160 The *multinodal cyme offers no fixed rule in the spirals of its nodes. **1840** Smart, **Multinodate*, or *Multinodous* (many-knotted). **1727** Bailey vol. II, **Multinodous*, full of Knots. **1874** *Q. Jrnl. Microsc. Sci.* XIV. 97 Greef regards *Pelomyxa* as a multicellular, or, rather, *multinuclear amœboid organism. **1882** Vines tr. *Sachs' Bot.* 946 The multinuclear bast-fibres and laticiferous cells of various Phanerogams. **1877** Huxley *Anat. Inv. Anim.* xii. 659 Unicellular organisms, which occasionally become multicellular, or at any rate *multinucleate, by the multiplication of the nucleus. **1873** T. H. Green *Introd. Pathol.* (ed. 2) 211 A *Multinucleated Cell from a Grey Miliary Tubercle of the Lung in a case of Acute Tuberculosis. **1882** *Nature* XXV. 523 The sixth internodal cell might be multinuclear, with *multinucleolar nuclei. **1849** Balfour *Man. Bot.* §765 Ovary sessile, 3-lobed, 1-celled, *multiovular. **1856** Mayne *Expos. Lex.*, *Multiovulatus*, applied to the cells or compartments of the ovary when they contain a great many ovules: *multi-ovulate. **1881** *Linn. Soc. Jrnl., Bot.* XVIII. 267 Ovary linear, multiovulate. **1831** Macgillivray tr. *Richard's Elem. Bot.* 184 [The spikelet] may be..*multipaleaceous,.. as in some species of *Uniola*. **1870** Rolleston *Anim. Life* p. lxxxiv, The mouth is constituted by a *multiperforate branchial skeleton. **1928** *Funk's Stand. Dict.*, Multiperforated. **1957** *Jrnl. Brit. Interplanetary Soc.* XVI. 207 It is for such reasons as these that the more complicated multiperforated charge..has been developed, which can have small propellent thickness between the perforations without reducing the loading density, and which has little unused propellent at the end of burning. **1875** Bennett & Dyer tr. *Sachs' Bot.* 195 Whole systems of shoots frequently have the appearance of *multi-pinnate leaves. **1850** Cayley *Math. Papers* (1889) I. 505 The developable which is the envelope of such a system [of *n* different planes] may be termed a '*multiplanar developable'. **1913** O. C. Gruner *Biol. Blood-Cells* iv. 191 At certain times the wandering cell becomes stationary... In place of migration..it settles down as an essentially *multi-potential or indifferent cell. **1939** Dible & Davie *Path.* viii. 152 If the germinal cells for a tumour be split off at this stage, only those tissues can be represented in the growth which are proper to the layer from which these cells have come. Such cells are multipotential but not totipotential. **1966** *Cancer* XIX. 1/1 We have designated these types of tumors as primitive multipotential primary sarcomas of bone:..'multipotential' because each shows differentiation along multiple lines (i.e. bone, cartilage, blood vessels, etc.). **1973** *Nature* 2 Mar. 20/2 The finding of multipotential haemopoietic stem cells (that is, cells capable of becoming any of the mature blood cell types, lymphoid or myeloid) in early mouse embryonic thymus. **1846** Dana *Zooph.* vii. (1848) 113 Cells *multiradiate. **1878** Bell tr. *Gegenbaur's Comp. Anat.* 105 The acicular structures, which are combined together in various ways to form multiradiate stars. **1840** Smart, **Multiradiated*. **1819** Lindley tr. *Richard's Obs. Fruits & Seeds* 48 Some.. botanists..have regarded such tubercles as so many radicles, and have attributed to these genera a *multiradicular embryo. **1878** Bell tr. *Gegenbaur's Comp. Anat.* 272 [In the Hemiptera] the fore-gut, which is frequently *multisacculate. **1870** H. A. Nicholson *Man. Zool.* 289 The..*multisegmentate 'cirri' of the adult [Cirripede]. **1881** *Athenæum* 18 June 818/1 A central *multisegmented axis. **1857** M. J. Berkeley *Cryptog. Bot.* §199 The filiform *multiseptate antheridia. **1838** G. Johnston *Brit. Zoophytes* 287 *Flustra Murrayana*, cells *multiserial, ovate. **1872** H. A. Nicholson *Palæont.* 325 In the Pycnodonts the teeth are multiserial. **1870** Rolleston *Anim. Life* 71 The cells..are arranged *multiserially in parallel longitudinal rows. **1870** Hooker *Stud. Flora* 187 Arctium..Pappus-hairs *multi-seriate. **1933** *Tropical Woods* XXXVI. 10 Heterogeneous Ray.—A xylem ray composed of cells of different morphological types. (Typically, with the cells of the multiseriate part radially elongated.) **1965** K. Esau *Plant Anat.* (ed. 2) vi. 138 A ray may be one cell wide and one cell high in the beginning; later, the initial divides or more initials are added to the first. The ray thus increases in height and may increase in width if multiseriate rays are characteristic of the plant. *Ibid.* xvii. 485 A well-known example of a multiseriate epidermis is the velamen of air roots of tropical Orchidaceae. **1686** *Phil. Trans.* XVI. 287 The *Multisiliquose or corniculated Herbs, which after each Flower bear many Pods or horned Seed Vessels. **1706** Phillips (ed. Kersey) s.v. *Corniculate Plants*, They are also termed *Multisiliquous. **1966** *Proc. 4th Symposium Remote Sensing Environment* (Univ. Mich., U.S. Govt. AD 638-919) 135 Much additional information is needed before *multispectral photography and other remote sensors can be..incorporated into operational urban information centers. **1971** *New Scientist* 27 Apr. 256/2 Placing the Earth under the most detailed observation with multispectral cameras. **1973** L. F. Curtis in Cruise & Newman *Photogr. Techniques Sci. Res.* ii. 101 Photographic analysis of the data obtained in multispectral studies may include colour enhancement techniques which aim to emphasize the tonal differences between objects. **1887** Bentley *Man. Bot.* (ed. 5) 334 The fruit or pericarp is ..*multi-spermous. **1902** *Proc. Zool. Soc.* 210 In one of the two specimens [of sponges] in the collection..there are a few *multispicular strands in the otherwise very regular unispicular meshwork. **1900** *Proc. Zool. Soc.* 139 The meshes of the reticulum are *multispiculate. **1852** Dana *Crust.* I. 538 Carapax *multispinous. **1839** Sowerby *Conch. Man.* 66 **Multispiral*, applied to a shell when the spire consists of numerous whorls; or to an operculum of numerous volutions. **1899** *Fortn. Rev.* LXV. 122 Arrangements of multi-spiral springs [etc.]. **1952** W. R. Ashby *Design for Brain* xvii. 182 S. 9/4 showed the necessity for ultrastability; is the hypothesis of *multistability equally necessary? **1962** A. Battersby *Guide to Stock Control* vii. 65 The effect of this sort of control by interconnected systems is called 'multi-stability' by cyberneticians. **1952** W. R. Ashby *Design for Brain* xvi. 171 To study the interactions of these two properties we might start by examining the properties of an ultrastable system whose main variables are all part-functions. But it has been found simpler to start by considering a system defined thus: a *multistable system consists of many ultrastable systems joined main variable to main variable, all the main variables being part-functions. *Ibid.* xvii. 179 The concept of the 'multistable' system clearly refers primarily to the nervous system. **1966** J. Singh *Gt. Ideas Information Theory, Lang. & Cybernetics* (1967) xiv. 221 Every animal is thus built up of a number of ultrastable subsystems organized with the possibility of dispersion of behavior. Such a multistable system can therefore adapt its behavior to settle in a stable resting state in a much shorter time than a single ultrastable system of the kind considered earlier. **1961** *Nature* 11 Mar. 833/1 *Multi-stranded deoxyribonucleic acid as determined by X-irradiation. **1970** *New Scientist* 17 Dec. 496/2 The antitumour effects of multistranded RNA which have been reported recently. **1842** Brande *Dict. Sci.*, etc., **Multi-striate*. **1856** Mayne *Expos. Lex.*, *Multisulcatus*..*multi-sulcate. **1840** Smart, **Multisulcated*. **1846** Dana *Zooph.* (1848) 698 Polyps *multitentaculate. **1883** W. H. Flower in *Encycl. Brit.* XV. 376/1 Two small molars with low *multituberculated crowns. **1862** Smiles *Engineers* III. 100 Without the steam-blast..the advantages of the *multitubular boiler (afterwards invented) could never have been fairly tested. **1874** J. Geoghegan *Silk in India* 28 In 1866 experiments were tried..with so-called Japan bivoltine and *multivoltine seed. **1883** G. Watt *Econ. Prod. India* III. 66 The multi-voltine worms are confined chiefly to Bengal, where they produce three chief crops.

b. In general use (mostly nonce-words): as ***multi-authored***, ***-barrelled***, ***-bladed***, ***-branched***, ***-centred***, ***-componential***, ***-consonantal***, ***-cored***, ***-directional***, ***-engined***, ***-ethnic***, ***-faced***, ***-faceted***, ***-geminal***, ***-generational***, ***-holed***, ***-hued***, ***-manned***, ***-marbled***, ***-pointed***, ***-sectional***, ***-sectioned***, ***-secular***, ***-segmental***, ***-spired***, ***-syllabic***, ***-threaded***, ***-toned***, ***-tribal***, ***-valued***, ***-volumed***; occas. with advb. force, as ***multi-ramified***. **multi'fistular** [L. *fistula*], consisting of many pipes. **multi'fluvian** [L. *fluvius*], having many rivers flowing into it. **multi'furcate**, forked in many directions. **multi'medial**, coming through many media. **multi'monstrous**, consisting of many monstrosities. **multi'personal**, comprising several personalities. **'multiplaned**, having or occupying several planes (cf. MULTIPLANE *sb.* and *a.*). **multi'sensual**, of many meanings. **multi'taped**, recorded from several (magnetic) tapes played simultaneously. **multi'titular**, having many titles.

1964 K. Winetrout in I. L. Horowitz *New Sociol.* 159 *The Lonely Crowd* is *multi-authored and *Faces in the Crowd* a research team product. **1974** *Nature* 22 Feb. 581/1 It suffers from the usual disadvantage of a multi-authored book in which no editorial attempt has been made to avoid redundancies and overlap. **1944** *Horizon* Oct. 225 'Moaning Minnies' (*multi-barrelled mortars). **1897** Mary Kingsley *W. Africa* 455 The *multi-bladed, real throwing knives of some middle Congo tribes. **1862** *Temple Bar* VI. 266 The lofty and *multi-branched genealogical tree. **1957** K. A. Wittfogel *Oriental Despotism* iii. 50 In contrast to the controlled state of *multicentered societies, the state of the single-centered hydraulic society was a veritable apparatus state. **1973** *Sci. Amer.* Apr. 90/2 Bruno's belief in a centerless or multicentered universe was derived from.. Nicholas of Cusa. **1971** *Archivum Linguisticum* II. 59 Cf. [*make up*] (*sc.* with cosmetics or greasepaint) (verb) and [*make-up*] (noun),..examples whose *multi-componential character as idioms is partly revealed by the difference of tonicity or accentuation corresponding to the grammatical distinction indicated. **1974** *Nature* 7 June 571/2 The survival curve of HVS is multicomponential after treatment with heat as well as after treatment with formaldehyde. **1948** D. Diringer *Alphabet* ii. 63 They did not employ it [*sc.* the alphabet] when they could use word-signs or *multi-consonantal phonograms. **1965** *Language* XLI. 346 Such multiconsonantal clusters as /mb/ and /ngb/ are merely graphic and represent consonants that are phonemically unitary. **1974** D. Kyle *Raft of Swords* ii. 14 Loop after loop of insulated *multi cored copper wire. **1942** *Illuminating Engin. Nomencl. & Photometric Stand.* (Illuminating Engin. Soc. U.S.) (ASA Z7.1-1942) 27 *Multidirectional illumination on a surface is that produced by several separated light sources of relatively small area. It is characterized by the fact that a small opaque object placed near the illuminated surface casts several shadows. **1964** *Discovery* Oct. 6/2 Control of a vast and complex multi-directional communications network. **1972** *Geo Abstr.* C. 368 (*heading*) Problems of multi-directional development of automobile transport. **1917** *Jrnl. R. Aeronaut. Soc.* XXI. 320 In the case of most single-engined aeroplanes or seaplanes a fuselage of circular cross-section is admirable... This is not so, however, in the case of *multi-engined aircraft, in which the power plant units are placed away from the body of the machine. **1931** C. Day Lewis *From Feathers to Iron* 14 Bodies we have, fabric and frame designed To take the stress of love, Buoyant on gust, multi-engined. **1967** *Jane's Surface Skimmer Systems 1967–68* 121/2 A drive pad at the rear of the primary box enables the engines of a multi-engined aircraft to be coupled together by spanwise shafting. **1967** 'Malcolm X' in A. Chapman *New Black Voices* (1972) We Afro-Americans..are not opposed to *multi-ethnic associations in any walk of life. **1969** *Alberta Hist. Rev.* Autumn 10/2 Both were born in remote wilderness conditions and embraced multi-ethnic populations. **1821** Southey *Vis. Judgem.* v. 70 Caitiffs, are ye dumb? cried the *multifaced Demon in anger. **1885** E. Dannreuther in Grove *Dict. Mus.* IV. 366 This is the central question, the multifaced problem he set himself to solve. **1870** Rolleston *Anim. Life* p. cxi, The larger *multifacetted eyes. **1892** *Pictorial World* 2 Jan. 311/1 The multi-faceted mind of the German Aristophanes. **1965** H. I. Ansoff *Corporate Strategy* (1968) i. 15 The nature of decisions is multifaceted and continually variable. **1971** *Computers & Humanities* VI. 38 Paralleling this trend toward the multifaceted department articulating with almost all the traditional disciplines is the emergence of the divisional course. **1728** North *Mem. Music* (1846) 51 The organon hydraulicon distinguisht the *multifistular engine. **1807** J. Barlow *Columb.* I. 514 Thy capes, Virginia,..guard secure thy *multifluvian Bay. **1816** Bentham *Chrestom.* Wks. 1843 VIII. 95 Why *bifurcate* rather than **multifurcate*? **1922** Joyce *Ulysses* 404 Recorded instances of *multigeminal..births. **1965** *New Society* 1 Apr. 25/2 Subjects from *multi-generational households have better scores. **1972** P. Laslett *Household & Family in Past Time* 7 A high proportion of multigenerational extended families among the remaining Dutch peasantry in the 1950s. **1953** *Lancet* 12 Sept. 540/1 A *multi-holed catheter had been passed. **1963** A. J. Hall *Textile Sci.* ii. 47 It is pumped at a uniform rate through multi-holed spinnerets into the coagulating bath. **1804** Fessenden *Orig. Poems* (1806) 17 The flame cinctur'd, *multihu'd arch in the sky. **1927** *Daily Express* 13 July 5/2 The hidden wiring of the multi-hued electric lights. **1971** *Sci. Amer.* Oct. 43/1 (Advt.),

'Philippine Birds' contains 569 illustrations.. portraying the multi-hued birds. **1973** *Islander* (Victoria, B.C.) 1 July 2/1 Multihued confetti of clouds drifted across the sky. **1961** *Life* 3 Mar. 33/1 The Russians will follow their manned orbiter.. with a *multimanned moon orbiter.. and space station. **1967** *Observer* 5 Nov. 4/5 A multi-manned expedition around the moon and back to earth. **1902** HARDY *Poems of Past & Present* 40 *Multimarbled Genova the Proud. **1802–12** BENTHAM *Ration. Judic. Evid.* (1827) III. 438 For species.. of *multimedial evidence, we have simple (composed either of multi-personal alone.. or of transcriptural alone), and complex. **1647** WARD *Simp. Cobl.* 21 Such a *multi-monstrous maufrey of heteroclytes and quicquidlibets. **1802–12** *Multipersonal [see *multimedial*]. **1899** C. F. D'ARCY *Ideal. & Theol.* iv. 153 Christianity teaches us to think of God as multipersonal unity. **1909** *Westm. Gaz.* 23 Mar. 4/2 The *multi-planed helicopter has been abandoned for the biplane. **1959** M. T. WILLIAMS *Art of Jazz* (1960) xii. 110 The nation's misery was mirrored in every facet of its multi-planed existence. **1902** R. W. CHAMBERS *Maids of Paradise* vi. 104 He was engaged in constructing a *multi-pointed paper star. **1816** T. L. PEACOCK *Headlong Hall* i, Any of the last-named *multiramified families. **1961** Y. OLSSON *On Syntax Eng. Verb* ii. 33 A classification can be made of the sentences of the language..: I. *multi-sectional (consisting of two or more Sections). **1964** *Gloss. Letterpress Rotary Printing Terms* (*B.S.I.*) 22 *Multi-sectioned newspapers or magazines. **1922** JOYCE *Ulysses* 655 The *multisecular stability of its primeval basin. **1901** C. P. STEINMETZ *Theoret. Elem. Electr. Engin.* 122 A closed coil armature, connected with a *multisegmental commutator. **1955** *Trans. Philol. Soc. 1954* 68 We may.. classify phonemic features by reference to the *types* of unit, of which they are constituents ..; in this way we may establish a broad distinction between (*a*) 'uni-segmental' features, i.e. such as combine within single phonemes, and (*b*) 'multi-segmental' features, i.e. such as can only be extracted from more complex units (syllables, morphemes, words, constructions, or sentences). **1811–31** BENTHAM *Logic* Wks. 1843 VIII. 249 *Multisensual, by reason of analogy. **1884** *Punch* 20 Sept. 141 Vast, *multi-spired, thick-roof'd.. is London. **1909** *Cent. Dict.* Suppl., *Multisyllabic. **1953** N. TINBERGEN *Herring Gull's World* ii. 10 The most elaborate call of the Herring Gull's repertoire is the multisyllabic call. **1972** F. KNEBEL *Dark Horse* (1973) xix. 294 He had long ago passed the point where he sought to impress bewildered laymen by scattering multisyllabic medical terms about. **1955** L. FEATHER *Encycl. Jazz* vii. 245 The unique tonal effects obtained from these *multi-taped, multi-speed novelties sold many millions of Capitol records. **1962** *John o' London's* 16 Aug. 162/4 Not all the tracks are multi-taped. **1844** *Civil Eng. & Arch. Jrnl.* VII. 236/1 '*Multi-threaded'.. screws. **1864** WEBSTER, **Multi-titular*. **1843** LYTTON *Last Bar.* II. i, Blended with these *multitoned discords. **1949** I. DEUTSCHER *Stalin* iii. 69 The *multi-tribal cities of the Caucasus. **1934** *Mind* XLIII. 200 Whatever is a proposition of the two-valued logic is recognized as a proposition within the *multi-valued 'logic' and *vice versa*. **1965** N. CHOMSKY *Aspects of Theory of Syntax* iv. 171 Regarding each of the dimensions of the system of paradigms as a multivalued feature, [etc.]. **1963** *Times Lit. Suppl.* 10 May 348/4 *Multi-volumed books.

2. Prefixed to a sb. either with adjectival sense = 'multiple, manifold', or with adverbial sense = 'in many ways or directions'. **,multibillio'naire**, one who is worth many billions of money. **,multicolline'arity** *Statistics*, the existence of a perfect linear correlation between a set of variables when the regression of some dependent variable on them is being investigated. **'multicycle**, (*a*) a cycle having more than three wheels; (*b*) a cycle for two or more riders. **multifœ'tation**, pregnancy with (*a*) more than one fœtus, or (*b*) more than two fœtuses. **multilo'cation**, location in many places at the same time. **,multimillio'naire**, one who is worth many millions of money. **multi-'negative** *Printing*, an array of many similar images in negative form used in the printing of small items several at a time by photolithography; similarly **multi-'positive**. **† multiro'tation** *Chem.* [a. G. *multirotation* (Parcus & Tollens 1890, in *Ann. d. Chem.* CCLVII. 161)] = MUTAROTATION. **multi'specialist**, a specialist in many subjects. **'multisyllable**, a polysyllable. **† multi'theism**, polytheism.

1906 'MARK TWAIN' in *North Amer. Rev.* Sept. 322 There would not be any *multi-billionaire alive, perhaps, who would be able to buy a full set. **1934** R. FRISCH *Statistical Confluence Analysis* xi. 75 There exist two or more independent linear relations between the systematic parts of these variates, but.. we are not aware of this *multicollinearity. **1972** T. H. & R. J. WONNACOTT *Introd. Statistics for Business & Econ.* xiii. 296 Suppose demand for a group of goods is being related to prices and income, with the overall price index being the first independent variable. Suppose aggregate income measured in money terms is the second independent variable. If this is real income multiplied by the same price index, the problem of multicollinearity may become a serious one. The solution is to use real income, rather than money income, as the second independent variable. **1887** *Longman's Mag.* July 271 Composite or *multi-cycles, carrying two or more passengers. **1898** *Field* 6 Aug. 275 This record stood until the 27th ult., when H. W. Payne, assisted by two multicycles as pacemakers, reduced this time to 1 min. 39⅗ sec. **1857** DUNGLISON *Dict. Med.*, **Multi-fœtation*. **1891** *Syd. Soc. Lex.* **1865** PUSEY *Truth Eng. Ch.* 169 A *multilocation (i.e. a contemporaneous presence in different portions of space) of Mary, according to her flesh. **1893** *Month* Apr. 483 The multi-location of one substance in separate parts of space. **1858** O. W. HOLMES *Aut. Breakf.-t.* x. (1895) 250 The *multi-millionaires sent him a trifle, it was said, to buy another eye with. **1921** Multi-millionaire [see CORONA[2]]. **1972** F. KNEBEL *Dark Horse* (1973) ix. 120 You got multi-millionaires who don't pay more than two or three per cent of their income in taxes. **1933** N. MONTAGUE in W. Atkins *Art & Pract. Printing* III. xii. 95 *Multi-negatives have become an economic necessity in the case of printing by photo-lithography such things as stamps, coupons, playing cards, and small labels. **1933** N. MONTAGUE in W. Atkins *Art & Pract. Printing* III. xii. 96 The 'H.L.' step and repeat projecting machine.. is designed for the production of multi-negatives or positives. **1967** E. CHAMBERS *Photolitho-Offset* vi. 70 The automatic operation can be commenced at any part of the layout and an exposure made to any position on the multi-negative. **1971** D. POTTER *Brit. Eliz. Stamps* ii. 23 In the first stages of printing a *multipositive is prepared, from which the printing cylinders are made. **1904** J. WELLS *J. H. Wilson* xiv. 118 Dr. Wilson might fairly be called a *multi-specialist. **1890** *Jrnl. Chem. Soc.* LVIII. 1084 The authors propose to employ the term '*multi-rotation' to denote the change.. of rotatory power which takes place in a sugar solution, from immediately after its preparation in the cold until constant rotation is attained. **1904** J. W. MELLOR *Chem. Statics & Dynamics* 224 The influence of acids upon the rate of multirotation of sugars. **1935** TIPSON & STILLER in Harrow & Sherwin *Textbk. Biochem.* ii. 43 In the course of time other sugars were examined, and it was found that the rotation is not necessarily halved, so the phenomenon was named multirotation. **1659** [O. WALKER] *Instr. Art Oratory* 38 A *multisyllable better answers a monosyllable precedent, than a monosyllable a multisyllable. **1719** DE FOE *Crusoe* II. (Globe) 585 For.. Idolatry, and *Multitheism no People in the World ever went beyond them.

3. Prefixed to a sb. forming a compound used attrib. with the force of a parasynthetic adj.; e.g. ***multicharge***, (of a cannon) capable of containing several charges; ***multicoil***, consisting of many coils. (Compounds of this type are occas. used predicatively, as in quot. 1947 for *multifactor* and quot. 1970 for *multifont*.) Typical examples include: ***multiaperture***, ***-author***, ***-band***, ***-bed***, ***-billion***, ***-blade***, ***-car***, ***-centre***, ***-class***, ***-component***, ***-cycle*** (cf. *multicyclic* in 1 a), ***-cylinder***, ***-day***, ***-element***, ***-engine***, ***-family***, ***-floor***, ***-image***, ***-jet***, ***-lane***, ***-lens***, ***-man***, ***-megaton***, ***-microphone***, ***-million***, ***-part***, ***-pin***, ***-plate***, ***-reel***, ***-role***, ***-row***, ***-screen***, ***-seat***, ***-step***, ***-syllable***, ***-track***, ***-tube***, ***-vane***, ***-vitamin***, ***-volume***, ***-way***, ***-word***. Also **multi-'access**, pertaining to, involving, or being a computer that may be used simultaneously by independent operators at a number of terminals; **multi'channel**, employing or possessing many communication or television channels (CHANNEL *sb.*[1] 9 d); also = *multi-track* above; **multi'circuit**, supplying or containing many electric circuits; **'multicore**, having many cores; applied *spec.* to an electric cable (cf. CORE *sb.*[1] 12); **multi-e'lectrode**, possessing or involving several electrodes; applied *spec.* to a valve in which there are two or more sets of electrodes, associated with separate electron beams, within a single envelope; **multi'factor** = *multifactorial* in 1 a; **multi'faculty**, (of an institution of higher education) possessing several faculties; **multi'filament**, containing or composed of several filaments; applied *spec.* to a yarn made up of many fine threads; also *absol.*, a multifilament yarn; **'multiflash**, (*a*) *Photogr.* made with two or more flash-bulbs operated simultaneously; (*b*) applied to a process or apparatus for desalinating sea-water in several stages in which water is 'flashed', i.e. converted suddenly into steam, at successively lower pressures; **'multifont**, pertaining to or possessing the ability (of a machine) to read characters of several different 'fonts' (founts) or designs; **'multifuel**, capable of running on more than one kind of fuel; **'multigerm** *Agric.*, (of a sugar-beet variety or seed produced by it) having or consisting of more than one seed in each seed ball (cf. *monogerm* adj. s.v. MONO- 1); **'multigrade** (see quot. 1972); **'multipath** *Telecommunications*, involving (the receipt of) radio signals that have travelled from a single source by several paths; **'multipoint**, having or serving many points; applied *spec.* to a water-heater serving a number of hot-water taps; **'multistart** *Engin.* (see quot. 1940); **'multiwall**, having many walls; applied *spec.* to a sack or large bag made of several layers of strong paper that are usu. attached to one another along the bottom and the side folds.

1966 *Guardian* 4 May 20/3 By the end of the seventies in Britain there will be more than 300,000 people interested in *multi-access computers. **1967** *Economist* 4 Mar. 850/3 This will mean hierarchies of powerful and less powerful multi-access computers linked throughout the country with hundreds of terminals and consoles connected to them from commerce, industry and research establishments. **1968** *Times* 1 Nov. 23/5 Multi-access computing needs data-links between users and computers. **1971** R. A. WISBEY *Computer in Lit. & Ling. Res.* 191 The Atlas multi-access system makes it possible to create and manipulate files of information from remote consoles and to use these files for the initiation of jobs on the Atlas computer. **1966** *Electronics* 14 Nov. 25 Honeywell spokesmen will not disclose details of the new design, beyond saying that it used conventional ferrite cores with one hole, not *multiaperture cores. **1968** *New Scientist* 15 Feb. 360/2 The elements, called MADs (multiaperture devices), are specially shaped ferrite discs.. which act as very fast switches. **1973** *Nature* 9 Feb. 412/1 As is inevitable in any such *multi-author work, the individual chapters vary considerably in scope. **1969** *Sci. Jrnl.* June 64 Vertical aerial view of part of the Carrizo Plains, California, at near right was taken using ordinary Ektachrome film and reveals little trace of the phenomena rendered starkly visible in the enhanced *multiband photograph at far right. **1971** *Flying* Apr. 90/1 About our portable multi-band radio. **1964** G. L. COHEN *What's Wrong with Hospitals?* i. 24 To the archetypal American patient of the medical magazines, there is no disgrace in entering a '*multi-bed ward'. **1963** *Observer* 31 Mar. 27/3 A background of *multi-billion defence spending. **1971** *New Scientist* 28 Jan. 184 What would be the practical and scientific benefits of a multibillion dollar space station? **1910** *Westm. Gaz.* 24 Mar. 5/2 This is the Pitter *multi-blade propellor, which.. is claimed to give an enormous thrust at low speeds. **1960** *Farmer & Stockbreeder* 1 Mar. 70 The multi-blade fan located in front of the engine has an output of up to 40,000 cu ft per min. **1962** *Economist* 11 Aug. 526/1 The proportion of *multi-car families is continuing to rise. **1965** PHILLIPS & WILLIAMS *Inorg. Chem.* I. xi. 403 Metals and metal-like hydrides are similarly electron-deficient... The electrons are thought to be in molecular orbitals embracing all the atoms in the structure, i.e. *multi-centre rather than two-centre orbitals. **1930** *Engineering* 31 Oct. 541/2 It is still the only *multi-channel radio-telephone service in the world. **1955** *Ann. Reg. 1954* 402 There were on exhibition at the radio show.. many television receivers designed for two-band or multi-channel reception. **1962** *Science Survey* III. 315 Indeed one can conceive of such a system in which a multi-channel magnetic tape carries the programme of the plant. **1966** *Punch* 20 July 101/2 The United States, where of course there's multi-channel TV operating more or less round the clock. **1883** *Standard* 21 Sept. 5/3 Haskell's accelerating *multi-charge cannon. *a* **1894** C. G. ROSSETTI *Divers Worlds, The Earth shall tremble* iii, The *multichord Thrilled harp of heaven. **1909** *Cent. Dict.* Suppl., **Multicircuit*, having a multiple circuit... *Multicircuit generator*, an electric generator, as for the supplying of arc-lights, which is connected with and feeds several parallel circuits. **1969** *Jane's Freight Containers 1968–69* 536/2 An a.c. drive motor with single and multi-circuit generators built as one unit. **1970** *Sci. Amer.* Feb. 28/2 One obstacle.. was that a multicircuit chip would have to incorporate logic gates of several different types and all would have to function perfectly. **1961** *Guardian* 16 June 6/5 The rise of the anonymous, *multi-class mass audience. **1877** *Elem. Lect. Electricity* 19 *Multi-coil Galvanometer. This is a galvanometer with three distinct coils of wire. **1934** WEBSTER, Multicomponent. **1966** D. G. BRANDON *Mod. Techniques Metallogr.* iii. 125 Identifying the elements in a *multicomponent sample. **1971** C. PLACEK (*title*) Multi-component fibers. **1908** *Westm. Gaz.* 6 Feb. 4/2 The high-tension wires are moulded in one, forming a *multicore cable. **1957** *Railway Mag.* Nov. 760/2 A prototype length of special 'thin'-type multi-core cable was used for certain indication circuits. **1961** *New Left Rev.* Jan.–Feb. 8/1 A multi-core city is gradually taking shape. **1903** *Public Opinion* 8 Oct. 471/1 The *multi-course dinner. **1916** C. A. COTTON in *Geogr. Rev.* I. 39 The diagrams.. represent stages in the growth of a composite (i.e., two-cycle or *multi-cycle) delta. **1918** —— in *Ibid.* VI. 320 In a previously published article the writer called attention to the occurrence of multicycle fault coasts. **1962** *Gloss. Terms Automatic Data Processing* (*B.S.I.*) 91 *Multi-cycle feeding*, a method of processing punched cards in which several fields of a single card are read sequentially on successive machine cycles... The principal use is as a card-saving stratagem when printing names and addresses. **1966** J. C. PUGH in G. H. Dury *Ess. Geomorphol.* 127 Multi-cycle bornhardts can also be found in the form of dome-on-dome residuals. **1884** KNIGHT *Dict. Mech.* Suppl., **Multi-cylinder Engine*, a steam engine with a plurality of cylinders. **1904** *Sci. Abstr.* VII. 1080 (*heading*) Multi-cylinder motors. **1909** *Westm. Gaz.* 10 June 4/2 Of the twenty-five pretty little machines which will career round the twenty-three-mile circuit.., no fewer than seventeen are fitted with four-cylinder engines, which shows.. the progress that has been made in the multi-cylinder car. **1969** *Jane's Freight Containers 1968–69* 495/3 Insulated flexi-van multi-cylinder high pressure gas holder. **1973** *Nature* 23 Mar. 217/1 By use [in their motor cycles] of multi-cylinder engines, overhead camshafts and such devices as electric starting motors, they have been able to sell products which are in many ways superior to those of British manufacturers. **1971** *Canad. Antiques Collector* May 10/1 These field studies extend up to a week with the *multi-day visitors accommodated economically in camps, lodges, schools and private homes. **1973** C. BONINGTON *Next Horizon* v. 85 He was not interested in the multi-day epic, or the highly technical rock-climb. **1926** *Wireless World* 26 May 722/1 (*heading*) The *multi-electrode valve. **1963** Multi-electrode [see DEKATRON]. **1965** *Math. in Biol. & Med.* (Med. Res. Council) IV. 139 Is it possible to recognize automatically particular waveforms in a single channel of a multi-electrode recording [of an electro-encephalogram]? **1961** Y. OLSSON *On Syntax Eng. Verb* iv. 85 The 'genitive' is a *multi-element term for PRE. **1970** *New Scientist* 24 Dec. 554/2 The Marconi Company.. developed a high-gain multi-element vhf aerial. **1934** WEBSTER, Multiengine. **1961** *Economist* 25 Nov. 830/2 Rolls-Royce immediately started hawking its competing *multi-engine system round the international market. **1934** R. FRISCH *Statistical Confluence Analysis* vii. 49 We get the special hypotheses regarding the correlation co-efficients on which Spearman's two factor and Thurstone's *multifactor theory are built. **1947** F. A. E. CREW *Genetics Rel. Clin. Med.* v. 84 There is the possibility that certain abnormal characterisations are themselves multifactor in nature. **1966** A. BATTERSBY *Math. in Managem.* iii. 68 The bonus is to be paid at the rate of one shilling for each ton of production in excess of 160... The manager.. undertakes [in addition] to apply a penalty of 10 shillings for a fall of 1 point in the yield, and a corresponding bonus for an increase. Such a scheme is called a 'multi-factor incentive'. **1961** *Technology* Feb. 36/4 The C.A.T.s.. should become *multi-faculty institutions with the proportion of science and social studies increased. **1968** *Economist* 13 Apr. 42/1 The schools are to be reduced by amalgamation from twelve to six, and each is to be closely associated with a multi-faculty institution of the University of London. **1965** G. McInnes *Road to Gundagai* xiv. 249 The enormous *multi-family picnics that took place. **1972** *Real Estate Rev.* Winter 73/2 The Federal Housing Administration then began requiring its field offices to report on the number of minorities occupying federally assisted multifamily housing. **1937** W. Watson *Textile Design & Colour* (ed. 4) 437 The diameter of each orifice is about 0·1 mm. for ordinary yarns, and may be as small as 0·06 mm. for fine denier *multi-filament yarns. **1940** *Chambers's Techn. Dict.* 562/2 *Multi-filament lamp*, an electric filament lamp having more than one filament in the same bulb, so that failure of one filament will not cause the lamp to be extinguished. **1944** *Textile Manufacturer* July 306/1 We made 150/150 yarn of that type but the multifilaments could not compensate for the inherent harsh character of hosiery made from it. **1968** E. Miller *Textiles* 70 Multifilament yarns give more flexibility and cover, the finer and more numerous the filaments are in the yarn the better it is in this respect. **1945** Webster Add., *Multiflash. **1956** *Nature* 21 Jan. 109/2 (*caption*) Multiflash photographs ..of a typical water-entry trajectory. **1964** *Listener* 21 May 835/1 The new 'multi-flash' distillation process was first realized in this country, and more than two-thirds of all the installations in the world are British. **1971** *Chem. Abstr.* 17 May 195/2 Multiflash evapn. for concg. solns., and producing fresh water. **1938** *Archit. Rev.* LXXXIII. 118/2 A *multifloor scheme was devised which, besides allowing high economy of site area, gave other advantages of even greater moment. **1960** *News Chron.* 7 Oct. 8/5 Multi-floor garages. **1838** *Civil Eng. & Arch. Jrnl.* I. 121/1 the *multiflue boiler of Mr. Booth. **1961** *Proc. IRE* XLIX. 185/2 Extensions of the notions described will result in improved *multifont recognition and in gains toward the isolation of the character separation problem. **1969** *Computers & Humanities* IV. 83 Of all devices for speeding the preparation of text for machines, none has been awaited ..with more confidence than some sort of fast, multifont, full page scanner, more appropriately called an optical character recognition (OCR) machine. **1970** *Ibid.* V. 75 The Scan-Data 300 is genuinely multifont. **1959** *Engineering* 9 Jan. 45/1 (*heading*) *Multi-fuel engines. **1965** *Economist* 22 May 941/2 The Wankel could come in here, with possibly only marginal disadvantages over available multi-fuel engines. **1778** [W. Marshall] *Minutes Agric.* 11 Sept. an. 1774 It [*sc.* an implement] is *multifurrow—the number may be increased or decreased at pleasure. **1884** Knight *Dict. Mech.* Suppl., *Multi-furrow Plow*, one having several bodies for plowing two or more furrows at once. **1950** *Proc. Amer. Soc. Sugar Beet Technologists* VI. 160 (*heading*) Embryology of mono- and *multigerm fruits in the genus Beta L. **1962** *Times* 21 May 18/5 The monogerm seed which is still being bred and selected to take the place of the multi-germ seed now used. **1959** *Motor Manual* (ed. 36) x. 237 The '*multi-grade' engine oils now available..cover a range of ratings. **1972** *Materials & Technol.* IV. ii. 68 Modern motor oils with good viscosity/temperature characteristics may meet the requirements of several SAE [*sc.* Society of Automotive Engineers] grades and are termed multigrade oils (e.g. 10W/30). **1974** *Drive* Autumn 56 Fast-moving engine parts 'snip up' ordinary multigrade oils like scissors. **1864** *Daily Tel.* 11 Apr. 3/2 The *multigroove rifling. **1962** *Punch* 17 Jan. 133/3 Technicians..explain..what you can and cannot do with a *multi-image lens [in television]. **1969** *Focal Encycl. Film & Television Techniques* 472/2 Multi-image films make use of expanding and diminishing pictures. **1963** *Daily Tel.* 21 Nov. 16 The experimental application of *multi-jet techniques for lifting transport aircraft vertically. **1966** *McGraw-Hill Yearbk. Sci. & Technol.* 411/2 The multi-jet configuration permits higher speeds..than single-jet turbines. **1974** *Encycl. Brit. Macropædia* XVIII. 637/1 The large transport aircraft, now almost exclusively of multijet design. **1961** *Times* 12 Dec. 14/3 A conservative British driver might envisage a *multi-lane nightmare in a wonderland of flyovers and freeways. **1966** *Times* 28 Feb. (Canada Suppl.) p. viii/5 Vancouver's west end, looking northwards over the multi-lane bridge. **1936** *Discovery* Aug. 237/1 This unique camera..is intended for mapping from a higher altitude than has ever before been practical with *multi-lens equipment. **1948** E. Raisz *Gen. Cartogr.* (ed. 2) xix. 194/1 The largest multilens camera is the nine-lens camera of the U.S. Coast and Geodetic Survey. **1951** J. M. Fraser *Psychol.* xv. 189 Wherever a number of people are involved in one task at the same time, a *multi-man chart can be used to record the task of each individual. **1967** Multi-man [see ejection 1 d]. **1958** J. Blish *Case of Conscience* I. vi. 58 The prettiest *multimegaton explosion you ever saw. **1965** H. Kahn *On Escalation* x. 198 Multimegaton weapons appeared to be unusable for any rational, and even for many irrational, purposes. **1941** *B.B.C. Gloss. Broadcasting Terms* 19 **Multi-microphone technique*, method of production in which several microphones, with outputs centralized in a mixer, are used either simultaneously or in succession to reproduce sounds from a single studio or hall. **1957** Manvell & Huntley *Technique Film Music* iv. 194 In England some years ago it was fashionable to use a multi-microphone technique, in which..considerable physical separation between different sections of the orchestra was necessary to enable each microphone to record only that section which it was intended to cover. **1962** A. Nisbett *Technique Sound Studio* iii. 61 If a close balance is adopted in a multi-microphone mix, artificial 'echo' may be added. **1948** *Amer. Jrnl. Roentgenology* LIX. 771/2 *Multimillion volt beta rays and multimillion volt roentgen rays in the treatment of cancer. **1966** *Times* 28 Feb. (Canada Suppl.) p. ix/4 It is a multi-million dollar operation. **1974** *Listener* 23 May 652/2 Multi-million pound shopping precincts. **1928** *Daily Express* 4 May 2/3 The powers given under the Electricity Supply Act of 1926 'to introduce what are known as *multi-part tariffs, whereby a consumer, who is willing to use energy for a number of purposes, may pay a fixed charge yearly and then pay a low running charge per unit'. **1895** *Century Mag.* Aug. 635/1 *Multi-partizan government leads inevitably to greater and more diversified partizanship. **1936** *Proc. IRE* XXIV. 912 It is..extreme high order harmonic distortion which makes the reception of frequency modulation over a *multipath medium far more distorted than the reception of amplitude modulation over the same medium. **1966** *Electronics* 3 Oct. 174 There are three vhf propagation problems that must be considered in designing the Aerocom satellite: fading caused by Faraday rotation, ionospheric fluctuation and sea-water multipath fades. **1970** J. Earl *Tuners & Amplifiers* iii. 75 Multipath interference can severely disturb stereo reception. **1963** *Thorn Electr. Industr. Group Profile* 16 *Multi-pin electrical connectors. **1964** R. F. Ficchi *Electr. Interference* v. 72 The package units are less reliable than the individual units. The dependence of [*read* on] multi-pin connectors which have a relatively high failure rate is the cause. **1948** *Motor Manual* (ed. 33) vii. 121 The *multi-plate clutch, in which two sets of metal discs were arranged alternately in sandwich fashion. One set was attached to the driving shaft, and the other..to the driven shaft. When a spring was permitted to force them all tightly together, they gripped firmly; but when the spring was restrained by the driver, one set of discs could slip round without turning the others. *Ibid.* 135 For top gear,..there is a separate clutch (sometimes of the multi-plate type) inside the gearbox. **1963** Bird & Hutton-Stott *Veteran Motor Car* 253 Transmission: Multiplate clutch, 4 speeds and reverse, shaft. **1971** *Engineering* Apr. 49 (*caption*) This picture shows the multiplate construction of the differential capacitor probe fitted to the gauging head. **1905** *Trans. Amer. Inst. Electr. Engin.* XXIII. 209 It seems as though the latter class of advantages might be obtained as readily and more simply and cheaply by the use of *multi-point control-switches, used in parallel with the ordinary ones. **1931** *Conc. Househ. Encycl.* 531/2 (*caption*) Automatic water heater for multi-point service. **1956** *Bk. Good Housek.* (Good Housek. Inst.) (new ed.) ix. 96/1 Multi-point heaters are now available to fit under a draining-board. **1964** M. Laski in S. Nowell-Smith *Edwardian England* iv. 160 The bathroom [was] served by..a multi-point pressure heater (the first..came on the market in 1899). **1971** B. Scharf *Engin. & its Lang.* x. 82 The cutting tools used on machine tools may be conveniently classified as single-point and multi-point tools. **1929** *Encycl. Brit.* XV. 856/2 Multireel pictures began to appear in 1909... A year later screen history was made by releasing *multireel pictures in their full length. **1881** *Nature* XXV. 198 Our *multireflex arrangement for creating greater sensitiveness. **1970** *Times* 4 Sept. (Aviation Suppl.) p. iii/1 They include..the RB 199 turbofan for the Anglo-German MRCA-75 *multi-role combat aircraft. **1958** *Chambers's Techn. Dict.* 996/1 **Multi-row radial engine*, a radial aero-engine with two or more rows of cylinders. **1971** *Power Farming* Mar. 11/1 For beans, Herbert had come up with a multi-row harvester which not only reduced the time in the field, but caused less damage. **1967** *Economist* 21 Oct. 267/1 A film in the very latest *multiscreen technique extolled the opportunities for everyone in this blossoming province. **1973** *Times* 5 Oct. 25/2 The highlight is the multiscreen show—consisting of what the layman would describe as a cinema screen divided into six parts with different but related films showing on each at the same time. **1958** *Times* 11 Nov. 8/1 The electoral system chosen for Algeria is that of the *multi-seat constituency. **1967** *Jane's Surface Skimmer Systems 1967–68* 112/1 Then work began on the Yard's first multi-seat passenger craft. **1778** [W. Marshall] *Minutes Agric.* 8 Jan. an. 1776 A *multi-soil Farm. **1884** *Cyclist* 13 Feb. 252/1 A new *multispeed gearing. **1940** *Chambers's Techn. Dict.* 564/1 **Multi-start worm*, a worm in which two or more helical threads are used in order to obtain a larger pitch and hence a higher velocity ratio of the drive. **1971** B. Scharf *Engin. & its Lang.* xii. 158 With single-start worms, lead equals pitch, but on multi-start worms, it amounts to pitch × number of starts (i.e. number of thread sections in a plane at right angles to the axis). **1961** G. R. Choppin *Exper. Nucl. Chem.* xi. 182 If the labeled compound is the end product of a *multistep synthesis, in order to obtain a higher final yield, it is best to achieve the labeling at as late a point in the synthesis as possible. **1964** *English Studies* XLV. 383 The difference between a normal one-step process and..the multi-step process..is so great that [etc.]. **1964** *Language* XL. 176 *Multisyllable words where a syllabic split in the written word occurs in the sequence vowel-consonant-consonant-vowel. **1958** J. Moir *High Quality Sound Reproduction* xviii. 545 The film standards used were those previously adopted for *multi-track recording in the studios. **1959** W. S. Sharps *Dict. Cinematogr.* 113/1 *Multitrack recording system*, the system employed for the recording of a multiple sound track. **1969** *Time* 29 Aug. 47 Recording studios also offer new technical means of composing, through such devices as the echo chamber, multi-track recording and tape superimposition. **1935** *Discovery* Feb. 43/2 The *multi-tube parachute rocket used for the Harz Mountain experiments. **1959** *Times* 23 Sept. 4 (Advt.), The Oldham Pg battery is unique in possessing a patented double-sleeve multi-tube positive plate. **1909** *Cent. Dict.* Suppl., *Multivane. **1963** R. R. A. Higham *Handbk. Papermaking* ii. 25 Situated in the trough [of the hydrapulper] is a multivane rotor, driven by a vertical shaft. **1942** *Endeavour* I. 32/1 On the matter of *multivitamin treatment, there are different schools of thought. *Ibid.* 32/2 No multivitamin 'pill'..can at present replace a mixed all-round diet. **1960** *Women's Own* 19 Mar. 25/3 A course of multi-vitamin tablets are a wise investment. **1968** M. Pyke *Food & Society* ii. 17 But it is different when a manufacturer advertises that..expensive multivitamin tablets protect the well-fed people who can afford them against deficiency diseases they will never experience. **1938** L. M. Harrod *Librarians' Gloss.* 104 **Multi-volume book*, a book in more than one volume. **1962** Y. Malkiel in Householder & Saporta *Probl. Lexicogr.* 15 Multi-volume encyclopedias shot through..with genuinely lexical entries. **1940** *Dict. Paper* (Amer. Paper & Pulp Assoc.) 234 **Multiwall-bag paper*, normally, a 40- or 50-pound..kraft paper. **1946** *Nature* 6 July 32/1 A review of literature on the acoustics of building, preparatory to carrying out experimental work with particular reference to multiwall units. **1955** *Times* 5 July (Paper Suppl.) p. iii/5 In little more than twenty-five years the development of the multi-wall paper sack..has established new standards of efficiency, convenience and cleanliness in the packaging of powdered and granular products. **1967** *Times Rev. Industry* May 82/1 As cement production grew, so did the use of multiwall sacks. **1974** *Columbia* (S. Carolina) *Record* 25 Apr. 9-D/1 The paper in question is used in multiwall bags, common in grocery stores. **1961** *B.S.I. News* Aug. 16/2 It was agreed that *multi-way adapters would not be permitted. **1967** *Gloss. Terms Materials Handling (B.S.I.)* III. 10 *Multi-way valve*, a rotatable chamber having a central inlet, and one outlet which can be positioned in line with any one of several radially spaced conveying lines. **1961** R. B. Long *Sentence & its Parts* i. 15 Many kinds of words and *multi-word units function as adjuncts. **1966** G. N. Leech *Eng. in Advertising* ii. 22 Idioms are treated as multi-word lexical items.

multiar ('mʌltɪɑː(r)). *Electronics.* [f. multi- + *ar*, of unknown origin.] A circuit which produces an output signal when a varying voltage applied at one input exceeds an adjustable constant voltage applied at a second input, and which consists of a simple regenerative circuit with a diode and a pulse transformer in the feedback loop.

1946 *Jrnl. Inst. Electr. Engin.* XCIII. IIIA. 321/1 The Multiar.. may be made to generate a delayed marker by utilizing the time-base waveform itself. *Ibid.* 1197/2 Two or more complete pick offs of the type described can be operated from a single sawtooth without mutual interaction, and for this reason the circuit is often called the 'Multiar'. **1953** *Electronic Engin.* XXV. 404 The discriminators consist of ten multiars, each with an individual H.T. supply. **1965** Millman & Taub *Pulse, Digital & Switching Waveforms* xvi. 625 The tube multiar is not useful for positive-going signals because multiple oscillations are obtained. However, a multiar constructed with a *p-n-p* transistor can be used if the input is a positive-going signal.

† **multibibe.** *Obs.*$^{-0}$ [ad. L. *multibib-us*, f. *multi-* + *-bibus* drinking, *bibĕre* to drink.]

1727 Bailey vol. II, *Multibibe*, one that drinks much, a great Drinker.

multibladed to **-carinated**: see multi- 1 a, b.

multicavous, *a. rare*$^{-0}$. [f. L. *multicav-us* (f. *multus* multi- + *cavus* hollow) + -ous.]

1721 Bailey, *Multicavous*, full of Holes. [Hence in Johnson, etc.].

multicellular to **multicoil**: see multi- 1 a, 3.

† **multicolorate,** *a. Obs.* [f. L. *multicolor*, late L. *multicolōrus* + -ate^{2}.] Multi-coloured.

1651 Biggs *New Disp.* ¶233 However oftentimes a multicolorate bloud by the Court-ship of iterated bloud-lettings may be sent forth.

'multi-colour, *sb.* and *a.* [multi- 2, 3.]

1. a. The condition of being many-coloured.

a **1849** Poe *Landscape Garden* Wks. 1864 IV. 340 In the multiform of the tree, and in the multicolor of the flower.

b. *pl.* Many or various colours.

1901 *Daily Chron.* 14 Dec. 8/4 Bars of applied silk done in multi-colours.

2. a. *attrib.* Applied to printing in many colours or a machine for such printing. **b.** *adj.* = next.

1881 *Macm. Mag.* XLIV. 388 Hawkweed topped all the multi-colour weeds. **1884** Knight *Dict. Mech.* Suppl., *Multi-color Printing Press*, a chromatic printing press. **1888** Jacobi *Printers' Vocab.*, *Multicolour letters.*—Characters cut in separate pieces for working in two or more colours.

'multi-coloured, *a.* [multi- 1.] Of many or various colours; many-coloured.

1845 Hirst *Poems* 65 Butterflies on every floweret wave their multi-coloured wings. **1859** Sala *Tw. round Clock* (1861) 417 Multicoloured streamers of attenuated ribbon. **1899** *Allbutt's Syst. Med.* VIII. 465 A rare but striking development of the ring formation is the production of multicoloured concentric circles.

'multi-colouredness. [f. multi-coloured *a.* + -ness.] The condition or quality of being multi-coloured.

1953 G. E. M. Anscombe tr. *Wittgenstein's Philos. Investigations* §47 Multi-colouredness is one kind of complexity.

multi-corneal, -costate: see multi- 1.

multicultural (mʌltɪ'kʌltjʊərəl), *a.* [multi- 1 + cultural *a.* 2.] Of or pertaining to a society consisting of varied cultural groups.

1941 *N.Y. Herald-Tribune Books* 27 July 3 A fervent sermon against nationalism, national prejudice and behavior in favor of a 'multicultural' way of life. **1959** *Times* 18 June (Suppl.) p. iv/4 This multi-cultural, multi-lingual society [of Montreal]..is one of the most cosmopolitan in the world. **1966** *Economist* 22 Jan. 273/2 For the provision of troops and police [to Rhodesia], consideration should be given to states which are multi-cultural (e.g., Canada) or multiracial (e.g., Trinidad, Jamaica, and New Zealand). **1970** P. K. C. Millins (*title*) Education in a multicultural society. **1973** *Daily Tel.* 20 July 17 Although Britain has a multi-cultural society, where are the black faces among television announcers, newscasters and sports commentators? **1975** *Globe & Mail* (Toronto) 21 May 5/1 Trustee Daniel Leckie, chairman of the work group, puts it this way: 'Morally, legally and pragmatically we are bound to adopt a thoroughly multicultural approach toward public education in Toronto.'

Hence **multi'culturalism**.

1965 *Prelim. Rep. R. Comm. Bilingualism & Biculturalism* (Canada) iii. 46 The answer they often gave was 'multiculturalism', or, more elaborately, 'the Canadian mosaic'. **1971** *Daily Colonist* (Victoria, B.C.) 9 Oct. 5/2 A policy of multiculturalism within a bilingual framework commends itself to the government as the most suitable means of assuring the cultural freedom of Canadians. **1972** *Times* 12 Dec. 17/6 The country [*sc.* Canada] faces complex and unresolved problems of..bilingualism and multi-culturalism. **1973** *Stornoway Gaz.* 30 June 9/4 A Gaelic Society that has outgrown its original meeting place in just a few short years and enabled the Gaels to meet the new and promising challenge of Multiculturalism.

multidialectal (mʌltɪdaɪəˈlɛktəl), *a.* [f. MULTI- + DIALECTAL *a.*] Proficient in speaking or comprehending more than two dialects. So **multidiaˈlectalism**.

1964 *English Studies* XLV. 27 The individual will acquire either a new dialect, or a new accent, or both. This does not mean..that he thereby loses his former variety of English, but simply that he becomes 'multi-dialectal' in English. **1965** A. H. MARCKWARDT in *Language* XLI. 146 Certainly a fourteenth-century Englishman with Chaucer's range of experience would have been multidialectal. **1971** *Language* XLVII. 194 They show..that command of heterogeneous structure is not a matter of multidialectalism or performance, but a necessary part of unilingual linguistic competence. **1975** *Amer. Speech 1972* XLVII. 290 Kurath accepts multidialectalism as a linguistic fact.

multidisciplinary (mʌltɪdɪsɪˈplɪnərɪ), *a.* [f. MULTI- + DISCIPLINARY *a.*] Combining many academic approaches, fields, or methods.

1949 [see *family-oriented* adj.]. **1961** *Times* 13 June 2/4 Senior member of a multi-disciplinary unit. **1965** *Math. in Biol. & Med.* (Med. Res. Council) p. vii, This is no new problem for a multidisciplinary subject like medical research. **1972** *Physics Bull.* Feb. 81/1 Interplay between different branches.. follows the wider multi-disciplinary trend between branches of science. **1974** *Nature* 10 May 195/1 This is an outstanding, balanced and humane multidisciplinary book which is much more than an introduction to psychology.

Also **multiˈdisciplined** *a.*

1950 *Brit. Jrnl. Delinquency* I. 151 For the purposes of this Summer School it was agreed that groups should be 'multi-disciplined'. **1953** A. K. C. OTTAWAY *Educ. & Society* viii. 144 This kind of collaboration has been called the 'multi-disciplined approach'. **1972** *Accountant* 6 Apr. 441/2 The Chartered Institutes should leave the provision of higher qualifications to other multi-disciplined specialist bodies.

multi-electrode to **-faculty:** see MULTI- 1, 2, 3.

multifarious (mʌltɪˈfɛərɪəs), *a.* (*sb.*) [f. late L. *multifāri-us* (class.L. *multifāriam* adv.) + -OUS.]

1. Having great variety or diversity; much diversified; (with pl. sb.) many and various.

1593 NASHE *Christ's T.* 38 The Scripture thou madest a too-to compounde Cabalisticall substaunce of, by canonizing such a multifarious Genealogie of Comments. **1617** SIR T. LAKE in *Fortescue Papers* (Camden) 36 The title is multifarious and the contents multiplicious. *a* **1652** J. SMITH *Sel. Disc.* i. 20 That complex and multifarious man that is made up of soul and body. **1655–87** H. MORE *App. Antid.* (1712) 194 This Idea is not free from the intanglement of multifarious Contradictions in the conception thereof. **1779** JOHNSON *L.P., Pope* (1868) 375 His reading, though his favourite authors are not known, appears to have been sufficiently extensive and multifarious. **1790** BURKE *Fr. Rev.* 65 That multifarious thing called a state. **1826** GOOD *Bk. Nat.* (1834) I. 111 The component parts of the cemented rocks are often very multifarious. **1850** GROTE *Greece* II. lxvi. (1862) VI. 1 Two years of cruel and multifarious suffering. **1884** F. TEMPLE *Relat. Relig. & Sci.* iv. (1885) 99 The things themselves which thus change are as multifarious as the changes which they undergo.

b. *Bot.* (See quot.)

1838 BARTON & CASTLE *Brit. Flora Med.* II. Gloss., *Multifarious*, very numerous; or arranged in many rows.

2. *Law.* 'Improperly joining in one bill distinct matters, and thereby confounding them' (Story).

1838 STORY *Equity Pleadings* v. 186. **1872** *Law Rep.* Chanc. 7 App. 463 The bill is multifarious. Each Defendant has a separate defence, and the cases of all cannot be united in the same record.

3. *sb.* In Kantian philosophy = MANIFOLD *sb.* 2 a.

1819 J. RICHARDSON *Kant's Logic* Introd. 46 Distinctness itself may be two-fold: First, a sensual one. This consists in the consciousness of the multifarious by intuition. **1836** J. W. SEMPLE *Kant's Metaphysic of Ethic* Introd. li. *note.* **1837** SIR W. HAMILTON *Metaph.* xlvi. (1870) II. 509 The principal function of the Understanding, out of the multifarious presented to it, to form a whole.

multiˈfariously, *adv.* [-LY[2].] In a multifarious manner; with great variety or diversity; in many and various ways.

1657 TOMLINSON *Renou's Disp.* 502 This syrupe is multifariously made. **1692** BENTLEY *Serm.* (1724) v. 194 If only xxiv parts..may be so multifariously placed and ordered,..as to make many Millions of Millions of differing Rows. **1763** W. LEWIS *Phil. Comm. Arts* 91 The mutual relations of bodies are multifariously modified by the circumstances in which the subjects are applied to one another. **1864** BURTON *Scot Abr.* II. i. 116 Another multifariously endowed Scottish physician, Walter Donaldson. **1885** *Law Times* LXXIX. 58/2 The person.. may sell it, lease it, and deal with it multifariously under the Act.

multiˈfariousness. [-NESS.] The state or quality of being multifarious; multiplied diversity.

1687 NORRIS *Coll. Misc.* 439 According to the multifariousness of imitability, so are the possibilities of Being. **1849** ROBERTSON *Serm.* Ser. I. ii. (1856) I. 28 Multifariousness of knowledge is commonly opposed to depth. **1893** *Nation* LVI. 14/3 The multifariousness of the workings of French upon our language.

b. *Law.* (See MULTIFARIOUS *a.* 2.)

1838 STORY *Equity Pleadings* v. 184. **1843** *Law Jrnl. Rep.* XII. I. 89 A demurrer, which had been filed upon two grounds, multifariousness and want of parties. **1876** *Law Rep.* 3 Chanc. Div. 370 Multifariousness..has ceased to be an objection by the express enactment of the Judicature Act.

†**multifary,** *a. Obs.* In 5 -phary(e. [ad. L. *multifāri-us*, med.L. *-phārius.*] Multifarious.

? *a* **1412** LYDG. *Two Merch.* 530 'O, out on neede of malys multipharye', He gan to crye. **1436** *Libel Eng. Policy* in *Pol. Poems* (Rolls) II. 181 As though wee sent into the londe of Fraunce Tenne thousande peple, men of gode puissaunce, To werre unto her hynderynge multiphary.

multiferous (mʌlˈtɪfərəs), *a. rare*[−0]. [f. L. *multifer* or mod.L. *multiferus*: see MULTI- and -FEROUS.] (See quots.)

1656 BLOUNT *Glossogr.*, *Multiferous*, bearing much or many; fruitful. **1721** in BAILEY. **1856** MAYNE *Expos. Lex.*, *Multiferus, Bot.*, employed by De Candolle to characterize vegetables which bear flowers and fruits many times in the course of a year: multiferous. **1866** in *Treas. Bot.*

multifid (ˈmʌltɪfɪd), *a. Bot.* and *Zool.* [ad. L. *multifid-us*, f. *multus* MULTI- + *fid-*, stem of *findĕre* to cleave.] Having many divisions; cleft or divided into many parts. Also *Comb.*

1752 J. HILL *Hist. Anim.* 23 The short and multifid-tailed monoculus. **1760** J. LEE *Introd. Bot.* II. xxxi. (1765) 153 *Cucurbica*, with multifid Leaves. **1835** KIRBY *Hab. & Inst. Anim.* I. App. 359 The lubricous, multifid, and constantly moving organs. **1877** HUXLEY *Anat. Inv. Anim.* viii. 471 A simple, bifid, or multifid fold of the integument.

Hence **ˈmultifidly** *adv.*, with multifid divisions.

1840 PAXTON *Bot. Dict.*, *Multifidly-pinnatifid*; a leaf is so called when it is pinnately-lobed, and these lobes are again divided into many parts. **1857** *Moore's Handbk. Brit. Ferns* (ed. 3) 187 The rachis bifidly or multifidly divided towards the apex.

mulˈtifido-, used as combining form of MULTIFID; = MULTIFIDLY.

1871 W. A. LEIGHTON *Lichen-flora* 152 Multifido-laciniate.

multifidous (mʌlˈtɪfɪdəs), *a.* [f. L. *multifidus* MULTIFID + -OUS.] = prec.: said *esp.* of feet, or of animals having such feet.

1646 SIR T. BROWNE *Pseud. Ep.* III. xxvii. 175 Those animalls..which are multiparous and multifidous, that is, which have many at a litter, and have also their feet divided into many portions. **1715** *Phil. Trans.* XXIX. 307 Quadrupeds, Viviparous (multifidous and bifidous) and Oviparous. **1856** W. CLARK *van der Hoeven's Zool.* I. 48 Lorica globose or oval..emitting from the terminal aperture processes of the animal variable, multifidous.

multifistular to **-flash:** see MULTI- 1 a, b.

‖**multiflora** (mʌltɪˈflɔərə). [L. fem. (sc. *rosa*) of *multiflōrus* MULTIFLOROUS.] In full, ***multiflora rose.*** A rose belonging to the species *Rosa multiflora*, which is native to Japan and bears clusters of white or pink flowers, or one of the varieties developed from it; also used *attrib.* to designate a plant bearing several flowers on one stem.

1829 *Western Monthly Rev.* III. 57 It is literally embowered in vines of the multiflora rose. **1839** 'PENCIL' *White Sulphur Papers* 82 A small arbor is covered with the multiflora rose and honey-suckle. **1852** [see MONTHLY *sb.* 3]. **1869** HOLE *Roses* 127 Nor am I acquainted..with any garden which has space to spare for the Multiflora or for the Hybrid Climbing Roses. **1890** *Harper's Mag.* Jan. 282/1 A multiflora rose, entangled with honey-suckle, clambered up the squat chimney. **1913** H. H. THOMAS *Rose Bk.* iii. 16, I am making a somewhat apologetic introduction of the multiflora roses. **1934** *Times Educ. Suppl.* 24 Nov. p. iv/1 Mermaid, one of the best of modern roses in leaf, flower, and length of flowering season when it is grafted on the *multiflora* stock, deserves to head the analysis of climbing and rambling roses. **1955** C. C. HURST in G. S. Thomas *Old Shrub Roses* ix. 91 Guillot..planted some of these Japanese Multifloras in his nursery. **1971** N. YOUNG *Complete Rosarian* xii. 217 The one unquestionable advantage of the multiflora stock is the fact that it is less prone to throw up suckers than any of the others. **1972** *Daily Tel.* 14 Oct. 8/2 If you are out for a real display in the ground, you might think of using the new multiflora tulips which have only lately turned up from Holland.

multifloral (mʌltɪˈflɔərəl), *a. Bot.* [Formed as next + -AL[1].] = next.

1875 BENNETT & DYER tr. *Sachs' Bot.* 431 The formation of multifloral inflorescences of peculiar form being characteristic of the more highly developed structure of Angiosperms.

multiflorous (mʌltɪˈflɔərəs), *a. Bot.* [f. late L. *multiflōr-us* (f. *multus* MULTI- + *flōr-, flōs* flower) + -OUS.] Of a stalk: Bearing many (i.e. more than three) flowers.

1760 J. LEE *Introd. Bot.* III. iv. (1765) 172 Uniflorous, Biflorous, Triflorous, or Multiflorous Peduncles. **1831** MACGILLIVRAY tr. *Richard's Elem. Bot.* 180.

multi-flue to **-fœtation:** see MULTI- 1 b, 2, 3.

multifoil (ˈmʌltɪfɔɪl). *Arch.* [f. MULTI- 2 + FOIL *sb.*[1]] An ornament consisting of many (i.e. more than five) foils. Also *attrib.* or *adj.*

1835 [see FOIL *sb.*[1] 2 b]. **1848** B. WEBB *Cont. Ecclesiol.* x. 419 There are multifoils with reliefs of angels singing. **1849** FREEMAN *Archit.* 278 The strange multifoil shape which is a peculiarity of the Arabian architecture of Spain.

Hence **ˈmultifoiled** *a*, composed of many foils.

1851 RUSKIN *Stones Venice* I. viii. §15 Multifoiled shafts are seldom true grouped shafts.

multifold (ˈmʌltɪfəʊld), *a.* [f. MULTI- + -FOLD, after *manifold.*] Manifold.

1806 T. MAURICE *Ind. Antiq.* I. 64 A first essay.. composed..amidst multifold disappointment. **1825** COLERIDGE *Lit. Rem.* (1836) II. 334 The multifold application of faculties common to man and brute animals. **1877** RUSKIN *Fors Clav.* lxxviii. 161 Machinery for multifold killing.

multifoliate, -foliolate: see MULTI- 1 a.

multiform (ˈmʌltɪfɔːm), *a.* and *sb.* [a. F. *multiforme* or ad. L. *multiform-is*: see MULTI- and -FORM.] **A.** *adj.* **a.** Having many forms, shapes, or appearances; highly diversified in form; of many and various forms or kinds.

1603 FLORIO *Montaigne* III. iii. (1632) 458 Life is a motion unequall, irregular and multiforme. **1667** MILTON *P.L.* v. 182 Aire, and ye Elements..that in quaternion run Perpetual Circle, multiform. **1744** HARRIS *Three Treat.* i. (1765) 32 Human Life—a Compound of various and multiform Actions. **1784** COWPER *Task* II. 287 The shifts and turns, Th' expedients and inventions, multiform, To which the mind resorts. *a* **1817** T. DWIGHT *Trav. New Eng.*, etc. (1821) I. 509 The multiform brogue, which salutes the ears of a traveller in..New-York. **1859** DARWIN *Orig. Spec.* v. 131 The variations..so common and multiform in organic beings under domestication. **1895** *Army & Navy Co-op. Soc.* Price List No. 62. 1649 Multiform or Lounge [Hat]. **1903** H. JAMES *Ambassadors* xvi. 146 The question of where, among packed accumulations, so multiform a wedge would be able to enter. Were seventy volumes in red-and-gold to be..the fruit of his mission? **1955** *Times* 21 July 7/5 It includes a model, drawings, and photographs of the multiform playhouse which the Questors Theatre at Ealing hopes to build and which could be adapted to five different types of stage.

b. *Math.* (See quot.)

1893 A. R. FORSYTH *Theory of Functions* 15 If a function have more than one value for any given value of the variable, or if its value can be changed by modifying the path in which the variable reaches that given value, the function is called multiform.

B. *sb.* That which is multiform; that which exhibits many and various forms. Also, multiform character, multiformity.

a **1849** POE *Landscape Garden* Wks. 1864 IV. 340 In the multiform of the tree, and in the multicolor of the flower. **1852** H. ROGERS *Ecl. Faith* (1853) 123 When I attempt..to seek the elusive unity in the infinite multiform. **1856** MRS. BROWNING *Aur. Leigh* III. 9 If He spoke To Peter then, He speaks to us the same; The word suits many different martyrdoms, And signifies a multiform of death. **1913** D. H. LAWRENCE *Love Poems* 37 You who are twisted in grief like crumpled beech-leaves,..who fall to earth At last like a bean-pod: what are you, oh multiform?

Hence **ˈmultiformness** *rare*[−0], multiformity.

1727 in BAILEY vol. II.

multiˈformity. [ad. late L. *multiformitās*, f. *multiformis* (see prec.). Cf. F. *multiformité.*] The condition or character of being multiform; diversity or variety of form, shape, or appearance.

1589 PUTTENHAM *Eng. Poesie* I. viii. (Arb.) 34 So is that part [the imagination]..in his much multiformitie vniforme, that is well proportioned. **1605** BACON *Adv. Learn.* II. 64 Contention hath been mooued..touching an Vniformitie of Methode in Multiformitie of Matter. **1613** PURCHAS *Pilgrimage* To Rdr., Barking out a multiformitie of oathes, like hellish Cerberi. **1720** J. JOHNSON *Collect. Laws*, etc. *Ch. Eng.* I. Pref. p. xvii, Which created Confusion and Multiformity in the Church. *a* **1834** COLERIDGE *Notes & Lect.* (1849) I. 105 The characters in this play are either impersonated out of Shakspeare's own multiformity..or [etc.]. **1862** MERIVALE *Rom. Emp.* lxiv. (1865) VIII. 77 The immensity and multiformity of Nature. **1899** *Allbutt's Syst. Med.* VII. 56 The multiformity and frequent latency of the disease.

multiˈformous, *a. rare.* [f. L. *multiform-is* MULTIFORM + -OUS.] Multiform.

a **1670** HACKET *Cent. Serm.* (1675) 171 His justice was multiformous in all the actions of his life. *a* **1670** —— *Abp. Williams* I. (1692) 204 His [Buckingham's] multiformous places compelled such a swarm of suitors to hum about him that [etc.]. **1847–54** WEBSTER (citing Taylor).

mulˈtiforous, *a. rare*[−0]. [f. L. *multifor-is, -us* (f. *multus* MULTI- + *foris* door, opening).]

1721 BAILEY, *Multiforous*, having many Holes. **1856** MAYNE *Expos. Lex.*, *Multiforous, Zool.*,..pierced by a great number of holes, as the *Asterias multifora*: multiforous.

multiˈfunctional, *a.* Also **multi-functional.** [MULTI- 1 b.] Having or fulfilling many functions.

1941 *Industrial & Engin. Chem.* XXXIII. 351/1 The effectiveness of the multifunctional addition agents is improved by the introduction of metal substituents, particularly in respect to antioxidant value. **1946** *Thorpe's Dict. Appl. Chem.* (ed. 4) VII. 391/2 Multifunctional Additives.—Such compounds combine the properties of power-point depressants, viscosity-index improvers and detergency. **1957** *Essays in Crit.* VII. 21 Shakespeare utilizes his multifunctional character, Edgar. **1959** BENN & PETERS *Social Princ. & Democratic State* xii. 255 The family was once a multi-functional organization within which men and women found their work, amusements, and religion under patriarchal government. **1972** *Nature* 28 Jan. 187/2 Dr Walter Marshall, director of the Atomic Energy Research Establishment at Harwell, described his establishment as a 'multi-functional' laboratory.

So **multiˈfunction** *attrib.* [MULTI- 3].

1967 *Electronics* 6 Mar. 67/2 The company already has a contract for the beam-forming subsystem of the Nike-X multifunction array radar.

multifurcate to **-generic**: see MULTI-.

multi'generous, *a. rare*$^{-0}$. [f. L. *multigener-us* (f. *multus* MULTI- + *gener-*, *genus* kind) + -OUS.]
1721 BAILEY, *Multigenerous*, of many Kinds.

multigerm to **-granulate**: see MULTI- 3, 1.

Multigraph ('mʌltɪgrɑːf, -æ-). Also **multigraph**. [f. MULTI- + -GRAPH.] The proprietary name of a small printing machine which uses specially cast type fitted in to grooves on a rotating cylinder. Also *attrib.* So **'multigraphed** *ppl. a.*, printed by a machine of this type.
1905 *Typewriter Trade Jrnl.* Jan. 17/1 Those who were not able to attend the recent show at Madison Square Garden, missed the opportunity of seeing the 'Multigraph', a machine for producing multiple copies of typewritten work. **1908** *Busy Man's Mag.* May 154/1 The multigraph operated by an office boy or girl really typewrites letters individually, but does it at a speed of 2,000 letters per hour. **1921** *Glasgow Herald* 12 Apr. 5 The Gammeter Multigraph, shown by the International Multigraph Co... is an office machine capable of turning out actual printing at over 4000 impressions per hour. **1925** *Daily Tel.* 13 May 20/5 (Advt.), Experienced multigraph operator and stationery buyer required by City firm. **1936** *Brit. Birds* XXX. 32 Explanatory text.. is supplied in a multigraphed brochure. **1967** KARCH & BUBER *Offset Processes* 546 Multigraph—A duplicator which prints from specially cast type.

multigravida (mʌltɪ'grævɪdə). *Obstetrics.* Pl. **-idas**, **-idæ**. [f. MULTI- after PRIMIGRAVIDA.] A pregnant woman who has had at least one previous pregnancy (or at least two) (formerly less specific: see quots. 1890, 1900).
1890 BILLINGS *Med. Dict.* II. 175/1 *Multigravida*, a woman who has been pregnant more than once. **1900** DORLAND *Med. Dict.* 399/2 *Multigravida*, a woman who has often been pregnant. **1938** A. L. MUDALIAR *Clin. Obstetr.* II. v. 30 Marked changes take place in the breasts consequent upon pregnancy, and such changes are more obvious in primigravidæ than in multigravidæ. **1943** W. SHAW *Textbk. Midwifery* viii. 146 In normal cases the average duration of the first stage of labour in a primigravida is between twelve and fifteen hours, whereas in a multigravida the duration is usually very much shorter. **1958** *Observer* 3 Aug. 10/5 Nice young upper-middle-class multigravida harassed by children. **1959** *Amer. Jrnl. Obstetr. & Gynecol.* LXXVII. 104 In multigravidas there is practically no distress caused by difficult labor or head pressure in the second stage (although both are seen where the previous pregnancies have been only abortions). **1972** E. C. HUGHES *Obstetr.-Gynecol. Terminol.* 331 A multigravida is a woman who is pregnant and who has been pregnant more than one time.

multihull ('mʌltɪhʌl). [f. MULTI- 2 + HULL *sb.*[2]] A boat with more than one hull; freq. *attrib.* Also **'multihulled** *a.*
1956 *Amat. Yacht Res. Soc. Publ.* No. 10. 4 In spite of the fact that multihulled craft have received such little attention .. there is enough interest on the part of amateurs to bring about a high degree of development. **1960** R. B. HARRIS *Mod. Sailing Catamarans* 9 By derivation it [*sc.* catamaran] could include any multihulled craft. With all respect for the many fine existing multihull sailing craft.., this book is concerned only with the twin-hulled sailing craft. **1963** E. F. COTTER *Sailing & Racing Catamarans* ii. 11 Beginning in the late 'Forties, new interest in multi-hulls appeared in widely scattered locations. **1969** C. E. JONES *People in Boats* 129/2 Multihulls are normally sloop or ketch-rigged, but occasionally other types of sail have been tried. **1972** *Observer* 11 June 18/7 If it was multihull weather I would back Tom Follett. *Ibid.*, I don't see another multihull which will outperform her.

multi'lateral, *a.* [MULTI- 1. Cf. med.L. *multilaterus* (Boeth.), *multilaterālis* (Duns Scotus).]
1. *Geom.* Having many (i.e. more than four) sides; = MANY-SIDED 1.
1696 PHILLIPS, *Multilateral*, all Figures that have more than four Right Lines. *a* **1696** SCARBURGH *Euclid* (1705) 27 After the division of strait-lin'd Figures.. into Trilateral.. and Multilateral, Euclide begins [etc.]. **1766** *Complete Farmer* s.v. *Surveying* 7 E 4/2 A regular polygon, otherwise called a regular multangular, or multilateral figure. **1862** TODHUNTER *Euclid* Def. 23 Multilateral figures, or polygons, [bounded] by more than four straight lines. **1875** BENNETT & DYER tr. *Sachs' Bot.* 765 Multilateral erect stems.
2. *fig.* = MANY-SIDED 2.
1784 SIR W. JONES in *Burke's Corr.* (1844) III. 31 The charter of justice.. makes me multilateral; it gives me an equity side, a law side, an ecclesiastical side, a crown side, an admiralty side. **1869** J. F. CLARKE *Brahmanism* in *Atlantic Monthly* May 561/1 The whole poem represents the multilateral character of Hinduism.
3. (See quot. 1802-12) *spec.* Pertaining to or concerning three or more countries, esp. of the trade and financial agreements made by them, or of the control of (part of) their armed forces by a supranational authority.
1802-12 BENTHAM *Ration. Judic. Evid.* (1827) II. 495 In the case of a bilateral or multilateral deed, viz. to which there are parties more than one. **1946** *Jrnl. R. Aeronaut. Soc.* L. 734/1 These agreements were mostly bilateral, and few were multilateral. **1948** *Hansard Commons* 29 Jan. 1290 The Opposition are asking us to support a conception of multilateral trade to which the Government have paid lip-service. **1955** *Times* 29 June 9/3 The west, he [*sc.* J. F. Dulles] said, had worked out the first effective system of multilateral arms control the world had ever known. **1957** *Economist* 30 Nov. 807/1 Commercial and financial relations.. can move on to a fully multilateral basis. **1960** *Times Lit. Suppl.* 27 May 334/1 The elaborate build-up of good will by multilateral visits between the heads of government. **1963** [see MULTINATIONAL *a.* and *sb.*].
4. *Educ.* Of a school providing for two or more types of secondary education; also *ellipt.* as *sb.*, a school of this kind. Cf. COMPREHENSIVE *a.* 1 d.
1938 *Rep. Consultative Comm. Secondary Educ.* (H.M.S.O.) p. xix, We use the term 'multilateral' to describe a school which by means of separate streams would provide for all types of secondary education with the exception of that provided by Junior Technical Schools. **1947** [see COMPREHENSIVE *a.* 1 d]. **1956** *Times Educ. Suppl.* 27 Apr. 536/3 The case against big multilateral schools has been so often put that it needs no repetition. **1959** *Punch* 17 June 797/1 He saw it in his mind's eye.. as a vast multilateral school bringing instruction in basket-weaving and psychology to all the scattered villages of the hilly north. **1967** *Listener* 13 July 41/2 Soon the multilaterals were being called comprehensive and one or two big authorities were actually building a few.
Hence **multi'lateralism**, the quality of being multilateral (sense 3); **multi'lateralist** *a.* and *sb.*, (one) advocating multilateral disarmament; **multi'lateralize** *v.*, to embrace in an agreement amongst many parties; so **multi,laterali'zation**, the integration of armed forces under supranational authority; **multi'laterally** *adv.*, so as to make a multilateral figure; also, amongst three or more parties; **multi'lateralness**, the condition or quality of being many-sided.
1731 BAILEY vol. II, *Multilateralness.* **1847** TULK tr. *Oken's Physiophilos.* 222 The spiriform ranks higher. In it the stem is manifestly differenced more multilaterally. **1879** *Haeckel's Evol. Man* I. viii. 214 Granular entodermcells, which, by mutual pressure, are flattened multilaterally. **1928** *Glasgow Herald* 13 June 10/6 M. Briand insisted specifically on the term 'war of aggression' after first talking generically of all war. The reason was the transformation of bilateralism into multilateralism. **1940** *Economist* 20 July 94/1 This element of multilateralism will in future be introduced by appropriate amendments to the Regulations governing each Special Account agreement. **1950** *Sun* (Baltimore) 19 June 10/4 Dr. Dalton says their move to abolish quotas and multilateralize commerce among the nations is really an incitement to class hatred. **1951** *Ann. Reg. 1950* 47 It [*sc.* the European Payments Scheme] was a step towards the complete multilateral system of payments desired by America, and was part of the plan to progress towards world economic multilateralism. **1957** *Essays & Stud.* New Ser. X. 7 No one would willingly admit to our vocabulary so unprepossessing and nebulous a word as *multilateralization*. **1960** *News Chron.* 7 Oct. 6/3 How ought we 'multilateralist' Labour MPs to vote on defence? **1960** *Guardian* 11 Oct. 11/1, I am resolutely opposed to urging any member of the Labour party to resign because he is a unilateralist or a multilateralist. *Ibid.* 22 Oct. 1/1 Mr Harold Wilson.. declared that the issue was not multilateralism versus unilateralism, but unity versus civil war. **1964** *Listener* 30 July 169/2 The British Government has recently suggested the mixed manning, the multilateralization, of the so-called tactical nuclear weapons now in western Europe. **1965** *Economist* 17 July 207 The Germans still don't want to non-proliferate until they've been multilateralised. **1972** *Sci. Amer.* Apr. 17/2 Government representatives from East and West met.., bilaterally and multilaterally, to discuss increased trade. **1973** *Current Hist.* May 202/1 Yugoslavia supports the convening of a European Security Conference, which would multilateralize the European territorial status quo.

multilayer ('mʌltɪleɪə(r)), *a.* and *sb.* Also **multi-layer**. [f. MULTI- 3, 2 + LAYER *sb.*]
A. *adj.* Composed of or taking place in many or several layers.
1923 *Daily Mail* 28 Apr. 5 Modern amateur practice has run violently in the direction of those compact multilayer coils called 'basket', 'pancake', or 'honeycomb' coils. **1932** J. W. MCBAIN *Sorption of Gases & Vapours by Solids* x. 325 (*heading*) Monomolecular, multilayer and classical thick films. **1960** *Farmer & Stockbreeder* 29 Mar. 77/1 The front-mounted one.. can be used for multi-layer stacking in the barn. **1966** R. J. ROSS *Television Film Engin.* xii. 452 The multilayer Kodachrome film was first developed in a normal negative developer to produce silver images.
B. *sb.* A structure or film composed of many or several layers, *spec.* of more than one monolayer.
1932 J. W. MCBAIN *Sorption of Gases & Vapours by Solids* x. 326 No such excitement would be aroused by a demonstration of the actual occurrence of multilayers deriving from the second hypothesis. **1963** R. R. A. HIGHAM *Handbk. Papermaking* viii. 214 Laminating machines are used to apply an adhesive to single or multi-layers of paper which are then bonded together by heat to form one ply. **1966** D. G. BRANDON *Mod. Techniques Metallogr.* i. 34 Films may be prepared from diele[c]tric multilayers (usually alternating zinc sulphide with magnesium fluoride). **1975** *Nature* 24 July 297/1 Its bottom is formed of multilayers of salt deposits separated by films of sand and gypsum.
So **'multilayered** *a.* [MULTI- 1 b].
1935 *Anat. Rec.* LXI. 391 Multilayered follicles were increasing in number and as many as ten or twelve granulosa layers surrounded the ova. **1959** *Biol. Abstr.* XXXIV. 1163/2 (*heading*) The multilayered tube wall as [a] model for the aorta. **1974** *Tetrahedron Lett.* 1573 We have previously described the synthesis of multilayered [2.2] metacyclophanes by way of the Stevens rearrangement.

'multilevel, *a.* Also **multi-level**. [MULTI- 3.] Having, involving, or operating on several levels (in any sense). Also *ellipt.* as *sb.*, a multilevel set of apartments.
1952 *Los Angeles Examiner* 19 Mar. III. 1 (*caption*) Multi-level apartment hotel is planned as the center for the development. **1959** G. TROUP *Masers* iv. 50 One multilevel excitation method is that known as 'optical pumping'. **1959** *Sunday Times* 12 Apr. 21/6 America welcomed the one-storey 'ranch' house and the 'split level'. Today, the development builders, who can find new names for old things, are trumpeting the 'multi level'. **1960** *Guardian* 17 Mar. 9/5 Multi-level traffic to separate vehicles from pedestrians. **1961** L. MUMFORD *City in Hist.* viii. 208 The new marketplaces at Coventry and Harlow, with their upper tiers of shops and offices, are.. only a recovery of the admirable Roman multi-level plan. **1964** E. A. NIDA *Toward Sci. Transl.* v. 80 When such vertical divisions are multilevel, that is to say, when the cuts extend through several layers, they mark very important distinctions in the language. **1969** *Jane's Freight Containers 1968-69* 121/3 Unloading automobiles from multi-level cars. **1972** *Village Voice* (N.Y.) 1 June 82/3 (Advt.), Unusual multi-levels. Charming bedroom apts. **1973** *Times* 5 Oct. (Safety Suppl.) p. ii, Junctions are multilevel and local roads.. are carried over or under their dual carriageways.
So **multi-'levelled** *a.* [MULTI- 1 b].
1948 *Hudson Rev.* I. I. 117 But precisely because it is a poem—compact, symbolic, multileveled, all details woven elaborately into the meaning pattern—it cannot be totally accounted for as yet. **1962** M. MCLUHAN *Gutenberg Galaxy* 103 When only the eye is engaged, the multi-levelled gestures and resonances of Senecan oral action are quite impertinent. **1964** E. BACH *Introd. Transformational Gram.* iv. 58 A multileveled theory such as is necessary for describing a natural language. **1968** A. LOMAX *Folk Song Style & Culture* iv. 95 The overall impact of the African style is multileveled, multiparted, highly integrated, multi-textured, gregarious, and playful-voiced.

multilineal (mʌltɪ'lɪnɪəl), *a.* [f. MULTI- + LINEAL *a.*] Having many lines; *spec.* denoting a kinship system which includes relationships derived from parents, grandparents, etc., of both father and mother. Hence **multiline'ality**, the fact of multilineal kinship.
a **1800** STEEVENS *Note on Shaks. Twel. N.* III. iii, This Map is multilineal in the extreme, and is the first in which the Eastern Islands are included. **1882** OGILVIE, *Multilineal, multilinear*, having many lines. **1943** T. PARSONS in *Amer. Anthropologist* XLV. 26 Since the same principle of lack of distinction by sex of intervening relative applies to still higher ascendant generations—the four great- and eight great-great-grandfathers—it is perhaps more accurate to speak of a 'multilineal' than a 'bilateral' system. **1956** R. FIRTH *Two Stud. Kinship in London* 16 The 'multilineal' American family. *Ibid.* 17 It is in this way that the conversion of bilateralism into multilineality occurs. **1965** G. P. MURDOCK *Culture & Society* xiii. 179 The 'multilineal' of Parsons.. is inappropriate since.. many such systems, including the American, are not in fact 'lineal' in any sense.

multilinear: see MULTI- 1 a.

multilingual (mʌltɪ'lɪŋgwəl), *a.* and *sb.* [f. MULTI- + L. *lingu(a* tongue, language + -AL.]
A. *adj.* Speaking, characterized by, or written in many languages.
1838 *Fraser's Mag.* XVII. 122 The art of multilingual quotation is no mark of reading. **1880** WESTCOTT *Speaker's Comm., John* xix. 20 Such multilingual inscriptions were not uncommon in the Roman provinces. **1958** *Listener* 2 Jan. 5/2 Indonesia.. is multi-racial and multilingual. **1960** E. DELAVENAY *Introd. Machine Transl.* vi. 96 This Cambridge research leads in the direction of a new kind of bilingual or multilingual dictionaries. **1968** *Amer. Speech* XLIII. 127 How is the language variance in multilingual communities best explained?
B. *sb.* One who speaks many languages.
1959 J. C. CATFORD in Quirk & Smith *Teaching of English* vi. 164 Strictly speaking, the alternative use of more than two languages is 'multilingualism' and the persons involved are 'multilingual' (adj.) or 'multilinguals' (n.). **1964** E. PALMER tr. *Martinet's Elem. Gen. Ling.* v. 160 These are the bilingual speakers, or if they possess more than two codes, the multilinguals, whatever degree of perfection they may achieve in handling each of the said languages. **1968** *Amer. Speech* XLIII. 127 What theoretical model most appropriately describes the individual multilingual's speech?
Hence **multi'lingually** *adv.*; **multi'lingualism**, the ability to speak many languages; the use of many languages; **multi'linguist** = MULTILINGUAL *sb.*
1923 W. J. LOCKE *Lengthened Shadow* 187 A white-haired white-moustached multilinguist by the name of Soussouki. **1940** *Q. Jrnl. Speech* Oct. 394 Problems confronting the speech therapist in the Union are legion, resulting from racial inequalities, multi-lingualism, [etc.]. **1953** U. WEINREICH in *Publ. Ling. Circle N.Y.* I. 1 Unless otherwise specified, all remarks about bilingualism apply as well to multilingualism, the practice of using alternately three or more languages. **1956** *Essays in Crit.* VI. 67 Fr. Jarret-Kerr is dealing with creative artists who worked in Spanish, Italian, Russian and French—and he confesses himself no multilinguist. **1958** *Times Rev. Industry* June 76/1 Working principles are explained multi-lingually through loudspeakers. **1968** J. A. FISHMAN *Readings Sociol. of Lang.* 12 Multilingualism has long been a topic recognized by sociologists, linguists, anthropologists, and others as shedding light on many aspects of language learning. **1972** *Sci. Amer.* Sept. 78/1 Bilingualism or multilingualism.. cannot be rigidly separated from interdialectal fluctuations. **1972** *Physics Bull.* Dec. 136/2 It [*sc.* a European *Physics Bulletin*] would have to be printed multilingually, and would be an extremely expensive exercise. **1973** *Archivum Linguisticum* IV. 55 Another way of putting this is to refer to one of the most common questions faced by those wishing to make sense of multilingualism—how many languages are there here, and how many dialects? **1974** *Daily Tel.* 10 July 18 An Oxford graduate and multilinguist, Saunders worked at the Treasury and the Coal Board.

Multilith ('mʌltɪlɪθ). Also **multilith**. [f. MULTI- + LITH(OGRAPH *sb.*] The proprietary name of a small, offset-lithographic, printing machine.

Also *attrib.* So **'multilithed** *ppl. a.*, printed by a machine of this kind.

1933 *Profit Making Up-to-Date* (Addressograph-Multigraph Corp.) 81 Multilith greatly reduces the necessity of type composition. **1936** *Business Office Training Course* (Addressograph-Multigraph Corp.) xi. 97 The latest addition to the Multigraph line is the 'Multilith'. This term applies to the simplified process of 'offset lithography' developed by the Multigraph Company. **1937** *Geogr. Jrnl.* LXXXIX. 403 Multilith photographer. **1951** *Archivum Linguisticum* III. 106 From 1942 dates the journal *Studies in Linguistics*..published..at first in mimeographed and later in multilithed form. **1965** *Times Lit. Suppl.* 14 Jan. 25/4 A new multilithed newsletter called *Cultural Events in Africa* is appearing monthly. **1968** *Globe & Mail* (Toronto) 13 Jan. 48/2 (Advt.), Pressman..—knowledge of multilith an advantage. **1974** *Oxf. Univ. Gaz.* 19 Dec. 373/1 (Advt.), Academic, literary, and other typing. .. Multilith duplicating.

multi-loculated: see MULTI- 2.

multi-lo'quacious, *a.* = MULTILOQUENT.

1819 *Metropolis* II. 179 A fat, elderly gentleman, multi-loquacious, and who speaks very fast.

multiloquence (mʌl'tɪləkwəns). *rare.* [ad. late L. *multiloquentia*: see MULTI- and LOQUENCY.] Much speaking; talkativeness; use of many words.

1760 'J. COPYWELL' [W. Woty] *Shrubs of Parnassus* 147 Where Clamour wages war with Sense, And Oratory centres in Multiloquence. **1846** WORCESTER (citing J. Q. Adams). **1893** *Temple Bar* XCVII. 625 He would invariably flounder astray in his own multiloquence.

So **mul'tiloquent** [cf. LOQUENT], **multi'loquious** (whence **multi'loquiousness**), **mul'tiloquous** [L. *multiloqu-us*] *adjs.*, given to much talking, talkative; **mul'tiloquy** [L. *multiloqui-um*] = MULTILOQUENCE.

1656 BLOUNT *Glossogr.*, **Multiloquent*, full of speech, that hath many words. **1891** S. MOSTYN *Curatica* 77 He ventured more than once to silence even the multiloquent Babbleton. **1640** QUARLES *Enchir.* (1641) II. xxvi, With three sorts of men enter no serious friendship: The Ingratefull man; the *Multiloquious man; the Coward. **1727** BAILEY vol. II, **Multiloquiousness*, talkativeness. **1658** PHILLIPS. **1664** *New Haven Col. Rec.* (1858) II. 530 In your large scedule and *multiloquous penings. **1542** BECON *Pathw. Prayer* xxxiii, Yᵉ *multiloquie & manner of bablyng in prayers, which the Ethnickes & Infidels dyd vse. **1677** GALE *Crt. Gentiles* III. 205 In Battologie there are two vices, (1) vain repetition of the same words, (2) Multiloquie or much speaking. **1700** ASTRY tr. *Saavedra-Faxardo* I. 81 Multiloquy makes their Words unregarded. **1721** BAILEY, *Multiloquy*, talkativeness.

multimacular to **-marbled**: see MULTI-.

multi-'media, *a.* [f. MULTI- + MEDIA[2].] Designating or pertaining to a form of artistic, educational, or commercial communication in which more than one medium is used. Hence as *sb.*

1962 *Times* 26 Feb. (Canada Suppl.) p. xviii/4 The first prong is a multi-media publicity campaign to encourage school children..to obtain adequate educational qualifications. **1962** *Listener* 5 Apr. 603/3 Both Futurists and Dadaists had a keen interest in multi-media art, in breaking down the technical and formal self-sufficiency of the work of art. **1968** *Sun* (Baltimore) 4 July A. 16/3 The notes of one conference we attended a few weeks ago..show that speakers were using such terms..as..multi-media and multi-mode curriculum. **1970** *Times* 28 Apr. 7 Late night performances of the Military Tattoo and of the multimedia rock musical *Stomp*. **1970** D. BERGEN in *Americana Ann.* 420 Multimedia information centers with print and audiovisual materials. **1971** *Black Scholar* Jan. 20/2 As originator of the practice of reading poetry to jazz, he not only stitched backwards and forward in his lineage and idiom, but wrought a new force in the now obscenely exaggerated concept of multi-media. **1974** *News & Press* (Darlington, S. Carolina) 25 Apr. 9/7 Hooser creates a multi-media effect that draws the viewer into the picture.

multimer ('mʌltɪmə(r)). *Chem.* [f. MULTI- + -MER.] An aggregate of molecules held together by relatively weak bonds, such as hydrogen bonds.

1959 M. DAVIES in D. Hadži *Hydrogen Bonding* 560 The use of the term 'polymer' for the associated molecules formed from stable monomers by hydrogen bonding, etc., seems objectionable, and it is suggested that the equivalent, self-explanatory term 'multimer' be used in these circumstances. **1967** *Arch. Biochem. & Biophysics* CXX. 158 (*heading*) Studies on protein multimers. **1972** H.-G. ELIAS in M. B. Huglin *Light Scattering from Polymer Solutions* ix. 399 A unimer of molecular weight M_1 will multimerize to a multimer with a degree of multimerization N.

Hence **multi'meric** *a.*; also **,multimeri'zation**, the formation of multimers; **'multimerize** (or *mul'timerize*) *v. intr.*, to associate to form a multimer or multimers; **'multimerized**, **'multimerizing** *ppl. adjs.*

1971 *Arch. Biochem. & Biophysics* CXLII. 329/1 The experimental basis for supposing that high pressure disaggregates multimeric proteins is already well established. **1972** H.-G. ELIAS in M. B. Huglin *Light Scattering from Polymer Solutions* ix. 451 It is believed that multimerizations occur preferentially in thermodynamically poor solvents as expressed for polyvinyl chloride solutions. *Ibid.* 398 For the multimerized material, we shall use the following nomenclature. *Ibid.* 400 In light scattering studies of multimerizing solutes, many different concentration dependences of the reciprocal apparent weight average molecular weights may be observed. *Ibid.* 441 Cellulose nitrates multimerize in ethanol at temperatures above 20° C. **1973** *Microbios* VII. 53 (*heading*) The multimeric nature of NADPH-nitrate reductase from *Aspergillus nidulans*. **1973** *Nature* 24 Aug. 528/3 Chapter 9 deals with the problems of aggregation or multimerization.

multimeter ('mʌltɪmiːtə(r)). *Electr.* [f. MULTI- 2 + METER *sb.*[3]] An instrument designed to measure voltage, current, and usu. resistance, often over several different ranges of value.

The word *Multimeter* is registered as a proprietary name in the U.S.

1910 *Hawkins' Electr. Dict.* 292/1 *Multi-meter*, a 'universal' electronic measuring instrument designed to serve the purpose of a voltmeter, ammeter, ohmmeter, ground detector and Wheatstone bridge. **1926** *Jrnl. Sci. Instruments* III. 346 The vacuum-tube multimeter has three ranges as a voltmeter, and six ranges as an ammeter for each range of the voltmeter. **1929** *Official Gaz.* (U.S. Patent Office) 5 Mar. 23/2 Rawson Electrical Instrument Company, Cambridge, Mass... *Multimeter* for Electric Meters. Claims use since latter part of 1919. **1967** *Electronics* 6 Mar. 117/1 The Instrumentation division of Fairchild Camera & Instrument Corp. has brought the price of a multimeter down to $249. **1971** *Nature* 12 Feb. 482/1 The 1970 resistance measurements were made with a digital multimeter (Fluke '8100A') to the same accuracy as the 1969 measurements. **1975** *Physics Bull.* Jan. 28/2 Sinclair Radionics new DM2 digital multimeter provides the facilities of the conventional multimeter: AC and DC voltage, AC and DC current ranges and resistance measurements, in a portable instrument.

multimillionaire: see MULTI- 2.

multimodal (mʌltɪ'məʊdəl), *a.* Also (with hyphen) **multi-modal**. [f. MULTI- 1 a + MOD(E *sb.* + -AL.] **a.** Of a frequency curve or distribution: having several modes or maxima (MODE *sb.* 7 c). Of a property: occurring among different individuals in accordance with such a distribution.

1902 *Biometrika* I. 305 A frequency distribution with more than one true mode is multi-modal. **1932** J. S. HUXLEY *Probl. Relative Growth* VII. i. 210 The body-length for males is irregular, multimodal and skew. **1959** SCHUELL & JENKINS in Saporta & Bastian *Psycholinguistics* (1961) 436/1 The distribution of scores on each test was plotted for the 100-patient sample... Only a few tests yielded irregular multi-modal distributions. **1962** *Lancet* 26 May 1090/1 In both cases distributions in two of the six age-groups are irregular..and of a form which might readily be interpreted as multimodal or bimodal.

b. Characterized by several different modes of occurrence or activity.

1928 D. B. LEARY *Mod. Psychol.* 128 The so-called multi-modal theory..assumes that there are several distinct types of intelligent conduct. **1968** W. A. STEWART in J. A. Fishman *Readings Sociol. of Lang.* (1968) 534 When a language has come to be used in more than one country and has..developed multimodal standardization, the form of standardization prevalent in any one country may [etc.]. **1969** *Jane's Freight Containers 1968–69* 32/3 As shippers adjust to the advantages of an integrated, multi-modal transportation system.

Hence **multi'modalism** (*rare*), **,multimo'dality**, the property or quality of being multimodal.

1902 *Biometrika* I. 305 Much of the multimodalism interpreted in the case of flowers as polymorphism is due either to misinterpretation.., i.e. is not true multimodalism ..or..is due to some heterogeneity..introduced by the gatherer. **1932** J. S. HUXLEY *Probl. Relative Growth* ii. 78 There is a slight tendency to multimodality..in the male body-length frequency curve. **1972** *Comprehensive Psychiatry* XIII. 391 (*heading*) Impact of a multi-modality treatment program for heroin addicts. **1973** D. NELKIN *Methadone Maintenance* i. 24 'Multimodality', an expression coined by Dr. Jaffe, which refers to a concept of rehabilitation that coordinates within a single administrative structure all varieties of approaches to addiction.

multimodous, *a.* [f. L. *multimod-us* (f. *multus* MULTI- + *modus* MODE *sb.*) + -OUS.]

1727 BAILEY vol. II, *Multimodous*, of divers Sorts, fashions or manner.

multimonstrous to **-nodous**: see MULTI- 1.

multinational (mʌltɪ'næʃənəl), *a.* and *sb.* [f. MULTI- + NATIONAL *a.* and *sb.*]

A. *adj.* **a.** Comprising or pertaining to many nationalities or ethnic groups. **b.** Possessing branches, factories, offices, etc., in many countries. **B.** *sb.* A multinational company. So **multi'nationally** *adv.*; **multi'nationalism**, the realm of multinational companies.

1926 *Time* 17 May 14 A majority of the multi-national citizens of what is now Hungary. **1940** *Mind* XLIX. 117 Their inequality makes for an intrinsic instability in their relations which causes one to regret the passing of the multi-national Empires, like Austria and Russia, with their stabilising effect. **1957** *Times Lit. Suppl.* 25 Oct. 635/2 The volume contains in fact five separate essays—on the beginnings of the American nation..on the problems of a multi-national nation [etc.]. **1961** *New Scientist* 23 Mar. 733/1 There will be an important multi-national programme of space research, starting in 1962. **1962** *Economist* 15 Dec. 1108/3 Assignments to multinational organisations should be up-graded. **1963** *Guardian* 19 Mar. 11/4 A multinational force would be one composed of Service units already in existence... Multilateral would mean manning.., for example, Polaris surface ships with mixed crews. **1964** *Economist* 17 Oct. 271/2 Very few such companies..seem..to think 'multi-nationally'. **1968** *Listener* 12 Dec. 783/1 The multinational firm transcends national boundaries..through the establishment of subsidiaries in foreign countries. **1971** C. TUGENDHAT (*title*) The multinationals. **1971** *Rand Daily Mail* 4 Dec. 12/2 There are plans for extra senates and supra-parliaments and multinational assemblies. **1972** *Listener* 18 May 652/2 Yours is a multinational group. What are the prospects for multinationalism? **1973** *Daily Tel.* (Colour Suppl.) 22 June 23/2 The five multi-national pilots—as her name implies the Europa is a truly European airship. **1975** *Bookseller* 18 Jan. 155/1 (Advt.), To manipulate the takeover of the Holmes Motor Corporation by an American multi-national and to destroy a rival spying network.

multinomial (mʌltɪ'nəʊmɪəl), *a.* and *sb. Alg.* Also 7 **-nomall**. [f. MULTI- after *binomial*. Cf. F. *multinome* sb., †*multinomie* adj.] **A.** *adj.* Of an expression: Consisting of many (i.e. more than two) terms connected by the signs + or −.

multinomial theorem, a theorem discovered by De Moivre for the expression of any power of a multinomial without actual involution.

1608 R. NORTON tr. *Stevin's La Disme* D, Ptolome and Iohannes Monta-regio haue not described their Tables of Arches, Chords, or Sines, in extreme perfection (as possibly they might haue done by Multinomall numbers) [orig. *nombres multinomies*]. **1697** *Phil. Trans.* XIX. 619 The infinite Number Multinomial. **1704** [see POLYNOMIAL A. 1]. **1706** W. JONES *Syn. Palmar. Matheseos* 42 When the Dividend and Divisor are Multinomial Quantities..there may be a Common Multiplier of both. **1742** MᶜLAURIN *Fluxions* II. 761 An investigation of the binomial and multinomial theorems. **1858** TODHUNTER *Algebra* xxxvii. §530 By applying the multinomial theorem to find the coefficients of other powers of *x*. **1904** *Jrnl. Math.* Ser. II. II. 478 The deficient multinomial expansion $\{x_1 + x_2 + x_3 + \dots\}^p$.

B. *sb.* A multinomial expression.

1674 JEAKE *Arith.* (1696) 294 Where the composition hath more than two parts, the Compound is called a Polynomial or a Multinomial. **1697** *Phil. Trans.* XIX. 619 A Method of Raising an infinite Multinomial to any given Power... By Mr. Ab. De Moivre. **1742** MᶜLAURIN *Fluxions* II. 608 Mr. De Moivre's theorem for raising a multinomial to any power of the index *n*. **1858** TODHUNTER *Algebra* xxxvii. §528 The expansion of the proposed multinomial.

multinominal (mʌltɪ'nɒmɪnəl), *a.* [f. L. *multinōmin-is* (f. *multus* MULTI- + *nōmin-*, *nōmen* name) + -AL[1].] Having many names; polyonymous.

1656 BLOUNT *Glossogr.* **1822** T. TAYLOR *Apuleius* XI. 281 The divine mandates of the multinominal Goddess. **1855** M. BRIDGES *Pop. Mod. Hist.* xx. 462 At these places he crushed..the multinominal and heroic legions of his enemies.

So †**multi'nominous** *a.*

a **1615** DONNE *Ess.* (1651) 101 How multinominous is the father in law of Moses? *a* **1631** —— *Paradoxes* (1652) 52 Why is Venus-star multinominous, called both Hesperus and Vesper?

multinuclear: see MULTI- 1 a.

multi-occu'pation. [MULTI- 2.] Occupation of a house by more than one family, with shared kitchen or sanitary facilities. Hence **multi-'occupy** *v. trans.*, to tenant (a house) with more than one family with such shared facilities; to place (tenants) in such a house; **multi-'occupied** *ppl. a.* Cf. *multiple occupancy*, *occupation* (s.v. MULTIPLE *a.* 2 c).

1963 *Guardian* 30 Mar. 2/2 A graduated percentage addition to the rateable value of houses in multi-occupation. **1965** *Ibid.* 3 Sept. 20/8 For every house multi-occupied by Pakistanis..there are many more multi-occupied by Irish. **1967** *Economist* 14 Oct. 177/1 Improvement grants are not available for multi-occupied houses. **1970** *Guardian* 31 July 9/1 The borough council is..planning to multi-occupy its emergency homeless in..a tenement building built in 1878. **1972** *Ibid.* 26 June 7/3 If families are evicted from multi-occupation property, they tend to move to the next street. **1973** C. MULLARD *Black Brit.* xiii. 164 There is still no national code in existence. If there were, multi-occupation and other housing problems would be non-issues.

multip, colloq. abbrev. MULTIPARA.

1948 MENCKEN *Amer. Lang.* Suppl. II. xi. 756 *Primip*, a mother having her first child... At subsequent deliveries she is a *multip*,..or a *para-two*, *three*, etc. **1967** *Midwives Chron.* Apr. 115/1 The risks to the grande multip cover pregnancy and labour and puerperium.

multipacket ('mʌltɪpækɪt). [f. MULTI- + PACKET *sb.*] A cargo boat built in two parts, having the propulsion unit and crew quarters at one end and one or more cargo units at the other. Also *attrib.*

1965 *Daily Express* 11 Nov. 17/2 A design for a cargo ship that splits in half has passed Ministry of Transport tests... The design, called the Multi-packet, has been developed by a Liverpool firm. **1967** *New Scientist* 28 Dec. 743/3 The multipacket vessel can enter harbour, deposit a fully laden cargo unit at the quayside, and depart with a different unit—all within a matter of hours. *Ibid.* 744/1 The greatest technical difficulty to be overcome in the new design is that of connecting and disconnecting the multipacket units quickly and easily.

multipaleaceous: see MULTI- 1.

‖**multipara** (mʌl'tɪpərə). *Obstetrics.* Pl. **-paras, -paræ**. [mod.L., fem. of *multiparus*: see MULTI- and -PAROUS.] A woman who has borne more than one child. Freq. used (in contrast to *primipara*) to include pregnant women with a single previous delivery, the forthcoming birth being anticipated in the enumeration.

1860 [see PRIMIPAROUS *a.*]. **1872** T. G. THOMAS *Dis. Women* (ed. 3) 76 Should the case be one of a multipara, the cylinder may be introduced without pain. **1879** J. M. DUNCAN *Clin. Lect. Dis. Women* xix. 209 Procidentia is.. more likely to occur to a multipara than a primipara. **1890** tr. *F. Winckel's Textbk. Obstetr.* III. v. 112 It is by no means easy to distinguish a multipara from a primipara, especially when the previous pregnancy took place many years before. **1938** A. L. MUDALIAR *Clin. Obstetr.* II. vi. 35 In multiparæ the changes in the breasts are not of much diagnostic value, because pregnancy may take place in a lactating woman. **1958** J. R. WILLSON et al. *Obstetr. & Gynecol.* xxviii. 321 In primigravidas the cervix is usually well effaced before the contractions of true labor begin, but preparation of the cervix in multiparas differs slightly. **1967** J. B. LAWSON in Lawson & Stewart *Obstetr. & Gynaecol. in Tropics* i. 5 None of the risks of high parity.. are unique to grande multiparae (para 5 and above) but are commoner in this group. **1972** E. C. HUGHES *Obstetr.-Gynecol. Terminol.* vii. 333 A multipara is a woman who has given birth two or more times to an infant or infants, alive or dead, weighing 500 gm or more.

multi'parient, *a.* [See MULTI- and PARIENT *a.*] = next 1.

1822 GOOD *Study Med.* IV. 233 While some women produce thus rapidly in single succession, there are others that are multiparient. **1851** RAMSBOTHAM *Obst. Med. & Surg.* (ed. 3) 49 If one ovary only is removed from a multiparient animal, she becomes less fruitful.

multiparous (mʌl'tɪpərəs), *a.* [f. mod.L. *multipar-us*: see MULTI- and -PAROUS.]

1. Bringing forth many young at a birth; pertaining to or characterized by this kind of parturition.

1646 SIR T. BROWNE *Pseud. Ep.* III. xv. 141 It is not denied there have been bicipitous Serpents with the head at each extream,.. which double formations do often happen unto multiparous generations. *Ibid.* 175 [see MULTIFIDOUS]. **1691** RAY *Creation* (1692) 106 Multiparous quadrupeds, as Dogs, as Swine, are furnished with a multitude of Paps. **1782** A. MONRO *Compar. Anat.* (ed. 3) 31 In bitches and other multiparous animals. **1829** *Good's Study Med.* V. 225 *Parodynia Pluralis.* Multiparous Labour. **1839–47** *Todd's Cycl. Anat.* III. 315/1 The oviducts are shorter.. in the uniparous Kangaroo, than in the multiparous Opossums. **1870** ROLLESTON *Anim. Life* 8 The multiparous character of the order [Rodentia].

2. That is a multipara; of or pertaining to a woman who has borne more than one child.

1860 TANNER *Pregnancy* ii. 78 The multiparous organ [*sc.* uterus] is in every respect rather larger and heavier. **1897** *Allbutt's Syst. Med.* II. 572 In the case of children of the multiparous, no less than 16 proved insusceptible to vaccination.

3. *Bot.* Applied to a cyme that has many axes.

1880 A. GRAY *Struct. Bot.* 152 Bravais distinguishes cymes as multiparous, with three or more lateral axes; biparous [etc.].

Hence **multi'parity** [see PARITY[2]].

1890 *Cent. Dict.* **1905** *Brit. Med. Jrnl.* 16 Sept. 42 Woman is in a state of transition from multiparity to uniparity.

multipartite (mʌltɪ'pɑːtaɪt), *a.* [ad. L. *multipartīt-us*: see MULTI- and PARTITE *a.*] Divided into many parts; having many divisions.

1721 in BAILEY. **1775** JENKINSON *Brit. Plants* Gloss. **1811–31** BENTHAM *Logic* Wks. 1843 VIII. 253/1 Strict division is bipartite; loose division is multipartite. **1819** *Pantologia* s.v., Multipartite Corol,.. Multipartite leaf... Divided into several parts almost to the bottom. **1872** OLIVER *Elem. Bot.* II. 153 Meadow Geranium.. with multipartite stipulate leaves. **1891** tr. *Harnack's Diff. & Int. Calc.* 367 All the curves constituting the multipartite boundary of a domain. **1898** *Allbutt's Syst. Med.* V. 638 The ordinary 'multinucleated' leucocytes, or more correctly, those with multipartite nucleus.

multi-partizan: see MULTI- 3.

multi-'party, *a. Polit.* [f. MULTI- + PARTY *sb.* 6.] Comprising several parties or members of several parties; of an electoral or political system which results in the formation of three or more influential parties.

1909 *Englishwoman* Apr. 325 The suffrage societies, nominally non-party and really multi-party in their composition. **1935** R. BASSETT *Essent. Parl. Democracy* ii. 43 Under the multi-party conditions prevalent in most continental parliamentary regimes, it is almost certain that no single party will be able to secure a working majority. **1954** B. & R. NORTH tr. *Duverger's Pol. Parties* II. i. 229 The typology of the multi-party system is difficult to establish. **1956** J. KLEIN *Study of Groups* 161 A democratic country with a multi-party system. **1958** A. LEISERSON *Parties & Politics* ix. 358 The multiparty system operates quite differently in a three-party situation.. from the way it does when there are five or six fairly identifiable party groupings. **1963** *Ann. Reg. 1963* 204 Dr Raúl Leoni.. stated that his party would try to form a multi-party coalition. **1970** B. M. BARRY *Sociologists, Economists & Democracy* v. 125 In a multi-party system, the parties are more precise but it is more difficult to tell what one is doing by voting for one.

Hence **multi-'partism, multi-'partyism**, a political system in which the major interest groups of the electorate are reflected in three or more influential parties. Also ***multi-partist*** adj.

1946 F. A. OGG *European Govt. & Politics* (rev. ed.) xlv. 901 The error would lie in failure to remember.. the total absence of anything approaching Western multi-partyism. **1954** B. & R. NORTH tr. *Duverger's Pol. Parties* II. i. 229 In this sense multi-partism is fairly characteristic of Western Europe, Great Britain excepted but Ireland included. *Ibid.* iii. 393 Great Britain and the Dominions, under a two-party system, are profoundly dissimilar from Continental countries under a multi-partist system. **1962** S. E. FINER *Man on Horseback* xii. 236 In Indonesia, where the sole unifying force in government is the personality of Sukarno, his recent activities provide a grotesque commentary on multi-partyism in a new and divided state. **1967** J. J. LINZ in Lipset & Rokkan *Party Syst. & Voter Alignments* 259 (*heading*) The transition from extreme multipartism to polarized conflict and civil war. **1971** D. W. RAE *Pol. Consequences Electoral Laws* (rev. ed.) iii. 53 An extreme case of 'multi-partism', with, say, ten parties, each polling about one tenth of the total vote.

multiped, -pede ('mʌltɪpɛd, -piːd), *sb.* and *a.* Now *rare.* [ad. L. *multiped-*, *-pēs* sb. and adj., *multipeda* sb., f. *multus* MULTI- + *pēs* foot.]

A. *sb.* A many-footed creature; †*spec.* a woodlouse.

1601 HOLLAND *Pliny* II. 378 A liniment made with the creepers called Sowes or Multipedes. **1670** LISTER in *Phil. Trans.* V. 2067 The Long and Round-bodied read-coloured Julus, distinguished from all other Multipeds, in that their innumerable legs are as small as hair, and white. **1713** DERHAM *Phys.-Theol.* IX. i. (1714) 406 *note*, It is a wonderful pretty Mechanism observable in the going of Multipedes, as the *Juli, Scolopendræ*, &c. **1860** *Temple Bar* I. 127 Those multipeds have the advantage over quadrupeds. **1861** *Fraser's Mag.* Dec. 766 A blood-thirsty swarm of brown broad backed multipeds.

B. *adj.* Many-footed.

1736 H. BROOKE *Univ. Beauty* v. 110 All the wondrous train, Who plung'd recluse in silent caverns sleep; Or multipede, Earth's leafy verdure creep. **1798** G. WAKEFIELD *Lett. Sir J. Scott* 18 Every fellow-creature, biped, quadruped, or multiped. **1828–32** WEBSTER, *Multiped.* **1850** OGILVIE, *Multipede.*

So **multipedous** (mʌl'tɪpɪdəs) *a.*, pertaining to or characteristic of many-footed animals.

1713 DERHAM *Phys.-Theol.* IX. i. (1714) 406 Motion.. Vermicular, or Sinuous.. or the Multipedous, or any other Way. **1851** *Fraser's Mag.* XLIII. 211 This subcuticular multipedous mode of going through the world.

multiperforate, -personal: see MULTI- 1.

'multiphase, *a.* [MULTI- 3.] Having or producing two or more phases; in *Electr.* = POLYPHASE *a.*

1890 *Century Dict.*, *Multi-phase*, having many phases, in any sense of that word. **1892** S. P. THOMPSON *Dynamo-Electr. Mach.* 687 Motors.. requiring multiphase currents. **1895–6** *Cal. Univ. Nebraska* 97 Single and multiphase dynamos. **1916** W. H. N. JAMES *Alternating Currents* v. 87 The relative merits of single and multiphase systems depend upon the purpose to which the power is to be applied. **1946** *Nature* 31 Aug. 307/2 The electrolytic polishing of multi-phase metals is usually more difficult than that of single-phase metals owing to differing properties.. of the different phases. **1966** D. G. BRANDON *Mod. Techniques Metallogr.* ii. 82 Absorption contrast arises from variations in chemical composition and hence provides information about the composition and distribution of phases in a multiphase alloy.

So **'multiphased** *a.*, occurring in several stages.

1970 *Sci. Amer.* Feb. 103/3 The effect of laser irradiation on the cells varied with the stage of mitosis, the multiphased process of cell division.

multiphasic (mʌltɪ'feɪzɪk), *a.* [f. MULTI- 1 a + PHAS(E + -IC.] Applied to tests or investigations designed to reveal various phases or aspects of personality, health, etc.

1940 *Psychol. Bull.* XXXVII. 425 The Multiphasic Personality Schedule is a group of 504 items for administration to adults. **1958** M. ARGYLE *Relig. Behaviour* viii. 87 Brown and Lowe (1915) tested a large number of students on the Minnesota Multiphasic Personality Inventory (MMPI) and found that a group of Bible students —who would be extreme Protestants—scored high on hysteria. **1968** *Daily Tel.* 22 Nov. 25/4 Multiphasic screening could disclose much potential sickness and make possible early treatment. **1971** *Brit. Med. Bull.* XXVII. 6/1 In a multiphasic programme the individual will be subjected to a number of tests within a short space of time.

multiplane ('mʌltɪpleɪn), *sb.* and *a.* [f. MULTI- 2, 3 + PLANE *sb.*[3]] **A.** *sb.* An aeroplane or glider having several 'planes' or main supporting surfaces placed one above another. Also *attrib.* or as *adj.*

1909 A. BERGET *Conquest of Air* II. ii. 139 Will the aeroplane be a 'monoplane' or 'multiplane'? *Ibid.* 147 The arrangement employed.. is 'partitioning'.. and applies to multiplane aeroplanes. **1928** *Jrnl. R. Aeronaut. Soc.* XXXII. 145 The method of obtaining the reduction of drag for a multiplane is described. **1939** C. H. L. NEEDHAM *Aircraft Design* I. vi. 74 When two or more planes are situated one above the other, so as to form biplane, triplane or multiplane arrangements, the low pressure region over the top of the lower wing is closely adjacent to the high pressure area below the upper wing. **1960** C. H. GIBBS-SMITH *Aeroplane* 337 Wenham was the first to build.. a multiplane aeroplane, a full-size glider with five wings. **1969** K. MUNSON *Pioneer Aircraft 1903–14* 154/2 In 1904 appeared the first man-carrying multiplane (Phillips I). This had a framework of twenty rigid blade sustainers. **1973** *Country Life* 11 Oct. 1074 In 1903 a multiplane, somewhat similar to the one built in 1893, was constructed and taken to Essex for trials.

B. *adj.* Involving or occupying several distinct planes or layers (not necessarily horizontal); applied *spec.* in *Cinemat.* to a technique employed to give an enhanced impression of perspective.

1909, etc. [see A above]. **1948** E. LINDGREN *Art of Film* vii. 127 Objects in different planes will appear to move at different speeds according to their distance from the camera lens.. and the relationship between these various movements can.. suggest almost a three-dimensional effect; this is the principle behind the multiplane technique now employed in the making of cartoon films. **1955** J. CAUNTER *How to do Tricks in Amat. Films* 65 To give the effect of maximum perspective to a background scene you will have to divide it into more than one layer of scenery... This is the multiplane principle. **1959** HALAS & MANVELL *Technique Film Animation* ii. 28 Now the animation studios have their own specialized cameras.. capable of photographing multi-plane images with back lighting. **1961** G. MILLERSON *Technique Television Production* xix. 362 Multiplane captions. Here the caption is comprised of several transparent or cut-out layers, and by revealing or obscuring these layers, we can add or remove detail to order. **1969** *Daily Tel.* 7 Feb. 21/6 A clever white multiplane set is used for the projection of slides and movie-film, either bathing the stage in dazzling colour or else enthroning unexpected VIPs.

multiple ('mʌltɪp(ə)l), *a.* and *sb.* Also 6 *Sc.* multipill (?), 8 (*rare*) multuple. [a. F. *multiple*, ad. late L. *multiplus* (cf. *duplus* DOUBLE) = L. *multiplex* (see MULTIPLEX). The word is rare before the 19th c. exc. in A. 1 and B. 2.]

A. *adj.*

1. *Math.* **a.** That is a multiple (see B. 2); †that is some multiple *of.*

1714 BARROW *Euclid* VII. Def. 20 Numbers are proportionall, when the first is as multiple of the second, as the third is of the fourth. **1727–52** CHAMBERS *Cycl.* s.v., Multiple ratio, or proportion, is that which is between multiple numbers. **1888** *Encycl. Brit.* XXIII. 564/2 *marg.*, Formulæ for multiple and sub-multiple angles.

b. ***multiple proportion, ratio***: the proportion or ratio existing between a quantity and some multiple of it, or between several multiples of it. ***law of multiple proportions*** (Chem.): see quot. 1876.

1704 J. HARRIS *Lex. Techn.* I, *Multiple Proportion*, is when the Antecedent being divided by the Consequent, the Quotient is more than Unity. **1795** HUTTON *Math. Dict.* s.v., Duple, triple, &c. ratios; as also subduples, subtriples, &c., are so many species of Multiple and Submultiple ratios. **1837** WHEWELL *Hist. Induct. Sci.* I. 151 Dalton's ideas concerning multiple proportions. **1876** ARMSTRONG in *Encycl. Brit.* V. 468/1 It is often the case that elements combine together in several proportions; whenever this occurs the several proportions in which the one element unites with the other invariably bear a simple relation to one another. Thus 1 part by weight of hydrogen unites with 8 parts by weight of oxygen, forming water, and with 16 or 8 × 2 parts of oxygen, forming peroxide of hydrogen... This law is known as the law of combination in multiple proportions.

c. *Printing.* ***multiple mark*** (see quot.).

1888 JACOBI *Printers' Vocab.*, *Multiple mark.*—A sign in arithmetic, thus ×.

2. a. Consisting of or characterized by many parts, elements, or individual components; having many origins, results, influences, issues, or the like; manifold. With pl. sb.: Many and various.

1647 N. BACON *Disc. Govt. Eng.* I. vii. 25 That Kings should bow down their necks under the double or rather multiple yoke of Pope and Archbishops. **1662** PETTY *Taxes* x. §13 Why should not the solvent thieves and cheats be rather punished with multiple restitutions than death, pillory, whipping, &c.? *a* **1734** NORTH *Lives* (1826) I. 427 It introduced two reports instead of one, and multiple attendances. **1831** CARLYLE *Sart. Res.* I. vii. (1858) 29 Doublets of fustian, under which lie multiple ruffs of cloth. **1859** DARWIN in *Life & Lett.* (1887) II. 230 You overrate the importance of the multiple origin of dogs. **1876** *Haeckel's Hist. Creation* II. 45 The multiple, or polyphyletic, hypothesis of descent. **1879** THOMSON & TAIT *Nat. Phil.* I. I. §327 This problem is essentially determinate, but generally has multiple solutions. **1886** *Sat. Rev.* 12 June 801/1 The intention of the Government to abolish the multiple vote which now belongs to the larger ratepayers.

b. ***multiple shop, store***: one of several shops of the same kind belonging to the same firm, opened in different localities. Cf. *chain store.*

1903 J. HAZELIP *Multiple-Shop Accounts* 1 There is considerable difference in the class of business carried on by multiple-shop firms. **1909** *Westm. Gaz.* 10 May 9/4 Some of the multiple shops.. have been retailing at 9s. 4d. sugar which has cost them 14s. 7½d. to buy. **1927** *Daily Tel.* 14 Mar. 4/7 The multiple shops.. have reduced their prices in accord with the drop in wholesale prices. **1929** E. GILL *Art-Nonsense* 315 Politics and social guidance are left to.. novelists, multiple-store keepers, manufacturers of motor-cars. **1959** *Times Lit. Suppl.* 4 Sept. 504/3 *An Introduction to Music* is another of what might be called the multiple-stores books which aim to provide everything for the music-lover. **1963** N. MARSH *Dead Water* (1964) ii. 46 There's a rash of boarding establishments and a multiple store. **1965** *Modern Law Rev.* XXVIII. 553 The new multiple shops and shopping centres in both the United States and England. **1972** N. MARSH *Tied up in Tinsel* vi. 140 There's no joy down your way: big multiple stores robbery.

c. ***multiple occupancy, occupation*** = MULTI-OCCUPATION.

1971 *Guardian* 11 June 12/3 There is a certain amount of substandard accommodation largely created through multiple occupation. **1973** *Times* 26 July 4/6 Probably 100 to 120 families are breaking the regulations applicable to multiple occupancy houses. **1975** *Times* 30 Aug. 13/6 Perhaps Mr Cutler.. would like to relax controls on houses in multiple occupation so that even more people can share a bath.

3. In technical use: **a.** *Anat.*, *Zool.*, and *Bot.* ***multiple allele*** or ***allelomorph***: any allele which is located at a genetic locus known to have three or more alleles; ***multiple factor***: any gene which acts in concert with other, non-allelic, genes to control the expression of a character; ***multiple fission***: the division of a cell into more than two daughter-cells. †**b.** *Chem.* Of salts: Containing many 'ingredients' or radicals. **c.** *Astron.* (***multiple star***: a cluster of stars forming apparently one system.) **d.** *Path.* Involving many parts, etc. ***multiple myeloma*** [tr. G. *multiples myelom* (J. von Rustizky 1873, in *Deutsche Zeitschr. f. Chirurgie* III. 163)], = MYELOMATOSIS; ***multiple sclerosis***, a chronic, progressive, demyelinating disease in which sclerosis occurs in patches in the brain and spinal cord, which chiefly affects young adults, and is often manifested initially as mild attacks with varying symptoms followed later by successive remissions (often long-lasting) and relapses, but typically leading to weakness and paresis of the lower limbs, intention tremors in the upper limbs, disturbed sight and speech, emotional changes, and mental deterioration; also called *disseminated sclerosis*. **e.** *Physics.* (***multiple echo***, ***image***: see quots.) **f.** *Electr.* (***multiple arc***: a compound electric circuit; ***multiple telegraphy***: a system by which many messages may be sent over the same wire.) **g.** Applied to mechanical contrivances or operations in which there are many parts of the same kind or in which the same action is many times repeated. **h.** *Math.* (See quots.) **i.** In the Kantian philosophy: That is a manifold. *rare.* **j.** *Statistics.* Involving the joint effect on the variable under investigation of two or more other variables. **k.** ***multiple use***: = MULTI-USE *a.*

a. 1752 J. HILL *Hist. Anim.* 20 The Monoculus, with multiple and capillaceous antennæ. **1831** MACGILLIVRAY tr. *Richard's Elem. Bot.* 109 The bulb is sometimes simple... Or it is multiple, when several small bulbs are found collected under the same envelope. *Ibid.* 319 Multiple fruits are those which result from the aggregation of several pistils contained in the same flower. **1848** *Quain's Anat.* (ed. 5) 972 The fangs of all the molar teeth are multiple. **1887** BENTLEY *Man. Bot.* (ed. 5) 239 The corolla is usually composed of but one whorl of petals,.. but in some flowers there are two or more whorls.. in which case it is called multiple. **1912** E. A. MINCHIN *Introd. Study Protozoa* vii. 120 In most cases, probably, of multiple fission the nucleus contains a centriole, and.. the centriole multiplies by fission a number of times without the nucleus as a whole becoming divided. **1913** *Amer. Naturalist* XLVII. 234 (*heading*) The Himalayan rabbit case, with some considerations on multiple allelomorphs. **1915** R. PEARL *Modes Res. Genetics* i. 21 In recent developments of Mendelian theory it has been a common practice to assume the existence of multiple factors as the causal agents of a single character. **1938** A. F. SHULL *Heredity* (ed. 3) xi. 103 (*heading*) Multiple alleles. **1945** E. ALTENBURG *Genetics* v. 83 Members of several gene pairs which act in a cumulative way on a trait are known as multiple factors. **1948** *Nature* 30 Oct. 684/1 (*heading*) Multiple allelomorphs in colour vision. **1971** J. Z. YOUNG *Introd. Study Man* xl. 585 Fourteen different systems of blood antigen genes are known... The most familiar of them are three multiple alleles known as G^A, G^B, and G, the first two being both dominant to G. These genes are often called simply *A, B,* and *O.* **1972** *Proc. Nat. Acad. Sci.* LXIX. 2346/1 Organisms dividing by multiple fission can be used to study the initiation and control of cytokinesis, because those unique events essential to cytokinesis are separated from events of the cell cycle that pertain to DNA synthesis, mitosis, or cytoplasmic growth.

b. 1797 *Encycl. Brit.* (ed. 3) XVI. 628/2 M. Magellan thinks, that the aphronitrum is not only a triple but a multiple salt. **1865** MANSFIELD *Salts* 55 A double salt will be indicated by a single cross,.. the cross being repeated for multiple salts of higher degree.

c. 1850 J. P. NICHOL *Archit. Heavens* 207 Multiple stars and groups like the Pleiades. *Ibid.* Contents p. xxi, Multiple systems. **1867** H. MACMILLAN *Bible Teachings* i. (1870) 17 The double and multiple stars shine with differently-coloured light.

d. 1851 PAGET *Lect. Tumours* vii. 78 Multiple ossifications of tendons, muscles, and other tissues. **1872** T. BRYANT *Pract. Surg.* 255 Sometimes they [*sc.* sublingual cysts] are multiple, and on several occasions on opening one cyst I have seen a second within. **1877** tr. *von Ziemssen's Cycl. Med.* XII. 708 Abscess of the brain is either single or multiple. *Ibid.* 852 Multiple cerebro-spinal sclerosis. **1887** *Brit. Med. Jrnl.* 26 Mar. 681/1 Multiple Peripheral (Alcoholic) Neuritis in Women. **1885** J. ROSS *Handbk. Dis. Nervous Syst.* xx. 674 (*heading*) Multiple sclerosis of the brain and spinal cord (disseminated or insular sclerosis). **1897** *Trans. Path. Soc.* XLVIII. 169 (*heading*) General lymphadenomatosis of bones, one form of 'multiple myeloma'. **1904** Multiple myeloma [see MYELOMATOSIS]. **1917** *Jrnl. Nervous & Mental Dis.* XLV. 454 In multiple sclerosis we had been in the habit of considering the disease incurable and although there might be a remission for a number of months or years, it could not be looked upon as a cure. **1957** S. L. ROBBINS *Textbk. Path.* xxxii. 1311/2 Studies on animals with injections of nervous tissue and adjuvants may yet prove to be important in multiple sclerosis, but no worker has yet reproduced a convincing replica of the disease. **1961** *Lancet* 5 Aug. 290/1 On paper electrophoresis, macroglobulinæmic sera yield patterns which are indistinguishable from those found in multiple myeloma. **1966** Multiple myeloma [see MYELOMATOSIS]. **1971** *New Scientist* 7 Jan. 6/1 Multiple sclerosis is the commonest disease of the nervous system in northern Europe and the USA. **1972** C. E. SEIVERD *Hematol. for Med. Technologists* (ed. 4) xxxvii. 667 Myeloma means marrow tumor; thus, multiple myeloma may be interpreted as simply meaning many tumors of the bone marrow. Multiple myeloma is also referred to by the following terms; myelome, plasmocytoma, plasma cell myeloma, myelomatosis, and Kahler's disease.

e. 1727–52 CHAMBERS *Cycl.* s.v. *Echo*, A multiple echo may be made, by so placing the echoing bodies, at unequal distances, as that they may reflect all one way. **1863** ATKINSON tr. *Ganot's Nat. Philos.* §193 Multiple echoes are those which repeat the same sound several times; this is the case when two opposite surfaces.. successively reflect sound.

f. 1873 F. JENKIN *Electr. & Magn.* iv. §7 With a long circuit of great external resistance large cells, or many of them joined in multiple arc, will fail to give us strong currents. **1877** *Athenæum* 21 July 84/1 An apparatus designed for multiple telegraphy, in which vibrations from a number of forks at the sending end were to be taken up by corresponding forks at the other end. **1879** G. PRESCOTT *Sp. Telephone* 50 A practical system of multiple telegraphy. **1888** *Encycl. Brit.* XXIII. 124/1 Delaunay's multiple telegraph.

g. 1875 KNIGHT *Dict. Mech.* 1496/2 *Multiple bolt*, an arrangement by which a number of bolts are simultaneously moved. **1879** *Engineering* XXVII. 506 Multiple wood-boring machine. *Ibid.* XXVIII. 195 Multiple drilling machine for rails. **1891** *Syd. Soc. Lex.*, *Multiple staining*, dyeing tissues for microscopical examination with more than one staining agent.

h. 1841 D. F. GREGORY *Ex. Diff. & Int. Calc.* xi. 460 Multiplication of several definite integrals together, so as to obtain a multiple integral. **1842** DE MORGAN *Diff. & Int. Calc.* 379 Multiple points are those in which two or more branches of the curve pass through the same point. **1879** SALMON *Higher Plane Curves* 32 A curve may.. have multiple tangents; or, in other words, that there may be lines which touch the curve in two or more points, or which have with the curve a contact of the second or higher order.

i. 1839 *Penny Cycl.* XIII. 176/1 The multiple matter presented by experience. *Ibid.* 176/2 The matter of mathematics is the multiple object of space and time.

j. 1903 *Phil. Trans. R. Soc.* A. CC. 3 (*heading*) On the fundamental theorem in multiple correlation. **1938** A. E. WAUGH *Elem. Statistical Method* xi. 318 Problems that involve the determination of the relationship between one variable and several other variables acting together are called problems of multiple correlation. *Ibid.* 321 The multiple-regression equation must obviously be altered so that we can account for changes in all the independent variables. **1958** M. ARGYLE *Relig. Behaviour* iii. 18 An alternative procedure for estimating the relative weight of different variables influencing percentages is multiple regression. **1971** *Brit. Med. Bull.* XXVII. 22/1 A multiple regression study showed that.. both water calcium and rainfall made significant contributions to the variance of cardiovascular death-rates between the towns studied. **1972** T. H. & R. J. WONNACOTT *Introd. Statistics for Business & Econ.* xiv. 350 Whereas the partial correlations measure the significance of regressors one by one, the multiple correlation *R* measures the significance of all the regressors at once.

k. 1969 *Gloss. for Landscape Work* (*B.S.I.*) v. 16 *Multiple use*, the use of land for more than one purpose, resulting in a modification in the methods of maintenance, for example, water catchment areas also used for cattle grazing or for forestry. **1969** *Jane's Freight Containers 1968–69* 505 (*caption*) SALwall.. incorporates a multiple-use double wall.

4. *Comb.* **a.** as ***multiple-valued*** adj.; **multiple-annular**, of many rings; (*b*) in phr. with sb. used attrib., as ***multiple contact switch***; **multiple-colour**, **-cylinder**, **-phase** = MULTI-COLOUR, etc.

1902 *Scotsman* 3 Jan. 7/6 A wonderfully complex, spiral, or *multiple-annular, nebula. **1899** *Daily News* 16 Feb. 5/1 His scheme of *multiple-colour illumination. **1889** *Electr. Engineer* 19 Apr. 310 The secondary coil is sub-divided into a number of sections connected with a *multiple contact switch. **1888** J. F. WILSON & D. GREY *Mod. Printing Mach.* x. 201 The large *multiple-cylinder machine erected by Colonel Hoe in 1848 for the Parisian daily paper *La Patrie.* **1891** *Times* 28 Sept. 13/6 A self-exciting *multiple-phase alternator of 80 volts electromotive force. **1878** *Encycl. Brit.* XVI. 731/2 (art. *Money*) When the state fixes the ratio between these metals a new system has come into existence, which has been called the *multiple tender system. **1882** MINCHIN *Unipl. Kinemat.* 197 Hence we do not get a *multiple-valued potential at *Q.*

b. ***multiple-beam***; **multiple-access** = *multi-access* (MULTI- 3); **multiple-aspect**, applied to a colour-light railway signal capable of displaying at least three aspects; **multiple-choice**, applied to an educational or psychological test in which the subject is asked to select his answer from several items; **multiple-disc**, applied to a kind of friction clutch consisting of a row of co-axial discs, fixed alternately to the driving and the driven parts, which may be brought in contact to transmit the drive from the one to the other; **multiple-unit**, of, pertaining to, or designating a train having a number of coaches provided with engines all of which can be controlled by a single driver; also as *sb.*, a coach of this kind.

1966 *New Scientist* 27 Oct. 160/3 This valuable experience.. has.. enabled us to take in our stride the 'multiple-access' problem of how to serve a large number of control consoles apparently simultaneously. **1970** O. DOPPING *Computers & Data Processing* ix. 130 A control program for a multiple access system must be able to identify a subscriber who requires service, find out which program he needs, and put him in the queue, if any. **1932** *Proc. Inst. Railway Signal Engin.* I. 57 (*heading*) Railway colour light signalling in relation to manual block and multiple aspect signals. **1963** KICHENSIDE & WILLIAMS *Brit. Railway Signalling* iii. 24 In colour-light areas, a multiple-aspect signal cannot display a 'green——clear' indication unless the next signal is showing at least a 'caution' if not a 'clear' aspect also. *Ibid.* 25 In colour-light areas.. every multiple-aspect signal serves as a distant, home and starting signal at the same time. **1970** *Railway World* Dec. 524 Multiple-aspect colour-light signalling with continuous track circuiting will be installed. **1945** *Proc. R. Soc.* A. CLXXXIV. 41 A multiple beam interferometric procedure.. can be used as a powerful method for revealing the details of the surface topography of approximately flat crystal planes. **1966** D. G. BRANDON *Mod. Techniques Metallogr.* i. 25 This may be done most simply by placing a half-silvered plate in contact with the specimen, when either two-beam or multiple-beam interference patterns may be obtained. **1928** ORLEANS & SEALY *Objective Tests* xiii. 220 Facility in framing optional answers for a multiple-choice question comes with practice. **1959** J. BARZUN *House of Intellect* 268 A basic defect of multiple choice tests: that they call for choices but not for reasons for choices. **1967** *Observer* 26 Nov. 1/4 In the American 'multiple-choice' examinations the candidate marks one of a number of possible responses to a question, instead of writing an essay on it. **1906**, **1909** Multiple disc [see *disc-clutch* (DISC *sb.* 8)]. **1967** *Jane's Surface Skimmer Systems 1967–68* 124/1 Flange-mounted converter automatically changing over from multiple-disc clutch.. to converter, operation, then again operation through multiple-disc clutch when moving on foils. **1902** *Encycl. Brit.* XXVIII. 93/1 The train operated by two or more motor cars under a common secondary control. This.. is called the 'multiple unit system'. **1955** *Oxf. Jun. Encycl.* VIII. 366/2 In Britain 'in-built' motive-power units have proved more popular than separate locomotives. These have 'multiple-unit' control, that is, one driver can control the current supply and braking throughout the whole train. **1967** *Economist* 21 Jan. 202/1 In October 1965 an agreement was reached between the railway management and the unions on single-manning for passenger and long-distance freight locomotives (and multiple-unit trains that have no loco as such). **1970** *Railway World* Dec. 540 At times of peak traffic, nine-car formations composed of two three-car multiple-units and three additional trailers are often seen.

c. Special collocations: **multiple birth** *Med.*, the birth of more than one child at a single confinement; **multiple exposure** *Photogr.*, the repeated exposure of the same frame of a film so as to produce superimposed images; **multiple image**, a composite image comprising two or more superimposed or adjacent images originally distinct (e.g. resulting from the repeated reflection of light, the reception of television signals that have travelled from the transmitter by different paths, or the simultaneous showing of several scenes on a cinema screen); **multiple personality** *Psychol.*, a dissociative condition in which an individual's personality is apparently split into two or more sub-personalities, each of which may become dominant and then is relatively distinct and complete; **multiple pregnancy** *Med.*, a pregnancy which would normally result in a multiple birth; **multiple resistance** *Med.*, resistance of a micro-organism to the action of more than one antibiotic; so ***multiple-resistant*** adj.; **multiple shift** *Industry*, a double or treble shift (sense 12); freq. *attrib.*; **multiple switchboard** *Teleph.* (see quot. 1932); **multiple twin**, (*a*) *Telephony*, a cable with a number of cores each of which consists of four wires arranged as two twisted pairs twisted together; usu. *attrib.*; (*b*) *Cryst.*, a twinned crystal composed of alternating lamellæ whose relative orientations are all governed by the same twin law; **multiple valve** *Electronics*, a multi-electrode valve.

1826 *Edin. Jrnl. Med. Sci.* II. 366 (*heading*) Memoir upon multiple or twin births. **1841** *Lancet* 9 Jan. 549/1 (*heading*) Statistics of multiple births. **1966** *Amer. Jrnl. Obstetr. & Gynecol.* XCIV. 490 (*heading*) Pregnancies following treatment with human gonadotropins with special reference to the problem of multiple births. **1968** *Guardian* 3 Oct. 9/2 Multiple births, enormously distressing to the mothers..; are becoming rarer. **1971** HELLMAN & PRITCHARD *Williams' Obstetr.* (ed. 14) xxv. 657 Some marriages appear to have an inordinately high frequency of multiple births. Greulich reported the case of a 35-year-old mother who in nine births delivered six pairs of two-egg twins and three single children. **1923** F. A. TALBOT *Moving Pict.* xxvii. 382 The perfection of the various devices for accomplishing multiple exposures rendered this manifestation of novelty in photography.. easy of ready accomplishment. **1968** *Listener* 18 Jan. 81/2 Multiple-exposure photograph of American mechanical claw used for scraping up samples of the moon's surface. **1863** ATKINSON tr. *Ganot's Nat. Philos.* §416 Multiple images formed by glass mirrors. **1963** A. F. ABBOTT *Ordinary Level Physics* xxv. 313 (*heading*) Multiple images formed by a thick glass mirror. **1965** Multiple image [see FREEZE *v.* 4 f]. **1971** *Gloss. Electrotechnical, Power Terms* (*B.S.I.*) III. iii. 23 *Multiple image; double image; ghost*, a defect apparent in reproduction in which an additional outline (ghost), or succession of outlines (multiple image), of prominent features of a picture may be observed displaced from the correct position of the outline by a noticeable amount. **1972** L. D. GIANNETTI *Understanding Movies* iii. 100 Multiple images, widely seen at Expo 67, will probably be the next modification of editing... Multiple image film-making does not intensify a movie's sense of realism,.. but tends to emphasize the expressionistic aspects of film art. **1901** *Proc. Soc. Psychical Res.* XV. 466 Cases of multiple personality are not very uncommon, but, so far as I know, no attempt has been made to determine the relation which the different personalities bear to each other. **1906** M. PRINCE *Dissociation of Personality* i. 3 The disintegration resulting in multiple personality is only a functional dissociation of that complex organization which constitutes a normal self. **1942** 'M. Innes' *Daffodil Affair* I. 38 'And did you say dissociation?' 'Yes. What is sometimes called multiple personality.' **1967** M. Argyle *Psychol. Interpersonal Behaviour* iii. 56 Everyone has a number of 'sub-personalities'..—cases of multiple personality are an extreme of what is universal. **1857** Bullock tr. *Cazeaux' Midwifery* 238 The term, compound or multiple pregnancy, has been applied to that in which two or more fœtuses are enclosed in the uterine cavity. **1964** *Obstetr. & Gynecol.* XXIV. 819 (*heading*) Size and number of umbilical vessels, a study of multiple pregnancy in man and the armadillo. **1952** S. K. R. Clarke et al. in *Lancet* 7 June 1132/1 Besides these organisms, called here 'completely resistant', there have appeared staphylococci with what may be called 'multiple resistance'—i.e. resistant to several of these drugs. **1960** *Brit. Med. Jrnl.* 2 Jan. 11/2 It cannot be assumed..that multiple resistance and enhanced virulence are necessarily associated. **1972** *Med. Microbiol. & Immunol.* CLVII. 142 (*heading*) Antimicrobial resistance of the genera *Proteus, Providencia* and *Serratia* with special reference to multiple resistance patterns. **1960** *Brit. Med. Jrnl.* 2 Jan. 17/1, 23 of the fatal infections were due to multiple-resistant strains. **1961** *Lancet* 29 July 248/2 It would prevent the selection and breeding of multiple-resistant strains. **1926** *Rep. R. Comm. Coal Industry* I. 175 in *Parl. Papers* (Cmd. 2600) XIV. 1 (*heading*) Advantages of multiple shifts. **1946** M. Dobb *Wages* (rev. ed.) iii. 62 Where it is practicable to introduce a multiple-shift system—two or three working-shifts a day instead of one—the same economy could be obtained together with the employment of additional workers. **1964** T. W. McRae *Impact of Computers on Accounting* vii. 208 Costs arising out of multiple-shift working. **1891** J. Poole *Pract. Telephone Handbk.* viii. 148 (*heading*) Multiple switch-boards. **1932** T. E. Herbert in E. Molloy *Pract. Electr. Engin.* V. 1865/2 A switchboard in which the subscribers' circuits are repeated at several points so as to make each subscriber accessible to every operator is known as a multiple switchboard. **1969** S. F. Smith *Telephony & Telegr. A* iv. 98 The need for a series type of multiple connexion which these jacks require on a multiple switchboard has certain disadvantages. **1922** *Encycl. Brit.* XXXII. 709/1 In..the 'multiple twin cable' the centre of yarn is dispensed with, and the cable consists of a number of 4-wire cores. **1932** *Amer. Mineralogist* XVII. 360 The diamond multiple twin..is from South Africa. **1959** J. W. Freebody *Telegr.* vi. 173/2 With the multiple-twin type [of cable] the paper insulated conductors are first twisted into pairs and two such pairs are then twisted together to form the two pair core or quad. **1966** *McGraw-Hill Encycl. Sci. & Technol.* V. 208/1 The width of the lamellae in multiple twins of plagioclases is usually about 1 mm and smaller. **1929** *Wireless World* 6 Mar. (*heading*) A Loewe multiple valve for mains operation. **1968** *Radio Communication Handbk.* (ed. 4) ii. 20/1 The trend is to make radio equipment as compact as possible and it is therefore convenient to take advantage of the special multiple valves which have more than one unit contained in a single envelope.

B. *sb.*

†**1.** = multiplie. *Sc. Obs.* (Perh. an error.)

1577–95 *Descr. Isles Scot.* in Skene *Celtic Scot.* (1880) III. App. 437 In all the small burnis of this Ile are multipill of salmond and other fisches.

2. a. *Math.* A quantity which contains another quantity some number of times without remainder. Thus, 4 is a multiple of 2; 6, of 2 and of 3.

least or ***lowest common multiple*** (L.C.M.): the least quantity that contains two or more quantities some number of times without remainder; e.g. 12 is the L.C.M. of 2, 3, and 4.

1685 tr. *Milliet's Elem. Euclid* v. 209 If the multiple of the first exceed that of the second, the multiple of the third will also exceed that of the fourth. *a* **1696** Scarburgh *Euclid* (1705) 181 If the Antecedent be not..a Multiple of the Consequent. **1818** Hallam *Mid. Ages* viii. i. (1819) II. 401 The preference given to twelve, or some multiple of it, in fixing the number..of judges. **1823** J. Mitchell *Dict. Math. & Phys. Sci.* s.v., To find the least common Multiple of several Numbers. **1856** Kane *Arct. Expl.* II. vii. 81 Their breadth either twelve, twenty-four, thirty-six, or some other multiple of twelve paces.

b. In chemical use (cf. A. 2 b).

1812 Sir H. Davy *Chem. Philos.* 112 If one number be employed to denote the smallest quantity in which a body combines, all other quantities of the same body will be multiples of this number. **1857** Miller *Elem. Chem., Org.* (1862) III. 28 Containing a certain additional number of multiples of the hydrocarbon C_2H_2. **1881** Lubbock in *Nature* 1 Sept. 409/2 Nearly all atomic weights are simple multiples of the atomic weight of hydrogen.

c. *fig.*

1858 J. Martineau *Stud. Chr.* 171 According as we..take each man as an integer, of which the race is a multiple [etc.]. **1869** Lecky *Europ. Mor.* (1877) I. 89 No multiple of the pleasure of eating pastry can be an equivalent to the pleasure derived from a generous action.

3. In the Kantian philosophy = manifold *sb.* 2 a.

1839 *Penny Cycl.* XIII. 176/1 The understanding, which subsumes the given multiple into unity.

4. *Teleph.* **a.** A section of a multiple switchboard containing one jack for each subscriber.

1905 A. C. Booth in M. Maclean *Mod. Electr. Pract.* VI. iii. ii. 110 The line shown..is already engaged by the insertion of a plug on the first multiple. **1948** J. Atkinson *Herbert & Procter's Telephony* (new ed.) I. x. 195/1 In general, a multiple is designed so that the best compromise between vertical and horizontal reach is obtained when the switchboard is equipped with the ultimate number of lines.

b. ***in multiple.*** Of calling jacks: (connected) between the same pairs of wires, so enabling the same connection to be made at different points.

1943 A. L. Albert *Fund. Telephony* viii. 174 The calling jacks of each section must be connected in parallel or multiple with the calling jacks of every other section. **1969** S. F. Smith *Telephony & Telegr. A* iv. 98 The bush of the jack will be connected to the exchange battery via the plug inserted in one of the other jacks with which it is connected in multiple.

5. A multiple shop or store (see A. 2 b above).

1951 in Partridge *Dict. Slang* (ed. 4) 1115/1. **1957** *Economist* 5 Oct. 60/1 The multiples have also been ahead in adjusting their range of shoe styles. **1966** *New Statesman* 29 July 156/1 A businessman, stating..that he had sold 'self-owned multiple to avoid capital gains tax'. **1972** *House & Garden* Feb. 100/4 Some of the small merchants..do a good business with Cape growths. The large multiples..are missing the opportunity.

6. An inexpensive work of art mass-producible by industrial methods.

1968 *Times* 26 Mar. 7 The artist who becomes interested in multiples takes the first step towards involving himself with the demands of technology. **1970** [see graphic *sb.* 3]. **1971** P. Dickinson *Sleep & his Brother* ii. 36 The one touch of art—a bronze and bulbous paperweight, vaguely post-Brancusi—had the look of one of a large issue of multiples. **1973** J. A. Walker *Gloss. Art, Archit. & Design since 1945* 141 The idea of Multiples was first suggested by Agam and Jean Tinguely. They put their idea to the Parisian gallery dealer Denise René in 1955 but none were produced until 1962.

multiple (ˈmʌltɪp(ə)l), *v.* *Teleph.* [f. multiple *a.* and *sb.*] *trans.* To make (a circuit) accessible to operators at more than one point on a switchboard or switchboards; to provide or employ duplicates of (a device) for this purpose.

1906 Bell & Wilson *Pract. Telephony* (ed. 4) ix. 108 At the outgoing end the lines are multipled three times on every two sections, so that every operator has every line almost directly in front of her. **1932** T. Sherratt in J. A. Fleming *Electr. Educator* (ed. 2) III. 1194/1 The trunks are multipled to the contacts of a number of line switches, so that several subscribers can gain access to the same trunks. **1942** Knight & Prickett *Poole's Telephone Handbk.* (ed. 8) xii. 312 Each answering jack and lamp is multipled every four, six, or twelve panels according to traffic requirements. **1969** S. F. Smith *Telephony & Telegr. A* iv. 96 It is sufficient..to multiple the jacks without also multipling the calling indicators or lamps.

multiple, variant of multiplie *Sc. Obs.*

†**multiplee.** *Math. Obs.* [? f. multiple + -ee (with vague meaning).] A partial product. Also (? *erron.*) a multiple.

1660 J. Moore *Arithm.* i. 50 (*Division*) In this example I set 568 on the [Napier's] bones, which gives me the severall Multiplées. **1674** Jeake *Arith.* (1696) 23 Under all these lines of production sometime called Multiplees..draw another right line. **1706** Phillips (ed. Kersey), *Multiplee*, is a greater Number that contains a less, a certain Number of Times without any Remainder.

ˌmultipleˈpoinding. *Scots Law.* [See poind *v.*] An action raised by the holder of a fund or property to which there are several claimants, who are thereby required to come together and settle their claims in court.

1693 Stair *Instit.* iii. i. (ed. 2) 376 Seing he ought to have raised a Process of multiple poinding, calling the Debitor and all the Arresters or Assigneys to dispute their several Rights. **1753** *Scots Mag.* May 258/1 A multiple-poinding was brought by the heritors. **1824** Scott *Redgauntlet* let. xiii, How can he bring a Multiplepoinding, the very summons of which sets forth, that the pursuer does owe certain monies, which he is desirous to pay by warrant of a judge? **1890** *Daily News* 30 Jan. 4/2 In the action of Multiplepoinding defending before the Lords of Council and Session, at the instance of Henry Calder..and others the sole trustees..acting under the Trust Disposition and Settlement, granted by Alexander Robertson,..and Mrs. Catherine Robertson,..Pursuers and Real Raisers.

multiplet (ˈmʌltɪplət). [f. multiple *a.* and *sb.* + -et, after *doublet, triplet.*] **a.** A group of lines in a spectrum that are close together and spaced approximately in accordance with a simple rule; a group of related levels in an atom that differ slightly in energy, esp. a group in which this is due to differing relative orientations of either the electronic spin and orbital angular momenta, giving different values of the quantum number *J* (in the case of fine structure), or the electronic and nuclear angular momenta, giving different values of the quantum number *F* (in the case of hyperfine structure).

1922 M. A. Catalán in *Phil. Trans. R. Soc.* A. CCXXIII. 147 As will be seen later there are many 'groups' of lines in the manganese spectrum with similar structure to that of the foregoing 'group', and for this form of regularity the name 'multiplet' is suggested. **1929** *Trans. Faraday Soc.* XXV. 672 Next, the coupling between spin momenta of the electrons gave a 'resultant' spin vector *S*, which determined the multiplicity. The multiplicity was given by $R = 2S + 1$, if *S* was measured in units of $h/2\pi$. Finally, the components of a multiplet were regarded as determined by the coupling between the resultant *L* vector and the resultant *S* vector. **1942** [see fine structure 1 a]. **1959** *Sci. News* LIII. 87 In order to interpret all the observations, such as the multiplet structure of spectral lines.., it has to be assumed that the electron has, independently of its orbital motion, an intrinsic angular momentum and a magnetic moment. **1967** W. R. Hindmarsh *Atomic Spectra* v. 50 A quantum number *F* can be ascribed to each hyperfine level such that the number increases by one from one level to the next and..the separation between two successive levels is..*AF* where *A* is a constant for a hyperfine multiplet. **1971** A. G. Sharkey in R. I. Reed *Recent Topics Mass Spectrometry* 128 High-resolution mass spectrometry is unique in providing a precise mass from which a molecular formula can be derived. The basis of the high-resolution technique is the ability of the instrument to resolve multiplets, having the same nominal mass but differing in precise mass.

b. A group of sub-atomic particles that are alike as regards the values of the various quantum numbers except for the third component of isospin (and hence charge), which is different for each particle and has one of the $2I + 1$ values $0, \pm\frac{1}{2}, \pm 1, \ldots, \pm I$ ($I = 0$ or half-integral); also, a larger group (also called a supermultiplet) composed of a number of such charge multiplets, each likewise characterized by a different value of hypercharge (or strangeness) but having the same spin and the same parity.

In quots. 1937 more a *transf.* use of prec. sense.

1937 *Physical Rev.* LI. 106 The structure of the multiplets of nuclear terms is investigated, using as a first approximation a Hamiltonian which does not involve the ordinary spin and corresponds to equal forces between all nuclear constituents, protons and neutrons. The multiplets turn out to have a rather complicated structure, instead of the *S* of atomic spectroscopy, one has three quantum numbers *S, T, Y*. *Ibid.* 117/1 Every one of these six states can be doubly occupied, with a particle $\tau = 1$ and $\tau = -1$ (neutron or proton). The half sum of the τ is denoted by T_ζ and the different T_ζ from $-T$ to T united into a multiplet. **1954** *Proc. Nat. Acad. Sci.* XL. 490 In discussing baryon states we used the intuitive argument of approximate mass degeneracy in a multiplet. **1956** [see hypercharge]. **1964** *New Scientist* 20 Feb. 458/3 The particles appear in groups, or 'multiplets', of particles of different charge but very nearly equal mass. **1965** *Ibid.* 18 Mar. 738/3 Just as in the theory of SU(2) the particles are arranged in multiplets, but now they are distinguished within a multiplet by both their charge and hypercharge. The SU(3) symmetry relates not just the proton and neutron one to another, but includes also in one multiplet the six particles known as hyperons. **1970** [see isospin]. **1970** D. B. Lichtenberg *Unitary Symmetry & Elem. Particles* iii. 34 The $2I + 1$ different charge states of a particle with isospin *I* constitute a multiplet. However, since isospin is not an exact symmetry, the different states are not exactly degenerate in energy. It is often said under such circumstances that different members of the multiplet are different particles, rather than different states of the same particle. **1973** L. J. Tassie *Physics Elem. Particles* iv. 39 We now consider the three pions π^-, π^0, π^+ as a charge multiplet or isospin multiplet of multiplicity $2I + 1 = 3$ yielding $I = 1$. We identify the $I_3 = +1$ state as the π^+; $I_3 = 0$ as the π^0; $I_3 = -1$ as the π^-. *Ibid.* xi. 134 The arrangement of *N*, Λ, Σ and Ξ into one multiplet, an octet.., is illustrated in Fig. 49.1. The mass splittings between the different isospin multiplets in the octet are about 20 times the mass splitting within isospin multiplets.

multiplex (ˈmʌltɪplɛks), *a.* and *sb.* †Pl. multiplices (*Math.*). [a. L. *multiplex*, f. *multus* multi- + *-plex* = -fold.] **A.** *adj.*

†**1.** *Math.* **a.** ***multiplex to, of***: that is some multiple of. *Obs.*

1570 Billingsley *Euclid* v. 126 b, Multiplex is a greater magnitude in respect of the lesse, when the lesse measureth the greater. As the line CD..is multiplex to the lyne AB. **1651** T. Rudd *Euclide* 185 How multiplex one magnitude is to one, so multiplex are all the magnitudes, to all. **1660** Barrow *Euclid* vi. Prop. 1 The triangle ACH is as multiplex of the triangle ACB, as the base HC is of the base BC. **1690** Leybourn *Curs. Math.* 211 Where AB 3 measureth CD 9, and therefore 9 is Multiplex to 3.

†**b.** ***multiplex proportion***, multiple proportion.

1557 Recorde *Whetst.* B iv b, There is one kinde of proportion, that is named multiplex, or manyfolde. **1609** Dowland *Ornith. Microl.* 62 The Proportions, which make Musicall Consonances, are sixe..three in the Multiplex Kind,..3 in the super particular. **1709–29** V. Mandey *Syst. Math., Arith.* 35 *Proportion Multiplex*, is the Habitude of a greater Number to a lesser, when the greater Number contains the lesser some times exactly. **1788** T. Taylor *Proclus* I. 49 All the multiplex and super-particular proportions which they [*sc.* numbers] contain.

2. = manifold *a.* 1, 2; multiple *a.* 2, 3.

1676 Grew *Anat. Flowers* ii. §21 The reason why the Figure of the Flower is more multiplex, than that of the Leaf. **1822** T. L. Peacock *Maid Marian* i, The whole complex and multiplex detail of the noble science of dinner. **1837** Carlyle *Fr. Rev.* (1872) III. i. viii. 54 Vehicles of all forms:..carriages, single, double and multiplex. **1838** —— *Sart. Res.* iii. x, Their raiment..is fastened together by a multiplex combination of buttons, thrums, and skewers. **1879** Farrar *St. Paul* I. 10 Brief and scattered letters out of the multiplex correspondence of a varied life. **1886** Pater *Ess. fr. Guardian* (1896) 25 So multiplex is the result that minds of quite opposite type might well discover in these pages their own special thought or humour.

3. In technical use. (Cf. multiple *a.* 3.)

a. *Bot.* Having many parts of the same kind together. Of a corolla: Having petals lying over each other in folds. **b.** *Electr.* = multiple *a.* 3 f. More widely in *Telecommunications*, applied to processes and equipment for transmitting two or more independent signals or programmes (to be later separated and recovered) simultaneously over a single wire or channel, and to a composite signal so formed. **c.** *Philos.* = multiple *a.* 3 i. **d.** *Path.* = multiple *a.* 3 d.

a. 1819 *Pantologia* s.v., *Multiplex Corol.* **1856** Henslow *Dict. Bot. Terms* 111 *Multiplex*, where many of the same parts or organs occur together.

b. 1873 M. Gally *Brit. Pat.* 1395 17 Apr. 13 My Invention has particular reference to 'multiplex telegraphy', or the employment of a number of operators sending without conflict a number of different messages upon a single wire. **1883** *Jrnl. Franklin Inst.* CXVI. 479 In the multiplex [system], as I myself have seen, an instantaneous change in the resistance of the line equal to five hundred miles, may be made without practically affecting the synchronous movement of the distributors. **1886** *Rep. Brit. Ass.* 812 Multiplex Telegraphy. By W. H. Preece, F.R.S. **1895–6** *Cal. Univ. Nebraska* 102 Telegraphy and Telephony. Single, duplex, quadruplex, and multiplex systems. **1934** [see COAXIAL *a.* 2c]. **1962** A. NISBETT *Technique Sound Studio* 261 Multiplex radio transmissions and the single groove of a stereo disc each contain more than one channel. **1970** J. EARL *Tuners & Amplifiers* ii. 47 Multiplex signal.. consists of 19kHz pilot-tone, the A + B mono information and sidebands of the A − B stereo information (the.. subcarrier.. having been suppressed at the transmitter). **1973** *Mod. Railways* Jan. 12/2 Interlockings within three or four miles of Bristol are operated by individual circuits... Beyond this distance electronic time division multiplex equipment is used.

c. **1838** tr. *Kant's Crit. Pure Reason* Explan. Terms 648 Diverse, Multifarious, Multiplex, Various, (*Mannichfaltig*).

d. **1899** *Allbutt's Syst. Med.* VIII. 895 Eyelid xanthoma differs essentially in structure from the multiplex variety.

B. *sb.*

†**1.** *Math.* = MULTIPLE *sb.* 2. *Obs.*

1570 BILLINGSLEY *Euclid* v. 132 For the multiplex of 3.. ye shall haue 18. **1651** T. RUDD *Euclide* 183 When equimultiplices being taken, the multiplex of the first exceedeth the multiplex of the second.. then [etc.]. *Ibid.* 195 Like parts of multiplices.. have one and the same proportion. **1695** ALINGHAM *Geom. Epit.* 61 The double, treble, (or any other Multiplex..) of two quantities are in the same reason as the Quantities themselves.

2. In the Kantian philosophy: = MANIFOLD *sb.* 2a.

1836 J. W. SEMPLE *Kant's Metaphysic of Ethic* Introd. p. li. *note*, Even Space and Time, though singulars *a priori*, do, so far forth as they consist of *partes extra partes*, exhibit a multiplex.

3. *Electr.* A multiplex system or signal.

1959 J. W. FREEBODY *Telegr.* ii. 50/2 This printer was used in connexion with the Murray multiplex. **1967** *Technology Week* 20 Feb. 4/2 Initial experiments with time-division multiplex have convinced Comsat Corp. that satellite transmission does not produce insuperable synchronization problems. **1970** *Toronto Daily Star* 24 Sept. 26/1 (Advt.), It ..tapes for multiplex and even makes 'sound with sound' recordings. **1973** HILLS & EVANS *Telecommunications Syst. Design* I. iv. 92 Modern equipment has group and supergroup limiters applied to the signal prior to their assembly into the higher multiplex.

multiplex ('mʌltɪplɛks), *v.* [f. the sb.] *trans.* To incorporate into a multiplex signal or system.

1925 C. A. WRIGHT *Telephone Communication* xiii. 317 The terminal equipment required to multiplex a telephone line is costly and its use is, consequently, justified only with long lines. **1955** *Sci. News Let.* 5 Mar. 158/2 You may soon be able to hear programs from your local FM station—minus commercials—in buses.. and on the job. This is just one of the possibilities of a system being considered.. that would allow FM stations to 'multiplex' their broadcasts. In the process, two separate signals would be sent from the same tower using the same radio frequencies. **1966** *McGraw-Hill Encycl. Sci. & Technol.* V. 352/2 When communication channels are multiplexed by time division, a number of messages is propagated over a common transmitting medium by allocating different time intervals in sequence for the transmission of each message. **1969** *Sci. Jrnl.* Dec. 42/3 A colour TV system multiplexes (by frequency division) video, colour and sound information. **1972** *Sci. Amer.* Sept. 120/3 The T1 carrier of the Bell Telephone System, which multiplexes 24 speech signals, is a typical example of a pulse-code-modulation (PCM) system.

Hence '**multiplexed** *ppl. a.*; '**multiplexing** *vbl. sb.* Also '**multiplexer, -or**, a device which multiplexes.

1955 *Sci. News Let.* 5 Mar. 158/3 Multiplexing is only practical on FM broadcasts because at present there are too many technical difficulties in splitting up AM programs. **1957** *Electronic Engin.* XXIX. 159/1 The information received from, say, two channels of the multiplexor are admitted serially to the clamping circuit. **1964** *Ann. N.Y. Acad. Sci.* CXV. 574 Multiplexers can be sequential sampling devices, or electronic commutators, which sample each channel in turn cyclically. **1969** *Sci. Jrnl.* Dec. 42 This spacing of the different signals over adjacent frequency ranges of the communication channel is called frequency-division multiplexing. *Ibid.* (*caption*) Frequency spectrum of a frequency division multiplexed channel shows how.. five carriers.. are each surrounded by sidebands. **1970** O. DOPPING *Computers & Data Processing* viii. 121 A multiplexor channel has its own facilities for sharing its time between different slow input/output operations. **1973** *Physics Bull.* July 413/3 A multiplexed hologram is produced from the sequence of exposures on the cine film.

'**multipliable**, *a.* [f. MULTIPLY *v.* + -ABLE. So in Fr.] Capable of being multiplied.

1625 BP. HALL *Medit.* III. lxxviii. Wks. 62 Good deeds are very fruitfull; and not so much of their nature, as of Gods blessing, multipliable. **1678** CUDWORTH *Intell. Syst.* I. v. 776 It is Indivisibly and Vnmultipliedly, and Illocally.. present with that which is naturally Divisible and Multipliable, and in a Place. **1706** PHILLIPS (ed. Kersey), *Multipliable*, or *Multiplicable*. **1865** RUSKIN *Sesame* i. §32 There is bread, sweet as honey,.. in a good book; and the family must be poor indeed which, once in their lives, cannot, for such multipliable barley-loaves, pay their baker's bill.

Hence '**multipliableness** (Bailey vol. II, 1727).

†'**multipliant**, *a.* (and *sb.*) *Arith. Obs.* [a. F. *multipliant*, pres. pple. of *multiplier* to MULTIPLY.] As adj. in ***number multipliant*** and absol. as sb.: = MULTIPLIER 2.

c **1430** *Art Nombryng* (E.E.T.S.) 10 Euery figure of the nombre multipliant is to be brought to the last save one nombre to be multipliede, til me come to the first of the multipliant.

multiplicability (ˌmʌltɪplɪkə'bɪlɪtɪ). *rare.* [f. next: see -ITY.] Capability of being multiplied.

1677 [see next]. **1851** RUSKIN *Stones Venice* I. App. xvii. 393 *note*, Of course mere multiplicability, as of an engraving, does not diminish the intrinsic value of the work.

multiplicable ('mʌltɪplɪkəb(ə)l), *a.* [ad. L. *multiplicābil-is*, f. *multiplicāre* to MULTIPLY.]

1. Capable of being multiplied; multipliable.

1471 RIPLEY *Comp. Alch.* in Ashm. (1652) 111 Eche thing multiplicable is in hys kinde. **1596** BELL *Surv. Popery* III. viii. 336 They that pray are innumerable and multiplicable into infinit *in potentia*. **1654** JER. TAYLOR *Real Pres.* 221 How then can Christs body be supposed to be multiplicable? **1677** GALE *Crt. Gentiles* IV. 250 If a singular is not multiplicable, then whatever agrees to any thing as singular admits not of multiplicabilitie. **1826** BENTHAM in *Westm. Rev.* VI. 497 Of all multiplicable beings,—among those in whose instance the practice of that rule of arithmetic is most mischievous, are locusts. **1851** RUSKIN *Stones Venice* I. App. xvii. 393 As noble.. as coins can be, or common cast bronzes, and such other multiplicable things.

†**2.** In active sense: Capable of multiplying (in the alchemical sense). *Obs.*

1471 RIPLEY *Comp. Alch.* in Ashm. (1652) 188 Then hast thou a Medcyn of the thyrd order of hys owne kynde Multyplycable.

multiplicand (ˌmʌltɪplɪ'kænd, 'mʌltɪplɪkænd). *Math.* [ad. L. *multiplicand-us*, gerundive of *multiplicāre* to MULTIPLY. Cf. F. *multiplicande* (16th c.).] The quantity to be multiplied: correlative to *multiplier*.

1594 BLUNDEVIL *Exerc.* I. iv. (1636) 9 The multiplicand, which must alwayes stand above. **1674** JEAKE *Arith.* (1696) 23 Multiply every figure of the Multiplicand by the multiplying digit. **1798** HUTTON *Course Math.* (1806) I. 32 Set the multiplier under the lowest denomination of the multiplicand, and draw a line below it. **1859** B. SMITH *Arith. & Algebra* (ed. 6) 11 The number to be repeated or added to itself, is called the Multiplicand. **1875** *Encycl. Brit.* II. 528/1 The process of multiplication by a single digit—by 8, for instance—is nothing but an abridgement of the operation of writing the multiplicand eight times and adding.

multiplicate ('mʌltɪplɪkət, mʌl'tɪplɪkət), *a.* and *sb.* Now *rare.* [ad. L. *multiplicāt-us*, pa. pple. of *multiplicāre* to MULTIPLY.]

A. *adj.* † Multiplied, increased (*obs.*); manifold; of many parts, elements, or sections; multiplex.

1432–50 tr. *Higden* (Rolls) I. 191 The chiefe cite of whom is Athenas, where study was somme tyme multiplicate. *Ibid.* III. 467 Lyke as the reason of the wittes of man is multiplicate [orig. *multiplex*], so he is mutable. **1656** HOBBES *Six Lessons* Wks. 1845 VII. 301 The proportions of the ordinate lines beginning at the vertex were triplicate, or otherwise multiplicate of the proportions of the intercepted parts of the diameter. **1664** *Phil. Trans.* I. 30 A Multiplicate Refraction of the rays of Light. **1713** DERHAM *Phys. Theol.* 95 There is another thing considerable in this multiplicate Number of the Eye; and that is, that the Object seen is not multiplied. **1802–12** BENTHAM *Ration. Judic. Evid.* (1827) II. 450 Multiplicate scription, or transcription: penning many scripts of exactly the same tenor. **1822** GOOD *Study Med.* IV. 233 Multiplicate Labour. *Ibid. marg.*, Multiplicate fertility. **1863** DANA in *Amer. Jrnl. Sci.* XXXVI. 333 The multiplicate Myriapods.

absol. **1846** GREENER *Sci. Gunnery* 174 An arrangement of leverage partaking of the multiplicate.

b. *Bot.* = MULTIPLEX *a.* 3a.

1760 J. LEE *Introd. Bot.* I. xx. (1765) 53 Flowers are said to be Multiplicate, when by the Increase of the Corolla only a Part of the Stamina are excluded. **1816** KEITH *Phys. Bot.* I. 117 Sometimes the pistil.. is multiplicate, that is when the flower produces more than one.

c. *Math.* (See quot.)

1868 A. SANDEMAN *Pelicotetics* 201 The ratio compounded of ratios that are all the same as one another is called the Multiplicate Compound Ratio of any one of these ratios.

B. *sb.* **a.** ***in multiplicate***: in many exactly corresponding copies or reproductions. **b.** One of many exact copies (of a document, etc.).

1858 A. J. B. BERESFORD HOPE in *Cambr. Ess.* 22 He offers it [*sc.* his report], copied in multiplicate, under the expressive name of flimsy. **1889** *Pall Mall G.* 24 Sept. 1/3 It was his habit to write a synopsis or *scenario* of his novels... This was in later years, when it was necessary to send multiplicates to the various subscribers to his syndicates.

†'**multiplicated**, *pa. pple. Obs.* [f. L. *multiplicātus* (see prec.) + -ED[1].] Folded many times.

1638 SIR T. HERBERT *Trav.* (ed. 2) 232 Their cap (or helmet) was a Tyara of linen multiplicated.

So †'**multiplicating** *ppl. a.*, multiplying.

1661 LOVELL *Hist. Anim. & Min.* Introd. c2 The life is more tenacious.. in those that have long bodies and many feet,.. by reason of the multiplicating part of their originall.

multiplication (ˌmʌltɪplɪ'keɪʃən). [a. F. *multiplication* (12th c.), ad. L. *multiplicātiōn-em*, n. of action f. *multiplicāre* to MULTIPLY.]

1. a. The act or process of multiplying, or increasing the quantity or amount of, a thing; the state of being multiplied or increased. Now *rare* exc. as coloured by sense 3.

c **1384** CHAUCER *H. Fame* II. 312 (Fairf. MS.) Euerych ayre other stereth More and more and speche vpbereth.. Ay through multiplicacion Til hyt be atte house of Fame. *c* **1450** LOVELICH *Grail* xlviii. 364 Thus there As Alle these good men sete, Fulfylled they were with Alle Manere of Mete; but in place as the Synneris were, Non Multiplicacion was not there. **1593** R. HARVEY *Philad.* 104 The ouerthrow of contraries is the generation of concord, and multiplication of consent. **1626** BACON *New Atl.* (1900) 41 Wee represent also all Multiplications of Light, which wee carry to great Distance. **1644** EVELYN *Diary* 17 Nov., Looking-glasses, which render a strange multiplication of things resembling divers most richly-furnish'd roomes. **1758** JOHNSON *Idler* No. 85 ¶1 One of the peculiarities which distinguish the present age is the multiplication of books. **1863** E. V. NEALE *Anal. Th. & Nat.* 37 The cottage becomes a mansion, the mansion a palace, the palace a town, simply by the multiplication of its parts. **1881** WESTCOTT & HORT *Grk. N.T.* Introd. §8 Repeated transcription involves multiplication of error. **1888** BRACKENBURY *Field Works* 46 The.. strength of the defence consisted in.. Multiplication of tiers of fire [etc.].

b. of words. (Cf. MULTIPLY *v.* 1b.)

1651 HOBBES *Leviath.* II. xxx. 182 Multiplication of words in the body of the Law, is multiplication of ambiguity. **1709** BERKELEY *Th. Vision* §134 Wks. 1871 I. 97 No multiplication of words will ever suffice to make them understand the truth. **1709** STRYPE *Ann. Ref.* I. xxxviii. 396 After a multiplication of language on both sides, Malvisier departed.

2. Propagation of animals and plants.

1387 TREVISA *Higden* (Rolls) I. 255 þere is more multiplicacioun and encrese of men and children in þe norþ contray þan in þe south. **1398** —— *Barth. De P.R.* XVII. ii. (1495) 595 Some trees haue multyplycacyon by graffynge of stockes. **1426** LYDG. in *Pol. Poems* (Rolls) II. 140 That he may se his generacioun Unto the forteth multiplicacioun Victoriously for to regnen here. **1662** STILLINGFL. *Orig. Sacræ* III. iv. §9 Wee have yet cause to beleeve that there was a more than ordinary multiplication in the posterity of Noah after the flood. **1838** *Penny Cycl.* XI. 18/2 The artificial multiplication of that species in gardens. **1845** MILL *Diss. & Disc.* II. 198 If.. it is intended that the law.. should assume a control over the multiplication of the people.

3. *Math.* **a.** The process of finding the quantity produced (see PRODUCT) by the summation of a given quantity (called the *multiplicand*) taken as many times as there are units in another given quantity (called the *multiplier*); or, in the case of a fractional multiplier, of finding the same fraction of the multiplicand as the multiplier is of unity.

compound multiplication: †(*a*) see quot. 1706; (*b*) see quot. 1859 and COMPOUND *a.* 2b (*b*). ***simple***, †***single multiplication***: see quots. 1706, 1854.

1390 GOWER *Conf.* III. 89 Be which [*sc.* Arithmetic] multiplicacioun Is mad and diminucioun Of sommes. *c* **1425** *Crafte Nombrynge* (E.E.T.S.) 21 Multiplicacioun is a bryngynge to-geder of 2 thynges in on nombur, þe quych on nombur contynes so mony tymes on, howe mony tymes þere ben vnytees in þe nowmbre of þat 2, as twyes 4 is 8. **1542** RECORDE *Gr. Artes* (1575) 122 Multiplication is suche an operation, that by two summes produceth the thirde. **1690** LEYBOURN *Curs. Math.* 14 Multiplication may be fitly termed a Compendium of Addition. **1706** PHILLIPS (ed. 6) s.v., *Single Multiplication* is when the Numbers given, consist each of them of one only Figure; as if 5 were to be multiply'd by 3, 9 by 6. *Ibid.* s.v., *Compound Multiplication*, is when either one or both Numbers given, consist of more Figures than one; as if 134 were to be multiply'd by 2, or 1232 by 23. *Ibid.* s.v., In Geometry, Multiplication, changes the Species or Kind; Thus a Right-line multiply'd by a Right-line, produces a Rectangle, or Plane; and that Rectangle, multiply'd again by another Line, produces a Solid. **1854** *Orr's Circ. Sci., Math.* 10 When the quantities are.. all of one denomination, the operation is called *simple* multiplication. *Ibid.* 162 The sign × placed between two quantities denotes the multiplication of those quantities together. **1859** B. SMITH *Arith. & Algebra* (ed. 6) 111 Compound Multiplication is the method of finding the amount of any proposed compound number, that is, of any number composed of different denominations.

fig. **1699** SOUTH *Serm.* (1823) III. 355 Society and converse.. being a kind of multiplication of himself into every person of the company he converses with.

†**b.** ***table of multiplication***, multiplication table.

1594 BLUNDEVIL *Exerc.* I. iv. (1636) 10 Before I teach you the true order of multiplying, I thinke it good to set you downe a Table of Multiplication. **1706** W. JONES *Syn. Palmar. Matheseos* 18 All the variety that can happen.. is express'd in the following Table of Multiplication.

†**c.** Used for: Product. *Obs. rare*$^{-1}$.

1586 T. B. *La Primaud. Fr. Acad.* (1587) 531 The number of 63. which is the multiplication of seven by nine.

d. In *Higher Algebra*, used in extended sense for: The successive application of operators.

1843 SIR W. R. HAMILTON in *Trans. Royal Irish Acad.* (1848) XXI. 257 We have now the system of the two equations, $q'' = q'q$; $q_{''} = qq'$; q'' and $q_{''}$ being those two distinct quaternion products which arise from the multiplication of the same two quaternion factors, q and q', with two different arrangements of those factors.

†**4.** *Alch.* The art of 'multiplying'. *Obs.*

1390 GOWER *Conf.* II. 88 This Ston.. makth multiplicacioun Of gold, and the fixacioun It causeth. **1471** RIPLEY *Comp. Alch.* XI. i. in Ashm. (1652) 181 Multyplycacyon.. ys.. dyfynyd, Augmentacyon yt ys of that Elixer indede, In goodnes, in quantyte, both for Whyt and Rede. **1543** [see MULTIPLY *v.* 6]. **1584** R. SCOT *Discov. Witchcr.* XIV. i. (1886) 294 The art or rather the craft of Alcumystrie, otherwise called Multiplication. **1612** WOODALL *Surg. Mate* Wks. (1653) 273 Multiplication by projection, is of a body amalgamated from 7. to 10. from 10. to 50. from 50. to 100. &c. according to the force and quantity of the tincture. *a* **1661** FULLER *Worthies* (1662) III. 204 **1696** in PHILLIPS.

5. *Bot.* Increase in the number of whorls or in the number of organs in a whorl.

1849 BALFOUR *Man. Bot.* §653 *Multiplication*, or an increase of the number of parts, gives rise to changes in plants. *Ibid.*, Multiplication causes a repetition of successive whorls, which still follow the law of alternation. **1880** A. GRAY *Struct. Bot.* vi. §3 (ed. 6) 179.

6. *attrib.*: **multiplication constant** or **factor** *Nuclear Physics*, in nuclear fission, the ratio by which the number of neutrons increases during a period equal to the lifetime of a neutron; **multiplication sign**, the sign × placed between two quantities to denote their multiplication; also *fig.*; **multiplication table**, a table of products of factors taken in pairs, usually beginning with 'twice one are two' (2 × 1 = 2) and going up to some assumed limit. (See also 3 b.)

1956 A. H. COMPTON *Atomic Quest* 137 These 'delayed' neutrons..make the difference between a multiplication constant of less than one and greater than one. **1962** *Newnes Conc. Encycl. Nucl. Energy* 111/1 The actual number of neutrons per fission varies considerably, but has an average value of 2·5. This is a high enough gain per cycle to suggest that a chain-reacting system of uranium could be made with a multiplication constant of at least unity. **1941** E. FERMI *Coll. Papers* (1965) II. 89 The chain reaction may reach a steady state only when the multiplication factor of the neutrons (including neutron losses due to diffusion outside of the reacting mass) is equal to 1. **1974** *Encycl. Brit. Macropædia* XIII. 305/1 If a fission bomb is to be made, the multiplication factor must be as large as possible. **1907** W. D. EGGAR *Elem. Algebra* i. 4 When a number is written in front of a bracket without a sign following it, thus 10(6 + 5), the multiplication sign is understood, just as when we write 10*a*. **1908** W. OWEN *Let.* 20 July (1967) 46 Best love, and a 'multiplication sign' (×) from your ever loving W. **1973** P. M. AITCHISON et al. *Form Two Maths.* vi. 67 Remember that a multiplication sign connects factors. **1674** JEAKE *Arith.* (1696) 22 To learn by heart the Table commonly called Multiplication Table. **1709** J. WARD *Yng. Math. Guide* I. ii. §4 (1734) 15 Multiplication Table. **1864** BOWEN *Logic* xi. 356 Our conclusions..are as absolute as the truths of the multiplication-table. **1871** *Routledge's Ev. Boy's Ann.* 277 Some young scamp who has learned the whole multiplication table of mischief..before he can repeat the sevens' column in arithmetic.

Hence **multipli'cational** *a.*

1868 A. SANDEMAN *Pelicotetics* 47 The laws of multiplicational equivalence.

multiplicative ('mʌltɪplɪkətɪv), *a.* and *sb.* [ad. med.L. *multiplicātīv-us*, f. *multiplicāt-*, ppl. stem of *multiplicāre* to MULTIPLY: see -IVE.]

a. Tending to multiply or increase; having the power or property of multiplying.

1653 R. G. tr. *Bacon's Hist. Winds* 350 It is a Diffusive, Communicative, Transitive and Multiplicative Motion. **1670** CLARKE *Nat. Hist. Nitre* 18 The form of Minerals is multiplicative of it self in a dispos'd matter, and proper place. **1765** *Univ. Mag.* XXXVII. 236/1 The plague.. proves the multiplicative power of those spirits. **1863** DANA in *Amer. Jrnl. Sci.* XXXVI. 325 The abnormal number of segments under the multiplicative method may arise from a self-subdivision of enlarging normal segments. **1868** A. SANDEMAN *Pelicotetics* 24 By finding the products in backward order the multiplicative and the additive parts of the process may be carried on together.

b. *Gram.* Applied to numerals that express 'so many times'. Also *sb.*, a multiplicative numeral.

1727–52 CHAMBERS *Cycl.*, *Multiplicatives.* See *Numerals.* **1863** W. SMITH *Gram. Lat. Lang.* §71. 33 Multiplicative Numerals end in -plex. **1872** MORRIS *Hist. Outl. Eng. Accid.* §134 Multiplicatives are expressed..By adjectives, with suffix -*fold* [etc.]. **1886** T. LE M. DOUSE *Gothic of Ulfilas* 149 'Multiplicative' adjs. are formed by adding *falpa-*, '-fold' to the cardinals. **1928** H. POUTSMA *Gram. Late Mod. Eng.* (ed. 2) iv. 304 The multiplicatives *double, treble, quadruple.*

So **'multiplicatively** *adv.*

1895 in *Funk's Stand. Dict.* **1914** C. D. BROAD *Perception* iii. 180 The strengthening of probability takes place multiplicatively. **1973** *Nature* 23 Feb. 513/1 The latter possibility has an attractive feature, namely that Misner's mechanism, and the one described here would operate simultaneously, the two effects combining multiplicatively.

multiplicator ('mʌltɪplɪkeɪtə(r)). [late L., agent-n. f. *multiplicāre* to MULTIPLY.]

1. *Math.* = MULTIPLIER 2. Now *rare* or *Obs.*

1542 [see MULTIPLIER 2]. **1579** DIGGES *Stratiot.* 4 The lesse is named the Multiplicator or Multiplyer, the other summe, or number to be multiplyed. **1690** LEYBOURN *Curs. Math.* 146 The Summ of the Logarithms of the Multiplicand, and of the Multiplicator, is equal to the Logarithm of the Product. **1734** J. WARD *Yng. Math. Guide* App. of Gauging 435 If any one would rather work by Multiplication than by Division, he may..change any Divisor into a Multiplicator. **1828** *Blackw. Mag.* XXIV. 320 The sign of a thousand with that of the proper multiplicator ..showed the number slain. **1923** *Glasgow Herald* 16 Oct. 7 In Cologne order was restored on Friday night... The price 'Multiplicator', which played a large part in creating the agitation, has been lowered from 1,800,000,000..to 400,000,000.

2. a. *Electr.* and *Magn.* = MULTIPLIER 4.

1823 *Q. Jrnl. Sci.* XVI. 124 It is this which constitutes the electro-magnetic multiplicator. **1876** *Catal. Spec. Collect. Sci. Apparatus S. Kens. Mus.* (1877) 1049 Multiplicator, according to Schweigger, for thermo-electrical currents.

b. In a galvanometer, a flat coil of conducting wire for multiplying the effect of the current.

1884 in KNIGHT *Dict. Mech.*

†**multiplicature.** *Obs. rare*$^{-1}$. [MULTI- 2.] The condition of having many folds.

1671 GREW *Anat. Plants* I. iv. §16 We have the Multiplicature; as in Gooseberries,..the Plaits being not only divers in the same Leaf, but..each Leaf gather'd up in five, seven, or more Foulds.

†**multi'plicious**, *a. Obs.* [f. L. *multiplici-*, *multiplex*: see MULTIPLEX and -OUS.] Multiplex.

1617 [see MULTIFARIOUS 1]. **1646** SIR T. BROWNE *Pseud. Ep.* III. xv. 141 That animall is not one, but multiplicious or many, which hath a duplicity or gemination of principall parts. **1660** STANLEY *Hist. Philos.* IX. §1. iv, From the symbolical use of numbers, proceeded a multiplicious variety of names. **1713** DERHAM *Phys. Theol.* IV. iv. 138 Its Apparatus [*sc.* of the nose]..is not so multiplicious as of the Eye.

Hence †**multi'pliciously** *adv.*

1646 SIR T. BROWNE *Pseud. Ep.* VII. ii. 343 The seed conveigheth with it not onely the extract and single Idea of every part, whereby it transmits their perfections or infirmities, but double and over againe; whereby sometimes it multipliciously delineates the same, as in Twins in mixed and numerous generations.

multiplicity (mʌltɪ'plɪsɪtɪ). [ad. L. *multiplicitās*, f. *multiplic-*, MULTIPLEX.]

1. a. The quality or condition of being multiplex or manifold; manifold variety.

1597 MORLEY *Introd. Mus.* Annot. *4, By this, which in *dupla* and *tripla* is spoken, may all other things concerning proportions of multiplicity be easily vnderstoode. **1607** TOPSELL *Four-f. Beasts* (1658) 113 Cerberus himself with his three heads signified the multiplicity of Devils. **1659** PEARSON *Creed* 641 The infinity of the devine essence is incapable of multiplicity. **1701** GREW *Cosmol. Sacra* I. v. 25 As the manifold Variation of the Parts, so the Multiplicity of the Use of each Part, is very wonderful. **1825** MACAULAY *Ess.*, *Milton*, With the greatest precision and multiplicity in its details. **1873** SYMONDS *Grk. Poets* ix. 297 The Greek Drama owed its power to the qualities of regularity and simplicity: the strength of the modern lies in subtlety and multiplicity. **1884** J. R. SEELEY in *Contemp. Rev.* Nov. 654 In Nature..the unity is much less obvious than the multiplicity.

b. An instance of this.

1587 GOLDING *De Mornay* ii. (1592) 14 Of vnitie or one in nombering, proceedeth..all the multiplicities..we see. **1602** WARNER *Alb. Eng.* XIII. lxxviii. (1612) 323 Of one all Multiplicities, Formes, Harmonies,..Be..produced and begot. **1646** GAULE *Cases Consc.* 11 Haply..at some purer Times of the Church, a Witch may not then and there be found..at least wise.., not in those Multitudes, or Multiplicities. **1878** STUBBS *Const. Hist.* III. xxi. 567 The diversities and multiplicities of legal usages.

c. In the Kantian philosophy = MANIFOLD *sb.* 2 a.

1839 *Penny Cycl.* XIII. 176/1 The consciousness of the individual in this multiplicity is effected by the imagination, which combines them into a whole.

d. In technical use (cf. MULTIPLE *a.* 3).

1841 J. J. SYLVESTER in *Lond. Phil. Mag.* XVIII. 136, I use the word *multiplicity* to denote a number, and distinguish between the total and partial multiplicities of the roots of an algebraic equation. **1851** PAGET *Lect. Tumours* vi. 70 Multiplicity is sufficiently marked in the cases of the hands and feet. **1872** T. BRYANT *Pract. Surg.* 735 These black cancers have..one peculiarity, and that is in their tendency to multiplicity. **1887** CAYLEY *Math. Papers* (1897) XII. 463 We might..have symbols of indefinite multiplicity (*x*, *y*, *z*, *w*,..), including within them all finite multiplicities, viz. (*x*, *y*) meaning (*x*, *y*, *O*, *O*,..).

e. *Physics.* The number of components (whether one or several) in a multiplet; *spec.* (*a*) the quantity $2S + 1$, where S is the spin quantum number of a term; (*b*) the quantity $2I + 1$, where I is the isospin of a charge multiplet.

1923 H. L. BROSE tr. *Sommerfeld's Atomic Struct. & Spectral Lines* vi. 385 Those terms are defined as similar which have the same multiplicity and the same azimuthal quantum number. **1929** [see MULTIPLET a]. **1934** H. E. WHITE *Introd. Atomic Spectra* xiv. 248 It is found experimentally that the multiplicities of the levels belonging to a given spectrum will either be all even or all odd. *Ibid.* 249 Spectral terms arising from successive elements in the periodic table alternate between even and odd multiplicities. **1948** G. R. HARRISON et al. *Pract. Spectroscopy* x. 241 For two electrons, $S = 0$ or 1, depending on whether the two spins are antiparallel or parallel. Hence atomic spectra that arise from two electrons (helium and the alkaline-earth metals Be, Mg, Ca, Sr, and Ba) can have multiplicities of 1 (that is, no splitting of levels because of spin) or 3 (splitting of each level into three). **1964** *Sci. Amer.* Feb. 82/2 The number of different charge states in a multiplet, or its 'multiplicity' (*M*), is directly related to the isotopic-spin quantum number I by the equation $M = 2I + 1$. **1972** *Physics Bull.* Feb. 92/1 A further interesting feature which these multiplets illustrate is the greater bonding of the states of lower multiplicity. **1973** [see MULTIPLET b].

f. *Biol.* The ratio of the number of infective particles to the number of susceptible cells; usu. in phr. ***multiplicity of infection.***

1947 *Proc. Nat. Acad. Sci.* XXXIII. 259 (*heading*) Dependence of the probability of reactivation on the multiplicity of infection. **1957** *Virology* III. 286 Luria (1947) found that cells of *Escherichia coli* B which had been infected with more than one inactivated particle of phage T2, or other members of the T group of coliphages, yielded active phage. He called this 'multiplicity reactivation'. **1964** W. HAYES *Genetics of Bacteria & their Viruses* xvi. 367 If a suspension of virulent phage is added to a growing culture of sensitive bacteria in broth, so that the number of phage particles exceeds the number of bacteria (multiplicity of infection = > 1),..the culture becomes clear, as a result of the infection and lysis of virtually all the bacteria. **1974** *Nature* 11 Oct. 542/1 Chang cells in suspension were infected at an input multiplicity of 10. *Ibid.* 543/2 Addition of VSV or EMC virus at a multiplicity of infection of 1.

2. a. ***the multiplicity of***: the great number of, the very many or numerous. Similarly ***a, such (a), this,*** etc., ***multiplicity of.***

1598 DALLINGTON *Meth. Trav.* X 3 Such multiplicity of words he hath. **1627** DRAYTON *Moone-Calfe* Poems 162 That on the Stationers Stall, who passing lookes, To see the multiplicity of Bookes, That pester it. **1659** SLINGSBY *Diary* (1836) 356 T'was all the night as bright as day with the multiplisity of bone fires. **1659** PEARSON *Creed* 384 The coronary thorns..did..pierce his..temples to a multiplicity of pains, by their numerous acuminations. **1710** STEELE *Tatler* No. 176 ¶8, I..am distracted with such a Multiplicity of entertaining Objects, that I am lost in the Variety. **1847** C. BRONTË *J. Eyre* v, Like one who had always a multiplicity of tasks on hand. **1860** G. PRESCOTT *Electr. Telegr.* 243 A few large bells would be preferable to this multiplicity of smaller ones. **1885** J. PAYN *Talk of Town* II. 138 It was not the least like a dressing-room except that it had a multiplicity of mirrors.

b. with collective sing. sb.

1601 HOLLAND *Pliny* I. 504 In that one significant word (*Cariosa*) hee said more than could be expressed possibly by any multiplicity of language whatsoeuer. *a* **1656** HALES *Gold. Rem.* (1673) 5 These places that are so fertile..of interpretation, and yeild a multiplicity of sense. **1749** FIELDING *Tom Jones* XII. x, I was so hurried, and drove and tore with the multiplicity of business. **1876** F. HARRISON *Choice of Bks.* iv. (1886) 90 Since which date, let us trust, the multiplicity of print and the habits of desultory reading have considerably abated.

†**c.** Without article or qualifying word. *Obs.*

1629 LE GRYS tr. *Barclay's Argenis* 188 Argenis being confounded with multiplicity of griefs. *a* **1734** NORTH *Life Dr. J. North* (1744) 240 After he was grown old and much worn by Multiplicity of Business. **1769** E. BANCROFT *Guiana* 378 Multiplicity of law-suits are universally allowed to be detrimental to new countries.

†**3.** ***the multiplicity of***: the majority of. *Obs.*

1639 in Nalson *Coll. Gt. Aff. State* (1682) I. 279 The Multiplicity of the People are mean conditioned.

†**multiplie.** *Sc. Obs.* Also 5 -ple, -plye. [app. a. OF. *moltepli*, *multepli* multiplication (Godefroy), vbl. sb. f. *multiplier* to MULTIPLY.] Multitude; great numbers or quantity.

c **1470** HENRY *Wallace* IX. 1707 'Dicson', he said, 'wait thow thair multiple?' 'Iij thowsand men thair power mycht nocht be'. *Ibid.* XI. 13 The Sotheroun fled fra him on athir sid To Burdeous, in gret multiplye. **1549** *Compl. Scot.* i. 23 Quhilk causit..my een to be cum obscure throucht the multiplie of salt teyris. **1596** DALRYMPLE tr. *Leslie's Hist. Scot.* I. 7 In sum places is funde multiplie of Tinne.

multiplied ('mʌltɪplaɪd), *ppl. a.* (*sb.*) [f. MULTIPLY *v.* + -ED^1.] Made many, much, or more; increased in number or quantity; manifold.

1463–4 *Rolls of Parlt.* V. 503/1 Wherthurgh the Citees.. mowe..be multiplied inhabitations, and restored to their auncien..prosperite. **1585** T. WASHINGTON tr. *Nicholay's Voy.* Ep. Ded., Olde men.., by reason of their multiplied yeeres, are to be released. **1613** PURCHAS *Pilgrimage* III. xvii. (1614) 334 Another Caue..which terrifieth those that enter with the multiplied sounds of Cymbals and vncouth minstrelsie. **1646** H. P. *Medit. Seige* 35 Their varied and multiplyed dangers. **1669–70** PEPYS *Let. to Capt. Elliot* 3 Mar., I pray you to accept..my hearty thanks for your multiplied kindness. **1783** *Dodsley's Ann. Reg.* (1785) 22/2 Orders were written and dispatched in multiplied copies to the different military stations. **1784** COWPER *Task* II. 597 Our habits, costlier than Lucullus wore, And by caprice, as multiplied as his. **1804** JAS. MAITLAND *Public Wealth* (1819) 274 The multiplied relations which the varied distributions of property create. **1841** D'ISRAELI *Amen. Lit.* (1867) 307 The poems of Surrey were often read, as their multiplied editions show. **1865** LYELL *Elem. Geol.* 576 Others again have the number of segments excessively multiplied as in *Paradoxides.*

b. *Math.*; †occas. as *sb.* = MULTIPLICAND.

1579 DIGGES *Stratioticos* 6 Place the Digitte 4 vnder 7 the thirde of your multiplyed number. **1660** BARROW *Euclid* VII. Def. 15 In every multiplication a unitie is to the multiplier, as the multiplied is to the product. *a* **1696** SCARBURGH *Euclid* (1705) 219 If a number multiplying two numbers make some numbers, their Products shall have the same proportion with the multiplied numbers.

c. *Bot.* = MULTIPLEX *a.* 3 a.

1777 ROBSON *Brit. Flora* v. 20. **1793** MARTYN *Lang. Bot.* s.v., According to the number of rows in a multiplied corolla.

multiplier ('mʌltɪplaɪə(r)). [f. MULTIPLY *v.* + -ER^1. Cf. F. *multiplieur* (16th c.).]

1. a. One who or a thing which multiplies or causes something to increase.

1470–85 MALORY *Arthur* XIV. viii. 652 That same man is an enchaunter and a multyplyer of wordes. **1477** CAXTON *Dictes* 11 b, Loue..thoo that be the grete multiplyers, that is to saye, the commones that labour the erth. *a* **1548** HALL *Chron.*, *Hen. V*, 43 b, Money the multiplier of iniquitie. **1667** *Causes Decay Chr. Piety* v. 81 Broils and quarrels, which are alone the great accumulators and multipliers of injuries. **1694** MOTTEUX *Rabelais* IV. xlvi. 180 Multiplyers of Law-suits. **1835** J. HODGSON *Hist. Northumb.* III. III. p. iv, Doubt and uncertainty are great multipliers of words. **1870** SPENCER *Princ. Psychol.* I. 35 At the surface of the body, where the extremities of nerve-fibres are so placed as to be most easily disturbed, we..find..multipliers of disturbances.

b. A (great) breeder. ? *Obs. rare.*

1661 J. CHILDREY *Brit. Baconica* 19 The Pilchard is a little fish, and a great multiplier.

2. a. *Math.* The quantity by which another (the *multiplicand*) is multiplied.

1542 RECORDE *Gr. Artes* F vii b, The multiplier or multiplicatour, that is to say, the numbre by which multiplication is made. **1674** JEAKE *Arith.* (1696) 23 Then take the second figure of the Multiplier, and proceed..as before. **1706** W. JONES *Syn. Palmar. Matheseos* 17 Both Multiplicand and Multiplier are call'd Factors. **1798** HUTTON *Course Math.* (1806) I. 13 We shall multiply all the parts of the multiplicand by all the parts of the multiplier. **1854** *Orr's Circ. Sci., Math.* 163 A figure, or number, prefixed to a letter, as a multiplier, is called the coefficient of that letter.

b. *Econ.* (See quot. 1964.)

1936 J. M. KEYNES *Gen. Theory Employment* x. 113 A definite ratio, to be called the *Multiplier*, can be established between income and investment and..between the total employment and the employment directly employed on investment. **1940** G. CROWTHER *Outl. Money* v. 157 In the upward process, the change in the National Income necessary to restore balance and reverse the trend [downwards] may be very many times larger than the original discrepancy... Thus a small original change results in a large ultimate change in the National Income. The ratio between them is usually known as the 'multiplier'. **1963** *Economist* 9 Feb. 481/2 A direct injection of £500 million of new Government spending can sometimes increase total national spending by £1,000 million (i.e. a multiplier of two). **1964** GOULD & KOLB *Dict. Social Sci.* 449/1 *Multiplier*... The term denotes the process (or the index, or coefficient, measuring such a process) whereby initial changes within economic systems (e.g. changes in the levels of investment) have cumulative and, in principle, measurable effects upon the system, its components and its equilibrium.

c. ***multiplier effect***, an effect such as could be assessed in terms of the economic multiplier.

1957 R. K. MERTON *Student-Physician* 14 Such an experimental institution for medical education would have multiplier-effects. **1963** *Economist* 16 Feb. 619/1 The multiplier effect..of an injection of purchasing power into personal incomes..is unlikely to exceed unity and may be as low as 0·7. **1964** T. W. MCRAE *Impact of Computers on Accounting* vii. 211 Such improvement will have a 'multiplier effect'. **1965** *Listener* 16 Sept. 405/2 What we can do is to concentrate our help where it will have the highest multiplier effect.

†**3.** One who performs the alchemical process of multiplication; hence, a false coiner. *Obs.*

c **1420** LYDG. *Assembly of Gods* 681 False vsurers, Multyplyers, coyn wasshers & clyppers. **1477** NORTON *Ord. Alch.* in Ashm. (1652) 17 The Multiplier doth him beguile With his faire promise. *c* **1515** *Cocke Lorell's B.* 8 Golde smythes, and grote clypper, Multyplyers, and clothe thyckers. **1560** DAUS tr. *Sleidane's Comm.* 119 Farre exceadinge all the Alcumisticall multipliers that ever were.

4. a. *Electr.* and *Magn.* An instrument used for multiplying or increasing by repetition the intensity of a force, current, etc. so as to make it appreciable or mensurable. Cf. THERMO-MULTIPLIER.

1795 T. CAVALLO *Compl. Treat. Electr.* (ed. 3) III. 98 With this machine, which..we shall call the Multiplier of Electricity, the accumulation of the communicated power does not advance..so quick as with the doubler. *Ibid.* 106, I shall now describe a few experiments made with this multiplier. **1823** *Ann. Philos.* June 436 M. Schweigger's electromagnetic Multiplier. **1858** NOAD *Man. Electr.* I. 66 Of the various instruments that have been termed 'multipliers' and 'doublers' we shall only describe the multiplier of Cavallo. **1877** ROSENTHAL *Phys. Muscles & Nerves* 150 The nerve..exhibits a difference which the multiplier is incapable of indicating. **1938** J. B. HOAG *Electron & Nucl. Physics* vi. 127 In another form of multiplier tube, electrons are oscillated back and forth between two surfaces which are good secondary emitters... At each impact of the electrons with the cathode surfaces, the number of electrons is appreciably multiplied. **1940**, etc. [see *electron multiplier* s.v. ELECTRON[2] 2 b]. **1950** K. HENNEY *Radio Engin. Handbk.* (ed. 4) xiii. 558 The multiplier phototube has a number of advantages compared with a phototube and separate amplifier. **1973** *McGraw-Hill Yearbk. Sci. & Technol.* 333/1 Because fewer gain stages with higher interstage voltages are needed, the speed of the multipliers has been improved, greatly increasing their usefulness for applications such as laser optical communications.

b. = MULTIPLICATOR 2 b.

In recent Dicts.

5. *Angling.* A multiplying-reel (see MULTIPLYING *ppl. a.* b, quot. 1856).

1867 F. FRANCIS *Angling* i. (1880) 15 The best reels..are the plain reels... Do not have a multiplier, even at a gift. **1875** 'STONEHENGE' *Brit. Rural Sports* I. v. iv. §3. 349 Though the multiplier is very pretty in theory, yet it is constantly failing in practice. **1897** *Outing* XXX. 262/1 On my reel, finest and most powerful of multipliers, I carried a thousand feet of line.

6. An arithmometer for performing calculations in multiplication.

1875 KNIGHT *Dict. Mech.* **1969** J. J. SPARKES *Transistor Switching* viii. 200 In the accumulator of this multiplier it is convenient to use flip-flops..which have two separate logic and pulse inputs per flip-flop. *Ibid.* 201 The multiplier circuit operates as follows. **1972** *Daily Tel.* 5 Apr. 10 (Advt.), The world's fastest and smoothest mechanical multiplier. Operates at 360 rpm, lists 10 columns and totals 11.

multiply ('mʌltɪplaɪ), *v.* Forms: 3-5 multe-, 4-6 multy-, (6 moulti-, moulty-); 3-6 -plie, -plye, 4-5 -pli(i); 4- multiply. [a. OF. (mod.F.) *multiplier*, ad. L. *multiplicāre*, f. *multiplic-*, MULTIPLEX.]

1. *trans.* To cause to become much, many, or more; to make many or manifold; to augment the number, amount, or quantity of. Now *rare* except as coloured by sense 5.

a **1275** *Prov. Ælfred* 675 in *O.E. Misc.* 137 Ac nim þe to þe a stable mon, þat word and dede bi-sette con, and multeplien heure god. *a* **1340** HAMPOLE *Psalter* xi. 1 A haly man that sees the vanyte of the warld multiplid. *c* **1386** CHAUCER *Melib.* ¶774 Swete wordes multiplien & encressen frendes. *c* **1400** *26 Pol. Poems* 148 In salt see I sayled well wyde ffor to multiply my tresoure. **1462** *Litt. Red Bk. Bristol* (1900) II. 128 Suche..Allions beth gretely multeplied and encreased within the Town. **1535** COVERDALE *Bel & Dr.* G, Peace be multiplied with you. **1648** WILKINS *Math. Magic* I. vii. 50 These Pulleys may be multiplyed according to sundry different situations. **1694** ADDISON *Poems, Virgil* Wks. 1726 I. 30 Till into seven it multiplies its stream. **1788** GIBBON *Decl. & F.* lvii. V. 661 The activity of the emperor seemed to multiply his presence. **1833** TENNYSON *Poems* 76 And all things that she [*sc.* my soul] saw, she multiplied, A manyfaced glass. **1858** GREENER *Gunnery* 155 Elongating the fibres and multiplying their number to an indefinite extent. **1872** ATKINSON tr. *Ganot's Nat. Philos.* §671 By coiling the copper wire in the direction of the needle..the action of the current has been multiplied. **1878** JEVONS *Primer Pol. Econ.* 21 Public libraries, museums, picture galleries and like institutions all multiply utility.

b. To use or utter a multiplicity of (words, etc.). ***to multiply words***: † (*a*) to be loquacious; (*b*) to be verbose.

1340 *Ayenb.* 218 Huanne þe multepliest þine benes ich nelle none y-here. **1382** WYCLIF *Job* xxxv. 16 Job..withoute kunnynge woordis multiplieth. ? **1520** tr. *Dial. Creat. Moral.* xii. D ij, This vale..brak owte and multyplyed greate wordis agayne the hyll. **1529** in *Vicary's Anat.* (1888) App. xiv. 258 No man..shall multiplye langage yn the Courte tyme. **1530** PALSGR. 641/2, I multiplye langage with one, as folkes do that chyde togyther. **1568** GRAFTON *Chron.* II. 100 When they had thus multiplied talke vpon both sydes. **1652** [see MULTIPLYING *vbl. sb.* 1]. **1726** SWIFT GULLIVER II. vii, They avoid nothing more than multiplying unnecessary Words, or using various Expressions. **1818** CRUISE *Digest* (ed. 2) VI. 444 What he meant by the said premises was evident, and could not have been rendered clearer by saying *all* the said premises, though it might have served to multiply words.

c. In const. of the type ***to multiply evil upon evil***, to add evil to evil, accumulate instances of evil.

1477 EARL RIVERS (Caxton) *Dictes* 74 b, And he sawe a long mayde that lerned to wryte, of whom he sayde that me multiplied euyl vpon euyll. **1625** BP. HALL *Medit.* III. xc. Wks. 65 It is a damnable iniquitie in man, to multiplie one sinne vpon another. **1830** TENNYSON *Poet* 33 Thus truth was multiplied on truth.

d. To adduce a large number of (instances, etc.).

1716 ADDISON *Freeholder* No. 6 ¶3 'Tis unnecessary to multiply Instances of this nature. **1845** *Encycl. Metrop.* II. 899/1 These explicit declarations against heresy might be multiplied to almost any extent. **1860** TYNDALL *Glac.* II. xxxii. 418 Instances of this kind might be multiplied.

†**e.** Const. inf. (A Hebraism.) *Obs.*

a **1340** HAMPOLE *Psalter* Cant. 500 Willis noght multiply to speke heghe thyngis. **1649** BP. REYNOLDS *Hosea* v. 12 He multiplyeth to pardon. **1684** BUNYAN *Pilgr.* II. 9 He taketh delight to multiply to pardon offences.

†**f.** To increase the intensity of; *occas.* to magnify optically. *Obs.*

1398 TREVISA *Barth. De P.R.* XVIII. xci. (1495) 840 The frogge multyplyeth his voyce whan he dooth his nether jowe somdeale in the water and strykyth the vpper jowe. *a* **1586** SIDNEY *Arcadia* III. (1629) 249 His eies saw no terrour, nor eare heard any martiall sound, but that they multiplied the hidiousnesse of it to his mated mind. **1626** BACON *New Atl.* (1900) 42 Wee Multiply Smells, which may seeme strange. **1651** J. CLEVELAND *Wks.* C 5 Just as an Optique Glasse contracts the sight At one end, but when turn'd doth multiply't.

2. *intr.* To become of great number or quantity; to be increased or augmented by accumulation or repetition.

c **1330** *Spec. Gy de Warewyke* 1009 Almesdede fordoþe þi synne..And þi god shal multiplie. **13..** *E.E. Allit. P.* B. 278 Euelez on erþe..grewen & multyplyed mony-folde. *c* **1412** HOCCLEVE *De Reg. Princ.* 5195 By concorde, smale þinges multiplien. **1412-20** LYDG. *Chron. Troy* II. 4376 þat þoruȝ þe worlde þe fyr gan multiplie. *c* **1470** HENRY *Wallace* VIII. 1002 He saw the Sothroun multipliand mayr. **1588** KYD *Househ. Phil.* Wks. (1901) 280 Much more may riches multiply that consist in bare money then [etc.]. **1666** MARVELL *Corr.* iii. Wks. (Grosart) II. 188 Busynesse does so multiply of late that I can scarce snatch time to write to you. **1781** GIBBON *Decl. & F.* xix. II. 127 Reduced to an humble station by the prudence of Constantine, they [*sc.* eunuchs] multiplied in the palaces of his degenerate sons. **1842** MANNING *Serm.* i. (1848) I. 7 As sin has multiplied in its extent, so it would seem also to have become more intense. **1858** KINGSLEY *Lett.* (1878) I. 21 The flame increased—multiplied—at one point after another.

†**b.** *transf.* To accrue as interest. *Obs. rare*$^{-1}$.

c **1440** *Alphabet of Tales* 525/25 At it sulde be lent in vsurie iij yere after his decese, and at þai sulde gyff for his sawle all þat multiplied þerof.

†**c.** *intr.* and *pass.* To be abundantly provided *with*. *Obs.*

a **1533** LD. BERNERS *Gold. Bk. M. Aurel.* (1546) E, Oure senate faylethe of meke and wyse Senatours, and multiplieth with these serpentines. **1588** KYD *Househ. Phil.* Wks. (1901) 265 That wealth whereby we should expect to haue our houses so distinguished and multiplyed with offycers.

†**3.** *trans.* To increase (a family, etc.) by natural generation or procreation (freq. in *pass.*); to cause (the earth) to become populous. *Obs.* or *arch.*

a **1300** *Cursor M.* 2647 Abram,..Multipli þi sede i sall. **1375** *Creation* 510 in Horstm. *Altengl. Leg.* (1878) 130 þeȝ..broȝten forþ mo [children], þe worlde to multiply. *c* **1400** MAUNDEV. (Roxb.) xx. 89 Waxez and beese multiplied and fillez þe erthe. **1474** CAXTON *Chesse* III. i. (1883) 76 Whan Adam their fader maried them for to multiplye yᵉ erthe of hys lignye. **1538** STARKEY *England* II. i. 146 The way and mean to suffyce, multyply, and encrese them [*sc.* the people] agayn to a conuenyent nombur, ys only natural generatyon. **1673** TEMPLE *Ess. on Ireland* Wks. 1731 I. 110 People are multiplied in a Country by the Temper of the Climate, favourable to Generation. **1712** ADDISON *Spect.* No. 413 ¶5 That all Creatures might be tempted to multiply their Kind. **1784** COWPER *Task* v. 221 When man was multiplied and spread abroad In tribes and clans.

absol. **1393** LANGL. *P. Pl.* C. XIX. 226 A man with-oute a make myghte nat wel of kynde Multeplie.

b. To breed (animals); to propagate (plants). †Also (of the parts of a plant), to produce by propagation, to cause to grow.

1471 RIPLEY *Comp. Alch.* XI. v. in Ashm. (1652) 182 The Tre of Hermes..Of whych one Pepyn a thowsand wyll Multyply. **1599** [see MULTIPLYING *vbl. sb.* 1]. **1707** *Curios. in Husb. & Gard.* 197 The Method of Multiplying Plants by Layers. **1760** J. LEE *Bot.* III. iii. (1810) 416 The Trunk, which serves to multiply the herb, and leads immediately from the root to the fructification. **1796** H. HUNTER tr. *St. Pierre's Stud. Nat.* (1799) III. 659 They could themselves drain marshes, clear waste lands, multiply flocks. **1833** *Penny Cycl.* I. 61/1 Most of them may be multiplied by cuttings struck in silver sand. **1857** BALFOUR *Cycl. India* 1184 This is a large Mango multiplied at Mergui.

4. *intr.* To increase in number by natural generation or procreation (occas. by artificial means).

a **1300** *Cursor M.* 638 Drightin þam blessed, and bad þam brede, And multipli in þar sede. **1390** GOWER *Conf.* II. 344 Hou god to man be weie of kinde Hath set the world to multeplie. **1413** *Pilgr. Sowle* (Caxton) v. xiv. (1859) 80 Whiche fisshes he putte in the stewe, where they haue spawned and multyplyed. *c* **1420** LYDG. *Assembly of Gods* 1717 Isys was callyd the Goddesse Of Frute, for she fyrst made hit multyply By the meane of gryffyng. **1535** COVERDALE *Job* xii. 23 He both increaseth the people, and destroyeth them: He maketh them to multiplie, and dryueth them awaye. **1665** SIR T. HERBERT *Trav.* (1677) 57 The Priests thereupon throw Rice upon their heads, praying that they may multiply as Rice. **1719** DE FOE *Crusoe* I. (Globe) 183 As for my Cats, they multiply'd. **1844** H. H. WILSON *Brit. India* II. 83 Under a climate more congenial..the descendants of a northern race may be able to aggregate and multiply. **1883** DARWIN in *Pall Mall G.* 7 Dec. 11/2 Multiply, vary; let the strongest live and the weakest die.

5. *trans.* (*Math.*) To operate upon (a given quantity, called the *multiplicand*) with another quantity (called the *multiplier*) so as to produce a quantity (called the *product*) having the same ratio to the multiplicand as the multiplier has to unity. In *Higher Algebra*, to apply an operator to (an operand).

c **1391** CHAUCER *Astrol.* II. §41 a, þan loke how moche space of feet ys be-twen þe and þe tour, & multiplie þat be 12. *c* **1400** MAUNDEV. (Roxb.) xx. 92 Now be þise all multiplied CCC. tymes and LX. **1594** BLUNDEVIL *Exerc.* I. iv. 5 b, Whensoeuer you haue to multiply one number by another. **1610** W. FOLKINGHAM *Art of Survey* II. viii. 62 Multiply the Basall Area by 6. **1635** J. BABINGTON *Geometry* 34 Let the line AB be given to be multiplyed by the line CD. **1706** W. JONES *Syn. Palmar. Matheseos* 20 Multiply each Figure of the Multiplicand, by each Figure of the Multiplier. **1825** J. NICHOLSON *Operat. Mechanic* 293 A force equal to 20 cwt. multiplied by 2304. **1842** DE MORGAN *Int. & Diff. Calc.* 11 What is *a* multiplied by $\frac{1}{1000}$? The answer is *a* taken the thousandth part of a time, or the thousandth part of *a*. **1858** BRIGHT *Sp., Reform* 27 Oct. (1869) 281 The annual income of the estate multiplied by the number of years which..he may be expected to live. **1885** W. K. CLIFFORD *Common Sense of Exact Sci.* 201 If a vector step be multiplied by itself, the product is zero; that is, AP . AP = $(AP)^2$ = 0.

transf. and *fig.* **1611** SHAKS. *Wint. T.* I. ii. 7 Like a Cypher (Yet standing in rich place) I multiply With one we thanke you, many thousands moe, That goe before it. **1891** MEREDITH *One of our Conq.* xviii, You have multiplied your investment by ten.

b. ***to multiply*** (one quantity) ***into***, † ***in*** (another); ***to multiply*** (two quantities) ***together***: to find the product of the two quantities.

1557 RECORDE *Whetst.* E ij b, 1225. And so moche doeth there arise by .35. multiplied into it self. **1571** DIGGES *Pantom.* I. vi. C iij b, The firste multiplied in the fourth, produceth a quantitie equall to that which is made by multiplication of the seconde in the thirde. **1610** W. FOLKINGHAM *Art of Survey* II. viii. 61 Multiply the perpendicular in the demibase. **1690** LEYBOURN *Curs. Math.* 15 The numbers to be multiplied must be set one under another. **1709** J. WARD *Yng. Math. Guide* (1734) 340 Multiply the Base of the given Triangle into Half its perpendicular Height. *Ibid.* 439 Multiply the Two Diameters (*viz.* the Length and Breadth) together. **1812** PLAYFAIR *Nat. Phil.* I. 110 The weight multiplied into the height to which it is raised. **1885** LEUDESDORF *Cremona's Proj. Geom.* 283 If these equations be multiplied together.

c. *intr.* To perform the process of multiplication.

1579 DIGGES *Stratioticos* 4 To multiplie, is to find of two Numbers a number product the one in the other augmented. **1652** *News fr. Low Countr.* 8 Podex can..Adde, Multiply, Subtract, Divide. **1798** HUTTON *Course Math.* (1806) I. 13 The number you multiply by, or the number of repetitions, is the Multiplier. **1840** LARDNER *Geom.* 102 If we require the area, we have only to multiply by 3·14.

d. Said of the multiplier (*trans.* and *intr.*).

c **1425** *Crafte Nombrynge* (E.E.T.S.) 21 Numerus multiplicans. Anglice, þe nombur multipliynge. **1570** BILLINGSLEY *Euclid* 214 b, If a number multiplieng himselfe produce a cube number: then is that number also a cube number. **1704** J. HARRIS *Lex. Techn.* II. s.v. *Multiplication*, Negatives multiplying Positives, must produce Negatives. **1709** J. WARD *Yng. Math. Guide* I. ii. (1734) 14 When the Number Multiplied is so often Added to itself, as there are Units in the Number Multiplying. **1859** SALMON *Higher Alg.* 70 The terms multiplying *xy* must be a_3a_0 and a_2a_1.

†**6.** *Alch.* (*trans.* and *intr.*) To increase the precious metals, as by transmutation of the baser metals. Also *intr.* (for *pass.*), said of the precious metals. *Obs.*

c **1386** CHAUCER *Can. Yeom. Prol. & T.* 848 A man may lightly lerne, if he have aught, To multiplye, and bringe his good to naught. **1390** Gower *Conf.* II. 84 Thei founden thilke experience, Which cleped is Alconomie, Whereof the Selver multeplie Thei made and ek the gold also. **1477** Norton *Ord. Alch.* in Ashm. (1652) 17 Saying how they can Multiplie Gold and Silver. *Ibid.* 18 When such men promise to Multiplie, They compasse to doe some Villony. *Ibid.*, Upon Nature thei falsely lye For Mettalls doe not Multiplie. **1543** tr. *Act 5 Hen. IV*, c. 4 It is ordeyned..that none from hensforth shall vse to multiplie golde or syluer, nor vse the craft of multiplication. **1592** Lyly *Gallathea* III. iii, An arte quoth you, that one multiplieth so much all day, that he wanteth money to buy meate at night? **1650** Evelyn *Diary* 14 Dec., An impostor that had like to have impos'd upon us a pretended secret of multiplying gold. **1688** *Act 1 Will. & Mary*, c. 30 [citing Act 5 Hen. IV].

multiply ('mʌltɪplɪ), *adv.* [f. multiple + -ly².] In a multiple manner; many ways or times, or more than once. *spec.* in *Math.* ***multiply connected*** (see quot. 1893); ***multiply-periodic***, having many periods.

The use of a following hyphen is similar to that described at well *adv.* VII.

1881 Maxwell *Electr. & Magn.* I. 120 If the region *s* is doubly or multiply connected. **1892** *Mind* I. 353 The rules for the synthesis of multiply-quantified propositions follow immediately from those for the synthesis of singly-quantified propositions. **1893** A. R. Forsyth *Theory of Functions* 315 A surface is simply connected, if it be resolved into two distinct pieces by every cross-cut; but if there be any cross-cut, which does not resolve it into distinct pieces, the surface is multiply connected. *Ibid.* 464 Functions which are multiply-periodic. **1922** F. W. Aston *Isotopes* 71 These multiply-charged clusters give most reliable values of mass. **1932** Lewis & Langford *Symbolic Logic* ix. 301 A hierarchy..is involved in multiply-general propositions and functions. **1962** W. & M. Kneale *Devel. of Logic* ii. 112 Two distinct quantifiers are required, as in the statement '*Some* man does not possess *all* knowledge', and multiply general statements are quite common in science and philosophy, e.g. '*Every* event has *a* cause'. **1963** B. Fozard *Instrumentation Nucl. Reactors* ii. 12 In many cases only one electron is separated from the parent atom in an ionising process but cases occur where several electrons are emitted and the atom is said to be multiply ionised. **1966** D. G. Brandon *Mod. Techniques Metallogr.* iv. 204 The ions will be multiply-charged. **1971** *Jrnl. Gen. Psychol.* LXXXV. 165 Almost no studies have been specifically directed to the detection of the relative power of the different kinds of categories into which words seem to be multiply encoded.

multi-ply, *sb.* and *a.* [f. multi- + ply *sb.*, plywood.] **A.** *sb.* Plywood comprising more than three layers. **B.** *adj.* Designating textiles, etc., formed by having several threads or webs twisted together; also denoting paper comprising several layers.

1940 *Chambers's Techn. Dict.* 563/2 *Multi-ply*, plywood formed of more than three layers of wood. **1950** *Gloss. Aeronaut. Terms* (B.S.I.) 1. 49 *Multi-ply fabric*, fabric formed of more than one ply. **1951** *Archit. Rev.* CIX. 159 (*caption*) Multi-ply was developed during the war for aircraft propellers. **1962** *Times* 3 Dec. (Agric. Suppl.) p. vii/5 The multi-ply paper sack. **1963** A. J. Hall *Textile Sci.* i. 9 The threads may be single or consist of two, three, or more single threads twisted together to give what are often termed *folded* or *multi-ply* threads. **1966** A. W. Lewis *Gloss. Woodworking Terms* 52 Laminated boards..include plywood, multi-ply, laminboard, [etc.].

multiplye, variant of multiplie *Sc.*

'multiplying, *vbl. sb.* [-ing¹.]

1. = multiplication, in various senses.

c **1380** Wyclif *Sel. Wks.* III. 37 In covetise of multipliinge of richessis. *c* **1384** Chaucer *H. Fame* II. 293 (Fairf. MS.) Fro roundel [to] compas Eche aboute other goynge, Caused of othres sterynge And multiplyinge euer moo. *c* **1386** —— *Pard. T.* 46 He shal have multiplying of his greyn. *a* **1400** in Halliwell *Rara Mathem.* (1841) 58 Þan al þat comes of þ at multiplyeng departe þou by þe noumbre of þe poyntes of þe vmbre. **1474** Caxton *Chesse* III. i. (1883) 77 The multiplynge of his goodes temporell. **1549** Latimer *3rd Serm. bef. Edw. VI* (Arb.) 87 *marg.*, These mixtures and multiplyinges are theft. **1553** *Acts Privy Counc.* (N.S.) IV. 254 Informacions, lettres and examinacions towching Whalley's accusacion for multiplying. **1599** Dubravius (*title*) A new Booke of good Husbandry... Conteining the order..of making of Fish-pondes, with the breeding, preserving, and multiplying of the Carpe [etc.]. **1625** Bacon *Ess., Seditions & Troubles* (Arb.) 405 The Multiplying of Nobilitie, and other Degrees of Qualitie. **1652** J. Chetwind in Harington *Briefe View* Ep. Ded., This Authour..hath avoyded the needlesse multiplying of words. **1659** Milton *Civ. Power in Eccl. Causes* Wks. 1851 V. 332 The multiplying and the aggravating of sin to them both. **1707** *Curios. in Husb. & Gard.* 129 These four last Observations for the multiplying of Corn. **1800** Lamb *Let. to Coleridge* 6 Aug., I cram all I can in, to save a multiplying of letters. **1855** Bain *Senses & Int.* II. ii. §12 (1864) 201 The multiplying of points of contact, by our having a plurality of fingers.

¶ **b.** Alleged term for a 'company' of husbands.

1486 *Bk. St. Albans* fvij, A Multiplieng of husbondis.

2. *attrib.*: ***multiplying way*** (? nonce-use), = 'family way' (see family 10 b).

1599 T. M[oufet] *Silkwormes* 47 What made thee shew thy multiplying pride, More in these egges, then all the egges beside? **1739** Mrs. Delany in *Life & Corr.* (1861) II. 53 Duchess is very well, though in a multiplying way.

'multiplying, *ppl. a.* [-ing².] That multiplies. † ***multiplying of***: tending to multiply.

a **1425** *Cursor M.* 2348 (Trin.) More..þen þe graueles in þe see So multeplynge [*earlier texts* untelland] shulde þei be. **1601** Shaks. *All's Well* v. iii. 102 Platus himselfe, That knowes the tinct and multiplying med'cine. **1611** Bible *Wisd.* iv. 3 The multiplying brood of the vngodly shall not thriue. **1646** H. Lawrence *Comm. Angells* 64 Such punishments..are multiplying of evill infinitely, if God prevent not. **1690** Child *Disc. Trade* (1698) 23 Interest.. which is of so prodigious a multiplying nature, that it must of necessity make the lenders monstrous rich. **1709** J. Ward *Yng. Math. Guide* I. vi. (1734) 72 The Multiplying Fraction is less than an Unite or 1. **1855** Bp. Wilberforce in R. I. Wilberforce *Life* (1881) II. vii. 287 Oh! our multiplying embarrassments from concessions and inconsistencies. **1877** Besant & Rice *Harp & Cr.* viii. 60 What time the *placens uxor* expects her husband to return with wavering step and multiplying eye.

b. in the names of instruments and machines having devices for increasing the number of movements, images, etc. Also ***multiplying-machine***, a machine for performing mechanically the arithmetical process of multiplication. (See Knight *Dict. Mech.* and *Suppl.*)

1823 *Ann. Philos.* June 437 The multiplying wire [in Schweigger's Multiplier] is of plated copper. **1839** T. C. Hofland *Brit. Angler's Man.* i. (1841) 6 The multiplying reel was formerly much used, but, from its liability to be out of order [etc.]. **1849** Noad *Electricity* (ed. 3) 396 Rapid horizontal motion is then given to the coil by means of a multiplying wheel. **1856** 'Stonehenge' *Brit. Rural Sports* I. §621. 234/2 Multiplying-reels, in which, by the introduction of machinery, the barrel is made to travel several times to the single revolution of the handle. **1876** Tait *Rec. Adv. Phys. Sci.* iv, An arrangement..consisting of a driving wheel and multiplying gear, by which I can communicate an extremely great velocity of rotation to this copper disc. **1882** Nares *Seamanship* (ed. 6) 53 *Multiplying sheaves.*—Are sometimes fitted to blocks where much friction takes place. **1889** *Nature* 21 Nov. 71/2 A multiplying apparatus which determines..in one function, the product of a number by each figure of the multiplier.

Hence † **'multiplyingly** *adv.*, manifoldly.

1483 Caxton *Gold. Leg.* 346 b/2 They suffrid in many maners prouffitably constantly and multyplyengly.

'multiplying-glass.

† **1.** A magnifying-glass. Also *fig. Obs.*

Cf. multiply *v.* 1 f.

1628 Feltham *Resolves* II. xxxv, On our sicke beds, [hee] shewes vs all our sinnes in multiplying Glasses. *c* **1640** *Capt. Underwitt* I. in Bullen *O. Pl.* II. 336, I wod not have a man ..so much a dwarfe that I must use a multiplying glass to know the proportion of his limbes. **1656** Cowley *Misc., Ode of Wit* ii, Some things do through our Judgment pass As through a Multiplying Glass. **1680** S. Mather *Irenicum* 19 The blind prophane world, who pretend to take offence at our divisions, looking upon them in the multiplying Glasses of their own enmity, and so accounting every difference in Religion to be a different Religion.

2. A toy consisting of a concave glass or lens, the surface of which is cut into numerous facets so as to give as many reflexions of the object observed. Also *fig.*

1671 Foulis *Hist. Romish Treasons* (1681) 60 As for Bellarmine, you may look through him like a Multiplying-glass and perceive multitudes of people. **1688** Holme *Armoury* III. ix. 375/1 Multiplying Glasses, that makes one things [*sic*] seem many. **1701** Norris *Ideal World* I. ii. 50 So many reproductions of one thing, like the image of the same face repeated in a multiplying glass. **1764** J. Ferguson *Lect.* 147 The multiplying glass is made by grinding down the round side..of a convex glass..into several flat surface[s]. **1831** Brewster *Optics* xxxix. 329 Natural multiplying glasses may be found among transparent minerals which are crossed with veins oppositely crystallised. **1862–7** *J. Wylde's Circ. Sci.* I. 60/2.

multi-point, -pointed: see multi- 3, 1.

multipolar (mʌltɪ'pəʊlə(r)), *a.* [f. multi- + polar *a.*] Having or pertaining to many poles.

a. *Anat.* Of a nerve cell: having many processes.

1859 *Todd's Cycl. Anat.* V. 443/2 Of the ganglia, it is exclusively the sympathetic which are made up of multipolar ganglion-cells. **1885** *Encycl. Brit.* XIX. 27/2 The cells of the spinal ganglia are usually rounded; those of the sympathetic more angular; those of the spinal cord multipolar. **1948** A. Brodal *Neurol. Anat.* xi. 354 The autonomic ganglion cells in most of the ganglia of the sympathetic trunk and in the peripheral ganglia are usually multipolar and are characterized by possessing numerous and long dendrites. **1964** J. Z. Young *Model of Brain* xix. 307 Multipolar amacrines are numerous in the cell islands of the optic lobes.

b. *Electr.* Of electrical machinery: having more than one pair of magnetic poles in the system of field magnets.

1884 Higgs *Magn. Dyn. Electr. Mach.* 259 Formerly, in multipolar machines there were as many brushes as poles. **1903** [see *bar winding* (bar *sb.*¹ 30)]. **1964** N. N. Hancock *Matrix Analysis of Electr. Machinery* v. 72 To apply the results to multipolar machines it will be necessary to reduce the speed and to increase the torque according to the number of pole-pairs.

c. *Cytology.* Having or involving more than two spindle poles.

1894 *Ann. Bot.* VIII. 313 Nuclear divisions with multipolar spindles. **1896** E. B. Wilson *Cell* ii. 68 The abnormal forms of mitoses are arranged by Hausemann in two general groups, as follows: (1) asymmetrical mitoses,.. and (2) multipolar mitoses. **1912** E. A. Minchin *Introd. Study Protozoa* vii. 120 In cases where the division of the nucleus is of the karyokinetic type, repeated divisions of the centriole result in the formation of a complicated multipolar mitotic figure, leading to a multiple division of the nucleus. **1937** M. J. D. White *Chromosomes* ii. 19 In many cells such as those of cancerous tissues and in Sea-Urchin eggs which have been fertilized several times as a result of polyspermy, multipolar spindles with a number of equatorial planes intersecting one another are found; there may be as many as 12 poles and 6 equatorial planes. **1950** *Hereditas* XXXVI. 393 (*heading*) Multipolar spindles in human cancer cells.

d. Consisting of, or divided into, more than two (political or other) alliances, ententes, parties, etc.

1968 *Guardian* 4 Dec. 4/6 The most profound challenge to American policy will be..to develop some concept of order in a world which is bipolar militarily but multipolar politically. **1969** S. Henig in Henig & Pinder *European Pol. Parties* 502 The country-by-country chapters have indicated a threefold classification between bipolar, unipolar and multipolar party systems. In bipolar systems.. government will be dominated either by the two parties singly..or by both together in a 'big coalition'. In a unipolar system..the norm is for one party to be easily the largest legislative group... In multipolar systems, neither one nor two parties are dominant even to the extent of always emerging the strongest from succeeding elections. **1975** *Times* 7 Apr. 14/2 Kissinger['s]..concept of a multipolar world, where major powers could compete and cooperate simultaneously.

multipolarity (mʌltɪpəʊ'lærɪtɪ). [f. prec. + -ity.] **a.** Multipolar quality or state.

1947 *Hereditas* XXXIII. 468 The anaphases...all showed serious disturbances, lagging chromosomes, multipolarity ..and so on. **1950** *Ibid.* XXXVI. 395 Multipolarity seems.. to be fairly independent of the chromosome number in that highly polyploid bipolar as well as multipolar configurations which contain low chromosome numbers are found. **1968** *Guardian* 4 Dec. 2/3 NATO..has yet to adjust to the political multipolarity of the late sixties. **1969** *Punch* 5 Mar. 329/2 Henry Kissinger..has already summed up the Soames affair as an example of 'political multipolarity', spoken of the problems of 'a pluralist world'... All good stuff, if we knew what it meant.

b. *Physics.* The highest order of multipole associated with a state or phenomenon.

1955 *Physical Rev.* XCVIII. 1198/1 (*heading*) Multipolarity of gamma transitions in F^{19} and Na^{23} by Coulomb excitation. **1973** *Nature* 31 Aug. 541/1 There have been speculations that other giant resonances with other multipolarities might exist; for example, quadrupole motions in which the nucleon distributions oscillate between prolate and oblate shapes with quadrupole deformations.

multipole ('mʌltɪpəʊl), *sb.* and *a.* *Physics.* [f. multi- 2 + pole *sb.*²] **A.** *sb.* A system of 2^l monopoles ($l = 1, 2, 3, \ldots$) with no net charge or pole strength and no moment of a lower order than l (cf. moment *sb.* 8 c); the dipole ($l = 1$) is often treated as a special case and the quadrupole ($l = 2$) regarded as the multipole of lowest order. Freq. *attrib.* or as *adj.*, esp. designating electromagnetic radiation of the kind produced by a multipole with a moment varying sinusoidally in magnitude.

In quot. 1916 this may not be the precise sense.

1916 *Jrnl. Amer. Chem. Soc.* XXXVIII. 764 One or more electrons are held by sufficiently weak constraints so that they may..in the extreme case pass altogether to another atom, thus producing in the molecule a bipole or multipole of high electrical moment. **1929** *Physical Rev.* XXXIV. 1252 Since m must change by ± 1,..the transition $j = 0 \rightarrow j = 0$ cannot occur for multipole radiation. **1932** J. H. Van Vleck *Theory Electr. & Magn. Susceptibilities* i. 12 The omitted terms are sometimes characterized as representing 'multipoles'. The omitted term in ϕ of lowest order, for instance, is..Nq/R^3, where q is the 'quadrupole moment'. **1950** D. Halliday *Introd. Nucl. Physics* ii. 57 If $|\Delta I| = 1$ the multipole order is 2 and we have..a dipole transition; if $|\Delta I| = 2$, the multipole order is 4 and we have a quadrupole transition. **1952** Blatt & Weisskopf *Theoret. Nucl. Physics* xii. 586 The electric multipole fields have non-vanishing radial components of **E**, and the magnetic multipole fields have non-vanishing radial components of **H**. The angular momentum carried by one quantum of multipole radiation is $\hbar l$, with z component $\hbar m$. Electric and magnetic multipole radiation of order l, m carry the same angular momentum but differ through their parity. *Ibid.* 587 Any arbitrary field **E**(r), **H**(r) which obeys the free-space Maxwell equations can be expanded in terms of multipoles. **1962** Corson & Lorrain *Introd. Electromagn. Fields* ii. 52 For the general multipole, characterized by the letter l, the potential varies as $1/r^{l+1}$. **1970** [see moment *sb.* 8 c].

B. *adj.* (Freq. written **multi-pole**.) Designed to close or open several circuits simultaneously.

1927 *Wireless World* 22 June 786/3 It is sometimes recommended that a multi-pole switch should be fitted in order to switch off both batteries. **1934** *Pract. Wireless* IV. 667/3 This multi-pole switch converts the usual panel-controlled push-pull action into a lateral movement. **1962** G. A. T. Burdett *Automatic Control Handbk.* iii. 24 The multi-pole type of control switch is a double break changeover switch especially designed for the switching of squirrel-cage motors.

multi-po'sition, *a.* [f. multi- + position *sb.*] Usable or placeable in more than one position. So **multi-po'sitional** *a.*

1944 *Illustr. Aviation Encycl.* (Aviation Research Associates) 143/2 *Multiposition propeller*: see *controllable pitch propeller*. **1948** F. J. Murray *Theory Math. Machines* (ed. 2) i. 3 Another method of indicating the digit which appears in a decimal place in a counter is by means of a multiposition switch. **1961** Y. Olsson *On Syntax Eng. Verb* iv. 82 A nucleus counts as multi-positional not only if it is identical in all of the Positions in which it occurs, but also if it is combined with a non-nuclear element. **1969** *Jane's Freight Containers 1968–69* 472 (*caption*) Duramin 30 ft ISO Container with side-loading facility and 'Sal-wall' lining (for multi-position load anchorage). **1971** *Power Farming* Mar. 69/2, 5 ft convertible hay or silage flail mower, straw chopper and haulm pulveriser. Easily adaptable, multi-position wheels.

multipotent (mʌlˈtɪpətənt), *a.* *rare.* [f. L. *multipotent-*, *-potens*: see MULTI- and POTENT.] Having much power; very powerful.
1606 SHAKS. *Tr. & Cr.* IV. v. 129 Ioue multipotent. **1632** LITHGOW *Trav.* VI. 239 Thousands famished, and put to the sword within this multipotent City, by Vespasian. **1656** BLOUNT *Glossogr.* **1889** TALMAGE in *Voice* (N.Y.) 28 Feb., I leave this imperial and multipotent numeral seven where the Bible leaves it.

multiˈpresence. [ad. mod.L. *multipræsentia*: see MULTI- and PRESENCE.] The fact or faculty of being present in many places at once.
1614 BP. HALL *No Peace with Rome* §17 That exploded opinion of transubstantiation, and (which is the root of it) the multi-presence of Christs body. **1727** DE FOE *Hist. Appar.* iv. (1840) 31 He has invisibility and multipresence, as a spirit has. **1885** SCHAFF *Christ & Christ.* 75 The mediæval schoolmen .. ascribe .. a miraculous multipresence to his body and blood in the sacrament of the altar.
So **multiˈpresent** *a.*, having the property of multipresence.
1882-3 *Schaff's Encycl. Relig. Knowl.* III. 2415/2 The glorified body is not omnipresent, but multipresent.

multiˈprocessing, *vbl. sb.* *Computers.* [f. MULTI- 2.] Processing by a number of processors sharing a common memory and common peripherals.
1961 *Communications Assoc. Computing Machinery* Oct. 421/1 Multiprocessing is defined here as the sharing of a common memory and all peripheral equipment by two or more processor units. **1967** C. J. DUNCAN in Cox & Grose *Organiz. Bibliogr. Rec. by Computer* II. 47 The decision as to whether to run the composing machine on-line or off-line will..depend upon the size of the machine, what multiprocessing facilities are available, and the precise machine configuration and loading. **1969** P. B. JORDAIN *Condensed Computer Encycl.* 327 The Honeywell 800 was an early powerful multiprocessing computer. It was equivalent to 8 conventional computers sharing a common memory. A hardware/software executive coordinated the eight processes to ensure efficient operation.
So **multiˈprocessor,** a processor capable of performing multiprocessing; usu. *attrib.*
1961 *Communications Assoc. Computing Machinery* Oct. 421 (*heading*) Problems of storage allocation in a multiprocessor multiprogrammed system. **1965** A. G. FAVRET *Introd. Digital Computer Applic.* xvi. 233 In multiprocessor systems the executive routines must be capable of allocating tasks among different processors or deciding which of several inquiries should be given priority. **1970** O. DOPPING *Computers & Data Processing* vi. 97 Two or more computer systems can be interconnected electrically to form a multi-processor system. *Ibid.*, The multi-processor alternative has the advantage that the capacity of the faster machine is always on tap also during input and output operations. **1971** *New Scientist* 25 Feb. 425/2 The 6000 models are well equipped with communications gear, and multi-processor configurations have interconnected memory units and multiplexors as well as processors.

multiˈprogramming, *vbl. sb.* *Computers.* [MULTI- 2.] The execution of two or more independent programs concurrently.
1959 *Communications Assoc. Computing Machinery* Nov. 15/1 The normal requirement in multiprogramming is to communicate with a particular program and at the same time allow all other programs to proceed... We now desire to stop a *program* rather than the *machine.* **1965** A. G. FAVRET *Introd. Digital Computer Applic.* xvi. 234 Multiprogramming techniques will probably also be used in some industrial process control applications where one computer is utilized to control several different processes on a time-shared basis. **1970** A. CAMERON et al. *Computers & Old Eng. Concordances* 25 You can do a run on a 360, of course, without tying up the entire 360 through..something called multi-programming. **1973** MURRILL & SMITH *Introd. Computer Sci.* vii. 260 The objective of multi-programming is to maintain two or more programs in memory simultaneously so that the processor can be working on one program while it is waiting for an input or output operation to be completed in the other program.
So **multiˈprogram, multiˈprogrammed** *adjs.* [MULTI- 3, 1], designed for or pertaining to multiprogramming.
1959 *Proc. Eastern Joint Computer Conf.* Dec. 75 (*heading*) Arithmetic and control in a multiprogram computer. *Ibid.* 80/2 The amount of work which can be accomplished per second..is, of course, increased enormously in a multi-programmed design. **1961** Multiprogrammed [see MULTIPROCESSOR]. **1964** T. W. MCRAE *Impact of Computers on Accounting* vii. 209 By far the most interesting development..has been the introduction of multi-programme machines, which can process a number of jobs at the same time. **1967** H. HELLERMAN *Digital Computer System Princ.* ii. 107 In multiprogrammed systems it [*sc.* a control program] also resolves all conflicts among problem programs for calls on common facilities and ensures privacy among the several users that may be sharing these facilities. *Ibid.* viii. 345 The major impetus for storage protection arises in multiprogram sharing of processor storage.

multi-ˈpurpose, *a.* [f. MULTI- + PURPOSE *sb.*] Serving, or intended to serve, many purposes; performing many duties.
1935 *Sci. Amer.* Sept. 164 It is capable of handling much larger signal voltages than the diodes incorporated in the multi-purpose type of glass tube. **1937** *New Republic* 6 Jan. 292 The multipurpose TVA dams. **1939** *Electronics* June 48/1 (*title*) Multi-purpose Midget Tubes. **1943** J. S. HUXLEY *TVA* xviii. 134 A co-operative, unified, multi-purpose undertaking. **1950** *Mind* LIX. 422 An all-round multi-purpose classification. **1959** *Listener* 12 Nov. 810/2 The use of what is now known..as the 'generalist' or 'multi-purpose' worker at village level. **1960** *Farmer & Stockbreeder* 8 Mar. 68 The only multi-purpose oil to be tested by the National Institute of Agricultural Engineering. **1965** *English Studies* XLVI. 30 While it [*sc.* þe] is a multivalent form it is not a multi-purpose form. **1972** *Jrnl. Social Psychol.* LXXXVII. 154 The multipurpose role inner city mothers often assume may explain this [observation] in part. **1972** M. SHEPPARD *Taman Indera* 65 A long multi-purpose head-cloth of red or blue cotton. **1973** *Country Life* 28 June 1904/1 A new multi-purpose mistblower, suitable for crops of all kinds. **1974** *Daily Tel.* (Colour Suppl.) 29 Nov. 72 Many rooms are multi-purpose, and the use to which they are put by family or friends should be analysed before making any decisions.

multi-ˈracial, multiracial, *a.* Of, pertaining to, or comprising several races, peoples, or ethnic groups; characterized by the coexistence or co-operation of individual members of such groups on amicable and equal terms. Also *fig.* So **multi-ˈracially** *adv.*
1923 *Overseas* Sept. 45 The interests of modern civilisation and, I think, Christian ethics, are better expressed in large, bi-racial or multi-racial States,..where racialism is accounted a public curse rather than a civic virtue. **1933** E. B. REUTER in E. S. Bogardus *Social Probl. & Social Processes* 96 The type of accommodation made is of course an individual matter, but the forms that it takes are ..those familiar in other bi-racial or multi-racial political areas. **1947** *Forum* (Johannesburg) X. I. 25/1 We, as a multi-racial society, have had our differences, while sharp antagonisms unfortunately exist today. **1957** L. F. R. WILLIAMS *State of Israel* 209 The unifying influence which this hostility is exerting upon Israel's multiracial population. **1957** *Economist* 19 Oct. 204/2 He triumphantly created the first multiracial government in Africa at the height of Mau Mau. **1958** *Times Lit. Suppl.* 10 Jan. 21/2 One feels the pleasant relief of a man living a multi-racial life away from the colour bar. **1959** *New Statesman* 28 Feb. 300/1 But it is his attack on the multi-racial clothing industry—involving the dismissal and replacement of 35,000 non-whites—that has frightened the coloured people especially. **1963** *Economist* 30 Nov. 887/3 Such a multi-racially-run world. **1966** *Listener* 6 Oct. 499/3 Closer contact between..the university worker and the industrial scientist, to make a truly 'multi-racial' commonwealth of scholarship. **1972** T. LILLEY *K Section* ix. 40 The Dock Labourers' Union was one of the biggest... Multi-racial, it owed allegiance only to itself.

multi-ˈracialism, multiracialism. [f. prec. + -ISM.] The condition or quality of being multi-racial; *spec.*, the conception of a state in which members of different races, peoples, or ethnic groups live on amicable and equal terms. So **multi-ˈracialist, multiracialist,** an advocate of multi-racial governments or societies.
1958 *Economist* 3 May 396/2 Its professed multi-racialism was bound to appear an attempt to entrench separate racial streams. **1959** *Manch. Guardian* 25 July 5/3 The concept of partnership or multi-racialism [in Kenya]. **1960** *Guardian* 25 June 5/5 Mr. Blundell is a convinced multi-racialist. **1962** *Times* 4 Jan. 9/2 Britain is pushing the Federation towards a multiracialism that will end in African control. **1962** *Punch* 28 Nov. 758/1 Uncle Tom, a born multi-racialist. **1964** *Ann. Reg. 1963* 326 In September, another Coloured man..escaped to Swaziland..hoping.. to represent the case for multi-racialism in South African sport. **1972** *Guardian* 8 Feb. 13/8 Multi-racialism here [*sc.* in Senegal] is not just an experiment. It is a proven fact.

multi-radiate to **-sacculate**: see MULTI- 1 a, 3.

multiscience (mʌlˈtɪʃəns). [f. L. *multus* MULTI- + *scientia* SCIENCE.] Knowledge of many things. So **mulˈtiscient** *a.* (in recent Dicts.); †**mulˈtiscious** *a.* [f. L. *multisci-us*], 'knowing much, skilful' (Blount *Glossogr.* 1656).
a **1834** COLERIDGE *Church & State* (1839) 226 *note*, Multiscience (or a variety and quantity of acquired knowledge) does not teach intelligence.

multisect (ˈmʌltɪsɛkt), *a.* *Ent.* [f. mod.L. *multisect-us*, f. *multus* MULTI- + *sectus*, pa. pple. of *secāre* to cut.] (See quot.)
1826 KIRBY & SP. *Entomol.* xlvi. IV. 305 Multisect (*Multisectum*). When an insect appears to have no distinct trunk and abdomen, but is divided into numerous segments.

multiˈsect, *v.* *rare*$^{-0}$. [f. MULTI- + L. *sect-*, ppl. stem of *secāre* to cut.] *trans.* To divide into many parts (*Century Dict.*). Also **multiˈsection** (*rare*$^{-1}$), division into many parts.
1862 MASSON in *Macm. Mag.* Dec. 85 On the plan of multisection, as well as on that of trisection, bisection.

multi-segmentate to **-siliquose**: see MULTI- 1.

ˈmultisided, *a.* [f. MULTI- + SIDED *ppl. a.*] = MANY-SIDED *a.* So **multiˈsidedness.**
1903 A. W. PATTERSON *Schumann* xvii. 202 The multi-sidedness of Schumann's genius. **1963** *Times* 30 May 9/6 The first floor elevation has a sawtooth plan with adjoining windows set at an angle to each other so that occupants can look through into each other's rooms, which may disconcert an ambassador seeking privacy; and the resulting multisided rooms may prove awkward in use.

multisoil: see MULTI-.

multisonant (mʌlˈtɪsənənt), *a.* *rare.* [f. L. *multison-us* + -ANT. See MULTI- and SONANT.] Having many sounds; sounding much.
1656 BLOUNT *Glossogr.*, *Multisonant*, that hath many or great sounds, that makes a great noise. **1821** *Tales of my Landlord* I. 241 The multisonant dash of ocean's billows. **1888** *Harper's Mag.* Oct. 741/1 The multicolored, multisonant stream rushes by.
So **mulˈtisonous** *a.*
1905 *Westm. Gaz.* 29 Dec. 2/1 The multisonous voices of winds and sea and forest.

multi-spermous to **-stable**: see MULTI-.

ˈmultistage, *a.* Also **multi-stage.** [f. MULTI- 3 + STAGE *sb.*] Consisting of, occurring in, or involving several stages (cf. STAGE *sb.* IV).
1904 *Engineering News* LI. 324/3 The pumps shown and described in the following are multi-stage turbine pumps. **1911** A. M. GREENE *Pumping Machinery* xiii. 522 (*heading*) Multi-stage compression. **1920** *Wireless World* Jan. 574/2 (*heading*) The design of multi-stage amplifiers using three-electrode thermionic valves. **1944** [see *intercool* vb. s.v. INTERCOOLING *vbl. sb.*]. **1946** *Nature* 5 Oct. 464/2 It was admitted that these ranges might be attained by the employment of multi-stage rockets. **1962** F. I. ORDWAY et al. *Basic Astronautics* x. 400 Large boosters..are being designed for use as the initial stage of a multistage space carrier vehicle. **1962** SIMPSON & RICHARDS *Physical Princ. Junction Transistors* xi. 246 We shall be concerned with typical intermediate stages in a multistage amplifier and not with unusual impedance matching arrangements at the input and output. **1963** R. R. A. HIGHAM *Handbk. Papermaking* vi. 139 Either single- or multi-stage bleaching may be carried out according to the conditions. **1971** *Brit. Med. Bull.* XXVII. 68/2 Multi-centric hypotheses [of the origin of cancer] have not proved as popular as multi-stage hypotheses, or theories which assume that a change from a normal cell to a malignant cell takes place in stages. **1971** B. SCHARF *Engin. & its Lang.* xv. 207 Multi-stage turbines may be compound, i.e. they have both impulse and reaction stages.
b. *spec.* in *Statistics.* Applied to sampling carried out in a number of stages, the sample obtained at each stage being divided into smaller units and taken as the population for the next stage of sampling.
1949 F. YATES *Sampling Methods for Censuses & Surveys* iii. 34 Multi-stage sampling introduces a flexibility into sampling which is lacking in the simpler methods. **1966** KENDALL & STUART *Advanced Theory Statistics* III. xxxix. 204 The motive for multi-stage sampling is almost invariably to reduce costs rather than reduce variance directly; the additional resources can, of course, be applied to an increase in sample size. **1973** F. E. FISCHER *Fund. Statistical Concepts* ix. 215 The extensive survey work which precedes every national election..is a perfect example of multistage sampling.
So **ˈmultistaged** *ppl. a.* [MULTI- 1].
1965 *Times Lit. Suppl.* 25 Nov. 1051/1 It is like a Greek tragedy in which the Furies have been replaced by a multi-staged rocket.

multiˈstage, *v.* Also mulˈtistage. [f. prec.] *trans.* To make multistaged. So **multiˈstaging** *vbl. sb.*, the use of several stages.
1911 A. M. GREENE *Pumping Machinery* xiii. 523 Since it is not possible to bring the curve of compression close enough to the isothermal, a method of multi-staging the compression has to be devised. **1944** A. H. CHURCH *Centrifugal Pumps & Blowers* vi. 128 If the total head to be developed by a pump is too large for a single stage to handle, multistaging is resorted to. **1972** *Physics Bull.* Oct. 591/2 In general one would like a higher overall pressure ratio and this can be obtained by multistaging.

multi-ˈstory, -ˈstorey, *a.* [f. MULTI- + STORY *sb.*², STOREY.] Of many storeys or floors. So **multi-ˈstoried, -ˈstoreyed** *a.*
1918 *N.Y. Times Mag.* 16 June 4 The stenographers..are here from multi-storied city skyscrapers. **1918** L. GALLOWAY *Office Management* (1919) 50 In a multistory factory building the location of the office within the factory itself vitally affects the efficiency of the clerical force. **1946** *Nature* 3 Aug. 152/2 The framed multi-story construction, to be advocated both on architectural grounds and for blast resistance. *Ibid.* 28 Sept. 439/1 The first remedy was to provide adequate car parks, underground, at ground level, and in multi-storied buildings. **1955** *Times* 31 Aug. 11/6 Rehousing..will create a total overspill of from 35,000 to 54,000, depending on the extent to which multi-storey flats are erected as the old and crumbling tenements come down. **1958** *Manch. Guardian Weekly* 7 Aug. 6/4 The sooner we have more meters the sooner the chaos in our streets will disappear—especially if the profits on metered parking are translated into proper garages and multi-storey parks. **1964** J. SUMMERSON *Classical Lang. Archit.* ii. 15 A building which..is multi-storeyed. **1973** *Times* 28 Feb. (Victoria Centre, Nottingham, Suppl.) p. i/1 The Victoria Centre, Nottingham's new £10m multi-storey shopping centre, is, according to its developers..the biggest of its type in Europe. **1975** J. SYMONS *Three Pipe Problem* xviii. 208 The car was in a multi-storey park.

multi-ˈtasking, *sb.* and *a.* *Computing.* Also **multitasking.** [MULTI- 2.] **A.** *sb.* The concurrent execution of a number of different tasks or jobs, as by interleaving or multiprocessing. **B.** *adj.* Able to do multi-tasking.
1966 *Datamation* Sept. 68 (*heading*) Configuring multi-tasking systems. *Ibid.* 68/1 Multi-tasking is defined as the use of a single CPU for the simultaneous processing of two or more jobs. **1978** *Pract. Computing* July-Aug. 24/2 The whole package is designed to run under RT/68, a real-time multi-tasking operating system. **1979** *Personal Computer World* Nov. 56/3 They are well used to multi-user, multitasking systems incorporating hard discs. **1981** *Kilobaud Microcomputing* June 35/2 The traditional method, multitasking, uses a single central processing unit ..to handle the programs for all of the users. **1983** *Your Computer* (Austral.) May 37/3 The MBC 1000 is also multi-user and multi-tasking. **1986** *What Micro?* Apr. 48/2 It

offers..a small taste of multi-tasking—you can order printing to go on while you're editing another piece of text.

Also **multi-'task** *a.*, involving multi-tasking, able to do multi-tasking.

1969 P. B. JORDAIN *Condensed Computer Encycl.* 328 Multitask operation extends beyond ordinary multiprogramming in that it allows a single copy of a program module to be used by more than one task. **1979** *Personal Computer World* Nov. 32 (Advt.), Together..we'll be demonstrating the Microstar 45 Plus multi-user, multi-task computer system in operation. **1983** *Austral. Personal Computer* Dec. 6/1 'Multi-task' systems, where one user at one micro can actually be doing three or four things at once.

multi-'tier, *a.* [f. MULTI- + TIER *sb.*[1]] Having or comprising several tiers or layers. So **multi-'tiered** *a.*; **multi-'tiering** *vbl. sb.*, arrangement in tiers or layers.

1952 *Flow Q.* Jan. 4 A multi-tier conveyor. **1957** *Textile Terms & Definitions* (Textile Inst.) (ed. 3) 67 *Multi-tier loom*, a loom with a batten having several rows of shuttles. **1958** T. LANDAU *Encycl. Librarianship* 283/2 The *multi-tier stack*... This system ensures a maximum storage space. Many of these stacks are several tiers high and are connected by book lifts, and occasionally by passenger lifts. **1960** (*title*) The power gain of multi-tiered VHF transmitting aerials (B.B.C. Engin. Monogr. 31). **1965** K. D. METCALF *Planning Academic & Research Library Buildings* viii. 134/2 Multi-tier book stacks hold themselves up. Each level of stack supports the levels above... A multitier stack provided about as concentrated shelving space as could be found until one or another of the recently developed compact-shelving arrangements began to be used. **1968** *Punch* 27 Nov. 786/2 Dear Public, You've had the Two-Tier System. Now for our fabulous Multi-Tier System, with *Flavorlik*, the new Soft-Centre stamps in *nine exciting flavours*. **1971** *Engineering* Apr. 63/2 If required, the machine will carry out multi-tiering and sleeve-wrapping.

multituberculate (ˌmʌltɪtjuːˈbɜːkjʊlət), *sb.* and *a. Palæont.* [ad. mod.L. name of order *Multituberculata* (E. D. Cope 1884, in *Amer. Naturalist* XVIII. 687), f. MULTI- + TUBERCULATE *a.*] A small fossil mammal of the order Multituberculata, characterized by teeth bearing many cusps arranged in two or three rows. Also as *adj.*, pertaining to or resembling an animal of this type.

1884 E. D. COPE in *Amer. Naturalist* XVIII. 687 The extinct marsupials belong to three types, as distinguished by the form of their superior molar teeth. These are trituberculate, quadrituberculate, or multituberculate. **1888** *Q. Jrnl. Microsc. Sci.* XXIX. 20 The multituberculate molar teeth of Myrmecobius. **1898** A. S. WOODWARD *Outl. Vertebr. Palæont.* 248 There is also some reason to suspect that other double-rooted multituberculate teeth from the Rhætic of Europe, commonly claimed as mammalian, may be similarly interpreted [as reptilian]. **1926** *Amer. Jrnl. Sci.* CCXI. 228 (*title*) The Multituberculates as living animals. **1933** A. S. ROMER *Vertebr. Paleont.* xiii. 257 The multituberculates had the longest history of any known mammalian order, for they appeared in the Triassic as the oldest known forms of mammals and persisted through into the Lower Eocene. **1969** *Sci. Jrnl.* 38/2 Entire skulls, including the basicranial region, of multituberculates have so far been found only in the Palaeocene genus *Ptilodus*, known from North America.

multitude (ˈmʌltɪtjuːd). [a. F. *multitude* (13th c.), or ad. L. *multitūdo*, *-tūdin-*, f. *multus* much, many: see -TUDE.]

1. The character, quality, or condition of being many; numerousness; great number. Also, number whether great or small.

In the common biblical (Hebraistic) phrase ***the multitude of*** = 'the many, the numerous', the meaning of the sb. varies between senses 1 and 2.

a **1325** *Prose Psalter* li. 7 He hoped in þe multitude of his riches. **1375** BARBOUR *Bruce* II. 330 For multitud mais na victory. *c* **1450** tr. *De Imitatione* III. xxiii. 93 Be þou blessed, þat hast done þys godenes wiþ þi seruaunt after þe multitude of þi mercy. *c* **1460** G. ASHBY *Dicta Philos.* 8 Truste nat oonly in men is multitude. **1560** BIBLE (Geneva) *Ps.* xxxvii. 11 Meeke men..shall haue their delite in the multitude of peace. **1577** B. GOOGE *Heresbach's Husb.* I. (1586) 8 Riches are not to be measured by their multitude. **1611** BIBLE *Josh.* xi. 4 Euen as the sand that is vpon the Sea-shore in multitude. **1650** BULWER *Anthropomet.* 230 That which fails in magnitude is called smal; as that which in multitude, few. **1734** tr. *Rollin's Anc. Hist.* IV. 208 Valour and not multitude determines the success of arms. **1774** WARTON *Hist. Eng. Poetry* Diss. ii. k 2 William the conqueror permitted great numbers of Jews..to settle in England... Their multitude soon encreased. **1868** TENNYSON *Lucretius* 168 Or do they fly..like the flakes In a fall of snow, and so press in, perforce, Of multitude? **1869** RUSKIN *Q. of Air* §121 The strength of the nation is in its multitude, not in its territory.

2. A great number, a host, a 'crowd' (*of* persons or things). Freq. qualified by *great*. Often *ellipt.* = multitude of men, etc. in question. **a.** *sing.*

The sing. was formerly often used (without article) where the pl. is now idiomatic, esp. in *great multitude*.

a **1340** HAMPOLE *Psalter* xxiii. 6 Swilk is the getynge [L. *generacio*], that is, multitud of tha that sekis him. **1340** —— *Pr. Consc.* 5113 And with him grete multitude sal come Of angels. *c* **1375** *Sc. Leg. Saints* xi. (*Symon & Judas*) 299 Of serpentis a multytude. **1390** GOWER *Conf.* I. 220 This Perseüs..With al his multitude rod. **1470–85** MALORY *Arthur* I. xvi. 58 It was pyte on to behold that multitude of the people that fledde. **1508** DUNBAR *Tua Mariit Wemen* 73 To manifest my makdome to multitude of pepill. **1586** A. DAY *Eng. Secretary* II. (1625) 34 Having..heaped on thy head a multitude of favours. **1651** HOBBES *Leviath.* I. ii. 50 A multitude of actions done by a multitude of men. **1667** MILTON *P.L.* x. 554 Imagining For one forbidden Tree a multitude Now ris'n. **1703** MAUNDRELL *Journ. to Euphrates* (1732) 2 Here are a multitude of Subterraneous Aqueducts. **1778** MISS BURNEY *Evelina* xxiv. (1791) II. 150 She asked Mr. Lovel a multitude of questions. **1872** MORLEY *Voltaire* (1886) 5 It was he who conveyed to his generation in a multitude of forms the consciousness..of..the rights of human intelligence.

b. *pl.* Great numbers, hosts, 'crowds'.

1596 SHAKS. *1 Hen. IV*, III. ii. 143 For euery Honor sitting on his Helme, Would they were multitudes. **1683** SALMON *Doron Med.* I. 333 Multitudes of words bring much error. **1781** COWPER *Retirem.* 158 The waves o'ertake them in their serious play, And ev'ry hour sweeps multitudes away. **1860** TYNDALL *Glaciers* II. xxiv. 357 Multitudes of such little explosions must be heard upon a glacier. **1875** C. F. WOOD *Yachting Cruise* vi. 143 Multitudes of barnacles.

†**c.** A great quantity (of something). *Obs.*

c **1400** *Lanfranc's Cirurg.* 98 If þ at greet multitude of blood lettiþ. *a* **1400–50** *Alexander* 69 Slik was þe multitude of mast so mekil & so thike, þat [etc.]. **1529** S. FISH *Supplic. Beggers* (1871) 2 What a multitude of money gather the pardoners in a yere? **1604** E. G[RIMSTONE] *D'Acosta's Hist. Indies* III. xvii. 175 The multitude of waters that runne into it, quench this smoake and fire. **1677** YARRANTON *Eng. Improv.* 134 Here is cheap Corn, good Corn, and a multitude of it. **1777** CHATHAM *Sp. on Address* 18 Nov., All this disgraceful danger, this multitude of misery.

3. A large gathering of people; a mass of people collected in one place; a throng.

1382 WYCLIF *Ezek.* xvi. 40 And thei shulen lede to vpon thee a multitude [Vulg. *multitudinem*], and thei shulen stoone thee. **1390** GOWER *Conf.* III. 217 The nyht suiende he schop to gon This multitude to assaile. *a* **1400–50** *Alexander* 104 Emang þe multitude of men quare mane ere togeder. **1538** STARKEY *England* I. ii. 51 To the intent that thys multytude of pepul and hole commynalty,..may..relygyously worschype God. **1581** LAMBARDE *Eiren.* I. xvii. 133 Three or more in one companie (which the lawe properly calleth a multitude). **1593** SHAKS. *2 Hen. VI*, v. i. 94 Thou are not King: Not fit to gouerne and rule multitudes. **1682** DRYDEN & LEE *Dk. Guise* IV. i. (1683) 39 A Multitude's a Bulky Coward. **1774** GOLDSM. *Nat. Hist.* (1776) II. 355 Our horses would scarcely, in this manner,..continue their speed, without a rider, through the midst of a multitude. **1784** COWPER *Task* VI. 100 Books are..spells, By which the magic art of shrewder wits Holds an unthinking multitude enthrall'd. **1828** WHATELY *Rhet.* in *Encycl. Metrop.* I. 300/1 A skilful orator's being able to rouse ..the passions of a multitude. **1862** BP. WORDSWORTH *Hymn*, '*Hark, the sound of holy voices*' i, Multitude, which none can number, Like the stars, in glory stands.

4. With *the*: 'The many', the populace, the common people.

1535 COVERDALE *Ps.* xxx. 13, I haue herde the blasphemy of the multitude: euery man abhorreth me. *a* **1586** [see MANY-HEADED]. **1588** SHAKS. *L.L.L.* v. i. 95 In the posteriors of this day, which the rude multitude call the after-noone. **1607** —— *Cor.* II. iii. 18 I. *Cit.*.. He himselfe stucke not to call vs the many-headed Multitude. *a* **1637** B. JONSON *Discoveries* (1640) 130 Jests that are true and naturall, seldome raise laughter with the beast, the multitude. **1671** MILTON *Samson* 696 The unjust tribunals,..condemnation of the ingrateful multitude. **1708** SHAFTESB. *Charac.* (1727) I. 76 To affect a superiority over the Vulgar, and to despise the Multitude. **1769** *Junius Lett.* i. 2 The multitude, in all countries, are patient to a certain point. **1843** RUSKIN *Mod. Paint.* I. 2 *note*, The multitude is the only proper judge of those arts whose end is to move the multitude.

multitudi'narious, *a. rare*$^{-1}$. [f. L. type **multitūdināri-us*, f. *multitūdin-*: see MULTITUDE and -ARIOUS.] Multitudinous.

So **multi'tudinary** *a. rare*$^{-0}$ (Worcester 1846, citing Mitford).

1810 *Splendid Follies* I. 188 Don't talk to me..my ideas are multitudinarious.

†**multitudine.** *Obs.* [a. OF. *multitudine*, or ad. L. *multitūdinem* MULTITUDE.] Multitude.

1547 BOORDE *Brev. Health* iii. (1557) 8 Knowledge, by the whiche wilfull Abhorsion maye come of the multitudenes of the flowers of a woman. **1556** *Chron. Gr. Friars* (Camden) 84 The Scottes toke a grete multitudyne of the Ynglych pepulle. *c* **1610** *Women Saints* (1886) 48 Being much terrified with the noise of the multitudine pursuing them.

multitudinism (mʌltɪˈtjuːdɪnɪz(ə)m). [f. L. *multitūdin-*, *multitūdo* MULTITUDE + -ISM, after Fr.] The principle according to which the interests of multitudes are placed before those of individuals, *esp.* in religion.

1860 H. B. WILSON in *Ess. & Rev.* 146 The Comte Léon de Gasparin..laid it down..that the individualist principle supplies the true basis of the Church, and that by inaugurating the union between Church and State Constantine introduced the false..principle of Multitudinism. **1866** *Contemp. Rev.* I. 92 The vicious multitudinism of the great public schools. **1870** *Ibid.* XIV. 390 Sentimental multitudinism, seeking to base itself on a loose humanitarianism.

Hence **multi'tudinist, multitudi'nistic** *adjs.*, favouring such a doctrine or principle.

1860 H. B. WILSON in *Ess. & Rev.* 159 To the multitudinist principle are due the great external victories which the Christian name has hitherto won. **1862** W. J. IRONS in *Replies to Ess. & Rev.* 226 Whether primitive Christianity..was 'multitudinistic',..or whether it was 'exclusive' and sought access to the individual conscience of the few.

multitudi'nosity. [f. MULTITUDINOUS: see -OSITY.] Multitudinousness.

1840 *Blackw. Mag.* XLVIII. 762 A fiery man..must be goaded into madness..by the multitudinosity of absurdities. **1939** R. A. KNOX *Let Dons Delight* vi. 161 For all that, sheer multitudinosity has power to oppress the mind.

multitudinous (mʌltɪˈtjuːdɪnəs), *a.* [f. L. *multitūdin-*, *multitūdo* MULTITUDE + -OUS.]

1. a. with pl. sb.: Existing in multitudes or great numbers; very numerous.

1629 DONNE *Serm.* (1649) II. xxviii. 242 The foundation of all, the Trinity, undermined by those numerous, those multitudinous Anthills of Socinians. **1644** HEYLIN *Stumblingblock* Tracts (1681) 723 The more multitudinous and united the Petitioners are, the more like to speed. **1650** *Descr. Fut. Hist. Europe* 23 Confounding..the multitudinous Pagans and Idolaters fighting against Christians. **1800** COLERIDGE *Talleyrand to Ld. Granville* 46 It argues, my Lord! of fine thoughts such a brood in us To split and divide into heads multitudinous. **1805** SOUTHEY *Madoc* II. xxv. Poems V. 367 The lesser fowls Flock multitudinous in heaven. **1846** TRENCH *Mirac.* Prelim. Ess. iv. 45 The multitudinous races of animals which people this world.

b. with collective sb.: Consisting of a multitude or great number of individuals.

1606 DEKKER *Sev. Sins* II. (Arb.) 20 In a State so multitudinous, where so many flocks of people must be fed. *a* **1662** HEYLIN *Laud* (1668) 70 The Puritan faction, which was grown multitudinous and strong. **1837** HALLAM *Hist. Lit.* I. vi. §35 A more multitudinous brood of sectaries. **1840** H. AINSWORTH *Tower of London* (1862) 212 When this multitudinous and confused assemblage had nearly filled the inclosure. **1882** A. W. WARD *Dickens* v. 112 Never before had his versatility..filled his canvas with so multitudinous and so various a host of personages.

c. with sing. sb.: Existing in or exhibiting a multitude of forms; having many elements or features; arising from or involving a multitude.

Often applied to bodies of sound which are varied in volume and tone.

1656 BLOUNT *Glossogr.*, *Multitudinous*, pertaining to a multitude; that hath a great..number, or great store of. *a* **1734** NORTH *Lives* (1826) III. 155 The abuses in the management of the royal navy, and the multitudinous fraud that corroded there. **1820** L. HUNT *Indicator* No. 20 (1822) I. 155 It was the rocks of an isle beyond Inistore, which made that multitudinous roaring of the wind. **1850** HAWTHORNE *Scarlet L.* Introd. (1879) 12 The pavement..has not..been worn by any multitudinous resort of business. **1858** KINGSLEY *Lett.* (1878) I. 21 The multitudinous moan and wail of the lost spirits. **1874** R. TYRWHITT *Sketch Club* p. vii, Multitudinous murder of tame pheasants. **1891** HARDY *Tess* xxxii, From the whole extent of the invisible vale came a multitudinous intonation.

d. Said of the ocean or any mass of water with reference to its great bulk or (after the ἀνήριθμον γέλασμα of Æschylus) to its innumerable ripples.

1605 SHAKS. *Macb.* II. ii. 62 This my Hand will rather The multitudinous Seas incarnardine. *a* **1794** SIR W. JONES *Hymn to Narayena* Wks. 1799 VI. 370 The waters flow'd,..Diffusive, multitudinous, profound. **1817** MOORE *Lalla Rookh, Veiled Prophet* (1854) 79 The multitudinous torrent. **1850** BLACKIE *Æschylus* II. 21 And of ocean waves The multitudinous laughter. **1860** W. COLLINS *Woman in White* I. 185 The multitudinous glory of the leaping waves.

e. Thronged or crowded (*with*). *poet.*

1820 SHELLEY *Prometh. Unb.* I. 5 Regard this Earth Made multitudinous with thy slaves. **1871** BROWNING *Balaust.* 1328 To live In a home multitudinous with herds.

f. *nonce-use.* Immensely productive or prolific.

1816 T. L. PEACOCK *Headlong Hall* iii, Two very multitudinous versifiers, Mr. Nightshade and Mr. Mac Laurel.

2. Of or pertaining to 'the multitude'. *rare*$^{-1}$.

1607 SHAKS. *Cor.* III. i. 156 At once plucke out The Multitudinous Tongue, let them not licke The sweet which is their poyson.

multi'tudinously, *adv.* [-LY[2].] In a multitudinous manner; in multitudes.

1859 MEREDITH *R. Feverel* iv, The rooms were dark, dark as the prognostics multitudinously hinted by the disappointed..guests. **1861** J. G. SHEPPARD *Fall Rome* iii. 125 They march multitudinously, openly, and incautiously, straight against the enemy. **1878** BROWNING *La Saisiaz* 44 Multitudinously wretched.

multi'tudinousness. [-NESS.] The character or condition of being multitudinous.

1653 GAUDEN *Hierasp.* To Rdr. a 2 b, The eminency of the first, the mediocrity of the second, and the meannesse yet multitudinousnesse of the third. *a* **1662** HEYLIN *Laud* (1668) 132 He had observed the multitudinousness of his Fathers Chaplains. **1830** *Blackw. Mag.* XXVIII. 147 Shakspeare rightly called him [*sc.* the sea] 'multitudinous'. But in spite of his multitudinousness [etc.]. **1876** *Fam. Herald* 7 Oct. 366/1 The multitudinousness of God's mercies. **1890** *Spectator* 11 Jan., Thinking grows..tired with the multitudinousness of the new subjects for thought.

multi-'use, *a.* [f. MULTI- + USE *sb.*]

1952 *Bull. Amer. Inst. Archit.* VI. IV. 11 The multi-use classroom was used to provide for as many as 4 or 5 different functions within a single space. **1960** *Farmer & Stockbreeder* 29 Mar. 125/1 It has been developed from 10 full years of American 'know-how' and British experience into the ideal multi-use machine for any size of farm. **1964** *Daily Tel.* 30 Jan. 19/1 (*heading*) 'Multi-use' policy 'best for Britain's canals'. **1971** P. GRESSWELL *Environment* 181 Examples of multi-use park design, and good maintenance, are the great London parks.

multi-'user, *a.* [f. MULTI- 3 + USER[1].] Having many users; *spec.* (of a computer, etc.) able to be used by more than one person and accessed from more than one terminal concurrently. Cf. *multi-access* s.v. MULTI- 3.

1964 *Communications Assoc. Computing Machinery* VII. 527/1 In the multiuser system it is important to provide a means of filing source and machine language programs on auxiliary storage. **1964** *Daily Tel.* 30 Jan. 14/2 It rejects the transport theory for the 'multi-user' conception. **1969** *Jane's Freight Containers 1968–69* 183/1 Berth No. 43—Multi-user container berth. **1974** *BP Shield Internat.* Oct. 9/1 (*caption*) The multi-user container berth at Tilbury. **1978** *Pract. Computing* July–Aug. 31/3 On the stand will be the multi-user, dual disk system based on the Altair 800B. **1983** *80 Microcomputing* Feb. 42/3 Such a system will cut up the RAM memory to enable up to three different programs to run simultaneously. Thus the system will not only be multi-user but also multitasking. **1985** *Personal Computer World* Feb. 24/1 (Advt.), Comart Communicator multi-user systems have expandability built in.

multivagant (mʌlˈtɪvəgənt), *a. rare.* [f. L. *multivag-us*: see MULTI- and VAGANT.] Wandering much.

1656 BLOUNT *Glossogr.*, *Multivagant*, wandring or straying much abroad. **1895** MONKSHOOD in *Working Men's Coll. Jrnl.* Jan. 164 Mulvaney, the multivagant, who holds the picture-place in the Kipling pantheon.

So **mulˈtivagous** *a.* $rare^{-0}$.

1727 in BAILEY vol. II.

multivalent (mʌltɪˈveɪlənt, mʌlˈtɪvələnt), *a.* and *sb. Chem.* [See MULTI- 1.] **A.** *adj.* **1. a.** Having many degrees of valency.

1874 J. P. COOKE *New Chem.* 278 Hydrates of multivalent radicals.

b. *Med.* Of an antigen or antibody: having several sites at which it can become attached to an antibody or antigen, respectively.

1934 *Harvey Lect.* XXVIII. 198 In this way it has been possible to show that antigen and antibody in this system, too, are multivalent with respect to each other—that is, that the composition of the precipitate varies according to the relative proportions of the reactants. **1948** KABAT & MAYER *Exper. Immunochem.* iii. 67 The immunochemist..has found it more useful to..consider the visible agglutination as an indication that the antigen particles are linked together by antibody molecules to form aggregates as a result of the combination of multivalent antibody with multivalent antigen on the particle surface. **1963** HUMPHREY & WHITE *Immunol. for Students of Med.* vi. 185 The combination in multiple proportions depends upon the fact that both antigen and antibody are multivalent. Antibody valencies are restricted to two per molecule but antigen valencies may exceed 200, although they are more usually around 5 to 10 per molecule.

2. *Cytology.* That is (part of) a multivalent.

1929 *Jrnl. Genetics* XXI. 41 The whole process by which multivalent combinations arise has been followed only in the tulips. **1937** C. D. DARLINGTON *Recent Adv. Cytol.* (ed. 2) iv. 129 The result seems to depend on..the distribution of the chiasmata in the multivalent chromosome. **1967** *Biol. Abstr.* XLVIII. 983/1 (*heading*) Multivalent associations in oocytes of *Triturus helveticus helveticus*.

3. *gen.* Having many applications, meanings, or values.

1933 *Mind* XLII. 484, I propose to call words which can enter sentences in more than one sense multivalent words. **1952** *Essays in Crit.* II. 99 It is unnecessary to heap up detailed parallels for the reader..; our object is to indicate their multivalent mode of functioning. **1963** *Listener* 31 Jan. 213/2 Spenser's allegory is sometimes naïve, often multivalent, and often, indeed, non-existent. **1971** *Archivum Linguisticum* II. 59 Interrogative form considered in the abstract is as multivalent as the flection *-s* and is variously used..for suggestions.., exclamations.., and so on.

B. *sb. Cytology.* An association of three or more completely or partly homologous chromosomes during the first division of meiosis.

1929 *Jrnl. Genetics* XXI. 12 At post-diplotene stages associations of three, four and five chromosomes are found, clearly the forerunners of the metaphase multivalents. **1937** M. J. D. WHITE *Chromosomes* v. 82 The frequency of formation of multivalents in polyploids varies a great deal and apparently depends in part on the length of the chromosomes and in part on the rapidity of zygotene pairing. **1959** *Biol. Abstr.* XXXIV. 12/1 Multivalent formation and 'secondary association' in the meiotic stages of autotetraploid races of Lycopersicon Mill. **1971** *Nature* 9 Apr. 390/1 Though most of the chromosomes are associated as bivalents, a few multivalents are present.

Hence **mulˈtivalence**, **-ˈvalency** the state or condition of being multivalent; also (after AMBIVALENCE), the property of having many meanings or interpretations.

a **1881** BARRATT *Phys. Metempiric* (1883) 64 Multi-valency of atoms. **1882** OGILVIE *Suppl.*, *Multivalence.* **1933** *Mind* XLII. 49 The solution of these paradoxes lies in the ambiguity... Multivalence would be better. Because it is a multiplicity of use not of meaning. **1937** *Jrnl. Immunol.* XXXII. 119 (*heading*) On the mutual multivalence of toxin and antitoxin. **1940** *Jrnl. Amer. Chem. Soc.* LXII. 2646/1 (*heading*) The bivalence of antibodies and the multivalence of antigens. **1963** HUMPHREY & WHITE *Immunol. for Students of Med.* vi. 218 The so-called 'sandwich' technique for the detection of antibody..employs a primary layer of a dilute solution of unlabelled antigen. After reacting for 30 minutes or so, this is rinsed off..and then exposed to specific fluorescein-labelled antibody. Such a method depends upon the multivalency of the antigen. **1965** *English Studies* XLVI. 28 This very multivalence..is the crux of a mythological interpretation, by which such a general mother-goddess may be associated with almost anything on earth and sea.

multivallate (mʌltɪˈvæleɪt, -ət), *a.* [f. MULTI- + VALLATE *a.*] Having encircling ramparts which form multiple lines of defence. Cf. BIVALLATE *a.* Also **multivaˈllation**.

1948 *Archaeol. Jrnl.* CV. 50 The best developed barbicans are found in multivallate camps. **1954** *Bull. Board Celtic Stud.* XV. 74 Multivallate 'camps' with various types of lateral or oblique entrance. **1963** [see BIVALLATE *a.*]. **1963** E. S. WOOD *Collins Field Guide Archaeol.* II. ii. 169 The chief areas of multivallation are the south-west..and Wessex.

multivalve (ˈmʌltɪvælv), *a.* and *sb.* [ad. mod.L. *multivalvis* (cf. Linnæus's division *Multivalvia*): see MULTI- and VALVE. In French 1752.]

A. *adj.* **a.** *Conch.* Having many valves, as the chitons and the acorn-shells.

1755 *Gentl. Mag.* XXV. 32. **1774** GOLDSM. *Nat. Hist.* VII. 61 Multivalve Shell-fish may be considered as animals shut up in round boxes. **1828** STARK *Elem. Nat. Hist.* II. 122 The shell of the Cirripeda is always multivalve. **1877** HUXLEY *Anat. Inv. Anim.* vi. 291 The former firmly fixed by the base of its multivalve conical shell.

b. *Bot.* and *Ent.* (See quots.)

1819 SAMOUELLE *Entomol. Compend.* 353 Rostrum.. Multivalve, forming a tube by means of many valves uniting. **1819** *Pantologia, Multivalve glume*... Having more than two valves. **1826** KIRBY & SP. *Entomol.* IV. 373 Tail of the female without a terebrant, or pungent multivalve ovipositor. **1831** MACGILLIVRAY tr. *Richard's Elem. Bot.* 274 A Pericarp is..Multivalve, when it divides into a greater number of valves or distinct segments.

c. *Electronics.* Having many thermionic valves.

1920 *Wireless World* Jan. 574/2 More than one valve may be connected in cascade to form a multi-valve amplifier. **1957** *Ibid.* July 310 (*heading*) Multi-valve cathode follower circuits.

B. *sb.* A multivalve shell; an animal having such a shell (as a chiton or an acorn-shell).

1753 CHAMBERS *Cycl. Supp.* **1776** DA COSTA *Elem. Conchol.* 242 Multivalves. Shells composed of many pieces or valves. **1851** WOODWARD *Mollusca* 36 Most of the multivalves of old authors were articulate animals.

Also **multiˈvalvate** ($rare^{-0}$), **ˈmultivalved**, **multiˈvalvular** *adjs.* = MULTIVALVE *a.*

1891 *Syd. Soc. Lex.*, **Multivalvate*, having more than two valves. **1758** ELLIS in *Phil. Trans.* L. 846 A *multivalved shell, composed of unequal valves. **1774** GOLDSM. *Nat. Hist.* VII. 18 The Multivalved [shell-fish], or those of the Acorn-shell Kind. **1826** GOOD *Bk. Nat.* II. 20 Of the multivalved testaceous worms..there are but three known species, the chiton, the lepas..and the phloas. **1760** J. LEE *Introd. Bot.* II. xxxiii. (1765) 159 *Antirrhinum*, with *multivalvular Fruit. **1849** BALFOUR *Man. Bot.* §530 The fruit being univalvular, bivalvular, or multivalvular, &c., according as there are one, two, or many valves.

multiˈvariant, *a.* [f. MULTI- + VARIANT *a.* and *sb.*] Influenced by or taking account of several variables; †*spec.* (of a chemical system) having more than two degrees of freedom (*obs.*).

1902 J. E. TREVOR in *Jrnl. Physical Chem.* VI. 136, I would ..suggest..that when the variance is successively zero, one, two, three, and more than two, the system be said to be in an Invariant, Univariant, Bivariant, Trivariant, Multivariant, state. **1904** *Ibid.* VIII. 491 The indifferent points of a bivariant or multivariant system form a series analogous to the series of states of equilibrium of a univariant system. **1953** A. K. C. OTTAWAY *Educ. & Society* iii. 47 Enough should have been said to indicate the multiplicity of factors which must be considered in any analysis of social change. That is why the concept of causation is so dangerous in social science; because we are dealing with multi-variant phenomena. **1959** *Biol. Abstr.* XXXIV. 561/2 (*heading*) The application of multivariant analysis to the physical characteristics of Guarao and Caribe Indians.

multiˈvariate, *a. Statistics.* [f. MULTI- + VARIATE *sb.*] Involving or having two or more variates or variables.

1928 *Biometrika* XXA. 32 (*heading*) The generalised product moment distribution in samples from a normal multivariate population. **1939** *Proc. Cambr. Philos. Soc.* XXXV. 180 (*heading*) A note on tests of significance in multivariate analysis. **1958** *Economist* 29 Nov. 782 The multi-variate linear regression technique..is satisfactory only if the explanatory variables vary independently of each other or if the degree of interaction between two or more of them can be measured and allowed for. This is certainly not the case in milk production and it was for this reason that the technique was rejected. **1967** C. BERNERS-LEE in Wills & Yearsley *Handbk. Managem. Technol.* i. 7 Procedures like multivariate regression analysis require a great deal of computation when more than a small number of variables are involved. **1968** R. A. BRADLEY in *Internat. Encycl. Social Sci.* X. 527/1 Multivariate analysis in statistics is devoted to the summarization, representation, and interpretation of data when more than one characteristic of each sample unit is measured. **1972** *Computer Jrnl.* XV. 215/2 Evaluation of the error matrix is therefore reduced to the evaluation of a multivariate polynomial at a number of points. **1973** *Nature* 16 Mar. 210/3 Altogether, the theory of multi-variate distributions poses the most difficult problems in mathematical statistics.

multivarious (mʌltɪˈvɛərɪəs), *a.* Now *rare.* [f. MULTI- + L. *vari-us* (see VARIOUS *a.*), as literal equivalent of Gr. πολυποίκιλος 'much-variegated, manifold' (L. & Sc.).] Manifold and diverse.

1620 FEATLY *Clavis Myst.* vi. (1636) 69 That manifold, or (to make a new compound to translate a compound), in the Originall multivarious wisedome [πολυποίκιλος Eph. iii. 10]. **1644** MAXWELL *Prerog. Chr. Kings* 24 God in Scripture, by frequent, pregnant, and multivarious expressions, hath so vindicated to himselfe the making and constituting of Kings [etc.]. **1678** CUDWORTH *Intell. Syst.* I. iv. §16. 293 From.. One Supreme Deity altogether proceeds the Genesis of the multivarious matter. **1832** FR. A. KEMBLE *Let.* in *Rec. Girlhood* (1878) III. 244 Multitudinous and multivarious beasts of prey. **1903** *Academy* 31 Oct. 462/1 Multi-various gossip about the London localities he knew best.

So † **multivaˈriety**.

1601 [BP. W. BARLOW] *Defence* 79 That multi-varietie of Gods wisdome. [Cf. 1620 above.]

multiˈversant, *a.* [f. MULTI- + pr. pple. of L. *versāre*, frequent. of *vertĕre* to turn.] Protean.

1828–32 WEBSTER (citing *Jrnl. Sci.*).

ˈmultiverse. [f. UNIVERSE by substituting MULTI- for UNI-.] An alternative suggested for the word UNIVERSE in order to indicate the absence of order or of a single ruling and guiding power.

1895 W. JAMES *Will to Believe* (1897) 43 Visible nature is all plasticity and indifference,—a moral multiverse, as one might call it, and not a moral universe. **1904** *Daily News* 11 Oct. 3 [Reporting Sir O. Lodge], The only possible alternative was to regard the universe as a result of random chance and capricious disorder, not a cosmos or universe at all, but rather a 'multiverse'. **1920** CHESTERTON *New Jerusalem* viii. 163 When I told a distinguished psychologist ..that I differed from his view of the universe, he answered, 'Why universe? Why should it not be a multiverse?' **1957** *Times Lit. Suppl.* 11 Oct. 602/1 It is precisely Mr Powys's ever-present contact with the vital, or spiritual, principles within the universe which enables him to explore with so uncanny a penetration the deeper problems of that comparatively small section of the universe—or as he would say multiverse—which constitutes man. **1959** N. N. HOLLAND *First Mod. Comedies* 128 Out of this 'pluralistic multiverse', as Robert Oppenheimer has recently called it. **1975** C. BURT *ESP & Psychol.* ii. 34 Modern physics presents us with a heterogeneous multiverse, in place of the homogeneous universe of Newton and Laplace.

multiversity (mʌltɪˈvɜːsɪtɪ). Chiefly *U.S.* [f. MULTI- + UNI)VERSITY *sb.*] A very large university comprising many different departments and activities.

1963 C. KERR *Uses of University* i. 42 The multiversity is in the main stream of events. To the teacher and the researcher have been added the consultant and the administrator. Teaching is less central than it once was for most faculty members; research has become more important. **1966** *Economist* 14 May 713/1 For the second year in succession Dr Clark Kerr, the president of the University of California, has been bitterly attacked for permitting too much freedom by a subcommittee of the State Legislature, which finances this great, sprawling 'multi-versity'. **1968** *Guardian* 30 Nov. 2/3 The inevitable transformation of universities everywhere into 'multi-versities' is being achieved with appalling birth pangs in the University of California, which a dozen years ago had two campuses and now has 10. **1969** C. DAVIDSON in Cockburn & Blackburn *Student Power* 337 Transforming the academic landscape into what we now call the 'multi-versity'. **1969** *Nature* 13 Dec. 1064/1 By the mid-sixties, the result..was clearly an overloading of the university system as a 'multiversity', to use the word of one of its first victims, Clark Kerr. **1971** *Wall Street Jrnl.* 12 Jan. 1/1 They don't like the way it has grown from a sleepy teachers' college of 3,000 students in 1950 to its present status as a giant, cosmopolitan 'multiversity'.

ˌmultiviˈbrator. *Electronics.* [ad. F. *multivibrateur* (Abraham & Bloch 1919, in *Compt. Rend.* CLXVIII. 1107), f. *multi-* MULTI- + *vibrateur* VIBRATOR.] A device that consists of two amplifying valves or transistors, each with its output connected to the input of the other, and produces an oscillatory signal rich in harmonics and capable of being triggered and stabilized by an applied sinusoidal signal of slightly higher frequency (the form of the coupling determining the resonant frequency of the device and whether it is astable, bistable, or monostable).

1919 *Sci. Abstr.* B. XXII. 287 The source of oscillations which has been found very successful in operation has been called a 'multivibrator'. It possesses, besides the fundamental wave-length, all the harmonics from 1 up to two or three hundred. **1940** *Amat. Radio Handbk.* (ed. 2) xiv. 219/1 A multi-vibrator operating on 10 kc can be readily locked by a few volts..of 100 kc frequency, and the harmonics of the multivibrator stage will produce carrier frequencies spaced throughout the radio-frequency spectrum at 10 kc intervals with a precision equal to that of the locking source. **1969** J. J. SPARKES *Transistor Switching* iii. 52 The multivibrator can, of course, produce square waves as well as rectangular waves simply by ensuring symmetry between the two halves of the circuit. **1971** J. H. SMITH *Digital Logic* iv. 75 Digital systems frequently need a multivibrator, or at least a source of continuous signals.

multivious (mʌlˈtɪvɪəs), *a.* [f. L. *multivi-us* (f. *multus* MULTI- + *via* way) + -OUS.] Having many ways; going or leading in many directions.

1656 BLOUNT *Glossogr.*, *Multivious*, that hath many ways, manifold. **1721** in BAILEY. **1850** D. THOMAS *Crisis of Being* vi. 97 The sinner is often perplexed amidst the multivious and conflicting directions that are given. **1880** BESANT & RICE *Seamy Side* xx, The young clerks..were dispersed, multivious, in quest of food.

multivocal (mʌlˈtɪvəkəl), *a.* and *sb.* [f. L. *multus* MULTI- + *voc-āre* to call, after *univocal*, *equivocal*.] **a.** *adj.* Susceptible of many interpretations or meanings. **b.** *sb.* A word of such a kind. Hence **mulˈtivocalness**.

1810 COLERIDGE in *Lit. Rem.* (1836) III. 55 Whenever I meet with an ambiguous or multivocal word. **1862** F. HALL *Hindu Philos. Syst.* 82 'Nature', in such a sense, or *swabhâva*, is one of the classical acceptations of the multivocal *prakṛiti*. **1873** —— *Mod. Eng.* 95 *note*, *Respect*, a word comparable, for its multivocalness, with the Latin *ratio*. *Ibid.* 169 Among the various blemishes which may disfigure a language, none..is more unphilosophical than multivocals.

mul'tivolent, *a. rare*$^{-0}$. [f. L. *multivol-us*: see MULTI- and VOLENT.]

1656 BLOUNT *Glossogr.*, *Multivolent*, of many or divers minds, mutable, wishing one while this, and another, that.

multivoltine: see MULTI- 1 a.

multocular (mʌl'tɒkjʊlə(r)), *a.* [f. L. *mult-us* MULT(I- + *ocul-us* eye + -AR.] Having many eyes. See also quot. 1887.

1713 DERHAM *Phys.-Theol.* VIII. iii. 401 Flies, &c. are Multocular, having as many Eyes as there are Perforations in their Corneæ. **1887** tr. *Nägeli & Schwendener's Microscope* 48 For some time past English and French opticians have made multocular Microscopes, by which several persons are enabled to observe one and the same object simultaneously. **1891** *Syd. Soc. Lex.*, *Multocular*, having many eyes.

'multo-scribbling, *ppl. a.* [f. *multo-* used as comb. form of L. *multus* in sense 'much'.] That scribbles a great deal.

1822 BYRON *Vis. Judgem.* lxv, Thus spoke the Demon (late call'd 'multi-faced' By multo-scribbling Southey).

multre, obs. form of MULTURE.

†**multum** ('mʌltəm). *Brewing. Obs.* [? A use of L. *multum*, neut. of *multus* much.] (See quots.)

1820 *Blackw. Mag.* VI. 545 Another substance composed of extract of quassia and liquorice juice, and used by fraudulent brewers to economise both malt and hops is technically called *multum*. **1829** *Art of Brewing* (Libr. Usef. Knowl.) I. 31/2 A compound termed *multum* was (or *is*) a mixture of opium and other ingredients, which sold about ten years ago, at five or six shillings a pound, when what was called an *extract of cocculus* was charged at a guinea and a-half. **1844** HOBLYN *Dict. Med.*, *Hard multum*, or Black extract, is a preparation made from Cocculus Indicus, and used by brewers to impart an intoxicating quality to beer.

‖**multum in parvo** ('mʌltəm ɪn 'pɑːvəʊ). [L. *multum*, neut. of *multus* much; *in*, prep.; *parvō*, abl. sing. of *parvus* little.] A great deal in a small compass. Also *attrib.* applied to articles of small bulk but of great comprehensiveness.

1732 *(title)* Multum in Parvo; or, the Jubilee of Jubilees. **1825** [S. MAUNDER] *title*, The Little Lexicon; or, Multum in Parvo of the English Language. **1836** MARRYAT *Three Cutters* i, This is the kitchen: is it not admirably arranged? What a *multum in parvo*! **1861** *(title)* Multum in Parvo Series. **1876** T. HARDY *Ethelberta* xliii, A multum-in-parvo pocket-knife.

multungulate (mʌl'tʌŋgjʊlət), *a.* and *sb.* [ad. mod.L. *multungulāt-us*, f. *multus* MULT(I- + *ungula* hoof: see -ATE².] **a.** *adj.* Having more than two functional hoofs; belonging to the order *Multungulata*. **b.** *pl.* An animal of this order.

1839-47 *Todd's Cycl. Anat.* III. 237/1 Aristotle divides them [*sc.* ungulates] into, 1st, *Polyschidæ*, or multungulates ..2d, the *Dischidæ*, or bisulcates,.. 3d, the *Aschidæ*, or solidungulate quadrupeds. **1863** DANA *Man. Geol.* 423 Multungulates, having three or five toes, as the Tapir,.. Rhinoceros..Palæotherium. **1866** BRANDE & COX *Dict. Sci.*, etc. II. 593/2 *Multungulate*..when a quadruped has the hoof divided into more than two parts.

†**'multuous**, *a. Obs. rare*$^{-1}$. [irreg. f. L. *multus* much + -UOUS. Cf. *multeous*.] Numerous.

1589 WARNER *Alb. Eng.* Prose Add. 165 In respect of their multuous Armies.

multure ('mʌltjʊə(r), -tʃə(r)), *sb.* Forms: 4-5 **multir**, 5 **-yr**, *Sc.* **mowter**, 5-7 **molter**, 5-9 **multer**, 6 **-ur**, **multrar**, **myltour**, 7 **mou(l)ture**; *Sc.* and *dial.* 5-9 **moulter**, 7-9 **moulture**, **mooter**, 8 **multur**, **mu'ter**, 9 **multre**, etc. (see E.D.D.); 5- **multure**, 7- **mulcture**. [a. OF. *molture*, *moulture*, mod.F. *mouture*:—med.L. *molitūra*, f. *molit-*, *molĕre* to grind. The form *mulcture* is due to association with MULCT.]

1. a. A toll consisting of a proportion of the grain carried or of the flour made, paid to the proprietor or tenant of a mill for the privilege of having corn ground at it. **b.** The right to exact this toll.

c **1300** [see *multure-greve* below]. *c* **1450** *Eng. Misc.* (Surtees) 61 All maner of mesurys of yᵉ mylne that thai take multyr with. **1478** *Acta Audit.* (1839) 59/1 Johne boid.. summond..for þe multʳ of þe teind schaf at dalmusternach. **1565-6** *Reg. Privy Council Scot.* I. 428 The landis of.. Braidley, with the myln and multuris of the samyn. **1622** *Extr. Burgh Rec. Stirling* (1887) 157 Nor yit that their be ony alteratioun..of the quantitie of the multure or knaifshep that presentlie is payed. **1628** COKE *On Litt.* 47 A rent cannot be reserued..out of any incorporeall inheritance, as ..mulcture of a Mill. **1641** BEST *Farm. Bks.* (Surtees) 103 Or else the fault is in the miller that taketh more mowter then is his due. **1681** STAIR *Instit.* I. xvii. §15 When a Superiour gives out Lands upon condition of Thirlage, the Multures are part of the *reddendo* or price. **1747** *Act 20 Geo. II*, c. 43 §17 Recovery of Multures or Services payable or prestable to their Mills. **1788** W. MARSHALL *Yorksh.* II. 342 *Mooter.* **1820** SCOTT *Monast.* viii, The Dame Glendinning had always paid her multure and knaveship duly. **1851** *Jrnl. R. Agric. Soc.* XII. I. 132 When farmers get oats made into meal for the use of their families and servants, the miller retains as multure 8¾ lbs. (a Scotch peck) for every boll (140 lbs.) of meal produced.

c. In proverbial expressions.

1607 R. C[AREW] tr. *Estienne's World of Wonders* 302 To bring the moulter to their mill. **1623** BP. SANDERSON *Serm.* 11 June (1689) 114 It were a lamentable thing if these men should be..maintained by the Magistrates..of purpose to bring Moulter to their own Mills. **1653** URQUHART *Rabelais* I. xi. 55 Out of one sack he would take two moutures or fees for grinding. **1820** [see MEAL *sb.*¹ 3 a].

¶**d.** Used (by confusion with *mult*, MULCT *sb.*) for: A fine.

1533 BELLENDEN *Livy* IV. xiii. (S.T.S.) II. 93 To promulgate ane law richt plesand to þe pepil concernyng the estimatioun of multuris [orig. *multarum*].

2. *attrib.*: †**multure-ark**, a chest or box in which the multure was deposited (cf. dial. *multure-chest*); †**multure-corn**, corn taken in payment of multure; hence often = an inferior or mixed kind of corn; **multure dish** *dial.*, a vessel for measuring or collecting the multure; †**multure grave, greve** [see GRAVE *sb.*³, GRIEVE], the steward who had charge of the multure; †**multure meal** = 1 a; †**multure oath**, an oath to the effect that multure had been paid.

1483 *Cath. Angl.* 246/2 A *Multer arke, *emolimentarium*. **1546** *Yks. Chantry Surv.* (Surtees) II. 246 The xᵗʰ of the *multer co[r]ne of Skipton Mylnez. **1592** *Nottingham Rec.* IV. 237 A busshell of multure corne. **1611** COTGR., *Bled barnage*, Meslin, or moulture corne. **1619** J. KING *Serm. 11 Apr.* 37 Ezekiel (Ezech. 4) lieth and sleepeth vpon his left and right side, and maketh him bread of moulter corne. **1625** F. MARKHAM *Bk. Honour* II. viii. §2, I can compare these wretched Clownes..to nothing but poore Moulter Corne, which this Milstone of knighthood grinds to dust, to feed dogs. **1483** *Cath. Angl.* 246/2 A *Multer dische, *metreta, tessera*. **1636** W. SAMPSON *Vow-breaker* II. i. D, Oh the Mooter dish, the Millers thumbe and the maide behinde the Hopper. *a* **1800** in M. A. Richardson *Local Hist. Table Bk.* Leg. Div. (1844) II. 136 The moutar dish was nearly fou iv a' kinds iv grain but yits. **1547** *Multer fre [see MULTURE *v.*]. **1651** *MS. Agreement, Treeton mill, co. York*, [The tenant] shall have his corn ground at Treeton mill moulter free and free to the hopper. ? *a* **1800** in Buchan *Ball.* (1828) II. 126 When ye come to my father's mill, Ye shall grind muture free. *c* **1300** *Durh. Treas. Misc. Cart.* No. 6592 Ricardo le *Multirgreue de Werke. **1479** *Hexham Priory* (Surtees) II. 77 Sub pœna perditionis totius grani versus lez multir-grafe. **1566** *Cal. Laing Charters* (1899) 205 [The oatmeal called the] *multure meill [of the granter's mill of Denny]. **1480** *Peebles Charters*, etc. 207 To atteiche the maltmen that duellis within the fredome of burgh to the nixt court for to mak and gif ane *multer aith for the termes bygane.

Hence †**'multure** *v.* [cf. OF. *multurer* in both senses], (*a*) to grind; (*b*) to exact the toll of multure from.

c **1450** *Eng. Misc.* (Surtees) 60 When j qwharter wheytt is sald for iiij s., than schall yᵉ corne be multyrd at yᵉ xvj vessell. **1547** *Aberdeen Reg.* (1844) I. 250 It is lesum to ws to grind and multur our cornis..at the mill of Gilcamstoun, multur fre. **1582** [see MULTURER].

multurer ('mʌltjʊərə(r)). Also 6 **multarar**, **multrar**, **multerair**. [f. prec. + -ER¹.] One who pays toll for the grinding of his corn at a mill.

1580 *Rec. Elgin* (New Spalding Cl.) I. 156 James Cuming, multarar at the auld miln of Elgin. **1582** *Cal. Laing Charters* (1899) 258 The multraris to haif ane pec and the fermoraris twa bollis ay quhill the aucht chaldyr be multrit. **1702** in J. Paterson *Hist. Regal. Musselburgh* (1857) 39 That..the multurer shall draw the multures at the milnes in maner underwritten. *a* **1768** ERSKINE *Inst. Law Scot.* II. ix. (1773) 314 The multure is a quantity of grain..due to the proprietor of the mill, or his tacksman, the multurer, for manufacturing the corns. **1838** W. BELL *Dict. Law Scot.* 665 The competition there may be with other mills to which the outsucken multurers have access.

multyn, obs. pa. pple. of MELT *v.*

†**'mulvel.** *Obs.* Forms: 4-5 (8 *Hist.*) **mulvel(l**, **-well(e**, **molle-**, **mullewelle**, (8 *Hist.* **mulvil**); 4 **milewel**, **milvele**, **mylwel**, 6 **millwell**, 7 **myll(e)well**; 4 **melewell**, **melvel**, 5-7 **mellwell**, (8 *Hist.* **melwel**); 6 **myllwyn**, 7 **milwyn**. [a. AF. *muluelle* (latinized *mulvellus*, 13th c.), OF. *muluel* (Godef.), prob. an altered form of *muruel*, *moruel*, dim. of *morue* (Walloon *molue*) cod: see MORRHUA. Cf. MORHWELL.] = COD *sb.*³

1338 in Dugdale *Monasticon* (1819) II. 584/1 In codelyngis et haddockis emptis iijˢ vjᵈ... In green mulvellis xvᵈ. *c* **1340** *Durham Acc. Rolls* (Surtees) 36 In xx Milueles salsis, viij s. **1387** TREVISA *Higden* (Rolls) I. 423 In þe oþer [pond] is perche and trouȝtis,.. So fareþ as wel In Albania þe Milewel [*v.r.* meluel, mylwel]. *c* **1460** J. RUSSELL *Bk. Nurture* 555 Salt samoun Congur, grone fische boþe lynge & myllewelle. **1577** J. DEE *Gen. & Rare Mem.* 24 For his Majesty to be Souerayn Lord of the Fishing of Myllwyn and Codd, there [*sc.* Ireland]. **1603** OWEN *Pembrokeshire* (1892) 123 Myllwell otherwise called codde. **1661** LOVELL *Hist. Anim. & Min.* 232 Cod fish..is a great Sea-whiting, called also a Keeling or Melwel. **1674** RAY *Coll. Words* 33 *Milwyn*; *Lancash.* Greenfish. **1755** JOHNSON, *Melwel*, a kind of fish. *attrib.* *c* **1430** *Two Cookery-bks.* 16 Take..Freysshe Mylwell hedys. *Ibid.* 61 Mulwyl taylys.

†**mulwine.** *Obs. rare*$^{-1}$. ? A drinking bout.

1607 MIDDLETON *Phœnix* H 4, You have made vs wayte a goodly time for you,..you are in your Rowses & Mulwines a poxe on you.

muly, var. MULEY *a.*³

mulyer, obs. form of MULIER *a.*

mum (mʌm), *sb.*¹, *int.*, and *a.* Forms: 4-6 **mom(me**, 6 **mume**, 6-7 **mumme**, 7 **mumbe**, 8 **mumm**, 5- **mum**. [Echoic; cf. G. *mumm*.]

A. *sb.*

†**1.** An inarticulate sound made with closed lips, esp. as an indication of inability or unwillingness to speak. Also, in negative or hypothetical context = '(not) the slightest word'. Sometimes with omission of *not*: 'not a word'. *Obs.*

1377 LANGL. *P. Pl.* B. Prol. 115 Thow myȝtest better mete the myste on Maluerne hulles, Than gete a momme of here mouthe but money were shewed. *c* **1460** *Towneley Myst.* xxi. 172 Though thi lyppis be stokyn yit myght thou say, mom. *a* **1500** *London Lickpenny* (MS. Harl. 542) iv, He would not geve me a momme of his mouthe. **1532** MORE *Confut. Tindale* Wks. 641/2 Tyndall neuer brought out yet eyther boke, lefe, or lyne to proue vs..that euer the ceremonies that he calleth now dumme, spake euer in old tyme so much as a mumme. **1651** LILLY *Chas. I* (1774) 235 The Common Council assembled: but mum could he get there, for the word London-Derry was then fresh in every mans mouth.

2. Refusal to speak, silence. *colloq.*

1562 J. HEYWOOD *Prov. & Epigr.* (1867) 163 Mum hath a grace in thee far more than speeche. **1678** BUTLER *Hud.* III. ii. 1494 Entrust it under solemn Vows Of Mum, and Silence, and the Rose. **1890** *Pall Mall G.* 7 Jan. 1/2 If the policy of 'mum' continues.

b. *attrib.*

1711 ADDISON *Spect.* No. 9 ¶6 The Mum Club (as I am informed) is an Institution of the same Nature, and as great an Enemy to Noise. **1797** T. PARK *Sonn.* 66 Doom'd by more severe mishap, To the mum-penance of La Trappe.

†**c.** A contest at 'playing mum' (see C. b). *Obs.*

1779 JOHNSON *Let. to Mrs. Thrale* 10 Mar., So, dear Madam, it is a mumm to see who will speak first.

†**3.** A silent person. (Cf. MOME *sb.*³) *Obs.*

1666 LOCKE *Let. to J. Alford* in *Gentl. Mag.* (1797) LXVII. I. 97, I do not in this advise you to be either a mumbe or morose. **1807-8** W. IRVING *Salmag.* (1824) 156 These silent members are..denominated orator mums.

B. *int.* A command to be silent or secret; 'hush!' 'silence!' 'not a word!' Also in phrases, †***mum for that*** (obs.), ***mum's the word***.

? **1399** *Title of poem* (= *'Rich. Redeles'*) cited by Bale *Index* (Anecd. Oxon.), Mum, soth-segger! **1568** FULWELL *Like will to Like* E iij, No more woords but mum & stand a while aside. **1605** SHAKS. *Lear* I. iv. 215 Mum, mum, he that keepes nor crust, nor crum, Weary of all, shall want some. **1687** MONTAGUE & PRIOR *Hind & P. Transv.* 7 It has cost me some pains to clear Her Title. Well but Mum for that, Mr. Smith. *a* **1704** T. BROWN *Walk round Lond.*, *Coffee-Houses* Wks. 1709 III. III. 39 But Mum's the Word—for who wou'd speak their Mind among Tarrs and commissioners. **1705** VANBRUGH *Country-Ho.* II, What does she play her jests upon me too?—but, mum, he laughs best that laughs last. *a* **1814** *Woman's Will* I. ii. in *New Brit. Theatre* IV. 47 The reason is obvious—But mum for that. **1852** MISS MULOCK *Agatha's Husb.* xxii, As to Cornwall,.. between you and me, Mrs. Harper, mum's the word. **1892** W. S. GILBERT *Mountebanks* I, But, mum! I must be discreet.

C. *adj.* Strictly silent or secret, not saying a word. Sometimes quasi-*adv.*, as ***to stand mum***, etc. *colloq.* (now somewhat *arch.* exc. *dial.*)

1521 in Foxe *A. & M.* (1583) 824/1 These comming to the Church..would say no prayers, but did sitte mumme..lyke beastes. *c* **1530** REDFORD *Play Wit & Sci.* (1848) 33 Let us not stay here muet and mum. **1600** HOLLAND *Livy* XXXII. xx. 820 When the publick cryer calleth you to give your opinions, ye are mum and mute. **1626-7** in *Crt. & Times Chas. I* (1848) I. 96 Wonder not the great duke bore him out, and all stood mum. **1788** COWPER *Pity Poor Africans* 5, I pity them [*sc.* slaves] greatly, but I must be mum, For how could we do without sugar and rum? **1834** *Tait's Mag.* I. 421/2 Sing mum till the public affair is over. **1894** R. BRIDGES *Feast of Bacchus* II. 709 Don't stand there mum. **1894** WEYMAN *Under Red Robe* i, I turned and they met my eye; and they were as mum as mice.

b. ***to play mum***: to be silent. (Cf. MUMBUDGET, MUMCHANCE.)

1532 MORE *Confut. Tindale* Wks. 412/2 Yet would he play mumme too, and neyther by himselfe nor his holy spiryte vouchesaufe to speake anye one woorde vnto them. **1625** *Gonsalvio's Sp. Inquis.* 19 Which fetch of theirs whoso will wisely and warily auoid, must take heed he play mumme, and speak not one word, but premeditated..afore hand.

mum (mʌm), *sb.*² Now chiefly *Hist.* Also 7 **mumme**, 9 **mumm**. [a. G. *mumme*, recorded from the end of the 15th c.

Adelung's assertion, that this beer was so called from the name of Christian Mumme, who was a brewer at Brunswick *c.* 1487, is discredited by M. Heyne. Kluge quotes from G. Baist the remark that the word resembles It. *mommo*, a child's word for drink.]

A kind of beer originally brewed in Brunswick.

Largely imported into England in the 17th and 18th c.; now mentioned only *Hist.* and in customs tariffs.

1640 GLAPTHORNE *Wallenstein* III. iii, I thinke you'r drunk With Lubecks beere or Brunswicks Mum. **1677** YARRANTON *Eng. Improv.* 118 The Mum at Brunswick is made of Wheat, and the Wheat that it is made of, is brought from..Magdenburg, and Shenibank..; when it comes to Brunswick it is Malted, and so made into Mum... But the Mum at Brunswick is a Medicine, and drinks very nauseous, ..that which makes it good..is its being long at Sea. **1756** NUGENT *Gr. Tour, Germany* II. 243 The chief trade of the inhabitants [of Brunswick] is in tanning leather, and in brewing mum from a malt made of barley, with a small mixture of wheat, well hopped. *Ibid.*, What they call ship-mum, is scarce drinkable, till it has purged itself at sea. **1851** THACKERAY *Eng. Hum.*, *Steele* (1853) 119 This boy.. exhibited an early fondness and capacity for drinking mum and sack. **1861** —— *Four Georges* i, I fancy the..burghers over their beer and mumm, rising up, cap in hand, as the cavalcade passes. **1894** *Act 57 & 58 Vict.* c. 30 §25 The duties of Customs now payable on beer of the descriptions called mum, spruce, or black beer, imported into Great Britain or Ireland.

†**b.** *attrib.* and *Comb.*, as ***mum-barrel, -beer; mum-begotten, -coloured*** adjs.; **mum-catchup** (see quot. 1769); **mum-glass,** (*a*) a glass used for drinking mum; (*b*) a slang name for the MONUMENT; **mum-house,** a house for the sale of mum. *Obs.*

1682-3 in *Hedges' Diary* (Hakl. Soc.) II. 272, I sent you by Capt. Heath one *mum barril with mangoes. **1672** SIR J. FOULIS *Acc. Bk.* 15 June (S.H.S.) 7 For a pint of *mum bear ..0. 8. 0. **1782-3** W. F. MARTYN *Geog. Mag.* II. 152 German exports to foreign countries are corn, tobacco.. mum beer [etc.]. **1699** T. BROWN *Life Erasmus* in R. L'Estrange *Erasmus Colloq.* (1725) B j, The Modern Dutch writers, who visit Frankfort Fair, once a Year, with two or three stupid *Mum-begotten Dissertations. **1769** MRS. RAFFALD *Eng. Housekpr.* (1778) 339 To make *Mum Catchup. To a quart of old mum put four ounces of anchovies, of mace, and nutmegs sliced, one ounce, of cloves, and black pepper half an ounce, boil it till it is reduced one third. **1702** *Phil. Trans.* XXIII. 1369 This Liquor was *Mum-coloured. **1684** R. WALLER *Nat. Exper.* 8 A tall Cup in the shape of a *Mum-glass. *a* **1700** B. E. *Dict. Cant. Crew, Mum-glass,* the Monument, erected..in Memory of the..Fire 1666. **1664** PEPYS *Diary* 3 May, I went..to the Fleece, a *mum-house in Leadenhall, and there drank mum.

mum (mʌm), *sb.*³ *dial.* and *colloq.* [Shortened form of MUMMY *sb.*²] **1. a.** A 'pet' name for 'mother'.

1823 MOOR *Suffolk Words* 242 Where's your mum? **1876** R. M. JEPHSON *He would be a Soldier* xviii, I saw the mum anxiously inquiring of her son who I was. **1876** C. M. YONGE *Three Brides* I. xvi. 274 You'll never do anything with my Governor..you should hear him and the Mum talking. **1955** M. ALLINGHAM *Beckoning Lady* vi. 88 Charlie Luke has a mum too, hasn't he? **1956** I. BROMIGE *Enchanted Garden* III. iii. 140 This will be our first holiday without the children for a good many years. It'll be good to be with Laurie as a wife and not a mum for a short time. **1960** *News Chron.* 8 Feb. 3/4 The mums from Manchester and Mitcham dressed up in their Sunday best..had to listen to the principal's report. **1966** AUDEN *About House* 15 The flesh Mum formulated. **1973** A. S. NEILL *Neill! Neill! Orange Peel!* II. 223 Many married men address their wives as Mum.

b. *Sociol.* Used *spec.* to designate the working-class mother who is a dominating influence in the lives of her children, even in their adulthood and marriage.

1957 YOUNG & WILLMOTT *Family & Kinship in East London* iii. 34 Where Mum plays so large a part in the lives of her descendants, she should be honoured for what she does... Since her status as 'Mum' is so high, it is derogatory to call her by any other name. **1958** M. KERR *People of Ship Street* ii. 22 The first characteristic which emerges clearly in this group is the central figure of the Mum. Whatever her personal qualities she is the focus of all the family activities. **1958** *Spectator* 30 May 710/2 The Mum restricts her son-in-law's roles and most of the men in the neighbourhood seem to suffer accordingly. **1958** *Listener* 11 Sept. 395/2 Many families who have been moved out of Bethnal Green..are in most cases perfectly wretched. They crave for their old associations, for Mum, the familiar pub, their pets and the old cosy squalor. **1959** *Ibid.* 4 June 981/2 There is, however, some difference of opinion in the field of 'Mum' sociology.

c. Colloq. phr. ***to be mum,*** etc. = *to be mother* (see MOTHER *sb.*¹ 3 e).

1962 N. FREELING *Love in Amsterdam* I. 37 'I'll be Mum,' he said, and poured the coffee. **1965** J. POTTER *Death in Office* xv. 147, I did the chores as mum..the tea-tray ploy was one of the standard fitness tests for prospective employees.

2. *Comb.*, as **mum figure** *colloq.*, one who represents the attributes of a mother; = *mother figure.*

1959 'N. BLAKE' *Widow's Cruise* 23 I'm a Mum figure—everyone coughs it up in my lap. **1960** *Times Lit. Suppl.* 16 Sept. 589/1 His wife is a shadowy mum-figure who collects for good causes.

mum (mʌm), *sb.*⁴ Abbrev. of CHRYSANTHEMUM. Also **'mum.**

1924 A. M. MARTINEAU *Gardening in Sunny Lands* ii. 38 The gardeners call chrysanthemums 'mums'. **1949** [see CUKE]. **1965** J. PHILIPS *Black Glass City* II. 62 A basket of bright-colored fall flowers..mums and asters. **1967** 'E. QUEEN' *Face to Face* lxiii. 197 The enormous basket-spray of shaggy 'mums. **1967** *Times* 4 Apr. 18/1 (Advt.), Captivating Meteor Mums... These chrysanthemums..cascade into bloom in August. **1975** M. H. CLARK *Where are Children?* i. 16 The window boxes..were filled with yellow and champagne mums.

mum (mʌm), *v.* [f. MUM *int.* or *sb.*¹ Cf. G. *mummen* to mutter; also = sense 4 below.]

†**1.** *trans.* To silence; to put to silence. *Obs.*

1399 LANGL. *Rich. Redeles* III. 337 He was..y-Mummyd on þe mouthe and manaced to þe deth. **1594** ? PEELE *Battle of Alcazar* I. Prol., Like those that were by kind of murther mumd. **1654** GAYTON *Pleas. Notes* III. viii. 123 If it were possible they would muzle his mouth; but Gines is mumm'd presently.

†**2.** *intr.* To make an inarticulate sound with closed lips, indicating inability to speak; hence, to keep silence. *Obs.*

c **1440** *Promp. Parv.* 348/2 Mummyn, as þey þat noȝt speke, *mutio.* *a* **1548** HALL *Chron., Rich. III,* 32 b, Whiche thynge yf it had bene trewe..euery goode and naturall childe would have rather mummed at, then to have blasted abroade. **1576** GASGOIGNE *Steele Gl.* (Arb.) 83 Better mumme, than meddle ouermuch. **1637** SHIRLEY *Example* IV. ii, *Jacinta...* I may reward your silence. *Vainman...* And when must I Begin to mum?

†**3.** To utter a faint sound; to whisper. *Obs.*

c **1460** *Towneley Myst.* viii. 188 If thou can nother muf nor mom, I shalle shelde the from shame. **1570** *Satir. Poems Reform.* xii. 166 3e dar not mum quhill Saidlar cum To se quhat Ingland sendis. *c* **1680** *Roxb. Ball.* (1887) VI. 370 They dare not mumm, if we say all's our own.

4. To act in dumb-show; to play as a mummer.

1530 PALSGR. 642/1, I mumme in a mummynge, *je mumme...* Lette us go mumme to nyght in womens apparayle. **1554** *Act Merch. Co.* in Mackenzie *Newcastle* II. 665 *note,* [Apprentices are not] to daunse, dyse, carde or mum, or use any gyttirnes. **1606** *Choice, Chance,* etc. (1881) 50 After they had masked and mummed, away they went. **1837** CARLYLE *Fr. Rev.* II. I. x, When a whole People goes mumming and miming. **1900** LD. ROSEBERY *Napoleon* vi. 89 The characters who mum to Offenbach's music.

mum, vulgar var. MA'AM.

mumbe, obs. f. MUM.

mumble ('mʌmb(ə)l), *sb.* [f. MUMBLE *v.*] A mumbled indistinct utterance or sound.

1902 *Westm. Gaz.* 20 Sept. 1/3 A series of mumbles and grunts. **1904** KIPLING *Traffics & Discov.* 308 A mumble of bees and broken voices that might have been the doves. **1905** SIR F. TREVES *Other Side of Lantern* III. i. (1906) 193 The contented mumble of the river.

mumble ('mʌmb(ə)l), *v.* Forms: 4 **momele,** 5 **momell, -(b)yll,** 5–6 **momble, mumbyll,** 6 **mumbil, -bell,** *Sc.* **mumbill, mummyll,** 6–8 *Sc.* **mumle,** 7 *Sc.* **mummil,** 6– **mumble.** [ME. *momele,* frequentative formation on MUM *int.*; cf. Du. *mommelen, mummelen,* G. *mummeln,* Sw. *mumla,* Da. *mumle,* and MAMBLE.]

1. *intr.* To speak indistinctly, or with the lips partly closed; to mutter. In early use: †To babble.

1362 LANGL. *P. Pl.* A. v. 21 Of þis Matere I mihte Momele [*B-text* mamely] ful longe. *c* **1440** *York Myst.* xxvii. 106 My fellows momellis þame emang. **1590** SPENSER *F.Q.* I. i. 42 He mumbled soft, but would not all his silence breake. **1683** KENNETT tr. *Erasm. on Folly* 107 The Auditors all wondred and some mumbled to themselves. **1879** BROWNING *Halbert & Hob* 64 So tottered, muttered, mumbled he, till he died. **1902** A. LANG *Hist. Scot.* II. xiii. 352 He heard the old woman mumbling to herself.

b. *transf.* and *fig.*

1842 EMERSON *Lect. Transcend.* Wks. (Bohn) II. 291 Church and old book mumble and ritualize to an unheeding ..mind. **1893** BARING-GOULD *Cheap-Jack Z.* I. 9 The organ was still mumbling and tooting.

2. *trans.* To utter in subdued or indistinct tones. Sometimes with mixture of sense 4.

c **1440** *Jacob's Well* xxiii. 154 It are þei, þat whanne þei are wrothe..momyll þe deuelys bedys. **1530** PALSGR. 642/1 He mumbleth his wordes, byd hym speke out playnly. **1626** L. OWEN *Spec. Jesuit.* 17 By one meanes or other, he learned to mumble a Masse. **1748** J. MASON *Elocut.* 10 When a person mumbles, or (as we say) clips or swallows his Words. **1771** SMOLLETT *Humph. Cl.* 13 July, He affirmed, that we mumbled our speech with our lips and teeth. **1861** HUGHES *Tom Brown at Oxf.* vii, Tom mumbled something to the effect that it was by no means necessary.

b. With †*forth, out, over,* †*up.*

1538 STARKEY *England* I. iv. 132 Mumblyng vp a certayn nombur of wordys no thyng vnderstonde. *a* **1555** LYNDESAY *Tragedie* 385 Thay be clokit vp in clerkis arraye,..And mummyll ouer ane pair of maglit matenis. **1555** T. WASHINGTON tr. *Nicholay's Voy.* III. xxi. 110 b, [They] goe to bathe..mumbling out certaine long prayers. **1658** tr. *Porta's Nat. Magic* xx. 407 Then they mumble forth some words. **1787** MME. D'ARBLAY *Diary* 18 Jan., I..mumbled out my own little compliment. **1834** GREVILLE *Mem.* 1 Dec. (1875) III. xxv. 166 The priest mumbles over the prayers.

†**c.** To whisper, utter furtively. *Obs.*

c **1539** HEN. VIII in Fiddes *Wolsey* II. (1726) 140, I dare be bolder with you then a great many that mumbell it abroad.

3. *intr.* To eat in a slow, ineffective manner; to chew or bite softly, as with toothless gums.

c **1325** *Pol. Songs* (1839) 238 The knave crommeth is crop Er the cok crawe; He momeleth ant moccheth Ant marreth is mawe. **1530** PALSGR. 642/1 Se yonder olde trot howe she mumbleth:..*comment elle masche en belyn.* **1561** AWDELAY *Frat. Vacab.* (1869) 8 Sitting as it were alone, mumblyng on a crust. **1620** MIDDLETON *Chaste Maid* I. i. 109, I have teeth, sir; I need not mumble yet this forty years. **1748** RICHARDSON *Clarissa* (1811) IV. v. 21 Take ye that thistle to mumble upon. **1833** MARRYAT *P. Simple* i, As proud, and, alas! as unconscious as the calf with gilded horns, who plays and mumbles with the flowers of the garland.

†**b.** *fig.*

a **1651** CALDERWOOD *Hist. Kirk* (Wodrow Soc.) III. 302 George Bishop of Murrey was a whole winter mummilling upon his papers, and had not his sermon *per cœur* when all was done.

4. *trans.* To bite or chew with toothless gums, or without making much use of the teeth.

1591 LYLY *Endym.* IV. ii. 55 Tis a stately occupation to stande..in a cold Morning, and to haue his nose bytten with frost, before hys baite be mumbled with a Fish. **1664** ETHEREDGE *Comical Revenge* III. iv, My Master pick'd him Up before a Puppit-show, mumbling a half-penny Custard. **1693** DRYDEN *Juvenal* x. (1697) 261 And Gums unarm'd to mumble Meat in vain. **1719** D'URFEY *Pills* (1872) III. 73 They're able enough to mumble a Pudding. **1826** SCOTT *Woodst.* xxviii, A child mumbling ginger-bread. **1847** LYTTON *Lucretia* II. Prol., His glove fell to the ground, and his spaniel mumbled it into shreds.

b. *transf.* and *fig.*

1695 CONGREVE *Love for L.* Prol. 35 As Asses Thistles, Poets mumble Wit, And dare not bite, for fear of being bit. **1864** LOWELL *Fireside Trav.* 291 The sea laps and mumbles the soft roots of the hills. **1883** A. FORBES in *Fortn. Rev.* 1 Nov. 673 A victim which she [France] was to be allowed only to mumble, not utterly to rend.

c. *transf.* To fondle with the lips.

1668 ETHEREDGE *She Would if She Could* I. ii, A right bred greyhound can as well forbear running after a hare..as I can mumbling a pretty wench. **1695** CONGREVE *Love for L.* v. i, Give me t'other hand, and I'll mumble 'em and kiss 'em till they melt in my mouth. **1884** READE *Jilt* 7 She drew away the hand he was mumbling.

†**5.** To maul, handle roughly, maltreat. Also, to bungle, handle clumsily. *Obs.*

1628 FORD *Lover's Mel.* v. i, He has mumbled his nose, that 'tis as big as a great cod-piece. **1638** —— *Lady's Trial* II. ii, 'Tis said..that a' has firk'd And mumbled the roguy Turks. **1672** WYCHERLEY *Love in Wood* III. iv, I have beat him out of the pit. I do so mumble these prating, censorious fellows they call wits, when I meet with them! **1709** STEELE *Tatler* No. 50 ¶ 11, [I] shall leave you to be mumbled by the learned and very ingenious Author of a late Book. **1721-2** AMHERST *Terræ Fil.* No. 44 (1754) 233 This was..a circumstance..that might be handsomely touch'd upon in a dedication. Let us see how our bungler mumbles it. **1753** H. WALPOLE *Let. to Conway* 24 May, Mr. Fox mumbled the Chancellor and his lawyers.

†**b.** ***to mumble up:*** to tumble together. *Obs.*

1673 RAY *Journ. Low C.*, etc. 496 Mercers never tie up anything they sell, and if they allow paper, they only rudely mumble up the commodities in it.

6. *Cookery.* (See quot.)

1728 E. SMITH *Compl. Housew.* (ed. 2) 12 To mumble Rabbets and Chickens... When they are half boiled..tear the Flesh from the Bones of the Rabbet in small flakes, and put it into the Stew-pan again with a very little of the Liquor it was boiled in,..when 'tis enough shake in a little Flour, and thicken it up with Butter. Serve it on Sippets. **1879** [see MUMBLED *a.* 2].

†**7.** *Comb.*, as **mumblecrust,** in plays, the surname or nickname of a toothless person or a beggar; **mumble-matins,** a nickname for a Romish priest; **mumble-news,** a tale-bearer. *Obs.*

a **1553** UDALL *Royster D.* I. iii. (Arb.) 20 Madge Mumblecrust. **1560** PILKINGTON *Expos. Aggeus* (1562) 41 Howe can they be learned, havinge none to teache them but Sir John Mumble-matins? **1588** SHAKS. *L.L.L.* v. ii. 464 Some carry-tale,..Some mumble-newes,..Told our intents before. **1603** DEKKER & CHETTLE *Grissil* IV. ii. (Shaks. Soc.) 66 *Beggar.* Jack Mumblecrust, steal no penny loaves.

mumblebee ('mʌmb(ə)lbiː). *local.* A kind of boat.

1891 *Devon County Standard* 14 Mar. 3/2 The Bluebell drove foul of the mumblebee Faith. *Ibid.*, The mumble bees Energy and Laura Mildred were also brought in. **1898** ANSTED *Dict. Sea Terms, Mumbleby* or *Mumblebee,* a name applied by Brixham fishermen to a boat midway in size between a *hooker* and a *trawler.*

'mumbled, *ppl. a.* [f. MUMBLE *v.* + -ED¹.]

1. Spoken in an indistinct voice.

1545 BRINKLOW *Compl.* 6 The mombled and mynsed Masse. **1638** D. MITCHELL *Let.* in Ld. Hailes *Memor.* (1766) II. 37, I have been..followed with many mumbled threatnings behind my back. **1841** D'ISRAELI *Amen. Lit.* (1867) 325 The Romanists had reduced their whole devotion to a mumbled ritual and a mechanical service.

2. ***mumbled eggs:*** buttered or scrambled eggs. (Cf. MUMBLE *v.* 6.)

1879 MRS. A. E. JAMES *Ind. Househ. Managem.* 88 Mumbled eggs, or 'rumble-tumble'.

mumble-fubbles, variant of MUBBLE-FUBBLES.

mumble-jumble ('mʌmb(ə)l,dʒʌmb(ə)l), *v. nonce-wd.* [f. MUMBLE *v.* + JUMBLE *v.*] *trans.* To speak indistinctly and incoherently.

1833 MARRYAT *P. Simple* xvii, I mumbled-jumbled something or other, half Spanish and half English.

mumblement ('mʌmb(ə)lmənt). [f. MUMBLE *v.* + -MENT.] The action of mumbling; something mumbled or muttered.

1595 COPLEY *Wits, Fits, & Fancies* 175 Such his mumblement being ouer-heard came afterwardes in question to his danger. **1837** CARLYLE *Fr. Rev.* III. III. viii, Lasource answered with some vague painful mumblement. **1862** —— *Fredk. Gt.* XI. v. (1872) IV. 76 Getting no.. answer,..getting only some vague mumblement as good as none.

mumbler ('mʌmblə(r)). [f. MUMBLE *v.* + -ER¹.] One who speaks indistinctly or in muffled tones.

1543 BALE *Yet a Course,* etc. 88 b, Masse momblers, holye water swyngers [etc.]. *a* **1550** in *Anglia* (1903) Jan. 204 For a syngar,..Momelers, foreskippers, ouerskippers *sunt tria mala.* **1694** MOTTEUX *Rabelais* IV. lxiv. (1737) 260 Mumblers of *Ave Marias.* **1891** *Ch. Times* 27 Nov. 1167/2 The mumblers, who think it a Catholic custom to make the Consecration inaudible.

mumble-the-peg. Now *U.S.* Also 9 **mumble-peg,** and *erron.* 7- **mumbledepeg,** 7- etc. **mumblety-peg,** 9 **mumble-te-peg.** A boys' game in which each player in turn throws a knife from a series of positions, continuing until he fails to make the blade stick in the ground. Hence **mumblety-pegging** *vbl. sb.*

The unsuccessful player is compelled to draw out of the ground with his teeth a peg which the others have driven in with a certain number of blows with the handle of the knife.

In Antrim the game is said to have been played with a fork instead of a knife (see E.D.D.). In Scotland it is locally called 'knifie'.

1627 W. HAWKINS *Apollo Shroving* Prol. 5 Nor scourgetop, nor Trusse, nor Leape-frog, nor Nine holes, nor Mumble the pegge. *a* **1652** BROME *New Acad.* II. Wks. 1873 II. 33 At Mumbledepeg I will so firk her. **1883** E. INGERSOLL in *Harper's Mag.* Jan. 201/1 It'll take more mumble-te-peg 'n you're worth, I reckon, to pull it out! **1891** A. WELCKER *Wild West* 14 He..would play any game whatever, even down to 'mumble-peg', if money was at stake. **1895** *Century Mag.* Aug. 543/1 Those mysterious and irresistible forces which..bind all boyish hearts to play mumble-the-peg at the due time. **1931** *Sun* (Baltimore) 18 Feb. 8/7 In my boyhood the spring was ushered in by children rolling hoops, spinning tops, skipping rope, playing mumblety-pegs. **1932** *Ibid.* 17 Sept. 10/7 The Park will attempt next week to match this week's golf tournament with a grand quoit pitchin' and mumblety-peggin' contest. **1938** M. K. RAWLINGS *Yearling* vii. 64 Jody and Fodder-wing lost interest in the talk and went into a corner to play mumbledepeg. Ma Baxter would never have allowed pocket knives to be flipped into her clean smooth floors. **1963** T. PYNCHON *V.* x. 298 They found two more musicians playing mumbledypeg with clam knives.

mumbling (ˈmʌmblɪŋ), *vbl. sb.* [f. MUMBLE *v.* + -ING[1].] The action of the vb. MUMBLE.

c **1400** *Destr. Troy* 1864 Me meruellis of þi momlyng & þi mad wordes. **1533** MORE *Debell. Salem* Wks. 1021/1 Consider..what wisedome the man hath shewed, in makyng such a mumbling of chaunging spyrytuall rulers into prelates. *a* **1553** UDALL *Royster D.* I. iii. (Arb.) 20 Olde browne bread crustes must haue much good mumblyng. **1621** BURTON *Anat. Mel.*, Democr. to Rdr. (1624) 24 Praying in gibberish, & mumbling of beads. **1878** BROWNING *Poets Croisic* xc, From his lips a sort of mumbling fell of who was to be kicked.

mumbling (ˈmʌmblɪŋ), *ppl. a.* [f. MUMBLE *v.* + -ING[2].] That mumbles.

c **1440** *York Myst.* xxxi. 305 Þou mummeland myghtyng. **1579** TOMSON *Calvin's Serm. Tim.* 187/1 True it is, that the Papists will pray in a mumbling and babling sort. **1693** DRYDEN *Juvenal* x. (1697) 268 For the Boys a mumbling Vow she sends. **1703** *Lond. Gaz.* No. 3904/4 A mumbling Speech, his upper Teeth before double. **1876** GEO. ELIOT *Dan. Der.* i, There was a faint, mumbling smile about the lips of the old woman.

Hence ˈ**mumblingly** *adv.*, in a mumbling manner.

1748 RICHARDSON *Clarissa* (1811) V. viii. 88 Mumblingly hoarse. **1872** 'L. CARROLL' *Through Looking-Gl.* (1898) 102 [He] muttered mumblingly and low As if his mouth were full of dough.

ˌ**mumbo-ˈjum.** ? *Obs.* [App. shortened from next.] A kind of punch made of rum and other alcoholic ingredients.

1837 T. HOOK *Jack Brag* xv, A certain quantity of the West Indian mumbo-jum.

mumbo jumbo (ˌmʌmbəʊ ˈdʒʌmbəʊ). Also (esp. in sense 1) with capital initials. [Of unknown origin.

Canon Robinson states that no light on the word can be obtained from the languages of the Niger region, to which the accounts of Moore and Park relate. The Kongo *nzambi*, god, might conceivably have suggested a reduplicating jingle like 'Mumbo Jumbo', but on geographical grounds this is an unlikely source.]

1. A grotesque idol said to have been worshipped by certain tribes or associations of Negroes.

1738 F. MOORE *Trav. Afr.* 40 A dreadful Bugbear to the Women, call'd Mumbo-Jumbo, which is what keeps the Women in awe. *Ibid.* 116 At Night, I was visited by a Mumbo Jumbo, an Idol, which is among the Mundingoes a kind of cunning Mystery... This is a Thing invented by the Men to keep their Wives in awe. **1799** M. PARK *Trav. Africa* iv. (ed. 2) 39 A sort of masquerade habit..which I was told ..belonged to Mumbo Jumbo. This is a strange bugbear.. much employed by the Pagan natives in keeping their women in subjection. **1837** HOOD *Ode to Rae Wilson* xxiv, You might have been High Priest to Mumbo-Jumbo. **1873** LELAND *Egypt. Sketch-Bk.* 83 The Savage, suggestive of wild African Mumbo-Jumbo,..will have vanished.

2. *transf.* **a.** An object of unintelligent veneration.

1847 EMERSON *Repr. Men, Goethe* Wks. (Bohn) I. 384 The ambitious and mercenary bring their last new mumbo-jumbo, whether tariff,..railroad, Romanism, mesmerism, or California. **1876** GEO. ELIOT *Dan. Der.* xxviii, The name of Mompert had become a sort of Mumbo-jumbo.

b. Obscure or meaningless talk or writing; nonsense. Also *ellipt.* as **mumbo**.

1896 FARMER & HENLEY *Slang* IV. 386/2 *Mumbo-Jumbo*, 2. (colloquial).—Unmeaning jargon. **1931** E. POUND *Let.* 27 Dec. (1971) 237 The continuation [of a magazine] can be called Poetry, Second Series, or new series, if that hackneyed term is still big heap mumbo on the lake shore. **1938** *Sun* (Baltimore) 16 Nov. 10/1 The Orson Welles mumbo jumbo of a few weeks ago has revived talk of greater public control over this form of communication. **1955** *Times* 2 May 17/3 A mumbo jumbo of meaningless words and phrases. **1969** M. PEI *Words in Sheep's Clothing* (1970) vii. 54 Mumbo jumbo developed by educators to confound the public in general and inquisitive parents in particular. **1973** *Sunday Express* 29 July 12/3 There is a great deal of unnecessary mumbo talked. **1975** *Times* 14 Aug. 14/5 Labour's elected representatives..mouth the mumbo-jumbo of capitalism: 'The pound must be kept strong', 'We must all buy British'.

3. *attrib.* and *Comb.*

1870 LOWELL *Wks.* (1890) III. 354 *note*, The Mumbo-Jumbo revenge in Collins's ode. **1895** ELWORTHY *Evil Eye* 402 Formulæ to be uttered in mumbo-jumbo incantation.

Hence **mumbo-ˈjumboism**, worship of a mumbo jumbo.

1883 E. THRING *Theory & Pract. Teaching* 127 The civilized Mumbo-jumboism which thinks it can award over a whole kingdom the palm of mind.

ˌ**mumˈbudget.** †**1.** = MUM *int.*, *a.*, and *sb.*[1] *Obs.*

Perh. orig. the name of some children's game in which silence was required.

a **1564** BECON *Display. Pop. Mass* Wks. III. 47b, Nowe ye playe mumme budget and scilence glumme. *a* **1566** R. EDWARDS *Damon & Pithias* (1571) C iij b, But mumbouget for Carisophus I espie In haste to come hether. [**1598** SHAKS. *Merry W.* v. ii. 6, I come to her in white, and cry Mum; she cries Budget, and by that we know one another.] **1611** COTGR., *Demeurer court*, to play at Mumbudget, or be at a Nonplus. **1622** MABBE tr. *Aleman's Guzman D'Alf.* I. (1630) 146, I was Mum-budget, and durst not open my lips to him..in that businesse. **1663** BUTLER *Hud.* I. iii. 208 Have these Bones ratled, and this Head So often in thy quarrel bled? Nor did I ever winch or grudge it, For thy dear sake. (Quoth she) Mum budget.

2. Phr. *to come mumbudgeting* 'to come clandestinely, secretly' (*E.D.D.*). (See also quot. 1909.) *dial.*

1872 HARDY *Under Greenwood Tree* I. II. ii. 115 There was this to be said for him, that you were quite sure he'd never come mumbudgeting to see ye, just as you were in the middle of your work, and put you out with his anxious trouble about you. *Ibid.* II. IV. ii. 110 Now, don't come mumbudgeting so close again. **1909** *Daily Chron.* 30 Apr. 6/5 In Mr. Hardy's 'Under the Greenwood Tree'.. mumbudgeting..seems to mean rather 'fussily', a sense in which the word budget is still used in the Midlands. **1939** N. MARSH *Overture to Death* xiii. 139 Whatever be the matter with you, then, mum-budgeting so close to my apron strings?

¶ **3.** With allusion to BUDGET *sb.*

a **1630** J. TAYLOR (Water P.) *A Bawd* Wks. 1630 II. 97 The magazin of taciturnitie, the mumbudget of silens, the cloath-bag of councell.

mumchance (ˈmʌmtʃɑːns, -æ-), *sb.* and *a.* Forms: 6 mom(me)cha(u)nce, mumchaunce, *Sc.* mwmschance, 6–7 mumschance, 7 mummechaunce, 6– mumchance. [a. MLG. *mummenschanze*, *-kanze* a certain game of dice, also, a masked serenade (= MDu. *mommecanse*, mod.G. *mummen-*, *mummschanz*), f. *mummen* MUM *v.* + *schanz* a. F. *chance*: see CHANCE *sb.*]

A. *sb.*

†**1.** A dicing game resembling hazard. *Obs.*

1528 ROY *Rede me* (Arb.) 60 To playe at the cardes and dyce Some of theym are nothynge nyce Both at hasard and momchaunce. **1607** DEKKER & WEBSTER *Westw. Hoe* II. ii, I thoght I had bin at Mum-chance my bones ratled so with iaunting? **1656** HARRINGTON *Oceana* (1658) 116 Do you conceive they will be better pleased when they shall be told, that upon like occasions you are at Mum-chance or Stool-ball?

†**2.** *to play mumchance*: *fig.* or *allusively*, to preserve a dogged silence. *Obs.*

1550 BALE *Eng. Votaries* II. 107b, He played momme chaunce and wolde make none answere. **1552** HULOET, Mumchaunce or silence.

†**3.** Masquerade; mumming. *Obs.*

1557–75 *Diurn. Occurr.* (Bannatyne Cl.) 87 At evin our soueranis maid the maskrie and mumschance, in the quhilk the quenis grace, and all hir Maries and ladies were all cled in men's apperrell. **1581–2** *Burgh Rec. Edinb.* (1882) IV. 229 Jhone Gilleis, doctour in Jhone Blakis schole, oblist himself nocht to pas in mwmschance after supper to mak playes or vse siclyke vaniteis heirafter. **1591** R. BRUCE *Serm.* vi. M 8, They haue..gone to mumchances, mumries & vnknawin language.

4. In similative phrases: One who acts in dumb show. Hence, one who has nothing to say, a 'dummy'. Also as quasi-proper name, as the type of a silent person. Now only *dial.*

1694 ECHARD *Plautus* 114 Why stand ye like a Mum-chance? What are ye tongue-ty'd? *a* **1700** B. E. *Dict. Cant. Crew*, *Mum-chance*, one that sits mute. He looks like Mum-chance that was Hang'd for saying of nothing. **1786** MACKENZIE *Lounger* No. 90 ¶ 2 The poor creature..sat as silent as mum-chance.

B. *adj.* Silent; 'tongue-tied'.

1681 T. FLATMAN *Heraclitus Ridens* No. 49 (1713) II. 60 Conscience, that was so clamorous before, is Mumchance, and says nothing to the Matter. **1823** LAMB *Elia* Ser. II. *New Yr.'s Coming of Age*, Singling out poor Twenty Ninth of February that had sate all this while mumchance at the side-board. **1892** *Spectator* 13 Feb. 229/2 Why are the pulpits alone to remain mumchance under penalties? **1897** *Daily Tel.* 11 Mar. 5/5 The man or woman who can sit 'mumchance'..over a well-acted farce do not deserve to be ranked in the noble army of all-embracing playgoers. **1900** WEYMAN *Sophia* i, Such a mumchance fool as the girl herself is. **1903** G. B. SHAW *Man & Superman* IV. 167, I couldn't sit mumchance and have everything put on me. **1957** L. DURRELL *Justine* II. 133 For my part I remained always stupefied and mumchance at all the avenues opened up by these thoughts. **1971** F. MEYNELL *My Lives* iv. 42 In a room of awesome vastness with a phalanx of dons at the distant end of it, I was mum-chance.

†ˈ**mumchance,** *v.* *Obs. rare*[−1]. [f. prec. Cf. MDu. *mommecansen*.] *intr.* To masquerade.

1606 BIRNIE *Kirk-Buriall* (1833) 10 [At funerals] in steed of mourning in the dust, as they did oft-tymes, we mumchance and mourgean in such dilicate duilles.

ˈ**mumchanceness.** [f. MUMCHANCE *a.* + -NESS.] Silence, reticence. Also **mumchanciness.**

1910 'A. HOPE' *Second String* xxi. 435 Perhaps his very mum-chanceness was his saving. Glib protestations would have smacked too strongly of the principal to commend the agent. **1920** J. JOYCE *Let.* 29 Aug. (1966) III. 17, I am much inconvenienced by their cursed mumchanciness.

mume, obs. form of MUM.

mu-meson (ˌmjuːˈmiːzɒn, -ˈmɛzɒn). *Nuclear Physics.* Also **mu meson.** [f. MU + MESON[3].] The original name for the MUON. (Freq. written *μ-meson.*)

[**1947** LATTES, OCCHIALINI, & POWELL in *Nature* 4 Oct. 455/1 There is, therefore, good evidence for the production of a single homogeneous group of secondary mesons... It is convenient to refer to this process..as the *μ*-decay. We represent the primary mesons by the symbol *π*, and the secondary by *μ*. *Ibid.* 455/2 (*heading*) Evidence of a difference in mass of *π*- and *μ*-mesons.] **1952** B. ROSSI *High-Energy Particles* 566/1 Mu-mesons. **1953** *Jrnl. Brit. Interplanetary Soc.* XII. 203 The final remnants of cosmic-radiation which we observe at sea level are mainly electrons, mu-mesons, gamma rays and a proportionately small component of protons and neutrons. **1969** *Times* 2 Jan. 16/2 The measurements may indicate a means of distinguishing between mu mesons and electrons on grounds other than the difference of mass between the two particles.

Hence **mu-ˈmesic, -meˈsonic** *adjs.* = MUONIC *a.*

1954 *Physical Rev.* XCIV. 1619/1 Mu-mesonic energy levels. **1957** *Ann. Rev. Nuclear Sci.* VII. 17 (*heading*) Mu mesonic X-rays. *Ibid.* 495 (Index), Mumesic atoms. **1964** W. E. JONES tr. *A. A. Sokolov's Elementary Particles* vi. 52 Since muons are similar to electrons in their properties.., they may form mu-mesic atoms, where the principal role is played by electrical forces, just as in the normal atom. **1969** *New Scientist* 9 Oct. 63/2 The quadrupole moments derived from mu-mesic X-rays can be used to check the reliability of standard calculations in atomic physics.

Mumetal (ˈmjuːmɛtəl). Also **Mu-metal**, and with small initial. [f. MU (*μ* being conventionally used to denote permeability) + METAL *sb.* (and *a.*).] The proprietary name of an alloy of iron that contains approximately 75–78 per cent nickel, 4–6 per cent copper, and 1½–2 per cent chromium by weight and is a useful material for transformer cores and magnetic shields because of its high permeability and low hysteresis loss in weak magnetic fields.

1924 *Trade Marks Jrnl.* 16 Apr. 858 Mumetal... Metallic alloys, unwrought or partly wrought. The Telegraph Construction and Maintenance Company, Limited,.. London,..manufacturers. **1925** *Jrnl. Iron & Steel Inst.* CXII. 74 The first commercial application of high-frequency melting in Europe was made by a British firm for the preparation of nickel-iron alloys for submarine cables. The research work..quickly resulted in the preparation of a series of alloys known under the name of 'Mumetal'. **1932** *Discovery* May 142/1 Pure iron, silicon-iron, permalloy, and mumetal are used because they can be magnetized and demagnetized without loss. **1945** *Electronic Engin.* XVII. 384 (*caption*) Recorder unit showing tube enclosed in Mu-metal screen. **1966** *New Scientist* 18 Aug. 351/3 The enclosures were formed of a material (mu-metal) which screens off the Earth's field. **1973** *Physics Bull.* Dec. 719/2 Until now conventional recording heads have had cores of a soft magnetic material, typically ferrite or laminated mumetal.

mumey, -ie, -ifie, obs. ff. MUMMY, MUMMIFY.

mumia, -al, var. forms of MUMMIA, MUMMIAL.

mumle, mumm, obs. ff. MUMBLE, MUM.

Mumm (mʊm). The proprietary name of the champagne produced by the firm of Mumm in Rheims.

[**1851** C. REDDING *Hist. Mod. Wines* (ed. 3) vi. 106 The great complaint against Champagne wine has been that it cannot be obtained of a uniform quality... To remedy this evil..Mumm, Geisler & Co., at Rheims, provided tuns holding twelve thousand litres each.] **1885** *Christie's Auction Catal.* 18 Dec. 17 Three dozens of Champagne, 1868, Mumm. **1907** C. E. HAWKER *Chats about Wine* 87 Such names as Cliquot,..Mumm, Pommery, Roederer, etc., will occur to everyone as carrying with them a guarantee of high-class quality and excellence. **1928** E. WAUGH *Decline & Fall* v. 188 The wedding..was to take place in church with all the barbaric concomitants of bridesmaids, Mendelssohn and Mumm. **1967** 'L. BLACK' *Two Ladies in Verona* x. 161 A bottle of Mumm Cordon Rouge. I leave the year to you. **1975** J. SYMONS *Three Pipe Problem* xii. 87 'Glass of Mumm, delicious.'..'I shouldn't have thought you could have seen the name.' 'Only the corner of the label. The Mumm label is distinctive.'

mummachog, variant of MUMMYCHOG.

mummanize: see MUMMIANIZE *v.* *Obs.*

mummary(e, obs. forms of MUMMERY.

mumme, obs. form of MUM, MUMMY.

mummer (ˈmʌmə(r)), *sb.* Also 5 *Sc.* mumre, 5–6 mummar, 6–7 mommer. [a. OF. *momeur*, *-eor* (early mod.F. *mommeur* Cotgr.), f. *momer* (prob. of Teut. origin) = MUM *v.*]

†**1.** One who mutters or murmurs. *Obs.*

c **1440** *Promp. Parv.* 348/2 Mummar, *mussator*. *a* **1548** HALL *Chron.*, *Hen. V* 35b, A neglecter of my dutye, a secrete mummer of suche thynges whiche touche both the inheritance of your croune and the honor of your realme.

2. †An actor in a dumb show (*obs.*); one who takes a part in a mumming; *spec.* (see quot. 1829). Also *transf.* and *fig.*

1502 ARNOLDE *Chron.* (1811) 17 Outake mommers and our [? *read* other] mynstrels. **1511–12** *Act 3 Hen. VIII*, c. 9 §1 Persones..wyth Vysoures..disgysed or apparelde as Mommers. *c* **1550** BALE *K. Johan* (Camden) 17 And over all this ye have browght in a rabyll Of latyne mummers and sects desseyvabyll. *a* **1566** R. EDWARDS *Damon & Pithias* (1571) Cj b, As farre as I see they be Mummers, for nought they say, For the moste parte, what soeuer you aske them. **1648** *Hunting of Fox* 24 Like mommers in a mask, make a fair shew, but speak nothing. **1728** POPE *Dunc.* III. 108 Peel'd, patch'd, and pye-bald, linsey-woolsey brothers Grave mummers! sleeveless some, and shirtless others. **1829** J. HUNTER *Hallamsh. Gloss.* 67 *Mummers*. This is the name of parties of youths who go about at Christmas fantastically dressed, performing a short dramatic piece of which St. George is the hero. **1873** 'OUIDA' *Pascarel* I. 16 Some sporting of a band of mummers headed by a scarlet Mefistofelo.

b. *slang* and *contemptuously*. A 'play-actor'.

1840 CARLYLE *Heroes* vi. (1841) 369, I, for one, will not call the man a Hypocrite! Hypocrite, mummer, the life of him a mere theatricality..? **1861** [see MUMMING *vbl. sb.* 2 c]. **1895** J. HOLLINGSHEAD *My Lifetime* I. xv. 141 The poor played-out mummer..could not complete his task.

Hence **'mummerdom**, the theatrical world.

1893 K. GRAHAME *Pagan Ess.* 71 Our poor erring brothers and sisters..of Mummerdom.

mummer ('mʌmə(r)), *v.* [See MUMMER 2.] To take part in a mumming. So **'mummering** *vbl. sb.* = MUMMING *vbl. sb.* 2.

1884 F. MADAN in *Bodleian Libr. MS. Eng. Poet. c.* 17 39 Christmas mummering at Ducklington, Oxon. **1964** L. DIACK *Labrador Nurse* II. xiii. 70 From Christmas Day to Twelfth Night..was the season for 'Mummering' or 'Janny-ing'. There was much dressing up and disguising, and parties went round from house to house to entertain and have fun. **1969** L. J. CHIARAMONTE in Halpert & Story *Christmas Mumming in Newfoundland* 91 The single male mummer..does not always accept a drink at the houses he mummers in. **1969** WIDDOWSON & HALPERT in *Ibid.* 147 Disguise is a central element in Christmas mummering throughout Newfoundland.

Mummerset ('mʌməsɛt). Also **Mummersetshire.** [Modelled on *Somerset(shire)*, and perh. influenced by MUMMER.] An imaginary rustic county in the West of England, and its dialect, invented by actors.

1951 J. B. PRIESTLEY *Festival at Farbridge* II. ii. 219 'Az tew Papular Antertainment,' he drawled in his best Mummerset. **1952** GRANVILLE *Dict. Theatrical Terms* 120 An adviser on regional dialect helps the cast to reach a mean which has earned the jocular nickname *Mummersetshire*, or actor's dialect. **1957** [see HONESTLY *adv.* 2 b]. **1961** *Punch* 15 Mar. 411/2 Stage yokels from Mummerset. **1961** *Times* 19 June 13/4 How long must we wait for a dialect dictionary in one combined volume with pronunciations in Barsetshire and Mummerset? **1965** *Listener* 25 Oct. 640/3 The characters did speak real dialect, and not Mummerset. **1966** D. BLAKELOCK *Eleanor* x. 77 That exaggerated, bogus country dialect known to actors as 'Mummerset'. **1966** C. MACKENZIE *Paper Lives* viii. 114 Nowadays you can't be sure if they *are* eggs, even when somebody on television says they are in B.B.C. Mummerset. **1968** N. MARSH *Clutch of Constables* viii. 203, I sat in the Northumberland Arms.. listening to the dullest brand of Mummerset-type gossip. **1970** *Guardian* 26 Mar. 11/3 The straight English is often sloppy and soft; and throughout there is often a damp sprinkling of mummersetshire such as was never heard or spoken. **1971** *Times* 16 Feb. 10/2 Philip Grout's production selflessly follows the spirit of the piece: it is all Mummerset and wagging bottoms, slack jaws and graceless tussles. **1975** *Times Lit. Suppl.* 28 Feb. 220/2 Ordinary people in British war films became more than lovable Cockneys, Mummerset rustics, or Bunny Doyle Northerners full of blunt common sense.

mummery ('mʌmərɪ). Forms: 6 **mummary(e, mumry, momerie, -y, mommerye,** 6–7 **mummerie,** 6–8 **mommery,** 6– **mummery.** [a. OF. *mommerie*, F. *momerie* (= Sp. *momeria*, early mod.Du. *mommerije* Kilian, G. *mummerei*), f. *momeur* MUMMER *sb.*: see -Y.]

1. A performance of mummers. †*in mummery*, in fancy dress.

1530 PALSGR. 246/1 Mommery, *mommerie*. **1533** MORE *Debell. Salem* Wks. 975/1 This good man playeth as though he came in in a mummary, for any one worde he saith. **1565** JEWEL *Repl. Harding* (1611) 358 Their holy One of Rome.. burnt that most Reuerend Father D. Cranmer at Rome in a mummery. **1592** [KYD] *Sol. & Pers.* II. i. 191 Prouide me foure Visards, foure Gownes, a boxe, and a Drumme; for I intend to go in mummery. **1653** H. COGAN tr. *Pinto's Trav.* xxiii. 86 Divers mummeries of several inventions were represented. **1719** FENTON *Prol. to Southerne's Spartan Dame* 18 Your Fathers..Disdain'd the Mummery of Foreign Strollers. **1820** W. IRVING *Sketch Bk.* II. 130 *note*, Masquings or mummeries were favourite sports at Christmas in old times.

2. *transf.* Ridiculous ceremonial or 'play-acting'; an instance of this. Often applied to religious ritual regarded as silly or hypocritical.

1549 ALLEN *Jude's Par. Rev.* x. 1–4 Pompous byshops and monkyshe mumry. **1641** MILTON *Animadv.* Wks. 1851 III. 243 She's invisible under the lock and key of the Prelates.., they onely are..the go-betweens of this trim devis'd mummery. **1663** COWLEY *Ess. in Verse & Prose, Agric.* (1669) 101 The Heathen Religion, which consisted all in Mommery and Madness. **1749** FIELDING *Tom Jones* VIII. i, Elves and fairies, and other such mummery. **1773** BRYDONE *Sicily* xx. (1809) 206 There is so much nonsense and mummery in their worship, that they are afraid lest strangers should believe they are serious. **1828** MACAULAY *Ess., Hallam* (1897) 60 From this compromise the Church of England sprang... Her worship is not disfigured by mummery. **1836** HOR. SMITH *Tin Trump.* I. 14 What miserable mummery are private theatricals! **1864** BURTON *Scot Abr.* I. v. 278 Those rags of Popish mummeries which Elizabeth permitted to hang round the Reformation in England.

†**mumme-tree.** *Obs. rare*⁻¹. = *tree nightshade*: see NIGHTSHADE 2.

1629 PARKINSON *Parad.* 432 But some Latine asses corrupting the Latine word *Amomum*, doe call it the Mumme tree.

mummey, obs. form of MUMMY *sb.*[1]

†**'mummia.** *Obs.* Forms: α. 5 **momyan, momyn;** β. 6–7 **momia, mummia, mumma,** 6–9 **mumia.** [a. med.L. *mumia, momia*: cf. MUMMY.]

1. = MUMMY 1.

1486 *Bk. St. Albans* C iij, Take momyan oderwise called momyn, among Poticaries. **1583** *Rates Custom Ho.* D iij, Mumma the pound iiii d. **1594** PLAT *Jewell-ho.* I. 13 Their flesh so embalmed is called Mumia. **1612** WEBSTER *White Devil* I. i, Your followers Haue swallowed you like Mummia. **1619** BERT *Hawks* 106 If you will giue any thing else, let it be Mumma beaten into powder and so giuen with her meate. **1657** *Physical Dict.*, *Mumia*, a thing like pitch sold at the apothecaries; some affirm it's taken out of old tombs.

b. *transf.* and *fig.*

1601 B. JONSON *Poetaster* II. i, Looke here, my sweet wife; I am mum, my deare mummia, my balsamum, my spermacete. **1654** GAYTON *Pleas. Notes* III. ii. 71 Consolidating..his Body of Errantry into a gumme and moving Mummia.

2. (See quot.)

1841 MAUNDER *Sci. & Lit. Treas.*, *Mumia*, in mineralogy, a sort of bitumen, or mineral pitch, which is soft and tough, like shoemaker's wax, when the weather is warm, but brittle, like pitch, in cold weather. It is found in Persia, where it is highly valued.

3. = MUMMY *sb.*[1] 2 a.

1727–41 CHAMBERS *Cycl.* s.v. *Transplantation*, Here the patient's excrement is the magnet, and the vital spirit of the plant arising from the seed is the mumia which the magnet receives.

Hence †**'mummial** *a.*, of the nature of mummia.

1650 CHARLETON *Paradoxes* Prol. 13 The incomparable Balsamicall or Mumiall Virtue of vitriol. **1694** SALMON *Bate's Dispens.* (1713) 68/1 A Kind of Mummial Balsam.

†**'mummianize,** *v. Obs.* Also (? *erron.*) **mummanize.** [f. MUMMIA + -AN + -IZE. (Cf. *momyan*, 15th c. form of MUMMIA.)] *trans.* **a.** To embalm as a mummy. **b.** To transform to mummy. Hence **'mummianized** *ppl. a.*

1593 NASHE *Christs T.* Ep. Ded., A handfull of Ierusalems mummianized earth..I here..offer vp at your feete. **1613** J. DAVIES *Muses Teares* C 3 b, Deere Vault, that veil'st him, mummanize his Corse, Till it arise in Heauen to be crown'd. **1631** R. H. *Arraignm. Whole Creature* xi. §1. 99 A glorious Sepulcher, layd over with brasse,..yet within full of dead Sculs..and mummiamized [*sic*] Earth.

mummie, obs. form of MUMMY *sb.*[1]

mummied ('mʌmɪd), *a.* [f. MUMMY + -ED[1].]

1. Mummified; converted into a mummy.

1611 in *Coryat's Crudities* Panegyr. Verses, Thinke them happy when may be shewed for a penny..The mummied princes, and Cæsar's wine yet i' Dover. **1842** LYTTON *Zanoni* v. i, The mummied and royal dead. **1900** PETRIE *Dendereh* 59 *Cercopithecus sabæus* Linn. One mummied specimen.

2. *transf.* and *fig.*

1862 B. TAYLOR *Poet's Jrnl. 3rd Even.* Poems (1866) 50 Shelved around us lie The mummied authors.

3. Of a fruit: brown and dry as a result of brown rot disease, caused by a fungus of the genus *Sclerotinia*.

1909 B. M. DUGGAR *Fungous Diseases of Plants* xi. 190 These mummied fruits are the chief sources of infection the following season, under ordinary conditions. **1935** *Bull. Min. Agric. & Fish.* LXXXVIII. 1 A fruit so infected [with a fungus of the genus *Sclerotinia*], instead of disintegrating becomes dried up and 'mummied'.

mummification (mʌmɪfɪ'keɪʃən). [f. MUMMIFY *v.* (see -FICATION) after F. *momification*.]

1. The process of mummifying or the condition of being mummied. Also *fig.*

1800 tr. *Lagrange's Chem.* II. 430 Mummification, the means by which saints were fabricated, is a thing not uncommon. **1887** J. H. MCCARTHY in *Gentl. Mag.* Mar. 297 If indeed the epithet 'Chinese', as applied to such a condition of torpidity of mummification, be not an insult to the Celestial empire.

2. *Path.* A drying of the animal tissues.

1857 BULLOCK *Cazeaux' Midwif.* 251 At other times, it seems to have undergone a kind of mummification, a complete drying up. **1873** T. H. GREEN *Introd. Pathol.* (ed. 2) 11 The limb..may dry up..and become converted into a black shrunken mass, which undergoes but little further change:—this constitutes Dry Gangrene or Mummification.

mummified ('mʌmɪfaɪd), *a.* [f. MUMMIFY *v.* + -ED[1].] **1.** In senses of the verb.

1859 KINGSLEY *Misc.* (1860) II. 295 An old dry weather-bleared, mummified chrysalis of a man. **1863** READE *Hard Cash* III. 315 Creeping awestruck round that mummified figure seated dead on his pool of sovereigns. **1883** [see MUMMIFY *v.* 3]. **1905** *Athenæum* 21 Oct. 545/3 The mummified fauna of ancient Egypt. **1905** SIR F. TREVES *Other Side of Lantern* VI. iii. (1906) 416 Mummified shrubs which have still a semblance of life.

2. Of a fruit: = MUMMIED *a.* 3.

1928 F. T. BROOKS *Plant Diseases* xi. 143 In New Zealand apothecia [of *Sclerotinia laxa*] are only found where mummified fruits have been buried in hard, compact soil. **1973** H. MARTIN *Scientific Princ. Crop Protection* (ed. 6) xv. 537 For the control of the brown-rot of stone fruits (*Sclerotinia* spp.) the removal and burning of diseased twigs and mummified fruits is of great importance.

mummiform ('mʌmɪfɔːm), *a.* Also 9 **mumiform.** [ad. F. *mumiforme*, mod.L. *mumiformis* (Latreille), f. *mumia* MUMMY *sb.*: see -FORM.] Resembling, or shaped like, a mummy; *spec.* applied to the pupæ of the Lepidoptera.

1856 in MAYNE *Expos. Lex.* 728/2. **1887** A. B. EDWARDS *Maspero's Egypt. Archæol.* 279 The mummiform type of sarcophagus is rarely met with.

mummify ('mʌmɪfaɪ), *v.* [ad. F. *momifier* to make into mummy, f. *momie* MUMMY: see -FY.]

1. *trans.* To make into a mummy; to preserve (the bodies of animals) by embalming and drying. Also, to dry into the semblance of a mummy.

1628 WITHER *Brit. Rememb.* 44, I could bide Shut up untill my Flesh were Mummy-fi'd. **1794** BLUMENBACH in *Phil. Trans.* LXXXIV. 185 The practice of mummifying their dead bodies. **1883** STEVENSON *Silverado Sq.* 245, I came suddenly upon his innocent body, lying mummified by the dry air and sun: a pigmy kangaroo.

2. *transf.* and *fig.*

1646 J. HALL *Poems* 58 Thou..shalt more long remaine Still mummifi'd within the hearts of men. **1661** EVELYN *Fumifugium* I. 13 So corrosive is this Smoake about the City, that if one would hang up Gammons of Bacon..or other Flesh to fume,..it will so Mummifie, drye up, wast and burn it that it suddainly crumbles away. **1880** SAYCE in *Nature* 26 Feb. 406 Can anything, therefore, be more absurd than an endeavour to mummify an extinct phase of pronunciation.

3. *Path.* Of tissues or organs: To shrivel or dry up.

1883 J. COATS *Man. Pathol.* 750 In these cases the fœtus shrivels and becomes mummified... In the mummified fœtus the various tissues may be recognized years after. **1899** *Allbutt's Syst. Med.* VI. 587 Two-thirds of the palmar surface [of the index finger] were black and mummified.

Hence **'mummifying** *vbl. sb.* and *ppl. a.*

1836 J. M. GULLY *Magendie's Formul.* (ed. 2) 199 This substance might be the mummifying principle of pyroligneous acid. **1866** LAING *Preh. Rem. Caithn.* 42 Some highly artificial modes of interment, like mummyfying or burning.

mumming ('mʌmɪŋ), *vbl. sb.* Also 5 **mommyng(e,** 5–6 **mummynge,** 6 **mumminge,** *Sc.* **muming,** 7 **moming.** [f. MUM *v.* + -ING[1].]

†**1.** Inarticulate murmuring; indistinct speech.

c **1440** *Promp. Parv.* 348/2 Mummynge, *mussacio, vel mussatus*. **1573** TWYNE *Æneid* XI. Hh ij b, Scarse had the legates done, when mumblynge mumminge [orig. *varius fremor*] much doth rise.

2. The action of disguising oneself; *spec.* the action of taking part in the representation of a mummers' play. Chiefly in phr. *to go a mumming*. Also, a performance of mummers.

c **1465** *Eng. Chron.* (Camden) 20 The erlle of Salisbury, the erl of Gloucestre and othir mo of thair assent were accordid to make a mommyng to the Kyng. **1546** LANGLEY *Pol. Verg. De Invent.* v. ii. 100 b, The disguising and muming that is vsed in Christemas tyme..came oute of the feaste of Pallas. **1648** GAGE *West Ind.* 152 A goodly mumming and silent stage play. **1725** BOURNE in Brand *Pop. Antiq.* xvi. (1777) 191 There is another Custom observed at this Time, which is called among us Mumming. **1801** STRUTT *Sports & Past.* III. vi. 222 A sport common among the ancients..consisted in mummings and disguisements. **1864** BURTON *Scot Abr.* I. v. 309 While the children thus went a-mumming..the fathers took to drinking.

attrib. **1828** SCOTT *F.M. Perth* xi, How I am to convey her out of this crowd..in such a mumming habit.

b. *transf.* and *fig.* Often with contemptuous reference to religious ceremonial.

1528 TINDALE *Obed. Chr. Man* 69 b, They thinke that they have done abundauntly ynough for God..yif they be present once in a daye at soch mummynge. **1565** STAPLETON *Fortr. Faith* 132 They..practise in consecrated places their schismaticall mumming. **1848** KINGSLEY *Saint's Trag.* III. i. 168 'Tis no time for mumming.

c. (Cf. MUMMER *sb.* 2.)

1861 MAYHEW *Lond. Labour* III. 139/2 We call strolling acting 'mumming', and the actors 'mummers'. All spouting is mumming.

†**3.** *to make a mumming of*: to treat with levity or contempt. *Obs.*

1523 SKELTON *Garl. Laurel* 200 Men of suche maters make but a mummynge.

mumming ('mʌmɪŋ), *ppl. a.* [f. MUM *v.* + -ING[2].] That 'mums' in various senses of the verb.

1582 T. WATSON *Centurie of Loue* l, Fortune..Who like a mumming mate so throwes the Dice. **1602** *2nd Pt. Return fr. Parnass.* IV. ii. (Arb.) 56 And all the grisly sprights of griping hell, With mumming looke hath dogd thee since thy birth. **1851** JUDD *Margaret* I. xvi. (1874) 144 She enacted sundry grimaces, uttered mumming sentences. **1879** MCCARTHY *Own Times* I. xiii. 313 Their wild mumming way.

†'**mummish**, *a. Obs.* [f. MUM *sb.*[1] + -ISH. Cf. MOMISH.] Of the nature of mummery.

1563 *Homilies* II, *Receiv. Sacram.* I. 214 What hath ben the cause of this mummyshe massyng, but the ignoraunce hereof?

mummock ('mʌmək), var. of MAMMOCK *sb.* (see E.D.D.), a shred, scrap.

Used by Hood for the sake of a ludicrous rime to *stomach*.

1839 HOOD *On Pawning Watch* xi, I haven't a rag or a mummock To fetch me a chop or a steak.

mum-mumble (mʌm'mʌmb(ə)l).

Onomatopœic variant of MUMBLE *v.*, perhaps under the influence of MUM *v.*

1917 R. GRAVES *Fairies & Fusiliers* 75 From which the ancient poet was mum-mumbling A song about some Lovers at a Fair. **1956** H. GOLD *Man who was not with It* (1965) xxxi. 292 This was our first fret-fingered, mum-mumbling babe.

mummy ('mʌmɪ), *sb.*[1] Forms: 5-7 mum(m)ie, 6-7 mumme, 7 mum(m)ey, mummi, 7-8 mommy, 8 mumy, 7- mummy. [a. F. *momie*, †*mumie* (= Sp., Pg. *momia*, It. *mommia*), ad. med.L. *mumia*, a. Arab. *mūmiyā* an embalmed body, a mummy, f. *mūm* wax (used in embalming).]

1. a. A medicinal preparation of the substance of mummies; hence, an unctuous liquid or gum used medicinally. *Obs.* exc. *Hist.*

c **1400** *Lanfranc's Cirurg.* 153 Take..mirre, sarcocol, mummie [*v.r.* mumie] of ech ʒ. ss...& leie it on þe nucha. **1525** tr. *Jerome of Brunswick's Surg.* xciii. Riv, Take.. Mumie .vi. barley cornes heuy. **1599** HAKLUYT *Voy.* II. I. 201 And these dead bodies are the Mummie which the Phisitians and Apothecaries doe against our willes make vs to swallow. **1656** BLOUNT *Glossogr.*, *Mumie* or *Mummie*.. is digged out of the Graves..of those bodies that were embalmed, and is called Arabian Mummie. The second kind is onely an equal mixture of the Jews Lime and Bitumen [etc.]. **1727** SWIFT *Further Acc. Curll* Wks. 1755 III. I. 161 The mummy of some deceased moderator of the general assembly in Scotland to be taken inwardly as an effectual antidote against Antichrist. **1786** tr. *Beckford's Vathek* (1868) 43 My taste for dead bodies and every thing like mummy is decided.

†**b.** Used jocularly for: Dead flesh; body in which life is extinct. *Obs.*

1598 SHAKS. *Merry W.* III. v. 18 The water swelles a man; and what a thing should I haue beene, when I had beene swel'd? I should haue beene a Mountaine of Mummie. **1622** FLETCHER *Sea Voy.* III. i, You shall grow mumey rascals.

c. A pulpy substance or mass. Chiefly in *to beat*, etc., ***to a mummy*** (earlier, ***to mummy***).

1601 SIR W. CORNWALLIS *Disc. Seneca* (1631) 6, I believe the hanging of one man to worke better effect among men, then twenty made into mummy. **1736** AINSWORTH *Lat. Dict.*, To beat one to a mummy, *Pugnis* vel *plagis aliquem valde contundere*. **1747-96** MRS. GLASSE *Cookery* vi. 130 It must be very thick and dry, and the rice not boiled to a mummy. **1796** MORSE *Amer. Geog.* II. 680 The most horrible machines, calculated for grinding to mummy those unhappy criminals. **1834** *Tracts for Times* No. 22. 2 These little mountaineers [*viz.* Scotch ponies] got in at a weak place in the hedge..and trod the garden, as one may say, to a mummy. **1890** *Leeds Mercury* 28 May 5/7 John Crow.. stated that..her face appeared to be smashed to a 'mummy'.

d. *fig.*

1642 FULLER *Holy & Prof. St.* v. xvii. 426 Many men are murdered merely for their wealth, that other men may make mummey of the fat of their estates. **1790** BURKE *Fr. Rev.* Wks. V. 414 With these philosophick financiers, this universal medicine made of church mummy is to cure all the evils of the state.

†**e.** Dried or desiccated meat. *Obs.*

1672 JOSSELYN *New Eng. Rarities* 11 Our way..is to make Mummy of them [*sc.* Wobbles], that is, to salt them well, and dry them in an earthen pot well glazed in an Oven.

2. In various transferred or extended uses.

†**a.** A sovereign remedy. Also, in Paracelsus' use (see quot. 1727-41). *Obs.*

1598 SYLVESTER *Du Bartas* II. I. *Eden* 254 Or holy Nectar..Or blest Ambrosia..Or else Nepenthe..Or Mummie? or Elixir..? No, none of these. **1605** TIMME *Quersit.* III. 168 This worke is very admirable; by which the true numie [*read* mumie], the uniuersal medicine, and the true balsam conseruing and restoring nature, is made. **1658** J. ROBINSON *Endoxa* x. 52 Here was no mummie of the Wound, nor Mundane Soul required. **1671** BLAGRAVE *Astrol. Physic* 157 How by the Magnet of ones Body to extract a Spiritual Mummy whereby to cure most Diseases incident unto the body of Man. **1727-41** CHAMBERS *Cycl.*, *Mummy*, is also used by some physicians for I know not what implanted spirit, found chiefly in carcasses, when the infused spirit is fled. The infused spirit is sometimes also called mummy in living subjects.

b. A medicinal bituminous drug obtained from Arabia and the East.

1601 HOLLAND *Pliny* II. 183 Of Pissasphalt or Mummie. **1638** SIR T. HERBERT *Trav.* (ed. 2) 129 Most remarkable, is a precious liquor or mummy growing here... It distills (in June only) from the top of those stupendious mountaines every yeere about five ounces. **1727** A. HAMILTON *New Acc. E. Ind.* I. iii. 42 The Country, of itself, affords or produces very few valuable Commodities, besides Coffee, and some Drugs, such as Myrrh, ..some Gum Arabick and Mummy.

†**c.** *Gardening.* A kind of wax used in the transplanting and grafting of trees. *Obs.*

1721 BRADLEY *Philos. Acc. Wks. Nat.* 173, I have taken notice of a new invented Method of transplanting Trees with Safety, by means of a Vegetable Mummy. **1759** ELLIS in *Phil. Trans.* LI. 211 Gardeners grafting mummy, consisting of a mixture of bees-wax, rosin, and pitch. **1789** *Trans. Soc. Arts* (ed. 2) II. 97 Water..which mixing with the earth naturally adhering to their roots, forms of itself a kind of mummy.

d. A rich brown bituminous pigment.

1854 FAIRHOLT *Dict. Terms Art*, *Mummy*, a bituminous substance employed by painters as a rich brown tint... The better kinds of mummy form useful grey tints mixed with ultramarine [etc.]. **1885** J. S. TAYLOR *Field's Chromatogr.* 160 Mummy varies exceedingly in its composition and properties... It is only used as an oil-colour.

3. a. The body of a human being or animal embalmed (according to the ancient Egyptian or some analogous method) as a preparation for burial.

1615 G. SANDYS *Trav.* 133 The Mummes (lying in a place where many generations haue had their sepultures) not far above Memphis. **1650** BULWER *Anthropomet.* 167 The Egyptians..were wont of old to guild the nails of the Dead, as appears by their Mummies. *c* **1710** *Mack Gregory's Advt.* 2 The Burial-Places of the Mommies near Memphis. **1841** BELLAMY in *Rep. Brit. Assoc.* II. 75 Description of two Peruvian Mummies. **1900** PETRIE *Dendereh* 59 Mr. Thomas has kindly sent me the following identifications of the animal mummies from the catacombs. *Ibid.*, *Herpestes ichneumon* L. An imperfect mummy.

b. *transf.* and *fig.*

1668 DRYDEN *Albumazar* Prol. 29 These..Dare with the mummies of the Muses play, And make love to them the Egyptian way. **1844** KINGLAKE *Eöthen* vi. (1878) 85 A mere oriental, who for creative purposes is a thing dead and dry —a mental mummy. **1876** L. STEPHEN *Eng. Th. in 18th C.* II. XII. vii. 435 The old theological dogmas had become mere mummies.

c. A human or animal body desiccated by exposure to sun or air. Also applied to the frozen carcase of an animal imbedded in prehistoric ice.

1727-41 CHAMBERS *Cycl.* s.v. *Mummy*, There are two kinds of bodies denominated mummies.—The first are only carcasses, dried by the heat of the sun. **1866** BUCKLAND *Curios. Nat. Hist.* Ser. III. II. 47 Since then I saw..another guano mummy described..as follows:—'This mummy was brought to Liverpool from Possession Island, western coast of Africa [etc.]'. **1875** W. H. DALL in Beach *Indian Misc.* (1877) 349 Most of the [Alaskan] mummies were wrapped up in skins or matting.

d. *Stock Exchange slang pl.* Egyptian securities.

1903 *Westm. Gaz.* 17 Feb. 11/1 Certain prophets were busy over 'Mummies' months ago.

e. An apple, plum, or other fruit of the family Rosaceæ, made brown and desiccated by the brown rot disease caused by a fungus of the genus *Sclerotinia*.

1909 B. M. DUGGAR *Fungous Diseases of Plants* xi. 190 The fruit which has decayed may fall to the ground or hang upon trees, gradually shrinking with evaporation each to a crumpled dried mass, generally known as a mummy. **1952** E. RAMSDEN tr. *Gram & Weber's Plant Diseases* ii. 153/2 Similar mummies that have fallen and remained on or near the surface of the soil may very rarely produce clusters of small brown-stalked cup-shaped apothecia.

4. *attrib.* and *Comb.*: **a.** simple attrib., as ***mummy-dust***, ***-hunter***; (in sense 'mummified'), as ***mummy-matron***; **b.** similative, as ***mummy-dead***, ***mummy-like***, ***-looking***, ***-shaped*** adjs.; **c.** special comb.: **mummy brown**, a shade of brown akin to that of the pigment mummy; **mummy-case**, the case of wood or papier-mâché (usually decorated with hieroglyphics) in which Egyptian mummies were enclosed; also *fig.*; **mummy disease**, a disease of mushrooms of uncertain ætiology, indicated by the dying back of young plants, or the distorted shape and hardened gills of older ones; **mummy-pits** *pl.*, the catacombs in which the Egyptian mummies were interred; **mummy-wheat**, a variety of wheat cultivated in Egypt, and said to have been grown from grains found in mummy-cases.

1886 R. RIDGWAY *Nomenclature of Colors for Naturalists* II. 92 *Mummy Brown, a bright brown color, nearly intermediate in tint between burnt umber and raw umber. **1930** MAERZ & PAUL *Dict. Color* 168/1 *Mummy Brown*, R[idgway] has a color by this name, 15 c 8, which is simply a somewhat reduced tone of the pigment known as 'mummy'. *a* **1936** KIPLING *Something of Myself* (1937) i. 13 A tube of 'Mummy Brown'. **1949** *Dict. Colours for Interior Decoration* (Brit. Colour Council) III. 18/2 Mummy Brown, see Clove Brown. **1830** GEN. P. THOMPSON *Exerc.* (1842) I. 274 The sermon would have been in its right place, if it had been found in a *mummy-case. **1922** JOYCE *Ulysses* 191 Coffined thoughts around me, in mummy cases, embalmed in spice of words. **1922** L. MUMFORD *City Devel.* (1946) i. 9 What remained of the provincial town in New England was a mummy-case. **1939** W. B. YEATS *Last Poems* 20 Everything else withered and *mummy-dead. **1942** TUCKER & ROUTIEN in *Res. Bull. Missouri Agric. Exper. Station* No. 358. 3 The common name '*mummy disease' was suggested by Dr. [A. M.] Klingman. It is quite appropriate for the symptoms that develop in white strains or varieties, and with Dr. Klingman's permission, will be used here. **1950** R. L. O. JACKSON *Mushroom Growing* vii. 66 The Americans have a similar disease called Mummy Disease, which spreads at an alarming rate, and which they think is caused by a virus, but so far this is of doubtful occurrence in this country. **1969** R. GENDERS *Mushroom Growing for Everyone* xiv. 198 Mummy disease. For long this has been a source of worry to American growers but only since 1950 has it become known to British growers. **1922** E. SITWELL *Facade* 13 When the moon's hurdy-gurdy wheeze Grinds out her slow *mummy-dust. **1738** *Common Sense* II. 267 The Expence the Nation is at..for maintaining our Foreign Ministers, Travellers, and *Mummy-Hunters. **1807-8** W. IRVING *Salmag.* (1824) 86 A trio of as odd, runty, *mummy-looking originals as ever Hogarth fancied. **1624** MIDDLETON *Game at Chess* IV. ii, To three olde *Mummey-Matrons, I haue promis'd The Mother-ship 'oth Maids. **1645** EVELYN *Diary* 5 Aug., The Captaine presented me with a stone he lately brought from Grand Cairo, which he tooke from the *Mummy-pitts. **1841** EMERSON *Ess.* Ser. I. i. (1876) 17 Belzoni digs and measures in the mummy-pits and pyramids of Thebes. **1842** TUPPER in *Literary Gaz.* 18 June 425/1 As you took so lively an interest in my resuscitated *mummy-wheat.

Hence (*nonce-wds.*) '**mummydom**, '**mummyhood**, the condition of being a mummy.

1796 H. WALPOLE *Let. to Miss Berry* 24 Aug., I..shall remain, I believe, in my mummyhood. **1888** MRS. LYNN LINTON *Thro' Long Night* I. iv, His strange old-world way, vivified from mummydom only by excessive embarrassment.

mummy ('mʌmɪ), *sb.*[2] Formerly *dial.* Also **mummie.** [Childish alteration of MAMMY[1]. Cf. MUM *sb.*[3]] **1.** A child's word for mother.

1784 J. CULLUM *Hist. Hawsted* iii. 172 *Mummy*, corrupted from mamma. **1839** C. CLARK *J. Noakes & Mary Styles* 26 Wor I to 'list My mummy, how 'tood shock her! **1898** *Eliz. & Germ. Gard.* (1899) 51 'What a funny mummy!' she said, evidently much amused. **1903** *Punch* 30 Sept. 231 Mummy dear, of course Uncle Jack is coming to meet us by a Circle Train, isn't he? **1914** 'BARTIMEUS' *Naval Occasions* ix. 68 Thank you, mummie darling. **1933** E. A. ROBERTSON *Ordinary Families* ii. 39 'Mummy, did you put in my straw hat?' came Marnie's adenoidal whine from upstairs. 'Oh, mummy, you always say yes. Sure you did? Mum*mee*!' **1974** M. PENOYRE *Breach of Security* v. 26 Oh, mummy, you're going out... I'd hoped you were going to..read me a story.

2. Phr. **mummy's boy** = *mother's boy* (MOTHER *sb.*[1] 16 a).

1927 E. BOWEN *Hotel* xv. 177 None of us seem to be making much impression on young Ronald... Did you ever see such a Mummy's boy! **1945** E. TAYLOR *At Mrs Lippincote's* xxi. 180 What a mummy's boy Norman sounds. **1967** 'H. CALVIN' *Nice Friendly Town* iv. 49 'Are you a mummy's boy?' 'No,' I said 'but she's a sonny's mum.' **1968** 'P. HOBSON' *Titty's Dead* xv. 152 You're not a man at all. Just a mummy's boy. **1975** W. J. BURLEY *Wycliffe* xi. 173 'What sort of boy was he?'..'Quiet. A bit of a mummy's boy.'

†'**mummy**, *a. Obs.* [f. MUM *sb.* + -Y.]

? Resembling mum; thick.

1743 *Lond. & Country Brew.* III. (ed. 2) 238 To recover thick, mummy Drink that is acid... Rack a Vessel of mummy Beer into two Casks, and fill them up with new Beer brewed not so strong and it is a Cure.

mummy ('mʌmɪ), *v.* [f. MUMMY *sb.*[1]] *trans.* To mummify; to make into a mummy. Also *transf.* and *fig.*

1620 SHELTON *Quix.* (1746) III. i. 2 Whom they found.. so dry'd and withered up, as if his flesh had been mummy'd. **1842** MRS. BROWNING *Grk. Chr. Poets* iv, It is better..to think out one true thought..than to mummy our benumbed souls with the circumvolutions of twenty thousand books. **1866** BUCKLAND *Curios. Nat. Hist.* Ser. III. I. 125 Your lifeless..carcases mummied in ice and lying in marble state on fishmongers' slabs. **1880** *Atlantic Monthly* Aug. 252 The Egyptians mummied all sorts of sacred brutes, including bulls, cats and crocodiles.

mummy apple, var. *mammee-apple* (MAMMEE 3).

mummychog ('mʌmɪtʃɒg). *U.S.* Also 9 **mumma-**, **mummichog.** [American Indian; a plural form, spelt *moamitteaug* in Roger Williams's Narragansett vocabulary (1643).] = KILLIFISH.

1787 PENNANT *Suppl. Arct. Zool.* 149 Inhabits New York, where it is known by the Indian name of Mummy Chog. **1859** BARTLETT *Dict. Amer.*, *Mummachog* (genus *Fundulus*), the popular name of the Barred Killifish of naturalists. **1884** GOODE, etc. *Nat. Hist. Aquatic Anim.* 449 The fishermen there [*sc.* on the Connecticut coast] call them [*sc.* mullets] by the name of 'Bluefish Mummichog'.

'**mummy-cloth.**

1. The cloth in which Egyptian mummies were wrapped.

1843 WATHEN *Arts, Antiq. & Chronol. Egypt* 143 Painted mummy-cloths, scarabei [etc.].

2. *U.S.* Used as a trade name for certain modern fabrics more or less resembling the material used for mummy-cloths. Also *momie-cloth* and *ellipt.*

1881 C. C. HARRISON *Woman's Handiwork* I. 46 (*heading*) Raw silk momie cloth, for draperies,..fifty inches wide, at $3.50... Cotton momie cloth..in all the new shades for $1.10,..Basket momie cloth, in woollen, costs $3. **1886** *Ann. Rep. Smithsonian Inst.* (1889) II. 652 Mummy cloth. **1890** in *Century Dict.* **1895** *Montgomery Ward Catal.* 4/2 Blade Crepon..similar to Momie or Armure. **1960** CUNNINGTON & BEARD *Dict. Eng. Costume* 264/2 *Momie cloth*,..of cotton or silk warp and woollen weft, resembling a fine crepe; usually black and used for mourning.

mummyll, obs. Sc. form of MUMBLE.

mump (mʌmp), *sb.* and *a.* Also 6-7 **mumpe.** [Symbolical of the movements of the lips made in pronouncing the word. Cf. MUMP *v.* and MUM *int.*

With sense 1 cf. Icel. *mumpaskælur* grimace with the mouth, *mumpr* curly beard (Björn Halldórson).]

A. *sb.*

†**1.** A grimace, 'mouth'. *Obs.*

1592 Nashe *P. Penilesse* 22 b, Now he is no body that cannot drinke..with leapes, gloues, mumpes, fro[l]ickes, and a thousand such dominiering inuentions. **1611** Cotgr., *Monnoye de Singe*, Moes, mumps, mouthes. **1635** [Glapthorne] *Lady Mother* I. i. in Bullen *O. Pl.* II. 106 Gallants now court their Mistress with mumps & mows as apes and monkes doe.

2. *pl.* **mumps** (now construed as *sing.*). An acute specific contagious disease characterized by inflammation and swelling of the parotid and salivary glands.

1598 Florio, *Recchione*, a disease or swelling in the necke called the mumps. **1758** Gooch *Cases Surg.* 17 A Species of tumor called by the common people the Mumps. **1864** J. Martineau in *Nat. Rev.* Nov. 274 The contagion of chickenpox and mumps.

3. *pl.* A fit of melancholy or ill-humour; 'sulks'.

1599 Nashe *Lenten Stuffe* 45 The sunne was so in his mumps vppon it, that it was almost noone before hee could goe to cart that day. **1671** Skinner *Etymol. Ling. Angl.* s.v., He has the Mumps, *pro Irasci, Indignari tacitâ præsertim Iracundiâ.* **1861** *Under the Spell* III. 109, I keep Kitty from getting the 'mumps'.

4. A block of peat.

1951 B. Lawrence *Somerset Jrnl.* 62 The blackish brown peat is cut in large slabs, called mumps. **1953** A. Jobson *Household & Country Crafts* vii. 84 Each piece of peat was cut to a uniform size. One man cut the blocks or 'mumps', and another carried them away to dry. **1962** *Amateur Gardening* 5 May 1/4 A 'mump' is a block of peat 10 in × 9 in × 9 in.

†**B.** *adj.* ? Drunk.

1599 Porter *Angry Wom. Abingt.* (Percy Soc.) 48 What though he be mump, misled, blind, or as it were?

mump (mʌmp), *v.*[1] [Related to mump *sb.*

Cf. Icel. *mumpa* to take into the mouth, eat greedily (Björn Halldórsson), Norw. *mumpa* to fill the mouth too full, to mumble (in eating), Du. *mompelen* (rarely poet. *mompen*) to mumble (in utterance), early mod.G. *mumpfen, mumpfelen* to mumble (in eating).]

†**1.** *trans.* To utter with imperfect articulation, as a toothless person; to mumble, mutter. Also with *out*. *Obs.*

a **1586** Sidney *Arcadia* iv. (1622) 407 Mumping out her hoarse chafe, shee gaue him the wooden salutation you heard of. **1694** 'Musophilus' *Posie for Lovers* 5 The Godly Bedlam..Mump't out her Scorn, and grumbled Holy Words. **1773** Goldsm. *She Stoops to Conq.* Epil., Old men, whose trade is Still to gallant and dangle with the ladies, Who mump their passion.

2. *intr.* †**a.** To grimace with the lips; to grin. Also *transf.* and *fig.* *Obs.*

1589 *Pappe w. Hatchet* Lyly's Wks. 1902 III. 406/7, I will make him mumpe, mow, and chatter. **1664** Cotton *Scarron.* I. 50 Venus, at that, wrigling and mumping, Cries, pray young man, leave of your frumping. **1719** D'Urfey *Pills* VI. 198 She [*sc.* a rabbit] mumps like an Ape. **1754** Richardson *Grandison* (1781) VI. ix. 33 Aunt Nell.. chuckled and mumped for joy.

b. To assume a demure or melancholy expression of countenance (see mumping *ppl. a.*); to be silent and sullen; to sulk, mope. *arch.* Also † *to mump it.*

c **1610** *Lady Compton* in Grose & Astle *Antiq. Rep.* (1808) III. 438, I would have two Gentlewomen... It is an indecent thing for a Gentlewoman to stand mumping alone, when God have blessed their Lord and Lady with a great Estate. **1675** Han. Woolley *Gentlewoman's Comp.* 69 Do not mump it, mince it, nor bridle the head, as if you either disliked the meat, or the company. **1825** Scott *Betrothed* xvii, These antiquated dames went mumping about with much affected indifference. **1837** T. Hook *Jack Brag* vi, How would you like to sit moping and mumping all alone. **1883** Stevenson *Lett.* (1901) I. vi. 304 It is better to enjoy a novel than to mump.

3. a. *intr.* To mumble with the gums; to move the jaws as if mumbling food; to munch, nibble. Also const. *at, on, upon*. *Obs.* exc. *dial.*

1596 Nashe *Saffron-Walden* Ded. C 3, Spend but a quarter so much time in mumping vppon Gabrielisme. **1615** J. Taylor (Water P.) *Urania* xlix. Wks. (1630) I. 5/2 When hee's..Not a tooth left to mumpe on beanes and pease: Then this Companion..Will let thee haue this Palfray. **1629** Davenant *Albovine* iv. i, Were my lean Jaws unmuffled you should see me mump, like a Matron that had lost her teeth. **1748** Smollett *Rod. Rand.* (1760) I. xi. 67 When he mumped or spoke, they [*sc.* his nose and chin] approached one another like a pair of nut-crackers. **1880** J. Nicol *Poems & Songs* 167 Jack and Pat, and Owen and Sandy, Mumping and crumping away at the candy.

†**b.** *trans.* To chew with toothless gums, or turn over and over in the mouth. *Obs.*

1599 Nashe *Lenten Stuffe* 47 Down she sunk to the ground, as dead as a door naile, and neuer mumpt crust after. **1818** Mrs. Sherwood *Fairchild Fam.* xxv, Miss Puss stood..mumping her parsley, after the manner of hares. **1838** *Fraser's Mag.* XVII. 117 Here, Doctor, mump it with satisfied tooth.

mump (mʌmp), *v.*[2] *colloq.* (orig. *slang.*) [prob. a. Du. *mompen* to cheat; connexion with prec. is doubtful. Sense 2 may belong to mump *v.*[1]]

†**1.** *trans.* To overreach, cheat. Const. *of, out of.* Also, 'to disappoint' (Phillips, ed. Kersey, 1706).

Very common in the second half of the 17th c.

1651 *Fuller's Abel Rediv., Colet* (1867) I. 124 Intending thereby to mump Colet, who..never wrote a verse in his life. **1668** Kirkman *Eng. Rogue* ii. xvi. 143 No sooner had I ended my Maunding, thinking to mump the Farmer out of some money,..but he [etc.]. **1676** Wycherley *Gent. Dancing Master* iv. (1735) 84 He is..some debauched person, who will mump you of your daughter. **1682** Mrs. Behn *City Heiress* 59 How finely I had been mumpt now, if I had not shew'd your Ladyship trick for trick. *a* **1734** North *Exam.* I. ii. §150 They..let Indictments go, depending on the Petit-Jury for the Acquittal..but, in that also, they were mumped, as will appear.

2. a. *intr.* To beg; †to play the parasite, to 'sponge' on others. **b.** *trans.* To obtain by begging or 'sponging'. **c.** To visit (a house) in the course of a begging round.

1673 [Implied in mumper]. **1685** F. Spence *House of Medici* 251 His..Presupposition, That they were so earnest for admittance, onely to mump [orig. *mandier*] the onely Voice they wanted for him. **1706** Phillips (ed. Kersey), To *Mump*,..to beg, to spunge upon. **1728** *Brice's Weekly Jrnl.* (Exeter) 27 Sept., Some of the Villains..had the no Conscience to rob a..Beggar-woman of a few Half-pence she had been mumping. **1738** Weddell *Voy. up Thames* 86 A giddy Heir..who is often glad to mump a Dinner of which Nature had ordained him the Giver. **1808** E. S. Barrett *Miss-led General* 37 Was it becoming the sons of the lord of the Manor to go..mumping from their tenants, to relieve an irreclaimable spendthrift? **1855** Macaulay *Hist. Eng.* xiv. IV. 260 One prince came mumping to them annually with a lamentable story about his distresses. **1866** *Temple Bar* XVII. 183 Having 'mumped' a small shop and several private houses.

mumper ('mʌmpə(r)). *Obs.* exc. *dial.* or *slang.* (See E.D.D.) [f. mump *v.*[2] + -er[1].]

A beggar, mendicant. Also, †one who 'sponges' on others.

1673 R. Head *Canting Acad.* 79 *Mumpers* are both Male and Female, a Gentiler sort of Beggars, for they scorn to beg for food, but money or cloaths. **1690** *Secret Hist. Chas. II & Jas. II* 69 The Commons..readily voted the Royal Mumper no less than one million two hunder'd and fifty thousand Pounds. **1736** Ainsworth *Lat. Dict.*, A mumper of a dinner, *Parasitus, cœnipeta.* **1755** *Mem. Capt. P. Drake* iii. 25, I..from a Mumper at Cottages became a Guest at the best Inns. **1766** H. Walpole *Lett.* 9 Feb. (1892) IV. 476 It is below such a nation as England to trouble its head whether an old mumper at Rome calls a wretched fugitive *Rè d' Inghilterra* or *Principe di Galles.* **1882** *Sydney Slang Dict.* 6/1 *Mumper*, beggar. **1967** *Economist* 30 Sept. 1172/1 This is the total number of 'travellers'—Romanies; mixed-blood 'past-rats' and 'didcois'; 'mumpers', who have no Romany blood; and (mostly Irish) tinkers—recorded by a Ministry of Housing census. **1972** *Countryman* Autumn 86 Beside the gypsies there are many other pickers—tramps, mumpers, all sorts.

mumping ('mʌmpɪŋ), *vbl. sb.*[1] *Obs.* exc. *dial.* [f. mump *v.*[1] + -ing[1].] The action of grimacing.

1611 Cotgr., *Minauderies*, foolish trickes, apish pranks, mumpings, mowings. **1721** Kelly *Scot. Prov.* 183, I know your meaning, by your mumping. *a* **1734** North *Exam.* I. iii §46 We are to understand his Meaning by his Mumping.

'**mumping,** *vbl. sb.*[2] [f. mump *v.*[2] + -ing[1].] Begging. ***mumping-day*** (see quot. 1817).

1694 Motteux *Rabelais* iv. xiii, He spyed Tickletoby afar off, coming home from mumping. **1816** Dunkin *Hist. Bicester* 270 The..singular custom..on the morrow after Christmas-day,..usually denominated *Mumping*. **1817** Fosbroke *Brit. Monachism* 74 St. Thomas's Day. On this day, called Mumping-day, the poor in Herefordshire go around the parishes, begging corn, &c.

mumping ('mʌmpɪŋ), *ppl. a.*[1] [f. mump *v.*[1] + -ing[2].] In senses of the verb: †Mumbling, toothless (*obs.*); grimacing, assuming a demure, sanctimonious, or miserable aspect of countenance.

1594 Nashe *Terrors of Night* Wks. (Grosart) III. 255 Aged mumping beldams. **1611** Cotgr., *Morgue*,..the mumping aspect of one that would seeme grauer then he is. *a* **1720** Sheffield (Dk. Buckhm.) *Wks.* (1753) I. 78 Puss transform'd, sat like a mumping bride. **1797** Burke *Regic. Peace* iii. Wks. VIII. 274 Our embassy 'of shreds and patches' with all its mumping cant. **1820** Lamb *Elia* I. *Two Races of Men*, To say *no* to a poor petitionary rogue (your bastard borrower) who, by his mumping visnomy, tells you, that he expects nothing better. **1826** Hood *Last Man* 109 But the beggar man made a mumping face, And knocked at every gate. **1869** Lowell *Cathedral* 647 Superannuate forms and mumping shams.

'**mumping,** *ppl. a.*[2] [f. mump *v.*[2] + -ing[2].] Begging.

1829 Lytton *Disowned* 8 And wherever we rove, we feed on the cove Who gibes at the mumping crew. **1883** G. A. Sala in *Illustr. Lond. News* 17 Nov. 475/3 Although the tramp when hard pressed solicits alms or food, he is not a 'mumping' or professional beggar.

mumpish ('mʌmpɪʃ), *a.* [f. mump *sb.* or *v.*[1] + -ish.] Sullenly angry; depressed in spirits.

1721 Bailey, *Mumpish*, angry, and silent withal. **1846** E. B. Barrett in *Lett. R. Browning & E. B. B.* (1899) II. 491 Mumpish! The expression proved a displeasure. Yet I am sure that I have shown as little sullenness as was possible.

Hence '**mumpishly** *adv.* (Webster 1847–54). '**mumpishness** (Bailey, vol. II. 1727).

†**mumps.** *Obs.* [? Short for mumpsimus 1 b; or connected with mump *v.*[1] 3.] A term of contempt or mock endearment for a woman.

1598–9 B. Jonson *Case is Altered* ii. ii, Diuine Mumps, prety Pastorella. *a* **1616** Beaum. & Fl. *Scornf. Lady* v. i, Not such another as I was, Mumps; nor will not be. **1695** tr. *Martial* ii. xli. 106 Weep, if you're prudent, old mumps.

mumps: see mump *sb.*

†**mumpsick,** *a.* *Obs.* *rare*[−0]. [f. mump *sb.* + sick *a.*] Having erysipelas.

1599 Minsheu *Span. Dict.*, *Esipulado*, mumpsicke

mumpsimus ('mʌmpsɪməs). [In allusion to the story (in R. Pace *De Fructu*, 1517, p. 80) of an illiterate English priest, who when corrected for reading 'quod in ore *mumpsimus*' in the Mass, replied, 'I will not change my old mumpsimus for your new sumpsimus'.]

†**1.** One who obstinately adheres to old ways, in spite of the clearest evidence that they are wrong; an ignorant and bigoted opponent of reform. *Obs.*

1530 Tindale *Pract. Prelates* H v, The chauncelars of englond..which be all lawers and other doctoures mumsimusses of diuinyte were called vpp sodenlye to dispute the mater. **1553** Underhill in *Narr. Reform.* (Camden Soc.) 141 Yff yow loke amonge the pristes in Poolles, ye shall fynde some old mumsymussis ther.

¶**b.** Used as a vague term of contempt: An 'old fogey'. ? Also = mumps. (In quots. 1596 and 1691 app. associated with mump *v.*[1]) *Obs.*

1575 Gascoigne *Posies, Supposes* ii And if this olde Mumpsimus..should win hir, then may I say,..farewel the sight of my Polynesta. **1596** Lodge *Wits Miserie* 37 The next of this progenie is Vnlawfull lucre, looke what a handsome Mumpsimus shee is, will you know her profession? **1691** Shadwell *Scowrers* i. i, *Eugenia*. [To Priscilla, her governess.] Did she so, old mumpsimus. [Cf. *ibid.*, Mutter no more under thy Gums, old Sybil.] **1815** *Zeluca* I. 336 He showed me into a room with some mumpsimuses.

2. A traditional custom or notion obstinately adhered to however unreasonable it is shown to be.

1545 Hen. VIII *Parl. Sp.* 24 Dec. in Hall *Chron., Hen. VIII* (1550) 261 b, Some be to styff in their old *Mumpsimus*, other be to busy and curious in their newe *Sumpsimus*. **1669** Penn *No Cross* ii. §9 (1682) 35 A by-rote *Mumpsimus*, a dull and insipid Formality, made up of corporal bowings and Cringings. **1862** Keble in Liddon, etc. *Pusey* (1897) IV. i. 25, I still hold to my old mumpsimus that the Prayer Book being what it is we cannot be unchurched by mere abuse or default of discipline.

3. *attrib.*, quasi-*adj.* Stupidly conservative.

1680 R. Bolron *Narrative* 9 The Jesuits..are the most Zealous for the propagation of their Religion in their old Mumpsimus Way. **1821** Syd. Smith *Wks.* (1859) I. 330/2 All the fat and sleek people..the mumpsimus, and 'well as we are' people, are perfectly outrageous at being compelled to do their duty.

mumry, obs. form of mummery.

mums (mʌmz), shortened form of mumsy *sb.* and *a.*

1939 L. M. Montgomery *Anne of Ingleside* xxix. 195 It is God who makes everything beautiful, but we can help Him out a bit, can't we, Mums? **1942** J. Cary *To be Pilgrim* cxviii. 254 'How are you really, Johnny?'..'Very hungry, Mums darling.' **1942** T. Bailey *Pink Camellia* ii. 18 Say you don't hate me, Mums. **1948** D. Ballantyne *Cunninghams* 8 Dear Mums, I received your ever welcome letter. **1968** 'R. Llewellyn' *End of Rug* (1969) xv. 123 You were always the tough one, Dads... I think I've got more of Mums. She'd cry over a hurt dog.

mumschance, obs. form of mumchance *sb.*

mumsy ('mʌmzɪ), *sb.* and *a.* Also **mumsey**. [f. mum *sb.*[3] + -sy.] **A.** *sb.* A playful variant of mummy *sb.*[2] **B.** *adj.* = maternal *a.* (a playful use).

1876 C. M. Yonge *Three Brides* I. xvi. 274 'Well,' says Mumsey, 'it is not what was thought the thing for ladies in my time.' **1916** *Farmer's Wife* Mar. 248/1 'Dear old motherkins!' 'Good old Mumsy!' **1927** M. Ostenso *Mad Carews* (1928) vii. 93 'Hello, Mumsey!' she greeted her mother. **1953** A. Christie *Pocket Full of Rye* xxvii. 184 Poor Mumsy, she was so devoted to Dad, you know. **1961** 'T. Hinde' *For Good of Company* i. 15 They're all three tucked up in one great big mumsy bed. **1970** 'W. Haggard' *Hardliners* vi. 64 The nurse..was a West Indian woman, large and mumsy. **1972** J. McClure *Caterpillar Cop* ii. 16 To hell with them and all that crap about mumsy-love.

mumu, var. muu-muu.

mun, *sb.*[1] *dial.* and *slang.* Also 7 munne, 7–9 munn, 8–9 mund. [a. ON. *munn-r*: see mouth *sb.* Cf. mompyns, munpynnys.] **a.** *dial.* The mouth (see E.D.D.). **b.** *slang. pl.* The jaws, 'chops', face.

13.. *E.E. Allit. P.* C. 44 Much maugre his mun, he mot nede suffer. **1665** R. Head *Eng. Rogue* I. iv, *Munns*, the Face. **1760** Foote *Minor* I (1767) 31 Why, you jade, you look as rosy this morning, I must have a smack at your muns. **1847** Halliwell s.v., A common cry at Coventry on Good Friday is—One a penny, two a penny, hot cross buns, Butter them and sugar them and put them in your muns. **1859** Matsell *Vocabulum* (Farmer), *Mund*. The mouth. *Munds*. The face.

†**mun,** *sb.*[2] *Obs.* *rare*[−1]. One of a class of street-ruffians in the seventeenth century.

1691 Shadwell *Scowrers* I. i. 3 Why I knew the Hectors, and before them the Muns and the Titire Tu's, they were brave fellows indeed. **1849** Macaulay *Hist. Eng.* iii. I. 361.

mun, *v.* *north.* and *midl.* Forms: *Pres. ind. sing.* and *pl.* 3– mun, 3–6 (9 *dial.*) mon, mone, 6 monn, moun. *Pres. subj.* 3 mune. *Pa. t.* 3 (Ormin) munnde, 3–5 mund(e, mond(e, (4 muond). See also maun. [a. ON. *monu, munu* (1st and 3rd sing. *mon, mun*, 1st pl. *monum, munum*; pa. t. *munda*), a preterite-pres. verb used as an auxiliary of the future tense = shall, will. The prehistoric sense was doubtless 'to intend' (Indo-Germanic root *men-*: *mon-*: *mn-* to think: see MIND *sb.*); ON. has a slightly differentiated form (inf. *mona, muna*) with the sense 'to remember': see MONE *v.*

In ON. the pres. sing. has a variant *man*: see MAUN *v.* In mod. Eng. dialects the pa. t. appears to be represented by *mud*, coincident in form with a frequent unstressed variant of the past tense of MAY *v.*; the two auxiliaries have therefore partly coalesced in the pa. t.

The combination of *mun* with a negative has various contracted forms, the most frequent being *mon't* (məʊnt). See E.D.D. s.vv. *Mud, Mun.*]

An auxiliary verb, followed by inf. without *to*. In mod. dialects equivalent to 'must'; in early use sometimes with the sense 'shall' (pa. t. = 'should', 'would').

c **1200** ORMIN 1967 Forr ȝiff mann mihhte wurrþenn warr þatt ȝho wiþþ childe wære,.. ȝho munnde affterr þe laȝheboc To dæþe ben istanedd. *Ibid.* 7927 Forr iwhillc mann birrþ ..beon.. offdredd, þatt all hiss gode dede Ne mune himm nohht beon god inoh To berrȝhenn himm fra pine. *a* **1300** *Cursor M.* 1105 þai thoght þat kynd him mond forbede To haf don suilk an ogli dede. *c* **1300** *Havelok* 840, I wene that we deye mone For hunger, þis dere is so strong. *a* **1350** *St. Laurence* 231 in Horstm. *Altengl. Leg.* (1881) 110 Decius þan him umbi-thoght How saint Laurence munde be schent. *c* **1420** *Avow. Arth.* xxiv, And thou mun pay my rawunsun, Gawan, with thi leue. *c* **1440** *Alphabet of Tales* 5 For þan I monde make mekull sorow. *a* **1553** UDALL *Royster D.* 4th Song (Arb.) 87, I mun be maried a Sunday. **1598** B. JONSON *Ev. Man in Hum.* I. i, Slid a gentleman mun show himselfe like a gentleman. **1688** SHADWELL *Sq. Alsatia* I. i. 5 What will awd Maaster say to this? I mun ne'er see the Face of him I wot. *a* **1721** PRIOR *Song* (1st line), Since, Moggy, I mun bid adieu, How can I help despairing? **1864** TENNYSON *North. Farmer* (*Old Style*) xvii, An' if I mun doy I mun doy.

b. with ellipsis of a vb. of motion.

c **1435** *Torr. Portugal* 1113 Sir, he said, I trow, she mone To the prynce off Aragon. *c* **1475** *Rauf Coilȝear* 425 Thow mon to Paris to the King.

mun, dial. var. *mon, man*: see MAN *sb.*[1] 4 e.

mun, *pronoun* (= them, him, it, etc.): see E.D.D.

mun, variant of MONE *v. Obs.*, remember.

mun: see MON[3], MUN.

munc, obs. form of MONK.

†**Mun'cerian.** *Obs.* Also 6 **Munseran**. [ad. mod.L. *Munceriān-us*, f. the name of *Muncerus* or Münzer.] One of the sect of Anabaptists, which arose in Germany under Thomas Münzer in 1521.

c **1559** R. HALL *Life Fisher* (1655) 222 From you are sprung Zuinglius, Munserans, or Patimontans, and a number of Hereticks mo. **1560** DAUS tr. *Sleidane's Comm.* 57 The madness of the Muncerians. **1727-41** CHAMBERS *Cycl.* s.v. *Anabaptists.*

munch (mʌn(t)ʃ), *sb.* [f. MUNCH *v.*] **a.** An act of munching. **b.** Something to eat; a meal (*dial.* and *jocular*).

a **1816** T. THOMPSON *Canny Newcastle* 53 Wiv a' the stravagin aw wanted a munch. **1897** BLACKMORE *Dariel* xlvii, The unfortunate starver.. tore the cake from Cator. In a moment it was gone, almost without a munch.

munch (mʌn(t)ʃ), *v.* Forms: 4-6 **monche**, 6 **manche**, 6-7 **mounch(e**, (9 **mounch**), 7-8 **maunch**, 6- **munch**. [App. onomatopœic (cf. CRAUNCH, CRUNCH); possibly suggested partly by MANGE *v.*]

1. *trans.* To eat with continuous and noticeable action of the jaws. Said of persons audibly masticating food which offers resistance to the teeth, and of cattle chewing their fodder. Also with *up*.

c **1374** CHAUCER *Troylus* I. 914 And some wolde monche [*v.rr.* muche, mucche, meche] hir mete alone. *a* **1518** SKELTON *Magnyf.* 2009 Nowe must you monche mamockes and lumpes of brede. **1530** PALSGR. 632/2, I manche, I eate gredylye, *je briffe*. Are you nat a shamed to manche your meate thus lyke a carter. **1540** —— *Acolastus* H iij b, I.. mounche vp browne breade. **1590** SHAKS. *Mids. N.* IV. i. 35, I could munch your good dry Oates. **1691** WOOD *Ath. Oxon.* II. 315 Maunching a roll of bread. **1798** JOANNA BAILLIE *Tryal* v. ii, You munch it up as expeditiously as a bit of plum-cake. **1810** *Splendid Follies* I. 180 As he mounched a large mouthful of macaroons. **1871** L. STEPHEN *Playgr. Eur.* iii. (1894) 75 He sat.. calmly munching bread and cheese.

transf. **1853** MISS E. S. SHEPPARD *Ch. Auchester* III. 55 The baby, who had been munching my finger all the time we talked. **1871** ROSSETTI *Last Confession* 521 He munched her neck with kisses.

2. *intr.* and *absol.* Also with *away*.

1530 PALSGR. 640/1 It is no good fellowes touche to stande monching in a cornar whan he hath a good morcell. **1605** SHAKS. *Macb.* I. iii. 5 A Saylors Wife had Chestnuts in her Lappe, And mouncht, & mouncht, and mouncht. **1690** DRYDEN *Don Sebastian* III. ii, No, 'tis the Son of a Mare that's broken loose, and munching upon the Melons. **1883** GILMOUR *Mongols* (1884) 108 Buy so much fodder and let the animal munch away at it half the night.

b. To work the jaws up and down, as old toothless people do in talking.

1848 DICKENS *Dombey* xxvii, 'Let me tell your fortune, my pretty lady', said the old woman, munching with her jaws.

Hence '**munching** *vbl. sb.* and *ppl. a.*

1568 *Hist. Jacob & Esau* II. iv. D j, Dinner at this time a day? Nothing with thee, but dinner and mounching alway. **1823** BYRON *Juan* XI. lxvi, Where there is neither fruit nor flower Enough to gratify a bee's slight munchings. **1835** MISS SEDGWICK *Linwoods* (1873) I. 46 Raisons and almonds, which served.. as munching for her companions.

Munchausen (mʌn'tʃɔːzən). The name of Baron Munchausen (in Ger. form Münchhausen), the hero of a pseudo-autobiographical narrative of impossible adventures, written in English by the German Rudolf Eric Raspe (1785): used to denote an extravagantly mendacious story of marvellous adventure. Hence **Mun'chausen** *v.* (*nonce-wd.*) *trans.*, to recount with extravagant exaggeration; **Mun'chausenish** *a.*, **Mun'chausenism.**

1850 *Fraser's Mag.* XLI. 411 Herodotus.. has been accused of all sorts of Munchausenisms. **1854** L. LLOYD *Scandin. Adv.* II. 252 Before setting them down as regular 'Munchausens'. **1865** *Sat. Rev.* 9 Nov. 587 A Munchausenish turn for the marvellous. **1895** J. G. MILLAIS *Breath fr. Veldt* (1899) 336 My readers may think I have caricatured and 'Munchausened' the.. tomfoolery of these clowns of the desert.

b. Used *attrib.* and in the possessive with reference to a syndrome in which the patient repeatedly feigns a dramatic or severe illness so as to obtain hospital treatment (see quot. 1951).

1951 R. ASHER in *Lancet* 10 Feb. 339/1 Munchausen's syndrome... Here is described a common syndrome which most doctors have seen, but about which little has been written. Like the famous Baron von Munchausen, the persons affected have always travelled widely; and their stories, like those attributed to him, are both dramatic and untruthful. Accordingly the syndrome is respectfully dedicated to the baron, and named after him. **1959** *Perspect. Biol. & Med.* II. 347 The peripatetic medical vagrant, the itinerant fabricator of a nearly perfect facsimile of serious illness—the victim of Munchausen's syndrome. **1967** *Amer. Jrnl. Med.* XLIII. 579/2 This complex of factors.. distinguishes the Munchausen patient from the malingerer, hypochondriac, hysteric, self-mutilator and drug addict, with all of which the diagnosis of Munchausen's syndrome has been confused in the past. **1967** *Cecil-Loeb Textbk. Med.* (ed. 12) 1453/2 The only ones who can be called malingerers with any confidence are some self-mutilating patients and the remarkable pathological liars, picturesquely called examples of the Münchhausen syndrome, who travel from hospital to hospital gaining admission by means of dramatic acts of illness.

muncheel (mʌn'tʃiːl). *Anglo-Ind.* Also **manjeel, munsheel, munchil.** [a. Malayālam *manjīl.*] A kind of hammock-litter used on the southwest coast of India.

1808 in C. Buchanan *Chr. Researches* (1819) 171 We proceed thither in our Manjeels. **1885** G. S. FORBES *Wild Life in Canara* 7, I.. travelled by land in a munchil.

munchene, variant of MINCHEN *Obs.*

muncher ('mʌn(t)ʃə(r)). [f. MUNCH *v.* + -ER[1].] One who munches.

1755 in JOHNSON. **1879** F. HARRISON *Choice Bks.* iv. (1886) 79 These munchers of vapid memoirs and monotonous tales.

'**munchet.** [? f. MUNCH *sb.* + -ET[1]. Cf. *hunchet.*] A small piece (of bread).

1845 THACKERAY *Leg. Rhine* iii, Munchets of bread, smeared with the same delicious condiment.

Munchi ('mʊntʃɪ), *sb.* and *a.* Also **Midsi, Mitshi, Munshi.** [Native name.] **A.** *sb.* **a.** A Negro people living in Nigeria near the junction of the Niger and Benue rivers; a member of this people. **b.** The language of this people. **B.** *adj.* Of or pertaining to this people.

1854 S. A. CROWTHER *Jrnl. Expedition Niger* (1855) ii. 61 There is a tribe on the south bank called Mitshi. They have been represented all along as a wild people and wicked archers. **1883** R. N. CUST *Sk. Mod. Lang. Afr.* I. xi. 231 Michi, Midsi, Mbidsi is the language spoken by a tribe dwelling on the Left or South Bank of the Binué. **1892** A. F. MOCKLER-FERRYMAN *Up Niger* iv. 76 The Mitshis are a difficult people to deal with, since they acknowledge no one as head of the tribe, and live in independent families, fearing no one, yet feared by all foreign tribes. *Ibid.*, There was a sort of feeling of relief among our crew when.. we had left the Mitshi country. **1905** C. PARTRIDGE *Cross River Natives* v. 89 This angle is peopled by the fierce Munchis or Mitshis, a warlike pagan tribe dreaded by their enemies on account of the deadly poison with which they smear their arrows. **1908** *Daily Chron.* 12 Nov. 5/6 At least one-half of the Munchi country is now open to trade. **1913** F. W. H. MIGEOD *Lang. West Afr.* II. xxi. 324 The fact of its being found in Munshi is of special interest... This dual connection, having in view the actual numerals which are similar, brings Munshi into touch with languages far to the west. **1933** J. CARY *American Visitor* viii. 96 When you say pagans, do you mean the Munchis.. or the Kukuruku?

munchie ('mʌn(t)ʃɪ). [f. MUNCH *v.* + -IE.] **a.** A light meal; the name given to any type of food. *slang.* **b.** In *pl.* Hunger induced after ingesting marijuana; also a snack eaten to satisfy this hunger. *U.S. slang.*

In quot. 1917 a family name for a kind of chocolate.

1917 W. OWEN *Let.* 21 Feb. (1967) 437 All I really want is Cigarettes, Munchie, and *plain Cadbury's.* **1959** I. & P. OPIE *Lore & Lang. Schoolch.* ix. 163 Food in general is referred to as 'bait'.. 'grub', or 'grubber', 'munchie', [etc.]. **1962** *Austral. Women's Weekly* Suppl. 24 Oct. 3/3 *Munchie*, any type of food. **1971** E. E. LANDY *Underground Dict.* 136 *Munchies*, hunger introduced by marijuana—eg. *I have the munchies.* **1971** *Current Slang.* (Univ. S. Dakota) VI. 8 *Munchies*, snacks to be eaten after smoking marijuana. **1972** *Dict. Contemp. & Colloquial Usage* (Eng.-Lang. Inst. Amer.) 20 *Munchie*, a snack; food to nibble on. **1973** *Times* 7 Feb. 16/1 There are.. munchies (to be hungry usually after ingesting marijuana).

munchil, variant of MUNCHEEL.

†'**munchin.** *Obs. rare.* [? f. MUNCH *v.*, after NUNCHEON. Cf. next.] A lunch or small repast.

a **1666** C. HOOLE *Sch. Colloquies* (1688) 61 My Bever (or Munchin).

munchion, *v. Obs. rare.* [? f. MUNCH *v.*, after *nuncheon.* Cf. MUNCHIN.] *intr.* ? To munch.

1611 COTGR. s.v. *Manger, Manger son pain en son sac*, to snudge it, or munchion alone in a corner.

munck(e, -ckey, obs. ff. MONK, MONKEY.

mun(ck)corn(e, variant forms of MONGCORN.

†**mund.** *Obs.* [OE. *mund* fem. = OFris. *mund* masc. guardianship, guardian, OS. *mund* hand, OHG. *munt* fem. hand, protection, masc. protector, ON. *mund* fem. hand, *mund-r* masc. sum paid by a bridegroom for his bride.]

1. A hand or palm, as a measure of length.

The primary sense 'hand' (part of the body) is not found later than OE.

a **900** *O.E. Martyrol.* 27 Mar. 52 Stænen bed seofon fota lang ond þrym mundum hierre þonne þæs huses flor. *c* **1205** LAY. 21994 He is end-longe feouwer & sixti munden.

2. Protection, guardianship.

a **1023** WULFSTAN *Hom.* xxviii. (Napier) 132 ȝe orsorȝe wuniað on lande.. under mynre munde. *c* **1205** LAY. 10518, & hælden me to munde a þire aȝere hond. **1861** MAINE *Anc. Law* v. (1876) 145 All the Germanic immigrants seem to have recognised a corporate union of the family under the *mund*, or authority of a patriarchal chief.

3. A guardian, protector.

a **1064** *Charter of Eadweard* in Kemble *Codex Dipl.* VI. 203 Ðat he beo ðærto ȝeheald & mund under me. *c* **1205** LAY. 23246 Of me þu scalt halden and habben me to munde.

mund, var. MUN *sb.*[1], MOUND *sb.*[1] and [2].

mund(e, obs. variant forms of MIND *sb.*[1]

Munda ('mʊndə), *sb.* and *a.* [Native word.] **A.** *sb.* **a.** A member of an ancient Indian people of pre-Aryan stock which was overrun by invading Caucasians and Mongols and which survives in present times as primitive tribes living in north-eastern India. **b.** The name given to the language group which includes the dialects of the Mundas and is believed to belong to the Austroasiatic family of languages. **B.** *adj.* Of or pertaining to the Mundas or their language. Cf. KOLARIAN.

1847 B. H. HODGSON *On Aborigines of India* iii. 150 Among the Kôls, I have seen *many* Oraons and Múndas nearly black. **1854** M. MÜLLER in C. C. J. Bunsen *Christianity & Mankind* III. 437 These people, called themselves 'Munda', which as an old ethnic name, I have adopted for the common appellation of the aboriginal Koles. .. It is said that the Mundas and Uraons lived peaceably together until the Brahmans reached their country. *Ibid.* 438 The dictionaries of the Munda and Tamulian languages differ more than should be the case with cognate dialects. **1866** *Jrnl. Asiatic Soc. Bengal* XXXV. II. (Special Number) 26 There are.. 'moondahs' and Santals.. speaking dialects of a language very different from the Dravidian. **1872** E. T. DALTON *Descr. Ethnol. Bengal* vii. 163 The people I am now about to describe comprise the Múndáris or Múndas of Chútia Nágpúr proper. **1877** A. H. KEANE tr. *Hovelacque's Sci. of Lang.* iv. 138 *Munda.* The language of the Kols, or Kolhs (south-west of Calcutta), would seem, like Sinhalese, to be independent of the Dravidian group. **1888** *Encycl. Brit.* XXIII. 41/2 There are scattered remnants of a still earlier population of India (Mundas, Kolarians), whose race characteristics.. do not so essentially differ from those of the Dravidians. **1904** G. A. GRIERSON *Linguistic Survey of India* II. 1 The Muṇḍā order is subject, object, verb, while in Khassi and Mōn it is subject, verb, object. **1912** S. C. ROY *Mundas & their Country* i. 16 The site of the original home of the Mundas will perhaps ever remain hidden from view in the mist of ages. **1933** [see AUSTRIC *a.*]. **1956** J. WHATMOUGH *Language* ii. 30 Munda is now found chiefly in the eastern Himalayas and in isolated regions in the Central Provinces. **1970** YAMADA RYUJI *Cultural Formation of Mundas* I. i. 13 The Mundas, together with several other Austroasiatic peoples in India, are called an agricultural people. **1975** *Amer. Speech 1972* XLVII. 289 The Indo-Aryan languages have acquired various structural features from the Dravidian and Munda languages spoken by the subjected peoples.

†'**mundal,** *a. Obs. rare.* [ad. med.L. *mundāl-is*, f. *mund-us* world. Cf. MUNDIAL.] Mundane, worldly.

1614 SIR T. DALE in Capt. Smith *Virginia* IV. (1624) 117 Leauing all contenting pleasures and mundall delights, to reside here with much turmoile. **1631** CAPT. SMITH *Advt. Planters* 33 They have builded many pretty Villages, faire houses, and Chapels, which are growne good Benefices of 120. pounds a yeare, besides their owne mundall industry.

¶ ? Taken as *sb.* = the world (i.e. this earth).

1534 *Coventry Corpus Chr. Plays* ii. 187 From the hy pales and blys eyuerlastyng Downe into this wale and meserabull mvndall [*MS. fragm.* Down into the vale off this mezerabull mundall].

mundane ('mʌndeɪn, mʌn'deɪn), *a.* (*sb.*) Forms: 5 mondeyne, 5–6 mondayn(e, mundayne, 6 mondain, mundain(e, 7 mundan, 6– mundane. [a. F. *mondain* (12–13th c.), ad. L. *mundān-us*, f. *mundus* world.]

1. Belonging to this world (i.e. the earth as contrasted with heaven); worldly; earthly.

In early use (till 1550) often following its sb., and sometimes taking *s* in the pl.

1475 *Bk. Noblesse* (Roxb.) 70 He saide that fortune and felicite mondeyne was joyned and knyt withe his vertue and noblesse roiall. **1509** BARCLAY *Shyp of Folys* 67 b, Alas oft goddes goodes.. Of suche folys is wastyd.. In great folyes mundaynes and outrage. *a* **1652** J. SMITH *Sel. Disc.* i. 21 Entangled with the birdlime of fleshly passions and mundane vanity. *a* **1720** SEWEL *Hist. Quakers* (1795) I. II. 146 By a singular and very strange turn of mundane affairs. **1869** MOZLEY *Univ. Serm.* ii. (1876) 50 Not like the goodness which feeds upon mundane motives and is weak and sickly.

b. Belonging to the 'world' as distinguished from the church. Of literature: Secular. *rare.*

1848 W. H. KELLY tr. *L. Blanc's Hist. Ten Y.* II. 532 It [Talleyrand's reconciliation to the church] was matter of inexpressible surprise and pain to the more mundane portion of the prince's intimate acquaintances. **1865** M. ARNOLD *Ess. Crit.* vi. (1875) 245 The beginnings of the mundane poetry of the Italians are in Sicily.

c. Belonging to the world of fashion. [= F. *mondain*.]

1904 *Edin. Rev.* Oct. 298 The Athénée and the Nouveautés.. the favourite resorts of 'mundane' pleasure-seekers.

2. Pertaining to the cosmos or universe; cosmic.

mundane soul, spirit: the *anima mundi* of the Platonists (ἡ τοῦ κόσμου ψυχή, ἡ κοσμικὴ ψυχή in Proclus).

1642 H. MORE *Song of Soul* II. III. i. 18 We have the sight Of what the Mundane spirit suffereth By colours, figures, or inherent light. **1665** GLANVILL *Scepsis Sci.* xxiv. 147 The Platonicall Hypothesis of a Mundane Soul. **1692** BENTLEY *Boyle Lect.* vii. (1693) 7 The Atoms or Particles which now constitute Heaven and Earth, being once separate and diffused in the Mundane Space, like the supposed Chaos, could never [etc.]. **1872** MOZLEY *Mirac.* (ed. 3) Pref. 24 The idea of God as the Supreme Mundane Being.

b. ***mundane egg***: in Indian and other cosmogonies, a primordial egg from which the world was hatched.

1684, 1789 [see ORPHIC 1 b]. **1841** ELPHINSTONE *Hist. Ind.* I. I. iv. 75 From this seed sprung the mundane egg, in which the Supreme Being was himself born in the form of Brahmá.

c. ***mundane era***, an era reckoned from the time of the creation of the world.

1892 E. M. THOMPSON *Gr. & Lat. Palæogr.* Add. 323 To reduce the Mundane era of Constantinople to the Christian era.

3. *Astrol.* Pertaining to the horizon and not to the ecliptic or zodiac; chiefly in ***mundane aspect, parallel***.

1687 J. BISHOP *Marrow Astrol.* II. 33 At which time the ☽ was directed to a mundane parallel of ♃. *Ibid.* 76 Narrowly observe all the Aspects, as well those in the World, as those in the Zodiack, for many times a Zodiacal Aspect may promise good in the Business, when there may be a Mundane Aspect will frustrate the good promised by the other. **1819** J. WILSON *Dict. Astrol.* 295 *Mundane Aspects*, distances in the world measured by the semiarc wholly independent of the zodiac.

4. *Nat. Hist.* Used by Darwin for: Found in all parts of the world, widely distributed.

1844 DARWIN in *Life & Lett.* (1887) II. 25 The Owl is mundane, and many of the species have very wide ranges.

†**5.** *sb.* A dweller in this world. *Obs. rare*$^{-1}$.

1517 H. WATSON *Ship of Fools* Prol. A ij b, By the shyppe we maye vnderstande yᵉ folyes and erroures that the mondaynes are in, by the se this present worlde.

Hence **mun'danely** *adv.*, **mun'daneness**.

1727 BAILEY vol. II, *Mundaneness*, worldliness. **1824** LANDOR *Imag. Conv.* ii. Wks. 1846 I. 46 The greatest of stakes, mundanely speaking, is the stake of reputation. **1886** MYERS in Gurney, etc. *Phantasms of Living* II. 294 This very mundaneness of the apparition is precisely what was to be expected.

mundanity (mʌn'dænɪtɪ). Also 7 -eity, 20 mondanity. [a. F. *mondanité* or ad. med.L. **mundānitā-tem*: see MUNDANE and -ITY.] **a.** The quality or fact of being mundane; worldliness; †in *pl.*, worldly affections or proclivities.

1502 *Ord. Crysten Men* (W. de W. 1506) IV. xxi. 254 The mundanytes that she sawe.. to habounde in the sayd courte. **1647** TRAPP *Comm. Eph.* ii. 2 The mundaneity or worldlinesse of the world. **1648** W. MOUNTAGUE *Devout Ess.* I. xx. §1. 376 The love of mundanity, wherein do indeed reside the vital Spirits of the body of Sin. **1888** MRS. H. WARD *R. Elsmere* II. xvi, He could have blessed her for the tone, for the escape into common mundanity. **1959** *Listener* 30 July 173/2 The outward mundanity of the master's life. **1963** *Movie* July–Aug. 20/2 The presentation of the torture sequences horrifies by its casual mundanity. **1972** *Daily Tel.* 27 Apr. 8/6 Nothing could be further removed from the mundanities of sausage and haddock than the subject of this book of circumferential recollections. **1974** *Nature* 17 May 199/2 It may mean the moral support that leads to a government grant, permission to work abroad for a spell or even such mundanities as the price of an airline ticket.

b. The characteristics of the fashionable world.

1892 *Nation* (N.Y.) 27 Oct. 324/2 Mr. Sidgwick.. carries an air of distinction and mundanity in his style. **1911** MRS. H. WARD *Case of Richard Meynell* xii. 242 With her grey hair, and her plain widow's dress, she threw her sister's charming mondanity into bright relief.

†**mun'dation.** *Obs.* [ad. L. *mundātiōn-em*, f. *mundāre* to cleanse, f. *mund-us* clean.] The action of cleansing or state of being cleansed.

1633 T. ADAMS *Exp. 2 Peter* iii. 10 Every day we gather new stains; for the mundation whereof there is another fountain provided. **1678** R. R[USSELL] tr. *Geber* II. I. IV. viii. 104 Such as its Mundation (or cleansing) shall be, such will be its Perfection. **1755** in JOHNSON.

mundatory ('mʌndətərɪ), *a.* and *sb.* [ad. L. *mundātōri-us*, f. *mundāre*: see prec.] **A.** *adj.* Having the property or quality of cleansing. *rare.*

1706 PHILLIPS (ed. Kersey), *Mundificative* or *Mundatory Medicines*,.. Medicines that are proper for the cleansing of Ulcers. **1755** in JOHNSON.

B. *sb.* A means or implement of cleansing. *rare.*

1859 R. F. BURTON *Centr. Afr.* in *Jrnl. Geog. Soc.* XXIX. 323 They have, however, no mundatories; the African skin does not wash well.

b. *Eccl.* A purificator or purificatory.

1674 BLOUNT *Glossogr.* (ed. 4), *Mundatory*, the same with *Purificatory*. **1884–5** *Cath. Dict.*, *Mundatory* or *Purificatory*.

Munday, munde, obs. ff. MONDAY, MIND.

mundel, variant of MANDIL.

1721 C. KING *Brit. Merch.* I. 301, 3 Toyletts, 20 Pieces of Mundels, 2 Barbary Aprons.

'mundial, *a. Obs. rare.* [a. OF. *mon-*, *mundial*, or ad. eccl. L. *mundiāl-is*, f. *mundus* world.] Mundane, worldly.

1560 ROLLAND *Crt. Venus* I. 744 Man to desaif with foull lust mundiall. **1619** W. SCLATER *Exp. 1 Thess.* (1630) 191 Saint Augustine notes of Friendship foure kinds... Thirdly Mundiall, where the tye is profit... Discontinuance in euill abateth Mundiall Friendship.

mundic ('mʌndɪk). Also 7–8 mundick, (8 mundik, mondic). [Prob. Celtic Cornish, but the original form is uncertain; *maen teg*, 'pretty stone' has been conjectured.] Cornish miners' name for iron pyrites, or pyrites in general. Also *attrib.*

1671 [see MAXY]. **1681** GREW *Musæum* III. I. ii. 272 Marcasite, or Yellow Mundick. *Ibid.* v. 307 A Mundick-Spar; consisting of tabulated or flat and square Crystals. **1855** J. R. LEIFCHILD *Cornwall Mines* 219 The yellow copper ore, at present so valued,.. was in fact cast aside as 'mundic'. **1880** BARING-GOULD *Preachers' Pocket* 239 Now and then a glittering particle of mundic cheats their hopes; but of gold.. they.. have none.

Hence **'mundicky** *a.*, full of mundic.

1814 W. PHILLIPS in *Trans. Geol. Soc.* II. 117 A.. mundicky.. Load.

†**mundicative**, erron. f. MUNDIFICATIVE *sb.*

1587 LEVINS *Pathw. Health* (1632) 106 For a wound in the head a good mundicatiffe. **1643** J. STEER tr. *Exp. Chyrurg.* xvi. 66 Make thereof a Mundicative. **1891** *Syd. Soc. Lex.*

†**mundi'cidious**, *a.* [f. L. *mund-us* world, after *homicidious*.] World-destroying.

1647 WARD *Simp. Cobler* (1843) 21 A vacuum and an exorbitancy are mundicidious evils.

mun'dificant. *rare*$^{-0}$. [ad. L. *mundificant-em*, pr. pple. of *mundificāre* to MUNDIFY.] A cleansing medicament.

1842 BRANDE *Dict. Sci.*, etc., *Mundificant*, a term applied in old pharmacy to certain healing and cleansing ointments and plasters. [Hence in later Dicts.]

mundifi'cation. ? *Obs.* [a. F. *mondification* (16th c.), or ad. med.L. *mundificātiōn-em*, n. of action f. *mundificāre* to MUNDIFY.]

1. The action of mundifying, cleansing, or deterging; the state of being mundified. Chiefly *Med.* (e.g. of wounds, ulcers).

1543 TRAHERON *Vigo's Chirurg.* II. ii. 16 After mundification, ye must incarnate the place. **1672** WISEMAN *Wounds* 26 This is done by universal Regiment and Digestion, with Mundification, that a new flesh may be made to fill the Cavity. **1810** BERESFORD *Bibliosophia*, etc. 102 The unparalleled difficulty of effectuating this mighty mundification.

fig. **1610** HEALEY *St. Aug. Citie of God* XXI. xxiii. 861 Those holy men.. did not enuy the mundification [L. *mundationem*] and beatitude of those spirits.

†**2.** *concr.* ? A purified preparation.

1603 LODGE *Treat. Plague* I 3, Take of the mundification of rozen, and put it vppon the saide sores.

†**mundificative**, *a.* and *sb. Med. Obs.* Also 5 -atif. [a. OF. *mon-*, *mundificatif* (*a.* and *sb.*), or ad. med.L. *mundificātīv-us*, f. *mundificāre* to MUNDIFY: see -IVE.] **A.** *adj.* Having power to cleanse (the body, a sore, etc.); detersive.

a **1400–50** *Stockh. Med. MS.* 13 Mu[n]dificatif clister. **1509** BARCLAY *Shyp of Folys* (1570) 165 Purging it with playsters mundificatiue. **1646** SIR T. BROWNE *Pseud. Ep.* I. xi. 46 We finde that gall is very mundificative, and was a proper medicine to cleere the eyes of Tobit. **1676** WORLIDGE *Cyder* (1691) 13 Wines that proceed from the vine being of a corroborative and mundificative nature. **1727–41** CHAMBERS *Cycl.* s.v., Mundificative plaisters, or unguents.

B. *sb.* A cleansing or detersive medicine.

c **1400** *Lanfranc's Cirurg.* 37 We musten clense þe wounde wiþ þis mundificatif. *Ibid.* 81 On of þe mundificatiuis of ony which þat schal be told in þe antidotarie. **1543** TRAHERON *Vigo's Chirurg.* II. ii. 16 After the digestyve, ye must clense the place wyth a mundificatyve of Syrupe of Roses. **1643** J. STEER tr. *Exp. Chyrurg.* viii. 35 A mundificative of the juice of Smallege doth very much clense putrid Vlcers. **1676** WISEMAN *Surg.* I. vii. 43, I continued the Mundificative and Cerote, and dressed it every other day. **1727–41** CHAMBERS *Cycl.*, *Mundificatives*, or *Mundifyers*.

†**'mundified**, *ppl. a. Obs.* [f. MUNDIFY *v.* + -ED[1].] Cleansed; *spec.* freed from husk or other integument.

1558 WARDE tr. *Alexis' Secr.* (1568) 3 Pine apple kernelles mondified. **1580** BLUNDEVIL *Order Curing Horses Dis.* v. 4 b, Giue him.. barlie faire sifted, and well sodden, and also mundified, that is to saie, the huske pulled awaie, like as when you blanch Almonds. **1725** BRADLEY *Fam. Dict.* s.v. *Cough*, The Patient may take a Spoonful of mundify'd Barley. **1736** BAILEY *Housh. Dict.* 365 Give him also gentle purges of mundified cassia.

†**'mundifier.** *Obs.* [f. MUNDIFY *v.* + -ER[1].] One who, or a thing which, mundifies; a cleansing medicament.

1603 LODGE *Treat. Plague* I 3 b, Make an ointment thereof, for it is a mundifier. **1630** J. TAYLOR (Water P.) *Praise Clean Linen* Ded., Wks. II. 165 Hee is a mender and you are a mundifier... Your Art is to keepe our bodies sweet and cleane. **1695** J. EDWARDS *Perfect. Script.* 192 Smegmaticks mundifiers, cleansers, adorners, are useful. **1727–41** CHAMBERS *Cycl.*, *Mundificatives*, or *Mundifyers*, in medicine, denote cleansers, purifyers, or detergents.

mundify ('mʌndɪfaɪ), *v.* Now *rare* or *Obs.* Also 6–7 mondify. [a. F. *mondifier* (14th c.), or ad. L. *mundificāre*, f. *mund-us* clean: see -FY.]

1. *trans.* To cleanse, purify. *lit.* and *fig.*

1504 LADY MARGARET tr. *De Imitatione* IV. xii. 276 It behoueth the to mundifye and clense the habytacion of thy herte fro all synnes. **1646** SIR T. BROWNE *Pseud. Ep.* VI. xii. 335 Fire.. refines those bodies which will never bee mundified by water. **1660** F. BROOKE tr. *Le Blanc's Trav.* 189 My companion was forced to pay for mundifying the Cistern. **1748** RICHARDSON *Clarissa* (1811) VII. lx. 237 Mundified or purified from my past iniquities. **1819** CRABBE *T. of Hall* XIX. 258 Whatever stains were theirs, let them reside In that pure place, and they were mundified.

b. *intr.* for *refl.* To make oneself neat or smart.

1699 ED. S——CY *Country Gentl. Vade-mecum* 29 He.. at least forces him [*sc.* a Beau].. to steer to the next Barber's Shop, to new Rig and Mundifie.

2. *trans.* In medical use: To free (the body, blood, a wound, ulcer, etc.) from noxious matter; to cleanse, deterge.

1528 PAYNEL *Salerne's Regim.* Y ij, Pipper.. mundifieth the lightis. **1597** GERARDE *Herbal* II. viii. 189 The juice thereof mundifieth corrupt and filthie vlcers. **1646** SIR T. BROWNE *Pseud. Ep.* VII. vii. 352 The graines of the Apples of Mandrakes mundifie the Matrix. **1758** J. B. *Le Dran's Observ. Surg.* (1771) *147 The Flesh ought.. to.. be well mundified. **1854** BADHAM *Halieut.* 384 To scour and mundify the guts.

absol. **1541** R. COPLAND *Guydon's Formul.* U ij, The incarnatyfe helpes that brede flesshe and mundyfye. **1610** MARKHAM *Masterp.* II. clxxiii. 483 Antimonuum.. mundifieth and purgeth. **1710** T. FULLER *Pharm. Extemp.* 119 It [the Electuary].. mundifies, dries, heals.

Hence **'mundifying** *vbl. sb.* and *ppl. a.*

1579 BAKER *Guydon's Quest. Chirurg.* 184 A mundifyng Vnguent for inueterate vlcers. **1610** HEALEY *St. Aug. Citie of God* X. xxxii. (1620) 385 The mundifying of proficients. **1626** BACON *Sylva* §65 Abstersive and Mundifying Clysters. **1631** R. H. *Arraignm. Whole Creature* ix. 65 The mundifying waters of the Word. **1712** *Bibl. Anat.* II. 203 The Ulcer.. healed entirely.. by the use of a mundifying and drying Collyry.

mundik, obs. form of MUNDIC.

mundil, variant of MANDIL, turban.

mundilion, ? erron. variant of MODILLION.

1667 PRIMATT *City & C. Build.* 70 A fair Stone-colour laid in Oyl for.. Shop-windows and Mundilions.

munditial (mʌn'dɪʃəl), *a.* [f. L. *munditia* cleanliness (f. *mundus* clean) + -AL[1].] ? Relating to cleansing or purifying.

1876 A. B. EVANS *Refl. Midday Commun.* xvi. (1880) 102, I have set this commandment.. side by side with the Sacramental and Munditial mandates.

†**mun'divagant**, *a. Obs.*$^{-0}$ [f. L. *mund-us* world + *vagant-em*, pres. pple. of *vagārī* to roam: cf. L. *mundivagus* and see -ANT[1].] (See quot.)

1656 BLOUNT *Glossogr.*, *Mundivagant*, wandring through the world. **1721** in BAILEY. **1755** in JOHNSON.

mundle ('mʌnd(ə)l). *dial.* Also 9 mungle. A stick used for stirring.

1551–60 in H. Hall *Soc. Eliz. Age* (1887) 152 In the Kytchyn.. a great mundle. **1688** R. HOLME *Armoury* III. xx. (Roxb.) 247/1 The Third, is called a Padle or Mundle, it is like an old spade without its Iron shooe, all wood. **1879** MISS JACKSON *Shropsh. Word-bk.* **1886** *Chesh. Gloss.*

mundul, variant (in Dicts.) of MANDIL.

mun'dung. *Obs. rare.* Shortened form of next.

1712 ? KING *Bibliotheca* in Nichols *Sel. Collect. Poems* (1780) III. 57 For vile mundung and fumy ale, Incense and odours, now exhale.

†**mun'dungus.** *Obs.* Forms: *α.* 7–8 mundungo; *β.* 7– mundungus (7 mundungo's, -gos, -gas,

mondongas). [A jocular use of Sp. *mondongo* tripe, black-pudding (see MONDONGO).]

†**1.** Offal, refuse. *Obs. rare.*

1637 BASTWICK *Litany* I. 10 Those Fishmongers that haue bought and sold Christs best fishes..and made them the mundungus and garbridge both of sea and land and the off-scouring of all things. **1786** 'A. PASQUIN' *Childr. Thespis* I. (1792) 83 Thus scarceness gives value to dirt and mundungus, And dignifies that Nature meant as a fungus. **1834** BECKFORD *Italy* II. 198 What is so liberally paid for by the..people as a rarity of exquisite relish, should not be suffered to turn mundungus.

2. Bad-smelling tobacco. Also *attrib.*

α. **1641** J. TAYLOR (Water P.) *Compl. M. Tenterhooke* (1877), [Kinds of Tobacco] Bermudas, Providentia, Shallow-congo, And the most part of all the rest (Mundungo). **1647** *M. Corbet's Learned Sp.* 3 Infernal stinking Smoaks of Mundungo [1681 p. 2 Mundungus]. **1700** J. BROME *Trav.* iii. (1707) 180 They are great lovers of Tobacco, and a little Mundungo will make them at any time very serviceable.

β. *a* **1652** BROME *Covent Gard.* I. Wks. 1873 II. 14, I must have tother glass to wash him out of my mouth, he furs it worse then Mondongas Tobacco. **1659** *Lady Alimony* II. ii. B 4, One Sir Gregory Shapeless, a Mundungo's Monopolist, ..who had smook'd himself into a Mercenary title of Knightship. **1671** SHADWELL *Humorists* III. 41 With a Glass of Windy-Bottle-Ale in one hand, and a Pipe of Mundungus in the other. **1678** BUTLER *Hud.* III. ii. 1006 After h' had ministred a Dose Of Snuff-Mundungus, to his Nose. **1688** R. HOLME *Armoury* III. xxii. (Roxb.) 273/2 Selling..that for good tobacco, which is none at all, or else the worst of all Mundungasses. **1767** S. PATERSON *Another Trav.* I. 192 The Flemish tobacco is the poorest Mundungus in the world. **1785** GROSE *Dict. Vulg. Tongue*, *Mundungus*, bad or rank tobacco. **1824** SCOTT *St. Ronan's* xxxii, Her jet black cutty pipe, from which she soon sent..clouds of vile mundungus vapour. **1840** B. E. HILL *Pinch—of Snuff* 54 He might..get rid of any dull flavourless mundungus under the title of Russell's Rappee. **1901** G. GISSING *Our Fr. Charlatan* 137, 'Here's a new mixture, my own blending,..I see your pipe is empty'... 'I stick to my own mundungus; any novelty disturbs my thoughts'.

mune, variant of MIN *sb.*[1] *Obs.*, MONE *v. Obs.*

munec, obs. form of MONK.

munechene, variant of MINCHEN *Obs.*

†'**munec-lif.** *Obs.* [OE. *munuclif*: see MONK and LIFE. Cf. ON. *múnklifi* and COTLIF.] A monastery.

In the OE. version of Bæda IV. iii. the word is used in the etymological sense 'monastic life' (orig. *monastica vita*).

c **893** K. ÆLFRED *Oros.* VI. xxiv. 290 Hic..sende on Egypte & het toweorpan eal fra munuclif þe his broðor ær ʒestaþelade. *c* **1000** ÆLFRIC *Hom.* (Th.) II. 506 He arærde him munuclif..þat mynster he ʒeloʒode mid wellybbendum mannum. *c* **1200** *Ormin* 6292 þatt lif þatt iss i muneclif Iss shadd fra ʒure swinnkess, & itt iss all an oþerr lif & hehhre lif & bettre. *c* **1205** LAY. 29717 At Bangor wes a munecclif. *Ibid.* 32218 ʒeond chirchen & ʒeond muneccliuen.

munegen, variant of MING *v. Obs.*

muneke, munen, obs. ff. MONK, MIN *v.*

Munendai, obs. form of MONDAY.

†'**muneral**, *a. Obs.* [ad. late L. *mūnerālis* (recorded in the sense 'relating to presents'), f. *mūner-*, *mūnus* present, gift, also office, official duty.] Pertaining to office or duty.

1606 BP. W. BARLOW *Serm.* 21 *Sept.* C, As if the calling Episcopall were a Numeral, not a Munerall function. **1625** T. ADAMS *Visitation Serm.* Wks. (1629) 933 To be a Bishop then, is not a Numerall, but a Munerall function.

†'**munerary**, *a. Obs.* [ad. L. *mūnerārius*, f. *mūner-*, *mūnus* gift: see prec. and -ARY.] Of or pertaining to gifts, having the nature of a gift.

1721 in BAILEY; and in mod. Dicts.

†'**munerate**, *v. Obs.*$^{-0}$ [f. L. *mūnerāt-*, ppl. stem of *mūnerāre*, *-ārī*, f. *mūner-*, *mūnus* gift.] (See quot.)

1656 BLOUNT *Glossogr.*, *Munerate*, to reward or recompence.

†**mune'ration.** *Obs.*$^{-0}$ [ad. late L. *mūnerātiōn-em*, f. *mūnerāre*: see prec.]

1658 PHILLIPS, *Muneration*,..a recompencing or rewarding.

munetere, obs. form of MINTER.

mung, moong (mʌŋ, muːŋ). [Hindī *mūng*.] Either of two legumes, native to India, the seeds of which are an important food: (*a*) *Phaseolus mungo*; also, the fibre of this plant, of which mats are made; (*b*) in full ***mung bean***, *Phaseolus aureus*.

1800 *Misc. Tracts* in *Asiat. Ann. Reg.* 299/1 The stalks of the Oord are hispid in a less degree than those of the Moong. **1866** LIVINGSTONE *Last Jrnls.* (1873) I. ii. 34 A large basket of soroko, or, as they call it in India, 'mung'. **1868** B. H. POWELL *Handbk. Econ. Products of Punjab* I. 239/1 Másh, múng and channa (gram), are the pulses most in use. **19..** *Mod. Trade List*, Moong mats. **1884** tr. *A. de Candolle's Orig. Cultivated Plants* v. 346 Green Gram or Múng—.. A species commonly cultivated in India and in the Nile Valley. **1916** C. J. BAMBER *Plants of Punjab* 600 *Phaseolus mungo*... Mung... Cultivated for its seeds which are eaten as *dal*. **1955** *New Biol.* XIX. 101 Mung bean preparations given succinate consumed oxygen at one-third of the rate shown by the tissue they were derived from. **1960** J. ORGAN *Rare Veg.* iv. 79 There are two kinds of bean used for sprouting, the Soy bean (*Soja max*) and the Mung bean (*Phaseolus aureus*). **1969** *Oxf. Bk. Food Plants* 38/2 Green Gram (*Phaseolus aureus*) is often known by the Indian name of 'mung' and is probably native to India... In China and the United States it is also used to produce bean sprouts.. which are popular in certain dishes.

mung, var. of MONG *sb.*[1]

‖**munga**[1] ('mʌŋgə). The Bonnet Macaque, *Macacus sinicus*, of southern India.

1843 J. E. GRAY *List Spec. Mammalia Brit. Mus.* 7. **1884–5** *Stand. Nat. Hist.* (1888) V. 516.

munga[2] ('mʌŋgə). *Austral.*, *N.Z.*, and *Forces' slang.* Also **manga, munger, mungey, mungy.** [Said to be f. F. *manger* to eat.] (See quots.) Also *attrib.*

Quot. 1907 may not belong here.

1907 'Q' *Major Vigoureux* xxii. 218 Annet, Linnet, and Matthew Henry sat..and watched their friend Jan eat his mid-morning snack—or 'mungey', as it is called in the Islands. **1919** W. H. DOWNING *Digger Dialects* 34 *Mungy* (Fr., Manger)—Food; a meal. **1925** FRASER & GIBBONS *Soldier & Sailor Words* 161 *Mungy wallah*, a man employed in the Cook House. **1929** *Papers Michigan Acad. Sci. & Arts* X. 309/2 *Mungey*, food in general. **1942** C. BARRETT *On Wallaby* iv. 70 Those munger vendors did a roaring trade. *Ibid.* vii. 152 There were rush-baskets full of mysterious munger; bricks of sugar, bubbly discs of native bread, and piles of vegetables. **1943** *2 N.Z.E.F. Times* 25 Oct. 11 He argued quite a lot until munga time. **1947** D. M. DAVIN *For Rest of Lives* 75 [The Cook] swore he'd give them some good manga to go off with. **1949** 'THE SARGE' *Excuse Feet* ix. 102 Herbert felt quite sure she would have put on a much better act for a bit of army *munga*. *Ibid.* 157 *Munga*, food. **1959** S. H. COURTIER *Death in Dream Time* vi. 69 Come an' get your munga. **1970** *N.Z. Listener* 12 Oct. 12/4 Certainly do feel hungry. How about a plate of steak and eggs now? Or a rich, smoking mutton chop? A man has to eat. White or brown, everyone scoffs the same munga. **1971** *Sunday Mail* (Brisbane) 24 Oct. 42/4 After the munga Ian showed me his cocktail bit.

Mungal, -ian, obs. ff. MONGOL, MONGOLIAN.

mungaree (mən'dʒɑːriː). *slang.* Also **mungaree, mungare(er, munjari,** †**numgare.** [ad. It. *mangiare* to eat.] Food.

1861 H. MAYHEW *London Labour* III. 139/2 We [*sc.* strolling actors] call breakfast, dinner, tea, supper, all of them 'numgare'. **1889** *Answers* 11 May 374 Broken meat and scraps of bread ('Bull and Munjari' they are called). **1942** C. BARRETT *On Wallaby* iv. 64 Chameleons..are insectivorous and get their own mungaree (food). **1944** L. GLASSOP *We were Rats* iv. xlvi. 252 Wailed the [Cairene] woman. 'Gibbit *bucksheesh*. Gibbit *mungareer*.'

mungcorn(e, variant forms of MONGCORN.

†**munge**, *v. Obs.* [ad. L. *mungĕre* = *ēmungĕre* EMUNGE.] *trans.* To wipe (a person's nose); *fig.* to cheat.

1660 *Eng. Monarchy Freest St. in World* 7 They munged the peoples Noses, and publiquely pickt their pockets.

munge(n, variant forms of MING *v. Obs.*

mungeet, variant of MUNJEET.

munger, -erell, obs. ff. MONGER, MONGREL.

mungo[1] ('mʌŋgəʊ). Also 8 **mungos.** [var. of MONGOOSE.

Kæmpfer (*Amœn. Exotic.*, 1712, p. 574) says that the Portuguese called the animal *mungo* and the plant *raje mungo* i.e. 'mungo root'.]

†**1.** = MONGOOSE 1. *Obs.*

1752 J. HILL *Hist. Anim.* 549 *Mustela griseo et albido variegata*... The tabbied Mungo. *Ibid.* 550 Ray and some others..call it *Viverra Indica quæ Mungo Lusitanis, Mungathia Ceylonensibus*; we call it the Mungo or Mungose. **1775** MARTYN *Elem. Nat. Hist.* I. I. 30 Pharaoh's Rat or Mungo. *Viverra Ichneumon.* **1845** *Encycl. Metrop.* XX. 236/2 This animal is known in India, of which it is a native, by the name of *Mungo* or *Mungutia*.

2. ***mungo-root*** (also in recent Dicts. *mungo*): the plant *Ophiorhiza Mungos*, supposed to be a strong antidote against the poison of snakes.

1738 MORTIMER in *Phil. Trans.* XL. 442 The two famous Antidotes, the Mungos-root, and the Serpentine-stone. **1762** B. STILLINGFL. tr. *Gedner's Use of Curios.* in *Misc. Tracts* 192 *note*, As soon as this serpent appears the weesel attacks him, and if she chances to be bit by him, she immediately runs to find a certain vegetable; upon eating which she returns, and renews the fight. The Indians are of opinion, that this plant is the mungos. **1838** *Penny Cycl.* XII. 429/2 The story of the *Ichneumon Mungo*..having recourse to the plant *Hampaddu Tanah*, or Mungo root, as an antidote when bitten by serpents.

†'**mungo**[2]. ? *slang. Obs.* ? A person of position, a 'swell'.

1770 [COLMAN] in *Oxford Mag.* IV. 229/1 But in the year 1770 the ladies of the first quality, the Mungoes, the superiors of the times, have abrogated [*printed* arrogated] the old Salic laws of libertinism, and openly set up a tavern in profest rivalry of Boodle's, Arthur's, and Almack's.

†'**mungo**[3]. *Obs.* [See quot. 1769.] A typical name for a Black slave. Hence, a Negro.

1769 H. WALPOLE *Mem. Geo. III* (1794) III. 211 Dyson, as usual was..ill-treated by the Opposition; Colonel Barré, the day before, having baptized him by the name of *Mungo*, a black slave in a new farce called *The Padlock*, who is described as employed by everybody in all jobs and servile offices. **1794** *Times* 12 Feb. 3/2 The manner in which the Black business was settled,..was this:—The husband.. desired his wife to go where she pleased, (after she said she'd live with no one but the Black) and Mungo was taken by a press gang. **1798** *Monthly Mag.* Mar. 184/1 Might not New Yorkers give encouragement to the poor Scotch and Irish emigrants..and thus totally do away the mungo and the tawney breeds? **1839** COL. HAWKER *Diary* (1893) II. 163 *note*, Heatley, the trumpet major,..and Fitzhenry, an old mungo and pupil of mine on the tambourine.

mungo[4] ('mʌŋgəʊ). Also **mongoe.** [Of obscure origin.

The story (obviously a figment) commonly told to account for the word is that when the first sample of the article was made, the foreman said 'It won't go', to which the master replied 'But it *mun go*' (i.e. must go).

Possibly the Scotch Christian name *Mungo* (in Yorkshire often used as a name for dogs) may have been applied to the material in jocular allusion to *mung*, MONG *sb.*[1], mixture, mixed meal.]

A fabric made from the short fibres recovered from old hardwoven or felted material. Also *attrib.*

1857 *Post Office Directory Yorks.* 1001 Mungo Merchants and Dealers [40 entries]. **1858** *Brit. Assoc. Rept.* 160 A large quantity of rag wool called shoddy and mungo imported from Germany. **1860** S. JUBB *Shoddy-trade* 19 The principal part of a rag machine is the swift..; the coarser set swifts are used to grind soft rags into shoddy; the finer set ones, to tear cloth rags into mungo. *Ibid.* 32 Mungo rag is either old or new. **1862** *Catal. Internat. Exhib.* II. XXI. 28 Shoddy and mungo, made from woollen rags. **1864** *Times* 19 Mar. 7/2 D. Illingworth and Son, Leeds, mungo manufacturers. **1879** *Cassell's Techn. Educ.* IV. 261/1 Technically speaking soft woollen rags..are converted into 'shoddy' and hard and fine woollen rags..into 'mungo'. **1884** *Cassell's Family Mag.* Feb. 155/2 A great many people are..occupied in cutting out the seams and button-holes of old cloth clothes... These are called *mongoe-cutters*, and the prepared woollen rags are known as *mongoe*. **1961** BLACKSHAW & BRIGHTMAN *Dict. Dyeing & Textile Printing* 116 *Mungo*, the poorest grade of *shoddy*, being that obtained from rags, etc., and from materials which have been felted. **1968** [see FIBRO, FIBRO 1].

mun'gofa. = GOPHER *sb.*[1] 3.

1836 J. E. HOLBROOK *N. Amer. Herpetol.* I. 41 *Testudo polyphemus*—Daudin. Synonymes... Gopher and Mungofa, *Vulgo*. **1844** J. E. GRAY *Catal. Tortoises*, etc. *Brit. Mus.* 4 The Gopher or Mungofa. *Testudo Gopher.* **1879** *Encycl. Brit.* X. 780/1 The flesh of the gopher or mungofa.. is considered excellent eating.

mungoos(e, mungos: see MONGOOSE, MUNGO[1].

mungrel(l, -il(l, obs. forms of MONGREL.

‖**munguba.** Also **monguba.** [Tupi.] A South American silk-cotton tree, *Bombax Munguba*.

1863 BATES *Nat. Amazons* i. (1864) 7 In the rainy season, when the monguba trees shed their leaves. **1866** *Treas. Bot.* 155/1 *Bombax Munguba* is a smooth-stemmed tree about eighty or one hundred feet high, commonly found on the banks of the Amazon river and the Rio Negro, where the natives call it Munguba.

Mungul, obs. form of MONGOL.

'**mungy**, *a. Obs.* exc. *dial.* [Perh. an altered form of MUGGY (which, however, does not occur in our quots. before 1730).]

†**1.** Dark, gloomy. *Obs.*

1632 VICARS tr. *Virgil* III. 81 Mungy clouds o'respread the skie most black. **1635** QUARLES *Embl.* V. v, Disperse these plague-distilling Clouds, and cleare My mungy Soule into a glorious day.

2. = MUGGY *a.* 1.

1658 EVELYN *Fr. Gard.* (1675) 4 The rotten sticks and mungy stuff to be found under old wood-piles. **1664** —— *Sylva* (1679) 10 Scatter a little mungy, half-rotten Littier, Fearn, Bean-hame, or old Leaves among them. **1707** MORTIMER *Husb.* 384 Round the Stem of the Tree to raise a small Hill about two Foot thick,..which cover with Stones, Tiles, or mungy Straw, to keep it moist.

3. Of weather: Muggy (see E.D.D.).

1815 *Monthly Mag.* XXXIX. 125 Essex Dialect..*Mongy*, Foggy.

‖**muni** ('mʊniː). *Hinduism* and *Jainism.* Also **moonee.** [a. Skr. *múni* impulse, eagerness (?), one moved by inward impulse, a seer, saint, etc., f. *man* to think.] An inspired or holy man; a sage; an ascetic or hermit.

1785 C. WILKINS tr. *Bhăgvăt-Gēētā* ii. 41 A man is said to be confirmed in wisdom, when he forsaketh every desire which entereth into his heart, and of himself is happy, and contented in himself... Such a wise man is called a *Mōōnĕē*. **1796** [see DHARMA]. **1811** W. WARD *Acct. of Hindoos* II. 46 How the moonees instruct their disciples in the different kinds of learning. **1828** H. H. WILSON in *Asiatick Res.* XVI. 18 The *Chárvákas* were so named from one of their teachers, the Muni Chárváka. **1854** M. MÜLLER in C. C. J. Bunsen *Christianity & Mankind* III. 285 The Turanian life is no longer a family life, or the life of a troglodyte Muni. **1866** E. T. DALTON in *Jrnl. Asiatic Soc. of Bengal* XXXV. II. (Special Number) 160 There is no tradition even of the 'Munis' having sought retreats amongst its rocks or by its waterfalls for their devotional exercises. **1875** MONIER-WILLIAMS *Indian Wisdom* x. 260 Let him remain without fire, without habitation, feeding on roots and fruits, practising the vow of a Muni. **1949** A. DANIÉLOU *N. Indian Music* I. ii. 39 Matañgā Muni considers that the word deśhī (worldly) applies to all earthly music. **1969** W. R. TRASK tr. *Eliade's Yoga* (ed. 2) viii. 327 Let us recall the *muni* of the *Rg-Veda* who, 'in the intoxication of ecstasy', mounted the 'chariot of the winds'. **1971** *Illus. Weekly India* 11 Apr. 17/1 The Jain Munis believe that the body is a great source of sin and must be subjugated and won over. **1972** P. Holroyde *Indian Music* iii. 74 The most famous of all their musical theoreticians: Bharata Muni.

muniall, obs. form of MONIAL *sb.*²

† **ˈmuniate**, *v. Obs.* [Badly f. L. *mūni-o, mūnīre* to fortify + -ATE.] *trans.* To fortify.

1657 Tomlinson *Renou's Disp.* 190 An Epitheme thus confected, will muniate and preserve the heart.

Munich (ˈmjuːnɪk). [G. *München.*] The name of the capital of Bavaria used with reference to a meeting of representatives of Germany, Great Britain, France, and Italy on 29 September 1938, when (by the Munich Agreement) the Sudetenland of N. Czechoslovakia was ceded to Germany; also *transf.* as a typical example of dishonourable appeasement. Hence **Muniˈcheer**, **ˈMunichite**, advocates of such an appeasement policy. Also **ˈMunichism**, such a policy. Also *attrib.*

1938 H. Nicolson *Diary* 8 Oct. (1966) I. 376 Go up to Leicester. Bertie Jarvis says that I have put the women's vote against me by abusing Munich. **1939** *Ann. Reg. 1938* 76 The Prime Minister followed with his defence of the Munich Agreement. **1939** A. Huxley *After Many a Summer* I. viii. 106 These last months, since the *Anschluss* and Munich, one had found that political discussion was one of the unpleasant things it was wise to avoid. **1939** L. MacNeice *Autumn Jrnl.* 36 Glory to God for Munich. **1941** *Amer. Speech* XVI. 66/1–2 *Munichism*..'the spirit of the surrender at Munich; appeasement'. **1942** *R.A.F. Jrnl.* 27 June 13 They do not enter into discussions with dishonourable men..; they have always known the real futility of 'Munichs'. **1942** *Sun* (Baltimore) 5 Aug. 4 (*heading*) Writer finds people hostile to war officialdom, Commons and Municheers. **1944** H. G. Wells *'42 to '44* 76 The misconduct of the war from Munich onward. **1950** A. Wilson *Such Darling Dodos* 88 Tony was not..unpatriotic, but he had been a great Munichite. **1955** *Ann. Reg. 1954* 24 A further complication..was the absence of normal diplomatic relations between a number of countries... Someone had to provide a channel of communication, even at the risk of being called a 'Municheer'. **1957** R. W. Zandvoort in *Wiener Beiträge* LXV. 281 *Munich*..giving rise to the words *Municheers* and *anti-Municheers*. **1958** *Spectator* 6 June 735/2 The pressure put upon President Benes to accept the Munich agreement. **1960** C. Day Lewis *Buried Day* v. 97 The hallucinatory and irresponsible Munich period. **1962** M. Foot *Aneurin Bevan* I. ix. 285 At Bridgwater, Vernon Bartlett,..won a spectacular victory in the teeth of all the 'peace' propaganda of the Munichites. **1967** *Listener* 5 Oct. 422/3 There are analogies from history—another Munich, another Dunkirk [etc.]—although historians assure us that history never repeats itself. **1973** K. Giles *File on Death* i. 7 Some of the most valuable men in this country were..Men of Munich, vulgarly so called. Now..we have little Munichs every week.

municion, obs. form of MUNITION.

municipal (mjuːˈnɪsɪpəl), *a.* and *sb.* Also α. 6 municipale, 6–7 municipall, municiple; β. 7 municipial(l. [a. L. *mūnicipālis*, f. *mūnicip-*, *mūniceps* member of a MUNICIPIUM, f. *mūni-a* pl., civic offices (cogn. w. *mūner-*, *mūnus*: see MUNERAL) + root of *capĕre* to take. Cf. F., Sp., Pg. *municipal*, It. *munizipale*.

The form *municipial*, common in 17th c., is due either to regarding the word as a derivative of *mūnicipium*, or to uncertainty as to the proper form of a derivative from *mūniceps*.]

A. *adj.*

1. a. Pertaining to the internal affairs of a state as distinguished from its foreign relations. Originally and still chiefly in the phrase ***municipal law***, the law of a particular state, as distinguished from international law or the law of nations (see also quot. 1959). So ***municipal rights, jurisdiction***, etc.

c **1540** tr. *Pol. Verg. Eng. Hist.* (Camden) I. 11 But the Englishe people use the propre and municipall lawes. **1565** *Reg. Privy Council Scot.* I. 332 Sic kynd of gudis as be the lawis municipal of this realme are expres forbidden. **1691** Wood *Ath. Oxon.* I. 23 He retired to Greys Inn in Holbourn to obtain knowledge in the municipal Law. **1740** W. Douglass *Disc. Curr. Brit. Plant. Amer.* 4 Every Country or Society have their own peculiar Regulations, which may be called their Municipal, or By-Laws in Trade. **1765** Blackstone *Comm.* I. Introd. ii. 44 Municipal or civil law: that is, the rule by which particular districts, communities, or nations are governed. **1806** Vesey *Reports* VI. 699 Notwithstanding the Union, for all the municipal jurisdiction of the Great Seal,..the countries remain as distinct, as formerly. **1861** *Sat. Rev.* 7 Dec. 580 Finding accidentally in the course of her search deserters from her navy on board, she claimed the municipal right of bringing them back to the service from which they had escaped. **1959** Jowitt *Dict. Eng. Law* II. 1201/1 *Municipal law*, that which pertains solely to the citizens and inhabitants of a State, and is thus distinguished from political law and the law of nations. **1965** *Mod. Law Review* XXVIII. 626 There is a useful review of municipal decisions which points to some areas of prospective conflict between community law and municipal law. **1971** *Ibid.* XXXIV. 602 A miscellany of other changes in United Kingdom law will have to be introduced in order to bring municipal law into closer harmony with Community law.

b. *transf.* Belonging to one place only; having narrow limits. [Cf. late L. *dii municipes*, gods whose worship is confined to particular localities.]

1631 Massinger *Emperor East* I. ii, Whose beames of iustice like the Sun extend Their light, and heate to strangers, and are not Municipall, or confinde. **1856** Emerson *Eng. Traits, Lit.* Wks. (Bohn) II. 109 The essays, the fiction, and the poetry of the day have the like municipal limits.

2. a. Pertaining to the local self-government or corporate government of a city or town.

In common use only from the 19th c.

1600 W. Watson *Decacordon* (1602) 43 A very hotch potch of omnium githerum,..politicall, liberall, mechanicall, municipiall, irregular, and all without order. **1604** R. Cawdrey *Table Alph.*, *Municipall*, priuately belonging to a freeman, or burgesse of a cittie. **1656** Blount *Glossogr.*, *Municipial, Municipal*, proper or peculiar to one onely City, or to the right of Freedom in a City. **1727–41** Chambers *Cycl.*, *Municipal officers*, are those elected to defend the interests of cities, their rights and privileges, and to maintain order and good policy; as mayors, sheriffs, consuls, bailiffs, &c. **1845** *Encycl. Metrop.* XIII. 569/2 After incredible efforts, the communes succeeded in obtaining a share in the municipal government. **1846** McCulloch *Acc. Brit. Empire* (1854) II. 197 Little or no change took place in the municipal constitution of corporations. **1864** *Chamb. Encycl.* VI. 611/2 By granting or renewing to them municipal charters. **1898** *Westm. Gaz.* 2 July 2/3 There is just now an interesting municipal tramway development in the Midlands.

b. ***municipal borough***: see quots.

1868 *Act 31 & 32 Vict.* c. 41 §2 In this Act..The Term 'Municipal Borough' means a Place subject to the Provisions of the Act of [5 & 6 Will. IV, c. 76]. **1889** *Act 52 & 53 Vict.* c. 63 §15 The expression ' municipal borough' shall mean, as respects England and Wales, any place for the time being subject to the Municipal Corporations Act, 1882.

3. *Roman Hist.* Of or pertaining to a MUNICIPIUM; hence contemptuously, provincial.

1618 Bolton *Florus* (1636) 228 Every Army of our most Valiant, and most Loyall Fellowes had under each ensigne those municipall bad members, and monsters of men. **1658** W. Burton *Itin. Anton.* 149 They were not any part of that Imperial body till favourably received by municipial priviledge into the freedom. **1850** Merivale *Rom. Emp.* ii. (1865) I. 61 The nobles looked with secret disdain upon his municipal extraction, his plebeian descent and recent nobility.

B. *sb.*

1. *Roman Hist.* An inhabitant of a municipium (tr. L. *municeps*).

1727–41 Chambers *Cycl.* s.v. *Municipal*, In the Roman law, municipal denotes a person vested with the rights and privileges of a Roman citizen. **1853** Merivale *Rom. Rep.* vii. (1807) 189 He was personally little known, being a new man, a municipal of Arpinum, without family distinctions. **1887** Cory *Lett. & Jrnls.* (1897) 524 Livy bears witness to the character of the Romans, including the municipals.

‖2. [Fr.: short for *garde municipale*.] A member of the Municipal Guard (F. *garde municipale*), a body of soldiers under the control of the municipality of Paris.

1837 Carlyle *Fr. Rev.* II. vi. vi, Is it not a happiness for many a Municipal that he can wash his hands of such a business. **1841** Thackeray *2nd Funeral Napoleon* iii. 64 These were followed by a regiment, a detachment of the municipals, on foot.

†3. *pl.* = Municipal laws. *Obs.*

1586 Ferne *Blaz. Gentrie* To Gent. Inner Temple, It might turne to some disparagement of my knowledge in the common lawes and municiples of our country.

municipalism (mjuːˈnɪsɪpəlɪz(ə)m). [f. MUNICIPAL *a.* + -ISM.] a. Devotion to the interests of one's municipality; municipal or local patriotism in contradistinction to national patriotism. b. Municipal institutions generally; also, preference for the municipal as opposed to the centralizing principle in local government.

1851 Gallenga *Italy* 41 That the provincialism, or *particularismus* (to use a German expression), of rival seats of government,..has nothing to do with the fierce rancours of ancient municipalism. **1875** Merivale *Gen. Hist. Rome* lxxx. (1877) 689 The narrow ideas of patriotic duty, by which they had fostered their intense municipalism, were rapidly obliterated. **1897** *Encycl. Soc. Reform* 905 Municipalism may be defined as the theory, or the practice of the theory, that it is wise to extend the functions of the municipality. **1898** *Daily News* 13 Dec. 8/3 Mr. Sidney Webb has been studying 'Municipalism',..with characteristic zeal in the United States, Australia, and New Zealand.

municipalist (mjuːˈnɪsɪpəlɪst). [f. MUNICIPAL *a.* + -IST.] a. One who advocates the extension of the range of municipal action or control; e.g. an advocate of municipal trading. b. One who is skilled or experienced in municipal administration.

1859 (*title*) The Municipalist, New York. **1899** *Westm. Gaz.* 10 Apr. 9/2 The Municipalists in the United States scored several notable successes at the recent elections. **1904** *Daily Chron.* 20 Apr. 4/4 It was odd to hear the son of the great municipalist attacking, in his father's presence, the municipalities for their heavy borrowings.

municipality (mjuːnɪsɪˈpælɪtɪ). [a. F. *municipalité*, f. *municipal*: see MUNICIPAL.]

1. A town, city, or district possessed of privileges of local self-government, also applied to its inhabitants collectively.

Somewhat *rare* exc. with reference to foreign countries (as France or Italy) where the word is the regular name of an administrative unit. 'In New Orleans, a district of the city corresponding to a ward' (Webster 1847).

1790 Burke *Fr. Rev.* Sel. Wks. II. 143 The municipalities had taken an alarm. **1841** Lewis *On Govt. Dependencies* 71 *note*, A body of public functionaries may preside for certain purposes over a district (as a county, department, municipality, or borough). **1865** Maffei *Brigand Life* II. 47 In the municipality of Bisaccia..the only boys' school was a miserable place which hardly deserved the name.

2. The governing body of a town or district having municipal institutions (usually, the Mayor and Corporation).

1795 Hel. M. Williams *Lett. on France* I. 170 (Jod.) We afterwards obtained our liberty by means of the municipality to whom we were unknown. **1800** Wellington in Gurw. *Desp.* (1834) I. 262 They might for a time be under the inspection of the municipality (to use a French phrase). **1836** Alison *Hist. Europe* xlii. §8 (1849–50) VII. 91 To the great disappointment of the municipality and people. **1885** *Pall Mall G.* 18 Nov. 4/2 If the new municipality provide these, then the supply of the inferior water of the companies may be purchased if desired.

3. A MUNICIPIUM.

a **1805** Murphy *Sallust* (1807) 196 If by your authority you oblige the municipalities to receive the prisoners. **1872** E. W. Robertson *Hist. Ess.* 237 The Municipality, from uniting the advantages of self-government with the privileges of citizenship, became the most favoured form of colony.

4. Government on municipal principles; municipal institutions.

187. E. A. Freeman in L. Stephen *Lett. J. R. Green* (1902) 214 Here [in Italy] was municipality on its grandest scale.

municipalization (mjuːnɪsɪpəlaɪˈzeɪʃən). [-ATION.] The action of the verb MUNICIPALIZE.

1884 J. Rae in *Contemp. Rev.* Feb. 296 The municipalization of ground rents. **1890** G. B. Shaw *Fabian Ess. Socialism* 51 The further municipalization of the gas industry is proceeding with great rapidity. **1958** *Economist* 13 Dec. 967/2 When Labour's election manifesto two weeks ago turned its back on the party's previous extraordinary scheme for the compulsory municipalisation of virtually all rented houses, Conservative propagandists growled angrily like a dog that was being deprived of a bone. **1970** *Internat. & Compar. Law Quarterly* 4th Ser. XIX. II. 211 The Dutch have..a system of nationalisation of housing with 85 per cent of all housing in municipal ownership. Nor is this a development occasioned by wartime devastation, as municipalisation can be traced back to a statute of 1905. **1972** *Guardian* 2 Nov. 12/4 Anthony Crosland..puts the case for the large-scale municipalisation of low-income rented housing. **1974** *Daily Tel.* 12 Jan. 5/2 The 'municipalisation' of privately rented property—except where the owner-occupier shares a house with a tenant—would be encouraged.

municipalize (mjuːˈnɪsɪpəlaɪz), *v.* [f. MUNICIPAL *a.* + -IZE.] *trans.* To bring under municipal ownership or control; to endow (a city, etc.) with municipal institutions.

1880 W. M. Torrens in *19th Cent.* Nov. 770 A measure for municipalising London. **1893** E. S. L. Buckland in *Westm. Rev.* Feb. 127 Now, when men are so anxious to municipalise our institutions. **1903** L. Darwin *Municipal Trade* 3 The different kinds of enterprises which have..been extensively municipalised. **1955** *Times* 1 June 7/2 The first action of the revolutionaries was to abolish, without compensation, all private ownership of land; a little later most urban dwellings were 'municipalized'. **1973** *Times* 25 Sept. 17/2 The programme of municipalization includes the building societies... It also includes the expensive commitment to municipalize rented housing.

municipalizer (mjuːˈnɪsɪpəlaɪzə(r)). [f. MUNICIPALIZE *v.* + -ER¹.] One who favours municipal control of public services, institutions, and the like; = MUNICIPALIST a.

1908 G. B. Shaw *Commonsense of Municipal Trading* p. ix, The most..disinterested of them would..become ardent municipalizers. **1928** *Weekly Dispatch* 24 June 9/3 Within the movement there are (1) prohibitionists,..(2) municipalisers; (3) advocates of State ownership and control.

municipally (mjuːˈnɪsɪpəlɪ), *adv.* [f. MUNICIPAL *a.* + -LY².] a. With regard to a municipality or municipal affairs.

a **1842** Arnold *Hist. Rome* (1843) III. 8 At the beginning of the second Punic war Capua..was beyond all doubt municipally independent. **1888** *Pall Mall G.* 9 May 6/2 General Boulanger has been municipally returned for three Communes in the Department of Lozère.

b. *Comb.*, as ***municipally-owned*** adj.

1898 E. Howard *To-Morrow* vi. 65 It may be found—especially on municipally-owned land—that the field of municipal activity may grow so as to embrace a very large area, and yet the municipality claim no rigid monopoly. **1972** *Guardian* 4 Dec. 6/8 Hull Corporation..runs the only municipally-owned telephone service in the country.

municipial(l, obs. forms of MUNICIPAL.

‖**municipio** (mjuːnɪˈsɪpɪəʊ, -ˈtʃɪpɪəʊ). [Sp. and It.] A municipality; a corporation, a town council. Also *attrib.*

1896 G. Bell *Let.* 14 Apr. (1927) I. 35 The Municipio appeared in splendid gondolas hung with streamers. **1938** E. Hemingway *Fifth Column* (1939) 275 No one will make any trouble for me in Cortina. I know them all at the municipio. **1948** K. Davis *Human Society* 317 The *municipios* of Latin America (somewhat similar to our New England townships). **1965** *Language* XLI. 471 All are natives of the large municipio town of Xochistlahuaca, Guerrero. **1972** *Country Life* 2 Mar. 508/1 French is as much in evidence as Italian [in Valle d'Aosta]...it strikes one as odd seeing the word *Mairie* over an Italian Municipio.

‖**municipium** (mjuːnɪˈsɪpɪəm). *Roman Ant.* Pl. **municipia**. [L. *mūnicipium*, f. *mūnicip-*, *mūniceps*: see MUNICIPAL.] A city whose citizens had the privileges of Roman citizens.

1720 STRYPE *Stow's Surv.* I. i. 7/1 Nor is there any Reason to think the Romans built the City of London where there was neither a Colony nor a Municipium. **1727** LARDNER *Wks.* (1838) I. 79 *Municipia* were towns, or cities, which had the citizenship of Rome bestowed upon them, and yet still lived according to their own laws and constitutions. **1861** PEARSON *Early & Mid. Ages Eng.* 184 A Roman colonia or municipium had consisted pretty generally of two main classes, the servile, and the free, who might by courtesy be called the self-governing.

municiple, obs. form of MUNICIPAL.

municipy (mjuːˈnɪsɪpɪ). *rare.* [ad. L. *municipium*: see MUNICIPIUM.]

†**a.** = MUNICIPIUM. **b.** A municipality.

1579 TWYNE *Phisicke agst. Fort.* II. Ep. Ded. 160b, The actes and lawes of certeine Municipies or freedomes haue bene such,..that they haue perished with their authours. **1882** W. CORY *Mod. Eng. Hist.* II. 431 A parish was not a municipy or corporation..the Legislature quietly created federal municipies called Boards of Guardians, capable of..buying manorial or trust lands.

†**muˈniferous**, *a. Obs.* [f. late L. *mūnifer* (f. *mūn-us* gift + *-fer* bearing) + -OUS.] (See quot.)

1656 BLOUNT *Glossogr.*, *Muniferous*,..that carries a gift.

†**muˈnific**, *a. Obs.* [a. L. *mūnific-us*, f. *mūn-us* gift: see MUNERAL and -FIC.] = MUNIFICENT. So †**muniˈfical** *a.*

1603 KNOLLES *Hist. Turks* (1621) 931 With trumpets, drums, peales of ordinance, and all other signes of munificall and joyfull entertainment. **1656** BLOUNT *Glossogr.*, *Munifical*, (*munificus*), bountiful, liberal. **1754** T. BLACKLOCK *Hymn Div. Love* vi, To thee, munific, ever-flaming Love! One endless hymn united nature sings.

†**muˈnificate**, *v. Obs.* [f. L. *mūnificāt-*, *mūnificāre*, f. *mūnific-us*: see prec.] (See quot.)

1623 COCKERAM, *Munificate*, to inrich.

†**munifiˈcation**. *Obs.* [f. MUNIFY *v.*: see -FICATION.] Protection; defence.

1653 R. SANDERS *Physiogn.* b iij, Against the most hostile shafts of envy, I shall not need much munification.

munificence (mjuːˈnɪfɪsəns). [a. F. *munificence*, ad. L. *mūnificentia*, f. *mūnificent-*: see MUNIFICENT *a.*] The quality of being munificent; splendid liberality in giving.

1555 EDEN *Decades* 93 To persuade hym of the..munificence..of owre men. **1581** MULCASTER *Positions* xxxviii. (1887) 170 That benefit, which the munificence of nature hath liberally bestowed on him. **1685** PETTY *Last Will* in *Tracts* (1769) p. ix, I would advise my wife in this case, to spend her whole 1587 *l.* per ann. that is to say, on her own entertainment, charity, and munificence. **1793** *Blackstone's Comm.* I. viii. 286 *note*, Though this was a splendid instance of royal munificence, yet it's operation is slow and inconsiderable. **1845** M. PATTISON *Ess.* (1889) I. 12 The miracles and power of the saint called forth the devotion and munificence of the people. **1892** GLADSTONE in *Daily News* 5 Dec. 3/4, I am sure that Liverpool, while it continues to amass wealth, will not fall behind in the necessary concomitant to redeem wealth from degradation—the quality of munificence.

†**muˈnificency**. *Obs.* Also 6 **-entie**, **munefycencie**. [ad. L. *mūnificentia*: see prec.] = MUNIFICENCE. Also, an instance of munificence.

c **1540** tr. *Pol. Verg. Eng. Hist.* (Camden) I. 83 Lucius..consecratinge to Christe suche temples as weare erected for the idolls of the jentiles, largelie adorned them with his munificentie. **1576** WOOLTON *Chr. Manual* F vj, Munefycencie, lyberalytie, and hospytalyty. **1613** SHERLEY *Trav. Persia* 83 Why should hee not giue time to the growing of his better fortunes, by your Maiesties Munificencies and fauours. **1615** G. SANDYS *Trav.* 93 Whatsoever here is estimable, proceedeth from the Munificency of this River. **1651** G. W. tr. *Cowel's Inst.* 114 Either by the munificency of our Kings, or by the too much negligency of our Common-wealth.

munificent (mjuːˈnɪfɪsənt), *a.* [f. L. *mūnificent-*, derivation-stem of *mūnificus*: see MUNIFIC *a.*

Not in Fr.; the form was suggested by *magnificent* and the other words of similar ending, and by *munificence*.]

Of persons: Splendidly generous in gifts, bountiful. Of actions, gifts: Characterized by munificence.

1583 HAYES *Gilbert's Voy.* in Hakluyt (1589) 680 Imitating the nature of the munificent God. **1607** B. JONSON *Volpone* I. iii, You are too munificent. **1649** *Alcoran* 27 God promiseth to you his grace and mercie; he is munificent, and omniscient. **1682** SIR T. BROWNE *Chr. Mor.* I. §5 Think it not enough to be Liberal, but Munificent. **1765** BLACKSTONE *Comm.* I. Introd. i. 27 Our munificent benefactor Mr. Viner. **1815** W. H. IRELAND *Scribbleomania* 200 *note*, Chaucer, and his munificent friend and patron John of Gaunt. **1849** MACAULAY *Hist. Eng.* vi. II. 78 Perhaps none of the munificent subscriptions of our own age has borne so great a proportion to the means of the nation. **1868** MILMAN *St. Paul's* xiii. 332 Laud..was munificent, almost magnificent. **1893** R. T. JEFFREY *Visits to Calvary* 147 A munificent marriage settlement has been made for you.

munificently (mjuːˈnɪfɪsəntlɪ), *adv.* [f. MUNIFICENT *a.* + -LY².] In a munificent manner; with splendid generosity.

1594 NASHE *Unfort. Trav.* G j, Some large summes of monie..which I knew not how better to imploy..than by spending it munificently vnder your name. **1628** BP. HALL *Old Relig.* vi. §2. 48 That God doth graciously accept, and munificently recompence our good workes. **1874** GREEN *Short Hist.* vi. §5. 317 Henry had munificently rewarded his services to the crown.

Hence †**muˈnificentness**. *Obs.*⁻⁰

1727 BAILEY vol. II, *Munificentness*, Liberality, Bountifulness.

†**munifience**. *Obs.* [Badly f. MUNIFY + -ENCE.] Fortification, defence.

1596 SPENSER *F.Q.* II. x. 15 Untill that Locrine for his Realmes defence, Did head against them make and strong munifience [*so ed.* 1596; *ed.* 1590 *has* munificence].

†**ˈmunify**, *v. Obs.* [irreg. f. L. *mūni-o* (inf. *mūnīre*) to fortify + -FY.] *trans.* To fortify; to provide with defences. Hence **ˈmunified** *ppl. a.*

1603 DRAYTON *Bar. Wars* II. xxxiv, The King assayles, the Barons munify'd. **1611** SPEED *Hist. Gt. Brit.* IX. viii. 27 Though many well munified places were fetched off without any resistance. **1635** HEYWOOD *Hierarch.* 609 The Diuell..replied that he..had no power to enter, the place being so munified and defended by his holy supplications.

muniment (ˈmjuːnɪmənt). Forms: 5 **minement**, **munyment(e**, 5–6 **munimente**, 6 **minumente**, **myniment**, 6–8 **miniment**, 7 **munument**, **mynamente**, 4– **muniment**. [a. OF. *muniment* (AF., in sense 1, *Rolls Parlt.* an. 1315), ad. L. *mūnīmentum* fortification, defence (in med.Latin title-deed, etc., as sense 1 below), f. *mūnī-re*: see MUNITE *v.* and -MENT.]

1. A document (such as a title-deed, charter, etc.) preserved as evidence in defence of rights or privileges belonging to a person, family, or corporation. Chiefly in *collective plural*.

Formerly sometimes confused with MONUMENT *sb.* 2.

1433 *Rolls of Parlt.* IV. 479/1 Alle the Munimentes that longeth to the Cominalte of the seid Town. *c* **1470** HARDING *Chron.* Proëm. xxvii, I haue seen of it the muniment, Vnder seale wryten. **1485** *Rolls of Parlt.* VI. 295/2 All Evidences, Deeds and Minements, concerning the said Mannors. **1503–4** *Act 19 Hen. VII*, c. 35 §2 All the evydences chartrez and munymentes concernyng the premysses. **1552** HULOET, *Rolles* or lyke places, where minumentes or recordes be kepte. **1594** WEST *2nd Pt. Symbol.*, *Chancerie* §105 The said deedes, evidences, escriptes, writings, and myniments. **1620** in *Eng. Gilds* (1870) 287 The ancient recordes and mynamentes, not onely of the towne, but also of other societies in other remote places of the kingdome. **1776** *Trial of Nundocomar* 32/2 Among the other records and muniments. **1845** LD. CAMPBELL *Chancellors* (1857) I. xiii. 194 The roll of his domestic expenses, preserved among the muniments of the bishopric. **1893** FOWLER *Hist. C.C.C.* (O.H.S.) 198 The various muniments, i.e. title-deeds or evidences relating to the College property.

2. Anything serving as a means of defence or protection. Now *rare*.

1546 LANGLEY *Pol. Verg. De Invent.* Pref. 2 For both Beastes and Birdes have..weapons as Hornes tuskes and other like munimentes to resist their foes. **1578** BANISTER *Hist. Man* I. 6 The Bones..which to the brayne, in their construction, are so safe a muniment. **1629** B. JONSON *On Poems Sir J. Beaumont*, Though I confesse a Beaumonts Booke to bee The Bound, and Frontire of our Poetrie; And doth deserue all muniments of praise, That Art, or Ingine, on the strength can raise. **1650** BULWER *Anthropomet.* 130 Others conceive one use of the Beard was for a munument. **1677** PLOT *Oxfordsh.* 339 These Fora, or places of Judicature (by the Danes called Tings), seem always to have had their muniments of stone. **1830** *Examiner* 163/2 Truth is the simple muniment with which every power used for evil may be met. **1860** EMERSON *Cond. Life*, *Worship* Wks. (Bohn) II. 403 We cannot spare the coarsest muniment of virtue.

†**b.** [Cf. F. *munir* to furnish (with); also MUNITION.] *pl.* Things with which a person or place is provided; furnishings. *Obs.*

1485 CAXTON *St. Wenefr.* 24 The couent that were gone oute cladde them with precious ornamentes of the chirche..and dredde not a lytell that the ornamentes and munymentis shold be sore hurte by the fallyng of the rayne. **1596** SPENSER *F.Q.* IV. viii. 6 By chance he certaine miniments forth drew, Which yet with him as relickes did abide. **1607** SHAKS. *Cor.* I. i. 122 Our Steed the Legge, the Tongue our Trumpeter, With other Muniments and petty helpes In this our Fabricke. **1852** MUNDY *Our Antipodes* (1857) 6 Where the receiving-rooms and bed-rooms contain little beyond the muniments necessary for sitting and lying.

3. *attrib.*, as ***muniment-chest***, ***-house***, ***-room***; also **muniment deed**, a title-deed.

1870 F. R. WILSON *Ch. Lindisf.* 114 In this chamber is a large carved *muniment chest. *a* **1864** HAWTHORNE *Sept. Felton* (1879) 162 Have you..no *muniment deed? **1656** BLOUNT *Glossogr.*, A **Muniment house* (in Cathedral, or Collegiate Churches, Castles, Colledges or such like) is a house or little room of strength, purposely made for keeping the Seal, Plate, Evidences, Charters, &c. of such Church, Colledge, &c., such Evidences being called in Law *Muniments*. **1661** WOOD *Life* 18 Mar. (O.H.S.) I. 384 Dʳ. Wallis sent for A. W. to com to him, then in the *muniment-room in the School Tower. **1899** A. CLARK *Wood's Oxford* (O.H.S.) III. 105 In the muniment-room of the Dean and Chapter of Lincoln.

†**ˈmunion**. *Mil. Obs. rare.* [a. F. *moignon* stump: see MONION.] The trunnion of a gun.

1646 ELDRED *Gunners Glasse* 104 The knobs of the mettal at each side of the Peece are called the Tronions or Munions.

munion, variant of MUNNION.

†**ˈmunish**, *v. Obs.*⁻¹ [f. F. *muniss-*, lengthened stem of *munir*:—L. *mūnīre*: see MUNITE *v.*] *trans.* To fortify, provide with means of defence.

1633 J. DONE *Hist. Septuagint* 69 It is scituated neare to the Temple in a most faire seate munished with many towers made of Stones of extreame greatnesse.

munishon, obs. form of MUNITION.

muˈnite, *v. Obs.* exc. *Hist. Pa. pple.* 5–6 **munyte**, 7 **munite**. [f. L. *mūnīt-*, ppl. stem of *mūnīre* to wall round, fortify, secure, earlier *mœnīre*, f. *mœnia* pl., walls, ramparts; cogn. w. *mūrus* (earlier *mœrus*) wall.] *trans.* To fortify, strengthen, protect. Hence †**muˈnited** *ppl. a.*, †**muˈniting** *vbl. sb.*

c **1420** *Pallad. on Husb.* VI. 223 Other condite hem kepe in pottes clene With pyk munyte & couching throute alway. **1533** *St. Papers Hen. VIII* (1830) I. 411 *note*, The fortresses and havens to be fortifyed and munyted. **1578** BANISTER *Hist. Man.* I. 6 The head..in whose propper angles they are ..strongly munited from all externe and accidentall iniuries. **1603** FLORIO *Montaigne* I. xlvii. (1632) 154 He had the better leasure to..strengthen Townes, to munite Castles [etc.]. **1624** QUARLES *Sion's Sonn.* xx. 14 An yvorie Tower, In..munited power. **1625** BACON *Ess.*, *Unity in Relig.* (Arb.) 431 Men must beware, that in the Procuring, or Muniting, of Religious Vnity, they doe not Dissolue and Deface the Lawes of Charity. **1657** EARL MONM. tr. *Paruta's Pol. Disc.* 170 His Enemy is in the Dominions, in a well munited seat. **1665** J. WEBB *Stone-Heng* 150 It was not unusual..to munite the *Tumuli* of their Dead with such empalements. **1696** PHILLIPS (ed. 5), *Munite*, fenced, made strong.

munition (mjuːˈnɪʃən), *sb.* Forms: 5 **munycion**, 5–6 **monysion**, **-yon**, 5–7 **municion**, 6 **monition**, **monycion**, **munishon**, **munitione**, **-tioun(e**, **munycyon**, 6– **munition**. [a. F. *munition*, ad.L. *mūnītiōn-em*, f. *mūnīre*: see MUNITE *v.*]

†**1. a.** The action of fortifying or defending, fortification. *lit.* and *fig.* **b.** *concr.* A fortification, defensive structure or work; anything that serves as a defence or protection. *Obs.*

1533 BELLENDEN *Livy* I. iii. (S.T.S.) 22 Sic thingis done, he garnist mont palentyne, quhare he was nurist, with strang mvnitioun. *c* **1540** tr. *Pol. Verg. Eng. Hist.* (Camden) I. 259 Leavinge a garrison for the munition of the porte hee hasted into Denmarcke. **1555** EDEN *Decades* 121 The situation of the place hath no natural munition or defense. **1565** CALFHILL *Answ. Treat. Crosse* 39 Let vs enter into the walled cities, The battayles of the Heretiques doe arise, Let the munitions of Christ holde vs. **1613** PURCHAS *Pilgrimage* (1614) 598 The inhabitants..haue the middest of the Groue fortified with a triple wall. The first munition containeth the Kings Pallace; the second [etc.]. *a* **1619** DANIEL *On Death Earl of Devon.* 351 With what munition he did fortifie His heart. *a* **1619** FOTHERBY *Atheom.* II. vii. §4 (1622) 268 The fortification and munition of their Towne. **1675** T. TURNOR *Bankers & Creditors* (ed. 2) 39 Such was the Care of our Ancestors..in the Munition and Fencing about of their Rights and Properties. *a* **1716** SOUTH *Serm.* (1744) VII. iv. 75 The inward firmness of one must be corroborated by the exterior munitions of the other. **1791** COWPER *Iliad* I. 357 Whose might, the chief munition is of all our host. **1816** KIRBY & SP. *Entomol.* xvii. (1818) II. 27 [Ants] unite more intimately for defence against some common enemy, and to raise works of munition that may resist his attack.

2. a. *sing.* and *pl.* Military stores; = AMMUNITION 1. Often more explicitly ***munition(s of war***. Also *colloq.*, the production of munitions; munition-work. ***Ministry of Munitions***: a ministry which from 1915 to 1921 controlled the manufacture and supply of munitions. So ***Minister of Munitions***.

In the 16–17th c. the sing. was often used *spec.* (= *ammunition* in the present restricted sense) for what is used in charging firearms and ordnance, as powder, shot, shell, etc.

a **1533** LD. BERNERS *Huon* xx. 58 A grete shyppe,..wel furnyshyd with bysket, wynes and flesshe,..and with monysyons of warre. **1544** in R. G. Marsden *Sel. Pl. Crt. Adm.* (1894) I. 140 All the victelles powder and monycions of the shippe. **1560** DAUS tr. *Sleidane's Comm.* 56 They were neyther sufficiently furnished of munition nor weapons. **1565** COOPER *Thesaurus*, *Armaturæ duplices*,..Souldiours hauyng double munition. **1575** CHURCHYARD *Chippes* (1817) 154 No maruel though, their hearts within did quaile Who did..behold Their powlder fayld, theyr water waxed skant Their hope is smal, that doth munishon want. **1616** BULLOKAR *Eng. Expos.*, *Munition*, great Ordinance for the warre, great shot. **1624** CAPT. SMITH *Virginia* IV. 163 We had of Tooles, Armes, and Munition sufficient. *a* **1639** SPOTTISWOOD *Hist. Ch. Scot.* II. (1677) 81 Right against it was all the munition of the Castle planted. **1642** *Petition in Ho. Lords* 16 Apr. in Clarendon *Hist. Reb.* V. §55 Armes, and Munition for defence of this Kingdom. **1727–41** CHAMBERS *Cycl.*, *Munition*, or *Ammunition*, the provisions wherewith any place is furnished in order for defence; or wherewith a vessel is stocked for a voyage; or [those] that follow a camp for its subsistence. **1818** COBBETT *Pol. Reg.* XXXIII 200 The President states..that they have given aid to neither of the parties in men, money, ships or munitions of war. **1825** SCOTT *Talism.* xx, De Vaux having been sent to Ascalon to bring up reinforcements and supplies of military munition. **1836** W. IRVING *Astoria* I. 302 The company was to fit them out, and keep them supplied with the requisite equipments and munitions, and they were to yield one half of the produce of their hunting and trapping. **1868** ROGERS *Pol. Econ.* xvii. (1876) 227 Gunpowder, firearms, or any other commodity which may be brought within the definition of munitions of war. **1915** *Times* 26 May 9/6 The Prime Minister has decided that a new Department shall be created, to be called the Ministry of Munitions. **1915** *Act 5 & 6 Geo. V* c. 54 §4 If the Minister of Munitions considers it expedient..that any establishment in which munitions work is carried on should be subject to the special provisions, [etc.]. **1917** HALL CAINE *Our Girls* i. 11 By permission of Mr. Montague, the Minister of Munitions.. we are at the gates of the great Arsenal. **1917** *Dalton* (Lancs.) *Guardian* 28 Apr. 3/5 He had been sent to munitions, and had not been out to the front. **1924** B. GILBERT *Bly Market* 66, I expect..you'll be leaving the schooling and go to the munitions. **1925** D. CARNEGIE *Hist. Munitions Supply in Canada* xxvi. 251 Mr. H. E. Morgan..was sent out to Canada from the Ministry of Munitions. **1935** A. J. CRONIN *Stars look Down* II. vii. 301 There was a future in munitions. .. They were going to put up a line of sheds..filling sheds. **1957** *Encycl. Brit.* XV. 963/1 On the formation of the first wartime coalition government in 1915, a major change in organization was made by setting up a ministry of munitions, with David Lloyd George as the first minister.

transf. and *fig.* **1560** DAUS tr. *Sleidane's Comm.* 233 That olde enemye of mankynde..layeth to all hys munition. **1625** B. JONSON *Staple of N.* I. iii, Here Master Picklocke, Sir, your man o' Law, And learn'd Atturney, has sent you a Bag of munition. *a* **1633** AUSTIN *Medit.* (1635) 101 Take (after) from the Bodie, all the Munition, that armes, and makes it strong in resisting. **1857** HUGHES *Tom Brown* II. iv, They carry all their munitions [for birds' nesting] into calling-over.

†**b.** ? Apparatus. *Obs.*

1477 EARL RIVERS (Caxton) *Dictes* 33 Holding in his honde a flabotomye of [? *read* or] munycion for latyng blood.

†**3.** ? A granted right or privilege; = MUNITY.

1461 *Rolls of Parlt.* V. 489/2 Corporacions, Municions,.. Annexions, Unyons, severauncez from Shires.

†**4.** ? The action of providing, provision. *Obs.*

1480 *Wardr. Acc. Edw. IV* (1830) 113 Also for to make into the same his saide grete Warderobe monysion of all maner of stuff. **1642** LD. SAYE & SELE *Sp. in Parlt.* 25 Feb. 3 This munition of such formes upon all men.

5. *attrib.* and *Comb.*: ***munition factory, girl, -maker, -making, work, worker, works***; also ***munitions work, worker***; **munition bread** [F. *pain de munition*] = *ammunition bread*; **munition house** = *ammunition house*; **munition ship** (see quots.); †**munition-wine**, wine supplied to soldiers.

1629 *S'hertogenbosh* 50 The Gouernours diuided also *mu[n]ition bread amongst the needy Burgers. **1867** SMYTH *Sailor's Word-bk.*, *Munition bread*, contract or commissariat bread. **1909** *Westm. Gaz.* 9 Oct. 2/2 In 1895 he visited the chief firearm and *munition factories of France. **1921** G. A. B. DEWAR *Great Munition Feat* v. 112 The notion that a munition factory was a place full of shirkers and profiteers is grossly ignorant. **1916** M. COSENS (*title*) Lloyd George's *munition girls. **1918** *Daily Mirror* 12 Nov. 6/2 Soldiers, sailors, munition girls and mere civilians clung on anywhere. **1569** *Burgh Rec. Edin.* (1875) III. 263 To put in the samyn [pikis] in the townys *mvnition hous quhair thay war of before. **1916** *Home Companion* 12 Aug. 16/1 This is my last chat to you, little mother *munition-makers. **1916** 'B. CABLE' *Doing their Bit* 24 No man or lathe or tool that can be turned to *munition-making is possibly doing anything else. **1706** PHILLIPS (ed. Kersey), **Munition-Ships*, such Vessels as are employ'd to carry ammunition &c. and to tend upon a Fleet of Men of War. **1867** SMYTH *Sailor's Word-bk.*, *Munition ships*, those which carry the naval stores for a fleet, as distinguished from the victuallers. **1603** FLORIO *Montaigne* I. xxxv, So hard frosts, that their *munition-wines were faine to be cut and broken with hatchets. **1916** 'B. CABLE' *Doing their Bit* 40 Anything less promising of *munition work it would be hard to find. **1918** *Times* 27 Mar. 3/1 These are all chapters in the romance of munitions work in the Midlands. **1915** *Daily Sketch* 18 Aug. 2 (*heading*) Badges for the volunteer *munition worker. **1915** W. OWEN *Let.* 16 Oct. (1967) 359 Dr. Rayner says I should become a Munitions Worker at Birmingham. **1925** D. CARNEGIE *Hist. Munitions Supply in Canada* xxvi. 250 One manufacturer said that it cost him approximately $300 to train each munition worker. **1957** *Encycl. Brit.* XV. 964/1 Specialist ladies were set up to deal with the health of munitions workers, especially women. **1917** W. OWEN *Let.* 7 Sept. (1967) 491 The other owner of a large *Munition Works. **1932** H. SIMPSON *Boomerang* xvi. 436 The women were haring off to munition-works at five pounds a week. **1940** G. D. H. & M. COLE (*title*) Murder at the munition works.

munition (mjuːˈnɪʃən), *v.* [f. MUNITION *sb.* Cf. F. *munitionner* (16th c. in Littré).]

1. *trans.* To supply with munitions of war.

1578–9 *Reg. Privy Council Scot.* III. 79 The citie of Carlisle, with ane strong castell and citidaill thairin, weill munitioned. **1640** GENT *Knave in Gr.* I. i. Bij, A Leaguer cannot be planted, mann'd, victuall'd, and munition'd with a small magazine. **1651** HOWELL *Venice* 102 Twelve Gallies ready rigg'd and munition'd, which his Holiness shall mann for the service of the League. **1888** M. MORRIS *Claverhouse* viii. 144 The castles of Stirling and Edinburgh were munitioned for war. **1895** *N. Amer. Rev.* Mar. 375 England has strongly fortified and completely munitioned stations at Halifax and St. John's.

2. To furnish (a room). *rare.*

1877 *Hon. Miss Ferrard* II. ii. 131 Helena's room was very differently munitioned from the pretty chamber she had left.

3. *intr.* To do munition work; to work in a munition factory.

1916 'B. CABLE' *Doing their Bit* 23 A man cast for a commission and refused for the ranks a year ago on account of his eyes has 'gone munitioning'.

munitioneer (mjuːnɪʃəˈnɪə(r)). [f. MUNITION *sb.* + -EER.] A worker in a munition factory.

1916 E. V. LUCAS *Vermilion Box* 254 In the need for copper there is quite a good price for engraved plates, and theirs have been weeded out for the munitioneers. **1919** *Athenæum* 23 May 360/1 'Trinitrotoluene', which the munitioneers shortened to T.N.T. **1927** W. DEEPING *Kitty* xxvii. 342 The men..returned to a land that was not full of heroes... The voice of the yellow dog was heard in it, the snarl of the ex-munitioneer. **1940** *New Statesman* 19 Oct. 376 The munitioneer can see no difference in the management or control of his factory.

munitioner (mjuːˈnɪʃənə(r)). *rare* [f. MUNITION *sb.* or *v.* + -ER[1]. Cf. F. *munitionnaire.*] †**a.** One who supplies military stores, a commissary. *Obs.* **b.** One who has the custody of ammunition. **c.** = MUNITIONEER; a maker of ammunition.

1632 HOLLAND *Cyrupædia* 141 The order of the Pioners, merchants and trades-men, artizanes and munitioners. **1888** RODWAY & WATT *Chron. Hist. Guiana* I. 9 By some accident the whole stock of gunpowder exploded. Juan Martinez, the munitioner, or Captain of Artillery, was charged with negligence. **1917** *Graphic* 30 June 806 (*caption*) The King with his munitioners.

munitionette (mjuːnɪʃəˈnɛt). *colloq.* [f. MUNITION *sb.* + -ETTE.] A female worker in a munition factory.

1915 *Daily Sketch* 9 Nov. 13/1 (*heading*) Munitionettes who receive threepence an hour. **1917** *Daily News* 17 May 3/1 A shell-shop filled with blue-clad mob-capped cheering munitionettes. **1919** *Punch* 7 May 366/2 Work for the ex-munitionette drawing unemployment pay. **1935** A. J. CRONIN *Stars look Down* II. xiii. 381 He had taken a little flutter with a munitionette from the Wirtley Works.

munitionless (mjuːˈnɪʃənlɪs), *a.* [MUNITION *sb.* + -LESS.] Not provided with munitions.

1927 W. S. CHURCHILL *World Crisis 1916–18* I. 224 The mastered agony of the munitionless retreat, the slowly regathered forces;..has he no share in these?

munitionment (mjuːˈnɪʃənmənt). [f. MUNITION *v.* + -MENT.] Provision with or supply of munitions; munitions collectively.

1915 H. BELLOC in *Land & Water* 29 May 10*/1 If the Austro-German forces under the effect of superior munitionment for the heavy pieces do pierce their opponent's line. **1917** [see GUNNING *vbl. sb.* 3]. **1929** J. BUCHAN *Courts of Morning* I. 133 Science has now created a norm of weapon and munitionment, which is substantially the same for all armies. **1930** H. JACKSON *Anatomy of Bibliomania* I. VIII. v. 167 Whether they have proved successful as armour or not, they [*sc.* Bibles] are no despicable munitionment of war in other respects.

†**muˈnitor.** *Obs. rare*[−1]. [a. L. *mūnītor*, agent-n. f. *mūnīre*: see MUNITE *v.*] One who works on fortifications.

1669 LEYBOURN in Sturmy *Mariner's Mag.* Commend. Verses, And the Munitor hither may resort For Rules whereby to Fabricate his Fort.

munity[1] (ˈmjuːnɪtɪ). Now *rare.* [App. a quasi-etymological alteration (as if from L. *mūnīre* to fortify, confirm) of IMMUNITY; the word being misapprehended in the positive sense 'privilege', the negative prefix seemed inappropriate.] A granted right or privilege; = MUNITION 3.

See also the spurious MUNITY[2], originating in a quot. from Mountague (1648).

1467–8 *Rolls of Parlt.* V. 597/1 Libertees, Fraunchises, Muniteez, Possessions,..and all other thinges in eny of the said Letters Patentes conteyned. **1640** [H. PARKER] *Case Ship Money* 12 These all in some sense may bee called Munities, or indemnities, belonging to the sacred person of the King. **1644** —— *Jus Pop.* 46 It appears by the story of Rehoboam that the people might capitulate for just Munities. **1856** OLMSTED *Slave States* 446 It is in those elements of character which should forever prevent us from trusting him with equal social munities with ourselves.

[**munity**[2]. Explained as: Security, freedom. Error for MUTINY.

[**1648** W. MOUNTAGUE *Devout Ess.* I. 35 Devotion..doth rather compose the mutiny [*misprinted* munity, *corrected in Errata*], then infringe the true liberty of our affections.] **1818** TODD [quoting this as 'munity']. Hence in **1864** WEBSTER, and some later Dicts.]

munjack, obs. form of MANJAK.

1699 DAMPIER *Voy.* II. II. 130 Munjack is a sort of Pitch or Bitumen, which we find in lumps.

munjak, variant of MUNTJAK.

‖**munjeet** (mʌnˈdʒiːt). Also **manjit, mungeet, munjeeth.** [Bengālī *manjīth* (Hindī *majīth*).] The Bengal Madder, *Rubia cordifolia* (formerly *Munjista*); the roots of this plant used in dyeing.

Also erroneously applied to the roots of *Morinda citrifolia* and *M. tinctoria* (Bentley *Man. Bot.*, ed. 5, 1883).

1813 E. BANCROFT *Perm. Colours* II. 278 More recently.. it has acquired in the Company's Sale Catalogues, the name of manjit and mungeet. **1819** *Act 59 Geo. III*, c. 52 (Rates Inwards), Madder or Munjeet. **1846** LINDLEY *Veg. Kingd.* 770 The roots of Rubia cordifolia..yield the Madder of Bengal, and form even an article of the export commerce to Europe, under the name of Munjeeth.

attrib. **1864** Munjeet-garancine [see MUNJISTIN].

munjistin (mʌnˈdʒɪstɪn). *Chem.* [f. mod.L. *Munjist-a*, Roxburgh's specific name of the *munjeet* + -IN.] An orange colouring matter contained in munjeet.

1863 STENHOUSE in *Proc. Roy. Soc. Lond.* XII. 634 Munjistine exists in munjeet in considerable quantity, and can therefore be easily obtained. **1864** —— *ibid.* XIII. 86 When the greater part of the munjistine is removed from munjeet-garancine by boiling water.

munk(e, obs. forms of MONK.

munk-corn, obs. form of MONGCORN.

munk(k)ey, -kye, obs. forms of MONKEY.

Munmoth, obs. form of MONMOUTH.

munn(e, variant forms of MUN *sb.*[1]

munne, variant of MIN *v.*[2] *Obs.*

munnion (ˈmʌnjən). *Arch.* Forms: 6 **munnyon,** 7 **minion,** 7–8 **monion,** (7 **monyon**), 8–9 **munion,** 7– **munnion.** [Alteration of *munial* MONIAL.] = MULLION.

1593–4 in Swayne *Sarum Churchw. Acc.* (1896) 299 Settinge vp of 26 foote of newe Mvnnyons, 13*s.* **1617** in Willis and Clark *Cambridge* (1886) I. 205 The iames and minions to be of white stone. **1679** MOXON *Mech. Exerc.* IX. 170 The upright Posts that divide the several Lights in a Window-frame, are called Munnions. **1762** in *Phil. Trans.* LII. 513 The glass not only suffered, but the monions were greatly damaged. **1823** P. NICHOLSON *Pract. Build.* 566 The window-frames, of oak, consist of a Munnion, Transom and bars. **1839** STONEHOUSE *Axholme* 293 The stone work in the munions, &c., of the clearstory were renewed. **1883** CLARK RUSSELL *Sailors' Lang.*, *Munions*, the pieces between the lights in the galleries of ships in former times.

munnt, Munonday, obs. ff. MOUNT, MONDAY.

munpynnys, variant of MOMPYNS *Obs.*

a **1529** SKELTON *Howe Douty Dk. of Albany*, etc. 293, I shrewe thy Scottishe lugges, Thy munpynnys, and thy crag.

Munro (mʌnˈrəʊ). *Mountaineering.* Name applied to Scottish mountains of at least 3,000 feet after Sir H. T. *Munro*, who published a list of all such peaks in the Journal of the Scottish Mountaineering Club for 1891.

1903 *Jrnl. Scottish Mountaineering Club* VII. 366 The view from the top was magnificent, all the big Munros in the neighbourhood showing up clear and resplendent. **1972** D. HASTON *In High Places* i. 3 These [*sc.* 'the bigger hills of Scotland'] are relatively small, mostly around 3,000 feet, and called 'Munros'. **1973** SILLAR & MEYLER *Skye* x. 188 Between then [*sc.* 1889] and 1891 H. T. Munro—later Sir Hugh Munro—listed Scottish peaks over 3,000 ft... These are known among Scottish mountaineers as 'Munros'.

munsel, obs. form of MANZIL.

Munsell (ˈmʌnsəl). The name of the American Albert H. *Munsell* (1858–1918), used *attrib.* in connection with his classification of colours by means of the three quantities hue, 'value' (lightness or brightness), and chroma, each of which can be assigned, for any particular colour, a numerical value on prescribed scales.

1905 H. E. CLIFFORD in A. H. Munsell *Color Notation* 4 The Munsell photometer..is an instrument of wide range, high precision, and great sensitiveness, and permits the valuations which are necessary in his system to be accurately made. **1913** [see *colour-balance* (COLOUR *sb.*[1] 18)]. **1937** *Discovery* Oct. 325/2 Other well-known systems besides Ostwald's, such as the American 'Munsell' colour-system. **1950** *Psychol. Abstr.* XXIV. 278/2 The key indicates the Munsell notation for each of the Ridgway color names. **1954** *Archit. Rev.* CXV. 198/2 The following colours from the Munsell range were used: putty-colour on metal panels below windows, [etc.]. **1957, 1959** [see CHROMA]. **1964** H. HODGES *Artifacts* xvii. 196 Colour readings using the Munsell Chart are, perhaps, most useful when considering the variation of firing conditions in a large sample of sherds of similar composition. **1971** *Jrnl. Gen. Psychol.* LXXXIV. 24 Ball is beginning to trace saturation changes in monochromatic input, employing Munsell Color Chips as matching targets.

munshee, -i: see MOONSHEE.

munsheel, variant of MUNCHEEL.

munshy, obs. variant of MOONSHEE.

1801 *Encycl. Brit.* Suppl. II. 283/1.

munsif: see MOONSIFF.

Munster (ˈmʊnstə(r)). Also **Muenster, Münster.** The name of a town in the Haut-Rhin Department of France used *attrib.* and *absol.* to designate a strongly flavoured, semi-soft cheese made in the Munster valley.

1902 *Encycl. Brit.* XXV. 336/2 Cows are grazed on the S. Vosges in summer and large quantities of cheese (Münster cheese) are made and exported. **1946** G. MILLAR *Horned Pigeon* xvii. 245 A fat chicken, a bottle of Burgundy, and a Münster cheese. **1947** M. GIVEN *Encycl. Cooking* I. 661 Muenster... Ripened 2 or 3 months to develop pronounced flavour. **1954** H. SMITH *Classical Recipes of World* 379 Munster, a French semi-hard, whole-milk fermented cheese. **1960** E. DAVID *French Provincial Cooking* 34 A little bowl of caraway seeds came with the Münster, a strong, rich, creamy textured cheese which, at the right stage of ripeness, is one of the great cheeses of France. *Ibid.* 87 The Münster cheese of Alsace. **1971** *Sunday Times* (Colour Suppl.) 28 Mar. 34/2 The softer a Münster looks the creamier it will be.

munster, obs. form of MINSTER[1], MUSTER.

munstral, obs. form of MINSTREL.

munt (mʊnt). *S. Afr.* and *Rhodesian slang.* [ad. Bantu *umuntu*, sing. of *abantu* (see BANTU *a.* and *sb.*), lit. a person, black person, servant.] A Black African: usu. as a term of contempt.

[**1926** G. CALLAWAY *Fellowship of Veld* iii. 25 To the Native the qualities which go to make up *ubuntu*, the qualities which make an *umntu* (person), are largely social. **1937** E. G. MALHERBE *Educational Adaptations in Changing Society* xx. 500 Standard of development will be judged by the extent to which the Native has ceased to be an Umuntu and has become a European.] **1948** O. WALKER *Kaffirs are Lively* 77 It's the towns that muck the *munt* up. **1953** N. GORDIMER *Lying Days* I. iii. 35 Man, there's a whole lota niggers round Ockerts', all over the garden and in the street and everywhere. Just a lot of munts from the Compound. **1962** *New Statesman* 24 Aug. 218/1 The old 'munt', as the African is still widely and insultingly termed. **1964** *Listener* 13 Feb. 257/1 His friends were muttering..about 'cheeky munts', which is the insulting white Rhodesian term for Africans. **1972** P. DRISCOLL *Wilby Conspiracy* (1973) xxiv. 309, I used the whistle too, of course, but those two munts in the truck didn't even hear it.

munt, obs. form of MINT *v.*[1], MOUNT.

†**'munter.** *Sc. Obs.* [a. F. *montre* watch. Cf. MONTRA *slang.*] A watch.

1634-5 BRERETON *Trav.* (Chetham Soc.) 188 Speech in Scotland. We call here a clock a knock, a watch a munter. **1644** *Sc. Acts Chas. I* (1819) VI. 152/1 Clocks, Watches, and Munters.

muntibank, obs. form of MOUNTEBANK *sb.*

muntin (ˈmʌntɪn). *Building.* Forms: 4 **mountayne,** 7 **mountan, moontan,** 7-9 **munton,** 8 **montan,** 9 **muntin, -ing.** [By-form of MONTANT with *t* dropped.] A central vertical piece between two panels, the side pieces being called *stiles.*

[**1330-2** in J. T. Smith *Antiq. Westminster* (1807) 207 Six pieces of timber, called mountaynes, ready prepared for the said chapel.] **1611** COTGR., *Montant*, a Mountan; an vpright beame, or post in building. **1688** R. HOLME *Armoury* III. xiv. (Roxb.) 15/2 The Rome well wanscoted about either with Moontan and panells, or carved as the old fashion was. **1703** T. N. *City & C. Purchaser* 28 Stiles, Rails, and Montans are of different breadths. **1774** GOSTLING *Walk Canterb.* xxv. 101 *note*, For example, by Gothic windows I mean those where the lights are narrow, and divided by muntons of stone. **1823** P. NICHOLSON *Pract. Build.* 228 Muntins or Montants.—The vertical pieces of the frame of a door between the stiles. **1850** *Parker's Gloss. Archit.* s.v., English joiners apply the term *muntin* to the intermediate upright bars of framing, and call the outside uprights *styles.*

muntjak (ˈmʌntdʒæk). Also **mintjac, munjak, muntjac(k.** [a. Sunda *minchek* (Rigg *Sunda Dict.*).] A small south-Asian deer of the genus *Muntiacus*, which has been introduced into parts of western Europe.

1798 NEMNICH *Polygl. Lex.* v. 835 Muntjack *Cervus Muntjac.* **1838** *Penny Cycl.* XV. 430/1 Such a conformation exists in some of the males of the *Cervidæ*, the Munjak for instance. **1880** *Encycl. Brit.* XIII. 602/2 The kidang or mintjac (*Cervulus muntjac*). **1891** FLOWER & LYDEKKER *Introd. Mammals* 316 The native name Muntjac has been generally adopted in Europe for a small group of Deer indigenous to the southern and eastern parts of Asia and the adjacent islands, which are separated by very marked characters from all their allies. **1939** *Geogr. Jrnl.* XCIV. 429 The Chinese tufted muntjac, or Mickie's tufted deer. **1965** D. MORRIS *Mammals* 384 Muntjacs are usually found singly or in pairs in the thick undergrowth. **1971** *Guardian* 8 Dec. 12/2, I have had the sad task of identifying the corpse of a Muntjac. **1973** *Country Life* 29 Nov. 1763/3 Besides red deer and roe, muntjac have also recently been reported among the Thetford trees.

attrib. **1838** *Proc. Zool. Soc.* VI. 105 A new species of Muntjac Deer, which lately died at the Gardens. **1963** *Times* 13 Mar. 14/7 A muntjac buck ventured into a well-populated corner of Hertfordshire to lie up beneath a hedge of holly in a secluded garden.

munton, variant of MUNTIN.

Muntz (mʌnts). The name of George Frederick *Muntz* (1794-1857), English political reformer and metallurgist, used (now always in ***Muntz metal***) to designate a type of brass he patented (*Brit. Pat. 6325* (1832), *11,410* (1846)) that contains about 55-64 per cent of copper (often with 1 per cent or more of lead), can be readily hot-worked, and is used esp. in shipbuilding.

1842 *Minutes Proc. Inst. Civil Engineers* 69 The 'Muntz' metal..is now being extensively used. **1860** *Chambers's Encycl.* I. 159/1 Muntz sheathing-metal, 16 [parts] copper and 10⅔ zinc. *c* **1865** J. WYLDE *Circle of Sciences* I. 376/1 An alloy of copper,..called Muntz's metal, is..employed for sheathing ships' bottoms. **1866** H. E. ROSCOE *Less. Elem. Chemistry* xxv. 217 The yellow, or muntz metal, used for the sheathing of ships, contains sixty per cent. of copper. **1887** D. A. LOW *Introd. Machine Drawing & Design* xiv. 58 The piston..is attached to a Muntz metal piston rod. **1930** *Engineering* 17 Jan. 68/2 Details of the water cut-offs, consisting of a combination of Muntz metal plates, asphalte and iron sheeting. **1963** *Listener* 17 Jan. 114/2 The Cutty Sark Society is offering an original sheet of Muntz metal [from the hull of the ship] to anyone who pays for a new one. **1969** E. N. SIMONS *Dict. Alloys* 112 Typical Muntz Metal parts are heavy plates, bolting and valve stems, heat-exchanger tubes, hot forgings, and brazing rods for copper alloys and cast iron.

munuc(h, obs. forms of MONK.

munument, obs. form of MUNIMENT.

Mununday, obs. form of MONDAY.

munye, munzel, -il, muohwa, variant forms of MING *v. Obs.*, MANZIL, MAHWA.

munyeroo (ˌmʌnjəˈruː). *Austral.* Also **munyeru.** [Aboriginal name.] A small, succulent herb, *Claytonia balonnensis*, of the family Portulacaceæ; also, the paste made from its ground seeds mixed with water, formerly used as food by Aborigines in central Australia.

1896 E. C. STIRLING in B. Spencer *Rep. Horn Sci. Exped. Central Austral.* IV. 56 In these districts 'Mŭnyeru' takes the place of the spore cases of 'Nardoo'.., which is so much used in the Barcoo and other districts to the south and east. **1934** A. RUSSELL *Tramp-Royal in Wild Austral.* xx. 127 The munyeroo, a form of pigweed, was also plentiful... The natives collect the seed in large quantities and pound it into flour for bread; they also eat the leaves fresh, both as a food and to relieve thirst. **1935** *Bulletin* (Sydney) 1 May 20/2 The succulent leaves of the munyeroo and parakylia, which the birds feed upon, provide sufficient moisture for their needs. **1941** I. L. IDRIESS *Great Boomerang* xxiii. 174 Some passing shower has fallen here, and the yellow gold is the munyeroo plant in flower. **1956** *Landfall* X. 97 Small black and brown munyeru seeds.

muon (ˈmjuːɒn). *Nuclear Physics.* [f. MU(-MESON + -ON[1].] A lepton that appears to be almost identical to the electron, except for being unstable and having a mass about 207 times greater, and is the chief constituent of cosmic radiation at the surface of the earth. (Orig. called a mu-meson, but now no longer classed as a meson.)

1953 *Sci. News Let.* 3 Jan. 14/1 About 20 or so particles exist in or can be knocked out of the atoms. Some of these are well-known oldtimers, like the electron... Others are new and stranger, like the pions, the muons, the V-particles. **1958** *Engineering* 4 Apr. 430/2 The fusion of hydrogen and deuterium (p − D reaction) catalysed by negative muons. The part played by the muon is to bind the two nuclei in a mesic molecular ion, so bringing them close enough together for fusion to occur. **1961** *Guardian* 21 Jan. 2/4 Muons were first discovered in the naturally occurring cosmic rays and identified precisely in 1947..at Bristol University. **1968** M. S. LIVINGSTON *Particle Physics* iv. 74 Muons are the 'penetrating' component of the ionizing particles in cosmic radiation observed beneath great layers of earth in salt mines. *Ibid.*, Slow μ^- muons can also displace electrons in atomic orbits and form temporarily stable atoms... Eventually, the muon decays into an electron and two neutrinos. **1968** *Times* 28 Nov. 14/1 The muons are created by the collision of cosmic rays with matter in the upper atmosphere of the earth. **1972** *Nature* 14 July 86/1 The mass difference of the electron and muon poses one of the inscrutable problems of particle physics. Except for the mass difference the muon does not appear to be any different from the electron. **1974** *Ibid.* 2 Aug. 377/2 Muons are more penetrating than any other charged particles.

b. Special Comb.: **muon number**, a quantum number assigned to sub-atomic particles that is ±1 for muons and their neutrinos and 0 for other particles and is conserved in all known interactions.

1961 *Physical Rev.* CXXIII. 1439/2 The possibility of essentially imaginary relative parities can only arise when some quantum number (here, muon number) is multiplicatively conserved. **1970** D. B. LICHTENBERG *Unitary Symmetry* i. 7 Other important symmetries are the invariances under gauge transformations. These symmetries are associated with conservation of charge Q, baryon number B, and two lepton numbers, the electron number L_e and the muon number L_μ.

Hence **mu'onic** *a.*, of, pertaining to, or involving a muon, or an atom having a negative muon orbiting the nucleus.

1955 S. S. SCHWEBER et al. *Mesons & Fields* II. 369 The same considerations lead to the conclusion that the two neutrinos ejected in μ decay are like neutrinos, even though a Dirac theory of neutrinos opens the possibility that one is an anti-neutrino... Such conclusions are important in calculating expectations for the muonic processes. **1965** *New Scientist* 1 July 36/1 Studies of the so-called 'muonic' X-ray spectra do not call for high energies. **1969** *Sci. Jrnl.* July 44/1 In a dense material, a muon is slowed down to a velocity corresponding to 1 keV in about 1 nanosecond, after which it is captured into a 'Bohr orbit', forming a hydrogen-like atom known as a muonic atom. **1972** *Physics Bull.* Mar. 149/2 Muonic molecules are systems in which a negative muon binds together two nuclei. Some examples are $(p\mu^-p)^+$, $(p\mu^-d)^+$, and $(d\mu^-d)^+$, and in practice only such ionic states are of interest. **1972** *Sci. Amer.* Nov. 104/3 The behavior of muonic atoms has provided much information about the structure of the nucleus, particularly about the distribution of protons within nuclei.

muonium (mjuːˈəʊnɪəm). *Nuclear Physics.* [f. MUON + -IUM, after POSITRONIUM.] A short-lived neutral system, analogous to an atom, consisting of a (usu. positive) muon bound to an electron.

1957 FRIEDMAN & TELEGDI in *Physical Rev.* CV. 1681/2, μ^+ can form 'muonium', i.e. (μ^+e^-). **1960** *Physical Rev. Lett.* V. 63/1 The present Letter reports the formation of muonium in pure argon gas. *Ibid.*, Muonium..can be formed when a positive muon is slowed down in matter and captures an electron from an atom in the stopping material. **1964** S. DEBENEDETTI *Nuclear Interactions* viii. 593 The absence of muonium annihilation, despite the fact that both muons and electrons behave separately as simple Dirac particles, furnishes further evidence for the basic difference between electrons and muons. **1970** G. K. WOODGATE *Elem. Atomic Struct.* ii. 20 The equation therefore applies to all the hydrogenic atoms hydrogen, deuterium, tritium, muonium, positronium, etc.

muphti(e, obs. form of MUFTI.

Muppet (ˈmʌpɪt). orig. *U.S.* Also with lower-case initial. [Coined by their creator, J. Henson (b. 1936); prob. f. PUPPET, perh. influenced by MARIONETTE: but see quot. 1978.] A proprietary name for any of a number of glove and rod puppets and marionettes (chiefly representing animals) first popularized in the children's television programme *Sesame Street*, and for playthings depicting them.

1970 *Globe & Mail* (Toronto) 26 Sept. 24/3 The muppet puppets..are among the most engaging of Sesame Street's characters. **1972** *Official Gaz.* (U.S. Patent Office) 26 Sept. TM221/1 Muppets, Inc., New York... Muppet. For puppets... First use on or about Sept. 22, 1971. *Ibid.* 3 Oct. TM35/2 Muppets, Inc., New York... The Muppets. For entertainment services featuring puppets and large animated animals and creatures... First use August 1954. **1972** *Trade Marks Jrnl.* 18 Oct. 2082/1 Muppets..Paper.. and cardboard articles..printed matter..plastic substances for modelling; kits..for molding and modelling; boxes.. pencils..satchels for scholars. Muppets, Inc..., New York. *Ibid.* 1 Nov. 2188/2 Muppets..Games..playthings; and balls... Muppets, Inc.,..New York. **1977** *Private Eye* 13 May 11/4 As we open the door we can imagine Freud himself sitting behind the desk with a Muppet on his knee. **1978** *Time* 25 Dec. 71/1 Henson..says that 'muppet' was simply a word that sounded good to him. The sound combination of puppet and marionette is merely an explanation that happens to sound logical. **1986** *Christian Science Monitor* 16 Jan. 27/4 Black-tie banquet with all the beloved Muppets, plus star clips.

muquaddam, variant of MOKADDAM.

mur, obs. form of MIRE *sb.*[1]

c **1275** *XI Pains of Hell* 150 in *O.E. Misc.* 151 Half heo doþ in o fur And half in-to a froren mur.

mur, obs. f. MOOR *sb.*[1]; var. MURE *a.*, MURR.

muræna, murena (mjʊˈriːnə). Also anglicized 6-8 **murene.** [a. L. *mūræna*, *mūrēna* sea-eel, lamprey, a. Gr. *μύραινα*, also *σμύραινα*, a fem. formation on *μύρος*, *σμῦρος* sea-eel. Cf. F. *murène* (whence perh. the form *murene* above), Sp. *morena*, Pg. *moreia* (whence MORAY), It. *murena.*] In early use applied vaguely as the name of a kind of eel mentioned by ancient writers. Now usually, a fish of the genus *Muræna*, the type of the family *Murænidæ* or Eels.

1555 EDEN *Decades* 200 Manates & murene & many other fysshes which haue no names. **1601** HOLLAND *Pliny* I. 248 Hee caused certain slaues condemned to die, to be put into the stewes where these Lampreies or Murænes were kept. **1753** CHAMBERS *Cycl. Supp.* s.v., The *Muræna* and lamprey, called by the Latin authors, *lampetra*, are two very different fishes. **1835** SIR J. ROSS *Narr. 2nd Voy.* xlvii. 620 Could we have dug out of Herculaneum or Pompeii..a muræna fattened on Syrian slaves. **1899** *Pop. Sci. Monthly* Sept. 685 Murenas are only eaten by the negroes.

murænoid (mjʊˈriːnɔɪd), *a.* and *sb.* Also **murenoid.** [f. MURÆN-A + -OID.]

a. *adj.* Belonging to the family *Murænidæ* of fishes (see prec.). **b.** *sb.* A murænoid fish.

1848 OWEN in *Times* 14 Nov. 9/1 Both..like other murænoid fishes and the known small sea snake (*hydrophis*) swim by undulatory movements of the body. **1849** CRAIG, *Murenoids*, a family of Apodal fishes, including the true eels. **1859-62** RICHARDSON, etc. *Mus. Nat. Hist.* II. 140 Family III—Murænoids (*Murænædæ* [sic]).

murage (ˈmjʊərɪdʒ). Now *Hist.* [a. OF. *murage*, in med.L. *mūrāgium*, f. F. *mur* wall: see MURE *sb.* and -AGE.]

1. A toll or tax levied for the building or repairing of the walls of a town; also, in mod. use, ***murage duty.*** Also the right granted to a town for the levying of such a toll.

[**1275** *Stat. Westm. 3 Edw. I*, c. 31 Des Citeins e des Burgeys a ki le Rey ou son piere ad grante Murage, por lor vile enclore.] **1423** *Cov. Leet Bk.* (E.E.T.S.) 59 þat Mold Lichefeld pay to þe murage of this cite aftur þe lond þat she holdithe, & no oþer wyse. *c* **1440** *Jacob's Well* iv. 29 To paye toll, pyckage, murage, or grondage. **1502** *Arnolde's Chron.* (1811) 22 We haue grauntyd for vs and for our eyers to our citezens yt they..be quyt for euer of pauage pontage and murage by al our reame. **1636** PRYNNE *Remonstr. agst. Shipmoney* 8 Kings of England cannot by their Prerogative ..grant Murage, or any other such Tallage to any by Patent. *a* **1676** HALE *Narr. Customes* iii. in S. A. Moore *Foreshore* (1888) 337 These two sorts of taxes. (1) Murage: for the wallinge in of a port so that it may bee safe against invasion of forren enemyes [etc.]. (2) Kaiage or wharfage. **1794** W. HUTCHINSON *Hist. Cumbld.* I. Gloss., *Murage*, a toll taken for a cart or horse laden going through a walled city or town for repairing the walls thereof. **1810** LYSONS *Magna Brit.* II. II. 581 Another ancient office is that of the murengers [of Chester], whose duty it is to receive the murage duties, and superintend their expenditure in the repair of the walls. **1851** *Orig. Paroch. Scot.* I. 467 In the same year..the same King granted to his burgesses of Rokesburgh liberty to raise a yearly murage from saleable commodities brought into the town in order to enclose it for the greater security of the same and the parts adjacent.

†2. The building of walls; also a system of defensive walls (cf. OF. *murage* a wall). *Obs. rare.*

1553 in *10th Rep. Hist. MSS. Comm.* App. v. 414 Massons workinge.. uppon the workes of muradge and pavadge. **1600** HOLLAND *Livy* XXXIV. xxxviii. 875 This Sparta in times past stood without murage. And the tyrants of late daies had built walles against the open flattes and plaine fields.

murager: see MURENGER.

‖**muraji** (mu'ra:dʒi). Also, with prefixed *ō-* 'great'. [Jap.] In early imperial Japan, one of the hereditary titles for a family or clan (cf. KABANE) who claimed their descent from other gods than the divine ancestors of the emperor. Also, **ō-muraji**, the representative of this family when he was entrusted with affairs of state.

1901 F. BRINKLEY *Japan* I. iii. 53 Such titles as 'great body' (*omi*), 'master of the multitude' (*muraji*), 'honourable intermediary' (*nakatomi*) and so on, were employed as terms of respect, and ultimately passed into use as official titles. *Ibid.*, The head of the clan then came to be distinguished by the prefix *O* (great or senior); as *O-mi* (the senior honourable person), *O-muraji* (the great master of the multitude), and so on. **1931** G. B. SANSOM *Japan* I. ii. 37 The *ō-muraji*, territorial administrative officers of high rank who traced their descent from gods other than the divine ancestors of the emperor. *Ibid.* 39 It became the custom to describe the more important members of a clan or corporation by the name of their hereditary office or by some honorific title granted by the court. Thus we have *muraji*, which means 'leader of a group'. **1964** *Japan* (Unesco) (ed. 2) i. 16/2 The clans.. had *kabane* (hereditary family title), to show the status of their families. *Kabane* were divided into *omi*, *muraji*, *kimi*, *atai*, *obito*, *miyatsuko* and *fubito*. **1970** J. W. HALL *Japan from Prehist. to Mod. Times* v. 37 Spokesmen chiefs, *Ō-omi* and *Ō-muraji*, were named to serve as chief ministers of state.

'**mural**, *sb.* Forms: 5 muraill, -ayl(le, 6 mural, *Sc. pl.* muralȝeis. [a. F. *muraille*:—Com. Rom. *muralia* (repr. L. *mūrālia* neut. pl. of *mūrālis* MURAL *a.*, taken as fem. sing.: see -AL[1] 5); cf. Sp. *muralla*, Pg. *muralha*, It. *muraglia*; also OF. *murail*, Pr. *muralh* masc.] †**1.** A wall. *Obs.*

Modern editors have introduced the word, by a doubtful conjecture into the text of Shaks. *Mids. N.* v. i. 208, where the folio has 'Now is the morall [? *read* wall] downe'. The Quartos have the unmeaning reading 'Now is the moon vsed'.

1471 CAXTON *Recuyell* (Sommer) II. 404 He sawe his enemies that hasted hem to come vnto the muraill & wallis with ladders. **1481** —— *Godeffroy* iii. 21 He shewid to hym ..a parte of the muraylles whiche were thenne yet apperyng. **1485** —— *Chas. Gt.* 142 In suche wyse that the grete quarters of the murayl & walles fyl and tombled doun to the erthe. **1513** DOUGLAS *Æneis* x. i. 53 Amyd the clos muralȝeis and paill, And doubill dykis, quhou thai thame assail. **1555** EDEN *Decades* 336 In folowyng this order of woorke in the pourgynge and diuydynge of golde, it shall not bee requisite as in other maner of practises, to bee at greate charges by reason of many men which shall be needefull, with manye murals [orig. *di tante muraglie*], fornaces, fiers, and dyuers artificers.

2. [Short for *mural painting* (MURAL *a.*[1] 2 a).] A painting executed on a wall or ceiling as part of a scheme of decoration. So ***mural painter***. orig. *U.S.*

1921 *Quill* Mar. 23 I'm doing big things... 'They satisfy' and such outdoor murals. **1929** *Arts & Decoration* Oct. 63 (*heading*) Arresting murals of classic inspiration in the Long Island home of F. Russell. **1931** H. CRANE *Let.* 4 Nov. (1965) 385 He's fundamentally a mural painter, and even his smaller paintings have a tremendous *scale*. **1936** R. E. SHERWOOD *Idiot's Delight* II. i. 76 He has been out in Australia doing colossal murals for some government building. **1946** H. FEIBUSCH *Mural Painting* 15 H. J. K. Tisdall, the mural painter, helped me with his wide knowledge of technique and materials. **1949** F. MACLEAN *Eastern Approaches* I. ii. 18 The Customs' building [in the frontier station of Negoreloye].. was a fine big, bright room, decorated with murals depicting scenes from Soviet life. **1954** T. GUNN *Fighting Terms* 43 Turn your closed eyes to see upon these walls A mural scratched there by an earlier man. **1964** MRS. L. B. JOHNSON *White House Diary* 17 July (1970) 181 There was a great mural in the Library by Thomas Hare Benton. **1973** F. TAUBES *Painter's Dict. of Materials & Methods* 159 Only a certain portion of a large mural can be completed in one day's work. **1974** *Impressionism* (R. Acad.) 32/2 Saint-Sulpice murals, completed 1861, were a revelation for young artists.

mural ('mjʊərəl), *a.*[1] Also 6–7 murall, 7 -ell. [a. F. *mural* (*coronne murail* 14th c. in Hatz.-Darm.), cf. Sp., Pg. *mural*, It. *murale*; ad. L. *mūrāl-is* belonging to a wall, f. *mūr-us* wall: see MURE and -AL[1].]

1. a. Of or pertaining to a wall; resembling a wall.

mural diagraph (see quot. 1829); so ***mural alphabet***, an alphabet the letters of which are represented by knocks and scratches on the wall through which the message or conversation is being sent. ***mural tower*** (see quot. 1844).

1586 WARNER *Alb. Eng.* II. viii. (1612) 35 Prouiding therefore murall workes, they threaten hot assault. **1624** WOTTON *Archit.* I. 14 Adding much beautie & strength to the Murall Angles, where they fall gracefully into an indented Worke. **1667** MILTON *P.L.* VI. 879 And soon repaird Her mural breach, returning whence it rowl'd. **1738** GLOVER *Leonidas* v. 551 Like the mural strength Of some proud city bulwark'd round. **1774** PENNANT *Tour Scotl. in 1772*, 120 The rocks which on both sides are perfectly mural and equidistant. **1807** J. BARLOW *Columb.* II. 244 Three cities gay their mural towers unfold. **1829** J. SWAIM (*title*) The Mural Diagraph, or the art of conversing through a wall. **1844** G. T. CLARK in *Archæol. Jrnl.* I. 102 The walls [of Edwardian castles] were strengthened by 'mural', or towers projecting inwards,.. and 'buttress-towers' projecting outwards. **1851** RICHARDSON *Geol.* vi. (1855) 153 A mural escarpment is one of a steeper and more perpendicular character. **1860** G. PRESCOTT *Electr. Telegr.* xxi. 420 The dots of the Mural alphabet are represented by knocks on the wall, and the lines by scratches. **1860** HARTWIG *Sea & Wond.* i. 5 Bold mural coasts, rising precipitously from the deep sea. **1880** HAUGHTON *Phys. Geog.* ii. 71 A margin of lofty unbroken mural precipices nowhere less than 12,000 feet in height.

b. *Roman Antiq.* **mural crown** (= *corona muralis*): an embattled crown, conferred upon the soldier who first scaled the wall of a besieged town. So also ***mural coronet, garland, wreath***, etc. In extended use, any embattled crown (e.g. that which the goddess Cybele is portrayed as wearing; also *Her.*).

1546 LANGLEY *Pol. Verg. De Invent.* II. xi. 54 The mural or wal croune that was geuen to him that scaled firste the walles. **1572** BOSSEWELL *Armorie* II. 77 b, One is named a Crowne murall. **1600** HOLLAND *Livy* VI. 231 Two goodly murall garlands [bestowed upon Manlius] for scaling and entering upon the wals first. **1629** MASSINGER *Picture* II. ii, All rewards And signes of honour, as the Ciuicke garland, The murall wreath, the enemies prime horse,.. To him alone are proper. **1751** JOHNSON *Rambler* N. 85 ⁋2 He toils without the hope of mural or civick garlands. **1851** HELPS *Comp. Solit.* iv. (1874) 54 One in rich vesture, superb, with what seems like a mural crown on her head.

Comb. **1872** HOWELLS *Wedd. Journ.* (1892) 297 The mighty rock, mural-crowned.

2. a. Placed, fixed, or executed on a wall.

1561 EDEN *Arte Nauig.* II. xvi. 43 b, You wyll make a mural dial. **1837** HOWITT *Rur. Life* VI. xvi. (1862) 584 The mural tablets to the memory of departed rectors. **1842** GWILT *Archit.* Gloss. s.v., An arch inserted or attached to a wall is called a *mural arch*; and columns placed within or against a wall are called *mural columns*. **1850** MRS. JAMESON *Leg. Monast. Ord.* (1863) 171 A fragment of mural painting preserved in the Christian Museum in the Vatican. **1872** JENKINSON *Guide Eng. Lakes* (1879) 186 Isel church is a small, ancient building, containing.. some mural inscriptions. **1916** H. F. OSBORN *Men of Old Stone Age* 316 This Art.. is also mural or parietal.., consisting of drawings, engravings, paintings and bas-reliefs on the walls of caverns and grottos.

†**b.** Of a fruit-tree: Growing against, and fastened to, a wall. Also of the fruit. *Obs.*

1664 EVELYN *Kal. Hort., July* 70 Mural-trees. *Ibid. Oct.* 76 Plant dry Trees.., Standard, Mural, or Shrubs. **1709** *Phil. Trans.* XXVI. 469 The Sap of our finer mural Fruit-Trees, as of Peaches, Nectarines, Apricocks, &c. **1731** *Gentl. Mag.* I. 40 The Nectarine and like delicate mural Fruit. *absol.* **1669** EVELYN *Kal. Hort., Mar.* (ed. 9) 30 Now is the best time for pruning young Murals.

c. *Astr.* In ***mural arch***, 'a wall, or walled arch, placed exactly in the plane of the meridian ...for the fixing of a large quadrant, sextant, or other instrument, to observe the meridian altitudes, &c., of the heavenly bodies' (Chambers *Cycl.* 1752); hence ***mural arc, circle, quadrant***, etc., an arc, circle, quadrant, etc., placed on such a wall; they have been superseded by the *transit-circle*.

1727–41 CHAMBERS *Cycl.* s.v., Tycho Brahe was the first who used a mural-arch in his observations. **1786** *Phil. Trans.* LXXVI. 5 In the year 1689, Mr. Flamsteed compleated his mural arc at Greenwich. **1812** WOODHOUSE *Astron.* vi. 25 When the quadrant is fixed to the side of a vertical wall in the plane of the meridian, it is called a mural quadrant. **1867–77** G. F. CHAMBERS *Astron.* VII. vi. 696 The Mural Circle consists of a graduated circle furnished with a suitable telescope and very firmly fixed to a wall (*murus*) in the plane of the meridian.

3. *Phys.* and *Path.* Belonging to or connected with the wall of the body or of any of its cavities. Cf. PARIETAL.

1884 BARNES *Syst. Obstetric Med. & Surg.* I. 329 Parietal, ..mural, interstitial or tubo-uterine gestation. **1898** *Allbutt's Syst. Med.* V. 866 Other parts of the endocardium may be affected also (mural endocarditis). **1899** *Ibid.* VI. 161 A thrombus formed from the circulating blood is at first parietal or mural.

†'**mural**, *a.*[2] *Obs. rare*[−1]. [Badly f. L. *mur-ia* brine (see MURIATIC *a.*) + -AL[1].] = MURIATIC *a.*

1742 PERRY in *Phil. Trans.* XLII. 51 This [hot spring] Water.. contains.. a mural Salt of a limy Quality.

'**mural**, *a.*[3] *Path. rare*[−0]. [a. F. *mural*, badly f. *mûre* mulberry: see -AL[1].] In ***mural calculus*** = 'mulberry calculus' (see MULBERRY 6).

1857 DUNGLISON *Med. Dict.*, *Mural*, vesical calculi are so called, when rugous and covered with tubercles or asperities.

'**muralled**, *a.* [f. MURAL *a.*[1] + -ED[2].] **1.** Made into a mural crown. *rare.*

1706 J. PHILIPS *Cerealia* 104 Ardent to deck his brows with mural'd gold, Or civic wreath of oak, the victors meed.

2. Decorated with murals. Cf. MURAL *sb.* 2.

1962 *UCLA Librarian* (Los Angeles) 25 May 106 The oaken walls and muraled ceiling of the drawing room were pulsing with sweet sound. **1967** A. WEST in *Coast to Coast 1965–6* 218 Stella watched the shadows.. as they bobbed on the muralled wall.

murally ('mjʊərəlɪ), *adv. rare.* [f. MURAL *a.*[1] + -LY[2].] **a.** With a mural crown. **b.** By means of walls or septa. **c.** On or from a wall.

1855 BAILEY *Spir. Leg.* in *Mystic*, etc. 107 Where Balkh Mother of cities, murally encrowned Mourns. **1872** E. TUCKERMAN *Genera Lichenum* 138 The passage from colourless spores with entire spore-cells, to brown spores with at length murally divided spore-cells. **1882** SALA in *Illustr. Lond. News* 16 Sept. 295/2 A sprig of 'Pellitory of the wall' murally plucked from Fountains Abbey. **1895** F. FOWLER in *Forum* (N.Y.) Feb. 687 Hotels.. that have been ornamented murally by some of the best-known painters.

muramic (mjʊə'ræmɪk), *a. Biochem.* [f. L. *mūr-us* wall + AM(INE + -IC.] ***muramic acid***: an amino-sugar, $C_9H_{17}NO_7$, which is present in combined form in the cell walls of bacteria and in bacterial spores.

1957 *Nature* 27 Apr. 841/2 An acidic hexosamine, first found in a product from bacterial spores, which Strange has provisionally characterized as 3-O-α-carboxyethyl hexosamine and has named 'muramic acid'. **1969** [see MUREIN]. **1973** *Physiol. Plant Path.* III. 366 Muramic acid and glucosamine are less stable to acid hydrolysis than are amino acids.

muran, obs. form of MURRAIN.

Murano (mjʊ'rɑ:nəʊ). The name of an island close to Venice, on which the manufactories of Venetian glass are situated. Used *attrib.* Hence **Mura'nese** *a.*, belonging to Murano.

1879 A. NESBITT in *Encycl. Brit.* X. 653/2 In 1428 a Muranese artificer set up a furnace in the same city [Venice]. **1883** J. PATON *Ibid.* XVI. 500/1 The products of the Murano glass-houses quickly supplanted the mirrors of polished metal. **1908** *Outlook* 4 Jan. 17/1 Of very ancient Muranese stock, Carpaccio was born most probably in 1455.

†**murated**, *a. rare*[−0]. [f. L. *mūrāt-us* walled + -ED[1].] (See quot.)

1727 BAILEY vol. II, *Murated*, walled, encompassed with Walls.

Murathee, variant of MAHRATTI.

Muratorian (mjʊərə'tɔərɪən), *a.* [f. *Muratori* (see below) + -AN.] Of or pertaining to L. A. Muratori (1672–1750), an Italian scholar. Usually in **Muratorian fragment** (or **canon**), the earliest Western canon of the N.T. (of about 170 A.D.), edited by Muratori in his *Antiquitates Italicæ*.

1855 WESTCOTT *Canon N.T.* ii. §11. 235 The Muratorian Fragment on the Canon. *Ibid.* 586 (Index), Muratorian Canon 235. **1875** LIGHTFOOT *Comm. Col.* 358 A mention of such an epistle occurs as early as the Muratorian fragment.

†**muray**. *Obs. rare*[−1]. [ad. OF. *murail* wall: see MURAL *sb.*] A fortification, wall.

13.. *K. Alis.* 6228 (Bodl. MS.), He þer cas Butumay Of Meopante þat touȝ clay Wiþ pylers of metal stronge þat ben an hundreþ feet longe And made swiche a stronge Muray þat neuer in tyl domesday þer ne shal shipp out passe Neiþer more ne þe lasse.

muray, variant of MORAY.

murayl(le, variant forms of MURAL *sb. Obs.*

murberien, obs. pl. form of MULBERRY.

murburne, -byrn, obs. forms of MOOR-BURN.

murc(k, variant forms of MURK *sb.*[2]

‖**murchana** ('mɜ:tʃənɑ:). Also **murcchana, murchhana**. [a. Skr. *mūrchanā* modulation.] (See quots.)

1891 C. R. DAY *Music in S. India* ii. 23 The s'rutis are arranged in their different svâras, or intervals of the scale, according to the 'murchanas'. Of what these murchanas consisted is very doubtful. *Ibid.* iv. 41 The following short melodies.. show as much as possible the full murchanas of their respective râgas. **1914** [see JATI, JÂTI]. **1921** H. A. POPLEY *Music of India* vi. 85 We shall notice.. the graced notes, these being called in the north Mūrchanā. **1954** *Grove's Dict. Mus.* (ed. 5) IV. 457/1 Now it is clear that the *Sa-grâma* and the *Ma-grâma* are modes of one another. All the same, the Indian theory considers them as separate entities and derives seven octave scales (*mūrchanās*) from each of them. **1968** *Indian Mus. Jrnl.* V. 54 The term '*mūrcchanā*'. In the early sources this refers to an octave-species within a basic tuning-system... One or two 17th-century *śāstra-s*, on the other hand, use the term '*mūrcchanā*' ..to refer to that 'pitch-area' within which the phrases of a *rāga* operate. **1972** P. HOLROYDE *Indian Music* 274 *Murchhana*... The word has been variously used: (a) It is the ancient name for the early modes in Indian music before the raga system emerged. (b) According to Popley's book,.. murchhana in South India refers to ascending and descending varna or graph-like grace movements. (c) According to Tagore the murchhana is the extending of the note 'to another in the ascending as well as the descending scale (like an *appoggiatura*) without any intermediate break in the disposition of the srutis in the interval'.

†**murche**. *Obs. rare*[−1]. A dwarf.

c **1440** *Promp. Parv.* 348/2 Murche, lytyll man. *Nanus, vel navus.*

murchisonite ('mɜ:tʃɪsənaɪt). *Min.* [f. name of Sir Roderick Impey *Murchison* (1792–1871) + -ITE.] A variety of orthoclase of flesh-red colour, resembling pertite.

1827 A. LEVY in *Philos. Mag.* Ser. II. I. 452, I shall propose for the substance I have described the name of Murchisonite, in compliment to the gentleman who first directed my attention to it. **1883** M. F. HEDDLE in *Encycl. Brit.* XVI. 419/2 *Amazon Stone*.. and *Murchisonite*, golden or greyish yellow, from Arran and Dawlish, are varieties [of *Common Felspar*].

†'**murcid**, *a. Obs. rare*⁻⁰. [ad. late L. *murcid-us* slothful. Cf. MURCOUS *a.*] 'Cowardly, unadvised, slothful' (Blount *Glossogr.* 1656).

murcok(e, obs. forms of MOOR-COCK.

†'**murcous**, *a. Obs. rare*⁻¹. [f. late L. *murc-us* (Amm. Marc.) one who cuts off his thumb to escape military service + -OUS.] Having the thumb cut off.

1684 tr. *Bonet's Merc. Compit.* XIV. 475 When Surgeons do not handle [whitlows] as they should..they render their Patients murcous.

murder ('mɜːdə(r)), *sb.* Forms: α. 1 morþor, -ur, 3–4 morþre, 3–4, 6 murthre, 4 myrþer, 4–6 murthir, morther, 5 *Sc.* murthour, murthyr, 5–6 murthur, 6 mwrther, *Sc.* morthour, 4–9 (now *dial.* and *Hist.* or *arch.*) murther; β. 3–5 murdre, 4–5 moerdre, 4–6 mordre, 5 moordre, 6 murdur, mourdre, 6– murder. [OE. *morðor* neut. (with pl. of masc. form *morþras*) = Goth. *maurþr* neut.:—OTeut. **murþrom*:—pre-Teut. **mrtro-m*, f. root **mer-*: *mor-*: *mr-* to die, whence L. *morī* to die, *mors* (*morti-*) death, Gr. μορτός, βροτός mortal, Skr. *mṛ* to die, *mará* masc., *mṛti* fem., death, *márta* mortal, OSl. *mĭrĕti*, Lith. *mirti* to die, Welsh *marw*, Irish *marþ* dead.

The word has not been found in any Teut. lang. but Eng. and Gothic, but that it existed in continental WGer. is evident, as it is the source of OF. *murdre*, *murtre* (mod.F. *meurtre*) and of med.L. *mordrum*, *murdrum*, and OHG. had the derivative *murdren* MURDER *v.* All the Teut. langs. exc. Gothic possessed a synonymous word from the same root with different suffix: OE. *morð* neut., masc. (MURTH¹), OS. *morð* neut., OFris. *morth*, *mord* neut., MDu. *mort*, *mord* neut. (Du. *moord*), OHG. *mord* (MHG. *mort*, mod.G. *mord*), ON. *morð* neut.:—OTeut. **murþo-*:—pre-Teut. **mrto-*.

The change of original *ð* into *d* (contrary to the general tendency to change *d* into *ð* before syllabic *r*) was prob. due to the influence of the AF. *murdre*, *moerdre* and the Law Latin *murdrum*.]

1. a. The most heinous kind of criminal homicide; also, an instance of this. In *English* (also *Sc.* and *U.S.*) *Law*, defined as the unlawful killing of a human being with malice aforethought; often more explicitly ***wilful murder***.

In OE. the word could be applied to any homicide that was strongly reprobated (it had also the senses 'great wickedness', 'deadly injury', 'torment'). More strictly, however, it denoted *secret* murder, which in Germanic antiquity was alone regarded as (in the modern sense) a crime, open homicide being considered a private wrong calling for blood-revenge or compensation. Even under Edward I, Britton explains the AF. *murdre* only as felonious homicide of which both the perpetrator and the victim are unidentified. The 'malice aforethought' which enters into the legal definition of murder, does not (as now interpreted) admit of any summary definition. Until the Homicide Act of 1957, a person might even be guilty of 'wilful murder' without intending the death of the victim, as when death resulted from an unlawful act which the doer knew to be likely to cause the death of some one, or from injuries inflicted to facilitate the commission of certain offences. By this act, 'murder' was extended to include death resulting from an intention to cause grievous bodily harm. It is essential to 'murder' that the perpetrator be of sound mind, and (in England, though not in Scotland) that death should ensue within a year and a day after the act presumed to have caused it. In British law no degrees of guilt are recognized in murder; in the U.S. the law distinguishes 'murder in the first degree' (where there are no mitigating circumstances) and 'murder in the second degree' (though this distinction does not obtain in all States).

α. *Beowulf* 2055 þara banena byre..morðres ʒylpeð. **971** *Blickl. Hom.* 63 Maniʒe men wenaþ þæt morþor sy seo mæste synne. **13..** *Cursor M.* 1072 (Gött.) Again abel her raised a strijf, wid murther he broght his broþer o lijf. *a* **1375** *Ibid.* 1121 (Fairf.) þar-wiþ come our creatour for-to speke wiþ þat traytour [Cain] of þat myrþer [*earlier texts* murth] and þat tresoun. **1423** JAS. I *Kingis Q.* clvii, The wolf, that of the murthir noght say[is] 'ho!' **1535** COVERDALE *Mark* xv. 7 There was in preson with the sedicious, one called Barrabas, which in the vproure had committed murthur. **1588** SHAKS. *Tit. A.* IV. iv. 54 His traytrous Sonnes, That dy'd by law for murther of our Brother. **1649** BP. REYNOLDS *Hosea* ii. 77 Jezebel binds her self by an oath unto murther. **1726** BUTLER *Serm. Rolls* viii. 151 But let us suppose a Person guilty of Murther. **1836** LYTTON *Athens* (1837) II. 342 In despotic Persia all history dies away in the dark recesses and sanguinary murthers of a palace governed by eunuchs and defended but by slaves.

β. ? *a* **1366** CHAUCER *Rom. Rose* 1136 He wende to have reproved be Of thefte or mordre, if that he Hadde in his stable an hakeney. **1390** GOWER *Conf.* I. 270 Than se so gret a moerdre wroght Upon the blod which gulteth noght. **1470–85** MALORY *Arthur* IV. xv. 118 He gaf them londes and charged hem neuer to doo outragyousyte nor mordre. **1604** SHAKS. *Oth.* I. ii. 3 Though in the trade of Warre I haue slaine men, Yet do I hold it very stuffe o'th'conscience To do no contriu'd Murder. **1671** MILTON *Samson* 1186 Hadst thou not committed Notorious murder on those thirty men At Askalon. **1782** PRIESTLEY *Corrupt. Chr.* II. IX. 152 Ten years penance [was] enjoined for a murder. **1855** MACAULAY *Hist. Eng.* xviii. IV. 211 The peal and flash of gun after gun gave notice, from three different parts of the valley at once, that murder was doing. **1891** C. ROBERTS *Adrift Amer.* 107 The farmer lived..for 48 hours; however he lived long enough to make it only murder in the second degree.

fig. **1809** MALKIN *Gil Blas* III. iii. ¶6 This brutal importunity is downright murder to one's feelings.

b. Proverb. ***murder will out*** (also ***murder cannot be hid***, etc.). ***the murder is out***: said when something is suddenly revealed or explained.

13.. *Cursor M.* 1084 (Gött.) For-þi men sais into þis tyde, Is no man þat murthir may hide. *c* **1386** CHAUCER *Nun's Pr. T.* 232 Mordre wol out that se we day by day. **1433** LYDG. *St. Edmund* II. 225 in Horstm. *Altengl. Leg.* (1881) 400 Moordre wil out, thouh it abide a while. **1596** SHAKS. *Merch. V.* II. ii. 83 Murder cannot be hid long. **1706** FARQUHAR *Recruiting Officer* III. i, Now the murder's out. **1852** DICKENS *Bleak Ho.* xxviii, Sir Leicester's cousins, in the remotest degree, are so many Murders, in the respect that they 'will out'.

c. Often applied to a death-sentence of a tribunal, killing of men in war, or any other action causing destruction of human life, which is regarded as morally wicked, whether legal or not. ***judicial murder***: see JUDICIAL *a.* 1.

1551 TURNER *Herbal* I. Prol. A iij b, By occasyon of thys boke euery man, nay euery old wyfe will presume not without the mordre of many, to practyse Phisick. **1662** STILLINGFL. *Orig. Sacræ* II. ix. §11. 276 Condemn them for the Murther of Socrates. **1665** DRYDEN *Ind. Emperor* V. ii. (1668) 60 Slaughter grows murder when it goes too far, And makes a Massacre what was a War. *a* **1674** CLARENDON *Hist. Reb.* XI. §244 This unparalleled murder and parricide was committed upon the 30th of January. **1790** BURKE *Fr. Rev.* 108 The actual murder of the king and queen, and their child, was wanting to the other auspicious circumstances of this 'beautiful day'. The actual murder of the bishops..was also wanting. **1849** MACAULAY *Hist. Eng.* iv. I. 487 Murder by false testimony is therefore the most aggravated species of murder. **1858** W. ARNOT *Laws fr. Heav. for Life on Earth* Ser. II. xiii. 104 [War] is, rather than does, murder.

d. *personified.*

1593 SHAKS. *Rich. II*, I. ii. 21 His summer leafes all vaded By Enuies hand, and Murders bloody axe. **1812** SHELLEY *Devil's Walk* xxvi, The hell-hounds, Murder, Want and Woe, Forever hungering, flocked around.

e. Phr. ***to get away with murder***: see GET *v.* 61 c.

f. An excellent or marvellous person or thing. *U.S. slang.*

1940 *Music Makers* May 37/3 *Murder*, something excellent or terrific... 'That's solid murder, gate!' **1943** M. SHULMAN *Barefoot Boy* ix. 90 We got on the dance floor just as a Benny Goodman record started to play. 'Oh, B.G.!' cried Noblesse... 'Man, he's murder, Jack.' **1948** H. L. MENCKEN *Amer. Lang.* Suppl. II. 707 The vocabulary of the jazz addict is largely identical with that of the jazz performer ...anything excellent is *killer-diller*, *murder* or *Dracula*. **1970** C. MAJOR *Dict. Afro-Amer. Slang* 83 *Murder*, (1930's–40's) excellent; the best.

†**2.** Used without moral reprobation: Terrible slaughter, destruction of life. *Obs.*

1297 R. GLOUC. (Rolls) 11717, & sir simond was aslawe & is folk al to grounde More murþre [*v.r.* morþre] ʒare nas in so lute stounde Vor þere was werst simond de mountfort aslawe alas & sir henri his sone [etc.]. **1412–20** LYDG. *Chron. Troy* III. xxii. (1513) O v, Pryamus..suche a mordre gan vpon them make That many grekes lay dede on the playne. *c* **1449** PECOCK *Repr.* V. vi. (Rolls) 516 Sowdiers wagid into Fraunce for to make miche morther of blood. **1590** *Disc. Sp. Fleet inv. Eng.* 23 The same day..the L. Henrie Seimer and sir William Winter did so thoroughly beate two Spanish Galeons..that they were inforced to withdraw themselues to the coast of Flanders, where forsomuch as they were in a very euill taking, as well in respect of the murther of their men, as the manifolde leakes of their ships, they were surprised, and without fight rifeled by the Zelanders.

3. As a cry or exclamation uttered by one who thinks or pretends to think himself or some one else in danger of murder. Also, in trivial use, as a comic ejaculation of horror. ***to cry blue murder*** (*slang*): to make an extravagant outcry or lamentation; also ***blue murder***, a loud or alarming noise, a great commotion, din, or disturbance; used in intensive phrases as ***like blue murder***, at a terrific pace, at top speed (*colloq.*).

c **1470** HENRYSON *Mor. Fab.* IV. (*Fox & Cock*) xiii. 478 The wedow hard, and..Seand the cace, scho sichit and gaif an schout: 'How, murthour, hay! with ane hiddious beir, Allace, now lost is gentill chantecleir!' **1604** SHAKS. *Oth.* V. i. 27, I am maym'd for euer: Helpe hoa: Murther, murther. **1788** BURNS *Epigr. on Elphinstone's Martial*, Heard'st thou that groan—proceed no further; 'Twas laurelled Martial roaring murther! **1837** LOVER *Rory O'More* xlvi, Pooh! pooh!—murdher! there's not a dhrop o' wather in the pot. **1859** HOTTEN *Dict. Slang* 8 *Blue-murder*, a desperate or alarming cry. *c* **1874** D. BOUCICAULT in M. R. Booth *Eng. Plays of 19th Cent.* (1969) II. 228 They were standing by and thrying to screech blue murdher. 'Stop their mouths,' said a voice. **1887** 'J. S. WINTER' in *Eng. Illustr. Mag.* Dec. 179 The dingy person dropped his victim and howled what the half-dozen officers..afterwards graphically described as 'blue murder'. **1893** G. B. SHAW in *World* 10 May 28/2 What it [*sc.* the slow movement of Stanford's Irish Symphony] does end in is blue murder. **1900** POLLOK & THOM *Sports Burma* iii. 78 The foolish beast would not budge, but kept yelling 'blue murder' whilst the bull was cruelly punishing her. **1914** *Evening News* 1 Oct. 2/1 They were off down the road like blue murder. **1921** G. B. SHAW *Back to Methuselah* II. 84 You couldnt produce it. There would be blue murder. It's out of the question. **1959** 'A. GILBERT' *Death takes Wife* xiii. 164 Corpses don't yell blue murder.

4. *Hist.* Used occas. to render Anglo-Latin *murdrum*: The fine imposed, in the 12th and 13th c., on the hundred in which a 'murder' (i.e. felonious homicide of an unknown by an unknown person: see note under sense 1) had been committed.

1823 LINGARD *Hist. Eng.* (1854) I. 247 [Norman Conquest]. In legal language the penalty was denominated the 'murder'.

5. In *fig.* and hyperbolic use: (an act of) destruction or spoliation supposed to be tantamount to murder. Also in weakened senses: a situation or condition that is very unpleasant or undesirable.

1857 TROLLOPE *Barchester Towers* II. ii. 37 This cellar is perfectly abominable. It would be murder to put a bottle of wine into it till it has been roofed, walled, and floored... Goodenough never had a glass of wine that any man could drink. **1878** 'R. BOLDREWOOD' *Ups & Downs* ix. 90 What a murder that one should have all these hundredweights of nails,.. and forests of posts and wallpates to get all over again! **1924** KIPLING *Debits & Credits* (1926) 316, I was never keen on bombin' myself... But bombin'-instruction's murder! **1951** J. B. PRIESTLEY *Festival at Farbridge* II. ii. 255 Cook's gone, and it's murder trying to do it all myself. **1956** A. J. LERNER *My Fair Lady* (1958) I. i. 8 By right she should be taken out and hung For the cold-blooded murder of the English tongue! **1960** H. PINTER *Room* in *Birthday Party*, etc. 105 *Rose.* You look cold. *Mrs Sands.* It's murder out. Have you been out? **1965** M. BRADBURY *Stepping Westward* i. 64 Private life was simple enough, but the communal centres were murder. **1973** A. ROSS *Dunfermline Affair* 69 An old hip injury... Not so bad when I'm just walking..but murder climbing stairs.

6. A popular parlour or children's game for a number of participants, which involves a mock murder hunt, led by a 'detective', to find the 'murderer' of one who is playing dead, having been 'murdered' in the dark. Also called **murders, the murder game, murder in the dark.**

1933 PHILLIPS & WESTALL *Bk. Indoor Games* iv. 276 To give as good an idea of 'Murder' as we can, we will describe in narrative form an actual game. **1934** N. MARSH *Man lay Dead* i. 14 Silly games are played... It's going to be Murders this time. *Ibid.* 20 Are we really going to play the Murder Game? **1937** M. HILLIS *Orchids on your Budget* (1938) vi. 103 You can still serve refreshments after bingo played for pennies or the murder game. **1948** C. DAY LEWIS *Otterbury Incident* v. 59 We'd get him interested if we made a detective job of it—sort of Murder Game. **1964** R. JEFFRIES *Embarrassing Death* xii. 147 Did you ever play the game 'Murder'?.. Everybody but the murderer must tell the truth: the murderer may lie. **1972** G. BRANDRETH *Party Games* 24 Murder in the Dark. 6 or more players. A chilling game, definitely not for those with weak hearts.

7. *attrib.* and *Comb.*, simple attrib., as ***murder bout, case, charge, film, -fine*** (= sense 4), ***gun, hunt, -haunt, -oath, story, -tool, trial, victim, weapon***; objective, as ***murder-aiming, -darting*** adjs.; instrumental, as ***murder-wasted***; **murder bag** (see quot. 1938); **murder book (file, log)**, a book or file in which are kept details of a police investigation of a murder; **murder game**: see sense 6; **murder inquiry**, a police investigation into a case of murder; **murder investigation** = *murder inquiry*; **murder-man**, (*a*) a murderer; (*b*) a writer of murder stories; cf. MURDERMONGER; **murder mystery**, a mysterious murder; *spec.* a murder story in which the murderer's identity is concealed by a complicated plot until the dénouement; **murder one** *U.S. colloq.*, (a charge of) first-degree murder; **murder rap** *slang* (orig. *U.S.*), a charge of murder; **murder room**, after the discovery of a murder, a (nearby) room used as a centre for directing a police inquiry into the crime; **murder squad**, a division of the police appointed to investigate crimes of murder.

1789 BURNS *On Seeing Wounded Hare* i, Blasted be thy *murder-aiming eye! **1938** F. D. SHARPE *S. of Flying Squad* vi. 65 In the Superintendent's office at Scotland Yard repose two plain cowhide bags... They are the *Murder Bags which contain all the tools which a detective is likely to need in solving a major crime. **1962** 'J. BELL' *Crime in our Time* v. iii. 156 He takes with him all the necessary apparatus for a detailed examination on the spot, the so-called 'murder bag'. **1972** 'A. GARVE' *Case of Robert Quarry* I. i. 8 Methodically checking the contents of his murder bag. **1972** J. WAINWRIGHT *Requiem for Loser* viii. 162 The final write-up would be bound into a single volume, called 'The *Murder Book'. **1973** Murder Book [see *murder log* below]. **1906** HARDY *Dynasts* II. VI. vii. 298 Bonaparte and Alexander..Are closing to a mutual *murder-bout. **1930** A. CHRISTIE *Murder at Vicarage* xv. 118, I should never have suspected that Hawes would take such a keen interest in the details of a *murder case. **1974** M. BIRMINGHAM *You can help Me* iii. 52 This is a murder case... To answer a few questions will hardly hurt her. **1937** 'M. INNES' *Hamlet, Revenge!* III. v. 297 There is nobody..who would wish to incriminate me in a *murder charge. **1974** *Times* 15 Feb. 1/3 (*heading*) Murder charge after London shooting. **1972** J. WAINWRIGHT *Requiem for Loser* viii. 162 The enquiry was still 'The *Murder Enquiry'. **1973** Murder enquiry [see *murder log* below]. **1967** W. KEENAN *Lonely Beat* iv. 39 He picked up the thick *murder file... The reports were in chronological order. **1973** Murder File [see *murder log* below]. **1947** M. GILBERT *Close Quarters* xvi. 244 It was a *murder film. **1898** E. JENKS in *Contemp. Rev.* Dec. 884 The three neighbouring villages must pay the *murder-fine. **1939** E. S. GARDNER *D.A. draws Circle* (1940) v. 57 'What are they, Doug, finger-prints?' 'Yes, on the *murder gun.' **1968** *Observer* 28 Apr. 8/2 (*heading*) *Murder-hunt police appeal to motorists. **1937** 'M. INNES' *Hamlet, Revenge!* III. i. 220 The scene..suggested..a riot rather than a *murder-investigation. **1973** R. LEWIS *Blood Money* iii. 28 This is a murder investigation. Give me your assistance. **1972** J. WAINWRIGHT *Requiem for Loser* viii. 162 The log was still

'The *Murder Log'. **1973** —— *High-Class Kill* 123 Bits and pieces which are part of a murder enquiry—the Murder File, the Murder Log..and the Murder Book. *c* **1412** HOCCLEVE *De Reg. Princ.* 3166 Bet it is to sle þe *mordreman, Than suffre hym regnë. *c* **1420** *Virgin's Compl.* 32 in *Pol. Rel. & L. Poems* (1903) 239, I criede on deth, 'why wilt þu fle? Cum, sle his moder, þu morder man!' **1889** Murder-man [see *blood-curdler* (BLOOD *sb.* 20)]. **1900** ADE *Fables in Slang* 198 The Book that begins with a *Murder Mystery. **1960** AUDEN *Homage to Clio* 26 The sin of Gluttony Is ranked among the Deadly Seven, but in murder mysteries One can be sure the gourmet Didn't do it. **1973** A. MACVICAR *Painted Doll Affair* vi. 68, I bought two of the paperbacks described as 'murder mysteries'. **1975** *Times* 22 Sept. 11/5 They..worked out a scheme about two lexicographers involved in a murder mystery. *c* **1470** HENRYSON *Mor. Fab.* XIII. (*Frog & Mouse*) xiii, Bot gif thou sweir to me the *murthour aith But fraude or gile to bring me ouer this flude But hurt or harme. *Ibid.* xvi, Thow swore the murthour aith richt now, that I. **1971** 'H. HOWARD' *Murder One* xiv. 177 Murray's going to stand trial charged with *murder one. **1972** G. V. HIGGINS *Friends of Eddie Coyle* xxvi. 162 The three of them're up on murder one, they're gonna be having a hearing this afternoon. **1929** D. HAMMETT *Dain Curse* (1930) xv. 169 He hasn't a chance in the world of hanging *murder-raps on them. **1972** J. POTTER *Going West* 57 Sergeant O'Leary said how about pulling her in on a murder rap. **1968** P. N. WALKER *Carnaby & Gaolbreakers* xv. 143 I'd like a room set aside as a *Murder Room. **1972** G. SERENY *Case of Mary Bell* I. iii. 38 The 'Murder Room' at Newcastle's West End Police..was a hive of activity all night. **1929** M. A. GILL *Underworld Slang*, **Murder squad*, police who investigate murders. **1958** S. HYLAND *Who goes Hang?* xlv. 220 A straightforward fact ..accepted by Macaulay and his murder squad. **1972** C. DRUMMOND *Death at Bar* iii. 84 Sergeant Reed had retired from the pub before the City of London murder squad arrived. **1831** M. EDGEWORTH *Let.* 16 Mar. (1971) 490 Rogers..told me..a capital *murder-story. **1929** F. N. HART *Hide in Dark* i. 27 It's despicable to tell a murder story with the lights on. **1843** CARLYLE *Past & Pr.* III. x, Fighting with steel *murder-tools is surely a much uglier operation than Working, take it how you will. **1888** KIPLING *Let.* 2 May in C. E. Carrington *R. Kipling* (1955) v. 97 He has been concerned in most of the more distinguished *murder trials of the past twenty years. **1973** D. WESTHEIMER *Going Public* iii. 42 Lee went to the *Houston Post* and looked through back issues, studying murders and murder trials. **1971** *Guardian* 11 Dec. 10/5 The weekly number of *murder victims [in India] is 283. **1870** MORRIS *Earthly Par.* III. IV. 30 Of Sigurd, who the dragon slew Upon the *murder-wasted heath. **1959** M. GILBERT *Blood & Judgment* vii. 71 He had turned up..the *murder weapon, ready furnished with a print of the murderer. **1962** K. ORVIS *Damned & Destroyed* xii. 84 Fay's cap of heroin burned like a murder-weapon in my pocket. **1973** R. LEWIS *Blood Money* iv. 36 Frust.. confirmed that..the poker..is the murder weapon.

murder ('mɜːdə(r)), *v.* Forms: *α.* OE. (a-, for-, of-) myrþrian, 3–4 morþre, 3–5 murthre, 4 mirþer, 5 morþere, 4, 6 murthur, 4–6 morther, 5 mourther, 6 (myrther), murthir, 3–8, (9 *dial.*) murther; *β.* 4–5 mo(u)rdre, morder, moerdre, 4–6 murdre, (5 moorderyn), 6 mordir, 4– murder. [OE. (*a-*, *for-*, *of-*) *myrðrian* = OHG. *murdran* (MHG. *ermurderen*, *-morderen*, mod.G. *mördern*), Goth. *maurþrjan*:—OTeut. **murþrjan*, f. **murþro-* MURDER *sb.*

It is doubtful whether the OE. verb survived into ME., or whether the ME. vb. is wholly a new formation on the sb. In any case many of the forms show assimilation to the sb. Cf. OF. *mordrir*, *murdrir*, *murtrir* to murder (mod.F. *meurtrir* to bruise), Anglo-Latin *murdrāre*.]

1. a. *trans.* To kill (a human being) unlawfully with malice aforethought; in early use often with the additional notion of concealment of the offence (see MURDER *sb.* 1); to kill wickedly, inhumanly, or barbarously.

α. **1297** R. GLOUC. (Rolls) 2383 þe kinges 3onge breþeren aurel & ambrose Dradde vor hor eritage ymorþred to be. *a* **1300** *Cursor M.* 1116 (Cott.) [God] will þat he bii þe vttrage, þat murþerhed [*Fairf.* mirþerret, *Gött.* murtherrt, *Trin.* murþereþ] sua is ane ymage. **1362** LANGL. *P. Pl.* A. IV. 42 He meyntenеþ his Men to Morþere myn owne. *c* **1440** *York Myst.* xl. 91 How þei mourthered þat man þat we of mene. **1536** WRIOTHESLEY *Chron.* (Camden) I. 59 The Abbott of Towre Hill, being my[r]therd. **1673** RAY *Journ. Low C.* 399 There be..cut-throats ready to murther any man for a small piece of mony. **1757** BURKE *Abridgm. Eng. Hist.* III. viii. Wks. X. 511 All historians are..agreed that he murthered his nephew.

β. *c* **1330** R. BRUNNE *Chron. Wace* (Rolls) 5310 Greffes hym mordred for enuye. **1390** GOWER *Conf.* I. 344 To take and moerdre of his malice This child. *c* **1440** *Promp. Parv.* 342/2 Moorderyn, or prively kyllyn, *sicario.* **1530** PALSGR. 642/1, I murdre, I kyll or slee a man in his bedde or at unwares, *je meurdrys.* **1647** CLARENDON *Hist. Reb.* IV. §119 If he had not been seasonably rescued, it was believed they would have murderd him. **1828** SCOTT *F.M. Perth* xxxii, I have slain—murdered, if you will—my late master. **1855** MACAULAY *Hist. Eng.* xviii. IV. 212 Hamilton murdered the old man in cold blood. **1861** *Times* 23 July, The charge is not merely that you killed your wife, but that you murdered her, by which is meant that you killed her with deliberate intention so to do.

†**b.** with adverbial extension. *Obs.*

1572 *Satir. Poems Reform.* xxxi. 37 For innocents ar murtherit downe, without remors, in land and towne.

c. *refl.* To commit suicide or self-murder.

c **1369** CHAUCER *Dethe Blaunche* 724 (Fairf.) Thogh..ye for sorwe mordred your selve. *c* **1565** in *Hakluyt's Voy.* (1904) VI. 331 The condemned person..launcing his body a crosse from the breast downe all the belly murthereth himselfe. **1629** J. COLE *Of Death* 33 The man that murdereth himselfe, after the committing of the sin, hath not any time of repentence. **1827** MACAULAY *Ess., Machiav.* (1865) I. 37/1 Othello murders his wife;..he ends by murdering himself.

d. To slaughter in a terrible manner, to massacre.

†Also with complement expressing the result: ***to murder to death.***

c **1350** *Will. Palerne* 2859 So harde sautes to þe cite were 3euen, þat þe komli kerneles were to-clatered wiþ engines, & mani of here mi3thi men murdred to deþe. *c* **1400** *Destr. Troy* 10701 Paris with pyne was pricket at his hert, To se his men so be mard, & murtherit to dethe. *Ibid.* 11141 There murtherit were mony of the mayn troiens. **1876** TENNYSON *Harold* v. i, They turn on the pursuer, horse against foot, They murder all that follow.

e. In fig. and hyperbolic uses. In the 18th c. occas. †to torment, torture.

a **1225** *Ancr. R.* 310 þu uniselie sunfule! þo þu, þuruh deaðliche sunne, murðredest Godes spuse, þet is, þi soule. *c* **1394** *P. Pl. Crede* 666 Boþe þey wiln & þei wolden y-worþen so grete To passen any mans mi3t to morþeren þe soules. **1592** SHAKS. *Ven. & Ad.* 502 Thy eyes' shrowd tutor, that hard heart of thine, Hath taught them scornfull tricks, & such disdaine That they haue murdred this poore heart of mine. **1605** —— *Macb.* II. ii. 36 Macbeth does murther Sleepe, the innocent Sleepe. **1711** in *10th Rep. Hist. MSS. Comm.* App. v. 186 It is inexpressible, how well he prepared for his long departure, his desired exit; murdering all hearts, who viewed him in that state. **1712–13** SWIFT *Jrnl. to Stella* 18 Mar., Dilly murders us with his *if* puns. **1776** J. ADAMS *Wks.* (1854) IX. 421 Your motion..for sending ambassadors to France with conditional instructions, was murdered. **1796** SOUTHEY *Lett. fr. Spain* (1799) 221 There is not a part of the civilized world where the female mind is not murdered by the customs of society. **1884** W. C. SMITH *Kildrostan* 48 Suspicion murders love, and from its death Come anguish and remorse.

f. *transf.* with an animal as subject or object.

14.., **1523** [cf. MURDERING *vbl. sb.*]. **1597** SHAKS. *2 Hen. IV*, IV. v. 79 Like the Bees,..wee bring it to the Hiue; And like the Bees, are murthered for our paines. **1600** J. PORY tr. *Leo's Africa* IX. 337 If the elephant chanceth to breake through the hedge, he murthereth as many men as he can finde. **1863** W. C. BALDWIN *Afr. Hunting* vi. 192, I found Swartz and the Kaffirs exulting over a cow and young heifer, which they had murdered among them in about twelve shots.

g. *absol.* To perform the act of murdering; to commit murder.

1535 COVERDALE *Jer.* vii. 9 When ye haue stollen, murthured, committed aduoutrie, and periury. **1597** SHAKS. *2 Hen. IV*, IV. v. 126 Haue you a Ruffian that will sweare? drinke? dance? Reuell the night? Rob? Murder? and commit The oldest sinnes, the newest kinde of wayes? **1646** SIR J. TEMPLE *Irish Rebell.* (1746) 193 The Names of such as murthered, this Examinant knoweth not. *a* **1762** LADY M. W. MONTAGU, etc. *Verses to Imitator of Horace* 103 For tho' in law, to murder be to kill, In equity the murder's in the will. **1857** J. HYDE *Mormonism* vii. 181 These men will fight, lie, rob, murder for Mormonism if commanded. **1910** *New Mag.* Nov. 224/2 Yes. I am the man who murders for the king.

h. *colloq.*, as a jocular threat.

1939 JOYCE *Finnegans Wake* III. 460 So don't keep me now for a good boy for the love of my fragrant saint, you villain, ..or I'll first murder you. **1942** T. RATTIGAN *Flare Path* II. ii. 66 *Patricia.* You're ill. I'm going to ring up a doctor. *Teddy.* I'll murder you if you do.

2. To spoil by bad execution, representation, or pronunciation, etc.

1644–7 CLEVELAND *Char. Lond. Diurn.* 4 Thus, they kill a man over and over, as Hopkins and Sternhold murder the Psalmes, with another to the same. *c* **1693** *Ad Populum Phaleræ* II. ii. 25 The Sense too oft is murder'd by the Sound. **1728** MORGAN *Algiers* II. 213 The Spaniards most corruptly and most abusively murder and confound several Letters. **1751** WESLEY *2nd Let. to Author Enthus. Methodists* 2 In your Second [section], you cite (and murder) four or five Lines from one of my Journals. **1830** MARRYAT *King's Own* xlv, Don't kill Billy; it's bad enough to have murdered Shakspeare. **1861** WHYTE MELVILLE *Good for N.* I. 199 Bella..insisted on her teacher sitting down with her to roast chicken when they ought to have been murdering a duet.

3. To consume or spend (time) unprofitably.

1712 ADDISON *Spect.* No. 371 ⁋8 A different kind of Men, who are the Pests of all polite Conversation, and murder Time as much as either of the two former. **1756** WASHINGTON *Lett.* Writ. 1889 I. 241 If the hurry of business ..will admit of an opportunity to murder a little time in writing to me, I should receive the favour as a mark of.. esteem. **1764** *Mem. G. Psalmanazar* 95 Thus having murdered, as I may say, another year, we were dismissed. **1791–1823** D'ISRAELI *Cur. Lit.* (1866) 255/2 Murdering time by a constant round of giddy dissipation. **1827** SCOTT *Jrnl.* 8 Aug., It kills time, or rather murders it, this company-keeping.

4. To mangle cruelly. [Cf. F. *meurtrir* to bruise.]

1876 TENNYSON *Harold* v. ii, They have so maim'd and murder'd all his face There is no man can swear to him.

5. *slang.* To defeat (an opponent or rival) totally or conclusively, esp. at a game or sport.

1952 G. TALBOT in Wentworth & Flexner *Dict. Amer. Slang* (1960) 349/2 The National Leaguers..eat up southpaws. They murdered them all season. **1973** 'J. PATRICK' *Glasgow Gang Observed* v. 49 Mick had stepped in and challenged Bertie to a 'square-go'. 'Mick murdered him, man,' Tim recalled. **1974** *Observer* 24 Feb. 23/7 If the passing had got any worse, a team of corporals' grandmothers would have murdered them. They ran like fugitives from a church parade.

murderable ('mɜːdərəb(ə)l), *a.* [f. MURDER *v.* + -ABLE.] Giving cause for murder, provoking or inviting murder.

1920 D. H. LAWRENCE *Women in Love* ii. 32 A murderee is a man who is murderable. And a man who is murderable is a man who in a profound, if hidden lust, desires to be murdered. **1927** *Sunday Express* 21 Aug. 10/4 This tendency to associate unpopular opinions with murderable offences seems to be an increasing one on both sides of the Atlantic. **1966** *New Statesman* 18 Mar. 377/1 They had made good, and they *were* good; pre-eminently, they had achieved 'security'. And hence the immediate public terror caused by their murder: the least murderable people in the world, if they could be murdered, then anyone could be murdered.

†'**murderably,** *adv.* *Obs.* *rare*[−1]. In 5 *Sc.* **murtherabily.** [f. MURDER *sb.* (*murther*) + -ABLE + -LY[2].] Murderously, by way of murder.

1456 SIR G. HAYE *Law of Arms* (S.T.S.) 260 Quhat ever he be that slais a man murtherabily and secretly.

†'**murderdom.** *Obs.* *rare*[−1]. [f. MURDER *sb.*, after *martyrdom.*] The practice of murdering.

1525 in *St. Papers Hen. VIII*, IV. 419 *note*, Yair cruell tiranny and murthirdome of cristin pepill.

murdered ('mɜːdəd), *ppl. a.* [f. MURDER *v.* + -ED[1].] In senses of the verb.

c **1402** LYDG. *Compl. Bl. Knt.* xli, How may thou see thus in thy presence, Without mercy, murdred innocence? **1588** SHAKS. *Tit. A.* II. iii. 300 Some bring the murthered body, some the murtherers. **1697** DRYDEN *Virg. Georg.* IV. 657 For Crimes, not his, the Lover lost his Life, And at thy Hands requires his murther'd Wife. **1742** YOUNG *Nt. Th.* v. 195 Hail, precious moments! stoln from the black waste Of murder'd time! **1765** FALCONER *Demagogue* 52 Nor murder'd reputation marks his way. **1849** MACAULAY *Hist. Eng.* v. I. 663 The head of the murdered magistrate was placed over the Guildhall. **1876** 'OUIDA' *Winter City* vii, I don't like murdered languages.

murderee (mɜːdə'riː). [f. MURDER *v.* + -EE[1].] A person who is murdered. Also, a person whose character and disposition suggest the passive qualities of an easy victim of murder.

1920 D. H. LAWRENCE *Women in Love* ii. 32 It takes two people to make a murder: a murderer and a murderee. And a murderee is a man who is murderable. **1925** *New Yorker* 28 Mar. 13/2 Some day, somebody is going to write a mystery story in which the murderee will be a swell guy. **1928** F. T. JESSE *Trial of S. H. Dougal* 4 The potential murderer has met the born murderee. **1928** A. HUXLEY *Point Counter Point* xii. 209 He's the real type of murderee ..the obvious victim; he fairly invites maltreatment. **1939** —— *After Many a Summer* 20 You're probably the sort of person that invites persecution. A bit of a murderee..as well as a scholar and a gentleman. **1958** S. HYLAND *Who goes Hang?* xii. 59, I don't *know* who the murdered man, the 'murderee', was. **1970** *Times Lit. Suppl.* 7 Aug. 883/1 This one hinges on the killing of one of those fiendishly attractive girls who, fictionally at least, are so often murderees. **1973** K. GILES *File on Death* vi. 151 Title wasn't much chop however you look at him, a murderee if ever I investigated one. **1974** *Sunday Times* 31 Mar. 52/3 TV Film..about Elizabeth Montgomery set up as possible next murderee in a storm.

murderer ('mɜːdərə(r)). [Partly f. MURDER *v.* + -ER[1]; partly a. AF. *mordreour*, *murdreour* (*-drere*), agent-n. f. *mordrer*, *mordrir* = MURDER *v.*]

1. One who murders or is guilty of a murder (see MURDER *sb.*[1] 1).

α. *a* **1300** *Cursor M.* 23112 þe first range mast stincand, sal be o wreches mistruand; þat renaid ar traiturs and fals, Murthereres [*Fairf.* man mirþeres] and monsuorn als. **1470–85** MALORY *Arthur* VII. xiv. 233 A saide she they were good knyghtes but they were murtherers. *c* **1515** *Cocke Lorell's B.* 11 There were theues, hores, and baudes; w[t] mortherers. **1560** DAUS tr. *Sleidane's Comm.* 235 The Murtherer standyng behynd his backe, letteth dryve at him with an hatchet. **1605** SHAKS. *Macb.* I. vii. 15 First, as I am his Kinsman, and his Subiect, Strong both against the Deed: Then, as his Host, Who should against his Murtherer shut the doore, Not beare the knife my self. **1741** MIDDLETON *Cicero* I. I. 54 Roscius prosecuted the Murtherer for damages. **1775** ADAIR *Amer. Ind.* 158 The Cheerake..still observe that law so inviolably, as to allow their beloved town the privilege of protecting a wilful murtherer.

β. *c* **1385** CHAUCER *L.G.W.* 2387 *Philomene* (Cambr. MS.) He wil nat for his shame Don so as Tereus to lese his name Ne serve 3ow as a morderour [*v.r.* morderere, -roure, -erour, murderour] or a knaue. **1390** GOWER *Conf.* III. 340 Slain is the moerdrer and moerdrice. *c* **1440** *Promp. Parv.* 342/2 Moord(e)rare (*K.*, *P.* morederar), *sicarius.* **1471** CAXTON *Recuyell* (Sommer) I. 63, Y had leuer to be murdrid than a murdrere. **1509** FISHER *Funeral Serm. Hen. VII*, Wks. (1876) 272 King Dauid.., all be it he had ben an auoutrer & murdrer also, yet [etc.]. **1621** DONNE *Serm.* xv. (1640) I. 149 A Sheriffe that should burne him, who were condemned to be hanged, were a murderer, though that man must have dyed. **1781** GIBBON *Decl. & F.* xx. III. 139 *note*, Those female captives, who gave their charms, and even their hearts, to the murderers of their fathers, brothers, &c. **1841** ELPHINSTONE *Hist. India* I. App. III. 445 Alexander.. proceeded in pursuit of one of the murderers of Darius to the royal city of the Zarangæi. **1849** MACAULAY *Hist. Eng.* iv. I. 487 The false witness..is, in truth the worst of murderers. **1865** DICKENS *Mut. Fr.* I. iv, We have got a murderer for a tenant.

b. *transf.* and *fig.*

c **1381** CHAUCER *Parl. Foules* 353 (Camb. MS.) The swalwe mortherere of the foulis smale That makyn hony of flouris frosche & newe. *c* **1585** R. BROWNE *Answ. Cartwright* 15 The sinner is the murtherer of his owne soule. **1600** SHAKS. *A.Y.L.* III. v. 19 Lye not, to say mine eyes are murtherers. **1611** BIBLE *1 John* iii. 15 Whosoeuer hateth his brother, is a murtherer. **1738** *Gentl. Mag.* VIII. 208/2 King Alfred, who hang'd 44 Judges in one Year, as Murtherers of the Law. **1797** GODWIN *Enquirer* I. iii. 17 It is the unrelenting murderer of hope and gaiety.

†**2.** A small cannon or mortar (see quot. 1704).

1497 *Naval Acc. Hen. VII* (1896) 338 Morderers of yron ..ij. **1563** in Nicolson & Burn *Westmoreld. & Cumbld.* (1777) II. 223 In the Citadel... Small serpentines 2, fowlers

2, murderers 2. **1617** J. TAYLOR (Water-P.) *Dolphins Danger* Wks. 1630 III. 33/1 The Dolphin..hauing..some 19 pieces of Ordnance, and 9 Murtherers. **1628** R. NORTON *Gunner* xiv. 59 Morter Peeces, Square Murtherers, Tortles, and Pettards are the sorts of the fourth kind of Ordnance. **1634** *Relat. Ld. Baltimore's Plantation* (1865) 20 We haue built a strong Fort & Palizado, and haue mounted vpon it one good piece of Ordnance, and 4 Murderers. **1670** *Lond. Gaz.* No. 436/1 This week the same Fregats took another prize from the Turks being a vessel of 6 Guns 4 Murtherers and 60 men. **1704** J. HARRIS *Lex. Techn.* I, *Murderers*, are small Pieces of Ordnance, either of Brass or Iron, having *Chambers* (that is Charges made of Brass or Iron) put in at their Breeches: They are mostly used at Sea at the Bulk-heads of the Fore-castle, Half-deck, or Steeridge, in order to clear the Decks when an Enemy boards the Ship; they are fastned and traversed by a Pintle, which is put into a Stock.

†3. A dagger or knife. *Obs. rare*⁻¹.

c **1510** *Robt. Deuyll* in Thoms *Prose Rom.* (1828) I. 10 Robert gate a murderer or bodkin, and thrast his mayster in the bely that his guttes fell at his fete, and so fell downe deed to the erth.

†4. (See quot.) *Obs. rare*⁻⁰.

1690 EVELYN *Mundus Muliebris, Fop Dict.* 19 *Meurtrieres*. Murderers; a certain Knot in the Hair, which ties and unites the Curls.

5. An instrument used for catching codfish.

1883 R. M. FERGUSSON *Rambles in Far North* xii. 79 There is a method of catching deep-sea cod..by means of an instrument called a 'murderer',..consisting of a long bar of lead measuring about eighteen inches, with numerous hooks attached, and suspended at the end of a long strong line. This instrument is towed at the stern of the fishing boat, and by its means many a large cod bids farewell to the Pentland Firth. **1883** *Fisheries Exhib. Catal.* 12 'Murderer' for catching Codfish.

6. *attrib.* and *Comb.*

1592 *Arden of Feversham* III. i. E 1, Beset With murtherer theeues that came to rifle me. **1594** KYD *Cornelia* III. ii. 37 The sword Which murdrer-like against thy selfe he drawes.

murderess ('mɜːdərɪs). Also 4 moerdrice, 6–7 murdress(e, murtheress(e. [f. MURDER(ER) + -ESS. Cf. OF. *morderesse*.

Gower's *moerdrice* is properly a distinct word, imitating Fr. forms like *emperice*: see EMPRESS.]

A woman that commits murder.

1390 GOWER *Conf.* I. 346 Sche that was an homicide And of hire oghne lord Moerdrice. **1588** A. MARTEN *Exhort. H.M. Faithf. Subj.* A 3 b, Athalea..was slayne..as a murtheresse of her owne children. *c* **1605** ROWLEY *Birth Merl.* v. ii, Thou murderess of a king. **1632** J. HAYWARD tr. *Biondi's Eromena* 19 What want you woman will you be your owne murtheresse? **1677** MRS. BEHN *Abdelazer* I. iii, Hold! hold, inhumane Murdress; What hast thou done, most barbarous of thy sex? **1804** SOUTHEY in *Ann. Rev.* II. 531 The parents, therefore, believe her to be the murderess, and prepare a fire to burn her. **1871** B. TAYLOR *Faust* (1875) I. v. 87 Then laughed the murderess in her glee.

¶ In C. James *Milit. Dict.* (1802) and in later Dicts. *murdress* is given equivalent to MEURTRIÈRE.

murdering ('mɜːdərɪŋ), *vbl. sb.* [f. MURDER *v.* + -ING¹.] The action of the verb MURDER; also, an act of committing murder.

c **1386** CHAUCER *Knt.'s T.* 1143 The treson of the mordring in the bedde. *c* **1440** *Promp. Parv.* 342/2 Moorderynge, *sicariacio, sicariatus*. **1585** T. WASHINGTON tr. *Nicholay's Voy.* IV. xxxvi. 160 [The] cruel murthering of their ancient citizens. **1629** J. COLE *Of Death* 32 The murthering of a mans selfe to eschew any calamity or sorrow, doth not argue any valour, but cowardise rather. **1828** P. CUNNINGHAM *N.S. Wales* (ed. 3) II. 28 They..usually continue their murderings until, in retaliation, blood is expiated by blood.

transf. **14..** *Noble Bk. Cookry* (1882) 86 Tak a goos of a nyght and a day murdring and chope hir in the wort in the same manner. **1523** FITZHERB. *Husb.* §51 Put not to many shepe in a penne at one tyme..for feare of murtheryng or ouer pressyng of their felowes.

†b. In passive sense. *Obs.*

1472–5 *Rolls of Parlt.* VI. 160/1 [The witnesses said they dared not to present the truth] for drede of murd[r]yng, and to be myscheved in their owne houses. **1600** J. JANE in *Hakluyt's Voy.* III. 844 The Captaine being in danger of murthering, was constrained to vse leuitie.

†c. *attrib.*: **murdering battery** (see quot.); **murdering shot**, shot used in a 'murdering piece'.

1628 R. NORTON *Gunner* x. 52 Peeces that either shoote stone shot, Fireballes, Murthering Shot, or els no shot at all. **1727–51** CHAMBERS *Cycl.* s.v. *Battery, Battery de revers*, or *murdering battery*, is one that plays on the back of any place: and being placed on an eminence, sees into it.

'murdering, *ppl. a.* [f. MURDER *v.* + -ING².] That murders or commits murder. *lit.* and *fig.*

1550 LEVER *Serm.* (Arb.) 38 As pickinge theft, is lesse then murtheryng robrye: so [etc.]. *c* **1560** (*title*) Orations of Arsanes agaynst Philip the trecherous kyng of Macedone;.. and of Scanderberg prayeng ayde of Christian Princes agaynst periurous murderyng Mahumet [etc.]. **1593** SHAKS. *2 Hen. VI*, III. ii. 324 Their cheefest Prospect, murd'ring Basiliskes. **1666** DRYDEN *Ann. Mirab.* lv, His murdering guns a loud defiance roar. **1676** HOBBES *Iliad* v. 415 Mars, bloody, murthering Mars. **1760** *Ann. Reg.* 11 These murdering wars which cut off so many experienced officers. **1790** J. B. MORETON *Mann. W. Ind.* 183 He horsewhips and shoots you dead with a murdering infamous tongue. **1859** W. COLLINS *'Blow up with the Brig!'*, I struggled hard to force my eyes from the slow, murdering flame.

†b. Of bait; cf. KILLING *ppl. a.* 1 b. *Obs. rare*⁻¹.

1681 CHETHAM *Angler's Vade-m.* iv. §26 (1689) 57 In the month of April, for Trouts, that 'tis A Murthering Bait.

Hence †**'murderingly** *adv.*

1662 J. SPARROW tr. *Behme's Rem. Wks., 1st Apol. Balth. Tylcken* 1 Venomously, spitefully, hatefully, murtheringly.

murdering piece. *Obs.* [See PIECE *sb.* 11.]

1. = MURDERER 2.

1602 SHAKS. *Ham.* IV. v. 95 O my deere Gertrude, this, Like to a murdering Peece in many places, Giues me superfluous death. **1603** KNOLLES *Hist. Turks* (1621) 851 And seeing them that were gathered together into the market place..to fight as men altogether desperat, he caused certain murthering pieces to be bent upon them. **1655** E. TERRY *Voy. E. India* 163 Mann'd she was but with ten men, and had only one small murdering-peece within her.

fig. **1617** MIDDLETON & ROWLEY *Fair Quarrel* II. i, There is not such another murdering-piece In all the stock of calumny.

¶ 2. Used by Burke for: A picture of carnage. Cf. *battle-piece*: see PIECE *sb.* 17 b.

1797 BURKE *Regic. Peace* iii. Wks. VIII. 309 A far more cruel 'murdering piece' than had ever entered into the imagination of painter or poet.

murderish ('mɜːdərɪʃ), *a. rare.* [f. MURDER *sb.* + -ISH.] Murderous.

1550 W. LYNNE *Carion's Cron.* 262 b, Perceyuyng the craft and papisticall murderysh harte of his brother. **1904** E. F. BENSON *Challoners* ix, Did you ever see such a murderish-looking woman?

†**'murderment.** *Obs. rare.* [f. MURDER *v.* + -MENT.] The act of murdering.

c **1425** *Cursor M.* 19716 (Trin.), Niȝte or day whenne þei myȝt spie Bi murþerment to do him diȝe. **1548** UDALL *Erasm. Par. Luke* iv. 52 The slaughter and murdremente of howe manye persones. **1600** FAIRFAX *Tasso* II. ii, To her came message of the murderment.

murdermonger ('mɜːdə,mʌŋgə(r)). [f. MURDER *sb.* + MONGER¹.] A dealer in murder, a professional murderer. So *fig.*, a writer of murder stories; fem. (*nonce-wd.*) **murder-mongeress.** Also **murder-mongering** *vbl. sb.*, the purveying of news or stories of murder.

a **1889** in Barrère & Leland *Dict. Slang* (1889) I. 139/1 The only one who is annoyed is our own special murder-monger, who has got several blood-curdlers of English extraction up his sleeve. **1900** M. HEWLETT *Richard Yea-and-Nay* II. vi. 299 She knew something of the Marquess, her cousin. Any ally of his must be a murdermonger. **1957** O. NASH *You can't get there from Here* 97, I repeat that one book by this murder-mongeress [*sc.* Agatha Christie] Will last you as long as the Library of Congress. **1967** *Punch* 4 Oct. 524/3 You may think that the enormous sums of money spent on murder-mongering by the newspapers have bred up a lamentable race of scribes.

murderous ('mɜːdərəs), *a.* [f. MURDER *sb.*¹ + -OUS. Cf. OF. *mordreux*.]

1. Of persons: Guilty of murder (? *obs.*); capable of or bent on committing murder. Also *transf.* of weapons, physical agents, etc.

1535 COVERDALE *Zeph.* ii. 5 Wo vnto you yᵗ dwel vpon the see coost, ye murthurous people. *a* **1586** SIDNEY *Ps.* v. ii, Thou, the Lord, in endless hatred hast The murd'rous man. **1588** SHAKS. *Tit. A.* IV. ii. 88 Stay murtherous villaines, will you kill your brother? **1594** —— *Rich. III*, I. ii. 94 Queene Margaret saw Thy murd'rous Faulchion smoaking in his blood. **1671** MILTON *P.R.* II. 76 Enforc't to flye Thence into Egypt, till the Murd'rous King Were dead, who sought his life. **1689** *Col. Rec. Pennsylv.* I. 252 He was pleased to direct that ye murtherous woman's sentence should proceed. **1719** WATTS *Hymns & Spir. Songs* II. lxxxiv. (1725) 206 The rich Flood of purple Gore Their murth'rous Weapons dy'd. **1720** J. HUGHES *Siege Damascus* v. ii, Too well I know thee now, O murd'rous fiend! **1811** PINKERTON *Petral.* II. 496 In different parts around the mountain, powerful murtherous vapours, of a mephitic nature, were exhaled. **1837** J. H. NEWMAN *Par. Serm.* (ed. 2) III. ii. 22 Saved from the murderous Egyptians in his infancy. **1884** A. J. E. WILSON *Vashti* iii, Putting her fingers in her ears that she might not hear the bubbling of the murderous water, she shut her eyes and sprang into the pond.

2. Of the nature of murder; characteristic of or involving murder.

1593 SHAKS. *2 Hen. VI*, V. i. 185 Who can be bound by any solemne vow To do a murd'rous deede. **1660** *Trial Regic.* 53 Suppose..they should have agreed upon such a Murtherous Act. **1764** GOLDSM. *Trav.* 416 Where beasts with man divided empire claim, And the brown Indian marks with murderous aim. **1877** MRS. OLIPHANT *Makers Flor.* iv. 93 The Florence of the historians..in which so many murderous encounters..were always going on.

3. *Comb.*

1654 GATAKER *Disc. Apol.* 62 This..murtherous-minded man. **1835** JAMES *Gipsy* i, 'This is a murderous-looking spot', said Colonel Manners.

Hence **'murderously** *adv.*, **'murderousness.**

1611 SPEED *Theat. Gt. Brit.* xl. 79/1 Oswy King of Northumberland..was murtherously made away. *a* **1639** W. WHATELEY *Prototypes* II. xxix. (1640) 133 Take heede of these vices, Envy, murderousnesse, hard-heartednesse, cruelty. **1844** L. HUNT *Poems* 163 Some, whom feeble love's excess, Through terror, tempts to murderousness. **1885** *Manch. Exam.* 26 June 5/7 He was attacked and murderously assaulted by two men.

murdre, obs. form of MURDER *sb.* and *v.*

†**'murdres**, *v. Sc. Obs.* Forms: α. 4 mwrthrys, 5 murthrys; β. 6 murdreis, murdris, murdres. [ad. OF. *murdriss-*, *mordriss-*, lengthened stem of *murdrir*, *mordrir* MURDER *v.* Cf. MURTRISH *v.* (The α forms are due to assimilation to *murther* MURDER *sb.*)] = MURDER *v.*

α. *c* **1375** *Sc. Leg. Saints* xxii. (*Laurentius*) 92 He had as a wykyt mane Mwrth[r]yst his lord. *c* **1425** WYNTOUN *Cron.* VI. ix. 63 (1795) I. 176 In Murrawe syne he murthrysyd was.

β. *c* **1507** DUNBAR *Poems* xxxiii. 30 In pottingry he wrocht grit pyne, He murdreist mony in medecyne. **1508** —— *Tua Mariit Wemen* 212 Apone sic materis I mus[e], at myd-nyght, full oft, And murnys so in my mynd, I murdris my selfin. **1545** in Tytler *Hist. Scot.* (1864) II. 349 *note*, The Lord Maclane's fader was cruellie murdressit..be Sir John Campbell of Calder. *a* **1578** LINDESAY (Pitscottie) *Chron. Scot.* (S.T.S.) II. 83 They murdrest him to the deid. **1585–86** *Reg. Privy Council Scot.* IV. 57 Maist schamefullie to murdreis him. **1598** *Ibid.* V. 443 To have murdreist him be way of hamesuckin.

†**'murdresar.** *Sc. Obs.* [f. prec. + -AR³.] = MURDERER 1 and 2.

1529 LYNDESAY *Compl.* 363 Men murdresaris, and commoun theiffis, In to that court gat, all, releiffis. **1536** BELLENDEN *Chron. Scot.* IX. xxv. (1821) II. 116 The murdresaris at last war takin. **1549** *Compl. Scot.* vi. 41 Mak reddy ȝour cannons, culuerene,..murdresaris.

†**'murdrier.** *Obs. rare*⁻¹. [a. OF. *murdrier* (mod.F. *meurtrier*), f. *murdre* MURDER *sb.*] = MURDERER.

1481 CAXTON *Godeffroy* x. 32 The contrees were ful of theues and of murdriers.

murdris, variant of MURDRES *v. Obs.*

murdur, obs. form of MURDER *sb.*

†**mure**, *sb. Obs.* [a. F. *mur*:—L. *mūrum* (*mūrus*).]

1. A wall. Also *transf.* and *fig.*

1471 CAXTON *Recuyell* (Sommer) I. 271 He..fortefied the Cyte of Troye with mures & towrs. *a* **1552** LELAND *Itin.* (1768) II. 79 Rogerus le Poure..cast a great Dike without it, and made a false Mure without the Dike. **1577** SETTLE *Frobisher's 2nd Voy.* in Hakluyt (1589) 624 At our first comming the streights seemed to be shut vp with a long mure of yce. **1597** SHAKS. *2 Hen. IV*, IV. iv. 119. **1651** JER. TAYLOR *Clerus Dom.* 3 There was never any people but had their Priests..and kept holy things within a mure.

2. quasi-*adj.* in ***crown-mure*** = mural crown; also Comb. in ***mure-crowned*** adj. *rare*⁻¹.

1682 WHELER *Journ. Greece* III. 238 Another I saw..of silver, with a Mure-crowned Head. *Ibid.* 264 A Figure, with a Crown-mure, with these Letters about it.

mure, *a. Obs.* exc. *dial.* (East Angl.: see E.D.D.) Also **mewre, meure, moyre, mur, meuer.** [a. OF. *meür*, *meüre*, mod.F. *mûr*, *mûre* ripe, mature.] **a.** Grave, modest, DEMURE. **b.** Mature (in phrase ***mure deliberation***).

c **1440** *Jacob's Well* xli. 254 Þe secunde fote in brede [of frenschip] is benignite, þat is, to suffere, & to be mure, & noȝt veniable, ne holde wratthe in herte. **1442** T. BECKINGTON *Corr.* (Rolls) II. 215 By commune and mure deliberacion t'acertaine your said Mageste of such inconvenients as [etc.]. *c* **1450** *St. Cuthbert* (Surtees) 7678 Moyre and sobyr in worde and dede. *c* **1500** *Melusine* xxiv. 160 He purueyed of remede by good & meure deliberacion of his counseill.

c. *Comb.*: **mure-hearted** *a.* (*dial.*), tender-hearted (see E.D.D.).

mure (mjʊə(r)), *v.* Forms: 6 **mowre**, 5– **mure**. *Pa. pple.* 4 **mwryt**, 5 **mewred**, 5–6 **muryd(e**, 6 **murid, muryed.** [a. F. *murer*:—L. *mūrāre*, f. *mūrus* MURE *sb.*]

1. *trans.* To wall in, to surround with a wall or walls; to fortify. = IMMURE *v.* 1. Also with *up*, *in*.

c **1440** MAUNDEV. (1839) xxvii. 277 He had let muren alle the mountayne aboute with a stronge walle and a fair. **1494** FABYAN *Chron.* v. cxl. 126 Howsis, Castellis, and townes strongely muryd. **1503** HAWES *Examp. Vir.* XII. 215 But sapyence with her wordes me mured With walles of comfort makynge me mery. **1653** URQUHART *Rabelais* I. lii, All other Abbies are strongly walled and mured about. **1780** VON TROIL *Iceland* 189 This bath, which is large enough to contain 50 persons at one time, is mured in with a wall of basalt.

2. To block up, or build up (a door, gate, etc.), by means of bricks and mortar, stones, etc. Also with *up*.

1375 BARBOUR *Bruce* IV. 164 Thai or day, throu mekill pane, Had mwryt vp the ȝet agane. **1523** LD. BERNERS *Froiss.* I. cccxcviii. 689 Let vs enclose ourselfe in this towne, and mure vp all our gates. **1673** BP. S. PARKER *Reproof Reh. Transp.* 519 Mure up your school doors. **1807** J. BARLOW *Columb.* VII. 632 There lodge their tons of powder and retire, Mure the dread passage, wave the fatal fire.

transf. and *fig.* **1581** MULCASTER *Positions* (1887) 69 Such fleshy parts..do..as it were mure up, and stop the passage. **1596** SPENSER *F.Q.* VI. xii. 34 He tooke a muzzel strong Of surest yron..: Therewith he mured up his mouth along.

b. To wall up the doors of; to stop the means of access to. With *up*.

1550 SIR R. BOWES in Hodgson *Hist. Northumbld.* (1828) III. II. 200 The said utter courde were best, as me think, to be mowred upp. **1672** MARVELL *Reh. Transp.* I. 124 Why not adjourn the Term, mure up Westminster-hall [etc.].

3. To shut up or enclose within walls; to imprison; to confine as in a prison or fortress. = IMMURE *v.* 2. Also with *up*.

In some examples the vb. app. refers to the alleged walling up in cells of anchorites (who were fed through a hole in the wall) and of persons condemned to perish by famine.

a **1450** *Knt. de La Tour* (1906) 73 He kylde hym, and dyde his wyf to be mewred and putte in pryson perpetuel. **1530** PALSGR. 642/1 It is a payne to be mured up in a stone wall lyke an anker. **1611** BIBLE *Josh.* x. *heading*, The fiue Kings are mured in a caue. **1670** tr. *Bernier's Mogol Emp.* (1676) I. 179 The Women were mured up, where they dyed of hunger and misery. **1799** in *Spirit Pub. Jrnls.* III. 104 Some youth, one mur'd in squalid city jails. **1847** MARRYAT *Childr. N. Forest* xxvi, [They] are not a little tired of being mured up in the cottage. **1888** AMÉLIE RIVES *Quick or Dead* vii. (1889) 82 They could never voluntarily have mured themselves in labyrinths of brick and stone during these late autumn days.

b. *refl.* To shut oneself *up*.

1608 BP. HALL *Epist.* I. v, An English-man, so madly devout, that he had wilfully mur'd up himselfe as an Anachoret. **1893** BLACK *Handsome Humes* I. i. 16 She said it was a pity he mured himself up in his college at Oxford.

mure, obs. f. MARE *sb.*[1], MIRE, MOOR *sb.*[1], MYRRH.

mureburne, -cok, obs. ff. MOOR-BURN, -COCK.

mureed, var. MURID.

murein ('mjʊəri:n). *Biochem.* [f. L. *mūr-us* wall + *-ein*, after PROTEIN.] A polymeric substance whose molecules consist of mucopolysaccharide chains interlinked with short peptide chains and which is an important structural component of the cell walls of many bacteria.

1964 WEIDEL & PELZER in *Adv. Enzymol.* XXVI. 195 The new type of polymer from which bacterial sacculi are tailored. We propose the term 'murein'.., in analogy to the trivial name 'protein'. Various other designations presently in use, like 'mucocomplex' or 'mucopolymer', have little to recommend them because they would fit a variety of chemically rather different structures. The term 'mucopeptide' which has also been proposed, appears to be somewhat misleading for a polymer which is..at least as much a polysaccharide as it is a (poly)peptide. **1969** W. G. MURRELL in Gould & Hurst *Bacterial Spore* vii. 236 All spore mureins so far studied..differ from known cell wall polymers in having..a two- to three-fold excess of glucosamine or muramic acid residues over glutamic acid or DAP residues. **1969** *New Scientist* 10 July 64/1 Murein contains an amino sugar, muramic acid, which is not found in higher organisms, and also several amino acids in the unusual D-configuration. **1972** *Nature* 3 Mar. 10/1 The bacterial cell wall is bounded by a fragile cytoplasmic membrane... This is surrounded by, or interwoven with, a more rigid cell wall..built up from a limited number of constituents and known variously as mucopeptide, peptidoglycan or murein.

murell, obs. form of MURAL *a.*[1]

†**'murely**, *adv. Obs.* Also 5 **meuerly, meurely.** [f. MURE *a.* + -LY[2].] Demurely; considerately.

c **1400** *Destr. Troy* 12431 The maidon to tho mighty meuerly saide [etc.]. *c* **1430** LYDG. *Min. Poems* (Percy Soc.) 10, vij. virgens..of ther cheris aperid murely. **1474** CAXTON *Chesse* III. ii, He ought to do no thyng ayenst his wylle, But to do al thyng nobly, meurely, fermely & honestly.

murene, obs. form of MURÆNA.

†**'murenger.** *Obs.* Forms: α. 6 **murager.** β. 6–9 **murenger, muringer.** [ME. *murager*, f. MURAGE; for the later insertion of *n* cf. *passenger*, *messenger*.] An officer whose duty it was to keep the walls of a city in repair.

α. **1506** in *Munic. Corpor. Rep.* (1835) IV. 2622 [The charter of Henry VII provides that the mayor and citizens of Chester, may yearly choose..two citizens to be overseers of the walls,..called Muragers.] ? **1580** in *9th Rep. Hist. MSS. Comm.* App. I. 305/1 [Oath for burgesses of Great Yarmouth, for their..election of] muragers.

β. *c* **1600** WEBB in D. King *Vale-Royall* (1656) II. 18 The special care whereof [the wall], belongeth to certain Officers yearly..elected..called the Maringers [sic], being usually, of the most antient Aldermen of the said City. **1682** THORESBY *Diary* (1830) I. 122 The walls [of Chester] are kept in excellent repair by the Muringers. **1815** W. PRICE *Hist. Oswestry* 86 The corporation of Oswestry consists of a mayor,..coroner, murenger, town-clerk [etc.]. **1883** in Picton *L'pool Munic. Rec.* I. 188 A muringer is mentioned amongst the officers in the reign of Philip and Mary.

mureþe, obs. form of MIRTH.

murex ('mjʊərɛks). Pl. **murices** ('mjʊərɪsi:z), also **murexes.** [a. L. *mūrex* (pl. *mūricēs*); prob. cogn. w. Gr. μύαξ (:—prehistoric ***musak-**) sea-mussel.] A kind of shell-fish, the animal of which yields a purple dye.

1589 GREENE *Tullies Loue* (1616) E 2 b, [Will] no color content your eye, but such as is stained by the fish *Murex*? **1698** M. LISTER *Journ. Paris* (1699) 74 There were but few Shells; but amongst them there was a Murex which dies purple. **1757** DYER *Fleece* II. 599 He beheld The wounded murex strike a purple stain. **1851** WOODWARD *Mollusca* I. 106 The murices appear to form only one-third of a whirl annually. **1889** WESTGARTH *Austral. Progr.* 316 Spinous murexes went in basketfuls for a shilling.

attrib. **1605** B. JONSON *Masque of Blackness*, All hauing their lights burning out of whelks, or murex shells.

murexan ('mjʊərɛksən). *Chem.* Also **murexane.** [f. MUREX + -AN.] Purpuric acid.

1838 R. D. THOMSON in *Brit. Ann. for 1839* (ed. R. D. Thomson) 384 Murexan. When murexid is dissolved in boiling water, and the solution mixed with muriatic [etc.]. **1841** *Penny Cycl.* XIX. 135/2 Murexane.

murexide ('mjʊərɛksaɪd). *Chem.* Also **murexid.** [f. MUREX + -IDE.] Purpurate of ammonia. Also *attrib.*

1838 R. D. THOMSON in *Brit. Ann. for 1839* (ed. R. D. Thomson) 383 Murexid, or purpurate of ammonia of Prout. **1841** BRANDE *Chem.* (ed. 5) 1384 Murexid.—This term has been applied by Liebig and Wöhler to Dr. Prout's purpurate of ammonia. **1875** *Ure's Dict. Arts* III. 378 The murexide colours are very fresh and brilliant. **1876** G. B. GOODE *Anim. Resources U.S.* 93 Series of murexides, or purpurate of ammonia dyes, made from guano. **1885** W. ROBERTS *Urin. & Renal Dis.* iii. (ed. 4) 68 A bright violet hue (murexid) is instantly developed.

mureyn(e, obs. forms of MURRAIN *sb.*

murg, variant of MARG.

murgeon ('mɜːdʒən), *sb.*[1] Now *dial.* Also 5 **margon,** 7 **murgion,** 8 **mergin, mudgeon.** [Of obscure origin; cf. dial. *morge* (Chesh.) *mudge* (Linc.) of similar meaning.] †Dirt, refuse, dregs (*obs.*); wet peaty soil; the mortar and cement of old walls.

a **1400–50** *Alexander* 628 It come noȝt a kyng son ȝe knaw wele to sytt Doune in margon & molle emange othire schrewis. **1607** NORDEN *Surv. Dial.* IV. 229 Many fetch Moore-earth or Murgion from the riuer between Colebrooke and Uxbridge. **1750** G. HUGHES *Barbadoes* *251 Some..Vapours that arose from the Mudgeon or Dregs of the Liquor. **1787** W. MARSHALL *Norfolk* (1795) I. 30 Another specimen of manure much coveted here is 'mergin'—that is the rubbish of old buildings.

murgeon ('mɜːdʒən), *sb.*[2] Now only *Sc.* Also 6 **morgeowne.** [Of obscure origin.] *pl.* Grimaces, bodily antics.

1500–20 DUNBAR *Poems* liii. 38 Scho maid sic morgeownis with hir hippis, For lauchter nain mycht hald thair lippis. *a* **1585** MONTGOMERIE *Flyting* 495 With mudȝons, and murgeons, and mouing the braine, They lay it, they lift it [etc.]. **1695** J. SAGE *Fundam. Charter Presbyt.* Pref. (1697) n 2, If their Mein had resembled so much as the Murgeons of an Ape, I could have pardon'd him. **1858** RAMSAY *Remin.* Ser. I. (1860) 174 He..gars them fissle, and loup, and mak murgeons to please the great fowk.

Comb. **1824** SCOTT *St. Ronan's* ii, Down cam masons and murgeon-makers, and preachers and player-folk.

murgeon ('mɜːdʒən), *v. Sc.* Also 6 **murion,** 7 **mourgean, murgean.** [f. MURGEON *sb.*[2]] *trans.*

a. To make grimaces at (a person). Also *absol.* to grimace. **b.** pseudo-*arch.* To murmur, mutter.

15.. *Christ's Kirk Gr.* 29 (Bannatyne MS.) Scho skornit Jok and skraipit at him, And mvrionit him with mokkis. **1606** BIRNIE *Kirk-Buriall* (1833) 2 The world, who..hes beene accustomed to murgean and apishly to imitate the kirks holy ceremonies. *Ibid.* 10 In steed of mourning in the dust..we mumchance and mourgean in such dilicate duilles, that [etc.]. **1837** J. M. WILSON *Hist. T. Borders* III. 304 How he..murgeoned his Cameronian aiths as he saw their smolt spirits scour awa to heaven like fire flaughts!

murgion, obs. form of MURGEON *sb.*[1]

murgullie: see MARGULLIE.

murhþe, obs. form of MIRTH.

murhwa, variant of MURWA.

muri, obs. form of MERRY.

Muria ('mjʊərɪə), *sb.* and *a.* Also **Morea, Moria.** [Native word.] **A.** *sb.* A member of a hill people of Bastar in India, a division of the Gonds. Cf. GOND *sb.* and *a.* **B.** *adj.* Of or pertaining to this people.

1861 *Selections from Records of Govt. of India* (*Foreign Dept.*) xxx. 8 The Moreas are distributed over the north of the dependency and the vicinity of Jugdulpore, and the Marias to the south and west of it. *a* **1863** S. HISLOP *Aboriginal Tribes of Central Provinces* (1866) i. 22 *Moria Gonds.* These are more civilized than the Márias. *Ibid.* i. 23, I do not possess detailed information regarding the mythology of the Morias. **1877** V. BALL *Jrnl.* 18 Mar. in *Jungle Life in India* (1880) xiii. 620 According to the Dewan, the following are the names of the principal of these races; they are said to possess distinct languages: Bhatra, Muria (= Gond), Purji, Gudwa (or Gudaba), Jhoria, and Mariah or Meriah. **1938** W. V. GRIGSON *Maria Gonds of Bastar* I. iii. 37 In 1931 the tribes enumerated as Gonds in the previous three censuses were separately enumerated under the names Bhattra, Gond, Maria, Muria, Koya and Parja. **1968** P. C. AGARWAL *Human Geogr. Bastar District* xiii. 258 Burha Deo is the principal deity of the Muria tribe. **1971** [see GOND *sb.* and *a.*].

muriacite ('mjʊərɪəsaɪt). *Min.* [ad. G. *muriacit* (1795), irreg. f. L. *muria*: see MURIATE and -ITE.] = ANHYDRITE.

1799 KIRWAN *Geol. Ess.* 144 Muriacite..consists of 27 per cent gypsum, 14 common salt, 5 mild calx, and 53 of micaceous sand. **1883** HEDDLE in *Encycl. Brit.* XVI. 400/1.

muriate ('mjʊərɪət), *sb. Chem.* Also 8–9 **muriat.** [a. F. *muriate*, f. *muriatique* MURIATIC. See -ATE[1] 1 c.] Old name, still current *Comm.*, for CHLORIDE.

1790 R. KERR tr. *Lavoisier's Elem. Chem.* 231 Muriat of barytes. **1791** MACIE in *Phil. Trans.* LXXXI. 376 A small quantity of muriate of tartar. **1869** PHILLIPS *Vesuv.* iv. 99 The usual ammoniacal and other muriates were collected.

muriate ('mjʊərɪeɪt), *v. rare.* [f. L. *muria* brine + -ATE[3].] *trans.* To pickle in brine.

1699 EVELYN *Acetaria* 22 Gerckems muriated with the seeds of Dill, and the Mango Pickle are for the Winter. **1859** R. F. BURTON *Centr. Afr.* in *Jrnl. Geog. Soc.* XXIX. 243 Minnows of many varieties, which simply sun-dried, or muriated if salt can be afforded, find their way far east.

muriated ('mjʊərɪeɪtɪd), *ppl. a.* [f. MURIATE *sb.* or *v.* + -ED.] †**a.** *Chem.* Combined with chlorine. ***muriated iron, lead***, etc. = chloride of iron, etc. **b.** Impregnated with a chloride or chlorides.

1789 A. CRAWFORD in *Med. Commun.* II. 349 Saturated solutions of the muriated iron and muriated barytes. **1841** R. HUNT *Art Photogr.* 11 Muriated Paper. **1892–3** *Rep. U.S. Geol. Surv.* in *Nature* 12 Mar. (1896) 439 Mineral springs.. divided into sulphated and muriated. **1896** *Allbutt's Syst. Med.* I. 324 Muriated Alkaline Waters.

muriatic (mjʊərɪ'ætɪk), *a.* [ad. L. *muriātic-us* pickled in brine, f. *muria* brine. Cf. F. *muriatique.*]

1. Pertaining to, or of the nature of, brine or salt; consisting of or containing brine. ? *Obs.*

1675 GREW *Disc. Tasts Plants* i. §22 Muriatick [taste], is Saltness joyned with some Pungency, as in common Salt. **1732** ARBUTHNOT *Rules of Diet* in *Aliments*, etc. 380 If the Scurvy be entirely Muriatick, proceeding from a Diet of salt Flesh or Fish. **1818** SCOTT *Let. to Ld. Montagu* 12 Nov. in Lockhart *Life*, The Duke is under the influence of the muriatic bath. **1830** LINDLEY *Nat. Syst. Bot.* 60 The leaves of *Ammannia vesicatoria* have a strong muriatic smell.

2. *Chem.* = MARINE *a.* 1 b, as in ***muriatic acid***, hydrochloric acid (still current *Comm.*); †***muriatic salt***, a chloride; †***muriatic ether***, chloric ether.

1676 GREW *Essential & Mar. Salts of Plants* i. §2 The Imitation of Nature, in producing a Marine, or Muriatick Salt out of the Lixivial Salt of a Plant. **1790** R. KERR tr. *Lavoisier's Elem. Chem.* 231 Table of the Combinations of Muriatic Acid. **1797** *Encycl. Brit.* (ed. 3) XII. 98/1 Muriatic copper, or marine salt of copper. **1850** *Fownes' Chem.* (ed. 3) 416 A volatile, oily, colourless liquid,..long known under the name of heavy muriatic ether. **1874** CARPENTER *Ment. Phys.* I. ii. (1879) 55 Some irritating vapour (such as that of ammonia or muriatic acid).

†**3.** Containing magnesium. ***muriatic earth***, magnesia. (Only in Kirwan?) *Obs.*

1796 KIRWAN *Elem. Min.* (ed. 2) I. 7 Magnesia, or Muriatic Earth. *Ibid.* 144 Muriatic Genus. Under this head I include not only those earths and stones in which magnesia predominates, but also those in which the siliceous earth predominates, if magnesia be, next after this, the most copious ingredient.

muria'tiferous, *a. Geol.* ? *Obs.* [f. MURIATE *sb.* + -(I)FEROUS.] Yielding salt or other chloride (not in economically valuable quantity).

1823 tr. *Humboldt's Superposition of Rocks* 324 Muriatiferous clay containing zechstein. **1832** DE LA BECHE *Geol. Man.* (ed. 2) 247 Most frequently the marly clays are merely muriatiferous; an abundance of salt..being more rare.

muricate ('mjʊərɪkət), *a. Bot.* and *Zool.* [ad. L. *mūricāt-us* shaped like the murex, f. *mūric-* MUREX.] Furnished with sharp points, studded with short hard excrescences. † Also (*rarely*) terminating in a long sharp point, like the murex.

1661 LOVELL *Hist. Anim. & Min.* Introd., The *turbines*, are great..angulous, muricate, or pentedactyls. **1777** ROBSON *Brit. Flora* 35 Of the pericarpy. *Muricate*, covered with sharp points, as in Xanthium. **1870** HOOKER *Stud. Flora* 162 *Anthriscus vulgaris*... Fruit..ovoid, muricate.

Hence **'muricately** *adv.*, in ***muricately-hispid*** (see quot.). Also **muricato-hispid** in the same sense.

1829 LOUDON *Encycl. Plants* 811 Stem muricato-hispid. *Ibid.* 1101. **1840** PAXTON *Bot. Dict.*, *Muricately-hispid*, covered with short, sharp, stiff bristles.

muricated ('mjʊərɪkeɪtɪd), *a.* [f. prec. + -ED.] = MURICATE.

In quot. 1707 used as an epithet of the points or protuberances themselves.

1707 SLOANE *Jamaica* I. 52 All along there were a great many asperities, muricated prickles, or small eminencies. *Ibid.* 53 The surface of this is..very rough with small muricated hollow tubercles. **1776** E. M. DA COSTA *Elem. Conchol.* 29 A Muricated, or Thorny Escallop or Spondyle. **1851** WOODWARD *Mollusca* I. 131 Shell..smooth or muricated. **1876** HARLEY *Mat. Med.* (ed. 6) 580 Carpels with five..minute muricated ridges.

murices, pl. of MUREX.

muricid ('mjʊərɪsɪd). [ad. mod.L. *Mūricid-æ*, f. *mūric-* MUREX.] A member of the family *Muricidæ* of molluscs, typified by the genus *Murex.*

1861 CARPENTER in *Rep. Smithsonian Inst. for 1860*, 207 The Cerites..were classed with the Muricids by Lamarck.

muriciform (mjʊə'rɪsɪfɔːm), *a.* [f. L. *mūric-* MUREX + -(I)FORM.] Resembling a murex or one of the *Muricidæ*.

1843 *Penny Cycl.* XXVI. 446/1 Muriciform type.

'muricite. [f. L. *mūric-* MUREX + -ITE.] A fossil murex.

1828–32 in WEBSTER.

muricoid ('mjʊərɪkɔɪd), *a. Zool.* [f. L. *mūric-* MUREX + -OID.] Resembling a murex, or what pertains to a murex.

1890 *Century Dict.*, *Muricoid operculum*, an operculum having a subapical nucleus. **1895** A. H. COOKE *Molluscs* (Camb. Nat. Hist. III.) 222 A very aberrant radula, not of the common muricoid type.

muriculate (mjʊə'rɪkjʊlət), *a. Bot.* [ad. mod.L. *mūriculāt-us*, f. L. *mūricul-us* small murex + -ATE. Cf. F. *muriculé*.] Minutely muricate.

1848 T. MOORE *Handbk. Brit. Ferns* (1857) 61 Spores somewhat muriculate.

murid (mjʊə'riːd). Also **mooreed**, **mureed**. [Arab. *murīd*.] A follower of a Muslim pir; a disciple; a member of the second order of the Sufi 'way', aspiring to join the third order.

1815 J. MALCOM *Hist. Persia* II. xxii. 396 The person who makes the attempt [for the third class of Sufiism] must be a holy mooreed or disciple, who.. has already made a progress that has placed him above the necessity of the common usages and forms of established religion. **1885** T. P. HUGHES *Dict. Islam* 421/2 *Murid*,.. 'one who is desirous or willing'. A disciple of some *murshid*, or leader, of a mystic order. Any student of divinity. **1929** E. D. ROSS tr. *H. Lammens's Islām* vi. 129 The *murīd* or novice aspiring to be admitted into the congregation. *Ibid.* 135 Admission into a *ṭarīqa* is preceded by a period of trial or noviciate, called *irāda*; whence the name *murīd* given to the *Sūfī* aspirant. **1967** F. RAHMAN *Islam* ix. 154 The absolute authority of the Sūfī leader, called Shaykh.. over his disciples called *faqīr*,.. *darwīsh*, *murīd*.. or *ikhwān*.

murid, variant of MOORIT *dial.*

†**'muride.** *Chem. Obs.* [a. F. *muride*, f. L. *muria*: see MURIATE and -IDE.] (See quot.)

1844 HOBLYN *Dict. Med.*, *Muride*, the name first given to bromine, from its being an ingredient of sea-water.

Muridism (mjʊə'riːdɪz(ə)m). [f. MURID + -ISM.] A revival movement in Islam encouraging the rising of Muslims against their religious and political opponents.

1866 *Chambers's Encycl.* VIII. 656/2 He was one of the zealous disciples of Kasi-Mollah, the great apostle of Muridism. **1875** C. HENEAGE tr. *Von Thielmann's Caucasus, Persia & Turkey* I. iv. 261 This movement, designated Muridism from the name Murid.. borne by the initiated, constitutes one of the greatest events in the modern history of Islamism. *Ibid.* 262 The growth of Muridism was to the Russians a matter of fearful import. **1895** *Macmillan's Mag.* July 217/1 It was called Muridism, and was mainly if not avowedly borrowed from Sufism; it was held to be a strictly orthodox form of the Mahommedan religion. **1931** *Times Lit. Suppl.* 12 Feb. 111/2 The doctrine of Muridism united the Mohamedan sects in a common crusade against the Russians. **1973** HOWAT & TAYLOR *Dict. World Hist.* 1034/2 *Muridism*, Muslim mystical.. movement originating in Shirvan in the 18th cent... The movement reached its peak under the third imam.. and manifested strong egalitarian tendencies.

murie, obs. form of MERRY.

muriform ('mjʊərɪfɔːm), *a.*[1] *Bot.* [ad. mod.L. *mūriformis*, f. *mūr-us* wall + *forma* shape: see -FORM.] Epithet for cellular cells consisting of flattened cells so arranged as to resemble the courses of bricks or stones in a wall.

1832 LINDLEY *Introd. Bot.* 63 Medullary rays.. are composed of a muriform cellular tissue. **1871** W. A. LEIGHTON *Lichen-Flora* 346 Spores muriform, fuscous. *Ibid.* 349 Spores muriform, colourless.

muriform, *a.*[2] *Med. rare*$^{-0}$. [a. F. *mûriforme* (in Littré), f. *mûre* mulberry: see -FORM.] Resembling a mulberry (*Syd. Soc. Lex.* 1891).

'muriform *a.*[3] *rare*$^{-0}$. [f. L. *mūr-*, *mūs* mouse + -(I)FORM.] 'Mouse-like or murine in form; myomorphic' (*Cent. Dict.* 1890).

murillo, var. MORILLO.

murine ('mjʊəraɪn, -rɪn), *a.* and *sb.* Also 7 murin. [ad. L. *mūrīn-us*, f. *mūr-*, *mūs* mouse.]

A. *adj.* **a.** Resembling a mouse; of or belonging to the family *Muridæ* or the sub-family *Murinæ*.

1607 TOPSELL *Four-f. Beasts* 506 The Murin wantonnesse of Xenophon. **1796** STEDMAN *Surinam* II. xxii. 144 A murine or mouse oppossum. **1877** COUES & ALLEN *N. Amer. Rod.* 7 Sigmodont rats..; highly murine in general aspect.

b. Affecting mice or rats; esp. in ***murine typhus*** [tr. F. *typhus murin* (C. Nicolle et al. 1932, in *Compt. Rend.* CXCIV. 1706)].

1933 *Biol. Abstr.* VII. 395/1 The name 'historic typhus' is proposed for the African (Old-World) form, and 'murine' typhus for the other 2. **1940** *Jrnl. Exper. Med.* LXXII. 417 In marked contrast to the white mouse and cotton rat, the murine virus induces no symptoms whatever.. in other rodents. **1947** J. C. SNYDER in F. H. Top et al. *Communicable Diseases* (ed. 2) lix. 879 Unlike the human body louse, which suffers a fatal infection with typhus, the rat flea is unharmed by the multiplication of murine typhus rickettsiae in its tissues. **1955** *Sci. Amer.* Jan. 74/3 Murine typhus, which occurs in many parts of the world including the U.S., is comparatively mild but closely related to epidemic typhus; an attack by one confers immunity against recovery against both. **1970** PASSMORE & ROBSON *Compan. Med. Stud.* II. xviii. 86/1 *Rickettsia prowazekii* is responsible for epidemic typhus, which is transmitted by lice. *R. mooserii* [sic] causes the milder endemic murine typhus, primarily a disease of rats, amongst which it is spread by the rat flea. *Ibid.* xix. 51/2 Murine typhus is not lethal to rats and hence is not accompanied by deviation of rat fleas to man on the scale found in murine bubonic plague.

B. *sb.* A member of the family *Muridæ* or of the sub-family *Murinæ*.

1879 *Cassell's Nat. Hist.* III. 112 These, although true Murines, have a very Rabbit-like character.

murine, error (? after L. *muria* brine) or misprint for MARINE *v.*

1656 MARNETTÈ *Perf. Cook* II. 24 To murine Carps. **1688** R. HOLME *Armoury* III. 83/2 Murine, or Marinate, is to pickle any sort of Fish, for to keep them.

†**'muring**, *vbl. sb. Obs.* [f. MURE *sb.* or *v.* + -ING[1].] Wall-building.

1624 WOTTON *Archit.* I. 27 Wals are either entire.. or intermitted;.. The entire Muring is by Writers diuersely distinguished. **1658** in PHILLIPS. **1703** tr. *Perrault's Abridgm. Vitruvius* I. i. 2 The Friezes imitate the Muring [orig. *la maçonnerie*], that is betwixt the ends of the Beams that are directly over the Pillars. **1721** in BAILEY.

muringer: see MURENGER.

'murinoid, *a. rare*$^{-1}$. [f. MURINE + -OID.] Resembling the mouse or its allies.

1864 H. ALLEN *Bats N. Amer.* (Smithsonian Misc. Collect.) 78 The Murinoid group of bats.

†**murio-.** *Chem.* [f. L. *muria*: see MURIATE.] = CHLORO-[2].

1799 SIR H. DAVY in Beddoes *Contrib. Phys. & Med. Knowl.* 115 The murionitric phosacid. **1823** W. PHILLIPS *Introd. Min.* (ed. 3) 343 Murio-carbonate of lead. **1845** in *Proc. Amer. Philos. Soc.* IV. 212 Murio-phosphate of lead.

murk, mirk (mɜːk), *sb.*[1] Forms: 1 **mirce, myrce,** 4 **merck, myrke,** 4–5 **merk(e, mirke,** 5–9 **mirk,** 6 **myrk,** 6, 9 **mark,** 7 **murke,** 7– **murk.** [OE. *mirce* str. neut., related to MURK *a.* Cf. ON. *myrkr*, genit. *myrkrs* (Sw. *mörker*), *myrkve* wk. masc. (Da. *mørke*).]

1. Darkness. *lit.* and *fig.* Now chiefly *Sc.*

a **1000** *Daniel* 448 (Gr.) Se ðe hie of ðam mirce ȝeneredе. *c* **1220** *Bestiary* 443 Ledeð mann to helle merk. **1303** R. BRUNNE *Handl. Synne* 2164 ȝyf þou brake euer any kyrke, On day, or yn nyȝht, yn myrke [*Dulwich MS.* in the merke]. *c* **1440** *York Myst.* xxxvii. 53 I spake of folke in mirke walkand. **1567** *Gude & Godlie B.* (S.T.S.) 107 Nor thé perturb in mark nor lycht. **1585** *Reg. Privy Council Scot.* IV. 28 The diet of the proclamatioun is in the mirk of the mone. **1601** SHAKS. *All's Well* II. i. 166 Ere twice in murke and occidentall dampe Moist Hesperus hath quench'd her sleepy Lampe. **1791** BURNS *Tam O'Shanter* 31 She prophesy'd that, late or soon, Thou would be found deep drown'd in Doon; Or catch'd wi' warlocks i' the mirk. **1852** LONGF. *Jewish Cemetery at Newport* ix, They lived in.. lanes obscure,.. in mirk and mire. **1858** CARLYLE *Fredk. Gt.* VI. i. (1872) II. 138 Aloft from the murk of commonplace rise glancings of a starry splendour. **1904** HEWLETT *Queen's Quair* I. vii. 94 In the grey mirk.. Lethington and his master came to rouse her.

2. Thick or murky air or vapour. Also *fig.*

a **1300** *Cursor M.* 23669 Ne mist ne merck ne na maner O weder to þe werld to der. **1846** LONGF. in *Life* (1891) II. 68 We came out in the murk and rain. **1891** E. FIELD *Western Verse* 34 A song of the land of murk and mist.

murk (mɜːk), *sb.*[2] Also 7–9 **murc,** 8 **murck,** 9 **mirk.** [? var. of MARC.] = MARC.

1676 WORLIDGE *Cyder* 91 In case you resolve to adde water to your Murc,.. then you need not press it too hard; for your Cider will then be the worse. **1750** W. ELLIS *Mod. Husbandm.* VII. II. 124 The Lees or Murk of the pressing [of walnuts]. **1845** *Encycl. Metrop.* XXV. 1275/2 When all the juice is received by the operation of treading, the skins, stems, and seeds, or as it is properly called, the murk, is submitted to great pressure.

murk, mirk (mɜːk), *a.* Now *dial.* (*Sc.*) and *poet.* or *arch.* Forms: 1 **mirce, myrce,** 3 **mirc,** 3–5 **merk,** 3–7 **mirke,** 4 **merck,** 4–5 **merke,** 4–6 **myrk,** 4–7 **myrke,** 5 **marke,** 6, 8, 9 **mark,** 4– **mirk,** 7– **murk.** [OE. *mirce* = OS. *mirki*, ON. *myrk-r* (inflected *myrkv-*; Sw. *mörk*, Da. *mørk*) :—OTeut. **merkwjo-*, **merkwi-*. Outside Teut. no certain cognates have been found.

It is usually assumed that the existing word is from ON., on the ground that OE. *mirce* should have yielded **mirch*; but it cannot be affirmed that OE. *c* from *kw* would not have remained as (k). Cf. *thick*:—OE. *þicce*.

The prevailing spelling in Scottish writers is *mirk*; the modern poetic use, being chiefly imitated from Sc., usually has this spelling; the independent use by English writers associates the word with *murky*, whence the form *murk*.]

1. Obscure, deficient in light, dark.

a. Of night, day, the weather, etc. **mirk night** *Sc.*, the darkest part of the night [cf. ON. *myrk-nætti*]. **mirk Monday** *Sc.*, the day of the great solar eclipse of 29 Mar. (= 8th April N.S.) 1652.

c **1300** *Havelok* 404 On the mirke nith to shine. *c* **1400** *Rom. Rose* 5339 Take eclips right as the mone, Whan.. The shadowe maketh her bemis merke. *c* **1450** *St. Cuthbert* (Surtees) 7136 þai rest in Iarow, whils it was myrke. **1549** *Compl. Scot.* vi. 38 I did spaceir vp ande doune but sleipe, the maist part of the mark nycht. *a* **1578** LINDESAY (Pitscottie) *Chron. Scot.* (S.T.S.) I. 405 The night was grow-and mark wpoun thame. **1647** HERRICK *Noble Numbers, To his Conscience*, That in the mirk and tonguelesse night, Wanton I may. *c* **1767** *Archæologia* I. 230 *note*, The great Solar eclipse, vulgarly called the Mirk Monday. **1781** BURNS *My Nanie, O* ii, The night's baith mirk and rainy, O. *a* **1884** CALVERLEY *Lit. Rem.* (1885) 206 Murk night seemed lately fair-complexioned day.

b. Of places.

Beowulf 1405 Gang ofer grundas ȝeȝnum for ofer myrcan mor. **1340** HAMPOLE *Pr. Consc.* 456 þar duellid man in a myrk dungeon. *c* **1475** *Rauf Coilȝear* 22 Amang thay myrk Montanis sa madlie thay mer. **1533** BELLENDEN tr. *Livy* I. vi. (S.T.S.) I. 38 In ane myrk and obscure place. **1792** BURNS *My Ain Kind Dearie* ii, In mirkest glen, at mid-night hour, I'd rove, and ne'er be eerie O. **1821** BYRON *Juan* IV. xxxiii, Mirk The sharp rocks look'd below. **1844** MRS. BROWNING *Sonn., Work & Contempl.*, These temples mirk.

c. Of air, etc.: Darkened; *esp.* darkened by mist; hence, misty, dense.

c **1375** *Sc. Leg. Saints* xiii. (*Marcus*) 177 Sa wondire myrke become þe ayr, þat before wes clere and fayre. **1609** HOLLAND *Amm. Marcell.* 88 A hideous bleakenesse of a thicke and mirke mist settled upon the ground. *a* **1839** PRAED *Poems* (1864) II. 353 Mirk was the air. **1888** LOWELL *Black Preacher* 38 Fingers long fleshless the bell-ropes work, The chimes peal muffled with sea-mists mirk.

d. *fig.* in various applications: †Atrociously wicked (*obs.*); obscure, hard to understand; gloomy, depressing; unenlightened.

a **1000** *Phœnix* 457 (Gr.) Fæder on fultum, forð onetteð, lænan lifes leahtras dwæscep, mirce mandæde. *a* **1300** *Cursor M.* 26105 And þar-wit-al sum questiones We sal vndo þe merk resons. *c* **1425** *Hampole's Psalter* Metr. Pref. 18 þe sentence is ful merke. **1579** SPENSER *Sheph. Cal.* Sept. 103 Such myster saying me seemeth to mirke. **1725** RAMSAY *Gentle Sheph.* IV. ii, Mirk despair Made me think life was little worth. **1855** BAILEY *Spir. Leg. in Mystic*, etc. 102 That variable orb, now great with love, And hope, now murk and mean with slavish fear.

†**2.** Having the sight obscured; dim. *Obs.*

c **1220** *Bestiary* 95 Or he it biðenken can, hise eȝen weren mirke. *c* **1460** *Towneley Myst.* xvii. 33 Myn ees are woren both marke and blynd.

3. Dark in colour. *rare.*

c **1250** *Gen. & Ex.* 286 And euerilc on ðat helden wid him, ðo wurðen mirc, and swart, and dim. *a* **1300** *E.E. Psalter* xvii. 13 Mirke watres þat ware ofe hewe. *a* **1849** H. COLERIDGE *Poems* (1850) II. 34 No fault of thine.. Clothes thee in weed of penance, murk and dun. **1898** W. K. JOHNSON *Terra Tenebr.* 139 Round thee the murk and passionate wave Its waste of foam in vain would fling.

murk, mirk (mɜːk), *v.* Forms: see MURK *a.* [f. MURK *a.* Cf. ON. *myrkva* to grow dark (possibly the source).]

†**1.** *intr.* To grow dark. *Obs.*

1320–30 *Horn. Ch.* 81 When that even bicam,.. It bigan to mirke. *c* **1400** *Destr. Troy* 7809 The night was so nighe,.. merkit the mountayns & mores aboute. **1633** J. FISHER *True Trojans* III. ix, Gif night gars the welkin merk.

2. *trans.* To darken, obscure. *lit.* and *fig.* Also to blacken, smudge.

a **1340** HAMPOLE *Psalter* cxxxviii. 11 Myrknes sall noght be myrked of þe. *c* **1450** *Cov. Myst.* xxii. (Shaks. Soc.) 207 With sum myst his wittys to merke. **1725** RAMSAY *Gentle Sheph.* III. iii, Soon the fleecy clouds mirk a' the skies. **1791** J. LEARMONT *Poems* 23 Their sordit sauls mirk't Britain's glory. **1907** *Daily News* 6 Sept. 6 Happy mites, most of them, for all the dirt which murked their countenances.

Hence **'murking** *ppl. a.*, becoming dark.

1535 STEWART *Cron. Scot.* (Rolls) III. 318 Quyetlie about the myrkand nycht,.. on to the wall he staw.

†**'murken**, *v. Obs.* Forms: 4 **merkin, mircken, mirken, -in, mourken,** 5 **merken,** 6 **myrken.** [f. MURK *a.* + -EN[5].] *intr.* To become murk or dark.

a **1300** *Cursor M.* 1764 Sun and mone þeir bemes hide, Merkind oueral þis werld wide. **13..** *E.E. Allit. P.* B. 1760 Mourkenes þe mery weder, & þe myst dryues. *c* **1400** *Destr. Troy* 7350 All merknet the mountens & mores aboute. **1513** DOUGLAS *Æneis* XI. xv. 131 All thyng dymmis and myrknys me about.

†**'murkful**, *a. rare. Obs.* In 4 **markefull, merkeful, merkful,** 6 **mirkful.** [f. MURK *sb.* + -FUL[1].] Full of darkness.

13.. *Cursor M.* 17863 (Arundel MS.) As we were stad in merkful [*v.r.* markefull, merkeful] stalle. **1520** NISBET *N.T. in Scots* Luke xi. 34 Al the body salbe mirkful.

murkily, -ness: see under MURKY *a.*

murkish ('mɜːkɪʃ), *a.* [f. MURK *a.* + -ISH[1].] Somewhat murky, dark.

1869 STEVENSON *Let.* 18 June in *Scribner's Mag.* XXV. 41/2 The dawn, orange and yellow and red, waxing brighter above a row of murkish clouds.

'murklins, *adv. Obs.* exc. *dial.* (see E.D.D.). Also 6 **marklynis,** 9 **mirklins.** [f. MURK *a.* + -LING[2].] In the dark.

1568 *Satir. Poems Reform.* xlviii. 56 Weill may thay brukit, thay neid not to lukit, Bot graip it marklynis be the grund. **1674** RAY *N.C. Words* 34 *Murklins*: in the dark.

'murkly, *adv. rare*$^{-1}$. [f. MURK *a.* + -LY[2].] Darkly; obscurely.

13.. *Cursor M.* 9278 (Gött.) Bot ȝit þat folk.. until oþer said 'quat may þis be So wonderly mirkly [*c* **1425** *Trin.* merkely] spekes he?'

murkness, mirkness ('mɜːknɪs). [f. MURK *a.* + -NESS.] **a.** Darkness. *lit.* and *fig.* (now only *Sc.*). **b.** Intense darkness caused by vapour or smoke; murkiness (*rare*).

c **1250** *Gen. & Ex.* 3104 Miȝte non egipcien Abuten him for mirknesse sen. *a* **1300** *Cursor M.* 15860 Nu er yee cummen to tak me, Als in mercknes o night. **1393** LANGL. *P. Pl.* C. XXI. 141 In menynge þat man shal fro meorknesse beo drawe. *c* **1400** *Destr. Troy* 13159 A myst & a merknes mynget wit rayn. **1456** SIR G. HAYE *Law Arms* (S.T.S.) 28 That ilke myrknes, of the quhilk the sternis was blekkit.

1581 N. BURNE *Disput.* Ep. Ded. aiv b, The Ministeris of mirknes. *a* **1670** SPALDING *Troub. Chas. I* (Bannatyne Club) II. 310 So they pairt, the ane army fra the uther, throw mirknes of nicht. **1849** *Reverberations* I. 16 Thro' the mist and thro' the murkness Travels the great human soul. **1889** SKRINE *Mem. E. Thring* 158 Four legs and a tail were heaved into the mirkness.

murkoke, obs. form of MOOR-COCK.

murksome, mirksome (ˈmɜːksəm), *a. rare.* [f. MURK *sb.* + -SOME.] Dark, obscure. Hence **ˈmurksomeness**.

1590 SPENSER *F.Q.* I. v. 28 Through mirkesome aire her ready way she makes. **1600** FAIRFAX *Tasso* XIII. v, There in silence deafe and mirksome shade. **1625** BP. MOUNTAGU *App. Cæsar* 75 You can easily foord over all the depths therof, and cleerly comprehend all the darkest mirksomenesse therin. **1642** H. MORE *Song Soul* II. I. iv. 2 That all that springs from hence should be resolv'd Into this mirksome sourse, *first matter* hight. **1794** BURNS *Bonie Lass Made the Bed to Me* i, The mirksome night did me enfauld. **1855–9** SINGLETON *Virgil* II. 141 Confined in darkness and a mirksome jail.

murky (ˈmɜːkɪ), *sb. Mus.* (See quots.)

1876 STAINER & BARRETT *Dict. Mus. Terms, Murky*, a piece of harpsichord music, having a bass consisting of broken octaves. **1897** *Riemann's Dict. Mus., Murkys* (Murky Bass), a term applied to broken octaves in accompaniment... Also pieces with such basses.

murky (ˈmɜːkɪ), *a. rare* before 17th c. Also 4, 8–9 **mirky**, 6–7 **murkie**. [f. MURK *sb.* + -Y.]

1. Of places: Excessively dark or gloomy.

a **1340** HAMPOLE *Psalter* lxxxvii. 6 þai set me in þe nether lake: in mirky stedes & in shado of dede. **1605** SHAKS. *Macb.* v. i. 41 Hell is murky. **1610** —— *Temp.* IV. i. 25 With such loue, as 'tis now the murkiest den..shall neuer melt Mine honor into lust. **1791** COWPER *Odyss.* x. 626 Haste to Pluto's murky abode. **1816** KEATS '*O Solitude!*' 3 O Solitude! if I must with thee dwell, Let it not be among the jumbled heap Of murky buildings. **1871** R. ELLIS tr. *Catullus* iii. 11 Now he wendeth along the mirky pathway, Whence, they tell us, is hopeless all returning. **1888** BURGON *Lives 12 Gd. Men* II. ix. 183 The ante-chapel..that afternoon happened to be exceptionally murky.

fig. **1840** DICKENS *Barn. Rudge* lxxiii, As through the narrow crevice of one good deed in a murky life of guilt.

2. Of air, mist, clouds, etc.: Thick, dark. Of gloom, darkness: Intense.

1667 MILTON *P.L.* x. 280 So sented the grim Feature, and upturn'd His Nostril wide into the murkie Air. **1718** ROWE tr. *Lucan* VI. 965 Black Clouds and murky Fogs involve her Head. **1725** POPE *Odyss.* XII. 475 When lo! a murky cloud the Thund'rer forms. **1814** SCOTT *Wav.* xvi, The path was altogether indiscernible in the murky darkness which surrounded them. **1818** BYRON *Ch. Har.* IV. xxxiv, Making the sun like blood, the earth a tomb, The tomb a hell, and hell itself a murkier gloom. **1859** JEPHSON *Brittany* i. 2 A county notorious even in England for its murky atmosphere.

3. Very dark in colour.

1791 W. GILPIN *Forest Scenery* I. 86 Its dark, murky hue is unpleasing. **1881** CABLE *Mme. Delphine* ii, The *gens de couleur*.., with 'Ichabod' legible on their murky foreheads.

4. Dirty, grimy.

1798 BLOOMFIELD *Farmer's Boy, Summer* 199 To ride in murky state the panting Steed.

5. Of looks: Sullen, cheerless, gloomy.

1841 MISS SEDGWICK *Lett. Abr.* I. 172 They would advance with downcast eyes and murky looks. **1856** R. S. HAWKER in *Life & Lett.* ix. (1905) 152 They left, looking very murky.

6. Phr. ***the murky past***: confused or 'dubious' happenings at a previous time; an obscure episode or period. Cf. PAST *sb.* 2.

1917 'CONTACT' *Airman's Outings* 141 At times the R.F.C. pilot, like the man with the murky past, is constrained to have clouds for a covering against attack. **1963** J. CLEUGH *Love locked Out* 11 St. Augustine, tormented by the murky past which had preceded his appointment as bishop of Hippo in North Africa. **1966** *Oxf. Univ. Gaz.* 23 Dec. 432/2 If I may go back into the murky past,..these sort of powers ..would..have been used at least to influence planning.. described..as precipitate and ill-considered.

Hence **ˈmurkily** *adv.*, **ˈmurkiness**.

1813 BYRON *Corsair* I. ix, As if within that murkiness of mind Work'd feelings fearful, and yet undefined. **1835** *Fraser's Mag.* XII. 572 Look adown that sullen stream, flowing murkily and more murkily between its resplendent quays. **1837** CARLYLE *Fr. Rev.* I. IV. iv, Is it not rather the very murkiness, and atmospheric suffocation, that brings the lightning and the light?

†**murl**, *v. Obs.* exc. *dial.* Also **mirl, murle**. [Of obscure origin: possibly a derivative of OE. *mearu* soft.] *intr.* and *trans.* To crumble; *fig.* to cause to decay. Cf MARL *v.*[1] 3.

c **1500** *Priests of Peblis* (Laing) 313 Thair manheid, and thair mense, this gait thay murle. **1600** SURFLET *Country Farm* III. i. 424 Ground..which murleth easily in breaking and stirring it with your fingers. **1641** BEST *Farm. Bks.* (Surtees) 62 That is founde to doe more harme then good, for it causeth the waxe to murle. **1691** RAY *N.C. Words* 50 To *Murl*, to crumble. **1897** P. H. HUNTER *J. Armiger's Revenge* ii. 27 He didna tak' a subjec' an' mirl it a' down to wee crumbs, that got lost in a body's pooch.

murleon, obs. form of MERLIN *sb.*[1]

murlie, obs. form of MURLY.

†**ˈmurlimews**, *sb. pl. Obs. rare.* Also 6 **mearlew muse**, 6–7 **murlemews**. [An arbitrary formation.] Foolish gestures or antics.

1583 GOLDING *Calvin on Deut.* xxii. 131 The Papistes.. fiske about after their foolish ceremonies and after murlimewes of their owne making [Fr. orig. *et apres tant d'agios qu'ils font*]. **1593** HOLLYBAND *Dict., Agyos* or *Agios*, blessings and crossings which the papisticall priests doe vse in their holy water, to make a mearlew muse. **1600** [? LYLY] *Maides Metam.* III. i. E 2 Good maister wizard, leaue these murlemewes, and tell Mopso plainly, whether Gemulo.. shall win the loue of the faire shepheardesse..or not.

murlin (ˈmɜːlɪn). *Sc.* Also 8 **murlain**, 9 **murlan**. [Cf. Gael. *mùrlan, mùrlag* of the same meaning.] A round narrow-mouthed basket.

17.. *Song, 'The Boatie Rows'* in Johnson *Mus. Museum* (1794) V. 439 And lightsome be her heart that bears The Murlain and the creel. **1855** OGILVIE Suppl., *Murlan*, or *Murlin*, a round, narrow-mouthed basket (Scotch).

murling (ˈmɜːlɪŋ), *ppl. a.* [f. MURL *v.* + -ING.] Crumbling; friable.

1610 W. FOLKINGHAM *Art of Survey* I. viii. 19 A blackish moulde which is light, deepe, fat, sweet in taste and odour, murling, plyable, mellow, of moderate warmth. **1819** W. TENNANT *Papistry Storm'd* (1827) 76 He disinterr'd their murlin' banes, And grund them into powther sma'.

murlon, obs. form of MERLIN.

a **1566** R. EDWARDS *Damon & Pithias* (1571) F j b.

murly (ˈmɜːlɪ), *a.* Also **murlie**. [f. MURL *v.* + -Y.] Of earth: Crumbly, friable.

1600 SURFLET *Country Farm* III. xx. 470 And as concerning the earth..that it be such as is verie murly, temperate [etc.]. **1610** W. FOLKINGHAM *Art of Survey* I. xi. 36 Onyons..thriue well in a red short, murly and moistish earth. **1838** MARY HOWITT *Birds & Fl., Childhood* xvi, The gentian blue on the murly hill And the snap-dragon white and yellow.

murmanite (ˈmɜːmənaɪt). *Min.* [ad. Russ. *murmanit* (A. E. Fersman 1923, in *Doklady Ross. Akad. Nauk* 63), f. *Murman*, name of a shore on the north of the Kola peninsula in Russia + *-it* -ITE[1].] A hydrated silicate of sodium and titanium with lesser and variable amounts of manganese, zirconium, iron, calcium, and niobium, which is found as violet monoclinic crystals.

1924 *Mineral. Abstr.* II. 263 Various new primary occurrences were found for..a new mineral murmanite from Alluaiva, Angvunsiok, and Sengischorr. **1951** *Ibid.* XI. 240 Recalculation of analyses of murmanite..suggests a formula $(Na_2,Ca)TiSiO_5{\cdot}xH_2O$ analogous to that of sphene. **1968** I. KOSTOV *Mineralogy* II. v. 298 Murmanite and lomonosovite form a complete isomorphous series and are monoclinic like sphene and fersmanite.

†**murmell**. *Sc. Obs.* [Cf. OF. *mormeler* to murmur, G. *murmeln* to murmur, *murmel* (obs.) murmuring.] Murmuring.

1535 LYNDESAY *Satyre* 2521 And, for till saif vs fra murmell, Schone, Diligence, fetch vs Gude-counsell. *Ibid.* 2538 Gif vs ȝour counsell, How we sall slaik the greit murmell Of pure peopill.

murmur (ˈmɜːmə(r)), *sb.* Forms: 4–7 **murmure**, 4–5 **mormur**, **-or**, 4–6, 8 **murmour**, 5, 7 **murmer**, 7 **murmor**, 4– **murmur**. [a. F. *murmure* masc. (12th c. in Hatz.-Darm.), n. of action f. *murmurer* to MURMUR. Cf. Pr. *murmuri*, Sp. *murmúrio*, *mormuréo*, It. *mormorio*.

The Eng. sb. coincides in form with the L. *murmur*, by which some of its senses may have been directly influenced.]

1. a. Subdued continuous or continuously repeated sound; an instance of this. Now *rare* exc. in ***the murmur of*** (a brook, the waves, etc.).

c **1400** MAUNDEV. (1839) xxviii. 281 In that Vale, heren men often tyme..grete Murmures and Noyses. **1523** SKELTON *Garl. Laurel* 270 With that there come in..A murmur of mynstrels. *c* **1586** C'TESS PEMBROKE *Ps.* XLVI. ii, Lo, a river streaming joy, With purling murmur safelie slides. **1592** SHAKS. *Ven. & Ad.* 706 Ech shadow makes him stop, ech murmour stay. **1602** MARSTON *Antonio's Rev.* v. iii, Making lowde murmur, with confused dinne. **1774** GOLDSM. *Nat. Hist.* (1776) I. 96 The murmur of a troubled sea. **1853** M. ARNOLD *Scholar-Gipsy* ii, All the live murmur of a summer's day. **1864** TENNYSON *En. Ard.* 688 Finding neither light nor murmur there. **1884** W. C. SMITH *Kildrostan* 48 The murmur of the running brooks.

b. *Path.* A sound of this kind (whether normal or morbid) heard in auscultation.

1833 J. FORBES in *Cycl. Pract. Med.* I. 241/1 [Auscultation.] When the valve [of the heart], not closing accurately, admits of regurgitation, a murmur accompanies the first sound. **1851** WALSHE *Dis. Lungs & Heart* 73 The sounds discoverable by auscultation of the breathing-apparatus in the state of health are:—(A) The respiratory murmurs; and (B) the resonance of the voice. *Ibid.* 212 Sounds of adventitious origin and properties produced either within or on the surface of the heart, are termed Murmurs. **1876** BRISTOWE *Theory & Pract. Med.* (1878) 561 Distinct pulsatile tumours, attended with more or less thrill and often with a murmur.

2. †**a.** The expression of discontent or anger by inarticulate complaint; muttered or indistinct complaint, grumbling or repining. *Obs.* **b.** An instance of this; an act of murmuring or repining; a subdued expression of discontent.

c **1381** CHAUCER *Parl. Foules* 520 Nature, which that alway had an ere To murmour of the lewednes behinde, With facound voys seide, 'hold your tonges there!' *c* **1386** —— *Pars. T.* ¶432 Murmure eek is ofte amonges seruauntz that grucchen whan hir souereyns bidden hem doon leueful thynges. **1390** GOWER *Conf.* I. 89 In myn herte I am desesed: With many a Murmur, god it wot. *c* **1477** CAXTON *Jason* 69 And [they] began to make grete bewaylinges and murmure upon Appollo. **1513** MORE *Rich. III* in Grafton *Chron.* (1568) II. 767 Done..to none other intent but to bring all the Lordes in an obloquy and murmour of the people. **1639** S. DU VERGER tr. *Camus' Admir. Events* 127 He endeavoured..to avoyde scandall, murmur, and the punishment wherewith the Judge threatned him. **1681** DRYDEN *Span. Friar* IV. ii. 54 Some discontents there are; some idle murmurs. **1709** STEELE *Tatler* No. 95 ¶1 Persons in the married State..pine away their Days, by looking upon the same Condition in Anguish and Murmur. **1742** YOUNG *Nt. Th.* VII. 732 Instinct, than reason, makes more wholesome meals, And sends all marring murmur far away. **1838** J. L. STEPHENS *Trav. Greece*, etc. 24/1, I should have ..given up the remnant of my stock of borrowed money without a murmur. **1874** STUBBS *Const. Hist.* I. xii. 472 The murmurs of the people reached the king in Normandy.

†**3.** Rumour. ***in murmur***: 'whispered about'.

1601 SHAKS. *Twel. N.* I. ii. 32 'Twas fresh in murmure.. That he did seeke the loue of faire Oliuia. **1760–72** H. BROOKE *Fool of Qual.* (1809) IV. 37 Some murmur of these matters may come to her ear.

4. A softly or gently spoken word or sentence; subdued or nearly inarticulate speech.

a **1674** CLARENDON *Hist. Reb.* XI. §201 That kind of Murmur which usually shews how the House stands inclined. **1773** GOLDSM. *Stoops to Conq.* IV. Wks. (Globe) 668/1 What billing, exchanging stolen glances, and broken murmurs? **1863** GEO. ELIOT *Romola* xii, His speech was the softest murmur. **1877** J. D. CHAMBERS *Div. Worship* 88 Whilst in Choir let there be no murmur heard among the Clerks.

5. *Comb.* **murmur diphthong**, a diphthong ending with a weak (murmur) vowel; **murmur vowel**, a glide or weak vowel, a SCHWA.

1892 H. SWEET *New Eng. Gram.* I. 234 There is another class of *murmur diphthongs* ending in (ə), as in *hear, here* (hiə), *fare, faire* (feə). **1933** O. JESPERSEN *Essentials Eng. Gram.* ii. 26 There are three kinds of diphthongs in English: (1) full (long-distance) diphthongs... (2) slow (short-distance) diphthongs... (3) murmur-diphthongs ending in the indistinct central vowel [ə]: [iə] as in *peer*, [ɛə] as in *pair*, [etc.]. **1965** A. D. CORDTS *Phonics* xii. 228 Today every basic reading system..recognizes the 'short' and 'long' vowel sounds, the diphthongs, the so-called murmur diphthongs and 'digraphs', [etc.]. **1910** Murmur vowel [see BACK *a.* 1 c]. **1924** W. J. SEDGEFIELD in Mawer & Stenton *Introd. Survey Eng. Place-Names* I. II. i. 8 The vowel that was distinctly pronounced loses under the secondary stress its clear character and becomes either the obscure sound called by phoneticians the 'murmur-vowel' [ə] or an indistinct [i]. **1957** S. POTTER *Mod. Linguistics* i. 27 The inhabitants of Birmingham..call their city [bəːmɪŋgəm], but Londoners call it [bəːmɪŋəm]... Midlanders raise the velum against the wall of the pharynx and make a plosion with the back of the tongue upon it before passing from agma to the murmur-vowel, whereas the people of London keep the nasal pharynx open at this juncture. **1966** A. WIJK *Rules of Pronunciation for Eng. Lang.* iv. 64 The murmur vowel is.. very common in both open and closed syllables when the stress falls on the immediately following syllable.

murmur (ˈmɜːmə(r)), *v.* Forms: 4, 6 **murmure**, 6 **mormour**, **murmour(e**, **-more**, 5– **murmur**. [a. F. *murmurer* (= Sp. *murmurar*, *mormurar*, Pg. *murmurar*, It. *mormorare*, *murmurare*), ad. L. *murmurāre*, f. *murmur* rumbling noise, murmur, a reduplicated onomatopœic formation. Cf. OHG. *murmurôn*, *murmulôn* (perh. from Latin; MHG., mod.G. *murmeln*) to murmur, Gr. *μορμύρειν* to boil up (as the waves), Skr. *marmara* rustling sound.]

1. *intr.* To make, produce, or emit a low continuous sound.

c **1386** CHAUCER *Sqr.'s T.* 196 They murmureden as dooth a swarm of Been. *c* **1430** *Pilgr. Lyf Manhode* IV. xiii, (1869) 182 Howndes gon abayinge up on him, murmuringe with here teth. **1589** GREENE *Menaphon* (Arb.) 45 All the companie began to murmure, and euery man to prepare his eye for so miraculous an obiect. **1712** ADDISON *Spect.* No. 393 ¶2, I have not heard a Bird sing, nor a Brook murmur. **1802** COLERIDGE *Picture* 56 Listening only to the pebbly brook That murmurs with a dead, yet tinkling sound. **1873** BLACK *Pr. Thule* xiv, Their conversation murmured around her unheeding ears. **1898** W. K. JOHNSON *Terra Tenebr.* 107 Where the tall pine-trees murmur round the homestead.

2. To complain or repine in low muttered tones; to give vent to an inarticulate discontent, to grumble. Often with *at*, *against*.

1474 CAXTON *Chesse* II. v. 61 The peple murmur and ryse agayn theyr lord. **1525** WARHAM in Ellis *Orig. Lett.* Ser. III. I. 371 It hathe been shewed me..that the people sore grudgethe and murmureth. *a* **1548** HALL *Chron., Hen. VI* 175 b, The capitaines of his Nauy murmured against hym. *Ibid., Edw. IV* 239 b, Dyd oppugne, and wyth yll woordes murmur at the doyng thereof. **1665** MANLEY *Grotius' Low C. Warres* 443 The multitude hereupon, murmured cruelly against Count Solmes. **1769** GOLDSM. *Hist. Rome* (1786) II. 11 Those veteran legions..began to murmur, for not having received the rewards which they had expected. **1860** WARTER *Sea-board* II. 161 He was never heard to murmur.

3. *trans.* To utter (sounds, words) in a low voice and indistinctly. Also with *out*.

1535 COVERDALE *John* vii. 32 And it came to the Pharises eares, that yͤ people murmured soch thinges of him. **1596** SHAKS. *1 Hen. IV*, II. iii. 51, I be thee haue watcht, And heard thee murmore tales of Iron Warres. **1799** WORDSW. *Poet's Epitaph* 39 He murmurs near the running brooks A music sweeter than their own. **1834** LYTTON *Pompeii* III. i, He is murmuring curses on the temple, be sure. **1837** DICKENS *Pickw.* xxviii. 304 Gabriel murmured out something about its being very pretty. **1894** A. CONAN DOYLE *Mem. Sh. Holmes* 41 My lips were parted to murmur out some sleepy words of surprise or remonstrance. **1897** MRS. RAYNER *Type-writer Girl* x. 111 A clerk..murmured something inaudible about 'conditions of sale'.

†**4.** *Sc.* To complain or grumble against, to animadvert upon the actions of; to accuse. *Obs.*

1478 *Rental Bk. Cupar-Angus* (1879) I. 209 Nevyr to murmur Abbot na conuent or ellis frely to gyfe our his tak. **1518** *Burgh Rec. Edin.* (1869) I. 178 He was hevely murmurit be the saidis provest..and communite of diuers gret faltis and wrangis. *Ibid.*, Gif thai had murmurit him without caus thai to be ponist siclyke. **1676** Sir J. Lauder *Hist. Notices Sc. Affairs* (Bannatyne Cl.) 120 Any who, without reason, misrepresented or murmured Judges and Magistrats for doing their offices.

murmuracion, -yon(e, var. ff. murmuration.

† **murmurant**, *a. Obs.* [a. F. *murmurant* (16th c. Littré), pr. pple. of *murmurer* murmur *v.*: see -ant.] = murmuring *ppl. a.*

1669 Holder *Elem. Speech* 53 Vocal or Murmurant. **1681** H. More in Glanvill *Sadducismus* Postscr. 33 Wizzards.. that speak with a querulous murmurant or mussitant voice.

murmu'ration. Forms: 4-6 **murmuracion**, 5 **mormeracyone**, **murmeracion**, 5-6 **murmuracyon**, 6 *Sc.* **murmuratioun**, 5- **murmuration**. [a. F. *murmuration* (= Pr. *murmuratio*, Sp. *mur-, mormuracion*, Pg. *murmuração*, It. *mormorazione*), a. L. *murmurātiōn-em*, n. of action from *murmurāre* to murmur.]

1. The action of murmuring; utterance of low continuous sounds; complaining, grumbling; complaint. Also with *a* and in *pl.*

c **1386** Chaucer *Pars. T.* ¶425 After bakbityng cometh gruchchyng or Murmuracion, and somtyme it spryngeth of Inpacience agayns god, and somtyme agayns man. *c* **1400** Maundev. (Roxb.) viii. 29 þai made murmuracion agaynes him by cause of thrist. **1536** Cranmer in Burnet *Hist. Ref.* (1829) I. 403 If he find in your most noble heart..that your grace, without murmuration and overmuch heaviness, do accept all adversities [etc.]. **1541** Paynel *Catiline* vii. 11 Cicero rose vp and ryght sharpely rebuked Q. Mutius:.. with many and fauourable murmurations of the hole senate therunto. **1641** R. B. K. *Parallel Liturgy w. Mass-bk.* 44 The reformed Church counts the secret murmuration of their Canon and words of consecration a very vile..practice. *a* **1653** Binning *Serm.* (1845) 205 The murmurations of the people in the wilderness. **1687** Sir J. Lauder (of Fountainhall) *Hist. Notices Sc. Affairs* (1848) 775 They most not stand near the witnesses when they depone, nor interrupt them by murmurations or susurrings. **1908** *Westm. Gaz.* 5 Aug. 2/1 The plaints and murmurations of these Randlords for the grievances which they clamoured to have redressed.

¶ **2.** A term for a flock (of starlings).

One of many alleged group terms cited in the first source: revived and popularized in the 20th c.

c **1470** in *Hors Shepe & G.* etc. (Caxton 1479, Roxb. repr.) 30 A murmeracion of stares. **1932** Auden in *New Statesman* 16 July 69/1 Patterns a murmuration of starlings Rising in joy over wolds unwittingly weave. **1938** *Times* 6 Jan. 15/5 Great murmurations of starlings are often represented as a peculiar phenomenon of our own times. **1946** M. Peake *Titus Groan* 306 The clearing ended where a derelict stone building..held back a grove of leafless elms, where a murmuration of starlings was gathered. **1966** *Sunday Mail Mag.* (Brisbane) 6 Mar. 6/4 Starlings when they're on the wing have to labor under the collective title of murmuration.

† **murmu'rator.** *Obs.* Also 7 **murmerator**. [a. late L. *murmurātor*, agent-n. f. *murmurāre* to murmur.] A murmurer, detractor.

1670 *Conclave wherein Clement VIII was elected Pope* 30 Having banished from his company all men that were deceitful, factious, adulators, murmurators. **1689** 'Philopolites' *Grumblet. Crew* 3, I cannot see what should hinder the going down of this new Oath; especially, with a great many of the debauched Sort of these Murmerators.

murmure, obs. form of murmur *sb.* and *v.*

murmured ('mɜːməd), *ppl. a.* [f. murmur *v.* + -ed[1].] Faintly uttered. ***murmured vowel*** = *murmur vowel*; also, a vowel-sound uttered with slow vibration of free vocal chords.

1800 Campbell *The 'Name Unknown'* 26 Thy murmured vows shall yet be mine. **1828** Scott *F.M. Perth* xxiii, Henry Smith stepped forward, amidst the murmured applauses of his fellow-citizens. **1885-94** R. Bridges *Eros & Psyche* Sept. xviii, And with him sweet Euphrosynè, attent Upon his murmur'd wants. **1933** L. Bloomfield *Language* vi. 102 Some languages..distinguish different voice-qualities, such as *muffled* vowels, *murmured* vowels, with slow vibration of the vocal chords, or *whispered* vowels. **1952** R. Jakobson et al. *Preliminaries to Speech Analysis* ii. 26 It is highly questionable whether there are languages in which..there actually is a..distinctive opposition of voiced and murmured vowels. **1966** M. Pei *Gloss. Linguistic Terminol.* 173 Vowels of weakly stressed syllables are sometimes murmured (reduced vowels), and they tend to lose their identity, contrary to fully voiced and whispered vowels.

murmurer ('mɜːmərə(r)). [f. murmur *v.* + -er[1].] One who murmurs; esp. one who complains against constituted authority.

1526 *Pilgr. Perf.* (W. de W. 1531) 107 b, Curynge the scrupulous persone..and mendyng the impacyent and murmurer. **1530** Tindale *Prol. Levit.*, Those murmurars agenst god as sone as they repented were healed of their deadly woundes. **1613** Shaks. *Hen. VIII*, ii. ii. 131 Heau'ns peace be with him:..for liuing Murmurers, There's places of rebuke. *a* **1770** Akenside *Ode* i. iii, Th' industrious bee.. Sweet murmurer! **1874** Green *Short Hist.* viii. §10. 579 The few murmurers were weeded from its ranks by a careful remodelling.

† **'murmurhead.** *Obs. rare*[−1]. [f. murmur *sb.* + -head.] Murmuring spirit; discontent.

c **1475** *Partenay* 3603 Most fals traytour And fals forsworn in-ded, Replet with uices, full of murmurhed.

murmuring ('mɜːmərɪŋ), *vbl. sb.* [f. murmur *v.* + -ing[1].] The action of the vb. murmur; an instance of this.

c **1384** Chaucer *H. Fame* iii. 434, I herd a noyse aprochen blyve That ferd as been don in an hive..Ryghte suche a maner murmuryng For al the world hyt semed me. **1515** Barclay *Eglogues* ii. (1570) B iv, One reacheth the bread with grutch and murmuring. **1535** Coverdale *Phil.* ii. 14 Do all thinges without murmurynges, and disputinges. *c* **1550** Lloyd *Treas. Health, Aphor.* a viij, If they which haue certayne murmuryng and wynd in theyr belyes, haue greate paynes in the loynes, they shal haue moyst deiections. **1590** Spenser *F.Q.* i. i. 23 But with his clownish hands their tender wings He brusheth oft, and oft doth mar their murmurings. *a* **1639** Wotton *Life Dk. Buckhm.* (1642) 22 He found..but smothered murmurings for the losse of so many gallant Gentlemen. **1737** *Gentl. Mag.* VII. 598/2 The Attempting to enforce any such Thing by a Law, would raise a most general Discontent and Murmuring. **1804** J. Grahame *Sabbath* 426 The murmuring So gentle of the brook. **1906** *Edin. Rev.* July 123 The night is full of..the murmurings of spring.

murmuring ('mɜːmərɪŋ), *ppl. a.* [f. murmur *v.* + -ing[2].] That murmurs, in various senses.

1530 Palsgr. 319/1 Murmuryng, grutchynge as folkes that be nat contented, *murmuratif*. **1590** Spenser *F.Q.* ii. v. 30 A gentle streame, whose murmuring wave did play Emongst the pumy stones. **1600** Shaks. *A.Y.L.* iv. iii. 80 The ranke of Oziers, by the murmuring streame. **1645** Evelyn *Diary* June, The..rock out of which Moses brought water to the murmuring Israelites. **1665** Dryden *Ind. Emp.* iv. iii. (Song), Hark, hark, the Waters fall, fall, fall: And with a murmuring Sound..To gentle Slumbers call. **1699** Garth *Dispensary* ii. 2 The ev'ning Breeze Begun to whisper through the murm'ring Trees. **1799** Sheridan *Pizarro* iv. i, O'er her unshelled brood the murmuring ringdove sits. **1863** Woolner *My Beautiful Lady* 119 Where the summer lay On honeyed murmuring limes.

Hence **'murmuringly** *adv.*

1611 Cotgr., *Murmurantement*, murmuringly. **1843** *Tait's Mag.* X. 558 The wing-stirr'd air shook murmuringly. **1876** Bancroft *Hist. U.S.* V. x. 443 Greene ..wrote murmuringly to Washington, that the fort might have kept the enemy at bay.

murmurish ('mɜːmərɪʃ), *a.* [f. murmur *sb.* + -ish[1].] Approaching the sound of a murmur.

1851 Walshe *Dis. Lungs & Heart* 204 The..sound..is, in fact, murmurish, without being actually converted into a murmur. **1889** *Lancet* 12 Jan. 78/1 A definite murmur was heard in forty-five cases,..and in six others the first sound was murmurish.

murmurless ('mɜːməlɪs). [f. murmur *sb.* + -less.] Without murmur.

1862 Walshe *Dis. Heart* (ed. 3) Index 550 Murmurless aneurismal sacs.

murmurous ('mɜːmərəs), *a.* [f. murmur *sb.* + -ous.]

1. Characterized or accompanied by subdued continuous sound; abounding in or characterized by murmurs.

1582 Stanyhurst *Æneis* i. (Arb.) 25 Where through nyne channels with mountayns murmerus hurring Rough the sea floas forward. **1590** Spenser *F.Q.* ii. xi. 32. **1659** H. More *Immort. Soul* iii. xvii. (1662) 219 A joynt groaning of a multitude together, mingled with a murmurous admiration. **1726** Pope *Odyss.* xx. 19 Round his swol'n heart the murm'rous fury rowls. **1819** Keats *Ode to Nightingale* v, The murmurous haunt of flies on summer eves. **1886** Const. F. Woolson *East Angels* ix. 176 The waves..flowed softly up the beach..with a rippling murmurous sound. quasi-*adv.* **1871** R. Ellis tr. *Catullus* lxiv. 263 Often a trumpeter horn blew murmurous, hoarsely resounding.

† **2.** Complaining, grumbling. *Obs.*

1592 Stow *Ann.* 691 This yeere many murmurous tales ranne in the citye betweene the earle of Warwike and the Queenes blood. **1702** C. Mather *Magn. Chr.* vi. v. (1852) 384 The judgments of God upon the murmurous Israelites.

Hence **'murmurously** *adv.*, **'murmurousness**.

1851 Mrs. Browning *Casa Guidi Wind.* ii. xxii, And murmurously the ebbing waters grit The little pebbles. **1890** *Chamb. Jrnl.* 13 Sept. 592/2 Murmurously low Falls the sad rhythm of old Ocean's tread. **1903** *Westm. Gaz.* 5 Oct. 2/1 Two streams of water flow..into stone basins, lulling one with a sleepy murmurousness.

murn, obs. and dial. form of mourn *sb.* and *v.*[1]

murning, var. murrnong.

murnival(l: see mournival.

muromontite (mjʊərəʊ'mɒntaɪt). *Min.* [a. G. *muromontit* (Kerndt 1848), f. mod.L. *Mūromontium*, Mauersberg in Saxony, where it was found: see -ite.] A mineral akin to allanite.

1854 Dana *Syst. Min.* (ed. 4) II. 210 With Allanite belong probably Bodenite..and Muromontite.

murot, variant of marrot.

'Murphy[1], illiterate perversion of Morpheus.

1748 Smollett *Rod. Rand.* xvi. (1760) I. 110 When Murfy sends his puppies to the heys of slipping mortals. **1841** Marryat *Poacher* xi, We dropped into the arms of Murfy. **1890** G. Stables *For England*, etc. xiii. 194 It's the nightmare I'll be having..as soon as I'm in the arms av Murphy.

Murphy[2] ('mɜːfɪ). *slang.* [Jocular uses of a common Irish surname.]

† **1.** ***Murphy's countenance***: 'a pig's face'.

1812 J. H. Vaux *Flash Dict.*

2. Also **murphy**, etc. A potato.

1811 *Lex. Balatron.*, *Murphies*, potatoes. **1827** Egan *Anecd. Turf* 151 Mathews relished the Irish stews and murpheys with greater goût. *a* **1845** Hood *To Henrietta* vii, No, no, they have no murphies there, for supper or for lunch. **1857** Hughes *Tom Brown* i. vi, She bakes such stunning murphies.

3. ***Murphy's law***: a name humorously given to various aphoristic expressions of the apparent perverseness and unreasonableness of things (see quots.). orig. *U.S.*

1958 *Nation* (N.Y.) 7 June 506/1 There is an old military maxim known as Murphy's Law which asserts that wherever there is a bolt to be turned, someday there will be someone to turn it the wrong way. **1961** Leeds & Weinberg *Computer Programming Fund.* viii. 241 What we desire is the presentation of the information in such an accurate and complete form that the reader will be able to use the subroutine correctly without hesitation or question. Recalling 'Murphy's law'—'If something can go wrong or be misinterpreted, it will'—should be enough stimulus for the goals we desire. **1962** J. Glenn in *Into Orbit* 85 We blamed human errors like this on what aviation engineers call 'Murphy's Law'. 'Murphy' was a fictitious character who appeared in a series of educational cartoons put out by the U.S. Navy... Murphy was a careless, all-thumbs mechanic who was prone to make such mistakes as installing a propeller backwards. **1970** *Sci. Amer.* June 143 Recently.. I learned of a governing principle known as Murphy's first law of biology. It states: 'Under any given set of environmental conditions an experimental animal behaves as it damn well pleases.' **1972** *Oxf. Times* 22 Sept. 12/7 That malign influence which presides over human and typographical enterprises, and which is sometimes described as Murphy's Law ('Things are out to get us'). **1973** G. Hart *Right from Start* i. 45 According to Murphy's law, if the worst possible thing can happen, it will. **1974** *N.Y. Times Mag.* 8 Sept. 33/1 'If anything can go wrong, it will,' says Murphy's Law.

4. Name given (in full, ***Murphy game***) to a confidence trick in which the victim is duped by unfulfilled promises of money or sex, etc. So ***Murphy man***, one who practises confidence tricks of this kind; ***to Murphy*** v. trans., to dupe, to swindle by means of such a trick. *U.S. slang.*

1959 *Washington Post* 2 Oct. B 8/1 The 'Murphy game' is ..a confidence game... The victim or 'pigeon' is lured by promises of a woman and then given..paper cut to bill size, in an envelope exchanged for the victim's cash. **1965** *N.Y. Times* 6 Apr. 1/3 Mayor Smitherman..and..a Selma lawyer..were 'murphyed' by the Negro confidence man at 2:30 a.m. today. **1965** *Time* 16 Apr. 16 'The Murphy game' is underworld argot for a slick maneuver in which a victim puts his cash in an envelope and gives it to the con man, who makes a fast sleight-of-hand switch and hands back an identical envelope stuffed with newspaper strips. **1966** *N.Y. Times* 4 Sept. iv. 5 Everybody should have a car... How are you going to get it?.. You know, you can get it playing the Murphy. **1968** W. Labov et al. in A. Dundes *Mother Wit* (1973) 331 The right of a hand of some murphy man. **1970** C. Major *Dict. Afro-Amer. Slang* 83 *Murphy*, a con game played on innocent (especially white) men who are expecting sex with a prostitute (usually black). **1972** T. Kochman *Rappin' & Stylin' Out* 244 An adept hustler who was playing the 'murphy' game on a white trick. **1972** J. Mills *Report to Commissioner* 52, I thought he was a complainant...some school kid who'd been Murpheyed. *Ibid.* 55 We stop in a bar..and it's filled with pimps, Murphy men, guys like that.

Murphy[3] ('mɜːfɪ). *N. Amer.* The name of William Lawrence *Murphy* (1876–1959), American manufacturer, used *attrib.* in ***Murphy bed***, any of various types of folding beds, developed from an original design by Murphy.

1925 *Small Home* Mar. 31 (Advt.), The closet off the living-room has been equipped with a Murphy Bed. **1930** *N.Y. Times* 2 Mar. xiii. 10/2 (Advt.), Apartments Unfurnished... 40s East—Most charming one-room apartment in town; restaurant, telephone service, Murphy beds: $78.50. **1969** L. Hellman *Unfinished Woman* vi. 63 They lived in the Murphy-bed, modern apartments that were already the slums off Hollywood Boulevard. **1974** *Apartment Life* May E2/2 The concealed wall bed, best known as a Murphy bed in the 1930s, is coming out of the woodwork again.

† **murr**, *sb. Obs.* Forms: 5 **myrr**, 5-7 **murre**, 6 **morre**, 6-7 **mur**, 7 **murrhe**, 7-8 **murrh**, 8 **murrh**. [Of obscure origin: possibly onomatopœic.] A severe form of catarrh; an attack of this.

c **1420** ? Lydg. *Assembly of Gods* 329 He ratelyd in the throte as he had the murre. **1451** *Paston Lett.* I. 224 On of the tallest younge men of this parysch lyth syke and hath a grete myrr. **1533** Elyot *Cast. Helthe* (1541) 3 b, The brayne exceding in cold hath The head disposed..to pooses and murres. **1561** Hollybush *Hom. Apoth.* 3 If the head doth ake by reason of a morre or runninge. **1603** Florio *Montaigne* iii. xii. 620 With them a..consumption of the lungs, is but an ordinary cough..: A pleurisie but a cold or murre. **1612** Cotta *Disc. Dang. Pract. Phys.* ii. i. 81 Old men surprised with murrhes and distillations. **1630** J. Taylor (Water P.) *Urania* lviii, On his death bed grunting like a hog: And almost speechlesse with his rattling Murr. **1655** Moufet & Bennet *Heath's Impr.* (1746) 208 The Milk of any Beast chewing the Cud..is very ill for Rhums, Murs, Coughs [etc.]. **1756** C. Lucas *Ess. Waters* I. 181 Hence, the Murr or stuffing of the Head, Rheums, or Catarrhs..are so rife amongst us.

murr (mɜː(r)), *v. Obs.* exc. *dial.* [Echoic.] *intr.* To make a harsh noise; in *Sc.* = PURR.

1662 *Tryal Sir H. Vane* 87 Then the Trumpets were ordered to sound or murre in his face, with a contemptible noise, to hinder his being heard. **1807** HOGG *Mount. Bard, Sandy Tod* 80 Sandy heard a noise, like baudrons Murring i' the bed at e'en.

murr, variant of MURRE.

‖**murra** (ˈmʌrə). *Roman Antiq.* Also **murrha, myrrha.** [L. *murra* = late Gr. μορρία or μόρρια. Cf. MURRHINE.] A substance of which precious vases and other vessels were made.

1598 GRENEWEY *Tacitus, Ann.* VI. xxviii. (1622) 131 Hauing taken vp a certaine waight of the stone Murrha. **1606** HOLLAND *Sueton.* 68 On cup of the pretious stone Myrrha [*margin* Or Murrha]. **1781** GIBBON *Decl. & F.* xxxi. III. 206 *note*, The fragile vessels of chrystal and *murra*, which last is almost proved..to mean the procelain of China and Japan.

murrage, -raie, obs. ff. MURAGE, MURREY.

murrain (ˈmʌrɪn), *sb.* and *a.* Forms: 4–5 moryne, 4–6 mor(e)yn(e, 5 morayne, morein, muran, murreyne, 5–6 moren, 6 morraine, -eine, -eyn(e, moryen, murrayne, -ein, murryn, 6–7 moraine, murraine, -en, -ion, 7 murain, murrin, myrren, 7– murrain. [a. F. *morine* (12th–13th c. in Hatz.-Darm.; AF. *moryn* 1321–2 in *Rolls of Parl.*; Anglo-L. *morina* 13th c.) = Sp. *morriña*, Pg. *morrinha* cattle plague, commonly regarded as a derivative of L. *mori* to die; cf. It. *moria* plague.] **A.** *sb.*

†**1.** Plague, pestilence. *Obs.*

c **1330** R. BRUNNE *Chron. Wace* (Rolls) 16453 What for moryne, what for dere, ffewe þer wore þat might liue here. *c* **1340** [see MANQUALM]. **1430–40** LYDG. *Bochas* III. xx. (1494) m vj, Nye all his people was slayne in that moreyne. *a* **1548** HALL *Chron., Hen. VIII* 177 b, Famyn and pestilence or a morreyn wherof the people died in euery place. **1613** PURCHAS *Pilgrimage* (1614) 161 A murren, procured..by Iewish exorcismes intending a plague to the men.

fig. **1581** J. BELL *Haddon's Answ. Osor.* 265 b, There be many noble men..that are not coathed as yet with this Lutheran moraine.

†**b.** In imprecations: ***a murrain of (it), murrain meet them, murrain on (one)***, may a murrain or pestilence fall upon (some one). Also in exclamations of anger: ***with a murrain, what a (the) murrain, how a murrain***. *Obs.*

a **1530** HEYWOOD *Weather* (Brandl) 523 A myller wyth a moryn and a myschyefe, Who wolde be a myller as good be a thefe. *c* **1560** INGELEND *Disobed. Child* C j, What a Murryn I say, what a noyse doest thou make? *c* **1560** [RICHARDES] *Misogonus* I. iii. 12 A moringe lighte one that foules face of thine! **1575** *Gamm. Gurton* I. iii, How a murryon came this chaunce. **1606** SHAKS. *Tr. & Cr.* II. i. 20 A red Murren o'th thy Iades trickes. **1607** DEKKER & WEBSTER *Westw. Hoe* IV. i, *Luce.* Who am I? *Tent.* What the Murrion care I who you are. **1607** TOURNEUR *Rev. Trag.* III. vi, A murren meete 'em! **1611** *Tarlton's Jests* (1638) A 2 b, A murren of that face. **1624** DAVENPORT *City Nightcap* IV. (1661) 36 Marry come up with a murren, from whence came you tro, ha? **1705** VANBRUGH *Confed.* I. i, What the murrain have they to do with quality? **1711** STEELE *Spect.* No. 113 ¶3 At last, with a Murrain to her, she cast her bewitching Eye upon me.

2. An epizootic disease in cattle.

1421 *Coventry Leet Bk.* (E.E.T.S.) 25 We commaund þat no bocher sell noo beestis of moren, ne no roten Schep. *c* **1450** *Merlin* 3 Thei..tolde their maister the mervelle of the moreyn, that was fallen a-monge the bestes. **1514** BARCLAY *Cyt. & Uplondyshm.* (Percy Soc.) 37 Why lose we our sede, our labour, and expence? Where cometh moryen, & grevous pestylence? **1577** B. GOOGE *Heresbach's Husb.* III. (1586) 129 b, The Pestilence, or Murraine, is a common name, but there are diuers kindes of it. **1670** MILTON *Hist. Eng.* VI. Wks. 1851 V. 241 The next year..was calamitous, bringing strange fluxes upon men, and murren upon Cattel. **1715** GARTH *Claremont* 162 In fillets bound, a hallow'd band Taught how to tend the flocks,..Could tell what murrains in what months begun, And how the seasons travell'd with the Sun. **1758** R. BROWN *Compl. Farmer* (1759) 28 For the Garget, Plague, or Murrain in Bulls, Cows or Oxen. **1846** J. BAXTER *Libr. Pract. Agric.* (ed. 4) II. 145 The early stage even of murrain is one of fever. **1884** G. FLEMING in *Encycl. Brit.* XVII. 57/2 It is now an established fact that murrains are all infectious.

b. *transf.*

1657 S. PURCHAS *Pol. Flying-Ins.* 130 The murrain among bees is very rare. **1817** *Sporting Mag.* L. 261 The roup, the gargut and the murrain, are terms often applied indiscriminately to the diseases of fowls. **1880** DISRAELI *Endym.* III. xiv. 141 A murrain had fallen over the whole of the potato crops in England.

†**3.** Flesh of animals that have died of disease; also in wider sense, dead flesh, carrion. *Obs.*

1382 WYCLIF *Jer.* vii. 33 And ben shal the moreyn [Vulg. *morticinum populi*] of this puple in to mete to the foules of heuene, and to the bestus of erthe. *c* **1610** in Gutch *Coll. Cur.* II. 15 That he bring no rotten flesh, no myrren, no sufferers, but lawful and wholesome for man's body.

†**b.** As a term of contempt (*nonce-use*).

1632 MASSINGER & FIELD *Fatal Dowry* III. i, If our fresh wits cannot turne the plots Of such a mouldy murrion on it selfe.

†**4.** Mortality (usually, by pestilence); *occas.* slaughter. *Obs.*

1387 TREVISA *Higden* (Rolls) I. 387 Also Beda..seiþ: Pestilens of moreyn bare doun Hibernia. *c* **1400** *Laud Troy Bk.* 5708 He cleff Gregeis as men do swyn, He made of hem gret moryn. **1530** PALSGR. 246/1 Moreyne dethe, *mortalité*; *mourine*. **1547–64** BAULDWIN *Mor. Philos.* (Palfr.) 32 The Athenians, being consumed with warres & morraine of people, to augment the city, decreed that euery man should haue two wiues. *a* **1632** T. TAYLOR *God's Judgem.* I. II. xl. (1642) 303 By the murraine of men by pestilence..the tillage of the earth was put off.

5. *attrib.* and *Comb.*: **a.** simple attrib., as ***murrain cattle, flock, sheep; murrain-rotted*** adj.

c **1490** CAXTON *Rule St. Benet* aa viij b, They shall departe from the congregacyon, leest that suche a moreyne shepe empoysen and enfecte the residue of yᵉ flocke. **1590** SHAKS. *Mids. N.* II. i. 97 Crowes are fatted with the murrion flocke. **1900** H. SUTCLIFFE *Shameless Wayne* xix, Clear the pens of yond murrain-rotted ewes. **1902** *Westm. Gaz.* 1 May 8/2 Tuberculous people and murrain cattle.

b. instrumental, as †**murrain-strike** *v.* (nonce-wd.), to infect with murrain.

1613 HEYWOOD *Silver Age* III. i. H 1 b, Il'e breake thy plowes, thy Oxen murren-strike.

†**B.** *adj.* Ill-conditioned, 'plaguy'. Also quasi-*adv.* as an intensive, 'confoundedly'. *Obs.*

1575 *Gamm. Gurton* II. iv, It is a murrion crafty drab, and froward to be pleased. *Ibid.* III. iv, Ich know thars not..A muryner cat than Gyb is, betwixt the Tems and Tyne. **1591** HARINGTON *Orl. Fur.* XII. xxxiv, Thou foole and murren lier. **1664** VISCT. FALKLAND *Marriage Nt.* III. i. 25 That same's a murrain wise boy, if you mark him. **1728** VANBR. & CIB. *Prov. Husb.* I. 17 My Lady was in such murrain haste to be here, that set out she would.

Hence **ˈmurrained** *a.*, infected with murrain. †**ˈmurrainly** *adv.*, 'plaguily'.

1548 L. SHEPHERD *John Bon* (1808) 6 Ye are morenly well learned I se by your recknynge That ye wyll not forget such an eluyshe thynge. **1575** *Gamm. Gurton* III. ii, And yead bene here, cham sure yould murrenly ha wondred! **1831** TRELAWNY *Adv. Younger Son* xciv, The Europeans..died like murrained sheep.

murrain, obs. form of MORION[1].

murram (ˈmʌrəm). Also **murrum.** [Native name.] A hard lateritic material associated with soils with impeded drainage in tropical Africa and locally used as road metal.

1925 *Dollar Mag.* Sept. 120 What first catches the attention..of eyes weary of murrum or black cotton soil..is the soothing greennesss. **1932** G. W. ROBINSON *Soils* iii. 59 In certain types of tropical soils, with impeded drainage, the deposition of iron oxides may result in the development of highly indurated concretionary material, known in Africa as 'murram'. **1935** *Soil Res.* IV. 192 Towards the foot of the slopes are murram soils. **1959** E. HUXLEY *Flame Trees of Thika* i. 7 A plain whose soil was largely murram, a coarse red gravel that baked hard and supported only thin, wiry grass, sad-looking thorn trees and tortured-branched erythrinas. **1961** *Engineering* 2 June 765 A variable thickness of murrum (a tough clay bound gravel). **1963** A. SMITH *Throw out Two Hands* vi. 71 The heavens open in their own African fashion to turn the murram roads into sloshy causeways. **1971** D. CREED *Trial of Lobo Icheka* vii. 78 In the town centre the wide murram road was a bedlam of activity.

murram, murray, obs. ff. MARRAM, MURREY[1].

Murray[1] (ˈmʌrɪ). Any of the series of guide-books, or of time-tables of all railway trains running in Great Britain, issued by John *Murray* (1808–92) or by his successors. Also in the possessive, and *fig.* So **ˈMurray-less** *a.*

1845 THACKERAY *Leg. Rhine* in *G. Cruikshank's Table-Bk.* Sept. 198 Crowds of English,..armed with Murray's guide-books. **1846** R. FORD *Gatherings from Spain* viii. 86 A solitary wanderer..can read the book of Spain..dwelling on what he likes, and skipping what he does not, as with a red Murray. **1847** [see BRADSHAW]. **1862** MRS. GASKELL *Let.* 23 July (1966) 927 We stopped all night in a clean hotel... It is not down in Murray, but ought to be for its cleanliness, civility, and moderate charges. **1864** *Daily Tel.* 26 Sept. 5/1, I hope he found his 'Murray' again, for one would not willingly see him wandering..Murray-less and unguarded. **1885** RUSKIN *Praeterita* I. vi. 183 Murray..did not exist in those days; the courier was a private Murray. **1898** H. G. WELLS *Let.* 22 Jan. in *G. Gissing & H. G. Wells* (1961) 77 The more I see of these Murrays the more I settle to Rome. **1925** A. HUXLEY *Along the Road* I. 42 Old guide-books..make excellent travelling-companions. An early Murray is a treasure. **1961** *Economist* 18 Mar. 1047/2 Murray's ABC Time-Table (now a pocketbook..) which sells 75,000 monthly in its two editions for Glasgow and Edinburgh. **1961** E. M. FORSTER *Alexandria* (ed. 3) p. xv, I have always respected guidebooks—particularly the earlier Baedekers and Murrays.

ˈMurray[2]. The name of the main river of a large river-system of south-eastern Australia, used *attrib.* to designate plants or animals native to this region, as **Murray cod**, a large carnivorous food-fish, *Maccullochella macquariensis*, of the family Serranidæ; **Murray lily**, a bulbous plant, *Crinum flaccidum*, belonging to the family Amaryllidaceæ and bearing white, lily-like flowers; also called the Darling lily; **Murray perch** = CALLOP; **Murray (river) pine**, a cypress pine, *Callitris glauca.*

1875 *Encycl. Brit.* III. 112/2 A very fine fresh-water fish is the Murray cod. **1911** C. E. W. BEAN '*Dreadnought' of Darling* xxxiv. 301 The Murray and the Darling and their tributaries contain a certain large, sluggish fish, which rather reminds one of a big carp, very delicious... They call him the Murray cod. **1952** D. STIVENS in *Coast to Coast 1951–2* The bunyip..was about ten feet long with a body like a Murray cod with gleaming golden-yellow scales. **1966** Murray cod [see CALLOP]. **1877** F. VON MÜLLER *Introd. Botanic Teachings* xx. 119 This showy genus Crinum furnishes also Victoria with a beautiful species, the *Murray Lily* (Crinum flaccidum), not however to be found away from the Murray-River southward. **1962** J. H. WILLIS *Handbk. to Plants in Victoria* I. 326 Murray Lily (Darling Lily, Macquarie Crinum)..on a few sandy inundated flats along the Murray R. flood-plain. **1880** G. WALCH *Victoria in 1880* 124 (Morris), Our noble old 1400-mile river, the Murray..produces..that finny monster, the Murray cod, together with his less bulky, equally flavourless congener, the Murray perch. **1951** T. C. ROUGHLEY *Fish Austral.* 147 In New South Wales it [*sc.* the callop, *Plectroplites ambiguus*] was until recently referred to as golden perch or yellowbelly, ..in Queensland and Western Australia as Murray perch. **1877** F. VON MÜLLER *Introd. Bot. Teachings* 38 Frenela or Callitris verrucosa,..known by the name Murray-Pine. **1933** *Bulletin* (Sydney) 4 Jan. 17 Is nothing to be done in methodical reafforestation with Murray pine... A beautiful timber white-ant and rot resistant, and its dark rosewood heart and soft cream subcortical layers. **1951** *Dict. Gardening* (R. Hort. Soc.) I. 362/1 *C[allitris] glauca.* Murray River Pine. Up to 100 ft... Widely distributed. The wood is in constant use in Australia. **1966** 'J. HACKSTON' *Father clears Out* 100 The solitary Murray Pine in the college paddock was flinging itself about like a windjammer in a gale. **1967** A. M. BLOMBERY *Guide to Native Austral. Plants* 225 Murray Pine. A tree with spreading light-green branches, and cones tending to be longer than broad when ripe.

Murrayism (ˈmʌrɪɪz(ə)m). [f. MURRAY[1] + -ISM.] **a.** A mode of expression reminiscent of a guide-book published by Murray. **b.** A tourist's fondness for Murray's guide-books.

1846 in *Downside Rev.* (1945) LXIII. 216 That Rome should be called the Metropolis of Art..'from the miracles of art which it contains' is a Murrayism. **1865** *Daily Tel.* 27 Sept. 7/3, I saw yesterday in the Tribune a British couple who had brought to the races 'Murray's Handbook'. I think Murrayism can scarcely go further.

Murray Valley. The name of the valley of the Murray River (see MURRAY[2]), used *attrib.* to designate a severe form of encephalitis and also the mosquito-borne virus that causes it.

1951 *Med. Jrnl. Australia* I. 526/1 A severe human encephalitis of virus origin spread diffusely along the Murray Valley during the early months of 1951. This has been provisionally referred to as Murray Valley encephalitis (MVE). **1955** *Sci. Amer.* Mar. 65/2 The New York laboratory decided to employ the neutralization test to compare each of the 11 new viruses with various other insect-borne viruses, such as the agents of yellow fever, dengue, louping ill, Murray Valley fever, Russian encephalitis, [etc.]. **1966** WRIGHT & SYMMERS *Systemic Path.* II. xxxiv. 1207/1 Epidemics of encephalitis occurred in Australia in 1912, 1918, 1922 and 1926... It is probable that these epidemics were outbreaks of the disease that has become known as Murray Valley fever. **1974** *Sydney Morning Herald* 6 Feb. 7 (*heading*) Mystery of the Murray Valley virus.

murre (mɜː(r)). Also 8 **merre**, 8–9 **murr**, 9 **mur, muir.** [Of obscure origin: cf. MARROT.

Fleming (*Brit. Anim.*, 1828, p. 134), and later writers, give a form *murse*, probably due to a misprint or misreading.]

A name applied to **a.** several species of GUILLEMOT, esp. of the genus *Uria*; **b.** the RAZOR-BILL, *Alca torda*. Also *attrib.*

1602 G. ARCHER in Purchas *Pilgrims* IV. 1647 Pettrels, Cootes, Hagbuts, Pengwins, Murres, Gannets, Cormorants, Guls, [etc.]. **1662** RAY *Three Itin.* III. 187 We saw..some of the young murres, a bird, black on the head and back, white under the breast and belly, and hath a sharp and black bill. **1681** GREW *Musæum* I. iv. iii. 72 The Auk, Rasor-Bill, or Murre. **1706** PHILLIPS (ed. Kersey), *Murrbird*, a kind of Bird. **1778** *Eng. Gazetteer* (ed. 2) s.v. *Pembrokeshire*, The razor-bill is the merre of Cornwall. **1845** WHITTIER *Fishermen* iii, And the noisy murr are flying, Like black scuds, overhead. **1876** GOODE *Anim. Resources U.S.* 11 Loons, grebes, auks, puffins, guillemot, murres.

murre, var. MURR; obs. f. MURREY, MYRRH.

murreie, murrel, obs. ff. MURREY, MOREL *sb.*[3]

murrelet (ˈmɜːlɪt). [f. MURRE + -LET.] A small species of auk, of the family *Alcidæ*.

1872 COUES *Key N. Amer. Birds* 344 *Brachyrhamphus marmoratus*... Marbled Guillemot, or Murrelet. *Ibid.*, Kittlitz's Murrelet.

murrell, murren: see MOREL *sb.*[3], MURRAIN.

murren, murreowne, obs. ff. MORION[1].

murrey (ˈmʌrɪ), *sb.*[1] and *a.* Now only *Hist.* and *arch.* Forms: 5 murreye, morrey(e, morreey, 5–6 murre, 5–8 murray, 5–9 murry, 6 mour(r)ey, -ye, -ie, -eie, -aie, morra, 7 muroy, 5– murrey. [a. OF. *moré* adj. and sb., *morée* fem. sb., murrey colour, murrey-coloured cloth, ad. med.L. *mōrātus, mōrāta*, f. L. *mōrum* mulberry.]

A. *sb.*

1. A colour like that of the mulberry; a purple-red or blood-colour. Also, cloth of this colour.

In some modern books 'murrey' is given as the name of a heraldic tincture; but Leigh and Guillim mention it only as the popular name for the colour heraldically termed *sanguine*.

[**1380** in *Test. Karleol.* (1893) 138, j Kirtill cum capucio de murre.] *c* **1412** HOCCLEVE *De Reg. Princ.* 695 And where be my gounes of scarlet, Sanguyn, murreye, & blewes sadde & lighte. *c* **1461** *E.E. Misc.* (Warton Club) 90 ȝoure flote is made for ȝoure sangweyns and also for ȝour violettes and ȝoure violettes sadder thanne ȝoure morreys. **1462** *Paston Lett.* II. 103 Your son wolle have to hys jakets murry and tany. *c* **1483** CAXTON *Dialogues* 14/38 *Entrepers moret*, Sad blew morreey. **1530** in W. H. Turner *Select. Rec. Oxford*

(1880) 68 A Goune of mourrey. **1587** HARRISON *England* II. xxi. 211/1 The die thereof contendeth with skarlet, murreie, and purple. **1640** HABINGTON *Edw. IV* 165 Five hundred Commoners in murrey receiv'd him. **1657** R. LIGON *Barbadoes* 68 The rinde smooth, with various greens, interlac'd with murries, yellowes, and faint carnations. **1745** P. THOMAS *Jrnl. Anson's Voy.* 93 Their [the Vicunnas] colour is almost Murrey. **1834** PLANCHÉ *Brit. Costume* xiii. 200 Murrey and blue were the colours of the house of York.

¶ 2. Used allusively for MUREX. *rare*$^{-1}$.

1579 TWYNE *Phisicke agst. Fort.* I. xx. 26 For thee the Tyrian Murrey swimmeth, or Purple fishe.

B. *adj.* Of a purplish-red colour; murrey-coloured. †***murrey kersey***: used as a term of contempt for a woman.

1403 *Mann. & Househ. Exp.* (Roxb.) 216 For ij. peyre off morrey hosyn ffor my mastyr, xiiij.s. **1599** B. JONSON *Ev. Man out of Hum.* IV. vi, I had on a gold cable hatband.. which I wore about a murrey French hat. **1607** MIDDLETON *Michaelm. Term* I. i, Let her pass me; I'll take no notice of her,—scurvy murrey kersey. **1625** in Rymer *Foedera* (1726) XVIII. 240 One Plate of Goulde,.. with a Case of Murrey Velvet. **1677** GREW *Colours Plants* I. §15 The larger Buds are purple or murrey, and the open Flowers, blew. **1840** H. AINSWORTH *Tower of London* I. i. 4 Doublets of murrey and blue cloth. **1847** G. HUME *Firstlings of Fancy* 17 The sharpened verge of a dark murrey cloud.

†**b.** Of the complexion: Sanguine. *Obs. rare*$^{-1}$.

1623 COCKERAM II, A murrey Complexion.

†**c.** In the name of a variety of nectarine.

1664 EVELYN *Kal. Hort., Aug.* 72 Nectarines. The Muroy Nectarine, Tawny, Red Roman, [etc.]. **1685–90** TEMPLE *Ess. Gard.* Wks. 1720 I. 183 The only good Nectorins are the Murry and the French... Of the Murry there are several Sorts, but being all hard, they are seldom well ripened with us. **1767** ABERCROMBIE *Ev. Man his own Gard.* (1803) 674/1 *Nectarines*.. Elruge, Temple, Murrey, Brugnion.

†**'murrey**, *sb.*[2] *Cookery. Obs.* In 5 murreye, morreye. [App. an Eng. subst. use of OF. *moré* (see MURREY *sb.*[1]) in the sense flavoured with mulberries.] A stew or 'compote' of veal, etc., prepared with mulberries.

c **1430** *Two Cookery-bks.* 28 Murreye.—Take Molberys, & wryng hem þorwe a cloþ e; nym Vele [etc.]. *Ibid.*, A rede Morreye.—Take Molberys, and wrynge a gode hepe of hem þorw a cloþ; nym Vele [etc.].

murrey, variant of MORAY.

†**murrey colour.** = MURREY *sb.*[1] I.

1537 *Bury Wills* (Camden) 133 A cote of murre color. **1573** *Art of Limming* (1588) 8 If thou wilt put to a good quantity of Synapour a little portion of blacke.. you shall make thereof a sanguine or Murrye colour. **1786** W. GILPIN *Lakes Cumbld.* (1808) II. xvii. 39 A species of white lychen ..which..had been found very useful in dying a murray-colour. **1849** MRS. MERRIFIELD *Orig. Treat. Paint. in Oil* I. Introd. vi. 186 *Morello di ferro*, probably some ore of iron, burnt until it assumes a morello or murrey colour.

Hence **murrey-coloured** *a.*

1657 W. COLES *Adam in Eden* xl. 80 Small purple or murrey coloured Flowers. *c* **1714** POPE, etc. *Mem. M. Scriblerus* I. vi. (1741) 24 A waistcoat of murrey-colour'd sattin. **1886** T. HARDY *Mayor Casterbr.* ix, Henchard's house was..fronted with murrey-coloured old brick.

murreyne, var. MORIAN *Obs.*; obs. f. MURRAIN.

murrh(e, variant forms of MURR *sb. Obs.*

murrhine ('mʌrɪn, -aɪn), *a.* and *sb.* Also murrine (in Dicts.); *β.* myrrhine. [ad. L. *murr(h)inus*, f. *murra* (see MURRA); cf. late Gr. *μόρρινος* (used subst. in fem. *μορρίνη*), f. *μορρία*, *μόρρια*. The form *myrrhine* represents the corrupt readings L. *myrrhinus*, late Gr. *μύρρινος*, which occur in some editions of the texts.]

A. *adj.* Made of or pertaining to murra. ***murrhine glass***: a modern fancy name for a delicate ware brought from the East, and made of fluor-spar.

a. **1579** TWYNE *Phisicke agst. Fort.* I. xxxviii. 56 A man myght see the pryce of one Murrhine stone to be at seuentie talentes. **1715** tr. *Pancirollus' Rerum Mem.* I. I. vii. 19 The Wine may grow warm, from the Colour of the Murrhine Cup. **1805** D. MACPHERSON *Ann. Comm.* I. 170 Murrhine stones from Ozenè. **1886** *Temple Bar* LXXVIII. 198 It has the pigeon's-neck lustre of the murrhine vase.

β. **1606** G. W[ODCOCKE] *Lives Emperors* in *Hist. Ivstine* Gg2, Golden and christaline, Myrrhine vessels and pottes. **1671** MILTON *P.R.* IV. 119 Crystal and Myrrhine cups imboss'd with Gems. **1832** GELL *Pompeiana* I. vi. 98 The myrrhine vases..which were in such request. **1885** PATER *Marius* I. 60 'Like jeweller's work! like a myrrhine vase!' admirers said of his writing.

B. *sb.* A murrhine vase.

1852 ANDREWS *Lat.-Eng. Lex.*, *Myrrhina*..murrhine vases, murrhines. **1879** LEWIS & SHORT, *Murrina* or *myrrina* ..murrine vases, murrines.

Murrian, obs. form of MORIAN, MORION[1].

murrie, obs. form of MURREY.

murrin, murrion(n: obs. ff. MORION[1], MURRAIN, MORIAN.

murrit, variant of MOORIT *dial.*

murrnong ('mɜːnɒŋ). *Austral.* Also mirrn'yong, murning. [Aboriginal name.] A yellow-flowered native herb, *Microseris lanceolata* (also called *M. scapigera*), of the family Compositæ, resembling a dandelion but having clusters of small tuberous roots, formerly used as food by the Aborigines.

1852 J. MORGAN *Life W. Buckley* 85 There was another sort of food very useful to me; this was a particular kind of root the natives call Murning—in shape, and size, and flavour, very much resembling the radish. **1878** R. BROUGH SMYTH *Aborigines Victoria* I. 209 *Murr-nong* or *Mirr-n'yong*, a kind of yam (*Microseris Forsteri*), was usually very plentiful and found in the spring and early summer, and was dug out of the earth by the women and children... The root is small, in taste rather sweet, not unpleasant, and perhaps more like a radish than a potato. **1889** J. H. MAIDEN *Useful Native Plants of Australia* 45 *Microseris Forsteri*... 'Murr-nong' or 'Mirr n'yong', of the aboriginals of New South Wales and Victoria. The tubers were largely used as food by the aboriginals. They are sweet and milky, and in flavour resemble the cocoa-nut. **1965** *Austral. Encycl.* II. 494/1 The most familiar native member of the tribe [*sc.* Compositae] is *Microseris lanceolata* (syn. *M. scapigera*), the 'yam', 'yam daisy', or 'murrnong' of the aborigines, who used its tuberous roots for food.

Murrumbidgee (mʌrəm'bɪdʒiː). The name of a river in southern New South Wales used *attrib.* in various Austral. slang collocations, as **Murrumbidgee jam** (see quot. 1943); **Murrumbidgee w(h)aler**, a swagman who camped in the region of the Murrumbidgee or other river, regarded as a classic type of indolent person; so **Murrumbidgee whaling**.

1873 J. C. F. JOHNSON *Christmas on Carringa* 16 Men when on the tramp through the Riverina country often carry a piece of twine and a hook to catch cod or black-fish. This is termed Murrumbidgee Whaling. **1878** 'IRONBARK' *Southerly Busters* 177 Murrumbidgee whalers are a class of loafers who work for about six months in the year—*i.e.*, during shearing and harvest, and camp the rest of the time in bends of rivers, and live by fishing and begging. **1885** *Australasian Printers' Keepsake* 72 [He] eyed Bob very suspiciously, muttering 'spieler' and 'Murrumbidgee whaler'. **1943** BAKER *Dict. Austral. Slang* (ed. 3) 52 *Murrumbidgee jam*, brown sugar moistened with cold tea and spread on damper. **1953** A. RUSSELL *Murray Walkabout* 147 He was a 'Murrumbidgee whaler', the river prototype of the tramping sundowner. **1969** *Sunday Truth* (Brisbane) 2 Nov. 34/1 The so-called Murrumbidgee whalers roamed the inland rivers, particularly for about 50 years from the 1880s, and caught cod which they sold to hotels and farms.

murry, variant of MORAY, MURREY.

murryon, mursail: see MORION[1], MESAIL.

murse, erron. form of MURRE.

murssell, obs. form of MORSEL.

†**murth**[1], **morth.** *Obs.* Forms: 1–3, 5 morð (morth), 4–5 murth(e. [OE. *morð* str. neut. and masc. = OFris. *morth*, *mord*, OS. *morð* (MLG., MDu. *mort*, Du. *moora*), OHG. *mord* neut. and masc. (MHG. *mort*, G. *mord*), ON. *morð*:—OTeut. **murþo*[m], *-o-z*, cogn. w. L. *mort-*, *mors* death. (Cf. MURDER *sb.*)] Murder, slaughter.

c **893** K. ÆLFRED *Oros.* I. viii. 40 þonne hi swylc ʒeblot & swylc morð donde wæron swylc her ær beforan sæde. *c* **1205** LAY. 19739 Hu heo mihten þene king mid morðe aquellen. *Ibid.* 28715 þat heo wolden..for saken Modredes sune þæ þat morð wrohte. *a* **1300** *Cursor M.* 1072 A-gain abel he raysed strijf, Wit murth he did his broiþer o lijf. *a* **1400–50** *Alexander* 1279 þe morth of all þe Messedone[s] and of þe many grekis. *c* **1400** *Destr. Troy* 5983 Full mekull was the murthe, & mony were ded.

b. *Comb.*, as **morth burning** [cf. MHG. *mortbrennen*], incendiarism; **morth game**, murderous play, murder; **morth spel**, murder.

c **1205** LAY. 19654 Mid morð-spelle þene king aquellen. *Ibid.* 22908 Moni þer feollen for heore muchele mode morðgomen wrohten. *a* **1300** *Cursor M.* 27838 O couaitise.. cums..morth brinning, manslaghter, and suik.

murth[2] (mɜːθ). *north.* Also (in E.D.D.) morth. [? a. ON. *mergð*, f. *marg-r* many.] A great quantity, plenty, abundance.

1674 RAY *N.C. Words* 34 A *Murth* of corn: abundance of corn. **1855** W. BROOKE *Eastford* 76, I think we should have had a murth of it this year, but the summer has been a little too cold, and Indian corn must have a hot sun. **1882** *Lanc. Gloss.*, *Murth*, a large quantity or number. Another form of *mort*.

murþ(e, obs. forms of MIRTH.

†**'murther**[1]. *Sc. Obs. rare.* Forms: 1 myrðra, 4 murthire, 6 murther. [OE. *myrðra*:—prehistoric **murþrjon-* f. **murþro-* MURDER *sb.*] = MURDERER I.

a **900** tr. *Bæda's Hist.* II. viii. [ix.] (1890) 124 Se myrðra.. se þe hine ʒewundade. *c* **1375** *Sc. Leg. Saints* iii. (*Andreas*) 81 Ane woman þat wedyt was wilfully with ane murthire. **1596** DALRYMPLE tr. *Leslie's Hist. Scotl.* III. (S.T.S.) 193 The cytharist, and the vthir twa murtheris, war takne.

†**'murther**[2]. *Obs. rare*$^{-0}$. [? a perversion of MORTAR *sb.*[1] 3 after MURDER *sb.* (cf. MURDERER 2).] ? = MORTAR *sb.*[1] 3.

1688 R. HOLME *Armoury* III. xviii. (Roxb.) 138/1 They are of some called Murthers and slings or sling peeces, because they are slung in their holds to turne any way.

murther, -ir, -our, -re, -ur, obs. ff. MURDER.

murtheris, -ys, var. ff. MURDRES *v. Sc. Obs.*

†**'murtrish**, *v. Obs. rare*$^{-1}$. [ad. OF. *murtriss-*, lengthened stem of *murtrir* to MURDER. Cf. MURDRES *v.*] = MURDER *v.*

c **1489** CAXTON *Sonnes of Aymon* x. 264 How had ye the hert for to see vs murtrished in your presence?

‖**muru** ('muːruː). *Obs. N.Z.* [Maori.] (See quot. 1863).

1836 J. A. WILSON *Jrnl.* 24 Aug. in *Missionary Life & Work in N.Z.* (1889) III. 48 We were told the events which led to the burning of the mission station, and the *muru* which followed. **1863** F. E. MANING *Old N.Z.* vii. 96 There were in the old times two great institutions..in Maori land—the *Tapu* and the *Muru*. Pakehas..called the *muru* simply 'robbery'... But I speak of the regular legalized and established system of plundering, as penalty for offences. **1905** W. B. *Where White Man Treads* 32 Hiakai.., forgetting the rules of muru, crashed it [*sc.* the tomahawk] into his enemy's skull. **1921** H. GUTHRIE-SMITH *Tutira* xxvii. 267 Neither..was *muru* an institution likely..to foster foresight. **1949** P. BUCK *Coming of Maori* (1950) III. vi. 421 The custom of *muru* (raiding) was sometimes employed by visitors if a death was due to accident.

muru(h)ðe, obs. forms of MIRTH.

‖**murumuru** ('muːruː'muːruː). [Tupi.] A Brazilian palm, *Astrocaryum murumuru*, whose stem is covered with black spines. Also *attrib.*

1853 A. R. WALLACE *Palm Trees of Amazon* 101 On the Upper Amazon cattle eat the fruits of the Murumurú, wandering about for days in the forest to procure it. **1860** MAYNE REID *Odd People* 135 These thorns are the spines of the 'murumuru', or 'pupunha' palm. **1927** R. R. GATES *Botanist in Amazon Valley* vi. 134 We stopped again to take on a canoe load of murumuru nuts. They are sometimes burned in the furnaces and they burn rather like charcoal. **1961** P. B. TOMLINSON *Anat. Monocotyledons* II. 142 *Astrocaryum murumuru* (Murumuru Palm), *A. tucuma* (Tucum Palm), and other spp. are included in a list of Brazilian palms yielding vegetable oils.

‖**murus gallicus** ('mjʊərəs 'gælɪkəs). [L. 'Gaulish wall' (Caesar *De Bello Gallico* VII. xxiii).] A type of late Iron Age Celtic fort having stone walls bound by horizontally placed timber frames. Also called *Gaulish* or *Gallic wall* (*fort*).

1947 J. & C. HAWKES *Prehist. Britain* 265 The specially constructed type known as the Gallic Fort in which stone walls are bound with timber (*murus gallicus*). **1947** *Proc. Prehistoric Soc.* XIII. 16 Moreover the distribution of 'murus gallicus' forts is strictly complementary to, and mutually exclusive with, that of the brochs. **1953** R. J. C. ATKINSON *Field Archaeol.* (ed. 2) ii. 62 Walls of *murus gallicus* type have in addition internal timbering. **1963** *Field Archaeol.* (Ordnance Survey) (ed. 4) 71 This work must not be confused with the special type of timber reinforcement (*murus gallicus*) which it resembles and which is reported by Caesar as frequent among the Gaulish forts which he assaulted. **1970** BRAY & TRUMP *Dict. Archaeol.* 233/2 One specialized form of timber-laced rampart, the *murus gallicus* or Gaulish wall, was encountered by Caesar during his campaigns against the Celtic tribes.

Murut ('muːrət). Also **Marut.** [f. Bajau *belud* hill.] A member of a primitive Dyak people originally inhabiting the hill country in the interior of North Borneo, although now more widely scattered; the language of this people. Also *attrib.* or as *adj.*

1846 H. KEPPEL *Expedition to Borneo* II. viii. 171 The Murut inhabits the interior of Borneo Proper. They are not tattooed,..and have a peculiar dialect. **1846**, etc. [see KAYAN]. **1848** F. S. MARRYAT *Borneo & Indian Archipelago* 111 The whole space was covered with naked savages. These were the Maruts, a tribe of Dyaks who live in the mountains. **1881** J. HATTON *New Ceylon* iii. 81 The interior of the country is inhabited by the descendants of the aboriginal population, called variously Muruts, Dusuns, or Ida'an. **1896** H. L. ROTH *Natives of Sarawak & Brit. N. Borneo* I. p. xx, British North Borneo has been less fortunate with the Muruts. **1923** *Blackw. Mag.* July 49/2 The Mûruts are not a warlike or courageous people. **1929** O. RUTTER *Pagans of N. Borneo* ii. 31 Speaking generally, the Muruts may be said to inhabit the hilly country of the interior of North Borneo. **1939** A. KEITH *Land below Wind* xi. 197 Here was a Murut headman in only a loincloth. *Ibid.* 198 Arusap called to them in Murut. **1968** *Encycl. Brit.* XV. 1012/2 The Muruts..are..abandoning their communal houses in favour of private dwellings.

murva: see MOORVA.

‖**murwa** ('mɜːwə). Also **murhwa.** [Hindī dial. *maruwā*.] A kind of millet, *Eleusine coracana*. Also, a fermented liquor brewed from this.

1847 *Nat. Encycl.* I. 236 Some..grains of Hindustan, as.. moong, oord, and murhwa. **1861** BENTLEY *Man. Bot.* 698 A kind of beer, called murwa or millet. **1862** [see MAND].

mury(e, muryn, obs. ff. MERRY, MURRAIN.

murza, variant of MIRZA.

Mus' (mʌs), dial. abbrev. of MISTER *sb.*[2] or MASTER *sb.*[1]

1875 W. D. PARISH *Dict. Sussex Dial.* s.v. *Master*. 'Master' is quite a distinct title from 'Mr.', which is always pronounced Mus, thus,—*Mus* Smith is the employer. *Master* Smith is the man he employs. **1906** KIPLING *Puck of Pook's Hill* 224 Oh, Mus' Reynolds, Mus' Reynolds... If I knowed all was inside your head, I'd know something wuth knowin'. **1917** —— *Diversity of Creatures* 68 Whoever pays the taxes old Mus' Hobden owns the land.

mus, var. MUSS *dial.*, mouth; obs. f. MOUSE.

‖**musa**^{1} (ˈmjuːzə). Pl. musæ, musas. [mod.L., from Arabic: see MUSE *sb.*^{4}] In early use, the plantain or banana tree (see MUSE *sb.*^{4}). Now only *Bot.*, a plant of the genus including the plantain tree (*M. paradisiaca*), the banana. Also *attrib.*

[**1578**: see MUSE *sb.*^{4}] **1832** MACGILLIVRAY tr. *Humboldt's Trav.* (1836) III. 46 Groups of musae and dragon-trees. **1877** P. L. SIMMONDS *Trop. Agric.* 455 Plants of the *Musa* tribe. *Ibid.* 466 Experience will soon determine which variety of *Musa* is most valuable for producing fibre. **1881** *Encycl. Brit.* XII. 261/2 Many palms, some tree ferns, and the noble Musas..do fairly well.

musa^2 (ˈmjuːzə). *Radio.* Also **MUSA, Musa.** [Acronym: see quot. 1937.] A radio aerial consisting of a number of rhombic elements in an end-fire array and giving a beam that is varied in direction by varying the phase relations between the elements.

1937 FRIIS & FELDMAN in *Bell System Techn. Jrnl.* XVI. 340 The word MUSA is coined from the initial letters of 'multiple unit steerable antenna'. **1940** *Ibid.* XIX. 309 The principal parts of the two musa receivers occupy three rows of bays each about 25 feet long and 11½ feet high. **1946** *Nature* 10 Aug. 190/1 Vertical angles were measured on transmissions from Rugby received at Holmdel with 'Musa' equipment. **1966** *McGraw-Hill Encycl. Sci. & Technol.* I. 447/2 The multiple unit steerable antenna, abbreviated MUSA,..has a directional pattern 1° wide at 18 Mc.

musaasa, var. MSASA.

musaceous (mjuːˈzeɪʃəs), *a.* [f. mod.L. *Mūsāceæ*, f. MUSA^1: see -ACEOUS.] Pertaining to the N.O. *Musaceæ*, of which *Musa* is the typical genus.

1852 TH. ROSS *Humboldt's Trav.* I. xiii. 429 A plant of the musaceous family.

musack, variant of MUSSUCK.

musad (ˈmjuːzæd). [f. MUSA^1 + -AD.] A plant of the order *Musaceæ*.

1846 LINDLEY *Veg. Kingd.* 163 *Musaceæ*. Musads.

musadene, obs. form of MUSCADINE^1.

musæum, obs. form of MUSEUM.

musaic(k, -al, etc.: see MOSAIC, -AL.

musak, variant of MUSSUCK.

Musak, erron. var. MUZAK.

musal (ˈmjuːzəl), *a.* [f. MUSE *sb.*^{1} + -AL^1.] 'Relating to the Muse, relating to poetry; poetical'.

1860 in WORCESTER (citing *Ec. Rev.*); and in later Dicts.

musal, obs. form of MUZZLE.

musalche(e, variant forms of MUSSALCHEE.

musalit, musall, obs. ff. MUZZLED, MUZZLE.

†**musall.** *Sc. Obs. rare.* ? = MIZZEN.

1535 STEWART *Cron. Scot.* (Rolls) I. 20 [see FUK]. *Ibid.* 373 Tha led thame in with musall, fuk, and mane.

Musalman, variant of MUSSULMAN.

musang (mjuːˈsæŋ). In 8 **moosang.** [a. Malay *mūsang* wild cat.] A PARADOXURE, or Palm-Civet; esp. *Paradoxurus musanga* (or *hermaphroditus*).

1783 MARSDEN *Sumatra* 94 Pole cat: moosang. **1840** *Cuvier's Anim. Kingd.* 93 Various species of Musang have been named as separate subgenera. **1884** STERNDALE *Mammalia India* 215 Genus Paradoxurus—The Musangs. *Ibid.* 217 *Paradoxurus..Grayii*, the Hill Musang. *Ibid.* 220 *Paradoxurus zeylanicus.* The Golden Musang.

musar. *Hist.* [Perh. a misinterpretation of OF. *musars* pl. of *musard* (see MUSARD), as if f. *muse* bagpipe.] (See quots.)

1776 SIR J. HAWKINS *Hist. Mus.* II. 44 About the end of the tenth century there sprang up in Provence certain professions of men called Troubadours, or Trouverres, Jongleours, Cantadours, Violars, and Musars. *Ibid.*, The Cantadours..were clearly singers of songs and ballads, as were also the Musars. **1782** BURNEY *Hist. Mus.* II. 233 At this period [12th c.] Violars, or performers on the Vielle and Viol; Juglars, or Flute-players; Musars, or players on other instruments;..abounded all over Europe.

musarabic, variant of MOZARABIC.

†**musard.** *Obs.* Forms: 4–5 **musard(e, 5 -erde, 4 mosard.** [a. F. *musard* (OF. also *musart*), f. *muser* MUSE *v.*: see -ARD. Cf. It. *musardo.*] A dreamer, foolish trifler.

13.. *Guy Warw.* (A.) 380 Ich wene þou art a fole musard! *c* **1330** R. BRUNNE *Chron.* (1810) 229 Comen is þe Sarazin.. Clad in cloþes fyn, himself is a mosard. *c* **1400** *Rom. Rose* 4034 Alle men wole holde thee for musarde, That debonair have founden thee. *c* **1450** *Merlin* xii. 183 And we ne do but as musardes. *c* **1489** CAXTON *Sonnes of Aymon* vii. 171 The kyng Charlemagn maketh vs lyke fooles and holdeth vs for nyce & musardes.

†**musardry.** *Obs.* Also **mosardry.** [a. OF. *musarderie*, f. *musard*: see prec. and -ERY.] Idle dreaming, sloth.

a **1400–50** *Alexander* 4486 Of..many foule synnes, Maumentry & manslatir, mosardry & pride. **1438** *Bk. Alexander Gt.* (Bann.) 107 To leif foly And all murning of musardry. **1513** DOUGLAS *Æneis* IV. Prol. 16 ȝour curius thochtis quhat bot musardry?

†**musardy.** *Obs. rare*$^{-1}$. [a. OF. *musardie*, f. *musard*: see MUSARD and -Y.] Foolish dreaming.

1481 CAXTON *Godeffroy* cxviii. 179 This is a moch folyssh pyte that thou hast, And I see the in a grete musardye.

Mus.B., Mus.Bac. Abbreviations of mod.L. *Musicæ Baccalaureus* 'bachelor of music'.

muscabell, muscadel, -della: see MUSCATEL.

Muscadet (ˈmʊskədeɪ). [f. the name of the Muscadet grape from which it is made.] A white wine made in the Loire valley near Nantes.

1920 A. L. SIMON *Blood of Grape* ix. 221 Muscadet white wines are in no way objectionable, and in no way fine. **1951** R. POSTGATE *Plain Man's Guide to Wine* iv. 88 A white wine called Muscadet, from the grape used in it. **1966** H. JOHNSON *Wine* 103 Nobody claims greatness for Muscadet, and yet it is one of the most useful of the lesser wines of France. **1969** R. HUTCHINGS *Lucky in Jeopardy* 21 In lieu of the Hock the Squire usually selects with a curry meal we had a bottle of *Muscadet*, which went down very refreshingly on our scorched palates. **1971** *Guardian* 13 Aug. 9/4 Three magnums, one of Rosé, one of Burgundy, one of Muscadet, from which you could help yourself.

‖**muscadin** (myskadɛ̃). [Fr.: a transferred use of *muscadin*, musk-comfit: see MUSCADINE^2.] A Parisian term for: A dandy, exquisite. Hence applied in contempt to the members of a moderate party in the French Revolution (about 1794–6), composed chiefly of young men of the upper middle class.

1794 C. PIGOT *Female Jockey Club* 98 It is a general complaint amongst our elegant *muscadins* and *muscadines* who frequent her Ladyship's assemblies. **1822** BYRON *Juan* VIII. cxxiv, Cockneys of London! Muscadins of Paris! **1827** SCOTT *Napoleon* III. 70 *note*, *Muscadins*, fops—a phrase applied to the better class of *sans culottes.* **1844** DISRAELI *Coningsby* IV. xv, Little do your 'muscadins' of Paris, and your dandies of London,..suspect [etc.].

attrib. **1795** BURKE *Regic. Peace* iv. (1892) 293 The Committee for Foreign Affairs..stunk so abominably, that no *Muscadin* Ambassador..could come within ten yards of them.

muscadine^1 (ˈmʌskədaɪn, -ɪn). Forms: 6 **muskadyn(e, (musca-, muskedyne, moscadyn, musadene, 6–7 muskadine, 7 -den, muskedine, muscadin), 6– muscadine.** [Of somewhat obscure origin; not found in Fr. (cf., however, MUSCADIN and MUSCADINE^2); prob. an English formation on Pr. *muscat*, fem. *muscade* (see MUSCATEL) + -INE.

Cf. It. '*moscatini*, certain grapes, peares and apricocks so called' (Florio 1598).]

1. In full ***muscadine-wine.*** = MUSCATEL 1. *Obs.* exc. *Hist.*

1541 *Rutland MSS.* (1905) IV. 310 For a galon and a pynte..of muskadyne, xviij d. *Ibid.* 324 A rwndlett off Musadene. **1542** UDALL *Erasm. Apoph.* 137b, Well fauoured or beautyfull stroumpettes he auoched to bee like vnto bastarde or muscadyne. **1593** NASHE *Christ's T.* 32 Buts of Sack and Muscadine. **1607** DEKKER & MARSTON *Northw. Hoe* IV. D.'s Wks. 1873 III. 54 *Bel...* How tooke he this drench downe. *May.* Like Egs and Muscadine, at a gulp. **1660** PEPYS *Diary* 19 Nov., And so he and I to the Sun and I did give him a morning draft of Muscadine. **1763** SMOLLETT *Trav.* (1766) I. xii. 210 The village of St. Laurent, famous for its Muscadine wines. **1851** LONGF. *Gold. Leg.* IV. *Convent of Hirschau*, The beautiful town that gives us wine With the fragrant odour of Muscadine. **1889** DOYLE *Micah Clarke* 72 Three flasks of most excellent muscadine.

2. In full ***muscadine grape.*** The name of several varieties of grape having the flavour or odour of musk; also, a vine bearing a variety of this grape.

1611 FLORIO, *Moscatello*, the Muskadine grape. **1629** PARKINSON *Parad.* 563 The white Muscadine Grape is a verie great Grape. The redde Muscadine is as great as the white. **1664** EVELYN *Kal. Hort.*, *Aug.* 72 Other Fruit. Cluster-grape, Muscadine, Corinths, [etc.]. **1706** LONDON & WISE *Retir'd Gard.* I. 20 This Exposition is fit only for Muscadines, Fig-trees and the like. **1719** —— *Compl. Gard.* 156 In moderate Climates the Muscadine Grape requires a South Wall. **1856** GRAY *Man. Bot.* (1860) 78 *Vitis vulpina*, L. (Muscadine or Southern Fox-Grape). **1860** HOGG *Fruit Man.* 97 Black Muscadine... This is an excellent grape, and has a trace of musky aroma in its flavour. *Ibid.* 114 Royal Muscadine. *Ibid.*, The White Muscadine of some authors is the Early Chasselas. **1874** LANIER *Poems, Corn* (1892) 18 Long Muscadines Rich-wreathe the spacious foreheads of great pines.

†**3.** A variety of pear. = MUSCATEL 4. *Obs.*

1755 in JOHNSON; and in some later Dicts.

4. quasi-*adj.* Resembling muscadine wine.

1646 SIR T. BROWNE *Pseud. Ep.* VI. xii. 336 Most decoctions of astringent plants..doe leave in the liquor a deep and Muscadine red.

†**ˈmuscadine**^{2}. *Obs.* Also 7 **muskedine, muskadine, musquedine.** [ad. F. *muscadin*, alteration of *muscardin*, ad. It. *moscardino*: see MOSCARDINO.] A sweetmeat perfumed with musk.

1665 MAY *Accompl. Cook* (ed. 2) 271 To make Muskedines, called Rising Comfits or Kissing Comfits. *Index*, Musquedines. **1696** SALMON *Fam. Dict.* (ed. 2), Muskadines, to make. **1706** PHILLIPS (ed. Kersey), *Muscadine*,..a sort of Sugar-Work made by Confectioners.

ˈmuscadine^3. *rare*$^{-1}$. [A quasi-Fr. fem. f. MUSCADIN.] A Parisian lady of fashion.

1794 [see MUSCADIN].

†**muˈscado**^{1}. *Obs. rare.* App. some weapon; ? a musket.

1592 *Arden of Feversham* III. vi. F 2, Zounds I hate them as I hate a toade, That cary a muscado in their tongue And scarce a hurting weapon in their hand.

†**muˈscado**^{2}. Some kind of herb: ? musk.

1612 DRAYTON *Poly-olb.* XV. 197 At Bridals..They hot Muscado oft with milder Maudlin cast.

‖**muscæ** (ˈmʌsiː). [Lat., nom. pl. of *musca* fly.] Specks which appear to float before the eyes; in full ***muscæ volitantes*** [L. *volitantēs*, pr. pple. of *volitāre* to fly about].

[**1753** CHAMBERS *Cycl. Supp.*, *Muscæ Volitantes*, dark, irregular veins and spots, seeming to fly before the eyes.., especially on looking at bright objects.] **1797** BROUGHAM in *Phil. Trans.* LXXXVII. 372 Those floating specks so often observed on the surface of the eye..called 'muscæ volitantes'. **1879** *St. George's Hosp. Rep.* IX. 531 Patients with muscæ. **1879** HARLAN *Eyesight* v. 61 'Muscae' may be made evident in any eye by looking through a small pin-hole in a card at a bright light.

muscal (ˈmʌskəl), *a.* and *sb.* [ad. mod.L. *Muscālēs* pl., f. *musc-us* moss: see -AL^1.]

A. *adj.* in ***muscal alliance***, a group of plants comprising the mosses. **B.** *sb.* A plant of this 'alliance'.

1846 LINDLEY *Veget. Kingd.* 54 Muscales.—The Muscal Alliance. *Ibid.* 56 Natural Orders of Muscals.

muscal(l)onge, variant forms of MUSKELLUNGE.

muscalmon, var. *musk-almond*: see MUSK *sb.*

†**muscane**, *a. Sc. Obs.* Also **muskane.** [Of doubtful origin; cf. Gael. *mosgain* 'having dry-rot, as wood' (McAlpine), Irish *mosgán* 'rotten, decayed' (O'Reilly); also Norw. *mosken* of the same meaning, and MOSKER *v.*] Of wood: Rotten, decaying.

Warner mistook the word in the Bellenden passage for the name of a kind of wood.

1501 DOUGLAS *Pal. Hon.* I. iii, Not throw the soyl bot muskane treis sproutit. *Ibid.* xix, I agane maist like ane elriche grume Crap in the muskane aikin stok misharrit. **1536** BELLENDEN *Cron. Scot.* (1821) II. 152 Ilk ane of thame had in thair hand ane club of muscane tre, quhilk kest ane uncouth glance, with the fische scalis, in the mirk. **1606** WARNER *Alb. Eng.* XIV. xc. (1612) 366 A club of Muscane in one hand,..For naturally that wood in darke giues Shine.

muscanonge, variant of MUSKELLUNGE.

†**muscardin.** *Obs. rare.* [a. F. *muscardin* (Buffon).] The dormouse, *Myoxus avellanarius.*

1774 GOLDSM. *Nat. Hist.* IV. 76 The greater dormouse, which Mr. Buffon calls the Loir; the middle..the Lerot; the less, which he denominates the Muscardin.

muscardine (mʌˈskɑːdiːn). [a. F. *muscardine.*] A disease incident to silkworms, caused by the development of a vegetable parasite or fungus in the body of the caterpillar. Also *attrib.*

1846 LINDLEY *Veget. Kingd.* 32 The Muscardine, which is so destructive to silkworms. **1890** W. P. BALL *Effects Use & Disuse* 108 The muscardine silkworm disease.

Hence **ˈmuscardined** *a.* [-ED^2], affected with muscardine.

1888 E. A. BUTLER *Silkworms* 72 The muscardined caterpillar..usually perishes before forming its cocoon.

‖**muscari** (mʌˈskɛərɪ, -raɪ). Also 6 **muscarie**, 7 (?) **muscaris**, 8 **muscaria**, 7–8 **muscary.** [mod.L. *muscari*, given by Clusius 1601 as one of the names by which the plant was known at Constantinople.

It would seem therefore to represent a mod.Gr. *μοσκάρι, dim. of μόσκος musk: the flowers have a musk-like odour. Clusius says that another name was *muschoromi* or *muscurimi* (? μόσκος Ῥωμαῖος 'Roman musk'), and that (in Italy) some called it *muschio greco.*]

A genus of bulbous plants belonging to the hyacinth tribe of *Liliaceæ*; a plant of this genus, esp. *Muscari botryoides*, the grape hyacinth.

1597 GERARDE *Herbal* I. lxxii. §1. 105 Yellow Muscarie hath fiue or sixe long leaues spread vpon the ground. **1664** EVELYN *Kal. Hort. June* 69 You may now take up all such.. Flower-roots..as..Martagon, Muscaris, Dens Caninus, &c. **1688** R. HOLME *Armoury* II. 66/2 The Muscary or Musk Grape flower. **1721** MORTIMER *Husb.* (ed. 5) II. 225 Muscaries or Grape-flowers. **1741** *Compl. Fam.-Piece* II. iii. 367 Muscaria's, great Snow-drops, Dwarf-flag. **1894** *Westm. Gaz.* 19 Apr. 7/2 There were azaleas,..spireas, muscaris, snowflakes, tuberoses [etc.].

muscariform (mʌˈskɛərɪfɔːm), *a. Bot.* Also **muscariiform.** [ad. mod.L. *muscāriform-is*, f. L. *muscāri-um* fly-brush (f. *musca* fly): see -FORM.]

Of an organ: Furnished with hairs so as to resemble a brush.
1839 LINDLEY *Introd. Bot.* (ed. 3) Index. **1866** *Treas. Bot.*

muscarine ('mʌskərɪn, -iːn). *Chem.* Also †**muscarin**. [ad. G. *muscarin* (Schmiedeberg & Koppe *Das Muscarin* (1869) 2, f. L. *muscārius* (see MUSCARIOUS *a.*): see -INE[5].] A quaternary ammonium base, $C_9H_{21}NO_3$, which is a poisonous alkaloid found in the fungus *Amanita muscaria* and which produces copious secretion by the mucous and sweat glands, nausea, vomiting, contraction of the pupils, and laboured respiration.
1872 *Jrnl. Chem. Soc.* XXV. 830 The physiological action of muscarine is antagonistic to that of atropine. **1878** tr. *von Ziemssen's Cycl. Med.* XVII. 936 Muscarine contracts the pupils. *Ibid.*, Muscarine-poisoning. **1910** *Practitioner* June 824 Putrefactive organisms split up proteins into.. ptomaines—neurin, cholin, muscarin, cadaverin, [etc.]. **1914** DALE & EWINS in *Jrnl. Physiol.* XLVIII. p. xxv, The choline esters hitherto examined, while showing the peripheral 'muscarine' action in small doses, show in larger doses.. a nicotine-like action. **1940** H. A. MCGUIGAN *Appl. Pharmacol.* 576 The action of pilocarpine and muscarine.. seems to be on the parasympathetic nerve endings and not directly on the gland cell. **1951** J. STEINBECK *Log from 'Sea of Cortez'* (1958) 124 Muscarine, the active poisonous principle of *Amanita muscaria* and other fungi. **1951** A. GROLLMAN *Pharmacol. & Therap.* xiii. 246 Muscarine has never been used in medical practice because its powerful parasympathomimetic effects are so generalized as to make it impossible to elicit the desired effects in any given organ. **1961** *Q. Rev.* XV. 154 The story of muscarine revolves round the presentation of three formulae, two erroneous ones $C_3H_{14}O_2N^+$ and $C_3H_{18}O_2N^+$, and the correct one $C_9H_{20}O_2N^+$.

Hence **musca'rinic** *a.*, resembling (that of) muscarine; capable of responding to muscarine; **musca'rinically** *adv.*, in a muscarinic manner.
1941 GOODMAN & GILMAN *Pharmacol. Basis Therapeutics* xix. 339 The nicotinic and muscarinic actions of acetylcholine can be strikingly demonstrated on the intestinal tract of.. the tench. **1961** *Nature* 25 Feb. 673/1 Observed differences in the muscarinic activities of the above isomers is [*sic*] therefore explicable in terms of differences in their fit at the muscarinic receptors. **1971** *Ibid.* 16 Apr. 444/1 The muscarinically, weakly active substrates of acetylcholinesterase, acetylthiocholine.. and acetylselenocholine.. are antiplanar at $\tau 2$ and $\tau 3$ both in crystals and in solution. **1974** *Canad. Jrnl. Physiol. & Pharmacol.* LII. 332/2 An alternative explanation.. is based on the concepts that there exist separate binding subsites on the muscarinic receptor to accommodate the polar and nonpolar side chains of muscarinic agonists [etc.].

mu'scarious, *a.* *rare*$^{-0}$. [f. L. *muscāri-us* (f. *musca* fly) + -OUS.] Of or belonging to flies.
1856 in MAYNE *Expos. Lex.* **1891** in *Syd. Soc. Lex.*

muscarium[1] (mʌ'skeərɪəm). [f. L. *muscus* moss + -ARIUM, after *herbarium*, *rosarium*, etc.] A place where mosses are grown.
1853 C. M'INTOSH *Bk. Garden* I. 667/1 The fernery and muscarium.—A garden for the cultivation of ferns and mosses is not often met with.

mu'scarium[2]. *nonce-wd.* [f. L. *musca* fly + -ARIUM.] (See quot.)
1872 O. W. HOLMES *Poet Breakf.-t* ix, Here is my *muscarium*, my home for house-flies.

†**muscary**. *Bot. Obs. rare*$^{-1}$. [ad. L. *muscāri-um* fly-brush.] = UMBEL.
1657 TOMLINSON *Renou's Disp.* I. xxvi. 239 Of Fennel... It is a kind of ferulaceous Plant..; its muscary or top, round, patulous, broad, and circulated.

muscary: see MUSCARI.

muscat ('mʌskæt). Forms: 6 *Sc.* **musticat**, 7 **muscatt**, (8 **muscate**, 9 **muschat**), 7– **muscat**. [a. F. *muscat* adj. (also ellipt. as sb.), a. Pr. *muscat* adj. = It. *moscato* having the flavour of musk:—late L. **muscātus*, f. *musc-us* MUSK *sb.*]

1. In full *muscat wine*. = MUSCATEL 1.
a **1578** LINDESAY (Pitscottie) *Chron. Scot.* (S.T.S.) I. 337 All kynd of drink, as aill, mallvesie, musticat [etc.]. *a* **1747** HOLDSWORTH *Rem. Virg.* (1768) 119 This is practised about Trani in Apulia, where they make excellent Muscat. **1756** NUGENT *Gr. Tour, France* IV. 253 The little town of Frontignan, famous for its muscate wine. **1816** ACCUM *Chem. Tests* (1818) 190 Various wines and spirituous liquors —Cape muschat. **1888** *Encycl. Brit.* XXIV. 610/1 Of these [Neopolitan wines] the best known are Lacryma Christi.., several descriptions of good class Muscat wine [etc.].

2. In full *muscat grape*. A variety of grape; also the vine producing it. = MUSCADINE[1] 2.
1655 *Com. Hist. Francion* XI. 3 He said.. that the Muscats he did eat were so great, that only one grain of them was enough to make all England to be perpetually drunk. **1682** S. WILSON *Carolina* 17 The Lords Proprietors have taken care to send plants of the Rhenish,.. Muscatt, Madera, and Spanish grapes. **1719** LONDON & WISE *Compl. Gard.* 229 Muscats, are a kind of Grapes..; there are three sorts of them viz. white, red, and black. **1855** C. M'INTOSH *Bk. Garden* II. 620/2 Muscats.. in no way differ as to pruning from other vines. **1882** *Garden* 4 Feb. 87/3 To insure the perfect keeping of Muscats.. they should be quite ripe by the end of August.

†**3.** A kind of peach; also, a kind of pear. *Obs.*
1664 EVELYN *Kal. Hort.*, *July* 20 Peaches.. Newington, Violet-muscat, Rambouillet. **1675** C. COTTON *Planters Manual* 50 The Rousselet, and the little Muscat of the Summer-Pears. **1707** MORTIMER *Husb.*, *Kal.* July, [Peaches.] Muscat. **1741** *Compl. Fam.-Piece* II. iii. 400 Pears .. Green Sugar,.. Verte longue, Long-stalked Muscat,.. and others.

4. A fungus, *Agaricus albellus*.
1887 HAY *Brit. Fungi* 86 *Agaricus albellus*; *Tricholoma albella*; The Muscat.

5. *attrib.* and *Comb.*, as *muscat flavour*; *muscat-flavoured* adj.; **muscat-house**, a hot-house for the cultivation of the muscat grape; **muscat rose** [F. *rose muscate*], the musk rose. Also *muscat grape*, *wine* (see above).
1707 *Curios. in Husb. & Gard.* 146 When the Flowers begin to appear on the white Muscat Rose-Bushes. **1860** HOGG *Fruit Man.* 110 [Grapes.] Muscat of Alexandria... Flesh.. with a fine Muscat flavour. **1888** *Encycl. Brit.* XXIV. 610/2 The Hungarian vineyards.. produce Muscat-flavoured wines. **1855** C. M'INTOSH *Bk. Garden* II. 620/2 Many err in keeping their Muscat-house at too high a temperature.

muscat, variant of MUSK-CAT.

muscat, -eer, obs. forms of MUSKET, -EER.

muscatel, muscadel (mʌskə'tɛl, -'dɛl). Forms: α. 4–5 **muskadelle**, (5 **-cadelle**), 5–8 **muscadell**, (6 **-cadle**, 7 **-cadall**, 6 **mosscadell**), 6–7 **muskadel(l**, (6 **-kadyll**, **-kedele**, *Sc.* **-kedall**), 5– **muscadel**, 6– **muscatel**. β. 6 **muscaldella**, **-tello**, 7 **moscadelli**, **muscitella**, 9 **moscatello**. [a. OF. *muscadel*, *muscatel*, a. Pr. **muscadel*, dim. of *muscat*: see MUSCAT. The β forms come from the equivalent It. *moscadello*, *moscatello*. Cf. Sp., Pg. *moscatel.*]

1. A strong sweet wine made from the muscat or similar grape.
The name is now applied to several wines, both white and red, made in Europe, Australia, and California.
? *a* **1400** *Morte Arth.* 236 Malvesye and muskadelle, þase mervelyous drynkes, Raykede fulle raythely in rossete cowpes. **1464** *Mann. & Househ. Exp.* (Roxb.) 251 For a quarte of muskadelle, at mastyr Hoys, iiij. d. **1526** *Pilgr. Perf.* (W. de W. 1531) 53 b, There groweth the myghty swete wynes as malueseys, tyeres, & muscadels. **1535** COVERDALE *Isa.* xxvii. 2 At the same tyme shal men synge of the vynyarde of Muscatel. **1590** MARLOWE *2nd Pt. Tamburl.* IV. iv, You shal.. drinke in pailes the strongest Muscadell. **1596** SHAKS. *Tam. Shr.* III. ii. 174. **1634** R. H. *Salernes Regim.* 42 The moderate dulce or sweet wine is chosen, and not that that is exceeding dulce, as Muskadell. **1704** *Collect. Voy.* (Churchill) III. 8/1 The Wines are.. generous..: The best kind is the Muscatel. **1785** J. PHILLIPS *Treat. Inland. Navig.* p. vii, Muscadell wines. **1867** *Australasian* 9 Feb. 186/1 Australian Wines in the Indian Market... The Muscatel has plenty of body. **1892** E. REEVES *Homeward Bound* 92 S——h's Special Old Port,.. at 35*s.* per dozen,.. and their ladies' muscatel at 25*s.* **1958** A. L. SIMON *Dict. Wines, Spirits, & Liqueurs* 117 *Muscatel*, the name of a sweet fortified wine made in California. Also, in England, that of a cheap, sweet, white, sparkling wine, usually flavoured with elderberry flowers essence. **1967** A. LICHINE *Encycl. Wines & Spirits* 374/1 In California a regrettable quantity of fortified wine known as 'Muscatel' is sold as a substitute for spirits.
β. **1554–5** *Burgh Rec. Edin.* (1871) II. 283, xvj quarts wyne muscaldella. **1605** B. JONSON *Volpone* II. ii, What auayles your rich man to haue his magazines stuft with Moscadelli? **1632** LITHGOW *Trav* I. 15 The.. wine that is drunke in Rome, is.. Albano, Muscatello, Sheranino. **1683** PEPYS *Diary at Tangier* in *Life*, etc. (1841) I. 430 The soldiers.. had staved all his wine, not only good white-wine,.. but canary and muscatella. **1833** C. REDDING *Mod. Wines* 241 Their sweet wines the Italians call Abbocati; their dry they denominate Asciati. Of the former kind are the Moscatello, Aleatico [etc.]. *Ibid.* 246 Moscatello wines.

2. A variety of grape (in full *muscatel grape*); also the vine bearing it. = MUSCADINE 2.
1517 [see MALVOISIE 2]. **1565** COOPER *Thesaurus* s.v. *Apianus*, The muscadell grape. **1601** HOLLAND *Pliny* I. 407 As touching the Muscadell Vines, Apianæ, they tooke that name of Bees, which are so much delighted in them... These Muscadell grapes like wel and loue cold countries. **1699** EVELYN *Kal. Hort.* (ed. 9) 174 [A catalogue of.. excellent Fruit-Trees.] Vines.. Muscatell, Black, White, excellent. **1763** MILLS *Pract. Husb.* IV. 371 The chasselas, otherwise called muscadel. **1851** C. REDDING *Mod. Wines* (ed. 3) 201 The large white Muscatel grape. **1854** LONGF. *Catawba Wine* ii, The Muscadel That bask in our garden alleys. **1886** *Encycl. Brit.* XX. 258/2 Raisins.. are prepared from a variety of muscatel grape.
β. **1707** MORTIMER *Husb.* 556 The Muscadella.. is a White Grape, not so big as the Muscadine.

3. *pl.* In full *muscatel raisins*. Raisins prepared from the muscatel grape, Malaga raisins.
1652 HEYLIN *Cosmogr.* II. 267 Cephalenia... Plentifull in .. Muscadels. **1833** C. REDDING *Mod. Wines* 187 The first [gathering of Malaga grapes].. furnishes the Muscatel raisins. **1870** YEATS *Nat. Hist. Comm.* II. i. (1872) 181 We receive.. fine Muscatels, or sun-dried raisins,.. from Malaga.

†**4.** A variety of pear. *Obs.*
1555 EDEN *Decades* 198 The frute is much lyke the muscadell peares of the Ilande of Sicilie. **1617** MORYSON *Itin.* III. 77 The Muskadel peare is very delicate, especially when it is dried. **1741** *Compl. Fam.-Piece* II. iii. 383 And these Pears;.. Jargonelle, Muscadella [etc.].

†**musca'telline**, *a. Obs. rare*$^{-1}$. [f. MUSCATEL: see -INE.] Resembling muscatel wine.
1673 *Phil. Trans.* VIII. 6022 As for the Smel, that wine is very fragrant, muscatellin and aromatic.

muscath, -att, -at(t)ier, obs. ff. MUSKET, -EER.

muscato, obs. form of MOSQUITO.

muscavado, obs. form of MUSCOVADO.

muscel, muscelin: see MUSSEL, MUSLIN.

muscelite, variant of MUSCULITE.

muscellage, -ing: see MUCILAGE, MUSCLING.

Muscelman, obs. form of MUSSULMAN.

muscelto, musceto, musch: see MISTLETOE, MOSQUITO, MUSK.

muschachoe, -adoe, -atoe: see MUSTACHIO.

muschat: see MUSCAT.

musche, variant of MUSH *Obs.*

‖**Muschelkalk** ('mʊʃ(ə)lkalk). *Geol.* [Ger., f. *muschel* mussel + *kalk* lime.] A limestone bed belonging to the red sandstone formation of Germany.
1833 LYELL *Princ. Geol.* III. 326 One group.. the Muschelkalk of the Germans, which has no precise equivalent among the English strata. **1836** T. THOMSON *Min., Geol.*, etc. II. 139. **1876** PAGE *Adv. Text-Bk. Geol.* xvi. 286 Shelly fossiliferous limestone known as the Muschelkalk.

muscheron, obs. form of MUSHROOM.

†**muschet**. *Obs. rare*$^{-1}$. [a. some OF. var. of *musguette*, *muguette*, altered form of (*noix*) *muscate*, *muscade*, a. Pr. *muscada*:—late L. **muscāta* (fem.) musk-scented, f. *musc-us* musk.] *nut muschet*: nutmeg.
c **1400** tr. *Secreta Secret.*, *Gov. Lordsh.* 85 Tak.. of nottys muschet, oon vnce.

muscheto, obs. form of MOSQUITO.

muschid, variant of MASJID.
1814 W. BROWN *Hist. Prop. Chr.* II. 546.

muschilongoe, variant of MUSKELLUNGE.

muschrumpe, obs. form of MUSHROOM.

muschyl, obs. form of MUSSEL.

muscicapine (mʌ'sɪkəpɪn), *a.* [f. mod.L. *Muscicapa* (f. *musca* fly + *cap-ĕre* to catch) + -INE.] Pertaining to the genus *Muscicapa* of birds, the type of the group *Muscicapidæ* or flycatchers.
1885 P. L. SCLATER in *Ibis* 17 On the Muscicapine Genus *Chasiempis*.

muscicolous (mʌ'sɪkələs), *a.* [f. mod.L. **muscicol-a* inhabitant of moss (f. *musc-us* moss + *col-ĕre* to inhabit) + -OUS.] Living in, or inhabiting, the mosses; growing on mosses.
1856 in MAYNE *Expos. Lex.* **1879** in STORMONTH *Man. Sci. Terms.*

So also '**muscicole** (also as *sb.*), **mu'scicoline** *adjs.* (with the same meaning).
1890 in *Century Dict.* **1965** B. E. FREEMAN tr. *Vandel's Biospeleology* ix. 110 These two species are commonplace muscicoles.

muscid ('mʌssɪd), *a.* and *sb.* [f. mod.L. *Muscidæ*, f. *musca* fly: see -ID.] **a.** *adj.* Of or pertaining to the dipterous family *Muscidæ*, or flesh-flies. **b.** *sb.* One of the *Muscidæ*.
1895 D. SHARP *Insects* I. (Camb. Nat. Hist. V.) 163 The transformations and physiological processes of the Muscid Diptera. **1896** J. B. SMITH in *Trans. Amer. Philos. Soc.* (1898) XIX. 185 In most of the Muscid flies we find [etc.]. *Ibid.* 189 The labellate tip of the Muscid proboscis. **1899** D. SHARP *Insects* II. (Camb. Nat. Hist. VI.) 504 Brauer associates Conopidae with Acalyptrate Muscids, and calls the group Holometopa.

muscien, obs. form of MUSICIAN.

musciform ('mʌsɪfɔːm), *a.*[1] [a. mod.L. *musciform-is*, f. *musca* fly: see -FORM.] Resembling a fly.
In some recent Dicts.

'**musciform**, *a.*[2] [f. L. *musc-us* moss.] Resembling a moss (*Syd. Soc. Lex.* 1891).

muscil(l)age, obs. forms of MUCILAGE.

muscite ('mʌssaɪt). *Palæont.* [ad. mod.L. *Muscītēs* (T. Thomson *Min., Geol.*, etc., 1836, II. 288), f. L. *musc-us* moss + -ITE.] A fossil plant of the moss family found chiefly in amber.
1859 PAGE *Geol. Terms*, *Muscites*, a general term for fossil plants of the Moss family. In recent Dicts.

muscke, musckle, obs. ff. MUSK, MUSCLE *sb.*

musclade, variant of MUSCULADE *Obs.*

muscle ('mʌs(ə)l), *sb.* Forms: 6–7 **muscule**, **muskle**, (6 **muskel**, **-il**, **musckle**, 7 **muskell**), **mustle**, 6– **muscle**. [a. F. *muscle*, or directly ad. L. *mūsculus*, dim. of *mūs* mouse, the form of certain muscles having some resemblance to that of a mouse. Cf. MOUSE *sb.* 8.

The word is found in all the Rom. langs.: Pr. *muscle*, *moscle*, Sp. *músculo* (also in the popular form *muslo* thigh), Pg. *musculo*, It. *muscolo*; also in the mod. Teut. langs., Ger., Du., Da., Sw. *muskel*.]

1. *Anat.* and *Phys.* Any one of the contractile fibrous bands or bundles, having the function of producing movement in the animal body, which conjointly make up the muscular system.

They are termed *voluntary* or *involuntary* according as they are or are not controlled by, the will; those which combine in some degree the functions of both are termed *mixed*.

1533 ELYOT *Cast. Helthe* (1539) 50 b, He kepeth his arme stedfast, inforcing thervnto the sinewes & muscules. **1548–77** VICARY *Anat.* ii. (1888) 20 This Corde is associated with a simple flesh, and so therof is made a brawne or a muskel. **1596** SPENSER *Astroph.* xx, It both bone and muscles ryved quight. **1615** CROOKE *Body of Man* 741 Contraction is the proper and ingenit action of the Muscle. **1701** GREW *Cosm. Sacra* I. v. §3. 23 In an Urchan the Skin is assisted with a strong Muscule closely adhering to it all along the Back. **1814** SCOTT *Wav.* x, He was a tall, thin, athletic figure,..with every muscle rendered as tough as whip-cord by constant exercise. **1879** tr. *Hæckel's Evol. Man* II. xxii. 274 In most lower animals, especially in Worms, we find that the muscles form a simple, thin, flesh-layer immediately below the outer skin-covering.

b. Phr. ***not to move a muscle***: to be perfectly motionless. ***to control, govern one's muscles***: to refrain from laughter.

1792 MARY WOLLSTONECR. *Rights Wom.* iv. 121 So ludicrous..do these ceremonies appear to me that I scarcely am able to govern my muscles. **1889** O'REILLY *50 Yrs. on Trail* 322, I stayed quite still and never moved a muscle.

2. *collect.* That part of the animal body which is composed of muscles or muscular fibre; also, muscular tissue. Also *Phys.*, the substance of which muscles are composed.

It is the chief constituent of 'flesh' in the animal body and of 'meat' in animal food.

1781 COWPER *Table-talk* 219 His form..Proportion'd well, half muscle and half bone. **1858** CARPENTER *Veg. Phys.* §4 A property peculiar to organised structure, and especially manifested in that form of it which is called muscle. **1866** ODLING *Anim. Chem.* 105 *note*, One gramme of muscle should furnish [etc.]. **1871** TYNDALL *Fragm. Sci.* (1879) II. xiv. 349 The combustion of muscle may be made to produce all these effects.

b. Used for: The exercise of the muscular as opposed to the 'mental' faculties.

1850 CARLYLE *Latter-d. Pamph.* vi. (1872) 209 It is not by rude force, either of muscle or of will, that one man can govern twenty men. **1883** GOODE *Fish. Indust. U.S.* 24 The shad fisheries of the South are prosecuted chiefly by the use of negro muscle.

3. *transf.* and *fig.*

1598 TOFTE *Alba* (1880) 95 Ah do not (Surgion like) Anatomise Each muskle of my griefe in cruell wise. **1864** TENNYSON *Aylmer's F.* 180 A grasp Having the warmth and muscle of the heart. **1878** R. W. DALE *Lect. Preach.* ii. 28 The muscles of their mind have degenerated. **1897** MARY KINGSLEY *W. Africa* 396 Wild fig-trees, with their muscles showing through the skin like our own beech-trees' muscles do.

b. Force, violence; an act, or the threat, of violence; fear inspired by force; intimidation; a person employed to use or threaten violence (freq. in *collect.* pl.); strength; influence, the exertion of economic or political influence. Phr. ***on the muscle*** (see quot. 1950). *slang* (orig. *U.S.*).

1930 *Amer. Mercury* Dec. 457/1 *On the muscle*, angry, quarrelsome. 'He busts up to me strictly on the muscle. So I let him have it.' **1931** *Detective Fiction Weekly* 5 Sept. 436/1 When the police drag his name into every gang killing or big shot feud he makes no denial. This circumstance has given Madden that terrorizing thing known in the underworld as 'muscle'. **1935** C. F. COE *G-Man* ii. 26 Winky and Palmy ain't hot for the muscle. **1942** *Detective Fiction Weekly* May 58/1 You were the best muscle in the whole crowd, Julio. **1950** H. E. GOLDIN *Dict. Amer. Underworld Lingo* 143/2 *On the muscle*. 1. By strong-arm methods; engaged in any criminal activity requiring strong-arm methods. 2. Acquired without paying as the result of a reputation for violence... 3. Belligerent. **1959** *Alfred Hitchcock's Mystery Mag.* Feb. 71/1 Skreen visited..the organization's punitive department. He gave one of the muscles the name of a pusher who'd taken a junkie's credit. **1962** *Cosmopolitan* Aug. 108/3 A female decoy to set Shanley up and adequate muscle to take care of him. *Ibid.* 122/1 'What kind of people were they?'.. 'They were muscle.' **1968** B. TURNER *Sex Trap* v. 30 Free women, a rent-free pad, and all the muscle you need to keep the things running smoothly. **1968** [see *black power* (BLACK *a.* 19)]. **1973** H. NIELSEN *Severed Key* xvi. 173 The muscle on the trucks.. were free-lancers.

4. *attrib.* and *Comb.* **a.** simple attrib., esp. *Anat.* and *Path.*, as ***muscle atrophy, bundle, fibre, power, rigidity, strain, tissue, twitch, work***.

1896 *Allbutt's Syst. Med.* I. 381 *Muscle-atrophy. **1899** *Ibid.* VI. 465 The individual fibres and the *muscle bundles become separated from one another; lastly the muscle fibres themselves become opaque. **1876** tr. *Wagner's Gen. Pathol.* 298 *Muscle-fibres suffer like changes. **1937** *Jrnl. R. Aeronaut. Soc.* XLI. 1092 The third part deals with the practical side of flying..autogiros, helicopters, *muscle power flight, etc. **1959** *Daily Tel.* 2 Nov. 1/2 There has been increasing interest recently in the possibility of achieving sustained flight by the use of muscle power only. **1968** *Brit. Med. Bull.* XXIV. 189/1 Machines through the ages have been principally concerned with deploying muscle power more effectively. **1901** OSLER *Pract. Med.* i. 25 There may be early *muscle rigidity. **1935** *Mind* XLIV. 353 We know by inference that *muscle-strain in our eyes (for instance) is a part-cause of our headache. **1878** BELL tr. *Gegenbaur's Comp. Anat.* 32 There are two varieties of this form of *muscle-tissue. **1899** *Allbutt's Syst. Med.* VI. 523 A simple *muscle-twitch. **1887** SMILES *Life & Labour* 303 Heavy brain-work..is more exhausting than *muscle-work.

b. objective, as ***muscle-kneading, -making*** adj., ***-relaxant*** adj. and sb., ***-relaxing*** adj., ***-training***.

1896 *Allbutt's Syst. Med.* I. 385 No hesitation need be felt in using muscle-kneading. **1894** *Outing* (U.S.) XXIV. 69/1 Muscle-making food. **1951** *New Biol.* XI. 101 The muscle-relaxant drugs, which are sometimes given in addition to anaesthetics in surgery. **1968** W. C. BOWMAN et al. *Textbk. Pharmacol.* xxii. 613 Mephenesin is useful as a muscle relaxant in the treatment of tetanus. **1947** *Lancet* 18 Jan. 97/1 (*heading*) Muscle-relaxing action of myanesin. **1960** R. W. MARKS *Dymaxion World of Fuller* 94 All the sanitary and muscle-relaxing effects of other types of bathing could be effected without the use of any bathroom. **1969** D. B. TAYLOR in J. A. Bevan *Essent. Pharmacol.* xvii. 162 The neuromuscular junction of voluntary muscle..is.. the site of action of a group of valuable muscle-relaxing drugs. **1869** 'MARK TWAIN' *Innoc. Abr.* 622 Who shall say it is not a muscle-training pastime, climbing the pyramids?

c. instrumental and locative, as ***muscle-monger, -worker; muscle-tired*** adj.

a **1849** H. COLERIDGE *Ess.* (1851) I. 188 That disgusting pedantry which some modern muscle-mongers have brought from the dissecting-room. **1878** HOLBROOK *Hyg. Brain* 92 A brain-worker rarely eats as much as a muscle-worker. **1899** *Scribner's Mag.* XXV. 102/2 Brain-weary, muscle-tired men.

d. Special combinations: **muscle acid**, an acid obtained by the oxidation of flesh; **muscle-bound** *a.*, having the muscles stiff and enlarged, esp. as a result of too much exercise or training; also *fig.*; **muscle car** *N. Amer. slang* = HOT ROD; **muscle case**, each of the segments of a muscle fibre as observed by Krause; also **muscle casket** (*Syd. Soc. Lex.* 1891); **muscle cell**, the element from which muscular tissue is derived; **muscle clot** = MYOSIN; **muscle column**, (*a*) Kölliker's name for a fibril of muscular fibre; (*b*) = *muscle-prism* (Cent. Dict. 1890); **muscle corpuscle**, a nucleus of a muscle fibre; **muscle current** *Electro-physiol.*, the flow of electrical current which occurs on connecting different points of a muscle; **muscle curve**, a curve indicating the amount of muscle-contraction as recorded by the myograph; **muscle epithelium** = MYOBLAST (*Syd. Soc. Lex.*); **muscle-feeling** = *muscular sense* (ibid.); **muscle fibrin**, Liebig's term for what is now known as SYNTONIN; **muscle-flexing** *a.*, demonstrating aggression or strength; **muscle force**, the force or power of human agency; **muscle juice** = *muscle plasma* (Syd. Soc. Lex.); **muscle notch** *Ent.* (see quot.); **muscle nucleus**, a nucleus or central part of a muscle fibre; **muscle plasm, plasma**, a filtrate obtained from living muscle after freezing, mincing, and mixing it with salted snow; **muscle plate** (see quot. 1882); **muscle prism**, (*a*) a prismatic section of muscle fibre; (*b*) the prismatic mass of muscle rods composing the dark disk of a muscle case; **muscle reading**, thought reading by the interpretation of muscular movements; **muscle rhombus**, a rhomboid section of muscular fibre; **muscle rods** *pl.*, Krause's term for the fine rod-like lines running through the dark streak of muscular fibre; **muscle sense** = *muscular sense*; also, the sense of position or movement, kinæsthesia (but see quots.); now more commonly used than *muscular sense*; **muscle serum**, the fluid remaining after coagulation of the myosin from muscle plasma; **muscle spindle** [tr. G. *muskelspindel* (W. Kühne 1863, in *Arch. f. path. Anat. u. Physiol.* XXVII. 528)], any of numerous small sensory organs within muscle, which consist of a bundle of intrafusal muscle fibres richly supplied with nerves and enclosed in a capsule and which respond to passive stretching and active contraction of the muscle; **muscle sugar** = INOSITE; **muscle tone** = *muscle sound*; **muscle tumour** = MYOMA (Dunglison *Med. Lex.* 1876); †**muscle vein** *Anat.*, cf. *musculous vein* (MUSCULOUS *a.* 3, quot. 1656); **muscle wasting** = *muscular atrophy*.

1866 ODLING *Anim. Chem.* 113 *Muscle-acids. **1879** W. BLAIKIE *How to get Strong* i. 18 Scarce any man grows earlier *muscle-bound [than the coal-heaver], for few backs do so much hard work. **1909** *Westm. Gaz.* 8 June 9/2, I have met many cases where an unintelligent use of such exercises has ..so thickened the muscles as to lead to the condition known as being 'muscle-bound'. **1918** *Nation* (N.Y.) 7 Feb. 133/2 There has been a curious sense of leisureliness, of muscle-bound movement. **1946** R. G. COLLINGWOOD *Idea of Hist.* iv. 189 German historians, muscle-bound in their struggle with the facts. **1973** J. WAMBAUGH *Blue Knight* ii. 32, I stopped by the arcade and saw a big muscle-bound fruit hustler standing there. **1969** *Time* (Canad. ed.) 16 May 98/1 It is a hyped-up Mustang—one of Ford's fast-moving contenders in what Detroit calls 'the *muscle-car' market, where the best sales pitch is neck-snapping acceleration. **1970** *Wall Street Jrnl.* 16 July 1/6 Two of the insurers' major targets are high-horsepower 'muscle' cars and fragile bumpers that offer little protection in minor accidents. **1974** *Weekend Mag.* (Montreal) 16 Mar. 2/1 But lower drinking ages have crippled the high school dope trade throughout Canada, the big Detroit muscle cars have been displaced by Vivas, MGBs and even Jeeps, and everywhere long hair for boys and short skirts for girls are right out of it. **1975** *Daily Colonist* (Victoria, B.C.) 26 Feb. 17/4 The spokesman said 'muscle cars' , today's terms for hot rods, had used the stretch up to several times a month. **1885** SCHÄFER *Essentials Histol.* 63 Diagrammatical Representation of a *muscle-case. **1891** *Syd. Soc. Lex.*, **Muscle-cells.* **1893** TUCKEY tr. *Hatschek's Amphioxus* 137 Muscle cells. **1872** HUXLEY *Physiol.* vii. 159 Myosin (or *muscle-clot as it is sometimes called). **1882** *Quain's Elem. Anat.* (ed. 9) II. 127 Kölliker was led to term the structures formerly known as fibrils '*muscle-columns'. **1882** *Muscle-corpuscle [see *muscle-nuclei*]. **1881** tr. *Rosenthal's Muscles & Nerves* Index, *Muscle current. **1877** FOSTER *Phys.* I. ii. 36 A *Muscle-curve obtained by means of the Pendulum Myographion. **1890** W. JAMES *Princ. Psychol.* II. xx. 198 *Muscle-feeling belongs to that class of general sensations which tell us of our inner states. **1961** *Times* 6 Dec. 17/5 Annoyance at the chest-beating, *muscle-flexing, tear-jerking banality of some moments in the second part [of an opera]. **1973** J. ROSSITER *Manipulators* xi. 112 Christou was turned over to you as a sort of muscle-flexing exercise. To prove I could do it. **1897** M. MATHER *Ruskin* 91 He would use all this *muscle-force [of men] ere he utilized the forces of nature. **1876** DUNGLISON *Med. Lex.*, **Muscle Juice.* **1826** KIRBY & SP. *Entomol.* III. xxxiv. 527 The Myoglyphides, or *muscle-notches, are sinuses..in the posterior margin of the upper side of the head. **1882** *Quain's Elem. Anat.* (ed. 9) II. 123 *Muscle-nuclei or muscle-corpuscles. **1877** FOSTER *Phys.* I. ii. 32 The slightly opalescent filtrate or *muscle-plasma as it is called, is at first quite fluid. **1874** F. M. BALFOUR in *Q. Jrnl. Microscop. Sci.* XIV. 350 *Muscle-plates. **1882** *Quain's Elem. Anat.* (ed. 9) II. 132 Most of the voluntary muscles of the body are developed from a series of portions of mesoderm..termed the muscle-plates. **1881** *Muscle prism [see *muscle-rhombus*]. **1879** BEARD in *Proc. Soc. Psych. Res.* (1882) I. 17 It was shewn that mind-reading so-called, was really *muscle-reading. **1881** tr. *Rosenthal's Muscles & Nerves* xi. 194 In such a *muscle-rhombus, the distribution of the tensions..is much more complex. **1877** FOSTER *Phys.* I. ii. 32 *Muscle-rods. **1895** E. B. TITCHENER in *Amer. Jrnl. Psychol.* VII. 83 *Muskelsinn*, *muscle sense. **1933** HEWER & SANDES *Introd. Study Nervous System* (ed. 2) II. i. 71 The sensations produced are those of 'muscle sense', stereognosis, vibratory sense, and a sense of pressure-pain. **1938** R. S. WOODWORTH *Exper. Psychol.* xix. 454 The traditional 'sense of touch' has been broken up by experiment into at least five senses. The first to be split off, early in the nineteenth century, was the muscle sense, kinesthesis. **1968** J. J. GIBSON *Senses considered as Perceptual Systems* vi. 111 The so-called muscle-sense should probably be ascribed no role in detecting the spatial postures and movements of the body, and therefore it had better not be called a sense. **1971** *Jrnl. Gen. Psychol.* Jan. 147 Formerly, kinesthesis was the so-called 'muscle sense'. Now it is known that receptors in joints mediate the appreciation of limb position. **1873** RALFE *Phys. Chem.* 119 *Muscle serum..yields..1·5 per cent. of fat. **1894** C. S. SHERRINGTON in *Jrnl. Physiol.* XVII. 238 He [*sc.* Kühne] designated the bundles simply in virtue of their shape, *muscle-spindles, 'muskel-spindeln', the name adopted here as the most suitable of all that have been applied. **1972** P. B. C. MATTHEWS *Mammalian Muscle Receptors* i. 47 With the exception of a few muscles innervated by cranial nerves, muscle spindles have now been found in every striated muscle of every species of mammal in which they have been appropriately sought. **1974** BERGMAN & AFIFI *Atlas Microsc. Anat.* vi. 140 Muscle spindles are found within skeletal muscles. Each spindle is formed of two to ten small muscle fibers, the intrafusal fibers, enclosed within a sheath of connective tissue which is pierced by nerve fibers. **1857** MILLER *Elem. Chem.* (1862) III. 783 Inosite, or *Muscle Sugar. **1704** J. HARRIS *Lex. Techn.* I, **Muscle Vein*, this Vein is Two-fold, the Superior and the Inferior. **1899** *Allbutt's Syst. Med.* VII. 460 Evidence of rapid *muscle wasting.

muscle ('mʌs(ə)l), *v.* [f. the sb.] **1.** *trans.* To move by the exercise of muscular force. *U.S. dial.* and *colloq.*

1913 H. KEPHART *Our Southern Highlanders* xiii. 262 We can muscle this log up. **1969** *New Yorker* 14 June 62/2 Graebner muscles one down the line so fast that Ashe's volley makes a high, awkward parabola. **1974** J. WAINWRIGHT *Hard Hit* 33 The refuse cart is collecting the empties... Three guys..are muscling the bins around.

2. To coerce by violence or by economic or political pressure. *slang* (orig. *U.S. underworld*).

1929 *Chicago Tribune* 18 Jan. 21/4 A certain gentleman in the illicit spirits business was accosted by two sinister characters, who 'muscled' him,..removing from his wallet the sum of $150. **1935** C. F. COE *G-Man* viii. 142 Mebbe it's a new mob. If they're musclin' Rap, it won't be long before they're musclin' us too. **1950** H. E. GOLDIN *Dict. Amer. Underworld Lingo* 143/2 *Muscle out*, to expel by force or threat of force an individual or gang from any racket or area. **1953** in Wentworth & Flexner *Dict. Amer. Slang* (1960) 349/2 If she persists,..she'll be muscled out of the [Free German Youth] movement. **1958** *Time* (Atlantic ed.) 13 Oct. 15/1 The old Union Pacific and Central Pacific railroads had once muscled each other. **1967** *Wall Street Jrnl.* 24 Apr. 32/1 Are aggressive underworld operators beginning to achieve some success in muscling a beachhead among the nation's established securities markets? **1971** *N.Y. Law Jrnl.* 23 Nov. 4/2 Big brewers may be illegally muscling small ones through predatory pricing—that is deliberately using below-cost pricing methods to force competitors out of the market.

3. *intr.* With *in* or *in on* (occas. *into*). To introduce oneself into the business, criminal activities, sphere of influence, etc., of another or others, by force or fraud; to enter forcibly, or uninvited. *slang* (orig. *U.S. underworld*). So **muscling-in** *vbl. sb.*

1929 W. R. BURNETT *Little Caesar* v. iii. 171 If you think you can muscle into this joint you're off your nut. *Ibid.* v. 182 You know, I been watching you ever since you muscled in on Sam Vettori. **1929** E. D. SULLIVAN *Look at Chicago* (1930) iv. 50 When the beer organization, which is trying to muscle in, arrives with its delivery, there is a scene reminiscent of the Fall of Port Arthur. **1931** G. IRWIN *Amer. Tramp & Underworld Slang* 133 *Muscle*, to use force or intimidation so as to secure a share in a 'racket' or graft, or to force one's way into an enterprise or gang by threat of violence. Also 'muscle in'. **1931** F. D. PASLEY (*title*) Muscling in. **1932** WODEHOUSE *Hot Water* vi. 123 You muscle in here, pretending to be the Vicomte de Blissac. **1932** *Observer* 26 June 13/3, I began to feel that he could probably beat Lindrum at billiards and muscle in on Al Capone. **1934** J. O'HARA *Appointment in Samarra* (1935) i. 13 So the feminine members had muscled in on the smoking-room. **1934** DYLAN THOMAS *18 Poems* 20, I would not fear the muscling-in of love If I were tickled by the urchin hungers. **1940** WODEHOUSE *Eggs, Beans & Crumpets* 57 Beetles tried to muscle in between his collar and his neck. *Ibid.* 99 And no more muscling in and trying to dictate the policy of the 'Uncle Joe To His Chickabiddies' page? **1942** E. WAUGH *Put out More Flags* iii. 162 You're muscling in on my territory. **1955** *Times Lit. Suppl.* 22 July 415/3 The technical secondary school is failing to challenge the grammar school, which is muscling-in on the occupations to which it primarily looks. **1963** N. MARSH *Dead Water* (1964) vii. 182 Far be me from it—I mean it from me—to muscle in where I'm not wanted. **1973** J. WAINWRIGHT *Devil you Don't* 30 'The Ponderosa' was his spread and no cheap, jumped-up, fiddle-foot was gonna muscle in.

4. To make one's way by employing muscular strength.

1961 in WEBSTER. **1972** D. HASTON *In High Places* i. 7 He [*sc.* the leader in a rock-climb] doesn't just find something for his hands and muscle up with scrabbling feet. Climbing should be a balanced set of movements.

muscle, obs. form of MUSSEL.

muscled (ˈmʌs(ə)ld), *a.* [f. MUSCLE *sb.* + -ED².] Furnished or endowed with muscle. Chiefly with adj. or adv. prefixed, as ***full-, well-muscled***, etc.

1644 in *Bulwer's Chirol.* a 4, See here appeares a Hand.. And marke how well 'tis muscled. *a* **1732** GAY *Arachne* 172 In a strong satyr's muscled form he came. **1868** NETTLESHIP *Browning* 219 The full-armed, full-muscled god will be ready to do battle. **1889** *Harper's Mag.* Nov. 851/2 They are slight, well built, and generally well muscled.

muscleless (ˈmʌs(ə)llɪs), *a.* [f. MUSCLE *sb.* + -LESS.] Destitute of muscle.

1841 R. OASTLER *Fleet Papers* I. 289 The head is sick.., the limbs are muscleless. **1867** *Lond. Rev.* 23 Mar. 337/1 Speculations..as boneless and as muscleless as the dummies in a tailor's window.

ˈmuscle man. *slang* (orig. *U.S.*). Also **muscle-man, muscleman.** [f. MUSCLE + MAN *sb.*¹]

a. A person who employs or threatens violence on behalf of a professional criminal, or who commits crimes of violence without instigation. **b.** Used to denote a paragon of powerful physique. **c.** *fig.*

1929 HOSTETTER & BEESLEY *It's a Racket!* 232 'Muscle Men' are those who 'muscle' their way. **1931** *Times Lit. Suppl.* 19 Feb. 125/1 O'Banion with the comment 'To hell with the Sicilians!' set his muscle-men moving. *Ibid.* 24 Sept. 728/3 Pinkerton's detectives were the most respectable of numerous bands of hired 'muscle men'. **1932** *Sun* (Baltimore) 23 Nov. 10/2 This country wants a frontal attack on the powerful citadel of muscle-men made rich by illegal beer. **1948** *Daily Mail* 21 Jan. 2/5 Princess MacFarlane..makes presents of boots to all the poor children, touring from slum to slum in a fast black saloon packed with muscle-men. **1952** S. KAUFMANN *Philanderer* (1953) xiv. 235 The other kind was the muscle men. You know, right off the farm where they were lifting tractors with one hand. **1953** W. BURROUGHS *Junkie* (1972) vii. 65 Bert was known as a muscleman. He was a heavy-set, round-faced, deceptively soft-looking young man who specialized in strong-arm routines and 'shakes'. **1960** *Times Lit. Suppl.* 27 May 333/3 *St. Petersburg*..was published..under the comparatively liberal tyranny of the Tsar and proscribed by Zhdanov, Stalin's literary muscle-man. **1962** A. HUXLEY *Island* xiii. 206 Little muscle-men and muscle-women—children with tendencies towards aggressiveness and love of power. **1966** 'C. KEITH' *Elusive Epicure* (1968) v. 76 If there is such a thing as a California type it's the big muscleman with a rather simple mind. **1968** P. OLIVER *Screening Blues* iv. 134 With the considerable returns accruing from operating policy wheels the racket came under the control of syndicates with muscle-men and hired gunmen ensuring that their 'rights' were protected. **1975** *Times* 26 Sept. 10/3 Auditions for 'the muscle man with a voice like a bird' [*sc.* Tarzan] will start soon.

†**ˈmuscling.** *Obs.* [f. MUSCLE *sb.* + -ING¹.]

1. The delineation or representation of the muscles in Painting or Sculpture.

1709 SHAFTESB. *Charac.* (1711) II. 186 A good Piece, the Painters say, must have good Muscling as well as Colouring and Drapery. *a* **1720** GRAHAM in Walpole *Vertue's Anecd. Paint.* (1765) III. 4 He..understood the anatomic part of painting,..following it so close, that he was very apt to make the muscelling too strong and prominent.

2. *transf.* Working of the muscles. ? *nonce-use.*

1760–72 H. BROOKE *Fool of Qual.* (1809) II. 116 Surprise, gratitude, ecstasy flashed from her eyes, and gave a joyous flush to the muscling of her aspect.

muscly (ˈmʌs(ə)lɪ), *a. rare.* Also 6 muskelly, 7 *Dicts.* **muskely, musculie, muskly.** [f. MUSCLE *sb.* + -Y.] Composed of muscle; exhibiting great muscular development.

1594 T. B. *La Primaud. Fr. Acad.* II. 97 The tongue then is a fleshy & muscly member. **1602** *Withals' Dict.* 404 Muskely, or of muscles. *a* **1745** SWIFT *Poems* Wks. 1784 VIII. 232 The muscly swelling breast Where the Loves and Graces rest. **1879** BROWNING *Halbert & Hob* 27 The muscly mass from neck to shoulder-blade.

muscobado, variant of MUSCOVADO.

muscod, variant of MUSK-COD.

muscoid (ˈmʌskɔɪd), *a.* and *sb.* [f. L. *musc-us* moss: see -OID.] **a.** *adj.* Resembling moss; moss-like; **b.** *sb.* A muscoid plant.

1841 WEBSTER, *Muscoid, a.* in *botany*, moss-like; resembling moss. *Muscoid, n.* A moss-like plant. **1879** in STORMONTH *Man. Sci. Terms.* [the adj.].

muscologist (mʌˈskɒlədʒɪst). [Formed as next: see -IST.] = BRYOLOGIST.

1818 HOOKER & TAYLOR *Muscologia Britannica* 91 Eminent muscologists. **1854** STARK *Brit. Mosses* 19 These are known to Muscologists as cauline and perichætial. *Ibid.* 55 Dillenius, the celebrated British muscologist. **1897** *Naturalist* 132 Muscologists in all parts of the world.

muscology (mʌˈskɒlədʒɪ). [ad. mod.L. *muscologia*, f. L. *musc-us* moss: see -OLOGY. Cf. F. *muscologie.*] = BRYOLOGY.

[**1818** HOOKER & TAYLOR (*title*) Muscologia Britannica; containing the Mosses..systematically arranged and described. *Ibid.* Introd. p. i, The Muscologia is a subject comparatively new.] *Ibid.* p. ii, In so few parts of Europe has the Muscology of the country been fully investigated. *Ibid.* p. vii, The student of Muscology. **1868** TRIPP *Brit. Mosses* 30 The muscology of a district may be improved by these means.

Hence **muscoˈlogic, muscoˈlogical** *adjs.*, of or pertaining to muscology.

1872 in LATHAM *Dict.* **1891** in *Syd. Soc. Lex.*

muˈscophilous, *a.* [f. L. *musc-us* moss + -PHIL + -OUS.] That flourishes among mosses.

1856 MAYNE *Expos. Lex.*, *Muscophilus*,..muscophilous; whence in *Syd. Soc. Lex.* 1891.

muscose (ˈmʌskəʊs), *a.* [ad. L. *muscōs-us*, f. *muscus* moss: see -OSE.] Of the nature of or resembling moss; moss-like.

1707 SLOANE *Jamaica* I. 124 The flowers..being brownish, very small, muscose [etc.]. *Ibid.* 125 Small muscose flowers. **1817** *Chron.* in *Ann. Reg.* 42/1 The hollows in her hull contain a quantity of fine black muscose mud.

Hence †**muˈscoseness** (Bailey vol. II, 1727), †**muˈscosity**, 'mossiness' (Blount *Glossogr.*, 1656).

muscot, variant of MESQUITA *Obs.*

muscous (ˈmʌskəs), *a. rare*—⁰. [ad. L. *muscōsus*, f. *musc-us* moss: see -OUS.] (See quot.)

1658 PHILLIPS, *Muscous*, mossy, or full of mosse. **1721** in BAILEY. **1891** in *Syd. Soc. Lex.*

muscovado (mʌskəʊˈvɑːdəʊ). Also 7–8 **muscavado**, (8 **musco-, muskavada, muscovad**, 9 **masca-, mascobado**). [a. Sp. *mascabado* adj., (sugar) of lowest quality. Cf. F. *mascovade* (1667 in Littré) now *moscouade.*] In full ***muscovado sugar***: Raw or unrefined sugar obtained from the juice of the sugar cane by evaporation and draining off the molasses.

1642 *Rates Merchandizes* 32 Sugar, Candy brown.. Candy white..Muscovados the hundred weight. **1657** R. LIGON *Barbadoes* (1673) 85 The Sugars they made, were but base Muscavadoes,..so moist, and full of molosses, and so ill cur'd. *Ibid.* 86 Good Muscavado Sugar. **1689** *Lond. Gaz.* No. 2512/4 Casks of Surinam Muscovado Sugars. **1770–4** A. HUNTER *Georg. Ess.* (1803) I. 419 The best brown sugar of St. Thomas, commonly called Moscovad. **1776** ADAM SMITH *W.N.* I. xi. (1869) I. 166 The brown or muskavada sugars imported from our colonies. **1828** *Register Debates Congress* IV. I. 780 Brown sugar (in which description is comprehended mascabado). **1887** *Encycl. Brit.* XXII. 626/1 The molasses is drained away from the crystallized raw sugar... The sugar so obtained is the muscovado of the sugar-refiners. **1903** *Longm. Mag.* Nov. 76 Mascobado, a natural brown sugar, is that which is allowed to drain off without 'claying'.

†**Muˈscovian**, *a.* and *sb. Obs.* Also **Mos-.** [f. mod.L. *Muscovia, Moscovia* MUSCOVY + -AN.]

a. *adj.* Belonging to Muscovy. ***Muscovian glass, rat***: see MUSCOVY. **b.** *sb.* A Muscovite.

1577 B. GOOGE *Heresbach's Husb.* I. (1586) 31 b, The Russians and Moscouians. *a* **1578** LINDESAY (Pitscottie) *Chron. Scot.* (S.T.S.) II. 306 Men of weir..to help the King of Swaden aganes the Muscovianis. **1579** LODGE *Reply to Gosson* 20 Your Muscouian straungers, your Scithian monsters. **1617** MIDDLETON *Hon. & Industry* Wks. (Bullen) VII. 302 A Russian or Muscovian. **1634** SIR T. HERBERT *Trav.* 106 Casements of broad cleere Muscouian glasse. **1655** J. OWEN *Vind. Evang.* Pref. 17 The Assembly of States, was called against the Muscovians. **1657** *North's Plutarch, Add. Lives* (1676) 80 The Moscovian Language. **1664** E. BROWNE in *Sir T. Browne's Wks.* (1836) I. 47 Mr. Gibbs gave mee a Moscovian rat's skin. *a* **1691** BOYLE *Hist. Air* (1692) 187 Whether Muscovian ice be..harder than English ice.

Muscovite (ˈmʌskəvaɪt), *sb.*¹ and *a.* Now chiefly *Hist.* or *arch.* Also 6 **Moschovite, Muscovit,** 6–8 **Moscovite.** [ad. mod.L. *Mus-, Moscovīta*, f. *Mus-, Moscovia* MUSCOVY: see -ITE. Cf. F. *Muscovite.*] **A.** *sb.* A native or an inhabitant of Muscovy or Moscow; a Russian.

1555 EDEN *Decades* 256 b, They were cauled Moscouites of the chiefe citie of al the prouince named Moscouia or Mosca. **1570** DEE *Math. Pref.* a iv, The wide Empire of the Moschouite. **1588** SHAKS. *L.L.L.* v. ii. 121, 303 Muscouites. *Ibid.* 265 Twentie adieus my frozen Muscouits [rimes with 'wits']. **1635** PAGITT *Christianogr.* (1639) 47 Of the Greeke Communion are the Muscovites, the Russes in Poland [etc.]. **1700** PRIOR *Carmen Seculare* 272 The young Muscovite, the mighty Head, Whose Sov'reign Terror forty Nations dread. **1788** PRIESTLEY *Lect. Hist.* v. lxv. 523 The Moscovites..were as jealous as any people in the south. **1877** D. M. WALLACE *Russia* xxv. 386 No wonder the Muscovites were scandalized by his conduct. **1905** *Daily Chron.* 11 Mar. 4/4 These may have been part and parcel of the plans of the Japanese commanders, deliberately devised to throw dust in the eyes of the Muscovite. **1961** in WEBSTER. **1973** J. SHUB *Moscow by Nightmare* x. 113 Are you one of those Muscovites who feel Leningrad is just a provincial town? **1975** *Times* 8 Mar. 13/3 Muscovites expect journalists to strengthen good will between our countries.

B. *adj.* Of or pertaining to Muscovy or its inhabitants, Russian.

1601 R. JOHNSON *Kingd. & Commw.* (1603) 168 Certaine English men sayling by the Moscouite sea,..haue pierced euen to Cathaia. **1657** *North's Plutarch*, Add. Lives (1676) 80 The Moscovite Language. **1797** *Encycl. Brit.* (ed. 3) XVI. 574/1 The Muscovite priests use exorcisms at the administration of baptism. **1821** SHELLEY *Hellas* 528 That Christian hound, the Muscovite Ambassador. **1835** ALISON *Hist. Europe* (1847) IV. 54 The frontier of the Muscovite dominions.

muscovite (ˈmʌskəvaɪt), *sb.*² *Min.* [f. the name *Muscovy (glass)*: see MUSCOVY and -ITE.] Common mica. Hence **ˌmuscovitiˈzation**, conversion into muscovite; **ˈmuscovitized** *ppl. a.*

1850 J. D. DANA *Syst. Min.* (ed. 3) v. v. 356 Muscovite, *D[ana].* **1862** —— *Man. Geol.* §56. 56 Muscovite, or common mica, is a potash-mica. **1883** *Encycl. Brit.* XVI. 413/1 Muscovite (Muscovy-Glass)... Crystals over a yard in diameter in China, where it is used for windows. **1909** *Cent. Dict.* Suppl., Muscovitization. **1930** *Trans. Geol. Soc. S. Africa* XXXII. 145 Since, however, albitization on an extensive scale generally accompanies the muscovitization, both processes in part merely involve a mutual exchange of alkali-radicles. **1944** *Q. Jrnl. Geol. Soc.* XCIX. 118 In slices they show..scattered plates of partly chloritized or muscovitized biotite. **1956** E. W. HEINRICH *Microsc. Petrogr.* ii. 28 Deuteric changes are..muscovitization of biotite [etc.]. **1965** G. J. WILLIAMS *Econ. Geol. N.Z.* xiii. 200/1 The granite in the general area of the Tin Range is more or less muscovitized.

†**ˈMuscoviter.** *Obs.* [f. MUSCOVITE¹ + -ER.] A Muscovite.

1650 GENTILIS *Considerations* 225 If Gustavus..had not bin intangled in the Muscoviters and Polish wars. **1671** CROWNE *Juliana* I. 8 The Muscoviters invaded us.

†**ˈMuscovitish**, *a. Obs. rare.* [f. MUSCOVITE *sb.*¹ + -ISH.] Muscovite.

1684 *Scanderbeg Rediv.* v. 105 Romadanowski the Muscovitish General.

Muscovy (ˈmʌskəvɪ). Also 6 **Muskovie**, 7 **muskevia, Muscovia.** [a. F. *Muscovie*, earlier *Moscovie*, ad. mod.L. *Moscovia*, f. Russian *Moskova* Moscow.] The name of the principality of Moscow, applied by extension to Russia generally.

I. 1. Used attrib. or quasi-*adj.* in the name of things belonging to, orginating or produced in and obtained from Muscovy, as **Muscovy hide, leather**, Russia leather; †**Muscovy glass**, common mica; also, sometimes, = TALC; †**Muscovy lantern**, one furnished with Muscovy glass; **Muscovy talc** = *Muscovy glass.*

1573 in Cunningham *Revels at Crt.* (1842) 42 Muskovie glasse. **1604** MARSTON & WEBSTER *Malcontent* I. vii, She were an excellent Lady, but that hir face peeleth like Muscouie glasse. **1606** DEKKER *Newes fr. Hell* F 4 b, A wise man might haue taken it for the Snuffe of a candle in a Muscouie Lanthorne. *a* **1618** *Rates Merchandizes* H 3 b, Red Hides, or Muscouia hides. *Ibid.* I, Muscouia Leather. *Ibid.* L 4 b, Spruce or Muscouia yearne. **1624** BOYLE in *Lismore Papers* (1886) II. 143, I receaved from Sir Wᵐ Hull 30 redd muskevia hydes. **1753** CHAMBERS *Cycl. Supp.* s.v. *Talc, Muscovy talc*, a kind of foliaceous body, well known by the English name of isinglass. **1796** KIRWAN *Elem. Min.* (ed. 2) I. 211 Mr. Sage found muscovy glass infusible in the strongest heat. **1811** PINKERTON *Petral.* II. 16 Talc has sometimes been called Muscovy glass. **1825** J. NICHOLSON *Operat. Mechanic* 740 Substituting varnished metallic gauze in the room of Muscovy talc, a kind of mica.

II. Uses due to misinterpretation or perversion of designations connected with MUSK *sb.*

2. A species of Crane's-bill or Geranium, *Erodium moschatum.*

1688 R. HOLME *Armoury* II. 103/2 Knotted Cranes Bill... This smelleth sweet like musk, and therefore is of many Flowerists, called Muscovy. **1731** MILLER *Gard. Dict.*, *Geranium..Moschatum.* Musked Crane's-bill or Moscovy. **1796** in WITHERING *Brit. Plants* (ed. 3) III. 609.

3. = MUSK-RAT.

1693 RAY *Synopsis Quadrup.* etc. 217 *Mus Aquaticus*.. The Muscovy or Musk Rat. **1781** PENNANT *Hist. Quadrup.* II. 476.

4. Muscovy duck (also *ellipt.*, as *Muscovy*), (*a*) = MUSK-DUCK 1; (*b*) = MUSK-DUCK 2.

1657 R. LIGON *Barbadoes* 35 Muscovia-Ducks..larded with the fat of this Porke..are an excellent bak'd-meat. **1712** E. COOKE *Voy. S. Sea* 150 Muscovy Ducks. **1821** GALT *Ann. Parish* xiii, He brought a Muscovy duck to Lady M. **1822** J. CAMPBELL *Trav. S. Afr. 2nd Journey* I. xiv. 148 We halted at the side of a lake, when one of our people brought down four wild ducks by one shot, and another found eight Muscovy ducks' eggs, as large as those of a turkey. **1863** W. C. BALDWIN *Afr. Hunting* v. 114 A fat Muscovy duck..is not a bad subject to work on. **1911** C. E. W. BEAN *'Dreadnought' of Darling* ii. 26 They fairly rushed the cargo into her... Japanese onions, condensed milk, tomato sauce, Worcestershire relish, half a dozen hens, and a dozen Muscovy ducks. **1953** *Amer. Speech* XXVIII. 276 In this type of folk naming, the domesticated varieties of ducks also are not wholly neglected, the large Muscovy, with distinctive head adornment, suggesting the scoters, sizable among wild ducks and with unusually shaped and colored bills. All of our three species are known as bay muscoveys [*sic*] in Maryland. **1956** *Nigerian Field* XXI. 108 The presence of the Muscovy duck in Africa has never been satisfactorily explained. The bird is indigenous to the Americas, hence its presence in Africa as a domesticated fowl must be due to the activity of man. **1972** *Country Life* 2 Mar. 489/1 The China goose can't stand up to the muscovy and retreats before him.

muscul, obs. form of MUSSEL *sb.*

†**musculade**. *Obs.* Also musclade. [? a derivative of F. *muscle* MUSSEL.] ? Mussel sauce.

c **1460** J. RUSSELL *Bk. Nurture* 821 Flowndurs, gogeons, muskels, menuce in sewe,..Musclade in wortes, musclade of almonds for states fulle dewe. *Ibid.* 719. **1513** *Bk. Keryunge* in *Babees Bk.* 166 To go to sewynge of fysshe: musculade. *Ibid.* 167.

†'**musculage**. *Obs.* In 6 mussulage. [f. L. *mŭscul-us* MUSCLE *sb.* + -AGE.] ? = MUSCULATURE.

1547 BOORDE *Brev. Health* ccxliii. 83 Muscles or mussulages, the whiche be lytle straynes descendynge from the head to the necke and face and other partes.

muscular ('mʌskjʊlə(r)), *a.* [ad. mod.L. **muscŭlār-is*, f. *mŭscul-us* MUSCLE *sb.* Cf. F. *musculaire.*]

1. a. Of or belonging to muscle or the muscles. ***muscular feeling, sensation*** (see quot. 1829). ***muscular sense***: the faculty of muscular sensation; by some modern psychologists recognized as an independent 'sense', but popularly regarded as a particular application of the sense of 'touch'. ***muscular sound***: the sound produced by the contraction of a muscle; so ***muscular murmur***, etc.

1685 *Willis' Lond. Pract. Physic* Pref., His Tract..Of Muscular Motion. **1701** GREW *Cosm. Sacra* I. iv. §14. 19 Upon these [parallel fibres] the far greater stress of the Muscular Action doth depend. **1809** *Med. Jrnl.* XXI. 457 Some modern theories upon the cause of muscular contraction. **1829** JAS. MILL *Hum. Mind* I. vii. 31 Muscular sensations, or those feelings which accompany the action of the muscles. *Ibid.* 33 In most cases of the muscular feelings, there is..great complexity. **1837** *Rep. Brit. Assoc.* V. 268 Muscular sound, or the resonance attending sudden muscular contraction [of the heart]. **1838–9** FR. A. KEMBLE *Resid. Georgia* (1863) 13 Diseases of the muscular and nervous systems. **1840** SWAINSON *Malacology* 399 Muscular Impressions: those indented marks in acephalous bivalves, indicating the insertion of those muscles by which the animal is attached to its shell. **1864** *Reader* No. 88. 304/3 Experiments on the muscular susurrus. **1875** LEWES *Probl. Life & Mind* II. VI. iv. 481 If I contract my muscles, a peculiar feeling is produced in me by the muscular sense. **1880** HAUGHTON *Phys. Geog.* vi. 270 *note*, The Scaly Ant-eaters are closely related to the South American Ant-eaters, even in minute details of muscular structure. **1881** tr. *Rosenthal's Muscles & Nerves* iii. 43 This muscular note clearly shows that vibrations must occur within the muscle. **1892** GREENER *Breech Loader* 202 The muscular sense may be trained: it enables sportsmen to judge accurately of distances, as letter-sorters and others judge of weights to a nicety.

b. Of diseases, etc.: Affecting the muscles. ***muscular dystrophy***, any of a group of hereditary disorders (or these disorders collectively) marked by the progressive wasting and weakening of some muscles owing (apparently) to some defect of the muscles themselves.

1727–41 CHAMBERS *Cycl.* s.v. *Consumption*, An universal, or muscular consumption. **1807** *Med. Jrnl.* XVII. 269 Diseases..of a muscular nature. **1886** Muscular dystrophy [see *dystrophy* s.v. DYS-]. **1896** *Daily News* 1 Feb. 3/1 The very general prevalence of muscular rheumatism. **1932** W. BOYD *Text-bk. Path.* xxx. 840 The muscular dystrophies have several clinical divisions, but the basic pathology is the same... The large muscles concerned with fixation (shoulder, girdle, hip) are chiefly affected, the small muscles concerned with active movement (hand, etc.) usually escaping. This is the opposite to what occurs in progressive muscular atrophy. **1939** DIBLE & DAVIE *Pathology* lviii. 896 (*heading*) The myopathies or muscular dystrophies. **1961** R. D. BAKER *Essent. Path.* xi. 275 In muscular dystrophy the atrophy is due to changes in the muscle fibers themselves... In muscular atrophy the primary change is in the nerves which supply the muscles or in the cord or brain. **1961** *Lancet* 9 Sept. 601/1 We have recently come across a family where five members suffered from muscular dystrophy, inherited apparently as an autosomal or X-linked dominant. **1973** *Nature* 1 June 287/1 The traditional concept that muscular dystrophy is a 'primary degenerative myopathy' has recently been challenged, and the suggestion put forward that the disease may..have a neural basis.

2. Composed of or of the nature of muscle; also, forming a constituent of muscle. ***muscular stomach*** (of a bird): one with muscular walls, as distinguished from a 'glandular' stomach. ***muscular tumour***: see MYOMA.

1681 GREW *Compar. Anat.* i. 3 The Muscular Fibers [of the gullet of a cat]..plainly Platted. *Ibid.* ii. 7 The Fibers of the Muscular Membrane. *Ibid.* iii. 14 Separated by a Muscular Ligament. *Ibid.* viii. 32 He [the Cassowary] hath no Gizard (as hath the Ostrich); yet a thick Muscular Stomach. **1704** F. FULLER *Med. Gymn.* (1711) Pref., The Muscular and Nervous Parts acquire..great Strength..by Exercises. **1851** WOODWARD *Mollusca* 6 The mollusca are animals with soft bodies, enveloped in a muscular skin. **1876** BRISTOWE *Th. & Pract. Med.* (1878) 494 The muscular walls of the heart are liable to many changes. **1888** A. FLINT *Hum. Phys.* (ed. 4) 470 A fluid, called the muscular juice.

3. a. Of an animal body, a limb, etc.: Characterized by muscle, having well-developed muscles.

1736 THOMSON *Liberty* IV. 146 The spreading Shoulders, muscular, and broad. **1838** JAMES *Robber* i, They were.. muscular and finely proportioned. **1859** GEO. ELIOT *A. Bede* xix, Look at this broad-shouldered man with the bare muscular arms.

Comb. **1784** COWPER *Task* v. 15 The muscular proportion'd limb Transformed to a lean shank.

b. ***muscular Christianity***: A term applied (from about 1857) to the ideal of religious character exhibited in the writings of Charles Kingsley. (See quot. 1858.) Also ***muscular Christian***; so ***muscular-Christian*** adj.

1857 *Sat. Rev.* 21 Feb. 176/1 We all know by this time what is the task that Mr. Kingsley has made specially his own—it is that of spreading the knowledge and fostering the love of a muscular Christianity. **1858** *Edin. Rev.* Jan. CVII. 190 It is a school of which Mr. Kingsley is the ablest doctor; and its doctrine has been described fairly and cleverly as 'muscular Christianity'. The principal characteristics of the writer whose works earned this burlesque though expressive description, are his deep sense of the sacredness of all the ordinary relations and the common duties of life, and the vigour with which he contends..for the great importance and value of animal spirits, physcial strength, and a hearty enjoyment of all the pursuits and accomplishments which are connected with them. **1858** *Tait's Edin. Mag.* XXV. 101/1 Here our muscular Christian insinuates that [etc.]. **1858** KINGSLEY *Let.* 19 Oct. in *Lett. & Mem. Life* (1883) 213 [To a clergyman who, in a review, had called him 'a muscular Christian'.] You have used that, to me, painful, if not offensive, term, 'Muscular Christianity'. **1865** —— *David* i. 5. **1880** DISRAELI *Endym.* xiv, Nigel..was also a sportsman. His Christianity was muscular. **1966** *Listener* 27 Oct. 613/2 That muscular Christian, Welldon, who was his headmaster and housemaster at Harrow,..always appreciated his [*sc.* Churchill's] merits. **1970** T. HILTON *Pre-Raphaelites* v. 133 The tone of the place [*sc.* the Working Men's College] was heavily muscular-Christian. **1975** J. BLACKBURN *Mister Brown's Bodies* xviii. 151 Great hulking fellows... Muscular Christians to a man.

4. Having regard to muscle or the use of muscle.

1828 SCOTT *F. M. Perth* ii, The air of personal health and muscular strength, which the whole frame indicated. **1848** MILL *Pol. Econ.* I. i. §1. 29 Labour is either bodily or mental; or, to express the distinction more comprehensively, either muscular or nervous. **1858** GREENER *Gunnery* 323 It would vary according to muscular development, the weight and height of the sportsman.

fig. **1853** LYTTON *My Novel* IX. xvi, No mind becomes muscular without rude and early exercise. **1862** *Illustr. Lond. News* 11 Jan. 51/1 A narrowness of chest which somebody has said is a defect fatal to muscular statesmanship.

Hence '**muscularly** *adv.*

1847–54 in WEBSTER. **1881** *Daily Tel.* 8 Apr. 5/2 The only way..to settle which is the better of the pair is to fight it out muscularly once a year on the Thames. **1883** *Harper's Mag.* Jan. 201/1, I do not know any..motions more muscularly graceful than those of the chopper's.

muscularis mucosæ (mʌskju:'lɑ:rɪs mju:'kəʊsi:). *Anat.* [mod.L., f. mod.L. *muscŭlāris* MUSCULAR + *mūcōsæ*, gen. (?) of MUCOSA: the term may be a shortening of *lamina muscularis mucosæ*.] A thin layer of smooth muscle fibres in certain mucous membranes. Also *ellipt.*, as **muscularis**.

[**1854** BUSK & HUXLEY tr. *Kölliker's Man. Human Histol.* II. 89 We find a dense, continuous, reddish layer 0·022–0·044''' in thickness, (Brücke) the muscular layer of the mucous membrane.] **1867** *Quain's Anat.* (ed. 7) III. p. cxcix, The deepest layer of the alimentary mucous membrane..is formed throughout by non-striated muscular tissue, and is named muscularis mucosæ. **1892** C. S. MINOT *Human Embryol.* (1897) i. 2 It is commonly asserted that the muscular coat of the uterus is largely made up of the hypertrophied muscularis mucosæ. **1959** N. ANDREW *Textbk. Compar. Histol.* vi. 280 In man the entire length of the intestine shows an inner circular and an outer longitudinal layer of muscularis mucosae. **1974** *Nature* 15 Mar. 238/1 Strips of gastric mucosa (dissected free of the underlying muscularis) were removed from (barbiturate-)anaesthetised adult mongrel dogs.

muscularity (mʌskju:'lærɪtɪ). [f. mod.L. *muscŭlār-is* MUSCULAR + -ITY.] The quality or state of being muscular.

1. The fact of consisting of muscles, or of having well-developed muscles.

1681 GREW *Musæum* I. v. i. 102 Their [*sc.* the guts of a sturgeon] great thickness and muscularity. **1793** YOUNG in *Phil. Trans.* LXXXIII. 173 Such an arrangement of fibres can be accounted for on no other supposition than that of muscularity. **1824** *Hist. Murder of Weare* 230 The body was remarkable for its muscularity and symmetry. **1874** CARPENTER *Ment. Phys.* I. ii. (1879) 31 The muscularity of the walls of the Arteries.

2. Muscular strength or vigour.

1859 SMILES *Self-Help* x. 258 The cultivation of muscularity. **1876** L. STEPHEN *Hours in Library* II. 341 The modern taste for muscularity.

3. The quality of being cognizable by the 'muscular sense'. *rare.*

1868 BAIN *Ment. & Mor. Sci.* II. i. 95 The other element of Touch is Muscularity; the weight, hardness, size, and form of things, are tested and remembered principally by the muscles of the hand and arm.

muscularize ('mʌskjʊləraɪz), *v.* [f. MUSCULAR + -IZE.] *trans.* To make muscular. Hence '**muscularized** *ppl. a.*

1848 LOWELL *Biglow P.* Poems 1890 II. 7 A..gentleman with infinite faculty of sermonizing, muscularized by long practice. **1896** *Godey's Mag.* Apr. 447/1 Garments that reveal rather than conceal the muscularized limbs.

†'**musculary**, *a. Obs. rare.* [ad. F. *musculaire*: see MUSCULAR and -ARY.] = MUSCULAR *a.*

1679 tr. *Willis' Pharmac. Rationalis* Pref., The Nervous and Musculary and Glandulous Membranes. *Ibid.* I. VI. iii. 129 What we have discoursed..concerning the Musculary Motion. **1683** SNAPE *Anat. Horse* II. vii. (1686) 81 Musculary or fleshy Fibres.

†'**musculated**, *ppl. a. Obs. rare*$^{-0}$. [f. L. *mūscul-us* MUSCLE *sb.* + -ATE[2] + -ED[1].] 'Having or consisting of muscles' (Bailey, vol. II, 1731).

musculation (mʌskju:'leɪʃən). *rare.* [a. F. *musculation*, f. L. *mūsculus*: see MUSCLE *sb.* and -ATION.] **a.** The function of muscular movement. **b.** The disposition or arrangement of muscles.

1857 DUNGLISON *Med. Lex.* s.v. *Locomotion*, It [*sc.* the word *locomotion*], as well as *musculation* has also been used for the function of animal movements. **1875** LEWES *Probl. Life & Mind* Ser. I. II. 498 It is not by Touch, Taste, Hearing, Smelling, Musculation, &c., that we can explain astronomical..and biological phenomena. **1892** *Temple Bar* Oct. 188 The anatomy of the body does not provide for the musculation of wings.

musculature ('mʌskjʊlətjʊə(r)). [a. F. *musculature*, f. L. *mūscul-us* MUSCLE *sb.*] The muscular system of the whole body or of one of its organs.

1875 E. R. LANKESTER in *Q. Jrnl. Microscop. Sci.* XV. 262 The ventral musculature. **1888** ROLLESTON & JACKSON *Anim. Life* 633 The jaw apparatus and the digestive tract have their special musculature. **1898** H. G. WELLS *War of Worlds* II. ii. 208 Bipeds, with flimsy siliceous skeletons and feeble musculature.

muscule, -ie, obs. ff. MUSCLE *sb.*, MUSSEL, MUSCLY.

musculin ('mʌskju:lɪn). *Chem.* Also -ine. [f. L. *mūscul-us* MUSCLE *sb.* + -INE.] The basis of animal muscle; syntonin; also, see quot. 1891.

1864 WEBSTER, *Musculine*. **1866** A. FLINT *Physiol. Man* I. 90 Musculine. This semi-solid organic principle is peculiar to the muscular tissue. *Ibid.* 91 Musculine, in combination with inorganic substances, goes to form the muscles. **1891** HALLIBURTON *Chem. Physiol.* 413 Paramyosinogen. *Note.* Termed musculin by Hammarsten.

†'**musculite**. *Geol. Obs.* Also 8 **muscullite**, 9 **muscelite**. [f. L. *mūscul-us* MUSSEL + -ITE.] A fossil mussel shell; a mytilite.

1681 GREW *Musæum* III. I. i. 264 A sort of Musculites fill'd with Earth. **1799** KIRWAN *Geol. Ess.* 132 Only turbinites were found in the one, and in the other only chamites, or muscullites. *Ibid.* 243 Impressions of reeds or fern, sometimes of musculites, mytilites, &c., are found on it [shale]. **1829** *Glover's Hist. Derby* I. 98 Occasionally the anomia and muscelite shells are met with in shale.

muscull, obs. form of MUSCLE *sb.*, MUSSEL.

musculo- ('mʌskju:ləʊ), combining form of L. *mūsculus* MUSCLE *sb.*, chiefly in *Anat.* and *Phys.* terms, as **musculo-ar'terial** *a.*, pertaining to the muscular and arterial systems; **musculo-'cellular** *a.*, partly muscular and partly cellular; **musculo-cu'taneous** *a.*, belonging or relating to muscles and skin; **musculo'fascial** *a.*, of or pertaining to both a muscle and its associated fasciæ; **musculo-liga'mentous** *a.*, composed of muscle and ligament; **musculo-'membranous** *a.*, composed of musculous membrane; **musculo-'pallial** *a.*, belonging to the muscles and pallium of a mollusc; **musculo-'phrenic** *a.*, pertaining to the muscular portion of the diaphragm; **musculo-ra'chidean** *a.*, relating to the muscles of the spine (*Syd. Soc. Lex.*); **musculo'skeletal** *a.*, of, pertaining to, or involving both muscular and skeletal structures; **musculo-'spiral** *a.*, 'relating to muscle and to a spiral' (*Ibid.*); esp. in ***musculo-spiral nerve***, the largest branch of the brachial plexus, which winds spirally round the humerus; also used as *sb. attrib.* in ***musculo-spiral paralysis***; **musculo-'tendinous** *a.*, partly muscular and partly tendinous.

1825 COLERIDGE *Aids Refl.* (1848) I. 85 The muscular life in the insect, and the *musculo-arterial in the bird. **1835–6** *Todd's Cycl. Anat.* I. 381 That circular *musculo-cellular tissue which surrounds the cervix. *Ibid.* 148/2 The *musculo-cutaneous nerve. **1949** *New Gould Med. Dict.* 647/1 *Musculofascial*, consisting of both *muscular and fascial elements, as in an amputation flap. **1950** *Jrnl. Amer. Med. Assoc.* 25 Feb. 557/2 (*heading*) Musculofascial pain. *Ibid.* 559/1 A sharp, slender needle may be introduced into musculofascial tissues without harm. **1964** L. Martin *Clin. Endocrinol.* (ed. 4) iii. 115 The musculo-fascial cone behind the eye. **1835–6** Owen in *Todd's Cycl. Anat.* I. 526/2 The dense *musculo-ligamentous sheath, which incloses the mandibles [in the Nautilus]. **1835** Kirby *Hab. & Inst. Anim.* II. xx. 324 A large *musculo-membranous pocket. **1885** Gibson in *Trans. R. Soc. Edin.* (1887) XXXII. 628 The visceral ganglia..give off two important nerves..first, externally, the *musculo-pallial nerve..; and, internally, the splanchnic nerve. **1840** E. Wilson *Anat. Vade M.* (1842) 290 The *Musculo-phrenic artery winds along the attachment of the diaphragm to the ribs. **1944** Dorland & Miller *Med. Dict.* (ed. 20) 947/1 *Musculoskeletal. **1962** D. Nichols *Echinoderms* iii. 54 Burrowing is apparently effected by musculo-skeletal methods rather than by digging with spines and tube-feet. **1971** *Brit. Med. Bull.* XXVII. 82/2 Rheumatic complaints..are presumed to stem from..the supporting structures of the locomotor or musculoskeletal system. **1972** *Lancet* 2 Sept. 449/1 (*heading*) Musculoskeletal disorders associated with type-IV hyperlipoproteinæmia. **1836–9** Todd *Cycl. Anat.* II. 160/1 This groove [in the humerus] indicates the spiral course..of the *musculo-spiral or radial nerve. **1873** Mivart *Elem. Anat.* 148 An oblique groove (called musculo spiral). **1899** *Allbutt's Syst. Med.* VI. 536 Musculo-spiral paralysis. *Ibid.* VIII. 9 The physician then examines the nerve-trunks..by means of gentle pressure..on the musculo-spirals. **1866** *Proc. Roy. Soc.* No. 86. 244 *Musculo-tendinous slip from *flexor pollicis longus* to indicial portion of *profundus*.

musculose (ˈmʌskjuːləʊs), *a. rare*⁻¹. [ad. L. *mūsculōs-us*: see musculous *a.* and -ose.] Composed of or full of muscular fibre; musculous.

1729 T. Dale *Freind's Emmenol.* x. (1752) 107 The musculose Coat of the trachea.

†**muscu'losity.** *Obs.* [f. L. *mūsculōs-us* (see next) + -ity.] The state of being musculous.

1601 Holland *Pliny* II. 109 They have..only a certaine musculositie at the ends..of their branches, much like to the tender buds of Asparagus. **1721** Bailey, *Musculosity*, bigness of muscles. **1864** in Webster; and in later Dicts.

†**'musculous,** *a. Obs.* [ad. L. *mūsculōs-us*, f. *mūscul-us*: see muscle *sb.* and -ous.]

1. Full of or composed of muscle or muscles. *musculous stomach*: cf. muscular *a.* 2.

1541 R. Copland *Guydon's Quest. Chirurg.* C iij, The other is flesshe musculous or lacertous. **1644** Digby *Nat. Bodies* xxxv. §8. 302 It is a musculous membrane. **1720** Quincy tr. *Hodges' Acc. Plague* 118 The musculous Flesh was..wasted.

b. *transf.* of vegetable tissue.

1601 Holland *Pliny* II. 18 The Elecampane hath a root shorter than the Skirwirts or Parsnips.., but more musculous and fuller as it were of brawne.

2. Characterized by muscular development. = muscular *a.* 3.

1609 Holland *Amm. Marcell.* xxx. ix. 397 His bodie was well brawned, musculous & strong. **1668** Culpepper & Cole *Barthol. Anat.* iv. viii. 165, I have sometimes seen..in a musculous man, one triangular muscle [etc.]. **1704** Swift *T. Tub* xi. (1711) 196 He had a Tongue so musculous and subtle, that he could twist it up into his Nose. **1775** Johnson *Journ. West. Isl., Col*, They are indeed musculous and strong.

3. Of or belonging to muscle or a muscle.

1653 H. More *Antid. Ath.* ii. xii. (1712) 79 The *Tunicallvea* has a Musculous power, and can dilate and contract..the Pupil. **1656** Blount *Glossogr.* s.v. *Vein*, *Musculous vein*, the first branch of the flanck veins, tearmed thus because it communicates it self with divers muscles. **1713** Derham *Phys.-Theol.* i. i. 10 *note*, In the Coat of this Bladder is a Musculous Power to contract it. **1758** J. S. *Le Dran's Observ. Surg.* (1771) Dict. C c iij b, *Myodes Platysma*, a Musculous Expansion.

Hence †**'musculousness**, 'largeness or fulness of muscles' (Bailey, vol. II, 1727).

Mus.D. Abbreviation of mod.Latin *Musicæ Doctor*, doctor of music.

1786 Wolcot (P. Pindar) *Bozzy & Piozzi* i. Wks. 1794 I. 332 Of Music's College form'd to be a Fellow, Fit for Mus.D. or Maestro di Capella. **1818** Scott *Rob Roy* iv, The ..ditty,..which I still prefer to all the opera airs ever minted by the capricious brain of an Italian Mus.D.

muse (mjuːz), *sb.*[1] Also 6 muze. [a. F. *muse*, ad. L. *mūsa*, a. Gr. μοῦσα (Doric μῶσα, μῶα, Æolic μοῖσα):—pre-Hellenic **montya*, f. Indogermanic root **mon-* (:*men-*: *mn-*) to think, remember, etc.: see mind *sb.*]

1. *Mythology.* **a.** (Now usually with capital.) One of nine sister-goddesses, the offspring of Zeus and Mnemosyne (Memory), regarded as the inspirers of learning and the arts, esp. of poetry and music.

In Greek antiquity there were other accounts as to the number of the Muses and of their parentage. The names of the nine Muses appear first in Hesiod, who says that Calliope is the chief of them. Later mythologists assigned to each of the Muses a particular class of functions, which, however, are less definitely limited than they appear in modern allusive use, where Clio is the Muse of history, Thalia of comedy, Melpomene of tragedy, Euterpe of music, and Terpsichore of dancing. The other names, Erato, Polyhymnia, Urania, and Calliope, are rarely mentioned in modern literature, as they have no well-known association with any particular branch of art or knowledge. Urania (lit. 'the heavenly'; in formal lists the Muse of astronomy) is invoked by Milton (*P.L.* vii.), who explains that he means not the fabled goddess of mythology, but the true celestial source of inspiration.

c **1384** Chaucer *H. Fame* iii. 309 So songe the myghty Muse, she That cleped ys caliope. *a* **1400–50** *Alexander* 2113 þe muses [*Dubl. MS.* musys] of musike. **1539** Taverner *Erasm. Prov.* (1552) 13 The doores of the muses be wythout enuye, that is to say, lerned persons ought frely..admyt other unto them yᵗ desire to be taught. **1632** Milton *Penseroso* 47 Spare Fast, that..hears the Muses..round about Joves Altar sing. **1714** *Spect.* No. 632 ¶ 1 Herodotus has in the same manner adapted his Books to the Number of the Muses. **1749** Fielding *Tom Jones* ii. vi, If the historic Muse hath entrusted me with any secrets, I will by no means be guilty of discovering them till she shall give me leave. **1803** Campbell *Stanzas to Painting* 7, I bless thee, Promethean muse! And call thee brightest of the Nine. **1813** Northcote *Sir J. Reynolds* (1818) I. 246 Sir Joshua..never ..even marked his own name, except in the instance of Mrs. Siddons's portrait as the Tragic Muse. **1847** Tennyson *Princess* ii. 377, I learnt more from her in a flash, Than if my brainpan were an empty hull, And every Muse tumbled a science in.

b. In classical poetry *the Muse* is often invoked or referred to as if only one Muse were recognized. Hence often in modern poetic use (cf. 2 a).

1629 Milton *Christ's Nativ.* iii, Say Heav'nly Muse, shall not thy sacred vein Afford a present to the Infant God? **1714** Tickell *Spect.* No. 620 Whom shall the Muse from out the shining Throng Select to heighten and adorn her Song? **1842** Tennyson *Will Waterproof* 9 No vain libation to the Muse, But may she still be kind.

c. As represented in painting or sculpture.

1756–7 tr. *Keysler's Trav.* (1760) II. 368 The two muses, under one of which is the word vrania, are good pieces. **1847** Tennyson *Princess* ii. 13 The Muses and the Graces, group'd in threes, Enring'd a billowing fountain in the midst.

d. *transf.*

a **1695** A. Wood *Athenæ Oxon.* (1721) II. 1036 Dr. Killigrew had a Daughter named Anne, a Grace for Beauty, and a Muse for Wit.

2. (With capital or small initial, according to the degree of personification.) **a.** Chiefly with a possessive: The inspiring goddess of a particular poet. Hence, a poet's particular genius, the character of his style and spirit.

c **1374** Chaucer *Troylus* ii. Proeme 9 O lady myn þat called art Cleo, Thow be my speed fro þis forth and my muse, To ryme wel þis book til I haue do. **1390** Gower *Conf.* III. 384 My muse doth me forto wite. **1576** Gascoigne *Steele Gl.* (Arb.) 53 As though my muze were mute and durst not sing. **1628** Milton *Vac. Exerc.* 53 But fie my wandring Muse how thou dost stray! **1868** Freeman *Norm. Conq.* (1877) II. vii. 159 The Biographer now deems it a fitting occasion to call on his muse to set forth the sufferings of the innocent.

b. *the Muse*: poetry personified, as an object of devotion. So *the Muses*: the liberal arts, 'polite literature'.

1755 Johnson *Dict.* Pref. B j, The votaries of the northern muses. **1776** Gibbon *Decl. & F.* x. (1869) I. 206 The barbarians became masters of the native seat of the muses and the arts. **1785–1821** Ritson (*title*) The Caledonian Muse; a Chronological Selection of Scotish Poetry. **1806** Pye *Ode for New Yr.* in *Times* 18 Jan., Weak is the loudest lay the Muse can sing, His deeds of valour to record. **1838** Thirlwall *Greece* II. xi. 58 The leisure of his retirement from public life was to the last devoted to the muses.

c. *transf.* Used for: One under the guidance of a Muse, a poet.

1615 G. Sandys *Trav.* 4 That memorable Sea-battle [at Lepanto]..sung by a crowned Muse [i.e. James I of England]. **1637** Milton *Lycidas* 19 So may som gentle Muse With lucky words favour my destin'd Urn, And as he passes turn, And bid fair peace be to my sable shrowd. **1803** H. K. White *Clifton Grove* Ded., The following trifling effusions of a very youthful muse. **1905** *Athenæum* 19 Aug. 233/2 The stately mansion built by that attenuated but majestic muse Mrs. Montagu.

d. In phr. *the tenth Muse*, a muse of inspiration figured as being added to the nine of classical mythology.

1650 A. Bradstreet (*title*) The tenth Muse lately sprung up in America, or Severall poems, compiled with great variety of wit and learning. *c* **1838** C. J. Mathews in M. R. Booth *Eng. Plays of 19th Cent.* (1973) IV. 125 Tell her from me that she's a second Venus, a tenth Muse, a fourth Grace. **1855** A. Trollope *Warden* xiv. 220 It was here that Tom Towers lived, and cultivated with eminent success the tenth Muse who now governs the periodical press. **1957** H. Read (*title*) The tenth Muse: essays in criticism. **1973** *Guardian* 29 June 15/4 Poet confronts poet..they 'talked shop like a tenth muse'.

†**3.** A song. *Obs.*

a **1529** Skelton *Replyc.* 337 For all his armony In metricall muses.

4. *attrib.* and *Comb.*, as †*muse-man*, †*-monger*, †*-sucker*; *muse-bit*, *-descended*, *-discovered*, *-haunted*, *-inspired*, *-led*, *-like*, *-loved*, *-rid*, *-ridden*, adjs.

1770 Armstrong *Sk.* II. Misc. II. 274 A *muse-bit blockhead. **1749** West *Odes Pindar* (1753) I. 53 The *Muse-descended Song. **1656** Cowley *Pindar. Odes, 2nd Olympique* vii, The *Muse-discovered World of Islands Fortunate. **1871** R. Ellis tr. *Catullus* lxi. 27 Leave the Thespian hollow-arch'd Rock, *muse-haunted, Aonian. **1660** Waller *To King, upon Happy Return* 117 The *Muse-inspired train Triumph, and raise their drooping heads again. **1759** Mason *Caractacus, To Hurd* 14 Oft my *Muse-led steps did'st thou behold. **1711** Shaftesb. *Charac.* (1737) I. 317 They wou'd..add their graces and attractive charms to what is most harmonious, *muse-like, and divine in human life. **1624** A. Holland in J. Davies *Scourge Paper-Persecutors* 2 Each drिueling Lozel now..Starts vp a sudden *Muse-man, and streight throws A Packe of Epigrams into the light. **1608** Day *Hum. out of Br.* Ded. (1881) 3 The Iron-pated *Muse-mongers about the towne. **1728** Pope *Dunc.* ii. 33 No meagre, *muse-rid mope, adust and thin. **1697** Collier *Ess. Mor. Subj.* ii. To Rdr. (1709) 5 To be *Muse-ridden at this rate is somewhat hard. **1604** Middleton *Father Hubburd's T.* Wks. (Bullen) VIII. 52 You never give the poor *Muse-suckers a penny.

muse (mjuːz), *sb.*[2] Also 6–7 muze. Somewhat *arch.* [f. muse *v.* Cf. OF. *muse* amusement, waste of time, deception.] †**a.** The action of musing; profound meditation or abstraction (*obs.*). **b.** An instance of this, a fit of abstraction; now only in *sing.* †*(to be) in one's muses*: in a state of abstraction (*obs.*). †**c.** *to be at a muse*: to be perplexed or uncertain; to 'wonder' (*whether*, *how*, *what*, etc.). *Obs.*

c **1475** *Partenay* 3431 In pensif muses hym faste beseying, He rest noght to ryde, so to Maillers cam. **1544** Patten *Exped. Scotl.* Pref. a iv, I haue bene often at a great muse with my selfe, whither the kynges Maiestie [etc.]. **1565** Cooper *Thesaurus* s.v. *Cogitatio*, To be in a deepe muse. **1578** Banister *Hist. Man* iv. 55 When a man by earnest study or muse vnto him selfe, vpon any earnest or waighty matter [etc.]. **1579** Lyly *Euphues* (Arb.) 94 His Lady, whome he finding in hir muses, began pleasantly to salute. *a* **1586** Sidney *Arcadia* ii. (1622) 113 In this depth of muzes, and diuers sorts of discourses, would shee rauingly haue remained, but that [etc.]. **1626–7** in *Crt. & Times Chas. I* (1848) I. 251 For the duke and our fleet, we are now all at a muse what should become of them. **1667** Milton *P.L.* vii. 52 He..was fill'd With admiration, and deep Muse to heare Of things so high and strange. **1701** Norris *Ideal World* i. ii. 73 Such a profound muse as when we are said to think upon nothing. *a* **1713** Ellwood *Autobiog.* (1714) 234 He made me no Answer, but sate some time in a Muse. **1751** R. Paltock *P. Wilkins* (1884) II. 279 'Sir', says I, after a seeming muse for some time, 'what should you think of Oniwheske [for a wife]?' **1871** Browning *Balaust.* 2682 Where she dwells Forever in a muse. **1889** Stevenson *Master of B.* ii, He would fall into a deep muse over our accounts.

†**muse,** *sb.*[3] [a. OF. *muse*; by Fr. scholars regarded as identical with *muse* muse *sb.*[1], or as a verbal noun f. the cognate med.L. *mūsāre* to play music. Cf. cornemuse.] A bagpipe.

The explanation in quot. 1782, which alone appears in modern Dicts., seems to be a pseudo-etymological guess connecting the word with OF. *muse* muzzle.

1426 Lydg. *De Guil. Pilgr.* 14304 Bombardys and cornemusys, Thys ffloutys ek, with sotyl musys. **1484** Caxton *Fables of Æsop* vi. vii, Whanne I pyped and played of my muse or bag pype ye dayned ne wold not daunse. [**1782** Burney *Hist. Mus.* II. 270 *note*, The Muse is the muzzle or tube of a bag-pipe, without the bellows.]

†**muse,** *sb.*[4] *Obs.* Forms: 6 mose, mouse, (? *pl.* mowsies), mouce, 6–7 muse. [Utimately a. Arab. *mauz*, *mauzah* banana.] The fruit of the plantain or banana (see musa[1]). Also *attrib.*

1578 Lyte *Dodoens* vi. xxxviii. 704 Of Musa or Mose tree. The Mose tree leaues be so great and large, that one may easyly wrap a childe..in them. **1585** T. Washington tr. *Nicholay's Voy.* i. xvi. 17 b, Apples of paradice, which they call muses. **1588** Hickok tr. *Frederick's Voy.* 18 Laden with fruite, as with Mouces which we call Adams apples. *Marg.* The Mowsies is a kind of fruite growing in clusters and are 5 or 6 inches long a peece. *c* **1602** in Purchas *Pilgrims* (1625) II. 1617 At Damiatta..are great gardens, full of Adams figs, ..these are also called Mouses.

muse (mjuːz), *v.* Forms: 4 mwse, 4–5 moyse, 5 mouse, mowse, mewse, musee, muse, mose, 6 muze, *Sc.* mus(s, 4– muse. [a. F. *muser* (12th c. in Hatz.-Darm.), to waste time, trifle, in OF. also to muse, meditate = Pr. *musar*, It. *musare* to stare about, idle, loiter.

Prob. a derivative of the Rom. word represented by It. *muso*, OF. *muse* muzzle (cf. Florio's explanation of It. *musare*, 'to hould ones musle or snout in the aire'), the primary allusion being to the action of 'a dog sniffing the air when in doubt as to the scent' (Skeat). Possibly the sense 'to meditate' may be due to the influence of L. *mūsa* muse *sb.*[1] Cf. med.L. *mūsāre* to play music.]

I. *intr.*

1. a. To be absorbed in thought; to meditate continuously in silence; to ponder. Const. *of*, *on*, *upon*, †*in*. †In early use occas. with *inf.* of purpose.

1340 *Ayenb.* 104 Þer-uore ich þe rede wel þet þou ne musy naȝt to moche hit uor to zeche. **1362** Langl. *P. Pl.* A. xi. 137 Þe more I muse þeron þe mistiloker hit [Theology] semeþ. *c* **1375** *Sc. Leg. Saints* l. (*Katerine*) 111 Þu suld moyse here & merwall, of hewine & erth. **1390** Gower *Conf.* I. 320 Thus fulofte there he sat To muse in his philosophie. *c* **1430** Lydg. *Min. Poems* (Percy Soc.) 144 Austyn gan muse in his oppynyoun, To fynde a mene the sowle for to save. *c* **1460** Sir R. Ros *La Belle Dame* 202 He mused sore, to conquere his desire. *c* **1489** Caxton *Blanchardyn* xliii. 162 He was musyng vpon þᵉ werke. **1490** —— *Eneydos* xxxvii. 126 Whan kynge Latyne hadde mused a lytyll in hym selfe he ansuered. **1535** Coverdale *Ps.* xxxviii. 3 Whyle I was thus musynge, the fyre kyndled. **1607** Earl Stirling *J. Cæsar* iv. i, Who muse of many things, resolve of none. **1634** W. Tirwhyt tr. *Balzac's Lett.* (vol. I.) 400 If I muse but two houres on the bankes of the Tyber, I am as understanding as if I had studied eight days. **1732** Berkeley *Alciphr.* iii. §1 Alciphron, having mused a while, answered [etc.]. **1781** Cowper *Retirem.* 376 And cultivate a taste for ancient song, Catching its ardour as I mus'd along. **1816** J. Wilson *City of Plague* ii. ii. 169 The sorrowful Still love to muse on all distressful things. **1833** Ht. Martineau *Berkeley the Banker* i. i, Her father paused to muse. **1901** 'Lucas Malet' *Sir R.*

Calmady VI. xi, Lady Calmady.. musing of many matters.. slowly went the length of the terrace. **1906** *Outlook* 14 July 42/2 In Imperial politics he decided.. while other men were musing and hesitating.

quasi-*trans.* **1781** COWPER *Truth* 441 Sorrow might muse herself to madness then.

b. With dependent question.

1390 GOWER *Conf.* I. 282 Whan that I muse And thenke how sche me wol refuse, I am with anger so bestad, For al this world mihte I be glad. *a* **1555** RIDLEY *Conf. with Latimer* (1556) e 7, I haue begonne.. to muse with myselfe, howe the dartes of the olde enemye maye be borne of. *a* **1713** ELLWOOD *Autobiog.* (1714) 21, I.. stood.. musing with my self what Course to take.

†**c.** In proverbial phr.: (see quot.). *Obs.*

a **1700** B. E. *Dict. Cant. Crew* s.v. *Corn, He measures my Corn by his own Bushel, he muses as he uses*, he thinks me Bad because he is so himself.

d. To say or murmur meditatively.

1834 A. MARSH *Two Old Men's Tales* II. xviii. 224 'But what can I promise? I who have nothing,' mused she, 'and am now penniless.' **1843** DICKENS *Christmas Carol* 32 'You must have been very slow about it, Jacob.'.. 'Slow!' the Ghost repeated. 'Seven years dead,' mused Scrooge 'And travelling all the time?' **1881** MRS. J. H. RIDDELL *Senior Partner* I. vii. 150 'That's strange,' mused Mr. McCullagh; 'and you getting on for thirty year of age.' **1922** JOYCE *Ulysses* 212 Amused Buck Mulligan mused in pleasant murmur with himself, selfnodding: 'A pleased bottom.'

2. With dependent question: To be at a loss to discover; to ask oneself meditatively, to 'wonder' (*what, how*, etc.). Now *rare*.

c **1380** WYCLIF *Wks.* (1880) 35 But here men musen whi prelatis ben so redy to curs in here owne cause. *c* **1407** LYDG. *Reson & Sens.* 2893 Musyng, what hyt myghte be That she so straungely spake to me. **1513** MORE *Rich. III* in Grafton *Chron.* (1568) II. 785 Whyle men mused what the matter ment. *a* **1562** CAVENDISH *Wolsey* (1893) 34 It made all the noble men.. and gentil-women to muse what it [*sc.* the firing of guns] shold mean, commyng so sodenly. **1581** *Pettie* tr. *Guazzo's Civ. Conv.* III. (1586) 161 b, Which maketh me much muse how it should be so. **1791** COWPER *Odyss.* xx. 41, I muse How single as I am I shall assail These shameless suitors. **1853** M. ARNOLD *Sohrab & Rustum* 347 Ah me, I muse what this young fox may mean!

3. a. To be affected with astonishment or surprise; to wonder, marvel. Const. *at*, †*of*, †*to*. Now *rare* (*poet.*).

1340 *Ayenb.* 47 Ofte hy sseaweþ and diȝteþ ham þe more quaynteliche and þe more honesteliche uor to maki musi þe foles to ham. **1340** HAMPOLE *Pr. Consc.* 6266 A grete wondir.. þat in swa short tyme.. He mught.. discusse al thyng; Bot of þis suld nane muse, lered ne lewed, For als grete wondirs has God shewed. *c* **1450** *Mirour Saluacioun* 3837 The aungeles with outen meseure thise thinges musyd seyng. **1526** *Pilgr. Perf.* (W. de W. 1531) 6 Some persons perauenture wyll muse or meruayle. **1530** PALSGR. 443/1, I muse at it to se how he bandeth hymselfe with your enemyes. *a* **1548** HALL *Chron.*, *Edw. IV* 234 The Frenchmen their at not a littell mused. **1605** SHAKS. *Macb.* III. iv. 85 Do not muse at me my most worthy Friends. **1641** MILTON *Prel. Episc.* Wks. 1851 III. 83 We need no longer muse at the spreading of many idle traditions. **1859** TENNYSON *Elaine* 1261 Then came the fine Gawain and wonder'd at her, And Lancelot later came and mused at her.

†**b.** With clause or *inf.* expressing the occasion for wonder. *Obs.*

1530 CROMWELL in Merriman *Life & Lett.* (1902) I. 328, I much muse that your Grace should so think. **1579** LYLY *Euphues* (Arb.) 178 Thou wilt muse Philautus to heere Euphues to preach, who of late had more minde to serue his Lady then to worshippe his Lorde. **1593** SHAKS. *2 Hen. VI*, III. i. 1, I muse my Lord of Gloster is not come. **1599** Q. ELIZ. in Harington *Nugæ Ant.* (1804) I. 304 We cannot but muse that you shoulde recite that circumstance. **1631** DEKKER *Match Mee* III. Wks. 1873 IV. 180, I muse thou art so poore. **1632** *Thomas of Reading* in Thoms *E.E. Prose Rom.* (1858) I. 135, I muse thou canst indure this vile beseeming seruitude.

†**c.** To be a matter of wonder. *Obs.*

c **1460** *Towneley Myst.* iv. 12 Wheder ar all oure elders went? This musys mekill in my thoght.

4. To gaze meditatively; to look thoughtfully or intently. Const. *on, upon*, †*in*.

?*a* **1366** CHAUCER *Rom. Rose* 1527 He so musede in the welle, That.. He lovede his owne shadowe. **1390** GOWER *Conf.* II. 128 It [his cofre] schal noght after ben unstoken, Bot whanne him list to have a syhte Of gold.. That he ther on mai loke and muse. *c* **1430** *Pol. Rel. & L. Songs* (1866) 148 As y stood musynge on þe moone. *c* **1450** LOVELICH *Grail* xliv. 570 Faste towardis hym gan he to Muse, And vppon hym sette his hors hed. *c* **1470** *Gol. & Gaw.* 1231 Ilk man may.. muse in his myrrour. **1639** N. N. tr. *Du Bosq's Compl. Woman* I. 63, I have heretofore a long time mused on the Statue of Venus made by Phidias. **1711** STEELE *Spect.* No. 113 ¶ 1 This was the Place wherein I used to muse upon her. **1798** WORDSW. *Night-piece* 26 The mind.. Is left to muse upon the solemn scene. **1820** W. IRVING *Sketch Bk.* I. 69 For some time Rip lay musing on this scene. **183**. J. H. NEWMAN *Ch. Fathers* (1840) 232 He began to eye and muse upon the great bishop of Milan.

†**5.** To wait or look expectantly. *Obs.*

a **1450** *Knt. de La Tour* (1906) 45 She.. wolde no more make folke to mouse after her, but wolde be sonner arraied and atte the chirche thanne ani other.

†**6.** To murmur; to grumble, complain. *Obs.*

1382 WYCLIF *2 Sam.* xii. 19 Whanne thanne Dauid hadde herd his seruauntis musynge [Vulg. *mussitantes*]. *c* **1430** LYDG. *Min. Poems* (Percy Soc.) 17 Wiche ought of resone the devise to excuse, To alle tho that wold ageyn it ffroune or muse. **1549–62** STERNHOLD & H. *Ps.* ii. 1 Why did the Jewish people muse, Seeing all is but vaine? **1598** SHAKS. *Merry W.* v. v. 253 Well, I will muse no further: Mr Fenton, Heauen giue you many, many merry dayes.

II. *trans.*

7. To ponder over, reflect upon; to contemplate, meditate. Now *rare*.

c **1395** *Plowman's Tale* 89 He mused his matter in mesure. *c* **1460** METHAM *Wks.* (E.E.T.S.) 64/1714 Ys this the loue that we haue musyd so offt? **1724** RAMSAY *Vision* i, I wandert waif and wae, Musand our main mischaunce. **1730** THOMSON *Hymn on Seasons* 121 Come then, expressive Silence, muse his praise. **1826** DISRAELI *Viv. Grey* II. i, The poet was absent, for he was musing a sonnet. **1878** B. TAYLOR *Deukalion* I. iii, What musest thou?

transf. and *fig.* **1850** MRS. BROWNING *Romaunt of Page* xi, His large eyes seemed to muse a smile.

†**8.** To murmur discontentedly. *Obs.*

1388 WYCLIF *John* vii. 32 Farisees herden the puple musinge [1382 grucchinge, Vulg. *murmurantem*] of hym these thingis. **1402** HOCCLEVE *Letter of Cupid* 238 Yt shal not ben in her elleccion the foulest slutte of al a tovne refuse, yf that me lyst, for al that they can muse.

†**9.** To excogitate. *Obs.*

a **1375** *Cursor M.* 2267 (Fairf.) þer ware al þe speche mused þat now ar in þis werlde vsed.

†**10.** To marvel at. *Obs.*

1567 *Gude & Godlie Ball.* (S.T.S.) 165 Musing greitlie in my mynde, The folie that is in mankynde. **1610** SHAKS. *Temp.* III. iii. 36, I cannot too much muse Such shapes, such gesture, and such sound.

†**11.** To bewilder, puzzle. *Obs.*

1673 *S'too him Bayes* 58 But that that most muses me is this.

muse, var. MEUSE; obs. f. MEWS, MOSS.

museacall, variant of MOSAICAL *a.*[1] *Obs.*

‖**museau** (myzo). *colloq.* [Fr., lit. 'muzzle, snout (of animal)'.] A person's face.

1915 D. H. LAWRENCE *Rainbow* xv. 423 You've got a *museau*, not a face. **1922** —— *England, my England* 228 A young man of twenty-two, with a fresh, jaunty *museau*. **1925** —— *St. Mawr* 7 She, with her odd little *museau*, not exactly pretty, but very attractive. **1955** *Essays in Criticism* V. 79 Lou, with her gipsy wildness, her animal *museau*.

mused (mjuːzd), *a.* [f. MUSE *v.*[1] + -ED.] Bemused, fuddled.

1842 TENNYSON *Will Waterpr.* 74 Head-waiter, honour'd by the guest Half-mused, or reeling ripe.

†**musedode**. *Obs. rare*⁻¹. [f. *muse* MOUSE *sb.* (cf. '*Vermicularis*, herba muris', Diefenbach); the second element may be = mod. dial. *dud* teat.] Some herb; perh. the stonecrop, *Sedum acre*.

c **1450** *Alphita* (Anecd. Oxon.) 190/1 *Vermicularis maior*, tetroselio idem g. tatesoriz, ang. andrede uel musedode.

‖**musée** ('mjuːzeɪ, ‖myze). Also **musee**. [Fr., ad. L. *mūsēum*.] **1.** = MUSEUM.

1660 in C. Innes *Sk. Early Scot. Hist.* (1861) 452 The studie or musee belonging thereto. **1861** C. M. YONGE *Young Stepmother* xvii. 233, I shall be most happy to introduce you into my *atelier* and show you my notes on the various *Musées*. **1885** H. JAMES *Little Tour in France* xv. 102 Of course I had time to go to the Musée; the more so that I have a weakness for provincial museums. **1924** R. FRY *Let.* 27 June (1972) II. 553 I've.. seen the much vaunted Musée here [*sc.* in Montpellier]. It's badly lit and worse hung. **1944** *Amer. N. & Q.* Aug. 72/2 In compiling material on the dime museum I could not help being struck with what seems to have been a showman's affectation—the almost universal use of *musee* for *museum*. **1970** B. WHELPTON *Painter's Paris* vii. 107 The Musée Cernuschi.. houses a superb collection of the art of China.

2. musée imaginaire (‖imaʒinɛr) [Fr., lit. 'imaginary museum']: an imaginary collection of all the works of human artifice.

[**1947** A. MALRAUX *Musée Imaginaire* 17 Un Musée imaginaire sans précédent s'est ouvert, qui va pousser à l'extrême l'intellectualisation commencée par l'incomplète confrontation des vrais musées; répondant à l'appel de ceux-ci, les arts plastiques ont inventé leur imprimerie.] **1959** *Twentieth Century* Oct. 262 He [*sc.* the culture-vulture].. haunts the limbo of the *musée imaginaire*, where all cultures and styles coexist. **1960** *Ibid.* Sept. 275 In Audenesque abstraction lies the power to keep us from.. the object labelled and dismissed in the *musée imaginaire*. **1962** *Listener* 8 Mar. 431/1 We are no longer bewildered by the 'matter' of civilizations now that the *musée imaginaire* has accustomed us to the quick pounce on the artifact that illumines a lost world. **1967** *Ibid.* 7 Sept. 293/2 Dallagret has gone for.. a kind of *musée imaginaire* sealed in polythene.

museful ('mjuːzfʊl), *a.* [f. MUSE *sb.*[2] + -FUL.] Absorbed in thought; thoughtful, pensive.

a **1618** SYLVESTER *Maiden's Blush* 185 In musefull care his Joseph calls hee quicke. **1700** DRYDEN *Pal. & Arc.* I. 541 Full of museful Mopings, which presage The loss of Reason. *a* **1810** C. B. BROWN *Carwin*, etc. (1822) II. 52 She was sitting in a museful posture. **1885** G. MEREDITH *Diana of Crossways* i, She is apt to spin it out of a museful mind, at her toilette, or by the lonely fire.

Hence '**musefully** *adv.*, in a museful manner.

1885 G. MEREDITH *Diana of Crossways* III. xiv. 276 Musefully listening, nursing a thought.

musehont: see MOUSE-HUNT[1].

musel, obs. f. MUZZLE; var. MESEL *Obs.*

'**museless**, *a. rare.* [f. MUSE *sb.*[1] + -LESS; in imitation of Gr. ἄμουσος, 'unpolished, inelegant, rude, gross' (L. & Sc.).] Without learning; uncultured. Also, uninspired.

1644 MILTON *Areop.* (Arb.) 36 It is to be wonder'd how museless and unbookish they were, minding nought but the feats of Warre. **1819** SHELLEY *Cyclops* 489 He [Cyclops] is coming,.. Drunken, museless, awkward, yelling, Far along his rocky dwelling. **1877** RUSKIN *Fors Clav.* lxxiii. 16 The museless cry of the multitude. **1882** G. M. HOPKINS *Let.* 4 Nov. (1955) 159 My mind is dull and museless. **1958** P. L. FERMOR *Mani* i. 6 Nothing in the grace and the enchantment of all this could remind one of museless and unbookish Sparta.

Hence '**muselessness**.

1877 RUSKIN *Fors Clav.* lxxxiii. 360 That Deadly Muselessness of the Cameronian leaders.

musell, obs. form of MUZZLE *v.*

musellim (mʊ'sɛlɪm). *Hist.* Forms: α. 7 **musellem**, 8 **mosolem**, 9 **musselim, musellim**; β. **mutsel(l)im**. [Arab. *musallim*, lit. paymaster, act. pple. of *sallama* to pay, 2nd conjug. of *salama*. The β forms represent *mutasallim*, the pple. of the 5th conjug. of the same verb.] A Turkish officer, the lieutenant of a pasha.

α. **1687** A. LOVELL tr. *Thevenot's Trav.* 193 A Convoy of three hundred Horse, and two hundred Foot, under the Command of the Musellem. **1703** MAUNDRELL *Journ. Jerus.* 29 Mar. (1721) 78 The Mosolem or Governour of the City. **1813** BYRON *Bride Abydos* I. xii, More ill-got wealth, a meaner soul Holds not a Musselim's control. **1847** MRS. A. KERR tr. *Ranke's Hist. Servia* 348 The power which.. had been conceded to his Musellims.

β. **1844** KITTO *Phys. Hist. Palestine* vi. 161 Its fisheries were.. rented of the Mutsellim of Szaffad by some fishermen of that town. **1855** OGILVIE *Suppl.* Mutselim.

Muselman, obs. form of MUSSELMAN.

†'**musen**, *v. Obs. rare*⁻¹. [? a. MHG. *mûsen* (inf.) in the same sense: see MOULT *v.*] = MEW *v.*[1] 2.

1623 COCKERAM, *Pollard*, is a Stagge.. hauing cast his head,.. then he is said to musen. **1658** PHILLIPS, *Musen*, a term among Hunters, is when a Stag.. casts his Head.

museography (mjuːziː'ɒgrəfɪ). [f. Gr. μουσεῖον MUSEUM: see -GRAPHY.] The systematic description of the contents of museums. Also = MUSEOLOGY.

1904 D. MURRAY *Museums* II. 15 Museography. **1953** *Times* 4 Mar. 9/6 An exhibition that is certainly a remarkable example of showmanship or, as it is now called, museography. **1973** *Guardian* 20 Jan. 10/2 French museography has improved.

So **muse'ographer, muse'ographist**, one who describes the contents of museums systematically; also **museo'graphical** *a.*

1776 DA COSTA *Elem. Conchol.* 57 Most of the naturalists and museographists have included Shells in their works. **1880** *Athenæum* 9 Oct. 470/3 Between the museographers and the pure historians works of art are in danger of becoming transformed into scientific specimens. **1935** R. B. PERRY *Tht. & Char. of W. James* I. ix. 176 He had no archaeological or museographical interest.

museology (mjuːziː'ɒlədʒɪ). [Formed as prec.: see -OLOGY.] The science of arranging museums.

1885 *Science* 31 July 82/1 Devices.. in which museology has been notably advanced by us. **1887** HYATT in *Proc. Boston Soc. Nat. Hist.* 4 May 361 The first of the Guides to the Society's Museum.. is an experiment of considerable importance in Museology. **1904** D. MURRAY *Museums* II. 41. **1946** *Nature* 9 Nov. 678/2 Another interesting connexion with the University of Chicago is the establishment of university classes in museology in the Department of Anthropology of the Museum. **1957** G. CLARK *Archaeology & Society* (ed. 3) i. 36 Prehistoric archaeology was virtually a branch of museology. **1973** *Nature* 21–28 Dec. 541/1 Dr. Carmichael also achieved renown as a science administrator in the worlds of academia, museology and government.

Hence **museo'logical** *a.*; **muse'ologist**, one versed in museology.

1899 *Nat. Science* Sept. 171 The museum as a whole is painfully suggestive of what museologists call 'the fat boy'. **1949** K. CLARK *Landscape into Art* 137 Cézanne's *petite sensation* was transformed into the most cerebral and museological of all styles—cubism. **1960** *Spectator* 4 Nov. 693 Modern methods of reproduction and museological arrangement. **1970** *Times* 18 Mar. 11/7, I.. would rather enjoy the image of myself as a kind of museological Hell's Angel or Jesse James.

†**muser**[1]. *Obs. rare*⁻¹. [Of obscure origin; possibly an error.] (See quot.)

a **1548** HALL *Chron.*, *Hen. VIII* 9 b, In the frount of the chafron was a goodly plume set full of musers or trimblyng spangles of gold.

muser[2] ('mjuːzə(r)). In 4 musure. [f. MUSE *v.* + -ER[1]; the earlier form is a. OF. *museor.*] One who muses; one engaged in thought or meditation. Also, †a designer or schemer (*obs.*).

1382 WYCLIF *Isa.* xxix. 24 The musures [Vulg. *mussitatores*] shul lerne the lawe. **1551** RECORDE *Cast. Knowl.* Ded. (1556) 2 The musers of mischeif wrought muche to the contrary. **1597** J. PAYNE *Royal Exch.* 38 There ys another sorte.., who be greate musers on Gods longe suffringe. **1677** GALE *Crt. Gentiles* II. IV. 87 Was it not a great Saying.. The greatest Musers are the best Artists? **1755** JOHNSON, *Muser*,.. one who muses; one apt to be absent of mind. **1828** J. STERLING *Ess. & Tales* (1848) II. 75 The sound of tumult or of fear Rouses the muser's lazy ear. **1887** STEVENSON *House Beautiful*, Oft [shall] the morning muser see Larks rising from the broomy lea.

muserde, musere: see MUSARD, MOUSE-EAR.

muserole, -roll, variant forms of MUSROL.

†**'musery**[1]. *Obs. rare*$^{-1}$. [a. OF. *muserie*, f. *muser* MUSE *v.*] An amusement, pastime.

*c*1430 *Pilgr. Lyf Manhode* II. lxix. (1869) 102 Pleyinge.. at dees, at merelles, and manye oothere museryes.

'musery[2]. *rare*$^{-1}$. [MUS(E *sb.*[1] + -ERY.] The work of the Muses.

1869 G. MEREDITH *Let.* 19 Dec. (1970) I. 407 Why, this stuff is not the Muse, it's Musery.

muset[1] ('mju:zɪt). *Obs.* exc. *dial.* Also 6 musit, 7 musett, 9 *dial.* mussit. [a. OF. *mucette, mussette*, 'a little hole, corner, or hoord to hide things in' (Cotgr.), f. *muce, musse*: see MEUSE.] = MEUSE *sb.* 1. Also, a hare's 'form'.

1592 SHAKS. *Ven. & Ad.* 683 The many musits through the which he goes, Are like a laberinth to amaze his foes. **1595** MARKHAM *Gentl. Acad.* 32 We terme.. the places through the which she [*sc.* the hare] goeth to releefe, her muset. **1600** HOLLAND *Livy* XXXVIII. xlix. 1015 To prevent those Thracian theeves that they should not hide themselves within their peakish holes & ordinarie covert musets. **1653** CHISENHALE *Cath. Hist.* Ep. Ded. A 4, The Author.. had no sooner escaped out of the English sheep-fold, but straightway he discovers the Muset thorow which he stole. **1688** R. HOLME *Armoury* II 134/2 A Hare [is lodged] in his Forme or Musett.

attrib. **1594** BARNFIELD *Affect. Sheph.* II. xi. (Arb.) 13 Or with Hare-pypes (set in a muset hole) Wilt thou deceave the deep-earth-delving Coney?

†**muset**[2]. *Obs. rare*$^{-1}$. [a. OF. *muset*, also *musette* shrew-mouse.] A shrew-mouse.

1601 HOLLAND *Pliny* II. 375 Against the biting of these musets or hardi-shrews [L. *muris aranei morsibus*].

musette (mju:'zɛt). [a. F. *musette*, dim. of OF. *muse*: see MUSE *sb.*[3]]

1. A kind of bagpipe.

1390 GOWER *Conf.* III. 365 Bot yit herde I no pipe there To make noise in mannes Ere, Bot the Musette I myhte knowe. **1811** BUSBY *Dict. Mus.* (ed. 3), *Musars*, the name given to certain itinerant musicians who performed on the Musette. **1905** *Edin. Rev.* Apr. 321 The sound of pipes and musettes.

2. A soft pastoral air imitating the sound of the bagpipe; a dance for which this music served.

1811 BUSBY *Dict. Mus.* (ed. 3), *Musette*, the name of an air generally written in common-time... Dances were formerly invented of a similar cast, and which were also called Musettes. **1879** STAINER *Music of Bible* 119 A piece of music written in the style of bagpipe music came.. to be called a musette. **1893** *Times* 21 Dec. 14/2 The lively gavotte, with its cleverly-scored musette.

3. A reed stop on an organ.

1825 DANNELEY *Encycl. Mus.*, *Musette*, an organ stop made of pewter, of the reed kind and of eight feet; called by the Germans *sackpfeife*. **1855** HOPKINS *Organ* 328 The Madelaine, Paris... Clavier de Récit Expressif... Muzette. *Ibid.* 333 Abbeville... Pedal, 6 Stops... Musette. **1888** tr. *Locher's Explan. Organ Stops* 63 *Schalmei*, a soft reed stop.. generally labelled Musette in French organs.

4. A small and simple variety of oboe (*Cent. Dict.* 1890).

1895 *Army & Navy Price List* 15 Sept. 1659 Musettes... Oboes [etc.].

5. In full, ***musette bag***. A type of canvas haversack. orig. *Mil.*

1923 E. HEMINGWAY *Three Stories* 13 The young gentleman had a musette over his shoulder. **1934** WEBSTER, Musette bag. **1943** [see *flight bag* (FLIGHT *sb.*[1] 14)]. **1949** A. HAYES *Girl on Via Flaminia* iii. 38 He got up from the bed and went to the table where he had placed the musette bag. He began to unbuckle the straps. **1955** J. THOMAS *No Banners* xxiii. 229 Alfred had the Sten gun in a canvas *musette* tied with string and slung over his shoulder. **1961** J. HELLER *Catch-22* (1962) xiii. 130 Major—de Coverely.. packed his musette bag, commandeered a plane and.. had himself flown to that city to rent two apartments. **1965** *Sun* 3 Nov. 11/5 The musette, or featherweight knapsack from the Continent, has largely replaced the saddlebag. **1968** *Amer. Hist. Illustrated* July (rear cover), The diary stayed behind in his musette bag.

museum (mju:'zɪəm). Also 7–8 **musæum**, 8 **muséum**; 9 *pl.* **musea**, now usu. **museums**. [a. L. *mūsēum*, ad. Gr. μουσεῖον a seat of the Muses, f. μοῦσα MUSE *sb.*[1] Cf. F. *musée* masc., Sp., Pg., It. *museo*.]

1. a. *Hist.* (with capital M.) The university building erected at Alexandria by Ptolemy Soter.

1615 G. SANDYS *Trav.* 111 That famous Musæum founded by Philadelphus. **1869** RAWLINSON *Anc. Hist.* 236 The 'Museum', or university building, comprised chambers for the Professors.

†b. *gen.* A building or apartment dedicated to the pursuit of learning or the arts; a 'home of the Muses'; a scholar's 'study'. *Obs.*

*c*1645 HOWELL *Lett.* (1655) I. VI. xx. 265 To my Honoured Friend and Fa. Mr. Ben Johnson. I thank you for the last *regalo* you gave me at your Musæum, and for the good company. **1675** in Willis & Clark *Cambridge* (1886) III. 42 A Legacy of five hundred pounds towards the building a Musæum, or commencement house. **1706** PHILLIPS (ed. Kersey), *Museum*, a Study or Library; also a College or Publick Place for the Resort of Learned Men. **1757** MRS. GRIFFITH *Lett. Henry & Frances* (1767) II. 82 It gives me uneasiness, in my musæum, when any sentiment or criticism occurs to me, that I cannot immediately communicate it to you. **1760** C. JOHNSTON *Chrysal* (1783) I. xvi. 92 He waited on the Virtuoso, and.. was immediately admitted to an audience in his musæum.

2. a. A building or portion of a building used as a repository for the preservation and exhibition of objects illustrative of antiquities, natural history, fine and industrial art, or some particular branch of any of these subjects, either generally or with reference to a definite region or period. Also applied to the collection of objects itself.

Although a 'museum' may include a library (as does the British Museum) or a picture gallery, the word is not in ordinary Eng. use applied to an institution of which either of these is the sole or the most prominent feature. On the continent the corresponding word is often used with reference to a collection of works of painting or sculpture, and when so used is rendered 'museum' in English.

1683 *Phil. Trans.* XIII. 108 Mr. Ashmole's Musæum at Oxford. **1706** PHILLIPS (ed. Kersey) s.v., The *Museum* or *Ashmole's Museum*, a neat Building in the City of Oxford. **1710** HEARNE *Collect.* (O.H.S.) III. 35 Mr. Lhuyd of the Muséum. **1771** SMOLLETT *Humph. Cl.* 2 June, Let. ii, I have seen the British Museum; which is a noble collection. **1778** MISS BURNEY *Evelina* (1791) I. xxiii. 129 [He] changed the subject to Cox's Museum, and asked what we thought of it? **1816** T. D. WHITAKER *Loidis & Elmete* 124 It would perhaps be difficult for all the musea of the kingdom to find half a dozen originals [of the wax impressions of seals] of the same date. **1863** LYELL *Antiq. Man* 10 Swords and shields of that metal, now in the Museum of Copenhagen. **1893** M. HOWE *Honor* 320, I was expected to give ten thousand to the Art Museum. **1936** *S.P.E. Tract* XLV. 176 There are.. a few English words whose meaning in the United States corresponds more closely to that of their French counterparts than to their meaning in England; e.g. ..*museum*. **1950** [see GALLERY *sb.* 6]. **1975** *Times* 27 Sept. 14/6 The first railway museum in Britain was opened.. at York in 1928.

b. *attrib.* and *Comb.*, as ***museum-goer, interest, specimen, -value***; **museum piece**, an object suitable for exhibition in a museum; also *transf.* (usu. with derogatory sense).

1930 *Times Educ. Suppl.* 23 Aug. 362/2 April is the general 'peak' month for museum-goers. **1971** *Daily Tel.* 11 June 16 An admission charge would not of course greatly deter the habitual museum-goer. **1933** P. GODFREY *Back-Stage* xiv. 180 The attempt of recent years to stage a music-hall revival has unearthed a few shaky veterans of variety, who have little more than a museum interest for the post-War generation. **1901** *Brit. Chess Mag.* XXI. 351 The more stately carved pieces (named for the sake of distinction 'museum-pieces'). **1908** R. FRY *Let.* 12 Dec. (1972) I. 306 It would be a great Museum piece, but.. the price is high for Ribera. **1920** W. J. LOCKE *House of Baltazar* iii. 31 Quong Ho was admitted to be a museum-piece of discretion. **1923** J. GALSWORTHY *Captures* 228, I felt as if I had a priceless museum piece which a single stumble might shatter to fragments. **1928** —— *Swan Song* I. xi. 82 The girl and her brother had been museum pieces, two Americans without money to speak of. **1936** L. MACNEICE tr. *Aeschylus' Agamemnon* Pref. 8 It is my hope that the play emerges as a play and not as a museum piece. **1949** B. A. BOTKIN *Treas. S. Folklore* I. i. 4 What saves these relics of the past from being mere museum-pieces is their symbolic and often living relation to the culture of the region. **1955** *Amer. Speech* XXX. 94 *Museum piece*,.. an old truck. **1960** H. NICOLSON *Let.* 22 Sept. (1968) 385, I had to lunch with such a bore... He is a museum piece; it is like seeing a railway-engine of 1854. **1964** D. VARADAY *Gara-Yaka* v. 48 He.. handed over his rifle, an ancient muzzle-loading museum piece. **1974** P. ERDMAN *Silver Bears* xv. 153, I am looked upon as a mildly amusing curiosity—even a museum piece. **1899** *Allbutt's Syst. Med.* VI. 257 The museum specimen of a uterus of a much quoted case. **1893** COLLINGWOOD *Ruskin* I. 143 Flaws and interruptions destroy the museum-value of a mineral.

3. *transf.* and *fig.*

1753 HERVEY *Theron & Aspasia* (1755) I. i. 13 The boundless Musæum of the Universe. **1846** E. FITZGERALD *Lett.* (1889) I. 166 A heathy promontory there, good museum for conversation on old poets, &c. **1849** THACKERAY *Pendennis* I. xxiv. 228 Miss Blanche.. had quite a little museum of locks of hair in her treasure-chest. **1894** H. DRUMMOND *Ascent Man* 106 The physical body of Man ..is.. a museum of obsolete anatomies.

mu'seuming, *vbl. sb. colloq.* [f. MUSEUM + -ING[1].] The action of inspecting museums.

1838 OWEN in *Life* (1894) I. 139 We steam to Bonn; there a day or two museuming, and then for Home.

mu'seumish, *a. colloq.* [f. MUSEUM + -ISH[1].] Resembling a museum or its exhibits.

1926 D. H. LAWRENCE *Let.* (1932) 657, I wouldn't care to live in Assisi.. it's too museumish, not enough life in it now. **1937** *Observer* 5 Sept. 13/3, I must confess that I went to 'Ghosts' with some apprehension. Might not these unhappy far-off things seem too far off; might not the echo of battles long ago bring a museumish air to theatre walls?

mush (mʌʃ), *sb.*[1] Also (sense 3 d) **moosh**, 20 *dial.* **mosh**. [App. an onomatopœic alteration of MASH *sb.*[1]; sense 3 and the related MUSH *v.*[2] are prob. old, though not recorded till the 19th c. Sense 1 and 3 b may have been affected by Du. *moes*, formerly used in these senses.]

1. *N. Amer.* A kind of porridge made with meal (chiefly of maize) boiled in water or milk until it thickens. Freq. in phr. ***mush and milk***.

1671 J. HARDY *Last Voy. to Bermudas* 11 Indian corn.. Which being groun'd and boyl'd, Mush they make Their hungry Servants Hunger for to slake. **1745** E. KIMBER *Itinerant Observations Amer.* (1878) 34 The meaner Sort you find little else but Water amongst, when their Cyder is spent, Mush and Milk, or Molasses, Homine,.. and Fish, are their principal Diet. **1814** BRACKENRIDGE *Jrnl.* in *Views Louisiana* 202 A pot of mush for supper, with a pound of tallow in it. **1817** in *Essex Inst. Hist. Coll.* (1866) VIII. 244 They.. gave me a supper of mush and milk. **1828** COBBETT *Treat. Cobbett's Corn* ix. §156 Taking off a lump of the mush at the time, and putting it in the milk, you take up a spoonful at a time, having a little milk along with it; and this is called mush and milk. **1866** 'MARK TWAIN' *Lett. fr. Hawaii* (1967) 210 I'm disgusted with these mush-and-milk preacher travels. **1893** KATE SANBORN *Truthf. Wom. in S. California* 37 The old greenhorn above who had his supper of mush and milk. **1895** *Montgomery Ward Catal.* 534/1 China Oatmeal or Mush and Milk Set.. cream pitcher, bowl and plate.

2. *dial.* A kind of iron-ore found in concretionary masses.

1686 PLOT *Staffordsh.* iv. §17. 159 Mush the best of all [Iron-Ore].. many times fill'd with a briske sweet liquor which the Workmen drink greedily.

3. a. Anything soft and pulpy. Also, anything reduced to or resembling a mass of powder. Chiefly *dial.*

1824 MACTAGGART *Gallovid. Encycl.*, *Mush*, a vast of matters tossed together, such as straw, grain, hay, chaff, &c. **1841** EMERSON *Man the Reformer* Wks. (Bohn) II. 247 A poor fungus or mushroom.. that seemed nothing but a soft mush or jelly. **1847** HALLIWELL, *Mush*, anything mashed. **1855** ROBINSON *Whitby Gloss.*, *Mush*, any thing decayed to a state of powder. **1878** E. W. CLARK *Life Japan* 76 The rice field is stirred up into a perfect mush of mud. **1914** D. H. LAWRENCE *Widowing of Mrs. Holroyd* III. 74 One of my sons ..was shot till 'is shoulder was all of a mosh.

b. *U.S.* 'Fish ground up; chum; pomace; stosh' (*Cent. Dict.* 1890).

c. *transf.* and *fig.*

1841–4 EMERSON *Ess.*, *Friendship* Wks. (Bohn) I. 88, I hate, where I looked for.. a manly resistance, to find a mush of concession. **1856** MRS. CARLYLE *Lett.* (1883) II. 297 Stewed into mush, hearing a popular preacher. **1876** BESANT & RICE *Gold. Butterfly* xviii, Bringing everlasting disgrace on our town with such mush as that.

d. *slang.* The mouth or face. Freq. pronounced (mʊʃ) and with spelling **moosh**.

1859 G. W. MATSELL *Vocabulum* 127 *Mush*, the mouth. **1906** E. DYSON *Fact'ry 'Ands* xv. 202 Er stream iv water.. takes Fuzzy fair in the mush, heels him over. **1914** JACKSON & HELLYER *Vocab. Criminal Slang* 60 *Moosh, mush*,.. the human face... Also the mouth... Example: 'He's got a harp moosh,' i.e., Irish. **1919** *Dialect Notes* V. 66 *Mush*, the mouth. 'Stop his mush and give us a rest.' **1932** J. T. FARRELL *Young Lonigan* I. i. 20 That time he had pasted Weary in the mush with an icy snow-ball. **1953** K. TENNANT *Joyful Condemned* x. 88, I don't usually go round pushing my moosh into anyone's business. **1959** I. JEFFERIES *Thirteen Days* i. 18 He said if anybody opened his mush, he'd kill 'em. **1966** 'L. LANE' *ABZ of Scouse* 71 'Ey you wit' ther maggerty moosh. **1971** B. W. ALDISS *Soldier Erect* 53 My regret was that I had not given Wally a bunch of fives in the mush while I had the chance. *Ibid.* 194, I hit him smack in the mush. Not very hard but pleasureably hard. My right fist did not hurt a great deal—not as much as his face hurt him. **1972** K. BONFIGLIOLI *Don't point that Thing at Me* iv. 34 You ought to see his moosh, where I hit him, it's a treat, honest. **1974** T. BARLING *Shooter Man* i. 12 A big grin all over his ugly mush.

e. *Surfing slang.* The foam produced when a wave breaks.

1969 *Surfer* IX. 57 Hardy rides and cuts out as the shoulder flattens to mush. **1970** *Surf '70* (N.Z.) 13/2 If there is any flat mush the board tends to stop and lose its turning ability. **1971** *Studies in English* (Univ. Cape Town) Feb. 28 When a surfer is tired, he catches a wave all the way in. For the last part of the distance he will be riding the frommel; the soup; white water; the mush.

4. *Radio.* Interference or noise heard as a hissing or the sound (ʃ); *spec.* (see quot. 1924).

1924 *Harmsworth's Wireless Encycl.* II. 1456 *Mush*, term used for the irregular intermediate frequencies set up by an arc transmitter which interfere with the fundamental wavelengths. **1927** [see BACKGROUND *sb.* 3]. **1928** *Observer* 1 July 4/4 In listening to very faint signals from a great distance a limit is put by the 'mush' and statics and other noises brought in from the aerial. **1952** *Electronic Engin.* XXIV. 120 Unwanted low frequency fluctuations of high frequency 'mush'. **1971** *Daily Mail* 17 Nov. 9/3 Were subjected to a continuous 'hissing noise', or 'electronic mush'.

5. *attrib.* and *Comb.*, as (sense 1) ***mush pan, pot***; **mush-head**, a person of a yielding disposition; one lacking in firmness; so ***mush-headed*** adj.; **mush-ice**, water only partly frozen, ice mixed with water; **mush-sugar**, a mixture of syrup and crystals of sugar.

1890 BARRÈRE & LELAND *Dict. Slang* II. 77/2 *Mush-head* (American), a stupid, witless fellow. **1919** H. L. WILSON *Ma Pettengill* ii. 63, I up and told her flat she could never run a boarding-house and make it pay; that no woman could who hadn't learned to say 'No!' and she was too much of a mushhead for that. **1932** *Screenland* Apr. 70/1 She has married the poor little mush-head that had been wished upon her. **1914** R. CULLUM *Way of Strong* III. viii. 294 The game isn't worth it, fighting this mush-headed crowd who have to get other folks to think for 'em. **1815** *Niles' Weekly Reg.* IX. 201/2 You may, by digging down three feet, take a pole sixty feet long and with the strength of your hands run it down the whole length, and find no termination of what is called the mush ice. **1907** J. LONDON *White Fang* 202 The fall of the year, when the first snows were falling and mush-ice was running in the river. **1966** R. M. PATTERSON *Trail* 86 They came.. poling and tracking against the slowly drifting mush ice of the fall. **1847** J. S. ROBB *Squatter Life* 59 Betsy Jones' Tumble in the Mush Pan. **1940** H. H. HATCHER *Buckeye Country* 173 When his self-made paste-board hat fell to pieces.. he covered his head with his mush pan. **1847** H. HOWE *Hist. Coll. Ohio* 432 Johnny, who wore on his head a tin utensil which answered both as a cap and a mush pot, filled it with water and quenched the fire. **1868** *Rep. Iowa Agric. Soc.* 1867 178 When sugar is contemplated, White Imphee is.. the best, as all I have made went to thick mush sugar immediately.

mush (mʌʃ), *sb.*[2] *slang.* [Shortened form of MUSHROOM.]

1. An umbrella. Chiefly *attrib.* in **mush-faker** = *mushroom-faker.* So **mush-faking** *vbl. sb.*

1821 HAGGART *Life* 56 Tommy Twenty, a mush toper feeker. **1851** MAYHEW *Lond. Labour* II. 127 The term [Mushroom-fakers]..has become very generally condensed among those who carry on the trade—they are now mush-fakers. **1856** MAYHEW *Gt. World Lond.* 6 note, The mouth has come to be styled the 'tater-trap';..umbrellas, 'mushrooms' (or, briefly, 'mush');..and so on. **1893** P. H. EMERSON *Signor Lippo* xx. 91 My old man..got his dudder by chinay-faking and mush-faking.

2. A 'small' cab-proprietor; a cab-driver who owns one, two, or three cabs. So **'musher** in the same sense. **'mushing** *vbl. sb.*, cab-owning on a small scale.

1887 *Globe* 22 Apr. 3 A musher, or a struggler, is a man who drives a horse and cab which is his own property, and his only 'lot'. *Ibid.*, 'Mushing' in the cab-trade is another word for 'struggling'. **1892** *Labour Commission* Gloss., *Little mushes*, term applied to those in the cab-driving industry who drive their own vehicles. **1902** *Academy* 27 Dec. 706/2 A Mush is the owner of 3 or 4 cabs.

mush (mʌʃ), *sb.*[3] [f. MUSH *v.*[3]] A journey made through snow with a dog-sledge.

1910 R. SERVICE *Trail of '98* 341, I was still weak from my illness and my long mush had wearied me. **1926** *Glasgow Herald* 8 Mar. 10/7 From Hudson in northern Ontario it is a twelve-day 'mush' for men and dogs over the frozen sub-arctic prairie to the Red Lake district. **1965** *Kingston* (Ont.) *Whig-Standard* 8 Feb. 8/6 It's 'Mush, Mush' time for Owner-driver Vern Zoschke and his Dogs.

mush (mʊʃ, mʌʃ), *sb.*[4] *Mil. slang.* Also **moosh.** [? f. MUSH *v.*[2]] A guardroom or cell; a military prison. Also (*Austral.*), prison food.

1917 W. MUIR *Observations of Orderly* xiv. 228 If one of those 'hooks' [*sc.* pilferers] were caught, he would be first 'rammed in the mush' (put in the guardroom). **1919** *Athenæum* 8 Aug. 727/2 When a man was 'run in' the guardroom he was in 'clink' or in 'moosh'. **1933** E. PARTRIDGE *Words, Words, Words!* III. 204 *Mush*, sometimes spelt and pronounced *moosh*..denotes guard-room or cell(s). **1943** HUNT & PRINGLE *Service Slang* 46 *Mush*, the *glasshouse* or guardroom. **1945** BAKER *Austral. Lang.* vii. 141 Jail food is *moosh*.

mush (mʊʃ), *sb.*[5] *slang.* Also **moosh.** [Orig. uncertain.] Man, 'chap'; hence also as a term of address.

1936 J. CURTIS *Gilt Kid* v. 53 I'm a bit of a coring mush, myself. **1943** *Police Jrnl.* Mar. 69 *Moosh*, a person, an individual. **1950** P. TEMPEST *Lag's Lexicon* 137 '*Moosh*' is used more as a greeting: 'Hullo, Moosh.' **1961** J. STROUD *Touch & Go* xvii. 183 Waiter!.. Look, moosh, this is cold. **1961** J. MACLAREN-ROSS *Doomsday Book* vii. 76 Long's you don't go laughing in the wrong place, mush. **1966** *New Statesman* 23 Dec. 934/3 My old woman's gone to Paris with a black moosh. **1968** A. DIMENT *Bang Bang Birds* v. 57 So this mush is running a string of..houses of ill-repute... So what? **1972** J. BROWN *Chancer* i. 12 Look, moosh, you'll strip off or I'll take them off you.

mush (mʌʃ), *sb.*[6] *slang.* Shortened f. MOUSTACHE, MUSTACHE *sb.*

1967 C. DRUMMOND *Death at Furlong Post* xv. 181 Take my oath it's he..with his hair parted..and the mush shaved off his lip. **1969** K. GILES *Death cracks Bottle* xiii. 172 He read one of these Service ads... You know, a young bloke with a mush telling troops to go plunging into the jungle.

†**mush,** *a. Obs.* In 6 **musche.** [f. MUSH *v.*[1]] = MUSHED *ppl. a.*

1578 *Inv. R. Wardrobe* (1815) 228 Ane [doublet]..of blak musche taffetie.

mush (mʌʃ), *v.*[1] *Sc.* Also 6–7 **musche.** [? a. OF. *moucher* to cut, trim.] *trans.* 'To cut out with a stamp, to nick or notch, to make into flounces. (Commonly applied to grave-clothes)' (Jam.); to 'puff'. Hence **mushed** *ppl. a.*, puffed. **'mushing** *vbl. sb.*, one of many nicks or notches stamped upon a garment for ornament.

1578 *Inv. R. Wardrobe* (1815) 231 Ane quheit hieland mantill. Certane pecis of muschet arming furing. **1615** in *Thanes of Cawdor* (Spald. Club) 240 Item 3 quarteris of reid bukkram to musche out the sleivis xv s. **1684** SIR J. LAUDER *Hist. Notices Sc. Affairs* (1848) 538 Many other things ware spoke of as sumptuous and prodigall, viz.,..mushed-out silks, and flored hoods. **1752** J. LOUTHIAN *Form of Process* (ed. 2) 9 The Justice-General's [Robe] being lined with Ermine for Distinction, and the Justice-Clerk's being distinguished by Outcuttings or Mushings.

mush (mʌʃ), *v.*[2] *dial.* Also 9 **mosh.** [Onomatopœic alteration of MASH *v.*, suggestive of duller sound made in pounding something soft. Cf. the earlier MUSH *sb.*[1]] *trans.* and *intr.* 'To crush, pulverize, crumble; to mash, to reduce to pulp; to crumble or decay away' (E.D.D.).

1781 HUTTON *Tour to Caves* (ed. 2) 93 *Mush*, to crush, or crumble. **1848** A. B. EVANS *Leicestershire Words* 58, I thought that she would have moshed her children then and there. **1855** ROBINSON *Whitby Gloss.*, *To Mush*, to crumble, to moulder. **1861** GEO. ELIOT *Silas M.* vii. 111 'Folks as had the devil to back 'em were not likely to be so mushed' as poor Silas was.

mush (mʌʃ), *v.*[3] [Apparently f. Fr. *marchez* or *marchons*, imp. of *marcher* to advance, the command given to sled dogs; cf. MUSH *sb.*[3]] Also const. *on.* **a.** *intr.* To travel on foot through the snow with a dog-sledge (said also of the dogs); *trans.* to drive dogs through the snow.

[**1862** R. KENNICOTT *Jrnl.* in J. A. James *First Sci. Explor. Russian Amer.* (1942) 130 My dogs are *dogs*! and we will *mouche* very likely, after all.] **1897** *Medicine Hat* (Alberta) *News* 30 Sept. 7/4 It is laughable to hear the driver yell, 'Mush, Mush,' at them. **1900** J. LONDON *Son of Wolf* 5 'Come, mush on there, you poor sore-footed brutes!' he murmured. **1903** *Sun* (N.Y.) 22 Nov., His little boat was cut out, and then he started to 'mush' back over the ice. **1904** S. E. WHITE *Silent Places* xvii. 180 'Mush! Mush on!' shouted Sam. The four dogs leaned into their collars. **1914** R. CULLUM *Way of Strong* I. i. 1 Five great sled dogs crouched in their harness. They were waiting the long familiar command to 'mush'; an order they had not heard since the previous winter. **1927** *Brit. Weekly* 13 Jan. 409/2 They were mushing on to a new strike. **1932** *Sun* (Baltimore) 15 Jan. 1/5 Through a raging blizzard McDowell mushed a dog team the eighty miles to Aklavik. **1934** *Beaver* Sept. 26 Constable Lee and his Indian interpreter, Albert, came mushing up with a jingle of bells from Fort Providence to pay their annual visit to trappers in the bush. **1947** *Mazama* Dec. 6/2 Norris left Mt. McKinley Park station on 11 April and mushed his dog team to Base Camp arriving 15 April. **1963** R. D. SYMONS *Many Trails* 198 And hurry! Hurry! Before it is too late—mush, mush on—the whip cracks hysterically. **1966** *Kingston* (Ont.) *Whig-Standard* 25 Feb. 12/1 There hasn't been so much excitement over sled-dogs in the north since Leonard Sepala mushed through the land of the midnight sun.

b. *transf.* To travel (through snow or ice).

1898 W. N. ROBERTSON *Yukon Memories* 210 You think all the while you are nearing the top, and 'mush on', like viewing a ship at sea. **1906** 'O. HENRY' *Four Million* 106 I never got off the train since I mushed out of Seattle, and I'm hungry. **1958** P. BERTON *Klondike Fever* 19 He thought nothing of making a present of his trousers to a pantless native and mushing home in his red flannels. **1966** *Globe & Mail* (Toronto) 24 Jan. 17/8, I then struck out to mush to the nearest bus stop.

Hence **'mushing** *vbl. sb.*

1904 *Prof. Papers U.S. Geol. Survey* No. 20. 15 In 'mushing', the best progress is made in relatively cool weather. **1930** W. N. ROBERTSON *Yukon Memories* viii. 114 There is a lingering feeling that the monotonous *mushing* along has not been devoid of its pleasures. **1966** *Kingston* (Ont.) *Whig-Standard* 25 Feb. 12/1 Wilfrid Charles is regarded as a sure-pop betting cinch to retain the mushing title.

mush (mʌʃ), *v.*[4] *colloq.* [f. MUSH *sb.*[1] 3.] Const. *in.* To sink into a soft surface.

1948 N. SHUTE *No Highway* ii. 41 The landing was a hazardous one because of the alternate thaw and freeze: the skis [of the aircraft] mushed in beneath the icy crust. **1962** J. GLENN in *Into Orbit* 13, I..skimmed right over the top of a rice paddy—almost mushing into it.

musha ('mʌʃə), *int.* [a. Irish *maiseadh*, lit. 'if it is so'.] An exclamation of surprise used by Irish speakers.

1831 LOVER *Leg. & Stor. Irel.* 3 Musha, thin, do you tell me so? **1837** —— *Rory O'More* xlvi, Musha! but you're the very sowl of good nature. **1898** J. D. BRAYSHAW *Slum Silhouettes* 15 Oh, musha! the divil a drown ye'll drown, Murty Hooligan, while there's hemp for the sowing. **1933** DAVIES & THOMSON tr. *O'Sullivan's Twenty Years A-Growing* i. 7 Ah, musha, youth is a queer thing.

mushal, -chee, var. ff. MUSSAL, -CHEE.

mushato(e, mushe, obs. ff. MUSTACHIO, MUCH.

musher ('mʌʃə(r)). [f. MUSH *v.*[3] + -ER[1].] A person who mushes; one who travels through snow on foot (with a dog-sledge). Also *fig.*

c **1900** *Western Miner* (1963) Mar. 30/1 Way up north there's a rail road... It followed the tracks of the mushers, Where they grasped the rocks for a hold. **1902** L. MCKEE *Land of Nome* 178, I felt that I had received a very high compliment..when an old-timer in the party..told me that I was a 'musher from hell'. **1925** *Chambers's Jrnl.* July 456/2 Those far northern regions are inaccessible..except to the most hardy and expert 'mushers'. **1948** *Time* 19 July 34/3 Klondike Mike, the greatest of the mushers, the sourdough who struck it rich and kept his poke, is a living legend. **1973** *Islander* (Victoria, B.C.) 20 May 3/1 Art Fraser, owner and musher of the dog team, was my guide.

mushere, obs. form of MOUSE-EAR.

musherom, -on, -oom, etc.: see MUSHROOM.

mushie ('mʌʃɪ). Austral. colloq. shortening of MUSHROOM *sb.* 1.

1935 O. P. MEYER *Four of Us* 52, I don't see many mushies yet. **1972** *Sunday Mail* (Brisbane) 9 Jan. 5/2 Mushies are seldom sold, and are grown so easily from cow manure.. that they're usually given away.

mushily ('mʌʃɪlɪ), *adv.* [f. MUSHY *a.* + -LY[2].] In a soft or mushy manner.

1896 'MARK TWAIN' in *Harper's Mag.* Jan. 296/2 The column of inert mortality sank mushily to the ground. **1910** 'O. HENRY' *Strictly Business* xvi. 187 'A cool hundred,' said Fuzzy thoughtfully and mushily. *a* **1935** T. E. LAWRENCE *Mint* (1955) II. xiv. 138 A black east wind froze the sweat mushily over our skins. **1971** 'D. SHANNON' *Ringer* (1972) ix. 147 'That I did,' confirmed Mr. Gebhart mushily. ''Scuse me—get my teeth—.'

mushiness ('mʌʃɪnɪs). *colloq.* [f. MUSHY *a.* + -NESS.] The condition of being soft or pulpy; also *fig.*, sentimental character, weakness, sloppiness.

1890 SARAH J. DUNCAN *Soc. Departure* 221 The unutterable mushiness of the 'bullock's heart' [fruit]. **1893** 'M. RUTHERFORD' *Cath. Furze* II. xiv. 70 Partly this distressing weakness is due to the absence of a clear conviction that we are right;..but frequently it is simple mushiness of character. **1946** A. L. BACHARACH *Brit. Music of our Time* xv. 197 One is perhaps disconcerted by an harmonic mushiness—he was especially fond of the now much-abused chords of the seventh and ninth. **1962** *Yale Rev.* June 540 Pound puts Joyce with Hueffer, diametrically opposite to 'the softness and mushiness of the neo-symbolist movement'.

‖**mushla** ('mʌʃlɔː). Also 7 **mushelaw,** 7–9 **mishlaw.** [Mosquito *mushla* (A. Henderson).] A fermented liquor from plantain, cassava, maize, etc.

1697 DAMPIER *Voy.* xi. 314 The Moskito Indians will take a ripe Plantain and roast it; then take a pint and half of Water in a Calabash, and squeeze the Plantain in pieces with their hands, mixing it with the Water; then they drink it all off together: this they call Mishlaw. *c* **1699** M. W. *Mosqueto Indians* in *Collect. Voy.* (Churchill 1732) VI. 293 Their plantain drink they call Mushelaw. **1827** O. W. ROBERTS *Voy. Centr. Amer.* 128 Preparations were making for a grand feast and mishlaw drink. **1842** T. YOUNG *Narr. Resid. Mosquito Shore* iii. 33 It is a custom to let their quarrels rest until they get inflamed by their filthy mushla.

mush-melon, -millian, obs. ff. MUSK-MELON.

'mushrat. = MUSK-RAT 1, 2. *N. Amer.*

1890 *Dialect Notes* I. 74 *Mushrat*, the muskrat or musquash. **1901** R. CONNOR *Man from Glengarry* 19 The Glengarry men..despised the Murphy gang as sawlogmen; 'log-rollers' or 'mushrats' they called them. **1939** W. FAULKNER *Wild Palms* 218 If I took aboard every floating sardine can you sonabitchin mushrats want me to I wouldn't even have room forrard for a leadsman. **1939** T. H. RADDALL *Pied Piper* 45 An' I'm goin' to play hell with you, you game-poachin', fish-spearin', wood-stealin' ol' mushrat! **1954** C. BRUCE *Channel Shore* 18 Stan was carrying on..talk of mushrats and rabbit-snaring. **1954** *Encounter* Oct. 3/2 All the lesser beasts—coon and possum and beaver and mink and mushrat (not muskrat: mushrat); they were still there.

mushroom ('mʌʃruːm), *sb.* Forms: α. 5 **musseroun,** 5–7 **muscheron,** 6 **mus(s)heron, mousheroun,** 7 **mucheron (muceron),** 8 **mushroon;** β. 6 **musherom, mousherom, mushrum(m)e, -romme, (mushorme),** 6–7 **mushrum, -rom,** 7 **muschrom(be, (mes-, musrume, mustrome),** 7 **musheroom, mushroome,** 6– **mushroom;** γ. 6 **moshrump, (mushrumpt), moushrimpe,** 6–7 **mus(c)hrump(e, mushrompe, (mustrump);** δ. 6 **mushrubbe,** 7 **mushrub.** See also MOUSSERON. [a. F. *mousseron* (OF. *moisseron*, 1389 in Hatz.-Darm.), usually held to be a derivative of *mousse* moss.]

1. In early use, a fungus of any of the larger 'umbrella-shaped' species, to which the names *toad's hat* and *toadstool* were also applied indiscriminately. Now commonly restricted to the common edible mushroom, *Agaricus campestris*, or to this and species that closely resemble it in general appearance. Some apply *mushroom* to any fungus supposed to be edible, and *toadstool* to any that is believed to be deleterious. Certain botanical writers have used the word as equivalent to FUNGUS. The mushroom is a proverbial type of rapid growth.

14.. *Voc.* in Wr.-Wülcker 597/13 *Mussetum*, musserouns. *c* **1440** *Promp. Parv.* 349/1 Muscheron, toodys hatte, *boletus*, *fungus*. **1533** ELYOT *Cast. Helthe* (1539) 89 Beware of musherons,..and al other thinges, whiche wyll sone putrifie. **1563** HYLL *Art Garden.* (1593) 30 The Toad stooles or Mushrooms, which grow out of the Walnut tree, and bee stiffe and hard. **1595** SOUTHWELL *Poems* (Grosart) 69 He that high grouth on cedars did bestowe, Gave also lowly mushrumpes [*v.r.* mushrumpts] leave to growe. **1612** W. PARKES *Curtaine-Dr.* 20 That Cædar..Vnder whose girdle, nay beneath whose knee, The little Mesrumes louingly agree. **1656** MARNETTE *Perf. Cook* I. 312 With Sparagus, with Hartichokes, with Muscherons, with Cream [etc.]. **1732** ARBUTHNOT *Rules of Diet* in *Aliments*, etc. I. 258 Mushrooms contain an Oil of a volatile Salt. **1818** KEATS *Endym.* IV. 234 For wine we left our heath, and yellow brooms, And cold mushrooms. **1846** LINDLEY *Veg. Kingd.* 37 In Paris none [*i.e.* no fungi] are permitted to appear in the markets except the common Truffle, Morel, and Mushroom. **1887** BENTLEY *Bot.* (ed. 5) 378 Fungi or Mushrooms.

2. *fig.* **a.** A person or family that has suddenly sprung into notice; an upstart. Also applied to a city, an institution, etc., that is of sudden growth.

a **1593** MARLOWE *Edw. II* (1598) C 1 b, A night growne mushrump, Such a one as my Lord of Cornewall is. **1622** *Interpreter* A 3 b, He may not..seeme to shrinke, withdraw, giue way, whilst other mushrumpes doe the state betray. **1651** HOWELL *Venice* 204 Which Commonwealths may be sayed to have bin but Mushrumps in point of duration. **1721** AMHERST *Terræ Fil.* No. 13 (1754) 66, I hear them scornfully call a rising great man an upstart, a mushroom, and a thing of yesterday. **1787** BENTHAM *Def. Usury* xiii. 179 Sheffield is an old oak; Birmingham is a mushroom. **1864** BURTON *Scot Abr.* I. ii. 96 The Stewarts..were mere mushrooms beside the descendants of the Guelphs.

†**b.** A contemptible person. *Obs.*

1594 ? GREENE *Selimus* Wks. (Grosart) XIV. 282 Summon a parley sirs, that we may know Whether these Mushroms here will yeeld or no. **1676** D'URFEY *Mad. Fickle* II. i, Come Ladies, I'le be your Gaurdian; Let these Musrumes stand if they dare. **1680** D. GRANVILLE in *Life* (1902) 224, I will make a filthy bustle before I dye among the Clergy of the nation, as contemptible a mushrump and silly ignoramus as some do make me. **1769** *Public Advertiser* 4 Oct. 2/2 A gouty Mushroom of an Earl from the West.

†**c.** An excrescence. *Obs. rare.*

1648 PRYNNE *Plea for Lords* 2 They are..the Exorbitances and Mushromes of Prerogative, the Wenns of just Government.

†**d.** A spontaneous growth. *Obs.*

1670 C. GATAKER in *Gataker's Antid. Errour* Ep. Ded. A ij b, Who endeavour to forget that they are Gods offspring, and would fain be taken for the Mushrooms of Chance.

3. *transf.* Something shaped like a mushroom. †**a.** In ornamental waterworks (see quot.). *Obs.*

1712 J. JAMES tr. *Le Blond's Gardening* 214 Mushrooms are a sort of inverted Bowl-dishes, cut with Scales on the upper Part, over which the Water falls into the Bason below.

b. = *mushroom anchor* (see 6 c).

1890 *Nature* 10 Apr. 539 A temporary light-vessel is substituted,..but probably before her mushroom bites the ground it has dragged somewhat.

c. *Archit.* A reinforced concrete pillar that broadens out towards the top, with the reinforcing rods passing upwards and outwards into a reinforced concrete slab forming part of the floor above, which is thereby supported by the pillars without the use of beams. Freq. *attrib.*

1907 *Western Architect* May 51/1 The essential feature of this new construction is the formation of a so-called mushroom at the top of each column, by extending its reinforcing rods, laterally, some four feet or more out into the slab in a radial direction and supporting on these, ring rods, which, in turn, carry the lighter reinforcement for the slab construction. **1927** T. P. BENNETT *Archit. Design in Concrete* 14 A scheme similar in principle has been employed in a number of factory buildings, and has acquired the name of 'Mushroom' construction. **1936** *Archit. Rev.* LXXX. 113/1 (*caption*) These conditions have been met by an adaptation of the 'mushroom' floor slab type of construction. Each floor consists of a reinforced concrete slab, 10 ins. thick, supported on external wall columns, spaced 21 ft. centre to centre, and two internal columns with mushroom caps. **1941** S. GIEDION *Space, Time & Archit.* VI. 374 The American engineer C. A. P. Turner had been experimenting with the mushroom system a year before Maillart, but the Swiss engineer had employed slabs as basic elements in bridges since the beginning of the century. **1963** tr. *Hatje's Encycl. Mod. Archit.* 182/2 His [*sc.* Robert Maillart's] most important invention in the field of high structures was made in 1908 with mushroom slab construction, which he used for the first time on a large scale in 1910. **1969** W. R. DALZELL *Architecture* 41 (*caption*) Reinforced concrete mushrooms support slab constructions.

d. A cloud (of smoke, fire, etc.) that spreads upwards and outwards.

1916 J. BUCHAN *Greenmantle* xxi. 291 There was the dull shock of an explosion and a mushroom of red earth. **1924** A. J. SMALL *Frozen Gold* iv. 110 A sudden, abrupt mushroom of smoke spread out above the building on the uprush of air. **1945** *N.Y. Times* 26 Sept. 16/6 At first it was a giant column that soon took the shape of a supramundane mushroom. **1952** G. WILSON *Julien Ware* xvi. 129 He..pulled energetically at the stem until a mushroom of smoke hung above his head. **1954** *Amer. Speech* xxix. 275 *Mushroom*, a fire which, reaching a ceiling and finding no outlet, starts to spread out and burn downward.

e. A mushroom-shaped implement used in darning.

1931 'R. CROMPTON' *William's Crowded Hours* viii. 172 The cavity through which both her fist and the darning 'mushroom' slipped so unavailingly. **1931** R. H. HEATON *Perfect Hostess* 95 Little comforts for the work-basket... Ribbon threader. Mushroom for darning. **1969** E. H. PINTO *Treen* vii. 134 Cabbage pressers..are larger versions of 'mushroom' darners, usually with the button end about 5 in. in diameter.

4. a. *slang.* An umbrella.

1856 [see MUSH *sb.*[2] 1]. **1871** 'M. LEGRAND' *Cambr. Freshm.* 87 Mr. Pokyr said he would take care of my umbrella—'mushroom' was the term he used.

b. *colloq.* A low-crowned circular hat, esp. a lady's straw hat with down-curving brim.

1865 *Hotten's Slang Dict.*, *Mushroom*, an inelegant round hat worn by demure ladies. **1896** GEORGIANA M. STISTED *Capt. Sir R. F. Burton* xi. 265 Many a pretty face.. surmounted by the 'mushroom' or 'pork-pie'. **1898** *Westm. Gaz.* 21 Apr. 3/2 The mushroom..is a quite round straw with a low crown. **1902** *Ibid.* 31 May 2/1 Mimi's costume consisted of a short holland overall and a brown straw mushroom.

5. = *mushroom-colour* (see 6 c).

1884 *West. Daily Press* 25 Apr. 7/6 The fanciful shade of mushroom. **1903** *Westm. Gaz.* 10 Sept. 4/2 A shade called mushroom..a fascinating sober and unusual tone.

6. *attrib.* and *Comb.* **a.** simple attrib., as ***mushroom-juice, -ketchup (-catchup), lip, minaret, omelette, pickle, -sauce, sculpture***; parasynthetic and similative ***mushroom-coloured, -like, -shaped*** adjs.

1748 *Mushroom juice [see KETCHUP]. **1808** MRS. RUNDELL *Dom. Cookery* (1824) 168 *Mushroom Ketchup. **1839** T. C. HOFLAND *Brit. Angler's Man.* viii. (1841) 147 Mushroom catchup. **1753** CHAMBERS *Cycl. Supp.* s.v. *Heath-moss*, The brown *mushroom-like *Coralloides.* **1962** D. HARDEN *Phoenicians* xi. 150 In tombs at Carthage jugs with *mushroom or trefoil lips abounded. **1930** R. CAMPBELL *Adamastor* 50 Their *mushroom minarets and toadstool towers. **1892** *Encycl. Pract. Cookery* I. XIII. 961/2 *Mushroom omelet—Either fresh or canned mushrooms may be used for this. **1954** G. M. LAPOLLA *Mushroom Cooking* 78 Mushroom omelette. One way of using mushroom stems. **1972** P. D. JAMES *Unsuitable Job for Woman* iv. 137 She made herself a mushroom omelette. **1747** H. GLASSE *Art of Cookery* ii. 35 Add a Spoonful of *Mushroom Pickle, pickled Mushrooms, or fresh, if you have them. **1911** W. OWEN *Let.* 25 Sept. (1967) 85 In the kitchen making mushroom pickle. **1747** H. GLASSE *Art of Cookery* ii. 35 To make *Mushroom-Sauce for White Fowls of all Sorts. **1771** MRS. HAYWOOD *New Present* 46 Mushroom Sauce. **1845** ELIZA ACTON *Mod. Cookery* 118 White Mushroom Sauce. **1970** *Washington Post* 30 Sept. B 1/5 This holy *mushroom sculpture of gray volcanic stone is part of the pre-Columbian art exhibit. **1835–6** *Todd's Cycl. Anat.* I. 39/2 The principal organ of motion in the pulmograda is the large..*mushroom-shaped disc.

b. *attrib.* quasi-*adj.* with the sense: Resembling a mushroom in rapidity of development or growth or in brief duration of existence; upstart; ephemeral.

1599 B. JONSON *Ev. Man out of Hum.* I. ii, These mushrompe gentlemen, That shoot vp in a night to place and worship. **1647** CLARENDON *Hist. Reb.* VI. §293 This was the end of that mushrump-army, which grew up and perished so soon that [etc.]. **1703** SAVAGE *Lett. Antients* lxviii. 207 A Mushrome Love sprung from a transitory View. **1707** E. FILMER *Defence Plays* 130 A new, upstart, Mushroom Sect, sprung from their own filthy Dunghill. **1818–60** WHATELY *Comm.-pl. Bk.* (1864) 145 He outlived his own mushroom-reputation. **1887** *Westm. Rev.* June 269 Radical millionaires, and mushroom aristocrats.

c. Special combinations: **mushroom anchor**, a mooring anchor having a saucer-shaped head upon a central shaft; **mushroom-bed**, a bed of horse-dung and fine earth specially prepared for mushroom growing; **mushroom city**, = *mushroom town* (below); **mushroom cloud**, the cloud of smoke that forms above the site of a nuclear explosion, with the characteristic shape of a tall pillar with a broad, flattish top; also *fig.*; (cf. sense 3 d); **mushroom colour**, a pale pinkish colour resembling that of a mushroom; so **mushroom-coloured** *a.*; †**mushroom-coral** = FUNGITE; **mushroom earth**, earth containing mushroom spawn; **mushroom-faker** *slang*, an itinerant umbrella-mender; **mushroom-flap** *obs.*, the cap of a common mushroom when fully opened; †**mushroom gall** (see quot.); **mushroom-grown** *a.*, sprung up spontaneously like mushrooms; **mushroom growth**, rapid growth like that of a mushroom; **mushroom hall** *dial.*, a house or hut erected by stealth (see quot.); **mushroom hat** = sense 4 b; **mushroom head**, (*a*) a kind of 'head' for a church bell; (*b*) the nose-plate on the inner part of the breech-plug of a breech-loading cannon (*Cent. Dict.* 1890); **mushroom-headed** *a.* (see quot.); **mushroom house**, a house specially constructed for growing mushrooms; **mushroom loaf** (see LOAF *sb.*[1] 2 d); **mushroom-man** (see quot.); **mushroom powder**, dried mushrooms powdered to serve as a flavouring; **mushroom-ring** = FAIRY-RING; **mushroom spawn**, the vegetative mycelium of mushrooms, usually embedded in an earthy matrix; **mushroom-stone** = FUNGITE; **mushroom sugar**, mannite derived from fungi; **mushroom town**, a town that has sprung up rapidly; **mushroom valve**, a lift valve whose moving element somewhat resembles a mushroom in shape.

1845 *Encycl. Metrop.* XIV. 548/1 An anchor of a very peculiar kind is employed to secure the vessels..; it is technically called the **mushroom anchor.* **1763** MILLS *Syst. Pract. Husb.* IV. 186 The spawn of mushrooms may be procured at almost any time, by those who have not already had *mushroom-beds in their gardens. **1860** H. GREELEY *Overland Journey* 140 A rush of three or four hundred, mainly men of broken fortunes from the dead *mushroom 'cities' of Nebraska and Kansas. **1948** P. JOHNSTON *Gold Rush* 42/1 By April 1850, Downieville had become a mushroom city of large proportions with a population of about 5000. **1958** *Spectator* 17 Jan. 63/1 If Europe is not to go up in a *mushroom cloud we must find an area of agreement with the Soviet Union. **1964** M. GOWING *Britain & Atomic Energy* ix. 267 Dr Penney was one of the scientific observers who saw the mushroom cloud rise from the ruins of Nagasaki. **1965** *Spectator* 5 Feb. 167/1 Hatred grows to mushroom-cloud proportions. **1900** *Westm. Gaz.* 16 Aug. 3/1 It is as near as you can get to it unless you say *mushroom-colour. **1904** *Daily Chron.* 13 Feb. 8/5 A..skirt of delicate *mushroom-coloured face cloth. **1681** GREW *Musæum* III. I. iii. 280 *Mushroom-Coral. *Fungites.* So called from a little likeness it hath to a Toad-Stool. **1731** MILLER *Gard. Dict.* s.v. *Mushrooms*, You should put in some of the Knobs of *Mushroom Earth, about six Inches asunder. **1839** H. BRANDON *Poverty, Mendicity & Crime* 164/1 **Mushroom fakers*, itinerant umbrella makers and repairers. **1851** MAYHEW *Lond. Labour* II. 127/2 The mushroom-fakers will repair any umbrella on the owner's premises. **1747** H. GLASSE *Art of Cookery* xi. 121 Two Quarts of the large *Mushroom Flaps rubbed to Pieces. **1861** MRS. BEETON *Bk. Househ. Managem.* 226 Choose full-grown mushroom-flaps, and take care they are perfectly fresh-gathered. **1753** CHAMBERS *Cycl. Suppl.*, **Mushroom Galls*..a name given by authors to a small species of galls very common on the leaves of the oak in September and October. **1827** G. HIGGINS *Celtic Druids* 86, I have no experience of *mushroom-grown men. **1911** E. WALLACE *Sanders of River* viii. 108 These secret societies he knew well enough... He knew their *mushroom growth; how they rose from nothingness with rituals and practices ready-made. **1931** *Economist* 2 May 944/2 Thus has terminated the career of a bank which enjoyed a mushroom growth immediately after the war. **1872** R. HEATH *Eng. Peasant* (1893) 145 It was a notion held among the peasantry in olden times, that he who could in one night erect a '*Mushroom Hall'..without hindrance from the officials of the manor, had obtained a copyhold right to the land. **1879** C. M. YONGE *Magnum Bonum* I. xi. 206 She looked up under her brown *mushroom hat. **1888** —— *Beechcroft at Rockstone* iv. 73 A..lady in a mushroom hat. **1897** *Westm. Gaz.* 17 June 3/2, 'The mushroom hat', the peculiar genius of which shape dwells in that coy droop of the brim. **1912** [see ABLOW *adv.* or *pred. a.*]. **1963** *Guardian* 29 Jan. 7/7 Dots..come on giant mushroom hats. **1872** ELLACOMBE *Bells of Ch.* in *Ch. Bells Devon* viii. 393 The bell being turned a quarter round by the button or *mushroom head by which it is hung. **1899** *Westm. Gaz.* 30 Nov. 4/2 Over this is placed a block of steel called the mushroom head. **1839** LINDLEY *Introd. Bot.* III. (ed. 3) 454 *Mushroom-headed; cylindrical, having a rounded, convex, overhanging extremity. **1875** PITT-RIVERS in *Proc. R. Inst. Gt. Brit.* VII. 514 We see [in the plate] the mushroom-headed waddy, with its projecting ridge flattened, then [in a later stage of development] curved. **1817** NEILL in *Edin. Encycl.* XI. 238/2 A *mushroom-house, constructed on Oldacre's plan. **1892** *Labour Commission* Gloss., **Mushroom-men*, men, having very little or no capital, who hire looms and start to compete in the cotton industry, on the principle that they have all to gain and nothing to lose. **1747** MRS. GLASSE *Cookery* xi. 122 To make *Mushroom Powder. **1807** WOLLASTON in *Phil. Trans.* XCVII. 138, I cut a groove..along the diameter of a *mushroom-ring. **1753** CHAMBERS *Cycl. Supp.* s.v. *Mushroom*, Into this [trench]..should be put in the knobs of *Mushroom spawn. **1850** PEREIRA *Elem. Mat. Med. & Therap.* (ed. 3) II. I. 952 Mushroom spawn is the name given by gardeners to the white branching cottony fibres (*mycelia*) which form the so-called root of the mushroom. **1668** CHARLETON *Onomasticon* 267 *Fungites*..Mushrum-stone. **1840** PEREIRA *Elem. Mat. Med.* II. 572 *Mushroom sugar has been found identical with mannite. **1819** R. L. MASON *Diary* 9 Dec. in *Narr. in Pioneer West* (1915) 66 Those *mushroom towns in a short time will produce their own death. **1938** H. ASBURY *Sucker's Prog.* 310 The invasion reached its peak with..the building of the trans-continental railroads which the gamblers followed step by step, carrying on their thieving business in every mushroom town that sprang up along the route. **1957** *Economist* 12 Oct. 105/2 These peasants turned workers..are the most interesting feature of the whole Polish social landscape. The mushroom town..displays the problem in a nutshell. **1877** *Design & Work* 7 July 114/3 Exhaust valve, consisting of ordinary *mushroom valve. **1924** S. G. WHEELER *Marine Engin.* I. vii. 102 Occasionally steam engines are controlled by 'mushroom' valves like internal combustion engines. **1966** J. A. DOLAN *Motor Vehicle Technol.* I. ix. 91 The valves used in motor vehicle engines are called poppet or mushroom valves.

mushroom (ˈmʌʃruːm), *v.* [f. MUSHROOM *sb.*]

1. *trans.* To elevate (a person) in social position with great suddenness. *nonce-use.*

1747 RICHARDSON *Clarissa* (1749) I. xl. 270 None but the prosperous upstart mushroom'd into rank (another of his peculiars) was arrogantly proud of it.

2. a. *intr.* Of rifle-bullets: To expand and flatten. Occas. with *out.* **b.** *trans.* To cause (a bullet) to 'mushroom'.

1893 SELOUS *Trav. S.E. Africa* 431 Such a bullet will mushroom on striking an animal. **1896** *Westm. Gaz.* 16 Dec. 6/3 The bullet was either mushroomed or the nickel shell and lead had parted company. **1900** *Brit. Med. Jrnl.* No. 2054. 1158 The result is that the lead mushrooms out.

3. *intr.* To gather mushrooms. Chiefly in pr. pple. or gerund.

1894 *Westm. Gaz.* 2 Jan. 7/2 While walking across a field mushrooming. **1901** *Essex Weekly News* 25 Oct. 3/3 He had been 'mushrooming'.

4. *intr.* To rise like a mushroom; to expand or increase rapidly; also const. *up, out.* Freq. *fig.*

1903 *Sun* (N.Y.) 2 Nov. 3 The flames had gone up the stairs to the very top of the house, and had then 'mushroomed' out, as the firemen say. **1911** *Ithaca Jrnl.* 10 Aug., The flames mushroomed from the shaft on all floors above. **1937** D. L. SAYERS *Busman's Honeymoon* v. 97 The loosened soot of centuries came plunging in a mad cascade down the chimney; it met the floor with a soft and deadly violence and mushroomed up in a Stygian cloud. **1947** J. C. RICH *Materials & Methods of Sculpture* ix. 249 If the end [of the chisel] receiving the impact of the carving hammer is too soft, it will quickly 'mushroom'. *Ibid.* ix. 261 The untempered ends of working chisels will frequently begin to mushroom..after repeated hammer blows. **1959** *Daily Tel.* 1 Dec. 11/8 A private Bill, promoted by the L.C.C.; it is intended to secure greater control of clubs which have 'mushroomed' into existence in recent years. **1962** *Listener* 9 Aug. 223/2 His characters are huge, they mushroom out one after the other and yet the plays aren't shapeless. **1972** *Language* XLVIII. 429 The number of publishing companies, both in Europe and North America, which have prepared new editions of primary sources [in linguistics] has mushroomed.

ˈmushroomed, *ppl. a.* [f. MUSHROOM *sb.* and *v.* + -ED.]

†**1.** *Cookery.* ? Dressed with mushrooms. *Obs.*

1821 COMBE *Wife* III. 390 Broil'd ham and a nice mushroom'd chicken.

2. Overgrown with mushrooms.

1885 MRS. CADDY *Footsteps Jeanne D' Arc* (1886) 9 The path turns downwards..across the mushroomed meadows.

3. Of rifle-bullets: Expanded and flattened.

1901 *Wide World Mag.* VIII. 160/1 The 'mushroomed' bullet was dug out of the earth.

ˈmushroomer. [f. MUSHROOM *v.* + -ER[1].] One who gathers mushrooms.

1885 *Illustr. Lond. News* 26 Sept. 331 One of the provincial advertisers calls such persons 'mushroomers'. **1898** CADMAN *H. Druidale* 175 I'll teach those mushroomers to keep out of my meadow.

mu'shroomic, *a. nonce-wd.* [f. MUSHROOM *sb.* + -IC.] 'Upstart'. (Cf. MUSHROOM *sb.* 6 b.)

1859 G. MEREDITH *R. Feverel* xvi, There were names historic and names mushroomic.

'mushrooming, *vbl. sb.* [f. MUSHROOM *v.* + -ING[1].] **a.** The gathering of mushrooms.

1900 *Westm. Gaz.* 16 Aug. 3/1 Mushrooming. The mushrooming is the event of our day.

b. The flattening and expansion (of bullets).

1900 *Daily News* 14 May 3/6 Soft-nosed bullets..appear to have been freely used by the Boers, as 10 per cent. of the wounds were caused by the 'mushrooming' of the core of the bullet.

c. Growth like that of a mushroom, as regards shape (cf. b) or rapidity. Freq. *fig.* Also as *ppl. a.*

1947 J. C. RICH *Materials & Methods of Sculpture* ix. 251 For fashioning chisels... It is advisable to cut the chisel blanks 1 to 2½ extra inches in length, since the occasional fracturing of a point, a mushrooming of the end receiving the hammer blows, and repeated sharpening will slowly shorten the total length. **1954** *Encounter* June 13/1 Over the past decade there has been a fantastic mushrooming of arts and crafts hobbies. **1957** *Listener* 12 Sept. 379/1 Economic changes..have brought..Africans into new jobs and opportunities, and into mushrooming new towns. **1968** A. DIMENT *Great Spy Race* x. 186 The mushrooming fireball of exploding petrol. **1968** *Brit. Med. Bull.* XXIV. 189/1 Recent mushrooming of activity and interest in this subject. **1972** K. S. ROUNDHILL *Prescription for Today's Missionary* 11 Positions for foreign teachers in the mushrooming educational programmes..are often available.

'mushroomy, *a.* [f. MUSHROOM *sb.* + -Y.] Like a mushroom.

1860 O. W. HOLMES *Elsie V.* vii, A large house of some pretensions to architectural display, namely, unnecessarily projecting eaves, giving it a mushroomy aspect. **1895** *Outing* (U.S.) XXVI. 42/2 These portable roof trees, though in shape mushroomy, have nothing else of the *parvenu* about them.

mushrub(be, -rum(pe, etc.: see MUSHROOM.

mushy ('mʌʃɪ), *a. colloq.* [f. MUSH *sb.*[1] + -Y.] **1.** Soft, pulpy; also *fig.*

1839 *Southern Lit. Messenger* V. 209/2, I soon recognized old *Noth Calinur* in their nasal mushy pronunciation. **1880** 'MARK TWAIN' *Tramp Abr.* xxvi. 267 Mushy, slushy early spring roads. **1883** *Pall Mall G.* 18 Sept. 12/1 It is poured into a machine in a thick, mushy state. **1952** M. TRIPP *Faith is Windsock* ii. 34 Unfortunately reception was indistinct and towns showed vague and mushy, making identification acutely difficult. **1962** *Which?* (Suppl.) July 86/2 Its handling was described as 'mushy' and our drivers said that it tended to 'wallow' in corners.

2. *fig.* Tender, sentimental, insipid. Also as *adv.*

1870 *Nation* (N.Y.) 3 Feb. 67 The death penalty is disappearing, like some better things, before a kind of mushy and unthinking doubt of its morality and expediency. **1876** GEO. ELIOT *Dan Der.* xlvi, She's not mushy, but her heart is tender. **1913** G. STRATTON-PORTER *Laddie* vii. 220 They formed a circle around Sally and Peter and as mushy as ever they could they sang, 'As sure as the grass grows around the stump, You are my darling sugar lump,' while they danced. **1928** G. B. SHAW *Intell. Woman's Guide Socialism* 458 You may..be a sharp, cynical sort of person; or you may be a nice, mushy, amiable, goodnatured one. **1951** J. D. SALINGER *Catcher in Rye* xvi. 137 She sings it very Dixieland and whore-house, and it doesn't sound at all mushy. **1971** WODEHOUSE *Much Obliged, Jeeves* i. 7 [Marriage] wouldn't have fitted in with my plans at all, she though physically in the pin-up class, being as mushy a character as ever broke biscuit. **1974** L. LAMB *Man in Mist* i. 12 Some mushy mag. She calls that a book!

3. (See quots. and cf. MUSH *sb.*[1] 4.)

1924 *Harmsworth's Wireless Encycl.* II. 1456 A mushy note is one which is not absolutely definite or clear cut, and so hard to read. It is a note received by the heterodyne method when damped wires or modulated continuous waves are being received. **1937** *Printers' Ink Monthly* May 39/3 *Mushy*, poor musical definition of an orchestral pickup.

4. *Surfing.* (See quots.)

1967 J. SEVERSON *Great Surfing* Gloss., *Mushy*, a slow, sloppy wave that has little power. **1969** *Surfer* IX. No. 6, 69 My little board's good for mushy waves, but when it's five foot or over and fast, I use the other. **1972** R. ABBOTT *Science of Surfing* v. 83 It is sometimes possible to 'beat' breaking sections, although this is easiest if the waves are 'mushy'.

music ('mju:zɪk), *sb.* Forms: 3–5 **musik**, 3–6 **musike**, 4 **musyce**, **musiqe**, 4–6 **musyk(e**, 4–7 **musique**, 5 **musy(c)que**, **-icque**, 6 **musyck**, *Sc.* **mwseik**, 6–7 **musick(e**, 7 **musiq**, 5– **music**. [a. F. *musique* (12th c. in Hatz.-Darm.), ad. L. *mūsica*, ad. Gr. μουσική (*sc.* τέχνη) lit. 'the art of the Muse' (fem. of μουσικός pertaining to the Muse or Muses, f. μοῦσα MUSE *sb.*[1]), applied *gen.* to artistic culture, poetry, etc., but also *spec.* to music.

Cf. Pr. *muzica*, Sp. *música*, Pg., It. *musica*; also G. *musik* (MHG. *museke*, OHG. *musica*), Du. *muziek*, Da., Sw. *musik*.]

1. That one of the fine arts which is concerned with the combination of sounds with a view to beauty of form and the expression of emotion; also, the science of the laws or principles (of melody, harmony, rhythm, etc.) by which this art is regulated.

Considered as an art, music has two distinct branches, the art of the composer and that of the executant. The word is often used with special reference to the executive branch, and to instrumental execution rather than vocal; thus, the designation of 'a teacher of music' is usually apprehended to mean one who teaches the art of playing on some instrument.

c **1250** *Gen. & Ex.* 460 Wit of musike, wel he knew. **1390** GOWER *Conf.* III. 90 The science of Musique, That techeth upon Armonie A man to make melodie. **1481** CAXTON *Myrr.* I. xii. 37 Of this science of musyque cometh alle attemperaunce. **1570** DEE *Math. Pref.* d iij, An Architect (sayth he [*sc.* Vitruvius]) ought to..haue heard Philosophers, haue skill of Musike, not ignorant of Physike [etc.]. **1638** *Burgh Rec. Glasgow* (1876) I. 388 That na maner of persone sould be permittit to teitch musik within this burgh..except [etc.]. **1711** ADDISON *Spect.* No. 29 ¶ 13 Musick, Architecture, and Painting..are to deduce their Laws and Rules from the general Sense and Taste of Mankind. **1827** WHATELY *Logic* i. (ed. 2) 18 There must have been..musical compositions previous to the science of Music. **1884** MACFARREN in *Encycl. Brit.* XVII. 77/1 Music ..is that one of the fine arts which appropriates the phenomena of sound to the purposes of poetry.

personified. *c* **1374** CHAUCER *Boeth.* II. pr. i. 31 (Camb. MS.) And with rethorice com forth Musyce A damysel of oure hous. **1509** HAWES *Past. Pleas.* xviii. (Percy Soc.) 77 Than forth so went good Counsell and I,..By Musykes toure walked most goodly. **1747** COLLINS *Passions* 1 When Music, Heav'nly Maid, was young.

2. a. Sounds in melodic or harmonic combination, whether produced by voice or instruments. † *in (good, true) music*: in tune.

† *broken music*: see BROKEN *ppl. a.* 16. *music of the spheres*: see SPHERE.

c **1381** CHAUCER *Parl. Foules* 62 The melodye herde he That comyth of thilke speris thryes thre That welle is of musik. **1390** GOWER *Conf.* I. 58 In wommanysshe vois thei singe, With notes..of such musike, Wherof the Schipes thei beswike. *c* **1400** *Destr. Troy* 13277 The myrthe of þaire mowthes musyk was like. **1471** CAXTON *Recuyell* (Sommer) II. 536 That made grete feste of theyr comyng in many manyers of Instrumentis of musycque. *a* **1500** *Flower & Leaf* 132 The Armony And sweet accord was in so good musyk, That the voice to angels most was lyk. *a* **1535** *Frere & Boye* 98 in Hazl. *E.P.P.* III. 65 A pype thou shalte haue also, In true musyke it shall go. **1588** BYRD *Ps., Sonn. & Songs* Pref. note, There is not any Musicke of Instruments whatsoeuer, comparable to that which is made of the voyces of Men. **1591** SHAKS. *Two Gent.* IV. ii. 31 Now must we to her window, And giue some euening Musique to her eare. **1611** A. STAFFORD *Niobe* 113 Thou deseruest a Quire of ancient Bards to sing thy praises; who, with their musickes melody, might expresse thy soules harmonie. **1613** *Purchas Pilgrimage* (1614) 308 With their voyces and cimbals, they make pleasant musicke. **1629** MILTON *Hymn Nativ.* xii. 117 Such Musick (as 'tis said) Before was never made. **1643** EVELYN *Diary* 24 Dec., I was entertain'd with the church musiq. **1697** CONGREVE *Mourn. Bride* I. i, Musick has Charms to sooth a savage Breast. **1769** GRAY *Installation Ode* 63 Sweet music's melting fall. **1886** C. E. PASCOE *London of To-day* xi. (ed. 3) 112 The music of the military and other bands is unusually excellent.

b. *transf.* Applied, e.g., to the song of birds, the murmur of running water, the euphony of spoken words, etc., *spec.* the cry of hounds on seeing the chase. Also in ironical collocations.

1590 SPENSER *F.Q.* II. vi. 25 She, more sweete then any bird on bough, Would..strive to passe..Their native musicke by her skilful art. **1593** G. FLETCHER *Licia* Sonn. xiv, My love lay sleeping, where birdes musicke made. **1617** MORYSON *Itin.* III. 28 Clashing of swords was then daily musicke in every street. **1653** WALTON *Angler* i. 12 What music doth a pack of dogs then make. **1687** A. LOVELL tr. *Thevenot's Trav.* I. 225 With that another Volley of great and small Shot: When this Musick had lasted about an Hour, they [etc.]. **1751** JOHNSON *Rambler* No. 88 ¶ 7 Milton, whose ear had been accustomed..to the music of the ancient tongues. **1808** SKURRAY *Bidcombe Hill* 9 The cheerful music of the opening hounds. **1836** W. IRVING *Astoria* III. 25 Musquitoes, which, with their stings and their music, set all sleep at defiance. **1858** R. S. SURTEES *Ask Mamma* xxxviii, The music of the hounds.

c. *fig.* in various applications, esp. something which it is a delight to hear. † *to step music*, to step with rhythmical grace.

a **1586** SIDNEY *Arcadia* II. (1629) 166 What Histories might euer make my fame yeeld so sweet a Musick to my eares..as that [etc.]? **1590** SHAKS. *Com. Err.* II. ii. 116 The time was once, when thou vn-vrg'd wouldst vow, That neuer words were musicke to thine eare,..Vnlesse I spake..to thee. **1611** —— *Wint. T.* IV. iv. 529 It is my Fathers Musicke To speake your deeds. *a* **1668** DAVENANT *Fair Favorite* v. i, I shall now be kil'd, Even with the musick of her voice. **1760–72** H. BROOKE *Fool of Qual.* (1809) III. 152 The performers stepped music, their action was grace. **1813** BYRON *Br. Abydos* I. vi, The mind, the Music breathing from her face. **1850** TENNYSON *In Mem.* xcvi, Perplext in faith, but pure in deeds, At last he beat his music out.

d. A kind of music. *lit.* and *fig.*

1584 POWEL *Lloyd's Cambria* 191 The second sort of them are plaiers vpon instruments, cheefelie the Harpe and the Crowth: whose musike for the most part came to Wales with the said Gruffyth ap Conan. **1664** PEPYS *Diary* 5 Oct., After three hours' stay it [the 'arched viall'] could not be fixed in tune: and so they were fain to go to some other musique of instruments. **1799** WORDSW. *Poet's Epitaph* 40 He murmurs near the running brooks A music sweeter than their own. **1822** BEDDOES *Bride's Trag* II. i, That is Love: 'Tis he that acts the nightingale, the thrush, And all the living musics. **1866** RUSKIN *Eth. Dust* IV. (1883) 60 All one's life is a music, if one touches the notes rightly and in time. **1883** STEVENSON *Silverado Sq.* (1886) 22 The stirring sunlight, and the growing vines..made a pleasant music for the mind.

3. Sounds in melodic or harmonic combination as devised by a composer; musical composition. ***to set to music***: to provide (a poem, etc.) with music to which it may be sung.

1607 T. HUME (*title*) Captain Humes Poeticall Musicke principally made for two basse-viols. **1697** MOTTEUX (*title*) The Loves of Mars and Venus. A Play set to Music. **1711** ADDISON *Spect.* No. 18 ¶ 2 That nothing is capable of being well set to Musick, that is not Nonsense. **1762** COLMAN *Mus. Lady* I. 15 (Stage-direction), Tunes the instrument, and turns over several pieces of music. **1763** J. BROWN *Poetry & Mus.* xiii. 223 If the Poet select and adapt proper Music to his Poem. **1898** SHUTTLEWORTH in *Daily News* 19 Nov. 6/3 The words attached to the music cannot make it sacred or profane.

†**4.** A piece of music composed or performed.

a **1586** SIDNEY *Arcadia* III. (1629) 247 Musickes at her window, and especially such Musickes, as might..call the mind to thinke of sorrow, and think of it with sweetnesse. **1589** PUTTENHAM *Eng. Poesie* II. x. (Arb.) 96 Vnlesse it be in small and popular Musickes song by these *Cantabanqui* vpon benches and barrels heads. **1611** SHAKS. *Cymb.* II. iii. 44, I haue assayl'd her with Musickes, but she vouchsafes no notice. **1668** SHADWELL *Sullen Lovers* II. Wks. 1720 I. 43, I came to present my Lady Vaine with a musick I have made. **1674** *Playford's Skill Mus.* 46 Exclamations may be used in all Passionate Musicks.

5. A company of musicians; the company of musicians attached to a military force; a 'band of music' (see BAND *sb.*[2] 4). [Cf. F. *musique*.] *Obs.* exc. in military use.

a **1586** SIDNEY *Arcadia* III. (1629) 235 The musick entring alone into the Lodge, the Ladies were all desirous to see from whence so pleasant a guest was come. **1588** SHAKS. *L.L.L.* V. ii. 211 Play musicke then: nay you must doe it soone. *Ibid.* 216 The musick playes, vouchsafe some motion to it. **1633** MARMION *Antiquary* II. i, Julia, go throw the Music a reward. **1666** PEPYS *Diary* 19 Dec., He says many of the musique are ready to starve, they being five years behind hand for their wages. **1711–12** SWIFT *Jrnl. to Stella* 8 Feb., A scoundrel dog, one of the Queen's music, a German. **1770** *Ann. Reg.* 102 The music of the chapel performed several Italian airs. **1847** *Infantry Man.* (1854) 75 The drummers and music are in the rear.

†**6.** Musical instruments. *Obs.*

1644 EVELYN *Diary* 1 Apr., Here also young gentlemen are taught to fence, daunce, play on musiq [etc.]. **1661** OGILBY *His Majesty's Entertainm.* 16 On the East-side, Winde-Musick. **1752** W. & J. HALFPENNY *Rur. Archit. in Chinese Taste* I. 6 A Room, wherein Musicians may be secreted (and play on soft Musick to the agreeable Surprize of Strangers). *a* **1800** S. PEGGE *Anecd. Eng. Lang.* (1814) 147 A fond Mother..will exultingly tell you that Miss 'learned herself to play upon the Musick'. **1816** KEATS *To C. C. Clarke* 113 What time you were before the music sitting, And the rich notes to each sensation fitting.

7. The written or printed score of a musical composition; such scores collectively; musical composition as represented by the usual graphic symbols.

1655 (*title*) Parthenia, or the Mayden-head of the First Musick that ever was Printed for the Virginals. **1884** *Encycl. Brit.* XVII. 87/2 Schütz wrote music to a translation of Peri's *Dafne*. **1886** GRESSWELL *How to play Fiddle* 70 The music must be placed on a stand, so that it can be seen without stooping. **1895** *Westm. Gaz.* 31 Dec. 3/2 We alone ..print over a ton weight of music week by week.

†**8.** *pl.* The short keys (now black) on the keyboard of an organ. *Obs.*

1694 W. HOLDER *Harmony* 156 The Breves representing the Tones of the broad Gradual Keys of an Organ; the Semibreves representing the Narrow Upper Keys, which are usually called Musicks.

9. A species of noctuid moth.

[? From the resemblance of its markings to written music.]

1832 J. RENNIE *Conspect. Butterfl. & M.* 65 The Music (*Xylophasia lithoxylea*, Stephens).

10. *U.S. colloq.* **a.** 'Lively speech or action; liveliness; excited wrangling, excitement'. **b.** 'Diversion; sport; also, sense of the ridiculous. In this sense apparently confused with *amuse*' (*Cent. Dict.* 1890). Cf. MUSICAL 8.

1859 BARTLETT *Dict. Amer.*, *Music*, amusement, fun. 'Jim is a right clever fellow; there is a great deal of music in him.' **18..** *Lett. fr. the South* in Schele de Vere *Americanisms* (1872) 618 Jake is not without his vein of fun, music they call it down here.

11. Phrases (*slang* or *colloq.*). † ***to make ill music***, † ***the music's paid*** (see quot. *a* 1700); ***to face the music***, to face boldly the consequences of one's actions; to accept the inevitable without hesitation; ***music while you work***: continuous light music played to workers, esp. in factories; ***to make (beautiful) music (together)***: to have sexual intercourse.

a **1700** B. E. *Dict. Cant. Crew*, *Musick. It makes ill Musick*, of any unwelcome... News... *The Musick's paid*, the Watch-word among High-way-men, to let the Company they were to Rob, alone, in return to some Courtesy. **1850** *Congress. Globe* App. 4 Mar. 324/3 There should be no skulking or dodging..every man should 'face the music'. *a* **1851** J. F. COOPER in Schele de Vere *Americanisms* (1872) 601 Rabelais' unpleasant 'quarter' is by our more picturesque people called *facing the music*. **1857** *Worcester* (Mass.) *Spy* 22 Sept. (Bartlett) A strong determination to face the music is everywhere manifested. **1897** RHODES in *Westm. Gaz.* 6 Jan. 5/1, I will not refer to the vulgar colloquialism that I was afraid to face the music. **1920** R. MACAULAY *Potterism* III. viii. 140 If Gideon didn't shove him, he's nothing to be afraid of in our talk, and if he did he'll have to face the music. **1940** *Radio Times* 21 June 3/2 This coming week there will be, twice every day, half-an-hour's music meant specially for factory-workers..under the title 'Music while you work'. **1958** J. BETJEMAN *Coll. Poems* 227 Though 'Music while you work' is now our wont, It's not so nice as 'Music while you don't'. **1958** 'J. BYROM' *Or be he Dead* xv. 186 So the old bitch *did* recognize me! Mrs Kernan and I were pretty sure she had. That's why we did a bunk so hastily, leaving Byron to face the bill and the music. **1960** R. POUND *Selfridge* ii. 40 One of the first applications of the music-while-you-work incentive to modern labour. **1967** F. MULLALLY *Prizewinner* vii. 117 He could say good-bye to any hope of making music later on with the Swede. **1968** S. E. ELLACOTT *Everyday Things in*

England 1914-68 xi. 162 The factory system of 'music while you work'..was introduced during the Second World War ..in munitions factories. In mechanical, repetitive jobs lively music helped production. **1969** H. NIELSEN *Darkest Hour* xxi. 238 You and Buddy can make beautiful music together. **1972** C. SHORT *Naked Skier* xxi. 115, I think we should make music together.

12. Flexibility or 'give' in the shaft of a golf club. *rare.*

1890 H. G. HUTCHINSON *Golf* iii. 57 A heavy head may bring just the right amount of life—of what Tom Morris calls 'music'—out of a very stiff shaft. **1903** W. J. TRAVIS *Pract. Golf* (rev. ed.) ix. 111 The man with a less rapid swing will get equally as long a ball by using a more supple shaft. The more 'music' there is in the shaft, however, the greater is the liability to slice or pull.

13. *attrib.* and *Comb.* **a.** simple attrib., as ***music cabinet, critic, -desk, -folio, -lesson, -man, -master, -meeting, -mistress, -monger, -night, -rack, -rest, -room, -school, -score, -sheet, -shop, -stand, -stool, -track.*** **b.** objective, instrumental, etc., as ***music-lover, -maker, -making, -publisher, -seller; music-drawing, flowing, -footed, -hungry, -loving, -mad, -panting, -sounding, -stirring, -stunned, -tongued*** adjs.

1883 *Heal & Son Catal.* Sept. 216 *Music Cabinet, Walnut or Ebonised. **1911** *Daily Colonist* (Victoria, B.C.) 22 Apr. 4/4 It does not matter to us what style of piano you may have we can give you a music cabinet style to harmonize. **1901** G. B. SHAW *Three Plays for Puritans* p. v, The difference between the leisure of a Persian cat and the labor of a cockney cab horse is not greater than the difference between the official weekly or fortnightly play-goings of the theatre critic and the restless daily rushing to and fro of the *music critic. **1956** AUDEN & KALLMAN *Magic Flute* (1957) 58 That is changed Since music-critics learned to feel 'estranged'. **1835** DICKENS *Sk. Boz, Mistaken Milliner*, 'Tap-tap-tap', went the leader's bow on the *music-desk. **1788** COWPER *Stanzas for* 1788, 12 The *musick-drawing bow. **1820** SHELLEY *Hymn Mercury* lxxxiii, I Present thee with this *music-flowing shell. **1858** SIMMONDS *Dict. Trade*, **Music-folio, Music-wrapper*, a case or book for holding loose music. **1607** CHAPMAN *Bussy d'Ambois* v. i, Thy *musique-footed horse. **1950** A. LOMAX *Mister Jelly Roll* iv. 181 A gang of *music-hungry, life-hungry white kids. **1835** MARRYAT *Pacha* iii, The *music-lesson was over. **1933** *Maclean's Mag.* 15 July 32/4 *Music lovers will thrill at the music of His Majesty's Scots Guards, and thirty other bands. **1963** AUDEN *Dyer's Hand* 507 That great music-lover, Bernard Shaw. **1870** D. J. KIRWAN *Palace & Hovel* xxxiv. 493 Theatre going and *music-loving people. **1776** BURNEY *Hist. Mus.* (1789) I. Pref. 11 A great genius *music-mad. **1864** BROWNING *Dramatis Personae* 49 Schumann's our *music maker now. **1955** N. CARDUS in H. van Thal *Fanfare for E. Newman* iii. 34 The composer's physiology as music-maker. **1946** *Music-making [see sense 13 c below]. **1963** *Times* 12 Feb. 14/4 A recital which had more of the air of a friendly music-making at home than the deadly earnest aspiration usually encountered on this platform. **1866** CARLYLE *Inaug. Addr.* 193 Our painters, poets and *music-men. **1937** H. G. WELLS *Brynhild* v. 61 The brightest and best producers, directors,..cutters, music-men. **1950** L. BENNETT *Anancy Stories & Dial. Verse* 40 Once upon a time Cockroach was a very good music-man an everybody wat have a dance always want Bredda Cockroach fe play fe dem. **1958** *Spectator* 10 Jan. 38/1 Mrs. Legge is what music-men call the flipover. *c*1630 B. JONSON *Expost. w. Inigo Jones* 63 He now is come To be the *music-master: tabler too. **1693** C. DRYDEN *D.'s Juvenal* VII. (1697) 179 Now look into the Musick-Master's Gains. **1845** *Ainsworth's Mag.* VII. 507, I see your ladyship's music-master..in the carriage. **1664** PEPYS *Diary* 5 Oct., To the *Musique-meeting at the Post-office, where I was once before. **1769** GRAY in *Corr. w. Nicholls* (1843) 97 Mr. Reinholt, and Miss Thomas, great names at Salisbury and Gloster music-meeting. **1861** WHYTE MELVILLE *Good for N.* I. 200 Paler and paler grew the *music-mistress's cheek. **1784** J. POTTER *Virtuous Villagers* I. 100 *Music-monger. **1686** WILDING in *Collect.* (O.H.S.) I. 264 At ye *Musick-night..000206. **1859** GEO. ELIOT *A. Bede* xxi, On music-nights it was apparent that patience could never be an easy virtue to him. **1819** SHELLEY *Prometh. Unb.* II. ii. 29 [A nightingale] Sick with sweet love, droops dying away On its mate's *music-panting bosom. **1848** *Knickerbocker* XXXI. 450 Mr. Joseph F. Atwill, one of our most popular *music-publishers..is issuing..a musical publication of rare interest. **1885** *List of Subscribers, Classified* (United Telephone Co.) (ed. 6) 157 Music publishers and sellers..Boosey & Co. **1919** WODEHOUSE *Damsel in Distress* xvi. 199 She was a stenographer in a music-publisher's office when we first met. **1855** *Knickerbocker* XLV. 136 You hide behind the *music-rack while Miss Mince passes. **1879** G. MEREDITH *Egoist* xxiv, She went to the music-rack and gave the song unasked. **1892** *Pall Mall G.* 2 Mar. 2/1 A rickety piano, with a Beethoven Symphony open on the *music-rest. **1922** JOYCE *Ulysses* 691 It's musicrest supporting the music..for voice and piano of *Love's Old Sweet Song*. **1638** *Burgh Rec. Glasgow* (1876) I. 388 Seing that the *musik schooll is altogidder dekayit within this burgh. **1801** T. BUSBY *Dict. Music*, **Music-seller*, one who buys and sells music..likewise all kinds of musical instruments. **1811** JANE AUSTEN *Sense & Sens.* I. xvii. 216 Booksellers, music-sellers, and print-shops. **1914** W. OWEN *Let.* c 3 July (1967) 264 Practically all my *Music Sheets.. have been stolen! *c*1760 in Dryden *Alexander's Feast* (title-page), Set to Musick by Mr. Handel. Edinburgh, sold by Robert Bremner, at his *Musick-shop, at the Harp and Hautboy. **1818** LADY MORGAN *Autobiog.* (1859) 204 He declared he would go..to all the old music-shops to try and find it. **1925** E., O., & S. SITWELL *Poor Young People* 20 To *music-sounding moonlight. **1762** G. COLMAN *Musical Lady* II. 39 Away with your *music-stands. **1887** I. R. *Lady's Ranche Life Montana* 11, I bought a sofa..and music-stand. **1819** SHELLEY *Prometh. Unb.* I. i. 777 The *music-stirring motion of its soft and busy feet. **1834** DICKENS *Sk. Boz* (1836). 1st Ser. I. 206 Mr. Wisbottle was describing semi-circles on the *music-stool. **1879** F. W. ROBINSON *Coward Consc.* II. xv, Slitherwick..sat down on the music-stool. **1902** CONRAD *Youth* 314 He swung half round on the music-stool, listening with his fingertips at rest on the keyboard. **1975** *Country Life* 2 Oct. 852/1 The wood's great weight also recommended it for pillar furniture: ranging from tea-poy to music stool. *a*1930 D. H. LAWRENCE *Sex, Literature & Censorship* (1955) 114 The dream of our pathetic, *music-stunned young girl of today. **1819** SHELLEY *Prometh. Unb.* II. ii. 42 Echoes, *music-tongued, which draw..All spirits on that secret way. **1953** K. REISZ *Technique Film Editing* III. xii. 187 It is most important that the dubbing editor should be able to cross fade from the dialogue to the *music track at any time.

c. *attrib.* or quasi-*adj.* in the sense MUSICAL *a.*

1602 SHAKS. *Ham.* III. i. 164, I..That suck'd the Honie of his Musicke Vowes. **1605** *1st Pt. Ieronimo* II. iv. 35 Clap a siluer tongue Within this pallat, that..I may..Haue euery sillable a musick stop. **1657** THORNLEY tr. *Longus' Daphnis & Chloe* 142 Her Singing Limbs. The Earth buried them, preserving to them still their musick-property. **1669** GALE *Ct. Gentiles* I. II. iii. 30 Many music Instruments had obteined a Barbaric name. **1877** G. B. SHAW *How to become Mus. Critic* (1960) 19 Tristan and Isolde, a music drama which, in order of development, is the latest of Wagner's works. **1885** —— *Ibid.* 91 His allegorical music-play Die Zauberflöte. **1903** R. HUGHES *Musical Guide* I. 207/2 Music-drama. An opera (particularly of the Wagnerian School) in which the text and the action determine the music, and are not interrupted by set arias, duets, etc. **1935** *Discovery* Sept. 250/2 This..building..is now the scene of the Triennial Music Festivals. **1946** MEZZROW & WOLFE *Really Blues* viii. 117 We had a ritual for these music-appreciation classes. **1946** *Penguin Music Mag.* Dec. 10 Since the early eighteenth century the music festival has been one of the most important and sustaining influences in English music-making. **1947** A. EINSTEIN *Music in Romantic Era* xvi. 227 Wagner..considered himself, justifiably, not as a pure musician, but as a music-dramatist. **1966** *Listener* 5 May 663/2 Puccini's *Madama Butterfly*, his only opera that may lay claim to be called a psychological music drama. **1975** *Country Life* 2 Oct. 846/1 Wagner's great works are music-dramas rather than operas in the old sense.

d. Special combinations: †**music-band**, a 'band of music'; **music-bells** *Sc.* = CARILLON 1; **music-book**, a book containing written or printed music-scores; **music-box**, †(*a*) a barrel-organ; (*b*) = *musical box* (see MUSICAL *a.* 10); (*c*) jocularly, a pianoforte; **music case**, (*a*) a container (see CASE *sb.*[2] 9) in which the component parts of a fount of music type are arranged before being set; (*b*) a container for sheet music; **music centre**, a stereophonic system combining record-player, radio, and cassette tape recorder in a single unit, usu. with separate loudspeakers; **music-club**, a club for promoting the practice of music; **music-demy** (see quot. 1859); **music gallery**, a gallery in a church or hall for the accommodation of the musicians; †**music-girl**, a female professional singer; **music-grinder**, an itinerant street musician (see GRIND *v.*[1] 7); **music-hall**, a hall used for musical performances; *spec.* a hall licensed for singing, dancing, and other entertainments exclusive of dramatic performances; also *attrib.*; so **music-hallish, music-hally** *adjs.*, suggestive of a music-hall; †**music-house**, (*a*) the room in a theatre, etc., in which the musicians sat (cf. *music-room*); (*b*) a public hall or saloon for musical performances; **music-licence**, a magistrates' licence to give vocal and instrumental entertainments in a public building or apartment; **music line**, a line (LINE *sb.*[2] 1 e) whose transmission characteristics are good enough for the transmission of music, and along which programme material is usually sent; **music-loft** = *organ-loft* (see ORGAN *sb.*[1] 8); **music-paper**, paper ruled for writing music upon (see quot. 1859); **music-pen** (see quot. 1840); **music-plate**, a metal alloy composed of antimony, tin, and lead; **music-roll**, (*a*) a receptacle for the carriage of rolled-up sheet music; (*b*) a roll, usually of perforated paper, used in a pianola or player-piano or similar instrument; **music-room**, a room in which music is performed; †*spec.* a room at the side of a theatre-stage in which the musicians sat; †**music-shell**, one of several species of gasteropodous molluscs of the family *Volutidæ*, esp. *Voluta musica*, characterized by markings on the shell resembling written music; **music-smith**, a mechanic who makes the metal parts for pianofortes, organs, etc.; †**music speech**, an oration formerly part of the proceedings at the Encænia at Oxford; †**music-stamper**, a kind of bat; **music type**, a fount of type, including several hundred pieces, used for the typographic printing of music, as distinguished from the use of engraved plates; also *attrib.*; **music-wire**, steel wire such as is used for stringed musical instruments.

1812 J. WILSON *Isle of Palms* IV. 442 The *music bands both near and far Are playing. **1856** OLMSTED *Slave States* 552 Music bands, composed of negroes. **1818** *Gentl. Mag.* LXXXVIII. II. 398 These carillons have been introduced into Scotland..where they are called *musick-bells. **1597** MORLEY *Introd. Mus.* 1 *Musicke bookes..being brought to the table: the mistresse of the house presented mee with a part, earnestly requesting mee to sing. **1895** 'MERRIMAN' *Grey Lady* I. ix, The Spaniard opened the music-book and indicated the page. **1773** GOLDSM. *Stoops to Conq.* I. i, Little Aminadab that grinds the *music box. **1844** MARG. FULLER *Wom. 19th C.* (1862) 258 Music-boxes, which you can wind up to play their set of tunes. **1849** THACKERAY *Pendennis* liv, There was a piano in Mr. Sibwright's chamber.., and at this music-box, as Mr. Warrington called it, Laura..played and sang. **1841** W. SAVAGE *Dict. Art of Printing* 487 All that I shall attempt is to give the plan of a pair of *Music Cases, with the characters. **1890** *Cent. Dict.*, Music-case. **1894** *Amer. Dict. Printing & Bookmaking* 383/2 *Music cases*, special cases of a complicated character employed in composing type-music. **1924** *Southward's Mod. Printing* (ed. 5) I. v. 41 Music Cases. This class of case has to be made to suit the founts of different founders, who vary in the number of characters they cast. **1960** K. AMIS *Take Girl like You* ii. 27 Jenny..fetched her music case, with books and not music in, from the classroom. **1974** *Hi Fi for Pleasure* Jan. 15 Model G 2601 KL..is a *music centre with everything. **1975** *Gramophone* Nov. 958/2 Decca's Compact 4 music centre now incorporates long wave in its tuner section. **1975** *Which?* Dec. 356/3 Most music centres are designed to be sold with one set of loudspeakers only. **1740** R. VERNEY *Let.* 11 Nov. in M. M. Verney *Verney Lett.* (1930) II. xxix. 185 Mr. Millward on returning..from the inn at East Claydon, where there is a *Musicck [*sic*] Club instituted, fell down. **1801** STRUTT *Sports & Past.* IV. i. §3 There were also music-clubs, or private meetings for the practise of music. **1946** *Penguin Music Mag.* Dec. 7 Gramophone societies and music clubs which flourish all over the country. **1859** *Stationers' Hand-bk.* 74 **Music Demy*, see short demy. *Ibid.* 82 Short Demy, a white thick soft paper, used by music publishers for printing music, 21 by $14\frac{1}{2}$ inches. **1794** SIR C. MALET in J. Forbes *Or. Mem.* (1813) III. 106 Opposite to it [was] the nobut khani, or *music-gallery. **1835** *Court Mag.* VI. 117/2 The good rector casts up to the music-gallery a look..of expostulation. **1765** G. COLMAN *Terence, Eunuch* III. ii, Are you fond of me For sending you that *musick-girl? **1852** *Chamb. Jrnl.* 27 Mar. 197/1 (art.) *Music-grinders of the Metropolis. **1842** DICKENS *Amer. Notes* iii. (1850) 21/1 The pupils all repaired ..to a spacious *music-hall,..and listened..to a voluntary on the organ. **1857** J. E. RITCHIE *Night Side London* 145 The new Music Hall, Hungerford Market. **1870** D. J. KIRWAN *Palace & Hovel* xxxiv. 503 A popular street and music-hall song. **1885** W. S. GILBERT *Mikado* II. 35 The music-hall singer attends a series Of masses and fugues and 'ops' By Bach. **1927** J. ADAMS *Errors in School* 112 His music-hall cluster. **1959** *New Statesman* 25 Apr. 574/3 The opening of the prison scene is made the occasion for an interminable drunken charade which destroys the balance of an act that is precarious enough in its original form—all for the sake of a primitive music-hall joke repeated at least a dozen times without variation. **1975** J. WAINWRIGHT *Square Dance* 248 You dress outrageously and you behave like a music-hall comedian. **1893** M. BEERBOHM *Let.* Sept. (1964) 60 A good many common *music-hallish people were standing in front of me. **1930** *Observer* 30 Mar. 15 The patriotic song of 1900 should have been sung by someone more robust and music-hallish than the cute and charming Miss Ada-May. **1889** G. B. SHAW *London Music in 1888–89* (1937) 211 The inferior theatre orchestra is *music-hally, blatant, thumping, out of tune. **1923** A. CHRISTIE *Murder on Links* xxii. 251 Their voices were..rather thin and music-hally, but attractive. **1602** MARSTON *Antonio's Rev.* v. v. K 1 b, While the measure is dauncing, Andrugios ghost is placed betwixt the *musick houses. **1605** in Cunningham *Revels at Crt.* (1842) 207 The musike house att yᵉ Court. **1612** *Ibid.* 214 A Musik house dore in the hall & a doore for the Musik house in the Bancketing house. **1697** DAMPIER *Voy.* (1729) I. 361 John Thacker..had formerly learnt to Dance in the Musick-houses about Wapping. **1714** MANDEVILLE *Fab. Bees* (1725) I. 468 The musick-houses at Amsterdam,..than which nothing can be more harmless. **1858** SIMMONDS *Dict. Trade*, **Music-licence*, a permission from the magistrates to hold concerts and vocal entertainments, &c. at a room or house. **1941** *B.B.C. Gloss. Broadcasting Terms* 20 *Music line. **1962** A. NISBETT *Technique Sound Studio* 246 A control line..is a telephone circuit on which programme details may be discussed, and is so called to distinguish it from the broad band (i.e. high quality) 'music line' along which programme is fed. **1858** SIMMONDS *Dict. Trade*, **Music-loft*, a raised balcony or gallery for a band. **1769** BARRINGTON in *Phil. Trans.* LX. 63 He..was left only with *music-paper, and the words of an oratorio. **1859** *Stationers' Hand-bk.* 74 *Music Paper*, royal drawing paper, in the 4to size, ruled with the musical stave of five lines. **1840** LARDNER *Geom.* iii. 35 These lines [*sc.* of the stave] are sometimes drawn upon paper by an instrument called a *music pen, consisting of five points at distances corresponding to the distances between the lines. **1839** URE *Dict. Arts* 51 Its [*i.e.* antimony] chief employment now is in medicine, and in making the alloys called type metal, stereotype metal, *music plates, and Britannia metal. **1890** *Cent. Dict.*, *Music-roll. **1890–1** *T. Eaton & Co. Catal.* Fall & Winter 42/1 Music rolls, in leather... Music rolls, in plush. **1906** *Bazaar, Exch. & Mart* Suppl. 3 Oct. 1322/1 Kastner's upright grand auto-piano for sale,..played by hand or by music rolls. **1907** *Yesterday's Shopping* (1969) 399/3 *Music rolls.* American cloth, lined cloth—1/5. **1913** *Strand Mag.* Jan. 13 (Advt.), For all player-pianos 'Songola' music rolls. **1608** DEKKER *Belman Lond.* B 2 b, Vpon euerie branch sat a consort of singers, so that euerie tree shewed like a *Musick roome. **1630** MIDDLETON *Chaste Maid* v. K 2 b, While all the Company seeme to weepe and mourne, there is a sad Song in the Musicke-Roome. **1692** R. L'ESTRANGE *Fables* clxxvi. 147 A Man that had a very Course Voice, but an Excellent Musique-Room, would be still Practising in that Chamber, for the Advantage of the Eccho. **1842** P. CUNNINGHAM *Revels at Crt.* 223 In other plans are boxes for the nobility, and in one the situation of the music room is clear enough; viz. at the side of the stage. **1875** 'MARK TWAIN' *Sketches New & Old* 307 We shall have billard-rooms [*sic*], card-rooms, music-rooms. **1928** 'SAPPER' *Female of Species* x. 173 The music-room appeared to be so-called because there was no trace of any musical instrument in it. **1942** E. BLOM *Music in England* vi. 92 In 1713 a dancing-master named Hickford opened a music room..where the celebrities of the day appeared. **1975** *Listener* 6 Nov. 608/3 My fourth new stopwatch..fell to the tiled floor of our music-room from my nerveless fingers. *c*1711 PETIVER *Gazophyl.* VI. lvi, Small Indian *Music-Shell. **1843** *Penny Cycl.* XXVI. 444/1

Musicales, the Music Shells. Consisting of *Volutæ ebræa, musica*, &c. **1858** SIMMONDS *Dict. Trade*, **Music-smith*, a workman who makes the metal parts for pianofortes, &c. *a* **1704** T. BROWN *Wks.* (1709) III. III. 94 (*title*) Prologue to a *Musick Speech had in the Theatre in Oxford. **1709** STEELE *Tatler* No. 45 ¶5 The Nymphs of this City [Oxford] are disappointed of a luscious Musick-Speech. **1713** PETIVER *Aquat. Anim. Amboinæ* 3 Vespertilio... *Musick-Stamper. **1825** T. C. HANSARD *Typographia* Index 11, Music type. **1841** W. SAVAGE *Dict. Art of Printing* 488 (*caption*) C. Hancock's plan of cases for Hughes' *music type. **1858** SIMMONDS *Dict. Trade, Music-type*, the symbols or notes of music, cast for printing from. **1875** SOUTHWARD *Dict. Typogr., Music types*, moveable types used in producing music. **1892** A. POWELL *Southward's Pract. Printing* (ed. 4) xxxi. 292 Most of the letter-founders supply music types. **1923** W. GAMBLE *Music Engraving & Printing* xv. 169 The setting up of music type is a difficult and tedious operation. **1934** C. LAMBERT *Music Ho!* 11 There are few technical terms and no music-type illustrations. **1968** *Listener* 27 June 845/2 To demonstrate this [*sc.* the shapes of this plain-chant melody] would need music-type. **1823** J. BADCOCK *Dom. Amusem.* 150 With small *musick-wire, cut your making into cakes.

music ('mju:zɪk), *v.* [f. MUSIC *sb.*] In various nonce-uses: **a.** *trans.* To influence by music; to train in music. **b.** To set to music, describe musically. **c.** *intr.* To produce music; entertain oneself with music.

1713 *Gentl. Instructed* I. Suppl. iv. (ed. 5) p. xli, A Man must have a mean Valuation of Christ to leave him for a Touch upon an Instrument, and a faint Idea of future Torments to be fiddled and musick'd into Hell. **1788** E. JERNINGHAM in *Jern. Lett.* (1896) I. 46, I suppose you have been reading, drawing, and musiking. *a* **1814** *Sixteen & Sixty* in *New Brit. Theatre* IV. 387 There be Miss Bore'em a musicing already. **1861** J. PYCROFT *Agony Point* xii. (1862) 142 The girls..have not only been Frenched, and Musicked, and Deportmented,..but they have also had [etc.]. **1876** T. S. EGAN tr. *Heine's Atta Troll*, etc. 221 The young one musicked and trilled. **1897** *Nat. Observ.* 27 Feb. 414 The authors,..after having 'musicked' mysticism in *Le Rêve*..treat now in *Messidor* the labour question. **1900** W. A. ELLIS *Wagner* I. 198 We met, ate, and even music-ed together once in Leipzig.

‖**musica** ('mju:zɪkə). [L., = music.] Used in special collocations to designate different kinds of music or musical techniques, as **musica ficta**, in contrapuntal music of the 10th to 16th centuries, the introduction by the singer of conventional chromatically altered tones to avoid unacceptable intervals; **musica figurata**, (*a*) contrapuntal music in which the different melodic strands move more or less independently; (*b*) plainsong with decorated melody; **musica plana** = *cantus firmus*; plainsong; **musica reservata** (see quot. 1972).

1740 J. GRASSINEAU *Musical Dict.* 154 *Musica Figuralis, Figurata*, or *Colorata*, figurate music, wherein the notes are of different values, and the motions various, now slow then quick. **1801** T. BUSBY *Dict. Music, Musica ficta*,..the name given by Franchinus and other musical writers, to the first deviations from the old ecclesiastical modes. **1886** W. S. ROCKSTRO *Hist. Mus.* 482 The Rules of..Musica ficta.. enable us to supply, with certainty, the accidental Sharps and Flats, which the older writers omitted. **1940** G. REESE *Music in Middle Ages* (1941) v. 121 Not until the 13th century did *musica plana* etc. come to connote music in free rhythm as distinguished from measured music, as do the English words 'plainsong' and 'plainchant'. **1944** W. APEL *Harvard Dict. Mus.* 467/2 *Musica reservata* denotes the Renaissance-like clarity, balance, and expressiveness, the full-blooded humanism of the Josquin period, in contrast to the abstract and mysterious transcendentalism of the earlier masters. **1954** A. HUGHES in *New Oxf. Hist. Music* II. xi. 370 The position which called for such a system as *musica ficta* is as simple as the processes of its working out are complex. It is the problem of the tritone. **1954** G. REESE *Music in Renaissance* ix. 512 The expression '*musica reservata*' has become one of the problems of music history. **1963** R. DONINGTON *Interpretation of Early Music* iv. 67 *D* minor, which we notate with a signature of one flat, grew out of the Dorian mode when its leading note, *C*, became habitually sharpened by the workings of *musica ficta*. **1968** *Listener* 23 May 676/2 His [*sc.* Palestrina's] Mass saves music, convinces the Pope that a regression to *musica plana*, plainsong, at the indiscriminate expense of *musica figurata* (the later, florid polyphonic style of the early Flemish composers) would be wrong—wrong metaphysically. **1972** *Composer & Conductor* Aug. 1/1 'Musica reservata'..lends itself to diametrically opposite definitions. Some musicologists describe it as music made suitable for popular use, while others regard 'musica reservata' as literally 'reserved for connoisseurs'.

musical ('mju:zɪkəl), *a.* (and *sb.*) [a. F. *musical* (14th c. in Hatz.-Darm.), ad. med.L. *mūsicālis* (Albertus Magnus *c* 1250), f. L. *mūsica* MUSIC *sb.*] **A.** *adj.*

1. Of or belonging to music.

musical instrument: see INSTRUMENT *sb.* 3. ***musical ear***: see EAR *sb.*[1] 5.

c **1420** LYDG. *Thebes* (E.E.T.S.) 222 The musycal, the lusty instrument, I mene the harpe most melodious, yove to this kynge be Mercurius. **1526** *Pilgr. Perf.* (W. de W. 1531) 7 b, Whiche..passeth all yᵉ armony of this worlde, bothe musycall instrumentes & voyce of man. **1613** PURCHAS *Pilgrimage* (1614) 324 Marsyas roamed with her, who after, being ouercome in a Musicall contention of Apollo, was flayed quicke. **1726** SWIFT *Gulliver* III. ii, He gave me the names and descriptions of all their musical instruments. **1790** SHERIDAN *Let.* in T. Moore *Life R. B. Sheridan* (1825) 468 We had a very pleasant musical party last night at Lord Erskine's. **1791** F. BURNEY *Jrnl.* Dec. (1972) I. 95 We have spent a charming Musical Evening at Mr. Burney's. **1814** J. MAYNE *Jrnl.* 7 Nov. (1909) x. 183 Countess Cardelli, who has agreeable musical parties at her house every Sunday evening. **1841** ELPHINSTONE *Hist. Ind.* I. 297 Musical science is said to have declined like all others. **1885** *List of Subscribers, Classified* (United Telephone Co.) (ed. 6) 157 Musical instrument makers..Chappell & Co. **1892** *Law Times, Weekly Notes* 188/1 The defendant had a musical evening regularly once a week. **1926** *Punch* 10 Nov. p. iii (Advt.), Recreation for yourself—Dance Parties—Musical Evenings. **1964** W. L. GOODMAN *Hist. Woodworking Tools* 92 These small block planes were very useful to violin and other musical-instrument makers.

2. Having the nature or characteristics of music; tuneful, melodious, harmonious; pleasing in sound, euphonious. Of sounds: Such as are used in music; having the nature of 'tones', as distinguished from mere 'noises'.

c **1430** LYDG. *Min. Poems* (Percy Soc.) 157 The unycorn, by musical swetnesse, Atween too maydenys is take and hath a fal. **1509** HAWES *Past. Pleas* xvi. (Percy Soc.) 76 The lytle byrdes swetely dyd syng With tunes musicall in the fayre mornyng. **1590** SHAKS. *Mids. N.* IV. i. 115 Marke the musicall confusion Of hounds and eccho in coniunction. *a* **1668** DAVENANT *Entertainm. Rutland Ho.* Poems (1672) 344 Would he not have you Cough but..with a musical concordance to the rest that have taken cold? **1720** J. WELWOOD in Rowe *Lucan* Pref. 43 The Versification [is] both musical and adapted to the subject. **1858** HAWTHORNE *Fr. & It. Note-Bks.* (1871) II. 310 The murmur of their voices took a musical tone. **1897** *Allbutt's Syst. Med.* III. 43 A murmur which began as a soft, gentle, blowing sound.. may..increase to a loud musical bruit in the course of a single week. **1873** BROWNING *Red. Cott. Nt.-cap* 402 What is this..makes The musicalest buzzing at my ear?

fig. **1643** PRYNNE *Sov. Power Parl.* App. 77 Out of which things, the moderate and musicall state of the Commonweale which we enjoy, is moulded and made up. **1818** BYRON *Ch. Har.* IV. clvi, Vastness which grows—but grows to harmonise—All musical in its immensities. **1892** SYMONDS *Michel Angelo* (1899) II. 5 No edifice..is..more musical in linear proportion than the Church of S. Andrea at Mantua.

3. Fond of or skilled in music.

c **1420** LYDG. *Assembly of Gods* 401 And as a poet musykall made he melody. **1596** SHAKS. *1 Hen. IV*, III. i. 237 *Hotsp.* Now I perceiue the Deuill vnderstands Welsh,..Byrlady hee's a good Musitian. *Lady.* Then would you be nothing but Musicall, For you are altogether gouerned by humors. **1685** DRYDEN *Alb. & Alban.* Pref. 6 The English I confess, are not altogether so Musical as the French. **1832** JEKYLL *Corr.* (1894) 294 At night we had four musical artistes. **1896** MRS. CAFFYN *Quaker Grandmother* 67 What! Do you take me for a musical person?

†**4.** *Math.* = HARMONIC *a.* 5 a. *Obs.*

1594 BLUNDEVIL *Exerc.* I. xxii. (1597) 23 Of Musicall proportion called in Latine *Harmoniaca proportio.* **1806** HUTTON *Course Math.* I. 119 Musical Proportion is when, of three numbers, the first has the same proportion to the third, as the difference between the first and second, has to the difference between the second and third. *Ibid.*, When numbers are in musical progression, their reciprocals are in arithmetical progression.

†**5.** Of or pertaining to the muses. *Obs.*

1490 CAXTON *Eneydos* 4 He hath redde the ix. muses, and vnderstande theyr musicalle scyences.

6. Set to or accompanied by music.

1685 DRYDEN *Alb. & Alban.* Pref. 2 The Italians..have not only invented, but brought to perfection, this sort of Dramatique Musical Entertainment. **1697** MOTTEUX *Loves of Mars & Venus* Pref., This Musical Play or Masque. **1791** H. WALPOLE *Let. to Miss Mary Berry* 28 June, Frank North ..has a musical comedy at the Little Haymarket, and coldly received. **1904** MRS. A. TWEEDIE *Behind Footlights* xvi. 292 For some forthcoming musical comedy.

7. *slang.* Applied to a horse with defective respiration; that is a 'roarer'.

1900 HAYES *Among Horses in Russia* Introd. 8 His skewbald Joseph, who was a beautifully shaped hunter,.. though musical.

8. *U.S.* Amusing; ridiculous. Cf. MUSIC *sb.* 10.

1816 PICKERING *Vocab. Words Amer.* 135 They would say of a man of humour, He is very musical. **1859** BARTLETT *Dict. Amer., Musical*, amusing. New England.

9. *Comb.*, as ***musical-headed*** adj.

1587 HARRISON *England* II. vi. (1877), The nobilitie.. whose cookes are for the most part musicall-headed Frenchmen.

10. Special collocations: **musical appreciation**, informed response to music; **musical arms**, a modification of the game of musical chairs (see quot.); **musical box**, a mechanical musical instrument consisting of a revolving toothed cylinder working upon a resonant comb-like metal plate; also *transf.* and *fig.*; **musical bumps**, a game similar to musical chairs, in which the competitors sit down on the floor or ground when the music stops and the last person to sit is out of the game; also *fig.*; **musical chairs**, a competitive parlour game in which a number of persons walk to music round a smaller number of chairs and each tries to secure a seat when the music stops, or an outdoor game on the same principle played on horseback; also *attrib.* and *fig.*; **musical chime**, a set of bells arranged to play a tune, a carillon; **musical clock**, a clock which produces short tunes at regular intervals; **musical comedy**, a light dramatic piece, on stage or in a cinema, consisting of dialogue, songs, and dancing, connected by a slight plot; also *fig.*; **musical director**, the conductor of the orchestra of a theatre, either for opera or for plays; **musical dramatist**, a composer of music-dramas (see MUSIC *sb.* 13 c); **musical drive**, an exhibition of horsemanship by a military unit in which the horses pull along the military equipment to the accompaniment of music; **musical festival** = FESTIVAL *sb.* 1 b; **musical fright** = *musical chairs*; **musical glasses** = HARMONICA 1 a; **musical ride** (see quot.); **musical saw**, a hand-saw held between the knees and 'played' with a violin bow; **musical shell** = *music-shell*; **musical snuff-box**, a snuff-box containing a small musical instrument worked by machinery; **musical watch**, a watch which incorporates a comb and cylinder mechanism to produce a tune at specified times.

1929 *Jrnl. Abnormal Psychol.* XXIV. 75 It is possible..in the teaching of '*musical appreciation' to inculcate dogmas about what is symbolized by certain musical combinations. **1947** C. GRAY *Contingencies & Other Essays* i. 20 The recognition of the truth..has brought about in recent years the development of an activity known as 'musical appreciation', which aims at fostering a love of music among the populace by means of broadcast lectures, evening classes, elementary handbooks and textbooks, educational gramophone records, and so forth; by teaching music, in a word, in very much the same way as one would teach any other subject in the educational curriculum. **1955** P. VINCENT in H. van Thal *Fanfare for Ernest Newman* 174 The courses of musical appreciation that have been taught in schools these last twenty years or so. **1962** M. SARGENT *Outline of Music* p. v, I believe this 'Outline' to be more thorough than many popular books on musical appreciation. **1924** D. C. MINTER *Children's Parties* x. 137 *Musical arms. This game is played in the same way as Musical Chairs, without, however, using chairs. [**1821** M. WILMOT *Let.* 16 Apr. (1935) 105 The musical bonbon box, and other trifles to *amuse* the children.] **1829** A. ROYALL *Pennsylvania* I. 10 A small wooden *musical box..by mechanical invention produced the name of any capital town you called for. **1840** HOOD *Kilmansegg, Misery* v, Toy, and trinket, and musical box. **1878** STATHAM in Grove *Dict. Mus.* I. 311 The 'musical-box' toy, which is in fact a carillon on a minute scale, playing on vibrating tongues. **1925** T. E. LAWRENCE *Let.* 3 Nov. (1938) 486 Our hut now has a little musical box. **1925** E. SITWELL *Poetry & Criticism* 21 No time for darkness there, excepting in the cubes of their musical-box brains. **1932** S. G. HEDGES *Indoor & Community Games* vi. 76 **Musical Bumps*... All march round in single file, while the pianist plays... When the music stops everyone must flop down on the floor—and the one who 'bumps' last falls out of the game. **1967** E. GRIERSON *Crime of One's Own* xi. 92 He..went a few paces and stopped abruptly—the technique one used at the piano to defeat too proficient children at a game of Musical Bumps. **1974** *Listener* 18 July 85/3 England may not be the world champions at soccer, but we are definitely past-masters at musical bumps. **1877** *Cassell's Family Mag.* Dec. 41/1 When there is a piano, '*Musical Chairs' played in the usual way..is quite as interesting. **1916** 'PETER' *Trench Yarns* 25 We had to get the men through the danger zone by a sort of musical-chairs rush. They came slowly up to the entrance, and then dashed in and round the corner into safety behind the bricks. **1933** A. BLEWITT *Ponies & Children* viii. 121 Musical Chairs—the posts are stuck in a small circle, one less than the number of competitors, who have to canter in a wide circle, led by a grown-up on horseback. **1939** R. S. SUMMERHAYS *Riding for All* xiv. 87 The almost inevitable event at all gymkhanas is musical chairs. **1950** G. BRENAN *Face of Spain* x. 202 The Spanish economic system is like a game of musical chairs, in which there are only half as many seats as there are performers. **1973** E. PAGE *Fortnight by Sea* v. 52 How rapidly the years slipped by, with what speed the game of musical chairs was played, how swiftly one was forced out of one role and into another. **1974** *Times* 16 Jan. 12/3 President Bourguiba..was still in the mood of playing musical chairs with his Prime Ministers. **1798** CRUTTWELL *Univ. Gazetteer* (1808) s.v. *Birmingham*, In each steeple is a set of *musical chimes. **1747** H. WALPOLE *Let. To Mann* 10 Nov., Don't you see that *musical clock? **1939** S. SPENDER tr. *E. Toller's Pastor Hall* I. 54 Even the *musical clock is afraid of being denounced. **1765** R. CUMBERLAND (*title*) The summer's tale: a *musical comedy of three acts. **1791, 1904** Musical comedy [see sense 6]. **1910** 'SAKI' in *Bystander* 7 Dec. 484/1 Noted lights of the musical-comedy stage. **1923** A. HUXLEY *Antic Hay* iii. 35 He looked..positively soldierly in his black jacket and his musical comedy trousers. **1957** *New Yorker* 12 Jan. 34/1 It was her favorite kind of film, a musical comedy in full color. **1967** *Listener* 3 Aug. 138/1, I thought I'd start in musical comedy,..carry on training as a dancer and singer. **1829** H. FOOTE *Compan. to Theatres* 147 Covent Garden—Season 1828–9... *Musical Director and Composer—Mr H. R. Bishop. **1902** W. H. CHANTREY *Theatre Accounts* 73 All reasonable requirements from time to time made by the Manager, and the directors of the Musical Director or Stage Manager. **1885** G. B. SHAW *How to become Mus. Critic* (1960) 73 The most subtle and profound of all *musical dramatists. **1963** *Listener* 3 Jan. 45/1 Compared with the microcosm created by the greatest musical dramatists his [*sc.* Puccini's] world is limited in subject-matter. **1930** *Times Educ. Suppl.* 31 May 1/3 The *musical drive by 'J' Battery, Royal Horse Artillery, was carried out at the gallop. **1852** DICKENS *Our Bore* in *Househ. Words* 9 Oct. 75/1 He was at the Norwich *musical festival. **1879** 'L. HOFFMANN' *Drawing-room Amusements* 24 *Musical Fright. **1766** GOLDSM. *Vic. W.* ix, They would talk of nothing but..pictures, taste, Shakespeare, and the *musical glasses. **1876** STAINER & BARRETT *Dict. Mus. Terms, Musical glasses*, a series of goblets of graduated sizes fixed in a case. The tone is produced by the friction of the fingers of the player on the edge of the glass. **1886** C. E. PASCOE *London of To-day* xviii. (ed. 3) 180 An exhibition of equestrian skill of the Life or Horse Guards, known as a *Musical Ride. This 'Musical Ride' is a kind of equestrian dance executed with extraordinary precision. **1960** C. DAY LEWIS *Buried Day* v. 93, I seen this regiment..performing their intricate 'musical ride', with guns and limbers, at the Naval and Military Tournament. **1927** *Melody Maker* Aug.

773/2 In the combination are two performers on *musical saw, which novelty, says Mr. Haggleton, always goes down well with his audience. **1946** R. Blesh *Shining Trumpets* (1949) v. 104 Exotic instruments may be utilized as well, such as harmonica, kazoo, jug, washboard, wood blocks and musical saw. **1957** W. C. Handy *Father of Blues* x. 139 The technique..was similar to that used in playing musical saws. **1958** A. Jacobs *New Dict. Mus.* 231 Mayuzumi..has written..music..including..'Tonepleromas 55' for wind and percussion instruments and musical saw. **1973** J. Wainwright *Devil you Don't* 22 Rawlings will have you warbling *La Traviata*, backwards..with musical saw accompaniment. **1666** J. Davies *Hist. Caribby Isles* 125 It may be called the *Musical-shell, because on the out-side of it there are blackish lines, full of notes. **1823** J. Badcock *Dom. Amusem.* 66 Pocket Organ, or *Musical Snuff-box. **1899** F. J. Britten *Old Clocks & Watches* 148 *Musical watches of large size with moving figures were a favourite conceit among French makers during the latter part of the eighteenth century. **1952** T. P. C. Cuss *Watches* xi. 145 On earlier musical watches—at the end of the eighteenth century—a pinned cylinder took the place of the disc. **1954** *Grove's Dict. Mus.* (ed. 5) V. 1018/2 Musical watches..were made, usually in Switzerland, at the beginning of the 19th century... There might be one tune..or, more rarely, an air and variation. **1973** *Watches in Usher Coll.* 12 Musical watch with tiny cylinder playing on 13 teeth.

B. *sb.*

†**1. a.** *pl.* Musical instruments. **b.** A musical performance. *Obs.*

c **1500** in Grose *Antiq. Rep.* (1809) IV. 408 All theys musycalls well handilled and orderide in ther kynde Gevithe soundes of swetnes. **1579** Spenser *Sheph. Cal.* May 28 Tho to the greene Wood they speeden hem all, To fetchen home May with their musicall.

2. a. A musical party. **b.** A musical person.

1823 D'Israeli *Cur. Lit.* Ser. II. I. 401 Such fashionable cant terms as 'theatricals', and 'musicals', invented by the flippant Topham. **1861** *Sat. Rev.* 21 Sept. 297 A luminous constellation of musicals has risen over Hereford. **1887** *Cornh. Mag.* June 632 Dull dinners and afternoon musicals completed the list of outside amusements.

3. A film or a theatrical piece (not opera or operetta) of which music is an essential element.

1938 *Chatelaine* Jan. 50/2 You can guess what it's about without my telling you—it's a musical. **1940** *Illustr. London News* CXCVI. 464/1 Some of these 'musicals' have proved extremely popular. **1944** [see *cover-girl*]. **1954** T. S. Eliot *Confidential Clerk* II. 47 *Lucasta*:..But what about taking me to a concert? *Colby*: Only the other day I invited you... *Lucasta*: To go to see that American Musical! **1959** *Listener* 13 Aug. 259/1 A Novello musical. **1973** *Ibid.* 14 June 815/2 Musicals..exist in a far from splendid isolation, endlessly repeating the tricks which once worked.

‖**musicale** (myzikal). *U.S.* [ellipt. use of F. *musicale* (fem. of *musical* adj.) for *soirée* or *matinée musicale*.] A musical party or reunion.

1883 A. B. Blake in *Harper's Mag.* 905/1 It was to be a musicale. **1896** *Cosmopolitan* XX. 408/2 The ladies' receptions are of a different character. Some are musicales.

musicality (mjuːzɪˈkælɪtɪ). [f. musical *a.* + -ity.] The quality or character of being musical.

1853 Miss E. S. Sheppard *Ch. Auchester* III. 65 A third, so deficient in natural musicality that he did not like my playing! **1877** Browning *Agamemnon* Pref. 6 There is abundant musicality elsewhere, but nowhere else than in his poem the ideas of the poet.

musicalization (mjuːzɪkəlaɪˈzeɪʃən). [f. next + -ation.] The expression or rendering of an art (other than music) in the style or manner of music; the action or process of musicalizing.

1928 A. Huxley *Point Counter Point* xxii. 408 The musicalization of fiction. **1930** H. Read *Julien Benda & New Humanism* 14 The cult of vagueness, the musicalisation of all the arts, the general subjectivism and romanticism. **1971** *Listener* 15 Apr. 473/3 The facts behind this 'musicalisation' of our culture..are fairly obvious. But the underlying motives are..complex.

musicalize (ˈmjuːzɪkəlaɪz), *v.* [f. musical *a.* + -ize.] *trans.* To set (a novel, play, or poem) to music; to express or render (an art other than music) in the style or manner of music.

1919 *N.Y. Times* 20 July IV. 2/6 'Kitty Mackaye'..is another play which is about to be musicalized. **1928** *Sunday Express* 19 Aug. 5/4 He prepared a musicalised version of the ..play. **1947** *Penguin Music Mag.* Dec. 72 The art of musicalising films rather than filming music. **1957** Manvell & Huntley *Technique Film Music* 284 Benjamin Britten had proved particularly adroit at musicalizing the rhythm and intonation of speech beyond their actual use in a vocal line. **1962** *Listener* 3 May 761/2 It was Huxley who showed, in *Point Counter Point*, how fiction could be musicalized. **1966** *New Statesman* 20 May 736/2 Usually with Zukofsky you get..a poem intricately musicalised (he is much affected by Bach's contrapuntal patterns).

musically (ˈmjuːzɪkəlɪ), *adv.* [f. musical *a.* + -ly².] In a musical manner; in accordance with the rules or requirements of music. Also *transf.*

1477 Norton *Ord. Alch.* v. in Ashm. *Theat. Chem. Brit.* (1652) 60 Joyne your Elements Musically, For two causes, one is for Melody. **1577** Northbrooke *Dicing* (1843) 109 In weddings they were wont to playe musically. **1663** Boyle *Usef. Exp. Nat. Philos.* II. xv. 260 That a Sound..may powerfully operate upon the Blood and Spirits, I, who am very Musically given, have divers times observ'd in my self. **1746–7** Hervey *Medit.* (1818) 252 A melody..far more musically pleasing than sweet Philomela's sweetest strains. **1854** Malden in *Philol. Soc. Trans.* 19 Such a line would be measured musically by four measures or bars. **1885** *L'pool Daily Post* 7 May 5/3 Mr. Ball took snuff with all his friends, sneezing musically after each pinch.

b. *Comb.*, as ***musically-falling***, ***-rhythmical*** adjs.

1740 Dyer *Ruins of Rome* 14 Thine too those musically-falling Founts To slake the clammy Lip. **1878** C. & M. C. Clarke *Recoll. Writers* 179 Miss Lamb promised to..hear her read poetry with the due musically-rhythmical intonation.

musicalness (ˈmjuːzɪkəlnɪs). [f. musical *a.* + -ness.] The quality of being musical.

1678 Cudworth *Intell. Syst.* I. v. 759 Matter.. perpetually remains, and all other things whatsoever are but ..passions and affections and dispositions thereof, as musicalness and unmusicalness, in respect of Socrates. **1756–82** J. Warton *Ess. Pope* (ed. 4) I. vi. 305 The peculiar musicalness of the first of these lines. **1881** A. Austin in *Macm. Mag.* XLIII. 402 Musicalness is unquestionably the most noticeable mark..of his own verse.

musicassette (mjuːzɪkæˈsɛt). [f. music *sb.* + cassette.] A tape cassette of prerecorded music.

1966 *Melody Maker* 8 Oct. 13/1 Musicassettes are with us. .. What exactly is a musicassette? It's the size of a bar of chocolate..and the tape is permanently housed inside the cassette. **1968** *Sat. Rev.* (U.S.) 25 May 50 As yet, of course, musicassettes are more for the uncritical listener to popular music. **1971** *Hi-Fi Sound* Feb. 12 (Advt.), Announcing the new professional musicassette library starting early in 1971. **1975** *Gramophone* Jan. 1293 (Advt.), A stereo musicassette player need not be expensive.

musicaster (ˈmjuːzɪkæstə(r)). [f. L. *mūsic-us* musician (see music) + -aster.] A musician of mediocre capacity.

1838 *Fraser's Mag.* XVII. 468 You may find a musicaster calling himself Smyth, a poetaster, Smythe.

†**ˈmusicate**, *v. Obs.* [f. ppl. stem of late L. *mūsicāre*, f. *mūsica* music.] *trans.* To set to music.

1614 *Declar. Pfaltzgrave's Faith* x. 180 It was alwaies so ordered that the text, which was musicated, was withall sung in the natiue language and was vnderstood by euery one.

musicen, obs. form of musician.

musician (mjuːˈzɪʃən). Forms: 4 musiceen, musucien, 4–6 musicien, 5 musi-, musycyen, 6 musicen, musyssyon, 6–7 musicion, -tian, -tion, 5– musician. [a. F. *musicien* (Oresme, 14th c.), f. L. *mūsic-a* music: cf. *physician*.]

1. One skilled in the science or practice of music.

c **1374** Chaucer *Boeth.* II. pr. vi. 42 (Camb. MS.) Also Musike maketh Musuciens and phisike maketh phisissiens. **1494** Fabyan *Chron.* II. xlvi. 29 Bledgaret, a cunnynge musician. **1553** Becon *Reliques of Rome* (1563) 116 b, Pope Vitalian being a lustye singer and freshe couragious musition hymself, brought into the church pricksong descant, & all kynde of..melodye. **1555** W. Watreman *Fardle Facions* II. xii. 280 Musicens (whiche encludeth singing and plaieng). **1604** Shaks. *Oth.* IV. i. 199 An admirable Musician. Oh she will sing the Sauagenesse out of a Beare. **1864** Browning *Abt Vogler* 88 The rest may reason and welcome: 'tis we musicians know. **1873** Helps *Anim. & Mast.* iv. (1875) 88, I knew a cat who..had the nicest perception as to who was the best musician in the room.

2. A professional performer of music, esp. of instrumental music. Also *transf.* and *fig.*

c **1450** Holland *Howlat* 756 All thus our lady thai lovit, with lyking and lyst, Menstralis and musicianis, mo than I mene may. **1553** Eden *Treat. Newe Ind.* (Arb.) 25 Al the musicions and minstrels..playe on theyr instrumentes. *a* **1649** Drumm. of Hawth. *Poems* Wks. (1711) 12/2 The wing'd Musicians did salute the Morne. *a* **1653** Binning *Serm.* (1845) 595 Christ and His ministers are the musicians that do apply their songs to catch men's ears and hearts. **1759** Robertson *Hist. Scotl.* III. Wks. 1813 I. 246 He was the son of a musician in Turin. **1880** Newton in *Encycl. Brit.* XI. 209/1 The notes of the hen [of the Pine-Grosbeak] may be deemed to qualify her as a musician of no small merit.

3. *Comb.*, as ***musician-like*** adj., ***musician-wise*** adv.; **musician thrush** (see quot. 1783).

1783 Latham *Gen. Synopsis Birds* II. I. 80 Musician Thrush... Le Musicien de Cayenne. *Ibid.*, It is much regarded for its song, which is so fine as to entitle it to the name of *Musician* among the inhabitants [Cayenne]. **1829** *Examiner* 68/1 It is..a very musician-like piece. **1897** Kipling *Captains Courageous* ix. 185 He swept his hand musician-wise through his hair.

Hence **muˈsicianess**, a female musician.

1829 Moore in *Mem.* (1854) VI. 35 Authors and authoresses, musicians and musicianesses.

musicianer (mjuːˈzɪʃənə(r)). Now *rare* in educated use. Forms: 6 *Sc.* musicinar, musecenar, 6–7 musicioner, 6–8 musitianer, 6–9 musitioner, 7– musicianer. [f. musician + -er¹.] = musician.

1540 *Records of Elgin* (New Spald. Cl. 1903) I. 47 The toun consentit to giff to John Kyntor, musicinar, ane croun of the sone for his seruice. **1609** *Househ. Bk. Earls Cumbld.* in Whitaker *Hist. Craven* (1812) 318 Payd to the musitioners which were appointed to play at Londesbro'. **1683** Tryon *Way to Health* 13 The most skilfulest Musicianer in the World can make no harmony, if his Instrument be not in tune. **1801** tr. *Gabrielli's Mysterious Husb.* II. 47 Those scrawls musicianers set before them to look at while playing. **1843** Thackeray *Irish Sk.-Bk.* (1857) 90 There were three girls..tossing their arms about to the tunes of three musicianers. **1899** Somerville & Ross *Irish R. M.* 294 Here, Yates! you're a sort of musicianer yourself!

musicianly (mjuːˈzɪʃənlɪ), *a.* [f. musician + -ly¹.] Characteristic or worthy of a skilled musician.

1864 Litchfield in *Reader* No. 97. 585/2 Her musicianly singing. **1897** *Oxford Mag.* 10 Feb. 185/2 Mr. A. Bent gave very musicianly renderings of Beethoven's Violin Sonata.

musicianship (mjuːˈzɪʃənʃɪp). [f. musician + -ship.] Skill as a musician.

1867 Macfarren *Harmony* (1892) 127 The otherwise manifested musicianship of him who made it. **1903** A. W. Patterson *Schumann* iv. 45 Surely a sufficient guarantee of his creative musicianship. **1930** *Times Educ. Suppl.* 2 Aug. 338/3 Miniatures full of dainty musicianship. **1959** *Times* 2 Feb. 1/4 The holder of the post will also be responsible for General Musicianship classes. **1970** P. Oliver *Savannah Syncopators* 98 But if blues singers appeal because of these talents as well as their musicianship, they are, like the *griots*, frequently considered as lazy, lacking in industry and job application.

musicien, -ion, obs. forms of musician.

musicist (ˈmjuːzɪsɪst). *rare.* [f. music + -ist.] = musician.

1873 M. Collins *Squire Silchester* II. xvi. 205 A famous trio—painter, poet, musicist.

†**ˈmusicker.** *Obs. rare.* [f. music + -er¹.] = musician.

14.. *Nom.* in Wr.-Wülcker 681/34 *Hic musicus*, a musyker. *c* **1425** *St. Christina* xxvi. in *Anglia* VIII. 129/33 þat songe..passed alle þe uoyses and Instrumentis of musikers or mynstralles. **1781** *Westm. Mag.* IX. 233 Whenever he [Charles Wesley] was called to play to a stranger, he would ask, in a word of his own, 'is he a musicker?'

musicless (ˈmjuːzɪklɪs), *a.* [f. music + -less.] Wanting taste or capacity for music; unmusical; also, without music.

1615 G. Sandys *Trav.* 172 Their musicklesse instruments are fannes of brasse, hung about with rings. **1854** Freeman in W. R. W. Stephens *Life & Lett.* (1895) I. 168, I, poor musicless brute, don't know the Hypo-Lydian from Cambridge New. **1873** Miss Broughton *Nancy* II. 173 In many musicless waltzings..we have learned to fit each other's step exactly.

†**ˈmusicness.** *Obs.* [f. music + -ness.] The quality of being musical.

1633 Nabbes *Tottenham Court* III. iii, *Iam.* Shall we dance, gentlemen? Musicknesse, and let activenesse freeze! Shall I use you sweet Mistris? *Wife.* Kindly sir, or I am waspish.

musico (ˈmuːzɪkəʊ). [a. It. *musico*, ad. L. *mūsicus*: see music.] A musician.

1821 Byron *Juan* IV. lxxxvi, The musico is but a crack'd old basin.

musico- (ˈmjuːzɪkəʊ), used as combining form of L. *mūsicus* in terms denoting the association of music with various arts or sciences, as ***musico-dramatic***, ***-mechanical***, ***-medico-artistic***, ***-philosophical***, ***-poetic*** adjs.; or (rarely) describing a person devoted to musical pursuits, as in ***musico-fanatic***; also, **musico-mania**, an excessive fondness for music; **musicophobia**, hatred of music.

1888 *Q. Rev.* CLXVII. 66 His [Wagner's] operas.. represented an entirely new type of *musico-dramatic art. **1844** J. T. Hewlett *Parsons & W.* viii, A friend of mine, a *musico-fanatic. **1855** Dunglison *Dict. Med.* 581/1 **Musicomania*, *Musomania*, a variety of monomania in which the passion for music is carried to such an extent as to derange the intellectual faculties. **1840** *Penny Cycl.* XVII. 2/2 As some description of it [the Apollonicon] may hereafter be found useful, as a part of *musico-mechanical history, we refer the reader to the article Apollonicon. **1796** Burney *Mem. Metastasio* II. 408, I am extremely delighted by the attentive perusal of the *musico-philosophical letters. **1903** F. W. H. Myers *Human Personality* I. 466 At church the sound of the organ terrified him. In this case we see agoraphobia, *musicophobia, &c. **1839** Longf. *Hyperion* IV. iv, Of course, my *Musico-poetic laboratory is an attic.

musicogenic (mjuːzɪkəʊˈdʒɛnɪk), *a. Path.* [f. musico- + -genic.] Applied to a form of epilepsy in which attacks are precipitated by the hearing of music, and to the attacks themselves.

1937 M. Critchley in *Brain* LX. 13 The aim of this paper is to describe the occurrence of epileptiform attacks in factual association with the hearing of music... Opportunity has since brought to notice a series of such cases of 'musicogenic epilepsy' (or 'musicolepsia'). **1962** *Jrnl. Amer. Med. Assoc.* 17 Feb. 503/1, 44 patients with musicogenic epilepsy have been reported in the literature. **1972** Boshes & Gibbs *Epilepsy Handbk.* (ed. 2) xiii. 61 Musicogenic seizures are extremely rare; the patient is usually an adult who is musically orientated.

musicographer (mjuːzɪˈkɒgrəfə(r)). *rare.* [f. Gr. μουσική music: see -grapher. Cf. F. *musicographe*.] A writer on musical subjects.

1884 *Leeds Mercury* 23 Apr. 3 England knows no musicographer whose writings are read with more general interest.

musicography (mjuːzɪˈkɒgrəfɪ). [f. Gr. μουσική music + -γραφία writing.] The science or art of writing music; musical notation.

1839 De Stains *Phonegraphy* 17 Part 2nd. Musicography. The following pages relate to music, for the writing of which are proposed seven distinct signs.

musicological (mjuːzɪkəˈlɒdʒɪkəl), *a.* [f. MUSICOLOGY: see -ICAL.] Of or pertaining to musicology. Hence **musicoˈlogically** *adv.*

1915 W. S. PRATT in *Musical Quarterly* I. 1 Several handy derivatives, such as 'musicologist'..'musicological', and the like. **1941** G. HAYDON *Introd. Musicology* i. 1 By no means everything written about music qualifies as musicological literature, but only that which exhibits an acceptable quality of scholarship. **1959** D. COOKE *Lang. Music* p. x, We concern ourselves more and more with parochial affairs—technical analyses and musicological *minutiae*—and pride ourselves on our detached, dehumanized approach. **1966** *New Statesman* 23 Sept. 451/2 Musicologically, they are.. scrupulous. **1969** *Daily Tel.* 12 Apr. 13 Musicologically sensational and musically highly enjoyable was Alan Hacker's performance on the basset clarinet of Mozart's Concerto, K. 622. **1970** P. OLIVER *Savannah Syncopators* 95 Musicological analyses of the blues have scarcely been undertaken to date. **1973** *Listener* 1 Mar. 286/2 Musicologically-inhibited people catalogue Caruso's liberties as heinous sins.

musicologist (mjuːzɪˈkɒlədʒɪst). [f. next: see -OLOGIST.] One who studies or practises musicology.

1915 [see MUSICOLOGICAL *a.*]. **1927** *Observer* 20 Feb. 18/2 The widest co-operation has..been secured from French, Spanish, German, and other foreign musicologists. **1930** *Music & Lett.* Apr. 138 The distinguished list of English musicologists. **1944** W. APEL *Harvard Dict. Mus.* 474/1 The men who undertook to 'discover Bach'..were musicologists in the true sense of the word. **1955** F. TOYE in H. van Thal *Fanfare for E. Newman* xi. 164 Who fifty years ago could have imagined that a musicologist of the calibre of Sir Donald Tovey should sponsor the performance of such an intrinsically popular opera as *Il Trovatore*? **1973** *Oxf. Mag.* 1 June 4/1 The members of the Faculty of Music are for the most part primarily musicologists.

musicology (mjuːzɪˈkɒlədʒɪ). [ad. F. *musicologie* or f. MUSIC *sb.* + -OLOGY.] The systematic study of music as opposed to the art of composition and performance; *esp.* academic research in music.

1909 M. S. LOGAN (*title*) Musicology. **1915** W. S. PRATT in *Musical Quarterly* I. 3 'Musicology', if it is to rank with other comprehensive sciences, must include every conceivable scientific discussion of musical topics. **1919** *Proc. Mus. Assoc. 1918–19* 106 The foundations of Musicology are the documents, manuscripts or printed music of past times. **1928** *Music & Lett.* Apr. 108 The most valuable piece of musicology is the treatment of the six motets. **1937** R. H. LOWIE *Hist. Ethnological Theory* xiv. 255 Comparative musicology..rose to a new plane with phonographic recordings. **1941** G. HAYDON *Introd. Musicology* i. 7 Musicology, following the lead of philosophy, adopts the epistemological concepts of space and time, and divides its subject matter under the two main headings *systematic* and *historical*. **1958** *Times Lit. Suppl.* 4 July 384/1 Only since the turn of the century has musicology been accepted fully and internationally as an independent branch of scholarship.

musicophile (ˈmjuːzɪkəʊfaɪl). [f. MUSICO- + -PHIL, -PHILE.] One who professes love of music.

1931 J. JOYCE *Let.* 3 Jan. (1957) 298 The wealthy musicophiles in London and New York who control the destinies of opera in those cities.

†ˈ**musicry.** *Obs.* [f. MUSIC + -RY.] The art of music.

1599 MARSTON *Sco. Villanie* III. xi, Shall all the world of Fidlers follow mee, Relying on my voice in musickrie?

Musigny (ˈmysiːniː). The name of a vineyard in the commune of Chambolle-Musigny in the Côte d'Or department of France used *attrib.* and *absol.* to designate the red Burgundy produced there.

1833 C. REDDING *Mod. Wines* v. 112 To recapitulate the wines of the Côte d'Or: the finest Burgundies are Romanée-Conti [etc.]. Of the second class, Chambolle, Musigny [etc.] among the red wines. **1907** *Yesterday's Shopping* (1969) 97/1 Burgundy—Musigny—Vintage 1899—Per doz. bots. 52/0. **1932** A. E. HOUSMAN *Let.* 31 May (1971) 321 The Sommelier insisted on Chambolle-Musigny 1921, which was most excellent. **1966** H. JOHNSON *Wine* 191 Musigny.. lingers and spreads in your mouth, making what French tasters call 'the peacock's tail' with its bouquet of flavours and flavours within flavours. **1967** A. LICHINE *Encycl. Wines & Spirits* 374/2 In a good year the wines, in addition to their ..feminine delicacy, have an incomparable bouquet... A fine estate-bottled Musigny can be expected..to profit enormously from imprisonment in the bottle.

musik(e, -ell, -er, obs. ff. MUSIC, -AL, -ICKER.

musilage, -idge, variant forms of MUCILAGE.

Musilman, obs. form of MUSSULMAN.

musimon, obs. form of MUSMON.

musing (ˈmjuːzɪŋ), *vbl. sb.* [f. MUSE *v.* + -ING[1].]

†**1.** Complaining, complaint. *Obs.*

1388 WYCLIF *Acts* xxviii. 29 Jewis wenten out fro hym, and hadden myche questioun, eithir musyng, among hem silf. **1500–20** DUNBAR *Poems* lxxv. 40 ȝour mvsing wald perss ane hairt of stane.

2. Thoughtful abstraction; the act of meditating or pondering.

c **1440** *Generydes* 491 Generydes stode still in grete musyng. **1594** CAREW *Huarte's Exam. Wits* (1616) 87 True it is, that much muzing, to some doth good, and to some harme. **1671** MILTON *P.R.* IV. 249 The sound Of Bees industrious murmur oft invites To studious musing. **1760–72** H. BROOKE *Fool of Qual.* (1809) IV. 80 His auditors continued in a kind of respectful musing. **1830** J. H. NEWMAN in *Lett. & Corr.* (1891) I. 229 Is not this the meaning of musing—namely, thinking about something or other, we cannot tell what?

b. A fit of thoughtful abstraction; a meditation.

1530 PALSGR. 530/2, I dumpe, I fall In a dumpe or musyng upon thynges, *je me amuse*. **1658–9** *Burton's Diary* (1828) IV. 242, I see the House in a great musing. **1711** ADDISON *Spect.* No. 7 ¶1 In the midst of these my Musings she desired me to reach her a little Salt upon the Point of my Knife. **1861** DORA GREENWELL *Poems* 171 Fed With golden musings by our friend that read From out thy chosen Poet.

musing (ˈmjuːzɪŋ), *ppl. a.* [f. MUSE *v.* + -ING[2].] Given to or characterized by meditation; contemplative; meditative; dreamy.

c **1450** J. METHAM *Wks.* (E.E.T.S.) 13 But nowe let alle this musyng matere pase. **1530** PALSGR. 247/1 Musyng felowe, *musart*. **1632** MILTON *Penseroso* 38 Com, but keep thy wonted state, With eev'n step, and musing gate. **1792** S. ROGERS *Pleas. Mem.* II. 179 The musing pilgrim. **1888** F. HUME *Mme. Midas* I. ii, 'She's a clever woman', observed Slivers, at length, in a musing sort of tone.

Hence ˈ**musingly** *adv.*, in a musing manner.

1611 FLORIO, *Accigliare*,..to looke staringlie or musinglie. **1886** STEVENSON *Kidnapped* xix, 'There's one thing', said Alan, musingly, 'that naebody kens his name'.

musing, obs. variant of MEUSING.

musion (ˈmjuːsɪɒn). *Her. Obs.* exc. *Hist.* [Of unknown origin; perh. arbitrarily f. L. *mūs* mouse.] The wild cat.

1572 BOSSEWELL *Armorie* II. 56 On a chiefe Pearle, a Musion or Catte, Gardant, Ermines. **1880** *Encycl. Brit.* XI. 699/2 The musion was the emblem of Burgundy.

musique, obs. form of MUSIC.

‖**musique concrète** (myzik kɔ̃krɛt). [Fr. (P. Schaeffer *À la recherche d'une musique concrète* (1952)).] = *concrete music* (CONCRETE *a.* and *sb.* A. 7). Also semi-anglicized as ***musique concrete***, and *fig.*

1952 *Time* 10 Nov. 95/1 Last summer the U.S. got a taste of creative recording in France's *musique concrète*, a compilation of natural sounds..recorded on tape, cut and spliced at patterns to make a composition. **1953** *Musical Quarterly* XXXIX. Oct. 608 A special session was devoted to Pierre Schaeffer's *Musique concrète* and Elektronische Musik developed in the studio laboratories of the Cologne Rundfunk. **1954** *Gramophone Record Rev.* Apr. 297 These experiments come to mind after studying the so-called *Musique Concrète* broadcast recently in the Third Programme. **1957** *Electronic Engin.* XXIX. 350 The recent Musique Concrete in France. To quote a reviewer of records 'This is neither music nor concrete'. **1958** *Oxf. Mag.* 8 May 410/1 The *musique concrète* of dishwasher, duplicator and the pneumatic drills of Restoration Oxford, Thalia shuts her pretty mouth. **1962** A. NISBETT *Technique Sound Studio* xi. 191 *Musique concrète* transformations. **1970** *New Scientist* 30 July 221/2 Modern office workers partial to John Cage and *musique concrète*.

†ˈ**musist.** *Obs. rare*[−1]. [f. MUSE *sb.*[1] + -IST.] A votary of the Muses.

1606 WARNER *Alb. Eng.* XIV. To Rdr. (1612) 331 The Musists, though themselues they please, Their Dotage els finds Meede nor Ease.

musit, variant of MUSET.

musitian, -ion, obs. forms of MUSICIAN.

musive (ˈmjuːsɪv), *a.* and *sb.* [a. F. *musif, -ive*, ad. late L. *mūsivus*: see MOSAIC *a.*[1]]

A. *adj.* = MOSAIC *a.*[1] 1. Now *rare* or *Obs.*

1506 GUYLFORDE *Pilgr.* (Camden) 37 The vaughtes be garnysshed with gold and byse with dyuers storyes of as subtyll musyn [? *read* musyu] werke as maye be. *Ibid.*, Of the sayde musyn werke. **1658** W. BURTON *Itin. Anton.* 91 Their very Poets scoffed at the Musive work of the pavements. **1813** J. FORSYTH *Remarks Excurs. Italy* 174 The musive work here exhibits a few grim old saints.

†**b.** ***musive gold*** = mosaic gold, late L. *aurum musivum*. *Obs.*

1796 KIRWAN *Elem. Min.* (ed. 2) II. 512 Mr. Wolfe found musive gold insoluble in acids.

B. *sb.* †**1.** = MOSAIC *sb.* 1.

1622 PEACHAM *Compl. Gent.* 118 The Grecians brought the Art of working in Musive, or Mosaique, to Venice. **1658** W. BURTON *Itin. Anton.* 156 The magnificent Acts of Statuarie, Founding, Mowlding, Musive, and Graving.

2. A species of noctuid moth.

1832 J. RENNIE *Conspect. Butterfl. & M.* 56 The Musive (*Graphiphora musiva*, Ochsenheimer).

musjid, variant of MASJID.

musk (mʌsk), *sb.* Forms: 4–7 **muske**, 6 **moske**, 7 **musch(e, mosk, (musque)**, 7–8 **mosch**, 5– **musk.** Also 4 in Latin forms **musco** (*abl.*), **muscum** (*accus.*). [a. F. *musc* (13th c. in Hatz.-Darm.) = Pr. *musc*, Sp., It. *musco* (also *muschio*), ad. late L. *muscus* (4–5th c.), med.L. *mos(c)hus*, late Gr. *μόσκος, μόσχος* (5–6th c.), prob. a. Pers. *mušk*, whence Arab. *misk* (whence, with Arab. prefixed article, Sp. *almizcle*, Pg. *almiscle*, *almiscar*); the ultimate source is perh. Sk. *muṣka* (Hindī *mušk*) scrotum, testicle.

The continental Teut. langs. have adopted the med.L. forms: G. *moschus*, Du., Sw. *myskus*, Da. *moskus, muskus*; obsolete forms are G. *mosch, musch*, Du. *musch*.]

1. a. An odoriferous, reddish-brown substance, secreted in a gland or sac by the male musk-deer. It has a very powerful and enduring odour, and is used as the basis of many perfumes, and in medicine as a stimulant and antispasmodic. Also applied occas. to substances of similar odour secreted by certain other animals.

1398 TREVISA *Barth. De P.R.* XVII. xix. (Tollem. MS.), Also of boxe beþ boxes made to kepe in muske and oþer spicerye. *c* **1400** *Lanfranc's Cirurg.* 196 If his herte quake, þan ȝeue him tiriaca maior wiþ a litil musco ouþer hoot wijn. **1471** RIPLEY *Comp. Alch.* XI. ii. in *Ashm.* (1652) 181 As musk in Pygments, and other spycys mo. **1555** EDEN *Decades* 108 They lefte a very sweete sauour behynde them sweeter then muske. **1620** J. MASON *New-found-land* 4 And a small beast like a Ferret whose excrement is Muske. **1656** RIDGLEY *Pract. Physick* 47 Hares runnet, and a little Musch. **1710** STEELE *Tatler* No. 103 ¶15 Perfumed so strongly with Musk that I was almost overcome with the Scent. **1798** W. YONGE in Beddoes *Contrib. Phys. & Med. Knowl.* (1799) 292 With mosch and valerian in larger doses. **1865** DICKENS *Mut. Fr.* I. xv, A grain of musk will scent a drawer for many years. **1870** YEATS *Nat. Hist. Comm.* III. (1872) 278 Musk is known in commerce under two forms—as Tonquin or Thibet musk, which is the most valuable, and Siberian, Kabardinian, or Russian musk, of inferior quality.

b. *pl.*

c **1570** WREN in *Hakluyt's Voy.* (1599) II. II. 59 The Negros answered againe, they had ciuet, muske, gold and graines. **1594** T. B. *La Primaud. Fr. Acad.* II. 120 But nowe they must haue muskes and perfumes.

c. An artificial preparation imitating musk.

1658 SIR T. BROWNE *Gard. Cyrus* iii, Animall-musk, seems to excell the vegetable. **1840** PEREIRA *Elem. Mat. Med.* II. 1397, I have seen several artificial pods of musk which have been imported from Canton. T. W. C. Martius ..calls this artificial kind Wampo musk. **1840** *Penny Cycl.* XVI. 27/2 An artificial musk is sometimes made with nitric acid and oil of amber.

d. An aromatic odour, resembling that of musk.

1855 TENNYSON *Maud* I. XXII. i, And the woodbine spices are wafted abroad, And the musk of the rose is blown.

2. An animal which produces 'musk', now usually the MUSK-DEER, sometimes called ***Tibet*** (or ***pouched***) ***musk***; also applied (with defining word) to other animals resembling the musk-deer, or possessing a musky smell.

c **1470** HENRYSON *Mor. Fab.* v. (*Parl. Beasts*) xviii, The marmisset the mowdewart..The musk, the litill mous [etc.]. **1611** FLORIO, *Lattitio*, a kind of Muske or Ziuet-cat. **1771** PENNANT *Synopsis Quadrup.* 58 Brasilian Musk. *Ibid.* 59 Indian Musk... Meminna... Inhabits Ceylon. *Ibid.*, Guinea Musk. **1781** —— *Hist. Quadrupeds* I. 112 Tibet Musk, of the form of a roebuck. **1801** SHAW *Gen. Zool.* II. II. 254 Pygmy Musk. *Moschus Pygmæus*... It is a native of many parts of the East Indies [etc.]. **1843** GRAY *List Mammalia Brit. Mus.* 172 The Musk. *Moschus moschiferus* Linn. *Ibid.*, The Kabarga or Siberian Musk. *Ibid.*, The White-bellied Musk. *Ibid.*, The Golden-eyed Musk. **1879** E. P. WRIGHT *Anim. Life* 155 In the musk the fur is thick and elastic, fit for a cold country. The males have an odoriferous gland in the middle of their abdomen.

3. a. A name for various plants having a musky odour; short for *musk-hyacinth, -mallow, okro, -tree*; in England now chiefly applied to *Mimulus moschatus* = *musk-plant* (b).

1731 MILLER *Gard. Dict.* s.v. *Geranium*, The 16th Sort [Musked Crane's-bill] is preserved in many gardens, for the sweet Scent its Leaves afford when rubb'd between the Fingers, which occasion'd its being called Musk, or Muscovy. **1786** ABERCROMBIE *Arrangem.* 74/1 in *Gard. Assist.*, (Muscaria) or musk hyacinth. Blue musk. Ash coloured musk. Purple musk. **1819** KEATS *Isabella* xi, Close in a bower of hyacinth and musk. **1866** *Treas. Bot.*, Musk, *Mimulus moschatus*; also *Erodium moschatum*. **1886** J. BONWICK in *Encycl. Brit.* XX. 174/1 Their [the Queenslander's] red cedar is the *Cedrela Goona*;..ebony, the *Malba*; musk, the *Marlea* [etc.]. **1897–8** BRITTON & BROWN *Amer. Flora*, Musk, *Malva moschata*.

b. Short for *musk apple, pear*.

1708 J. PHILIPS *Cyder* I. 31 But how with equal Numbers shall we match The Musk's surpassing Worth! **1731** MILLER *Gard. Dict.* s.v. *Pyrus* §9 Orange Musquée, *i.e.* The Orange Musk. **1741** *Compl. Fam.-Piece* II. iii. 388 Pears.. Orange Musk,..Jargonelle [etc.]. **1786** ABERCROMBIE *Arrangem.* 11 in *Gard. Assist.*, [Pears] Little musk.

4. *attrib.* and *Comb.* **a.** Obvious combinations, as ***musk-animal, -colour, trade***; (sense 3) ***musk-pot***; = flavoured or scented with musk, as ***musk-cake, -comfit, †fruit, julep, lozenge, plum, -sugar***. Also ***musk-coloured, -like, -perfumed, -scented*** adjs.

1693 DALE *Pharmacol.* 626 Animal Moschiferum... The *Musk Animal. **1706** *Closet of Rarities* (Nares), To make *musk-cakes, take half a pound of red roses,..add four grains of musk; mix them well to a thickness, make them into cakes and dry them in the sun. **1654** WHITELOCKE *Jrnl. Swed. Emb.* (1772) II. 179 A plain suit of..english cloth of *musk colour. **1681** GREW *Musæum* I. VII. ii. 164 'Tis about two inches long. Of a dark brown or Musk-colour. **1685** *Lond. Gaz.* No. 2072/4 He was habited in a Musk colour Cloth Coat. **1684** *Ibid.* No. 1944/4 A Petticoat of *Musk coloured Silk. **1598** FLORIO, *Moscadino*, a kinde of *muske comfets. **1638** BAKER tr. *Balzac's Lett.* (vol. III.) 55 For I have not yet medled with any of the *Musque fruits, which I hope you shall eat. **1775** ASH, **Musk julep*... A julep in which there is an infusion of musk. **1803** *Med. Jrnl.* IX. 498 It gives out a strong aromatic *musk-like smell. **1895** *Army & Navy Price List* 15 Sept. 702/2 *Musk Lozenges per box, 0/9. **1922** JOYCE *Ulysses* 11 Phantasmal mirth, folded away: *muskperfumed. *a* **1643** W. CARTWRIGHT *Siedge* IV. v, I've ..Kept *Musk-plums in my Mouth continually. **1859** G.

MEREDITH *R. Feverel* ix, The farmer pointed at some *musk-pots in the window. **1671** *Phil. Trans.* VI. 3002 Another *Musk-sented Insect. **1891** O. WILDE *Picture of Dorian Gray* (ed. 2) xv. 272 He bathed his hands and forehead with a cool musk-scented vinegar. **1937** *Discovery* Feb. 53/2 A musk-scented lady. **1957** R. CAMPBELL *Coll. Poems* II. 98 Musk-scented lace and fans of ostrich plume. **1696** SALMON *Fam. Dict.* (ed. 2), *Musk-Sugar, to Make. **1677** J. PHILLIPS tr. *Tavernier's Trav.* II. 153 Fearing that the cheats and adulterations of Musk would spoil the *Musk-Trade.

b. In various names for the receptacle in the musk-deer (or other animal) which contains the musk. See also MUSK-BAG, -COD.

1681 GREW *Musæum* I. II. ii. 22 The *Musk Bladder or Bag is about three inches long. **1837** M. DONOVAN *Dom. Econ.* II. 155 The removal of the *musk glands [in the crocodile] is absolutely necessary, as otherwise the flesh would be insupportable. **1888–91** BLANFORD *Mammalia India* 553 Many musk-deer are snared in nooses, others shot to secure the '*musk-pod', which is an article of commerce. **1834** tr. *Cuvier's Anim. Kingd.* I. 166 The other Musks have no *musk-pouch. **1840** PEREIRA *Elem. Mat. Med.* II. 1395 The *musk sac is of an oval form [etc.].

c. In the names of plants having a musky odour (frequently translating mod.Latin *moschatus*), as **musk carnation**, the clove-gilliflower; **musk cranesbill**, *Erodium moschatum*; **musk** (†**wood**) **crowfoot**, *Adoxa Moschatellina*; **musk-flower** = *musk-plant* (*b*); **musk geranium** = *musk cranesbill*; †**musk-gillyflower**, the clove-gilliflower; †**musk-grape** (**-flower**), **-hyacinth**, one of the grape-hyacinths, *Muscari moschatum*; **musk-mallow**, (*a*) *Malva moschata*; (*b*) = next; **musk okro**, *Hibiscus Abelmoschus*; **musk orchis**, *Herminium Monorchis*; **musk-plant**, †(*a*) = *musk okro*; (*b*) *Mimulus moschatus*; (*c*) = *musk mallow* (*a*); **musk-root**, 'the Sumbul root, derived from *Euryangium Sumbul*; also the Spikenard, *Nardostachys Jatamansi*; and *Adoxa Moschatellina*' (Treas. Bot. 1866); †**musk-scabious**, ? *Scabiosa atropurpurea*; **musk-seed**, the seed of *Hibiscus Abelmoschus*; **musk thistle**, the thistle *Carduus mutans*. Also MUSK-MELON, -ROSE, -TREE, -WOOD.

1866 M. ARNOLD *Thyrsis* vii, Soon will the *musk carnations break and swell. **1785** MARTYN *Rousseau's Bot.* xxiv. (1794) 337 Very like this is *Musk Cranesbill.. easily known by its musky odour. **1688** R. HOLME *Armoury* II. 103 *Musk-wood Crowfoot hath the leaf divided [etc.]. **1855** MISS PRATT *Flower. Pl.* III. 91 Tuberous Moschatell... It has several rustic names, as.. Hollow-root, and Musk-Crowfoot. **1852** *Cottage Gard. Dict.* (Johnson) 623 *Musk-flower, *Mimulus moschatus*. **1845–50** MRS. LINCOLN *Lect. Bot.* App. 101/2 *Erodium moschatum*, (*musk geranium). **1607** TOPSELL *Hist. Four-f. Beasts* (1658) 430 There be divers herbs which smell sweet like musk, as Angelica, Dorsis, *Musk-gilliflowers, *Musk grapes. **1598** FLORIO, *Muscorini*, *muske grape floure[s]. **1629** PARKINSON *Parad.* xi. 112 *Muske Iacinth. **1731** MILLER *Gard. Dict.*, *Muscari*, .. Musk-Hyacinth or Grape-flower, of a worn-out purple-greenish Colour. **1785** MARTYN *Rousseau's Bot.* xxiv. (1794) 342 Another wild species called *Musk Mallow. **1882** *Garden* 15 July 38/2 The White Musk Mallow [is] a charming British wild flower. **1756** P. BROWNE *Nat. Hist. Jamaica* (1789) 285 The *Musk Okro. The seeds of this plant.. have a strong and perfect smell of musk. **1731** MILLER *Gard. Dict.*, *Orchis*; *odorata moschata, sive Monorchis*. The Yellow Sweet or *Musk Orchis. **1785** MARTYN *Rousseau's Bot.* xxiv. (1794) 344 The *Musk plant of the West Indies is another species of Hibiscus; its kidney-shaped seeds have a very strong smell of musk. **1852** *Cottage Gard. Dict.* (Johnson) 607/1 *Mimulus moschatus* (Musk-plant). **1897–8** BRITTON & BROWN *Amer. Flora*, Musk-plant, a. *Mimulus moschatus*; b. *Malva moschata*. **1844** *Chem. Gaz.* II. 68 On *Radix Sumbul*, the Persian *Musk Root. **1706** PHILLIPS (ed. Kersey), **Musk-scabious*, a kind of Herb. **1731** MILLER *Gard. Dict.* s.v. *Scabiosa*, The Indian or Musk Scabious's are preserv'd for the Beauty and sweet Scent of their Flowers. **1712** tr. *Pomet's Hist. Drugs* I. 15 This Plant grows likewise in Egypt, where it is called *Musk-seed. **1873** *Beeton's Dict. Comm.* s.v., The musk-seed brought from the island of Martinico is accounted better than any other. **1731** MILLER *Gard. Dict.*, *Carduus*; *nutans*... The *Musk, or Nodding Thistle.

d. In the names of varieties of fruits having a musky smell or taste, as ***musk-apple***, ***cherry***, ***peach***, ***pear***; cf. MUSK *sb.* 3 b.

1611 COTGR. s.v. *Muscadelle*, *Pomme muscadelle*, a Muske apple. *Ibid.*, *Muscateline*, the Muske Peare; the smallest, sweetest, and soonest ripe of all other Peares. **1629** PARKINSON *Parad.* 583 The Muske Nectorin.. both smelleth and eateth as if the fruit were steeped in Muske. **1679** EVELYN *Kal. Hort.*, *Aug.* (ed. 5) 22 Man Peach,.. Musk Peach [etc.]. **1786** ABERCROMBIE *Arrangem.* 12 in *Gard. Assist.*, Principal Varieties [of Pears],.. Musk blanquette,.. Musk robine. **1884** HOGG *Fruit Man.* (ed. 5) 621 Pears... Musk Drone. See Bourdon Musqué.

e. In various names for MUSK-OX, as ***musk-bison***, ***buffalo***, ***sheep***; also ***musk bull***, ***cattle***, ***cow***.

1792 PENNANT *Arct. Zool.* I. Plate vii, Musk Bull and Cow. *Ibid.* II. Index, Bison or Ox, musk. **1823** BYRON *Juan* XII. lxxxii, Where the musk-bull browses. **1876** DAVIS *Polaris Exp.* 126 A long hunt for musk-cattle. **1877** A. R. WALLACE in *Encycl. Brit.* VII. 275/1 The musk-sheep (*Ovibos*).

f. In the names of animals having a musky odour, as † **musk ant**, 'the name given by Lister and Ray to a peculiar species of ant, which is of the number of the perfumed insects' (Chambers *Cycl. Supp.* 1753); † **musk-beaver** = MUSK-RAT 1; **musk-beetle**, a capricorn beetle, *Callichroma moschata*; **musk-cavy**, the PILORI; † **musk-fly** = *musk-beetle*; † **musk-goat** = MUSK-DEER; † **musk-goat-chafer** = *musk-beetle*; † **musk-hog**, the peccary; † **musk-insect** = *musk-beetle*; **musk-kangaroo**, a very small, rat-like, arboreal kangaroo, *Hypsiprymnodon moschatus*; **musk lorikeet**, an Australian parrot, *Glossopsitta concinna*; = *musk-parrakeet*; **musk-mole**, a Mongolian mole, *Scaptochirus moschatus* (Cent. Dict. 1890); **musk-parrakeet** (see quot.); **musk-shrew**, the Indian musk-rat (see MUSK-RAT 2); **musk-tortoise**, **-turtle**, a small American freshwater turtle, *Aromochelys odorata*; **musk-weasel**, any viverrine carnivore. See also MUSK-CAT, -DEER, -DUCK, -OX, -RAT.

1671 *Phil. Trans.* VI. 3002 A *Musk-Ant.. observed by me. **1771** PENNANT *Synopsis Quadrup.* 259 *Musk Beaver. **1753** CHAMBERS *Cycl. Supp.*, *Musk-Insect*, a term used by some to express the capricorn, or *Musk beetle. **1864–5** WOOD *Homes without H.* viii. (1868) 174 The Musk Beetle (*Cerambyx moschatus*). **1823** CRABB *Technol. Dict.* s.v. *Musk*, *Musk Cavy, the *Mus pilorides* of Linnæus. **1665** HUBERT *Catal. Rarities* 40 A dark green coloured flie called the *Musk flie, for his odoriferous sent when he is a live. **1601** HOLLAND *Pliny* II. 87 *marg.*, Plinie neuer heard of the *Musk-goats nor Ciuet cats in these daies. **1668** CHARLETON *Onomasticon* 8 *Capra Moschi*, the Musk Goat. **1681** GREW *Musæum* I. VII. ii. 164 The *Musk-Goat-Chafer. *Capricornus odoratus*... While it lives, and for sometime after its death, It hath a fragrant smell; from whence the Name. **1773** *Gentl. Mag.* XLIII. 219 The Mexican *Musk-Hog. **1671** *Phil. Trans.* VI. 3002 Two or three more *Musk Insects. **1894** LYDEKKER *Marsupialia* 73 The *Musk-Kangaroos. Genus *Hypsiprymnodon*. *Ibid.*, The remarkable creature known, from its strong scent, as the Musk-Kangaroo. **1901** A. J. CAMPBELL *Nests & Eggs Austral. Birds* 596, I have observed many nests of the *Musk Lorikeet in Victoria. **1966** EASTMAN & HUNT *Parrots of Australia* 32 Musk lorikeet... Pleasant strong musky odour associated with this Lorikeet. **1848** GOULD *Birds Australia* V. pl. 52 *Trichoglossus concinnus*, Vig. and Horsf. Musky Parrakeet... *Musk Parrakeet, Colonists. **1834** ROGET *Anim. & Veg. Phys.* II. 135 The *Sorex moschatus*, or *musk shrew. **1888** BLANFORD *Mammalia India* 233 *Crocidura murina*, the brown musk Shrew. *Ibid.* 236 *Crocidura cærulea*, the grey musk Shrew. **1885** *Stand. Nat. Hist.* (1888) III. 452 *Aromochelys odorata* is a small turtle found in pools.. and known as the *musk-turtle, besides other savory names. **1835** SWAINSON *Nat. Hist. & Classif. Quadrup.* 361 *Viverrinæ*. *Musk-Weasels.

musk, *v. rare.* [f. MUSK *sb.*] *trans.* To perfume with or as with musk.

1632 SHERWOOD, *To Muske*, perfume with Muske, *Musquer* [1611 COTGR. has 'bemuske', see BE- 6 b]. **1791** E. DARWIN *Bot. Gard.* I. 6 Musk'd in the rose's lap fresh dews they shed. *Ibid.* 138 The Nymph.. Each tangled braid with glistening teeth unbinds And with the floating treasure musks the winds.

muskadel(l, -delle, dyll: see MUSCATEL.

muskaden, -dine, -dyn(e: see MUSCADINE[1].

muskalinge, -allonge, -allunge, -alo(u)nge, var. ff. MUSKELLUNGE.

†**'musk-'almond.** *Sc. Obs.* In quot. *muscalmon*. A kind of sweetmeat.

1822 GALT *Sir A. Wylie* I. iii. 31 The muscalmons were declared to be as big as doos' eggs.

muskane, variant of MUSCANE *a. Obs.*

muskat, variant of MUSK-CAT.

muskateire, obs. form of MUSKETEER.

muskatoon, obs. form of MUSKETOON.

muskavada, obs. form of MUSCOVADO.

muskaye, obs. form of MOSQUE.

'musk-bag.

1. The bag or gland containing musk in various animals, esp. the Musk-deer.

1681 GREW *Musæum* I. II. ii. 22 The Musk Bladder or Bag is about three inches long. **1877** J. GIBSON in *Encycl. Brit.* VII. 25/1 The Musk Deer.. differs from the true deer in the absence of horns, and in the presence of the musk-bag.

†**2.** A small bag containing musk and other perfumes, etc. *Obs. rare.*

1706 *Closet of Rarities* (Nares), To make musk-bags to lay among your cloaths.—Take the flowers of lavender-cotton six ounces [etc.].. dry them and beat them to powder, and lay them in a bag wherein musk has been.

†**'musk-ball.** *Obs.* [BALL *sb.*[1]]

1. A 'ball' or receptacle for musk. Cf. *must-ball*: see MUST *sb.*[2]

1423 *Rolls of Parlt.* IV. 219 Item, 1 Muskball d'or. **1463** *Bury Wills* (Camden) 35 My muske bal of gold. **1550** BALE *Image Both Ch.* III. xviii. B b ij, Their vessels of Yuory comprehendeth all.. their combes, their muske balles, their pomander pottes [etc.].

2. A ball of soap scented with musk.

1589 RIDER *Bibl. Schol.* 979 A muske ball, *pastillus orbiculus*. **1594** GREENE & LODGE *Looking Glasse* (1598) B 2 b, We neuer vse any musk-balls to wash him with. **1719** *Accomplish'd Female Instructor* (Nares), Curious musk-balls, to carry about one, or to lay in any place. Let the groundwork be fine flower of almonds, and Castle-soap, each a like quantity, seare the soap thin [etc.].

attrib. **1594** BARNFIELD *Affect. Sheph.* II. xxvi. (Arb.) 16 Sell thy sweet breath to th' daintie Musk-ball-makers.

†**'musk-cat.** *Obs.* Forms: see MUSK *sb.* and CAT *sb.*[1]; also 6–7 **musket**, 7 **muscat**, **muskat**. 'The animal from which musk is got' (J.); usually, the MUSK-DEER. Cf. CIVET-CAT.

1551 GESNER *Hist. Anim.* I. 787 Angli muske [dicunt]: & animal muske catte,.. quod nomen zibethi animali potius conueniret. **1553** EDEN *Treat. Newe Ind.* (Arb.) 25 In this region are founde many muskecattes. **1601** SHAKS. *All's Well* v. ii. 21 Heere is a purre of Fortunes sir, or of Fortunes Cat, but not a Muscat. **1607** mus-kat [see MOSCHAT]. *a* **1631** DONNE *Elegie* Poems (1633) 149 As the sweet sweat of Roses in a Still, As that which from chaf'd muskats [*v.r.* muskets] pores doth trill. **1638** SIR T. HERBERT *Trav.* (ed. 2) 322 The Musk Cat here also convenes and may merit a ca'tagraph. **1794** Z. MACAULAY in *Life & Lett.* iv. (1900) 67 [Referring to Sierra Leone.] Some of the sailors were.. in the act of killing a beautiful musk-cat, which they afterwards ate.

b. *transf.* as a term of reproach to a fop (cf. MUSK-COD 2); also applied to a courtesan.

c **1566** *Merie Tales of Skelton* in *Wks.* (1843) I. p. lx, Skelton dyd keepe a musket at Dys, vpon the which he was complayned on to the bishop of Norwych. **1586** WHITNEY *Choice of Emblems* 79 Heare Lais fine, doth braue it on the stage, With muskecattes sweete, and all shee coulde desire. **1599** B. JONSON *Ev. Man out of Hum.* II. i. (1600) D 4, Hee sleepes with a muske Cat euery night. **1607** TOURNEUR *Rev. Trag.* I. iii. (1608) B 3, How dost, sweete Muskcat, When shall we lie togither? **1777** SHERIDAN *Trip Scarb.* III. i, Thou essence-bottle, thou musk-cat!

c. *attrib.*

1609 *Ev. Woman in Hum.* III. i. in Bullen *O. Pl.* IV, I can smell him half a mile ere hee come at me, indeede hee weares a Musk-cat—what call ye it? **1651** CLEVELAND *Poems* 6 Whose language is a Tax, whose Musk-cat verse Voids nought but flowers for thy Muses here.

†**'musk-cod.** *Obs.* Forms: see MUSK *sb.* and COD. Also 7 **muscod.** [COD *sb.*[1]]

1. = MUSK-BAG 1.

1672 BLOME *Descr. Jamaica* 29 They [*sc.* Allegators] have in them Musk-codds, which are stronger scented then those of the East-Indies. **1721** [see COD *sb.*[1] 1 b.]

2. *transf.* A scented fop.

1599 B. JONSON *Ev. Man out of Hum.* V. vi, I beleeue, muske-cod. I beleeue you. **1634** S. R. *Noble Soldier* II. i. in Bullen *O. Pl.* I. 277, I begge, you whorson muscod! my petition Is written on my bosome in red wounds.

'musk-deer. A small hornless ruminant (*Moschus moschiferus*) of Central Asia, the male of which yields the perfume called 'musk' (see MUSK *sb.* 1). Applied also to the other members of the family *Moschinæ*, and to the family *Tragulidæ*, or chevrotains, which are horned and have no musk-bags.

1681 GREW *Musæum* I. II. ii. 21 The Musk Deer. **1770** GRAY *Corr. w. Nicholls* (1843) 113 Are her subjects all civet-cats and musk-deer? **1865** MATHIAS *Sport in Himalayas* 122 The musk-deer (called by the natives moosknafar) inhabits thick, dense, scrubby jungle... Their presence in a jungle may always be known by the musky odour of their droppings. **1893** LYDEKKER *Horns & Hoofs* 330 The musk-deer, or kastura, as it is termed in Hindustani, is so well known to all Himalayan sportsmen, that [etc.].

'musk-duck.

1. A tropical American duck, *Cairina moschata*, erroneously called the *Muscovy* and *Barbary duck*.

It is now domesticated and is larger than the common duck.

1774 GOLDSM. *Nat. Hist.* (1776) VI. 130 The Muscovy duck, or, more properly speaking, the Musk Duck, so called from a supposed musky smell,.. a native of Africa. **1824** *Shaw's Gen. Zool.* XII. II. 81 They have obtained the name of Musk-duck from their musky smell. **1877** NEWTON in *Encycl. Brit.* VII. 506/2 The Musk-duck (*Cairina*) of South America, which is often domesticated and in that condition will produce fertile hybrids with the common Duck.

2. An Australian duck, *Biziura lobata*, so called from the musky odour of the male.

1834 *Proc. Zool. Soc.* II. 19 A specimen was exhibited of the Musk Duck of New Holland, *Hydrobates lobatus* Temm. **1880** MRS. MEREDITH *Tasmanian Friends & Foes* 159 That's a musk duck... The whole bird has a strange odour of musk, rendering it quite uneatable.

musked (mʌskt), *a.* Now *rare* or *arch.* Also 7 **musket.** [f. MUSK *sb.* + -ED[2].] Flavoured, or perfumed with musk; tasting like musk.

Often in names of plants and fruits (sometimes translating mod.L. *moschātus*).

1576 BAKER *Jewell of Health* 227 b, Add.. of sublimed wyne vj pyntes, of Rose-water Musked one pynt and a halfe. **1597** GERARDE *Herbal* II. cccxliv. 795 Musked Cranes bill hath many weake and feeble branches trailing vpon the grounde. *Ibid.* 796 It is called.. *Geranium moscatum*: in English Musked Storkes bill, and Cranes bill. **1614** DRUMM. OF HAWTH. *Sonn.* '*Alexis here she stay'd*', Shee set her by these musket Eglantines. **1694** SALMON *Bate's Dispens.* (1713) 591/2 The musked Julep against Fits of the Mother. **1706** LONDON & WISE *Retir'd Gard.* I. I. xi. 51 Abricots of the best Sort, whereof two must be musked. **1731** MILLER *Gard. Dict.* s.v. *Geranium* §16 Musked Crane's-bill or Moscovy. **1753** ARMSTRONG *Taste* 96 But hear their Raptures o'er some specious Rhime Dub'd by the musk'd and greasy Mob sublime. **1802** W. FORSYTH *Fruit Trees* vii. (1824) 179 Its colour red and yellow, its flesh tender and musked. **1852** R. S. SURTEES *Sponge's Sp. Tour* lxvi. (1893) 349 A musked cambric handkerchief.

muskedall, -dele, obs. forms of MUSCATEL.

muskedine: see MUSCADINE.

muskeet, variant of MESQUITE.

muskeeto, obs. form of MOSQUITO.

muskeg (ˈmʌskɛg). *Canadian.* Also **muskeag.** [Cree Indian; corresp. to Odjibway *mashkig*, Abnaki *mskakw*.] A kind of bog: see quots.

1865 VISCT. MILTON & W. B. CHEADLE *N.W. Passage by Land* 207 Muskegs—or level swamps—the surface of which is covered with a mossy crust five, or six inches in thickness, while a thick growth of pines and the fallen timber add to the difficulties of the road. **1886** *Times* 24 Sept. 7 A 'muskeg' is a lake bearing on its surface a thick growth of decayed vegetable matter and peat, in layers made year after year. **1899** *Blackw. Mag.* Mar. 541/2 A thick forest of tall pines with patches of bad muskeag, or marsh. **1904** M. ROBERTS *Bianca's Caprice* 143 Beyond the Prairie lay the muskeg, the barren lands of Northern Canada.

Hence **muˈskeggy** *a.*, abounding in muskegs.

1894 *Blackw. Mag.* June 802 Muskeggy prairies of varying size. **1903** A. C. P. HAGGARD *Sporting Yarns* 98 After a while this prairie..developed into muskeggy swamp.

muskeito(r, obs. forms of MOSQUITO.

muskel(e, -ell, obs. ff. MUSCLE *sb.*, MUSSEL.

muskellunge (ˈmʌskəlʌndʒ). Also 8 maskinunga, muschilongoe, muskinunge, 9 masquinongé, -ongy, masquenonger, muscanonge, maskinonge, maskinongé, -ongy, maskenozha; masc-, maskal(l)onge, muscal(l)onge, masculonge, muskallunge, -al(l)onge, -alounge, -elunge, maskelonge, masque alonge; *Dicts.* maskalunge, muskullonge, -alinge, -elunjeh, moskalonge, etc. [Odjibwa; spelt *mackinonge*, *micikinonge* by Cuoq *Lexique de la langue algonquine* (where *c* represents (ʃ)). According to Cuoq, f. *mac*, *mici* great + *kinonge* pike; according to Baraga the first element is *mask* ugly.

The varieties of form are partly due to diversities of native dialect, partly to a French popular etymology which took the word as *masque long* or *masque allongé*, 'long mask'.]

A large pike, *Esox masquinongy*, inhabiting the Great Lakes of North America, valued as a food-fish.

1794 S. WILLIAMS *Vermont* 122 The Pike or Pickerel abounds much in Lake Champlain. It is there called by the name of Muschilongoe. **1796** MORSE *Amer. Geog.* I. 352 Maskinungas, a very large species of pickerel. **1798** I. ALLEN *Hist. Vermont* 13. **1809** A. HENRY *Trav.* 30 Among the pike, is to be included the species, called, by the Indians, masquinongé. **1836** J. RICHARDSON *Fauna Bor. Amer.* III. 127 *Esox estor* (Le Sueur), The Maskinongé. **1855** LONGF. *Hiawatha* VIII, And he said to the Kenozha, To the Pike, the Maskenozha. **1868** LOSSING *The Hudson* 61 Lake George.. abounds with fine fish, the largest and most delicious being the Masque alonge. **1884** G. B. GOODE, etc. *Nat. Hist. Aquat. Anim.* I. 466 At Sacket's Harbor very few Muskellunge are caught. **1894** *Outing* XXIV. 454/1 A dinner of muscallonge steaks. **1899** *Pall Mall Mag.* Apr. 445 The big trout and maskinonge were stirring themselves in the depths of the lake. **1946** *Wisconsin State Jrnl.* 18 July 1/4 Gen. Dwight D. 'Ike' Eisenhower and his four brothers all continued their fishing luck Wednesday when they hit the jack pot with a muskellunge each. **1959** E. TUNIS *Indians* 40/2 Not to be despised, however, was the big pike called muskellunge by the Algonquins, the name it still bears. **1963** *Globe & Mail* (Toronto) 13 Apr. 5/6 He is also an officer of the Outdoor Writers of Canada and only in one respect might he come into conflict with his companions on that body—by using the U.S. term muskellunge instead of the accepted, original Canadian name, maskinonge. **1970** R. LOWELL *Notebk.* 251 Each night, a star, gold-on-black, a muskellunge, Dies in the highest sphere that never dies.

muskely, -elly, obs. forms of MUSCLY.

musket[1] (ˈmʌskɪt). *Obs.* exc. *Hist.* Also 5 muskyte, 5–7 muskett(e, 7 musquet. [a. ONF. *musket* (AF. pl. *muskez*, 1332 in *Litt. Cant.* I. ccccxli. 486), *mousquet*, Central OF. *mouchet* (mod.Fr. corruptly *émouchet*) = It. *moschetto* a small kind of sparrowhawk.

The word has the form of a dim. of Com. Rom. *mosca*:—L. *musca* fly: cf. It. *moscardo* of the same meaning. Some scholars regard the name as alluding to the diminutive size of the bird, others as meaning 'speckled' comparing F. *moucheter* to mark with spots like flies or fly-specks.]

The male of the sparrowhawk.

c **1425** *Voc.* in Wr.-Wülcker 641/14 *Hic capus*, muskett. *c* **1475** *Pict. Voc.* ibid. 761/6 *Hic capus*, a muskyte. **1486** *Bk. St. Albans* b v b, Tho that kepe Sperhawkys and muskettys ben called Speruiteris. **1581** DERRICKE *Image Irel.* D ij b, Then the Iacke and Musket laste, by whom the birds are vext. **1614** MARKHAM *Cheap Husb.*, *Of Hawkes* i. 135 The Gos-hawke and her Tercell, The Sparrow-Hawke Musket, and such like. **1687** DRYDEN *Hind & P.* III. 1119 The Musquet and the Coystrel were too weak. **1688** R. HOLME *Armoury* II. 236/1 A Musket is the Male of a Spar-hawk or Sparrow-hawk.

musket[2] (ˈmʌskɪt). Forms: 6 mosquet, muscat, 6–7 muskett(e, 7 muscatt(e, musquatte, 7–9 musquet, 6– musket. [a. F. *mousquet* (in 16th c. also *mousquette* fem.), ad. It. *moschetto*, orig. a kind of sparrowhawk (see MUSKET[1]). With regard to the practice of naming species of firearms from birds of prey, cf. *falcon*, *falconet*, *saker*.]

1. A hand-gun of the kind with which infantry soldiers are armed.

Originally applied to the matchlock, and in the 18th c. still sometimes distinguished from the 'firelock' or 'fusee'. (From early examples it appears that arrows as well as bullets were discharged from muskets.) Subsequently it became the general name for the infantry gun, whatever its construction. This use still survives, but as the modern gun is commonly (and in the Army Regulations) called by the specific term *rifle*, there is a tendency to restrict *musket* to the obsolete forms of the weapon.

c **1587** SIR R. KNYGHTLEY in *Buccleuch MSS.* (Hist. MSS. Comm.) I. 225 Muskettes and calleevers and holebertes shall be provided for this company. **1590** SIR J. SMYTH (*title*) Certain Discourses,..concerning the formes and effects of divers sorts of weapons,..and chiefly, of the Mosquet, the Caliver and the Long-bow. **1595** R. JOHNSON *7 Champions* II. (1608) O j, Like unto an arrow forced from a musket. **1598** BARRET *Theor. Warres* II. i. 27 One good musket may be accounted for two calliuers. **1639** *Burgh Rec. Glasgow* (1876) I. 400, 32 musquattis at £9 16*s.* 8*d.* the peice. **1672** CAPT. T. VENN *Milit. Obs. Art Drilling* ii. 34 The Musquet is to be rested at the sentinel posture. **1727–52** CHAMBERS *Cycl.*, *Musket*, or Musquet, properly a fire-arm borne on the shoulder, and used in war; to be fired by the application of a lighted match... At present they are little used save in the defence of places; fusees, or fire-locks, having taken their place. **1764** *Mem. G. Psalmanazar* 153 He had too great a regard for me, to send me with them to carry a brown musket. **1844** H. H. WILSON *Brit. India* III. 126 Five or six men, armed with musquets and ginjals. **1876** VOYLE & STEVENSON *Milit. Dict.* (ed. 3) s.v., The musket, as it is still called, has been brought to great perfection in the rifled small-arm of the present day.

2. *attrib.* and *Comb.*, as ***musket ammunition***, ***ball***, ***barrel***, ***bullet***, ***butt***, ***charge***, ***flint***, ***range***, ***reach***, ***stock***; ***musket-armed***, ***-like***, ***-proof*** adjs. Also **musket-arrow**, a short arrow discharged from a musket; **musket basket** (see quot. 1704); **musket powder**, the kind of gunpowder used for small-arms; **musket-rest**, a forked staff to support the heavy musket in use before the middle of the 17th century; **musket-slit**, a slit in a wall through which a musket may be fired.

1810 WELLINGTON *Let.* 12 June in Gurw. *Desp.* (1836) VI. 188 The state of the *musket ammunition..is not so bad as [etc.]. **1885** H. M. STANLEY *Congo* I. 388 Its one-story block-house..impregnable to *musket-armed natives. **159.** in Meyrick *Ant. Armour* (1824) III. 67 *Musket arrowes with 22 shefe to be newfethered. **1867** SMYTH *Sailor's Word-bk.*, *Musket arrows*, used in our early fleets, and for conveying notices in 1815. **1725** DE FOE *Voy. round World* (1840) 165 We returned the salute with our *musket-ball. **1825** J. NEALE *Bro. Jonathan* III. 109 A musket-ball had gone thro' both legs. **1644** EVELYN *Diary* 27 Feb., Two extravagant musqueteeres shot us with a streme of water from their *musket barrells. **1688** CAPT. J. S. *Fortification* 125 *Musket-Baskets, or smaller Gabions. **1704** J. HARRIS *Lex. Techn.* I, *Musket-Baskets*, in Fortification, are Baskets of about a Foot and half high... They are filled with Earth, and are set on low Parapets or Breast-works,..that the Musketeers may fire between them at the Enemy. **1598** BARRET *Theor. Warres* 167 It is not so light a matter to skirmish among the *musket bullet. **1813** SCOTT *Rokeby* VI. xxxiii, Sword, halberd, *musket-but. **1859** J. GRANT *Leg. Black Watch* (Rtldg.) 374 Stunned by a blow from a musket-butt. *c* **1610** MIDDLETON, etc. *Widow* IV. ii, I'll send him a whole *musket-charge of gunpowder. **1743** BULKELEY & CUMMINS *Voy. S. Seas* 102 Twelve *Musket-Flints. **1892** GREENER *Breechloader* 71 Guns quite plain, almost *musket-like in their outward appearance. **1644** NYE *Gunnery* (1647) 5 The *Musket Powder is now commonly made of Saltpetre five parts, one part of Brimstone, and one of Cole. **1880** *Encycl. Brit.* XI. 319/1 It was the custom for the fine grain or musket powder to contain a larger proportion of saltpetre than that for cannon. **1601** R. JOHNSON *Kingd. & Commw.* (1603) 92 The horsemen were all armed, many of whose curasses were heigh *musket proofe. **1603** in Meyrick *Ant. Armour* (1824) III. 81 Two blacke armors of muskett proofe. **1622** SIR R. HAWKINS *Observ. Voy. S. Sea* lxvi. 164 The vpper worke of their shippes being Muskets proofe. **1863** YONGE *Brit. Navy* II. 437 A musket-proof stockade. **1834–47** J. S. MACAULAY *Field Fortif.* (1581) 141 Villages commanded by the neighbouring ground, within *musket-range. **1646** H. P. *Medit. Seige* 23 To be gall'd with their small shot, if they be within *musket reach. **1598** B. JONSON *Ev. Man in H.* II. v, He will neuer come within the signe of it, the sight of a cassock, or a *musket-rest againe. **1856** MAYHEW *Rhine* 225 You perceive *musket-slits hemming you in on every side. **1833** *Penny Cycl.* I. 77/1 Its wood is so hard as to be in request for the manufacture of *musket-stocks.

musket, variant of MUSK-CAT.

musketa, obs. form of MOSQUITO.

musketade (mʌskɪˈteɪd). Also 7 musquetad. [f. MUSKET[2] + -ADE, after F. *mousquetade*.] A continued discharge of muskets; an attack with muskets. So **muskeˈtading** *vbl. sb.*

1655 FLECKNOE *Relat. 10 Yrs. Trav.* 12 Your young Gallants..talk of nothing but Rampards and Parapats, Musquetads, Estramacons, and Canonads. **1865** CARLYLE *Fredk. Gt.* XX. vii. (1872) IX. 144 Broglio truly has burst-out into enormous cannonade, musketade and cavalry-work. *Ibid.* xii. 228 Most furious cannonading, musketading; and seemingly no end to it.

musketeer (mʌskɪˈtɪə(r)). Forms: 6 mosquettier, musketire, 6–7 musketear(e, muscat(t)ier, 6–8 musket(t)ier, musquetier, 7 muscateer, muskat(e)ire, musketer(e, musketteer(e, musketter, musqueteir(e, musquetiere, musquetteer, -ier, 7–9 musqueteer, 6– musketeer. See also MOUSQUETAIRE. [f. MUSKET[2] + -EER[1], after F. *mousquetaire*, It. *moschettiere*. Cf. Sp. *mosquetero*.]

a. *Hist.* A soldier armed with a musket.

1590 MARLOWE *2nd Pt. Tamburl.* III. ii, It must haue.. Parapets to hide the Muscatiers. **1590** SIR J. SMYTH *Disc. Weapons* 10 b, Mosquettiers. **1598** BARRET *Theor. Warres* III. i. 35 The musketier is to cary his musket vpon his left or right shoulder. **1604** E. GRIMSTONE *Hist. Siege Ostend* 170 In them were 2500 musketers and small shott. **1639** *Conceits, Clinches, Flashes & Whimzies* No. 121 Muscattiers of all other Souldiers are the most lazie: for they are alwayes at their rest. **1663** BUTLER *Hud.* I. ii. 567 Did they coyn Piss-pots, Bowls, and Flaggons, Int' Officers of Horse and Dragoons; And into Pikes and Musqueteers Stamp Beakers, Cups, and Porringers? **1689** *Andros Tracts* I. 175 Except he would accept of a Guard of Two Muskateires to wayte upon him. **1707** *Reflex. upon Ridicule* 74 'Tis not for a Commander to act the Part of a Musquetier. **1777** WATSON *Philip II*, XIII. (1839) 257 On the left his cavalry, flanked by a body of musqueteers. **1814** SCOTT *Wav.* xxxv, Waverley, having mounted his horse, with a musketeer leading it [etc.].

b. ***musketeer gauntlet***, ***glove***: see MOUSQUETAIRE 2.

1922 JOYCE *Ulysses* 458 Fawn musketeer gauntlets. **1968** *Guardian* 26 July 7/3 There were musketeer gloves and gaiters of sequins.

musketo(e, obs. forms of MOSQUITO.

musketoon (mʌskɪˈtuːn). *Obs.* exc. *Hist.* Also 7 musquetoon, musquettoon, 7–9 muskatoon. [a. F. *mousqueton*, ad. It. *moschettone*, f. *moschetto* MUSKET[2]: see -OON.]

1. A kind of musket, short and with a large bore.

1650 R. STAPYLTON *Strada's Low C. Warres* VI. 31, 15 Supernumeraryes, armed with Musketoons, and Rests. **1655** MRQ. WORCESTER *Cent. Inv.* §67 A..way..for Musquettoons fastened to the Pummel of the Saddle so that a Common Trooper cannot misse to charge them, with twenty or thirty Bullets at a time, even in full Career. **1684** OTWAY *Atheist* II. i, Stand Centinel..with Musquetoons and Blunderbusses. **1772** SIMES *Milit. Guide* s.v. *Blunderbuss*, Blunderbuss is a short fire arm with a large bore... The shortest sort of them are called musquetoons. **1800** in *Spirit Pub. Jrnls.* IV. 22 The construction of the musquetoon, or wall piece. **1889** DOYLE *Micah Clarke* 152 Your musquetoon should be sloped upon your shoulder.

2. A soldier armed with a musketoon.

1638 SIR T. HERBERT *Trav.* (ed. 2) 232 Three hundred thousand horse, and seventy thousand good musquetoons. **1670** G. H. *Hist. Cardinals* II. III. 185 Forty Souldiers a horseback, drawn by order out of his Majesties Musquetoons.

3. *Comb.*: **musketoon pistol**, a smaller kind of musketoon.

1695 *Lond. Gaz.* No. 3055/4 At his late Dwelling-House ..are to be sold..Musketoons, and Musketoon Pistols.

muskeˈtooner. [f. MUSKETOON + -ER[1].] = MUSKETOON 2.

1925 *Chambers's Jrnl.* June 339/2, I felt a tearing blow above my right hip and I knew that the kneeling musketooner had touched me.

musketry (ˈmʌskɪtrɪ). Also 7–8 musquetry. [ad. F. *mousqueterie*, f. *mousquet*: see MUSKET[2] and -ERY, -RY.]

1. Muskets collectively.

Chiefly in ***discharge***, ***fire of musketry*** (passing into sense 2).

1646 ELDRED *Gunners Glasse* 136 The Musquetry and Hargubusry. **1777** W. DALRYMPLE *Trav. Sp. & Port.* civ, Joined together by a wall with loopholes, defencible only by musquetry. **1790** BEATSON *Nav. & Mil. Mem.* 222 When, pouring upon them the whole fire of their cannon and musquetry, almost every shot took place. **1884** F. M. CRAWFORD *Rom. Singer* I. 28 Which he fired out of his mouth like discharges of musketry.

2. The fire of muskets.

1756 WASHINGTON *Lett.* Writ. 1889 I. 322 A garrison which was only intended to defend the stores, and might be protected by 100 against musketry. **1796** H. HUNTER tr. *St.-Pierre's Stud. Nat.* (1799) II. 224 The sound of musquetry ought to be prohibited at least around the haunts of the harmless cattle. **1866** NEALE *Sequences & Hymns* 105 The quicker ring of musketry.

3. The art or science of manipulating small arms.

1854 J. C. KENNEDY *Theory Musketry* (1855) Introd., The following course of Instruction in the Theory of Musketry, was arranged for the use of the School of Musketry at Hythe. **1876** VOYLE & STEVENSON *Milit. Dict.* (ed. 3) s.v., To go through the annual course of musketry, under the regimental instructor.

4. Troops armed with muskets.

1772 NUGENT tr. *Hist. Fr. Gerund* III. vi. 563 With what applause the whole juvenile musquetry received this harangue of the prating..young thing of a theologist. **1902** A. LANG *Hist. Scot.* II. i. 9 Gamboa, a Spaniard (the Scots had no musketry), was captain of 200 mounted musketeers.

5. *attrib.*, as in ***musketry action***, ***drill***, ***fire***, ***instruction***, ***instructor***, ***powder***.

1875 CLERY *Min. Tact.* x. (1877) 122 Marcognet's column of eight battalions was engaged in a *musketry action with two battalions of Pack's brigade. **1859** *Musketry Instr.* 55 *Musketry Drill and Practice Return. **1852** CHESNEY *Observ. Fire-Arms 300 marg.*, Batteries of artillery supposed to be put hors de combat by *musketry fire. **1859** (*title*) Regulations for conducting the *Musketry Instruction of the Army. **1876** VOYLE & STEVENSON *Milit. Dict.* (ed. 3),

**Musketry Instructor. Ibid.*, **Musketry Powder* comprises the powders used with small-arms and pistols.

musket shot.
1. Shot fired from a musket; also, a musket-ball.
1590 SIR J. SMYTH *Disc. Weapons* 15 In giuing their volees of Mosquet shot but onlie twelue scores. **1621** BURTON *Anat. Mel.* I. ii. I. iii. (1651) 50 Such as shall endure a Rapiers point, musket shot, and never to be wounded. **1755** WASHINGTON *Lett.* Writ. 1889 I. 193, I have also impressed wagons and sent them..for flour, musket-shots, and flints. **1884** PAE *Eustace* 143 The musket-shot flew like hail.
2. The range of a musket.
1617 MORYSON *Itin.* I. 228 From hence a Musket shot, or little more, is another house, which [etc.]. **1669** STAYNRED *Fortification* 2, 720 Foot, being within Musket-shot. **1719** DE FOE *Crusoe* II. (Globe ed.) 404 Our Men came within two Musket Shot of them. **1844** *Regul. & Ord. Army* 274 An unexpected obstacle within point-blank Musket-shot of the place attacked.

muskett(i)er, obs. forms of MUSKETEER.

musketto, obs. form of MOSQUITO.

muskewashe, obs. form of MUSQUASH.

muskia, muskie, obs. forms of MOSQUE.

†**'muskified,** *ppl. a. Obs.* [f. MUSK *sb.* + -IFY + -ED[1].] Scented with or steeped in musk.
1677 *Compleat Servant-Maid* 105 Muskified Bisquet boyled. **1689** MOYLE *Sea Chyrurg.* II. xxiii. 78 Spirit Otalgicus dropt warm into the Ears morning and evening and Muskified Cotton after it.

muskil, obs. form of MUSCLE *sb.*, MUSSEL.

†**'muskin**[1]. *Obs.* [a. OF. *mus(e)quin* pretty face, sweetheart, *musquine* sweetheart.] **a.** A pretty face. **b.** A term of endearment for a woman.
1530 PALSGR. 247/1 Muskyn, a proper visage, *musquin.* **1538** BALE *Thre Lawes* B iv b, The woman hath a wytt,..My muskyne and my mullye, My gelouer and my cullye, Yea, myne owne swete hart of Golde.

†**'muskin**[2], var. or erron. form of MISKEN.
1657 BECK *Univ. Char.* I 2, A muskin, vid. Titmouse. **1658** ROWLAND tr. *Moufet's Theat. Ins.* 901 To destroy the Muskin or Titmouse.

†**'muskin**[3]. *slang. Obs.* exc. in allusive use. (See quot. 1756.)
1756 JOHNSON *Connoisseur* No. 138 ¶6 Those who..call a man a cabbage,..an odd fish, and an unaccountable muskin, should never come into company without an interpreter. **1922** JOYCE *Ulysses* 395 The embraces of some unaccountable muskin.

muskiness: see after MUSKY *a.*

musking, obs. variant of MUTCHKIN.

musking-place. A place where weasels or kindred animals deposit musk.
1920 *Chambers's Jrnl.* May 291/2 The wolves have their calling-posts, the beavers have their castor-signs, the weasels have their musking-places.

†**'muskings,** *sb. pl. Obs. rare* [Cf. dial (Northamp.) *musk* vb., 'of pigs, to rout about among and pick up loose or stray corn'.]
? Sweepings (of barns, etc.) used for feeding pigs.
1649 BLITHE *Eng. Improv.* xx. 117 Their cornish Muskings they cast into the great yard,..and all Muskings forth of their Barnes, and of their Courts.

muskinunge, obs. form of MUSKELLUNGE.

†**'muskish,** *a. Obs.* [f. MUSK *sb.* + -ISH.] Somewhat musky. *Comb.*: **muskish-minded** *a.*
1601 DENT *Pathw. Heaven* 67 Let all carnall worldlings, and muskish minded men lay this to heart. **1707** MORTIMER *Husb.* (1721) II. 296 Small Pears having something of a muskish Flavour. **1725** BRADLEY *Fam. Dict.* s.v. *Peach*, When ripe [they] have a muskish Taste.

muskle, -ly, obs. ff. MUSCLE *sb.*, MUSSEL, MUSCLY.

musk melon. Forms: see MUSK *sb.* and MELON[1]; also 6 **mush-millian,** 7 **mus milion, mellon,** 9 **mush-melon.** [f. MUSK *sb.*
The name seems to have originally belonged to an oriental melon (Du. *muscus-meloen, moscadelmeloen*, Dodoens) which has a musky scent, and to have been transferred to the common melon by mistake.]
1. The MELON, *Cucumis Melo.* (Applied both to the fruit and the plant producing it.)
1573 TUSSER *Husb.* (1878) 94 Musk million, in April and May. **1578** LYTE *Dodoens* v. xxxi. 590 In Frenche, Melon.. in Englishe, Melons and muske Melons. **1591** HORSEY *Trav.* (Hakl. Soc.) 253 My water to dress my meat withall was poisoned, my drincke and herbs and mush-millians sent poisoned. **1648** GAGE *West Ind.* 61 Bigger then our biggest Muskmillians in England. **1694** PENN in *Academy* (1896) 11 Jan. 36/3 Water and mus mellons. **1766** W. STORK *Acc. East Florida* 48 The vines,..water and musk-melons, are indigenous plants of East-Florida. **1825** MOTLEY *Corr.* (1889) I. i. 4 We have..planted a good many things, such as corn, radishes, water and musk melons, etc. **1884** BOURKE *Snake Dance of Moquis* xxxi. 354 We feasted heartily on mush-melons and clabber.
attrib. **1649** *Survey Manor of Wimbledon* in *Archæologia* X. 432 There is a muskmilion ground trenched, manured, and very well ordered for the groweth of musmilions, which borders, herbes, flowers, and musmilion ground, wee valew to bee worth £3 0 0. **1708** E. COOK *Sot-weed Factor* (1865) 19 Musmillion vine.
2. ? Allusively for 'scented millions'.
1662 M. W. *Marriage Broaker* I. ii. 10 Musk-millions of rich gallants will besiege Her Fort; and my cake's dowe.

Muskogean (ˌmʌskəʊˈgiːən, mʌˈskəʊgɪən). Also **Muskhogean.** [f. MUSKOGEE.] An Indian language family in south-eastern N. Amer., consisting of the Creek-Seminole, Hitchiti-Mikasuki, Alabawa-Koasati, Apalachee, and Choctaw-Chickasaw languages. Also *attrib.* or as *adj.*
1891 J. W. POWELL in *7th Ann. Rep. Bureau Ethnol.* 94 (*heading*) Muskhogean family. **1907** F. W. HODGE *Hand-bk. Amer. Indians* I. 962/2 The Muskhogean population at the time of first contact with Europeans has been estimated at 50,000. **1932** *Times Lit. Suppl.* 8 Sept. 624/3 Forming part of the Muskhogean culture area east of the Mississippi. **1933** [see CREEK *sb.*[3]]. **1940** *Language* XVI. 142 Curiously enough ..certain other Muskogean languages closely related to Muskogee do employ gemination as a grammatical process. **1959** E. TUNIS *Indians* 19/2 Remnants of the temple-mound culture survived into historical times among the Muskhogean Indians of the Southeast. **1972** *Language* XLVIII. 845 Hockett exemplifies 3a with 'Arunta.., Muskogean (except Creek-Seminole).., and Wishram'.

Muskogee (mʌˈskəʊgiː). Also **Muscogee, Muskhogee, Muskhokee, Muskogi, Muskohge.** [f. Creek *maskóki*, perh. of Algonquian origin.] The name of a group of N. American Indians, consisting mainly of Creek Indians; also the language spoken by them; also *attrib.*
1775 J. ADAIR *Hist. Amer. Indians* 161, I had a conversation..with several of the more intelligent Muskohge traders. *Ibid.* 392 A Muskohge warrior..got to a bramble swamp. *Ibid.* 430 The Cherokees and Muscogees still observe that old custom. **1836** *Trans. Amer. Antiq. Soc.* II. 94 The Muskhogees are the prevailing nation... The Hitchittees..speak a dialect of the Muskhogee. **1868** [see CREEK *sb.*[3]]. **1907** F. W. HODGE *Handbk. Amer. Indians* I. 962/2 The recognized languages of the stock..are as follows:..Muskogee (including almost half the Creek confederacy, and its offshoot, the Seminole). **1948** D. DIRINGER *Alphabet* I. x. 183 The Muskhokee dialect is the principal dialect of the Muskhogean group; politically, the Muskhokee were the dominant tribe of the Creek Confederacy. **1949** E. A. NIDA *Morphology* (ed. 2) vi. 159 Muskogee has some verbs of rather irregular formation which indicate differences of singular, dual, and plural subjects. **1959** E. TUNIS *Indians* 70/2 The principal tribe was the Muskhogee, called Creeks by the English.

Muskovie, obs. form of MUSCOVY.

'musk-ox. A ruminant, *Ovibos moschatus*, formerly existing in all arctic regions, but now only in Arctic America; it evolves a strong odour of musk. Also *attrib.*
1744 A. DOBBS *Countries Adjacent to Hudson's Bay* 18 Betwixt these Rivers is a kind of Ox, called the Musk Ox, which smells at some Time in the Year so strong of Musk, that it cannot be eat. **1835** SIR J. ROSS *Narr. 2nd Voy.* xvi. 252 They further informed us that there were plenty of musk oxen on the hills to the southward. **1892** W. PIKE *North. Canada* 65 We scattered over the country, hoping to find a band of musk-ox.

muskquash, -quass, obs. forms of MUSQUASH.

'musk-rat.
1. **a.** A large acquatic rodent, *Fiber zibethicus*, common throughout N. America, so called from its musky smell. Also called MUSQUASH and ONDATRA.
1620 *Observ. Silkwormes* D 2 b, Muske Rats skins, two shillings a dozen: the cods of them will serue for good perfumes. **1714** LAWSON *Hist. Carolina* 120 Musk Rats frequent fresh Streams and no other; as the Bever does. He has a Cod of Musk, which is valuable, as is likewise his Fur. **1892** W. PIKE *North. Canada* 25 Musk-rats swam in all the little creeks and lakes.
b. *U.S.* A nickname for the inhabitants of low-lying districts, esp. the St. Clair Flats (Michigan).
1845 in C. Cist *Cincinnati Misc.* 240 The inhabitants of.. Delaware [are called] Muskrats. **1857** in *Archiv Stud. neu. Spr.* XXII. 162 (citing *Atlantis* II. 645). **1890** *Century Mag.* July 369/2 Her grandmother..having a profound contempt for the 'muskrats' as the Flats people are generally called.
c. The fur or skin of the musk-rat.
1879 *Encycl. Brit.* IX. 838/2 *Musk-Rat.*—A well-known fur in North America. **1902** *Scotsman* 3 Jan. 7/5 Musk-rat is the least costly, being worth only about 2*d.*
2. Applied to other rat-like animals having a musky odour. **a.** In India and Sri Lanka (Ceylon), the shrews *Crocidura murina* and *C. cærulea.* **b.** The DESMAN. **c.** The PILORI (cf. *musk-cavy*). **d.** A viverrine quadruped, the South African genet, *Genetta felina* (in recent Dicts.). **e.** The musk-kangaroo, *Hypsiprymnodon moschatus.*
1681 R. KNOX *Hist. Ceylon* 31 They have a sort of Rats, they call Musk-Rats, because they smell strong of Musk. **1774** GOLDSM. *Nat. Hist.* (1824) II. 92 The musk rat. Of these animals of the rat kind, but with a musky smell, there are also three distinctions..; the Ondatra, the Desman, and the Pilori. **1785** *Gentl. Mag.* LV. I. 204 A little animal, very frequent in these parts, totally unknown I believe, to other countries. It is called here [Russia] the Musk-rat. **1813** J. FORBES *Orient. Mem.* I. 41 The musk-rats [at Bombay].. have a most disagreeable smell. **1836** [see PILORI]. **1884** STERNDALE *Mamm. India & Ceylon* 83 *Sorex cærulescens.* The common Musk Shrew, better known as Musk-rat. **1892** J. D. OGILBY *Catal. Austral. Mamm.* 38 *Hypsiprymnodon moschatus* Ramsay (1876). Australian Musk Rat.
3. *attrib.*: ***musk-rat burrow, cap, skin, study***; **musk-rat house,** the 'house' or burrow of the American musk-rat; **musk-rat weed,** a tall American meadow-plant, *Thalictrum polygamum* (formerly *T. Cornuti*).
1870 *Amer. Naturalist* IV. 385 This fish, when the bank was carelessly approached, would withdraw to a deserted muskrat burrow. **1916** C. A. EASTMAN *From Deep Woods to Civilization* 101 We saw that they were colored troopers, wearing buffalo overcoats and muskrat caps. **1962** W. STEGNER *Wolf Willow* III. iii. 230 Crouching in the trench in his muskrat cap, he looked like some digging animal. **1837** W. IRVING *Capt. Bonneville* I. 277 They found the swamp full of 'muskrat houses'. **1939** *Beaver* June 10 Older men remembered when the muskrat houses had been so thick that the marsh looked like a hayfield in coils. **1962** W. STEGNER *Wolf Willow* III. ii. 150 They had seen muskrat houses built six feet high in the sloughs—and when the rats built high you could depend on a hard winter. **1642** in *Archives of Maryland* (1887) IV. 99, 2. musk-rat skins. **1796** E. P. SIMCOE *Diary* (1911) 315 We..slept well,..but the smell of musk-rat skins..was disagreeable. **1823** in T. L. McKenney *Memoirs* (1846) I. App. 296 Furs and other articles..to wit,..2,500 muskrat skins, [etc.]. **1939** *Amer. Midland Naturalist* XXI. 514 (*title*) Central Wisconsin muskrat study. **1897–8** BRITTON & BROWN *Amer. Flora*, Muskrat weed, *Thalictrum polygamum.*

'musk-'rose. [So called from its musky odour; cf. F. *rose muscade* and the botanical name.] A rambling rose (*Rosa moschata*), having large fragrant white flowers, in panicled clusters.
1577 B. GOOGE *Heresbach's Husb.* II. (1586) 66 b *marg.*, Muske-roses. **1590** SHAKS. *Mids. N.* II. i. 252. **1625** BACON *Ess., Gardens* (Arb.) 556 In May and Iune, come..Roses of all kinds, except the Muske, which comes later. **1637** MILTON *Lycidas* 146. **1707** MORTIMER *Husb.* (1721) II. 165 The Spanish Musk Rose. *a* **1763** SHENSTONE *Elegies* xviii. 10, I steal the musk rose from the scented brake. **1837** RIVERS *Rose Amateur's Guide* 86 The Blush Musk, or Fraser's Musk, or *Rosa Fraserii*, is not quite a pure Musk Rose. *Ibid.*, The Ranunculus, or new White Musk, is merely an improved variety of the old, or original Musk Rose. **1842** TENNYSON *Gardener's Dau.* 189 Then for roses, moss or musk, To grace my city rooms.
attrib. **1590** SHAKS. *Mids. N.* II. ii. 3 Some to kill Cankers in the muske rose buds.

musk squash, obs. form of MUSQUASH.

'musk-tree. A name given to various Oceanic trees or shrubs, from the scent of their leaves or timber. **a.** The shrub *Marlea vitiense* (N. O. *Cornaceæ*), with edible nuts. **b.** A tree of the genus *Olearia*, formerly *Aster, Eurybia* (N. O. *Compositæ*), esp. the Silver-leaved Musk-tree, *O. argophylla*, and the Dwarf Musk-tree, *O. viscosa.*
1848 MRS. PERRY *Let.* in Goodman *Ch. in Victoria* (1892) 71 Also there is some pretty underwood, a good deal of the musk-tree—which is very different from our musk-plant, growing quite into a shrub and having a leaf like the laurel in shape. **1866** *Treas. Bot.* 479/1 The silver-leaved Musk tree, *Eurybia argophylla*, is a Tasmanian plant, attaining a height of twenty to twenty-five feet, with a girth of three feet. **1888** MRS. M'CANN *Poet. Wks.* 143 The musk tree scents the evening air Far down the leafy vale.

muskullonge: see MUSKELLUNGE.

muskwash, variant of MUSQUASH.

'musk-wood.
1. A name given to several trees having a musky smell. **a.** A low fragrant resinous tree, *Trichilia moschata* (often called *Moschoxylon Swartzii*), a native of Jamaica. **b.** Species of *Guarea*, esp. *G. Swartzii.* **c.** The silver-leaved musk-tree, *Olearia argophylla*, of New South Wales and Tasmania.
1725 SLOANE *Jamaica* II. 24 Musk-wood. This tree in respect of its sweet smell I reduce hither. **1794** BARHAM *Hortus Amer.* 107 Musk-Wood. This is vulgarly and commonly called *alligator-wood.* **1863** *Chamb. Encycl.* V. 127/1 *Guarea grandifolia* is called Musk-wood in some of the islands of the West Indies; the bark smelling so strongly of musk, that it may be used as a perfume. **1866** *Treas. Bot.*, *Musk-wood* of Jamaica. *Moschoxylum Swartzii*; also *Guarea Swartzii.* —of New South Wales and Tasmania. *Eurybia argophylla.*
2. (See quot.)
1891 *Syd. Soc. Lex.*, *Muskwood*, the name of a bark obtained from Syria, and supposed to be the product of the liquid storax tree. It has an agreeable balsamic smell.

†**'musk-worm.** *Obs.* Perh. = *musk-beetle* (MUSK *sb.* 4 e); applied to a dealer in perfumes.
1599 B. JONSON *Cynthia's Rev.* v. iv. Wks. (1616) 246 What coyle these muske-wormes [*printed* mukse-wormes] take, to purchase anothers delight? for themselues, who beare the odours, haue euer the least sence of them.

'musky, *sb.*[1] A playful shortening of MUSK-RAT (sense 1).
1884 *Chamb. Jrnl.* 1 Nov. 704/1, I saw the dead musky being carried off.

musky ('mʌskɪ), *sb.*[2] Also **muskie**. Short for *muskallonge* (see MASKINONGE).

1894 *Outing* (U.S.) XXIV. 453/1 We were then all ready for old musky to begin his real fight. **1902** *Scribner's Mag.* XXXI. 534 The familiar term, with which sportsmen have come to know him, the musky. **1928** *Game Fishes of Canada* 12 The next most definite cult among the anglers are those who devote themselves to muskies. **1936** G. CLARK *Which we Did* i. 20 Jimmie Frise..was successfully commissaried by me to our favorite muskie water for the closing day of the season. **1962** *Times* 12 Apr. 7/3 Waterways full of bass, northern pike and muskies. **1968** *Globe & Mail* (Toronto) 3 Feb. 40/1 They recaptured these previously marked fish: 13 walleyes, three smallmouth bass, 11 largemouth bass, but not one musky. **1975** G. V. HIGGINS *City on Hill* ix. 215, I should spend my days..going after muskies and telling lies when I didn't catch any.

musky ('mʌskɪ), *a.* Also 7 **muskie**. [f. MUSK *sb.* + -Y.]

1. Smelling, or tasting of musk; having a taste or smell like that of musk; perfumed with musk.

c **1610** ROWLANDS *Terrible Batt.* 13 A Muskie-Gentle, we did visit then, A Silken Gallant. **1613** PURCHAS *Pilgrimage* (1614) 502 Muske is made of a certaine beast called Gudderi, ..which once in the Moone sheddeth his muskie bloud. **1634** MILTON *Comus* 989 West winds, with musky wing About the cedar'n alleys fling Nard, and Cassia's balmy smels. **1769** SIR W. JONES *Palace Fortune* Poems, etc. (1777) 15 The floating ringlets of his musky hair. **1830** LINDLEY *Nat. Syst. Bot.* 34 The musky seeds of *Hibiscus Abelmoschus.* **1849** THACKERAY *Pendennis* xxv, Holding a most musky pocket-handkerchief up to his face. **1888** *Graphic* 21 Jan. 54 The musky flesh of the animal [*sc.* a crocodile].

fig. **1858** EMERSON *Lett. & Soc. Aims, Persian Poetry* Wks. (Bohn) III. 247 The garden flowers are never wanting in these musky verses. **1901** HENLEY in *Pall Mall Mag.* Oct. 262 [Rossetti] His musky, strenuous, high-piled achievements in words.

b. As a specific name for animals and plants.

1781 PENNANT *Hist. Quadrup.* II. 476 Shrew, Musky... Muscovy or Musk rat. **1822** *Hortus Anglicus* II. 82 *Ajuga Iva.* Musky Bugle. **1885** *Cassell's Encycl. Dict.*, Musky-mole, *Scaptochirus moschatus.* [= *musk-mole*: see MUSK *sb.* 4 e.]

2. Of an odour, taste, etc.

1613 PURCHAS *Pilgrimage* (1614) 775 Some rich sables of muskie sent. **1688** R. HOLME *Armoury* II. 47/2 A Musk Pear ..is..of a Musky Taste. **1746** HERVEY *Medit.* (1818) 107 The musky flavour of the apricot. **1862** BURTON *Bk. Hunter* I. 44 A sort of indistinct slightly musky perfume, like that said to frequent Oriental bazaars. **1897** MARY KINGSLEY *W. Africa* 228 It does not remove the musky taste from crocodile.

Comb. **1831** TENNYSON *Anacreontics* in *Germ* 131 With roses musky-breathed. **1866** *Treas. Bot.* s.v. *Adoxa,* The musky-scented flowers.

Hence **'muskiness**, the quality of being musky; a musky odour or taste.

1727 in BAILEY vol. II. **1755** in JOHNSON; and in later Dicts.

muskyl, -yll(e, obs. forms of MUSSEL.

muskyte, -kyto, obs. ff. MUSKET[1], MOSQUITO.

musle, obs. form of MUZZLE.

muslege, -idge, obs. forms of MUCILAGE.

Musleman, obs. form of MUSSULMAN.

musli, var. MUESLI.

Muslim ('mʊzlɪm, 'mʌzlɪm, 'mʌs-), *sb.* and *a.* Also 7–9 **Moslim**, 8– **Moslem** ('mɒzləm), 9 (**Mooslim**). [a. Arab. *muslim,* active pple. of *aslama,* of which the noun of action is *islām*: see ISLAM.]

A. *sb.* One who professes Islam; a Muhammadan; in mod. use *spec.* = *Black Muslim.*

1615 BEDWELL *Arab. Trudg., Moslim,* or *Mussliman,*..is one that is instructed in the beleefe of the Mohammetanes. **1788** GIBBON *Decl. & F.* lviii. VI. 48 The Moslems soon found, that..resistance was impotent. **1816** BYRON *Siege Cor.* ii, The crescent shines Along the Moslem's leaguering lines. **1836** LANE *Mod. Egypt.* I. iii. 97 The public worship of the Mooslims. **1841** —— *Arab. Nts.* I. 59 The Muslim holds that he is to be admitted into heaven only by the mercy of God, on account of his faith. **1877** J. E. CARPENTER tr. *Tiele's Hist. Relig.* 99 The severe asceticism in which the Moslims were soon to rival Christians and Buddhists. **1903** G. W. FORREST *Cities of India* iii. 66 All the Muslim wants is a courtyard with a tank for ablution [etc.]. **1955** *Times* 3 May 9/4 Lahore witnessed the astonishing sight of hundreds of Sikhs of all people being fêted by Muslims. **1961** [see *Black Muslim* s.v. BLACK *a.* 19]. **1969** *Sunday Standard* (Bombay) 3 Aug. 1/8 The promised equal opportunities to Buddhists and Muslims in Ladakh had not materialised so far. **1971** *Black Scholar* June 52/1 Submission to democratic centralism instead of the egoism that sent him first against his Muslims. **1972** J. MILLS *Report to Commissioner* 120 They [*sc.* Black Panthers] aren't like the Muslims. **1973** *Jewish Chron.* 9 Feb. 11/2 The basic credo of the Muslims is a hatred of Whites.

¶ The form **Moslemin** [repr. the Arab. pl. (oblique case) *muslimīn*] is sometimes used for the plural, and occasionally in error for the singular (with a pl. *Moslemins*). Some writers have employed the singular form as a plural or collective.

1819 T. HOPE *Anastasius* (1820) I. i. 10 Upon this principle they cringed to the ground to every Moslemin they met. *Ibid.* ii. 41 The lion at whose roar Moslemen trembled. **1836** LYTTON *Athens* (1837) II. 147 They might have..seen that opening paradise in immortality below, which the Moslemin beheld in anticipation above. **1840** MACAULAY *Ess., Clive* (1897) 512 The recurrence of this solemn season excites the fiercest and saddest emotions in the bosoms of the devout Moslem of India. **1840** CARLYLE *Heroes* ii. 104 All Moslem are bound to study it [the Koran]. **1847** DISRAELI *Tancred* v. iv, The Ansarey..are not Moslemin. **1854** MILMAN *Lat. Chr.* IV. ii. (1864) II. 209 Jonas..led the conquering Moslemins in pursuit of the fugitives from Damascus. **1905** *Mission. Rec. United Free Ch.* Jan. 23/2 A few Muslim and Hindus..were also present.

B. *adj.* **a.** Of or pertaining to the Muslims; Muhammadan.

1777 J. RICHARDSON *Dict. Persian, Arab.*, etc., Dissert. 24/2 An open scoffer at the Moslem faith. **1788** GIBBON *Decl. & F.* lxiv. VI. 294 The most powerful of the Moslem princes. **1812** BYRON *Ch. Har.* II. lxiv, The pilgrim..gazed around on Moslem luxury. **1841** E. ROBINSON *Bibl. Res. Palestine* I. 352 The tract around this tank [the Upper Pool] ..is occupied as a Muslim cemetery. **1877** A. B. EDWARDS *Up Nile* ii. 25 The mosque of Sultan Hassan,..perhaps the most beautiful in the Moslem world. **1905** *Athenæum* 7 Jan. 15/3 Whereof the Muslim writers..of course say nothing. **1907** SIR W. M. RAMSAY in *Expositor* Oct. 318 The lower town is now purely Moslem. **1968** *E. African Law Jrnl.* IV. 17 The establishment of special courts to deal exclusively with Muslim law is peculiar in East Africa to Kenya and Zanzibar. **1970** *Times* 3 Apr. (Arab League Suppl.) p. iii/1 The Indians are the only large non-Muslim group, besides Christian Arabs and Europeans.

¶ The plural form **Moslemin** (see A) occurs appositively or as adj.

1844 DISRAELI *Coningsby* IV. x, The Moslemin Arabs.

b. Muslim (or **Moslem**) **League**, in full **All India Muslim League**, a Muslim political organization founded in India in 1906 whose demands in 1940 for an independent Muslim state led to the establishment of Pakistan; so **Muslim Leaguer**.

1907 *Times* 2 Jan. 3/1 Resolved [on 30 Dec. 1906], that this meeting, composed of Musulmans from all parts of India, assembled at Dacca, decides that a political association be formed, styled the All India Moslem League. **1913** *Times* 31 Oct. 7/4 The All-India Moslem League..Mr. Ameer Ali has tendered his resignation of the presidentship of the London All-India Moslem League..and his Highness the Aga Khan..will retire from the headship of the League in India. **1955** *Times* 7 July 9/2 The Muslim League did not win a majority, but remains the largest single party. **1971** *Hindustan Times Weekly* (New Delhi) 4 Apr. 7/1 Besides the Congress (N)..it includes such disparate elements as..the Muslim League. **1972** *Guardian* 5 Feb. 11/5 Muslim Leaguers are helpless now.

Hence **Mus'limic** *a.* = MUSLIM *a.*; **'Muslimism**, the religion of the Muslims, Islam, Muhammadanism; **'Muslimite** = MUSLIM *sb.* (in quot. used as adj.); **'Muslimize** *v. trans.*, to convert to Muslimism, hence **'Muslimized** *ppl. a.*

1777 J. RICHARDSON *Dict. Persian, Arab.*, etc., Dissert. 6/1 Moslemism. *a* **1835** MOTHERWELL *Poet. Wks.* (1847) 71 On thunders the might Of the Moslemite war. **1845** E. WARBURTON *Crescent & Cross* I. 310 These captives are all christians when caught, but are immediately Moslemised. **1872** T. L. CUYLER *Heart-Th.* 82 Christ is in the Missionary Church. He is not in heathenism, or in Moslemism, or in Rome. **1898** *Daily Chron.* 25 Feb. 6/3 Colonel Trotter remarked that the Moslemized towns were in advance of the pagan. **1903** *19th Cent.* Mar. 387 The countries and peoples of the Moslemic East.

muslin ('mʌzlɪn). Forms: 7 **muslina, muscelin, muzlin**, 7–8 **musling**, 8 **musselin, musslin, mussolin**, 8– **muslin**. [a. F. *mousseline,* ad. It. *mussolina, -ino* (whence the obs. Eng. forms *muslina, mussolin*), f. *Mussolo* (also used as appellative = muslin) the town of Mosul (in Arabic *mauçil*), where muslin was formerly made. Cf. Sp. *muselina,* G. *musselin,* from Fr. or It.

In the 13th c. the OF. *mosulin* was applied to 'cloth of silk and gold' made at Mosul (Marco Polo).]

1. The general name for the most delicately woven cotton fabrics, including many varieties, used for ladies' dresses, curtains, hangings, etc. Also *occas.* a dress made of this; *pl.* muslin skirts.

1609 W. BIDDULPH in T. Lavender *Trav.* 43 A little towne called Muscla, from whence the inhabitants..bring a kinde of linnen cloath called Muslina to Aleppo. **1682** *True Protest. Mercury* No. 110. 2/2 One Lac'd Cravat of Muzlin. **1706** *Lond. Gaz.* No. 4269/4, 7 Pieces of strip'd Muslings, and one Piece of plain. *c* **1794** *Search after Perfection* II. iv. in *New Brit. Theatre* (1814) III. 54 O mercy on us, if they have not cut to pieces my mistress's new gold muslin. **1848** THACKERAY *Van. Fair* ii, She insisted upon Rebecca accepting..a sweet sprigged muslin, which was too small for her now. **1849** LYELL *2nd Visit U.S.* (1850) II. 332 Embroidered muslin, of the finest and costliest kind, is much worn. **1860** SALA *Badd. Peerage* I. xv 268 The niece of Manuel Harispe disdained to answer, but with an indignant flutter of her muslins, brushed past her uncle and out of the room. **1882** MISS BRADDON *Mt. Royal* II. iv. 53 Inside the tapestry there was a screen of soft muslin.

b. 'In some parts of the United States, cotton cloth used for shirts, other articles of wearing apparel, bedding, etc.' (*Cent. Dict.* 1890).

1872 SCHELE DE VERE *Americanisms* 71 A story is told of a gentleman in Philadelphia, who ordered muslin shirts in Boston, and although reminded of the unsuitableness of that material..insisted upon his order, as he had always worn muslin, meaning cotton-shirting.

c. muslin-de-laine = *mousseline-de-laine*: see MOUSSELINE 1 b.

1862 Muslin-de-laines [see DELAINE *a*].

2. *slang.* The fair sex. *a bit of muslin,* a woman or girl.

1823 MONCRIEFF *Tom & Jerry* I. i, You've got a bit of muslin on the sly, have you? **1850** THACKERAY *Pendennis* li. [l.], That was a pretty bit of muslin hanging on your arm —who was she? **1884** H. SMART *From Post to Finish* xvii. (1885) 128 Keep clear of muslin for the next six or seven years. It's brought as many of your profession to grief as spirits.

3. *Naut. slang.* 'Canvas', sails collectively.

1822 *Blackw. Mag.* XI. 429 She shewed as little muslin as the weather required. **1894** *Outing* (U.S.) XXIV. 295/2 When we got that fair wind we piled the muslin on her.

4. = *muslin-moth* (in 5 b).

1819 G. SAMOUELLE *Entomol. Compend.* 248 *Arctia mendica* (muslin). **1869** E. NEWMAN *Brit. Moths* 27 The Round-winged Muslin (*Nudaria Senex*). *Ibid.*, The Muslin *Nudaria mundana.*

5. *attrib.* and *Comb.* **a.** simple *attrib.* or *adj.* Made or consisting of muslin.

1684 A. SYMSON *Geogr. Collect.* (S.H.S.) II. 87 It is an excellent place for whitening or bleeching of Linnen, holland and Muzlin Webbs. **1704** *Lond. Gaz.* No. 3981/4 A fine new Flourish'd Muslin Apron. **1721** AMHERST *Terræ Fil.* No. 46 (1754) 247 With..long muslin neckcloths run with red at the bottom. **1880** 'OUIDA' *Moths* I. 33 She rose, shook her muslin breakfast-wrapper about her impatiently.

b. Special combinations: as †**muslin calico**, ? = sense 1; **muslin glass** = MOUSSELINE 2; **muslin grounds** (see quot.); **muslin kail** *Sc.* [? named in allusion to its thinness], broth composed simply of water, shelled barley, and greens (Jam.); **muslin moth**, a name given to certain moths with semi-transparent wings; **muslin wheel** (see quot. 1830).

1705 *Lond. Gaz.* No. 4146/4 *Muslin Callicoes 131 Pieces. **1884** KNIGHT *Dict. Mech., Suppl.*, **Muslin glass*... Glass blown very thin. **1882** CAULFEILD & SAWARD *Dict. Needlework,* **Muslin Grounds*..is a description of Gingham. **1785** BURNS *To Jas. Smith* xxiv, I'll sit down o'er my scanty meal, Be't water-brose, or *muslin-kail, Wi' cheerfu' face. **1869** E. NEWMAN *Brit. Moths* 34 The *Muslin Moth (*Arctia mendica*). **1903** W. F. KIRBY *Europ. Butterflies & M.* Plate xxv, *Spilosoma Mendica* —Spotted Muslin Moth. **1830** J. KENNEDY *Misc. Pap. Manuf. Lanc.* (1849) 56 Crompton's machine was called the..*Muslin Wheel, because its capabilities rendered it available for yarn for making muslins.

muslined ('mʌzlɪnd), *a.* [f. MUSLIN + -ED[2].] Draped with or dressed in muslin.

1883 HOWELLS *Woman's Reason* xviii. II. 134 The pretty chintzed and muslined room. **1891** T. HARDY *Tess* vii, The muslined form of Tess could be seen standing still.

muslinet (mʌzlɪ'nɛt). Also **muslinette**. [f. MUSLIN + -ET[1].] See quot. 1882. Also *attrib.*

1787 BP. THURLOW in Hatfield *Hist. Notices Doncaster* (1866) I. 330 Mrs. Thurlow..has determined to put herself into a dress made out of the piece of muslinette you were so good as to present her. **1803** in *Spirit Publ. Jrnls.* (1804) VII. 59 Muslinets or dimities. **1879** 'EDNA LYALL' *Won by Waiting* xxxvi, Putting on a clean muslinette apron and bib, [she] took her place by the bed. **1882** CAULFEILD & SAWARD *Dict. Needlework, Muslinette,* a thick variety of muslin, resembling a Brilliant; employed for infants' clothing and for dressing gowns.

musling, musman, obs. ff. MUSLIN, MUSMON.

musmé, -me, variant forms of MOUSMEE.

musmon ('mʌsmɒn). Also 7 **musmone**, 7–8 **musimon**, 8–9 **musman**, 9 **mousmon**. [a. L. *mūsimon-* (Pliny), late Gr. μούσμων (Strabo).] A name for the MOUFLON.

1601 HOLLAND *Pliny* I. 228 There is in Spaine, but especially in the Isle Corsica, a kind of Musmones, not altogether vnlike to sheep. **1688** R. HOLME *Armoury* II. 175/1 A Musimon.—This Beast is engendered of a She-Goat and a Ram... Some term it a..Musmon. **1776** PENNANT *Brit. Zool.* (ed. 4) I. 27 *note,* Having thrice within these few years had opportunity of examining the Musimon, we found that [etc.]. **1794** *Sporting Mag.* III. 64 The Mouflon or Musman has been classed both of the sheep and the goat kind. **1887** FREEMAN in Stephens *Life & Lett.* (1895) II. 361 A mouflon or a mousmon who has not a thick armour of wool.

‖**musnud** ('mʌsnʌd). [Urdū *masnad,* a. Arab. *misnad,* f. *sanada* to lean against.] A seat made of cushions, esp. one used as a throne by the native princes of India.

1763 R. ORME *Hist. Milit. Trans.* I. IV. 254 Salabat-jing.. went through the ceremony of sitting on the Musnud or throne in public. *c* **1804** MRS. SHERWOOD in *Life* xvii. (1847) 295 The Nawaub was sitting..on a musnud encircled with cushions. **1890** G. HOOPER *Wellington* 45 The Hindoo gentleman, to his delight and astonishment, was placed on the musnud.

musolin, obs. form of MUSLIN.

musomania (mju:zəʊ'meɪnɪə). [f. Gr. μοῦσ-α muse + μανία madness.] = MUSICOMANIA.

1855 [see MUSICOMANIA under MUSICO-].

†**muso'mastix.** *nonce-wd. Obs.* [f. Gr. μοῦσ-α MUSE: see -MASTIX.] An enemy of the Muses.

1586 *Praise of Mus.* 64 Is it not enough for any malicious Musomastix to take his pen and write I ly..?

†'**muson.** *Hunting. Obs.* [a. OF. *muison* change, moulting.] The shed horns of a deer. In quot. 1663 used jocularly for 'horns'.

a **1552** LELAND *Itin.* (1769) III. 55 Fisschar men hath divers tymes taken up with theyr Nettes yn Torrebay Musons of Hartes. **1663** KILLIGREW *Parson's Wedd.* v. iv. 152 We shall have that damn'd Courtier pluck on his shooes with the Parsons Musons.

muson, variant of MOISON *Obs.*

musoola, obs. form of MASSOOLA(H.

musophobist (mjuː'zɒfəbɪst). *nonce-wd.* [f. Gr. *μοῦσ-α* MUSE *sb.*[1]: see -PHOBIST.] One who regards poetry with suspicious dislike.

1880 SWINBURNE *Misc.* (1886) 49 But, be it said with leave of our most illustrious Musophobist, they are equalled at their best if not excelled [etc.].

musoun, variant of MOISON *Obs.*

musquash ('mʌskwɒʃ). Forms: α. 7–8 **mussascus;** β. 7 **muskewashe, muskquash, muske quashe, musquashes, musk-quass, musquass, musquosh,** 8 **musk squash,** 9 **muskwash,** 7– **musquash.** [a. Abnaki *muskwessu* (Rasler *Abnaki Dict.* 1691) or the equivalent in other Algonkin dialects; the form *mussascus* prob. belongs to the Powhatan (Virginian) dialect.]

1. = MUSK-RAT[1].

1624 CAPT. SMITH *Virginia* II. 27 A Mussascus is a beast of the forme and nature of our water Rats, but many of them smell exceedingly strongly of Muske. *Ibid.* 216 Martins, Fitches, Musquassus, and diuers other sorts of Vermin whose names I know not. **1633** *New Hampsh. Prov. Papers* (1867) I. 71, 2 otters and 4 musquosh. **1674** JOSSELYN *Voy. New Eng.* 86 The Musquashes is a small Beast that lives in shallow ponds. **1765** T. HUTCHINSON *Hist. Mass.* I. 471 Musquashes, and even Bevers, were not much regarded, until the English..encouraged the pursuit of them. **1773** *Hist. Brit. Dom. in N. Amer.* VII. iii. 135 The mussascus, a sort of water rat, that smells like musk. **1782** CREVECŒUR *Lett.* 252 The casualties that generally happen either by inundations or the musk squash. **1812** J. SMYTH *Pract. of Customs* (1821) 221 Musquash, or Musk Rat, is a diminutive of the Beaver, which is to be met with in North America. **1848** THOREAU *Maine W.* (1894) 105 Musquash are their principal food on these expeditions. **1872** SCHELE DE VERE *Americanisms* 371 In the Northern States it [the musk-rat] is generally called Musquash, from its general Indian designation.

2. The fur of the musquash.

1884 *York Herald* 26 Aug. 1/2 [advt.] Fur Capes, in all the most Fashionable Furs, including..Musquash. **1903** *Westm. Gaz.* 17 Sept. 4/2 Musquash is a brown fur.

3. *attrib.* and *Comb.*, as ***musquash fur, hole, skin***; **musquash house** = *musk-rat house*; **musquash poison,** the plant *Cicuta maculata* (Britton & Brown *American Flora*); **musquash-root** (see quots.); **musquash sealskin,** imitation sealskin made from musquash; **musquash weed,** (*a*) = *musquash root*; (*b*) = *musk-rat weed*.

1876 GOODE *Anim. Resources U.S.* 74 *Musquash fur used in felting. **1835–40** HALIBURTON *Clockm.* Ser. I. xxiii, I thought it was like Uncle Peleg's *musquash hole, and that no soul could ever find the bottom of. **1857** THOREAU *Maine W.* (1894) 283 What increased the resemblance was one old *musquash house almost afloat. **1807** *Massachusetts Spy* 22 July (Th.), Five children were lately poisoned in Scipio (New York) by eating Wild Parsnip or *Musquash Root. **1857** [see *beaver-poison*]. **1859** BARTLETT *Dict. Amer.*, *Musquash root* (Cicuta maculata), an umbelliferous plant and deadly poison. **1866** *Treas. Bot.*, *Musquash root*, an American name for *Cicuta maculata*; also *Claytonia acutiflora*. **1940** E. EARLY *New England Sampler* 309 The Indian had told his grandmother..of a decoction of Cowbane (called Musquash Root) that would make a woman forever sterile. **1902** *Westm. Gaz.* 18 Dec. 4/2 One is really just as well off with the *musquash sealskin. **1828** *Lights & Shades* I. 211 Chattered with the broker about *musquash skins,..and gum arabic. **1767** *Massachusetts Gaz.* 21 May 3/1 Persons (especially Children) would do well to beware of this Weed. It is called wild Hemlock by some, and *Musquash Weed by others. **1892** *Jrnl. Amer. Folk Lore* V. 91 *Thalictrum polygamum*, muskrat-weed; musquash weed. **1907** A. B. LYONS *Plant Names* (ed. 2) 457 T[halictrum] polygamum... Celandine, Muskrat-weed, Musquash-weed.

musquatte, obs. form of MUSKET *sb.*[2]

musquaw ('mʌskwɔː). [Cree Indian.

The corresponding Odjibwa form is used by Longfellow *Hiawatha* ii, 'The Mishe-*Mokwa*, He the Great Bear of the mountains.']

An American name for the Black Bear.

1861 WOOD *Nat. Hist.* I. 397 The grisley Bear and the Musquaw or Black Bear. **1902** *Pearson's Mag.* June 665 The American Musquaw bear.

musquedine, var. MUSCADINE[2] *Obs.*

musqueet, ? variant of MESQUITE.

1808 PIKE *Sources Mississ.* III. (1810) 272 Here commenced the oak timber, it having been musqueet in general from Saint Antonio.

musque(e)to, -quit(t)o(e: see MOSQUITO.

musquet, obs. form of MUSKET *sb.*[1] and *sb.*[2]

musquetaire, variant of MOUSQUETAIRE.

musquet(t)eer, -eir, -ier, obs. ff. MUSKETEER.

musquet(t)oon, variant forms of MUSKETOON.

Musquito, var. MISKITO *a.* and *sb.*

musquosh, obs. form of MUSQUASH.

†'**musrol.** *Obs.* Forms: 6 **mouseroll, muzroule,** 7 **mus(e)role, mustroll, muzrole,** 7–8 **muse-roll,** 7–9 **musroll,** 8 **muss-rol,** 8– **musrol.** [a. F. *muserolle*, ad. It. *museruola*, f. *muso* muzzle.] The nose-band of a bridle.

1551 T. WILSON *Logike* 76 There remaineth a wicked inclination, the same must alwaies be brideled and kept in, even with the terror of the law, as though it were a mouse-roll. **1589** *Pappe w. Hatchet* in *Lyly's Wks.* (1902) III. 410 Thou shalt be broken as Prosper broke his horses, with a muzroule, portmouth, and a martingall. **1609** BLUNDEVIL *Art of Riding* 11 b, He praiseth much yͤ Musroll, saying that if yͤ horse doe naturally keep his mouth close together, that then it cannot hurt him. **1679** T. KIRKE *Mod. Acc. Scot.* 6 Their Bridles have not Bitts, but a kind of Musroll of two pieces of wood. **1797** *Encycl. Brit.* (ed. 3) X. 594 *Martingale*, ..a thong of leather, fastened to one end of the girths under a horse's belly, and at the other end to the muss-rol. **1833** J. HOLLAND *Manuf. Metal* II. 312 The snaffle..is derived from the old musrol or watering bit.

muss (mʌs), *sb.*[1] *Obs.* exc. *dial.* (see E.D.D.) Also 6–7 **musse.** [Of obscure origin.

Cotgrave 1611 has 'the game called *musse*' as one of the senses of F. *mousche* (now *mouche*) lit. a fly. Although *mouche* is the name of more than one game (see Littré) the sense 'scramble' has not been shown to occur in Fr., and it is probable that Cotgrave's explanation was suggested merely by the similarity of sound in the Eng. word.]

A game in which small objects are thrown down to be scrambled for; a scramble. Also *transf.*

1591 PERCIVALL *Sp. Dict.*, *Rebatina*, scrambling, a musse, a sudden skirmish. **1598** FLORIO, *Buschetta*, a play at musse, as children vse. **1606** SHAKS. *Ant. & Cl.* III. xiii. 91 When I cried hoa, Like Boyes vnto a musse, Kings would start forth, And cry, your will. **1623** MIDDLETON & ROWLEY *Spanish Gipsy* II. (1653) C 3, They'l throw down Gold in Musses. **1678** DRYDEN *Prol. to Shadwell's True Widow* 20 Bauble and cap no sooner are thrown down, But there's a muss of more than half the town. *a* **1734** NORTH *Examen* II. iv. §149 (1740) 311 All this Business was but a confused Muss of Oates and his Men falling foul upon one another.

muss (mʌs), *sb.*[2] Now *dial.* Also 6 **mus, musse.** [Perh. a. OF. *muse* mouth, muzzle.] A playful word for: Mouth. (See also E.D.D.)

a **1529** SKELTON *P. Sparowe* 362 Many a prety kusse Had I of his swete musse. —— *Sp. Parrot* 270 Now kus me, Parrot,..Goddys blessyng lyght on thy swete lyttyll mus!

† **muss,** *sb.*[3] *Obs.* [Perh. the same word as prec.: cf. the double sense of MUSKIN[1].] A term of endearment.

1598 FLORIO, *Pupo*, a pigsneye, a sweet-hart, a prettie musse, a daintie mop [etc.]. **1598** B. JONSON *Ev. Man in Hum.* II. iii, Sweete hart will you come in to breakfast... I pray thee (good Musse) we stay for you... What ayle you sweet hart, are you not well, speake good Musse. *Ibid.* v.i, Nay kisse me sweet musse.

muss (mʌs), *sb.*[4] *dial.* and *U.S.* [App. an onomatopœic alteration of MESS *sb.*

Sense 1 may belong to MUSS *sb.*[1]; cf. quot. *a* 1734 under that word.]

1. A disturbance, row. *Obs.*

1830 *Constellation* (N.Y.) 11/3 I've been in many a *scrape* before, but never such a *muss*! **1838** *N.Y. Advertiser & Express* 17 Feb. 4/6 The complainant testified that there was a 'muss' in Chatham Street. **1840** C. F. HOFFMAN *Greyslaer* I. II. iv. 206 That's just what I told Red Wolfert when he showed signs of kicking up a muss. **1848** DURIVAGE *Stray Subj.* 138 You're eternally kicking up a muss with somebody. **1857** BORTHWICK *Three Yrs. California* 153, I got into a 'muss' down at the store last night, and was whipped. **1862** LOWELL *Biglow P.* Ser. II. iii. 61 When Satan sets himself to work to raise his very bes' muss, He scatters roun' onscriptur'l views relatin' to Ones'mus. **1864** O. L. JACKSON *Colonel's Diary* (1922) 135 We have just had quite a muss [preceding the battle of Kenesaw Mt.]. **1873** 'MARK TWAIN' & WARNER *Gilded Age* 267 That gentleman delivered the young aspirant for a muss one of his elegant little left-handers. **1903** A. H. LEWIS *Boss* 19 It was nothin' but a cheap muss on the pier.

2. A state of untidiness; a muddle, mess.

1840 C. F. HOFFMAN *Greyslaer* II. III. iv. 142 All this muss is of Wat Bradshawe's cooking. **1842** *Spirit of Times* (Philad.) 22 Jan. (Th.), I upset my table, spilt my ink, and knocked down my books, making a deuced muss. **1843** MRS. L. M. CHILD *Lett. fr. New York* 129 (Bartlett) 'My head aches', said he; 'they have put my mind and body both into a confounded muss'. **1870** MRS. WHITNEY *We Girls* vi. (1874) 128 That is the difference between work and muss. **1890** *Anthony's Photogr. Bull.* III. 177 He has received many a lecture from his much enduring wife, for the awful muss which he has made. **1970** *Toronto Daily Star* 24 Sept. 40/1 (Advt.), Here's your cartridge... Instant loading. No muss or fuss. **1972** M. MEAD *Blackberry Winter* ix. 103 The first year Miss Abbott, the head of the dormitory apartments, described us as 'a mental and moral muss', and we accepted this with a kind of wicked glee.

† **muss,** *v.*[1] *Obs.* In 7 **musse.** [ad. L. *mussāre.*] *intr.* To mutter or murmur indistinctly.

1645 PAGITT *Heresiogr.* (1661) 86 They dare not so much as whisper or as much as musse against it.

muss (mʌs), *v.*[2] *dial.* and *U.S.* [f. MUSS *sb.*[4]]

1. *trans.* To make untidy; to crumple, to ruffle; to smear, mess; to entangle, confuse. Also with *up*. Hence **mussed** *ppl. a.*; also ***mussed-up***.

1837 in *Amer. Speech* (1965) XL. 127 Wish he muss imself [*sic*] up well and arty. *a* **1850** *Dow's Serm.* I. 151 (Bartlett) See that beautiful girl [the morning after a ball]; her hair mussed and mossy, except what lies in the bureau. **1856** W. T. SHERMAN in *Century Mag.* Dec. (1891) 297 The mayor, ..a large, good man, but as usual so mussed up and involved in old business that he could do nothing. **1865** MRS. WHITNEY *Gayworthys* 129, I don't like bran-new things. I want my dress to be mussed a little. **1876** HOLLAND *Sev. Oaks* xxi. 304 O don't! Mr. Fenton; you'll muss her hair. **1888** *Detroit Free Press* (Farmer), Neither of us got two winks of sleep during the night on the car... We reached Chicago in a mussed up condition. **1893** SALTUS *Madam Sapphira* 61 There, don't muss me up. **1902** C. J. C. HYNE *Mr. Horrocks Purser* 57 If Boy Austen..contrived to get badly mussed up with an undesirable woman [etc.]. **1907** C. E. MULFORD *Bar-20* v. 47, I paid twenty wheels for that [*sc.* a hat] eight years ago, and I don't want it mussed none. **1909** *Philad. Publ. Ledger* 24 June 7/6 (Advt.), Lot 3..Some four hundred soiled or mussed waists, in white lawn & lingerie. **1925** D. H. LAWRENCE *Death of Porcupine* 112 The really quick, Tolstoi loved to kill them off or muss them over. **1930** 'R. CROMPTON' *William's Happy Days* iii. 66 Trampling over his doorstep and 'mussing up' everything. **1955** W. GADDIS *Recognitions* II. ii. 351 The wind hit him,..mussing his hair from behind. **1973** D. WESTHEIMER *Going Public* ii. 28 Only a little mussed, the kid says! I'm not leaving looking like something the cat dragged in.

2. *intr.* To busy oneself in a confused, unmethodical, and ineffective manner. = MUDDLE *v.* 6.

1876 BESANT & RICE *Gold. Butterfly* x, I might meddle and muss till I busted up the whole concern.

mussak, variant of MUSSUCK.

‖**mussal** (mʌ'sɑːl). *Anglo-Indian.* Also **mosaul, mus(s)aul, mushal.** [Urdū (Arabic) *maš'al.*] A torch. Also, a torch-bearer, MUSSALCHEE.

1698 FRYER *Acc. E. India & P.* 34 The Duties march like Furies, with their lighted Mussals in their hands. **1751** in *Hedges' Diary* (Hakl.) II. 11 Oil 2 rs. Mussaul 1,,8. **1810** T. WILLIAMSON *E. India Vade M.* I. 219 The mosaul, or flambeau, consists of old rags, wrapped very closely round a small stick. **1852** *Life Bombay* 23 The Musaul, or lamp-lighter. **1872** E. BRADDON *Life in India* v. 161 The mussal is invariably carried so that we get the full benefit of the glare and smell.

‖**mussalchee** (mʌ'sɑːltʃiː). *Anglo-Indian.* Forms: 7 **massalgee, mossalagee,** 8 **mossoljee, mussaulche,** 9 **massaulchee, mosaulchy, musalche(e, mushalchee, mussalgee,** 9– **mussalchee.** [Urdū; f. *maš'al* MUSSAL with Turkish suffix.] A torch-bearer.

1610 FINCH in Purchas *Pilgrims* (1625) I. 432 He always had in seruice fiue hundred Massalgees. **1751** in *Hedges' Diary* (Hakl.) II. 11 Servants' Wages. 8 Frosses 11. 6 Mussaulches 12. 1 Barber 3,,4,,9. **1793** HODGES *Trav. India* 17 With two additional men or boys, to carry baggage and lights in the night, called mossoljees. *c* **1803** MRS. SHERWOOD in *Life* xvi. (1847) 278 A Mussalchee; his business is to wash dishes, carry a lantern, and, in fact, wait upon the Kitmutghaur. **1810** T. WILLIAMSON *E. India Vade M.* I. 218 Few mosaulchies are allowed more than five rupees monthly. **1839** MALCOM *Trav.* (1840) 20/1 One cooley to carry the baggage, and a musalche. **1907** *Blackw. Mag.* Sept. 423/1 Each carriage was met, as night fell, by mussalchees or torchbearers.

Mussalman, -mone, obs. ff. MUSSULMAN.

mussascus, obs. form of MUSQUASH.

mussaul, variant of MUSSAL.

mussel ('mʌs(ə)l), *sb.* Forms: 1 **muscelle, muscle, musle, mucxle, muxle,** 4–6 **muscule,** 4–7 **muskle,** 4–9 **muscle,** 5 **moscle, moscolle, moskyll, muschyl, muskele, muskyl, musselle, musshell, mustul,** (*pl.* **mwskollz**), 5–6 **muscul(l, mussil(le,** 5–7 **muskel,** 6 **muskil, mussil(le,** 7 **(mistle), mussell, mustell,** 8 **muscel,** 7– **mussel.** [OE. *muscle*, etc., wk. fem., corresp. to MLG. *mussel*, MDu. *mosscele* (Du. *mossel*), OHG. *muscula* (MHG. *muschele*, mod.G. *muschel*), a. late L. *muscula* (also *musla*, whence F. *moule*), altered form of L. *mūsculus* dim. of *mūs* mouse.]

1. A bivalve mollusc belonging to either of the two families *Mytilacea* (Sea Mussels) and *Unionacea* (Fresh-water Mussels).

horse mussel: see HORSE *sb.* ***pearl mussel***: see PEARL.

a **1000** ÆLFRIC *Colloq.* in Wr.-Wülcker 94/13 Muslan, *musculas*. *c* **1050** *Voc.* ibid. 447/38 *Musculus*, muscle. **1307–8** *Durham Acc. Rolls* (Surtees) 4 In muscles emptis in villa. *c* **1374** CHAUCER *Boeth.* v. pr. v. 131 (Camb. MS.) As oystrys and musculis and other swiche shelle fyssh of the see. **1387–8** T. USK *Test. Love* II. xii. (Skeat) l. 32 Thilke Margarite thou desirest, was closed in a muskle, with a blewe shell. **1393** LANGL. *P. Pl.* C. x. 94 A ferthyng-worth of muscles Were a feste for suche folke. *c* **1420** *Liber Cocorum* (1862) 46 Fyrst sethe thy mustuls. **1485** *Cely Papers* (Camden) 178 Item pᵈ for brede & mwskollz for the schype iiijᵈ. *a* **1529** SKELTON *E. Rummyng* 556 Garnyshed was her snout Wyth here and there a puscull, Lyke to a scabbyd muscull. **1555** EDEN *Decades* 93 Sea musculs are engendred of such quantitie, that many of them are as brode as buckelers. **1603** OWEN *Pembrokeshire* (1892) 120 The Ryver muskles are not for meate. **1610** SHAKS. *Temp.* I. ii. 463 Thy food shall be The fresh-brooke Mussels. **1661** J. CHILDREY *Brit. Baconica* 174 The Pearl-bearing Muskles are found upon this shore. **1697** DAMPIER *Voy.* (1729) I. 173 Here are a great many Perewincles and Muscles. **1740** JOHNSON *Sir F. Drake* Wks. IV. 434 The shell of a muscle of prodigious size. **1806** *Gazetteer Scotl.* (ed. 2) 547 In the Dovan there are sometimes found mussels containing small pearls. **1810** Lamb *Let. to B. Montagu* 12 July, How much more dignified leisure hath a mussel glued to his unpassable rocky limit two inch square! **1875** Huxley & Martin *Elem. Biol.* (1883) 107 Under the name of 'Fresh-water Mussel' two distinct kinds of animals..are included; namely, the *Anodonta* and two or three kinds of *Unio*.

2. A fossil bivalve shell found in ironstone bands in coal. See *mussel band*.

1834–5 J. Phillips *Geol.* in *Encycl. Metrop.* VI. 592/1 Coals..with bands of 'muscles'.

3. = mussel plum.

1718 Mrs. Eales *Receipts* 29 They will blue as well as the Muscles and better than the black Pear-Plums.

4. *attrib.* and *Comb.*, as ***mussel dredge***, ***extract***, ***gatherer***, ***gathering***, ***monger***, ***-opener***, ***poisoning***, ***-pooled***, ***sauce***, ***soup***, ***-spawn***, †***taker***; **mussel band** *Geol.* (see quot. 1883); **mussel-bank**, **-bed**, a layer of mussels at the bottom of the sea; **mussel bind** = *mussel band*; †**mussel boat**, ? a mussel-shell used by children as a toy boat; **mussel crab**, a pea-crab (*Pinnotheres maculatus*), dwelling as a messmate within the shell of the edible mussel (*Funk's Standard Dict.* 1895); **mussel-cracker**, (*a*) (see quot. 1845); (*b*) = biskop; **mussel-crusher** = *mussel-cracker* (b); **mussel digger** *U.S.*, (*a*) a name for the California grey whale; (*b*) a machine for digging mussel mud (Funk); **mussel duck**, the scaup duck, *Fuligula marila*; **mussel eater**, (*a*) one who is in the habit of eating mussels; (*b*) *U.S.* the buffalo perch, *Aplodinotus grunniens*, of the Mississippi valley (*Cent. Dict.* 1890); **mussel farm**, a place set apart for breeding mussels; **mussel man**, one who gathers mussels; **mussel mud**, mud abounding in mussels; **mussel pecker**, **picker**, the oyster catcher, *Hæmatopus ostralegus*; **mussel rake**, a rake used for gathering mussels; †**mussel rock**, ? a rock containing fossil mussel-shells; **mussel scale**, an insect having the shape of a small mussel-shell, which attacks the bark of apple-trees; **mussel scalp**, a mussel-bed; †**mussel stone**, a fossil mussel-shell.

1834–5 J. Phillips *Geol.* in *Encycl. Metrop.* VI. 590/1 Iron-stone courses are most plentiful in the middle and lower part, where also lie the '*muscle bands'. **1883** Gresley *Coal Mining Gloss.*, *Mussel band*, a bed of clay ironstone containing fossil bivalve shells, anthracosia, &c. **1634** W. Wood *New Eng. Prosp.* (1865) 47 The Bay..will be all flatts for two miles together, upon which is great store of *Muscle-banckes, and Clam bancks. **1774** Goldsm. *Nat. Hist.* VII. 47 It requires a year for the peopling a *muscle-bed. **1869** G. C. Scott *Fishing in Amer. Waters* 90 At the right time of tide, the locations of the mussel-beds are plainly indicated. **1854** F. C. Bakewell *Geol.* 34 Argillaceous layers, containing numerous shells of fresh-water muscles, called by the miners '*Muscle-bind'. *a* **1590** *Marr. Wit & Wisd.* ii. (Shaks. Soc.) 13 So we ware both put into a *mussellbote, And came saling in a sowes yeare ouer sea into Kent. **1612** R. Daborne *Chr. turn'd Turke* 353 Poore fishers brat, that neuer didst aspire Aboue a musle boat. **1845** *Zoologist* III. 1171 *Hæmatopus ostralegus.* Vulgarly termed by the Hartlepool fishermen *mussel-cracker. **1905** *East London* (Cape Province) *Dispatch* 6 Nov. 7/4 Judging by the enormous incisors, and the perfect pavement of rounded molars with which the jaws of these white steenbras are armed, these fish live largely upon shell-fish, hence the local name *mussel cracker* and the Durban name *mussel crusher.* **1930** C. L. Biden *Sea-Angling Fishes of Cape* xviii. 256 Mussel-Crusher or Mussel-Cracker. **1951** *Cape Times* 7 Feb. 2/5 Twenty-five mussel-crackers and ten blou stompkop were landed. **1953** J. L. B. Smith *Sea Fishes S. Afr.* (ed. 2) 502 The name 'Musselcracker' is applied in South Africa mainly to 2 fishes, *Sparodon durbanensis* and *Cymatoceps nasutus*, both of which develop massive jaws and powerful teeth. **1973** *Stand. Encycl. S. Afr.* VIII. 14/1 The musselcracker or mussel-crusher (*Cymatoceps nasutus*) is one of the best-known angling fishes in South Africa... The jaws are very powerful, with canine teeth in front and molars behind... Their flesh is coarse, but the head is a delicacy. The young are silvery, yellow and black; the adults are dark, and develop a curious fleshy nose. **1905**, etc. *Mussel-crusher [see *mussel-cracker* above]. **1860** *Merc. Marine Mag.* VII. 213 It being difficult to capture them, they have a variety of names among whalemen, as..'*Muscle-digger', 'Hard-head', &c. **1883** *Fisheries Exhib. Catal.* 13 *Mussel Dredge. **1864** Atkinson *Provinc. Names Birds*, *Mussel Duck... Scaup Duck. *Fuligula marila.* **1886** *Gentl. Mag.* Apr. 407 Once or twice in a lifetime, the *mussel-eater is 'musseled', i.e. poisoned more or less dangerously. **1899** *Allbutt's Syst. Med.* VIII. 492 After the intravascular injection of peptone or leech-extract, or crab or *mussel-extract. **1868** *Rep. U.S. Commissioner Agric.* (1869) 320 A *muscle farm near Rochelle has been cultivated, it is claimed, for hundreds of years. **1859** A. J. Munby *Diary* 18 July (1972) 38, I met the *mussel gatherers..fine young women with brown bare limbs. **1884** *Harper's Mag.* Nov. 842/1 The gay idlers..don the costume of the mussel-gatherer. **1862** *Chamb. Encycl.* IV. 516/2 In the river Earn ..*muscle-gathering is quite a trade. **1459** *Maldon (Essex) Court-Rolls* Bundle 34. No. 3, Johannes Morell, *muskylman. **1552** Huloet, Muskleman, *conchyta.* **1623** Fletcher *Rule a Wife* iv. i, Here's a chaine of whitings eyes for pearles, A *mussellmonger would have made a better. **1791** Huddesford *Salmag.* 111 Musclemongers and oystermen, crimps, and coal-heavers. **1774** J. Adams in *Fam. Lett.* (1876) 18 But I long more still to see the procuring more sea-weed, and *muscle mud, and sand, etc. **1825** *Prince Edward Island Register* (Charlottetown) 23 Aug. 1/1 Plenty of manure [is] at hand, either kelp, seaweed, mussle-mud, [etc.]. **1851** J. F. W. Johnston *Notes on N. Amer.* II. 151 Mussel-mud,..or sea-mud full of mussels, abounds in the Bay of St Andrews... This is an excellent fertilising substance... But the most apparently singular way of using it is to put it, with the mussels still living, into the turnip-drills, where it gives alone an excellent crop of turnips. **1973** *Canadian Antiques Collector* Jan.–Feb. 64/1 Of special value [as fertilizer] was the 'deep, black, stinking mud', better known as 'mussel-mud'—which lay thick in the beds of the Island's many tidal estuaries. **1909** *Daily Chron.* 25 Sept. 7/6 (Advt.), Oyster and *mussel opener (young) wanted for evenings. **1885** Swainson *Prov. Names Birds* 188 *Mussel pecker. **1889** H. Saunders *Man.* 543 A common name [for the Oyster-catcher] is 'Sea Pie'.. another equally appropriate term being '*Mussel-picker'. **1946** Dylan Thomas *Deaths & Entrances* 9 The *mussel pooled and the heron Priested shore. **1899** *Allbutt's Syst. Med.* VIII. 494 Urticaria is occasionally symptomatic of grave conditions, such as *mussell poisoning, infective fevers [etc.]. **1883** *Fisheries Exhib. Catal.* 293 A *Mussel rake. **1681** Grew *Musæum* iii. i. 265 A Piece of white *Muscle-Rock. *Musculites Saxum.* **1747** Mrs. Glasse *Cookery* ix. 88 *Muscle-Sauce made thus is very good. **1853** *Zoologist* XI. 3862 With an especial reference to the '*mussel-scale' of the apple. **1552** Huloet, *Muskleskalp. **1593** *Minutes of Culross Council*, To be given to George Bruer for the ancarage and mussel-scalp. **1879** H. Stevenson in R. Lubbock *Fauna Norf.* Mem. 15 The sandy flats and mussel-scalps of that portion of the coast. **1896** J. H. Crawford *Wild Life Scotl.* 271 The punt lingered opposite the mud flats, or mussel-scaups exposed by the tide. **1771** Mrs. Haywood *New Present* 39 *Mussel Soup. **1902** *Chambers's Jrnl.* May 277/2 Some seasons the *mussel-spawn is pretty much in evidence here. **1681** Grew *Musæum* iii. i. 264 The *Muscle-Stone. *Musculites.* *c* **1515** *Cocke Lorell's B.* 5 Steuen mesyll mouthe *muskyll taker.

mussel ('mʌs(ə)l), *v.* [f. mussel *sb.*] In *passive*: To be poisoned by eating mussels.

1857 Dunglison *Dict. Med.* s.v. *Mytilus edulis*, One affected with such phenomena is said, occasionally, to be musselled. **1886** *Gentl. Mag.* Apr. 407 Once or twice in a lifetime, the mussel-eater is 'musseled', i.e. poisoned more or less dangerously.

mussel(e, -lle, obs. forms of morsel.

mussel(l, obs. forms of muzzle.

musselege, obs. form of mucilage.

musselim, variant of musellim.

musselin, -olin, obs. forms of muslin.

Musselman(n, obs. forms of Mussulman.

mussel plum. [Named from its resemblance in shape and colour to a mussel-shell.] A dark purple variety of plum. Also *attrib.* in ***mussel-plum cheese***.

1626 Bacon *Sylva* §509 The Muscle-Plumme, the Damasin Plumme [etc.]. **1657** Austen *Fruit Trees* (ed. 2) 57, I esteeme the Mustle Plum one of the best. **1676** Worlidge *Cyder* (1691) 220 The Muscle-plum one of the best of plums. **1729** Langley *Pomona* 89 The Bruxel Apricot..is best propagated on the Muscle-Plumb Stock. **1808** Mrs. Rundell *Dom. Cookery* (1824) 313 Mussel-plum Cheese. **1881** *Encycl. Brit.* XII. 275/2 The Mussel, Brussels, St. Julien, and Pear plums.

'mussel-shell. The shell of a mussel.

c **725** *Corpus Gloss.* 863 *Conca*, musclan scel. **1387–8** T. Usk *Test. Love* iii. i. (Skeat) l. 45 On the see sides in the more Britain in muskle shelles of the heuenly dewe the best ben engendred. **1584** R. Scot *Discov. Witchcr.* i. iv. (1886) 8 They can saile in an egge shell, a cockle or muscle shell. **1681** Grew *Musæum* i. vi. ii. 148 The Natives of Brasile use Muscle-shells for Spoons and Knives. **1707** *Curios. in Husb. & Gard.* 312 As thin as a Muscle-Shell. **1829** *Glover's Hist. Derby* I. 95 A stratum of muscle shells. **1873** Browning *Red Cott. Nt.-cap* 34 Granite and muscle-shell are ground alike To glittering paste.

b. *nonce-use.* One who gapes like a mussel-shell.

1598 Shaks. *Merry W.* iv. v. 29 *Simp.* Pray you Sir, was't not the Wise-woman of Brainford? *Fal.* I marry was it (Mussel-shell) what would you with her?

†**'musser.** *Obs.* [If not a misprint for *musset*, prob. f. *musse* meuse + -er[1].] = muset.

1611 Barrey *Ram Alley* ii. i. C 2, We can finde..the mussers, formes and holes, You yong men vse.

musshell, mussil, obs. forms of mussel.

mussiek, variant of mussuck.

mussilage, obs. form of mucilage.

Mussilman, obs. form of Mussulman.

mussit, *dial.* form of muset.

†**'mussitant**, *a. Obs.* [a. L. *mussitant-em*, pr. pple. of *mussitāre*: see next.] Speaking in an undertone; muttering, murmuring.

1681 [see murmurant].

†**mussitate**, *v. Obs.* [f. ppl. stem of L. *mussitāre*, freq. of *mussāre* to mutter.] *intr.* To mutter.

1626 Minsheu *Ductor* (ed. 2) 484 To *Mussitate*, or mutter betweene the teeth. **1652** Gaule *Magastrom.* 59 It did still muscitate [sic] in dark corners. **1721** Bailey, To *mussitate*, to mutter often.

mussitation (mʌsɪ'teɪʃən). [ad. late L. *mussitātiōn-em*, n. of action f. *mussitāre*: see prec.] Muttering; murmuring.

1649 Roberts *Clavis Bibl.* 443 *marg.*, A mussitation, or low prayer. **1734** A. Young *Idol. Corrupt.* II. 144 The Murmur, or Mussitation, which Liquor makes that is pent up in a Bottle. **1891** *Syd. Soc. Lex.*, *Mussitation*,.. Muttering; a morbid symptom consisting in movement of the lips of the sick without the production of sound or of articulate sounds, or a muttering with a very low voice.

mussite ('mʌsaɪt). *Min.* [Named by Bonvoisin in 1806 from the *Mussa* Alp, Tyrol, its locality: see -ite.] Obs. synonym of diopside.

1819 Bakewell *Introd. Min.* 304 Diopside, Mussite and Alalite, are names given to certain minerals found in the plain of Mussa, and at Ala in Piedmont. **1883** *Encycl. Brit.* XVI. 416/1.

Mussleman, variant of Mussulman.

mussoey, mussoi, variant forms of massoy.

Mussolini (mʌsəʊ'li:ni:). [Name of Benito *Mussolini* (1883–1945), prime minister of Italy and leader of the Fascist Party in Italy.] One who embodies the characteristics of Mussolini; also *attrib.* So **Mussolini-'esque**, **Musso'linian** *adjs.*, of, pertaining to, characteristic of, or (somewhat) resembling Mussolini; **Musso'linism**, the political principles or policy of Mussolini or of the Fascist Party in Italy.

1924 *Glasgow Herald* 29 Jan. 9 Signor Mussolini..said that he was unable to accept the antithesis that some people wished to create between Fascism and Mussolinism. *Ibid.* 30 June 11 The working classes needed to be warned against the establishment of 'Mussolinism' in this country. **1928** H. G. Wells *Way World is Going* ii. 15 The consolidation and reconstruction of China..has not gone on under the direction of some strong-jowled hero of the Diaz or Mussolini type. **1928** *Daily Express* 21 Nov. 19 Mr. [J. W. H. T.] Douglas' stern, unbending look always interests me. So does his Mussolini-esque and frequent call of 'Fight!' **1932** H. Nicolson *Diary* 15 Mar. (1966) 112 Tom does not wish to end it, being still obsessed by Mussolinian ideas. **1936** [see Hitler]. **1946** R. Capell *Simiomata* ii. 86 There are still Mussolinian Italians with the Germans. **1959** *Guardian* 16 Oct. 11/3 He..fails to acknowledge that there were many more sides to 'Mussolinism' than the less creditable later period. **1970** R. A. H. Robinson *Origins of Franco's Spain* iii. 134 The policies of Gil Robles meant 'the enslavement, in Mussoliniesque style, of the proletariat'.

mussoola(h, variant forms of masoola(h.

muss-rol, variant of musrol.

‖**mussuck** ('mʌsək). *Anglo-Indian.* Forms: 7 mussocke, 9 musak, (? *corruptly*) **muskatt**, **mussak**, **mussiek**, **mussoch**, **mussuck**, **musuk**. [Hindī *maçak.*] A leather water-bag; usually, one made of the whole skin of a goat.

1610 Finch in Purchas *Pilgrims* (1625) I. 427 A Mussocke of water being sold for a Rupia. **1802** *Misc. Ess.* in *Ann. Reg.* 814/1 The troops from India brought Muskatts or leather bags to contain the water in. **1840** A. Abbott in C. R. Low *Afghan War* (1879) 133 At Kooner I had a raft of fifty 'mussucks', very badly put together and with scarcely any timber on it. **1867** A. L. Adams *Wand. Nat. India* 59 When the cooling effects of a mussiek of water refreshed us for our breakfast.

attrib. **1895** *Westm. Gaz.* 15 May 3/1 In the meantime Mussoch rafts, *i.e.*, rafts supported by inflated goats' skins, were improvised to transport men from one bank to the other, worked by native boatmen.

mussulage, variant of musculage.

mussulah, variant of massoola(h.

Mussulman ('mʌsəlmən), *sb.* and *a.* Forms: 6, 9 **muselman**, 7 **moussiliman**, **mulsulman**, **muscelman**, **musilman**, **musleman**, **mussalman**, **mussalmone**, **mussilman**, 7–9 **musalman**, **musselman**, **mussleman**, **musulman**, 9 **moosulman**, **musselmann**, **mussulmaun**, 7– **mussulman**. *pl.* **-mans**. *Catachrestic pl.* 7–9 **-men**. [a. Pers. *musulmān*, primarily an adj. f. Pers. (a. Arab.) *muslim*: see Muslim. Cf. med.L. *mulsumānus* (Aragon, 12th c.), F. *musulman* (fem. *-an*), Sp. *musulman*, *-mano*, Pg. *musulmão*, It. *musulmano*, G. *muselmann*.]

A. *sb.* **1.** A Muslim. Now *arch.*

1563–83 Foxe *A. & M.* 759/2 And if it chaunce a Christian being on horsebacke, to meet or passe by a Musulman, that is a Turkish priest [etc.]. **1585** T. Washington tr. *Nicholay's Voy.* ii. xxi. 59 No Muselmans shall enter into their Mosques, without they be first wel washed and purified. **1615** Bedwell *Moham. Imp.* i. §9 The Musselmans..do exercise themselues in feats of armes. **1632** Lithgow *Trav.* v. 206 They call themselues Musilmans, to wit, good beleeuers. **1653** H. Cogan tr. *Pinto's Trav.* xv. 51 Saying that it was not lawful for any to enjoy the blessings of God, but the holy and just Moussilimans, such as they were. **1687** *Lond. Gaz.* No. 2237/1 The Caimacan to raise money for the War, had sent to all the rich Musselmen. **1788** Gibbon *Decl. & F.* l. V. 212 Prayer, fasting, and alms, are the religious duties of a Musulman. **1800** Wellington in Gurw. *Desp.* (1837) I. 76 There are 4 musselmenn upon the island of Seringapatan. **1888** Allnutt *Cambr. Univ. Serm.* 15 Mar. *Cambr. Rev.* p. lxii, We have only to look at the character of the prayers which every pious Musalman daily offers up.

2. [tr. G. *muselmann.*] *pl.* **Mussulmans**, **Mussulmen** [G. *muselmänner*]. Under the Third Reich, an inhabitant of a concentration camp or extermination camp who had reached a state of physical and emotional exhaustion in which he displayed fatalism and loss of initiative.

[**1950** H. NORDEN tr. *E. Kogon's Theory & Practice of Hell* xviii. 214 Not all the prisoners were what came to be known as 'Moslems', men who were physically and mentally broken, who allowed anything to be done to them.] **1953** G. REITLINGER *Final Solution* xvii. 458 Most of those who died were just *Mussulmen*, the camp slang word for a walking skeleton wrapped up in a bit of blanket. The journey from Auschwitz,..for days on end in open trucks, freezing and without food, was alone sufficient to make a *Mussulman*. **1959** M. LEVIN *Eva* 224 These..were the creatures called mussulmans..in the last stage, when they reacted only as brute animals. **1975** N. FREELING *What are Bugles blowing For?* xxvii. 169 The man..has let himself die. It is a phenomenon similar to what was seen in the camps... The Musselmen they were called.

B. *adj.* Of or pertaining to Muslims. Now *arch.*

1684 tr. *Travernier's Trav.* II. 46 If it [Persia] were.. really sensible of Piety and the Musal-Man Faith. **1698** FRYER *Acc. E. India & P.* 91 Here are a sort of bold, lusty, and most an end, drunken Beggars, of the Musslemen Cast. **1788** GIBBON *Decl. & F.* l. V. 212 The gravest of the Musulman doctors imitate the modesty of their master. **1817** BYRON *Beppo* lxxxi, Less in the Mussulman than Christian way. **1883** F. DAY *Indian Fish* 17 A Mussalman tribe, composed of immigrants from Arabia.

Hence **Mussul'manic**, †**'Mussulmanish** *adjs.* = MUSSULMAN *a.*; **'Mussulmanism** (now *rare*), Muhammadanism; ‖**Mussulmanlik** [Turkish *musulmānlik*], the Mussulman faith, Islam; †**'Mussulmanlike** *a.*, Muslim; **'Mussulmanly** *adv.* (*rare*$^{-0}$), in the manner of Mussulmans (Craig 1849); †**'Mussulmans** *Anglo-Indian* [cf. MOORS], the Urdū language.

1599 HAKLUYT *Voy.* II. 159 As well in..Constantinople, as in other places of your Musulmanlike Empire. **1625** PURCHAS *Pilgrims* II. ix. xv. 1610 From that time the Mussulmanlick beganne, that is, the true Beliefe. **1638** SIR T. HERBERT *Trav.* (ed. 2) 272 Hee dyed Anno Domini 273, and before the Hegira or Mussulmanish accompt 347. **1731** BAILEY vol. II. (ed. 2), Mussulmanism, *Mahometanism*. **1767** J. RENNELL *MS. Let.* in Yule 448/1 But the politest Language is the Moors or Mussulmans and Persian. **1800** *Chron.* in *Asiat. Ann. Reg.* 53/2 The leopard, with a true Mussulmanic aversion for swine's flesh, rather avoided this animal. *Ibid., Misc. Tr.* 123/2 Several of the Mussulmans assert that Ally was the first person who embraced Mussulmanism. **1865** *Morn. Star* 6 Mar., Rare as are conversions from Mussulmanism to Christianity,..yet fewer still are the instances in which the proselytes to either faith are women. **1900** *Dundee Advert.* 29 Nov. 4 Mussulmanic theology.

†**Mussulmin**, repr. Arab. *muslimīn* pl. (See MUSLIM.)

1679 L. ADDISON *1st St. Mahumedism* 96 The Musulmin are very metaphorical in expressing themselves in the description of their Faith. *Ibid.* 97.

Mussulwoman ('mʌsəlwʊmən). *Humorous.* A female Mussulman. Hence **Mussulwomanish** *a.*

1668 DRYDEN *Even. Love* III. i, *Jac.* A Mussulman, at your service. *Wild.* A Musselwoman, say you? **1817** BYRON *Beppo* lxxvii, The poor dear Mussulwomen whom I mention. **1840** HOOD *Kilmansegg, Her Fancy Ball* xxiv, And Lady K. nid-nodded her head, Lapp'd in a turban fancy-bred,..Some Mussul-womanish mystery. **1854** *Tait's Mag.* XXI. 136 Amidst the shrieks of the terrified Mussulwoman.

mussurana (mʊsə'rɑːnə). [ad. Pg. *muçurana* f. Tupi, cord.] A Brazilian colubrid snake, *Clelia clelia*.

1914 T. ROOSEVELT *Through Brazilian Wilderness* i. 14 The most formidable enemy of the many dangerous Brazilian snakes is a non-poisonous, entirely harmless, rather uncommon Brazilian snake, the mussurana. **1934** *Discovery* July 207/2 A cannibal snake, known in Brazil as the Mussurana..though harmless to men and animals, lives entirely on other snakes to whose venom it is immune. **1964** G. VEVERS tr. *Vogel's Reptiles & Amphibians* xiii. 162 In Brazil there is a handsome snake, much-loved and protected, which feeds, although not exclusively, on other snakes, particularly poisonous ones. This is the Mussurana, *Clelia clelia*, which is frequently depicted in the act of eating a Jararaca or other poisonous snake. It reaches a length of 7½ ft., is typically a metallic black, although the young are pale, and it lives on the ground. **1970** *East African Standard* 23 Jan. 6/4 The Mussurana, or snake-eater, feeds on deadly snakes, particularly the lethal Fer-de-lance.

mussy ('mʌsɪ), *a.* *U.S.* [f. MUSS *sb.*[4] + -Y.] Untidy, rumpled, tousled. Hence **'mussiness**.

1859 BARTLETT *Dict. Amer., Mussy.* 1. Disarranged, disordered, tumbled;..2...Smeary, dirty, nasty. **1869** *N.Y. Independent* 25 Mar. (Cent.), A general appearance of mussiness, characteristic of the man. **1873** W. S. MAYO *Never Again* viii. 101 A warm but somewhat mussy victorine of cat-skin that encircled her neck. **1896** *Peterson Mag.* VI. 330/2 A trunkful of limp, mussy, bedraggled gowns.

mussy, obs. variant of MUZZY *a.*

mussy, dial. var. MERCY *sb.* Cf. LAWK, LAWKS, *int.*

1823 E. MOOR *Suffolk Words & Phr.* 243 Mussy on us. **1881** J. C. HARRIS *Nights with Uncle Remus* (1883) xii. 67 For mussy sake gin 'im a walkin'-cane. **1903** P. L. DUNBAR *In Old Plantation Days* 63 Lawd a' mussy, 'pon my soul, an' you one of de faifful ol' de flock! **1909** *Dialect Notes* III. 344 Lawsy mussy (pon my soul). **1935** *Scribner's Mag.* Feb. 120/2 Hab mussy, Jedus!.. When a bullbat go lak dat he diggin' a grabe.

must (mʌst), *sb.*[1] Also 3–4, 9 **most**, 4–7 **muste**, 5 **moste**, 7 **moust**. [ad. L. *must-um*, orig. neut. (sc. *vinum*) of *mustus* adj., new, fresh. Cf. OHG. (MHG. and mod.G.) *most*, OF. *moust* (F. *moût*), Sp., Pg., It. *mosto*.]

1. New wine; the juice of the grape either unfermented or before the fermentation is completed. Also *new must*.

c **888** K. ÆLFRED *Boeth.* v. §2 Ne meaht þu win wringan on mide winter, þeah ðe wel lyste wearmes mustes. *c* **1205** LAY. 8723 Nes þer neouþer win ne must [*c* **1275** most]. *a* **1300** *Cursor M.* 18968 'Drunken,' þai said, 'o must ar þai.' **1377** LANGL. *P. Pl.* B. XVIII. 368 May no drynke me moiste ne my thruste slake, Tyl þe vendage falle in þe vale of iose-phath, Þat I drynke riȝte ripe must [*MS. R.* most: **1393** *C. text* most] *resureccio mortuorum.* **1481** CAXTON *Myrr.* II. x. 89 The clustres of grapes ben so grete and so full of Muste that [etc.]. **1548** UDALL *Erasm. Par. Luke* v. 73 Will put newe muste into old bottelles. **1671** MILTON *P.R.* IV. 16 Or as a swarm of flies in vintage time, About the wine-press where sweet moust is pour'd, Beat off, returns as oft with humming sound. **1677** W. HARRIS tr. *Lemery's Course Chem.* 246 Wine is nothing else but the Muste, or Juyce of ripe Grapes, whose Spirituous parts are disingaged, and set at liberty in the Fermentation. **1775** R. CHANDLER *Trav. Asia M.* (1825) I. 213 We stopped at Mersenet..which afforded us a dish of boiled wheat, and some must of wine. **1813** SIR H. DAVY *Agric. Chem.* iii. (1814) 130 When this juice [of the grape], or must, as it is commonly called is exposed to the temperature of about 70°, the fermentation begins. **1874** SYMONDS *Sk. Italy & Greece* (1898) I. xi. 210 Men..are treading the red must into vats and tuns.

pl. **1601** HOLLAND *Pliny* II. 150 As touching Musts or new wines. **1634** R. H. *Salernes Regim.* 73 Inconveniences that breed by drinking of new Wine or Musts. **1888** *Pall Mall G.* 23 Jan. 7/1 Musts which twenty years ago readily sold for from 80 to 90 pesetas per hectolitre now sell for 13 or 14 pesetas.

b. *transf.* and *fig.*

1563 MAN *Musculus' Commonpl.* 153 Els the Jewes might haue with good reason preferred the old wine of Moses lawe, aboue the new must of the doctrine of Christ. **1656** BLOUNT *Glossogr., Must*,..any thing fresh or new. **1850** NEALE *Med. Hymns* (1867) 115 From the Cross's pole of glory Flows the must of ancient story In the Church's winevat stored. **1865** SWINBURNE *Rococo* 40 The blood red must of pain.

†**c.** *in (the) must, on the must*: said of wine while still in process of fermentation. Also *fig.* *Obs.*

1533 ELYOT *Cast. Helthe* I. 13 b, Wyne in muste or sowre. **1594** PLAT *Jewell-ho.* II. 16 Rhenish wine in the muste. **1634** MASSINGER *Very Woman* III. v, 'Tis wine; I sure 'tis wine! excellent strong wine! I'th must I take it. *a* **1661** FULLER *Worthies* (1662) I. 8 Which hath made his Holynesse the more cautious, to canonize none whilest their memories are on the Must, immediately after their Deaths. *a* **1700** DRYDEN *Baucis & Philemon* 111 The Wine..Still working in the Must, and lately press'd.

†**2. a.** Any juice or liquor undergoing or prepared for undergoing alcoholic fermentation. *Obs.*

1382 WYCLIF *Song Sol.* viii. 2, I shal ȝyue thee drinken of spiced win, and of the must of my poumgarnetes [Vulg. *mustum malorum*]. **1708** J. PHILIPS *Cyder* I. 5 The Must, of pallid Hue, declares the Soil Devoid of Spirit.

b. *dial.* The pulp of apples or pears after the juice has been pressed out in making cider or perry.

1670 in *Evelyn's Pomona*, etc. (ed. 2) 63 To preserve the Must (which is the bruised Fruit) from straining through the Crib when they apply the Skrews. **1794** J. CLARK *Agric. Heref.* 40 Drawing the stone on its edge..over the fruit in the trough, until it is reduced into a kind of paste, provincially *must*. **1897** *Evesham Jrnl.* 16 Jan. (E.D.D.), There can be no doubt about the must being highly acceptable in a winter of food scarcity [for cattle].

c. 'The pulp of potatoes prepared for fermentation' (*Cent. Dict.* 1890).

†**3.** A variety of cider-apple. *Obs.*

1664 BEALE in Evelyn *Pomona*, etc. 26 We should prefer a peculiar Cider-fruit, which in Herefordshire are generally called Musts; (both the Apple and the Liquor and the Pulpe together in the contusion) as from the Latine *Mustum.* **1707** MORTIMER *Husb.* (1721) II. 327 The best sorts [of apples] for Cyder are found to be the Redstreak, the White Must, the Green Must [etc.]. **1764** *Museum Rust.* II. x. 37.

4. *attrib.*, as *must-maker, -making, -tub, -tun, -vat*; †**must-month**, September.

1598 SYLVESTER *Du Bartas* II. ii. IV. *Columnes* 404 In Must-Month [orig. *au mois donne-vin*], the Beam Stands equi-poiz'd in equi-poizing them [*sc.* day and night]. **1853** URE *Dict. Arts* I. 700 A little red precipitate of mercury, when added to the must-tun, stopped the fermentation. **1862** M. B. EDWARDS *John & I*, I. xii. 254 Cider or most making. *Ibid.* 255 John looked at the geese-stuffers—I at the most makers. **1870** *Auctioneer's Catal.* in Miss Jackson *Shropsh. Word-bk.*, Must-tub. ['The tub into which the apple-pulp is put, in the process of cider-making.']

†**must**, *sb.*[2] *Sc. Obs.* Forms: 5 **moist**, 6–7 **muist**, 6, 9 **must**. [a. OF. *must* (15th c. in *pomme de must* must-ball), var. of *musc* MUSK.] **a.** Musk; also *attrib.* in *must-ball, -box*. **b.** (See quot. 1808.)

1488 *Inv. R. Wardrobe* (1815) 5 Item, twa tuthpikis of gold, with a chenye, a perle & erepike, a moist ball of gold [etc.]. **1513** DOUGLAS *Æneis* XII. Prol. 148 Must, myr, aloes, or confectioun. *a* **1585** MONTGOMERIE *Flyting* 15 Thy smell was sa fell, and stronger than muist. *a* **1693** M. BRUCE *Good News Evil T.* (1708) 68, I carry a little Muist-box (which is the Word of God) in my Bosom, and when I meet with the ill Air of ill company, that's like to gar me Swarf, I besmell my self with the sweet savour of it. **1808** JAMIESON, *Must*, an old term, applied by the vulgar to hair-powder, or flour used for this purpose. S. Perhaps it might anciently receive this name as being scented with *musk*, S. *must.* **1843** M. A. RICHARDSON *Local Hist. Table-bk.* VI. 272 Their necks deep-pierc'd, with must abound.

must (mʌst), *sb.*[3] [? Back-formation from MUSTY *a.*: cf. MUST *v.*] Mustiness; mould.

1602 WARNER *Alb. Eng.* XIII. lxxviii. (1612) 322 By Rot, Must, Sowernes, Fruits, Corne, Wine good-Quallities forgo. **1693** EVELYN *De la Quint. Compl. Gard.* I. 88 A kind of Cellar, which is never without some Taste of Must. **1743** *Lond. & Country Brew.* IV. (ed. 2) 261 Water naturally breeds a Must, which is a Sort of Mushroom. **1778** [W. MARSHALL] *Minutes Agric.* 15 July an. 1777, I am in hopes that it will act as an antiputrescent, and preserve it from mould and must. **1827** HOOD *Ode to Melancholy* 116 Like the sweet blossoms of the May, Whose fragrance ends in must. **1852** H. MAYHEW in Visct. Ingestre *Meliora* Ser. I. 279 There was a smell of must and dry rot that told of damp and imperfect ventilation. **1855** DICKENS *Dorrit* II. x, The gloom and must and dust of the whole tenement were secret. **1867** J. HOGG *Microsc.* II. i. 298 From this stage it readily passes to that of must and mildew. **1897** *Literature* 11 Dec. 233/2 His notes..savour of dryness and must.

fig. **1633** P. FLETCHER *Purple Isl.* VIII. xxxii, Such was his minde, tainted with idle must. **1869** LYNCH *Ch. & State* 23 If you defile by the dust and must and rust of time the holiest pages of the Bible.

must, *sb.*[4] The verb MUST used for the nonce as a noun in obvious applications.

1603 DEKKER, etc. *Grissil* IV. ii, Must is for kings, And low obedience for low underlings. **1611** BEAUM. & FL. *King & no King* IV. iii, 1 *Sw.* I, this must be granted. 2 *Sw.* Still this must? 1 *Sw.* I say this must be granted. 2 *Sw.* I, give me the must again, brother, you palter. **1616** B. JONSON *Devil an Ass* III. iii. 209 *Mer.* You must. *Eve.* Must I? Doe you your musts, Sir, I'll doe mine. **1736** AINSWORTH *Lat. Dict.* s.v. *Away*, Away with this must, *aufer mihi oportet*. **1768–74** TUCKER *Lt. Nat.* (1834) II. 680 There is no *must* in the case, but they may and ought to be forborne. **1876** GEO. ELIOT *Dan. Der.* III. xxiii, In uttering these three terrible *musts*, Klesmer lifted up three long fingers in succession. **1885** *Pall Mall G.* 17 Jan. 1/1 The absolute Must of Duty and of Right.

b. Something that must be done, possessed, considered, etc.; a necessity. orig. *U.S.*

1892 *Dialect Notes* I. 205 An article marked with the word *must* is spoken of as a *must*, or emphatically—if there is absolutely no way of keeping it out of the paper—as a *dead must*. **1941** *Amer. Speech* XVI. 67/1 The *dirndl*, a dress which was a 'must' for every woman in 1937. **1948** 'J. TEY' *Franchise Affair* xxi. 239 The Feathers—one of the 'musts' of American visitors to Britain—was..famous. **1951** 'J. WYNDHAM' *Day of Triffids* v. 103 It was close on midnight when we had finished adding our own secondary wants to the list of musts. **1957** R. HOGGART *Uses of Literacy* x. 250 These valuable books are *musts* for *you*. **1960** *House & Garden* Mar. 136 Nature in Schweppshire is a top must, is actively encouraged. **1973** *Guardian* 30 Mar. 2/4 A film and a song made the Trevi Fountain a 'must' for tourists.

c. *attrib.* and *Comb.* Essential, mandatory, obligatory. *colloq.* (orig. *U.S.*).

1912 M. NICHOLSON *Hoosier Chron.* 180 His gratification at being able to write 'must' matter for both sides of a prominent journal. **1937** *Amer. Speech* XII. 8 Roosevelt.. was called..The New Deal Caesar who specialized in must-legislation. **1939** *Canadian Forum* June 94/2 This is a *must* book. **1941** *Britannia & Eve* Sept. 4/1 They had come to accept the fact that mails and government-priority 'must' passengers monopolised the flying boats. **1952** *Manch. Guardian Weekly* 27 Nov. 3/2 A list of suggestions which he [*sc.* Senator Taft] had marked as either 'must' or 'optional' legislation. **1959** *New Statesman* 10 Jan. 32/2 A struggle of some interest..is now taking place among those women's periodicals..which are still 'must-reading' for debutantes with any claim to literacy. **1973** *Black World* May 69/2 His forthcoming paper is a 'must-read'.

†**must**, *a.*[1] *Obs. rare.* Forms: 5 **moste**, 6 **must**. [ad. L. (*vinum*) *must-um*: see MUST *sb.*[1]] Of wine: New, unfermented.

c **1440** *Gesta Rom.* xxi. 337 (Cambr. MS.) Gyf me A draught of thi wyne moste. **1559** MORWYNG *Evonym.* 383 Siething the medicines with the wyne whyle it is must and new.

†**must**, *a.*[2] *rare*$^{-1}$. [Cf. MUSTY *a.*] ? Sour.

1547 BOORDE *Brev. Health* ccclxxxi. 122 His stomake is turned and must, or els is redy to perbreake or to vomyt.

must (mʌst), *a.*[3] and *sb.*[5] Also **musth** (moost). [a. Urdū *mast*, a. Pers. *mast* lit. 'intoxicated'.]

A. *adj.* Applied to male animals, as elephants and camels, in a state of dangerous frenzy to which they are subject at irregular intervals. Phr. *to go must*.

1871 FORSYTH *Highl. India* 287 She is not subject to the danger of becoming 'must' and uncontrollable, as male elephants do periodically after a certain age. **1887** KIPLING *Departmental Ditties* (1888) 21 The Commissariat *hathee* had—forgive the rhyme—gone *musth*. **1895** MRS. B. M. CROKER *Village Tales* (1896) 89 A 'must' elephant.

transf. **1893** *Sat. Rev.* 2 Dec. 611 Mr. Labouchere 'went must' on the Matabele business.

B. *sb.*

1. The condition or state of being 'must'.

1878 J. GIBSON in *Encycl. Brit.* VIII. 124/1 An elephant in 'must', as this frenzied condition is termed, is regarded as the most dangerous of animals. **1901** *Wide World Mag.* VIII. 194/1 A huge, tuskless elephant, in a state of must or periodical madness. **1959** M. PUGH *Chancer* 35 He suffered from the recurring nightmare that his cameras would go on musth and stampede out of the studios at the second he was due on the air. **1972** *New York* 1 May 10/3 In twenty seconds she can go from emotional neutral to the fury of an elephant in musth. **1973** *Nature* 2 Nov. 17/2 The madness of the animal 'on musth' causes other elephants to avoid him.

attrib. **1882** *Times Law Rep.* 8 Mar., After Elephants arrived at the age of 21 they became dangerous at certain seasons, called 'Must' or 'Moost Season'. **1890** Baker *Wild Beasts* I. 46 The approach of the 'must' period is.. perceived by a peculiar exudation of an oily nature.

2. 'An elephant in must'.
In recent Dicts.

must (mʌst), *v.*¹ Forms: 1 **móste**, 2–6 **moste**, **muste**, 3–6 **most**, 4 **mast**, 5 **moost**, 6 *Sc.* **moist**, 3– **must**. *2nd sing.* 1 **móstes**, **móstest**, 2–3 **mostes**, 2–5 **mostest**, 5 **mustest**, 5– **must**. *Plural* 1 **móstan**, **-on**, **-un**, 4–5 **moston**, 3–5 **mosten**, 4–5 **mostyn**, **mustyn**, 6 **musten**, 3–5 **most(e**, 3– **must**. [OE. *móste*, pl. *móston*, subj. *mósten*, pa. t. of *mót* pret.-pres., MOTE *v.*] An auxiliary of predication, followed by the infinitive (without *to*).

†**I.** The past tense of MOTE *v. Obs.*

1. In the sense of MOTE *v.* 1, expressing permission or possibility. **a.** Past ind. = might, was able or permitted to, could. Chiefly with negative expressed or implied.

Beowulf 3100 þenden he burhwelan brucan moste. *c* **1000** Ælfric *Gram.* xliv. (Z.) 264 *Tibi licuit* ðu mostest. *c* **1175** *Lamb. Hom.* 9 3ef þu sungedest toward þine drihtene and me hit mihte witen, nouþer gold ne seoluer no moste gan for þe. *c* **1225** *Ancr. R.* 260 Of al þe brode eorðe ne moste he habben a grot, forte deien uppon. *c* **1275** *XI Pains of Hell* 190 in *O.E. Misc.* 152 For heo nolden beon ischriven þe hwile þat hi mosten lyuen. *c* **1290** *S. Eng. Leg.* I. 352/243 þo þis bodi ne moste beo ifounde in Engelonde. *c* **1384** Chaucer *H. Fame* III. 1004 They wer a-cheked bothe two And neyther of hem most out goo. ?*a* **1400** *Arthur* 570 Mordred fly toward Londoun, He most not come in þe toun. *c* **1400** *Laud Troy Bk.* 17535 He.. bad hem mak Be-twene hem of Grece—iff thei moste—A fynal pes, what-so it coste.

b. Past subj., in petitions, final clauses, wishes, and the like = might, should, might be permitted to.

Occas. with omission of inf. of vb. of motion (cf. 8 a).

c **893** K. Ælfred *Oros.* v. ix. 232 And eft wæron biddende þæt Metellus to Rome moste. *a* **900** Cynewulf *Crist* 1388 þæt ðu mostes wealdan worulde ȝesceaftum. *c* **1205** Lay. 19880 He bad þe to fultume þene milde godes sune, þat þu mostes wel don. *c* **1250** *Gen. & Ex.* 2624 Iakobeð wente bliðe agen, ðat ȝhe ðe cildes [*MS.* gildes] fostre muste ben. *c* **1305** *St. Andrew* 75 in *E.E.P.* (1862) 100 Hail beo þu, swete Rode, he seide: swettest of alle treo þat þu wiþ mie louerdes lymes ihalewed mostest beo. *c* **1350** *Will. Palerne* 3978 þe king bisouȝt þe quene,.. þat he most se his sone. **1362** Langl. *P. Pl.* A. VIII. 23 And for þei sworen bi heore soule—'so God hem moste helpe!'—Aȝeyn heore clene Concience, heore catel to sulle. *c* **1386** Chaucer *Clerk's T.* 494 Mekely she to the sergeant preyde.. That she moste kisse hire child er þat it deyde. *c* **1400** *Brut* cxii. 114 If ȝe wolde consent and grant þat y most her haue.

2. In the sense of MOTE *v.* 2, expressing necessity or obligation. **a.** Past ind. = had to, was obliged to, it was necessary that (I) should.

Occas. with omission of inf. of vb. of motion (cf. 8 a).

Beowulf 1939 þæt hit sceadenmæl scyran moste, cwealmbealu cyðan. *a* **1000** *Fallen Angels* 108 Ær ic moste in ðeossum atolan æðele ȝebidan. *c* **1205** Lay. 9904 þider him come sonde ut of þissen londe þæt.. he mosten [*sic*] cume sone to his kine-dome. *a* **1225** *Leg. Kath.* 1564 Bicom to þet te king, Maxence, moste fearen. *a* **1300** *Cursor M.* 2249 Wit cord and plum þai wroght sa hei, þe hette o þe sun moght þai noght drei, þar-for most þai þam hide Bath wit hors and camel hide. *a* **1300** *Vox & Wolf* 85 in Hazl. *E.P.P.* I. 60 A-doun he moste, he wes therinne. *c* **1350** *Will. Palerne* 1052 þanne seiȝ þei no socour but sunder þanne þei moste. *c* **1384** Chaucer *H. Fame* I. 187 And seyde he most vnto Itayle. **1390** Gower *Conf.* I. 119 The day was wonder hot withalle, And such a thurst was on him falle, That he moste owther deie or drinke. **1450** in *Four C. Eng. Lett.* (1880) 4 And they seyd he most speke with here master. **1471** Caxton *Recuyell* (Sommer) I. 33 How dardanus slew his broder iasius by trayson wherfore he moste departe out of the contre.

b. Past subj. = should or would be obliged to .., would of necessity...

c **1386** Chaucer *Sqr.'s T.* 30, I moste been a Rethor excellent That koude hise colours longynge for that Art If he sholde hire discryuen euery part. *Ibid.* 434 For wel she wiste The ffaukon moste fallen fro the twiste, Whan þat it swowned next for lakke of blood.

II. Used as a pres. tense, and hence (under certain conditions) as a past tense corresponding to this.

The use as a present arose from the practice of employing the past subj. as a moderate, cautious, or polite substitute for the present indicative. The modern use as a past tense coincides with sense 2, but app. does not historically descend from it, exc. that the preterital use in *must needs* (see NEED, NEEDS *advs.*) may perhaps represent a continuous survival.

3. a. Equivalent to the older MOTE *v.* 2, expressing necessity: Am (is, are) obliged or required to; have (has) to; it is necessary that (I, you, he, it, etc.) should. In the second person, *must* now chiefly expresses a command or an insistent request or counsel; in the third person it tends to be restricted to the expression of a necessity which is either imposed by the will of the speaker, or relative to some specified end, or enunciated as a general proposition.

a **1300** *Cursor M.* 5018 Yee most [*Gött.* must] yow hast on your fare. *a* **1300** *K. Horn* (Laud MS.) 1254 Reymyld, qwad horn, ich moste wende To þe wodes hende. *c* **1386** Chaucer *Wife's Prol.* 440 Oon of vs two moste bowen doutelees And sith a man is moore resonable Than wooman is, ye moste ben suffrable. **1426** Lydg. *De Guil. Pilgr.* 2955 Consydre how thow art ysett Vnder a-nother, and soget To hym, and mvstest hym obeye. **1548–9** (Mar.) *Bk. Com. Prayer, Athan. Creed*, He therefore that will bee saued: must thus thinke of the trinitie. **1579** Gosson *Sch. Abuse* (Arb.) 56 The Thracians when they must pass ouer frosen streames, sende out theyr Wolues. **1606** Shaks. *Tr. & Cr.* III. ii. 45 What are you gone againe, you must be watcht ere you be made tame, must you? **1738** Swift *Pol. Conversat.* Wks. VI. 253 Tom, you must go with us to Lady Smart's to Breakfast. **1768** Bickerstaff *Padlock* I. ii. (1824) 4 *Diego* (Unseen, puts on a large padlock) That must do till I get a larger. **1776** *Trial of Nundocomar* 16/1 The books must be produced, as we cannot receive parole evidence of their contents. **1799** E. Du Bois *Piece Family Biog.* III. 203 Well, since it seems that it must be so, I do acquiesce in it. **1810** Syd. Smith *Wks.* (1850) 188/1 It must be remembered, that [etc.]. **1891** *Law Times* XC. 441/2 The judges criticise Parliament, and they in their turn must accept criticism upon their order.

b. Used to express a fixed or certain futurity. *I must* = I am fated or certain to..., I shall certainly or inevitably...

a **1400–50** *Alexander* 707 Thik & thraly am I thrett & thole must I sone þe slauughter of my awne sonn. **1526** Tindale *John* iii. 30 He must increace: and I muste decreace. **1592** Shaks. *Rom. & Jul.* IV. i. 48, I heare thou must, and nothing may prorogue it, On Thursday next be married to this Countie. **1697** Dryden *Virg. Georg.* IV. 372 Crowds of dead, that never must return To their lov'd Hives. **1771** Smollett *Humph. Cl.* 28 Apr. i, My wooll will suffer for want of grace, and I must be a loser on all sides. **1892** Ld. Esher in *Law Times Rep.* LXVII. 211/1 The sewage matter .. goes along a sewer which must carry it into the stream, unless it is intercepted on the way.

c. In expressions like ***I must say*** = I cannot help saying. Also in explanatory clauses, as ***you must know*** or ***understand*** = you ought to be informed, I would have you know. ***if you must know***: used to introduce information provided against the judgement or inclination of the speaker.

1563–83 Foxe *A. & M.* 988/1 You must vnderstand, through the Citie of Rome, runneth a famous Riuer, called Tiber. **1581** Pettie tr. *Guazzo's Civ. Conv.* II. (1586) 111, I must saye, that your taste differeth much from mine. **1599** Q. Eliz. *Let.* in Moryson *Itin.* (1617) II. 40 We must therefore let you know, that as it cannot be ignorance, so it cannot be want of meanes. **1711** Addison *Spect.* No. 40, ¶1, I must allow, that there are very noble Tragedies, which have been framed upon the other Plan. **1713** —— *Guard.* No. 97 ¶1 Now you must know, sir, my face is as white as chalk. **1721** Amherst *Terræ Fil.* No. 34 (1754) 181 He.. gave me a glass of each to taste; which, I must say, was excellent ale indeed. [**1818** Scott *Heart Midl.* xxix, in *Tales of My Landlord* 2nd ser. III. iv. 104 He's in Gaffer Gabblewood's wheat-close, an ye maun ken.] **1861** Hughes *Tom Brown at Oxf.* II. x. 193 Well, if you must know, I never saw her before yesterday. **1871** M. Arnold *Friendship's Garland* 169 The *Morning Star*, I must say, does its duty nobly. **1875** Jowett *Plato* (ed. 2) II. 49, I must beg to be absolved from the promise. **1885** *Boy's Own Paper* 28 Mar. 403/2 Well, if you must know, it's our boat. **1902** H. James *Wings of Dove* xxxiii. 511 Well, if you must know—and I want you to be clear about it—I didn't even seriously think of a denial to her face. **1927** C. Asquith *Black Cap* 250 'If you must know,' she had said, 'well, you've got dirty nails, haven't you? Look.' **1951** J. D. Salinger *Catcher in Rye* xix. 173 Girl lives in the Village. Sculptress. If you must know. **1972** 'G. Harding' *Skytrap* ii. 39 If you must know, I wanted to be kissed gently.

d. As a past tense: Was obliged, had to; it was necessary that (I, he, it, etc.) should.

In modern use confined to instances of oblique narration, and of the virtual oblique narration in which the speaker has in his mind what might have been said or thought at the time. To say 'I must go to London yesterday' would now be a ludicrous blunder.

1691 Shadwell *Scowrers* I. i. 3 In those days a man could not go from the Rose Tavern to the Piazza once, but he must venture his life twice. **1720** Welton *Suffer. Son of God* I. viii 204 Thou wast but just come into the World, when, presently, Thou must Away, and take thy Flight into Egypt. **1781** C. Johnston *Hist. J. Juniper* II. 13 He said he must e'en be content to stay where he was. **1785** Cowper *Let. to Newton* 27 Aug., I foresaw plainly this inconvenience: that, in writing to him on such an occasion, I must almost unavoidably make self and self's book the subject. **1802** Wordsw. *Sonn., 'Once did She hold'* 8 She was a Maiden City, bright and free;.. And, when She took unto herself a Mate, She must espouse the everlasting Sea. **1840** Carlyle *Heroes* v. (1841) 260 If you wanted to know what Abelard knew, you must go and listen to Abelard. **1845** E. FitzGerald *Lett.* (1889) I. 154 Poussin must spend his life in Italy before he could paint as he did. **1849** Macaulay *Hist. Eng.* i. I. 50 It was necessary to make a choice. The government must either submit to Rome, or must obtain the aid of the Protestants. *Ibid.* v. 619 Yet a few hours of gloomy seclusion, and he must die a violent and shameful death. **1894** J. T. Fowler *Adamnan* Introd. 74 He could not bear to be idle.. he must always be doing something.

e. As a past or historical present tense, *must* is sometimes used satirically or indignantly with reference to some foolish or annoying action or some untoward event. Now *colloq.*

1390 Gower *Conf.* II. 145 Whan that the lord comth hom ayein, The janglere moste somwhat sein. **1605** Shaks. *Macb.* IV. iii. 212 And I must be from thence? My wife kil'd too? *Mod. Colloq.* The fool must needs go and quarrel with his only friend. Just when I was busiest, that bore C. must come in and waste three hours. As soon as I had recovered from my illness, what must I do but break my leg?

4. In the first person, *must* often expresses an insistent demand or a firm resolve on the part of the speaker. Hence also in the second and third persons, rendering sentiments imputed to others.

a **1425** *Cursor M.* 6569 (Trin.) Who made þis calf I most [*other texts* I wald] him ken. **1509** Barclay *Shyp of Folys* (1874) II. 98 Nowe Carles are nat content with one grange Nore one ferme place, such is theyr insolence They must haue many. **1530** Palsgr. 642/2, I muste be prayed.. to do a thynge, *je me veulx prier*. **1673** Dryden *Marr. à-la-Mode* IV. iii. 60, I must, and will go. **1798** Joanna Baillie *Tryal* v. i. Softly, Mariane; let us leave this room, if you must laugh, for he will overhear you. **1827** Wordsw. *Lit. Crit.* (1905) 258 He is not content with a ring and a bracelet, but he must have rings in the ears, rings on the nose—rings everywhere.

5. As *must* has no pa. pple., the need of a past conditional has been supplied by placing the principal verb in the perfect infinitive. Thus ***I must have seen it*** = I should (in the case supposed) necessarily have seen it; ***I must have done it*** = I should have had to do it, or have been obliged to do it.

c **1460** *Towneley Myst.* xxx. 180 Bot, sir, I tell you before, had domysday oght tarid, We must haue biggid hell more, the warld is so warid. **1526** Tindale *Heb.* xii. 20 Yf a beast had touched the mountayne, hit must have bene stoned. **1621** Donne *Serm.* xv. (1640) I. 149 A Sheriffe that should burne him, who were condemned to be hanged, were a murderer, though that man must have dyed. **1695** Dryden *Parallel Poetry & Painting* Ess. (ed. Ker) II. 146 Whereas if I had chosen a noon-day light for them, somewhat must have been discovered which would rather have moved our hatred than our pity. **1714** Swift *Pres. St. Affairs* Wks. 1755 II. I. 212 Had this point been steadily pursued.. there must probably have been an end of faction. **1815** Jane Austen *Emma* vii, Indeed, Harriet, it would have been a severe pang to lose you; but it must have been. You would have thrown yourself out of all good society. I must have given you up. **1896** *Law Times Rep.* LXXIII. 616/1 If he had looked he must have seen the light of the approaching train. **1896** F. S. Boas *Shaks. & Predec.* 384 *note*, Had it [*Hamlet*] been in existence.. before 1598, it must have been mentioned by Meres.

6. a. Expressing the inferred or presumed certainty of a fact; either (with present inf.) relating to the present time, as in ***you must be aware of this*** = I cannot doubt that you are aware of this; or (with perfect inf.) relating to the past, as in ***he must have done it*** = it is to be concluded that he did it.

Sometimes expressing an inference which will be rendered necessary if some particular assumption is made, as in *if he says so, it must be true; if he really did it, he must have been mad.*

1652 Evelyn *Ess. 1st Bk. Lucretius* (1656) 164 The continent must be incorporeal, the contained corporeal. **1673** Dryden *Marr.-à-la-Mode* I. i. 8 Your friend? then he must needs be of much merit. **1762** Goldsm. *Cit. W.* lxxi, This must have been a sad shock to the poor disconsolate parent. **1768** Sterne *Sent. Journ.* (1775) I. 61 (*Pulse*), I am sure you must have one of the best pulses of any woman in the world. **1768** Goldsm. *Good-n. Man* III. (*ad fin.*), But, come, the letter I wait for must be almost finished. **1800** Wordsw. *Hart-leap Well* 141 What thoughts must through the creature's brain have past! **1809** Malkin *Gil Blas* IV. x. ¶8 Such a house must belong to some family above the common. **1833** Coleridge *Table-t.* 4 Jan., Yet the shipping interest, who must know where the shoe pinches, complain to this day. **1879** G. Meredith *Egoist* xxxvi, How you must enjoy a spell of dulness! **1887** Hall Caine *Coleridge* 123 Coleridge must have earned a substantial sum by these lectures. **1891** E. Peacock *N. Brendon* I. 54 He must be an old man. **1903** Morley *Gladstone* I. Pref. Note, Between two and three hundred thousand written papers of one sort or another must have passed under my view.

b. In oblique past tense.

1726 Swift *Gulliver* IV. iii, He replied, That I must needs be mistaken. *Ibid.*, After which he said, it was plain I must be a perfect Yahoo. **1834** *Tait's Mag.* I. 13/1 All was shut up in darkness, and must have been so for some hours.

†**c.** Formerly ***must be*** was occas. used for ***must have been*** = presumably was. *Obs.*

1733 Tull *Horse-hoeing Husb.* xv. 203 Whilst the Roman Empire was in its Glory.. its Price must be then very high.

7. In ***must not*** (whether present or pa. t.) the negative, though formally belonging to the auxiliary, has the same effect as if it belonged to the following infinitive. ***I must not*** = I am not allowed to, I am obliged not to, etc. (sometimes, I will not permit myself to).

The coincidence with the negative use of sense 1 and of MOTE *v.* 1 is merely accidental.

1583 Fulke *Defense* xxii. 512 We must not.. drawe places of Scripture vnto Christ, which by the holy Ghost had an other meaning. **1594** Shaks. *Rich. III*, III. i. 106 *York.* And therefore is he idle? *Glo.* O my faire Cousin, I must not say so. **1601** —— *All's Well* II. v. 64 You must not meruaile Helen at my course. **1606** —— *Ant. & Cl.* I. iv. 10, I must not thinke There are, euils enow to darken all his goodnesse. **1607** —— *Cor.* I. i. 43 You must in no way say he is couetous. **1741** Richardson *Pamela* II. 362, I will love you dearly; but I mustn't love my Uncle. Why so? said he. **1760–72** H. Brooke *Fool of Qual.* (1809) III. 102 You must not enter any door of the lower story.. for there our domestics inhabit. **1832** Tennyson *Death of Old Year* 6 Old year, you must not die;.. Old year, you shall not die. **1882** 'Leslie Keith' *Alasnam's Lady* III. 279, 'I suppose I mustn't touch the precious papers?' she was saying. **1902** 'Mrs. Alexander' *Stronger than Love* v, I must not sit here talking.

8. Elliptical uses. **a.** With ellipsis of a verb of motion. Now *arch.*

c **1386** Chaucer *Man of Law's T.* 184 Allas vn to the Barbre nacion I moste goon. **1393** Langl. *P. Pl.* C. XVIII. 225 A medecine moste þer-to, þat myghte amende þe prelates. *c* **1425** *Cast. Persev.* 3038 in *Macro Plays* 167 For, wrechyd sowle, þou muste to helle. **1611** Shaks. *Cymb.* III. v. 2 My Emperor hath wrote, I must from hence. **1638** Junius *Paint. Ancients* 60 With Poëts.. out it must whatsoever they have conceived. **1720** [see 3 d]. **1731** Swift *To Gay*, His work is done, the minister must out. **1884**

TENNYSON *Becket* III. ii, Seeing he must to Westminster and crown Young Henry there to-morrow. **1889** *Macm. Mag* May 77 This shamefacedness will be thought mere folly of course in these days when everything must to the papers.

b. With ellipsis of infinitive to be supplied from the context.

Freq. in impers. phrases with *needs*: see NEEDS *adv.* d.

1297 R. GLOUC. (Rolls) 1223 þo was al þe court anuyd, as he moste nede. *c* **1400** *Destr. Troy* 1691 Then meuyt to his mynde, as yt most nede, þat [etc.]. **1591** SHAKS. *Two Gent.* II. ii. 2 *Pro.* Haue patience, gentle Iulia. *Iul.* I must where is no remedy. **1604** [see NEEDS *adv.* d]. **1607** SHAKS. *Cor.* III. ii. 97 *Com.* I thinke 'twill serue. if he can thereto frame his spirit. *Volum.* He must, and will. **1692** R. L'ESTRANGE *Fables* cclxxii. 238 'Tis Good.. to run no more Risque of the Main Chance, then of Necessity Must. **1712** SWIFT *Jrnl. to Stella* 21 Dec., I dined with Lord Treasurer, and must again to-morrow. **1734**, **1821**, **1871** [see NEEDS *adv.* d]. **1838** J. P. KENNEDY *Rob of the Bowl* ix. (1866) 77 Indeed, I must not and cannot, playmates. **1863** EMERSON *Voluntaries* iii. 15 When Duty whispers low, *Thou must*, The youth replies, *I can.* **1876** TENNYSON *Harold* v. i, I have not spoken to the king One word; and one I must. Farewell! **1882** *Wheel World* May 12 There's no compulsion; only you must. **1886** [see DRIVE *v.* B. 1 b].

9. *dial.* In questions = may, shall. Also *if I must* = if I may. Cf. MOTE *v.* 1.

a **1796** PEGGE *Derbicisms* (E.D.S.) 46 (s.v. *Mun*), Also, *must* for may, as, 'I will go if I must'. **1889** *N.W. Linc. Gloss.* s.v., Must I goä oot wi' Jaane, muther; we'll be back e' time to get teä ready. **1896** *Hetton-le-Hole Gloss.* s.v., 'Would you like your milk to drink, Mr. P.?' 'Yes, please'. 'Must I bring you't, then?'

†**III. 10.** *impers.* (with personal object.) It behoves (or behoved), it is (or was) necessary for (a person) to. [Cf. Fr. *il me faut*; also ME. *me oughte*, OUGHT *v.*]

a **1300** *Cursor M.* 10671 In his seruis me most ai lend Bituixand to mi liues end. *c* **1350** *Ipomadon* 8275 (Kölbing) My lyff now muste me tyne. *Ibid.* 8409 Ipomadon saw, that nedys hym moste. *c* **1386** CHAUCER *Can. Yeom. Prol. & T.* 393 Vs moste putte oure good in auenture. *c* **1400** MAUNDEV. (Roxb.) xxiv. 112 He.. feled wele.. þat him most nedez dye þeroff. *c* **1440** *Jacob's Well* 211 ȝif þou fynde a thyng þat is noȝt þin, þe muste restore it. **1471** CAXTON *Recuyell* (Sommer) I. 27 For of force me muste obeye the kyng.

must, *v.*[2] *Obs.* exc. *dial.* [? Back-formation from MUSTY.]

1. *intr.* 'To grow mouldy' (J.) or 'musty'; to contract a musty or sour smell.

1530 PALSGR. 642/2, I muste as breed dothe, *je moysys. Ibid.*, I muste or foyste, as a vessel dothe, *je moysis.* **1577** HARRISON *England* II. xviii. (1877) I. 299 Till it [the corn] must and putrifie. **1648** GAGE *West Ind.* xviii. 135 The Wheat will not keep long without musting and breeding a worm called Gurgojo. **1707** MORTIMER *Husb.* 103 In wet Weather it [*sc.* barley] will be inclined to sprout or must. **1769** MRS. RAFFALD *Eng. Housekpr.* (1778) 103 Dry it often with a cloth to keep it from musting. **1888** *Berksh. Gloss.*, Them pots o' jam be beginnin' to must.

2. *trans.* 'To mould; to make mouldy' (J.) *rare.*

1707 MORTIMER *Husb.* 111 Some Granaries.. are subject, against wet Weather, to give and be moist, which is very bad for Corn, and will must it. **1892** *Harper's Mag.* June 98/2 Barley.. has no dews or rains to bleach or 'must' it when it is ripening.

†**must**, *v.*[3] *Sc. Obs.* Also 8–9 muist, 9 moust. [f. MUST *sb.*[2]] *trans.* To powder with 'must' or hair-powder.

1751 H. BLYDE *Contract* 4 Sae I.. muisted my head, and made ready a clean. **1808** J. MAYNE *Siller Gun* III. xxiii. [IV. xix], Tho' muisted is your carrot pash. **1816** SCOTT *Antiq.* x, Would ye creesh his bonny brown hair wi' your nasty ulyie, and then moust it like the auld minister's wig?

must (mʌst), *v.*[4] *Anglo-Indian.* [f. MUST *a.*[3]] *intr.* To 'go must'.

1893 KIPLING *Many Invent.*, *My Lord Elephant* 43 'As when one o' they native king's elephants *musted* last June.'

musta, must'a' ('mʌstə), a representation of the colloq. or vulgar pronunciation of *must have* (MUST *v.*[1] 5).

1903 P. L. DUNBAR *In Old Plantation Days* 266 It must 'a' been P'ovidence that directed bofe yo' min's in de same channel. **1927** M. OSTENSO *Mad Carews* (1929) v. 93 You're late... Must'a' stayed at the Phillips' till it was dark. **1938** M. RICHARDSON in B. A. Botkin *Treas. S. Folklore* (1949) III. i. 443 One of the other guards musta told him to bring it in. **1965** J. WAINWRIGHT *Death in Sleeping City* II. 104 They killed—Tommo. They musta—killed Tommo. **1973** *Black World* Jan. 62/2 They laid me out real good... Musta used up most of the insurance money.

mustac: see MOUSTAC.

mustaccio, mustacheo, obs. ff. MUSTACHIO.

mustache: see MOUSTACHE.

mustachio (mʊ'stɑːʃəʊ, -æ-, məs-). Pl. **mustachios** (-ʃəʊz). Forms: α. (*from It. and Sp.*) 6 (mostacchi *It. pl.*), mustachyo(e, (*quasi-Lat.* mostachium), 6–7 mustaccio, mostacho, 6–9 mustachoe, 7 mustatioe, mustacheo, mostachoe, 7–8 mustacho, 7, 9 moustachio, 8 mustacio, 8–9 mustachioe, 6– mustachio; β. (*corrupt forms*) 6 moucheacheo, muschachoe, muchache, 6–7 mouchache, 7 mochachoe; 6 mowchatowe, mutchatoe, mutchado, 6–7 muschatoe, 7 m(o)uchato(e, mushato(e, mochatoe, muchate, mus(t)chadoe, mochedoe, monchato(e, munchattoe; mouthchato; 8 mouthacho. [Adopted in 16th c., partly from Sp. *mostacho*, and partly from its source, It. *mostaccio* moustache, also face, snout, *mostacchio* moustache (cf. Albanian *mustakes*, Rumanian *mustate* moustache), a derivative of Gr. *μυστακ-*, *μύσταξ* masc. (also *βύσταξ*) moustache, a Doric word, commonly believed (notwithstanding the difference both in meaning and in gender) to be a dialectal variant of *μάσταξ* fem., mouth, jaws.

In the 16–17th c. the word appears in a multitude of corrupt forms due to imperfect apprehension or recollection of the sound. Some of them suggest a pseudo-etymological association with Sp. *muchacho* boy.

In the sing. the word is almost or entirely obsolete, being superseded by MOUSTACHE; but the plural *mustachios* has considerable currency, sometimes occurring in books that have *moustache* in the singular. With regard to the pronunciation of the first syllable cf. MOUSTACHE.]

1. The hair on the upper lip: = MOUSTACHE 1 a.

α. **1551** W. THOMAS tr. *Barbaro's Trav. Persia* (1873) 35 They suffer their mostacchi to growe a quarter of a yarde longer than their beardes. [*marg.*] Mostacchi is the berde of the vpper lyppe. **1588** SHAKS. *L.L.L.* v. i. 110 It will please his Grace.. sometime to.. dallie with my excrement, with my mustachio. **1598** FLORIO, *Mostaccio, Mostazzo*, a face, a snout, a mostacho. **1603** DEKKER *Wonderfull Yeare* B 2, The Souldier.. had brisseld vp the quills of his stiffe Porcupine mustachio. **1612** SHELTON *Quix.* II. x. (1620) 63 Her beautie .. was infinitely increased by a Moale she had vpon her lippe, like a Mostacho, with seuen or eight red haires like threeds of gold, and aboue a handfull long. **1621** J. TAYLOR (Water-P.) *Superb. Flagellum* C 8, Some their mustatioes of such length doe keepe, That very well they may a maunger sweepe. **1650** R. STAPYLTON *Strada's Low C. Warres* v. 110 They [the covenanters] began to cut their beards, leaving onely great mustachios, turned up like Turks. **1712** BUDGELL *Spect.* No. 331 ¶11 A distinct Treatise, which I keep by me in Manuscript, upon the Mustachoe. **1728** MORGAN *Algiers* II. iv. 271 Twirling his starched Mustachio. **1796** MORSE *Amer. Geog.* II. 392 The court of Madrid has of late been at great pains to clear their upper lip of mustachoes. **1811** WELLINGTON in Gurw. *Desp.* (1837) VII. 319 Almost all the artillerymen wore mustachios, which I think is contrary to your orders. **1852** LONGF. *Emperor's Bird's Nest* v, As he twirled his gray mustachio.

β. **1565** WILLES in *Hakluyt's Voy.* (1599) II. II. 85 Sauage men.. with huge beards and monstrous muchaches. **1583** STUBBES *Anat. Abus.* II. (1882) 50 It is a world to consider, how their mowchatowes must be preserued and laid out, from one cheke to another, yea, almost from one eare to another. **1592** *Arden of Feversham* II. i. 54 His chinne was bare, but on his vpper lippe A mutchado, which he wound about his eare. **1596** SPENSER *State Irel.* Wks. (Globe) 635/1 To cutt of all theyr beardes close, save only theyr muschachoes which they weare long. **1615** BRATHWAIT *Strappado*, The Epistle Dedicatorie. To all.. Ladies, Monkies.. and Catomitoes,.. false-haires, periwigges, mouchatoes:.. and Shee-painters. Send I greeting [etc.]. **1631** R. H. *Arraignm. Whole Creature* xv. §3. 263 Entertaining of Taylers, Barbers, Perfumers, to teach them how to cut their beards: weare their Love-locks: turne vp their Mushatoes [etc.].

b. The hair on one side of the upper lip: = MOUSTACHE 1 b.

α. **1579** G. HARVEY *Letter-bk.* (Camden) 61 The clippings of your thris-honorable mustachyoes. **1592** LYLY *Midas* III. ii, Wil you haue.. your mustachoes sharp? **1598** R. HAYDOCKE tr. *Lomazzo* I. 30 Those long haires.. vpon the vpper lip, the mostachiums. **1638** BAKER tr. *Balzac's Lett.* (vol. III.) 108 The Cavalier.. consists wholly of a Pickdevant, and two Mustachoes. **1668** R. L'ESTRANGE *Vis. Quev.* (1708) 88 He was a little severe upon his Guides, for disordering his Mustachoes. **1719** DE FOE *Crusoe* I. 177 Of these Mustachioes or Whiskers, I will not say they were long enough to hang my Hat upon them; but [etc.]. **1787** *Gentl. Mag.* Nov. 952/1 The face [on a coin] is without a beard, but hath mustacios on the upper lip. **1825–9** MRS. SHERWOOD *Lady of Manor* IV. xxiii. 15 A pair of large mustachoes. **1884** W. S. GILBERT *Princess Ida*, He grew moustachios.

β. **1579** J. JONES *Preserv. Bodie & Soule* I. xviii. 32 The space betweene the Nose ende and the vpper lippe, whence the heare groweth,.. and is termed after the Spanishe phrase Moucheacheos. **1592** GREENE *Upst. Courtier* D 4, The barber.. asketh.. if it be his pleasure to haue.. his mustachios [1620, D 2 b mouchaches] fostered to turne about his eares like the branches of a vine. **1615** BRATHWAIT *Strappado* (1878) 108 His peak't munchattoes. **1620** J. PYPER tr. *Hist. Astrea* I. II. 19 The haire, the eye-browes, the mouthchatos, the beard. **1648–58** HEXHAM, *De Knevelbaerdt*, the Muschadoes on the upper-lipp. **1650** TRAPP *Comm. Lev.* xiii. 45 *A covering upon his upper lip.* His mouchaches, that by his breath hee might not infect others. ? **1651** in H. Cary *Mem. Gt. Civil War* (1842) II. 446 The king being told who it was, replied merrily, 'I did not like his starched mouchates'. **1688** R. HOLME *Armoury* II. 391/1 The British Beard hath long Mochedoes on the higher lip hanging down either side the chin, all the rest of the face being bare. **1706** E. WARD *Wooden World Diss.* (1708) 104 If you find him with Mouthacho's, he is certainly a Size above ordinary in his own Conceit.

†**c.** Plural form with sing. construction. *Obs.*

c **1592** MARLOWE *Jew of Malta* IV. (1633) H j, A fellow Met me with a muschatoes like a Rauens wing. **1612** N. FIELD *Woman is a Weathercock* v. i, *Abra...* And a huge Mustachios? *Neu.* A verie Turkes.

d. = MOUSTACHE 1 c.

1612 SHELTON *Quix.* I. III. vi. (1652) 39 b, Torralua the Sheepheardesse.. was a round wench,.. and drew somewhat neere to a man, for shee had Mochachoes.

e. A false moustache. Also with *a* and *pl.*

1622 tr. *Luna's Pursuit Lazarillo* 30 Foure of them.. came and tooke me vp, and.. put me on a Beard, not forgetting the great Mustachios, and a Perewig made of Mosse, that made me shew like a wild man in a Garden. **1716** ADDISON *Freeholder* No. 7 ¶2 They.. clapt him on a huge pair of Mustachoes to frighten his people with. **1902** SNAITH *Wayfarers* xvii, Attaching.. a pair of moustachios to his upper lip.

†**2.** *pl.* The hair on the lip of an animal; †the 'whiskers' of a cat. Also, the awn or bristles of certain grasses; = BEARD *sb.* 6. *Obs.*

1591 SYLVESTER *Du Bartas* I. iii. 811 Here for our food, Millions of flow'ry grains, With long Mustachoes, wave upon the Plains. **1634** S. R. *Noble Soldier* II. i. in Bullen *O. Pl.* I. 276 My Barbour.. poak'd out My Tuskes more stiffe than are a cats muschatoes. **1635** BRATHWAIT *Arcad. Pr.* 219 An ambitious fire-flye.. fals down, and cingeth his braving mouchate's for his labour. **1651** H. MORE *Second Lash* in *Enthus. Tri.*, etc. (1656) 214 Have you made sport with the mustacho's of it in the figure of a mouse? **1665** HOOKE *Microgr.* 157 The Mustacheos of a Cat. **1693** SIR T. P. BLOUNT *Nat. Hist.* 9 The Civet-Cat.. hath.. Mustachios like a Cat. **1790** BRUCE *Trav. Source Nile* V. 138 He [the Fennec] had strong thick mustachoes.

3. *attrib.* and *Comb.*, as ***mustachio-twiddler***; †**mustachio beard**, a moustache.

1566 DRANT *Horace, Sat.* I. ii. B ij, Fashions, in nottynge of the heare,.. and mustacho beardes. **1848** THACKERAY *Van. Fair* xiv, Said the moustachio-twiddler.

mustachioed (mʊ'stɑːʃəʊd, -æ-, məs-), *a.* [f. MUSTACHIO + -ED[2].] = MOUSTACHED.

1827 LYTTON *Pelham* xi, A most superbly mustachioed German. **1835** WILLIS *Pencillings* II. xlv. 51 A hundred indolent-looking,.. mustachoed, and withal very handsome men. **1852** SMEDLEY *L. Arundel* xxxviii, Singing duets.. with a palefaced moustachioed puppy. *a* **1864** HAWTHORNE *Amer. Note-bks.* (1879) I. 84 A dark mustachioed face.

mustachis, -us, obs. pl. forms of MOUSTACHE.

mustach(y)o(e, -acio: see MUSTACHIO.

‖**mustafina** (mʌstə'fiːnə). Also musteefino, -phina. [App. a derivative of MUSTEE; the last part, if not arbitrary, may perh. represent Sp. *fino* FINE *a.*] The offspring of a mustee and a white.

a **1818** M. G. LEWIS *Jrnl. W. Ind.* (1834) 106 The child of a mustee by a white man is called a musteefino. **1825** *Gentl. Mag.* XCV. I. 6 The fifth descent, viz. from a white and musteephina, is white by law, and of free birth. **1833** MARRYAT *P. Simple* xxxi, I believe.. the mustee and white [make] the mustafina, or one sixteenth black. **1872** SCHELE DE VERE *Americanisms* 115.

mustage, obs. form of MOUSTACHE.

‖**mustaiba** (mʌstə'iːbə). Also **mostahiba, mosatahiba.** [Brazilian Pg. *mostahiba* (a Tupi word).] A close-grained Brazilian wood.

1843 HOLTZAPFFEL *Turning*, etc. I. 94 Mustaiba, from the Brazils and Rio Janeiro... is used at Sheffield for the handles of glaziers' and other knives [etc.].., it is known in England as Mosatahiba. **1858** SIMMONDS *Dict. Trade.* **1866** *Treas. Bot.*, *Mostahiba*, a hard Brazilian wood.

mustang ('mʌstæŋ). Also **mestang.** [App. a confusion of two synonymous Sp. words, *mestengo* (now *mesteño*) and *mostrenco*.

Minsheu *Sp. Dict.* (1599) gives '*Mestengo* or *Mostrenco*, a strayer'. The *Novísimo Diccionario* (1888) has both words as adjs., with the explanation 'Wild, having no master: said of horses and cattle'. *Mesteño* appears to be a derivative of *mesta*, an association of graziers; one of the functions of these associations being the appropriation of the wild cattle that have attached themselves to the herds (*Novís. Dicc.*). The derivation of *mostrenco* is obscure.]

1. a. The wild or half-wild horse of the American plains, esp. of Mexico and California; descended from the stock introduced by the Spanish conquerors. Also *attrib.* as ***mustang horse, mare, pony.***

1808 PIKE *Sources Mississ.* III. 273 Passed several herds of mustangs or wild horses. **1821** S. AUSTIN *Jrnl.* 5 Sept. in *Texas State Hist. Assoc. Q.* (1904) VII. 300 Mustang horses very plenty saw at least.. 150. **1834** A. PIKE *Prose Sk. & Poems* 74 Lewis & Irwin obtained young and unbroken wild horses, (or, as the hunters call them, mestangs). **1837** W. IRVING *Capt. Bonneville* II. xix. 28 She was mounted on a mestang or half wild horse. **1884** *Encycl. Brit.* XVII. 14/2 The Mexican mule, bred by a male ass of a mustang mare, is also a very hardy, strong, and useful animal. **1888** B. HARTE *Cressy* ii. (1889) I. 66 Hank and Jim ain't been off their mustangs since sun up. **1890** GUNTER *Miss Nobody* v, Sure-footed as these mustang ponies generally are. **1941** *Sun* (Baltimore) 30 July 7/6 A Spanish vessel loaded with Mustang horses was shipwrecked years ago.

b. *transf.* Applied to an Australian wild or unbroken horse.

1890 'R. BOLDREWOOD' *Col. Reformer* (1891) 315 Their time was spent in running in these swift and half-wild mustangs. *Ibid.* 318 His stud of Australian Arabs.. would be sold for the price of bush mustangs.

2. In full ***Mustang grape***: A small red grape, *Vitis candicans*, of Texas.

1846 J. GREGG *Diary* 27 Sept. (1941) I. v. 239 There is a large species, called by the Americans, the *Mustang grape* which very much resembles the Muscadine of the western country, except in growing in large bunches or racemes. **1854** LONGF. *Catawba Wine* iii, The red Mustang, Whose clusters hang O'er the waves of the Colorado. **1903** A. ADAMS *Log of Cow-boy* 6 Along the river grew endless quantities of Mustang grapes. **1951** *Dict. Gardening* (R. Hort. Soc.) IV. 2250/2 *V[itis] candicans.* Mustang Grape. Vigorous high climber.

3. *slang.* An officer in the U.S. services who has been promoted from the ranks; in quots. 1847: a volunteer officer as distinct from a regular-army officer.

1847 G. B. McClellan *Mexican War Diary* 2 Jan. (1917) 23 'Mind, Mr. Smith,' said the old Mustang [*sc.* General Patterson] the night before, 'mind and appear as early as possible, so that you may not delay us'—all this with that air of dignity and importance so peculiarly characteristic of Mustangs. *Ibid.* 4 Jan. 43, I have repeatedly seen a Second Lieutenant of the regular army exercise more authority over the Volunteers..than a Mustang General. [**1874** L. P. A. d'Orléans *Hist. Guerre Civile en Amérique* I. 35 Le surnom dérisoire de *mustang*..qu'il appliquait aux volontaires inexpérimentés avant l'épreuve commune.] **1931** *Leatherneck* Feb. 13 We have three..mustangs, two of whom are..completing their probationary periods. **1939** J. B. Connolly *Navy Men* 172 He was a 'mustang'—up from the enlisted ranks. **1950** *Time* 11 Dec. 22 A mustang who had worked his way up from the ranks in 13 years of service. **1953** M. Dibner *Deep Six* v. 35 A damned 'mustang'. Never went to the Academy or anything. **1962** *Amer. Speech* XXXVII. 288 *Mustang*, a self-made man, i.e., a Marine officer who started as a private instead of as a second lieutenant. **1971** *N.Y. Times Mag.* 5 Sept. 11 The most decorated enlisted man in the Korean War—the mustang everybody thought was the perfect combat commander.

mustanger ('mʌstæŋgə(r)). *Western U.S.* Also **moustanguer.** [f. MUSTANG + -ER[1].] One who catches or entraps mustangs.

1856 Olmsted *Journ. Texas* viii. 443 The business of entrapping them [*sc.* mustangs] has given rise to a class of men called 'mustangers', composed of runaway vagabonds and outlaws of all nations. **1874** Lady Herbert tr. *Hübner's Ramble* I. vii. (1878) 79 Others moustanguers; and their little Indian horses or moustangs.

mustard ('mʌstəd), *sb.* Forms: 3 **mustart**, 3–5 **mostard**, 4–6 **mustarde**, 5–7 **musterd**, 6 **musterde**, **mudsterd**, 4– **mustard**. [a. OF. *moustarde*, *mostarde* (mod.F. *moutarde*) = Pr., Catal., Pg., It. *mostarda*, Rumanian *mostar*, f. Com. Rom. *mosto* MUST *sb.*[1], whence Catal. *mostassa*, *mostalla*, Sp. *mostaza* mustard (as a condiment), Sp. *mostear* to spread mustard on. The name etymologically belongs to the condiment as originally prepared by making the ground seeds into a paste with must.

The Fr. word has been adopted into several Teut. langs., in some instances with assimilation of the ending to native suffixes: MDu. *mostaert* (Du. *mostaard*), MLG. *mostert*, *mustert*, MHG. *mostert*, *musthart* (G. *mostert*, *mostrich*).]

1. a. The seeds of black and white mustard (see sense 2) ground or pounded to a powder (often with admixture of other substances), sometimes called ***flour of mustard***; also, this substance as made into a paste by the addition of water or vinegar, and serving as a condiment of extreme pungency, or applied to the skin as a rubefacient in the form of a poultice or plaster.

oil of mustard: a fixed oil obtained from mustard-seeds by pressure. ***essence of mustard***: a volatile oil distilled from black mustard-seed; also, the commercial name of an embrocation containing mustard and other ingredients.

1289 *Househ. Exp. R. De Swinfield* (Camden) I. 19 In mostard .iiij.*d.* *a* **1300** *Siriz* 279 in Mätzner *Altengl. Sprachpr.* 111/1 Pepir nou shalt thou eten, This mustart shal ben thi mete. **13..** *Metr. Hom.* (Vernon MS.) in *Archiv Stud. neu. Spr.* LVII. 308 Summe smered hire Mouþ wt oute with grounden Mustard. *c* **1460** J. Russell *Bk. Nurture* 686 Furst set forthe mustard & brawne of boore. **1532** More *Confut. Tindale* Wks. 582/1 And now when hys argument is all made vp, ye shal find it as full of reason as an egge full of mustarde. **1642** Fuller *Holy & Prof. St.* III. ii. 156 Some think their conceits, like mustard, not good except they bite. **1786** Abercrombie *Gard. Assist.* Mar. 75 Flour of mustard. *a* **1834** Coleridge in *Sir H. Davy's Rem.* (1858) 80, I..having seen in an advertisement something about essence of mustard curing the most obstinate cases of rheumatism. **1838** T. Thomson *Chem. Org. Bodies* 439 Oil of Mustard..is expressed from the seeds of the *sinapis alba* and *nigra*. *Ibid.* 902 *note*, The mustard of the shops is said to be often mixed with wheat flour and cayenne pepper to heighten the flavour. **1867** Bloxam *Chem.* 479 The essence of mustard and that of horseradish are composed of $C_8H_5NS_2$.

b. With prefixed place-name or local adj., indicating varieties of manufacture or preparation.

In the 16–17th c. Tewkesbury was the chief seat of mustard manufacture in England, but this industry is not now practised there.

1591 Nashe *Saffron Walden* D 4 b, A messe of Tewksbury mustard. **1597** Shaks. *2 Hen. IV*, II. vi. 262 His Wit is as thicke as Tewkesburie Mustard. **1834** McCulloch *Dict. Comm.* (ed. 2) 810 Mustard..was formerly extensively cultivated in Durham, but it is now seldom seen in that county. At present it is principally raised in the neighbourhood of York,..and being manufactured in the city of York, is afterwards sold under the name of Durham mustard. **1842** *Penny Cycl.* XXII. 36/2 French mustard for the table is often prepared with vinegar.

c. *fig.*

1546 J. Heywood *Prov.* (1867) 44 Where her woordes seemd hony,..Now are they mustard. **1832** L. Hunt *Sir R. Esher* (1850) 126 As if the fighting they were going to have was not mustard enough to their beef.

d. *transf.* Applied to substances resembling mustard (prepared for the table) in appearance.

1582 Hester *Secr. Phiorav.* III. lxx. 96 Take this hearbe [Millefoil]..and put thereunto Bedellium, Frankensence, and common oile, and make thereof as it were a Mustarde.

e. *proverbial phrases*: esp. with reference to the pungency of mustard.

The use of ***keen as mustard*** is anticipated by the expression ***keenest mustard*** in quot. 1658 s.v. KEEN *a.* (*adv.*) 4.

1659 [see STRONG *a.* 15 b]. **1672** W. Walker *Parœmiologia* 25/1 As keen as mustard. **1679** 'T. Ticklefoot' *Clod-Pate's Ghost* 4/2 You shall see a man as hot as Mustard against Plot and Plotters. *a* **1732** Gay *Songs & Ball., New Song of New Similes*, My passion is as mustard strong. *a* **1886** Hobart *Sk. Life* (1887) 53, I returned, keen as mustard, to my ship. **1916** 'B. Cable' *Doing their Bit* ii. 36 They get as keen as mustard on it. **1932** R. Aldington *Soft Answers* 185 His famous Uncle Harold..had unfortunately died insolvent, owing to being as keen as mustard on the form of the Empire's horses and the forms of the Empire's barmaids. **1938** N. Marsh *Artists in Crime* ii. 13 He's as keen as mustard,..and he can talk of nothing but his work.

f. The colour of the condiment, usu. a brownish-yellow. Also *attrib.* or as *adj.* Cf. *mustard-coloured*, *-yellow* adjs.

1848 [see DANDIE DINMONT]. **1922** Joyce *Ulysses* 226 She stared at the large poster of Marie Kendall... Mustard hair and dauby cheeks. **1923** *Daily Mail* 17 Apr. 7 (Advt.), In shades of Jade, Mustard, Cherry, Nigger or Grey. **1951** E. Paul *Springtime in Paris* ii. 33 Most of the young coloured men, yellow, brown, snuff, mustard or ginger in hue, had white girls with them. **1965** J. Gale *Clean Young Englishman* III. 101, I wore my demobilisation suede shoes and a mustard ferreting coat. **1969** G. Macbeth *War Quartets* 60, I rose against a full moon, sharp in mustard light. **1971** *Vogue* 15 Sept. 129/2 Coats..colours: orange, mustard, brick, royal.

g. In fig. phrases: that which enhances the flavour of anything, or adds piquancy or zest; the best of anything. Phr. ***to cut the mustard***: to accomplish, to succeed, to make good; to come up to expectations, to meet requirements. *slang* (chiefly *U.S.*).

1903 A. Adams *Log Cowboy* xv. 237 For fear they were not the proper mustard, he had that dog man sue him in court for the balance, so as to make him prove the pedigree. **1904** 'O. Henry' *Cabbages & Kings* vi. 101 I'm not headlined in the bills, but I'm the mustard in the salad dressing just the same. **1905** 'H. McHugh' *You can search Me* 17 Petroskinski is a discovery of mine, and he's all to the mustard. **1907** 'O. Henry' *Trimmed Lamp* 217 Why don't you invite him if he's so much to the mustard? **1907** —— *Heart of West* x. 163, I looked around and found a proposition that exactly cut the mustard. **1909** —— *Roads of Destiny* 99 'She cut the mustard,' he said, 'all right.' **1922** C. Sandburg *Slabs of Sunburnt West* 7 Kid each other... Tell each other you're all to the mustard. **1923** Wodehouse *Inimitable Jeeves* iv. 41 Never before had I encountered a curate so genuinely all to the mustard. **1930** —— *Very Good, Jeeves* iii. 70 Life at this juncture seemed pretty well all to the mustard. **1960** J. Mitford *Hons & Rebels* ix. 56 Perhaps I could get a job as a maid in somebody's house..but Idden convinced me I would never cut the mustard at this occupation. **1966** 'J. Hackston' *Father clears Out* 114 Nell was all to the mustard. On her first Sunday afternoon she sat with young Bob Marlow..and, when it was Herby Carter's Sunday, went for a spin with him in his..jinker... For Tom..she sat in the old creek-bed. **1968** *Down Beat* 7 Mar. 18/1 There, in the Apple, his skill was tested in competition with the established ones. If he couldn't cut the mustard, he became part of the anonymous mob. **1974** *Citizen* (Ottawa) 24 Aug. 78 What if it doesn't work out? What if I'm bored with it? What if I'm no good at it? What if I just can't cut the mustard?

h. As quasi-*adj.*: very good, keen, enthusiastic; thorough. Also (*fig.*) hot, pungent.

1925 E. Wallace *King by Night* ix. 41 That fellow is mustard. **1931** T. Lyell *Slang, Phrase & Idiom* 537 *To be mustard*, to be excellent at anything. It must never be used of the female sex. **1936** Wodehouse *Laughing Gas* xvii. 186 Avoid actors. They are mustard. **1959** *Times* 19 June 16/3 He [a batsman] is mustard on anything a trifle short of a length. **1960** L. Cooper *Accomplices* I. vi. 62 He showed me..an extract from a report from..the F.B.I. There wasn't much of it but what there was was mustard. **1966** L. Southworth *Felon in Disguise* ix. 131 He could see the couple and what they were doing. 'Blimey, she's mustard,' he thought. **1972** *Daily Express* 4 July 6/8 Britain is particularly hot on calculus. The Russians and the East Germans are mustard on the theory of numbers and on solid geometry. **1973** 'B. Mather' *Snowline* xix. 231 You can wash out South Africa... They're mustard there. You couldn't smuggle in a grain of wheat. **1973** J. Wainwright *Touch of Malice* 62 'Careful, Charlie,' warned Sanderson quietly. 'He's mustard.' 'Not mustard,' said Ripley. 'Dynamite—'.

2. a. The name of several species of cruciferous plants forming the Linnæan genus *Sinapis*, but now included in the genus *Brassica*; esp. *B. nigra*, the black (or brown) mustard, and *B. alba*, the white mustard (see 2 c).

Also *B. arvensis*, wild (field or corn) mustard (also called CHARLOCK); *B. juncea*, Indian (Russian or Sarepta) mustard; *B. Pekinensis*, Pekin mustard.

1340 *Ayenb.* 143 Þet zed o mostard is wel smal ac hit is wel strang and wel bitinde uor hit is hot ine þe uerþe degre ase ziggeþ þise fisiciens. *c* **1440** *Promp. Parv.* 349/1 Mustard, or warlok, or se(n)vyne, herbe.., *sinapis*. **1570** Pena & L'Obel *Stirp. Adversaria* (1576) 67 Sinapi sativvm Erucæ, aut Rapifolium... *Ang.* Mudsterd, Senbeye. **1597** Gerarde *Herbal* II. ix. 190 *Sinapi syluestre.* Wilde Mustard. **1691** Ray *Creation* II. (1692) 73 As for the Mustard that sprung up in the Isle of Ely,..yet might it have been brought down in the Channels by the Floods. **1731** Miller *Gard. Dict.* s.v. *Sinapi*, The Species are; 1... Common or Red Mustard. 2... Garden or White Mustard. 3... Indian Mustard, with a Lettuce leaf. **1817** Neill in *Edin. Encycl.* XI. 274/2 White mustard (*Sinapis alba*)..is cultivated only as a small salad, and is used while in the seed-leaf, along with cresses. **1856** Gray *Man. Bot.* (1860) 36 *Sinapis arvensis*, L. (Field Mustard. Charlock.) **1875** *Encycl. Brit.* I. 384/1 The brown mustard is grown solely for its seeds, which yield the well-known condiment. **1884** *Ibid.* XVII. 112/2 Of these [species] the principal are the Black or Brown Mustard, *Brassica nigra* (*Sinapis nigra*, L.), the White Mustard, *Brassica alba*, and the Sarepta Mustard, *B. juncea*.

b. Applied with defining word to various other (chiefly cruciferous) plants, resembling or supposed to resemble mustard in appearance, taste, etc.

bastard mustard = *false mustard*. †**candy mustard** = CANDYTUFT. **false mustard**, *Polanisia Graveolens* (formerly *Cleome dodecandria*). †**Grecian mustard**, some plant of the N.O. *Thlaspideæ* ('*Thlaspi Græcum*', Gerarde). **old man's mustard**, *Achillea Millefolium* (Britten and Holland). †**peasant's mustard** = *boor's mustard* (see BOOR 4). **poor man's mustard**, *Alliaria officinalis* (Britten and Holland). **wild mustard**, (*a*) see 2; (*b*) *Raphanus Raphanistrum* (Britten and Holland); †(*c*) applied apparently to various mustards, as Treacle mustard, and Hedge mustard. See also BOOR'S, BUCKLER, CHURL'S, CLOWN'S, DISH, GARLIC, GREEN, HEDGE, KNAVE'S, MITHRIDATE, TANSY, TOWER, TREACLE, WORMSEED-*mustard*, etc.

1597 Gerarde *Herbal* II. xix. 206 Grecian Mustard hath many leaues spread vpon the ground, like those of the common Daisie. *Ibid.* Buckler Mustard... Small buckler Mustard. *Ibid.* xx. 207 Candie Mustarde excelleth all the rest. *Ibid.* xxi. 209 Pesants Mustarde. *Ibid.* Yellowe Mustard. *Ibid.* White Treacle Mustard. *Ibid.* 211 Thornie mustarde groweth vp to the height of fower cubites. **1611** Cotgr., *Moustarde sauvage*, treacle Mustard, wild Mustard, wild Sene. **1633** *Gerarde's Herbal* II. xxi. 266 Round leaued Mustard hath many large leaues laid flat vpon the ground like the leaues of the wilde Cabbage. **1760** J. Lee *Introd. Bot.* App. 320 Mustard, Bastard, *Cleome*. **1845–50** Mrs. Lincoln *Lect. Bot.* App. 144/1 *Polanisia..graveolens*, (false mustard..). **1853** G. Johnston *Nat. Hist. E. Bord.* I. 35 *Sinapis arvensis*. Wild Mustard.—Cornfields.

c. ***mustard and cress***: the plants white mustard and cress (*Lepidium sativum*) used in the seed-leaf as a salad herb; also *fig.* and *attrib.*

Sometimes grown in fancy pots, etc., as an ornament.

1824 Loudon *Encycl. Gard.* (ed. 2) §4029 Rape is cultivated in gardens as a small salad herb, to be..used in cresses and mustard. **1827** Hone *Table Bk.* I. 607 An ingenious contrivance to make mustard and cress seeds grow in pleasant forms over vessels and basketwork. **1831** Manning *Let.* 3 Apr. in *Life* I. 76 Six months of this rustic vegetation, and my cerebellum would put forth mustard and cress. *Mod.* Mustard and cress sandwiches.

3. a. = *mustard gas* (see sense 4 c).

1918 *Jrnl. Amer. Med. Assoc.* 7 Dec. 1911/2 (*heading*) Mustard (yellow cross) burns. **1937** A. M. Prentiss *Chem. in War* ii. 50 If sufficient effort is expended in finding more efficient ways of using it, mustard will undoubtedly yield far greater results. **1966** *Science* 5 Apr. 409/1 Mustard, *bis*(*β*-chloroethyl)sulfide, shared interest with a series of nitrogenous analogues. **1966** *McGraw-Hill Encycl. Sci. & Technol.* III. 44/2 Wet or perspiring skin absorbs more mustard than does dry skin.

b. *Pharm.* Any of the group of substances that contains mustard gas and the nitrogen mustards (cf. NITROGEN b).

1946 *Science* 5 Apr. 412/1 The oxidation of pyruvate by brain brei was significantly inhibited by sulfur mustard. **1964** *Brit. Med. Bull.* XX. 91/1 The biological alkylating agents..include the sulphur and nitrogen mustards, epoxides, [etc.]. **1970** *Nature* 6 June 897/1 Quinacrine mustard makes part of the human *Y* chromosome fluoresce particularly brightly.

4. *attrib.* and *Comb.* **a.** attrib. quasi-*adj.* Of the nature of mustard, pungent.

1598 Marston *Sco. Villanie* I. ii, Sharp mustard rime, To purge the snottery of our slimie time.

b. Obvious *Comb.*, as ***mustard †-box***, ***†-breaker***, ***-coloured*** (adj.), ***flour***, ***-keen*** (adj.), ***-maker***, ***-mill***, ***†quern***, ***spoon***, ***spoonful***, ***-yellow***; also in various names of appliances in which mustard is used remedially, as ***mustard-plaster***, ***-poultice*** (also vb. trans.), ***vomit***.

1687 *Lond. Gaz.* No. 2296/4 A Sugar Box, a Pepper Box, and a *Mustard Box without mark. **1410** *Will of Durem* (Somerset Ho.), *Mustard brekers. **1886** Mrs. Lynn Linton *P. Carew* xxiv, A *mustard-coloured envelope. **1884** *Encycl. Brit.* XVII. 113/1 The mustard papers commonly used as rubefacients and vesicants are made from *mustard flour entirely deprived of its fixed oil. **1935** G. Heyer *Death in Stocks* iii. 29 I'd had a letter from Arnold, and they were instantly *mustard-keen to see it. **1968** 'J. J. Marric' *Gideon's River* xviii. 162 Singleton's got the frogmen out already, the Warbler says he's mustard-keen. *c* **1483** Caxton *Dialogues* 42/21 Nycholas the *mustard-maker. **1533** More *Debell. Salem* i. Wks. 933/2 A musterde maker in Cambridge. **1609** *Ev. Woman in Hum.* I. i. in Bullen *O. Pl.* IV, I had as leef have heard the grinding of a *Mustard-Mill. **1810** E. Weeton *Let.* 25 Feb. (1969) I. 235 *Mustard plasters and bottles of warm water were applied to the feet. **1866** S. Thomson *Dict. Dom. Med.* 356 The well known mustard plaster or cataplasm. **1869** 'Mark Twain' *Sketches New & Old* (1875) 46 That mustard-plaster of a newspaper. **1909** *Westm. Gaz.* 23 Dec. 4/1 It had lapels that were far too wide,..being what some tailors called 'the mustard-plaster type'. **1975** D. Delman *One Man's Murder* v. 95 Let me go home early to a mustard plaster. **1802** *Med. Jrnl.* VIII. 31 *Mustard poultices were applied to his feet. **1858** Dickens *Let. to Miss Hogarth* 18 Aug., I got home at half-past ten, and mustard-poulticed and barley-watered myself tremendously. **1356** in Riley *Memor. Lond.* (1868) 284 *Mustarde quernes. **1694** Salmon *Bate's Dispens.* (1713) 129/2 Let them be ground in a Mustard-Quern. **1890** *Anthony's Photogr. Bull.* III. 195 About a *mustard spoonful of dry pyro. **1737** Monro in *Med. Ess. Edinb.* (ed. 2) II. 303 Her Disease seemed..at last to be almost cured by the Use of *Mustard Vomits. **1904** *Daily Chron.* 30 Mar. 8/2 A certain shade of *mustard-yellow.

c. Special combinations: as **mustard ball**, †(*a*) mustard made into a ball; (*b*) *dial.* (see quot. 1888); **mustard beetle**, a beetle destructive to mustard plants; †**mustard-bowl**, a wooden bowl in which mustard-seed was pounded, proverbially referred to as the instrument for producing stage thunder; **mustard bush**, *Austral.* (see quot. 1965); **mustard cloth, leaf, paper**, cloth or paper coated with mustard, etc. and used as a sinapism; **mustard gas**, dichlorodiethylsulphide, $(ClCH_2CH_2)_2S$, a colourless, oily liquid which is a powerful poison and vesicant, acting directly on the skin, and which was first used in warfare by the Germans in 1917, at Ypres; **mustard-oil**, an oil obtained from mustard seed; **mustard shrub**, a West Indian shrub, *Capparis ferruginea*, bearing pungent berries; **mustard-stone** *Sc.*, a stone on or with which to beat or pound mustard seed; †**mustard-token**, app. a token given to purchasers of mustard, entitling them to a small repayment when a certain number have been accumulated; also *transf.* as a term of contempt; **mustard-tree**, (*a*) the mustard of the N.T., described as a 'tree' (see MUSTARD SEED 1); (*b*) *Austral.* = *mustard bush*; **mustard weevil**, a weevil which damages the white mustard plant, *Ceutorhyncus contractus*; **mustard whey**, a medicinal preparation of mustard (see quot.).

1679 OATES *Narr. Popish Plot* 48 The Deponent saith, that by Tewxbury *Mustard-balls, we are to understand, Fire-balls. **1790** W. DYDE *Tewkesbury* ii. 5 Tewkesbury..was likewise remarkable for its mustard balls, which being very pungent, have occasioned this proverb,..'He looks as if he lived on Tewkesbury mustard'. **1888** *Sheffield Gloss.*, *Mustard-ball*, a leaden ball used in making sauce from sorrel and in bruising mustard seeds, &c. **1890** MISS E. A. ORMEROD *Injur. Insects* (ed. 2) 151 *Mustard Beetle ('Black Jack'), *Phædon betulæ* Linn. **1728** POPE *Dunc.* II. 226 'Tis yours to shake the soul With Thunder rumbling from the *mustard-bowl. **1764** H. WALPOLE *Let. to Earl of Hertford* 6 Feb., Lord North in vain rumbled about his mustard-bowl, and endeavoured alone to outroar a whole party. **1933** *Bulletin* (Sydney) 7 June 25/2 Another hardy northwesterner is the *mustard bush. It is of dwarf habit, with a dense growth of leaves relished by sheep. **1965** *Austral. Encycl.* II. 263/1 The mustard-bush or mustard-tree (*Apophyllum anomalum*), an almost leafless tree with small fragrant flowers, is an inland species whose young shoots have a somewhat mustard-like flavour; in spite of its wiry nature it is much relished by stock. **1897** *Trans. Amer. Pediatric Soc.* IX. 101 He applied warm *mustard cloths to the body and extremities. **1917** *Nation* (N.Y.) 15 Nov. 524/2 The Germans have just invented a new and particularly powerful weapon in their so-called '*mustard gas'. **1934** *Discovery* Feb. 32/1 As far as can be judged from the sample of casualties officially studied, one in thirty-eight of the British casualties from 'mustard gas' died and about one in four hundred was incapacitated for six months or longer. **1937** J. M. MURRY *Necessity of Pacifism* v. 76 The sword of the Lord is broken in men's hands... The mustard-gas of the Almighty—it cannot be. **1973** G. BEARE *Snake on Grave* xxvi. 160 Less than fifty years ago this place was a sea of blood and mud..scoured and sterilised by mustard gas. **1879** MRS. A. E. JAMES *Ind. Househ. Managem.* 23 *Mustard leaves in a tin case. **1900** EVA C. E. LÜCKES *Gen. Nursing* x. (ed. 2) 129 Mustard leaves that are procured from a chemist are nearly always used now in preference to plasters. **1850** *Fownes' Man. Chem.* (ed. 3) 539 *Mustard-oil. **1888** *Sat. Rev.* 11 Aug. 174 And what is a fish or a vegetable curry without mustard-oil? **1874** GARROD & BAXTER *Mat. Med.* (1880) 209 *Mustard Paper. **1756** P. BROWNE *Jamaica* 247 The *Mustard Shrub. This plant is..strongly impregnated with an acrid volatile salt, like most of the mustard tribe, among whom it ought to be placed. *a* **1550** *Freiris Berwik* 556 in *Dunbar's Poems* (S.T.S.) 303 He was sa ferce he fell owttour the sek, And brak his heid vpoun ane *mustard stane. **1600** DEKKER *Shoomakers Holyday* (1610) B4b, Peace you crackt groates, you *mustard tokens, disquiet not the braue souldier. **1622** MASSINGER & DEKKER *Virg. Mart.* II. iii, Ile rather part from the fat of them, then from a mustard-tokens worth of Argent. **1844** *Asiatic Jrnl.* Ser. III. III. 92 Prof. Royle read a paper on the *mustard-tree of Scripture. **1893** *Times* 5 June 8/2 Miss E. A. Ormerod issues a note of warning that we are likely to have this year a widespread attack of the *mustard weevil. **1789** W. BUCHAN *Dom. Med.* App. (1790) 705 *Mustard Whey. Take milk and water, of each a pint; bruised mustard-seed, an ounce and a half. Boil them together till the curd is perfectly separated; afterwards strain the whey through a cloth.

'mustard, *v. rare.* [f. MUSTARD *sb.*] *trans.* To spread or season with mustard.

1851 MAYHEW *Lond. Labour* II. 227 This sort of meat, sometimes profusely mustarded, is often eaten in the beer-shops with thick 'shives' of bread.

mustardavelles, -dybiles, variant forms of MUSTERDEVILLERS.

'mustarder. *Hist.* [mod. a. AF. *mustarder* (1301 in *Rolls Parlt.* I 250; common in 14th c.) = F. *moutardier*: see MUSTARD *sb.* and -ER[2].] A maker of or a dealer in mustard.

1805 R. YATES *Hist. St. Edmund's Bury* 203 Squenelarii, Basket-keepers. Mustarder. **1866** ROGERS *Agric. & Prices* I. iv. 104 The following trades are also enumerated..cooper.. barber, mustarder, woolcomber.

mustardevillys, var. MUSTERDEVILLERS.

'mustard-pot. A pot or cruet for holding table mustard.

In Wyclif's sarcastic phrase (which was often echoed by Protestant controversialists in the 16–17th c.) the word seems to mean a jar for keeping a supply of mustard ready mixed (covered with parchment to exclude the air).

c **1380** WYCLIF *Serm.* Sel. Wks. I. 381 þese lettris mai do good for to covere mostard pottis, but not þus to wynne men blis. **1580** FULKE *Retentive, Dang. Rock* xviii. 299 Their learned workes shall liue and be in honor, when the Popes decretalls..shall stoppe mustard pottes. **1603** H. CROSSE *Vertues Commw.* (1878) 109 If they set forth any notable booke of diuinitie, humanitie, or such like, they are in no request, but to stop musterd-pots. **1610–11** in Halliwell *Anc. Invent.* (1854) 70 Item, two musterd pottes. *a* **1745** SWIFT *Direct. Serv.*, *Gen.* Wks. 1751 XIV. 14 You may conveniently stick your Candle in a Bottle,..a twisted Napkin, a Mustard-Pot, an Inkhorn [etc.]. **17..** R. GRAVES *Fable* in Dodsley *Coll. Poems* (1782) V. 73 The pepper, Tom assigned his lot With vinegar, and mustard-pot.

mustard seed. Forms: see MUSTARD *sb.* and SEED *sb.* Also 7 **muster seed.**

1. The seed of mustard. Also *attrib.* and *fig.*

The 'mustard-seed' (κόκκος σινάπεως) of the N.T., spoken of as producing a 'tree' (Matt. xiii. 31), is prob. the seed of the black mustard (*Brassica nigra*), which in Palestine grows to a great height. Some commentators have identified it with the tree *Salvadora persica*, which does not suit the description of it as a 'herb'.

1390–1 *Earl Derby's Exp.* (Camden) 22 Pro j bz. de mustardseed iij s. **14..** *Stockh. Med. MS.* II. 467 in *Anglia* XVIII. 318 A greyn of mustard-seed [in weight]. **1660** *Act 12 Chas. II*, c. 4 (Rates) Muster seed the c li...x s. **1763** MILLS *Syst. Pract. Husb.* IV. 129 Another sort..produces the seeds which are commonly sold under the appellation of Durham mustard-seed. **1847** W. DARLINGTON *Amer. Weeds* (1860) 47 The skin of the White Mustard seeds contains a large amount of mucilaginous matter. **1884** *Encycl. Brit.* XVII. 113/1 The mustard-seed imported from the East Indies is also largely composed of *Brassica juncea*. **1887** MOLONEY *Forestry W. Afr.* 274 *Brassica juncea*... Herb cultivated abundantly in India for the seeds, which yield mustard-seed oil. **1926** C. VAN VECHTEN *Nigger Heaven* 286 *Mustard-seed*: see high yellow (= mulatto). **1952** DYLAN THOMAS *Coll. Poems* 170 In the mustardseed sun.

fig. **1700** CONGREVE *Way of World* IV. ix, Thou dost bite, my dear Mustard-seed.

†**2.** The plant mustard = MUSTARD *sb.* 2. Also with defining word. Cf. MUSTARD *sb.* 2b. *Obs.*

1523 FITZHERB. *Husb.* §20 Kedlokes hath a leafe lyke rapes,..and groweth in al maner corne, and hath small coddes, and groweth lyke mustard sede. **1578** LYTE *Dodoens* v. lv. 618 *Sinapi sylvestre.* Wilde Mustarde seede. *Ibid.* 619 The first kind is called..in English, White Senuie, & white Mustarde sede. *a* **1614** DONNE *Βιαθανατος* 184 As much as a graine of Musterseed is enough to remove mountaines. **1626** BACON *Sylva* §582 Some Herbs are but Annuall,..As Borrage,..Tobacco, Mustard-Seed, and all kinds of Corne. **1681** GREW *Musæum* II. III. iii. 235 The lesser Champaine Treacle Mustard-Seed. *Thlaspios Campestris.*

3. *U.S.* A very fine shot used for shooting birds with the least injury to the plumage.

1809 T. G. FESSENDEN *Pills Poetical* 8 Her single good gun loaded with mustard seed shot. **1844** *Knickerbocker* XXIII. 440 None of the fine mustard-seed or robin, but the heavy duck-shot. **1884** COUES *Key N. Amer. Birds* (ed. 2) 4 Use 'mustard-seed', or 'dust-shot', as it is variously called... A small bird..may be riddled with mustard-seed and yet be preservable.

mustardvillars, var. MUSTERDEVILLERS.

mustardy ('mʌstədɪ), *a.* [f. MUSTARD *sb.* + -Y.] Resembling or covered with mustard.

1852 R. S. SURTEES *Sponge's Sp. Tour* (1893) 203 The dirty, egg-stained, mustardy copy of *Bell's Life*. **1861** THORNBURY *Turner* (1862) II. 342 A mustardy yellow. **1911** W. J. LOCKE *Glory Clementina Wing* xix. 280 Her ill-fitting mustardy brown stuff skirt. **1936** W. JAMES *Gangways & Corridors* vi. 69 There was a hideous affair of mustardy yellow diagonal serge. **1975** *Times* 5 July 11/3 The plate of crudités, with a mustardy mayonnaise dip.

mustatioe, mustchadoe, obs. ff. MUSTACHIO.

must-be ('mʌstbi:). [f. MUST *v.*[1] + BE *v.*] The inevitable, what is fated to happen.

1907 *Cambr. Hist. Eng. Lit.* I. 4 The must-be often helps an undoomed man when he is brave. **1922** D. H. LAWRENCE *Aaron's Rod* 242 A ghastly atmosphere of must-be. **1970** R. LOWELL *Notebk.* 177 Hope is the must-be, the tomb of a small child.

must deviles, variant of MUSTERDEVILLERS.

mustechee, musteese, obs. ff. MESTIZO.

1600 in *Hedges' Diary* (Hakl.) II. 209 It's alsoe of very ill consequence that your Covenant servants should intermarry with any of the people of the Country or those of mixed Race or Mustechees.

†**'musted**, *ppl. a.*[1] *Sc. Obs.* Also mousted, **muisted, moosted, -et.** [f. MUST *sb.*[2] or *v.*[3] + -ED.] Powdered with 'must' or hair powder.

1814 SCOTT *Wav.* xxxvi, The carle..wi' the black coat and the mousted head. **1824** —— *Redgauntlet* Let. x, Muisted hair.

†**'musted**, *ppl. a.*[2] *Obs. rare*[−1]. In 7 moosted. [f. MUST *v.*[2] + -ED[1].] Mouldy.

1632 LITHGOW *Trav.* x. 457 No food..but three ounces of moosted browne bread.

mustee (mʌ'sti:), **mestee** (mɛ'sti:). Also 8 **mæsti, meste, musty,** 9 **mesti, musti,** (*erron.* **muster**). [Corruptly a. Sp. *mestizo* (pronounced mes'tiθo): see MESTIZO.] The offspring of a white and a quadroon; also, loosely, a half-caste.

1699 in Wheeler *Madras in Old. Time* (1861) I. 356 Wives of Freemen..Mustees. 2. **1712** W. ROGERS *Voy.* (1718) 203 The Mustees, begot by Spaniards on Indian women. **1781** *Hicky's Bengal Gaz.* 24 Feb. (Yule), A Slave Boy..pretty white or colour of Musty. **1783** MARSDEN *Sumatra* 40 They are in general lighter than the Mestees, or half breed, of the rest of India. **1796** STEDMAN *Surinam* (1813) I. xii. 309 The Samboe dark, and the Mulatto brown, The Mæsti fair. **1802** C. JAMES *Milit. Dict.*, *Musti*, one born of a Mulatto father or mother and a white father or mother. **1813** *Sporting Mag.* XLII. 211 The Government have multiplied the difficulties for Europeans mixing with Creoles or Mestis. **1825** *Gentl. Mag.* XCV. I. 6 The third descent, from a white and quadroon, is called a muster. **1865** WHYTE MELVILLE *Cerise* (1866) II. vii. 103 Those Portuguese rovers, and the mustee who commanded them.

attrib. **1829** MARRYAT *F. Mildmay* xviii, A class of women, born of white fathers and mustee or mulatto women.

mustelid ('mʌsti:lɪd). [f. mod.L. family name *Mustelidæ*, f. L. *mustēla* weasel, adopted as the name of a genus by Linnæus (*Systema Naturæ* (ed. 10, 1758) I. 582): see -ID[3].] A small carnivorous mammal of the family Mustelidæ, which includes weasels, stoats, badgers, mink, and others. Cf. MUSTELINE *sb.*[1]

1910 H. F. OSBORN *Age of Mammals* iv. 259 The mustelids were becoming more numerous [in the Miocene]. **1933** A. S. ROMER *Vertebrate Paleontology* xv. 291 Continued emphasis on a flesh-eating diet has..resulted in the retention of well-developed shearing teeth in the greater number of mustelids. **1953** *New Biol.* XIV. 120 Most mustelids and wild dogs and cats do not [have fleas]. **1968** A. S. ROMER *Procession of Life* xv. 247 The mustelids tend to be relatively small in size, short of leg, and primarily forest-dwellers in habitat. **1972** T. A. VAUGHAN *Mammalogy* XII. 201/1 Most mustelids aggressively search for prey in burrows, crevices, or dense cover. **1975** *Nature* 20 Mar. 187/1 Other interesting elements of the fauna include..a new species of gomphothere, a canid, a mellivorine mustelid.

mustelidan (mʌ'stɛlɪdən). [f. mod.L. *Mustēlid-æ* (f. *Mustēlus* a genus of dog-fishes, altered from L. *mustēla* weasel) + -AN.] A shark of the family *Mustelidæ*, typified by the genus *Mustelus*.

1859–62 SIR J. RICHARDSON, etc. *Mus. Nat. Hist.* II. 165 Mustelidans (*Mustelidæ*).

musteline ('mʌstɪlɪn), *a.*[1] and *sb.*[1] [ad. L. *mustēlīn-us* (*mustellīnus*), of or belonging to a weasel, f. *mustēla* (*mustella*) weasel.] **A.** *adj.* Of, pertaining to, or characteristic of the subfamily *Mustelinæ*, or the family *Mustelidæ*, the weasels or martens, typified by the genus *Mustela*.

1656 BLOUNT *Glossogr.*, *Musteline*, of or like a Weesel. **1828–32** WEBSTER, *Musteline*, pertaining to the weasel or animals of the genus Mustela; as, a musteline color; the musteline genus. **1849–52** OWEN *Teeth* in *Todd's Cycl. Anat.* IV. 914/2 The most aquatic..of the Musteline quadrupeds, viz., the sea-otter. **1891** FLOWER & LYDEKKER *Mammals* 567 Weasel-like (Musteline) forms.

B. *sb.* A musteline animal.

1891 FLOWER & LYDEKKER *Mammals* 570 The brain.. differs from that of *Lutra* and other Mustelines.

musteline, *a.*[2] and *sb.*[2] [f. mod.L. *Mustēl-us* (see MUSTELIDAN) + -INE[1].] **a.** *adj.* Of or pertaining to the *Mustelinæ*, a subfamily of dogfishes or small sharks. **b.** *sb.* A musteline fish.

1890 in *Century Dict.*

mustelinous ('mʌstɪlaɪnəs), *a.* [Formed as MUSTELINE *a.*[1] + -OUS.] = MUSTELINE *a.*[1]

1856 MAYNE *Expos. Lex.*, *Mustelinus*, applied by Desmarest and Gray to a Family (*Mustelini*,..) of the *Mammifera*, having the *Mustela* for their type: mustelinous.

mustell, obs. form of MUSSEL.

†**mustelle.** *Obs. rare*[−1]. [a. F. *mustelle* in the original of this passage.] A weasel.

1487 CAXTON *Bk. Gd. Manners* I. xiv. (W. de W. *c.* 1515) E j b.

musteloid ('mʌstɪlɔɪd), *a.* and *sb.* [f. mod.L. *Mustēl-a* (see MUSTELINE *a.*[1] + -OID.] **A.** *adj.* Pertaining to the family *Mustelidæ* or weasel-like animals. **B.** *sb.* A musteloid animal.

1891 FLOWER & LYDEKKER *Mammals* 590 The Musteloid type.

mustenaunce, corruption of MONSTRANCE.

1479–81 *Rec. St. Mary at Hill* 101 For mendyng of the mustenaunce crosse.

'musteous, *a. rare*[−0]. [f. L. *musteus* belonging to or like must; f. *mustum*: see MUST *sb.*[1] and -EOUS.] 'Sweet as must, like must' (Ash, 1775).

muster ('mʌstə(r)), *sb.*[1] Forms: α. 4–5 **moustre,** 4–6 **mustre,** 5 **mostre, muster, mowstre,** (*pl.* **mustres, mustrez**), 5–6 **moster, mouster, mustour(e, musture,** 6 **mowster, moystere, mustere.** β. 5 **mo(u)nstre,** 6 **mounster.** [ME. *mostre, moustre*, a. OF. *mostre, moustre* fem. (later in learned form *monstre* fem., whence mod.F. *montre*) = Sp. *muestra*, Pg., It., *mostra*, a Com. Rom. verbal noun f. *mostrare* to show:—L. *monstrāre*.

In the sense 'pattern', 'sample', the word passed from OF. into the Teut. langs. as MHG. (mod.G.) *muster*, MDu., MLG. *monster, munster* (mod.Du. *monster*).]

†**1.** The action, or an act, of showing; manifestation; exhibition, display. *to do muster*: to show one's mettle, give proof of prowess. *Obs.*

c **1380** WYCLIF *Serm.* Sel. Wks. II. 360 For þei abiden surely þe shewyng of oure Lord Jesus Crist [tr. 1 Cor. i. 7, *expectantibus revelationem Domini nostri Jesu Christi*]. For þei shal be knowun at domesday,..þat þei ben of Cristis secte, and shulen be taken in after his mustre. **1436** *Pol. Poems* (Rolls) II. 148 Thow clepest thi selfe duc, whan woltow ryse Ande in pleyne felde do mustre with thi lance? *c* **1477** CAXTON *Jason* 104 The noble and riche flees wherof Iason made mustre fro ferre. *c* **1520** *Treat. Galaunt* (W. de W., repr. 1860) 19 Small gyrdynge in the waste, with all theyr other mustur. **1538** LATIMER *Let.* 13 June *Serm. & Rem.* (Parker Soc.) 395 She herself, with her old sister of Walsingham [and other images]..would make a jolly muster in Smithfield; they would not be all day in burning. **1577** HELLOWES *Gueuara's Chron.* 45 At these dayes the pillers giue a muster vpon the fierce waters: declaring the pryde of his power. **1581** MULCASTER *Positions* xxxvii. (1887) 151 They begin to make some muster and shew of their learning. **1603** OWEN *Pembrokeshire* (1892) 80 Wyndowes of this stone would make the like varietie and muster to the eye. **1602** CAREW *Surv. Cornwall* I. (1723) 75 b, You shall hardly find an assembly of boyes in Deuon or Cornwall, where the most vntowardly amongst them, will not as readily giue you a muster of this exercise [*sc.* wrestling], as you are prone to require it. *a* **1661** FULLER *Worthies* (1662) I. xvi. 50 [tr. Record of Hen. V] He that useth such Arms or Coats of Arms, shall on the day of his Muster [orig. *die Monstrationis suæ*] manifestly shew..by virtue of whose gift he enjoyeth the same.

2. A pattern, specimen, example. Now only *Comm.*, a pattern, sample.

In mod. use confined to certain particular branches of commerce or particular localities (used, e.g. in the Sheffield cutlery trade, and by British merchants in Asia).

c **1369** CHAUCER *Dethe Blaunche* 912 Trewly she Was hir chefe patrone of beaute And chefe ensample of al hir [*sc.* Nature's] werke And moustre [*MS. Fairfax*, moūstre, *i.e.* mounstre]. **1387–8** T. USK *Test. Love* II. vi. (Skeat) l. 86 They shulde hete, nat dignite, but moustre of badnesse and mayntenour of shrewes. **1578** T. N. tr. *Conq. W. India* 223 To have knowledge of the rivers and mines of gold, and to bring a moster of the same. **1582** HAKLUYT *Voy.* (1599) II. 162 You shall send home into this realme certain Mowsters or pieces of Shew to be brought to the Diershall. **1613** J. MAY *Declar. Est. Clothing* v. 26 They haue a practize..to shut in a fine woofe at both ends of their cloth, which serveth for a muster to shewe. **1698** FRYER *Acc. E. India & P.* 84 Merchants bringing and receiving Musters. **1727** A. HAMILTON *New Acc. E. Ind.* I. v. 45, I shewed him the Musters of my Goods. **1821** SCOTT *Kenilw.* xvi, Your suit should succeed, being..founded in justice and honour, and Elizabeth being the very muster of both. **1879** *China Overland Trade Rep.* XXIII. No. 12. 2/3 A few musters of new Teas have been shewn.

3. a. An act of mustering (soldiers, sailors, etc.); an assembling of men for inspection, ascertainment or verification of numbers, introduction into service, exercise, or the like. Phrase, *to make, take a muster*.

† *to make one's muster*: to muster or review one's men; also, to present oneself for inspection.

c **1400** MAUNDEV. (1839) xxii. 234 And when the firste thousand is thus passed, and hathe made his mostre, he withdrawethe him on that o syde. **1419** *Ordin. War* xiii. in *Black Bk. Adm.* (Rolls) I. 463 That noman be so hardy to have other men at his mustrez, than tho that be with hym self withold for the same voiage. *c* **1450** *Merlin* 658 The kynge..made a mustre of armed peple. *c* **1489** CAXTON *Sonnes of Aymon* viii. 187 The kyng Charlemagne began for to make hys mustres, for to know how much people that he had. **1513** BRADSHAW *St. Werburge* I. 227 In musture and in batayle euer the pryce haue they The kynges grace to serue. **1536** BELLENDEN *Cron. Scot.* xv. xiii. (1821) II. 441 The Erle of Ros come, with mony folkis, to Perth, and maid his mowster to the king. *a* **1548** HALL *Chron., Hen. VI* 185 The people of the erles parte, beyng in their muster in Sainct Jhons felde..: sodaynly the lord Fawconbridge, whiche toke the musters, wisely declared to the multitude, the offences and breaches of the late agremente. **1553** T. WILSON *Rhet.* 80 Metellus toke muster and required Cesar to be there. **1560** DAUS tr. *Sleidane's Comm.* 467 That the kyng of England wold hire eight thousande horsemen,..& that mounsters [orig. *delectus*] shoulde be take in sondry places. **1568** GRAFTON *Chron.* II. 327 The Lorde Percye caused all his companie..to make their Musters, and they found them selues to be the number of three thousand men of armes, and vij thousande Archers. *c* **1586** C'TESS PEMBROKE *Ps.* LXXXVII. iii, Iehova this account shall make, When he of his shall muster take. **1601** B. JONSON *Ev. Man in Hum.* (Qo. 1) III. ii, No signior, as I remember you seru'd on a great horse, last generall muster. **1632** LITHGOW *Trav.* III. 89 The Candeots..make muster euery eight day, before the Seriant-maiors. **1667** TEMPLE *Let.* 21 May, Wks. 1720 I. 34 The Levies here and Musters go on with all the Care and Speed this Government is capable of. **1726–31** TINDAL *Rapin's Hist. Eng.* XVII. (1743) II. 89 They took a muster and found their Army amounted to four thousand Foot, and six hundred Horse. **1816** SCOTT *Old Mort.* ii, Frequent musters and assemblies of the people, both for military exercise and for sports and pastimes, were appointed by authority. **1849** COBDEN *Speeches* 86 In addition to these, the pensioners are liable to muster and drill. **1864** *Chamb. Encycl.* VI. 637/1 *Muster* ..is a calling over of the names of all the men composing a regiment or a ship's company. *Ibid.*, In regiments of the line, a muster is taken on the 24th of each month; in ships of war, weekly. **1874** GREEN *Short Hist.* vii. §6. 410 Catholic lords led their tenantry to the muster at Tilbury.

transf. *a* **1533** LD. BERNERS *Gold. Bk. M. Aurel.* (1546) Mm j b, The daie of forgettynge maketh the muster of my thoughtes. **1539** TONSTALL *Serm. Palm. Sund.* E vij, If a muster shulde be taken of swearers. **1796** BURKE *Regic. Peace* i. Wks. VIII. 140 In divisions..we are to make a muster of our strength.

b. Phr. *to pass muster*, earlier † *to pass* (*the*) *musters*: orig. *Mil.* to undergo muster or review without censure; hence *transf.* and *fig.* to bear examination or inspection, to come up to the required standard, to be above, or go free from, censure; to succeed, be accepted (*as* or *for* the possessor of certain qualities).

1575 GASCOIGNE *Making of Verse* in *Steele Gl.*, etc. (Arb.) 35 And yet the latter verse is neyther true nor pleasant, and the first verse may passe the musters. **1598** *Acts Privy Council* XXIX. 21 You must have spetiall care that not wone (*sic*) dwellers, victuallers, horsboyes, hirelinges or vagrant *pasvolentes* do offer to passe musters in the bandes. **1627** CAPT. SMITH *Seaman's Gram.* xii. 56 Such a Ship..might well passe muster for a man of warre. **1673** *Articles & Rules for better Govt. of H.M. Forces* xliv, No Muster-Master shall knowingly let any pass the Musters, but such as are qualified. **1689** *Lond. Gaz.* No. 2426/4 The new Regiment Commanded by the Prince de Steinhuise has pass'd Muster. **1738** SWIFT *Pol. Conversat.* 42 She may pass Muster well enough. **1855** THACKERAY *Newcomes* II. 106 Enough good looks to make her pass muster. **1882** MRS. RIDDELL *Pr. Wales' Gard.-Party* 266 Perhaps if her lot had been cast in the present day she might have more than passed muster.

c. Phrase. *in muster*: mustered, assembled for inspection.

1820 BYRON *Mar. Fal.* IV. ii, Are all the people of our house in muster? **1869** MRS. STOWE *Old Town Folks* xlv. (1870) 510 There was a splendid lunch laid out in the parlour, with all the old silver in muster.

† **d.** *master of the musters, commissary of the musters*: = MUSTER-MASTER. *Obs.*

1548 PATTEN *Exped. Scot.* A j b, Syr George Blaag, and Syr Thomas Holcroft, Commissioners of the mousters. **1633** T. STAFFORD *Pac. Hib.* I. xxi. 121 The Commissaries of the Musters. **1647** SPRIGGE *Anglia Rediv.* (1854) 327 Commissary-general Stane, commissary-general of the Musters. **1785** G. A. BELLAMY *Apology* III. 49 He had been named..deputy Commissary to the musters. **1802** C. JAMES *Milit. Dict.* s.v. *Commissary-*, Commissary-general of the musters, or muster-master general.

e. *false muster*: a fraudulent presentation at a muster, or a fraudulent inclusion in a muster-roll, of men who are not available for service. Formerly often *fig.*

1665 MANLEY *Grotius' Low C. Warres* 197 What with Death, and running away, and what with the Captains false Musters, they hardly arose to that Number. **1686** SOUTH *Serm.* (1697) II. ix. 418 It is this Plague of the World, Deception, which takes wrong Measures, and makes false Musters almost in every Thing. **1727–52** CHAMBERS *Cycl.* s.v. *Muster, False Muster*, is when such men pass in review, as are not actually listed as soldiers. **1790** WESLEY *Wks.* (1872) IV. 493 Still I complain of false musters. **1801** WELLINGTON in Gurw. *Desp.* (1837) I. 326 Our friend, the Commissary, has been guilty of making false musters, as appears in the clearest manner. **1817** JAS. MILL *Brit. India* II. IV. viii. 274 He excelled in deceiving the government with false musters and accounts.

† **f.** Payment given to soldiers at a muster.

1662 J. DAVIES tr. *Olearius' Voy. Ambass.* 351 While he was in those parts, he pay'd his Army twelve Musters together. **1670** COTTON *Espernon* II. VIII. 398 During which time the Army had receiv'd five Musters, and yet complain'd of being ill us'd.

g. *Austral.* and *N.Z.* A collecting of stock (cattle, sheep, etc.) by riding round the scattered herd and driving it together.

1841 S. REVANS *Lett.* I. 90 (MS.), I am not yet confident of the mode in which flock and stock musters will be dealt with by the natives. **1867** LADY BARKER *Station Life in N.Z.* (1870) xx. 173 It is impossible to estimate our loss until the grand muster at shearing. **1884** 'R. BOLDREWOOD' *Melb. Mem.* xiii. 95 All the stockmen in the country came cheerfully to his muster. **1884** [see Dict.]. **1892** W. E. SWANTON *Notes on N.Z.* ii. 97 Previous to the shearing, there is the general muster, which means the rounding up and bringing in of all the sheep, good or bad, on the 'run'. **1898** —— *Rom. Canvas Town* 135 The brandings and musters went on all right. **1946** F. D. DAVISON *Dusty* ix. 90 The paddock..was not the easiest in the world to lift sheep from, but Tom had a feeling..that the count would show a clean muster. **1950** *N.Z. Jrnl. Agric.* Oct. 348/3 After the marking muster musterers proceed to the high country and muster wethers. **1956** *Coast to Coast 1955–6* 35 Whole country's gone dead since muster. **1961** B. CRUMP *Hang on Minute Mate* 75 We're starting the shearing muster in a few days. **1963** *Times* 12 Mar. p. xii/7 (*caption*) A muster of merinos for shearing on Benangaroo, a 40,000 acre sheep and cattle property near Coolac, in the southern tablelands of New South Wales.

4. The number (of persons or things) mustered or assembled on a particular occasion; an assembly, collection.

1382 WYCLIF *1 Kings* v. 13 And king Salomon chees werkmen of al Israel; and the moustre [Vulg. *indictio*] was thretti thousandis of men. **1401** J. HANARD in Ellis *Orig. Lett.* Ser. II. I. 16 And Oweyn ys moster a Monday was..viij Mill. and xij^{xx}. spers. **1483** in *10th Rep. Hist. MSS. Comm.* App. v. 317 What so ever parson..will make assemble congregation or moustre of people. **1577** B. GOOGE *Heresbach's Husb.* I. (1586) 12 The double number of them makes the muster the greater. **1810** *Sporting Mag.* XXXVI. 145 A tolerable muster of amateurs and boxing gentry. **1863** W. C. BALDWIN *Afr. Hunting* viii. 325 We set off, a strong muster, two days ago, to hunt part of the forest in which the elephants stand. **1890** 'R. BOLDREWOOD' *Col. Reformer* (1891) 236 I've never seen half, or quarter the muster we've got here lately.

5. A muster-roll. †Also, a census report.

1565 GARGRAVE in J. J. Cartwright *Chapters Yorksh. Hist.* (1872) 15, I have ben at York, wher I taryed untyll Tuysday last to have receyvyd the bokes of musters. **1612** BACON *Ess.*, *Greatness of Kingdoms* (Arb.) 470 The population may appeare by Musters, and the number and greatnesse of Cities and Towns by Carts and Mappes. **1748** *Anson's Voy.* I. i. 5 He knew by the musters that his squadron wanted three hundred seamen of their complement. **1840** DICKENS *Barn. Rudge* xl, I..got put down upon the muster.

¶**6.** Alleged term for: A company (of peacocks).

[The notion is that of sense 1, 'show, display'.]

c **1470** in Lydg. *Hors, Shepe & G.* etc. (Caxton 1479, Roxb. repr.) 30 A muster of pecoks. [Hence 1486 in *Bk. St. Albans* F vj; and in many later works which copy the list of terms there given.] **1820** W. IRVING *Sketch Bk.*, *Christmas Day* (1865) 259 Master Simon..told me that, according to the most ancient and approved treatise on hunting, I must say a *muster* of peacocks.

† **7.** Some astronomical instrument. *Obs. rare*$^{-1}$.

Perh. a dial, clock; cf. F. *montre* watch, It. *mostra* 'a watch or a dyall of the sunne' (Florio).

a **1400–50** *Alexander* 130 Quadrentis coruen all of quyte siluyre.., Mustours & mekil quat mare þen a littill.

8. *muster out*: the action of 'mustering out'; discharge from service. *U.S.*

1892 LEE *Hist. Columbus, Ohio* II. 146 The Fourth Ohio Infantry..returned for muster out, Jun. 12. **1899** *U.S. Statutes* 12 Jan. XXX. 784 All matters pertaining to the muster out of volunteers.

9. *attrib.* and *Comb.*: *muster-day*, *-drum*, *-field*, *-ground*, *-parade*, *-place*; **muster-card** *Comm.*, a pattern-card; † **muster file**, a muster-roll; † **muster maker**, ? the reviewing officer at a muster; † **muster mistress** *humorous*, a female muster-master; **muster paper**, 'a description of paper supplied from the dockyards, ruled and headed, for making ships' books' (Smyth *Sailor's Word-bk.* 1867); **muster party**, *Austral.*, an expedition undertaken for the purpose of 'mustering' cattle on a run. Also MUSTER-BOOK, -MASTER, -ROLL.

1576 GASCOIGNE *Steele Gl.* (Arb.) 63 When *muster day, and foughten fielde are odde. *a* **1660** *Contemp. Hist. Irel.* (Ir. Archæol. Soc.) II. 162 The Major tellinge him he would putt him nexte mustar daye in the heade of a selecte regiment of horse. **1875** *Encycl. Brit.* II. 562/1 The conscripts then took the military oath, *sacramentum*, and were dismissed until the appointed muster-day. **1849** AYTOUN *Scheik of Sinai* ii, Each morning, in the market-place, The *muster-drum is beat. **1838** B. DRAKE *Tales* 179 Our sons..assembling in the '*muster field', divide themselves into armies, and pelt each other with Buckeye balls. **1601** SHAKS. *All's Well* IV. iii. 189 So that the *muster file, rotten and sound, vppon my life amounts not to fifteene thousand pole. **1798** *Deb. Congress U.S.* 15 May (1851) 1707 At the *muster ground on the Commons of Portsmouth. **1876** BANCROFT *Hist. U.S.* VI. xxxvii. 184 The chosen muster-ground of the most various elements of human culture brought together by men. **1586** EARL LEYCESTER *Corr.* (Camden) 278 But, betwene the auditor and the *muster-maker, you will easilie find the faults. **1599** CHAPMAN *Hum. Dayes Myrth* E 1 b, He was taken learning tricks at old Lucilas house the *muster mistris of all the smock-tearers in Paris. **1876** VOYLE & STEVENSON *Milit. Dict.* (ed. 3) s.v. *Muster Roll*, The Queen's Regulations lay down that the presence of the commanding officer is necessary on all *muster parades. **1890** 'R. BOLDREWOOD' *Col. Reformer* (1891) 118 These *muster parties were extremely congenial to Mr. Neuchamp's tastes and tendencies. **1810** SCOTT *Lady of L.* III. xii, The *muster-place be Lanrick mead.

† **'muster**, *sb.*² *Obs.* Also 6 **mowster**. Short for MUSTERDEVILLERS.

1466 *Mann. & Househ. Exp.* (Roxb.) 170 Item, my mastyr owyth hym for ij. yerdes of must'. **1500** *Inv.* in *Ann. Reg.* (1768) *Antiq.* 137 A coarse single gown of muster. **1504** *Will of Broumfeld* (Somerset Ho.), A coote cloth of Mowster. **1549** *Act 3 & 4 Edw. VI*, c. 2 §1 Russetes, Musters, Marbles, Grayes, Royes, and suche lyke colors.

muster ('mʌstə(r)), *v.*¹ Forms: α. 3–6 **mustre**, 4–5 **mostre**, 5 **mostere**, **mouster**, **mustere**, **-ir**, **-yr**, 5–6 **moustre**, 6 **must(o)ure**, **mustyrre**, 4– **muster**; β. (? 5 **monstre**), 6 **monster**, **mounster**. [ad. OF. *mostrer*, *moustrer* (later, in learned form *monstrer*, whence mod.F. *montrer* to show) = Pr., Sp., Pg. *mostrar*, It. *mostrare*:—L. *monstrāre* to show. Cf. M.Du., Du. *monsteren*, MHG., mod.G. *mustern* to muster.

The β type is doubtful for the 15th c., as *u* and *n* are usually indistinguishable in MSS. of that date. For the 16th c., though some instances might be due to misprints, the existence of the type is proved by the spelling *mounster*. In military use the form with *n* may have been due to the influence of Du. *monsteren*.]

† **1. a.** *trans.* To show, to show forth, display, exhibit; to show up, report, tell, explain. Sometimes with clause as obj. *Obs.*

a **1300** *Cursor M.* 9512 þat suilk a man cuth think in thoght þat mustre þat mercle moght? *Ibid.* 25523 þat ilk time þou mistred [*sic*] þe, Suet iesu! wit hert sa fre, To maria magdalene. *c* **1330** R. BRUNNE *Chron.* (1810) 309 To þe pape of Rome þei mostred þer resoun. **13..** *Evang. Nicod.* 51 in *Archiv Stud. neu. Spr.* LIII. 392 His miracles musters his myght. *c* **1400** *Rule St. Benet* 2 In þis sentence mustirs sain benet us hu we sal lede ure lif. *c* **1440** *York Myst.* i. 145 Ande in my fyrste makyng to mustyr my mighte,..I byd in my blyssyng ȝhe aungels gyf lyghte. *c* **1450** *Merlin* xxii. 407 So dide Galashin that often was he shewed, and mustred, with the fynger on bothe sides. **1471** CAXTON *Recuyell* (Sommer) I. 145 In mustryng and shewyng your corayges. *a* **1548** HALL *Chron., Hen. VIII* 73 b, Anticke images of gold..mounsteryng their countenaunces towardes the enteryng of the palaice. **1622** R. HAWKINS *Voy. S. Sea* lix. 139 If they had come to boord with the Spanish high-charged ships, it is not to be doubted but they would have mustred themselues better, then those which could not with their prowesse nor props, haue reached to their wastes.

† **b.** ? To set an example of. *Obs.*

1601 SHAKS. *All's Well* II. i. 55 They weare themselues in the cap of the time, there do muster true gate, eat, speake, and moue vnder the influence of the most receiued starre.

†**c.** *intr.* for *refl.* To show, to appear, to be displayed; to make a (good, bad, etc.) appearance.

c **1412** HOCCLEVE *De Reg. Princ.* 415 Vndir an old pore habyt regneþ oft Grete vertu, þogh it moustre porely. *c* **1430** LYDG. *Min. Poems* (Percy Soc.) 3 So this citee with lawde, preyse, and glorye, For joy moustered lyke the sone beme, To yeve ensample thorowouȝt this reme. **1513** DOUGLAS *Æneis* X. xiii. 31 Sik like Mezentius mustyrris in the feyld, With huge armour, baith speyr, helm, and scheyld. *Ibid.* XII. vi. 41 And haltandly in his cart for the nanis He skippis vp and musturis wantonly. **1533** BELLENDEN *Livy* III. iii. (S.T.S.) I. 251 For þe nobill palacis and towris musturit so aufully within þe ciete, þat þai drewe þe myndis of equis and wolchis fra all segeing. **1565** CALFHILL *Answ. Martiall* ix. 167b, When the Papists beholde the work of their owne hands, the Crosse it self, fayre mustering in yͤ church, which might peraduenture haue bene a logge for the chimney. **1578** LYTE *Dodoens* VI. i. 653 When these buddes do open and spreade, the sweete and pleasant Roses do muster and shewe foorth of colour white. **1597** BACON *Ess., Coulers Good & Evill* v. (Arb.) 144 And this maketh the greater shew if it be done without order, for confusion maketh things muster more.

2. a. *trans.* To collect or assemble (*primarily* soldiers) for ascertainment or verification of numbers, inspection as to condition and equipment, exercise, display, or introduction into service. Also † *to muster their arms*: of an army, to appear in armed array. Also *absol.*

c **1420** LYDG. *Thebes* III. in *Chaucer's Wks.* (1561) 373 Soche a nombre gadred in to one Of worthy knightes, neuer aforn was sein, Whan they in feere, were moustred in a plein. *c* **1440** *Promp. Parv.* 349/2 Musteryn, or gadyr togedur, *commonstro, coaduno.* *c* **1450** *Merlin* xxvii. 560 Thei moustred and assembled all the peple that thei myght gete. **1530** PALSGR. 643/1, I muster, I take the muster of men, as a capytayne doth, *je fais les monstres.* What place wyll you sygne to muster your folkes in. *a* **1548** HALL *Chron., Hen. VI* 164b, How busy he was in mustering, how diligent in setting forward. **1557** *Act 4 & 5 Philip & Mary*, c. 3 §1 Commaundment hathe bene given..to divers..persons to muster their Majesties People..and to levie a nombre of them for the Service of their Majesties. **1560** DAUS tr. *Sleidane's Comm.* 137b, This man would have also footemen ready monstered. **1593** SHAKS. *3 Hen. VI*, II. i. 112, I then in London,.. Muster'd my Soldiers. **1613** R. C. *Table Alph.* (ed. 3), *Muster*, take view of men, in armour. **1647** N. BACON *Disc. Govt.* I. xxii. (1739) 40 They mustered their Arms once every year both in Towns and Hundreds. **1682** BUNYAN *Holy War* iii. 52 When the King had mustered his Forces (for it is he that mustereth the Host to the Battel), he gave [etc.]. **1799** *Med. Jrnl.* I. 93 On Sundays, when they were mustered by the commanding officer. **1865** W. G. PALGRAVE *Arabia* II. 275 Before long he had mustered and equipped about thirty frigates. **1879** FROUDE *Cæsar* xv. 241 All sides were mustering their forces in view of an impending fight. **1894** J. T. FOWLER *Adamnan* Introd. 61 The Clan Neill, mustered by Columba himself.

fig. **1700** BLACKMORE *Paraphr. Job* xv. 67 She'll draw her Troops of Terrors in array, Muster her Griefs, and horrid War display.

†**b.** *refl.*

1535 COVERDALE *Isa.* viii. 9 Mustre you and gather you, take youre councel together. **1568** GRAFTON *Chron.* II. 327 So that at the last they mustered themselues and they were aboue ten thousand men. **1594** T. B. *La Primaud. Fr. Acad.* II. *Seneca*, Those lewde and lasciuious bookes, which haue mustered themselues of late yeeres in Pauls Churchyard, as chosen souldiers ready to fight vnder the deuils banner. *c* **1642** TWYNE in *Wood's Life* (O.H.S.) I. 60 That afternoone they mustered themselves in the fields.

c. *intr.* for *refl.* Of an army, etc.: To come together for inspection, exercise, or preparation for service.

c **1450** LOVELICH *Grail* xlv. 150 Eche Man In his beste Aray, To-forn him they Mostred þere þat day. **1471** CAXTON *Recuyell* (Sommer) I. 143 Whan alle thassamble had mustryd and were gaderd to gyder. **1523** LD. BERNERS *Froiss.* I. ccliv. 154 They went & mostred before the bastide of Arde. **1530** PALSGR. 643/1, I muster, as men do that shall go to a felde. **1535** COVERDALE *1 Kings* xx. 27 The children of Israel mustured,..and wente to mete them, and pitched their tentes ouer against them. **1593** SHAKS. *Lucr.* 720 Besides his soules faire temple is defaced, To whose weake ruines muster troopes of cares. **1775** A. COOKE in Sparks *Corr. Amer. Rev.* (1853) I. 19 The country round were alarmed and mustering. **1849** MACAULAY *Hist. Eng.* ii. I. 186 At every conventicle they mustered in arms. **1874** GREEN *Short Hist.* iii. §7. 152 The royal army had already mustered in great force at the King's summons.

transf. and *fig.* **1593** SHAKS. *Lucr.* 442 Whose ranks of blew vains..mustring to the quiet Cabinet, Where their deare gouernesse and ladie lies, Do tell her shee is dreadfullie beset. **1611** MURE *Misc. Poems* i. 88 A field of fancies musterd in my mynd. **1689** H. PITMAN *Relat.* 23 When the young ones [*i.e.* turtle] are hatcht, they musters out of their Cells and marches into the Sea. **1700** BLACKMORE *Paraphr. Job* xxxvi. 158 Recruits of Vapours which arise, Drawn from the Sea to muster in the Skys.

†**d.** *trans.* To enlist, enroll. *Obs.*

1439 *Rolls of Parlt.* V. 32/2 And so have mustred and entred in of record the Kyngs Souldeours. **1587** GOLDING *De Mornay* xxx. (1592) 483 Because he yelded his soule vnto death, & did muster himself among the transgressers. **1611** SHAKS. *Cymb.* IV. iv. 10 Newnesse Of Clotens death (we being not knowne, not muster'd Among the Bands) may driue vs to a render Where we haue liu'd. **1748** SMOLLETT *Rod. Rand.* xxvii, I had been rated on the books, and mustered as surgeon's mate.

e. To call the roll of. Now chiefly *Naut.*

to muster in (U.S.): to muster (a watch) at the time of going on duty.

1670 EACHARD *Cont. Clergy* 48 He falls a fighting with his text,..then he musters all again, to see what word was lost, or lam'd in the skirmish. **1820** SCORESBY *Acc. Arctic Reg.* II. 199 When the crew have been mustered by the proper officer of the customs, and paid a month's wages in advance. **1835** SIR J. ROSS *Narr. 2nd Voy.* iv. 43 The ship's company was mustered. **1840** R. H. DANA *Bef. Mast* xxiii, The Carpenter sometimes mustered in the starboard watch. **1867** SMYTH *Sailor's Word-bk., Muster the watch*, a duty performed nightly at 8 p.m., and repeated when the watch is relieved up to 4 a.m.

†**f.** To take the census of. *Obs.*

1565 COOPER *Thesaurus, Censor*,..one that valueth or mustreth. **1636** BRATHWAIT *Rom. Emp.* 13 In the eigth yeere of his reigne hee mustred the City.

g. Of an army, etc.: To comprise, to number.

1837 W. IRVING *Capt. Bonneville* III. 6 The whole garrison mustered but six or eight men. **1851** HUSSEY *Papal Power* i. 2 Formed a Synod of their own, mustering about 80. **1907** *Athenæum* 18 May 597/2 Davout's corps..defeated a force comprising the choicest part of the Prussian army, and mustering nearly double its numbers.

h. *U.S. to muster in, to muster into (the) service*: to enroll as recruits. *to muster out (of service)*: to summon together in order to discharge from service; to discharge, pay off (soldiers).

1834 J. A. WAKEFIELD *Hist. War* 93 The place appointed for us to be discharged at (or mustered out of the service of the United States). **1862** *U.S. Statutes* XII. 339 No person under the age of eighteen shall be mustered into the United States service. **1864** SALA in *Daily Tel.* 25 Feb., Drunken or dishonest subalterns who have been 'mustered out'— *i.e.*, expelled the army for misconduct.

i. To produce for inspection.

1904 *19th Cent.* June 1033 The bluejacket may at any moment be called on to muster his kit.

3. a. To collect, bring together (persons or things); esp. to bring forward from one's own stores. Often in phrases (*I, he*, etc.) *can muster* (such or such a number or amount); *as many as* (*I*, etc.) *can muster.*

c **1586** C'TESS PEMBROKE *Ps.* LXXXI. i, Muster hither musicks joyes, Lute, and lyre, and tabretts noise. **1692** R. L'ESTRANGE *Fables* xxxiii. 32 A Daw that had a mind to be Sparkish, Trick'd himself up with all the Gay-Feathers he could Muster together. **1743** BULKELEY & CUMMINS *Voy. S. Seas* 16 All the Hands we could muster in both Watches, Officers included, were but twelve. **1748** *Anson's Voy.* II. ii. 135 All the..remnants of old sails that could be mustered. **1793** SMEATON *Edystone L.* §286, I melted down all the pewter plates and dishes that we could muster on board the buss. **1832** HT. MARTINEAU *Ireland* ii. 16 A respectable addition was made by them to the few shillings Sullivan had been able to muster. **1835** J. P. KENNEDY *Horse Shoe R.* ii, I mustered my horse and gun, and some decent clothes. **1838** THIRLWALL *Greece* II. 333 The Platæans could only muster 600. **1838** *Lett. fr. Madras* (1843) 172 We cannot muster many volumes yet. **1841** LYTTON *Nt. & Morn.* I. iv, With your wife's fortune, you muster 200*l* a-year. **1855** MACAULAY *Hist. Eng.* xii. III. 175 A procession of twenty coaches belonging to public functionaries was mustered.

b. *fig.* To summon, gather up (one's thoughts, courage, strength, etc.).

1588 SHAKS. *L.L.L.* v. ii. 85 Muster your Wits, stand in your owne defence. **1671** MILTON *Samson* 402 Mustring all her wiles. **1742** YOUNG *Nt. Th.* VIII. 1319 They scarce can swallow their ebullient spleen, Scarce muster patience to support the farce. **1814** SCOTT *Wav.* xv, Cantering his white pony down the avenue with all the speed it could muster. **1840** DICKENS *Barn. Rudge* xxv, At length you have mustered heart to visit the old place. **1849** C. BRONTE *Shirley* I. vi. 119 Mr. Moore's dark face mustered colour; his lips smiled [etc.]. **1863** W. C. BALDWIN *Afr. Hunting* vii. 289, I re-mounted, mustered a canter, by dint of great persuasion. **1876** TREVELYAN *Macaulay* II. xv. 478 He mustered strength to dictate a letter.

4. *intr.* To assemble, gather together in a body. (Cf. 2c *transf.* and *fig.*)

1603 SHAKS. *Meas. for M.* II. iv. 20 Oh, heauens Why doe's my bloud thus muster to my heart. **1687** A. LOVELL tr. *Thevenot's Trav.* I. 57 They burn Incense about him, which they say scares away Evil Spirits and Devils, who otherwise would muster about the [dead] Body. **1820** SCOTT *Abbot* iii, I think he comes of gentle blood—see how it musters in his face at your injurious reproof. **1869** LOWELL *Gold Egg* xxv, What marvels manifold, Seemed silently to muster! **1886** C. E. PASCOE *London of To-day* xviii. (ed. 3) 159 The members of the Four-in-Hand and Coaching clubs muster in great force.

†**5.** *trans.* To pass in review, to 'take stock of'.

a **1625** FLETCHER & MASS. *Cust. Country* v. v, With what a greedy hawkes eye she beholds me? Marke how she musters all my parts.

6. *Austral.* and *N.Z.* To collect stock (cattle, sheep, etc.) together for counting, shearing, drafting, branding, etc. Also with *off* and *up*, and with place as obj.

1846 C. J. PHARAZYN *Jrnl.* 23 June 45 (MS.), Assisted in mustering Ewes and Lambs into Stock-Yard. **1852** J. R. CLOUGH *Diary* 4 May in J. Deans *Pioneers of Canterbury* (1937) 292 Port Philip men just arrived..and two of the survey men mustered the cattle this day. **1858** MCCOMBIE *Hist. Victoria* vii. 89 Takere..had attacked Mr. Bolden when mustering his stock. **1860** *St. Leonard's Jrnl.* 31 July, To muster stragglers off Isolated Hill. **1867** LADY BARKER *Station Life in N.Z.* (1870) xvi. 122 It is very difficult to 'muster' these ranges. **1875** WOOD & LAPHAM *Waiting for Mail* 29 Mustering cattle. **1878** E. S. ELWELL *Boy Colonists* 208 They all started from the hut to muster off 'Nob' mountain. **1930** L. G. D. ACLAND *Early Canterbury Runs* vii. 164 The country had never been stocked... [They] had once mustered it..and got about 300 wild sheep off it. **1934** A. RUSSELL *Tramp-Royal in Wild Australia* xxiii. 210 Here we loosed the herd and went east to muster up another section of the run. **1946** F. D. DAVISON *Dusty* vi. 65 There were a lot of sheep to be done, to be mustered from the paddock and brought to yard and shears. **1947** P. NEWTON *Wayleggo* (1949) 12 The musterer's job is to muster the sheep off such country into the respective homesteads. **1950** *N.Z. Jrnl. Agric.* Oct. 349/3 While the hill wethers are being shorn the ewes and lambs are being mustered on the various blocks and are brought in.

absol. **1874** A. BATHGATE *Colonial Experiences* vii. 80 A shepherd, while out mustering, descried the errant steed on a small plateau. **1878** E. S. ELWELL *Boy Colonists* 173 Walker's men never mustered beyond the 'Saddle'. **1892** HORNUNG *Under Two Skies* 41 All hands were away mustering in a distant paddock. **1944** F. CLUNE *Red Heart* 18, I found Bob Buck out mustering.

7. *intr.* To pass muster *for.*

1820 LAMB *Elia* Ser. I. *Oxford in Vac.*, I longed to coat him in russia, and assign him his place. He might have mustered for a tall Scapula.

8. muster up. a. To assemble or bring together (troops) for battle, etc.

c **1592** MARLOWE *Massacre Paris* II. iii. B 7, Ile muster vp an army secretly. **1593** SHAKS. *3 Hen. VI*, IV. viii. 18 In Oxfordshire shalt muster vp thy friends. **1621** BURTON *Anat. Mel.* III. ii. II. i. (1651) 450 They press and muster up wenches as we do soldiers. **1700** S. L. tr. *Fryke's Voy. E. Ind.* 305 We were muster'd up, and received the next day two months Pay. **1790** BEATSON *Nav. & Mil. Mem.* I. 185 Mr Hodge..mustered up about three hundred volunteers. **1891** C. ROBERTS *Adrift Amer.* 190 The few Indians.. returned..with all of the tribe that they could muster up.

b. *fig.* To summon up, gather up, to marshal.

1628 PRYNNE *Cens. Cozens* 10 Which I shall enumerate and muster vp in order. **1662** *Bk. Com. Prayer* Pref., The old Objections mustered up. **1743** R. BLAIR *Grave* 79 Whilst busy-meddling Memory..musters up The past Endearments of their softer Hours. **1777** PRIESTLEY *Matt. & Spir.* (1782) I. xvi. 188 Dʳ Oswald..has mustered up all his logic to invalidate it. **1813** SCOTT *Let.* 6 Nov., A very large river..is at this moment mustering up all its waters with a voice like distant thunder. **1893** SELOUS *Trav. S.E. Africa* 111 She had mustered up courage to speak to him.

muster, *v.*[2] *dial.* ? *Obs.* [Of Scandinavian origin: cf. Norw. *mustra* to whisper, mumble, to chatter continually (Ross), Icel. *muskra* to murmur, maunder (Vigf.).] (See quots.) Hence **'mustering** *vbl. sb.* Also † **'musterer**[1].

c **1440** *Promp. Parv.* 349/2 Must(e)ryn, or qwysp(e)ryn privyly (or rummuelon, *infra*; *H.* whyspryn), *mussito.* *Ibid.* 436/2 Romelynge, or privy mysteryngе (*P.* preuy mustringe), *ruminacio, mussitacio.* **1496** *Dives & Paup.* (W. de W.) v. iv. 199/2 What is susurro that is called a musterer. It is a preuy rowner, that pryuely telleth false tales amonges the people for to make dyscencyon. **1825** JAMIESON, *Muster*, to talk with exceeding volubility. Clydes. **1847** HALLIWELL, *Mustir*, to talk together privately.

'muster-book. A book in which military forces are registered. Also, on a man-of-war, a book containing the names of the crew.

1587 GOLDING *De Mornay* (1592) 99 The beginning thereof is nothing els but a Musterbooke of names. **1597** SHAKS. *2 Hen. IV*, III. ii. 146 Wee haue a number of shadowes to fill vppe the Muster-Booke. **1643** DAVENANT *Unfort. Lovers* III. i, All that I read is in the Muster-book. **1702** *Roy. Declar.* 1 June in *Lond. Gaz.* No. 3815/3 [They] are..Required..to cause the said List to be Examined, by the Muster-Book of such Man of War. **1867** SMYTH *Sailor's Word-bk., Muster-book*, a copy of a ship of war's open list, drawn up for the use of the clerk of the check, in calling over the crew.

fig. **1561** DAUS tr. *Bullinger on Apoc.* (1573) 296 All the Saintes, which before the commyng of Christ are written in the registers of the heauenly muster booke.

musterd(e, obs. forms of MUSTARD *sb.*

† **musterdevillers.** *Obs.* Forms: 5 **mostyrdewyk** (?), **mister-, mustrevilers, mowster devylers, must deviles, musterler** (?), **musterdelyre, musterdevyle, musturdevylers, musterdevylers, -illers, -elers, -il(l)es, -yles, -yllys, -ilous, muster dewyllers, mustardevillys, mostar de velis, mustarddybiles, mustardvillars, mustardavelles, mustyrddevyllers, moster develers, 5–6 musterdevilers, 6 mustredevyles, musterdevilys, muster de villois.** See also MUSTER *sb.*[2] [From the name of the town now called Montivilliers, in Normandy.

The name (in med.L. *Monasterium Villare*) appears in 1550 as *Musterdevillers* (Coke *Deb. betw. Heralds* §108); 15th c. forms are *Moustervillers* (in *Paston Lett.* I. p. lxxix), *Mustirvilers* (ibid. p. 8).]

A kind of mixed grey woollen cloth, much used in the fourteenth and fifteenth centuries.

1400 in *Cely Papers* (1900) 56, I have a gowyn clothe of mostyrdewyk of my lordes leveray for you. **1428** in Rymer *Foedera* (1710) X. 391 Duas Pecias de Russeto Mustrevilers. **1467** *Will of Bate* (Somerset Ho.), Of colour of musterdevillers. **1494** *Will Maude Parterich* (25 Feb.) P.C.C., 23 Vox, My Musterler gowne coler and cuffis lyned with velwett. **1523** *Test. Ebor.* (Surtees) V. 171 My musterdevilys gowne furride with shankkes. **1564** *Burgh Rec. Edin.* (1875) III. 187 Thai nor nane of thame..sall lit ony maner of cullouris of muster de villois.

mustered ('mʌstəd), *ppl. a.* [f. MUSTER *v.*[1] + -ED[1].] Gathered together; collected; assembled.

1638 G. SANDYS *Paraphr. Job* (1648) 54 Know'st thou how God collects the Must'red Clouds, How in their darknesse hee his lightning shrouds? **1697** DRYDEN *Virg. Georg.* IV. 626 Himself their Herdsman, on the middle Mount, Takes of his muster'd Flocks a just Account.

musterer[1]: see MUSTER *v.*[2]

musterer^2 ('mʌstərə(r)). *Austral.* and *N.Z.* [f. MUSTER *v.*^{1} (sense 6) + -ER^1.] One who musters sheep or cattle.

1863 E. C. CHUDLEIGH *Diary* 19 Dec. in Richards *Diary of E. R. Chudleigh* (1950) 114 All the musterers dogs have come home. **1872** LADY BARKER in D. M. Davin *N.Z. Short Stories* (1953) 20 Of course Christmas Day would be a complete holiday, and we had invited shearers and musterers, and all the odd hands which flock to a station at shearing-time, to come up to our house. **1892** W. E. SWANTON *Notes on N.Z.* ii. 97 To accomplish this [muster], ..on large 'runs' additional hands called 'musterers' have to be engaged. **1947** [see MUSTER *v.*^{1} 6]. **1961** B. CRUMP *Hang on Minute Mate* 73 I'm short of a couple of musterers, if you're interested. Done any sheep work before? **1970** *Telegraph* (Brisbane) 4 July 2/1 Lawrence Ryan..worked as a musterer on a South Queensland cattle station 20 years ago.

mustering ('mʌstərɪŋ), *vbl. sb.* [f. MUSTER *v.*^{1} + -ING^1.] **a.** The action of the vb. MUSTER in various senses; an instance of this.

c **1440** LYDG. *Hors, Shepe & G.* 66 Withouten hors what were here mustrynges? *c* **1440** *Promp. Parv.* 349/2 Musterynge, or gaderynge togeder of men to be schewyde, ..*coadunacio*. **1560** DAUS tr. *Sleidane's Comm.* 246 They commaund Scherteline..to invade the enemies that wer in mustering underneth the Alpes. **1601** B. JONSON *Poetaster* v. iii, Hee's one that hath had the mustring or conuoy of a companie. **1769** FALCONER *Dict. Marine* (1780), *Mustering*, the act of calling over a list of the whole ship's company, or any..detachment thereof, who are..summoned to answer by their names on the occasion. **1835** W. IRVING *Tour Prairies* xxvi. 231 A general mustering of our horses took place. **1860** G. DUPPA *Station Diary* Oct. in S. S. Crawford *Sheep & Sheepmen of Canterbury* (1949) v. 47 To collect stragglers for a second mustering. **1874** A. BATHGATE *Colonial Experiences* xv. 206 Life on a sheep-station is rather a dull one. There are periodical 'musterings' and other duties to be attended to. **1878** E. S. ELWELL *Boy Colonists* 172 The mode of mustering adopted by Ernest was this. **1888** *Sat. Rev.* 8 Dec. 668 He knew..what the heavy mustering on the Opposition benches meant. **1911** C. E. W. BEAN *'Dreadnought' of Darling* xviii. 172 There was the operation of mustering going on as clear and plain as if the hillside were a mile distant. **1968** K. WEATHERLY *Roo Shooter* 95 Tales told in a bush pub; tales of droving, mustering.

b. *attrib.*

1736 AINSWORTH *Lat. Dict.*, A mustering place, *diribitorium*. **1745** J. HEMPSTEAD *Diary* 6 May (1901) 442 The 1st & 2d Company are viewing Arms &c. Mustering Day through the Colony. **1817** CHALMERS *Astron. Disc.* vi. (1852) 138 On some field of mustering competition, have monarchs met. **1841** *Southern Lit. Messenger* VII. 768/1 Who should I see..but Mr. Jim Guest himself, in..mustering jacket and trowsers, and tarpaulin hat. **1878** E. S. ELWELL *Boy Colonists* 169 In mustering times Ernest used to set some of the huge boulders on the sides of its cliffs rolling. **1899** *Scribner's Mag.* XXV. 7/1 The mustering-places for the regiment were appointed in New Mexico. **1930** L. G. D. ACLAND *Early Canterbury Runs* vi. 138 More stories were told of him in shearers' huts and mustering camps than of any other runholder. **1953** O. E. MIDDLETON in C. K. Stead *N.Z. Short Stories* (1966) 186 See him coming in from the back country at mustering-time.

mustering ('mʌstərɪŋ), *ppl. a.* [f. MUSTER *v.*^{1} + -ING^2.] That musters, in senses of the vb.

1594 GREENE & LODGE *Looking-Gl.* (1598) A 4, Like the mustering breath of Æolus That ouerturnes the pines of Libanon. **1758** J. BLAKE *Plan Mar. Syst.* 24 Let each be signed by the aforesaid mustering-officer. **1874** SYMONDS *Sk. Italy & Greece* (1898) I. xi. 211 Mustering storm-clouds blue with rain. **1897** P. WARUNG *Tales Old Regime* 110 So that his attitude should not appear strange to the mustering officer.

musterler, (?) variant of MUSTERDEVILLERS.

'muster-master. Now only *Hist.*

1. An officer who was responsible for the accuracy of the muster-roll of some portion of an army. Also, in dockyards (see quot. 1815); formerly, in penal settlements, the official charged with keeping the muster-roll of convicts. ***muster-master general*** (also ***chief muster-master***): see quot. 1802.

1579 DIGGES *Stratiot.* 102 He may admonish the Muster Mayster and Treasurer. **1598** BARRET *Theor. Warres* II. i. 24 We haue Muster-masters appointed in euerie Shiere. **1622** F. MARKHAM *Bk. War* IV. i. 122 Muster-Masters..are very odious vnto Captaines; for in seruing of his Prince truly, and in mustering strickly he wipeth much vndue profit from the Captaine. **1662** STILLINGFL. *Orig. Sacr.* III. ii. §11 As though he had been Muster-Master-Generall at that great Rendes-vous. **1666** MARVELL *Corr.* Wks. (Grosart) II. 190 That all muster-masters lose their places, who shall muster any that have not taken the oaths and the sacrament. **1667** PEPYS *Diary* 18 Jan., A letter from the Duke of York commanding our payment of no wages to any of the muster-masters of the fleet. **1702** *Lond. Gaz.* No. 3825/3 Her Majesty has been pleased to constitute the Rt. Hon. the Lord Walden Commissary-General of the Musters, and chief Muster-master of Her Majesty's Forces. **1707** *Ibid.* No. 4310/2 Her Majesty has been..pleased..to ..appoint Michael Hyde Esq; Commissary and Mustermaster-General of all the Forces. **1775** *Mass. Prov. Congr.* 6 May (1823) 199 Muster masters in the Massachusetts army, whose business it shall be to pass muster on every soldier that shall be enlisted into said army. **1802** C. JAMES *Milit. Dict.*, *Muster-master-general*, *Commissary-general* of the Musters, one who takes account of every regiment, their number, horses, arms, &c. **1815** *Falconer's Dict. Marine* (ed. Burney), *Muster-master*, in royal dock-yards a person appointed by the Navy Board to call over the lists of all his Majesty's ship's companies in the different ports; as also the artificers working on board, in order to prevent false musters. **1896** *Peterson's Mag.* (U.S.) VI. 288/1 Washington directed Colonel James Glover and Muster-Master-General Moyland to co-operate with the Board of Admiralty.

fig. **1600** W. WATSON *Decacordon* (1602) 287 Their ringleader, and muster-master father Parsons. **1662** STILLINGFL. *Orig. Sacr.* III. ii. 449 Lucretius gives us in so exact an account of the several courses the Atoms took up in disposing themselves into bodyes, as though he had been Muster-Master-General at that great Rendes-vous.

¶**2.** Used incorrectly for 'drill-sergeant'.

1711 STEELE *Spect.* No. 134 ¶4 A new sort of Muster-master, who teaches Ladies the whole Exercise of the Fan.

Hence **'mustermastership**.

1664–5 PEPYS *Diary* 12 Mar., We talked also of getting W. Howe to be put into the Muster-Mastershipp in the roome of Creed. **1763** H. WALPOLE *Let. to Earl of Hertford* 2 Dec., Mr. Calcraft being turned out yesterday, from some muster-mastership.

'muster-roll.

1. An official list of the officers and men **a.** in an army or some particular division of it; **b.** in a ship's company.

a. 1640 in Rushw. *Hist. Coll.* III. (1692) I. 143 They are likewise to present unto the House some fit way for a perfect Muster-Roll to be made of the King's Army. **1673** *Articles & Rules for better Govt. of H.M. Forces* xli, No Man shall presume to present himself to the Muster, to be Inrolled in the Muster-Rolls, by a counterfeit or wrong Name. **1712** STEELE *Spect.* No. 444 ¶4 He shews the Muster-Roll, which confirms that he was in his Imperial Majesty's Troops. **1781** GIBBON *Decl. & F.* xvii. II. 47 Inscribed on the muster-roll of their numerous armies. **1844** THIRLWALL *Greece* lxiv. VIII. 308 He was obliged to fill up the muster-rolls with boys of sixteen. **1853** STOCQUELER *Milit. Encycl.* s.v., The muster-rolls are called over on the 24th of each month, when every individual answers to his name. **1888** PLUMPTRE *Ken* I. 162 It was believed..that pay was drawn for the troops on the strength of false muster rolls.

b. 1809 *St. Papers* in *Ann. Reg.* 757/2 If such a vessel is not provided with a muster-roll of the crew. **1867** SMYTH *Sailor's Word-bk.*, *Muster-roll*, a document kept by the master of every British vessel, specifying the name, age, quality, and country of every person of the ship's company.

2. *transf.* and *fig.*

1605 BACON *Adv. Learn.* II. xvi. §7 It may bee thought I seeke to make a great Muster-Rowle of Sciences. **1737** POPE *Hor. Epist.* II. i. 124 Tho' but, perhaps, a muster-roll of Names. **1858** BRIGHT *Sp., Reform* 21 Dec. (1876) 305 One of the brightest names in the muster-roll of English worthies. **1875** MCLAREN *Serm.* Ser. II. viii. 147 The muster-roll of heroes of faith in the Epistle to the Hebrews.

3. *Naut.* The reading of the muster-roll; roll-call.

1833 MARRYAT *P. Simple* xx, Having waited the usual hour before the governor's house, to answer to our muster-roll, and to be stared at, we were dismissed. **1869** W. S. GILBERT *Bab Ball., Nancy Bell* 36 And only ten of the *Nancy's* men Said 'Here!' to the muster roll.

†**muster-yong.** *Obs.* [? a. G. **musterjunge*, f. *muster* MUSTER *sb.*^{1} + *junge* boy.] ? A boy fraudulently entered on a muster-roll.

1635 BARRIFFE *Milit. Discipl.* cxx. (1643) 415 Besides all Officers, Muster-yongs and Pasvolants.

mustesa, -ezo, obs. forms of MESTIZO.

musth, variant of MUST *a.*^{3}

musticat, mustice, obs. ff. MUSCAT, MESTIZO.

mustify ('mʌstɪfaɪ), *v. slang.* [f. MUSTY *a.*^{2} + -FY.] *trans.* To make musty or mouldy.

1847 MRS. GORE *Castles in Air* xxi. II. 201 Should I, in my own country, have dreamed of mustifying myself by a humdrum dinner in..Bloomsbury Square?

mustily ('mʌstɪlɪ), *adv. rare.* [f. MUSTY *a.*^{2} + -LY^2.]

a. In a musty or mouldy manner. †**b.** Dully; ill-humouredly. *Obs.*

a **1620** FLETCHER & MASS. *False One* III. ii, These Cloaths smell mustily. **1620** MIDDLETON *World tost at Tennis* Induct., I meane, why so melancholy, thou lookst, mustily, me thinkes. *Rich.* Doe I so? and yet I dwell in sweeter ayre Then you. **1675** COTTON *Burlesque upon B.* 102 Apollo, what's the matter, pray, You look so mustily to day. **1755** JOHNSON, *Mustily*,..Mouldily.

mustiness ('mʌstɪnɪs). [f. MUSTY *a.*^{2} + -NESS.]

1. The state, condition or quality of being musty; 'mould; damp foulness' (J.).

1526–30 in Grose *Antiq. Rep.* (1808) II. 205 The said page to make fires for the eyres and mustenes of the said chambers. **1664** EVELYN *Kal. Hort., Oct.* (1679) 26 Keeping them [seeds] dry, and free from mustiness. **1888** MRS. H. WARD *R. Elsmere* vii, The peculiar clean mustiness of the room only just opened for the summer season.

fig. **1894** *Nation* (N.Y.) 19 July 47/1 The same impression of mystery, of vagueness, of mediaeval mustiness and superstition is made by these dramas as by the others.

†**2.** Crossness; ill-humour. *Obs. rare.*

a **1619** FLETCHER *Bonduca* I. ii, Any mirth, and any way, of any subject, Junius, is better then unmanly mustinesse. **1734** MRS. E. MONTAGU *Lett.* (1809) I. 14 That he might have put it in his book of drawings among the faces that express the several passions; but he has none that express mustiness.

mustir, mustizo, obs. ff. MUSTER, MESTIZO.

†**mustle**, *v. Obs. rare*$^{-0}$. [Cf. MUSTER *v.*^{2}; also RUSTLE *v.*] *intr.* To murmur, make a noise.

1570 LEVINS *Manip.* 194/12 To Mustle, *strepere*.

mustle, obs. form of MUSCLE *sb.*

mustour(e, mustre, obs. forms of MUSTER.

mustredevyles, variant of MUSTERDEVILLERS.

mustrol, variant of MUSROL.

mustrump, mustul: see MUSHROOM, MUSSEL.

†**'mustulent**, *a. Obs. rare.* [a. L. *mustulent-us*, f. *mustum* MUST *sb.*^{1}: see -ULENT.] Abounding in must; resembling must; also *jocularly*, 'vinous'.

1592 R. D. *Hypnerotomachia* 3 In mustulent Autume. **1611** COTGR. s.v. *Visage*, *Visage de pressurier*, a mustulent, or maumsie face. **1656** BLOUNT *Glossogr.*, *Mustulent*, sweet as Must; also fresh, new, green.

musture, obs. form of MUSTER.

†**'musty**, *a.*^{1} ? *Obs. rare.* [f. MUST *sb.*^{1} + -Y.] Of, pertaining to, or made with must or new wine; in a state of must or newness.

c **1420** *Pallad. on Husb.* XI. 525 Now..vse this ferment ffor musty breed whom this wol condiment. **1599** MINSHEU *Span. Dict.*, *Mostóso*, mustie, of sweet wine. **1802** BEDDOES *Hygëia* VIII. 32 New musty liquors remain at least equally strong for a time.

musty ('mʌstɪ), *a.*^{2} (and *sb.*) [Of obscure origin. Prob. in some way related to MOISTY, MOIST adjs., the *oi* of which represents OF. *u.*]

1. 'Mouldy; spoiled with damp; moist and fetid' (J.).

1530 PALSGR. 730/1 Sprede your corne abrode, it wyll vaxe musty els. **1532** MORE *Confut. Tindale* Wks. 649/2 When his wordes be wel sifted, men shall find little fine flowre in them, but all very mustie branne. **1604** T. M. *Black Bk.* in *Middleton's Wks.* (Bullen) VIII. 28 Away I scudded in the musty moth-eaten habit. **1605** SHAKS. *Lear* IV. vii. 40 And was't thou faine..To houell thee with Swine and Rogues forlorne, In short, and musty straw? **1653** WALTON *Angler* xiv. 199 Have your worms well scowred, and not kept in sowre or mustie moss. **1693–4** GIBSON in *Lett. Lit. Men* (Camden) 216 Old musty papers are but ill company for neat cloaths and white hands. **1707** MORTIMER *Husb.* 108 The Buyers are usually furnished with musty bad Corn from Foreign Parts. **1865** DICKENS *Mut. Fr.* III. xi, An early public-house, haunted by unsavoury smells of musty hay. **1874** BURNAND *My time* xiv. 120 She walked into the study amongst the old musty books. **1897** *Allbutt's Syst. Med.* II. 792 The damage done by the use of musty grain as food falls upon the nervous system.

b. Of food, liquors, etc.: Having a mouldy or decayed smell or taste. Of a cask, bottle, etc.: Stale-smelling, fusty.

1530 PALSGR. 319/1 Mustye as a vessel is or wyne or any other vitayle, *moysy*. **1577** *Patent Roll 19 Eliz.* IX, Corrupte and mustie butter. **1599** B. JONSON *Ev. Man out of Hum.* I. ii, He looks like a mustie bottle. **1599** SHAKS. *Much Ado* I. i. 50 You had musty victuall. **1681** NEVILE *Plato Rediv.* 233 If you have a musty Vessel, and by consequence dislike the Beer which comes out of it. **1732** POPE *Hor. Sat.* II. ii. 67 Nor lets, like Naevius, every error pass, The musty wine, foul cloth, or greasy glass. **1738** SWIFT *Pol. Conversat.* 141 This Venison is musty. **1799** G. SMITH *Laboratory* I. 433 To correct a musty Taste in Wine. **1802** *Med. Jrnl.* VIII. 479 In cleansing musty casks. **1891** *Daily News* 5 Mar. 7/2 The puddings were occasionally made with sour milk and musty eggs. *Ibid.*, A custard..which was sloppy and musty.

c. Of rooms, atmosphere, etc.: Having the unpleasant faint odour suggestive of mouldiness or decay.

1577 HARRISON *England* II. vi. (1877) I. 156 Beare with me ..that lead thee..into a mustie malthouse. **1599** SHAKS. *Much Ado* I. iii. 61 Being entertain'd for a perfumer, as I was smoaking a musty roome, comes me the Prince and Claudio. **1683** TRYON *Way to Health* 592 Do not all Houses and Places grow musty..if the Air be any way prevented by Window-shutters..that it cannot have its free egress and regress? **1797** GODWIN *Enquirer* II. iv. 208 The very air.. feels musty.

2. *fig.* **a.** Of immaterial things, ideas, etc.: 'Stale; spoiled with age' (J.); that has lost its newness or interest; antiquated, disused, old-fashioned.

1592 NASHE *P. Penilesse* (ed. 2) 14, I know many wise Gentlemen of this musty vocation [Antiquaries]. **1602** SHAKS. *Ham.* III. ii. 359 But while the grasse growes, the Prouerbe is something musty. **1683** BURNET tr. *More's Utopia* (1685) 38 Some old musty laws. **1763–5** CHURCHILL *Journey* Poems 1769 II. 7 Read musty lectures on Benevolence. **1806–7** J. BERESFORD *Miseries Hum. Life* (1826) II. xxxix, Your newspapers delayed..till..all their intelligence is musty. **1900** H. SUTCLIFFE *Shameless Wayne* xxv, Each buried legend of his house, each musty tale of wrongs suffered and repaid came back to mind.

b. Of persons: 'Dull; heavy; wanting activity; wanting practice in the occurrences of life' (J.); antiquated, 'mouldy'.

1637 SANDERSON *Serm.* (1681) II. 81 They settle upon their own dregs, and grow muddy and musty with long ease. **1665** BRATHWAIT *Comment Two Tales* (Chaucer Soc.) 48 How is it, you old musty Dotard, that with a sorrow you hide the keys of your Chests from me? **1712** ADDISON *Spect.* No. 482 ¶2 Being married to a Bookish Man, who has no Knowledge of the World, she is forced..to spirit him up now and then, that he may not grow musty, and unfit for Conversation. **1745** FIELDING *True Patriot* Wks. 1775 IX. 298 None but a musty moralist..would have condemned such behaviour. *a* **1763** BYROM *Poetaster* 24 Then he..of old musty Bards mumbles over the Names. **1824** W. IRVING *T. Trav.* II. viii. 86 A little rusty, musty old fellow, always griping among ruins. **1883** *Gd. Words* 183 The doctors say we get musty and fusty if we stay in one place.

†3. Ill-humoured, peevish, sullen. *Obs.* exc. *dial.*

1620 SHELTON *Quix.* II. xlviii. 313 The ill-wounded Don Quixote was exceeding musty and melancholy, with his Face bound vp and scarred. **1622** FLETCHER *Span. Curate* IV. iii, He is monstrous vexed and musty at my chessplay. **1672** SHADWELL *Miser* I. Wks. 1720 III. 9 What a Devil makes thee in so musty a humour? *c* **1728** EARL OF AILESBURY *Mem.* (1890) 691 He was very musty because I would not catch at the bait and be his bubble. **1760** FOOTE *Minor* II. (1767) 45 Here comes the musty trader, running over with remonstrances. I must banter the cit.

4. *Comb.*, as ***musty-fusty, -smelling, walled*** adjs.

1857 W. COLLINS *Dead Secret* IV. iv, In that old part of the house it is what you call *musty-fusty. **1897** MRS. E. L. VOYNICH *Gadfly* (1904) 22/1 Corridors, and stairs, all more or less *musty-smelling. **1751** *Female Foundling* II. 135 An old, *musty walled Chapel.

†B. *sb.* A kind of snuff having a musty flavour.

1709 STEELE *Tatler* No. 27 ¶11 I'll call at Charles's, and know the Shape of his Snuff-Box... I ought to be informed, whether he takes Spanish or Musty. *Ibid.* No. 79 ¶3, I made her resign her snuff-box for ever, and half drown herself with washing away the stench of the musty.

musty (ˈmʌstɪ), *a.*[3] *rare.* [f. MUST *sb.*[5] or *a.*[3] + -Y.] = MUST *a.*[3]

1868 *Morn. Star* 6 Jan., The twentieth [elephant] was so vicious and 'musty'. **1882** FLOYER *Unexpl. Baluchistan* 57 The two 'musty' camels.

†ˈ**musty**, *v. Obs.* [f. MUSTY *a.*[2]]

1. *intr.* To become musty. *lit.* and *fig.*

1631 GOUGE *God's Arrows* II. §22. 160 Corne.. being so heaped together.. mustieth, putrifieth, and is made unfit for use. **1633** SHIRLEY *Gamester* II. ii, But I may lose it ere I go to bed. Dost think 't shall musty? What's a hundred pound? **1702** T. BROWN *Lett. Dead to Living* (1707) II. 68 You.. keep your Reputation musty'ng upon an old Foundation, which is ready to sink.

2. *trans.* To render or make musty or mouldy.

1707 MORTIMER *Husb.* (1721) I. 61 It [the wheat] was mustied and spoiled with lying so long in the Ground.

musty: see MUSTEE.

mustyr(re: see MUSTER *v.*

mustyrddevyllers, obs. f. MUSTERDEVILLERS.

musuk, musulman: see MUSSUCK, MUSSULMAN.

musume(e, -më, -mé, variant forms of MOUSMEE.

musure, musycke, obs. ff. MUSER[2], MOSAIC.

musycyen, -yssyon, obs. forms of MUSICIAN.

mut, obs. form of MOOT *v.*[1], MOTE *v.*[1], MUTE *sb.*

mut, var. MUTT.

‖**muta** (ˈmjuːtə). [It. *muta* imp. = change.] In *Music*, a direction to the player (see quots.).

1876 STAINER & BARRETT *Dict. Musical Terms* 298/2 *Muta*, a direction to a player on a horn, trumpet, etc., or on drums, to change the *key* of his instrument. **1880** GROVE *Dict. Mus.* II. 439/1 A word often seen attached to Horn parts—'muta in E♭', 'muta in B', etc., meaning simply 'change to E♭ or B♭', etc. **1938** *Oxf. Compan. Music* 602/2 *Muta D in C* means 'change tuning from D to C'. **1959** *Collins' Music Encycl.* 446/1 *Muta*,.. a direction to the performer found in parts for wind instruments and timpani, indicating either a change of instrument,.. or a change of crook,.. or a change of tuning.

muta, var. MOOTAH, MOOTER.

†**muˈtabilate**, *v. Obs. rare*$^{-1}$. [f. L. *mūtābil-is* MUTABLE *a.* + -ATE.] *trans.* To change.

?**1685** T. BROWN *Adv. Oates* Wks. 1730 IV. 245 It is a Folly.. to.. yield to Melancholly; for 'twill mutabilate poor Nature's Light, And turn it's Day into a gloomy Night.

mutability (mjuːtəˈbɪlɪtɪ). [a. F. *mutabilité*, ad. L. *mūtābilitās*: see next and -ITY.]

1. Disposition to change, variableness, inconstancy.

c **1374** CHAUCER *Troylus* I. 851 Now sith hire whiel by no way may soiorne, what wastow if hire mutabilite Ryght as þi seluen list wol don by the. **1412–20** LYDG. *Troy Bk.* I. v. (1513) C j b, They saye that chaunge and mutabylyte Apropred ben to femynyte. *a* **1548** HALL *Chron., Edw. IV* 191 The Duke of Somerset, was incontinently, for his greate mutabilitie and lightnes, behedded at Exam. **1662** STILLINGFL. *Orig. Sacr.* II. vii. §1 It would argue mutability in God to revoke that Law, and establish another instead of it. **1711** ADDISON *Spect.* No. 162 ¶6 This Mutability of Temper and Inconsistency with our selves is the greatest Weakness of human Nature, so [etc.]. **1838** THIRLWALL *Greece* III. xviii. 77 He had himself experienced the mutability of the public taste. **1883** LINDA VILLARI *Machiavelli & Times* II. i. III. 242 Of his easy mutability we find proofs in two of the various *Discorsi* written by him [*sc.* Guicciardini].

2. a. Liability to change.

1432–50 tr. *Higden* (Rolls) III. 223 For truly the firste trawthe whiche is God may not be where mutabilite is founde. **1570–6** LAMBARDE *Peramb. Kent* (1826) 433 That heavenly kingdome, which is not subject to mutabilitie or chaunge. **1594** HOOKER *Eccl. Pol.* I. ii. §6 The law whereby he worketh is eternall, and therefore can haue no shew or cullor of mutabilitie. **1622** BP. HALL *Contempl., O.T.* XVI. iv, How slippery are the stations of earthly honors, and subject to continuall mutabilitie. **1791** COWPER *Yardley Oak* 70 What exhibitions various hath the world Witness'd of mutability in all That we account most durable below! **1860** TYNDALL *Glac.* II. xxvii. 389, I endeavoured to satisfy myself of the mutability which had been ascribed to them [*i.e.* the veins in glaciers].

b. An instance of this.

1549 *Compl. Scot.* i. 20 Prosperus men prouidis nocht to resist the occasions of the mutabiliteis. **1598** YONG *Diana* 67 What place is there so strong, where one may be safe from the mutabilities of time? **1648** CHAS. I *Declar.* 22 Nov. *Wks.* (1662) 293 It is the humour of those who are of this Weather-cock-like disposition to love nothing but mutabilities. **1711** SHAFTESB. *Misc. Refl.* II. iii. Charact. III. 95 We Islanders, fam'd for other Mutabilitys, are particularly noted for the Variableness.. of our Weather. **1873** SYMONDS *Grk. Poets* iii. 78 Simonides moralizes upon the mutabilities of life. **1888** PLUMPTRE *Ken* I. p. xi. *note*, One could scarcely find a more striking instance of the mutabilities of history.

3. *Biol.* The tendency to undergo, or capacity for undergoing, mutation.

1908 J. A. THOMSON *Heredity* iii. 92 It is possible that the prolific multiplication in a new environment may have had something to do with the awakening of the impulsive mutability [in *Œnothera lamarckiana*]. **1916** *Genetics* I. 606 (*heading*) Mutability in different species of Drosophila. **1929** *Proc. Nat. Acad. Sci.* XV. 834 That gene.. does not influence the mutability of the miniature-gamma gene. **1958** *Nature* 11 Oct. 984/1 The sites in each segment have been plotted in order of decreasing mutability for each mutagen. **1974** *Ibid.* 9 Aug. 493/2 There was no significant difference in mutability between the two strains.

mutable (ˈmjuːtəb(ə)l), *a.* and *sb.* Also 5 muitable. [ad. L. *mūtābil-is* changeable, f. *mūtāre* to change: see -ABLE.] A. *adj.*

1. a. Liable or subject to change or alteration.

c **1374** CHAUCER *Boeth.* IV. pr. vi. 107 (Camb. MS.) The whiche destynal causes, whan they passen owt fro the bygynnynges of the vnmoeuable puruyaunce, it mot nedes be þat they ne be nat Mutable. **1456** in *Coventry Corpus Chr. Plays* 117 With-oute whom [i.e. Fortune], sithen non playnly can prosper, That in this muitable lyfe ar nowe procedyng, I am come thurgh love. **1515** BARCLAY *Egloges* IV. (1570) C vj b/2, Protheus.. Mutable of figure oft times in one houre. **1594** HOOKER *Eccl. Pol.* I. xv. §1 Although no lawes but positiue be mutable, yet all are not mutable which be positiue. **1646** SIR T. BROWNE *Pseud. Ep.* VI. vii. 306 There is no East and West in Nature; nor are those absolute and invariable, but respective and mutable points. **1709** STEELE *Tatler* No. 39 ¶15 The Use of Clothes continues, though the Fashion of them has been mutable. **1783** LATHAM *Gen. Synopsis Birds* II. I. 347 Mutable Flycatcher. *Muscicapa mutata.* **1824** MISS FERRIER *Inher.* xc, Her mutable countenance had now all the fixedness and paleness of marble. **1902** A. LANG *Hist. Scot.* II. xvi. 428 Like all other laws those of the Kirk proved to be mutable.

absol. **1847** EMERSON *Repr. Men, Montaigne* Wks. (Bohn) I. 352 Let a man learn to look for the permanent in the mutable and fleeting.

b. *Gram.* Subject to mutation.

1707 LHUYD *Archæol. Brit.* 300 The Consonants are divided into Mutable and Immutable. The Mutable are such as by the Addition of an h, or else by a full point (.) above them, either alter or lose their Pronunciation, as b, c [etc.]. **1837** G. PHILLIPS *Syriac Gram.* 28 Nouns of many syllables, the last of which is mutable, are exemplified in the following Table. **1843** W. NEILSON *Irish Gram.* 5 The sounds of the mutable consonants, when aspirated, differ materially from those which they receive, when simple.

2. Inconstant in mind, will, or disposition; fickle; variable. Now somewhat *rare.*

1412–20 LYDG. *Troy Bk.* I. v. (1513) C j b, Theyr hertes be so freell and vnstable Namely in youthe so meuynge and mutable That [etc.]. *a* **1548** HALL *Chron., Edw. IV* 191 b, Least the sight.. might.. also wyn the hartes of the mutable commonaltie. *Ibid., Rich. III* 48 The mutable mynde of quene Elyzabeth. **1625** K. LONG tr. *Barclay's Argenis* IV. vii. 260 They call Fortune whatsoever is doubtfull.. and for this cause they feigne her a mutable and blind Goddesse. **1795** SOUTHEY *Joan of Arc* III. 85 Paris with her servile sons, A headstrong, mutable, ferocious race, Bow'd to the invader's yoke. **1818** BYRON *Ch. Har.* IV. cvi, A child Most mutable in wishes but in mind A wit as various. **1860** MOTLEY *Netherl.* (1868) I. vii. 468 Ever variable and mutable as woman, Elizabeth was perplexing and baffling to her counsellors. **1871** DARWIN *Desc. Man* II. xix. 339 The most fertile imagination and the most mutable caprice have created the fashions of painting, as well as those of garments.

3. *Biol.* Capable of undergoing mutation; liable to undergo mutation frequently.

1905 F. E. CLEMENTS *Res. Methods in Ecol.* 319 *Mutable*, able to produce mutants. **1908** J. A. THOMSON *Heredity* iii. 91 There he [*sc.* de Vries] found his long-looked-for mutable plant, an evening primrose (*Œnothera lamarckiana*). **1928** *Genetics* XIII. 360 To designate a character showing frequent heritable changes, the terms 'mutable', or 'frequently mutating' will be used. **1941** *Nature* 22 Mar. 356/2 We have carried out an experiment with a mutable gene which produces coloured spots on the petals and stems of *Portulaca grandiflora*. **1972** *Molecular & General Genetics* CXIV. 144 (*heading*) The genetics of a new mutable allele at the *white* locus in *Drosophila melanogaster*.

B. *sb.*

1. *pl.* Things capable of change. *Obs. rare*$^{-1}$.

1652 GAULE *Magastrom.* 150 Having its inherance in movables or mutables.

2. A mutable consonant (see A. 1 b).

1821 O'REILLY *Irish Dict.* Introd. 2 The division of the consonants into mutables and immutables. **1843** W. NEILSON *Irish Gram* 4 [Letters] capable of aspiration, or mutables.

Hence ˈ**mutably** *adv.*, in a mutable manner; so as to be capable of change; also, with constant change or variation; ˈ**mutableness** (now *rare*), mutability.

1481 BOTONER *Tulle Old Age* (Caxton) b 3, The mutablenes & euyl dysposicion of men hit is so grete in oure dayes. **1582** BATMAN *Barth. De P.R.* v. vi. 39 If yᵉ eie be to much mouing it betokeneth.. mutablenesse of affection. **1646** E. F. *Marrow Mod. Divin.* (ed. 2) 13 Though he and his will were both good, yet were they mutably good. *a* **1677** MANTON *Serm. Ps. cxix* verse 123 (1681) 832 Every man is, or may be a liar, because of the mutableness of his Nature. **1703** J. BARRETT *Analecta* 32 How little valuable are all Worldly things, that are so unstable!.. their mutableness would take off so much as would leave them of little Value. **1755** in JOHNSON. **1796** KIRWAN *Elem. Min.* (ed. 2) I. 509. Rather greasy; often in some positions mutably resplendent.

mutage (ˈmjuːtɪdʒ). [a. F. *mutage*, f. *muter*: see MUTE *v.*[4]] The process of muting wine. Cf. MUTE *v.*[4]

1839 in URE *Dict. Arts.*

mutagen (ˈmjuːtədʒən). *Biol.* [f. MUTA(TION + -GEN.] An agent that causes mutation.

1946 *Proc. R. Soc. Edin.* B. LXII. 220 In unpublished experiments with chemical mutagens, a significant change in the rate of induced lethals was recorded. **1952** *New Biol.* XII. 86 Certain chemical substances, or penetrating radiation such as ultra-violet or X-rays, may increase the mutation rate considerably. Those agents, called 'mutagens', are at present being intensively studied. **1971** J. Z. YOUNG *Introd. Study Man* xxviii. 393 Another implication of the randomness of the effects of mutagens is that no amount of them is too small to be biologically irrelevant.

mutagenesis (mjuːtəˈdʒɛnəsɪs). *Biol.* [f. MUTA(TION + -GENESIS.] The production or origination of mutations.

1953 *Nature* 21 Nov. 964/1 (*heading*) Chemical mutagenesis in bacteriophage *T* 2. **1961** *Jrnl. Molecular Biol.* III. 121 (*heading*) The theory of mutagenesis. **1972** *Heredity* XXIX. 203 (*heading*) Gamma ray mutagenesis in a strain of *Escherichia coli* deficient in DNA polymerase I.

mutagenic (mjuːtəˈdʒɛnɪk). *Biol.* [f. MUTA(TION + -GENIC.] Causing or capable of causing mutation.

1946 *Proc. R. Soc. Edin.* B. LXII. 211 Muller's classical discovery in 1927 of the mutagenic action of X-rays has provided an extremely useful tool for studying the nature of gene mutation and chromosome breakage. **1952** *New Biol.* XII. 87 All known mutagenic agents also damage the cell. **1959** *New Scientist* 20 Aug. 219/1 Plant geneticists.. now combine mutagenic radiations and chemicals with the classic techniques of plant breeding to produce novel plants. **1971** *Nature* 1 Oct. 296/3 Dr Mary Lyon.. argued that the radiation from nuclear fall-out is likely to be less mutagenic than the medical use of X-rays. **1974** *Times* 11 Jan. 16/1 The 'mutagenic' effect of lead compounds.

Hence **mutageˈnicity**, the property of being mutagenic.

1956 *New Biol.* XX. 30 Different types of radiation were tested for mutagenicity. **1970** *Nature* 30 May 800/1 The concern felt by many scientists about the potential mutagenicity of the ever increasing number of synthetic chemicals in the environment. **1972** *Guardian* 15 Dec. 7/4 Evidence of mutagenicity in a chemical compound is a danger signal.

mutagenize (ˈmjuːtədʒənaɪz), *v. Biol.* [f. MUTAGEN + -IZE.] *trans.* To treat (cells or organisms) with mutagenic agents; also *absol.* So ˈ**mutagenized** *ppl. a.*

1966 *Virology* XXIX. 339/1 The mutants were produced by mutagenizing with hydroxylamine. *Ibid.* 339/2 A mutagenized phage stock was prepared. **1969** A. M. CAMPBELL *Episomes* ii. 16 From a mutagenized lysogenic culture, some bacteria can be recovered that are no longer lysogenic. **1970** *Nature* 31 Oct. 414/2 Mutagenized stocks of virus. **1972** *Ibid.* 18 Feb. 363/3 Instead of mutagenizing stocks of transforming virus.. [they] took mouse 3T3 cells.. and.. selected for cells which behave at 32° C as typical transformants.

†ˈ**mutal**, *a. Obs. rare*$^{-1}$. [irreg. f. L. *mūt-āre* to change + -AL[1].] Changeable.

a **1562** G. CAVENDISH *Wolsey*, etc. (1825) II. 139 Fortune.. Which is of nature bothe cruel and mutall.

mutalali, var. MUDALALI.

mutanize, obs. form of MUTINIZE.

mutant (ˈmjuːtənt), *sb.* and *a. Biol.* [ad. L. *mutant-em* pr. pple. of *mūtāre* (see MUTATE *v.*).]

A. *sb.* An individual (or, formerly, a species or form) which has arisen by or undergone mutation, or which carries a mutant gene (in *Science Fiction*, usu. an individual with freak or grossly abnormal anatomy, abilities, etc.); also, a mutant gene.

1901 *Rep. Brit. Assoc. Adv. Sci.* 848 Two genera of Conifers which are in a period of spontaneous generation, a period in which they do form mutants, to use the terminology of de Vries, which mutants *may* be true to seed. **1919** T. H. MORGAN *Physical Basis Heredity* xx. 249 Of the twelve dominant mutants that have appeared in *Drosophila* each appeared at first in a single individual. **1919** *Jrnl. Exper. Zool.* XXVIII. 363 By aid of these two dominants it is very easy to determine in a single experiment whether a given mutant is in the second or third chromosome. **1929** *Encycl. Brit.* VI. 947/1 There is a mutant or sport of the fruit fly with black coloration of the body. **1930** R. A. FISHER *Genetical Theory Nat. Select.* i. 13 Under the blending theory of inheritance, every individual was regarded as a mutant. **1954** 'J. CHRISTOPHER' *22nd Century* 140 You really can produce a breed of telepathic mutants that will supplant us? **1955** 'J. WYNDHAM' *Chrysalids* ii. 21 The nearest approach to decoration was a number of wooden panels with sayings..burnt into them... Blessed is the norm, and... Watch thou for the mutant! **1962** [see *hypomorph* s.v. HYPO- II]. **1969** *Nature* 18 Oct. 272/1 (*heading*) Vitamin K-deficient mutants of bacteria. **1974** *Encycl. Brit. Macropædia* XII. 756/1 Better strains of *Penicillium* and other industrial fungi..have been raised from artificially produced mutants.

fig. **1971** *Time* 7 June 7/1 An ominous new mutant of the American tragedy in Viet Nam... The troops who became addicted to heroin while serving in SE Asia.

B. *adj.* Having the attributes of a mutant; produced by mutation.

1903 *Amer. Naturalist* XXXVII. 740 The form, habit and behavior of some of the mutant forms discovered by de Vries seventeen years ago. **1928** *Genetics* XIII. 389 In this work two mutant characters have been studied. *Ibid.* 392 The sex-ratio in the mutant stock is normal. **1930** R. A. FISHER *Genetical Theory Nat. Select.* i. 11 In domestication..the rigour of Natural Selection [is] relaxed so that mutant types can survive. **1955** *Bull. Atomic Sci.* June 215/3 There is evidence that a mutant gene frequently does produce some disability of the individual who carries it. **1973** *Nature* 9 Feb. 368/2 Mutant cells resistant to particular drugs..are being routinely used today by somatic cell geneticists.

mutarotation (mju:tərəˈteɪʃən). *Chem.* [f. L. *mūtā-re* to change + ROTATION.] The change of optical activity with time exhibited by the solutions of some compounds (esp. sugars) after being made up. (Orig. called *multirotation* (MULTI- 2).)

1899 T. M. LOWRY in *Jrnl. Chem. Soc.* LXXV. 213 The essential feature of the phenomenon, however, is the *change* of rotatory power which takes place in the freshly prepared solution, and the term 'mutarotation' may, therefore, be used with advantage to include all those cases in which such a change occurs without reference either to the sign or to the relative magnitude of the initial and final rotations. **1937** *Chem. Rev.* XXI. 65 The brucine salt..was found..to exhibit definite mutarotation. **1971** *Jrnl. Gen. Psychol.* LXXXV. 116 Each quantity of the sugar solution was refrigerated for a day before use at room temperature to allow adequate time for mutarotations.

So **mutaroˈtational** *a.*, of, or of the nature of, mutarotation. Also **mutaroˈtate** *v. intr.*, to exhibit mutarotation; **mutaroˈtating** *ppl. a.*

1930 *Jrnl. Chem. Soc.* II. 2618 These two interconvertible, mutarotating forms of mannose are thus assigned different ring structures. **1951** I. L. FINAR *Org. Chem.* I. xviii. 372 These glycosides..do not undergo many of the reactions of the sugars, *e.g.*, they show no reducing properties, they do not mutarotate, etc. **1971** N. L. ALLINGER et al. *Org. Chem.* xxvii. 701 Monosaccharides commonly mutarotate. **1971** M. F. MALLETTE et al. *Introd. Biochem.* v. 145 Because the acetals of carbohydrates are kinetically stable, they do not undergo mutarotational changes. **1973** *Biochemistry* (Easton, Pa.) XII. 2544/1 If the enzyme..promoted instability by distorting the ring, the mutarotational rate would be enhanced.

mutasarrif, var. MUTESSARIF.

mutase (ˈmju:teɪz, -s). *Biochem.* [a. G. *mutase* (J. Parnas, at the suggestion of F. Hofmeister, in *Biochem. Zeitschr.* (1910) XXVIII. 284), f. L. *mūt-āre* to change: see -ASE.] **a.** Any enzyme which brings about a dismutation reaction.

1914 [see DEHYDRASE a]. **1943** SUMNER & SOMERS *Chem. & Methods Enzymes* xvii. 298 Aldehyde mutase brings about the Cannizzaro reaction. Here, two molecules of an aldehyde undergo an oxido-reduction.

b. Any enzyme which brings about the transfer of a phosphate group from one carbon atom to another in a molecule.

1938 *Jrnl. Biol. Chem.* CXXIV. 552 Mannose-1-phosphate and galactose-1-phosphate, synthetically prepared, were not converted to the respective 6-esters by muscle, liver, or yeast mutase, with or without the addition of accelerating ions. **1964** CORI & BROWN in Florkin & Stotz *Comprehensive Biochem.* XV. vi. 212 In a system consisting of hexokinase, mutase and phosphorylase, glucose could be converted to glycogen, provided that the inorganic phosphate formed in the phosphorylase reaction was removed by barium ions. **1970** R. W. MCGILVERY *Biochemistry* xv. 292 The sequence begins by a freely reversible mutase reaction, in which the phosphate group of glucose-6-phosphate is transferred to form glucose-1-phosphate.

mutassarif, mutasserif, varr. MUTESSARIF.

mutate (ˈmju:teɪt), *a.* and *sb.* [ad. L. *mūtāt-us*, pa. pple. of *mūtāre* to change.]

A. *adj. Bot.* Changed. *rare*$^{-0}$.

1840 in PAXTON *Bot. Dict.*

B. *sb.* **1.** *Gram.* A form having a mutated vowel.

1875–6 H. SWEET in *Trans. Philol. Soc.* 558 Several of the words given above may also be mutates, such as *ded, sed, gredig.*

2. *Chess.* (See quot. 1970.)

1922 HUME & WHITE *Good Companion Two-Mover* 297 We shall see that the term changed mate block (or 'mutate', as Brian Harley has suggested) is often indefinite in that it may include or exclude added mate features according to the individuality of separate problems. **1924** FEAST & WHITE *Simple Two-Move Themes* 62 The changed-mate waiters, or Mutates,..classify more readily. *Ibid.* 66 Every type of mating strategy discussed in Part III may theoretically be treated in Mutate form. **1931** B. HARLEY *Mate in Two Moves* ii. 20 We now come to the last of the big groups into which the two-mover can be divided: the Complete Block both before and after the Key, which changes one or more mates: that is, the Complete Block-Change, or, as I have christened it for short, the Mutate. **1959** B. J. HORTON *Dict. Mod. Chess* 85/1 He [*sc.* Brian Harley] did much to popularize the 'mutate' in his regular chess columns. **1962** K. S. HOWARD *Amer. Two-Move Chess Problem* 11 More than any other type of problem, the attractiveness of a mutate is dependent on the excellence of its construction. *Ibid.* 12 Wurzburg in No. 133 utilizes a mutate setting to show a charming illustration of a Bristol withdrawal key. **1970** J. M. RICE *ABC of Chess Problems* 182 Mutate is the term given to a complete-block problem in which White, with no mere waiting-move at his disposal, is forced to abandon one or more of his set mates and introduce new replies to Black's defences.

mutate (mju:ˈteɪt), *v.* [f. L. *mūtāt-*, ppl. stem of *mūtāre* (:—older **moitāre*, f. root **moi-* to change, whence MEAN *a.*[1]): see -ATE.] **1. a.** *intr.* To undergo change, be transmuted. Now only *Gram.* to undergo mutation. **b.** *trans.* (*Gram.*) To cause mutation of (a sound).

1818 J. BROWN *Psyche* 53 Since men of rank, when they mutate From one into another state, Assume the nature most allied To that which they must throw aside.

2. *Biol.* **a.** *intr.* To undergo mutation.

1913 *Amer. Naturalist* XLVII. 12 A mutation need not be a loss, and..a recessive may revert in the sense that it may mutate. *Ibid.* 68 There is in *Œnothera lamarckiana* a tendency to mutate in certain definite directions generation after generation. **1926** [see MUTATING *ppl. a.*]. **1951** E. HAMILTON *Star Kings* xix. 145 They're creatures of this crazy planet... I think they were human once—human colonists who mutated under radioactive influence. **1972** *Sci. Amer.* Apr. 65/2 We have no reason to think the gene for cytochrome *c* mutates more slowly than the gene for hemoglobin. **1974** *Nature* 1 Feb. 261/1 The evolution of enzymes in bacteria is studied by introducing novel substrates and selecting strains that have mutated to be able to use these substrates.

b. *trans.* To cause (genetic material) to undergo mutation.

1961 *Jrnl. Molecular Biol.* III. 142 There are many genetic sites which can be mutated by HA. **1972** *Nature* 14 Apr. 326/1 Clearly, in at least some phage genes certain segments of DNA are more readily mutated than others.

Hence **muˈtated** *ppl. a.*, having undergone mutation; **muˈtating** *ppl. a.*, undergoing mutation.

1875–6 H. SWEET in *Trans. Philol. Soc.* 549 It is extremely probable that all subjunctives originally had mutated vowels. **1903** *Amer. Naturalist* XXXVII. 739 This particular factor in distinguishing between fluctuating and mutating variability therefore becomes a safe one, when it is modified to make mutating variability include only newly acquired and transmissible qualities. **1913** *Ibid.* XLVII. 71 Such study should be continued for many years, breeding.. from some highly mutating stock. **1919** T. H. MORGAN *Physical Basis Heredity* xx. 248 When these are recessive it is probable..that the actual mutation occurred several generations before the mutated genes came together to produce the mutant character. **1926** *Proc. Nat. Acad. Sci.* XII. 687 The first frequently mutating character observed in *Drosophila virilis* was the body 'reddish', which was found to mutate frequently to wild type. **1945** *Genetics* XXX. 497 From outcrossing flies of the mutating cultures to those of normal cultures (Reed-sport) the results..in table 2 were obtained. **1964** *Jrnl. Molecular Biol.* IX. 352 (*heading*) Identification of the altered bases in mutated single-stranded DNA. **1967** *Biol. Abstr.* XLVIII. 3217/1 (*heading*) Notes on mutant forms among Philippine plants. IV. A case of a 'recurrently mutating' banana. **1973** *Guardian* 18 May 18/1 There are reports of mutated fish in the lagoon and radiation sickness from eating the fish.

mutation (mju:ˈteɪʃən). [a. F. *mutacion* (13th c. in Littré), *-ation*, ad. L. *mūtātiōn-em*, n. of action f. *mūtāre* to change: see MUTATE and -ATION.]

1. a. The action or process of changing; alteration or change in form or qualities.

c **1374** CHAUCER *Boeth.* Pr. vi. 18 (Camb. MS.), ffor-thi wenestow þat þise Mutacyouns of fortune fletyn with-owte gouernor. **1426** LYDG. *De Guil. Pilgr.* 3280 To maken.. That merveyllous mutacion, Bred in-to flesshe, wyn in-to blood. *c* **1430** *Pilgr. Lyf Manhode* I. xli. (1869) 24 Al mutacioun that is doon in haste j hate. *c* **1522** BP. FOX in Ellis *Orig. Lett.* Ser. II. II. 4 Thestate & condicion of the Toune & Marches of Calis & other Fortryses within the same, & of theyr ruynes, decayes, mutacyons, and alteracions, fro the auncyent estatuz and ordinances [etc.]. **1523** LD. BERNERS *Froiss.* I. clv. 187 It is come to the kynges knowledge, howe that his subgettes ar sore greued by reason of the mutacyon of y[e] moneys. **1605** SHAKS. *Lear* IV. i. 11 O world! But that thy strange mutations make vs hate thee Life would not yeelde to age. **1655** G. S. in Hartlib *Ref. Commw. Bees* 21, I took the pain to observe and collect the Generation of several Insects, with their various mutations from kind to kind. **1776** BURNEY *Hist. Mus.* (1789) I. iv. 54 The Mutations or changes incident to melody which in modern music we should call..modulation. *a* **1849** HOR. SMITH *Addr. Mummy* ix, Since first thy form was in this box extended We have above ground seen some strange mutations. **1892** STEVENSON & L. OSBOURNE *Wrecker* vi, More than three years had intervened almost without mutation in that stationary household.

†**b.** Changeableness. *Obs.*

a **1548** HALL *Chron., Edw. IV* (1550) 23 Suche is ye mutacyon of the common people, lyke a rede wyth euery wind is agitable and flexible.

†**c.** Change in government, revolution. Also, ? revolt, insurrection. *Obs.*

In the sense 'revolt' the word may be a. OF. *meutacion*, f. *meute* riot, uproar (see MUTE *sb.*[3]).

a **1470** TIPTOFT *Cæsar* x. (1530) 12 He douted lest in his absence there shuld arise some chaunge or mutacyon in Fraunce. **1660** MILTON *Free Commw.* Wks. 1851 V. 432 We had bin then by this time firmly rooted past fear of Commotions or Mutations. **1737** WHISTON *Josephus, Hist.* I. xvi. §5 He..exacted the tribute..as a penalty for the mutations they had made in the country.

†**2.** *concr.* (*Roman Antiq.*) As rendering of L. *mutatio* (see quot. 1610). *Obs.*

1610 HOLLAND *Camden's Brit.* I. 65 Also Mutations; for so they called in that age, the places where strangers, as they journeied did change their post-horses [etc.]. **1677** PLOT *Oxfordsh.* 326 Pillars of stone, whereon they inscribed the distances from the regal Cities, Stations, and Mutations.

3. *Mus.* **a.** In mediæval solmization: The change from one hexachord to another involving a change of the syllable applied to a given note.

1597 MORLEY *Introd. Mus.* Annot., Mutation is the leauing of one name of a note and taking another in the same sound. **1609** DOULAND *Ornith. Microl.* 16 To a Musitian.. Mutation is..the putting of one concord for another in the same Key. **1760** *Phil. Trans.* LI. 743 The author is speaking of the sixth division of harmonic, which was mutation. **1807** ROBINSON *Archæol. Græca* v. xxiii. 534 In music the Greeks distinguished..rhythmus, mutations, and melopœia.

b. ***mutation stop***: a stop whose pipes produce tones one-fifth or a major third above the proper pitch of the key struck, or above one of its octaves. So ***mutation rank***.

1855 HOPKINS *Organ* 110 Mutation or Filling-up Stops do not give a sound corresponding with the key pressed down; but some sound g on the C key, others e. **1881** C. A. EDWARDS *Organs* 153 The proper balancing of the foundation and mutation ranks.

c. In violin-playing: 'The shifting of the hand from one position to another' (*Cent. Dict.* 1890).

4. *Gram.* **a.** In the Celtic languages, a change of an initial consonant, depending on the grammatical (or, prehistorically, on the phonetic) character of the preceding word.

1843 *Proc. Philol. Soc.* I. 124 That remarkable system of initial mutations of consonants which distinguishes the Celtic languages from all others in Europe. **1904** *Athenæum* 5 Nov. 621/3 If Welsh loses its mutations as South Wales is doing slightly, we shall be sorry.

b. = UMLAUT.

1875–6 H. SWEET in *Trans. Philol. Soc.* 558 The mutation of original *ā*, which is written *æ* in WS. *Ibid.* 567 The most marked distinction between A[nglo-] F[risian] and O[ld] S[axon] is the want of 'umlaut' or mutation in the latter. **1887** SKEAT *Princ. Eng. Etymol.* Ser. I. 211 In many instances, the original vowel of the root has suffered both mutation and gradation.

Comb. **1892** SWEET *Eng. Gramm.* I. 315 The following mutation-plurals are still in common use.

5. *Law.* **a.** In French law (see quot. 1856). Also Comb. (in Canada) ***mutation-fine***.

1825 *Act 6 Geo. IV*, c. 59 §5 Every..droit de lods et ventes, and mutation fine of every description [Lower Canada]. **1856** BOUVIER *Amer. Law Dict.* (ed. 6) II. 195 *Mutation*, French law... Applied to designate the change which takes place in the property of a thing in its transmission from one person to another... It is nearly synonymous with transfer.

b. ***mutation of libel*** (see quot. 1856).

1685 CONSETT *Pract. Spirit. Courts* III. i. §2 (1700) 82 We now come to the other part of *Mynsinger* his purpose (*Scil.*) the mutation or changing of Libels; *mutare Libellum*, to change the Libel, is to vary and alter the substance of it. **1856** BOUVIER *Amer. Law Dict.* (ed. 6) II. 195 *Mutation of libel*, practice. An amendment allowed to a libel, by which there is an alteration of the substance of the libel.

6. *Biology.* **a.** The process whereby detectable and heritable changes in genetic material arise; also, formerly, a process by which de Vries (*Die Mutationstheorie* (1901–3)) supposed a new species to be suddenly produced by a departure from the parent type (in contrast with *variation*). **b.** A change of this kind in the genetic material. **c.** An individual (or, more rarely, an assemblage of like individuals) which has been produced by this process; a mutant.

1894 W. B. SCOTT in *Amer. Jrnl. Sci.* Nov. 372 Bateson's results..emphasize strongly the difference between variation and that steady advance along certain definite lines which Waagen called mutation. **1901** *Jrnl. R. Microsc. Soc.* 439 Quite distinct from these are those abrupt..variations ..which sometimes occur, and of which de Vries records a remarkable instance in the genus *Œnothera*. For such variations de Vries proposes the term *mutations*. **1904** *Westm. Gaz.* 23 Apr. 12/3 It is with the origin of the minor species that the De Vries Mutation Theory is concerned. **1905** in *Q. Jrnl. Geol. Soc.* LXI. *Proc.* p. lxxiii, A mutation, in the palaeontological and original sense, may be defined as a contemporaneous assemblage of individuals united by specific identity of structure *inter se*, and by common descent from a known pre-existing species, from which they differ in some minute but constant character or characters. **1907** *Athenæum* 31 Aug. 242/1 The theory of mutation.. assumes that a species has its birth, its lifetime, and its death, even as an individual, and that throughout its life it remains one and the same. By a mutation it does not change itself, but simply produces a new type. The mutation 'is allied to its ancestor as a branch is to a tree'. **1919** *Jrnl. Exper. Zool.* XXVIII. 381 In our opinion, the attempted distinctions between 'saltations', 'mutations', and 'variations of slight degree' have led rather to confusion of thought than to clearer thinking. To us these are all a single class, 'mutations', and the term carries no restrictions of degree, covering the most extreme as well as the slightest detectable inherited variation. **1925** *Genetics* X. 117 If one thinks of mutations as being simply inherited changes, it becomes necessary to distinguish changes that involve whole chromosomes.., changes that involve several adjacent genes .., and what have been called 'point-mutations' or 'gene-mutations'. **1928, 1930** [see *gene mutation* s.v. GENE[1] 2]. **1955** *Sci. News Let.* 25 June 409 Many mutations are lethal. If man-made irradiation increases the mutation rate, the result is sure to be harmful. **1955** *Sci. Amer.* July 74/2 Reproduction is one of the two essential features of life.

Mutation is the other. **1957** I. Asimov *Naked Sun* (1958) xi. 145 Even the best gene analysis of parents can't assure that all gene permutations and combinations will be favourable, to say nothing of the possibility of mutations. That's our big concern, the unexpected mutation. **1965** A. H. Sturtevant *Hist. Genetics* x. 62 It is ironic that few of the original mutations observed by de Vries in Oenothera would now be called mutations. **1971** J. Z. Young *Introd. Study Man* xxviii. 392 The cause of mutation is some faulty copying during replication of the DNA. This..will be inherited only if it occurs in the line of the germ cells. Mutations elsewhere in the body are called somatic mutations... The accumulation of somatic mutations may produce some of the diseases of old age. **1972** [see Mendelian *sb.*]. **1974** *Sci. Amer.* Sept. 82 (*caption*) One-gene mutation is responsible for the difference between the beta chain of a normal hemoglobin molecule..and that of hemoglobin *S*, the variant form responsible for sickle-cell anemia.

7. Special Comb.: **mutation mink**, a mink belonging to a mutant strain with a fur colour different from the normal; fur or a garment made from the skin of such a mink; **mutation pressure**, a tendency for recurring mutation (rather than selection) to alter the frequency of a particular allele within a population; **mutation rate**, the rate at which gene mutations occur (see quot. 1971); **mutation theory**, the theory of de Vries concerning the origin of new species (see 6 a).

1942 H. Bock in *Amer. Fur Breeder* Oct. 14 (*title*) *Mutation mink and their use in coats. **1945** R. G. Hodgson *Mink Book* (ed. 2) 41 Mutation mink got their start in the United States..and the Silverblu..was the important mink to give the industry something to think about. **1956** J. G. Links *Book of Fur* 166 The mutation mink names Silverblu, Aleutian, Royal Pastel..each representing a different mutation which had been developed since the original Silverblu. **1958** *Vogue* Jan. 12 Natural pale beige mutation mink. **1966** R. Serjeant *Mink on my Shoulder* xi. 152 To the fur trade and perhaps also to the general public, the mutation mink means a mink of an abnormal colour or fur pattern that can be repeated at will. **1931** *Genetics* XVI. 100 (*heading*) *Mutation pressure. **1962** D. J. Merrell *Evol. & Genetics* xxiv. 237 Theoretically mutation pressure alone could bring about evolution. **1930** R. A. Fisher *Genetical Theory Nat. Select.* vi. 122 If..the *mutation rates..are high enough to maintain any considerable genetic diversity, it will only be the best adapted genotypes which can become the ancestors of future generations. **1948** *Proc. R. Soc.* B. CXXXV. 168 It follows that human mutation rates are about twice those of *Drosophila* per nuclear division, and about one two-hundredth of those of *Drosophila* per day. **1971** Levitan & Montagu *Textbk. Human Genetics* xvii. 649 Mutation rates are usually stated in terms of the number of changed genes per locus per generation. **1904** *Mutation theory [see sense 6 above]. **1912** *Amer. Naturalist* XLVI. 359 We can distinguish and trace the history of these quantitative variations from generation to generation only when the differences between them are of some size. This has led many to think that only variations of some size are inherited (the mutation theory) and others to deny that such variations can be increased in size by selection. **1962** D. J. Merrell *Evol. & Genetics* xxi. 213 In the very early days of genetics de Vries (1902) proposed the mutation theory of evolution as an alternative to the theory of natural selection.

mutational (mjuːˈteɪʃənəl), *a.* *Biol.* [f. mutation + -al.] Of or pertaining to mutation.

1904 *Nature* 25 Feb. 386/2 De Vries's 'mutational' variations. **1931** E. B. Ford *Mendelism & Evolution* iv. 72 This criticism omits all reference to an important condition of the theory: the size of the mutational steps involved. **1955** *Bull. Atomic Sci.* June 210/2 No exposure [to radiation] is so tiny that it does not carry its corresponding mutational risk. **1964** G. H. Haggis et al. *Introd. Molecular Biol.* p. xi, Recent refinements in genetic analysis..have made it possible to relate mutational events to modification of nucleic acid structure.

Hence **muˈtationally** *adv.*, as a result of mutation.

1934 in Webster. **1960** *Biochim. & Biophys. Acta* XLIII. 288 (*heading*) The similar properties of tryptophan synthetase and a mutationally altered enzyme in *Neurospora crassa*. **1971** *Nature* 24 Dec. 443/3 Strains of *E. coli* with mutationally altered ribosomal proteins.

mutationist (mjuːˈteɪʃənɪst). [f. mutation + -ist.] One who stresses the importance of mutation as a factor in the evolution of new forms or species.

1904 *Science* 10 June 881/2 It might be inferred that Lamarckians and Darwinians are..regarded as believers in adaptiveness as a factor in evolution, and mutationists are necessarily supposed to hold the opposite view. **1909** *Fabian News* XX. 76/1 The mad mutationist who claims that evolution takes place by mutation only. **1911** A. D. Darbishire *Breeding & Mendelian Discov.* 4 The point at issue between the Selectionist..and the Mutationist.

‖**mutatis mutandis** (mjuːˈtɑːtɪs mjuːˈtændɪs), *adv. phr.* [L., f. *mutatis*, *mutandis*, ablative pl. respectively of pa. pple. and gerundive of *mūtāre* to change.] 'Things being changed that have to be changed', i.e. with the necessary changes; with due alteration of details (in comparing cases).

1498 *Coventry Leet Bk.* (1909) 595 And like billes, mutatis mutandis, were put In ayenst Gloucestre & Worcestre. **1615** T. Bone *Let.* 9 Nov. in J. P. Collier *Egerton Papers* (1840) 472 The very same (*mutatis mutandis* onely) weere put in practize by Foreman. **1666** *Phil. Trans. R. Soc.* I. 289 The like may be fitted to Mars in other positions, *mutatis mutandis*; and so for the other Planets. **1710** Swift *Tale Tub* (ed. 5) Author's Apology sig. a1, I know nothing more contemptible in a Writer than the Character of a Plagiary; which he here fixes at a venture, and this, not for a Passage, but a whole Discourse, taken out from another Book only *mutatis mutandis*. **1753** Chesterfield in *World* 14 June 146 The utility of this invention extends, *mutatis mutandis*, to whatever can be the subject of letters. **1817** Coleridge *Biogr. Lit.* I. xiii. 288 The actual application of the positions which had so wonderfully enlarged the discoveries of geometry, mutatis mutandis, to philosophical subjects. **1877** *Trans. Connecticut Acad. Arts & Sci.* III. 345 The same may be said, *mutatis mutandis*, of the other symbols of the same type. **1892** [see homosexual *a.* and *sb.* A.]. **1931** *Times Lit. Suppl.* 23 July 570/2 *Mutatis mutandis*, one might trace a succession from the seventeenth-century divine and Fellow of the Royal Society..to the well-known modern names in philosophy. **1955** *Times* 11 July 13/6 *Mutatis mutandis* these lucid words still apply to the exertions of Russian historians carrying on the same tradition. **1962** S. E. Finer *Man on Horseback* ii. 6 What is said of the army here is to be taken also to apply, *mutatis mutandis*, to the air force and the navy. **1973** *Times* 13 Dec. 18/2 *Mutatis mutandis*, we are going to face a series of enforceable demands by the 'undeveloped' nations, equivalent to the Arabs' demand for higher pay for their oil.

mutative (ˈmjuːtətɪv), *a.* [a. OF. *mutatif* (1493 Godef.), a. med.L. *mūtātīv-us* f. *mūtāt-*, ppl. stem of *mūtāre* to change: see -ative.]

1. Of or pertaining to change or mutation.

1743 [see metabolic *a.* 1]. **1907** *Athenæum* 31 Aug. 242/3 Whilst wheat, oats, peas, and vetches are still..in a mutative state or period, barley is now in a period of stability.

2. Given to change, changeable.

1818 *Blackw. Mag.* III. 533 He is neither so mutative and *dissimilis sibi* as Odoherty.

‖**mutato nomine** (mjuːˈtɑːtəʊ ˈnəʊmɪneɪ), *advb. phr.* [L., f. *mutato*, ablative sing. of pa. pple. of *mūtāre* to change + *nomine*, ablative sing. of *nōmen* name.] 'The name being changed': applicable in a transferred context if the name of the person, place, etc., is altered accordingly.

The original phrase (cited in quot. 1621) quotes Horace *Sat.* I. i. 69.

1621 Burton *Anat. Mel.* (Democritus to Reader) 37 Accounting it an excellent thing..to make our selues merry with other mens obliquities, when as he himselfe is more faultie than the rest, *mutato nomine de ta fabula narratur*, he may take himselfe by the nose for a foole. *a* **1661** Fuller *Worthies* (1662) Lincs. 153 Which Proverb, *Mutato Nomine*, is used in other Counties. **1828** J. S. Mill in *Westm. Rev.* IX. 146 Nobody would pretend that a man unacquainted with the properties of simple substances would be perfectly capable of performing such an analysis, or that the knowledge of the ultimate elements of bodies was of no service to the chemist. The same observations apply, *mutato nomine*, to the logician, and the syllogism. **1840** J. B. Fraser *Koordistan* II. vi. 152 The words of Burns, *mutato nomine*, describe their country exactly. **1860** Thackeray in *Cornhill Mag.* May 632 A score of such queer names and titles I have smiled at in America. And, *mutato nomine*?

muˈtator. [a. L. *mūtātor*, agent-noun f. *mūtāre* to change.] †**1.** One who changes. *Obs. rare*$^{-1}$.

1632 [see plantator 1].

2. *Biol.* Any gene which increases the mutation rate of other genes. Usu. *attrib.*, esp. in ***mutator gene***.

1943 *Proc. Nat. Acad. Sci.* XXIX. 138 In determining the abnormal mutation rate we shall consider only those cultures which have given at least one sex-linked recessive, since this is the only indication of the presence of the 'Mutator' gene in the mother. **1945** *Genetics* XXX. 496 Recently, high mutation frequency in a strain of *D. pseudoobscura*, race B, was found to be due to a dominant mutator. **1970** *Jrnl. Molecular Biol.* L. 129 Mutator genes cause a generalized increase in mutation rate. They have been identified in a variety of organisms, including phage and bacteria.

mutatory (ˈmjuːtətərɪ), *a.* [ad. mod.L. type **mūtātōri-us*: see prec. and -ory.] Changing; mutable; variable.

In recent Dicts.

mutazalite, variant form of motazilite.

mutch (mʌtʃ). *dial.* Also *Sc.* 5 mwch, 5–6 much, 7 moche. [a. MDu. *mutse* (mod.Du. *muts*) = MGH., mod.G. *mütse*; prob. a shortened form of MDu. *amutse*, *almutse*, MHG. *armuz*, *almuz*, med.L. *almutia*, F. *aumusse*, Pr. *aumussa*, Sp. *almucio* amice[2]; the origin of the Rom. word, which meant a covering for head and shoulders worn by canons, is obscure. Cf. mozzetta.]

†**1.** *Sc.* A night covering for the head. Often ***night mutch***. *Obs.*

1473 *Acc. Ld. High Treas. Scot.* (1877) I. 39, v elne of Holland claith for sarkis and muchis. *Ibid.* 40, ij elne of lawne for my Lordis muchis. **1474** *Ibid.* 27, j elne of Hollande clath for mwchis to the King. *Ibid.* 41, viij elne of Hollande clath for sarkis and mwchys. **1503** *Ibid.* (1900) II. 211 Item, for thre muches brocht hame be him to the King. **1612** *Sc. Bk. Customs* in *Halyburton's Ledger* (1867) 322 Mutches called nycht mutches of linning plane..nycht mutches embrodered with gold and siluer. *a* **1670** Spalding *Troub. Chas. I* (Spald. Club) II. 388 He had on his heid ane white perllit mvtche. **1831** Shennan *Tales* 75 (E.D.D.) Even her night-mutch did appear: The vera plaits aboon her brow.

2. A cap or coif, usually of linen, worn by women and young children. Also *attrib.*

1634–5 Brereton *Trav.* (Chetham Soc.) 188 We call here ..a cap, a mutch, if it be linen. **1724** Ramsay *Tea-t. Misc.* (1762) 9 Their toys and mutches were sae clean, They glanced in our ladses' een. **1822** Galt *Provost* xxxvi, Mrs. Fenton, with her mutch off,..was seen trying to sunder the challengers and the champions. **1884** Q. Victoria *More Leaves* 113 The old mother, Mrs. Brown, in her white mutch,..and a few neighbours stood round the room. **1894** Crockett *Lilac Sunbonnet* 36 The 'mutch' box lined with pale green paper.

Hence **ˈmutchless** *a.*, without a cap.

1826 J. Wilson *Noct. Ambr.* Wks. 1855 I. 216 The mutchless mawsie flings herself frae the tap step.

mutchado, -atoe: see moustache, mustachio.

mutcher, dial. variant of moocher.

mutchkin (ˈmʌtʃkɪn). *Sc.* Also 6 mych-, mutskin, musking, 7 mutchin, mwching, 8 mutchken, -kine, muchkin. [a. early mod.Du. *mudseken* (now *mutsje*), app. an irregular diminutive of *mud*(*de* mud *sb.*[2]] A measure of capacity for liquids (or for dry substances of a powdery or granular character); the fourth part of the old Scots pint, or about three-quarters of an imperial pint.

? **1425** *Sc. Acts Jas. I* (1814) II. 12 Quhilkis makis..of þe new mete now ordanit ix pyntis & three muchekynis. **1508** *Acc. Ld. High Treas. Scot.* (1902) IV. 113 Item, to Pieris the payntour, for glew,..thre mychkinnis olye, calk, for the chapell. **1591** in *Thanes of Cawdor* (Spald. Club) 200 Item thrie muskingis aquavitye xv *s.* **1603** *Rec. Convent. Roy. Burghs Scot.* (1870) II. 157 Ilk burgh..caus mak and haue all thair mesouris of stovpeis of quart, pynt, choping, and mwching,..conformeable to the jadge and stovpe of Sterling. **1632** Lithgow *Trav.* x. 478 With Wine, a mutchkin, thrice a weeke Pack'd in her pocket. **1769** *De Foe's Tour Gt. Brit.* (ed. 7) IV. 252 Boys and Girls, coming ..to sell us Whortle-berries,..sold to every one of us near a Mutchkin for a Baubee. **1756** Mrs. Calderwood *Jrnl.* (1884) 85 The proportion..was like our mutchkin of salt to twenty pound weight of butter. **1814** Scott *Wav.* xxxix, He whistled the 'Bob of Dumblain', under the influence of half a mutchkin of brandy. *a* **1884** Peerie *Nugæ Eccles.* I. 24 Another mutchkin, Dibble.

b. *Comb.*, as ***mutchkin cap***, ***stoup***, ***tin***.

1721 Ramsay *Ode to Ph*—— iii, That mutchkin stoup it hauds but dribs. **1786** Burns *Earnest Cry* 7 Paint Scotland greetan owre her thrissle; Her mutchkin stowp as toom's a whissle. *a* **1791** Grose *Olio* (1796) 115 Paddy lifted a muchkin tin..and threw it at the narrator. **1823** Galt *Gilhaize* xiv, A smith came in for a mutchkin-cap of ale.

mute (mjuːt), *a.* and *sb.*[1] Forms: α. 4–5 **muwet**, 4–6 **mewet**, **muet**, 5 **mwet**, **muyt**, 6 **muete**; β. 5 **mut**, 6– **mute**. [ME. *muet* (*mewet*, *muwet*), a. F. *muet*:—popular L. **mūtettus* dim. of L. *mūtus*. In the 16th c. the word was assimilated in spelling and pronunciation to L. *mūtus* (whence OF. *mu*, Pr. *mut*, Sp. *mudo*, It. *muto*).]

A. *adj.*

1. a. Not emitting articulate sound; silent.

to stand mute (***of malice***): in *Law*, to refuse deliberately to plead.

c **1374** Chaucer *Troylus* v. 194 She..stod forth mewet [*v.r.* muwet] mylde and mansuete. *c* **1450** *Merlin* 172 Thei were alle stille and mewet as though thei hadde be dombe. **1513** More *Rich. III* in Grafton *Chron.* (1568) II. 784 She [was]..neither mute, nor full of bable. **1543–4** *Act 35 Hen. VIII*, c. 5 If any person..stand muet or wilnot directly answere to the same offences. **1547** [see malice *sb.* 6]. **1605** Bacon *Adv. Learn.* I. vii. §3 When Counsellors and seruants stand mute and silent. *a* **1674** Clarendon *Hist. Reb.* xi. §234 He could not be so ignorant as not to know what judgment the law pronounced against those who stood mute, and obstinately refused to plead. **1750** Gray *Elegy* xv, Some mute inglorious Milton here may rest. **1772** *Act 12 Geo. III*, c. 20 Such Person so standing Mute..shall be convicted of the Felony or Piracy charged in such Indictment or Appeal. **1866** M. Arnold *Thyrsis* xxii, Which task'd thy pipe too sore, and tired thy throat—It fail'd, and thou wast mute! **1906** *Westm. Gaz.* 26 May 12/1 At the Middlesex Sessions on Saturday..a young woman..was found by the jury to be standing mute of malice. *Ibid.*, It was not till 1827 that it was enacted that a plea of not guilty should be entered for a prisoner who stood mute of malice.

b. *transf.* in the sense: Not emitting sound; not manifesting sound. ***mute swan***: the common swan, *Cygnus olor*.

1513 More *Rich. III* in Grafton *Chron.* (1568) II. 794 All was still and muete, and not one worde aunswered to. *c* **1600** Shaks. *Sonn.* xcvii, For sommer and his pleasures waite on thee, And thou away, the very birds are mute. **1615** G. Sandys *Trav.* 117 The water..passing along with a mute and vnspeedy current. **1653** Walton *Angler* i. 17 The children of Israel..having hung up their then mute Instruments..sate down. **1774** G. White *Selborne* 14 Feb., The martin..is rather a mute bird. **1785** Pennant *Arct. Zool.* II. 543 Mute Swan. *Ibid.* 542 *note*, We change the name of the Tame Swan into Mute, as..this species emits no sound. **1790** Bruce *Trav. Source Nile* III. 55 The sky-lark is here, but is mute the whole year, till the first rains fall in November. **1810** Scott *Lady of L.* I. xv, The groves are still and mute! **1849** C. Bronte *Shirley* x, Mute was the room,—mute the house. **1849** M. Arnold *Obermann* ii, Behind are the abandoned baths Mute in their meadows lone. **1884** Wood in *Sunday Mag.* May 306/1 The descendants of Mute Swans, Greylag Geese and Wild Ducks.

c. Proverbial phrases. ***as mute as a fish*** or ***fishes*** (and dialectically, ***as mute as a mackerel***, ***maid***, ***mouse***, ***poker***, ***statue***, ***stone***).

c **1407** Lydg. *Reson & Sens.* 6267 They be as Muet as a stone. *c* **1440** *Compleynt* 50 in *Temple of Glas* 59 A tunge I haue, but wordys none, But stonde mut as any stone. **1576** Gascoigne *Steele Gl.* (Arb.) 67 Be thou eke as mewet as a mayde. **1620** Melton *Astrolog.* 38 What wife he shall haue ..whether she shall be as mute as a Fish, or haue a tongue as loude as a Fish-Wife. **1621–3** Middleton & Rowley *Changeling* III. iii, Be silent, mute, Mute as a statue. **1760**

FOOTE *Minor* I. (1767) 20 *Sir Will.* You can be secret as well as serviceable? *Shift.* Mute as a mackerel. **1781** C. JOHNSTON *Hist. J. Juniper* II. 141 The Nabob's friends.. had stood all this while as mute as fishes. **1807** in *Spirit Publ. Jrnls.* XI. 3 The members as mute as fishes gaping for loaves. **1844** DICKENS *Mart. Chuz.* xxviii, Damme, sir, if he wasn't as mute as a poker. **1881** BESANT & RICE *Chapl. of Fleet* I. v, They one and all.. became suddenly as mute as mice.

2. a. Destitute of the faculty of speech; dumb. Also *absol.*

1377 LANGL. *P. Pl.* B. xvi. 111 Bothe meseles & mute and in the menysoun blody, Ofte he heled suche he ne helde it for no maistrye. **1483** CAXTON *Gold. Leg.* 117b/1 Zoe.. whyche had ben muet & dombe vii yere by a sekenes that she had. **1649** *Alcoran* 176 They shall be infamous, deaf, mute, and blinde, and condemned to the flames of hell, because they are wicked. **1651** G. W. tr. *Cowel's Inst.* 173 He that is mute can neither Covenant nor promise, since he cannot speak nor utter words congruous to a Covenant. **1815** SCOTT *Ld. of Isles* III. xxiii, For though from earliest childhood mute, The lad can deftly touch the lute. **1899** *Allbutt's Syst. Med.* VII. 418 The leading peculiarities of hysterical mutism are these... The subjects of this disability are completely mute.

b. Applied to the lower animals as lacking the power of articulate speech. Cf. DUMB *a.* 1 b.

1667 MILTON *P.L.* IX. 557 Beasts, whom God on thir Creation-Day Created mute to all articulat sound. **1678** R. L'ESTRANGE *Seneca's Mor., Anger* vii. (1692) 392 A Brutal Folly, to be Offended at a Mute Animal. **1845** FORD *Handbk. Spain* I. 35 Oaths.. seem to be considered as the only language the mute creation can comprehend.

3. Temporarily bereft of the power of speech.

1483 CAXTON *Gold. Leg.* 271/2 The blessyd Berthylmewe .. entryd in to the temple.. and made the deuylle soo muet that he gat noo remembraunce to them that adoured hym. **1576** FLEMING *Panopl. Epist.* 418 Noble men at their meetinges should not be mute and tong-tyed. **1651** HOBBES *Leviath.* I. xvi. 83 This number is no Representative; because.. it becomes oftentimes.. a mute Person, and unapt .. for the government of a Multitude. **1706** E. WARD *Wooden World Diss.* (1708) 28 Then he's struck mute. **1781** COWPER *Conversat.* 352 The fear of being silent makes us mute. **1887** BOWEN *Virg. Æneid* III. 298 Mute with wonder I stood.

4. a. Of things or action: Not characterized by or attended with speech or vocal utterance.

1599 SHAKS. *Hen. V*, I. i. 49 When he speakes,.. the mute Wonder lurketh in mens eares. **1700** DRYDEN *Sigism. & Guisc.* 684 Mute solemn Sorrow, free from Female Noise. **1802** COLERIDGE *Hymn bef. Sunrise* 26 Mute thanks and secret ecstasy. **1871** MACDUFF *Mem. Patmos* ix. 121 The four and twenty Elders prostrate themselves in mute adoration. **1898** FLOR. MONTGOMERY *Tony* 15 Their mute appealing expression.

b. *transf.*

1627 SIR R. COTTON *View Reign Hen. III* 45 In himselfe hee reformed his naturall Errors, Princes Manners though a mute law haue more of life and vigour then those of letters. **1788** GIBBON *Decl. & F.* l. V. 185 The jurisdiction of the magistrate was mute and impotent. **1782** W. GILPIN *River Wye* 91 He will work them up with such colours, mute, or vivid, as best accord with the general tone of his landscape.

5. *Gram.* and *Phonetics.* **a.** Of a consonant: Produced by an entire interruption of the passage of breath, or by the complete closure of the organs of the mouth; 'stopped'.

After late L. *mūtus*, Gr. ἄφωνος.

1589 PUTTENHAM *Eng. Poesie* II. xiii. (Arb.) 135 The vowell is alwayes more easily deliuered then the consonant: and of consonants, the liquide more then the mute. **1688** R. HOLME *Armoury* III. 408/1, T.. is a mute Letter, and sounded through the Teeth.

†**b.** Of a consonant: Voiceless. *Obs.*

1668 WILKINS *Real Char.* 369 (*Zh*) the sonorous Consonant, and (*Sh*) its correspondent mute... The first being vocal, the other mute.

c. Of a letter: Not pronounced, silent.

1638 BRATHWAIT *Barnabees Jrnl.* (1818) 181 What tho' graves become acute too? What tho' accents become mute too? **1840** *Proc. Philol. Soc.* III. 6 It gradually was established.. that when a mute *e* followed a single consonant the preceding vowel was a long one.

6. *Astrol.* (see quot. 1696).

1658 GADBURY *Doctr. Nativities* 39 Some Signs there are which be termed mute... If any of the mute Signs ascend in a Nativity [etc.]. **1696** PHILLIPS (ed. 5), *Mute Signs*, are those which are denominated from Creatures that have no Voice, as *Cancer, Scorpio, Pisces*; and in Nativities, when the Significators therein do spoil or cause some Impediment in the Speech of him that is born. **1819** J. WILSON *Dict. Astrol.* 296 *Mute Signs*, they are called dumb signs by the Arabians, and are said to have an effect on the native's speech, and cause dumbness.

7. *Sporting.* Not giving tongue (said of hounds while hunting). ***to run mute***, to follow the chase without giving tongue.

1677 COX *Gentl. Recr.* (ed. 2) 17 When Hounds or Beagles run long without opening or making any cry, we say, they run Mute. **1843** SURTEES *Handley Cross* v. 101 A short sharp chirp is borne on the breeze; it is Heroine all but running mute. **1855** 'STONEHENGE' *Brit. Sports* IV. 119 The defects which should especially be avoided are—first,.. 'babbling'; secondly, mute running. *Ibid.*, 'Babbling', 'mute running', and 'skirting', are dependent upon a defect in breeding. **1897** *Encycl. Sport* I. 582 *Mute*, silent, the hounds going too fast to speak. Some hounds are naturally mute.

8. Of wine: (See quot.) Cf. MUTE *v.*[4]

1801 *Tilloch's Philos. Mag.* X. 151 In Languedoc, a kind of wine is made of white grapes called mute wine, which is employed to sulphur others... This wine never ferments, and for that reason is called mute wine.

9. Said of metals that do not ring when struck.

1806 TURTON tr. *Linn. Syst. Nat.* VII. Expl. Terms. **1841** MAUNDER *Sci. & Lit. Treas.* (1848) 487/2.

10. *Comb.*

1639 S. DU VERGER tr. *Camus' Admir. Events* 311 Mute-strucken with this lustre.. he remained quite astonished. **1660** *Trial Regic.* 53 This Mute-man fortuned to see the Murtherer of his Father. **1728–46** THOMSON *Spring* 162 Herds and flocks Drop the dry sprig, and, mute-imploring, eye The falling verdure. **1746** SMOLLETT *Advice* 41 Bribe him, to feast my mute-imploring eye, With some proud lord, who smiles a gracious lie! **1850** BROWNING *Christmas Eve* xx. 62 Stumbling, mute-mazed, at nature's chance.

B. *sb.*

1. *Phonetics.* [See A. 5.] An element of speech formed by a position of the vocal organs such as stops the passage of the breath, or entirely interrupts the sound; a stopped consonant, a 'stop'.

1530 PALSGR. Introd. 20 Theyr consonantes be devyded in to mutes & liquides or semivocalles. **1656** BLOUNT *Glossogr.*, Mutes (*mutæ*), these letters *b, c, d, g, h, k, p, q, t*, are so called, because they have no sound, without the assistance of a vowel. **1887** *Encycl. Brit.* XXII. 383/1 In Indian languages (pʻ) would be felt as a final post-aspirated mute.

allusively. **1654** TRAPP *Comm. Job* xxxii. (1657) 280 We use to say, That at meetings young men should be Mutes, and old men Vowels.

†**2.** ***in mute***, in an undertone. *Obs.*

c **1530** *Crt. of Love* 148 In mewet spak I, so that noght astert, By no condicion, word that might be herd.

3. A person precluded by nature, mutilation, or employment from the exercise of speech.

a. A dumb person; one deprived of the power of articulate speech owing to some congenital or pathological infirmity.

1615 G. SANDYS *Trav.* 74 Fifty Mutes he hath borne deafe and dumbe. **1660** *Trial Regic.* 53, I have heard a story of a Mute, that was born Mute. **1713** SWIFT *Cadenus & Vanessa* Wks. 1755 III. II. 25 Love can with speech inspire a mute. **1823** SCOTT *Peveril* xvi, The pretty mute was mistress of several little accomplishments. **1837** HT. MARTINEAU *Soc. Amer.* III. 335 In.. Hancock.. there are only 3 persons between 14 and 21 who cannot read and write; and they are mutes. **1899** *Allbutt's Syst. Med.* VIII. 109 The hysterical mute expresses himself in writing easily and correctly.

transf. **1775** GIBBON *Priv. Lett.* 25 Feb. (1896) I. 251, I am still a Mute; it is more tremendous than I imagined; the great speakers fill me with despair, the bad ones with terror. **1841** D'ISRAELI *Amen. Lit.* (1867) 687 The mute who cannot speak at a dinner or on the hustings, is eloquent in a pamphlet.

b. An actor on the stage whose part is performed only in dumb-show.

1579 W. WILKINSON *Confut. Familye of Loue* 32 Mutes vpon a stage called forth to fill vp a roome and make a shew. **1604** DEKKER *Kings' Entertainm.* Cj, The Personages (as well Mutes as Speakers) in this Pageant were these. **1765** E. THOMPSON *Meretriciad* (ed. 6) 48 Behind him waddles a theatric Mute. **1787** MME. D'ARBLAY *Diary* 18 Jan., It made me feel, once more.. like a mute upon the stage. **1884** *Truth* 13 Mar. 376/2 The sea-green robes of a beautiful mute in Mr. Gilbert's topsy-turvy plays.

c. In oriental countries: A dumb house-servant or janitor; usually one who has been deliberately deprived of the power of speech.

1599 SHAKS. *Hen. V*, I. ii. 232 Our graue Like Turkish mute, shall haue a tonguelesse mouth. **1603** KNOLLES *Hist. Turks* (1621) 763 Hee saw seauen Muts (these are strong men, bereft of their speech, whom the Turkish tyrants haue always in readinesse, the more secretly to execute their bloody butcherie). **1735** SOMERVILLE *Chase* III. 393 As his Guard of Mutes On the great Sultan wait. **1825** MACAULAY *Ess., Milton* (1897) 25 The mutes who throng their antechambers.

†**d.** *Law.* One who refuses to plead to an indictment. *Obs.* (Cf. MUTE *a.* 1 *note.*)

1659 FULLER *App. Inj. Innoc.* I. iii. 3 In our Common Law, Mutes at the Bar, who would not plead to the Indictment, are Adjudged guilty. **1660** *Trial Regic.* 31 He, that doth refuse to put himself upon his Legal Trial of God, and the Countrey, is a Mute in Law. **1738** NEAL *Hist. Purit.* IV. 187 Judgment was given against him as a Mute.

e. A professional attendant at a funeral; a hired 'mourner'.

1762–71 H. WALPOLE *Vertue's Anecd. Paint.* (1786) II. 219 Forty gentlemen.. submitted to wait as mutes with their backs against the wall of the chamber where the body laid in state. **1842** *Literary Gaz.* 31 Dec. 897/2 There he saw the two mutes and the hearse at the door. **1892** STEVENSON & L. OSBOURNE *Wrecker* I. 23 Those who had met at the depôt like a pair of mutes, sat down to table with holiday faces. **1962** WODEHOUSE *Service with Smile* I. 16 That's why she slinks about the place like a funeral mute, is it?

4. *Mus.* **a.** A clip of metal, wood or ivory that can be placed over the bridge of a violin or similar stringed instrument to deaden the resonance without affecting the vibration of the strings.

1811 BUSBY *Dict. Music* (ed. 3). **1894** *Pall Mall Mag.* Feb. 590 He played it over a dozen times with the mute on his violin after she had gone to rest.

b. A pear-shaped leather pad or piece of metal which can be inserted into the bell of a metal wind-instrument to check the emission of sound.

1841 *Musical World* Apr. 247 A mute is a piece of brass formed to fit the inside of the bell of a trumpet. **1845** E. HOLMES *Mozart* 176 The mutes which soften the tone of brass instruments.

5. *Cinemat.* A positive or negative film print which has no synchronous sound-track. Also *attrib.* or as *adj.*

1933 A. BRUNEL *Filmcraft* 161 *Mute*, the negative or positive of the pictorial image. **1953** K. REISZ *Technique Film Editing* 281 *Mute negative*, picture negative of a sound film, without the sound-track. *Mute print*, positive print of the picture part of a sound film without the sound track. **1963** E. LINDGREN *Art of Film* (ed. 2) ii. 37 We now have two lengths of negative film, one known as the mute negative (or picture negative or action negative) and the other known as the sound negative. The projection print is made by printing these two negatives on to a single positive film. **1969** W. RUTHERFORD *Gallows Set* ii. 27 We're filming him tomorrow morning... And we're doing a bit of mute, showing him going up to the gate. *Ibid.* iv. 53 There's.. a couple of cans on shipbuilding, mostly mute but with a bit of sound.

6. *Comb.*, as ***mute-like*** adj.; **mute-closure** (*Phonetics*), closure of the oral passage so as to form a mute.

1875 WHITNEY *Life Lang.* iv. 62 These are the only mute-closures found in English, or French, or German. **1889** CLARK RUSSELL *Marooned* xvii, There is really no need for such a mute-like face as yours.

†**mute**, *sb.*[2] *Obs.* Also 6 **meute**, 6–7 **mewte**, 7 **mut, muite**, 8 **mewt**. [f. MUTE *v.*[1] Cf. F. *émeut* of the same meaning.]

1. The action of 'muting'; *concr.* (*sing.* and *pl.*) dung (of birds).

1575 TURBERV. *Falconrie* 116 If hir mewtes bee cleane and white. **1596** HARINGTON *Metam. Ajax* 31 You have a speciall regard to obserue, if she [*sc.* the hawk] make a cleane mute. **1614** MARKHAM *Cheap Husb.* 140 If your Hawke.. get any inward bruise, which you shall know by the blacknesse or bloodinesse of their muts, you shall then annoynt her meat .. with Sperma-Cœtæ till her mutes be cleare againe. **1645** G. DANIEL *Poems* Wks. (Grosart) II. 45 Like a Falcon.. Check'd by my bonds, I fall, And lime my Selfe, in all The muite and Slime. **1706** PHILLIPS (ed. Kersey), *Mute*, dung, especially of Birds. **1727** BRADLEY *Fam. Dict.* s.v. *Apostume*, They must be held on the Fist until they have made one or two Mewts. **1820** SCORESBY *Acc. Arctic Reg.* I. 426 The reddish colour.. is given by the mute of birds.

2. A kind of slimy discharge, as mucus.

1578 LYTE *Dodoens* III. cxiii. 306 It doth mundifie and clense the breast of all cold meutes or flegme.

†**mute**, *sb.*[3] *Obs.* Also 4 **mut**, 9 **meute**. [a. OF. *muete, meute* (mod.F. *meute*):—popular L. **movita*, verbal noun f. L. *movēre* to MOVE. Cf. med.L. *mota* (from OFr.).]

1. A pack of hounds.

13.. *Gaw. & Gr. Knt.* 1720 Thenne watz hit lif vpon list to lyþen þe houndez, When alle þe mute hade hym met, menged to-geder. *c* **1410** *Master of Game* (MS. Digby 182) xxxv, þanne shulde þe sergeant of þe mute of þe herte houndes.. make alle hem of þe office.. hardell þeire houndes. **1486** *Bk. St. Albans* F vj b, A Mute of houndes. **1664** *Spelman's Gloss.*, *Mute*, a Kenel or Crie of Hounds. **1688** R. HOLME *Armoury* II. 132/1 Hounds 16 [are] a Kennell of Hounds, or a Mute.

2. The cry of hounds working.

13.. *Gaw. & Gr. Knt.* 1915 Hit watz þe myriest mute þat euer men herde. *c* **1350** *Will. Palerne* 2192 Alle men þat mut herde of þe muri houndes, seweden after ful swiþe to se þat mury chace.

¶**3.** Misused for MEW *sb.*[2] 1.

The mistake seems to have arisen from confusion with the med.L. *mūta* mew for hawks.

1854 MILMAN *Lat. Chr.* VII. i. III. 117 The cloisters became.. the kennels of their hounds, the meutes of their hawks.

mute (mjuːt), *sb.*[4] *dial.* A kind of mule.

In some districts applied to the offspring of a mare and an ass (the 'mule' properly so called), and in others to that of the she-ass and stallion (the 'hinny').

1843 BORROW *Bible in Spain* xxiii, Gigantic and heavily-laden mutes and mules. **1895** *Daily News* 23 July 2/2 The most curious 'donkey' was a 'mute'. *Ibid.*, The mute was said to be nine years old.

mute (mjuːt), *v.*[1] *Obs.* exc. *dial.* Also 6, 8 **mewt**. [a. OF. *muetir* (*mutir* Cotgr. 1611), aphetic form of *esmeutir*, earlier *esmeltir*.

The ulterior origin is obscure; the Teut. *smelt-* to melt, SMELT *v.*, would suit the form, but the affinity of sense is not very close.]

Of a bird, esp. a hawk: **a.** *intr.* To void the fæces. **b.** *trans.* To discharge as fæces.

c **1450** *Bk. Hawking* in *Rel. Ant.* I. 296 Ye schull say that your hawke mutith and not sclisith. **1486** *Bk. St. Albans* C viij, She mutith when she auoydith hir order. *a* **1529** SKELTON *Ware the Hauke* 62 The hawke.. mutid there a chase Vpon my corporas face. **1575** TURBERV. *Falconrie* 61 A greene seere of hir foote,.. large panell, and able to slyse farre from hir when she mewteth. **1611** BIBLE *Tobit* ii. 10 Mine eyes being open, the Sparrowes muted warme doung into mine eyes. **1622** tr. *Luna's Pursuit Lazarillo* ix. 74 Aske a Philosopher why Flyes vpon a white thing doe mute black, and contrariwise, vpon a black, white. **1679** CROWNE *Amb. Statesm.* III. 38 Flying rumours, which like birds Soaring at random, mute on any head. **1698** B. BULLIVANT in *Phil. Trans.* XX. 168 It [*sc.* the bird] muted the Honey pure. **1727** BRADLEY *Fam. Dict.* s.v. *Back-worm*, Make 'em into a Pill, which give her in the Morning so soon as she has cast, and after she has mewted it clean away, then give her good hot Meat. **1774** G. WHITE *Selborne* 28 Sept., When they [*sc.* swifts] mute.. they raise their wings. **1820** *Blackw. Mag.* VII. 676 Sir Dick gave the dung that he ventures to mute on The glories of Europe, our Wellesley and Newton.

†**mute**, *v.*[2] *Obs.* [Of obscure origin: perh. a. L. *mūtīre* to murmur. The identity of the word in the various quots. is uncertain.] *intr.* To

murmur. Hence '**muting** *vbl. sb.*, murmuring discontent.

In quot. 1542 perh. a mistake for *mutining*, or possibly a. MDu. *muytinge* insurrection.

1542 *Fabyan's Chron.* VII. 486/2 And in this yere [1524–5] ..[was] a mutyng in Norfolke & Suffolke for payment of money. **1570** FOXE *A. & M.* (ed. 2) I. 365/2 Muche lesse durst poore subiectes once mute agaynst hym. *Ibid.* 659/2 The kyngdome of the Pope and his members..began to be so strong, that none durst styrre or once mute agaynst them. *a* **1639** SPOTTISWOOD *Hist. Ch. Scot.* (1677) III. 124 They perceived a secret muting in their own Army. **1642** D. ROGERS *Naaman* 519 That none should be so daring or presumptuous, as once to mute or quetch, if they once proclaime their will. **1643** R. BAILLIE *Lett.* (1841) II. 91 Mr. Harie Guthrie made no dinne. His letter was a wand above his head to discipline him, if he should mute. **1644** *Ibid.* 147 This was read openlie in the face of the Assemblie, and in the eares of the Independents, who durst not mute against it. **1655** FULLER *Ch. Hist.* XI. xvii. 162 That murmuring and muting against Princes differ only in degree, not in kinde.

mute (mjuːt), *v.*³ [f. MUTE *a.*]

† **1.** *intr.* (See quot.) *Obs.*⁻⁰

Perh. *mute* may be a mistake for *run mute*, which appears in later edd. of Phillips.

1678 PHILLIPS (ed. 4), *Mute*,..also when Hounds run long, without making any cry they are said to mute.

2. *trans.* To deaden or subdue the sound of: *spec.* in *Music*, to muffle the sound of (a musical instrument). Also *fig.*

1883 F. CORDER in Grove *Dict. Mus.* III. 637 Berlioz muted the clarinet by enveloping the bell in a bag of chamois leather. *Ibid.*, Violins are muted either by placing a wooden or brass instrument upon the bridge. **1891** G. MEREDITH *One of our Conq.* III. viii. 148 The tone of neutral colour that, as in sound, muted splendour. **1891** *Times* 22 Oct. 14/2 The strings are muted, and, yet..the woodwind is always to be kept in subjection to them. **1906** MAX PEMBERTON *Hundred Days* 101 A heavy Indian carpet muted the footsteps of the Emperor as he paced it.

b. To silence.

1891 G. MEREDITH *One of our Conq.* II. v. 129 They are spirited on, patted, subdued, muted, raised, rushed anew, away, held in hand.

mute (mjuːt), *v.*⁴ *Wine-making.* [f. F. *muter*, f. L. *mūtus* dumb (cf. MUTE *a.*).] *trans.* To check the fermentation of (must). Hence '**muted** *a.*¹; '**muting** *vbl. sb.*

1839 URE *Dict. Arts* 1203 If *must*, so *muted*, is boiled into a syrup within a week or ten days, it retains no sulphureous odour. A very slight muting would suffice for the most fermentable cane-juice. **1853** *Ibid.* (ed. 4) I. 155 The muted wines.

mute, variant of MEWT *v.*

a **1529** SKELTON *Sp. Parrot* 26 Lyke your pus cate, Parrot can mute and cry In Lattyn, in Ebrew, Araby, and Caldey.

mute, obs. form of MOOT *sb.*¹, *v.*¹, MOULT *v.*

muted *a.*¹: see MUTE *v.*⁴

muted ('mjuːtɪd), *a.*² [f. MUTE *v.*³ + -ED¹.] Rendered mute, silent; muffled. *spec.* Of music or musical instruments: Having the sound muffled. Also in extended use; *spec.* of colour = SUBDUED *ppl. a.* 2.

1861 *Sat. Rev.* 14 Dec. 611 There is a pleasing effect by the muted violins. **1879** G. MEREDITH *Egoist* III. ii. 50 That low muted tone of the very heart, impossible to deride. **1897** *Edin. Rev.* Apr. 316 It is only a muted melancholy. **1905** HOWELLS *London Films* 93 The muted Sunday streets. **1939** M. B. PICKEN *Language of Fashion* 101/3 Muted, subdued or toned down. Often applied to colours. **1950** *Britannica Bk. of Year* 682/2 *Muted*, of lighting, subdued. **1958** *Oxf. Mail* 9 July 6/2 Sea colours—aquamarine, sapphire blue, muted green. **1964** *Daily Tel.* 7 Feb. 16/2 'It is unlikely that the development of public expenditure on the scale implied will leave much scope for a reduction in taxation.' This muted sentence..must often come to people's minds as they read of new commitments. **1964** MRS. L. B. JOHNSON *White House Diary* 17 July (1970) 181 *My* West is muted brown and green and gray. **1968** *Jazz Monthly* Nov. 23/1 Davis uses that distinctive hard-edged smokey-centred muted tone. **1974** *Impressionism* (R. Acad.) 45/2 He uses a very restricted colour-range to convey an overcast snow-effect—muted blues and greens set off against grey and white.

Hence '**mutedly** *adv.*

1891 G. MEREDITH *One of our Conq.* II. viii. 212 Now and then mutedly ebullient at the mouth.

mutely ('mjuːtlɪ), *adv.* [f. MUTE *a.* + -LY².] In a mute or silent manner.

1628 MILTON *Vac. Exerc.* 6 Hail, native Language, that.. mad'st imperfect words..slide through my infant-lips, Driving dumb Silence from the portal door, Where he had mutely sat two years before! **1687** DRYDEN *Hind & P.* I. 535 The rest amazed, Stood mutely still, and on the stranger gazed. **1863** WOOLNER *My Beautiful Lady* 42 Her mutely gracious ways. **1884** F. M. CRAWFORD *Rom. Singer* i, Nino sat mutely by, as we smoked.

mutener, obs. form of MUTINEER.

muteness ('mjuːtnɪs). [-NESS.] The quality or condition of being mute or silent.

1590 H. BARROW in *Confer.* iii. 65 Here Mr. Cooper was smitten with mutenes. **1643** MILTON *Divorce* I. iii. 8 The bashful mutenes of a virgin. **1821** LAMB *Elia* Ser. I. *Quakers' Meeting.* What is the stillness of the desert, compared with this place? What the uncommunicating muteness of fishes? **1852** SEIDEL *Organ* 138 If the foot of a wood pipe be very badly worm-eaten,..muteness of the pipe will be the consequence. **1898** *Atlantic Monthly* LXXXII. 480/1 Terror and absolute muteness reign in the house.

b. Said of hounds: The habit of being 'tongueless' when the occasion requires 'cries'.

1881 *Encycl. Brit.* XII. 315/2 Lastly, they must be free from certain faults, such as muteness, babbling, and skirting.

mutenie, -ye, obs. forms of MUTINY *sb.*

mu'ter, mutere, obs. ff. MULTURE, MOOTER.

† **mutess**, *v. Obs. rare.* Also 5 **muteyse**. [a. OF. *mutiss-*, *muetir* MUTE *v.*¹] = MUTE *v.*¹

1486 *Bk. St. Albans* A iij b, An euell callid the Cray..that is whan an hawke may not muteyse. *Ibid.* A vj b, Ye shall say yowre hawke mutessith or mutith and not sklysith.

‖ **mutessarif** (muːtə'sariːf). Also **mutasarrif, mutassarif, mutasserif, mutesarrif, mutussarif.** [Turk., ad. Arab. *mutaṣarrif* governor of a sanjak.] In the Ottoman Empire and Iraq, a governor of a province.

1875 *Encycl. Brit.* III. 446/2 Batum..is now the seat of a *mutessarif*, or deputy-governor. **1900** G. BELL *Let.* 2 May (1927) I. 87 There has come a telegram from Damascus to bid me say the Mutussarif fears for the safety of your presence. **1914** T. E. LAWRENCE *Let.* June (1938) 174 All the Consuls & Valis & Kaims & Mutasarrifs & Commandants came out also. **1919** R. WEBB *Let.* 28 June in M. Llewellyn Smith *Ionian Vision* (1973) vi. 106 We were gradually getting the bad Valis, Mutessarifs, &c, removed. **1921** *Blackw. Mag.* June 705/2 A few of the political officers remain in the new capacity of Adviser to an Arab Mutassarif. **1933** *Times Lit. Suppl.* 9 Nov. 760/2 It was in Jerusalem that he was able to watch the simple methods of Rauf Pasha, then Mutessarif of El Kuds. **1969** D. WALDER *Chanak* xi. 199 The Mutessarif of Chanak (a combination of English mayor and French prefect) had taken over the Sanjak. **1972** D. DAKIN *Unification of Greece* viii. 116 The *mutessarifs* (provincial governors) were, if Christian, to have Moslem assessors, and, if Moslems, then Christian assessors.

muth, variant of MATH².

muthafucka, muthafukka, muthafucking, varr. *mother-fucker*, *mother-fucking* ppl. adj. (MOTHER *sb.*¹ 17 a).

1969 H. R. BROWN *Die Nigger, Die* ii. 29 The dirty muthafucka. **1969** R. D. TAYLOR *Drum Song* in A. Chapman *New Black Voices* (1972) 312 Ain't that blackmuthafukka beautiful. **1971** *Black World* Mar. 54/2 The best muthafucking thing that done ever happened to me.

muthologic, -ical, etc.: see MYTHOLOGIC, etc.

muti ('muːtɪ). *S. Afr.* Also 9 **booti, mooti.** [ad. Zulu *umuthi* tree, plant, medicine.] Medicine; a medicinal charm (used esp. by a medicine-man or witch-doctor).

1831 W. B. BOYCE *Jrnl.* 23 June in A. Steedman *Wanderings & Adventures in S. Afr.* (1835) II. 282 He mentioned the report of Mr. Shepstone having sent men on horseback to plant booti (bewitching matter) upon his place. **1891** R. MONTEIRO *Delagoa Bay* viii. 172 They [*sc.* the Kaffirs] don't mind saying some are used as 'mooti', physic. **1911** *State* Dec. 659 (Pettman), He produced a few pinches of powder from the *muti* bag suspended round his neck. **1947** *Cape Times* 10 May 1/1 It was thought that the plant had been killed out by witchdoctors, who consider it an important ingredient of a powerful muti. **1957** J. PACKER *Nor Moon by Night* xviii. 176 He may have made *muti* of that boy's eyes and tongue. *Ibid.* xxvi. 234 This *muti* is like the bite of a cobra—it makes a man sleep. **1971** *Sunday Times* (Johannesburg) 28 Mar. 20/3 The club which has often used the rolling of the bones to forecast the results of vital matches need some new 'muti' to revive their form.

mutic ('mjuːtɪk), *a. Bot.* and *Ent.* [a. L. *muticus* (see MUTICOUS *a.*). Cf. F. *mutique.*] = MUTILATE *a.* 3. **a.** *Bot.* Without a point or beard, muticous. **b.** *Ent.* Wanting spines.

1777 ROBSON *Brit. Flora* 25 Of the calyx. Mutic, without awns. **1842** LOUDON *Encycl. Trees & Shrubs* Index, *Mutic*, pointless; a term opposed to mucro. **1861** HAGEN *Syn. Neuroptera N. Amer.* 341 *Mutic*, unarmed, i.e. without spines, &c.

muticate ('mjuːtɪkeɪt), *a. Zool. rare*⁻¹. [Formed as next + -ATE.] = MUTILATE *a.* 3.

1860 OWEN *Palæont.* 311 Both form and structure are compatible with the hoofless muticate type of herbivorous Mammal, as shown by the Manatee.

muticous ('mjuːtɪkəs), *a. Bot.* [f. early L. *muticus* awnless (Varro *De Re Rust.* I. xlviii) + -OUS.] Without point or awn, beardless.

1856 MAYNE *Expos. Lex.*, *Muticus*, *Bot.*, without the arista or awn; beardless, muticous. **1874** R. BROWN *Man. Bot.* 609 *Muticous*, destitute of a terminal point. **1881** *Jrnl. Bot.* X. 12 Not unlike a muticous form of *Tortula unguiculata.*

mutil, obs. form of MUTULE.

mutilate ('mjuːtɪlət), *sb.* [Subst. use of next adj.] A member of the *Mutilata*, the lowest division of Megasthenes in Dana's classification of Mammalia, comprising those with 'mutilate' limbs; a cetacean or sirenian.

1862 DANA *Man. Geol.* 423 *note*, Mutilates. The limbs short and paddle-like for swimming. **1863** [see MEGASTHENE].

mutilate ('mjuːtɪlət), *a.* Also 6 *Sc.* **mutilat, mutillait.** [ad. L. *mutilāt-us*, pa. pple. of *mutilāre* to MUTILATE.]

1. Of a human body: Wanting or deprived of one or more of its members; mutilated; of a limb, rendered imperfect by mutilation. *Obs.* exc. *poet.*

1532 FRITH *Mirror* (1626) 44 Wee..are much bound to him, that he hath giuen to vs our perfect members:..yet.. wee are much bound vnto him, although he hath made vs imperfect & mutilate. **1540–1** ELYOT *Image Gov.* 71 He beheld a great noumbre of persons, some..mutilate of their membres. **1563–4** *Reg. Privy Council Scot.* I. 269 In caise any of thame..happynnis to be hurt, mutilat, or slane. **1646** SIR T. BROWNE *Pseud. Ep.* VII. ii. 342 Criples mutilate in their owne persons, do come out perfect in their generations. **1795** SOUTHEY *Maid of Orleans* I. 82 Imaged forms Of saints and warlike chiefs, moss-canker'd now And mutilate, lay strewn upon the ground. **1814** CARY *Dante, Inf.* xxviii. 60 Another shade, Pierc'd in the throat, his nostrils mutilate.

2. Of things: Having some part destroyed or wanting. *Obs.* exc. *poet.*

c **1560** [BANNATYNE] in *A. Scott's Poems* (E.E.T.S.) 1 To Rdr., My copeis awld, mankit, and mvtillait. **1567** J. SANFORD tr. *Epictetus* 6 The instrument being mutilate and vnperfect. **1644** HAMMOND *Conscience* §71. 38 The maimed mutilate obedience, the compounding betwixt God and Satan. **1673** [R. LEIGH] *Transp. Reh.* 57 The story as he has castrated it is so mutilate and deficient. **1814** SOUTHEY *Roderick* XVIII, Mutilate..Of royal rites was this solemnity.

3. *Nat. Hist.* Deficient in some part common to the species or to closely related species, or possessing it only in an imperfect or modified form.

1760 J. LEE *Introd. Bot.* I. xx. (1765) 61 Mutilate Flowers are the reverse of Luxuriant. Linnæus confines the Term to those Flowers only that want the Corollæ, though they ought to be furnished with it. **1826** KIRBY & SP. *Entomol.* IV. xlvi. 333 Mutilate (*Mutilata*). When they [the elytra] appear unnaturally short or curtailed as if mutilated. **1848** MAUNDER *Treas. Nat. Hist.* 796. **1890** *Century Dict.*, *Mutilate*, deprived of hind limbs, as a cetacean or a sirenian.

Hence † '**mutilateness** *rare*⁻¹.

1599 A. M. tr. *Gabelhouer's Bk. Physicke* 199/1 It will prævent the mutilatenes of anye persone.

mutilate ('mjuːtɪleɪt), *v.* Also 6 **mutulate**, 7 *Sc.* **mittellate.** [f. L. *mutilāt-*, ppl. stem of *mutilāre* to cut or lop off; f. *mutil-us* maimed (? = Gr. μύτιλος or μίτυλος, hornless): see -ATE¹.]

1. *trans.* To deprive (a person or animal) of a limb or some principal organ of the body; to cut off or otherwise destroy the use of (a limb or organ). *spec.* in *Scots Law*: cf. MUTILATION.

1562 [implied in MUTILATING *vbl. sb.*]. **1609** SKENE *Reg. Maj.* (1774) 395 (tr. *Stat. Rob. II*, c. 11) Gif ane man mutilats ane other, or wounds, or beates him, be forthocht felonie. **1616** BULLOKAR *Eng. Expos.*, *Mutilate*, to maime, cut off, or make lame. **1646** SIR T. BROWNE *Pseud. Ep.* VII. ii. 342 Such as fearing to concede a monstrosity, or mutilate the integrity of Adam, preventively conceive the creation of thirteene ribs. **1685** SIR J. LAUDER *Chron. Notes Sc. Affairs* (1822) 135 M'Alla, skiper in Leith, sues before the Councill John Reid, skiper there, for mittellating him. **1838** THIRLWALL *Greece* IV. 337 The Greeks..mutilated the slain. **1839** *Ibid.* VI. 295 He was condemned to be mutilated, ..in his nose and ears. **1854** MILMAN *Lat. Chr.* IV. viii. (1864) II. 396 They were blinded, or mutilated by the loss of their tongues. **1866** ROGERS *Agric. & Prices* I. xxi. 525 Sheep-dogs were purposely mutilated in order to prevent their running game down.

absol. **1805** *Med. Jrnl.* XIV. 54 A high variolous susceptibility, which..when excited by art [*i.e.* by vaccination]..very often mutilates, and very often destroys.

fig. **15..** *Narr. Reformation* (Camden) 238 The said scholemaster so appalled..the tender and fyne wittes of his scholers, whose memories were also therby so mutilated and wounded, that [etc.]. **1841** MYERS *Cath. Th.* III. §50. 196 Let a man sit down to the study of the Bible..mutilating no endowment of his understanding.

2. To render (a thing, esp. a record, book, etc.) imperfect by cutting off or destroying a part.

1534 MORE *Treat. Passion* Wks. 1291/1, I wil not in any worde wyllinglye, mangle or mutulate that honourable mans worke. **1637–50** ROW *Hist. Kirk* (Wodrow Soc.) 65 The maters being relating to Bishops, it is easie to espy who did mutilat the Register. **1701** GREW *Cosm. Sacra* V. I. §40. 289 The Scriptures are hereby [*sc.* the various Lections], neither Mutilated, nor Depraved. **1824** DIBDIN *Libr. Comp.* 681 Which [book-leaves] have been dreadfully devoured or mutilated by..some..animal. **1902** A. LANG *Hist. Scot.* II. ix. 208 The deposition of Bowton was mutilated, to shield Murray's associates.

Hence '**mutilating** *vbl. sb.* and *ppl. a.*

1562 *Reg. Privy Council Scot.* I. 218 The Tolbuith..in the quhilk he wes wardit, for the cruell onsetting upoun James Lord Ogilvy and mutilating of him of his rycht arme. **1677** GILPIN *Demonol.* (1867) 402 The misrepresentation and abuse of it, as may be seen..in his clipping and mutilating of it. **1826** E. IRVING *Babylon* I. II. 125 No other book..hath been permitted to escape the violent or mutilating hands of their inquisitory acts. **1827** STEUART *Planter's G.* (1828) 140 The Mutilating system [of transplanting trees], now generally prevalent. *Ibid.*, A planter, according to the Mutilating method,..then proceeds to lighten and lop the top. **1905** TUCKWELL *Remin. Rad. Parson* xiii. 189 The mutilating process became intolerable at last, and I gently dropped out of the journal.

mutilated ('mjuːtɪleɪtɪd), *ppl. a.* [f. MUTILATE *v.* + -ED¹.]

1. = MUTILATE *a.* 1; also, *rarely*, castrated.

1597 A. M. tr. *Guillemeau's Fr. Chirurg.* *iv, Wounded & mutilatede persons. **1790** BURKE *Fr. Rev.* 106 The most splendid palace in the world, which they left..strewed with

..mutilated carcases. **1812** BYRON *Ch. Har.* II. lviii, The lively, supple Greek; And swarthy Nubia's mutilated son. **1860** TYNDALL *Glac.* II. xvii. 315 Mutilated statuary. **1870** ROLLESTON *Anim. Life* Introd. 67 Some..portion of the mutilated organ or limb should be left *in situ*.

2. Of things: Having some part cut off or destroyed; wanting some portion essential to completeness.

1628 LE GRYS tr. *Barclay's Argenis* 93 Thou mayest yet see the Cities as it were mutilated, the roofes and pinnacles of the Temples being broken downe. **1771** MACKENZIE *Man Feel.* xl. 264 Harley's own story, from the mutilated passages I have mentioned..I found to have been simple to excess. **1784** COWPER *Task.* I. 774 Folly such as your's..Has made ..Our arch of empire..A mutilated structure, soon to fall. **1862** BURTON *Bk. Hunter* (1863) 43 A call by a public library to replace a mutilated book with a new copy. **1875** DARWIN *Insectiv. Pl.* xiii. 319 This mutilated leaf..re-expanded in two days. **1878** BOSW. SMITH *Carthage* 340 He was encouraged to make aggressions on her mutilated territory.

3. Special applications. (See quots.)

1693 tr. *Blancard's Phys. Dict.* (ed. 2), *Myurus*, a mutilated Pulse, increasing or decreasing gradually. **1696** PHILLIPS (ed. 5), *Mutilated*, otherwise called Azimene Degrees, are certain degrees in several Signs, that threaten the Native that has them Ascending, with Lameness [etc.]. **1727–41** CHAMBERS *Cycl.* s.v. *Corniche*, Mutilated Corniche is that whose projecture is omitted, or else interrupted, right to the larmier, or reduced into a platband with a cimatium. *Ibid.*, *Mutilated Roof.* Sometimes it is cut, or mutilated, that is, consists of a true and a false roof which is laid over the former: this last is particularly called a mansard. **1793** MARTYN *Lang. Bot.* (1796) s.v. *Mutilatus*, A mutilated flower. Not producing a corolla, when it ought regularly to do it. **1802** C. JAMES *Milit. Dict.* s.v., A battalion is said to be mutilated, when its divisions, &c., stand unequal. **1875** KNIGHT *Dict. Mech.*, *Mutilated Wheel*, a wheel, from a part of the perimeter of which the cogs are removed.

mutilation (mjuːtɪˈleɪʃən). Also 6 *Sc.* **mutilatioun.** [a. L. *mutilātiōn-em*, n. of action f. *mutilāre* to MUTILATE. Cf. F. *mutilation.*]

1. The action of depriving (a person or animal) of a limb or of the use of a limb; the excision or maiming (of a limb or bodily organ); also, an instance of the action; *rarely* a mutilated condition.

1646 SIR T. BROWNE *Pseud. Ep.* VII. ii. 342 We observe that mutilations are not transmitted from father unto son; the blind begetting such as can see [etc.]. **1651** HOBBES *Leviath.* II. xxvii. 160 Mutilation of a limbe, [is a] greater [Crime], than the spoyling a man of his goods. *a* **1716** SOUTH *Serm.* (1744) X. viii. 239 When a man is in imminent danger of the mutilation of a leg or an arm. **1769** BLACKSTONE *Comm.* IV. 370 Some punishments..occasion a mutilation or dismembring, by cutting off the hand or ears. **1849** MACAULAY *Hist. Eng.* v. I. 569 Many of them were also sentenced to mutilation. On a single day the hangman of Edinburgh cut off the ears of thirty-five prisoners. **1867** FREEMAN *Norm. Conq.* (1877) I. v. 371 There he put on shore the hostages..having first subjected them to various mutilations, as the loss of hands, ears and noses. **1883** GREEN *Conq. Eng.* v. 227 The laws against mutilation of cattle.

b. *Scots Law.* The action of disabling or wounding (a person) in his members as distinguished from 'demembration'.

1525 *Extracts Aberd. Reg.* (1844) I. 113 The cruell slauchteris, mutilatiounis, and hurts doyne amang thame under silence of nycht, be thair neychbours about. **1546** *Ibid.* 230 Tuching the hurting and bluid draving of the said Amrouse Tailzeour, and mutilation of him of his left hand. **1555** *Burgh Rec. Stirling* (1887) 65 Thai wer acquyt..of mutilatioun of the lard of Cragingelt. **1609** [see DEMEMBRATION]. **1699** SIR A. SETON (*title*) A Treatise of mutilation and demembration and their punishments. **1797** *Encycl. Brit.* (ed. 3) IX. 720/2 [Law of Scotland.] Mutilation, or the disabling of a member, is punished at the discretion of the judge. **1838** in *Bell's Dict. Law Scotl.*

c. *spec.* Castration.

1727–41 CHAMBERS *Cycl.* s.v., Mutilation is sometimes also used in a more immediate manner for 'castration'. **1828–54** in WEBSTER. **1850** in OGILVIE. In some recent Dicts.

2. The action of rendering (a thing) imperfect by excision or destruction of one or more of its parts; also, an instance of this.

1638 SIR T. HERBERT *Trav.* (ed. 2) 117 Making the ships their object (after a great mutilation of shrowds and masts) they sunk the..Fleet. **1659** PEARSON *Creed* II. 136 All the originall letters in the name Hoseah are preserved in that of Joshua:..this alteration was not made by..diminution or mutilation; but by addition. **1867** DICKENS *Lett.* (1880) II. 270, I have no more power to stop that mutilation of my books than you have. **1874** H. R. REYNOLDS *John Bapt.* ii. 69 Very numerous other omissions and mutilations are notified by Tertullian. **1875** WHITNEY *Life Lang.* iv. 55 Another consequence of the same difference of accent is the greater mutilation of the radical part of the word in the Romanic languages..than in the Germanic.

mutilative (ˈmjuːtɪlətɪv), *a. nonce-wd.* [f. MUTILATE *v.* + -IVE.] Causing mutilation.

1883 LYON PLAYFAIR in *Times* 20 June 11 This fatal and mutilative disease [*sc.* small-pox].

mutilator (ˈmjuːtɪleɪtə(r)). Also 7 -er. [a. L. *mutilātor*, agent-n. f. *mutilāre* to MUTILATE.] One who mutilates.

1637–50 ROW *Hist. Kirk* (Wodrow Soc.) 181 That hurters and mutilaters of ministers may once at last be taken. **1767** BUSH *Hibernia Cur.* To Rdr. (1769) 12 That class of hireling pedagogal priggs, the abridgers, or rather mutilators of our civil history. **1820** LAMB *Elia* Ser. I. *Two Races Men*, I mean your borrowers of books—those mutilators of collections,.. and creators of odd volumes. **1828** SCOTT *F.M. Perth* vii, Our townsman..did far wrong to cut off a gentleman's hand for such a harmless pleasantry, and the town may be brought to a heavy fine for it, unless we secure the person of the mutilator. **1874** L. STEPHEN *Hours in Library* (1892) I. iii. 111 Bentley was..the tasteless mutilator of Milton.

† **mutile**, *v. Obs. rare*⁻¹. [ad. F. *mutiler*, ad. L. *mutilāre*: see MUTILATE *v.* and MITTLE *v.*] *trans.* To mutilate.

a **1618** SYLVESTER *Spectacles* xxxii, Hee sees high Archs, huge shining Heaps of Stone Maim'd, mutil'd, murder'd, by yeers wasteful teen.

mutillait, obs. Sc. form of MUTILATE *a.*

mutillid (mjuːˈtɪlɪd), *sb.* and *a.* [f. mod.L. family name *Mutillidæ*, f. generic name *Mutilla* (Linnæus *Systema Naturæ* (ed. 10, 1758) I. 582): see -ID³.] **A.** *sb.* A solitary, parasitic, fossorial wasp of the family Mutillidæ, including insects also known as velvet ants, whose bodies are covered with fine hair. **B.** *adj.* Pertaining to or resembling an insect of this type.

1910 W. M. WHEELER *Ants* xiv. 244 Existing mutillids, however, present two highly specialized characters..: they are, so far as is known, parasitic and their females are wingless. **1913** [see CLERID *a.* and *sb.*]. **1971** E. O. WILSON *Insect Societies* xviii. 338/1 Several observers..have witnessed guard bees protecting their nests against mutillid wasps and ants. **1972** L. E. CHADWICK tr. *Linsenmaier's Insects of World* 299/1 The mutillids chirp with a sound like that of boiling water.

mutilo, obs. form of MUTULE.

† **mutilous**, *a. Obs.* [f. L. *mutil-us* (see MUTILATE *v.*) + -OUS.] Of things: Mutilated, imperfect.

1649 JER. TAYLOR *Gt. Exemp.* II. Disc. vi. 17 Our faith is commonly lame, mutilous and imperfect. **1653** ASHWELL *Fides Apost.* 160 A mutilous member or defective Article. **1660** tr. *Amyraldus' Treat. conc. Relig.* III. ix. 503 Some mutilous monuments and the foundation of some old castle. **1692** RAY *Disc.* II. iv. 112 In all other figured Fossils it is observed that they are never found mutilous broken or imperfect. *a* **1707** WILLARD *Body of Divinity* ccxlii. (1726) 880/2 Divers do make these two [petition and thanksgiving] to be the parts of prayer,..as if it were mutilous without them both.

Hence † **ˈmutilously** *adv.*, † **ˈmutilousness.**

1648 E. SPARKE *Ep. Ded.* to *Shute's Sarah & Hagar*, While thus mutilously they render him. **1668** WILKINS *Real Char.* II. viii. §1. 198 Mutilousness.

† **mutiˈnado.** *Obs.* [Pseudo-Sp. formation on MUTINE *v.*: see -ADO. Cf. Sp. *amotinado* mutineer.] A mutineer.

1604 E. GRIMSTONE *Hist. Siege Ostend* 218 The mutinadoes..had the point. **1611** SPEED *Hist. Gt. Brit.* IX. xx. §27. 735/2 This vnfortunate Prince, hauing..incurred extreme hatred with many of the Nobility and people laboured with King Henry..to make an accord betweene him and his Mutinadoes.

† **mutine**, *sb.* and *a.*¹ *Obs.* Also 6 **mutyne, mutin.** [a. F. *mutin* adj. rebellious, mutinous, sb. rebel, mutineer; also in 16th c. rebellion, mutiny; corresponding to Sp. *motin*, Pg. *motim* rebellion, mutiny:—Rom. **movitino*, f. popular L. **movita*: see MUTE *sb.*²] **A.** *sb.*

1. Popular disturbance or tumult; rebellion, mutiny.

1560 DAUS tr. *Sleidane's Comm.* 426 b, In the selfe same momente, whan that heate and mutine began to ryse..was brought a remedy, and all the tempeste appeased. **1579** *Guisian Ambas.* A iv, The Fyre and Flame of..mutynes and tumultes. **1600** FAIRFAX *Tasso* I. i. 1 His soldiers wilde (to braules and mutines prest) Reduced he to peace.

2. A turbulent or rebellious person; a mutineer.

1581 SAVILE *Tacitus, Hist.* II. xvii. (1591) 83 Otho went out, & hauing rebuked the principal mutins, returning againe [etc.]. **1595** SHAKS. *John* II. i. 378 Your Royall presences be rul'd by mee, Do like the Mutines of Ierusalem, Be friends a-while. **1604** E. GRIMSTONE *Hist. Siege Ostend* 6 The mutines of Isabella fort were pacified.

B. *adj.* Turbulent, mutinous. *Obs. rare*⁻¹.

1587 T. HUGHES *Misfort. Arthur* Introd., Our industrie maintaineth..The Commons libertie and each mans right; Supresseth mutin force and practicke fraude. **1598** [R. CAREW] *Herrings Tayle* A 2 b, On traytor sea, and mid the mutine [*printed* mutiue] windes.

‖ **mutine** (mytin), *a.*² [Fr., fem. of *mutin* adj.: see prec.] Of a girl or woman: Rebellious, unsubmissive.

1870 MISS BROUGHTON *Red as Rose* I. 50 Essie..looking excessively mutine and ill-humoured. **1877** MRS. FORRESTER *Mignon* I. 112 Mignon's face assumes an unmistakeably mutine look.

† **mutine**, *v. Obs.* Also 6–7 **mutin.** [a. F. *mutiner*, f. *mutin*: see MUTINE *sb.* Cf. Sp., Pg. *amotinar*, It. *ammutinare.*]

1. *intr.* To rise in revolt against authority; to rebel, mutiny.

1555, 1559 [implied in MUTINING *vbl. sb.*]. **1560** DAUS tr. *Sleidane's Comm.* 41 b, Nowe that a subsidie is to be gathered..for the Turkishe warre, men do grudge and mutine. **1581** SAVILE *Tacitus, Hist.* I. xviii. (1591) 45 The soldiers mutin and charge the Centurions and Tribunes with treason. **1597** BEARD *Theatre God's Judgem.* (1612) 227 Thus they backbited and slaundered Moses, and mutined against him. **1609** B. JONSON *Sil. Wom.* I. iii, Then [he] railes at his fortunes, stamps, and mutines, why he is not made a counsellor. **1641** MILTON *Ch. Govt.* II. 65 This.. plainly accuses them to be no lawful members of the house, if they thus perpetually mutine against their own body. **1650** HOWELL *Giraffi's Rev. Naples* I. 12 There came no fruit at all, because the shopkeepers had mutined and agreed not to buy any fruit. **1692** O. WALKER *Grk. & Rom. Hist.* 257 When the Legions mutined in the East, and threatned to kill him.

fig. **1602** SHAKS. *Ham.* III. iv. 83 Rebellious Hell, If thou canst mutine in a Matrons bones, To flaming youth, let Vertue be as waxe, And melt in her owne fire. **1620** BRATHWAIT *Five Senses* ii. 10 There is no discord so harsh to a good eare, as the discord of the affections; when they mutine one against another. **1642** BP. MORTON *Presentm. Schismatic* 23 In these times the hand and foot both mutine cause they are not eyes.

† **b.** *trans.* To think or say mutinously. *Obs.*

1545 *St. Papers Hen. VIII* (1849) X. 272 What so ever the Venecians have in tymes passed mutined of thEmpereours procedinges with them.

2. *trans.* To incite to revolt.

1600 E. BLOUNT tr. *Conestaggio* 169 A yoong licentious man, who had mutined the people. **1606** *Rep. Disc. Supreme Power* 34 Pope John..mutined the people against the Emperour. **1613** PURCHAS *Pilgrimage* (1614) 386 Ferrat Can ..writeth to the Rebels, offering..to mutine the Kings armie.

Hence † **ˈmutined** *ppl. a.*, † **ˈmutining** *vbl. sb.* and *ppl. a.*

1555 W. WATREMAN *Fardle Facions* II. xi. 247 Among them is no mutinyng, no vproures, no sturres. **1559** *Fabyan's Chron.* VII. 564/1 In this yere..was a certayne mutenyng traiterouslye attempted aboute Wadharst in Southsex. **1577–87** HOLINSHED *Hist. Eng.* IV. xxx. *Chron.* I. 67/2 Imperiall robes which he neuer..put..on in lawfull wise, but..was put into them by the mutining souldiers. **1602** MARSTON *Antonio's Rev.* III. ii, Alas my son's distraught. Sweete boy appease Thy mutining affections. **1604** E. GRIMSTONE *Hist. Siege Ostend* 41 There shall be abated..what they shall disburse for the..entertainment of the mutined Souldiers. **1659** *Parl. Speech Other Ho.* 8 The People..were loath their fellow-Mutineer, for no other virtue but Mutining, should come to be advanced to be their Master. **1670** MILTON *Hist. Eng.* II. 95 The giddy favour of a mutining rout is as dangerous as their furie.

mutinee, obs. form of MUTINY.

mutineer (mjuːtɪˈnɪə(r)), *sb.* Also 7 -ier, -yer. [a. F. *mutinier* (16th c.), f. *mutin*: see MUTINE *sb.*] One who revolts against or openly resists the authority of a superior; *spec.* one guilty of mutiny as defined in Military and Naval law.

1610 SHAKS. *Temp.* III. ii. 40 Keepe a good tongue in your head: If you proue a mutineere, the next Tree. **1630** *R. Johnson's Kingd. & Commw.* 34 Spinola hath made great use of a secret of warre, how in scarcitie of moneys to awe these mutiniers. **1654** EARL MONM. tr. *Bentivoglio's Warrs of Flanders* 108 The mutinyers were contented to receive a donative of four payes. **1743** BULKELEY & CUMMINS *Voy. S. Seas* Pref. 17 The very Person who accused us, was the Ringleader and chief Mutineer. **1821** SHELLEY *Hellas* 191 Silence those mutineers—that drunken crew, That crowd about the pilot in the storm. **1838–9** HALLAM *Hist. Lit.* IV. IV. iii. §100. 121 He stands forth as a mutineer against authority. **1857** KEITH YOUNG *Delhi* (1902) 11, 12th May. Mutineers from Meerut have seized the bridge at Delhi.

mutineer (mjuːtɪˈnɪə(r)), *v.* [f. prec.] *intr.* To mutiny. Hence **mutiˈneering** *vbl. sb.* and *ppl. a.*

1682 SIR J. LAUDER *Hist. Notices Sc. Affairs* (1848) 375 The Lord Nairne and some others mutineered, and alledged ..ther was no law could oblidge them to afternoons meetings. **1684** *Ibid.* 561 A souldier..is shot..for..giving a blow to his serjeant. This is strict military discipline against mutineering. **1709** STEELE *Tatler* No. 60 ¶9 To quell mutineering Captains. **1856** DE QUINCEY *Confess.* 9 Through the gloomy vigils of his prison, you hear muttered growls of impotent mutineering. **1889** CLARK RUSSELL *Marooned* xix, We don't mean to be laid hold of, and charged with mutineering.

† **mutiner.** *Obs.* Also 7 **mutener.** [f. MUTINE *v.* + -ER¹. Cf. MUTINEER.] A turbulent, rebellious, or mutinous person; a mutineer.

1569 STOCKER tr. *Diod. Sic.* II. xxix. 81 He put to death the principall mutiners. **1589** *Pappe w. Hatchet* A iv, These mutiners in Church matters, must haue their mouthes bungd with iests, not arguments. **1602** SEGAR *Hon., Mil. & Civ.* I. iii. 5 According to discipline Militarie, [to] compell Muteners to obedience and order. *a* **1677** BARROW *Serm.* (1686) III. 277 They [*sc.* seducers] were..murmurers, complainers, or conjunctly discontented mutiners.

† **mutinery.** *Obs. rare*⁻¹. [ad. OF. *mutinerie*, f. *mutin* MUTINE *sb.*] Mutiny.

1563 FOXE *A. & M.* 696 b, The better instruction of your hyghnes people to..hatred of rebellion and mutinery.

† **mutinewe.** *Obs. rare*⁻¹. [If not some error, prob. f. MUTINE *sb.* or *v.* after *retinue*, *revenue.*]

c **1540** tr. *Pol. Verg. Eng. Hist.* (Camden No. 29) 14 A mutinewe [*sic MS.*] rose sodainly thereof and every man forsooke the campe and departed.

muting (ˈmjuːtɪŋ), *vbl. sb.*¹ [f. MUTE *v.*¹ + -ING¹.] **a.** The action of the vb. MUTE¹.

1613–16 W. BROWNE *Brit. Past.* I. i. 20 The Stock-doue and the Blackbird..Whose muting on those trees doe make to grow Rots curing Hyphear. **1641** MILTON *Animadv.* 31 This..livelesse Colossus, that..is subject to the muting of every Sparrow.

b. *concr.* That which is muted; 'droppings'.

1614 MARKHAM *Cheap Husb.* II. xvii. 144 The signes [of the priuie euill in Hawkes] are..foule blacke muteings. **1615** LATHAM *Falconry* Explan. Wds., *Mvting* is the.. ordure which comes from Hawkes. **1725** BRADLEY *Fam.*

Dict. s.v. *Pheasant Pouts*, Their principal Haunts..may easily be known by..their Mutings. **1847** COUCH *Illustr. Instinct* xiii. 239 Many birds will carefully remove the mutings of the young from the neighbourhood of their nest.

muting, *vbl. sb.*²: see MUTE *v.*²

muting (ˈmjuːtɪŋ), *vbl. sb.*³ [f. MUTE *v.*³ + -ING¹.] **a.** The action of the verb MUTE *v.*³ Also *attrib.*

1881 *Times* 25 Oct. 11/4 The mysterious glamour thrown over the whole by the muting of the strings. **1885** *Encycl. Brit.* XIX. 70/2 A surding or muting effect produced by impeding the vibration of the strings.

b. *Electronics.* The automatic suppression of the output of an amplifier when the input signal falls below some predetermined level. Freq. *attrib.*

1936 W. T. COCKING *Wireless Servicing Man.* xv. 168 In practically all cases muting is obtained by arranging for a valve to apply a large bias to the last I.F. valve, the detector, or the first L.F. valve in the absence of a carrier, so that the stage is rendered inoperative. **1959** H. N. GANT *Mobile Radio Telephones* ii. 51 Receivers for mobile radio telephony have very large amplification and the transmitter to which they are tuned is only on when a message is to be passed, so there are long periods when the receiver produces only noise, in the form of a loud roaring sound. To prevent this annoyance the more complex receivers often incorporate a muting or squelch circuit to cut off the receiver output in the absence of the signal. **1970** J. EARL *Tuners & Amplifiers* ii. 39 The diodes and four transistors..give a.g.c. for the FET in the f.m. front-end, a potential for the tuning meter and inter-station muting.

muting, obs. form of MOULTING *ppl. a.*

1578 *Mirr. Mag.*, *Vter Pendragon* xv, For her disport my Ladye coulde procure The wretched winges of this my muting minde, Restlesse to seeke her emptie fiste to finde.

mutinie, -ier, obs. ff. MUTINY, MUTINEER.

†**muˈtinious**, *a. Obs. rare*⁻¹. [f. MUTINY *sb.* + -OUS.] Mutinous.

1663 *Short Surv. Pres. Ministry* 38 They..did not run into Mutinious and Rebellious routes.

†**ˈmutinist.** *Obs. rare*⁻¹. [f. MUTINE + -IST.] A mutineer.

1616 J. LANE *Contn. Sqr.'s T.* x. 616 Mutinistes [**1630** mutiners] and wronge doers all hee hates.

mutinize (ˈmjuːtɪnaɪz), *v.* Now *arch.* Also 7 mutanize. [f. MUTINE *sb.* + -IZE.] †**a.** *intr.* To mutiny (*obs.*). **b.** *trans.* To cause mutiny in.

1605 *Play Stucley* L j, False Abdelmeleck mortally is sick, ..His soldiers mutinise. **1606** G. W[OODCOCKE] tr. *Justine* VI. 30 b, His souldiers mutanized much against him. **1841** *Blackw. Mag.* XLIX. 470/2 They know them [*sc.* propagandist principles] to be most apt to mutinize and convulse kingdoms.

Hence **ˈmutinizing** *ppl. a.*

1830 *Westm. Rev.* XIII. 446 Were this our learned Reformist to add to his collection of mutinizing professors one on the art and science of Nomography.

mutinous (ˈmjuːtɪnəs), *a.* [f. MUTINE + -OUS.]

1. Of persons, their attributes, etc.: Given to mutiny, rebellious.

1578 T. N. tr. *Conq. W. India* Pref. 2 Heere also is described how to use and correct the stubborn and mutinous persons. **1605** BACON *Adv. Learn.* I. ii. §8 Learning doth make the minds of men..pliant to gouernment; whereas Ignorance makes them..mutinous. **1665** SIR T. HERBERT *Trav.* (1677) 251 Finding that neither by threats nor promises he could allay the mutinous humour of the Camp. **1677** WOOD *Life* 14 Dec. (O.H.S.) II. 395 A..report that the Masters should be put out of the Convocation house, because that they in the election of orator had proved mutinous. *a* **1715** BURNET *Own Time* (1766) I. 141 He was mutinous when out of power. **1820** SHELLEY *Œd. Tyr.* I. 98 The troops grow mutinous. **1828** SCOTT *F.M. Perth* xiii, Let us take counsel in friendly fashion, rather than resemble a mutinous crew of mariners in a sinking vessel. **1880** MCCARTHY *Own Times* III. xxxii. 48 A mutinous spirit began to spread itself abroad. **1882** PEBODY *Eng. Journalism* xxiii. 178 Sir Robert Peel found that, with the Press at his back, he could defy even his own mutinous followers to turn him out of office.

†**b.** Turbulent, contentious. *Obs.*

1589 NASHE *Pref. Greene's Menaphon* (Arb.) 15 Which makes our Poets vndermeale Muses so mutinous, as euerie stanzo they pen after dinner, is full poynted with a stabbe. **1596** —— *Saffron Walden* L j b, He is verie seditious and mutinous in conuersation, picking quarrells with euerie man that [etc.]. **1596** SPENSER *F.Q.* v. ix. 48 Then brought he forth Sedition, breeding stryfe In troublous wits, and mutinous uprore. **1608** D. T[UVIL] *Ess. Pol. & Mor.* 2 Mutinous and turbulent assemblies. **1621** T. WILLIAMSON tr. *Goulart's Wise Vieillard* 77 Quarrell-some, mutinous, and mad-braine-sicke persons.

c. *absol.* as *pl.* Mutinous persons.

a **1627** HAYWARD *Edw. VI* (1630) 116 Charge [was] giuen that the lawes of England should be administred & the mutinous be seuerely suppressed [in Ireland]. *a* **1687** WALLER *Maid's Trag. Alter'd* Poems (1712) 206 Lend me your Guards, that if Perswasion fail, Force may against the Mutinous prevail.

d. *transf.* and *fig.* of the elements, passions, etc.

1610 SHAKS. *Temp.* v. i. 42, I haue..call'd forth the mutenous windes. **1633** HEYWOOD *Eng. Trav.* IV. Wks. 1874 IV. 69 There are in this disturbed braine of mine So many mutinous fancies. **1635-56** COWLEY *Davideis* I. 8 His mutinous waters hurry to the War, And Troops of Waves come rolling from afar. **1695** LD. PRESTON *Boeth.* I. 34 The mutinous Passions of Grief, Anger, and Sadness do.. distract thee. **1820** SHELLEY *Ode to Naples* 55 Elysian City, which to calm enchantest The mutinous air and sea! **1821** —— *Hellas* 156 By dreadful abstinence And conquering penance of the mutinous flesh. *Ibid.* 884 Mutinous passions, and conflicting fears.

2. Of the nature of or proceeding from mutiny; characterized by or expressing mutiny.

1592 *Nobody & Someb.* (1877) B 4 b, Goe thou in secrete ..Bring scandalls on the rich, raise mutinous lyes Vpon the state. **1593** SHAKS. *3 Hen. VI*, II. v. 90 What stratagems,.. Erroneous, mutinous, and unnatural, This deadly quarrel daily doth beget! **1609** HOLLAND *Amm. Marcell.* xv. v. 39 Terrified were we with the mutinous grumbling..of the souldiors. **1647** CLARENDON *Hist. Reb.* I. §53 For the late license of printing all mutinous and seditious discourses was not yet in fashion. **1717** LADY M. W. MONTAGU *Let. to Pope* 12 Feb., They..demanded justice in a mutinous way. **1857** KEITH YOUNG *Delhi* (1902) 3 What think you of the mutinous proceedings of the Native regiments? **1865** DICKENS *Mut. Fr.* III. i, Fledgeby appeared to be on the verge of some mutinous expressions.

3. [After F. *air mutin.*] = MUTINE *a.*²

1882 J. STURGIS *Dick's Wand.* III. xxix, She continued to regard him with a pretty mutinous look. *Ibid.* IV. xliv, 'Oh, I like flirtations,' said Miss Holcroft with her little mutinous air—'other people's flirtations'.

Hence **ˈmutinously** *adv.*, **ˈmutinousness.**

a **1586** SIDNEY *Arcadia* II. (1891) 195 A people, in nature mutinously prowde. **1629** JACKSON *Creed* VI. II. xx. §2 The mutinousness of the Souldiers. **1702** ECHARD *Eccl. Hist.* (1710) 11 They mutinously cry'd out for a king. **1859** THACKERAY *Virgin.* II. xiv. 114 She had behaved so mutinously.

mutiny (ˈmjuːtɪnɪ), *sb.* Forms: 6 mutinee, mutenye, (-inye, -yny, -enie), 6-7 mutinie, (7 muttenie), 6- mutiny. [f. MUTINE *v.* or *sb.* + -Y, ? after *felony*. Cf. the earlier MUTINERY, MUTINEWE.]

1. Open revolt against constituted authority; now chiefly *spec.* revolt on the part of a disciplined body (esp. military or naval) or a section of it against its officers; behaviour subversive of discipline, mutinous conduct.

1579 FENTON *Guicciard.* I. (1599) 33 Townes would fall into tumults, men would draw into mutinie [*printed* munitie]. **1591** SHAKS. *1 Hen. VI*, I. i. 160 The Earle of Salisbury craueth supply, And hardly keepes his men from mutinie. **1633** BP. HALL *Occas. Medit.* xlvii. (ed. 3) 115 Wee cannot quench hot and unruly desires in youth without some mutiny, & rebellious opposition. **1648** C. WALKER *Hist. Independ.* I. 34 *margin*, The Army put into mutiny against the Parliament. **1673** *Articles & Rules for better Govt. of H.M. Forces* xv, No Officer or Souldier shall utter any words tending to Sedition, Mutiny, or Uproar. **1743** BULKELEY & CUMMINS *Voy. S. Seas* Pref. 17 We were.. advised..not to return to our Country, lest we should suffer Death for Mutiny. **1780** COWPER *Table T.* 452 He gives the word, and mutiny soon roars In all her gates. **1821** SHELLEY *Hellas* 570 His name..Holds our besieging army like a spell In prey to famine, pest, and mutiny. **1857** KEITH YOUNG *Delhi* (1902) 11, 15th May. Hear a rumour of the Goorkha corps..in open mutiny, and refusing to march. **1889** CLARK RUSSELL *Marooned* xiii, The crew are in a state of mutiny.

b. In particularized sense: A mutinous revolt; a rebellion of a considerable number of soldiers, sailors, or other persons in subordinate position, against those set in authority over them.

the Indian Mutiny, a revolt of the native troops of Bengal in 1857-8.

1581 SAVILE *Tacitus, Hist.* I. xviii. (1591) 45 A mutinee of the Gard-soldiers. **1583** STUBBES *Anat. Abus.* II. (1882) 4 Mutenies, wars, and ciuill dissentions. **1591** SHAKS. *1 Hen. VI*, v. i. 62 Ile..sacke this Country with a mutiny. **1647** CLARENDON *Hist. Reb.* I. §87 Mutinies in the fleet and army, under pretence of their want of pay. **1688** *Act 1 Will. & Mary* c. 5 §2 Every Person being in Their Majestyes Service ..who shall..Joyne in any Mutiny or Sedition in the Army. **1789** BRAND *Hist. Newcastle* II. 304 The coal-trade at Newcastle was for some time put a stop to by a mutiny of the keelmen. **1835** MARRYAT *Jac. Faithf.* xxix, We have had a regular mutiny, and attempt to take the ship from me. **1901** *Scotsman* 9 Mar. 8/3 The Irish mutiny in the House of Commons has been suppressed.

c. In attrib. uses; often with the meaning 'that took part in or was present during the Indian Mutiny'.

Mutiny Act, an Act, passed annually from 1689 to 1879, authorizing the crown to frame 'Articles of War' dealing with offences against discipline in the military and naval forces and the constitution of courts-martial. It is now embodied in the Army Act, 1881. So also ***mutiny bill.***

1731-2 EARL OF STRAFFORD *Sp.* in *Hist. & Proc. Ho. Lords* (1742) IV. 61, I am entirely against this Bill, or any Mutiny-Bill; because it is the turning of our Civil Government into a Military Government. **1765** BLACKSTONE *Comm.* I. 409 By the annual mutiny acts, a soldier may be arrested for a debt which [etc.]. **1857** KEITH YOUNG *Delhi* (1902) 3, 28th March.—At work all the morning at that mutiny case. **1895** KIPLING *2nd Jungle Bk.* 114, I was a Mutiny baby, as they call it. **1903** *Daily Chron.* 3 Jan. 5/6 Last night the Mutiny veterans..held a special dinner at the camp.

†**2.** Discord, contention; a state of discord, a dispute, quarrel. Phrase, *in* or *at* (*a*) *mutiny*. *Obs.*

1567 FENTON *Trag. Disc.* I. 34 b, He..(besides a thousand pettie mutynies that fall out in housekeping,) escapeth seldom without a sprit of grudge or cyuill discension, disturbynge hys quiet. **1588** SHAKS. *L.L.L.* I. i. 170 A man of complements whom right and wrong Haue chose as vmpire of their mutinie. **1589** GREENE *Menaphon* I 4, He found all the Swaines in a mutinie about the recouery of their beautifull Paragon. **1592** —— *Disput.* 35 At this pleasant Tale all the boord was at a mutinie, and they said the gentleman did passing wisely. **1592** SHAKS. *Rom. & Jul.* I. v. 82 Youle make a Mutinie among the Guests. **1593** —— *Lucr.* 1153 So with her selfe is shee in mutinie, To liue or die which of the twaine were better. **1605** *Play Stucley* F 4 b, Are then Molucco and his brother king, At ciuill mutinie among themselves. **1632** LITHGOW *Trav.* x. 474 What mutinies and malice, are dayly among your Monasteries, each envying anothers priuiledge. **1643** in *10th Rep. Hist. MSS. Comm.* App. v. 494 Such..persons..may absent.. themselves.., least that theare may be any muttenie or disorder in the said companies or meetinges. **1667** MILTON *P.L.* II. 926 Then if..these Elements In mutinie had from her Axle torn The stedfast Earth.

mutiny (ˈmjuːtɪnɪ), *v.* [f. MUTINY *sb.*]

1. *intr.* To commit the offence of mutiny; to rise in revolt *against* (rarely †*upon*); to refuse submission to discipline or obedience to the lawful command of a superior, *esp.* in the military and naval services.

1584 *Leycesters Commw.* 53 Cal you but to minde..when her Ma..did wyth-draw, but a litle her wounted fauour.. towardes him: did not al the Court as it were, mutinie presentlie? **1600** SHAKS. *A.Y.L.* I. i. 24 The spirit of my Father, which I thinke is within mee, begins to mutinie against this seruitude. **1679** in Ellis *Orig. Lett.* Ser. III. IV. 309 The Duke of Albemarle..daily expected the army in London would mutiny upon him for want of pay. **1688** *Act 1 Will. & Mary* c. 5 (*title*) An Act for punishing Officers or Soldiers who shall Mutiny or Desert Their Majestyes Service. **1761** HUME *Hist. Eng.* III. lx. 294 Dundalk..was delivered up by the troops who mutinied against their governor. **1814** SCOTT *Wav.* xiv, Saunders..began to mutiny against the labour for which he now scarce received thanks. **1864** *Spectator* 24 Dec. 1467 The shopmen..found out..that their life was a little too like life on slave plantation ..and at last they mutinied. **1875** JOWETT *Plato* (ed. 2) III. 372 They mutiny and take possession of the ship.

†**b.** Conjugated with *to be*. *Obs. rare.*

1648 GAGE *West Ind.* vi. 19 Wee..thereby guessed at the truth that the Barbarians were mutinied. **1656** EARL MONM. tr. *Boccalini's Advts. fr. Parnass.* 56 Their Scouts..brought back word, that the whole Militia of Janisaries were mutinied against the Ottaman Monarchy.

c. *fig.*

1594 SHAKS. *Rich. III*, I. iv. 142 'Tis a blushing shame-fac'd spirit [*i.e.* conscience], that mutinies in a mans bosom: It filles a man full of Obstacles. **1751** JOHNSON *Rambler* No. 133 ⁋4 The powers of pleasure mutiny for employment. **1795** SOUTHEY *Maid of Orleans* II. 361 Temperate Myself, no blood that mutinied,..I sent abroad Murder and Rape. *a* **1822** SHELLEY *Chas. I*, II. 144 The baser elements Had mutinied against the golden sun That kindles them to harmony.

†**d.** To contend or strive (*with*); to quarrel.

1593 SHAKS. *Rich. II*, II. i. 28 All too late comes counsell to be heard, Where will doth mutiny with wits regard. **1606** —— *Ant. & Cl.* III. xi. 13 My very haires do mutiny: for the white Reproue the browne for rashnesse, and they them For feare. **1603** KNOLLES *Hist. Turks* (1621) 152 The Catalonians began to mutinie among themselues.

†**2.** *trans.* To cause to mutiny or rebel *against*.

1643 PRYNNE *Sov. Power Parlt.* App. 39 The Duke of Guise..mutinies the Citizens against the King. **1648** C. WALKER *Hist. Independ.* I. 34 Cromwell..by mutinying the Army against the Parliament, made them his owne.

Hence **ˈmutinied** *ppl. a.*, **ˈmutinying** *vbl. sb.* and *ppl. a.*

1600 *St. Papers, Domestic* 447 The Archduke, having reclaimed his mutinied Spaniards..left the Infanta at Ghent. **16..** F. DAVISON *Ps.* lxxiii, Leaue mutyniing, and rest secure. **1665** MANLEY *Grotius' Low C. Warres* 321 This mad mutinying frenzy was..among all the Garrisons of Germany. **1671** W. PERWICH *Despatches* (1903) 137 The Newfoundland's ships..will..loose their season..through the obstinacy of the mutinyed seamen. *a* **1716** SOUTH *Serm.* (1842) III. 372 The mutinying of the army about St. Albans. **1873** *Daily News* 26 Aug., The mutinied regiments of Iberia.

mutish (ˈmjuːtɪʃ), *a. nonce-wd.* [f. MUTE *sb.*¹ + -ISH.] Somewhat like a mute.

1865 *Cornh. Mag.* Sept. 310 This dress..gave him the appearance of one of the mutes..of an economic funeral company. This mutish-looking gentleman..was [etc.].

mutism¹ (ˈmjuːtɪz(ə)m). [ad. F. *mutisme* (1741 in Hatz.-Darm.), f. L. *mūt-us*: see MUTE *a.* and -ISM.] **a.** The state or condition of being mute; the refraining from speech, silence; lack of the faculty of speech, or inability to produce articulate sounds, dumbness. Also *fig.*

1824 W. E. ANDREWS *Crit. Rev. Fox's Bk. Martyrs.* I. 365 The term of his mutism was expected with impatience. **1851** WALSHE *Dis. Lungs & Heart* 392 Cases of this affection [*sc.* tuberculous meningitis]..in which a peculiar form of mutism formed a striking symptom. **1853** C. BRONTE *Villette* xxviii, Paulina was awed by the savants, but not quite to mutism. **1859** MAX MÜLLER *Sci. Lang.* Ser. I. ii. (1864) 32 Man must have lived for a time in a state of mutism. **1873** *Nature* 27 Feb. 323/2, I know of two instances where perfect mutism accompanied the deafness in cats. **1882** SALA *America Revisited* I. ix. 138 Behind the counter was a very paragon of mutism in the shape of an hotel clerk. **1891** *Temple Bar* May 114 She all at once broke through her mutism and plied me with questions. **1894** A. GRIFFITHS *Secrets Prison House* II. IV. viii. 220 There was no other outlet but confession or obstinate mutism. **1899** [see MUTE *a.* 2]. **1969** P. ANDERSON in Cockburn & Blackburn *Student Power* 215 Given the complete mutism of the past, any such initial attempt will inevitably suffer from errors, lapses, [etc.]. **1975** *N.Y. Times Book Rev.* 8 June VII. 21/3 All we can hope is..that the innumerable poems..will not give us nausea, or a new, science-inspired dose of mutism.

b. In *Psychol.* used (in contrast to *aphonia*) to imply the absence of any ascertainable defect of the vocal organs and hence a cause that is primarily psychological rather than physiological.

1892 D. H. Tuke *Dict. Psychol. Med.* II. 827/2 *Mutism*, dumbness from mental defect or disorder. In addition to the cases of Deaf-Dumbness.., mutism occurs in the course of various mental disorders, as Mental Stupor, Delusional Insanity, &c. **1930** *Internat. Jrnl. Psychoanal.* XI. 185 (*title*) On the physiology of hysterical aphonia and mutism. **1940** *Amer. Jrnl. Psychiatry* XCVI. 1445 In psychotic patients mutism is often associated with other manifestations of negativism. **1961** W. R. Brain *Speech Disorders* vii. 107 Mutism is the term applied to a complete loss of speech in a conscious patient in the absence of organic disease of the nervous system. **1972** S. Cashdan *Abnormal Psychol.* ii. 50 In extreme cases, social withdrawal leads to mutism (refusal to speak) and regression (acting in infantile ways).

mutism[2] (ˈmjuːtɪz(ə)m). [ad. F. *mutisme*, f. *muter*: see MUTE *v.* and -ISM.] = MUTAGE.

1853 Ure *Dict. Arts* I. 155 Wines which have been subjected to mutism.

muto- (ˈmjuːtəʊ). Assumed as combining form of L. *mūtāre* to change, in the following technical terms. **ˈmutograph**, an apparatus for taking a series of photographs of objects in motion; hence **ˈmutograph** *v. trans.*, to portray with this apparatus. **ˈmutoscope**, an apparatus for exhibiting a scene recorded by the mutograph, which may be seen by looking through an aperture and turning a handle at the side of the instrument; hence **mutoˈscopic** *a.*, also **ˈmutoscope** *v.*

1897 *Sci. Amer.* 17 Apr. 248/2 The 'mutograph' and 'mutoscope', are the inventions of Mr. Herman Casler... The machine with which the original pictures are taken..is known as the 'mutograph', nearly following the Latin and Greek words signifying 'changing delineation'. *Ibid.* 249/1 Prints..for use in the..mutoscope machines. *Ibid.* 249/2 A series of 'mutograph' pictures. **1899** *Westm. Gaz.* 11 Feb. 7/2 The Biograph and Mutoscope are two inventions for the reproduction of objects in motion. The negatives of views for use in both are produced by the Mutograph, a camera by which from 3,000 to 4,000 separate photographs can be taken per minute. *Ibid.* 3 Aug. 3/1 The impression that we have been indulging in a mutoscopic debauch. *Ibid.* 21 Sept. 4/1 Efforts are to be made to get Mr. Chamberlain and Lord Selborne to be 'mutoscoped' on their way to the Cabinet Council to-morrow. **1901** *World's Work* Aug. 1057/2 Prints made from the film are mounted consecutively about a cylinder. As the cylinder is revolved the mounted pictures are held back by a stop, and snap past the eye so that the illusion is of a continuous motion picture. Encased in a box and with the automatic penny-in-the-slot attachment the mutoscope is ready for its common commercial use. **1902** S. Smith *Life Work* xlv. 464 Pictures and mutoscopic exhibitions which corrupted the young wholesale. **1922** Joyce *Ulysses* 362 Mutoscope pictures in Capel street: for men only. **1969** *Jabez Elliott* (Ringwood, Hants.) *Miscellany Catal.* No. 6. 7 A little booklet or pad..of 82 photographs of two girls dancing. When the leaves are flicked over the dancers spring to life... These little books, called Mutoscopes, were popular in the early days of the Cinema.

muton (ˈmjuːtɒn). *Biol.* [f. MUT(ATION + -ON[1].] The smallest element of the genetic material (supposedly a single pair of nucleotides) which when altered can give rise to a mutant individual.

1957 S. Benzer in McElroy & Glass *Symp. Chem. Basis Heredity* 71 The unit of mutation, the 'muton', will be defined as the smallest element that, when altered, can give rise to a mutant form of the organism. **1959** [see CISTRON]. **1970** Ambrose & Easty *Cell Biol.* x. 356 It seems probable that the smallest unit of recombination (the recon) has in fact the same dimensions as the smallest unit of mutation (the muton), that is a single nucleotide base pair in the DNA molecule. **1971** J. Z. Young *Introd. Study Man* iii. 53 Mutation may occur by the change of any single base and these are thus the letters of the genetic language (also known as mutons).

muton, -oun, -own, obs. forms of MUTTON.

mutsel(l)im: see MUSELLIM.

mutsenigo, variant of MOCCENIGO.

mutsha, mutshi, varr. MOOCHA.

mutskinn, obs. form of MUTCHKIN.

mutt (mʌt). *slang* (orig. *U.S.*). Also mut. [abbrev. *mutton-head* (MUTTON 9 b] **a.** One who is stupid, ignorant, awkward, blundering, incompetent, or the like; a blockhead, dullard, or fool; also, non-pejoratively, a person, fellow.

1901 'H. McHugh' *Down Line* 79, I knew that Clara Jane would cancel the contract with the mutt that mixed in just as soon as she saw the automobile snap. **1910** O. Johnson *Varmint* 377 Engaged to that Ver Planck fellow that was hanging around. I think he's a mutt. **1915** Wodehouse *Psmith, Journalist* xvi. 116 This ain't him. This is some other mutt. **1920** *Blackw. Mag.* Feb. 176/2 Dougal, the elder brother, was a quiet, inoffensive kind of a mutt. **1926** *Spectator* 1 May 813/1 Not doubting the poor mutt's love for her. **1929** [see GOOP]. **1942** 'M. Innes' *Daffodil Affair* iv. 146 Why couldn't you keep to the racket, you poor mut, and leave tinkering alone! **1955** W. Gaddis *Recognitions* II. vii. 597 Got to look up a mutt named Chavenay. **1972** *Police Rev.* 10 Nov. 1444/2 Some male driver—poor mutt!—will be fiddling with the jack. **1973** D. May *Laughter in Djakarta* xii. 203 The poor mutt must have driven it along the bank.

b. A term of contempt applied to a dog, *esp.* a mongrel.

Quot. 1904 refers to a horse.

1904 *Outing* XLV. 170/2 Watch that mut curl up out there. **1906** H. Green *Actors' Boarding House* 335 A fellow can't leave nothin' on his bed without that mutt chawin' it up! **1911** R. W. Chambers *Common Law* x. 310 Now fat old woman..Arrive to exercise their various dogs; And 'round and 'round the little mutts all run. **1927** *Ladies' Home Jrnl.* Dec. 4/1 Be careful the mutt doesn't get into a race with a caterpillar some day, and die of heart collapse. **1932** *Sun* (Baltimore) 15 Oct. 20/5 There are people who especially desire a mutt dog. **1949** *Sat. Even. Post* 16 Apr. 44/2 That cat! That mutt! they fight it out And back and forth they shuttle. **1970** *New Yorker* 29 Aug. 50/3 The cast includes a Sheepdog.., a Mutt Bitch. **1972** C. Weston *Poor, Poor Ophelia* (1973) vi. 29 Two barefoot hippies were sharing a bag of potato chips with a happy-looking mutt.

c. Phr. ***Mutt and Jeff*** [from the names of two characters called *Mutt* and *Jeff*, one tall and the other short, in a popular cartoon series by H. C. Fisher (1884–1954), American cartoonist]. (*a*) A stupid pair of men; stupid dialogue; (*b*) (see quot. 1943); (*c*) as *adj.*, deaf.

1917 E. E. Cummings *Let.* 4 June (1969) 26 By failing to get up..I escaped departing with the bums mutts and jeffs (not to say ginks, slobs, and punks) who came over with us. **1937** M. Huxley in A. Huxley *Lett.* (1969) 426 A sort of Mutt and Jeff on war and peace and religion. **1937** Partridge *Dict. Slang* 545/2 *Mutt and Jeff*, the British War Medal and Victory Medal: military: 1918. **1943** C. H. Ward-Jackson *It's a Piece of Cake* 43 *Mutt and Jeff*, the King George V silver Jubilee and the Edward VIII Coronation medals, or ribbons, worn together; or the 1918 Victory and Overseas medals or ribbons worn together. **1949** *Sun* (Baltimore) 10 Dec. 24/5 Richard ——, identified as the taller man in the recent series of 'Mutt and Jeff' robberies here, yesterday pleaded guilty to armed robbery. **1960** J. Franklyn *Dict. Rhyming Slang* 98/2 *Mutt & Jeff*, deaf. 20 C. Current in the theatrical world, and formed on the names of the two famous stripcartoon characters. **1973** *Washington Post* 21 Nov. C2 The women..call the two cops..'Mutt and Jeff'. Who is Jeff? 'The white one..Mutt is always being kicked around. Jeff makes him do all the work.' **1974** D. Seaman *The Bomb* xx. 200 He silently named them Mutt and Jeff. One [man] stood well over six feet..while the other barely reached to his mate's armpits.

mutt, variant of MATH[2]; obs. form of MOTE *v.*[1]

muttenie, obs. form of MUTINY.

mutter (ˈmʌtə(r)), *sb.*[1] [f. MUTTER *v.*[1]] The act of muttering; a low indistinct utterance.

1634 Milton *Comus* 817 Without his rod revers't And backward mutters of dissevering power, We cannot free the Lady. **1874** Spurgeon *Treas. Dav.* Ps. xcviii. 6 That chill mutter..which is now so commonly the substitute for earnest congregational singing. **1875** A. R. Hope *My Schoolboy Fr.* 146, I gave an inaudible mutter.

mutter (ˈmʌtə(r)), *sb.*[2] [Hindī *matar.*] An Indian variety of pea, sometimes used in this country as fodder for cattle.

1884 W. Williams *Princ. & Pract. Vet. Med.* (ed. 4) 298 An Indian pea.., called in Liverpool Indian mutters. *Ibid.*, Horses commenced to die very suddenly some time after the owners had commenced to use the mutters.

mutter (ˈmʌtə(r)), *v.*[1] Forms: 4–5 **moter(e, mot(t)re, 5–6 muttre, 6 muttor, 6– mutter.** [Prob. an onomatopœic formation with frequentative suffix -ER[5]; cf. G. dial. *muttern* to mutter, *motter* sb. a muttering; also MUSTER *v.*[2]]

1. *intr.* To speak in low tones, with the mouth nearly closed, so that one's words are barely audible.

1388 Wyclif *2 Sam.* xii. 19 Whanne Dauid hadde herd his seruauntis spekynge priueli, ether moterynge [1382 musynge, Vulg. *mussitantes*]. **1568** Grafton *Chron.* II. 301 Therewith the French men beganne to muttor, and sayde among themselues, the prince had spoken nobly. **1598** Drayton *Heroic. Ep.* xvii. 15 Mine eyes..thought report too niggardly had spard; And stroocken dumbe with wonder, did but mutter, Conceiuing more then she had words to vtter. **1611** Bible *Isa.* viii. 19 Seeke..vnto wizards that peepe and that mutter. **1642** Fuller *Holy & Prof. St.* II. xxi. 134 He heard his men muttering amongst themselves of the strength and greatnesse of the Town. **1692** R. L'Estrange *Fables* ccxix. 192 The Wolfe went Muttering away upon't. **1717** Pope *Iliad* x. 527 The Head, yet speaking, mutter'd as it fell. **1855** Bain *Senses & Int.* III. i. §8 (1864) 345 Some persons of weak or incontinent nerves can hardly think without muttering—they talk to themselves. **1860** Holland *Miss Gilbert* ii, At not infrequent intervals she heard her little brother moaning and muttering in his sleep.

b. *esp.* To speak in low indistinct tones expressive of dissatisfaction which one dare not utter more openly; to murmur, complain, grumble. Const. *against*, *at*.

a **1548** Hall *Chron., Hen. VI* 121 Certain souldiors.. beganne to mutter and murmure against the kyng and his counsaill. **1575–85** Abp. Sandys *Serm.* ii. 26 The worthie magistrate Moses was muttered against. **1621** T. Williamson tr. *Goulart's Wise Vieillard* 70 They..doe mutter at, and finde fault with euery thing that is spoken or done. **1692** Washington tr. *Milton's Def. Pop.* ii. M.'s Wks. 1851 VII. 66 The People must not dare to mutter. **1706** E. Ward *Wooden World Diss.* (1708) 27 Oft does he mutter at the Partialities of the Board. **1720** De Foe *Capt. Singleton* xiii. (1840) 228 Our men muttered a little at this; but I pacified them. **1856** Emerson *Eng. Traits, Wealth* Wks. (Bohn) II. 71 Whether it were not possible to make a spinner that would not rebel, nor mutter, nor scowl, nor strike for wages?

c. *transf.* To make a low rumbling sound.

1797 Mrs. Radcliffe *Italian* i, Like distant thunder muttering imperfectly from the clouds. **1858** Hawthorne *Fr. & It. Note-bks.* II. 50 The thunder muttered and grumbled.

2. *trans.* To utter with imperfect articulation and in a low tone. Also *fig.* to express or say in secret.

c **1374** Chaucer *Troylus* II. 492 (541) With that he smoot his heed adoun anoon, And gan to motre [*v.rr.* motere, mottre, muttre], I not what trewly. *a* **1586** Sidney *Ps.* II. i, What do theis people meane, To mutter murmurs vaine? **1593** Shaks. *3 Hen. VI*, I. i. 165 What mutter you, or what conspire you Lords? **1604** —— *Oth.* III. iii. 417 There are a kinde of men, So loose of Soule, that in their sleepes will mutter their Affayres. **1645** Pagitt *Heresiogr.* Ep. Ded., Who have their Prayers in their owne tongue, and mutter them not in latine as the Romists doe. **1724** Ramsay *Vision* ix, Revenge is muttert be ilk clan. **1750** Gray *Elegy* 106 Mutt'ring his wayward fancies he would rove. **1856** Sir B. Brodie *Psychol. Inq.* I. iii. 100, I knew a gentleman who was accustomed to mutter certain words to himself..even in the midst of company.

b. with obj. clause.

1555 Eden *Decades* 21 The people..muttered amonge them selues that owre nation hadde trowbled the elementes. **1561** T. Norton *Calvin's Inst.* I. xiii. (1634) 46 Arrius saith that Christ is God, but he muttereth that he was created. **1622** Bacon *Hen. VII* 163 They muttered extremely, that it was a thing not to be suffered. **1623** Meade in Ellis *Orig. Lett.* Ser. I. III. 151 Yet its muttered the Match will be. **1849** Macaulay *Hist. Eng.* ii. I. 230 Some who had always professed the doctrine of nonresistance in its full extent were now heard to mutter that there was one limitation to that doctrine.

c. ***to mutter over***: to recite in low indistinct tones, to mumble.

1810 Scott *Lady of L.* III. iv, And much, 'twas said, of heathen lore Mix'd in the charms he mutter'd o'er. **1817** Moore *Lalla R.* (1824) 175 To mutter o'er some text of God, Engraven on his reeking sword.

d. *transf.* (Cf. 1 c.)

1667 Milton *P.L.* IX. 1002 Skie lowr'd, and muttering Thunder, som sad drops Wept at compleating of the mortal Sin Original.

ˈmutter, *v.*[2] ? Variant of MOULTER *v.*[1]

1609 Butler *Fem. Monarchie* vi. §22 If you feele it [*sc.* leg-honey] betweene your warme fingers, it muttereth apart, where wax sticketh fast togither.

mutteˈration. *nonce-wd.* [See -ATION.] The action of muttering.

1753 Richardson *Grandison* (1811) IV. xxxvii. 283 So the night past off, with prayings, hopings, and a little *mutteration.* (Allow me that word, or find me a better.)

muttered (ˈmʌtəd), *ppl. a.* [f. MUTTER *v.*[1] + -ED[1].] Uttered indistinctly and in low tones.

1701 Addison *Epil. to G. Granville's Brit. Enchantress*, Where sounding Strings and artful Voices fail, The charming Rod and mutter'd Spells prevail. **1856** Emerson *Eng. Traits, Char.* Wks. (Bohn) II. 60 It is done in the dark, and with muttered malediction. **1888** H. Smart *Master of Rathkelly* xxiii, And now came a low muttered conference between McDermot and his companions.

mutterer (ˈmʌtərə(r)). [f. MUTTER *v.*[1] + -ER[1].] One who mutters.

1552 Huloet, Muttrer, *susurro.* **1671** H. Foulis *Hist. Rom. Treasons* (1681) 88 These mutterers of King-murthering. *a* **1677** Barrow *Decalogue* ix. *Creed*, etc. (1697) 432 The words of a mutterer, saith the Wise man, are as wounds [*Prov.* xviii. 8]. **1854** H. Miller *Sch. & Schm.* xviii. (1860) 197/1 He was a mutterer of charms, and a watcher of omens.

muttering (ˈmʌtərɪŋ), *vbl. sb.* [-ING[1].] The action of the verb MUTTER.

1513 More *Rich. III* in Grafton *Chron.* (1568) II. 777 Yet then began there, here and there some maner of mutteryng amongest the people. **1538** Bale *Thre Lawes* E vij b, The lorde doth not regarde Your mangy mutterynge. **1613** W. Browne *Brit. Past.* I. ii. (*ad fin.*), The roaring voyce of winds,..Nor all the muttring of the sullen waues. **1667–68** Pepys *Diary* 17 Feb., Some mutterings I did hear of dissolving the Parliament. **1760–72** H. Brooke *Fool of Qual.* (1809) III. 89, I heard secret treadings and mutterings. **1856** Froude *Hist. Eng.* (1858) I. v. 468 The mutterings of discontent had developed into plain open treason. **1904** A. R. Whitham *Ep. Consolations* i. 10 Already the mutterings of the distant storm might be heard. **1971** *Guardian* 14 Jan. 1/3 There may be some feminine muttering that in promoting the 'Woman's Guardian' we are perpetuating the idea of the female ghetto.

ˈmuttering, *ppl. a.* [-ING[2].] That mutters.

1567 Maplet *Gr. Forest* 112 Let muttring Mutius take heede least he be serued with the same sawce Virgil requited Bauius and Meuius. **1660** Ingelo *Bentiv. & Ur.* II. (1682) 143 The muttering Fiends obey'd. **1712** Steele *Spect.* No. 266 ¶2 In a muttering Voice, as if between Soliloquy and speaking out. **1842** J. Wilson *Chr. North* (1857) II. 13 The muttering thunder seems to have changed its place. **1843** R. J. Graves *Syst. Clin. Med.* xiv. 147 A low muttering delirium. **1917** T. S. Eliot *Prufrock & other Observations* 9 Certain half-deserted streets The muttering retreats Of restless nights in one-night cheap hotels. **1927** Joyce *She weeps over Rahoon* in *Pomes Penyeach*, The moongrey nettles, the black mould And muttering rain.

Hence **ˈmutteringly** *adv.*

c **1681** Hickeringill *Trimmer* vi. Wks. 1716 I. 388 It was a business (than which) nothing is more discours'd of (mutteringly) at this day. **1741** Richardson *Pamela* I. 69, I said something mutteringly, and he vow'd he would hear it. **1847** De Quincey *Sp. Mil. Nun* Wks. 1854 III. 53 Mutteringly she put that question to herself.

†ˈmutterous, *a. rare*[−1]. [f. MUTTER *sb.*[1] + -OUS.] Full of muttering sound; murmurous.

1582 Stanyhurst *Æneis* I. (Arb.) 31 Lyke bees..That.. toyle with mutterus humbling. *Ibid.* III. 73 With rumbling mutterus eccho.

mutt-eye ('mʌtaɪ). *Austral. slang.* [Orig. unknown.] (Cut) corn.

1946 K. Tennant *Lost Haven* (1947) x. 135 Five sacks of potatoes, three of mutt-eyes, another three of pumpkins. **1966** Baker *Austral. Lang.* (ed. 2) iv. 84 Bull's eyes, fried eggs; mutt eyes, corn; frog's eyes, boiled sago.

‖**mutti** ('mʊtɪ). [G., f. *mutter* mother.] A childish or familiar form of 'mother' (used in German-speaking countries).

1906 M. A. von Arnim *Princess Priscilla's Fortnight* ii. 32 She's a witch—Mutti, she's a witch! **1939** C. Isherwood *Goodbye to Berlin* 169 'Poor little Mummy, little Mutti, little Mutchen,' he crooned. **1967** A. Wilson *No Laughing Matter* iii. 314 And as for Mutti—strange little bent witch-like lady! **1972** *Guardian* 29 July 3/5 An announcement from ..the lifeguards. 'Achtung, achtung—morning gymnastics for the ladies...' And off go the Muttis to trim their waistlines, while father relaxes.

mutton ('mʌt(ə)n). Forms: 4 moltoun; 3–5 motoun, 4 motone, 5 motene, 5–6 motonne, mot(t)on, mouton, 5–7 muton, 6 muttoun, mot(t)en, mutown, mutten, 5– mutton. [ME. *motoun*, *moton* (rarely *moltoun*), a. OF. *moton*, rarely *molton* (mod.F. *mouton*) = Pr. *multó-s*, Catal. *multo*, OSp. *moton*, It. *montone*, Venetian *moltone*:—med.L. (8th c.) *multōn-em*, prob. f. Gaulish **multo-s* (OIrish *molt* ram, Welsh *mollt*, Cornish *mols*, Breton *maout*).

Some scholars have conjectured that med.L. *multōnem* is a metathetic form of *mutilōnem* (of which Du Cange has one example) f. L. *mutilus* in the sense 'deprived of horns' or in the sense 'castrated'; Diez compares mod. Pr. *cabro mouta* corresponding to L. *capra mutila* hornless goat. But it seems very unlikely that the Celtic forms can be unconnected; if they are from popular Latin the adoption must have taken place at a very early period.]

1. The flesh of sheep, used as food.

c **1290** *S. Eng. Leg.* I. 472/344 Huy nomen with heom in heore schip at þat hem was leof, Gies and hennes, craunes and swannes and porc, motoun and beof. *c* **1375** *Sc. Leg. Saints* xxv. (*Julian*) 114 Sancte Julyane.. In til his tyme wes na glotone, na wont wes nocht to ete motone. *c* **1420** *Liber Cocorum* (1862) 46 Take fresshe brothe of motene clene. *c* **1450** *Two Cookery-bks.* 72 Stwed Mutton. Take faire Mutton that hath ben roste,.. and mynce it faire. *c* **1460** J. Russell *Bk. Nurture* 533 Mustard is meete for brawne beef, or powdred motoun. **1533** More *Answ. Poysoned Bk.* Wks. 1059/1 Men bye bief or moten out of the bouchers shoppes. *a* **1575** Gascoigne *Posies, Hearbes* 147 Fiue flocks of sheepe coulde scarce mainteine good mutton for his house. **1620** Venner *Via Recta* iii. 50 Of Mutton.. that is the best, which is of an yeere or two olde. **1710–11** Swift *Jrnl. to Stella* 19 Mar., They.. had a breast of mutton and a pint of wine. **1848** Clough *Bothie* v, Racing home for the eight o'clock mutton. **1870** Yeats *Nat. Hist. Comm.* i. v. 49 Welsh sheep are small, but the mutton is renowned for the delicacy of its flavour. **1897** 'Merriman' *In Kedar's Tents* x, The steaming dish of mutton and vegetables.

2. a. A sheep; *esp.* one intended to be eaten. Now only *jocular*.

1338 R. Brunne *Chron.* (1810) 174 A bouke of a motoun. **1390** Gower *Conf.* I. 39 The Wolf in pes with the Moltoun. **1481** Caxton *Godeffroy* clvii. 231 Oxen, Kyen, Motons and other vytaylles. **1565** Lady Lovat in Fraser *Polichron.* (S.H.S.) 153 With twa mutowns yearly price of the pice thratin s. iiij d. **1615** G. Sandys *Trav.* 37 Moldavia and Valachia do serve them with beeves and muttons. **1692** R. L'Estrange *Fables* ccccclxxxv. 461 The Sheep in this Fable was clearly too hard for the Two Doctors; and we find all those Reasonings to be true in the World, which the Mutton Alleges in the Fiction. **1795** Cowper *Needless Alarm* 81 A mutton, statelier than the rest, A ram, the ewes and wethers, sad, address'd. **1833** *Penny Cycl.* I. 448/2 The word *mutton* is sometimes used [in America], as it once was in England, to signify a sheep. **1839** Thackeray *Leg. St. Sophia of Kioff*, A humble company of pious men, Like muttons in a pen.

b. The carcass of a sheep. *Obs.* or *arch.*

1607 Topsell *Hist. Four-f. Beasts* (1658) 482 In many places they salt their Muttons when they are killed, and so eat them out of the pickle. **1625** B. Jonson *Staple of N.* ii. iv, Goes to the Butchers, fetches in a muton. **1703** Dampier *Voy.* III. i. 108, I was presented with half a Mutton. **1863** Hawthorne *Our Old Home* (1864) II. 189 There were butchers shops.. presenting no such generously fattened carcases as Englishmen love to gaze at in the market, no stupendous halves of mighty beeves, no dead hogs or muttons.

†**c.** *spec.* A wether, castrated ram. *Obs.*

14.. *Voc.* in Wr.-Wülcker 597/10 *Multo*, a wether or a moton. **1609** Skene *Reg. Maj.* ii. 135 Ane man taken with reid hand, with ane sheip, or muton, or with ane calfe,.. sould not be put to death, bot sald be scurged. **1655** Moufet & Bennet *Health's Improv.* (1746) 143 Ewes and Rams are subject to far more Maladies than Muttons.

†**3.** *Sc.* Used as a term of contempt for a man.

1508 Dunbar *Flyting* 241 Mauch muttoun, vyle buttoun, peilit gluttoun, air to Hilhouse. *c* **1560** A. Scott *Poems* (S.T.S.) xxx. 32 Quha bene w[t] beistly lust abusit, I hald him bot ane muttoun.

4. *slang.* Food for lust; loose women, prostitutes. Also ***laced mutton***: see laced *ppl. a.* 5. So, the genital organs of a woman; copulation; phr. ***to hawk one's mutton***, (of a woman) to seek a lover, to solicit (cf. *hawking* ppl. a. s.v. hawk *v.*[2]). See also mutton-monger.

a **1518** Skelton *Magnyf.* 2265 And from thens to the halfe strete, To get vs there some freshe mete. Why, is there any store of rawe motton? **1538** Bale *Thre Lawes* B iv b, What wylt thu fall to mutton?.. Ranke loue is full of heate. *c* **1590** Greene *Fr. Bacon* (1630) H i b, The old lecher hath gotten holy mutton to him, a Nunne, my Lord. *c* **1590** Marlowe *Faustus* (1604) C 4 b, I am one that loues an inch of raw Mutton better then an ell of fride stock fish, and the first letter of my name beginnes with leachery. **1636** Heywood *Love's Mistr.* ii. i. Wks. 1874 V. 113 Lord of lamentations, ..Mounsieur of mutton-lac'd. *a* **1700** B. E. *Dict. Cant. Crew, Mutton-in-long-coats*, Women. **1864** Hotten *Slang Dict.* (ed. 3) 184 *Mutton*, a contemptuous term for a woman of bad character... In that class of English society which does not lay any claim to refinement, a fond lover is often spoken of as being 'fond of his mutton'. **1937** Partridge *Dict. Slang* 380/2 Hawk one's mutton. **1939** H. Hodge *Cab, Sir?* v. 53 He can't quite believe she hawks her mutton in hexagonal horn-rimmed spectacles. **1964** N. Freeling *Double-Barrel* ii. viii. 65 In the army we used to say, of such and such a girl, nurse, waaf, whatever she was, 'That one hawks her mutton.' **1973** 'J. Patrick' *Glasgow Gang Observed* vii. 73 They're aw cows hawkin' their mutton.

†**5.** Short for *mutton-candle* (see 9 b). *Obs.*

1841 J. T. Hewlett *Parish Clerk* III. 174 A flight of sparrows.. would flutter into the chapel and fan out the muttons with their wings. **1859** Thackeray *Virgin.* xxv, Let us.. bless Mr. Price and other Luciferous benefactors of mankind, for banishing the abominable mutton of our youth.

6. *Stock Exchange.* (See quots.)

1881 *Daily News* 1 Feb. 3/1 The tithes and muttons (as the tax on live stock is called) bring in 200,000 liras. **1887** Atkin *House Scraps* 16 *Muttons*, Turks 1873. **1896** Farmer & Henley *Slang* s.v., *Mutton* in *pl.* (Stock Exchanges).—The Turkish loans of 1865 and 1873. (From being in part secured on the sheep-tax.)

7. In various phrases. ***as dead as mutton***: quite dead. ***to take*** (or ***eat***) ***a bit of*** (or ***one's***) ***mutton with***: to dine with. ***to return to one's muttons*** (jocular), to return to the matter in hand (after F. *revenons à nos moutons*); so, ***to resume one's muttons***; conversely, ***to stick to one's muttons***. ***mutton dressed as lamb***: an elderly or middle-aged woman dressed (coiffured, painted, etc.) as though she were young. ***to be one's muttons*** (N.Z.): see quot. 1941.

1714 Mandeville *Fab. Bees* (1733) II. 43 If you will come and eat a bit of mutton with me tomorrow, I'll see no body but yourself. **1821** M. Edgeworth *Let.* 19 Dec. (1971) 297, I think he is winning.. the heart of Lady Caroline—But to return to my muttons. **1838** Thackeray *2nd Lect. Fine Arts* Wks. 1900 XIII. 280 But let us return to our muttons. **1838** Col. Hawker *Diary* (1893) II. 141, I shot him [a swan] as dead as mutton. **1856** Reade *Never too Late* xii, Will you eat your mutton with me to-day, Palmer? **1880** Disraeli *Endym.* lxxvi, Will you take your mutton with me? **1895** Kipling *Brushwood Boy* in *Day's Work* (1898) 348 Look at young Davies makin' an ass of himself over mutton-dressed-as-lamb old enough to be his mother! **1903** A. Bennett *Leonora* iii. 72, I shall have to return to my muttons directly. **1922** Joyce *Ulysses* 541 *Passée.* Mutton dressed as lamb. **1930** *Punch* 28 May 606/3 Both houses, having dealt with the Whitsuntide holidays, resumed their muttons. **1933** *Sun* (Baltimore) 3 Mar. 6/7 Let's stick to our muttons, old man radio, and make it music alone. **1937** D. L. Sayers *Busman's Honeymoon* xv. 307 Aggie Twitterton. Runs arter 'im like an old cat... At '*er* age! Mutton dressed as lamb. **1940** *National Education* (Wellington, N.Z.) Feb. 17 Milk, however, is small Charlie's muttons. **1941** Baker *N.Z. Slang* vi. 54 The farming community has given us [this century] another useful expression in *our muttons*. When we speak of something *being our muttons* or *a person's muttons* we mean that it is regarded with particular favour, that we like it especially well. **1943** A. Hastings *Bright Conversations* 24 Stick to your muttons, and don't talk tripe. **1967** V. S. Naipaul *Mimic Men* i. iii. 41 Our middle-aged ladies, mutton dressed as lamb, as our barman says. **1974** N. Marsh *Black as he's Painted* i. 31, I digress... Shall we return to our muttons?

8. *Printing.* = *mutton quad* (mutton 9 b).

1938 *Amer. Speech* XIII. 270 An em quad is a space the square of the type body... In the shop.. frequently called muttons or monkeys. **1960** G. A. Glaister *Gloss. Book* 122/2 The popular name for an em quad is mutton.

9. a. *attrib.*, as ***mutton*** †***-bouk*** Sc., ***-chine, -cutlet, -gravy, -pasty, -pie,*** †***-steak, -suet.***

1524 *Burgh Rec. Stirling* (1887) 20 Ane *mutton buke. **1712** Prior *Extemp. Invitation to Earl of Oxford* 4 If They can Dine On Bacon-Ham, and *Mutton-chine. **1730** Swift *Lady's Dressing Room* 99 *Mutton-Cutlets, prime of Meat. **1860** Sala *Badd. Peerage* xx. II. 44 The whiskers confined to the mutton cutlet form and size. **1675** Han. Woolley *Gentlew. Comp.* 139 With some *Mutton-gravy, beat or shake them well together in the Pan. **1775** Ash, **Muttonpasty*, a muttonpie. **1900** Sutcliffe *Shameless Wayne* iii, A breakfast of mutton-pasty and ham. **1696** Salmon *Fam. Dict.* (ed. 2), *Mutton-Pye. **1712** Addison *Spect.* No. 367 ¶4 They [sheets of the 'Spectator'].. make a good Foundation for a Mutton pye. **1805** Surr *Winter in Lond.* (1806) I. 196 An old mutton-pie man was run over as he was crossing Piccadilly. **1728** Ramsay *Fables, Miser & Minos* 4 Frae his hoords he doughtna take As much would buy a *mutton-stake. **1706** London & Wise *Retir'd Gard.* I. 85 An Ounce and a half of *Mutton Suet. **1844** Stephens *Bk. Farm* II. 107 Mutton-suet is used in the manufacture of common candles.

b. Special combinations: **mutton-bone**, (*a*) the bone remaining from a joint of mutton; (*b*) quasi-*arch.*, app. the game of knuckle-bone; †**mutton-broker** = mutton-monger; **mutton-broth**, a broth made from mutton; **mutton-candle**, a candle made of mutton-fat (see 5); **mutton cloth** (see quot. 1957); †**mutton-cumber** [? after *cowcumber* = cucumber], some kind of cucumber; †**mutton-driver**, a sheep-stealer; **mutton-faced** *a.*, having a face suggestive of mutton (as a term of abuse); **mutton fat**, (*a*) the fat of mutton; also *attrib.*; (*b*) = *mutton-candle*; in full, ***mutton-fat candle***; (*c*) used *attrib.* and *absol.* of jade to designate a creamy white colour valued highly by connoisseurs; **mutton-fist** *slang*, (*a*) a large red coarse hand, also applied to a person having such a hand; (*b*) a printer's index-hand (Jacobi *Printers' Vocab.* 1888); **mutton-fisted** *a.*, clumsy, heavy-handed; also *fig.*; † **mutton haft**, ? a knife-handle of sheep's bone; **mutton-ham**, (*a*) the thigh of a sheep cured in the same fashion as ham; (*b*) a sail used in certain fishing-smacks in America, so ***mutton-ham boat***; **mutton-head** orig. *U.S.*, a dull, stupid person; **mutton-headed** *a. slang* and *dial.*, dull, stupid; **mutton-leg sleeve** = *leg-of-mutton sleeve*; †**mutton-light**, a mutton-candle; **mutton measles**, 'the cysticercus of the flesh of the sheep; probably the larval form of *Tænia tenella*' (*Syd. Soc. Lex.* 1891); **mutton quad** *Printers' slang*, an em quad; †**mutton-saddle**, ? a saddle of mutton; **mutton-sheep**, ? a sheep bred for meat, not for wool; **mutton-snapper** *West Indian*, 'a large fish of the *Mesoprion* genus' (Smyth *Sailor's Word-bk.* 1867); †**mutton-tea**, ? mutton-broth, cf. *beef-tea*; **mutton-thumper** *U.S. slang*, 'a bungling bookbinder' (*Cent. Dict.* 1890); †**mutton tugger**, ? a whore-monger; †**mutton-water**, ? mutton-broth; **mutton-wood**, 'a composite tree (*Olearia Colensoi*) of New Zealand;—so called because it grows on islands frequented by mutton-birds' (Webster's *Suppl.* 1902). See also mutton-bird, mutton-chop, mutton-fish, mutton-monger.

1785 Wolcot (P. Pindar) *Lyric Odes* xi. (1786) 31 The curs.. Show'd anxiousness about the *mutton bone. **1843** Thackeray *Men's Wives, Dennis Haggarty's Wife*, A dirty table-cloth was laid for dinner, some bottles of porter and a cold mutton-bone being laid out on a rickety grand-piano hard by. **1849** James *Woodman* xxxv, Two of his servants were engaged in the ancient game of mutton-bones. **1694** Motteux *Rabelais* (1737) V. 217 Procurers, and *Mutton-Brokers. **1655** J. Phillips *Satyr agst. Hypocrites* 14 Nor was it *mutton-broth, nor veal broth neither. **1881** Besant & Rice *Chapl. of Fleet* i. xiii, Have a cup of mutton-broth for him when he wakes. **1848** Thackeray *Van. Fair* v, If a pound of *mutton-candles cost sevenpence-halfpenny, how much [etc.]. **1923** *Daily Mail* 12 Mar. 2 (Advt.), Stockinette is white *mutton cloth in its new form, and everyone knows there is nothing to beat it for any kind of cleaning or polishing. **1957** *Textile Terms & Definitions* (Textile Inst.) (ed. 3) 67 *Mutton cloth*, a plain-knitted fabric of loose texture, usually cotton, made on a multi-feeder circular knitting machine. **1695** W. Westmacott *Script. Herb.* 47 Cucumbers or *Mutton-cumbers.. being so commonly known. **1508** Dunbar *Flyting* 246 *Muttoun dryver, girnall ryver, 3ad-swyvar, fowll fell the. **1892** Stevenson & Osbourne *Wrecker* xii. 193 'You ——, ——, little, *mutton-faced Dutchman,' Nares would bawl. **1863** Le Fanu *House by Churchyard* (ed. 2) III. 127 The *mutton-fat wanted snuffing. **1864** Le Fanu *Uncle Silas* III. xvii. 259 The imperfect light of our mutton-fat candle. **1900** A. R. Colquhoun *The 'Overland' to China* viii. 163 The mutton-fat dips which they are intended to burn are only lighted for a few minutes in each month. **1912** B. Laufer *Jade* xii. 328 A brown-red tinge passing into light-yellow shades is strewn over a background of a glossy white which the Chinese designate as mutton-fat. **1920** 'K. Mansfield' *Let.* 20 May (1928) II. 34 A flamingo in a cage made of mutton-fat jade. **1935** [see Ch'ien Lung]. **1936** J. Goette *Jade Lore* vi. 104 White jade from Central Asia.. shows a greater range than does the Burmese. The native connoisseur has always put great emphasis on what he terms mutton fat. **1969** F. Koval tr. *O. Luzzatto-Bilitz's Antique Jade* 46 White jade which is slightly translucent and opalescent is called by the Chinese 'Mutton-Fat Jade'. **1664** Cotton *Scarron.* i. 18 Lifting his *Mutton-fists to th' skies. **1865** *Hotten's Slang Dict.*, *Mutton-fist*, an uncomplimentary title for any one having a large coarse red hand. **1918** *Mutton-fisted [see *ham-handed* adj. (ham *sb.*[1] 3)]. **1927** *Observer* 27 Nov. 6 A critic of his central sound sense.. and mutton-fisted manner of calling a spade a spade. **1934** *Times Lit. Suppl.* 22 Nov. 813/2 But he [*sc.* a hunter] was naturally a little headstrong, and a mutton-fisted stable-boy speedily made of him an incurable puller. **1965** D. Francis *For Kicks* ix. 120, I worked in a slovenly fashion and rode.. like a mutton-fisted clod. **1668** Dryden *Even. Love* iv. iii, Here's the sixpenny whittle you gave me, with the *mutton haft. *a* **1791** Grose *Olio, Grumbler* xvi. (1796) 68 A fine plate of *mutton-ham was next set on the table. **1839** *Mag. Dom. Econ.* IV. 119 The mutton hams cured in the highlands of Scotland and at the Cape of Good Hope. **1899** *Atlantic Monthly* Aug. 197 (*title of art.*) In a *mutton-ham boat. *Ibid.*, Her mutton-ham fluttered as white as new cotton around her single mast. I more than once sought to learn why Albemarle and Pamlico fishing smacks call their huge sails 'mutton-ham'. **1803** T. G. Fessenden *Terrible Tractoration* (ed. 2) iv. 159 And couldst thou, pertinacious B—, But maul these *mutton heads, most sadly. **1825** J. Neal *Bro. Jonathan* I. 99 Peace, mutton-head! **1928** D. H. Lawrence *Woman who rode Away* 209 That *fool*, Joe, standing there like a mutton-head! **1938** H. Nicolson *Let.* 11 July (1966) 349, I suppose that some mutton-head might say [etc.]. **1960** I. Wallach *Absence of Cello* 160 I'm neither an oaf, a boor, or a muttonhead. **1972** 'J. & E. Bonett' *No Time to Kill* xi. 148 Bone-heads, that's what you are. Mutton-heads. Idiots. **1768** *Woman of Honor* III. 29 A poor *mutton-headed flock, ready to follow any bell-weather. **1897** G. Bartram *People of Clopton* ii. 49 He were sich a mutton-headed fool theer were no valley in ootwittin' him. **1934** Wodehouse *Right Ho, Jeeves* xix. 242 She had caused all the trouble by her mutton-headed behaviour in saying 'Yes' instead of 'No'. **1942** E. Paul *Narrow St.* xx. 164 A mutton-headed obstinate father. **1830** *Ladies' Mag.* III. 183 Think of such terms as **mutton leg sleeves*, for example. **1845** *Lowell* (Mass.) *Offering* V. 201 Here is a piece of the first dress I ever saw, cut with what were called 'mutton-leg' sleeves. **1922** JOYCE *Ulysses* 431 In ..widow Twankey's blouse with muttonleg sleeves buttoned behind. **1795** WOLCOT (P. Pindar) *Pindariana* Wks. 1812 IV. 180 Nay while a *mutton-light remains A sun with us no credit gains But yields to every Farthing Candle. **1871** *Amer. Encycl. Printing* (ed. Ringwalt), **Mutton Quad*, a slang term, in English printing-offices, for em quad. **1761** ARMSTRONG *Day, Epist. J. Wilkes* 160 But let me ne'er of *mutton-saddle eat. **1842** LD. WESTERN in Bischoff *Woollen Manuf.* (1842) II. 380 A request..that I would fairly try how far it was possible, to make them into *mutton sheep. **1786** R. WILLAN in *Med. Commun.* II. 117 He had this day some *mutton tea. *c* **1600** in Wood *Life* (O.H.S.) I. 293 [The Oxford colleges are] the nurseries of wickedness, the nests of *mutton tuggers, the dens of formall droanes. **1768** in *Med. Observ.* (1772) IV. 62 She had thrown up some *mutton-water which had been prescribed for common drink.

mutton, variant of MOUTON (French coin).

'mutton-bird. *Austral.* and *N.Z.* **1. a.** Either of two species of the genus *Puffinus*, in New Zealand the sooty shearwater *P. griseus*, and in Australia the short-tailed shearwater *P. tenuirostris*. **b.** An Antarctic petrel of the genus *Pterodroma*. Also *attrib.*

1824 LATHAM *Gen. Hist. Birds* X. 176 This [Petrel] we believe is the species called in Norfolk Island, Mutton Bird; probably from the flesh having somewhat of the flavour of that meat. **1846** G. H. HAYDON *Five Yrs. Australia Felix* 47 (Morris), The mutton-bird, or sooty petrel..is about the size of the wood-pigeon of England, and is of a dark colour. These birds are migratory, and are to be seen ranging over the surface of the great southern ocean far from land... Many millions of these birds are destroyed annually for the sake of their feathers and the oil of the young. **1864–5** WOOD *Homes without H.* ii. (1868) 63 The ground resembles a rabbit warren, being everywhere undermined by the burrows of the Mutton Bird (*Puffinus brevicaudus*) the size of a pigeon. **1898** F. T. BULLEN *Cruise Cachalot* 358 'Mutton birds'. This latter delicacy is a great staple of their [*sc.* the Maories'] flesh food... When it is being cooked in the usual way, *i.e.* by grilling, it smells exactly like a piece of roasting mutton. **1905** W. B. *Where White Man Treads* 202 The other day as we opened the mutton-bird burrows, I heard you remonstrate with our lads. **1911** A. E. MACK *Bush Days* 110 On the surface of the water sat a mutton-bird. **1944** A. RUSSELL *Bush Ways* v. 27 The mutton birds make underground nesting burrows. **1954** A. MOOREHEAD *Rum Jungle* ix. 133 It is usually in a gale (known as the 'mutton bird gale')..that the main swarm suddenly appears. **1963** B. PEARSON *Coal Flat* xxii. 375 Mrs Torere brought out..a half-kerosene tin of cooked mutton-birds preserved in fat. **1965** *Courier-Mail* (Brisbane) 24 Mar. 2/7 Mutton bird rookeries can be found on the coasts. **1970** *Southerly* XXX. 226 The children saw countless thousands of mutton birds passing over the farm, returning from ocean wanderings north of the equator to their nesting colonies on the Bass Strait coasts.

2. a. mutton-bird scrub, tree *N.Z.*, an evergreen shrub or small tree, *Senecio reinoldii*, of the family Compositæ, bearing dark green leaves and clusters of small yellow flowers.

1898 MORRIS *Austral Eng.* 310/1 Mutton-bird Tree..so called because the mutton-birds, especially in Foveaux Straits, New Zealand, are fond of sitting under it. **1906** LAING & BLACKWELL *Plants N.Z.* 438 *S[enecio] rotundifolius* is the mutton-bird scrub of Stewart Island. Its leaves are much used by tourists for post cards, the white tomentum of the underside affording a suitable surface for writing. **1963** POOLE & ADAMS *Trees & Shrubs N.Z.* 200 *S[enecio] reinoldii* Endl. Mutton-bird scrub. Shrub or small tree reaching 10 m.

b. *slang.* In full, ***mutton-bird eater.*** (See quot. 1937). Loosely, any Tasmanian.

1937 PARTRIDGE *Dict. Slang* 546/1 *Mutton-Bird* (gen. pl.), a resident in North Tasmania: Southern Tasmanians'. **1941** BAKER *Dict. Austral. Slang* 48 *Mutton-bird*, a resident of Northern Tasmania. Also, 'mutton-bird eater'.

So **mutton-birder**, one who catches mutton-birds in season; one who is engaged in the preparation of mutton-birds for the market. Also **'mutton-birding** *vbl. sb.*

1881 G. WALCH *Victoria in 1880* 49 Armed with a piece of stout curved wire, fastened at the end of a long stick, the mutton-birder fishes in the holes for his prize. *Ibid.*, One of the sports of the neighbourhood is 'mutton-birding'. **1900** *N.Z. Illustr. Mag.* II. 919 Mutton-birding on Stewart Island. **1965** *Austral. Encycl.* VI. 234B (*caption*) A mutton-birder's hut, with casks of dressed and salted mutton-bird carcasses.

ˌmutton-'chop.

1. a. A piece of mutton for broiling or frying, usually a division of the loin containing one rib (having the end of the bone chopped off) and half the vertebra to which it is attached.

1720 SWIFT *To Stella* Wks. 1755 III. II. 184 A slice of bread and mutton-chop. **1758** JOHNSON *Idler* No. 33 ⁋25 Could get nothing but mutton-chops off the worst end. **1789** FARLEY *Lond. Art of Cookery* (ed. 6) 59 Mutton Chops. Take a loin of mutton, and cut chops from it about half an inch thick. **1848** DICKENS *Dombey* viii, Mrs. Pipchin made a special repast of mutton-chops.

attrib. *a* **1860** ALB. SMITH *Lond. Med. Student* (1861) 103 A lot of cups, egg-shells, mutton-chop bones, and pewter spoons flew up in the air.

b. *pl. slang.*

1865 *Hotten's Slang Dict.*, *Mutton-chops*, a sheep's-head.

2. In full ***mutton-chop whisker***: a side whisker shaped like a mutton-chop, i.e. narrow at the top and broad and rounded at the bottom (usu. in *pl.*). So ***mutton-chop whiskered*** adj.

1865 *Reader* No. 121. 456/2 Mutton-chop whiskers. **1875** [see BURNSIDE, BURNSIDE]. **1878** BESANT & RICE *Celia's Arb.* ii, His whiskers..were cut to the old-fashioned regulation 'mutton-chop', very much like what has now come into fashion again. **1882** MISS BRADDON *Mt. Royal* II. x. 216 Where Leonard sat, burly, florid, black-haired, mutton-chop whiskered. **1904** D. C. MURRAY *V.C.* 13 The clean-trimmed hirsute mutton-chop on either side the heavy jowl combined to make him intensely respectable to look at. **1972** J. WAMBAUGH *Blue Knight* (1973) vi. 83 Some of the boys had mutton-chops and moustaches. **1973** 'D. JORDAN' *Nile Green* xxiv. 97 The mutton-chop whiskered auctioneer. **1975** J. SYMONS *Three Pipe Problem* iii. 24 A square honest face framed by mutton-chop whiskers.

muttoned ('mʌt(ə)nd), *a.* [f. MUTTON + -ED[2].] Of a sheep: Having flesh (of a specified quality); having the legs covered with flesh.

1847 *Jrnl. R. Agric. Soc.* VIII. II. 432 The nicest muttoned sheep fed in Northumberland. **1871** *Daily News* 7 Dec., Their sheep show beautiful forequarters and are muttoned down to the hocks.

'mutton-fish.

1. A name for various American and West Indian sea-fish, esp. the eel-like *Zoarces anguillaris.*

1735 MORTIMER in *Phil. Trans.* XXXIX. 112 The Mutton-Fish. This is reckon'd one of the most delicate Fish of the Bahama Islands. **1754** CATESBY *Nat. Hist. Carol.* II. 25. **1884** GOODE, etc. *Nat. Hist. Aquat. Anim.* 247 The Mutton-fish *Zoarces anguillaris*..is occasionally eaten by the Cape Ann fishermen, by whom it is known as the Mutton-fish, the name referring to a supposed resemblance of its flesh to mutton.

2. *Austral.* (The flesh of) a shell-fish of the genus *Haliotis*, esp. *H. iris*; = PAUA.

1840 J. S. POLACK *Manners & Customs of New Zealanders* II. xvi. 176 The *paua*, (mutton-fish) shell. **1843** E. DIEFFENBACH *Travels in N.Z.* II. x. 239 *Haliotis iris*... Inhabits New Zealand... The 'mutton-fish' of the colonists; eaten boiled, but very tough. **1874** A. BATHGATE *Colonial Experiences* xvii. 245 The beautiful iridescent shell of the mutton-fish..is not uncommon in the south. **1882** J. E. TENISON-WOODS *Fish & Fisheries N.S. Wales* 92 Then mutton fish were speared. This is the ear shell-fish (*Haliotis nævosa*), which was eagerly bought by the Chinese merchants. **1898** MORRIS *Austral Eng.*, *Mutton-fish*, a marine univalve mollusc, *Haliotis nævosa*, Martyn: so called from its flavour when cooked. **1944** *Living off Land* ii. 30 In the case of molluscs like mutton fish, cook until most of the natural moisture has boiled out of the shell. **1956** M. WEST *Gallows on Sand* ix. 98 The ecology of *Haliotus asinina*—mutton-fish to you. **1959** W. G. MCCLYMONT *Explor. N.Z.* (ed. 2) 42 They lived on mutton fish.

3. *U.S.* A kind of medusa.

1884 *Stand. Nat. Hist.* (1888) I. 93 One of the most abundant medusæ at times in the neighborhood of the Florida Keys is a Discophore, called by naturalists *Linerges*, and known to fishermen there as the 'thimble-fish', 'mutton-fish thimble', [etc.]. *Ibid.* Index, Mutton-fish 93.

'muttonhood. *jocular.* [f. MUTTON + -HOOD.] The state of being mutton as opposed to lamb.

1841 J. T. HEWLETT *Parish Clerk* I. 59 When they grew up to adolescent muttonhood. **1887** *Sat. Rev.* 8 Jan. 48 Mutton that is standing with reluctant feet where muttonhood and lambhood meet.

muttoniness ('mʌt(ə)nɪnɪs). *rare*[−1]. [f. MUTTONY *a.* + -NESS.] Muttony quality.

1882 'ANNIE THOMAS' *Allerton T.* III. ix. 164, I like to have my animal..dressed in such a way that its original beefiness or muttoniness is completely disguised.

mutton-monger. *slang.* [f. MUTTON (sense 4) + MONGER.]

1. A whoremonger. Now *Obs.* or *rare.*

1532 MORE *Confut. Tindale* Wks. 366/1 Motenmongers, priapistes, ydolaters, whoremaisters. **1542** UDALL *Erasm. Apoph.* 151 b, One Didymo (who..had in euery bodyes mouth a veraye eiuil name of beeyng a muttonmoungre). **1600** *Look About You* H 4, Ah old Muttonmonger I beleeue heer's worke towards. *a* **1700** B. E. *Dict. Cant. Crew*, *Mutton-monger*, a Lover of Women; also a Sheep-stealer. **1923** J. MANCHON *Le Slang* 201 A mutton-monger, un coureur de filles.

†**2.** A great eater of mutton; also, a sheep-stealer. *Obs.*

1649 W. M. *Wandering Jew* (1857) 42 He is a curse to Pasties; a Tormentor of Poultry,..a terrible Sheep-biter; a horrible Mutton-monger, a Gorbelly-Glutton. **1664** COTTON *Scarron.* I. 34 Yet scarce could satisfie their hungers, These Trojans were such Mutton-mongers. *a* **1700** [see 1].

†**muttonship.** *Obs.* [f. MUTTON + -SHIP.] ***your muttonship***: as a mock title (see MUTTON 4).

1632 BROME *North. Lass* II. iv, How got your Rotten Muttonship into this Lions case?

muttony ('mʌt(ə)nɪ), *a.* [f. MUTTON + -Y.] Having the quality of mutton.

1858 R. S. SURTEES *Ask Mamma* lxxv. 329 He had killed a south-down,—not one of your modern muttoney-lambs, but an honest, home-fed, four-year-old. **1881** R. GRANT WHITE *Engl. Without & Within* 101 There it was mutton which was mutton, and yet was not muttony.

mutual ('mjuːtjuːəl), *a.* and *sb.* Also 6 **mutuel.** [a. F. *mutuel* (from 14th c.) = Sp. *mutual*, f. L. *mūtu-us* borrowed, reciprocal:—prehistoric **moitwo-*, f. root **moi-* to change. Cf. Gr. (Sicilian) μοῖτον ἀντὶ μοίτου, tit for tat; also L. *mūtāre* (see MUTATION).

OF. had *mutu* = Sp. *mútuo*, Pg., It. *mutuo*.]

A. *adj.* **1. a.** Of relations, sentiments, actions: Possessed, entertained, or performed by each (of two persons, things, classes, etc.) towards or with regard to the other; reciprocal. *spec.* in ***mutual aid, deterrence.***

1477 NORTON *Ord. Alch.* Introd., in Ashm. (1652) 5 In mutuall love. **1539** CROMWELL in Merriman *Life & Lett.* (1902) II. 303 His highnes wold be glad..to entre a liege for mutual ayde on bothe sydes in cace of nede to be given. *a* **1614** D. DYKE *Myst. Self-deceiving* (ed. 8) 71 When wee imbrace one another, there is a mutuall hold on both sides. **1681** VISCT. STAIR *Inst. Law Scot.* I. iii. §9. 26 Though frequently such Obligations in mutual Contracts, are conceived by way of provision or condition. **1709** SHAFTESB. *Charac.* (1711) I. II. 113 'Tis in War that mutual Succour is most given, mutual Danger run, and common Affection most exerted. **1729** *Act 2 Geo. II*, c. 22 §13 Where there are mutual Debts between the Plaintiff and Defendant. **1816** WHEATON *Cases Supr. Crt. U.S.* I. 279 The Mutual Assurance Society *v.* Watts' Executor. **1838** W. BELL *Dict. Law Scot.* 667 There is no contract, whether mutual or unilateral, which is binding without a *consensus in idem placitum*, expressed or implied. *Ibid.*, In the case of mutual and onerous entails, the prohibitions are effectual against the creditors of the entailer. **1848** WHARTON *Law Lex.*, *Mutual Testament*, a will made by two persons who leave their effects reciprocally to the survivor. **1849** MACAULAY *Hist. Eng.* i. I. 84 Between him and his subjects there could be nothing of the nature of mutual contract. **1871** B. STEWART *Heat* §43 The tendency of heat in crystals is to increase the mutual distance of the molecules. **1881** JOWETT *Thucyd.* I. 174 Mutual fear is the only solid basis of alliance. **1894** H. DRUMMOND *Ascent Man* 303 Organisms which give mutual aid survive and people the world with their kind. **1912** J. S. HUXLEY *Individual in Animal Kingdom* v. 135 Mutual aid (though it implies mutual dependence) establishes minimum waste. *Ibid.* vi. 154 The ideals of active harmony and mutual aid as the best means to power and progress. **1927** —— *Religion without Revelation* i. 49 Permanent facts of human existence—..suffering, mutual aid, comradeship, physical and moral growth. **1943** *New Statesman* 20 Nov. 326 Lease lend, now officially named 'Mutual Aid', is giving rise to a great deal of discussion in the United States. **1955** *Ann. Reg. 1954* 149 Canada had previously made 400 Sabres available to the R.A.F. as part of the mutual aid programme. **1955** *Bull. Atomic Sci.* Jan. 16/1 In the non-Communist world a new formula is gaining more and more popularity—'mutual deterrence' by the consideration of the opponent's retaliatory power. **1966** SCHWARZ & HADIK *Strategic Terminology* 61 *Mutual deterrence*, situation obtaining between nuclear powers when each is deterred from attacking the other (i.e., launching a first strike) because the damage expected to result from the victim's retaliation (second strike) would be unacceptable.

b. Qualifying personal designations of relationship, friendship, or hostility, to indicate that the relation or sentiment is mutual.

a **1562** G. CAVENDISH *Wolsey* (1893) 221 Yt is..the especyall cause of all my travell into this contrie..to spend my lyfe with you as a very father, and a mutuall brother. **1639** GLAPTHORNE *Argalus* IV. Wks. 1874 I. 53 But Amphialus, Since we are mutuall friends,..I'le make thee my full Executour. **1719** ABP. KING in Ellis *Orig. Lett.* Ser. II. IV. 315 Common friends are not allowed to be common friends, but all obliged to declare themselves mutual enemies. **1813** SHELLEY *Q. Mab* III. 172 For kings And subjects, mutual foes, for ever play A losing game into each other's hands.

c. ***mutual admiration society***: a satirical designation for a coterie of persons who are accused of over-estimating each other's merits. Also ***mutual admiration gang.***

1851 THOREAU *Jrnl.* 27 Feb. in *Early Spring in Massachusetts* (1881) 16 It is the hip-hip-hurrah and mutual admiration society style. **1858** O. W. HOLMES *Aut. Breakf.-t.* i, All generous companies of artists, authors, philanthropists, men of science, are, or ought to be, Societies of Mutual Admiration. *Ibid.*, Who can tell what we owe to the Mutual Admiration Society of which Shakspeare, and Ben Jonson, and Beaumont and Fletcher were members? **1880** L. STEPHEN *Pope* 50 That body was not more free than other mutual admiration societies from the desire to impose its own prejudices on the public. **1920** G. B. SHAW *How to become Musical Critic* (1960) 313 A ridiculous little mutual-admiration gang of snobs. **1953** G. HOUGH *Romantic Poets* v. 160 Keats would have been better off at this stage..without so many ladies, or with ladies of a different kind; and some of the familiar sonnets suggest a small and rather silly mutual admiration society. **1969** G. BATTISCOMBE *Queen Alexandra* x. 139 Seldom can there have been a more devoted family: the unkind might even have called them a mutual admiration society.

¶ **d.** quasi-*ellipt.* Pertaining to or characterized by some (implied) mutual action or relation.

mutual terms, principles: used to describe a business arrangement between two parties, in which exchange of services takes the place of money payments. ***mutual fund*** *U.S.*, a unit trust; also *attrib.*; hence ***mutual funding.***

1848 THACKERAY *Van. Fair* v, He was admitted into Dr. Swishtail's academy upon what are called 'mutual-principles'—that is to say, the expenses of his board and schooling were defrayed by his father in goods, not money. **1880** *Encycl. Brit.* XIII. 173/2 These bodies [life assurance companies] have been of three kinds—(1) the purely *mutual* offices, in which the assured themselves constitute the society; (2) *proprietary* offices..; and (3) the *mixed* offices. **1950** J. C. CLENDENIN *Introd. to Investments* 600 (*Index*) Mutual funds (*see* Open-end companies). **1958** *Spectator* 18 July 108/1 In the United States, total investment in Mutual Funds (the American term for unit trusts) stands at over £3,000 million. **1962** S. STRAND *Marketing Dict.* 472 *Mutual Funds Market*, the daily buying and selling transactions of the shares of mutual funds. Companies selling mutual funds are listed on the financial pages of newspapers. **1969** *Times* 30 Apr. 28/3 As a Mutual Society all our profits must go to our policyholders. *Ibid.* 5 May (Suppl.) p. vi/3 The average turnover of mutual fund portfolios rose..to 43 per cent. **1972** *Daily Tel.* 4 Nov. 28/4 By lending those funds on mortgage, the [building] societies, which are mutual and non profit-making, pass on the benefit of the short-term cost of money to long-term borrowers. **1973** *Times* 18 May 29/2 Expanding industries such as insurance or mutual funding.

e. *Electr.* Applied to quantities and properties that depend equally and symmetrically on two circuits or circuit elements and represent an effect on either of a certain kind of change in the other; esp. ***mutual inductance*** (see INDUCTANCE), ***induction***.

1865 J. C. MAXWELL in *Phil. Trans. R. Soc.* CLV. 507 To find the coefficient (M) of mutual induction between two circular linear conductors in parallel planes. **1886**, etc. [see INDUCTANCE]. **1896** F. BEDELL *Princ. Transformer* iii. 37 The relation between two circuits is strictly a mutual one, the coefficient of mutual induction having the same value with either circuit as primary or secondary. **1931** MOYER & WOSTREL *Radio Handbk.* VII. 395 In most circuits, the coupling between the input and output circuits is adjusted by changing the mutual reactance. **1959** B. J. LEY et al. *Linear Circuit Anal.* iii. 150 The coefficients Y_{11}, Y_{22},.., Y_{nn} of the principal diagonal terms were called self-admittances and the off-diagonal coefficients Y_{hk} $(h \neq k)$ were called the mutual admittances... To find the mutual admittance Y_{12} we examine the term $Y_{12}(j\omega)\mathbf{V}_2$ in the first equation of Eqs. (3–69). This term represents the phasor current leaving node 1 when nodes 1, 3,.., *n* are grounded and node 2 has a phasor voltage $\mathbf{V}_2$. **1969** A. M. HOWATSON *Princ. Appl. Electr.* v. 100 The impedance Z_{12} is, physically, the voltage produced in mesh 1 due to unit current flowing in mesh 2. It is called the open-circuit transfer impedance or mutual impedance of mesh 2 to mesh 1, and because $Z_{12} = Z_{21}$ it is also that from mesh 1 to mesh 2.

f. *Electronics.* ***mutual conductance***, the ratio of the change in the anode current of a valve to the change of grid voltage causing it, the anode voltage being held constant; so ***mutual characteristic***, a characteristic curve representing the variation of anode current with grid voltage at constant anode voltage.

1918 L. A. HAZELTINE in *Proc. IRE* VI. 64 The effectiveness of the audion as a relay depends primarily on the slope of the characteristic curve. This slope, being the quotient of a current by a voltage associated therewith, is of the dimensions of a conductance and may be called the mutual conductance of the grid towards the plate. **1933** K. HENNEY *Radio Engin. Handbk.* VIII. 195 The mutual characteristic, or transfer characteristic of the tube, shows the effect of the grid voltage upon the plate current. **1942** *Electronic Engin.* XIV. 734/1 The alternating potential is applied to control the electron stream at a point where the electron velocity is low, thereby producing a positive feedback which increases the effective mutual conductance of the valve. **1962** D. F. SHAW *Introd. Electronics* xi. 212 The value of g_m is low when I_a is very small but after an initial curvature the mutual characteristics are almost linear and parallel. **1963** B. FOZARD *Instrumentation Nuclear Reactors* x. 116 At middle frequencies where the undesirable effects of the various capacitances are negligible the gain is g_mR where g_m is the mutual conductance of the valve and *R* is the effective anode load resistance.

2. Respective; belonging to each respectively.

In some of the examples there is a mixture of sense 1, the notion being that of a reciprocal relation between each of the persons and what belongs to the other.

1548 UDALL, etc. *Erasm., Par. Acts* 37 b. Euen so the lorde prepared, in theyr mutuall vision, eache one for other [Saul & Ananias]. **1652** LOVEDAY tr. *Calprenede's Cassandra* III. 207 The tears that were shed on both sides in the remembrance of their mutuall losses. **1755** J. SHEBBEARE *Lydia* (1769) I. 44 Pressing each other to their bosoms in silence, they again unclasped their mutual arms. **1796** *Hist. Ned Evans* II. 152 The time would not allow them to enter into minute details of their mutual adventures. **1818** HOBHOUSE *Hist. Illustr.* (ed. 2) 59 Perhaps we shall find both the one and the other to have been more active despoilers than has been confessed by their mutual apologists. **1837** BEDFORD in *Life Southey* (1850) VI. 353, I cannot believe the difference in your mutual years can create any strong line of demarcation between you.

†**3.** Of intercourse: Intimate. *Obs.*

1603 SHAKS. *Meas. for M.* I. ii. 158 But it chances The stealth of our most mutuall entertainment With Character too grosse, is writ on Juliet. **1659** H. L'ESTRANGE *Alliance Div. Off.* 292 The society and conversation could not be so mutual between them. **1749** FIELDING *Tom Jones* XVII. iii, Two families.. between whom there has always existed so mutual an intercourse and good harmony.

4. Pertaining to both parties; common.

a. Of things, actions, sentiments.

Now regarded as incorrect.

1591 SHAKS. *Two Gent.* V. iv. 173 That done, our day of marriage shall be yours One Feast, one house, one mutuall happinesse. **1596** —— *Merch. V.* V. i. 77 If.. any ayre of musicke touch their eares, You shall perceiue them make a mutuall stand. **1631** BRATHWAIT *Eng. Gentlew.* 125 Those daughters of Scedasus of Leuctra,.. conceiuing a mutuall sorrow for their lost Virginity, became resolute actors in their owne Tragedy. **1797** MRS. A. M. BENNETT *Beggar Girl* (1813) II. 45 The major hinted at their mutual obligations to Mrs. Walsingham. **1802–12** BENTHAM *Ration. Judic. Evid.* (1827) V. 204 Under the mutual appellative *self-regarding*, both self-serving and self-disserving are comprized. ?**1820** BYRON *Let. to Murray* (1821) 9 Mr. Hobhouse was desirous that I should express our mutual opinion of Pope. **1831** SCOTT *Ct. Robt.* xv, Their apartments were contiguous, but the communication between them was cut off for the night by the mutual door being locked and barred. **1882** F. J. FURNIVALL in *Digby Myst.* (E.E.T.S.) Ded. 2 A reminder of the days when his [*i.e.* Shakspere's] triumphant art was the subject of our mutual work.

b. Qualifying a personal designation expressive of a relation.

Commonly censured as incorrect, but still often used in the collocations ***mutual friend, mutual acquaintance***, on account of the ambiguity of *common*, which is the only adj. correctly expressing the intended meaning. Expressions like ***mutual father, mutual child***, formerly not uncommon, would now sound strange.

1632 SIR T. HAWKINS tr. *Mathieu's Unhappy Prosperitie* 22 Hee turneth himselfe towards his wife, conjureth her by the love he had borne her,.. and by their mutuall children, a little to humble her spirit. **1658** G. STARKEY *Pyrotechny* Ded., My good fortune first by the occasion of our mutual Friend, Dr. Robert Child. **1723** LADY M. W. MONTAGU *Lett., to C'tess Mar* (1887) I. 346 Our mutual acquaintance are exceedingly dispersed. **1778** BURKE *Corr.* 24 Dec. (1844) II. 251 Our mutual friend, John Bourke. **1786** MRS. A. M. BENNETT *Juvenile Indiscr.* V. 86 The eldest I sent for home, to superintend my domestic affairs, before our mutual darling had compleated her education. **1802** *Noble Wanderers* II. 199 Her sister Ismena had succeeded to their mutual father, Astamanes. **1825** SCOTT *Fam. Lett.* 15 Oct., Our mutual friend Mr. Wright. **1867** GEO. ELIOT in Cross *Life* (1885) III. 20 Don't write unless you have a real desire to gossip with me a little about yourself and our mutual friends. **1883** L. OLIPHANT *Altiora Peto* I. 93 We had no mutual relations to talk about.

†**c.** Having the specified character in common.

1794 GODWIN *Cal. Williams* 265 He talked of the injustice of which we were mutual victims, without bitterness.

†**5.** Responsive. *Obs.*

1657 COKAINE *Obstinate Lady* III. ii, Love is a passion not to be withstood, And, until hearts be mutual, never good. **1809** CAMPBELL *Gertr. Wyom.* I. x, When fate had reft his mutual heart:.. and Gertrude climb'd a widow'd father's knee. **1816** BYRON *Ch. Har.* III. xxiv, Who then could guess If ever more should meet those mutual eyes. **1850** MRS. BROWNING *Poet's Vow* IV. xii, The old nurse looked within her eyes, Whose mutual look was gone.

6. *Comb.* with the sense 'mutually', as ***mutual-dependent, -kindling, -melting*** adjs.

a **1743** SAVAGE *'Happy the Man'* iv, Who, melting on thy mutual-melting breast, Entranc'd enjoys love's whole luxurious charms, Is all a God. **1786** BURNS *Lament* ix, Love's luxurious pulse beat high,.. To mark the mutual-kindling eye. **1895** W. H. HUDSON *Spencer's Philos.* 172 Thus remaining unintegrated into the great organization of mutual-dependent parts which constitutes society.

B. *sb.* **a.** = *mutual friend*. **b.** = *mutual fund* (MUTUAL *a.* 1 d).

1901 KIPLING *Kim* xii. 314 The wire came in about what our mutual friend said he had hidden... I meet our mutual at Delhi on the way back. **1971** *Financial Mail* (Johannesburg) 26 Feb. 690/1 Some mutual fund men.. are once again pressing the Registrar for permission to go ahead with those property mutuals.

mutualism ('mjuːtjuːəlɪz(ə)m). [f. MUTUAL *a.* + -ISM. Cf. F. *mutuellisme* (see 1 b).]

1. a. The doctrine that individual and collective well-being is attainable only by mutual dependence. Esp. in connection with the theory of non-profit credit and voluntary association for the exchange of services advocated by P. J. Proudhon (1809–65). **b.** [after F. *mutuellisme*.] The system of the association of 'mutualists' at Lyons.

1849 C. DANA *Proudhon* (1896) 36 But how can they gain possession of this instrument [*sc.* capital]? By the organization of credit, on the principle of reciprocity or mutualism, if we may use a new word. *Ibid.* 40 Mutualism of credit, or credit at cost. **1863** J. WEISS *Life & Corr. Parker* I. 106 A mutualism to secure culture and material welfare. **1873** MORLEY *Rousseau* II. xii. 190 Those schemes of Mutualism, and all the other shapes of collective action for a common social good. **1892** SCHÄFFLE *Impossibility Soc. Democr.* 17 Socialism, communism,.. anarchism, mutualism [etc.]. **1929** *Amer. Jrnl. Sociol.* XXXIV. 783 By 'mutualism' Proudhon meant a practice of voluntary association for strictly specified and limited purposes. **1968** *Internat. Encycl. Soc. Sci.* XII. 606/1 Federalism, that is, mutualism transferred into the realm of politics, is the solution.

2. *Biol.* A condition of symbiosis in which two associated organisms contribute mutually to the well-being of each other. By some writers applied esp. to such a relationship that (*a*) is not necessary for the survival or reproduction of the organisms involved, or else (*b*) is necessary for one or both of the organisms. Also *transf.*

1876 *Beneden's Anim. Parasites* 83 It is often very difficult to say where commensalism ends and mutualism begins. **1949** W. C. ALLEE et al. *Princ. Animal Ecol.* xxxv. 711/1 Varying degrees of mutualism exist, from a slight benefit to a remarkable interdependence of both species in the partnership. **1953** *Parasitology* XLII. 261 Symbiosis can be broadly divided into the three well-recognized categories: commensalism (where the host is for all practical purposes unaffected by the presence of the symbiote), parasitism (where the host is injured), and mutualism (where the host is benefited). **1956** T. W. H. CAMERON *Parasites & Parasitism* 231 Commensalism, in turn, grades into mutualism, which implies a certain benefit by the host from the presence of the invader, but the association is not an essential one. **1962** J. D. SMYTH *Introd. Animal Parasitol.* i. 6 An association in which both associates benefit has long been referred to as mutualism by some authors and symbiosis by others... *Symbiosis* could.. broadly be used to include all the different kinds of relationship which exist in nature. By usage, however, it has come to be restricted to associations.. in which the participating species are dependent on each other for existence... In cases of mutualism, on the other hand, the association is not obligatory to existence. **1962** K. F. LAGLER et al. *Ichthyol.* xiv. 436 [Among fishes] instances of mutualism (symbiosis) are not clearly known; this is the relationship in which neither of two species can reproduce or grow in the absence of the other. **1963** C. J. MCCALL in A. Dundes *Mother Wit* (1973) 420 The relationship is rather one of mutualism, in that it is latently eufunctional for both institutions. **1967** M. E. HALE *Biol. Lichens* v. 70 *Mutualism.* This term describes a mutually beneficial relationship where one or both components may be dependent on the association for survival. **1970** *Nature* 5 Sept. 1001/1 The commonest species, *Remora remora*, is an active cleaner, and the mutualistic relationship between fish and host is strong, but the mutualism is less strong in other species.

mutualist ('mjuːtjuːəlɪst), *sb.* (and *a.*) [f. MUTUAL *a.* + -IST. Cf. F. *mutuelliste* (= 1 b), *mutualiste* member of a mutual assurance society.]

1. a. An advocate of mutualism. Also *attrib.* or as *adj.* **b.** A member of a corporation of labour masters at Lyons.

1848 W. H. KELLY tr. *L. Blanc's Hist. Ten Y.* II. 258 Several Lyonese republicans.. had been the first to interfere between the manufacturers and the mutualists. *Ibid.*, The executive council of the mutualists.. ordered the workmen to resume their suspended labours, and was obeyed. **1892** SCHÄFFLE *Impossibility Soc. Democr.* 11 Some so-called mutualists depend for everything on a brotherly reciprocity. **1909** F. LAWTON *3rd French Republic* xiv. 320 From 1852 onwards, the Mutualist movement extended rapidly. **1929** *Amer. Jrnl. Sociol.* XXXIV. 783 Let exchange take place directly within each 'mutualist' association. **1948** M. NOMAD in F. Gross *European Ideologies* viii. 329 Proudhon's 'mutualist anarchism', with its panacea of a 'People's Bank'. **1969** A. RITTER *Pol. Thought Proudhon* v. 130 The units of a mutualist society are not only to be equal in power; they are also to differ in their occupations, personalities, ideas, inclinations.

2. *Biol.* One of two organisms which mutually live on each other. Cf. MUTUALISM.

1876 *Beneden's Anim. Parasites* 84 Every colony of campanulariæ or sertulariæ lodges a crowd of messmates and mutualists. **1894** J. WEIR in *Amer. Naturalist* Aug. 713, I mean by the term mutualist, an animal which gives a *quid pro quo* or specific beneficial service to the host which affords it sustenance and domicile.

mutualistic (mjuːtjuːə'lɪstɪk), *a.* [f. MUTUALIST + -IC.] Exhibiting or characteristic of mutualism (esp. sense 2).

1885 *Anarchist* 15 Sept. 2/2 He shews how two principles pervade human society—one mutualistic, which leads to equality, the other, antagonistic, which destroys it. **1911** J. G. MCINTOSH *Manuf. Varnishes* III. 291 Giard does not see that the ants are enemies of the cochineal... Their relations are mutualistic and in no way predatory. **1936** *New Phytologist* XXXV. 129 The presence of the fungus in a mycorrhizal association is to be regarded as an example of controlled parasitic attack and has no mutualistic significance. **1967** V. AHMADJIAN *Lichen Symbiosis* iv. 78 To say that all lichens are mutualistic is as wrong as saying that all are parasitic. **1970** [see MUTUALISM 2]. **1974** *Nature* 18 Oct. 574/2 Mortimer Starr (University of California, Davis) produced a new classificatory scheme which has the virtue of both clarifying and thinking about the phenomenon and indicating where further experimental work is required—to decide, for example, whether a symbiotic association is mutualistic or obligately parasitic in this respect.

Hence **mutua'listically** *adv.*

1949 W. C. ALLEE et al. *Princ. Anim. Ecol.* xvii. 251 There does not appear to be any development of a strict taxonomic relation like that in so many examples of mutualistically paired species in which pollination is involved. **1967** V. AHMADJIAN *Lichen Symbiosis* iv. 78 In some *Collema* lichens the fungal hyphae periodically destroy certain parts of the algal colony while living mutualistically with the rest.

mutuality (ˌmjuːtjuː'ælɪtɪ). [f. MUTUAL *a.* + -ITY: cf. F. *mutualité*.]

1. a. The quality or condition of being mutual; reciprocity.

a **1586** SIDNEY *Arcadia* III. (1622) 347 There is no sweeter tast of friendship, then the coupling of soules in this mutualitie either of condoling, or comforting. *a* **1635** SIBBES *Confer. Christ & Mary* (1656) 77 We have not comfort, because we do not make him ours by a spirit of mutuality. **1782** PAINE *Let. Abbé Raynal* (1791) 43 A mutuality of wants have formed the individuals of each country into a kind of national society. **1892** *Times* 8 Feb. 5/2 In future the.. South American Republics must look for protection and mutuality of interests.. only among themselves.

b. *Law.* A condition of things under which two parties are mutually bound to perform certain reciprocal duties.

1845 STEPHEN *Comm. Laws Eng.* (1874) II. 55 There is.. a distinction between a promise and a contract; for the latter involves the idea of mutuality which the former does not. **1847** C. G. ADDISON *Law of Contracts* I. i. (1883) 14 The mutuality of the obligation is the very essence of all contracts founded upon mutual promises. **1848** WHARTON *Law Lex.*, *Mutuality*, reciprocation; an acting in return. **1884** BOWEN in *Law Times Rep.* 24 May 380/1, I will not say whether there was sufficient mutuality between the parties to make what was done between them binding or not.

c. A system of organizing conditions of work by agreement between the workmen involved and the employer; also ***mutuality system***.

1968 *Sunday Tel.* 20 Oct. 19/2 The employers team pressed the unions to surrender the 'mutuality' system. **1970** *Guardian* 4 Dec. 15 'Mutuality'.. means that the rates for each job have to be 'mutually agreed' on the shop floor where they are to be carried out and by the people who will perform the tasks. **1972** *Times* 27 Jan. 14/5 The agreement had that degree of mutuality to bring it within the set-off provisions of section 31. *Ibid.* 7 Nov. 19/3 The management has also conceded a large measure of 'mutuality', the arrangement under which shop floor representatives retain bargaining rights on many shop floor working conditions.

2. Interchange of acts of goodwill; intimacy.

1604 SHAKS. *Oth.* II. i. 267 (1st Qo.) They met so neere with their lips that their breathes embrac'd together. When these mutualities [*Folios* mutabilities] so marshall the way, hand at hand, comes the maine exercise [etc.]. **1628** EARLE *Microcosm., Plausible Man* (Arb.) 59 Hee loues not deeper mutualities, because he would not take sides. **1867**

BUSHNELL *Mor. Uses Dark Th.* 207 Gathered at their firesides in domestic mutualities and pleasures.

3. *Biol.* The rendering of mutual services by organisms in the condition of symbiosis; cf. MUTUALISM 2.

1876 *Beneden's Anim. Parasites* Introd. 18 The services of many of these [animals] are rewarded either in protection or in kind, and mutuality can well be exercised at the same time as hospitality. *Ibid.* 24.

mutualize (ˈmjuːtjuːəlaɪz), *v.* [f. MUTUAL *a.* + -IZE.] *trans.* †**a.** To give and receive in return; to reciprocate. *Obs.* **b.** To organize on the 'mutual' system. Hence **mutualiˈzation**.

1812 in *Spirit Pub. Jrnls.* XVI. 360 Pledges shall have been mutualized, and those solemn assurances reciprocated, which..can only be violated by the unprincipled. **1905** *Daily News* 23 June 7/2 The report advocates complete mutualisation, with elimination of stock by purchase at a price only commensurate with the dividends. **1930** *Economist* 12 Apr. 825/2 It was created four years ago in connection with the 'mutualisation' of the company. **1951** *Ann. Reg. 1950* 5 It [*sc.* the party programme] was followed, two days later, by proposals for 'mutualization', rather than nationalization, of industrial assurance. **1955** *Times* 28 May 9/1 With the return of the Conservative Government measures of re-nationalization, of fresh nationalization, and of mutualization are no longer risks to be discounted, however vaguely, as contingencies just round the corner. **1960** *Times* 15 Jan. 17/2 Yesterday it [*sc.* the Canada Life Assurance Company] asked to be removed from the list because it had completed its 'mutualization' programme by purchasing all its own shares outstanding.

mutually (ˈmjuːtjuːəlɪ), *adv.* [f. MUTUAL *a.* + -LY².]

1. a. With mutual action or sentiment; in a mutual relation; reciprocally. Freq. in phr. *mutually exclusive*.

c **1540** tr. *Pol. Verg. Eng. Hist.* (Camden, No. 29) 8 They marched forward, and, drawing their blades mutually, ranne together with great cryes. **1542** UDALL *Erasm. Apoph.* 211 b, The honest opinion yͤ the subiectes haue of their kyng and the hertie good wille of the prince mutually toward his subiectes. *c* **1590** MARLOWE *Faust* (1604) C 2, As are the elements, such are the spheares, Mutually folded in each others orbe. **1682** NORRIS *Hierocles* 27 We mutually promote each other in the advantages of virtue. **1751** HARRIS *Hermes* Wks. (1841) 178 And thus is it that interrogatives and relatives mutually pass into each other. **1816** G. S. FABER *Orig. Pagan Idol.* III. 4 These again are said to be mutually the same with each other. **1847** C. BRONTË *J. Eyre* iv, We mutually embraced. **1874** W. WALLACE tr. *Hegel's Logic* ii. 30 Sense..is individual, and as the individual (which, reduced to its simplest terms, is the atom) is also a member of a series, sensible existence presents a number of mutually exclusive units. **1893** LIDDON, etc. *Life Pusey* I. xv. 348 If a good life always meant a true creed, many mutually contradictory errors would be true. **1908** A. BENNETT *Jrnl.* 5 Jan. (1932) I. 274 Every day's experience shows the folly of mutually-exclusive generalisations concerning two countries. **1969** D. C. HAGUE *Managerial Economics* vii. 141 To be drawn up correctly, our list of probabilities must be such that if any one event occurs, this automatically rules out the possibility that any other event in the same list could also occur. The events will then be mutually exclusive.

†**b.** In return; as one side of a reciprocal action. *Obs.*

1598 SHAKS. *Merry W.* IV. vi. 10, I haue acquainted you With the deare loue I beare to faire Anne Page, Who, mutually, hath answer'd my affection,..Euen to my wish. **1699** BENTLEY *Phal.* 247 This Account..establishes and is mutually establish'd by the Testimony of Suidas. **1704** NEWTON *Opticks* III. i. (1721) 345 Pellucid Substances act upon the Rays of Light at a distance..and the Rays mutually agitate the Parts of those Substances at a distance.

2. In mutual co-operation or companionship; by mutual agreement; jointly, in common.

1598 SHAKS. *Merry W.* V. v. 103 Pinch him (Fairies) mutually: Pinch him for his villanie. **1603** —— *Meas. for M.* II. iii. 27 *Duke.* So then it seemes your most offence full act Was mutually committed. *Jul.* Mutually. **1653** WALTON *Angler* xi. 197 They mutually labour to cover it with the same sand. **1735** LD. LYTTELTON *Lett. fr. Persian* (ed. 3) I. 141, I wou'd restore her back again to him untouch'd; or in case they shou'd mutually desire it, carry her with me to my Seraglio in the East. **1784** J. POTTER *Virtuous Villagers* I. 35 You have my free consent to marry, if you and she mutually wish it. **1786** MRS. A. M. BENNETT *Juvenile Indiscr.* II. 157 The loss we mutually sustained in the early death of our parents. *a* **1817** T. DWIGHT *Trav. New Eng.*, etc. (1821) II. 187 The prisoners then began to walk within their room, at the same pace with that of their watchman: the sound of their feet being mutually heard.

†**3.** By both parties respectively. *Obs.*

1632 LITHGOW *Trav.* x. 460 The Gouernours interrogation and my Confession being mutually subscribed.

mutualness (ˈmjuːtjuːəlnɪs). [f. MUTUAL *a.* + -NESS.] The quality of being mutual.

1620 T. GRANGER *Div. Logike* 119 Here mutualnesse in friendship is explicated by the equall. **1886** P. BROOKS in *Life* (1900) II. 542 Here there is the perfect mutualness, the absolute..harmony of the Father and the Son.

mutuary (ˈmjuːtjuːərɪ). *Civil Law.* [ad. L. *mūtuāri-us*, f. *mūtu-us* borrowed: see MUTUAL *a.* and -ARY.] (See quot. 1856.)

1839 [see MUTUUM]. **1856** BOUVIER *Amer. Law Dict.* (ed. 6) II. 196 *Mutuary*, [in] contracts, a person who borrows personal chattels to be consumed by him, and returned to the lender in kind.

†**ˈmutuate**, *v.* *Obs.* [f. L. *mūtuāt-*, ppl. stem of *mūtuārī* to borrow; f. *mūtu-us*: see MUTUAL *a.* and -ATE³.] *trans.* To borrow. Hence †**ˈmutuated** *ppl. a.*, †**ˈmutuating** *vbl. sb.*

a **1548** HALL *Chron., Hen. VII* 27 b, Dyuerse lordes..had mutuate and borowed dyverse and sondy summes of money. **1595** M. MOSSE *Arraign. Usurie* 39 Mutuating and Accommodating: how they differ. *Ibid.* 40 These two kindes of lending which..we call mutuating and accommodating, doe differ in these two poyntes. **1597** A. M. tr. *Guillemeau's Fr. Chirurg.* *iv b, I am not the man which liveth by an other mans mutuated supellectilles. **1657** TOMLINSON *Renou's Disp.* 218 They mutuate their odour..from the places through which they permeate. **1684** T. GODDARD *Plato's Demon* 288 This mutuated or fide-commissary power which he [*sc.* 'our Author'] hath placed in the King. **1689** G. HARVEY *Curing Dis. by Expect.* ii. 7 From their Subjects many Trades are observed to mutuate their distinction; from Physick the Physician. **1716** M. DAVIES *Athen. Brit.* II. Ded. to King, This one only Latin mutuated Pentameter Verse, viz. *Principis est Virtus maxima, nosse Suos.*

mutuation (mjuːtjuːˈeɪʃən). [ad. L. *mūtuātiōn-em*, n. of action f. *mūtuārī*: see MUTUATE *v.*] An act of lending or borrowing. Also *fig.*

1604 DOWNAM *Lect. Ps.* 15. v. 151 Wherefore the contract of vsurie is nothing else but illiberall mutuation, and may thus briefely bee defined: Vsurie is mutuation, or lending for gaine. **1649** BP. HALL *Cases Consc.* (1650) 24 In both there seems to be a valuation of time: which whether in case of mutuation, or sale, may justly be suspected for unlawful. **1778** HALHED *Bengal Gram.* Pref. 3, I have been astonished to find the similitude of Shanscrit words with those..of Latin and Greek: and these not in technical and metaphorical terms, which the mutuation of refined arts and improved manners might have occasionally introduced; but [etc.]. **1827** G. S. FABER *Orig. Expiat. Sacr.* 197 Such a mutuation necessarily supposes a knowledge of the sabbatical seventh day.

†**mutuaˈtitial**, *a.* and *sb.* *Obs. rare*⁻¹. [f. L. *mūtuātīti-us* (f. *mūtuārī*: see MUTUATE *v.*) + -AL¹.] **A.** *adj.* Borrowed. **B.** *sb.* Something borrowed.

1654 VILVAIN *Epit. Ess.* vi, *Mutuatitial Essais.* The Sixth ..Century of Mutuatitials.

†**mutuaˈtitious**, *a.* *Obs. rare.* [f. L. *mūtuātīti-us*, f. *mūtuārī* to borrow: see MUTUATE *v.* and -ITIOUS.] Borrowed; taken from some other.

1625 N. CARPENTER *Geog. Del.* I. iv. (1635) 87 The Peripatetickes..distinguishing the motions of the Planets into a proper or naturall, and accidentall or mutuaticious. **1664** H. MORE *Antid. Idolatry* x. 134 The mutuatitious Good works of their pretended Holy men and women. **1813** T. BUSBY *Lucretius* II. v. Comm. p. xv, With regard to their light: Metrodorus thought it mutuatitious, and borrowed of the sun.

mutuel (mytɥɛl, ˈmjuːtjuːəl). Chiefly *N. Amer.* shortening of PARI MUTUEL. Freq. *attrib.* and in *pl.* Also *transf.* (see quot. 1949).

1908 *Westm. Gaz.* 12 Dec. 16/2 In France last year 320,000,000 francs passed through the 'mutuel'. **1926** *Daily Colonist* (Victoria, B.C.) 23 July 10/5 Returns from the 'mutuels' show that British Columbians are betting as much as ever, or more so, at the Vancouver races. **1938** D. RUNYON *Furthermore* vi. 113 Then I see Herbie start for the mutuels windows. **1944** *Sun* (Baltimore) 21 Sept. 17/4 The mutuel machines will do close to a $400,000,000 business around New York tracks this season. **1949** *Amer. Speech* XXIV. 193/1 *Race mutuels*, a number game in which the winning number is derived from the racing results of any well-known race track. **1968** *Globe & Mail* (Toronto) 13 Jan. 40/8 The better class horses would attract more patrons who..would accelerate the mutuels play. **1972** *N.Y. Times* 1 June 56/1 The scramble had handled $659,439..meaning the scramble accounted for 8.45 per cent of the mutuel business. **1974** *New Yorker* 25 Feb. 86/2 Serious horseplayers will be sorry to hear..that the take from the mutuels will again be seventeen per cent.

mutule (ˈmjuːtjuːl). *Arch.* Also 6 mutilo, *pl.* **mutuli**, 7–8 **mutil**. [a. F. *mutule* (It. *mutulo*), ad. L. *mūtulus* modillion.] The modillion proper to the cornice in the Doric order; a projection upon the soffit of the Doric corona.

1563 SHUTE *Archit.* B iij, [If he] should make ymages..for pillers and make ouer their heade Mutilos, and Coronas. *Ibid.* D iv b, Vitruuius..doth describe the beginning of Mutuli to be necessarie. **1664** EVELYN tr. *Freart's Archit.* I. xiii. 36 The Gotique Order..has compos'd certain lame figur'd Mutils or Corbells in stead of Cartouzes. *Ibid.*, *Acc. Archit.* 137 Mutules..have their name from their defect, as being made thinner and more abated below than above. **1703** tr. *Perrault's Abridgm. Vitruvius* 37 The Corinthian Modillions are imitated by the Mutils of the Dorick Order. **1727–41** CHAMBERS *Cycl.* s.v., The mutules in the Doric answer to the triglyphs, which are under them. **1843** WATHEN *Arts, Antiq. & Chronol. Egypt* 181 Above the architrave of the porch is a cornice ornamented with long mutules or brackets. **1862** MRS. SPEID *Last Years Ind.* 187 The stone triglyphs and mutules of the Doric order.

‖**mutum** (ˈmuːtəm). [Native name.]
= CURASSOW.

1863 [see CURASSOW]. **1933** P. FLEMING *Brazilian Adventure* I. xvi. 137 Sometimes we got a *mutum*, a big black and white turkey with a speckled crest. **1964** A. L. THOMSON *New Dict. Birds* 175/2 The Razorbilled Curassow *Mitu mitu*, which is called 'mutum' by the Brazilians, is black with a bluish sheen in both sexes, with brown on the belly, and with a high narrow frontal comb of the same red colour as the bill; it weighs about 7¾ lb. (3500 grams) and inhabits the Amazon region and northern Brazil.

†**ˈmutuous**, *a.* *Obs.* [f. L. *mūtu-us* MUTUAL + -OUS.] = MUTUAL *a.* Hence **ˈmutuously** *adv.*

1683 E. HOOKER *Pref. Pordage's Mystic Div.* 91 The opportune interposition of prudent indulgence, mutuous toleration and grand moderation. *Ibid.* 52 Such like words evn Religionists too often use in Repartées, mutuously.

†**ˈmutuum.** *Civil Law.* *Obs.* [a. L. *mūtuum* a loan, neut. of *mūtuus* borrowed.] A contract under which such things are lent as are consumed in the use, or which cannot be used without their extinction or alienation.

1486 *Materials Reign Hen. VII* (Rolls) I. 267 That ye, in the boke called the pele doo entre a mutuum..of the forsaide D.ccclxxvii. li. ix. s. ii. d. **1681** VISCT. STAIR *Inst. Law Scot.* I. x. §17. 127 Loan comprehendeth both the Contracts in the Law called *mutuum* and *commodatum*; by the former a thing Fungible is freely given, for the like to be restored in the same kind and quantity, though not the same individual. **1839** STORY *Bailments* §47. 34 A deposit differs from what is called in the civil law a *mutuum*, for there the identical thing lent is not to be returned, but another thing of the same kind, quality, nature or value. In the latter case, the property passes immediately to the mutuary.

muu-muu (ˈmuːmuː). Also **mumu**. [Hawaiian *mu'u mu'u* lit. cut off, from the fact that the yoke was originally omitted.] A woman's loose-fitting dress, usually brightly coloured and patterned, which originated in Hawaii as a local adaptation of the 'Mother Hubbard' dress provided by the missionaries.

1923 C. LONDON *New Hawaii* xv. 250 Not far off..swam a dozen men and women. They wore respectively loincloths and white or red muumuus. **1930** D. BLANDING *Hula Moons* 40 Helen being a woman, put on a yellow *mumu*, a cross between a flour sack and an old-fashioned nightie. *Mumus* were designed by the well-intentioned missionary ladies..as a covering for the Hawaiian women, in the early days when a few flowers sufficed for a garment. **1959** M. JANSMA *Wandering Malihini* ii. 33 A Hawaiian lady, costumed in an attractive *muumuu*,..sang to us songs of welcome and love. **1960** [see HOLOKU]. **1962** O. RUHEN *Tangaroa's Godchild* xvi. 230 The missionary..invented the Mother Hubbard, from which the muu-muu is derived, to cover the glorious voluptuous bodies of the earth's most beautiful women. **1964** *Daily Mail* 21 Jan. 3/3 Mu-mus or Mother Hubbards describes the beachwear better. **1964** *Sunday Truth* (Brisbane) 19 July 21/7 The new cafe at Brisbane airport is to give a typical Australian welcome..by means of waiters wearing Hawaiian shirts, waitresses with muu-muus and a background aborigine motif. **1964** *Asia Mag.* 16 Aug. 5 (*caption*) A blonde Caucasian girl wears the long muumuu of the islands. **1966** 'O. MILLS' *Enemies of Bride* viii. 76 It was Madeleine, tousle haired, in a short mu-mu with..Ella in a still shorter mu-mu. **1969** C. ARMSTRONG *Seven Seats to Moon* xi. 105 Nanjo with..a blue muumuu concealing her bathing suit..came..and curled herself on the floor.

muvable, obs. form of MOVABLE.

‖**muvule** (muːˈv(j)uːliː). Also **mvula, mvule, mvuli**. [a. Luganda *muvule*, Kiswahili *mvule*.] The East African name for IROKO. Also *attrib.*

1911 *Encycl. Brit.* XXVI. 397/1 The largest timber tree [in Tanganyika] is the mvule, which attains vast dimensions, its trunk supplying the natives with the dug-out canoes with which they navigate the lake. **1940** W. J. EGGELING *Indigenous Trees of Uganda Protectorate* 131 Muvule is a tree of great importance to the timber trade of Uganda. **1947** *E. African Ann.* 1946–7 82/1 In the shade of an immense *mvuli* tree, an old man..is sitting. **1962** *Times* 9 Oct. (Uganda Suppl.) p. viii/4 Giant muvule trees (African teak). **1966** B. KIMENYE *Kalasanda Revisited* 77 Hunched over the heavy, old-fashioned mvule desk, they set about answering the numerous personal questions. **1966** C. SWEENEY *Scurrying Bush* ii. 31 Here and there a *Mvule* tree soared upwards.., the smooth, sheer trunks branchless for the first sixty or seventy feet. **1973** *Daily Colonist* (Victoria, B.C.) 2 May 1/7 Livingstone's heart was buried under a mvula tree in Chipundu.

muvver (ˈmʌvə(r)). Representation of a Cockney or childish pronunciation of MOTHER *sb.*¹

1888 KIPLING *Wee Willie Winkie* 5, I don't fink I'll ever want to kiss big girls, nor no one, 'cept my muvver. **1898** J. D. BRAYSHAW *Slum Silhouettes* 118 A tanner for muvver, an' tuppence for me. **1899** [see KIP *v.*²]. **1924** R. MACAULAY *Orphan Island* viii. 79 Going shopping for my muvver. **1931** S. JAMESON *Richer Dust* xviii. 516, I kep' the letter you wrote poor muvver after you was married. **1958** J. TOWNSEND *Young Devils* x. 83 Andrews has gone to get 'is muvver's washing.

muwe, obs. form of MEW *sb.*², *v.*¹ and MUID.

muwe(n, muwes, obs. ff. MAY *v.*¹, MEWS.

muwet, obs. form of MUTE *sb.*

muwyer, variant of MOWYER *Obs.*

mux (mʌks), *v.* *dial.* and *U.S. local.* [Of obscure formation; cf. MUSS *v.*², MUCK *v.*, and dial. *mucksy* dirty.] = MUCK *v.* 4.

1806 *Balance* (Hudson, N.Y.) 26 Aug. 272 (Th.), To do observance, make obliging mention, Wink lovingly, mux chastity away. **1859** BARTLETT *Dict. Amer.* (ed. 2) 287 To *mux* is much used in New England for *muss*; as, 'Don't *mux* my crinoline.' **1869** BLACKMORE *Lorna Doone* III. x. 157 By vice of mismanagement on the part of my mother, and Nicholas Snowe, who had thoroughly muxed up everything. **1877** J. M. BAILEY *They all do It* 22 Stop muxin' that bread! ..you've eaten enough for twenty people. I shan't have you muxing and gauming up the victuals. **1914** *Dialect Notes* IV. 77 *Mux*, to handle, paw over, maul. **1934** *West Virginia Rev.* Dec. 78/1 One may hear *muxed* in certain sections of West Virginia now and then... It is a term synonymous to *messed up*, rather than a form of mixed.

mux (mʌks), *sb. U.S. local.* [f. the vb.] A disordered or muddled state; = MUCK *sb.*[1] 4.

1848 in *Amer. Speech* (1935) X. 41/1 'In a mux.' Confused, disarranged. **1865** E. STODDARD *Two Men* iv. 28, I knew you would come back. Now we are in a mux. **1890** *Cent. Dict.*, *Mux*, work performed in an awkward or improper manner; a botch; a mess; as, he made a mux of it. **1910** *Dialect Notes* III. 454 *Mux*, confusion, 'all in a mux'.

muy(e, muyd, obs. ff. MUID, MOOD *sb.*[1]

muyezin, obs. form of MUEZZIN.

muyle, muynde, obs. ff. MULE, MIND *sb.*

muyre, muys(e, obs. ff. MIRE, MOUSE.

muyson, variant of MOISON.

Muzak ('mju:zæk). Also *erron.* **Musak.** [Cf. MUSIC *sb.*] The proprietary name of a system of piped music for factories, restaurants, supermarkets, etc.; also used loosely, with small initial, to designate recorded light background music generally. Also *attrib.* or as *adj.* Hence (nonce-wds.) **'muzakal** *a.*, **'muzakman.** Hence as *v. trans.*, to introduce Muzak to; to equip for the relaying of Muzak; to play in the style of Muzak; so **'Muzaked** *ppl. a.*

1938 *Trade Marks Jrnl.* 11 May 572/1 Muzak... Instruments and apparatus and parts thereof.. for use in the wireless transmission and reception of signals and pictures. Rediffusion Limited,.. London,.. engineers. **1946** *Ibid.* 27 Mar. 152/1 Muzak... Records of sound, light or electric signals; and instruments and apparatus and parts thereof.. for the production of and reproduction from such records. Rediffusion Limited,.. London,.. manufacturers. **1954** *Official Gaz.* (U.S. Patent Office) 21 Sept. 497/2 Muzak Corporation.. *Muzak.* For transmitting from central locations specially programmed background music to stores, restaurants, homes, hotels, banks, [etc.]. **1959** *Observer* 21 June 10/5 Several firms have already arranged to receive Muzak in the factories. *Ibid.*, Executives in the brave new muzakal world will have a new and special privilege: they alone will be able to switch it off. **1960** *Guardian* 9 May 5/7 Canned music, or Muzak.. will to-day ooze into yet another corner of the world. **1961** *Times Lit. Suppl.* 30 June 396/2 The comfortable times before Musak (relayed music) and large-scale cultural enterprise took over. **1965** *Listener* 17 June 898/2 We shall have muzak wherever we go. **1966** AUDEN *About House* 62 The radio in students' cars, Musak at breakfast. **1968** *Times* 29 Nov. p. xi/1 If muzak be the food of love, no wonder it is commonly to be found.. among the frozen mint-flavoured peas and the crinkle-cut chips. *Ibid.* p. xi/2 In my sort of terms this is what makes it all sound the same, though that is heresy to a professional muzak-man. **1969** *Listener* 8 May 661/1 Mifune.. walks along a beach to the sound of a Bach chorale, muzak-ed. **1970** M. MOORCOCK *Chinese Agent* xiii. 87 He made the cab stop outside Hennekeys' recently repainted and muzaked pub. **1971** *Daily Tel.* (Colour Suppl.) 11 June 20/3 When subjects were doing a simple manual assembly task, the 'Muzaked' group's output was 17 per cent. up on a 'silent' group. **1971** *New Scientist* 17 June 707/2 The volume has to be kept down to Muzak level so as not to interfere with.. conversation. **1974** *N.Y. Times* 17 Aug. 17/2 'We needed a catchy name and the best known trade name at that time was Kodak,' explained U. V. (Bing) Muscio, current president. 'So we just combined Kodak and music and got Muzak.'

Muzarab(ic, variant forms of MOZARAB(IC.

Muzbi, Muz(hu)bee, varr. MAZHABI.

muze, obs. form of MUSE, MEWS.

muzell, muzhik, var. ff. MUZZLE, MOUJIK.

muzle(d, -lin, obs. ff. MUZZLE(D, MUSLIN.

muzro(u)le, variant forms of MUSROL.

muzz (mʌz), *sb. slang.* Also 8-9 **muz.** [Belongs to next.] One who 'muzzes' over books. Cf. MUG *sb.*[6] 2.

1788 *Trifler* No. 5. 56 The diligence exercised in improving my mental abilities, brought upon me the almost indelible stigma of a Muz. **1807** *Spirit Pub. Jrnls.* (1809) XII. 305, I often wish you had been with us, though we do quiz you for a reading muz. **1899** W. K. R. BEDFORD *Outcomes Old Oxford* 86, I don't mind memoirs, but I hate a muzz.

muzz (mʌz), *v. slang.* [Of obscure origin; the relation to MUZZY *a.* is uncertain.

The word may be in part a grotesque alteration of MUSE *v.*; cf. *bemuse.*]

1. *intr.* To study intently: to 'mug'. Const. *over.*

1775 S. J. PRATT *Liberal Opin.* lxxxv. (1783) III. 134 Curse that Thomas,.. for ever muzzing over a musty book. **1815** *Zeluca* I. 356 To see you muzzing over a game of chess. **1829** SCOTT *Jrnl.* 26 Jan., I muzzed on—I can call it little better—with *Anne of Geierstein.* **1902** *Daily Chron.* 19 Mar. 3/3 To work overmuch at Eton is to 'sap',.. at Westminster it is to 'muzz'.

2. *trans.* To render 'muzzy'; to fuddle. Cf. MUZZLE *v.*[2]

a **1787** 'FRED. PHILON' *He would be a Soldier* IV. i, *Caleb.* A choice companion he is; only apt to get muzzed too soon. **1794** J. WILLIAMS *Shrove Tuesday* 6 When the nocturnal orgie'd muzz'd his brain. **1865** *Sat. Rev.* 17 June 727/1 A certain judge was in the habit of muzzing himself by plenteous libations. **1882** H. BRADSHAW in Prothero *Mem.* viii. (1888) 259 A very heavy cold on me.. muzzed my head.

3. *intr.* To loiter aimlessly; to 'hang about'. Cf. MUSS *v.*[2] 2.

1779 MME. D'ARBLAY *Diary* 11 Jan., If you but knew.. who I shall see to-night, you would not dare keep me muzzing here. **1794** J. WILLIAMS *Parental Didactics* 18 And that high royal corps snug and sublime, Who muz majestic in the court ycleped Crane.

Hence **muzzed** *a.*, fuddled. **'muzzing** *ppl. a.*, that studies hard, 'mugging'.

1793 J. BERESFORD in W. Roberts *Looker-on* No. 54 (1794) II. 311 Hunt out some college cell, Where muzzing quizzes mutter monkish schemes. **1836** *Comic Almanack* Mar. (1870) 48 While Harlequin, half muzz'd with wine, Don't care a rush for Columbine. **1851** OWEN in *Life* (1894) I. 352 At Westminster.. he is in a class of very sharp and hard-working, or as he calls it, muzzing boys.

muzzel(l, obs. forms of MUZZLE.

muzzily ('mʌzɪlɪ), *adv.* [f. MUZZY *a.* + -LY[2].] In a 'muzzy' manner.

1903 *Sat. Rev.* 5 Dec. 700/2 They maunder muzzily on, these wastrels.

muzziness ('mʌzɪnɪs). [f. MUZZY *a.* + -NESS.] The condition of being muzzy.

1814 MOORE *Mem.* (1853) II. 37 You must excuse the muzziness you may have detected throughout this epistle. **1834** BECKFORD *Italy* I. Advt. p. ii, The intellectual muzziness of the past. **1847** *Brit. & For. Med. Rev.* XXIII. 553 A slight feeling of muzziness in the head. **1858** HOGG *Life Shelley* II. 416 An abiding.. muzziness.. inspired with.. strong.. ale. **1900** A. C. BENSON *E. W. Benson* I. iv. 129 He used to speak.. of the muzziness of head that this [*sc.* quinine].. had produced in him.

muzzle ('mʌz(ə)l), *sb.*[1] Forms: 4-6 **mosel,** 5 **mosle, mosol, -ul, -yl,** (**mor-, murselle**), 5-6 **mosell, moosle,** *Sc.* **mussal,** 5-7 **mussel,** 6 **mo(u)ssell, mousil, moozle, moozzell, musell, -yll,** (**mowseale**), **mezell** (?), *Sc.* **misel(l, -al(l, musal(l,** 4-7 **mozell,** 6-7 **mousel(l, moosel(l, mussell, musle, muzzell,** 6-8 **muzle,** 7 **muzel,** *Sc.* **myssel(l,** 7-8 **muzzel,** 6- **muzzle.** [a. OF. *musel, muzel, mousel, muisel* (12-13th c.), mod.F. *museau*:—med.L. *mūsellum*, dim. of med.L. *mūsus* (8th c. in Du Cange) or *mūsum* (whence Pr. *mus, muus*, OSp. *mus*, It. *muso*), of uncertain origin, but perh. connected with F. *muser* (see MUSE *v.*[1], *note*) and its cognates. (OF. had *muse, mouse* fem. = muzzle.)

Diez and others, connecting OF. *musel* with Pr. *mursel, morsel* (cf. the occas. 15th c. forms in Eng., also Breton *morzeel* beside *muzel*, muzzle), have assumed as the common etymon a pop. L. **morsellus*, dim. of *morsus* bite (cf. late L. *jūsum* from L. *deorsum*), but this involves serious difficulties.]

I. 1. The projecting part of the head of an animal which includes the nose and mouth.

c **1410** *Master of Game* (MS. Digby 182) xxxi, þe other beloweth lowe.. stoupynge with þe heede and þe musell towarde þe erthe. *c* **1430** *Pilgr. Lyf Manhode* III. xlviii. (1869) 161 It is figured as a swyn that in þe eerthe hath his morselle [*v.r.* murselle]. *c* **1489** CAXTON *Sonnes of Aymon* xxvi. 561 The horse.. smote his mussell in to the erth. **1533** MORE *Debell. Salem* Wks. 993/1 A mastyffe hath.. a great mosel and a thycke boystous body. **1587** MASCALL *Govt. Cattle, Sheep* (1596) 228 There is also another scabbinesse which chanceth somtimes on the mousels of sheepe. **1649** OGILBY *Virg. Georg.* III. (1684) 104 Some from the Dams hinder the tender Kid, And with hard Muzzles from the Pap forbid. **1685** *Lond. Gaz.* No. 2062. 2/2 A dark bay Gelding.. with a brown Musle. **1797** *Encycl. Brit.* (ed. 3) IX. 501/1 The head of a chamæleon is not unlike that of a fish... The muzzle is blunt. **1851** MAYNE REID *Scalp Hunt.* iii, A dark-brown stallion with black legs, and muzzle like the withered fern. **1877** J. A. ALLEN *Amer. Bison* 445 An adult measures about nine feet from the muzzle to the insertion of the tail.

b. *transf.* Contemptuously or jocularly applied to the part of the human face including the nose and chin.

1426 LYDG. *DeGuil. Pilgr.* 22753 Hyt semyth.. By lyfftynge vp off thy mosel, That thow pleyest the ape wel. *a* **1586** SIDNEY *Arcadia* II. (1622) 107 But euer and anon turning her muzzell towards mee, shee threw such a prospect vpon me, as might well haue giuen a surfet to any weake louers stomacke. *a* **1700** DRYDEN tr. *Ovid's Art of Love* I. 582 Of a black muzzle, and long beard, beware. **1829** SCOTT *Jrnl.* 25 Mar., The dry old rogue twisting his muzzle into an infernal grin. **1850** THACKERAY *Pendennis* lxi, Your black muzzle, old George, is the only face I should see.

c. *slang.* (See quot.)

a **1700** B. E. *Dict. Cant. Crew*, *Muzzle*, a Beard (usually) long and nasty.

d. = MUFFLE *sb.*[2] 1.

1870 DUBOIS *Cosmop. Cookery* 188 Muzzle (mufle) of beef with curry.

2. That end of a fire-arm from which the shot is discharged; *spec.* in a cannon, the part extending from the astragal to the extreme end mouldings.

1566 *Inv. R. Wardr.* (1815) 170 Item, sex missellis of irne. **1624** CAPT. SMITH *Virginia* v. 179 The powder by carelesnesse was tumbled downe vnder the mussels of the two peeces. **1633** T. STAFFORD *Pac. Hib.* I. ix. (1821) 116 That the peece.. should be abased at the tayle, and elevated at the musle. **1698** FRYER *Acc. E. India & P.* 37 Over the Gates five Guns run out their Muzzels. **1711** SWIFT *Jrnl. to Stella* 9 May, They fought at sword and pistol this morning in Tuttle Fields, their pistols so near that the muzzles touched. **1855** MACAULAY *Hist. Eng.* xiii. III. 361 The soldiers were still fumbling with the muzzles of their guns and the handles of their bayonets. **1892** GREENER *Breech-Loader* 107 The gun.. should not be left muzzle-up or muzzle-down against a wall, a gate, or a tree.

b. *charged* (*crammed*) *to the muzzle*: loaded, filled, or 'stuffed' *with.*

1807-8 W. IRVING *Salmag.* (1811) II. 63 Every body seems charged to the muzzle with gun-powder;—every eye flashes fire-works and torpedoes. **1859** G. MEREDITH *R. Feverel* vi, So instead of beating about and setting the boy on the alert at all points, crammed to the muzzle with lies, he just said [etc.]. **1875** M. PATTISON *Casaubon* 69 Casaubon had, in this way, solicited Leunclavius in a letter charged to the muzzle with gratifying compliments.

†3. The nozzle of a pair of bellows. *Obs.*

1726 SWIFT *Gulliver* III. v, He had a large Pair of Bellows, with a long slender Muzzle of Ivory.

4. *Agric.* = BRIDLE *sb.* 5 d.

1765 A. DICKSON *Treat. Agric.* (ed. 2) 200 There is another thing supposed also to belong to the plough, and that is the bridle or muzzle. **1840** J. BUEL *Farmer's Comp.* 142 By setting the muzzle higher up in the index of the beam.

5. The mouth at the base of a cooking-place.

1874 BEDFORD *Sailor's Pocket Bk.* vii. 206 They [*sc.* cooking places] should be in rear of.. the arms; the simplest form is a trench dug in a line with the wind..; depth, about a foot at the muzzle decreasing to 3 inches at the chimney.

II. 6. A contrivance, usually consisting of an arrangement of straps or wires, put over an animal's mouth to prevent it from biting, eating, or rooting.

c **1386** CHAUCER *Knt.'s T.* 1293 White Alauntz.. folwed hym, with mosel faste ybounde. *c* **1440** *Promp. Parv.* 344/2 Moosle, or mosul for a nette [= neat], *oristrigium.* **1523** *MS. Acc. St. John's Hosp., Canterb.*, For a mezell for a calf. **1556** WITHALS *Dict.* (1568) 15 b/1 A moosle that letteth dogges to bite. **1596** SPENSER *F.Q.* VI. xii. 34 He tooke a muzzel strong Of surest yron, made with many a lincke. **1635** MARKHAM *Faithf. Farrier* 78 The Horse having stood all night on the Mussell or at the empty Racke. **1697** DRYDEN *Virg. Georg.* III. 611 Some, when the Kids their Dams too deeply drain, With Gags and Muzzles their soft Mouths restrain. **1774** GOLDSM. *Nat. Hist.* (1776) III. 361 It often happens.. that the ferret disengages itself of its muzzel, and then it is most commonly lost, unless it be dug out. **1856** 'STONEHENGE' *Brit. Sports* I. III. v. §457 Many young dogs are such savage fighters or biters, as to require the muzzle always on at exercise. *Ibid.* II. I. vi. §72 Some very gross feeders requiring the muzzle on immediately after their last feed of corn over night.

fig. **1597** SHAKS. *2 Hen. IV*, IV. v. 132 For the Fift Harry, from curb'd License pluckes The muzzle of Restraint. **1644** [H. PARKER] *Jus Pop.* 60 So to inure Rome to the snaffle, and break the Senate to the musle. **1802** LADY JERNINGHAM in *J. Lett.* (1896) I. 210 Doctor Jenner is.. to have a premium.. for having Discovered so useful a muzzle for.. the small Pox. **1901** *Scotsman* 5 Mar. 8/3 The self-imposed muzzle which he has worn for the last five years no longer prevents him from taking part in the military debates.

b. An ornamental piece of armour covering a horse's nose.

1860 J. HEWITT *Anc. Armour* III. 667 Steel muzzles elaborately wrought in open-work. **1870** A. DEMMIN *Weapons of War* 350 The muzzle, which was placed over the nostrils.. could be of no use in war.

c. The face-piece of an inhaler.

1899 *Allbutt's Syst. Med.* VI. 55 The naso-oral muzzle must never be used.

†7. *Sc.* A veil, face-cloth. (Cf. MUZZLE *v.*[1] 3 b.) *Obs.*

1603 *Philotus* xxvii, 3our Veluote hat, 3our Hude of Stait, 3our Myssell quhen 3e gang to gait. **1605** *Burgh Rec. Glasgow* (1876) I. 237 That thai gang vpone the calsay syd with thair mussellis on thair faice, and clopperis.

III. 8. *attrib.* and *Comb.*, as (sense 1) **muzzle-bone,** (sense 2) **muzzle-astragal, -end, moulding, rope, stopper;** **muzzle chops,** nickname for a man with prominent nose and mouth; **muzzle-lashings** (see quot.); **muzzle-loader,** a gun that is loaded at the muzzle (opp. to *breech-loader*); so **muzzle-loading** *ppl. a.*; **muzzle-peg,** a contrivance to keep the nose of a dog raised while hunting game; hence **muzzle-pegged** *a.*; **muzzle-ring,** the moulding of greatest circumference encircling the muzzle of a gun; **muzzle-sight,** a sight placed at or near the muzzle of a gun; **† muzzle-scab,** a disease in sheep; **muzzle velocity,** the velocity at which a projectile leaves the piece from which it is fired.

1769 FALCONER *Dict. Marine* (1780) I 3 b, The *muzzle-astragal and fillets. **1845** *Encycl. Metrop.* VII. 366/2 In the *Ornithorhynque* the *Muzzle-bones are flat. **1611** MIDDLETON & DEKKER *Roaring Girl* III. iii, This old *muzzle chops should be he, By the fellowes discription. **1875** *Ure's Dict. Arts* II. 376 The coil.. is struck down vertically with its *muzzle end upon the anvil. **1889** KIPLING *Barrack-r. Ballads, East & West* 69 The Colonel's son a pistol drew and held it muzzle-end. **1815** BURNEY *Falconer's Dict. Marine* 290/2 **Muzzle-lashings*, are two and a half inch ropes, about four or five fathoms in length, used to lash the muzzles of guns, so as to confine them to the upper part of the ports. **1858** GREENER *Gunnery* 331 There is no possibility of a breech-loader ever shooting equal to a well-constructed *muzzle loader. *Ibid.* 333 The celebrated trial of Breech versus *Muzzle-loading fire-arms, which took place in April last. **1721** BAILEY, **Muzzle mouldings* (of a Gun) is the Ornament round the Muzzle. **1819** T. B. JOHNSON *Shooter's Comp.* 85 Your young dog.. will perhaps take the wind of himself, and hunt with his nose elevated. Should this not be the case, recourse must be had to the *muzzle peg. *Ibid.* 27 The Russian Pointer.. runs.. his nose close to the ground (if not *muzzle-pegged). **1626** CAPT. SMITH *Accid. Yng. Seamen* 32 *Mousell rings at her mouth. **1692** *Capt. Smith's Seaman's Gram.* II. vi. 94 The Muzzle Ring, or Cornice. **1858** GREENER *Gunnery* 99 Six outside staves of great dimensions, which, at the muzzle ring, pass through openings in the muzzle ring. **1879** *Man. Artill. Exerc.* VII.

vii. 508 A clove hitch is made with the centre of the *muzzle rope round the fid. **1726** *Dict. Rust.* (ed. 3), **Mousel-scab*, a Distemper that sometimes attends Sheep and young Teggs. *c* **1860** H. Stuart *Seaman's Catech.* 11 On the barrel is the ..*muzzle sight. **1844** *Regul. & Ord. Army* 96 *note*, *Muzzle-Stoppers. **1879** *Man. Artill. Exerc.* 8 The longer the projectile, the less perfectly it is centred, the lower its *muzzle velocity [etc.].

muzzle ('mʌz(ə)l), *sb.*[2] [ad. G. *Mosel*, Du. *Moezel* = Moselle, where cf. the 18th c. form *mossel.*] Moselle wine.

1853 Jerdan *Autobiog.* IV. xiii. 243 We sat down to excellent rotten cabbage, but washed down with sensible muzzle and schnaps. *Ibid.* 244 The bumpers of muzzle.

†'**muzzle,** *a. Obs.* Also 7 mussel. = muzzled *ppl. a.*[2]

1691 *Lond. Gaz.* No. 2652/4 A little Man,..having a Mussel Beard. **1813** Gen. P. Thompson *Let.* 26 Jan. (MS.), A brown muzzle horse; which upon examination I found by no means to intend a horse with a brown muzzle, but a horse that reflects brown-muzzle rays... A brown-muzzle horse therefore is a horse of a brinded or mingled brown.

'**muzzle,** *v.*[1] Forms: see the sb. [f. muzzle *sb.*[1] Cf. F. *museler*.]

1. a. *intr.* To thrust out the muzzle or nose; to feel, smell, or root about with the muzzle. (Cf. nuzzle.)

c **1489** Caxton *Sonnes of Aymon* xix. 426 They felle where thei wente, musselinge in the grounde as hogges. **15..** *Johan the Euangelyst* 499 And yf the grounde be slypper and slydynge In faythe I fall downe moselynge. **1581** J. Bell *Haddon's Answ. Osor.* 80 Lyke a most filthy hogge mooselyng in the durtie swinesty of Epicure. **1598** Barckley *Felic. Man* iv. 330 The Beare came..muzling about his mouth and nose, finding that he breathed not [etc.]. **1607** Hieron *Wks.* I. 156 If we euer be like swine, muzling in the ground. **1679** Rusden *Further Disc. Bees* ix. 91, I and others have found that an hogg musling in an Hive hath been the best way of dressing it. **1844** Stephens *Bk. Farm* II. 701 Every pig takes its own place right earnestly, and muzzles away at the udder.

†**b.** *fig.* To 'growl' or murmur *at*.

1581 J. Bell *Haddon's Answ. Osor.* ii. 68 Our Syr Ierome sets vp his bristles & although he know my meaning, yet mooseleth at the wordes.

2. a. *trans.* To bring the muzzle or snout close to.

a **1600** *Constancy of True Love* xi. in J. P. Collier *Roxb. Ball.* (1847) 94 The lyon..Ran where I left my garment first;..And having musled thus the same [etc.]. **1692** R. L'Estrange *Fables* ccxxvii. 199 The Bear comes directly up to Him, Muzzles, and Smells to him.

†**b.** To root about or amongst. *Obs.*

1617 *Presentm.* in *Essex Rev.* XV. 48 His church pale, broken down, lett in hogges and other cattle, which mussells and spoyles the churchyard. **1733** Tull *Horse-hoeing Husb.* xx. 288 Had there been Oaks in the Place, I should rather have thought that Tillage perform'd by a Race of the first Teachers of it, in muzzling Acorns than by Plows.

†**c.** 'To fondle with the mouth close. A low word' (J.). Cf. mousle *v. Obs.*

1692 R. L'Estrange *Fables* ccxix. 192 The Nurse..was Then Muzzling and Cokesing of it. **1697** Vanbrugh *Relapse* i. (1708) 12 Ah, you young hot lusty Thief, let me muzzle you—[*Kissing*]. **1708** Mrs. Centlivre *Busie Body* iii. 34, I will, Chargee, so muzle, and tuzle, and hug thee.

3. a. To put a muzzle on (an animal or its mouth); to prevent by means of a muzzle from biting, etc.

c **1470** in *Som. & Devon N. & Q.* (1905) IX. 303 The saide Dogge beying owte of chayne was mosolyd. **1519** *Surtees Misc.* (1888) 34 They shall mosell their dogges. **1526** Tindale *1 Cor.* ix. 9 Thou shalt not mosell the mouth of the oxe. **1530** Palsgr. 642/2, I wolde advyse you musyll your dogge, for he is called peryllous. **1565** Cooper *Thesaurus*, *Fiscella*, a thing made with twigges and strynges to moosell beastes that thei mought not bite yong springes. **1597** Drayton *Heroic. Ep.* 49 b, Or who will muzzell that vnruly Beare? **1627** Hakewill *Apol.* ii. v. §4 He that made a dry path through the red sea, musled the mouthes of the Lyons. **1753** *Scots Mag.* Feb. 100/1 All the dogs..to be..muzzled. **1820** Scott *Abbot* xix, Large stag-hounds, or wolf-dogs.. carefully muzzled to prevent accidents to passengers. **1856** Kane *Arct. Expl.* I. xxix. 390 Completely muzzled with a line fastened by a running knot between her jaws and the back of her head. **1873** G. C. Davies *Mount. & Mere* xxii. 194 It is best to muzzle ferrets.

b. *fig.*

1611 Shaks. *Wint. T.* i. ii. 156 My dagger muzzel'd, Least it should bite it's Master. **1613** —— *Hen. VIII*, i. i. 121 This Butchers Curre is venom'd-mouth'd, and I Haue not the power to muzzle him. **1622** Bp. Hall *Contempl., N.T.* iii. v, It is thine onely mercy, O God, that hath chained and muzled up this band-dog. **1631** R. Bolton *Comf. Affl. Consc.* i. (1635) 6 He is everlastingly musled by an Almighty arme, from ever doing them any deadly hurt. **1700** Dryden *Prol. to Pilgrim* 2 How wretched is the fate of those who write! Brought muzzled to the stage, for fear they bite. **1884** Pae *Eustace* 87, I have the power not only to muzzle him, but draw his teeth.

c. *transf.* To close (a fishing-net).

1876 F. Francis *Bk. Angling* (ed. 4) xii. 438 The Esk..is a fine river, and would be finer if the Solway stake nets were only muzzled.

†**4.** *transf.* To muffle; *Sc.* to veil, mask (the face). *Obs.*

1426 Lydg. *De Guil. Pilgr.* 17184 Thys lady, with hyr corbyd bak, Was y-moselyd with that sak. **1457** *Sc. Acts Jas. II* (1814) II. 49/2 At na woman cum to þe kirk nor mercat wt hir face musalyt or couerit þt scho may not be kende. **1582** *Reg. Privy Council Scot.* III. 525 Scho fand the foirsaid nowmer of personis accowterit in maner foirsaid, all mussallit. **1590** *Ibid.* IV. 533 They wer unknawne to him, thay being missallit.

fig. **1589** R. Bruce *Serm.* iv. (1590) O 3, They that are this way misseled vp in thair saull, of all men in the earth they are maist miserable.

5. To restrain from speaking, impose silence upon. †**a.** Phr. ***to muzzle* (*up*) *the mouth of*** (a person).

1531 Tindale *Exp. 1 John* (1538) 42 b, Who..wold put his heade in ye Romysh byshops haltre that so moseleth mens mouthes, that they can not open them. **1569** *Reg. Privy Council Scot.* I. 680 It plesit the Almichtie to brydill and musall up the mouth of Sathan. *a* **1586** Sidney *Ps.* xxxix. i, I muzzle will my mouth while in the sight I do abide of wicked wight. **1642** *Prince Rupert's Declaration* 4 Have they not by imprisonment or threats muzzeled the mouthes of the most grave and learnedst Preachers of London? **1737** Whiston *Josephus, Hist.* Pref. (1777) §5 Their tongues loosed..for law suits, but quite muzzled up when they are to write history.

b. with person as obj.

1545 Brinklow *Compl.* xvi. (1874) 40 Shal not he than do a Christen preacher wrong,..that moselyth hym for the space of whole .xij. monthes? **1577–87** Holinshed *Chron.* II. 16/2 There is nothing that ought to moozzell vp anie one from rebuking other nations. **1825** Syd. Smith *Wks.* (1867) II. 200 What establishment can muzzle its fools and lunatics. **1878** Seeley *Stein* III. 370 The best way of muzzling him was to take him into the Austrian service. **1888** Bryce *Amer. Commw.* xi. I. 145 Congress has other means of muzzling an ambitious chief magistrate.

6. *Naut.* †**a.** ***to lie muzzled***: (of a ship) to remain inactive. So ***to muzzle oneself***: to cease from action. *Obs.* **b.** In yachting use: To take in (a sail).

1697 Dampier *Voy.* (1699) 83 We saw a Ship..: We lay muzled to let her come up with us, for we supposed her to be a Spanish Ship. **1726** Shelvocke *Voy. round World* 195 Their fire had little or no effect, all stood fast with us, and they muzzled themselves. **1745** *Gentl. Mag.* July 352 The Lion's rigging being cut to pieces,..all her lower masts and topmasts shot thro' in many places, so that she lay muzzled in the sea, and could do nothing with her sails. **1884** E. F. Knight *Cruise of Falcon* I. iii. 30, I had to call up the watch below to muzzle the sail. **1895** *Outing* (U.S.) XXVI. 46/1 Muzzle it, man the down-haul!

†**7.** To render ineffective or inoperative. *Obs.*

1706 Baynard in Sir J. Floyer *Hot & Cold Bath.* ii. 250 Whilst they [*sc.* the salts] are swimming in the Fluid, they are muzzled and invelloped in the clammy and glutinous Parts.

8. To muffle (bells). Now *dial.*

1708 *Lond. Gaz.* No. 4489/2 The Bells were muzled, and rang as for a Funeral the whole Evening. **1883** *Almondbury & Huddersf. Gloss.*, *Muzzle*, used for *muffle*, in regard to the church bells.

9. *slang.* To hit on the mouth; hence, to thrash.

1851 Mayhew *Lond. Labour* I. 16/1 It is often said in admiration of such a man that 'he could muzzle half a dozen bobbies before breakfast'. **1859** *Hotten's Slang Dict.*, *Muzzle*, to fight or thrash. **1888** 'R. Boldrewood' *Robbery under Arms* II. vi. 106 Jim and I jumped off and muzzled him.

10. *slang.* To take, 'bag'.

1890 'R. Boldrewood' *Col. Reformer* ix, I thought, Sir, as you'd like a snack, so I muzzled enough grub for two. **1897** Barrère & Leland *Dict. Slang*, *Muzzle*, to get, to take.

'**muzzle,** *v.*[2] *dial.* [app. connected with muzz *v.* and muzzy.] **a.** *trans.* To make 'muzzy'; to fuddle. **b.** *intr.* To drink to excess (1828 in *Craven Gloss.*).

1796 Charlotte Smith *Marchmont* III. 43 Gads my life, if I don't believe though that the cheating sly rascal put summot in my drink,..I becomed all of a sudden as muzzled! as muzzled! **1856** Miss Yonge *Daisy Chain* ii. ix, You have read yourself into a maze,..what Mary calls, muzzling your head.

Hence '**muzzling** *vbl. sb.*

1828 *Craven Gloss.* **1866** Motley *Corr.* (1889) II. 222 From his point of view all our guzzlings and muzzlings must seem reprehensible.

muzzled ('mʌz(ə)ld), *ppl. a.*[1] [f. muzzle *sb.*[1] or *v.*[1] + -ed.]

1. Wearing a muzzle.

1530 in *Ancestor* (Oct. 1904) 182 A beyres hede sable mouseled geules. *a* **1550** in Baring-Gould & Twigge *West. Armory* (1898) 4, 3 beares' heads erased arg: musled or. **1595** Shaks. *John* ii. i. 249. **1716** Gay *Trivia* ii. 408 Led by the nostril, walks the muzzled bear. **1850** Mrs. Jameson *Leg. Monast. Ord.* (1863) 110 Three bears' heads muzzled.

fig. **1647** May *Hist. Parl.* i. vii. 73 They would faine be at something were like the Masse that will not bite; a muzzled Religion. **1647** Trapp *Comm. Rom.* iii. 20 Those misled and muzled souls. **1789** Burns *Elegy on* 1788 vi, Thou now hast got thy daddy's chair, Nae hand-cuff'd, mizzl'd, hapshackl'd Regent, But, like himsel', a full free agent.

†**2.** Muffled; veiled; masked. *Obs.*

1581 in Tytler *Hist. Scotl.* (1864) IV. 38 Certain 'musselled men'. **1582** *Reg. Privy Council Scot.* III. 495 Certane uther musalit men on horsback, in weirlike maner, with pistolettis. **1588** Churchyard *Spark Friendship* C 3 b, The musled faces couered with counterfaite good maners.

†**muzzled,** *ppl. a.*[2] *Obs.* Also 7 muzzeld. [? repr. OF. *meslé*, pa. pple. of *mesler* to mingle, mix (see meddle, mell *v.*). Cf. muzzle *a.*] ? Speckled with white or grey.

1630 *Tinker of Turvey* 12 His blacke lockes dangling downe, Curl'd and knotty muzzeld beard. **1858** Lytton *What will he do* ii. iv, It [*sc.* a horse] was a dark muzzled brown.

'**muzzler.** [f. muzzle *sb.*[1] and *v.*[1] + -er[1].]

1. One who muzzles animals. (In quot. *fig.*)

1653 A. Wilson *Inconst. Ladie* iii. i. (1814) 49, I must not be raind vp, by a tame musler, That shall confine my freedome to his winks.

2. *Pugilism.* A blow on the mouth.

1811 *Lex. Balatron.* s.v., The milling cove tipped the cull a muzzler. **1819** *Sporting Mag.* III. 231 Smith placed that which seemed to be a muzzler upon his adversary's jaw.

3. A muzzle-loading gun.

1872 W. Cory *Lett. & Jrnls.* (1897) 292 There is a muzzler here with which you can shoot the half-dozen pheasants.

4. *Naut.* (See quot. 1878.)

1878 D. Kemp *Yacht & Boat Sailing* 359/2 *Muzzler*, a wind that blows directly down a vessel's intended course. Synonymous with 'nose ender'. **1893** Sloane-Stanley *Remin. Midshipm. Life* xxxiii. 448 The following morning there was a nice breeze, but a dead muzzler.

'**muzzling,** *vbl. sb.* [f. muzzle *v.*[1] + -ing[1].]

1. The action of putting a muzzle on an animal. Often *attrib.*, as ***muzzling order***.

1579 Fulke *Heskins' Parl.* 9 The moosling of the oxe, that treadeth the corne. **1886** *Sat. Rev.* 22 May 712 Sir Charles Warren has done wisely in extending the Muzzling Order of his predecessor. *Ibid.*, To enforce muzzling for an adequate period in every parish in the island.

†**b.** *fig.* ? Putting to silence. *Obs.*

1575 R. B. *Appius & Virg.* in Dodsley *O. Pl.* (1827) XII. 350 Here is naught els but railing of words out of reason, Now tugging, now tattling, now musling in season.

2. *Pugilism.* Hitting on the mouth.

1819 *Sporting Mag.* IV. 179 He went to work at the muzzling system.

muzzy ('mʌzɪ), *a. colloq.* and *dial.* Also 8–9 mussy. [Perh. a later form of mossy *a.* in sense 5. But cf. dial. *mosey* = mouldy, rotten, muggy, hazy, stupefied with liquor; also mosy *a.*, downy. The chronological relations with muzz *v.*[1] and muzzle *v.*[2] are uncertain.]

1. a. Of persons, their actions, manner, etc.: Dull, stupid, spiritless; also, mentally hazy.

1728–9 Mrs. Delany in *Life & Corr.* (1861) I. 195 When I returned from the duchess of Norfolk's assembly, (muzzy enough, not having met with agreeable conversation). **1761** J. Hawkesworth *Edgar & Emmeline* 7 What, always muzzy, with a dismal countenance as long as a taylor's bill! **1817** Keats *Lett.* 15 Apr., I don't feel inclined to write any more at present for I feel rather muzzy. **1827** Scott *Jrnl.* 28 Feb., Discontinuing smoking..leaves me less muzzy after dinner. **1849** Thackeray *Pendennis* xxxi, We may expect that his view of the past will be rather muzzy. **1883** *Sat. Rev.* 10 Nov. 586 A sentimental Celt may regard himself, in his muzzy Celtic way, as being an ill-treated rightful heir of any land which chances to belong to a 'Saxon'.

b. Of places, times, etc.: Dull, gloomy.

1727–8 Mrs. Delany in *Life & Corr.* (1861) I. 159 The town is mussy, though very full. I have not been at an assemblée this winter. **1754** A. Murphy *Gray's-Inn Jrnl.* No. 80 Sunday the most muzzy Day in the year. **1770** Foote *Lame Lover* i. Wks. 1799 II. 60 A damn'd muzzy dinner at Boodle's. **1821** Coleridge in *Blackw. Mag.* X. 253 Here have I been sitting, this whole long-lagging, muzzy, mizly morning.

c. *transf.* Blurred, indistinct in form, etc.

1832 W. Irving in *Life & Lett.* (1866) III. 26 His form is still fine on the stage, but his countenance is muzzy and indistinct. **1867** *Art Jrnl.* XXIX. 123/3 The execution..is vague and muzzy to a fault. **1899** *Contemp. Rev.* June 830 A growing tendency to see everything blurred and muzzy.

2. Stupid with excess of liquor.

1775 T. Campbell *Diary* in Napier *Johnsoniana* (1884) 223 We went to the Coffee house in the evening, where almost all the gownsmen we saw were tipsy... The next night also, we went to another Coffee house, and there the scene was only shifted, all muzzy. **1849** Thackeray *Pendennis* v, His muzzy, whiskified brain. **1852** R. S. Surtees *Sponge's Sp. Tour* lix, Leather, though somewhat muzzy, was sufficiently sober to be able to deliver this message. **1892** J. Payn *Mod. Whittington* II. 133 He was 'muzzy' in the morning; he was 'elevated' in the afternoon; but at six o'clock, punctually, he was drunk.

3. *Comb.*, as **muzzy-headedness**, a fuddled or intoxicated condition.

1930 R. H. Mottram *Europa's Beast* vii. 169 Cocktails were sheer silliness, a short cut to muzzy-headedness.

mvula, mvule, mvuli, varr. muvule.

Mwami ('mwɑːmɪ). [Native title, = chief.] The royal title of the former kings of Ruanda and Urundi in Africa.

On independence in 1962 Rwanda (formerly Ruanda) became a republic; Burundi (formerly Urundi) remained a monarchy until 1966 when the Mwami was deposed by a coup.

1890 H. M. Stanley *In Darkest Africa* x. 246 The chief was styled Mwani. **1923** *Glasgow Herald* 30 Jan. 12 The Mwami or Sultan of Ruanda..was assisted in his administration of the country by a state religion, and he was in a sense the personification of the deity Imana. **1959** *Times* 9 Nov. 8/6 The Mwami (Paramount Chief) of Ruanda sent a letter..expressing regret that he is unable to come to Brussels, where he was to have been received by the king, with the Mwami of Urundi, in private audience. **1970** A. T. Grove *Africa South of Sahara* (ed. 2) xi. 201/2 In Burundi the dead Mwami was sewed into the skin of a black bull for burial.

mwbill, Sc. var. moble.

mwchin, var. moochin.

mwde, obs. f. mud.

mwe, obs. f. mew *sb.*[2], *v.*[1]

Mweru, var. MERU *sb.* and *a.*

mwlat, var. MULET.

mwncke, mwnk, obs. ff. MONK.

mwre, obs. Sc. f. MOOR *sb.*[1], obs. f. MURE *v.*

mwrthrys, var. MURDRES.

mwskoll, obs. f. MUSSEL.

my (maɪ, *unstressed* mɪ), *poss. adj.* Also 2–6 mi, (4 mii, 6 mye), 9 *dial.* moy, etc. *β.* (unstressed forms) 3–6 (also 9 in representations of Irish speech) me, 8 m', 9 *dial.* ma, etc. [early ME. *mī*, reduced form of *mīn* (see MINE *poss. pron.*), used orig. before consonants except *h*, but occurring before vowels in northern texts as early as the beginning of the 14th c. and ultimately becoming the universal possessive adj. of the 1st pers. sing. in prose use.]

1. Of or belonging to me; that I have, hold, or possess. The possessive genitive of I *pron.*

For the functions of the possessive see HIS *poss. pron.* B. 2.

α. *a* **1175** *Cott. Hom.* 225, Ic wille settan mi wed betwuxe me and eow. *c* **1175** *Lamb. Hom.* 157 Wa is mine saule þet mi lif þus longe ilest. *a* **1240** *Lofsong* in *O.E. Hom.* I. 213 Mi leofmonnes luft erm halt up min heaued. *c* **1290** *St. Cristopher* 40 in *S. Eng. Leg.* I. 272, Ich am a man opon mi seruiz and noman serui i-nelle Bote my louerd. *a* **1300** *Cursor M.* 4487 Me-thoght i bare A lepe.. Wit bred þat i bar on mi heued [*Gött.* mj, *Fairf.* my, *Trin.* myn heued]. *a* **1300–1400** *Ibid.* 13568 (Gött.) Mi eien tua [*other texts* min, myne]. *c* **1320** *Sir Tristr.* 2997 Mi wille ȝif y miȝt gete, þat leuedi wold y se. **1423** JAS. I *Kingis Q.* cxv, How long think thay to stand in my disdeyne. **1470–85** MALORY *Arthur* IV. xv. 139 And lete hym wete I can doo more whan I see my tyme. **1516** *Test. Ebor.* (Surtees) VI. 1 To pray for my soull and myn ancestres. *c* **1550** CHEKE *Mark* i. 7 Mi stronger commeth after me, yᵉ latchet of whoos schoo J am not worthi to bow down and louse. **1592** R. GREENE *Blacke Bookes Messenger* Wks. (Grosart) XI. 34 Euery one.. almost disdained my companie. **1602** SHAKS. *Ham.* v. i. 264 A Ministring Angell shall my Sister be. **1622** MABBE tr. *Aleman's Guzman d' Alf.* 280 That they might conferre it on a Gentlemans sonne of good ranke.. but my Iunior. **1721** STRYPE *Eccl. Mem.* II. I. xxiii. 188 Yet can I not, without some touch of my estimation,.. satisfy the result herein presently. **1722** DE FOE *Col. Jack* (1840) 156 It is my aversion, it fills my.. soul with horror. **1788** GIBBON *Decl. & F.* IV. Pref. p. vi, My time will now be my own. **1855** M. ARNOLD *Balder Dead* I. 106 Who will bear my hateful sight in Heaven? **1864** TENNYSON *North. Farmer* I. xiv, I done my duty by Squoire an' I done my duty by all [*ed.* 1875 *has* moy]. **1888** STEVENSON *Black Arrow* II. iii, It is my murderer in the secret passage. **1895** KEKEWICH in *Law Times Rep.* LXIII. 663/2, I do not think I am precluded.. from forming my own conclusion on this point.

β. *a* **1250** *Owl & Night.* 869 (Cott.) For al me song is of longinge. **13..** *Sir Beues* (A.) 2583 And ȝhe wile, for me sake, Cristendome at þe take. *c* **1400** *Cursor M.* 20704 (Brit. Mus. Add. MS.) Ther on schal ligge me modre deere. *c* **1560** A. SCOTT *Poems* (1902) xv. 22 Now lat me lady do quhat evir scho will. **1712** ARBUTHNOT *John Bull* II. xviii, *J. Bull.* I shall have it to m'own self? *L. Baboon.* To thy n'own self. **1832** W. STEPHENSON *Gateshead Local Poems* 37 He'll end ma days as sure as death. **1888** H. SMART *Master of Rathkelly* I. xv. 223 I'll just keep me oiye on that Cassidy.

¶ Down to the 16th c. *my* often resulted from the transference of the *n* of *mine* to the accompanying sb. or adj. (See N 3 b, NAIN, NAUNT, NOWN, NUNCLE.)

1535 in *Lett. Suppress. Monasteries* (Camden) 51 A pore pryery, a fundacion off my nawynsetres.

b. Prefixed to *lord*, *lady* (see LADY *sb.* 6 a, LORD *sb.* 15); hence *my lady*, *my lord* vbs., to address as 'my lady', 'my lord'. So *my* NABS.

c **1330** *Amis & Amil.* 1228 Mi lord the duke, he seyd anon, For schame lete tho leuedis gon. **1395** *E.E. Wills* (1882) 7 To praye diuine seruice for my lordes soule Sir Thomas West. *c* **1412** HOCCLEVE *De Reg. Princ.* 1381 Men mote hir clepe 'my lady chaungeabil'. **1470** *Paston Lett.* II. 412 He sente to my Lady of Norff. by John Bernard only for my mater. **1655** FULLER *Ch. Hist.* IX. 149 To the Lord Treasurer. My singular good Lord [etc.]. **1684** LADY R. RUSSELL *Lett.* 20 Apr. (1807) 28, I hear my Lord Gainsborough and my Lady will be shortly at Chilten. **1771** SMOLLETT *Humph. Cl.* Let. to Sir W. Phillips 8 Aug., Ma lords and gentlemen. **1831** [see LORD *sb.* 15 c]. **1834** MARRYAT *P. Simple* xiv, To find myself .. my lorded this and my lorded that, every minute. **1849** —— *Valerie* vii, 'Don't flare up, my lady.' 'Don't my lady me.' **1886** *Blackw. Mag.* Aug. 223 To make the grievous mistake of 'my-ludding' the counsel. **1887** W. S. GILBERT *Ruddigore* 11, Whose middle-class lives are embarrassed by wives Who long to parade as 'My Lady'.

c. Used with vague application (cf. HIS *poss. pron.* B. 2 b, OUR B. 1 d). Also with ethical force in certain playful or ironical idiomatic collocations.

1592 MORYSON *Let.* in *Itin.* (1617) I. 37, I knew where my Gentlemans shooe wrung him. **1653** H. MORE *Antid. Ath.* II. i. (1712) 37, I would have my Atheist to take Shipping with me. **1667** DRYDEN & DK. NEWCASTLE *Sir M. Mar-all* II. 20 *Sir John.* Dost thou not know the Contents on't? *Landl.* Yes, as well as I do my *Pater noster*. **1755** SMOLLETT tr. *Gil Blas* VII. i, I lay in ambush.. and, sure enough, perceived my man enter. **1799** H. K. WHITE *Let. to bro. Neville*, I leave [the office] at eight in the evening; then attend my Latin until nine. **1808** COL. HAWKER *Diary* (1893) I. 13, I brought down my bird every shot. **1817** COLERIDGE *Biog. Lit.* x. (1907) I. 116 My taper man of lights listened with.. praise-worthy patience.

2. Used vocatively. **a.** Prefixed affectionately to terms of relationship or endearment; also, affectionately or compassionately, or in a jocular or merely familiar tone, to certain designations which are otherwise rarely used vocatively, as in ***my man, my boy, my good fellow, my poor man.*** (See also DEAR *a.*[1] 2 b, c, for the use as prefixed to that adj.)

In modern English it is not (as in some languages) the rule of ordinary speech to prefix *my* to terms of relationship (*father, mother, brother,* etc.) used vocatively; the use belongs to impassioned literary language. *Son* and *daughter*, however, are exceptions; and the omission of *my* before the vocative *friend* is somewhat *arch.* or *rhetorical*.

a **1225** *Ancr. R.* 98 Cum to me, mi leofmon, mi kulure, mi schene, mi veire spuse. *c* **1386** CHAUCER *Miller's T.* 513 My faire brid, my swete cinamome, Awaketh, lemman myn. **1388** WYCLIF *Prov.* i. 10 Mi sone, if synneris flateren thee, assente thou not to hem. **1582** STANYHURST *Æneis* III. (Arb.) 86 Take, myeboy, theese tokens by myn owne hands finnished holye. **1767** S. PATERSON *Another Trav.* I. 425 My good gentlemen and lady-connoisseurs. **1816** SCOTT *Antiq.* viii, 'Farewell, my father!' murmured Isabella. **1875** JOWETT *Plato* (ed. 2) I. 26 But consider how monstrous this is, my friend.

b. *esp.* in ***my dear (dearest), my love***, etc. (see these words); hence ***my dear*** vb., to address as 'my dear'; etc.

1807–8 W. IRVING *Salmag.* (1824) 96 Mrs. Cockloft began 'my dearing' it as fast as tongue could move. **1830** MISS MITFORD *Village* Ser. IV. 93 All through her childhood, the tiny heiress.. was my-deared, petted, fondled. **1848** THACKERAY *Van. Fair* xlv, They my-loved and my-deared each other assiduously. **1855** —— *Newcomes* lix, Miss Ethel and my wife.. 'my-dearesting' each other with that female fervour [etc.].

c. Prefixed (without intervening adj.) to the name of the person addressed: (*a*) *poet.* as a latinism, expressing intimate friendship (*obs.* or *arch.*); (*b*) in the language of fervid affection.

1732 POPE *Ess. Man* i. 1 Awake, my St. John! **1793** COWPER *To Mary* 16 Thy sight now seconds not thy will, My Mary!

3. In ejaculations, as ***my eye! my God! my gracious! my stars! my word!*** etc. (see these words); whence (elliptically) ***my!*** or ***oh, my!***, which is common (esp. *U.S.*) as a mild exclamation of surprise; also ***oh-my*** vb., to say 'oh, my!'

1707 J. STEVENS *Quevedo's Com. Wks.* (1709) 350 Such Words and Sayings are a Discredit to your self..: As for Instance,.. my Whither d'ye go. **1825** JAMIESON *Suppl.*, *My*, interj. Denoting great surprise, Roxb. **1840** MRS. TROLLOPE *Widow Married* xi, What a bonnet!—my! **1849** MRS. CARLYLE *Lett.* II. 69 When she did take in the immense fact, oh, my! if she didn't show feeling enough. **1883** 'MARK TWAIN' *Life on Mississippi* xvii, My, what a race I've had! **1893** BARING-GOULD *Cheap Jack Zita* i. 10 The servant maids.. were listening and.. oh-mying over the bargains.

†**4. a.** ***my (un)witting***: with (without) my knowledge. (Cf. F. *à mon escient.*) *Obs.*

c **1450** *Merlin* 12 Yef euer man, my witynge, hadde to do with me. **1470** *Paston Lett.* II. 412 He sente to my Lady of Norff.. my onwetyng.

b. ***my lane*** (see LONE *a.* 6 b): by myself. *Sc.*

1724 RAMSAY *Vision* i, Mylane I wandert waif and wae. **1818** HOGG *Brownie of Bodsbeck* I. xi. 219 Ony thing but a bogle face to face at midnight, an' me a' my lane.

5. In names of games.

1621 J. TAYLOR (Water P.) *Motto* D 4, At Primefisto.. at My-sow-pigg'd, and.. Looke about ye. **1732** MRS. DELANY *Life & Corr.* (1861) I. 385 Played at my lady's hole, supped, and went early to bed. **1770** MME. D'ARBLAY *Early Diary* 20 Apr., Mr. Seton and myself declined playing—I never do but at Pope Joan, Commerce, or My Sow's Pig'd!

‖**mya** (ˈmaɪə). *Zool.* Pl. **myæ, myas.** [mod.L. (Linnæus 1758), prob. an alteration of Gr. μῦ-ς mussel; Linnæus has *myes* as a plural.] A bivalve of a genus formerly of wide extent, but now restricted to the Gaper or Soft Clam (*M. arenaria*) and closely resembling species.

[**1777** PENNANT *Brit. Zool.* IV. 78 *Mya*, Gaper... A bivalve shell gaping at one end.] **1797** *Encycl. Brit.* (ed. 3) XII. 561/2 The margaritifera; or pearl mya. **1841** *Penny Cycl.* XIX. 143/2 The Myæ live buried in sandy beaches, wherein they often lie with the tube just projecting. **1854** WOODWARD *Mollusca* 317 The Myas frequent soft bottoms.

myal (ˈmaɪəl). [perh. of West African origin.] Only in attrib. use denoting persons or things associated with the practice of MYALISM: see quots.

1774 E. LONG *Hist. Jamaica* II. 416 Not long since, some of these execrable wretches in Jamaica, introduced what they called the myal dance, and established a kind of society, into which they invited all they could. The lure hung out was, that every Negroe, initiated into the myal society, would be invulnerable by the white men. *Ibid.* 417 One of these myal men.. gave him a wonderful account of the powerful effects produced by the myal infusion. **1843** PHILLIPPO *Jamaica* 249 *note*, The author once saw a negro suffering from a gum-boil, who persisted in affirming that the Myal Doctor had extracted a snake from the affected part. **1851** G. BLYTH *Remin. Miss. Life* iv. 174 The doctor or Myal-man is resorted to that he may neutralise the power of the Obeah-man. *Ibid.* 175 They became excited and frenzied singing Myall songs.

‖**myalgia** (maɪˈældʒɪə). *Path.* [mod.L., f. Gr. μῦ-ς muscle + -αλγία, ἄλγος pain.] A morbid condition of a muscle, characterized by pain and tenderness; muscular rheumatism. Hence **myalgic** (maɪˈældʒɪk) *a.*, of the nature of, characterized by, or affected with myalgia.

1860 T. INMAN *On Myalgia* Pref. p. viii, The Author was guided to the choice of the word 'Myalgia'—first, because it had a familiar look about it, as resembling neuralgia; secondly, because it implied no other theory than that the muscles were the seats of pain. *Ibid.* 187 Is the heart subject to myalgic affections? **1880** A. FLINT *Princ. Med.* 803 Neuralgia affecting sensory nerves in muscular organs may be distinguished as myalgia. **1897** *Allbutt's Syst. Med.* III. 1 The word [Rheumatism].. has now become a convenient term for embracing myalgic, neurotic and arthritic pain.

myalism (ˈmaɪəlɪz(ə)m). [f. MYAL + -ISM.] A kind of sorcery or witchcraft practised in the West Indies and other countries.

1843 PHILLIPPO *Jamaica* 248 Myalism, as well as Fetishism, were constituent parts of Obeism. **1873** W. J. GARDNER *Hist. Jamaica* 191 Of late years Myalism has generally been regarded as an art by which that of the Obeah man could be counteracted. **1874** [see OBEAHISM].

Hence **myalist** (ˈmaɪəlɪst), one who practises myalism. Also *attrib.*

1851 G. BLYTH *Remin. Miss. Life* iv. 175 Sometimes the Myalists meet in large companies, generally at night. **1889** P. A. BRUCE *Plant. Negro* viii. 123 A Myalist outbreak meant the repression of the malignant influences of Obeah.

myall[1] (ˈmaɪəl). [Native name: Bigambel (Dumaresque River) *mail* the blacks (a black = *namail*).] An aboriginal of Australia who has not come under the influence of white civilization.

1835 in T. L. Mitchell *Exped. East. Australia* (1839) I. App. 353 The smoke from fires of the Myall blacks. **1839** T. L. MITCHELL *Ibid.* I. 20 The natives who remain in a savage state.. are named '*myalls*' by their half civilized brethren. **1890** 'R. BOLDREWOOD' *Col. Reformer* (1891) 202 A lot of half-tamed naked Myalls, as yet hardly to be trusted. **1898** —— *Rom. Canvas Town* 145 If murder doesn't come of it, I'm a myall black fellow.

myall[2] (ˈmaɪəl). [Native name: Kamilaroi (Hunter River) *maiāl*.] Any Australian acacia, esp. *Acacia pendula* or *A. homalophylla* (which yields a useful hard scented wood). Also, the wood of these trees.

1845 J. O. BALFOUR *Sketch N.S. Wales* 38 The Myall-tree .. is the most picturesque tree of New South Wales. **1852** MUNDY *Antipodes* I. x. 316 Dandy amateur bushmen have the handle of their stock-whip made of the *Myâl*, *Acacia pendula*, or violet wood. **1859** H. KINGSLEY *G. Hamlyn* v, A man that's seen a naked old hag of a gin ride away on a myall-bough. **1880** *Silver's Handbk. Australia* 275 Stringy bark is useful for boards.. myall for pipes. **1890** 'R. BOLDREWOOD' *Col. Reformer* (1891) 400 The boundless ocean-plains.. where the saltbush grows, and the myall and the mulgah. **1893** J. A. BARRY *Steve Brown's Bunyip* 277 The myall ashes still glowed redly.

†**'myance.** *Sc. Obs.* [Altered form of *moyens*, pl. of MOYEN *sb.*[1], with assimilation of the last syllable to the suffix -ANCE.]

1. Means, resources; agency, intercession, influence exerted on behalf of another: see MOYEN *sb.*[1]

1500–20 DUNBAR *Poems* xxxiii. 36 He wald haif, for a nicht to byd, A haiknay and the hurtmanis hyd, So meikle he was of myance [*riming with* sciens, gyans, gardeviance]. **1545** *Reg. Privy Council Scot.* I. 4 Throw suppli myance and favour of the King of Ingland. **1550** *Ibid.* 109 Diverse oure Soverane Ladyis legis makis myance that the samin [coins] hes passage. *a* **1585** MONTGOMERIE *Flyting* 71 Trot, tyke, to a tow, mandrage but myance.

¶ **2.** ? Information, intelligence.

1561 *Diurn. Occurr.* (Bannatyne Cl.) 70 The said erle havand myance thairof, rasit his freindis.

myand, -ane, myar: see MOYEN, MIRE.

‖**myasthenia** (maɪəsˈθiːnɪə). [mod.L. *myasthenia*, f. Gr. μῦ-ς muscle + ἀσθενεία weakness.] Muscular weakness. Hence **myas'thenic** *a.*

1856 MAYNE *Expos. Lex.*, *Myasthenia*.. *Myasthenicus*,.. myasthenic. **1902** *Brit. Med. Jrnl.* 31 May 1323 The girl's distressing nervous sensitiveness made impossible.. an attempt to obtain the myasthenic reaction.

myasthenia gravis (maɪəsˌθiːnɪə ˈgrævɪs). *Med.* [mod.L., shortening of *myasthenia gravis pseudoparalytica* (F. Jolly 1895, in *Berliner klin. Wochenschr.* 7 Jan. 7/1), f. MYASTHENIA + L. *gravis* severe, grave.] A rare chronic disease, occurring chiefly in young adults, that is characterized by muscular weakness unaccompanied by atrophy, with temporary paresis following exertion, and is caused by a defect in the mechanism which converts a nervous impulse into a muscular contraction.

1900 CAMPBELL & BRAMWELL in *Brain* XXIII. 278 The disease has received various names. The earlier cases were published as 'cases of bulbar paralysis without discoverable anatomical changes'... Strümpell introduced the term 'Asthenic bulbar palsy'... Other names which have been employed are 'general profound myasthenia', 'Erb's disease', the 'Erb-Goldflam' and the 'Hoppe-Goldflam-symptom-complex'. Jolly has proposed the term 'myasthenia gravis pseudo-paralytica', and this, or for short 'myasthenia gravis', appears to us the most suitable and convenient hitherto suggested. **1939** W. HAYMAKER tr. *R. Bing's Textbk. Nerv. Dis.* v. 182 Myasthenia gravis occasionally appears in more than one member of a family. **1961** *Lancet* 5 Aug. 281/2 The clinical diagnosis of myasthenia gravis is usually easy. **1970** *Toronto Daily Star* 24 Sept. 1/4 The twins have myasthenia gravis, a disease that killed their brother Richard last year when he was 6 months old. Excitement of any kind..can set off the choking, gasping attacks. **1974** Passmore & Robson *Compan. Med. Stud.* III. xxxiv. 31/2 Myasthenia gravis is also associated with an immunological disturbance.

†**myce**, *v. Obs.* Also **myse**. [? a. OF. **micier*, *michier* (now dial.) to crumble, slice small, f. *miche* (see MICHE *sb.*[1]).] *trans.* To cut up small.

1381 in *Forme of Cury* (1780) 93 Nym onyons and myce hem riȝt smal. *Ibid.* 95 Myse bred and schepys talwe as gret as dyses. *c* **1450** *Two Cookery-bks.* 71 Take fressh brawne, and myce it small. *Ibid.* 75 Putte the mary therein, and myced dates And streberies.

myce, obs. pl. of MOUSE *sb.*

mycel, obs. form of MICKLE.

mycelial (maɪˈsiːlɪəl), *a. Bot.* [f. MYCELI-UM + -AL[1].] Consisting of or characterized by mycelium.

1870 Bastian in *Nature* 30 June 173/2 Ordinary mycelial filaments. **1882** *Jrnl. Microscop. Sci.* Jan. 6 A mycelial thread. **1894** *Times* 13 Dec. 11/5 *Eurotium Oryzæ*, a mycelial plant of the *Aspergillus* family.

So **myˈcelian, myˈcelioid** *adjs.*

1857 M. J. Berkeley *Cryptog. Bot.* §226, I have..found a *Cyphella* on the hardest gravel stones, where the fine mycelioid threads, by which it was attached [etc.]. **1887** W. Phillips *Brit. Discomycetes* 147 The fully developed cups are much more rare than the green mycelioid state. **1891** *Syd. Soc. Lex.*, *Mycelian*, relating to *Mycelium*.

‖**mycelium** (maɪˈsiːlɪəm). *Bot.* [mod.L. (Fries 1832), f. Gr. μύκης mushroom + -IUM, with intercalated *l* (? after *epithēlium*).] The vegetative part of the thallus of fungi, consisting of white filamentous tubes (hyphæ); the spawn of mushrooms.

1836 M. J. Berkeley *Fungi* 28* *Sporidia*.., at first covered by the converging *flocci* of the *mycelium*. **1847** Johnston in *Proc. Berw. Nat. Club* II. No. 5. 214 The decumbent filaments of this Mould form a cobweb-like mycelium. **1875** Huxley & Martin *Pract. Biol.* v. 34 As all the ramifying hyphæ proceed from the spore as a centre, their development gives rise..to a delicate stellate mycelium.

Mycenæan (maɪsɪˈniːən), *a.* and *sb.* [f. L. *Mycēnæ-us* (f. *Mycēnæ*) + -AN.] **A.** *adj.* Of or belonging to Mycenæ, an ancient Greek city in the Argive plain, and *esp.* the kind of civilization, culture, or art of which it was the centre. **B.** *sb.* A native or inhabitant of Mycenæ. Also, the language used by the Greeks of the Mycenæan Age.

[**1598** Chapman *Iliad* vii. 157 The king himself that rules the rich Mycenian land.] **1797** *Encycl. Brit.* (ed. 3) XII. 562/2 The Mycenæans, sending 80 men, partook with the Lacedæmonians in the glory acquired at Thermopylæ. **1842** Mure *Tour in Greece* II. 167 The Mycenæan structure [*sc.* the Treasury of Atreus] has..the advantage of being in a nearly perfect state of preservation. **1896** *Nat. Sci.* Dec. 353 Mycenæan culture was permeated by Oriental elements. **1930** Magoffin & Davis *Romance of Archaeol.* ii. 31 Mycenaean civilization could now be seen to be the mainland exotic of which Minoan island civilization had been the stem and the flower. **1956** Ventris & Chadwick *Documents in Mycenaean Gk.* i. iii. 74 There seems as yet to be little certain indication which dissociates Mycenaean from the Aeolic group. **1958** J. Chadwick *Decipherment of Linear B* v. 73 The name Mycenaean, originally a label for the culture of the Greek mainland in the Late Helladic period, is now generally extended to the Linear B script and the dialect it contains. **1965** *Language* XLI. 314 Antonio Tovar..comes out..against the Porzig-Risch thesis that Mycenaean represents a form of 'Southern Greek'. **1968** *Encycl. Brit.* XXII. 975/2 The dialect (conventionally known as Mycenaean) is the oldest Greek known and belongs to the Achaean subdivision. **1968** P. Martin tr. *Pallottino's Meaning of Archaeol.* 160 The people of the Mycenaean civilization..were neither more nor less than the forebears of the Greeks of history. **1971** L. A. Boger *Dict. World Pottery & Porcelain* 235/2 The style of painting on the early Mycenaean vases is almost exactly like Minoan Floral and Marine styles. **1972** M. Magnusson *Introducing Archaeol.* iii. 34 Schliemann was convinced he had found the graves of Homer's Mycenean royal family, the graves of murdered Agamemnon and his companions.

mycetal (maɪˈsiːtəl). *Bot.* [f. Gr. μυκητ-, μύκης mushroom + -AL[1].] (See quot.)

1857 M. J. Berkeley *Cryptog. Bot.* §63, I shall..consider Algals, or Hydrophytes, as forming the first grand group; and for the second, propose the name of Mycetals, comprising..Fungals and Lichens.

‖**mycetes** (maɪˈsiːtiːz), *sb. pl. Biol.* [mod.L., ad. Gr. μύκητες, pl. of μύκης mushroom, fungus.] The group of minute vegetable organisms commonly known as microbes. Hence **myˈcetic** *a.*

1876 tr. *von Ziemssen's Cycl. Med.* I. 254 If..the mycetic germ of a pestilence is supplanted..by a pathogenetic protomyces. *Ibid.* 399 A very strong proof of the possible dissemination of cholera mycetes by the air. **1896** *Allbutt's Syst. Med.* I. 504 Others have singled out the schizomycetes as mycetes or microbes.

myceto- (maɪˈsiːtəʊ, maɪsɪˈtɒ), before a vowel **mycet-**, combining form of Gr. μύκης mushroom, used in various scientific terms: **myˌcetogeˈnetic, myceˈtogenous** *adjs.*, produced by mushrooms. **myceˈtology** (see quots.). **myceˈtophagous** [-PHAGOUS] *a.* = FUNGIVOROUS *a.* **myceˈtophilid, -philoid** *a.* and *sb.* [Gr. -φίλος loving], belonging to, a member of, the family *Mycetophilidæ* or fungus midges. ‖**mycetoˈzoa**, a group of fungoid organisms, consisting chiefly of the Myxomycetes; also **mycetoˈzoan**, ‖ **-ˈzoon**, a member of this group.

1887 tr. *De Bary's Fungi*, etc. 368 These phenomena of deformation by Fungi may be termed *mycetogenetic metamorphosis. *Ibid.* 369 All these *mycetogenous deformations. **1856** Mayne *Expos. Lex.*, *Mycetologia*,..a treatise or dissertation on the mushrooms: *mycetology. **1879** *Encycl. Brit.* IX. 827/2 Mycetology, or more commonly mycology, the science of fungi. **1906** J. B. Smith *Explanation of Terms used in Entomology* 86 *Mycetophagous: feeding upon fungi. **1920** *Amer. Naturalist* LIV. 314 Many of these mycetophagous insects undoubtedly show a very close association with certain species of fungi. **1946** C. T. Brues *Insect Dietary* v. 193 Mycetophagous insects..are abundant. **1957** Snell & Dick *Gloss. Mycology* 101/1 Mycetophagous. Fungivorous; eating fungi. **1974** *Sci. Amer.* Apr. 128/3 Mycetophagous Breeding in the Australian Dung Beetle, *Onthophagus Dunningi*, G. F. Bornemissza. **1899** Sharp in *Camb. Nat. Hist., Insects* II. 463 The larva of *Mycetobia pallipes*..gives rise..to an ordinary *Mycetophilid fly. **1880** Saville Kent *Infusoria* I. 41 The group of the Myxomycetes or *Mycetozoa. **1885** E. R. Lankester in *Encycl. Brit.* XIX. 832/1 It indeed seems not at all improbable that..the Mycetozoa represent more closely than any other living forms the original ancestors of the whole organic world. **1881** T. Gill in *Smithsonian Rep.* 414 *Mycetozoans. **1888** Rolleston & Jackson *Anim. Life* 908 The spore of a Mycetozoan is a minute spherical or oval body. **1885** E. R. Lankester in *Encycl. Brit.* XIX. 832/1 The naked protoplasm of the *Mycetozoon's plasmodium.

mycetocyte (maɪˈsiːtəʊsaɪt). *Zool.* [ad. G. *mycetocyt* (K. Šulc 1911, in *Sitzungsber. d. k. böhm. Ges. f. Wissensch.* (*Math.-naturw. Classe*) *Jahrg. 1910* III. 10): see MYCETO- and -CYTE.] Any of the large cells found in some insects, either aggregated into a mycetome or not, which contain symbiotic micro-organisms, esp. yeasts.

1924 *Philippine Jrnl. Sci.* XXIV. 157 In this species there are no specialized 'mycetoms' or 'mycetocytes', as in the aphids. **1946** E. A. Steinhaus *Insect Microbiol.* iv. 198 The number of mycetocytes present in each individual aphid ranges from about 60 to 70. **1952** *Science* 25 Apr. 459/1 All aphids, except very old ones, contain numerous large cells in the body cavity (mycetocytes) containing many more or less spherical intracellular particles. **1973** W. S. Romoser *Sci. Entomol.* iii. 72 In many cases the microbes present are passed from generation to generation. In some insects in which this occurs specialized cells, mycetocytes, and the tissues composed of these cells, mycetomes, can be found associated with the gut, fat body, or, appropriately, the gonads.

‖**mycetoma** (maɪsɪˈtəʊmə). *Path.* [mod.L., f. Gr. μυκητ-, μύκης mushroom + -ωμα (cf. *sarcoma*).] A fungoid disease of the foot (or hand). Hence **myceˈtomatous** *a.*, affected with mycetoma.

1874 H. V. Carter (*title*) On Mycetoma or the fungus disease of India. **1892** *Lancet* 16 July 170/1 The actinomycotic nature..of the black variety of mycetoma. **1897** *Allbutt's Syst. Med.* II. 90 Mycetoma or Madura foot. **1898** P. Manson *Trop. Dis.* xxxvii, A mycetomatous foot or hand.

mycetome (ˈmaɪsɪtəʊm). *Zool.* Also **mycetom**. [ad. G. *mycetom* (K. Šulc 1911, in *Sitzungsber. d. k. böhm. Ges. f. Wissensch.* (*Math.-naturw. Classe*) *Jahrg. 1910* III. 10): see MYCETO- and -OME.] An organ in some insects consisting of an aggregation of mycetocytes.

1924 *Philippine Jrnl. Sci.* XXIV. 143 (*heading*) Studies on the embryogeny and postnatal development of the Aphididæ with special reference to the history of the 'symbiotic organ', or 'mycetom'. **1946** E. A. Steinhaus *Insect Microbiol.* iv. 190 In 1850 Leydig observed certain organs in aphids which have subsequently been called 'symbiotic organs', 'pseudovitelli', 'green bodies', 'bacteriotomes', and 'mycetoms' or 'mycetomes'. **1946** *Nature* 30 Nov. 795/2 These insects would starve for lack of nitrogenous food were it not for mycetome symbiosis with *Azotobacter*. **1973** [see MYCETOCYTE].

mych, myche, mychel, mycht: see MITCH *v.*, MUCH, MICKLE, MICHAEL, MIGHT.

-mycin (ˈmaɪsɪn), *suffix. Pharmacol.* [f. Gr. μύκης fungus + -IN[1].] Used to form the names of antibiotic compounds derived from fungi, usu. with part of the generic name or specific epithet of the fungus, as ACTINOMYCIN, ERYTHROMYCIN, STREPTOMYCIN, etc.

myck(e, mycle, obs. forms of MEEK, MICKLE.

myco- (ˈmaɪkəʊ), irreg. combining form (for MYCETO-) of Gr. μύκης fungus, used in chemical and botanical terms: **mycoˈdextrin, -ˈinulin**, substances analogous to dextrin and inulin (respectively) found in the truffle *Elaphomyces granulatus*. **mycoˈmysticism**, mystical sensations induced by drugs extracted from mushrooms; so **mycoˈmystical** *a.* **mycoˈprotein**, the albuminoid which is the principal constituent of the protoplasm of the cell. ‖ **ˈmycothrix** [Gr. θρίξ hair] = LEPTOTHRIX. **ˌmycotoxiˈcosis** [-OSIS], a pathological condition caused by a mycotoxin. **mycoˈtoxin**, any toxic substance produced by a fungus.

1891 *Syd. Soc. Lex.*, **Mycodextrin*. **1872** Watts *Dict. Chem.* Suppl., **Myco-inulin*. $C^{12}H^{22}O^{11}H^2O$. **1962** A. Huxley *Island* ix. 141 Neurotheology, metachemistry, *mycomysticism. *Ibid.* 156 The local panel of medical and *mycomystical experts. **1885** Klein *Micro-Org.* 34 A kind of protoplasm, the *mycoprotein of Nencki. **1876** *Wagner's Gen. Path.* 90 Cells..united by transverse division into short moniliform filaments of two or more members (*mycothrix, torula-forms). **1948** M. V. Gorlenko in *Amer. Rev. Soviet Med.* V. 164 The moulds..are ubiquitous and not particular as to the substrate upon which they grow. This circumstance, as well as the toxicity, suggests that equine stachybotriotoxicosis is not induced by *Stachybotrys alternans* alone, but may be caused also by other moulds. The disease may be appropriately called *mycotoxicosis. **1957** *Rev. Med. & Vet. Mycol.* II. 502 Mycotoxicoses..are stated to be causing great losses among farm animals in the U.S.S.R. **1968** *Prog. Industr. Microbiol.* VII. 156 Alimentary toxic aleukia..appears to be the only mycotoxicosis other than ergotism to have directly affected major segments of human populations. **1962** *Adv. Vet. Sci.* VII. 335 If *mycotoxins are indeed present in such grain, sufficient levels of toxin may be added to the mixed feed to be harmful to animals fed thereon. **1974** *Daily Tel.* 26 Mar. 16 The mycotoxins enter the food chain and accumulate in man through his use of milk, eggs, poultry or meat.

mycobacterium (maɪkəʊbækˈtɪərɪəm). [mod.L. (Lehmann & Neumann *Atlas und Grundriss der Bakteriologie* (1896) II. 108), f. MYCO- + BACTERIUM.] A saprophytic or parasitic bacterium of the genus so called, which includes those causing tuberculosis, leprosy, and other diseases in man and other animals; also, a bacterium of the family Mycobacteriaceæ.

1909 E. R. Stitt *Pract. Bacteriol.* vii. 66 (*heading*) Study and identification of bacteria. Mycobacteria and corynebacteria. **1949** H. W. Florey et al. *Antibiotics* I. iv. 211 The sensitivity to antibiotics of the slow-growing mycobacteria, notably various strains of the tubercle bacillus, has been studied. **1962** *Lancet* 1 Dec. 1153/1 Disease resembling tuberculosis..may be produced by mycobacteria other than tubercle bacilli. **1973** R. G. Krueger et al. *Introd. Microbiol.* iii. 62/2 Many types of mycobacteria occur as free-living organisms in soil, water, and dairy products... Some mycobacteria are parasites of animals in which they may cause disease, including tuberculosis.

mycobiont (maɪkəʊˈbaɪɒnt). *Bot.* [f. MYCO- + Gr. βιουντ-, pr. pple. stem of βιοῦν to live, f. βίος life.] The fungal component of a lichen; any fungus which is associated with an alga to form a lichen.

1957 G. D. Scott in *Nature* 2 Mar. 486/2 Three new terms are here proposed... They are:..(2) 'mycobiont', applicable to a fungus in association with an alga in the formation of a lichen. **1961** *Science* 10 Mar. 700/2 In our investigation, 11 pure cultures of mycobionts were tested for active compounds. **1969** *Ecology* L. 744/2 In the laboratory the lichen organization breaks down and either the phycobiont..or the mycobiont..overgrows the other partner. **1973** *Phytochemistry* XII. 2249 (*heading*) Sterols of the mycobiont and phycobiont isolated from the lichen *Xanthoria parietina*.

‖**mycoderma** (maɪkəʊˈdɜːmə). Also (in sense 2) **ˈmycoderm**. [mod.L.: see MYCO- and DERMA.]

1. A genus of fermentation-fungi, as that which forms the mother of vinegar (*Mycoderma aceti*).

1846 Lindley *Veget. Kingd.* 44. **1849** Balfour *Man. Bot.* §1125 Peculiar species of Mycoderma are developed in vinegar, in yeast, and in flour. **1887** tr. *De Bary's Fungi*, etc. 250 With free admission of air the sprouts are frequently elongated cylindrical shoots (the 'Chalara-' and Mycoderma-form).

2. A pellicle or membrane formed by certain bacteria, as on the surface of liquids that have become 'mothery'.

1854 C. H. Jones & Siev. *Pathol. Anat.* v. 199 The mycoderm of favus. **1861** H. Macmillan *Footn. Page Nat.* 238 These mycodermata, as they are called, of ulcerated and mucous surfaces.

Hence **mycoˈdermatoid, -ˈdermatous** [Gr. δερματ-, δέρμα: see DERMA], **-ˈdermic** *adjs.*, of, pertaining to, or consisting of mycoderms.

1847 *Todd's Cycl. Anat.* IV. i. 144/1 Mycodermatous vegetations occur as elements of the crust of porrigo favosa. **1849** Balfour *Man. Bot.* §1126 Some mycodermatous Fungi are connected with certain cutaneous.. diseases. **1882** Ogilvie, *Mycodermic*. **1890** *Century Dict.*, *Mycodermatoid*.

mycology (maɪˈkɒlədʒɪ). [ad. mod.L. *mycologia*: see MYCO- and -LOGY.] That branch of botany which treats of fungi; also, the mycological features of a district or country.

1836 M. J. Berkeley *Fungi* 7* The immense advances which have of late years been made in the study of Mycology. **1845** Lindley *Veget. Kingd.* 37 The African Mycology is remarkable for the varied forms it produces amongst the puff-balls and allied genera. **1885** G. S. Woodhead & A. W. Hare (*title*), Pathological Mycology. An Enquiry into the Etiology of Infective Diseases.

Hence **myco'logic, -'logical** *adjs.*, pertaining to or connected with mycology or the study of fungi; hence **myco'logically** *adv.*; **my'cologist**, one who studies or is versed in fungi.

1836 M. J. BERKELEY *Fungi* 7* That most excellent mycologist, Schweinitz. **1838** *Penny Cycl.* XI. 19/2 The mycological system of Fries. **1846** WORCESTER, *Mycologic*. **1875** COOKE *Fungi* xiii. 269 The mycologic vegetation of a country. *Ibid.* 281 A great portion of this country is mycologically unknown. **1903** *Westm. Rev.* 30 Nov. 2/1 The Director..is a botanist; the Assistant-Director..is a mycologist. **1933** *Jrnl. R. Hort. Soc.* LVIII. II. 266 Dr. Downson..resigned his appointment as mycologist to the Government of Tasmania. **1967** M. E. HALE *Biol. Lichens* ii. 33 The definition of the term stroma, however, has not yet been settled even among mycologists.

mycophage ('maɪkəʊfeɪdʒ). [f. MYCO- + -PHAGE.] One who or that which eats fungi.

1958 *Times Lit. Suppl.* 19 Dec. 742/1 Why do the English and the Celts fear all but the cultivated mushroom, while Slavs and Italians are enthusiastic mycophages? **1965** B. E. FREEMAN tr. *Vandel's Biospeleology* xix. 328 It is generally impossible to classify a cavernicole as a humiphage, xylophage, mycophage, coprophage, or necrophage.

mycophagy (maɪ'kɒfədʒɪ). [See MYCO- and -PHAGY.] The eating of fungi; esp. of those species usually neglected or avoided. Hence **my'cophagist**, one who practises mycophagy; also, an animal that eats fungi; **my'cophagous** *a.* = *mycetophagous* adj. (s.v. MYCETO-).

1861 H. MACMILLAN *Footn. Page Nat.* 262 The dung and fly Agaric, whose loathsome and poisonous properties are such as to deter the most devoted mycophagist from their use. **1865** *Reader* 30 Sept. 368/2 Mycophagy, a grand name for what West of England boys call eating 'twoad's meeyat'. **1901** *Nation* 11 Apr. 295/3 'The Mushroom Book' introduces the beginner..to the most important edible and poisonous forms, placing him quickly in possession of the facts most important to the successful mycophagist. **1919** *Trans. Brit. Mycol. Soc.* VI. 355 *(title)* The red squirrel of North America as a mycophagist. **1922** *Ibid.* VIII. 84 *(title)* Some observations on the mycophagous propensities of slugs. **1939** *Bull. Torrey Bot. Club* LXVI. 1 *(title)* The Snail *Polygyra thyroidus* as a mycophagist. *Ibid.* 5 *P. thyroidus* is decidedly mycophagous in regard to its food preferences. **1950** A. P. KELLEY *Mycotrophy in Plants* xi. 151 As Frank continued to study mycorrhizae, he saw digestion of the mycelium and was led to develop another idea which may be termed 'mycophagy'. According to this concept, the 'fungus-eating plants' are able to draw their victim into the protoplasm,..and finally to digest it.

mycophilic (maɪkəʊ'fɪlɪk), *a.* [f. MYCO- + -PHILIC.] Fond of mushrooms; feeding upon mushrooms.

1972 *Times Lit. Suppl.* 25 Feb. 211/1 (Advt.), A favourite with mushroom-hunting enthusiasts and mycophilic epicures.

mycophobia (maɪkəʊ'fəʊbɪə). [f. MYCO- + -PHOBIA.] (See quot. 1962.) So **myco'phobic** *a.*

1958 *Times Lit. Suppl.* 19 Dec. 742/2 The mycophobic hate was back again,..and everything which is not the cultivated mushroom is now banished as 'toadstools'. **1962** *Spectator* 22 June 834/2 Mycophobia, i.e. unreasoning fear of mushrooms.

mycoplasma (maɪkəʊ'plæzmə). *Biol.* Pl. **-plasmas, -plasmata.** [mod.L. (J. Nowak 1929 in *Ann. de l'Inst. Pasteur* XLIII. 1349): see MYCO- and PLASMA.] An individual belonging to the genus *Mycoplasma*, comprising a group of pleomorphic, Gram-negative organisms which are much smaller than, and lack the cell wall of, bacteria but, unlike viruses, are capable of growth in artificial media, and which in nature are nearly all animal parasites though only a few are proven pathogens; also called a pleuropneumonia-like organism or PPLO.

[**1955** *Internat. Bull. Bacteriol. Nomenclature & Taxonomy* V. 15 *(heading)* Mycoplasma peripneumoniae. Nowak 1929... The generic name *Mycoplasma* was validly published. The older generic names *Asterococcus*, *Coccobacillus*, and *Micromyces* are unavailable. As next in priority sequence *Mycoplasma* apparently is, therefore, the legitimate name of the genus... It should be noted that.. the later *Borrelomyces* is more commonly accepted. However, unless some later name is conserved by international action, *Mycoplasma* probably should be recognized as correct.] **1960** *Ann. Rev. Microbiol.* XIV. 140 *(heading)* Nutrition, metabolism, and pathogenicity of mycoplasmas. **1963** *New Scientist* 25 Apr. 200/2 We know, too, of organisms (the mycoplasmata) which multiply inside cells. **1970** AMBROSE & EASTY *Cell Biol.* i. 7 The smallest free-living organisms are the mycoplasmas. These minute cells, the smallest of which are only 1,000 Å in diameter, have been isolated from soil and have been identified as the infective agent in various animal infections. **1971** *Nature* 22 Jan. 231/3 Mycoplasmas also share another important characteristic with bacteria and other cells; they are susceptible to infection by viruses. **1973** *Times* 14 July 1/2 In the United States the term 'viral pneumonia' usually means a lung infection with mycoplasma, an organism intermediate between bacteria and viruses.

So **myco'plasmal** *a.*, of, pertaining to, or caused by mycoplasmas.

1960 *Ann. Rev. Microbiol.* XIV. 154 Mycoplasmal infection of the trachea. **1972** *Science* 5 May 504/2 The structure of the mycoplasmal cell. **1974** *Nature* 31 May 422/1 No viral or mycoplasmal contamination was detected.

mycorrhiza (maɪkəʊ'raɪzə). *Bot.* Pl. **-æ** (-iː) or **-s.** Also **mycorhiza.** [a. mod.L. *mycorhiza* (A. B. Frank 1885, in *Ber. Deutsch. Bot. Ges.* III. 129), f. MYCO- + Gr. ῥίζα root.] A symbiotic or slightly pathogenic fungus growing in association with the roots of a plant. Also *attrib.* Hence **myco'rrhizal** *a.*

1895 W. R. FISHER in *Schlich's Man. Forestry* IV. III. ii. 376 This altered root with its matted coating of mycelium receives the name mycorhiza, and the fungus has the power of absorbing nutritive matter from the soil and conveying it to the roots of the host. **1898** tr. *Strasburger's Bot.* 210 Judging from the results of culture experiments made with these plants without mycorrhiza. **1900** *Nature* 28 June 201/2 All known species of mycorhizal fungi. **1916** *Nature* 2 Nov. 172/1 The abhorrence of lime by the humus-loving rhododendrons appears to be intimately connected with the mycorrhiza, the symbiotic fungus which lives in association with the roots of the rhododendron and heath family. **1924** J. A. THOMSON *Science Old & New* xxvii. 148 In many cases ..the partner fungus or mycorhiza confines itself to the outside of the root, forming a dense, absorbing feltwork... The fungus absorbs water and salts and organic materials from the soil and passes these on to the tree; the benefit it gets in return is a supply of carbohydrates from the root. **1926** TANSLEY & CHIPP *Study of Vegetation* ix. 158 Etymologically the word mycorrhiza refers to the fungus-root combination. *Ibid.*, Mycorrhizal fungi may be divided roughly into endotrophic and ectotrophic. **1927** *Forestry* I. 115 Mycorrhiza formation and the mycotrophic habit are of the first importance to trees growing in humus soils. **1934** *Ibid.* VIII. 97 Coralloid clusters of short thick rootlets (mycorrhizas) varying in colour with that of the associated mycelium. **1955** *Jrnl. Ecol.* XLIII. 408 The results of experiments performed with excised mycorrhizal roots may not necessarily be directly applied to mycorrhizas attached to parent trees. **1967** *Punch* 24 May 766/3 The orchid seedling, having no green leaves, depends for its food on the phenomenon of mycorhiza, an association with a resident fungus that is less of a coming together for mutual benefit than an unending war wherein the opposing forces are so perfectly balanced there is no victor, no vanquished. **1967** M. E. HALE *Biol. Lichens* v. 69 Mycorrhizal fungi associated with the roots of trees. **1973** *Nature* 7 Dec. 366/2 The necessity (or not) of raising nursery seedlings under conditions conducive to mycorrhizal infection, are discussed.

‖**mycosis** (maɪ'kəʊsɪs). *Path.* Also **myk-.** [f. Gr. μύκης (see MYCO-) + -OSIS.] The presence of parasitic fungi in or on any part of the body, or the disease caused thereby. Hence **mycotic** (maɪ'kɒtɪk) *a.*, characterized by mycosis.

1876 tr. *Wagner's Gen. Pathol.* 268 The character of diphtheria is most probably a mykosis. **1877** tr. *von Ziemssen's Cycl. Med.* XII. 573 Some cases [of meningitis] have been recognised to be of mycotic origin. **1880** A. FLINT *Princ. Med.* 97 A form of intestinal mycosis.

mycotrophy (maɪ'kɒtrəfɪ). *Bot.* [a. G. *mykotrophie* (R. Falck 1923, in *Mykologische Untersuchungen und Berichte* II. 49), f. MYCO- + Gr. τροφή nourishment: see -Y[3].] The state of certain plants which have mycorrhizæ growing in association with their roots, possibly as an aid in the assimilation of nutrients. So **myco'trophic** *a.*

1927 *Forestry* I. 115 Defining mycotrophy as the capacity to assimilate organic compounds through the agency of specific root fungi, Falck reviews the historical evidence bearing on the significance of mycorrhiza. **1927** [see MYCORRHIZA]. **1930** *Nature* 9 July 80/1 The mycotrophic habit has been shown to be of wide occurrence in many families of plants. **1959** J. L. HARLEY *Biol. Mycorrhiza* i. 6 The mycotrophy of the Ericales is described because it now appears to have something in common with the ectotrophic mycorrhizas of forest trees. *Ibid.* xi. 172 *(heading)* Other mycotrophic plants with septate endophytes.

mycterism ('mɪktərɪz(ə)m). *rare.* [ad. Gr. μυκτηρισμός, f. μυκτηρίζειν to sneer at, f. μυκτήρ nose.] A gibe or scoff.

1593 R. HARVEY *Philad.* 8, I may well say, notwithstanding your trifling mycterisme, that [etc.]. **1678** PHILLIPS, *Mycterisme*, a disdainful gibe, or scoff; in Rhetorick, it is taken for a more secret and close kind of Sarcasm. **1900** SAINTSBURY *Hist. Crit.* I. 301 Quintilian.. observes that..the Greeks call certain kinds of allegory, sarcasm, asteism [etc.]..to which it may be well to add mycterism, a kind of derision which is dissembled, but not altogether concealed.

myctophid ('mɪktəfɪd), *sb.* and *a.* *Zool.* [f. mod.L. family name *Myctophidæ*, f. the generic name *Myctophum* (C. S. Rafinesque *Indice d'Ittiologia Siciliana* (1810) 56), f. Gr. μυκτήρ nose + ὄφις snake: see -ID[3].] A small, marine, deep-water fish of the family Myctophidæ, distinguished by luminous organs along its sides; also called lantern-fish. Also as *adj.*, of or pertaining to this family of fishes.

1931 J. R. NORMAN *Hist. Fishes* viii. 151 In the Myctophids or Lantern-fishes (*Myctophidae*) the photophores are fewer in number. **1956** A. HARDY *Open Sea* xii. 233 There are a great many different species of myctophids, but most are very similar in appearance. *Ibid.* 245 *(caption)* A myctophid Lantern-fish *Myctophum punctatum*. **1971** *Nature* 29 Oct. 623/2 The myctophids, or lantern fishes..are among the most common and widely distributed deep-sea fishes known.

mycul(le, obs. forms of MICKLE.

mydaleine (maɪ'deɪlɪɪn). [f. Gr. μυδαλέος dripping, wet + -INE[5].] A poisonous ptomaine obtained from putrid flesh, etc.

1887 A. M. BROWN *Anim. Alkaloids* 37 The action of mydaleine on the animal economy is very interesting. **1897** *Allbutt's Syst. Med.* II. 788 Mydaleine, which has been obtained from the human cadaver.

myd(d)ai, etc., obs. ff. MIDDAY.

mydde: see MEAD *sb.*[2], MID.

myddel, etc., obs. ff. MIDDLE.

myddes, var. MIDS.

mydding, myddoe, middrefe: see MIDDEN, MEADOW, MIDRIFF.

myde: see MID, MIDE, MEED.

mydemyst, mydes, (-is), mydew, myding: see MIDMOST, MIDS, MEADOW, MIDDEN.

mydle, obs. f. MEDDLE, MIDDLE.

‖**mydriasis** (mɪdrɪ'eɪsɪs). *Path.* [late L. *mydriāsis* (Celsus), a. Gr. μυδρίᾱσις, Ionic -ησις.] Excessive dilatation of the pupil of the eye.

[**1657** *Physical Dict.*, *Midriasis*.] **1805** *Med. Jrnl.* XIV. 402 Under the term *mydriasis*, the older writers have comprehended a morbid affection of the iris, and of the retina. **1849–52** *Todd's Cycl. Anat.* IV. II. 1466/1 Mydriasis ..renders the individual more or less presbyopic.

mydriatic (mɪdrɪ'ætɪk), *a.* and *sb.* [f. prec.: see -ATIC.] **a.** *adj.* Pertaining to, or causing, mydriasis. **b.** *sb.* A drug that produces mydriasis.

1855 DUNGLISON *Med. Lex.* **1863** *Syd. Soc. Year-bk.* 444 On the Antagonistic Effects of Opium and the Mydriatics. **1864** tr. *Donders' Anom. Accomm. Eye* 590 The ancients.. were acquainted with the mydriatic action of some plants.

mydrid, mydrif, mydrun, mydwe, mydyng: see MIDRED, MIDRIFF, MIDGERN, MEADOW, MIDDEN.

†**mye**, *v. Obs.* [a. OF. *mier* (recorded only as refl.) to crumble, f. *mie*:—L. *mīca* crumb.] *trans.* To crumble, grate (bread).

a **1310** in Wright *Lyric P.* xxxix. 111 Thah me teone with hym þat myn teh [= teþ] mye. **13..** in *Rel. Ant.* I. 51 Al this mye smal, and farse the catte within. *c* **1420** *Liber Cocorum* (1862) 8 Take mylke of almondes, lay hit anone With myed bred. **1483** *Cath. Angl.* 239/1 To Mye brede, *micare, interrere*.

myeld, obs. form of MILD.

‖**myelencephalon** (ˌmaɪəlɛn'sɛfəlɒn). *Anat.* [f. Gr. μυελός, -όν marrow + ENCEPHALON.]

a. The cerebro-spinal axis or system (Owen). **b.** The medulla oblongata (Huxley). So **myelence'phalic** *a.*, pertaining to or connected with the myelencephalon; **myelen'cephalous** *a.*, (*a*) = *myelencephalic*; (*b*) pertaining to the sub-kingdom *Myelencephala* (Owen) or vertebrates.

[**1843** OWEN *Lect. Comp. Anat.*, *Invertebrates* 12 The sub-kingdom *Vertebrata*, or *Myelencephala*.] **1846** —— *Lect. Anat. Vertebrate Anim.* I. *Fishes* 46 The perfect type of that primary segment of the myelencephalous skeleton. **1866** —— *Anat. Vertebr.* I. 268 Myelencephalon of Fishes. **1866** *Ibid.* III. 79 The myelencephalic columns. **1871** HUXLEY *Anat. Vert.* 72 All the other cerebral nerves originate in the posterior division of the hind-brain—the myelencephalon.

myelin[1], **-ine** ('maɪəlɪn). [a. G. *myelin*, f. Gr. μυελός marrow: see -IN, -INE.]

1. *Chem.* Virchow's term for a fatty substance obtainable from various animal tissues (e.g. brain-substance, yolk of egg), and also from some vegetable tissues. Also *attrib.*

1867 *Syd. Soc. Bienn. Retrosp.* 11 The peculiar substance termed by Virchow, myeline substance..appears to be derivable from protagon. **1867** *Jrnl. Anat.* I. 359 So-called Myeline-forms (rounded and elongated bodies with double contours, resembling nerve-tubes). **1887** tr. *De Bary's Fungi*, etc. 300 The motile formations observed in Beneke's myelin (protagon-mixtures).

2. *Anat.* The medullary sheath of nerve-fibres, or white substance of Schwann. Also *attrib.*

1873 A. FLINT *Physiol. Man, Nervous Syst.* i. 21 The medullary substance..is called by various names; as myeline, white substance of Schwann, medullary sheath. **1896** *Allbutt's Syst. Med.* I. 176 The nerve fibres..undergo changes in the myelin sheath similar to degeneration.

Hence **'myelinate, 'myelinated** *adjs.*, (of nerve-fibres) furnished with myelin; **myeli'nation**, the process of development of the medullary sheath of nerves in the embryo (*Syd. Soc. Lex.* 1891); **mye'linic** *a.*, of or containing myelin; **myelini'zation** = *myelination*; **'myelinize** *v. trans.*, to furnish with myelin; **ˌmyelino-neu'ritis**, inflammation of the medullary sheath of nerves.

1894 *Lancet* 3 Nov. 1037/1 In a muscular nerve trunk from one-third to one-half of the *myelinate fibres are from cells of the spinal root ganglion. **1899** *Allbutt's Syst. Med.* VII. 75 An exceedingly small group of *myelinated fibres. *Ibid.* 732 The changes in the cortex begin at a stage prior to the *myelination of the pyramidal fibres. **1900** *Lancet* 18 Aug. 529 The order of succession in the *myelinisation of the projection centres and the association centres. **1903** *Contemp. Rev.* Sept. 389 When the child plays it is literally organising its brain, *myelinising its mind-machine. **1876** tr. *Wagner's Gen. Pathol.* 329 Neither protagon.. nor one of its products of decomposition.. arising from the action of alkalies furnish of themselves *myelinic forms. **1897** *Allbutt's Syst. Med.* II. 979 *Myelino-neuritis such as is met with in disseminated sclerosis.

myelin² (ˈmaɪəlɪn). *Min.* Also -ine. [a. G. *myelin* (Breithaupt), ad. Gr. μυέλινος marrowy, f. μυελ-ός marrow.] A yellowish- or reddish-white variety of kaolin; so called from its appearance.

1854 Dana *Min.* 250 Myelin of Breithaupt (Talksteinmark) is from Rochlitz.

myelitis (maɪəˈlaɪtɪs). *Path.* [mod.L., f. myel-on + -itis.] Inflammation of the spinal cord.

1835 R. B. Todd in *Cycl. Pract. Med.* IV. 640/2 Inflammation of the spinal marrow called by Harles and Ollivièr *myelitis.* **1887** *Brit. Med. Jrnl.* 26 Mar. 680/1 Sections of the cord from a case of acute central myelitis.

Hence **myelitic** (maɪəˈlɪtɪk) *a.*

1856 Mayne *Expos. Lex., Myeliticus,*.. myelitic. **1899** *Allbutt's Syst. Med.* VII. 15 Acute myelitic ataxy.

myel(l)mas, obs. forms of Michaelmas.

myelo- (ˈmaɪələʊ, maɪəˈlɒ), before a vowel **myel-**, combining f. Gr. μυελός, μυελόν (see myelon), used in many medical and chemical terms, of which the following are typical examples: **ˈmyelocone** [Gr. κονίς dust]: see quots. **myeˈloidic, myeˈloidin**: see quot. 1872. **ˌmyeloˈmargarin,** a fatty substance obtained by Köhler from the tissue of the central nervous system. **ˌmyelomonoˈcytic** *a.*, designating that form of leukæmia which is characterized by the presence in the circulating blood of myeloid cells of both the monocytic and the myelocytic series. **myeˈlopathy,** disease of the spinal cord; hence **ˌmyeloˈpathic** *a.* **ˈmyeloplaque, ˈmyeloplax** [Gr. πλάξ anything flat and broad] = osteoclast (*a*). **ˈmyeloplast** [-plast] = prec.; hence **ˌmyeloˈplastic** *a.*, connected with myeloplasts. **ˌmyeloproˈliferative** *a.*, characterized by or pertaining to the proliferation of cells of or derived from the bone marrow; esp. in ***myeloproliferative syndrome*** (see quot. 1974).

1878 Kingzett *Anim. Chem.* 267 Kühn gave to one of the principles of the brain the name of cerebrine, and to another that of *myelokon. **1891** *Syd. Soc. Lex., Myelocone,* term employed by Couerbe for a fatty substance obtained from the cerebral structures and which consists chiefly of pulverulent stearine. **1872** Watts *Dict. Chem.* Suppl., **Myeloïdin* and **Myeloïdic acid.* These names are given by Köhler.. to two phosphoretted bodies which he has extracted from brain. **1876** tr. *Wagner's Gen. Pathol.* 329 His [*sc.* Köhler's] *myelomargarin. **1958** Dameshek & Gunz *Leukemia* viii. 161 (*heading*) '*Myelo-monocytic' leukemia. **1960** F. G. J. Hayhoe *Leukaemia* ii. 13 A mixed picture of early monocytic and myelocytic cells is seen, and this variety is called acute myelo-monocytic leukaemia or the Naegeli type of acute leukaemia. **1972** *Nature* 4 Feb. 274/2 High levels of urinary lysozyme activity were observed in acute monocytic and myelomonocytic leukaemia. **1897** *Allbutt's Syst. Med.* IV. 83 The atrophy of muscle may be *myelopathic, and have a central spinal origin. **1891** *Syd. Soc. Lex.*, **Myelopathy.* **1899** *Allbutt's Syst. Med.* VII. 207 Progressive spinal muscular atrophy (Progressive myelopathy, wasting palsy). **1877** Schäfer *Histol.* 93 Another element to be found in the marrow is.. the *myeloplaque or ostoclast. **1891** *Syd. Soc. Lex.* **Myeloplasts*... Large multinucleated protoplasmic masses or giant cells, found in the marrow of bones. **1874** H. V. Carter *Mycetoma* 42 An alteration of the bones produced by a diathesis, such as he supposes to belong to the *myeloplastic formations generally. **1866** A. Flint *Princ. Med.* 51 **Myeoloplaxes* [sic], cells in the marrow of bones. **1876** tr. *Wagner's Gen. Pathol.* 389 So-called mother-cells with daughter-cells—giant-cells, myeloplaxes. **1951** W. Dameshek in *Blood* VI. 372 (*heading*) Some speculations on the *myeloproliferative syndromes. **1962** *Lancet* 19 May 1044/2 The levels were generally normal in various other conditions—kidney disease,.. acute or chronic liver disease, and neoplastic or myeloproliferative disease. **1974** R. P. Custer *Atlas Blood & Bone Marrow* (ed. 2) xix. 383/1 The term 'myeloproliferative syndrome' was suggested by Dameshek to include a heterogeneous group of disorders characterized by proliferation of any or all cell lines indigenous to the bone marrow at some time during the course of the disease.

myeloblast (ˈmaɪələʊblɑːst, -æ-). *Anat.* [a. G. *myeloblast* (O. Naegeli 1900, in *Deutsche med. Wochenschr.* 3 May 289/1): see myelo- and -blast.] Any of the immature cells (approximately 15 microns in diameter, with large nuclei and a small amount of densely staining cytoplasm) which are confined to the bone marrow, appearing in the circulating blood only in pathological states, and which, according to the so-called monophyletic (unitary) theory of hæmopoiesis, are the precursors of all other myeloid cells of the blood and bone marrow, or, according to the diphyletic (dualistic) or polyphyletic theories, are the precursors only of the myelocytes and of cells derived from them.

1904 F. P. Foster *Appleton's Med. Dict.* 1395/1 Myeloblast. **1909** R. J. M. Buchanan *Blood in Health & Dis.* viii. 143 Nägeli termed them 'myeloblasts'. **1911** W. K. Hunter *Rec. Adv. Hæmatol.* 30 Both the neutrophile and the eosinophile myelocyte are, according to Ehrlich, originally derived from a cell to which the name myeloblast has been given. **1961** *Lancet* 19 Aug. 434/2 The leucoerythroblastosis persisted, although granulocyte precursors, occasionally including myeloblasts, became more numerous than the nucleated red cells in the peripheral blood. **1968** Passmore & Robson *Compan. Med. Studies* I. xxvi. 11/2 After birth, the production of the granulocytic white cells takes place only in the red marrow. .. The first stage of development is the myeloblast.

So **myeloˈblastic** *a.*, of, pertaining to, or involving myeloblasts; **ˌmyeloblaˈstosis** [-osis], the condition of having large numbers of myeloblasts in the bone marrow and circulating blood.

1916 L. F. Barker *Monographic Med.* III. 214 The cells of these myeloblastic proliferations. **1924** *Jrnl. Exper. Med.* XL. 845 (*heading*) Studies on the maturation of myeloblasts into myelocytes and on amitotic cell division in the peripheral blood in subacute myeloblastic leucemia. **1937** Kracke & Garver *Dis. Blood* v. 65 A true myeloblastosis, in which the myeloblast is the predominant cell type in both the bone marrow and peripheral blood, occurs only in the terminal, exacerbation stage of chronic myelosis and in acute myeloblastic leukemia. **1938** H. Downey *Handbk. Hematol.* III. xxv. 2014 They [*sc.* the cells] are clearly of the myeloblastic type. **1965** *New Scientist* 17 June 800/2 The three main leukaemias of poultry—lymphomatosis, erythroblastosis and myeloblastosis—are caused by filterable transmissible agents. **1974** Passmore & Robson *Compan. Med. Studies* III. xxi. 62/1 (*table*) Acute myeloblastic leukaemia.

myelocele (ˈmaɪələʊsiːl). Also (erron.) -cœle. [f. myelo- + Gr. κήλη tumour, *esp.* rupture, hernia.] **1.** *Path.* **a.** = myelomeningocele. **b.** Spina bifida in which tissue of the spinal cord lies exposed over part of its length, without protrusion as a swelling; an area of neural tissue so exposed.

1875 Jones & Sieveking *Path. Anat.* (ed. 2) xii. 290 The protruded sac contains some portion of the spinal cord itself, forming the so-called myelocele. **1922** *Brain* XLV. 44 Myelocele... Here.. segments of the medullary folds have remained open and the neural ectoderm lies exposed on the surface of the body as a ribbon of delicate tissue down the mid-dorsal line. **1924** J. A. Foote *Dis. New-Born* x. 140 Myelocele, or meningo-myelocele, is the name given to the tumor when the spinal cord itself is concerned in the embryonic fissure. **1952** J. E. Morison *Foetal & Neonatal Path.* xiv. 247 Especially when the tissues are infected a myelocoele may be incorrectly described as a myelomeningocoele. **1963** [see myelomeningocele]. **1974** Passmore & Robson *Compan. Med. Stud.* III. xxxvi. 9/2 The [spinal] cord may be fully exposed, usually for a length of several segments without any covering from the dura mater, forming a myelocoele.

2. *Anat.* Var. of myelocœle.

myelocœle (ˈmaɪələʊsiːl). Also -cele, -cœl. [f. myelo- + -*cœle* (f. Gr. κοιλία cavity of the body: cf. cœlo-¹).] **1.** *Anat.* The central canal of the spinal cord.

1885 B. G. Wilder in *N.Y. Med. Jrnl.* 21 Mar. 326/2 (*caption*) Schematic representation of the cavities of the brain and myelon... Encephalocoele. Myelocoele. Neurocoele. **1896** —— in *Jrnl. Compar. Neurol.* VI. 318 (*table*) Myelocele. **1940** *Chambers's Techn. Dict.* 566/1 *Myelocoel,* the central canal of the spinal cord. **1972** T. W. Jenkins *Funct. Mammalian Neuroanat.* ii. 15/1 The lumen of this division (metacoele) joins the myelocoele without any line of demarcation so that both form the fourth ventricle.

2. *Path.* Var. of myelocele.

myelocyte (ˈmaɪələʊsaɪt). [f. myelo- + -cyte.] **1.** The nucleus of a ganglionic nerve-cell.

1866 A. Flint *Princ. Med.* 51 *Myeolocytes* [sic], or cells found in the substance of the brain, the spinal cord, and in one of the beds of the retina. **1889** *Nature* 21 Nov. 72/1 The nervous elements termed myelocytes.

2. A cell generally confined to the bone marrow (appearing in the circulating blood only in pathological states) which is smaller than the myeloblast from which it derives, which when mature has neutrophil, eosinophil, and basophil cytoplasmic granules, and which is the precursor of the polymorphonuclear leucocyte of the circulating blood.

1891 *Johns Hopkins Hosp. Bull.* II. 87/1 These elements seem never to acquire the power of amoeboid movement which the polynuclear cells possess. They appear to arise in the marrow and have been called by Ehrlich 'myelocytes'. **1911** [see myeloblast]. **1962** *Gray's Anat.* (ed. 33) 65 Myeloblasts divide and give rise to smaller cells, the myelocytes. **1968** Passmore & Robson *Compan. Med. Studies* I. xxvi. 12/1 The myelocyte is a smaller cell with a round nucleus.

So **myeloˈcytic** *a.*, of, pertaining to, or involving myelocytes.

1896 *Boston Med. & Surg. Jrnl.* 2 Jan. 6/1 The shape of the myelocytic nucleus.. is generally to be contrasted with that of the 'polynuclear' cell. **1972** *Science* 20 Oct. 304/1 Tumor cells derived from patients with both acute lymphocytic and acute myelocytic leukemia.

myelogenetic (ˌmaɪələʊdʒɪˈnɛtɪk), *a.* [f. myelo- + genetic *a.*] Concerned with the development of the spinal cord.

1900 *Lancet* 18 Aug. 529/1 The myelogenetic method which investigated the details of the central fibres by tracing the history of their development.

myelogenic (ˌmaɪələʊˈdʒɛnɪk), *a.* [f. myelo- + -genic.] Derived from or originating in the bone marrow. Also **myeˈlogenous** *a.*

1875 C. H. Jones & Siev. *Pathol. Anat.* ii. 74 The form [of leuchæmia] which arises from an affection of the osseous medulla.. has been called the myelogenous by Neumann. **1876** tr. *Wagner's Gen. Pathol.* 515 A myelogenic cystosarcoma myxomatodes of the bones of the head. **1904** *Brit. Med. Jrnl.* 10 Sept. 605 Myelogenous leukæmia is rare.

myelogram (ˈmaɪələʊgræm). *Med.* [f. myelo- + -gram.] **1.** A radiograph obtained by myelography.

1937 *Arch. Neurol. & Psychiatry* (Chicago) XXXVIII. 1126 The method of injection of air and the roentgen technic are discussed and five air myelograms shown. **1942** *Surg., Gynecol. & Obstetr.* LXXV. 735/2 The myelogram.. demonstrated a tumor which had invaded the upper thoracic subarachnoid space. **1974** *Daily Colonist* (Victoria, B.C.) 19 Sept. 2/1, I had a whiplash and am being told a myelogram is the only way to determine if I have a ruptured disc.

2. (A list of) the proportions of the various cells in a sample of bone marrow.

1940 *Biol. Abstr.* XIV. 1635/1 Sternal puncture may also aid in diagnosis through modifications of the myelogram. **1949** *Jrnl. Clin. Path.* II. 8/1 Most workers perform differential counts on marrow films, and by presenting the data in the form of a 'myelogram' express the incidence of the various cell types as percentages. **1956** E. Ponder tr. *M. Bessis's Cytol. Blood & Blood-Forming Organs* vii. 172 Some include megakaryocytes in the myelogram, while others do not.

myelography (maɪəˈlɒgrəfɪ). *Med.* [f. myelo- + -graphy.] Radiography of the spinal chord after injection of a contrast medium (often air) into the subarachnoid space.

1937 *Arch. Neurol. & Psychiatry* (Chicago) XXXVIII. 1126 This report is based on 10 cases of lesions of the spinal canal in which the level of the block was found by air myelography. **1943** *Amer. Jrnl. Med. Sci.* CCVI. 691 If.. a protruded intervertebral disk in the lumbar region is suspected air myelography should be used. **1969** N. A. Lewtas in D. Sutton *Textbk. Radiol.* lxiii. 1134/2 Myelography of spinal tumours is best performed as a pre-operative examination.

Hence **myeloˈgraphic** *a.*, observed using myelography; **myeloˈgraphically** *adv.*, by myelography.

1940 H. K. Pancoast et al. *Head & Neck in Roentgen Diagnosis* xii. 892 If there is a difference in the localization of tumors by neurologic and myelographic findings, the possibility of multiple tumors occurring within the spinal chord should be considered. **1950** *Med. Radiogr. & Photogr.* XXVI. 27 To demonstrate myelographically the lesions.., 6 cubic centimeters of *Pantopaque* were injected into the lumbar subarachnoid space. **1957** *Trans. Amer. Neurol. Assoc.* LXXXI. 171 (*heading*) Myelographically demonstrated cervical intervertebral discs, co-existing with tumors. **1969** N. A. Lewtas in D. Sutton *Textbk. Radiol.* lxiii. 1142/1 There are four principal myelographic signs of disc prolapse.

myeloid (ˈmaɪələɪd), *a.* [f. Gr. μυελ-ός marrow + -oid.] Resembling marrow, as ***myeloid tumour***; of or pertaining to marrow, as ***myeloid cell.*** Also, of, pertaining to, or involving myeloid cells.

1857 *Trans. Path. Soc. Lond.* VIII. 346 Large Myeloid Tumour in the Head of the Humerus. **1875** C. H. Jones & Siev. *Pathol. Anat.* 320 The myeloid cells or 'myeloplaxes' of bone. **1887** *Brit. Med. Jrnl.* 26 Feb. 458/1 A myeloid sarcoma growing from the centre of the first metatarsal bone. **1927, 1961** [see erythroid *a.* 2]. **1966** Wright & Symmers *Systemic Path.* I. iv. 179/2 Leukaemias may arise from any of the stem cells of the leucopoietic series, and the three most frequent types may be classified as myeloid, lymphatic and monocytic. **1971** *Brit. Med. Bull.* XXVII. 66/1 Leukaemia, in the acute and in the chronic myeloid forms, is the type of malignancy which is most frequently induced by whole-body exposures of several hundred rads.

myeloma (maɪəˈləʊmə). *Path.* Pl. **-omas, -omata.** [f. myel(o- + -oma.] A tumour composed of bone-marrow cells (see quots.); *spec.* (*a*) (the tumour found in) myelomatosis; (*b*) a giant-cell sarcoma.

1857 Mayne *Expos. Lex.* 736/1 *Myeloma,* term for a medullary tumour or enlargement. **1894** *Med. News* (Philadelphia) LXV. 239/1 (*heading*) Myeloma: report of a case. **1900** Dorland *Med. Dict.* 419/2 *Myeloma,* (1) any medullary tumor; (2) giant-cell sarcoma; (3) a slow-growing tumor of a tendinous sheath containing myeloplaxes. **1902** *Encycl. Medica* XII. 449 Myelomata are rare tumours after the age of twenty-five. **1914** *Lancet* 28 Nov. 1236/2 This large class [*sc.* giant-cell sarcoma] is made up of two groups of cases: (1) the myeloid sarcomata, myelomata of some authors; and (2) the malignant giant-cell sarcomata. **1922** J. Ewing *Neoplastic Dis.* (ed. 2) xviii. 256 Giant-cell sarcoma of tendon sheaths and aponeuroses.—The specific structure and benign clinical course of a group of giant-cell sarcomas of tendon sheaths of the hand and feet have long been recognized. They have been fully described, especially by French observers, under the terms 'myeloma' or 'xanthosarcoma' (Gross, Paquet, Reverdin, Heurteaux, Spiess, Lit.). **1948** R. A. Willis *Path. Tumours* xliii. 680 The changing views regarding the nature of this tumour [*sc.*

osteoclastoma or giant-cell tumour of bone] have resulted in a diverse and confusing terminology—'myeloma', 'myeloid sarcoma', 'tumeur à myéloplaxes', 'benign giant-cell tumour', 'osteoclastoma', and 'chronic (non-suppurative) hemorrhagic osteomyelitis', being only some of the names applied to it. 'Myeloma' and 'myeloid' should be discarded, for the tumours are unrelated to the haemopoietic tumours of bone marrow, and in particular are quite distinct from the lesions of myelomatosis. **1966** WRIGHT & SYMMERS *Systemic Path.* I. iv. 185/2 Sometimes myelomas produce extramedullary masses in the viscera. **1967** *New Scientist* 4 May 276/3 The other source of information..about antibody structure has been the discovery of diseases, called myelomas, in which molecules, chemically similar to the immune globulins but without known antibody activity, are produced in the blood of patients suffering from a cancer-like proliferation of cells in the bone marrow and bloodstream. **1970** PASSMORE & ROBSON *Compan. Med. Stud.* II. xxviii. 4/2 An important tumour affecting the bone marrow is the plasma cell myeloma (myelomatosis or multiple myeloma). In this disease the bone marrow becomes packed with plasma cells.

myelomatosis (ˌmaɪələʊməˈtəʊsɪs). *Path.* [f. *myelomat-* (taken as stem of MYELOMA) + -OSIS.] A malignant proliferation of plasma cells causing numerous accumulations of them to form in the bone marrow and abnormal proteins to be present in the blood and urine.

1904 *Jrnl. Path. & Bacteriol.* IX. 173 At the necropsy the bone marrow of all the bones examined was found to be more or less affected by a diffuse sarcoma-like growth of rounded or polyhedral mononuclear cells—a form of 'multiple myeloma' or 'myelomatosis'. **1906** *Jrnl. Amer. Med. Assoc.* 16 June 1893/2 Hoffmann defines myelomatosis as the multiple development of malignant tumors in the bone marrow, originating in hyperplasia of one of the cellular elements of the mother soil [*sic:* ? *read* cell] (lymphocyte, myelocyte, plasma cell). **1961** *Lancet* 16 Sept. 639/2 Neither in myelomatosis in man nor in any of the plasmacytomas of mice..do we ever regularly observe a direct Coombs test or signs of hæmolytic anæmia. **1966** WRIGHT & SYMMERS *Systemic Path.* II. xxxix. 1419/2 Myelomatosis or multiple myeloma is a neoplastic condition originating from the bone marrow.

myelomeningocele (ˌmaɪələʊmiːˈnɪŋgəʊsiːl). *Path.* Also (erron.) -cœle. [f. MYELO- + *meningocele* s.v. MENINGO-.] Spina bifida in which tissue of the spinal cord and its investing membranes (the meninges) protrudes through the cleft, forming a rounded swelling of the skin usu. slightly above the base of the spine; the tissue so protruding. Also called *meningomyelocele*; cf. MYELOCELE.

1889 *Buck's Handbk. Med. Sci.* VIII. 471/2 In myelomeningocele the external wall of the sac consists not of dura mater but of pia mater turned inside out. **1924, 1952** [see MYELOCELE 1]. **1963** *Cecil-Loeb Textbk. Med.* (ed. 11) 1581/1 Myelocele involves a lesser defect of the meninges [than meningocele] with exposure of the spinal cord, but without cystic protrusion. Myelomeningocele is characterized by an incorporation of the spinal nerve roots and cord in the sac of a meningocele. **1974** PASSMORE & ROBSON *Compan. Med. Stud.* III. xxxvi. 9/2 There may be a developmental failure of the spinal cord and then the flat neural plate with its exposed central canal is liable to be involved with the sac and form a myelomeningocoele.

‖**myelon** (ˈmaɪəlɒn). *Anat.* [a. Gr. μυελόν, late var. of μυελός marrow.] Owen's name for the spinal cord. Hence **ˈmyelonal, myeˈlonic** *adjs.*

1846 OWEN *Lect. Anat. Vertebrate Anim.* I. *Fishes* 172 This part is called the 'brain' or encephalon: the rest of the axis I term the 'myelon'. *Ibid.* 174 At the bottom of the ventricle the myelonal canal is exposed. **1883** E. R. LANKESTER in *Encycl. Brit.* XVI. 680/2 The retina of the Molluscan cephalic eye,..unlike that of the Vertebrate myelonic eye, is essentially a modified area of the general epiderm.

myelosis (maɪəˈləʊsɪs). *Path.* Pl. **myeloses.** [f. MYEL(O- + -OSIS.] **1.** The formation of a tumour of the spinal cord.

1891 in *Syd. Soc. Lex.* **1900** in DORLAND *Med. Dict.*

2. The proliferation of blood-cell precursors in the bone marrow.

1916 L. F. BARKER *Monographic Med.* III. 213 (*heading*) Acute myeloid leukemia. (Acute leukemic myelosis.) **1922** V. ELLERMANN *Leucosis Fowls* i. 9 Schnidde's shorter and correcter words, myelosis and lymphadenosis, are now used in several text-books. **1952** *Blood* VII. 767 The term erythremic myelosis is used to indicate the parallelism with the leukemic myeloses. **1974** PASSMORE & ROBSON *Compan. Med. Stud.* III. xxi. 72/2 Pure erythraemic myelosis, di Guglielmo's syndrome, is rare, and is characterized by intense and bizarre proliferation of red cell precursors, which escape into the peripheral blood. *Ibid.* 73/1 Megakaryocytic myelosis is probably a variant of chronic myeloid leukaemia, as the clinical picture, course and prognosis are similar, and it usually terminates with definite evidence of myeloid leukaemia.

myere, obs. f. MERE, MIRE; var. MYOUR.

myery, obs. f. MIRY.

myes(se, obs. pl. MOUSE.

‖**mygale** (ˈmɪgəliː). Also 4 migale, mygal. [late L., a. Gr. μῡγαλῆ.]

1. The shrew-mouse.

1382 WYCLIF *Lev.* xi. 30 A mygal [Vulg. *mygale*], that is a beeste born trecherows to bigile, and moost gloterous. **1398** TREVISA *Barth. De P.R.* XVIII. lxxiv. (Bodl. MS.), The firette hatte Migale and is a litel beste as it were a wesel. **1828** SIR J. G. WILKINSON *Mat. Hierogl.* [13] The sacred animal of Buto is said to have been the mygale or shrew-mouse.

2. *Zool.* A genus of large hairy spiders of America; a spider of this genus, *e.g.* the bird-spider (*M. avicularia*). [Named by Latreille 1802.]

1834 *Cuvier's Anim. Kingd.* III. 287 This Mygale—*Aranea avicularia*..—is about an inch and a half long. **1843** OWEN *Lect. Anat. Invertebrate Anim.* I. 255 In the Mygale a third ganglion of very small size is formed. **1890** *Daily News* 20 Sept. 5/4 The huge Brazilian mygale.

Hence **ˈmygaloid** *a.*, belonging to the genus *Mygale* or family *Mygalidæ*.

1893 MINCHIN in *Nat. Sci.* III. 123 A large mygaloid spider.

myg(h)e, myghele, -ell, obs. ff. MIDGE, MICHAEL.

myȝt(e, myght(e: see MID, MIGHT, MITE.

mygnyon, mygrame, -eym, -ime, obs. ff. MINION, MEGRIM.

mygth, myhel, myhth: see MIGHT, MICHAEL.

myiasis (maɪˈeɪsɪs). *Path.* Also **myasis.** [mod.L., f. Gr. μυῖα fly + -ASIS.] Injury inflicted by dipterous larvæ on the human body.

1837 F. W. HOPE in *Trans. Entom. Soc.* (1839) II. 259 The genera producing *Myasis*, or fly-disease. **1899** SHARP in *Camb. Nat. Hist., Insects* II. 512 The various attacks of Dipterous larvæ on man have received the general name of 'myiasis'. **1904** *Brit. Med. Jrnl.* 17 Dec. 1641 Dr. J. W. Stephens showed the larvae and flies of myiasis.

myilde, myir, myis, myist, myit: see MILD, MIRE, MOUSE, MIST, MITE.

Mykames, myke, mykel, -il(l, obs. ff. MICHAELMAS, MEEK, MICKLE.

mykkis, Sc. pl. of MICHE *sb.*[2] *Obs.*

mykkylle, mykle, mykul, -yl(l, obs. ff. MICKLE.

mykylmes, obs. f. MICHAELMAS.

Mylar (ˈmaɪlɑː(r)). Also **mylar.** A proprietary name for a polyester which is the condensation product of ethylene glycol and terephthalic acid and is used in the form of films having high strength and heat resistance.

1954 *Trade Marks Jrnl.* 3 Nov. 1110/1 Mylar... Non-mouldable plastics in the form of films for use as a substitute for glass; and electrical insulating materials. E. I. Du Pont de Nemours and Company.., Wilmington, State of Delaware, United States of America; manufacturers. **1962** *New Scientist* 5 Apr. 796/2 A self-inflating balloon made of aluminized mylar was launched in August, 1960. **1966** *McGraw-Hill Encycl. Sci. & Technol.* VIII. 38/1 The tape used in magnetic recording consists of a plastic base with a coating of magnetic oxide. The base material of Mylar or cellulose acetate varies in thickness from 0·0007 to 0·0015 in. **1973** *Daily Colonist* (Victoria, B.C.) 16 May 1/3 Another possibility..is for astronauts to envelop the spaceship with a giant sheet of mylar, an insulating material.

mylded: see MILE *v.*

myldrop, obs. f. MELDROP *Sc.*

myle: see MIL, MILE, MOIL.

myleed: see MILE *v.*

Myleran (ˈmaɪləræn). *Pharm.* A proprietary name for 1,4-di(methanesulphonyloxy)butane, $C_6H_4O_6S_2$, which is a cytotoxic agent with a selective action on bone marrow and is used in the treatment of myeloid leukæmia.

1952 *Trade Marks Jrnl.* 12 Nov. 1049/1 Myleran... The Wellcome Foundation Limited, .. London, .. manufacturing chemists. **1953** *Lancet* 31 Jan. 207/2 'Myleran'..showed an intense inhibitory effect on the growth of the Walker rat carcinoma 256. **1959** *Progr. Hematol.* II. 227 With Myleran,..the margin between the therapeutic dose and the toxic dose, producing irreversible aplastic change in the bone marrow, is relatively narrow. **1968** *Internat. Pharmacol. Abstr.* V. 1509 A 26-year-old woman had to be treated with busulphan (Myleran), 2–8 mg. daily during the first to sixth and 19–30th weeks of pregnancy because of chronic myeloid leukemia.

myles, -ies, var. MILDS.

mylie, obs. f. MILE *sb.*[2]

myliobatid (mɪlɪˈɒbətɪd). *Zool.* [ad. mod.L. *Myliobatidæ*, f. Gr. μυλίας millstone + βατίς skate.] A fish of the family *Myliobatidæ* (eagle-rays).

1859–62 RICHARDSON, etc. *Mus. Nat. Hist.* II. 168/1.

†**myll.** *Obs.* [Related to MILE *v.*] ? A stripe or orphrey.

a **1500** in *Archæol.* LII. 213 The blew myllys do serve for boyth the vygylles of seynt Edward synglarly. **1540** *Invent.* in *Trans. Lond. & Mdsx. Archæol. Soc.* IV. 329, ij tuncyles without stolles and phanams of blewe velvett enbrotheryd with anteloppes and mylles of gold.

myll-: see MIL(L-.

myllan, obs. f. MILAN[1]; var. MILAN[2] *Obs.*

myllaner, etc., obs. ff. MILLINER *sb.*

mylle, obs. f. MILE *sb.*[1]

myllen, obs. ff. MILAN[1], MILL *sb.*[1]

myllewell, var. MULVEL.

mylleyn, obs. f. MILAN[1].

myllin soole: see MILLENSOLE.

myllyant, obs. f. MILLION.

myln(e, obs. ff. MILL *sb.*

mylnar, -er(e, obs. ff. MILLER[1].

mylnard, obs. f. MILLWARD.

‖**mylodon** (ˈmaɪlədɒn). [mod.L., f. Gr. μύλη, μύλο-ς mill, millstone, molar + ὀδοντ-, ὀδούς tooth.] A genus of gigantic extinct sloths from the Pleistocene, having teeth more or less cylindrical; an animal of this genus. So **mylodont** (ˈmaɪlədɒnt); also used *adj.* = belonging to the genus *Mylodon*.

1839 *Penny Cycl.* XV. 70/1 Mylodon (Owen). A genus of Edentate Megatherioids. **1840** OWEN in *Zool. Voy. Beagle* I. 72 The Mylodon..holds an intermediate place between the Ai and the great Armadillo. **1850** KINGSLEY *Alton Locke* xxxvi, A mylodon among South American forests. **1899** *Nat. Sci.* XIV. 266 Mylodonts were known to have been contemporaneous with man in other parts of Argentina farther north. *Ibid.* 267 The claw is of a mylodont..type.

†**ˈmyloglosse,** *a. Obs.* In 7 *erron.* myleo-. [ad. mod.L. *myloglōss-us*: see next.]

1669 HOLDER *Elem. Speech* 49 The Tongue being held in that posture onely by the force of the Geneoglosse or Myleoglosse Muscles.

‖**myloglossus** (maɪləʊˈglɒsəs). *Anat.* [mod.L. *myloglōssus* (sc. *musculus*), f. Gr. μύλη, μύλο-ς millstone, molar + γλῶσσα tongue.] A muscular slip accessory to the styloglossus, passing from the angle of the jaw to the tongue.

[**1693** tr. *Blancard's Phys. Dict.* (ed. 2), *Myloglossum.*] **1756** *Winslow's Anat. Hum. Body* II. 339 The Mylo-Glossi are small fleshy Planes situated transversely, one on each side, between the Ramus of the lower Jaw, and the Basis of the Tongue. **1843** WILKINSON tr. *Swedenborg's Anim. Kingd.* I. i. 19 The mylo-glossus of some authors is a part of the mylo-hyoideus.

mylohyoid (maɪləʊˈhaɪɔɪd), *a.* and *sb.* (Earlier in L. form ‖**mylohyoideus.**) [ad. mod.L. *mylohyoīdeus* (Riolanus), f. Gr. μύλη, -ος (see prec.) + ὑοειδής HYOID.] **a.** *adj.* Connected with the lower jaw and the hyoid bone; esp. ***mylohyoid muscle***, a flat triangular muscle forming a large part of the muscular floor of the mouth. Also **mylohyoiˈdean** *a.* **b.** *sb.* The mylohyoid muscle.

1694 W. COWPER *Myotomia Ref.* 76 *Mylohyoideus.* Though Falloppius and his Followers make this a Pair of Muscles, It seems not to be divisible without apparent Violence. **1804** ABERNETHY *Surg. Obs.* (1827) 35 The mylohyoideus muscle. **1838** W. J. E. WILSON *Anat. Vade M.* 220 The Inferior dental nerve..gives off but one branch, the mylo-hyoidean. *Ibid.*, The external surface of the mylo-hyoid muscle. **1840** OWEN in *Zool. Voy. Beagle* I. 72 The mylo-hyoid ridge. **1843** WILKINSON tr. *Swedenborg's Anim. Kingd.* I. i. 20 The mylo-hyoideus arises broad but thin from the base of the lower jaw. **1866** *Proc. R. Irish Acad.* IX. 460 Inseparably connected to the mylohyoid of its own side. **1891** *Syd. Soc. Lex., Mylohyoïdean ridge.*

mylonite (ˈmaɪlənaɪt). *Geol.* [f. Gr. μυλών mill + -ITE.] A siliceous schist resulting from the crushing of quartzose rocks. Hence **myloˈnitic** *a.*, **ˈmylonized** *ppl. a.*, applied to such rocks; **ˌmylonitiˈzation, myloniˈzation,** the formation of mylonite; **ˈmylonitize** *v. trans.*, to convert into mylonite; **ˈmylonitized** *ppl. a.* = MYLONIZED *ppl. a.*

1886 *Rep. Brit. Assoc.* 1026 The gneisses and pegmatites ..are crushed, dragged, and ground out into a finely laminated schist (mylonite). **1888** HATCH *Gloss.* in Teall *Brit. Petrogr.* 440 *Mylonitic.* **1901** *Nature* 19 Sept. 513/1 All these mylonised rocks show a characteristic striping on the divisional planes. **1910** *Trans. Edin. Geol. Soc.* IX. Spec. Part 'The Thrust-Masses in the Western District of the Dolomites' i. 18 The actual shear-plane is occupied by a finely mylonitized, greenish tuffoid material. *Ibid.* 19 The rock material immediately below the inturned ends is Porphyrite finely mylonitized into a tuff. **1913** B. N. PEACH et al. *Geol. Central Ross-shire* (Mem. Geol. Surv. Scot.) iii. 13 It would appear that the mylonisation of the gneiss is probably due to the passage over it of the great mass of rock brought forward by the Moine thrust-plane. *Ibid.* 112/2 (Index), Mylonitisation. **1926** H. H. READ et al. *Geol. Strath Oykell & Lower Loch Shin* (Mem. Geol. Surv. Scot.) iii. 24 The intrusion is truncated by thrust-planes, and its rocks show evidence of shattering and mylonisation. **1956** E. W. HEINRICH *Microsc. Petrogr.* vii. 187 Such rocks as gabbros and peridotites may also be mylonitized. **1970** *New Scientist* 7 May 275/2 The rocks are crushed, smashed and sheared into an extremely fine grained powder, in a process called mylonization. **1971** *Scott. Jrnl. Geol.* VII. 311 At the western edge of the Moine Nappe mylonitization is the earliest recognizable tectonic event..and involves Cambrian rocks.

mylse, var. MILCE.

mylt(e: see MELT *v.*

myluel, -well, var. MULVEL.

mylvart, obs. f. MILLWARD.

mylyng: see MILE *v.*

mylyon, obs. f. MELON.

myn: see MIN, MINE.

myna: see MINA.

mynace, -asse, obs. ff. MENACE *v.*

mynah, -eh, var. MINA².

mynament, obs. f. MUNIMENT.

mynd(e, obs. Sc. ff. MINE *sb.*¹

mynde, var. pa. pple. MENG *v.*

myndoure, obs. Sc. f. MINER.

myne: see MIN, MINE.

mynekin: see MINCHEN.

Mynerfe, -erff, -erve, obs. ff. MINERVA.

mynes(ch, essh, obs. ff. MINISH.

my-ness. *nonce-wd.* Self-centredness.

1662 J. Chandler *Van Helmont's Oriat.* To Rdr., It comprehends all things, which man in his Own-ness, Selfish-ness and My-ness,..cannot understand.

mynewe, variant of MING *v. Obs.*

† **myne-ye-ple.** *Obs.* [Of obscure origin and meaning. Prof. Skeat has suggested derivation from OF. *manople* gauntlet.]

14.. *Chevy Chase* 62 (MS. Ashm. 48, lf. 16 b) Thorowe ryche male and myne ye ple many sterne yᵉ strocke done streght. **14..** *Eger & Grime* 1025 (Percy fol.), Through rich many & myny plee the red blood blemished both their blee. [*Bp. Percy's note*: It shd be Mail & many plie. See Reliques, vol. I. pag. 10, ver. 21 & Glos.].

myng(e, variant forms of MENG *v.*

‖ **mynheer** (maɪnˈhɛːr, məˈnɛːr). Also 7 **mynhere, menheir**, 7–8 **minheer**, 8 **miin heer**, 9 **mynher**, 9– (*S.Afr.*) **meneer**. [Du. *mijnheer*, Afrikaans *meneer*, f. *mijn* my + *heer* lord, master (see HER *sb.*).] The courteous form of address or title of courtesy corresponding in Dutch to 'sir', 'Mr.'; hence, a Dutchman, an Afrikaaner.

1652 in *Nicholas Papers* (Camden 1886) 308 Myn Heer Capel. **1654** Gayton *Pleas. Notes* 236 True Myn-here (quoth Steepen Malten) we shall not heare of this againe. **1678** J. Phillips tr. *Tavernier's Trav.* II. I. vii. 49 Menheir Velant, chief of the Holland-Factory at Agra. **1701** C. Wooley *Jrnl. New York* (1860) 58 Frederick Philips, the richest Miin Heer in that place. **1711** *Spectator* No. 5 ⁋5 He afterwards proceeds to call Minheer Hendel, the Orpheus of our Age. **1782** Cowper *To Lady Austen* (12 Aug.), 'Tis thus I spend my moments here, And wish myself a Dutch mynheer. **1886** *All Year Round* 14 Aug. 35 Mynheer, as clever at a trick as a Yank or a Jap. **1939** S. Cloete *Watch for Dawn* i. 5 What are these questions that you torment me with, meneer? **1946** *Cape Times* 16 Nov. 4 Meneer is a strange man. **1948** *Cape Argus* 9 Aug. 9/5 The meneer found those spoons... Mr. Erlank swung back to the constable. 'Did you find spoons there?' he asked. **1970** G. Croudace *Scarlet Bikini* vii. 79 I'm listening, *meneer*.

transf. **1819** Scott *Ivanhoe* i, Mynheer Calf, too, becomes Monsieur de Veau.

Hence **myn'heerify** *v. nonce-wd.*, to study Dutch.

1804 Southey *Let. to Lieut. Southey* 12 Sept., I am learning Dutch, and wish you were here..to mynheerify with me.

myniment, obs. form of MUNIMENT.

mynye, variant of MING *v. Obs.*

myo- (ˈmaɪəʊ), combining f. Gr. *μῦς* (gen. *μυό-ς*) muscle, in many scientific terms (of which the most important will be found as Main words). **'myoblast** [-BLAST], a cell which gives rise to muscular elements; hence **myo'blastic** *a.* (in recent Dicts.); **myo'chemistry**, the chemistry of muscle; ‖**'myochrome** [Gr. *χρῶμα* colour], Thudichum's name for the colouring matter of red muscle (cf. *myohæmatin*); **myo'clonic** *a.* [cf. CLONIC], pertaining to or affected with myoclonus; ‖**my'oclonus** [Gr. *κλόνος* violent confused motion], convulsive action of the muscles; **'myocœl(e** [Gr. *κοῖλος* hollow], **myo'cœlom(e**, the cavity in the centre of a myotome in an early stage; hence **myocœ'lomic** *a.*; ‖**myo'comma** (*pl.* **-'commata, 'commas**) [Gr. *κόμμα* segment], one of the lateral flakes into which the muscular system of fishes and other lower vertebrates is divided; **'myocyte** [Gr. *κύτος* cell], a contractile fibre cell or layer in some sponges and protozoans; **'myodome** [Gr. *δόμος* house, chamber], a cavity in the skull of most teleostean fishes for the reception of the rectus muscles of the eye; **myody'namics** *sb. pl.*, that branch of science which treats of muscular contraction; **myodynami'ometer, -dyna'mometer**, an instrument for measuring muscular force; **myoepi'thelial** *a.*, (of an animal cell) having characters of both a muscular and an epithelial cell; so **myoepi'thelium**, a tissue composed of such cells; *spec.* the contractile cells outside the epithelium of some mammalian glands, e.g. in the breast; ‖**myofi'broma**, a tumour consisting of muscular and fibrous tissue; **myo'filament**, any of the elongated threads, revealed by the electron microscope, which are arranged side by side in bundles to form a myofibril and of which there are two kinds in an ordered arrangement, viz. thick filaments composed of myosin molecules and thin filaments composed of actin molecules; also, one of the related filaments of smooth muscle; **myo'genesis**, the formation of muscular tissue; **myo'genic, my'ogenous** *adjs.*, produced by or arising in the muscles; **myo'hæmatin**, MacMunn's name for the colouring matter of red muscle; **myohæmo'globin** *Biochem.* = MYOGLOBIN; **myo-inositol** (usu. with *myo-* in italics) (see INOSITOL); ‖**myo'lemma** [LEMMA²], a delicate membranous sheath enveloping each fibril of muscular tissue; ‖**myoli'poma**, a tumour containing adipose tissue and muscular tissue (*Syd. Soc. Lex.* 1891); **'myomere** [Gr. *μέρος* part], a myotome; hence **myo'meric** *a.*; **myo'metrium** *Anat.* [Gr. *μήτρα* womb], the muscular coat of the uterus, which forms the bulk of the wall of that organ and surrounds the endometrium; tissue from this muscular coat; so **myo'metrial** *a.*; **'myoneme** *Biol.* [Gr. *νῆμα* thread], any of the minute contractile filaments found in the cytoplasm of many protozoa; **myo'neural** *a. Physiol.*, neuromuscular; having characteristics of both muscular and nervous tissue; **my'onymy** [Gr. *-ωνυμία, ὄνομα* name], nomenclature of muscles; **'myophan(e** *a.* [Gr. *-φανής* appearing, *φαίνειν* to appear], having a striated appearance as of muscle; **'myophone** [Gr. *φωνή* sound], an adaptation of the microphone for measuring the sound of contracting muscles; **'myophore** [-PHORE], an apparatus for the attachment of muscles in certain mollusks; hence **my'ophorous** *a.* (in recent Dicts.); **myo'physical** *a.*, relating to myophysics; **myo'physics**, the physics of muscle, the science concerned with muscular action; **'myoplasm** *Anat.* [f. mod.L. *myoplasma* (coined in Ger. by P. Schiefferdecker 1905, in *Sitzungsber. d. niederrhein. Ges. f. Natur- und Heilkunde zu Bonn 1904* B. 90)], the cytoplasm or sarcoplasm of a muscle cell; hence **myo'plasmic** *a.*; **myo'polar** *a.*, relating to muscular polarity; **myosar'coma**, a tumour consisting partly of muscular and partly of sarcomatous tissue; hence **myosar'comatous** *a.* (in recent Dicts.); **myoscle'rotic** *a.*, involving hardening of the muscles; **'myoscope** [-SCOPE], an instrument for observing muscular contraction; **'myospasm**, ‖**myo'spasmus**, spasm or cramp of a muscle; **myo'tatic** *a. Physiol.* [Gr. *τατικ-ός* exerting tension (f. *τείνειν* to stretch)], applied to a muscular contraction (usu. a reflex) that occurs as a result of the stretching of the muscle; **'myotube** *Biol.* [ad. Sp. *myotubo* (J. F. Tello 1917, in *Trabajos d. Lab. de Investig. biol. de la Univ. de Madrid* XV. 122)], a cylindrical cell that develops from myoblasts during the formation of a muscle fibre (see quots. 1960, 1972).

1884 Hyatt in *Proc. Boston Soc. Nat. Hist.* 5 Mar. 121 The action of the lateral *myoblasts in moving an elongated vermiform animal. **1962** *Lancet* 1 Dec. 1165/1, I still wonder if two hours' instruction in pathological *myochemistry will help the candidate. **1968** *Nature* 2 Nov. 433/2 (*heading*) New myochemistry. **1872** Thudichum *Chem. Phys.* 37 A coloured albuminous matter, *myochrome, identical with hemato-crystalline. **1899** *Allbutt's Syst. Med.* VII. 889 The *myoclonic spasm may manifest itself in the weakness of overwork. **1883** in *Brain* VII. 569 Rhythmical *Myoclonus. **1889** E. R. Lankester in *Q. Jrnl. Microsc. Sci.* XXIX. 393 The fin-rays, the cavities of which are part of the *myocœl. *Ibid.* 377 The *myocœlomic pouches or intramuscular lymph-spaces of the head. **1846** Owen *Lect. Anat. Vertebrate Anim.* I. *Fishes* 164 The fibres of each *myocomma of the trunk run straight and nearly horizontally from one septum to the next. **1880** Günther *Fishes* 94 The aponeurotic septa between the myocommas. **1887** Sollas in *Encycl. Brit.* XXII. 419/2 Contractile fibre cells or *myocytes occur in all the higher sponges. **1888** *Amer. Naturalist* Apr. 358 [In mail-cheeked fishes] *Myodome undeveloped, the cranial cavity being closed in front. **1855** Dunglison *Med. Lex.*, *Myodynamics*, see Muscular contraction. **1861** *Syd. Soc. Year-bk. Med.* 30 The Myodynamics of the heart and blood-vessels. **1855** Dunglison *Med. Lex.*, *Dynamometer*, **Myodynamiometer*, **Myodynamometer*... An instrument contrived by M. Regnier. **1881** F. M. Balfour *Compar. Embryol.* II. 550 In all the Coelenterata, except the Ctenophora, the contractile elements of the body wall consist of filiform processes of ectodermal or entodermal epithelial cells. The elements provided with these processes, which were first discovered by Kleinenberg, are known as *myo-epithelial cells. **1904** *Nature* 3 Mar. 431/1 At certain stages complete continuity could be observed between motor nerve trunk and the protoplasmic body of the myoepithelial cell. **1973** R. P. Gould in G. H. Bourne *Structure & Function Muscle* (ed. 2) II. iv. 192 These are known as myoepithelial, basal, or basket cells, and they are able to act like smooth muscle cells and so aid movement of the secretion into the excretory ducts. **1892** F. P. Foster *Med. Dict.* IV. 2367/1 *Myo-epithelium. **1943** *Amer. Jrnl. Path.* XIX. 474 Myoepithelium can be demonstrated in the male breast of gynecomastia when the ducts are developed. **1961** L. Martin *Clinical Endocrinol.* (ed. 3) i. 16 The act of suckling appears to provoke a reflex secretion of oxytocin whereby the myoepithelium surrounding the alveoli of the breast is stimulated to contract and the milk ducts are simultaneously kept open. **1888** *Brit. Med. Jrnl.* 24 Nov. 1182 Uterine *Myofibroma. **1949** *Jrnl. Clin. Invest.* XXVIII. 770/1 (*heading*) *Myofilaments and myofibrils of cardiac muscle. **1970** *Nature* 11 Apr. 180/1 Two to eight cells in each complete transverse section contain what appear to be sparse myofilaments and probably represent degenerate muscle cells. **1973** *Hewer's Textbk. Histol.* (ed. 9) x. 119 Although the fibrous proteins actin and myosin can both be isolated from smooth muscle fibres it is not yet clear what their exact relationship is to the longitudinally orientated myofilaments observed in these cells. **1876** Dunglison *Med. Lex.*, *Paralysis*, **Myogenic*... Partial muscular paralysis dating from very early life. **1904** *Brit. Med. Jrnl.* 17 Sept. 682 Is conduction in the heart due to muscle or nerve —is it myogenic or neurogenic? **1891** *Syd. Soc. Lex.*, *Myogenesis. **1921** *Amer. Jrnl. Physiol.* LVIII. 182 (*heading*) Tension of differential growth as a stimulus to myogenesis. **1956** *Biol. Bull.* CXI. 303 This relationship prompted a re-examination of the situation in amphibian embryos, where it has been claimed that the notochord is essential to somitic myogenesis. **1974** *Nature* 10 May 106/1 In ways not anticipated, myogenesis has yoked in an uneasy alliance muscle biochemistry, molecular genetics and cell differentiation. **1885** *Proc. R. Soc.* XXXIX. 248 The name ..of *myohæmatin [is proposed] for the intrinsic pigment in striped muscle, which belongs to the same series [*sc.* that of histohæmatins]. **1924** *Myohemoglobin [see COPROPORPHYRIN]. **1934** M. Bodansky *Introd. Physical Chem.* (ed. 3) xviii. 608 Muscle hemoglobin (myohemoglobin, myoglobin) has been isolated in crystalline form. **1953** J. Hunt *Ascent of Everest* 274 Myohaemoglobin is an oxygen-carrying pigment similar to haemoglobin. **1951** H. G. Fletcher et al. in *Jrnl. Org. Chem.* XVI. 1241 It is suggested that, since the substance [sc. *meso*-inositol] was first discovered in muscle..and was at one time called 'muscle sugar', it is better called **myo*-inositol. **1965** *Adv. Biochem.* XXXIV. 85 As a degradation product of phytoglycolipid, a complex lipid found in a variety of seed phosphatides, 2-α-D-glucopyranosyl-*myo*-inositol was obtained. **1840** W. J. E. Wilson *Anat. Vade M.* 132 A number of ultimate fibrils enclosed in a delicate sheath or *myolema [*sic*]. **1899** *Allbutt's Syst. Med.* VI. 916 This [congenital lipoma] may be associated with spina bifida and sometimes contains striated muscle fibre (*myolipoma). **1887** Hubrecht in *Q. Jrnl. Microsc. Sci.* XXVII. 614 An arrangement in distinct *myomeres. **1889** *Athenæum* 12 Jan. 47/2 The *myomeric value of the gill-slits and of the nerves which fork over them. **1943** L. R. Wharton *Gynecology* xxxvii. 542 The prognosis in *myometrial sarcoma is poor. **1974** Passmore & Robson *Compan. Med. Stud.* III. xl. 16/2 Drugs used in labour should not depress myometrial contractility. **1900** Dorland *Med. Dict.* 421/1 **Myometrium*, the muscular substance of the uterus. **1907** *Practitioner* Dec. 792 The myometrium contained many thick-walled blood-vessels. **1956** *Nature* 10 Mar. 478/2 Progesterone..prevents..œstrogen-induced growth of the myometrium. **1965** *Science* 1 Oct. 67/2 Samples of myometrium were obtained from the uteri of five adult females undergoing hysterectomies. **1901** G. N. Calkins *Protozoa* ii. 38 The outside is covered by living membranes which may become complicated by the addition of muscular fibrils (*myonemes). **1973** E. Vivier in G. H. Bourne *Structure & Function Muscle* (ed. 2) II. iii. 182 The best characterized myonemes have chiefly been identified in ciliates, in which their structure recalls that of smooth muscle fibers of Metazoa cells. **1905** *Jrnl. Physiol.* XXXII. 436 But when plain muscle developes connection with sympathetic nerves it must at the *myoneural junction acquire a mechanism that can receive the nervous impulse. **1960** G. H. Bourne *Struct. & Function Muscle* I. ii. 48 It has been suggested that the iridial muscles are really myoneural elements rather than true smooth muscle cells. **1963** *Lancet* 19 Jan. 153/1 They also showed that the myoneural junction of a neonatal infant behaves in many respects like that of a patient with myasthenia gravis. **1885** Wilder in *Jrnl. Nerv. Dis.* XII. 271 A *myonymy which is..inapplicable to the same parts in many animals. **1880** Saville Kent *Infusoria* I. 58 The muscular or *myophan layer. **1889** Preece & Maier *Telephone* 467 Applied to a muscle, the same instrument [Boudet's microphone] becomes an excellent *myophone. It indicates the normal muscular sound. **1895** *Camb. Nat. Hist.* III. 274 In *Septifer* the anterior adductor muscle is carried on a sort of shelf or *myophore. **1891** *Syd. Soc. Lex.*, **Myophysical laws*, the laws governing muscular action. **1892** *Monist* II. 276 Myophysical and psycho-physical questions. **1881** G. S. Hall *German Culture* 221

Our conclusion is not likely to be affected by any solution of such..questions of *myophysics as the pre-existence of muscular currents. **1907** *Alienist & Neurologist* XXVIII. 58 The author [*sc.* Schiefferdecker] suggests a number of new terms. The indifferent protoplasm becomes '*myoplasm' as soon as the cell is plainly recognizable as a muscle cell. **1933** *Physiol. Rev.* XIII. 302 Since the myofibrils represent differentiation products of the original myoplasm, it would seem in accord with a more precise terminology to speak of intra- and interfibrillar sarcoplasm; or, perhaps even better, the protoplasm of the fibrils (sarcostyles) might be designated sarcoplasm, that of the interfibrillar regions myoplasm. **1952** *Jrnl. Physiol.* CXVIII. 348 The aim..was to measure the myoplasm resistance and the membrane resistance and capacity in Purkinje fibres of the mammalian heart. **1975** *Nature* 10 Jan. 97/2 The action potential on the surface membrane depolarises the T-system within the fibre, which in turn triggers the release of Ca^{2+} into the myoplasm from its internal storage site, the sarcoplasmic reticulum. **1970** T. TOMITA in E. Bülbring et al. *Smooth Muscle* vii. 207 The *myoplasmic resistance was measured by means of double micro-electrodes in one arm of a bridge circuit. **1975** *Nature* 10 Jan. 100/2 If the ionic current causing this presumed SR potential change was primarily carried by Ca^{2+} moving from one side of the SR to the other, it is interesting to note how much increase in total myoplasmic Ca^{2+} would correspond to a 135 mV potential change. **1888** *Amer. Jrnl. Psychol.* I. 185 Correcting for the movement of the indifference point along the *myopolar tract. **1891** *Syd. Soc. Lex.*, *Myopolar*, a term applied to the direction of the electric current in electrotonic experiments when the nerve is stimulated between the electronising electrodes and the muscle. **1876** tr. *Wagner's Gen. Pathol.* 420 Rhabdomyoma, *myoma striocellulare*, *myosarcoma, true myoma. **1873** A. FLINT *Princ. Med.* 720 Pseudo-Hypertrophic, or *Myo-sclerotic, Paralysis. **1876–7** *S. Kens. Mus. Catal. Sci. App.* No. 3803 Double *Myoscope for the examination and demonstration of the laws of muscular contraction. **1856** MAYNE *Expos. Lex.*, *Myospasmus*,..a *myospasm. **1881** W. R. GOWERS *Epilepsy*, etc. 100 The *myotatic irritability of the muscles is lost. **1881** —— *Diagn. Dis. Spinal Cord* (ed. 2) ii. 29 It seems..desirable to discard the term 'tendon-reflex' altogether... They may be termed 'tendon-muscular phenomena', but the intervention of tendons is not necessary for their production; the one condition which all have in common is that passive tension is essential for their occurrence, and they may more accurately be termed myotatic contractions. **1924** LIDDELL & SHERRINGTON in *Proc. R. Soc.* B. XCVI. 240 Gowers, in 1881, proposed for the 'tendon-phenomena', then not commonly accepted as reflex, the term 'myotatic contractions'... His suggested adjective would suitably apply to the reflexes brought forward in this paper... Myotatic reflexes could embrace stretch-reflexes in general, including 'jerk' and 'clonus', which we regard as fractional forms of the complete and fully functional myotatic reflex. **1972** J. A. WILSON *Princ. Animal Physiol.* xi. 438/1 The peak of reflex tension in a myotatic reflex occurs at the time of completion of the stretch movement. *Ibid.* 438/2 When the foot of a spinal dog is raised so that the leg is flexed, the leg muscles respond with an extensor thrust—a myotatic reflex. **1933** M. FERNÁN-NÚÑEZ tr. *S. Ramón-Cajal's Histology* xvi. 280 The periphery of the cells exhibits a striated cortex, which goes on successively enlarging. In the axis resides a string of nuclei, as well as an undifferentiated protoplasmic cord (*D*); the ensemble finally represents tubes of contractile material filled with the protoplasm and nuclei (*myotubes of Tello). **1960** L. PICKEN *Organization of Cells* vii. 295 By the fourth day of incubation, the multinucleate coenocytic cells (derived from the spindle-shaped, uninucleate myoblasts) have developed a peripheral layer of myofibrils, embedded in sarcoplasm, and a linear series of nuclei occupying the cell axis. These cylindrical cells are conveniently distinguished as a particular stage in the development of the muscle fibres, namely as 'myotubes'. From the seventh day after their appearance, the myotubes begin to multiply by longitudinal fission... The formation of a secondary is prepared by nuclear fission, leading to the formation of a second linear series of nuclei; round which new myofibrils form. **1972** D. A. FISCHMAN in G. H. Bourne *Structure & Function Muscle* (ed. 2) I. iii. 107 The myotube is here defined as the multinucleated syncitium which results from the cytoplasmic fusion of myoblasts. The term is purely descriptive, for it only implies an immature muscle fiber in which the myofibrils are, in general, circumferentially distributed within the cell, and the nuclei occupy the core or central zone of the syncitium. **1973** *Nature* 3 Aug. 253/3 From the fourth to the sixth day of incubation, motor nerve fibres invade the limb-bud muscles [of the chick embryo], and the first myotubes appear.

myocardiac (maɪəʊˈkɑːdɪæk), *a.* [f. MYO- + CARDIAC *a.*] Of or pertaining to the myocardium; myocardial.

1908 *Practitioner* Oct. 610 As the author says, myocardiac deficiency is the chief indication for the Nauheim treatment. **1940** A. HUXLEY *Let.* 7 July (1969) 454, I am still under the weather with..myocardiac weakness.

‖**myocardium** (maɪəʊˈkɑːdɪəm). [mod.L., f. Gr. μυ(ο)- MYO- + καρδία heart.] The muscular substance of the heart. Hence **myoˈcardial** *a.* Also ˌ**myocarˈditis**, inflammation of the myocardium; whence ˌ**myocarˈditic** *a.*

1866 A. FLINT *Princ. Med.* 279 Myocarditis. **1868** *Trans. Path. Soc. Lond.* XIX. 195 Concurrent pericarditis, myocarditis, and endocarditis. **1879** *St. George's Hosp. Rep.* IX. 405 Abscess of the myocardium. **1880** FLINT *Princ. Med.* 332 To differentiate the different myocardial lesions. **1896** *Allbutt's Syst. Med.* I. 816 Myocarditic changes.

myoctonic (maɪəʊˈktɒnɪk), *a. Chem.* [f. Gr. μυοκτόν-ος, f. μυ(ο)-, μῦς mouse + -κτόνος slaying: see -IC.] The name of a highly poisonous acid obtained from *Palicourea Marcgravii.* So **myˈoctonine**, an alkaloid obtained from *Aconitum lycoctonum*; hence **myoctoˈninic** *a.* = MYOCTONIC.

1872 WATTS *Dict. Chem.* Suppl., *Myoctonic acid.* **1887** *Brit. Med. Jrnl.* 15 Jan. 123 Myoctonine is one of the two substances extracted from aconitum lycoctonum by MM. Dragendorff and Spohn. **1891** *Syd. Soc. Lex.*, *Myoctoninic.*

myoelectric (maɪəʊɪˈlɛktrɪk), *a.* Also (with hyphen) **myo-electric**. [f. MYO- + ELECTRIC *a.*] Applied to (apparatus or techniques using) the currents produced in the body which would normally cause muscular contraction and relaxation.

1955 *Jrnl. Bone & Joint Surg.* XXXVII-B. 506 (*heading*) The use of myo-electric currents in the operation of prostheses. **1963** *Aerospace Med.* XXXIV. 267/1 By attempting to move his arms, the pilot generates muscle action potentials, or myoelectric signals, which may be utilized as a control source. **1964** *New Scientist* 12 Mar. 668/2 A powered prosthetic device with myoelectric control. **1965** D. FRANCIS *Odds Against* xx. 246 The myo-electric arm..worked entirely by harnessing the tiny electric currents generated in one's own remaining muscles. **1972** *Science* 12 May 607/3 The design of myoelectric artificial aids for the physically handicapped.

Hence **myoeˈlectrically** *adv.*

1964 *New Scientist* 12 Mar. 671/1 A Russian team..has introduced a myoelectrically controlled hand. **1970** *Ibid.* 5 Mar. 477/1 We constructed in 1966 a myoelectrically controlled hand and arm unit.

myofibril (maɪəʊˈfaɪbrɪl). *Anat.* Also in mod. L. form **myofibrilla** (pl. **-fibrillæ**). [f. MYO- + FIBRIL, FIBRILLA.] Any of the elongated cylindrical threads, about one micrometre thick, which arranged side by side in a bundle constitute the contractile components of a striated muscle fibre.

1898 *Jrnl. R. Microsc. Soc.* 64 The muscle-cell produces conducting substance (myofibrils). **1913** DORLAND *Med. Dict.* (ed. 7) 605/1 *Myofibril, myofibrilla*, a muscle-fibril. **1928** *Biol. Abstr.* II. 804/1 The author compares his results on the origin and formation of myofibrillae in striated muscles with those of other investigators. **1933** *Physiol. Rev.* XIII. 318 Thus far it has been assumed that myofibrils are actual morphologic entities. **1960** G. H. BOURNE *Struct. & Function Muscle* I. ii. 34 Hogue (1937) demonstrated cross striated myofibrillae in living cultures of cardiac muscle cells. Microdissection of fresh muscle fibers as a means of demonstrating myofibrils is exceedingly difficult. **1968** *New Scientist* 11 Jan. 70/1 Normal skeletal muscle..is composed of parallel fibres averaging 70 micrometres in diameter. These are in turn made up from hundreds of fine myofibrils, one to two micrometres thick, running the whole length of the fibre. **1970** AMBROSE & EASTY *Cell Biol.* xi. 370 The myofibril is itself composed of fine filaments.

Hence **myoˈfibrillar** *a.*

1927 *Biol. Abstr.* I. 861/1 Cerebellar ataxia [is due] to loss of 'myofibrillar perceptions'. **1956** *Anatomical Rec.* CXXV. 483 Lacking the regular myofibrillar organization of striated muscles, these filaments appear to span the cell as a loose bundle. **1972** D. A. FISCHMAN in G. H. Bourne *Structure & Function Muscle* (ed. 2) I. iii. 117 Probably no aspect of muscle differentiation has elicited as much interest with biologists as the problem of myofibrillar biosynthesis and assembly.

myogen (ˈmaɪədʒən). *Biochem.* [a. G. *myogen* (O. von Fürth 1895, in *Arch. f. exper. Path. und Pharm.* XXXVI. 274), f. *myo(sino)gen* MYOSINOGEN.] A mixture of albumins (varying between species) extracted from skeletal muscle plasma; crystalline substances obtained from such mixtures have been designated ***myogen A***, *B, I, II*, etc.

1896 *Jrnl. Chem. Soc.* LXX. II. 48 The proteids in the muscle plasma are three in number, namely paramyosinogen.., myosinogen or myogen 77 to 83 per cent. of the total proteïd, and traces of serum albumin. **1939** *Biochem. Jrnl.* XXXIII. 1342 Baranowski..has recently obtained from rabbit muscle extract a crystalline protein, which he has named myogen A. **1970** R. E. SCOPES in E. J. Briskey et al. *Physiol. & Biochem. of Muscle as Food* II. xxii. 472 It is now clear that..myogen A (when prepared from rabbit muscle) consisted of cocrystallized α-glycerophosphate dehydrogenase (α-GPDH) and aldolase... It has since been shown that pig myogen A is a different enzyme, lactate dehydrogenase. *Ibid.*, Myogens I and II from fish sarcoplasms..have been crystallised;.. neither is related to the myogen A of rabbit.

myoglobin (maɪəˈgləʊbɪn). *Biochem.* [a. G. *myoglobin* (H. Günther 1921, in *Virchows Arch. f. path. Anat. und Physiol.* CCXXX. 150), f. *myo-* MYO- + *globin* GLOBIN.] A red protein responsible for the transport of oxygen in muscle cells, which differs from hæmoglobin in containing only one hæm group and one peptide chain in its molecule (instead of four of each) and in having a much greater affinity for oxygen.

1925 *Proc. R. Soc.* B. XCVIII. 332 This difference does not justify, however, the introduction of the names 'myochrome' or 'myoglobin' for muscle hæmoglobin proposed respectively by Mörner and Günther. **1956** *New Biol.* XXI. 45 Muscles contain myoglobin, a compound related to haemoglobin which takes up oxygen released by haemoglobin..and stores it for use in time of oxygen shortage. **1958** *Manch. Guardian Weekly* 2 Oct. 12 J. C. Kendrew's molecular model of myoglobin, derived from the first successful X-ray analysis of a protein molecule ever to be made, aroused tremendous interest at the Congress [of Biochemistry at Vienna]. **1968** PASSMORE & ROBSON *Compan. Med. Stud.* I. xv. 11/2 Myoglobin can pick up and store in the cells the oxygen brought by the blood even when the circulation is too inadequate to maintain a high oxygen tension in the tissue fluid interposed between capillaries and muscle cells.

myogram (ˈmaɪəgræm). [f. MYO- + -GRAM, after next.] A tracing made by a myograph.

1890 *Century Dict.* **1899** *Allbutt's Syst. Med.* VI. 519 Its [the knee-jerk's] myogram shows it to be a simple twitch.

myograph (ˈmaɪəgrɑːf, -æ-). [f. MYO- + -GRAPH.] An instrument for taking tracings of muscular contractions and relaxations. So **myoˈgraphion** [Gr. γραφεῖον pencil, graving tool].

1867 *Jrnl. Anat.* I. 158 With both Pflüger's and Du Bois' instruments muscles must be cut out and fixed to them, with Marey's myograph this is unnecessary. Marey terms the instrument 'myographic forceps'. *Ibid.*, We have already two Myographions, Pflüger's and Du Bois Reymond's; to these Marey has added a third. **1876–7** *S. Kens. Mus. Catal. Sci. App.* No. 3798 Rosenthal's Rotating Myographion.

myoˈgraphic, -ical, *adjs.* [f. prec. or next + -IC, -ICAL.] Pertaining to or produced by the myograph; also, pertaining to myography.

1808 BARCLAY *Muscular Motions* 438 Showing more than usual anxiety to point out some myographical errors. **1846** WORCESTER, *Myographic.* **1867** [see prec.]. **1885** *Brain* VII. 569 Myographic tracings.

myography (maɪˈɒgrəfɪ). *rare*⁻⁰. [f. MYO- + -GRAPHY.] A description of muscles; the descriptive science of muscles. Hence **myˈographer, myˈographist**, one who is skilled in myography.

1721 BAILEY, *Myography.* **1836** SMART, *Myographist.* **1890** *Century Dict.*, *Myographer.*

myoid (ˈmaɪɔɪd), *a.* and *sb.* [f. MY(O- + -OID.]

A. *adj.* Resembling muscle; composed of muscular tissue.

1857 DUNGLISON *Dict. Med. Sci.* (rev. ed.) 616/1 *Myoid*, an epithet given to tumours composed of fibre cells or muscular fibres of organic life. **1970** *Amer. Jrnl. Anat.* CXXIX. 399 (*heading*) Myoid elements in the mammalian nephron. *Ibid.* 399/1 This procedure revealed myoid features in the nephric tubules. **1973** *Anatomical Rec.* CLXXVII. 525 (*heading*) Myoid cells in the capsule of the adrenal gland and in monolayers derived from cultured adrenal capsules.

B. *sb.* [perh. a different word.] A structural part of the cones and rods of the retina.

1900 *Lancet* 7 July 7/2 The cell-body, traced from the cuticular end, begins as a distinct granular protoplasmic swelling, called the myoid. **1961** S. DUKE-ELDER *Syst. Ophthalmol.* II. iii. 241 In man and other mammals the inner segment of the rod is an elongated slightly barrel-shaped structure, homogeneous in appearance, made up of two elements, an outer ellipsoid and an inner myoid. **1972** *Vision Res.* XII. 1841 (*heading*) Optical function of myoids. *Ibid.*, The myoid is a cylindrical part of the photoreceptor connecting the region of the cell containing its nucleus with the region containing the ellipsoid.

myoidal (maɪˈɔɪdəl), *a. rare*⁻¹. [f. Gr. μῦ-ς mouse + -OIDAL. Cf. Gr. μυώδης.] Mouse-like.

1847 TULK tr. *Oken's Physiophilos.* 640.

myology (maɪˈɒlədʒɪ). [ad. mod.L. *myologia*: see MYO- and -LOGY.] **a.** The science of muscles; that part of anatomy which treats of the muscles. **b.** A myological description; the myological features or muscular anatomy of a particular animal or part of the body.

1649 BULWER *Pathomyot.* Pref. 3 A Book which all Anatomists kisse with reverence, as conteining the Oracles of Myologie. **1699** *Phil. Trans.* XXI. 132 If we are allowed to multiply Muscles from their appearance in various Subjects, we shall never arrive to a perfect Myology. **1713** DERHAM *Phys.-Theol.* VII. ii. (1714) 357 *note*, Steno thus concludes his Myology of the Eagle. **1796** SOUTHEY *Lett. fr. Spain* (1799) 477 Myology, Neurology, and Splanchnology. **1885** *Gentl. Mag.* Sept. 281 From considerations of.. myology and osteology, the Screamer cannot be placed along with the Anserine birds.

Hence **myoˈlogic, -ˈlogical** *adjs.*, pertaining to or concerned with myology; **myˈologist**, one who studies or is expert in myology.

1808 BARCLAY *Muscular Motions* 370 By..numberless combinations of flexions [etc.]..the human body may exhibit phenomena calculated to astonish the myologist himself. **1836** SMART, *Myological*, pertaining to myology. **1860** WORCESTER, *Myologic* (citing *Penny Cycl.*). **1862** *Syd. Soc. Year-bk. Med.* 16 Myological enquiries.

‖**myoma** (maɪˈəʊmə). *Path.* [mod.L., f. Gr. μῦ-ς muscle + -ωμα (cf. σάρκωμα SARCOMA).] A tumour composed of muscular tissue.

1875 C. H. JONES & SIEV. *Pathol. Anat.* 151 Tumours consisting of smooth muscular fibre..have recently received the name of *myoma* or *fibromyoma*. **1899** *Allbutt's Syst. Med.* VIII. 51 The case of a woman, forty years of age, the subject of myoma of the uterus.

Hence **myˈomatous** *a.*, pertaining to a myoma; **myoˈmotomy**, the removal of a uterine myoma by abdominal section (*Syd. Soc. Lex.* 1891).

1876 GROSS *Dis. Bladder*, etc. 266 A myomatous fibroma. **1887** *Brit. Med. Jrnl.* 14 May 1045/2 An enormous uterine tumour of the spongy myomatous variety. **1900** *Ibid.* No. 2053 Epit. Current Lit. 71 Myomotomy for Calcified fibroma.

myomancy (ˈmaɪəmænsɪ). [f. Gr. μυ(ο)-, μῦς mouse + μαντεία -MANCY.] Divination by the movements of mice.

1727–52 CHAMBERS *Cycl.* s.v., Some authors hold myomancy to be one of the most ancient kinds of divination; and think it is on this account that Isaiah, lxvi. 17, reckons mice among the abominable things of the idolater. **1855** SMEDLEY *Occult Sci.* 335.

myomectomy (maɪəʊˈmɛktəmɪ). *Surg.* [f. MYOM(A + -ECTOMY.] Excision of a myoma, esp. in the uterus.

1886 *Buck's Handbk. Med. Sci.* III. 811/2 The operation of myomectomy..is another product of the fertile mind of Schröder. It has been termed by him myomotomy, but for the sake of greater exactness the other term is to be preferred. **1900** *Lancet* 18 Aug. 501/1 Myomectomy should always be done when it was possible to save the uterus. **1908** *Practitioner* Oct. 608 Vaginal myomectomy. **1974** PASSMORE & ROBSON *Compan. Med. Stud.* III. xxviii. 46/1 Myomectomy is the treatment of choice in cases where it is desirable to preserve the uterus for future pregnancies.

myomorph (ˈmaɪəmɔːf). *Zool.* [ad. mod.L. *Myomorpha*, f. Gr. μυ(ο)-, μῦς mouse + μορφή shape.] A rodent of the division *Myomorpha* (including mice, rats, dormice, etc.). So **myoˈmorphic, -ˈmorphine** *adjs.*, belonging to or characteristic of these rodents.

187. *Cassell's Nat. Hist.* III. 102 The Dormice..fall under the definition of the Myomorphic section. **1887** HEILPRIN *Distrib. Anim.* 357 Of the non-murine families of myomorphs the dormice (Myoxidæ) and mole-rats (Spalacidæ) belong to the Old World exclusively. **1898** *Proc. Zool. Soc.* 29 Nov. 860 In *Dipus* the incisors are capable of separation and approximation as in most myomorphine rodents.

‖**myon** (mjən). Also **myen**. [Korean.] A Korean administrative unit approximately equivalent to a rural district or township. Also *attrib.*

1898 I. L. BISHOP *Korea & her Neighbours* II. xxxii. 203 The country is now divided into districts (*Kun*), each *Kun* containing a number of *myen* or cantons, each of which includes a number of *ni* or villages. **1951** C. OSGOOD *Koreans & their Culture* ii. 20 The kun..comprises a series of myŏn, or townships, of which there are said to be currently fourteen in Kanghwa Kun. **1972** P. M. BARTZ *South Korea* 48/2 From provincial governor to rural *myon* chief and city mayor to *dong* head, officials are appointed, not elected. **1972** *Korea Herald* 17 Nov. 1/6 Detailed work on formulation of a plan to construct one factory in each of 770 selected eups and myons throughout the country..began yesterday.

myone, myoner: see MOYEN, MINER.

myonicity (maɪəʊˈnɪsɪtɪ). [f. Gr. μυών cluster of muscle + -ICITY.] Muscular contractility.

1866 [see NEURICITY].

myopathy (maɪˈɒpəθɪ). *Path.* [ad. mod.L. *myopathi-a*: see MYO- + -PATHY.] Disease of the muscles. Hence **myoˈpathic** *a.*

1849 CRAIG, *Myopathy*, a morbid condition of the muscles. **1856** MAYNE *Expos. Lex.*, *Myopathicus*,..of or belonging to *Myopathia*: myopathic. **1877** tr. *von Ziemssen's Cycl. Med.* XVI. 86 All the maladies included in the group of rheumatic myopathies. **1880** A. FLINT *Princ. Med.* 770 A myopathic paralysis. **1897** [see NEURO-PATHIC].

myope (ˈmaɪəʊp), *sb.* (*a.*) [a. F. *myope*, ad. late L. *myōp-*, *myōps*, a. Gr. μυωπ-, μύωψ, MYOPS.] A short-sighted person.

1728 CHAMBERS *Cycl.* (ed. 2) s.v. *Eye*, It is not, however, myopes and old men alone that would..have their vision.. very near or very remote. **1849–52** *Todd's Cycl. Anat.* IV. II. 1463/2 Myopes..read with more ease in partial darkness than those whose sight is perfect. **1887** [see MYOPIC].

fig. **1870** O. W. HOLMES *Mech. Thought & Morals* (1871) 19 Intellectual myopes, near-sighted specialists.

b. *adj.* Myopic.

1892 'H. S. MERRIMAN' *Slave of Lamp*, xv, His face..was the face of a hawk, with the contracted myope vision characteristic of that bird.

‖**myopia** (maɪˈəʊpɪə). [mod.L., a. late Gr. μυωπία, f. μύωψ MYOPS.] Short-sightedness.

[**1693** tr. *Blancard's Phys. Dict.* (ed. 2).] **1727–52** CHAMBERS *Cycl.* s.v., The myopia is owing to the too great convexity of the ball of the eye. **1803** *Med. Jrnl.* IX. 141 The structure of his eyes..being naturally such as to dispose him to myopia. **1895** ZANGWILL *Master* III. ii. 294 There's money in myopia and diseases of the eye generally.

fig. **1801** CHARLOTTE SMITH *Lett. Solit. Wand.* I. 280 Those who have what you justly called the myopia of the mind. **1891** O. W. HOLMES *Poet Breakf.-t.* Pref. p. viii, The kind of partial blindness which belongs to intellectual myopia.

myopic (maɪˈɒpɪk), *a.* (*sb.*) *Path.* [f. MYOPE or MYOPIA + -IC.] **a.** Of, relating to, or affected with myopia; short-sighted; near-sighted.

1800 YOUNG in *Phil. Trans.* XCI. 36 The focal length of spectacles required for myopic or presbyopic eyes. **1846** MRS. GORE *Eng. Char.* (1852) 91 He was repeatedly required at his own balls to call up carriages..for fashionable ladies, myopic enough to mistake him for his delegate. **1849–52** *Todd's Cycl. Anat.* IV. 1467/1 The French glasses, whether presbyopic or myopic. **1887** *Brit. Med. Jrnl.* 21 May 1120/1 This treatment is safe in myopes who have attained the age of puberty, and have not large myopic crescents.

fig. **1891** MEREDITH *One of our Conq.* III. i. 8 Your Moralist is a myopic preacher. **1955** *Sci. Amer.* Oct. 103/1 Until Maupertuis's death in 1759 Voltaire did not relent in his flood of unmerciful, unscrupulous and myopic ridicule. **1972** G. DURRELL *Catch me a Colobus* v. 82 For some considerable time I had been endeavouring to persuade the BBC to film an animal-collecting trip, but they had been very myopic about the whole thing. **1975** *Times* 3 July 15/2 The Inner London Education Authority..appears to share this myopic vision of the troubles at North London Polytechnic.

b. *absol.* and *sb.*

1883 *Encycl. Brit.* XVI. 259/1 For the myopic who can see an object clearly at 4 inches distance. *Ibid.* XVII. 785/1 All myopics should work in a good light.

So **myˈopical** *a.*; hence **myˈopically** *adv.*, like a short-sighted person.

1748 *Phil. Trans.* XLV. 413 The Eye is myopical, and she sees the right Side of Objects a little darkened. **1830** *Fraser's Mag.* II. 95 A myopical..race, of most Lilliputian vision. **1901** G. GISSING *Our Friend the Charlatan* x, He..blinked myopically at his visitors before rising.

myopism (ˈmaɪəpɪz(ə)m). [f. Gr. μυωπ-, μύωψ MYOPS + -ISM.] = MYOPIA.

1822 W. DUNLAP *Mem. C. B. Brown* 31 He had discovered by accident, that he was afflicted with a myopism. **1860** C. W. KING *Antique Gems* i. 34 Myopism is still in Italy almost a distinct peculiarity of aristocratic birth. **1880** 'OUIDA' *Moths* viii. 100 Lady Stout was one of those happy people who only see just so much as they wish to see. It is the most comfortable of all myopisms.

‖**myops** (ˈmaɪɒps). Also 8 **miops**. [late L., a. Gr. μύωψ, f. μύειν to shut + ὤψ eye.] A short-sighted person (*lit.* and *fig.*).

[**1693** tr. *Blancard's Phys. Dict.* (ed. 2).] **1798** *Founders Fr. Repub.* II. 174 Being a *miops*, he was obliged to wear spectacles. **1801** CHARLOTTE SMITH *Lett. Solit. Wand.* I. 280, I feel that I have been a myops in the present instance.

‖**myopsis** (maɪˈɒpsɪs). *Path.* [mod.L., incorrectly f. Gr. μυῖα fly and ὄψις sight.] A disease of the eyes in which *muscæ volitantes* are seen. Also (in anglicized form) **ˈmyopsy**.

1860 WORCESTER, *Myopsy.* **1864** WEBSTER, *Myopsis.*

myoptic (maɪˈɒptɪk), *a.* [f. MYOPE or MYOPY after Gr. ὀπτικός OPTIC.] = MYOPIC.

1849 *Blackw. Mag.* LXVI. 104 Such dismal domiciles were only fit resorts for the myoptic bat. **1866** ATKINSON *Ganot's Physics* §521 Persons who see only at a very short distance are called myoptic.

myopy (ˈmaɪəʊpɪ). [ad. mod.L. *myōpia*: see MYOPIA.] Myopia, shortsightedness.

1854 CT. EDW. DE WARREN tr. *de Saulcy's Dead Sea* II. 273 Was this done as a preservation against ophthalmia, or as a remedy for myopy? **1879** MRS. LYNN LINTON *Under Which Lord?* III. iv. 93 Mrs. Everett made a cold bow, and, afflicted with sudden myopy, did not see the hand held out. **1880** LE CONTE *Sight* 50 Myopy is a structural defect.

myosin (ˈmaɪəsɪn). *Chem.* Also **-ine**. [f. Gr. μῦ-ς muscle + -OSE[2] + -IN[1].] The chief ingredient of the clot formed on coagulation of muscle-plasma.

vegetable myosin or *myosin-globulin* is found, with vitellin, in maize, oats, peas, etc.

1869 E. A. PARKES *Pract. Hygiene* (ed. 3) 158 The nitrogenous aliments are blood-fibrine, muscle-fibrine or syntonin, myosin [etc.]. **1887** BENTLEY *Man. Bot.* 37 The proteids exist in these grains as globulins, which hitherto have been known only to occur in animals, that is, as myosin-globulin and vitellin-globulin.

Hence **myoˈsinogen**, a proteid of muscle-plasma.

1891 *Syd. Soc. Lex.* **1896** *Allbutt's Syst. Med.* I. 171 Several very important albuminous substances, for example, myosinogen and fibrinogen, are coagulated at 56° C.

myosis: see MIOSIS.

‖**myositis** (maɪəˈsaɪtɪs). *Path.* [irreg. f. Gr. μυός, genit. of μῦς muscle + -ITIS.] Inflammation of a muscle; myitis.

1819 *Pantologia.* **1834** BARLOW in *Cycl. Pract. Med.* III. 598/1 Sagar..describes two diseases, a chronic one ranged in the class *Dolores*, order *Vagi*; and an acute under the specific name of myositis.

Hence **myoˈsitic** *a.* (*Syd. Soc. Lex.* 1891).

myosote (ˈmaɪəsəʊt). [ad. L. *myosōtis* (see next).] The forget-me-not, *Myosotis palustris*.

1879 *Encycl. Brit.* IX. 414/1 The common or true Forget-me-not, the Water Myosote. **1890** R. BRIDGES *Shorter Poems* II. 5 And laden barges float By banks of myosote.

‖**myosotis** (maɪəˈsəʊtɪs). [L., a. Gr. μυοσωτίς, f. μυός, gen. of μῦς mouse + ὠτ-, οὖς ear.]

†**1.** The mouse-ear, *Hieracium Pilosella*. *Obs.*

1706 PHILLIPS (ed. 6), *Myosota* or *Myosotis*, the Herb Mouse-ear, or Bloud-strange. **1753** CHAMBERS *Cycl.* Suppl. s.v., The broad-leaved Alpine Myosotis.

2. A plant of the genus *Myosotis*.

1857 MISS PRATT *Flower. Pl.* IV. 46 In the Netherlands this Myosotis is often made into a syrup.

myotic, var. MIOTIC *a.* and *sb.*

myotility (maɪəʊˈtɪlɪtɪ). *Phys.* [irreg. f. MYO- + *-tility* (cf. *motility*, *contractility*), after F. *myotilité*.] A term used variously for muscular force, power of contraction, or contractility.

1830 R. KNOX *Béclard's Anat.* §667 The muscles possess an active power or property, commonly designated under the names of muscular irritability, muscular force, or myotility [orig. Fr. *myotilité*]. **1891** in *Syd. Soc. Lex.*

myotome (ˈmaɪətəʊm). [f. MYO- + Gr. τομή section, and -τόμος cutting: see -TOME.]

1. *Anat.* A muscular segment or metamere.

1856 GOODSIR in *Edin. New Philos. Jrnl.* (1857) V. 122 For the muscular system I employ the terms Myome, Myotome, Synmyotome. **1872** HUMPHRY *Myology* 7 The transverse inscriptions or sclerotomes which..divide the lateral muscles into so many 'myotomes'. **1894** GADOW & ABBOTT in *Phil. Trans.* CLXXXVI. 182 The original protovertebræ are now differentiated into sklerotomes..and into myotomes.

2. *Surg.* An instrument for dividing muscle.

1846 BRITTAN tr. *Malgaigne's Man. Oper. Surg.* 289 To destroy the corresponding septum of the muscular sheath, and thus enlarge the subconjunctival space in which the myotome is to act.

myotomic (maɪəˈtɒmɪk), *a.* [f. MYOTOME or MYOTOM-Y.] Pertaining to myotomy or a myotome.

1856 MAYNE *Expos. Lex.*, *Myotomicus*... Of or belonging to *Myotomia*: myotomic. **1897** *Nature* 7 Oct. 555/2 The myotomic sacs remain monodermic on their outer face.

†**myotomist** (maɪˈɒtəmɪst). *Obs.* [f. MYOTOMY + -IST.] A professor of muscular anatomy.

1649 BULWER *Pathomyot.* II. i. 97 The other Muscles..are like to retaine their old names, unlesse some..Myotomist be pleased to take pitty of their private Condition.

myotomy (maɪˈɒtəmɪ). [ad. mod.L. *myotomia*, f. Gr. μυ(ο)-, μῦ-ς muscle + τομή, -τομία cutting.]

1. Dissection of muscles; muscular anatomy.

1676 RAY *Corr.* (1848) 123 Mr. Willughby himself hath left a myotome [*sic*] of a swan. **1727–52** CHAMBERS *Cycl.*, *Myotomy*, *myotomia*, an anatomical dissection, or demonstration of the muscles.

2. The surgical division of a muscle.

1871 *Brit. Med. Jrnl.* 18 Nov. 578 On Intraocular Myotomy. By Augustin Prichard. **1878** tr. *von Ziemssen's Cycl. Med.* XIV. 852 The defect may..be due to an habitual spasm of the genioglossi,..which may necessitate myotomy.

myotonia (maɪəˈtəʊnɪə). *Path.* [mod.L., f. MYO- + Gr. τόν-ος TONE *sb.* + -IA[1].]

1. The inability to relax voluntary muscle for a period following its use; any condition characterized by this.

1898 *Jrnl. Nerv. & Mental Dis.* XXV. 509, I think it proper to assign all such cases to the one clinical category of myotonia. *Ibid.* 510 Cases which show symptoms of organic disease..can at once be excluded from the group of myotonias. **1905** *Ibid.* XXIX. 416 Myotonia appears to have been used also in the collective sense. Hochsinger describes as myotonia of infancy the persistent hypertonicity of the flexors, and diagnosticates it from tetany, but if myotonia is used as an inclusive term it is a question if it should not cover tetany itself, while if it is used in the narrow sense it has been preëmpted by Thomsen's disease. **1948** F. B. CARLSEN tr. *Thomasen's Myotonia* ii. 15 There is a definite difference in the ages at which the myotonia in Thomsen's disease..on the one hand, and dystrophia myotonica on the other, manifests itself. **1963** CAUGHEY & MYRIANTHOPOULOS *Dystrophia Myotonica* p. x, Her father was a London professional man who had myotonia of the grip. **1970** MASTERS & JOHNSON *Human Sexual Inadequacy* viii. 220 Specific evidence has been accumulated of the incidence of both myotonia and vasocongestion in the female's pelvis as she responds physiologically to sex-tension elevation.

2. In the (usu. mod.L) names of specific diseases in which myotonia is a prominent feature, as: **a. myotonia congenita** [A. Strümpell 1881, in *Berliner klin. Wochenschr.* 28 Feb. 121/2], **congenital myotonia** (*rare*), a rare hereditary disease manifested soon after birth and characterized by myotonia but without muscular wasting or other symptoms. Also called THOMSEN'S DISEASE.

1886 *Brain* IX. 113 The eighth article..makes confusion worse confounded by using another term, viz. dysmyotonie congénitale, almost adopting Strumpell's term, congenital myotonia. **1887** *Jrnl. Nerv. & Mental Dis.* XIV. 129 (*heading*) Thomsen's disease (myotonia congenita). **1963** CAUGHEY & MYRIANTHOPOULOS *Dystrophia Myotonica* xviii. 216 Myotonia congenita..was described in detail in 1876 by Dr. Asmus Julius Thomsen who was himself affected and in whose family it had occurred for five generations. **1974** J. T. HUGHES *Path. Muscle* iv. 76 In contrast to myotonia congenita and paramyotonia congenita, dystrophia myotonica is frequently diagnosed.

b. myotonia atrophica [tr. F. *myotonie atrophique* (G. Rossolimo 1902, in *Nouvelle Iconographie de la Salpêtrière* XV. 63)], a hereditary condition characterized esp. by myotonia, muscular wasting, cataracts, frontal baldness, and gonadal atrophy. Also called *dystrophia myotonica*.

1908 *Jrnl. Nerv. & Mental Dis.* XXXV. 269 Myotonia atrophica is an extremely rare affection. **1963** CAUGHEY & MYRIANTHOPOULOS *Dystrophia Myotonica* p. viii, Dystrophia myotonica has been known as myotonia atrophica, Steinert's disease, dystrophia myotonica or myotonic dystrophy. **1974** J. N. WALTON *Disorders Voluntary Muscle* (ed. 3) xv. 595 Dystrophia myotonica (myotonia atrophica) was described by Steinert (1909) and Batten and Gibb (1909).

myotonic (maɪə'tɒnɪk), *a.* *Path.* [f. MYO- + TONIC *a.*] Producing, exhibiting, or characteristic of myotonia.

1887 A. DE WATTEVILLE tr. *H. von Ziemssen's Handbk. Therap.* VI. 213 The Myotonic Electrical Reaction. **1887** *Jrnl. Nerv. & Mental Dis.* XIV. 129 Those [cases] which, although showing the principal symptoms, the 'myotonic disorder of the muscles', still..cannot be considered as true cases of Thomsen's disease. **1887** *Lancet* 14 May 973/2 'Myotonic contractions', which has also been suggested, has the advantage of avoiding prejudice of the question whether the condition is always congenital. **1909** *Brain* XXXII. 190 The muscles did not give the myotonic reaction as described by Erb in Thomsen's disease. **1948** F. B. CARLSEN tr. *Thomasen's Myotonia* ii. 18 Myotonic patients may often play the piano without difficulty. **1963** CAUGHEY & MYRIANTHOPOULOS *Dystrophia Myotonica* ii. 20 Brown and Harvey (1939) examined myotonic goats electromyographically.

† **myour.** *Obs.* Also 4 miour(e, 5 myoure, -owre, -ure, -ere. [a. OF. *mieur*, *miur*, f. *mier* MYE *v.* + *-eur*, -OUR.] A bread-grater.

1316–17 *Durham Acc. Rolls* 513 In 1 Mioure et 1 Scomur ..10d. *c* **1420** *Voc.* in Wr.-Wülcker 660/23 *Hoc micatorium*, myowre. **1485** *Inv.* in *Ripon Ch. Acts* (Surtees) 370, j myour pro pane micando.

† **mype.** *Obs. local.* [a. north. Welsh *maip* turnip.] A parsnip.

Gerarde, who seems to be the only independent authority for the word, was a native of Cheshire.

1597 GERARDE *Herbal* II. ccclxxxviii. 871 The old writers ..have called this wilde Parsnep by the name of *Elaphoboscum*: that of the garden we do call Parsneps and Mypes. **1600** SURFLET *Country Farm* II. xxxv. 244 Parsneps, mypes, carrets,..are sowen al after one fashion. **1665** LOVELL *Herbal* (ed. 2) 296 Mypes, see Parsneps.

myr, myrabolam, myrac(ke, myraltie, myravid: see MIRE *sb.*[1], MYROBALAN, MIRACH, MAYORALTY, MARAVEDI.

myrcene ('mɜːsiːn). *Chem.* [f. mod.L. *Myrc-ia*, name of a genus of tropical trees and shrubs + -ENE.] 2-Methyl-6-methylene-2, 7-octadiene, $C_{10}H_{16}$, a liquid terpene found in bay, hop, and other essential oils.

1895 POWER & KLEBER in *Pharmaceut. Rundschau* XIII. 61/1 As this body is not identical with any of the known terpenes, we propose for it the name *myrcene*. **1926** H. FINNEMORE *Essential Oils* lviii. 528 When 1 part of myrcene was heated..with 3 parts of glacial acetic acid and 1/50 part of 50 per cent sulphuric acid, an oil of lavender-like odour was obtained. **1953** I. A. PREECE *Biochem. Brewing* ix. 254 The myrcene content of a hop sample might well prove to be an outstanding factor in determining the storage characteristics of that sample. **1969** *Daily Tel.* 16 Sept. 21/2 The disaster tank..had contained myrcene, an oil closely allied to turpentine, which in certain circumstances can turn into a sticky residue with a low flashpoint.

myrhorr: see MIRROR.

myria- ('mɪrɪə), rarely **myrio-**, before a vowel **myri-**, used as combining form of Gr. μυριάς MYRIAD (or μυρίος countless, μυρίοι 10,000).

1. With the meaning 'ten thousand', in names of weights and measures of the metric system: **'myriagram(me, 'myrialitre, 'myriametre, 'myriare** = 10,000 grammes, litres, metres, ares.

1804 *Ann. Reg.* 612 A bridge..will shorten the route from Paris to Cherbourg by some myriameters. **1810** *Naval Chron.* XXIV. 301 Myriagram = 20 lb. 7 oz. 58 gr. *Ibid.*, Myriar, square kilometer. **1811** P. KELLY *Univ. Cambist* I. 154 The words Decagramme, Hectogramme, Kilogramme, and Myriagramme, express 10, 100, 1,000, 10,000 Grammmes. *Ibid.* II. 268 Myriometre... Myriolitre... Myriogramme. **1871** C. DAVIS *Metric Syst.* I. 11 The myriametre, equal to nearly 6 and one-fourth miles.

2. With the meaning 'very numerous': **myria'canthous** *a.* [Gr. ἄκανθος thorn], having very many spines; **myri'amerous** *a.* [Gr. μέρος part], having very many segments; **myri'anthous** *a.* [Gr. ἄνθος flower], bearing very many flowers.

1856 MAYNE *Expos. Lex.*, *Myriacanthus*,..that which has numerous spines, as the *Bouria myriacantha*,.. myriacanthous. *Ibid.*, *Myriamerus*... Applied by Blainville to the *Chetopoda*, which have many segments, rings, or articulations,..myriamerous. *Ibid.*, *Myrianthus*... Having very numerous flowers, as the *Hypericum myrianthum*: myrianthous. **1882** OGILVIE, *Myriacanthous*,..myriad-spined; specifically, of or belonging to the genus Myriacanthus.

myriad ('mɪrɪəd), *sb.* and *a.* Also 6–7 -ade, 7 miriad(e, myrriad. [ad. med.L. *myriad-*, *myrias*, a. Gr. μυριαδ-, μυριάς, f. μυρίος countless, μυρίοι ten thousand. Cf. F. *myriade.*] **A.** *sb.*

1. a. As a numeral: Ten thousand.

(Chiefly in translations from Greek or Latin, or in reference to the Greek numeral system.)

1555 EDEN *Decades* (Arb.) 159 *marg.*, One myriade is ten thousande. **1621** BURTON *Anat. Mel.* II. iii. III. (1651) 326 Rome..vaunted her self of two myriades of inhabitants. **1663** *Hanmer's Anc. Eccl. Hist.* 39 When the Historiographer had collected the number of them that perished by sword and famine, he reporteth that it mounted to a hundred and ten Myriads [*edd.* 1577, 1585 myllions, millions]. **1734** tr. *Rollin's Anc. Hist.* (1827) II. III. 159 One single myriad of talents of silver is worth 30,000,000 of French money. **1836** THIRLWALL *Greece* II. 289 That 4000 men from Peloponnesus had fought at Thermopylæ with 300 myriads. **1881** N. T. *Acts* xxi. 20 How many thousands [*marg.* Gr. myriads].

† **b.** *ellipt.* for: A myriad of coins of some understood value. *Obs.*

1601 R. JOHNSON *Kingd. & Commw.* (1603) 74 [They] pay little lesse then two myriades and a half of ordinary reuenue. **1632** MASSINGER *City Madam* IV. i, Make it up a thousand, And I will fit him with such tools as shall Bring in a miriad.

2. *transf.* **a.** (*pl.*) Countless numbers, hosts (*of*).

1555 EDEN *Decades* (Arb.) 159 It is a miserable thynge to hear how many myriades of men these..devourers of mans flesshe haue consumed. **1570** DEE *Math. Pref.* *iij, Who can Imagine the Myriades of sundry Cases..tried and concluded by the forenamed Rules, onely? **1660** EVELYN *Diary* 29 May, Myriads of people flocking [to London], even so far as from Rochester. **1762** FALCONER *Shipwr.* I. 66 Where winged deaths in dreadful myriads fly. **1803** WELLINGTON in Gurw. *Desp.* (1835) II. 251, I hope to be able to strike a blow against their myriads of horse in a few days. **1875** HELPS *Soc. Press.* iii. 50 Amidst the myriads of planets with which the universe is probably peopled.

b. *sing.* in same sense.

1850 ROBERTSON *Serm.* Ser. III. x. 124 A myriad of different universes. **1864** TENNYSON *Aylmer's F.* 436 That codeless myriad of precedent. **1875** *Ure's Dict. Arts* III. 324 Like a myriad of tubes.

3. *absol.* **a.** Countless numbers of men, animals, or inanimate things (to be inferred from the context).

1559 AYLMER *Harborowe* B 3 b, A sclender pollycie to make so many Myriades to flee. **1667** MILTON *P.L.* I. 87 Who..Cloth'd with transcendent brightness didst outshine Myriads though bright. **1727–46** THOMSON *Summer* 1030 Where putrefaction into life ferments, And breathes destructive myriads. **1784** COWPER *Task* v. 77 How find the myriads that in summer cheer The hills and vallies with their ceaseless songs, Due sustenance? **1842** BORROW *Bible in Sp.* xxx, This now desolate bay had once resounded with the voices of myriads. **1877** C. GEIKIE *Christ* II. xlix. 279 He might..repair this error..if He went up now and showed His power before the assembled myriads of Israel.

b. *sing.* in same sense.

a **1718** T. PARNELL *Solomon* Posth. Wks. (1858) 161 His lofty stature, where a Myriad shine, O'ertops, and speaks a majesty divine. **1724** GAY *Captives* v. (1772) 64 The silver moon, And all the starry myriad that attend her.

B. *adj.*

1. a. Existing in myriads; of indefinitely great number; countless, innumerable. Chiefly *poet.*

a **1800** COLERIDGE *Hymn to Earth* 28 Myriad myriads of lives teem'd forth from the mighty embracement. **1817** SHELLEY *Rev. Islam* v. 1725 The City's moonlit spires and myriad lamps. **1830** TENNYSON *Ode to Memory* iv, Thou of the many tongues, the myriad eyes! **1850** ROBERTSON *Serm.* Ser. III. i. (1872) 5 Myriad, countless curses. **1886** W. W. STORY *Fiammetta* 189 The crickets were trilling a myriad infinitesimal bells in the grasses.

b. with *sing. sb.*: Consisting of myriads. Also, having a myriad phases or aspects.

[**1817**: see 3.] *a* **1854** H. REED *Lect. Brit. Poets* v. (1857) 187 The myriad mind of Shakspeare. **1873** SYMONDS *Grk. Poets* ix. 281 Prometheus when he described the myriad laughter of the dimpling waves [etc.]. **1874** MAHAFFY *Soc. Life Greece* ix. 289 The myriad life of the Peiræus. **1876** PAGE *Adv. Text-bk. Geol.* iii. 67 A home for itself and its myriad progeny.

2. As a numeral (cf. A. 1). *rare.*

1875 MERIVALE *Gen. Hist. Rome* lxii. (1877) 504 A capital sum of four myriad millions of sesterces.

3. *Comb.*: chiefly parasynthetic, as ***myriad-accomplished, -handed, -islanded -jewelled, -limbed, -minded, -mirrored, -voiced, -wrinkled*** etc.; also advb., as ***myriad-flaking, -murmuring, -times, -tinkling, -wise*** etc.

1909 'MARK TWAIN' *Is Shakes. Dead?* 67 The man who wrote the plays was not merely myriad-minded, but also myriad-accomplished. **1957** R. CAMPBELL *Coll. Poems* II. 106 The Heliades, The myriad-flaking snowstorm of whose boughs Is never still. **1872** SYMONDS *Introd. Study Dante* viii. 255 A myriad-handed foe. **1922** JOYCE *Ulysses* 48 Tides, myriadislanded, within her. **1909** E. POUND *Personae* 43 Unless it were to make the halo round each one Appear more myriad-jewelled marvellous. **1923** D. H. LAWRENCE *Birds, Beasts & Flowers* 41 Nude fig-tree... Rather like an octopus, but strange and sweet-myriad-limbed octopus. **1817** COLERIDGE *Biog. Lit.* xv, Our myriad-minded Shakespeare [*note*, ἀνὴρ μυριόνους]. **1916** BLUNDEN *Harbingers* 12 And wed me with the myriad-minded man. **1968** *Jrnl. Mus. Acad. Madras* XXXIX. 9 Tyagaraja can truly be said to be myriad-minded. **1921** W. DE LA MARE *Veil* 52 Their myriad-mirrored eyes Great day reflect. **1872** SYMONDS *Introd. Study Dante* vii. 231 Homer, large, liberal, and myriad-murmuring as the sea. **1860** FARRAR *Orig. Lang.* (1865) 65 The myriad-ravelled intricacy of sensuous impressions. **1864** TENNYSON *Boädicea* 42 The myriad-rolling ocean. **1879** FARRAR *St. Paul* I. 10 A myriad-sided character. **1944** BLUNDEN *Shells by Stream* 26 We may glide Over a myriad-times extended sea And land of life abundant. *a* **1918** W. OWEN *Coll. Poems* (1963) 127 The myriad-tinkling flocks. **1883** J. G. WHITTIER *What Traveller Said* in *Bay of Seven Islands* 48, I dread the myriad-voiced strain. **1859** MARY HOWITT *Marion's Pilgr.* v. iv, Traffic, myriad-wheeled. **1917** D. H. LAWRENCE *Look! We have come Through!* 120 Its oneness veers Out myriad-wise. **1859** TENNYSON *Idylls of King: Elaine* 156 Then came an old, dumb, myriad-wrinkled man. **1942** W. FAULKNER *Go down, Moses* iii. 75 Then he saw the myriad-wrinkled face.

† **'myriaded,** *a.* *Obs. rare*[−1]. [f. MYRIAD + -ED[2].] Countless.

1667 WATERHOUSE *Fire of London* 123 We have not been worthy of the least of those Myriaded ones [*sc.* mercies] that we have enjoyed.

'myriadfold, *a.* and *sb.* [f. MYRIAD + -FOLD.] **A.** *adj.* Countless, innumerable; having innumerable aspects or features.

1870–4 J. THOMSON *City Dreadf. Nt.* XVI. vi, Through sequences and changes myriadfold. **1881** TYNDALL *Floating Matter of Air* 78 These media declare themselves to be crowded with particles—not hypothetical, not potential, but actual and myriadfold in numbers.

B. *sb.* Only advb., with indef. article: ***a myriadfold***, an infinite amount (more *than* or *beyond*).

a **1711** KEN *Hymns Evang.* Poet. Wks. I. 254 A Myriadfold an Angel flies, Swifter than Morning Splendor gilds the Skies. **1890** J. MARTINEAU *Auth. in Relig.* IV. iv. 567 The fields and gardens will yield their produce a myriadfold beyond all experience.

myriadth ('mɪrɪədθ), *a.* [f. MYRIAD + -TH[1].] That is a very minute (properly, a ten-thousandth) part of a whole.

1824 LANDOR *Imag. Conv.*, *Aristoteles & Callisthenes* Wks. 1853 I. 232/2 A myriad of conquerors is not worth the myriadth part of a wise and virtuous man. **1873** M. COLLINS *Squire Silchester* II. iv. 41 The myriadth division of one beat of Time's inaudible pulse.

† **'myriagon.** *Obs. rare*[−1]. [f. MYRIA- + -GON.] A geometrical figure having 10,000 sides.

1674 BOYLE *Corpusc. Philos.* 34 Pentagons, Chiliagons, Myriagons, and innumerable other Polygons.

myriagram(me, -litre, etc.: see MYRIA-.

† **'myriander,** *a.* *Obs. rare*[−1]. [a. F. *myriandre* (Rabelais), ad. Gr. μυρίανδρος, f. μυρίοι 10,000 + ἀνδρ-, ἀνήρ man.] Having 10,000 men.

a **1693** *Urquhart's Rabelais* III. li, The Chiliander and Myriander Ships launched from their Stations.

myriapod ('mɪrɪəpɒd), *a.* and *sb.* Also **myrio-**. [ad. mod.L. *Myriapoda* (see next).]

a. *adj.* Having very numerous legs; *spec.* pertaining to or having the characteristics of the *Myriapoda*. **b.** *sb.* One of the *Myriapoda.*

1826 KIRBY & SP. *Entomol.* xxviii. III. 22 *note*, Though the octopod and myriapod insects breathe by tracheæ. *Ibid.* 40 The Myriapods exceed most insects in the vast elongation of their body. **1865** THOREAU *Cape Cod* ix. 187 A venomous-looking, long, narrow worm, one of the myriapods. **1877** HUXLEY *Anat. Inv. Anim.* vii. 396 The myriapod larva..is essentially different from an insect larva. **1880** T. GILL in *Smithsonian Rep.* 352 A distinct order of Myriopods.

‖ **Myriapoda** (mɪrɪ'æpədə). Also **Myrio-**. [mod.L., f. Gr. μυριάς (see MYRIA-) + ποδ-, πούς foot. Cf. Gr. μυριόπους myriad-footed.] A class of arthropodous animals, comprising the centipedes and millipedes. Hence **myri'apodan** *a.*, **myri'apodous** *a.*, = MYRIAPOD *a.*

1828 STARK *Elem. Nat. Hist.* II. 208 The Myriapoda.. approach the insects in the organization of their respiratory apparatus. **1841** T. R. JONES *Anim. Kingd.* 225 The Myriapoda [*ed.* **1871** Myriopoda] may be divided into two families, originally indicated by Linnæus: the *Julidæ*, or millepedes, and the *Scolopendridæ*, or centipedes. **1856** MAYNE *Expos. Lex.*, *Myriapodus*,..myriapodous. **1887** S. H. SCUDDER in *Proc. Boston Soc. Nat. Hist.* 4 May 373 The supposed Myriapodan genus Trichiulus.

myriapodal (mɪrɪ'æpədəl), *a.* [f. MYRIAPODA + -AL.] = MYRIAPOD *a.*

1893 *Rep. U.S. Nat. Mus. 1892* 258 Comparatively little can ever be known concerning the probably great abundance of Insect, Arachnid, and Myriapodal life of former geological time.

'myriarch. *rare.* [ad. Gr. μυριάρχης, μυρίαρχος, f. μυρίοι ten thousand + -άρχης, ἀρχός ruler.] A commander of ten thousand men.

1632 HOLLAND *Cyrupædia* 69 Then, called he togither the Myriarches [*marg.* Colonels, or leaders of ten thousand], the Chiliarches [etc.]. **1656** BLOUNT *Glossogr.*, *Myriarck.*

So **'myriarchy** [after *chiliarchy*], government by ten thousand rulers.

1650 R. HOLLINGWORTH *Exerc. Usurped Powers* 18 Not an heptarchy, but a chiliarchy, or myriarchy might follow.

† **'myriate,** *a.* *Obs.*[−1] [f. Gr. μυρίοι 10,000 + -ATE[2].] That is a ten-thousandth part; infinitesimal.

1665 GLANVILL *Def. Van. Dogm.* 38 He that supposeth all the..parts of a Worm..to be actually contain'd, though in myriate and indivisible proportions, in a drop of dew.

‖ **myrica** (mɪ'raɪkə). [L., a. Gr. μυρίκη.]

1. The tamarisk.

1706 PHILLIPS (ed. 6), *Myrica* or *Myrice*, a low Shrub, call'd Tamarisk. **1819** SHELLEY *Let. to T. L. Peacock* 25 Feb., The cytisus,..the myrtle, and the myrica [at Naples]. **1855** MISS PRATT *Flower. Pl.* II. 305 *Tamarix Anglica* (Common Tamarisk)... It is the Myrica of the Greeks and Romans.

2. A Linnæan genus of shrubs mostly furnished with glands having aromatic secretions; a plant of this genus, e.g. *Myrica Gale*, the bog myrtle.

1797 *Encycl. Brit.* (ed. 3) XII. 566/1 Wax-bearing myrica, or candleberry myrtle. **1826** CARRINGTON *Dartmoor* 69 Upon his [*sc.* the Dart's] banks..Nature's hand has thrown the odorous Myrica.

3. *attrib.* **myrica-tallow, -wax** = myrtle-wax. **1862** *Amer. Jrnl. Sci.* Ser. II. XXXIII. 320 As a substitute for bees-wax in the manufacture of candles, the Myrica wax appears to be worthy of more attention than it has yet received. **1865** WATTS *Dict. Chem., Myrica-tallow*, myrtle-wax.

myricaceous (mɪrɪˈkeɪʃəs), *a.* [f. mod.L. *Myricāce-æ* + -EOUS.] Belonging to the N.O. *Myricaceæ* (consisting of the single genus *Myrica*).
In some recent Dicts.

myricic (maɪˈrɪsɪk), *a.* [f. MYRICA + -IC.] In *myricic alcohol*, myricyl alcohol (*Syd. Soc. Lex.* 1891).

myricin (mɪˈraɪsɪn, ˈmɪ-, ˈmaɪərɪsɪn). *Chem.* Also -ine. [f. MYRICA + -IN[1].] That part of beeswax which is insoluble in boiling alcohol. **1821** URE *Dict. Chem., Myricin.* The ingredient of wax which remains after digestion with alcohol. **1856** LETHEBY in *Orr's Circ. Sci., Pract. Chem.* 460 Chinese wax is entirely free from myricine. **1874** GARROD & BAXTER *Mat. Med.* 409 Wax is separable by means of alcohol into three portions: myricine,..cerotic acid..and ceroleine.

myricyl (mɪˈraɪsɪl, ˈmɪrɪsɪl). *Chem.* [f. MYRICA + -YL.] = MELISSYL. Chiefly *attrib.* in ***myricyl alcohol***; also **myriˈcylic** *a.* in the same sense. **1865** WATTS *Dict. Chem., Myricyl*, Hydrate of. Melissic alcohol, Melissin. **1868** *Fownes' Chem.* (ed. 10) 633 Myricyl Alcohol..is obtained from myricin. *Ibid.* 731 Palmitic acid exists also as..myricyl palmitate. **1905** *Daily Chron.* 10 Mar. 8/5 Myricylic alcohol.

myrie, obs. form of MERRY, MIRY.

‖**myringitis** (mɪrɪnˈdʒaɪtɪs). *Path.* [mod.L., f. *myringa, myrinx* membrana tympani + -ITIS.] Inflammation of the membrana tympani. **1856** MAYNE *Expos. Lex.* **1874** ROOSA *Dis. Ear* 222, Independent or primary myringitis.

myringotome (mɪˈrɪŋgətəʊm). *Surg.* [f. mod.L. *myringa* + -τόμος cutting, τέμνειν to cut.] An instrument for perforating the membrana tympani. So **myrinˈgotomy**, perforation of the membrana tympani. **1879** *St. George's Hosp. Rep.* IX. 765 The patient then came down to Brighton, with a view of having myringotomy performed. **1895** *Arnold's Catal. Surg. Instr.* 174 Myringotome.

myriogramme, etc.: see MYRIA- I.

myriological (ˌmɪrɪəˈlɒdʒɪkəl), *a.* [f. MYRIOLOGUE + -ICAL.] Pertaining to a myriologue. **1847–54** WEBSTER.

myriologist (mɪrɪˈɒlədʒɪst). Also *erron.* **myria-**. [Formed as next + -IST.] One who sings or composes a myriologue. **1847–54** WEBSTER. **1869** TOZER *Highl. Turkey* II. 241 In some places there are found women who are professed myriologists. **1885** R. F. BURTON *Thousand Nights* I. 137 *note*, English wants the word for the præfica or myrialogist.

myriologue (ˈmɪrɪəlɒg). [ad. mod.Gr. μυριολόγι(ον), corrupted f. μοιρολόγι(ον), f. μοῖρα fate + λόγος speech. Cf. *moirologist.*] An extemporaneous funeral song, composed and sung by a woman. **1824** *New Monthly Mag.* XI. 141 The myriologues (or laments) which are uttered on these occasions have all the characters of inspiration. **1863** MARY HOWITT tr. *F. Bremer's Greece* I. v. 136 The myriologues or songs for the dead. **1869** TOZER *Highl. Turkey* II. 229.

myriophyllite (mɪrɪəˈfɪlaɪt), *a.* [f. Gr. μυρίος countless + φύλλον leaf + -ITE.] (See quot.) **1882** OGILVIE, *Myriophyllite*, a kind of fossil root, with numerous fibres, found in the coal-measures.

myriophyllous (mɪrɪəˈfɪləs), *a. Bot.* [Formed as prec. + -ITE.] Having a very large number of leaves or leaflets. **1856** MAYNE *Expos. Lex.*

myriopod, variant of MYRIAPOD.

myriorama (mɪrɪəˈræmə, -ˈɑːmə). [f. Gr. μυρίος countless + ὅρᾱμα view. Cf. *panorama.*]

a. A picture made of a number of separate sections which are capable of being combined in numerous ways so as to form different scenes. **1824** (*title*) Myriorama, a collection of many thousand landscapes designed by Mr. Clark on 16 oblong cards. **1832** *Encycl. Amer.* IX. 116 *Myriorama*,.. a sort of landscape kaleidoscope recently invented by Brés, of Paris, and improved by Clark, of London... With 16 cards 20,922,789,888,000 changes may be made.

b. An entertainment consisting of a succession of a large number of views. **1901** *Westm. Gaz.* 7 Dec. 5/2 The School Board has paid for the admission of 2,000 children to a myriorama. **1901** *Scotsman* 12 Mar. 7/3 Mr. C. W. Poole..opened a short season's engagement with his myrioramic entertainment.

myrioscope (ˈmɪrɪəskəʊp). [f. Gr. μυρίο-ς countless: see -SCOPE.] (See quot.) **1875** KNIGHT *Dict. Mech.* 1504/2 *Myrioscope*, this is a variation of the kaleidoscope, and..depends upon the multiplication of images, which coalesce in such manner as to form a geometrical pattern.

myriotheism (ˈmɪrɪəθiːɪz(ə)m). *rare*[−1]. [f. Gr. μυρίο-ς countless + θε-ός god + -ISM.] Belief in, or worship of, an infinity of gods. **1818** COLERIDGE in *Lit. Rem.* (1838) III. 183 See the influence of the surrounding myriotheism in the *dea Mors*!

myristic (maɪ-, mɪˈrɪstɪk), *a. Chem.* [f. med.L. (*nux*) *myristica* (Diefenbach), adopted by Linnæus as the generic name of the nutmeg-tree, f. Gr. μυρίζειν to anoint.] ***myristic acid***: a fatty acid found in nutmeg-oil and other vegetable and animal fats. Hence **myˈristate**, a salt of myristic acid. **1848** BRANDE *Man. Chem.* 1263 Nutmeg butter consists of three fatty substances, two of which are soluble, but the third nearly insoluble in common alcohol; this latter has been termed Myristine; when purified..it may be rendered nearly colorless and inodorous, and is then a compound of glycerine with myristic acid. *Ibid.*, Myristate of potassa,.. Myristate of baryta. **1868** *Fownes' Chem.* (ed. 10) 730 Myristic Acid..occurs as a glyceride in Nutmeg-butter and Otoba fat. *Ibid.* 731 The myristates of the alkali-metals..are soluble in water.

So **myˈristicene**, the terpene obtained from volatile oil of nutmeg. **myˈristicin**: see quots. **myˈristicol**, an oxygenated oil forming the chief constitutent of volatile oil of nutmeg. **myˈristin**, the glyceride of myristic acid. **myˈristone**, a crystalline substance obtained by the distillation of calcium myristate. **1872** J. H. GLADSTONE in *Jrnl. Chem. Soc.* Ser. II. X. 3 I would suggest the following:—Hydrocarbon from Nutmeg *Myristicene. **1839** URE *Dict. Arts* 908 The oil of mace, lets fall, after a certain time, a concrete oil under the form of a crystalline crust, called by John *myristicine. **1876** HARLEY *Mat. Med.* (ed. 6) 464 Oil of Nutmeg contains..several fatty acids in combination with glycerin, the most considerable of which is myristicin. **1872** J. H. GLADSTONE in *Jrnl. Chem. Soc.* Ser. II. X. 11 *Myristicol. **1848** *Myristine [see MYRISTIC]. **1868** *Fownes' Chem.* (ed. 10) 731 Myristin..is obtained by pressing nutmegs between hot plates. **1854** R. D. THOMSON *Cycl. Chem.*, *Myristone.

myrk(e, etc., obs. forms of MURK, etc.

myrmecic (mɜːˈmiːsɪk), *a. rare*[−1]. [f. Gr. μυρμηκ-, μύρμηξ ant + -IC.] Ant-like. **1905** H. W. & F. G. FOWLER tr. *Lucian* III. 137 They no doubt have, on their modest myrmecic scale, their architects and politicians.

myrmeco- (ˈmɜːmɪkəʊ, -ˈkɒ, mɜːˈmiːkəʊ), combining form of Gr. μυρμηκ-, μύρμηξ, ant, used in a few scientific terms. **myrmecoˈlogical** *a.*, pertaining to myrmecology. **myrmeˈcologist**, a student or professor of myrmecology. **myrmeˈcology**, the department of study concerned with ants. **myrmeˈcophagid**, **myrmeˈcophagine**, a member of the genus *Myrmecophaga* [Gr. -φάγος eating], family *Myrmecophagidæ*, or sub-family *Myrmecophaginæ* of ant-eaters. **myrmeˈcophagous** *a.*, ant-eating, belonging to the genus *Myrmecophaga*. **myrˈmecophile**, a myrmecophilous insect. **myrmeˈcophilous** *a.*, applied (*a*) to insects that live in ant-hills, (*b*) to plants living symbiotically with ants or fertilized by them. **myrmeˈcophilism, -phily**, the condition of being myrmecophilous. **myrmecoˈphobic** *a.*, refusing the society of ants. **myrˈmecophyte**, a myrmecophilous plant. **1886** *Nature* 7 Jan. 240 *Myrmecological studies, by Herr G. Adlerz. **1901** W. M. WHEELER in *Amer. Naturalist* XXXV. 432 It thus becomes necessary to review much that is well known to the *myrmecologist. **1972** *Sci. Amer.* Sept. 193/1 Forty-five years ago the American myrmecologist William Morton Wheeler wrote a volume with a very similar title, the fruit of his lifetime study of ants. **1885** *Riverside Nat. Hist.* (1888) V. 66 These accessory articulations are well exemplified in the Dasypodids and *Myrmecophagids. *Ibid.* 59 The palatines and pterygoids of the two sides not meeting as they do in the *Myrmecophagines. **1840** OWEN in *Zool. Voy. Beagle* I. 87 The cervical vertebræ do actually differ in two *myrmecophagous species. **1898** *Nat. Sci.* May 326 The larvae at the same time both myrmecoid and myrmecophagous. **1898** *Nat. Sci.* May 324 The progeny (eggs, larvae and nymphs)..can also be utilised by the *myrmecophiles. **1927** H. ST. J. K. DONISTHORPE *Guests of British Ants* p. xv, A large number of creatures do manage to live in or near ants' nests. Such creatures when associated with, and not merely present with ants, are known as *myrmecophiles. **1959** E. F. LINSSEN *Beetles Brit. Is.* I. 47 Certain beetles are known as myrmecophiles (ant-lovers) from their association with ants. The name *myrmecophilism has been given to this curious habit. **1866** *Intell. Observ.* No. 56. 128 Other *myrmecophilous coleoptera. **1888** *Nature* 20 Dec. 172 Myrmecophilous plants. **1898** *Nat. Sci.* May 325 The search for the liquids secreted by Aphides does not usually constitute a true case of *myrmecophily. **1897** *Pop. Sci. Monthly* L. 829 The plant, becoming *myrmecophobic..achieves an economy of nutritive forces. **1902** J. M. COULTER *Plant Studies* 162 Very definite arrangements are made by certain plants for harboring ants, which in turn guard them against the attack of leaf-cutting insects and other foes. These plants are called *Myrmecophytes.

‖**Myrmecobius** (mɜːmɪˈkəʊbɪəs). Also anglicized **myrmecobe** (in Dicts.). [mod.L. (Waterhouse, *Proc. Zool. Soc.*, July 1836), a. Gr. μυρμηκόβιος, f. μυρμηκ(ο)-, -μηξ ant + -βιος living, βιοῦν to live.] A genus of insectivorous marsupials, typical of the sub-family *Myrmecobiinæ*; an animal of this genus. **1838** OWEN in *Trans. Geol. Soc.* Ser. II. (1842) VI. 64 The Phascolothere resembles the *Myrmecobius* more than it does the Opossum. **1841** WATERHOUSE *Marsupialia* 145 Banded Myrmecobius..Red Myrmecobius. **1887** HEILPRIN *Distrib. Anim.* 99 The native ant-eater, or striped myrmecobius.

Hence **myrmeˈcobian**, an animal of this genus. **1839–47** *Todd's Cycl. Anat.* III. 260/1 The Myrmecobians..shelter themselves in the hollows of trees.

myrmecoid (ˈmɜːmɪkɔɪd), *a. rare.* [ad. Gr. μυρμηκοειδ-ής, f. Gr. μύρμηξ ant.] Ant-like. **1861** *Eng. Wom. Dom. Mag.* III. 59 It was observed by a very ancient and learned individual, that the sluggard might imbibe information by inspecting the regularity of myrmecoid evolutions. **1898** *Nat. Sci.* May 326 Myrmecoid animals can be protected by this resemblance..against insectivorous birds which do not eat ants.

myrmekite (ˈmɜːmɪkaɪt). *Petrogr.* [ad. G. *myrmekit* (J. J. Sederholm 1897, in *Bull. de la Commission géol. de la Finlande* I. VI. 113), f. Gr. μυρμηκ-ιά anthill, wart + *-it* -ITE[1].] An intergrowth of plagioclase with drops or wormlike forms of quartz. **1916** *Bull. de la Commission géol. de la Finlande* IX. XLVIII. 1 The intergrowth of plagioclase and 'vermicular' quartz.. I have called *myrmekite*. *Ibid.*, I prefer to write *myrmekite*, as analogous to poikilite etc., instead of myrmecite. **1926** H. H. READ et al. *Geol. Strath Oykell & Lower Loch Shin* (Mem. Geol. Surv. Scot.) vi. 154 In slice..the pinkish medium-grained rock is seen to be composed of quartz, oligoclase, and myrmekite. **1967** *Mineral Mag.* XXXVI. 491 Myrmekite and the other vermicular textures all appear to lack any specific crystallographic or lattice co-relationship between the vermicular and host mineral.

Hence **myrmeˈkitic** *a.*, of the nature of or containing myrmekite; **ˌmyrmekitiˈzation**, conversion into myrmekite; a myrmekitic state. **1916** *Bull. de la Commission géol. de la Finlande* IX. XLVIII. 120 Myrmekitic intergrowths may occasionally originate like the minerals crystallising in a molten magma, not as crystalloblastic minerals. *Ibid.* 118 The myrmekitization and the formation of the biotite are here obviously independent phenomena. **1944** *Q. Jrnl. Geol. Soc.* XCIX. 118 The plagioclase is sericitized and its larger plates show myrmekitic margins. **1964** *Amer. Mineral.* XLIX. 50 The myrmekite type I..is formed by the myrmekitization of plagioclase already in the rock. **1972** *Mineral. Mag.* XXXVIII. 573 Microprobe and optical measurements have shown the myrmekitic plagioclase of such intergrowths to be very similar compositionally to non-myrmekitic plagioclase.

myrmeleon (mɜːˈmiːlɪən). [mod.L. (Linnæus), contracted f. *myrmēcoleōn*, in med.L. *mirmicoleon* (a. Gr. μυρμηκολέων, f. μύρμηξ ant + λέων lion).] A genus of *Myrmeleon(t)idæ*; a member of this genus, an ant-lion. **1802** BINGLEY *Anim. Biog.* (1813) III. 241 The Common Myrmeleon, or Ant-lion. **1840** J. O. WESTWOOD *Introd. Mod. Classif. Insects* II. 41 Larva of Myrmeleon. **1885** C. F. HOLDER *Marvels Anim. Life* 207 We shall find in the sandy spots..the myrmeleon.

myrmicine (ˈmɜːmɪsaɪn), *a. Ent.* [ad. mod.L. *Myrmicinæ*, f. *Myrmica* (Latreille, f. Gr. μύρμηκ-, -μηξ ant): see -INE.] Of or belonging to the sub-family *Myrmicinæ* of stinging ants. **188.** *Cassell's Nat. Hist.* V. 381 The Turf Ant (*Formica flava*) is often found occupying one side of its hillock, with a colony of another Myrmicine Ant (*Myrmica scabrinodis*) comfortably established on the other.

myrmidon (ˈmɜːmɪdən). Forms: α. 5 **mirmydane, -en, myrmaidon, murmindone, -mondon,** 5, 7 **mer-,** 5, 8 **mir-, myrmydon,** 6 **myr-,** 6–7 **mir-,** 7–8 **mermidon,** 7– **myrmidon.** β. 5 **mi-, myrondone, mi-, myrundone.** [ad. L. *Myrmidon-es* pl., a. Gr. Μυρμιδόνες.]

1. (With capital M.) One of a warlike race of men inhabiting ancient Thessaly, whom, according to the Homeric story, Achilles led to the siege of Troy (*Iliad* II. 684).

α. *c* **1400** *Laud Troy Bk.* 4597 Achilles cam thenne faste saylande With alle his gode Mirmydanes. *Ibid.* 7353 Achilles with his Murmindones. *c* **1400** *Destr. Troy* 8666 The Myrmaidons, his men, þaire maistur can take. **1598** MARSTON *Sco. Villanie* III. viii, What Mirmidon, or hard Dolopian, What sauage minded rude Cyclopian? **1606** SHAKS. *Tr. & Cr.* v. viii. 13 On Myrmidons, cry you all a maine, Achilles hath the mighty Hector slaine. *a* **1618** SYLVESTER *Woodmans Bear* lxxv, Marble-hearted Mermidon. **1715** POPE *Iliad* I. 238 Go, threat thy earth-born Myrmidons. **1833** *Penny Cycl.* I. 84/2 [Achilles] allowed his friend..Patroclus..to lead the Myrmidons, his followers, out to battle.

β. **1412–20** LYDG. *Chron. Troy* II. 8574 þe..ferse Achille Arїued is with his knyȝtes alle, Mirundones whom men are wont to calle. **1471** CAXTON *Recuyell* (ed. Sommer) 574 And then arryued the right stronge Achilles with his myrondones. *Ibid.* 634 Mirondones. *Ibid.* 635 Myrundones.

b. Used of Achilles himself.

1606 SHAKS. *Tr. & Cr.* I. iii. 378 For that will physicke the great Myrmidon, Who broyles in lowd applause.

2. *transf.* A soldier of (one's) body-guard; a faithful follower or servant. ? *Obs.*

Cf. SHAKS. *Tr. & Cr.* v. vii. 1.

c **1610** BEAUM. & FL. *Philaster* v. iv, We are thy Mirmidons, thy Guard, thy Rorers. **1640** GLAPTHORNE *Wallenstein* II. ii, Fall on my Mirmidon, While we retreat. **1698** FARQUHAR *Love & Bottle* III. ii, Now, my myrmidons, fall on. **1748** RICHARDSON *Clarissa* III. xiii. 88 Who knows what consequences might have follow'd upon..my projected visit, followed by my Myrmidons? **1820** T. HOPE *Anast.* (ed. 2) III. xiii. 332 Part of my myrmidons hid their apparatus and persons near the quarter which I meant to alarm. **1821** SCOTT *Kenilw.* i, Which produced the following dialogue, betwixt the myrmidons of the bonny Black Bear [*sc.* hostler and tapster].

3. An unscrupulously faithful follower or hireling; a hired ruffian; a base attendant.

1649 MILTON *Eikon.* iv. 30 He sallied out from Whitehall, with those trusty Myrmidons, to block up..the House of Commons. **1666** PEPYS *Diary* 12 July (1877) IV. 14 He spoke contemptibly of Holmes and his mermidons, that came to take down the ships from hence. **1749** FIELDING *Tom Jones* XV. v, The Door flew open, and in came Squire Western, with his Parson, and a Set of Myrmidons at his Heels. **1816** T. L. PEACOCK *Headlong Hall* ii, His myrmidon on this occasion was a little rednosed butler. **1874** FARRAR *Christ* II. lx. 372 Herod and his corrupt hybrid myrmidons 'set Him at nought'.

transf. **1839** in *Spirit Metrop. Conserv. Press* (1840) II. 463 Acts which..are not only being perpetrated by British ministers, but are openly confessed and unblushingly gloried in by their myrmidons of the press. **1860** RUSSELL *Diary India* II. vii. 142 The Southern who harried their glens with his canine myrmidons in the evil days ere King Jamie annexed England to Scotland.

b. Chiefly ***myrmidon of the law, of justice***: applied contemptuously to a policeman, bailiff, or other inferior administrative officer of the law.

a **1700** B. E. *Dict. Cant. Crew, Myrmidons*, the Constable's Attendants..; also the Watchmen. **1714** *Spectator* No. 616 ¶4, I have just left the Right Worshipful and his Myrmidons about a Sneaker of Five Gallons. **1809** BYRON *Bards & Rev.* 467 Bow-street Myrmidons. **1840** DICKENS *Barn. Rudge* lxvi, His complaint should be..fully stated..to all the inferior myrmidons of justice. **1863** *Conf. of Ticket of Leave Man* 160 Lest my foes, the myrmidons of the law, should track the golden stream back to its sources.

myrmidonian (mɜːmɪˈdəʊnɪən), *a.* [f. MYRMIDON + -IAN.]

1. Of, pertaining to, or characteristic of the Myrmidons.

1624 in Bedell *Lett.* ii. 48 All those Myrmidonian fights and bloudie encounters. **1632** LITHGOW *Trav.* II. 72 That Mirmidonian Phillip, and these Epirean worthies, Pyrhus and Scanderberg. **1717** POPE *Iliad* IX. 244 The Myrmidonian tents and vessels. **1804** J. LARWOOD *No Gun Boats* 18 Every bark would become a Trojan Horse..the myrmidonian cohorts would issue from its fatal carcase.

¶ **2.** Used for: Pertaining to ants.

[Pseudo-etymological association with Gr. μύρμηξ ant.]

1747 GOULD *Eng. Ants* 106 The Myrmidonian and Jet Settlements are particularly delighted with Juices. **1818** KIRBY & SP. *Entomol.* xvii. (ed. 2) II. 72 As the exploits of frogs and mice were the theme of Homer's muse, so..might I celebrate..the exhibition of Myrmidonian valour.

† **myrmidonize**, *v.* *Obs. rare*$^{-1}$. [f. MYRMIDON + -IZE.] *trans.* To make callous.

1593 NASHE *Christ's T.* 25 She hath steeled my soft impressiue hart, and mirmidoniz'd myne eies.

myrobalan (maɪˈrɒbələn). Forms: α. 6–8 **miro-**, (7 **mera-**, **muro-**), 6– **myro-**, **mira-**, **myra-**; (6 **-bolon**), 6–7 (9) **-bolane**, (7 **-balane**, 9 **-balam**, **-um**, **-bolam**, **-um**), 6– **-bolan**, **-balan**. β. 7 **mira-**, **marablane**. [a. F. *myrobolan* (= It., Sp. *mirabolano*, Pg. *myra-*) or its source L. *myrobalanum*, a. Gr. μυροβάλανος (1) perh. the ben-nut, (2) in mod. Gr., emblic, f. μύρο-ν unguent, balsam + βάλανος acorn, date, ben-nut.

Known colloq. amongst dyers as *m'rabs*.]

1. The astringent plum-like fruit of species of *Terminalia* (N.O. *Combretaceæ*), e.g. *T. Bellerica* (see BELLERIC), *T. Chebula* (see CHEBULE, CHEBULIC), *T. citrina*: formerly used medicinally, but now chiefly in dyeing, tanning, and ink-making. **emblic myrobalan**: see EMBLIC.

α. **1530** PALSGR. 245/2 Mirabolon a frute, *mirabolan.* **1533** ELYOT *Cast. Helthe* (1541) 68 Myrobolanes, callyd Kebuli. *c* **1540** in *Vicary's Anat.* (1888) 226 Putt therto of mirobolane cytrine pouldered, one vnce. **1562** BULLEIN *Bulwarke, Bk. Simples* (1579) 62 Who so vseth to eate often of Myrobalans being condite, shall not seeme olde, sayth Mesue. **1610** B. JONSON *Alch.* IV. ii, Shee melts Like a Myrobalane. **1611** COTGR., *Myrobalan citrin*, the yellow, or Citron Myrobalan. **1626** BACON *Sylva* §644 There be Fruits, that are Sweet before they be Ripe; As Myrabolanes. **1712** tr. *Pomet's Hist. Drugs* I. 141 The Indian Myrobalans are small long Fruit, of the Size of a Child's Finger End. **1803** *Phil. Trans.* XCIII. 267 The infusion of Myrobalans from the East Indies, differed from the other astringent infusions. **1883** *Madras Mail* 5 Dec. 21/1 It is only when the ruling price of myrabolams is too high that inferior tanning materials are in request. **1899** F. T. BULLEN *Log Sea-waif* 205 Indian produce, of which cotton, linseed, and myrabolums formed the staple.

β. **1617** MINSHEU *Ductor* 8264 *Mirablane.* [*Ibid.* 8510 *Myrabalane*, 8514 *Murobolane.*] **1624** FORD & DEKKER *Sun's Darling* II. i, Marmalades,..ponadoes, marablane [etc.].

2. A variety of plum.

1664 [see PRIMORDIAL *sb.* 2]. **1767** ABERCROMBIE *Ev. Man his own Gardener* (1803) 673/1 Plums..Myrobalan, Apricot plum [etc.]. **1860** HOGG *Fruit Man.* 232 Plums..Cherry (Early Scarlet..Myrobalan).

3. *attrib.*, as ***myrobalan tree***; † **myrobalan ben**, † **date**, the ben-nut; **myrobalan plum**, † (*a*) = sense 1; (*b*) = sense 2.

1706 PHILLIPS (ed. Kersey), *Myrobalanum*, a Fruit, call'd by Apothecaries *Myrobalan Ben, or the Nut of Egypt. **1601** HOLLAND *Pliny* XII. xxii. II. 163 Of the *Myrabolan Date. **1598** FLORIO, *Citrino*,..a kinde of *mirabolane plum. **1708** [see EMBLIC]. **1731** MILLER *Gard. Dict.*, *Prunus*; *fructu rotundo, nigro-purpureo*... Myrabolan Plum. **1555** EDEN *Decades* (Arb.) 100 A greate multitude of certeine beastes..creping as thicke as antes aboute the *myrobolane trees.

† **ˈmyron.** *Obs.* App. a servant, underling.

c **1440** *York Myst.* xxx. 139 Loke þat no man nor no myron of myne..be neghand me nere. *Ibid.* 147; xxxiii. 62.

myronic (maɪˈrɒnɪk), *a.* *Chem.* [ad. F. *myronique* (Bussy), f. μύρον unguent, perfume.] In ***myronic acid***, an acid obtained from black mustard. Hence **ˈmyronate**, a salt of myronic acid.

1840 PEREIRA *Elem. Nat. Med.* 1267 Myronic acid. *Ibid.* The alkaline myronates are crystallizable. **1873** HOOKER tr. *le Maout & Decaisne's Bot.* 232 Black mustard..contains a fixed..oil..This volatile oil..is produced by the action of a peculiar albumine (myrosine) on the myronic acid contained in the seed.

† **myˈropolist.** *Obs.* [f. Gr. μυροπώλης (f. μύρο-ν ointment + -πώλης seller, πωλεῖν to sell) + -IST.] A dealer in ointments or perfumery.

1656 BLOUNT *Glossogr.*, *Myropolist*, a seller of sweet Oyls, Ointments or Perfumes. [Hence in Phillips, Bailey, and later Dicts.] **1657** TOMLINSON *Renou's Disp.* 689 He that handled or sold them [*sc.* unguents] was called an Unguentary and Myropolist.

myrosin (ˈmaɪərəsɪn). *Chem.* Also **-ine**, **-yne**. [ad. F. *myrosyne* (Bussy), f. Gr. μύρο-ν unguent, perfume + *-yne* (= -IN, -INE), with intercalated *s*.] A nitrogenous ferment contained in the seeds of black mustard.

1840 PEREIRA *Elem. Mat. Med.* 1267 Black mustard contains myronate of potash, myrosyne, fixed oil [etc.]. **1873** [see MYRONIC]. **1874** GARROD & BAXTER *Mat. Med.* 145 The zymotic action of..yeast, diastase,..and myrosin.

myrospermin (maɪərəʊˈspɜːmɪn). *Chem.* Also **-ine**. [f. mod.L. *Myrosperm-um* (f. Gr. μύρο-ν balsam + σπέρμα seed) + -IN.] (See quot.)

1842 [see MYROXOCARPIN].

myrour(e, **-owre**, obs. forms of MIRROR *sb.*

myroxocarpin (maɪˌrɒksəʊˈkɑːpɪn). *Chem.* [f. mod.L. *Myrox(ylon)* + CARPIN.] A crystallizable substance obtained from white Peru balsam, *Myroxylon* (now *Myrospermum*) *peruiferum*. So **myroˈxylic** *a.*, **myˈroxyline** (see quots.).

1842 PEREIRA *Elem. Mat. Med.* 1561 Richter asserts that oil of balsam of Peru is composed of two distinct oils;—one, called myrospermine, which is soluble in alcohol; the other, termed myroxiline, insoluble in alcohol. **1848** BRANDE *Man. Chem.* 1391 By the action of an alcoholic solution of potassa upon *cinnameine*, Plantamour obtained a compound which he has designated Myroxylic acid. **1854** R. D. THOMSON *Cycl. Chem.*, *Myroxocarpine.*

myrr, **myrren**: see MURR, MURRAIN.

myrrh[1] (mɜː(r)). Forms: 1 **myrra**, **murra**, 1, 4 **murre**, 1–6 **myrre**, 2–6 **mirre**, 4 **merre**, **mirr**, 4–5 **myre**, 4, 6 **mir**, 5 **mere**, **myr**, 5–6 **myrr**, 5–7 **myrrhe**, 6–7 **mirrh**, **myrrhe**, 7– **myrrh**. Also in L. form 4 **mirra**, 6–8 **myrrha**. [OE. *myrra*, *myrre*, *murra* = OS. *myrra* (MDu. *myrre*, *mirre*, Du. *mirre*), OHG. *myrrâ*, *mirrâ*, *murrâ*, (MHG. *mirre*, G. *myrrhe*), ON. *mirra*; also OF. *mirre* (11th c.), mod.F. *myrrhe*, It., Sp. *mirra*:—L. *murra*, *murrha*, *myrrha*, a. Gr. μύρρα, of Semitic origin (Arab. *murr*, Heb. *mōr*).]

1. A gum-resin produced by several species of *Commiphora* (*Balsamodendron*), esp. *C. Myrrha* (see 2): used for perfumery and as an ingredient in incense. Also *Med.*, the tincture made from this.

In early use almost always with reference to the offering of myrrh by the Magi to our Lord.

c **825** *Vesp. Ps.* xliv. 9 Myrre & dropa & smiring. *c* **975** *Rushw. Gosp.* Matt. ii. 11, & ontynden heora goldhord brohtun him lac gold recils & murra [*Ags. Gosp.* myrre, *Hatton Gosp.* mirre]. *c* **1000** ÆLFRIC *Hom.* (Th.) I. 118 Myrra deð..þæt þæt deade flæsc eaðelice ne rotað. *c* **1200** *Trin. Coll. Hom.* 45 Gold bicumeð to kinge. Recheles to gode. mirre to deaðliche men. *a* **1300** *Cursor M.* 11502 Attropa gaf gift o mir, A smerl o selcuth bitturnes. *c* **1386** CHAUCER *Knt.'s T.* 2080 And garlandes hangynge with ful many a flour, The Mirre, thencens, with al so greet odour. *c* **1450** MYRC *Festial* 49 Myrre ys an oynement þat kepyth ded bodyes from rotyng. ? **1550** BALE *Image Both Ch.* I. ii. D. v, The odoriferous myrrha geueth forth the swete smelle of all good christen workes. **1652** CRASHAW *Carmen Deo Nostro* Wks. (1904) 198 Mountains of myrrh, and Beds of species. **1672** WISEMAN *Wounds* II. i. 2 Put a Pea in the middle of it, with Tincture of Myrrhe and Honey of Roses. **1797** *Encycl. Brit.* (ed. 3) XII. 572 The Troglodite myrrh was superior to every species of Arabian myrrh. **1803** *Med. Jrnl.* IX. 270 A mixture of three drachms of myrrh, one drachm and a half of balsamus Peruvianus or canadensis [etc.]. **1835** *Penny Cycl.* III. 345/1 Myrrh in sorts is the term applied to various inferior and adulterated kinds. **1851** LONGF. *Gold. Leg.*, *Nativity* vi, Another goblet! quick! and stir, Pomegranate juice and drops of myrrh..therein!

† **2.** Any shrub or tree that yields the gum-resin, esp. *Commiphora* (*Balsamodendron*) *Myrrha*.

c **1402** LYDG. *Compl. Bl. Knt.* 66, I saw ther Daphne..The myrre also, that wepeth ever of kinde. *a* **1450–1530** *Myrr. our Ladye* 285 Myrre is a tree that groweth fyue cubytes in lengthe. **1603** DRAYTON *Heroic. Ep.* iv. 141 Turn'd into a Myrrhe, Whose dropping Liquor ever weepes for her. **1634** MILTON *Comus* 937 With Groves of myrrhe, and cinnamon.

3. *attrib.* as ***myrrh-bush***, ***-posy***, ***-wine***; ***myrrh-breathing***, ***-distilling*** adjs.; **myrrh resin** (see quot.); **myrrh-seed**, a book-name for *Myrospermum pubescens*; **myrrh-shrub** = sense 2; † **myrrh wine**, myrrhed wine. See also MYRRH-TREE.

1616 R. C. *Times' Whistle* 1112 One kisse From thy *mirre-breathing mouth. **1605** DRAYTON *Idea* liii, Sweet mirrh-breathing Zephire. **1833** TENNYSON *Lotos Eaters* 103 Yonder amber light, Which will not leave the *myrrh-bush on the height. **1624** QUARLES *Sion's Sonn.* (1714) 354, I Op'd my Door, my *Myrrh-distilling Door. **1749** LAVINGTON *Enthus. Meth. & Papists* II. (1754) 8 Christ gaue her so large a share of the *Myrrh-posy of his Passion, that frequently under an Alienation of her Senses she would throw herself on her Back on the Ground. **1854** R. D. THOMSON *Cycl. Chem.*, *Myrrh Resin... Obtained from myrrh by alcohol; yellowish-brown, hard and brittle. **1866** *Treas. Bot.* II. 772/2 *Myrrh-seed, *Myrospermum pubescens*. **1876** HARLEY *Mat. Med.* (ed. 6) 666 *Balsamodendron Myrrha.* The *Myrrh Shrub. **1878** H. M. STANLEY *Dark Cont.* II. xii. 350 Where the myrrh and bdellium shrubs exhaled their fragrance. **1609** BP. HALL *Passion Serm.* Wks. (1625) 425 S. Marke calls this draught, οἶνον ἐσμυρνισμένον, *Myrrh-wine.

myrrh[2] (mɜː(r)). [ad. late L. *myrrhis*, *murris* (see MYRRHIS).] The aromatic plant, *Myrrhis odorata* (N.O. *Umbelliferæ*), Sweet Cicely.

1597 GERARDE *Herbal* II. cccxcix. 82 Great Cheruill, or Myrrhe. **1638** RAWLEY tr. *Bacon's Life & Death* (1650) 32 These yield a Robust heat, especially..Valerian, Myrrhe, Pepper-wort, Elder-flowers, Garden-chervile. **1741** *Compl. Fam.-Piece* II. iii. 378 Your Myrrhs should likewise now have frequent Water given them. **1852** JOHNSON *Cottage Gard. Dict.*, *Myrrhis*... This is the British Myrrh, formerly used in various ways. **1886** BRITTEN & HOLLAND *Plant-n.*, Myrrh, *Myrrhis odorata*,..Cumb.; Aberdeensh.

ˈmyrrhate, *sb.* [f. MYRRH-IC + -ATE[1].] A salt of myrrhic acid.

1840 [see MYRRHIC].

† **ˈmyrrhate**, *a.* *Obs. rare*$^{-1}$. [ad. L. *myrrhāt-us*, f. *myrrha* MYRRH[1]: see -ATE[2].] = MYRRHED *a.*

1659 HAMMOND *On Ps.* lx. 3 Thou hast made us to drink the wine of astonishment. [Paraphrase:] Thou hast..given us a myrrhate draught.

† **ˈmyrrhean**, *a.* *Obs. rare*$^{-0}$. [f. L. *myrrheus* (f. *myrrha* MYRRH[1]) + -AN.] (See quot.)

1656 BLOUNT *Glossogr.*, *Myrrhine*, *Myrrhean*..of myrrhe, made of myrrhe, seasoned with myrrhe.

myrrhed (mɜːd), *ppl. a. rare.* [f. MYRRH[1] + -ED, after L. *myrrhātus*.] **a.** Mixed with myrrh.

c **1450** *Mirour Saluacioun* xxv. (Roxb.) 92 And thas gyves myrred wyne to Jhū crist forto drinke Y[t] heresies vndere coloure of trewth to teche folk swynke. **1620** J. HAYWARD *Sanct. Troub. Soul* II. ix. 221 And first they offered him myrrhed wine, which was a composition..to dull..the seuere sence of death. **1905** D. SMITH *Days of His Flesh* xlix. 492 *note*, The offering of the myrrhed wine to Jesus before the crucifixion.

b. Sprinkled with myrrh.

1609 S. W. *Marie Magd. Funerall Teares* 29 To vnwrap so mangled a bodie out of mirrhed cloathes, without tearing of any skinne, or leauing on any mirrhe, is..impossible.

myrrhic (ˈmɜːrɪk, ˈmɪrɪk), *a.* [f. MYRRH[1] + -IC.] In ***myrrhic acid***, a substance obtained by heating the resin of myrrh.

1840 PEREIRA *Elem. Mat. Med.* 1189 Hard resin (myrrhic acid ?)..soluble in caustic alkalies, forming resinates (myrrhates ?). **1848** BRANDE *Man. Chem.* 1584.

ˈmyrrhin. *Chem.* [f. MYRRH[1] + -IN.] That part of myrrh which is soluble in alcohol.

1845 *Chem. Gaz.* III. 265 The resin of myrrh..is..a neutral resin, and may be called Myrrhine. **1865** WATTS *Dict. Chem.*

myrrhine, *a.*[1] and *sb.*: see MURRHINE.

† **ˈmyrrhine**, *a.*[2] *Obs.*$^{-0}$ [ad. L. *myrrhin-us*, f. *myrrha* MYRRH[1]: see -INE.] = MYRRHEAN.

1656 [see MYRRHEAN].

‖ **myrrhis** (ˈmɜːrɪs, ˈmɪrɪs). [late L., a. Gr. μυρρίς.] = MYRRH[2]. (Now only as generic name.)

1548 TURNER *Names Herbes* (E.D.S.) 54 Myrrhis is called in Cambrygeshyre casshes, in other places mockecheruel. **1601** HOLLAND *Pliny* II. 202 Myrrhis, which some call Smyrrhiza, others Myrrha, is passing like vnto Hemlocke. **1706** PHILLIPS (ed. Kersey), *Myrrhis*, Mock-Chervil.

myrrhite ('mɜːraɪt, 'mɪ-). Also 6-7 mirrite. [ad. L. *myrrhītēs*, a. Gr. μυρρίτης (sc. λίθος), f. μύρρα MYRRH[1]: see -ITE.] Murrhine stone.

1567 MAPLET *Gr. Forest* I. 15 The Mirrite is a Gem, both in taste and colour like to Myrrhe. 1688 HOLME *Armoury* II. 40/2. 1855 OGILVIE Suppl., *Myrrhite*, a kind of precious stone.

myrrhol ('mɜːrɒl, 'mɪrɒl). *Chem.* (Also -ole.) [f. MYRRH[1] + -OL.] (See quot.)

1845 *Chem. Gaz.* III. 265 The distilled oil of myrrh (Myrrhole). 1865 WATTS *Dict. Chem.* s.v. *Myrrh*.

myrrhophore ('mɜːrəfɔə(r), 'mɪrə-). [ad. Gr. *μυρροφόρος, f. μύρρα MYRRH[1] + -φόρος bearing, φέρειν to bear.] (See quot. 1848 and *Mark* xvi. 1.)

1848 MRS. JAMESON *Sacr. & Leg. Art* (1850) 218 The women who carry the spices and perfumes to the tomb of Jesus are called in Greek Art, the Myrrhophores. 1899 *Reliquary* Jan. 44 The three boxes containing the sweet spices prepared by the Myrrhophores to anoint our Saviour.

'myrrh-tree. [MYRRH[1].] = MYRRH[1] 2.

In MSS. of the Wycliffite Bible *myrre tree* occurs in several places as a variant reading for *myrte tree*.

1382 WYCLIF *Gen.* xliii. 11 The licoure of myrre tree, and of therebynt, and of almaundis. *a* 1400 *Propr. Sanct.* in *Archiv Stud. neu. Spr.* LXXXI. 301 Mirre-tre þat ȝiueþ two-maner gummes. 1567 MAPLET *Gr. Forest* 52 The Mirhe tree, sayth Plinie, groweth in the pastures and woods of Arabia. 1601 LYLY *Love's Metam.* I. ii. 103 Cinyras that with furie followed his daughter Mirrha, till shee was chaunged to a Mirre tree. 1797 *Encycl. Brit.* (ed. 3) XII. 571/2 The myrrh-tree..is a native of Abexim in Ethiopia. 1867 TRISTRAM *Nat. Hist. Bible* xii. 365 Many modern travellers have noticed the Myrrh tree both in Arabia Felix (Saba) and in Eastern Africa.

myrrhy ('mɜːrɪ), *a.* [f. MYRRH[1] + -Y[1].] Smelling like or redolent of myrrh. Also *Comb.*, as ***myrrhy-threaded***.

1842 BROWNING *Waring* vi, Some pigeon, from the myrrhy lands, Rapt by the whirlblast to fierce Scythian strands. 1857 *Chamb. Jrnl.* VII. 224 The sweet myrrhy buds that grow on the wood-apple. 1860 SIR T. MARTIN *Horace* 135 Her myrrhy hair [*Carm.* III. iv. 22 *murreum..crinem*]. 1865 G. M. HOPKINS *Poems* (1967) 21 For sackcloth and frieze And the ever-fretting shirt of punishment Give myrrhy-threaded golden folds of ease.

myrriad, myrrour(e, obs. ff. MYRIAD, MIRROR.

myrsen: see MEERSCHAUM.

†**myrt.** *Obs.* Also 5 mirte, 6 myrte, 7 mirt. [ad. L. *myrt-us*, a. Gr. μύρτος. Cf. F. *myrte*, It., Sp., Pg. *mirto*.] = MYRTLE.

1382 WYCLIF *Isa.* lv. 13 For the nettle shal growe the tre that is clepid myrt. *c* 1420 *Pallad. on Husb.* III. 1094 Six sester old wyn do to mirtes bayis v pound. *c* 1550 LLOYD *Treas. Health* c 8 Syrupes of myrte, of licorise, of Calamente. 1589 FLEMING *Virg. Georg.* I. 26 The frutes of bloudie myrts. 1615 BRATHWAIT *Strappado* (1878) 170 Sweet-breath'd Sicamour and Mirt.

b. *attrib.* (see also MYRT-TREE).

1535 COVERDALE *2 Esdras* (= *Neh.*) viii. 15 Pynebraunches, Myrtbraunches, Palmebraunches. 1561 HOLLYBUSH *Hom. Apoth.* 40 b, Stype Myrte berries in oyle of Violettes. 1562 TURNER *Herbal* II. 61 The brothe of Myrtilles or Myrte sedes.

myrtaceous (mɜː'teɪʃəs), *a. Bot.* [f. mod.L. *Myrtāce-æ*, fem. pl. of late L. *myrtāceus* (Celsus), f. *myrt-us* MYRT: see -ACEOUS.] Of the N.O. *Myrtaceæ*, to which the myrtle belongs.

1835 *Penny Cycl.* III. 123/2 Myrtaceous plants with white blossoms. 1866 *Treas. Bot.* 773/1 A myrtaceous tree.

myrtal ('mɜːtəl), *a.* and *sb.* [ad. mod.L. *myrtāl-is*, f. *myrt-us* MYRT + -AL[1].] **A.** *adj.* Belonging to Lindley's 'alliance' *Myrtales*, consisting of the myrtles and allied plants. **B.** *sb.* A plant of this 'alliance'.

1846 LINDLEY *Veget. Kingd.* 716 The Myrtal Alliance. *Ibid.* 722 An instance of the approach of Myrtals to the Asteral Alliance. *Ibid.* 726 Myrtal Exogens.

myrtene ('mɜːtiːn). *Chem.* [f. L. *myrt-us* MYRT + -ENE.] The terpene from volatile oil of myrtle.

1872 J. H. GLADSTONE in *Jrnl. Chem. Soc.* Ser. II. X. 3, I would suggest the following:—..Hydrocarbon from Myrtle. Myrtene.

myrther, obs. form of MURDER.

myrti'foliate, *a. rare*[−1]. [f. L. *myrt-us* MYRT + *folium* leaf + -ATE[2].] Myrtle-leaved.

1693 *Phil. Trans.* XVII. 619 A pretty Myrtifoliate Alnus.

myrtiform ('mɜːtɪfɔːm), *a. Anat.* [ad. mod.L. *myrtiform-is*, f. *myrt-us* MYRT.] Of the shape of a myrtle-berry; in ***myrtiform caruncle, fossa.***

1840 W. J. E. WILSON *Anat. Vade M.* (1842) 34 The myrtiform fossa is divided from the canine fossa by a perpendicular ridge. 1857 BULLOCK tr. *Cazeaux' Midwifery* 48 The myrtiform caruncles.

†**'myrtine,** *a. Obs.* [ad. late L. *myrtin-us* (in *oleum myrtinum*), f. *myrt-us* MYRT: see -INE.] Of myrtle.

(Erroneously used in the first quot.)

1382 WYCLIF *Esther* ii. 12 So onli that sixe monethis thei shulde ben enoynt with myrtine oile [Vulg. *oleo myrrhino*]. 1545 RAYNOLD *Byrth Mankynde* 81 Take oyle Myrtine, oyle of rooses, of eche iiii. ounces.

†**'myrtite.** *Obs.* [ad. late L. *myrtītēs*, a. Gr. μυρτίτης (οἶνος).] Myrtle wine.

c 1420 *Pallad. on Husb.* III. 1093 Sone in this mone ek mirtite is to make. 1607 TOPSELL *Four-f. Beasts* 49 Drunke with vineger, it is good against al venim of Serpents.. against the Lizzards with Mirtite.

myrtle ('mɜːt(ə)l), *sb.* Forms: 5 mirtille, -ylle, 6 mirt-, myrtel(l, -ylle, 6-8 mirtle, 7 mertle, mert-, mirt-, myrtil(l, 6- myrtle. [a. OF. *mirt-*, *myrtille*, fem. (1) myrtle-berry, (2) bilberry, whortleberry, also *myrtil*, masc. (= It. *mirtillo* myrtle-berry), ad. popular L. **myrtilla*, *-us*, dim. of L. *myrta*, *myrtus* MYRT.]

†**1.** The fruit or berry of the myrtle tree. *Obs.*

c 1400 *Lanfranc's Cirurg.* 53 Poudre of mirtillis. 1526 *Gt. Herbal* cclxvii. (1529) P ij b, Mirte is a lytell tre so called, the whiche tre bereth a fruyte that is named Myrtylles. 1578 LYTE *Dodoens* 462 Barley giuen with Mirtels, or wine,.. stoppeth the running of the belly. 1657 COLES *Adam in E.* lxxi. 135 Being boyled in red Wine with Pomegranat Rinds, and Myrtills, it stayeth the Lask. 1732 LEDIARD *Sethos* II. x. 426 Boxes of myrtles and oranges.

2. a. A plant of the genus *Myrtus* (N.O. *Myrtaceæ*), esp. *M. communis*, the Common Myrtle, a shrub growing abundantly in Southern Europe, having shiny evergreen leaves and white sweet-scented flowers, and now used chiefly in perfumery.

The myrtle was held sacred to Venus and is used as an emblem of love.

1562 TURNER *Herbal* II. 60 b, Dioscorides maketh ii. sortes of sowen or set myrtel trees... But other writers make yet mo kyndes of Myrtilles. 1590 C'TESS PEMBROKE *Antonie* 68 Since then the Baies so well thy forehead knewe To Venus mirtles yeelded haue their place. 1611 BIBLE *Isa.* xli. 19, I will plant in the wildernes..the Myrtle, and the Oyle tree. 1639 S. DU VERGER tr. *Camus' Admir. Events* 14 The palmes of my valour, and mirtles of my incomparable love. 1667 MILTON *P.L.* IV. 262 The fringed Bank with Myrtle crownd. 1768 PENNANT *Brit. Zool.* II. 255 Myrtles flourish in the open air during the whole year. 1784 COWPER *Task* III. 570 The spiry myrtle with unwith'ring leaf. 1846 LINDLEY *Veget. Kingd.* 737 Even the berries of the common Myrtle are esteemed in the Greek Archipelago, especially a sort with white fruit. 1864 TENNYSON *Islet* 19 Fairily-delicate palaces shine Mixt with myrtle and clad with vine.

b. With qualifying word, applied to various species of the genus *Myrtus*, and other myrtaceous genera, and (esp. in Australasia and U.S.) to plants of other Natural Orders resembling *Myrtus*.

crape, fringe, Jew's, peach myrtle: see these words. See also Miller *Gard. Dict.*, Morris *Austral Eng.*, and Britton & Brown *Amer. Flora*.

1578 LYTE *Dodoens* VI. xiii. 674 This herbe is called..in English, Kneeholme,..and Petigree, also we may cal it yᵉ wilde Myrtel. 1597 GERARDE *Herbal* III. lxvii. 1226 Another kinde of Myrtill, called *Myrtus minor*, or noble Myrtill. 1601 Ground-myrtle [see GROUND *sb.* 18 c]. 1607 TOPSELL *Four-f. Beasts* 132 The seede of blacke mirtle. 1753 CHAMBERS *Cycl.* Suppl. s.v. *Myrtus*, The broad-leaved Roman Myrtle. 1843 W. BAXTER *Brit. Phænog. Bot.* VI. 474 *Ruscus aculeatus*. Prickly Butcher's Broom... Wild Myrtle. Prickly Petigree. 1845-50 MRS. LINCOLN *Lect. Bot.* v. 118 *Leiophyllum.. buxifolium* (sand myrtle). 1852 MUNDY *Antipodes* I. ii. 76 The South Sea myrtle, or Leptospermum. 1884 SARGENT *Rep. Forests N. Amer.* (10th Census IX) 41 *Ceanothus thyrsifolius*... Blue Myrtle.

c. Applied to plants of the genus *Myrica*: (*a*) **bog myrtle, Dutch myrtle,** Sweet Gale, *Myrica Gale*; (*b*) CANDLEBERRY *myrtle*, WAX-*myrtle*, q.v.

1597 GERARDE *Herbal* III. lxviii. 1228 *Myrtus Brabantica* ..Gaule, sweete Willow, or Dutch Myrtle tree. *Ibid.*, Gaule or the wilde Myrtle. 1797 *Encycl. Brit.* (ed. 3) XII. 573/2 Broad leaved Dutch myrtle, with spear-shaped, sharp pointed, dark-green leaves. 1826 CARRINGTON *Dartmoor* 176 Holne Chace..in swampy spots abounding with the myrica gale or Devonshire myrtle. 1866 *Treas. Bot.* 770/1 *M[yrica] Gale*, the Sweet Gale or Bog Myrtle,..the badge of the Campbells.

3. Short for *myrtle-green*.

1872 [see HUNTER 5 d]. 1884 *Christian World* 17 Jan. 52/1 Very rich Brocaded Plush..in Myrtle. 1897 'SARAH GRAND' *Beth Bk.* xxxix, Her white silk trimmed with myrtle.

†**4.** A kind of snuff. *Obs.*

1715 *Lond. Gaz.* No. 5394/4 Neat Mirtle Barcelona, at 1 s. per Ounce.

5. *attrib.* and *Comb.*, as ***myrtle band, bark, blossom, bough, bower, branch, bud, bush, crown, flower, grove, leaf, oil, shade, shrub, spray, sprig, twig, walk, wand, wreath; myrtle-leaved, -like*** adjs.; **myrtle bilberry** (see quot.); **myrtle bird** (U.S.), *Dendroica* (*Silvicola*) *coronata*, which feeds on the berries of the candleberry myrtle; **myrtle-bloom,** a myrtaceous plant; **myrtle candle,** a candle of myrtle-wax; **myrtle flag, grass,** *Acorus Calamus*; **myrtle green,** a shade of green like that of myrtle leaves; **myrtle-greener,** one who is dressed in myrtle green; **myrtle-of-the-river,** a large evergreen shrub, *Calyptranthes zuzygium*, of the family Myrtaceæ, native to Jamaica and bearing panicles of white flowers; **myrtle sedge** = *myrtle flag*; †**myrtle spurge,** a species of spurge having leaves like those of the myrtle; †**myrtle thrush,** ? nonce-transl. of Fr. (see quot.); **myrtle warbler** = *myrtle bird*; **myrtle wax,** wax produced by the candleberry myrtle, *Myrica cerifera*; **myrtle wine,** wine made from myrtle-berries.

1667 MILTON *P.L.* IX. 431 Them she upstaies Gently with *Mirtle band. 1864 *Chamb. Encycl.* VI. 641/2 *Myrtle bark is used for tanning in many parts of the south of Europe. 1849 *Rural Cycl.* III. 538/1 *Myrtle Bilberry,—botanically *Vaccinium Myrtillus*. 1808-13 A. WILSON *Amer. Ornith.* (1831) II. 130 Yellow-rump Warbler... As December's snows come on, they retreat to the lower countries of the southern States, where..I found them..among the myrtles, from which circumstance, they were usually called, in that quarter, *myrtle birds. 1857 THOREAU *Autumn* (1894) 137, I see many myrtle birds now about the house. 1846 LINDLEY *Veget. Kingd.* 718 To *Myrtleblooms and Melastomads they [*sc.* Myrobalans] are related through Memecylon. 1817 SHELLEY *Rev. Islam* III. xxxiv. 6 The *myrtle-blossoms starring the dim grove. 1781 COWPER *Anti-Thelyphth.* 174 His steed..Whose bridle..Hung not far off upon a *myrtle bough. 1784 —— *Task* II. 215 Ausonia's..*myrtle bow'rs. 1611 BIBLE *Neh.* viii. 15 Pine branches, and *Myrtle branches. 1846 LINDLEY *Veget. Kingd.* 737 *Myrtle buds and berries. 1555 PHAER *Æneid* III. (1558) 49 With roddes vpright & braunches thick a *myrtyl bushe ther grew. 1791 JEFFERSON in *Harper's Mag.* (1885) Mar. 535/2 *Myrtle candles of last year out. 1813 SCOTT *Trierm.* I. xvi, One wreath'd them with a *myrtle crown. 1796 WITHERING *Brit. Plants* (ed. 3) II. 344 *Myrtle Flag. Sweet Smelling Flag, or Calamus. Sweet *Myrtle-grass. 1684 R. WALLER *Nat. Exper.* 85 *Mirtle Flower water. ? 1793 COLERIDGE *Lines Autumnal Even.* 52 Love..in Joy's red nectar dips His myrtle flower. 1858 R. S. SURTEES *Ask Mamma* 134 The Major in..a *myrtle-green coat. 1925 E., O., & S. SITWELL *Poor Young People* 2 The colours most in favour are marine Blue Louise, gris bois, grenate, myrtle green. 1858 R. S. SURTEES *Ask Mamma* 155 While the *myrtle-greeners and others distribute themselves..here, there, and everywhere. 1592 SHAKS. *Ven. & Ad.* 865 This said, she hasteth to a *myrtle grove. 1601 HOLLAND *Pliny* XXIII. ix, The powder of drie *Myrtle leaves. 1606 SHAKS. *Ant. & Cl.* III. xii. 9 The Morne-dew on the Mertle leafe. 1688 HOLME *Armoury* III. xii. 437/1 The Mirtle Leaf Pen-Knife, it is a Pen-Knife with two edges, resembling a Mirtle Leaf, or rather a Javeline head. 1849 M. ARNOLD *Mod. Sappho* 49 Hast thou with myrtle-leaf crown'd him, O Pleasure? 1731 MILLER *Gard. Dict.* s.v. *Rhus*, The *Myrtle-leav'd Sumach. 1753 CHAMBERS *Cycl.* Suppl. s.v. *Thymelæa*, Hoary *myrtle-like leaves. 1859 W. S. COLEMAN *Woodlands* (1866) 141 The yellow-green leaves..give out their myrtle-like odour. 1919 *Ann. Rep. Board of Regents Smithsonian Inst. 1917* 384 The *myrtle-of-the-river..with opposite glossy leaves and clusters of fruit resembling blueberries. 1924 J. A. THOMSON *Science Old & New* v. 27 Even the names transport us into a land of pure delight—the paradise tree, the myrtle-of-the-river, the marlberry, and the bois-fidèle. 1601 HOLLAND *Pliny* II. Table, *Mirtle oyle. 1611 COTGR. s.v. *Myrtin*, *Huile myrtin*, Mirtle oyle; oyle extracted from Mirtle leaues. 1855 PRATT *Flower. Pl.* V. 324 Sweet Sedge ..in some country places it is called *Myrtle Sedge. 1596 B. GRIFFIN in *Pass. Pilgr.* xi, Venus with Adonis sitting by her, Vnder a *Mirtle shade. 1611 COTGR., *Meurte sauvage*, the wild Mirtle tree, or *Mirtle shrub. 1562 TURNER *Herbal* II. 154, I knowe no English name for it [*sc.* Myrtites], but it may be called *myrtel spourge. 1707 *Curios. in Husb. & Gard.* 154 The Wood-Spurge, the Cipress-Spurge, and the Mirtle-Spurge. 1611 COTGR. s.v. *Meurte*, *Oiseau de meurte*, a *Mirtle Thrush. 1601 HOLLAND *Pliny* XV. xxix, Rings made of *Myrtle twigs. 1802 COLERIDGE *Picture* 27 No *myrtle-walks are these. 1629 MILTON *Hymn Nativ.* iii, And waving wide her *mirtle wand. 1892 B. TORREY *Footpath-Way* 95 Not so was it with the *myrtle warblers. 1947 *Proc. Iowa Acad. Sci.* LIV. 379 Myrtle Warbler..is often a late migrant, for a warbler. 1963 R. D. SYMONS *Many Trails* ii. 17 Small birds that at first glance look like myrtle warblers. 1763 *Ann. Reg.* 54 Candles, *myrtle wax, 14 boxes. 1766 STORK *Acc. E. Florida* 48 The myrtle-wax shrub is, without doubt, the most useful of the spontaneous growth of America. 1597 GERARDE *Herbal* III. lxvii. 1227 Wine is made of Myrtle berries..this is called *Vinum Myrteum*, or *Myrtites*, *Myrtle wine. 1864 *Chamb. Encycl.* VI. 641/2 A Myrtle wine, called *Myrtidanum*, is made in Tuscany. 1784 COWPER *Task* II. 229 Who sell their laurel for a *myrtle wreath, And love when they should fight.

'myrtle, *v. Obs.* or *dial.* In 5 myrtil, 9 mirtle. [f. **murt* (cf. TO-MURT in *E.E. Allit. P.* C. 150) + -LE 3.] *intr.* To fall to pieces, crumble away.

c 1400 *Destr. Troy* 4301 All maumentre in myddelerthe myrtlit to peses. *Ibid.* 4312 Bothe Mawhownus & maumettes myrtild in peces. 1828 *Craven Gloss.*, *Mirtle*, to waste away, crumble.

'myrtle-berry. a. The fruit of the myrtle (*Myrtus*). **b.** The bilberry or whortleberry. (Cf. OF. *myrtille*.) **c.** ***myrtle-berry wax*** = myrtle-wax.

1579 LANGHAM *Gard. Health* (1633) 400 Myrtle beries are very good for them that spit, vomit, or pisse bloud. 1638 RAWLEY tr. *Bacon's Life & Death* (1650) 50 Unctuous and Comfortable things are, Saffron, Mastick, Myrrhe, and Myrtle-Berries. 1660 *Act 12 Chas. II*, c. 4 Mertle berries the pound—js. 1718 QUINCY *Compl. Disp.* 100 Myrtle-Berries are very rough and astringent. 1751 *Gent. Mag.* Feb. 52/1 The plants of Skiddow are the myrtle berries, generally called black-berries, the *vitis idæa* of Dioscorides. 1888 *Encycl. Brit.* XXIV. 459/2 Myrtle-Berry Wax is obtained from the fruit of several species of Myrica.

'myrtle-tree. = MYRTLE 2 a and c. (Cf. MYRT-TREE.)

1548 TURNER *Names Herbes* (E.D.S.) 54 Myrtus is called ..in english a myrtle tree, or a myrt tree. **1590** SPENSER *F.Q.* III. v. 40. **1611** COTGR., *Meurte de Brabant*, the sweet shrub Gaule, or sweet Willow; the Dutch Mirtle tree. **1611** BIBLE *Isa.* lv. 13 In stead of the brier shall come vp the Myrtle tree. **1748** *Anson's Voy.* II. i. 117 There are none of them of a size to yield any considerable timber, except the myrtle-trees which are the largest on the Island. **1849** AYTOUN *Poems, Scheik of Sinai* v, Amidst the dark-green masses Of the flowering myrtle-trees.

myrtly ('mɜːtlɪ), *a.* [f. MYRTLE *sb.* + -Y[1].] Containing myrtles or redolent of myrtle.

1882 G. F. ARMSTRONG *Garland fr. Greece* 135 Every brake And myrtly jungle seemed to undulate With motions of strange beings.

†**myrt-tree.** *Obs.* Also 6 myrtre(e. [See MYRT.] = MYRTLE 2 a and b.

In second quot. used erron. (cf. note s.v. MYRRH-TREE).

1382 WYCLIF *2 Esdras* (= *Neh.*) viii. 15 The braunchis of myrt tree. **1388** —— *Esther* ii. 12 So oneli that thei weren anoyntid with oile of myrt tre [*oleo myrrhino*] bi sixe monethis. *c* **1510** BARCLAY *Mirr. Gd. Manners* (1570) F iij, The Myrtree and Orange by sea bankes doth growe. **1562** TURNER *Herbal* II. 60 b, The Wild Myrte tre, which is called in Englishe bochers brome. **1580** LYLY *Euphues* (Arb.) 364 And in this poynt they [*sc.* women] are not vnlike vnto the Mirt [*ed.* 1581 Mirre] Tree. **1616** SURFL. & MARKH. *Country Farm* 290 The Myrt-tree, which craueth the same ground.. that the Myrtle-tree, as being a kind of wild Myrtle-tree.

attrib. **1513** DOUGLAS *Æneis* VI. vii. *heading*, Eneas..fand quene Dido in the myrtre schaw.

Myrtynmes, obs. f. MARTINMAS.

myry, obs. f. MERRY, MIRY.

myrytayne, obs. f. MARITIME.

mys, mys-: see MISS, MIS-.

myscelto, -towe, -tyne, obs. ff. MISTLETOE.

myscha(u)nt(e, -chea(u)nt(e, var. MESCHANT *Obs.*

†**myse.** *Obs.* [Form and origin doubtful.] Applied to the 'lice' (Vulg. *sciniphes*, LXX. σκνῖφες) of the third plague of Egypt.

c **1440** *York Myst.* xi. 273 Lorde, grete myses bothe morn and none Bytis vs full bittirlye. [*c* **1460** *Towneley Myst.* viii. 286 Greatte mystis.]

myse, obs. pl. MOUSE *sb.*

mysegging, obs. form of MISSAYING.

myself (maɪ'sɛlf, mɪ'sɛlf), *pron.* Forms (see also SELF): *α.* 1 me siolf, sylf, 2–3 meseolf, 3 me sellf (*Ormin*), seolfan, suluen, 4–6 meself, (6 mee-). *β.* 3 mi-, myseolf, (-ve), -sulf, (-ve), 3–4 miself, 4–5 mi-, 4–6 myselve(n, (5 -syllf, -silven, -seluon, -yn, 6 selfin, sellf), 5–7 my-selfe, 4– myself. *γ. dial.* 6 -sell, 8–9 mysel', mysel, mesel, mysen, etc. (see E.D.D.). [orig. ME *acc.-dat. pron.* + SELF (q.v.); in OE. in two distinct constructions (see notes to senses 1 and 5). The transition from the form *meself* to *myself* was prob. due, partly to unstressing and obscuring of the vowel of *mē* (*mē'self, mĕ'self, mi'self*), partly to the analogy of *herself*, in which *her* was felt as a possessive genitive.]

I. Emphatic uses.

1. a. In apposition with the subject-pronoun *I*: In my own person; for my part.

In OE. *ic me self*, where *me* is a kind of ethical dative and the uninflected *self* is in apposition with *ic*.

α. **853** in Earle *Land-charters* 343 Ealle ða ȝerihte ða ic meseolf ær ahte. *c* **1200** ORMIN 16242, I me sellf shall reȝȝsenn itt þe þridde daȝȝ off dæþe. *c* **1205** LAY. 3214 Ne bidde ich nanne maðmes, me seolf ich habben inoȝe. *a* **1225** *St. Marher.* 11 Ich me seolf smelle of þe swote ihū swottre þen euer ani þing þ is on eorðe. *a* **1300** *Cursor M.* 5768 'Ga forth,' he said, 'wit-vten dred, For i me-self sal þe lede.' *c* **1330** *Amis & Amil.* 850 Y seighe it meself this ich day. **1576** FLEMING *Panopl. Epist.* 66, I mee selfe stoode in neede of a comforter.

β. *c* **1205** LAY. 8816 Ah ich mi seolf neore & mine gode cnihtes i-numen weoren ure king. **1297** R. GLOUC. (Rolls) 8361 Icholle to hom..& wiþinne vif dawes mid hom be mi sulf in bataile. *c* **1350** *Will. Palerne* 722 Mi-self knowe ich nouȝt mi ken ne mi kontre noiþer. **1390** GOWER *Conf.* I. 43, I am miselven on of tho, Which to this Scole am underfonge. *c* **1400** MAUNDEV. (1839) xx. 221 He schalle not trowe it lightly: and treuly, no more did I my self, til I saughe it. *c* **1440** *Alph. Tales* lvii. 42 Nowder of þies two did itt, I did it my selfe. **1535** COVERDALE *Jer.* xxi. 5, I my selff will fight agaynst you. **1601** SHAKS. *Jul. C.* III. i. 236, I will my selfe into the Pulpit first. **1682** DRYDEN & LEE *Dk. Guise* I. i. (1683) 5, I will my self to Court. **1776** *Trial of Nundocomar* 92/1 Mohun Persaud..knew as little of Persian as I did myself. **1887** CARROLL *Game of Logic* i. § 1. 4 If there are any: I haven't seen many, myself. **1890** 'R. BOLDREWOOD' *Col. Reformer* (1891) 320 Judge Shortcharge may be right, or he may be wrong, but he decides. I go for the judge myself.

γ. **1500–20** DUNBAR *Poems* lx. 71 Gif I be ane of thay my sell. **1790** MRS. WHEELER *Westmld. Dial.* 50, I dunnet mitch heed me sel. **1864** TENNYSON *Northern Farmer* viii, Theer wur a boggle in it, I often 'eärd 'um mysen.

†**b.** ***myself one***, or ***alone***: by myself. Also (*rare*) simply ***myself***. *Obs.*

c **1275** *Wom. Samaria* 31 in *O.E. Misc.* 85, I nabbe, heo seyde, nenne were, ich am my seolf al one. *c* **1325** *Song of Merci* 21 in *E.E.P.* (1862) 119 Ful stille .i. stod my self al on. *c* **1485** *E.E. Misc.* (Warton Club) 43 Bi a forrest as I gane fare, Walkyng al myselvene alone. **1535** COVERDALE *Deut.* i. 9, I am not able to beare you my self alone. [So **1611**.] *c* **1540** *Pilgryms Tale* 168 in Thynne *Animadv.* (1875) 82 For that I was my-selue, & company had non. **1600** SHAKS. *A.Y.L.* III. ii. 269, I had as liefe haue beene my selfe alone.

c. In apposition with *me. rare.*

13.. *R. Glouc. Chron.* (1724) 30 (MS. B), Ac for me my self, ich wol soþ segge of þis dede.

2. By ellipsis of *I, myself* comes to be used as a nominative. **a.** as simple subject. Now only *poet.*

The verb in concord is usually in the 1st person sing., †but occas. in the 3rd.

c **1350** *Will. Palerne* 543 Nay! sertes my-selue schal him neuer telle. *c* **1369** CHAUCER *Dethe Blaunche* 34 My-selven can not telle why The sooth. *c* **1386** —— *Wife's Prol.* 175 (Harl. MS.) My self haþ [*Ellesm.* haue, *other* 5 *MSS.* hath] ben þe whippe. **1450** *Rolls of Parlt.* V. 176/1 Myself hath be armed in the Kynges daies. **1588** SHAKS. *Tit. A.* IV. iv. 74 My selfe hath often heard them say,..That Lucius banishment was wrongfully. **1601** —— *Jul. C.* IV. iii. 171 My selfe haue Letters of the selfe-same Tenure. **1634** T. WHALLEY in *Ussher's Lett.* (1686) 602 My self only think it not improbable, but that he might live there some Years. **1756** TOLDERVY *Hist. 2 Orphans* II. 59 Myself has received singular favours from the hands of the doctors Mead and Monro! **1859** FITZGERALD tr. *Omar* xxvii, Myself when young did eagerly frequent Doctor and Saint. **1864** BROWNING *Death in Desert* Wks. 1896 I. 591/2 Before the point was mooted, 'What is God?' No savage man inquired, 'What am myself?'

b. As part of a compound subject or predicate, and after *than, as.* Also as simple predicate.

Except at the beginning of an enumeration, or as simple predicate, *myself* in this use now expresses no special emphasis, being preferred in order to avoid the awkwardness of *I*.

c **1386** CHAUCER *Prol.* 546 Ther was also a Reve and a Millere,..A Maunciple, and my-self. **1606** SHAKS. *Ant. & Cl.* II. v. 83 These hands do lacke Nobility, that they strike A meaner then my selfe. **1748** RICHARDSON *Clarissa* III. xxiii. 136 Enough to make a better man than myself..run into madness. **1866** *Good Words* Aug. 544/2 One of our party and myself started on an expedition.

3. Substituted for ME as the object of a verb or governed by a preposition.

The use of *myself* as the sole or the first-mentioned object of a verb is now *arch.* In an enumeration, when not occupying the first place, it does not now express any special emphasis, being in this position commonly preferred to *me*.

c **1205** LAY. 493 Mine þralles i mire þeode me suluen [*c* **1275** mi-seolue] þretiað. *c* **1350** *Will. Palerne* 1175 þe londes þat he has he holdes of mi-selue. **1377** LANGL. *P. Pl.* B. XVI. 46 *Liberum arbitrium*..þat is lieutenant to loken it wel by leue of my-selue. *c* **1400** *Destr. Troy* 13177 Two sons ..of the same kynges,..sesit my selfe, & my sure felow. **1500–20** DUNBAR *Poems* xxxiv. 19 Thow salbe merchand for my sell, Renunce thy God and cum to me. **1593** SHAKS. *2 Hen. VI*, III. ii. 59 And for my selfe, Foe as he was to me, [etc.]. **1789** BURNS *To Dr. Blacklock* ii, He tauld mysel' by word o' mouth, He'd tak' my letter. **1809** MALKIN *Gil Blas* v. i. ⁋ 18 Membrilla has neither chick nor child but myself. **1812** (*title*) The History of Myself and my Friend: a Novel. **1842** BORROW *Bible in Sp.* xxxviii, Several of the ultra-popish bishops..had denounced the Bible, the Bible Society, and myself. **1856** RUSKIN *Mod. Paint.* IV. v. xx. § 1 To myself, mountains are the beginning and the end of all natural scenery.

4. a. (passing into *sb.*) My being or personality; my own or very self. † ***another myself*** [after L. *alter ego*]: a second self, said of an intimate friend (cf. I *pron.* 4 b).

1526 *Pilgr. Perf.* (W. de W. 1531) 1 b, My wytte is gross, my selfe rude, and my tonge very barbarouse. **1574** HELLOWES tr. *Gueuara's Fam. Ep.* (1577) 113, I bewaile the death of my friend, which is another my selfe. **1592** SHAKS. *Rom. & Jul.* II. ii. 49 And for thy name which is no part of thee, Take all my selfe. **1599** B. JONSON *Cynthia's Rev.* I. iv. (1616) 194 Your sweet disposition to trauaile..hath made you another my-selfe in mine eye. **1667** MILTON *P.L.* v. 95 Best Image of my self and dearer half. **1690** LOCKE *Hum. Und.* II. xxvi. (1695) 188 That consciousness whereby I am my self to my self. **1768–74** TUCKER *Lt. Nat.* (1834) I. 302 There might have been two myselves some thousands of miles apart. **1859** FITZGERALD tr. *Omar* xx, To-morrow I may be Myself with Yesterday's Sev'n thousand Years. **1864** JEAN INGELOW *Poems* 23 O, let me be myself! But where, O where,..Shall the myself be found? **1871** R. W. DALE *Commandm.* vi. 156 My life is not so sacred as myself.

b. ***to be myself, to feel like myself***: to be, or feel as if I were, in my normal condition of body or mind.

1777 *Johnsoniana* 51, I am not at all myself this morning. *a* **1845** HOOD *Lamia* i. 82, I was not quite myself—(not what I am). **1886** BESANT *Childr. Gibeon* II. xix, It gave me such a shake as I never had before; I haven't felt like myself ever since.

II. Reflexive uses.

5. As direct or indirect obj., in acc. and inf. const., or in dependence on a prep. (Orig. only emphatic refl., but now in general use, replacing the refl. *me*, which is now only *arch.*: cf. ME *pron.* 5.) Also in phr. ***says I to myself.***

In OE. recorded only in the acc., *self* being in concord with *me*.

837 *Will* in Thorpe *Dipl. Angl.* (1865) 476 Ic wille ærist me siolfne Gode allmehtȝum forȝeofan to ðere stowe æt Cristes cirican. *c* **1000** ÆLFRIC *Gen.* xxii. 16 Ic swerige þurh me sylfne, sæde se ælmihtiȝa. *c* **1205** LAY. 828 Iche wlle þesne king læden mid me seolfan [*c* **1275** mi seolue]. **1297** R. GLOUC. (Rolls) 9285, & wanne ich am encheson of such peril ywis Verst icholle þer inne do mi sulue. **1390** GOWER *Conf.* I. 280, I am so with miselven wroth. **1484** CAXTON *Fables of Æsop* III. ii, By cause that I..fayned my self to be a medycyn. **1535** COVERDALE *Gen.* iii. 10, I hyd my self. **1551–6** R. ROBINSON tr. *More's Utopia* (Arb.) 13 Such spare houres as..I..cold..winne to me self. **1624** CAPT. SMITH *Virginia* III. viii. 76 The loue I beare you, doth cause me thus nakedly to forget my selfe. **1671** MILTON *P.R.* I. 204 Myself I thought Born to that end. **1711** ADDISON *Spect.* No. 26 ⁋ 1, I very often walk by my self in Westminster Abbey. **1720** [see SAY *v.*[1] B. 3 b ¶]. **1759** JOHNSON *Idler* No. 55 ⁋ 4, I acquainted myself with the black inhabitants of metallic caverns. **1811** (*title*) Thinks I to myself: a Novel. **1825** LAMB *Elia* II. *The Superannuated Man*, I had foolishly given a handle against myself. **1855** DICKENS *Let. to Leigh Hunt* in *Cornh. Mag.* May (1892) 505, I..reject all engagements, to have my time to myself. **1891** KIPLING *Light that Failed* v, I'm not going to belong to anybody except myself. **1920** J. LEE *Penitent* in *Northern Numbers* 81 As I lay in the trenches at Noove Chapelle,..Sez I to mysel', sez I to mysel':—Billy, me boy, here's the end o' you.

mysell, var. MEASLE *a.*; dial. f. MYSELF.

myselry, var. MESELRY.

myselue(n, -on, etc., obs. ff. MYSELF.

myse mase, obs. f. MIZMAZE.

mysen, dial. f. MYSELF.

mysentery, obs. f. MESENTERY.

mysetente: see MISTEND.

myseuse, obs. f. MISUSE *v.*

myshef, -evouse, obs. ff. MISCHIEF, MISCHIEVOUS.

Mysian ('mɪsɪən), *sb.* and *a.* [f. L. *Mysia*, Gr. Μυσία Mysia + -AN.] **A.** *sb.* **a.** A native or inhabitant of ancient Mysia in north-west Asia Minor. **b.** The language of Mysia. **B.** *adj.* Of or pertaining to ancient Mysia, its inhabitants or its language.

1555 [see BULGARIAN *a.* and *sb.*]. **1601** HOLLAND tr. *Pliny's Nat. Hist.* v. xxx. 110 Teuthrania, which the Mysians in old time held. **1834** J. S. MILL in *Monthly Repos.* VIII. 837 The most despised of all foreign nations. Witness the phrase Μυσῶν λεία, the spoil of the Mysians, applied to any people so poor in spirit, that even the unwarlike Mysians could plunder them with impunity. **1844** A. W. KINGLAKE *Eothen* iii. 54, I saw, and acknowledged the snowy crown of the Mysian Olympus! **1884** *Encycl. Brit.* XVII. 122/2 Ancient writers all agree in describing the Mysians as a distinct people,..though they never appear in history as an independent nation. *Ibid.*, 123/1 The only relic of the Mysian language is a very short inscription,..supposed to be in the Mysian dialect. *a* **1936** A. E. HOUSMAN *Coll. Poems* (1939) 216 Up the Mysian entry wending, Lydians, Lydians, what is yon? **1939** L. H. GRAY *Foundations of Language* 383 Of *Mysian* we may have a scanty inscription of the fourth or third century B.C., consisting of five lines. **1948** D. DIRINGER *Alphabet* 466 Some scholars mention a Mysian, a Cilician and a Cappadocian alphabet. **1954** PEI & GAYNOR *Dict. Linguistics* 142 *Mysian*, an extinct language, once spoken in Asia Minor... A language of undetermined linguistic affinities, classified as Asianic. **1972** W. B. LOCKWOOD *Panorama Indo-Europ. Languages* 174 In Asia Minor, Mysian is said to have been a living language in the sixth century. **1974** *Encycl. Brit. Micropædia* VII. 151/3 The Mysians..were mentioned by Homer as primitive allies of the Trojans.

mysid ('maɪsɪd). [f. mod.L. family name *Mysidæ*, f. the generic name MYSIS (P. A. Latreille in C. S. Sonnini *Buffon's Hist. Nat. Insectes & Crustacés* (1802) III. 36): see -ID[3].] A small shrimp-like crustacean of the family Mysidæ or the suborder Mysidacea; an opossum-shrimp. Also *attrib.*

1941 STEINBECK & RICKETTS *Sea of Cortez* xv. 152 That night we rigged a lamp..and hung it close down to the water... Pelagic isopods and mysids immediately swarmed to the illuminated circle. **1956** A. HARDY *Open Sea* xiii. 254 Many ostracods and copepods, and at least one mysid, are known to flash brightly. **1961** *New Scientist* 15 June 661/1 Small marine crustaceans, called mysids, would orientate themselves preferentially at right angles to the direction of polarization of vertical light. **1965** B. E. FREEMAN tr. *Vandel's Biospeleology* ix. 117 The mysids are mainly marine Crustacea. **1969** A. WHEELER *Fishes Brit. Is. & N.-W. Europe* 133/2 The 'whitebait herring', i.e. those in their first year,..eat crustacea, the copepod *Calanus*, the larvae of acorn barnacles, mysid shrimps, and the eggs and larvae of decapods and amphipods.

‖**Mysis** ('maɪsɪs). [mod.L. (Latreille 1802), perh. a. Gr. μύσις closing of lips or eyes.] The typical genus of *Mysidæ* or opossum-shrimps.

1842 *Penny Cycl.* XXIII. 80/2 The second pair of antennæ are inserted below the preceding, as in *Mysis.* **1891** *Daily News* 29 Jan. 5/2 The shrimp-like mysis.

b. Used *attrib.* to denote the stage of certain decapods in which they resemble the genus *Mysis.*

1865 *Q. Jrnl. Sci.* II. 508 This Zöea-phase afterwards gives place to one which can only be called a *Mysis*-phase. **1872** DARWIN *Orig. Spec.* xiv. 390 The mysis-stage.

myskelen, obs. f. MASLIN[2].

myskidyd: see MISGUIDED.

myslary, var. MESELRY.

myslen, obs. f. MASLIN[2].

Mysoline ('maɪsəliːn). *Pharm.* Also **mysoline**. A proprietary name for primidone.

1949 *Trade Marks Jrnl.* 12 Oct. 901/2 Mysoline... Pharmaceutical substances for human and veterinary use; sanitary substances and disinfectants;..Imperial Chemical (Pharmaceuticals) Limited,..Slough, Buckinghamshire, England; manufacturers and merchants. **1958** J. H. BURNS *Lect. Notes Pharmacol.* (ed. 5) 52 Primidone (Mysoline) is the most effective agent for the form of epilepsy known as 'grand mal'. **1966** *Economist* 30 Apr. 512 Other drugs that ICI hope will attract a large market are..the anti-epileptic Mysoline and the long-established anti-malarial Paludrine. **1973** *Clin. Chim. Acta* XLIV. 383 Both mysoline and phenytoin subjects show a more severely raised GGTP level than those treated with phenobarbitone.

mysomer, obs. f. MID-SUMMER.

myson, obs. f. MIZEN.

‖**mysophobia** (maɪsə'fəʊbɪə). [mod.L., f. Gr. μύσος neut., uncleanness: see -PHOBIA.] Morbid dread of dirt or defilement.

1879 W. A. HAMMOND & W. J. MORTON *Neurol. Contrib.* No. 1. **1899** *Allbutt's Syst. Med.* VII. 878.

Mysore ('maɪsɔə(r)). The former name of a state in southern India (now Karnataka), used to designate coffee produced there.

1907 *Yesterday's Shopping* (1969) 2 The Mocha and Mysore mixed in equal quantities are recommended for best Coffee. *c* **1938** *Fortnum & Mason Catal.* 7/2 Coffees... 'Mysore'. **1951** W. H. BRINDLEY in W. G. Copsey *Modern Grocer* (ed. 5) II. viii. 97 The best quality and most widely known coffees from India are Mysores... Mysores are now full-bodied in cup, but often a little rough and dry on the palate. **1965** L. DEIGHTON *Action Cook Bk.* 132/2 Here are some good combinations: Costa Rica with Tanganyika (Chagga); Mocha mixed with Mysore.

Mysorean (maɪsə'riːən), *sb.* and *a.* [See prec.] **A.** *sb.* A native or inhabitant of Mysore. **B.** *adj.* Of or pertaining to Mysore.

1871 C. M. YONGE *Pioneers & Founders* iii. 61 The Mysoreans complained that the English promises had not been kept. **1932** *Times Lit. Suppl.* 3 Mar. 159/4 A photograph of Mysorean industrial life. **1968** *Jrnl. Mus. Acad. Madras* XXXIX. 74 Kangari Radhakrishnaiya..is believed to have been a Mysorean.

mysorin (maɪ'sɔərɪn). *Min.* [ad. F. *mysorine* (Beudant), f. *Mysore*: see MYSORE.] Anhydrous ortho-carbonate of copper, found in Mysore.

1839 URE *Dict. Arts* 336. **1854** DANA *Syst. Min.* (ed. 4) II. 458 Mysorin... Color blackish-brown, when pure.

mysose, obs. f. MISUSE *v.*

myspeak to **myspend**: see MIS-SPEAK to MIS-SPEND.

myspylle, var. MESPILE.

myss, obs. f. MISS; obs. pl. of MOUSE.

myssanger, obs. f. MESSENGER.

myssell, obs. f. MEASLE.

mysselyng, obs. f. MIZZLING.

myssen, etc., obs. ff. MIZEN.

myssis, obs. f. MISEASE.

myssomere(e, obs. ff. MID-SUMMER.

myssour,-uyr, obs. Sc. ff. MEASURE.

myssyfe, etc., obs. ff. MISSIVE.

myst (mɪst). [ad. L. *mysta*, *mystēs* (see MYSTES). Cf. F. *myste* (Rabelais).] A priest of the mysteries; one who is initiated into mysteries.

a **1693** *Urquhart's Rabelais* III. xlviii. 385 Those Mysts and Flamens. **1849** GROTE *Greece* II. lxv. (1862) V. 589 Kleokritus—herald of the Mysts or communicants in the Eleusinian mysteries. **1856** R. A. VAUGHAN *Mystics* (1860) I. 15 The disciple admitted to these was a philosophical myst, or mystic.

myst, obs. f. *might* (see MAY *v.*[1] 2 b *note*); obs. f. MIST, MOST; see MYSE.

mystacal ('mɪstəkəl), *a.* [f. Gr. μυστακ-, μύσταξ MYSTAX + -AL[1].] = MOUSTACHIAL.

1888 P. L. SCLATER *Argentine Ornith.* I. 200 A mystacal stripe formed of white spots with faint black edgings.

mystacial (mɪ'steɪʃ(ɪ)əl), *a.* Also **mystachial**. [Formed as prec. + -IAL.] = prec.

1782 A. MONRO *Compar. Anat.* (ed. 3) 92 The mystachial [suture], which reaches..from the lower part of the *septum narium* to between the two middle *dentes incisores*. **1842** *Jrnl. Asiatic Soc. Bengal* (1844) XIII. I. 68 Mystacial regions defined by black. **1888** [see MOUSTACHIAL].

mystacine ('mɪstəsaɪn), *a.* and *sb.* [ad. mod.L. *mystacin-us*, f. Gr. μυστακ-, μύσταξ MOUSTACHE: see -INE.] **a.** *adj.* Having a fringe of hairs or moustachial streak above the mouth; *spec.* belonging to the genus *Mystacina* or group *Mystacinæ* of bats. So **mysta'cinous** *a.* **b.** *sb.* A bat of this genus or group.

1839 J. O. WESTWOOD *Introd. Mod. Classif. Insects* I. Gen. Syn. 143 Mouth mystacinous. **1876** *Van Beneden's Anim. Parasites* 251 The bat..*Vespertilio mystacinus*, harbours..the *Rictularia plagiostoma*... We have never met with this nematode in the mystacines of Belgium.

mystacocete ('mɪstəkəʊsiːt). *Zool.* [ad. mod.L. *Mystacocēt-us*, f. Gr. μυστακ(ο)-, μύσταξ upper lip, moustache + κῆτος whale. (App. formed as a correction of the unmeaning *mysticētus* MYSTICETE[1].)] A cetacean of the sub-order *Mystacoceti* or whale-bone whales (opposed to *Odontoceti*).

1883 W. H. FLOWER in *Encycl. Brit.* XV. 393/1 The Mystacocetes appear at first sight to be the most specialized and aberrant of the existing *Cetacea*.

mystagogic (mɪstə'gɒdʒɪk), *a.* [ad. late L. *mystagōgic-us*, Gr. μυσταγωγικός, f. μυσταγωγός MYSTAGOGUE.] Pertaining to a mystagogue or mystagogy; relating to instruction in mysteries.

Used chiefly in englishings of St. Cyril of Jerusalem's μυσταγωγικαὶ κατηχήσεις.

1631 J. BURGES *Answ. Rejoined, Lawfuln. Kneeling* 90, I will adde one Testimony more out of the Mystagogick catechisme of Cyrill. **1693** W. W. tr. *Dupin's Eccl. Hist.* II. 107 There are 5 others, called Mystagogick Lectures. **1871** TYLOR *Prim. Cult.* II. 387. **1900** *Dublin Rev.* Apr. 261 The Testament includes a mystagogic instruction containing a far more..explicit statement of the Christian mysteries.

mystagogical (mɪstə'gɒdʒɪkəl), *a.* [Formed as prec.: see -ICAL.] = prec.

1624 BP. MOUNTAGU *Immed. Addr.* 91 Cyril of Ierusalem, if yet hee be the Author of those Mystagogical Catechismes vnder his name. **1644** DIGBY *Nat. Soul* Concl. 464 The mystagogicall illuminations of the great Areopagite. **1693** W. W. tr. *Dupin's Eccl. Hist.* II. 108 The 5 Mystagogical Catechisms. **1826** G. S. FABER *Diffic. Romanism* (1853) 249. **1853** R. I. WILBERFORCE *Doctr. Holy Eucharist* (ed. 2) 64.

Hence **mysta'gogically** *adv.*, as a mystagogue.

1836 *Fraser's Mag.* XIII. 488 That truly wonderful poet mystagogically represents the scribes of the periodical press.

mystagogue ('mɪstəgɒg). Also 7 **mysto-**, **mista-**; 6 **-goge**. [ad. L. *mystagōg-us*, a. Gr. μυσταγωγός, f. μύστης MYSTES + ἀγωγος leading, ἄγειν to lead. Cf. F. *mystagogue* (16th c.).]

1. In Ancient Greece: One who gave preparatory instruction to candidates for initiation into the Eleusinian or other mysteries. Hence *gen.*, one who introduces to religious mysteries, a hierophant; a teacher of mystical doctrines.

a **1550** *Image Hypocr.* IV. 139 in Skelton's Wks. (1843) II. 440/2 Mockinge mystagoges. **1682** tr. *Bonet's Merc. Compit.* Ep. Ded., The Egyptians..the first Mystogogues of all the Learning and Religion of the Ancients. **1711** G. HICKES *Two Treat. Chr. Priesth.* (1847) II. 10 A mystagogue is a priest who is a teacher of mysteries. **1751** LAVINGTON *Enthus. Meth. & Papists* III. 336 The famous Porphyry, who was more a Philosopher than a Mistagogue. **1831** CARLYLE *Sart. Res.* III. x, Some..individual named Pelham, who seems to be a Mystagogue, and leading Teacher and Preacher of the Sect. **1845** J. H. NEWMAN *Ess. Devel. Chr. Doctr.* vi. §2. 342 Clement speaks of heretical teachers..becoming mystagogues of misbelief. **1856** R. A. VAUGHAN *Mystics* (1860) I. 94 The Church is the great Mystagogue. **1891** R. BUCHANAN *Coming Terror* 344 The raving mystagogues of the East.

†**2.** One who keeps church relics and shows them to strangers. *rare*$^{-0}$.

1656 BLOUNT *Glossogr.*

mystagoguery (ˌmɪstə'gɒgərɪ). [f. MYSTAGOGU(E + -ERY.] = MYSTAGOGY (in trivial or *transf.* sense).

1927 *Observer* 17 July 6 The mystagoguery of weak human beings. **1963** *Times Lit. Suppl.* 4 Jan. 4/5 But mystagoguery like this will not earn for Indian art the friends it so much needs. **1966** *New Statesman* 2 Dec. 838/1 It works out as practically a capitulation..to the literary mystagoguery of France and the United States.

mystagogy ('mɪstəgɒdʒɪ). [ad. L. *mystagōgi-a*, a. Gr. μυσταγωγία, f. μυσταγωγός MYSTAGOGUE.] Initiation, or instruction preparatory to initiation into mysteries.

1579 FULKE *Heskins' Parl.* 399 He [*sc.* Gregory Nazianzen] calleth it [the sacrament]..a holy and heauenly mystagogie. **1660** INGELO *Bentiv. & Ur.* II. (1682) 172 He was so bold also to institute an obscene Mystagogy. **1876** R. P. KNIGHT *Symbolic Lang.* 11 *note*, All theology among the Greeks is the outbirth of the Orphic Mystagogy. **1882–3** *Schaff's Encycl. Relig. Knowl.* II. 1602 Mystagogy..is applied..in the Greek Church, to the sacraments.

‖**mystax** ('mɪstæks). *Ent.* [L., a. Gr. μύσταξ (see MOUSTACHE).] A line of stiff hairs or bristles above the mouth-cavity, as in certain *Diptera*.

1860 F. WALKER in *Linn. Soc. Jrnl.* (1861) V. 234 *Laphria replens*..mystax with a few black bristles.

mysteir, obs. form of MISTER *sb.*[1]

mysteltew, obs. form of MISTLETOE.

mysterial (mɪ'stɪərɪəl), *a.* Now *rare.* [ad. late L. *mystēriālis* (cf. *mystēriāliter* in Vulg.), f. *mystērium* MYSTERY[1]. Cf. OF. *mysterial.*] Mysterious; †mystical.

[*c* **1425**: implied in the adv.] *a* **1529** SKELTON *Replyc.* 366 Howe there is a spyrituall, And a mysteriall, And a mysticall Effecte energiall. **1630** B. JONSON *Love's Triumph* (1641) 149 Beauty and Loue, whose story is mysteriall. **1633** W. AMES *Fresh Suit agst. Ceremonies* I. 107 Except there be some mysteriall distinction understood betwixt Canons and Lawes. **1675** O. WALKER, etc. *Paraphr. St. Paul* 79 *note*, The mysterial unity of Matrimony, by which two become one flesh. **1839** J. ROGERS *Antipopopr.* xiii. §2. 289 There is something mysterial and darkly declared. **1879** 'JULIAN HOME' *Sk. Camb.* 37 Mysterial music faintly breaks.

Hence † **my'sterially** *adv.*, mystically.

c **1425** *Found. St. Bartholomew's* (E.E.T.S.) 7 The deuyl, the whiche in Ezechiel mysterially ys callid the grete egle.

mysteriarch (mɪ'stɪərɪɑːk). [ad. eccl. L. *mystēriarch-ēs*, a. Gr. μυστηριάρχ-ης, f. μυστήρι-ον MYSTERY[1] + -άρχης ruling, ἄρχειν to rule.] One who presides over mysteries.

1656 BLOUNT *Glossogr.*, *Mysteriarck.* *a* **1839** GALT *Demon Destiny* III. 22 Anon she saw a veil'd mysteriarch come. **1894** *Academy* 27 Aug. 137/2 It is she who gives our Lady the rapt gaze of a Mysteriarch.

† **myste'rifical**, *a.* *Obs.*$^{-1}$ [f. L. *mystērium* MYSTERY[1]: see -FICAL.] 'Creating' a mystery.

1607 R. C[AREW] tr. *Estienne's World of Wonders* 272 This strange, mysticall, or mysterificall manner of sacrifice.

mysterioso (mɪstɪərɪ'əʊsəʊ), *a.* [ad. It. *misterioso* adj., mysterious.] Of music: executed in a mysterious manner. Also *transf.* as *sb.*

1953 in H. E. Vizetelly *New Internat. Year Book 1952* 619 *Mysterioso*, a motion-picture, radio or television program which depends upon the element of mystery for its effect. **1957** S. DANCE in S. Traill *Concerning Jazz* 44 In mysterioso numbers suitable for accompanying the more exotic dances in the night-clubs.., there was evoked what was considered a 'jungle' atmosphere. **1957** MANVELL & HUNTLEY *Technique Film Music* ii. 28 The theme is played twice on strings pizzicato, with suitable mysterioso embellishments. **1967** J. SEVERSON *Great Surfing* Gloss., *Mysterioso*, an 'adornment' or surf trick popular in the late fifties... The stance is with the surfer bending over, hiding his head in his hands.

mysteriosophy (mɪstɪərɪ'ɒsəfɪ). [f. Gr. μυστήριο-ν MYSTERY[1] + σοφία wisdom.] A system of doctrine concerning mysteries.

1894 BUCHANAN tr. *Harnack's Hist. Dogma* I. App. III. 354 Philosophy in Iamblichus becomes a theurgic mysteriosophy, spiritualism. **1899** INGE *Christian Mysticism* i. 4 The Neoplatonists, who found in the existing mysteriosophy a discipline..congenial to their speculative views.

mysterious (mɪ'stɪərɪəs), *a.* [f. L. *mystērium* MYSTERY[1] + OUS. Cf. F. *mystérieux.*]

1. Full of or fraught with mystery; wrapt in mystery; hidden from human knowledge or understanding; impossible or difficult to explain, solve, or discover; of obscure origin, nature, or purpose.

1622 MASSINGER & DEKKER *Virgin Martyr* IV. i. H2b, Turne ore all the volumes Of your mysterious Æsculapian science. **1632** MILTON *Penseroso* 147 Som strange mysterious dream. **1653** WALTON *Compl. Angler* 163 And as their breeding, so are their decayes also very mysterious. **1738** GRAY *Tasso* 56 Euphrates' font, and Nile's mysterious head. **1770** *Lett. Junius* xxxvi. 171 Your conduct has been mysterious as well as contemptible. **1849** MACAULAY *Hist. Eng.* vi. II. 153 Patrick and Jane had been seen going in at that mysterious door which led to Chiffinch's apartments. **1853** E. K. KANE *Grinnell Exped.* i. (1856) 13 It is a mysterious sea, that has baffled for centuries the research of navigators. **1893** *Sat. Rev.* 29 July 130 Certain of the chief inhabitants of the village..are discussing at the inn the mysterious death of the Squire.

b. Of words, language.

1616 BULLOKAR *Eng. Expos.*, *Mysterious*, darke spoken in a mystery, hard to vnderstand. **1667** MILTON *P.L.* x. 173 God at last To Satan first in sin his doom apply'd Though in mysterious terms. **1791** MRS. RADCLIFFE *Rom. Forest* ii, The sound of his steps..seemed like the mysterious accents of the dead. **1797** —— *Italian* xvii, A few mysterious words having been exchanged. **1816** SHELLEY *Mont Blanc* 76 The wilderness has a mysterious tongue Which teaches awful doubt.

c. Of God, religion, rites.

1624 GATAKER *Transubst.* 94 The..Mysterie, or mysterious rite, as the word there vsed properly importeth. **1667** MILTON *P.L.* IV. 750 Haile wedded Love, mysterious Law. **1773** COWPER *Olney Hymns* III. xv, God moves in a mysterious way His wonders to perform. **1857** P. FREEMAN *Princ. Div. Serv.* II. 14 In almost all cases in which a mysterious truth is propounded by Almighty God for our acceptance. **1881** P. BROOKS *Candle of the Lord* xviii. 311 To the Christian, God is mysterious because He is radiant with infinite truth.

2. Of persons: †**a.** Dealing with or versed in mysteries; using occult arts. *Obs.* **b.** Whose movements are full of mystery; delighting in mystery.

1620 J. MELTON *Astrologaster* Ded. to E. Melton, The Misterious Egyptians..would excellently with their Pensils in liuely cullors..the ful shape & portraiture of a Hart, a Lyon, Lamb, or Hare. **1634** MILTON *Comus* 130 Mysterious Dame That ne're art call'd, but when the Dragon woom Of Stygian darknes spets her thickest gloom. **1789** E. DARWIN *Bot. Gard.* II. 24 You taught mysterious Bacon to explore

Metallic veins. **1842** LYTTON *Zanoni* I. v, Accompanying this mysterious Zanoni. **1874** W. BLACK *Pr. Thule* ii, Sheila ..is romantic and mysterious, and believes in..dreams.

3. a. That is due to a mystery. *rare.*

1667 MILTON *P.L.* VIII. 599 Though higher of the genial Bed by far, And with mysterious reverence I deem.

b. Having a sense of mystery. *rare.*

1897 KIPLING *Capt. Cour.* i. 5 It makes me feel mysterious to pass that butler's pantry place.

4. *Comb.*: **mysterious-spoken** *a.*, having a mysterious manner of speaking.

1837 DICKENS *Pickwick* xxii, An important-looking, sharp-nosed, mysterious-spoken personage.

my'steriously, *adv.* [f. prec. + -LY².] In a mysterious manner; in or as in a mystery.

1638 SIR T. HERBERT *Trav.* (ed. 2) 171 Mahomitan Princes are terrible crafty or mysteriously politicious. **1667** MILTON *P.L.* III. 516 Each Stair mysteriously was meant. *a* **1716** SOUTH *Serm.* (1744) VIII. v. 141 The blood of that son..so mysteriously, and yet so really, conveyed to us. **1738** WARBURTON *Div. Legat.* II. iv. (1846) 200 Every thing in these rites was mysteriously conducted, and under the most solemn obligations to secrecy. **1797** MRS. RADCLIFFE *Italian* vii, What but spirit could have quitted this vault so mysteriously? **1842** S. LOVER *Handy Andy* xxi, The mysteriously-sentimental and imaginative school. **1851** HELPS *Comp. Solit.* i. 8 *note*, Physicians' prescriptions may have a better effect for being expressed mysteriously, but legal matters cannot surely be made too clear. **1861** GEO. ELIOT *Silas M.* iii, The rich..accepted gout and apoplexy as things that ran mysteriously in respectable families.

mysteriousness (mɪˈstɪərɪəsnɪs). [-NESS.]

1. The quality or condition of being mysterious or a mystery; the quality of being shrouded in mystery or obscurity: applied chiefly to the mysteries of religion.

1649 ROBERTS *Clavis Bibl.* 381 The mysteriousnesse and difficulty of the Book. **1664** H. MORE *Myst. Iniq.* 212 Profound veneration, which Obscurity and Mysteriousness conciliates to all Truths. **1754** SHERLOCK *Disc.* I. I. II. 65 The Mysteriousness of the whole Proceeding arises only from hence, That our finite Minds cannot comprehend the Reasons and Limits of the divine Justice. **1834** J. H. NEWMAN *Par. Serm.* I. xvi. 242 Such being the necessary mysteriousness of Scripture doctrine. **1883** F. M. PEARD *Contrad.* I. 2 Blue and shadowy depths suggested a soft mysteriousness.

†**b.** Applied to the Eucharist. *Obs.*

1650 JER. TAYLOR *Holy Living* iv. §10. 347 The celebration of the holy Sacrament is the great mysteriousnesse of the Christian religion. **1660** —— *Worthy Commun.* i. §5. 95 Those great appelatives with which..the most eminent Saints of God use to..invest the great mysteriousness.

2. The behaviour or attitude of one who makes a mystery of a matter.

1784 JOHNSON in *Johnsoniana* (1836) 407 Nothing ends more fatally than mysteriousness in trifles. **1791–1823** D'ISRAELI *Cur. Lit.* (1858) III. 332 Elizabeth all her life had persevered in an obstinate mysteriousness respecting the succession. **1886** *Manch. Exam.* 13 Jan. 5/1 There is an air of constitutional mysteriousness about them.

mysterium (mɪˈstɪərɪəm). *Astr.* [f. MYSTER(IOUS *a.* + -IUM.] A hypothetical substance to which a galactic radio emission at 1665 megahertz was attributed until it was identified as an exceptionally strong component of a set of four lines emitted by the hydroxyl radical.

1965 H. WEAVER et al. in *Nature* 2 Oct. 30/1 There is no known identification of the strong emission line at 1,665 Mc/s... We shall speak of this unidentified line as arising from 'mysterium'. *Ibid.* 30/2 Our observations indicate that 'mysterium' is found in strong H II regions, but not in all strong H II regions. **1967** *Science* 25 Aug. 885/1 Mysterium has now been identified as OH. **1974** G. L. VERSCHUUR *Invisible Universe* ix. 77 How do we now know that the mysterium signals are in fact OH lines?

‖**mysterium tremendum** (mɪˈstɪərɪəm trɛˈmɛndəm). [L., = tremendous mystery.] A term used to express the overwhelming awe and sense of unknowable mystery felt by those to whom this aspect of God or of being is revealed.

1923 J. W. HARVEY tr. *R. Otto's Idea of Holy* iv. 12 We shall find we are dealing with something for which there is only one appropriate expression, *mysterium tremendum*. *Ibid.* v. 25 We gave to the object to which the numinous consciousness is directed the name 'mysterium tremendum'. **1957** J. S. HUXLEY *Relig. without Revelation* (rev. ed.) ii. 32 The *mysterium tremendum* of religion. **1963** A. HUXLEY *Let.* 17 Feb. (1969) 949 One..opens oneself up receptively to the *Mysterium tremendum et fascinans* within and without. **1968** *Times* 15 Oct. 11/4 Should we not beware of the mysterium tremendum, the Wrath of God. **1971** *Nature* 13 Aug. 450/2 Their inter-relationship [*sc.* that of biology and physical-chemical research] seems to me to represent one of the deepest questions man can ask, a real *mysterium tremendum*.

†**mysterize** (ˈmɪstəraɪz), *v. Obs.* [f. MYSTERY¹ + -IZE.] **a.** *trans.* To interpret mystically.

1650 SIR T. BROWNE *Pseud. Ep.* v. x. 212 The Cabalists, ..mysterizing their ensignes, doe make the particular ones of the twelve Tribes, accommodable unto the twelve signes in the Zodiack.

b. *intr.* To make mysteries of things.

1845 T. COOPER *Purg. Suic.* I. lxxii, To mysterize I scorn.

Hence ˈ**mysterizingness**.

1817 T. FORSTER *Observ. Infl. Atmosphere* ix. 46 How prone we are to abuse the natural instincts of hope, and mysterizingness.

mystery¹ (ˈmɪstərɪ). Forms: 4 mystri, 4, 6 -y, 4–6 mist-, mysterye, 4–7 -ie, 5–9 mistery, 6 mystyry, mistirie, mistrie, mysteri, 4– mystery. [a. AF. *misterie (OF. mistere, mod.F. mystère masc.), = It. misterio, mistero, Sp. misterio, Pg. mysterio, ad. L. mystērium, a. Gr. μυστήριον, f. *mūs-, root of μύειν to close (the lips or eyes): cf. μύστης MYSTES.

In classical Greek μυστήριον occurs chiefly in plural, denoting certain secret religious ceremonies (the most famous being those of Demeter at Eleusis) which were allowed to be witnessed only by the initiated, who were sworn never to disclose their nature. (See sense 9 below.) In the LXX the word occurs only in Daniel and the Apocrypha, where it has the sense of 'secret purpose or counsel' (esp. of a king or of God). This sense is found in the N.T., where the word also means sometimes a religious truth long kept secret, but now revealed through Christ to his Church, and sometimes anything that has a symbolic significance. In later Christian Greek μυστήριον became equivalent to SACRAMENT (in several passages the Vulgate renders it by *sacramentum*, even when it means only 'secret'; in other passages *mysterium* is retained). In OF. and English the Christian senses of the word naturally appear earliest.]

I. Theological uses.

†**1. a.** ***in*** **or** ***through his mystery***: in or by its mystical presence. **b.** ***in*** **(*a*)** ***mystery***: mystically.

c **1315** SHOREHAM *Poems* I. 672 Ac one gode aryȝt hyt nomeþ, þat body ine hys mysterye. ? **14..** *Plowman's Tale* 1219 His flesh and blood, through his mystry, Is there, in the forme of brede. **1526** *Pilgr. Perf.* (1531) 31 God hath no suche bodyly membres, as this texte [*Exodus* xxxiii. 23] to the lettre dothe pretende to shewe: but all this was done in great mistery. **1533** FRITH *Answ. More* E 4 For we do yt not actualiye in dede, but onlye in a misterie. **1560** DAUS tr. *Sleidane's Comm.* 118 Whiche place..is to be understande in a mistery [L. *mystice*]. **1628** *Field's Of the Church* III. App. 205 The crucified body of Christ thy sonne, which is here present in mystery, and sacrament.

2. A religious truth known only from divine revelation; usually (cf. sense 5), a doctrine of the faith involving difficulties which human reason is incapable of solving.

1382 WYCLIF *Rom.* xvi. 25 The revelacioun of mysterie holdun stille..in tymes euerlastynge; the which mysterie is now maad opyn by scripturis of prophetes. *c* **1430** LYDG. *Min. Poems* (Percy Soc.) 238 Al mysteryes of the oold and newe lawe. **1513** DOUGLAS *Æneis* VI. Prol. 143 The glorius modir..Quhilk of hir natur consavit Criste, and buir Al hail the misteris of the Trinite. **1549** *Bk. Com. Prayer, Litany*, By the misterye of thy holy incarnacion,..Good Lorde deliuer vs. *a* **1568** ASCHAM *Scholem.* I. (Arb.) 82 They counte as Fables, the holie misteries of Christian Religion. **1597** HOOKER *Eccl. Pol.* v. lii. §1 This diuine mysterie [of the Incarnation] is more true then plaine. **1720** SWIFT *Let. to Yng. Clergyman* Wks. 1751 V. 24, I do not find, that you are any where directed in the Canons or Articles to attempt explaining the Mysteries of the Christian Religion. **1784** COWPER *Task* II. 528 'Tis revelation satisfies all doubts, Explains all mysteries, except her own. **1855** BREWSTER *Newton* II. xxiv. 359 The investigation of the sacred mysteries, while it prepared his own mind for its final destiny, was calculated to promote the spiritual interests of thousands. **1894** ILLINGWORTH *Personality* iii. 68 In the presence of a fact which..was a mystery—a thing which could be apprehended when revealed, but could neither be comprehended nor discovered.

3. A religious ordinance or rite, *esp.* a sacramental rite of the Christian religion; *spec.* (*pl.*) the Eucharist; *occas.* the consecrated elements.

1506 *Ord. Crysten Men* (W. de W.) I. iii. C 8 Many of the mysteryes afore sayd be done at the chirche dore and not within yᵉ chirche. *c* **1532** DU WES *Introd. Fr.* in *Palsgr.* 1064 The mystery of the masse. **1549** *Bk. Com. Prayer, Matrimony*, O God, which hast consecrated the state of matrimonie, to such an excellent misterie, that in it is signified and represented the spiritual mariage & vnitie betwixte Christ and his church. *Ibid., Communion*, Wee moste hartely thanke thee, for that thou hast vouchsafed to feede vs in these holy Misteries [**1552** to fede vs, whiche haue duely receiued these holy misteries]. **1662** J. DAVIES tr. *Mandelslo's Trav.* 30 His mouth and nose were covered with a linen cloth, lest the impurity of his breath should profane the mystry. **1687** A. LOVELL tr. *Thevenot's Trav.* I. 189 But seeing there is no Mystery in that Chappel, it is left without any Lamp, nay without any cross too. **1693** W. W. tr. *Dupin's Eccl. Hist.* II. 108 *note*, Concerning the Holy Mysteries of the Altar. **1737** WESLEY in *Wks.* (1872) I. 54, I will administer to you the mysteries of God. **1850** NEALE *Hist. East. Ch.* I. 1013 In proceeding to the consideration of the three next mysteries of the Eastern Church, penance, matrimonial coronation, and the prayer-oil. **1854** MILMAN *Lat. Chr.* III. vii. (1864) II. 155 Within [the sacred edifices] were the reliques of the tutelar saint, the mysteries and the presence of the Redeemer.

4. An incident in the life of our Lord or of the Saints regarded as an object of commemoration in the Christian church or as having a mystical significance. Hence, each of the fifteen divisions of the rosary corresponding to the 'mysteries of redemption'.

1655 JER. TAYLOR *Golden Grove* 57 Meditate on the passion of our blessed Saviour and all the mysteries of our Redemption. *Ibid.* 59 Upon the Holy-days..let the matter of your meditations be according to the mystery of the day. **1687** A. LOVELL tr. *Thevenot's Trav.* I. 195 We went in Procession through all the Sanctuaries of the great Church, where all the mysteries of the Passion were represented to the Life. **1705** NELSON *Fest. & Fasts* Prelim. Instr. 8 If we commemorate any Mystery of our Redemption. **1835** *Penny Cycl.* IV. 79/1 A chaplet..divided into three sets, white, red, and damask roses, corresponding to the joyful, sorrowful, and glorious mysteries. **1852** MRS. JAMESON *Leg. Madonna* Introd. p. lxi, Another cycle of subjects consists of the fifteen Mysteries of the Rosary.

II. Non-theological uses.

5. a. A hidden or secret thing; a matter unexplained or inexplicable; something beyond human knowledge or comprehension; a riddle or enigma.

13.. *E.E. Allit. P.* A. 1194 To þat pryncez paye hade I ay bente..To mo of his mysterys I hade ben dryuen. **1382** WYCLIF *Dan.* ii. 27 The mysterie whiche the kyng axith, the wise men..mown not shewe to the kyng. *c* **1400** *Apol. Loll.* 44 Daniel, ouercomer of lyowns, saw misteris of priui þingis. *c* **1550** CHEKE *Matt.* xiii. 11 A mysteri is a secret and an hiden thing, which ought not to be schewed abrood. **1598** B. JONSON *Ev. Man in Hum.* II. ii, To meditate Vpon the difference of mans estate: Where is deciphered to true iudgements eye A deep, conceald, and precious misterie. **1638** JUNIUS *Paint. Ancients* 27 The great interpreter of the mysteries of Nature. **1731** BAILEY vol. II, *Mysteries* (in *Numbers*), the number 5 multiplied by 5, makes 25; and 4 multiplied by 4, makes 16; and 3 multiplied by 3, makes 9; but 9 and 16 is equal to 25. **1742** YOUNG *Nt. Th.* VII. 501 'Tis immortality decyphers man, And opens all the myst'ries of his make. **1821** BYRON *Two Fosc.* II. i, *Doge.* I am what you behold. *Mar.* And that's a mystery. **1836** MACGILLIVRAY *Trav. Humboldt* xviii. 246 There are mysteries in the affections and hatreds of animals. **1867** DK. ARGYLL *Reign of Law* i. 15 The relation in which God stands to those rules of His government which are called 'laws', is, of course, an inscrutable mystery to us. **1869** FREEMAN *Norm. Conq.* (1875) III. xii. 85 There was a mystery about the marriage. **1870** DICKENS (*title*) The Mystery of Edwin Drood. **1892** WESTCOTT *Gospel of Life* 1 [Christianity] does not introduce fresh mysteries into the world: it meets mysteries which already exist.

†**b.** A personal secret. *Obs.*

1529 MORE *Dyaloge* I. Wks. 124/2 Let yᵉ knowlege of the father alone therefore amonge our wifes misteryes. **1602** SHAKS. *Ham.* III. ii. 382 You would pluck out the heart of my Mysterie. **1604** —— *Oth.* IV. ii. 30. **1617** MORYSON *Itin.* I. 13 The servant answered that the old woman was in bed and that he knew not the mystery, whether any eggs were in the house or no.

c. A political or diplomatic secret; a secret of state. *Obs.* exc. as a contextual use of the general sense. [Cf. F. *mystère d'état.*]

a **1618** RALEIGH *Maxims of State* (1642) 9 Mysteries or Sophismes of State, are certaine secret practizes, either for the avoiding of danger; or averting such effects as tend to the preservation of the present State, as it is set or founded. **1622** BACON *Hen. VII* 43 Touching the Mysterie of reannexing of the Duchy of Britainie to the Crowne of France..the Ambassadours bare aloofe from it. **1658–9** CHALONER in *Burton's Diary* (1828) III. 130 Every secretary ought to write what is to pass a Parliament, not as he writes his mysteries. *a* **1704** T. BROWN *Praise Poverty* Wks. 1730 I. 89 Half-politicians maxims called mysteries of state. **1857** BUCKLE *Civiliz.* I. xii 668 They heard..mysteries of state and mysteries of creed unfolded..to the popular gaze.

d. ***to make a mystery of***: to treat as a secret; to keep (a thing) secret in order to make an impression. [Cf. F. *faire* (*un*) *mystère de.*]

1634 W. TIRWHYT tr. *Balzac's Lett.* III. x. 248, I cannot.. make of euery meane matter a mystery by whispering it in the eare. **1687** A. LOVELL tr. *Thevenot's Trav.* I. 2 Making a mystery of nothing, and frankly discoursing with any man upon what Subject he proposes. **1720** OZELL tr. *Vertot's Rom. Rep.* I. IV. 196 The Consuls always made a Mystery to the People of those first Elements of their Juris-Prudence. **1834** HT. MARTINEAU *Farrers* iii. 35 He made no mysteries, but told all that he was asked to tell. **1839** URE *Dict. Arts* 578 As manufacturers make no mystery of this matter, any person may have an opportunity of inspecting the operation. **1841** BORROW *Zincali* I. ii. 1 58 Nor did he make a mystery of his knowledge, but publicly boasted of it.

¶**e.** The biblical phrase ***mystery of iniquity*** [Vulg. *Mysterium iniquitatis*, Gr. τὸ μυστήριον τῆς ἀνομίας], by association with various senses of this word, has been used in many different applications.

1382 WYCLIF *2 Thess.* ii. 7 Forwhi the mysterie, or priuyte, of wickidnesse worchith now [**1526** TINDALE the mistery off iniquytie]. **1545** BALE (*title*) A mysterye of inyqyte contayned within the heretycall Genealogye of Ponce Pantolabus. **1613** PURCHAS *Pilgrimage* (1614) 571 If I might, with the Readers patience, I would adde somewhat of their Mysterie of iniquitie, and the mysticall sense of this iniquitie. **1647** N. BACON *Disc. Govt. Eng.* vii. 24 If God had not given them over to thraldom under that mistery of iniquity, of sinful man aspiring into the place of God. **1756** BURKE *Vind. Nat. Soc.* 38 The Whole of this Mystery of Iniquity is called the Reason of State. **1855** MACAULAY *Hist. Eng.* xvii. IV. 52 This mystery of iniquity [*sc.* a plot against William III] has..been gradually unveiling. **1884** *Pall Mall G.* 28 Aug. 3/2 The great city [of London] is full of many mysteries—not a few of them..mysteries of iniquity.

6. In generalized sense. **a.** The condition or property of being secret or obscure; mysteriousness. Also, mysteries collectively, mysterious matter.

Phrase, ***wrapped in mystery***.

1601 SHAKS. *All's Well* v. iii. 103 Platus himselfe,..Hath not in natures mysterie more science, Then I haue in this Ring. **1742** YOUNG *Nt. Th.* VII. 134 And virtue vies with hope in mystery. **1788** REID *Aristotle's Log.* iv. §2. 74 This is the mystery contained in the vowels of those barbarous words. **1818** COLERIDGE *Friend* I. xiii. 161 The mystery and the dignity of our human nature. **1835** THIRLWALL *Greece* vi. I. 247 The origin of the Homeric poetry is wrapt in mystery. **1856** KINGSLEY *Lett.* (1878) I. 467 Everywhere, skin deep below our boasted science, we are brought up short by mystery impalpable. **1865** G. MACDONALD *A. Forbes* 18 In all the enhancing mystery of candlelight. **1883**

H. Drummond *Nat. Law in Spir. W.* Introd. 28 A Science without mystery is unknown; a Religion without mystery is absurd.

b. The behaviour or attitude of mind of one who makes a secret of things (often intrinsically unimportant) usually for the purpose of exercising undue power or influence.

1692 Dryden *St. Euremont's Ess.* 309 Questions, which should be handled with a great deal of Mystery and Secrecy. **1726** Swift *Gulliver* II. vii, He professed..to..despise all Mystery, Refinement, and Intrigue, either in a Prince or a Minister. **1821** Byron *Mar. Fal.* III. ii, Israel, speak; what means this mystery? **1832** tr. *Sismondi's Ital. Rep.* ix. 218 The senate joined to this rigour the perfidy and mystery which characterise an aristocracy.

†**7.** Obscure or mysterious reason; hidden or mystic meaning. *Obs.*

14.. in *Tundale's Vis.* (1843) 134 Grete mystery is in both tweyne: The toon [turtle] comendyd for his chastite And the tother [dove]..Is symple and meke. **1432–50** tr. *Higden* (Rolls) III. 103 Seynte Mathewe th' Euangeliste assignethe xiiij. generaciones, for the cause of a certeyne mistery [Trevisa: som priue menynge]. **1591** Harington *Orl. Fur.* Pref. ¶iv, The ancient Poets haue..wrapped..in their writings diuers..meanings, which they call the sences or mysteries thereof. **1598** Barret *Theor. Warres* IV. i. 100 Is there any meaning or misterie in marching the left or right side shot before in the vantgard? **1658** Sir T. Browne *Hydriot.* iii. 30 Most [urns] imitate a circular figure.. whether from any mystery, best duration or capacity, were but a conjecture. **1687** A. Lovell tr. *Thevenot's Trav.* I. 82 Nor shall I speak of their Sacerdotal Vestments, which have their Mysteries.

8. An action or practice about which there is, or is supposed to be, some secrecy; a 'secret' or highly technical operation in a trade or art. Now often *trivial*. (Cf. MYSTERY[2] 2a and b.)

1594 Greene & Lodge *Looking Gl.* (1598) B 2, He was the first man that euer instructed me in the mysterie of a pot of Ale. **1607** Norden *Surv. Dial.* I. 6 And of whom such land is holden, the same is called the Lord of that land after a sort [etc.]..as if you be so willing as you seeme to talke of these mysteries, you shall anon perceiue. **1617** Moryson *Itin.* III. 80 They forbad the English..to dwell in Poland..lest they should..find the mysteries of the trade. **1706** E. Ward *Wooden World Diss.* (1708) 61 The Mystery of his Art and Science, consists in a long List of Fustian Words and Phrases. **1719** De Foe *Crusoe* I. 263, I let him into the Mystery, for such it was to him, of Gunpowder and Bullet. **1808** Han. More *Cœlebs* I. xxi. 305 No man is allowed to set up in an ordinary trade till he has served a long apprenticeship to its mysteries. **1827** Disraeli *Viv. Grey* V. v, The mysteries of rouge et noir. **1837** —— *Venetia* I. ix, Harassed with all the mysteries of packing.

9. a. Chiefly *pl.* In the religious systems of Ancient Greece, Rome, Egypt, etc., certain secret rites to which only the initiated were admitted.

1643 [see Eleusinian]. **1738** Warburton *Div. Legat.* II. iv. (1846) 194 The first and original Mysteries, of which we have any sure account, were those of Isis and Osiris in Egypt. **1849** Grote *Greece* II. lxiv. (1862) V. 484 Until that day of the month Boedromion (about the beginning of September) when the Eleusinian mysteries were celebrated.

b. The secrets of freemasonry.

1738 J. Anderson *Const. Fratern. Free Masons* 150 The G. Master shall ask his Deputy, if he..finds the Candidate Master well skill'd in the Noble Science and the Royal Art, and duly instructed in our Mysteries? **1872** C. I. Paton *Freemasonry* II. i. 50 Every candidate for initiation into the mysteries of Freemasonry.

10. Used by modern writers (after F. *mystère*, med.L. *mystērium*) as a name for the miracle-play.

A distinction has been drawn by some writers between 'mystery' and 'miracle-play' (see quot. 1875), but this is not generally accepted.

[This sense has been often erroneously referred to MYSTERY[2] on the ground of the undoubted fact that the miracle-plays were often acted by the mysteries or trade guilds.]

1744 Dodsley *O. Pl.* I. Pref. p. xiii, The mysteries only represented in a senseless manner some miraculous History from the Old or New Testament. **1773** J. Hawkins *Orig. Eng. Drama* Pref. p. vii, One of the first improvements on the old Mystery was the Allegorical Play, or Morality. **1821** Scott *Kenilw.* xvii, My wife, sir, hath played the devil ere now, in a Mystery, in Queen Mary's time. **1838** Prescott *Ferd. & Is.* xx. (1846) II. 211 The sacred plays, or mysteries, so popular throughout Europe, in the middle ages. **1875** A. W. Ward *Eng. Dram. Lit.* I. 23 Properly speaking, Mysteries deal with Gospel events only... Miracle Plays, on the other hand, are concerned with incidents derived from the legends of the saints of the Church.

11. = MEDICINE *sb.* 4, 4b. (Cf. *mystery-man.*)

1841 Catlin *N. Amer. Indians* I. xii. 87 The whole village ..with..its medicines (or mysteries) and scalp-poles waving over my head. *Ibid.* xv. 106, I..have been regularly installed medicine or mystery.

12. In technical use. **a.** A kind of fly for salmon fishing. **b.** An alloy of platinum, tin, and copper, imitating gold. **c.** A kind of plum cake. **d.** Shortened form of *bag of mystery* (BAG *sb.* 18b). *slang.* **e.** A girl newly arrived in a town or city; a girl with no fixed address; a young or inexperienced prostitute. *slang.* **f.** A mystery story.

a. 1867 F. Francis *Angling* xi. (1880) 427 No. 1 is called The Mystery. **1902** *Encycl. Brit.* XXV. 446/1 Lightly dressed flies..such as the Sun-fly and the Mystery.

b. 1885 *Standard* 8 Apr. 6/4 There was not a particle of gold in it. It was made of a composition called 'mystery', composed of platinum, tin, and copper.

c. 1889 R. Wells *Bread & Biscuit Baker's Assist.* 58 Mystery or Cheap Plum Cake at 3*d.* per lb. 8 lbs. of common flour, 3 lbs. of brown sugar, 1 lb. of lard [etc.].

d. *a* **1890** G. Horncastle in Barrère & Leland *Dict. Slang* (1890) II. 79/2 The peelers I scorn and defy, While strings of these *mysteries* I wave round my head, And then to the people I cry, 'Sassidges, oh, sassidges! Oh, beef and pork and German!'

e. 1937 J. Worby *Other Half* 278 *Mystery*, a girl who is down and out, come to town to look for a job. **1955** C. H. Rolph *Women of Streets* x. 120 When you're a new girl they call you a 'mystery'. And you're a mystery until you've been here three or four years. Then you become a 'history'. **1960** *Observer* 28 Feb. 23/4 Many teddys, tearaways and mysteries (drifting girls) are put off by the typical orthodox youth club. **1960** C. MacInnes *Mr Love & Justice* 19 'All those men. Maybe two or three a day...' 'Two or three? Are you kidding? What you take me for—a mystery?' **1962** R. Cook *Crust on its Uppers* (1964) iv. 37 'I Saw a Human Monster in My Bedroom, says Teenager'..means the little mystery's woken up when she wasn't supposed to. **1967** M. M. Glatt et al. *Drug Scene* 117 *Mystery*, girl (young) having left home on arrival in London. **1974** G. F. Newman *Price* v. 169 Instead of calling a couple of mysteries, he called a cab.

f. 1973 *Directory of Dealers in Secondhand & Antiquarian Bks. in Brit. Isles 1973–75* 111 Fantasy, scientific romance, Gothic novel, mystery and detective.

III. 13. *attrib.*, as ***mystery-monger***, ***-priest***; ***mystery-mongering*** adj. and sb.; ***mystery-piety***; **mystery-bag** = *bag of mystery* (BAG *sb.* 18b); **mystery gold** = 11b; **mystery-man**, (*a*) one who works or has to do with 'mysteries', *esp.* a conjuror, a medicine-man; (*b*) a man about whom little is known; **mystery-play** = sense 10; **mystery-religion** (see quot. 1967); **mystery ship**, an armed and camouflaged merchantman used in the war of 1914–18 as a decoy or to destroy submarines; **mystery story**, a detective or crime story; **mystery tour**, a pleasure trip for which there is no advance announcement of the places to be visited; **mystery train**, a train taking passengers on a mystery tour; **mystery trip** = *mystery tour*; **mystery woman**, a woman about whom little is known; **mystery writer**, a writer of mystery stories.

1889 *Sportsman* 2 Feb. 4/1 But the '*mystery-bags' of Sieur X, if we are to believe the common report, were far from being fragrant. This gentleman has been sentenced to six months' imprisonment for 'making sausages of tainted meat'. **1887** J. Hutchison *Pract. Banking* III. 681 *note*, A great number of spurious sovereigns and half-sovereigns are in circulation... Those made of '*mystery gold'..stand the tests of the ordinary acids. **1841** Catlin *N. Amer. Indians* I. vi. 39 Their physicians, who are also medicine (or *mystery) men. **1865** J. Bright in *Daily Tel.* 13 July, Mr. Disraeli.. is what among a tribe of Indians would be called the 'mystery man'. **1910** *Encycl. Brit.* III. 570/1 'Adventurer', as applied to Disraeli, was a mere term of abuse. 'Mystery-man' had much of the same intention, but in a blameless though not in a happy sense it was true of him to the end of his days. **1933** H. G. Wells *Shape of Things to Come* I. 112 That Mystery Man of Mystery Men, Sir Basil Zaharoff, the armaments salesman. **1972** G. Lyall *Blame Dead* ii. 10 You sounded a bit of a mystery man in those stories this morning —they'll want to know more. **1772** Nugent *Hist. Fr. Gerund* II. 362 He was..a whisperer, and a *mystery-monger. **1885** *Expositor* 1 Sept. 191 We are no muttering mystery-mongers. **1901** W. James *Mem. & Stud.* (1911) vii. 150 With all these things, infected by their previous *mystery-mongering discoverers, even our best friends had rather avoid complicity. **1912** Mrs. R. Davids *Buddhism* i. 20 There is no evidence..that this late recourse to writing was due to any mystery-mongering or esotericism. **1939** Dylan Thomas *Let.* 29 Sept. (1966) 240 Censorship and conscription, mystery-mongering and umbrella-worship. **1939** P. S. Watson tr. *Nygren's Agape & Eros* II. II. iii. 355 Neoplatonism..to a large extent bears the stamp of *Mystery-piety. **1852** Yonge *Cameos* IV. ix. (1877) 108 Keillar was summoned before Cardinal Beaton..for having written a *mystery-play. **1751** Lavington *Enthus. Meth. & Papists* III. 385 Jannes and Jambrees, who opposed Moses.. when the Jews were expelled Egypt, were Egyptian *Mystery-Priests. **1913** H. A. A. Kennedy *St. Paul & Mystery-Religions* III. 69 There are special strains of religious thought and feeling more or less common to all the *Mystery-Religions, such as that of regeneration (in some sense) and union or communion with deity. *Ibid.* 86 This connection with Dionysus leads us into the heart of conceptions typical for mystery-religion, the conception of union with the Divine and attainment of undying life. **1925** S. Angus *Mystery-Religions & Christianity* ii. 45 A Mystery-Religion was (1) a religion of symbolism which, through myth and allegory, iconic representations, blazing lights and dense darkness, liturgies and sacramental acts, and suggestion..provoked in the initiate a mystical experience conducing to *palingenesia* (regeneration), the object of every initiation. *Ibid.* 50 II. A Mystery-Religion was a religion of Redemption which professed to remove estrangement between man and God. *Ibid.* 52 III. The Mystery-Religions were systems of *Gnosis* akin, and forming a stage to, those movements to which the name of Gnosticism became attached. **1967** D. T. Kauffman *Dict. Relig. Terms* 322/1 *Mystery religions*, secret cults in pre-Christian Greek and Roman culture, as well as in areas of Egypt and Asia... The mystery religions included the Orphic, Eleusinian, Mithraic. **1914** *Daily Mail* (Greater Manchester ed.) 7/4 The grey, gaunt outline of the *mystery ship took definite shape. **1925** Mystery ship [see DECOY *sb.*[2] 6]. **1975** B. Meyrick *Behind Light* xvi. 207 The crew of Mystery Ship 51 listened as the warning boom of their foghorn echoed..through..the Dover Straits. **1908** Chesterton *All Things Considered* 115 *Mystery stories are very popular, especially when sold at sixpence. **1932** H. Crane *Let.* 20 Mar. (1965) 404 Even the suspense of the usual mystery story utilizes that device. **1934** Mystery story [see *crime-story*]. **1974** A. Price *Other Paths* I. vii. 86 You've been holding on to the book... I can't wait to hear your mystery story. **1947** J. Betjeman in *Strand Mag.* Aug. 41 The morning paddle, then the *mystery tour By motor-coach inland this afternoon. **1973** C. Bonington *Next Horizon* vii. 105 Climbing with Tom Patey was a kind of Magical Mystery Tour, in which no one, except perhaps himself, knew what was coming next. **1933** H. A. Piehler *England for Everyman* 35 Recent enterprises include '*mystery' trains for hikers, bound for unknown destinations, and circular tours by special trains through beautiful scenery. **1958** *Listener* 23 Oct. 653/2 An enterprising char-à-banc proprietor advertised '*mystery trips'. **1913** R. C. Praed (*title*) The *mystery woman. **1922** M. Arlen *Piracy* 321 The *Daily Mail* at once called her a 'mystery woman'. **1974** 'A. Gilbert' *Nice Little Killing* ix. 127 It was something she couldn't afford to be made public. .. Mrs Brown was the original mystery woman. **1942** *Amer. Speech* XVII. 3 Most of this [*sc.* slang and cant] I have excluded,..because it is already rather thoroughly recorded in the special dictionaries, out of which, no doubt, the *mystery-writers took it in the first place. **1973** *N.Y. Times* 1 Aug. 37/1 Good mystery writers have always known that man himself is the greatest mystery of all.

mystery[2] ('mɪstərɪ). Forms: as in prec. Also 9 *arch.* **mistery**. [ad. med.L. *misterium*, altered form of *ministerium* (MISTER *sb.*[1]) by confusion with *mystērium* MYSTERY[1]. In senses 2–4 there was prob. confusion with *maistrie*, MASTERY.

In med.L. *mistera* was a form commonly used with senses 2 and 3.]

†**1. a.** Service, occupation; office, ministry. *Obs.*

c **1386** Chaucer *Pars. T.* ¶821 Preestes been aungeles, as by the dignitee of hir misterye. **1432–50** tr. *Higden* (Rolls) V. 195 Paphnucius goenge to visitte a broþer laborynge in infirmite, causede the sonne to stonde stille thro his preyer, un tille that he hade fullefillede his mistery. **1509** Fisher *Funeral Serm. C'tess Richmond* Wks. (1876) 309 [She] was borne vp in to the countre aboue with the blessyd aungelles deputed..to that holy mystery. *a* **1533** Ld. Berners *Gold. Bk. M. Aurel.* K vii b, None should be taken from the misterie and office that he occupied.

†**b.** Something helpful. *Obs.*

1581 Mulcaster *Positions* xxxiv. 122 We..may not neglect so great a misterie for our owne health, as exercise is.

2. a. Handicraft; craft, art; (one's) trade, profession, or calling. Now *arch.*

The identity of the word in the first quot. is doubtful; cf. the variants.

a **1375** *Cursor M.* 13142 (Fairf.) Ho daunsed & sange to tumble with-al,..for ho sa wele hir mystri [*Cott.* mister, *Gött.* maistri] couþe. *c* **1440** *Gesta Rom.* xliii. 171 (Harl. MS.) He sente messageris..to loke yf eny swiche myght be founde, þat coude make swiche a shirte, but they coude fynde noon, but that they wer..vncunnynge in the mystery. **1536** Cromwell in Merriman *Life & Lett.* (1902) II. 27 Brought up in some good literature occupacion or misterie. *c* **1550** *Disc. Common Weal Eng.* (1893) 128 Bristowe had a greate trade by making of poyntes, and was the cheifest misterie that was exercised in the towne. **1594** West *2nd Pt. Symbol.* §220 Unto the name of the partie indicted must be vnited the addition of his estate, degree, or misterie. **1609** Tourneur *Funeralle Poeme* Wks. 1878 I. 179 And out of his owne morall character He might have learn'd his mysterie of warre. **1612** Woodall *Surg. Mate* Wks. (1653) Pref. 1 That noble Science or Mystery of the healing mans body. **1647** Clarendon *Hist. Reb.* IV. §41 That great and admirable mystery, the Law. *a* **1661** Fuller *Worthies* (1662) I. xvi. 48 Seeing the whole mistery of Heraldry dwells more in the region of fancie, than judgment. **1727–52** Chambers *Cycl.*, *Additions of Mystery*, are such as scrivener, painter, mason, and the like. **1756** Burke *Vind. Nat. Soc.* 33 The Invention of Men has been sharpening and improving the Mystery of Murder. **1800** Coleridge *Piccolom.* I. ii, The sum of war's whole trade and mystery. **1827** Hallam *Const. Hist.* vi. (1876) I. 326 Those arts of management which his successors have always reckoned so essential a part of their mystery. **1872** Tennyson *Last Tourn.* 327 Thy Paynim bard Had such a mastery of his mystery That he could harp his wife up out of hell. **1889** 'Mark Twain' *Conn. Yank.* xxxii. 367 A good blacksmith..[offered]..to..teach him the trade—or 'mystery', as Dowley called it. **1957** *Listener* 25 July 141/1 We usually start with some sort of prejudice against the verse-writer who is better known as a writer of prose: there is a (very proper) feeling that the two are different mysteries.

b. ***art and mystery***: a formula usually employed in the indentures by which apprentices are bound to a trade; also *transf.* (Cf. MYSTERY[1] 8.)

1627 *Borough Deeds Maldon* (Essex) Bundle 148 No. 5 [To] instruct the said John Wormell in the said science mistery and trade of a woollen draper. **1660** R. May (*title*) The Accomplisht Cook, or the art and mystery of cookery [etc.]. **1680** Cotton (*title*) The Compleat Gamester... To which is Added, The Arts and Mysteries of Riding [etc.]. **1765** Blackstone *Comm.* I. 426 This is usually done to persons of trade, in order to learn their art and mystery. **1856** Bouvier *Law Dict.* II. 196/2 Masters..bind themselves in the indentures with their apprentices to teach them their art, trade, and mystery.

†**c.** Skill, art. *Obs.*

1601 Shaks. *All's Well* III. VI. 68 If you thinke your mysterie in stratagem, can bring this instrument of honour againe into his natiue quarter. **1624** Ford & Dekker *Sun's Darling* IV. i. (1656) 33 Mistery there, like to another nature, Confects the substance of the choisest fruits, In a rich candy. **1661** T. Campion *Setting of Mus.* in Playford *Skill Mus.* (1662) 95 We must consider whether the Bass doth rise or fall, for in that consists the mystery.

3. A trade guild or company. *arch.* or *Hist.*

14.. *Rolls of Parlt.* V. 390/2 By the sight of Men of the same Misterie. ?*a* **1500** *Chester Pl.* (E.E.T.S.) Banes 59 That by twentye fower occupations, artes, craftes or misterie, these pagente shulde be played. **1530** in S. Young *Ann. Barber-Surgeons* (1890) 579 The Maisters and Wardens of the misterie or Crafte of Barbor Surgions of the

Citie of London. **1553** in Hakluyt *Voy.* (1589) 259 M. Sebastian Cabota.. gouernour of the mysterie and companie of the Marchants aduenturers. **1618** in Rymer *Fœdera* (1710) XVII. 78 The Master and Wardens of the Misterie of Stationers. **1708** J. CHAMBERLAYNE *St. Gt. Brit.* I. III. x. 29 Each Company or Mystery hath a Master annually chosen from among themselves. **1823** SCOTT *Quentin D.* xix, President of the mystery of the workers in iron.

4. *attrib.*: †**mystery-man** *nonce-wd.* (see quot.).

1626 BACON *New Atl.* (1650) 33 Wee have Three that Collect the Experiments of all Mechanicall Arts; And also of Liberall Sciences; [etc.]... These we [*sc.* the people of 'New Atlantis'] call Mystery-men.

‖**mystes** ('mɪstiːz). [L., a. Gr. μύστης, agent-n. f. *mūs-, root of μύειν to close (the lips or eyes): the primary sense is prob. 'one vowed to keep silence'. Cf. Gr. μυεῖν (μυέειν) to initiate into mysteries.] One initiated into mysteries.

1676 GLANVILL *Ess. Philos. & Relig.* IV. 41 Abraham (as Grotius collects from Ancient History) a great Mystes in the Knowledge of the Stars. **1677** B. RIVELEY *Serm. Funeral Bp. Norwich* 26 There are few kinds of Literature but he was a *Mystes* in them. **1778** APTHORP *Lett. on Prev. Christ.* (1778) 360 After having undergone the formalities, the aspirant became a *mystes*. **1904** *Expositor* Apr. 256 The instructions were given to the *mystes* [etc.].

mysti, obs. form of MISTY.

mystic ('mɪstɪk), *a.* and *sb.* Forms: 4 **mystyke, -ik,** 5 **-ike,** 4 **mistyk,** 6 **-ik,** 7 **mysticke, -ique, misticke, -ique,** 7–8 **-ick, mystick,** 4– **mystic.** [a. OF., F. *mystique* = It. *mistico*, Sp. *místico*, Pg. *mystico*, ad. L. *mysticus*, a. Gr. μυστικός, f. μύστης MYSTES.] A. *adj.*

1. a. Spiritually allegorical or symbolical; of the nature of, or characteristic of, a sacred mystery; pertaining to the mysteries of the faith. Also (more definitely) = MYSTICAL *a.* 1, but now somewhat rhetorical in tone.

1382 WYCLIF *Bible, Ep. Jerome* vii, James, Petre, Joon, Jude, seuene epistlis maden as wel mistik as redi [orig. *tam mysticas quam succinctas*]. **1490** CAXTON *Eneydos* ix. 37 To rendre theym from theyr lacyuyte, in-to pudike, mystike, and shamefaste chastyte. **1535** JOYE *Apol. Tindale* (Arb.) 36 Not in a mistik allegory. **1552** ABP. HAMILTON *Catech.* (1884) 16 The haly kirk is callit the mistike bodye and spouse of Christ. **1577** B. GOOGE *Heresbach's Husb.* II. 69 b, The holy Scripture dooth teache a more hygher and mysticall [orig. *reconditam*] consyderation. **1648** J. BEAUMONT *Psyche* VII. xcii, For genuine Divinity Shall be engag'd, but in a mistick fashion, In all the bus'ness of his Generation. **1656** COWLEY *Davideis* II. 48 Thy right hand does hold The mystick Scepter of a Cross of Gold. **1827** KEBLE *Chr. Y., Tues. in Whitsun week*, The mystic Dove Hovering His gracious brow above. **1849** CASWALL *Lyra Cath.* 55 Offerings of mystic meaning!—Incense doth the God disclose [etc.]. **1879** FARRAR *St. Paul* I. 3 The mystic union of the soul with Christ.

b. ***mystic testament*** [= F. *testament mystique*]: in the law of Louisiana, a sealed testament.

1856 BOUVIER *Law Dict.* II. 581/1 A mystic testament is also called a solemn testament, because it requires more formality than a nuncupative testament. **1888** *Encycl. Brit.* XXIV. 574/1 A special form of will, borrowed from Roman law, called the mystic or sealed will.

2. Pertaining to the ancient religious mysteries or to other occult rites or practices; occult, esoteric.

1615 G. SANDYS *Trav.* 79 Drinke three, or three thrice told, A mysticke law of old. **1627** DRAYTON *Moone-Calfe, Bat. Agincourt*, etc. 175 When turning ouer his most mistique bookes, Into the secrets of his Art he lookes. **1643** MILTON *Divorce* II. iv. Wks. 1851 IV. 73 Their filthines was hid, but the mystick reason thereof known to their Sages. **1648** HERRICK *Hesper., His Fare-well to Sack*, 'Tis thou, alone, who with thy Mistick Fan, Work'st more then Wisdome, Art, or Nature can. **1725** POPE *Odyss.* XI. 59 And mutter'd vows, and mystick song apply'd To griesly Pluto, and his gloomy bride. **1785** BURNS *Addr. Deil* xiv, When Masons' mystic word an' grip, In storms an' tempests raise you up. **1805** SCOTT *Last Minstr.* v. xxvii, Car'd not the Ladye to betray Her mystic arts in view of day. **1835** THIRLWALL *Greece* I. iii. 65 The mystic rites of Demeter. **1875** MANSEL *Gnostic Heresies* iii. 41 Some of these.. prepare a bridal chamber, and perform certain mystic rites of initiation.

†3. Secret, concealed. *Obs.* (Cf. MYSTICAL 4.)

a **1625** FLETCHER *Noble Gent.* IV. v. (1647) 42/2 These are but illusions to give couller To your most misticke leacherie! **1697** DRYDEN *Virg. Æneid* I. 357, I have search'd the mystic rolls of Fate [L. *fatorum arcana*].

4. The distinctive epithet of that branch of theology which relates to the direct communion of the soul with God; hence, pertaining to or connected with this branch of theology. Now *rare*; cf. MYSTICAL 5.

1639 N. N. tr. *Du Bosq's Compl. Woman* II. 29 Saint Bridget hath written so well of the Mistick Theology, that even the learnedest men admire her doctrine. **1727–52** CHAMBERS *Cycl.*, *Mystic theology* denotes a refined and sublime kind of divinity, professed by the mystics. **1765** MACLAINE tr. *Mosheim's Eccl. Hist.* Cent. xiii. II. iii. §4 The Mystic doctors carried this visionary method of interpreting scripture to the greatest height. **1854** MILMAN *Lat. Chr.* VIII. v, The difficult and mystic work which bore the name of Dionysius the Areopagite.

5. a. Of hidden meaning or nature; enigmatical, mysterious. (Cf. MYSTICAL 2.)

a **1631** DONNE *Elegies* viii. Poems (1633) 55 Foole, thou didst not understand The mystique language of the eye nor hand. **1693** J. EDWARDS *Author. O. & N. Test.* I. 187 The antient Sages and Philosophers were obscure and mystick in their Stile. **1727** DE FOE *Syst. Mag.* I. iii. 66 These mystick Characters were the Original of all the Hyeroglyphick Writing. **1791** MRS. RADCLIFFE *Rom. Forest* (1820) II. 61 Her mind.. rejected the mystic and turbulent promptings of imagination. **1807** tr. *Three Germans* I. 48 He sighed for the explanation to Holstein's mystic conduct. **1810** SIR A. BOSWELL *Edinb.* Poet. Wks. (1871) 53 [In the game of hopscotch] There, on the pavement, mystic forms are chalk'd. **1819** SCOTT *Ivanhoe* xxxviii, Is there no leech here who can tell us the ingredients of this mystic unguent? **1874** BLACK *Pr. Thule* iii, The room, too, in which this mystic Princess sat, was strange and wonderful.

b. In recent use: Inspiring an awed sense of mystery.

1842 TENNYSON *Morte d'Arth.* 144 An arm Clothed in white samite, mystic, wonderful. **1852** MRS. STOWE *Uncle Tom's C.* xxxvi. 249 At midnight—strange, mystic hour, when the veil between the frail present and the eternal future grows thin. **1875** JOWETT *Plato* (ed. 2) I. 380 Such is the mystic voice which is always murmuring in his ears.

B. *sb.*

†1. Mystical meaning; mystical representation.

c **1315** SHOREHAM *Poems* I. 630 Cryst and hijs membrys, men, O body beþe ine mystyke. *Ibid.* 837 To þe folke þat torneþ al to cryst Ine þe body of mystyke. *Ibid.* 2157 Þys ylke bok þe mistyk ys Of þese sacrementis.

2. Originally, a 'mystic doctor', an exponent of mystical theology; also, one who maintains the validity and the supreme importance of mystical theology. Hence, in extended application: One who, whether Christian or non-Christian, seeks by contemplation and self-surrender to obtain union with or absorption into the Deity, or who believes in the possibility of the spiritual apprehension of truths that are inaccessible to the understanding.

1679 PENN *Addr. Prot.* II. (1692) 146 Taulerus, Thomas a Kempis, and othere Misticks in that Communion. **1714** R. FIDDES *Pract. Disc.* II. 380 Those mysticks who would discard the passions of hope and fear. **1765** MACLAINE tr. *Mosheim's Eccl. Hist.* Cent. xv. I. i. §11 The Mystics were defended against their adversaries, the Dialecticians, partly by the Platonics. **1781** COWPER *Truth* 128 An Indian mystic. **1856** VAUGHAN *Mystics* I. Pref. p. v, The way in which mystics reduced themselves to utter inactivity. **1875** JOWETT *Plato* (ed. 2) III. 595 He is no mystic or ascetic seeking absorption in the divine nature. **1899** INGE *Chr. Mysticism* vii. 258 To the true mystic, life itself is a sacrament.

3. *occas.* One initiated into mysteries.

1859 KINGSLEY *Misc.* I. 327 A mystic—according to the Greek etymology—should signify one who is initiated into mysteries. **1871** JOWETT *Plato* I. 381 This was the meaning of the founders of the mysteries when they said, 'Many are the wand bearers but few are the mystics.'

Hence '**mysticness**.

1912 F. LAWRENCE *Let.* in A. Huxley *Lett. D. H. Lawrence* (1932) 75 Her weird mysticness throws a veil over her.

mystic: see MYSTICK.

mystical ('mɪstɪkəl), *a.* Also 5–8 **misti-,** 6 **myste-, mysty-.** [Formed as MYSTIC *a.*: see -ICAL.]

1. Having a certain spiritual character or import by virtue of a connexion or union with God transcending human comprehension: said esp. with reference to the Church as the Body of Christ, and to sacramental ordinances. (Cf. MYSTIC *a.* 1.)

1529 MORE *Suppl. Soulys* Wks. 327/2 Christes mistical body that is his church. **1549** *Bk. Com. Prayer, Communion*, All they whyche bee of the misticall body of thy sonne. **1550** SENONOYS tr. *Godly Saiyngs* (1846) 118 The mystycal or sacramental breade. **1597** HOOKER *Eccl. Pol.* v. lxvii. §7 A true.. participation of Christ, who thereby imparteth himselfe.. as a misticall head vnto euery soule that receiueth him. **1633** G. HERBERT *Temple, Ch., Superl.*, Approach, and taste The churches mysticall repast. **1660** COKE *Power & Subj.* 77 These two individual persons, by the law of God, are made one mystical person, of which the husband is head. **1845** *Encycl. Metrop.* II. 901/1 This mystical body, the Catholic Church. **1864** NEALE *Seaton. Poems* 165 They eat the mystical supper.

b. (Spiritually) allegorical or symbolical.

? *a* **1500** *Chester Pl.* (E.E.T.S.) viii. 333 Dauid.. prophesied that kinges from Tharsis and Araby with misticall giftes shall come and present that Lord. **1529** MORE *Dyaloge* I. Wks. 160/2 The misticall gestures and seremonies vsed in the masse. **1530** PALSGR. Introd. p. xvi, The nombre of thre, whiche of all other is most.. mystycall. **1555** SAUNDERS *Let.* in *Coverdale's Lett. Martyrs* (1564) 204 Though he stand behynd the wal and hyde himselfe (as Salomon saieth in his mystical ballade). **1655** FULLER *Ch. Hist.* III. xi. 12 To make up the rotundity of so sacred, and mystical a number. **1690** T. BURNET *Th. Earth* III. Concl. 113 'Tis plain to me in the Apocalypse, that Mystical Babylon is to be consum'd by fire. **1861** E. GARBETT *Bible & its Critics* i. 32 The mystical horseman in the Apocalypse.

c. In the interpretation of Scripture, applied to the spiritual or allegorical sense which is held to underlie the obvious or literal meaning.

1526 *Pilgr. Perf.* (W. de W. 1531) 4 b, Leest he wolde lene all togyder to the litteral sense of scripture, and not to yᵉ spiritual or mistical sense. **1553** WILSON *Rhet.* 62 b, Some do use after the literal sense to gather a misticall understandyng. **1662–3** SOUTH *Serm.* (1727) V. 53, I profess not myself either skilled, or delighted, in mystical Interpretations of Scripture. **1860** PUSEY *Min. Proph.* 620 S. Jerome gives here the mystical meaning.

2. Having an unseen, unknown, or mysterious origin, character, effect, or influence; of dark import, obscure meaning, or occult influence. Now *rare* or *Obs.* (Cf. MYSTIC *a.* 5.)

a **1500–34** *Coventry Corpus Chr. Plays* (1902) 12/341 Were mystecall vnto youre heryng,—Of the natevete off a kyng. **1533** ELYOT *Cast. Helthe* (1539) 33 In the serchyng out of secrete and misticall thynges, their wyttes excellyd. **1587** GOLDING *De Mornay* (1592) Ep. Ded. p. v, Least the matters which in some cases are misticall enough of themselues by reason of their owne profoundnesse, might haue ben made more obscure. **1643** J. M. *Sov. Salve* 21 While they mature.. such their mysticall and pernicious designes. **1727** SHUCKFORD *Hist. World* I. Pref. p. l, Instead of supporting them with Reason and Argument, they had them expressed in mystical Sentences. **1743** BULKELEY & CUMMINS *Voy. S. Seas* 104 [He] has not only traduc'd us, but made the whole affair so dark and mystical, that [etc.]. **1824** MISS FERRIER *Inher.* xxxiv, Struck with the mystical fragments of speech she had bestowed on him. **1829** SCOTT *Anne of G.* i, I would.. we had that mystical needle which mariners talk of. **1848** LYTTON *Harold* x. i, That illness had been both preceded and followed by mystical presentiments of the evil days [etc.].

†b. Of a person: Obscure in speech or in style.

1471 RIPLEY *Comp. Alch.* in Ashm. (1652) 111 Though I dare not here plainly the knot unbinde, Yet in my writeing I wyll not be so Mysticall, But that [etc.]. **1613** PURCHAS *Pilgrimage* (1614) 18 Such mysticall Mist-all and Misse-all Interpreters. **1626** BACON *Sylva* §96 A Physitian, that would be Mysticall, prescribeth, for the Cure of the Rheume, that a Man should walk Continually upon a Camomill-alley; Meaning, that he should put Camomill within his Socks.

3. Connected with mysterious or occult rites or practices. (Cf. MYSTIC *a.* 2.)

1577 tr. *Bullinger's Decades* III. vi. 386/2 Their mysticall apparaile, & their sundrie offices. **1582** STANYHURST *Æneis* II. (Arb.) 48 Too you for wytnesse do I cal; you mystical altars. **1667** MILTON *P.L.* v. 620 Mystical dance, which yonder starrie Spheare Of Planets and of fixt in all her Wheeles Resembles nearest. **1740** LADY HARTFORD *Corr.* (1806) II. 10 The Court and army danced what they called a mystical dance. **1801** CAMPBELL *Lochiel's Warn.* 55 'Tis the sunset of life gives me mystical lore, And coming events cast their shadows before. **1869** F. W. NEWMAN *Misc.* 192 Their smell when burnt, and the mystical cloud of smoke, were universally esteemed.

†4. Secret, unavowed, concealed; = MYSTIC *a.* 3.

1611 *Second Maiden's Trag.* II. i. in Hazl. *Dodsley* X. 419 Confess, thou mystical panderess! *a* **1687** PETTY *Pol. Anat.* (1691) 38 This is the State of the External and Apparent Government of Ireland... But the Internal and Mystical Government of Ireland is thus.

5. = MYSTIC *a.* 4. Also, pertaining to or characteristic of mystics (see MYSTIC *sb.* 2); relating to, or of the nature of, mysticism.

1613 PURCHAS *Pilgrimage* (1614) 572 So many are the interpretations in their mysticall Theologie, that Truth must needs be absent, which is but One. **1647** CRESSY *Exomologesis* lxxv. 635 Mysticall Theology being nothing else in generall but certaine rules by the practise whereof a vertuous Christian might atteine to a nearer.. conversation with God. **1655** FULLER *Ch. Hist.* IX. xvi. 179 His soul imployed in mysticall meditations. *c* **1710** BURNET *Autobiogr.* in *Suppl. Hist.* (1902) 473 With my ascetick course of life I joined the reading all the Misticall Authors I could find; in particular all Teresa's works. **1841** D'ISRAELI *Amen. Lit.* (1859) II. 50 The mystical Pythagoras, and the allegorising Plato. **1844** W. G. WARD *Ideal of Chr. Ch.* 326 Mystical theology is the ascetic theology of those, who are unusually advanced in the Christian course, and leading a life of unearthly and noble sanctity. **1884** *Encycl. Brit.* XVII. 129/2 The intuition or ecstasy or mystical swoon which appears alike among the Hindus, the Neo-Platonists, and the mediæval saints. **1904** ILLINGWORTH *Chr. Char.* ix. 182 Both [St. Paul and St. John] were men the basis of whose life was profoundly mystical.

mysticality (mɪstɪ'kælɪtɪ). *rare.* [f. prec. + -ITY.] Mysticalness.

1834 *Fraser's Mag.* X. 425 There is a fashion of mysticality in modern writers of verse which is in very bad taste. **1902** *Daily Chron.* 1 Nov. 3 Those who care for 'mysticality'—as an American writer would say.

mystically ('mɪstɪkəlɪ), *adv.* [-LY².]

1. In a mystic manner or sense; with mystic or symbolical meaning or representation. (With reference to spiritual things.)

1552 HULOET, Misticallye, *typice.* **1579** FULKE *Heskins's Parl.* 227 Euen as we are the bodies and members of Christ, and that is spiritually and mystically. **1583** FOXE *A. & M.* II. 2001/2 *The fat priest.* I pray the what is mistically? *Wood.* I take mistically to be the fayth that is in vs, that the world seeth not, but God onely. **1646** SIR T. BROWNE *Pseud. Ep.* 297 He.. that was mystically slaine in Abel. **1671** FLAVEL *Fount. of Life* v. Wks. 1701 I. 34/1 [The union] of two distinct Natures, and Persons; by one Spirit, Mystically. *a* **1711** KEN *Preparatives* Poet. Wks. 1721 IV. 97 When Saints of all their Sins releas'd On Jesus mystically feast. **1895** SALMOND *Chr. Doctr. Immortality* v. ii. 534 In virtue of their being mystically or representatively in Christ as their Head.

†b. *transf.* and *gen.* Symbolically, metaphorically, figuratively. *Obs.*

1586 W. WEBBE *Eng. Poetrie* (Arb.) 23 They supposed all wisedome.. to be included mystically in that diuine instinction, wherewith they thought their *Vates* to bee inspyred. *c* **1590** GREENE *Fr. Bacon* (1630) A 4 b, Why he doth speake mysticallye. **1670** PETTUS *Fodinæ Reg.* Introd., Moses in writing the History of the Creation did mystically teach the whole progress of the Metallick Art. *a* **1688** CUDWORTH *Immut. Mor.* (1731) 58 He doth not mean Mystically in this, but Physically.

2. Mysteriously, obscurely, incomprehensibly. (Often used vaguely.)

1517 WATSON tr. *Barclay's Shyp of Folys* A ij, I desyre alway and appetyteth newe inuencyons compyled mystycally. *a* **1536** TINDALE *Briefe Decl. Sacr.* (? 1550) D ij, Many of the olde doctors spake so mistycallye that they seame sometymes to affirme plainly, that it is but bred and wine only..and sometyme that it is hys very body and bloud. **1589** WARNER *Alb. Eng.* IV. xxi. 89 Some such are mistically domme. **1651** CARTWRIGHT *Cert. Relig.* I. 3 Your Lordship speaks mystically, will it please you to be plain a little? **1693** CONGREVE *Old Bach.* IV. xii, Still mystically senseless and impudent. **1799** SICKELMORE *Agnes & Leonora* I. 57 They adjourned to the stable, to review the beast that had been so mystically introduced. **1884** SEELEY in *Contemp. Rev.* Oct. 494 Faust..was..as mystically, as awfully sombre as any of those plays of Calderon.

†**b.** *Eccl.* In a low or inaudible voice, secretly.

1657 SPARROW *Bk. Common Prayer* 102 The Priest should say it μυστικῶς secretly and mystically.

3. With mystic rites. *rare.*

1817 COLERIDGE *Sibyl. Leaves* (1859) 241, I have arrows mystically dipt.

mysticalness (ˈmɪstɪkəlnɪs). *rare.* [-NESS.] The quality or condition of being mystical.

1608 *2nd Pt. Def. of Ministers' Reasons Refus. Subscr.* 78 Those bookes..have..as greate a promyse of blessing vpon the reading of them, notwithstanding their mysticalnes, as any other. **1614** JACKSON *Creed* III. 246 Marke the mysticalnesse of this speech. **1816** J. GILCHRIST *Philos. Etym.* p. v, Abstruseness and ingenious mysticalness.

mysticete[1] (ˈmɪstɪsiːt). Formerly also in L. form. [ad. mod.L. *mysticētus*, a. Gr. μυστίκητος (in old edd. of Aristotle *Hist. Anim.* III. xii, where mod. edd. read ὁ μῦς τὸ κῆτος, 'the "mouse" (*i.e.* the whale so called)').

The identity of the animal referred to by Aristotle has not been determined. In old Latin translations μυστίκητος was rendered *musculus piscis* and was thus associated with the animal so named by Pliny ('the whale's guide').]

1. The Arctic Right Whale, *Balæna mysticetus.*

[**1797** *Encycl. Brit.* (ed. 3) II. 754/2 *Balæna*..1. The mysticetus, or common whale.] **1815** W. SCORESBY in *Mem. Wernerian Soc.* (1818) II. 263 The huge Mysticetus, or Whalebone Whale. **1820** —— *Acc. Arctic Reg.* I. 459 The colour of the Mysticetus is velvet-black, grey,..and white, with a tinge of yellow. **1835–6** *Todd's Cycl. Anat.* I. 567/2 The Mysticete, or common Whalebone-Whale. **1894** *Athenæum* 3 Nov. 599/3 The 'Old Greenland Sea', where the mysticete had formerly been slain in such prodigious numbers.

2. One of the *Mysticete* (see next); a whalebone whale or mystacocete.

1876 *Van Beneden's Anim. Parasites* 58 The singular mysticete recently distinguished by the name of *Rhachianectes glaucus.* **1885** J. G. WOOD in *Longm. Mag.* Mar. 549 The Greenland whale (*Balæna mysticetus*), the type of the Mysticetes.

‖**mysticete**[2] (mɪstɪˈsiːtiː), *sb. pl.* [mod.L., a. Gr. *μυστικήτη, pl. of μυστίκητος (see prec.).] The suborder of cetaceans consisting of the whalebone whales: opposed to the *Denticete* or toothed whales. Cf. MYSTACOCETE.

(Used by Scoresby app. only as pl. of *mysticetus.*)

1820 W. SCORESBY *Acc. Arctic Reg.* II. 211 The difference of proportion existing between the heads and bodies of some mysticete. **1864** J. E. GRAY in *Proc. Zool. Soc.* 198 [Cetacea] Sub-order I. Cete..Sect. I. Mysticete... [p. 231] Sect. II. Denticete.

mysticism (ˈmɪstɪsɪz(ə)m). [f. MYSTIC + -ISM. Cf. F. *mysticisme*, G. *mysticismus.*]

1. The opinions, mental tendencies, or habits of thought and feeling, characteristic of mystics; mystical doctrines or spirit; belief in the possibility of union with the Divine nature by means of ecstatic contemplation; reliance on spiritual intuition or exalted feeling as the means of acquiring knowledge of mysteries inaccessible to intellectual apprehension.

1736 H. COVENTRY *Philemon* Conv. I. II. 59 How much nobler a Field of Exercise..are the seraphic Entertainments of Mysticism and Extasy than the mean and ordinary Practice of a mere earthly and common Virtue! **1765** MACLAINE tr. *Mosheim's Eccl. Hist.* Cent. XVII. II. I. i. §51 This female apostle of Mysticism [*sc.* Madame Guyon] derived all her ideas of religion from the feelings of her own heart. **1839** HALLAM *Lit. Eur.* IV. iii. §55 IV. 230 The scepticism of Malebranche is merely ancillary to his mysticism. **1845** S. AUSTIN *Ranke's Hist. Ref.* III. 95 He was not only susceptible of the sublimest mysticism, but his whole soul was steeped in it. **1890** *Guardian* 25 June 1030 He makes no attempt to show..that the Mysticism of Swedenborg is the only alternative to the Agnosticism of Professor Huxley. **1899** INGE *Chr. Mysticism* ii. 44 The Gospel of St. John..is the charter of Christian Mysticism.

2. As a term of reproach. **a.** From the hostile point of view, mysticism implies self-delusion or dreamy confusion of thought; hence the term is often applied loosely to any religious belief to which these evil qualities are imputed. **b.** Sometimes applied to philosophical or scientific theories alleged to involve the assumption of occult qualities or mysterious agencies of which no rational account can be given.

1763 WARBURTON *Doctr. Grace* III. ii. Wks. 1788 IV. 706 With an incredible appetite devouring the trash dropt from every species of Mysticism. **1763** WESLEY *Jrnl.* 28 Aug. (1827) III. 140 The same poison of Mysticism has.. extinguished the last spark of life. **1825** COLERIDGE *Aids Refl.* 381 The grounding of any theory or belief on accidents and anomalies of individual sensations or fancies, and the use of peculiar terms invented or perverted from their ordinary significations, for the purpose of expressing these idiosyncracies, and pretended facts of interior consciousness, I name Mysticism. **1838** PRESCOTT *Ferd. & Is.* viii. (1846) I. 367 An acute and subtile perception was often clouded by mysticism and abstraction. **1855** M. PATTISON in *Oxford Ess.* 258 That deluge of crude speculation and vague mysticism which pervades the philosophical and religious literature of the day. **1899** *Allbutt's Syst. Med.* VIII. 120 The terrorism, revivalism, mysticism, or self-concentration which sometimes pose as religion.

mysticismus: see -ISMUS.

mysticist (ˈmɪstɪsɪst). *rare*[−1]. [f. MYSTIC + -IST.] An advocate of mystical interpretation.

1860 WILLIAMS in *Ess. & Rev.* 64 The later mysticists charitably prayed for Hillel, because his expositions had been historical.

mysticity (mɪˈstɪsɪtɪ). [f. MYSTIC + -ITY, after F. *mysticité.*] The quality of being mystic or mystical.

1760 *Chron.* in *Ann. Reg.* 108/2 [transl. French] That zeal, that *Mysticity*, those extraordinary follies, which one would think proper only for the dark and barbarous ages. **1834** MEDWIN *Angler in Wales* II. 1, I will endeavour to 'make note' of their tenets, though many of them escaped me through their mysticity. **1885** PATER *Marius* I. 115 Flavian had caught something of..the sonorous organ-music of the medieval Latin, and therewithal something of its unction and mysticity of spirit. **1891** *Temple Bar* Mar. 434 The mysticity of the place being merely Leonardesque.

mysticize (ˈmɪstɪsaɪz), *v.* [f. MYSTIC *a.* + -IZE.] *trans.* To render mystical; to introduce a mystical element into, give a mystic meaning to.

1680 DODWELL *On Sanchoniathon* (1691) 66 By Mysticizing the Κοσμογονία of Moses to a sense not very distant from that received among the wisest Philosophers. **1827** G. S. FABER *Sacr. Cal. Prophecy* (1844) I. 49 They thus agree in the point of mysticising the prophetic day. **1830** S. R. MAITLAND *Twelve Hundred & Sixty Days* 46 You are obliged to get rid of the days, and to mysticise all the periods. **1903** *Jrnl. Hellenic Stud.* XXIII. 313 Not even an Orphic attempted to mysticize the shovel or the fork.

Hence ˈ**mysticizing** *ppl. a.*

1842 G. S. FABER *Prov. Lett.* (1844) II. 23 His fancifully mysticising plan of a cathedral. **1879** FARRAR *St. Paul* II. xxxvii. 227 St. Paul's methods..involve a mysticising idealisation of 1,500 years of history.

mystick (ˈmɪstɪk). [ad. F. *mistic, -ique*: see MISTICO.] = MISTICO.

1828 W. IRVING *Visit to Palos* in *Life & Voy. C. Columbus* (1849) III. 459 Two or three picturesque barks, called mystics, with long latine sails. *Ibid.* 460.

ˈ**mysticly**, *adv. rare.* [f. MYSTIC *a.* + -LY[2].] Mystically.

c **1450** *Mirour Saluacioun* (Roxb.) 20 Of this doghtere some tyme sange Salomon mistikly. **1868** MORRIS *Earthly Par.* (1870) I. I. 389 Nor shall he keep his man's shape more, when he First feels the iron wrought so mysticly.

ˈ**mystico-**, combining form of Gr. μυστικό-ς MYSTIC, denoting 'partly mystical and partly ...', or 'mystically', as ***mystico-humanitarian, -oriental, -religious*** adjs.

1861 *Chamb. Encycl.* II. 212/1 His *Biblia Pauperum*, or 'Poor Man's Bible', is a mystico-allegoric explanation of the plain contents of the sacred books. **1932** R. CAMPBELL *Taurine Provence* 53 Our modern mystico-humanitarian scientists who are merely barbarians. **1893** A. BEARDSLEY *Let. c* June (1971) 50, I am going to do a full page illustration of the wonderful and gorgeous *Song of Songs*, in mystico-Oriental style. **1834** J. S. MILL tr. *Plato's Phædrus* in *Monthly Repos.* VIII. 636 There are two sorts of madness; one coming from human disease, the other from a divine influence. This last we divided into four kinds: viz., prophetic inspiration..; mystico-religious, (τελεστική,) to Bacchus; poetic, to the Muses; and finally, that of which we are speaking, the inspiration or enthusiasm of Love. **1846** GROTE *Greece* I. xx. II. 160 The mystico-religious poetry of Greece. **1899** *Allbutt's Syst. Med.* VIII. 196 Psychopaths of the litigious, erotic, and jealous, mystico-religious and other types.

mystific (mɪˈstɪfɪk). *rare*[−1]. [f. after MISTIFY: see -FIC.] A mystifier; one given to mystification.

a **1849** POE *Mystification* Wks. 1864 IV. 253 In no instance before that of which I speak, have I known the habitual mystific escape the natural consequences of his manœuvres.

So **myˈstifically** *adv.*, in a mistifying manner.

1880 MISS BROUGHTON *Second Thoughts* I. I. ii. 29 'Let us look at it, Gill', says the squire, taking the card in his turn, and also mystifically reading it.

mystification (ˌmɪstɪfɪˈkeɪʃən). [ad. F. *mystification*, n. of action of *mystifier* MYSTIFY *v.*[2]]

1. The action of mystifying a person, playing upon his credulity, or throwing dust in his eyes.

1815 *Paris Chit-chat* (1816) III. 163 Old recollections.. made me an excellent subject for mystification. **1826** J. GILCHRIST *Lect.* 52 Special pleading of advocates, whose main talent is quibbling and mystification. **1874** L. STEPHEN *Hours in Library* (1892) I. i. 10 He was punished for assuming a character for purposes of mystification. **1885** *Manch. Exam.* 10 Apr. 5/2 The whole manifesto..was regarded by the public as a piece of grandiloquent mystification.

b. An instance of this.

1817 *Edin. Rev.* XXVIII. 382 Having amused himself with a mystification (or what is in England vulgarly called a hoax). **1823** *New Monthly Mag.* VIII. 122 Of all the mystifications with which man is acquainted, Voltaire thought life itself the greatest. **1876** BLACK *Madcap Violet* xv. 138 The sweetheart is impatient of these mystifications, and wishes her to promise to marry him.

2. The condition or fact of being mystified.

1817 SCOTT 1 Jan. in *Fam. Lett.* (1894) I. xiii. 399 The mystification of those who would see very far into the mill-stone is sufficiently diverting. **1836–7** DICKENS *Sk. by Boz, Tuggs's at Ramsgate*, The Tuggs's went to bed..in a state of considerable mystification and perplexity. **1884** F. M. CRAWFORD *Rom. Singer* II. i. 4 They never left Italy at all, it seems. I am rather mystified, and I hate mystification.

mystificator (ˈmɪstɪfɪˌkeɪtə(r)). *rare.* [ad. F. *mystificateur*, f. *mystifier* MYSTIFY *v.*[2]] A mystifier.

1823 *New Monthly Mag.* VIII. 122 Lawyers, physicians, and divines, are mystificators of the first order. **1898** *Westm. Gaz.* 4 Oct. 2/1 A special word or two with regard to Lockwood as a mystificator.

So ˈ**mystificatory** *a.*, mystifying.

1830 *Westm. Rev.* XII. 270 [Coleridge's] confidences to Captain Medwin and Mr. Leigh Hunt, were..of this mystificatory class. **1830** *Fraser's Mag.* II. 492 Your verses ..say all this, only in much more mystificatory language. **1927** C. E. MONTAGUE *Right off Map* viii. 68 This mystificatory drug had been working to some effect on the people of Ria's City.

mystified (ˈmɪstɪfaɪd), *ppl. a.* [f. MYSTIFY *v.*[2]]

1. Bewildered, puzzled, perplexed.

1863 *Conf. Ticket of Leave Man* 142 Having..slipped a couple of sovereigns into the hand of the bewildered and mystified Sergeant Jobson. **1902** *Munsey's Mag.* XXVI. 586/2 What have you two in your heads? asked the mystified lady.

2. Made obscure.

1869 FREEMAN *Norm. Conq.* III. xii. 182 The intentionally mystified language of the Biographer.

mystifier (ˈmɪstɪfaɪə(r)). [f. MYSTIFY *v.*[2] + -ER[1].] One who mystifies by practical joking or otherwise. Also, one who or a thing which causes perplexity or bewilderment.

1823 *New Monthly Mag.* VIII. 116 In our own history, Oliver Cromwell shines the prince of mystifiers. **1856** FARADAY in H. B. Jones *Life* (1870) II. 366 That phrase *polarity* in its present undefined state is a great mystifier. **1859** HARE *Guesses* (ed. 5) 213 He is not a mystic, but a mystifier. **1886** *Pall Mall G.* 23 June 1/1 If Demos is mystified much longer he will vote against his mystifier.

mystify (ˈmɪstɪfaɪ), *v.*[1] *rare.* Also 8 mist-. [f. MIST *sb.* or MISTY *a.* + -FY.] Only in pa. pple.: Beclouded, befogged (*lit.* and *fig.*).

a **1734** NORTH *Life Ld. Keeper North* (1742) 79 His Lordship was not so mistified, by his Amour, as not to discern these Arts. **1819** BYRON *Juan* II. xii, When gazing on them, mystified by distance, We enter on our nautical existence. **1833** R. H. FROUDE *Rem.* (1838) I. 284 As we went up, every thing was mystified and cloudy.

mystify (ˈmɪstɪfaɪ), *v.*[2] (Also mist-.) [ad. F. *mystifier* (1772 in Hatz.-Darm.), irreg. f. *mystère* MYSTERY[1] or *mystique* MYSTIC: see -FY.

Often associated with Eng. *mist*: cf. prec.]

1. To bewilder or perplex intentionally; to play on the credulity of; to hoax, humbug.

1814 HAZLITT *Pol. Ess.* (1819) 73 The noble Secretary *mistified* the house, as he had himself been *mistified* by his highness of Benevento. **1816** SOUTHEY *Ess.* (1832) I. 262 He was sometimes thus wantonly imposed upon, or, to use a word which seems now to be naturalized, thus *mystified.* **1818** *Blackw. Mag.* IV. 222 To bewilder, or, in the French phrase, to *mistify* the attentive world. **1863** COWDEN CLARKE *Shaks. Char.* 200 She has a tilt at him, jeering, joking, mystifying, obfuscating him. **1873** DIXON *Two Queens* IV. vii. I. 218 Puebla was to choose his words—to hint at dark intrigues—to mystify the council.

absol. **1837** *Fraser's Mag.* XV. 339 We would not swear that she was not secretly quizzing and mystifying all the time.

2. Of impersonal agencies: To bewilder, cause perplexity to. Chiefly *pass.*

1823 *Spirit Publ. Jrnls.* (1825) 293 The poor lad seemed quite mystified with his strange adventures. **1837** DICKENS *Pickw.* iii, Mr. Pickwick, who was considerably mystified by this very unpolite by-play. **1876** *N. Amer. Rev.* CXXIII. 112 This view led to positive evil in the observations of the late transit by mystifying the observers.

3. To wrap up or involve in mystery; to make mystical; to interpret mystically.

1829 I. TAYLOR *Enthus.* ix. 237 The practice of mystifying the Scriptures must be named as an especial characteristic of monkish religion. **1855** W. IRVING *Wolfert's Roost* i, The fabulous age, in which vulgar fact becomes mystified, and tinted up with delectable fiction. **1855** MILMAN *Lat. Chr.* VIII. viii. V. 22 *note* d, The early life of Becket has been mystified..by the imaginative tendencies of the age immediately following his own.

4. To involve in obscurity; to obscure the meaning or character of.

1827 SOUTHEY *Let. to H. Taylor* 12 Apr., The metapoliticians have dealt with their branch of policy as the metaphysicians have with their branch of philosophy,—they have muddied and mystified it. **1828** C. WORDSW. *Chas. I*, 20 Why bring this perplexity into one of the simplest things in the world, by the only means through which it could be mystified? **1874** SPURGEON *Treas. Dav.* Ps. xcviii. 2 We abhor those who mystify it [*sc.* the gospel].

Hence ˈ**mystifying** *sb.* and *ppl. a.*; ˈ**mystifyingly** *adv.*

1818 T. L. Peacock *Nightmare Abbey* xi, All this mystifying and blue-devilling of society. **1825** Scott *Diary* in Lockhart *Life* (1837) VI. 132 Another of Byron's peculiarities was the love of mystifying. *c* **1827** Coleridge in *Blackw. Mag.* (1882) CXXXI. 119 Such a mystifying cant of Hylozoism [etc.]. **1862** Thornbury *Turner* I. 317 The lines may be in Dibdin—I never could find them; but such is the mystifying fun Turner was so fond of. **1934** Webster, *Mystifying*. **1953** in Botkin & Harlow *Treas. Railroad Folklore* 508 The Delaware and Hudson came tooling up from Pennsylvania with what it mystifyingly called 'Standard gauge; 6 foot and 4 foot, 3 inches'. **1966** *English Studies* XLVII. 19 A conjunction which appears mystifyingly vexing. **1973** *Daily Tel.* 2 Mar. 15/2 *The Wrath of Goď* (Empire Two, 'X') would seem to parody that novel, mystifyingly, I would say, to most people.

† **mystill.** *Obs. rare*⁻¹. [ad. mod.L. *mistilio*, f. *mist-us* mixed.] = Maslin².

1463 *Bury Wills* (Camden) 16 To eche grome and page vj d. and peyre bedys of mystill.

mystiltyne, obs. f. Maslin¹.

mystily, obs. f. Mistily.

mystique (mɪˈstiːk). [F. *mystique*: see Mystic *a.* and *sb.*] The atmosphere of mystery and veneration investing some doctrines, arts, professions, or personages; any professional skill or technique which is designed to mystify and impress the layman.

1891 E. Dowson *Let.* 10 May (1967) 197 Its curious mixture of French technique & the mystique of Rossetti. **1940** *Economist* 14 Sept. 330/1 It is assumed that the only policy which can counter the Hitlerian *mystique* is that of 'European Revolution' which has a *mystique* of its own. **1940** *Time* 21 Oct. 94/2 In the '30s Ernest Hemingway expounded the *mystique* of bullfighting in *Death in the Afternoon*. **1943** H. Read *Politics of Unpolitical* ii. 27 But I do not claim that the principle of equality is a rational doctrine. On the contrary, it is an irrational dogma, a *mystique*. **1949** 'G. Orwell' *Nineteen Eighty-Four* II. 211 All the beliefs, habits, tastes, emotions, mental attitudes that characterize our time are really designed to sustain the mystique of the Party. **1951** *Observer* 2 Dec. 4/6 The 'mystique' built up around him [*sc.* Stalin] has become a genuine outlet for the Russian religious instinct. **1951** *Sunday Times* 16 Dec. 4 True, the new style [of the Civil Servant] has its own mystique, and the Mr. Alphabet Precis today prides himself on knowing when to write 'Dear' and when 'My dear' [etc.]. **1952** M. Muggeridge in A. Mayor tr. *Ciano's Diaries 1937–8* p. viii, The strange mixture of bombast, lies, cynicism and sincerity which furnished its [*sc.* the Fascist Regime's] mystique. **1952** A. Powell *Buyer's Market* 141 Money, with its multifarious imagery and restrictive mystique. **1955** H. Spring *These Lovers fled Away* 316 Talk to me about wine. To me it's something I drink... But to them it's a mystique. **1958** *Times* 25 Apr. 3/1 There is a mystique about violins, especially old violins. **1958** *Spectator* 20 June 813/1 His System has been.. damned by lazy actors as a rarefied mystique. **1959** *Times Lit. Suppl.* 15 May 284/5 The particular virtue of this account is that it shows how the task was done and thereby disposes of its *mystique* without destroying the belief that it was a miracle. **1960** *Times* 7 Jan. 13/2 Flying, both the *mystique* and the technicalities of it, plays its part, too, in the Egyptian stories. **1972** *Guardian* 3 Nov. 12/4 The City, of course, talks its own language and this has helped to add to the mystique.

mystlyone, obs. f. Maslin².

mystorne, obs. f. Misturn.

mysz, obs. pl. Mouse *sb.*

myszen, obs, f. Mizen.

myt, obs. f. Mite².

mytan, -ayne, etc., obs. ff. Mitten *sb.*

mytche, obs. f. Much.

myten, etc., var. Miting; obs. ff. Mitten *sb.*

myter, obs. f. Metre, Mitre.

myth (mɪθ), *sb.* Also (*c* 1840–65) **mythe.** [ad. mod.L. *mȳthus*: see Mythus. Cf. F. *mythe.*

The pronunc. (maɪθ), formerly prevalent, is still sometimes heard. The corresponding spelling *mythe* was affected by Grote and Max Müller (among others). Cf. also the following:—

1838 T. Keightley *Mythol.* (ed. 2) 1 Mythology is the science which treats of the *mythes*.. current among a people. **1846** —— *Notes on Bucol. & Georg. Virg.* p. vii, From the Greek μῦθος I have made the word *mȳthe*, in which however no one has followed me, the form generally adopted being *mȳth*.]

1. a. A purely fictitious narrative usually involving supernatural persons, actions, or events, and embodying some popular idea concerning natural or historical phenomena.

Properly distinguished from *allegory* and from *legend* (which implies a nucleus of fact) but often used vaguely to include any narrative having fictitious elements. For the Platonic myth see quot. 1905.

1830 *Westm. Rev.* XII. 44 These two stories are very good illustrations of the origin of myths, by means of which, even the most natural sentiment is traced to its cause in the circumstances of fabulous history. **1849** Miss Mulock *Ogilvies* II. ii. 20 There is a German fairy fable of the Elle-women, who are all fair in front, but if you walk round them hollow as a piece of stamped leather. Perhaps this is a myth of young-lady-hood. **1856** Max Müller *Chips* (1880) II. xvi. 84 Many mythes have thus been transferred to real persons, by a mere similarity of name. **1856** E. M. Cope in *Cambr. Ess.* 147 One of those myths or fables in which.. Plato shadows forth the future condition of the human soul. **1866** *Edin. Rev.* CXXIII. 312 The celebrated mythe or apologue called 'The Choice of Hercules', one of the most impressive exhortations in ancient literature to a life of labour and self-denial. **1899** Baring-Gould *Vicar of Morwenstow* vii. 195 It is chronicled in an old Armenian myth that the wise men of the East were none other than the three sons of Noe. **1905** J. A. Stewart *Myths of Plato* 1 The Myth is a fanciful tale, sometimes traditional, sometimes newly invented, with which Socrates or some other interlocutor interrupts or concludes the argumentative conversation in which the movement of the [Platonic] Drama mainly consists. *Ibid.* 2 The Platonic Myth is not illustrative—it is not Allegory rendering pictorially results already obtained.

b. in generalized use. Also, an untrue or popular tale, a rumour (*colloq.*).

1840 W. H. Mill *Observ.* I. 118 The same non-historical region of philosophical myth. **1846** Grote *Greece* I. i. I. 67 It is neither history nor allegory, but simple mythe or legend. **1854** Geo. Eliot *Let.* 23 Oct. (1954) II. 179 Of course many silly myths are already afloat about me, in addition to the truth, which of itself would be thought matter for scandal. **1885** Clodd *Myths & Dr.* 7 Myth was the product of man's emotion and imagination, acted upon by his surroundings. **1939** J. S. Huxley *'Race' in Europe* 28 Napoleon, Shakespeare, Einstein, Galileo—a dozen great names spring to mind which in themselves should be enough to disperse the Nordic myth. The word *myth* is used advisedly, since this belief frequently plays a semi-religious role, as basis for a creed of passionate racialism. **1940** C. S. Lewis *Problem of Pain* v. 64, I offer the following picture —a 'myth' in the Socratic sense, a not unlikely tale. **1941** H. G. Wells *You can't be too Careful* v. i. 240 As the New Deal unfolded, American myth and reality began to take on an increasing parallelism with Europe. **1950** *Scot. Jrnl. Theol.* III. 37 To this inner fellowship of disciples the 'mystery' of the Kingdom of God is disclosed, whereas to outsiders this same Kingdom remains veiled in parables, remains, that is, a figure of speech, a colourful vision, an imaginative dream, or, as we might say, a myth. **1959** *Listener* 31 Dec. 1171/2 The theme of *Sacrilege in Malaya*.. is that any institution of this kind needs some myth, that is some nonsense, to make it work. **1961** *Ibid.* 2 Nov. 739/2 Disraeli set himself to recreate a national political party out of the wreckage of Peel's following. A new myth had to be evolved. **1963** *Brit. Jrnl. Sociol.* XIV. 27 We use *myth* in a sense a little different from the popular one. To us it does not mean an untrue or impossible tale, but a tale which is told to justify some aspect of social order or of human experience. **1973** *Times* 13 Nov. 6/6 There is a myth going around that there are an awful lot of empty houses in Windsor Great Park. *Ibid.* 4 Dec. 7/4 Egypt's decision to sit at the table with Israel would 'shatter the myth' surrounding Israel's constant call for 'direct negotiations'.

2. A fictitious or imaginary person or object.

1849 Lytton *Caxtons* x. iii, As for Mrs. Primmins's bones, they had been myths these twenty years. **1874** Sayce *Compar. Philol.* iv. 165 The pronominal root is a philological myth. **1888** *Times* (weekly ed.) 3 Feb. 9/3 Parliamentary control was a myth.

3. *attrib.* and *Comb.*, as *myth-addict*, *-addiction*, *-criticism*, *-maker*, *-monger*, *-pattern*, *-play*, *-removal*, *-stage*, *-system*, *-talk*, *-transcriber*; *myth-bound*, *-creating*, *-destroying*, *-haunted*, *-making* (also vbl. sb.), *-producing*, *-provoking* adjs.; **myth-history** (see Mythistory).

1945 Koestler *Yogi & Commissar* II. i. 133 Almost every discussion with myth-addicts, whether public or private, is doomed to failure. **1954** —— *Invisible Writing* ii. 31 It does not matter by what name one calls this mental process—double-think, controlled schizophrenia, myth addiction, or semantic perversion. **1964** *Economist* 8 Aug. 551/2 Trying to educate the myth-bound Americans. **1874** H. R. Reynolds *John Bapt.* ii. 74 The myth-creating tendencies of the age. **1846** Grote *Greece* I. i. I. 75 The Athenian mythe-creators. **1957** N. Frye *Anat. Criticism* 72 The most conspicuous today being fantastical learning, or myth criticism. **1949** Koestler *Insight & Outlook* x. 153 The only [myth] which his myth-destroying genius embodied into his system. **1940** G. Barker *Lament & Triumph* 33 The Avalon haven I have in the grave Is now myth-haunted by God like Arthur. **1871** Tylor *Prim. Cult.* I. 20 That the earliest myth-maker arose and flourished among more civilized nations. **1961** *Guardian* 22 Sept. 10/5 The myth-makers are always quick to produce a propaganda image of the Leader. **1972** *Listener* 10 Aug. 183/1 Why did Buonarroti, who had started life as a court page, become a professional revolutionary and myth-maker, to bore historians for the next 130 years? **1865** Tylor *Early Hist. Man.* xi. 308 The myth-making power of the human mind. **1881** J. Royce *Let.* 28 Dec. in R. B. Perry *Tht. & Char. of W. James* (1935) I. 791 Ontology, whereby I mean any positive theory of an external reality as such, is of necessity myth-making. **1965** *Times Lit. Suppl.* 25 Nov. 1068/4 The myth-making gestures in her work. **1974** *Listener* 24 Jan. 111/3 There is..no causal connection between art and revolution.. to suppose there is one is to take a step towards mythmaking. **1961** *Ibid.* 28 Sept. 479/3 They find their natural allies in the political myth-mongers and the political gangsters. **1951** M. McLuhan *Mech. Bride* 5/2 This urgent appetite to have the cake and eat it, too, is widely prevalent in the myth patterns.. of industrial society. **1957** N. Frye *Anat. Criticism* 282 The scriptural play is a form of a spectacular dramatic genre which we may provisionally call a 'myth-play'. **1954** Koestler *Invisible Writing* xxxvi. 390 An indication of the deep, myth-producing forces that were and still are at work. **1966** *Punch* 26 Jan. 139/1 Author explores the myth-provoking north-west coast of Spain. **1951** Myth-removal [see Demythologize *v.*]. **1950** *Scot. Jrnl. Theol.* III. 39 We have seen that.. Christians are to.. get beyond the myth-stage of spiritual understanding. **1953** A. K. C. Ottaway *Education & Society* 42 Every society is held together by a myth-system. **1970** *Jrnl. Ecumen. Studies* VII. 822/1 In this essay, Gilkey is the theologian who establishes guidelines for myth-talk. **1924** D. H. Lawrence in *N.Y. Times Mag.* 26 Oct. 3/2 White people always, or nearly always write sentimentally about the Indians—all of them, anthropologists, and myth-transcribers and all.

† **myth**, *a. Obs.* [var. of Methe *a.*] Gentle.

c **1320** R. Brunne *Medit.* 156 So meke and so myþe [*Bodl. MS.* miþi] a mayster to tray. *c* **1450** Holland *Howlat* 693 All war merschallit to meit meikly and myth.

† **myth**, *v.*¹ *Sc. Obs.* [a. ON. *miða.*]

1. *trans.* To show.

13.. *Guy Warw.* (1883) p. 396 Þer nis no tong may telle in tale þe ioie þat was at þat bridale Wiþ menske & mirþe to miþe. *c* **1470** *Gol. & Gaw.* 871 Thoght he wes myghtles, his mercy can he thair myth. **1501** Douglas *Pal. Hon.* I. lxvii, Gif that my spreit was blyith, The fewerous hew intill my face did myith All my male eis. **1513** —— *Æneis* IX. vii. 14 The brycht helm in twynkland sterny nycht Mythis [Virgil *prodidit*] Eurilly with bemys schynand lycht.

2. To mark, notice.

c **1470** Henry *Wallace* v. 664 Scho durst nocht weill in presens till him kyth, Full sor scho dred or Sotheron wald him myth.

† **myth**, *v.*² *Sc. Obs. rare.* [var. Meith *v.*] *trans.* To measure.

1513 Douglas *Æneis* VIII. Prol. 40 The myllar mythis the multur wyth a met scant.

myth, obs. f. Might, Mite², var. Mithe *v. Obs.*

myther, var. Moider *v. dial.*

mythic (ˈmɪθɪk), *a.* [ad. late L. *mȳthic-us*, a. Gr. μυθ-ικός, f. μῦθος Mythus: see -ic. Cf. F. *mythique.*] = Mythical.

1669 Gale *Crt. Gentiles* I. II. i. 2 Mythic, or Fabulous, Theologie, at first broached by the Poets. **1699** Baker *Refl. Learning* x. 110 The times before these were the Mythic Ages, and are all Fable. **1775** J. Bryant *Mythol.* II. 97 The mythic heroes of Egypt. **1825** Coleridge *Lit. Rem.* (1836) II. 335 While yet poesy, in all its several species of verse, music, statuary, &c. continued mythic. **1840** W. H. Mill *Observ.* I. 7 To show.. the incredibility of his mythic theory as applied to the Gospels. **1866** Kingsley *Herew.* xviii. 344 *note*, Langebek.. tries.. to rationalize the mythic pedigree of Earl Siward Digre. **1881** *Ch. Times* No. 967. 513 To reject the Gospels themselves as mythic.

mythical (ˈmɪθɪkəl), *a.* [f. late L. *mȳthicus*: see prec. and -ical.]

1. Of the nature of, consisting of, or based on a myth or myths.

1678 Cudworth *Intell. Syst.* I. iv. 438 M. Terentius Varro.. distinguished Three Kinds of Theology, the First Mythical or Fabulous, the Second Physical or Natural, and the Last Civil or Popular. **1830** Tufnell & Lewis tr. *C. O. Müller's Doric Race* p. iv, The term *mythus*, and its derivative mythical, which have been naturalized by the German writers. **1832** *Philol. Mus.* I. 108 Mythical legends. **1850** Maurice *Mor. & Met. Philos.* (ed. 2) v. 67 The biography of Zerduscht.. is altogether confused and mythical. **1878** Gladstone *Prim. Homer* 10 A tradition, perhaps true, perhaps mythical, grew up, of Homer's blindness.

b. *transf.* Having no foundation in fact; fictitious.

1870 Disraeli *Lothair* xxxii. 169 Her influence is mythical. **1889** *Academy* 15 June 411 The account of pheasants being captured by poachers lighting sulphur under their roosting-trees appears very mythical.

2. Of persons or times: Belonging to a period of which the accounts handed down are of the nature of myths; existing only in myth.

1678 Cudworth *Intell. Syst.* i. iv. 712 This is an Old opinion derived down all along from the Heroick times (or, the Mythical Age). **1835** Thirlwall *Greece* ix. I. 347 He seems to have been a rhetorical historian, who selected this half mythical subject. **1846** Grote *Greece* I. i. I. 1 The mythical world of the Greeks opens with the gods, anterior as well as superior to man. **1865** Seeley *Ecce Homo* v. 43 Any theory which would represent them [*sc.* miracles] as due entirely to the imagination of his followers or of a later age .. leaves Christ a personage as mythical as Hercules. **1892** J. Tait *Mind in Matter* 308 That Jesus Christ was no creature of the imagination or mythical aftergrowth.

3. Of writers, their methods: Dealing with or involving the use of myths.

1874 H. R. Reynolds *John Bapt.* i. §3. 20 If the narrative were free from all suspicion of mythical handling. **1888** *Atlantic Monthly* Aug. 211/2 The grave Thucydides, least mythical of historians.

b. Applied to theories or views which regard narratives of supernatural events as myths.

1874 Rogers *Orig. Bible* i. 36 The theory which attempts to account for their belief [*i.e.* in miracles] on mythical principles. **1887** *Encycl. Brit.* XXII. 592/1 The mythical theory that the Christ of the Gospels.. was the unintentional creation of the early Christian Messianic expectation.

Hence ˈ**mythicalism**, attachment to or belief in myths.

1896 *Fortn. Rev.* Apr. 633 All superstition, mythicalism, other-worldism, and all that savours of obscurantism.

mythically (ˈmɪθɪkəlɪ), *adv.* [f. prec. + -ly².] In a mythical manner; by means of myths.

1817 Coleridge *Biogr. Lit.* (1907) I. ix. 100 The philosopher who cannot utter the whole truth without conveying falsehood.. is constrained to express himself either *mythically* or equivocally. **1846** Geo. Eliot tr. *Strauss's Life of Jesus* II. II. ix. 425 The two narratives in the Old Testament are to be understood mythically. **1875** *Encycl. Brit.* II. 57/1 Ideas mythically expressed and explained. **1877** Freeman *Norm. Conq.* I. App. 772 A dispute between Robert and Cnut which could be connected, even mythically, with Cnut's death and Robert's pilgrimage.

mythicism (ˈmɪθɪsɪz(ə)m). [f. MYTHIC + -ISM.] The principle of attributing a mythical character to narratives of supernatural events.

1840 W. H. MILL *Observ.* I. Pref. 8 The anti-historic mythicism of Strauss.

Hence **mythicist** (ˈmɪθɪsɪst), an exponent of mythicism or mythical theories.

1871 FARRAR *Witn. Hist.* ii. 74 No mythicist surely could have made what has been called the damaging admission that faith was an essential to their operation [*sc.* of miracles]. **1874** H. R. REYNOLDS *John Bapt.* v. §3. 332 Here we encounter the stiffest antagonism of the rationalist, the materialist, and the mythicist.

mythicize (ˈmɪθɪsaɪz), *v.* [f. MYTHIC + -IZE.] *trans.* To turn into myth; to interpret mythically.

1840 W. H. MILL *Observ.* I. 58 Christ's death..his resurrection..are so mythicized as to drop the substance, making them 'no individual, but a divine and eternal history'. **1863** *Sat. Rev.* 199 An English Bunsen or Strauss ..may mythicize or transcendentalize either the Old Testament or the New. **1891** T. K. CHEYNE *Orig. Psalter* 323 The storm-wind (mythicized sometimes as the cherub).

Hence **ˈmythicized** *ppl. a.*; **ˈmythicizing** *vbl. sb.* and *ppl. a.* Also **ˈmythicizer**.

1840 W. H. MILL. *Observ.* I. 4 The prepossession..with which the recent mythicizer of the Gospel undertakes his task. *Ibid.* 24 That mythicizing process. **1871** FARRAR *Witn. Hist.* i. 25 If the Resurrection be merely a spiritual idea, or a mythicised hallucination. **1893** FAIRBAIRN *Christ in Mod. Theol.* I. II. iii. §4. 271 The unconsciously creative mythicizing imagination.

ˈmythico-, combining form of Gr. μυθικό-ς MYTHIC, used in the sense 'mythical and..'.

1840 W. H. MILL *Observ.* (1861) 110 Our champion of mythico-philosophical interpretation. **1855** LEWIS *Credib. Rom. Hist.* II. 508 Mythico-historical narrative. **1895** A. NUTT in Kuno Meyer *Voy. Bran* I. 101 The mythico-romantic literature of the Irish. *Ibid.* 196 A mythico-topographical survey of Ireland.

mythifiˈcation. *rare*$^{-1}$. [f. MYTH *sb.* + -(I)FICATION.] The construction of myth.

1865 tr. *Strauss's New Life of Jesus* I. Introd. 126 Most especially have I represented the Gospel of John..as the culminating point of the evangelical mythification.

mythify (ˈmɪθɪfaɪ), *v. rare.* [f. MYTHIF(ICATION: see -IFY.] To construct a myth or myths about.

1906 *Critic* Feb. 161/1 The truth is that no distinguished actor in modern history has been so recklessly mythified as the great diplomatist [*sc.* Talleyrand]. **1951** AUDEN *Nones* (1952) 50 We have time To misrepresent, excuse, deny, Mythify, use this event While, under a hotel bed, in prison, Down wrong turnings, its meaning Waits for our lives.

mythism (ˈmɪθɪz(ə)m). [f. MYTH *sb.* + -ISM.] = MYTHICISM. So **ˈmythist** = MYTHICIST; **ˈmythize** *v.* = MYTHICIZE *v.*

1840 CARLYLE *Heroes* i. (1858) 204 He is careful not to insinuate that the old Greek Mythists had any notion of lecturing about the 'Philosophy of Criticism!' **1840** W. H. MILL *Observ.* (1861) 172 On the system of the mythists, these purely Jewish circumstances of the Nativity should have been told by the Hebrew Gospel. **1848** BROWNSON *Wks.* (1884) V. 256 The pure Evangelicism promised you has degenerated into pietism, mythism, rationalism. **1851** G. S. FABER *Many Mansions* 329 Some would parabolise, or rather indeed (to use the more proper term) mythise, the.. statements in the Book of Job.

mythistory. *rare.* [ad. late L. *mȳthistoria*, a. Gr. μυθιστορία, f. μῦθος MYTH *sb.* + ἱστορία HISTORY.] (See quot. 1731.)

1731 BAILEY vol. II, *Mythistory*, an history mingled with false fables and tales. [Hence as *myth-history* in Worcester 1846 and subsequent Dicts.] **1972** *Times* 8 June 16/4 The reason for Eton's interest in Jane [Shore] is that, in the barnacle-encrustation of legend and mythistory that has grown up around her in the past 500 years, she is said to have used her influence with Edward to save Eton from destruction.

mythless (ˈmɪθlɪs), *a.* [f. MYTH *sb.* + -LESS.] Without a myth.

1924 C. K. OGDEN tr. *Vaihinger's Philos. of 'As If'* 343 The myth..we have lost 'in the abstract character of our mythless existence'. **1936** *Times Lit. Suppl.* 14 Mar. 218/2 In Conrad he finds another writer with an heroic conception of life, but one that is austere, mythless, without veneration for the deep forces of Nature.

mytho- (ˈmaɪθəʊ, ˈmɪθəʊ, mɪˈθɒ), combining f. Gr. μῦθος MYTH, as in MYTHOLOGY, etc. A few compounds of occasional occurrence are placed here: **ˈmythoclast** [Gr. -κλαστης breaker], one who destroys or casts discredit upon myths; hence **mythoˈclastic** *a.* **mythoˈgenesis**, the production of myths. **myˈthogony** [Gr. -γονία creation], the study of the origin of myths; hence **mythoˈgonic** *a.* **ˌmythoheˈroic** *a.*, concerned with mythical heroes. **ˌmytho-hiˈstoric** *a.*, involving a mixture of myth and history. **ˈmythomane** = *mythomaniac*; also *attrib.* **mythoˈmania**, the condition or tendencies of a mythomaniac. **mythoˈmaniac**, (*a*) one who is 'mad on' myths; (*b*) one who has an abnormal or pathological tendency to lie or exaggerate; also as *adj.* **myˈthometer**, a standard by which myths judged. **myˈthonomy** (see quots.); **mythoˈpastoral** *a.*, combining mythic and pastoral elements. **mythoˈpœia** = MYTHOPŒISM †**ˈmythoplasm**, the fabrication of myths. **ˌmytho-theˈology**, theology based on myth.

1890 *Sat. Rev.* 4 Oct. 392 To give the *mythoclast his due. **1881** *Spectator* 15 Oct. 1309/2 In this *mythoklastic age. **1887** *Mind* XII. 623 The cause of the extraordinary development in man of '*mythogenesis'. **1889** *N. & Q.* Ser. VII. VII. Advt. p. iv, The *mythogonic hypothesis presented by Professor Max Müller and other philologists. *Ibid.*, The author draws a sharp distinction between *mythogony and mythology. **1841** *Fraser's Mag.* XXIV. 129 In the *mytho-heroic poems, the great Heraclide family enjoyed all that fame which mythic poetry can give. **1878** T. SINCLAIR *Mount* vii. 167 Æschylus..is almost wholly epical or mytho-heroic. **1838** T. KEIGHTLEY *Mythol.* (ed. 2) 304 Grecian history—of which the..*mytho-historic portion commences with the Dorian migration. **1954** *Encounter* Dec. 77/2 [Socialism is to be] treated as the way to that abolition of 'injustice' whose necessary existence in any human society these *mythomanes find intolerable. **1959** *Ibid.* June 79/1 The mythomanes seized the new means of communication. **1962** *Punch* 26 Sept. 464/3 A mythomane tart with a line in imaginary family grandeur. **1975** *Times* 2 May 11/8 *Paper Tiger*.. is a modest..entertainment, with David Niven as a pathological mythomane who..finds himself obliged to live up to his fantasies. **1909** *Cent. Dict.* Suppl., *Mythomania. **1955** *Antiquity* XXIX. 197 Deception for the mere fun of deceiving—a sort of mythomania. **1958** *New Statesman* 6 Sept. 311/1 As for the formal principle on which the New Critics plumed themselves, it cannot be said that they ever applied it with any consistency or finesse; and lately it has been giving way to mythomania and symbol-hunting. **1973** *Times Lit. Suppl.* 30 Nov. 1476/1 It proves to have no resemblance to the sculpture, and the assertion is seen as a manifestation of mythomania. **1857** *Fraser's Mag.* LVI. 88 *note*, When it is the fashion to insist that almost every one and everything bygone is a myth..we would humbly remind the *mythomaniacs that [etc.]. **1922** W. S. MAUGHAM *Writer's Notebk.* (1949) 186 She is not only a liar, she is a mythomaniac who will invent malicious stories that have no foundation in fact. **1961** *Times* 15 June 17/3 Mary ends up sadder, if less mythomaniac, than she began. **1973** C. MCCARRY *Miernik Dossier* (1974) 90, I regarded Miernik as a mythomaniac... I did not believe in the existence of the sister. **1890** *Sat. Rev.* 4 Oct. 392 Even Elia's dissertation on the origin of the crackling is gravely brought under the ..*mythometer of this degree of positive critic. **1882** *Amer. Naturalist* Oct. 829 Mythography... Mythology... *Mythonomy. **1890** *Cent. Dict.*, *Mythonomy*, the deductive and predictive stage of mythology. **1939** C. S. LEWIS *Lett.* (1966) 163 We now need a new word for 'the science of the nature of myths'... Would 'mythonomy' do? **1838** *Blackw. Mag.* XXXIV. 716 The *mythopastoral class of Sanscrit plays. **1731** BAILEY vol. II, **Mythoplasm*, a fabulous narration of history. **1959** H. BLOOM *Shelley's Mythmaking* i. 8, I do not claim that *all* of Shelley's major and mature poems are *mythopoeic, especially in the precise and narrow sense of mythopoeia that I insist upon here. **1970** *Listener* 30 July 154/2 Science is not immune to mythopoeia. **1927** J. S. HUXLEY *Relig. without Revelation* vi. 191 They possess a vague and elastic *mytho-theology. **1932** R. KNOX *Broadcast Minds* iv. 72 They had ancestors..to whom that mytho-theology was real.

mythogenic (mɪθəʊˈdʒɛnɪk), *a.* [f. MYTHO- + -GENIC.] Myth-forming; of or pertaining to the creation of myths.

1964 *Economist* 8 Feb. 511/2 The mythogenic dragons of the golden age of steam. **1970** *Time* 5 Oct. 73 Religion has cut itself off from its 'principal sources of nourishment—the soul, the symbolic and mythogenic process, the psychic energy resources'.

mythograph (ˈmɪθəgrɑːf, -æ-). [See next.] = next.

1891 tr. *De la Saussaye's Man. Sci. of Relig.* xxv. 207 The saying of an anonymous mythograph.

mythographer (mɪˈθɒgrəfə(r)). [f. Gr. μυθογράφ-ος: see MYTH *sb.* and -GRAPHER.] A writer or narrator of myths.

1660 STANLEY *Hist. Philos.* IX. xv. (1687) 502/2 Those Mythographers, who..feigned three Women who made use of one Eye amongst them. **1669** GALE *Crt. Gentiles* I. III. vi. 72 Many of the first Mythographers confound the Universal Deluge, with that particular Floud of Deucalion. **1778** WARTON *Hist. Poetry* II. Emend. E3, Fulgentius, Boccacio's favorite mythographer. **1846** GROTE *Greece* I. vi. I. 208 The genealogy just given of Œneus..seems to have been followed generally by the mythographers. **1891** R. ELLIS in *Class. Rev.* V. 457/2 Apollodorus (the Mythographer).

mythographic (mɪθəʊˈgræfɪk), *a.* [f. MYTHOGRAPHY + -IC.] Of or pertaining to the representation of mythical subjects in art, literature, etc. So **mythoˈgraphical** *a.*

1939 TILLYARD & LEWIS *Personal Heresy* v. 120 Between Aristotle and the modern mythographical school of Miss Maud Bodkin, Professor Wilson Knight, and Professor D. G. Jame, we find almost nothing. **1955** R. GRAVES *Crowning Privilege* iii. 42 The death of Marvan's pig is a mythographic way of recording the murder of inspired poetry by a new-fangled academicism. **1965** *Listener* 2 Dec. 902/1 A mythographic fantasy *The Complaint of Nature*, diffuse and heady with virtuoso language. **1968** J. A. W. BENNETT *Chaucer's Book of Fame* i. 17 The attraction of this mythographical tradition for Chaucer results in a Venus very different from the divinity he had found described in the *Roman de la Rose*.

mythographist (mɪˈθɒgrəfɪst). [f. next + -IST.] One who practises mythography.

1890 *Sat. Rev.* 12 Apr. 454 The limited space afforded by coins and gems is, from one point of view, an advantage to the mythographist.

mythography (mɪˈθɒgrəfɪ). [ad. Gr. μυθογραφί-α: see MYTHO- and -GRAPHY.] Representation or expression of myths in plastic art.

1851 NEWTON in Ruskin *Stones Venice* I. 401 In the language of Greek mythography, the wave pattern and the Mæander are sometimes used singly for the idea of water. **1881** *Academy* 12 Nov. 359/2 One essential condition of mythography has been almost wholly neglected,—we mean the dualistic aspect of every myth in its relations to art and literature respectively.

mythologem (mɪθəʊˈləʊdʒəm). Also **muthologema.** [ad. Gr. μυθολόγημα.] A mythical story; a fundamental theme or motif of myth.

1884 *Jrnl. Hellenic Stud.* V. 236 The apotheosis of Homer and his marriage with Hebè..do not properly belong to the Homeric era, but to the *mutholegema* of later times. **1939** L. BLOOMFIELD in C. F. Hockett *Bloomfield Anthol.* (1970) 424 Any normal human being could analyze this mythologem of 'metrical convenience'. **1961** *Times Lit. Suppl.* 27 Jan. 56/3 Professor Kerényi..repeatedly inquired of Mann his views on particular images and mythologems. **1973** G. POCOCK *Corneille & Racine* 305 This passion is not merely sexual, but is linked more generally with what, to use a modern mythologem, we would call the unconscious.

mythologer (mɪˈθɒlədʒə(r)). [f. L. *mȳtholog-us*, a. Gr. μυθολόγ-ος: see MYTHO- and -LOGER.] A mythologist.

1610 HOLLAND *Camden's Brit.* I. 207 If it be true as Mythologers [*marg.* Expounders of Morall Tales] affirme, that there was neuer any Hercules. **1680** DODWELL *On Sanchoniathon* (1691) 107 The most Antient and most Popular Opinions are most likely to have been intended by the Mythologers. **1835** THIRLWALL *Greece* ii. I. 39 Later mythologers attributed a more numerous offspring to Lycaon. **1874** MAHAFFY *Soc. Life Greece* xi. 323 The popular views of the comparative mythologers.

mythologian (mɪθəˈləʊdʒɪən). *rare.* [Formed as prec. + -IAN.] A mythologist.

1613 PURCHAS *Pilgrimage* (1614) 568 Typhon neuer hewd Osiris into so many pieces as these vaine Theologians and Mythologians haue done. *a* **1693** *Urquhart's Rabelais* III. li. 411 Our ablest Mythologians. **1863** MAX MÜLLER *Sci. Lang.* Ser. II. (1864) xi. 519 Quite opposed to this, the solar theory, is that proposed by Professor Kuhn, and adopted by the most eminent mythologians of Germany, which may be called the meteorological theory.

mythologic (mɪθəˈlɒdʒɪk), *a.* and *sb.* [Formed as next: see -IC.] **A.** *adj.* = MYTHOLOGICAL.

1664 BUTLER *Hud.* II. i. 444 Though Love be all the worlds pretence, Mony's the Mythologic fence, The real substance of the shadow. **1669** GALE *Crt. of Gentiles* I. I. ii. 8 Mythologick Traditions of the first chap: of Genesis. **1728** SHUCKFORD *Hist. World* IV. 214 Such Schemes and Representations [*sc.* of the Deities] could not be made, until the Mythologic Times. **1784** COWPER *Tiroc.* 197 Taught at schools much mythologic stuff, But sound religion sparingly enough. **1847–8** DE QUINCEY *Protestantism* Wks. 1858 VIII. 163 The gay mythologic religion of Greece. **1871** TYLOR *Prim. Cult.* I. 84 So thoroughly does riddle-making belong to the mythologic stage of thought, that [etc.]. **1878** GLADSTONE *Prim. Homer* vi. 77 A great mythologic drama.

†**B.** *sb.* A mythological personage or narrative.

a **1631** DONNE *Paradoxes* (1652) 52 So is she [*sc.* Venus] joyned in Commission with all Mythologicks, with Juno [etc.]. **1669** GALE *Crt. Gentiles* I. II. iii. 31 Not only the stories of Moses, but of others also, lie hid in the Mythologics of Bacchus.

Hence †**mythoˈlogicly** *adv.* (*rare*$^{-0}$.)

1611 COTGR., *Mithologiquement*, mithologikely; by a morall exposition of fables.

mythological (mɪθəˈlɒdʒɪkəl), *a.* Also 7 **muth.** [f. late L. *mȳthologic-us*, a. Gr. μυθολογικ-ός, f. μυθολογία MYTHOLOGY: see ICAL.] Of or belonging to mythology; based upon or of the nature of mythology or mythical narrative; having reference to a myth or myths.

1614 RALEIGH *Hist. World* II. xvi. 474 The Mythologicall interpretation of these I purposely omit, as..no lesse perplexed than the labours [of Hercules] themselues. **1696** WHISTON *Th. Earth* 2 Asserting it [sc. *Genesis*] to be a meer Popular, Parabolick, or Mythological relation. **1794** SULLIVAN *View Nat.* V. 182 This mythological dogma of the Scandinavians. **1837** WHEWELL *Hist. Induct. Sci.* (1857) II. 181 The mythological nomenclature of planets. **1856** MAX MÜLLER *Chips* (1867) II. 10 A kind of Eocene period, commonly called the Mythological or Mythopœic Age. **1858** GLADSTONE *Homer* II. 265 The mythological absorption of the Sun in Apollo.

b. Applied to writers of myths.

a **1656** USSHER *Ann.* (1658) 21 This Rameses..is by Muthological writers surnamed Neptunus.

c. Treated of or celebrated in mythology.

1807 G. CHALMERS *Caledonia* I. I. i. 9 Sesostris is another mythological conqueror **1876** BESANT & RICE *Gold. Butterfly* I. iii. 66 Cornelius began to regret his allusion to the mythological maid, for his classical memory failed.

mythoˈlogically, *adv.* [f. prec. + -LY².] In a mythological manner; in relation to or according to mythology; by means of myths.

1659 B. JONES (*title*) Hermælogium: or an essay at the rationality of the Art of Speaking. As a supplement to Lillie's Grammar. Philosophically, mythologically, and emblematically offered by B.J. **1693** *Phil. Trans.* XVII. 803 So that plain Writing was before Mythologick; and 'tis probable those that have it Mythologically, had it before pure. **1776** BURNEY *Hist. Mus.* I. 255 *note*, Etymologies; which, like fungous excrescences, spring up from old Hebrew roots, mythologically cultivated. **1858** GLADSTONE *Homer* II. 137 The whole conception of Apollo and Minerva, if it be viewed mythologically, is full of inexplicable anomaly. **1873** SYMONDS *Grk. Poets* vii. 193 In the Prometheus the fundamental moral law of Nemesis..is expressed mythologically, as abstract and ideal.

mythologist (mɪˈθɒlədʒɪst). [f. L. *mȳthologus*, Gr. μυθολόγ-ος (f. μῦθο-ς MYTHUS + -λόγος: see -LOGUE) + -IST.]

1. A writer of myths.

1642 A. ROSSE *Mel Heliconium* 104 Other Mythologists have other conceits. **1645** BP. HALL *Three Tract., Peace-maker* §26 It is no marvell that (as our Mythologists tell us of old) Discord took it ill that she was not called to the banquet of the Celestiall powers. **1662** STILLINGFL. *Orig. Sacræ* I. iv. §2 This Orpheus by Mythologists is usually called the son of Calliope. **1709** STEELE *Tatler* No. 49 ¶3 The Figures which the ancient Mythologists and Poets put upon Love. **1794** G. ADAMS *Nat. & Exp. Philos.* III. xxv. 55 This invisible and formless being..was by ancient poets and mythologists pourtrayed by Saturn. **18..** LAMB *Spec. from Fuller* 538 *note*, That Fabulous Natural History, where poets and mythologists found the Phœnix and the Unicorn. **1830** TUFNELL & LEWIS tr. *C. O. Müller's Doric Race* p. vi, The imagination of the mythologist was 'a chartered libertine'.

2. One who is versed in myths or mythology. ***comparative mythologist***: an expert in comparative mythology.

1631 HEYLIN *St. George* II. viii. 310 *Omnis fabula* (as the Mythologists affirme) *fundatur in Historia*. **1693** J. EDWARDS *Author. O. & N. Test.* I. 206 Vossius, or Bochart, or any other Mythologist. *a* **1704** T. BROWN *Comm.-pl. Bk.* Wks. 1709 III. II. 129 Mythologists..are mighty Unravellers of the Fables of the old Ethnicks. **1844** EMERSON *Ess.* Ser. II. i. 12 In the old mythology, mythologists observe, defects are ascribed to divine natures. **1856** MAX MÜLLER *Chips* (1880) II. xvi. 85 The first duty of the mythologist is..to reduce each mythe to its primitive unsystematic form. **1865** TYLOR *Early Hist. Man.* i. 3 The new school of Comparative Mythologists in Germany and England.

mythologize (mɪˈθɒlədʒaɪz), *v.* [ad. F. *mythologiser*, f. *mythologie* MYTHOLOGY: see -IZE.]

†**1.** *trans.* To interpret (a story, fable) with regard to its mythological features; to expound the symbolism of. *Obs.*

1603 FLORIO *Montaigne* II. x. (1632) 227 Most of Æsopes fables have divers senses... Those which Mythologize them, chuse some kinde of colour well-suting with the fable. **1632** SANDYS (*title*) Ovid's Metamorphosis Englished, Mythologiz'd, and Represented in Figures. **1649** OGILBY tr. *Virg. Æn.* I. 46 *note*. [Pallas], Goddess of Wisdom, born of Jove's Brain; by Macrobius..mythologiz'd, the Vertue of the Sun deriv'd from the highest part of the Sky. **1704** SWIFT *T. Tub*, Pref. Wks. 1751 I 11 This Parable was immediately mythologised. The Whale was interpreted to be Hobbes's *Leviathan* [etc.]. **1727** WARBURTON *Tracts* (1789) 108 How one of their own Fables is here mythologized and explained.

2. *intr.* To relate a myth or myths; to construct a mythology. Also const. clause.

1609 HOLLAND *Amm. Marcell.* d 2, Natalis Comes of this fabulous narration doth mythologize in this maner. **1669** GALE *Crt. Gentiles* I. II. i. 10 Noah his three sons divided the world; so did Saturnes... Thus they mythologised. **1718** *Freethinker* No. 88 ¶13 While the Writer thus gravely mythologizes on so odd an Adventure. **1753** SHUCKFORD *Hist. World, Creation* Pref. (1810) II. 324 They mythologized that five gods were now born, Osiris, Orus, Typho, Isis, and Nepthe. **1848** MARIOTTI *Italy* II. iv. 118 What can the poet hope by mythologising on well-defined historical events? **1883** *Sat. Rev.* 10 Nov. 607 As to Mr. Brown's examination of the character and legend of Circe, we are constrained to say that with all his industry, he is.. mythologizing on a mistaken method.

b. *trans.* To relate (something fictitious). *rare.*

1851 *Fraser's Mag.* XLIII. 410/1 That Hunter had been mythologizing..something to Benson's discredit.

3. To represent or express mythologically. *rare.*

1678 CUDWORTH *Intell. Syst.* I. ii. §20. 83 What the Poets fable of Tantalus in Hell..is nothing to that true fear which men have of a Deity..in this life, which indeed was the very thing mythologized in it. **1902** *Q. Rev.* Oct. 481 The whirling wind..has been mythologised into a demon.

4. *trans.* To make mythical; to convert into myth or mythology; to mythicize.

1847 J. W. DONALDSON *Vind. Protest. Princ.* 67 The task which he [*sc.* Strauss] undertook, of mythologizing the evangelical history. **1878** EMERSON *Misc. Papers, Sov. Ethics* Wks. (Bohn) III. 381 Our religion..respects and mythologizes some one time and place, and person.

Hence **myˈthologizing** *vbl. sb.* and *ppl. a.*

1778 POTTER *Æschylus*, To Mrs. Montague (1808) p. xxvi, They [*sc.* the Greek writers] were indeed enough acquainted with Egypt to acquire from thence a turn for mythologizing. **1858** MAX MÜLLER *Chips* (1867) II. xvii. 154 Crime itself was called, in the later mythologizing language, the daughter of Night. **1873** SYMONDS *Grk. Poets* Ser. II. v. (1876) 132 The polytheistic and mythologising instincts of the race. **1880** *Encycl. Brit.* XIII. 399/1 Barren mythologizings.

mythologizer (mɪˈθɒlədʒaɪzə(r)). *rare.* Also 7 **mith-**. [f. prec. + -ER¹.] One who or something which mythologizes.

1641 *Relation Answ. Earl of Strafford* 89 The 100 handed Gyant Briareus (whom the Mithologizers of Poems use as a Type of the Multitude). **1870** LOWELL *Among my Bks., Witchcraft* 83 Imagination, has always been, and still is..the great mythologizer.

ˈmythologue. *rare*⁻¹. [app. f. Gr. μῦθο-ς MYTHUS + λόγος: see -LOGUE.] A mythical story.

1792 GEDDES *Bible* I. Pref. p. xi, May we not..consider his history of the Fall as an excellent mythologue, to account for the origin of human evil.

mythology (mɪˈθɒlədʒɪ). Also 5 **meth-**, 7 **muth-**, **mythio-**, **mith-**. [a. F. *mythologie* or ad. late L. *mȳthologia*, a. Gr. μυθολογία: see MYTHO- and -LOGY.]

†**1. a.** The exposition of myths; the interpretation of a fable. *Obs.*

1412–20 LYDG. *Chron. Troy* II. 2487 Þis god..Schewed hym silf in his apparence, Liche as he is discriued in Fulgence, In þe book of his methologies. **1656** BLOUNT *Glossogr.*, *Mythologie*, a declaration of fables, an expounding or moralizing upon a tale.

†**b.** Symbolical meaning (of a fable, etc.). *Obs.*

1603 HOLLAND *Plutarch's Mor.* 1302 The Muthology of this fable..accordeth covertly, with the trueth of Nature. **1680** W. DE BRITAINE *Hum. Prud.* §27. 89 A Country Man in Spain coming to an Image enshrined,..You need not (quoth he) be so proud, for we have known you from a Plumb-Tree: Have a care you do not find the Mythology in your self. *a* **1704** BROWN *New Maxims Conv.* Wks. 1711 IV. 11 It has been an old Remark..that *Opinio* is of the Feminine Gender... The Grammatical Observation is not worth a Farthing, but a wholesome Mythology's couched under it. *a* **1734** NORTH *Lives, Sir Dudley North* (1742) 152 Those [sc. *Whig* and *Tory*] were the Appellatives; but the Mythology was Seditious and Loyal.

2. a. A mythical story. *rare.* †Formerly in wider use: A parable, allegory.

1603 HOLLAND *Plutarch's Mor.* Explan. Words, *Mythologie*, a fabulous Narration: or the delivery of matters by way of fables and tales. **1610** —— *Camden's Brit.* II. 220 By which prety fable..is covertly couched by a Mythiology that there lie hidden in these Ilands, veines or mines of Mettals. **1640** BP. REYNOLDS *Passions* iv. 21 Wee finde some roome in the holy Scriptures for Mythologies; as that of the Vine, the Fig-tree, and the Bramble. **1654** VILVAIN *Epit. Ess.* v. 88 Any Poetasters may make the like Mythologies from Esops Fables. **1664** MORE *Myst. Iniq.* Apol. x. 566 Such as Allegorize away the History of Christ into an heartless Mythology. **1873** SYMONDS *Grk. Poets* i. 2 We call Mythologies those poems of pure thought and fancy, cadenced not in words, but in living imagery,..mirrors of the mind of nascent nations.

b. In generalized use, without article.

1646 SIR T. BROWNE *Pseud. Ep.* I. viii. 30 All which [*sc.* the relations of Sir J. Maundeville] may..afforde commendable mythologie, but..containeth impossibilities, and things inconsistent with truth. **1692** BENTLEY *Boyle Lect.* ii. 37 The Modesty of Mythology deserves to be commended... 'Tis once upon a time, in the Days of Yore, and in the Land of Vtopia. **1727** SWIFT *Wonder of Wonders* Wks. 1751 V. 80 The Heathen Religion is mostly couched under Mythology. **1843** PRESCOTT *Mexico* I. iii. (1850) I. 45 Mythology may be regarded as the poetry of religion,—or rather as the poetic development of the religious principle in a primitive age. **1845** S. AUSTIN *Ranke's Hist. Ref.* I. 291 Erasmus adopted the idea of the Italians,—that the sciences were to be learned from the ancients.., mythology from Ovid [etc.].

3. A body of myths, esp. that relating to a particular person, or belonging to the religious literature or tradition of a country or people.

1781 GIBBON *Decl. & F.* xxviii. III. 101 The monarchy of heaven, already clouded by metaphysical subtleties, was degraded by the introduction of a popular mythology. **1830** H. N. COLERIDGE *Grk. Poets* 74 The Mythology..of the Iliad, purely pagan as it is. **1856** EMERSON *Eng. Traits, Race*, The songs of Merlin, and the tender and delicious mythology of Arthur. **1880** H. PHILLIPS *Worship of Sun* 5 In the Indian mythology the worship of Surya is the same as that of Helios or Here.

transf. **1821** LAMB *Elia* I. *Old Benchers Inner T.*, Fantastic forms..who made up to me—to my childish eyes—the mythology of the Temple. **1949** 'G. ORWELL' *Nineteen Eighty-Four* II. 155 She only questioned the teachings of the Party when they in some way touched upon her own life. Often she was ready to accept the official mythology. **1961** *Listener* 24 Aug. 281/2 This is an antidote to militarism which does not exist in western 'mythology'. **1965** M. SCHOFIELD *Sexual Behaviour of Young People* I. i. 9 The frequent articles in the press and the radio and TV programmes tend to create a teenage mythology. **1975** *Times* 22 Sept. 13/2 Not all private [pension] schemes were in fact as generous as popular mythology suggested.

4. That department of knowledge which deals with myths.

1836 SMART, *Mythology*,..the science of those fables which constitute the religious system and the poetical machinery of the ancient Greeks and Romans. **1864** *Chamb. Encycl.* VI. 646/2 The science of comparative mythology.

mythopœic (mɪθəʊˈpiːɪk), *a.* [f. Gr. μυθοποι-ός (f. μῦθο-ς MYTHUS + ποιεῖν to make) + -IC.] Myth-making; productive of myths; pertaining to the creation of myths.

1846 GROTE *Greece* I. i. I. 84 The commanding functions of the Supreme God..was a potent stimulus to the mythopœic activity. *Ibid.* xvi. 472 The mythopœic fertility of the Greeks. **1874** SAYCE *Compar. Philol.* ix. 376 The mythopœic age is the period of primitive unconscious childhood and barbarism. **1898** A. LANG *Making of Relig.* App. 367 The romantic and 'marvellous' circumstances are mythopœic accretions due to Dr. Janet's own memory or fancy.

So **mythoˈpœism**, the making of myths; **mythoˈpœist**, a myth-maker.

1873 SYMONDS *Grk. Poets* i. 2 Decayed, disintegrated, dilapidated phrases, the meaning of which had been lost to the first mythopoeists. **1899** *Eng. Hist. Rev.* Apr. 226 The spirit of mythopœism is always active.

mythopoem (ˈmɪθəʊpəʊɪm). [f. MYTHO- + POEM, after prec. words.] A mythical poem. So **ˌmythopoˈesis**, the making or construction of myths. **ˈmythopoet**, a poetical writer of myths. **ˌmythopoˈetic** *a.* = MYTHOPŒIC; so **mythopoˈetical** *a.* **mythoˈpoetize** *v.*, *intr.* to produce myths. **ˈmythopoetry**, mythological poetry.

1882 *Fraser's Mag.* XXVI. 376 Here, for me at least, the *mythopoem of the lagoons was humanised; the spirit of the salt-water lakes had appeared to me. **1882** KEARY *Outl. Prim. Belief* 320 *note* 3 It is in keeping with the principles of *mythopoesis that Calypso's land..should be in the midst of the sea. **1873** SYMONDS *Grk. Poets* Ser. II. vi. (1876) 158 There is nothing dead, devoid of soul, in the world of this arch-*mythopoet [Æschylus]. **1880** *Academy* 26 June 470 The *mythopoetic faculty has already been busy with the name of one whose actual life was more strange than fiction itself. **1965** *Philos. Rev.* LXXIV. 548 Wheelwright is engaged not in metaphysical but in mythopoetic investigation. **1970** J. O. LOVE (*title*) Worlds in consciousness: mythopoetic thought in the novels of Virginia Woolf. **1972** *Times Lit. Suppl.* 7 Apr. 381/2 This mythopoetic quality. **1900** R. FRY in *Monthly Rev.* Dec. 152 In such periods the magnifying *mythopoetical effect, which for us comes only with time, takes place at once, and swells their contemporaries to heroic proportions. **1959** B. BERNARDI *Mugwe, a Failing Prophet* iii. 52 It constitutes a typical instance of mythopoetical amalgamation. **1893** *Pall Mall Mag.* II. 346 If we watch the process of *mythopoetising in our daily life. **1869** *Contemp. Rev.* XII. 67 This costume..becomes his dominant token in subsequent *mythopoetry. **1878** SYMONDS *Shelley* v. 122 The strife is now removed into the region of abstractions, vivified by mythopoetry.

‖**mythos** (ˈmaɪθɒs). In 8 *pl.* **mythoi**. [late L., a. Gr. μῦθος.] = MYTHUS.

1753 SHUCKFORD *Hist. World, Creation* Pref. (1810) II. 327 Of this sort we generally find the *mythoi* told of them. **1803** G. S. FABER *Cabiri* I. 324, I cannot but be persuaded that the poem of Homer at least is a mere mythos. **1865** MILL *Comte* 27 A God concerning whom no mythos..had yet been invented. **1876** *Contemp. Rev.* June 113 The.. mythos of Demeter and Persephoné. **1946** 'G. ORWELL' in *Polemic* Jan. 6 The poisonous effect of the Russian *mythos* on English intellectual life. **1957** N. FRYE *Anatomy of Criticism* 52 *Mythoi* or plot-formulas. **1974** *Sat. Rev. World* (U.S.) 2 Nov. 30/2 The same mythos of violence that was indigenous to..the American West.

Mythra, obs. form of MITHRAS, MITRA.

‖**mythus** (ˈmaɪθəs). [mod.L. = late L. *mȳthos* (see MYTHOS).] = MYTH *sb.* 1.

1825 COLERIDGE *Lit. Rem.* (1836) II. 335 This the most venerable, and perhaps most ancient of the Grecian *mythi*, is a philosopheme. **1831** CARLYLE *Misc.* (1840) III. 229 The rudest heart quails with awe at the wild mythus of *Faust*. **1841** R. C. TRENCH *Parables* 4 The Parable is different from the Mythus, inasmuch as in the Mythus, the truth and that which is only the vehicle of the truth are wholly blended together. **1850** THACKERAY *Pendennis* II. xxiii. 237 Conscience! What is conscience?.. What is public or private faith? Mythuses alike enveloped in enormous tradition. **1892** *Athenæum* 24 Sept. 410/3 They consist of mythus and tradition intermingled and intertangled.

mytilacean (mɪtɪˈleɪʃən), *a.* and *sb.* *Zool.* [f. mod.L. *Mytilācea* (-*eæ*), f. *mȳtil-us*: see MYTILUS and -ACEAN.] **A.** *adj.* Belonging to the family *Mytilaceæ*. **B.** *sb.* A member of this family; a mussel-like animal.

1839 *Penny Cycl.* XIV. 318/1 Family of Mytilaceans.

So **mytiˈlaceous** *a.* = prec. adj.

1856 MAYNE *Expos. Lex.* **1891** *Syd. Soc. Lex.*

Mytilenæan, Mytilenean, Mytilenian (mɪtɪˈliːnɪən, mɪtɪlɛˈniːən), *sb.* and *a.* [f. L. *Mytilenæus*, Gr. Μυτιληναῖος Mytilenæan.]

A. *sb.* A native or inhabitant of Mytilene, the ancient city and modern capital of the Aegean island of Lesbos. **B.** *adj.* Of or pertaining to Mytilene or its inhabitants.

The form Μιτυληναῖος (L. *Mitylenæus*) also is attested by ancient sources, and is sometimes followed by modern writers in the form *Mitylen(a)ean*. The name of the modern city is frequently transliterated *Mitilini*.

1550 T. NICOLLS tr. *Thucydides' Hystory* III. iii. fol. lxxii, The sayde Mytilenians. **1601** HOLLAND tr. *Pliny's Nat. Hist.* v. xxx. 110 Acheleum..founded first by the Mityleneans. **1790** W. MITFORD *Hist. Greece* II. xv. 227 The principal Mitylenæans had sent offers to the Lacedæmonian administration to renounce the Athenian. *Ibid.* 228 The whole Mitylenæan people would go in procession out of the city. **1900** J. B. BURY *Hist. Greece* x. 413 The Mytilenaeans received secret intelligence and postponed the feast. **1911** *Encycl. Brit.* XIX. 887/1 This base coinage..ceases about 450 B.C., when the Mytilenaean silver begins. *Ibid.* XXI. 73/2 An assembly was held and under the invective of Cleon it was decided to kill all male Mytileneans of military age. **1945** G. B. GRUNDY *Fifty-Five Years at Oxford* xiv. 221 He could not have supposed that any reader of his history who read the Mytilenian Debate or the Melian Dialogue would regard the Funeral Oration as being a picture of a political ..life..at Athens. **1965** T. T. B. RYDER *Koine Eirene* iv. 77 The Athenian people voted a decree of thanks to the Mytileneans for their services in the war against the Spartans. **1968** V. EHRENBERG *From Solon to Socrates* viii. 359 In the Mytilenean debate..Cleon attacks rhetoric. **1972** R. MEIGGS *Athenian Empire* iii. 47 We may prefer the different motivation he attributes to the Mytilenaeans. *Ibid.* xvii. 312 A rich Mytilenaean left two daughters. **1974**

Guardian 11 Nov. 4/6 Life is rough for the Mytilenians at present.

mytiliform (maɪˈtɪlɪfɔːm), *a.* [f. MYTILUS: see -FORM.] Mussel-shaped; mytiloid.

1854 WOODWARD *Mollusca* 265 Shell equivalve, mytiliform.

mytilite (ˈmɪtɪlaɪt). *Geol.* Also 8 **mytul-**. [f. MYTIL-US: see -ITE.] A fossil mussel-shell.

1794 KIRWAN *Elem. Min.* (ed. 2) I. 81 Compact Limestone..frequently abounds with..pectinites, gryphites, mytulites, &c. **1811** PINKERTON *Petral.* I. 254 In a specimen [of argillite] from Hessia, mytilites occur.

†**ˈmytilod.** *Obs.* [ad. mod.L. *mȳtilōdēs*, f. MYTIL-US: see -ODE[1].]

1708 *Phil. Trans.* XXVI. 79 Mytiloides, The Mytilod, or Sea Muscle-stone.

mytiloid (ˈmɪtɪlɔɪd), *a.* and *sb.* [f. MYTIL-US + -OID.] **a.** *adj.* Mussel-like; belonging to the family *Mytilidæ*. **b.** *sb.* A member of this family; a mussel.

1847 TULK tr. *Oken's Physiophilos.* 594 Fam. 4. Mytiloid, Locust-Crabs. **1882** OGILVIE, *Mytiloid*, a term applied to shells resembling in character that of the mussel.

mytilotoxine (ˌmɪtɪləʊˈtɒksɪn). *Chem.* [f. *mytilo-*, MYTILUS + TOXIN(E.] A leucomaine found in the common mussel, isolated by Brieger.

1887 A. M. BROWN *Anim. Alkaloids* 104.

‖**Mytilus** (ˈmɪtɪləs). [mod.L. *mȳtilus*, after L. *mȳtilus, mītulus, mūtulus* (whence late Gr. μυτίλος) sea-mussel.] A genus of bivalves, now comprising the marine mussels.

1817 J. BRADBURY *Trav. Amer.* 257 It has exactly the appearance of marine rocks, perforated by *Mytilus*, or *Rugosus*. **1843** OWEN *Lect. Comp. Anat. Invertebrates* I. 284 *note*, The nervous system of the Mytilus. **1878** BELL tr. *Gegenbaur's Comp. Anat.* 329 Pecten, Lima,..Mytilus have an organ of this kind.

‖**myxa** (ˈmɪksə). [L. (fem. sing.).] The Indian tree *Cordia Myxa*, having a mucilaginous and emollient fruit; also, the fruit of this tree, the sebesten. (Cf. MYXE.)

[**1706** PHILLIPS (ed. 6), *Myxa*,..a sort of Prunes or Plums, like Damsins.] **1865** J. H. INGRAHAM *Pillar of Fire* (1872) 122 In this garden there was also the wine-giving myxa. **1891** *Syd. Soc. Lex.*, *Myxæ*, the fruits of *Cordia myxa*.

myxamœba (mɪksəˈmiːbə). Also **myxo-amœba**. Pl. **-æ**. [f. MYXO- + AMŒBA.] In a slime mould of the division Myxomycota, a cell lacking flagella but capable of amœboid movement. So **myxaˈmœboid** *a.*

1875 BENNETT & DYER tr. *Sachs' Bot.* 10 In the Myxomycetes the swarm-spores (Myxo-amœbæ)..coalesce gradually in great numbers. **1887** H. E. F. GARNSEY tr. *A. de Bary's Compar. Morphol. & Biol. Fungi* viii. 423 Swarm-cells with purely amoeboid motion have been unnecessarily distinguished by the name of myxamoebae. **1888** ROLLESTON & JACKSON *Anim. Life* 908 *Myxamœba.* **1927** GWYNNE-VAUGHAN & BARNES *Structure & Development of Fungi* 45 In early stages of development they [*sc.* Myxomycetes] appear as small, naked uninucleate amoebae, the myxamoebae. *Ibid.*, Eventually multiplication ceases, the zoospores resume the myxamoeboid form and fuse in pairs. **1947** F. A. & F. T. WOLF *Fungi* I. iv. 40 In moist weather the spore walls open to emit swarm cells (myxamoebae), which ingest bacteria and fungus spores, assimilate them, and grow to become a large, multinucleate, naked mass of protoplasm (plasmodium). **1968** H. HARRIS *Nucleus & Cytoplasm* vi. 118 The experiments.. demonstrate the failure of high concentrations of actinomycin D to inhibit decisive events in the differentiation of colonial myxamoebae. **1971** P. H. B. TALBOT *Princ. Fungal Taxonomy* viii. 100 A myxamoeba may put out flagella and become a swarmer, or a swarmer may retract its flagella and become a myxamoeba.

myxcion, obs. form of MIXTION.

†**myxe.** *Obs.* Also **mixe**. [ad. late L. *myxa* neut. pl. (Palladius) = late Gr. μύξα.] A kind of damson or plum. (Cf. MYXA.)

c **1420** *Pallad. on Husb.* III. 1032 Now curneles of mixe [*v.r.* myxe] hit is to keste In molde in sum vessell.

‖**Myxine** (mɪkˈsaɪniː). [mod.L. *Myxīnē* (Linnæus), app. alteration of Gr. μυξῖνος slime-fish, f. μύξα slime.] A genus of cyclostomous fishes having very slimy eel-shaped bodies, which are frequently found in the bodies of other fishes (e.g. cod); a fish of this genus, a hag-fish or borer.

1836 YARRELL *Brit. Fishes* II. 463 As a British fish, the Myxine occurs most frequently on the eastern coast. **1882** TENISON-WOODS *Fish & Fisheries N.S. Wales* 3 *Cyclostomata*, or Lampreys and Myxines.

myxinoid (ˈmɪksɪnɔɪd), *a.* and *sb. Ichthyol.* [f. MYXINE + -OID.] **a.** *adj.* Pertaining to or having the characters of the family *Myxinidæ* (typical genus MYXINE) of cyclostomous fishes. **b.** A fish of this family.

1846 OWEN *Lect. Anat. Vertebrate Anim.* I. *Fishes* 46 In 1837, I separated the Lampreys, Myxinoids, and Lancelets, under the name *Dermopteri*. *Ibid.* 51 The Myxinoid fishes. *Ibid.* 72 A complex system of peculiarly Myxinoid cartilages. **1871** HUXLEY *Anat. Vert.* 73 In the Myxinoid fishes there are no motor nerves of the eyeball.

myxne, obs. form of MIXEN.

myxo (ˈmɪksəʊ). Abbrev. of MYXOMATOSIS.

1953 S. J. BAKER *Australia Speaks* 105 Another popular Australian speech habit is to truncate a word and add the suffix *o*. Among words..which fall into this category..are ..*myxo*, the disease myxomatosis, used to kill off rabbits; [etc.]. **1961** PARTRIDGE *Dict. Slang* Suppl. 1193/2 Myxo. Myxomatosis: Australian: since ca. 1945... But, since ca. 1950, also current in Great Britain. **1967** J. MORRISON in *Coast to Coast 1965–6* 135 The myxo'll look after the rabbits. **1970** M. TARMEY *Skinman* i. 22 They reckon myxo'll spread quite a bit this summer.

myxo- (ˈmɪksəʊ), also before a vowel **myx-**, combining form of Gr. μύξα slime, mucus, occurring in a number of scientific terms. ‖**myxœˈdema**, a disease characterized by the conversion of the connective tissue into a gelatinous substance and destruction of the thyroid gland; hence **myxœˈdematous**, **-œˈdemic** *adjs.* ‖**myxofiˈbroma**: see quot.; hence **myxofiˈbromatous** *a.* ‖**myxogastres** (-ˈgæstriːz) [Gr. γαστήρ belly], an earlier name of the Myxomycetes; hence **myxoˈgastrous** *a.* ‖**myxogliˈoma**: see quot. **myxomyˈcetal**, **-myˈcetan** *adjs.*, pertaining to or characteristic of the Myxomycetes. **ˈmyxomyˌcete**, one of the Myxomycetes. ‖**ˌmyxomyˈcetes** *sb. pl.*, the slime-moulds or slime-fungi, a group of organisms usually referred to the Mycetozoa; hence **myxomyˈcetous** *a.* **ˈmyxopod** [Gr. ποδ-, πούς foot], a protozoan possessing pseudopodia; also as adj. = **myˈxopodous** (*Cent. Dict.* 1890). ‖**myxosarˈcoma**, a tumour composed of myxomatous and sarcomatous tissue; hence **myxosarˈcomatous** *a.* **ˈmyxospore**, **myˈxosporous** *a.* (see quot.).

1877 ORD in *Med.-Chirurg. Trans.* (1878) LXI. 71, I propose to give the name of *Myxoedema to the affection. **1897** *Allbutt's Syst. Med.* III. 319 The effects of myxœdema ..can be removed by the administration of thyroid extract. **1887** *Brit. Med. Jrnl.* 19 Mar. 632/2 The *myxœdematous and other undoubtedly metaplastic processes. **1898** J. HUTCHINSON *Archives of Surg.* IX. 351 Her own description of her *myxœdemic symptoms is that she became yellow or creamy looking with habitually bluish lips. **1856** MAYNE *Expos. Lex*, **Myxofibroma*, a non-malignant tumour consisting of delicate myxomatous connective tissue, intermixed with which are coarser bundles of fibrous tissue. **1897** *Allbutt's Syst. Med.* III. 713 A large *myxofibromatous polypus. **1838** M. J. BERKELEY in *Ann. Nat. Hist.* I. 97 The group *Myxogastres, as Fries remarks, differ in their singular vegetation from all other Fungi. **1866** *Treas. Bot.* II. 774/2 *Myxogastrous Fungi. **1878** tr. *von Ziemssen's Cycl. Pract. Med.* XIII. 750 **Myxoglioma*..is to be regarded as a variety of glioma. It is a bright red, translucent, viscid tumor. **1902** *Brit. Med. Jrnl.* 19 July 223 *Myxomycetal spores. **1880** SAVILLE KENT *Infusoria* I. App. 470 The developmental phenomena of several *Myxomycetan types. **1877** HUXLEY *Anat. Inv. Anim.* 5 Another *Myxomycete, *Æthalium septicum*. *Ibid.* 44 Zoospores of **Myxomycetes*. **1882** OGILVIE, **Myxomycetous*, pertaining to the Myxomycetæ. **1875** HUXLEY in *Encycl. Brit.* II. 50/1 In one state, each of these *Monera* is a **myxopod*, that is, is provided with longer or shorter pseudopodia as locomotive organs. **1877** —— *Anat. Inv. Anim.* ii. 81 After swimming about for a while, these mastigopods draw in their flagella, and become creeping myxopods. **1872** T. BRYANT *Pract. Surg.* 747 They [*sc.* the round-celled kinds of sarcoma] are common in *myxo- or glio- or lympho-sarcoma. **1897** *Trans. Amer. Pediatric Soc.* IX. 156 Congenital sarcomata of the skin..are mostly spindle-shaped, or *myxosarcomatous. **1854** *Encycl. Brit.* (ed. 8) V. 147/1 The organs of reproduction of Fungi are spores... When spores are produced..in the midst of a gelatinous mass, without any evident organization, they are called *Myxospores.., the plants being *myxosporous.

myxobacterium (mɪksəbækˈtɪərɪəm). Also **myxobacter**. [ad. mod.L. *Myxobacter* (R. Thaxter 1892, in *Bot. Gaz.* XVII. 403), f. MYXO- + BACTERIUM.] A slime bacterium of the order Myxobacterales, which includes predominantly saprophytic bacteria having a vegetative state in which the unicellular rods are embedded in slime to produce thin, flat colonies, and forming spores, often in distinct fruiting bodies. So **myxobacˈterial** *a.*, of or pertaining to an organism of this kind.

1932 D. E. JOHNSON in *Jrnl. Bacteriol.* XXIV. 340 Other cultures had the characteristics of the vegetative stage of Myxobacteria. **1946** *Nature* 23 Nov. 745/1 The lytic effect of certain myxobacteria upon the true bacteria (eubacteria) has been known for some years. **1949** H. W. FLOREY et al. *Antibiotics* I. i. 40 Three other bacteria..were inhibitory to *Ustilago*, a non-sporing rod, a motile sporing rod, and a myxobacterium. **1957** R. S. BREED et al. *Bergey's Man. Determinative Bacteriol.* (ed. 7) 854 In the vegetative condition, myxobacters consist of unicellular rods which occur in two characteristic shapes. *Ibid.* 855 The myxobacterial colony, also sometimes designated as a swarm or pseudoplasmodium, consists characteristically of a flat, thin mass of vegetative cells which spreads rapidly. **1961** *New Scientist* 16 Mar. 669/1 The predators [in the soil] include also myxo-bacteria, giant rhizopods, acrasieae and others. **1973** R. G. KRUEGER et al. *Introd. Microbiol.* iii. 60/1 Myxobacteria grow as individual cells that are typically embedded in a mass of slime they produce during growth. *Ibid.* 60/2 In soil and in dung, myxobacteria are active in the degradation of complex organic materials.

myxococcus (mɪksəˈkɒkəs). [mod.L., f. MYXO- + COCCUS.] A myxobacterium of the genus so called. Also *attrib.* So **myxoˈcoccal** *a.*, of or pertaining to an organism of this kind.

1892 R. THAXTER in *Bot. Gaz.* XVII. 396 In forms like Myxococcus, in which the rods are somewhat scattered, the first preparation for spore production..consists in the appearance of groups of rods moving with a circular tendency. [*Ibid.* 403 Myxococcus n. gen. – Rods slender, curved, swarming together after a vegetative period.] **1932** *Jrnl. Bacteriol.* XXIV. 337 There is some variation in the ability of Myxococcus cultures to fruit on the same types of media. **1946** *Nature* 23 Nov. 745/1 The growth of the myxococcus concerned..results in the production of a true non-enzymic antibiotic substance. *Ibid.*, An inoculum of myxococcal microcysts. **1973** R. G. KRUEGER et al. *Introd. Microbiol.* iii. 61/1 Representatives of the *Myxococcus* group behave in a fashion that requires response of vegetative cells to the presence and behavior of other vegetative cells of the same type.

‖**myxoma** (mɪkˈsəʊmə). *Path.* Pl. **myˈxomata**. [mod.L., f. Gr. μύξα mucus, after *sarcōma*.] A tumour consisting of mucous or gelatinous tissue.

1870 *Brit. Med. Jrnl.* II. July to Dec., Index. **1872** T. BRYANT *Pract. Surg.* 748 Many myxomata show opaque spots composed of true adipose tissue.

attrib. **1897** *Allbutt's Syst. Med.* IV. 688 Although I have examined some hundreds of specimens [of nasal polypus] I have never succeeded in finding a true myxoma cell.

Hence **myxomatous** (mɪkˈsəʊmətəs) *a.*, pertaining to or affected with myxoma.

1872 T. BRYANT *Pract. Surg.* 713 A fibro-cellular, myxomatous, fibro-nucleated, or fibro-plastic tumour. **1875** tr. *von Ziemssen's Cycl. Med.* X. 226 Myxomatous degeneration.

myxomatosis (ˌmɪksəməˈtəʊsɪs). [f. *myxomat-* (taken as stem of MYXOMA) + -OSIS, as tr. G. *myxomkrankheit* (G. Sanarelli 1898, in *Centralbl. für Bakteriol.* XXIII. 871).] A highly infectious virus disease of rabbits, originally detected in Brazil but now occurring elsewhere, characterized by fever, swelling of the mucous membranes, and the presence of myxomata; the disease has been artificially introduced into several countries to reduce rabbit populations. Also *attrib.* and *transf.* So **myˈxomatized** *ppl. a.*, infected with myxomatosis.

1927 *Proc. Soc. Exper. Biol. & Med.* XXIV. 436 The point of particular interest concerning the myxomatosis of rabbits..is the fact that both epithelial tissue and connective tissue is affected. **1938** *Nature* 16 Apr. 682/2 A field test is now in progress of the virus of myxomatosis, as an agent in reducing rabbit population. **1953** *Times* 20 Oct. 5/4 The Ministry of Agriculture and Fisheries announced yesterday that in the past week myxomatosis, a virus disease of rabbits, was discovered near Edenbridge, Kent. **1953** A. UPFIELD *Murder must Wait* v. 44 'Was the child raised on cow's milk?' ..'No, of course not. It wouldn't do, what with cows feeding off the same grass as myxomatised rabbits and things.' **1955** *Sci. News Let.* 5 Feb. 88/3 Myxomatosis..is threatening to wipe out the European rabbit. **1955** *Sci. Amer.* May 32/1 The myxomatosis virus..was recently introduced in France by a doctor who wished to get rid of the rabbits on his estate, and..the disease soon spread over most of Western Europe. **1958** *Times* 6 Jan. 5/6 Rabbit numbers are increasing in many parts of the country, although isolated outbreaks of myxomatosis have lately occurred in over 30 counties... It seems that myxomatosis is now in a weakened strain. **1966** [see COLUMNARIS]. **1968** M. PYKE *Food & Society* v. 59 The farmers.., for their own ends, had introduced the disease, myxomatosis, to exterminate the rabbits, which previously kept the brush in check. **1972** R. ADAMS *Watership Down* ii. 8 He had coolly ..stood firm during the terrible onslaught of the myxomatosis.

myxophycean (mɪksəʊˈfaɪsiːən), *a.* [f. mod.L. name of class *Myxophyceæ*, f. MYXO- + Gr. φῦκος seaweed + *-eæ* suffix designating the class (cf. -ACEÆ).] Belonging or pertaining to the Myxophyceæ or Cyanophyceæ, a class of unicellular or filamentous blue-green algae.

1939 G. W. PRESCOTT in F. R. Moulton *Probl. Lake Biol.* 74/1 The greatest pests [in water blooms] are Myxophycean species. **1957** *New Biol.* XXIII. 96 In many respects there is a great similarity between this Myxophycean poison [of *Microcystis aeruginosa*] and that of the Death Cap mushroom, *Amanita phalloides*. **1964** *Oceanogr. & Marine Biol.* II. 214 This internal environment affects the proportion of the Myxophycean endophytes [of *Codium bursa*].

myxovirus (ˈmɪksəʊvaɪərəs). *Biol.* [mod.L., f. MYXO- (see quot. 1954) + VIRUS.] Any of a group of related viruses that includes the influenza virus (see quot. 1966). (At first the term was used to include the paramyxoviruses, later regarded as a separate group.)

[**1954** *Nature* 3 Apr. 621/1 The group name *Myxovirus* for viruses related to influenza was intended to indicate that the viruses in question have a particular kind of affinity for certain mucins.] **1955** *Virology* I. 180 When tests are made with fowl red cells it has not been shown that the same receptors are involved as with other *Myxoviruses.* **1962** C. H. ANDREWES in *Adv. Virus Res.* IX. 285 The known myxoviruses are: 1. True influenzas... 2. Paramyxoviruses. .. The viruses of the second group differ from the 'true influenzas' in their larger, more variable size, in the absence of filamentous forms (except for NDV) and in normally producing hemolysins as well as hemagglutinins... 3. Viruses possibly related to myxoviruses—measles, distemper, rinderpest. **1966** J. E. PRIER *Basic Med. Virol.* x. 247/1 In effect then, a new definition of the myxovirus group has emerged that is oriented around these biophysical characteristics: (*a*) a size range of 80 to 300 mμ..; (*b*) possession of a coiled ribonucleoprotein inner helix surrounded by an envelope studded with projections; and (*c*) the presence of lipid as an essential constituent of the virus particle. **1968** H. HARRIS *Nucleus & Cytoplasm* v. 90 The virus used in this work was the 'Sendai' virus, a member of the para-influenza group of myxoviruses. **1974** *Sci. Amer.* Feb. 33/2 Myxoviruses (influenza viruses) and paramyxoviruses..have a set of genes that encodes the manufacture of several viral proteins.

myxson, obs. f. MIXEN.

myxte, var. MIXT *v.*

myxtioun, myxyon, obs. ff. MIXTION.

myxy ('mɪksɪ). Colloq. shortening of MYXOMATOSIS. Also *attrib.* or as *adj.*, suffering from myxomatosis.

1961 R. JEFFRIES *Evidence of Accused* i. 15 Rabbits..were slowly returning after the second scourge of myxy. **1962** — *Exhibit No. Thirteen* x. 97 He'd paid a quid for a myxy rabbit which he'd dropped about the warren. **1973** *Daily Tel.* 22 Oct. 18 It is our custom to shoot any 'myxy' rabbits sitting out in the last stages of this horrible disease.

myyld, obs. f. MILD *a.*

myys, obs. pl. MOUSE.

myzont ('maɪzɒnt), *a.* and *sb. Zool.* [ad. Gr. μυζοντ-, pres. ppl. stem. of μύζειν to suck.] = MARSIPOBRANCH, MARSIPOBRANCHIATE *a.* and *sb.*

1882 T. GILL in *Proc. U.S. Nat. Mus.* V. 516 The Myzonts or Marsipobranchiates. **1891-** (in recent Dicts.).

‖**myzostoma** (maɪ'zɒstəmə). *Zool.* Also (anglicized) '**myzostome.** [f. Gr. μύζειν to suck + στόμα mouth.] One of an order (*Myzostomata* or *Myzostomida*) of small worms parasitic on crinoids, having disc-like bodies provided with suckers. So **my'zostomid**; also **myzo'stomatous, my'zostomous** *adjs.*, belonging to this order (in recent Dicts.).

1876 *Van Beneden's Anim. Parasites* 42 One of the most curious of these worms is the *Myzostoma*... These myzostomes resemble trematode worms. **1885** *Nature* 5 Nov. 8/2, I have found *Myzostoma*-cysts or other modifications of the pinnule-joints on individuals from Torquay [etc.]. **1902** *Encycl. Brit.* XXXIII. 885/2 Full-grown Myzostomids are hermaphrodite.

N

N (ɛn), the fourteenth letter of the modern, and thirteenth of the ancient Roman alphabet, represents historically the Greek *nū* and the Semitic *nun*. The earlier Greek forms were ᴎ and ᴎ, corresponding to the Phœnician 𐤍. The sound usually denoted by the letter is a voiced nasal consonant with front closure (the point of the tongue touching the teeth or the fore part of the palate). It is, however, also capable of being used as a sonant or vowel, here denoted by ((ə)n), as in *bidden* (ˈbɪd(ə)n), *bitten* (ˈbɪt(ə)n), *slacken* (ˈslæk(ə)n). With one or other of these values the letter is very frequent in English, and is silent only in a few cases at the end of syllables after *l* and *m*, as *kiln*, *damn*, *condemn*, *contemn*, *limn*, *hymn*, *solemn*, *column*.

Before the sounds (g) and (k) the letter *n* is also employed in English to denote a nasal with back tongue-closure, in this dictionary distinguished as (ŋ), as in *finger* (ˈfɪŋgə(r)), *think* (θɪŋk). When not followed by these sounds, this back-nasal is expressed by the digraph *ng*, as in *hang* (hæŋ), *sing*, *song*. (On the difference in pronunciation between *finger* and *singer*, etc., see the note to the letter G.)

In Scottish texts of the 15–16th centuries the change of Latin and French *gn* to *ng* is frequently represented in the spelling of such words as *sing* sign, *ring*, *reng* reign, and *ngn* is common between vowels, as *resingnit* resigned, *mangnitude*, etc.

2. In OE. *n* is very frequent as the terminal letter of inflectional syllables, as in the *-an* of the infinitive and the oblique cases of weak nouns. In southern texts this *n* is always retained, but in the north it appears to have been generally dropped by the middle of the 10th century. In ME. the retention or dropping of the letter varied in the different midland and southern dialects. On the other hand, the *-en* of strong past pples., which became *-ë* in southern dialects, was retained in the north as in modern English.

In inflectional syllables (as in *reading*, *writing*, etc.) *-ng* has in many dialects been reduced to *n*, and this pronunciation (usually called 'dropping one's *g*'s') may sometimes be heard even from educated speakers.

3. In ME. the *n* of the indefinite article *an* is frequently transferred to a following word beginning with a vowel (while a converse process has given such forms as *adder*, *apron*, and *auger*). The forms thus produced occasionally alliterate with words properly beginning with *n*, and in one or two cases (as *newt* and *nickname*) have finally established themselves in the language. The following are examples of the practice from ME. and early modern texts.

c **1220** *Bestiary* 503 in *O.E. Misc.* 16 Tu wuldes seien..ðat it were a neilond. *a* **1400–50** *Alexander* 1066 Alexander.. him a narawe hent. *c* **1420** *Anturs Arth.* 349 (Irel. MS.) This is a nayre and a knyȝt. *c* **1420** *Avow. Arth.* xv, As he neghet bi a noke. *c* **1420** J. PAGE *Siege Rouen* (Camden) 18 A negge at ixd. a nappyle at xd. **1448** *Paston Lett.* I. 74 On..smot hym on the hede with a nege [= edge] tole. **1519** *Knaresborough Wills* (Surtees) I. 8 To Richard Hardestie.. a nox. **1532** in Marsden *Sel. Pleas Crt. Adm.* (Selden) 37 It shall be lefull for the said master to take in a nable lodysman. **1573** TUSSER *Husb.* (1878) 36 An ax and a nads. **1609** *MS. Acc. St. John's Hosp., Canterb.*, For sending a letter to Lonndon and the retorning of a nanser.

b. A similar transference also takes place with the *n* of *myn*, mine, and *þin*, *thyn*, thine. (See also OWN *a.* 1 ϵ, NAIN, NAUNT, NEAM, NUNCLE.)

c **1320** *Sir Tristr.* 921 Mark, mi nem, to se. *Ibid.* 2150 Mark, þi nem. *Ibid.* 2135 Sweet ysonde, þi nare! **13..** *Gaw. & Gr. Knt.* 2467 Þerfore I eþe þe..to com to þy naunt. *a* **1400–50** *Alexander* 1356 (D), I vndertake it..tyre is þi nawne. *c* **1420** *Sir Amadace* (Camden) liii, I haue a doȝtur, that my nayre ho isse. **1439** *E.E. Wills* (1882) 118 My Noych with my Baleys. *c* **1530** REDFORDE *Wit & Science* (1848) 21 Foorth shal I bete thy narse, now. **1545** *Test. Ebor.* VI. 225, I give to my nawnte..the graie horse.

c. More rarely the *n* is derived from the old dative of the def. article: see ALE 2 and NONCE[1].

a **1330** *Rowland & V.* 389 At þe nende of þritti niȝt. *Ibid.* 581 When it com to þe neue.

B. I. 1. The letter used to represent the sound.

c **1000** ÆLFRIC *Gram.* (Z.) 6 Semivocales syndon seofan, *f, l, m, n, r, s, x.* **1530** PALSGR. *Introd.* p. xix, M, N, and R.. never lese theyr sounde,..excepte only N, whan he commeth in the thyrde parson plurell of verbes after E. *c* **1620** A. HUME *Brit. Tongue* 12 The top of the tongue stryking on the inward teeth formes d, l, n, r, s, t, and z. **1668** WILKINS *Real Char.* III. xii. 367 The reason why this Letter N, and L, and R, are for the most part, both in Greek and Latin immutable. **1710** STEELE & ADDISON *Tatler* No. 260 ¶5 Which would..pronounce the Letters M. or N. and in short, do all the Functions of a Genuine and Natural Nose. **1727–38** CHAMBERS *Cycl.* N, In the French the *n* is frequently a mere nasal vowel. **1841** LATHAM *Eng. Lang.* 108 Of the Liquids it may be predicated..that *n* is allied to the Series *t.* **1886** K. OLIPHANT *New English* I. 257 The *n* is prefixed, as in *neke name* for *eke name*.

b. In *Printing* used as a unit of measurement (freq. EN: cf. EM); also ***n-quadrat***.

1683 MOXON *Mech. Exerc., Printing* xiii. ¶1 Some [types] are n thick; that is to say, n Quadrat thick, viz. half so thick as the Body is high. **1824** J. JOHNSON *Typogr.* II. 65 The use of the n-quadrat in spacing must be guided by circumstances. *Ibid.* 138 We always indent an m and an n, or even two m's. **1892** *Academy* 3 Sept. 199/3, 49,000 American ems (equal to 98,000 English ens).

c. Used with reference to its shape.

1897 *Allbutt's Syst. Med.* III. 810 The loops being..made to assume the outline of the letter N. *Ibid.*, In one case where N-like bends were produced. **1899** J. G. MILLAIS *Breath fr. Veldt* 55 The birds alighting in the background are represented in their usual N-shaped formation.

2. Used to indicate that the name of a person is to be inserted by the reader or speaker. †Also put instead of a particular day.

c **1000** *Oratio Poetica* 1 in *Be Domes Dæge* 36 Thænne gemiltsað þe N...ðeoda þrym-Cyningc. **14..** *Eng. Fragm. Med. Service-Bks.* 6, I. N. take the N. to myn wedded wyf. *c* **1440** MYRC *Festial* 260 Such a day N. ȝe schull haue Seynt Lukes day. **1552** *Bk. Com. Prayer, Priv. Baptism*, Yf thou be not baptysed already, N, I baptyse thee in the name of the Father [etc.]. **1574** *Reg. Privy Council Scot.* II. 402, I, N, now electit Provest (or Baillie) of the Burgh.

3. Used as a distinguishing letter, to denote one of a series of things, a point in a diagram, etc.

1677 MOXON *Mech. Exerc.* 28 Fasten these staples as at NN to the Main-plate. **1733** TULL *Horse-Hoeing Husb.* xxi. (Dubl.) 301 The Plow-Tail consists of the Beam N; the Coulter O [etc.]. **1797** *Encycl. Brit.* (ed. 3) XI. 723/1 At N is a dove-tailed piece of brass. **1873** SKEAT *Piers Plowman* Pref. p. xlvii, I had intended to collate it, denoting it by the letter N. **1884** *Pall Mall G.* 14 Aug. 10/1 The two policemen connected with the N division.

4. a. In *Math.* used to indicate an indefinite number. ***to the nth (power)***, to any required power; hence *fig.* to any extent, to the utmost. Also used in place of *bi-*, *di-*, *tri-*, etc., in words (e.g. ***n-ary***).

1852 SMEDLEY *L. Arundel* xxiii, Minerva was great upon the occasion; starched to the *n*th. **1873** G. SALMON *Treat. Higher Plane Curves* (ed. 2) p. xi, Number of points which determine a *n*-ic. **1885** *Pall Mall G.* 21 Mar. 1/2 It is the *n*th power of man. **1897** *Edin. Rev.* July 4 The Neapolitan..is an Italian to the *n*th degree. **1903** B. RUSSELL *Princ. Math.* xxxvii. 310 Even an *n*-dimensional series of such terms..is still denumerable. **1924** GALSWORTHY *White Monkey* ix. 193 For the *n*th time it inspired in him a certain liking and confidence. **1940** W. V. QUINE *Math. Logic* 42 The truth table for an *n*-ary mode of composition appears as in Table 3. *Ibid.* 225 A range of *n*-argument functionality..is itself an *n*-adic relation. **1940** W. DE LA MARE *Pleasures & Speculations* 223 Its children's children to the n-th generation. **1954** I. M. COPI *Symbolic Logic* ix. 306 A dyadic or triadic or *n*-adic relation. **1956** F. POHL *Alternating Currents* (1966) 85 Spaceships ran from point to point in n-dimensional hyperspace. **1963** *Dict. U.S. Mil. Terms* (U.S. Dept. Defense) 156 *Nth country*,..the next country of a series to acquire nuclear powers. **1964** E. BACH *Introd. Transformational Gram.* vii. 154 Relations..are accordingly named dyadic, triadic, (or, for *n* terms, *n*-adic) or binary, ternary, and so on. *Ibid.* 155 A relation is the set of ordered pairs (triples, *n*-tuples) for which it holds. **1965** PATTERSON & RUTHERFORD *Elem. Abstract Algebra* v. 156 A vector space, namely the set..of all ordered *n*-tuples $a = [a_1, .., a_n]$ of elements from a field *F.* **1972** H. B. ENDERTON *Mathematical Introd. Logic* i. 50 An *n*-ary connective symbol combines with *n* wffs to produce a new wff. **1974** *Observer* (Colour Suppl.) 1 Sept. 10/1 (Advt.), This is where the standby duty crews wait, in full flying clothing, ready for the off. N-number of aircrew will always be there—24 hours a day, 365 days a year.

b. In *Physics* and *Chem.* *n* represents the principal quantum number of an electronic orbit in an atom, which determines the energy of the orbit (to the first order) and can take the values 1, 2, 3,...(corresponding to increasing energy). In molecular spectroscopy *n* was introduced to denote the vibrational quantum number of a diatomic molecule (now usu. replaced by *v*), and later (as *N*) the total angular momentum, apart from spin, of diatomic and polyatomic molecules (see also quot. 1962[1]).

1914 N. BOHR in *Phil. Mag.* XXVII. [507 According to Balmer, Rydberg, and Ritz the frequency of the lines in the line-spectrum of an element can be expressed by the formula $\nu = f_r(n_1) - f_s(n_2)$, where n_1 and n_2 are whole numbers and $f_1, f_2, \ldots$ a series of functions of *n*, which can be expressed by $f_r(n) = (K/n^2)\phi_r(n)$, where *K* is a universal constant and ϕ a function which for large values of *n* approaches the value unity.] *Ibid.* 508 We shall assume that this spectrum is emitted by a system possessing a series of stationary states in which, corresponding to the *n*th state, the energy, omitting the arbitrary constant, is given by $A_n = -hK/n^2$. *Ibid.* 509 For $n = 1$, corresponding to the normal state of the atom, we get [etc.]. **1920** *Sci. Abstr.* A. XXIII. 423 If the nuclei are related in a quasi-elastic manner to the equilibrium positions, then the energy values for a diatomic non-rotating molecule are the same as for a Planck oscillator, namely: $E = nh\omega$, where *n* denotes the quantum number for the atomic oscillation. **1922** A. D. UDDEN tr. *Bohr's Theory of Spectra* III. i. 67 This quantum number which will always be denoted by *n* will therefore be called the 'principal quantum number'. **1926** E. C. KEMBLE et al. in *Bull. Nat. Res. Council* No. 57. 5 Some discrepancies in minor details of notation will be found from chapter to chapter in this report. The following major items, however, have been followed consistently:..Vibrational quantum number for diatomic molecule: *n.* **1951** D. BOHM *Quantum Theory* xv. 348 *n* = the principal quantum number..defined as one plus the total number of nodal surfaces in the wave function. **1953** *Jrnl. Optical Soc. Amer.* XLIII. 425/1 [Report of Sub-committee of the Joint Commission for Spectroscopy.] Notation for diatomic molecules... *N.* Total angular momentum of the electrons and nuclei, excluding spin... Replaces former *K.* **1962** P. J. & B. DURRANT *Introd. Adv. Inorg. Chem.* vii. 207 The angular momentum due to the rotation of the [diatomic] molecule about an axis at right angles to the internuclear axis is denoted by N. **1962** J. POTTER tr. *Messiah's Quantum Mech.* II. xxi. 964 Each quantum number *n* represents the number of vibrational quanta relative to a particular normal mode of vibration. **1966** G. HERZBERG *Molecular Spectra & Molecular Struct.* III. i. 73 For $^3\Sigma$ states each rotational level except the one with $N = 0$ is split into three component levels.. corresponding to $J = N + 1, N, N - 1$, respectively. **1973** J. YARWOOD *Atomic & Nuclear Physics* vi. 188 The quantum mechanical treatment [of the one-electron atom] introduces the integral principal quantum number *n* which..decides the total energy of the system, the quantum number *l* which ..has any integral value between 0 and $(n - 1)$, and the azimuthal magnetic quantum number m_l which is an integer having $(2l + 1)$ values between $+ l$ and $- l$.

5. ***n-declension***, the 'weak' declension of Teutonic nouns and adjectives, in which the stem ends in *n*; so ***n-stem***, ***n-plural***.

1843 *Proc. Philol. Soc.* I. 73 The *n* declension..makes its appearance in many of the Indo-European languages, besides the Gothic. **1866** MORRIS *Ayenb. Inwyt* p. xxxv, They are remnants of the *n* declension. **1886** T. M. DOUSE *Introd. Gothic* p. x, Consonant Declensions; *n*-stems. **1894** V. HENRY *Comp. Gram. Engl. & Germ.* 236 The *n*-plural requires no explanation.

6. ***N-rays*** (originally ***n-rays***), a form of radiation app. identified in 1903 by R. Blondlot of the University of Nancy, from the initial letter of which the name is derived. ***N[1]-rays*** (originally ***n_1-rays***), another form of radiation, having, in some respects, the opposite effects. [Soon after their alleged discovery it was concluded that such rays do not exist and Blondlot's work was in error.]

1903 *Nature* LXVIII. 119/2 The name *n*-rays is suggested for these radiations. *Ibid.* 578/1 Several papers on the so-called N rays discovered by M. Blondlot are printed in the *Journal de Physique* for August. **1904** —— LXIX. 455/2 The n_1-rays, described in the previous note, have exactly the opposite effect. **1906** *Nature* 1 Mar. 413/1 It would be interesting to know whether anyone has obtained success in repeating the latest experiment designed to show the objective reality of the *n*-rays. **1925** A. HUXLEY *Let.* 25 Jan. (1969) 241 You remember the unanimously favourable verdict in favour of N rays? **1941** W. SEABROOK *Doctor Wood: Mod. Wizard of Laboratory* xvii. 234 According to Blondlot, the rays were given off spontaneously by many metals. A piece of paper, very feebly illuminated, could be used as a detector, for, wonder of wonders, when the N rays fell upon the eye they increased its ability to see objects in a nearly dark room. **1973** *Nature* 12 Oct. 344/2 The protracted error immortalised in scores of publications can be due only to psychological (self-deception), not to chemical causes. The 'anomalous' water belongs to the category exemplified by the N rays of Blondlot.

†7. *Radiology.* A unit of neutron dosage (see quot. 1942). *Obs.*

1942 AEBERSOLD & LAWRENCE in *Ann. Rev. Physiol.* IV. 36 In this laboratory, a standard Victoreen *r*-meter with a 100r condenser-chamber is used. The unit of fast neutron exposure is arbitrarily taken as that amount which produces the same reading with this meter as a roentgen of x-ray. Thus an *n* of fast neutrons produces inside this 100r Victoreen thimble chamber the same amount of ionization as produced by an *r* of x-rays. **1948** E. PATERSON in R. Paterson *Treatment of Malignant Dis. by Radium & X-Rays* xxxiii. 593 The *n* unit has fulfilled a useful function, however, in demonstrating differences in effect between X- or gamma-radiation and neutrons when ratios of the dosage required to produce effects are compared.

II. Abbreviations. **1. N.** = various proper names, as Nathaniel, Nicholas, Noah, etc.; N, naira (formerly, £N, Nigerian pound); N., Nationalist; N (*Chem.*), Nitrogen; N, nuclear; **n.** (*Gram.*), noun, neuter; **N.A.**, National Academician (*U.S.*); **N.A.A.C.P.**, National Association for the Advancement of Colored People (*U.S.*); **N.A.A.S.**, National Agricultural

Advisory Service; **N.A.B.**, National Assistance Board; **N.A.C.A.**, National Advisory Committee for Aeronautics (*U.S.*); **NAD(P)**, nicotinamide-adenine dinucleotide (phosphate); **N.B.**, New Brunswick; **N.B.C.**, National Broadcasting Corporation (*U.S.*); **N.B.G.**, no bloody good (cf. *N.G.*); **N.C.B.**, National Coal Board; **N.C.O.**, non-commissioned officer; **N.C.R.**, no carbon required, the registered trade-name for paper chemically treated so that the pressure of writing or typing alone produces duplicate copies without the use of carbon paper between sheets; **n.d.**, **N.D.**, no date; **N.D.C.**, National Defence Contribution; **N.D.P.**, National Democratic Party (*Canad.*); **NEB**, National Enterprise Board; **N.E.B.**, New English Bible; **N.E.D.**, New English Dictionary; **N.E.D.(C.)**, National Economic Development (Council); **N.F.**, National Front; **N.F.**, New Franc (nouveau franc); **N.F.**, Norman French; **N.F.S.**, National Fire Service; **N.F.T.**, National Film Theatre; **N.G.**, **n.g.**, no go, no good (the latter is the current use, cf. *N.B.G.*); **N.H.I.**, National Health Insurance; **N.H.S.**, National Health Service; **NIC**, **Nic** (also with pronunc. nɪk), newly industrialized (or industrializing) country; **NIMBY**, **nimby**, orig. *U.S.* (with pronunc. ˈnɪmbɪ), 'not in my backyard', a slogan expressing objection to the siting of something considered unpleasant, such as nuclear waste, in one's own locality; freq. *attrib.*; **NIR** [f. the initials of Russ. *Nauchno-Issledovatel'skaya Rabota* scientific research work], a colour television system developed in Russia, similar to SECAM; **N.I.R.A.**, National Industrial Recovery Act (*U.S.*); **N.K.V.D.** [Russ. *Naródnyĭ Komissariát Vnútrennikh Del*], Soviet Commissariat of Internal Affairs, replacing the Ogpu; **N.l.**, North latitude; **N.L.F.**, National Liberation Front; **NNI**, noise and number index (see NOISE *sb.* 3 d); **N.O.**, Natural Order; Naval Officer; **N.O.R.A.D.**, North American Air Defence; **N.O.W.**, National Organization for Women (*U.S.*); **N.P.**, Notary Public; **n.p.** (see quot. 1952); also, not paginated; **N.P.D.** [G. *Nationaldemokratische Partei Deutschlands*], National Democratic Party of Germany; **N.P.L.**, National Physical Laboratory; **N.P.V.**, Net Present Value; **N.R.A.**, National Recovery Administration (*U.S.*); **N.R.D.C.**, National Research Development Corporation; **N.S.**, New Style; **N.S.** (*Banking*) not sufficient; **N.S.P.C.A.**, National Society for the Prevention of Cruelty to Animals; **N.S.P.C.C.**, National Society for the Prevention of Cruelty to Children; **N.S.W.**, New South Wales (*Austral.*); **N.T.**, New Testament; **N.T.**, Northern Territory (*Austral.*); **N.T.S.C.**, National Television System Committee (*U.S.*); **N.U.M.**, National Union of Mineworkers; **N.U.R.**, National Union of Railwaymen; **N.U.S.**, National Union of Students; **N.U.T.**, National Union of Teachers; **N.Y.S.E.**, New York Stock Exchange.

See also N.A.A.F.I., N.A.L.G.O., N.A.S.A., N.A.T.O., N.A.T.S.O.P.A., N.E.P., Nibmar, N.I.C., N-P-N, N.U.P.E. (as main entries).

1789 J. Brown *Sel. Rem.* (1807) 155 It is neither *N. nor F. nor P. that I either fear or trust. **1960** *Brit. Exports & Exchange Restrictions* (Swiss Bank Corporation) May 108, 1 Nigerian Pound = 20 Shillings. 1£*N = 1£stg. **1973** *Times* 1 Oct. (Nigeria Suppl.) p. xi/3 Each member would be paid N120 a month. **1958** *Oxford Mail* 19 July 1/2 Beirut battle group is part of *N-weapon division... U.S. paratroopers.. equipped with tactical nuclear weapons. **1958** *Observer* 2 Nov. 6/1 Plenty of Aldermaston badges, with their semaphore symbol of ND—nuclear disarmament. **1883** *Harper's Mag.* Nov. 843/2 He enjoys..the unusual distinction of being an *N.A. and an A.R.A. **1910** *Crisis* Nov. 12 (*heading*) The *N.A.A.C.P. **1974** *Black Panther* 16 Mar. 4/4 The NAACP filed its first suit attacking segregation and discrimination in education on March 15, 1933, against the University of North Carolina. **1948** *Sci. News* VI. 48 The *N.A.A.S., which is the only body giving advice on the whole of agriculture. **1971** *Arable Farmer* Feb. 70/1 A nationwide series recently completed by NAAS, of 77 experiments testing nitrogen, phosphate and potash rates for spring barley. **1953** B. Abel-Smith *Reform of Social Security* 27 Malingering is very hard to detect, as the *N.A.B. is constantly aware. *Ibid.*, We might keep our whole system on a flat rate basis but take the N.A.B. level as representing the community's present definition of subsistence. **1969** *Listener* 12 June 834/3 In Northborough ..mothers were not allowed to collect the father's weekly contribution..through the NAB. **1922** *Aviation* 13 Nov. 665/1 (*heading*) *N.A.C.A. For National Air Policy. **1970** N. Armstrong et al. *First on Moon* i. 17 Vaguely co-ordinated by something called NACA—the National Advisory Committee for Aeronautics. **1961** *Biochem. Jrnl.* LXXX. 322/1 *NAD formation almost certainly involves nucleophilic attack on the α-phosphorus of ATP. **1964** W. G. Smith *Allergy & Tissue Metabolism* viii. 85 The resulting α-β- unsaturated acid is reduced to its saturated counterpart by an enzyme which requires the reduced form of NADP. **1970** R. W. McGilvery *Biochemistry* xvi. 319 In general, NADP is used as an electron carrier for reductive syntheses, such as the formation of fatty acids.., whereas NAD is used more in the processes of energy production. *a* **1912** W. T. Rogers *Dict. Abbrev.* (1913) 133/1 **N.B.*... New Brunswick. **1929** F. W. Wallace *Rec. Canad. Shipping* 2 *Abyssinia*, ship, 833 tons. Built 1868, St. John, N.B. **1973** *Fisheries Fact Sheet* (Environment Canada Fisheries & Marine Service) No. 1. 1 (*caption*) Purse seining in Baie des Chaleurs, N.B. **1950** G. Marx *Let.* 7 Nov. in *Groucho Lett.* (1967) 75, I heard you on the *NBC radio show. **1969** *Listener* 13 Nov. 667/1 The Duke of Edinburgh 'met the press' recently on America's NBC network. **1903** R. Bedford *True Eyes* xxxiv. 195 So see here—this place is *N.B.G., Billy, me man. Let's do what I say—sell everythin' an' clear. **1929** C. Mackenzie *Three Couriers* II. v. 180 Crowder messing about with a typewriter? O.K. Crowder outside an office? N.B.G. **1956** A. Wilson *Anglo-Saxon Attitudes* II. iii. 369 Those Barkers were n.b.g.: I saw quite a lot of their dishonesty at Melpham. **1973** G. Mitchell *Murder of Busy Lizzie* iii. 42 Bang goes our reason for coming here... She said it was N.B.G. and that seems to be just about right. **1948** *Coal* Dec. 12/2 There are many complaints and criticisms of the *N.C.B. It would be surprising if there were not. **1955** *Times* 3 Aug. 11/4 An official of the N.C.B. opencast executive said that the prospecting had shown the site to contain about 750,000 tons of good quality coal. **1963** *Times* 7 Feb. 13/4 It is essential not to impair the work at the N.C.B. which has made it possible to raise productivity four times above the national average. **1803–10** *Orderly Bks. of Manx Fencibles* in *Yn Lioar Manninagh* (1890) I. 152 Any party, consisting of 6 men or upwards, must have a *N.C.O...appointed to go with them. **1883** *Army Regulations* II. 102 Report on conviction of N.C.O. by civil power. **1915** *Cornhill Mag.* Mar. 388 Had a chat with my N.C.O.s. **1955** *Times* 11 May 6/7 Corporal J. R. Saunders, who receives the George Medal, was the n.c.o. in charge of fire fighting at the storage unit. **1973** K. Giles *File on Death* i. 5 Old top secrets.. guarded by superannuated N.C.O.s. **1954** in *Official Gaz.* (U.S. Patent Off.) (1955) 12 July 104/1 *NCR no carbon required paper. **1956** *Brit. Printer* Mar. 42/1 Since its appearance on the US market some 18 months ago, NCR paper..is now being manufactured in this country. The initials NCR represent not only the name of the manufacturers—the National Cash Register Co Ltd—but the particular characteristics of the paper (No Carbon Required). **1967** C. Wilson in Wills & Yearsley *Handbk. Management Technol.* 46 Copies of print-outs are obtained with carbon paper or NCR paper. The latter ('no carbon required') has a chemically coated surface activated by percussion. **1834** *William Pickering's Catal. Manuscripts & Bks.* 19 Angler's Guide...Lond. *n.d. **1879** *Blackwell's Catal.* No. 1. 10 Chappell's Old English Ditties..N.D. **1917** T. J. Wise *Bibliogr. Brontë Family* VI. 225 Museum of Brontë Relics.. A Descriptive Catalogue. (N.D., but *circa* 1890). **1952** J. Carter *ABC for Book-Collectors* 124 No date (n.d.). This term, unqualified, means that research has failed (or has not attempted) to establish even an approximate date for the book described. **1959** *N. & Q.* CCIV. 292/1 *A Chronicle History of Portsmouth* by Henry Slight (3d. edit., n.p., n.d.). **1937** *Times* 1 June 17/5 The present *N.D.C. scheme..imposes a high rate of tax on excess profits only. **1939** *Times* 4 Jan. 17/2 The figures in each case are struck after provisions for income-tax and N.D.C. **1961** *Edmonton* (Alta.) *Jrnl.* 4 Aug. 17/3 The *NDP organizers produced mimeographed songsheets complete with Tommy Douglas lyrics. **1972** *Maclean's Mag.* Mar. 12/2 The NDP..refused to have the issue even raised for discussion. **1973** J. Hart et al. *National Enterprise Board* (Labour Party Green Paper) i. 12 The *NEB would 'hold' all existing government shares in joint public-private firms. **1983** *Times* 30 June 15/2 The British Technology Group.. includes the NEB and the National Research Development Corporation (NRDC). **1961** *Theology* May 175 There is no need to give an account here of the principles and methods of the *N.E.B. **1980** G. B. Caird *Lang. & Imagery of Bible* I. iv. 97 Does the prophet (Isa. 13:5) foresee the devastation of the whole land (AV, NEB) or of the whole earth (JB)? **1904** A. S. Palmer in R. C. Trench *On Study of Words* (rev. ed.) 175 Dr. Murray decides in favour of this explanation, of unknown authorship, and so spurious, uncanonical,—**N.E.D.* **1961** *Essays & Studies* XIV. 35 Of the many accounts of the origin and progress of the dictionary, it may suffice to mention here the following: the *Preface* to Vol. 1 of *N.E.D.*, [etc.]. **1973** *Jrnl. Soc. Bibliogr. Nat. Hist.* VI. 229 The work is known familiarly as NED, OED, or even 'Murray'. **1975** *N. & Q. for Som. & Dorset* Sept. 127 The single reference cited under lug-fall in the *N.E.D.*..takes the definition a little further. **1962** *Daily Tel.* 9 Feb. 12/2 The *NEDC will not be a collection of amateurs or mere theorists. *Ibid.* 7 Mar. 12/2 The collective wisdom of 'NED'. **1964** M. Argyle *Psychol. & Social Probl.* xvi. 199 A new government advisory department, like N.E.D.C. or N.I.C. **1970** *Facts* (National Front) I. 3/3 (*caption*) *N.F. supports the Springboks. **1976** *Economist* 13 Mar. 18/1 The National Front vote, and the derisory failure of..the former NF leader, showed there is a small but steady support of 2–3% for the Front. **1984** S. Townsend *Growing Pains A. Mole* 22 Ms. Fossington-Gore shouted back, 'You're wearing a symbol of fascism, you nasty NF lout.' **1960** *British Exports & Exchange Restrictions* (Swiss Bank Corporation) May 55 Only spare parts from O.E.E.C. countries may be obtained through import certificates when the value is less than NF. 5,000. **1971** A. Diment *Think Inc.* ii. 28, I..added three $100 bills and two NF 1000 notes to the wad. **1942** *Daily Mirror* 25 Feb. 4/5 It will be necessary to enrol men under 41 for whole-time duties in the National Fire Service... Men over 25 when they registered will still be given an opportunity to express preference for the *NFS. **1947** *Science News* IV. 47 Four days after she disappeared a fire broke out in the cellar of the Baptist Church and a passing police officer called the N.F.S. **1965** *New Statesman* 19 Mar. 462/3 Ozu..made some 54 films, of which only nine have ever been seen in London and those only by assiduous patrons of the *NFT. **1969** *Listener* 24 July 125/1 Members of the NFT poured into their cinema to hear a discussion between Satyajit Ray and Lindsay Anderson. **1838** *Morning Post* (Boston) 25 June 2/3 They then went together to the plaintiff's to try to settle, but it was *n.g. **1840** *Daily Pennant* (St. Louis) 20 June (Th.), The bells, boys, and engines tried to get up a fire last night, but it was N.G. **1922** Joyce *Ulysses* 427 Fish and taters. N.g. **1972** 'L. Egan' *Paper Chase* (1973) x. 160 So that little ride on the merry-go-round was n.g. **1934** Foster & Taylor *National Health Insurance* xiv. 191 Enter on debit side of Cash Book and credit side of *N.H.I. Fund Current Account. **1958** *Spectator* 20 June 806/1 A doctor..wrote on what he called unjustified claims by his patients upon the N.H.I. **1948** *Lancet* 20 Nov. 823/3 Other doctors do not discriminate between private and *N.H.S. patients. *Ibid.* 4 Dec. 904/1 The pharmacist's principal trouble just now is over delay in payment of his accounts under the N.H.S. **1968** *Listener* 11 July 58/3 One of the hospital committee shown arguing in the NHS film whether or not it should refund the cost of a 7s 11d vest. **1975** *Guardian* 5 Nov. 14/5 There will be the equivalent of 2,500 to 3,000 more beds available for NHS use. **1978** *Economist* 10 June 84/1 The newly industrialising countries—those with a growing industrial base geared to exports—have an acronym, *Nics. **1980** *Sci. Amer.* Sept. 58/3 The N.I.C. and OPEC countries have about a fifth of the population of the developing countries other than China. **1986** *Courier-Mail* (Brisbane) 26 Aug. 32/1 South Korea, Taiwan and the two city-states of Singapore and Hong Kong are often known as NICs because they have been very successful at developing their economies and growing rapidly. **1980** *Christian Science Monitor* 6 Nov. B5/3 A secure landfill anywhere near them is anathema to most Americans today. It's an attitude referred to in the trade as *NIMBY—'not in my backyard'. **1986** *Times* 30 Apr. 12/6 Wakeham has become a convert to the Nimby..principle. A chief whip who thinks that nuclear waste is too dangerous for his constituency will find it hard to persuade other Tory MPs that it is safe for theirs. **1966** *Economist* 12 Feb. 628 This Russian-designed system offers the best prospect of a single acceptable colour television system for the whole of Europe... The Russians call the Soviet system *NIR. **1969** Carnt & Townsend *Colour Television* II. vii. 237 In April, 1963, the Non-linear NIR system had already been anticipated by B. W. B. Pethers of the BBC. This was some two years before the NIR system came to light, but at that time it was felt that NIR did not have any significant advantages over the other systems. **1933** *Sun* (Baltimore) 23 Aug. 1/3 'Threats, intimidation, compulsion, boycotts, blacklists and suppression of opinion,' he declared, 'were never contemplated by the *N.I.R.A. and, therefore, have no rightful place in the picture.' *Ibid.* 9 Sept. 1/2 The power of propaganda and the press has had few better illustrations than the way in which the so called 'Nira' is obscuring the other great Administration activities in Washington and in the country. **1942** V. Conolly *Soviet Asia* (Oxf. Pamphs. on World Affairs) 13 The *N.K.V.D. (Commissariat of Internal Affairs, former O.G.P.U.). **1945** Koestler *Yogi & Commissar* III. iii. 208 The deportees were called for..by the so-called 'Executive Troikas' of the N.K.V.D. **1973** T. Allbeury *Choice of Enemies* vi. 21 He was wearing an NKVD uniform. **1965** *New Society* 22 Apr. 259 Nguyen Huu Tho was made president of the *NLF. **1971** *Ink* 12 June 8/3 The delegates..would have been Thieu/Ky (S. Vietnam), Tho (NLF), Ho Chi Minh (N. Vietnam). **1972** H. Evans *Editing & Design: Newsman's English* vii. 147 When the report says the NLF, the deskman should write in 'the National Liberation Front, political arm of the Vietcong...' This does not offend the reader who knows and it helps the rest, which is most of us. There was at one time, anyway, another NLF—in Aden—and at another an FLN, in Algeria and France. **1963** *NNI [see NOISE *sb.* 3 d]. **1969** *Guardian* 5 Mar. 9/2 Within such an area noise levels would be 40 NNI. **1970** R. D. Ford *Introd. to Acoustics* vii. 144 An external NNI of 55 has been taken as the recommended limit in the vicinity of London Airport and householders exposed to more noise have been offered a special grant for soundproofing their homes. **1914** 'Bartimeus' *Naval Occasions* xvii. 144 That girl to-night —Molly—I suppose she has refused half a dozen *N.O.'s. **1916** G. Franklin *Naval Digression* I. xv. 136 Which brings to light another peculiarity of the average N.O.—how he can adopt a friendly 'hail-fellow-well-met' attitude to all and sundry and lose nothing in respect by it, even should they be ex-service men. **1958** M. Dickens *Man Overboard* i. 14 There'll be a lot of sharks about waiting for the innocent N.O. with his touching faith in human nature. **1959** *Roundel* June 3/1 Creation of the North American Air Defence Command by the governments of Canada and the United States was recognition..that air defence of the continent..is a single, common problem. *NORAD is a truly integrated, international Command—responsible to both the U.S. Joint Chiefs of Staff and the Canadian Chiefs of Staff Committee. **1970** *Toronto Daily Star* 24 Sept. 31/3 In NORAD we permitted American nuclear bombers to make provocative flights over Canadian territory. **1966** *N.Y. Times* 22 Nov. 44/1 *NOW..was formed three weeks ago in Washington to press for 'true equality for all women in America'. **1970** G. Greer *Female Eunuch* 296 When NOW was formed it was read into the Congressional record. **1973** *Times* 2 June 8/3 Betty Friedan..'founding mother' of NOW in 1966. **1882** Halkett & Laing *Dict. Anon. & Pseudon. Eng. Lit.* I. 122/1 Answer to the Declaration published by the Archbishop of Canterbury...*N.P., N.D. Octavo. Pp. 12. *a* **1912** W. T. Rogers *Dict. Abbrev.* (1913) 137/1 *n.p.*, no place (no printer's name). **1952** J. Carter *ABC for Book-Collectors* 124 No place, no printer, no publisher (indiscriminately or collectively shortened to n.p.). **1966** *Dawson's of Pall Mall Catal. No.* 162. 12 Cicero ..Laelius de amicitia. (n.p., n.d.) (Cologne..about 1467). **1969** N. B. Eales *Cole Library of Early Med. & Zool.* 330 The Complete Dictionary of Arts and Sciences... 2 vols. Fr., [4], vi, n.p. Pls. 1–11, 14–35, 40–42. **1966** *Guardian* 14 Mar. 21/8 The *NPD..won up to 10 per cent in some Bavarian towns. **1969** S. Hyland *Top Bloody Secret* ii. 125 The two people who..organised the first conference of the Neo-Nazi party, NPD. *a* **1912** W. T. Rogers *Dict. Abbrev.* (1913) 137/1 **N.P.L.*, National Physical Laboratory (Bushey, by Teddington). **1920** *Flight* XII. 1131/2 With regard to the staffs at the N.P.L. and at the R.A.E., he said he hoped that provision would be made to maintain these on an adequate scale. **1959** *Ann. Reg. 1958* 388 There was a scientific symposium at the National Physical Laboratory (N.P.L.), Teddington. **1964** *Economist* 26 Sept. 1195/1 Then DCF is no more use than *NPV. **1969** D. C. Hague *Managerial Econ.* II. vi. 128 If we..add together the sums of money in Column C, including the minus £1,000 for Year 0, we are left with a net amount of £10. This is known as the net present value (NPV) of the project. **1933** *N.Y. Times* 3 Aug. 16/4 The most vital issue in the whole National Recovery Program is, of course, the question whether we shall end up speaking of it as the NRA or the *N.R.A. People are saying NIRA and NRA but there is no denying the fact that there is a self-conscious air about it. **1933** G. ADE *Let.* 25 Aug. (1973) 170 The country editor.. need not ignore the N.R.A. or the Farm Relief Board or any of the agencies intended to bring us back to happier times. **1962** *Amer. Speech* XXXVII. 48 Many such letter groups have entered the American language as items of common exchange: *O.K.*.. *N.R.A.* **1954** F. A. BUTTRESS *World List Abbrev.* 186 *NRDC, National Research Development Corporation, 1 Tilney Street, London, W.1. **1959** *Engineering* 6 Feb. 182/3 If proof were required that NRDC's activities are useful and beneficial, it is provided by their profitability. **1967** *Jane's Surface Skimmer Systems 1967–68* 30/1 The Company has been granted an NRDC licence. **1698** PRIOR *Let. Earl Halifax*, Paris, the 9th Aug: *NS. **1709** STEELE *Tatler* No. 4 ¶5 They write from Saxony of the 13th Instant, N.S. **1900** *Westm. Gaz.* 30 June 9/3 It is generally sufficient.. that the bank has not returned cheques unpaid with the mystical letters 'N.S.' (not sufficient) in the corner. *a* **1912** W. T. ROGERS *Dict. Abbrev.* (1913) 137/2 **N.S.P.C.A.*, National Society for the Prevention of Cruelty to Animals. **1895** *Civil Rights for Children* (N.S.P.C.C.) (inside back cover), Mary P. Bolton Asst.-Sec., *N.S.P.C.C. **1963** *Social Work* Oct. 20/2 Some will emphasise the word 'neglect' and think in terms of an extended N.S.P.C.C. inspectorate. [**1852** T. CASS *Let.* 1 May in J. Deans *Pioneers of Canterbury* (1937) x. 221, I take the opportunity of sending you a few lines by way of *N.S. Wales, a cattle vessel leaving in a day or two.] **1889** H. C. RUSSELL (*title*) The source of the underground water in the western districts... (Read before the Royal Society of N.S.W., August 7, 1889.) **1909** B. STEVENS *Golden Treasury of Austral. Verse* 336 *Gidya*, a Queensland and N.S.W. aboriginal word for a tree of the acacia species. **1971** *Sunday Australian* 8 Aug. 3/1 Justice ministers in Victoria and NSW, said yesterday they were considering.. changes. **1866** tr. *Viner's Gramm. N.T. Dict.* (ed. 6) 14 The idiom of the *N.T. is.. a variety of the Greek language. *a* **1912** W. T. ROGERS *Dict. Abbrev.* (1913) 138/1 **N.T.*,.. Northern Territory, -ies (Australia). **1930** A. G. PRICE *Hist. & Problems of Northern Territory* 64 For labour in the N.T., see reports of Gilruth.. and Urquhart. **1969** *Northern Territory News* (Darwin) 11 July 3/3 The NT Police Commissioner.. wants breath-analyser tests introduced in the Territory. **1957** *B.B.C. Handbook* 136 The *N.T.S.C. system now in use for a public service in the United States of America. **1966** *Economist* 12 Feb. 628/2 The Americans manage to transmit colour from coast to coast by NTSC. **1948** *Ann. Reg. 1947* I. v. 90 The negotiations with the *N.U.M. on the method of working overtime.. languished. **1914** *Railway Mag.* Nov. 401/1 It was.. agreed that all existing contracts and conditions of service shall remain in operation,.. (signed) for General Managers' Committee:— .. for *N.U.R.:—.. for A.S.L.E.&F.:—. **1955** *Times* 2 May 12/7 The union have won the right to put their case without having representatives of the N.U.R. present. **1975** *Guardian* 17 June 26/8 The NUR executive threw the negotiating ball firmly back into Mr Wilson's court. **1924** *University* I. 21 F. G. Connor.. who attended as the representative of the English *N.U.S., described the constitution and development of the National Union of Students of England and Wales. **1973** J. H. M. SCOTT *Dons & Students* xii 145 The vice-chancellors turned it down, effectively siding with the NUS against it. **1889** *Schoolmaster* 4 May 634/1 In place of the familiar initials, N.U.E.T. we have the shorter, and let us hope the improved, form of *N.U.T... The objects of the N.U.E.T. remain the objects of the N.U.T. **1973** L. HOLCOMBE *Victorian Ladies at Work* iii. 39 The National Union of Teachers.. was organized in 1870... In 1911 the N.U.T. elected its first woman president. **1941** *Exchange* Feb. 3/1 'Secondary distribution!' That's a phrase to make the heart of any floor member of the New York Stock Exchange skip a beat. It means—in most cases, where *NYSE stocks are being distributed—that just so much business is not passing through the Exchange. **1964** *Financial Times* 25 Feb. 3/7 A special committee set up by the N.Y.S.E. **1973** *N.Y. Law Jrnl.* 4 Sept. 4/2 It might be possible to include all NYSE-listed securities.

b. N. = North; also **N.B.**, North Britain (Scotland); **N.E., NE.**, North-east, etc.; **N.W.**, North-west, esp. (usu. followed by a numeral) a London postal district.

1615 CAPT. ADAMS *Jrnl. Voy. Siam* 21 May, From 4 to 8, 1 l[eague] n. **1615** T. ROE *Jrnl.* 26 Mar. in *Embassy to Court of Gt. Mogul* (1899) I. 3 Wee.. saw land N.W. for the Canarye 8 leauges off. **1708** *Lond. Gaz.* No. 4418/3 The Wind was this Morning.. at six, at N., at eight at N.E. **1720** DE FOE *Capt. Singleton* vii. (1840) 131 As the course of the other rivers were N. by E. or N.N.E. the course of this lay N.N.W. **1769** FALCONER *Dict. Mar.* s.v. *Sailing*, The former [ship] steering E. *b* N. **1855** MAURY *Phys. Geog.* (ed. 2) 258 The wind is reported as prevailing.. from N. 3 times. **1857** J. A. SYMONDS *Let.* 1 Feb. (1967) I. 88 Sunday. Harrow *N.W.*.. You will wonder what N.W. means on the top of this page. It is in consequence of some Postal arrangements that those letters should be affixed to districts of London. **1899** W. J. LOCKE *White Dove* (1900) x. 151 Dr. Frodsham.. had.. [moved] from the house in Weymouth Street into the purer air of the N.W. district. **1965** *Listener* 27 May 792/1 Living with him was his beautiful companion, a Madame de Bargeton of N.W.3, something of a Madame Verdurin also. **1967** *Ibid.* 30 Nov. 733/2 Who could have littered the *Times* with bylines and signed columns and a woman's page so close to NW1's heart? **1971** A. BENNETT in D. Nathan *Laughtermakers* iv. 93, I did a series on television with sketches about this area, N.W.1, of which I am a part, and so in a sense it was making fun of myself. But it pinpointed something and since then N.W.1 has been used as a catchphrase to indicate Sunday supplement trendiness which people now find rather suspect.

2. N.B. = Lat. *nota bene*, 'note well'.

1673 RAY *Journ. Low C.* 163 NB. One of these Electors may nominate himself to any office. **1710** ADDISON *Tatler* No. 224 ¶5 Of late Years, the N.B. has been much in Fashion. **1755** HERVEY *Theron & Aspasio* I. xi. 415 'Behold.' He sets his N.B. on the passage. **1797** *Encycl. Brit.* (ed. 3) XI. 722/1 N.B. At the end of the tube G there is a lens for increasing the density of the rays. **1800** *Asiat. Ann. Reg.* II. 95/1 He.. ingeniously added a N.B. at the foot of the whole. **1861** G. H. LEWES *Jrnl.* 3–6 June in *Geo. Eliot's Lett.* (1954) III. 424 Reposed awhile and chatted (N.B. all the journey we have had fine talk with Trollope). **1965** I. FLEMING *Man with Golden Gun* iii. 40 Distinguishing marks: a third nipple about two inches below his left breast. (N.B. in Voodoo and allied local cults this is considered a sign of invulnerability and great sexual prowess.)

3. a. N (also rarely *N*, *n*) (*Chem.*) = NORMAL *a.* and *sb.* A. 2 b (i).

1863 F. SUTTON *Syst. Handbk. Volumetric Anal.* 165 Free iodine is.. very readily estimated by solution in iodide of potassium, and titration with N/10 hyposulphite. **1906** *Amer. Chem. Jrnl.* XXXV. 511 A saturated solution of silver chloride.. is only about 0·00001N. **1931** J. C. WARE *Analyt. Chem.* iv. 137 Test the solubility of a portion of the precipitate.. with 2 cc. 6*n* HNO_3. **1970** M. D. HAWKINS *Calculations in Volumetric & Gravimetric Anal.* 11. 35 The solution was titrated against 0·0908N potassium thiocyanate.

b. *n* (also rarely n) (*Chem.*) = NORMAL *a.* and *sb.* A. 2 b (ii).

1889 G. M'GOWAN tr. *A. Bernthsen's Text-bk. Org. Chem.* i. 44 From petroleum have been separated.. normal heptane, n-octane, n-nonane, and n-decane. **1938** L. F. FIESER in H. Gilman *Org. Chem.* I. ii. 53 The conversion of *n*-butylcyclopentane into *o*-ethyltoluene on dehydrogenation with palladium charcoal. **1971** N. L. ALLINGER et al. *Org. Chem.* iii. 28 One isomer, isobutane, has one carbon atom which is bound to three other carbons, and there is no such carbon atom in the other isomer, *n*-butane.

c. In *Physics N* is used to designate the series of X-ray emission lines of longer wavelength than the *M*-series obtained by exciting the atoms of any particular element (cf. M 5 a); these arise from electron transitions to the atomic orbit of fourth-lowest energy, of principal quantum number 4, which is thus termed the ***N-shell***, and electrons in this shell ***N-electrons***.

1911 [see M 5 a]. **1923** H. L. BROSE tr. *Sommerfeld's Atomic Structure & Spectral Lines* viii. 505 Our relativistic formula of the fine-structure.. furnishes us with a principle of sub-division for the multiplicity of M- and N-lines. *Ibid.* 507 Just as the M-shell belongs to the quantum-number 3, so does the N-shell to the quantum-number 4. **1948** LAPP & ANDREWS *Nuclear Radiation Physics* v. 74 In the heavier elements such as tungsten ($Z = 74$) the *N* shell is saturated with 32 electrons. **1967** G. L. CLARK *Handbk. X-Rays* i. 7 At still longer wavelengths *M*- and *N*-series lines have been measured only for heavier elements. **1968** *Physical Rev.* CLXVI. 944/1 Radiationless transitions are favored in low-*Z* elements and always dominate in the *M*, *N*, and higher shells for the ordinary Auger effect. **1970** E. P. BERTIN *Princ. & Pract. X-Ray Spectr. Anal.* i. 27 An electron having just enough energy to expel, say, an *LII* electron can also expel *LIII*, *M*, and *N* electrons, but not *LI* or *K* electrons.

d. N (*Physics*) = newton.

1951 *Symbols, Signs & Abbrev.* (R. Soc. Symbols Comm.) 14/2 Newton... N. **1973** KLEPPNER & KOLENKOW *Introd. Mechanics* ii. 84 Since $g = 9·8$ m/s², the weight of 1 kg mass is 9·8 N.

n-, in OE. and ME., the negative particle *ne* in combination with a word beginning with a vowel, *h*, or *w*, as *nam*, am not, *nis* is not, *nadde* had not, *nas* was not. See NE and NABBE, NAD, etc.

'n[1], **-n**, *dial.*, reduced enclitic form of the negative particle *not*, *no*, or *na*.

c **1750** in J. F. PALMER *Dev. Dial.* (1837) 6, I did'n care. *Ibid.*, I coud'n abide her vather. **1864** TENNYSON *North. Farmer* I. xvii, What atta stannin' theer fur, an' doesn bring ma the aäle?

'n[2], **'n'** (ən), colloq. shortening of AND *conj.*

Esp. common in *rock 'n' roll.*

1858 O. W. HOLMES in *Atlantic Monthly* Sept. 497/1 To beat the taown 'n' the keounty. **1906** E. DYSON *Fact'ry 'Ands* xvii. 233 Ther revolvin' arm was bent out, 'n' it got home a left lead 'n' er right cross. **1923** *Radio Times* 28 Sept. 23/2 Dance Programme.. One-step, 'By 'n' Bye'. **1925** C. R. COOPER (*title*) Lions 'n' tigers. **1928** F. HURST *President is Born* v. 67 God bless Mother 'n' Father. **1959** W. GOLDING *Free Fall* ii. 58 He was helmeted, assured, delicate at the rudder-bar and joystick in the fish-'n-chip smell of the engine oil. **1968** *Listener* 18 July 93/2 Tony Carruthers has turned the whole building into a prison to assist Charles Marowitz's production of a Canadian play about four boys having sex-'n-violence in a reformatory. **1971** *Black World* June 63/1 The President's tryin' his level best to bring more 'n more boys home all the time. **1973** J. WAINWRIGHT *Devil you Don't* 30 Dudley was mad.. but good 'n mad.

'n[3], *Lanc. dial.*, reduced form of *han* 'have'.

1864 R. A. ARNOLD *Hist. Cotton Famine* 302 That's o at we'n getten. *Ibid.* 304 Yo'n bin far enough to-day.

'n[4], colloq. reduced form of THAN *conj.*

1867 J. T. TROWBRIDGE *Darius Green* in *Oxf. Bk. Children's Verse* (1973) 262 The little chatterin', sassy wren, No bigger 'n my thumb. **1898** J. D. BRAYSHAW *Slum Silhouettes* 2 That on'y made Bill madder 'n ever. **1903** K. D. WIGGIN *Rebecca* i. 8 We've only just started on it,.. 'it's more 'n two hours'. **1910** C. E. MULFORD *Hopalong Cassidy* ix. 63 He hates Greasers worse 'n I do. **1973** 'J. ASHFORD' *Double Run* viii. 57 The duty would be more 'n Mr. Smith could pay if it's properly declared.

†**na**, *adv.*[1] and *conj.*[1] *Obs.* [OE. *ná*, f. *ne* NE + *á* ever (see A *adv.* and O *adv.*), giving normally *nā* in northern ME. and Sc., and *nō* (see NO *adv.*) in midland and southern dialects. But the *na* which actually appears in northern and Sc. texts seems rather to be an alteration of *ne* than a genuine survival of the old form.]

1. *adv.* Not, in no way, by no means.

Frequently used along with another negative, as *ne*.

Beowulf 1536 Swa sceal man don, þonne he.. na ymb his lif cearað. *c* **888** K. ÆLFRED *Boeth.* vii. §3 ʒif þæt þine aʒne welan wæron.. ne meahtest þu hi na forleosan. **971** *Blickl. Hom.* 33 Nolde he him na andswerian buton mid monþwærnesse. *c* **1000** *Ags. Gosp.* Matt. vii. 25 þær bleowun windas.. on þæt hus & hyt na ne feoll. *a* **1121** *O.E. Chron.* (Laud MS.) an. 1083 Hi.. wolden hiʒ utdraʒan, þaða hiʒ ne dorsten na utgan. *c* **1175** *Lamb. Hom.* 123 Ne nom he na alle þa þe þer inne weren. *c* **1205** LAY. 9294 þer he na ne come ʒif hit nere for swikedome. *c* **1350** *Will. Palerne* 1172, I na gult him neuer, to gif him enchesoun [etc.].

a **1300** *Cursor M.* 12847 Baptis þe na dar i noght. **13..** —— 16948 (Gött.), If i ʒu lije na [*Cott.* ne] sall. **1375** BARBOUR *Bruce* IX. 71 (Edinb. MS.), And that him sair repent sall he.. May fall, quhen he it mend na may. **1423** JAS. I *Kingis Q.* lxvii, Tho began myn axis and turment, To sene hir part, and folowe I na myght. **15..** in *Dunbar's Poems* (S.T.S.) 321, I dar noght speke, For I na dare, my hert it is so sare.

b. *na war (it)*, were it not, had it not been, but for (the fact *that*), etc.

1375 BARBOUR *Bruce* III. 642 He had bene tane but dout, Na war it that he [etc.]. *Ibid.* VI. 345, VII. 218, etc. *c* **1375** *Sc. Leg. Saints* Prol. 98 ʒet wald I,.. na var eld & falt of sycht, Of þe twelf apostolis spek now. *Ibid.* i. 528, etc.

c. *conj.* That.. not, but that. Also ***Deil na*** = 'May' (with negative following).

1375 BARBOUR *Bruce* V. 372 Of thretty was levit nane, Na thai war slane ilkane, or tane. *c* **1375** *Sc. Leg. Saints* xxxii. (*Justin*) 82 þat wes nocht sa priuely na it wes persawit in hy. **1456** SIR G. HAYE *Law Arms* (S.T.S.) 221 Quhat war he that had sa hard a hert na he wald have merci of thame..? **1533** GAU *Richt Vay* 12 Thay quhilk.. trowis noth na he wirkis al the guid warkis in thayme. **1786** BURNS *Earnest Cry* xvi, Deil na they never mair do guid, Play'd her that pliskie.

2. *conj.* Nor. Also, neither (only in early ME.).

c **1000** *O.E. Chron.* (Cant. MS.) an. 995 Naþer na of þam cinge na of þam folce. *c* **1131** *O.E. Chron.* (Laud MS.) an. 1131 þær man him held þæt he ne mihte na east na west. *c* **1205** LAY. 13344 Nis nan kine-lond na swa brad næ swa long. *Ibid.* 14165 Ah nulle ich castel na burh nane þe bitechen.

a **1300** *Cursor M.* 1962 Ete o.. nakin worme þat es made, Na o fouxul [*Gött.* Na foul] þat refes his liuelade. *Ibid.* 5780 þis es mi nam, na mar na less [*Gött.* more ne less]. **1375** BARBOUR *Bruce* I. 318 He wyst nocht quhat to do na say. *c* **1375** *Sc. Leg. Saints* xv. (*Barnabas*) 22 He was nocht dwelland with criste, na in þis warld vakand, na hard nothire, na saw his ded. **1456** SIR G. HAYE *Law Arms* (S.T.S.) 167 [They] nouthir had were to him, na he to thame. *c* **1470** HENRY *Wallace* I. 105 To thar men without thai mycht nocht wyn, Na thai to thaim. **1508** DUNBAR *Tua Mariit Wemen* 299 We na fallowis wer.. In fredome, na furth bering, na fairnes of persoune. **1535** STEWART *Cron. Scot.* II. 439 Quhilk hes no strenth.. Na dow to weild ane wapin with thair hand. **1786** BURNS *Twa Dogs* 16 Tho' he was o' high degree, The fient a pride na pride had he.

b. Used with another negative following.

1375 BARBOUR *Bruce* I. 230 A noble hart may haiff nane es, Na ellys nocht that may him ples, Gyff fredome failʒhe. *c* **1375** *Sc. Leg. Saints* i. (*Peter*) 6 þis petir.. vald neuir bow for aduersite, na for na perele þat mycht be. **1456** SIR G. HAYE *Law Arms* (S.T.S.) 26 He.. schewe in dede that he lufit it nocht na nane that delt with it. **1535** STEWART *Cron. Scot.* II. 205 For clerk or preist,.. Na for na bischop that wes in Britane.

c. With omission of preceding negative.

c **1375** *Sc. Leg. Saints* xxx. (*Theodora*) 631 For Ioy na solace bot thru þe, Na lykine in my hert ma be. **1456** SIR G. HAYE *Law Arms* (S.T.S.) 219 We may undo na gaynsay the commoun lawe.

na (nɑː), *adv.*[2] *Sc.* and *north. dial.* [repr. OE. *ná* (see prec.), and corresponding to the midland and southern NO. The pron. (nɑː) for (neɪ) has parallels in *twā*, *whā*.] No, used in answer to a question, to express dissent, etc.

1228 in *Mem. Ripon* (Surtees) I. 53 Per suum *na* vel suum *ya*. *c* **1375** *Sc. Leg. Saints* xxix. (*Placidas*) 600 þane cane þai at hym hertly spere.. gyf he wist quhare he was.. he sad: 'na'. *c* **1375** *Cursor M.* 766 (Fairf.), And wate þou quar-fore? na [*Cott.* nai, *Gött.* nay], ho sayde. *c* **1475** *Rauf Coilʒear* 79 Na, thank me not ouir airlie, for dreid that we threip. **1513** DOUGLAS *Æneis* VII. vi. 32 Hes nocht Troy all infyrit ʒit thame brynt? Na: all sic laboure is for nocht and tynt. **1596** DALRYMPLE tr. *Leslie's Hist. Scot.* VIII. 75 Na; nocht sa: bot he quhen pleises him selfe wil cum. **1725** RAMSAY *Gentle Sheph.* I. i, Na, Patie, na! I'm nae sic churlish beast. **1786** BURNS *To a Louse* iv, Na faith ye yet! ye'll no be right Till ye've got on it. **1816** SCOTT *Old Mort.* vii, Na, my leddy, it's no that. **1827** J. WILSON *Noct. Ambr.* Wks. 1855 I. 354 Na Sir—I canna say that I should. **1894** *Northumbld. Gloss.* s.v., 'Are ye gan win us?' 'Na'.

b. Doubled for the sake of emphasis.

1513 DOUGLAS *Æneis* I. Prol. 24 Na, na, nocht sua, bot knele quhen I thame heir. **1594** A. HUME *Treat. Conscience* iv. Wks. (S.T.S.) 104 Na, na, thy intention sall be na releuant defence vnto thee. **1682** PEDEN *Lord's Trumpet* 20 Na, na, sirs, love to God goes beyond all that. **1786** BURNS *Answ. Tailor* x, 'Na, na', quo' I, 'I'm no' for that'. **1815** SCOTT *Guy M.* xxiii, 'Had we not better.. dismount?' 'Na, na,.. we maun cross Dumple at no rate'. **1891** 'H. HALIBURTON' *Ochil Hills* 51 Na, na, my lad!

†**na**, *conj.*[2] *Sc. Obs.* [Of obscure origin: cf. NOR in the same sense. Examples of NE in this use are very rare.] Than.

1375 BARBOUR *Bruce* VI. 538 The lest party of thame twa Wes starkar fer na he. *c* **1375** *Sc. Leg. Saints* iii. (*Andrew*) 1103 þe fend wes away in hy, sonare na ony man cuth thynke. **1456** SIR G. HAYE *Law Arms* (S.T.S.) 53 [He] slewe of his menʒe ma na fourty thousand. *c* **1470** HENRY *Wallace* v. 388, I meyn fer mar the tynsell off my men, Na for my selff. **1508** DUNBAR *Tua Mariit Wemen* 295 Mar with wylis

I wan na wichtnes of handis. **1535** STEWART *Cron. Scot.* I. 271 Tha wald erar de Na with the Romanis to subdewit be.

b. Than if. *rare*$^{-1}$.

1456 SIR G. HAYE *Law Arms* (S.T.S.) 303 Quhen he cummys furthwart on thre festuale days,..all the peple.. press the mare to se him na he rade every day.

na (nə), *adv.*^{3} *Sc.* and *north. dial.* Also **-na.** [Enclitic form of NO *adv.* 'not', with obscuration of vowel owing to the absence of stress.] Not. Chiefly used with auxiliary verbs, as *canna*, *maunna*, *dinna*, *hasna*, etc.

1714 RAMSAY *John Cowper* 29 'Tis an ill wind that dis na blaw Some body good. **1725** —— *Gentle Sheph.* I. i, I needna mak sic speed. **1786** BURNS *Holy Fair* xiv, They canna sit for anger. **1793** —— *Wilt thou be my dearie?* If it winna, canna be. **1816** SCOTT *Old Mort.* i, Them that shame na to take upon themsells the persecuting name of..tories. *a* **1828** BEWICK *The Howdy* (1850) 13 [Thou] dis na leuk vara pleasd.

na, obs. variant of NAY.

naa, dial. variant of NO *a.* and *adv.*

N.A.A.F.I. ('næfɪ). Also **NAAFI**, **Naafi**, **Naffy**. The Navy, Army, and Air Force Institutes which run canteens, stores, etc., for service personnel; also, a canteen, restaurant, etc., run by this organization. Also *attrib.*

[**1921** *Times* 7 Jan. 7/3 The joint organization for the administration of canteens for the three Services, hitherto known as the Navy and Army Canteen Board, has been reconstituted with effect from January 1, 1921, under the title 'The Navy, Army, and Air Force Institutes'.] **1927** *Daily Express* 16 Mar. 9/2 Cheering workgirls surrounded the Prince of Wales when he visited the 'Naafi'.. headquarters in Kennington yesterday. **1928** J. FORTESCUE *Canteens in Brit. Army* 73 The general policy of the N.A.A.F.I. is to afford facilities to its members of all three services to purchase commodities of high quality at prices competitive with those of 'multiple' shops. **1937** PARTRIDGE *Dict. Slang* 548/2 *Nafy* or *Naffy*; properly *Naafi*; loosely *Narfy* (..pronounced thus by Indian Army officers). The canteen: naval and military: from ca. 1930. **1940** *War Weekly* 19 Jan. 409/3 N.A.A.F.I., or 'Naffy', as it is affectionately called by the troops. *Ibid.*, The 'Naffy' Institute is a comfortable, red-brick building. **1943** HUNT & PRINGLE *Service Slang* 47 *Naffy*, the services are supplied on land and sea by the N.A.A.F.I... There are fully equipped shops and grocery stores in addition to the station canteens and mobile canteens which serve outposts. *Naffytime*, the morning break. **1945** J. MACLAREN-ROSS in *Penguin New Writing* XXVI. 54 He'd dropped his notebook in a Naffy. **1945** PARTRIDGE *Dict. R.A.F. Slang* 40 *Naffy Romeo*, a ladies' man—addicted to treating W.A.A.F. personnel with Naffy refreshments. *Naffy gong*, 1939–43 star (medal). Since late 1943. **1948** A. M. TAYLOR *Lang. World War II* (rev. ed.) 135 The various NAAFI clubs were almost invariably called Naffies. **1959** 'M. AINSWORTH' *Murder is Catching* 10 Best if I drop you at the Naffy. **1959** *Times* 17 Jan. 8/4 Common rooms sometimes suggest more the Naafi than the bookman's study. **1959** *Spectator* 23 Jan. 127/3 The NAAFI Is a sort of caafi Where soldiers are rude About the food. **1972** *Oxford Times* 4 Aug. 5 Mr Lewin leaves Oxford for Belfast on Monday to take up an appointment as manager of a NAAFI club in the city. **1973** *Times* 14 May 11/5 Kafka and Brasso make a great double act with a NAAFI piano. **1974** R. GENTIL *Trained to Intrude* ii. 20 At that time Dover.., apart from the pubs and the NAAFI, offered very little comfort to the serviceman.

Naagoree, obs. form of NAGARI.

naam (nɑːm), *sb. Hist. Law.* Also **nam.** [OE. *naam*, *nám*, a. ON. *nám*, Goth. *-nêm* (in *andanêm*), related by ablaut to the vb. *niman* to take, NIM. Hence med.L. *namium*, *namum*. The ONF. *namps*, *nampt*, and med.L. *namptum*, *namtum*, *nantum* (see Du Cange), are prob. of Scand. origin.] The act of taking another's goods by way of distraint; goods or chattels taken in this way. (Cf. WITHERNAM.)

a **1035** *Laws Cnut* in Thorpe I. 386 Be naame. Ne nime nan man nane name, ne innan scire ne ut of scire, ær man hæbbe þriwa on hundrede his rihtes ȝebeden. *a* **1087** *Laws William I* in Du Cange s.v. *Namium*, Ne prenge hum Nam ni l'en Conté, ne defors, dici qu'il eit tres fois demanded dreit, el Undred, û el Conté. *c* **1290** BRITTON (1865) I. 173 Naam si est un general noun a avers et a chateus et a totes choses moebles qe hom put prendre en noun de destresce. **13..** HORNE *Mirror of Justices* (Selden) xxvi. 69 Une accioun mixte..qest appelle de naam. *Ibid.*, Naam nest autre chose qe renable destresce.

1611 COTGR., *Nampt*, a distresse, a beast or mouable distrained;..a distraining (in which sence our common Lawyers vse Naam). **1641** *Termes de la Ley* 208 Lawfull Naam is nothing else but a reasonable distresse. **1727–38** CHAMBERS *Cycl.* s.v. *Namium*, Prohibited Naam, is an unjust taking the cattle of another, or driving them to an unlawful place. **1785** in *Hist. York* II. 43 At the County Court..shall be holden Pleas of Naam, that are called *Replegiarum*. **1837** *Penny Cycl.* IX. 29/1 The modern distress is the 'naam', restricted to the taking of personal chattels. **1895** WHITTAKER tr. *Horne's Mirror of Justices* (Selden) xxvi. 70 A mixed action..which is called an action of naam.

Hence **naam** *v.* [AF. *naamer*], to distrain, to make distraint.

1895 WHITTAKER tr. *Horne's Mirror of Justices* (Selden) xxvi. 72 If any one be wrongfully naamed, you must distinguish whether this be done by those who are entitled to naam or by others.

naan, var. NAN^{3}.

naape, obs. form of NAPE.

naartj(i)e, varr. NARTJIE.

nab (næb), *sb.*^{1} Chiefly *north.* and *Sc.* Also 5, 9 **nabb**, 9 **knab.** [a. ON. *nabbr* and *nabbi*, a projecting peak or knoll: cf. Norw. dial. *nabb* and *nabbe*, 'nab' of a rock or hill, knag, pin, (tether-)peg, Sw. *nabb* (dial. *nabbe*), nab, promontory, prominence (MSw. *skogsnabb*, point of a wood).]

1. A projecting or jutting out part of a hill or rock; a peak or promontory; a rocky or outstanding hill, a summit, etc.

a **1400–50** *Alexander* 5494 He stekis þam vp with þar stoures in a straite lawe, And..in þe nabb speris [= 5496 in þe roche stoppis]. **1688** HICKES *Dict. Island.* 108 *Gnypa*, summitas rupis vel montis. *A. Bor.* a nabb. [Hence in Ray, 1691.] *a* **1800** *Old rhyme* in *Proc. Berw. Nat. Club* (1837) I. v. 149 St. Abb's upon the nabs, St. Helen's on the lea. **1828** G. YOUNG *Geol. Surv. Yorks.* 98 At Clayton point and other nabs to the south of Scarborough. **1843** COOPER *Sussex Gloss.*, *Nab*, the summit of a hill. **1855** ROBINSON *Whitby Gloss.*, *Nab*, a rocky projection from the land into the sea, as Saltwick Nab. **1877** DIXON *Diana, Lady Lyle* II. VII. i. 173 This nose of land starts up into a nab or peak, on which stands a feudal edifice.

attrib. **1891** ATKINSON *Moorland* 42 Soaring hill and deepening dale, abrupt nab-end and craggy wood.

b. A projecting tuft or clump.

1848 E. BRONTË *Wuthering Heights* xxi, Will you just turn this nab of heath, and walk into my house?

2. A projection or spur on the bolt of a lock (see first quot.). Also *attrib.*

1677 MOXON *Mech. Exerc.* 27 The Toe, or Nab of the Bolt, which rises..above the Straight on the Top of the Bolt: The Office of this Nab, is to receive the Bottom of the Bit of the Key, when in turning it about, it shoots the Bolt backward or forwards. *Ibid.* 28 The Nab end. **1797** *Encycl. Brit.* (ed. 3) X. 111/2 To the main plate [of a lock] belong the key-hole,..bolt-toe or bolt-knab. **1867** SMYTH *Sailor's Word-bk.*, *Nab*, the bolt-toe, or cock of a gun-lock.

b. The keeper of a door lock.

1875 KNIGHT *Dict. Mech.* 1505/1.

†**nab**, *sb.*^{2} *Obs. slang.* [Of uncertain origin: cf. the later NOB and KNOB in sense 1.]

1. The head. Also *Comb.*

1567 HARMAN *Caveat* 86, I tower that bene bouse makes nase nabes. I se that good drinke makes a dronken head. **1608** DEKKER *Lanth. & Candle Lt.* c iij b, The Ruffin cly the nab of the Harman beck. **1622** FLETCHER *Beggar's Bush* III. iv, I crown thy nab with a gage of benebowse. *a* **1700** B. E. *Dict. Cant. Crew*, *Nab-girder*, a Bridle.

b. The head of a stick. *rare*$^{-1}$.

1616 DEKKER *Lanth. & Candle Lt.* (ed. 2) P, He carries a short staffe..having in the Nab or head of it a Ferme (that is to say, a hole).

2. A hat.

1673 R. HEAD *Canting Acad.* 33 Cast our Nabs [*Fletcher* caps] and Cares away, This is beggars Holiday. **1688** SHADWELL *Sqr. Alsatia* II. Wks. 1720 IV. 47 Here's a Nabb! you never saw such a one in your Life... A rum Nabb: It is a Beaver of 5*l.* *a* **1700** B. E. *Dict. Cant. Crew*, *Pentice Nab*, a very broad-brim'd Hat. **1729** FIELDING *Pleas. Town* Wks. 1775 I. 223, I was..enquiring after you, when your boy brought your nab (Oh,..that the son of a King should pawn a hat!). **1754** —— *J. Wild* II. vi. There were..those who preferred the nab, or trencher hat, with the brim flapping over their eyes.

3. 'A coxcomb' (*a* 1700 B. E. *Dict. Cant. Crew*).

nab (næb), *sb.*^{3} [f. NAB *v.*^{1}]

1. *slang.* One who 'nabs'; a police officer.

1813 *British Press* 29 July 178 A nab stepp'd in and show'd his writ. **1852** JUDSON *Myst. New York* iv. (Farmer), I don't know..about no persuits, 'cept the nab's persuits. **1967** *New Yorker* 27 May 32/3, I talk him into splitting the scene and we start hitchhiking back down Sunset, and just like that the Nabs stop us for bumming rides. **1971** J. WAINWRIGHT *Dig Grave* 78 All the nabs in the world were in the downstairs front.

2. A snatch, bite. *rare.*

1867 F. H. LUDLOW *Little Brother* 47 And then [the dog] turned to see if there wasn't a chance of getting a nab at his plump little calves.

nab, *sb.*^{4} Sc. var. of NOB, a person of note.

Also written *knab*: see Jamieson and *Eng. Dial Dict.*

nab (næb), *v.*^{1} *slang* or *colloq.* Also 9 **knab.** [Of obscure origin: cf. NAP *v.*^{3} in the same sense.]

1. *trans.* To catch (a person) and take into custody; to apprehend or arrest; to catch, seize, or pounce upon (one) in wrong-doing.

1686 F. SPENCE tr. *Varillas' Ho. Medicis* 407 Verselli was nabb'd playing at dice. **1688** SHADWELL *Sqr. Alsatia* III. Wks. 1720 IV. 56 Our Suffolk Heir is nabb'd, for a small Business: and I must find him some Sham-bail. **1694** MOTTEUX *Rabelais* IV. xii, He sends to him one of these Catchpoles or Apparitors who nabs, or at least cites him, serves a Writ or Warrant upon him. **1748** SMOLLETT *Rod. Rand.* xxiii, They embraced the prisoner..and asked how long she had been nabb'd. **1768** GOLDSM. *Good-n. Man* III, Ay, but if so be a man's nabbed, you know. **1818** SCOTT *Hrt. Midl.* xxix, Don't keep chattering till some travellers come up to nab us. **1838** DICKENS *O. Twist* xliv, 'It..reminds you of being nabbed, does it?' said the Jew... 'Reminds me of being nabbed by the devil', returned Sikes. **1886** G. R. SIMS *Ring o' Bells* II. vi, Jack's in prison... Must have been nabbed while I was abroad.

b. To catch, in other applications.

a **1700** B. E. *Dict. Cant. Crew* s.v., *I'll Nab ye*, I'll have your Hat or Cap. **1742** RICHARDSON *Pamela* III. 335 Let's see, what have I said?—Ay, by my Soul, you have nabbed me cleverly. **1821** CLARE *Vill. Minstr.* I. 168 If Puss can't nab ye by the nose, I'll find a scheme..To save my bread.

2. To snatch or seize (a thing); to steal.

1814 *Sporting Mag.* XLIV. 47 All was lost, Save what was nabb'd to pay the cost. **1831** TRELAWNY *Adv. Younger Son* II. 68 As surly..as a bull-dog with his bone, when an impudent cur offers to knab it. **1851** MAYHEW *Lond. Lab.* I. 51/2 Mr. —— nabs the chance of putting his customers awake.

b. *intr.* To snatch *at* a thing.

1803 'CHRISTOPHER CAUSTIC' [Fessenden] *Terrible Tract.* I. (ed. 2) 43, I learnt these from as nice a rabbit As naturalist could wish to nab at.

3. *to nab the rust*: (see quots. and cf. *Eng. Dial. Dict.* s.v. *Nab*).

1801 *Sporting Mag.* XVIII. 101 To nab the rust; a jockey term for a horse that is restive. **1881** *Isle of Wight Gloss.*, *Nab the rust*, to be angry or sulky.

†**4.** 'To cog a die' (Phillips 1706). *Obs.*$^{-0}$

nab (næb), *v.*^{2} *dial.* [var. of KNAB *v.*]

1. *trans.* and *intr.* To bite gently, to nibble.

1678 BUTLER *Hud.* III. ii. 1457 To nab the itches of their sects, As jades do one another's necks. **1750** ELLIS *Sheph. Guide* 232 The sheep may nab and eat. **1775** ASH, *Nab*, to bite, to bite with repeated quick but gentle motion. **1891** *Hartland Gloss.*, *Nab*, to nibble or bite gently.

2. To speak affectedly. *rare*$^{-1}$. (Cf. GNAP *v.*, KNAP *v.*^{1} 4.)

1895 SARAH TYTLER *Macdonald Lass* iv, I would as soon face one of the cutters' captains, nabbing his English.

nab, in phr. *hab (or) nab*, etc.: see HAB.

nabal ('neɪbəl). [From the Hebrew proper name *Nābāl* in 1 Sam. xxv. 3, etc.] A churlish or miserly person. Also *attrib.*

1604 G. POWEL *Catholike's Supplic.* 127 The greedy Nabals & hold-fast Labans of the world. **1617** HIERON *Wks.* II. 397 Many a carnall man, many a Nabal, hath these temporall things in a large measure. **1825** SCOTT in Lockhart *Life* (1839) VII. 367 Nicol is certainly going to sell Faldonside, the Nabal asks £40,000—at least £5000 too much. **1871** W. ALEXANDER *Johnny Gibb* (1873) 192 'Nabal vratch', soliloquised Dawvid Hadden within himself.

Hence **'nabalism**, †**'nabalite**; †**naba'litic** *a.*

1645 PAGITT *Heresiogr.* (1661) 60 Ignorant Idiots, noddy Nabalites. **1659** GAUDEN *Tears Ch.* 35 It is a sin arguing a Nabalitick and vile heart. **1886** W. D. MACRAY *Pref. Chron. Abbat. Rameseiensis* p. xxix, The churlishness of the second abbot..is condemned not so much for its own Nabalism as for its shortsightedness.

nabal, variant of NABLE *Obs.*

nabam ('neɪbæm). *Chem.* [f. *Na*, the chemical symbol for sodium + bisdithiocar*bam*ate (see quot. 1950).] A water-soluble powder used as a fungicide, usu. as a spray with zinc sulphate as a stabilizer; $(NaS{\cdot}CS{\cdot}NH{\cdot}CH_2-)_2$.

1950 *Phytopathology* XL. 118 The Subcommittee on Fungicide Nomenclature of the American Phytopathological Society, cooperating with the Interdepartmental Committee on Pest Control, has selected common names for five commercially-available fungicidal chemicals which are useful in the control of various destructive plant diseases... *Nabam* for the fungicidal chemical, disodium ethylene bisdithiocarbamate. **1960** [see FERBAM]. **1967** L. H. PURDY in D. C. Torgeson *Fungicides* I. vii. 206 Nabam reacted with zinc sulfate was the first commercially used spray fungicide for in-the-row treatment control of cotton seedling diseases.

Nabatæan (næbə'tiːən), *sb.* and *a.* Also **Nabatean, Nabathæan, Nabathean.** [f. L. *Nabat(h)æ-us*, Gr. *Ναβαταῖ-ος*, *Ναβαθαῖ-ος* (cf. *Nebāṭu* the native name of the country) + -AN.]

A. *sb.* One of an ancient Arabian people; their language. **B.** *adj.* Of or pertaining to the Nabatæans.

1601 HOLLAND tr. *Pliny's Nat. Hist.* I. XII. xx. 374 The Troglodyte Nabathæans: who onely of the ancient Nabathæans, there setled and remained. **1875** *Encycl. Brit.* III. 411/2 Two forms of Shemitic writing (the Palmyrenian .., and the Sinaitic or Nabathæan). **1884** *Ibid.* XVII. 160/1 *Nabatæans*, a famous people of ancient Arabia. **1897** F. HOMMEL in H. von Hilprecht *Recent Res. in Bible Lands* 146 Between the decline of the Nabatean Empire and the appearance of Muhammad. **1898** E. CLODD *Tom Tit Tot* vi. 65 Ibn Khaldun..describes how the Nabathean sorcerers of the Lower Euphrates made an image of the person whom they plotted to destroy. **1911** *Encycl. Brit.* XXIV. 626/1 The language of this country was Nabataean. **1920** *Public Opinion* 9 July 42/3 Little did the ancient..Nabataeans imagine that a people called Americans would one day wander among the ruins of their proud city. **1931** *Times Lit. Suppl.* 29 Oct. 832/2 His new work..is intended to summarize all that is known on the subject of the Nabateans. *Ibid.*, The sources of Nabatean history. **1973** *Times* 9 June 11/7 A fragment of ancient Nabatean pottery. **1974** *Times* 21 Dec. 11/4 The Arava, stretching from the Dead Sea to Eilat, which has been virtually virgin soil since the days of the Nabateans.

†**nabbe, nabbeð, -eth,** have not, has not: see NE and HAVE *v.* A. 9. *Obs.*

Beowulf 1850 þæt þe Sæ-ȝeatas selran næbben cyning æniȝne. *c* **888** K. ÆLFRED *Boeth.* xvi. §3 Heora selfra nanne anwald nabbað. *Ibid.* xxxix. §5 Ic..ȝet næbbe þis ȝedon. **971** *Blickl. Hom.* 131 Ne mæȝ þæt ne beon þæt þa bearn.. langunga nabban. *c* **1175** *Lamb. Hom.* 31 Nabbe ic nawiht þer-of. *c* **1230** *Hali Meid.* 9 As gentille wimmen..þat nabbeð hwerwið buggen ham brudgume. *a* **1300** *Vox & Wolf* 39, I nabbe don her nout bote goed.

nabber (ˈnæbə(r)). *slang.* [f. NAB *v.*[1] + -ER[1].] One who 'nabs'; hence (*a*) a bailiff or constable; (*b*) a thief.

1810 *Splendid Follies* III. 118 Oxford, where..he might elude the pursuit of nabbers till daddy's heart relented. **1880** *Jamieson's Sc. Dict.*, *Nabber*, a pilferer, a thief.

nabbie (ˈnæbɪ). Also **nabby**. [? f. NOBBY *a.*] A type of Scottish boat used esp. in herring-fishing on Loch Fyne and in the Firth of Clyde, and originally having a raking mast, lug-sail and jib. Cf. NOBBY *sb.* 2.

1884 R. HOGARTH *Herring Fishery* 4 These boats were round-sterned—from fourteen to sixteen feet keel and about seven feet beam. It was not possible to go any distance to look for herrings in boats of this description. They were known by the name of 'nabbies'. **1907** *Yachting Monthly* IV. 366/1 It may interest 'M.I.N.A.' to know that he is quite correct in his use of the word 'nabbie' as applied to the present-day Loch Fyne type of fishing boat. **1955** *Mearns Leader* (Stonehaven) 17 June, 46 ft. 'Nabby' boat, *June Rose*, from Fisherrow. She is very well equipped and powered by a 66 h.p. Kelvin Diesel. **1959** P. NORTON *End of Voyage* 85 The Loch Fyne skiff or nabbie is a graceful bird-like craft.

nabby, Sc. variant of NOBBY *a.*

†**nab-cheat.** *Obs. Cant.* Also 6 **-chet, nob-chete.** [f. NAB *sb.*[2] + CHEAT *sb.*[1] 3.] A hat or cap.

c **1530** COPLAND *Hye Wey to Spyttel Hous* in Hazl. *E.P.P.* IV. 69 His watch shall feng a prounces nobchete. **1567** HARMAN *Caveat* 85, I towre the strummel trine vpon thy nabchet and Togman. **1622** FLETCHER *Beggar's Bush* II. i, Thus we throw up our nab-cheats first for joy, And then our filches.

nabe (neɪb). *U.S. slang.* [f. the pronunc. of NEIGHBOURHOOD.] A neighbourhood; *spec.* a local cinema. Also *attrib.*

1935 *Evening Sun* (Baltimore) 8 Apr. 17 On Sunday two powerful [box office pictures] were released to the nabes. **1937** *Amer. Speech* XII. 317/2 *Nabe*, neighborhood motion picture theatre. **1942** BERREY & VAN DEN BARK *Amer. Thes. Slang* §50/1 *Nabe, naborhood, neighb*, neighborhood. *Ibid.* §587/5 Nabe pichouse, a neighborhood motion-picture theater. **1961** A. BERKMAN *Singers' Gloss. Show Business* 61 Nabes..neighborhood movie houses. **1970** *New Yorker* 20 June 30/1 They picked an aging star, slapped together a moldy script, and sent the result out to the nabes. **1971** *Time* 8 Nov. 73/1 In Portland, where business is also dragging, the nabes (the trade term for the neighborhood houses) are now closed except on weekends.

Nabeshima (næbəˈʃiːmə). The name of a baronial family in feudal Japan used *attrib.* and *absol.* to designate the porcelain produced from the kilns established by this family in 1722 at Okawachi on the island of Kyushu in Japan.

1886 W. CHAFFERS *Marks Pott. & Porc.* (ed. 7) 412 Nabeshimayaki was made at Okawaji, painted principally in blue with plants, fishes, &c., distinct from the Hiradoyaki. **1902** F. BRINKLEY *Japan* VIII. ii. 95 The *Nabeshimayaki*, as the Okawachi manufactures were subsequently called, stands first among Japanese porcelains decorated with vitrifiable enamel. **1937** R. L. HOBSON *Handbk. Pott. & Porc. Far East* 163 The early Nabeshima porcelain is a good white ware with lustrous glaze of fine texture. **1965** S. JENYNS *Jap. Porcelain* vi. 230 Within their narrow range the saucer dishes of Nabeshima are technically as perfect as any porcelain that the Japanese were able to produce. **1967** H. H. SANDERS *World of Jap. Ceramics* 218 The old Nabeshima style is a flat bowl form with a high foot, which has a traditional blue-and-white comb-tooth pattern under the glaze and three underglaze blue patterns on the outside of the bowl. **1971** L. A. BOGER *Dict. World Pott. & Porc.* 237/1 Both the underglaze blue and the polychrome enameled Nabeshima are notable for the consummate skill with which the decorations have been applied, particularly the underglaze blue.

‖**nabi** (ˈnɑːbiː). Pl. **nebi'im.** [Heb. *nābhi* prophet.] **1.** *Theol.* One inspired to speak the word of God; a prophet, *spec.* a Hebrew prophet of the Old Testament.

[**1765** W. DODD in *Bible with Commentary* note on Gen. xx. verse 7 The Hebrew נביא *nebia*, signifies a person that speaks something in an eminent and extraordinary manner.] **1877** A. MILROY tr. *Kuenen's Prophets & Prophecy in Israel* iii. 63 The Nabi is, and cannot but be, an improvisatore. **1885** T. P. HUGHES *Dict. Islam* 427/1 *Nabī*, ..a prophet. One who has received direct inspiration..by means of an angel, or by the inspiration of the heart..; or has seen the things of God in a dream. *Ibid.* 475/2 According to Muhammadan writers a *nabi* is anyone directly inspired by God. **1900** W. W. SKEAT *Malay Magic* 99 Of the prophets (Nabi) there are an indefinite number. **1908** R. J. WILKINSON *Life & Customs* (Papers on Malay Subjects 3) I. 14 Other religions had prophets of their own who were nevertheless true prophets like *Nabi Isa*, the prophet of the Christians, and *Nabi Musa*, the prophet of the Siamese. **1918** *Encycl. Relig. & Ethics* X. 384/1 The true religion of Israel..traced its origin to those who bore the title *nabî*. *Ibid.* 384/2 In the Hebrew order of the OT books the *nᵉbî'îm* and the *hăkĕhāmîm* appear in different divisions. **1922** J. SKINNER *Prophecy & Religion* i. 4 Amos instances the raising up of *Nĕbî'îm* as a proof of Yahwe's peculiar love for Israel. **1961** B. VAWTER *Conscience of Israel* iv. 75 To him Amos was only a *nabi* like the many who grubbed out a living by devising oracles for clients.

2. *Art.* A member of a group of late 19th-century French post-impressionists, including Bonnard, Vuillard, Denis, and Sérusier, who followed the artistic theories of Gauguin.

1931 C'TESS DE LAUZANNE tr. *Basler & Kunstler's Post-Impressionists* xi. 52 All the 'Nabis', all the 'enflammés' who left the Jullian Academy, were attracted by the theories of..Paul Gauguin. **1945** GOLDWATER & TREVES *Artists on Art* (1947) 379 Sérusier gathered about him a group known as the *Nabis* which included..Denis, Bonnard, Vuillard, and later Maillol. **1959** *Listener* 22 Oct. 694/2 Felix Vallotton who worked in Paris and had relations with the Nabis. **1963** L. & E. HANSON *Post-Impressionists* xi. 277 They were..nicknamed the Nabis..because most of them wore beards, some were Jews and all were desperately earnest. **1963** *Times* 2 May 6/5 The 'Nabi' phase of French painting. **1969** M. BULLOCK tr. *Chassé's Nabis & their Period* i. 14 The Nabis soon became known as devotees of 'beautiful greys' and broken colours... When we try to outline Nabism, we always return in the end to the concept of fantasy and dream. **1971** tr. W. Verkade in J. Russell *Vuillard* 85 One day Sérusier said to me: 'Let's go and see the Nabi, Denis, at Saint-Germain.' **1972** L. LAMB *Picture Frame* ii. 24, I should guess that you have got hold of one of the Nabis... If you think it's a Vuillard, it probably *is*. **1973** *Times* 7 May 7/4 Art nouveau, the Nabis, the Pointillistes.

Hence **'nabi'ism, 'nabism.**

1922 J. SKINNER *Prophecy & Religion* i. 5 *Nabi'ism* had its unprogressive and degenerate representatives. **1969** [see sense 2 above].

nabla (ˈnæblə). *Math.* [a. Gr. *νάβλα*: see NABLE (and cf. quot. 1879 s.v. NEBEL).] = DEL.

The operator was introduced by Sir William Hamilton, who represented it by the symbol ◁. (In quot. 1837 he uses ∇′ as a symbol for any arbitrary function.)

[**1837** W. R. HAMILTON in *Trans. R. Irish Acad.* XVII. 236 Considering x as a function ψ of a new variable o' and performing any operation ∇′ with reference to the latter variable, $\nabla' f\psi(o') = \nabla' f(1 + \Delta)(\psi(o'))^{o}$. **1846** *Proc. R. Irish Acad.* III. 291 The following..general characteristic of operation $i\frac{d}{dx} + j\frac{d}{dy} + k\frac{d}{dz} = \lhd$, in which x, y, z are ordinary rectangular coordinates, while i, j, k are his [*sc.* Hamilton's] own coordinate imaginary units, appears to him to be one of great importance in many researches. **1847** W. R. HAMILTON in *Phil. Mag.* XXXI. 291 In the paper designed for Southampton..the characteristic was written ∇; but this more common sign has been so often used with other meanings, that it seems desirable to abstain from appropriating it to the new signification here proposed. **1853** —— *Lect. Quaternions* vii. 610 Introducing, for abridgment, as a new characteristic of operation, a symbol defined by the formula ◁ = [etc.].] **1884** W. THOMSON *Notes Lect. Molecular Dynamics & Wave Theory of Light at Johns Hopkins Univ.* x. 112 (MS.), I took the liberty of asking Professor Bell..whether he had a name for this symbol ∇^2; and he has mentioned to me *nabla*, a humorous suggestion of Maxwell's. It is the name of an Egyptian harp, which was of that shape. **1892** *Phil. Trans. R. Soc.* CLXXXIII. 431 Physical mathematics is very largely the mathematics of ∇. The name Nabla seems, therefore, ludicrously inefficient. **1939** D. E. RUTHERFORD *Vector Methods* iv. 50 A convenient method of writing grad ϕ is $\nabla\phi$, where ∇ (pronounced 'nabla') is defined as the vector operator $\nabla \equiv \mathbf{i}\frac{\partial}{\partial x} + \mathbf{j}\frac{\partial}{\partial y} + \mathbf{k}\frac{\partial}{\partial z}$. **1964** [see DEL]. **1969** L. YOUNG *Systems of Units in Electr. & Magn.* v. 63 The symbol nabla, ∇, is a vector differential operator.

†**'nable.** *Obs. rare.* Also 6 **nabal.** [ad. L. *nablum* (Vulg.; *nablium*, Ovid), ad. Gr. *νάβλα*, prob. of Phœnician origin, and so identical with Heb. *nēbel* which it is used to translate.] A Jewish instrument of music: see NEBEL.

1382 WYCLIF *1 Macc.* xiii. 51 With preisyng, and braunchis of palmes, and instrumentis of musik, and cymbalis, and nablis. **1546** LANGLEY tr. *Pol. Verg. de Invent.* I. xii. 23 b, The Prophet Dauid founde diuerse instrumentes as regals and Nabals. **1609** BIBLE (Douay) *1 Chron.* xv. 16 Singing men on musical instruments, to witte, on nables, and harpes, and cymbals. **1609** HEYWOOD *Brit. Troy* VII. iv, Nables and Regals holy Dauid found.

nablock, obs. form of NIBLICK *sb.*

†**'nabman.** *Obs. slang.* [f. NAB *v.*[2]] A police officer; a constable. (Cf. NAB *sb.*[3] 1.)

1823 in *Spirit Pub. Jrnls.* 201 For never were hearts, if the nabmen would let them, More formed to be jovial and light than our's.

nabob (ˈneɪbɒb). Also 7 **nawbob, nobob(b, nabab**; 8 **navob.** [= F. and Sp. *nabab*, Pg. *nababo*, ad. Urdū *nawwāb* deputy governor: see NAWAB and NAIB.]

1. The title of certain Muslim officials, who acted as deputy governors of provinces or districts in the Mogul Empire; an official thus designated; a governor of a town or district in India. Now *Hist.*

1612 R. COVERTE *Voy.* 36 An Earle is called a Nawbob, and they [*sc.* noblemen] are the chiefe men that attend on him. **1625** PURCHAS *Pilgrims* I. IV. 467 The Nabob, with fiftie or sixtie thousand people in his campe. **1687** *Lond. Gaz.* No. 2270/6 They took after that a great Ship belonging to the Nabob of Decca, in the River's mouth. **1764** CHURCHILL *Candidate* Poems II. 22 Nabobs themselves, allur'd by thy renown, Shall pay due homage to the English Crown. **1771** GOLDSM. *Hist. Eng.* IV. 375 The nabob whom the English supported, was reinstated in the government. **1817** JAS. MILL *Brit. India* I. III. iv. 621 *note*, The term Nabob, as equivalent to Subahdar, is very modern in Hindustan; and is said to have begun with Sujah Dowlah. **1858** J. B. NORTON *Topics* 34 The proclamation of Khan Bahadoor Khan.., who set himself up as nabob of that place, was put in evidence.

2. *transf.* A person of (†high rank or) great wealth; *spec.* one who returned from India with a large fortune acquired there; a very rich and luxurious person. Now *arch.*

1764 H. WALPOLE *Lett.* (1857) IV. 222 Mogul Pitt and Nabob Bute. **1773** FOOTE *Nabob* II, But, after all, Master Touchit, I am not so over-fond of these nabobs. **1796** STEDMAN *Surinam* II. 54 The customs and manner of living of these West-India nabobs. **1818** LADY MORGAN *Autobiog.* (1859) 35 Lady Cork..took us to dine at Sir George Cockerell's, the richest nabob in London. **1830** MACAULAY *Ess., Southey's Colloq.* (1851) I. 103 The glorified spirit of a great statesman and philosopher dawdling, like a bilious old nabob at a watering place. **1869** *Echo* 6 Feb., India may have ceased to grow nabobs as yellow as the gold mohurs they were wont to amass.

3. *attrib.* and *Comb.*, as ***nabob fortune, -hunting, -maker, -plunderer***; ***Nabob-land*** (= India).

1764 H. WALPOLE *Lett.* (1891) IV. 180 There is the devil to pay in Nabob-land, but I understand Indian histories no better than stocks. **1771** *Ann. Reg.* 91 This project may not be quite so noble as that of Nabob-hunting, but is certainly more commercial. **1775** MORTIMER *Ev. Man own Broker* 14 *note*, As to the nabob plunderers, these build palaces. **1795** BURNS *Heron Election Ball.* II. ii, As to his fine Nabob fortune, We'll e'en let this subject alane. **1862** BEVERIDGE *Hist. India* I. III. xii. 682 On these presents the nabob-makers of Calcutta were far more intent than on the interests of their employers.

†**4.** *U.S.* (See quot. 1806.) *Obs. rare*[−1].

1803 E. S. BOWNE *Girl's Life 80 Yrs. Ago* (1888) 151 Silk nabobs, plaided, colored and white, are much worn, very short waists, hair very plain. **1806** FESSENDEN *Orig. Poems* 36 Misses, squires, and gentlefolks, Call for Nabobs, hats, and cloaks. *Note.* Nabobs were a kind of outside garment formerly worn by the dashing belles of America.

Hence **na'bobery**, (*a*) a place frequented by nabobs; (*b*) the essential qualities of a nabob or nabobs; **na'bobical** *a.*, pertaining to a nabob; **'na,bobish** *a.*, of the nature of a nabob; **'na,bobishly** *adv.*, after the manner of a nabob; **'nabobism**, great wealth and luxury; **'nabobry**, the class of nabobs.

1834 *New Monthly Mag.* XL. 375 Such is the *nabobery into which Harley-street, Wimpole-street, and Gloucester-place, daily empty their precious stores of bilious humanity. **1852** W. M. SAVAGE *R. Medlicott* II. x, He reminds me of a nabob. Nabobbery itself. **1763** H. WALPOLE *Lett.* (1891) IV. 154 Not paying Lord Clive the three thousand pounds, which the Ministry had promised him in lieu of his *Nabobical annuity. **1865** *Fortn. Rev.* II. 31 There arose what were known in England as Indian families. These it is true were ridiculed as upstart, *nabobish, and so forth. **1894** *Forum* Aug. 739 He [*sc.* the Englishman] is *nabobishly extravagant in his expenditures upon horse-racing and hunting. **1884** *Homil. Monthly* Aug. 649 The banquets of *nabobism. **1777** M. MORGANN *Ess. Falstaff* 112 At a time when the whole body of the *Nabobry demands and requires defence.

nabobess (ˈneɪbɒbɪs). [f. prec. + -ESS[1].] A female nabob; the wife of a nabob.

1767 STERNE *Lett.* lxxxiii. § 1 He hopes..to see her eclipse all other Nabobesses..in wealth. **1779** BURGOYNE *Maid of the Oaks* IV. i, I will have no nabobs nor nabobesses in my family. **1807** in *Spirit Pub. Jrnls.* XI. 6, I wonder why that old Nabobess, Mrs. Hargrave, left him her immense fortune. **1847** *Mirror* June 354/2 Let me hope the nabobess will give me due notice.

nabobical, -ish(ly, -ism, -ry: see NABOB.

nabobship (ˈneɪbɒbʃɪp). [f. NABOB + -SHIP.]

1. The office or rank of a nabob; the position of being a nabob.

1753 *Lond. Mag.* in *Scots Mag.* Apr. 197/2 Mahomet was restored to the nabobship of Arcot. **1780** ORME *Hist. Indostan* I. 367 A Moorish dress distinguished likewise with ornaments peculiar to the Nabobship. **1808** *Edin. Rev.* XI. 463 The nabobship of the Carnatic has been vested in the present family for more than a half a century. **1876** GRANT *Hist. India* I. xxxii. 168/1 The latter..now succeeded to the nabobship of Oude.

2. The territory over which a nabob exercises jurisdiction; a district governed by a nabob.

1761 *Lond. Mag.* XXX. 183 Every nabob [has] the appointment of all the polygars in his nabobship. **1798** PENNANT *Hindoostan* II. 12 These provinces are now annexed to the great nabobship of the Carnatic. **1862** BEVERIDGE *Hist. India* I. III. ii. 412 Pondicherry..belonged nominally to the nabobship of Arcot.

nabocklish (naˈbɒklɪʃ), *int. Irish dial.* Also **nabochlish, na bocklish, naboklish.** [Ir. *na* not + *bac*, imp. sing. of *bacaim* 'I meddle' + *leis* with it: lit. 'don't meddle with it'.] Never mind! Leave it alone!

1841 C. J. LEVER *Charles O'Malley* I. ii. 10 Arrest him!—na bocklish—catch a weasel asleep. **1843** W. CARLETON *Traits & Stories Irish Peasantry* (new ed.) I. 341 But, *naboklish*! what'll ye have! **1867** P. KENNEDY *Banks of Boro* xxi. 129 But, *nabochlish*, we will find ourselves in the wrong box, maybe. **1917** J. MORLEY *Recollections* II. v. iii. 222 When I hear or read some malicious or injurious word in politics, I find real comfort in saying to myself '*Nabochlish*!' **1939** C. MORLEY *Kitty Foyle* xxix. 285 Like Pop said sometimes, nabocklish! which is Irish for let's not worry too much.

Nabokovian (næbəˈkɒfɪən, nəˈbɒkɒfɪən), *a.* [f. the name *Nabokov* (see below) + -IAN.] Of, pertaining to, resembling, or characteristic of the Russian-born novelist and poet Vladimir Nabokov (1899–1977) or his writings.

1959 *Observer* 1 Nov. 21/6 There is a Nabokovian poignancy in leaving such delicate things to be destroyed, as he says with a rueful smile, 'by such booted people'. **1965** *Times Lit. Suppl.* 28 Jan. 68/4 Mr. Nabokov's *Eugene Onegin* will be read not for the learning. It will be read for the brilliant fireworks of his prose and for the beauty of the Nabokovian phrase. **1968** *Punch* 25 Dec. 932/3 Mr. Stegner chooses instead to invest detail with significance, and he overwrites in truly Nabokovian manner. **1972** *Sat. Rev.* (U.S.) 10 June 68/2, I found myself searching for Nabokovian anagrams in the names. **1975** *Times Lit. Suppl.* 31 Oct. 1285/1 The narrative manner similarly alternates between abruptly functional stage or screen-direction and a Nabokovian obliquity in which words take on an energy of their own and skitter away from the matter in hand.

nabs (næbz). *slang.* Also 9 **knabs.** [Of obscure origin: cf. NIBS.] A term used with possessive pronouns as a slang or jocular designation of a person; ***my nabs*** = 'my gentleman', †myself. Also as *pl.*

a **1790** POTTER *New Dict. Cant, Nabs.* a person of either sex. **1812** J. H. VAUX *Flash Dict., His-nabs,* him, or himself, *Mynabs,* me, myself. **1823** in *Spirit Pub. Jrnls.* 248 Sought out the road where Toley's turnpike lay, And came upon his nabs just as he rose. **1851** MAYHEW *Lond. Labour* III. 149 (Hoppe), Your nabs sparkle my nabs a drop of bevare. **1895** EMERSON *Birds,* etc. 203, I do a bit of stuffing, and as sure as I get gutting a bird, in come my nabs and steal some.

nabut, obs. form of NOBBUT.

nacarat ('nækəræt). [F. *nacarat,* supposed to be ad. Sp. and Pg. *nacarado,* f. *nacar* nacre.

If this etym. is correct, the reference is to that species of pinna which is distinguished by its red colour; but the word has also a striking resemblance to Arab. *nakaʿat,* a red flower used in dyeing.]

1. A bright orange-red colour.

1727–38 CHAMBERS *Cycl.* s.v. *Dying,* Nacarat, or bright orange-red, is given with weld, and goats hair, boiled with potashes. **1839** URE *Dict. Arts* 874. **1853** C. BRONTE *Villette* xxix, A small box I had bought for its brilliancy, made of some tropic shell of the colour called 'nacarat'. **1854** R. H. PATTERSON *Ess. Hist. & Art* (1862) 33 We can never ally mahogany to vivid reds,.. and more particularly to orange-reds, such as scarlet, nacarat, and aurora.

2. (See quot.)

1839 URE *Dict. Arts* 874 The nacarat of Portugal or Bezetta is a crape or fine linen fabric, dyed fugitively of the above tint. **1875** KNIGHT *Dict. Mech.* 1505/1.

†**nacarine,** *a. Obs. rare*$^{-1}$. [f. *nacar-at* (see prec.) + -INE[1].] Red, reddish.

c **1643** LD. HERBERT *Autobiog.* (1886) 165 Every bout tied with a small ribbon of a naccarine, or the colour that the Knights of the Bath wear.

nace, variant of NAIS *a.,* NASE, nose.

nacelle. [a. F. *nacelle*:—late L. *nāvicella* (*naucella*), dim. of *nāvis* a ship.] †**1.** A small boat. *Obs. rare*$^{-1}$.

1483 CAXTON *Gold. Leg.* 141/1 The quene of thys contree wente for to playe on the ryuage of the see and byheld thys lytyl nacelle and the chyld therein.

2. [after the same uses in Fr.] **a.** The basket or gondola of a balloon or airship.

1901 *New Penny Mag.* XII. 440 The 'nacelle', or basket, from which.. the aeronaut directs his operations. **1909** *Aero* 13 July 117/2 The dirigible.. has a screw at either end of the nacelle or cradle. **1932** *Times* 27 May 13/7 The balloon with which the first ascent was made will be used, but a new *nacelle* will be constructed.

b. The cockpit of an aeroplane; hence, any streamlined structure on an aeroplane for housing something, esp. an engine.

1914 *Scotsman* 8 Sept. 2/7 (Advt.), The Henry Farman seaplane is a biplane of the pusher type... The pilot and passenger have comfortable quarters in a nacelle which is built out from the front of the machine. **1915** *War Illustr.* 10 July 494/2 The machine was apparently a gun-carrying 'pusher' biplane of the type in which the gunman sits right out in the nose of the boat-shaped body—or 'nacelle'. **1918** 'AVION' *Aeroplanes & Aero Engines* v. 59 The engine, tanks, crew, controls, and instruments are accommodated in a body known as the 'nacelle', above which the centre section [of the upper wing] is erected in the usual way. **1920** *Blackw. Mag.* Feb. 195/1 The spirit was not entering the tank, but spilling over the sides on to the floor of the nacelle. **1928** C. F. S. GAMBLE *Story N. Sea Air Station* i. 56 They could seat two persons in the covered-in *nacelle,* with the pilot in front. **1935** *Jrnl. R. Aeronaut. Soc.* XXXIX. 267 The full anti-drag rings and nacelle cowls merge into the wing. **1943** W. L. COWLEY *Aerodynamics of Aeroplane* iii. 53 The engine with a tractor propellor is sometimes placed.. in the nose of nacelles or egg-shaped bodies out on the wings. **1973** E. ARNOLD *Proving Ground* xxix. 309 The planes.. upended to show the twin nacelles of P-38s.

c. A similarly shaped structure on or in a motor vehicle.

1959 *Motor* 3 June 603/3 The furnishings belong to the polished walnut school, upon which is superimposed a hooded crackle-finish nacelle in front of the driver containing a full but oddly-framed set of instruments. **1967** E. RUDINGER *Consumer's Car Gloss.* (ed. 2) 71 *Nacelle,..* sometimes used to describe the moulding surrounding a car's lights or dashboard instruments. **1969** *Practical Motorist* Nov. 271/1 Instrumentation is restricted to an oblong speedometer with a small rev-counter perched atop the facia in a separate nacelle. **1970** *Daily Tel.* 7 Apr. 3/1 The Lotus 72's radiator has been moved from the nose and replaced by two smaller radiators mounted in nacelles on the sides of the car.

naceoun, obs. form of NATION.

nach, nâch, variants of NAUTCH.

nache (neɪtʃ). ? *Obs.* Also 7 **nach, natch.** [a. OF. *nache*:—pop. L. **natica,* f. *natis* buttock. Cf. NAGE.] The point of the rump in an ox or cow; the rump. Also ***nache-bone*** = NATCHBONE.

1523 FITZHERB. *Husb.* §57 If thou shalte bye fatte oxen.. se that they be soft.. vpon the hucbone, and the nache by the tayle. **1614** MARKHAM *Cheap Husb.* (1623) 89 Soft huckell bones, and a bigge nach [1668 natch], round and knotty. **1798** A. YOUNG *Ann. Agric.* XXX. 198 (Britten), [The catch or point of the rump is called] The nache in some writers; also the tail points by others. **1799** *View Agric. Lincoln* 299 Breadth of nache, eight inches below the tail setting on, 1 ft. 6 in. **1828** *Craven Gloss., Nache-bone,* rump bone.

Nachee, var. NATCHEZ.

‖**Nachlass** ('naːxlas). [G.] Unpublished writings left by an author after his death.

1842 J. S. MILL *Let.* Apr. in *Wks.* (1963) XIII. 515 She bids me .. to ask what you think of Otfried Müller's Nachlass as a subject for translation. **1948** *Mind* LVII. 382 The argument is supported throughout by cogent evidence from Kant's works. The quotations from the *Nachlass* and the *Opus Postumum* are especially valuable. *Ibid.* 524 It has the advantage of making his lectures far better material for publication than that found in the average professor's *Nachlass.* **1961** D. ROSS in Aristotle *De Anima* 49 The chapter is apparently a series of jottings which an early editor found in Aristotle's *Nachlass,* and put together so that nothing of the Master's should be lost.

Nachschlag ('naːxʃlaːk). *Mus.* [Ger., f. *nach* after + *schlag* blow, note.] A grace note which takes its value from that of the note preceding it.

1879 [see AGRÉMENT 2]. **1880** GROVE *Dict. Mus.* II. 441/2 In the works of the great masters the Nachschlag, though of very frequent occurrence, is almost invariably written out in notes of ordinary size. **1915** A. DOLMETSCH *Interpretation of Music of 17th & 18th Cents.* iv. 255 C. Ph. E. Bach incidentally mentions the *Nachschlag,* but only to condemn it. **1944** W. APEL *Harvard Dict. Mus.* 476/1 The ornamenting notes constitute a melodic movement away from the preceding note, and are to be performed as a part of this... Thus the Nachschlag is the exact opposite of the appoggiatura. **1960** E. BODKY *Interpretation of Bach's Keyboard Works* v. 180 In bar 20 this version leads to ugly parallel fifths, which Landshoff tries to avoid by changing the short appoggiaturas of bars 19 and 20 into *Nachschläge.*

nacht, obs. form of NIGHT, NAUGHT.

‖**Nachtlokal** ('nɑxtlokal). Pl. **nachtlokale.** [G.] A night-club. Also *attrib.*

1939 E. AMBLER *Mask of Dimitrios* v. 95 'She is the proprietress of a *Nachtlokal* called *La Vierge St. Marie.*' '*Nachtlokal*?' He grinned. 'Well, you could call it a night club.' **1954** P. BOTTOME *Against Whom?* xxiii. 173 Konrad, since it was his free evening, would be at a Nacht-Lokal dancing. **1968** D. HOPKINSON *Incense Tree* viii. 94 We went dancing together in the almost total darkness of a *Nachtlokal.* **1970** S. J. PERELMAN *Baby, it's Cold Inside* 227 Some grisly *Nachtlokal* in the Kurfürstendamm.

Nachtmaal: see NAGMAAL.

‖**nacht und nebel** (naxt ʊnt 'neːb(ə)l). [G.] The German for 'night and fog', used, freq. *attrib.,* of a situation characterized by mystery or obscurity.

The name of an infamous decree issued by the Nazis in December 1941.

1947 V. H. BERNSTEIN *Final Judgment* xviii. 240 *Nacht und Nebel* was issued over Hitler's signature, but Keitel issued several covering memoranda and interpretations. Indeed, the name of the Chief of the High Command was so closely identified with the order that it was sometimes referred to as the 'Keitel Decree'. **1963** *Times* 21 Feb. 12/5 This was *Tannhäuser* as a would-be music drama, set in a *Nacht und Nebel* thirteenth-century Germany, peopled by symbols and based on the orchestra. **1968** A. MARIN *Clash of Distant Thunder* (1969) i. 5 The transport camp.. where captured commandos and *Nacht und Nebel* prisoners were isolated. **1971** D. CORY *Sunburst* vi. 100 Country after country going under, disappearing in the mist of *Nacht und Nebel.* **1973** *Listener* 26 July 123/1 The indescribable verbal miasma, exhalations of *Nacht und Nebel,* that is Scientology's contribution to the encyclopaedia of religious knowledge.

nacio(u)n, obs. forms of NATION.

†**nack,** obs. variant of KNACK *sb.*[2]

1676 LADY FANSHAWE *Memoirs* (1829) 192 He sent me a very rich present of perfumes, skins, gloves, and purses embroidered, with other nacks of the same kind. **1747** RICHARDSON *Clarissa* (1811) I. 40 If he gets a nack of visiting her there. **1789** in Hatfield *Notices Doncaster* (1866) I. 82 Corruptors of youth who attend such places with gaming tables, dice, nacks, and other instruments.

†**nack,** obs. variant of KNACK *v.*

1570 FOXE *A. & M.* (ed. 2) 129 In bodkyn wise at him they nacke, They laugh to see him skippe.

nack, obs. variant of NOCK *v.*

nacker, var. KNACKER *sb.*[1]

'**nacket,** *sb.*[1] *Sc.* [app. ad. F. *naquet* 'the boy that serues, or stops the ball.. at Tennis; a.. Tennis Court-keeper's boy' (Cotgr.).]

†**a.** (See etym. note.) *Obs.* **b.** A pert, forward, smart boy.

1500–20 DUNBAR *Poems* xiv. 67 Sa mony rakkettis, sa mony ketche-pillaris, Sic ballis, sic nackettis, and sic tutivillaris. **1833** SANDS *Poems* 121 (E.D.D.), In there comes a little nackit. **1890** 'H. HALIBURTON' *In Scottish Fields* 135 He would rest content with.. referring to him as a 'nacket'.

'**nacket,** *sb.*[2] *Sc.* [var. of *nocket,* of obscure origin, current in Sc. and Northumb.: see *Eng. Dial. Dict.*] A snack or lunch: a slight repast.

1789 DAVIDSON *Seasons* 78 (Jam.). **1821** SCOTT *Pirate* xi, She could not but say, that the young gentleman's nacket looked very good.

'**nacky,** variant of KNACKY *a.*

1803 MARY CHARLTON *Wife & Mistress* III. 57 They're so nacky at winning folk's money. **1824** MISS FERRIER *Inher.* xv, Have you no nice, nacky, little handy work that you could be doing at?

nacoda(r, obs. forms of NAKHODA.

†**nacorne,** var. of NAKER. So †**nacorner,** nakerer. *Obs. rare*$^{-0}$.

c **1440** *Promp. Parv.* 350/1 Nacorne, ynstrument of mynstralsye, *nabulum. Ibid.,* Nacornere, *nabularius.*

nacre ('neɪkə(r)). Also 6 **nackre,** 7 **nacker, nakre,** 7–9 **naker.** [a. F. *nacre,* †*nacle* (1416; cf. med.L. *nacrum,* 1347 in Du Cange) = Sp. and Pg. *nacar,* It. *nacchera,* †*naccara,* med.L. *nacchara, nacara* (1295 in Du Cange), of uncertain, but prob. Oriental, origin.]

1. The pinna or sea-pen, or other shell-fish yielding mother-of-pearl.

1598 FLORIO, *Naccare*... Also the shell-fish which some call a nackre. **1601** HOLLAND *Pliny* IX. xlii. I. 261 The Nacre also called Pinnæ, is of the kind of Shell-fishes. It is.. never without a companion,.. which beareth the Nacre companie. **1658** HOOLE tr. *Comenius' Orb. Sensual.* (ed. 12) 46 The Oyster affordeth sweet meat,.. the Naker, pearls. **1687** A. LOVELL tr. *Thevenot's Trav.* II. 162 Every one of these Barks hath Men for Diving to the bottom of the Sea and picking up the Shell-fish or Nacres. **1727** *Philip Quarll* 188 Polishing the Rest of his Shells, some, as fine as tho' they had been Nakers of Pearl. **1777** PENNANT *Brit. Zool.* IV. 97 *Pinna,* nacre; its animal a Slug. **1834** GOOD *Bk. Nature* II. 17 Among the more elegant of this division is the nacre, pinna, or sea-pen.

attrib. **1605** SYLVESTER *Du Bartas* II. iii. III. (*Lawe*) 699 Tis a Valley paved (else) With golden sands, with Pearle, and Nacre-shels.

2. A smooth, shining, iridescent substance forming the inner layer in many shells; mother-of-pearl.

1718 OZELL tr. *Tournefort's Voy.* I. 178 It is a shining Naker within. **1755** *Gentl. Mag.* XXV. 32 Orient, the fine naker, or mother of pearle colour, which is seen on some shells. **1799** HATCHETT in *Phil. Trans.* LXXXIX. 316 Of the shells composed of nacre or mother of pearl, I selected the oyster. **1811** PINKERTON *Petral.* I. 414 These exquisite colours arise from the laminar naker, or what is commonly called mother-of-pearl, of a kind of nautilus. **1862** ANSTED *Channel Isl.* IV. xxii. 510 The iridescent nacre of the shell was used in this way. **1888** *Contemp. Rev.* May 690 A fine pearl is worth from one to eight pounds sterling a grain according to size, colour, and 'nacre'.

attrib. **1895** C. HOLLAND *Jap. Wife* 61 A flat shell, with lovely mother-of-pearl tints on its nacre hollow.

Hence '**nacred** *a.,* faced with, having the hues of, nacre; '**nacreness,** the qualities of nacre.

1755 *Gentl. Mag.* XXV. 82 This shell.. is finely nakered within. **1845** MACGILLIVRAY *Conchol. Text-bk.* 224 *Nacred,* pearly, perlaceous. **1862** F. HALL *Hindu Philos. Syst.* 169 Cognizing nacreness as the abstract nature of the thing beheld.

nacreous ('neɪkriːəs), *a.* [f. NACRE + -OUS.]

1. Consisting of or resembling nacre in substance.

1836–41 BRANDE *Chem.* 791 When heated, these crystals fuse,.. and, at a red heat, sublime, yielding nacreous scales. **1851** WOODWARD *Mollusca* iv. 38 The nacreous shells are formed by alternate layers of very thin membrane and carbonate of lime. **1875** BLAKE *Zool.* 242 The internal or nacreous stratum of a fossil bivalve shell.

2. Exhibiting the iridescent hues of nacre.

1854 MURCHISON *Siluria* ix. 196 The nacreous lustre of its interior. **1877** *Athenæum* 3 Nov. 572/2 A youth reclining on a cliff, contemplating a fan-like, nacreous mass of cloud. **1899** *Allbutt's Syst. Med.* VIII. 558 The nacreous aspect is preserved, and the affected area may look brilliantly white.

nacrine ('neɪkraɪn), *sb.* and *a.* [f. NACRE + -INE[1] and [4].] **a.** *sb.* The hue of nacre. **b.** *adj.* Of the nature of, belonging to, nacre.

1839–52 BAILEY *Festus* 508 Alternating with azure and all gems—Or as in nacrine blent in one soft blaze. **1862** F. HALL *Hindu Philos. Syst.* 246 Nacrine silver, which is nothing but nacre under the appearance of silver.

nacrite ('neɪkraɪt). *Min.* [f. NACRE + -ITE[1] 2: named by A. Brongniart, 1807.] A mineral occurring in pearly scales.

Thomson's *nacrite* is not the same as Brongniart's.

1808 ALLAN *Mineral Nomencl.* (ed. 2) s.v. **1816** JAMESON *Min.* (ed. 2) I. 524. **1836** T. THOMSON *Min., Geol.,* etc. I. 245 This mineral occurs usually in mica slate, taking the place of the mica; so that the rock.. constitutes a mixture of nacrite and quartz. **1876** HARLEY *Mat. Med.* (ed. 6) 127 Potash is found in most of the alkaline-earthy minerals, as mica, felspar, lepidolite, and nacrite.

nacrous ('neɪkrəs), *a.* [-OUS.] Nacreous.

1835–6 *Todd's Cycl. Anat.* I. 547/1 The shell is white, lined with a nacrous layer within. **1854** BADHAM *Halieutics* 212 The shot lustrous surface of the belly and sides is certainly nacrous.

So **nacry** ('neɪkrɪ), *a. rare.*

1859 RICHARDSON *Yarrell's Brit. Fishes* II. 234 The scales are small... The cheeks nacry and scaleless. *Ibid.* 296 The sands..were covered with its delicate nacry scales.

nacyon(e, obs. forms of NATION.

†**nad, nadde, nade**, had not: see NE and HAVE *v.* A. 9. *Obs.*

The forms are common from *c* 1300 to *c* 1430.
c **1275** LAY. 8013 Wei þat ich nadde bi war. *Ibid.* 19948 Nade Arthur nanne cok þat he nas kempe god. *a* **1300** *Cursor M.* 3281 He nadde rested but a þrowe. **13..** *Gaw. & Gr. Knt.* 724 Nade he ben duȝty..he hade ben ded. ?*a* **1366** CHAUCER *Rom. Rose* 458 She nadde on but a streit old sak. *c* **1400** *Beryn* 3902 Nad Geffrey & his wit ibe, wee had be distroyed. **1440** in *Wars Eng. in France* (Rolls) II. 450 It nad ben possible..but by such moyens. **1480** CAXTON *Chron. Eng.* ccxlii. 282 They wold haue done moche harme..nadde the maire..seced hem with fayre wordes.

‖**nada**[1] ('nɑːdə). *Hinduism.* Also **naad** (nɑːd). [Skr. *nādá* sound.] Inchoate or elemental sound considered as the source of all sounds and as a source of creation; the 'inner' sound of the body.

1913 'A. AVALON' *Tantra of Great Liberation* p. xxiii, It is Nāda..when there is a sound in which there is something like a connected or combined disposition of the letters. **1920** *Encycl. Relig. & Ethics* XI. 93/1 The Sāktas base their doctrines on the assumption that through Śiva and Sakti there is a drop, Bindu, formed which develops into a female element Nāda (sound), containing in itself the names of all things to be created. **1926** *Indian Art & Lett.* II. 79 Nāda as inchoate stressing sound is shown in the form of a crescent-moon on His [*sc.* Siva's] head. **1930** S. N. DASGUPTA *Yoga Philos.* ix. 269 This sound in the stage of pure varṇas is called nāda... But each varṇa vanishes as it is generated, as the sense of hearing has no power to hold them together. **1940** H. E. KENNEDY tr. *Marquès-Rivière's Tantrik Yoga* i. 20 Then there is *Laya Yoga*, based upon the contemplation of the inward parts (nâda), and produced by closing the ears. **1943** D. GASCOYNE *Poems 1937–1942* 50 The incoherent *Nada* of the seer. **1960** SWĀMĪ PRAJÑĀNANANDA *Hist. Dev. Indian Music* ii. 25 The *nāda* or causal sound is the basis or ground of music, and upon this primal ground all the phenomena of Indian music are built. **1960** KOESTLER *Lotus & Robot* I. ii. 99 The last stages before samadhi: the appearance of an 'inner light', and of various 'inner sounds' or nadas. **1968** *Indian Mus. Jrnl.* V. 8 Boundless is the ocean of *Nāda*. **1972** P. HOLROYDE *Indian Music* 274 *Naad* or *Nada*, literally 'resonant sound', but like most Sanskrit words its overtones are more than the literal and precise English. It is much more complex, implying 'vital power'.

‖**nada**[2] ('nada, 'naða). [Sp., = nothing, f. L. (*res*) *nata* thing born; small, insignificant thing.] Nothing; nothingness, non-existence; a state or condition as of non-existence.

1933 E. HEMINGWAY *Winner take Nothing* 23 It was all a nothing and a man was nothing too... He knew it all was nada y pues nada y nada y pues nada. Our nada who art in nada, nada be thy name. **1939** JOYCE *Finnegans Wake* 521 Vurry nothing, O potators... It amounts to nada in pounds or pence. **1947** *Horizon* XV. 160 The sleepless man—the man obsessed by death, by the meaninglessness of the world, by nothingness, by nada—is one of the recurring symbols in the works of Hemingway. **1962** *Spectator* 25 May 685/1 This sense of the endless *nada* lying beyond the phenomenological world. **1966** E. FIGES *Equinox* 145 A mess, or less than a mess: nothing, nichts, nada, niente, rien. **1974** *Punch* 25 Sept. 493/2 *Hudson*: Will there be anything else, old one? *Mr. Bellamy*: Nada, Hudson. Nada y pues nada y nada y pues nada.

nadder, naddre, etc., obs. forms of ADDER.

Na-Dene ('nɑːdə'neɪ). Also **Na-Déné, Nadene.** [f. Athapascan *na* cogn. with Haida *na* to dwell, Tlingit *na* people + Northern Athapascan *Dene* people.] The name given to a North American Indian linguistic family consisting of the Athapascan, Eyak, Haida, and Tlingit languages. Cf. ATHAPASCAN, HAIDA.

1915 E. SAPIR in *American Anthropologist* XVII. 534 (*title*) The Na-Dene languages, a preliminary report. *Ibid.* 535 In all Na-dene languages..a large number of stems is found consisting of consonant plus vowel plus consonant. **1932** W. L. GRAFF *Language & Languages* xi. 431 The most important North American branches: Eskimo,..Na-Dene. **1932** D. JENNESS *Indians of Canada* ii. 20 Philologists..have discovered no kinship among any of the eleven Canadian tongues, unless perhaps between Haida, Tlinkit, and Athapaskan, which Sapir would group together under the name of Nadene. **1954** PEI & GAYNOR *Dict. Linguistics* 143 *Na-Dene*, according to Rivet, a family of North American Indian languages, consisting of the Athapascan, Haida and Tlingit. **1957** *Encycl. Brit.* V. 138/1 The *Nadene* languages, probably the most specialized of all, are tone languages, and, while presenting a superficially 'polysynthetic' aspect, are built up, fundamentally, of monosyllabic elements of prevailingly nominal significance. **1965** *Canad. Jrnl. Linguistics* Spring 96 This would be exemplified, hypothetically, by a discovery that Haida does not belong with the other Na-Dene languages. *Ibid.* 97 Na-Dene..also remains essentially as organized by Sapir. **1968** H.-J. PINNOW in *Internat. Jrnl. Amer. Linguistics* XXXIV. 204 (*title*) Genetic relationship vs. borrowing in Na-Dene. **1970** C. LAIRD *Language in America* (1972) iv. 53 Speakers of Na-Dene..are today found in the lush Pacific Northwest. *Ibid.*, One of the Na-Dene languages.

Naderism ('neɪdərɪz(ə)m). [f. name of Ralph *Nader* (b. 1934), American lawyer + -ISM.] Public agitation for greater safety and higher quality in consumer goods.

1969 *Britannica Bk. of Year* (U.S.) 800/2 *Naderism*, a protest against defective consumer goods in the manner of the American lawyer Ralph Nader. **1970** *Americana Annual* 725 The phenomenon [*sc.* consumerism] was also called 'Naderism', because of the successful crusades of a young lawyer, Ralph Nader, against unsafe automobiles, industrial hazards, and environmental pollution. **1971** *Guardian* 9 Oct. 10/6 While Medawar is sold on Naderism for his own operation..he has not advised the CA to change their style. **1973** *Listener* 22 Mar. 380/2 It need not be doubted that Naderism, like the Civil Rights campaigns..is..religious in character.

nadir ('neɪdə(r)). *Astron.* Also 5 **naddyr**, 7 **nadyr.** [= F., Sp., Pg., and It. *nadir*, ad. Arab. *naḍīr* opposite to, over against (also used as *sb.*). In sense 2 used ellipt. for *naḍīr es-semt* 'opposite to the zenith'.]

†**1.** A point in the heavens diametrically opposite to some other point, esp. to the sun. Const. *of* and *to*. (See also quot. 1727–38.) *Obs.*

c **1391** CHAUCER *Astrol.* II. §6 The nadir of the sonne is thilke degree þat is opposit to the degree of the sonne, in the 7 signe, as thus, euery degree of aries bi ordre is nadir to euery degree of libra by ordre. *Ibid.* §36 þe bygynnyng of the 7 hows is nadir of the Assendent, & the bygynnyng of the 8 hows is nadir of the 2. **1598** SYLVESTER *Du Bartas* II. ii. IV. *Columnes* 644 In what bright starry Signe, th' Almighty dread Daye's Princely Planet's dayly billeted; In which his Nadir is. **1727–38** CHAMBERS *Cycl.* s.v., *Sun's Nadir* is the axis of the cone projected by the shadow of the earth; thus called, in regard that the axis being prolonged, gives a point in the ecliptic diametrically opposite to the sun.

2. The point of the heavens diametrically opposite to the zenith; the point directly under the observer. Also *attrib.*

c **1495** *The Epitaffe*, etc. in Skelton's Wks. 1843 II. 393 Creatures more maddyr In erthe the none wandreth atweene senit and naddyr. **1559** W. CUNNINGHAM *Cosmogr. Glasse* 40 Nadir [under the figure of the globe]. **1593** FALE *Art Dial.* 6 Above C. let Zenith be written, beneath D. Nadir. **1604** R. CAWDREY *Table Alph.* (1613), *Nadir*, the point directly vnder vs opposite to the Zenith. **1625** N. CARPENTER *Geog. Del.* I. v. 103 If the earth..bee placed neere the Nadir or midnight point, they will appeare greater in the East or West. **1727–38** CHAMBERS *Cycl.* s.v. *Zenith*, The nadir is the zenith to our antipodes, as our zenith is the nadir to them. **1815** J. SMITH *Panorama Sc. & Art* I. 516 All circles drawn through the zenith and nadir, are perpendicular to the horizon. *a* **1821** KEATS *Hyperion* I. 276 From the nadir deep Up to the zenith. **1859** TENNYSON *Merlin & V.* 347 May this hard earth cleave to the Nadir hell.

fig. *a* **1631** DONNE *Select.* (1840) 172, I can see him in the nadir, in the lowest dejection, and see how he works upon Joseph in the prison. **1675** TRAHERNE *Chr. Ethics* 408 [Humility] hath a nadir beneath it, a lower point in another heaven. **1693** CONGREVE *Double-Dealer* I. ii, You shall command me from the zenith to the nadir.

†**b.** *nadir to*, directly under. *Obs. rare.*

1634 SIR T. HERBERT *Trav.* 5 Note, that only then, when wee are Nadyr to the Sunne, we have no shadow. *Ibid.* 43 Muskat is a Citie..almost Nadyr to the crabbed Tropique.

3. *transf.* The lowest point (*of* anything); the place or time of greatest depression or degradation.

1793 H. WALPOLE *Let. to H. More* Wks. 1846 VI. 496 The nadir of contempt. **1837** HALLAM *Hist. Lit.* I. i. §4 *note*, The seventh century is the *nadir* of the human mind in Europe. **1865** W. G. PALGRAVE *Arabia* I. 361 The land, then at its very nadir in every respect. **1882** FARRAR *Early Chr.* II. 221 The Jewish and the heathen world, each at the nadir of their degradation and impiety.

attrib. **1814** *Sortes Horatianæ* 63 The black-letter of antiquity..has now, I think, reached its nadir point. **1858** CARLYLE *Fredk. Gt.* III. xvi. (1872) I. 239 This..is about the nadir-point of the Brandenburg-Hohenzollern History.

Hence '**nadiral** *a. rare*[−1]. [F. *nadiral.*]

1891 T. HARDY *Tess* xxv, Its transcendental aspirations..based on the geocentric view of things, a zenithal paradise, a nadiral hell.

nadorite ('nædəraɪt). *Min.* [Named in 1870 from its locality, Djebel *Nador*, in Algeria: see -ITE[1] 2.] A brown chlorantimonate of lead, occurring in orthorhombic crystals.

1872 DANA *Min.* App. I. 11 Nadorite [occurs]..in flattened tabular crystals. **1893** CHAPMAN *Blowpipe Practice* 160 Nadorite... Hitherto found only in calamine deposits.

nadrylle: see ADRYLLE *v.*

†**næ**, occas. ME. variant of NA *conj.*[1] *Obs.*

c **1205** LAY. 9680 Swa..nulle ich nauere mare..næ nauere mare heom senden gauel. *Ibid.* 9686.

nae, Sc. and north. var. of NA or NO, not.

1725 RAMSAY *Gentle Sheph.* I. i, Weel I kend she meant nae as she spak. **1755** R. FORBES *Ajax, Shop-bill* vi, We'll gar him say, he's nae outwitted. **1816** SCOTT *Old Mort.* vii, I see nae sae muckle difference atween the twa ways o't. **1838** HOWITT *Rur. Life* I. 312 I'll nae gie it thee.

nae, Sc. variant of NO *a.* and *adv.*

naebody, Sc. form of NOBODY.

nae-the-less, Sc. form of NATHELESS.

naething, Sc. form of NOTHING.

†**næve.** *Obs.* [ad. L. *næv-us* NÆVUS: cf. obs. F. *neve* (Cotgr.).] A spot or blemish.

1619 SCLATER *Exp. 1 Thess.* (1630) 229 The Image of God ..perhaps in them hath more næues and blemishes. **1649** DRYDEN *Elegy Ld. Hastings* 55 Was there no milder way but the small-pox,.. So many spots, like næves, our Venus soil? *a* **1697** AUBREY *Lives* (1898) II. 182 He was a tall, handsome, and bold man: but his naeve was that he was damnable proud.

nævoid ('niːvɔɪd), *a. Path.* [f. NÆV-US + -OID.] Of the nature of a nævus.

1876 *Trans. Clinical Soc.* IX. 53 The vascular appearance of the tumour..tended to confirm the belief that it was nævoid in character. **1899** J. HUTCHINSON in *Archives Surg.* X. 130 There probably existed somewhere in the vesiculæ a little nævoid or papillary growth.

næ'vose, *a. rare*[−0]. [f. as prec. + -OSE[1].] 'Spotted, freckled' (Webster 1847). So '**nævous** *a.* (*Cent. Dict.* 1890).

‖**nævus** ('niːvəs). *Path.* Also (chiefly *U.S.*) **nevus.** Pl. **nævi** ('niːvaɪ). [L.] A hypertrophied state of the blood-vessels of the skin, forming spots or elevations of a red or purplish colour, usually congenital; a mother's mark, a mole. ***nævus needle***, a surgical needle for removing a nævus (Knight 1884).

[**1693** tr. *Blancard's Phys. Dict.* (ed. 2), *Nævi*, Moles, certain native Spots, and are Two-fold, either plain, or protuberant. **1706** PHILLIPS (ed. Kersey), *Nævus*, a Mole, a natural Mark or Spot in the Body.] **1835–6** *Todd's Cycl. Anat.* I. 242/2 If the common mole be admitted under this class of nævi. *Ibid.* 243/1 The..characteristic of the third form of nævus. **1876** DUHRING *Dis. Skin* 41 Permanent vascular growths in the skin, as nævi. **1899** *Allbutt's Syst. Med.* VIII. 826 A nævus is a new growth consisting of a congeries of dilated freely communicating vessels, held together by connective tissue. **1913** *Jrnl. Amer. Med. Assoc.* 1 Feb. 341/1 (*heading*) Melanotic sarcomas resulting from irritation of pigmented nevi. **1961** R. D. BAKER *Essent. Path.* xx. 545 The word nevus has been used to designate skin blemishes of various sorts including 'birthmarks', but in current usage nevus means the ordinary mole of the skin. **1971** *Brit. Med. Bull.* XXVII. 69/1 Trivial congenital defects such as..pigmented or vascular naevi.

naf, have not: see HAVE *v.* A. 9.

naf(e, naff(e, obs. or dial. forms of NAVE.

†**naff(e.** *Obs. rare*[−0]. [Of obscure origin.] Some water-bird.

1570 LEVINS *Manip.* 9/17 A Naffe, a birde, *vria*. **1678** LITTLETON *Lat.-Eng. Dict.*, *Vria*, a bird called a naff. Naff, *mergus cirrhatus*.

naff (næf), *v. slang.* [Of uncertain origin: Partridge links the word tentatively with old backslang *naf* = *fan* (the female genitals: see FANNY[4] 2). Cf. EFF *v.* (perh. with metanalysis).] *intr.* A euphemistic substitution for FUCK *v.* Freq. used *imp.* with *off*: 'go away'.

1959 K. WATERHOUSE *Billy Liar* ii. 37 Naff off, Stamp, for Christ sake! **1975** CLEMENT & LA FRENAIS *Porridge* 63 'It's all been arranged, it's all set up, right? So naff off', I said. **1977** —— *Further Stir of Porridge* 178, I restrained him with an iron grip to the wrist. 'Naff off!' **1977** *Sounds* 9 July 16/1 Ain't never seen no dole queue, So naff off. **1977** *Custom Car* Nov. 30/1 'Go and get yourself naffed, you chauvinistic, capitalistic leper,' she rejoined sweetly, poking both index fingers into his eyes. **1982** *Sunday Times* 18 Apr. 1/4 Princess Anne..lost her temper with persistent photographers and told them to 'naff off'. **1985** S. LOWRY *Young Fogey Handbk.* ii. 30 'Salute'..does not mean naffing about in a tutu.

Hence '**naffing** *ppl. a.*, used as an intensive.

1959 K. WATERHOUSE *Billy Liar* 46 Well which one of them's got the naffing *engagement* ring? **1976** CLEMENT & LA FRENAIS *Another Stretch of Porridge* 16 Stealing your tin of naffing pineapple chunks? Not even my favourite fruit.

naff (næf), *a. slang.* [Origin unknown: app. not related to prec.

Cf. north. dial. *naffhead, naffin, naffy* 'a simpleton; a blockhead; an idiot' (*Eng. Dial. Dict.*); *niffy-naffy* adj. 'inconsequential, stupid' (*Gloss. Whitby* 1876); Sc. *nyaff* 'a term of contempt for any unpleasant or objectional person' (*Scot. Nat. Dict.*).]

Unfashionable, outmoded, or vulgar; unselfconsciously lacking style, socially inept; also, worthless, faulty, 'dud'.

1969 *It* 13–25 June 16/4 A lot of these bands are pretty naff anyway. **1970** *Sunday Tel.* (Brisbane) 22 Feb. 92/1, I have been to no less than three parties in the past two weeks which rejoiced in the naffest bit of social intercourse it has been my misfortune to witness. **1977** *Record Mirror* 17 Sept. 9/2 A really naff song that wouldn't get anywhere without Ringo's name on it. **1982** L. CODY *Bad Company* ii. 13 No electricity. .. I think it's just a naff battery connection. **1983** *Sunday Tel.* 21 Aug. 11/3 It is naff to call your house The Gables, Mon Repos, or Dunroamin'. **1985** *Times* 26 Mar. 11/1 Gaultier had turned everything that fashion most despises, what English youth calls 'naff', into high style.

Naffy, var. N.A.A.F.I.

nafre, obs. form of NEVER.

nag (næg), *sb.*[1] Forms: α. 5–7 **nagge**, 6–8 **nagg**, 5– **nag.** β. *north.* and *Sc.* 5–7 **nage**, 6– **naig** (neːg). γ. **neg.** [Of obscure origin: the corresponding Du. *neg* or *negge* has not been found earlier than Kilian, who gives 'Negghe *Holl. Fris.* Mannus, equus pumilus. *Ang.* nagghe'.]

1. A small riding horse or pony.

α. *c* **1400** *Destr. Troy* 7727 He neyt as a nagge, at his nose thrilles. *c* **1440** *Promp. Parv.* 350/1 Nagge, or lytylle beest, *bestula, equillus*. *c* **1489** CAXTON *Sonnes of Aymon* v. 133 He wente to Kyng Yons courte vpon a lytyll nagge. **1509** HAWES *Past. Pleas.* XXXII. (Percy Soc.) 157 Thus Correction, with her whyp did dryve The litle nagge. **1535** *Act 27 Hen. VIII*, c. 6 §1 Horses and nagges of small stature and value. **1598** BARRET *Theor. Warres* V. ii. 143 A pretie light horse, such as be our Northerne nagges. **1617** MORYSON *Itin.* I. 56 They have very little horses in these parts to draw the Waggons, like to the galloway nags of Scotland. **1641** BROME *Joviall Crew* IV. i, I prethee, good Friend, let our Nags be set up. **1709** PRIOR *Let. to Sir T. Hanmer* 4 Aug., If at Rischam fair any pretty nagg.. presented himself. **1732** BOLINGBROKE *Let. to Swift* 18 July, Get on Pegasus.. or mount the white nag in the Revelation. **1810** *Sporting Mag.* XXXVI. 232 The unequalled goodness of the English nag. **1840** DICKENS *Barn. Rudge* i, His nag gone lame in riding out here. **1879** BROWNING *Martin Relph* 130 Lend to a King's friend here your nag!

fig. *a* **1764** LLOYD *Fam. Ep.* Poet Wks. 1774 II. 58 As a plain nag, in homely phrase, I'll.. make a trot in easy rhime.

β. **1464** *Mann. & Househ. Exp.* (Roxb.) 195 Reynold Morgan on a bay nage of myn. **1471** *Paston Lett.* III. 12 That the horse may be kept well, .. and that Jakys nage have mete i-now also. **1532** *Test. Ebor.* (Surtees) VI. 34 Unto my moder a bay nage. **1572** *Satir. Poems Reform.* xxxii. 18 With our Naiggis to gane [= go] to Edinburgh. **1648** *Hamilton Papers* (Camden) 150 That litell nage that I was bringinge for the Prince. *a* **1774** FERGUSSON *Plainstanes & Cawsey* Poems (1845) 47 Whinstanes houkit frae the Craigs May thole the prancin feet o' naigs. **1785** BURNS *Ep. to J. Lapraik* II. ii, Dealing thro' amang the naigs Their ten-hours bite. **1814** SCOTT *Wav.* xxx, The casualties whilk may befall the puir naig while in your honour's service. **1887** SERVICE *Life Dr. Duguid* 260 Saddling his naig he sallied oot to seek her.

γ. *a* **1734** NORTH *Lives* (1826) I. 288 They [in Northumberland] were a comical sort of people, riding upon negs, as they call their small horses.

†**b.** *transf.* as a term of abuse. *Obs.*

1598 MARSTON *Sco. Villanie* B 2 Hence lewd nags away, Goe read each poast, .. Then to Priapus gardens. *Ibid.* E vii b, The witlesse sence Of these odde naggs, whose pates circumference Is fild with froth! **1606** SHAKS. *Ant. & Cl.* III. x. 10 Yon ribaudred Nagge of Egypt.. Hoists Sailes, and flyes.

2. *attrib.* and *Comb.*, as ***nag-bell***, ***-colt***, ***horse***, ***-tail***; also ***nag-tailed*** adj.

1619 in Ferguson & Nanson *Munic. Rec. Carlisle* (1887) 277 Mr. Maior.. shall call for.. the horse and nage bells with all expedytion. **1710** *Lond. Gaz.* No. 4701/4 Stoln or stray'd.., a brown Bay Nag-Colt. **1769** *Stratford Jubilee* I. i. 8 With relays of your nag-tailed bays. **1791** GILPIN *Forest Scenery* II. 256 The short dock everywhere disappeared... The nag-tail however still continued in use. *Ibid.*, The nag-tail is still seen in all genteel carriages. **1816** *Sporting Mag.* XLVIII. 239 A fall of 50*l.* per cent. has taken place in nag and hack horses.

nag, *sb.*[2], occas. variant of KNAG *sb.*[1]

a **1775** *Jock o' the Side* viii. in Child *Ballads* III. 481 They cut a tree with fifty nags [*v.r.* snags] upo' each side For to clim Newcastle wall.

nag (næg), *sb.*[3] [f. next.] The act of nagging; irritating language.

1894 *Westm. Gaz.* 26 Nov. 2/1 Its correspondent.. quotes in support a counter piece of nag in some German *Standard.* **1895** *Daily News* 14 Mar. 5/2 There is not a trace of 'nag' in their rejoinders. **1971** J. GARDNER *Every Night's a Bullfight* ix. 261 They had covered all their separate problems, yet the nag in Douglas's mind left him edgy about the box office situation. *Ibid.* x. 293 The added knowledge served to compound his growing nag of worry.

nag (næg), *v.* Also **nagg, knag, gnag.** [Orig. a dialect word, and prob. of Scand. origin: cf. Norw. and Sw. *nagga* (obs. Da. *nagge*) to gnaw, bite, nibble; to vex, irritate; to be painful (Færöese *nagga* to rub; obs. Icel. *nagga*, ? to complain), with the related sb. *nagg* (Da. *nag*) gnawing, remorse, rancour, pain, etc.

A LG. *naggen* in the sense 'to irritate, provoke, etc.' is also recorded in the 15th c. (in *Teuthonista*), and appears (along with *gnaggen*) to be still in use. In some northern Eng. dialects a variant *naig* (*knaig, gnaig*), recorded from 1781 onwards, occurs in the same senses as *nag*.]

1. *dial.* **a.** *trans.* and *intr.* To gnaw, to nibble.

1825 BROCKETT *N.C. Gloss.*, *Nag*, to gnaw at anything hard. **1854** MISS BAKER *Northampt. Gloss.* s.v., The child likes to gnag at a crust. **1869** *Lonsdale Gloss.*, *Nag*, to natter or nibble as a mouse. **1876** *Mid-Yorksh. Gloss.* s.v., Give t' dog a bone to nag.

b. *intr.* To keep up a dull gnawing pain; to ache persistently.

1836 [see NAGGING *ppl. a.* 1]. **1879** [see 4]. **1886** *Cheshire Gloss.* s.v., 'How's your face, now?' 'Well, it nags a bit'.

2. a. To be persistently worrying or irritating by continued fault-finding, scolding, or urging.

1828 *Craven Gloss.*, *Knag*, to wrangle, to quarrel, to raise peevish objections. **1859** B. JERROLD *Life Jerrold* 216 The servant writes.. to know whether Mrs. Squaw nags. **1863** *Sat. Rev.* 3 Oct., Man was formed to bully, as woman was formed to nag. **1880** SPURGEON *Ploughm. Pict.* 112 If they are always nagging and grumbling they will lose their hold of their children.

b. Const. *at* a person, etc.

1857 SIR F. PALGRAVE *Norm. & Eng.* II. 706 He was constantly.. knagging at Richard's power and prosperity. **1865** TROLLOPE *Belton Est.* xvii. 203 It's no good my mother nagging at me. **1894** BIRRELL *Ess.* xviii. 208 Authors and critics cannot help nagging at one another.

3. a. *trans.* To assail or annoy (a person) with persistent fault-finding or provocation; to irritate with continuous urging to something. Also *transf.* and *fig.*

1840 SPURDENS *Suppl. Forby* s.v., They tew mawthers are ollost nagging one another. **1849** ALB. SMITH *Pottleton Legacy* xxii, Not having anybody to abuse directly, they began to knag their brother. **1861** DIXON *Bacon* x. §9 When she again goes home to Westwood Park she nags and frets Sir John. **1874** LISLE CARR *Jud. Gwynne* I. iii. 75 In spite of his heroic stolidity and equanimity even when being nagged to desperation. **1921** *Challenge* 28 Oct. 375/1 He nags his brain into a state of consuming doubt, but dares not arrive at any conclusion. **1958** L. DURRELL *Balthazar* viii. 172 As I examined him a phone started to nag somewhere. **1960** *Times* 20 June 4/2 Laver, a fighter still nagged by his shoulder. **1963** *Times* 4 Mar. 5/1 Barrington was a little out of sorts with himself, and after Yuile.. had tied him down by curling the ball into the wind, Reid nagged him out. **1969** *Listener* 6 Mar. 324/1, I am told that R. P. Blackmur used to give a lecture on Jane Austen in which he explored her work in terms of the verb 'to nag' ('she nags out her plots').

b. To wear *out* by nagging.

1870 VERNEY *L. Lisle* xxvii, To have a tongue to nagg folk's lives out.

4. Used with repetition of the stem-syllable to express the persistency of the action.

1860 THACKERAY *Lovel* iii. 88 Is it pleasing to.. have your wife nagnagging you because she has not been invited..? **1879** MISS JACKSON *Shropsh. Word-bk.* s.v., The tuth-ache .. kep' nag, nag, naggin'.. till about four o'clock.

naga[1] ('nɑːgə). *India.* [Skr. *nāgá* serpent, snake.] In Hindu mythology, one of a race of serpent-demons, the offspring of Kadru and the sage Kasyapa, supposed to be the guardians of Patala or the regions under the earth.

1785 C. WILKINS tr. *Bhăgvăt-Gēētā* 151 The *Nāgs* are serpents fabled with many heads. **1810** E. MOOR *Hindu Pantheon* 391 On the other side of Nandi, or the bull, is Naga; his hooded head upreared; his length coiled under him. **1821** J. LEYDEN tr. *Malay Annals* ii. 21 'Make no noise,' said Malin, 'it is some great snake or naga.' **1828** H. H. WILSON in *Asiatick Researches* XVI. 462 Kulika is one of the eight chiefs of the *Nágas*, or serpents of *Pátála*. **1832** C. COLEMAN *Mythol. of Hindus* I. xiii. 254 The fifth lunar day of Sravana is held sacred to the Nagas. **1875** MONIER-WILLIAMS *Indian Wisdom* xiv. 430 All the Nāgas are described as having jewels in their heads. **1909** *Encycl. Relig. & Ethics* II. 809/1 Nāgas are figured on numberless sculptures all over India, and in popular tales they and their beautiful daughters play an important part. **1948** P. J. THOMAS *Epics, Myths & Legends of India* (ed. 3) x. 86 The Nagas are said to be.. mortal enemies of their half-brother Garuda. **1967** V. IONS *Indian Mythol.* 117/2 The Nagas called upon Vishnu to save them, and he descended to Patala in the form of Narmada (personification of a river). **1968** B. WALKER *Hindu World* II. 388 The Nāgas possess secrets little dreamt of by creatures living on the surface, and theirs is a realm of magic and magnificence.

Naga[2] ('nɑːgə). *India.* [a. Hindi *naṅga*, f. Skr. *nagná* cogn. w. NAKED *a.*] A naked mendicant belonging to any Hindu sect, *spec.* such an ascetic belonging to a Dadu Panthi subsect whose members are allowed to carry arms and serve as mercenaries.

1828 H. H. WILSON in *Asiatick Researches* XVI. 80 The *Dádu Pant'his* are of three classes... The *Nágas*, who carry arms, which they are willing to exercise for hire, and, amongst the Hindu princes, they have been considered as good soldiers. *Ibid.* 135 Nagas. All sects include a division under this denomination... They carry their secession from ordinary manners so far as to leave off every kind of covering. **1879** *Rajputana Gazetteer* II. 147 The Nágas of Jaipur are a sect of militant devotees belonging to the Dádu Panthi sect, who are enrolled in regiments to serve the State; they are vowed to celibacy and to arms. **1917** *Encycl. Relig. & Ethics* IX. 123/1 All these Jaipur Nāgās are vowed to celibacy, and their numbers are replenished by children placed by parents under their charge as disciples. **1939** C. VON FÜRER-HAIMENDORF *Naked Nagas* i. 7 A learned Brahmin.., when I told him of my plans to work among the Nagas, thought that I wanted to study people whose nakedness had religious grounds.

Naga[3] ('nɑːgə). *India.* [Of disputed origin: perh. f. Skr. *nága* mountain or f. Skr. *nagná* naked.] **a.** A member of a group of peoples living mainly in the Naga hills which divide Assam from Burma; a native or inhabitant of Nagaland. Also *attrib.* **b.** The Tibeto-Burman language of these tribes.

1837 J. M'COSH *Topography of Assam* xiv. 156 The next border tribes met with in proceeding westward are the Nagas... The Nagas go literally naked in their hills. **1841** W. ROBINSON *Descr. Acct. Asam* 380 The origin of the word Naga is unknown; but it has been supposed by some to have been derived from the Sanskrit.. and applied in derision to the people, from the paucity of their clothing. **1853** *Jrnl. Indian Archipelago* VII. 55 Several of the adjacent languages —Kyen, Heuma, Naga &c., have *v, f*, or both. **1872** *Jrnl. Asiatic Soc. Bengal* XLI. I. 84 The Rájah had first intended to fly to the Nága Hills, but from fear of our army, the Nágás would not afford him an asylum. **1890** KIPLING *Barrack-Room Ballads* (1892) 17 We've chivied the Naga an' Looshai, we've give the Afreedeeman fits. **1903** [see KACHIN]. **1928** C. DAWSON *Age of Gods* ix. 195 Assam and Manipur, where a degraded form of megalithic culture still survives among the Naga and Kachin tribes. **1939** C. VON FÜRER-HAIMENDORF *Naked Nagas* i. 7, I left Viceregal Lodge enriched.. in my knowledge of Naga cuisine. **1964** R. PERRY *World of Tiger* xiv. 207 A man-eater.. killed fifty-two Nagas in eight months. **1971** N. RUSTOMJI *Enchanted Frontiers* xvi. 257 At a mammoth meeting held by the Nagas at Mokokchung in October 1959, known as the Third Naga People's Convention, a demand was formulated for the constitution of the Naga hills as a new State within the Indian Union, to be named Nagaland. **1972** PRAKASH SINGH *Nagaland* i. 9 The appellation 'Naga' was quite foreign to the Nagas themselves until very recent times... The appellation 'Naga' was actually given to these hill tribes by the plains people. **1973** *Times* 14 Nov. 18/3 The Nagas are a group of 20 tribes of Sino-Tibetan origin, now numbering about half a million.

‖**nagaika** (nə'gaɪkə). Pl. **-kas, -ki.** [Russ., of Turkic origin.] A thick plaited whip used by Cossacks.

1842 tr. *J. G. Kohl's Russia* 410 The genuine Cossack of the steppe.. depends only on his well plaited *nagaika* or whip, with which he rarely fails to cut down a wolf, as with a sabre. **1914** N. JARINTZOFF *Russia: Country of Extremes* vii. 202 The *nagaiki* flashed in the air, heavily lashing people's faces. **1917** *Daily Chron* 22 June 1/4 The Cossacks.. drove off the agitators from the station with their nagaikas. **1928** F. UTLEY tr. *Astrov's Illustr. Hist. Russ. Rev.* I. x. 69 An old, grey-haired police officer.. gave the command: 'Charge with the *nagaikas!*' (whips).

nagana (nə'gɑːnə). [ad. Zulu *nakane.*] A disease of domestic animals in southern Africa, characterized by fever, lethargy, and œdematous swellings, and caused by the hæmoflagellate parasite *Trypanosoma brucei* which is transmitted by tsetse flies of the genus *Glossina*. Also *attrib.*

1895 D. BRUCE (*title*) Preliminary report on the tsetse fly-disease, or nagana, in Zululand. **1896** *Nature* 16 Apr. 567/1 Nagana pursues a much slower course in cattle than in horses. **1904** *Q. Rev.* July 120 The 'fly districts' where nagana disease is rife. **1904** *Brit. Med. Jrnl.* 20 Aug. 368 Nuttall of Cambridge.. experimented on the conveyance of the nagana trypanosome from sick to healthy animals. **1925** *Times* 29 Dec. 11/3 It was believed that wild game.. formed a permanent reservoir from which tsetses could convey 'nagana' to domestic stock. **1931** J. S. HUXLEY *What dare I Think?* i. 33 Human sleeping sickness and nagana disease of cattle, [are] transmitted by tsetse-flies. **1947** [see *horse-sickness* (HORSE *sb.* 28 a)]. **1965** *New Scientist* 26 Aug. 504/3 Wild game don't suffer from nagana, the tsetse-borne trypanosome disease that disastrously affects domestic cattle. **1970** JUBB & KENNEDY *Pathol. Domestic Animals* (ed. 2) I. iv. 324/1 *Trypanosoma brucei* is a cause of nagana in most domestic species in Africa, but man is refractory.

nagare, -ere, obs. forms of AUGER *sb.*[1]

‖**Nagari** ('nɑːgəriː), *a.* Also 8 **nagree, naagoree,** 9 **nagaree, naguree.** = DEVANAGARI (q.v.).

1776 *Trial of Nundocomar* 9/1, I have likewise.. a Nagree letter of attorney. **1786** SIR W. JONES *Let.* 27 Feb. *Mem.* (1835) II. 55 The characters.. are little more than the *nagari* letters inverted and rounded. **1846** J. T. THOMSON *Hindee Dict.* Pref. p. iii, A delay in preparing the Naguree types prevented its publication. **1872** MONIER-WILLIAMS *Sanskrit Dict.* Pref. 18 *note*, The present form of Nāgarī is thought to be little older than the tenth or eleventh century. **1891** *Jrnl. Asiatic Soc. Bengal* LIX. I. 81 Two very distinct classes of the ancient Nágari alphabet.

na-gat, obs. Sc. form of NO-GATE.

†**nage.** *Obs. rare*[−1]. [a. OF. *nage*, var. *nache*: see NACHE.] The buttock.

c **1320** LANGTOFT *Chron.* (Rolls) II. 248 The fote folk Put the Scottes in the polk And nackened thair nages.

nagelfluh ('nɑːgəlfluː). *Geol.* Also 9 **nagelflue,** and with capital initial. Pl. **-fluhe.** [a. G. *nagelfluh*, f. *nagel* NAIL *sb.* + Swiss Ger. *fluh* (S. Ger. dial. *flüe*) rock face.] A massive conglomerate which accompanies the molasse in the Swiss Alps and contains pebbles supposed to look like nail-heads.

1808 R. JAMESON *Syst. Mineral.* III. ix. 210 Nagelfluh. —This rock is usually composed of fragments of limestone, more or less rounded, and of various magnitudes, cemented together by a basis of calc-sinter. **1849** *Q. Jrnl. Geol. Soc.* V. 229 If the masses of nagelflue which constitute the Rigi mountain near Lucerne, and the still loftier Speer.. near Wesen be included in one group, their thickness must be enormous, certainly exceeding 6000 or 8000 feet. **1879** *Encycl. Brit.* X. 321/2 The well-known nagelflue of Switzerland.. can be shown from its fossil contents to be essentially a lacustrine formation. **1912** T. G. BONNEY *Building of Alps* i. 25 The gravels, the so-called Nagelfluhe, are occasionally fully a mile in thickness. **1962** L. C. KING *Morphology of Earth* iv. 98 The presence of conglomerates and breccias grading into arkoses shows the rapid erosion of adjacent highlands... Thus arose the coarse *Nagelfluh* outwash of the Alps which passes northward into finer grades of sediment.

nagged (nægd), *ppl. a.* [-ED[1].] That is subject to nagging. Hence, downtrodden, wearied, irritated, annoyed.

1893 K. D. WIGGIN *Polly Oliver's Problem* ix. 107 Existence was wearing a particularly dismal aspect on that afternoon... He felt 'nagged', injured, blue, out of sorts with fate. **1961** M. SPARK *Prime of Miss Jean Brodie* ii. 35 'Mary, don't you *want* to walk tidily?' 'Mary,' said Sandy, 'stop staring at the brown man.' The nagged child looked numbly at Sandy and tried to quicken her pace.

nagger ('nægə(r)). [-ER[1].] One who nags.

1881 *Spectator* 22 Jan. 109 The Irish are naggers. **1895** *Daily Tel.* 17 Jan. 5/3 Naggers always labour under imaginary grievances.

naggin, variant of NOGGIN.

nagging ('nægɪŋ), *vbl. sb.* [f. NAG *v.* + -ING[1].] The action of the verb; persistent annoyance, irritation, or fault-finding.

1855 SMEDLEY *H. Coverdale* lix, A process termed in the patois of.. kitchens.. 'nagging'. **1864** MISS YONGE *Trial* vii, His grumbling remarks.. too often.. were that sort of censure that is expressively called knagging. **1896** HARE *Story of my Life* I. ii. 167 Fits of naughtiness.. caused by the incessant 'nagging' I received.

nagging ('nægɪŋ), *ppl. a.* [f. NAG *v.* + -ING².] **1.** Of pain: Gnawing, aching persistently. Also of thirst.
1836 MRS. SHERWOOD *Henry Milner* III. iv, A person enduring a nagging tooth-ache. **1847** HALLIWELL, *Nagging-pain*, a slight but constant pain, as the toothache. **1906** E. DYSON *Fact'ry 'Ands* vi. 67 He sighed frequently; his nagging thirst got at him again.

2. a. Persistently annoying by petty fault-finding or irritation.
1869 MRS. HEATON *Dürer* I. iii. (1881) 61 A nagging tongue in a woman is not of such rare occurrence. **1874** LISLE CARR *Jud. Gwynne* I. i. 15 No nagging wife,..no chance of visitors. **1894** J. KNIGHT *Garrick* xiv. 274 Her letters are..those of a jealous, conceited, nagging woman.

b. Of the nature or character of nagging.
1883 *Congregationalist* Dec. 1036 A..disposition to a nagging criticism. **1884** SHARMAN *Hist. Swearing* iii. 41 They may place nagging obstacles in the way of its career. **1946** W. S. MAUGHAM *Then & Now* xxviii. 162 He had not the strength to withstand the nagging arguments of the others. **1953** R. MACAULAY *Let.* 11 Aug. (1961) 106, I think nagging doubts..would always from time to time raise their heads and disturb.

Hence **'naggingness.**
1898 *Daily News* 9 Nov. 8/4 Your remarks..are not a whit too strong, as her naggingness is becoming unbearable.

naggingly ('nægɪŋlɪ), *adv.* [f. NAGGING *ppl. a.* + -LY².] In a nagging or insistent way; in a persistently irritating, annoying, or exhausting manner.
1936 P. FLEMING *News from Tartary* vi. 98 Things had gone quietly, naggingly against us all the way. **1951** M. LEINSTER in D. Knight *100 Yrs. Sci. Fiction* (1969) 209 Haynes wished he could talk with him once more—talk sensibly, quietly, without..this naggingly demanding wonderment.

'naggish, *a.*¹ Also kn-. [f. NAG *v.* + -ISH.] Of a nagging character or type.
1885 J. W. EBSWORTH *Roxb. Ball.* V. 323 A knaggish persistence, as of a scolding but coquettish vixen.

naggish ('nægɪʃ), *a.*² [f. NAG *sb.*¹ + -ISH¹.] Of horses: suggestive of a nag; small, inferior.
a **1800** *Spirit Farmer's Museum* (1801) 204, I see some here in gay coats, mounted on naggish horses.

naggle ('næg(ə)l), *sb.* [f. the vb.] Pettiness.
1865 *Pall Mall G.* 8 Apr. 7 In these days of niggle and naggle, its force is apt to be miscalled coarseness by critics of a particular school.

naggle ('næg(ə)l), *v.* Also *dial.* gn-. [Frequentative of NAG *v.*] *intr.* To gnaw; to nag, quarrel, haggle, etc. Hence **'naggling** *vbl. sb.*
1869 *Lonsdale Gloss., Naggle*, to gnaw. **1884** *Manch. Exam.* 28 May 5/7 When..Lord Salisbury began to naggle about days [etc.]. **1884** HAWLEY *Wit, Wisdom & Philos. Richter* 114 Frivolous, giddy man needs some powerful shock to counteract his tendency to continual petty naggling. **1897** *Daily News* 5 July 3/4 They seemed to have been quarrelling and naggling a great deal.

† **'naggon.** *Obs. rare*⁻¹. = NAG *sb.*¹
1630 J. TAYLOR (Water-P.) *Wks.* (N.), Wert thou George with thy naggon, That foughtst with the draggon.

naggy ('nægɪ), *sb.* Also *Sc.* 8–9 **naigie** ('negɪ), 8 **nagie.** [dimin. of NAG *sb.*¹: see -IE, -Y.] A small nag, a pony. (See also *Shank's naggy*.)
1784 *Dick o' the Cow* lxii. in Child *Ballads* III. 468 Here is a white-footed nagie. **1793** BURNS *Bonnie Jean* ii, He had owsen, sheep, and kye, And wanton naigies nine or ten. **1828** *Sporting Mag.* XXI. 286 A black naggy, with a tail much longer than his height. **1894** BLACKMORE *Perlycross* 64 Then the naggie put his foot down.

naggy ('nægɪ), *a.*¹ Also kn-. [f. NAG *v.* + -Y¹.] Given to nagging; also *dial.* ill-natured, bad-tempered.
1697 CLELAND *Collect. Poems* 96 Their knaggie talking did up barme him, Their sharp reflections did much warm him. **1825** BROCKETT *N.C. Gloss., Knaggy*, testy, ill-humoured. *Ibid., Naggy*, irritable. **1855** A. MANNING *O. Chelsea Bunho.* xx. 326, I..wondered what on earth could have made me so knaggy and upsettish. **1887** *S. Cheshire Gloss.* s.v., That woman..is so naggy wi' everybody as gos near her.

naggy ('nægɪ), *a.*² [f. NAG *sb.*¹ + -Y¹.] Of horses: inferior in size or quality; naggish.
a **1861** T. WINTHROP *John Brent* (1883) vii. 54 The little villain's mount was a red roan, a Flat-head horse, rather naggy, but perfectly hardy and wiry.

nagher(e, varr. NAWER, nowhere. *Obs.*

naght, naȝt(e, obs. ff. NAUGHT, NIGHT *sb.*

naghtertale, obs. form of NIGHTERTALE.

‖**Nagmaal** ('naxma:l). *S. Afr.* Also **Nagtmaal, Nachtmaal.** [Afrikaans *nagmaal* (Du. *nachtmaal*), f. *nag* (Du. *nacht*) night + *maal* meal.] The Lord's Supper, or Holy Communion; also the Communion service, or the occasion on which the service is held.
1835 A. STEEDMAN *Wanderings S. Afr.* I. 184 During '*naacht-maal*' (the administration of the Lord's Supper,) the village becomes a scene of great bustle and activity. **1842** R. GODLONTON *Sk. Eastern Districts Cape G.H.* 50 The period for the quarterly administration of the sacrament, (or *nachtmaal*). **1852, 1871** [see DUTCH *a.* 2 b]. **1916** J. BUCHAN *Greenmantle* iii. 35 It was as slow as a vrouw coming from nachtmaal. **1925** *British Weekly* 25 Nov. 182/1 Shy young Dutchmen in 'nachtmaal' clothes. **1930** R. CAMPBELL *Adamastor* 23 The baboons..all their Simian dignity forgot Would hold a sort of Nagmaal on the spot. **1945** *Cape Argus* 7 Aug., The accident occurred while the..family were on their way to Nagmaal on Sunday. **1948** *Ibid.* 5 June (Mag. Sect.) 2/4 At nagtmaal the farmers drove in from miles around and opened up their little dorp dwellings. **1953** *Cape Times* 15 Apr. 13/4 They would be utter fools to put her there in broad daylight at *Nagmaal* time. **1974** *Sunday Times* (S. Afr.) 24 Nov. 5 Seldom-worn black suits bought decades before to last a lifetime of weddings, Nagmaals and funerals.

nagnail, dial. variant of AGNAIL.

Nago ('nɑ:gəʊ). [f. Ewe *anagó* a Yoruba Negro.] **a.** A member of an African Negro people, originally Yoruba-speaking, of whom many were taken to the Americas as slaves. **b.** The language of this people, now applied *spec.* to the lingua franca or pidgin form spoken by this people in Brazil. Also *attrib.* or as *adj.*
1775 *Jamaica Gaz.* 25 Mar., [A man] of the Nago country ..says his master died when he was a boy and has been run-away ever since. **1793** B. EDWARDS *Hist. Brit. Colonies in W. Indies* II. 73 Many of the Whidah Negroes are found to be circumcised... It is practised universally by the Nagoes. **1825** R. BICKELL *W. Indies* 43 Frank, a Nago, 5 ft 7¼ in. no brand-mark, country marks on his face. **1942** D. PIERSON *Negroes in Brazil* iii. 73 It is likely that Nagô was not maintained in a pure form but came to be a patois containing numerous elements from other African dialects as well as from Portuguese. **1949** *Caribbean Quarterly* I. i. 11, 33 were Nagoes..from the Slave Coast. **1968** W. J. SAMARIN in J. A. Fishman *Readings Sociol. of Lang.* 665 As linguistic curios a few others might be cited:..Nago, probably based on Yoruba and ultimately used only in certain Brazilian pseudo-African cults.

nagor ('neɪgɔ:(r)). [Arbitrarily named by Buffon (1764 *Hist. Nat.* XII. 326): see quot. 1780.] The Senegal antelope, *Cervicapra redunca*, having short horns with a forward curve.
1780 SMELLIE tr. *Buffon's Nat. Hist.* (1785) VII. 38 We have found, in the cabinet of M. Adanson,..a stuffed animal, which we called Nagor, on account of the resemblance of its horns to those of the nanguer. **1801** SHAW *Gen. Zool.* II. II. 361 The Nagor is chiefly found in that part of Senegal nearest the isle of Goree. **1834** *Penny Cycl.* II. 80/1 The Nagor, known only from the description of Adanson and the figure of Buffon. **1904** P. C. MITCHELL *Guide Zool. Gardens* 43 The Reed-Buck, the Nagor, and Roi Rhébok are different species of Cervicapra.

nagre, obs. variant of AUGER *sb.*¹

Nagree, obs. form of NAGARI.

nag's-head. [? f. NAG *sb.*¹] (See quots.)
1855 HOPKINS *Organ* xv. §283 The 'nag's-head swell', as the above early kind of swell was called, was not well designed. *Ibid.*, The nag's-head swell continued in use for upwards of half a century. **1881** *Grove's Dict. Mus.* III. 489/1 The original organ swell was the 'nagshead', a mere shutter, invented by Abraham Jordan in 1712.

nagsman ('nægzmən). [f. NAG *sb.*¹ + MAN *sb.*¹ 4 p.] A skilled horseman who is employed to train or show horses.
1891 W. A. KERR *Practical Horsemanship* x. 171 The nagsman who will ride him up and down the yard is pretty certain to be an artist in the saddle, one who, as he gets 'the office', rides either to sell or to buy. **1903** F. M. WARE *First-Hand Bits of Stable Lore* viii. 107 A 'nagsman' handling a green and raw horse may seem..to be rough in his treatment. **1952** R. S. SUMMERHAYS *Encycl. for Horsemen* 191/1 *Nagsman*, a horseman who, by his skill, rides to improve a horse, whether as a ride, or on account of some vice or bad manners. **1955** H. SMITH *Horseman through Six Reigns* xxi. 203 If the rider's body is still..it is generally a sign that the horse is a good ride, though an expert showman or nagsman can cover up a lot. **1959** *Times* 25 Apr. 9/3 What the P.T. instructor and the drill sergeant do for the recruit ..the nagsman does for the colt. **1963** E. H. EDWARDS *Saddlery* ix. 78 While it might be of assistance to the experienced nagsman, it could be very dangerous in other hands.

'nagster. *rare*⁻¹. [f. NAG *v.* + -STER.] A nagging female.
1873 BESANT & RICE *Little Girl* I. II. iv. 150 When she was in a bad temper, which was often, she was a Nagster.

Nagtmaal: see NAGMAAL.

'Nagualism. [f. Central American *nagual*, a guardian spirit, esp. some beast or bird, supposed to be inseparably attached to a person.] A system of superstition and mysticism practised by a secret sect or society formerly existing in Central America.
1883 BRINTON in *Folk-Lore Jrnl.* I. VIII. 249 The learned Abbé..is not entirely satisfied that animal magnetism, ventriloquism, and such trickery, can explain the mysteries of nagualism, as the Central American system of the black arts is termed. **1896** JEVONS *Introd. Hist. Relig.* xvi. 207 Nagualism is one of the ancient forms of worship, and consists in choosing an animal as the tutelary divinity of a child.

So **'Nagualist,** an adherent of Nagualism.
1894 *Science* 9 Mar. 136/2 The Nagualists were also adepts in occult art.

Naguree, variant of NAGARI.

'nagus. *north.* and *Sc. rare.* Also 9 **nagas.** [Of obscure origin.] A miserly person.
1508 DUNBAR *Flyting* 177 Nyse nagus, nipcaik, with thy schulderis narrow. **1882** *Lancs. Gloss., Nagas*, a greedy, stingy person.

nagyagite ('nædʒəgaɪt, 'nægjəgaɪt). *Min.* [f. *Nagyag* in Hungary, its locality; named by Haidinger in 1845.] Black telluride of lead.
1849 NICOL *Min.* 476 Nagyagite..in the open tube emits sulphurous acid. **1882** DANA *Min.* (ed. 4) 149 Nagyagite, or Foliated tellurium, is..foliated like graphite.

nah, nahte, ought not, had not; see OWE *v.* 5.

nah¹ (nɑ:), a representation of a colloq. or vulgar pronunciation of NOW *adv.* Also **na.**
1847 E. BRONTË *Wuthering Heights* II. v. 109 He'll hev his lad; und Aw mun tak him—soa nah yah knaw! **1907** SHAW *Major Barbara* II. 245 Wot prawce Selvytion nah? **1954** E. PANGBORN *Mirror for Observers* (1955) II. iv. 135 'Did you think I was sore?' 'You had a right to be.' 'Nah. Hold everything.' **1959** B. KOPS *Hamlet of Stepney Green* I. 108 Na Davey, what can I say to you? **1959** A. WESKER *Chicken Soup with Barley* I. i. 176 Two o'clock they plan to march —nah!

nah² (nɑ:), a representation of a colloq. or vulgar pronunciation of NO *adv.*³ Cf. NA *adv.*²
1920 C. SANDBURG *Smoke & Steel* 45 Nothin' ever sticks to my fingers, nah, nah, nothin' like that. **1950** *Astounding Sci. Fiction* Nov. 97 'I'll fight you,' offered Borklin. His huge fists closed. 'Nah—why? Wouldn't be a fight, anyway.' **1961** I. JEFFERIES *It wasn't Me!* iii. 46 'I don't need permission...' 'I think you do.' 'Nah,' I said. **1961** J. HELLER *Catch-22* (1962) xxxviii. 393 Havermeyer shook his head thoughtfully. 'Nah, I couldn't do that.' **1966** *New Society* 12 May 9/2 The waiter knows better. 'Nah, you don't want herrings, I'm gonna give you the soup.' **1973** *Time Out* 2–8 Mar. 13/2 Nah, she don't know.

‖**nahal** (nə'hɑ:l). Also with capital initial. [Heb., f. initials of *No'ar Ḥalutzi Loḥem*, Pioneer and Military Youth.] The name of a military youth organization in Israel, used to designate an agricultural settlement manned by members of this organization. Also *attrib.*
1963 D. R. ELSTON *Israel* ii. 79 *Nahal* members are under no compulsion to continue as agricultural settlers once their period of service is over. **1964** L. DEIGHTON *Funeral in Berlin* xlii. 272 Our people in the *nahals* have got to pack a punch. **1969** *Times* 15 Nov. 7/7 The J.N.F. directly promotes the Israeli war effort by helping to establish *nahal* military-agricultural colonies. **1972** I. T. NAAMANI *Israel* ix. 131 In 1950, Pioneer and Military Youth (Noar Halutzi Lohem, or Nahal) was founded. This was an organisation of young people who wished to serve in the army as units and later continue as a group to establish for themselves or help others establish agricultural settlements on the borders. Usually the members of Nahal received several months of intensive military training and then were assigned to a frontier village, where..they underwent rigid agricultural tutoring. **1973** *Guardian* 21 Apr. 3/6 It has always been an axiom of Israeli planning that borders must be peopled... The first 12 villages have already been established. All were started as 'nahal' settlements by young soldiers, combining military and agricultural training.

nahcolite ('nɑ:kəlaɪt, nɑ:'kəʊlaɪt). *Min.* [f. $NaHCO_3$, its chemical formula + -LITE.] Native sodium bicarbonate, found as colourless, transparent, monoclinic crystals.
1928 F. A. BANNISTER in *Nature* 1 Dec. 866/1 The name nahcolite is proposed for naturally occurring sodium bicarbonate. These incrustations were found lining the walls of a cuniculus near the Stufe di Nerone, Baia, Naples, Italy. **1929** —— in *Min. Mag.* XXII. 60 Dr. L. J. Spencer has very kindly suggested an ingenious name, *Nahcolite.* **1940** *Amer. Mineralogist* XXV. 777 The origin of nahcolite in the Stufe de [*sic*] Nerone and in a lava tunnel at Vesuvius can be easily explained by the action of CO_2 and water vapor upon thermonatrite or trona. **1971** *Prof. Papers U.S. Geol. Survey* No. 750-B. 194 This report describes a new analytical technique for determining the amount of nahcolite in oil shale.

naht, obs. form of NAUGHT.

Na'htchi, var. NATCHEZ.

Nahua, var. NAHUATL *sb.* and *a.*
1948 D. DIRINGER *Alphabet* 122 The Nahua civilization of Mexico. **1957** E. HYAMS *Speaking Garden* vi. 70 *Tumatl* is a Nahua word. **1962** *Listener* 23 Aug. 270/2 Mexico's own Nahua and Mayan cultures.

Nahuatl ('nɑ:wɑ:t(ə)l), *sb.* and *a.* Also **Nahuat, Nahuatla, Nahuatlac.** [f. Sp., f. Nahuatl.]
A. *sb.* **a.** A group of peoples of Southern Mexico and Central America which includes the Aztec; a member of these peoples. **b.** The Uto-Aztecan language of this people. **B.** *adj.* Of or pertaining to the Nahuatl people or their language.
1822 J. BLACK tr. *de Humboldt's Essay on Kingdom of New Spain* I. 138 The Toultecs,..the Acolhuas, and the Nahuatlacs, all spoke the same language as the Mexicans. **1873** A. LANG in *Fortnightly Rev.* May 624 The rite itself was actually practised by the Nahuatls in America. **1877** L. H. MORGAN *Ancient Society* II. vi. 181 The question of the organization of these, and the remaining Nahuatlac tribes of Mexico, in gentes will be considered in the next ensuing chapter. **1891** Z. NUTTALL *Atlatl or Spear-thrower of Ancient Mexicans* 6 The Nahuatl text of Sahagun's invaluable Manuscript Historia. **1902** *Encycl. Brit.* XXV. 373/2 The dominant [American] ethnic groups:—Eskimo,

on Arctic shores;..Nahuatla-Maya, Southern Mexico and Central America. **1915** E. SAPIR in *American Anthropologist* XVII. Jan.–Mar. 99 The total number of Southern Paiute consonants that have to be directly accounted for in terms of Nahuatl consonants is considerably less. **1921** —— *Language* iv. 70 The compounded object of a verb precedes the verbal element in..Nahuatl. **1948** C. L. B. HUBBARD *Dogs in Britain* xix. 215 The Aztecs (tribal name for the last Nahuatl immigrants into the Mexican valleys). **1971** *Language* XLVII. 737 The language as a whole, once called Mexicano, has more recently been referred to as Nahuatl (in some cases Nahuat). **1973** *Guardian* 23 Mar. 12/6, I was going to learn Nahuatl, the Aztec language, which some of the two-dollar whores could speak.

So **Nahuatlan**, the group of Nahuatl dialects; also as *adj*.

1902 *Encycl. Brit.* XXV. 374/1 The [linguistic] families of ..Middle America..:—..Nahuatlan, Mex.; Otomitlan [etc.]. **1933** L. BLOOMFIELD *Language* iv. 72 A *Uto-Aztecan* family has been proposed..to include..the great *Nahuatlan* family in Mexico, including *Aztec*... Beside Nahuatlan, we may mention the *Mayan* family in Yucatan. **1953** *Amer. Speech* XXVIII. 62 The ending *-an*..is used after vowels as well as after consonants..*Tibetan, Nahuatlan*, [etc.].

nai, obs. form of NAY *adv*.

Naia, variant of NAJA.

naiad (ˈnaɪæd, ˈnaɪæd). *Myth.* Also 7 nay-. [f. L. *Nāïad-*, Gr. Ναϊαδ-, stem of *Nāïas* Ναϊάς, related to νάειν to flow, νᾶμα running water, river, etc.] **1.** One of a number of beautiful young nymphs imagined as living in, and being the tutelary spirits of, rivers and springs; a river-nymph.

1610 SHAKS. *Temp.* IV. i. 128 You Nimphs cald Nayades of yᵉ windring brooks. **1622** DRAYTON *Poly-olb.* xx. 125 The boughs for garlands..Which the clear Naiads make them anadems withal. **1728–46** THOMSON *Seasons, Spring* 400 Down to the river, in whose ample wave Their little Naiads love to sport at large. **1784** COWPER *Task* I. 328 Between them weeps A little Naiad her impov'rish'd urn. *a* **1821** KEATS *Hyperion* I. 13 The Naiad 'mid her reeds Press'd her cold finger closer to her lips. **1850** LEITCH tr. *C.O. Müller's Anc. Art* §403 (ed. 2) 538 To the Nereids of the sea correspond the Naiads of the land. **1880** 'OUIDA' *Moths* I. 101 What nymph or Naiad have you found?

transf. **1876** R. F. BURTON *Gorilla L.* II. 256 A bubbling brook, a true naiad of the hills.

attrib. and *Comb.* **1820** SHELLEY *Sensit. Pl.* I. 21 The Naiad-like lily of the vale. **1865** MISS YONGE *Clever Wom.* viii, The naiad performances they shared together on the smooth bit of sandy shore.

2. *Ent.* = NYMPH *sb.* 3.

1918 J. H. COMSTOCK in *Ann. Ent. Soc. Amer.* XI. 224, I, therefore, propose the restriction of the term nymph to the designating of the early stages of insects with a gradual metamorphosis and the use of the term naiad for designating the immature stages of the Plecoptera, Odonata, and Ephemerida. **1930** W. J. LUCAS *Aquatic (Naiad) Stage Brit. Dragonflies* i. 1 The two stages in a dragonfly's life are no less strikingly unlike... Hence arises the necessity for the student of our dragonfly fauna to study and classify the naiads independently of the imagines. **1942** E. O. ESSIG *College Entomology* i. 11 Naiads of aquatic insects are frequently referred to as nymphs. **1972** SWAN & PAPP *Common Insects N. Amer.* xv. 171 Metamorphosis in the group [*sc.* the Odonata] is incomplete or gradual. The naiads or nymphs are important predators of mosquito larvae.

3. *Bot.* A submerged aquatic plant with linear leaves, belonging to the family Najadaceæ, which includes only one genus, *Najas* (or *Naias*).

1966 *Rhodora* LXVIII. 216 (*title*) Two new naiads from Illinois and distributional records of the Naiadaceae.

‖**naiades** (ˈnaɪədiːz, ˈnaɪədiːz). *Myth.* Also 7 nay-. [L. *Nāïadēs*, Gr. Ναϊάδες, pl. of *Nāïas*, Ναϊάς: see prec.] Naiads, river-nymphs.

1390 GOWER *Conf.* II. 172 And for the wodes in demeynes To kepe, tho ben Driades; Of freisshe welles Naiades. **1591** SPENSER *Virg. Gnat* 26 Ye Sisters, which the glorie bee Of the Pierian streames, fayre Naiades. **1613–16** W. BROWNE *Brit. Past.* II. iv, With all the Nayades that fish and swim. **1634** MILTON *Comus* 254 The Sirens three, Amid'st the flowry-kirtl'd Naiades. **1671** —— *P.R.* II. 355 Nymphs of Diana's train, and Naiades. **1791** COWPER *Odyss.* XIII. 121 A pleasant cave Umbrageous, to the nymphs devoted named The Naiades. **1820** SHELLEY *Witch Atl.* xxiii, The fountains where the Naiades bedew Their shining hair.

naiant (ˈneɪənt), *a. Her.* Also 6 **nayaunt, -ante**. [a. AF. **naiant, -aunt*, = OF. *noiant* (*noant, nouant*), pres. pple. of *noier, nouer, noer*:—L. *natāre* to swim.] Swimming. (See quots.)

1562 LEIGH *Armorie* (1597) 99 b, If he [a dolphin] were in Fesse, then you should saye, nayaunt. **1572** BOSSEWELL *Armorie* II. 65 The fielde is verte, a whale nayante Argente, pellettee Sable. **1610** GUILLIM *Heraldry* III. xxii. 167 All Fishes being borne Transuerse the Escocheon must in blazon be termed Naiant. **1661** MORGAN *Sph. Gentry* III. v. 51 Three Sea-horses naiant argent. **1704** J. HARRIS *Lex. Techn.* I, *Naiant*, or *Natant* (i.e. Swimming) is the proper Term in Heraldry, to Blazon Fishes in an Escutcheon, when they are drawn in an Horizontal Posture, Fess-wise, or Transversly across the Escutcheon. **1858** E. J. MILLINGTON *Heraldry* 346 The base water, therein a Salmon naiant. **1864** BOUTELL *Her. Hist. & Pop.* xiv. (ed. 3) 149 Another shield, azure, charged with three herrings naiant in pale arg.

‖**naib** (ˈnɑːɪb, ˈneɪɪb). Also 7 **neip**, 8 **niab**, 9 **naybe**. [Arab. *nā'ib* a deputy: cf. NABOB and NAWAB.] A deputy governor; a deputy.

1682 HEDGES *Diary* 11 Oct., Before the expiration of this time we were overtaken by yᵉ Caddie's Neip, yᵉ Meerbar's deputy. **1765** HOLWELL *Hist. Events Bengal* I. 53 This person was appointed Niab, or deputy governor of Orissa. **1773** *Gentl. Mag.* XLIII. 89 One Kissindas (Duan and Naib of Decca) had embarked himself. **1813** J. FORBES *Oriental Mem.* I. 259 The naib or vizier..met the chief in the inner court and conducted him to the hall of audience. **1865** *Sat. Rev.* 18 Feb. 201 Many such letters from his naibs or deputies..have passed through our hands. **1882** FLOYER *Unexpl. Baluchistan* 191 He answered that..if I were a naib, or perhaps a sultan, we should be brothers.

naic(k, variants of NAIK.

naice (neːs), *a.* Representation of an affected pronunc. of NICE *a.*; freq. joc. or derogatory.

1925 A. HUXLEY *Those Barren Leaves* II. iii. 112 'So naice, I always think, these Corner Houses,' says Mrs. Cloudesley. **1941** A. CHRISTIE *Evil under Sun* v. 82 Ay am sure it has always been the quayettest [*sc.* quietest] place imaginable! The people who come here are such naice people. **1950** *Spectator* 29 Sept. 354/2 If you want to read about nice people who are really nice and not in the least 'naice', you will enjoy..*Rain on the Wind*. **1962** J. CANNAN *All is Discovered* iii. 49 Having agreed..that it was a naice morning. **1973** *Observer* (Colour Suppl.) 17 June 46/4 The girls in well-cut tweeds from the 'naice' public schools.

naïd (ˈneɪɪd). *Myth.* [f. L. *Nāïd-*, Gr. Ναϊδ-, stem of *Nāïs* Ναΐς, var. of Ναϊάς: see NAIAD.]

†**1.** A naiad. *Obs. rare.*

1617 DRUMM. OF HAWTH. *Forth Feasting* A 3 b, O Naïd's deare, (said they) Napæas faire,..Nymphes which on Hills repaire. **1717** FENTON *Poems* 147 To this dear Solitude the Naïds bring Their faithful Urns to form a silver Spring.

2. *Zool.* A river-mussel. *rare.*

1851 WOODWARD *Manual of the Mollusca* 273 Like other fresh-water shells the Naïds are often extensively eroded by the carbonic acid dissolved in the water they inhabit.

naie, obs. form of NAY.

‖**naïf** (naif), *a.* Also **naif**, (6–7 **naife**). [F. *naïf*:—L. *nātīv-um*: see NAÏVE.]

1. a. Natural, artless, naïve.

1598 GALLOWAY in M. Napier *Mem. J. Napier* viii. (1834) 296 Not affectat, bot naturall and naife. [**1656** BLOUNT *Glossogr.*, *Naif* (Fr.), lively, quick, natural.] **1784** MME. D'ARBLAY *Diary* 15 Jan., I was half ready to laugh,—there was something so *naïf* in the complaint. **1807** SYD. SMITH *Wks.* (1850) 84 The naïf manner in which he speaks of the vestiges of ecclesiastical history. **1846** MILL *Diss. & Disc.* (1859) II. 298 The European mind had returned to something like the *naïf* unsuspecting faith of primitive times. **1885** *Manch. Exam.* 18 Feb. 3/2 Had these delightfully *naïf* sentences been written a century ago.

b. As *sb.*

1893 G. B. SHAW in *World* 10 May 28/2 You will sometimes find some naïf doing this, and verdantly assuming that *his* point of view commands the absolute truth. **1932** T. S. ELIOT *Sel. Ess.* 305 He [*sc.* Blake] becomes the apparent naïf, really the mature intelligence. **1968** L. DURRELL *Tunc* ii. 36 Somewhere inside she was a naïf—always a bad sign in a woman connected with politics and public life. **1975** *Times Lit. Suppl.* 20 June 701/1 The Bronowski who concluded this was no mathematical naïf... He had spent a whole decade as a senior lecturer in mathematics.

c. *Art.* See NAÏVE *a.* 1 c.

1947 M. MCCARTHY in *Partisan Rev.* XIV. 178 As in the case of the *naif* painters, his very faults, the crudity of his conceptions,..become part of the subject. **1955** —— *Charmed Life* (1956) iii. 58 If Warren had been a carpenter or a plumber, he could have made his marks as a *naif* painter. **1974** *Times* 7 Jan. 8/1 At the age of 39, Haddelsey is one of the world's leading *naif* painters.

†**2.** (See quots.) *Obs. rare.*

1656 BLOUNT *Glossogr.* s.v., Jewellers..when they speak of a Diamond that is perfect in all its properties, as in the water, shape, cleanness, &c...say tis a Naif Stone; others, account a Naif Stone, to be one that is found growing naturally in such perfection, as if it had been artificially cut. **1698** FRYER *Acc. E. India & P.* 213 Uncut Stones [diamonds] are distinguished in two sorts, Thick or Pointed, which are called Naife-Stones, and Flat Stones.

Hence **naˈïfly** *adv. rare.*

c **1655** SIDNEY in *19th Cent.* (1884) Jan. 64 Having noe other intention but to ease my troubled thoughts..by setting downe naifely the true state of my mind. **1887** *Sat. Rev.* 1 Oct. 443 The naïf and naïfly expressed vexation of the Irish Nationalist papers.

naif, variant of NEIF; obs. form of NIEVE.

naig, Sc. and north. variant of NAG *sb.*[1]

naigie, Sc. variant of NAGGY *sb.*

‖**naik** (ˈnɑːɪk, ˈneɪɪk). Forms: 6 **nayque**, 8, 9 **naigue**, 7, 9 **naig**; 6, 9 **naic**, 9 **naick**; 7– **naik**. [ad. Urdū *nā'ik*, Hindī *nāyak* leader, guide, chief, overseer, officer, etc.:—Skr. *nàyaka* leader.]

1. An Indian title of nobility or authority; a person so styled; a lord, prince, or governor.

1588 HICKOCK tr. *C. Frederick's Voy.* 16 b, The Naic, that is to saye the Lord of the Citie sent..to demand of them certaine Arabian horses. **1598** W. PHILLIP tr. *Linschoten's Voy.* 51 When they will honor a man..They giue him the title of Nayque, which signifieth a Capitaine. **1687** A. LOVELL tr. *Thevenot's Trav.* III. 105 There are many Naiques to the South of St. Thomas, who are Sovereigns. **1698** FRYER *Acc. E. India & P.* 38 The true Possessors of it are the English, instated therein by one of their Naiks, or Prince of the Gentues. **1809** VISCT. VALENTIA *Voy.* I. 398 All I could learn was that it was built by a Naig of the place. **1862** BEVERIDGE *Hist. India* I. II. iii. 271 The naik or governor of the district volunteering to build a fort.

2. A military officer; in later use, a corporal of native infantry.

1787 SIR A. CAMPBELL *Regul. Troops* 6 (Yule), A Troop of Native Cavalry on the present Establishment consists of 1 European subaltern,..4 Naigues,..and 68 Privates. **1816** 'QUIZ' *Grand Master* IV. 78 Jemadars, Havildars, Naiks, and Subadars. **1849** EASTWICK *Dry Leaves* 51 A naik and three (a corporal's party). **1895** *Westm. Gaz.* 14 Dec. 7/1 A gunner squad of one naik and fourteen gunners.

nail (neɪl), *sb.* Forms: 1 **næȝel, næȝl**, 2 **nayȝel**, 3 **neil(e**, 3–7 **nayle, naile**, 4–5 **nayll(e, naill(e**, 4–6 **nale**, (6–7 **neale**, 6 **neayle**), 4–7 **nayl**, 4– **nail**. [OE. *næȝel, næȝl* = OFris. *neil* (*nil*), OS. *nagal* (Du. *nagel*), OHG. *nagal, -el, -il* (MHG. *nagel, nail, neil*, G. *nagel*), ON. *nagl* (Sw. *nagel*, Da. *negl*, Icel. *nögl*), Goth. **nagls*, from a root **nag-* found also in Lith. *nâgas* nail, *nagà* hoof, OSl. *nogŭtĭ* (Russ. *nógotĭ*) nail, *noga* foot, and obscurely represented in L. *unguis*, OIr. *ingen*, Gr. ὄνυξ, ὄνυχος, OPers. *nāχun*, Skr. *nakhás*.

In the West Germ. languages the same form of the word is used in senses I and II, but in ON. the nail for fastening has the derivative form *nagle, nagli*, whence also Da. *nagle* (but Sw. *nagel*).]

I. 1. a. A hard, oval-shaped, protective covering of modified epidermis, formed upon the upper surface of the last phalanges of the fingers and toes in Man and the Quadrumana, and answering to the claws or hoofs of other animals and birds.

c **725** *Corpus Gloss.* (Hessels) U. 260 *Unguana*, næȝl. *c* **1000** *Laws Æthelbirht* in Thorpe I. 16 ȝif þuman næȝl of weorðeð, iii. scill. ȝebete. *Ibid.*, Æt þam neȝlum ȝehwylcun scilling. *c* **1000** ÆLFRIC *Hom.* II. 432 His feax weox swa swa wimmana, and his næȝlas swa swa earnes clawa. *c* **1055** *Byrhtferth's Handboc* in *Anglia* VIII. 326 Læt gan þæt ȝetæl ..þæt þu cume to þæs læstan fingres næȝle. *c* **1205** LAY. 21880 [They set] nailes to heore nebbe, þat æfter hit bledde. *a* **1225** *St. Marher.* 19 [They] bunden hire the tet [= that the] blod barst ut et te neiles. *c* **1300** *Havelok* 2163 His fet he kisten an hundred syþes, þe tos, þe nayles, and þe lithes. **1362** LANGL. *P. Pl.* A. VII. 56 He caste on his..Cokeres and his Coffus for Colde of his nayles. *c* **1430** LYDG. *Stans Puer* 49 Fro blaknes kepe weel þi nailis. *c* **1470** HENRY *Wallace* IX. 1924 His handis.. Off manlik mak, with nales gret and cler. *a* **1548** HALL *Chron., Hen. VI* 182 b, A scoldyng woman, whose weapon is onely her toungue and her nayles. **1590** SHAKS. *Mids. N.* III. ii. 298, I am not yet so low But that my nailes can reach vnto thine eyes. *a* **1631** DONNE *Poems* (1650) 139 She is all faire, but yet hath foule long nayles. **1682** DRYDEN *Mac-Fl.* 44 The lute still trembling underneath thy nail. **1707** J. STEVENS tr. *Quevedo's Com. Wks.* (1709) 350 Do not bite your Nails. **1774** GOLDSM. *Nat. Hist.* (1776) II. 285 The nails still continued perfect; and all the marks of the joints..remained perfectly visible. **1814** BYRON *Lara* II. vi, The bitter print of each convulsive nail. **1873** MIVART *Elem. Anat.* vii. 238 Our hair and nails are epidermal parts of the exoskeleton.

b. A similar growth on the toes of beasts and birds; a claw or talon. (See also quot. 1841.)

a **1100** *Eadwine's Cant. Psalt.* lxviii. 32 Ceælf ȝeong.. hornæs forðledende & neȝlæs *vel* clawa. *a* **1340** HAMPOLE *Psalter* lxviii. 36 Þe new kalf, forth bryngand hornes & nayles. *c* **1384** CHAUCER *H. Fame* II. 34 This Egle..Withyn hys sharpe nayles longe Me fleynge in a swappe he hente. **1398** TREVISA *Barth. De P.R.* XVIII. i. (Bodl. MS.), Nailles beþ nedefulle to kepe þe vttermoste parties and also for defence of many manere beestes. **1579** GOSSON *Sch. Abuse* (Arb.) 54 Lyons folde vp their nailes when they are in their dennes. **1661** LOVELL *Hist. Anim. & Min.* Isagoge b 1 b, The nailes are in all that have toes; but the ape's are imbricate, those of the rapacious aduncate: in others they are straight; as in doggs. **1727–38** CHAMBERS *Cycl.* s.v. *Animals*, Having the foot divided into Two parts or toes, having two nails, as the camel-kind. **1797** BEWICK *Brit. Birds* (1847) I. 373 The middle toe, including the nail, is about seven eighths of an inch. **1841** WATERHOUSE *Marsup.* 202 A tuft of long black hairs which conceal a nail, with which the tip of the tail is furnished. **1859** *Todd's Cycl. Anat.* V. 477/2 In the dog and cat..a bony plate extends from the last phalanx into the posterior fold of the nail. **1893** NEWTON *Dict. Birds* 89 The toes of most birds are protected by claws or flat nails, only in the Ostrich the outer toe has no nail.

2. Something resembling a nail in shape or colour: †**a.** A growth in the eye; a haw. *Obs.*

c **1410** *Master of Game* (MS. Digby 182) xii, Sometyme commeth to þe houndes sekenes in hir eyenn, for þer commeth a webbe..into þᵗ one syde of þe eye and is cleped an nayle. **1600** SURFLET *Countrie Farme* I. xxviii. 182 The naile in the eie shall be lifted vp with a little small needle of Iuorie, and then cut quite away with cisers. **1607** TOPSELL *Four-f. Beasts* (1658) 83 Pain and blindness in the eye, by reason of any skins, webs, or nails. **1656** RIDGLEY *Pract. Physick* 120 A Haw in the Eye is a little nail; it is a nervous membrane.

b. (See quot. 1578.) Now *rare* or *Obs.*

1562 TURNER *Herbal* II. 116 b, The iuyce oughte to be pressed out of the tender roses, after that whiche is named the nayle be cut awaye. **1578** LYTE *Dodoens* 655 The nayles, that is to say, the white endes of the leaues whereby they are fastened to the knappes..is called in Latine, *Vngues Rosarum*. **1611** COTGR., *Ongle d'une rose*, the nayle, root, or white bottome of the flower of a Rose. **1657** W. COLES *Adam in Eden* xix. 38 There be six parts in a Rose..as 1. The Leaves. 2. The Nails. [**1821** tr. *Decandolle & Sprengel's Philos. Plants* I. iii. 63 In a poly-petalous corolla, the smaller part of the petals, which often resembles a stalk, is called the nail (*unguis*), and the expanded part is called *lamina*.]

c. A nail-like excrescence, situated on the upper mandible of certain soft-billed birds.

1769 E. BANCROFT *Guiana* 171 The upper mandible being augmented with a nail. **1840** *Cuvier's Anim. Kingd.* 263 The bill is larger . . with always a white terminal nail to the upper mandible. *Ibid.*, Bill, generally blackish, with . . a black nail.

3. In allusive expressions or phrases:

a. ***a nail*** or ***nail's breadth*** (cf. L. *transversum unguem*), the smallest amount. Chiefly in negative expressions.

1538 BALE *Thre Lawes* 261 The see doth ebbe and flowe And varyeth not a nayle. **1637** GILLESPIE *Eng. Pop. Cerem.* II. i. 9 The position . . which we maintaine . ., and from which we will not departe the breadth of one naile, is this. **1639** S. DU VERGER tr. *Camus' Admir. Events* To Rdr. a 2 He may not swerve a nailes breadth. **1754** SMOLLETT *Quix.* (1803) IV. 45, I have a greater regard for a nail's breadth of my soul, than my whole body.

b. With verbs, as ***to bite, blow, pare one's nails.***

1577 *F. de Lisle's Legendarie* I viij b, This caused the Cardinal and the rest of his brethren to bite their nailes. **1579** TOMSON *Calvin's Serm. Tim.* 229/1 God must needes paire the nailes, as well of vs men as women, and vse violence against vs. **1600** HOLLAND *Livy* XLI. xxxiv. 938 It is nothing so good, . . to take downe the Ætolians and pare their nailes, as to looke unto Philip that he wax not too great. **1663** SOUTH *Serm.* 5 Nov. (1727) V. 221 So that the King, for any thing that he has to do in these Matters, may sit and blow his Nails; for use them otherwise, he cannot. **1809** MALKIN *Gil Blas* VII. xv, To pare his nails the closer, I had gone into the market, and informed myself of the prices. **1883** STEVENSON *Treas. Isl.* IV. xix, A man who has been three years biting his nails on a desert island . . can't expect to appear as sane as you or me.

c. ***from the tender nail*** (tr. L. *de tenero ungui*, Hor. *Odes* III. vi. 24), from early youth. ***to the*** or ***a nail*** (tr. L. *ad unguem*, Hor. *Sat.* I. v. 32), to a nicety, to perfection.

1603 HOLLAND *Plutarch's Mor.* 4 Loving them inwardly, and (as the proverbe saith) from their tender nailes. *c* **1611** CHAPMAN *Iliad* XXIII. 581 A tall huge man, that to the nail knew that rude sport of hand. *a* **1834** COLERIDGE *Notes Horace, Epist.* II. xv, Maenius is capital. The swell-feast buffoon to a nail. **1891** S. MOSTYN *Curatica* 43 My peroration was never extempore, but always prepared beforehand, and polished to the nail.

d. ***naked, nice, as my nail***: see the adjs.

e. ***tooth and nail***: see TOOTH.

II. 4. a. A small spike or piece of metal of varying length and thickness (generally furnished with a point and a broadened head, so as to be easily driven in by a hammer), used to fix one thing firmly to another, or as a peg from which something may be suspended, occasionally also as an ornament; rarely, a wooden peg (cf. *tree-nail*).

c **725** *Corpus Gloss.* (Hessels) P. 107 *Paxillum, palum*, naeȝl. *c* **893** K. ÆLFRED *Oros.* IV. i. 158 Hie namon treowu, & sloȝon on oþerne ende moniȝe scearpe isene næȝlas. *c* **900** tr. *Bæda's Hist.* III. xvii, Se liȝ þurhæt ða næȝlas . . ðe heo to ðam waȝe mid ȝefæstnod wæs. *c* **1000** *Sax. Leechd.* III. 212 Næȝelas ȝeseon anxsumnysse ȝetacnað. *a* **1225** *Leg. Kath.* 2151 [He] het . . þurhdriuen hire tittes wið irnene neiles. *c* **1300** *Havelok* 712 Þer-inne wantede nouth a nayl, þat euere he sholde þer-inne do. **1340** HAMPOLE *Pr. Consc.* 7709 Als nayles er in a whele with-out, þat with þe whele er turned obout. **13..** *Gaw. & Gr. Knt.* 603 Ryche golde naylez þat al glytered & glent as glem of þe sunne. *c* **1440** *Promp. Parv.* 350/2 Nayl of metalle, *clavus*. Nayle of tymbyr, *cavilla*. *c* **1483** CAXTON *Dialogues* 21 Gyrdellis with nayles of silver. **1526** *Pilgr. Perf.* (W. de W. 1531) 223 b, As a nayle, the moo knockes it hath the more sure it is fixed. **1560** DAUS tr. *Sleidane's Comm.* 283 b, That they should dryve in Iron nayles into the Canons and other great pieces. **1626** BACON *Sylva* §14 For handsomness sake, . . it were good you hang the upper Glass upon a Nail. **1687** A. LOVELL tr. *Thevenot's Trav.* I. 219 Our Rudder broke, which being quickly mended again with some Nails, we sailed only with a fore-sail. **1769** FALCONER *Dict. Marine* (1780) s.v., In the same sense our seamen say, every nail in her bottom is an anchor. **1813** SHELLEY *Q. Mab* v. 142 To mould a pin, or fabricate a nail! **1876** VOYLE & STEVENSON *Milit. Dict.* 268/2 Iron nails are either wrought, cast, or cut out of sheet-iron.

collect. **1430** *Rec. St. Mary at Hill* (1904) 72 Also for a c blak nayll vj d. Also for iij^{c} & half white nayll . . ij s xj d. **1573** TUSSER *Husb.* (1878) 36 A hatchet and bil, with hamer and englishe naile, sorted with skil.

b. In *transf.* and *fig.* senses.

a **1340** HAMPOLE *Psalter* ix. 15 [Thai] ere festid in ded of synn, with nailes of ill delite. *Ibid.* xii. 1 With þe naile of luf festid . . in Jesu crist. *c* **1386** CHAUCER *Reeve's Prol.* 23 For in oure wit ther stiketh ever a nayl. **1436** *Pol. Poems* (Rolls) II. 182 The nayle of thys conclusioun. **1586** T. B. *La Primaud. Fr. Acad.* I. (1594) 26 The soule, . . being filled with infinite perturbations, fastened in the midst of it with the naile of pleasure and griefe. **1649** E. REYNOLDS *Hosea* i. 33 Take . . this nayle . . out of my heart. **1684** *Contempl. St. Man* I. x. (1699) 108 Let him . . fix his Memory with a Thousand Nails. **1822** LAMB *Elia* Ser. II. *Confess. Drunkard*, The countless nails that rivet the chains of habit. **1893** SELOUS *Trav. S.E. Africa* 474, I set to work to do a trade with Lo Magondi, but found him a terribly hard nail.

c. Prov. ***one nail drives out another***, etc.

For purely figurative uses see 7 c.

1586 B. YOUNG *Guazzo's Civ. Conv.* IV. 191 One danger is expelled by an other, As one nayle is driuen out by an other. **1591** SHAKS. *Two Gent.* II. iv. 193 Euen as one heate, another heate expels, Or as one naile, by strength driues out another. **1607** —— *Cor.* IV. vii. 54 One fire driues out one fire; one Naile, one Naile. **1630** J. TAYLOR (Water P.) *Siege Jerusalem* Wks. 13/1 Thus as one nayle another out doth drive The Persians the Assyrians did deprive. **1900** *Athenæum* 27 Oct. 547/2 Nail drives out nail.

†**d.** Used as a mark to show the depth to which a coal-keel might be loaded. (Cf. NAIL *v.* 2 c.)

1651 *Rec. Comp. Hostmen Newcastle* (Surtees) 95 The Court was informed by Mr Raph Gray . . that they see two keeles of Coles of M^{r} —— Claverings, who had the Tweelve chalder nailes drowned. **1679** *Ibid.* 139 Custome-house officers threatens to seize the keiles that are measured by Stoke nales. **1695** *Act 6 & 7 Will. III*, c. 10 §7.

e. *Mining*. A blasting-needle.

1839 URE *Dict. Arts.* 836 When the hole is dry, and the charge of powder introduced, the nail, a small taper rod of copper, is inserted so as to reach the bottom of the hole.

5. a. In passages relating or alluding to the Crucifixion of Christ.

This is one of the most frequent contexts in which the word occurs in OE. and early ME.

a **900** CYNEWULF *Crist* 1109 Swa him mid næȝlum þurh-drifan . . þa hwitan honda. —— *Elene* 1109 Þær þa æðelestan . . hydde wæron . . næȝlas on eorðan. **971** *Blickl. Hom.* 91 He eac æteowde þa wunda & þara næȝla dolh. *c* **1000** *Ags. Gosp.* John xx. 25 Ne ȝelyfe ic buton . . ic do minne finger on ðære næȝela [*Hatton* nayȝelene] stede. *a* **1225** *Ancr. R.* 114 Godes honden weren ineiled oðe rode. Þurh þeo ilke neiles ich halse ou ancren [etc.]. *c* **1290** *S. Eng. Leg.* I. 16/503 Þe swete nayles al-so And þe swete burþene of godes sone. *c* **1325** *Chron. Eng.* 629 in Ritson *Metr. Rom.* II. 296 Ther-inne wes closed a nail gret That ede thurh godes fet. *c* **1400** MAUNDEV. (Roxb.) x. 39 Þe foure nayles þat Criste was nayled with. **1500–20** DUNBAR *Poems* lxxii. 107 Croce and nalis scharp, scurge, and lance. **1580** HAY *Demandes* in *Cath. Tract.* (S.T.S.) 58 He hes nocht the markes of his blissid fyve woundes, maid . . in his handes and feit be the nales. **1649** E. REYNOLDS *Hosea* i. 31 They felt the nails wherewith they had crucified Christ, sticking fast in their own hearts. **1756–7** tr. *Keysler's Trav.* (1760) I. 430 The faithful . . elevate their minds to Christ's passion, of which the nail is a memorial. **1869** LECKY *Europ. Mor.* iv. (1877) II. 250 The nails of the Cross . . were converted by the emperor into a helmet.

†**b.** Hence, probably, in oaths and forms of asseveration, as (*by*) ***nails***, (*by*) ***God's nails, his nails, 's nails.*** *Obs.*

These expressions, however, might also belong to (or may sometimes have been taken in) sense 1: see GOD *sb.* 14 a.

c **1386** CHAUCER *Doctor-Pardoner Link* 2 (C. 288) Our Hoste gan to swere as he were wood, 'Harrow!' quod he, 'by nayles and by blood!' *c* **1460** [see GOD *sb.* 14 a]. *c* **1530** COPLAND *Hye Wey to Spyttel Hous* 362 in Hazl. *E.P.P.* IV. 43 With horyble othes swerynge as they were wod, Armes, nayles, woundes. **1573** *New Custom* II. iii, His nails, I would plague them one way or another. **1604** DEKKER *Honest Whore* I. vii, Nailes, I think so, for thou telst me. *Ibid.* Sneales eate the foole. **1631** CHETTLE *Hoffmann* C, Well, and you were not my father,—s'nailes and I would not draw rather then put vp the foole.

6. *transf.* **a.** A defect in a stone. ? *Obs.*

1655 STANLEY *Hist. Philos.* II. (1701) 61/2 That the Stars are of a fiery Substance, invisible, Earthly Bodies intermixt with them; that they are inherent, as nails in Chrystal. **1727–38** CHAMBERS *Cycl.* s.v. *Marble*, There are two defects frequent in marbles . .; the one, what they sometimes call nails, answering to the knots in wood.

†**b.** *Med.* (See quots.) *Obs.*

1600 SURFLET *Countrie Farme* I. xii. 78 To ripen a naile, otherwise called a fellon or Cats-haire. **1634** T. JOHNSON *Parey's Chirurg.* XXII. xxxii. (1678) 516 Some call it [a carbuncle] a Nail, because it inferreth like pain as a Nail driven into the flesh. **1685** J. COOKE *Mellif. Chirurg.* IV. II. i. (ed. 4) 194 When it becomes so hard, and the Cornea round about being brawny, presseth it down, 'tis called *Elos, Clavus*, i.e. the Nail, being like a Nail-Head.

c. = BACKING *vbl. sb.* 11.

1797 *Statist. Acc. Scotl.* XIX. 207 The waft was chiefly spun by old women, and that only from backings or nails, as they were not able to card the wool.

d. (See quot. 1812.)

1812 J. H. VAUX *Flash Dict.* s.v., A person of an over-reaching, imposing disposition, is called a nail, a dead nail, a nailing rascal. **1874** S. BEAUCHAMP *Grantley Grange* I. 121 Murby is the 'deadest nail' in all the country.

7. In allusive phrases (chiefly with verbs):

a. ***to hit the*** (***right***) ***nail on the head***, to aim aright, to come at the very point of the matter, to say or do exactly the right thing.

a **1529** SKELTON *Col. Cloute* 34 And yf that he hyt The nayle on the hede, It standeth in no stede. **1559** W. CUNNINGHAM *Cosmogr. Glasse* 19 You hit the naile on the head (as the saying is). **1599** H. BUTTES *Dyets Drie Dinner* E vj, His chiefe pride resteth in hitting the nayle on the head with a quainte Epithite. **1654** WHITLOCK *Zootomia* 75 If in giving their judgments, forsooth, they have not hit the naile on the head. **1700** S. L. tr. *Fryke's Voy. E. Ind.* 327 At last they ignorantly hit the nail on the head, saying that the Devil was in him. **1760** MURPHY *Way to keep Him* II. ii. You have not hit the right nail on the head. **1809** MALKIN *Gil Blas* I. v. ⁋5 He hit the right nail on the head: for he let me do what I pleased. **1838** DICKENS *O. Twist* xlii, You've hit the right nail on the head, and are as safe here as you could be.

b. ***to drive the nail*** (***up***) ***to the head*** (or ***home***), to push a matter to a conclusion.

1560 DAUS tr. *Sleidane's Comm.* 278 b, Let hym have a respect to him selfe and his children . . and dryve not the nayle to the head. **1604** HIERON *Wks.* I. 536 He will be sure to driue the nailes of his exhortations to the head. **1650** TRAPP *Comm. Deut.* ix. 7 One knock after another, drives this naile home to the head. **1690** *Def. Dr. Walker* 6 But to drive the Nail home, take the Testimonial of Gervase Squire, Esq. **1897** F. BARRETT *Harding Scandal* xiv, He must drive the nail right home, . . by leaving no doubt in the minds of Denise and Thrale.

c. In miscellaneous phrases, esp. various applications of ***to drive*** (or ***clinch***) ***a nail***.

1548 UDALL *Erasm. Par. Luke* xii. 113 Leat therefore one nayle driue out another nayle. [Cf. 4 c.] **1581** PETTIE tr. *Guazzo's Civ. Conv.* II. (1586) 96 That fellow could not be without a reply to beate backe the nayle againe. **1623** F. RYVES in *Ussher's Lett.* (1686) 301 After a while, that Negotiation was hung up upon the Nail, in expectance of the Princes return. **1677** W. HUGHES *Man of Sin* II. iii. 53 To clinch the Nail, (for 'tis all one) in Prose this fashion [etc.]. **1687** R. L'ESTRANGE *Answ. Dissenter* 30 So he sets himself to the Driving of Another Naile. **1698** FRYER *Acc. E. India & P.* 357 They rather sought by one Nail to drive out another, than openly to denounce War against them. **1728** VANBR. & CIB. *Prov. Husb.* IV. i. 87 O she's mad for the Masquerade! it drives like a Nail, we want nothing now but a Parson, to clinch it. **1768–74** TUCKER *Lt. Nat.* (1834) II. 14 To gain any success, we must proceed with discretion . ., driving the nail that will go. **1809** MALKIN *Gil Blas* XI. xiii. ⁋4 A mischievous wind from the wrong quarter . . drives a nail into the very head of the expedition. [Cf. *Judges* iv. 21–22.] **1830** GALT *Lawrie T.* II. ii. (1849) 46 He was . . brisk at a bargain, so the nail was soon driven.

d. ***a nail in one's coffin***, something that hastens or contributes to the end of the person or thing referred to. Freq. used with ref. to drinking. (Cf. COFFIN *sb.* 3 d.)

1792 WOLCOT (P. Pindar) *Expost. Odes* xv, Care to our coffin adds a nail, no doubt. **1824** SCOTT *Redgauntlet* ch. xvi, Every minute he lies here is a nail in his coffin. **1884** *Illustr. Lond. News* 29 Nov. 526/3 'The Candidate' . . is one more nail in the coffin of slow acting.

8. ***on the nail.*** **a.** On the spot, at once, without the least delay. Chiefly used of making money payments.

The origin of the phrase is obscure, and it is not even certain that it belongs to this sense of *nail*. Though different in meaning, it may correspond to F. *sur l'ongle*, 'precisely, exactly' (cf. Du. *op den nagel*, G. *auf den nagel* in the same sense). The explanations associating it with certain pillars at the Exchange of Limerick or Bristol are too late to be of any authority in deciding the question.

1596 NASHE *Saffron Walden* Wks. (Grosart) III. 59 Tell me, haue you a minde to anie thing in the Doctors Booke! speake the word, and I will help you to it vpon the naile. **1600** HOLLAND *Livy* VI. xiv. 225 [He] paid the whole debt downe right on the naile, unto the creditour. **1632** MASSINGER *City Madam* I. i, A payment on the nail for a manor Late purchased by my master. **1668** R. STEELE *Husbandm. Calling* v. (1672) 127 Not I'le do it at my leisure, but upon the nail I restore him fourfold. **1694** ECHARD *Plautus* 90 I've occasion for a hundred Pounds down o' the Nail. **1720** SWIFT *Run on Bankers* Wks. 1755 IV. I. 22 We want our money on the nail. **1764** *Oxf. Sausage* 74, I on the Nail my Battels paid. **1804** MAR. EDGEWORTH *Pop. T., Will* ii, The bonnet's all I want, which I'll pay for on the nail. **1839** CARLETON *Fardorougha* (ed. 2) 424 Answer me that on the nail! **1887** A. BIRRELL *Obiter Dicta* Ser. II. 165 He . . paid for him on the nail with other people's money.

b. (Precise meaning not clear.)

1679 tr. *M. Mancini's Apol.* 96 While my Caleche . . ran all on the Nayl [F. *voloit*] by the Road, and I endeavour'd by travelling all night to repair my loss of time. **1750** W. ELLIS *Mod. Husbandm.* VI. I. 73 It is in their Power to forbear such Work till dry Weather favours their Design; and then Carts are drawn, as we call it on the Nail, without damaging their arable Lands.

c. In a fix or trap; neatly caught.

1810 JANE PORTER *Sc. Chiefs* xxx, 'We shall have the rogue on the nail yet', cried he.

d. In readiness.

1846 LANDOR *Exam. Shaks.* Wks. II. 276 He sighed too . . and had ne'er a word on the nail.

e. 'On the carpet', under discussion.

1886 W. T. STEAD in *Contemp. Rev.* May 666 The enormous advantage of being up to date, of discussing subjects that are, in the slang phrase, 'on the nail'. **1891** *Pall Mall G.* 18 Nov. 2/1 We must leave Spiritualism . . for Theosophy, a subject at present very much 'on the nail'.

9. *Sc.* **a.** ***to go*** (or ***be***) ***off at the nail***, to behave strangely, go (*or* be) off one's head.

1721 KELLY *Scot. Prov.* 173 He is gone off at the Nail . . means that he is gone out of all bounds of Reason. **1822** GALT *Sir A. Wylie* xlvii, I see ye're terrified, and think I'm going off at the nail. **1824** MISS FERRIER *Inher.* lix, They [*sc.* servants] are really going off at the nail. **1897** BEATTY *Secretar* xlix, That woman's aff at the nail.

b. ***off the nail***, not quite sober.

1822 GALT *Steamboat* 300, I was what you would call a thought aff the nail, by the which my sleep wasna just what it should have been.

10. In comparisons, as ***deaf as a nail, hard as nails, right as nails.***

a **1845** HOOD *Tale Trump.* viii, She was deaf as a nail—that you cannot hammer A meaning into, for all your clamour. **1862** HORLOCK *Country Gentl.* v, Hard as nails in condition. **1889** JESSOPP *Coming of Friars* v. 229 The old stewards of manors . . as a class . . were hard as nails. **1894** ASTLEY *50 Years Life* I. 225, I really believe, in a fortnight I shall be as right as nails.

III. 11. A measure of weight for wool, beef, etc., usually equal to eight pounds = CLOVE *sb.*^{3}; †also, a measure of land. Now only *south. dial.* (So MDu. and MHG. *nagel.*)

1429 *Rolls of Parlt.* IV. 352 A nail of Lambeswolle, is at the value of ix*d.* **1442** *Ibid.* V. 59/1 Half a pek and a nayle of Londe, Pasture and Hethe. **1455** *Ibid.* 335/2, m.ccxxvi sakkes and half sakke and xi naylis of Woll. *c* **1500** in Arnolde *Chron.* (1811) 101 And it conteyne more than xij naile than shal the Sheref take therfore as miche as of a sac of iij weis. **1530** PALSGR. 247/1 Nayle of woll. **1618** *Sussex Arch. Coll.* (1851) IV. 24 Paid 7*s.* to the hemp-dresser, for 14 nail of hemp-dressing. **1674** JEAKE *Arith.* (1696) 80 Beef, in 1 Nail, 8 Pounds of common use. **1681** WORLIDGE *Syst. Agric.* (ed. 2) 329 A Naile, in some places eight pound, in some seven pound, being [? a sixteenth] of a Hundred. **1836** COOPER *Sussex Gloss.*, *Nail*, eight pounds of beef or cheese.

12. A measure of length for cloth; $2\frac{1}{4}$ inches, or the sixteenth part of a yard. †Abbrev. ***nai.***

The precise origin of this sense is not clear. The use of *the nail* in early examples suggests that one sixteenth from the end of the yard-stick may have been marked by a nail.

1465 *Paston Lett.* II. 235 By me a quarter and the nayle therof for colers. **1480** *Wardr. Acc. Edw. IV* (1830) 117, ij yerds di' and a naille corse of blue silk. **1481–90** *Howard Househ. Bks.* (Roxb.) 417 Item .v. yardys mynus the nayle, welwet blake. **1536** *Act 28 Hen. VIII*, c. 4 §1 Euery..halfe piece of lockerams to be in bredth a hole yarde, lackyng a nayle of the yarde. **1562** LEIGH *Armorie* (1597) 77 A tippet of three nailes breadth. **1592** LYLY *Midas* v. ii, They be halfe a yeard broad, and a nayle. **1611** COTGR., *Vn sezieme d'aulne*, three ynches, and (as one Neale of the yard) the least diuision of the French ell. **1630** WINGATE *Arith.* 365, 205¾ yards or Ells, and 2 nai. **1681** *Lond. Gaz.* No. 1665/4 A parcel of Grey Searge, Yard and Nail broad. **1732** *Acc. Workhouses* 60 An ell and half of three quarters and nail wide linnen. **1822** BEDDOES *Bride's Trag.* I. ii, I've..written twenty yards, two nails, An inch and a quarter, cloth-measure, of sonnets.

IV. *attrib.* and *Comb.*

13. In sense 1. **a.** In the names of articles used for the care of the nails, as ***nail-brush***, ***enamel***, ***file***, ***-knife***, ***lacquer***, ***-pick***, ***polish***, ***†-sax***, ***scissors*** (also *transf.*), ***varnish***; ***nail buffer***, ***clipper(s***, ***-parer***, ***-picker***, ***polisher***, ***-scraper***.

1802 M. EDGEWORTH *Let.* in E. Inglis-Jones *Great Maria* (1959) iv. 65 Enter Miss Linwood who looks not unlike a strolling player... I *wish* she had a nail brush. **1807** J. BERESFORD *Mis. Hum. Life* 245 Using a nail-brush that would serve for a wool-comb. **1893** *Times* 14 Dec. 8/2 A plentiful supply of hot and cold water, soap, nail brushes, and towels. **1908** *Sears, Roebuck Catal.* 328/1 Solid Silver Nail Buffer, fancy handle, 4½ inches long. **1971** *Petticoat* 24 July 3/4 There are six appliances for the nails—two files, a nail buffer, cuticle stick, nail brush and callous remover. **1945** J. STEINBECK *Cannery Row* xvi. 67 Dora..was there to buy a pair of nail-clippers. **1969** *Sears, Roebuck Catal.* 869/3 Resco Nail Clipper. Helps guard hosiery, furniture, pet's paw-health. **1907** Nail enamel [see *nail polish* below]. **1913** *T. Eaton & Co. Catal.* Spring & Summer 177/3 Lustrite Nail Enamel..will produce a brilliant lustre. **1972** *Vogue* June Special 90 Blueberry Wine Nail Enamel. **1881** *Graphic* 21 May (back cover) (Advt.), Nail file. Cigar cutter. Scissors. **1894** *Country Gentlemen's Catal.* 173/2 Pair nail scissors, button-hook and nail-file. **1922** F. COURTENAY *Physical Beauty* 47 When you have shaped the external edge of the nails with a fine pair of scissors, finish with emery or a steel nail file. **1969** *Sears Catal.* Spring/Summer 397 Sapphire-coated Nail File... Two surfaces..one for shaping, one for finishing. *a* **1225** *Juliana* 56 Irnene gadien, kene te keoruen al þat ha rineð to as neil cniues. **1966** J. S. COX *Illustr. Dict. Hairdressing* 101/2 *Nail lacquer*, nitro-cellulose dissolved in Butyl Acetate and allied substances forming, when dry, a hard, tough, resistant film on the surface of the nail. **1973** J. ROSSITER *Manipulators* viii. 90 A cosmetician's display of nail lacquers and lipstick cases. **1974** *Harpers & Queen* Sept. 50/3 We want to change our nail lacquers as often as our clothes. **1683** WILDING in *Collect.* (O.H.S.) I. 257 For a nail-pearer. **1947** J. STEINBECK *Wayward Bus* xvii. 222 He took his gold nail-pick from his pocket and opened it and cleaned his nails. **1810** *Splendid Follies* I. 125 Tooth-brush, nail-picker, tongue-scraper. **1907** *Yesterday's Shopping* (1969) 538/3 Diamond Nail Enamel..box 0/10½... Electric Nail Polish..bot. 1/6. **1937** *Discovery* Mar. 86/1 It [*sc.* diatomite] is used in face powders and nail polishes. **1972** 'H. CARMICHAEL' *Naked to Grave* i. 15 A tiny bottle of pink nail polish and another of nail polish remover. **1897** *Sears, Roebuck Catal.* 435/2 Chamois Nail Polisher, fancy Solid Sterling Silver mountings. **1913** E. WHARTON *Custom of Country* I. i. 13 Mrs. Heeny, driving her nail-polisher cheeringly. *c* **1000** ÆLFRIC *Gloss.* in Wr.-Wülcker 142/23 *Nouaculum*, næȝlsex. *c* **1205** LAY. 30578 He igrap a nail sax felliche kene and wel iwhæt. **1810** *Splendid Follies* I. 10 Away too went combs and razor..; the wash-ball, the nail-scraper. **1854** J. E. MILLAIS *Let.* 5 June in M. Lutyens *Millais & Ruskins* (1967) 222, I have had to operate upon myself with a pair of nail scissors. **1860** *All Year Round* No. 52. 35, Combs and brushes, tweezers and nail-scissors. **1919** W. H. DOWNING *Digger Dial.* 35 *Nail scissors*, the crossed sword and baton worn as a badge of rank by a General. **1951** *Catal. of Exhibits, South Bank Exhib., Festival of Britain* 60/1 Baby's nail scissors..Cuticle nail scissors. **1926–7** *Army & Navy Stores Catal.* 495/2 'Elite' Nail Varnish..bot. 1/6. **1936** *Chem. Abstr.* XXX. 7784 Cosmetics in pharmacy... A discussion of face powders, foundation creams,..shampoos and nail varnishes. **1954** *Granta* 6 Nov. 23/2 One uses nail varnish the other not. **1972** *Vogue* Feb. 46/2 Nail Varnish, Revlon's Ultima II. **1974** *She* Jan. 63/4 Nail Varnish Remover pads, 14p for 17.

b. In various attributive uses, as ***nail-clippings***, ***-joint***, ***-parings***, ***†-reach***, ***-score***.

Also freq. in recent medical works in such combs. as ***nail-bed***, ***-cell***, ***-fold***, ***-follicle***, ***-groove***, ***-matrix***, ***-plate***, ***-root***, ***-substance***, ***-surface***, ***-tissue***, ***-wall***, etc.

a **1652** BROME *New Acad.* I. i, Let him take heed, he comes not in my Nayl-reach. **1834** *Penny Cycl.* II. 149/1 The index and middle fingers..being connected together as far as the nail-joint. **1859** *Todd's Cycl. Anat.* V. 477/1 They are enclosed within raised ridges of the whole integuments, the nail walls. **1875** ANDERSON *Norse Mythol.* 455 A mythical ship made of nail-parings. **1893** NEWTON *Dict. Birds* 89 A thickening of the Malpighian layer, which forms the 'nailbed' out of which the corneous cells grow. **1896** A. MORRISON *Child Jago* 45 Nail-scores, wide as the finger, striped her back. **1897** MARY KINGSLEY *W. Africa* 444 A bundle of finger, or other bones, nail-clippings, eyes, brains, &c.

c. Miscellaneous combs., as ***nail-biter***, ***-biting***, ***-cutting***, etc.; ***nail-bearing***, ***-like*** adjs.; **nail-tailed** *a.*, having a nail or spur on the tip of the tail; **nail-tailed wallaby** *Austral.*, a wallaby of the genus *Onychogalea*, distinguished by white stripes on the cheeks and at the top of each limb, and a horny nail near the end of the tail.

1840 *Cuvier's Anim. Kingd.* 261 The corneous portion is restricted to the nail-like extremity. **1841** WATERHOUSE *Marsup.* 201 Nail-bearing kangaroo, *Macropus unguifer*. **1863** GOULD *Mamm. Austr.* II. 52 *Onychogalea unguifer*, Nail-tailed Kangaroo. **1893** *Daily News* 5 July 5/5 Directing his attention..to the study of nail-biting. *Ibid.*, Eleven..were confirmed nail-biters. **1896** F. G. AFLALO *Sk. Nat. Hist. Austral.* i. 43 The Nail-tailed (*Onychogalea*) and Hare (*Lagorchestes*) Wallabies are wanting in Tasmania, though three species of each are found on the mainland. **1896** LYDEKKER *Marsupials* 49 The three species of Nail-tailed Wallabies, which are confined to Australia..form a well-marked group. **1899** *Westm. Gaz.* 8/2 The question whether nail-cutting is a surgical operation. **1941** KOESTLER *Scum of Earth* 151 But what was the symbolical meaning of all these ..nail-biting..figures? **1959** *Ann. Reg. 1958* 190 Sinclair Weeks said..that the outlook was 'far better than the nail-biting pessimists think'. **1970** W. D. L. RIDE *Guide Native Mammals Austral.* 53 Three species of rather strikingly marked wallabies are called nail-tailed wallabies because they possess a small dark horny nail, rather like a finger nail, hidden in the dark hair at the end of the slender tail. **1973** *Times* 2 Oct. 21/4 The next few weeks will be nail-biting ones for Leonard Grouse.

14. In sense 4. **a.** Attributive, as ***nail-apparatus***, ***boot***, ***†-chapman***, ***factory***, ***-hammer***, ***-length***, ***-machine***, ***mill***, ***-print***, ***-shank***, ***-shop***, ***-smith***, ***-trade***; **†nail-ball** (see quots.); **nail-blank**, an unfinished nail; **†nail-board** *Naut.* (meaning uncertain); **nail bomb**, a lethal weapon, used *esp.* by urban guerrillas, made from nails wrapped round a stick of gelignite; **nail-gall**, a nail-shaped gall produced on the leaves of lime and other trees by a mite of the genus *Phytoptus*; **nail-kag** or **-keg**, a small barrel containing nails; also (*U.S.*) a hat of a similar shape; **nail-money** (see quot.); **nail-plate**, **-strip**, a piece of iron from which nails are cut; **nail-stub**, a worn horse-shoe nail; a stub-nail; **nail-tumbler**, a part of the lock mechanism of a rifle; **nail violin** (see quot. 1959). See also NAIL-HEAD, -HOLE, -ROD, -TOOL, etc.

1839 URE *Dict. Arts* 875 The first *nail apparatus to which I shall particularly advert is due to Dr. Church. **1853** STOCQUELER *Mil. Encycl.*, *Nail Balls, a missile, consisting of a strong nail, with a ball thereto attached while in the act of casting. **1864** WEBSTER (citing Scott), *Nail-ball*, a round projectile with an iron pin protruding from it, to prevent its turning in the bore of the piece. **1875** KNIGHT *Dict. Mech.* 1509/1 The cutter enclosed in the box..forming the *nail-blank. **1971** *New Scientist* 26 Aug. 483/3 They will assess the effects on the elderly, the sick, children..of the explosives, *nail-bomb, indiscriminate rifle and machine gun fire. **1971** *Guardian* 11 Oct. 20/3 A boy of about 10 threw a nail bomb at troops in Belfast yesterday. **1973** R. CLUTTERBUCK *Protest & Urban Guerrilla* x. 111 The same unemployed teenage boys..turned out..almost every evening to throw stones and nail-bombs at army posts and patrols. **1973** 'I. DRUMMOND' *Jaws of Watchdog* x. 135 These revolutionaries were not the ill-shaven back-street throwers of nail-bombs. They were a disciplined corps. **1630** J. TAYLOR (Water P.) *Fight at Sea* Wks. III. 34/1 They stayed some halfe an houre ..tearing vp our *naile-bords vpon the Poope and the trap-hatch. **1923** D. H. LAWRENCE *Ladybird* 242 The other fellows with sticks and *nail-boots had now taken heart and were scrambling like crabs past our hero. **1685** DANGERFIELD *Mem.* 17 [Received] of a *Nail-Chapman 10s. **1833** H. BARNARD in *Maryland Hist. Mag.* (1918) XIII. 374, I found my old friend..who took me to see..a *nail factory [etc.]. **1879** *Encycl. Brit.* X. 46/1 The lime-leaf '*nail-galls' of *Phytoptus tiliae* closely resemble the 'trumpet-galls' formed on American vines by a species of Cecidomyia. **1951** *Dict. Gardening* (R. Hort. Soc.) III. 1345/1 Nail-galls. Galls on leaves of Lime and other trees somewhat resembling tin-tacks driven through the leaf tissues. They result from attacks of species of Phytoptus. **1872** 'MARK TWAIN' *Innoc. Abr.* xxvi. 194 They wear a cylindrical hat termed a '*nail-kag'. **1889** —— *Yankee Crt. K. Arthur* (1900) 6 A helmet on his head the size of a nail-keg with slits in it. **1839** URE *Dict. Arts* 876 The shears which cut the rod into *nail-lengths. **1819** E. DANA *Geogr. Sk. Western Country* 77 Zanesville is.. at the falls, whereon various mills are erected..including.. an oil mill, *nail machine, and woolen factory. **1853** URE *Dict. Arts* (ed. 4) II. 255 The nail machine consists essentially of a pair of cutting chisels or edges [etc.]. **1850** *Rep. Comm. Patents: Agric. 1849* (U.S. Dept. Agric.) 93 Within its present limits are about fifty cotton factories.. seven rolling, slitting, and *nail mills. **1801** STRUTT *Sports & Past.* III. i. 124 They also claimed every one of them six crowns as *nail money, for affixing the blazon of arms to the pavilions. **1797** in *Essex Inst. Hist. Coll.* (1918) LIV. 107 Agreed with Mr. Allen to work at eight shillings pr. ton.. cutting every kind of rods and dubble for iron hoops or *nail plates. **1810** in Ure *Dict. Arts* (1839) 875 The principal business of rolling and slitting-mills, is rolling nail plates. **1945** *Amer. Speech* XX. 115 Since the cut nail is an American invention, the word *nail-plate* must be of American origin. **1890** W. H. ST. J. HOPE in *Archaeol.* LII. 687 The left arm, with open hand, showing the *nail-print, is extended downwards. **1839** URE *Dict. Arts* 877 The *nail shank being still firmly held in the jaws of the vice. **1847** H. MILLER *First Impress. Eng.* viii. 146 Little brick houses, with a *nail-shop in each. **1611** COTGR., *Cloutier*, a nayler, a *nayle-smith. **1762** tr. *Busching's Syst. Geog.* IV. 388 It also contains many nail-smiths or nailers. **1869** *Echo* 22 Sept. 1/4 The nailsmith, like Othello, will 'find his occupation gone'. **1875** KNIGHT *Dict. Mech.* 1505/2 The *nail-strips are heated by being placed on their edges on red-hot coals. **1851** H. MELVILLE *Moby Dick* III. xxvii. 176 Look ye, blacksmith, these are the gathered *nail-stubbs of the steel shoes of racing horses. **1727** BOYER *Dict. Royal* II. s.v., The *Nail-trade,..*commerce de Cloux*. **1844** *Regul. & Ord. Army* 101 For *Nail-tumbler, new..3*d.* **1884** E. HERON-ALLEN *Violin-Making* v. 108 In the year 1740 a German musician, named Johann Wilde,..invented a curious instrument called a *Nail-violin. **1944** W. APEL *Harvard Dict. Mus.* 478/1 There exists a quartet by F. W. Rust for nail violin, two violins and cello. **1959** *Collins Mus. Encycl.* 448/2 *Nail Violin*... It consisted of a semicircular resonator of wood into which were driven U-shaped nails of graduated lengths. The sound was produced by a bow.

b. Objective and obj. gen., in names of persons, as ***nail-bearer***, ***-manufacturer***, ***-minder***, ***-tacker***, ***-tinner***, ***-weigher***, ***-worker***; or of apparatus, as ***nail-clincher***, ***-cutter***, ***-driver*** (also *transf.*), ***-extractor***, ***-passer***, ***-piercer***, ***-puller***, ***-selector***, etc.

1871 RUSKIN *Fors Clav.* I Feb. 5 Fors, the *Nail-bearer, means the strength of Lycurgus, or of Law. **1875** KNIGHT *Dict. Mech.* 1506/1 **Nail-clincher*, a blacksmith's tool for clinching the point end of a nail..against the hoof. *Ibid.* 1505/2 The American *nail-cutter was the first to cut the nails and swage the heads at one operation. **1823** J. F. COOPER *Pilot* I. viii. 106 The cannon, above which were painted the several quaint names of 'boxer', ..'exterminator', and '*nail-driver'. **1872** *Life of Bill Hickman* 54 (Th.), I had a nail-driver [*sc.* a horse], very swift, and no end to his bottom. **1839** URE *Dict. Arts* 875 Mr. Edward Hancorne,..*nail manufacturer, obtained a patent in October, 1828. **1884** *B'ham Daily Post* 24 Jan. 3/4 A small factory..wants a practical *Nail-minder. **1839** *Hereford Gloss.*, *Nail piercer*, or Nail percer, and corruptly, *Nail passer, a gimlet. **1890** BUCKMAN *Darke's Sojourn* xviii. 170 Nails, nail-passers and such-like, were poked in between the beams and the boards of the floor above. **1688** HOLME *Armoury* III. 295 This goeth under several names, as a Gimblet, a *Nail Piercer. **1713** CHESELDEN *Anat.* I. ii. (1726) 25 The passage..may be made..with a carpenters nail-piercer or gimblet. **1880** *Encycl. Brit.* (ed. 9) XI. 439/2 A very powerful modification..has lately been introduced into use under the name of the *nail-puller. **1884** KNIGHT *Dict. Mech.* Suppl. 626/2 **Nail Selector*, a machine, or an attachment to a nail-machine, to pick out perfect nails from headless and ill-formed nails. **1885** *Harper's Mag.* Jan. 284/1 The outer sole is applied by a '*nail-tacker'. **1819** *P.O. Lond. Direct.* 382 *Nail-tinners, and Manufacturers of Chain Hooks. **1832** *Lincoln Herald* 11 Sept. 2/4 An extraordinary affidavit of a *nail-weigher of Dudley. **1882** *Standard* 26 Dec. 2/3 He supplies..the *nail-workers with their sixty-pound bundles of iron.

c. Instrumental, as ***nail-bestudded***, ***-pierced***, ***-studded***; and similative, as ***nail-like***, ***-shaped***.

a **1777** FAWKES *Song of Deborah*, Low at her feet he bow'd his nail-pierc'd head. **1836–9** *Todd's Cycl. Anat.* II. 490/1 The secreting canals are..nail-shaped. **1844** MRS. BROWNING *Drama of Exile* Poems 1889 I. 99 Look out, O Jehovah, to this I bring before Thee, With a hand nail-pierced. **1855** GARROD *Mat. Med.* 152 The clove is a small, tapering, nail-like body. **1862** W. BARNES *Hwomely Rhymes* I. 185 The nail-bestudded woaken door. **1900** BARING-GOULD *Bk. Dartmoor* 229 A mediæval dwelling,..with its oak, nail-studded door and its panelled walls.

nail (neɪl), *v.* Forms: 1 (ȝe)næȝlan, 3 naȝȝlenn, neilen, 3–6 naylle(n), 4–7 nayle (5 naylyn); 3–4 naill(e, 3–7 naile, (5 nale), 4– nail. [OE. *næȝlan* = OS. *neglian*, MDu. *naghelen*, *neghelen* (Du. *nagelen*), OHG. *nagalen*, *negilen* (MHG. *nagelen*, *negelen*, G. *nageln*), ON. *negla* (*nagla*; Sw. *nagla*, Da. *nagle*), Goth. (*ga*)*nagljan*, f. *nagl-* NAIL *sb.*]

I. 1. *trans.* To fix or fasten (a person or thing) with nails *on* or *to* something else.

Early examples usually relate to the Crucifixion.

a. Const. *on* or *upon*.

c **950** *Lindisf. Gosp.* Matt. xxvii. 22 Cuoedon alle, 'sie ahoen *vel* fæste ȝenæȝlad on rode'. *c* **975** *Rushw. Gosp.* Matt. xxvii. 23 Heo swiðor cleopadun..'Siæ næȝled on rode'. *a* **1225** *Ancr. R.* 114 Godes honden weren ineiled oðe rode. *a* **1300** *Cursor M.* 14900 Til he was naild on þat tre. **1340** *Ayenb.* 263 Iesu Crist..ynayled a rode. **1390** GOWER *Conf.* III. 183 His skyn was schape al meete, And nayled on the same seete. *c* **1470** HENRY *Wallace* VII. 1153 On charnaill bandis [he] nald it full fast and sone. **1585** T. WASHINGTON tr. *Nicholay's Voy.* IV. xiii. 126 b, Two winges nayled vpon the target with two great yron nailes. **1679** MOXON *Mech. Exerc.* IX. 161 Instead of Nailing the Hindges upon the Door, they Rivet them on. **1828** D'ISRAELI *Chas. I*, I. vi. 157 The royal anathema was nailed on the Episcopal gate at London. **1847** TENNYSON *Princ.* II. 188 Take my life, And nail me like a weasel on a grange For warning.

b. Const. *to*.

c **1200** *Trin. Coll. Hom.* 21 His holie lichame was tospred on þe holie rode, and nailed þarto his fet and his honden. *c* **1290** *S. Eng. Leg.* I. 206/215 To grounde harde heo him caste..and to þe eorþe naileden him faste. *Ibid.* 222/96 Wiþ bole-huden stronge ynou ynailed þerto faste. *a* **1310** in Wright *Lyric P.* xxviii. 84 He was nailed to the tre. **1398** TREVISA *Barth. De P.R.* XVII. clxviii. (Bodl. MS.), The laþe is..nailed þwarte ouer to the rafters. **1430–40** LYDG. *Bochas* I. (1558) fol. 30 It is meryer a man to go at large, Than with yrons to be nailed to a blocke. **1523** FITZHERB. *Husb.* §3 The fenbrede is a thyn borde pynned or nayled moste commonly to the lyft syde of the shethe. **1560** DAUS tr. *Sleidane's Comm.* 62 What dyd he, when he was nayled to the Crosse. **1665** BOYLE *Occas. Refl.*, *Disc.* IV. iii. 63 By cutting off several of the parts of the Tree, and by Nailing many of the rest to the Wall. **1781** COWPER *Expost.* 220 They..Seized fast his hand,..and nailed it to the tree. **1819** SHELLEY *Prometh. Unb.* I. 20 Hung [I] not here Nailed to this wall of eagle-baffling mountain. **1884** *Law Times Rep.* LI. 161/2 An iron bracket nailed to the corner of the chimney.

refl. **1829** GEN. P. THOMPSON *Exerc.* (1842) I. 39 Glory and success nailed themselves to the republican standards.

c. Used in similes denoting extreme fixity.

1687 A. LOVELL tr. *Thevenot's Trav.* I. 72 They..sit as close as if they were nailed to the Horse. **1832** LYTTON *Eugene A.* I. ii, As steady on his seat as if he were nailed to it. **1866** MEREDITH *Vittoria* xi, He called to his coach-man to drive away, next to wait as if nailed to the spot.

d. In allusive phrases, as *to nail one's colours to the mast*, to adopt an unyielding attitude; *to nail to the counter*, to expose as false or spurious (in allusion to the shopkeepers' practice of dealing thus with bad coins); *to nail to the barn-door*, to exhibit after the manner of dead vermin.

1842 O. W. HOLMES *Med. Ess.* Wks. 1891 IX. 67 A few familiar facts..have been suffered to pass current so long that it is time they should be nailed to the counter. **1844** [see COLOUR *sb.* 7 d]. **1848** DICKENS *Dombey* v, Mrs. Chick had nailed her colours to the mast, and repeated 'I know it isn't'. **1890** *Spectator* 9 Aug., It was a good deed to nail all this to the counter. **1894** *N. & Q.* 8th Ser. V. 130/2 There are two other uses of the word *level* which should be nailed to 'N. & Q.'s' barn door.

2. a. To pierce or drive through with a nail or nails. Now *rare* or *Obs.*

c **1000** *Lambeth Ps.* xxi. 17 Hi dulfon *vel* næȝledun handa mine and fet mine. *a* **1300** *Fall & Passion* 67 in *E.E.P.* (1862) 14 Hi nailed him in hond an fete as ȝe mow al i-se. *c* **1460** *Towneley Myst.* xxvi. 416 Thrugh feete and handys nalyd was he. **1537** WRIOTHESLEY *Chron.* (1875) II. 100 John Daye..had one of his eares nayled, for seditious wordes speakinge of the Quenes Highnes. **1615** W. HULL *Mirrour* 87 Christ dyed being nayled hand and foote. **1671** MILTON *Samson* 990 Jael, who with inhospitable guile Smote Sisera sleeping through the Temples nail'd.

b. To fix or fasten with nails. Also with *about*, *in*, *together*, etc.

c **1250** *Gen. & Ex.* 564 Ðhre hundred elne was it long, Naild and sperd, ðig and strong. *a* **1300** *Cursor M.* 8242 A-boute þat tre a siluer cercle son naild he. *c* **1386** CHAUCER *Knt.'s T.* 1645 And eek squyeres Nailinge the speres, and helmes bokelinge. *c* **1386** —— *Clerk's Prol.* 29 He is now deed, and nayled in his chest. *a* **1400–50** *Alexander* 3376 If any Naue to it neȝe þat naylid is with iryn, þen cleuys it ay to þe clife carryg & othyre. **14..** *MS. Linc.* A. I. 17 f. 38 (Halliw.), At the nether ende of the pavisse he gart nayle a burde. **1495** *Naval Acc. Hen. VII* (1896) 155 For a c grete spykes of Iron for to nayle & fasteyn the seid plankes..at the dokke hedde. **1530** PALSGR. 643/1 Nayle this same with thre or foure nayles and than it is sure. *Ibid.*, I nayle in a thynge, *je encloue*. **1660** F. BROOKE tr. *Le Blanc's Trav.* 355 They built a little Bark, nailed with wooden pinnes. **1782** COWPER *Colubriad* 1 Close by the threshold of a door nailed fast Three kittens sat. **1836** THIRLWALL *Greece* xii. II. 112 Casting metal statues, which before had been formed of pieces wrought with the hammer, and nailed together. **1855** DELAMER *Kitch. Gard.* (1861) 175 Nail fig-tree branches in their places on the wall. **1890** BUCKMAN *Darke's Sojourn* 68 The draught [was] prevented by a small tarpaulin nailed across the opening.

c. To stud with (or as with) nails; to mark by driving in a nail. *rare.*

13.. *Gaw. & Gr. Knt.* 599 A sadel, þat glemed ful gayly ..Ay quere naylet ful nwe. *c* **1483** CAXTON *Dialogues* 31 A gyrdle nayled With silver weyeng xl pens. **1648** R. FANSHAW tr. *Past. Fido* III. ii. 91 Those Stars which nail Heav'ns pavement! **1695** *Act 6 & 7 Will. III*, c. 10 §3 The.. Commissioners shall..cause the said Keils and Boats so admeasured to be marked or nailed on each Side.

†**d.** *Mil.* (cf. 3 c). To render (a cannon) useless by driving a nail into the vent; to spike. *Obs.*

1598 BARRET *Theor. Wars* v. iv. 138 That the Ordinance be not nayled, nor the munition fiered. **1643** *True Informer* E I b, Some of their Ordnance were naild by the Kings Troopes the next morning after. **1690** J. MACKENZIE *Siege London-Derry* 17/1 The rest attending the Lord Kingston till they had broke the Trunnions, and nailed the heavier Guns. **1705** tr. *Bosman's Guinea* 28 Attempting to Fire upon the Enemy with our Cannon, I found them all nailed. **1759** ROBERTSON *Hist. Scot.* III. Wks. 1813 I. 175 The French.. broke their troops, nailed part of their cannon [etc.]. **1781** [see NAILING *vbl. sb.*].

e. *intr.* To work as a carpenter. (*U.S.*)

1885 WHITMAN in *N. Amer. Rev.* CXLI. 434 'What did you do before you was a snatcher?'..'Nailed'.

3. ***nail up***: **a.** To render fast, to close up firmly, by fixing with nails.

1530 PALSGR. 643/1 You muste seke some other waye, for this doore is nayled up. **1615** W. LAWSON *Country Housew. Gard.* (1626) 12 Take heede of a doore or window..of any other mans into your Orchard: yea, though it be nailed vp. **1629** WADSWORTH *Pilgr.* iv. 34 The Vice Admirall.. prepared himselfe for to fight,..nailing vp his decks. **1711** ADDISON *Spect.* No. 110 ¶5 The Door of one of his Chambers was nailed up. **1835** DICKENS *Sk. Boz, Mr. Watkins Tottle* i, He..actually nailed up the board, and locked the door on the outside. **1860** TYNDALL *Glac.* I. xxvii. 199 The hotel..was nailed up and forsaken.

fig. **1604** T. M. *Black Book* Moral, That heauen is..made so fast, naylde vp with many a Starre.

b. To fasten up or affix at some elevation by means of nails; to fasten with nails to a wall, etc.

1630 *R. Johnson's Kingd. & Commw.* 192 Who, if he have sacrificed an Oxe, useth to naile up the head and hornes at his gate. **1867** SMILES *Huguenots Eng.* iv. 83 This document was found nailed up on the Bishop of London's door. **1878** T. HARDY *Ret. Native* v. vi. (1890) 347 He had spent the time in..nailing up creepers.

†**c.** *Mil.* = 2 d. *Obs.*

1654 EARL MONM. tr. *Bentivoglio's Wars Flanders* 385 Coming to their Batteries, they unhorst some of their Peeces, they nail'd up some others. **1690** LUTTRELL *Brief Rel.* (1857) II. 37 They had also..burnt the town, took the fort and nailed up the guns. **1745** P. THOMAS *Jrnl. Anson's Voy.* 294 He ordered to nail up such of the Cannon as could be fought. **1763** SCRAFTON *Indostan* iii. (1770) 65 The plan of operations was, to nail up the cannon, and push at the head quarters. **1781** *Encycl. Brit.* (ed. 2) s.v. *Nailing*, Vimercalus..made use of his invention first in nailing up the artillery of Sigismund Malatesta.

4. ***nail down*** (cf. 7), to fix down with nails; to fasten down the lid of (a box) in this way.

1669 STURMY *Mariner's Mag.* v. xii. 64 They nail down Quoyners to the Fore-Trucks of heavy Guns. **1679** MOXON *Mech. Exerc.* IX. 156 Nail it firmly down with two Brads into every Joyst. **1834** MARRYAT *P. Simple* xlv, The trunks, which had been left open, were nailed down.

II. 5. a. To fix, fasten, make fast, as by means of nails; to secure. Now *rare* or *Obs.*

c **1386** CHAUCER *Clerk's T.* 1128 O noble wyves, ful of heigh prudence, Let noon humilitie your tonge naille. *c* **1407** LYDG. *Reson & Sens.* 6266 And kan nat speke a worde ageyn; Meknes hath so her tonge nayled. **1582** STANYHURST *Æneis* III. (Arb.) 71, I am named syr Polydor; with darts fel nayled heer vnder I lodge. **1622** J. BUROUGH in *Lett. Lit. Men* (Camden) 130 Wherein if I finde any thinge worth your Jewell house I will..make means to nayle them untill you may take further order. **1697** CONGREVE *Mourn. Bride* II. vi, Rivet and nail me where I stand, ye Pow'rs. **1794** GALLOWAY *Poems* II. 47 For behold the whole city was nailed fast asleep.

b. To clench, prove.

1785 BURNS *Death & Dr. Hornbook* i, Ev'n Ministers they hae been kenn'd..Great lies and nonsense baith to vend, And nail't wi' Scripture. **1902** 'MARK TWAIN' in *Harper's Mag.* Feb. 431/2 Nailing an alibi where it can't be budged.

6. a. To fix (a person or thing) firmly *to* something; *esp.* to pin (one) *to* or *on* the ground, etc., with a weapon. Also in *fig.* contexts.

1590 *Pasquil's Apol.* I. A iij b, Their attempt is still to nayle our best men to the wall with the speare of slaunder. **1602** MARSTON *Antonio's Rev.* Prol., A breast Nail'd to the earth with griefe. **1622** FLETCHER *Sea-Voy.* III. i, Take you arrows, And nail these monsters to the earth! **1691** HARTCLIFFE *Virtues* 101 To whose Fingers their Money is as it were glued and nailed. **1697** DRYDEN *Æneid* IX. 787 The second Shaft..pierc'd his Hand, and nail'd it to his side. **1835** LYTTON *Rienzi* I. i, Nailing him on the very sod where he had sate..not an hour ago. **1889** J. M. DUNCAN *Clin. Lect. Dis. Wom.* xxviii. (ed. 4) 228 Concave hardness is felt fixing or nailing the womb..to the region between the plane of the left ischium [etc.].

b. To fix, or keep (one) fixed, *to* or in a certain place, position or occupation, so that there is no possibility of leaving it.

c **1611** CHAPMAN *Iliad* xv. 140 This threat even nail'd him to his throne. **1624** DONNE *Devot.* 48 How shall they come to thee, whom thou hast nayled to their bedd? **1711** ADDISON *Spect.* No. 92 ¶6 Coquetilla begs me not to think of nailing Women upon their Knees with Manuals of Devotion. **1784** COWPER *Task* I. 500 Those Whose headaches nail them to a noonday bed. **1791** BENTHAM *Panopt.* 55 Supposing no sage regulations made by any body to nail them to this or that sort of work. **1828** *Lights & Shades* II. 147 He is a shopman, and nailed all day behind the counter. **1861** J. RUFFINI *Dr. Antonio* xxi, Found poor Sir John nailed fast by a fit of the gout.

c. To fix or fasten (the eyes, mind, etc.) *to* or *on* the object of one's attention.

1591 LYLY *Wks.* (1902) I. 424, I sawe an Oke, whose statelines nayled mine eies to the branches. **1760–72** H. BROOKE *Fool of Qual.* (1809) IV. 120 He nailed his eyes, as it were, on the face of Mr. Clinton. **1792** WOLCOT (P. Pindar) *Captive* Wks. III. 227 Where the pale pond'ring wretch, in thought profound, Nails to the murky floor his haggard eye. **1829** SCOTT in *Lockhart* (1839) IX. 304, I cannot nail my mind to one subject of contemplation. **1860** EMERSON *Cond. Life* vi. Wks. (Bohn) II. 407 The man whose eyes are nailed not on the nature of his act, but on the wages.

†**d.** To pin (one's faith) *to* something. *Obs.*$^{-1}$

1594 T. B. *La Primaud. Fr. Acad.* II. Ep. Rdr., They are cleane voyde of brayne, wit, and common sense, that nayle all their beliefe so fast to the sight of their bodily eyes.

7. a. To fix or pin (one) *down* to something.

1615 Z. BOYD *Let.* in *Zion's Flowers* (1855) Introd. 30 The Gentlemen of Saumure have at last nailed me down to them, and resolved..that I shall..be their property. **1707** NORRIS *Treat. Humility* iii. 104 Our bodies are as much nailed down to the earth by their own weight [etc.]. **1796** H. HUNTER tr. *St.-Pierre's Stud. Nat.* (1799) II. 58 Wherefore has not gravity nailed them down to the surface of the Earth? **1880** MEREDITH *Tragic Com.* (1881) 182 You see plainly she was nailed down to write the thing. **1893** G. ALLEN *Scallywag* i. 3 Isabel meant..to nail her down at once to the matter on hand.

refl. **1864** BURTON *Scot Abr.* II. i. 122 Johnson nailed himself down to the hexameter and pentameter.

b. *intr.* To bind oneself *down*. *rare*$^{-1}$.

1859 LONGF. in *Life* (1891) II. 386 George comes on Wednesdays; but..I cannot nail down to that day.

8. *slang.* **a.** To secure; to succeed in catching or getting hold of (a person or thing); to steal. Hence also, to arrest.

1760 FOOTE *Minor* II. Wks. 1799 I. 260 Some bidders are shy, and only advance with a nod; but I nail them. **1764** —— *Patron* i. ibid. I. 334 *Bev.* Fix the old fellow so that she may not be miss'd. *Sir Pet.* I'll nail him, I warrant. **1805** *Europ. Mag.* XLVII. 335, I had learnt..to plume myself upon nailing a job. **1812** J. H. VAUX *Flash Dict.* s.v., I nail'd the swell's montra in the push. **1847** THACKERAY *Brighton in 1847* i. Wks. 1886 XXIV. 134 [He] insisted on nailing me for dinner before he would leave me. **1883** STEVENSON *Treas. Isl.* iii, Lubbers as..want to nail what is another's. **1889** D. C. MURRAY *Dang. Catspaw* 245 We shall have to wait and nail them, sir, when we've proved complicity. **1918** [see CUT *sb.*[2] 24 d]. **1931** *Amer. Speech* VII. 111 They nailed me right on the border. **1969** C. F. BURKE *God is Beautiful, Man* (1970) 29 The cops..nail Ben for havin' the cup.

b. To catch (one) in some fix or difficulty.

1766 GOLDSM. *Vic. W.* xii, When they came to talk of places in town, you saw at once how I nailed them. **1810** J. CREEVEY in *C. Papers* (1904) I. vi. 125 So now the Ministers are nail'd. **1845** LD. CAMPBELL *Chancellors* xcv. (1857) IV. 309 The King and all the councillors were much tickled to see the wily chief Justice thus nailed.

†**c.** To cheat, get the better of (one). *Obs.*

1812 J. H. VAUX *Flash Dict.*, *Nail*, to nail a person is to over-reach or take advantage of him in the course of trade or traffic. **1819** *Sporting Mag.* IV. 209 He would undertake to 'blind', or 'nail' any keeper in the kingdom.

d. To succeed in hitting (a person).

1886 DOWDEN *Shelley* I. i. 24 To surround 'Mad Shelley' and 'nail' him with a ball..was a favourite pastime.

'nailage. *rare*$^{-1}$. [f. NAIL *v.* + -AGE.] The charge made by the Customs for nailing up a package of tobacco opened for inspection.

1766 W. GORDON *Gen. Counting-house* 204 Tobacco..at 2*d.* per lb...deducing nailage at 4 lb. per hhd.

nailbourne: see EYLEBOURN.

nailed (neɪld), *ppl. a.* [f. NAIL *v.* + -ED[1].]

1. Fastened, studded, or constructed with nails; having the form of nails (quot. 1853).

Beowulf 2023 Hio næȝled sinc hæleðum sealde. *c* **960** *O.E. Chron.* (Parker MS.) an. 937 ȝewitan him þa Norþmen næȝled cnearrum. *a* **1000** *Cædmon's Gen.* 1433 (Gr.), Hwonne hie of nearwe ofer næȝled bord..stæppan mosten. **1607** TOPSELL *Four-f. Beasts* (1658) 390 By touching the stick she bringeth down the pikes and sharp nailed boards upon her own body and back. **1657** G. THORNLEY *Daphnis & Chloe* 38 The Theeves had their Swords on, with their scaled and nailed Corslets. **1823** in Cobbett *Rur. Rides* (1885) I. 291 The parson could not attempt to begin, till the rattling of their nailed shoes ceased. **1853** HUMPHREYS *Coin-coll. Man.* xviii. 231 The letters termed by numismatists nailed letters...They have the addition of a small knob at the extremities. [**1885** J. B. DAVIDSON in *Athenæum* 3 Oct. 435/2 The Northmen fled in their nailed barks over the roaring sea back to Dublin and Ireland.]

b. With advbs., as ***nailed-on***; also ***nailed-up***, an epithet recently applied to dramas of loose construction without literary or artistic value.

1683 MOXON *Mech. Exerc., Printing* xxiv. ¶19 He.. doubles the loose half of the Leather over the remaining Nail'd-on half. **1894** *Westm. Gaz.* 24 Apr. 2/1 One of the most inept 'nailed up' dramas..that ever faced the footlights. **1895** *Times* (weekly ed.) 312/3 A sample of what the Americans call the 'nailed-up' drama.

2. Provided with (finger or toe) nails.

a **1300** *Body & Soul* in *Map's Poems* (Camden) 338 Scharpe clauwes, long nayled. *c* **1440** *Promp. Parv.* 350/2 Nayled, as fyngers, or toos [*P.* nayled on fyngers], *unguatus*. **1611** COTGR., *Onglé*, nayled; hoofed. **1828** *Lights & Shades* II. 192 Hands white, long-fingered, acorn-nailed. **1894** MRS. DYAN *All in Man's Keeping* (1899) 87 The long-nailed black hand of his..dusky attendant.

nailer ('neɪlə(r)). Forms: 5–7 nayler, 6–7 -or, 8–9 nailor, nailer. [f. NAIL *v.* + -ER[1].]

1. a. One who makes nails; a nail-maker.

c **1440** *York Myst.* xix. (*title*) The Gyrdillers and Naylers. **1538** LELAND *Itin.* (1769) IV. 114 There be many Smithes in the Towne..and a great many Naylors. **1611** COTGR., *Cloutier*, a nayler, a nayle-smith; a seller or maker of nayles. **1665** D. DUDLEY *Mettall. Martis* (1854) 39 Twenty thousand Smiths or Naylors at the least dwelling near these parts. **1723** *Lond. Gaz.* No. 6163/3 Edward Cooke,..by Trade a Nailor. **1776** ADAM SMITH *W.N.* I. i. I. 10 A smith ..whose..business has not been that of a nailer can seldom ..make more than eight hundred or a thousand nails in a day. **1831** J. HOLLAND *Manuf. Metal* I. 170 The nailors in general furnish them both better and cheaper than the smiths can make them. **1871** NAPHEYS *Prev. & Cure Dis.* I. viii. 224 Nailers' consumption, a form of chronic pneumonia.

appos. **1847** H. MILLER *First Impr. Eng.* viii. 145 The nailer-lads were frequently refused..permission.

b. In phrases ***like***, or ***as busy as, a nailer***.

1857 HOLLAND *Bay Path* x. 120 Yes, he did and he stuck to it like a nailer. **1899** *Harper's Mag.* Sept. 510 Thady.. bein' kept as busy as a nailer.

2. One who drives in nails.

1803 *Naval Chron.* IX. 73 The Tonnant..was coppered by several gangs of punchers and nailers.

3. *slang.* **a.** A marvellously good thing, animal, or person; an exceptionally good hand *at* something.

a **1818** MACNEILL *Poems* (1844) 50 A vet'ran Scot spoiled Egypt's plot; Ah, pangs,—that was a nailer. **1884** MRS. E. KENNARD *Right Sort* v. 48 That young roan mare who carried you so brilliantly through the run...She's a nailer! **1897** W. RYE *Norfolk Songs* 133 Edward, Lord Suffield was a nailer at sprint running.

b. [f. NAIL *v.* 8 a.] A policeman or detective.

c **1863** T. TAYLOR in M. R. Booth *Eng. Plays of 19th Cent.* (1969) II. 84 Then there's the Nailer's been after me... What, Hawkshaw, the 'cutest detective in the force? **1935** A. J. POLLOCK *Underworld Speaks* 79/1 *Nailer*, a uniformed police officer.

Hence **'naileress**, a female nail-maker. *rare.*

1847 H. MILLER *First Impr. Eng.* viii. 147 The two young naileresses were really very pretty.

nailery ('neɪlərɪ). [f. NAILER: see -ERY.] A place or workshop where nails are made.

a **1798** PENNANT (T.), Near the bridge is a large almshouse, and a vast nailery. **1802** JEFFERSON in *Harper's Mag.* (1885) Mar. 539/1 Profits of nailery. **1847** H. MILLER *First Impr. Eng.* viii. (1857) 132 The sole workers in the nailery were two fresh-coloured, good-looking young girls. **1895** *Edin. Rev.* July 223 The naileries, the shipping and the shopkeeping of his native town.

†**nailfast**, *a. Obs. rare.* [f. NAIL *sb.* + FAST *a.* Cf. MDu. *nagelvast*, MLG. *naelvast*, G. *nagelfest*, ON. *nagl(a)fastr* (Sw. *nagelfast*, Dan. *naglefast*).] Fastened with nails.

1428 *Will W. Ward* (Somerset Ho.), Ita quod nichil dict. rotefast vel naylefast inde capiat. **1640** *Will Cowper* ibid., All goods nailfast in the said house.

'nail-head. [f. NAIL *sb.* + HEAD *sb.*[1]]

1. The head of a nail. Also *fig.*

1683 MOXON *Mech. Exerc., Printing* x. ¶9 The Plate.. with the extuberancies of Nail-heads would hinder the free sliding of the Quoins. **1839** URE *Dict. Arts* 876 Compressing the metal into the shape of a nail-head. **1855** *Rambler* III. 239 Mr. Forster will have it that the language..scribbled on the rocks of the desert of Sinai, in the Egyptian hieroglyphics, and in the 'nail-head' letters of Assyria and Persia, is all one. **1948** D. DIRINGER *Alphabet* vi. 358 The vertical strokes ended with wedges or 'nailheads'; this script was therefore termed 'nail-headed'.

2. a. An ornament shaped like the head of a nail.

1836 PARKER *Gloss. Archit.* (1850) II. 47 The nail-head being an ornament easily cut, was much used in almost all periods of Norman work. **1892** *Daily News* 24 Oct. 3/2 A red cloth dress was bordered with gold braid with nail-heads of jet an inch or so apart. **1947** *Sun* (Baltimore) 31 Oct. 3/7 (Advt.), It can look dressed-up or casual with its gold-toned nailheads, oblong gold-toned buckle. **1973** *Philadelphia Inquirer* (Today Suppl.) 14 Oct. 14/1 (Advt.), Zip-front shirt jac with nailhead trim. **1974** *Sumter* (S. Carolina) *Daily Item* 24 Apr. (Belk Stroman Advts. Suppl.) 2 Denim shifts with nailheads, embroidery, polka dot or check trims!

b. *attrib.*, as ***nail-head moulding, ornament, pattern***.

1845 FREEMAN in *Proc. Archæol. Instit., Winchester* 5 Their rim is ornamented with the nail-head moulding. **1848** RICKMAN *Styles Archit. Eng.* App. 54 The nail-head, and toothed ornaments, though found in France, are by no means so abundant as in England. **1877** J. C. COX *Ch. Derbysh.* III. 319 The archway..resting on corbels having the nail-head pattern.

3. *Min.* **nail-head spar**, a variety of calc-spar in which the crystals resemble nail-heads.

1851 *Amer. Jrnl. Sci.* Ser. II. XII. 396 Calcspar..variety called Nail-head Spar. **1892** DANA *Min.* 266 Nail-head spar, a composite variety having its name from its form.

ˈnail-headed, *a.* [Cf. prec. and -ED[2].] Having a head like that of a nail; formed like a nail-head.

1801 HAGER *Babylon. Inscr.* 41 The nail-headed characters to be met with in Persia. *Ibid.* 43 An upright line with a nail-headed top. **1834** *Penny Cycl.* II. 397/2 The Babylonian characters, on account of their rude shape, are often called nail-headed. **1842** GWILT *Archit.* 1007 Nail-headed Moulding..so called from being formed by a series of projections resembling the heads of nails or square knobs. **1936** D. GASCOYNE *Man's Life is this Meat* 19 In my hand lies the same whispering, nail-headed dude, ever imploring the benefit of a hippograph. **1948** [see NAIL-HEAD 1].

ˈnail-hole. [f. NAIL *sb.* + HOLE *sb.*] A hole made to receive a nail; a hole caused by the removal of a nail.

1679 MOXON *Mech. Exerc.* IX. 161 The Nail-holes of the Hindge. **1691** T. H[ALE] *Acc. New Invent.* p. xxii, The great Nail-holes, which they use to spile up at stripping. **1725** BRADLEY *Fam. Dict.* s.v. *Shoeing*, Our Smiths..make..their Nails of a great Shouldering, by driving them over hard upon the Nail-hole. **1825** J. NICHOLSON *Operat. Mechanic* 640 All the nail-holes or other irregularities on the surface must be carefully stopped. **1851** MAYNE REID *Scalp Hunt.* xxvi. 190 We had stripped the shoes off the horses, filling the nail-holes with clay. **1875** *Carpentry & Join.* 79 The nail holes are subsequently filled with putty.

ˈnailing, *vbl. sb.* [f. NAIL *v.* + -ING[1].] The action of the verb in various senses; nail-making; the nails with which a thing is fastened.

a **1400** *Minor Poems fr. Vernon MS.* 625/466 Spere & spounge and sharp nayling. **1494-5** *Rec. St. Mary at Hill* (1904) 215 For nailyng & storyng of the beme. **1570** FOXE *A. & M.* (ed. 2) 2280/1 He did bynd this Ieffrey prentise vnto the craft of nayling. **1704** J. HARRIS *Lex. Techn.* I, *Nailing of Cannon*, is the driving of a Nail, or Iron Spike, by force into the Touchhole of a Piece of Artillery, so as to render it useless to the Enemy. **1781** *Encycl. Brit.* (ed. 2) s.v., One Gasper Vimercalus was the first who invented the nailing of cannon. *c* **1850** *Rudim. Navig.* (Weale) 135 Lead nails are small round-headed nails, for nailing of lead. **1880** L. WALLACE *Ben-Hur* VI. iv, All he could do was to wrench the board from its nailing.

Comb. **1543** *Richmond Wills* (Surtees) 43 Item ij nalyng hamers ij[d]. **1875** KNIGHT *Dict. Mech.* 1506/2 *Nailing-machine*.., a machine which acts automatically to drive the nails into shoe-soles.

b. *slang.* (See NAIL *v.* 8.)

1819 *Sporting Mag.* IV. 208 Snaring of hares, packing of game and 'nailing' of keepers. **1820** *Ibid.* VI. 79 Those lads ..care not for the expences of the tip provided there is no nailing.

ˈnailing, *ppl. a.* [f. NAIL *v.* + -ING[2].]

1. Fixing like a nail.

1887 T. A. TROLLOPE *What I remember* II. vii. 119 Dickens said, with nailing forefinger levelled at me, 'Give us that for *Household Words*'.

2. *slang.* †**a.** (See NAIL *sb.* 6 d.) *Obs.* **b.** Excellent, splendid. Also in adv. use, as ***nailing good***.

1883 *Pall Mall G.* 29 Mar. 4/1 He was a well-tried old dog, and we can have another nailing run out of him another day. **1884** MRS. E. KENNARD *Right Sort* x. 113 What a nailing good fencer to be sure!

nailing, obs. form of NEALING *vbl. sb.*

nailless (ˈneɪllɪs), *a.* [f. NAIL *sb.* + -LESS.] Destitute of nails; not provided with, or protected by, nails.

1847 *National Encycl.* I. 884 The thumbs were nailless. **1896** *Daily News* 24 Oct. 8/3 A pattern of the nailless horseshoe now under trial in..the German Army.

ˈnail-maker. [f. NAIL *sb.* + MAKER *sb.*] One who makes nails.

1530 PALSGR. 186 *Clovtier*, a nayle maker. **1755** JOHNSON, *Nailer*, one whose trade is to forge nails; a nail-maker. **1839** URE *Dict. Arts* 877 The same sorts of operations..as are usually performed by the hands of a nail-maker. **1884** W. H. GREENWOOD *Steel & Iron* x. 210 Nail rods are the square bars used by nail-makers.

ˈnail-making, *vbl. sb.* [f. NAIL *sb.* + MAKING *vbl. sb.*] The process of making nails. Also *attrib.*

c **1835** *Encycl. Metrop.* VIII. 688/1 Various patented inventions for nail-making machinery. **1875** KNIGHT *Dict. Mech.* 1508/2 Machinery for splitting rods for nail-making was first introduced in Sweden. **1887** P. MCNEILL *Blawearie* 153 Right and left at it we went as hard as nail-making.

ˈnail-punch. *Joinery.* [f. NAIL *sb.* + PUNCH *sb.*[1] 2.] A driving punch for nails.

1899 C. G. WHEELER *Woodworking for Beginners* (1900) xvi. 433 *Nail-Set, or Punch*.., for sinking nail-heads below the surface, is quite important, and it is well to have a large one and a fine one. **1951** *Practical Home Woodworking* ii. 36 A nail-punch has a flat 'point'. **1973** *Practical Woodworking* 34 It is sometimes necessary to drive the head of a nail well below the surface and to fill the resulting cavity with putty. .. Nail sets, or nail punches, as they are sometimes called are designed for this purpose.

ˈnail-rod. Also **nail rod, nailrod.** [f. NAIL *sb.* + ROD *sb.*]

1. a. A strip or rod of iron from which nails are cut.

1761 KINNERSLEY in *Phil. Trans.* LIII. 95 The conductor ..consisted of square iron nail rods. **1810** in Ure *Dict. Arts* (1839) 875 Rolling and slitting-mills..also serve to make nail rods. **1876** VOYLE & STEVENSON *Milit. Dict.* 268/2 Plates rolled for the purpose, and then slit by means of slitting rollers into nail rods. **1887** *Pall Mall Gaz.* 22 May 12/1 Rolled bar iron, and..nail rods.

fig. **1858** CARLYLE *Fredk. Gt.* VII. ix. (1872) II. 342 The thread-paper Duchess of Kendal.., poor old anatomy or lean human nailrod.

b. Without article, as a material.

1869 *Rep. Comm. Agric. 1868* (U.S. Dept. Agric.) 433 The most convenient method of destroying the bugs is by using a pair of tongs made of nail-rod. **1892** *Daily News* 15 Feb. 7/3 There is a good demand for nailrod. **1900** *Ibid.* 24 Sept. 8/7 Nail-rod and rivet-iron.

2. *transf.*, chiefly in Australasian use: Coarse dark tobacco in the form of a thin roll or stick.

1886 *N. Zealand Herald* 8 Nov. 7/3 Nailrod and 1lb bars ..with a full assortment of Havana..Cigars. **1890** A. J. VOGAN *Black Police* 200 He hands our black friend a piece of 'nailrod' with which to charge his evening pipe. **1896** H. LAWSON *While the Billy boils* 118 'You can give me half-a-pound of nailrod', he said, in a quiet tone. **1896** L. TRACY *Final War* xi. 77 Then joy prevailed, and the fumes of nail-rod mingled in the breeze with the strains of 'Annie Laurie'.

Nailsea (ˈneɪlsiː). The name of a town near Bristol, used to designate a style of glassware first made there in the late 18th century. Freq. *attrib.*

[**1897** A. HARTSHORNE *Old Eng. Glass* xix. 307 Nailsea, near Bristol, was another [source], with darker coloured glass, sometimes blue. **1907** E. DILLON *Glass* 368/2 (*index*) Nailsea glass-works.] **1910** D. WILMER *Early Eng. Glass* xi. 205 The manufacture of Nailsea glass continued until about the year 1873, some of the latest productions having gilt decoration. **1926** N. H. MOORE *Old Glass* I. 170 The Nailsea glass which is of interest to collectors shows specimens very beautiful in color, like the ornamental flasks which were Nailsea's chief product. **1960** H. HAYWARD *Antique Coll.* 195/1 *Nailsea glass*, the brownish-green glass speckled with white with which the name of Nailsea, near Bristol, is associated, was used on occasions for the making of wine-bottles, and sealed examples exist. **1961** E. M. ELVILLE *Collector's Dict. Glass* 140/1 Also described as 'Nailsea' are the peculiar love-tokens which were..made at all glassworks near coastal towns. **1966** J. LAVER *Victoriana* xiv. 173 (*caption*) Bottles decorated with loops of coloured glass, one of many varieties known as 'Nailsea'. **1971** *Guardian* 23 Mar. 32/8 Nailsea style coloured glass for sale..including walking sticks, bells, bottles, bellows.

ˈnail-set. *Joinery.* [f. NAIL *sb.* + SET *sb.*[1] 33.] = NAIL-PUNCH.

1899 [see NAIL-PUNCH]. **1927** R. A. FREEMAN *Certain Dr. Thorndyke* II. xviii, Carpenters don't fix mouldings on with screws. They use nails and punch them in with a 'nail-set' and stop the holes with putty. **1947** J. C. RICH *Materials & Methods Sculpture* vi. 170 The tools required for chasing may be purchased or fashioned by the sculptor either from tool steel,..or from small steel tools called nail sets. If nail-set tools are used it will be first necessary to remove or draw out the temper, prior to shaping the ends by means of filing into the desired forms. **1973** [see NAIL-PUNCH].

ˈnail-sick, *a.* *Naut.* [f. NAIL *sb.* + SICK *a.*] Leaky at the nail-holes. (Cf. IRON-SICK.)

1865 THOREAU *Cape Cod* viii. 145 Much smaller waves soon make a boat 'nail-sick', as the phrase is. **1879** T. WARDEN *Crossford* II. 73 As the little craft was old and nailsick, she made a good deal of water in the ordinary way.

†**ˈnail-tool.** *Obs.* [f. NAIL *sb.* + TOOL *sb.*] An instrument used in making nails.

1338 *Durham Acc. Rolls* (Surtees) 376 Item j magnus Nailtoll. **1483** *Cath. Angl.* 248/1 A Nayle tulle, *clavatorium*. **1584** *Knaresborough Wills* (Surtees) I. 145 All my naile tooles and all my hammers. **1637** *Ibid.* II. 160 One stiddie, one great naile toole, my hammers.

†**ˈnail-wort.** *Obs.* [f. NAIL *sb.* + WORT *sb.*] A name suggested by Gerarde for *Draba verna* and *Saxifraga tridactylites*, and by Cotgrave applied to *Paronychia*, with reference to their supposed efficacy in affections of the finger nails.

1597 GERARDE *Herbal* VI. iv. 500 There is another sort of Whitlow grasse or Naile woort, that is likewise a low or base herb, hauing a small tough roote. *Ibid.*, We may call them in English Naile woort, and Whitlowe grasse. **1611** COTGR., *Paronychie*, Whitlo-grasse, Nayle-wort (a weed).

naily (ˈneɪlɪ), *a.* *rare.* [f. NAIL *sb.* + -Y[1].] Studded with nails.

1604 T. M. *Black Bk.* Moral, How they grate with their hard nayly soales The stones in Fleet-streete. **1800** HURDIS *Fav. Village* 108 Lest..It drown his instep, and his naily shoe Drench with the chilling element below. **1865** *Englishman's Mag.* Oct. 290, I should recommend everything of the..nailiest in the way of boots.

naimcouth, Sc. var. NAMECOUTH *a. Obs.*

nain (neːn), *a.* *Sc.* Also 5 **nan**, 6, 8 **nane**. [See etym. note to OWN *a.*] (One's) own.

c **1375** *Sc. Leg. Saints* xliii. (*Cecilia*) 155 þar is na thing sa suet, think me, as my nan brothire. **1509** in *Munim. Univ. Glasguensis* (Maitland) 45 Mes of the Requiem..for my faderes saule..and myne nane saule. **1755** R. FORBES *Ajax, Shop Bill* vii, Fare may be had, for their nain wear, The starkest hose. **1816** SCOTT *Antiq.* xxix, A cusin o' his nain —Miss Eveline Neville. **1871** W. ALEXANDER *Johnny Gibb* ii, Ilka ane had their nain.

Hence **nainˈsel', -ˈsell**, (one's) own self; ***her nainsel'***, a phrase attributed to Highlanders in place of the first personal pronoun, and hence used as a designation for a Highlander.

c **1700** in Maidment *Pasquils* (1868) 314 Should..Heaven or Hell Make a man such a fool as forget him nain-sell? **1716** *Wodrow Corr.* (1843) II. 139 It's ower sheap; her nainsel no sell it so sheap. **1786** *Har'st Rig* lxxxix, Now dances Niel wi' little Nell, And canty Kate with hur nanesell. **1828** SCOTT *F.M. Perth* xxxiii, Her nainsell will never bid thee less, come by them how she can.

‖**nainsook** (ˈneɪnsʊk). [Urdū (Hindī) *nainsukh*, f. *nain* the eye + *sukh* pleasure.] A cotton fabric, a kind of muslin or jaconet, of Indian origin; a garment made of this. Also *attrib.*

1804 in *Spirit Pub. Jrnls.* VII. 59 Nor could I find a man in the whole parish who understood any thing about nainsooks and bandannoes. **1885** *Yng. Ladies' Jrnl.* 1 July 59/2 The embroidery may be worked on silk, nainsook muslin, or fine linen. **1892** *Monthly Packet* Dec. 636 Our whitest, coolest nainsooks..seemed best to suit the day.

naio (ˈnaɪəʊ). Also **naeo, naieo.** [Hawaiian.] An evergreen tree, *Myoporum sandwicense*, of the family Myoporaceæ, native to Hawaii and bearing clusters of pink or white flowers; also called bastard sandalwood, as its wood is fragrant. Cf. NGAIO.

1888 W. HILLEBRAND *Flora Hawaiian Islands* 339 The wood of the 'Naeo' or 'Naieo', most so that of the roots, becomes fragrant on drying. **1915** W. A. BRYAN *Nat. Hist. Hawaii* xvi. 222 The bastard sandalwood or naieo is a tree common on the summit of Kaala, and the higher forest belt generally. **1970** S. CARLQUIST *Hawaii* xv. 275 The naio, *Myoporum sandwicense*, is a common dry forest tree with relatives in New Zealand and on South Pacific islands.

naip(e)rie, obs. forms of NAPERY.

‖**Nair** (ˈnɑːɪr, nɛə(r)). Forms: α. 6–8 **nayre, naire**, 7– **nair**, 8–9 **naïr**, 20 **nayar**. β. 6–7 **nayro**, 7 **nairo**. [a. Sp. and Pg. *nayre, naire*, ad. Urdū (Hindī) *nāyar* or *nāyaṛ*. The source of the forms in *-o* is not clear.] A member of the noble and military caste in Malabar. Also *attrib.*

α. **1582** N. LICHEFIELD tr. *Castanheda's Conq. E. Ind.* I. xiv. 34 The house of the Nayres, which amongest the Malabars are Gentlemen. **1603** R. JOHNSON *Kingd. & Commw.* 174 Many of the Malaber princes..lay all their hopes and fortunes on the Nairs. **1660** F. BROOKE tr. *Le Blanc's Trav.* 56 The third part of them are Naires, or Gentlemen. **1796** H. HUNTER tr. *St.-Pierre's Stud. Nat.* (1799) I. 339 Their military is formed of the Nobility, called Naïrs, who possess the second rank in the State. **1845** STOCQUELER *Handbk. Brit. India* (1854) 299 The Nairs have great faith in their superhuman knowledge. **1888** G. SMITH *Stephen Hislop* iv. (1889) 98 A European officer of the Nair brigade felt aggrieved. **1911** *Encycl. Brit.* XIX. 318/2 *Nayar* .., a caste or tribe on the W. coast of S. India, who form the dominant race in Malabar. Traditionally they are soldiers, but many have taken to professions... Their total number in all India in 1901 was just over one million. **1922** *Edin. Rev.* Jan. 187 Even the Nayar, when he addresses a Brahman, must use the language of deprecation. **1955** M. GLUCKMAN *Custom & Conflict in Afr.* iii. 68 The father's rôle seems to have been reduced to a minimum among the Nayar castes of Malabar in India in the past.

transf. **1791** BURKE *Fr. Rev.* (1824) 188 Did the privileged nobility..deserve to be looked on as the Nayres or Mamelukes of this age..?

β. **1598** W. PHILIP tr. *Linschoten* (1885) I. 279 Noblemen called Nayros, which are souldiers that doe onely weare and handle arms. **1638** SIR T. HERBERT *Trav.* (ed. 2) 301 The Nayroes are his Lords; a sort of Mamaluck. **1698** FRYER *Acc. E. India & P.* 51 Each State having a Representative..to act according to the Votes of the Nairos Gentry.

naira (ˈnaɪrə). [See quots. 1972.] A unit of currency in Nigeria, equal to 100 kobo.

1972 *N.Y. Times* 9 Aug. 14 On Jan. 1, 1973, Nigeria will scrap her system of Nigerian pounds,..and begin a decimal currency system with units of money called the naira and the kobo... The name is adapted from the word Nigeria. **1972** *Times* 9 Oct. (Nigeria Suppl.) p. viii/4 The new currency being introduced by the Central Bank of Nigeria consists of naira and kobo. Kobo are coins and naira are notes. The origin of the names has not been fully explained, but naira is said to have been derived from the word Nigeria. *Ibid.*, The various denominations of the naira notes, which are now on display in public places, carry pictures showing various aspects of Nigeria's economic activities. The old Nigerian coins which they replace bear the head of the Queen of England. **1974** *Globe & Mail* (Toronto) 2 Oct. 7/3 A number of firms .. were allowed to stay on, provided they raised their capital to at least 200,000 Naira (roughly $350,000).

‖**naïs** (ˈneɪɪs). Pl. naïdes (ˈneɪɪdiːz). [L. *Nāïs*, Gr. *Ναΐς*: see NAÏD and NAIAD.]

1. *Mythol.* A river-nymph.

1697 DRYDEN *Æneid* XII. 215 King Turnus Sister .. by the grateful God, Now made the Nais of the neighb'ring Flood. **1697** —— *Virg. Past.* VI. 33 Ægle .. The fairest Nais of the neighbouring Flood. **1838** KEIGHTLEY *Mythol.* 238 Many a warrior who fought before Troy could boast descent from a Naïs or Nereis.

2. *Zool.* A small fresh-water worm allied to the earthworm.

1835–6 *Todd's Cycl. Anat.* I. 172/2 A naïs or an earth-worm cut in two .. will continue to live. **1870** NICHOLSON *Man. Zool.* xxix. (1875) 217 In this process the Naïs throws out a bud between two rings, at a point generally near the middle of the body.

nais, *a. rare.* Also 9 *Sc.* nace. [a. ON. *neiss*, related to *neisa* (Sw. *nesa*) shame.] Covered with shame; destitute.

Only in connexion with *naked*, as in ON. *nǫktan ok neisan* (acc.), *neiss er nǫkkviðr halr*.

a **1300** *Cursor M.* 989 (Cott.) Adam was out don nais and naked, In to þe land quar he was maked. *c* **1325** *Metr. Hom.* 52 For ef this thef mai us met .. He bes ful redi .. To .. mak us bathe nakid and nais. **1871** W. ALEXANDER *Johnny Gibb* xxi. 159 A peer [= poor] nace nyaukit beggar creatur.

naish, dial. var. of NESH *a.*, soft.

† **ˈnaissance.** *Obs. rare*⁻¹. [a. F. *naissance*: see next and -ANCE.] Origin, birth.

1490 CAXTON *Eneydos* 27 She wolde .. goo vnto the Royame of fenyce, the countrey of her nayssaunce and byrthe.

naissant (ˈneɪsənt), *a.* Also 6–7 nay-. [a. F. *naissant*, pres. pple. of *naître*:—Rom. **nascĕre*, L. *nascī* to be born: cf. NASCENT.]

1. *Her.* Of animals: Issuing from the middle of the fesse or other ordinary.

1572 BOSSEWELL *Armorie* II. 29 b, Gules and Sables parted per Fesse enuecked, thre lyons nayssant argente, crowned. **1610** GUILLIM *Heraldry* III. xv. 142 This Lion is said to be Naissant, because he seemeth to issue out of the wombe of the Fesse. **1704** J. HARRIS *Lex. Techn.* I. **1727–38** CHAMBERS *Cycl.* s.v., Naissant differs from issuant, in that the animal in the former case issues out at the middle, and in the latter at the bottom, of the shield, or charge. **1838** *Penny Cycl.* XII. 143/2 Beasts of prey are, according to their attitude, blazoned .. couchant, dormant, naissant [etc.]. **1864** BOUTELL *Her. Hist. & Pop.* x. (ed. 3) 60 A Lion Naissant is now borne upon a chief by the Baron Dormer.

2. That is in the act of springing up, coming into existence, or being produced. *rare.*

1885 LOWE *Bismarck* I. 184 A navy which should defend the naissant Empire's coasts. **1887** A. M. BROWN *Anim. Alkal.* 79 Naissant hydrogen reduces it to the state of hypoxanthine.

† **nait**, *sb. north.* and *Sc. Obs. rare.* Also 4 naite, 6 nate. [a. ON. *neyte*, *neyti* (Norw. *nöyte*, MSw. *-nöte*) use, etc.: related to *neyta* NAIT *v.*¹] **a.** Use, profit, advantage. **b.** Use, end, purpose.

a **1300** *Cursor M.* 22883 Agh we þer-on to seke resun Hu he dos alkin thing to nait. *Ibid.* 24746 Þof mans wijt [= wit] be neuer sa strait, Sco mai well bring it vnto nait. *c* **1475** *Rauf Coilȝear* 61, I defend that we fall in any fechtine; I had mekill mair nait sum freindschip to find. **1513** DOUGLAS *Æneis* IV. xii. 10 Furth scho drew the Troiane swerd, fute hait, A wappin was neuir wrocht for sic a nate.

† **nait**, *a. north.* and *Sc. Obs. rare.* Also 5 nayet. [a. ON. *neyt-r* fit for use, good: related to prec. and next.] Useful, good at need.

c **1400** *Destr. Troy* 1038 Nestor, a noble man, naitest in werre. *Ibid.* 3878 Non was so noble, ne of nait strenght, As Ector. [Also 8211, etc.] **1513** DOUGLAS *Æneis* XII. vii. 47 This Iapis sage .. wyth his nait handis tway Begouth for till exem, and till assay The wond.

† **nait**, *v.*¹ *Obs.* Also 4–5 naite, nayt(e, 5 (7, 9 *dial.*) nate. [a. ON. *neyta* (Norw. *nöyta*, Sw. *nöta*):—**nautjan*, f. **naut-* (cf. *naut* cattle, NOWT, *nautr* gift, companion), ablaut var. of **neut-*, whence Goth. *niutan*, ON. *njóta* (Sw. *njuta*), OE. *néotan* to enjoy.]

1. *trans.* To make use of, to use.

13.. *E.E. Allit. P.* B. 531 Vche fowle [took] to þe flyht þat fyþerez myȝt serue, Vche fysch to þe flod þat fynne couþe nayte. *a* **1400** *Sir Perc.* 185 Other gudez would scho nonne nayte; But with hir tuke a tryppe of gayte. *c* **1400** *Destr. Troy* 6031 All necessaries for þe night, þat þai naite shuld. *c* **1460** *Towneley Myst.* xxiii. 62 Loke that we haue that we shuld nate, For to hald this shrew strate. **1677** NICOLSON *Gloss.* in *Trans. R. Soc. Lit.* (1870) IX. 316 *Nate*, to use. **1807** STAGG *Poems* 48 Then brouce about nor tek sec preesin, To nate your awn.

b. To go over, recite, repeat. *rare.*

13.. *S. Erkenwolde* 119 in Horstm. *Altengl. Leg.* (1881) 268 Ser Erkenwolde .. welneghe al þe nyȝt hade naityd [*MS.* nattyd] his houres. **13..** *Gaw. & Gr. Knt.* 65 Loude crye was þer kest of clerkez & oþer, Nowel nayted o-newe, neuened ful ofte.

2. *refl.* To exert oneself. *rare.*

a **1400–50** *Alexander* 2518 For Alexander all-ways .. Naytis him-selfe in ilke nede, & so his name rysis. *Ibid.* 2968 [He] naytis him to ryse, Buskis him vp at a braide.

† **nait**, *v.*² *Obs. rare.* [a. ON. *neita*, f. *nei* NAY *adv.*] *trans.* To refuse, deny.

c **1374** CHAUCER *Boeth.* I. met. i. 1 (Camb. MS.), With how deef an Ere deth cruwel torneth a-wey fro wrecches and nayteth to closyn wepynge eyen. *c* **1386** —— *Pars. T.* ¶939 Ne he shal nat nayte ne denye his synne. *c* **1400** *Apol. Loll.* 77 As it schal be ȝeuen to him that is callid .., so it schal be naytid him þat offreþ himsilf. *c* **1440** *Promp. Parv.* 351/1 Naytyn, or denyyn, *nego, abnego, denego.*

naithless(e, obs. forms of NATHELESS.

† **ˈnaitly**, *adv. Obs.* Forms: 4–6 **naytly**, 5 **naytely**, **naitly**, **-li**, **nately**. [f. NAIT *a.* + -LY².] To some purpose; properly; thoroughly.

13.. *E.E. Allit. P.* B. 480 Ho hittez on þe euentyde & on þe ark sittez, Noe nymmez hir anon & naytly hir stauez. *a* **1400–50** *Alexander* 2896 Þis reuere .. on niȝtis so naytely it fresys, Till any powere to pas or preke on with stedis. *c* **1400** *Destr. Troy* 2427 Than naknet anon full naitly were all, And broght to me bare. [Also 2746, 6628, etc.] *c* **1460** *Towneley Myst.* xiii. 158 Bot nately Both oure dame and oure syre .. can nyp at oure hyre. **1513** DOUGLAS *Æneis* VIII. vii. 99 Sche .. hyr puir damysellis, as scho ma, Naytly exersis for to werk the lyne.

naïve (nɑːˈiːv, naɪˈiːv), *a.* Also **naive**. [a. F. *naïve*, fem. of *naïf* (see NAÏF and NEYF):—L. *nātīv-um* NATIVE *a.*

'The word being only imperfectly naturalized, the pronunciation is somewhat unsettled: the chief variations given in the leading Dicts. are (nɑːˈiːv), (ˈnɑːiːv), and (neɪˈiːv)' (*N.E.D.*, 1906).]

1. a. Natural, unaffected, simple, artless.

1654 DOROTHY OSBORNE *Lett.* (1903) 234 Though he makes his people say fine handsome things to one another, yet they are not easy and *naïve* like the French. **1673** DRYDEN *Marr. à la Mode* III. i, *Naive*! as how? *Phil.* Speaking of a thing that was naturally said; it was so *naive*. **1762** LLOYD *Poet. Wks.* (1774) II. 11 And *naïve* both (allow the phrase Which no one English word conveys). **1797** MME. D'ARBLAY *Diary* (1846) VI. 150 She related .. her arguments to dissuade him, and his *naïve* manner of combating them. **1817** LADY GRANVILLE *Lett.* (1894) I. 117 Her manner is .. delightful, she is very naïve. **1859** JEPHSON *Brittany* viii. 109 The naïve details which the popular ballad-maker delighted in. **1885** CLODD *Myths & Dr.* I. iii. 39 As belief in causality spread, men were not content to rest in the naïve explanations of an uncritical age.

b. Philos. ***naïve realism.*** Also ***naïf realism.*** [The fem. form, despite being adj. to a sb. which in Fr. is masc., has acquired currency in English.] The belief, attributed to non-philosophers, that the world is directly perceived as it really is, as contrasted with philosophical theories of sense-data, the subjectivity of colour, etc. So ***naïve realist.***

1882 W. JAMES *Will to Believe* (1897) 290 Even the most *naïf* realism will hardly pretend that the non-table as such exists *in se* after the same fashion as the table does. **1895** F. THILLY tr. *Paulsen's Introd. Philos.* II. i. 344 We start out from the popular conception whose standpoint is *naïve Realism.* **1897** B. RUSSELL *Ess. Found. Geometry* ii. 93 Those who have done most to further non-Euclidean Geometry —with the exception of Riemann, who was a disciple of Herbart—have usually inherited from Newton a naïve realism as regards absolute space. **1909** W. JAMES *Meaning of Truth* ii. 50 The reader will observe that the text is written from the point of view of *naïf* realism or common sense. **1914** C. D. BROAD *Perception* i. 1 We are going to begin from the position of naïf realism. It is true that our everyday view of the world is not quite naïvely realistic, but that is what it would like to be. **1932** [see ILLUSION 4 b]. **1932** H. H. PRICE *Perception* ii. 26 We ask a Naïve Realist what sort of thing it is whose existence he knows of. *Ibid.* iii. 61 The Naïve Realist conception of 'belonging to' would not have been saved. **1954** A. J. AYER *Philos. Ess.* vi. 142 The naïve realist is not in error. Naïve realism is not a false theory of perception: it is a refusal to play this sort of game. **1971** A. FLEW *Introd. Western Philos.* III. x. 346 The position supported by the uninstructed 'instincts and propensities of nature' is by instructing philosophers labelled contemptuously, 'Naïve Realism'.

c. ***naïve painter***: a painter who has not been trained in a formal manner; so ***naïve painting.*** Cf. NAÏF *a.* 1 c.

1957 *Observer* 3 Nov. 14/4 Naive or primitive painting is a discovery of the twentieth century... The innocent eyes of the often untaught naïve painters give an account of the world quite unhampered by preconceptions of what paintings of it should be like. **1961** *Spectator* 28 July 149 A very intense, fat little book on naïve painters, with Henri Rousseau as the grand point of departure. **1970** *Time* 9 Feb. 54 The United States possesses the oldest, the most original, and just about the most authentic naive painters.

2. *Biol.* and *Psychol.* Not having previously had a particular experience or been the subject of a particular experiment, *esp.* not having taken or received a particular drug; unconditioned. Const. *to.*

1940 *Amer. Jrnl. Psychol.* LIII. 46 (*heading*) Configurational properties considered 'good' by naïve subjects. **1961** *Jrnl. Agric. Sci.* LVII. 401 Assessments of bacon qualities by naïve and experienced judges using photographic reference standards. **1963** *Animal Behaviour* XI. 463 The naive female cat does not exhibit the complete mating pattern on the first opportunity for sexual behaviour. **1969** *Sci. Jrnl.* Sept. 42/1 When research subjects are volunteers who are naive to marihuana, an effective placebo is no problem. **1970** *Nature* 11 Apr. 119/1 Interesting social and psychological similarities and differences were revealed among three groups of subjects: marijuana naïve persons (N), persons not naïve to marijuana (NN) and chronic marijuana users (C). **1974** *Ibid.* 19 Apr. 697/1 Twenty experimentally naïve male albino Wistar rats .. were anaesthetised with ether.

naïvely (nɑːˈiːvlɪ, naɪˈiːvlɪ), *adv.* Also **naively**. [f. as prec. + -LY², after F. *naïvement.*]

† **1.** Naturally, true to nature. *Obs. rare.*

1640 SIR W. MURE *Counterbuff* 300 They'le surely trust these men, So Naive-lie represented by thy pen.

2. In a naïve manner; artlessly.

1705 POPE *Lett.* Wks. 1751 VII. 116 She helped Gay to the head, me to the middle, .. and cried very naively, I'll be content with my own tail. **1849** RUSKIN *Sev. Lamps* p. vi, The text .. sometimes naïvely describes as sublime or beautiful, features which the plate represents by a blot. **1874** L. STEPHEN *Hours Libr.* I. iv. 159 He .. enjoys his playthings too naïvely for the pleasure not to be a little contagious.

naïveness (nɑːˈiːvnɪs, naɪˈiːvnɪs). *rare.* Also naiveness. [f. NAÏVE *a.* + -NESS.] = NAÏVETY.

1949 KOESTLER *Insight & Outlook* 387 The reconquest of 'naiveness' is one of the periodic revolutions in painting. **1968** *Classical Q.* XVIII. 208 A weakness of the book .. is a certain naïveness of interpretation.

‖**naïveté** (naivte). [F.: see NAÏVE and -TY.]

1. An instance or case of artlessness; an artless action, remark, etc.

1673 DRYDEN *Marr. à la Mode* III. i, Such an innocent piece of simplicity; 'twas such a *naiveté*. **1756** H. WALPOLE *Let. to Mann* 18 Mar., I have nothing more to tell but a *naïveté* of my Lady Coventry. **1780** T. DAVIES *Life Garrick* I. x. 91 A kind of droll farce, full of ridiculous incidents, and certain bon mots, called naivetés. **1873** SYMONDS *Grk. Poets* xi. 390 The affection of the Greeks for the grasshopper is one of their most charming naïvetés.

2. The quality of being naïve; artlessness; absence of pretence or conventionality.

1725 LADY M. W. MONTAGU *Lett.* (1893) I. 482, I, .. with great naïveté, desired to explain with her on the subject. **1794** MRS. RADCLIFFE *Myst. Udolpho* xviii, Sometimes she was compelled to smile at the naïveté of Annette. **1814** SCOTT *Wav.* xxxii, He had a sort of naïveté and openness of demeanour. **1848** MRS. JAMESON *Sacr. & Leg. Art* (1850) 8 We have frequent examples of this naïveté of sentiment in the old mosaics. **1870** EMERSON *Soc. & Sol.* xii. 253 The naïveté of his eager preference of Cicero's opinions to King David's.

naïvety (nɑːˈiːvtɪ, naɪˈiːvtɪ). Also **naivety**. [Anglicized form of prec.] = NAÏVETÉ.

1708 tr. *Petronius Arbiter* Pref., The Simplicity and Naivety is not to be imitated. **1742** HUME *Ess., Simplicity in Writing* (1748) 260 The absurd Naivety of Sancho Pancho is represented in such inimitable Colours by Cervantes. [*Note*, Naivety, a Word which I have borrow'd from the French, and which is wanted in our Language.] **1798** W. TAYLOR in *Monthly Mag.* VI. 345 Three volumes .. display occasionally, a grace and a naivety seldom surpassed. **1841** CARLYLE *Misc.* (1857) IV. 232 Shrewd simplicities, naiveties, blundering ingenuities. **1898** *Expositor* Dec. 424 The .. simplicity or naivety of the language of that Gospel.

‖**Naja** (ˈneɪdʒə, ˈneɪjə). Also **naia**. [mod.L., f. Hindī *nāg* snake.] A genus of highly venomous snakes, comprising the species *N. tripudians* of India and *N. haje* of Africa; the Indian or African cobra; a snake belonging to either of these species.

1753 CHAMBERS *Cycl. Supp.* App., *Naia*, in zoology, the name of a species of Coluber. **1770** PENNANT *Ind. Zool.* 9 You dread the spring of the Tiger, or the mortal bite of the Naja. **1788** GRAY in *Phil. Trans.* LXXIX. 25, I need only mention the Naja, a species well known to be very venomous. **1840** *Penny Cycl.* XVI. 63/1 A gigantic hooded serpent .. which, he remarked, was not a *Naja*. **1888** *Riverside Nat. Hist.* III. 377 The fangs of the Naja are long and grooved.

nakare: see NAKER².

† **nake**, *a. Obs. rare.* Also **naken**. [ME. *nake(n)* = OFris. and MLG. *naken*: see the note to NAKED *a.*] Naked.

c **1320** *Cast. Love* 1655 When I was nake ȝe ȝeve me clothyng. *c* **1380** *Sir Ferumb.* 2744 Þe Sarasyns dude his helm a-down, & maked his hed al nake. **1393** LANGL. *P. Pl.* C. XXI. 51 [Þey] nailede hym with þre nayles naked [*v.r.* naken] on þe rode. *c* **1400** *Laud Troy Bk.* 7214 Kyng Thoas herte be-gan to qwake, He wende to be hanged al nake.

nake, *v. Obs.* (exc. *Sc.*) [Originally, and most commonly, in ppl. and pret. form *naked*, based directly on the adj., the *-ed* being apprehended as a verbal ending.] *trans.* To make naked, in various *lit.* and *fig.* senses; to bare, lay bare, strip, unsheathe, etc.

Benacian occurs once in OE., but *nacian* in Bosw.-Toller rests upon an erroneous reading (cf. *O.E. Martyrol.* 18).

c **1320** LANGTOFT *Chron.* (Rolls) II. 248 The fote folk Put the Scottes in the polk, And nackened [*B.* nakid] thair nages. *c* **1374** CHAUCER *Boeth.* IV. met. vii. (1868) 148 O nice men whi nake ȝe ȝoure bakkes as who seiþ. **1402** HOCCLEVE *Let. Cupid* 353 Oure first moder .. made al mankynde lese his lyberte, and naked yt of Ioye. *c* **1440** *Gesta Rom.* lxix. 313 (Harl. MS.), Thenne he nakid hire evene to þe smok. **1502** DOUGLAS *Pal. Hon.* I. i, Write thir frenesyis Quhilks of thy sempill cunning nakit the. **1606** WARNER *Alb. Eng.* XV. xciv. 376 Thus he nakt to her his heart. **1607** TOURNEUR *Rev. Trag.* V. i, Come, be ready: nake your swords; think of your wrongs! **1614** T. ADAMS *Sinner's Passing Bell* Wks. 1861 I. 339 Sickness hath .. naked him of his silks. **1887** SERVICE

Life Dr. Duguid 258 He naked his swurd, an' swure he would thole't nae langer.

refl. *c* **1375** *Sc. Leg. Saints* i. (*Peter*) 31 He bad nocht, bot hym nakyt swith. *c* **1412** HOCCLEVE *De Reg. Princ.* 3290 He nakid hym, and schewed hym as blyue. *c* **1430** *Pilgr. Lyf Manhode* I. v. (1869) 3 Eche wight onclothed him and naked him at the entringe. **1533** BELLENDEN *Livy* I. xi. (S.T.S.) I. 65 Ane parte þareof schamefully nakit þame self of þare wapynnys. *Ibid.* III. xix. II. 27 He nakit him of his abulȝementis.

naked ('neɪkɪd), *a.* and *sb.*[1] Forms: 1 naecad, nacod, -ud, naced, 2 næcod, nakod, 2- naked, (3 -edd, 3-5 -ede, 4 -ide, 4-6 -id, -yd), 6 nakt, 7 nak't; 4-6 naket, *Sc.* nakit, (6 nakkit), nakyt, 6 *Sc.* naiket, -it, -yt, -att, nakyt. [OE. *nacod*, *næcad*, = OFris. *naked*, *naket*, MDu. *naket*, *naect* (Du. *naakt*), MLG. *naket*, OHG. *nakot*, *naccot*, *nachot*, *nahhut*, etc. (MHG. *naket*, *nachet*, G. *nackt*), ON. *nǫkkviðr*, *neycquiðr* (also *nǫkð-*, *nǫkt-*, etc.; MSw. *nakudher*, *naqvidher*), Goth. *naqaþs*, *naqad-*, a participial derivative from the stem **naq-*:—pre-Teut. **nogʷ-*, which is also represented in OSl. *nagŭ* (Russ. *nagói*), Lith. *nŭgas*, Skr. *nagnás*, L. *nūdus* (:—**nogʷedos*), OIr. *nocht*.

The West Germ. languages have also forms ending in *-n*, *-nd*, or *-nt*, as OFris. *naken*, MDu. *nakent* (Du. dial. *nakend*), MLG. *naken(t*, MHG. *nackent*, *nachent* (G. *nackend*), ME. *nake(n*: the explanation of these is not clear. In Icel. *nakinn* (Norw. and Sw. *naken*, Da. *nögen*) the ending has been altered from *-iðr* on the analogy of such participles as *vakiðr*, *vakðr*, *vaktr*: *vakinn*.]

A. *adj.* **I. 1. a.** Unclothed, having no clothing upon the body, stripped to the skin, nude. †Also *occas.* having only an under-garment on.

c **850** *O.E. Martyrol.* (Herzfeld) 26 þa het he hi nacode lædan to sumum scandhuse. *c* **950** *Lindisf. Gosp.* Mark xiv. 52 He miððy forwarp [sindonem, &] nacod foreflæh from ðæm. *c* **1000** ÆLFRIC *Gen.* iii. 7 Hiȝ oncneowon þa, þæt hiȝ nacode wæron. *Ibid.* 10. *c* **1205** LAY. 6273 Nakede heo weoren and naðing ne rohten. *c* **1290** *S. Eng. Leg.* I. 27/45 Men vrne nakede al a-boute and wummen al-so. *c* **1369** CHAUCER *Dethe Blaunche* 125 Hyr women kaught hir vp anoon, And broghten hir in bed al naked. **1439** *E.E. Wills* (1882) 116 My Image to be made all naked, and nothyng on my hede but myn here cast bakwardys. *c* **1489** CAXTON *Sonnes of Aymon* i. 49 It is rayson that we take of oure goode gownes, and goo to the kynge naked. **1560** DAUS tr. *Sleidane's Comm.* 43 Then he is torned naked and decked againe with a laymans apparell. **1593** SHAKS. *Rich. II*, I. iii. 298 Who can..Wallow naked in December snow by thinking on fantasticke summers heate? **1608** ARMIN *Nest Ninn.* (1842) 24 To bed he goes; and Jemy euer used to lye naked, as is the use of a number. **1673** [R. LEIGH] *Transp. Reh.* 11 Innocence..is no less a stranger to the use of swords and guns then the naked Indian. **1719** DE FOE *Crusoe* II. (Globe) 498 We advanced a little Way farther, and behold, to our Astonishment, three Women naked..come flying. **1761** *Brit. Mag.* II. 445 The streets were..filled with naked people, some with shirts and shifts on only, and numbers without either. **1822** LAMB *Elia* Ser. I. *Decay of Beggars*, To be naked is to be so much nearer to the being a man, than to go in livery. **1870** MORRIS *Earthly Par.* III. IV. 17 Three damsels stood, naked from head to feet Save for the glory of their hair.

absol. *c* **1220** *Bestiary* 219 He fleð fro ðe so neddre fro de nakede. **1663** GERBIER *Counsel* d 6 b, The Inhabitants.. affecting no other livery then that of the first naked.

fig. **1560** DAUS tr. *Sleidane's Comm.* 59 b, Where they nowe appeare in theyr likenes, and are beholden naked with the eies of all men. **1579** W. WILKINSON *Confut. Familye of Love* 7 Christ commeth not bare or naked, but clothed and accompanied with all his mercies.

b. In comparisons, as ***naked as a needle***, ***a worm***, ***one's nail***, etc.

1377 LANGL. *P. Pl.* B. XII. 162 Take two stronge men, and in themese caste hem, And bothe naked as a nedle. *a* **1467** *Gregory's Chron.* (Camden) 211 The Lorde Schalys..was slayne at Synt Mary Overeyes.., and laye there dyspoyly nakyd as a worme. **1470-85** MALORY *Arthur* XI. i. 572 There syr launcelot toke the fayrest lady by the hand..and she was naked as a nedel. **1559** *Mirr. Mag.* (1563) B b vij, We..Were led in prysoners naked as my nayle. **1633** HEYWOOD *Eng. Trav.* II. i. C iij b, He..did..so Plucke them and Pull them till hee left them as naked as my Naile. **1654** E. GAYTON *Pleasant Notes Don Quixot* III. iv. 88 As naked and bare as a shorne Sheep, as we say in our English Proverbe. **1860** O. W. HOLMES *Prof. at Breakfast-Table* iii. 39 A friend..had a watch given him..with a loose silver case... You know them,—the cases that you hang on your thumb, while the.. real watch, lies in your hand as naked as a peeled apple. **1879-81** G. F. JACKSON *Shropshire Word-Bk.* 297 W'y yo' bin as naked as a robin. **1890** D. C. MURRAY *John Vale's Guardian* III. xxxviii. 215 Time was I wouldn't ha' married her..without her lands. You can send her now as naked as a robin, if you like. **1939** *N. & Q.* 15 July 42/1 As naked as a needle. **1943** *Amer. Speech* XVIII. 67/2 Naked as a jaybird. **1963** J. T. ROWLAND *North to Adventure* xi. 160 Tell us what you were doing, standing naked as a jaybird. **1974** *State* (Columbia, S. Carolina) 8 Mar. 1-B/1 Just a footnote to ask if there is any truth to the rumor that 'naked as a jaybird' is going to be amended to use 'gamecock'!

c. In the plant-names ***naked lady*** or ***ladies***, and ***naked boys***, popular appellations of the Meadow Saffron (*Colchicum autumnale*).

1668 WILKINS *Real Char.* II. iv. 74 Having naked flowers without any stem;.. Medow Saffron, Naked Lady. *a* **1691** AUBREY *Nat. Hist. Wilts* (1847) 51 Naked-boys (q. if not wild saffron) about Stocton. **1760** J. LEE *Introd. Bot.* App. 320 Naked Ladies, *Colchicum*. **1853** TYAS *Pop. Flowers* Ser. III. 2 The Autumnal Crocus, or Meadow Saffron..bears also the name of Naked Lady, from the fact of its pretty flowers presenting themselves without leaves. **1857** *N. & Q.* 2nd Ser. III. 254 In Herefordshire..and in Norfolk, the autumnal crocus..is called commonly..Naked-boys.

d. Of a horse or ass: Without harness or trappings; unsaddled, bare-backed.

c **1000** ÆLFRIC *Hom.* I. 210 He nolde on nacedum assan ridan. **1607** TOPSELL *Four-f. Beasts* (1658) 244 Bucephalus, ..so long as he was naked and without furniture,..would suffer any man to come on his back. **1833** DARWIN *Jrnl. Voy. Beagle* viii. (1839) 143 A naked man on a naked horse is a fine spectacle.

e. In printing, ***naked forme*** (see quots.).

1683-4 J. MOXON *Mech. Exerc. Printing* (1962) 347 *Naked Form*,..is when the Furniture is taken from about all sides of the Form. **1888** C. T. JACOBI *Printers' Vocab.* 86 *Naked forme*, a forme of type waiting for—or stripped of—furniture. **1960** G. A. GLAISTER *Gloss. Bk.* 144/1 A 'naked forme' consists of pages of type secured by page-cord; a 'dressed forme' is one of pages of type with furniture between and around them and the page-cord removed.

2. a. Of parts of the body: Not covered or protected by clothing; bare, exposed.

1340 *Ayenb.* 244 Wyþ-oute none nakede uisage onwriȝe. *c* **1375** *Sc. Leg. Saints* ii. (*Paul*) 918 Strakis one his nakit flesche with a swerd. **1390** GOWER *Conf.* II. 15 It lay in his nakede arm. **1601** SHAKS. *Jul. C.* IV. iii. 101 There is my Dagger, And heere my naked Breast. **1667** MILTON *P.L.* IV. 772 On thir naked limbs the flourie roof Showrd Roses. **1805** SCOTT *Last Minstr.* v. xxiii, His naked foot was dyed with red. **1856** KANE *Arct. Expl.* II. i. 24 He was.. scratching his naked skin.

b. ***naked bed***, orig. used with reference to the custom of sleeping entirely naked; in later use denoting the removal of the ordinary wearing apparel. Now *arch.*

c **1400** *Destr. Troy* 13803 As Vlixes the lorde lay for to slepe..on a night in his naked bed. **1503** HAWES *Examp. Virt.* I. vii, As I in my naked bedde was leyd. **1592** KYD *Sp. Trag.* II. v. 1 What out-cries pluck me from my naked bed ..? **1617** MORYSON *Itin.* I. 242, I had never lien in naked bed since I came from Venice,..having alwaies slept..in my doublet, with linnen breeches and stockings. **1666** PEPYS *Diary* 7 Sept., I went the first time into a naked bed, only my drawers on; and did sleep pretty well. **1699** R. L'ESTRANGE *Erasm. Colloq.* (1725) 190 He would sit in a Chair, but very rarely came into his naked bed. **1756** AMORY *Buncle* (1770) I. 94 This young lady went into naked bed in her cabbin. **1870** MRS. GORDON *Life Brewster* 297 Sir David exclaimed in horror 'What! go to your naked bed in the middle of the ocean?'

c. In *fig.* context, of things personified, of unembodied spirits, etc.

1599 SHAKS. *Hen. V*, v. ii. 34 Why that the naked, poore, and mangled Peace..Should not in this..Our fertile France, put vp her louely Visage? **1628** MILTON *Vac. Exerc.* 23, I have some naked thoughts that rove about. **1678** CUDWORTH *Intell. Syst.* 346 Pan being used not so much for the naked and abstract Deity, as the Deity as it were embodied in this Visible Corporeal World. **1722** WOLLASTON *Relig. Nat.* ix. 212 When the soul shall be disengaged from the gross matter..and..become naked spirit. **1816** SHELLEY *Daemon* II. 242 Before the naked powers that thro' the world Wander like winds have found a human home. **1833** TENNYSON *Two Voices* 374 If first I floated free, As naked essence must I be Incompetent of memory.

d. *transf.* Applied to qualities, actions, etc. in which nakedness is involved.

1667 MILTON *P.L.* IV. 290 With native Honour clad In naked Majestie [they] seemd Lords of all. **1728** POPE *Dunc.* II. 283 In naked majesty Oldmixon stands. **1788** GIBBON *Decl. & F.* xl. IV. 53 The naked scenes which Theodora was not ashamed to exhibit in the theatre. **1821** SHELLEY *Adonais* xxxi, He..Had gazed on Nature's naked loveliness. **1897** *Manch. Guard.* 9 Aug. 10/4 Say whether this is naked weight or weight in cycling costume.

3. a. Destitute of clothing (implying poverty and wretchedness). Also *occas.* of animals: Stripped of the usual warm covering.

c **850** *O.E. Martyrol.* (Herzfeld) 204 Him com onȝean an þearfende man nacod on cealdum wyntra. *c* **1000** *Ags. Gosp.* Matt. xxv. 36 Ic wæs nacud & ȝe me scryddon. *c* **1200** ORMIN 6164 þe birrþ claþenn nakedd mann. **1340** HAMPOLE *Pr. Consc.* 508 Naked we come hider, and bare And pure. **1362** LANGL. *P. Pl.* A. VII. 212 Alle manere of Men þat þou mayȝt aspye, þat neodi ben, or naket. *c* **1480** HENRYSON *Mor. Fab.* 1257 (*Sheep & Dog*), The Scheip..sauld the woll, he bure vpoun his bak;..Nakit and bair syne to the feild couth pas. **1551** CROWLEY *Pleas. & Pain* 29 Naked and bare, hauynge no clothes my fleshe to hyde. **1605** SHAKS. *Lear* III. iv. 28 Poore naked wretches..That bide the pelting of this pittilesse storme. **1697** DRYDEN *Virg. Georg.* III. 679 Short of their Wool, and naked from the Sheer.

absol. *a* **900** CYNEWULF *Crist* 1354 þonne ȝe..him hleoð ȝefon hingrendum hlaf & hræȝl nacedum. **971** *Blickl. Hom.* 213 He wolde..hingriȝendum mete syllan, & nacode scrydan. *a* **1225** *Leg. Kath.* 102 Ha..spende al þet oðer in neodfule & in nakede. *a* **1300** *Cursor M.* 20121 Naked and hungri sco cled & fede. *c* **1400** *Rule St. Benet* (Verse) 582 Cleth þe naked þat hase nede. **1500-20** DUNBAR *Poems* ix. 29, [I have not] Harbreit the wolsome, nor naikit cled att all. **1535** COVERDALE *Job* xxii. 6 Thou hast..robbed the naked of their clothinge. **1692** DRYDEN *Eleanora* 47 The afflicted came, The hunger-starved, the naked and the lame.

b. Bare or destitute of means. *rare.*

a **1625** FLETCHER *Hum. Lieut.* III. v, I am a poor man, naked, Yet something for remembrance,..gentlemen. **1719** DE FOE *Crusoe* II. (Globe) 507, I had been stripp'd naked, in a remote Country, and nothing to help myself. **1722** —— *Col. Jack* (1840) 165 Thus a naked planter has credit at his beginning. **1893** STEVENSON *Catriona* v, In the meanwhile I am held naked in my prison.

†4. a. Without weapons (or armour); unarmed.

1375 BARBOUR *Bruce* x. 431 He wes armyt and wes vycht, The tothir nakyt wes,..And had nocht for till stynt no strak. **1489** *Paston Lett.* III. 359 My seid Lord of Northumberland heryng..that they wer but naked men, addressed hym self towardes theym withoute eny harneys. **1553** T. WILSON *Rhet.* (1580) 95 This vilaine was armed, and the other man naked. **1596** DALRYMPLE tr. *Leslie's Hist. Scot.* III. 186 Baith the parties war vnarmet, or as we vse to speik, naked men. **1644** *Prerog. Anatomized* 4 It's hard usage,..because in time of peace, I walke unarm'd, to put me naked in the front of a Battell. **1727** DE FOE *Hist. Appar.* viii. 143, I scorn to take up a sword against a naked man. **1787** *Minor* III. ix. 186, I could not endure the idea of killing a naked man.

fig. **1693** WOOD *Life* (O.H.S.) IV. 49 He disarmes the author, then fights with him naked.

b. Without defence or protection; defenceless, unprotected; open or exposed *to* assault or injury.

1560 DAUS tr. *Sleidane's Comm.* 265 If they should leave their owne countrey naked,..others would take possession. **1603** R. JOHNSON *Kingd. & Commw.* 61 He is forced to keepe the greater part of those troupes at home, vnless he should lay naked his estates to infinite casualties. **1688** PENTON *Guard. Instr.* (1897) 18 Left naked to infinite temptations of doing nothing, or worse. **1751** JOHNSON *Rambler* No. 180 ¶3 As a small garrison must leave one part of an extensive fortress naked when an alarm calls them to another. **1822** SHELLEY *When the lamp is shattered* iv, Thine eagle home [will] Leave thee naked to laughter. **1863** COWDEN CLARKE *Shaks. Char.* xv. 373 Gaunt suddenly fell away from him..and left him naked to the tender mercies of his priestly enemies.

II. 5. a. Of a sword or other weapon: Not covered by a sheath; unsheathed.

Beowulf 539 Hæfdon swurd nacod..heard on handa. *c* **888** K. ÆLFRED *Boeth.* xxix. §1 Him ealne weȝ.. hangað nacod sweord ofer ðæm heafde be smale þræde. *c* **1205** LAY. 686 Bi þone toppe he hine nom..& his nakede sweord leide on his necke. **13..** *Sir Beues* (A.) 3648 þai..bete hire wiþ swerdes naked. **1390** GOWER *Conf.* I. 287 He..tok him..A naked swerd to bere on honde. *c* **1450** *Merlin* 409 The Ban and the kynge Bohors com on with swerdes naked in her handes. **1535** COVERDALE *Micah* v. 6 These shal subdue.. the londe of Nymrod with their naked weapens. **1599** SHAKS. *Hen. V*, IV. ii. 21 Scarce blood enough..To giue each naked Curtleax a stayne. **1634** PEACHAM *Gentl. Exerc.* II. v. 118 In her right hand a naked poniard. **1714** POPE *Epil. Rowe's J. Shore* 44 Many an honest man may copy Cato, Who ne'er saw naked sword. **1802** *Naval Chron.* VII. 83 Was not your sword naked? **1887** BOWEN *Virg. Æneid* II. 334 Naked steel and glittering blade Ready, and ranged for slaughter.

†b. Of the tongue: Thrust out, exposed. *Obs.*[−1]

c **725** *Corpus Gloss.* (Hessels) E 499 *Exserta lingua*, naecad tunge.

6. a. Free from concealment or reserve; plain, straightforward; outspoken, free. Now *rare.*

a **1225** *Ancr. R.* 316 Schrift ȝet schal beon naked, þet is, nakedliche imaked. *Ibid.*, þis nis nout naked schrift. *c* **1391** CHAUCER *Astrol.* Prol., This tretis..wole I shewe the under ful lihte rewles & naked wordes in englissh. **1602** *2nd Pt. Return fr. Parnass.* I. ii. 281 What cares he for modest close coucht termes... Giue him plaine naked words stript from their shirts. **1652** COTTERELL tr. *Calprenède's Cassandra* III. IV. (1676) 296 By this naked confession of my life. **1788** GIBBON *Decl. & F.* xl. IV. 53 *note*, A fragment of the Anecdotes, somewhat too naked, was suppressed by Alemannus. *c* **1789** —— *Mem.* (1857) 122 The most naked tale in my history is told by the Rev. Mr. Joseph Warton.

b. ***the naked truth***, the plain truth, without concealment or addition.

a **1585** MONTGOMERIE *Cherry & Slae* 1141, I..trewly tald the naikit truth To men that melld with me. **1663** BUTLER *Hud.* I. ii. 36 We shall tell The naked Truth of what befel. **1709** BERKELEY *Th. Vision* §120 It is scarce possible to deliver the naked and precise truth. **1843** R. J. GRAVES *Syst. Clin. Med.* xiv. 181, I have not deviated in the slightest degree from the strict and naked truth. **1889** JESSOPP *Coming of Friars* v. 242 An unmarried woman was a chattel... That is the naked truth.

c. ***naked force***, unconcealed, ruthless force.

1963 E. WILSON in *New Statesman* 6 Dec. 847/2 According to the United States State Department, Fidel Castro uses naked force in Cuba.

7. a. Exposed to view or examination; uncovered, stripped of all disguise or concealment.

1382 WYCLIF *Job* xxvi. 6 Nakid is helle beforn hym. *a* **1535** FISHER *Serm.* Wks. (1876) 401 All thinges be naked and open before his eyes. **1579** FULKE *Heskins' Parl.* 129 With a naked soule, and pure minde you beholde those thinges that are in heauen. **1611** BIBLE *Micah* i. 11 Passe yee away thou inhabitant of Saphir, hauing thy shame naked. **1672** MARVELL *Reh. Transp.* I. 96, I shall without Art write down his own Words..as they ly naked to the view of every Reader. **1703** ROWE *Ulyss.* II. i, My Friends, who view my naked Soul. **1781** COWPER *Expost.* 339 Darkness itself before His eye is light, And hell's close mischief naked in His sight. **1819** LADY CHARLEVILLE in Lady Morgan *Autobiog.* (1859) 272, I show you this to read my naked heart. **1875** JOWETT *Plato* (ed. 2) I. 11 Should we not ask him to show us his soul, naked and undisguised?

b. Plain, obvious, clear.

1589 T. COOPER *Admon.* 192 That considering the proofe to be naked in it selfe, thou mayest the better iudge of the strength thereof. **1855** MACAULAY *Hist. Eng.* xx. IV. 496 Chamberlayne laid his plan, in all its naked absurdity, before the Commons. **1884** *St. James's Gaz.* 12 Aug. 3/1 People..shut their eyes in the face of staring, naked, palpable facts.

III. 8. a. Bare, destitute, or devoid *of* something. †Also const. *from*.

c **897** K. ÆLFRED *Gregory's Past C.* lvi. 431 Se lyteȝa feond swa micle ieðlicor ðæt mod ȝewundað swa he hit onȝiet nacodre ðære byrnan wærscipes. *c* **1220** *Bestiary* 144 Ðanne ðe neddre is of his hid naked. *c* **1380** WYCLIF *Sel. Wks.* III. 199 But þouȝ here children ben nakid fro virtues in soule, þei chargen noþing. **1533** BELLENDEN *Livy* I. xi. (S.T.S.) I. 64 Mecius..was als nakit of manhede and curage as he was of faith. **1581** J. BELL *Haddon's Answ. Osor.* 149 Freewill is made naked of all maner merite. **1632** LITHGOW *Trav.* VIII. 361 The maritine Townes..being left halfe naked of defence. **1665-6** PEPYS *Diary* 19 Jan., It is a remarkable thing how infinitely naked..Covent Garden is..of people. **1709** STEELE *Tatler* No. 2 ¶3 They thought fit to leave him naked of the proper Means to make those Excellencies useful. **1788** GIBBON *Decl. & F.* lxxvii. VI. 629 The monuments of antiquity had been left naked of their precious ornaments.

b. Bare, lacking, or defective in some respect. *c* **1386** CHAUCER *Sec. Nun's T.* 486 If thou speke of moo, Thow liest; for thy power is full naked. **1549** *Compl. Scot.* Prol. 16 To condamp and repreif this raggit naykyt tracteit. **1622** BACON *Hen. VII* (1876) 37 Concerning which battle the relations that are left unto us are so naked and negligent [etc.]. **1692** DRYDEN *St. Euremont's Ess.* 340 The Pleasures of the Senses sometimes render despicable the Satisfactions of the Mind, as too dry, and too naked. **1817** COLERIDGE *Biog. Lit.* (Bohn) 210 The poem..is..written in language as unraised and naked as any perhaps in the two volumes.

c. Clean, clear, unfilled, unoccupied. **1643** PRYNNE *Sov. Power Parlt.* App. 205 Moreover, he hath sold..very many naked and unwritten Parchments. *c* **1660** SOUTH *Serm. John* vii. 17 (1715) I. 231 It finds the Mind naked, and unprepossessed with any former Notions. **1822** SYD. SMITH *Wks.* (1859) II. 1/1 It is a great point in any question to clear away encumbrances, and to make a naked circle about the object in dispute.

9. a. Devoid of trees or other vegetation; bare, barren, waste. †Of water: Having no weeds. [*c* **1385** CHAUCER *L.G.W.* Prol. 126 Forgeten had the erthe his pore estat Of winter, that him naked made and mat.] **1549** *Compl. Scot.* xi. 92 ȝe sal be compellit to laubir the naikyt feildis vitht ȝour auen handis to there proffet. **1615** G. SANDYS *Trav.* 227 So was I left alone on a naked promontorie right against the Citie. **1697** DRYDEN *Virg. Georg.* III. 716 We see the naked Alps, and thin Remains Of scatter'd Cotts. **1721** BRADLEY *Philos. Acc. Wks. Nat.* 180 They are better fed Fish, and much larger in such Ponds, than where they have only a naked Water. **1784** COWPER *Task* III. 773 Those naked acres. **1793** —— *A Tale* v, Sea-beaten rocks and naked shores. **1839** ALISON *Hist. Europe* (1849–50) VIII. liii. §3. 398 No forests clothe their sides; naked, they present their arid fronts to the shivering blasts. **1879** FARRAR *St. Paul* (1883) 206 The corruption which the ebbing tide..had left upon the naked sands.

b. Bare of leaves or foliage; leafless. **1591** SPENSER *Daphn.* xlviii, Let birds be silent on the naked spray. **1602** MARSTON *Antonio's Rev.* Prol., Wks. 1856 I. 71 Snarling gusts nibble the juyceles leaves, From the nak't shuddring branch. **1697** DRYDEN *Virg. Georg.* II. 562 When Storms have shed From Vines the hairy Honours of their Head;..Ev'n then the naked Vine he persecutes. **1784** COWPER *Task* VI. 141 These naked shoots, Barren as lances, among which the wind Makes wintry music. **1841** BROWNING *Pippa* i, How these tall Naked geraniums straggle! **1882** *Garden* 25 Feb. 135/2 Laurels and Hollies that have got naked at bottom should now be headed down.

c. Of ground, rock, etc.: Devoid of any covering or overlying matter; exposed. **1693** EVELYN *De la Quint. Compl. Gard.* II. 146 Some plants which our Climate is not capable naturally of producing in the naked Ground. **1759** MARTIN *Nat. Hist.* I. 15 The lower Parts, or Basis of the Rock lie intirely naked. **1776** G. SEMPLE *Building in Water* 3 The Workmen..built Part of the Piers..on Part of the Foundation..and the rest of them on the naked Bed of the River. **1797** *Encycl. Brit.* (ed. 3) II. 248/1 Whether we take this method or begin upon the naked floor [of the foundation]. **1855** MACAULAY *Hist. Eng.* xviii. IV. 191 Huge precipices of naked stone frown on both sides. **1887** W. PHILLIPS *Brit. Discomyc.* 70 [It grows] on the naked ground in damp and shady woods.

d. *naked fallow*, a 'bare' fallow, one on which no crop at all is grown (cf. FALLOW *sb.*[2]). So *naked fallowing*. **1805** R. W. DICKSON *Pract. Agric.* I. 364 Such soils as may ..require the aid of naked or summer fallowing. **1808** J. C. CURWEN *Hints Feeding Stock* 234 Though no friend to naked fallows, I was obliged [etc.]. **1840** J. BUEL *Farmer's Companion* 169 On substituting fallow crops for naked fallows. **1889** [see FALLOW *sb.* 2].

e. *transf.* of the wind: Bleak, cold. **1821** SHELLEY *Hellas* 293 A flock Of wild swans struggling with the naked storm. **1834** R. MUDIE *Feathered Tribes* (1841) I. 49 The black cock has the shelter of the bush when the naked wind blows.

10. a. Destitute of sails or tackle. *rare*. **1390** GOWER *Conf.* I. 183 [He] hath ordeined..A nakid Schip withoute stiere. *c* **1400** *Destr. Troy* 3701 All þere takyll was tynt, tylude ouer borde, The nauy wex nakit; noy was on honde. **1819** SHELLEY *Cyclops* 18, I myself stood on the beaked prow And fixed the naked mast.

b. Destitute of carpets, hangings, or similar furnishings; unfurnished. **1528** GARDINER in Burnet *Hist. Ref.* (ed. Pocock) I. 89 We pass three chambers all naked and unhanged. **1588** SHAKS. *L.L.L.* v. ii. 805 Go with speed To some forlorne and naked Hermitage. **1646** SIR T. BROWNE *Pseud. Ep.* 386 The spirits of many long before that time will finde but naked habitations. **1704** POPE *Windsor For.* 68 The hollow winds thro' naked temples roar. **1788** MME. D'ARBLAY *Diary* 1 Dec., He longed, he said, to cover all the naked, cold boards, to render them [the rooms] more habitable. **1822** GALT *Steam-boat* iv. 74 To cover the naked walls they had brought carpets from home. *a* **1834** COLERIDGE in *Rem.* (1836) II. 77 The stage in Shakspeare's time was a naked room with a blanket for a curtain.

c. *naked flooring*, the timbers which support the flooring boards. **1823** in CRABB *Technol. Dict.* **1825** J. NICHOLSON *Operat. Mechanic* 569 Naked flooring, for ball-rooms, should be framed very strong. **1847** SMEATON *Builder's Man.* 74 There are three kinds of naked flooring: single, double, and framed.

d. Devoid of ornament or facing of any kind; plain and bare. **1850** INKERSLEY *Styles Archit. France* 313 The enormous projection of the naked buttresses. **1879** STEVENSON *Trav. Donkey* 48 Here and there a few naked cottages and bleak fields. **1892** T. B. F. EMINSON *Epid. Pneumonia at Scotter* 12, Cesspools of naked brick.

11. a. Uncovered, unprotected, exposed. **1607** TOPSELL *Four-f. Beasts* (1658) 389 Moles want their sight, because they have not their eyes open and naked as other Beasts. **1771** BURKE *Corr.* (1844) I. 280, I always felt it on the naked nerve, and with the quickest, sorest sensibility. **1852** MRS. STOWE *Uncle Tom's C.* xi. 94 It seemed as if every blow cut into my naked heart. **1861** J. R. GREENE *Man. Anim. Kingd., Cœlent.* 94 In some *Plumulariæ* the gonophores appear to be naked. **1899** *Allbutt's Syst. Med.* VIII. 325 These changes are described as occurring.. in the ultimate naked fibrils.

b. Not placed within a case or receptacle; esp. *naked light* (also *attrib.*). *a* **1626** MIDDLETON *Mayor Queenb.* I. ii, Yes, sir, in lanterns; but I'll never trust candle naked again. **1839** URE *Dict. Arts* 1079 As the naked cage of Davy often gets red-hot with flame [etc.]. **1842** PARNELL *Chem. Anal.* (1845) 13 The crucible..should never be introduced naked into the fire. **1865** *Morn. Star* 3 Nov., The Use of Naked Lights in a Fiery Mine. **1886** *S.W. Lincolnsh. Gloss.* s.v., We don't reckon to take a nak'd light into the yard. **1929** R. GRAVES *Poems* 18 Then it's those naked-light instructions That the muctions plaster up. **1966** *Listener* 18 Aug. 237/1 The naked electric-light bulb had to be left on all day. **1971** *Chambers's Dict. Sci. & Technol.* 787/2 *Naked-light mine*, nonfiery mine, where safety lamps are not required.

c. *naked fire*, an open fire, one not closed in by any contrivance. ? *Obs.* **1673** GREW *Philos. Hist. Plants* (1682) 19 The strongest heat which a naked fire in that Furnace would produce. **1756** C. LUCAS *Ess. Waters* III. 68 It requires a naked fire to fuse it. **1800** tr. *Lagrange's Chem.* II. 189 Place the retort on a sand-bath, or a naked fire.

12. *Bot.* **a.** Of seeds: Not enclosed in a case or ovary; having no pericarp. **1578** LYTE *Dodoens* IV. viii. 461 The grayne..is naked, bare, and cleane. **1706** PHILLIPS (ed. Kersey), *Naked Seeds* .., such Seeds of Plants, as are not included in any Pod or Case. **1776–96** WITHERING *Brit. Plants* II. 179 Flowers of 1 petal, beneath, and 4 naked seeds. **1846–50** A. WOOD *Class-bk. Bot.* 52 Truly naked seeds are found in few plants. **1875** BENNETT & DYER tr. *Sachs' Bot.* 433 The cases are, however, not rare in which the seeds remain quite naked from first to last.

b. Of stalks, etc.: Destitute of leaves. Of leaves, etc.: Free from hairs; smooth, glabrous. **1721** BRADLEY *Philos. Acc. Wks. Nat.* 34 Plants, whose.. whole Foliate or naked Roots put forth every Spring their fresh Flower-Stalks. **1753** CHAMBERS *Cycl. Supp.* s.v. *Leaf*, Naked Leaf expresses a leaf whose surface is smooth and equal, without any particular marks. *Ibid.* s.v. *Stalk*, Naked stalk, one that has no leaves. **1776–96** WITHERING *Brit. Plants* II. 320 The barren branches naked and bent backwards. **1860** A. GRAY *Man. Bot.* 281 Flowers perfect, solitary or long naked scapes or peduncles.

c. In the specific names of varieties of grain having naked seeds, as *naked barley* and *naked oats*, or of plants with naked stems, as *naked broom-rape*. **1578** LYTE *Dodoens* IV. viii. 461 The naked or hulled Barley groweth in some places of Fraunce. **1678** SALMON *Pharm. Lond.* I. iv. 117 *Zeopyrum*, Naked Barley. **1707** MORTIMER *Husb.* (1721) I. 136 In Staffordshire..is a sort of red or naked Oats. **1764** *Museum Rust.* III. 151 The naked oat..I am told is very much cultivated in Cornwall. **1808** J. WALKER *Econ. Hist. Hebrides* I. 229 The naked oat..is so called, because the grain..falls naked from the head, like a grain of wheat. **1835** *Penny Cycl.* III. 166/2 The naked oat ..is found wild in many parts of Europe. **1838** *Ibid.* XII. 291/1 Naked Barley, a species but little cultivated now, is of unknown origin. **1860** A. GRAY *Man. Bot.* 281 *Aphyllon*, Naked Broom-rape.

13. a. *Zool.* Destitute of hair or scales; not defended by a shell. **1769** E. BANCROFT *Guiana* 134 A long tail, which is almost naked towards the end. **1828** STARK *Elem. Nat. Hist.* I. 364 Skin naked, with longitudinal folds. **1844** CARPENTER *Zool.* §573 The Cod tribe..have a long body..covered with soft scales,—the head, however, being naked. **1897** H. O. FORBES *Hand-bk. Primates* II. 199 The front, top, and sides of the head and face are nearly naked.

b. As the distinctive epithet of classes of animals (see quots.). **1601** HOLLAND *Pliny* XXIX. vi. II. 365 Naked snailes (I meane those that bee found without shells.) **1774** GOLDSM. *Nat. Hist.* (1776) VII. 112 Klein gives them a class..under the name of Naked Quadrupedes. **1828** STARK *Elem. Nat. Hist.* I. 364 Family III. Naked Serpents. **1834** MCMURTRIE *Cuvier's Anim. Kingd.* 270 The naked Acephala are not numerous. **1840** tr. *Cuvier's Anim. Kingd.* 336 We call those Mollusca *naked* in which the cloak is simply membranous or fleshy. **1851** WOODWARD *Mollusca* I. 62 The rest are termed 'naked cephalopods', because the shell is internal.

IV. 14. a. Left without any addition; not strengthened or increased in any way; bare, mere; †absolute. *c* **1000** ÆLFRIC *On New Test.* (Grein) 21 Nu miht þu wel witan, þæt weorc sprecan swiðor, þonne þa nacodon word. *c* **1380** WYCLIF *Wks.* (1880) 35 Whi schulde curatis pronounsen here breþeren a cursed for nakid lettris of syche coueitous prelatis. **1523** SKELTON *Garl. Laurel* 1205 Harde to make ought of that is nakid nought. **1552** ABP. HAMILTON *Catech.* (1884) 48 Thai that presumis owyr mekil of thair awin nakit frewill & gud deedis. *a* **1652** J. SMITH *Sel. Disc.* iv. 103 A naked perception of sensible impressions, without any work of reason. **1700** C. NESSE *Antid. Armin.* (1827) 17 Some grant..to the non-elect only a prescience or naked foresight. **1785** BURKE *Sp. Nabob Arcot* Wks. 1842 I. 319/2 On these principles he chooses to suppose..a naked possibility. **1837** T. JONES *Christian Warrior* III. xv. 77 He would make him believe that a naked Christ and a naked faith is quite enough. **1876** STAINER & BARRETT *Dict. Mus. Terms*, *Naked fourth*, the interval of a fourth without the addition of any other interval.

b. Not accompanied by, or overlaid with, remarks or comments; expressed in plain unadorned language. *c* **1400** *Cato's Mor.* 345 in *Cursor M.* 1673 þou wondris in þi witte þat I wrate þis writte in twa versis nakid. **1450–1530** *Myrr. our Ladye* 3 In many places where the nakyd letter.. ys not easy for symple soulles to vnderstonde; I expounde yt ..more openly. **1594** HOOKER *Eccl. Pol.* II. vii. §1 To draw all things unto the determination of bare and naked Scripture. **1655** S. ASHE *Funeral Serm. Gataker* 25 This I enlarge not by specifying instances, because the naked quotations may be sufficient. **1711** ADDISON *Spect.* No. 39 ¶6 The naked Thought of every Speech..divested of all its Tragick Ornaments. **1768** BLACKSTONE *Comm.* III. 377 Herein they state the naked facts, as they find them to be proved. **1835** THIRLWALL *Greece* iii. I. 65 This is the naked abstract of the tradition. **1878** O. W. HOLMES *Motley* xxiv. 226 One who felt himself wronged must not be expected to reason in naked syllogisms.

c. Not otherwise supported, assured, or confirmed. (Chiefly in legal use.) *c* **1380** WYCLIF *Sel. Wks.* III. 420 Sith þei supposen þat hor naked graunte is als myche worthe as graunte wiþ hor lettres. *c* **1555** HARPSFIELD *Divorce Hen. VIII* (Camden) 45 If the parties make but a naked and bare promise of affiance. **1616** T. GODWYN *Moses & Aaron* (1641) 257 The making of peace was a naked stipulation..for the laying aside of all hostile affections. **1681** STAIR *Inst. Law Scot.* 116 Whether it be a naked Paction or Promise, or a Mutual Contract. **1766** BLACKSTONE *Comm.* II. 195 The lowest and most imperfect degree of title consists in the mere naked possession, or actual occupation of the estate. **1818** CRUISE *Digest* (ed. 2) II. 455 Suppose a naked right, or a contingent remainder had descended. **1823** CRABB *Technol. Dict.*, *Nude contract*, a bare naked contract, without a consideration, which is void in law. **1871** DE VERE *Americanisms* 509 *Naked possessor*, is the odd title by which, in Texas and the Southwestern States, the occupant of a farm is known, who can show no title to his land. **1877** TENNYSON *Harold* II. ii, Thou art perfect in all honour! Thy naked word thy bond!

d. Not supported by proof or evidence. **1581** J. BELL *Haddon's Answ. Osor.* 43b, Unlesse you suppose, that with your naked clamorous affirmatives ye may expell them out of the Church. **1632** LITHGOW *Trav.* x. 457 Onely for a naked suspition, mistaking the honorable intention of the English. **1673** CAVE *Prim. Chr.* I. iv. 81 None were ever greater Enemies to a naked profession. **1817** JAS. MILL *Brit. India* II. v. vii. 603 For the evidence of these designs, Mr. Hastings presents his own naked assertion.

15. a. *naked eye*, the eye itself, unassisted by the microscope, telescope, or other aid to vision. So *naked sight*. **1664** POWER *Exp. Philos.* I. 17 Smaller than the smallest hair our naked eyes can discover. **1672** GREW *Anat. Veget.* iii. 77 As the Tract of these Pores appears to the naked Eye. **1711** ADDISON *Spect.* No. 121 ¶9 Such [creatures] as are bulky enough for the naked Eye to take hold of. **1789** MME. D'ARBLAY *Diary* 18 Jan., With my glass..I can see just as other people see with the naked eye. **1812** WOODHOUSE *Astron.* xxiii. 240 To the naked sight, or to unassisted vision. **1875** MANNING *Mission H. Ghost* xiii. 359 The naked eye cannot perceive them, but the power of the microscope reveals them.

b. *attrib.* Visible to the naked eye. **1876** *Trans. Clinical Soc.* IX. 138 The naked-eye characters being..characteristic. **1897** *Allbutt's Syst. Med.* III. 963 There was no naked-eye damage to the cord. **1908** *Westm. Gaz.* 11 Aug. 12/1 The other naked-eye planets are too near the sun to be visible. **1930** *Times Educ. Suppl.* 5 Jan. p. iv/3 Within the limit of the naked-eye visibility. **1965** *Listener* 20 May 741/1 Another naked-eye cluster is Præsepe in Cancer, now well placed during the evenings.

16. Undiluted, neat. *rare*$^{-1}$. **1824** SCOTT *Redgauntlet* let. xiii, I am drinking naked spirits, I think.

17. *Comb.*, as *naked-armed*, *-bladed*, *-eyed*, *-flowered*, *-flowering*, *-footed* (also adv.), *-handed* (also adv.), *-limbed*, *-nerved*, *-seeded*, *-tailed* adjs. Also **naked ape**, man, *Homo sapiens*; **naked-beard grass**, an American grass having an abortive flower; **naked boys, lady**, see sense A I. 1 c; †**naked-tail** (see quot.). **1967** D. MORRIS (*title*) The *naked ape. **1967** *Spectator* 10 Nov. 577/1 Even before man has destroyed all other animals to make more room for himself, the naked ape may well destroy himself also. **1973** W. BARLOW *Alexander Principle* iii. 33 The 'Naked Ape' has replaced Rousseau's 'Noble Savage'. **1891** T. HARDY *Tess* xxix, Tess had come out ..*naked-armed and jacketless. **1860** GRAY *Man. Bot.* 553 *Gymnopogon*. *Naked-beard Grass. **1856** MRS. BROWNING *Aur. Leigh* I. 330 And with two grey-steel *naked-bladed eyes Searched through my face. **1848** E. FORBES (*title*) A Monograph of the British *naked-eyed Medusæ. *Ibid.* 3 In the naked-eyed species. **1870** NICHOLSON *Man. Zool.* x. (1875) 119 The 'naked-eyed' Medusæ..are exceedingly elegant..when examined in a living condition. **1853** TYAS *Pop. Flowers* Ser. III. 2 The *Naked-flowered Crocus (*C. nudiflorus*) adorns the meadows..in the fall of the year. **1885** *Globe* 31 Jan. 1/5 Of the shrubs,..none is more kindly than the yellow naked-flowered jasmine. **1841** MACGILLIVRAY *Withering's Brit. Plants* 63 *C. nudiflorus*, *naked-flowering Crocus. **1855** MISS PRATT *Flower. Pl.* V. 233 Naked-flowering Saffron. **1923** D. H. LAWRENCE *Birds, Beasts & Flowers* 16 And yet the soul continuing, *naked-footed, ever more vividly embodied. **1848** *Sporting Life* 1 July 210/2 The savage..does not fear to encounter the dangers of his chase *naked-handed. **1869** WHITTIER *Hive at Gettysburg* in *Poetical Works* (1898) 380/2 And he who, lone and naked-handed, tore Those jaws of death apart. *a* **1930** D. H. LAWRENCE *Phoenix* (1936) III. 164 There the painted women dance..opposite the *naked-limbed men. **1933** DYLAN THOMAS *Let.* Nov. (1966) 48 It is typical of the..*naked-nerved..to emphasise its brutality. **1776** LEE *Botany* 415 (Jod.) *Gymnospermia*, *naked-seeded. **1845** *Encycl. Metrop.* XIV. 495/1 In Guiana is found the rabo pelado, or *naked-tail, a ravenous animal, of the vulpine species. **1841**

WATERHOUSE *Marsup.* 94 *Naked-tailed opossum, *Didelphys nudi-caudata.*

B. *sb.*[1]

1. ***the naked***: †**a.** The naked skin. *Obs. rare.*

a **1400–50** *Alexander* 4182 Quare it neȝes on þe nakid it noyis for euire. *c* **1400** *Destr. Troy* 6403 He shot þrough the shild & the shene maile,.. Hit neghit to þe nakid.

†**b.** *Art.* The nude. *Obs.*

1735 POPE *Ep. Lady* 188 Artists! who can paint or write, To draw the Naked is your true delight. **1753** HOGARTH *Anal. Beauty* xi. 91 The drapery.. helps to satisfy the eye,.. without depriving the beholder of any part of the beauties of the naked.

c. The face or plain surface of a wall, etc.

1726 LEONI *Alberti's Archit.* I. 66 Angles jutting out from the naked of the Wall. **1776** G. SEMPLE *Building in Water* 13 The Cutwaters.. extend 12 Feet each beyond the naked of the Bridge. **1823** P. NICHOLSON *Pract. Builder* 339 *Naked of a Wall*, the vertical or battering surface, whence all projectures arise. **1842** GWILT *Archit.* 1007.

†**2.** *Art.* A nude figure. *Obs.*

1622 PEACHAM *Compl. Gent.* II. xiii. (1634) 148 Hee excelled in Perspective, and above all other masters laboured in Nakeds. **1675** A. BROWNE *App. Art of Limning* 21 To understand how to make choice of a good Naked, and to draw it well.

†**naked,** *sb.*[2] *Obs. rare.* [f. prec.] Nakedness.

c **1000** ÆLFRIC *Deut.* xxviii. 48 Drihten asent hungor on eow and þurst and næcede. *c* **1470** HENRYSON *Orph. & Eur.* 529 For this dispyte quhen he was deid anon Was dampnyt .. To suffer hunger, thrist, nakit and cald.

†**'nakedhead.** *Obs.* In 4 **nakedhed(e, nakidhe(e)d.** [f. NAKED *a.* + -HEAD: cf. MDu. *naket-, naectheit* (Du. *naaktheid*), G. *nacktheit*, Sw. *nakenhet*, Da. *nögenhed.*] Nakedness.

a **1300** *Cursor M.* 23089 O naked-hed quen i drogh [h]arme, Yee gaf me clething. **13..** *K. Alis.* 7056 Ther is none.. for the nakedhed aschamed. *c* **1380** WYCLIF *Sel. Wks.* III. 47 Of þe caitifte of helle, of þe nakidheed fro al solace. **1382** —— *Jer.* ii. 25 Forfende thi foot fro nakidhed.

'nakedish, *a. rare.* [-ISH.] Somewhat naked.

1806 GALPINE *Brit. Bot.* 26 *Alopecurus*.. Glumes nakedish, united at their base.

'nakedize, *v.* [f. NAKED *a.* + -IZE.] **a.** *intr.* To go naked. **b.** *trans.* To make naked.

1858 HOGG *Shelley* II. 289 It was most manifest that the children liked to nakedize—such was the term of art—exceedingly. **1885** J. C. JEAFFRESON *Real Shelley* II. 192 The troop of nakedized children rushed downstairs.

nakedly ('neɪkɪdlɪ), *adv.* Also 3 **-liche,** 5 **-lye;** 4 **nakyd-,** 5 **nakidly.** [f. NAKED *a.* + -LY[2]: cf. MDu. *naectelike, -lic(k.*]

1. a. Without concealment or reserve; plainly, openly. (Common in 17th c.)

a **1225** *Ancr. R.* 316 Schrift ȝet schal beon naked, þet is, nakedliche imaked, and nout.. hendeliche ismoked. **1340** *Ayenb.* 174 He ssel zigge his zennes clyerliche and nakedliche. **1561** *Reg. Privy Council Scot.* I. 173 In sa fer as is allegit naketlie, that I ressavit.. and disponit the gudis. **1603** *Lismore Papers* Ser. II. (1887) I. 56 Laying nakedlie and feelinglie before his eies the danger of the action. **1643** *Myst. Iniq.* 43 The Catholike cause (which the King.. is induced to serve either nakedly, or cloathed with this pretence). **1682** SIR T. BROWNE *Chr. Mor.* (1716) 23 The Judge of all knoweth all, and every man will nakedly know himself. **1818** HALLAM *Mid. Ages* (1872) I. 402 Quarrels of private families ..sometimes.. were more nakedly conspicuous. **1846** GROTE *Greece* II. iv. (1862) II. 88 This supremacy was not claimed directly and nakedly.

b. Without addition or amplification; simply, barely.

1534 MORE *Comf. Trib.* II. Wks. 1205/1 Hard is it.. in many maner thinges, to.. affirme or denye, reproue or allow, a mater nakedlye proponed & put furth. **1560** BECON *New Catech.* Wks. 1564 I. 427 If we had ben without bodies, Christ wold haue geuen vnto vs those spirituall gifts, nakedly & simply. **1651** SAUNDERS *Plen. Poss.* 7 His meaning is.. nakedly what the words expresse. **1710** *Brit. Apollo* No. 40. 1/2 Our Church has Nakedly proposed them but left the Sense of them undetermined. **1741–3** WESLEY *Extr. Jrnl.* (1749) 22, I desired five or six to go with him to Justice Copeland, to whom they nakedly related the fact. **1809–10** COLERIDGE *Friend* (1865) 111 To state it nakedly is to confute it satisfactorily.

2. Without reference to, apart from, other things or circumstances. (Common in 17th c.)

c **1380** WYCLIF *Serm.* Sel. Wks. II. 231 þus shulde stiwardis of þe Chirche juge not nakydly bi þer wille, but sikerly aftir Goddis lawe. **1549** LATIMER *7th Serm. bef. Edw. VI* (Arb.) 207 Not the bare death, consideryng it so nakedly by it selfe. **1646** J. WHITAKER *Uzziah* 7 The acts of the unregenerate in themselves nakedly considered, some of them may be right. **1724** SWIFT *Drapier's Lett.* Wks. 1755 V. II. 67 Let us take the whole matter nakedly,.. without the refinements of some people. **1756** BURKE *Vind. Nat. Soc.* Wks. 1842 I. 8/2 When it is nakedly considered, and those matters which are apt to divert our attention from it.. are not taken into the account. **1873** *Speaker's Comm.* Ps. cxxxviii. 1 It is doubtful if the Hebrew word Elohim, used nakedly.., can have this meaning. **1884** LD. SELBORNE in *Law Rep.* 9 App. Cases 611 The question, therefore, is nakedly raised by this appeal.

3. In a naked, unclothed, or exposed manner; nudely. Also *fig.*

a **1440** *Found. St. Bartholomew's* (E.E.T.S.) 40 All thyng worldly [he] hadde forsake for the loue of criste, nakidly askapynge the wrake of this worlde. **1595** DANIEL *Civ. Wars* I. lxxx, This.. dazeleth all their clearest sighted eies, That they see not how nakedly they lie. *a* **1619** FLETCHER *Mad Lover* I. i, How have you borne yourself, how nakedly Laid your soul open. **1684** R. WALLER *Nat. Exper.* Pref. Truth, through the fine Web.. sometimes seems so plain and lively, that some might conclude, She was Nakedly Discovered. **1755** BURKE *Vind. Nat. Soc.* Wks. I. 71 Things which we pass by in their common dress, yet which shock us when they are nakedly represented. **1896** *Daily News* 5 Nov. 9/2 A.. man of about 30 years of age was indicted for nakedly exposing himself in a public place.

†**b.** Without means of defence. *Obs. rare.*

1562 PILKINGTON *Expos. Nehemiah* (1585) 64 Good men may also learne here not.. to goe nakedlie without weapon, to yeald them selues into their enemies hands. **1632** LITHGOW *Trav.* VIII. 362 Rash fellowes.. who will nakedly hazard themselues in knowne perrils, without Ordonance.

4. Barely, poorly, imperfectly; slightly. ? *Obs.*

1589 COOPER *Admon.* 120 They.. haue handled them so coldely, nakedly, and vnperfectly, that many haue bene grieued to heare them. **1634–5** BRERETON *Trav.* (Chetham Soc.) 156 My Lord of Kildare, who passed through them nakedly attended. *a* **1682** SIR T. BROWNE *Tracts* (1683) 6 The Reader, unacquainted with such Vegetables, or but nakedly knowing their natures.

nakedness ('neɪkɪdnɪs). [f. NAKED *a.* + -NESS.]

1. The state or condition of being unclothed or destitute of clothing. Also *transf.* a naked person.

c **1000** ÆLFRIC *Hom.* I. 392 On hungre & on ðurste,.. on cyle, & on nacednysse. —— *Gen.* ix. 23 Swa þæt hiȝ ne ȝesawon heora fæder nacednisse. *c* **1386** CHAUCER *Clerk's T.* 810 To yow broghte I noght elles.. But feyth and nakednesse and maydenhede. *a* **1425** *Cursor M.* 23089 (Trin.), Bi nakudnes whenne I toke harm wiþ cloþing ȝe made me warm. **1526** *Pilgr. Perf.* (W. de W. 1531) 8 Where shall be no sycknes, no necessite nor nakednes. **1573** L. LLOYD *Marrow of Hist.* (1653) 39 The women.., lifting up their cloaths, shewing their nakedness. **1617** MORYSON *Itin.* III. 172 A black vaile,.. through which the nakednesse of their shoulders.. may be seene. **1667** MILTON *P.L.* x. 217 As Father of his Familie he clad Thir nakedness with Skins of Beasts. *c* **1718** PRIOR *Pallas & Venus* 16 Thou to be strong must put off every dress; Thy only armour is thy nakedness. **1788** GIBBON *Decl. & F.* xliv. IV. 347 He concealed his nakedness with a linen towel. **1855** TENNYSON *Maud* I. x. i, Grimy nakedness dragging his trucks And laying his trams in a poison'd gloom. **1885** *Pall Mall G.* 20 May 3/1 The fair nakednesses who look down unabashed upon the well-dressed crowd.

b. Absence of cover or concealment; the state of a thing when not cloaked or disguised in any way; a feature requiring to be kept concealed.

1599 SHAKS. *Much Ado* IV. i. 177 Why seek'st thou then to couer with excuse, That which appeares in proper nakednesse? **1661** MARVELL *Corr.* Wks. (Grosart) II. 66, I would not tell you any tales, because there are nakednesses which it becomes us to cover if it be possible. **1768** STERNE *Sent. Journ., Passport*, I could wish.. to spy the nakedness of their hearts. **1820** SHELLEY *Liberty* xvi, Till in the nakedness of false and true They stand before their Lord. **1885** *Manch. Exam.* 30 Dec. 5/3 None of us have as yet gone to the length of avowing this design in all its nakedness.

c. Openness to attack; weakness. *rare.*

a **1591** H. SMITH *Serm.* (1866) II. 40 It grieves me.. to discover the nakedness of my countrymen. **1611** BIBLE *Gen.* xlii. 9 To see the nakednes of the land you are come.

2. Destitution; bareness, poverty.

1570–6 LAMBARDE *Peramb. Kent* (1826) 133 By decay of the haven.. it was brought in manner to miserable nakednesse and decay. **1631** WEEVER *Anc. Funeral Mon.* 315 This penury, nakednesse, and abiection. **1642** MILTON *Apol. Smect.* Wks. 1851 III. 310 The lofty nakednesse of your Latinizing Barbarian. **1742** FIELDING *J. Andrews* II. ii, He.. discovered the nakedness of his pockets. **1754** PITT *Lett. to Nephew* iv. 22 Exposing the nakedness and emptiness of the mind. **1853** KANE *Grinnell Exp.* xxix. (1856) 251 It is this nakedness of resources.. that makes our position one of bitterness. **1873** HAMERTON *Intell. Life* III. iv. 95 The result would be simple intellectual nakedness.

b. Bareness due to absence of vegetation, ornament, or other accessories.

1750 JOHNSON *Rambler* No. 80 ¶4 The nakedness and asperity of the wintry world. **1821** SHELLEY *Adonais* xlix, Where.. fragrant copses dress The bones of Desolation's nakedness. **1859** JEPHSON *Brittany* viii. 107 The broken arches.. and desolate nakedness of the cathedral.

3. Freedom from unnecessary ornament or refinement; simplicity. *rare.*

1617 MORYSON *Itin.* IV. IV. iii. 379 No people of Europe.. vseth lesse Ceremonyes,.. doing all such thinges without any ostentation, yea with great simplicity and nakednes. **1711** HEARNE *Collect.* (O.H.S.) III. 173 Much admiring the Simplicity and Nakedness of yᵉ Style. **1711** ADDISON *Spect.* No. 85 ¶4 Nature in her Simplicity and Nakedness.

4. Absence of hairs or scales.

1851 CARPENTER *Man. Phys.* (ed. 2) 397 This order.. is further distinguished.. by the softness and nakedness of the skin. **1873** MIVART *Elem. Anat.* vii. 243 In Batrachians.. we find a nakedness of skin greater even than in man.

†**'naken,** *v. Obs.* Forms: 3 **nacn(en),** 4–5 **nakn(en);** 4 **nacken, -in, nakkin, nakin,** 4–5 **nakyn, naken.** [app. f. *naken* NAKE *a.* + -EN[5].]

1. *trans.* To strip (a person) naked; to divest of clothing (or armour); to lay (part of the body) bare. Also *refl.*

a **1240** *Wohunge* in *O.E. Hom.* I. 283 A nu nacnes mon mi lef. *a* **1300** *Cursor M.* 4173 þai hent ioseph.. And nackend him and kest him dun. *a* **1350** *S. Anastasia* 140 in Horstm. *Altengl. Leg.* (1881) 27 þe Emperoure.. Gert nakkin þam al foure in fere. **1382** WYCLIF *1 Chron.* x. 9 Whanne thei haden spuylid hym.. and nakenyd fro armys. *c* **1440** *Alph. Tales* 84 He nakend þe tane of his legis. *c* **1440** *Gesta Rom.* lxiv. 277 (Harl. MS.), Do of and nakyn þe of all þi Clothing. **1483** *Cath. Angl.* 248/1 To Nakyn, *nudare.*

b. To strip or deprive one *of* something.

c **1430** *Pilgr. Lyf Manhode* I. xli. (1869) 25 Therfore j haue wrethe in myn herte whan ye.. nakenen me of my right.

2. To lay bare; to reveal or disclose.

a **1300** *Cursor M.* 27099 Alle þis werld.. es nackind forwit cristis ei. **1382** WYCLIF *Ecclus.* xix. 8 If ther is to thee gilte, wile thou not nakenen. —— *Isa.* xxii. 6 And Elam toc an arewe caas,.. and the target naknide the wal.

Hence †**'nakening** *vbl. sb. Obs.*

1382 WYCLIF *Ecclus.* xi. 29 In the ende of a man [there is] ful nakenyng of the werkis of hym. **1483** *Cath. Angl.* 248/2 A Nakynynge, *nudacio.*

naker ('neɪkə(r)), *sb.*[1] Now only *Hist.* Also 4–5 **nakere,** *gen. pl.* **nak(e)ryn,** 5 **nakyr,** 9 **nakir.** Cf. NACORNE and NAQUAIRE. [a. OF. *nacre, naquere, nakaire, nacaire,* etc. = It. *nacchera*, med.L. *nach-, nacara, nacaria*, med.Gr. ἀνάκαρα, ad. Arab. *naqārah*, Pers. *naqāra.* In English the word seems to have had real currency only in the 14th cent.] A kettle-drum.

13.. *E.E. Allit. P.* B. 1413 Ay þe nakeryn noyse, notes of pipes, Tymbres & tabornes tulket among. *a* **1352** MINOT *Poems* iv. 80 þe princes.. Gert nakers strike and trumpes blaw. *c* **1386** CHAUCER *Knight's T.* 1653 Pypes, trompes, nakers, and clariounes. *c* **1400** MAUNDEV. (Roxb.) xxxi. 138 þer es herd noyse as it ware of trumppes and tawburnez and nakers. *a* **1440** *Sir Degrev.* 1085 With trompe and with nakere And the scalmuse clere.

1819 SCOTT *Ivanhoe* xxx, A flourish of the Norman trumpets.. mingled with the deep and hollow clang of the nakers. **1891** *Cornh. Mag.* May 450 Every road.. resounded with nakir and trumpet.

Hence †**'naker** *v. intr.*, to beat upon nakers.

c **1400** *Laud Troy Bk.* 4699 Thei nakered, piped and blew, Vnto that the Cokkes crew.

†**naker,** *sb.*[2] *Obs. rare*$^{-0}$. [f. NAKE *v.* + -ER[1].] One who makes naked.

c **1440** *Promp. Parv.* 351/1 Nakare, or he þat spoylythe men of clothys, *denudator.*

naker, obs. form of NACRE.

†**'nakerer.** *Obs.* Also 4 **nakarer.** [f. NAKER *sb.*[1] + -ER[1].] A performer upon the naker.

1310–11 *MS. Cott. Nero* c. viii. lf. 87b, Rogerole Troumpour, Janino le Nakerer, Menestrallis Regis. *a* **1377** in *Househ. Ord.* (1790) 4 Mynstrelles—Nakerers. *c* **1400** *Siege Jerusalem* 852 (E.E.T.S.) With dynnyng of pipis, & þe nakerer' noyse.

†**na'kette.** *Obs. rare.* [Of obscure origin.] Some precious stone.

c **1460** *Emare* 94 Of crapowtes and nakette As thykke ar they sette. *Ibid.* 142 Wyth crapawtes and nakette, Thykke of stones ar they sette.

nakhlite ('nɑːklaɪt). *Geol.* [f. El *Nakhla* el Baharia, the village near Alexandria, Egypt, where the first known examples fell in 1911 + -ITE[1].] Any of a class of achondrites containing about 75 per cent ferroan diopside and 15 per cent olivine.

1916 [see HOWARDITE 2]. **1962** B. MASON *Meteorites* vii. 116 The diopside-olivine achondrites or nakhlites are represented by two meteorites, Lafayette (Indiana, U.S.A.) and Nakhla (Egypt). **1971** [see HOWARDITE 2].

Hence **nakh'litic** *a.*

1963 *Geochim. & Cosmochim. Acta* XXVII. 1077 Abundances of cadmium have been determined by neutron-activation analysis in 31 meteorites:.. 0·18 and 1·79 p.p.m. in two nakhlitic achondrites. **1971** P. R. BUSECK in B. Mason *Handbk. Elemental Abundances in Meteorites* 365 (*table*) Type.. Nakhlitic.

‖**nakhoda** ('nɑːkədɑː). Forms: 7 **nocheda, nockhoda, nohuda, nucquedah, nokayday, nockado; necoda, nahoda, nacoda,** 9 **nacodah, nakouda, nakhoda, nakhuda.** [a. Urdū (Persian) *nākhodā, nākhudā*, f. *nāw* boat, ship + *khudā* master.] The captain or master of an Indian boat or vessel.

1605 SARIS in Purchas *Pilgrims* I. IV. 385 The Nockhoda of the Iuncke alledged many rich parcells taken. **1611** MIDDLETON *Ibid.* I. III. 263 The Nohudas and Merchants in great feare of losse of their ship and goods. **1663** H. COGAN tr. *Pinto's Trav.* xiii. 42 The three Necodas of the Junks, so are the commanders of them called in that country. **1802** JAMES *Milit. Dict., Nakouda.* **1834** A. PRINSEP *Baboo* II. xii. 249 (Stf.), He laughed and told me I should see the Nakhoda in the evening. **1887** MRS. D. Dale *S. Australia* 244 The proas are owned by Malays, each one commanded by a head man or nacodah.

nakin, -kyn, variants of NO-KIN.

†**'naking,** *vbl. sb. Obs. rare*$^{-0}$. [f. NAKE *v.* + -ING[1].] The action of making naked.

c **1440** *Promp. Parv.* 351/1 Nakynge, or nakydnesse (or stryppyng), *nudacio, denudacio.*

‖**nakodo** (na'kodo). Also **nakohdo.** [Jap.] In Japan, one who acts as go-between in the arrangement of a marriage.

1890 B. H. CHAMBERLAIN *Things Japanese* 221 The conduct of the affair must be entrusted to a middleman (*nakōdo*)—some discreet married friend, who not only negotiates the marriage, but remains through life a sort of godfather to the young couple. **1895** L. HEARN *Out of East* viii. 258 He was a professional nakōdo, or match-maker, and was.. acting in the service of a wealthy rice dealer. **1902** —— *Kottō* x. 123 A majority of Japanese marriages, indeed, are arranged.. with the aid of a nakōdo. **1936** K. NOHARA *True Face of Japan* iv. 85 Although he receives monetary compensation for his services, the Nakohdo is not a professional marriage-broker.

nakquayre: see NAQUAIRE.

nakre, obs. form of NACRE.

nal, obs. form of AWL.

nala, var. NULLAH.

nald(e, would not: see NILL *v.*

nale, in phr. *at* (*the*) or *atte nale*: see ALE 2.

N.A.L.G.O., NALGO, Nalgo (ˈnælgəʊ). [Acronym f. the initial letters of *N*ational *A*ssociation of *L*ocal *G*overnment *O*fficers.] The name of a trade union of municipal, county, etc., local-government servants.

1909 *Municipal Jrnl.* 29 Oct. 896/2 A change in the Executive Offices of such an organization as the N.A.L.G.O. is always a matter of concern. **1957** *Times* 12 Nov. 8/1 A delegate conference of Nalgo health service branches will be held in London on Sunday. **1962** *Listener* 12 July 74/3 Pompous remarks about Nalgo and the T.U.C. **1975** *Guardian* 5 Nov. 8/8 The social workers, all members of NALGO, say that..the money could be better spent.

† **nall(e,** obs. forms of AWL.

14.. *Metr. Voc.* in Wr.-Wülcker 628 Baryngsexe, sole, nalle (*subula*), corduane. **1432-50** tr. *Higden* (Rolls) VIII. 249 Prikkede thro alle the body with nalles, neldes, and pynnes. **1496** *Fysshynge w. Angle* (1883) 14 Shomakers nalles in especyall the beste for grete fysshe. **1530** PALSGR. 247/1 Nall for a souter, *alesne.* **1564** [see AWL]. **1573** TUSSER *Husb.* (1878) 36 Hole bridle and saddle, whit lether and nall. **1632** [see AWL].

attrib. and *Comb.* **1530** PALSGR. 247/1 Nall maker, *faiseur dalesnes.* **1601** HOLLAND *Pliny* XI. xxxvii. I. 331 Like a shomakers Nall blade.

nalorphine (ˈnæləfiːn). *Pharm.* [f. *N-allyl*nor*morphine*, another name for the compound (see quot. 1953[2]).] A heterocyclic base, $C_{19}H_{21}NO_3$ (or its hydrobromide salt), which is very similar to morphine in chemical structure and is used as an antagonist for that drug and for other narcotics with a similar action.

1953 *Jrnl. Pharmacol. & Exper. Therap.* CIX. 157 N-allylnormorphine (nalorphine) has been shown to have a specific respiratory stimulating effect against the depression caused by morphine,..codeine, methadone. **1953** *Proc. R. Soc. Med.* XLVI. 927 *N*-Allylnormorphine is now officially called nalorphine... A methyl group is removed from the nitrogen [of morphine], hence the term NOR from the German 'Nitrogen ohne radicale'. An allyl group is substituted. **1967** *Martindale's Extra Pharmacopoeia* (ed. 25) 838 Given apart from narcotics, nalorphine may itself cause respiratory depression and disturbing psychotic effects. **1968** J. H. JAFFE in D. H. Efron *Psychopharmacol.* VIII. 854/1 Nalorphine has virtually no abuse potential; its subjective effects are not 'liked' by post-addicts; it does not relieve morphine withdrawal symptoms, but instead precipitates them, and when given over long periods in high doses it produces an atypical physical dependence in which withdrawal symptoms are not associated with craving. **1971** H. W. ELLIOTT in D. H. Clouet *Narcotic Drugs* xxvi. 484 The pharmacological basis for the nalorphine test is an antagonism between nalorphine and the morphine-like drugs, which can be detected by examining the pupil.

naloxone (næˈlɒksəʊn). *Pharm.* [f. *N-allyl*nor*oxymorphone*, an alternative name for the compound.] A heterocyclic base, $C_{19}H_{21}NO_4$ (or one of its salts), which resembles nalorphine in its chemical structure and antagonism to narcotics (see quot. 1968).

1964 *Amer. Jrnl. Med. Sci.* CCXLVII. 412 The n-allyl derivative of oxymorphone (Numorphan) has recently been synthesized and found to be a potent narcotic antagonist... It has also been suggested that this preparation (Naloxone), differs from other narcotic antagonists in that its administration simultaneously with a narcotic results in antagonism of the respiratory depression but not of the analgesia induced by the narcotic. **1968** *Clin. Pharmacol. & Therapeutics* IX. 215/1 Unlike nalorphine and cyclazocine, naloxone does not produce miosis, subjective effects, tolerance, or physical dependence. **1973** *Nature* 23 Mar. 228/3 Binding was demonstrated by incubating tissue homogenates with tritium-labelled naloxone, a potent antagonist which precipitates withdrawal in humans addicted to opiates.

† **nam,** am not: see NE and BE *v.* A. I. 1. *, *1 sing.*

c **825** *Vesp. Psalter* cxviii. 60 ȝearu ic eam & neam ȝedroefed. *c* **950** *Lindisf. Gosp.* Matt. iii. 11 His ȝesceoe nam [*Rushw.* næm] ic wyrðe beara. *c* **1200** ORMIN 10281 Namm I nohht Godess sune. *c* **1205** LAY. 14136 Næm [*c* 1275 nam] ich næuere bute care. *a* **1240** *Ureisun* in *O.E. Hom.* I. 185 Hwi nam ich in þin earmes. *c* **1305** *Edmund Conf.* 61 in *E.E.P.* (1862) 72 Nam ic þi felawe, quaþ þis child. **1390** GOWER *Conf.* I. 67 Seie I noght That I nam somdel for to wyte. *c* **1450** LOVELICH *Grail* xxxviii. 472 In non wyse nam I not so. **1575** GASCOIGNE *Flowers* Wks. 64, I nam..the wisest wight of all. **1576** —— *Steele Gl.* (Arb.) 50, I n'am a man, as some do thinke I am.

Nam (næm, nɑːm). Also **'Nam.** Colloq. abbrev. of *Vietnam.*

1969 *Time* 2 May 33/1 'Nam' or 'The Nam' is widely used by U.S. troops to refer to Vietnam. **1973** R. LUDLUM *Matlock Paper* vii. 66 The early days in 'Nam..those weeks of unreported combat. **1973** J. DI MONA *Last Man at Arlington* (1974) 198 [We] were a unit in 'Nam. **1974** *Publishers Weekly* 30 Dec. 93/3 Four Americans caught in Vietnam... The GIs become buddies in Germany... Now in 'Nam' they hope their camaraderie will be closer still.

† **nam,** variant of MNAM, mina. *Obs.*

1377 LANGL. *P. Pl.* B. VI. 241 Mathew..mouthed thise wordes, That *seruus nequam* had a nam.

nam, pledge: see NAAM.

nam, pa. t. of NIM *v. Obs.*

Nama (ˈnɑːmə), *a.* and *sb.* [Hottentot.]

A. *adj.* Pertaining to or designating one of the four main Hottentot tribes, found in Namaqualand in western South Africa. **B.** *sb.* **a.** A member of this tribe; these people collectively. **b.** Their language, a dialect of Hottentot. Hence **ˈNaman** *a.* and *sb.*

1864 W. H. I. BLEEK *Reynard the Fox in S. Afr.* p. xxix, To make our available stock of Nama Hottentot literature quite complete. **1881** T. HAHN *Tsuni-‖Goam* i. 3 In the Nama language, one of the Khoikhoi idioms, the Bushmen are called Sā-n (com. plur). *Ibid.* ii. 89, I afterwards made him a present of ammunition, and, as anxious as a Nama is to possess that most precious material, he said: 'No; you want to pay [for] my cow, and I shall not accept it.' **1908** T. G. TUCKER *Introd. Nat. Hist. Lang.* viii. 148 Hottentot dialects: viz. *Nama* (of the Namaqua) to the north-west, [etc.]. **1930** C. G. SELIGMAN *Races Afr.* ii. 34 The customary division of the Hottentots into four main groups—Naman, Korana, Gonaqua, and Old Cape Hottentots. **1944** M. OLDEVIG *Sunny Land* 51 Namas—or Hottentots. *Ibid.* 53 Three different Nama tribes. **1965** [see HOTTENTOT 2]. **1966** J. H. GREENBERG *Lang. Afr.* (ed. 2) 68 Nama Hottentot indicates the past by an element *go* (in the usual orthography). *Ibid.*, In Nama there is no phonemic distinction between *k* and *g*. **1974** *Times* 14 Jan. 4/6 They have intermarried with Coloured and Nama (Hottentot) people.

namable, variant of NAMEABLE *a.*

naman, -mon, variants of NO-MAN, no one.

† **ˈnamandly,** *adv.* In 4 **nom-**. [Cf. MDu. *namende-*, *namondelike*, G. *namentlich.*] Namely.

c **1375** *Cursor M.* 27282 (Fairf.) In spiring prest loke þou be sleye..in þakin þingis nomandeli [*Cott.* namly] þat is gaine kind in leccheri.

Namaqua (nəˈmɑːkwə), *a.* and *sb.* [Hottentot, f. *Nama* (see NAMA *a.* and *sb.*) + *-qua*, f. *khoi* man.] **1.** = NAMA *a.* and *sb.*

[**1668** O. DAPPER in I. Schapera *Early Cape Hottentots* (1933) 34 De Hottentots, genaemt *Namaquas*, leggen tegenwoordigh ontrent tachentigh of tuegentigh mÿlen oost-noord-oostwaerts van de kaep van goeder hope, maer zeer verre te landewaerts in.] **1670** J. OGILBY *Africa* 576 The chiefest people hitherto discover'd in this Southerly part of Africa, are the Gorachouqua's, Goringhaiqua's, Goringhaikona's, Kochoqua's,..Namaqua's, Heusaqua's, Brigoudins, and Hankumqua's. **1790** E. HELME tr. *Le Vaillant's Trav. Afr.* I. vii. 133, I had been assured there were some [*sc.* gazelles] in the country of the great *Namaquois.* **1806** J. BARROW *Voy. Cochinchina* 374 Their dwellings..are constructed on the same principle as those of the Namaqua Hottentots. **1822** W. J. BURCHELL *Trav. S. Afr.* I. 582 To the Hottentot Race are referable the tribes denominated Bushmen, the Namaquas, and Koras or Koraquas, as well as the Hottentots proper. **1822** [see GRIQUA *sb.* and *a.*]. **1849** E. E. NAPIER *Excursions S. Afr.* I. 53 The Dutch became gradually acquainted not only with numerous hordes of Hottentots, similar to those at the Cape; but likewise with a few varieties of the same race, such as the Namaquas. **1851** J. ANDERSON in G. M. Theal *Yellow & Dark-Skinned People Afr.* (1910) iii. 58 The signs of gender were almost identical in the Namaqua and the Egyptian. **1865** [see HOTTENTOT 2]. **1880** *Encycl. Brit.* XI. 731/2, 3000 Bushmen, 1500 Namaqua. **1930** I. SCHAPERA *Khoisan Peoples S. Afr.* I. ii. 48 The Great Namaqua were always the most northerly group of Hottentots, and probably formed the rearguard of their invasion of South Africa. **1932** *Times Lit. Suppl.* 15 Sept. 642/2 There was a little trouble with some Namaqua guides who suddenly refused to go any further. **1959** *Chambers's Encycl.* VII. 248/1 In south-west Africa many of the 15,000 Namaqua retain their Hamitic speech. **1972** *Stand. Encycl. S. Afr.* V. 607/1 The Nama (also called Naman or Namaqua) consisted of two groups: the Little Nama, living in the North-Western Cape south of the Orange River, and the Great Nama, living in South-West Africa.

2. Namaqua dove, a small, long-tailed dove, *Œna capensis*, found in Africa south of the Sudan; **Namaqua grouse, partridge, sandgrouse,** a terrestrial game bird, *Pterocles namaqua.*

1801 J. BARROW *Acct. Trav. S. Afr.* I. iv. 325 Along the road were numbers of that beautiful little pigeon, called here the Namaaqua dove, not larger than a sparrow. **1864** T. BAINES *Explor. S.-W. Afr.* v. 124 A pretty Namaqua dove fluttered about in abortive efforts to sip the water. **1905** J. DU PLESSIS *Thousand Miles in Afr.* 137 Little black-eyed Namaqua doves. **1947** J. STEVENSON-HAMILTON *Wild Life S. Afr.* xxxiv. 291 Doves... The little namaqua (*Oena capensis*) appears to be a winter migrant to the eastern Transvaal low country. **1972** *Shooting Times & Country Mag.* 27 May 24/2 Mourning, laughing and even tiny, wagtail-sized Namaque [*sic*] doves arrive to raid the crops. **1806** J. BARROW *Trav. S. Afr.* (ed. 2) I. iii. 219 Cape partridges and the Namaaqua grouse were equally plentiful. **1867** E. L. LAYARD *Birds S. Afr.* 277 Namaqua Grouse... Namaqua Patrys of Colonists. **1790** E. HELM tr. *Le Vaillant's Trav. Afr.* II. xxi. 434 The Hottentots of the colonies call them perdrix Namaquais, (Namaquai partridges). **1890** A. MARTIN *Home Life Ostrich Farm* xi. 227 The beautiful little 'Namaqua partridges'..are in reality a kind of grouse. **1936** E. L. GILL *First Guide S. Afr. Birds* 113 Namaqua Sandgrouse, Namaqua Partridge... Much the most widespread of the Sandgrouse in South Africa. **1972** Namaqua partridge [see KORHAAN]. **1893** H. A. BRYDEN *Gun & Camera S. Afr.* xxii. 477 The Namaqua sandgrouse [drinks] between eight and ten in the morning. **1962** MACKWORTH-PRAED & GRANT *Birds S. Third Afr.* 372 Namaqua Sandgrouse... Birds of the desert fringe. A common Sandgrouse of the drier parts of South Africa especially the western side.

‖ **namaskar** (nʌmʌˈskɑː(r)). *India.* Also **namashkar, namaskara.** [Hindi, ad. Skr. *namaskârá*, the greeting '*namas*', obeisance.] = NAMASTE *sb.*

1930 C. PARSONS *Mysore City* 88 Indian girls..making the silent and beautiful salutation of the 'namaskāra'—folded hands and bent head and bowing figure. **1948** *U.N. World* (N.Y.) Apr. 35 One by one they filed past, some doing *namaskar* (hands placed together in an attitude of prayer), others bowing low. **1966** J. & R. GODDEN *Two under Indian Sun* iv. 102 Instead of a handshake, he uses the namashkar, the graceful movement that means 'to take the other's dust upon you', hands joined together as if in prayer and raised to the forehead or the breast according to the rank or honour of the person saluted. **1967** SINGHA & MASSEY *Indian Dances* iii. 44 Indians always use joined palms for the namashkar, that is, when they greet anyone, but the position in which they are held indicates the status of the person greeted. **1969** R. SHANKAR *My Music* i. 12/1 The simplest gesture of the *namaskar*, or greeting (putting the hands palm to palm in front of the forehead and bowing). **1972** 'E. PETERS' *Death to Landlords!* viii. 113 Priya offered her *namaskar* shyly.

‖ **namaste** (ˈnɑːmæsteɪ), *sb.* and *int. India.* Also **namasthe.** [Hindi, ad. Skr. *námas*, bowing, obeisance + *te* dat. of *tuam*, you (sing.).]

A. *sb.* A salutatory gesture made by bringing the palms together before the face or chest and bowing. Also *attrib.*

1948 *Time* 16 Aug. 30 In response Nehru closed palms in front of his chest. This traditional Hindu *namasthe* (greeting) is as much a part of his public manner as was the V sign for Churchill. **1951** J. MASTERS *Nightrunners Bengal* vii. 97 She brought her palms together in front of her face and moved them up to her forehead and down again in the gesture called *namaste.* **1959** M. BRECHER *Nehru* 385 A young man stepped forward from the crowd and greeted Gandhi in the traditional *namaste* salutation, joining his hands palm to palm and bowing slightly. **1960** KOESTLER *Lotus & Robot* I. i. 52 A toothless Brahmin..walked in and, after a dignified *namaste*, hung a garland round my neck. **1965** E. LINTON *World in Grain of Sand* vii. 114, I shall be waiting for a letter from you. Namastes and love from Savitri. *Ibid.*, I join my hands in 'namaste' to you and Chander Kala. **1973** 'B. MATHER' *Snow Line* vii. 79 The namaste sign..is with the palms together as in prayer, head bowed reverently and nose touching the fingertips.

B. *int.* Used as a respectful greeting.

1967 D. C. COOKE *c/o American Embassy* (1968) ii. 21 '*Namaste*, Sahib,' the Sikh said. **1969** 'E. PETERS' *Mourning Raga* iii. 48 She pressed her hands together in reverence to him, and bowed her head..'Namaste!'

Hence **ˈnamaste** *v. intr.*, to give the *namaste* sign.

1969 J. K. GALBRAITH *Ambassador's Jrnl.* xxvi. 586 After we had shaken hands, waved, *namasted* and got on board, the crowd lined up by the plane and one of the engines failed to start. **1971** R. PARKES *Line of Fire* xi. 101 He namasted gravely. **1971** *Illustr. Weekly India* 18 Apr. 6 The crowds clustered there drew apart, respectfully '*namasteing*', as the big man at the wheel acknowledged their greetings and drove in.

naˈmation. *rare*—[0]. [ad. med.L. *namation-em*, f. *namare*, f. OE. *nám* NAAM.] (See quot.)

1706 PHILLIPS (ed. Kersey), *Namation*, (Law-Term) a distraining, or taking a Distress: In Scotland, it is taken for impounding. [Hence in later Dicts.]

namaycush (ˈnæmeɪkʌʃ). Also 8 **naym-**, 9 **namacush.** [American Indian; in Cree *numākoos*, Ojibway *namēgoss.*] The great lake trout (*Salvelinus namaycush*) of N. America.

1785 PENNANT *Arct. Zool.* II. Suppl. 139 Naymacush. Inhabits the lakes of Hudson's Bay. **1829** RICHARDSON *Fauna Bor. Amer.* III. 179 The namaycush is the tyrant of the lakes. **1888** G. B. GOODE *Amer. Fish* 468 The amateur is likely to confound the namaycush with the Siscowet. **1892** SHIELD *Amer. Game Fishes* 238 The namaycush reaches its greatest perfection in the Northern parts of Lakes Huron and Michigan.

namby-pamby (ˈnæmbɪˈpæmbɪ), *a.* and *sb.* [A fanciful formation on the name of *Ambrose* Philips (died 1749), author of pastorals ridiculed by Carey and Pope.

1726 CAREY (*title*) Namby Pamby. *Ibid.* 29 So the Nurses get by Heart Namby Pamby's Little Rhimes. **1733** POPE *Dunc.* III. 319 Beneath his reign shall..Namby Pamby [*ed.* 1, A—e P—s] be prefer'd for Wit.]

A. *adj.* **1.** Of style, compositions, actions, etc.: Weakly sentimental, insipidly pretty, affectedly or childishly simple.

1745 W. AYRE *Mem. Pope* II. 90 He us'd to write Verses on Infants, in a strange Stile, which Dean Swift calls the Namby Pamby Stile. **1791** BOSWELL *Johnson* I. 97 At a very advanced age he condescended to trifle in namby pamby rhymes. **1793** W. ROBERTS *Looker-on* No. 84 (1794) III. 351 Sweet smirking troops, In coats of green, and namby pamby pride. **1823** *Edin. Rev.* XXXIX. 73 Too many of these namby-pamby lyrics have still been allowed to remain. **1844** THACKERAY *Little Trav.* i. Wks. 1869 XXII. 181 Keyser has dwindled down into namby-pamby prettiness. **1882** MISS BRADDON *Mt. Royal* III. x. 191 He had just that small namby-pamby air which would suit Pauline's faint-hearted lover.

absol. **1874** L. STEPHEN *Hours in Library* (1892) II. ii. 64 That unlucky taste for the namby-pamby by which Wordsworth annoyed his contemporaries.

2. Of persons: Inclined to weak sentimentality, affected daintiness, or childish simplicity; of a weak or trifling character.

1774 *Westm. Mag.* II. 145 A namby-pamby Duke. **1774** T. DAVIES in *J. Granger's Lett.* (1805) 60 Certain namby-pamby people were never to be satisfied. **1840** THACKERAY *Paris Sk.-bk.* (1869) 47 The namby-pamby mystical German school [of painters]. **1848** —— *Van. Fair* xlii, She was a namby-pamby milk-and-water affected creature. **1883** *Fortn. Rev.* 1 Sept. 384 An amount of curious facts which namby-pamby travellers hesitate to tell.

B. *sb.* **1.** That which is marked by affected prettiness and feeble sentimentality; a composition of this kind.

a **1764** LLOYD *Cobbler of Cripplegate*, While namby-pamby thus you scribble. **1801** in *Spirit Pub. Jrnls.* V. 284 An ode which he has just composed in praise of Inanity, or Namby Pamby. **1814** T. L. PEACOCK *Wks.* (1875) III. 129 Mr. W. R. Spenser, a writer of fantastical namby-pambies. **1838** MACAULAY *Sir W. Temple* Ess. (ed. Montague) II. 260 Passages in which raillery and tenderness are mixed in a very engaging namby-pamby. **1894** SALA *Things I have seen* II. xiv. 135 The words in the songs.. were not always sickly namby-pamby.

2. A namby-pamby person.

1885 *Athenæum* 17 Oct. 498/1 He is excellent.. on Haydon *passim*; about the namby-pambies of the time he writes as becomes the author of the 'Book of Snobs'.

Hence **'namby-'pambical** *a.*, of a namby-pamby nature; **'namby-'pambics**, namby-pamby writing; **'namby-'pambiness**, weak sentimentality; **'namby-'pamby** *v.*, to talk namby-pamby to (one); **'namby-'pambyish** *a.*, somewhat namby-pamby.

1757 MRS. GRIFFITH *Lett. Henry & Frances* (1767) III. 130, I had never written Namby Pambicks in my Life. **1761** WESLEY *Wks.* (1872) XII. 122 Omit one or two [hymns]... They are namby-pambycal. **1809-12** MISS EDGEWORTH *Absentee* xvi, A lady of quality.. sends me.. her waiting gentlewoman to namby-pamby me. **1832** *Examiner* 517/1 The words.. are namby-pambyish. **1890** SAINTSBURY *Hist. Elizab. Lit.* iv. 138 The sweetness without namby-pambyness which Daniel had at constant command.

'namby-'pambyism. [f. prec. + -ISM.] Weak or insipid sentimentality; an instance of this.

1834 *Tait's Mag.* I 206/2 The namby-pambyisms of the 'Book of Beauty'. **1842** MRS. BROWNING *Grk. Chr. Poets* (1863) 187 The concentrate essence of namby-pambyism. **1867** HATTON *Tallants of Barton* iii, I hate to see such namby-pambyism.

name (neɪm), *sb.* Forms: *α.* 1 nama, 2- name, (5 *Sc.* nayme), 2-5 nam, (5 naam). *β.* 1 noma, 2 nome. [OE. *nama*, *nǫma* masc. = OFris. *nama*, *noma*, OS. *namo* (MDu. *name*, *naem*, Du. *naam*), OHG. *namo* (MHG. and G. *name*), Goth. *namô*; the original gender and the final *n* of the stem (see NEMN *v.*) is retained in ON. *nafn*, *namn* neut. (Sw. *namn*, Da. *navn*). Cognate forms occur in all the other Indo-European languages, as Skr. *nāman*, Gr. *ὄνομα*, L. *nōmen*, OIr. *ainm* (pl. *anmann*), OSl. *imę* (Russ. *imya*), etc.]

I. 1. a. The particular combination of sounds employed as the individual designation of a single person, animal, place, or thing.

α. *Beowulf* 78 [He] scop him Heort naman. *Ibid.* 343 Beowulf is min nama. **862** *Charter* 29 in *O.E. Texts* 439 Brocces ham ðes dennes nama. ðes oðres dennes nama sænget hryg. *a* **1000** *O.E. Chron.* an. 975 Eorla ealdor þæm wæs Eadweard nama. *a* **1122** *Ibid.* (Laud MS.) an. 1118 Iohan of Gaitan.. þam wæs oðer nama Gelasius. *c* **1200** *Trin. Coll. Hom.* 91 þat mai ech man understonden þe wot wat bitocneð þese tweie names betfage and ierusalem. *c* **1250** *Gen. & Ex.* 232 Name he gaf hire..; Issa was hire firste name. *c* **1320** *Sir Tristr.* 1216 Marchaund ich haue ben ay, Mi nam is tramtris. **1390** GOWER *Conf.* I. 191 The kinges Moder there lay, Whos rihte name was Domilde. *c* **1450** MYRC 138 Then may the fader.. Crysten the chylde and ȝeue hyt name. **1526** *Pilgr. Perf.* (W. de W. 1531) 24 Marke therin the citees names & other places in his mynde. **1560** DAUS tr. *Sleidane's Comm.* 406 A sonne named Henry.. the seventh of that name. **1598** SHAKS. *Merry W.* I. iv. 14 Peter Simple, you say your name is? **1651** HOBBES *Leviath.* III. xxxiv. 213 God needeth not to distinguish his Celestiall servants by names. **1710** POPE *Windsor For.* 339 The fam'd authors of his ancient name, The winding Isis, and the fruitful Thame. **1776** GIBBON *Decl. & F.* vi. I. 156 The name of Antoninus.. had been communicated by adoption to the dissolute Verus. **1818** SHELLEY *Julian* 584 The name Of Venice, and its aspect, was the same. **1897** H. PORTER in *Century Mag.* July 357 He would call them sometimes by their last names.

β. *c* **850** *Martyrol.* in *O.E. Texts* 177 His noma wæs Maximus. **971** *Blickl. Hom.* 161þæs noma wæs Zacharias. *c* **1175** *Lamb. Hom.* 83 þenne ne mihte noht hire sune habbe þene nome þet him wes iȝefen. *a* **1225** *Leg. Kath.* 444 Nat ich nowðer þi nome ne ich ne cnawe þi cun. *a* **1300** *K. Horn* (Harl. MS.) 214 Wel brouc þou þy nome ȝyng. **1362** LANGL. *P. Pl.* A. III. 3 The kyng clepet a clerke (I know not his nome). *c* **1420** *Chron. Vilod.* 687 Now wolly telle ȝow forther —more þe nomes of þe founders euerychon.

b. In Oxford and Cambridge use, in phrases denoting that the person continues, or ceases, to be an actual member of a college or hall.

1779-81 JOHNSON *L.P.*, *Shenstone*, He continued his name in the book ten years, though he took no degree. **1858** *Ordinances Univ. Cambr.* (1904) 257 His name not having been kept on the boards of his College. **1860** *Oxford Univ. Cal.* 140 Provided they have kept their name on the Books of some College or Hall.. for twenty-six Terms. **1860** HUGHES *Tom Brown at Oxf.* xxiv, Drysdale, anticipating his fate, took his name off before they sent for him.

c. *Stockbroking.* The ticket bearing the name of the purchaser of stock, handed over to the selling broker on name-day or ticket-day.

[**1891** G. H. STUTFIELD *Rules & Usages Stock Exchange* 59 When the issuer of the ticket is a broker,.. he has to insert the name of his client as the person into whose name the Stock is to be transferred.] **1907** POLEY & GOULD *Hist., Law & Pract. Stock Exchange* 178 It is called the ticket or name day because of the passing of tickets or names on that day. **1934** F. E. ARMSTRONG *Bk. Stock Exchange* x. 193 'Names' play an important part in the settlement of Stock Exchange transactions. **1968** J. D. HAMILTON *Stockbroking Today* I. iii. 89 Once in the office the names are sorted by the Names Department so that each name or batch of names matches a certain sale.. and where there is more than one ticket they are pinned together.

d. (*or*) *my name is not* ——, appended to a statement as an assertion of its truth.

1803 S. OWENSON *St. Clair* vi. 29 Sir Patrick will make the walls of the old Abbey ring again, or my name is not Michael M'Carty. **1898** J. D. BRAYSHAW *Slum Silhouettes* 220, I tell yer straight, if me an' Kitty don't make Soufend sit up, my name ain't Bill Brown. **1962** C. S. FORESTER *Hornblower & Hotspur* xiii. 174 We'll have a westerly gale, sir, or my name's not William Bush.

e. *to put*, or *write, someone's name down for*: to enter someone's name on a list of those interested in sharing in, acquiring, or taking part in a particular commodity or activity (cf. PUT *v.*[1] 41 i).

1819 M. EDGEWORTH *Let.* 2 Apr. (1971) 193 Lady Jersey .. told me she would put down our names and give me some tickets for Almacks. Of the 5 Patronesses she is supposed to rule. **1821** —— *Let.* 30 Oct. (1971) 248 The Colleges are now so full that a young mans name must be written down 3 or 4 years before he can hope to get in. **1824** [see PUT *v.*[1] 41 i]. **1969** *Guardian* 20 Mar. 20/3 Lord Linley, seven-year-old son of Princess Margaret and Lord Snowdon, had had his name put down for Eton. **1974** *Listener* 25 Apr. 525/3 Frances has her name down for Danesbury [Hospital] just in case something should happen to Ron.

f. *give it a name*: what would you like to drink?

1854 DICKENS *Hard T.* I. vi. 43 What thall it be, Thquire. .. Thall it be Therry? Give it a name, Thquire!.. have a glath of bitterth. *c* **1863** T. TAYLOR in M. R. Booth *Eng. Plays of 19th Cent.* (1969) II. 88, I hope you'll allow me to stand treat—give it a name, gentlemen... Thank you, I never drink with strangers. **1929** J. B. PRIESTLEY *Good Companions* I. vi. 235 The waiter collected orders and told Inigo to give it a name. **1931** T. R. G. LYELL *Slang* 540 'Well, boys, the drinks are on me! Give it a name!' **1951** J. B. PRIESTLEY *Festival at Farbridge* I. ii. 59 What are you drinking? Give it a name, chaps—there's everything here.

g. *to have one's name* (*and number*) *on it*: of a bullet, etc.: to be destined to kill a particular person.

1917 A. G. EMPEY *Over Top* 312 Tommy detests these mortars because.. he knows that it is only a matter of minutes before a German shell with his name and number on it will be knocking at his door. **1919** *Athenæum* 18 July 632/2 A soldier refers to the shell that kills him as 'having his name and number on it'. **1925** FRASER & GIBBONS *Soldier & Sailor Words* 163 *Name* (*or number*) *on, to have one's*, said of a bullet that hit a man; *i.e.*, that it was destined for him. **1958** R. STOREY *Touch it Light* in *Plays of Year* XVIII. 376 *Ted.* That farmer don't like us, sir. Ever since that bomb fell on his cowshed. *Og.* He thought it should have fallen on you? *Syd.* It had our name on it all right. **1973** D. FRANCIS *Slay-Ride* xii. 140 The bomb probably had my name on it in the first place.

h. *no names, no pack-drill*: phr. used to indicate that if nobody is named as being responsible, nobody can be blamed. Cf. *pack-drill* s.v. PACK *sb.*[1] 15 c.

1923 O. ONIONS *Peace in our Time* I. ii. 25 Men had a way of omitting the names of those of whom they spoke; no names no pack-drill. **1926** E. WALLACE *More Educated Evans* vii. 160 There's a certain party—no names no pack-drill—who's fairly doggin' me to get information. **1931** P. MACDONALD *Crime Conductor* I. i. 7 'Meaning?' said Cuthbertson. 'No names,' said Garth Johnson quickly, 'no pack drill!' **1955** M. ALLINGHAM *Beckoning Lady* ii. 32 It just means no name, no pack drill, and always speak well of them as has money to sue. **1962** 'B. GRAEME' *Undetective* iii. 32 'It's a lie, mister. Who told you?' 'No names, no pack drill.'

i. *to have one's name in lights*: to be a well-known actor and so have one's name displayed in lights outside the theatre.

1929 J. B. PRIESTLEY *Good Companions* II. i. 282 His determination to top the bill and have his name in electric lights. **1972** *Guardian* 15 Jan. 8/4, I couldn't wait to get up there with the best of them and see my name up in lights —topping the bill at the Palladium.

j. *the name of the game* (colloq.): the object or essence of an action, etc.

1966 *Legionary* (Ottawa) Oct. 36/1 Where the knight's concerned, quality is the name of the game. **1967** *Maclean's Mag.* Aug. 27/3 And if this means running up against slum landlords, do-nothing local councils or a hostile white community—well, that's the name of the game. **1970** G. JACKSON *Let.* in *Soledad Brother* (1971) 247 We should never make it easy for them—by relaxing—at this stage of the educational process. Examples are crucially important. Well that's the name of the game right now. **1972** *Jazz & Blues* Sept. 7/3 If I can make you feel like you want to holler on your horn then that's the name of the game man. **1972** *Times* 29 Sept. 11/1 The name of the game this week is survival. **1973** *Nature* 6 July 2/1 Call my bluff was the name of the game at last week's meeting of the International Whaling Commission.

2. a. The particular word or words used to denote any object of thought not considered in, or not possessed of, a purely individual character. *to call names*: see CALL *v.* 17 c.

c **1000** ÆLFRIC *Gen.* ii. 19 Ælc libbende nyten, swa swa Adam hit ȝeciȝde, swa ys hys nama. *c* **1175** *Lamb. Hom.* 115 Ðe king bið icoren to þan þe him cuð his noma. *c* **1250** *Gen. & Ex.* 222 Ilc kinnes beste of erðe boren,.. ðor gaf adam ilc here is name. *c* **1374** CHAUCER *Boeth.* III. pr. vi. (1868) 78 If þe name of gentilesse be referred to renoun and clernesse of linage. **1390** GOWER *Conf.* I. 13 For pride of thilke astat To bere a name of a prelat. *c* **1470** HENRY *Wallace* VIII. 472 Nayme off rewill on him he wald tak nayne. **1486** *Bk. St. Albans* D iij, Now foloys the naamys of all maner of hawkys. **1527** TINDALE *Doctr. Treat.* 116 That which is deserved is called (if thou wilt give him his right name) hire or wages. **1560** DAUS tr. *Sleidane's Comm.* 82 b, This is in dede yᵉ first original of the name of Protestauntes. **1590** SIR J. SMYTH *Disc. Weapons* 2 b, Their Ensignes also they will not call by that name, but by the name of Colours. **1615** W. LAWSON *Country Housew. Gard.* (1626) 18 It is hardly possible to misse in graffing so often, if your Gardiner be worth his name. **1634** MILTON *Comus* 628 He.. would.. shew me simples of a thousand names. **1667** —— *P.L.* VI. 174 Unjustly thou deprav'st it with the name Of Servitude. **1712** STEELE *Spect.* No. 374 ¶1 There is a Fault, which, tho' common, wants a Name. **1781** COWPER *Retirement* 723 Flowers by that name promiscuously we call. **1850** TENNYSON *In Mem.* cxi, Thus he bore without abuse The grand old name of gentleman. **1873** *Act 36 & 37 Vict.* c. 88 §22 The offence, by whatever name called, which if committed in England would be perjury.

†**b.** A title of rank or dignity. *Obs. rare.*

a **1548** HALL *Chron.*, *Hen. V* 75 b, Deprived of all honores, names, dignities and preheminences whiche he then had.

†**c.** *Gram.* A noun. *Obs.*

1563-7 BUCHANAN *Reform St. Andros* Wks. (S.T.S.) 8 The lawast class is for thayme that suld declin the namis, and the verbes actives, passives and anomales.

†**d.** *Arith.* Denomination. *Obs. rare.*

1714 CUNN *Treat. Fractions* 51 The Quote is that part of the Answer that is of that Name; then reduce the Remainder to the next inferior Name.

II. In pregnant senses, chiefly originating in Biblical uses based upon Hebrew modes of expression.

3. The name (sense 1) of God or Christ, with implication of divine nature and power inherent in it.

c **825** *Vesp. Psalter* viii. 2 Dryhten ur, hu wundurlic is noma ðin. *a* **850** *Lorica Prayer* in *O.E. Texts* 174 Daelniomende.. alra ðeara goda ðe ænig monn for his noman ȝedoeð. **971** *Blickl. Hom.* 103 His noman we sceolan weorþian mid wordum & mid dædum. *c* **1200** ORMIN 5342 þa shallt tu þurrh þe name off Crist Ben borrȝhenn att tin ende. *c* **1250** *Gen. & Ex.* 3497 Tac ðu nogt in idel min name. **1382** WYCLIF *Acts* xxvi. 9 Aȝens the name of Jhesu Nazarene, for to.. do manye contrarie thingis. *c* **1430** LYDG. *Min. Poems* (Percy Soc.) 237 Condigne laude nor comendacioun, Youe to this name ther can no tonge telle. **1526** *Pilgr. Perf.* (W. de W. 1531) 219 b, Thy holy name is inuocate & named vpon vs. **1560** DAUS tr. *Sleidane's Comm.* 43 They gave thankes to God yᵗ they should suffer for the glorie of his name. **1667** MILTON *P.L.* III. 412 Hail Son of God,.. thy Name Shall be the copious matter of my Song. **1738** WESLEY *Hymn*, *Thee we adore* i, Thee we adore Eternal Name. **1781** COWPER *Truth* 556 His own glorious rights he would disclaim, And man might safely trifle with his name. **1817** SHELLEY *Rev. Islam* x. xxvii, Our secret pride Has scorned thee, and thy worship, and thy name. **1850** TENNYSON *In Mem.* xxxvi, We yield all blessing to the name Of Him that made them current coin.

4. a. The name of a person (†or thing) with implication of the individual denoted by it.

1382 WYCLIF *Rev.* iii. 4 Thou hast a fewe names in Sardis, the whiche defouleden not her clothes. *a* **1400-50** *Alexander* 993 þare is na region ne rewme.. bot it sall my name loute. **1467-8** *Rolls of Parlt.* V. 574/2 Eny Acte made for the corporation or name of the Duchie of Lancastre. **1599** SHAKS. *Hen. V*, II. iv. 56 By the hand Of that black Name, Edward, black Prince of Wales. **1662** STILLINGFL. *Orig. Sacræ* I. iv. §11 Unless this might be any plea for his ignorance,.. that he had so many great names after him guilty of the same. **1700** DRYDEN *Pal. & Arc.* II. 504 There Samson was, with wiser Solomon, And all the mighty names by love undone. **1781** COWPER *Conversat.* 828 Echo learns politely to repeat The praise of names for ages obsolete. **1849-50** ALISON *Hist. Eur.* V. xxix. 208 Names since immortalised in the rolls of fame were.. assembled.. at the Tuileries.

b. The name (sense 1) of a person or group of persons, with implication of all the individuals bearing, or comprehended under, it; those having a certain name; hence, a family, clan, people.

1382 WYCLIF *Isa.* lxvi. 22 As newe heuenus and newe erthe.. so stonde shal ȝoure sed, and ȝoure name. **1559** in Froude *Hist. Eng.* (1863) VIII. 3 Whose blood they once shed, they lightly never cease killing all that name. **1588** SHAKS. *Tit. A.* II. iii. 183 Ah beastly creature, The blot and enemy to our generall name. **1601** —— *All's Well* I. iii. 162, I am from humble, he from honored name. **1667** MILTON *P.L.* IX. 142 Since I in one Night freed.. welnigh half Th' Angelic Name. **1690** *Lond. Gaz.* No. 2575/3 Three of the Heads of Clans, or Chiefs of a Name, are come in and submitted to him. **1781** COWPER *Expost.* 170 The favours poured upon the Jewish name. **1817** SHELLEY *Pr. Athan.* I. 30 Of an ancestral name the orphan chief. **1849** MACAULAY *Hist. Eng.* v. I. 547 All the clans hostile to the name of Campbell were set in motion.

5. a. The name (sense 1) of a person as mentioned by others with admiration or commendation; hence, the fame or reputation involved in a well-known name. *to have one's name up*, to be much spoken of.

c1320 *Sir Tristr.* 22 Of a kniȝt is þat y mene, His name it sprong wel wide. c1375 *Sc. Leg. Saints* xl. (*Ninian*) 479 Of þe bischope þe nam ran sa in al þe land to and fra. a1425 *Cursor M.* 12633 (Trin.), Fro þenne of ihesu sprong þe nome. 1603 Shaks. *Meas. for M.* ii. iv. 155 My vnsoild name, th' austeerenesse of my life. 1784 Cowper *Task* vi. 101 Some to the fascination of a name Surrender judgment hoodwinked. 1789 *Loiterer* No. 43. 4 The ill effects of possessing an extensive reputation, or as an old English Phrase expresses it, having one's name up. 1809 Malkin *Gil Blas* viii. x. ¶1 When once my name was up for a man after the Duke of Lerma's own heart, I had very soon my court about me. 1859 Tennyson *Vivien* 681 If they find Some stain or blemish in a name of note.

b. ***of no name, without*** (*a*) ***name***, implying obscurity and unimportance.

1611 Bible *Job* xxx. 8 They were children of fooles, yea children of base men [*marg.* men of no name]. 1671 Milton *Samson* 677 Nor do I name of men the common rout,.. Heads without name no more rememberd. 1697 Dryden *Æneid* vi. 1055 These shall then be Towns of mighty Fame; Tho' now they lye obscure; and Lands without a Name. 1821 Shelley *False Laurel & True* 7 One of the crowd thou art without a name.

c. A famous or notorious person, a celebrity; one whose name is well known. Also *attrib.* or as *adj.*, and in extended use, of a well-known group of people, esp. a jazz band (see *name band* below).

1611 Bible *Ezek.* xxiii. 10 She became famous [*marg.* a name] among women. 1826 Disraeli *Viv. Grey* iii. vii, Dr. Spix is a most excellent man, a most accurate traveller, quite a name. 1842 Tennyson *Ulysses* 11, I am become a name; For always roaming.. Much have I seen and known. 1936 *Variety* 17 June 32/1 The greatest 'names' in the industry, including the cream of its players. 1941 *Sun* (Baltimore) 28 July 11/5 Virtually all of the name horses in the land will be on the scene for the thirty-day meeting. 1943 *Ibid.* 14 Aug. 7/5 At least ten 'name' players, fellows like Gene Sarazen and Craig Wood and Byron Nelson and Walter Hagen, have assured Corcoran that they'd be available. 1945 L. Shelly *Jive Talk Dict.* 15/1 *Name*,.. most popular band at the moment. 1947 *Sat. Rev.* (U.S.) 11 Oct. 53/1 The growing group of record makers who.. turn.. to the reservoir of fine performing talent that.. lie outside the galaxy of first-rank star names. 1955 J. Betjeman in R. S. Thomas *Song at Year's Turning* 12 His publisher believed that a 'name' was needed to help sell the book. 1960 *20th Cent.* Apr. 342 A big factor in the sale of the more popular 'name' records is the personality cult. 1972 *Times* 12 Dec. 2/6 RIBA circles.. had feared that the former Secretary of State, Mr. Walker, would appoint a 'name' with glamour to a post where he would have had little real authority or influence. 1973 *Black World* Jan. 28/2 He has concerned himself with the promotional affairs of several 'name' theaters in the Cleveland area. 1973 *Times* 6 Feb. 7/3 There is a narrowing of the opportunities for 'name' designers (couture tailors). 1974 *Times Lit. Suppl.* 18 Jan. 50/3 Professor Eliade is what publishers like to call a 'name', and you cannot ignore him.

d. An underwriter at Lloyd's.

1885 G. van de Linde *Chartered Accountants' Students' Soc. Lect. Biogr. Lloyd's Policy* 10 The respective partners of Blank & Co.,.. head the policy by underwriting it to the extent of £10,000 between them, each name being respectively responsible for the amount against the signature. 1928 Wright & Fayle *Hist. Lloyd's* xxiii. 422 Let us consider the career of an underwriting 'Name', that is an Underwriting Member of Lloyd's represented by an Agent. 1937 R. Straus *Lloyd's* xi. 257 Marine underwriters.. offered themselves as 'Names' to those Underwriting Agents who specialised in non-marine risks. 1972 G. Lyall *Blame the Dead* iv. 23 He's a Name. *Ibid.* 24 That means a member; they call them Names. 1973 *Daily Tel.* 16 Oct. 3/7 Discussing evidence given earlier by her father, Dr Dugdale said he was a 'name' several times over at Lloyd's, concerned in shipping and aircraft insurance. He made her a 'name' ensuring her a great deal of capital and a very high income.

6. a. The reputation *of* some character or attribute. †Also const. with *inf.*, and *ellipt.* (quot. 1727).

a1300 *Cursor M.* 17472 Of men þai wan schenschip and schame, And of þar leute tint þe name. 1303 R. Brunne *Handl. Synne* 6842 Of large almes men ȝaue hym name. c1418 *Pol. Poems* (Rolls) II. 245 If hym lust to have a name Of pelour under ipocrasie. 1456 *Paston Lett.* I. 383 Consideryng the goode nome and fame of trouth.. the which I here of you. c1530 Ld. Berners *Arth. Lyt. Brit.* 283 Ye have the name to be the.. gentyllest of hearte of any lady now lyvynge. 1581 Pettie tr. *Guazzo's Civ. Conv.* i. (1586) 42 b, There are diuerse which thinke to get the name of pleasant conceited fellowes. 1601 Holland *Pliny* x. li. I. 297 He would have the name to eat the resemblers of mans voice. 1625 Bacon *Ess., Simulation* ¶2 The ablest Men.. haue had.. a name of Certainty, and Veracity. 1727 A. Hamilton *New Acc. E. Ind.* II. xxxiii. 16 The Name that it got.. stuck so fast to it, that none of it would go off at any Price. 1814 Nicholson *Country Lass* i. Wks. (1897) 41 Sic beauty, and the name o' siller, Gart wooers flock. 1894 *Law Times* XCVII. 384/1 No profession will lightly earn for itself the name of a profession of hireling suborners of perjury.

b. With *a* and *adj.* A fame or reputation of a specified kind.

1382 Wyclif *2 Sam.* vii. 9, I made to thee a greet name. 1382 —— *Prov.* xxii. 1 Better is a good name, than manye richessis. c1430 *Babees Bk.* 42 *note*, A good name menny folde ys more worthe then golde. 1500–20 Dunbar *Poems* lxxxii. 70 Keip ordour.. That ȝe may gett ane bettir name. 1546 [see ill *a.* 1 c]. 1599 Shaks. *Much Ado* iii. i. 98 He hath an excellent good name. 1625 Bacon *Ess., Riches* (Arb.) 237 A good Name, for good and faire dealing. a1674 Clarendon *Hist. Reb.* viii. (J.), The king's army.. had left no good name behind. 1738 Swift *Let. to Pope* 8 Aug., I have an ill name in the Post-office of both Kingdoms. 1784 Cowper *Task* ii. 759 Such expense.. buys the boy a name, That sits a stigma on his father's house. 1818 [see dog *sb.*[1] 15 h]. 1845 S. Austin *Ranke's Hist. Ref.* III. 473 If he were victorious, he would.. bequeath a great name to posterity.

c. (Usually in phr. ***to get*** or ***make*** (***oneself***) ***a name.***) A distinguished name; a reputation.

1382 Wyclif *2 Sam.* viii. 13 Forsothe Dauid made to hym a name, whanne he turnyde aȝen. c1407 Lydgate *Reas. & Sens.* 5832 This mayde.. Had a name and dyde excelle To pleyen at this noble play. 1509 Barclay *Shyp of Folys* (1874) II. 101 By cruell delynge he must hym get a name. 1535 Coverdale *Zeph.* iii. 20, I wil get you a name.. amonge all people of the earth. 1603 Shaks. *Meas. for M.* i. ii. 173 This new Gouernor.. for a name Now puts the.. Act Freshly on me: 'tis surely for a name. 1667 Milton *P.L.* xii. 45 They cast to build A Citie.. And get themselves a name. 1853 Lytton *My Novel* vi. xviii, Tell her that I am nameless, and will yet make a name. 1884 W. C. Smith *Kildrostan* 48 When you make yourself a name, As I am sure you will do.

†**d.** ***to bear*** or ***carry the name***, to have a reputation. *Obs.*

1470–85 Malory *Arthur* xii. ix. 605 There is none that bereth the name now but ye and syr Tristram. 1572 *Scholehouse Wom.* in Hazl. *E.P.P.* IV. 138 So they may be trimmed and fed of the best, They haue no remorce who beareth the name. 1601 Holland *Pliny* ix. xvii. I. 245 Our auncestours set more store by the Sturgeon, and it carried the name above all other fishes.

7. a. Without article: Repute, reputation, fame, distinction. Now *rare.*

c1375 *Leg. Rood* 124 [He] euill angerd was þat þis cristen king had name More þan he. 1382 Wyclif *Zeph.* iii. 20 Y shal ȝeue ȝou in to name, and in to herying to alle peplis of erthe. c1430 *How Gd. Wif* 75 in Hazl. *E.P.P.* I. 185 Gode name is golde worthe, my leue childe. c1477 Caxton *Jason* 33 My desir restith in two singuler thinges; that one is for to conquere name in armes. 1530 Palsgr. 247/2 Name, *renom.* 1597 Morley *Introd. Mus.* Pref., Not so much seeking thereby any name or glorie. 1601 Holland *Pliny* I. 419 Yea, and after that, the Falern wines were in name and called for. 1605 Bacon *Adv. Learn.* ii. xxiii. §5 Senators that had name and opinion for general wise men. 1859 Tennyson *Vivien* 63 He lay as dead And lost to life and use and name and fame.

b. ***of*** (***great***, etc.) ***name***, noted, distinguished, famous. Now usually with adj.

c1380 Wyclif *Wks.* (1880) 2 The firste two [sects] weren grete men of name and hauynge. 1415 *Pol. Poems* (Rolls) II. 126 Lordes of name an hunderde and mo Bitterly that bargayn bowght. a1548 Hall *Chron., Hen. VII* 23 b, The cytie.. conteyned an hundred and fifty thousand houses of name. 1577–87 Holinshed *Chron.* I. 152/1 Of the English side, there died two dukes.. with sundrie other men of name. 1625 Bacon *Ess., Travel* (Arb.) 523 Eminent Persons.. which are of great Name abroad. 1699 T. Baker *Refl. Learning* xiii. 160 In this kind Bartolus is of great name; whose Authority is.. valu'd.. amongst the Modern Lawyers. 1782 Cowper *Friendship* 85 Hence authors of illustrious name.. Are sadly prone to quarrel. 1816 Keatinge *Trav.* (1817) I. 33 Although the military architect may be one of high name. 1857 Church *Misc. Writ.* (1891) I. 16 It would be difficult, perhaps, to mention a writer of name who has more [faults].

8. One's repute or reputation, etc.; esp. ***one's*** (***good***) ***name.***

a1300 *Cursor M.* 28165 For his.. welth, his wytt, and his god name. c1385 Chaucer *L.G.W.* 1811 *Lucrece*, Thus thou shalt be ded & also lese Thyn name. c1450 *St. Cuthbert* (Surtees) 102 Gyfe he did, he lost his name. 1500–20 Dunbar *Poems* liv. 22 Quhai in felde receawes schame, And tynis thair his knychtlie name. 1526 *Pilgr. Perf.* (W. de W. 1531) 103 b, Defame hym, that is to saye, take his good name from hym. 1596 Shaks. *1 Hen. IV*, v. iv. 70 Would to heauen, Thy name in Armes, were now as great as mine. 1665 Boyle *Occas. Refl.* 5 Companies, where sometimes he may lose his good Name. 1705 tr. *Bosman's Guinea* 17 If the same Care was taken.. Guinea would soon lose its dreadful mortal Name. 1781 Cowper *Charity* 453 Flavia, most tender of her own good name. 1834 Medwin *Angler in Wales* II. 297 Daily, hourly came Fresh followers, lured by his success and name. 1859–64 Tennyson *Grandmother* 50, I love you so well that your good name is mine. 1874 Manning *Ess.* Ser. iii. 26 For the fair name of England, they are being blotted out of our history.

9. a. The mere appellation in contrast or opposition to the actual person or thing; reputation without correspondence in fact. †Also ***at name***, nominally, professedly; ***in name only, only in name***: of a marriage without sexual relations.

1382 Wyclif *Ecclus.* xxxvii. 1 Ther is a frend, bi only name a frend. —— *Rev.* iii. 1 Thou hast name, that thou lyuest, and thou art deed. 1483 Caxton *Gold. Leg.* 197/1 The holy vyrgyne.. wente to the sayne for to goo fetche at name somme vytaylles. 1601 Shaks. *All's Well* v. iii. 309 Tis but the shadow of a wife you see, The name, and not the thing. 1666–7 Stillingfl. *Serm.* Prov. xiv. 9 (1673) 29 Religion becomes but a meer name. 1727 Gay *Fables, Hare & Many Friends*, Friendship, like love, is but a name, Unless to one you stint the flame. 1784 Cowper *Tiroc.* 421 Well he plays his part, Christian in name, and infidel in heart. 1817 Jas. Mill *Brit. India* II. v. viii. 661 He well knew, that in the circumstances,.. a pension.. little or nothing differed from a name. 1851 Mayhew *Lond. Labour* I. 385 It has the name of being eighteen yards. 1867 E. Quincy in *Life Josiah Quincy* 481 The Law School, though in existence.. had but a name to live. 1888 *Green's Short Hist.* viii. §8. 571 The expulsion of the majority of the existing House reduced the Commons to a name. 1894 W. J. Locke *At Gate of Samaria* (1895) xxi. 245 Henceforward Thornton would be her husband only in name. 1972 A. Roudybush *Sybarite Death* (1974) xxi. 173, I married her.. but it never even occurred to me that our marriage would be other than a marriage in name only. 1975 R. Player *Let's talk of Graves* ii. 60 She had hated her husband and been his wife only in name.

b. ***in all but name***: of a situation or set of circumstances, existing but not officially acknowledged or recognized.

1934 J. E. Neale *Queen Elizabeth* xv. 251 In all but name the Papacy was at war with Elizabeth.

III. In prepositional phrases.

10. by name: a. Used with verbs of naming or calling, or (in later use) simply added to the proper appellation of a person, etc.

a900 Cynewulf *Elene* 755 Syndon tu on þam.. þe man Seraphin be naman hateð. a1000 *O.E. Chron.* an. 975 þone.. hatað wide cometa be naman cræftgleawe men. c1200 Ormin 1828 Summ we findenn o þe boc Enngell bi name nemmnedd. c1220 *Bestiary* 38 Ðat defte meiden, Marie bi name. 1382 Wyclif *1 Sam.* xvii. 23 That bastard man, Goliath bi name. a1425 *Cursor M.* 7370 (Trin.), Dauid he hette bi his name. 1590 Shaks. *Mids. N.* v. i. 157 It doth befall, That I, one Snowt (by name) present a wall. 1667 Milton *P.L.* vii. 536 Wherever thus created, for no place Is yet distinct by name. 1711 Addison *Spect.* No. 98 ¶3 A famous Monk, Thomas Conecte by Name. a1832 Scott in Lockhart *Life* (1900) I. 240 The last of my chargers.. was a high-spirited.. one, by name Daisy.

b. With verbs of calling upon, summoning, enumerating, or mentioning; or in enumeration of individuals.

c900 *Judith* 81 Heo.. ongan ða sweȝles Weard be naman nemnan. c1000 *Ags. Gosp.* John x. 3 þa sceap ȝehyrað his stefne, & he nemð his aȝene sceap be naman. a1122 *O.E. Chron.* (Laud MS.) an. 656 Ðet wæron be nam Ithamar biscop of Rofecestre [etc.]. a1300 *Cursor M.* 7388 His suns sex,.. All he did þam call be nam. *Ibid.* 12211 Of ilk a letter for to ask, Resune of ilkan bi name. 1393 Langl. *P. Pl.* C. ii. 4 A loueliche lady.. Cam down fro þat castel and calde me by name. c1400 *Destr. Troy* 37 Amonge þat menye,—to myn hym be nome,—Homer was holden haithill of dedis. 1431 in *Eng. Gilds* (1870) 276 First, ye Aldirman schal clepene vpe ij. men be name. 1606 Shaks. *Tr. & Cr.* i. ii. 199 Ile tel yu them all by their names. 1667 Milton *P.L.* x. 649 The Creator calling forth by name His mightie Angels gave them several charge. 1738 Pope *Epil. Sat.* ii. 10 None but you by Name the guilty lash. 1848 Thackeray *Van. Fair* xlii, She forgot to send any message of kindness to Lady O'Dowd.., and did not mention Glorvina by name.

†**c.** Used to direct special attention to something mentioned; hence, especially, particularly. *Obs.* Cf. namely *adv.* 1.

1583 Babington *Commandm.* (1590) 370 Wee will neuer, I feare, see the mischiefe of playing, and by name of Dicing. 1626 Bacon *Sylva* §666 It is strange.. that Dust helpeth the fruitfulness of Trees, and of Vines by name. 1660 Sharrock *Vegetables* 27 The seeds of divers Sowbreads, by name the Roman,.. doe the like.

d. With *know.* (*a*) Individually. (*b*) By repute only; not personally or actually.

1382 Wyclif *Exod.* xxxiii. 17 Thi silf Y haue knowe bi name. 1667 Milton *P.L.* xii. 577 Though all the Starrs Thou knewst by name. 1795–1814 Wordsw. *Excurs.* iv. 1226 Abhorrence and contempt are things He only knows by name. 1864 *Cornh. Mag.* X. 175 Sovereigns whom their subjects scarcely knew save by name.

11. in one's name, in the name of one:

a. In phrases expressing invocation of, reliance upon, or devotion to, the persons of the Godhead.

a900 Cynewulf *Christ* 413 þu ȝebletsad leofa, þe in Dryhtnes noman duȝeþum cwome. c950 *Lindisf. Gosp.* Matt. xxviii. 19 Fuluande hia in noma fadores & sunu & halȝes gastes. 971 *Blickl. Hom.* 141 Hie on þinum noman wunnon. c1200 Ormin 16813 He ne wass nohht ȝet O Cristess name fullhtnedd. a1225 *Leg. Kath.* 1442 Feole.. þoleden anan deað i þe nome of drihtin. a1300 *Cursor M.* 266 Now o þis prolog will we blin In crist nam our bok begin. c1315 Shoreham i. 248 Ich cristni þe ine þe uader name, And sone, and holy gostes. 1382 Wyclif *Matt.* xviii. 20 Where two or three shulen be gedrid in my name. 1413 *E.E. Wills* (1882) 21 In the name of god, Amen... I, Richard Ȝonge [etc.]. 1534 More *Comf. agst. Trib.* i. Wks. 1164/1 That in the name of Jesus euery knee bee bowed. 1596 Shaks. *1 Hen. IV*, iii. ii. 153 This, in the Name of Heauen, I promise here. 1738 Wesley *Ps.* vi. v, Or in the Name of Jesus, chase My Troublers all away.

b. In adjurations, orig. by solemn reference to God, Christ, or the saints, but latterly with various substitutions for the names of these, the phrase freq. becoming a mere ejaculation.

For examples of *a God's name*, see a *prep.*[1] 10.

c831 *Charter* 39 in *O.E. Texts* 446 Ic.. bebiade eadwealde.. an godes naman & an ealra his haliȝra ðet [etc.]. a900 *Durham Admon.* Ibid. 176 Ic eow halsiȝe on fæder naman & on suna naman. c1205 Lay. 10136 Luces þe king.. beð hine on godes nomen þat him god uðe. a1300 *Cursor M.* 11915 Vnto your kyth, on godds nam, I bidd yow þat yee nu wend ham. 1362 Langl. *P. Pl.* A. i. 71, [I] halsede hire in heiȝe nome er heo theonne ȝeode, What heo weore witerly. c1440 *Alph. Tales* 264 In þe Name, speke, þou yong childe, & tell if þis dekyn did þis trispas! 1470–85 Malory *Arthur* vii. viii. 224 In the deuyls name sayd the damoysel that suche a bawdy kechen knaue [etc.]. 1595 Shaks. *John* ii. i. 106 In the name of God How comes it then that thou art call'd a King? 1611 —— *Wint. T.* iii. iii. 105 Name of mercy, when was this, boy? 1626 Massinger *Roman Actor* iv. ii, In the name of wonder, What's Cæsar's purpose? 1642 [see goodness 5]. 1722 De Foe *Plague* (1884) 85 'Name of God go in. 1740 J. Clarke *Educ. Youth* (ed. 3) 16 In the Name of Wisdom, what is the Meaning? 1819 Shelley *Cenci* iv. i. 128 Earth, in the name of God, let her food be poison. 1861 Hughes *Tom Brown at Oxf.* ix, What in the name of fortune have they been doing to you? 1875 Jowett *Plato* (ed. 2) I. 212 What, in the name of goodness, do you come hither to teach?

c. Denoting the use of another's name to give authority or countenance to one's acts; or implying that the action is done on account or on behalf of some other person or persons. Hence, by contrast to this, ***in one's own name.***

1388 Wyclif *1 Kings* xxi. 8 Therefor sche wroot lettris in the name of Achab. 1405 *Rolls of Parlt.* III. 605/2 To fulfill all maner accordez..made..be..our Attournees, or be twa of them in oure name. **1444** *Ibid.* V. 108/2 To sue an Action of dette in his owne name. **1523** LD. BERNERS *Froiss.* I. 745 Ther was a cry made, in the kynges name, on payne of dethe [etc.]. *a* **1548** HALL *Chron., Hen. VIII* 64b, Sir Thomas More made a brief oracion in the name of the citee. **1631** GOUGE *God's Arrows* v. Ded. 406 You who in the name of the rest were Solliciters in this business. **1686** tr. *Chardin's Trav. Persia* 13 The Envoy, having the Grand Vizier's word in the Name of his Highness, return'd to Genoa. **1754** SHERLOCK *Disc.* (1759) I. i. 2 St. Peter, in the Name of all made answer, Lord, to whom shall we go? **1818** CRUISE *Digest* (ed. 2) II. 397 That the plaintiff could have no remedy at law, either in his own name, or in the names of the trustees. **1849** MACAULAY *Hist. Eng.* vi. II. 17 A speech which the Bishop of Valence, in the name of the Gallican clergy, addressed..to Lewis the Fourteenth. **1891** *Law Times Rep.* LXIII. 765/1 The defendants were liable as principals, as they had contracted in their own names.

d. = Under the character or designation of (some person or thing). Now *rare* or *Obs.*

1382 WYCLIF *Matt.* x. 41 He that resceyueth a prophete in the name of a prophete. *c* **1400** MAUNDEV. (1839) xv. 170 Thei brennen his Body in name of Penance. **1464** *Rolls of Parlt.* V. 560/1 [They] shall pay..cs in name of a payne. **1467-8** *Ibid.* 581/2 To have to hir for terme of hir life, in name of her Dower. **1548** HOOPER *Declar. Commandm.* ix. Wks. (1843) 372 To lose his head, in the name of a pain. **1598** SHAKS. *Merry W.* III. v. 101 To carry mee in the name of foule Cloathes to Datchet-lane. **1611** —— *Wint. T.* III. ii. 61 Which comes to me in name of Fault. **1642** tr. *Perkins' Prof. Bk.* iii. §209. 64 To deliver..the deed unto the feoffee in the name of seisin of the same land. **1796** SOUTHEY *Lett. fr. Spain* (1799) 418 These men lay the people under contribution in the name of alms.

e. Indicating the assigned ownership of a thing.

1850 *Punch* XVIII. 91 If a box of cigars has not been left here in the name of Adam Simpleton? **1888** *Law Times* LXXXV. 120/2 A sum of consols standing in the name of J. K.,..deceased.

†**12.** ***in name with***, mentioned in connexion with (one of the other sex). *Obs. rare.*

1565-73 *Durham Depos.* (Surtees) 256 Being at borde at the said Agnes house, then wedoo, and was in name with hir. **1575-6** *Ibid.* 284 She was then in name with one Francis Castell.

13. a. by the name of, called or known by, having, the name of. Now *colloq.* and *U.S.*

1676 *Life Father Sarpi* in *Brent's Counc. Trent* 42 A Nephew of his by the name of Maestro Santo. **1725** BERKELEY *Proposal* Wks. 1871 III. 230 A Charter for erecting a College by the name of St. Paul's College in Bermuda. **1841** THACKERAY *Sec. Funeral Napoleon* 3 A grocer living there by the name of Greenacre. **1883** CABLE *Old Creole Days* 35 A palish handsome woman, by the name —or going by the name—of Madame John. **1884** J. QUINCY *Figures of Past* 130 There was a captain by the name of Clark.

b. So *of the name of.*

1727-8 POPE *Let. to Swift* 23 Mar., A member of their Parliament, of the name of Jonathan Gulliver. **1843** *Richardson's Borderer's Table-bk.* Leg. Div. I. 116 A little crouse, chantin chieldie o' the name o' Tom Fenwick.

14. ***to one's name***, belonging to one.

1876 WHYTE MELVILLE *Katerfelto* vii, I have not a horse to my name.

IV. 15. *attrib.* and *Comb.*, as ***name-fancy***, ***-sound***; ***name-calling***, †***-cleping***, ***-giving***; ***name-giver***, ***-maker***, ***name-worthy*** adj.; 'bearing a name', as ***name-board***, ***-card***, ***-label***, ***-plate***, ***-ribbon***, ***-ring***, ***-tab***, ***-ticket***; 'well-known', of or pertaining to a name (sense 5 or 7), as ***name brand***, ***-worthy*** adj.; 'containing or intended for names', as ***name-book***, ***-scroll***; 'named after, or giving a name to, one', as ***name-daughter***, ***-father***, ***-flower***, ***-mamma***, ***-saint***, ***-sire*** (cf. NAME-CHILD, -SON); in *Logic*, as ***name-forming***, ***-matrix***, ***-relation***, ***-variable***; in *Linguistics*: consisting of or pertaining to a proper name, as ***name-element***, ***-form***, ***-giving***, ***-group***, ***-lore***, ***-stem***, ***-system***; **name-act**, a cabaret act performed by well-known performers; **name band**, a jazz or dance band that has made a name for itself; hence **name bandleader**; **name-bar** (see quot.); **name-calling** *vbl. sb.*, abusive language, mere abuse; hence **name-call** *v.*; †**name-device**, a rebus; **name-dropping** *vbl. sb.*, familiar mention of the names of distinguished people in order to imply one's own importance; also *attrib.*; hence (as a back-formation) **name-drop** *v.*, **name-dropper**; **name-droppingly** *adv.*; **name-part**, the part in a play from which it takes its name; also of a book, a ballet, etc.; **name-piece** = *name-poem*, *name-story*; **name-plate**, a metal plate bearing a name; *spec.* one attached to a piece of machinery, or displaying the name of a road or building; also *attrib.* and *fig.*; also as *vb.*; **name-poem**, the poem from which a volume of collected poems is named; **name-story**, the story from which a volume of collected short stories is named; **name-tag**, anything on which a name can be written, to identify the person or object to which it is fixed; **name-tape**, a piece of tape with a person's name woven into it or printed on it, fixed to a person's clothing for identification; hence **name-taped** *ppl. a.*; †**name-wizard**, one skilled in the mystical meaning of names.

1942 BERREY & VAN DEN BARK *Amer. Thes. Slang* §590/15 **Name act*, an act consisting of well-known players. **1949** L. FEATHER *Inside Be-Bop* iii. 21 The Berry Brothers and several other name acts. **1967** *Stage* 2 Mar. 21/4 (Advt.), Top groups required for one night stands. Name acts for winter season cabaret. **1936** *Amer. Mercury* XXXVIII. p.x/1 **Name band*, a band that has gotten the breaks (whether they're good or not). **1938** *Sat. Even. Post* 2 Apr. 9/1 We are to have an orchestra—'a name-band by all means'. *Ibid.* 9/3 At least $2500 for a name band. **1955** L. FEATHER *Encycl. Jazz* (1956) 122 His son..is also a drummer, heard w[ith] Erskine Hawkins and other name bands including Count Basie, '55. **1963** *Globe & Mail* (Toronto) 8 Jan. 5/1 Although its popularity declined with the passing of the name bands, Toronto's Palace Pier was still a busy, and apparently profitable operation until yesterday. **1958** P. GAMMOND *Decca Bk. Jazz* xix. 236 The year 1951 saw the return to Britain of pre-war '*name' bandleader, Roy Fox. **1884** F. J. BRITTEN *Watch & Clockm.* 180 **Name Bar*,..the bar carrying the upper end of a watch barrel arbor. **1846** YOUNG *Naut. Dict.* s.v. *Arch-board*, On this, or more commonly on a board called the *name-board, fitted above it, the ship's name is painted. **1939** AUDEN & ISHERWOOD *Journey to War* v. 121 On our left was a little station: we read its name-board, Ling Pao. **1955** J. COPE *Fair House* i. 24 The turn-off to the Boer farm was a gap in the bush at the roadside, no gate or fence or name-board. **1867** SMYTH *Sailor's Word-bk.* 491 **Name-Book*, a mustering list. *c* **1886** KIPLING *Departm. Ditties*, etc. (1899) 101 He keeps the Name Book. **1944** *Time* 7 Aug. 38/2 Five times in five minutes the cigaret-counter girl at a Walgreen store in Chicago repeated wearily, 'We have no *name brands.' **1853** DICKENS *Nobody's Story* in *Househ. Words* Extra Christmas No. 35/2 Such *name-calling and dirt-throwing. **1891** *Tablet* 10 Jan. 63 The most hopeless of all is that of name-calling. **1947** *Amer. Speech* XXII. 231/1 *Namecalling*, the attempt to put a person or thing in a bad light by attaching to him or it a word with unpleasant connotations. **1965** G. JACKSON *Let.* 16 Mar. in *Soledad Brother* (1971) 69, I have been subjected to the ordeal of hunger, thirst, name-calling, and other uncountable indignities. **1973** J. ROSSITER *Manipulators* v. 51 Perhaps.. you've been name-calling somebody. And they didn't like it. **1973** R. LUDLUM *Matlock Paper* xxvi. 222, I don't want to be responsible for indiscriminate name-calling, any wide-spread panic. **1975** *Verbatim* Feb. 4/1 The argument is a little uneven, for here it delivers a polemic against name-calling, there against grammar. **1798** MME. D'ARBLAY *Diary* VI. 202 Captain Dickenson, as his *name-card says. **1828** P. CUNNINGHAM *N.S. Wales* (ed. 3) II. 112 The name-cards are elegantly printed by our colonial press. **1907** *Yesterday's Shopping* (1969) 361/2 (Advt.), Menu and name cards. **1925** W. J. LOCKE *Great Pandolfo* ii. 23 The beautiful lady whose name he had not caught, because, in abstraction, she had turned her name card maddeningly upside down, took little or no interest in him. **1969** A. CADE *Turn up Stone* i. 25 Michael's experience in the Middle East had taught him the importance of the exchange of name cards in many countries. A man without a card was a man without an identity. **1387-8** T. USK *Test. Love* III. i. (Skeat) l. 102 In that denominacion I wol me acorde to other mens tonges, in that *name-cleping. **1809** GRANT *Lett. fr. Mountains* III. 212 My eldest girl is now staying here, and your *name-daughter with Duncan at the Fort. **1891** R. L. STEVENSON *Let.* Nov. (1899) II. 241, I shal begin to despair of everything but my name-daughter. **1631** WEEVER *Anc. Funeral Mon.* 277 An vsual fashion in former times..which they call rebus, or *name-deuises. **1955** J. D. SALINGER *Franny & Zooey* (1962) 25 There's an unwritten law that people in a certain social or financial bracket can *name-drop as much as they like just as long as they say something terribly disparaging about the person as soon as they've dropped his name. **1959** I. ROSS *Image Merchants* (1960) v. 94 Newsom does not even have to name-drop. The PR man who can avoid that indulgence has truly arrived. **1969** *Daily Tel.* 22 Aug. 18/3 Mr Walters can name-drop better than most when it comes to generals and film stars. **1947** *San Francisco Examiner* (Pict. Rev.) 7 Sept., Our newest menace. The *name dropper. **1959** *Woman's Own* 24 Jan. 31/1 One of my favourite snobs—the name-dropper. **1972** H. KEMELMAN *Monday the Rabbi took Off* xii. 84 He would be likely to point out important people to his son—the wife of the British consul, the American first secretary. He was no name-dropper, but he wanted so much to have his son think well of him. **1950** M. MCCARTHY *On Contrary* (1962) 186 The idea that it's smart to be in step, to be liberal or *avant-garde*, is conveyed through the *name-dropping of a Leo Lerman in *Mademoiselle*. **1951** L. Z. HOBSON *Celebrity* (1953) viii. 119 Rex Stout and Oscar Hammerstein... Conversational spice, he had been thinking; nobody could call it name-dropping. **1966** *Philos.* XLI. 359 Plus a wordy, name-dropping Introduction. **1973** *Times* 7 Feb. 4/5 (*heading*) Solicitors appalled by 'name-dropping' in courts. **1966** *Guardian* 30 Dec. 4/8 He becomes absorbed (*name droppingly so) into the ranks of the literati. **1922** E. EKWALL *Place-Names Lancs.* 62 It is probably a Scand. name..as *Brand* is hardly with certainty evidenced as an O.E. *name-element. **1932** E. WEEKLEY *Words & Names* ix. 134 From the name-element *mun*, thought, etc., were formed a number of names. **1937** *Harvard Univ. Summaries Ph.D. Theses* 272 The deuterotheme..is by far the more stable name-element in the late Germanic period. **1951** *Traditio* VII. 411 The second theme, *-ferth*..is obviously a metathesized form of *frith* (peace) which occurs in many Germanic names both as a first and second name element. **1865** LUBBOCK *Preh. Times* 471 In some tribes these *name-fancies take a different form. **1748** RICHARDSON *Clarissa* IV. 5 Knowest thou not, that I am a great *name-father? **1894** HALL CAINE *Manxman* VI. iv, Go to your god-father. He'd have been your name-father too if [etc.]. **1907** A. QUILLER-COUCH *Major Vigoureux* ii. 20 Glorious trumpet daffodils! ..Major [Narcisse] Vigoureux delighted in them. Were they not his *name-flower? **1927** *Observer* 24 Apr. 15 Marigold, its heroine, has the unaffected charm of her name-flower. **1946** B. BLOCH in *Language* XXII. 208 The non-past indicative form of a verb, an adjective, or the copula serves as the **name form*, used to refer collectively to all the members of a paradigm. **1951** TRAGER & SMITH *Outl. Eng. Struct.* 60 The uninflected or name-form is the base. **1970** *English Studies* LI. 445 The name-forms are arranged under OE phonemes. Thus under OE *ā* we find head-words like *āc*, *brād*, *rāp*. **1955** H. LEBLANC *Introd. Deductive Logic* 2 Semiotic quotes..are a *name-forming operator. **1956** J. H. WOODGER tr. *Tarski's Logic, Semantics, Metamath.* 161 Quotation marks provide an example of a name-forming functor with *one* sentence argument. **1957** A. N. PRIOR *Time & Modality* 119 Our *x*'s are given..by means of a name-forming operator on intervals. **1610** HOLLAND *Camden's Brit.* I. 7 Why the Britains should so much sticke unto their Brutus, as the *name-giuer of their Iland. **1881** A. J. EVANS in *Macm. Mag.* XLIII. 219 A great city,..the namegiver of this whole inland sea. **1863** A. B. GROSART *Small Sins* (ed. 2) 74 The insidious *name-giving to any sins of 'small sins'. **1864** MAX MÜLLER *Sci. Lang.* Ser. II. viii. (1868) 336 Locke never seems to have realised the intricacies of the names-giving process. **1898** E. CLODD *Tom Tit Tot* vi. 75 Mungo Park thus describes the name-giving ceremony among the Mandingo people. **1940** A. H. GARDINER *Theory of Proper Names* vi. 20 Certain name-givings..do not give rise to proper names. **1970** G. R. STEWART *Amer. Place-Names* p. xii, European scholars rarely concern themselves with the process of name-giving or its motives. **1950** H. L. LORIMER *Homer & Monuments* iv. 125 Apart from the negative evidence of the Pylos tablets, there is the fact..that certain series of signs in both groups form *name-groups which also occur at Knossos in the Palace script. **1963** *English Studies* XLIV. 32 Large name-groups with end-variation, e.g. *Cēolwald*, *-helm*, *-bald*, *-ward*, etc. **1910** *Westm. Gaz.* 14 Mar. 11/2 Affixing red *name-labels to their seats in the Council Chamber. **1928** D. H. LAWRENCE *Lady Chatterley* iv. 36 I'd be ashamed to see a woman walking round with my name-label on her. **1924** *Daughter of C. Patmore* iii. 36 At one time she is deep in heraldry and *name-lore. **1932** E. WEEKLEY *Words & Names* vii. 82 One of the puzzles of name-lore is the process by which the French name *Jacques* ..was early confused with *Jankin* or *Jenkin*. **1875** WHITNEY *Life Lang.* viii. 136 The claims of rival *name-makers are very sharply discussed. **1893** STEVENSON *Catriona* 370 That very fine great lady that is Barbara's *name-mamma. **1940** W. V. QUINE *Math. Logic* iii. 152 Such expressions might be classed as **name matrices*, for they are related to names as statement matrices are related to statements. **1894** *Westm. Gaz.* 11 Sept. 3/3 It had been intended..that Miss Letty Lind should take the *name part. **1936** *Times Lit. Suppl.* 25 Jan. 73/2 But Reid, after all, is in the 'name-part'. **1961** *Times* 5 Apr. 13/6 With Dame Margot Fonteyn in a memorable account of the name-part [of *Giselle*]. **1924** *Glasgow Herald* 24 Apr. 4 The *name-piece of the volume is a genealogical..account of this branch of the..family. **1882** OGILVIE, **Nameplate*, a metal plate bearing a person's name [etc.]. **1896** *Brit. & For. Bible Soc. Rep.* 156 Family Bible. .. With autograph and name-plate. **1904** *Electr. Rev.* 3 Sept. 327 The committee recommends that the ratings of generators and motors, except traction motors, be marked plainly on the name-plate. Two types of service are recommended, continuous working and intermittent working, and the name-plate must state to which service it relates. **1908** [see FINGER-POST *v.*]. **1967** *Gloss. Terms Builders' Hardware (B.S.I.)* IV. 17 *Name plate*, a plate.. bearing one or more words fixed to a door, gate or cupboard ..to convey information concerning contents, premises, business, profession or individuals. **1971** M. TAK *Truck Talk* 110 *Nameplate finders*, cab-mounted spotlights used to find an address on a building at night. **1972** *Village Voice* (N.Y.) 1 June 20/2 Fiction writers..start getting asked to do book reviews and being invited to name-plate cocktail parties. **1958** BLUNDEN *War Poets* 29 The *name-poem is one of the great achievements. **1956** R. CARNAP *Meaning & Necessity* (ed. 2) iii. 96 The method of the *name-relation is an alternative method of semantical analysis, more customary than the method of extension and intension. *Ibid.* 97 Following Russell and Church, I used the word 'denotes' for the name-relation in the first version of this book. However, in view of the ambiguity just described, I now prefer to avoid it. **1905** *Daily Chron.* 23 Feb. 6/5 *Name-ribbons may have to be changed. **1877** W. JONES *Finger-ring* 416 *Name rings are common in France. **1870** RUSKIN *Lect. Art* (1875) 148 His Christian name was John Baptist: he is here painting his *name-Saint. **1861** LYTTON & FANE *Tannhäuser* 37 Four pages..That held the *name-scrolls of the listed bards. **1852** *N. Brit. Rev.* Nov. 69 The Life of their *Name-sire, sent forth by the Cavendish Society. **1863** MELVILLE BELL *Princ. Speech* 148 The alphabetic or *name-sound of the letter O. **1924** MAWER & STENTON *Introd. Survey Eng. Place-Names* ix. 166 Recent investigation has shown that many Germanic *name-stems which are never recorded in England in historic times were still used by the Angles, Saxons and Jutes of the fifth and sixth centuries. **1953** K. JACKSON *Lang. & Hist. Early Brit.* I. 174 The name-stem *Maglocun* which appears both in Ogam and in Latin. **1927** *Observer* 24 Apr. 8/4 There is an air of strain, as if she were attempting—at any rate in the *name-story (the others are nearer her usual vein)—to achieve a high-flown style. **1936** *Times Lit. Suppl.* 25 Jan. 76/4 His 'name-story' is of a poor Australian woman who marries an Afghan trader. **1931** C. L'E. EWEN *Hist. Surnames* iii. 50 Fick concluded that the German *name-system exceeded in splendour..others of the Aryan group. **1937** *Harvard Univ. Summaries Ph.D. Theses* 271 The aim of this study is..to study the Old English dithematic name against the background of the general Germanic name-system. **1960** V. JENKINS *Lions Down Under* vi. 95 Mother was almost sewing on *name-tabs at the airport. **1973** P. O'DONNELL *Silver Mistress* ii. 25 The clothes..had tailor's name-tabs. **1946** W. S. KNICKERBOCKER *20th Cent. English* 333 Each may usurp the business of the other and lose thereby his special *name-tag. **1948** H. LAWRENCE *Death of Doll* x. 230 They did not want name tags pinned to their coat sleeves by Nick. **1953** A. UPFIELD *Murder Must Wait* iv. 36 On some of her clothes is a name tag with the initials P.R. overlaid on others which could be J.O. or J.U. **1958** C. WATSON *Coffin scarcely Used* xvii. 163 Purbright watched Gibbins going through pockets. 'Any name tags?' he asked. **1964** G. L. COHEN *What's Wrong with Hospitals?* i. 16 A parallel substitute for the spoken word is the system of name tags prevalent in America and gaining ground in Europe. 'It saves the staff from having to introduce themselves.' **1899** in A. Adburgham *Shops & Shopping* (1964) xxii. 261 *Name tapes. **1932** E. BOWEN *To North* v. 45 She stitched name-tapes on to her new summer-term outfit. **1964** —— *Little Girls* II. vii. 152 Her mackintosh, name-taped as St. Agatha's demanded. **1969** *Guardian* 1 Sept. 7/5 Those new-fangled printed heat-adhesive name tapes. **1971** M.

McCarthy *Birds of America* 49 Peter would have to have a haircut and name-tapes on his clothes. 1826 Miss Mitford *Village* Ser. II. (1863) 428 That identical black bag, with its *name-tickets. 1955 A. N. Prior *Formal Logic* 182 It would not be possible to lay it down..that in any thesis a description may be substituted for a *name-variable. 1957 —— *Time & Modality* 46 Q is enriched by name-variables, predicate variables, and quantifiers. 1963 O. Wojtasiewicz tr. *Łukasiewicz's Elem. Math. Logic* 103 We shall be concerned with a certain theory of name variables. 1605 Camden *Rem.* 35 An Onomanticall or *Name-wisard Iew. 1598 R. Haydocke tr. *Lomazzo* To Rdr., All the *name-worthy writers of the Arte of Painting. 1879 A. W. Ward *Chaucer* 190 Occleve, the only name-worthy poetical writer of the reign of Henry IV. 1903 *Chambers's Cycl. Eng. Lit.* (new ed.) III. 695/1 *The Growth of Love*, .. *Eros & Psyche* .., are amongst his nameworthy poems.

name (neɪm), *v.*[1] Forms: 1 (ʒe)namian, 2– name, 6 nayme, *Sc.* neame; 4–5 nome. *Pa. pple.* 4 y-namyd, 5 inamed, 4 *Sc.* nammyt, 6 namen. [OE. (*ʒe*)*namian* = OFris. *nama, noma, -ia*, OS. *namôn*, MDu., MHG. *namen*, f. *nama* NAME *sb.* The usual verb in OE. and ME. is *nemnan, nemnen* NEMN.]

I. 1. a. *trans.* To give a name or names to (persons, places, things, etc.); to call by some name.

c 1000 Ælfric *Gen.* ii. 20 Adam þa ʒenamode ealle nytenu heora namum. 1382 Wyclif *Eph.* iii. 15 The fadir of oure Lord Jhesu Crist, of whom ech fadirheed in heuenes and in erthe is named. *c* 1440 *Promp. Parv.* 351/1 Namyn, *nomino, denomino, cognomino.* 1483 *Cath. Angl.* 248/2 To Name; *appellare, baptizare.* 1535 Coverdale *Luke* ii. 21 His name was called Iesus, which was named of ye angell, before he was conceaued. 1548–9 *Bk. Com. Prayer, Baptism* 5 b, Then one of them shal name the childe, and dippe him in the water. 1608 Shaks. *Per.* III. iii. 13 My gentle babe Marina, Whom, for she was borne at sea, I haue named so. 1667 Milton *P.L.* XII. 326 Of the Royal Stock Of David (so I name this King). 1735 Pope *Donne Sat.* IV. 25 Behold! there came A thing which Adam had been pos'd to name. 1819 Shelley *Cyclops* 701 My father named me so. 1872 Ruskin *Eagle's Nest* §66 The stars already named and numbered are as many as we require to hear of.

b. Const. *after, from, for, to* (dial.), †*of*.

c 1450 Lovelich *Merlin* 991 (Kölbing), They..bad..that it named scholde ibe Aftyr his grant-fadyr. 1535 Coverdale *2 Chron.* vii. 13 To humble my people, which is named after my name. 1667 Milton *P.L.* II. 579 Cocytus, nam'd of lamentation loud Heard on the ruful stream. 1697 Dryden *Æneid* III. 28 Enos, nam'd from me, the City [I] call. 1800 Helena Wells *Const. Neville* I. 7 Louisa, who had been named for the mother of Mr. Hayman. 1826 [see FOR *prep.* 7 c]. 1842 R. I. Wilberforce *Rutilius & Lucius* 97 Porphyry,..whom, I suppose, you have named after the great philosopher. 1875 Lowell *Under Old Elm* VIII, Virginia, fitly named from England's manly queen! 1930 Ade *Let.* 20 Aug. (1973) 147 At one time he [*sc.* Peter VanRensselaer] owned thousands of acres in this region and the city of Rensselaer is named for him. 1933 S. Howard *Alien Corn* I. 14 We were just saying you must have been named for Wagner's Elsa. 1936 M. de la Roche *Whiteoak Harvest* vi. 95 You'll have children and perhaps..you'll name a little boy for me. 1957 *Northern Life* June 9/1 Saville Row was named for Col. Sir Geo. Saville, who commanded the garrison of the town [*sc.* Newcastle upon Tyne] in 1776–7 and lived in a house here. 1968 B. Foster *Changing Eng. Lang.* v. 226 A very typically American turn of phrase that is showing signs of headway in Britain is the replacing of 'named after' by 'named for'.

c. With the name as complement.

1390 Gower *Conf.* II. 17 And thus Iphis Thei namede him. 1526 *Pilgr. Perf.* (W. de W. 1531) 1 The cause why we name this treatyse the pilgrymage of perfeccion. 1582 N. Lichefield tr. *Castanheda's Conq. E. Ind.* I. ii. 6 Afterward they named it the Iland of Sancta Hælena. 1634 Milton *Comus* 58 A Son..Whom..she brought up and Comus nam'd. 1742 Pope *Dunc.* IV. 409, I rear'd this Flow'r,.. Then thron'd in glass, and named it Caroline. 1781 Cowper *Charity* 3 Whether we name thee Charity or Love. 1839 Keightley *Hist. Eng.* I. 52 The province was named Normandy from the Northmen. 1875 Jowett *Plato* (ed. 2) I. 441 There is a virtue, Simmias, which is named courage.

d. In *pa. pple.*

c 1400 *Destr. Troy* 7305 A lyuely yong knight,..nomet Boethes. 1490 Caxton *Eneydos* vi. 25 His sone, named pygmaleon, succeded hym. 1530 Palsgr. 643/2 Howe is he named more than Johan? 1605 Shaks. *Lear* I. i. 274, I..am most loth to call Your faults as they are named. 1667 Milton *P.L.* I. 80 One..Long after known in Palestine, and nam'd Beëlzebub. 1704 Pope *Windsor For.* 172 A rural nymph..the fair Lodona nam'd. 1781 Cowper *Charity* 550 That monument of ancient power, Named with emphatic dignity, the Tower. 1855 Macaulay *Hist. Eng.* xii. III. 151 Another brother, named Richard, had, in foreign service, gained some military experience.

2. a. To call by some title or epithet.

c 900 in Bouterwek *Screadunga* 18 Hwi namode Crist on his godspelle Abel rihtwisne toforan oþrum? *c* 1375 *Sc. Leg. Saints* i. (*Peter*) 550 Of þe blame, þat lytil befor tholit he Of thame namyt of galele. 1382 Wyclif *1 Macc.* x. 1 Alisaundre, son of Antiochus, that is named [*v.r.* y-namyd] noble. *c* 1477 Caxton *Jason* 6 Fro thenne forthon he named him his broder. 1535 Coverdale *Isa.* lxi. 6 Ye shalbe named the prestes of the Lorde. 1588 Shaks. *L.L.L.* I. ii. 18 As an appertinent title to your olde time, which we may name tough. 1631 Chettle *Hoffman* B 3 What though for this.. he was nam'd A prescript outlaw. 1732 Pope *Ess. Man* I. 282 Cease then, nor Order Imperfection name. 1818 Shelley *Silence* 2 Silence! Oh, well are Death and Sleep and Thou Three brethren named. 1869 Lynch *Church & State* 17 Name them bishops, or name them not bishops, you will still have chief men.

†**b.** In *pass.* To have a (good or bad) name; to be (well or ill) spoken of. *Obs. rare.*

1390 Gower *Conf.* I. 333 Sche, that hath evere be wel named. *Ibid.* III. 268 That in hir lif sche were schamed And I therof were evele named. *a* 1533 Ld. Berners *Gold. Bk. M. Aurel.* (1546) G b, My sonne in lawe is greatly desyred, loued and wel named amonge the common people.

†**c.** To give (one) the name (of being something); to allege or declare (a person or thing) *to be* something. *Obs.*

1470–85 Malory *Arthur* x. xlvi. 488 Corsabryn noysed her and named her that she was oute of her mynde. 1568 Grafton *Chron.* II. 342 Sir John Froyssart nameth one John Ball to be a chiefe Captaine. 1591 *Durham Depos.* (Surtees) 332 [He] did then jussell upon a strainger naymed to be a Duke. 1647 N. Bacon *Disc. Govt. Eng.* I. v. (1739) 13 Other obedience than this I do not know to be due to him whom you name to be Pope.

†**d.** In *pass.* To be said *to be*, etc. *Obs. rare*[−1].

1551 Recorde *Pathw. Knowl.* I. xxvii, The circle is not named to be drawen in a triangle, because it doth not touche the sides of the triangle.

3. To call (a person or thing) by the right name.

In *Sc.* use freq. with negative, implying that one has forgotten the name.

c 1450 *Merlin* 319 Gentill sir, cometh forth, for I can not yet yow namen. 1610 Shaks. *Temp.* I. ii. 335 Thou.. wouldst..teach me how To name the bigger Light and how the lesse. 1611 —— *Wint. T.* I. ii. 386 There is a sicknesse, Which puts some of vs in distemper, but I cannot name the Disease. 1786 Burns *Holy Fair* iv, I'm sure I've seen that bonie face, But yet I canna name ye. 1846 Keble *Lyra Innoc.* 24 Easier each hour the task will grow To name the unfolding flower.

II. 4. a. To nominate, designate, assign, or appoint (a person) to some office, duty, or position.

a 1000 *Laws Edw.* in Thorpe I. 158 ʒif he..ne mehte, þonne namede him man six men. *a* 1000 *Laws Æthelst.* ibid. 240 Beforan..his witum þe se cyng silf namode. *c* 1000 Ælfric *Hom.* II. 500 [Hi] wurdon ʒenamode to þam ylcan ʒewinne þe heora fæderas on wæron. 1430–40 Lydg. *Bochas* IX. xix. (1554) 27 How Robert duke of Normandy..was named to the crowne of Jerusalem. 1496–7 *Act 12 Hen. VII*, c. 13 §1 The seid orderours and assessours..shall name Collectours for the levye of the same aide. 1542–3 *Act 34 & 35 Hen. VIII*, c. 27 §56 Such persons, as shalbe named to be iustices of peace. 1552 *Reg. Privy Council Scot.* I. 130 Gif the Lord neames his tennent and chargis to mak him in reddiness to compeir. 1605 Shaks. *Macb.* II. iv. 31 He is already nam'd, and gone to Scone To be inuested. 1687 A. Lovell tr. *Thevenot's Trav.* I. 81 Hisouf Basha..was declared Mansoul, and Kaidar Zada named in his place. 1726 Wodrow *Corr.* (1843) III. 240 The Assembly came to the choice of the new Moderator, and Mr. Mitchell..was named by the Commissioner. 1799 Jefferson *Writ.* (ed. Ford) VII. 362 In the meantime, a consul general is named to St. Domingo. 1831 *Examiner* 563/1 A malignant Ministry ..names him to a Bishopric. 1874 Green *Short Hist.* viii. §10. 568 Though the members of the Council were originally named by him, each member was irremovable save by consent of the rest.

†**b.** To assign (an honour, etc.) *to* a person.

1523 Q. Margaret in Mrs. Wood *Lett. Illustr. Ladies* I. 301 The cause of this is about the benefices, for the governor hath named them to sundry persons, but he..holdeth them in his hands.

†**c.** *intr.* To vote. *Obs. rare*[−1].

1566 in Fowler *Hist. C.C.C.* (O.H.S.) 111 He hath lost his right of the Colledge for refusinge to name diffinitivelye in Mr. Belly's matter.

5. a. To mention, speak of, or specify (a person or persons, etc.) by name. †Also *absol.*

c 1000 Ælfric *Saints' Lives* viii. 165 Quintianus cwæð ..'ʒit þu namast Crist?' *Ibid.* ix. 37 Nu bidde ic þe..þæt þu nanne bryd-guman næfre me ne namiʒe. 1390 Gower *Conf.* I. 156 The knyht also, if I schal name, Danz Petro hihte. *a* 1425 *Cursor M.* 5162 (Trin.), Whenne iacob in bed þat lay herde Ioseph named þat day. *c* 1475 *Rauf Coilȝear* 503 He namit na mair the, Nor ane vther man to me. 1535 Coverdale *1 Sam.* xxviii. 8 Bringe me him vp whom I shal name vnto thee. 1560 Daus tr. *Sleidane's Comm.* 44 b, Herin he named no nation. 1590 Shaks. *Mids. N.* I. ii. 41 Now name the rest of the Players. 1630 *R. Johnson's Kingd. & Commw.* A 2 b, Some of our owne have beene more ingenuous, to name him when they quote him: and thats faire play. 1711 Steele *Spect.* No. 254 ¶5, I..never hear him named but with Pleasure and Emotion. 1791 Mrs. Radcliffe *Rom. Forest* viii, Theodore was not once named. 1817 W. Selwyn *Law Nisi Prius* (ed. 4) II. 949 If two ports of discharge are named in the policy [etc.]. 1855 Tennyson *Brook* 130 He took Her blind and shuddering puppies, naming each. 1875 Jowett *Plato* (ed. 2) I. 296 Tell me to whom among the Athenians he should go. Whom would you name?

transf. 1850 Tennyson *In Mem.* ii, Old Yew, which graspest at the stones That name the under-lying dead.

b. *refl.* To announce one's own name.

1597 Shaks. *2 Hen. IV*, II. ii. 120 Iohn Falstaffe Knight: (Euery man must know that, as oft as hee hath occasion to name himselfe). 1607 —— *Cor.* IV. v. 63 Necessitie commands me to name my selfe.

c. ***to name on*** (or ***in***) ***the same day*** (or †***of a day***), to bring into comparison or connexion. Only in negative and interrogative sentences.

c 1606 B. Jonson *Epigr.* cxxxi, They were not to be named on the same day. *a* 1641 Bp. Mountagu *Acts & Mon.* (1642) 37 But nor he (Abraham) nor he (David) to be named in the same day with our Saviour. 1694 Congreve *Double-Dealer* III. ii, *Sir Paul*... You may talk of my Lady Froth! *Care.* O, fy! fy! not to be named of a day. 1839 Lockhart *Scott* (1900) I. 275 That Scott..was not to be named as a table-companion in the same day with this or that master of.. dissertation.

d. Of the Speaker of the House of Commons: To indicate (a member) by name as guilty of disorderly conduct or disobedience to the chair.

1792 *Hansard's Parl. Hist.* XXX. 113 The Speaker.. stated that..he was now compelled to name the member that had given this interruption. 1810 *Sporting Mag.* XXXV. 302 The Speaker..felt very sorry that it would become his duty to name him. 1881 *Hansard's Parl. Deb.* CCLVIII. 68 *Mr. Speaker*, In the terms of the standing order, I Name you..as wilfully disregarding the authority of the Chair. 1928 [see LAST *a.* 1 f]. 1972 *Guardian* 11 Feb. 22/4 The Speaker failed to 'name' or suspend Miss Devlin after hitting Mr Maudling. *Ibid.* 15 Mar. 1/4 Mr Charles Loughlin, MP for Gloucestershire West, was named by the Deputy Speaker after telling him that he 'did not give a damn' whether Sir Robert did or did not listen to his point of order. In accordance with the usual custom, the Leader of the House..moved that Mr Loughlin be suspended.

e. ***name!*** Used in Parliamentary practice, or in imitation of this, to demand that a member be named, or that the name of some person alluded to by a speaker shall be given.

1817 *Parl. Deb.* 279 Loud cries of hear, hear, name, name, order. 1859 Reade *Love me Little* II. 244 Who told you that, aunt? Name; as they say in the House. 1866 Dickens *Mugby Junc.* iii, Miss Piff, trembling with indignation, called out; 'Name!'

f. To specify officially (someone) by name to whom certain political (usu. Communist) affiliations are imputed, esp. in South Africa under the Suppression of Communism Act, 1950, and in the U.S.A. during the period of McCarthyism.

1950 *Times* 9 Mar. 5/3 Senator McCarthy has been ordered by Senator Tydings..to name to-morrow the high State Department official who he has alleged in the Senate intervened to protect an employee who was regarded as a bad security risk. 1952 *Economist* 31 May 581/3 He [*sc.* Mr E. S. Sachs] has been 'named' by the Minister of Justice as a Communist under the Suppression of Communism Act. 1956 L. Kuper *Passive Resistance in S. Afr.* II. viii. 188 For most whites, a 'named' person bears a permanent social stigma; he is not acceptable as an employee, or in ordinary intercourse. 1957 S. Adler *Isolationist Impulse* xv. 460 He [*sc.* McCarthy] said he could name 205, or 57, or 81 Reds (the numbers usually varied with each harangue) in the State Department. *Ibid.* 461 He was unable to substantiate these charges by naming one Communist survivor of the Truman purge. 1958 G. M. Carter *Politics of Inequality* II. ii. 65 The Minister could then forbid those 'named' to take part in any specified organization. But the 'naming' process is not essential before taking action, for the Minister..can also prohibit any gathering if it appears to aid the objects of Communism.

g. To cite as co-respondent in a divorce petition.

1971 Yeldham & Carne *Rees's Divorce Handbk.* (ed. 4) ii. 27 Unless otherwise directed, where a wife's petition alleges adultery with a woman *named*, the alleged adultress must be made a respondent in this cause. 1971 A. Hunter *Gently at Gallop* ii. 11 Laing divorced her, naming Berney... Berney was named in another suit, and his first wife petitioned, using that as grounds... He's been named once or twice since then. 1972 *Guardian* 23 Dec. 24/5 The television actress, Linda Thorson..was named yesterday in a divorce suit.

6. a. To mention, speak of, or specify (a thing) by its name or usual designation.

1382 Wyclif *Eph.* v. 3 Fornycacioun..and al vnclennesse, or auarice, be not named in ȝou. 1390 Gower *Conf.* II. 84 Quikselver..the which..Is ferst of thilke fowre named. 1535 Coverdale *1 Cor.* v. 1 Soch whordome, as is not once named amonge the Heythen. 1591 Shaks. *1 Hen. VI*, I. i. 41 Name not Religion, for thou lou'st the Flesh. 1608 —— *Per.* v. iii. 33 Did you not name a tempest, A birth and death? 1671 Milton *Samson* 674 Nor do I name of men the common rout. 1732 Pope *Ess. Man* II. 193 Nor Virtue, male or female, can we name, But what will grow on Pride, or grow on Shame. 1781 Cowper *Conversat.* 496 The woes that fear or shame..forbade them once to name. 1819 Shelley *Cenci* IV. iv. 128 The crimes which mortal tongue dare never name. 1860 Pusey *Min. Proph.* 582 To name evil is a temptation to evil.

transf. 1599 Shaks. *Hen. V*, IV. Prol. 16 The Clocks doe towle And the third howre of drowsie Morning name.

b. To make mention of, to speak about (a fact, circumstance, etc.). †Also const. *on*.

1542 Udall *Erasm. Apoph.* 196 b, The same is named on diverse others as well as on Alexander. 1599 Shaks. *Hen. V*, IV. iii. 42 He..Will stand a tip-toe when this day is named. 1617 Moryson *Itin.* I. 228, I was troubled with loosenesse of body, whereof I made good use, as I shall hereafter shew, which makes me name it. 1669 Sturmy *Mariner's Mag.* IV. viii. 218 This Rule will not be impertinent to this Place, being not named before. 1719 De Foe *Crusoe* II. (Globe) 511 My Fellow-Traveller and I had different Notions. I do not name this to insist upon my own. 1729 Pope *Let. to Swift* 28 Nov., I was once displeas'd before at you, for complaining to Mr. * of my not having a pension, and am so again at your naming it to a certain Lord. 1874 Green *Short Hist.* ii. §8. 106 The measures we have named were only part of Henry's legislation.

c. To mention or cite as an instance.

1594 Shaks. *Rich. III*, IV. iv. 173 What comfortable houre canst thou name, That euer grac'd me with thy company? 1690 Locke *Hum. Und.* I. ii. §23, I would gladly have any one name that proposition whose terms or ideas were either of them innate.

d. To state, give particulars of.

1605 Shaks. *Lear* I. i. 73, I finde she names my very deede of loue: Onely she comes too short. 1735 Pope *Donne Sat.* IV. 162 He names the price for ev'ry office paid. 1850 Tennyson *In Mem.* xciii, Hear The wish too strong for words to name. 1864 —— *En. Ard.* 215 Annie, the ship I sail in passes here (He named the day).

e. Phr. ***you name it, I*** (or ***we***) ***have*** (or ***have done***) ***it*** (also with other verbs), everything that you can think of is available, has been done, etc.; also ellipt., ***you name it***.

1962 J. Braine *Life at Top* xviii. 213 You name the drink, we have it. 1964 M. S. Allwood *American & British* 137 *American.* You name it! *British*....or whatever you like.

1967 *Field & Stream* Aug. 63/2 Mallards, gadwall, partridge, quail—you name it—they're up here for the season every year. **1968** *Sun* (Baltimore) 18 Sept. A. 14/4 Bear Creek, Back River, you name it; the story is the same. **1969** N. FREELING *Tsing-Boum* vii. 45 What sort of world are they born into anywhere?—hunger, napalm, you name it and we've got it. **1969** *Rolling Stone* 28 June 17/3 I've written every kind of music there is. You name it, I've written it. All except one thing I couldn't do: rhythm and blues. **1972** D. LEES *Zodiac* 53 He's been a smuggler, a gun runner, a dope peddler—you name it. **1973** *Times* 6 Jan. 9/4 Bits of chicken, port, olive— you name it. *Ibid.* 22 Jan. 9/2 At that time the cops knew me. You name it, I'd done it. **1973** *Black Panther* 8 Sept. 17/1 I've seen police call people slur names such as nigger, mother fuckers, bitches, whores ..you name it, they had a name for it.

7. With cognate object: **a.** To utter or mention (the name of a person or thing).

1382 WYCLIF *2 Tim.* ii. 19 Ech man that nameth the name of the Lord. **1526** *Pilgr. Perf.* (W. de W. 1531) 219b, Thy holy name is inuocate & named vpon vs. **1588** SHAKS. *L.L.L.* III. i. 167 When tongues speak sweetly, then they name her name. **1715** DE FOE *Fam. Instruct.* I. i. (1841) I. 24 It is a.. profane thing to name his name on slight occasions. **1820** SHELLEY *Hymn Merc.* x, Still scoffing at the scandal, And naming his own name. **1864** TENNYSON *Aylmer's F.* 581 That night, that moment, when she named his name.

†**b.** To utter (a word); to say. *Obs.*

1588 SHAKS. *L.L.L.* v. ii. 239 *Du.* Will you vouchsafe with me to change a word? *Mar.* Name it. —— *Tit. A.* III. ii. 33 As if we should forget we had no hands, If Marcus did not name the word of hands. **1593** —— *3 Hen. VI*, v. v. 58 What's worse then Murtherer, that I may name it?

c. *to name no names*: to refrain from mentioning the names of the people involved in an incident, etc., in order to protect them; often with the implication that the hearer or reader could supply these names.

1792 F. BURNEY *Jrnl.* June (1972) I. 212 She desired he would name no names, but merely mention that some ladies had been frightened. **1843** DICKENS *Mart. Chuz.* (1844) iv. 46 Naming no names, and therefore hurting nobody but those whose consciences tell them they are alluded to. **1890** KIPLING *Soldiers Three* 12 Av coorse I will name no names, for there's wan that's an orf'cer's lady now, that was in ut. **1908** K. GRAHAME *Wind in Willows* iv. 89 The Wild Wood is pretty well populated by now; with all the usual lot, good, bad and indifferent—I name no names. **1919** BEERBOHM *Seven Men* 203 But now my sense of duty forces me To a departure from my custom of Naming no names. One name I must and shall Name. **1972** L. LAMB *Picture Frame* xiii. 107 You put that tale around, naming no names, at one o' your police smokers, you'll have 'em all rolling in the aisles.

8. To mention or specify as something desired, suggested, or decided upon; to appoint or fix (a sum, time, etc.). *to name the day*: of a woman, to fix her wedding day; also *transf.*

1593 SHAKS. *Rich. II*, IV. i. 304 *Rich.* Ile beg one Boone.. Shall I obtaine it? *Bull.* Name it, faire Cousin. **1594** —— *Rich. III*, III. iv. 19 But you, my Honorable Lords, may name the time. **1611** BIBLE *Gen.* xxiii. 16 Abraham weighed to Ephron the siluer, which he had named. **1638** EARL MANCH. in *Buccleuch MSS.* (Hist. MSS. Comm.) I. 278 To name 24*l.* a month..is so poor and mean an offer. **1766** GOLDSMITH *Vicar of Wakefield* I. xvii. 171 'Name, then, your day...' ..She again renewed her..promise of marrying Mr. Williams..and..that day month was fixed upon for her nuptials. **1778** MISS BURNEY *Evelina* lxxxi, If there is any thing I can name which he can do for me. **1835** DICKENS *Sk. Boz, Mr. Watkins Tottle* ii, I am quite sure that I never could..name the day to my future husband. **1841** —— *Let.* 25 Mar. (1969) II. 243 Chigwell, my dear fellow, is the greatest place in the world. Name your day for going. **1863** READE *Hard Cash* xxxiv, Then he made hot love to her, and pressed her hard to name the day. **1974** *Times* 9 Feb. 16/6 'Heath names the day,' shrilled the billboards yesterday. And an elderly couple on a bus said: 'It's about time he got married.'

†**name**, *v.*², obscure var. of NIM *v.*, to take.

c **1450** *St. Cuthbert* (Surtees) 310 þat a childe in his kyngdome Now late borne he myght him name.

name, pa. t. of NIM *v. Obs.*

nameable ('neɪməb(ə)l), *a.* Also namable. [f. NAME *v.*¹ + -ABLE.]

1. That admits of being named, or being called by a certain name.

1840 CARLYLE *Heroes* (1858) 299 This is the Heavenly Ideal (well named in Knox's time, and namable in all times, a revealed 'Will of God'). **1843** MILL *Logic* I. iii. §2 We shall commence with Feelings, the simplest class of nameable things. **1886** STEVENSON *Dr. Jekyll* 25 He gave an impression of deformity without any nameable malformation.

2. Worthy of being named; memorable.

1780 J. ADAMS *26 Lett. Revol. Amer.* (1789) 23 The sixth talk is to shew, 'that no person, in America, is of so much influence, power, or credit, that his death, or corruption, by English money, could be of any nameable consequence'. **1858** CARLYLE *Fredk. Gt.* III. xiv. I. 311 Donauwörth... A Town nameable in History ever since. **1865** *Ibid.* XVIII. x. V. 253 Möllendorf, nameable from that day forward.

Hence **namea'bility.**

1882 W. HOEY tr. *Oldenberg's Buddha* 230 The bases on which all nameability and all existence..rest.

'name-child. [f. NAME *sb.* 15 + CHILD.] One called after, or named out of regard for, another.

1845 MISS STRICKLAND *Queens of Eng.* VIII. 3 She was the darling of her..father, being the child of his old age, his name-child. **1876** SWINBURNE *Erechtheus* 877 The namechild of the lords of under earth.

transf. **1872** *Daily News* 12 Aug., The Bellerophon..the massive name-child of the old historic fighting ship.

†**namecouth**, *a. Obs.* Forms: 1 namcúð, 3-4 **namecouth**, (4 **-coþ**, **-kouþ**, 6 *Sc.* **-kouth**), 4-5 **namecouthe**, (4 **-kowþe**), 6 **naamkouth**, *Sc.* **naimcouth**; 1-3 **nomecuðe**, 4-5 **-kowthe**. [OE. *namcúð, nomecúð*: see NAME *sb.* and COUTH *a.*] Known by name, well known, famous.

a **1000** *Laws Ethelred* ix. 37 in Thorpe I. 348 On þam ȝemotan, þeah rædlice wurðan on namcuðan stowan. *c* **1000** ÆLFRIC in Assmann *Ags. Hom.* (1889) 85 Ða beoð heahfæderas, nomecuðe wæras. *Ibid.* 92 Sum rice cyning namcuð on worulde. *a* **1225** *Leg. Kath.* 537 Wittiest..& mest nomecuðe icud of alle clergies. *c* **1290** *S. Eng. Leg.* I. 467/181 To Marcile þe wynd heom drof, a gret name-couth cite. **1340-70** *Alex. & Dind.* 823 þe aþel king alexandre, ..þat noble is & name-kouþ. **1387** TREVISA *Higden* (Rolls) I. 43 Al þe worlde aboute haþ name kowthe sees þritty. **1413** *Pilgr. Sowle* (Caxton) v. i. (1859) 70 One of the seuene name couthe planetes, that ben cleped of clerkes sterres erratiks. **1513** DOUGLAS *Æneis* VI. i. 59 The naimcouth hous, that Laborinthus hait. [**1557** GRIMALDE in *Tottel's Misc.* (Arb.) 102 As in the famous woork, that Eneids hight The naamkouth Virgil hath set forth in sight.]

Hence †**namecouthhead.** *Obs. rare.*

1340 *Ayenb.* 25 Huanne he wilneþ and zekþ and porchaceþ los and namecouþhede.

†**namecund**, *a. Obs. rare*⁻¹. [Cf. NAMECOUTH and MDu. *name-, naemcond-*.] Famous.

c **1200** ORMIN 6863 þiss illke Balaam was an Full namecund prophete Onn alde daȝhess.

named (neɪmd), *ppl. a.* [f. NAME *v.*¹ + -ED¹.] **a.** Mentioned by name. (Usu. with *above-*, *before-*, *first-*, *last-*, etc.) **b.** Famous, distinguished, (highly) spoken of. *rare.* †**c.** Called by a certain name; so-called. *Obs.*

1467- [see BEFORE E. 1]. **1490-** [see FORE-NAMED]. **1530** PALSGR. 319/2 Noysed named or bruted, *fameux*. *c* **1530** L. Cox *Rhet.* (1899) 54 The excellent and moste hyghly named philosopher Plato. **1567** RASTELL (*title*) A brief Shew of the false wares packed together in the named *Apology of the Church of England*. **1592** WEST *1st Pt. Symbol.* I. §12a, Named contracts, be those which have a cause by law defined, and they are called by proper names. **1603-** [see AFORED. 1 b]. **1837** CARLYLE *Fr. Rev.* III. I. ii, The famed and named go; the nameless, if they have an accuser. **1847** *Infantry Man.* (1854) 89 The named file moves..on.

Hence †**'namedly** *adv.*, by name. *Obs. rare*⁻¹.

a **1641** BP. MOUNTAGU *Acts & Mon.* (1642) 221 Cicero speaks namedly of the Acrostichis.

name-day ('neɪmdeɪ). Also **name's-day.** [f. NAME *sb.* + DAY; in sense 1, after Du. *naamdag*, Da. *navndag*, or G. *namenstag*, Sw. *namnsdag*.]

1. The day sacred to the saint whose name one bears. (Used chiefly with reference to continental sovereigns.)

α. **1721** *Lond. Gaz.* No. 5980/2 Yesterday being the King of Sweden's Name-Day. **1777** ROBERTSON *Hist. Amer.* II. 433 Presents made to him on the anniversary of his Name-day (which is always observed as an high festival). **1812** LD. CATHCART in *Examiner* 12 Oct. 649/1 The accounts of the battle..reached the Emperor early on the morning of his name-day. **1865** *Pall Mall G.* 21 Sept. 9/1 Several promotions..were made at St. Petersburg on the occasion of the Emperor's name-day.

β. **1799** W. TOOKE *View Russian Emp.* I. 372 No one neglects to keep his birth and name's day, and those of his family. **1842** MOTLEY *Corr.* (1889) I. iv. 98 The day of the Emperor's fête (or day distinguished..as the name's-day of the Czar..). **1881** *Scribner's Mag.* Oct. 886/1 On the 5th of December, the name's-day of the Empress.

2. The day on which a child is named.

1880 MUIRHEAD *Ulpian* xv. §2 *note*, The name-day was the ninth for boys and the eighth for girls.

3. *Stock Exch.* The day on which the seller of registered securities receives from the buyer a ticket with the name and details of the person to whom the securities are to be transferred.

1885 P. CAMPBELL *Stock Exchange* 25 The second [account day] is called 'Name or Ticket Day', devoted by Brokers and Jobbers to concluding Investment operations by completing and delivering transfers. **1895** A. J. WILSON *Gloss. Colloq. Terms Stock Exchange* 170 Each settlement occupies three days—1st, 'contango day'..; 2nd, 'name day', when the names of buyers of registered securities are passed to the sellers; and 3rd, 'pay day'. **1907** [see NAME *sb.* 1 c]. **1941** DICE & EITEMAN *Stock Market* (ed. 2) x. 155 The second day of settlement is called 'ticket day' or 'name day.' On this day a broker who wishes delivery on stock that he has bought sends a ticket to his jobber, giving the name of the security. **1970** M. GREENER *Penguin Dict. Commerce* 325 Ticket day..is also sometimes called name day.

†**'namefy**, *v. nonce-wd.* [f. NAME *sb.* + -IFY.] *trans.* To mention by name.

1589 LYLY *Pappe w. Hatchet* Wks. 1902 III. 406 Name me? Mary, he and his shall bee namefied, that's it I thirst after, that name to name.

†**namel**, obs. aphet. form of ENAMEL.

1426 LYDG. *Pilgr. Life Man* 6686 Loo, her,..Off the syluer bellys clere, And off the namel ek yfere.

namele, obs. form of NAMELY *adv.*

nameless ('neɪmlɪs), *a.* Also 4-7 **nameles**, 6-7 **-lesse**. [ME. *namelēs* = MDu. *name-, naemloos* (Du. *name-, naamloos*), MHG. *namelôs* (G. *namenlos, namlos*), Da. *navnlös*, Sw. *namnlös*: see NAME *sb.* and -LESS.]

1. Not possessed of a (distinguished) name; devoid of name or fame; unknown by name; obscure, inglorious.

c **1311** *Pol. Songs* (Camden) 254 For fiht is fliht, the lond is nameles. *c* **1374** CHAUCER *Boeth.* IV. pr. v. (1868) 131 Exiled pore and nedy and nameles. **1582** STANYHURST *Æneis* II. (Arb.) 61 Prince Priamus..In shoare now namelesse dooth ly lyke a truncheon al headlesse. *a* **1616** BEAUM. & FL. *Bonduca* II. 1, When one is smother'd with a multitude, And crowded in amongst a nameless press. **1658** SIR T. BROWNE *Hydriot.* v. 75 To be namelesse in worthy deeds exceeds an infamous history. **1728** POPE *Dunc.* III. 157 Each Songster, Riddler, ev'ry nameless name. **1813** SCOTT *Rokeby* III. xviii, Maiden! a nameless life I lead, A nameless death I'll die. **1855** TENNYSON *Maud* I. IV. iii, I am nameless and poor. **1887** BOWEN *Virg. Æneid* VI. 505 Thou hadst laid thee to die on a heap of the nameless dead.

b. Not mentioned by name; left in obscurity.

a **1535** MORE *Rich. III*, Wks. 57 The other two were somwhat greter parsonages, & natheles of theyr humilite content to be nameles. **1667** MILTON *P.L.* VI. 380 Nameless in dark oblivion let them dwell. **1868** FREEMAN *Norm. Conq.* (1877) II. App. 545 The lands had been held by a nameless freeman.

2. Not specified by name, left unnamed, in order to avoid giving offence, or for some other reason.

c **1430** LYDG. *Min. Poems* (Percy Soc.) 31 Thou tolde me, ..That thou kneuhest one, nameles of me as nowhe. *a* **1529** SKELTON *Ware Hauke* 38 He shall be as now nameles, But he shall not be blameles. **1617** MORYSON *Itin.* III. 194 A great Prince of Germany (for good respect namelesse). **1653** WALTON *Angler* ii. 46 Another of the company that shall be nameless. **1711** STEELE *Spect.* No. 91 ¶1 The Loves of a Family in Town, which shall be nameless. **1800** MRS. HERVEY *Mourtray Fam.* II. 38 A certain person, who shall be nameless, is now engaged on Tower duty. **1875** JOWETT *Plato* (ed. 2) I. 489 On the authority of one who shall be nameless.

†**3.** Of a book, letter, etc.: Having no name attached to it, anonymous. *Obs.*

1529 MORE *Dyaloge* III. Wks. 223/1 For yᵉ boke is put forth namelesse, & was in the beginning rekened to be made by Tindal. **1643** PRYNNE in P. & Walker *Fiennes' Trial* 5, I received a Note..with a datelesse, namelesse Paper inclosed. **1667** SIR R. MORAY in *Lauderdale Papers* (Camden) II. 88 There is a Damned book come hither.. called Naphtali, or the Wrestlings of the Church of Scotland, &c. nameless. **1786** WESLEY *Wks.* (1872) IV. 339 One of the hearers wrote me a nameless letter upon it. **1822** GALT *Provost* xxx, I received a twenty-pound note in a nameless letter.

4. Whose name is not, or has not been, divulged; anonymous, unknown. Also const. *to.*

1591 SHAKS. *Two Gent.* II. i. 111, I haue writ your Letter Vnto the secret, nameles friend of yours. **1624** GATAKER *Transubst.* 36 On the false report of another namelesse author like to himselfe. **1697** STILLINGFL. *Disc. Trinity* 173 A certain nameless Socinian was the Author of them. *a* **1735** ATTERBURY *Serm.* (J.), Little credit is due to accusations of this kind, when they come from suspected, that is, from nameless pens. **1807** CRABBE *Hall of Just.* I. 33 Yet nameless let me plead—my name Would only wake the cry of scorn. **1855** MACAULAY *Hist. Eng.* xv. III. 576 The two nameless executioners who had done their office..on the scaffold. **1856** DE QUINCEY *Confess.* Wks. I. 226 A gang of Vandals (nameless, I thank heaven, to me).

absol. **1589** PUTTENHAM *Eng. Poesie* I. xxxi. (Arb.) 74 After whom followed Iohn Lydgate.., and that nameles, who wrote the Satyre called Piers Plowman.

5. a. Bearing no legitimate name.

1593 SHAKS. *Lucr.* 522 Thy issue blur'd with namelesse bastardie. **1693** DRYDEN *Juvenal* (1697) 157 And into Noble Families advance A Nameless Issue, the blind work of Chance. **1732** POPE *Ep. Cobham* 233 A rev'rend sire, whom want of grace Has made the father of a nameless race.

b. Having no name; unnamed.

1638 SIR T. HERBERT *Trav.* (ed. 2) 333 Iles for the greatest part namelesse and numberlesse. **1719** DE FOE *Crusoe* II. (Globe) 581 We began..to enter upon the vast nameless Desart. **1792** S. ROGERS *Pleas. Mem.* II. 209 A thousand nameless rills that shun the light. **1819** SHELLEY *Prometh. Unb.* I. 205 All the gods Are there, and all the powers of nameless worlds.

6. Of altars, tombs, etc.: Bearing no name or inscription.

1655 STANLEY *Hist. Philos.* I. (1701) 57/2 Nameless Altars, Monuments of that Expiation. *c* **1718** POPE *Epit. Rowe*, Beneath a rude and nameless stone he lies. **1859** MISS PROCTER *Legends & Lyr.* Ser. I. 104 Over a nameless grave.

7. That cannot be definitely named or described; inexpressible, indefinable.

1591 SHAKS. *Two Gent.* III. i. 319 She hath many namelesse vertues. **1593** —— *Rich. II*, II. ii. 40 What I cannot name, 'tis namelesse woe I wot. **1709** POPE *Ess. Crit.* 144 Music resembles Poetry, in each Are nameless graces which no methods teach. **1780** COWPER *Progr. Err.* 244 Are all the nameless sweets of friendship fled? **1817** SHELLEY *Rev. Islam* III. iv, When suddenly was blended With our repose a nameless sense of fear. **1850** TENNYSON *In Mem.* iv, Such clouds of nameless trouble cross All night below the darken'd eyes. **1887** RUSKIN *Præterita* II. 256 The nameless ailing of overwearied flesh.

8. That one shrinks from naming; unutterable; horrible, abominable.

1611 BIBLE *Wisd.* xiv. 27 Worshipping of idoles not to be named [*marg.* namelesse], is the beginning, the cause, and the end of all euill. *a* **1704** T. BROWN *Satire Woman* Wks. 1730 I. 56 Of impotent, still varying desires; And of ten thousand nameless vices more Is this vile idol made, which men adore. **1819** SHELLEY *Cenci* v. i. 44 Avenging such a nameless wrong As turns black parricide to piety. **1866** LIDDON *Bampton Lect.* vi. (1875) 308 Paganism allowed man to sink beneath a flood of nameless sensualities.

†**b.** ***nameless finger***, the middle finger. *Obs.*⁻¹

After L. *digitus impudicus* or *infamis*.

1584 R. SCOT *Discov. Witchcr.* XII. xviii. (1886) 223 Put thy nameles finger in the wound.

Hence **'namelessly** *adv.*, **'namelessness.**

1847 WEBSTER, *Namelessly*. **1861** MEREDITH *Evan Harrington* III. xi. 179 A bunch of the best flowers that could be got were..sent namelessly. **1866** DICKENS *Mugby Junc.* i, A youth with a bitter sense of his namelessness. **1885** *Spectator* 10 Jan. 51/1 The very namelessness helps to deepen the impression of remoteness.

nameli(ch, etc., obs. forms of NAMELY *adv.*

†**'nameling.** *Obs. rare*⁻¹. [f. NAME *sb.* + -LING.] *pl.* Persons bearing the same name.

1706 DE FOE *Jure Divino* II. 4 The Namelings fight, because the Clan commands.

namely ('neɪmlɪ), *a.* Now only *Sc.* [f. NAME *sb.* + -LY¹; in Sc. use probably after Gael. *ainmeil* from *ainm* name.] Distinguished, famous, notable (*for* a thing).

c **1440** *Promp. Parv.* 351/1 Namely, or singulere, *precipuus*. **1483** *Cath. Angl.* 248/2 Namely.., *precipuus*, *excipuus*.

1815 [MRS. JOHNSTONE] *Clan Albin* xiv, 'Nay, for that matter', said Moome, 'Skye was always namely for witches'. **1896** N. MUNRO *Lost Pibroch* (1902) 9, I will take you to one of your own trade, who is namely for music.

namely ('neɪmlɪ), *adv.* Forms: α. 2–4 **nomeliche**, 4–5 **nom(e)ly**. β. 3–4 **nameliche**, 4–5 **-lich**, 5 **-lych**; 4 **namlich(e**; 4 **namelike**, **namlik(e**, **-lic**. γ. 4–6 **namly**, (4 **-li**, **-le**, **nammeli**); 4 **namele**, 4–5 **-li**, 6 **-lye**, 6–7 **-lie**; 4– **namely**. [ME. *name-*, *nomeliche* = OFris. *nam-*, *nomlik*, MDu. *name-*, *naemlike*, *-lijc*, *-lic* (Du. *namelijk*), MLG. *nemelike(n*, *-lik* (hence Sw. *nemligen*, Da. *nemlig*), MHG. *nam(e)-*, *nem(e)lîche*, etc. (G. *nämlich*), ON. *nafnliga*, Icel. *nefnilega*: see NAME *sb.* and -LY².]

†**1.** Particularly, especially, above all. (Usually with preceding *and*.) *Obs.*

α. *c* **1175** *Lamb. Hom.* 139 Sunnedei ah efri cristenne Mon nomeliche to chirche cume. *a* **1225** *Leg. Kath.* 21 Him weox weorre on euch halue, & nomeliche in an lond Ylirie hatte. *c* **1325** *Chron. Eng.* 75 in Ritson *Metr. Rom.* II. 273 Al thyn honour were leid adoun, And nomeliche to thy lemmon. *c* **1375** *Lay-Folks Mass-Bk.* (MS. B.) 615, I thonk God of his godnesse, And nomely now of þis messe. *c* **1420** *Chron. Vilod.* 4496 Williham was a fulle sputusmon..And nomely bokke hunters in his tyme nad no rest.

β. *c* **1200** *Trin. Coll. Hom.* 51 Hie..folgeden here lichames wille, nameliche on two þigges, þat on was muðes mede, þat oðer hordom. *a* **1300** *Cursor M.* 14478 Oft þai on him soght to scam, And namlikest for þat resun, þat he vp-raised lazarum. **1387** TREVISA *Higden* (Rolls) VI. 295 A greet pestilence of reþeren destroyed wel nygh al Europa, and namliche Britayne. *c* **1449** PECOCK *Repr.* I. xviii. 110 A perilose thing is it forto appeire vntreuly a mannys name and namelich a prelatis name.

γ. *a* **1300** *Cursor M.* 4442 þus can godd help man in nede, Namli þat wil him luue and dred. **1362** LANGL. *P. Pl.* A. II. 115 Fauel..bad Gyle go to and ȝyue gold aboute, And namely to this notaries. *c* **1420** *Pallad. on Husb.* II. 131 Rude erthe and namly wodlond best is hold For pastynyng. *c* **1489** CAXTON *Sonnes of Aymon* iii. 72 Whan reynawde vnderstode the good wyll of his folke, & namly of his brethern [etc.]. **1542** UDALL *Erasm. Apoph.* 26 To bee pronounced by a philosophier and namely but such a philosophier as Socrates. **1608** TOPSELL *Serpents* (1658) 681, I finde some difference about the nature of this living creature, and namely whether it be a Serpent or a Fish. **1700** *New Hampsh. Prov. Papers* (1868) III. 327 Returning thanks.. for many blessings and favors..And, namely, for the enjoyment of the Gospel.

†**b.** Carefully, precisely. *Obs. rare.*

a **1400–50** *Alexander* 293 For any cas þat is to com to knaw if þe likis, I sall as namely ȝow neuyn as it ware nowe done. *Ibid.* 582 Latt him..norisch him as namely as he myne awyn warre.

†**c.** By name, individually. *Obs. rare.*

1551 ROBINSON *More's Utop.* II. (1895) 143 Wher to be present they onlye be constreined that be namelye chosen and appoynted to learnynge. **1588** J. UDALL *Demonstr. Disc.* (Arb.) 13 Neyther are the offices and officers, namely, and particularly expressed in the Scriptures.

†**2.** At least, at any rate. *Obs. rare.*

1387 TREVISA *Higden* (Rolls) V. 407 Assenteþ to me, nameliche, in þre þinges, ȝif ȝe willeþ nouȝt assente to me and [*v.r.* in] þe oþere. *c* **1449** PECOCK *Repr.* V. v. 511 A mannys fader and modir ben to him grettist benefetouris, or namelich lien in grettist wil forto be benefetouris to him.

3. To wit; that is to say; videlicet.

c **1450** *Merlin* 8 In that the feende repaireth moste, bothe in man and woman, namly, when they be in grete ire. **1535** COVERDALE *1 Kings* iii. 13 That thou hast not prayed for, haue I geuen the also, namely, ryches, and honoure. **1574** tr. *Marlorat's Apocalips* 28 That is to wit, whiche are already past: namely my passion and resurrection. **1617** MORYSON *Itin.* I. 242 My Host told me a strange thing, namely that in Alexandria of Ægypt..there was a Dovecote. **1682** NORRIS *Hierocles* 5 Namely, to consider what is meant by the Law and the Order of it. **1711** ADDISON *Spect.* No. 123 ⁋4 They both agreed upon an Exchange of Children, namely that the Boy should be bred up with Leontine as his Son [etc.]. **1798** WASHINGTON *Lett.* Writ. 1893 XIV. 99 It would then have been understood as it is at present, namely, that the gentlemen would rank in the order they are named. **1875** HELPS *Soc. Press.* iii. 48 The worst and most disheartening point..is this namely,—that the course of modern thought and modern life is set against these improvements.

†**b.** With *as*. For example. *Obs.*

1583 STUBBES *Anat. Abus.* II. (1882) 49 Almost all things, as namelie butter, cheese, fagots. **1600** J. PORY tr. *Leo's Africa* VIII. 307 There is most excellent outlandish linnen cloth to be sold, as namely fine cloth of cotton brought from Balabach. **1653** WALTON *Angler* vi. 141 There is more than one sort of them [*sc.* Salmon], as namely a Tecon.

namen, obs. pa. pple. of NAME *v.*, pa. t. pl. of NIM *v.*, to take.

namer ('neɪmə(r)). [f. NAME *v.*¹ + -ER¹.] One who, or that which, gives a name or names.

1627 DRAYTON *Agincourt* lxv, Skilfull Merlin, namer of that Towne [Caermarthen]. **1627** SPEED *England* xxxi. §8 Thirtie one Market-Townes..whereof Lincolne the Counties namer is chiefe. *a* **1853** ROBERTSON *Lect.* ii. (1858) 161 The poet has been called as the name imports, creator, namer, maker. **1869** BROWNING *Ring & Bk.* IX. 1371 Gaetano..newest namer for a thing so new.

namesake ('neɪmseɪk), *sb.* [f. NAME *sb.* The use of *sake* is peculiar, but the comb. may have originated in two persons or things being mentioned or coupled together 'for the *name's sake*': for examples of *name-sake* in this sense, see SAKE.] A person or thing having the same name as another.

1646 SIR T. BROWNE *Pseud. Ep.* 170 Nor [does] the Dog-fish at sea much more make out the Dog of the land, then that his cognominall or name-sake in the heavens. **1657** J. WATTS *Vindic. Church Eng.* 89, I shall here dehort you from being of Iohn and Iames, (though you are the name-sake of the one). **1712** ADDISON *Spect.* No. 482 ⁋2 Another.. subscribes herself Xantippe, and tells me, that she follows the Example of her Name-sake. **1797** MME. D'ARBLAY *Let.* June, It was a very sweet thought to make my little namesake write to me. **1826** SCOTT 26 Mar. in *Croker Papers* (1884) I. 319, I enclose a letter for your funny namesake and kinsman. **1867** FREEMAN *Norm. Conq.* (1877) I. iv. 182 The unhappy descendant and namesake of the great Emperor.

attrib. **1650** FULLER *Pisgah* II. 64 Looking southward behold the City of Nebo, at the foot of its namesake mountain. **1860** FORSTER *Gr. Remonstr.* 26 Postponing Luke to lucre; and setting more store by a handful of marks than by all the doctrines of their namesake saint.

Hence **'namesake** *v.*, to call by the same name; to name *after* one. *nonce-wd.*

1651 CLEVELAND *Poems* 5 Their name-sak'd signs in their strange character. **1836** HALIBURTON *Clockm.* (1838) p. ix, Here's a Book they've namesaked arter me.

namesmanship ('neɪmzmənʃɪp). *colloq.* [f. NAME *sb.* + -MANSHIP, after GAMESMANSHIP.] Skill in the use of influential names of people or objects; skill in name-dropping.

1964 *Amer. Speech* XXXIX. 225 Namesmanship at sea. **1967** *Economist* 28 Oct. p. xxii/2 Namesmanship has been in, in Sweden, since the appearance this summer of Mr Ake Ortmark's book on 'The Power Game in Sweden'.

'name-son. *Sc.* [f. NAME *sb.* 15 + SON *sb.*¹] A name-child of the male sex.

1760–1 SMOLLETT *Sir L. Greaves* xii, God for ever bless your honour: I am your name-son sure enough. **1824** MISS FERRIER *Inher.* xxvi, The Major was..flattered by the interest expressed for this little name-son. **1894** A. WHYTE *S. Rutherford* xi. 88 It is with the name-son..of this sturdy old saint that we have chiefly to do.

Namibia (nə'mɪbɪə). [f. *Namib* (a desert on the western coast of southern Africa) + -IA¹.] A name given to South-West Africa in 1968 by the United Nations in anticipation of its being released from the mandate granted to South Africa by the League of Nations in 1919 (see quots. 1968). Hence **Na'mibian** *sb.*, a native or inhabitant of Namibia; also *adj.*, of or pertaining to the land or people of Namibia.

1968 *Post* (S. Afr.) 4 Feb. 5 We are Namibians and not South Africans. **1968** *United Nations 22nd Session* Suppl. 16A 12 June 1/2 Resolution 2372... Proclaims that, in accordance with the desires of its people, South West Africa shall henceforth be known as 'Namibia'. *Ibid.* 2/1 The Council shall organize a training programme for Namibians. *Ibid.*, Reaffirms the inalienable right of the Namibian people to freedom and independence. **1970** R. HALL *South-West Afr.* (*Namibia*) 3 The Reverend Michael Scott..has won international respect by the tenacity of his fight..to sustain the rights of the Namibian peoples. **1973** *Times* 8 Mar. 6/3 Namibians prefer to be misgoverned or misruled by themselves rather than by others. **1973** *Guardian* 28 June 13/8 The Namibian strikes last year..secured important concessions. **1974** *Stand. Encycl. S. Afr.* X. 145/1 In United Nations circles the territory [*sc.* S.-W. Africa] is called Namibia, a designation derived from the name of the coastal desert, the Namib.

Namierian (neɪ'mɪərɪən), *sb.* and *a.* [f. the name of Sir Lewis B. *Namier* (1888–1960), British historian + -IAN.] **A.** *sb.* An adherent of the methods and theories of Sir L. Namier concerning the structure of, and research into, political history. **B.** *adj.* Of, pertaining to, illustrating, or concerning the historical theories or techniques of Namier.

1958 *Oxf. Mag.* 27 Feb. 330/2 The Namierian revolution in historical method, now a quarter of a century old, destroyed a long accepted view of the nature of political parties in the 18th century. *Ibid.* 332/1 If the party is of little importance, as the Namierians have proved, then [etc.]. **1961** *Encounter* XVI. 39/2 The general configuration of world history will continue to look much the same, whether one takes the Namierian or pre-Namierian view about the structure of politics in Britain in George III's reign. **1962** *Guardian* 6 July 6/5 The Namierian House of Commons. **1967** *Economist* 6 May 575/3 His expertise with the telescope at one moment and the microscope at another is quite Namierian.

So **'Namierite** *a.* and *sb.* in same sense. **Namieri'zation**, the application of Namier's methods and theories to a historical situation; hence **'Namierize** *v.*; **'Namierizing** *vbl. sb.*

1948 *Bull. Inst. Hist. Research* XXI. 123, I refer to the process, which I can only call, after its distinguished inventor, the 'Namierizing' of British History: the discovery and exploration of the personal side of parliamentary politics and the parliamentary groups which flourished and manoeuvred, formed, broke and reformed their alliances under cover of debates and constitutional dogmas. **1952** *John o' London's Weekly* 20 June, A really intensely detailed and penetrating piece of analysis is known to historians all over the world as a 'namierisation'. **1957** *Economist* 12 Oct. 120/1 The expression 'to namierise' is a deserved tribute to Sir Lewis's influence. **1958** *Listener* 17 Apr. 661/3 Surely namierite scholarship has..underlined the great differences ..between the political systems of the eighteenth century and our own. **1958** *N.Z. Listener* 5 Sept. 12/4 May one hope that in future volumes he will add a dash of Namierite bitters to the cocktail? **1960** *Observer* 28 Aug. 8/4 Essentially, Namierisation meant a rigorous substitution of accurate detail for the generalisations which had contented older historians. **1961** *Times Lit. Suppl.* 2 June 334/4 This..piece of Namierisation does not offer portraits of any individual members of the group. **1967** *Economist* 22 July 329/3 Are we not, in fact, with the nineteenth century, in danger of much the same kind of difficulties as Namierite zeal landed us in with the eighteenth? **1969** *Listener* 20 Mar. 388/3 A generation ago the Namierites were busy counting heads while the Clapham sect totted up the trade statistics. **1971** *Sunday Times* 30 May 31/4 To 'namierise' is now a well-known historical technique which has been applied—often with far less subtlety—in very different fields. It consists, essentially, of constructing multiple biographies of inarticulate men whose common but unconscious aims may be a force, even a determining force, in history. **1972** *New Society* 13 Apr. 51/2 It [*sc.* the Scarman inquiry into violence in Ulster in 1969] is the Namierisation of a nightmare in which ten people died, [etc.]. **1973** P. A. ALLUM *Politics & Society Post-War Naples* ix. 280 The disappearance of the monarchy left the Vatican as the major institutional support of the *status quo*. In consequence, the Christian Democrats became..a 'Court Party' in the Namierite sense.

naming ('neɪmɪŋ), *vbl. sb.* [f. NAME *v.*¹ + -ING¹.]

a. The action of the vb., in various senses, or the result of this.

a **1300** *K. Horn* (Laud MS.) 216 (220) 'Horn child', qwad þe king, 'Wel brouke þou þi naming'. **1482** *Rolls of Parlt.* VI. 204/2 Other Benefices of Cherchys, and namyng to the same. **1504–5** in Brand *Newcastle* (1789) I. 641 [A priest] to have the same service, the same namyng, appointment and assignment..as is above expressed. **1579** E. K. *Gloss. Spenser's Sheph. Cal.* Apr. 123 Neptune and Minerua stroue for the naming of the citie of Athens. **1665** SIR T. HERBERT *Trav.* (1677) 249 An infamous strumpet; not worth a naming the second time. **1766** ENTICK *London* IV. 52 They having had all along the naming of the weigh-master. **1831** CARLYLE *Sart. Res.* II. i, Poetry itself is no other, if thou consider it, than a right Naming. **1875** JOWETT *Plato* (ed. 2) IV. 276 Even in the infant the latent power of naming is almost immediately observable.

attrib. **1825** *Greenhouse Comp.* I. 204 Each being distinguished by its name written on a small naming-stick.

b. ***naming of parts***: the process of becoming acquainted, or of acquainting others, with the essentials of an unfamiliar object or topic.

1946 H. REED *Map of Verona* 22 To-day we have naming of parts. Yesterday We had daily cleaning. And tomorrow morning, We shall have what to do after firing. But to-day, To-day we have naming of parts. **1967** *Listener* 15 June 782/2 The Carnegie Report..begins with a very plain 'naming of parts', which is vital if the different forms of television are to be easily distinguished. **1967** *Punch* 26 July 135/2 We all know the experience, when we take up any new subject..of taking in..an enormous new naming-of-parts, so that we are able to make the distinctions the new subject demands. **1971** *Guardian* 29 Sept. 20/4 Many of the eruptions over topics like sex-education..spring..from a resistance to what may be summed up in the old grammarian's phrase, 'The naming of parts'. **1975** *Nature* 10 Apr. 483/1 (*heading*) Teleost ancestry, or naming of parts. *Ibid.* 483/3 Patterson has been meticulous in naming of parts, that is in tracing homologous structures throughout his series of fishes and naming them accordingly.

'namingly, *adv.* 'By name' (Webster 1847).

namle, -li, etc., obs. forms of NAMELY *adv.*

namma hole, var. GNAMMA HOLE.

nammet ('næmɪt). *dial.* Also -it, -ut. Var. of NUMMET, luncheon, slight meal. Also *attrib.*

1847 HALLIWELL. **1863** WISE *New Forest* 193 The labourer still..feels himself lear..before he eats his nammit. **1878** T. HARDY *Ret. Native* I. iii, I haven't seen the colour of drink since nammet-time to-day.

nammo(re, na-mo(re, obs. ff. NO MORE.

nam-nam, var. NUM-NUM.

na-mon, obs. form of NO MAN.

nampkyn, obs. form of NAPKIN.

Namurian (næ'm(j)uːrɪən), *a.* (*sb.*) *Geol.* [f. *Namur*, name of a town and province of southern Belgium + -IAN.] Of, pertaining to, or designating the lowest stage of the Upper Carboniferous in western Europe, lying above the Dinantian; also as *sb.*, the Namurian stage or epoch.

1915 C. Schuchert *Text-bk. Geol.* II. xl. 729 Kayser adds a third series, the Namurian (Namur, Belgium), which is referred to the base of the Middle Carboniferous. **1931** Gregory & Barrett *Gen. Stratigr.* vii. 118 Above the Dinantian [in Belgium] is a coarse sandstone, the great Grès d'Ardenne, corresponding to the Millstone Grit; it is called the Namurian. **1938** A. K. Wells *Outl. Hist. Geol.* 100 The normal facies of the Namurian Stage is deltaic. **1963** D. W. & E. E. Humphries tr. *Termier's Erosion & Sedimentation* xiii. 292 By the Namurian, subsidence had practically finished and the last reef phase passed into large biostromes. **1967** D. H. Rayner *Stratigr. Brit. Isles* vii. 200 It is also the type area of the Millstone Grit, where millstones were once fashioned out of the coarser sandstones... The sandstones ..probably represent a lesser proportion of Namurian time than their thickness at first sight suggests.

†**nan**[1]. *Obs.* exc. *arch.* [f. the female name *Nan*, familiar form of *Ann(e).*] A serving-maid.

c **1700** *Street Robberies Consider'd*, *Nan*, a maid of the house. **1725** *New Cant. Dict.*, *Nan*, a Maid-servant. **1922** Joyce *Ulysses* 46 Lambert Simnel, with a tail of nans and sutlers, a scullion crowned.

nan[2] (næn). *colloq.* [Prob. formed on granny, or a shortening of nana[1], nanna, nanny *sb.*[1]] A grandmother; occas., a children's nurse.

1940 N. Marsh *Surfeit of Lampreys* (1941) iii. 43 Nanny's hands..made a quick involuntary movement. 'You'll be all right, Nan,' added Henry. **1954** —— *Spinsters in Jeopardy* viii. 150 The new Nanny... I didn't think I had to have a Nan over here. **1955** E. Blishen *Roaring Boys* iii. 123 'Been to see my nan,' he growled. **1968** L. Berg *Risinghill* 45 Perhaps it is Nan's importance in Islington..that gives warmth and security to grandchildren. **1969** *Guardian* 15 Sept. 7/3 Her Mum and her Nan aren't a lot of help. **1975** *New Society* 18 Sept. 631/1 Jackie gets £1 a week off her grandmother, who owns a pub: 'My nan's got tons of money.' **1975** *Country Life* 13 Nov. 1277/2 I had a great, great grandmother who was a witch... Old Nan would remove the spell from a churn.

‖**nan**[3] (nɑːn). Also **naan.** [Hindi.] In Indian and Pakistani cooking, a type of leavened bread.

1967 *Guardian* 8 Dec. 8/4 North Indian or Pakistani [cooking] which depends on the clay oven called a tandoor, into which kebabs..and the special bread called nan are lowered and rapidly cooked. **1971** *Carry Singapore in your Pocket* (Singapore Tourist Promotion Board) (ed. 3) 31 One first-class Kashmiri restaurant..serves..a wide variety of naan and pilau prepared in Kashmiri style. **1972** 'E. Peters' *Death to Landlords!* iv. 76 The dough-cake type of bread called *nan.* **1973** *Times* 19 June (Bombay Suppl.) p. xv/3 Nan, a leavened bread dotted with poppy seed. **1973** *Sat. Rev. World* (U.S.) 18 Dec. 48/2 *Naan*, bread baked in a special oven by an Indian baker. **1974** R. Howe in Moraes & Howe *J. K. Galbraith introduces India* 189 It [*sc.* chicken] is eaten with the fingers accompanied by slabs of *nan roti*, a type of bread also made in the *tandur*.

nan, aphetic form of anan *int.*

1748 Foote *Knights* i. Wks. 1799 I. 67 Nan? what do you say? *Ibid.*, Nan? what? **1825** Brockett *N.C. Gloss.* **1836** Cooper *Sussex Gloss.* **1875** Miss Jackson *Shropsh. Word-bk.* s.v., *Nan* is very seldom used now; only a few of the aged folk seem to retain it.

nan, obs. f. none; obs. f. nain *Sc.*

nana[1], **nanna** (ˈnænə). Also **nan-nan.** Forms of address used by a child to a grandmother; occas., a children's nurse.

c **1844** E. Pepys *Diary* 8 Oct. in *Country Life* (1972) 9 Mar. 577/1, I cut Herbert's hand..he only said 'O, Emy you had better send for Nana.' *Ibid.* 25 Dec. 578/1 Mama rung the bell for Nana. **1869** C. M. Yonge *Release* ii. xi. 176 Poor dear Zélie..had been mother's nana. **1899** E. E. Cummings *Let.* 27 Nov. (1969) 3, I am sorry dear Nana but I will be a good boy. **1901** *Punch* 4 Dec. 405/2 Please, Nanna, don't turn on the dark. **1927** W. E. Collinson *Contemp. Eng.* 7 Children still use, as in the nineties, and long before, mummy, daddy, nanny or nanna, nursie. [**1928** Barrie *Peter Pan* i. in *Plays* 18 Nana the nurse..is a Newfoundland dog.] **1954** *Caribbean Q.* III. i. 5 The role of the *nana* or nurse in preserving folk songs, tales..herb lore is not to be under-estimated. **1958** M. Kerr *People of Ship Street* 48 The granny, or 'nin', or 'nanny', or 'nanna' or 'gran' as she is often called. **1959** D. Wallace *Richard & Lucy* xv. 210 A mewling toddler, clutching at her grandmother and weeping if Nan-nan were out of sight for more than a minute. **1959** *Woman's Own* 2 May 9/2 Cliffie..lived with his grandparents... Sometimes he would say..'I think I must go home today, thank you. Nana is expecting me.'

nana[2] (ˈnɑːnə). *slang* (chiefly *Austral.*). [Perh. f. banana.] **a.** A foolish person, a fool. **b.** The head. Also *attrib.*, as in ***nana haircut*** (see quot. 1941).

[**1894** A. B. Paterson 'Hughey's Dog' in C. Semmler *The World of 'Banjo' Paterson* (1967) 29 'Off his nanny again,' thought the boss, 'the sooner he goes the better.'] **1941** Baker *Dict. Austral. Slang* 48 *Nana (hair)cut*, a utilitarian haircut in which the back of the head is closely shaved. **1965** G. McInnes *Road to Gundagai* ix. 148 Although he was obviously a gent, he was not a 'tonk' or a 'nana'. **1967** *Coast to Coast 1965–66* 35 If you..horror of horrors, had a *nana* haircut. **1967** C. Drummond *Death at Furlong Post* xiii. 165 It seems if you have a bit of cash it snowballs unless you are a proper 'nana. **1968** J. Lock *Lady Policeman* iv. 41 Do we stand there like a 'nana' holding up our hands to stop invisible traffic? **1971** *TV Times* (Austral.) 18 Dec. 19/4 It's only the famous ones who get fired... They're the ones.. making..statements like 'The management is a nana'. **1972** M. Farhi *Pleasure of your Death* iii. 106 The answer, you 'nana. **1974** *Times* 22 Jan. 14/2 A frank admission that he had made a nana of himself. **1974** *Telegraph* (Brisbane) 22 Apr. 2/4 The baby started crying again. I did my nana and I hit him. **1975** *Australian* 8 Feb. 13 'We've all learned to laugh at ourselves and our predicament,' Trevor England said. 'If we hadn't we'd all be off our nanas.'

nanberry, -bury, dial. varr. of anbury.

1707 *Lond. Gaz.* No. 4325/4 A dark brown Gelding.., full aged, a Nanberry on the inside of the near Leg. **1876** F. K. Robinson *Gloss. Words used in Neighbourhood of Whitby* 129/1 *Nanberries*, s. pl. warty spots on the groin of a horse. **1883** A. Easther *Gloss. Dial. Almondbury & Huddersfield* 90 *Nanberry* or *Nanbury*, *sb.* a kind of wart formed on the bag of a cow. **1970** 'J. Herriot' *If only they could Talk* xxv. 152 They [*sc.* horses] did get those little dangling growths sometimes—nanberries, the farmers called them. **1973** —— *Let Sleeping Vets Lie* xiii. 113 Oh, and Mr. Ross said would you take some nanberries off a stirk's belly while you're here.

nance (næns). *slang.* = nancy[2].

1924 G. C. Henderson *Keys to Crookdom* 412 *Nance*, effeminate fellow, sissy man. Nance walk—walk like a woman. **1932** [see fag *sb.*[5]]. **1934** *Amer. Speech* IX. 27/1 *Nance*, an effeminate man. **1935** A. J. Pollock *Underworld Speaks* 79/1 *Nance*, a fairy; a male sexual pervert. **1941** B. Schulberg *What makes Sammy Run?* viii. 158 They were all so different—a titled Englishman and a famous poet and an aesthetic nance and a tough, drunken ex-reporter. **1957** J. G. Cozzens *By Love Possessed* (1958) ii. v. 450 Here; I'll sneak out the back. Nances and I don't get on. **1971** F. Forsyth *Day of Jackal* xx. 336 We're looking for a fellow who screwed the arse off a Baroness..not a couple of raving nances.

nancy[1] (ˈnænsɪ). Also **ananci, hanancy.** [ad. Tshi (Ashantee, etc.) *ananse* spider; *anansesem* spider-story.] ***nancy-story, -tale,*** a folk- or fairy tale of a type current among the Blacks in the Gold Coast and the West Indies.

[**1705** tr. *Bosman's Guinea* xvii. 332 The Negroes call this spider Ananse, and believe that the first Men were made by that Creature.]

a **1818** M. G. Lewis *Jrnl. W. Ind.* (1834) 253 The Negroes are very fond of what they call Nancy stories, part of which is related, and part sung. *Ibid.* 307 It seems to be an indispensable requisite for a Nancy-story, that it should contain a witch, or a duppy. **1891** Hartland *Sci. Fairy Tales* xi. 294 An ananci tale in which the heroine and her two sisters are changed into black cats. **1894** Alice Spinner *Study in Colour* ix. 80 She told her nancy stories. **1967** *Times* 24 June 11/5 Here in Guyana, the term 'a nancy story' is common everyday parlance for a far-fetched yarn or even a downright lie... A 'Nancy Story' is..one of the very few fragments of African culture which survived transplantation with the slaves.

nancy[2] (ˈnænsɪ). *slang.* Also **nancy-boy.** [orig. *Miss Nancy* (miss *sb.*[2] 2 b), f. pet-form of the female name *Ann.*] An effeminate man or boy; a homosexual. Also as *adj.* Hence ˈ**nancified** *ppl. a.*; ˈ**nancifully** *adv.*

1904 'No. 1500' *Life in Sing Sing* 251/1 Nancy, effeminate man. **1918** C. Mackenzie *Early Life Sylvia Scarlett* i. iv. 123 If you can let that nancified milksop mess you about, you can put up with me. **1930** E. Waugh *Vile Bodies* 36 Where's my Fairy Prince? Powdering hisself again, I suppose... Come here, Nancy, and put away the beauty cream. **1931** R. Campbell *Georgiad* ii. 36 Sharing out my last desires and fancies With tough old suffragettes and ageing nancies. *Ibid.* 42 Grim guards enough to awe the Nancy race. *Ibid.*, Their flag of truce they raise To bribe his laughter with their public praise, And all their little nancy husbands too. **1933** H. S. Walpole *Vanessa* iv. 723 But he isn't one of those, you know, or anything like that. Not a bit nancy. **1936** 'G. Orwell' *Keep Aspidistra Flying* i. 19 A youth..with gilded hair, tripped Nancifully in. **1937** —— *Road to Wigan Pier* ii. 35 You and I..and the Nancy poets ..—all of us *really* owe the comparative decency of our lives to poor drudges underground,..with their lungs full of coal dust. **1937** *Times* 25 Jan. 37/2 That nancyfied nonentity in the Foreign Office. **1937** E. Linklater *Juan in China* xxii. 288 You're a fop and a nancified civilian. **1947** L. Hastings *Dragons are Extra* x. 224 In the early part of the War I had occasional glimpses of an unfamiliar species known comprehensibly, I believe, as the Nancy Left. **1958** L. Durrell *Balthazar* ii. 31, I can't stand that Toto fellow. He's an open nancy-boy. **1967** K. Giles *Death & Mr. Prettyman* ii. 58 Beautiful smooth dark rum, not like that nancified white stuff you poms put in your cokes. **1974** L. Deighton *Spy Story* xv. 148 Pop music and nancy-boy actors.

nancy, narcissus: see sweet Nancy.

Nancy Dawson (ˈnænsɪ ˈdɔːsən). ? *Obs.* [See quot. 1890.] A sailor's dance or song; a nancy-boy.

1766 C. Anstey *New Bath Guide* ix. 64 With what Grace his Gloves he draws on, Claps, and calls up Nancy Dawson: Me thro' ev'ry Dance conducting. **1771** Smollett *Humph. Cl.* I. 176, I can dance a Welsh jig, and Nancy Dawson. *c* **1810** W. Hickey *Mem.* (1960) xxv. 418 The dragoons.. marched off..the fifes playing 'Nancy Dawson'. **1840** *Family Mag.* (Cincinnati) 332/2 She sailed through the waltz like an elephant dancing 'Nancy Dawson' in the ring of a menagerie. **1890** Barrère & Leland *Dict. Slang* II. 81/1 *Nancy Dawson*, a name for a molly, an effeminate youth, apathetic, &c... The original Nancy Dawson was a noted prostitute, on whom there is a song still current among sailors.

nancy-pretty. [Also called *none-so-pretty*: the one name is no doubt a corruption of the other.] A popular name in various districts for the plant London Pride.

1828–92 in various dial. glossaries (Northumb., Yks., Lanc., Som., Devon).

NAND (nænd). *Computers.* [f. *n(ot) and.*] A Boolean function of two or more variables that has the value zero when all of them are unity, and is otherwise unity; 'not..and..'. Usu. *attrib.*

1958 *IRE Trans. Electronic Computers* VII. 181/3 Using a positive logic (+ is identified with true and ONE) the circuit represents the binary NOR function, $\overline{A_1 + A_2} = B$. A negative logic (− is identified with true and ONE) results in the binary NAND function, $\overline{A_1 \cdot A_2} = B$. **1960** N. R. Scott *Analog & Digital Computer Technol.* x. 392 Of course, $A|B = \overline{A \cdot B}$; so this circuit is sometimes called a not and (or nand) circuit. **1966** *Electronics* 31 Oct. 42 The circuits used ..are transistor-transistor NAND logic. **1971** J. H. Smith *Digital Logic* iv. 48 Due to practical manufacturing reasons the NAND configuration forms the basis of the majority of integrated circuit systems. *Ibid.*, The action of the NAND is that it gives a *0* output when *all* its inputs are *1* signals.

Nandi (ˈnændɪ), *sb.*[1] [Skr., 'the happy one'.] In Hindu mythology, the name of the bull of Siva which is his vahan or vehicle, and symbolizes fertility; also, a figure or statue of Nandi.

1807 H. T. Colebrooke in *Asiatick Researches* IX. 425 Near it stands a bull, intended perhaps for the bull called *Nandí*, a constant attendant of Śiva. **1891** M. Monier-Williams *Brāhmanism & Hinduism* (ed. 4) xvii. 440 A shrine for the stone image of Siva's bull (nandi). **1910** *Encycl. Relig. & Ethics* III. 311/2 A represention of his sacred animal, the bull Nandī, is usually placed before him [*sc.* Siva]. **1953** *Antiquity* XXVII. 169 Worth mentioning also are some clay censers, the handle of one being ornamented with a nandi. **1969** *Hindu Weekly Mag.* (Madras) 3 Aug. p. ii/6 The majestic 'Nandi', the conventional vehicle of Lord Siva in front of the 'sanctum' in the forecourt.

Nandi (ˈnændɪ), *sb.*[2] and *a.* [Native name.]

A. *sb.* **a.** An East African people of mixed Nilotic, Hamitic, and Bantu origin which inhabits an area on the Uganda-Kenya border and has given its name to the Nandi plateau; a member of this people. **b.** The Nilotic language spoken by the Nandi and some neighbouring tribes. **B.** *adj.* Of or pertaining to this people or their language.

1885 J. Thomson *Through Masăi Land* (ed. 3) 469 From this place we could see the high forest region of Nandi... The Wa-nandi are allied in language and customs to the Wa-kamaria and Wa-elgeyo, though much braver and more warlike. **1902** H. H. Johnston *Uganda Protectorate* II. xix. 876 All the Nandi-speaking peoples except the Andorobo make *pottery*. *Ibid.* 882 The Nandi especially believe profoundly in the powers of their medicine men, and follow them implicitly. **1909** C. Eliot in A. C. Hollis *Nandi* p. xiv, Most of the wild hunting tribes called Dorobo speak a dialect of Nandi. *Ibid.* p. xxi, When a Nandi is ill, it is necessary to discover and propitiate the particular ancestor who has occasioned the disaster. **1909** *Westm. Gaz.* 3 Feb. 4/1 (*heading*) Nandi customs and folk-lore. **1930** C. G. Seligman *Races Afr.* vii. 163 The Nandi and Suk may be said to live in garden settlements, each man having his own homestead in or near his fields of grain. **1951** in E. E. Evans-Pritchard *Social Anthropol.* i. 12 (*thesis-title*) 'The political organization of the Nandi' (East Africa). **1964** A. N. Tucker in D. Abercrombie et al. *Daniel Jones* 445 The Nandi Group, comprising Nandi, Kipsigis, [etc.].

b. Nandi bear, a hypothetical animal resembling a bear, said to inhabit parts of East Africa.

1931 C. R. S. Pitman *Game Warden* xiv. 287 Tales of that elusive monster popularly known in Kenya as the 'Nandi bear' can boast a more substantial basis. **1937** *Discovery* Jan. 2/2 The Wandarobo name 'Keret' or 'Kerit' is applied to the lynx or caracal as well as to the mythical 'Nandi Bear'. **1950** *Sun* (Baltimore) 2 May 13/2 The curious Nandi bear..is often blamed for the killing of humans and domesticated animals in East Africa. Although scientific evaluation is lacking, native and white hunters alike claim to have encountered the beast; and several descriptions of the bearlike creature agree on its shambling gait, shaggy hair, little ears and long snout. **1956** *Nature* 10 Mar. 446/1 This animal may be the dreaded Nandi bear.

nandine (ˈnændɪn). *Zool.* [app. a native name.] A West African viverroid animal (*Nandinia binotata*), having rows of spots on the sides.

1843 J. E. Gray *Mammalia* 54. **1860** Wood *Illustr. Nat. Hist.* I. 245 We arrive at the pretty little creature which is known by the name of Nandine.

nandu (ˈnænduː). *Ornith.* Also **nandou.** [ad. Brazilian (Tupi-Guarani) *nhandú, ñandú.*] A variety of ostrich (*Rhea Americana*) peculiar to South America.

1840 *Cuvier's Anim. Kingd.* 233 The Nandou..or Ostrich of America, is about half the size of the African Ostrich. **1866** *Chambers's Encycl.* VI. 656/2 The Nandu is shy and wary, but is successfully hunted by the Indians.

nane, Sc. and north. f. none, obs. f. nain *Sc.*

nanes, obs. form of nonce[1].

Nanga (ˈnæŋgə). [Jap., abbrev. *Nanshuga*, f. *nanshu* southern China + *ga* painting, picture.] Used, chiefly *attrib.*, to designate an intellectual style of Japanese painting.

1958 M. L. Wolf *Dict. Painting* 188 *Nanga School*, in Japanese art, a style of painting depicting genre subjects in a manner of Chinese idealism. **1970** J. W. Hall *Japan from Prehist. to Mod. Times* x. 217 The property of the samurai class was the style of 'literati' painting (*bunjinga* or *nanga*).

1970 *Oxf. Compan. Art* 762/1 *Nanga School*, school of painting which arose in Japan at the end of the 17th c.,..and persisted until late in the 19th. *Ibid.* 762/2 The Nanga painters were not all amateurs, but they spurned the professional schools of their day... In general their work represented the art of the intelligentsia as opposed to Ukiyo-e, which was that of the people. **1970** *Ashmolean Mus. Rep. Visitors 1969* 43 a particularly desirable acquisition in connection with the Museum's collection of Nanga painting. **1972** *Times* 18 May 21/6 Ikeno Taiga's *Taigado Gafu*..made £400. This is one of the finest colour-printed Nanga books and extremely rare. It is dated 1803.

nangat(is, variants of NO-GATE(S *adv.*

†**'nanger**, *v. Obs. rare.* [f. ANGER *v.*, after NANGRY *a.*] *trans.* To make angry.

1675 WYCHERLEY *Country Wife* II. i, Why dost thou look so fropish? Who has nangered thee? *c* **1681** HICKERINGILL *Trimmer* ii. Wks. 1716 I. 368 Who, then has nanger'd thee? dear heart!

nangnail, dial. variant of *angnail* AGNAIL.

†**'nangry**, *a. Obs. rare.* [f. ANGRY *a.* with prothetic *n*: see N 3.] Angry.

1681 T. FLATMAN *Heraclitus Ridens* No. 39 (1713) I. 256 Oh, 'tis the featest little nangry Fool. *Ibid.* 261 Since the Maggot is so nangry, it shall be a Warning to Harry.

'nanguer. *Zool.* [See first quot.] A species of antelope formerly accepted by zoologists on the authority of Buffon.

1780 SMELLIE tr. *Buffon's Nat. Hist.* (1785) VI. 409 The ninth antilope is an animal, which, according to M. Adanson, is called *nangueur* or *nanguer* in Senegal. **1801** SHAW *Gen. Zool.* II. II. 360 The Red Antelope, or Nagor, is much allied to the Nanguer or Dama. **1835** E. T. BENNETT in *Trans. Zool. Soc.* I. 2 Pallas adopted the idea in his Monograph of the genus Antilope.., in which the Nanguer was introduced under the name of Antilope Dama, which it has ever since retained. **1868** *Nat. Encycl.* I. 809 To this group belongs the Mhorr Antelope.., the Nanguer (*A. dama*) of Senegal; and the Addra.

nanis, obs. Sc. and north. form of NONCE[1].

nanism ('neɪnɪz(ə)m). [ad. F. *nanisme* (Littré), f. L. *nān-us* (Gr. νᾶν-ος) dwarf + *-isme* -ISM.] The condition of being dwarfed; tendency to become stunted or dwarfed; an instance of this.

1856 MAYNE *Expos. Lex.* **1899** *Q. Rev.* July 277 Nanism is a feature common to all animals and plants in great altitudes and high latitudes.

So **'nanity** (see quot.). *nonce-wd.*

1892 JESSOPP in *Illustr. Lond. News* 26 Nov. 667/1 By nanity I understand the condition of those who labour under any abnormal deficiency.

nanization (neɪnaɪ'zeɪʃən). [f. ***nanize**, ad. F. *naniser* (1875 in Littré *Suppl.*): see NANISM.] The process of artificially dwarfing trees or plants.

1889 REIN *Industries Japan* 265 Dwarfing or Nanisation is the name which we give to the various operations for producing dwarfed forms.

nankeen (næn'kiːn), *sb.* (and *a.*) Also 8 **nankein**, 9 **-kin**, **-quin**, and with capital initial. [f. *Nankin* or *Nanking*, 'southern capital', the name of the chief city of the province of Kiangsu in China. Cf. F. and Du. *nankin*, G. *nanking*.]

1. A kind of cotton cloth, originally made at Nanking from a yellow variety of cotton, but now extensively manufactured from ordinary cotton and dyed yellow. Also *attrib.* with *cloth*.

1755 *Songs & Poems on Costume* (Percy Soc.) 239 Make his breeches of nankein, Most like nature, most like skin. **1801** *Encycl. Brit.* Suppl. II. 292/1 The colour of nankeen is natural, the down of which it is made being of the same yellow tinge with the cloth. **1826** J. F. COOPER *Last Mohic.* i, His nether garment was of yellow nankeen. **1878** J. H. GRAY *China* III. xxiii. 143 The cloth called nankin, generally written nankeen, is of the greatest durability.

attrib. *c* **1809** F. BUCHANAN in *Eastern India* III. 144 (Yule), Wool having the colour of nankeen cloth. **1839** URE *Dict. Arts* 877 Nankin cloth has been long imitated in perfection by our own manufacturers.

b. With *pl.* A kind or variety of this cloth.

1781 ABIGAIL ADAMS in *Fam. Lett.* (1876) 402 There are some articles, which come from India,..Bengals, nankeens, Persian silk. **1797** STAUNTON *Acc. Macartney's Embassy China* II. 425 The land in this neighbourhood..produces the cloth usually called Nankeens in Europe. **1842** BRANDE *Dict. Sci.*, etc. s.v., They are sometimes bleached, and then are called white nankeens. Imitation nankeens are manufactured at Manchester. **1858** HOMANS *Cycl. Commerce* 1387/2 The broad pieces called 'the Company's nankeens' are generally of a better quality than the narrow ones.

2. *attrib.* (passing into *adj.*) Made of nankeen.

1774 in Grosley *Obs. England* II. 142 His nankeen small-clothes were tied with 16 strings at each knee. **1795** ANDERSON *Narr. Embassy China* 70 The uniform of the soldiers consists of a large pair of loose, black nankeen trowsers. **1823** *Chron.* in *Ann. Reg.* 70/1 The female preacher had on a nankeen dress. **1885** J. PAYN *Talk of Town* I. 26 A dark blue coat with a short light waistcoat;..and nankeen breeches.

b. *pl.* Trousers made of nankeen.

1806–7 J. BERESFORD *Mis. Hum. Life* (1826) II. xi, Pushing through the very narrow path of a very long field of very high corn immediately after a very heavy rain:—nankeens. **1853** LYTTON *My Novel* I. ii, If you had my nankeens on.., and had fallen into a thicket of thistles.

3. A yellow or pale buff; the colour of nankeen.

1775 SHERIDAN *Duenna* II. iii, As for the dimity skin you told me of, I swear, 'tis a thorough nankeen as ever I saw! **1838** T. THOMSON *Chem. Org. Bodies* 934 This lichen, with soda, yields a yellow; with lime..a nankeen. **1882** *Garden* 18 Mar. 189/3 The colour is a beautiful nankeen.

4. *attrib.* or as *adj.*, denoting a yellow colour like that of nankeen.

1839 URE *Dict. Arts* 877 The following is the process for dyeing calico a nankin colour. **1868** *Chambers's Encycl.* VI. 656/2 Another..nankeen dye is produced by boiling annatto in a strong solution of pearl ashes. **1882** *Garden* 25 Nov. 469/3 The..petals being of a nankeen-yellow.

b. In the names of some Australian birds, as the ***nankeen bird***, ***crane***, or ***night-hawk***, and the ***nankeen hawk***. Also ***nankeen gum***, a species of eucalyptus, *E. populifolia*.

1804 CALEY in *Trans. Linn. Soc.* XV. 184, I saw no Nankeen Hawks this autumn. **1838** J. H. JAMES *Six Months S. Austral.* 202 Shooting one or two beautiful nankeen birds. **1872** C. H. EDEN *My wife and I in Queensland* 121 The nankeen crane (*Nycticorax caledonicus*), a very handsome, bright nankeen-coloured bird. **1889** MAIDEN *Native Plants* 506 This tree is..called 'Nankeen Gum' in Northern Australia, from the peculiar light-brown colour of the bark.

5. ***nankeen cotton***, the variety of cotton from which nankeen cloth was originally made.

1797 STAUNTON *Acc. Macartney's Embassy China* II. 425 It is asserted, that the seeds of the nankeen cotton degenerate..when transplanted to another province. **1865** *N. & Q.* 3rd Ser. VII. 474/2 A new species of cotton, called Nankeen, of a bright yellow colour and fine texture, is now raised in the United States.

6. A kind of Chinese porcelain. Also *attrib.*

1781 *Lionel & Clarissa* 7 Half-a-dozen plates, four Nankeen beakers, and a couple of shaking Mandarins. **1782** WEDGWOOD in *Phil. Trans.* LXXII. 322 The Dresden porcelain is more refractory than the common Chinese, but not equally so with the stone Nankeen. **1784** H. WALPOLE *Descr. Strawberry Hill* 8 A blue and white saucer with a landscape, of fine Nankin china. **1796** KIRWAN *Elem. Min.* (ed. 2) I. 52 Nankeen indeed even resists this heat. **1845** *Encycl. Metrop.* Index, Nankin porcelain. **1917** D. H. LAWRENCE *Phoenix II* (1968) 113 There were delicate blue Nankin cups. **1921** W. DE LA MARE *Mem. Midget* ii. 12 Dwarf trees..in green Nankin tubs. *Ibid.* xxiv. 157 A little masterpiece: and real old Nankin. **1957** MANKOWITZ & HAGGAR *Conc. Encycl. Eng. Pott. & Porc.* 161/2 Large quantities of porcelain decorated in blue were exported through this town [Nankin], hence the term 'Nankin Blue' or 'Nankin China' or simply 'Nankin'..a synonym for blue-and-white porcelain.

7. A kind of lace.

1865 F. B. PALLISER *Hist. Lace* xv. 199 It was not until 1745 that the blondes..made their appearance. The first silk used for the new production was of its natural colour, 'écrue', hence these laces were called 'nankins' or 'blondes'. **1882** Nankin [see BLOND *sb.* 2 b].

Hence **nan'keening**; **nanki'nett**.

1805 *Ann. Reg.* 682 Muslins, piquées, dimities, and nankinetts. *a* **1845** HOOD *To Lady on Dep. India* vi, Go to the land of muslin and nankeening.

nankin(s, variants of NO-KIN *Obs.*

nanman, obs. form of NO MAN.

nanmo(re, obs. forms of NO MORE.

nanna, nan-nan: see NANA[1].

†**'nannicock.** *Obs. rare*[−1]. (Sense obscure.)

1600 N. BRETON *Pasquils Fools-cap* C 4 b, Hee that doth wonder at a Weathercocke..And is in loue with euery Nannicocke.

nannofossil ('nænəʊfɒsɪl). *Geol.* [f. as next + FOSSIL *a.* and *sb.*] A fossil of a minute plankton organism.

1963 H. STRADNER in *Proc. 6th World Petroleum Congr.* I. 167/1 Nannofossils (minute calcareous elements of planktonic marine flagellates) were found in sediments younger than Triassic. *Ibid.*, A key for the determination of nannofossil assemblages is given. **1971** *Nature* 3 Sept. 46/1 The ophiolites in those deep-sea troughs were overlain by..radiolarian and nannofossil oozes. **1972** *Sci. Amer.* Dec. 33/2 The white ooze is a typical oceanic sediment, made up almost entirely of the skeletons of microfossils and nannofossils. **1974** *Nature* 13 Sept. 129/2 The chalk contains abundant nannofossils whose preservation is, unfortunately, somewhat marred by calcite overgrowths.

nannoplankton ('nænəʊ,plæŋktən). *Biol.* Also **nanoplankton.** [a. G. *nannoplankton* (H. Lohmann 1909, in *Verhandl. Deutsch. Zool. Ges.* XIX. 234), f. *nanno-*, used as comb. f. of Gr. νᾶνος, L. *nanus* dwarf + PLANKTON.] Very small forms of plankton.

1912 MURRAY & HJORT *Depths of Ocean* vi. 356 As far as quantity is concerned, the smallest plankton organisms, Lohmann's Nanno-plankton, play a far more important rôle than the whole of the other species caught in our silk nets. **1939** *Nature* 7 Oct. 643/1 There was a nannoplankton consisting entirely of very small flagellates. **1959** *New Biol.* XXIX. 40 Examination of marine nannoplankton, that is the very small plankton organisms which are not retained even by the finest nets, has shown the presence of many colourless forms related to the algae. **1966** R. S. WIMPENNY *Plankton of Sea* iii. 114 The water..is strained through a funnel of fine pipes which filter out the very small organisms of the nannoplankton. **1974** B. H. MCCONNAUGHEY *Introd. Marine Biol.* (ed. 2) i. 7/1 Nanoplankton is, then, simply a size designation that includes parts of both phytoplankton and zooplankton. Strictly speaking, the term nanoplankton is used for organisms ranging from 5 to 60 μm in size.

nanny ('nænɪ), *sb.*[1] Also **nannie.** [Appellative use of pet-form of the female name *Ann(e*: see -Y[6].] A child's form of address to a nurse; hence, a children's nurse. Also *transf.*, applied to a person or institution, etc., considered to be unduly protective or apprehensive. Also *attrib.* and *Comb.*

1795 LADY NEWDIGATE *Let.* in A. E. Newdigate-Newdegate *Cheverels* (1898) 154 Nanny Ashcroft got me y[e] most delightful & perfect Warm Sea Bath last night..after w[ch] I ate my Bason of Milk & went to Bed. **1861** A. HALLIDAY in H. Mayhew *London Labour* (1862) Extra vol. 418/2 An old woman..give me a lodging once for two years. We used to call her Nanny. **1864** *Chambers's Jrnl.* Sept. 506/1 Don't you know I'm a locomotive, and that you should always shunt yourself on to a siding when you hear *me* coming, Nanny? **1912** A. N. LYONS *Clara* i. 3 That little boy was..inured to the coming and going of 'nannies'. **1919** [see CIG]. **1955** T. H. PEAR *Eng. Social Differences* 273 The effect upon the Nannie-cultured Englishman, of two mothers. **1958** A. WILSON *Middle Age of Mrs Eliot* I. 98 He was so calm and soothing and nannylike that she wanted to hit him. **1959** *Listener* 23 Apr. 735/1 Barristers are handled rather like naughty children by their nanny chief clerks. *Ibid.* 2 July 31/2 They can be nursery memories reproducing folk memory: immemorial nanny-lore. *Ibid.* 9 July 49/1 An extraordinarily powerful old bureaucratic nanny..goes stalking up and down the United States, pouncing on people who are telling commercial fibs. **1961** J. WADE *Back to Life* iv. 35 Nan came in... Her nannie days were past. **1965** B. SWEET-ESCOTT *Baker St. Irreg.* v. 147 There was also a good deal of Nanny work we had to do for Professor Pyke... The professor suffered from the traditional absent-mindedness of his kind, and we were expected to keep track of him. **1972** *Times* 2 Aug. 26/1 (Advt.), Country loving nannie. **1973** 'M. INNES' *Appleby's Answer* xvii. 155 Blabbing for your old nanny—that's what you'll be. **1973** *Times* 31 May 10/2 Kicked upstairs by the knighted nannies of his Institute, Hamo is sent on a world tour. **1973** *Listener* 7 June 742/2 The top authorities..who regulate television should [be]..impervious to the huge army of self-appointed nannies. **1974** *Times* 2 Feb. 18/3 Our natural modesty led us to cheer on the rest with encouraging cries..while deprecating our own dazzling accomplishments in the way that Nanny would have wished. *Ibid.* 29 Mar. 19/6 Surely our English cousins, having themselves retired from being 'nanny to the world', must understand how we feel. **1974** J. MANN *Sticking Place* vi. 106 Lorna took Rachel by the arm in a nanny-like way.

Hence **'nannified** *ppl. a.*; **'nannify** *v.*; **'nanniness, 'nannyism; 'nannyish** *a.*

1959 *Punch* 8 Apr. 474/1 Of all the nannyisms that have constrained the English middle classes the most inhibiting has been that favourite injunction about not putting ideas into the child's head. **1960** *Guardian* 1 July 8/1 The ponified and nannified Children's Bookland created by middle-class writers. **1962** *Times* 8 Feb. 9/7 Easy for his opponents to smile tolerantly on Wilberforce and make him seem impossibly nannyish. **1962** *Listener* 13 Dec. 1024/1 Is free speech in this country to be nannified out of existence by official vanity? **1972** J. ROSSITER *Rope for General Dietz* iii. 34 The air of nannyish protectiveness she had possessed in her BEA uniform. **1973** *Times Lit. Suppl.* 8 June 647/2 Mr Davidson's gentle male nanniness, initiating charming boys only to lose them.

'nanny, *sb.*[2] Ellipt. for NANNY-GOAT.

1890 'R. BOLDREWOOD' *Col. Reformer* xxviii. 417 He did consider the nanny question and calculated whether a steamer load of those miniature milchers would not pay decently.

nanny ('nænɪ), *v.* [f. NANNY *sb.*[1]] To act in the manner of a nanny; to be unduly protective. Hence **'nannying** *vbl. sb.*

1954 J. TRENCH *Dishonoured Bones* ii. 46 Don't nanny me. **1963** *Economist* 6 July 41/3 Labour..would produce a less compulsively nannying piece of legislation. **1969** *Guardian* 11 June 11/7 Professional women get none of this obligatory nannying: their main grudge is inequalities of opportunity rather than of pay. **1971** J. OSBORNE *West of Suez* I. 35 Devoting all his time to Daddy and nannying him like he does. **1972** E. LONGFORD *Wellington: Pillar of State* iii. 31 In the short run, his five-year plan for nannying France—for such it soon seemed to be—could only damage the popularity of Wellington. **1974** E. DEWAR *Dying Business* ix. 110 There was no need for you to come nannying me.

nannygai ('nænɪgaɪ). *Austral.* Also **nannyghai, nennigai.** [Aboriginal name.] A large marine food fish, *Centroberyx affinis*, found off the south-eastern coast of Australia.

1871 A. OLIVER *Fisheries New South Wales* 5 Fish, common to our coast,..when properly smoked or corned, are far superior to any imported codfish or ling... Nothing can surpass a corned 'moorra nennigai'. **1882** J. E. TENISON-WOODS *Fish New South Wales* 52 The Nannygai... Colour, a most beautiful pink, with silver stripes on the body. **1896** *Badminton Mag.* III. 206 A great variety of large game fish ..the Nannyghai, the snapper, and a dark species of rock cod. **1896** F. G. AFLALO *Sk. Nat. Hist. Austral.* 199 The large-eyed, crimson Nannygai (*Beryx*), taken on the Schnapper grounds. **1947** *Coast to Coast 1946* 237 Morwong, rock-cod, nannygai and the rest, but not a real red fish among the lot. **1965** *Austral. Encycl.* VI. 240/1 Both [fishes] are wrongly called red snapper; the increasing use of this name in the fish trade for different species of nannygai is deprecated because of confusion with the true snapper. **1966** T. C. ROUGHLEY *Fish & Fisheries of Australia* (rev. ed.) 18 In some quarters..there was a prejudice against the nannygai,..and the New South Wales Fisheries Department therefore condoned the use of the name 'redfish' for it, and the sales were given a helpful impetus.

nanny-goat ('nænɪgəʊt). [f. the feminine name *Nanny*: cf. BILLY-GOAT.] **1.** A she-goat.

1788 T. DAY *Hist. Little Jack* (1820) 55 Telling me that my father was a beggar man and my mother a nanny-goat. **1857** DUFFERIN *Lett. High Lat.* (ed. 3) 250 We have purchased an ancient goat—a nanny-goat—so that we may be able to go a-milking upon occasion. **1888** FREEMAN in Stephens *Life* (1895) II. 388 A nanny-goat that I had.

2. An anecdote. *slang*.

1843 T. C. HALIBURTON *Attaché* 1st Ser. II. vii. 114 The old knight's got an anecdote.., and nanny-goats ain't picked up every day in country. *c* **1895** F. M. FORD *Let.* (1965) 8 That is a subject abt. which I have a nanny goat to commence the next chapter with & it is reserved.

3. *to get* (a person's) ***nanny-goat***: to get one's goat (see GOAT 3 c). Also, *to get* (a person's) ***nanny***. *slang*.

1914 R. LARDNER in *Sat. Even. Post* 15 Aug. 9/3 'Good night, Horseshoes!' he says. That got my nanny up this time. 'Shut up, you lucky stiff!' I says. **1928** E. WALLACE *Double* xi. 122 'She was most kind and gracious—recognised me in an instant. Didn't mention you, by the way,' he dug Dick in the ribs playfully. 'That's got your nanny-goat!' **1972** J. MINIFIE *Homesteader* xvii. 143 Take it easy, old boy. .. Don't let them get your nanny.

4. A totalisator. *slang*.

1961 PARTRIDGE *Dict. Slang* Suppl. 1194/2 *Nanny-goat*, totalisator... Rhyming on tote. **1970** *Daily Mail* 10 Mar. 8/6 The poor old ailing Tote—the Nanny Goat, as they call it.

'nanny-house. *rare*. [? f. the name *Nanny*.] (See quots.) Also ***nanny-shop***.

a **1700** B. E. *Dict. Cant. Crew, Nanny-house*, a Bawdy-house. **1825** BROCKETT *N.C. Gloss., Nanny-house, -shop*, a brothel. **1836** M. SCOTT *Cruise Midge* xix, A narrow turning to the right..that led amongst a nest of nanny houses, as they are called, inhabited by brown free people.

nano- ('nænəʊ-, 'neɪnəʊ-, 'nɑːnəʊ-), *prefix*. [f. L. *nan-us*, Gr. νᾶν-ος dwarf + -O.] Prefixed to the names of units to form the names of units 10^9 times smaller, i.e. one thousand-millionth part of them (symbol n), as ***nanoamp(ere, -farad, -gramme, -henry*** [HENRY[3]], ***-litre -metre, -mole*** [MOLE *sb.*[7]] (hence ***-molar*** adj.), ***-volt, -watt***; **'nanoequivalent**, one thousand-millionth of a gramme-equivalent. Also NANOSECOND.

1947 *Compt. Rend. de la 14me Conf.* (Union Internat. de Chimie) 115 The following prefixes to abbreviations for the names of units should be used to indicate the specified multiples or sub-multiples of these units:..n nano- 10^{-9} ×. **1952** *Wireless World* May 187/2 The prefixes 'pico' and 'nano' became popular in this country fifteen or twenty years ago, mostly through the technical publications of Philips and others, with 'pico' as favourite. **1973** *Nature* 23 Nov. 190/3 The transient currents generated are small (of the order of a few nanoamps) and flow for a very short time (of the order of 10 nanoseconds). **1962** *Flight Internat.* LXXXII. 634/2 Designers are talking in terms of nanoAmperes. **1967** *McGraw-Hill Yearbk. Sci. & Technol.* 146 Accuracy and precision [of coulometric analysis].. range from a few hundredths of a per cent at the hundred microequivalent level..to approximately 10% at the five nanoequivalent level. **1951** *Wireless World* Nov. 458/1 This is undesirable..if another metric value, the nF (nano-farad) could be accepted for one-milliardth of a farad... Originally introduced—so far as I know—in Germany and also used in other Continental countries before the war, this *nano* abbreviation is now, in the Indonesian PTT, as normal as *km* for length of wire. **1951** *Nature* 8 Dec. 1008/2 Most microanalytical needs are satisfied by the subunits milligram and microgram. This sequence has now been extended by the nanogram (ng = 10^{-9} g) and picogram (pg = 10^{-12} g). **1964** W. G. SMITH *Allergy & Tissue Metabolism* vii. 76 In man, 10^8 platelets contain 60 nanograms (0·06 mg.) of serotonin. **1975** *Nature* 11 Sept. 141/2 Nanogram quantities of DNP-D-GL induced anti-DNP antibody formation, while larger amounts prevented responses to DNP-conjugates, as previously reported. **1975** WILLIAMS & WILSON *Biologist's Guide to Princ. & Techniques Pract. Biochem.* i. 16 Response of isolated organs to nanogramme quantities of active substances has been obtained by this technique. **1968** *New Scientist* 29 Feb. 484/1 The capacitors ..are 28 microfarads, 5 nanohenries, 2 milliohms. **1974** *Nature* 26 Apr. 774/2 The use of injection experiments.. demands careful quantitative control over the injection of nanolitre volumes of material. **1963** *Calibration & Test Services* (Nat. Bureau of Standards Misc. Publ. 250) 41 Transmittances of these disks at wavelengths from 365 to 390 nm (nanometer, 10^{-9} meter)..will also be determined on request. **1970** *Sci. Jrnl.* Feb. 49/3 Usually points closer than one nanometre (10^{-9}m) can be separated with the electron microscope. **1971** *Sci. Amer.* Sept. 89/2 Blue light at a wavelength of 450 nanometers (a nanometer is a billionth of a meter). **1969** *Nature* 18 Oct. 221/1 They are of such high biological potency that nanomolar concentrations can produce well-marked effects. **1968** *McGraw-Hill Yearbk. Sci. & Technol.* 387/2 Conduction is blocked in isolated, desheathed frog sciatic nerves by a solution [of tetrodotoxin] containing about 3 nanomoles per liter. **1971** *Sci. Amer.* Sept. 98/2 Plants will increase photosynthesis with increasing concentration of carbon dioxide to at least three times the normal concentration of 12·5 nanomoles per cubic centimeter (·03 percent by volume). **1968** *New Scientist* 22 Aug. 391/1 The other problem is how to take just a few microvolts from the national standard of one volt, and to infer its correctness to a few parts of a nanovolt (10^{-9}V). **1968** *Sci. Amer.* Mar. 17 (Advt.), The new COS/MOS units..operate on nanowatts of power in the quiescent state.

nanoid ('neɪnɔɪd), *a. rare*⁻⁰. [f. L. *nān-us* dwarf + -OID.] Resembling a dwarf, dwarf-like.

1856 MAYNE *Expos. Lex.*

nanophanerophyte (ˌnænəʊ'fænərəʊfaɪt). [a. F. *nanophanérophyte* (C. Raunkiær 1905, in *Oversigt K. Danske Videnskabernes Selskabs Forhandl.* 352), f. NANO- + PHANEROPHYTE.] A shrub or sub-shrub between 25 cm and 2 m in height, bearing its resting buds above the surface of the soil.

1913 W. G. SMITH in *Jrnl. Ecol.* I. 17 Nanophanerophytes less than 2 m. high. **1932** FULLER & CONARD tr. *Braun-Blanquet's Plant Sociol.* xii. 293 The round, woody cushions ..are not to be classed with the cushion forms, because of the lignified shoots, but rather among the semishrubs and nanophanerophytes. **1960** N. POLUNIN *Introd. Plant Geogr.* iii. 94 Refinements may be used such as the subdivision of phanerophytes into nanophanerophytes (shrubs) in which the renewal buds lie less than 2 metres above ground, microphanerophytes [etc.].

nanoplankton, var. NANNOPLANKTON.

'nanosecond (see NANO-). [f. NANO- + SECOND *sb.*[1]] A unit of time equal to one thousand-millionth of a second.

1959 W. C. G. ORTEL in *IRE Trans. Electronic Computers* III. 265 (*heading*) Nanasecond logic by amplitude modulation at X band. [*Note*] Although the term *millimicrosecond* has attained some currency, the metric system provides the standard prefix *nano-*, (abbreviated n-), by which the decimal multiplier 10^{-9} may be denoted conveniently without multiple prefixes. **1960** *Times* 17 Feb. 2/6 Pulses of nanosecond duration are being studied by means of fast recording techniques and spectrographic methods. **1964** *Evening Standard* 30 Oct. 19/3 The latest computers are now doing their sums in 'nano-seconds'... According to General Sarnoff, former head of the Radio Corporation of America, 'A nano-second is to a second what a second is to 30 years'. **1966** [see GIGA-]. **1967** *New Statesman* 14 July 47/3 It takes a nanosecond for an electric signal to travel a foot. **1968** *Dataweek* 24 Jan. 1/3 The 9400 would appear to be slower than the IBM System/360 Model 25 (memory cycle of 600 nanoseconds per two bytes against IBM's 180 nanoseconds per 64 bytes) but faster than the ICT 1902A (3 microseconds per 24-bit word). **1972** *Sci. Amer.* Jan. 121/1 Present atomic clocks keep time to better than 100 nanoseconds per day.

Nansen passport. [f. name of Fridtjof *Nansen* (1861–1930), Norwegian diplomat and explorer, who was responsible for the issue of the papers described below.] A document of identification issued after the war of 1914–18 to a stateless person ineligible for a passport. Also *absol.*

1925 *Measures to help Refugees: Rep. 5th Comm. to 6th Assembly League of Nations* 1 After lengthy negotiations, the Refugee Service has secured recognition for the Nansen Passports from forty Governments in the case of Russians and from twenty-eight in the case of Armenians. **1932** J. B. C. WATKINS tr. *Sörensen's Saga F. Nansen* 285 Nansen called together representatives from the various governments to a meeting at Geneva in July 1922. Thirty-one were represented, and they accepted Nansen's proposal for an identification certificate for each refugee which could be used as a passport. Fifty-two governments have recognized these certificates, which are stamped with Nansen's picture and known as 'Nansen passports'. They may be obtained by Armenian, Chaldean, Turkish, and Syrian refugees. **1944** H. G. WELLS *'42 to '44* 50 The practical organization of the Nansen passports that were for a time a resort for the multitude of people who had lost their national standing through changes of boundaries and similar dislocations. **1958** *Spectator* 14 Feb. 209/2 The 'Nansen passport' was one result. **1975** L. DICKSON *Radclyffe Hall at Well of Loneliness* xvii. 215 Souline had only a 'Nansen', a letter of identity not a passport, allowing her to reside in France. *Ibid.* 220 The long process of obtaining for Souline British naturalization papers, a first step in which was to exchange her French 'Nansen' for an English 'Nansen'.

‖**nant** (nænt). [W.] A brook; a valley.

1862 G. BORROW *Wild Wales* II. xxxii. 368, I saw a small house close by a nant or dingle. **1883** G. ALLEN *Flowers & their Pedigrees* vi. 184 There was once a time when great glacial sheets spread over the combs and glens of Snowdonia, as they spread to-day over the nants of Chamounix. **1923** *Chamber's Jrnl.* 26 May 409/1 A hill-road scrambles through orchards and vineyards and across dashing *nants* (mountain torrents) to a lofty ledge of pasture-land.

Nantes, obs. form of NANTZ.

Nantgarw (nænt'gæruː). Also **Nantgarrow** (nænt'gærəʊ). The name of a village in Glamorgan, used to designate a translucent soft-paste porcelain produced between 1813 and 1920 at the Nantgarw pottery founded by William Billingsley and Samuel Walker.

1820 W. W. YOUNG *Diary* 28 Oct. in E. M. Nance *Pott. & Porc. Swansea & Nantgarw* (1942) 524 Put Advertisement for the Nantgarw China in *The Cambrian.* **1820** *Cambrian* 28 Oct. in *Ibid.* xiii. 395 (Advt.), For Sale by Auction... At the China Manufactory at Nantgarw on Wednesday the 8th day of November 1820. A Quantity of Nantgarw Porcelain; a considerable portion of this is enamelled and gilded in a superior style. **1849** L. W. DILLWYN *Let.* 5 June in J. Marryat *Coll. Hist. Pott. & Porc.* (1850) ix. 186/2, I believe that all the China with granulated fracture was marked 'Nantgarrow'. **1880** J. RANDALL *Hist. Madeley* 206 Employing agents in Paris to buy up Sevres china in white for the purpose of having it painted in London, as Nantgarw had been. **1948** W. D. JOHN *Nantgarw Porc.* iii. 53 Two glazes were used on the Nantgarw porcelain. **1964** M. KELLY *March to Gallows* i. 10 It wasn't an environment for highflown escape. Nantgarw china and French song, for example. **1973** *Times* 16 Oct. 4/8 The Welsh porcelain brought particularly competitive prices, with one Nantgarw plate painted with fruit and flowers at £714.

nantokite ('næntəkaɪt). *Min.* Also **nantoquite**. [f. *Nantoco* in Chile + -ITE 2 b.] A white chloride of copper found in granular masses.

1872 DANA *Min.* App. i. 11 Nantokite. .. Occurs in a copper vein with atacamite. **1893** CHAPMAN *Blowpipe Pract.* 188 Nantokite..often greenish externally.

Nantucketer (næn'tʌkɪtə(r)). [f. *Nantucket*, the name of an American island off the coast of Massachusetts + -ER[1].] A native or inhabitant of Nantucket.

1851 H. MELVILLE *Moby Dick* II. xli. 279 Now some Nantucketers rather distrust this historical story of Jonah and the whale. **1882** E. K. GODFREY *Island of Nantucket* 24 The Nantucketers seem to have a mania for bell-ringing. **1914** R. A. DOUGLAS-LITHGOW *Nantucket* xv. 296 A Nantucketer does not pull, he always 'hauls', he does not tie or fasten anything, he 'splices' it. **1935** *Amer. Speech* X. 38/1 The calm superiority of the Nantucketer is shown in the case of the school boy who began his composition thus: 'Napoleon was a great man..but he was an off-islander.' **1948** *Sat. Even. Post* 26 June 46/3 Russells had also played a part, along with Howlands and Rotches, who had been Nantucketers, in committing New Bedford to the gigantic gamble on whaling. **1974** *Sci. Amer.* Mar. 119/1 The yellowfin-tuna fishery on the Pacific Equator, worked only recently by American and Japanese long-liners, is plainly disclosed in the Nantucketers' logbooks.

Nantz (nænts), *sb.* (and *a.*) Now only *arch.* Also 7 **nantes**, 7–9 **nants**. [From the place of manufacture, *Nantes* on the Loire in France.] Brandy. Also freq. ***right Nantz***.

1684 J. HAYNES *Epil. Lacy's Sir H. Buffoon*, There's one's for a Cup of Nants. **1693** *Humours Town* 29 A Tost and Ale, or perhaps, a Cup of cool Nants. **1706** E. WARD *Wooden World Diss.* (1708) 99 His Superiors, whom nothing will go down with, under right Nantz or Rum. **1822** SCOTT *Pirate* i, The devout opinion that a cup of Geneva or Nantz was specific against all cares. **1831** TRELAWNY *Adv. Younger Son* III. 330 It..didn't make a man's inside water-proof, which good Nantz would. **1889** DOYLE *Micah Clarke* 50 Let us.. have a drop of the right Nants before we go.

attrib. **1696** VANBRUGH *Relapse* Pref., Drinking his mistress's health in Nantes brandy.

†**'nany**, *a. Obs.* [OE. *nǽniȝ*, f. *ne* NE + *ǽniȝ* ANY *a.*] Not any, no.

c **725** *Corpus Gloss.* (Hessels) N 198 *Nullo negotio*, nænȝe earbeðe. **805** *Charter* 34 in *O.E. Texts* 442 [þæt] næniȝ mon ..on nænȝe oðre halfe oncærrende sie. *a* **900** CYNEWULF *Crist* 39 Næniȝ efenlic þam..in worlde ȝewearð wifes ȝeeacnung. *c* **1000** *Boeth. Metr.* x. 53 Nat næniȝ mon hwær hi nu sindon. *c* **1200** ORMIN 59 Ne mihhte naniȝ mann.. Utbresten off þe deofless band.

nanys(e, obs. forms of NONCE[1].

naological (neɪəʊ'lɒdʒɪkəl), *a.* [f. next + -ICAL.] Pertaining to, connected with, naology.

1846 *Ecclesiologist* VI. 65 The pursuit of Naological studies..had afforded much amusement to a long and happy life. **1849** FREEMAN *Archit.* 57 They are for the most part rather 'naological' than architectural.

naology (neɪ'ɒlədʒɪ). [f. Gr. νᾱό-ς temple + -LOGY.] The study of sacred buildings.

1846 DUDLEY (*title*) Naology. **1846** *Ecclesiologist* VI. 65 The part with which we are not concerned..is far superior to that with which we are—Christian Naology.

na'ometry. *rare*⁻¹. [f. as prec. + -METRY.] (See quot.)

1626 B. JONSON *Staple of N.* III. ii, To calculate a time and halfe a time, and the whole time, according to Naömetry. *P. Iv.* What's that? *Tho.* The measuring o' the Temple.

‖**naos** ('neɪɒs). [a. Gr. νᾱός temple.] A temple; the inner cell or sanctuary of a temple.

1775 R. CHANDLER *Trav. Asia M.* 256 Over the entrance of the Naos was a vast stone. **1858** BIRCH *Anc. Pottery* I. 166 Sometimes the whole of a *naos*, or chapel, was constructed or tiles. **1895** SAYCE *Egypt* 208 Fragments of red granite from some gigantic naos.

†**nap**, *sb.*[1] *Obs.* Forms: 1 hnæp(p, 2–3 nep, 2–4 nap. [OE. *hnæp(p*, = OS. *nap* (MDu. and Du. *nap*), OHG. *(h)napf* (G. *napf*), of obscure origin. An OLG. **hnap* is the source of OF. *hanap* (see HANAP), and It. *nappo* may also be an adoption from Teutonic.] A drinking-cup or bowl.

c **1000** ÆLFRIC *Gloss.* in Wr.-Wülcker 123 *Ciatus*, hnæp. *Anthlia*, hnæp. *c* **1050** *Vocab.* ibid. 283 *Patera*, hnæpp. *c* **1070** in Earle *Land Charters*, etc. 250, vi mæsene sceala, & ii ȝebonede hnæppas. *a* **1100** in Napier *O.E. Glosses* I. 1847 *Poculi, i. calicis*, steapes, hnæppes. *c* **1200** *Trin. Coll. Hom.* 163 Hire nap [is] of mazere. *a* **1225** *Ancr. R.* 344 Ibroken nep oðer disch. *c* **1250** *Death* 107 in *O.E. Misc.* 174 Hwer beoð þine dihsches?.. Hwer beoþ þine nappes? *c* **1350** *Body & Soul* (Camden) 343, I nam nouther furst ne last That schal drynken of that nap.

nap (næp), *sb.*[2] Also 4–7 **nappe**, (7 **knap**, 8 **napp**). [f. NAP *v.*[1]] A short or light sleep, *esp.* one taken during the day; a doze.

13.. *Cursor M.* 7201 (Gött.), Bot sampson wakind of his nap, Of bandis he lete himseluen scap. *c* **1412** HOCCLEVE *Min. Poems* 63 It me reueth many a sleep & nap. *c* **1450** *St. Cuthbert* (Surtees) 7435 þan I wakynd of my nappe. **1530** PALSGR. 247/2 Nappe a lytell slepe, *repos.* **1596** SPENSER *F.Q.* IV. v. 42 If by fortune any litle nap Upon his heavie eye-lids chaunst to fall [etc.]. **1628** FORD *Lover's Mel.* II. ii, In his naps he never looks in a glass. **1680** OTWAY *Caius Marius* IV. i, I'll swear it wak'd me out of a sweet Nap. **1711** ADDISON *Spect.* No. 112 ¶3 If by chance he has been surprized into a short Nap at Sermon. **1787** MME. D'ARBLAY *Diary* 16 Aug., I sat up all night,.. not daring to trust to a nap for myself. **1848** DICKENS *Dombey* xxiii, He refreshed his mind with a nap. **1863** 'OUIDA' *Held in Bondage* (1870) 3 A suspicious appearance of having just tumbled out of a nap.

b. In verbal phrases, esp. ***to take a nap***.

c **1400** *Rom. Rose* 4005 He slombred, & a nappe he toke. **1548** UDALL *Erasm. Par. Mark* xiii. 88 Although the people doe sumtymes take a nappe. **1606** HOLLAND *Sueton.* 171 Otherwhiles he would catch a nap in the day time, as he sat to minister iustice. **1653** *Nissena* 28 He slept but a little.. though but for a very smal space he stole a nap. **1709** STEELE *Tatler* No. 52 ¶4 [He] seems to take a Nap with his Eyes open. **1787** JEFFERSON *Writ.* (1859) II. 246 The genius of invention and improvement in Europe seems to be absolutely taking a nap. **1863** GEO. ELIOT *Romola* i, You'll know better than to take your nap in street corners.

nap (næp), *sb.*[3] Also 5–6 **noppe**, 7 **nappe**, 8–9 **knap**. [a. MDu. or MLG. *noppe* (mod.G. and Da. *noppe*; Du. *nop*, Sw. *nopp*, Norw. *napp*; also Walloon *nope*, †*noppe*), sb. related to *noppen* NAP *v.*[2] There is no evidence for the OE. *hnoppa* given by Somner.]

1. a. Originally, the rough layer of projecting threads or fibres on the surface of a woollen or other textile fabric, requiring to be smoothed by shearing; in later use, a special surface given to cloth of various kinds by artificial raising of the short fibres, with subsequent cutting and smoothing; the pile.

c **1440** *Promp. Parv.* 358/1 Noppe of a clothe, *villus, tomentum*. **1495** *Act 11 Hen. VII*, c. 27 They pull of both the noppe and the coton of the same Fustians. **1526** SKELTON *Magnyf.* 453 Whan the noppe is rughe, it wolde be shorne. **1589** FLEMING *Virg. Georg.* IV. 69 They bring towels with nap shorne off (The floow or roughness shorne away for feare to hurt his handes). **1617** MORYSON *Itin.* III. 165 The nap of the cloth (and that somewhat course) being worne off, the ground plainely appears. **1710** SWIFT *Tatler* No. 238 ¶5 His only Coat, where Dust confus'd with Rain Roughen the Nap, and leave a mingled Stain. **1727–38** CHAMBERS *Cycl.* s.v. *Teazel*, To card, or draw out the wool or knap from the thread or ground of several kinds of cloths. **1805** J. LUCCOCK *Nat. Wool* 124 The principal object is to procure a long and well formed knap. **1841** BORROW *Zincali* I. v. I. 90 It is very old, torn, and threadbare, with no nap upon it. **1882** SALA *Amer. Revis.* (1885) 232 To destroy the nap on gentlemen's coats.

attrib. **1875** KNIGHT *Dict. Mech.* 1511/2 *Nap-warp*,.. in fustian weaving, the upper warp covering the main warp or nap.

fig. **1591** LYLY *Endym.* v. ii, You haue worne the nappe of your witte quite off, and made it thredbare. **1593** SHAKS. *2 Hen. VI*, IV. ii. 7 To dresse the Common-wealth, and turne it, and set a new nap vpon it. **1627** E. F. *Hist. Edw. II* (1686) 91 When the nap of this Project was fallen off. **1682** *Lenten Prol.* I in *3rd Collect. Poems* (1689) 26/1 Our Prologue-Wit grows flat: the Naps worn off.

b. The woolly substance removed from the surface of cloth by the process of shearing.

1780 A. YOUNG *Tour Irel.* I. 181 Large quantities of knap are constantly taken out of the machine.

c. With *pl.* A cloth having a nap on it.

1771 *Pennsylv. Gaz.* 26 Sept. 3/1 The Sale of a large Assortment of coarse and fine Broadcloths, Bearskins, Coatings, Naps. **1888** *Daily News* 3 Dec. 2/7 Some fair orders are being placed for the cheaper makes of tweeds, serges, naps, pilots, and curls.

d. Blankets or other covering used by a person sleeping in the open air. *Austral. slang.*

c **1905** in Stewart & Keesing *Old Bush Songs* (1957) 249 My nap is rather thin, But my rig is pretty good. **1918** C. FETHERSTONHAUGH *After Many Days* 279 That night he could not catch the donkey, and he had to camp without any 'nap' (blankets). **1926** L. C. E. GEE *Bushtracks & Goldfields* 41 The quarts were boiled and an after-dinner supply of coffee made, the 'nap' spread out on soft sandy spots, the two travellers reclined with pipes. **1933** R. B. PLOWMAN *Man from Oodnadatta* 2 The blackboy's nap (blankets, underproof sheet, etc.) filled in the rear compartment. **1934** A. RUSSELL *Tramp-Royal in Wild Austral.* vii. 54 Rolled in our 'nap' with the 'break' at our heads and the camp fire at our feet, we slept snug and comfortable. **1936** —— *Gone Nomad* iii. 15 Here I hobbled out my horse and built a fire, placing beside it my nap and sweat-soaked saddle for pillow. **1945** *Coast to Coast 1944* 157 If you carry enough nap, you goes hungry; if you carry enough tucker you sleeps cold.

2. *transf.* A surface, esp. of a soft or downy nature, resembling the nap of cloth.

1591 SPENSER *Muiopot.* 333 The velvet nap which on his wings doth lie. **1638** FORD *Fancies* v. ii, Frizzle or powder their hair, plain their eye-brows, set a nap on their cheeks. **1668** CULPEPPER & COLE *Barthol. Anat.* I. xiv. 33 The Liver in its hollow side, cloathed with its Coat and ragged Nap. **1776–96** WITHERING *Brit. Plants* IV. 165 In the young and unexpanded plants or buttons the pileus is covered with a knap or frize of a brown glutinous wool. **1856** KANE *Arct. Expl.* I. xxvii. 358 Feathers of young frosting gave a plush-like nap to its surface. **1891** T. HARDY *Tess* xliii, Every twig was covered with a white nap as of fur grown from the rind during the night.

3. The smooth and glossy surface of a beaver, felt, or silk hat.

1727–38 CHAMBERS *Cycl.* s.v. *Hat*, The hat.. is.. rubbed with pumice, to take off the coarser knap; then rubbed over afresh with seel-skin, to lay the knap still finer. **1838** DICKENS *Nich. Nick.* xxix, Mr. Folair twirled his old hat round upon his hand, and affected the extremest agony lest any of the nap should have been knocked off. **1862** THORNBURY *Turner* II. 319 A hat with the nap carefully brushed the wrong way.

†**nap**, *sb.*[4] *Obs rare*$^{-1}$. [Of obscure origin: cf. Norw. *napp*, a little tug or pull.] A draught.

14.. *Songs & Carols 15th C.* (Warton Club) 48 He tok that maydyn be the pap, And tok thereof a ryȝt god nap.

nap (næp), *sb.*[5] [abbrev. of *Napoleon*.]

1. A twenty-franc piece; = NAPOLEON 1.

1820 MOORE *Mem.* (1853) III. 99 Got forty pounds at the banker's and gave Mr. Lake his remaining three Naps. **1862** H. MARRYAT *Year in Sweden* II. 283 English sovereigns and French naps as common as halfpence.

2. a. A card game, in which each player receives five cards, and calls the number of tricks he expects to win; one who calls five is said to ***go nap***, and to ***make his nap*** if he succeeds in winning them all. ***nap hand***, a hand which will probably take all five tricks in the game of nap; a strong hand; also *fig.* Cf. NAPOLEON 4.

The game is often called ***half-penny, sixpenny***, etc. ***nap***, according to the amount paid for each 'point' staked.

1862 C. C. ROBINSON *Dial. Leeds* 371 He's a nap hand at his traade! **1879** MISS BRADDON *Vixen* III. 194 The younger members of the house party played Nap. **1887** BLACK *Sabina Zembra* xxi, It was sixpenny 'Nap' they were going to play. **1894** MASKELYNE *Sharps & Flats* 24 The dupe.. being rendered suspicious by the eagerness of those about him to wager that he would not make his Nap. **1899** *Captain* I. 369/2 He showed me the way to deal myself a 'nap' hand, no matter who shuffled the cards. **1955** *Radio Times* 22 Apr. 9/2 Both these races (run over the Rowley Mile) test three-year-olds in the spring and complete the 'nap hand' of classics.

b. Hence in phr. ***to go nap***, to stake all one can, to speculate heavily; also *fig.* In *Austral.* also used neg.

c **1884** GLOVER *Racing Life* 38 Look here, you go nap—now hear that? nap!—on Royal Angus. **1898** *Westm. Gaz.* 12 Feb. 6/1 The market is going nap on the British Tea Table. **1938** F. S. ANTHONY *Me & Gus* 8 That's why the girls go nap on you the way they do. **1955** P. WHITE *Tree of Man* (1956) vii. 80, I never went nap on the priests meself. **1957** D. NILAND *Call me when Cross turns Over* viii. 184 But he never went nap on the city, he said, and now he had done with it for good. **1959** *Times* 22 Dec. 3/2 That is the sort of thing that poses another problem within the selectors' main one—whether to go nap on the ability that they know a man has in him, or whether to go entirely on the evidence of trials. **1961** A. UPFIELD *Bony & White Savage* vii. 59 The woman who runs the bookshop knows we don't go nap on the sexy stuff. **1967** N. MARSH *Death at Dolphin* x. 256 When you get one of your hunches.. I reckon it's safe to go nap on it.

c. A tip that a horse or greyhound is the most likely to win; *spec.* (see quot. 1937). In full, ***nap selection***. Also, the horse or greyhound so tipped; a bet on such a horse or greyhound. *colloq.*

1895 *Starting Price* 30 Mar. 1/2 Our 'Outsider's' nap of Docker for the Hainton Stakes. **1926** *Westm. Gaz.* 20 July 1/4 The Whip, who yesterday gave Lightstep, Nap (won 3–1),.. continues to hold a strong lead in Naps over the selections of the other racing critics. **1927** W. E. COLLINSON *Contemp. Eng.* 30 He stars this one, and the horse so starred is the nap selection. **1937** E. RICKMAN *On & off Racecourse* ix. 195 Every racing writer gives a single 'nap' or starred selection each day. It is his idea of the most promising bet the programme affords. **1960** *Which?* Mar. 60/1 The figures in the table are based on the correspondent's 'nap' selection—the word comes from a card game—for each day's racing, the horse that he thinks is the best bet. **1971** *Post* (S. Afr., Cape ed.) 9 May 16/5 (Advt.), Information from 'Horseman' includes jackpots, naps, accumulators, duplas, quinellas, doubles.

†**nap**, *sb.*[6] *slang.* [f. NAP *v.*[3]] (See quots.)

a **1700** B. E. *Dict. Caut. Crew*, *Napper of Napps*, a Sheep-stealer. *c* **1700** *Street Robberies Consider'd*, *Nap*, an arrest.

nap (næp), *sb.*[7] *Theatr. slang.* [? variant of KNAP *sb.*[2] 1.] A pretended blow; esp. in phr. ***to give*** or ***take the nap***.

1851 MAYHEW *Lond. Labour* III. 139 (Hoppe), Then Pantaloon comes up.., and I give him the 'nap', and knock him on his back. **1877** *Era Almanack* 49, I don't think, though, I shall be able to take the nap much longer.

nap, *sb.*[8] Variant of KNAP *sb.*[1] 1.

1702 TONKIN in *Carew's Cornwall* (1811) 343 *note*, A large level piece of ground, which is higher than any other part of this fortification, it being the nap of the hill.

nap, *sb.*[9] *Sc.* [var. of *knap* KNOP *sb.*[1] 3.] A shin of beef.

1844 H. STEPHENS *Bk. Farm* II. 169 The nap or shin is analogous to the hough of the hind leg.

nap, *sb.*[10] *Sc.* Var. of *knap* KNOP, a tub.

1824 MACTAGGART *Gallovid. Encycl.* 78.

nap (næp), *v.*[1] Forms: 1 **hnapp-**, **hnæppian**, **(h)neap(p)-**, 2–6 **nappe**, (3 **nappi**, 5 **nappyn**), (5) 6– **nap**, (8 **knap**). [OE. *hnappian*, *hnæppian*, app. related to OHG. (*h*)*naffez-*, *naphez-*, *naffizan* 'dormitare'.] *intr.* To sleep lightly or for a brief time; to take a short sleep.

Formerly in more dignified use than at present, being frequently employed in renderings of Biblical passages.

c **825** *Vesp. Psalter* iii. 6 Ic hneappade & slepan ongon. *c* **897** K. ÆLFRED *Gregory's Past. C.* xxviii. 192 Ne slapiȝe no ðin eaȝan, ne ne hnappiȝen ðine bræwas. *c* **1000** *Ags. Gosp.* Matt. xxv. 5 Ða se brydguma ylde, þa hnappudon hiȝ ealle & slepun. *c* **1200** *Trin. Coll. Hom.* 201 Sume men slapeð faste, and sume nappeð. *a* **1225** *Ancr. R.* 324 þe þet nappeð upon helle brerde, he torpleð ofte al in er he lest wene. *c* **1275** LAY. 1219 So he gon nappi [*c* 1205 slomnen], þar after to slepe. **13..** *E.E. Allit. P.* C. 465 Quen hit neȝed to naȝt nappe hym bihoued. **1377** LANGL. *P. Pl.* B. v. 393, 'I most sitte', seyde the segge 'or elles shulde I nappe'. **1423** JAS. I *Kingis Q.* lx, Gif I hald my pes, than will sche nap. **1519** HORMAN *Vulg.* 88, I can not but nappe whyle he precheth. **1598** MARSTON *Pygmal.* v. 160 The boy did nap, Whereby bright Phœbus did great Mars intrap. **1647** TRAPP *Comm. Matt.* xxv. 5 They slept but half-asleep, they napped and nodded. **1719** D'URFEY *Pills* (1872) III. 103 On whose fair Hills.. The God of Love lay knapping. **1767** J. PENN *Sleepy Serm.* 23 It would, we think, be better for them to be found rather watching, than napping. **1819** SHELLEY *Peter Bell 3rd* II. iv, He.. On every side did perk and peer Till he saw Peter dead or napping. **1881** M. C. HAY *Missing* III. 118 Aunt Charlotte will nap a little.

fig. *a* **1050** *Liber Scintill.* (1889) 2 Hi hnappiað on ȝewilnungum & ȝelustfullungum flæsces. *c* **1380** WYCLIF *Wks.* (1880) 303 To þise sectis ceessiþ not þe iugement þat is now & bifore tymes, & here leesing nappiþ not. *c* **1449** PECOCK *Repr.* v. i. 478 Doom.. cesith not, and the perdicioun.. nappith not.

b. Phr. ***to take*** or ***catch (one) napping***, to find (one) asleep; also *fig.*, to take unawares or off one's guard, to surprise (a person).

1562 PILKINGTON *Expos. Neh.* (1585) 65 Our mortall enemie.. hopeth to speede at length, and take thee napping. **1610** HOLLAND *Camden's Brit.* II. 54 The most watchfull may sometimes bee taken napping. *a* **1659** BP. BROWNRIG *Serm.* (1674) II. vi. 62 How much more unbecoming is it, that the Sun of righteousness should take us napping? **1743** BULKELEY & CUMMINS *Voy. S. Seas.* 92 The Captain said, Very well, Gentlemen, you have caught me Napping. **1844** DISRAELI *Coningsby* VIII. iii, The Tory party is organised now; they will not catch us napping again. **1884** *Leeds Merc.* 30 Apr. 4/6 The truth is that the Government whips were caught napping, as they too often are.

c. ***nap-at-noon***, a popular name for plants of the goat's-beard family (*Tragopogon*), the flowers of which close during the morning.

1865 *Cornh. Mag.* July 34 The peasant christens his flowers after their habits. In the Midland counties the common goatsbeard is his 'nap-at-noon'.

nap (næp), *v.*[2] Also 5–6 **noppe**, 8 **knap**. [a. MDu. or MLG. *noppen* (Du. and G. *noppen*, Da. *noppe*, Sw. *noppa*, Norw. *nappa*; also Walloon *noper*, †*nopper*), of uncertain origin.]

†**1.** *trans.* To trim (cloth) by shearing the nap.

c **1483** CAXTON *Dialogues* 33 Clarisse the nopster can well her craft.. cloth for to noppe. **1483** *Cath. Angl.* 256/1 To Noppe; *detuberare*. **1582** BENTLEY *Mon. Matrones* 72 They have so shorne, nopped and turned Christ's garment.

2. To furnish with a nap; to raise a nap on.

1620 SHELTON *Quix.* III. xxxviii. 264 Had the Bayz been napp'd, every Grain of it would have been as big as your biggest Peas. **1685** *Lond. Gaz.* No. 2009/8 For Beautifying of Cloth,.. by Napping and Freezing the same without Honey, Mollosse, or any Moisture. **1727–38** CHAMBERS *Cycl.* s.v. *Cloth*, The cloth thus woven, scoured, knapped, and shorn, is sent to the dyer. **1852** MORFIT *Tanning & Currying* (1853) 534 To soften the fibres, and nap the surface without cutting the flesh off.

nap (næp), *v.*[3] *Cant* and *slang.* Also 7, 9 **knap**. [Cf. Sw. and Norw. *nappa*, Da. *nappe*, to snatch, snap, etc. The precise source and relationship to NAB *v.*[1] are not clear.]

1. *trans.* To seize, catch, or lay hold of (a person or thing); to take into custody; to nab, steal.

1673 in R. Head *Canting Acad.* 11 If the Cully naps us, And the Lurries from us take. *Ibid.* 192 Though he tip them the piks, they nap him agen. *a* **1700** B. E. *Dict. Cant. Crew*, *Nap the Wiper*, to Steal the Handkerchief. **1719** D'URFEY *Pills* (1872) IV. 320 But nap'd them in the Streets, By Dozens and Scores. **1812** J. H. VAUX *Flash Dict.* s.v. *Knap*, To *knap a clout*, is to steal a pocket-handkerchief. **1863** E. FARMER *Scrap Book* (ed. 3) 53 Hunting after sweets we nap some sours.

b. ***to nap it***, to 'catch it', to receive severe punishment, esp. in a boxing-match.

a **1700** B. E. *Dict. Cant. Crew* s.v., *You have Napt it*, you are Clapt, Sir. *Ibid.* s.v. *Nask*, *He Napt it at the Nask*, he was Lasht at Bridewell. **1820** *Blackw. Mag.* VIII. 81 Some entered the ring in a very bad condition.. and knapped it every round. **1821** *Sporting Mag.* VII. 274 Josh as usual napt it in the first part of the round.

†**2.** (See latest quots.) *Obs. rare*$^{-0}$.

1673 [see NAPPING *vbl. sb.*[3]]. **1680** HEAD & KIRKMAN *Eng. Rogue* IV. 210 Nothing could perswade him but that he was cheated of his Money, that he napt on him, and I know not what. **1688** HOLME *Armoury* III. xvi. (Roxb.) 64/2 Nap or Knap, or cog a die is the slurring it out of ones fingers. *a* **1700** B.E. *Dict. Cant. Crew*, *Nap*, by Cheating with the Dice to secure one Chance.

nap (næp), *v.*[4] [f. NAP *sb.*[5] 2c.] *trans.* To recommend (a horse or greyhound) as a likely winner.

1927 *Daily Express* 22 June 17/7 Great Chum napped for White City Cup Final. **1973** *Listener* 28 June 864/3 You start napping odds-on chances, and they get beaten just as easily as the others.

nap, variant of KNAP *v.*[1]

nap (in *hap or nap*): see HAB *adv.* 2.

Napa ('næpə). Also **nappa**. The name of a county, town, and valley in California, U.S.A., used *attrib.* and *ellipt.* to designate (*a*) leather prepared from sheep- or goat-skin by a special tawing process; (*b*) wine grown in the valley.

1883 R. L. STEVENSON *Silverado Squatters* 34 (*heading*) Napa wine. **1895** *Montgomery Ward Catal.* 289/3 Men's Smoke Napa Gauntlet. **1897** C. T. DAVIS *Manuf. Leather* (ed. 2) 275 The staking machine..can be adjusted to any kind of leather, including napa. **1903** L. A. FLEMMING *Pract. Tanning* 51 Coloring black Napa. Black Napa leather is generally colored blue on the flesh side. **1921** B. E. ELLIS *Gloves & Glove Trade* 58 'Nappa' gloves are made from tawed leathers. **1961** *Housewife* Apr. 59/1 Fawn nappa leather handbag. **1971** M. MCCARTHY *Birds of America* 157 Several glasses of Napa Valley wine. **1974** *Country Life* 21 Mar. 688/1 Slip-on mules in coloured nappa leather for £7.

napæa (nəˈpiːə). *rare.* Also 7 -ea. [a. L. *Napæa*, ad. Gr. *Ναπαία*, fem. of *ναπαῖος*, f. *νάπη* a wooded dell.] A nymph haunting wooded dells.

1612 SHELTON *Quix.* I. III. xi, O ye Napeas and Driades, which do wontedly inhabite the Thickets and Groues. **1617** DRUMM. OF HAWTH. *Forth Feasting* A 3 b, O Naïd's deare, (said they,) Napæas fair, O Nymphes of trees, Nymphes which on Hills repaire!

So **naˈpæad** (after *naiad* or *dryad*).

1818 L. HUNT *Foliage, The Nymphs* p. xi, And there are the Napeads—names till now Scarce known.

napæan (nəˈpiːən), *a. rare*$^{-1}$. [f. prec. + -AN.] Consisting of the Napæas.

1697 DRYDEN *Virg. Georg.* IV. 777 The soft Napæan race will soon repent Their Anger, and remit the Punishment.

napalm (næ-, ˈneɪpɑːm), *sb.* orig. *U.S.* [f. NA(PHTHENATE + PALM(ITATE (see quot. 1946).]

1. a. A thickening agent consisting essentially of aluminium salts of naphthenic acids and of the fatty acids of coconut oil. **b.** A thixotropic gel consisting of petrol and napalm (or some similar agent), used in flame-throwers and incendiary bombs; jellied petrol.

1942 in L. F. Fieser *Sci. Method* (1964) iv. 47 Novello and Harris will arrive..on Monday morning and deliver 7 small bombs and 7 large ones, each loaded with 100 grams of white phosphorus and with Napalm Polymer Gum prepared in gasoline. **1942** H. C. HOTTEL *Stud. Fuel Projection from Nozzles* (U.S. Govt. Res. Rep. PB 23769, 8 June) Summary, Very striking and extremely promising, however, is the enormous increase in range obtainable by the use of special materials, specifically a starch-water suspension and an incendiary gasoline gel known as Napalm. The latter can be projected three times as far in a one-eighth inch jet as can a conventional hydrocarbon fuel. **1946** L. F. FIESER et al. in *Industr. & Engin. Chem.* Aug. 769/1 It was next found (January 29, 1942) that a combination of aluminium naphthenate with the same 'aluminum palmitate' could be easily incorporated into gasoline to form a promising gel, and we termed this naphthenate-'palmitate' combination a Napalm gel. Subsequently it developed that the supposed 'aluminum palmitate' was actually the aluminum soap of the total fatty acids of coconut oil, and that the specific gelling quality is due to a high content of lauric, not palmitic, acid. **1951** KIRK & OTHMER *Encycl. Chem. Technol.* VI. 580 The U.S. uses a mixture of aluminum soaps, generally referred to as Napalm, as a thickening agent. A fuel of any desired consistency may be prepared by mixing the proper amount of Napalm with gasoline. **1952** R. CUTFORTH *Korean Reporter* xix. 174 He was no longer covered with a skin, but with a crust like crackling which broke easily. 'That's napalm,' said the doctor. **1953** *Armed Forces Chem. Jrnl.* (U.S.) July 8/2 The thickening agent, known popularly as napalm, gelled the gasoline to a honey-like consistency. **1964** L. F. FIESER *Sci. Method* ii. 27 On Feb. 14 [1942], we reported to NDRC development of two lines of gels that could be prepared by stirring with gasoline at room temperature. To one, made from aluminum *na*phthenate and 'aluminum *palm*itate', I gave the name Napalm. *Ibid.* 32 The most interesting sample, Napalm X-104, arrived on April 13, 1942... The material is a brownish, dry, nonsticky powder. When an amount of Napalm powder sufficient to produce a 12% solution is poured into gasoline and given one stir, solvation occurs rapidly and the swollen solvated particles soon fill the container with material of applesauce consistency... After aging for a few hours without attention, the gel reaches its final form, in which it is tough, strong, and sticky. **1966** *Chem. & Engin. News* 14 Mar. 24/3 An Air Force contract to supply 100 million pounds of the new napalm, which contains 50% polystyrene. *Ibid.*, Napalm-B, besides the 50% polystyrene, contains 25% benzene and 25% gasoline. It is replacing the soap-jelled gasoline napalm formulations of World War II and the Korean action. **1966** *Daily Tel.* 16 Aug. 17/3 Mrs. Anne Kerr, Labour M.P. for Rochester and Chatham, said in Tokyo today that the United States should withdraw from South Vietnam 'rather than drop napalm on innocent peasants'. **1967** *Freedomways* VII. 121 We saw a man who was a victim of napalm, and two women who had been tortured in Diem's prisons. **1968** [see INCENDIJEL]. **1968** V. W. SIDEL in S. Rose *Chem. & Biol. Warfare* iii. 46 The adhesiveness, prolonged burning time and high burning temperature of napalm favour third-degree burns, and such burns are likely to be deep and extensive. **1970** K. LYLE in A. Chapman *New Black Voices* (1972) 293 I-am-wishing for an hour of napalm on ALL Junior Chambers-of-Commerce.

2. *attrib.* and *Comb.*, as ***napalm bomb, -bombing, burn, gel, jelly.***

1945 *N.Y. Times* 17 Aug. 2/7 Only a few [new weapons] can be mentioned. Among them were:..the Napalm bomb—jellied gasoline with a detonator in a plane's detachable fuel tank. **1957** S. JAMESON *Cup of Tea for Mr. Thorgill* v. 41 All these years he has done harm—from a position of complete safety and comfort, like a pilot dropping napalm bombs. **1963** *Daily Tel.* 22 Aug. 10/2 The United Arab Republic..admits to using napalm bombs against the Royalist tribes. **1973** *Black Panther* 13 Oct. 14/2 He also charged that the Portuguese had been attacking them with tanks, napalm bombs and highly sophisticated and dangerous weapons supplied mostly by NATO countries. **1955** G. GREENE *Quiet American* 197 What I detest is napalm bombing... The poor devils are burnt alive, the flames go over them like water. **1959** *Times Lit. Suppl.* 23 Oct. 614/3 Fontane sees the war at close quarters—the heat, the dysentery, the napalm-bombing. **1952** *Times* 14 July 7/6 The napalm burns are not necessarily the most painful of wounds. **1968** *Listener* 8 Aug. 170/2 A televison shot of a patient suffering from napalm burns in Vietnam. **1946** Napalm gel [see 1]. **1968** V. W. SIDEL in S. Rose *Chem. & Biol. Warfare* iii. 46 The napalm gel proved far superior to the original rubber-based gel. **1966** *Daily Tel.* 2 Nov. 14/8 Pictures showing the full horror of burns in Vietnam caused by the diabolical napalm jelly of phosphorus and petrol.

napalm (næ-, ˈneɪpɑːm), *v.* [f. prec.] *trans.* To attack or destroy with napalm. Also *fig.* Hence **ˈnapalmed** *ppl. a.*, **ˈnapalming** *vbl. sb.*

1950 *N.Y. Times* 26 Sept. 2/7 Troops were napalmed when they were found hiding in caves at the dead end of a canyon. *Ibid.* 6 Nov. 2/2 Capt. Warren Nichols..dived down in a napalming attack on a concentration of Red troops. **1952** DYLAN THOMAS *Let.* 8 Oct. (1966) 378, I think it has something to do with what Our Side gives to people after it has napalmed them. **1966** *Punch* 12 Jan. 64/2 The nobility of our democracy obliges us to succour the people..not to napalm them down. **1966** *New Statesman* 26 Aug. 292/2 There is no patience left in Vietnam. It has been napalmed and shot away. **1967** *Observer* 10 Dec. 5/3 The Americans are very busy bombing, rocketing and napalming air fields. **1968** *Economist* 27 Apr. 21/1 The nationalists have no intention of occupying these stockades, since the villages that contain them would then be napalmed or razed. **1968** *Guardian* 1 Oct. 8/4 Napalmed peasants in Vietnam. **1969** R. PETRIE *Despatch of Dove* III. 155 How to get rid of poverty? Blow it up! Napalm it! **1972** *Village Voice* (N.Y.) 1 June 62/2 (Advt.), They said they wanted to napalm draft records instead of people.

nape (neɪp), *sb.*[1] Also 4 naape, 6 **naupe, nawpe.** [Of obscure origin. The entire absence of forms with initial *k* makes it difficult to connect the word with the app. synonymous OFris. (*hals*) *knap*. The variants *naupe*, *nawpe* also present difficulties; it is not clear whether they have any connexion with mod. north. dial. (*k*)*naup*, (*k*)*nope* the head or top of the head, a lump or swelling, a hillock.]

1. a. The back of the neck; that part of the body in man or animals which contains the first cervical vertebræ. (Now usually as in b.)

In early examples sometimes translating L. *vertex*.

13.. *K. Alis.* 1347 Felip was..Dedly woundid thorugh the nape. *c* **1330** R. BRUNNE *Chron.* (1810) 211 þe maufesours [were] ateynt, and cursed ouer þe nape. *a* **1400** *Prymer* (1891) 77 In to his naape his wickednesse schal falle down. *c* **1460** RUSSELL *Bk. Nurture* 455 Furst Kit owte þe nape in þe nek þe shuldurs before. **1582** STANYHURST *Æneis* II. (Arb.) 66, I twisted a wallet On my broad shoulders, my nape dyd I settle eke vnder. **1656** RIDGLEY *Pract. Physick* 256 Every morning rub hard the hinder part of the Head and Nape. **1762** HOOLE tr. *Tasso* XI. 317 In his right eye the fatal arrow drove,..And issu'd at his nape. **1808** *Med. Jrnl.* XIX. 446 These emunctories are put on the nape or occipital region. **1851** C. L. SMITH tr. *Tasso* III. xliv, On the nape and back he struck them dead.

attrib. **1883** *Fisheries Exhib. Catal.* 200 Apparatus used in the preparation of boneless fish, including mitre boxes, knives,..nape-hooks. **1888** O. THOMAS *Catal. Marsup.* 7 Nape-hairs directed backwards. **1922** JOYCE *Ulysses* 256 Stooping her fair pinnacles of hair, stooping, her tortoise napecomb showed.

b. Esp. in phr. ***the nape of the neck*** (†or *head*).

α. [*c* **1440** *Promp. Parv.* 351/1 Nape of an hedde, *occiput, cervix, vertex*.] **1530** PALSGR. 247/1 Nape of the necke, *fossette de la teste*. **1540** MORYSINE tr. *Vives' Introd. Wisd.* C vij, Kepe the nape of thy necke from colde. **1601** HOLLAND *Pliny* II. 119 It helpeth al the infirmities incident to the nape of the neck. **1649** BULWER *Pathomyot.* II. i. 44 If we put the index of our Hand about the pit of the hinder part of the head, or nape of the neck. **1768–74** TUCKER *Lt. Nat.* (1834) I. 447 As one catches up a dog by the nape of his neck. **1839** THIRLWALL *Greece* lii. VI. 287 A..stone which fell on the nape of his neck. **1872** BAKER *Nile Trib.* xiii. 230 The harpoon was sticking in the nape of the neck.

β. **1530** PALSGR. 247/2 Naupe of the heed, *canneau de col, la fossette de la teste*. **1541** R. COPLAND *Guydon's Quest. Chirurg.* N iij b, They are applyed in the nawpe of the necke, and kepeth the place of the cephalyke bledynge.

2. a. The fleshy part left projecting from the end of a fish's back after the head is removed. ? *Obs.*

1482 *Rolls of Parlt.* VI. 222/1 That the napes of the seid barelled fissh, shuld be no longer than the litell bone that sitteth upon the grete fyne.

b. The part of a fish next the head. *rare.*

1656 SIR J. MENNES & SMITH *Musarum Deliciæ* (ed. 2) 86 Then to a Nape of Ling he would invite Some Rascall Tapster. **1884** G. B. GOODE *Fisheries U.S.: Nat. Hist. Aquatic Anim.* 201 George's fish are very fat fish with white 'napes'.

†**nape**, *sb.*[2] *Obs. rare*$^{-1}$. [a. OF. *nape*, var. of *nappe*:—L. *mappa*: see NAPKIN.] A table-cloth.

c **1450** *Bk. Curtasye* 656 in *Babees Bk.* 199 þo ouer nape schalle dowbulle be layde.

†**nape**, *sb.*[3] *Obs. rare.* [ad. L. *nāpus*: cf. NEEP.] The name suggested by Turner, and used by some later writers, for the yellow turnip.

1562 TURNER *Herbal* II. (1568) 61 Napus is named in Greke *βουνιας*... It may be called a Nape or a yelow rape vntill we fynde out the olde Englishe name for it. **1600** SURFLET *Countrie Farme* II. xxxii. 240 Napes and nauets..are two diuers sorts..: the napes are greater and drawing toward a yellow colour..: nauets are lesse, white, and a great deale more sauorie. **1657** TOMLINSON *Renou's Disp.* 308 There are three differences of Napes or Rapes.

nape, *sb.*[4] *dial.* [perh. for *knape*: see KNAP *sb.*[1] 1, quot. 1538.] (See quot.)

1837 J. F. PALMER *Dialogue Devonsh. Dial.* Gloss., Where a rising ground falls off on either side, so as to form an ascending ridge, that ridge is called the nape.

nape, obs. variant of NEAP *dial.*

†**nape**, *v.*[1] *Obs.* Also 5 *inf.* napyn, 6 **nawpe.** [f. NAPE *sb.*[1] It is not clear whether the north. dial. (*k*)*naup*, (*k*)*nope*, to strike on the head, has any connexion with Palsgrave's *nawpe*.]

1. *trans.* To strike (a person) on the back of the neck. Also *transf.*

c **1440** *Promp. Parv.* 351/2 Napyn, or slen be the nape, *occipito*. **1530** PALSGR. 643/2, I nawpe one in the necke, I stryke one in the necke, *je accollette* and *je frappe au col*. **1549** LATIMER *3rd Serm. bef. Edw. VI* (Arb.) 76 He was taken and naped in ye head wyth the title of an heretique.

2. ? To cut (a fish) through the nape.

c **1450** *Two Cookery-bks.* 102 Take a troute, and nape him. *Ibid.* 105 Take a tenche, and nape him. **1482** *Rolls of Parlt.* VI. 222/2 Every Barell of fissh, which herafter shall be founde..medelled, naped, leyd double, or not boned nor splatted, accordyng to this Acte.

Hence †**ˈnaping** *vbl. sb. Obs.*

1495 *Act 11 Hen. VII*, c. 23 That every suche Gauger Packer and Sercher take no more for..his labour for bonyng napyng and packyng of a barell fisshe..[than] *jd.*

†**nape**, *v.*[2] *Obs.*$^{-1}$ (Precise sense obscure.)

c **1460** *Towneley Myst.* xxx. 575 Gederand and gredy, sore napand and nedy youre godys forto spare.

napea(d: see NAPÆA.

ˈnape-crest. *Ornith.* [f. NAPE *sb.*[1] + CREST *sb.*] *pl.* An African genus of scansorial birds.

1840 *Cuvier's Anim. Kingd.* 220 A third genus consists of the Nape-crests (*Chizæris*, Swainson), which have a rounded beak approaching that of some Trogons.

†**ˈnapell.** *Obs. rare.* [a. F. *napel* (16th c., Paré), or ad. med.L. *napellus*] = next.

1598 SYLVESTER *Du Bartas* II. i. III. *Furies* 179 Dead-laughing Apium, weeping Aconite,..Hot Napell, making lips and tongues to swell. *a* **1649** DRUMM. OF HAWTH. *Poems* (1656) 135 The Nightshade, Henbane, Napell, Aconite.

‖**naˈpellus.** *Bot.* [med.L. *napellus* (13–14th c. in Diefenbach), f. *nāpus* turnip.] The common aconite; monk's-hood, wolf's-bane.

1626 BACON *Sylva* §499 There is an old Tradition of a Maiden that was fed with Napellus (which is counted the Strongest poyson of all Vegetables). **1727–38** CHAMBERS *Cycl.* s.v. *Aconite*, The *Napellus*, thus called *a napo*, because its root resembled the turnep kind. **1797** *Encycl. Brit.* (ed. 3) I. 77/1 The napellus bears large blue flowers, which appear in August.

†**napelo.** *Obs. rare*$^{-1}$. [a. It. *napelo*, *nap*(*p*)*ello*, ad. med.L. *napellus*.] = prec.

1580 FRAMPTON *Monardes' Two Med. agst. Venome* 124 The Bezaar stone is..of great efficacie agaynst Napelo, the strongest of all venomes.

naperer (ˈneɪpərə(r)). *Obs.* exc. *Hist.* [f. NAPER-Y + -ER[1].] The person having charge of the royal table linen.

1494 FABYAN *Chron.* VII. 586 The lorde Gray Ruthyn, or Ryffyn, naperer. **1611** SPEED *Hist. Gt. Brit.* IX. xiii. §2. 712/2 Anne, late wife of Iohn de Hastings Earle of Pembroke..was admitted..to vse the office of Naperer. **1688** HOLME *Armoury* III. 42/2 Naperer, or Keeper of the Table Linnen. **1865** *Edin. Rev.* Apr. 339 Their..ancestors having held the same honourable office of royal naperer.

Naperian, variant of NAPIERIAN.

naperon, obs. form of APRON.

napery (ˈneɪpərɪ). Forms: 4–6 naprye, 5–6 -ry, 6–7 -rie, (5 nappre, 6 napre, 6–7 *Sc.* naiprie); 4–7 naperie, (7 napp-, *Sc.* naipp-), 5–7 -rye, (6 naparie, 7 -ry), 5– **napery.** [a. obs. F. *naperie* (*napperie*, 1400 in Godef.), f. *nape* (*nappe*) NAPE *sb.*[2] + -ERY.]

1. Linen used for various household purposes, esp. table linen. Now *rare* exc. *Sc.*

c **1380** WYCLIF *Wks.* (1880) 434 Dizschis & coupis of siluer & oþer vessel, & costly naprye. **1418** *E.E. Wills* (1882) 32 All my beddynge & naperie. *c* **1460** J. RUSSELL *Bk. Nurture* 238 The surnape ye shulle make..with a clothe vndir a dowble of riȝt feire napry. **1530** PALSGR. 457/1 Gyve me leave to bleche my naperye in your garden. **1578** T. N. tr. *Conq. W. India* 176 His Table clothes, napkins, and towels, were made of Cotten wooll, verie white and newe, for he was never served but once with that naperie. **1656** HEYLIN *Surv. France* 15 The napperie of the Table was..so foul and dirty, that I durst not conceive it had been washed above once. **1799** J. ROBERTSON *Agric. Perth* 382 Some weaving napery for the warehouses at Dunfermline. **1822** GALT *Provost* xxxviii, All the best of her sheets and napery. **1870** ROCK *Text. Fabr.* Introd. 75 Venetian linens, for fine towelling and napery in general.

attrib. and *Comb.* **1532** HERVET tr. *Xenophon's Househ.* (1768) 38 Shetes, towels, and all naprye ware by them selfes. **1615** BRATHWAIT *Strappado* (1878) 6 But this's not all Ile doe: Bacchus shall knowe His naprie-drawers shall not end it so. **1631** —— *Whimzies, Ruffian* 133 A kicke, I meane, from some surly Naprie groome, which serves in full discharge of his Commons. **1865** *Caledon. Merc.* 5 Sept., The officers then seized..two napery presses, a chest of drawers.

†b. Personal linen. *Obs.*

1598 E. GUILPIN *Skial.* A viij, [The] goodly show Of thyne apparraile and thy naperie. **1602** DEKKER *Honest Wh.* Wks. 1873 II. 41 Prithee put me into wholesome naperie.

2. †a. The charge or custody of the royal linen; the office of naperer. *Obs.*

a **1483** *Liber Niger* in *Househ. Ord.* (1790) 56 The steward takethe.. for his napery at the iiii principall festes of the yere ..in prises of lynyn clothe. **1601** F. TATE *Househ. Ord. Edw. II* (Chaucer Soc.) 27 A lawendere of the Naperie, who shal wash all manner of linnen cloth, appertaining to the office of the Naperie. **1628** COKE *On Litt.* 107b, To perform the office of the napery at his coronation.

b. A store-room for linen.

1819 HALLAM *Mid. Ages* II. ix. III. 427 *note*, The house consisted of a hall, parlour,..a napery, or linen room [etc.].

†3. The making up or manufacture of personal or household linen. *Obs. rare.*

1630 J. TAYLOR (Water P.) *Praise Clean Linen* Wks. II. 169/1 What were the function of the Linnen Draperye Or Sempsters admirable skill in Naperye? **1650** FULLER *Pisgah* IV. vi. §4 Kings Merchants..brought in linen-yarn.., Solomon so setting up Napery, and the manufacture of weaving.

4. (See quot.) *Obs. rare*$^{-0}$.

1688 HOLME *Armoury* III. 148/1 Napery—the working of Linnen in Painting according to the Foldings thereof.

†napet. *Obs.*$^{-0}$ [f. NAPE *sb.*^{2} + -ET^1.] Napkin.

c **1440** *Promp. Parv.* 351/2 Napet, or napekyn, *napella, manupiarium.*

†naphe. *Obs. rare*$^{-1}$. [a. F. *naphe, naffe* = Sp. *nafa, nefa,* It. *nanfa, lanfa,* ad. Arab. *nafḥa(h)* fragrance, perfume.] Orange-flower water.

1600 SURFLET *Countrie Farme* I. xii. 53 The water of Naphe drunke to the quantitie of sixe ounces, causeth the malignitie of the plague to breake foorth by sweates.

naphew, obs. form of NAVEW.

naphtha (ˈnæfθə, ˈnæpθə). Forms: 6 **napta,** 7 **neptha, nephta,** 6–7, 9 **naphta,** (9 **nafta**), 6– **naptha, naphtha.** See also NAPHTHE and NEFT(E. [a. L. *naphtha,* a. Gr. νάφθα (also νάφθας), possibly of Oriental origin (but Arab. and Pers. *nafṭ* is prob. from Greek); hence also It. and Sp. *nafta,* Pg. *naphta,* F. *naphte.*] **a.** A name originally applied to an inflammable volatile liquid (a constituent of asphalt and bitumen) issuing from the earth in certain localities; now extended to most of the inflammable oils obtained by dry distillation of organic substances, esp. coal, shale, and petroleum.

1572 J. JONES *Bathes* II. 13 As plenty of Naphta gathered in the aforesaid place doth shewe. **1577** FRAMPTON *Joyfull News* 84 Fountaines..of Petroleo, of Napta, of Sulphur. **1605** DANIEL *Queen's Arcadia* II. iv, Like Neptha that takes fire by sight of Fire. **1698** FRYER *Acc. E. India & P.* 333 From about Thirty Mountains near the same place.. springs the famous Naphtha. **1753** HANWAY *Trav.* (1762) I. IV. lvii. 264 There is also a white naptha on the peninsula of Apcheron, of a much thinner consistency. **1788** GIBBON *Decl. & F.* lii. V. 402 The principal ingredient of the Greek fire was the naptha, or liquid bitumen. **1838** T. THOMSON *Chem. Org. Bodies* 719 Persian naphtha, as it is collected on the spot, is very nearly, but not quite colourless. **1876** HARLEY *Mat. Med.* 99 Naphtha, whether obtained artificially or as a product of nature, is sometimes used medicinally.

fig. **1847** EMERSON *Poems, Dæmonic Love* Wks. (Bohn) I. 460 Deep..loving eyes, Flowed with naphtha fiery sweet.

b. *attrib.* and *Comb.*, as ***naphtha-fire, -fuel, -gas, -lamp, -ship, -spring, -vapour***; ***naphtha-bearing*** adj.; **naphtha-brown** (see quot. 1874); **naphtha engine** (see quot.); **naphtha launch,** a launch powered by a naphtha engine.

1909 *Westm. Gaz.* 2 Dec. 9/2 The leasing of certain areas of naphtha-bearing land contrary to existing regulations. **1874** CROOKES *Hand-bk. Dyeing* 208 The so-called naphtha-brown is merely the crude melt from the manufacture of magenta. **1892** P. BENJAMIN *Mod. Mechanism* 270 Naphtha-engines, which utilize naphtha both as the fuel under the boiler and as the fluid to be vaporized in the boiler and used in the engine, have recently come into somewhat extensive employment as motors for light launches. **1831** CARLYLE *Sart. Res.* II. v, Women, in whose placid veins circulates too little naphtha-fire. **1895** *Daily News* 25 Apr. 7/2 The annual consumption of naphtha fuel in Russia. **1877** *Scribner's Monthly* Nov. 3/1 It consists of a large reflector behind a common naphtha lamp and mounted upon the bow of the boat. **1899** 'Q' (QUILLER COUCH) *Ship of Stars* ii, Even the boy grew tired of the naphtha-lamps. **1887** *Forest & Stream* 8 Dec. 395/3 The success which the naphtha launch has attained in a very short time must be taken as very strong proof of the inherent excellence of the machine itself. **1903** *Mobile* (Alabama) *Advertiser* 2 Jan. 6/3 The big naphtha launch Stella arrived from up the Alabama river yesterday afternoon. **1923** H. E. WILLIAMS *Spinning Wheels & Homespun* xv. 182 There have been times when..skimming away in little naptha [*sic*] launches..has seemed an enviable lot. **1888** *Daily News* 28 Nov. 3/6 The Destruction of a Naphtha Ship. **1753** HANWAY *Trav.* (1762) I. IV. lvii. 264 Near this place..naptha-springs are found. **1825** T. THOMSON *1st Princ. Chem.* I. 153 To take care that the whole of it is consumed, and that none escapes under the form of naphtha vapour.

naph'thalamide. *Chem.* [f. NAPHTHAL-IN + AMIDE.] A former name of PHTHALIMIDE.

1838 T. THOMSON *Chem. Org. Bodies* 30 Naphthalamide ..may be obtained by heating naphthalate of ammonia in a retort. Water and ammonia are disengaged, and naphthalamide sublimes.

naph'thalamine. *Chem.* [f. as prec. + AMINE.] (See quot.)

1875 *Ure's Dict. Arts* III. 394 Naphthalamine, which is the base corresponding to aniline, is now manufactured in the same way as that body is from benzole. It yields beautiful commercial dyes.

'naphthalate. *Chem.* [f. as NAPHTHAL-IC + -ATE^4.] A salt of naphthalic acid. Now called PHTHALATE.

1838 T. THOMSON *Chem. Org. Bodies* 29 The alkaline naphthalates are very soluble in water.

naphthalene (ˈnæfθəliːn). *Chem.* Also formerly **naphthaline, -in** (-ɪn). [f. NAPHTHA + *-l-* + -ENE, -INE^5: named by Kidd.] A white crystalline substance, having a peculiar smell and pungent taste, usually obtained as a product in the distillation of coal-tar.

First noticed in 1819 by Garden (*Annals Phil.* XV. 74–5) and Brande (*Q. Jrnl. Sci.*, etc. VIII. 287).

α. **1821** KIDD in *Phil. Trans.* CXI. 209 Observations on Naphthaline, a peculiar substance resembling a concrete essential oil. **1836–41** BRANDE *Chem.* (ed. 5) 553 When chlorine is passed over naphthalin, heat is evolved. **1857** DUNGLISON *Med. Lex.* 619 When Coal-tar is subjected to distillation, naphthaline passes over after coal naphtha. **1889** *Lancet* 28 Sept. 659/2 Naphthalin finely powdered and well spread..has its disinfecting power increased. **1897** *Allbutt's Syst. Med.* III. 742 Naphtha-line is another useful intestinal disinfectant.

β. **1866** WATTS *Dict. Chem.* IV. 5 Naphthalene when pure consists of brilliant white scaly crystals. **1891** *Syd. Soc. Lex.* s.v. *Naphthalinum,* Naphthalene, in powder, obtained by dissolving the scaly crystals in alcohol.

attrib. **1872** WATTS *Dict. Chem.* 1st Suppl., Naphthalene Alcohol. **1874** tr. *Lommel's Light* 189 In Naphthalin red.. there are rays of low refrangibility. **1890** THORPE *Dict. Appl. Chem.* I. 233/2 This..is the saffranine of the naphthalene series. **1891** *Syd. Soc. Lex.* s.v. *Naphthalene,* This dye, together with naphthalin rose and naphthalin scarlet, are known as varieties of Magdala red.

naphthaleneacetic (ˌnæfθəliːnəˈsiːtɪk), *a.* [f. NAPHTHALENE + ACETIC *a.*] ***naphthaleneacetic acid***: either of the two crystalline compounds, $C_{10}H_7CH_2COOH$, obtained by replacing one of the hydrogen atoms of naphthalene by an acetic acid group; *spec.* α-naphthaleneacetic acid, which has the action of an auxin and is used to stimulate the rooting of plant cuttings, to initiate flowering of the pineapple, to prevent premature drop of fruit, and to improve the colour of apples.

1917 *Chem. Abstr.* XI. 3876/2 (Index), Naphthalene-acetic acids. **1936** *Contrib. Boyce Thompson Inst.* VIII. 78 Treating cuttings or shoots of *Ilex, Taxus, Pachysandra, Hibiscus, Acer,* and *Chrysanthemum* with preparations of indoleacetic, indolepropionic, indolebutyric, or naphthaleneacetic acids induced earlier rooting, increased the number of roots, and roots emerged from a greater area of stem tissue as compared with control cuttings. **1942** *Science* 22 May 536/1 Low concentrations of α-naphthaleneacetic acid (the compound used most extensively) applied as foliage sprays induced formation of inflorescences in advance of the normal period, but high concentrations..delayed flowering far beyond that of the controls. **1968** F. C. STEWARD *Growth & Organization in Plants* viii. 394 The application of auxin during the dark period eliminates the photoperiodic induction due to the dark period in a short-day plant like cocklebur. Auxins, whether IAA or a synthetic substitute like naphthalene acetic acid..are all active in this respect.

naphthalic (næfˈθælɪk), *a. Chem.* [f. as NAPHTHAL-ENE + -IC.] Pertaining to, or derived from, naphthalene; esp. ***naphthalic acid*** = *phthalic acid*: see PHTHALIC *a.*

1838 T. THOMSON *Chem. Org. Bodies* 27 Naphthalic acid was discovered and described by M. Laurent. **1859** *Chamb. Jrnl.* XI. 211 An abominable naphthalic fluid, which is to blind and suffocate the enemy.

naph'thalidine. *Chem.* [f. as prec. + -ID + -INE^5.] = NAPHTHYLAMINE.

1848 FOWNES *Elem. Chem.* (ed. 2) 503 Naphthalidam, perhaps better called naphthalidine, forms numerous crystallizable salts. **1857** MILLER *Elem. Chem., Org.* 574 Each compound yields an azotised base; naphthalidine, or naphthylamine..being that furnished from nitro-naphthalin.

naphthalize (ˈnæfθəlaɪz), *v.* [f. as NAPHTHAL-ENE + -IZE.] *trans.* To mingle, saturate, or impregnate with naphtha. Hence **'naphthalized** *ppl. a.*, **'naphthalizing** *vbl. sb.*

1842 *Mech. Mag.* XXXVI. 392 Naphthalizing Coal Gas. **1844** *Illustr. Lond. News* 30 Nov. 346/1 The advantages of naphthalised gas. *c* **1865** LETHEBY in *Orr's Circ. Sci.* I. 107/2 The other constituents of coal-naphtha..are not so fit for the purpose of naphthalising.

So **naphthali'zation.**

c **1865** LETHEBY in *Orr's Circ. Sci.* I. 125/2 The intensity of the light may be brought up to any degree by the usual process of naphthalisation.

'naphthalol. *Chem.* [-OL.] (See quot. 1897.)

1891 in *Syd. Soc. Lex.* **1897** *Allbutt's Syst. Med.* III. 742, β Naphthol and its compound with salicylic acid, called naphthalol or betol.

naph'thamein(e. *Chem.* [Cf. *naphthylamine.*] Naphthaline violet; a coal-tar colour, in the form of a light amorphous powder, obtained from naphthylamine.

1891 in *Syd. Soc. Lex.*

naphthaquinone, var. NAPHTHOQUINONE.

†'naphthe. *Obs.* In 4 **napte,** 7 **napthe, naphte.** [Cf. F. *naphte.*] Naphtha.

1382 WYCLIF *Dan.* iii. 46 To tende the fourneis with napte, herdis of hemp, and pitche. **1621** BURTON *Anat. Mel.* III. ii. II. i, His eyes are like a balance.., his affection tinder or napthe itself. **1662** J. DAVIES tr. *Olearius' Voy. Ambass.* 237 In these Fire-works, the Persians make use of white Naphte, which is a kind of Petreolum.

naphthene (ˈnæfθiːn). *Chem.* [ad. F. *naphtène*: in sense a, named by Pelletier & Walter 1840, in *Jrnl. de Pharm.* XXVI. 561; in sense b, coined afresh by Markovnikov & Oglobine 1884, in *Ann. de Chim. et de Physique* II. 447; cf. NAPHTHA + -ENE.] **†a.** A substance formerly thought to represent a liquid hydrocarbon contained in naphtha (now regarded as a mixture of hydrocarbons). *Obs.*

1849 CRAIG s.v. *Naphtha,* Native naphtha is composed of three liquids, namely—naphtha.., naphthene.., and naptholе [*sic*]. **1854** THOMSON *Cycl. Chem.* 378 Naphthene. $C_{16}H_{16}$. That portion of mineral naphtha which comes over second in distillation. **1857** MILLER *Elem. Chem., Org.* 581.

b. Any of a class of saturated cyclic hydrocarbons (including cyclopentane and cyclohexane) that are present in or obtained from petroleum.

1884 *Jrnl. Chem. Soc.* XLVI. 1276 Hydrocarbons of the C_nH_{2n} series, called by the authors naphthenes, constitute the principal part of Caucasian petroleum. **1921** J. S. CHAMBERLAIN *Textbk. Org. Chem.* 38 The saturated cyclic hydrocarbons known as naphthenes are characteristic of Russian (Baku) petroleum and are also found in that from Galicia. **1951** C. R. NOLLER *Chem. Org. Compounds* xxxix. 759 The saturated alicyclic hydrocarbons frequently are called cycloparaffins or cyclanes although petroleum technologists usually call them naphthenes because cyclopentane..and cyclohexane..and their homologs have been isolated from the naphtha fraction of petroleum. **1964** N. G. CLARK *Mod. Org. Chem.* v. 78 The naphthenes (a term used in the petroleum industry for the cyclic paraffins) are mainly cyclopentane and cyclohexane, and their simple derivatives.

naphthenic (næfˈθiːnɪk), *a. Chem.* [ad. F. *naphténique* (Markovnikov & Oglobine 1884, in *Ann. de Chim. et de Physique* II. 476), f. *naphtène* NAPHTHENE: see -IC.] **1.** ***naphthenic acid***: any of the carboxylic acids obtained in the refining of petroleum, esp. one derived from an alicyclic compound (as cyclohexane or cyclopentane); also, an unspecified mixture of such acids.

1894 *Jrnl. Chem. Soc.* LXVI. I. 532 The methyl salts of the lower natural naphthenic acids were prepared and fractionated with a view to isolate the methyl salt of heptanaphthenic acid (hexahydrobenzoic acid). **1932** *Jrnl. Amer. Chem. Soc.* LIV. 240 We observed that naphthenic acids are formed when linoleic acid is cracked under pressure. **1942** *Chem. Rev.* XXX. 100 The mixture of acids now known as naphthenic acid. **1946** S. B. ELLIOTT *Alkaline-Earth & Heavy-Metal Soaps* ii. 33 Naphthenic acids..are the raw materials from which some of the most important soaps are manufactured. **1957** VAN DER HAVE & VERVER *Petroleum* xiii. 383 The free naphthenic acids also find certain applications, for instance as wetting agents for the pigments used in printing inks and paints. **1966** *McGraw-Hill Encycl. Chem. Technol.* X. 47/2 Naphthenic acid production is about 16,000,000 lb annually.

2. Of, pertaining to, or containing naphthenes.

1931 *Engineering* 2 Jan. 1/2 Cyclohexane, a hydrocarbon of the naphthenic series. **1969** *Sci. Jrnl.* Nov. 32/2 The basic structure of bitumen is that of clusters of naphthenic and aromatic rings... It is called a naphthenic crude oil. **1974** *Sci. Amer.* Dec. 7 (Advt.), Up to this point, the best traction drive lubricants were naphthenic oils.

Hence **'naphthenate,** any of the salts of a naphthenic acid, some of which are used as paint driers, as fungicides, and in lubricants.

1899 *Jrnl. Chem. Soc.* LXXVI. I. 423 (*heading*) Properties of naphthenates and their qualitative distinction from salts of fatty acids. **1924** *Chem. Abstr.* XVIII. 2688 Al naphthenate forms a transparent, colorless, and porous mass which can be powdered; it has a water-proofing action. **1942** *Chem. Rev.* XXX. 103 In the case of castor machine oils, where increased..viscosity..is desired, various naphthenates have been used. **1960** E. L. DELMAR-MORGAN *Cruising Yacht Equipment & Navigation* xiii. 158 It is usually possible to see when power kerosene is deteriorating, by the fact that it becomes bright green in colour, as a result of the formation of copper naphthenate formed by the interaction of the fuel and the metal of a copper or brass tank. **1973** *Biol. Abstr.* LV. 6965/2 Potassium naphthenate significantly increased the ascorbic acid content of green pods of bush bean plants.

naphthol (ˈnæfθɒl). *Chem.* [f. NAPHTH-A + -OL.] One of two phenols of naphthalene, distinguished as α (*or* alpha) naphthol and β (*or* beta) naphthol; the latter is employed in the cure of skin-diseases and for other medical purposes. Also *attrib.*

1849 [see NAPHTHENE]. **1857** MILLER *Elem. Chem., Org.* 581. **1869** ROSCOE *Elem. Chem.* 422 On heating the aqueous solution of this body, a substance called naphthol, analogous to phenol is formed. **1881** *Athenæum* 10 Dec. 782/3 The action of cold sulphuric acid on β naphthol. **1899** *Allbutt's Syst. Med.* VIII. 611 A slight friction..with a 5 per cent naphthol ointment.

naphthoquinone (næfθəʊ'kwɪnəʊn). *Chem.* Also **naphtha-**. [f. NAPHTH(ALENE + -O + QUINONE.] Each of the six compounds, $C_{10}H_6O_2$, obtained (theoretically) by replacing two of the ≥ CH groups of naphthalene by carbonyl groups, *spec.* 1,4- (or α-)-naphthoquinone, a volatile yellow solid whose molecule forms part of the structure of vitamin K.

1870 *Jrnl. Chem. Soc.* XXIII. 446/2 (Index), Naphthoquinones. **1914** H. T. CLARKE *Introd. Study Org. Chem.* xxxiv. 417 The *ortho* quinone, β-naphthaquinone,..is a red crystalline solid, which decomposes at 115–120°. **1942** *Ann. Reg. 1941* 344 The four forms of vitamin K proved to be naphthoquinone derivatives. **1951** I. L. FINAR *Org. Chem.* I. xxix. 593 Theoretically, six naphthaquinones are possible... Only three are known, the 1:2-, 1:4- and 2:6-, but it appears that derivatives of 2:3-naphthaquinone have been prepared. **1966** *McGraw-Hill Encycl. Sci. & Technol.* XI. 194/2 The naphthoquinones are prepared by oxidation of the corresponding aminonaphthols.

'naphthous, *a.* [f. NAPHTH-A + -OUS.] Of the nature of naphtha.

a **1883** CHRISTISON *Life* (1885) I. 395 A naphthous fluid, which Gregory afterwards found to present a great resemblance to native naphtha. **1885** *Harper's Mag.* Feb. 494/2 Naphthous or petroleum mixtures.

'naphthyl. *Chem.* [f. NAPHTH-A + -YL.] The monatomic radical of naphthylamine. Also *Comb.*

1866 WATTS *Dict. Chem.* **1887** *Brit. Med. Jrnl.* 9 Apr. 800/1 Naphthyl-sulphite of soda is found in the urine of rabbits to which naphthalene has been administered.

naph'thylamine. *Chem.* Also -in. [f. as prec. + AMINE.] A crystalline substance produced by the action of ammonium sulphide, or acetic acid, on an alcoholic solution of nitronaphthaline.

1857 [see NAPHTHALIDINE]. **1863** FOWNES *Chem.* (ed. 9) 643 Naphthylamine forms numerous crystallizable salts. **1884** *Athenæum* 26 Mar. 433/1 Some sulphanilic acid with some hydrochlorate of naphthylamin [is] added.

naphthylic (næf'θɪlɪk), *a. Chem.* [f. as prec. + -IC.] Of or containing naphthyl, as in ***naphthylic alcohol*** = NAPHTHOL.

1883 *Times* 9 Mar., The two isomeric modifications of naphthylic alcohol known as alpha naphthol and beta naphthol.

'napier. *rare.* [f. NAP-ERY + -IER: cf. OF. *napier* (Godef.).] = NAPERER.

1880 BURTON *Reign Q. Anne* I. i. 39 The office of napier being attached to a manor held in grand sergeantry by a noble house.

Napierian (neɪ'pɪərɪən), *a.* Also **Naperian**. [f. the name of John *Napier* (see next) + -IAN.] Invented by Napier (see LOGARITHM).

1816 tr. *Lacroix's Diff. & Int. Calculus* 26 A system of logarithms, which we shall call Naperian, from the name of Naper their inventor. *c* **1865** *Orr's Circ. Sci.* I. 517/1 This number *e*..is called the base of the Napierian Logarithms.

Napier's bones. Also **Nepier's**, **Naper's**. [See def.] Narrow slips of bone, ivory, wood, or other material, divided into compartments marked with certain digits, and used to facilitate the operations of multiplication and division according to a method invented by John Napier of Merchiston (1550–1617). Also occas. called ***Napier's rods***.

The method was described by Napier in his book *Rabdologiæ seu Numerationis per Virgulas libri duo* (1615).

a **1658** CLEVELAND *On Ugly Woman* 15 Who would suppose..That crookt *et-cætera's* were Wrinkles, and Five Napiers Bones glew'd to a Wrist, an Hand. **1664** BUTLER *Hud.* II. iii. 1095 A moon-dial, with Napier's bones, And sev'ral constellation stones. **1678** PHILLIPS, *Nepiers Bones* or *Rods.* **1727–38** CHAMBERS *Cycl.* s.v. *Neper's.* **1834** *Edin. Rev.* LIX. 320 The method of calculation invented by Baron Napier,..since called Napier's bones. **1866** *Chambers's Encycl.* VI. 662/2 The contemporaneous invention of logarithms..caused Napier's bones to be overlooked, and they are now scarcely ever used.

napi'folious, *a. rare*$^{-0}$. [f. L. *nāpus* turnip + *folium* leaf.] 'Having leaves like the turnip; turnip-leaved'.

1856 MAYNE *Expos. Lex.*

napiform ('neɪpɪfɔːm), *a.* [f. L. *nāpus* turnip + -FORM.] Having the form, shape, or appearance of a turnip; esp. *Bot.* of roots.

1846–50 A. WOOD *Class-bk. Bot.* 64 The napiform (turnip-shaped) root is another variety of the fusiform. **1882** *Jrnl. Microsc. Sci.* Jan. 8 The *Teleutospore* is a very remarkable body..; when fully formed it is napiform. **1891** *Syd. Soc. Lex.*, Napiform cancer.

naping, *vbl. sb.*: see NAPE *v.*[1]

napkin ('næpkɪn), *sb.* Also 5–6 **napkyn**, 5 **namp-**, **nap(p)ekyn**, 6–7 **napking**, 9 *Sc.* **naipkin**; 6 *Sc.* **neap-**, **neipkyn**, 9 **neepkin**. [app. f. F. *nappe* NAPE *sb.*[2] + -KIN. There appears to be no trace of the form in MDu. or Flemish.]

1. a. A square piece of linen, used at meals to wipe the fingers or lips and to protect one's garments, or to serve certain dishes on; a table-napkin, serviette.

to take sheet and napkin, to sleep and eat (with one). ***to stick a napkin under one's chin***, to partake of a meal.

1420 *Inventory* in *Lincoln Chapter Acc. Bk.* A. 2. 30. f. 69, 2 nappekynnes 20d. *c* **1440** *Promp. Parv.* 351/2 Napet, or napekyn, *napella. a* **1483** *Liber Niger* in *Househ. Ord.* (1790) 83 All the basyns, ewears, cuppes & napkins. **1513** *Bk. Keruynge* in *Babees Bk.* (1868) 155 Laye your knyues, & set your brede,..your spones, and your napkyns fayre folden besyde your brede. **1555** WATREMAN *Fardle Facions* II. x. 215 Thei [Tartars] neither vse..table clothe ne napkin. **1617** MORYSON *Itin.* III. 116 the Hostesse..is tied to dresse his meate and give him napkins with like necessaries. **1653** MEWE in Hartlib *Common-w. Bees* (1655) 42 If you please to take a sheet and napkin with me for some time, we shall discourse of this. **1760** FOOTE *Minor* I. Wks. 1799 I. 237 There is not a buck or a turtle devoured within the bills of mortality, but there I may, if I please, stick a napkin under my chin. **1792** A. YOUNG *Trav. France* 277 The idea of dining without a napkin seems ridiculous to a Frenchman. **1841** LANE *Arab. Nts.* I. 123 Each person who is to partake of the repast receives a napkin. **1881** BESANT & RICE *Chapl. of Fleet* I. 149 These she laid on a plate, with bread and salt, and put the whole upon a napkin.

b. A similar piece of linen or other cloth used for other purposes; a small towel.

1687 A. LOVELL tr. *Thevenot's Trav.* I. 31 They spread you out a large napkin..upon the said benches, where you sit down. **1810** CLARKE *Trav. Russia* (1839) 102/1 They..present him with a basin, water, and a clean napkin, to wash his hands. **1875** JOWETT *Plato* (ed. 2) III. 656 Like a napkin, always..at hand to clean the mirror.

c. A rectangular piece of towelling or absorbent material used as a baby's undergarment by folding, drawing up between the legs, and fastening at the waist.

1845 MRS. GASKELL *Let.* (1966) 824 Meta is so neat & so knowing, only, handles wet napkins very gingerly. **1861** MRS. BEETON *Bk. Househ. Managem.* 1021 Soiled baby's napkins should be rolled up and put into a pan, when they should be washed out every morning. **1961** *Brit. Med. Dict.* 1212/1 The skin..is the more easily affected by the free ammonia liberated through the interaction of acid urine and badly washed napkins. **1974** *Janet Frazer Catal.* Spring & Summer 292/2 Fully-bleached terry napkins. Soft and absorbent... Size 24" × 24"..£3·35 (dozen).

2. a. A (pocket-)handkerchief. Now only *Sc.* and *north. dial.*

1530 PALSGR. 247/2 Napkyn for the nose, *movchover.* **1575** LANEHAM *Let.* (1871) 38 Out of hiz bozome drawne foorth a lappet of his napkin, edged with a blu lace. **1604** SHAKS. *Oth.* III. iii. 290, I am glad I haue found this Napkin: This was her first remembrance from the Moore. **1674** RAY *N.C. Words* 34 *Napkin*, a Pocket Hand-Kerchief, so called about Sheffield in Yorkshire. **1755** FORBES *Ajax, Shop Bill* 40 Napkins, as guid's in a' the land, to dight your nib. **1822** GALT *Sir A. Wylie* xiii, A ne'er-do-weel pocket-picker whuppet the napkin out of my pouch. **1884** D. GRANT *Lays* 87 She startit, wi' her napkin Pressed to lovely nose an 'een.

fig. **1648** GAGE *West Ind.* 1 What judicious eye, that will not be blinded with the napkin of ignorance [etc.].

Phr. **1570** FOXE *A. & M.* (ed. 2) 951/2 It maye well bee a Napkin for my Nose, but I will neuer be ashamed of it.

b. Used to render Gr. σουδάριον (L. *sūdārium*).

1526 TINDALE *Luke* xix. 20 Beholde here thy pounde, which I have kepte in a napkyn. —*John* xi. 44 His face was bounde with a napkyn. *Ibid.* xx. 7.

c. Hence in phrases ***to hide, lay up, wrap up***, etc. ***in a napkin***, in allusion to Luke xix. 20.

1598 R. C. *Household Gov.* Ep. Ded. 2 Or to hide my tallent in a napking. **1698** FRYER *Acc. E. India & P.* 112 This humour of laying up their Talent in a Napkin. **1768–74** TUCKER *Lt. Nat.* (1834) II. 101 We had best..wrap up our bibles as well as our talent of reason in a napkin. **1856** EMERSON *Eng. Traits, Wealth* Wks. (Bohn) II. 70 The headlong bias to utility will let no talent lie in a napkin. **1872** MORLEY *Voltaire* (1886) 7 He never counted truth a treasure to be discreetly hidden in a napkin.

3. *Sc.* A kerchief or neckerchief.

1787 BEATTIE *Scoticisms* 60 She had a red silk napkin on her head. **1845** STILL *Cottar's Sunday* 22 His napkin white she ties wi' cantie care.

4. *attrib.* and *Comb.*, as **†napkin-cap**, a small linen cap (*obs.*); **napkin-cheese**, cheese made by straining cream through a bag made of a napkin; **†napkin nook**, the corner of a handkerchief (*obs.*); **napkin-ring**, a ring placed on a table-napkin when rolled up; **nakpin-snatching** (see quot. 1823).

1583 *Leg. Bp. St. Androis* 819 Ten pundis stirling furth he tuike, And knit it in a neapkyn nucke. **1686** in *Narragansett Hist. Reg.* III. (1884–5) 105, 18 Napkins & 9 Napkin Rings. **1746** H. WALPOLE *Lett.* (1846) II. 154 He then took off his bag, coat, and waistcoat,..and after some trouble, put on a napkin-cap. **1823** EGAN *Grose's Dict. Vulg. Tongue*, *Napkin-snatching* or Fogle-hunting. Sneaking pocket-handkerchiefs. **1839** *Workwoman's Guide* 275 Checked Napkin Rings. **1865** *Pall Mall Gaz.* 22 May 4 Pastry, preserves, and napkincheeses of their own making. **1972** *Country Life* 21 Dec. 1755 This woven design, using sterling silver ribbons interwoven..is very attractive. There are napkin rings (ideal for a wedding present)... The napkin ring costs £20.

†'napkin, *v. Obs.* [f. prec. 2 c.] *trans.* To wrap *up* or hide in or as in a napkin.

1621 SANDERSON *Serm.* I. 191 Let every man beware of napkining up the talent, which was delivered him to trade withal. **1657** OWEN *Communion Father*, etc. II. x. Wks. 1851 II. 215 When others napkin their talents, as having to do with an austere master. *a* **1680** CHARNOCK *Attrib. God* (1834) II. 695 To napkin up a gift he hath bestowed..is to apply it to a wrong use.

napkined ('næpkɪnd), *ppl. a.* [f. NAPKIN *sb.* and *v.*] Wrapped up in, or covered with, a napkin; provided with, or served on, a napkin, etc. Also *transf.*

1756 RICHARDSON *Corr.* (1804) II. 92 The geniusses,..who studiously in many inexplicable plaits, wrap up their napkin'd talents. **1799** in *Spirit Pub. Jrnls.* III. 103 Or busy waiter ply his napkin'd care. **1822** *Blackw. Mag.* XI. 161 And napkin'd Aldermen May grudge the goût with which the bits descend. **1842** J. AITON *Domest. Econ.* (1857) 94 Who really enjoys the hot peppered soup, the cold napkined fish..? **1894** BLACKMORE *Perlycross* 155 Mrs. Gilham appearing with a napkin'd tray.

'napkining. Now *rare* or *Obs.* [f. NAPKIN *sb.* + -ING[1].] Material for napkins.

1640 in Entick *Lond.* (1767) II. 167 Damask for towelling and napkenning. **1696** J. F. *Merchant's Wareho.* 10 If you agree for the Napkenning, the Tabling is three times the bredth, and three times the price. **1714** *French Book Rates* 190 The Pieces of Napkining shall contain 4 Dozen each. **1812** J. SMYTH *Pract. of Customs* (1821) 131 Diaper Towelling and Napkining of the manufacture of Silesia.

naple, obs. form of APPLE *sb.*

naple, variant of NAVEL *sb. Obs.*

Naples ('neɪp(ə)lz). The name of a city in Southern Italy, used to designate various things in some way connected or associated with it.

1. †a. As an epithet of certain diseases: (see NEAPOLITAN *a.*). *Obs.*

1507 *Extr. Aberd. Reg.* (1844) I. 437 Item, that diligent inquisitioun be takin of ale infect personis with this strange seiknes of Nappillis. **1596** BARROUGH *Meth. Physick* (ed. 3) 361 The frenchmen at that siege got the buttons of Naples (as we terme them) which doth much annoy them at this day. **1656** *Roxb. Ball.* (1899) IX. c*, A Brewer may gett a Naples face.

b. ***fustian of Naples***: see FUSTIAN A. 1 c.

c. ***Naples biscuit*** or ***cake***. ? *Obs.*

1699 EVELYN *Acetaria* (1729) 53 Make them into Cakes or Loaves cut long-wise, in shape of Naples-Biscuit. **1760–72** H. BROOKE *Fool of Qual.* (1809) I. 131, I broke some Naples biscuit into a cup. *Ibid.* II. 6 He ordered up a bottle of sack and some Naples cakes. **1769** MRS. RAFFALD *Eng. Housekpr.* (1778) 261 A nutmeg and two Naples biscuits.

d. ***Star of Naples***, the Star of Bethlehem. ***Naples radish*** (see quot.). ***Naples spider***, the Tarantula.

1760 J. LEE *Introd. Bot.* App. 320 Naples, Star of, *Ornithogalum.* **1763** MILLS *Pract. Husb.* IV. 38 The Naples radish, which has a very white, round, small, and sweet root. **1840** HOOD *Kilmansegg, Birth* xvii, Even some old ones appear'd to have had A bite from the Naples Spider.

2. Naples yellow, a yellow pigment in the form of a fine powder, prepared from antimony, and originally manufactured at Naples; also, the colour produced by this.

1738 tr. *Lairesse & Fritsch's Art Painting* 159 With purple or Violet agrees Naples-yellow. **1774** in Willis & Clark *Cambr.* (1886) II. 42 To wash the plain parts of the Cieling and Walls in the Chapel a Naples yellow. **1801** *Encycl. Brit.* Suppl. II. 292/2 About the nature of the substance called Naples yellow there has been much diversity of opinion. **1839** T. H. FIELDING *Painting in Oil & Water Col.* 114 Naples Yellow is in great use at the present day.

napless ('næplɪs), *a.* [f. NAP *sb.*[3] + -LESS.] Having no nap, worn, thread-bare.

1596 NASHE *Saffron Walden* T 2 b, Those two [authors] he hath wrought reasonably vpon, hauing worne the first..napless. **1607** SHAKS. *Cor.* II. i. 250 Neuer would he Appear i' th' Market place, nor on him put The Naples Vesture of Humilitie. *a* **1763** SHENSTONE *Econ.* iii. Wks. 1764 I. 304 His only coat,..napless, as an heath..by fleecy myriads graz'd. **1812** COLMAN *Br. Grins, Two Parsons* lxxx, Brushed against his sleeve his napless hat. **1841** J. T. HEWLETT *Parish Clerk* II. 268 An old black coat, napless, not from frequent brushing, but continual wear.

Hence **'naplessness**.

1830 MRS. C. READE *Brown Hand* I. i. 41 She looks down at the carpet—not to sigh over its naplessness.

Napoleon (nə'pəʊlɪən). Also with lower-case initial. [a. F. *napoléon*, f. the Christian name of certain Emperors of the French, esp. *Napoleon I* (1769–1821).]

1. A gold coin issued by Napoleon I, of the value of twenty francs; a twenty-franc piece. ***double napoleon***, a forty-franc piece.

1814 SHELLEY in Dowden *Life* (1886) I. 445, I sold my watch, chain, etc., which brought eight napoleons, five francs. **1815** *Ann. Reg., Chron.* 104 The French generals and children gave him a double Napoleon each. **1823** BYRON *Juan* XV. vii, Bright as a new Napoleon from its mintage. **1887** RUSKIN *Præterita* II. 251 The little gems of picture cost a napoleon each.

2. A particular make of long boot. Also *attrib.*

1860 *All Year Round* No. 64. 331 A very excellent dress for mounted soldiers, is the ordinary hunting 'Napoleon' boot, pulled over trousers [etc.]. **1860** WHYTE MELVILLE *Mkt. Harb.* (1861) 58 They..caused one of his intimate friends who particularly piqued himself on 'boots', to..relapse into 'Napoleons' in disgust.

3. *U.S.* A particular kind of cannon.

1863 *Life Stonewall Jackson* 120 Pelham was sent forward with two guns, a Blakely and a Napoleon. **1880** *Harper's Mag.* May 917/1 The artillery is almost entirely the old brass Napoleon. **1897** *Outing* XXX. 80/1 These gun companies were each supplied with one 12-pounder Napoleon gun and one Gatling gun.

4. a. A card-game. See NAP *sb.*^{5} 2 a.

1876 'CAPT. CRAWLEY' *Card Player's Man.* 242 If..he declare five..he is said to go the Napoleon, whether he win or lose. **1887** *All Year Round* 5 Feb. 68 Euchre, finding its way back to Paris, was simplified..into Napoleon.

b. = NAP *sb.*^{5} 2 c.

1895 *Starting Price* 23 Mar. 1/1 With runious 'all day wires' and extortionately priced 'Napoleons' we will have nothing to do.

5. One resembling Napoleon I, esp. in having gained supremacy in his own sphere through ruthless ambition. Also *transf.*

1821 SHELLEY *Let.* 25 Sept. (1964) II. 353 He was a little Napoleon..with a dukedom instead of an empire for his theatre. **1866** J. BLACKWOOD *Let.* 2 Aug. in Geo. Eliot *Lett.* (1956) IV. 293 He is a Napoleon in his Trade is Truefitt. **1879** R. L. STEVENSON *Trav. with Donkey* 144, I had travelled hitherto through a dull district, and in the track of nothing more notable than the child-eating Beast of *Gévaudan*, the *Napoleon Buonaparte* of wolves. **1894** A. CONAN DOYLE *Mem. Sherlock Holmes* 260 He is the Napoleon of crime, Watson. He is the organizer of half that is evil and of nearly all that is undetected in this great city. He is a genius, a philosopher, an abstract thinker. **1907** I. ZANGWILL *Ghetto Comedies* 353 This, then, was the notorious multi-millionaire, 'the Napoleon in dollars'. **1932** Q. D. LEAVIS *Fiction & Reading Public* 312 Northcliffe, being the Napoleon of the Press, naturally disliked having to play second fiddle to the advertiser. **1939** T. S. ELIOT *Old Possum's Pract. Cats* 35 The Cat who all the time Just controls their operations: the Napoleon of Crime! **1969** *N.Y. Rev. Bks.* 18 Dec. 33/2 We had Napoleons of finance, Napoleons of industry, Napoleons of the betting ring. **1973** 'I. DRUMMOND' *Jaws of Watchdog* vi. 79 'Royston,' said Colly. 'What kind of a name is that for a Napoleon of crime?' **1975** *Times* 2 June 10 A Time Profile—General Vo Nguyen Giap—Communist Napoleon who conquered South Vietnam.

6. A type of rich cake made from layers of puff pastry filled with cream, custard, or jam. Also *attrib.*

1892 *Encycl. Pract. Cookery* I. 246/1 *Napoleon Cake.* Lay in a Napoleon-cake pan..a layer of puff paste, spread over that a layer of pastry cream, cover with puff paste, glaze the top with sugar, and bake. **1896** E. TURNER *Little Larrikin* xxviii. 342 In the centre were five white-iced Napoleons, ornamented with devices cut from silver tea-paper, this being the nearest the funds would stretch to wedding-cake. **1956** E. STARKIE *Diary* Sept. in J. Richardson *Enid Starkie* (1973) xxviii. 204 There was..every kind of cake, biscuit and sweet—the most succulent cake was called Napoleon! **1961** J. HELLER *Catch-22* (1962) xxiv. 249 Prune and cheese Danish from Copenhagen, éclairs, cream puffs, Napoleons and *petits fours* from Paris, Reims and Grenoble, [etc.]. **1968** A. BINKLEY *What shall I Cry?* 139 'You got more of those cakes?'.. Lenni handed him a box in which one napoleon remained. **1969** W. S. KUNICZAK *Sempinski Affair* (1970) vii. 69, I..felt my resolve melting like the Napoleon pastries on my plate. **1975** C. NESBITT *Little Love & Good Company* xvi. 201 A plate of luscious Napoleons oozing thick whipped-cream.

7. Used *attrib.* and *absol.* of brandy of supposed great age or special merit.

1930 J. DOS PASSOS *42nd Parallel* II. 207 They were sitting over Napoleon brandy in big bowlshaped glasses and cigars. **1967** C. CHURCHILL *World of Wines* x. 208 'Napoleon Brandy' ranks high among some of the more transparent promotional myths of the industry. **1967** A. LICHINE *Encycl. Wines* 214/2 The worst deception in Cognac brandies is the fraud and fakery connected with alleged 'Napoleon' brandy—but a distinction must be made between brandies pretending to derive from Napoleon's time, and the Napoleon style. **1968** C. FORSYTE *Murder with Minarets* vii. 42 They sat over their Napoleon after dinner. **1968** T. PARKER *People of Streets* 48 Could I have a glass of Napoleon brandy please? **1975** D. BEATY *Electric Train* 147 Liqueurs—two Napoleon brandies. Warm on her stomach.

Hence also **Napole'onic** *a.*, pertaining or relating to, connected with, characteristic of, Napoleon; **Napole'onically** *adv.*, after the manner of Napoleon; **Na'poleonism**, (*a*) the methods of government practised by Napoleon; *spec.* the assumption of absolute control over subject peoples or countries; (*b*) attachment to the policy or dynasty of the Napoleons; (*c*) conduct or behaviour resembling that of Napoleon; **Na'poleonist**, *sb.* an adherent of Napoleon or the Napoleonic dynasty; *a.* pertaining or attached to Napoleon; **Napoleo'nistic** *a.*, Napoleonic; **Na'poleonize** *v.*, to govern in the style of Napoleon.

1863 DICEY *Federal St.* II. 23 With that affectation of the *Napoleonic style he was so partial to. **1886** SWINBURNE *Misc.* 122 Tyrants of a type devoid even of Napoleonic pretention to glory. **1865** SALA in *Reader* 337/2 A moustache quite *Napoleonically spiked. **1892** *National Observer* 10 Dec. 80/2 His methods were Napoleonically simple. **1831** ARNOLD *Let.* in Stanley *Life* (1844) I. 266 To strangle in the birth the first symptoms of *Napoleonism. **1865** *Sat. Rev.* 14 Jan. 35/2 Napoleonism will be..at least an intermittent fever with the French. **1966** *New Statesman* 28 Oct. 828/1 The military life had the advantage of absorbing what could easily have been insidious at this stage: the premature dream of glory, the stupefying effects of youthful Napoleonism. **1969** *Sunday Times* 6 Apr. 27 Personal incompatibility.. and the traditional Latin American leader's custom of renouncing ultimate power as soon as he had won it (for fear of accusations of 'Napoleonism'), were less significant than the internal political and social divisions. **1970** *Guardian Weekly* 6 June 2 Without our nation standing up against Russia's modern day mad dog Napoleonism Europe itself would not remain independent through the 1970s. **1842** BRANDE *Dict. Sci.*, etc. 805/2 The unparalleled flatteries of the *Napoleonists. **1861** M. ARNOLD *Educ. France* 36 Disliked as a Napoleonist creation by the Bourbons. **1877** M. M. GRANT *Sun Maid* ii, His features were of the type *Napoleonistic. **1822** *Examiner* 355/1 France must again be *Napoleonized, that is to say, made once more essentially military. **1877** OWEN *Wellesley's Desp.* p. xxii, The complex ..antagonism of England and revolutionary and Napoleonized France.

na'poleonite. *Min.* [f. as NAPOLEON + -ITE^1.] A variety of feldspar, orthoclase.

1836 T. THOMSON *Min., Geol.* etc. I. 291 Felspar..: moonstone, napoleonite, necronite. **1866** WATTS *Dict. Chem.* IV.

napoo (nɑːˈpuː), *int.*, *a.*, and *v. colloq.* Also **na poo, napooh.** [Corruption of F. (*il n'y e*)*n a plus* there is no more.] **a.** *int.* Finished; gone; done for. **b.** *adj.* Finished; good for nothing; dead. **c.** *v. trans.* To finish, kill, or destroy.

1915 'I. HAY' *First Hundred Thousand* 302 You say 'Na pooh!' when you push your plate away after dinner... 'Poor Bill got na-poohed by a rifle-grenade yesterday.' **1917** W. J. LOCKE *Red Planet* xvi. 194 Instinctively I stretched out my hand. He laughed. 'Napoo. You must take it as gripped.' **1919** J. B. MORTON *Barber of Putney* xv. 253 'Can't do nothing,' said Curly, ''e's napoo.' *Ibid.* xviii. 301 Even if they themselves were na-pooed, they'd hate to think of the lousy Boche living in their home. **1925** N. VENNER *Imperfect Impostor* i. 6 If you haven't got a job to do, you're a washout. You might as well be napood right off. **1927** W. DEEPING *Kitty* xvi. 205 A man's phrase—a war-phrase—seemed to trickle into his head. Everything was na poo, a wash-out. His marriage—. **1936** F. CLUNE *Roaming round Darling* vi. 52 All the boys about here..have looked for money in the gullies, and the only thing they ever come across was a rum-keg—empty—'*Napoo*', like the Diggers used to say! **1943** J. B. PRIESTLEY *Daylight on Saturday* xxix. 228 You're as good as dead—just waitin' to stiffen. Fini—napoo! **1973** L. MEYNELL *Thirteen Trumpeters* v. 81 Prudence..fell down dead in the croupier's bag. Fini. Napoo.

nappa, var. NAPA.

nappe (næp). [a. F. *nappe* table-cloth, NAPE *sb.*^{2}] **1.** *Hydraulics.* A sheet of water falling over a weir or similar surface.

1892 MARICHAL & TRANTWINE tr. Bazin in *Proc. Engineers' Club Philadelphia* IX. 231 We now proceed to study the form of the sheet of water passing over the weir. [*translator's footnote*] For want of a convenient English equivalent, we shall designate this sheet by its very appropriate French name, the *nappe*, a name applied primarily to a table-cloth, the form of which..is well imitated by the sheet of water passing over the weir. *Ibid.* [*text*], The upper surface of the nappe has already been studied by certain experimenters. **1945** W. P. CREAGER et al. *Engin. for Dams* II. xi. 357 If the area below the lower nappe is filled with masonry, the shape of the sheet and the discharge will not be changed appreciably. **1966** F. M. HENDERSON *Open Channel Flow* vi. 177 If the nappe is contained within parallel walls downstream of the weir, it may well enclose the air between itself, walls, and floor.

2. *Geol.* A sheet of rock which has moved sideways over neighbouring strata, usu. as a result of overthrusting.

Earlier used in F. as *nappe de recouvrement* sheet of overlaying (e.g. *Bull. Soc. vaudoise des Sci. nat.* (1893) XXIX. 252).

1922 *Q. Jrnl. Geol. Soc.* LXXVIII. 87 In deciding upon the basal limit to be assigned to any particular nappe, one generally chooses some prominent thrustplane; failing this, one is entitled to select the axial plane of some recumbent anticline or syncline, according to local convenience. **1932** [see ALLOCHTHONOUS *a.*]. **1944** A. HOLMES *Princ. Physical Geol.* vi. 81 Tear faults are commonly developed in nappes, where they naturally arise if one part of a nappe has been driven forward further than the adjoining parts. **1970** LINTON & MOSELEY in *Cambr. Anc. Hist.* (ed. 3) I. i. i. 15 The Gulf of Oman, in which a series of 'nappes' or horizontally displaced rock sheets have been successively driven from north-east to south-west.

nappe, obs. form of NAP.

napped (næpt), *ppl. a.* Also 5 **noppyd**, 7 **nap'd, napp'd**, 7, 9 **napt.** [f. NAP *v.*^{2} Cf. Da. *noppet*, Norw. *nappad.*] Of cloth: Having a nap.

c **1440** *Promp. Parv.* 358/1 Noppyd, *villosus.* **1676** *Lond. Gaz.* No. 1137/4 One Sute of gray cloaths, the Coat nap'd. **1760–72** H. BROOKE *Fool of Qual.* (1809) II. 34 He..was dressed in a plain napped coat. **1848** BUCKLEY *Iliad* 295 A chest filled with garments, and napped tapestry.

transf. **1869** BLACKMORE *Lorna D.* (1891) 230 A branching stick, napped with moss all around the sides.

nappekyn, obs. form of NAPKIN *sb.*

napper^1 (ˈnæpə(r)). *rare.* [f. NAP *v.*^{1} + -ER^1.] One who naps or takes a nap.

c **1400** *Rowland & O.* 288 Cheualrye es fro hym gone, A nolde nappere als he were. **1728–31** *Lett. fr. Fog's Jrnl.* (1732) II. 103 These are all very moderate Nappers, compared to the famous Seven Sleepers.

napper^2 (ˈnæpə(r)). *rare.* [f. NAP *v.*^{2} + -ER^1.] One who raises the nap on cloth; a machine for this purpose.

1769 *Dubl. Mercury* 16 Sept. 2/2 The several cotteners and nappers in the city of Dublin. **1884** KNIGHT *Dict. Mech.* Suppl. 627/1 *Napper*, a machine for cleaning, napping, and surfacing hosiery goods.

†**ˈnapper**^{3}. *Obs. slang.* [f. NAP *v.*^{3} + -ER^1.] (See quots.)

1653 (*title*) A total Rout of a Pack of Knaves and Drabs, intituled..Nappers, Mobs and Spanners. *a* **1700** B. E. *Dict. Cant. Crew*, *Napper*, a Cheat, or Thief.

napper^4 (ˈnæpə(r)). *dial.* and *slang.* [Of obscure formation.] The head.

1785 GROSE *Dict. Vulgar T.* **1800** in *Spirit Pub. Jrnls.* IV. 274 By my soul your napper shall be broke. **1821** *Sporting Mag.* VIII. 233 He..run his napper against a stone wall. **1899** *Speaker* 9 Dec. 253/2 Wooly went off his napper. **1916** 'TAFFRAIL' *Pincher Martin* xii. 232 Yer kin be drownded in yer barth, or git a chimney-pot dropped on yer napper in a gale o' wind. **1936** F. CLUNE *Roaming round Darling* ix. 78 Half a score of Dubboites..waited with suspense and open mouths for a brick to fall back and crack the thrower on the napper. **1936** W. LAWSON *When Cobb & Co. was King* v. 81 Fell on his napper on a log. **1947** [see CONK *sb.*^{1} c]. **1959** G. M. WILSON *Shadows on Landing* vii. 78 If anyone ever asked for an orangeade bottle on his napper, Fruity did.

nappern, napperone, obs. or dial. ff. APRON.

nappie: see NAPPY *sb.* and *a.*

nappill, -yll, obs. forms of APPLE *sb.*

ˈnappiness. *rare*$^{-0}$. [f. NAPPY *a.*^{1} + -NESS.] The quality of being nappy; shagginess.

1611 COTGR., *Veleure*, shag, hairinesse, nappinesse.

napping (ˈnæpɪŋ), *vbl. sb.*^{1} [f. NAP *v.*^{1} + -ING^1.] The action of sleeping or taking a nap.

c **825** *Vesp. Psalter* cxxxi. 4 ȝif ic sellu slep eȝum minum oððe breȝum minum hneappunge. *a* **1380** *St. Aug.* 486 in Horstm. *Altengl. Leg.* (1878) 70 þou seist i schal slep and take napping sone. *c* **1440** *York Myst.* xxix. 84 Warne all wightis to be in pees, For I am late layde vnto napping. **1549** LATIMER *6th Serm. bef. Edw. VI* (Arb.) 166, I had rather ye should go a napping to the sermons, than not to go at al. **1846** LANDOR *Imag. Conv., Southey & Landor* Wks. II. 69 This really is no napping; it is heavy snoring.

ˈnapping, *vbl. sb.*^{2} [f. NAP *v.*^{2}] The action of raising a nap on cloth (also *attrib.*); the nap itself; the material employed for the nap of hats.

c **1440** *Promp. Parv.* 358/1 Noppynge, *villositas, villatura.* **1839** URE *Dict. Arts* 635 The first cover of beaver or napping ..is strewed equably over the body, and patted on with a brush. **1875** KNIGHT *Dict. Mech.* 1510/2 *Napping*, a sheet of partially felted fur... It becomes the nap of the hat. *Ibid.*, *Napping-machine*, a machine for raising the nap or pile on woollen and cotton fabrics.

ˈnapping, *vbl. sb.*^{3} [f. NAP *v.*^{3}: see also KNAPPING *vbl. sb.*] Cheating. Also *attrib.*

1673 R. HEAD *Canting Acad.* 97 What chance of the Dye is soonest thrown, in topping, slurring, palming, napping. **1700** T. BROWN tr. *Fresny's Amusem.* Wks. 1709 III. 71 Assisting the Frail square Dye with high and low Fullums, and other Napping Tricks.

napping, variant of KNAPPING *vbl. sb.*

napping (ˈnæpɪŋ), *ppl. a.* [f. NAP *v.*^{1} + -ING^2.] Taking a nap.

a **1650** in *Westm. Gaz.* (1901) 16 May 2/3 How can that Ship but dash on ev'ry shelf, Whose napping Pilot cannot guide himself? **1868** GEO. ELIOT *Sp. Gipsy* 243 Nay, I endure nought worse than napping sheep, When nimble birds uproot a fleecy lock To line their nest.

ˈnapping, *a. rare*$^{-1}$. = NAPPY *a.*^{2}

c **1685** *Debtford Plumb Cake* in *Bagford Ball.* (1876) 71 With each some Plumb Cake in her hand and Cup of good napping Ale.

ˈnappishness. *rare*$^{-1}$. [f. NAP *sb.*^{2} + -ISH + -NESS.] Sleepiness.

1851 H. MELVILLE *Whale* II. 59 What little nappishness remained in us altogether departed.

ˈnappist. *nonce-wd.* [f. NAP *sb.*^{5} 2 + -IST.] One who is in the habit of playing nap.

1894 MASKELYNE *Sharps & Flats* 123 As all 'Nappists' will admit.

nappy (ˈnæpɪ), *sb.*^{1} Also 9 **nappie.** [sb. use of NAPPY *a.*^{2}] Ale; liquor.

1743 *Lond. & Country Brew.* IV. (ed. 2) 283 A regaling Refreshment of good Nappy. **1753** G. BURTON in *Mem. Stukeley* (Surtees) I. 407 Nothing can fix his thoughts..but a bottle of old nog or nappy. **1820** CLARE *Rural Life* (ed. 3) 90 And while I've sixpence left I'll spend it In cheering nappy. **1882** J. WALKER *Auld Reekie* 78 Yonder toon, whase nappy broon Has won the proudest laurels.

nappy (ˈnæpɪ), *sb.*^{2} *N. Amer.* [Of obscure origin.] An earthenware or glass dish with sloping sides.

1873 MRS. WHITNEY *Other Girls* xxxiii, Kate..producing some nice little stone-ware nappies hot from the hot closet, transferred the food from the china to these. **1916** *Daily Colonist* (Victoria, B.C.) 1 July 2/1 (Advt.), If it's Cut Glass you want, then we have what you want. Berry Bowls, Bon-Bon Dishes, Nappies, [etc.]. **1969** *Northwest* (*Sunday Oregonian Mag.*) 14 Dec. 24/1 Faceted knife rests, nappies (those flat bottomed, slope-sided little dishes for relish and a myriad of other uses), vases, celery dishes, whatever your budget would support—these offered marriage fitting recognition.

nappy (ˈnæpɪ), *sb.*^{3} *colloq.* = NAPKIN *sb.* 1 c. Also *fig.*

1927 W. E. COLLINSON *Contemp. Eng.* 7 Mothers and nurses use pseudo-infantile forms like pinny (pinafore), nappy (napkin). **1938** S. SPENDER *Trial of Judge* II. 49 The babe's scream till the nurse brings its nappy. **1955** M. F. Gilbert *Sky High* viii. 118 He's got about as much sense as a baby that kicks its nappy off and then cries because it's sleeping in a puddle. **1959** *Economist* 6 June 921/2 An able minister..will need anything up to six months to get out of his administrative nappies. **1961** *Which?* Apr. 84/1 There are various types of nappy used in this country, including a T-shaped one made of gauze..and disposable nappies. **1972** Ld. Robens *Ten Year Stint* xvi. 322, I had been a Minister when John Eden was in his political nappies, but had never experienced such peculiar behaviour. **1973** *Guardian* 3 Feb. 24/2 The greatest pollution in this land..was..committed against women 'from the nappy to the coffin'.

b. *attrib.* and *Comb.*, as ***nappy-changing***, ***towel***; **nappy pin**, a curved safety pin used for fastening nappies; **nappy rash**, infantile erythema caused by persistent contact with urinary ammonia from a damp nappy; **nappy service**, a commercial laundry service for babies' nappies.

1970 D. Bagley *Running Blind* ii. 17 No nappy-changing for you. **1973** *Guardian* 23 May 9/3, I draw the line at nappy-changing, not because I am a man but because..I don't like suprises of that nature. **1966** *Olney Amsden & Sons Ltd. Price List* 1 *Nappy Pins*. Snaplock curved with enamelled safety cap. **1967** H. W. Sutherland *Magnie* i. 2 He saw Bridie stop and look across at him, a nappy pin in her mouth. **1972** J. Mann *Mrs. Knox's Profession* xv. 110 He wielded the tin of powder and the nappy pins with voluntary attentiveness. **1959** *Which?* Sept. 104/2 Do the synthetic detergents cause dermatitis, or don't they? And does a baby get nappy-rash if its nappies are washed in them? **1966** 'G. North' *Sergeant Sgt. Cluff* xvi. 128 An infant red in the face, tormented by nappy-rash, howled in a pram. **1967** *New Scientist* 25 May 449/3 What started out as an effective treatment for nappy rash in infants may now be an essential instrument of modern warfare. **1972** J. Wilson *Hide & Seek* ii. 34 A baby who had teething troubles and nappy rash. **1959** *Manch. Guardian* 8 July 5/5 The nappy service cost 2s 6d a dozen, three times a week. **1970** K. Giles *Death in Church* ii. 47 Auntie..switched me on to Nappy Service, six dozen delivered every morning. **1940** C. Day Lewis tr. *Virgil's Georgics* iv. 89 Her sisters washed his hands Duly with pure water and fetched the nappy towels.

nappy ('næpɪ), *a.*[1] Now *rare*. Also 5–6 noppy, 7 nappie, 8 knappy. [ad. MDu. *noppigh* (Du. *noppig*), or MLG. *noppich*, f. *noppe* NAP *sb.*[3]]

1. Having a nap; villous, downy, shaggy.

1499 *Promp. Parv.* 358/1 (P.) Noppy or wully, *villosus*. **1530** Palsgr. 319/2 Noppy as clothe is that hath a grosse woffe, *gros*. **1611** Cotgr., *Velu*, hairie, shag, nappie, or of a high nap. **1625** K. Long tr. *Barclay's Argenis* iii. iii. 155 The first troupe was of children, in white nappy garments. **1675** Hobbes *Odyssey* (1677) 36 Clothed with soft nappy cloak and coat. **1727** De Foe *Eng. Tradesm.* (1732) II. i. iv. 123 The French wore nappy [1745 knappy] and coarse [cloth]. **1776–96** Withering *Brit. Plants* IV. 197 Pileus rather conical, knappy, yellow. **1823** in *Spirit Pub. Jrnls.* 513 Neither its owner nor itself are any longer nappy. **1904** *Westm. Gaz.* 10 Nov. 4/2 The cloth was slightly nappy.

2. Fuzzy, kinky; used colloquially and freq. derogatorily of Negroes' hair. So **nappy-head**, a Negro; **nappy-haired, -headed** *adjs.* *U.S.*

1950 A. Lomax *Mister Jelly Roll* (1952) 80 Light-skinned Downtown shared the bandstand with 'real black and nappy-headed' Uptown. **1956** S. Longstreet *Real Jazz* xviii. 150 To call a man '*nappy*' is to say his hair is kinky—a real insult. **1962** E. Cleaver in A. Dundes *Mother Wit* (1973) 16/1 Good hair, bad hair, nappy hair. **1966** K. L. Morgan in *Ibid.* 606/2 They would come up with black nappy-haired babies. **1967** J. Taylor in A. Chapman *New Black Voices* (1972) 175 One of the new breed of nappy-haired, bangle-wearing nationalists. **1968** J. Pullum in P. Oliver *Screening Blues* iii. 92 Joe Pullum's high-pitched 'black gal, black gal, what makes your nappy head so hard?' **1971** *Black World* June 71/2 Her hair..was in the bushy style that the freedom riders had brought. They called it 'natural'; Bojack called it nappy. **1973** *Ibid.* Apr. 63 All them ol' nappy-heads runnin' up there tryin' to pull his clothes off.

nappy ('næpɪ), *a.*[2] Also 6 noppy, 6–7 nappie. [prob. a transferred use of prec.]

1. a. Of intoxicating liquors, chiefly ale: Having a head, foaming; heady, strong.

α. *a* **1529** Skelton *E. Rummyng* 102 She breweth noppy ale. *Ibid.* 557 This ale, sayde she, is noppy. **1568** Fulwell *Like will to Like* C ij, Heer is a pot of noppy good ale.

β. **1564** Bulleyn *Dial. agst. Pest.* (1573) 108 She had very good nappie ale. **1586** A. Day *Eng. Secretary* i. (1625) 110 His peculiar skill in discerning the nappie taste by the nut-brown colour of Seller-Ale on a frosty morning. **1630** Westcote *Devonshire* 393 It is famous to have..the nappiest ale that can be drunk. **1686** *Loyal Garland* (ed. 5) B 2 b, Let..nappy Ale be ever free To strangers that do come and go. **1714** Gay *Sheph. Week* ii. 56 With nappy Beer I to the Barn repair'd. **1807** Crabbe *Par. Reg.* iii. 869 Thy coat is thin.., It's worn to th' thread! but I have nappy beer. **1868** Lowell *To J. Bartlett* ix, May Horace send him Massic wine, And Burns Scotch drink, the nappiest.

fig. **1582** Stanyhurst *Æneis* Ded. (Arb.) 4 Such leauinges as wee haue of Ennius his ragged verses..sauoure soom-what nappy of thee spigget. **1592** Nashe *Four Lett. Confut.* 27 Plucking Elderton out of the ashes of his Ale, and not letting him inioy his nappie muse of ballad making.

b. Applied to a bottle or cup.

c **1700** in Maidment *Pasquils* (1868) 409 A bottle that is both whyte and nappie. **1789** Shirrefs *Poems* (1790) 214 [They] ca'd about the nappy cup, To keep their wanton spirits up.

2. Slightly intoxicated or exhilarated by drink.

1721 Amherst *Terræ Filius* No. 41. 216 So many Traitors we drank, it made my cranium nappy. **1776** *Patie's Wedding* in Herd *Coll. Songs* II. 191 When that the carles grew nappy, They danc'd as weel as they dow'd. **1825** in Brockett *N.C. Gloss.* **1882** in *Lancs Gloss.*

3. Of a horse: awkward, disobedient.

1924 G. Brooke *Horse-Sense* v. 36 There are horses that refuse from temper, generally called 'nappy horses'. **1952** R. S. Summerhays *Elem. Riding* (ed. 3) xii. 72 A 'nappy' horse is a horse which can be described as one who will not go forward, will often go sideways and sometimes backwards. **1960** *Times* 23 July 9/2 Do not give the pony more than 20 minutes of this or it will sicken him, and..he may turn nappy and start refusing. **1963** Bloodgood & Santini *Horseman's Dict.* 134 *Nappy (to be)*, for a horse to be inclined to shy or refuse suddenly and without warning. **1973** J. White *Norfolk Child* 131 My father..was utterly patient with every horse he rode, however nappy.

naprie, -y, etc., obs. forms of NAPERY.

napron(ne, -oun, -un(e, obs. ff. APRON.

napta, obs. form of NAPHTHA.

†**nap-taking**, *a.* *Obs. rare*$^{-1}$. [irreg. f. NAP *v.*[1]] That takes one napping; unexpected.

1602 Carew *Cornwall* 158 b, Besides such nap-taking assaults, spoylings, and firings haue in our forefathers daies, between vs and Fraunce, beene very common.

napte, napthe: see NAPHTHE.

naptha, variant of NAPHTHA.

napu ('nɑːpuː). [a. Malay *nāpu*.] The musk-deer of Java and Sumatra.

1820 Raffles in *Trans. Linn. Soc.* (1822) XIII. 261 *Moschus*. The Malays distinguish three species or varieties of this genus, viz. the Napu,..the Kanchil.., and the Pelandok. **1870** Nicholson *Man. Zool.* (1875) 614 The musk-gland is wanting in the Napu (*Moschus Javanicus*) of Java.

†**na'quaire**. *Obs. rare*. In 6 nak-, nauquayre. [a. F. *naquaire*, obs. var. of *nacaire*: see NAKER *sb.*[1]] A naker, kettledrum.

1523 Ld. Berners *Froiss.* I. cxlvii. 176 The kyng..entred into the towne with trumpets, tabours, nakquayres & hornyes. **1530** Palsgr. 247/2 Nauquayre a kynde of instrument, *naquair*.

na-quar, -quhare, obs. forms of NOWHERE.

na-quil(e, variants of NOWHILE *Obs.*

na-quiþer, obs. form of NOWHITHER.

nar, *a.* *Obs.* exc. *north. dial.* Forms: 1 nearra, neorra, nerra, nærra, 3–5 nerre, 4 nerr, 4, 6 ner; 6–7 narre, 7 narr, 6, 9 nar. Also *compar.* 4 nerrer, 6 (9) narer, 9 *dial.* narder; *superl.* 4–6 nerrest, (6 -ast), 6–7 narrest. [OE. *néarra* etc., comparative of *néah* NIGH; but in ME. perh. partly from ON. *nærre*, *nærri* adj. (see next). The ME. compar. *nerrer* and superl. *nerrest* have been formed on *nerre* as if it were a positive form.] Nearer, nigher.

1. In attributive use. (†In OE. also = later.) In mod. dial. only in ***nar horse***, ***leg***, ***side***, and occas. in other senses of the positive *near*.

c **893** K. Ælfred *Oros.* i. i, On hire westhealfe is seo us nearre Ægyptus. *c* **900** tr. *Bæda's Hist.* ii. xv, His ða nerran [*v.r.* nearran, neorran] tide wæron wyrsan þam ærran. *c* **975** *Rushw. Gosp.* Matt. xxi. 31 Se æftera *vel* nærra [L. *novissimus*]. *c* **1200** Ormin 15691 For þatt teȝȝ wærenn off hiss kinn & tærþurrh nerre breþre. *c* **1305** in *Pop. Treat. Sci.* 133 So that the sonne..schyneth on the nerre half in thulke that ner him is. **1429** *Rolls of Parlt.* IV. 342/2 Paied..atte a rather and nerre day. **1565** Cooper *Thesaurus* s.v. *Propius*, *Gradu sanguinis propior*, Nerre kinne. **1607** Markham *Caval.* ii. (1617) 5 The farre fore-foote, and the narre hinder foot. *Ibid.* iv. 9 You shall linke together his [the horse's] left legges, which we call his narre legges. **1659** *Indenture, Goosnargh, Lancs*, 2 closes..called narr or nearer croft and the further croft. **1736** ——, *Sheffield*, The narr stubbed piece,..the far stubbed piece. **1863** Atkinson *Prov. Danby*, *Nar-side*, the lefthand side (of a horse or team). **1871** E. Peacock *Ralf Skirl.* II. 108 A hos..brok' his nar fore-leg in two places. **1899** Dickinson & Prevost *Cumbld. Gloss.* s.v., The left-hand or nar horse walks on the land, when ploughing two abreast.

b. In superlative. Nearest.

c **1470** Henry *Wallace* ix. 421 Eftir he gaiff stayt to his nerrest ayr. **1500–20** Dunbar *Poems* xxxiii. 25 In Scotland than, the narrest way, He come. **1563** Winȝet *Four Scoir Thre Quest.* Wks. (S.T.S.) I. 96 Vsurping (as..hir Grace's nerrest freindis thocht) hir Hienes auctorite. **1596** Dalrymple tr. *Leslie's Hist. Scot.* Prol. 7 To the vse of thair nychtbours and nerrest natiouns. **1609** Skene *Reg. Maj.* 33 Some are narrest heires, some are farther.

2. In predicative use. Occas. const. *to*.

13.. *E.E. Allit. P.* A. 233 Ho was me nerre þen aunte or nece. **1362** Langl. *P. Pl.* A. xi. 250 ȝet am I neuere þe ner, for nouȝt I haue walkid. **1382** Wyclif *Ruth* iii. 12 Ne I denye me to be nyȝ, but there is another nerre than Y. **1413** *Pilgr. Sowle* (Caxton 1483) i. iii. 4 It semyd me moche more nerre than it was byfore. **1461** *Paston Lett.* I. 542 He answered ageyn in these wordes, 'Nere is my kyrtyl but nerre is my smok'. *a* **1542** Wyatt in *Tottel's Misc.* (Arb.) 58 Your sighes yow fet from farre,.. Yet ar ye nere the narre. **1579** Spenser *Sheph. Cal.* July 97 To Kerke the narre, to God more farre, has bene an old sayd sawe. **1868** Brierley *Irkdale* xiii. 198 (Lancs Gloss.), Letten somb'dy else be nar to him nor me.

b. In forms *nerrer*, etc. and in superlative.

c **1330** R. Brunne *Chron. Wace* (Rolls) 10626 His neuew he ys,..Of blod ys non nerrer þan he. **1340** Hampole *Pr. Consc.* 9237 Alle þas..When þai com þar sal be hym nerrest. Þe nerrer þat þai sal hym be [etc.]. **1570** *Satir. Poems Reform.* xii. 181 Feche Leuenox hame, ȝe haif nane narer nor he. **1869** Gibson *Folk-speech Cumbld.* 31 Mebbe I wad be narder t' truth.

nar, *adv.* (and *prep.*) *Obs.* exc. *north. dial.* and *Sc.* Forms: 4–5 nerre, 4–6 nerr, 5–6 ner; 4–7 narre, 5–6 nare, 5–6, 9 nar, 9 *dial.* naar, naur. Also *compar.* 4 nerrer, (5 -ere), nerþere, 5 narrere. [ME. *nerre*, ad. ON. *nærre*, *nærri* adv., 'nearer, near', compar. of *ná-* 'nigh', used only in combs. as *ná-búi* neighbour.]

1. Nearer, nigher, closer. (Cf. NEAR *adv.*[1])

a **1300** *Cursor M.* 12366 Þe folk stod and behild o-ferr, For leons durst þai cum na nerr. **13..** *E.E. Allit. P.* C. 85 At alle peryles, quoth þe prophete I aproche hit no nerre. **1390** Gower *Conf.* I. 314 This Flete..The bryghte fyres sih a ferr, And thei hem drowen nerr and nerr. *c* **1440** *York Myst.* ix. 62 Telle hym I wol come no narre. **1470–85** Malory *Arthur* xx. xxii. 838 Thenne Syr Launcelot stode nerre syr Gauwayn, and..doubled hys strokes. **1562** Cooper *Answ. Def. Truth* (1850) 52 That he might press upon you somewhat narre than other before had used. **1591** Harington *Orl. Fur.* ii. xlii, Still, as I approcht a little narre, More wonderfull the building doth appeare. **1703** Thoresby *Let. to Ray*, *Nar*, nearer. **1857** J. Scholes *Jaunt* 19 (Lancs Gloss.), Aw hardly know iv aw awt to ventur ony narr.

b. In forms *nerrer*, *narrer*, etc.

c **1375** *Sc. Leg. Saints* xvi. (*Magdalene*) 932 Þe bischape for rednes Durste cum na narrere. *c* **1380** Wyclif *Serm.* Sel. Wks. I. 63 Þei shulden sue Crist in poverte, nerrer þan oþir comounes. *Ibid.* II. 101 Ech man shulde sue him or ferþere or nerþere. *c* **1400** Maundev. (1839) iv. 30 Whoso wil..come nerrer to Jerusalem. *c* **1450** Lovelich *Grail* xlvi. 243 He dressed hym to haven a syhte, Nerrere than he scholde han do.

2. Near, nigh, close (to).

a **1300** *Cursor M.* 4551 Þan cald þe king ioseph nerr. *Ibid.* 17288 + 387 Als þai come narre þe castelle. *c* **1330** R. Brunne *Chron. Wace* (Rolls) 9610 He somounde firste þo til his werre, Þat deyned nought for Lot come nerre. *a* **1352** Minot *Poems* (ed. Hall) x. 15 Wight men of þe west neghed þam nerr. *c* **1470** *Gol. & Gaw.* 1017 Thair with the nobill in neid nyghit hym ner. **1519** Horman *Vulg.* 27 Sume se but narre. **1560** Rolland *Crt. Venus* i. 516 Sclander and schame euer to it drawis nar. **1596** Dalrymple tr. *Leslie's Hist. Scot.* Prol. 40 Sche..cumis nevir ner thame. **1647** H. More *Song of Soul* ii. App. lxxxii, Besides that firie flame that was so narre The Planets self. *a* **1833** R. Anderson *Cumbld. Ball.* (*c* 1850) 93 Lads aw nar us are weyld fops an fuils. **1867** Waugh *Owd Blanket* iv. 95 They begun a-drawin' nar to th' heawse.

b. Nearly, almost. *rare*.

13.. *Cursor M.* 7012 (Gött.), Fourti thousand of Israele, Of beniamyn nerr [*Cott.* negh] als fele. **1859** A. Whitehead *Leg Westmld.* 6 (E.D.D. s.v. *Near*), An flay'd poor Brittons nar to death. **1871** Alexander *Johnny Gibb* xviii. 136 A chap or twa, naar grippit braid i' the crood.

†**nar**, are not: see NE and BE *v.* *Obs.*

c **1330** R. Brunne *Chron. Wace* (Rolls) 7656 In al Saxonye nar [*v.r.* ere] non þem lyk. *Ibid.* 16501 Þat we nar [*v.r.* ne are] worþy a-geyn be cald To penaunce. *c* **1330** *Amis & Amil.* 597 Kinges sones..Nar non to gode to the.

†**nar**, were not, variant of NERE. *Obs.*

c **1320** *Sir Tristr.* 2464 So bliþe al bi dene Nar þai neuer are. *c* **1330** *Arth. & Merl.* 6137 (Kölbing), Þo nar þo wiþ king Arthour Bot to & fourti. *c* **1440** Lydg. *Hors, Shepe & G.* 112 The besi Marchant..Nar [*v.r.* Ner] shippis & hors coude make no cariage.

†**nar**, in ***nar nar***, an imitation of the growling of a dog (cf. NARR *v.*). *Obs. rare*$^{-1}$.

1509 Barclay *Shyp of Folys* (1570) 69 Though all be well, yet he none aunswere hath Saue the dogges letter, glowming with nar nar.

nar, variant of NER, nor. *Obs.*

Nara ('nɑːrə). [The name of a town in Central Honshu, Japan, capital of Japan A.D. 710–84.] Used *attrib.* to designate the Buddhist sculpture of the period of Japanese history during which Nara was the capital.

1902 F. Brinkley *Oriental Series: Japan* VII. i. 19 As to sculpture, the point of excellence to which it had been carried is attested by several statues which form part of the Nara temple relics. **1903** K. Okakura *Ideals of East* 112 The stone Buddhas of the Tin Tal in Ellora..are beautiful, with a self-contained grandeur and harmony of proportion. In them we find the sources of inspiration of the Tâng and Nara sculptures. **1955** Paine & Soper *Art & Archit. Japan* iv. 26 The earliest clay images of the Nara period are the groups of figures dating from 711 in the Pagoda of Hōryūji. **1970** *Oxf. Compan. Art* 609/2 During the Heian period..the trend was away from the realism of the Nara period.

narawe, obs. variant of ARROW.

narc (nɑːk). *U.S. slang.* Also **nark**. [abbrev. NARCOTIC *sb.* or *a.*] A federal, state, or local narcotics agent. Cf. NARCO.

1967 *N.Y. Times* 17 Oct. 44 Most speed freaks get to a point where they're seeing narks in the trees with cameras. **1968–70** *Current Slang* (Univ. S. Dakota) III–IV. 85 *Narc*, an official of the Narcotics Control Board. *Ibid.*, *Narco, or narc*, narcotics officer. (Drug users' jargon). **1970** E. Tidyman *Shaft* (1971) iv. 50 The police didn't frighten him. The Narcs didn't frighten him. **1972** J. Wambaugh *Blue Knight* (1973) vii. 114 A narco cop nailed him..the narcs busted in the pad. **1973** *Black Panther* 20 Oct. 15/1 Then I made contact for the ring with the narc agent. **1975** *New Yorker* 19 Feb. 96/3 Bo, a rookie detective..is so confused by the Department's manipulations that he doesn't guess that she is an undercover narc.

narceia (nɑːˈsiːə). *Chem.* [f. Gr. νάρκη numbness + -IA[1]: cf. next.] = NARCEINE.
1840 *Penny Cycl.* XVI. 87/2 The stronger and concentrated acids decompose narceia. **1857** MILLER *Elem. Chem., Org.* 277 The formula of narceia.. differs from that of ordinary narcotine, in containing four equivalents more of water. **1874** GARROD & BAXTER *Mat. Med.* 201 Narceia is very insoluble, and irritates the skin at the point of injection.

narceine (ˈnɑːsiːɪn, -aɪn). *Chem.* Also -in. [a. F. *narcéine* (Pelletier, 1832), f. Gr. νάρκη numbness, deadness: see -INE[5].] A bitter crystalline alkaloid obtained from opium, sometimes used in medicine as a substitute for morphia.
1834 *Cycl. Pract. Med.* III. 152/2 The active principles, the meconate of morphia, the narceine, and narcotina. **1864** *Syd. Soc. Year-bk. Med. for* 1863, 430 Codein, narceine and thebaine produce violent and even tetanic spasms. **1875** H. C. WOOD *Therap.* (1879) 229 Decidedly larger doses of narcein than of morphia are required to obtain any action.

narciss (nɑːˈsɪs). Also 6 -cyss, 6–9 -cisse. [ad. L. *Narciss-us* or a. F. *Narcisse.*] = NARCISSUS.
1586 W. WEBBE *Eng. Poetrie* (Arb.) 78 White violets sweete Nais plucks and bloomes fro the Poppies, Narcyss, and dyll flowres most sweete. **1597** GERARDE *Herbal* I. lxxxvi. 137 The mountain Rush leaved Narcisse with an indented or curled cup. **1660** SHARROCK *Vegetables* 80 Narcisses and Crocuses are commonly taken up first. **1825** HONE *Every-day Bk.* I. 18 Apr., Musk Narcisse, *Narcissus moschatus.* **1838** *Blackw. Mag.* XLIII. 255 Sappho's scant but blooming rose—the rich narciss of Melanippides. **1880** S. HIBBERD in *N. & Q.* 6th Ser. I. 412/2 In other sections of the narciss family, yellow is the predominant colour. *Ibid.* 413/1 This term is never applied to a narciss.

nar'cissine, *a.* [ad. L. *narcissin-us* (Pliny), ad. Gr. ναρκίσσινος.] **1.** Of or pertaining to the plant Narcissus. *rare*$^{-0}$.
1656 BLOUNT *Glossogr.* [hence in later Dicts.].
2. Resembling, or of the nature of, Narcissus (see NARCISSUS 2); loving or admiring oneself.
1813 E. S. BARRETT *Heroine* II. xxii. 77 Flinging off my bonnet, I shook my narcissine locks over my shoulders. **1911** BEERBOHM *Zuleika D.* ii. 15 Yet there was nothing Narcissine in her spirit. Her love for her own image was not cold æstheticism.

narcissism (nɑːˈsɪsɪz(ə)m). Chiefly *Psychol.* [f. the name of *Narcissus*, a beautiful youth who fell in love with his own reflection in a fountain (Ovid *Metam.* III. 370; subsequently referred to by Havelock Ellis in *Alienist & Neurologist* (1898) XIX. II. 280; the term *Narcissismus* was used by Näcke in *Die sexuellen Perversitäten* (1899)): see -ISM.] Self-love and admiration that find emotional satisfaction in self-contemplation; occas. (erron.) **'narcism.**
1822 COLERIDGE *Let.* 15 Jan. (1971) V. 196 Of course, I am glad to be able to correct my fears as far as public Balls, Concerts, and Time-murder in Narcissism. **1905** H. ELLIS *Stud. Psychol. Sex* IV. iii. 187, I have referred to the developed forms of this kind of self-contemplation.. and in this connection have alluded to the fable of Narcissus, whence Näcke has since devised the term Narcissism for this group of phenomena. **1922** J. RIVIERE tr. *Freud's Introd. Lect. Psycho-Anal.* xxiv. 347 It is probable that this *narcissism* is the universal original condition, out of which *object-love* develops later without thereby necessarily effecting a disappearance of the narcissism. **1938** H. A. MURRAY *Explorations in Personality* iii. 180 Narcism (or Egophilia) is technical for self-love. **1946** [see INTROJECTION 3 a]. **1955** H. MARCUSE *Eros & Civilization* (1969) viii. 169 The striking paradox that narcissism, normally understood as egotistic withdrawal from reality, here is connected with oneness with the universe, reveals the new depth of the conception. **1969** P. LOEWENBERG in B. B. Wolman *Psychoanal. Interpretation of Hist.* vi. 182 He [*sc.* Herzl] regressed to the stage of narcissism in which his only sexual object was his own ego and its fantasies. **1970** HINSIE & CAMPBELL *Psychiatric Dict.* (ed. 4) 487/2 *Narcism*, a shortened (and incorrect) form of narcissism.

narcissist (nɑːˈsɪsɪst). [f. as prec. + -IST.] A person affected with narcissism. Also *attrib.*
1930 B. RUSSELL *Conquest of Happiness* I. i. 22 A narcissist, ..inspired by the homage paid to great painters, may become an art student. **1934** C. DAY LEWIS *Hope for Poetry* vi. 32 We find, instead of criticism, long narcissist ramblings, the 'reviewer's' views on everything under the sun. **1953** *Essays in Crit.* III. 89 A narcissist indulgence in a 'phantasmal world' of self-reflection. **1958** *Times Lit. Suppl.* 24 Jan. 46/3 The doctrine here is that Shelley is a self-absorbed narcissist, yearning emptily and 'regressively' for death.

narcissistic (nɑːsɪˈsɪstɪk), *a.* [f. as prec. + -ISTIC.] Of or pertaining to narcissism; marked by excessive love of self.
1916 E. JONES tr. *Ferenczi's Contrib. Psycho-Anal.* 174, I was just striving to make clear to a patient her excessive ambition, arising from narcissistic fixation. **1922** J. RIVIERE tr. *Freud's Introd. Lect. Psycho-Anal.* xxiv. 347 Thus it appeared that auto-erotism was the sexual activity of the narcissistic phase of the direction of the Libido. **1935** S. SPENDER *Destructive Element* xv. 267 It was not a narcissistic desire to recover lost charms and innocence. **1964** *Economist* 23 May 801/2 Students.. would be vastly improved if they were a lot less frowsty and narcissistic. **1973** L. BELLAK et al. *Ego Functions* II. x. 159 Kernberg has discussed 'Barriers to Being in Love' from the standpoint of narcissistic personality features.

narcissistically (nɑːsɪˈsɪstɪkəlɪ), *adv.* [f. prec.: see -ICALLY.] In a narcissistic manner.
1925 T. DREISER *Amer. Trag.* (1926) I. I. xv. 112 She narcissistically painted her flight. **1962** *Times* 3 May 17/2 Some literary men seem almost narcissistically concerned with themselves and their art. **1968** *Daily Tel.* 13 Nov. 15/5 If you don't go for seeing yourself narcissistically reflected in the shimmering walls, there is the view of lacy trees outside. **1974** D. MEIRING *President Plan* x. 84 The father [was] bound narcissistically within the mirrors of his supposed professional importance.

narcissus (nɑːˈsɪsəs). [In sense 1, a. L. *narcissus* (Virgil, etc.), ad. Gr. νάρκισσος, acc. to Pliny and Plutarch f. νάρκη numbness, in reference to the heavy or narcotic effects produced by it; in sense 2: see NARCISSISM.] **1.** *Bot.* Pl. **narcissi** (and **narcissuses**). A genus of the order *Amaryllidaceæ*, containing many species; a plant of this genus; now esp. *Narcissus poeticus*, a bulbous plant, flowering in spring and bearing a heavily scented single white flower with an undivided corona edged with crimson and yellow.
1548 TURNER *Names Herbes* (E.D.S.) 55 Narcissus is of diuerse sortes. **1562** —— *Herbal* II. 62 Narcissus hath a narrow lefe, many together and fat. **1578** LYTE *Dodoens* 209 There are two very faire and beautifull kindes of Narcissus. **1596** NASHE *Saffron Walden* 73 Like the doure Narcissus, hauing flowres onely at the roote. **1613** DAVORS *Secrets of Angling* I. xxxvii, Red Hyacinth, and yealow Daffadill, Purple Narcissus, like the morning rayes. **1638** MILTON *Lycidas* 148 Wks. (ed. Todd) V. 58 *note*, Next, adde Narcissus that still weeps in vaine. *c* **1709** PRIOR *2nd Hymn Callimachus* 99 The yellow crocus there, and fair narcissus. **1797** *Encycl. Brit.* (ed. 3) XII. 635/1 The.. poetic daffodil, or common white narcissus, is well known. **1820** SHELLEY *Sensit. Pl.* I. 18 Narcissi, the fairest among them all. **1829** LANDOR *Imag. Conv., Epicurus*, etc. Wks. 1853 I. 503/1 Laden with hyacinths and narcissuses, anemones and jonquils. **1873** 'OUIDA' *Pascarel* I. 22 At every step they trampled a bright narcissus under foot.
Comb. **1885** *Cassell's Encycl. Dict.*, Narcissus-flowered Anemone, *Anemone narcissiflora*.
2. (With capital initial.) The name of a youth in classical mythology who died of self-love after seeing his reflection in water and was turned into the flower, used chiefly *attrib.* and *Comb.* allusively for: one who admires himself exclusively, one who resembles Narcissus in handsomeness.
1606 SHAKES. *Ant. & Cl.* II. v. 96 Go get thee hence, Had'st thou Narcissus in thy face to me, Thou would'st appeere most vgly. **1767** W. KENRICK tr. *Misc. Wks. J.J. Rousseau* II. 121 (*title*) Narcissus, or the self-admirer. A comedy. **1860** A. J. MUNBY *Diary* 10 Feb. in D. Hudson *Munby* (1972) 49 His face.. seemed to me weak and self-conscious; a Narcissus face. **1891** O. WILDE *Pict. Dorian Gray* i. 4 This young Adonis, who looks as if he was made of ivory and rose-leaves. Why, my dear Basil, he is a Narcissus. **1928** R. CAMPBELL *Wayzgoose* ii. 44 Here was a man—I thought it was a mess, A bottle-nosed Narcissus of the Press. **1929** D. H. LAWRENCE *Pornograhy & Obscenity* 26 The most emancipated bohemians.. are still utterly.. enclosed within the narcissus-masturbation circle. **1930** —— *A Propos Lady Chatterley* 23 Poor, self-conscious, uneasy, narcissus-monk as he was. **1935** A. HUXLEY *Let.* 20 Sept (1969) 397 Why is it that when one enters that [*sc.* theatrical] world, one always finds oneself with crooks, imbeciles, narcissus complexes? *a* **1963** C. S. LEWIS *Poems* (1964) 89 So should I quickly die Narcissus-like of want. **1964** M. MCLUHAN *Understanding Media* (1967) v. 66 The frontiers between forms that snap us out of the Narcissus-narcosis.
3. narcissus fly, a hover-fly, *Lampetia* (= *Merodon*) *equestris*, whose larva infests the bulbs of narcissus and other plants, causing them to rot.
1903 F. V. THEOBALD *First Rep. Econ. Entomol.* 107 A correspondent.. sent the larvæ of the Narcissus Fly, from Chertsey, with the following note: 'They play havoc with the narcissus bulbs and are evidently the maggot of some fly.' **1926** *Jrnl. Econ. Entomol.* XIX. 249 The observations were made on the larvae of the narcissus fly. **1951** COLYER & HAMMOND *Flies Brit. Isles* xii. 166 Our last example from the group is *Merodon equestris* F., the 'Large Bulb Fly' or 'Narcissus Fly', which is a serious pest to the horticulturalist. **1966** *Punch* 28 Sept. 485/3 There are in Britain some two hundred and twenty known varieties of hover fly, of which only the Narcissus flies are destructive (to narcissi, naturally).

narco (ˈnɑːkəʊ). U.S. slang abbrev. of *narcotic* or *narcotics*, used esp. (freq. *attrib.*) = NARC (see also quots.).
1955 *Amer. Speech* XXX. 87 *Narco*, the narcotic hospital in Lexington, Kentucky. **1958** J. & W. HAWKINS *Death Watch* 43 This informant is a thief, a narco or a four-bottle bum. **1960** *Sat. Rev.* (U.S.) 6 Feb. 11/3 The Beat Generation has marihuana and the ritual of dodging the 'narcos'—the narcotics squad. **1961** RIGNEY & SMITH *Real Bohemia* p. xvi, *Narco, the*, federal narcotics agents. **1964** *Manhunt* Mar. 67/2, I feel very strongly about helping narco violators. *Ibid.* 68/1 You've gone to bat on forty-three narcos *without a single acquittal!* **1968** *Wall St. Jrnl.* 19 Feb. 1/1 Students also have agitated against university acquiescence in the presence on the campus of 'narcos'—police agents seeking to make arrests for violations of narcotics laws, whose basic premises many of the students question. **1970** K. PLATT *Pushbutton Butterfly* (1971) xi. 126 Tina was in the drug racket... The narco squad might have had reason to suspect her. **1971** 'D. SHANNON' *Ringer* (1972) iii. 58 The pedigrees varied from burglary to narco dealing to rape. **1972** [see NARC].

narco- (ˈnɑːkəʊ). *Psychol.* [f. Gr. νάρκη numbness.] Prefixed to a sb. to indicate that use is made, in the treatment specified by the sb., of a drug (usu. a barbiturate such as amylobarbitone or thiopentone sodium) which, while inducing relaxation, facilitates the remembering and verbalizing of repressed emotional experiences. So ***narco-analysis***, ***-hypnosis*** (also ***-hypnotic*** adj.), ***-therapy***; ***narco-synthesis***, the acceptance into the conscious self of repressed emotional experiences revealed by the use of drugs.
1936 J. S. HORSLEY in *Jrnl. Mental Sci.* LXXXII. 416 Narco-analysis is an eclectic technique based on the observation that a combination of narcosis with psychotherapy is quicker and sometimes more effective than the formal methods of analytical psychology. **1943** —— (*title*) Narco-analysis. *Ibid.* i. 3 Clearly any title which suggests that a particular narcotic is essential to the technique is undesirable. Therefore I devised the term 'Narco-Analysis' which is inclusive of all such methods. **1973** E. RUDINGER *Treatm. & Care in Mental Illness* (rev. ed.) 161 Narco-analysis or abreaction is a treatment that is also available privately, but the drugs used and the nursing home fee have to be paid in addition to the psychiatrist's fee. **1949** A. HUXLEY *Let.* 21 Oct. (1969) 605 The world's rulers will discover that infant conditioning and narco-hypnosis are.. efficient. **1974** HAWKEY & BINGHAM *Wild Card* v. 51 McElroy was sufficiently promising a subject to be questioned under narco-hypnosis. **1949** A. HUXLEY *Let.* 9 Dec. (1969) 611 The latest in.. narco-hypnotic techniques. **1945** GRINKER & SPIEGEL *Men under Stress* III. v. 102 Here he underwent pentothal narcosynthesis and ventilated his intense anxiety. **1955** A. HUXLEY *Let.* 10 Jan. (1969) 720 Mescalin.. acts in the opposite way to narcosynthesis. **1958** [see ABREACTION]. **1963** *Times* 9 Mar. 8/1 It is believed to be the first instance in which narcosynthesis—a technique to help patients release suppressed or forgotten information—has ever been used for this purpose. **1966** P. POLATIN *Guide to Treatm. in Psychiatry* v. 50 Narcotherapy is most effective for acute anxiety states, conversion reactions and dissociative phenomena such as amnesias and fugues. **1968** S. LOEBL *Exploring the Mind* xv. 184 Hypnotherapy and narcotherapy, as these procedures are called, have by now become part of psychiatry's ever-growing therapeutic arsenal.

narcolepsy (ˈnɑːkəlɛpsɪ). *Path.* Also -lepsia. [First formed as F. *narcolepsie* (Gélineau 1880, in *Gaz. des Hôpitaux* LIII. 626/2), f. *narco-* as comb. form of Gr. νάρκη numbness + *-lepsy* as in EPILEPSY.] A nervous disease characterized by short and frequently recurring attacks of somnolence; also, the somnolent state which often precedes an attack of epilepsy.
1880 *Jrnl. Nervous & Mental Dis.* VII. 737 Dr. Gelineau [*sic*], *Gaz. des Hopitaux* [sic], Nos. 79 and 80, describes at length, and discusses a case in his practice which.. seems to be one of a new disease, for which he proposes the name 'Narcolepsy'. **1888** *Lancet* 28 Jan. 188/2 Narcolepsia consists in sudden attacks of deep sleep lasting some minutes. **1894** *Ibid.* 3 Nov. 1065/1 A case of narcolepsy, the subject being a soldier who suffered daily from sudden attacks of somnolence. **1898** *Pop. Sci. Monthly* LII. 558 Among rarer forms of pathological sleep the author discusses narcolepsy. **1928** *Brain* LI. 78 All narcolepsy is.. symptomatic, but at present we do not always know of what pathological or physiological condition it is thus symptomatic. **1969** *Sunday Times* 2 Nov. 10/3 It [*sc.* amphetamine] is the best drug of narcolepsy (uncontrollable attacks of sleeping). **1972** H. L. WILLIAMS in Brady & Nauta *Princ., Pract. & Positions Neuropsychiatric Res.* 454 It has been observed that patients with idiopathic narcolepsy frequently move directly from waking to REM sleep.

narcolept (ˈnɑːkəlɛpt). [Back-formation from next.] = NARCOLEPTIC *sb.*
1957 R. A. HEINLEIN *Door into Summer* (1960) iv. 54 I'm forever deprived, like a narcolept on a honeymoon. **1973** *Times Lit. Suppl.* 19 Oct. 1268/5 Like that later narcolept Edgar Allan Poe.

narcoleptic (nɑːkəʊˈlɛptɪk), *a.* and *sb.* [ad. F. *narcoleptique*; cf. EPILEPTIC *a.* and *sb.*]
A. *adj.* Characteristic of or affected with narcolepsy.
1904 G. S. HALL *Adolescence* I. 264 Sometimes a sense of fatigue, lassitude, and sleepiness, rarely narcoleptic, may supervene. **1912** *Jrnl. Nervous & Mental Dis.* XXXIX. 131 (*heading*) Adipose pituitary syndrome of Lannois with narcoleptic fits. **1949** *Progress Neurol. & Psychiatry* IV. 414 Narcoleptic sleep,.. major convulsions, or other 'epileptic' symptoms. **1960** *Arch. Gen. Psychiatry* III. 422/1 This narcoleptic patient is an intelligent 42-year-old married Negro male shipping clerk. **1972** *Ibid.* XXVI. 462/1 The narcoleptic sleep attack is more imperative but of shorter duration than diurnal hypersomniac sleep.
B. *sb.* A narcoleptic person.
1928 *Brain* LI. 84 The sleep of the narcoleptic is to be likened in all respects to normal, healthy sleep. **1957** *Proc. Mayo Clinic* XXXII. 324 A serious problem among the narcoleptics is the tendency to drowse when driving. **1972** *Arch. Gen. Psychiatry* XXVI. 457/2 Hypersomniacs do not fall asleep while eating, speaking, or walking, as narcoleptics do.

narcomania (ˌnɑːkəˈmeɪnɪə). *Path.* [f. *narco-* (see NARCOLEPSY) + -MANIA.]
An uncontrollable craving for narcotic drugs.
1888 N. KERR *Inebriety* 34, I propose to call this abnormal state, especially in its marked maniacal forms, by the comprehensive name—Narcomania. **1896** *Daily News* 19 June 6/3 No man is better acquainted with all developments of narcomania than Dr. Norman Kerr.

Hence **narco'maniac**, one who suffers from narcomania; **narco'maniacal** *a.*

1888 N. Kerr *Inebriety* Index, Narcomaniacs often driven against will. **1889** *Ibid.* (ed. 2) 74 Narcomaniacal untruth.

narcosis (nɑːˈkəʊsɪs). *Path.* [a. Gr. νάρκωσις, f. ναρκοῦν to benumb.] The production of a narcotic state (†or the quality of producing this); the operation or effects of narcotics upon the system; a state of insensibility. Also a psychologically therapeutic sleep artificially prolonged by the use of drugs. So *narcosis therapy*.

1693 tr. *Blancard's Phys. Dict.* (ed. 2), *Narcosis*, a privation of Sense as in a Palsie, or in taking of Opium, &c. **1697** *Phil. Trans.* XIX. 383 The Narcosis of Opium, for Example, is gone or separated, because the dryed juice.. smells not so strong. **1753** Chambers *Cycl. Supp.*, *Narcosis*, a stupefaction or insensible state, whether brought on by medicines, or happening from natural causes. **1863** *Macm. Mag.* Oct. 461 By Narcosis I.. mean exclusively the action of large doses of the substances called Narcotics upon the organism. **1872** Hamilton *Nervous Dis.* 72 This follows profound narcosis by alcohol or opium. **1936** [see *narco-analysis* s.v. narco-]. **1943** Curran & Guttmann *Psychological Med.* viii. 97 Probably the most humane method is to give continuous narcosis for the first few days after the drug [*sc.* morphine] has been withdrawn; but relapse is very frequent. **1945** Grinker & Spiegel *Men under Stress* iv. xvii. 394 At the present time, aside from the method of narcosis therapy (continuous sleep), the use of intravenous barbiturates is dignified by three different terms.

narcotia (nɑːˈkəʊʃ(ɪ)ə). [f. narcot-ic *a.* + -ia.] = narcotine.

1876 Harley *Mat. Med.* (ed. 6) 765 Opium contains from 6 to 8 per cent. of Narcotia or Narcotine.

narcotic (nɑːˈkɒtɪk), *sb. Med.* Also 4 ner-, 4–5 -ike, (-yke), 7–8 -ick. [ad. F. *narcotique* (14th c.), or med.L. *narcōtic-um*, Gr. ναρκωτικ-όν, neut. of ναρκωτικός: see next.] **1. a.** A substance which when swallowed, inhaled, or injected into the system induces drowsiness, sleep, stupefaction, or insensibility, according to its strength and the amount taken.

c **1385** Chaucer *L.G.W.* 2670 *Hypermnestra*, He shal slepe as longe as euere the leste, The narcotykis & opijs ben so stronge. *c* **1386** —— *Knt.'s T.* 614 With nercotikes and opie of Thebes fyn. **1412–20** Lydg. *Chron. Troy* ii. x, Narcotikes that cause men to slepe. **1655** Culpepper, etc. *Riverius* i. ii. 10 A sleeping Disease is got by the too frequent use of Medicines called Narcoticks, that do produce sleep. **1677** Plot *Oxfordsh.* 60 Boetius holds it to be a good narcotick, and that it safely may be given to procure sleep. **1702** J. Purcell *Cholick* (1714) 123 The Pain may be eas'd..by Anodins and Narcoticks. **1834** *Cycl. Pract. Med.* III. 149/2 The nerves most particularly affected by narcotics are the respiratory. **1846** J. Baxter *Libr. Pract. Agric.* (ed. 4) I. 405 The hop is a useful narcotic, and the smell of its flowers soporific. **1878** M. L. Holbrook *Hygiene Brain* 62 Take no narcotics to make you sleep.

b. In extended use: any drug which affects the mind in some way and is prohibited or under strict legal control in many countries owing to the social problems associated with its misuse, but which tends nevertheless to be extensively sold and used illegally. orig. *U.S.*

1926 *Rep. Drug Addiction in Calif.* (Calif. State Narcotic Comm.) 13 When used in this report, the term 'narcotics' or 'drugs' includes all of the following: Cocaine, opium, morphine, codeine, heroin, alpha eucaine, beta eucaine, flowering tops and leaves, extracts, tinctures, and other narcotic preparations of hemp or loco weed, Indian hemp, peyote, or chloral hydrate or any of the salts, derivatives or compounds of the foregoing substances. **1955** *U.S. Senate. Hearings* (1956) VIII. 4160 There are three groups into which the narcotics set forth in division 10 of the Health and Safety Code are divided: 1. Opiate group. 2. Cocaine, marihuana, and lophophora. 3. Synthetic group. **1972** *Daily Tel.* (Colour Suppl.) 11 Aug. 12/1 The Americans prefer the word 'narcotics', which although not entirely accurate—not all banned drugs cause narcosis—is better understood, so it will be used from here on. **1974** A. Goth *Med. Pharmacol.* (ed. 7) xxv. 300 In some state statutes the legal category 'narcotics' embraces the opiates, opiate-like drugs, marihuana, and cocaine. Medically defined, however, the term narcotic refers only to drugs having both a sedative and an analgesic action and is essentially restricted to the opiates and opiate-like drugs. *Ibid.* xxv. 304 Although marihuana is not medically a narcotic, it is classified legally as a narcotic in some states for purposes of control. **1974** *Encycl. Brit. Macropædia* V. 1049/2 Prejudice and ignorance have led to the labelling of all use of nonsanctioned drugs as addiction and of all drugs, when misused, as narcotics.

2. *attrib.* (freq. in *pl.*).

1926 *Proc. 1st World Conf. Narcotic Educ.* 111 How the police catch the crook or the narcotic dealer;..it is only when someone tells the police who the narcotic addict or peddler is that the police get them. *Ibid.* 227 The narcotic squad [in Philadelphia] was under the command of Captain Van Horn. **1929** *Narcotic Educ.* Jan. 46/1 To get sufficient evidence against John Smith it is necessary that a Government agent purchase narcotics from John Smith, but John Smith will only sell..for..$2,500 in advance... Where can a narcotic agent be found who has $2,500 to use? *Ibid.* Apr. 73/1 Out of the gray, neutral shadows cast by the murder of Arnold Rothstein, federal authorities forged a sturdy weapon expected to crush the most gigantic narcotic ring in the history of the illegal drug trade. **1951** *Manch. Guardian Weekly* 28 June 2/2 The State Legislature at Albany ordered an inquiry, which met last week. And this week the American Legion has followed it up with a 'narcotic clinic' of its own. **1953** *Conf. Drug Addiction among Adolescents* (N.Y. Acad. Med., Comm. Public Health Relations) II. 159 He..devised a plan..for the preventive and follow-up care of young narcotics addicts. **1953** W. Burroughs *Junkie* (1972) iii. 37 They found out the narcotics squad had a warrant for him sworn out by the State Inspector. **1963** *Listener* 4 Apr. 585/1 They were the bookies, and money lenders..and the narcotic pedlars. **1972** *Daily Tel.* 4 Sept. 3/1 A national Narcotics Bureau is to be set up in London next month to coordinate the activities of police drug squads in this country. **1973** *N.Y. Law Jrnl.* 19 June 4/5 The defendant argued that the offence itself, sale of dangerous drugs..made it 'appear' that he was a narcotics addict.

narcotic (nɑːˈkɒtɪk), *a.* Also 7–8 -ick(e, 8 -ique. [ad. med.L. *narcōtic-us* or Gr. ναρκωτικ-ός, f. ναρκοῦν to benumb, stupefy: see narcosis and -otic. Hence also F. *narcotique*.]

1. Of substances or their qualities: Having the effect of inducing stupor, sleep, or insensibility.

1601 Holland *Pliny* II. 103 This later Daffodil..stuffeth the head, for which narcoticke qualitie..it took the name in Greek Narcissus. *Ibid.*, *Explan. Words Art*, Narcoticke medicines be those that benum and stupifie with their coldnesse. **1651** French *Distill.* v. 116 Three parts of four of them are an insipid Narcotick flegme. *a* **1668** Davenant *Masque* Wks. (1673) 364 Injunctions are gone out..for the purging of the heavenly Beverage of a narcotique weed. **1742** *London & Country Brew.* i. (ed. 4) 47 The stupifying narcotic Qualities of the Yeast. **1799** *Med. Jrnl.* I. 161 The narcotic principle is contained chiefly in those vegetables which..have a direct tendency to induce sleep. **1804** *Ibid.* XII. 38 Hyosciamus, cicuta, and other narcotic and acrimonious plants. **1865** Kingsley *Herew.* iii, Stupid with mead made from narcotic heather honey.

b. *transf.* of persons, actions, qualities, etc.: Producing sleep or dullness.

1751 Johnson *Rambler* No. 89 ¶8 He that finds the frigid and narcotick infection beginning to seize him. *a* **1763** Shenstone *Economy* iii. 95 Pale, meagre, muse-rid wight! who reads in vain Narcotic volumes o'er. **1791** Boswell *Johnson* (1816) II. 109 That it endeavoured to infuse a narcotick indifference..into the minds of the people..is but too evident. **1855** Motley *Dutch Rep.* v. iv. (1866) 729 He ..habitually fell asleep at that horrible council-board,.. while the other murderers had found their work less narcotic. **1888** Lanciani *Anc. Rome* 113 To lose hours upon hours in listening to silly and narcotic lecturers.

2. Of the nature of narcosis.

1661 Lovell *Hist. Anim. & Min.* 335 It's cured..if malignant, venenate, and narcotick, by alexipharmicks, and roborants. **1834** *Cycl. Pract. Med.* III. 160/2 It is not the repetition of sound, but of the same sound, which produces the narcotic effect. **1863** M. Howitt tr. *Bremer's Greece* II. xii. 52 The want of animation and movement..exercises a slumberous, narcotic effect on the mind.

narcotical (nɑːˈkɒtɪkəl), *a.* Now *rare.* [f. prec. + -al[1].] Of a narcotic nature; soporific.

1587 Harmer tr. *Beza's Serm.* 421 Medicines which they call narcotical, that is to say such as benowme and ded the diseased. **1597** A. M. tr. *Guillemeau's Fr. Chirurg.* 49 b/2, We must endevoure to mitigate the payne with Narcoticall thinges. **1657** Tomlinson *Renou's Disp.* 113 Soft confections,..purging or narcoticall. **1695** Westmacott *Script. Herb.* 25 The Chymical Oyl of Box-wood [is].. look'd upon to be highly Narcotical. **1831** *Fraser's Mag.* III. 770 [He] drugged the readers..with narcotical essays upon currency.

Hence **nar'cotically** *adv.*; **nar'coticalness** (Ogilvie, 1850).

1654 Whitlock *Zootomia* 222 As those things do, that passe for narcotically cold. **1811** Byron *Hints fr. Hor.* 733 Hark to those notes, narcotically soft! The cobbler-laureats sing. **1890** *Blackw. Mag.* CLXVIII. 22/1 The oppressive atmosphere of a narcotically perfumed boudoir.

nar'coticism. *rare.* [f. narcotic *a.* + -ism.] Narcotism.

1822 *Monthly Mag.* LIII. 199/2 Those who eat them to excess were affected..with a kind of stupor and narcoticism. **1899** *Two Worlds* 6 Jan. 1/2 Souls who, in their earth life, allowed narcoticism to control them.

nar'coticness. *rare*$^{-1}$. [f. narcotic *a.* + -ness.] Narcoticalness.

1651 R. Child in *Hartlib's Legacy* (1655) 137 It taketh away the appetite, not by real satiating, but by its Narcoticknesse deluding nature. **1727** Bailey vol. II. [hence in later Dicts.], *Narcotickness*, stupifying..Quality.

nar,cotico-'acrid, *a.* and *sb. Med.* [f. *narcotico-* as combining form of narcotic *a.* + acrid *a.* Cf. F. *narcotico-âcre*.]

A. *adj.* Possessing both narcotic and acrid or irritant properties.

1835 *Cycl. Pract. Med.* IV. 230/1 The symptoms which characterize the narcotico-acrid poisons generally. **1854** *Encycl. Brit.* (ed. 8) V. 180/2 They have narcotico-acrid properties and are usually more or less poisonous. **1861** Bentley *Man. Bot.* 582 The plants of the order should be regarded with suspicion,..some act as narcotico-acrid poisons.

B. *sb.* An irritant narcotic poison.

1829 Christison *Treat. Poisons* (1832) 592 Some varieties of poisoning with the vegetable narcotico-acrids. **1840** *Penny Cycl.* XVI. 88/2 Many natural compounds have an acrid principle combined with the narcotic, and hence are termed narcotico-acrids.

So **nar,cotico-'irritant** *a.* (Ogilvie, 1882.)

'narcotina. *Chem.* ? *Obs.* [f. as next + -ina.] = narcotine.

1834 *Cycl. Pract. Med.* III. 152/2 Separating..the meconate of morphia, the narceine and narcotina. **1840** *Penny Cycl.* XVI. 87/2 A brilliant crystalline substance is left, which is the narcotina of the opium.

narcotine (ˈnɑːkətɪn, -aɪn). *Chem.* [f. narcot-ic *a.* + -ine[5], or a. F. *narcotine*.] A bitter crystalline alkaloid derived from opium (discovered by Derosne in 1803), sometimes used in medicine.

1823 Haden tr. *Majendie's Formulary* 28 If a grain of narcotine, dissolved in oil, be given to dogs, it produces a state of stupor. **1876** Harley *Mat. Med.* (ed. 6) 762 A solution of narcotine and hydrochlorate of papaverine.

narcotism (ˈnɑːkətɪz(ə)m). *Path.* [f. as prec. + -ism, or ad. F. *narcotisme*.]

1. The condition produced by narcotics; a state of stupor, somnolence, or insensibility.

1831 Davies *Mat. Med.* 296 During narcotism, the circulation is sometimes slightly accelerated, at others it is slower. **1859** R. F. Burton *Centr. Africa* in *Jrnl. Geog. Soc.* XXIX. 367 It affects the head, and produces an agreeable narcotism, followed by sound sleep. **1875** H. C. Wood *Therap.* (1879) 225 Whenever it is desired to produce very decided narcotism by..opium, the drug should always be given in liquid form.

b. The method of producing insensibility by narcotics.

1843 R. J. Graves *Syst. Clin. Med.* v. 69 You have lately seen an infusion of green tea useful in..narcotism. **1855** Ramsbotham *Obstet. Med.* 184 Siebold makes the same remark in reference to two forceps cases, in which he employed narcotism.

2. A morbid inclination to sleep.

1843 R. J. Graves *Syst. Clin. Med.* viii. 91 That tendency to narcotism..which is observed in every case of genuine typhus. **1897** *Trans. Amer. Pediatric Soc.* IX. 118 Pronounced narcotism and headache are..the most characteristic symptoms of his lithæmic attacks.

3. *transf.* The narcotic influence *of* something.

1867 Lowell *Wks.* (1890) II. 317 Lapped in waking dreams by the narcotism of an age of science. **1876** J. Ollive *Wooing of Até* III. xvi. 271 His musings were..softened by the genial narcotism of tobacco.

narcotist (ˈnɑːkətɪst). [f. as prec. + -ist.] One addicted to the use of narcotics.

1860 *All Year Round* No. 53. 61 There, though opium-eating is now unusual... I have seen the miserable narcotist lying staring at nothing. **1881** *Sat. Rev.* 5 Mar. 288 The narcotist who..finds himself unable to sleep without morphia or chloral.

narcoti'zation. [f. next + -ation.] The action of narcotizing; the state induced by narcotic poisoning.

1864 *Lond. Rev.* 6 Aug. 154/1 The irregularity of the circulation was like that described in M. Decaisne's cases of narcotization as produced by ordinary smoking. **1876** tr. *Wagner's Gen. Pathol.* 163 After narcotization of animals, there always arises dilatation of vessels.

narcotize (ˈnɑːkətaɪz), *v.* [f. narcot-ic *a.*]

1. *trans.* To bring or render insensible with a narcotic.

1843 R. J. Graves *Syst. Clin. Med.* xiv. 151 He was evidently deeply narcotised. **1859** R. F. Burton *Centr. Africa* in *Jrnl. Geog. Soc.* XXIX. 243 Near the coast the people narcotise fish with the juice of certain plants. **1899** *Allbutt's Syst. Med.* VII. 823 Giving morphia by hypodermic injection in such large doses as to keep the patient deeply narcotised.

refl. **1865** *Reader* 1 Apr. 374/3 They narcotize, but do not nicotinize themselves.

2. *transf.* To dull or deaden. Also *absol.*

1864 E. Sargent *Peculiar* II. 189 What wonder that he should narcotize his moral sense with the aroma of these social fascinations. **1876** Lowell *Among my Bks.* Ser. ii. 248 They rather narcotize than fortify. **1894** Du Maurier *Trilby* II. 252 He longed for his old brain-disease to come back and narcotise his trouble.

Hence **'narcotized** *ppl. a.*, **'narcotizing** *ppl. a.*

1851 H. Mayo *Pop. Superst.* (ed. 2) 138 The narcotising agent recommended by Mr. Jackson. **1863** B. Taylor *H. Thurston* xiv. 183 It surrounded each fair face with a nimbus, to the narcotized vision of youth. **1878** O. W. Holmes *Motley* 226 How much better is the restlessness of a noble ambition than the narcotized stupor of club-life.

nard (nɑːd), *sb.* Also 4–6 narde. [= OF. *narde* (mod.F. *nard*), ad. L. *nardus* (see nardus), ad. Gr. νάρδος, of Oriental origin: cf. Heb. *nērʼd* (pl. *nʼrādīm*), Arab. and Pers. *nārdīn*, Skr. *narada*, *nalada*.]

1. An aromatic balsam or ointment used by the ancients, derived from the plant of the same name (see sense 2, and cf. spikenard).

Chiefly in poetic use, or in echoes of N.T. passages.

1382 Wyclif *John* xii. 3 Marie took a pound of oynement spikenard, or trewe narde, precious. **1388** —— *Song Sol.* i. 11 Whanne the kyng was in his restyng place, my narde ȝaf his odour. *c* **1420** *Pallad. on Husb.* iv. 143 Her seed yf me reclyne In baume, or narde, or opi, daies thre. **1477** Norton *Ord. Alch.* v. in Ashm. (1652) 70 Amber, Narde, and Mirrhe. **1526** Skelton *Magnyf.* 2373 Your wordes be more sweter than ony precyous narde. **1554** Philpot *Exam. & Writ.* (Parker Soc.) 233 You have plentifully poured upon me your precious nard. **1601** Holland *Pliny* xii. xii. I. 364 The good..and true Nard is known by the lightnes, red colour, sweet smell, and the tast especially. **1647** Jer. Taylor *Lib. Proph.* Ep. Ded. 3 Whose lessons were softer than Nard, or the Juice of the Candian Olive. **1708** J. Philips *Cyder* ii. 53 Steams, than Myrrh or Nard more grateful. **1775** R. Chandler *Trav. Asia M.* (1825) I. 165 Mutianus..had many holes filled with nard to nourish and moisten it. **1835** BROWNING *Paracelsus* IV. 192 Heap cassia, sandal-buds and stripes Of labdanum, and aloe-balls, Smeared with dull nard. **1866** BRANDE & COX *Dict. Sci.* etc. II. 635/1 The Nard of the ancients..is now believed to have been the produce of a dwarf Valerianaceous herb.

Comb. **1696** PHILLIPS, *Nard-Plant*, that grows in the Indies,..sweet, and smelling like Galingale.

2. An aromatic plant, esp. that yielding the ointment used by the ancients (now usually supposed to be *Nardostachys Jatamansi*; cf. SPIKENARD).

1591 PERCIVALL *Sp. Dict.*, *Asarabacar*, a kinde of Narde, a kinde of foale foote. **1598** FLORIO, *Nigella*, the herbe Pepper-woort, narde or Coriander of Rome. **1626** BACON *Sylva* §616 There is a Kinde of Nard, in Creet,..that hath a Root hairy, like a Rough-footed-Doves foot. **1667** MILTON *P.L.* v. 293 He..now is come Into the blissful field, through Groves of Myrrhe And flouring Odours, Cassia, Nard, and Balme. **1855** SINGLETON *Virgil* I. 33 As much as lowly nard To beds of crimson roses,—in our mind So much Amyntas yieldeth unto thee.

3. With defining terms, as ***Celtic***, ***French***, ***Indian***, ***Italian***, ***mountain***, ***rustic nard***; also †***nard savage***.

1601 HOLLAND *Pliny* II. 88 As for the plant Saliunca or Nard Celtick [etc.]. *Ibid.* 104 Some haue taken rustick-Nard to be the root of Bacchar, and so named it: the which hath put me in mind of French Nard. **1611** FLORIO, *Nardo saluatico*, nard-sauage. **1678** SALMON *Pharm. Lond.* I. iv. 60 The male is the broad Italian Nard, (which is the sweeter) and is called Lavender. **1768** CROKER *Compl. Dict.* II. s.v., The Indian Nard..was formerly employed in the same intentions as the Celtic. **1799** G. SMITH *Laboratory* I. 432 The following drugs, viz. liquorish and celtic-nard. **1801** *Encycl. Brit.* Suppl. II. 293/2 The Protean plant Valerian, a sister of the Mountain and Celtic Nard. **1842** *Penny Cycl.* XXII. 347/2 It is curious that the Celtic and mountain nards are also Valerians.

4. Mat-grass (*Nardus stricta*). *rare*$^{-1}$.

1866 *Treas. Bot.* 777/2 The common Nard, or Matgrass..is a worthless grass for agricultural purposes.

Hence **nard** *v. trans.*, to anoint with nard.

1828 TENNYSON *Lover's Tale* I. 671 She took the body of my past delight, Narded..and balm'd it for herself.

nar'diferous, *a.* *rare*$^{-1}$. [f. L. *nardifer* + -OUS.] Bearing or producing nard.

1657 TOMLINSON *Renou's Disp.* 461 Bizantian Blatta..is long and strict, found in nardiferous lakes.

'nardine, *a.* *rare.* [ad. obs. F. *nardin* (Godef.), or L. *nardinus*, Gr. *νάρδινος*, f. *νάρδος* NARD.] Of or pertaining to nard; having the qualities of nard. †*oil nardine*, oil of nard.

c **1400** *Lanfranc's Cirurg.* 104 Anoynte his nolle & his necke wiþ hoote oynementis as wiþ oile of nardine. **1545** RAYNOLD *Byrth Mankynde* 78 Take oyle nardine, oyle of whyte lyllies, of eche an ounce and an halfe. **1828–32** WEBSTER cites *Asiatic Res.*

nardoo (nɑːˈduː, ˈnɑːduː). Also nardu. [Native Australian; also given as *ngárdū* and *ardoo*.]

1. The sporocarp of the plant *Marsilea quadrifolia*, used as food by the Australian aborigines; the flour made from this. Also *attrib.*

1861 H. J. WILLS in W. Howitt *Discov. Austral.* (1865) II. 248 Starvation on nardoo is by no means very unpleasant. **1861** KING *Ibid.* 252 The natives..gave in return some chewed pitchery and nardoo balls. **1862** KENDALL *Poems* 110 Lest unfriendly hands Should rob him of his hoard of wild nardoo. **1874** *Dusk Twilight Hour* 134 They fished and hunted for their food, And gathered nardoo.

2. The plant *Marsilea quadrifolia*, also called *clover-fern*.

1864 *Chambers's Encycl.* VI. 670/2 *Nardoo*, a plant of the acotyledonous natural order *Marsileaceæ*. **1889** LUMHOLTZ *Cannibals* 41 On the banks of the Thompson river I observed the well-known nardu (*Marsilea*).

attrib. **1865** W. HOWITT *Discov. Austral.* II. 247 They now began to inquire of the nardoo seed, imagining it the produce of a tree. **1866** *Treas. Bot.* 777/1 Nardoo fields, probably swampy places in which it abounds.

‖**nardus** (ˈnɑːdəs). Now *rare.* [L. *nardus*: see NARD *sb.*] Nard, spikenard (the ointment and plant). Also *attrib.* and *fig.*

971 *Blickl. Hom.* 73 Þær wæron þreo þa betstan [wyrta], ele, & nardus, & spica. **1398** TREVISA *Barth. De P.R.* XVII. cx. (1495) 672 Nardus is a lytyll herbe wyth pryckes and smellyth wel..and therof is treble manere kynde, Indica, Celtica, and Sirica. **1526** TINDALE *John* xii. 3 A pounde of oyntment called nardus. **1535** COVERDALE *Mark* xiv. 3 There came a woman which had a boxe of pure and costly Nardus oyntement. **1578** LYTE *Dodoens* 307 It is good to be poured into the eares with oyle of roses, or Nardus. **1600** FAIRFAX *Tasso* XVIII. xv, Vpon his brest and forehead gently blew The aire, that balme and nardus breath'd vnseene. **1720** STRYPE *Stow's Surv.* (1754) II. VI. ii. 597/2 Edward is dead,..A King, or fragrant Nardus hight, a gracious princely Peer. **1797** HOLCROFT tr. *Stolberg's Trav.* (ed. 2) III. lxxix. 217 They..scattered this valuable water of the nardus. **1842** *Penny Cycl.* XXII. 347/1 The first kind being called nardus, and distinguished into the Syrian and Indian varieties.

nare (nɛə(r)), *sb.* Now only *arch.* [ad. L. *nāris* (usu. in pl. *nārēs*: see NARES). Cf. OF. *nairre* (Godef.).]

†**1.** A nostril. *Obs.* (chiefly in 17th c. verse).

1398 TREVISA *Barth. De P.R.* XVII. cxii. (Bodl. MS.), Veynes & nares & þe pawme of the hondes..be bawmed þerwiþ. *a* **1616** B. JONSON *Epigr.*, *On famous Voy.* 133 For, yet, no nare was tainted, Nor thumb, nor finger, to the stop acquainted. **1663** BUTLER *Hud.* I. i. 742 There is a Machiavilian plot, (Tho' ev'ry nare olfact it not).

2. *spec.* A nostril of a hawk.

1486 *Bk. St. Albans* a v, With a penne put it in the hawkis nares Ones or twyes. *Ibid.* c vij, Thorogh her Nostrellis or hir nares. *c* **1575** *Perf. Bk. Sparhawkes* (1886) 6 Seare fayre: nares wyde: stalke short and bygg. **1614** LATHAM *Falconry* (1633) 131, I was inforced first to slit her with a knife, from her eare vnto her nare. **1614** MARKHAM *Cheap Husb.* II. VIII. xiii. 142 The Rheume is a continuall running or dropping at the Hawkes Nares. **1727** BRADLEY *Fam. Dict.* s.v. *Aposthume*, When the Nares of the Hawk are stuffed up..put some Drops thereof upon her Nares. **1840** BROWNING *Sordello* IV. 59 Who bade him bloody the spent osprey's nare? **1860** H. AINSWORTH *Ovingdean Grange* 61 Its keen-bent beak,..wide nares, and full black eye.

Comb. *c* **1450** *Bk. Hawking* (Harl. MS. 2340) 14 a, Coold..makith flume fall oute of þe brayne, [and] but if it have hastely help it wol stop his nare þrolles.

†**nare**, *a.* *Obs.* Forms: 1 **neara, neare**, 2 **nara**, 3–4 **nare**. [OE. *neara*, var. of *nearo* NARROW *a.*] Narrow.

In the collocation *narewei*, *nare wey*, which occurs in the *Moral Ode* 347 (Egerton text) and R. Glouc. *Chron.* 3312, the form may be due to elision of the *w* (in *narew*) before that of the word following.

c **888** K. ÆLFRED *Boeth.* xix, Behealde he..hu neara þære eorðan stede is, þeah heo us rum þince. *a* **900** *Kentish Gloss.* in Wr.-Wülcker 80 *Puteus angustus*, neare pyt. *c* **1000** *Ags. Gosp.* Matt. vii. 14 Eala hu neara [*Hatton* nara] & hu angsum is þæt ȝeat. *c* **1270** *S. E. Leg.* I. 304/157 þe hul..is sumdel nare [= 163 narv]. *Ibid.* 320/724 It lith..ibouwed ase an hare..for is In is sumdel nare. *c* **1315** SHOREHAM I. 1383 He a-uangeþ a crowet eke, And a towaylle nare.

†**nare**, were not: cf. NE and NERE. *Obs.*

a **1175** *Cott. Hom.* 223 Nare hio blinde ȝescapene. *c* **1200** *Moral Ode* 201 (Trin. Coll. MS.), Alle unhalðe þurh deað cam in þis middeneard..Nare noman elles dead. *c* **1374** CHAUCER *Boeth.* I. pr. iii. (1868) 10 Certis it nar[e] not leueful ne sittyng to philosophie [etc.].

†**narel(l**. *Obs.* *rare.* [a. OF. *narel (later *nareau*): see NARE *sb.* and -EL[2].] A nostril.

1486 *Bk. St. Albans* c vj b, Brynne the Narellis thourogh owte. **1611** COTGR., *Canolles*, a haukes Narell; one of the little holes whereat she draws in, and lets out, her breath. *Ibid.*, *Nareau*, a narell, or nosethrill.

narer, nearer: see NAR *a.*

‖**nares** (ˈnɛəriːz). *Anat.* [L. *nārēs*, pl. of *nāris*, NARE *sb.*, related to NASE *sb.*, nose.] *pl.* The nostrils or nasal passages.

1693 tr. *Blancard's Phys. Dict.* (ed. 2), *Nares*, the Nostrils. **1727–38** CHAMBERS *Cycl.* s.v. *Nose*, Divided in the middle by a third [bone]..into two partitions, called the *nares* or nostrils. **1753** —— *Cycl. Supp.* s.v., The *nares* of fish differ also in proportion. **1808–10** *Mem. Wernerian Soc.* I. viii. 140 The blowholes or nares were united at the posterior part into one tube. **1833** *Cycl. Pract. Med.* II. 104/1 The introduction of a cylindrical plug of lint through the anterior nares. **1873** MIVART *Elem. Anat.* 76 These openings are the hinder nostrils, or posterior nares.

nare-throlle: see NARE *sb.* 2.

nareu, -ewe, obs. ff. NARROW *a.* (and *v.*).

narf: see NARVE.

narghile, nargileh (ˈnɑːgɪleɪ). Also **-ghileh, -ghyle, -ghille, -gilé, -guilè.** *β.* **narghilly, -gilly,** (nɑːˈgɪlɪ). [= F. *narghileh*, *narguilé*, ad. Pers. (or Turk.) *nārgīleh*, f. Pers. *nārgīl*, coconut, of which the receptacle for the tobacco was originally made.] An Oriental tobacco-pipe in which the smoke passes through water before reaching the mouth: a HOOKAH.

α. **1839** MISS PARDOE *Beauties of Bosph.* 35 The *narghilè*, or water pipe,..which greatly resembles the hookah of Hindostan, is always filled with Shiraz tobacco. **1848** THACKERAY *Van. Fair* li, A Turkish officer..making believe to puff at a narghile. **1877** A. B. EDWARDS *Up Nile* xxi. 667 Gorgeous..narghilehs with long flexible tubes. **1897** GUNTER *Susan Turnbull* ii. 14 He enjoys his nargileh pipe.

β. **1847** DISRAELI *Tancred* III. ii, Inhaling through rose-water the..artificial flavour of the nargilly. **1871** M. COLLINS *Mrq. & Merch.* II. vii. 184 He is smoking his narghilly.

narȝwe, obs. form of NARROW *v.*

narhwal, obs. form of NARWHAL.

narial (ˈnɛərɪəl), *a.* *Anat.* [f. L. *nāri-s* nostril (see NARES) + -AL[1].] Belonging to the nares.

1870 FLOWER *Osteol. Mamm.* xi. 171 The edges of these greatly expanded narial apertures. **1881** OWEN in *Nature* XXIV. 499/2 The entry to the narial passage, or respiratory mouth as it may be called.

So **'naric** *a.* (*Cent. Dict.* 1890).

naricorn (ˈnɛərɪkɔːn). *Ornith.* [f. L. *nāri-s* nostril + *corn-ū* horn.] A horny covering protecting the nostrils in certain birds.

1866 COUES in *Proc. Philad. Acad. Nat. Sci.* 176 The 'naricorn' or rhinotheca is an irregularly convoluted little scroll, very thin and delicate in texture. *Ibid.*, When the naricorns are *in situ* the outer of these divisions..forms the most conspicuous part.

nariform (ˈnɛərɪfɔːm), *a.* [f. as prec. + -FORM.] (See quots.)

1846 DANA *Zooph.* (1848) 432 *Nariform*, a compressed calicle, resembling in shape a nose inverted. **1847** WEBSTER, *Nariform*, formed like the nose.

‖**narikin** (ˈnærɪkɪn). [Jap.] In Japan, a wealthy parvenu.

1920 *Glasgow Herald* 2 Sept. 7 'Narikin', or mushroom millionaires, have spent their rapidly amassed fortunes on extravagant living. **1923** in J. MANCHON *Le Slang* 203. **1933** *Times Lit. Suppl.* 16 Nov. 784/3 *Narikin*..as commonly used is..a term of reproach, applied to those *nouveaux riches* who made rapid fortunes as profiteers of the War. **1946** R. BENEDICT *Chrysanthemum & Sword* (1947) iv. 95 Narikin is often translated 'nouveau riche' but that does not do justice to the Japanese feeling... A narikin is a term taken from Japanese chess and means a pawn promoted to queen.

narine (ˈnɛəraɪn), *a.* [f. as NARIFORM *a.* + -INE.] 'Of or belonging to the nostrils' (Ogilvie, 1882).

naringin (nəˈrɪndʒɪn). *Chem.* [ad. G. *naringen* (E. Hoffmann, at the suggestion of Flückiger, 1879 in *Arch. der Pharm.* CCXIV. 140), f. *naringi*, given as Skr. for ORANGE *sb.*[1], *a.*: see -IN[1].] A bitter glucoside, $C_{27}H_{32}O_{14}$, of a tricyclic alcohol which is found in shaddock, grapefruit, and certain types of orange.

1879 *Jrnl. Chem. Soc.* XXXVI. 468 Naringin, the hesperidin of de Vrij, which is found in the fully developed buds of *Citrus decumana* to the amount of 2 per cent., is obtained from the residue left on distillation of the ethereal oil. **1926** *Biochem. Jrnl.* XX. 1305 Naringin, the specific glucoside of the grape-fruit, was found present in the rind and in alcoholic extracts of it. **1957** E. V. MILLER *Chem. Plants* viii. 113 Naringin is found in large quantities in the juice of immature grapefruits..and to a certain extent in the segment walls of mature fruits. **1970** *New Scientist* 1 Jan. 21/1 The most promising [sweetening] compounds are made from naringin isolated from grapefruit, hesperidin from sweet oranges and neohesperidin from Seville oranges.

nark (nɑːk), *sb.* *slang.* [Romany *nāk* nose.]

1. a. (See quot. 1894.)

1860 in Hotton *Slang Dict.* (ed. 2) 179. **1894** A. MORRISON *Mean Streets* 260 He resolved to..become a nark—a copper's nark—which is a police spy or informer. **1916** G. B. SHAW *Pygmalion* I. 110 It's a—well, it's a copper's nark, as you might say. What else would you call it? A sort of informer. **1933** AUDEN *Dance of Death* 37 Quick under the table, it's the 'tecs and their narks, O no, salute—it's Mr. Karl Marx. **1936** J. G. BRANDON *Pawnshop Murder* x. 90 Police 'narks', 'noses', and all such kindred brethren. **1954** [see GRASS *sb.*[1] 12]. **1968** *Listener* 19 Dec. 810/3 Don't do it.., he's a copper's nark. **1975** *Times* 9 Jan. 4/4 If it was thought we were coppers' narks it could endanger the lives of our film crews.

b. A policeman.

1891 F. W. CAREW *No. 747* vi. 65 If you don't turn up my fair share, I'll put the narks upon you. S'elp me never, I will. **1937** M. ALLINGHAM *Dancers in Mourning* xxvii. 327 There's a bunch o' narks at either end of the lane. **1959** A. SILLITOE *Loneliness of Long-Distance Runner* 27 Don't let that gate creak too much or you'll have the narks tuning-in. **1959** I. & P. OPIE *Lore & Lang. Schoolch.* xvii. 369 There are, in the London area, at least thirty nicknames current among boys... The Law, Nark or Narker, Nobby, [etc.]. *a* **1966** M. ALLINGHAM *Cargo of Eagles* (1968) v. 74 I've 'appened on a little something wot the official narks 'aven't cottoned to yet.

2. Freq. in *Austral.* and *N.Z.* **a.** A person who is annoying, unpleasant, obstructive, or quarrelsome. Cf. KNARK.

1846 *Swell's Night Guide* 68 They are the rankest narks vot ever God put guts into, or ever farted in a kickses case. **1898** *Bulletin* (Sydney) 17 Dec. (Red Page), An informer or mar-plot is a *nark* or *Jonah*. **1906** E. DYSON *Fact'ry 'Ands* i. 12 'Yeh know, Feathers, she's no bally nark; er bloke kin trust 'er,' he said. **1908** *Austral. Mag.* 1 Nov. 1251 *Nark*, a spoil-sport. **1918** *Aussie* Sept. 2/2 He appealed in vain to Madame... 'Orright, then, Madame, I can be a nark, too! I know where there's..fat, juicy frogs, and you wont get one of 'em!' **1925** FRASER & GIBBONS *Soldier & Sailor Words* 164 *Nark*, a bad-tempered man; a spoil-sport... Also, a man eager to curry favour by running about and doing odd jobs for a superior. **1928** V. PALMER *Man Hamilton* 94 'Oh, don't be a nark, Miss Byrne,' he coaxes her. **1933** F. CLUNE *Try Anything Once* 81 Lieutenant Hennessy fulfilled the most exacting requirements of what a 'nark' should be. **1937** PARTRIDGE *Dict. Slang* 551/2 *Nark*... A person on inquiry from head office: London clerks', managers', etc.: from before 1935. **1943** *Penguin New Writing* XVIII. 63 If I said anything..he'd go crook and tell me not to be a nark. **1959** I. & P. OPIE *Lore & Lang. Schoolch.* xviii. 391 'It is a way to get your own back on an old nark who has spoilt a game,' declares an Edinburgh 12-year-old. **1965** J. S. GUNN *Terminol. Shearing Industry* II. 6 *Nark*, a troublemaker who interrupts the rhythm of the shed. A nark shearer only hurts himself, but a shedhand or roller who does not keep the board clear can slow up the work of all men handling the fleece.

b. An annoying or unpleasant thing or situation; a source of astonishment or vexation.

1923 J. MANCHON *Le Slang* 203 *Nark*..(rare), rancune, une dent qu'on a contre quelqu'un. **1926** R. R. TERRY *Shanty Bk.* II. 25 When they went to church to say 'I will', the drummer got a nark. [*footnote*] *Nark*, a disagreeable surprise. **1937** N. MARSH *Vintage Murder* 114 It's a blooming nark, dinkum it is. **1947** *Book* (Christchurch, N.Z.) IX. 23 'It's a nark, isn't it,' she said. 'I thought you'd get by without the op.' **1948** R. ALLEY *Gung Ho* 16 Typhoid, malaria, and all the narks. **1966** P. MOLONEY *Plea for Mersey* 51 Not hardened junkies, when deprived of dope, Ere felt such anger, ere got such a nark As Scouseville driver seeking space to park.

nark (nɑːk), *v.* [f. the sb.] **1. a.** *trans.* To watch, look after. **b.** *intr.* To act as an informer. *slang.*

1859 in Hotten *Dict. Slang* 67. **1894** A. MORRISON *Mean Streets* 260 Hardly had he begun his narking when some of the..mob dropped on him. **1896** —— *Child Jago* 55 It was the sole commandment that ran there: 'Thou shalt not nark'.

2. *trans.* and *intr.* To annoy, exasperate, infuriate; to complain, grumble. Often in *pa. pple. slang* (freq. in *Austral.* and *N.Z.*) and *dial.*
1888 J. DALBY *Mayroyd of Mytholm* II. 45 That's just what he's ta'en to him for, just to nark Mayroyd. **1888** S. O. ADDY *Gloss. Words Sheffield* 155 *Narked*, vexed, angry... 'He wor narked about it.' **1896** H. LAWSON *Shearing of Cook's Dog* in *While Billy Boils* 167 The cook usually forgot all about it in an hour... But this time he didn't; he was 'narked' for three days. **1899** *Bulletin* (Sydney) 25 Feb. (Red Page), Tom was gettin' narked, so I tries to get him to turn in. **1908** E. J. BANFIELD *Confessions of Beachcomber* I. v. 174 He'll be a bit narked at having wasted a whole bloomin' day. **1916** *Anzac Book* 142 But wot narks us more than any Is to 'ear the sergeant say: 'The sea's too rough to land our stores; There ain't no jam today!' **1916** J. B. COOPER *Coo-oo-ee* xix. 299, I thought you would. That's very like the Tippinses to nark like that. **1930** *Bulletin* (Sydney) 19 Mar. 23/1 It was this that narked me most—'e couldn't see a joke. **1932** L. A. G. STRONG *Don Juan & Wheelbarrow* ix. 162 Is it true..that So-and-So is narked as the Cottage 'Ospital be over to 'Arraton, 'stead of here? **1940** F. SARGESON *Man & his Wife* (1944) 49 That got Tom narked. He told George he ought to be ashamed of himself for telling things like that. **1945** *Daily Sketch* 20 Apr. 2/2 Like you, I am all for personal liberty—and so no doubt are the inmates of Wormwood Scrubs—but the fact remains that so long as there is not economic freedom for everybody, what is the point of constantly narking about State-planning? **1947** D. M. DAVIN *Gorse blooms Pale* 78 It narked her that everyone was eating out of her hand except me. **1958** *Times Lit. Suppl.* 15 Aug. p. xxxii/3 This naturally brings out the worst in their opponents and in the resultant narking and name-calling the 'legitimate contention' is lost sight of. **1962** [see HALF *adv.* 3]. **1966** *Crescendo* Apr. 29/2 The narked comments of some respected musicians. **1968** *Daily Progress* (Charlottesville, Virginia) 11 July C.14/1 In Britain, to nark is to nag, scold, annoy or irritate. Mrs. Ewing, a vivacious blonde, narks mostly about home rule for Scotland. She has managed to irritate some members of Parliament and her election victory annoyed Prime Minister Harold Wilson's Labor party. **1970** *New Scientist* 23 July 190/2 The Chinese have naturally been somewhat narked at being left out of the fun. **1973** *Daily Tel.* 2 Nov. 15 If you feel especially narked about something, you can turn it into a theory of human behaviour.

3. *trans.* Usu. with *it.* To cease, desist, stop, terminate. Freq. in imp. *slang.*
1889 *Sporting Times* 29 June 1/3 And as terseness of expression was an art she'd studied well, She determined that her lady friend should nark it. **1925** in FRASER & GIBBONS *Soldier & Sailor Words* 164. **1933** *Bulletin* (Sydney) 1 Feb. 20 It was 'ard luck when a bloke narked the show. **1936** J. CURTIS *Gilt Kid* xvii. 175 Nark it for God's sake... You'll get us done, yelling around the gaff like that. **1943** M. HARRISON *Reported Safe Arrival* 12 There was a sharp interchange of: 'Nark it!' and 'Oo says so?' I think there had been an interchange of more than words had not the Orderly Officer then appeared. **1943** *R.A.F. Jrnl.* Aug. 30 Nark it, Flight,.. you sound like a penny uplift. **1959** I. & P. OPIE *Lore & Lang. Schoolch.* x. 199 Saying by the one being tortured: ''Ere, nark it.' **1973** N. GRAHAM *Murder in Dark Room* xxiii. 162 'Nark it,' I said. 'I want a little bit of information from you.'

narker ('nɑːkə(r)). *slang.* [f. NARK *v.* + -ER[1].] An informer; a policeman; one who complains or disparages.
1932 NORDHOFF & HALL *Mutiny on Bounty* iii. 39 The captain's 'narker' or spy among the men. **1937** *Sunday Dispatch* 7 Feb. 22/6 The narkers are at it again with their fancy explanation of our Test mistakes. **1959** [see NARK *sb.* 1 b]. **1959** A. SILLITOE *Loneliness of Long-Distance Runner* 28 I'd..screw my eyes up like I was on my way to the hospital, ..'Cancer,' I'd manage to say to Narker, which would make his slow punch-drunk brain suspect a thing or two. **1971** *Daily Tel.* 3 May 8/4 His motto will be to celebrate not denigrate, and I commend this to the legion of glib narkers who tend to monopolise the screen.

narks (nɑːks), *sb. pl.* Colloq. abbrev. of nitrogen *narc*osis.
1962 S. MILES *Underwater Med.* vii. 100 Unromantic British divers simply call it 'Narks'. **1967** 'J. PALMER' *Above & Below* i. 9 It's lucky the ship lies in such shallow water. We shan't get the 'narks'.

narky ('nɑːkɪ), *a. slang.* [f. NARK *sb.* 2 + -Y[1].] Irascible, vexed, bad-tempered, sarcastic.
1895 *Leeds Mercury Weekly Suppl.* 13 July 3/8 Doan't let's get narky ower it. **1898** B. KIRKBY *Lakeland Words* 105 He were a bit narky ower t' trottin' do. **1943** M. HARRISON *Reported Safe Arrival* 53 Harry was interested. 'Garn!' he said. 'Yer kiddin', Perfess [Professor]!.. Shakespeare, eh? Full of swearin', eh? I allus thought 'e wz fer school-kids and blokes like yew, Perfess. I don' mean nothin' narky: on'y 'e ain't the sort of bloke me and de Pen 'ud settle dahn to read a basin of, if yer get me meanin'?' **1958** L. DURRELL *Balthazar* ii. 33 Below the belt... Dirty. Cruel. Narky. **1958** [see DUCKY *sb.* 2]. **1970** *New Society* 5 Mar. 399/1 Shelter has incurred a lot of narky criticism since it announced its intention of setting up a chain of housing advisory centres. **1973** *Irish Times* 2 Mar. 14/5 My husband is narky in the house. If I was to bring heaven down it would not satisfy him.

‖**Narodnik** (nə'rɒdnɪk, ‖na'rodɲik). Also **narodnik**. Pl. **Narodniki, Narodniks**. [Russ., f. *narod* people + -NIK.] A supporter of the type of populist agrarian socialism originating amongst the Russian intelligentsia in the late 1860s which regarded the peasants and intelligentsia as the only revolutionary forces and denied the revolutionary role of the working class; one who tries to educate politically communities of rural or urban poor while sharing the conditions of their lives. Also *attrib.* and *transf.* Hence **Na'rodnikism**, the theory of making political power a reality for the masses.
1885 E. NOBLE *Russ. Revolt* 204 In the spring of 1877 the members of a revolutionary society called the 'Narodniki' (Party of the People) 'went to the people', establishing a large number of propaganda centres along the line of the Volga. **1904** G. DRAGE *Russ. Affairs* i. 51 A party arose who called themselves *Narodniki* (Nationalists). **1921** M. P. PRICE *My Reminisc. Russ. Revolution* ii. 27 The Narodniks therefore preached 'back to the land'. **1929** L. KRASSIN *Leonid Krassin* vii. 58 The Narodniki, the first organised agrarian party, welcomed..common possession of the soil. **1950** E. H. CARR *Bolshevik Revolution* I. I. i. 4 For the past thirty years [*sc.* 1868–98] the leading Russian revolutionaries had been the *narodniks*—a composite name for a succession of revolutionary groups believing in the theory of peasant revolution and in the practice of terrorism against members of the autocracy. *Ibid.* iii. 52 The peasantry remained for the Mensheviks an essentially anti-revolutionary force; any revolutionary policy which counted on its support was a reversion to the *narodnik* heresy of a peasant revolution. **1965** *New Statesman* 20 Aug. 240/1 Last year's Mississippi Summer Project..was..composed of young Southern Negroes and Northern students on the staff of the Student Non-Violent Co-ordinating Committee... They were the original *narodniks* of the movement. **1966** *Economist* 3 Sept. 887/2 A new *narodnik* movement, a fresh attempt by the intellectuals to 'go to the people'. **1969** J. SAUL in Ionescu & Gallner *Populism* 135 It may seem useful to lump together Russian Narodnikism and North American Populism..because both represent largely rural responses to..'capitalism' or 'modernization' or 'industrialization'. **1970** G. JACKSON *Let.* 25 Mar. in *Soledad Brother* (1971) 197 The dialectic between Narodnik and Nihilist should never break down. **1971** *Graphic* (Durban) 7 May 12/2 Her aunts were active in the populist narodniki movement [in Russia].

narow(e), -hede, -ly, -ness, obs. ff. NARROW *a.*, NARROWHEAD, etc.

narp (nɑːp). *slang.* [Origin unknown.] A shirt.
1839 H. BRANDON *Poverty, Mendicity & Crime* 164/1 *Narp*, a shirt. **1949** in PARTRIDGE *Dict. Underworld* 464/1.

narr (nɑː(r)), *v.* Now only *dial.* [Onomatopœic: cf. NAR and GNAR *v.*] *intr.* Of a dog: To snarl, growl. Also *transf.*
1509 BARCLAY *Shyp of Folys* (1570) 69 Narring with thy selfe, like as a dogge doth barke. **1530** PALSGR. 643/2, I narre, as a dogge dothe whan he is angred, *je rechine.* **1573** BARET *Alv.* s.v. *Grinne*, A grinning, or scornefull opening of ye mouth, as when a dog narreth. **1585** FETHERSTONE tr. *Calvin on Acts* xvii. 3. 409 The worship of the law, whereat the Jewes narre at this day like dogs.
1875 PARISH *Sussex Dial.*, *Narre*, to growl like a dog. **1894** *Northumbld. Gloss.*, *Narr*, to snarl, to find fault in a growling manner.

narr, obs. variant of NAR *a.*, nearer.

narra[1] ('nærə). *S. Afr.* Also **nara(s)**. [ad. Hottentot *'narab*.] A spiny shrub, *Acanthosicyos horrida*, of the family Cucurbitaceæ, found in arid regions of south-western Africa, distinguished by thorns, which replace the leaves of young plants, and yellow flowers; also, the large globular fruit of this plant. Also *attrib.*
1838 J. E. ALEXANDER *Expedition Interior Afr.* II. iii. 68 The 'naras was growing on little knolls of sand; the bushes were about four or five feet high, without leaves, and with apposite thorns on the light and dark green striped branches. **1853** F. GALTON *Narr. Explorer Trop. S. Afr.* i. 21, I have mentioned above the 'Nara, a prickly gourd, which..is the staple food of these Hottentots. **1881** T. HAHN *Tsuni-‖Goam* 101 !Naras.—This fruit is a *Cucurbitacea*, almost as large as a new-born child's head. The flesh of it is eaten raw, and the seeds are kept for the dry season, when there is no fruit. The seeds taste almost like almonds. **1946** L. G. GREEN *So Few are Free* (1948) xii. 165 The narra, a member of the melon family..sends its roots down through the dunes for fifty feet, if necessary, to find moisture... The ripe narra is full of edible seeds, which are treated in many ways by the Hottentots. Boiled, they make a porridge. Tough pancakes are formed by the narra fluid and stored for months. Narra beer may be brewed from the syrupy juice. **1959** G. JENKINS *Twist of Sand* xiii. 267 The trails of naras creeper would provide some sort of fuel. **1973** *Stand. Encycl. S. Afr.* VIII. 40/2 Naras (properly: narra)... Spiny, much-branched, prostrate shrub of the family *Cucurbitaceae*, found growing on sand-dunes in the dry coastal strip of South-West Africa.

narra[2] ('nɑːrə). [Tagalog.] The Filipino name for the south-east Asian tree, *Pterocarpus indicus*, of the family Leguminosæ, or its timber; = AMBOYNA. Also *attrib.*
1859 J. BOWRING *Visit to Philippine Islands* xv. 270 (*table*) Narra, or Naga, or Asang... Buildings, furniture, doors and windows. **1890** J. FOREMAN *Philippine Islands* xix. 371 Narra ..gives logs up to 35 feet long by 26 inches square. It is the Mahogany of the Philippines. **1911** *Philippine Bureau of Forestry Bull.* No. 10. 11. 35 The members of the Narra family mentioned here have simply or doubly compound leaves. *Ibid.*, Narra is found throughout the Philippines. *Ibid.* 36 Narra is the most common commercial name for the wood in the Philippines. **1929** *Amer. Speech* IV. 284 Of the native [Filipino] words, a few have already been accepted. ..*narra* and *camagon*, hard woods used in fine cabinet work. **1947** J. C. RICH *Materials & Methods Sculpture* x. 292 *Narra* is a Philippine wood related to the Andaman Islands' Padouk. It has a yellow to reddish-brown color and is not always available commercially. **1971** F. H. TITMUSS *Commercial Timbers of World* (ed. 4) 48 This [*sc.* amboyna, *Pterocarpus indicus*] is one of the most important export species of the Philippines (the wood being known as narra on the North American market).

narra, dial. variant of NE'ER *A.*

'narrable, *a. rare*$^{-0}$. (See quot.)
1623 COCKERAM I, *Narrable*, that which may be declared.

narracion, -cyon, obs. forms of NARRATION.

Narragansett (nærə'gænsət). Also **Nar(r)haganset, Nar(r)ohiganset(t)**, etc. [Algonquian *Naiaganset* people of the small point (of land).] **1.** An Algonquian people orig. living in New England; a member of this people. Also *attrib.*
1622 *Relation Eng. Plantation Plimoth, New Eng.* 44 They told us that if they were Narrohigganset men they would not trust them. **1637** T. MORTON *New Eng. Canaan* I. xiv. 45 The cause why these other Salvages of the Narohigansets, came into these parts, was to see what strength we were of. **1682** M. ROWLANDSON *Narr. Captivity among Indians* 5, I was sold to him by another Narrhaganset Indian. **1764** T. HUTCHINSON *Hist. Colony Mass.-Bay* I. 138 At first, the Naragansets gave kind words to the messengers. **1809** 'D. KNICKERBOCKER' *Hist. N.Y.* II. v. iv. 29 He has been secretly endeavoring to instigate the Narrohigansett (or Narraganset)..Indians. **1848** *Trans. Amer. Ethnol. Soc.* II. i. 77 (*table*) *Families*... Algonkins. *Languages* or *Dialects*... Narragansets. **1850** R. G. LATHAM *Nat. Hist. Varieties Man* 329 Algonkins... Narraganset.—Extinct. In 1674, in Rhode Island. **1871** C. M. YONGE *Pioneers & Founders* i. 8 The Pequots were..at war..with the Narragansets, or river Indians. **1933** L. BLOOMFIELD *Lang.* 72 The *Algonquian* family..includes the languages..of New England (..*Narraganset, Mohican*, and so on). **1945** C. M. WEBSTER *Town Meeting Country* 11 The Narragansetts on the west shores of Narragansett Bay. **1951** HEPBURN & LOGAN *New England* 84/1 The Old Narragansett Church is worth seeing.

2. In full, **Narragansett pacer** (or **pacing mare**): a breed of pacing horse (now extinct) which originated in Rhode Island.
1777 J. ADAMS in J. & A. Adams *Familiar Lett.* (1876) 272 We are looking about for American curiosities to send across the Atlantic as presents... Narraganset pacing mares, mooses, wood ducks,..have all been thought of. **1809** 'D. KNICKERBOCKER' *Hist. N.Y.* II. VII. iii. 194 A crafty man.. bargained him out of his..charger, leaving in place thereof a villainous, spavined, foundered, Narraganset pacer. **1826** J. F. COOPER *Last of Mohicans* I. ii. 18 Giving her Narraganset a smart cut of the whip. **1943** E. FORBES *Johnny Tremain* 92, I never saw a horse his color before... Narragansett breed. **1946** M. C. SELF *Horseman's Encycl.* 286 A noble breed of horses was developed, namely, the Narragansett Pacer. They are said to have had a smooth gliding motion..and were very popular..with the Virginia plantation owners. **1963** BLOODGOOD & SANTINI *Horseman's Dict.* 144 *Pacer*... Specifically: a Standardbred pacing horse descended from the Thoroughbred English stallion 'Messenger' and from the native, so-called Naragansett pacing mares.

narratable (næ'reɪtəb(ə)l), *a.* [f. NARRATE *v.* + -ABLE.] That can be narrated.
1852 DICKENS *Let. to J. White* 22 Nov., If you should think of any other idea narratable by an old man.

narratage ('nærətɪdʒ). [f. NARRATE *v.* + -AGE.] A technique used in films, plays, and on television in which one of the characters has the role of storyteller.
1948 E. LINDGREN *Art of Film* vi. 112 Other films.. employ a method known as *narratage*, in which one of the characters, usually a minor character in the film, is depicted as telling the story. **1954** *Encounter* Aug. 55/1 Here, still surviving in an age of redundant dialogue and, worse still, explanatory narratage, are stories really told in pictures.

narrate (næ'reɪt), *v.* [f. L. *narrāt-*, ppl. stem of *narrāre* to relate, recount, supposed to be for **gnārāre*, related to *gnārus* knowing, skilled, and thus ultimately allied to KNOW *v.*]
The earliest examples (1656) are prob. translations of Sp. *narrar*. Otherwise the word comes into English use only after 1750; Richardson and Johnson call it Scottish:—
1748 RICHARDSON *Clarissa* (1811) VI. 223 When I have least to narrate, to speak in the Scottish phrase, I am most diverting. **1755** JOHNSON, *Narrate*, to relate, to tell; a word only used in Scotland. **1813** *Q. Rev.* July 433 The style [of M^c^Crie's *Knox*] is..free from all modern affectation, excepting the abominable verb 'narrate', which must absolutely be proscribed in all good writing.

1. *trans.* To relate, recount, give an account of.
1656 S. HOLLAND tr. *Zara* (1719) 11 His Excellency.. narrates his several Encounters. *Ibid.* 136 It were needless to narrate what flouting..there was amongst the bundle of Knights. **1754** CAMBRIDGE in *World* No. 56 II. 192, I have listened to the tales..of senators who narrated the eloquence they never spoke! **1755** AMORY *Mem.* (1769) I. 299 Were I to give you the particulars of all these things, it would take up days to narrate. **1788** ANNA SEWARD *Lett.* (1811) I. 92 In narrating interesting facts, his comments.. often fatigue by their plenitude. **1804** SOUTHEY in *Ann. Rev.* II. 17 The discovery of Madeira is narrated with all the exaggerations of romance. **1823** BENTHAM *Not Paul* 308 On this occasion three principal events are narrated. **1875** JOWETT *Plato* (ed. 2) I. 399 The tale of the last hours of Socrates is narrated to Echecrates.

b. To speak the commentary of (a broadcast, film, exhibition, etc.).
1974 *Anderson* (S. Carolina) *Independent* 24 Apr. 1B/2 Rear Adm. Rice narrated a slide show depicting historical portions of Anderson. **1975** *Daily Tel.* 30 Oct. 6/6 The Prince of Wales introduces and narrates 'One Day in November', a £20,000 colour film about the work of the Royal British Legion.

2. *absol.* To give an account, make a relation.
1795 tr. *Mercier's Fragm. Pol. & Hist.* II. 439 They ought merely to narrate, to prove, and to conclude by a short recapitulation. **1830** CARLYLE *Misc.* (1857) II. 168 Most men speak only to narrate. **1843** MARRYAT *M. Violet* xxxiii, Any one on hearing him narrate would say the same.

Hence **na'rrated** *ppl. a.*, **na'rrating** *vbl. sb.* and *ppl. a.* Also **na'rrater**, narrator (*rare*).
1758 MRS. LENNOX *Henrietta* II. vii. (1761) I. 159 Here miss Woodby broke in upon the fair narrater. **1802** MRS. E. PARSONS *Myst. Visit* IV. 149, I cannot be so exact in the repetition as he was in the narrating. **1802–12** BENTHAM *Ration. Judic. Evid.* (1827) I. 57 The narrating witness in question speaks of some other person and not of himself. **1875** JOWETT *Plato* (ed. 2) IV. 121 Like the Protagoras . . it is a narrated dialogue.

narration (næˈreɪʃən). Also 5–6 **-cion**, 6 **-cyon**, **-tioun**, 6 *Sc.* **nerr-**. [a. F. *narration* (12–13th c.), or ad. L. *narrātiōn-em*, noun of action f. *narrāre* to NARRATE: see -ATION.]

1. The action of relating or recounting, or the fact of being recounted; an instance of this. †In early use esp. in phr. *to make narration*.
1432–50 tr. *Higden* (Rolls) II. 175 The ordre of the narracion of stories requirethe that the gestes of the worlde scholde be describede also. **1481** CAXTON *Myrr.* III. xix. 176 It behoueth ouer longe narracion that of alle them wolde descryue the gretenes. **1509** HAWES *Past. Pleas.* XXIV. (Percy Soc.) 108 Fantasy, and estymacyon truely, And memory, as I make narracyon, Eche upon other hath occupacyon. **1573** G. HARVEY *Letter-bk.* (Camden) 44 The short time I have wil scars suffice to make a simple and bare narration of things. **1594** T. B. *La Primaud. Fr. Acad.* II. 389 Our meaning is not to make any long particular narration. **1697** DRYDEN *Æneid* Ded. a j b, Narration, doubtless, preceded Acting, and gave Laws to it. **1823** BYRON *Juan* XIV. vii, This narrative is not meant for narration, But a mere airy and fantastic basis. **1844** MISS MITFORD in L'Estrange *Life* (1870) III. x. 189 Mr. Dickens wants the earnest good-faith in narration which makes Balzac so enchanting. **1870** LOWELL *Study Wind.* (1871) 191 [Dante] the great master of laconic narration.

b. That which is narrated or recounted; a story, narrative, account.
1432–50 tr. *Higden* (Rolls) II. 429 Whiche thynge was provede to haue bene after his narracion. **1482** *Monk of Evesham* (Arb.) 65 Let vs turne ageyne thys narracyon to thoes thynges the whyche we haue lefte oute. **1528** ROY *Rede me* (Arb.) 73 Olde wyves tales . . Which they call holy narracions. **1576** FLEMING *Panopl. Epist.* 255 Vppon vrgent necessitie, wee must . . leuen our Orations with historical narrations. **1624** CAPT. SMITH *Virginia* Ep. Ded. 2 Your Gratious hand . . hath given birth to the publication of this Narration. **1662** STILLINGFL. *Orig. Sacræ* III. i. §1 A Divine revelation then must be faithful and true in all its narrations. **1710** STEELE *Tatler* No. 20 ¶1 The following Narration is a sufficient Testimony of the Truth of this Observation. **1794** J. R. SULLIVAN *View Nat.* II. 214 It is a narration suited to the capacity of the people. **1859** BLACKWELL *Mallet's North. Antiq.* 76 That kind of narrations, in which truth is designedly blended with fable.

2. a. *Rhet.* That part of an oration in which the facts of the matter are stated (see quots.).
1509 HAWES *Past. Pleas.* x. (Percy Soc.) 34 Dysposicion, the true seconde parte Of rethorike, doth evermore dyrecte The maters . . As from a fayre parfit narracion. **1553** T. WILSON *Rhet.* 4 The narracion is a plain and manifest poynctyng of the matter, and an evident settyng furthe of all thynges that belong unto the same. **1586** A. DAY *Eng. Secretary* I. (1625) 23 The force hereof besides the Exordium comprehendeth chiefly a Narration. **1612** BRINSLEY *Lud. Lit.* xiii. (1627) 180 In their Narration, to the end the Auditors may fully understand the matter. **1727–38** CHAMBERS *Cycl.* s.v., The narration, according to the writers of rhetoric, makes the second part of a just speech, or harangue; viz. that immediately following the exordium. **1840** *Penny Cycl.* XVI. 468/2 Under disposition the various parts of an oration are discussed, viz. the exordium, narration [etc.].

b. The story related in a poem; the narrative part of a poem; a narrative passage in a drama.
1586 W. WEBBE *Eng. Poetrie* (Arb.) 88 The proposition or narration let it not be far fetched or vnlikely. **1668** DRYDEN *Dram. Poesy* Ess. (ed. Ker) I. 62 Not that I commend narrations in general,—but there are two sorts of them. One, of those things which are antecedent to the play [etc.]. **1727–38** CHAMBERS *Cycl.* s.v., In the drama, the narration is the whole of the piece; in the epopœia, it is only a part, though in effect it is the principal part, and the main body of the poem. **1783** BLAIR *Lect.* xlii. II. 425 In the narration of the Poet . . it is not material, whether he relate the whole story in his own character, or introduce some of his personages to relate any part of the action.

Hence **na'rrational** *a.*
1866 *Reader* 29 Sept. 823 These indications of his opinions are anachronisms from a narrational point of view. **1867** *Art Jrnl.* XXIX. 95/3 It is neither absolutely scientific, nor descriptive, nor narrational.

narrative (ˈnærətɪv), *sb.* [f. as next: cf. obs. F. *narratif, -ive* in same sense.]

1. *Sc. Law.* That part of a deed or document which contains a statement of the relevant or essential facts (cf. quot. 1838).
1561 *Reg. Privy Council Scot.* I. 189 Ordanis the wordis (at the lest) to be haldin pro deleto in the said summondis sa oft as the samyn is thairin, viz. in the narrative and conclusion. **1574** *Ibid.* II. 382 The haill narrative of the said supplicatioun [being] verefeit and understand to thair Lordships. **1681** STAIR *Instit.* I. x. §63. 148 He who craves regress had right when he changed any further then by the Narrative of the Excambion. *a* **1768** ERSKINE *Inst. Law Scot.* II. iii. §22 (1773) 189 After the name and designation of the granter, follows that clause in the charter called the narrative, or recital. **1838** W. BELL *Dict. Law Scot.* 669 The narrative describes the granter and the person in whose favour the deed is granted, and states the cause of granting.

2. An account or narration; a history, tale, story, recital (of facts, etc.).
1566–7 *Reg. Privy Council Scot.* I. 496 He . . wes fred and relevit . . upoun celerat and wrangus narrative without satisfactioun. **1622** BACON *Hen. VII* 53 Therefore by this Narratiue you now vnderstand the state of the Question. **1660** R. COKE *Power & Subj.* 36 Diodorus Siculus . . gives a narrative of the original government of the Egyptians. **1725** POPE *Odyss.* x. 537 Gushing tears the narrative confound. **1769** *Junius Lett.* xxx. (1788) 160 He shall find me ready to maintain the truth of my narrative. **1837** W. IRVING *Capt. Bonneville* I. 22 We shall now state a few particulars . . to prepare him for the circumstances of our narrative. **1895** J. H. ROUND in *Bookman* Oct. 25/2 This history . . is . . a straightforward, readable narrative.

3. (Without article.) The practice or act of narrating; something to narrate.
1748 CHESTERF. *Lett.* cxxxiv. (1872) I. 246 To have frequent recourse to narrative betrays great want of imagination. **1778** MISS BURNEY *Evelina* lx, What have I to write? Narrative does not offer, nor does a lively imagination supply the deficiency. **1781** COWPER *Conversat.* 217 The path of narrative with care pursue.

narrative (ˈnærətɪv), *a.* [ad. L. *narrātīv-us, -a, -um*, f. *narrāt-*: see NARRATE *v.* and -IVE, and cf. F. *narratif, -ive* (15th c.).]

1. That narrates or recounts; occupied or concerned with, having the character of, narration; *narrative line*, a consecutively developed story. Also in *Painting*.
1605 BACON *Adv. Learn.* II. iv. §3 The division of poesy which is aptest in the propriety thereof . . is into poesy narrative, representative, and allusive. *a* **1652** J. SMITH *Sel. Disc.* VI. 195 The representation of divine things by some sensible images or some narrative voice must needs be in them both. **1712** ADDISON *Spect.* No. 297 ¶6 The *Paradise Lost* is an Epic or a Narrative Poem. **1752** JOHNSON *Rambler* No. 188 ¶5 No style of conversation is more extensively acceptable than the narrative. **1844** L. HUNT *Imag. & Fancy* 20 The greatest of all narrative writers. **1864** BRYCE *Holy Rom. Emp.* Pref., A narrative history of the countries included in the Romano-Germanic Empire. **1902** R. FRY *Let.* 10 Oct. (1972) I. 196 Already he has Giovanni Bellini's *farmito* colours . . and he has too the pure narrative style . . of the great Venetians. **1962** R. G. HAGGAR *Dict. Art Terms* 221/1 Tissot painted admirable narrative pictures. **1962** *Listener* 22 Feb. 335/2 That rich outpouring of 'narrative' painting which began in England with the Bayeux tapestry, continued through the missals and Books of Hours, to be picked up again by Hogarth, Rowlandson, and Gillray. **1962** *Times* 1 Nov. 8/4 Supporting this narrative line is a cross section of Alf's social background. **1972** *Guardian* 16 Feb. 12/3, I pictured a story with every western cliche in it . . Why have a straight narrative line when everybody knows the story?

2. Given to narration; garrulous, talkative.
1681 LUTTRELL *Brief Rel.* (1857) I. 111 Mr. John Smith (called Narrative Smith). **1693** DRYDEN *Disc. Sat.* Ess. (ed. Ker) II. 30 The tattling quality of age, which, as Sir William D'Avenant says, is always narrative. **1725** POPE *Odyss.* III. 80 The Banquet done, the narrative old Man, Thus mild, the pleasing Conference began. **1742** YOUNG *Nt. Th.* VIII. 109 Man is the tale of narrative old Time. **1826** J. J. CONYBEARE *Illust. Anglo-Sax. Poetry* 68 The narrative old monarch proceeds to state that . . Heribald was accidentally killed.
fig. **1882** *Fraser's Mag.* XXVI. 503 There are the decayed taverns . . where stone and wood and lime are narrative of hoary antiquity.

Hence **'narratively** *adv.*, in a narrative manner; also, considered as a narrative.
1651 J. F[REAKE] *Agrippa's Occ. Philos.* To Rdr., I have writ many things, rather narratively then affirmatively. **1726** AYLIFFE *Parergon* 28 The words of all Judicial Acts are written Narratively. **1791** BURKE *App. Whigs* Wks. 1842 I. 518/2 Not in the way of argument, but narratively. **1863** P. DAVIDSON *Pentateuch Vind.* v. 154 The name Jehovah occurs in the first way or narratively, one hundred and sixteen times. **1883** *Ch. Times* XXI. 905/3 The details are historically valuable, but narratively dry.

narrator (næˈreɪtə(r)). [a. L. *narrātor*, agent-n. f. *narrāre* to NARRATE. Cf. F. *narrateur* (1552).]

a. One who narrates.
1611 COTGR., *Narrateur*, a Narrator, relater, declarer. **1625** BP. MONTAGU *App. Cæsar* 5 Hee is but a Narrator of other mens opinions. **1725** WATTS *Logic* (ed. 2) 268 Consider whether the Narrator be honest and faithful, as well as skilful. **1797** MRS. RADCLIFFE *Italian* ix, 'I tell you', replied the narrator [etc.]. **1803** W. TAYLOR in *Ann. Rev.* I. 301 Of such a narrator the very hostility is not oppressive. **1874** L. STEPHEN *Hours in Library* (1892) I. i. 43 He was simply a narrator of plain facts.

b. One who speaks a commentary in a broadcast or a film; hence also, a character who relates part of the plot of a play to the audience.
1941 *B.B.C. Gloss. Broadcasting Terms* 20 *Narrator*, person whose role is to deliver, in either his own or an assumed character, narrative passages in a radio-dramatic programme. **1948** E. LINDGREN *Art of Film* vi. 112 There may be . . portions [of film] . . in which we see the action of the story, but hear the words of the narrator, which thus become . . a form of commentary. **1955** *Radio Times* 22 Apr. 25/1 Bob Hope compères the . . Annual Awards . . Narrator, Leslie Mitchell. **1960** *Times* 3 Oct. 16/2 For Ahlsen clearly employs the 'narrator' technique in order to allow his protagonist not only to act out the dramatic scenes . . but also to speak his thoughts aloud in monologue form if not actually fire them into the auditorium. **1961** *Times* 23 May 15/1 It is the incidentals of Brecht's method—the narrator-characters half in, half outside the action . . which have . . proved capable of easy assimilation. **1973** D. GIFFORD *Brit. Film Catal. 1895–1970* 15 *Credits* . . Associate Producer . . Director . . Narrator [etc.].

narratory (ˈnærətərɪ), *a.* [ad. L. type **narrātōri-us*: see NARRATE *v.* and -ORY[1], and cf. It. *narratorio*, obs. F. *narratoire*.] Characterized by, inclined to, narration; of a narrative nature.
1586 A. DAY *Eng. Secretary* II. (1625) 59 The first whereof appeareth to be Narratory and Nunciatorie. **1649** ROBERTS *Clavis Bibl.* 540 The narratory description of the famine in brief. **1803** MME. D'ARBLAY *Let.* 23 Mar., I had hoped some return in some of your narratory letters in which I so delight. *a* **1853** W. JAY *Autobiogr.* (1855) i. 13 Such a work is devotional rather than narratory. **1887** J. HATTON *Old Ho. at Sandwich* III. xiv, By what may be called a forward narratory movement.

narratress (næˈreɪtrɪs). [f. NARRATE *v.* + -RESS.] A female narrator.
1798 SOTHEBY tr. *Wieland's Oberon* (1826) I. 142 Herself the proud narratress of the tale. **1855** BAGEHOT *Lit. Stud.* (1879) I. 301 The animated narratress of that not intrinsically melancholy legend.

So **na'rratrix**.
1809 R. SURTEES in *Scott's Fam. Lett.* (1894) I. 151 My narratrix is Elizabeth Cockburn, an old wife of Offerton. **1886** *Pall Mall G.* 16 Oct. 5 'But' says the narratrix, 'it was impossible for that lady to keep her Grace supplied with a new work each time she went to the . . library.'

narre, obs. variant of NAR *a.*, nearer.

narrest, nearest: see NAR *a.*

‖**narrischkeit** (ˈnɑːrɪʃkaɪt). [Yiddish *naarishkeit, narrishkeit*, ad. G. *närrischkeit*, f. *närrisch* foolish.] Foolishness, nonsense; that which is of no consequence.
1892 I. ZANGWILL *Childr. Ghetto* I. 179 What *Narrischkeit*! Why should he die? **1963** *Punch* 4 Dec. 803/1 The piece of *narrischkeit* currently being serialised.

narrow (ˈnærəʊ), *a.* and *sb.* Forms: 1 **nearu**, **-o**, **-uo**, **naru(u)**, **neruu**, 2 **nareu**, 3–4 **naru**, (3 **narv**), 4 **narw**, **narou**; 3 **neruh**, 4 **narouȝ**, **nargh**, 5 **narevh**, **narwh**, **narough**; 4–6 **narow(e**, **narrowe**, 6 *Sc.* **narraw**, 4– **narrow**. *Inflected.* 1 **nearwe**, **naarwe**, 3 **narrwe**, 3–4 **narwe**, 4 **narȝwe**; 1 **nearewe**, **-uwe**, 1, 3 **nearowe**, 2 **nærewe**, 2–3 **narewe**, 3 **nerewe**, **-uwe**. [OE. *nearu, nearo* (also *neara*: see NARE *a.*) = OS. *naru* narrow, MDu. *nare, naer* (Du. *naar*) unpleasant, dismal, sad, distressed, etc., Fris. *nâr* narrow. Not found in the other Teutonic languages, and of doubtful etymology.]

A. *adj.*

1. a. Having little breadth or width in comparison with the length; wanting in breadth; constricted.
Beowulf 1409 Ofereode þa æþelinga bearn . . stiȝe nearwe, enge anpaðas. *c* **893** K. ÆLFRED *Oros.* I. i. §32 Se sæ þe æȝðer is ȝe nearo ȝe hreoh. *c* **950** *Lindisf. Gosp.* Matt. xvi. 5 Mið ðy ȝecwomun ðeȝnas his ofer luh *vel* nearo sæ. **1154** *O.E. Chron.* (Laud MS.) an. 1137 Sume hi diden . . in an cæste þat was scort & nareu & undep. *c* **1200** *Trin. Coll. Hom.* 199 [The adder] cumeð to ane þurlede ston, and criepeð nedlinge þureh nerewe hole. *a* **1225** *Ancr. R.* 430 He . . went þe neruwe ende of þe horne to his owune muðe, & utward þene wide. *c* **1290** *S. Eng. Leg.* I. 212/424 Þis brugge . . was so narovȝ þat onneþe ani-þing miȝte þare-oppe sette ani fot. **1340** HAMPOLE *Pr. Consc.* 819 Þe lefte eghe . . semes les, And narower þan þe right eghe es. **1390** GOWER *Conf.* I. 98 Ther was no grace in the visage, Hir front was nargh, hir lockes hore. *c* **1400** MAUNDEV. (1839) v. 45 Egypt is a long Contree; but it is streyt, that is to seye narow. **1463** *Bury Wills* (Camden) 23 A long narevh table. **1526** *Pilgr. Perf.* (W. de W. 1531) 145 Her sekynge in yᵉ narowe lanes betokeneth [etc.]. **1592** SHAKS. *Rom. & Jul.* II. iv. 88 Oh here's a wit . . that stretches from an ynch narrow, to an ell broad. **1632** LITHGOW *Trav.* I. 22 Italy . . growing narrower, and narrower, till it shut out it selfe in two hornes. **1696** BP. PATRICK *Comm. Exod.* xxxix. (1697) 710 Then they cut off lesser, and narrower Wires. **1723** CHAMBERS tr. *Le Clerc's Treat. Archit.* I. 91 Make the lower Arch . . narrower than usual. **1756–7** tr. *Keysler's Trav.* (1760) II. 70 The streets are for the most part narrow and winding. **1815** J. SMITH *Panorama Sci. & Art* I. 292 The narrower the base . . the more easily may the body be overthrown. **1866** G. MACDONALD *Ann. Q. Neighb.* ix. (1878) 140 Up a straight, steep, narrow stair.

b. In fig. contexts, esp. *narrow way*, etc. (in ref. to Matt. vii. 14).
c **950** *Lindisf. Gosp.* Matt., Contents 17/14 Ðerh brad woeȝ moniȝe, ðerh neruu *vel* unrum hwon . . inngae ȝetrymes. *c* **1000** *Ags. Gosp.* Matt. vii. 14 Gangað inn þurh þæt nearwe ȝeat. *c* **1200** ORMIN 6208 Þa follȝhe ȝitt tatt narrwe stih þatt ledeþþ ȝunnc till heoffne. **12..** *Moral Ode* 339 (Egerton MS.), Laete we þe brode strete . . Go we þene narewe wei. *a* **1340** HAMPOLE *Psalter* cxviii. 35 Þis strete is þe narw way till heuen. **1382** WYCLIF *Matt.* vii. 14 How streit is the ȝate, and narowe the weye, that ledith to lijf. **1526** *Pilgr. Perf.* (W. de W. 1531) 18 In the strayte and narowe poynt of deth they descende to hell. **1551** ROBINSON tr. *More's Utop.* (1895) 10 An other is so narrow in [1556 betwene] the sholders, that he can beare no iestes nor tawntes. **1597** J. KING *On Jonas* (1618) 142 There is but a narrow path betwixt fire and water, as Esdras speaketh. **1606** SHAKS. *Tr. & Cr.* III. iii. 154 Honour trauels in a straight so narrow, Where one but goes a breast. **1682** SIR T. BROWNE *Chr. Mor.* I. §1 Tread softly and circumspectly in this . . narrow Path of Goodness. **1742** POPE *Dunc.* IV. 152 When Reason doubtful . . Points him two ways, the narrower is the better. **1780** COWPER *Progr. Err.* 118 Himself a wanderer from the narrow way.

c. In special applications, as *narrow axe* U.S., an axe used primarily for chopping, opp. BROAD-AXE; *narrowback* U.S, a citizen of the United States of Irish ancestry (see also quot. 1941);

narrow band Electr., a band (BAND *sb.*[2] 14) of frequencies lying within a narrow range; freq. *attrib.* (with hyphen); ***narrow boat***, a canal boat, *spec.* one not exceeding 7 feet in width or 72 feet in length; ***narrow cloth***, cloth under 52 inches wide; ***narrow-cut*** adj., applied to filters which transmit only a narrow band of wavelengths; ***narrow front*** (see quot. 1802); ***narrow goods***, braid, ribbons, and similar woven articles; †***narrow land***, one of the narrow strips into which open fields were divided; ***narrow money*** (Econ.), a measure of the amount of money available in an economic system, according to a narrow definition of money (e.g. M_0 or M_1: see M III. 9): contr. with *broad money* s.v. BROAD *a.* D. 2; ***narrow-range*** attrib., restricted in incidence or scope; ***narrow trade***, the trade in narrow goods; ***narrow wares***, narrow goods; ***narrow weaver***, a weaver of narrow cloth or goods; ***narrow work*** (see quot. 1851). See also NARROW GAUGE, SEAS.

1641 *Public Rec. Colony of Connecticut* (1850) I. 444 A broad axe, 2 *narrow axes, wimbell & chessells. **1854** THOREAU *Walden* 46, I went on for some days cutting and hewing timber.. with my narrow axe. **1941** J. SMILEY *Hash House Lingo* 39 **Narrow back*, dishwasher; cashier. **1957** *N.Y. Times* 29 Sept. X3 William Joseph Patrick (Pat) O'Brien, a Milwaukee-born Irishman or narrowback. **1966** *Publ. Amer. Dial. Soc.* 1964 XLII. 39 Irish informants use ..*narrowback* for a second generation Irishman who has neither the need, the desire nor the physical equipment to do the work his father had to do. **1975** G. V. HIGGINS *City on Hill* ii. 56 You went out and married the same kind of commoner he always was himself, and a narrowback to boot. **1956** *Nature* 28 Jan. 178/2 A *narrow-band tuned amplifier on 16 kc./s. **1962** A. NISBETT *Technique Sound Studio* 261 *Music line*, broad-band circuit for carrying programme (including speech), as distinct from a telephone line which may occupy only a narrow band. **1971** M. S. GHAUSI *Electronic Circuits* vii. 437 When extremely high *Q* and excellent stability are required in narrow-band bandpass filters, the use of crystal filters is practical. **1951** *Oxf. Jun. Encycl.* IV. 37/2 The *narrow boat, or 'monkey boat'.., is possibly the commonest craft on inland waterways in England... because the locks on the group of canals in the Midland counties.. can only pass a boat about 7 feet wide and 70 feet long. **1972** *Country Life* 13 Jan. 93/1 Only the deep draught of narrow boats can keep the canals open in the absence of proper dredging. **1975** *Times* 8 Mar. 10/6 Some of the older narrow boats with a three-foot draught are constantly ploughing through mud, for the canals are silted up. **1647** CLARENDON *Hist. Reb.* VI. §183 The Wealthy Manufacture there of Kerseys, and *narrow Cloaths. **1727** DE FOE *Eng. Tradesman* xxvi. (1841) I. 258 The narrow-cloths, in Yorkshire and Staffordshire. **1964** L. A. MANNHEIM tr. *Clauss & Meusel's Filter Pract.* 63 *(caption)* Absorption curve of a deep red filter (*narrow-cut type). **1969** *Focal Encycl. Photogr.* (rev. ed.) 615/1 Special narrow-cut tricolour filter sets are used to make indirect colour separation negatives from colour transparencies. **1802** JAMES *Milit. Dict.*, *Narrow Front*, a battalion, &c. is said to assume a *narrow front, when it goes from line into column. **1876** VOYLE & STEVENSON *Milit. Dict.* s.v. *Column*, The formation of troops.. in deep files and narrow front. **1888** *Daily News* 29 Oct. 2/7 There is a slight revival in cords, braids, and *narrow goods. **1640** *Conveyance of land, Lincolnsh.* (MS.), Et vnam selionem terre (anglice one *Narrow-land) in Scunthorpe. [**1979** *Jrnl. Money, Credit & Banking* XI. 99 Poole and Lieberman.. suggest that if the central bank attempts to control the level of narrowly defined money, which includes bank demand deposits and currency M_1, the optimal reserve requirement ratio against time deposits should be zero.] **1981** *Narrow money [see *broad money* s.v. BROAD *a.* D. 2]. **1983** *Times* 9 Nov. 17/4 The other target money measures are all well above the permitted range, with the narrow money aggregate, M_1, up 1·5 per cent last month. **1984** *Times* 10 May 19/2 The London Business School has rallied to the cause of the Government's much-maligned narrow money target: M_0 ... The new measure, which consists mainly of notes and coins in circulation as well as cash held by banks and banks' operational balances with the Bank of England, was introduced in the Budget to replace M_1 which had become distorted by developments in the banking sector. **1986** *Times* 19 Mar. 26/3 Changes in interest rates have a.. direct effect on narrow money. **1932** FAUCETT & MAKI *Study of Eng. Word-Values* 7 It is fair to require of all students of English a mastery of wide-range words but.. it is unfair standardizing of procedure to pass or fail students on their knowledge or lack of knowledge of *narrow-range words. **1964** E. ULDALL in D. Abercrombie et al. *Daniel Jones* 279 The narrow-range 'smooth' contours.. vary most often from one sentence to another. **1826** *Hist. Eur.* in *Ann. Reg.* 59/1 The *narrow-trade or that which consisted in the manufacture of ribbands. *c* **1645** in *Archaeologia* LII. 135 A hosyer & whole saleman for *narrow wares. **1767** *Ann. Reg.* 152/1 The engine weavers were supposed to be ruinous to the *narrow weavers. **1851** GREENWELL *Coal-trade Terms Northumb. & Durh.* 37 **Narrow Work*, excavations, 3 yards in width and under. **1875** J. H. COLLINS *Metal Mining* 52 In deeper workings it is desirable.. to lessen the proportions of 'narrow work', as the headings are called.

d. Of vowels, in contrast to *broad* or *wide*.

1844 *Proc. Philol. Soc.* I. 283 The Greek substituted a long and broad vowel for the short and narrow vowel of the nominative. **1890** SWEET *Prim. Spoken Engl.* 4 Each of the vowels.. is either *narrow* or *wide*, according as the tongue and uvula are tense.. or relaxed.

e. Denoting a type of phonetic transcription in which separate symbols are used to denote all identifiable features (phonemic and non-phonemic) of an utterance; opp. *broad*.

1877 [see BROAD *a.* 5 c]. **1908** H. SWEET *Sounds of English* 10 In comparing the sounds of a variety of languages.. we require a 'narrow', that is, a minutely accurate notation covering the whole field of possible sounds. **1933** *Amer. Speech* VIII. II. 49/2, I have never been able to understand how there might be any advantage whatever of *broad* over *narrow* transcription for English. **1961** Y. OLSSON *On Syntax Eng. Verb* ii. 20 The editing [when linguists transcribe] would not imply a greater crime than a phonetician using a broad, instead of a narrow, notation. **1964** D. ABERCROMBIE *Eng. Phonetic Texts* 35 It is.. convenient to use 'broad' as an equivalent of *simple phonemic*, and 'narrow' for any departure from this, either in the direction of comparative or in the direction of *allophonic*, or both together.

2. a. Of no great extent; small, limited in size; confined. ***narrow house***, the grave.

c **888** K. ÆLFRED *Boeth.* xix, He hine ne mæȝ furðum tobrædan Ofer þa nearwan eorðan ane [= *Metr.* x. 16 Ofer ðas nearowan.. eorðan sceatas]. *c* **1200** ORMIN 3687 Þatt illke child, tatt tær wass leȝȝd Inn an full naru cribbe. *c* **1230** *Hali Meid.* 42 Hwel he bið et hame, alle þine wide wanes þuncheð þe to nearewe. **1535** COVERDALE *2 Kings* vi. 1 The place where we dwell.. is to narow for vs. *a* **1548** HALL *Chron., Hen. VIII* 102 b, Certain Welshemen were lodged at a poore village named Cause, because in Caleys was verye narow lodgyng. **1617** MORYSON *Itin.* I. 204 The place being so narrow as shee could onely stand. **1663** BOYLE *Usef. Exp. Nat. Philos.* I. ii. 40 Consider how.. delicate a Workmanship must be employ'd to contrive into so narrow a compass the several Parts. **1697** DRYDEN *Virg. Georg.* IV. 124 With mighty Souls in narrow Bodies prest. **1752** HUME *Pol. Disc.* x. 197 What an astonishing multitude in so narrow a country as antient Greece. **1810** JANE PORTER *Scot. Chiefs* xi, Wallace's camp or the narrow house must be our prize. **1864** TENNYSON *En. Ard.* 177 His careful hand,—The space was narrow,—having order'd all.

b. Lying or pressing close; confining.

971 *Blickl. Hom.* 103 [Hie] wilnodan þæt he hie of þæm nearwan þeostrum alesde. *c* **1000** *Riddles* liii. 3 þa wæron ȝenumne nearwum bendum, ȝefeterade fæste togædre. **1297** R. GLOUC. (Rolls) 4299 Þe brutons gonne to fle, Ac þo hii come among narwe hegges hii stode aȝen anon. **1633** MAY *Hen. II*, VI. 508 He drawes his martiall forces vp, to presse With narrow siege the Towne of Limoges. *a* **1770** JORTIN *Serm.* (1771) II. xiv. 276 Our knowledge of God is confined in narrow bounds. **1793** COWPER *On Bill Mortality* iii, Life, within a narrow ring Of giddy joys comprised. **1821–2** SHELLEY *Chas. I*, IV. 45 A low dark roof, a damp and narrow wall. **1871** FREEMAN *Norm. Conq.* (1876) IV. xvii. 72 The immediate and permanent authority of both was confined within very narrow bounds.

3. a. Limited in range or scope; restricted.

1523 FITZHERB. *Husb.* §4 It is so narowe a point to know, that it is harde to make a man to vnderstande it by wrytynge. **1597** HOOKER *Eccl. Pol.* v. lxvii. §2 The question is yet driuen to a narrower issue. **1625** BACON *Ess., Viciss. Things* (Arb.) 569 As for the great Burnings by Lightnings, which are often in the West Indies, they are but narrow. **1690** LOCKE *Hum. Und.* IV. xi. §10 How foolish.. a thing it is for a Man of a narrow Knowledge.. to expect Demonstration.. in things not capable of it. **1709** POPE *Ess. Crit.* 61 One science only will one genius fit; So vast is art, so narrow human wit. **1771** *Junius Lett.* I. (1788) 271 His plan, I think, is too narrow. *a* **1806** H. K. WHITE *Poems* (1837) 36 Can the voice of narrow Fame repay The loss of health? **1871** FREEMAN *Norm. Conq.* (1876) IV. xiii. 234 The earldom of Northumberland in the narrower sense of the name was vacant.

b. Limited in amount; very small or poor.

1606 SHAKS. *Ant. & Cl.* III. iv. 8 Most narrow measure [he] lent me. **1668** R. STEELE *Husbandm. Calling* ix. (1672) 239 Let me rather have a narrow estate and wide soul. **1711** ADDISON *Spect.* No. 108 ⁋7 We find several Citizens that were launched into the World with narrow Fortunes. **1734** tr. *Rollin's Anc. Hist.* (1827) II. II. 112 His circumstances were very narrow. **1814** JANE AUSTEN *Lady Susan* iii. (1879) 208 In narrow circumstances it was proper to render her pecuniary assistance. **1819** SHELLEY *Cenci* II. ii. 12 He has wide wants, and narrow powers. **1846** MCCULLOCH *Acc. Brit. Empire* (1854) II. 677 The court overruled the objection, but only by the narrowest majority.

c. Of time: Short, brief. *rare.*

1611 CORYAT *Crudities* (1776) I. 144 Had I not beene brought into such a narrow compasse of time. **1646** SIR T. BROWNE *Pseud. Ep.* III. vi. 117 From this narrow time of gestation [may] ensue a.. smalnesse in the exclusion. **1819** SHELLEY *Cenci* V. iv. 100 Upon the giddy, sharp and narrow hour Tottering beneath us.

†**d.** (See quot.) *Obs. rare*$^{-0}$.

a **1700** B. E. *Dict. Cant. Crew* s.v., *'Tis all narrow*, said by the Butchers one to another when their Meat proves not so good as expected.

e. *Econ.* (See quots.)

1935 *Economist* 12 Oct. 712/2 Technically, markets remain 'narrow', and day-to-day price movements are correspondingly exaggerated. **1940** G. CROWTHER *Outl. Money* vii. 267 The market is at all times 'narrow', that is, quotations are available only for half a dozen of the most important currencies. **1962** S. STRAND *Marketing Dict.* 474 *Narrow market*, in the stock market, a dull trading session, generally limited to a few fields. **1965** J. L. HANSON *Dict. Econ.* 288/2 *Narrow market*, a term used more particularly of stock exchange securities of which there is only a small supply available in the market.

4. a. Sparing, close, parsimonious, mean. Now *dial.*

a **1225** *Ancr. R.* 430 Beoð large touward ham, þauh ȝe þe neruwure beon and te herdure to ou suluen. *a* **1586** SIDNEY *Arcadia* II. (1613) 156 To narrow breasts he comes all wrapt in gaine. **1596** DALRYMPLE tr. *Leslie's Hist. Scot.* IX. 261 Nouther.. ouer skairs, narraw, or gredie. **1659** A. HAY *Diary* (S.H.S.) 220 It was not expedient to me to buy from them becaus they are somquhat narrow. **1773** JOHNSON in *Boswell*, Archibald.. was narrow in his ordinary expenses. **1796** *Hist. Ned Evans* I. 146 He was.. so extremely narrow as to allow himself little more than the bare necessaries of life. **1821** GALT *Ann. Parish* iii, He was a narrow ailing man. **1897** J. GORDON *Vill. & Doctor* 72 It ain't as I was a narrer man.., I bain't mean.

b. Lacking in breadth of view or sympathy; narrow-souled, narrow-minded, illiberal, prejudiced, bigoted.

1664 POWER *Exp. Philos.* Pref. 6 They are but narrow Souls, and not worthy the name of Philosophers. **1724** A. COLLINS *Gr. Chr. Relig.* 9 Some Jews being so narrow as to think Circumcision.. necessary. **1760** FOOTE *Minor* I. Wks. 1799 I. 231 People who have their attention eternally fixed upon one object, can't help being a little narrow in their notions. **1825** MACAULAY *Ess., Milton* (1851) I. 22 The days of cold hearts and narrow minds. **1874** BLACKIE *Self-Cult.* 30 The merely professional man is always a narrow man.

c. So of actions, views, disposition, etc.

1657 in *Burton's Diary* (1828) II. 248 It is very narrow not to let it extend to the protestants elsewhere, as those in Munster. **1664** POWER *Exp. Philos.* I. 61 We have not those narrow conceptions of these subtle Spirits. **1711** ADDISON *Spect.* No. 126 ⁋9, I daily find more Instances of this narrow Party-Humour. **1781** GIBBON *Decl. & F.* xxx. III. 177 The events.. have undoubtedly been diminished by the narrow and imperfect view of the historians of the times. **1813** SHELLEY *Q. Mab* v. 163 Blunting the keenness of his spiritual sense With narrow schemings and unworthy cares. **1874** GREEN *Short Hist.* viii. §1. 452 There was nothing narrow or illiberal in his early training.

d. Exclusive.

1855 MACAULAY *Hist. Eng.* xviii. IV. 143 In no danger of falling under the dominion either of a despot or of a narrow oligarchy. **1871** FREEMAN *Norm. Conq.* (1876) IV. xviii. 208 An oligarchy not less proud and even more narrow than their brethren of Bern and Venice.

5. a. Strict, close, precise, careful.

a **1225** *Ancr. R.* 144 Þe sterke dom of domesdei—& so neruh mid alle. *Ibid.* 156 Hwo se wule ivinden et te neruwe domesmon merci & ore. **1552** in *Liturg. Serv. Q. Eliz.* (1847) 246 If thou shouldest enter into thy narrow judgment with me,.. I were never able to suffer it. **1579** FULKE *Confut. Sanders* 692 You are.. a narrowe vewer of such idle pictures. **1607** NORDEN *Surv. Dial.* I. 4 Millions.. are now dayly troubled with your so narrow looking thereinto. **1671** MILTON *P. R.* IV. 515 Thenceforth I thought thee worth my nearer view And narrower Scrutiny. **1710** ADDISON *Tatler* No. 162 ⁋2, I have made a narrow Search into the Nature of the old Roman Censors. **1751** SMOLLETT *Per. Pic.* xxx, Seeking to make a narrower inquiry.

b. *transf.* of the eyes, etc. (Partly in sense 1.)

1577 HARRISON *England* II. vi. (1877) I. 160 They sit still, pinking with their narrow eies. **1592** R. D. *Hypnerotomachia* 55 b, An extreame delight and desired nourishment unto a narrowe looke and greedie eye. **1611** BEAUM. & FL. *Philaster* III. i, I.. plac'd thee there To pry with narrow eyes into her deeds. **1876** GEO. ELIOT *Dan. Der.* xxix, Looking into her eyes with his narrow gaze.

6. Near, close. †**a.** Coming near the truth. *Obs.*

1551 T. WILSON *Logike* (1580) 37 Thei haue a narrowe gesse by all likelihoode, that the Hare was there a little before. **1679** EVELYN *Sylva* (ed. 3) 4 What some upon an accurate and narrow guess have not feared to pronounce.

†**b.** Of friendship: Close, intimate. *Obs. rare.*

1556 *Aurelio & Isab.* (1608) A iv, Remembring them bothe of their narrowe frendshippe. **1574** HELLOWES *Guevara's Fam. Ep.* (1584) 158 The Judge cannot holde narrow friendship with any man.

c. Of an escape: Barely effected.

1581 RICH *Farew.* E j b, She ioyed nothyng so muche in the narrowe escape she had made with life. **1749** FIELDING *Tom Jones* VIII. ix. *heading*, The lucky and narrow escape of Partridge. **1814** SCOTT *Wav.* xxx, He had made a narrow escape, however; the bullet had grazed his head. **1860** SALA *Baddington Peerage* xx, What's a narrow squeak, a close shave, to such as I am? **1874** STUBBS *Const. Hist.* I. viii. 223 The escape was a narrow one.

d. *Bowls.* (See quot.)

a **1700** B. E. *Dict. Cant. Crew*, *Narrow*, when the Biass of the Bowl holds too much. **1882** [see NARROW *adv.* 3].

7. *Comb.*, as ***narrow-backed, -beamed, -billed, -bladed, -bodied, -bottomed, -brained, -brimmed, -cast, -celled, -chested,*** †***-clothed, -compassed, -ended, -grated, -gutted, -heeled, -holed, -laced, -limited, -listed, -meshed, -muzzled, -nosed, -quartered, -shared, -shouldered, -sighted, -slitted, -slotted, -snouted, -sterned, -streeted, -throated, -toned, -topped, -verged, -visioned, -waisted, -wheeled.*** Also NARROW-EYED, -HEARTED, -MINDED, -NECKED, -SOULED, etc.

1847 YOUATT *Pig* 58 *Narrow-backed, flat-sided.. animals. **1927** *Observer* 14 Aug. 7/4 Agile, *narrow-beamed cars, with plenty of acceleration and 'safety-first' brake-power, are his ideal. **1895** *Funk's Stand. Dict.*, *Narrow-billed. **1909** A. E. MACK *Bush Calendar* 9 Birds breeding in August... Chalcococcyx basalis. Narrow-billed bronze cuckoo. **1953** D. A. BANNERMAN *Birds Brit. Isles* I. 299 There is much to be said in favour of retaining these broad-billed buntings, as distinct from the narrow-billed species, under the specific name *tschusii*. **1825** J. NICHOLSON *Operat. Mechanic* 465 Modelling it.. with a sharp *narrow-bladed knife. **1949** M. MEAD *Male & Female* vi. 133 The slender, *narrow-bodied of the Arapesh, Tchambuli, Swede, Eskimo, and Hottentot. **1963** *Times* 1 Feb. 14/5 This narrow-bodied look was extended to coats. **1707** MORTIMER *Husb.* (1721) I. 4 In a *narrow-bottom'd Ditch, if Cattle get into it, they cannot stand to turn themselves. **1777** WATSON in *Phil. Trans.* LXVIII. 876 Put it into a narrow-bottomed ale glass. **1860** EMERSON *Cond. Life, Consid.* Wks. (Bohn) II. 414 No shovel-handed, *narrow-brained.. stockingers. **1686** *Lond. Gaz.* No. 2145/4 A little *narrow-brim'd black Hat. **1778** [W. MARSHALL] *Minutes Agric.* 26 Mar. 1776, In these flutes sowed the seed *narrow-cast. **1884** BOWER & SCOTT *De Bary's Phaner.* 376 The periphery of the cylinder is occupied by a meristematic *narrow-celled ring. **1873** *Routledge's Yng. Gentlm. Mag.* 178/1 [He] made everybody else in the field look *narrow-chested. *c* **1412** HOCCLEVE *De Reg. Princ.* 540 If a wight vertuous, but *narwe clothid, To lordes curtes now of dayes go. **1647** H. MORE *Song of Soul* II. App. ciii, Within his *narrow-compast brains. **1877** HUXLEY & MARTIN *Elem. Biol.* 195 *Narrow-ended and broad-ended papillæ. **1791** MRS. RADCLIFFE *Rom. Forest* (1820) III. 280 Its heavy black walls, and *narrow-grated windows. **1903** *Dialect Notes* II. 299 (Cape Cod dial.) **Narrow gutted*, mean, ungenerous. **1903** *Eng. Dial. Dict.* IV. 228/2 *Narrow-gutted*, of horses.. weak in the loins. *Ibid.*, *Not*[*tinghamshire*]. A narrow-gutted brute. **1924** D. H. LAWRENCE *Let.* 29 Oct. (1962) II. 816 A narrow-gutted 'artist' with a stutter. **1965** G. J. WILLIAMS *Econ. Geol. N.Z.* xviii. 283/2 Unless the seam is narrow-gutted as at Kawakawa,..it seems certain that coal does not exist above the greywacke. **1615** MARKHAM *Country Contentm.* I. xix. 82 That Cock is said to be sharp heel'd or *narrow heel'd, which every time he riseth hitteth, and draweth blood of his adversary. **1531** ELYOT *Gov.* II. xiv, In a *narowe holed seeue they will stille abide with the good corne. **1882** MASSON in *Macm. Mag.* XLV. 251 Jeffrey's more *narrow-laced clientage of the blue-and-yellow. **1690** CHILD *Disc. Trade* Pref. (1698) 21 These trades..the Dutch interest of three per cent. and *narrow-limited companies in England, have beat us out of. **1603** *Burford Reg.* (Hist. MSS. Comm.), Various Collect. I. 72 Confecit..duos pannos laneos vocatos *narowe listed whites. **1884** BOWER & SCOTT *De Bary's Phaner.* 325 Bands of tissue, appearing irregularly *narrow-meshed in cross-section. **1869** TOZER *Highl. Turkey* II. 204 Lean-jawed, *narrow-muzzled animals. **1846** BRITTAN tr. *Malgaigne's Man. Oper. Surg.* 269 A little osseous projection..in *narrow-nosed people. **1884** J. TAIT *Mind in Matter* (1892) 61 Discussions about narrow-nosed apes. *a* **1618** RALEIGH *Royal Navy* 13 So will all *narrow quartered ships sinck after the Tayle. **1765** *Univ. Mag.* XXXVII. 33/2 He plowed them up with a *narrow-shared wheel-plow. **1649** G. DANIEL *Trinarch., Rich. II*, ccxcvii, Soe may the *Narrow-should'red Pigmey heave Mount Caucasus. **1708** BP. BERKELEY *Serm.* Wks. 1871 IV. 601 We *narrow-sighted mortals. **1905** J. LONDON *Jacket* (1915) xi. 90 His eyes..were cunning and..*narrow-slitted. **1923** KIPLING *Irish Guards in Gt. War* I. 234 The *narrow-slotted pill-boxes. **1897** GÜNTHER in Mary Kingsley *W. Africa* 708 Both the *narrow-snouted form..and the broad-snouted. **1755** JOHNSON, *Pink*,..a kind of heavy *narrow-sterned ship. **1858** HAWTHORNE *Fr. & It. Note-bks.* (1872) I. 41 A commercial city.., *narrow-streeted and sometimes pestilential. **1674** HICKMAN *Quinquart. Hist.* (ed. 2) 48, I see not what there is in these passages, which the most strait, *narrow-throated Calvinist may not swallow. **1865** M. ARNOLD *Ess. Crit.* Pref. 14 That powerful, but at present somewhat *narrow-toned organ, the modern Englishman. **1769** MRS. RAFFALD *Eng. Housekpr.* (1778) 355 When they are cold put them into *narrow-topped jars. *a* **1678** MARVELL *Garden* i, Some single herb or tree, Whose short and *narrow-verged shade Does prudently their toils upbraid. **1868** CROOM ROBERTSON in *Fortn. Rev.* Dec. 635 We are taunted with being a *narrow-visioned people. **1688** HOLME *Armoury* III. v. 237/2 The Gowns were broad-Shouldered, narrow-Wasted. **1881** *Daily Tel.* 5 July 2/1 A great narrow-waisted yawl, almost on her beam ends. **1758** *Ann. Reg.* I. 112/2 A *narrow wheeled waggon.

B. *sb.*

1. A narrow part, place, or thing; the narrow part of something. Also *fig.* Now *rare.*

13.. *Guy Warw.* (A.) 3493 Into þe narwe hij come, hem to lett. **1535** COVERDALE *2 Esdras* vii. 5 Yf he wente not thorow the narow, how might he come in to the brode? **1642** ROGERS *Naaman* 37 We cannot speed, because we still keep a breadth in his narrow, and in our afflictions are light-hearted. **1702** C. MATHER *Magn. Chr.* III. i. App. (1852) 339 When it came to the narrow of any question he would still profess himself conquered by Mr. Hooker's reason. **1742** RICHARDSON *De Foe's Tour Gt. Brit.* II. 270 We might also mention another Narrow; that is, the Minds of the Generality of its People.

2. *spec.* (Chiefly in *pl.*) **a.** A narrow part of a sound, strait, or river.

1633 T. JAMES *Voy.* 106 We were in the narrow of the Straight. **1665** *Lond. Gaz.* No. 5/4 Three or four Privateers are crusing in the Narrow. **1702** *Ibid.* No. 3844/4 In the Narrow off of Winterton. **1743** BULKELEY & CUMMINS *Voy. S. Seas* 145 At Four this Morning weighed, and steered E.N.E. for the Narrows. **1840** MARRYAT *Poor Jack* li, We should have been taken possession of by a privateer in the very narrows. **1883** STEVENSON *Silverado Sq.* 4 Through the narrows the tide bubbles, muddy like a river.

b. A narrow part of a pass or valley; a narrow way between mountains. (Chiefly *U.S.*)

1716 B. CHURCH *Hist. Philip's War* (1865) I. 23 They Marched until they came to the narrow of the Neck. **1768** C. BEATTY *Jrnl.* 16 We travelled up Juniata river,..through a bad road, to a place called the Narrows. **1788** M. CUTLER in *Life*, etc. (1888) I. 403 We passed the narrows or gaps of two ranges of high mountains. **1808** PIKE *Sources Mississ.* (1810) 175 A fine creek, which we followed through narrows in the mountains for about six miles.

c. A narrow part of a street.

1772 C. HUTTON *Bridges* 2 Streets..without narrows or crooked windings. **1866** CONINGTON *Æneid* 49 Some block the narrows of the street. **1882** *Daily News* 18 Aug. 3/1 Lives there the elderly man..who has not been sorely frightened by the risks encountered in those terrible narrows?

d. *Mining.* A narrow gallery.

1850 ANSTED *Elem. Geol.* §1106 These galleries are of different dimensions, the larger ones..are called broads, and they are intersected by other galleries at right-angles to them whose dimensions are not quite so large, and which are called narrows. **1883** GRESLEY *Gloss. Coal-mining* 173.

'narrow, *adv.* Now *rare.* Forms: 1 nearwe, 3 neruwe, 3–4 nar(e)we, 4–5 narow, (5 -oo), 6–8 narrow. [OE. *nearwe*, f. *nearu* NARROW *a.*]

†**1.** Closely, straitly, strictly. *Obs.*

Beowulf 976 Hyne sar hafað in nydgripe nearwe befongen. *a* **1000** *Boeth. Metr.* xxi. 5 Se ðe..sie nearwe ȝehefted mid þisses mæran middanȝeardes..lufe. *a* **1225** *Ancr. R.* 268 3if þu wult þet heo drede þe, hold hire nearuwe. *a* **1250** *Owl & Night.* 68 Alle ho the driveth honne,..And wel narewe the bi-ledet. *c* **1330** R. BRUNNE *Chron.* (1810) 16 Þe kyng was narow holden, his folk alle to dryuen. *c* **1385** CHAUCER *L.G.W.* 600 *Cleopatra*, Loue hadde..hym so narwe boundyn In his las. *c* **1460** *Towneley Myst.* xiii. 436 Thay will nyp vs fulle naroo. [**1667** MILTON *P.L.* VII. 21 Narrower bound Within the visible Diurnal Spheare.]

†**2.** Closely, carefully, keenly. *Obs.*

a **900** CYNEWULF *Elene* 1158 Þeodcwen ongan..secan nearwe ȝeneahhe, to hwan hio þa næȝlas..ȝedon meahte. *c* **1290** *Beket* 1745 in *S.E. Leg.* I. 156 Wel narewe þe king him gan bi-þenche to derne is luþere þouȝt. **1297** R. GLOUC. (Rolls) 5954 He biþoȝte him wel narwe ȝif þer miȝte be eny red. *c* **1386** CHAUCER *Merch. T.* 744 How excellent franchise In women is whan they hem narwe avise. *c* **1400** *Laud Troy Bk.* 15264 Many a way that lady soght And wel narwe sche hir be-thoght. **1412–20** LYDG. *Chron. Troy* III. xxii, To Hector he marked hath so narowe That he smote him euen amid the face. *c* **1592** GREENE *Wks.* (Rtldg.) 317/1 Looking more narrow by the fire's flame, I spied his quiver.

Comb. **1596** SHAKS. *Tam. Shr.* III. ii. 148 Wee'll ouer-reach..The narrow prying father.

3. Narrowly, in various senses; in a narrow or close manner.

c **1200** *Trin. Coll. Hom.* 213 Þe sullere doð narewere þane he sholde, and te biggere rumluker þan he sholde. **1377** LANGL. *P. Pl.* B. XIII. 371 3if I ȝede to the plow I pynched so narwe, That a fote-londe or a forwe fecchen I wolde. **1697** DRYDEN *Æneid* v. 675 Mnestheus..miss'd the Dove. Yet miss'd so narrow, that he cut the Cord. **1765** A. DICKSON *Treat. Agric.* (ed. 2) 274 If this kind of grass-ground is plowed..shallow and narrow. **1882** T. HARDY *Two on Tower* xxvii, 'I am not skilful', she said, 'I always bowl narrow'.

b. ***to fall narrow***, to fall short. ***to go narrow***, to keep the legs too close together. ? *Obs.*

1648 CRASHAW *Delights of Muses* Wks. (1904) 129 [He] ne're suffred yet his little arrow, Of Heavens high'st archies to fall narrow. **1697** *Lond. Gaz.* No. 3289/4 Lost..a Bayish dun Horse about 15 hands,..goes narrow. **1727** BAILEY, vol. II. s.v., A Horse is said to go narrow, when he does not take Ground enough, that does not bear far enough out, to the one Hand or to the other.

narrow ('nærəʊ), *v.* Forms: 1 nearwian, 4 narwe, narewe, nerewe, 5, 7– narrow. [OE. *nearwian*, f. *nearw-*, *nearu* NARROW *a.*; but in later use prob. a new formation directly from the adj. OE. had also *nyrwan* (= **niȝrwan*) and *ȝenyrwan* to compress, constrain, afflict, etc.]

1. *intr.* To become narrower, to decrease in width or breadth; to diminish, lessen, contract. Also with *down.*

a **1000** *Gen.* 1570 Sefa nearwode. *a* **1000** *Riming Poem* 37 Sinc searwade, sib nearwade. *c* **1330** R. BRUNNE *Chron. Wace* (Rolls) 4577 Brod & þykke þe gynnynge was, & euere hit nareweþ [*v.r.* nereweþ] rysande on heyght. **1387** TREVISA *Higden* (Rolls) I. 57 Þenne he narweþ to þe narwenesse of sex hondred paas. **1746** in *Acc. Fr. Settlem. N. Amer.* 20 Above that isle it narrows so, that before Quebec it is not above a mile wide. **1773** MRS. GRANT *Lett. fr. Mountains* (1813) I. xiii. 113 The glen..instead of narrowing,..grows broader as it retires. **1821** BYRON *Foscari* III. i. 410 The time narrows, signor. **1847** TENNYSON *Princ.* III. 180 Following up The river as it narrow'd to the hills. **1897** H. DRUMMOND *Ideal Life* 101 Have you ever noticed, how Christ's life narrowed? **1906** L. J. VANCE *Terence O'Rourke* II. ii. 214 Then it narrowed down to a mere contest of endurance.

2. a. *trans.* To make narrower; to reduce the breadth of (a thing); †also *fig.* to constrict, constrain, oppress. Also with *down* and *in.*

a **1000** *Riddles* xxvi. 10 Feleþ sona mines ȝemotes, seo þe mec nearwað, wif wundenlocc. *a* **1300** *E.E. Psalter* xxxiv. 5 Þai be als dust ogain wind..And louerdes aungel narwand þam. **1429** *Coventry Leet Bk.* (E.E.T.S.) 118 The meyre shuld go be all the brooke, & se where hit is narowed..or stopped. **1646** SIR T. BROWNE *Pseud. Ep.* 64 At the straits of Magellan, where the land is narrowed. **1768** *Conn. Col. Rec.* (1885) XIII. 52 By encroachments said road is so narrowed that it is rendered almost useless. **1796** MORSE *Amer. Geog.* I. 75 A northeast wind narrows the stream. **1834** McMURTRIE *Cuvier's Anim. Kingd.* 321 Abdomen nearly square, posteriorly narrowed. **1860** O. W. HOLMES *Elsie V.* (1887) 84 She narrowed her lids slightly. **1885** J. MORRIS *Kotaka* xi. 106 The entire force and volume of the Fuzikawa being here narrowed down to the width of the gorge. **1885** J. W. DAWSON *Egypt & Syria* ii. 39 It is just where the broad expanse of alluvium..is narrowed in by that great promontory. **1889** R. L. STEVENSON *Master of Ballantrae* iv. 122 The family was now so narrowed down (indeed, there were..just the father and the two sons) that it was possible to break the entail. **1899** *Allbutt's Syst. Med.* VIII. 835 The sweat-pores were obviously narrowed by pressure.

b. To limit or restrict; to make less or smaller; to contract; to reduce.

1674 *Govt. Tongue* 168 We see in all things how desuetude do's contract and narrow our faculties. **1706** STANHOPE *Paraphr.* III. 428 Subtle Glosses had narrowed the just extent of this Word. **1769** BURKE *Obs. Late St. Nation* Wks. II. 115 He has here pretty well narrowed the field of taxation. **1817** W. SELWYN *Law Nisi Prius* (ed. 4) II. 1083 A by-law,..if it narrow the number of those out of whom the election is to be made, is void. **1859** J. MARTINEAU *Ess.* (1866) I. 91 It greatly narrows the ground of difference. **1893** SIR R. BALL *Story of Sun* 282 This consideration narrows the search for the body.

c. To drive or press closer.

1814 SCOTT *Wav.* lxv, Eager to distress and narrow the posts of the enemy. **1864** TENNYSON *Boadicea* 39 Tho' the gathering enemy narrow thee.

narrow, dial. f. NE'ER A *adj. phr.*

narrowed ('nærəʊd), *ppl. a.* [f. NARROW *v.*] Contracted, lessened in breadth (*lit.* and *fig.*).

1599 DANIEL *Let. Octavia* Wks. 1717 I. 75 Yet oft our narrow'd Thoughts look more direct Than your loose Wisdoms. **1611** BIBLE *1 Kings* vi. 6 In the wall of the house hee made narrowed rests round about. **1798** ATWOOD in *Phil. Trans.* LXXXVIII. 204 It would be giving that term too narrowed a meaning. **1805–17** R. JAMESON *Char. Min.* (ed. 3) 199 Narrowed heavy-spar..is an oblique four-sided table. **1887** MEREDITH *Ballads & P.* 84 With a narrowed eye he peered.

narrower ('nærəʊə(r)). [f. as prec. + -ER[1].] One who, or that which, narrows or contracts.

1753 RICHARDSON *Grandison* III. xxi. 192, I do aver..that Love is a narrower of the heart. **1790** G. WALKER *Serm.* II. xxxi. 419 Half-taught philosophers..may reprobate it as the narrower of a christian's heart.

narrow-eyed, *a.* [NARROW *a.* 1 and 5.]

†**1.** Observing closely. *Obs. rare*$^{-1}$.

1599 B. JONSON *Ev. Man out of Hum.* II. vi, These narrow-ey'd decypherers..that will extort strange and abstruse meanings out of any subject.

2. Having narrow eyes. Also *fig.*

1607 MIDDLETON *Phœnix* II. iii. 147 They blind him with beer, and make him so narrow-eyed, that he winks naturally at all their knaveries. **1687** WOOD *Life* 5 Sept. (O.H.S.) III. 236 All the Chineses, Tartars, and all that part of the world was narrow-eyed. **1703** *Lond. Gaz.* No. 3942/4 A black slight Limb'd Mare,..narrow Ey'd. **1893** F. ADAMS *New Egypt* 160 The..obstinate, narrow-eyed, restless man!

narrow gauge. 1. The smaller distance from each other at which the two rails are laid on some railways, involving a corresponding narrowness of carriage. Freq. *attrib.* See GAUGE *sb.* 3.

Formerly applied to what is now the British standard gauge of 4 ft. 8½ in., as opposed to the BROAD GAUGE; now confined to gauges less than this, or than some corresponding standard.

1841 *Penny Cycl.* XIX. 256/1 Many who admit the inconvenience of the narrow gauge consider seven feet to be beyond the most advantageous width. **1844** SIR D. GOOCH *Diaries* 53 It became a fight between the broad-gauge companies and the narrow-gauge companies. **1889** G. FINDLAY *Eng. Railway* 117 A notable feature in the life of the Crewe works is the narrow-gauge railway... The gauge of this railway is 18 inches.

2. *Cinemat.* (See quot. 1959.) Cf. GAUGE, GAGE *sb.* 1.

1951 G. H. SEWELL *Amateur Film-Making* (ed. 2) xii. 115 It is not impossible that one day research will place in the hands of the narrow-gauge worker the means of obtaining fully stereoscopic pictures without undue difficulty. **1953** L. J. WHEELER *Princ. Cinematogr.* x. 283 It is interesting to note that the B.K.S. has officially adopted the term 'narrow gauge' [film] in preference to 'sub-standard'. **1959** W. S. SHARPS *Dict. Cinematogr.* 100/1 Ciné film is designated according to its width, 35 mm. film..being said to be of 'standard gauge'...the only other professional size of film..is 16 mm. wide and this is termed 'sub-standard', or 'narrow-gauge'.

†**'narrowhead**. *Obs.* [-HEAD.] Narrowness.

c **1440** *Promp. Parv.* 351/2 Narowhede, *strictura.*

narrow-hearted, *a.* [NARROW *a.* 4.] Mean, ungenerous, ignoble.

c **1200** *Trin. Coll. Hom.* 29 To þe narewe herted man on his þonke he seið..cune sume meðe þenne þu almesse makest. **1648** GAGE *West Ind.* Ded., See what wealth and honor they have lost by one of their narrow hearted Princes. *a* **1680** CHARNOCK *Attrib. God* (1834) II. 282 To fancy a God without it, is to fancy a miserable,..narrow-hearted..God. **1775** ADAIR *Amer. Ind.* 139 The Indians..ridicule the white people, as a tribe of narrow-hearted and dull-constitutioned animals.

Hence **narrow-'heartedness**.

1858 J. MARTINEAU *Stud. Chr.* 239 The false and dangerous position into which their churches have been brought by narrow-heartedness and insincerity. **1878** SPURGEON *Treas. Dav.* Ps. cviii. 5 David had none of..the narrow-heartedness of some nominal Christians.

narrowing ('nærəʊɪŋ), *vbl. sb.* [f. NARROW *v.*] The action of the vb., in various senses; the result of this; a narrowed place or part.

1611 BIBLE *1 Kings* vi. 6 Hee made narrowed rests [*marg.* Heb. narrowings, or, rebatements] round about. **1664** E. BUSHNELL *Compl. Shipwright* 13 At the Narrowing of the Floare, or other Circular lines. **1711** W. SUTHERLAND *Shipbuild. Assist.* 80 Narrowings or tapering Parallels of the lower part. **1769** FALCONER *Dict. Marine* (1780), *Facons*, the narrowing of a ship's floor afore and abaft. **1851** MAYNE REID *Scalp Hunt.* xli. 317 We placed ourselves to defend the ..second narrowing of the channel. **1871** BLACKIE *Four Phases Mor.* i. 107 *note*, Such a narrowing of the idea of religious duty..is most unphilosophical.

'narrowing, *ppl. a.* [f. as prec.] That narrows or contracts, in *trans.* and *intr.* senses.

1664 E. BUSHNELL *Compl. Shipwright* 13 The narrowing lines Abaft. **1827** KEBLE *Chr. Y. 22nd S. after Trin.*, Of his narrowing heart each year Heaven less and less will fill. **1843** PUSEY *Holy Euch.* 26 It will then seem..too refined and narrowing a distinction. **1879** FARRAR *St. Paul* (1883) 259 The narrowing valleys through which the rivers descend.

Hence **'narrowingness**.

1883 'VERNON LEE' in *Academy* 29 Dec. 426 Its tragic and sordid narrowingness.

narrowish ('nærəʊɪʃ), *a.* [f. NARROW *a.* + -ISH.] Somewhat narrow.

1823 R. H. FROUDE in *Rem.* (1838) I. 164 The parsonage is situated in a steep and narrowish glen. **1867** CARLYLE *Remin.* (1881) II. 334 Pope's partial failure I was prepared for; less for the narrowish limits visible in Milton and others. **1897** MARY KINGSLEY *W. Africa* 594 At the head of a rock ridge in a narrowish depression.

narrow-leaved, *a.* Also 7 leafed. That has narrow leaves. Chiefly in plant-names (see quots.).

1629 PARKINSON *Parad.* 182 It may fitly bee called a narrow leafed Flowerdeluce. **1658** SIR T. BROWNE *Gard. Cyrus* Wks. (Bohn) II. 548 Why coniferous trees are tenuifolious or narrow-leafed? **1754** CATESBY *Nat. Hist. Car.* I. 69 The narrow-leaved Candle-berry Myrtle. **1766** *Compl. Farmer* s.v. *Lavender*, There are two sorts, distinguished by the names of lavender spike, and common narrow leaved lavender. **1768** PENNANT *Brit. Zool.* (1776) I. 13 The narrow-leaved Plantane is greedily eat by horses and cows. **1833** in *Proc. Berw. Nat. Club* I. i. 29 Narrow-leaved Ever-lasting Pea. **1859** MISS PRATT *Brit. Grasses* 22 Narrow-leaved Cotton-grass. **1879** LUBBOCK *Sci. Lect.* ii. 46 Caterpillars which live on or among narrow-leaved plants.

narrowly ('nærəʊlɪ), *adv.* Forms: 1 nearo-, næro-, nearu-, 2 nearwelice, 3 neruhlic(h)e, narruliche; 5–6 naroly, (5 *Sc.* narro-, 6 -lye), narowly, (6 -lye, -lie, narrouly, -lie), 6–7 narrowlie, 5– narrowly, (6 -owe-). [OE. *nearolíce*, f. *nearo* NARROW *a.* + *-líce*, -LY², but in later use a new formation on the adj.]

1. Carefully, closely, with close attention.

c **897** K. ÆLFRED tr. *Gregory's Past. C.* xxi. 153 Maneȝu diȝlu ðing sindon nearolice to smeaȝeanne. *a* **1122** *O.E. Chron.* (Laud MS.) an. 1085 Swa swyðe nearwelice he hit lett ut aspyrian, þæt næs an ælpiȝ hide..þæt næs ȝesæt on his ȝewrite. *a* **1225** *Ancr. R.* 334 He seið, þet he nule nout so neruhliche demen ase ȝe siggeð. **1529** S. FISH *Supplic. Beggars* (1871) 2 They loke so narowly vppon theyre prouffittes, that the poore wyues must be countable to theym of euery tenth eg. **1581** SIDNEY *Apol. Poetrie* (Arb.) 43, I..more narrowly will examine his parts. **1617** MORYSON *Itin.* I. 186 Thinking that I had never a penny left, whom he had seen so narrowly searched. **1688** HOLME *Armoury* III. 348/1 If they be but narrowly looked into,..there will be but little difference found. **1709** ADDISON & STEELE *Tatler* No. 103 ¶ 11, I watched him narrowly for Six and Thirty Years. **1745** P. THOMAS *Jrnl. Anson's Voy* 120 You must search narrowly to discover it. **1806** A. DUNCAN *Nelson* 123 For the purpose of observing the enemy's motions more narrowly. **1885** *Manch. Exam.* 21 May 5/3 We are not concerned to inquire too narrowly which of the two parties is to blame.

†**b.** Deeply, firmly. *Obs. rare*⁻¹.

1494 FABYAN *Chron.* VI. cxcv 200 Enprynted so naroly [are] thyse verses in yᵉ boke of theyr conscyence.

2. In a contracted or confined manner.

c **1000** ÆLFRIC *Gen.* Prol. (Gr.) 24 Nu ys seo foresæde boc on maneȝum stowum swiðe nærolice ȝesett & þeah swiðe deoplice. *c* **1532** DU WES *Introd. Fr.* in *Palsgr.* 940 To reduce narowly, *coartér*. **1563** WINȜET tr. *Vincent. Lirin.* Wks. (S.T.S.) II. 45 Thai thingis..for strenthin of oure memorie, lat ws schortliar and mair narroulie reherse. **1582** STANYHURST *Æneis* I. (Arb.) 20 Rush do the winds forward through perst chinck narrolye whizling. **1847** W. E. STEELE *Field Bot.* 197 Leaves narrowly linear. **1887** W. PHILLIPS *Brit. Discomyc.* 140 Sporidia..narrowly fusiform or linear.

†**3.** Sparingly, parsimoniously. *Obs. rare.*

a **1225** *Ancr. R.* 414 Heo schal libben bi elmesse ase neruhliche ase heo euer mei. *a* **1275** *Prov. Ælfred* 519 in *O.E. Misc.* 133 Ne þeng þu neuere þi lif to narruliche leden. **1647** CLARENDON *Hist. Reb.* VI. §409 He gave over any pursuit in Court, and liv'd narrowly in the Country.

†**4.** Barely, scarcely. *Obs. rare.*

c **1375** *Sc. Leg. Saints* i. (*Peter*) 480 Narowly cuth he purchase Audience till he had sad his will. *Ibid.* xlvi. (*Anastas.*) 36 Publy strat kepyn til hir mad, Sa þat narroly fud scho had. *a* **1400–50** *Alexander* 1370 þat he fiches & firmes sa fast to þe wall, So nere vnethes at ane eld [= a needle] miȝt narowly betwene.

b. Only by a (very) little; only just.

1560 DAUS tr. *Sleidane's Comm.* 185 [He] escaped drowning verye narrowely. **1639** FULLER *Holy War* I. vi. (1840) 9 Tyrius mentioneth one memorable massacre, which they narrowly escaped. **1687** A. LOVELL tr. *Thevenot's Trav.* I. 75 They very narrowly missed being taken by the Christians. **1726** SWIFT *Gulliver* I. ii, One [arrow] very narrowly missed my left eye. **1774** *Misc. Ess.* in *Ann. Reg.* 159/2 She..very narrowly escaped being drowned. **1837** DE QUINCEY *Coleridge* Wks. 1862 II. 111 He will see how narrowly Dr. Watson missed this elevation. **1884** *Law Times Rep.* L. 113/2 He narrowly escaped falling into one of the ditches. **1885** *Manch. Exam.* 13 July 5/5 The match in the end was very narrowly won by Harrow.

†**5.** Closely, straitly. *Obs.*

1560 DAUS tr. *Sleidane's Comm.* 132 b, Nowe was the citie on every syde so narrowly and straightlye besieged. **1584** POWEL *Lloyd's Cambria* 86 The Northwales men..pursued Run so narrowlie, that all his Scottish shifts could not saue his life. **1642** ROGERS *Naaman* 31 The prodigall..was faine to be pursued so narrowly by the hand of God. **1707** *Lond. Gaz.* No. 4295/2 Which Place is..narrowly beset by the Troops.

6. Illiberally; strictly.

1708 SWIFT *Sent. Ch. Eng. Man* II. Wks. 1751 II. 83 He does not think the Church of England so narrowly calculated, that it cannot fall in with any regular species of Government. **1876** BANCROFT *Hist. U.S.* VI. lviii. 483 The narrowly selfish colonial policy. **1885** *Law Times* LXXX. 113/1 The Court held that the language of the Act is not to be read so narrowly.

narrow-minded, *a.* [NARROW *a.* 4.] Lacking in breadth of mind; incapable of broad views; illiberal, bigoted, prejudiced. Also *absol.*

1625 B. JONSON *Staple of News* v. i, A narrow minded man! my thoughts doe dwell All in a Lane, or line indeed. **1636** —— *Discov.* Wks. (Rtldg.) 743/2 He is a narrow-minded man, that affects a triumph in any glorious study. **1768–74** TUCKER *Lt. Nat.* (1834) II. 658 The rigorous and narrow-minded throw so many difficulties in the way of salvation. **1777** ROBERTSON *Hist. Amer.* (1783) II. 271 Where a narrow-minded bigotry appears in such close union with oppression and cruelty. **1830** HERSCHEL *Stud. Nat. Phil.* 7 The objection whch has been taken..by persons, well meaning perhaps, certainly narrow-minded. **1874** L. STEPHEN *Hours in Library* (1892) I. vii. 266 He shows to the full their narrow-minded hatred of the preceding century.

Hence **narrow-'mindedly** *adv.*

1827 HARE *Guesses* (1859) 276 Historians are apt to write ..presumptuously and narrowmindedly. **1884** *Q. Rev.* Apr. 328 The Chinaman shows himself less narrow-mindedly conservative.

narrow-'mindedness. [-NESS.] The fact or quality of being narrow-minded.

1646 BOYLE *Wks.* (1772) I. p. xxxiv, Persons that endeavour to put narrow-mindedness out of countenance, by the practice of so extensive a charity. **1748** HARTLEY *Observ. Man* II. ii. §33. 164 The Jews..being led thereto by the same Narrow-mindedness. **1768–74** TUCKER *Lt. Nat.* (1834) II. 114 The sources of narrow-mindedness, considered as a fault of the will. **1835** ARNOLD in Stanley *Life* (1844) II. viii. 16 The narrow-mindedness of every sect plays out its own play. **1889** G. FINDLAY *Eng. Railway* 6 Every weapon that the prejudice and narrow-mindedness of the many..could devise.

narrow-mouthed, *a.* [NARROW *a.* 1.]

1. a. Of vessels: Having a small mouth or opening.

1600 SHAKS. *A.Y.L.* III. ii. 211 As Wine comes out of a narrow-mouth'd bottle. **1629** GAULE *Pract. The.* 33 Because our Vessels are narrow mouthed, and take it in but by drops. **1754–64** SMELLIE *Midwifery* I. Introd. 8 This assertion he illustrates by the example of an olive in a narrow-mouthed jar. **1844** *Mem. Babylon. Princ.* II. 191, I seized one of the narrow-mouthed vessels used for drinking. **1910** W. DE LA MARE *Three Mulla-Mulgars* xvi. 247 Sipped slowly from their gurgling, narrow-mouthed bags or bottles. **1967** KARCH & BUBER *Offset Processes* vi. 248 When mixing solution 'A', 'B' or 'C' it is advisable to use a one gallon, narrow-mouthed bottle.

b. Denoting a form of spade.

1830 *Cumbld. Farm Rep.* 65 in *Lib. Usef. Kn., Husb.* III, A narrow-mouthed spade (technically called a spit).

†**2.** Of languages: (See quot.) *Obs. rare*⁻¹.

1667 *Phil. Trans.* II. 603 Those [languages] that are narrow-mouthed, and require but very slight Motions of the Lips and the other Organs of Speech.

narrow-necked, *a.* [NARROW *a.* 1.] Of vessels: Having a narrow neck.

1605 TIMME *Quersit.* III. 192 The end of a narrowe necked glasse. **1611** COTGR., *Vrne*, a narrow-necked pot..to.. keepe water in. **1727** POPE *Thoughts* Swift's Wks. 1751 V. 251 It is with narrow-souled People as with narrow-necked Bottles. **1815** J. SMITH *Panorama Sci. & Art* II. 212 A ready method of coating narrow necked jars. **1899** *Daily News* 6 Oct. 5/2 There have been found several long narrow-necked jars.

narrowness ('nærəʊnɪs). Also 6 narownes(se. [f. NARROW *a.* Cf. OE. *nearo-*, *nearunes*, narrowness, constraint, distress, etc.] The fact or quality of being narrow, in various senses.

1. Smallness from side to side; lack of breadth.

1530 PALSGR. 247/2 Narownesse, *estreissevr*. **1553** EDEN *Treat. Newe Ind.* (Arb.) 7 There is none other passage oute of the narownesse of the readde sea. **1596** DALRYMPLE tr. *Leslie's Hist. Scot.* Prol. 32 Farther beyonde lorne, the lande ..is driuen to a strait and gret narownes. **1627** CAPT. SMITH *Seaman's Gram.* ii. 4 According there to her breadth or narrownesse, we say she hath a narrow or broad buttocke. **1652** NEEDHAM tr. *Seiden's Mare Cl.* 132 There may som difference bee alleged onely from the largeness of the one and the narrowness of the other. **1722** DE FOE *Plague* Wks. (Bohn) V. 20 As many people as the narrowness of the place would permit to stop. **1803** *Med. Jrnl.* IX. 76 Cases..in which the narrowness or distortion of the pelvis was.. considerable. **1883** WACE *Gospel & Witn.* iv. 86 There would be something terrible..in the narrowness and straitness of the path which it marks out.

b. Small size or capacity of a place, etc.

1571 GOLDING *Calvin on Ps.* lxv. 5 Our narownesse is a let untoo us, that God cannot replenish us [etc.]. **1624** T. GODWIN *Moses & Aaron* I. (1641) 22 All Israel could not stand by, for the narrownesse of the place. *a* **1676** HALE *Prim. Orig. Man.* II. ix. (1677) 212 Which was considerable then, considering the narrowness of the City in those days. **1795** in *Ld. Auckland's Corr.* (1862) III. 296 The narrowness of my library alone..would hinder me from placing a collection of the 'Moniteur' in it.

2. Scantiness, limited amount *of* a thing.

1647–8 COTTERELL *Davila's Hist. Fr.* (1678) 11 Finding the narrowness of his fortune could not maintain the greatness of his birth. **1699** WANLEY in *Lett. Lit. Men* (Camden) 293 The narrowness of my time and paper will not permit me to trouble you much further. **1751** EARL ORRERY *Remarks Swift* (1752) 73 The narrowness of her income. **1824** W. IRVING *T. Trav.* I. 328 My father made me a tolerable allowance, notwithstanding the narrowness of his income.

b. Restricted range *of* an immaterial thing.

1641 MILTON *Ch. Govt.* I. i, To come within the narrownesse of household government, observation will shew us [etc.]. **1697** DRYDEN *Æneid* Ded. a 2 Those more amply treated, than the narrowness of the Drama can admit. **1741** WARBURTON *Div. Legat.* II. 146 The Pleonasm evidently arose from the Narrowness of a simple Language. **1818** MACAULAY in Trevelyan *Life* (1876) I. ii. 96 It was attributed to the narrowness of his reading. **1877** MRS. OLIPHANT *Makers Flor.* iii. 79 The narrowness of my opportunities..compels me to give up this.

3. Limited or small capacity *of* mind, understanding, etc.

1553 EDEN *Treat. Newe Ind.* (Arb.) 11 Suche as by the narownes of theyr vnderstandinge are not of capacitie to conceaue the causes and natures of thynges. **1626** BACON *Sylva* §290 To enlarge their Mindes to the Amplitude of the World; And not reduce the World to the Narrowness of their Mindes. **1647** CLARENDON *Hist. Reb.* II. §85 Every man ..by the narrowness of his understanding..contracted all his other affections to that one of Revenge. **1699** BURNET 39 *Art.* i. 32 The only difficulty..in apprehending this, has arisen from the Narrowness of Mens Minds. **1786** W. THOMSON *Watson's Philip III* (1839) 281 Whose thirst of vengeance was in proportion to the narrowness of his capacity. **1851** GALLENGA *Italy* 357 Even men of..rigid morality were..scarcely less dangerous, from the narrowness of their understanding. **1882** 'OUIDA' *Maremma* I. 200 It is this narrowness of the peasant mind which philosophers never fairly understand.

4. Deficiency in breadth or largeness *of* soul, mind, view, etc.

1645 HOWELL *Twelve Treat.* (1661) 352 The sense of poverty..brings along with it a narrownesse of soul. *a* **1665** J. GOODWIN *Filled w. the Spirit* (1867) 247 It will relieve you against the natural scantness and narrowness of your hearts. **1705** STANHOPE *Paraphr.* I. 12 The same Narrowness of Spirit, which tempts us not to satisfie all others. **1759** DILWORTH *Pope* 70 He hated a narrowness of soul in any party. **1793** SMEATON *Edystone L.* §296 The amazing narrowness of mind of some persons. **1830** D'ISRAELI *Chas. I*, III. iv. 57 If we are struck by the comprehension of his understanding, we may equally be so at the narrowness of his views. **1873** HAMERTON *Intell. Life* v. iii. 189 The narrowness of men's ideas in direct proportion to their parsimony in expenditure.

b. Without const., in same sense. Also *pl.*

1697 SIR T. P. BLOUNT *Ess.* 74 Which sort of narrowness I find many are subject to. **1734** BERKELEY *Analyst* Wks. 1871 III. 297 That prevailing narrowness and bigotry among many who pass for men of science. **1817** JAS. MILL *Brit. India* II. v. vi. 565 The narrowness which the mind contracts by habitual application to the practice of English law. **1889** RUSKIN *Præterita* III. 96 Norton saw all my weaknesses, measured all my narrownesses.

5. In miscellaneous uses of the adj.

1651 *Fuller's Abel Rediv., Luther* 52 Then complained he againe of the narrownesse of his breast. **1783** JOHNSON in *Boswell*, I was occasionally troubled with a fit of narrowness. **1871** BLACKIE *Four Phases Mor.* i. 98 The narrowness of the view which the inspection of a watch necessitates. **1884** *Truth* 13 Mar. 369/2 Considering the narrowness of the defeat..the tie should certainly be replayed.

narrow seas. Also 5 sea. [NARROW *a.* 1.]

1. The channels separating Great Britain from the adjacent continent and from Ireland.

14.. *Sailing Directions* (Hakl. Soc.) 21 And yif..ye be bounde into the narowe see..go your cours north est. *a* **1548** HALL *Chron., Rich. III* 49 b, He called home agaîne his shippes of warre whiche he had apoynted to kepe the narowe sees. **1562–3** *Royal Proclam.* 8 Feb., All marchauntes of all other nations, passynge through her narrowe Seas with theyr shippes and vessels. **1593** SHAKS. *3 Hen. VI*, I. i. 239 Sterne Falconbridge commands the Narrow Seas. **1630** *R. Johnson's Kingd. & Commw.* 198 In 88. upon short warning they rigged to the narrow seas 100. good men of warre. **1690** *Lond. Gaz.* No. 2574/1 Your Majesties Dominion of the Narrow Seas. **1721** PERRY *Daggenh. Breach* 22 Such cruising Ships.., who are appointed..to have their Station in the narrow Seas, between England and Ireland. **1754** *Ess. Manning Fleet* 45 As soon as they arrive within the Narrow Seas. **1807** *Edin. Rev.* XI. 17 Great Britain has the sovereignty of what are called the narrow seas. **1847** TENNYSON *Princ.* Concl. 70 God bless the narrow seas!

2. In other applications. *rare.*

1615 W. BEDWELL *Arab. Trudg., Giebel*, The mouth of the narrow seas..is after the Arabicke name vulgarly..called *Estrecho de Gibraltar*. **1627** CAPT. SMITH *Seaman's Gram.* x. 48 It may bee hee meant in some narrow Seas.

narrow-souled, *a.* [NARROW *a.* 4.] Lacking in breadth of view or feeling; ungenerous.

1641 MILTON *Animadv. Remonstr. Def.* i. Wks. 1851 III. 186 The shallow surview..of some mercenary, narrow souled, and illiterate chaplain. **1691** T. H[ALE] *Acc. New Invent.* p. iii, A peevish endeavour of some narrow-soul'd Men. **1766** FORDYCE *Serm. Yng. Wom.* (1767) II. xii. 201 She was none of those narrow-souled women.

absol. **1700** DRYDEN *Cymon & Iph.* 35 Love..To lib'ral Acts inlarg'd the narrow-Soul'd. **1768–74** TUCKER *Lt. Nat.* (1834) II. 545 Discovering daily new sources of solacement ..which the selfish and narrow-souled never can discern.

b. Mean, stingy. *north. dial.*

a **1700** B. E. *Dict. Cant. Crew* s.v. *Narrow*, *A Narrow-soul'd Fellow*, poor or Mean-spirited, stingy. **1828** *Craven Gloss.*, *Narrow-souled*, parsimonious, ungenerous.

narrow-spirited, *a.* [NARROW *a.* 4.] Mean-spirited, wanting in generous or liberal feelings.

1679 *Trial Langhorn* 14 He said he was a narrow Spirited, and a narrow Soul'd Physician. **1703** *Moderation a Virtue* 10 But the narrow-spirited Zealots prevailed. **1705** STANHOPE *Paraphr.* II. 275 Neither the Peevish,..nor the Selfish and Narrow-Spirited..are any of them charitable. **1768–74** TUCKER *Lt. Nat.* (1834) I. 357 We..shall find subjects to rejoice at which the selfish and narrow-spirited never know. **1818** SCOTT *Rob Roy* x, Qualities..modified by a narrow-spirited, but yet ardent patriotism.

Hence **narrow-'spiritedness.**

1709 CHANDLER *Effort agst. Bigotry* Ded. A 2 b, That narrow Spiritedness that is more or less the Fault of all Parties. *a* **1714** M. HENRY *Wks.* (ed. Fullarton) II. 356 That narrow spiritedness which confines religion and the church to our way and party.

†**'narrowth.** *Obs. rare*⁻¹. In 3 neruhðe. [f. NARROW *a.* + -TH¹.] Narrowness, constraint.

a **1225** *Ancr. R.* 378 þeos two þinges limpeð to ancre, neruhðe & bitternesse.

'narrowy, *a. rare*⁻¹. [-Y¹.] Narrowish.

1858 O. W. HOLMES *Aut. Breakf.-t.* (1883) 234 Some narrowy crapes of China silk.

narruliche, obs. form of NARROWLY.

narsarsukite (nɑːsɑːˈsʊkaɪt). *Min.* [f. *Narsarssauk*, *-suk*, name of a plain in SW. Greenland + -ITE[1].] A silicate and fluoride of sodium, iron, and titanium, $Na_2(Ti,Fe)Si_4(O,F)_{11}$, which is found as yellow tetragonal crystals.

1900 G. FLINK in *Meddelelser om Grønland* XXIV. 154 The new mineral..was the first that attracted my attention on Narsarsuk. None of the other new minerals has been found at so many different localities on the plateau or is so largely distributed there. It may therefore, more than any other mineral, be said to be characteristic of the place. On this ground I propose for it the name narsarsukite. **1935** *Amer. Mineralogist* XX. 598 The narsarsukite was seen only in the quartz veins in the roof rock and upper part on the intrusive. **1968** I. KOSTOV *Mineral.* II. 300 Baotite is a typical example of silicates with tetragonal rings of silicon tetrahedra [Si_4O_{12}]. Narsarsukite has similar rings but they are not isolated as in baotite but linked together along the tetragonal axis in a tube-like manner.

†**nart**, art not: see NE and BE *v.* A. I. 2. *Obs.*

*c***893** K. ÆLFRED *Boeth.* viii, þonne neart ðu þeah unȝesæliȝ. *c***950** *Lindisf. Gosp.* John xix. 12 Narð ðæs cæsares friond. *c***1200** ORMIN 4676 Loc nu ȝiff þatt tu narrt rihht wod. *c***1205** LAY. 13633 Nert þu na wimman swa sære to wepen. *c***1330** *Arth. & Merl.* 7498 (Kölbing), A, Mahoun!..þou nart no god worþ a slo. *c***1374** CHAUCER *Boeth.* I. pr. v. (1868) 23 þou nart nat put out of it. **1413** *Pilgr. Sowle* (Caxton 1483) IV. xx. 65 Why nart thou here?

narthecal (nɑːˈθiːkəl), *a. Eccl.* [f. *narthec-*, NARTHEX + -AL[1].] Of the nature of a narthex.

1866 *Ecclesiologist* XXVII. 32 The plan shows a western narthecal mass with central vestibule.

narthex (ˈnɑːθɛks). *Archæol.* [a. Gr. *νάρθηξ*, properly the name of a tall umbelliferous plant with a hollow stalk; also, a small case or casket for unguents, etc.; and in later use applied as in def. The synonymous L. *ferula* was used in the same sense (Du Cange).] A vestibule or portico stretching across the western end of some early Christian churches or basilicas, divided from the nave by a wall, screen, or railing, and set apart for the use of women, catechumens, penitents or other persons; an ante-nave.

1673 CAVE *Prim. Chr.* I. vi. 123 The Narthex..was that part of the church that lay next to the great door. **1723** BINGHAM *Antiq. Ch.* (1838) II. 401 This [*πρόναος*] in the modern Greek rituals is always called the Narthex, and is peculiarly allotted to the monks or women [etc.]. **1788** GIBBON *Decl. & F.* xl. IV. 93 From the sanctuary in the east to the nine western doors..and from thence into the *narthex* or exterior portico. **1846** R. HART *Eccl. Rec.* (ed. 2) 225 In the primitive church there was also a *Narthex* or ante-nave to the west. **1869** TOZER *Highl. Turkey* I. 79 These narthexes..seem originally to have been intended for catechumens and penitents. **1894** BARING-GOULD *Deserts S. France* I. 251 A church that consists of a narthex or vestibule, and a nave with three aisles.

nartjie (ˈnɑːtʃɪ, ˈnarci). *S. Afr.* Also **naartj(i)e, naatje(e), naretje.** [Afrikaans, f. Tamil *nārattai* citrus.] The tangerine or mandarin orange. Also *attrib.* and *transf.*

1790 E. HELME tr. *Le Vaillant's Trav. Afr.* I. ii. 23 The citrus and oranges (specially the sort called *naretyes* [sic]) are excellent. **1796** tr. *Le Vaillant's New Travels* I. 190 There is a kind of orange..called at the Cape *naretjes*, which, notwithstanding the smallness of its size, is sold at a higher rate. **1870** *Cape Monthly Mag.* Oct. 219 The 'nartjie', a dwarf orange. **1890** A. MARTIN *Home Life Ostrich Farm* xi. 211 Dutchmen..often bringing with them very good onions, oranges, *naatjes* or mandarines, nuts, dried peaches and figs. **1908** *Westm. Gaz.* 14 Aug. 4/3 The only orange now on the market here is the Cape 'naatjee'. **1909** *Daily Chron.* 15 June 4/3 The little Tangerine..and its bigger relative the Mandarin are called Naartjes in Natal. **1923** *Chambers's Jrnl.* Apr. 269/2 Oranges, nartjes and grape-fruit ripen during June, July and August. **1937** S. CLOETE *Turning Wheels* iii. 46 Others handled the seeds they had brought with them—..the pips of nartjes. *Ibid.* xiii. 210 Martha, your heart is like a naartjie. **1947** [see DENNEBOL]. **1949** A. WILSON *Wrong Set* 41 Oranges of all sizes..from the tiny nartjies, through tangerines and green mandarins to the great navel oranges. **1953** N. GORDIMER *Lying Days* III. xxvii. 276 'You've been eating a naartje,' I said. **1966** E. PALMER *Plains of Camdeboo* ii. 33 Fanny's pot-roasted venison and pou, her van der Hum made of brandy, syrup and naartjie peel, her pickled peaches,..are still remembered. **1967** *Punch* 5 July 17/1 Accept and enjoy a naartje off the tree. **1970** *Rand Daily Mail* 28 Feb. 7/4 Many South African words of Dutch or Afrikaans origin are now part of English usage even in other countries—..naartjie and mealie. **1971** *Sunday Express* (Johannesburg) 28 Mar. 11/4 Couldn't the orange [of air-hostesses' uniforms] be toned down a little and the blue be slightly deeper? No wonder the poor girls are referred to as naartjies. **1972** D. FRANCIS *Smokescreen* vii. 85 The *naartjies* turned out to be like large lumpy tangerines with green patches on the skin. **1974** *Sunday Times* (Johannesburg) 28 July 4/2 The record for the number of naartjies and oranges brought into the ground by spectators is held jointly by Ellis Park, Loftus Versfeld and Kings Park, a total of 200,000 citric fruit units being introduced at each ground. **1975** *Darling* (S. Afr.) 9 Apr. 95 You only feel a naartjie riding in the back of a truck with three drums of pig swill and a stack of moulting lucerne bales for company.

naruȝ, narw(e, obs. forms of NARROW.

†**narve.** *Obs. rare.* Also **narfe.** [perh. a variant of NERVE *sb.*] (See quots.)

1688 HOLME *Armoury* III. 92/2 *Narve*, sinews pulled to Threads, and glewed on the [saddle-] Tree to hold the Tree from cracking or breaking. *Ibid.* 345/1 The Narfe..is the sinews glewed on the Tree to strengthen it.

narwhal (ˈnɑːhwəl). Forms: α. 7 **narh-**, 8– **narwhale.** β. 8 **narhwal, -hual,** 8–9 **narwal, -whal.** γ. 8 **narv(h)al.** [= mod.Du. and G. *narwal*, mod.F. *narval* (1690), ad. Da. or Sw. *narhval* (f. *hval* WHALE), the relationship of which to ON. *náhvalr* is obscure. The latter appears to be formed on *ná-r*, corpse, and is usually supposed to refer to the colour of the skin.] A delphinoid cetacean (*Monodon monoceros*) inhabiting the Arctic seas, and remarkable as being without teeth except two in the upper mandible, one (sometimes both) of which develops into a spirally-twisted straight horn; the sea-unicorn.

α. **1658** SIR T. BROWNE *Pseud. Ep.* III. xxiii. (ed. 4) 205 Those long horns preserved..in many places, are but the teeth of Narh whales. **1747** *Gentl. Mag.* XVII. 174 They having..seen the skull of the Narwhale armed with two horns. **1787** HUNTER in *Phil. Trans.* LXXVII. 373 The..Spermaceti Whale, and the Monodon Monoceros, or Narwhale, have also fallen under my inspection. **1833** TENNYSON *Lotos Eaters* 152 (ed. 1), Where..the monstrous narwhale swalloweth His foamfountains in the sea. *c***1865** LETHEBY in *Orr's Circ. Sci.* I. 103/2 Even the Monodons or narwhales may be made to yield train-oil.

β. **1752** J. HILL *Hist. Anim.* 314 *Monodon*, the Unicorn-fish, or Nar-wal. **1762** tr. *Busching's Syst. Geog.* I. 490 The horn of the whale called Narwhal has been found in the earth. **1799** W. TOOKE *View Russian Emp.* III. 105 The Frozen Ocean, likewise, teems with the narhwal. **1820** W. SCORESBY *Acc. Arctic Reg.* I. 494 Narwals are quick, active, inoffensive animals. **1873** *Spectator* 23 Aug. 1067/2 The men sit in dead silence..watching for the narwhal, which are blowing near.

attrib. **1813** BINGLEY *Zool.* II. 1 Of the Narwal Tribe. **1866** KINGSLEY *Herew.* i. I. 79 The handle was..curiously bound with silver, and butted with narwhal ivory. **1875** F. T. BUCKLAND *Log-bk.* 286 Some suppose that the ivory bits ..were made of walrus or narwhal tusks.

γ. **1723** *Pres. St. Russia* II. 386 Who slit their Cheeks, and put the Bones of the Fish Narval into the Wound. **1728** SLOANE in *Phil. Trans.* XXXV. 460 The Tooth of a Sort of Whale in the Northern Seas called Narvhal.

nary (ˈnɛərɪ), *a.* Chiefly *U.S.* and *dial.* [var. of NE'ER A. The form is typically U.S., but app. occurs in some Eng. dialects, and is now used more widely outside the U.S.] Neither; no; not a; now almost always followed by the indef. article. Also (*U.S.*) ***nary (a) red*** or ***cent***, not a cent.

1746 N. WRIGHT *Jrnl.* 6 Aug. in *New England Hist. & Geneal. Reg.* (1848) II. 209 The Indians..escaped them, and there was no 'spile dunne on nary side'. **1821** *Mass. Spy* 14 Feb. (Th.), He asked her whether she was most fond of writing prose or poetry. 'Nary one,' says she, 'I writes small hand.' **1836** HALIBURTON *Clockm.* (1862) 113, I guess there ain't much to brag on nary way, damage done on both sides. **1848** LOWELL *Biglow P.* Ser. I. i, Slavery ain't o' nary color. *Ibid.* Ser. II. ii, Nary sounds but watch-dogs' false alarms. **1849** *Picayune* (New Orleans) 6 May 2/6 I'm goin' tew get my breakfuss yere, and not pay 'nary red' till I dew! **1856** *Knickerbocker* XLVII. 99 'Aint you gwine for to give us three dollars?' 'Nary a red!' sung out *Hart.* **1856** 'J. PHOENIX' *Phoenixiana* 125 Playin at billiards and monte Till they've nary red cent to ante. **1863** RUSSELL *Diary North & South* I. 168 Another..replied to the demand for so many thousand soldiers, 'Nary one'. **1872** G. P. BURNHAM *Mem. U.S. Secret Service* p. vii, *Nary red*, out of pocket; 'broke' of ready funds. **1893** MCCARTHY *Red Diamonds* I. 65 We hadn't nary cent to work it with. **1895** S. CRANE *Red Badge of Courage* x. 102 There's too much depending on me fer me t' die yit. No, sir! Nary die; I *can't*! **1906** *Dialect Notes* III. 147 (N.W. Arkansas) Nary a red. **1917** 'H. H. RICHARDSON' *Fortunes R. Mahony* IV. x. 379 She would discover a thousand drawbacks to his scheme, but nary a one of the incorporeal benefits he dreamed of reaping from it. **1920** E. O'NEILL *Beyond Horizon* I. ii. 36 They've been thick as thieves all their lives, with nary a quarrel I kin remember. **1932** *New Yorker* 9 Apr. 54/1 We flit hither and thither among the gadgets,..with nary a thought for the morrow. **1941** *Time* 6 Jan. 16/1 From the National Defense Advisory Commission,..there was nary a peep. **1971** M. TORRIE *Bismarck Herrings* xi. 156 'Were many turned out during her time?' asked Timothy. 'Nary a one,' replied Mrs. Baines. **1973** *New Society* 30 Aug. 522/3 You can wander around the cavernous vaults of the Law Courts in the Strand these days and come across nary a person. **1973** *People's Jrnl.* (Inverness & Northern Counties ed.) 1 Dec. 4/4 And there was nary a stranger on hand to be impressed! **1974** *Verbatim* Dec. 6/2 The computer that did all the dogwork gets nary a mention.

†**nas**, was not: see NE and BE *v.* A. 6. *Obs.*

*c***893** K. ÆLFRED *Boeth.* v. §1 He..næs nauht ȝedrefed. *c***1000** ÆLFRIC *Gen.* ii. 5 Man næs, þe þa eorðan worhte. *c***1175** *Lamb. Hom.* 81 In þisse world nas na laȝe. *c***1250** *Lutel soth Serm.* 16 in *O.E. Misc.* 186 So reusful dede idon neuer non nas. *c***1320** *Sir Tristr.* 161 Nas neuer non fairer fedde. *c***1374** CHAUCER *Boeth.* I. pr. vi. (1868) 27, I nas nat deceiued quod sche. *c***1420** *Chron. Vilod.* 416 Heyre of Westsex non other þere nasse. *c***1450** *Merlin* 220 Ther nas noon that was wounded to deth. *c***1570** *Pride & Lowl.* (1841) 8 So paynted and so coloured..Nas Floras land.

†**nas**, has not: see NE and HAVE *v.* *Obs.*

1579 SPENSER *Sheph. Cal.* May 61 For pittied is mishappe that nas remedie.

N.A.S.A., NASA, Nasa (ˈnæsə). [Acronym f. the initial letters of *N*ational *A*eronautics and *S*pace *A*dministration, set up in 1958.] A body responsible for organizing research in extraterrestrial space conducted by the United States.

1958 *Aviation Week* 14 Apr. 25/1 The President's recommendations and proposed legislation to create NASA, using NACA as a nucleus, were sent to Congress before the Easter recess. **1958** D. EISENHOWER in *N.Y. Times* 30 July 10/7 The present National Advisory Committee for Aeronautics..will provide the nucleus of the N.A.S.A. **1965** *Economist* 4 Sept. 873/2 The Manned Orbiting Laboratory, a project which President Johnson has decided to entrust not to Nasa but to the Air Force. **1969** *Times* 13 June 7/6 N.A.S.A.'s Apollo applications programme has reached an advanced stage of discussion.

nasal (ˈneɪzəl), *sb.* Also 7 **nazal.** [In sense 1, a. OF. *nasal*, var. *nasel* NASEL; in sense 2, ad. med.L. *nāsāle*; otherwise a subst. use of next.]

1. A nose-piece on a helmet. Cf. NASEL.

1480 CAXTON *Ovid's Met.* XII. xiv, Hector toke hym thenne by the nasal and drewe the helme over hys heed. **1656** BLOUNT *Glossogr.*, *Nazal*, the Nose-piece of a Helmet. **1828–41** TYTLER *Hist. Scot.* (1864) I. 320 The head, which is protected with a conical steel cap and a nasal. **1834** PLANCHÉ *Brit. Costume* 46 The Danish helmet, like the Saxon, had the nasal. **1869** BOUTELL *Arms & Armour* ix. 161 Iron hats..broad-brimmed and provided with a nasal.

†**2.** = ERRHINE 1 and 2. *Obs. rare.*

1601 HOLLAND *Pliny* Explan. Words, *Nasals* be Nose-tents. **1621** BURTON *Anat. Mel.* II. v. I. iv, Sneezing, masticatories, and nasals are generally received. **1632** tr. *Bruel's Praxis Med.* 7 A nasal or errhine of..Pepper-wort.

3. A nasal letter or sound.

1669 HOLDER *Elem. Speech* 59 In attempting to pronounce these two Consonants, as likewise the Nasals, and some of the vowels. **1773** KENRICK *Dict.*, *Gram.* ii. 4 All the mute consonants which are silent before a vowel, and gutturals, nasals or palatines after it. *a***1794** SIR W. JONES *Orthogr. Asiat. Words* Wks. 1799 I. 185 The liquid nasal follows these, being formed by the tongue and roots of the teeth, with..assistance from the other organ. **1844** *Proc. Philol. Soc.* I. 287 Although the Dutch rejects the nasal in the nominative. **1867** ELLIS *E.E. Pronunc.* I. iii. 67 We know how the present English stumble over the French nasals.

4. *Anat.* A nasal bone.

1854 OWEN in *Orr's Circ. Sci.* II. 53/1 The neural spine is usually single, sometimes cleft along the middle; it is the 'nasal'. **1873** MIVART *Elem. Anat.* 85 The nasals are small bones placed side by side above the nares.

nasal (ˈneɪzəl), *a.* Also 8 **nazal.** [ad. med.L. **nāsāl-is* (cf. It. *nasale*, Sp. *nasál*, F. *nasal*), f. *nās-us* nose: see -AL[1].]

1. Of, belonging or pertaining to, the nose.

Freq. in a large number of anatomical terms, as ***nasal artery, bone, cartilage, duct***, etc.

1656 BLOUNT *Glossogr.* s.v. *Vein*, *Nasal vein*, the nose vein, seated between the nostrils. **1726** MONRO *Anat. Bones* 89 Its nasal Process is connected to the nasal *Lamella ossis ethmoidis*. *Ibid.* 134 The nasal Bones are firm and solid. **1768** PARSONS in *Phil. Trans.* LVIII. 194 There does not appear any passage..but the mouth and nasal holes. **1826** S. COOPER *First Lines Surg.* (ed. 5) 319 Whenever the tears cannot pass freely through the nasal duct into the nose. **1855** HOLDEN *Hum. Osteol.* (1878) 131 The nasal fossæ open widely to the air in front through the nostrils. **1893** ALLEN *Handbk. Local Therap.* 113 The use of this agent, in the treatment of chronic nasal catarrh.

b. Of appliances: Used in connexion with the nose (see quots.).

1875 KNIGHT *Dict. Mech.* 1512/2 *Nasal Irrigator*, a syringe for nasal douches. *Ibid.*, *Nasal Speculum*, an instrument for distending the nostrils to expose the mucous membrane of the nose. **1895** *Arnold's Surg. Instr. Catal.* 214 Nasal Truss..for correcting deformities of the Nose.

2. Of speech-sounds: Produced, to a greater or less degree, by means of the nose.

1669 HOLDER *Elem. Speech* 45 There are but 3 Nasal Letters commonly in use. **1727–38** CHAMBERS *Cycl.* s.v. *N*, The N is a nasal consonant. **1776** BURNEY *Hist. Mus.* (1789) II. iv. 309 Why the French language should have so many nazal endings. **1855** D. FORBES *Hindust. Gram.* 6 At the end of a word..it generally has a nasal sound, like the French *n*. **1888** KING & COOKSON *Sounds & Inflexions* 105 The existence of nasal sonants is therefore a matter of hypothesis. **1890** H. SWEET *Primer Spoken Eng.* 1 In nasal sounds, such as *m*, the passage into the nose is left open.

b. Characterized by the presence, to an unusual or disagreeable extent, of sounds produced by means of the nose.

1669 HOLDER *Elem. Speech* 59 Some Nations may be found to have a peculiar Guttural or Nasal smatch in their Language. **1784** COWPER *Task* II. 436 Odious as a nasal twang Heard at conventicle. **1805** N. NICHOLLS in *Corr. w. Gray* (1843) 40 Mason replied instantly, in a surly, nasal tone. **1869** TOZER *Highl. Turkey* II. 253 The nasal character of the ecclesiastical music of that period. **1883** G. W. CURTIS in *Harper's Mag.* Dec. 13/2 They..worshipped God in ice-cold barns and with endless nasal prayers.

Comb. **1804** SOUTHEY in *Ann. Rev.* II. 528 The shibboleth of our nasal-twanged neighbour. **1894** 'MAX O'RELL' *J. Bull & Co.* 37 Half a dozen Samoans were joining in with their cracked nasal-sounding voices.

c. Used with reference to snoring.

1824 W. IRVING *T. Trav.* I. 8 The nasal communications of two or three..who, having been silent while awake, were ..indemnifying the company in their sleep. **1884** PAE *Eustace* 105 Certain vigorous nasal sounds gave token that he was in a deep slumber.

3. Received through the nose.

1832 G. DOWNES *Lett. Cont. Countries* I. 363, I had no nasal perception of any mephitic exhalation.

4. Provided with a nose-piece.

1824 MEYRICK *Anc. Armour* I. 26 He wears a nasal helmet, and a hauberk with tight sleeves.

Hence **ˈnasalism** = NASALITY. *rare*[−1].

1883 Oscar Wilde in *South. Times* 6 Oct. 4/2 The nasalism of the modern American had been retained from the Puritan Fathers. **1887** *Proc. R. Soc. Edin.* XXXII. 349 The Yankee nasalism is another familiar instance of the same kind. **1937** *Evening News* 23 Mar. 4/2 'We just dote on a good English accent,' she said, 'and we've got to get away from nasalism, our teacher says.'

nasality (neɪˈzælɪtɪ). [f. NASAL *a.* + -ITY: cf. F. *nasalité* (1767).] The quality of being nasal, *spec.* of utterance; an instance of this.

1776 J. Collier *Mus. Trav.* 25 A Clerk of the parish, who ..has the finest nasality, or nose-intonation, that ever was given to Psalm tune. *a* **1794** Sir W. Jones *Orthogr. Asiat. Words* Wks. 1807 III. 284 The Indian sound differs only in the greater nasality of the first letter. **1815** Byron *Let. to Moore* 8 Mar., Why do you always twit me with his vile Ebrew nasalities? **1859** Trollope *West Indies* xiii. (1860) 197 A nasal twang..quite distinct from the nasality of a Yankee. **1872** O. W. Holmes *Poet Breakf.-t.* i. (1885) 18, I can reproduce phonetically its vibrating nasalities.

nasalizable (ˈneɪzəlaɪzəb(ə)l), *a.* [f. NASALIZE *v.* + -ABLE.] Capable of being pronounced nasally.

1872 S. S. Haldeman *Pennsylvania Dutch* 11 This vowel being nasalisable.

nasalization (ˌneɪzəlaɪˈzeɪʃən). [f. next + -ATION; cf. F. *nasalisation.*] The action of nazalizing; the effect of this.

1855 tr. *Lepsius' Stand. Alph.* (1863) 58 The clear vowels are further capable of a peculiar alteration, that of nasalisation. **1856** *Trans. Philol. Soc.* 51 On the Nasalization of Initial Mutes in Welsh. **1879** Whitney *Sanskr. Gram.* 58 The nasalization of the alterant vowel.

nasalize (ˈneɪzəlaɪz), *v.* [f. NASAL *a.* + -IZE: cf. F. *nasaliser.*] **a.** *intr.* To speak nasally or through the nose. **b.** *trans.* To render nasal in pronunciation; to utter with a nasal sound. Hence **ˈnasalized** *ppl. a.*, **ˈnasalizing** *ppl. a.* and *vbl. sb.*

1846 in Worcester. **1859** R. F. Burton in *Jrnl. Geog. Soc.* XXIX. 337 Some such strongly-nasalized sound. **1868** G. Stephens *Runic Mon.* I. 257 The..slurring and nasalizing and falling-away of the N in the later Scandinavian dialects. **1888** H. Sweet *Eng. Sounds* 38 Nothing is more common than the nasalizing influence of a nasal on a preceding vowel.

nasally (ˈneɪzəlɪ), *adv.* [f. NASAL *a.* + LY^{2}.] In a nasal tone.

1847 in Webster. **1888** P. Fitzgerald *Fatal Zero* ix. 51 The lady added, very nasally, that what annoyed her was the English saying that the Americans talked through their noses.

Nasara: see NASRANI.

na-say, dial. variant of NAY-SAY.

†**nascal.** *Obs. rare.* [ad. med.L. *nascale*, of obscure origin.] A pessary or suppository.

The med.L. term also appears as *nascare, nastare, nascaplere, nastaplare*: see *Alphita* (Anecd. Oxon.) 123.

1640 Ferrand *Melanch.* 355 Women,..who may make use of..a Nascall or Pessary, composed of Castoreum mixed with Rue. **1661** Lovell *Hist. Anim. & Min.* 399 It is cured, in the paroxysme, by..nascals, discutients, rue [etc.].

Nascapee, Nascapi, varr. NASKAPI *a.* and *sb.*

ˈnascence. *rare.* [See next and -ENCE.] Birth.

1570 *Satir. Poems Reform.* xvii. 191 Our King..Quha our defence, in his nascence, Tuik haill in gouerning. **1892** *Echo* 28 Jan. 1/5 The renascence, or should we say nascence, of British sculpture is the joy of the artistic hour. **1901** *Science* 21 June 983/1 Formations often disappear through the agency of fires, floods, mankind, etc., in which cases new formations may arise by nascence.

nascency (ˈnæsənsɪ). [ad. L. *nascentia*: see next and -ENCY.] The process or fact of being born or brought into existence; birth.

1682 H. More *Annot. Glanvill's Lux O.* 90 A Spirit of Nature..to which belongs the Nascency or Generation of things. **1871** Earle *Philol. Eng. Tongue* iii. 167 In the nascency of geological ideas, a controversy flourished upon this question. **1873** B. Stewart *Conserv. Force* vii. 197 Under certain physical or chemical conditions, such as light, nascency [etc.].

nascent (ˈnæsənt), *a.* [ad. L. *nascent-, nascens*, pres. pple. of *nascī* to be born.]

1. In the act of being born or brought forth.

a **1624** R. Crackenthorp *Vigil. Dormitans* 188 In the first the Pope was but Antichrist nascent, in the second Antichrist crescent. **1679** C. Nesse *Antichrist* 64 Antichrist was nascent when Rome usurp'd authority first ouer all the churches. **1722** Wollaston *Relig. Nat.* v. 91 Formed at once in the first article of the nascent animalculum. **1774** Goldsm. *Nat. Hist.* (1776) VIII. 113 Some are found to place their eggs within the aurelia of some nascent insect. **1816** Kirby & Sp. *Entomol.* (1843) II. 349 Ensuring a due supply of food for the nascent larvæ. **1839-48** Bailey *Festus* xxxiv. 360 To seize the nascent souls Of men as they rerose from death to life. **1878** Gladstone *Prim. Homer* 100 The population, over whom the nascent babe was to reign.

2. *transf.* In the act or condition of coming into existence; just beginning to be; commencing to form, grow, or develop, etc.

a. of mathematical quantities.

1706 W. Jones *Syn. Palmar. Matheseos* 226 These Fluxions..are in the First Ratio of their Nascent Augments. **1766** Amory *Buncle* (1770) IV. 38 An adequate notion of a nascent or evanescent quantity. **1801** Young in *Phil. Trans.* XCII. 25 A partial undulation, filling up the nascent angle between the radii and the surface. **1821** Parr *Let.* Wks. 1828 VIII. 352 Your project of publishing sermons resembles a nascent arc.

b. of practices, institutions, qualities, or other abstract concepts.

In very frequent use in the 19th c., in a great variety of contexts.

1741 Warburton *Div. Legat.* II. 218 To support nascent Hero-worship. **1749** Berkeley *Let.* Wks. 1871 IV. 323, I recommended this nascent seminary to an English bishop. **1763** Gray *Let.* Poems (1775) 301 Imagination..reigns in all nascent societies of men. **1803** Syd. Smith *Wks.* (1850) 15 These symptoms of returning, or perhaps nascent purity in the mind of Mr. Lewis. **1818** G. S. Faber *Horæ Mosaicæ* I. 297 A person who was perplexed with a nascent infidelity. **1847** R. W. Hamilton *Rewards & Punishm.* v. (1853) 205 The nascent emotion acquires vigour. **1875** Maine *Hist. Inst.* ix. 278 Two alternative expedients were adopted by nascent law.

c. of material things or substances. (Common in scientific use, esp. in *Chem.* and *Zool.*) *spec.* applied to hydrogen that has just been released from a compound by electrolysis or chemical action (marked by its great reactivity and reducing power).

1802 Paley *Nat. Theol.* (1817) 60 That cartilage in truth is only nascent or imperfect bone. **1807** H. Davy in *Phil. Trans. R. Soc.* XCVII. 11 It was natural to account for both these appearances, from the combination of nascent oxygene and hydrogene respectively. **1826** —— in *Ibid.* CXVI. 388 Nascent hydrogen was not, as had been generally believed, the cause of the appearance of metals from metallic solutions. **1832** *Planting* 91 in *Lib. Usef. Kn., Husb.* III, *Nascent stem.*—The development of the stem of a seedling plant, just previous to the exhibition of the first leaves. **1849** Noad *Electricity* (ed. 3) 157 The oxides of copper and zinc reduced by the nascent hydrogen. **1862** Darwin *Orchids* vi. 268 These protuberances may be provisionally considered as nascent antennæ. **1877** Thomson *Voy. Challenger* I. ii. 141 They seem to thrive best among the elements of nascent limestones. **1959** *Proc. Nat. Acad. Sci.* XLV. 1441 Thus there is a protein component which is transiently associated with the ribosomes and has all the characteristics which would be expected in a compulsory precursor of the soluble proteins. It appears that this nascent protein is a polypeptide strand which is formed on the ribosome and is subsequently released as soluble protein. **1965** Phillips & Williams *Inorg. Chem.* I. xi. 412 Nascent hydrogen is an unstable form of hydrogen which has sufficient life or kinetic stability for it to be able to react with Po before it is transformed into normal H_2 molecules. Similarly, the hydrides of phosphorus, arsenic, and antimony can be made by the action of nascent hydrogen on soluble compounds of the element. **1974** *Nature* 1 Nov. 74/2 Experiments..have shown that nascent RNA chains have 5′-triphosphate termini.

3. ***nascent state***, the state of coming into existence, beginning to form, develop, etc. So ***nascent condition***.

1796 Kirwan *Elem. Min.* (ed. 2) I. 206 Inflammable air, in its nascent state. **1819** G. S. Faber *Dispensations* (1823) II. 213 Idolatry is plainly enough described as being only in a nascent state. **1830** Lyell *Princ. Geol.* I. ix. (1837) I. 230 Endeavouring to connect the phenomena..with a nascent condition of organic life. **1859** Darwin *Orig. Spec.* xiv. (1873) 398 It may..represent the nascent state of the wing. **1880** Cleminshaw *Wurtz' Atom. The.* 208 The peculiar activity of hydrogen and oxygen when in the nascent state.

4. ***nascent green***, a light green, like that of a young plant.

1839 Ure *Dict. Arts* 420 Yellow with blue [produces] green of a variety of shades; such as nascent green.

nascently (ˈnæsəntlɪ), *adv.* [f. NASCENT *a.* + -LY^{2}.] In a nascent manner; incipiently.

1890 W. James *Princ. Psychol.* I. ix. 258 Other processes discharge that ought as yet to be but nascently aroused. **1920** *Times Lit. Suppl.* 29 Apr. 264/2 Notions of the type of mana or orenda are of 'a nascently philosophic order'. **1936** White & Renner *Geogr.* xxiv. 517 The water present in volcanic and geyser eruptions is at least partially of magmatic origin. It is, in that event, nascently formed by the union of hydrogen and oxygen atoms, as these gases are liberated from hot magmatic materials deep in the earth.

nasche, obs. form of NESH *a.*, soft.

†**nase**, *sb. Obs.* Also 5 **nace, nasse.** [OE. *nasu* = MDu. *nase*, OHG. *nasa* fem., nose (MHG. *nase, nas*, G. *nase*), ON. *nǫs* (:—**nasu*) nostril (pl. *nasar*), related to Lith. *nósis*, OSl. *nosŭ* (Russ. *nos*), Skr. *nas-*, and with difference in vowel-grade to L. *nāsus* nose, *nārēs* nostrils, Skr. *nāsā* nose. The relationship to OE. *nosu* NOSE is obscure; see also NESE.] The nose.

a **1000** *Laws Ethelb.* in Thorpe *Laws* I. 14 ȝif nasu þyrel weorð. *Ibid.* 16 ȝif man oðerne mid fyste in naso slæhþ. *c* **1050** *Vocab.* in Wr.-Wülcker 264 *Columpna*, eall seo nasu. *Pirula*, forewerd nasu. **1390** Gower *Conf.* III. 202 His nase of and his lippes bothe He kutte. *c* **1400** *Destr. Troy* 7031 The noble kyng in the nase hade an euyll wound. *c* **1407** Lydg. *Reson & Sens.* 3553 Huge boolys of metal, With flavme..Which yssed out at nasse and mouthe. *c* **1440** Capgrave *Life St. Kath.* II. 1321 To ȝeue mankynd bothe nase, eye & tothe. [**1886** *Rochdale Gloss., Nase* (old), the nose.]

†**nase**, *a. Obs. Cant.* [Of obscure etym. Cf. NAZY.] Drunken, intoxicated; intoxicating (liquor).

a **1550** *Hye Way to Spittel Hous* in Hazl. *E.P.P.* IV. 69 With bousy cove maimed nace. *Ibid.*, For my watch it is nace gere. **1567** Harman *Caveat* (1869) 86 Now I tower that bene bouse makes nase nabes.

†**nase**, *adv. Obs. rare.* [f. NA *adv.*^{1} + *-se*, as in OE. *nese* no, *ȝese* yes.] Not, by no means.

c **1315** Shoreham I. 1862 Ne forþe þe moder þet hyt beer, Ne woldest þou nase y-faȝe. *Ibid.* 1873, 1890.

nase, variant of NAZE, headland.

naseberry (ˈneɪzbərɪ). Also 7 -bury, 9 knees-. [ad. Sp. or Pg. *néspera* medlar (Sp. *níspero* medlar-tree): see etym. note to MEDLE *sb.*] A West Indian tree (*Sapota Achras*) which yields an edible fruit called the Sapodilla plum. Also *attrib.*

1698 *Phil. Trans.* XIX. 435 The *Chrysodendros Americana*, or Star-apple, the Nasebury Tree. **1725** Sloane *Jamaica* II. 171 Naseberry. This tree riseth up with a streight trunc..about thirty foot high. **1753** Chambers *Cycl. Supp.* App., *Naseberry tree*, the English name of a distinct genus of plants, called by botanists Cainito, or Chrysophyllum. **1760** J. Lee *Introd. Bot.* App. 320 Naseberry-tree, *Sloanea.* **1849** Balfour *Man. Bot.* §937 *Achras Sapota*, and other species, furnish the Sappodilla Plum and Naseberry, well-known West Indian fruits. **1892** M. North *Recoll. Happy Life* I. 99 The Sapodilla or kneesberry whose fruit is about the size of an apple and tastes like a medlar.

†**naˈsee**, *a. Obs. rare*$^{-1}$. [ad. OF. *nasé*:—Romanic **nāsātu-s*, f. L. *nāsus* nose.] Having a mutilated nose.

c **1330** R. Brunne *Chron.* (1810) 168 His nese..he carfe at misauentoure... þei caled him þis toname, Statin þe nasee.

†**ˈnasel.** *Obs.* Also 5 **nasell.** [a. OF. *nasel* (11th c.):—late L. **nāsāle*: cf. NASAL *sb.* 1.] A part of the helmet serving as a guard for the nose.

c **1330** R. Brunne *Chron. Wace* (Rolls) 10043 A riche corounal wiþ perre,..þe nasel & bendeles of gold ful bryght. **13..** *Guy Warw.* (A.) 2288 His hauberk was al to-tore & his nasel avaled bifore. *c* **1400** *Rowland & O.* 465 Rowlande.. hittes hym on þe helme thanne, þat þe Nasell floghe full hye. *c* **1450** *Merlin* 329 The kynge Aroans helde hervy..by the nasell of the helme.

nash, dial. variant of NESH *a.*, soft.

nash, *v. slang.* [Etym. obscure.] (See quots.)

1812 J. H. Vaux *Flash Dict.*, *Nash*, to go away from, or quit, any place or company; speaking of a person who is gone, they say, he is nash'd. **1832** *Lincoln Herald* 18 Sept. 2/4 You had better nash (go away) unless you want to be nippered (taken into custody).

nashi, nashki, varr. NASKHI *sb. pl.*

†**nash-cloth**, an ash-cloth. *Obs. rare*$^{-0}$.

1611 Cotgr., *Charrié*, a Bucking-cloth, or Nash-cloth.

nash-gab, -gob. *Sc.* and *north. dial.* [f. dial. *nash* impertinence (cf. *snash*) + GAB *sb.*] Impertinent talk; a pert or gossiping person.

1816 Scott *Old Mort.* viii, The Philistines..are gaun to whirry awa' Mr. Henry, and a' wi' your nash-gab. **1818** —— *Rob Roy* xxvi, They hae coost up my kindred to Rob to me already—set up their nashgabs! **1843** *Richardson's Borderer's Table-bk., Leg. Div.* I. 116 The nashgob of a creature, Tom Fenwick, wins the haggis.

Nashiji (nəˈʃiːdʒɪ). Also **Nashidji** and with lower-case initial. [Jap., lit. 'pear ground'.] A Japanese lacquer containing gold or silver flakes. Also, the technique of decorating with this lacquer. Also *attrib.*

1881 J. J. Quin in *Trans. Asiatic Soc. of Japan* IX. 6 The kind of powdered gold lacquer called *nashiji*, from its resemblance to the spotted skin of a pear, was introduced about the beginning of the 10th century. *Ibid.* 7 The groundwork of this box is thick *nashiji*, inlaid with various coloured shells. **1889** J. J. Rein *Industries of Japan* III. iii. 352 Nashi-ji gets its name 'pear ground' from its use in a kind of surface decoration with coarse gold powder or its bronze substitute, which is said to be an imitation in colour of the Japanese pears. *Ibid.* 368 Nashi-ji is one of the most frequent and popular modes of surface decoration. The fine particles of gold dust and foil have at first a brownish yellow colour, but always with age become brighter and more brilliant, because of the greater transparency of the lacquer varnish. **1904** S. Hartmann *Japanese Art* vii. 247 At the beginning of the tenth century, the Nashidji lacquer, of a yellowish orange colour, sprinkled with gold. **1911** J. F. Blacker *ABC of Japanese Art* ix. 176 Now all *Nashiji* on articles intended for exportation is applied by workers in plain lacquer. The best *Nashiji*, the best *Togi-dashi*, the best *Honji*, have the first twenty-two processes alike. **1957** *Encycl. Brit.* XIII. 575/2 In Japanese lacquer, the following are the chief processes used:—*Nashiji* (pear-skin), small flakes of gold or silver sunk to various depths in the lacquer [etc.] **1975** *Country Life* 10 Apr. 907/1 The chests..were.. in *Hiramakie* in gold and grey lacquer on a *Nashiji* ground. .. *Nashiji* (pearskin) is a technique which can be traced back to AD 905, employing small flakes of gold and silver foil at different levels in the lacquer.

Nasho (ˈnæʃəʊ). *Austral. slang.* Abbrev. of 'national serviceman'; also, compulsory military training (discontinued in 1972).

1962 C. Rohan *Delinquents* 52 They..had supper with a couple of national servicemen... 'I'm not keen on Nashos,' she said. **1966** B. Beaver *You can't come Back* (1968) 5 Sam, the new one, was just eighteen and due for his Nasho training. **1966** *Bulletin* (Sydney) 23 Apr. 12/3 The bulk of the Nashos—how the Army loathes that term—have little time for the 'protests'. **1970** *Telegraph* (Brisbane) 8 July 16/3 (*heading*) RSL [*sc.* Returned Services League] wants full Nasho details.

Nashville ('næʃvɪl). The name of the capital city of Tennessee, U.S.A., used *attrib.* and *absol.* to designate a type of country-and-western music originating there.

1963 *Broadcasting* (U.S.) 28 Jan. 74/3 Bill Fuller..said, 'We play your Nashville numbers in Ireland and they like it because it's our kind of music.' *Ibid.* 78/2 Composer [Harlan] Howard..operates without the benefit of musical education. His 'Pick Me Up on Your Way Down' and scores of others are pure Nashville. **1968** *Sing Out!* Oct./Nov. 57/2 The songs are pleasant, though rarely distinctive (but, of course, that's Nashville). **1969** *Rolling Stone* 28 June 19/1 Along parallel lines a conservative approach to maintaining the Nashville sound could eventually backfire. **1973** *Nation Rev.* (Melbourne) 31 Aug.–6 Sept. 1459/1 The music is pure Nashville. **1975** *Hi-Fi Answers* Feb. 60/2 Musical styling ranges from the almost pure Nashville sound of 'Can't Go Back' to the rocking gospel tune of 'Let It Flow' and the convincing train beat of 'Sunshine Special'.

‖**nasi** ('nɑːsɪ). [Malay.] Cooked rice. Used usu. in *Comb.* to designate *spec.* dishes, as: **nasi br(i)yani** (brɪ'jɑːnɪ) [Malay *beriani, biani*], a type of pilau; **nasi goreng** (gɒ'rɛŋ), savoury fried rice with a variety of ingredients including meat and/or fish; **nasi Padang**, rice served as in Padang in Sumatra.

1894 N. B. Dennys *Descr. Dict. Brit. Malaya* 331 *Rice* (*padi* and *nasi*). **1900** W. W. Skeat *Malay Magic* v. 226 The rice is..then boiled so that it becomes *nasi* (cooked rice). **1958** *Catal. County Stores, Taunton* June 4 Nasi Goreng (Fried Rice with Pork)—a tin 4/-. **1963** *Times* 16 Feb. 5/5 *Nasi goreng* contains boiled rice, pork, curry powder, soy sauce, sliced omelette and tomatoes. **1971** *Carry Singapore in your Pocket* (Singapore Tourist Promotion Board) (ed. 3) 30 Malay and Indonesian type food is mainly of Sumatran origin and known as Nasi Padang. *Ibid.* 31 One first-class Kashmiri restaurant..serves nasi bryani. **1972** T. Lilley *K Section* xli 225 Lunch?..It's only nasi-goreng, but it'll fill a hole. **1972** *New Nation* (Singapore) 25 Nov. 7/5 The nasi briyani was of excellent consistency. **1972** R. McKie *Singapore* 109 Popular Indonesian and Malay food includes nasi Padang, after the town of Padang in Sumatra.

† **nasi'cornous**, *a. Obs. rare*$^{-1}$. [f. L. *nāsus* nose + *cornū* horn.] Having a horn on the nose.

1646 Sir T. Browne *Pseud. Ep.* 166 Some Unicornes wee will allow even among insects, as those foure kinds of nasicornous Beetles described by Muffetus.

nasiform ('neɪzɪfɔːm), *a. rare.* [f. as prec. + -form.] Having the form of a nose.

1752 J. Hill *Hist. Anim.* 211 The Cyprinus, with a nasiform snout. **1826** Kirby & Sp. *Entomol.* III. xxxi. 253 In the pupa of *Morpho Menelaus*..this nasiform prominence of the prothorax is extended into a long arched horn.

Nasik ('nɑːsɪk). [See def.] The name of a town in the presidency of Bombay (where the inventor, A. H. Frost, resided), used *attrib.* to designate certain elaborate 'magic' squares and cubes. Hence '**Nasikal**, '**Nasical** *a.*; **-ally** *adv.*

1866 P. Frost in *Q. Jrnl. Math.* VII. 94 To distinguish the squares..from the ordinary magic squares, I shall call them Nasik Squares, and his cubes Nasik Cubes. *Ibid.* 98 The squares about the same diagonals may be turned through any number of right angles..without destroying the Nasikal properties.

nasillate ('neɪzɪleɪt), *v. rare.* [f. F. *nasill-er* (f. L. *nāsus* nose) + -ate.] *intr.* To speak through the nose. So **nasi'llation**, nasal utterance.

1859 W. White *Northumbld. & Border* 464, I sang Yankee Doodle with appropriate nasillation. **1863** —— *Jrnl.* 5 Oct. (1898) 186 Maury..does not nasillate in speaking.

nasion ('neɪziːɒn). *Anat.* [a. F. *nasion* (P. Broca *Instruct. gén. pour les Recherches anthropol.* (ed. 2, 1879) iii. 143), f. L. *nās-us* nose: see -ion[2].] The centre of the fronto-nasal suture.

1889 *Buck's Handbk. Med. Sci.* VIII. 202/1 (*caption*) *N*, Nasion (junction of the nasal and frontal). **1934** F. Stark *Valleys of Assassins* I. ii. 193 The face is broken off just at the nasion, and only the ends of the molars are present. **1937** Glaister & Brash *Medico-Legal Aspects Ruxton Case* x. 154 The greatest discrepancy..can easily be accounted for by the difficulty of determining the exact position of nasion and prosthion in a portrait. **1971** *Nature* 30 July 311/1 The nasal length [of Olduvai hominid 24] from nasion to the left lateral lip of the nasal aperture is 42·5 mm and nasion to nasospinale 36·0 mm.

† **nask(in**. *Obs. Cant.* (See quots.)

1686 Higden *Juvenal Sat.* x. 38 Each heir by dice, drink, whores, or masking, Or Stistead brought into the Naskin [*note.* The cant. word for a Prison]. *a* **1700** B. E. *Dict. Cant. Crew, Nask*, or *Naskin*, a Prison or Bridewell.

Naskapi ('næskəpɪ), *a.* and *sb.* Also **Nascapee, -i, Nascopi(e), -upi, Nasquapee, Nescaupick.** [Native name.] **A.** *adj.* Pertaining to or designating an Indian people inhabiting northern Quebec and the interior of Labrador. **B.** *sb.* **a.** This people; a member of this people. **b.** Their language.

1774 G. Cartwright *Jrnl.* 18 June (1792) II. 9 Soon after our arrival there, two canoes of Nescaupick Indians came. **1779** —— *Jrnl.* 7 Mar. (1792) II. 418 My Nescaupick sled..was drawn by the two men, a bloodhound, and a Newfoundland dog. **1849** J. McLean *Notes 25 Years' Service Hudson's Bay* I. 305 The Nascopies, or mountaineers of Labrador, speak a mixture of Cree and Sauteaux, the former predominating. **1863** H. Y. Hind *Explor. Labrador Peninsula* I. iii. 30 On Father Laure's map..the Nasquapees are stated to occupy the country north of this lake under the name of Les Cuneskapi. **1908** *Catholic Encycl.* III. 229/2 To the east are the Micmac, Malecite, Abnaki, Nascapi, and the Montagnais of Labrador. **1934** D. Jenness *Indians of Canada* (ed. 2) xviii. 270 Two tribes (*Montagnais* 'Mountaineers'; *Naskapi* 'rude, uncivilized people') were the first to come into close contact with Europeans. *Ibid.* 271 Much of the Naskapi territory was open plateau covered with grasses and lichens. **1957** *Encycl. Brit.* XV. 741/2 North of the St. Lawrence, the Montagnais and Nascapee resemble the southern Algonkin. **1966** C. F. & F. M. Voegelin *Map N. Amer. Indian Lang.* (*caption*) Algonquian Family. 1. Cree-Montagnais-Naskapi. **1974** *Country Life* 4 Apr. 780/3 A painted deerskin coat of the Naskapi tribe.

‖**naskhi** ('næskiː), *sb. pl.* Also **nashi, nesk(h)i, niskhi**, etc. and with capital initial. [Arab. *naskī*, f. *nasaka* to copy.] The normal cursive Arabic script. Also *attrib.* or as *adj.*

1771 W. Jones *Gram. Pers. Lang.* 15 Our books are printed in the Niskhi hand, and all Arabick manuscripts, as well as most Persian and Turkish histories, are written in it; but the Persians write their poetical works in the Tâlik, which answers to the most elegant of our Italick hands. **1777** J. Richardson *Dict. Pers., Arab., & English* p. iii/1 In this character the Alcoran was originally written: it was afterwards improved under the denomination of Cufik; and continued in use till the appearance of the Niskhi, in the tenth century of our era... The Niskhi,..with some variation and corruption, is the same which now prevails in Arabia, Persia, India, and other Eastern countries. **1807** in W. Jones *Wks.* XIII. 416 *Zafar Námeh.* A most elegant history of Taimur, written in the Niskh character. **1820** J. G. Jackson *Acct. Timbuctoo & Housa* 350 The Arabs have various modes of writing, the principal of which is that used by the Koreish, the most learned of all the Western tribes, and is denominated the *Niskhi*, or upright character: if this is understood, the others may be easily comprehended. **1849** F. Madden tr. *Silvestre's Universal Palæogr.* I. 52 The Arabic Neskhi alphabet, already in use among the Arab tribes, was forced upon Persia with the Coran, and took the place of the ancient cuneiform and other writings. **1854** A. Sprenger *Catal. Arab., Pers. & Hindústány MSS. in Libraries of King of Oudh* I. 8 Copies are not frequent, yet there are five in the Moty Mahall. The best is written in Naskhy. **1879** C. Rieu *Catal. Pers. MSS. in Brit. Mus.* I. 7/2 The Coran in Arabic, with a Persian version written in small Nashki. **1880** *Encycl. Brit.* XIII. 117/2 Arabic epigraphy begins with the rise of Islam. Two systems of writing were used concomitantly, the Cufic or uncial, and the Neski or running hand. **1893** [see Kufic *a.*]. **1948** D. Diringer *Alphabet* 271 The two main branches of the Arabic script, Naskhi and Kufic. **1959** *Chambers's Encycl.* XII. 291/1 The earliest form of the North-Arabic script was the Kufic...in this script however many of the signs were inconveniently alike, and the so-called *Nashī*-script, in which diacritical points are used to distinguish similar letters, began to take its place as early as the 7th century A.D. **1970** *Oxf. Compan. Art* 634/1 Naskhi inscriptions are common in architecture and the decorative arts.

naskh-ta'lyq: see nastalik.

† '**nasky**, *a. Obs. rare*$^{-0}$. App. a var. of nasty.

1611 Cotgr., *Maulavé*, ill washed;..naskie, nastie.

Nasmyth ('neɪsmɪθ). The name of James *Nasmyth* (1808–1890), Scottish engineer, used *attrib.* and in the possessive to denote a form of hammer or pile-driver he invented, in which the falling weight is raised by steam pressure on a piston attached to it.

1845 *Jrnl. Franklin Inst.* XL. 283 Nasmyth's steam hammer for pile driving. *a* **1877** Knight *Dict. Mech.* III. 2348/2 Plate LXII shows the new Nasmyth steam-hammer at Woolwich, England. It is at present the largest and most powerful in the world. **1902** L. F. Vernon-Harcourt *Civil Engin.* iv. 56 Nasmyth's pile-driver is the oldest and best-known form of these machines. **1928** R. Bridges in H. Bradley *Coll. Papers* 43 A friend whose mind I used to compare to a Nasmyth's hammer, which can weld a ton of iron or crack a nut without crushing its kernel. **1945** R. Hargreaves *Enemy at Gate* 278 Bringing, in effect, a Nasmyth hammer to the task of cracking a walnut. **1963** A. F. Burstall *Hist. Mech. Engin.* vi. 207 Considerable improvements took place in forging, particularly after the invention of Nasmyth's steam hammer..in 1839.

Nasmyth's membrane ('neɪsmɪθ). *Anat.* [f. the name of Alexander *Nasmyth* (d. 1848), British dentist, who described the membrane in 1839.] A transient membrane covering the crown of young teeth; the primary enamel cuticle.

1853 *Q. Jrnl. Microsc. Sci.* I. 162 The layer is about 1-40th of an inch thick, and consists of an external delicate structureless Nasmyth's membrane. **1906** *Brit. Dental Jrnl.* XXVII. 1017 The interest at the time was centred on the condition of its Nasmyth's membrane. **1973** *Gray's Anat.* (ed. 35) 1235/2 The newly erupted enamel is covered by a two-layered structure (reduced enamel epithelium and primary cuticle). This is called Nasmyth's membrane.

naso- ('neɪzəʊ), modern combining form of L. *nāsus* nose, employed in a large number of anatomical or pathological terms relating to the nose in conjunction with some other part, as ***naso-ethmoidal, -frontal, -labial, -lachrymal, -malar, -maxillary, -oral, -palatal, -palatine, -pharyngeal, turbinal*** adjs. Also ***naso-antritis, -pharyngitis, -pharynx.*** **naso'ciliary**, applied to a branch of the ophthalmic nerve that supplies the skin and mucous membrane of the nose, the eyelids, and parts of the eyeball, and communicates with the ciliary ganglion; **nasopha'ryngeal** *a.*, of or pertaining to the nasopharynx, or the nose and the pharynx; '**nasopharynx**, the uppermost part of the pharynx, lying above the soft palate and communicating with the posterior nares.

Many other combs. of the same character, as ***naso-aural, -basal, -buccal***, etc. are given in the *Syd. Soc. Lex.* (1891).

1891 *Syd. Soc. Lex.*, **Naso-antritis*, inflammation of the mucous lining of the antrum and of the nose. **1895** *Quain's Elem. Anat.* (ed. 10) III. ii. 236 The nasal nerve (oculo-nasal or *naso-ciliary) enters the orbit between the heads of the external rectus muscle. **1968** Passmore & Robson *Compan. Med. Stud.* I. xxi. 10/2 The ophthalmic nerve..breaks up into its lacrimal, frontal and nasociliary branches while still within the wall of the cavernous sinus. **1883** Martin & Moale *Vertebr. Dissect.* 108 This is the *naso-ethmoidal cartilage. **1839–47** *Todd's Cycl. Anat.* III. 734/1 The ..*naso-frontal process [is regarded] as the basis for the lachrymal bone. **1876** Flower *Osteol. Mammalia* (ed. 2) 168 A rounded depression over the naso-frontal suture. **1836–9** *Todd's Cycl. Anat.* II. 223/1 The second [set], or *naso-labial fibres, are elevators of the upper lip. **1897** *Allbutt's Syst. Med.* IV. 716 The naso-labial fold is more or less obliterated. **1836–9** *Todd's Cycl. Anat.* II. 209/1 The lower aperture of the *naso-lachrymal canal. **1885** *Athenæum* 31 Jan. 156/1 A new index, the '*naso-malar index', was proposed. **1836–9** *Todd's Cycl. Anat.* II. 209/1 The anterior or *naso-maxillary border. **1899** *Albutt's Syst. Med.* VI. 55 The *naso-oral muzzle must never be used. **1854** Owen in *Orr's Circ. Sci.* II. 66/2 The prepalatal or *naso-palatal aperture. **1836–9** *Todd's Cycl. Anat.* II. 208/2 The..*naso-palatine surface is divided..by an horizontal plate of bone. **1881** Mivart *Cat* 74 The anterior termination of the anterior palatine canal transmitting the naso-palatine nerve. **1872** Cohen *Dis. Throat* 97 A pseudo-membranous deposit in the pharyngeal and *naso-pharyngeal region. **1884** M. Mackenzie *Dis. Throat & Nose* II. 251 This method of enlarging the naso-pharyngeal space. **1892** P. McBride *Dis. Throat, Nose & Ear* 281 Naso-pharyngeal Catarrh associated with Crust Formation.—As we have seen, crusts may exist in the naso-pharynx in cases of atrophic rhinitis. **1973** *Sci. Amer.* Oct. 32/3 As the term indicates, nasopharyngeal carcinoma originates in the nasal cavity, the pharynx and the rear of the oral cavity. **1896** *Allbutt's Syst. Med.* I. 334 Chronic *naso-pharyngitis..requires likewise alkaline muriated or saline waters. **1877** Burnett *Ear* 185 The arrival of the beak of the catheter in the *nasopharynx. **1902** D. J. Cunningham *Text-bk. Anat.* 981 This sheet [*sc.* the soft palate]..cuts into the cavity of the pharynx.., and, falling short of the posterior wall, incompletely divides it into two, namely, an upper part or naso-pharynx (pars nasalis), and a lower part or pharynx proper, which is further subdivided..into the oral pharynx..and the laryngeal pharynx. **1935** Imperatori & Burman *Dis. Nose & Throat* xxiv. 283 Most often neoplasms in the nasopharynx really have their origin in the nose but by their growth extend back into the nasopharynx. **1973** *Daily Colonist* (Victoria, B.C.) 3 Nov. 1/3 Snoring results from vibration of the soft tissues of the nasopharynx. **1876** Flower *Osteol. Mammalia* (ed. 2) 110 It is sometimes distinguished under the name of *nasoturbinal.

†**2.** Used in terms denoting nasal sounds, as ***naso-guttural, -spirital, -vocal.*** *Obs.*

1669 Holder *Elem. Speech* 59 Thus out of..36, casting out as useless..9 Naso-Spirituals, 6 Naso-Vocals, and 2 Spiritals, there remain 19 Consonants. *Ibid.* 75 Some may be found to take in some Letters, as the Ore-spirital L' R' and Naso-spirital M' N' Ng'. **1748** *Phil. Trans.* XLV. 406 The Power or Force..of the Naso-guttural *N*.

3. ***naso-ductility***, capacity of being led by the nose. *nonce-wd.*

1820 Coleridge in *Lit. Rem.* (1839) IV. 125 Let the reproach be shared between the Breath's fetid conscience and the nostrils' nasoductility.

nasogastric (neɪzəʊ'gæstrɪk), *a. Med.* [f. naso- + gastric *a.*] Reaching or supplying the stomach via the nose; effected via such a route.

1958 *Med. Ann. District of Columbia* XXVII. 331 (*heading*) Hypertonic dehydration complicating high protein nasogastric tube feeding. **1961** *Lancet* 2 Sept. 519/2 The uncritical use of naso-gastric suction in all upper abdominal cases should be reconsidered. **1964** *Ibid.* 26 Dec. 1351/1 The indwelling polyvinyl nasogastric tube scarcely disturbs the infant. **1974** Passmore & Robson *Compan. Med. Stud.* III. 10/1 Most nasogastric feeds are based on milk.

nasology (neɪ'zɒlədʒɪ). [f. as naso- + -logy.] The study of the nose or of noses. So **naso'logical** *a.*; **na'sologist**.

a **1854** S. Phillips *Ess. fr. Times* (1871) II. 336 Mr. Dickens is as deep in nasology as the learned Slawkenbergius. **1858** Lytton *What will He do* I. i, Characters..graphically portrayed, with a nasological illustration. **1899** *Daily News* 17 Feb. 4/7 What is your favourite perfume? asks the nasologist of his patient.

nason ('neɪsən). [Of obscure etym.] (See quot. 1855.)

1690 *Specification* in Grove *Dict. Mus.* (1880) II. 594/2 Choir Organ..Flute, of metal. Nason, of metal. **1694** *Ibid.*, Echoes of halfe stops;..Principal. Nason. **1855** Hopkins *Organ* ii. 118 Nason. This name is sometimes found applied in old organs to a wood-stopped Flute of 4-feet pitch on the Great Manual... It is generally a very quiet and sweet-toned Stop.

nasonite ('neɪsənaɪt). *Min.* [f. the name of Frank Lewis *Nason* (1856–1928), U.S. geologist + -ite[1].] A silicate and chloride of calcium and lead, $Ca_4Pb_6(Si_2O_7)_3Cl_2$, which forms hexagonal crystals and is found as white or grey granular masses.

1899 Penfield & Warren in *Amer. Jrnl. Sci.* clviii. 346 Hand specimens usually present a mottled or spotted appearance owing to numerous inclusions of yellow axinite and brown garnet, which are scattered rather uniformly through the massive nasonite. **1935** *Prof. Papers U.S. Geol. Survey* No. 180. 93/2 Nasonite commonly forms the matrix of glaucochroite crystals, and in the few specimens seen is also associated with garnet, axinite, and barite. **1971** *Amer. Mineralogist* LVI. 1177 If one imagines two unit cells of apatite superposed in the *c* direction.. and rotates one of them of 60° around the 6_3 axis, one obtains the unit cell of nasonite.

nasospinale (ˌneɪzəʊspɪˈnɑːliː). [app. mod.L., f. NASO- + late L. *spīnāle*, neut. of *spīnālis* SPINAL *a.*

So etymologized, e.g., in R. Martin *Lehrb. d. Anthrop.* (1914) 513. But cf. F. *naso-spinal* adj., used and prob. coined (as the fem. *naso-spinale*) by P. Broca (*Mém. de la Soc. d' Anthrop. de Paris* (1875) II. 72) as the epithet of a line 'de la racine du nez à la base de l'épine nasale'.]

The point of intersection of a line joining the lowest points on the anterior nasal apertures with the midsagittal plane.

1920 H. H. WILDER *Lab. Man. Anthropometry* i. 47 (*heading*) Nasospinale... This point is defined as a point (usually within the bone substance), where a line tangent to the two lateral curves of the lower margin of the piriform aperture crosses the median line. **1933** *Jrnl. R. Anthrop. Inst.* LXIII. 44 The definition of the nasospinale we have given above is an elaboration of that which was first given by Broca. **1949** H. SICHER *Oral Anat.* i. 97 The nasal profile angle is the angle formed by the line from nasion to nasospinale with the Frankfort horizontal. **1971** Nasospinale [see NASION].

Nasquapee, var. NASKAPI *a.* and *sb.*

Nasrani (næzˈrɑːnɪ). Also **Nasrany**, etc. Pl. **Nasara**, etc. [Arab. *Naṣrānī*, pl. *Naṣārā* cogn. with NAZARENE *a.* and *sb.*] A Christian, so called by Muslims; = NAZARENE *sb.* 1 b.

1583 J. NEWBERY *Let.* 15 July in Purchas *Pilgrimes* (1625) II. IX. xviii. 1643 In Aleppo I hired two Nastraynes, and one of them hath the Indian tongue. **1615** G. SANDYS *Relation* III. 153 On the twentieth of March with the rising Sunne we departed. A small remainder of that great Caruan; the Nostraines (so name they the Christians of the East) that rid vpon Mules and Asses being gone before. **1792** R. HERON tr. *Niebuhr's Trav. Arabia* II. XXVI. v. 242 In Arabia, the Christians are called *Nassara* or *Nusrani*. **1820** J. G. JACKSON *Acct. Timbuctoo & Housa* 510 It is not correct to assert that *Nasari is a general term*, applied to infidels in Muhamed; it is applied to Christians only. **1826** DENHAM & CLAPPERTON *Narrative* p. xxxi, You were the first man whose hand I ever touched—but they all said it did not signify with you, an *Insara* (a Christian). **1836** E. W. LANE *Account* II. iv. 52 The kelbs before removal from their original places are called *Nasa'ra* (or Christians, in the singular, *Nusra'nee*). **1844** J. H. DRUMMOND HAY *Western Barbary* xi. 76/2 The inhabitants rushed out from their houses to have a sight of the Ensara. **1888** C. M. DOUGHTY *Trav. Arabia Deserta* II. xvii. 514 When I responded,.. Sâlem exclaimed, 'Ullah! how truly the Nasrâny speaks!' **1905** *Jewish Encycl.* IX. 195/1 In the Koran also the Christians are called 'Al-Naṣ ara'. The name may be traced back to Nazareth, Jesus' birth-place. **1912** *Catholic Encycl.* XIV. 681/1 The St. Thomas Christians now prefer to be called *Nasrani* (Nazarenes), the designation given by the Mohammedans to all Christians. **1926** R. BELL *Origin Islam* v. 149 If we could be sure that *Ṣābi'īn* denoted the Christians of South Arabia, *Naṣārā* would then denote specially those of the north. But we shall not.. go far wrong in taking it as meant to denote Christians in general. The word Naṣārā is apparently derived from *Nazaraioi*, which is mentioned as the name of a Jewish-Christian sect. **1936** F. STARK *Southern Gates Arabia* iv. 40 About fifty children pursued, calling 'Nasrani' in a monotonous but not insulting way. **1937** R. BELL tr. *Qur'ān* I. xxii. 318/2 Those who have believed, those who have judaised, the Ṣābi'īn, the Naṣārā, the Magians, and the Polytheists—verily Allah will distinguish between them on the day of resurrection. **1958** L. DURRELL *Balthazar* iv. 87 He, a city-bred Alexandrian —almost a despised *Nasrany*—could out-shoot, out-talk and out-gallop.. them. **1963** *Times* 14 Feb. 14/7 They drew aside and conferred among themselves since a *Nasrani* or Christian is seldom met in their deserts.

Nass (næs). The name of a river in British Columbia, Canada, used *attrib.* to denote a branch of the Tsimshian people who inhabit the basin of this river, and whose native name is NISKA. Also as *sb.*, their language.

1829 J. S. GREEN in *Missionary Herald* (Boston, Mass.) (1830) XXVI. 344 The Nass Indians live on the continent. *Ibid.*, The Nass to my ear is harsh and disagreeable. **1911** F. BOAS *Handbk. Amer. Indian Lang.* I. 290 The system of vowels of Tsimshian is nearly the same as that of the Nass dialect. *Ibid.* 292 Many *u*-sounds of Tsimishian are *ī* or *ē* in Nass. [**1934** D. JENNESS *Indians of Canada* (ed. 2) ii. 18 The Tsimshian of the Nass and Skeena rivers. *Ibid.* xxi. 336 The Tsimshian ('people inside of the Skeena river'), were divided into three groups, the Tsimshian proper around the mouth of Skeena river, the Gitksan ('Skeena River people') farther up the same stream, and the Niska who inhabited the basin of Nass (Niska) river.]

nass(e, variants of NAS, was not. *Obs.*

nassa (ˈnæsə). [mod.L. (J. B. P. A. de Monet, Chevalier de Lamarck 1799, in *Mém. Soc. d'Hist. Nat. Paris* I. 71), f. L. *nassa* basket fish-trap.] The shell of a marine gastropod of the genus once so called, now included in the genus *Nassarius*; a basket shell; = DOG-WHELK. Also *attrib.*

1853 L. REEVE *Conchologia Iconica* XVI. s.v. *Nassa*, plate 1 The rough Nassa... A very elegantly coronated species, with the spine rising into a sharp turret. **1971** *World Archaeol.* III. 136 String bands to which cowrie or nassa shells are attached. **1974** S. P. DANCE *Encycl. Shells* 156/1 *Nassarius fossatus* Gould. Giant Western Nassa. Shell ovate. Conical spire, apex pointed.

Nassauvian (nəˈsɔːvɪən). Also **Nassavian**. [f. *Nassau*, capital city of the Bahama islands + -IAN.] A native or inhabitant of Nassau. Also *attrib.* or as *adj.*

1924 F. HOLMES *Bahamas during Gt. War* xii. 121 On May 29th [1917], greatly to the satisfaction of all Nassauvians, the Lighting Restrictions were.. suspended. **1928** R. A. CURRY *Bahamian Lore* vi. 64 Along the side-walks of Bay Street you will meet.. the Nassauvian in white clothes. **1961** I. FLEMING *Thunderball* xii. 126 A discussion about the merits of Nassavian labour... The Chief of Immigration and Customs was a sleek Nassavian with quick brown eyes. **1973** *Listener* 16 Aug. 202/2 Nassauvians generally have a care for their visitors' feelings.

nasse, obs. variant of ASS *sb.*, NASE.

nassella (næˈsɛlə). [mod.L. (E. Desvaux in C. Gay *Historia Física y Política de Chile*, *Botánica* (1853) VI. 263), f. L. *nassa* net + *-ella*, fem. of *-ellus*, diminutive suffix.] A coarse grass of the genus so called, native to Chile, but also found in other countries to which it has been introduced, esp. New Zealand, where it has become a troublesome weed. Also *attrib.*

[**1936** H. H. ALLAN *Introd. Grasses N.Z.* 118 *Nassella trichotoma*, a rather graceful tussocky species, somewhat resembling *Festuca novae-zelandiae* in habit, but with very different spikelets. Recently collected by Professor A. Wall on the Waipara River bed, and in the Omihi Valley, where it appears to be thoroughly established.] **1946** *Nature* 21 Dec. 920/1 Weed problems.. such as nassella, constitute a serious threat to good pasture land [in New Zealand]. **1950** *N.Z. Jrnl. Agric.* June 515/1 Nassella tussock... This insidious pest crept almost unawares on to some of our good pastoral country. **1966** G. W. TURNER *Eng. Lang. Austral. & N.Z.* viii. 172 In scientific language Latin botanical names often become general. The recently troublesome Nassella tussock has no more popular name. It is controlled in accordance with the Nassella Tussock Act of 1946 by Nassella Tussock Boards.

Nasserite (ˈnæsəraɪt). [f. the name of Gamel Abdel *Nasser* (1918–70), President of Egypt from 1956 to 1970 + -ITE¹.] A supporter of Nasser. Also *attrib.* or as *adj.* So **ˈNasserism**, the political principles or policy of Nasser; **ˈNasserist**, a Nasserite; also *attrib.* or as *adj.*

1958 *Times* 18 Mar. 11/3 The argument.. between the west-looking policy pursued by President Chamoun and M. Solh and the Nasserite policy espoused by some of the Opposition. **1958** *Observer* 20 July 10/2 We were prepared (as Sir Anthony Eden seemed to be at the time of Suez) to overthrow 'Nasserism' by force. **1958** *Economist* 26 July 300 It is obvious and well understood here that the coup in Iraq means a further link in the encirclement of Israel by Nasserist forces and thus increases Israel's military danger. **1958** *Times* 16 Dec. 9/6 The others are the Nasserists, the Communists, and Brigadier Kassem. **1959** *Daily Tel.* 24 Apr. 12/5 Five visiting Iraqi officers are reported to have recently investigated public feeling here, much to the concern of the Nasserites. **1965** M. SPARK *Mandelbaum Gate* iv. 105 Are you a nationalist?.. A Nasserite? **1966** *Economist* 5 Mar. 889/1 If this is not potential 'nasserite material', what is? **1968** *Ibid.* 3 Feb. 23/3 One hears a lot about 'Young Turks', 'Nasserists', and so on these days. **1969** J. MANDER *Static Society* viii. 225 We might say that Peron invented 'Nasserism' a decade before Nasser. **1971** *Guardian Weekly* 10 Apr. 7/1 Officially Sadat upholds the Nasserist orthodoxy. He told the Palestinians.. that there was no such thing as an Egyptian strategy or a Syrian strategy, but only an Arab strategy. **1973** HOWAT & TAYLOR *Dict. World Hist.* 1047/2 *Nasserism*, Western term used to denote first the policies of Egypt.. under President Abd Al-Nasir, and second, a generalized movement among Arabs.

nass-fish. [Of obscure origin.] = ANGLER¹ 2.

1880–4 DAY *Fishes Gt. Brit.* I. 64.

nassh(e, obs. variants of NESH *a.*, soft.

nast (nɑːst, -æ-). *dial.* [Back-formation from NASTY *a.*] Dirt, filth, foulness.

1789 MARSHALL *Rural Econ. Glouc.* I. 330 *Nast*, foulness; weeds in a fallow. **1839** *Hereford Gloss.*, *Nast*, dirt, nastiness. **1882–** in dial. glossaries (Lanc., Chesh., Warw., Worc., Glouc.). **1885** WESTALL *Old Factory* xxiv, I don't care about rooting and pottering among nast.

†**nast**, hast not: see NE and HAVE *v.* A. 9. *Obs.*

c **1290** *Beket* 760 in *S. Eng. Leg.* I. 228 On me nast þu power non swych destresse for-to do. *a* **1310** in Wright *Lyric P.* xxxvii. 102 Nast thou nothyng bote fyht, Whil thou art a lyve.

nast, knowest not: see NOT *v.*

‖**nastalik** (næstəˈliːk). Also **nastaliq**, **nestalik**, **nestaliq**, etc. [Pers., f. Arab. *nasḵi* NASKHI + *ta'līq* hanging.] A Persian cursive script, characterized by rounded forms and elongated horizontal strokes. Also called TALIQ.

1795 W. OUSELEY *Pers. Miscellanies* I. i. 7, I must here remark, that in India the Talik hand is generally called Nustaleek... Although used occasionally by the Arabian, and commonly by the Turkish penmen, yet it seems to be more particularly a favourite of the Persians. **1809** C. STEWART *Descr. Catal. Oriental Library of Late Tippoo Sultan of Mysore* 57/1 Octavo, Nastâlik Character, beautifully written. **1854** A. SPRENGER *Catal. Arab., Pers., & Hindústány MSS. in Libraries of King of Oudh* I. 89 Myr'imád of Qazwyn a most exquisite calligraph particularly in Naskh-ta'lyq. **1879** C. RIEU *Catal. Pers. MSS. in Brit. Mus.* I. 5/2 The texts.. are given in Arabic, and mostly accompanied with an interlinear Persian version in Nestalik. **1908** MAULAVI ABDUL MUQTADIR *Catal. Arab. & Pers. MSS. in Oriental Public Library at Bankipore*: *Pers. Poetry* 5 Written in a perfect Nasta'līq, in four columns, with one gold and two ornamental rules. **1913** *Encycl. Islām* I. 391/2 It was probably not until this later period that the *nesta'līḳ* arose (said to be a contraction of *nasḵhī* and *ta'līḳ*), a variation of *ta'līḳ*, from which it does not differ in any essential features. **1919** D. C. PHILLOTT *Higher Pers. Gram.* i. 36 The *nasta'līq*.. is a combination of the *naskh*.. or ordinary hand and the *ta'līq*..: it is a beautiful hand, chiefly used by the Persians for well-written manuscripts; but the modern Arabs call the Persian writing generally *ta'līq*. **1948** D. DIRINGER *Alphabet* 595/2 (*index*) Nesta'liq script; *see* Ta'liq. **1954** A. F. L. BEESTON *Catal. Addit. Pers. MSS. in Bodl. Libr.* 92/1 Main text and index in neat Naksh, the other pieces in Nastaᶜlīḳ. **1957** *Encycl. Brit.* XVII. 593/1 In this academy [*sc.* the Academy of Artistic Book-Production at Herat] the Persian texts were no longer written in *naskhi*, but in *nastaliq* an offshoot of the old cursive character, invented by the celebrated Mir Ali of Tabriz. **1966** HOSKING & MEREDITH-OWENS *Handbk. Asian Scripts* ii. 20 After 1600 there is a steady deterioration in *Nasta'līk* which becomes larger and coarser, whereas *Naskhī* gradually improves after this date. **1973** 'D. JORDAN' *Nile Green* xxiv. 99, I vaguely heard him expounding the difference between *naskhi* and *nasta'liq* script.

nastell: see ASTEL.

nastic (ˈnæstɪk), *a.* *Bot.* [a. G. *nastisch* (E. Strasburger *Lehrbuch der Botanik* (ed. 6, 1904) I. ii. 221), f. Gk. ναστ-ός pressed together + -IC.] Of movements of parts of plants: uninfluenced by the direction of an external stimulus.

1908 W. H. LANG tr. *Strasburger's Text-bk. Bot.* (ed. 3) 270 When.. the movement results from the internal disposition of the structure it is spoken of as nastic. **1912** *Ibid.* (ed. 4) 300 Nastic movements.. are curvatures which bring about a particular position in relation to the plant and not to the direction of the stimulus. **1929** J. C. BOSE *Growth & Tropic Movements Plants* xx. 216 If the movement be nastic, then the closure or the opening movement will remain the same, whether the organ be held in normal position or upside down. **1951** M. ABERCROMBIE et al. *Dict. Biol.* 150 Nastic movements are classified according to nature of stimulus, e.g. photonasty, response to alteration in light intensity, thermonasty, response to alteration in heat intensity, seismonasty, response to shock. **1965** BELL & COOMBE tr. *Strasburger's Textbk. Bot.* 380 Nastic movements, depending on growth differences on the two sides of the organ concerned, are seen particularly clearly in the perianth segments of the many flowers which open or close according to the temperature.

ˈnastify, *v.* *nonce-wd.* [f. NASTY *a.* + -FY.] *trans.* To make nasty.

1873 M. COLLINS *Miranda* II. 237 The makers will glaze, varnish, nastify paper to such an extent that writing on it is a perfect nuisance.

nastily (ˈnɑːstɪlɪ, -æ-), *adv.* [f. NASTY *a.* + -LY².] In a nasty manner or state; filthily; disagreeably, unpleasantly.

1611 COTGR., *Sordidement*, filthily, nastily, naughtily. **1616** SURFL. & MARKH. *Country Farme* VII. xxxviii. 701 The Badger.., finding his lodging so nastily beraied, presently.. forsakes the place. **1663** *Aron-bimn.* 68 The Houses of God could not be suffered to lie so Nastily.. were the true worship of God observed in them. **1741** RICHARDSON *Pamela* I. 239, I vexed her yesterday, because she talk'd nastily. **1775** MRS. J. HARRIS *Lett.* I. 302 He feeds nastily and ferociously, and eats quantities most unthankfully. **1858** HAWTHORNE *Fr. & It. Note-bks.* (1872) I. 52 Streets narrow.. and smelling nastily.

nastiness (ˈnɑːstɪnɪs, -æ-). [f. NASTY *a.* + -NESS.]

1. Filthiness or foulness of persons, places, or things; disagreeable dirtiness or want of cleanliness; an instance of this, a filthy act or habit.

1611 COTGR., *Souillarderie*, sluttishnesse, nastinesse, greasinesse. **1621** BURTON *Anat. Mel.* I. ii. II. v. (1651) 83 Through their own nastiness, and sluttishness,.. suffer their air to putrifie. **1679** PENN *Addr. Prot.* II. (1692) 201 The.. Tedious Imprisonments, even to Death it self, through nastiness of Dungeons. **1719** J. T. PHILLIPS tr. *Thirty-four Confer.* 324 Spitting in your Houses, and some other daily Nastinesses committed by you. **1737** L. CLARKE *Hist. Bible* (1740) I. I. 104 That which increased his Misery was the Nastiness of his Distemper, which rendered him.. loathsome to others. **1794** S. WILLIAMS *Hist. Vermont* 154 Nothing can exceed the nastiness that appears in their food. **1803** MALTHUS *Popul.* I. iv. (1817) I. 68 All voyagers agree with respect to the filth of the habitations, and the personal nastiness of the people.

b. That which is nasty; dirt, filth.

1611 COTGR., *Souillure*, soyle, filth, nastinesse. *c* **1645** HOWELL *Lett.* (1650) II. II. 8 Here one shall see nor dog, nor cat, nor cage, to cause any nastines within the body of the House. **1687** A. LOVELL tr. *Thevenot's Trav.* I. 30 They are not subject to that filth and nastiness which breed among our Hair, if we be not careful to comb it well. **1703** MAUNDRELL *Journ. Jerus.* (1721) 9 The Houses were all fill'd with Dirt and Nastiness. **1769** E. BANCROFT *Guiana* 219 When the Snake is killed, it must first be washed clean, and freed from all filth and nastiness. **1808** *Med. Jrnl.* XIX. 570 Where nastiness of every description, and putridity in its most loathsome forms, are to be found.

c. A filthy, disgusting, or repulsive thing.

1859 HUGHES *Scour. White Horse* vi. 124 Haven't you made me ill often enough with your nastinesses fifteen years ago? **1859** SALA *Tw. round Clock* (1861) 43 Snowy lump-sugar has been refined by means of unutterable nastinesses of a sanguineous nature. **1871** Miss Mulock *Fair France* ii. 52 No greasy nastinesses of stews.

2. Moral foulness or impurity; grossness, obscenity; talk or writing of this kind.

1700 Dryden *Pref. Fables* Wks. (Globe) 507 The nastiness of Plautus and Aristophanes. **1785** Reid *Intell. Powers* VIII. i. 491 By bad habits men may acquire a relish for nastiness. **1870** Lowell *Among my Bks.* Ser. I. (1873) 45 The common quality..of all Dryden's comedies is their nastiness.

3. Unpleasantness of flavour.

1868 *Atlantic Monthly* Mar. 264 That quality of unmitigated nastiness which so familiarly attests the genuineness of our Western doses. **1897** *Allbutt's Syst. Med.* III. 627 Such sense of taste as remains is only capable of perceiving a bitter nastiness.

Nastrayne, obs. var. Nasrani.

†**na'sturce.** *Obs. rare.* [a. F. *nasturce*, ad. L. *nasturtium*.] = nasturtium 2.

1693 [see caper *sb.*[1] 3]. **1706** Phillips (ed. Kersey), *Nasturces* or Capucin Capers, a kind of French Bean that gets up upon Branches, or Poles, which are near it. **1707** Mortimer *Husb.* (1721) II. 154 Nasturces, commonly called Capuchin Capers, are multiply'd only by the Seed.

na'sturtian. Also 8 **nastert-**, 9 **-ion.** [Corrupt form of next.] = nasturtium 2.

1740-1 Mrs. Delany *Life & Corr.* (1861) II. 147 Nastertians, ivy, honeysuckles.., and all sorts of twining flowers. **1769** Mrs. Raffald *Eng. Housekpr.* (1778) 351 Gather the nasturtian berries soon after the blossoms are gone off. **1845-50** Mrs. Lincoln *Lect. Bot.* 50 Orbicular, or the round leaf; the Nasturtion affords an example of this kind. **1883** *Harper's Mag.* July 167/2 Boxes of nasturtions and mignonette stand on the sills.

nasturtium (næˈstɜːʃ(ɪ)əm). Also 6-8 **-cium.** [a. L. *nasturtium*, so named, acc. to Pliny, from its pungency ('nomen accepit a narium tormento'): cf. F. *nasitort*.]

1. a. A genus of cruciferous plants having a pungent taste, of which the best-known representative is the Watercress (*N. officinale*); also, a plant belonging to this genus. Now only *Bot.*

1570 Foxe *A. & M.* 1156/2 This was some mery deuill, or els had eaten with his teeth some Nasturcium before. **1602** R. T. *Five Godlie Serm.* 101 The Nasturcium of the Persians ..I take to be a more precious and soueraigne plant than our common Cresses, although it be vulgarly deemed the same. **1664** Evelyn *Kal. Hort.* (1729) 195 Sow also..Cabbages, Cresses, Nasturtium, Fennel [etc.]. **1696** Phillips (ed. 5), *Nasturtium*, the name of a Plant, otherwise called Nosesmart, or Cresses. **1753** Chambers *Cycl. Supp.* s.v., The leaves of the nasturtiums are divided and cut into segments. **1797** *Encycl. Brit.* (ed. 3) XVII. 513/1 The nasturtium grows on the brinks of rivulets and water ditches. **1837** Wheelwright tr. *Aristophanes* II. 261 What prat'st thou of nasturtiums?

†**b.** *sweet nasturtium*: (see quot.). *Obs.*[−1]

1712 tr. *Pomet's Hist. Drugs* I. 21 It is call'd Cardamome, or sweet Nasturtium, because it has a smell much like the Nasturtium.

¶Used jocularly in place of *aspersion*.

1922 Joyce *Ulysses* 315 Don't cast your nasturtiums on my character. **1933** D. L. Sayers *Murder must Advertise* i. 22 He's been a long time in the firm and doesn't like any nasturtiums cast at it. **1970** *Guardian* 2 Feb. 9/4 No nasturtiums are cast upon anyone's actual hormones.

2. a. A trailing plant of the S. American genus *Tropæolum*, commonly cultivated in gardens for its showy orange-coloured flowers; Indian Cress.

Now usually denoting the larger species *Tropæolum majus*, introduced from Peru in 1686, but at first applied to *T. minus* (also from Peru), known in this country from 1596, and at first called *Nasturtium Indicum*.

[**1629** Parkinson *Parad.* v. 281 *Nasturtium Indicum*, by which name it is now generally..called. **1706** Phillips (ed. Kersey), *Nasturtium Indicum*, Indian Cresses, the Flowers of which smell, and look very pleasantly. **1741** *Compl. Fam.-Piece* II. iii. 369 Sow some Seeds of the *Nasturtium Indicum* upon Hot-beds.]

1704 Gardiner tr. *Rapin's Gardens* I. 34 The arm'd Nasturcium through each teeming Bed, With Trefoil intermingling Leaves, is spread. **1725** Bradley *Fam. Dict.* s.v. *Sallet*, The dry'd seeds of the Indian Nasturtium reduced to powder, finely bolted, and mix'd with a little leaven. **1789** Barker in *Phil. Trans.* LXXIX. 164 The nasturtiums were not cut off till after the middle of November. **1845-50** Mrs. Lincoln *Lect. Bot.* II. 78 The pollen of the Nasturtium. **1872** Oliver *Elem. Bot.* II. 154 Indian Cress,..called Garden Nasturtium.

attrib. **1747-96** Mrs. Glasse *Cookery* vi. 98 A few nasturtium flowers stuck here and there, look pretty. **1881** T. Hardy *Laodicean* VI. iii, The same nasturtium leaves that presented their faces to the passers without.

b. *Comb.* with names of colours, as ***nasturtium-red, -yellow***. Also *ellipt.* as the name of a colour.

1845 *Encycl. Metrop.* VIII. 465/1 Nasturtium.—Chrome yellow 24, flux 76. **1892** *Pall Mall G.* 19 May 1/3 The Eton jacket..opened over a blouse of nasturtium-yellow silk. **1896** *Daily News* 18 July 6/3 An oblong yoke of bright nasturtium-red velvet.

nasty (ˈnɑːstɪ, -æ-), *a.* Also 5 **naxty, -te,** 6, 8 (9 *Sc.*) **nesty,** 7 **gnastie, naustie.** [Of obscure origin: cf. Du. *nestig* (? MDu. *nistich*) foul, dirty, the history of which is also obscure. The early form *naxty* and Cotgrave's *nasky* may indicate a stem *nasc-*, which also appears in Sw. dial. *naskug*, *nasket* (Rietz) dirty, nasty, but the ultimate relationship of the forms is not clear.]

The original force of the word, denoting what is disgustingly dirty or foul, has been greatly toned down or altered in English use (see senses 3-5), but is retained in the United States, where *nasty* is not commonly used by polite speakers: cf. De Vere *Americanisms* (1871) 509 and R. G. White *England Without & Within* (1881) xvi. 386.

1. a. Foul, filthy, dirty, unclean, esp. to a disgusting degree; offensive through filth or dirt; characterized by the presence of, or contact with, filth or uncleanness.

In quot. 1477 prob. *transf.* and = filthy *a.* 4.

a **1400** *Pol. Rel. & L. Poems* 252 Nasty, sory, vnmiȝty. *c* **1420** *Anturs of Arth.* xv, Thus in dawngere and dole I downe and I duelle, Nasty [*v. rr.* naxty, naxte] and nedfulle, and nakede one nyghte. **1477** in Leadam *Sel. Cases Star Chamb.* (Selden Soc.) 2 The seid mysdoers..accompaigneth theym with many evyll disposed and nasty persones. **1548** Patten *Exped. Scotl.* D vij, A very slouuen saynt & belyke a nesty. **1576** Fleming *Panopl. Epist.* 356 Let vs spring out of our nastie nestes of sluggishnesse. **1587** —— *Contn. Holinshed* III. 1547/2 *marg.*, The mischiefe of nastie apparell. **1617** Moryson *Itin.* III. 162 The nastie filthinesse of the nation in generall. **1663** Boyle *Usef. Exp. Nat. Philos.* II. v. 152 Not to meddle with such nasty things as the grosser sort of humane Excrements. **1696** Bp. Patrick *Comm. Exod.* i. 14 In carrying Dung..into the Field, and such like nasty Services. **1710** Swift *Medit. Broomstick* Wks. 1755 II. I. 181 Destined to make other things clean and be nasty itself. **1745** P. Thomas *Jrnl. Anson's Voy.* 31 The ship..was in a very nasty condition. **1800** *Med. Jrnl.* IV. 110 Garments.. often grow rotten and infectious as they grow nasty. **1841** W. Spalding *Italy & It. Isl.* III. 168 Streets which are narrow, steep, and exceedingly nasty.

b. Morally filthy; indecent, obscene, esp. as ***nasty mind***.

a **1601** ? Marston *Pasquil & Kath.* II. 311 You forget your selfe to vse such jests, Such nastie ribauldrie, vpon my daughter. *c* **1648-50** Brathwait *Barnabees Jrnl.* II I4 A curmudgeon rich but nasty [*porobscænum*]. **1666** Bp. S. Parker *Free & Impart. Censure* (1667) 52 An intemperate sensuality is nasty. *a* **1731** Atterbury (J.), The greatest heap of nasty language that perhaps ever was put together. **1809** Malkin *Gil Blas* II. vii. ¶ 16 What an exhibition before my comrades! It was surrendering myself to all their nasty witticisms. **1873** E. E. Hale *Ups & Downs* x. 96 He hated it as a gentleman hates to hear a nasty story. **1914** G. B. Shaw *Misalliance* 16 Thats what theyre like: theyve nasty minds. With really nice good women a thing is either decent or indecent. **1930** W. S. Maugham *Cakes & Ale* xvii. 162 'Don't bother about it,' she said. 'He's got a nasty mind.' **1933** [see hot *a.* 6c]. **1942** Berrey & Van den Bark *Amer. Thes. Slang* § 295/1 *Nasty look*, a reproving look. **1969** M. Allingham *Case-Book* 29 One doesn't have to have a nasty mind to wonder.

2. Offensive to smell or taste; nauseous.

a **1548** Hall *Chron., Hen. VI* 135 The Lady Margaret.. was of suche nasty complexion and euill sauored breathe, that he abhorred her company. **1601** Weever *Mirr. Mart.* C j b, The aire's a gnastie old mans breath ill smelling. **1835** Marryat *Jac. Faithf.* xxii, For one good smell by the river's side, there be ten nasty ones. **1853** Kane *Grinnell Exp.* xxxiv. (1856) 306 Began using the remnant of our fetid bear's meat: nasty physic, but we will try it. **1885** *Law Times* LXXIX. 74/2 There was a nasty smell about the premises.

3. Of weather: Foul, dirty, wet, disagreeable.

1634 Sir T. Herbert *Trav.* 216 We..had little other or better weather then high stormes, nastie raines and lowd thunders. **1744** Fielding *Tumble-down Dick* Wks. 1784 III. 405 It is a cursed nasty morning. I wish we have not wet weather. **1776** S. J. Pratt *Pupil of Pleas.* (1777) I. 33 It's a nasty evening and not fit for walking. **1814** Jane Austen *Lett.* (1884) II. 222 It is a nasty day for everybody,..here is nothing but thickness and sleet. **1838** Dickens *Nich. Nick.* xiv, 'A nasty night, Mr. Noggs', said the man. **1892** *Daily Weather Rep.* 20 Dec., Variable breezes,..dull, nasty, probably some rain.

4. a. Offensive in some respect; disagreeable, unpleasant, objectionable, annoying.

In common use as a general epithet expressing dislike or annoyance.

1705 *Lond. Gaz.* No. 4106/4 Rob. Thomkins,..pale Faced, has nasty rough Hair. **1732** Fielding *Lottery* Wks. 1784 II. 131 Does not the nasty red colour go down out of my face? **1782** Mme. D'Arblay *Lett. & Diary* (1842) II. 191 How disagreeable these sacques are! I am so incommoded with these nasty ruffles! **1837** Landor *Pentameron* iii. Wks. 1853 II. 329/1 An Italian, a poet, write in French! What human ear can tolerate its nasty nasalities? **1844** Willis *Lady Jane* I. 259 My creditors They send their nasty bills in, once a year. **1888** *Poor Nellie* 280 They..had nasty little tricks of whispering unpalatable truths. **1961** [see equalizer d].

absol. **1884** Rae *Contemp. Socialism* 105 The taste of the *bourgeoisie* for the cheap and nasty.

b. Applied to persons (passing into 5).

1711 Swift *Lett.* (1767) III. 153 The little nasty lawyer that came up to me so sternly at the Castle the day I left Ireland. **1838** Dickens *Nich. Nick.* ix, 'He's a nasty stuck-up monkey',..said Mrs. Squeers. **1862** Trollope *Orley F.* I. 306 'Nasty, sly girl', said Lady Staveley to herself. **1865** Dickens *Mut. Fr.* I. iv, That nasty Lightwood feels it his duty [etc.].

c. Difficult to deal with; dangerous, bad.

1828 *Sporting Mag.* XXIII. 33 Mr. Russel hunts here, and I learnt that he is a nasty one to get away from. **1875** W. S. Hayward *Love agst. World* 11 This is a nasty ditch we are coming to. **1884** *Sat. Rev.* 14 June 783/2 There was outside of Harwich harbour a nasty sea.

d. Having unpleasant results; rather serious.

1880 'Ouida' *Moths* xxiii. It would be very funny if she gets a few 'nasty ones', as the boys say, herself. **1883** *Standard* 16 May 2/7 Mr. Grace..received a nasty blow on the finger. **1894** *Daily Tel.* 4 Jan. 5/4 Laid up.., owing to a nasty fall, sustained while hunting.

5. Ill-natured, ill-tempered, disagreeable (*to* another).

1825 Brockett *N.C. Gloss.*, *Nasty*, ill-natured, impatient, saucy. **1848** A. B. Evans *Leicestersh. Words*, *Nasty*, ill-tempered, cross, vexed. 'She got quite nasty'. **1858** S. Wilberforce *Sp. Missions* (1874) 78 The absence of toleration confines itself to a few nasty articles in newspapers. **1871** M. Collins *Mrq. & Merch.* I. ii. 83 He will take delight in being..nasty to a neighbour. **1874** Lisle Carr *Jud. Gwynne* I. iii. 71 Lest the headstrong William might turn nasty.

6. ***nasty man***, the one in a gang of garrotters who actually does the work.

1863 Trevelyan *Compet. Wallah* 20 Scheming to avoid, as best they can, The fell embraces of 'the nasty man'.

7. Phrases: ***a nasty piece*** (or ***bit***) ***of work*** (or ***goods***): an unpleasant or contemptible person; ***something nasty in the woodshed***, a traumatic experience or a concealed unpleasantness in a person's background.

1923 'Bartimeus' *Seaways* vii. 110 Nasty Bit of Work. I'd go and bash his head for two pins. **1928** 'M. Hoffe' *Many Waters* II. iv. 62 Edith shows in Mr. Rosel. He is really a rather nasty piece of work. **1932** S. Gibbons *Cold Comfort Farm* x. 141 When you were very small..you had seen something nasty in the woodshed. **1945** G. B. Grundy 55 *Yrs. at Oxf.* v. 87 Among the many pupils I had..there was only one I disliked. He was what is called a 'nasty piece of work'. **1949** 'M. Innes' *Journeying Boy* ix. 109 Nasty bit of work, isn't he?..Specialises in blackmailing adolescents. **1952** A. Christie *Mrs McGinty's Dead* xxvii. 184 She was a nasty bit of goods all right—children know. **1953** 'H. Cecil' *Nat. Causes* xix. 223 He was a nasty piece of work all right. A real blackmailer. **1959** *Sunday Times* 5 July 6/6 He enjoyed a temperate childhood: nothing nasty in his woodshed. **1959** *Listener* 3 Sept. 350/1 Although the idea is no longer entirely respectable (rather akin to 'something nasty in the woodshed'), we [etc.]. **1960** D. Fearon *Murder-on-Thames* xiv. 116 He was a nasty bit of work. I don't know that he actually had a criminal record, but the blighter stank of black market. **1968** B. Bainbridge *Another Part of Wood* ii. 70 They had all, Joseph, brother Trevor, the younger sister,..come across something nasty in the woodshed, mother or father or both, having it off with someone else. **1975** A. Christie *Curtain* v. 46 You do not like him?..What you call the nasty bit of goods.

8. *Comb.*, as ***nasty-minded*** adj.; ***nasty-mindedness***.

1921 D. Canfield *Brimming Cup* xiv. 236 A nasty-minded remark from somebody who didn't know what he was talking about. **1935** *Times Lit. Suppl.* 3 Oct. 613/3 A nasty-minded boy. **1972** 'J. & E. Bonett' *No Time to Kill* vii. 96, I don't want everybody to know about Greg and me. It's not that I'm ashamed... But nasty-minded people make it sound dirty. **1940** M. Marples *Public School Slang* p. x, For some reason food inspires a particular kind of satirical nasty-mindedness. **1960** *Encounter* Mar. 75/1 The nasty-mindedness of the Freudians.

'**nasty**, *v. Obs.* exc. *dial.* [f. prec.]

1. *trans.* (and *refl.*) To make nasty or dirty.

1728 T. Boston *Wks.* (1855) VI. 563 As willing to be washed as ever child ashamed of his nastying himself is. **1770** *Phil. Trans.* LX. 186 Salt is by no means to be used.. as it always will drop and nasty the plumage.

2. *intr.* To commit a nuisance.

1749 in Cramond *Church of Keith* 55 (E.D.D.), If any person shall be convicted..of nastying within the walls of the churchyard.

nasty (ˈnɑːstɪ, -æ-), *sb.*[1] [f. the adj.] **1.** (Freq. with capital initial.) Used as a jocular alteration of 'Nazi'.

1935 'R. Crompton' *William—the Detective* vi. 121 I'm jolly well not going to be called Her Hitler... I'll be called Him Hitler... Now I'm Him Hitler an' we four are the nasties. **1939** *Airman's Gaz.* Dec., All aircraft off duty being allowed to..view the stupendous, side-splitting entertainment provided by the Nasty Air Force and our Navy. *Ibid.*, All races won by the Nasties with a three mile start each time. **1940** H. G. Wells *Babes in Darkling Wood* IV. iii. 349 If it helps beat them Nastys,..I'll sit in the 'ole pond all day. **1942** *R.A.F. Jrnl.* 30 May 19 Ole Nasty can hit a hay-stack all right, but it's all he can hit. **1943** J. B. Priestley *Daylight on Saturday* xxi. 163 Cripes, ol' Nasty give us Phoney War all right, didn't 'e?

2. A nasty person; something nasty.

1935 'L. Luard' *Conquering Seas* 39 Fair is foul and foul is fair when Jack nasties step aboard. **1959** *Listener* 2 Apr. 609/2 For a Silver Wedding party there was such a grouping of nasties that one seemed to be involved in a misanthropist's nightmare. **1968** *Saturday Night* (Toronto) Feb. 27 Nasties—they're the newest social force, waiting in the wings to displace the last 1960s social force, the Flower People. They've always been around, the Nasties—disguised as merely unpleasant people. **1970** *Guardian* 8 Aug. 21 Nice nasties are de rigueur these days. **1971** *Ibid.* 22 Feb. 9/1 You come up against all manner of nasties in the woodshed: inadequacy, fear, alcoholism, ignorance, poverty, and hopelessness. **1973** H. Miller *Open City* xiv. 153 Here was a big nasty in a Crombie coat, standing right in the middle of her own living room. She was becoming very frightened. **1974** H. MacInnes *Climb to Lost World* ix. 145, I was convinced that there must be nasties in this territory, but..I found only one spider. **1975** *Country Life* 30 Jan. 257/3 It is the business of museums to present us with nasties as well as with fine things.

nasty (ˈnæstɪ), *sb.*[2] *Bot.* [a. G. *nastie* (E. Strasburger *Lehrbuch der Botanik* (ed. 6, 1904) I. ii. 221), f. Gk. ναστ-ός pressed together.] A nastic movement.

1936 J. B. Hill et al. *Bot.* ix. 228 Nasties are responses of bilaterally symmetrical organs like leaves and flower petals. **1955** *Sci. Amer.* Feb. 101/2 Nasties (or, more euphoniously, nastic movements) are among a plant's more beautiful motions: a typical example is the opening of a flower. They are the result of differing responses of different parts of the plant structure to the same external stimulus. **1965** Bell & Coombe tr. *Strasburger's Textbk. Bot.* 361 If, however, the direction of the movement is quite independent of that of the stimulus, but is determined solely by the structure of the organ, the movements are designated nasties.

nasute ('neɪsjuːt), *a.* (and *sb.*) Also 7 **nasut.** [ad. L. *nāsūt-us*, f. *nāsus* nose.]

†**1.** *fig.* Keen-scented, sagacious. *Obs.*

1653 GAUDEN *Hierasp.* 303 The names then of Clergy and Laity, in which the Nasuter Criticks of this age, sent something of pride. **1660** H. MORE *Myst. Godl.* VII. x. 320 Our modern Atheists, especially the more nasute sort of them. **1697** EVELYN *Numism.* vi. 212 If there be some so Nasute.. as to undertake the discrimination of.. Medals. **1707** T. BRAY *Bibl. Paroch.* (ed. 2) 34 *note*, This is a piece of Knowledge extremely slighted by such as would be accounted Nasute, Critical and Sagacious.

†**2.** Having a strong sense of smell. *Obs. rare*$^{-1}$.

1699 EVELYN *Acetaria* (1729) 132 They are commonly discovered, scented and rooted out by a nasute greedy Swine purposely brought up.

3. *Zool.* Nose-shaped or having a pronounced proboscis, esp. in reference to a caste of soldier termites of the genus *Nasutitermes.* Also as *sb.*, a termite of this caste.

1884 J. HALL in *Geol. Mag.* Dec. 560 In other forms [of lamellibranchiate molluscs], the anterior extremity becomes nasute or rostrate. **1926** R. J. TILLYARD *Insects Austral. & N.Z.* xi. 103 In the family Termitidae the soldiers are sometimes of the nasute type, i.e. they are provided with pear-shaped heads more or less produced anteriorly, above the mandibles, into a narrow, snout-like process. **1934** *Discovery* Nov. 307 (*caption*) Earthen mound built by nasute termites in northern Australia. **1963** A. W. LEFTWICH *Student's Dict. Zool.* 160 Nasutes. Soldier-termites: specialized forms within the genus *Nasutitermes*, able to defend the colony by discharging an acrid secretion from glands situated at the end of a long snout or rostrum. **1970** F. J. GAY in *Insects of Australia* (Commonwealth Sci. & Industr. Res. Organization) xv. 292/1 *Nasutitermes* is widely distributed throughout Australia, particularly in the northern half of the continent. The soldiers are the typical nasute type.

Hence †**nasuteness**, the quality of being nasute; sagacity. *Obs.*

1660 H. MORE *Myst. Godl.* VIII. ii. 365 Any man that has but a moderate nasuteness. **1685** —— *Curs. Refl. Baxter* Pref. A 2 An Ostentation of his singular Nasuteness.

nasutus (neɪ'sjuːtəs). Pl. nasuti. [L. *nāsūt-us*, f. *nāsus* nose.] = NASUTE *sb.*

1869 A. S. PACKARD *Guide to Study of Insects* 587 There also occur among workers [of certain termite species] certain individuals (Nasuti) which have the front of the head prolonged into a horn. **1895** D. SHARP in *Cambr. Nat. Hist.* V. xxi. 371 The prolongation and form of the head of these Nasuti may be fairly described as adaptation to useful ends. **1920** *Bull. U.S. Nat. Mus.* CVIII. 71 Two specimens [of *Nasutitermes costaricensis*] from Texas..; a dealated female and two nasuti.

nat, *sb.*¹ Now *north. dial.* Also 4–5 **natte,** 6–8 **natt,** 7 **knat.** [a. F. *natte*: see etym. note to MAT *sb.*¹] **a.** A mat. (Freq. in church-accounts.) **b.** *dial.* A straw mattress.

1361–2 *Durham Acc. Rolls* (Surtees) 385 Cum factura del nattes in coro. **1399** *Fabric Rolls York Minster* (Surtees) 17 In nattes emptis de Iohanne de Francia, 8*d.* **1426** LYDG. *De Guil. Pilgr.* 11264 Olde nattys ageyn he made. **1430–40** —— *Bochas* III. i. (1554) 69 A brode hat, rent out of nattes olde. **1483** *Cath. Angl.* 249/1 To make Nattes, *storiare.* **1597** *Vestry Bks.* (Surtees) 43 For makinge a natt for the wyves to knele on when they come to be churched. **1682** *Ibid.* 206 To George Newton for nats for the church, 3 *s.* **1730** *Finghall Churchw. Acc.* (MS.), For two Nats, 7*d.* **1744** *Ibid.*, Paid for a Natt 11*d.* **1788** W. MARSHALL *Yorksh.* Gloss, *Nat*, a straw mattress. **1876** in *Whitby Gloss.* **1877** in *N.W. Linc. Gloss.*

Comb. **1426** LYDG. *De Guil. Pilgr.* 11282 The nattemakere answerde ageyn. **1483** *Cath. Angl.* 249/1 A Natte maker, *storiator.* **1530** PALSGR. 247/2 Nat maker, *natier.*

Hence † **'natting,** matting. *Obs. rare*$^{-1}$.

1669 *Fabric Rolls York Minster* (Surtees) 348 For covering the seates with natting in the Dean's closet 1*s.*

Nat (næt), *sb.*² *India.* Also **Nut.** [Skr. *naṭa* dancer, actor, tumbler.] A member of an itinerant class of entertainers, fortune-tellers, and the like, found esp. in northern India, but coming from no tribe in particular. Also **'Nati,** the argot spoken by these people; also *attrib.* or as *adj.*

1801 D. RICHARDSON in *Asiatick Researches* VII. 457 Strictly speaking, these people might be denominated *players* or *actors*, from their Persian name of *Bazee-gur*,.. *juggler* or *tricker*; but the appellation of *Nut* extends to several tribes, and properly belongs to many more. **1855** H. H. WILSON *Gloss. Judicial & Revenue Terms* 369/2 *Naṭa*, *Naṭ*, or *Nuṭ*,..a dancer, an actor, a tumbler, a public performer; applied also to a tribe of vagrants who live by feats of dexterity, sleight of hand, fortune-telling and the like. **1896** W. CROOKE *Tribes & Castes N.-W. Provinces & Oudh* IV. 66 These Nats say that they came originally from Ratanpur and Bilāspur in the Central Provinces. *Ibid.* 70 Their domestic ceremonies are of the usual Nat type. **1908** *Encycl. Relig. & Ethics* I. 451/1 The ritual of the Nats, a tribe of wandering acrobats, is more remarkable. **1917** KIPLING *Eyes of Asia* (1918) 8 The nature of the enemy in this war is like the Nat (juggler) who is compelled to climb a pole for his belly's sake. **1922** G. A. GRIERSON *Ling. Survey India* XI. 121 Any tribe may be represented among the people acting as Naṭs. *Ibid.* 122 The great majority of Naṭī slang words..have been taken from the common Aryan vocabulary of Northern India.

nat (nɑːt), *sb.*³ [Burmese *nāt*, f. Skr. *nāthá* lord, protector.] **a.** In the animistic native religion of the Burmese people, a spirit or demon, a supernatural being.

1819 F. HAMILTON *Acct. Kingdom Nepal* I. i. 57 The Bhotiyas..worship all the spirits, that by the Burmas are called Nat. **1826** J. CONDER *Mod. Traveller: Birmah, Siam & Anam* 82 Carved images..are to be seen.., the supposed representatives of different *nats* or demons. **1828** *Asiatick Researches* XVI. 468 In Ava and Siam..in the existence of *Nats*, it is admitted, that other animated creatures than man and animals exist. **1858** C. T. WINTER *Six Months Brit. Burmah* i. 13 The Nats who guard the royal city, palace, and umbrella. **1878** C. J. F. S. FORBES *Brit. Burma* viii. 223 A man going on a journey through a forest, comes to a large and conspicuous tree..and places..an offering to the Nát of the tree. **1923** *Blackw. Mag.* Aug. 149/1 We had been talking..of folk-lore, superstitions, witches, djinns, nats, spookes, ghouls and other inventions of primitive man. **1934** 'G. ORWELL' *Burmese Days* xiv. 209 Sacrificing to the local god. Nats, they call them—a kind of dryad. **1959** C. OGBURN *Marauders* (1960) iv. 115 These were intended to propitiate, entice, or exorcise the nats, or forest spirits. **1968** O. WYND *Sumatra Seven Zero* i. 10 'Rubies..only come out of the ground when their protecting "nats" permit it.'.. 'What is a "nat"?'.. 'A Burmese spirit of the earth and air.' **1974** *Times* 30 Apr. 16/7 A Burmese journalist..asked if I would like to come with him to an evening of 'Nat' Dancing. To the Burmese the Nats are the multitudinous spirits that inhabit all natural phenomena and can exercise at will power over people and objects... The monks are tolerant of Nats: a good many of them are probably Nat-conscious themselves.

b. *Comb.*, as ***nat-worship***, ***-worshipper***.

1833 A. JUDSON *Let.* 29 Nov. in F. Wayland *Mem. A. Judson* (1853) II. 56 The best outward test is to have refrained from rum, nat-worship, &c. **1910** *Encycl. Relig. & Ethics* III. 21/1 The practical everyday religion of the Burmese peoples is Animism, called generally in Burmese 'Nat-worship'. **1965** M. NASH *Golden Road to Modernity* ix. 320 There is a system of animistic belief (nat worship) which is integrated with Buddhism and gives a villager a belief system reaching from hut to heaven and beyond. **1906** J. G. R. FORLONG *Faiths of Man* I. 257 Its [*sc.* Burma's] population in 1894 was..Nāt worshipers..420,000. **1923** *Blackw. Mag.* Feb. 183/2 They are all Nat or spirit worshippers.

Nat (næt), *sb.*⁴ [Abbrev. of NATIONAL *a.* and *sb.*, NATIONALIST.] A member of (*a*) the National Party in South Africa; (*b*) the Scottish or Welsh Nationalists.

In S. Afr. also = 'National'.

1934 W. SAINT-MANDÉ *Halcyon Days Afr.* ii. 24 Labour had done right to join forces with the Nats., for the Smuts government would gradually have reduced the white workers to slaves. **1958** *New Statesman* 22 Mar. 367/2 The movement..cannot lose momentum. The Nats must know this, unless the strain of continually having to defend an indefensible position has lost them their sanity. **1967** *Economist* 18 Mar. 1008/2 Both Scotland and Wales could in time do well. But the start of their national lives would be bleak... One cannot take seriously the present Nats who advocate freedom and promise prosperity in one breath. **1968** *Guardian* 20 Sept. 13/2 Jeremy Thorpe's overtures to the Celtic Nationalists... The Liberals would back the Nats on devolution. **1970** B. KNOX *Children of Mist* i. 23 Scot Nats? He'd met all kinds. **1971** *Sunday Times* (Johannesburg) 28 Mar. 2/2 The Transvaler, official organ of the Nat Party in the Transvaal. **1972** M. SINCLAIR *Norslag* ix. 73 'Weren't you with the...' 'Yes, I was an ardent Nat then.'.. MacCaig was already neatly pigeonholed. **1974** *Times* 22 Apr. 7/1 The white people.. will be voting overwhelmingly for Mr. Vorster's National Party... The average voter will..continue to vote 'Nat'. **1974** *Sunday Post* (Glasgow) 28 Apr. 5/5 And there are other Labour strongholds where it wouldn't need much of a swing to put in the Nats.

†**nat,** *adv. Obs.* Also 6 **natt.** [Reduced form of *naȝt* NAUGHT *adv.*] = NOT *adv.*

c **1385** CHAUCER *L.G.W.* Prol. 12 Men schal nat wenyn euery thyng a lye [etc.]. **1393** LANGL. *P. Pl.* C. III. 18 Layn nat yf ȝe knowen. *Ibid.* XIX. 251 Ich with-sat nat hus heste. **1402** HOCCLEVE *Let. Cupid* 46 That men shulde nat for her sake dey. *c* **1420** LYDG. *Assembly of Gods* 453 Yef she be examynyd she woll hit nat deny. *a* **1485** FORTESCUE *Wks.* (1869) 486 The fyle wereth, and after that is laide asyde as a thyng nat profitable. **1513** BRADSHAW *St. Werburge* II. 27 The notable actes of our fathers..(yf litterature were nat) myght nat nowe be tolde. **1536** *Lett. Suppress. Monast.* (Camden) 147, I colde natt then name them to you. **1575** *Gamm. Gurton* I. ii. 30 Nay; but ich saw such a wonder as ich saw nat this vii yere.

nat, variant of NOT *v.*, wot not. *Obs.*

nat, obs. form of NOT *a.*, hornless.

nata'bility. [f. L. *natābil-is*, f. *natāre* to swim + -ITY.] Capacity of floating.

1796 H. HUNTER tr. *St.-Pierre's Stud. Nat.* (1799) II. 153 The natability of aquatic seeds is, undoubtedly, proportioned to the length of the voyages which they have to perform.

natal ('neɪtəl), *a.*¹ and *sb.*¹ Also 4–7 **natall,** 5 **natale.** [ad. L. *nātāl-is* adj. and sb., f. *nāt-*, ppl. stem of *nasci* to be born, + *-ālis*: see -AL¹. Cf. F. *natal* adj. and sb. (15th c.).]

A. *adj.* †**1.** Presiding over birthdays or nativities.

c **1374** CHAUCER *Troylus* III. 150 Now nece myn, by natal Ioves fest, Were I a god, ye sholde sterve as yerne.

2. Of places: Native. Chiefly *poet.*

c **1420** *Pallad. on Husb.* XI. 130 And as for seed, in natal soil hit feede. **1436** *Pol. Poems* (Rolls) II. 167 The duke knewe that the townes thre Shulde have loste alle hys natale cuntree. *c* **1480** HENRYSON *Mor. Fab., Lion & Mouse* 51 My natall land is Rome withouttin nay. **1605** CAMDEN *Rem.* 108 Children tooke names from their natall places. **1632** LITHGOW *Trav.* x. 498 Where thence, (O natall place) my soule did coyle. **1725** POPE *Odyss.* I. 8 Safe with his friends to gain his natal shore. **1762** KAMES *Elem. Crit.* xix. (1833) 349 After a long voyage it was customary among the ancients to salute the natal soil. **1820** SHELLEY *Hymn Merc.* xxiv, He sought his natal mountain-peaks divine. **1855** TENNYSON *Daisy* 18 How young Columbus seem'd to rove, Yet present in his natal grove.

3. Of or pertaining to (one's) birth; connected with, or dating from, one's birth.

1447 BOKENHAM *Seyntys* (Roxb.) 9 The tytyl of hyr natal dygnyte In her yung age she dede forsake. **1589** PUTTENHAM *Eng. Poesie* I. xxiii. (Arb.) 61 Others for magnificence at the natiuities of Princes children..are called songs natall or *Genethliaca.* **1663** SANDERS *Palmistry* II. 31 Thy Natal Stars (meaning the Radical Position of the Heavens at thy Birth) promise thee happy success. **1817** SHELLEY *Rev. Islam* Ded. i, Ere my fame become A star among the stars.., If it indeed may cleave its natal gloom. **1866** G. MACDONALD *Ann. Q. Neighb.* xxxi. (1878) 533 A belief that the circumstances of one's natal position are not to be rudely handled. **1899** *Allbutt's Syst. Med.* VII. 733 The pre-natal and natal affections are readily distinguished from this disease.

fig. **1848** R. I. WILBERFORCE *Doctr. Incarnation* xiv, (1852) 383 In God only is Holiness... From this natal source does the principle of holiness extend itself through the creation. **1872** BLACKIE *Lays Highl.* 39 From the scriptured rock at ease I spell Creation's natal chapter.

b. ***natal hour*** or ***day***, the hour or day of one's birth; birthday. Also *fig.*

1704 PRIOR *Prol., Her Majesty's Birthday* 6 Thou, propitious star, whose sacred power Presided o'er the monarch's natal hour. **1729** T. COOKE *Tales*, etc. 55 O! Youth..on whom the kindest Ray Has shed an Influence from your natal Day. **1781** COWPER *Anti-Thelyphth.* 92 Hypothesis (for with such magic power Fancy endued her in her natal hour). **1853** KANE *Grinnell Exp.* xxv. (1856) 206 The natal day of the prince consort. **1875** WHITNEY *Life Lang.* viii. 135 The saint to whom his natal or christening day is sacred.

c. ***natal games***, ***ring*** (see quots.).

1727–38 CHAMBERS *Cycl.* s.v. *Natalis*, Natal Games were games introduced on the anniversaries of the birth-days of great men. *Ibid.*, Natal Ring..was a ring only worn on the birth-day. **1877** W. JONES *Finger-ring* 46 Perseus alludes to the natal ring in his first Satire.

d. Connected with one from birth.

1811 W. R. SPENCER *Poems* 97 My natal angel round my heart. **1879** LONG *Æneid* IX. 333 Who am all lost, if back Come not my Sire, by our great natal Gods.

B. *sb.* † **1.** [obs. F. *natal.*] A birthday-feast.

1484 CAXTON *Fables of Æsop* IV. xi, He would haue celebrated and holden a natall or a grete feste.

†**2.** *pl.* [L. *nātālēs.*] Birthday celebrations. *Obs.*

1597 BP. HALL *Sat.* III. iv, Were yesterday Polemon's natals kept? **1636** FITZ-GEFFREY *Blessed Birthday* (1881) 119 Why should not we with ioy resound and sing, The blessed Natals of our heauenly King?

natal ('neɪtəl), *a.*² [f. L. *nat-is* (see NATES) + -AL¹.] Of or pertaining to the nates or buttocks.

1870 H. A. NICHOLSON *Man. Zool.* lxxxiii. 556 The natal callosities are generally large and conspicuous.

Natal (nə'tɑːl), *sb.*² The name of a province of the Republic of South Africa used *attrib.* in:

1. Natal sore *Path.* = *oriental sore* s.v. ORIENTAL *a.* and *sb.* A. 3 b.

1852 C. BARTER *Dorp & Veld* ii. 13 The Natal sore, a very painful boil. **1855** J. W. COLENSO *Ten Weeks in Natal* 245 The Natal sores or boils..are such as I have known among my parishioners in Norfolk. **1915** O. S. ORMSBY *Pract. Treat. Dis. Skin* 360 As distinguished from the Natal sore, which was chiefly found in the lower part of that country, the veldt sore was most abundant in the high, barren tablelands. **1951** G. PANJA in R. B. H. Gradwohl *Clin. Trop. Med.* xxxiii. 641 Tropical Phagedenic Ulcer... Synonyms. .. Natal sore.

2. The names of plants and animals found there, as **Natal francolin**, *Francolinus natalensis*; **Natal lily**, a bulbous plant of the family Amaryllidaceæ, *Clivia miniata*, which bears clusters of scarlet flowers, or one of several species of *Crinum*; **Natal mahogany**, either of two evergreen timber trees, *Kiggelaria africana*, of the family Flacourtiaceæ, or *Trichilia emetica*, of the family Meliaceæ; **Natal plum**, one of several shrubs or trees bearing fruit resembling a plum, esp. a spiny evergreen shrub or small tree, *Carissa macrocarpa*, of the family Apocynaceæ, which bears tubular, white, fragrant flowers and an edible purple fruit.

1906 Natal francolin [see *coast-partridge* (COAST *sb.* 14)]. **1947** J. STEVENSON-HAMILTON *Wild Life S. Afr.* xxxii. 274 The Natal francolin (*Francolinus natalensis*)..may be recognized by its red bill and legs, and white breast with V-shaped black markings. **1855** *Cape of Good Hope Almanac & Ann. Reg. for 1856* 283 The Natal lily is the perfection of beauty and fragrance. **1859** R. J. MANN *Colony of Natal* viii. 152 Most places are commonly covered with another very beautiful amaryllid..which is termed *par excellence* the 'Natal lily'. The flowers of this striking plant are large white pink-ribbed bells, hanging in enormous bunches round the summit of the flower-stalk. **1962** WATT & BREYER-BRANDWIJK *Medicinal & Poisonous Plants S. & E. Afr.* (ed. 2) 1378/1 Crinum sp... Natal lily. **1904** H. STONE *Timbers of Commerce* 3 (*heading*) Natal Mahogany. Kiggelaria Dregeana. **1907** T. R. SIM *Forests & Forest Flora Cape Good Hope* 128 *Kiggelaria africana*, Wild Peach, Natal

Mahogany..does best in open forest. *Ibid.* 161 This tree [sc. *Trichilia emetica*]..is known in the Transkei as Cape Mahogany, Manuti Mahogany, or Natal Mahogany. **1973** PALMER & PITMAN *Trees S. Afr.* II. 1071 *Trichilia emetica* Vahl. Woodland mahogany, Natal mahogany... This is one of the widespread trees of Africa. **1859** R. J. MANN *Colony of Natal* viii. 158 The *Amatungulu* (Natal plum) is the berry of an evergreen periwinkle (*Vinca*) growing as a small shrub on the sea-coast lands. The fruit is about the size of a damson. **1876** H. BROOKS *Natal* v. 168 A plant..bearing a really valuable fruit which is familiarly known as the Natal plum. **1970** *Country Life* 17 Dec. 1230/3 Scarlet ixoras and the spiny carissa (Natal plum) are used as evergreen hedges. **1973** PALMER & PITMAN *Trees S. Afr.* III. 1901 *Carissa macrocarpa*... Amatungulu, Natal plum..is a common and often conspicuous species in coastal bush, on sand dunes and on the edges of coastal forest... Although it is often a low bush, it can grow into a small tree up to 4 m high, many-branched, spiny, with dense evergreen foliage.

Natalian (nəˈtɑːlɪən), *a.* and *sb.* [f. NATAL *sb.*[2] + -IAN.] **A.** *adj.* Of or pertaining to the province of Natal in South Africa. **B.** *sb.* A native or inhabitant of Natal.

1867 R. J. MANN in *Intellectual Observer* X. 186 In the year 1842,..the Dutchmen within the Natalian territory became subjects of the British Crown. **1870** A. LINDLEY *After Ophir* ii. 27 The Natalians carry their *penchant* for genteel and sonorous titles nearly as far as the Sicilians. **1878** [see JIMMY[2] 1]. **1897** J. BRYCE *Impressions S. Afr.* xviii. 359 The Natalians have..become the less energetic. **1928** R. CAMPBELL *Wayzgoose* i. 10 Seldom do suns such striking talent show As when they set Natalian woods aglow. **1935** S. DESMOND *Afr. Log* xxxix. 191 Throughout the day I see the lovely Natalian landscape roll past. **1960** *Guardian* 14 Oct. 12/5 Natalians are subjects of the Queen. **1973** *Sunday Times* (S. Afr.) 18 Feb. 2 An independent Natal has long been the dream of many White Natalians.

† **nataˈlitial**, *a.* and *sb. Obs.* [f. L. *nātālīti-us* (f. *nātālis* NATAL *a.*[1]) + -AL[1].]

A. *adj.* Belonging to or connected with one's birth or birthday.

1611 CORYAT *Crudities* 74 The Parish of Odcombe, my deare natalitiall place. **1641** J. JACKSON *True Evang. T.* III. 175 His natalitiall hymne was sung..by a Chore of Angels. **1679** EVELYN *Sylva* (1776) 630 We read in the life of Virgil how far his natalitial Poplar had outstripped the rest of its Contemporaries.

B. *sb.* [L. *nātālitia.*] A birthday celebration.

1652 SPARKE *Prim. Devot.* (1663) 84 Our funerals border on our natalitials.

† **nataˈlitious**, *a. Obs.* [f. as prec. + -OUS.]

1. = NATALITIAL *a.*

1646 BUCK *Rich. III* 78 It importeth no reason why those early and natalitious teeth should presage such horrour..to his birth. **1669** BADDELEY *Life Bp. Morton* 1 The natalicious and Birth-places of most Noble..Princes.

2. Concerned with one's children. *rare*[−1].

Not from the L. text, which has only *bellum internecivum.*

1654 R. CODRINGTON tr. *Iustine* XXVI. 353 The Gauls.. made a natalitious and an intrinsick war with..their children.

natality (nəˈtælɪtɪ). [f. NATAL *a.*[1] + -ITY. In recent use ad. F. *natalité.*]

1. Birth. *rare.*

1483 CAXTON *Gold. Leg.* 245/1 The passyng out of thys world of sayntes is not sayd deth of sayntes but natalyte. **1830** J. BADCOCK *Ess. Foote* in Foote's Wks. p. lxxvii, I should doubt whether Samuel Foote visited Truro more than once since the natality of Mr. Polwhele was proclaimed to his kindred.

2. Birth-rate; ratio of births to the population.

1888 MYERS *Sci. & Fut. Life* (1893) 104 The natality or rate of increase of different provinces of France. **1899** *Pop. Sci. Monthly* Sept. 673 The revival of religious ideas.. might have some effect on natality.

natant (ˈneɪtənt), *a.* [ad. L. *natant-em*, pres. pple. of *natāre*, freq. form of *nāre* to swim, float.] **a.** Swimming, floating. † **b.** Of the pulse: Buoyant. *Obs.*

1707 FLOYER *Physic. Pulse-Watch* 407 In a Disease from Water, if the Pulse be natant and great, 'tis a sign of Life. **1753** CHAMBERS *Cycl. Supp.* s.v. *Leaf*, Natant Leaf, one which floats upon the surface of the water. **1831** *Crayons fr. Commons* 63 He who natant still delights to lave His pliant members in the limpid wave.

Hence **ˈnatantly** *adv.*, 'swimmingly, floatingly' (Webster 1847).

Nataraja (ˌnætəˈrɑːdʒə). *India.* [Hindi, lit. 'prince of dancers', f. Skr. *naṭa* dancer, actor + *rājan* prince, king (see RAJA).] A name of Siva, the Hindu god of creation and dissolution, in his role as lord of the dance, when he symbolizes cosmic energy. Also, a figure depicting Siva as lord of the dance.

1911 V. A. SMITH *Hist. Fine Art India & Ceylon* vii. 249 The place of honour may be given to the spirited images of Siva as 'Natarāja', 'Lord of the Dance', the first of their kind to be found in Ceylon. *Ibid.* vii. 251 (*caption*) Bronze Siva Nataraja, 3 feet high. **1916** H. KRISHNA SASTRI *S. Indian Images Gods & Goddesses* iv. 77 Natarāja..is the well-known dancing form of god Siva. **1917** COOMARASWAMY & DUGGIRALA tr. *Mirror of Gesture* 15 The image of Śiva as dancer (Naṭarāja, Naṭeśa) and actor is everywhere conspicuous in Śaiva literature. **1918** A. COOMARASWAMY *Dance of Śiva* 66 Explorers of the infinitely great and infinitely small, we are worshippers of Naṭarāja still. **1968** *Indian Mining & Engin. Jrnl.* V. 40 God in his aspect of Naṭarāja, or Lord of the Dance. **1972** P. HOLROYDE *Indian Mus.* i. 42 That first artist who fashioned the Nataraja into a symbolic equation of energy.

† **natatile**, *a. Obs. rare*[−1]. [ad. L. *natātilis* (Tertullian), f. *natāt-*, ppl. stem of *natāre* to swim, + *-ilis*: see -ILE.] Able to swim.

1721 BAILEY. **1725** —— *Erasm. Colloq.* (1878) II. 147 A Natatile Beet do you say?.. Who ever heard of, or ever read the Name of a Swimming Beet?

natation (nəˈteɪʃən). Also 6 **nawtacyon**. [ad. L. *natātiōn-em*, n. of action f. *natāre* to swim. Cf. F. *natation.*] The action or art of swimming; also, †that which swims or floats.

1542 BOORDE *Dyetary* xiii. (1870) 265 Euery thyng that is vnctious..doth swymme aboue in the brynkes of the stomacke:..the excesse of suche nawtacyon or superfyce will ascend to the oryse [*v.r.* orifice] of the stomacke. **1623** COCKERAM I, *Natation*, a swimming. **1646** SIR T. BROWNE *Pseud. Ep.* 193 Other animalls..need no other way of motion, for natation in the water, then for progression upon the land. **1793** *Charac.* in *Ann. Reg.* 252/1 Had I remained in England and opened a school of natation. **1834** MCMURTRIE *Cuvier's Anim. Kingd.* 276 Here, as among the Vertebrata, we find the walk, the run, the leap, natation and flight. **1865** WELD *Last Wint. in Rome* 111 No Roman bathes in the Tiber now, and as for feats of natation [etc.].

Hence **naˈtational** *a.*, relating to swimming; **naˈtationist**, a swimmer.

1883 *Field* 22 Dec. 853 To take an active lead in matters natational. **1891** *Daily News* 17 Feb. 3/8 The question of supremacy between the nationists could be settled.

‖**Natatores** (neɪtəˈtɔəriːz). *Ornith.* [L., pl. of *natātor*, f. *natāre* to swim.] *pl.* An order of birds adapted for swimming, including ducks, geese, swans, pelicans, etc. (Named by Illiger, 1811.)

1823 VIGORS in *Trans. Linn. Soc.* XIV. 405 Five great primary divisions..of birds..: Natatores, or Webfooted Birds. **1855** DALLAS *Syst. Nat. Hist.* II. 156 The most striking character of the *Natatores*, or Swimming Birds is derived from the structure of the feet. **1870** GILLMORE tr. *Figuier's Reptiles & Birds* i. 210 The Natatores are obviously devoted, by their organisation, to an aquatic life. **1881** *Nature* XXIII. 365 The wading-birds and natatores.

natatorial (neɪtəˈtɔərɪəl), *a.* [f. as NATATORY *a.* + -AL[1].]

1. Of or belonging to swimming.

1816 T. L. PEACOCK *Headlong Hall* viii, Mr. Cranium, being utterly destitute of natatorial skill, was in imminent danger of final submersion. **1890** *Boston* (Mass.) *Jrnl.* 26 Mar. 2/4 One of the animals..came off victorious on account of superior natatorial powers.

b. Of organs: Adapted for swimming.

1823 VIGORS in *Trans. Linn. Soc.* XIV. 405 *note*, Podiceps has a true natatorial foot. **1870** H. A. NICHOLSON *Man. Zool.* 74 The gonocalyx..now serves as a natatorial organ. **1871** T. R. JONES *Anim. Kingd.* (ed. 4) 459 It..swims freely about by means of two natatorial feet.

2. Characterized by swimming; *esp.* in *Ornith.* of the order of birds called *Natatores.*

a. 1839 *Penny Cycl.* XIII. 334/2 The circle of the *Laridæ*, no less than that of the natatorial order, has now been traced. **1854** OWEN in *Orr's Circ. Sci.* II. 75/1 Natatorial birds sometimes need very extended flight. **1872** H. A. NICHOLSON *Palaeont.* 387 In many cases—especially amongst the Natatorial birds [etc.].

b. 1870 H. A. NICHOLSON *Man. Zool.* xxxii. 190 In the Natatorial Isopoda..the last pair of abdominal legs are expanded. **1892** *Working Men's Coll. Jrnl.* Oct. 126 When stocking an aquarium with natatorial insects, give these a separate department.

So **nataˈtorious** *a.* [-IOUS.]

1826 KIRBY & SP. *Entomol.* III. xxx. 171 The larva of *Agrion*, which in its tapering body and anal natatorious laminæ represents a shrimp.

natatorium (neɪtəˈtɔərɪəm). *N. Amer.* [L. *natātōrium* a place for swimming.] A swimming-pool.

1890 in WEBSTER. **1897** E. BELLAMY *Equality* x. 60, I propose..that we go over to the natatorium and take a plunge. **1900** *Amer. Jrnl. Sociol.* Jan. 473 A considerable number of Wellesley college girls..patronize the Brookline natatorium. **1907** *Amherst College Catal. 1907–08* 104 In the natatorium, swimming is taught by a competent instructor. Every student who on entering college cannot swim, is required to learn the first year. **1911** *Daily Colonist* (Victoria, B.C.) 2 Apr. 2/4 Pearl Moore came to her death by drowning in a pool at the Washington natatorium. **1921** *Ibid.* 6 Oct. 1/5 Plans have been completed for the immediate construction of an up-to-date natatorium in Vancouver. **1966** *Punch* 21 Dec. 921/2 Only in Texas, perhaps, will a man in search of somewhere to swim pick up the Yellow Pages and look under Natatoriums; the directory refers him to Swimming Pools. **1971** *Parks & Recreation* (U.S.) VI. 31 This modern natatorium demonstrated that using a vinyl-coated nylon air-supported structure as the roof in the winter and completely removing it in the summer is a desirable and effective arrangement.

natatory (ˈneɪtətərɪ), *sb.* [In sense 1, ad. late L. *natātōrium* sb., neut. of *natātōrius*: see next.]

† **1.** A swimming-bath, pool. *Obs.*

c **1400** MAUNDEV. (1839) viii. 93 Also streghte from Natatorie Siloe, is an Ymage of Ston. **1653** URQUHART *Rabelais* I. lv, On the out-side were placed the tilt-yard,.. the theater.., and Natatorie or place to swim in.

2. An organ used in swimming.

1852 DANA *Crust.* II. 878 The abdominal natatories are very small.

natatory (ˈneɪtətərɪ), *a.* [ad. late L. *natātōrius*: see NATATION and -ORY.]

1. Of organs: Adapted for or used in swimming or floating.

1799 *Brit. Critic* XIII. 212 When they feel the necessity of sleep, their natatory bladder is much inflated. **1835** KIRBY *Hab. & Inst. Anim.* I. vi. 197 It is said that they can render themselves heavy or light at pleasure, which some effect by means of a natatory vesicle. **1859** DARWIN *Orig. Spec.* xiv. (1873) 389 They have six pairs of beautifully constructed natatory legs. **1878** BELL *Gegenbaur's Comp. Anat.* 416 The natatory membrane of many Reptiles.

2. Of or belonging to swimming.

1836 E. HOWARD *R. Reefer* xix, I perfected my natatory studies (affected phraseology is the fashion). **1863** G. KEARLEY *Links in Chain* vii. 154 They are enabled to perform a sort of natatory movement. **1885** *Graphic* 24 Jan. 90/3 He had confidence in his own natatory skill.

3. Characterized by swimming.

1887 E. D. COPE *Orig. Fittest* 278 There is little doubt that the natatory Sirenian order was derived from it by a process of degradation. **1895** 'Q.' (QUILLER COUCH) *Wandering Heath* 95 Nereus..With his natatory daughters.

natch (nætʃ), *sb.* Now *dial.* Forms: 6 **natche**, 7 **nach**, 9 **natch.** [? var. of NOTCH.] A notch. Hence **natch** *v.*, to cut notches in; **natched**, notched, indented.

1570 LEVINS *Manip.* 38/7 A Natche, *incisura. Ibid.* 14 To Natche, *incidere.* **1578** LYTE *Dodoens* 43 Brounewurte hath ..leaues natched or dented rounde about. **1659** *New Haven Col. Rec.* (1858) II. 276 A gray mare..branded on yᵉ neare shoulder with an S, wᵗʰ a nach on yᵉ further eare. **1878–** in dial. glossaries, etc. (see *Eng. Dial. Dict.*).

natch (nætʃ), *adv.* Colloq. abbrev. of NATURALLY *adv.* orig. *U.S.*

1945 in L. SHELLY *Jive Talk Dict.* 15/1. **1946** *Sun* (Baltimore) 24 Sept. 3/3 (Advt.), Natch! Mom's gettin' both of us Hen self-starters... Baltimore's most popular 'first shoes for babies'. **1953** *New Yorker* 10 Jan. 21/3 Their disapproving papa..inserted a dime, which, he said, would otherwise have gone to buy them a Coca-Cola... Well, natch, this brought a twenty-dime return. **1957** P. WILDEBLOOD *Main Chance* 132 'You don't mean to say,' she whispered tragically, 'that we're going to eat?' 'Why, natch. We're going to have another drink first, though.' **1962** J. WAIN *Strike Father Dead* 60 We went in: Saloon Bar, natch. Lucille may have been Public Bar in her heart, but she was Saloon Bar on the outside. **1968** *N.Y. Times Bk. Rev.* 23 June VII. 1/3 The banning—in Boston, natch—of 'Fanny Hill' back in 1821. **1970** *Daily Tel.* (Colour Suppl.) 3 July 5/2 A crowd of opulent-looking masochists..were actually savouring this culinary surrealism and, natch, paying through the nose for it. **1971** A. DIMENT *Think Inc.* ii. 20 They blamed you, natch. **1973** *Times* 29 May 8/5, I went down to Bath to celebrate (along with the coronation of King Edgar, natch) the re-opening of the Assembly Rooms.

natch, variant of NAUTCH.

natch-bone. *rare.* [f. *natch*, var. of NACHE.] = AITCH-BONE.

1613 MARKHAM *Eng. Husbandman* II. II. vii. (1635) 81 His natch-bones which are on both sides the seting on of his taile. **1822** KITCHINER *Cook's Oracle* 151 We have also heard it called Natch-Bone. **1855** in OGILVIE *Suppl.*

Natchez (ˈnætʃɛz, ˈnɑːtʃiː). Also **Nachee**, **Naˈhtchi.** [Native name.] A North American Indian people of Mississippi; a member of this people; also, their language. Also *attrib.* or as *adj.*

1775 J. ADAIR *Hist. Amer. Indians* 86 In the year 1747, a Nachee warrior told me, that while one of their prophets was using his divine invocation for rain..he was killed with thunder on the spot. **1845** *Cherokee Advocate* (Tahlequah, Okla.) 24 Apr. 4/3 The tradition has been widely recorded, that the dominion of the Natchez once extended even to the Wabash. **1848** *Trans. Amer. Ethnol. Soc.* II. i. 77 (*table*) *Families*... Natchez. **1850** R. G. LATHAM *Nat. Hist. Varieties Man* 340 Disinterred skulls from the Natchez area. ..Such is a brief notice of the customs of the Natchez. **1890** J. G. FRAZER *Golden Bough* II. 382 The chief solemnity of the Natchez, an Indian tribe on the Lower Mississippi, was the Harvest Festival or the Festival of New Fire. **1891** *7th Ann. Rep. Bureau Amer. Ethnol. 1885–86* 96 The Shetimasha, the language of which is known from a vocabulary to be totally distinct..from the Na'htchi. *Ibid.* 97 The missionary..affirmed the affinity of the Taensa language to that of the Na'htchi... The Taensa language is considered to be a branch of the Na'htchi. **1949** M. MEAD *Male & Female* 396 This was done..by certain women in Natchez Indian society. **1959** E. TUNIS *Indians* 82/2 The Natchez were Muskhogeans who lived on the Mississippi River. **1965** *Canad. Jrnl. Ling.* Spring 99 An 'Eastern Group' comprising Siouan-Yuchi and Natchez-Muskogian. *Ibid.* 145 My Natchez informant..told about the great removal.

nate(ly, obs. forms of NAIT(LY.

† **ˈnated**, *a. Obs. rare*[−1]. (See quots.)

1628 FELTHAM *Resolves* II. xii. 31 How like a nated Sop, spunged, even to the cracking of a skinne? **1656** BLOUNT *Glossogr.* (citing Feltham), *Nated*, born, bred, brought forth, framed of nature.

† **naterelle**, variant of HATTREL *Obs.*

c **1440** *Promp. Parv.* 351/2 Naterelle, *idem quod* nape.

nates (ˈneɪtiːz), *sb. pl. Anat.* and *Med.* [a. L. *natēs*, pl. of *natis* rump, buttock.]

1. The buttocks, haunches.

1706 in PHILLIPS (ed. Kersey). **1754–64** SMELLIE *Midwifery* III. 101, I had several cases in which the nates presented. **1804** ABERNETHY *Surg. Obs.* 29 An adipose tumour growing beneath the skin of the nates. **1876** GROSS *Dis. Bladder*, etc. 261 A piece of oil-cloth, placed under the nates, will more effectually secure this object.

2. The anterior and larger pair of the optic lobes (*corpora quadrigemina*) of the brain.

1681 tr. *Willis' Rem. Med. Wks.* Vocab., *Nates*, two prominences in the brain, so called because in the form of buttocks. **1713** DERHAM *Phys.-Theol.* VI. ii. 361 The different magnitude of the Nates, and some other Parts of the Brain, in Beasts. **1756** *Gentl. Mag.* XXVI. 517/1 The nates too were very large and broad, and near two inches in length. **1840** G. V. ELLIS *Anat.* 47 The anterior pair,—the nates, larger than the posterior. **1899** *Allbutt's Syst. Med.* VII. 345 The anterior tubercles or nates are connected with the optic tracts.

3. The umbones of a bivalve shell (*Cent. Dict.*).

†**nath**, has not: see NE and HAVE *v.* A. 9. *Obs.*

a **1300** *Signs bef. Judgm.* 102 in *E.E.P.* (1862) 10 þe þing þat bodi no flesse naþ non. *a* **1310** in Wright *Lyric P.* xii. 42 Why, nath nout uch mon his? *c* **1330** *Arth. & Merl.* 9214 (Kölbing), He naþ non heued, þat nil it defende. **1362** LANGL. *P. Pl.* A. VI. 42 He with-halt non hyne his huire that he hit nath at euen. **1422** tr. *Secreta Secret., Priv. Priv.* 158 Of ydylnesse ne of folye he nath not to do.

nathe (neɪð). *Obs.* exc. *dial.* Also 6–7, 9 nath (næθ). [var. of NAVE (and *naff*): cf. the similar variation between RATHE *sb.*[2] and RAVE *sb.*[2]] The nave of a wheel.

1382 WYCLIF *Ecclus.* xxxiii. 5 The entrailes of a fool as the whel of a carre, and as a turnende ful axtre [*MS. C* nathe] the thenkingus of hym. *c* **1449** *Pol. Poems* (Rolls) II. 222 The Carte nathe is spokeles, For the counseille that he gaffe. **1523** FITZHERB. *Husb.* §5 The wheles..be made of nathes, spokes, fellyes, and dowles. **1649** BLITHE *Eng. Improv. Impr.* (1652) 167 Nathes or Hubs. *Ibid.* 200 Six spokes..fastned into a little short Hub or Nath. **1655** *Phillis of Scyros* (N.), The restlesse spokes, and whirling nathes, Of my eternal chariot. **1778** *Eng. Gazetteer* (ed. 2) s.v. *Field*, There were 80 pair of nathes for wheels cut out of it first. **1796** W. MARSHALL *Midl. Counties* Gloss. **1880–** in dial. glossaries (Northumb., Lanc., Sheffield, Staff., etc.).

natheless, nathless (ˈneɪθlɪs, ˈnæθlɪs), *adv.* (and *prep.*) Now only *arch.* Forms: α. 1 **na þe læs, naðe læs,** 3 **naðelas,** 4–5 **naþeles,** (4 -lese), 4–6 **natheles,** (4 -lees), 6– **natheless,** (6 -lesse, also 6 naithe-, naythelesse, 7 nay-the-less). β. 4–7 **nathles,** (4 **naþles**), 6–7 **nathlesse,** (6 naith-), 7 **nathless.** [f. OE. *ná* NA *adv.*[1] + *þe* (= *þý*) THE + *læs* LESS *adv.* Cf. NETHELESS and NOTHELESS.] Nevertheless, notwithstanding.

α. *c* **900** in Bouterwek *Screadunga* (1858) 22 þa na þe læs beseah Lothes wif underbæc. *a* **1122** *O.E. Chron.* (Laud MS.) an. 1011 Naðe læs for eallum þisum griðe..hi ferdon æghwider folc mælum. *c* **1200** *Vices & Virtues* 27 Ac naðelas ic wille, a godes half, ðat tu bie ȝewarned. *c* **1290** *Beket* 414 in *S. Eng. Leg.* I. 118 Ake naþeles is heorte bar euere to Thomas þer. ? *a* **1366** CHAUCER *Rom. Rose* 403 But natheles I trowe that she Was faire sumtyme, and fresh to se. *c* **1440** *Gesta Rom.* xlviii. 208 (Harl. MS.), Naþeles hit shall be don as thow wolt have hit. **1533** MORE *Apol.* 131 This Calanius beynge a senator, and natheles lenyng all vnto the people. **1596** SPENSER *Hymn Beauty* 159 Nathelesse the soule is faire and beauteous still. **1622** WITHER *Philarete* M 4 Yet I, poore I; must perish nay-the-lesse. **1748** RICHARDSON *Clarissa* (1768) II. 348 But she comes on very well nathelesse. **1816** SCOTT *Old Mort.* Introd., If it be..pretended that my information..is, natheless, incompetent to the task. **1867** MORRIS *Jason* IX. 228 Somewhat they doubted, natheless forth they passed.

β. *c* **1400** *Apol. Loll.* 4 þowe he be his seruaunt of dette & oblisching, naþles he is not his seruaunt in filling of werk. **1600** HOLLAND *Livy* XXIV. xix. 521 The enterprise, being a service of small consequence, and nath'lesse very dangerous. **1667** MILTON *P.L.* I. 299 The torrid Clime Smote on him sore..; Nathless he so endur'd. **1748** THOMSON *Cast. Indol.* II. xli, Nathless with feigned respect he bade give back The rabble rout. **1790** COLERIDGE *Devonshire Roads*, Nathless Revenge and Ire the Poet goad. **1814** SCOTT *Wav.* xxx, 'Indubitably', answered Mr. Cruickshanks;..'Nathless, if your honour—'. **1868** MORRIS *Earthly Par.* (1870) I. II. 554 Nathless by some few fathers old These tales about the place were told.

b. *prep.* In spite of, notwithstanding. *rare.*

1567 DRANT *Horace, Ep.* Ded., Wheras, nathles the wyt of the one and the port of the other, all theyre wyde fames hadd long ere this time bene drenched in the dust. **1802** MRS. RADCLIFFE *Gaston de Blondeville* Posth. Wks. 1826 III. 39 Yet could he not endure to behold him, nathless the expectations of most in the court. **1882** O'DONOVAN *Merv Oasis* I. 327 Nathless the dread which I had of these creatures, I was obliged to make a halt.

†**nathemo(re,** *adv. Obs.* Forms: α. 2 **naþema, naðemo,** 3 **na þe ma,** 4 **naþemo.** β. 2 **naðemore,** 6 **nathemore.** [f. as prec. + MO or MORE.] Never the more.

α. *c* **1127** *O.E. Chron.* (Laud MS.) an. 1127 Hit ofþuhte naþema ealle Frencisc & Englisc. *c* **1200** *Trin. Coll. Hom.* 83 þis wiðerfulle mannisshe..seð mine wunderliche deden and naðemo me ne leueð. *c* **1205** LAY. 4627 Nu we nuten na þe ma þat we ne speken wit ure ifæn. **1297** R. GLOUC. *Chron.* (Rolls) 5154 Ac souþsex ne laste noȝt longe, ne est sex naþemo. **1340** *Ayenb.* 41 Of þise zennes ne byeþ naȝt kuytte ..þo naþemo þet benimeþ oþer of hyaldeþ mid wrong. *a* **1400** *Song of Joy* (MS. Laud 622) 41 Ne aungel nys naþemo bot his messagere.

β. *c* **1200** *Trin. Coll. Hom.* 79 þe man..[that] ne wile seche after wreche & naðemore haten him þe him agilteð. **1590** SPENSER *F.Q.* I. viii. 13 But nathemore would that corageous swayne To her yeeld passage. **1596** —— *Hymn Beauty* 158 Yet nathemore is that faire beauties blame.

†**nather,** *conj. Obs.* [OE. *náðer, náðor*, var. of *nauðer, nawðer*: see NAUTHER.] Neither.

c **893** K. ÆLFRED *Oros.* III. i, Hie naþer næfdon siþþan ne heora namon ne heora anwealde. *c* **1000** ÆLFRIC in Assmann *Ags. Hom.* (1889) 70 Næron hi..naðor ne godes scep ne godes bearn þa ȝyt. *a* **1122** *O.E. Chron.* (Laud MS.) an. 1110 Naþer ne leoht..ne nan þing mid ealle of him wæs ȝesæwen. *c* **1200** *Moral Ode* 325 (Trin. Coll. MS.), Ne muȝe we werien naðer ne wið þurst ne wið hunger. *a* **1300** *Cursor M.* 11679 In þis wildernes es [water] nan, Naþer for vs ne for vr fee.

nather, -ir, obs. (chiefly *Sc.*) varr. of NEITHER.

nathing, obs. Sc. form of NOTHING.

nathir, obs. Sc. form of NETHER.

naþur-quar: see NOTHER-WHERE.

‖**natica** (ˈnætɪkə). *Zool.* [mod.L., perh. from med.L. *natica* buttock, f. L. *natis*: see NATES.] A genus of carnivorous sea-snails; a snail belonging to this genus.

1840 *Cuvier's Anim. Kingd.* 360 A broad notch or sinus.. distinguishes it from Natica and Nerita. **1851** WOODWARD *Mollusca* I. 47 The red spots on the naticas and nerites are commonly preserved in tertiary and oolitic fossils. **1874** WOOD *Nat. Hist.* 637 Our first example of this family is the Natica.

ˈ**naticide.** *rare*[−1]. [f. L. *nāt-us* or *nāt-a* child + -CIDE I.] One who kills his or her child.

1855 *Fraser's Mag.* LI. 255 The symptoms..indicating 'head disease' in the Esher adulteress and naticide.

naticoid (ˈnætɪkɔɪd), *a. Zool.* [f. NATICA + -OID.] Resembling (that of) Natica.

1851 WOODWARD *Mollusca* I. 135 Shell trochiform or naticoid. *Ibid.* 138 Shell naticoid, often eroded.

natif(e, -iff, obs. forms of NATIVE *sb.* and *a.*

natiform (ˈneɪtɪfɔːm), *a.* [f. L. *nat-is* (see NATES) + -(I)FORM.] Resembling or having the form of buttocks.

1681 tr. *Willis' Rem. Med. Wks.* Vocab., *Natiform*, in the form of a buttock. **1839–47** *Todd's Cycl. Anat.* III. 384/1 The natiform protuberances are unusually large. **1898** DAWSON WILLIAMS *Med. Dis. Inf.* 262 The skull assumes a peculiar and characteristic shape, to which the term natiform has been applied.

nation (ˈneɪʃən), *sb.*[1] Forms: 4 **naciun(e, -cioun,** 4–6 **nacion,** (4 -one), **-cyon,** (5 -one), 6 **natyon,** *Sc.* **natioun, naceoun,** 4– **nation.** [a. F. *nation*, †*nacion*, etc., ad. L. *natiōn-em* breed, stock, race, nation, f. *nāt-*, ppl. stem of *nascī* to be born. Cf. Sp. *nacion*, It. *nazione*.]

I. 1. a. An extensive aggregate of persons, so closely associated with each other by common descent, language, or history, as to form a distinct race or people, usually organized as a separate political state and occupying a definite territory.

In early examples the racial idea is usually stronger than the political; in recent use the notion of political unity and independence is more prominent.

a **1300** *Cursor M.* 241 Of Ingland the nacion Es Inglis man þar in commun. *Ibid.* 8225 All naciun and lede aght vr lauerd for to drede. *c* **1380** WYCLIF *Sel. Wks.* III. 393 þo gospels of Crist written in Englische, to moost lernyng of our nacioun. *c* **1386** CHAUCER *Man of Law's T.* 183 Allas! un-to the Barbre nacioun I moste anon. *c* **1460** FORTESCUE *Abs. & Lim. Mon.* iii. (1885) 115 The said kynge is compellid to make his armeys..of straungers, as Scottes, Spaynardes,..and of oþer nacions. **1494** FABYAN *Chron.* clxxxviii. 190 With a great hoost of Danys, and other straunge nacyons. **1538** STARKEY *England* I. iv. 106 To defend thys custume long vsyd in our reame and natyon. **1596** SHAKS. *Merch. V.* I. ii. 49 He hates our sacred Nation. **1625** N. CARPENTER *Geog. Del.* II. iii. (1635) 53 Wee shall obserue..a multitude of miserable and wretched nations. **1682** G. VERNON *Life Heylin* 74 In almost all Nations Christened, the sam Law has continued to this very time. **1753** FOOTE *Eng. in Paris* Epil., Wks. 1799 I. 31 Not a Buck, nor a Blood, through the whole English nation, But his roughness she'll soften. **1793** BURKE *Corr.* (1844) IV. 159 Every thing we have done is in the style of hostility to France, as a nation. **1852** TENNYSON *Ode Wellington* 4 Let us bury the Great Duke To the noise of the mourning of a mighty nation. **1872** FREEMAN *Gen. Sk. Europ. Hist.* xvii. §1 (1874) 349 In Switzerland four languages are spoken; yet the Swiss certainly make one nation. **1878** SEELEY *Stein* II. 20 When the state fell to pieces, the nation held together.

Comb. **1817–8** COBBETT *Resid. U.S.* (1822) 333 What should they run rambling about a nation-making for? **1878** GLADSTONE *Prim. Homer* vi. 77 His..was..a nation-making office. **1888** W. D. LIGHTHALL *Yng. Seigneur* 10 The people are the true nation-makers.

transf. **1658** SIR T. BROWNE *Hydriot.* v. 71 What time the persons of these Ossuaries entred the famous Nations of the dead. **1708** POPE *Ode St. Cecilia* 52 Love, strong as Death, the Poet led To the pale nations of the dead. **1725** —— *Odyss.* x. 627 To all the phantom nations of the dead.

b. A number of persons belonging to a particular nation; representatives of any nation.

1572 BOSSEWELL *Armorie* II. 23 Whiche heauenly signe so seene on bothe Nations, they of the Frenche [etc.]. **1725** DE FOE *Voy. round World* (1840) 190 It being express in his orders not to permit any nation..to come on shore and stay there. **1818** SHELLEY *Eugan. Hills* 261 Once remotest nations came To adore that sacred flame.

c. In the mediæval universities, a body of students belonging to a particular district, country, or group of countries, who formed a more or less independent community; still retained in the universities of Glasgow and Aberdeen, in connexion with the election of the Rector.

See Rashdall *Univ. Mid. Ages* (1895) I. 157, II. 367, etc. [*c* **1411** *St. Andrews Univ. Statute* (MS.), Item..statutum fuit ut omnino essent quatuor nationes. **1453** in *Munim. Univ. Glasg.* (Maitland) I. 6 Rectores.., decanos, procuratores nacionum, regentes, magistros et scolares. **1482** *Statutes* ibid. II. 6 Divisio Suppositorum per quatuor Naciones. **1593** in *Fasti Acad. Aberd.* (1889) I. 57 [Rector] eligatur per omnes Academiæ Suppositos divisos in quatuor Nationes.]

1664 in *Fasti Acad. Aberd.* (1898) II. 11 The colledge being fullie conveened and divided in four nationes..did.. nominat..procurators for electing of ane Rector. **1723** *Ibid.* 14 [The Principal, etc.] did..cause the whole students of the College divide themselves into the four Nations of Mar, Buchan, Murray, and Angus. **1735** *St. Andrews Univ. Records* (MS.), The Albane Nation met on Munday the 24th March. **1806** FORSYTH *Beauties Scotl.* IV. 92 [In St. Andrews] masters and students are divided, according to the place of their birth, into four nations. **1859** *Scottish Univ. Comm., Glasgow* Ord. 3 *Parl. Papers* (1863) XVI. 386 That in the Election of Rector.., the matriculated students shall vote, as at present, in four nations.

†**d.** A country, kingdom. *Obs. rare.*

1663 MARVELL *Corr.* Wks. (Grosart) II. 88 Courts of Merchants to be erected in some few of the considerablest ports of the nation. **1668** WALTON *Angler* I. xvii. (ed. 2) 226 There be divers kinds of Cadis or Case-worms, that are to be found in this Nation in several distinct Counties.

2. ***the nations.*** **a.** In and after Biblical use: The heathen nations, the Gentiles.

a **1340** HAMPOLE *Psalter* xvii. 53 þarfore i sall shrife til þe in nacyons lord. **1382** WYCLIF *Deut.* iv. 27 ȝe shulen dwelle fewe in the nacioums. **1398** TREVISA *Barth. De P.R.* III. v, Isider sayeþ þat anima, þe soule, haþ þe name by settynge of nationis. **1593** G. HARVEY *Pierce's Super.* 81 S. Paule..was ..omnisufficiently furnished to be a Doctour of the Nations. **1611** BIBLE *Deut.* iv. 27 And the Lord shall scatter you among the nations. **1656** MANASSEH BEN ISRAEL *Vind. Jud.* iii. §12 The holy Prophets made Prayers and Supplications for all Men, as well for the Nations as the Israelites.

b. The peoples of the earth; the population of the earth collectively.

1667 MILTON *P.L.* I. 598 As when the Sun..In dim Eclips disastrous twilight sheds On half the Nations. **1742** POPE *Dunc.* IV. 626 O sing, and hush the Nations with thy Song! **1796** H. HUNTER tr. *St.-Pierre's Stud. Nat.* (1799) III. 397 Egypt has attained a degree of power..which renders her the centre of the Nations. **1820** SHELLEY *Liberty* x, The trance In which, as in a tomb, the nations lay. **1842** TENNYSON *Locksley Hall* 124 There rain'd a ghastly dew From the nations' airy navies grappling in the central blue.

c. ***law of nations***: see LAW *sb.*[1] 4 c.

†**3.** Without article: Nationality. In phr. ***of English,*** etc. ***nation;*** ***of*** or ***by nation.*** *Obs.*

1375 BARBOUR *Bruce* I. 193 Schyrreffys and bailȝheys.. He maid off Inglis nation. *c* **1375** *Sc. Leg. Saints* xiv. (*Luke*) 2 Sancte lucas as of nacion syrus [= Syrian] was. **1500–20** DUNBAR *Poems* viii. 29 And namelie we of Scottis natioun,.. Forȝett we nevir into our orisoun To pray for him. **1579** FENTON *Guicciard.* v. (1618) 186 Brandano Constable of the Florentines, of nation a Lucquoys. **1641** EARL MONM. tr. *Biondi's Civil Wars* IV. 53 Though he were a Fleming by Nation, yet was hee not separated from the interest of France.

4. a. ***the nation***, the whole people of a country, freq. in contrast to some smaller or narrower body within it.

1602 SHAKS *Ham.* II. ii. 370 The Nation holds it no sinne, to tarre them to Controuersie. **1661** DRYDEN *On Coronation* 35 Loud shouts the nation's happiness proclaim. **1709** POPE *Ess. Crit.* 546 Then unbelieving priests reform'd the nation. **1796** H. HUNTER tr. *St.-Pierre's Stud. Nat.* (1799) III. 509 Wishes for the Nation. *c* **1812** JANE AUSTEN *Mansf. Park* (1851) 60 You are speaking of London, I am speaking of the nation at large. **1858** BRIGHT *Sp. B'ham* in *Times* 30 Oct. 9/5 The nation in every country dwells in the cottage. **1892** GLADSTONE in *Daily News* 12 July 3/7 Now..the nation votes and the nation rules.

b. ***two nations***: phr. used of two groups within a given nation divided from each other by marked social inequality; hence ***one nation***, a nation which is not divided by social inequalities.

1845 DISRAELI (*title*) Sybil, or The two nations. *Ibid.* I. II. v. 149 Two nations; between whom there is no intercourse and no sympathy; who are..ignorant of each other's habits, thoughts, and feelings..; who are formed by different breeding, are fed by different food,..and are not governed by the same laws... The Rich and the Poor. **1892** *Youth's Compan.* 8 Sept. 446/1 (*heading*) Salute to the Flag... I pledge allegiance to my Flag and the Republic for which it stands: one Nation indivisible, with Liberty and Justice for all. **1971** *Guardian* 19 Nov. 12/2 There are two nations now within schools... Social inequality is growing. **1973** *Times* 15 Oct. 17/6 The Disraelian doctrine of 'One Nation' has.. been in the past little more than an ideal or a pretence. **1974** *Times* 16 Oct. 14/6 God bless the squire and his relations; full speed astern to the Two Nations.

II. 5. †**a.** A family, kindred. *Obs. rare.*

c **1386** CHAUCER *Wife's T.* 212 Allas! that any of my nacioun Sholde ever so foule disparaged be! **1508** KENNEDIE *Flyting w. Dunbar* 411 Homage to Edward Langschankis maid thy kyn, In Dunbar thai ressauit him, the false nacione.

†**b.** The native population *of* a town or city.

1523 LD. BERNERS *Froiss.* I. ccxx. 284 Mo than sixscore, all yong men of the nacyon of yᵉ towne. *Ibid.* ccliv. 377 They of the nacion of the towne were taken to mercy.

†**c.** An Irish clan. *Obs.*

1584 in O'Flaherty *West Connaught* (1846) 390 He is, by her Majesties apointment, capten and chief both of his countrey and nacion.

d. A North American Indian people.

1650 *Archives of Maryland* (1883) I. 260 The Ports adjoyning are very much pestered with great Concourse of Indians of several nations. **1709** J. Lawson *New Voy. Carolina* 199 Two Nations of Indians here in Carolina were at war together. **1722** D. Coxe *Descr. Carolana* iv. 49 Near the Bottom of the Bay..is the fair River of the Miamihas (so call'd because upon it lives Part of a Nation bearing the same Name). **1740** in *South Carolina Hist. Soc. Coll.* (1887) IV. 83, I desire also that you will send me..the Indian presents, with power to distribute them, for much Depends on the Nations. **1763** in C. Gist's *Jrnls.* (1893) 196 Negocieatory maters with a number of Indian nations. **1775** in *Collect. Mass. Hist. Soc.* 3rd Ser. V. 75 The sachems and warriors of the Six Nations. **1836** W. Irving *Astoria* III. 24 There were white men residing with some of their nation. **1867** Parkman *Jesuits N. Amer.* xxxii. (1879) 426 That portion [of the Hurons] called the Tobacco Nation.

†**6. a.** A particular class, kind, or race of persons. Also ***man's nation***, human kind. *Obs.*

1382 Wyclif *Phil.* ii. 15 In the myddel of a schrewid nacioun and weyward. **1390** Gower *Conf.* II. 50 Among the gentil nacion Love is an occupacion. *Ibid.* I. 55 Out of mannes nacion Fro kynde thei be so miswent, That to the liknesse of Serpent Thei were bore. **1535** Coverdale 1 *Pet.* ii. 9 But ye are..that kyngly presthode, that holy nacion. *a* **1568** Ascham *Scholem.* II. (Arb.) 137 The worst of all, as Questionistes, and all the barbarous nation of scholemen. **1605** B. Jonson *Sejanus* I. ii, You are a subtile nation, you physicians! **1670–98** Lassels *Voy. Italy* I. 14 Civil education..makes even schoolboyes (an insolent Nation any where else) most respectfull to one another. *a* **1734** North *Exam.* Pref. (1740) 11 These are what the Compilers, a most useful Nation, hunt after.

†**b.** So of animals. *Obs.*

1590 Spenser *F. Q.* II. xii. 36 All the nation of unfortunate And fatall birds about them flocked were. **1594** —— *Astrophel* 98 There his welwoven toyles..He laid the brutish nation to enwrap. **1697** Dryden *Virg. Georg.* III. 806 The scaly Nations of the Sea profound. **1733** Pope *Ess. Man* III. 99 The nations of the field and wood. **1781** Cowper *Hope* 353 The screaming nations, hovering in mid air.

†**7.** *Astrol.* Nativity; nature. *Obs. rare*$^{-1}$.

1375 Barbour *Bruce* IV. 719 Gif thai men, that will study In the craft of astrology, Knaw all mennis nacioune.

8. A great number, a host *of* persons or things.

1762 Sterne *Tr. Shandy* V. xxi, The French had..a nation of hedges and copses..to cover them. **1765** *Ibid.* VII. xxi, What a nation of herbs he had procured.

9. *attrib.* and *Comb.* (see also sense 1 a *ad fin.*), as **nation-building**, the creation of a new nation, *spec.* a newly independent nation; hence **nation-builder**; **nation-state**, a sovereign state the members of which are also united by those ties such as language, common descent, etc., which constitute a nation; **nation-wide** *a.*, as wide as a nation; extending over, reaching, or affecting the whole nation; also as *adv.*

1907 *Collier's* 12 Jan. 7/2 Next week's issue will be our annual Automobile Number, and, in addition to general news and illustrations concerning the modern vehicle, it will give some lucid arguments for the automobile as a nation-builder. **1920** N. M. Butler *Is Amer. Worth Saving?* xvi. 285 (*heading*) Alexander Hamilton, nation-builder. **1933** P. S. Cleary (*title*) Australia's debt to Irish nation-builders. **1967** *Freedomways* VII. 167 These are the new lessons in old African history that are giving many present-day African nation builders a new consciousness of past achievements. **1913** N. M. Butler in *Educational Rev.* (N.Y.) Apr. 405 These six men are..the moving forces of the constructive nation-building of the American people. *Ibid.* 406 The most prominent in the galaxy of our nation-building heroes. **1928** *Daily Tel.* 4 Sept. 10/4 For such an enterprise of nation-building peace..is the essential condition. **1931** *Economist* 7 Mar. 486/1 One of the urgent needs of India is that the Provinces should have funds available for so-called 'nation building' services. **1971** *Sunday Nation* (Nairobi) 11 Apr. 3/2 The Ambassador advised the students to study hard and return home after graduating to play their part in nation-building. **1973** *Express* (Trinidad & Tobago) 7 Apr. 12/4 Unless we are prepared to..rid ourselves of our petty differences and general smallmindedness, we are not ready for nation building. **1918** J. A. R. Marriott *European Commonwealth* ii. 18 The ultimate genesis of the world conflict of to-day is sought..in..the existing European polity..based upon the recognition of the rights of a large number of Nation-States, entirely independent and nominally coequal. **1935** Huxley & Haddon *We Europeans* i. 11 The nation-state is a modern conception and product, the result of certain peculiar social and economic circumstances. *Ibid.* vi. 187 With the sixteenth century, nation-states of the modern type began to appear. **1945** H. Kohn *Idea of Nationalism* i. 19 Nationalism demands the nation-state; the creation of the nation-state strengthens nationalism. **1950** Theimer & Campbell *Encycl. World Politics* 301/2 Absolutism paved the way for the modern nation-state marked by sovereignty and the repudiation of any superior authority. **1959** *Encounter* July 75/1 Egypt is turning into a modern nation-state. **1971** *Black Scholar* June 29/1 As the cultural revolution and students become more politically sophisticated, the question of an independent black nation-state will become a popular demand. **1973** *Listener* 10 May 616/1 The nation state requires the idea of an entity along with other entities that are equal. **1915** *Munsey's Mag.* May 708/2 The nation-wide primary is coming. **1925** E. S. Jones *Christ of Indian Road* iii. 72 A year ago began a struggle in South India that has had nation-wide consequences. **1928** *Daily Express* 27 Apr. 1 In deciding to publish this most moving..narrative the 'Daily Express' embarks on a venture which will command nation-wide attention. **1958** *Economist* 1 Nov. 413/1 The one real issue of nation-wide importance which this campaign has produced concerns the trade unions. **1960** *Farmer & Stockbreeder* 15 Mar. 72/1 Perhaps F.M.C. could have done more if it hadn't started off on so wide a scale —nation-wide in fact. **1972** *Daily Tel.* 21 Jan. 1/7 Mr. Ian Smith, the Rhodesian Prime Minister, is to make a nationwide broadcast today. **1975** *Lamp* (Exxon Corporation) Winter 3/2 Now being telecast nationwide..each of these television messages pays tribute to an outstanding man or woman.

nation (ˈneɪʃən), *adv.*, *a.*, and *sb.*[2] *dial.* and *U.S.* Also **'nation, naation.** [A euphemistic abbreviation of DAMNATION. Cf. *tarnation.*]

A. *adv.* Very, extremely, etc.

1771 *Trial of Atticus* 26 He is a nation bawdy creature to talk. **1785** Grose *Dict. Vulgar T.*, *Nation*,..a vulgar term used in Kent, Sussex, and the adjacent countries, for very..; a nation long way. **1799** R. Warner *Walk. West. Counties* (1800) 105 My guide..had informed me I was to expect 'a nation strange road'. **1824** in *Spirit Pub. Jrnls.* (1825) 478 They takes 'nation good care to be set down at the turnpike. **1825** Brockett *N.C. Gloss.* [and in many later dial. glossaries]. **1859** Dickens *T. Two Cities* I. ii, 'I hope there ain't, but I can't make so nation sure of that', said the guard. **1873** J. Spilling *Molly Miggs*, etc. (1903) 69, I can't tell no one how naation riled I felt. **1884** 'Mark Twain' *Huck. Finn* xix. 186 Looky here, Bilgewater,..I'm nation sorry for you, but you ain't the only person that's had troubles like that.

B. *adj.* Very large, very great, etc.

1765 in Bartlett *Dict. Amer.* (1877) (ed. 4) 419, I believe, my friend, you're very right, They'll get a nation profit by it. **1828** *Craven Gloss.* s.v., There wor a nation seet o folk at kirk. **1836** Haliburton *Clockm.* (1862) 303 Niagara fall; what a nation sight of machinery that would carry. **1877** Banks *Glory* vii, I might not have been in such a nation hurry to jump from my cart. **1962** A. Jobson *Window in Suffolk* vi. 100 What a nation fule he wur tew be shure.

C. *sb.* In imprecations. Also *Comb.*

1775 *Yankee Doodle* in O. E. Winslow *Amer. Broadside Verse* (1930) 141/1 A swamping gun..makes a noise like father's gun, Only a nation louder. **1842** Pulman *Rustic Sk.* 31 Your [horse] is naation seyzid tall. **1880** *News & Press* (Cimarron, New Mexico) 23 Dec. 1/7 'Well, I've got the g.b.' 'The geebee, Thomas! What in the nation is that?' 'I've got the grand bounce.' **1881** T. Hardy *Laodicean* VI. iv, O nation!..if I were a man. **1884** 'Mark Twain' *Huck. Finn* xiii. 113 Why, how in the nation did they ever git into such a scrape? **1886** Elworthy *W. Som. Word-bk.* s.v. *Nation-seize*, Nation-seize thee! where's a bin bidin about to? **1918** J. C. Lincoln *Shavings* 213 Now how in the nation did I get it Wood?

national (ˈnæʃənəl), *a.* and *sb.* [a. F. *national* (16th c.), f. *nation* NATION *sb.*[1] + *-al* -AL[1]. Cf. It. *nazionale*, Sp. *nacional.*]

A. *adj.* **1. a.** Of or belonging to a (*or* the) nation; affecting, or shared by, the nation as a whole.

1597 Howson *Serm.* 24 Dec. 24 The Ciuill and Nationall lawes of anie Countrey. **1643** Caryl *Sacr. Cov.* 26 That which promotes personall holinesse, must needs promote Nationall holinesse. **1678** Marvell *Growth Popery* 39 This was a National Business if ever any were. **1730–1** Bolingbroke *Let. to Swift* Jan., National corruption must be purged by national calamities. **1743** Bolingbroke *Remarks Hist. Eng.* (1780) ii. 28 A Spirit of Liberty will be always and wholly concern'd about national Interests. **1790** Burke *Fr. Rev.* (1898) 31 The spirit of caution which predominated in the national councils. **1835** Thirlwall *Greece* vii. I. 253 The national festival of the *Pambœotia* was celebrated with games. **1856** Froude *Hist. Eng.* I. ii. 161 Their angry jealousy refused to tolerate longer a national dishonour. **1871** Freeman *Norm. Conq.* (1876) IV. xvii. 72 In the end national unity and national freedom appeared again in more perfect shapes. **1914** G. B. Shaw *Dark Lady of Sonnets* 132 The very stupid people who cannot see that a National Theatre is worth having for the sake of the National Soul. **1927** 'A. Hope' *Memories & Notes* xiv. 239, I went to Boston in company with Peter Dunne, whose 'Mr. Dooley' had already made him what the papers in the States call a 'national figure'. **1931** *Hansard Commons* 28 July 2217, I should take no exception to a small sum towards the preservation of such things as Hadrian's Wall and the other national monuments. *c* **1935** E. E. Cummings *Let.* 7 Jan. (1969) 134 Here lies a national hero (Who governed by fits and by starts). **1939** *Hansard Commons* 2 Sept. 232 In the national interest, having in mind the great inroads that war must..make on the youth of our nation, we should see..that some of our youth are left to carry on in the future. **1966** Tacheron & Udall *Job of Congressman* vii. 198 And then, you see, some of your friends back home say, 'Why, he is becoming a national figure.' **1966** *Oxf. Compan. Amer. Hist.* 560/1 National monuments include buildings, statues, homesteads, battlefields, cemeteries, and sites of historic, scenic, or political significance. **1969** Plano & Olton *Internat. Relations Dict.* vi. 128 When a state bases its foreign policy solely on the bedrock of national interest with little or no concern for universal moral principles, it can be described as pursuing a realistic in contradistinction to an idealistic policy. **1973** *Times* 17 Dec. 15/3 The NUM..cannot be totally indifferent to the national interest. **1973** *N.Y. Times* 22 June 35 One of the most successful codebreaking organizations of those post-war years was the National Security Agency. **1975** *Atlantic Monthly* Jan. 32/2 The Department of Defense could give no adequate definition of 'national security'.

b. Of troops, etc.: Maintained by a nation. (See also quot. 1802.)

1802 James *Milit. Dict.*, *National troops*, are those born in our own dominions, in opposition to foreigners. **1842** Borrow *Bible in Spain* xxxvi, The bookseller..was an officer in the national cavalry. **1876** Voyle & Stevenson *Milit. Dict.* 269/1 The national defences of a country consist, besides her armies and reserves, of the navy [etc.].

c. Of or belonging to the French Government during the time of the first Republic.

1793 Nelson in Nicolas *Disp.* (1845) I. 308 We..have taken nothing but a miserable National brig of eight guns. **1837** Carlyle *Fr. Rev.* III. vi. i, Most chopfallen, blue, enters the National Agent this Limbo whither he has sent so many.

d. Designating a B.B.C. radio service which operated during the 1930s. Also *ellipt.*

1931 *Daily Express* 22 Sept. 13/3 Tonight..on the National begin..the new poetry readings. **1938** W. Goatman *By-Ways of B.B.C.* viii. 81 Control-Room engineers are responsible..for controlling three separate programmes—National, Regional, and Empire. **1956** B. Paulu *Brit. Broadcasting* vii. 145 From 1930 to the outbreak of World War II, there was the National Service, uniform throughout the country, consisting mainly of London programs of national appeal. **1965** A. Briggs *Golden Age of Wireless* 36 By 1934..there was more light entertainment on the National than on the Regional service. **1971** D. G. Bridson *Prospero & Ariel* viii. 177 Back in the thirties, there had been two nation-wide broadcast programmes, the National and the Regional.

e. In the war of 1939–45 used to designate foodstuffs made to official specifications for nation-wide distribution, as ***national flour***, ***loaf***, etc.

1940 *Hansard Commons* 25 Jan. 810/2 All butter sold by the Ministry of Food is..described as 'National Butter'. **1941** *New Statesman* 16 Apr. 157 The bakers are equally reluctant to change their habits. They shake their heads with a mournful smile at mention of the national loaf. **1941** *Lancet* 15 Nov. 605/1 When the Medical Research Council drew up its second memorandum on national flour in the spring of 1941 it offered the nation something new. **1943** *Daily Tel.* 20 Dec. 3 National Milk-Cocoa—the new food drink evolved by the Ministry's scientific advisers—is already available to all factories and industrial undertakings in limited quantities. **1945** *ABC of Cookery* (Ministry of Food) vi. 20 National Household Milk is dried skim milk. *Ibid.* xix. 69 The best foods for iron are liver, eggs,..national or wholemeal bread and oatmeal. **1956** W. Thompson *Time off my Life* xix. 146, I couldn't stand the stuff they called 'national loaf' in the war.

2. a. Peculiar to the people of a particular country, characteristic or distinctive of a nation. †Also const. *unto*.

1625 Carpenter *Geog. Del.* II. xiv. (1635) 219 Who obserues not in all Nations certaine naturall or nationall vertues or vices. **1646** Sir T. Browne *Pseud. Ep.* 201 That an unsavoury odour is gentilitious or national unto the Jews. **1650** Bulwer *Anthropomet.* 81 In Perviana also, a great Nose is in request and National. **1796** H. Hunter tr. *St.-Pierre's Stud. Nat.* (1799) III. 236 They abjured the national prejudices which had rendered them..the enemies of other men. **1822** B. W. Procter *Diego de Montilla* xlv. 7 The dances I have named are national. **1858** Max Müller *Chips* (1880) III. i. 38 Truly national poetry exists only where there is a truly national life.

b. spec. ***national football*** (*Austral.*) = *Australian rules*; ***national game*** (see quots.: in quots. 1930 and 1963 the game is two-up.)

1828 *Oscotian* (ed. 2) I. 35 The day or two previous..gave employment for our youth, in adjusting the arrangements, necessary for the noble and national game, of Cricket. **1869** W. G. Beers (*title*) Lacrosse: the national game of Canada. **19..** *Primer Austral. Football* (Austral. National Football Council) 1 Youngsters who are keen to learn and understand the fundamentals of their National Football. **1912** Hilton & Smith *Royal & Anc. Game of Golf* 34 The Scots themselves have yielded to the softening influences of the South..and the change is reflected in their national game. **1930** L. W. Lower *Here's Luck* 70 He had a small piece of wood in his hand, on which were balanced two pennies. The national game was in progress. **1958** National football [see *Australian rules*]. **1963** F. Hardy *Legends from Benson's Valley* 108 The demise of the bookmakers increased attendance at the Sunday sessions of Australia's national game.

†**3. a.** Belonging to the same nation as oneself; compatriotic. *Obs. rare*$^{-1}$.

1632 Lithgow *Trav.* I. 20 In these parts a man can finde no worser enimie than his nationall supposed friend.

†**b.** Gentile; belonging to 'the nations', as opposed to the Jews. *Obs. rare*$^{-1}$.

1662 Pagitt *Heresiogr.* (ed. 6) 180 A National Saint, or a Saint of the Gentiles.

4. a. Patriotic; strongly upholding one's own nation.

1711 *Fingall MSS.* in *10th Rep. Hist. MSS. Comm.* App. V. 159 It showes in them an ingratitude to so national a man. **1797** Mrs. A. M. Bennett *Beggar Girl* (1813) II. 61 The fine old palace, the chamber,..were..severally explained by the national major. **1810** S. Green *Reformist* I. 243 Amongst other prejudices natural to a national Scotchman, he bore an inveterate hatred to the Irish. **1871** *Daily News* 7 Sept., He is intensely national... He believes that the Scots are the finest race in the world.

b. Devoted to the interests of the nation as a whole. Also *Comb.*

1801 J. Adams *Wks.* (1854) IX. 585 Too strongly infected with the spirit of party, to give much encouragement to men who are merely national. **1889** *Spectator* 9 Nov. 625/2 This signal encouragement to the national-minded Radicals of the United Kingdom.

5. In special collocations: ***National convention***, ***council***, ***debt***, ***synod*** (see the sbs.); **national anthem**, the hymn 'God save the King'; also, the words or music sung or played on similar occasions in other countries; **National Assembly**, an assembly consisting of representatives of a nation; spec. †(*a*) = *General Assembly* (see ASSEMBLY 5 b); (*b*) a synod of the Church in a particular nation; (*c*) the first of the revolutionary assemblies of France, in session 1789–91; also applied at various later dates to the popular assembly, and now to the two houses, the Senate and the Chamber of Deputies, when in joint session; **National Assistance**, a form of welfare payment combining Unemployment Assistance and Public Assitance, begun in 1948, administered by the **National Assistance Board**, and replaced in 1966 by Supplementary Benefits; **national bank**, a bank associated with the national finances; *U.S.*, a bank whose circulating notes are secured by United States bonds deposited with the government; **national cake** (see CAKE *sb.* 7b); **national character**, personality or cultural characteristics which seem to be wide-spread enough in a particular nation or racial group for generalizations to be made concerning either the whole group or individuals belonging to it; so **national characteristic**; **national church**, (*a*) a church consisting of a nation; (*b*) a church established by law in a particular nation; **National Front**, a political group in Britain with extreme reactionary views; **National Government**, a coalition government, esp. one in which party differences are subordinated to the national interest in times of crisis; also in the sense of a government free from external domination (see quot. 1943); **national guard**, an armed force existing in France at various times between 1789 and 1871; a member of this force; also (with capitals), in the United States, a militia force which may be used by its own state, e.g. for law enforcement, or by the Federal government as part of the U.S. army; **national health**, health as it concerns the nation as a whole; **National Health Service**, the comprehensive health service provided in Great Britain, initiated in 1946 and financed by taxation; freq. *ellipt.* as ***National Health***; **National Hunt Committee**, the body which controls steeplechasing and hurdle-racing in Great Britain; freq. *ellipt.* and *attrib.* as ***National Hunt***; **national income**: see INCOME *sb.*[1] 6a; **National Insurance** = INSURANCE 4e; also *attrib.*; **National Mark**, a mark designating grade for use on British agricultural produce; also *attrib.*; **national minority**, a minority group, belonging historically to another nationality, which feels itself or is felt to be culturally or racially separate from the majority in a country; **national park** = PARK *sb.* 2b; **national product**, the monetary value of all goods and services produced in a country in one year; cf. *gross national product* (s.v. GROSS *a.* and *sb.*[4] A. 6c); **National Republicans** *U.S.*, an early name for the Whig party; **National Savings**, a method of saving through investment in British Government securities, started in the war of 1914–18 as National War Savings; also applied to similar schemes in other countries; so ***National Savings Certificate***, etc.; **national school**, (*a*) a school conducted and supported to a greater or less extent by the state; (*b*) a school provided for under a system of state-aided education, esp. one of the type set up in Ireland after 1831 under the National System of Education; **national service**, a statutory obligation to serve in the armed forces for a specified period; hence **national serviceman**, one who is performing national service; **National Socialism**, the name adopted by Adolf Hitler for his doctrines of nationalism, racial purity, anti-Communism, and the all-powerful role of the State; so **National Socialist**, a member of the National Socialist Workers' Party led by Adolf Hitler after 1920; = NAZI *sb.*; also *attrib.*, of or pertaining to this party or to the doctrines of National Socialism; **National Society**, founded in 1811 to promote the education of the poor; **national theatre** (freq. with capital initials), a theatre endowed by the State; also ellipt., *the National*; **National Trust**, a trust for the preservation of places of historic interest or natural beauty in England, Wales, and N. Ireland, founded in 1893, incorporated in 1907, and supported by endowment and private subscription. Also NATIONAL GRID.

1819 SHELLEY (*title*) A New *National Anthem. **1837** LOCKHART *Scott* (1839) I. 305 Drowning the National Anthem in howls and hootings. **1876** VOYLE & STEVENSON *Milit. Dict.* 269/1 The playing of the national anthem is only due to those personages who are entitled, under the regulations, to a royal salute. **1621** *1st & 2nd Bk. Discipl. Ch. Scot.* 89 The *Nationall Assemblies of the Countrey, called commonly the Generall Assemblies. **1647** CLARENDON *Hist. Reb.* II. §8 That National or General Assemblies should be called only by the King's Authority. **1660** R. COKE *Power & Subj.* 219 The Emperors and Kings did convoke.. Provinciall and National Assemblies and Synods. **1790** BURKE *Fr. Rev.* (1898) 47 This..would appear perfectly unaccountable, if we did not consider the composition of the National Assembly. **1839** [see ASSEMBLY 5b]. **1948** *Act 11 & 12 Geo. VI* c. 29 §2 (*title*) *National Assistance Act, 1948. *Ibid.*, The National Assistance Board (hereafter in this Act referred to as 'the Board') shall exercise their functions in such manner as shall best promote the welfare of persons affected by the exercise thereof. **1958** *New Statesman* 27 Sept. 398/3 Few people are at a worse disadvantage than the man who is fresh from prison and is also homeless. National Assistance methods..must sometimes seem designed to assist such a man back into prison in the shortest possible time. **1959** J. BRAINE *Vodi* viii. 124 There isn't any dole for him. It's bankruptcy first and then National Assistance. **1968** J. LOCK *Lady Policeman* xviii. 152 The National Assistance Board telephoned. **1969** *Listener* 12 June 834/3 The women he has studied are the very poorest, depending almost entirely on National Assistance. **1838** *Democratic Rev.* I. 52 That portion of the plan..which involved a present non-committalism on the question of a *National Bank. **1858** HOMANS *Cycl. Comm.* 131/2 The directors of the National Bank proposed to the State banks a resumption of specie payments on the 21st February, 1817. **1896** *Daily News* 27 July 7/5 Mr. Sewall..being a national banker.. while they bitterly denounce national banks. **1778** HAMILTON *Wks.* (1886) VII. 542 It is of great consequence to preserve a *national character. **1863** *Home & Foreign Rev.* III. 549 Next to those who form the national taste and fix the national character, the greatest geniuses are those who corrupt them. **1908** KIPLING *Lett. of Travel* (1920) 144 'Hustle' does not sit well on the national character. **1967** M. ARGYLE *Psychol. Interpersonal Behaviour* iv. 82 If the people from some cultural group are consistently aggressive, [etc.] .., we *can* say that their norms are different; but it may be more useful to say that their level of motivation is different, and to regard this as a feature of their 'national character'. **1960** DUIJKER & FRIJDA *National Character* i. 4 The existence of a stereotype might give rise to a *national characteristic. **1651** BAXTER *Inf. Bapt.* 31 The Jews were a *Nationall Church. **1716** M. DAVIES *Athen. Brit.* II. 335 He is Low-Church..; such a one is a poor begging Convert from Popery or Presbytery to the National Church. **1832** ARNOLD in Stanley *Life* (1844) I. vi. 274, I cannot understand what is the good of a national Church if it be not to Christianize the nation. **1633** PRYNNE *1st Pt. Histriom.* 570, 54 ancient and moderne, generall, *nationall, provinciall Councels and Synodes. **1967** *Spearhead* Nov.–Dec. 6 (*caption*) On October 7th there took place..an event which may well prove to have historic significance in British politics. This was the first Annual General Meeting of Britain's new party, The *National Front. *c* **1970** *Facts: National Front* 2/3 When the National Front comes to power it will know well how to deal with the murderer and the thug. **1973** C. MULLARD *Black Brit.* III. viii. 91 White fascist groups like the National Front are lumped together with progressive, power-demanding groups like the Black People's Alliance. **1931** J. REITH *Diary* 24 Aug. (1975) i. 106 A wire..informed me that the Labour government had resigned, that MacDonald was prime minister of a *National government. **1931** *Economist* 17 Oct. 692/1 Sir John Simon..stated that..'if the broad base National Government finds it [*sc.* a tariff] necessary, I am not going on that ground to refuse to support the National Government.' **1936** J. A. SPENDER *Gt. Brit.: Empire & Commonwealth* IV. xliii. 512 National Government [in 1915] was the logical corollary of the party-truce. **1943** *Ann. Reg. 1942* 143 With the security of India threatened, we..should bring her people into full moral support..by conceding forthwith the demands for a 'National Government', with virtual independence of British authority. **1969** T. A. NEAL *Democracy & Responsibility* xviii. 223 Strong arguments may be marshalled to explain MacDonald's formation of the National Government. *Ibid.* xix. 230 In November of the same year [*sc.* 1935], the National Government was re-elected, with a total of 428 supporters in the House of Commons. **1793** *Observer* 27 Jan. in M. Miliband *Observer of 19th Cent.* (1966) i. 4 The train moved on with a slow pace from the Temple to the Boulevards, which were planted with cannon, and beset with *National Guards, drums beating, trumpets sounding, and colours flying. **1797** *Encycl. Brit.* (ed. 3) XVI. 158/1 The citizens..enrolling themselves as a militia for general defence, under the appellation of the national guard. **1814** WELLINGTON in Gurw. *Desp.* (1838) XI. 490 Captain Pierre Penne of the French National guards, who was taken prisoner on the frontier. **1847** *Santa Fé* (New Mexico) *Republican* 18 Dec. 3/1 Some National Guards that were at San Antonio had a small fight. **1848** W. H. KELLY tr. *L. Blanc's Hist. Ten Y.* I. 182 He set out in the uniform of a national guard. **1868** *N.Y. Herald* 4 July 6/1 The first division of the National Guard will parade. **1909** *World Today* Oct. 1099 While many of the American states designate their amateur soldiery as 'National Guards', the venerable Bay State still sticks to the thoroughly Yankee caption of 'militia'. **1966** *Oxf. Compan. Amer. Hist.* 530/1 *Militia*, now officially termed the National Guard in the U.S., is the body of armed forces within the states, formed by enlistments. **1973** *Freedomways* XIII. 14 The forces of state power (the police, the army, the National Guard) will be used. **1908** *National Health* I. 1. 18/2 (*heading*) The Women's *National Health Association of Great Britain. **1911** LLOYD GEORGE *Insurance of the People* 2 A few weeks ago I had the honour of introducing in the House of Commons a measure dealing with proposals for securing the national health. **1935** *Economist* 7 Sept. 456/2 The most important event..in the field of health during the reign was the creation of the scheme of National Health Insurance in 1912. **1946** *Act 9 & 10 Geo. VI* c. 81 (*title*) National Health Service Act. **1952** A. CHRISTIE *Mrs. McGinty's Dead* xii. 96 Nowadays even if you've got a chilblain you run to the doctor with it so as to get your money's worth out of the National Health. **1958** J. CANNAN *And be a Villain* i. 23 A doctor w'at was too taken up by 'is posh paying patients to trouble with a National 'Ealth kid. **1958** R. GRAVES in *Times Lit. Suppl.* 15 Aug. p. x/5 What is even worse, any slight mania or differentiating oddness..they now take along to the National Health psychiatrist, pleading to be de-thinged. **1958** *Listener* 30 Oct. 699/2 The workings of the National Health Service. **1966** J. S. COX *Illustr. Dict. Hairdressing* 102/1 *National Health wig*, a wig or other similar postiche of necessity supplied by a Wigmaker for a client whose health is said to be affected by lack of hair, to the order of the Ministry of Health. **1967** M. ARGYLE *Psychol. Interpersonal Behaviour* ix. 174 This [*sc.* counselling] is the most widely practised kind of psychotherapy—it is given by National Health Service psychiatrists in England. **1967** *Melody Maker* 27 May 5 With his bushy sideboards and National Health specs he resembled an animated Victorian watchmaker. **1973** J. PORTER *It's Murder with Dover* ii. 13 Gritting his National Health teeth, [he] limped off. **1866** C., J., & E. WEATHERBY *Racing Calendar for 1866. Races Past* p. vi, Advertisements and reports of Steeple Chases under the Grand *National Hunt Rules are included in the Sheet Calendar. **1873** C., J., E., & J. P. WEATHERBY *Racing Calendar, Steeple Chases Past, for Season 1872–73* p. xiii, Any person running a horse in contravention of this Rule shall (at the discretion of the Grand National Hunt Committee) be disqualified from ever running a horse where these rules are in force. *Ibid.* p. xxv, The following form of certificate is that approved by the National Hunt Committee. **1898** A. E. T. WATSON *Turf* ix. 173 Horses are usually put to jumping because for some reason or another their career on the flat has ceased to look promising, it having been so continually proved that failures under Jockey Club Rules were brilliant successes under the Rules of the National Hunt. **1902** *Encycl. Brit.* XXIX. 333/1 None other than thoroughbred horses are nowadays ever found in races run under the rules of the National Hunt Committee, the body which governs the sport of steeplechasing. **1935** *Encycl. Sports* 590/1 National Hunt Rules fix the opening of the steeplechasing season as July 1. **1963** BLOODGOOD & SANTINI *Horseman's Dict.* 152 *Point-to-point*, cross-country race for qualified hunters..ridden by amateurs..over a flagged natural hunting country; under the jurisdiction of the National Hunt (England). **1967** *Everyman's Encycl.* VI. 482/2 In 1866, as a result of the efforts of Lord Suffolk, Lord Coventry and the duke of Beaufort, the National Hunt Committee was formed as the authoritative governing body over steeplechasing. **1975** *Oxf. Compan. Sports & Games* 496/1 Over the years, the National Hunt season has gradually become longer, and the 1973–4 season began early in August and will end on 1 June. **1878** BLACKLEY in *19th Cent.* Nov. 834 (*title*) *National Insurance: A cheap, practical and popular means of abolishing poor rates. **1911** National insurance [see INSURANCE 4e]. **1913** *Q. Rev.* Apr. 510 The labourer has gained something in a pecuniary sense from..national insurance. **1922** *Encycl. Brit.* XXX. 998/2 A few doctors.. had started a new organization in opposition to the British Medical Association, called the National Insurance Practitioners Association. **1931** *Times Lit. Suppl.* 20 Aug. 626/3 The indebtedness of the national insurance fund has already risen. **1967** E. RUDINGER *Wills & Probate* 60 Matthew's father-in-law had also been receiving the state old age pension, or national insurance retirement pension, as it is properly called. **1968** *Brit. Med. Bull.* XXIV. 207/1 National Insurance records giving the dates on which patients left and returned to work. **1973** *Times* 13 Jan. 19/7 The National Insurance Scheme covers benefits payable by the State (through the Department of Health and Social Security) and covers pensions, widows' benefits, maternity benefits and sickness and unemployment benefits, together with certain minor benefits. **1928** *Times* 8 Aug. 12/3 The Minister of Agriculture and Fisheries has appointed a Committee, to be known as the *National Mark Committee, ..empowered to authorize the use of grade designation marks. *Ibid.*, An artistic and striking 'National Mark' has been designed,.. a silhouette map of South Britain with a circle inset bearing the words around the margin, 'Produce of England and Wales'. **1929** *Daily Express* 7 Nov. 3/4 There has been a greatly increased demand for British beef since the National Mark scheme was introduced. **1931** *Times* 17 Nov. (Suppl.) p. xiv/1 One mark, the National Mark, which is a trade mark registered in the name of the Minister of Agriculture, is being used for all graded produce of England and Wales. **1934** *Daily Tel.* 31 Dec. 14/4 The National Mark Scheme began eight years ago to encourage home producers. **1937** *Food Manufacture* Oct. 340 The National Mark Scheme for Fruit Products..has now been extended to include..fruit juices. **1921** R. W. SETON-WATSON in H. W. V. Temperley *Hist. Peace Conf. Paris* IV. 266 *National minorities shall enjoy equal rights. **1934** C. A. MACARTNEY (*title*) National states and national minorities. **1945** E. E. BROOKE tr. *Azcárate y Florez's League of Nations* p. vii, When those responsible for reconstructing Europe find themselves once again confronted by the difficulties which national minorities have created in the past. **1970** V. VAN DYKE *Human Rights, U.S. & World Community* II. v. 98 A recognition of 'the right of members of national minorities to carry on their own educational activities'. **1868** J. D. WHITNEY *Yosemite Bk.* i 22 The Yosemite Valley..has been made a *National public park and placed under the charge of the State of California. **1871** [see PARK *sb.* 2b]. **1872** *Publ. Colonial Soc. Mass.* VIII. 377 Congress, by an Act approved March 1, 1872, has set apart a tract of land near the head-waters of the Yellowstone River... The reservation so set apart is to be known as the 'Yellowstone National Park'. **1903** [see PARK *sb.* 2b]. **1933** *Discovery* Feb. 68/2 The creation of the great American national parks..has saved the bison from extinction. **1949** *Act 12 & 13 Geo. VI* c. 97 An Act to make provision for National Parks and the establishment of a National Parks Commission. **1950** R. N. HUTCHINS *National Parks & Access to Countryside Act* i. i. 3 New Zealand..has 10 National Parks and over 200 reserves and public domains. *Ibid.*, In England and Wales, the designation of a National Park will not affect the ownership of the land,..nor will any additional facilities for public access be made available merely by such definition. **1962** *Listener* 1 Mar. 373/1 The Planning Board or committee in charge of a national park has a statutory duty ..to 'preserve and enhance' the natural beauty of the landscape. **1974** *Times* 1 Apr. (Yorkshire & Humberside Suppl.) p. ix/1 Within reasonable driving distance of the Humber the choice lies between three national parks, a noble sprinkling of country estates and several attractive cathedral cities. **1945** S. KUZNETS *National Product in Wartime* I. ii. 7 Estimates of peacetime *national product assume that economic activity is to produce goods to satisfy ultimate consumers; that production is for man, not man for production. **1962** *Listener* 20 Dec. 1041/1 The French national product rose at a rate of no less than 8 per cent. a year. **1964** GOULD & KOLB *Dict. Social Sci.* 454/1 If a series of national product estimates for several years is divided by a price index, each year's national product being divided by the price index for that year, the resulting series is known as *deflated* or *real* national product. **1831** H. CLAY *Priv. Corr.* 308 By division between the Antis and the *National Republicans, the Jackson party may succeed. **1888** BRYCE *Amer. Commw.* II. III. liii. 333 The National Republican, ultimately the Whig party, represented many of the views of the former Federalists. [**1917** (*title*) National War Savings Committee... First annual report, in *Parl. Papers 1917–18* (Cd. 8516) XVIII. 703.] **1919** *Saving* 3 Dec. 138/2 The

Model Schemes suggested by the *National Savings Committee are of various forms. **1922** *Encycl. Brit.* XXXI. 369/2 The system of linking up National Savings certificates with local finance becomes, in effect, a national credit bank spread over the whole country. **1932** *Discovery* Nov. 374/2 The much abused Post Office . . has actually allowed it [*sc.* the Institute of Industrial Psychology] to redesign the National Savings Certificate. **1941** *Picture Post* 3 May 35/3 Buy National Savings Stamps—they cost 6d. and 2/6 each. . . When you have the right amount you convert them into National Savings Certificates—15/- each. **1964** A. WYKES *Gambling* x. 238 Offering a lottery ticket worth one mark . . for every eight marks deposited in national-savings accounts. **1972** *Times* 21 Nov. 19/6 Historically national savings have been treated as a poor relation to other investment media. **1819** *Gentl. Mag.* LXXXIX. II. 85 In 1812 there were 52 *National Schools. **1838** *Digest Evidence before Comm. Houses Lords & Commons, 1837, on National Syst. Educ. Ireland* ii. 25 She was highly gratified; indeed she was astonished; she could not have believed that in the national school the Bible was used at all. **1880** MISS BRADDON *Just as I am* li, My looks won't matter when I am a national school teacher. **1966** *New Statesman* 27 May 774/3 But certain schools, to be called perhaps National Schools, should be placed directly under the Department of Education. **1968** T. KINSELLA *Nightwalker* 65 But the authorities Used the National Schools to try to conquer The Irish national spirit. **1972** M. E. COLLINS *Ireland Three* vi. 49 The National Schools were free, but not compulsory. . . The National Schools, though in theory of mixed religion, were in practice, separate, and children of each religion went to their own schools. **1916** R. FRY *Let.* 25 Jan. (1972) II. 393, I don't think Ha talked to me of *national service. **1916** *Hansard Commons* 19 Dec. 1352 It is proposed to appoint at once a director of National Service, to be in charge of both the military and civil side of universal national service. **1939** *Ibid.* 2 Sept. 240 National Service (armed forces) Bill, 'to make provision for securing and controlling the enlistment of men for services in the armed forces of the Crown; and for purposes connected with the matter aforesaid, presented, accordingly, read the First time; and ordered to be printed. **1940** *Ann. Reg. 1939* 397 The National Service (Armed Forces) Act, which rendered liable for service in the forces all male persons between eighteen and forty-one. **1940** H. G. WELLS *Babes in Darkling Wood* I. i. 21 Romeo and Juliet weren't called on for national service. **1942** G. G. SLACK *Liability for National Service* I. i. 1 The Government powers of control over persons are, in relation to their liability for National Service, exercised by the Minister of Labour. **1944** J. S. HUXLEY *On Living in Revolution* 21 It is both probable and desirable that some form of National Service will continue after the war is over. **1958** M. KERR *People of Ship Street* iii. 29 The boys in between 18 and 20 are of course doing National Service. **1970** M. MOORCOCK *Chinese Agent* xiii. 87 He had avoided being called up for his National Service for two years and, when he had been called up, he'd managed to desert. **1949** *Times* 20 Oct. 5/5 The Secretary of State for War gave an assurance that no *national service man would be posted to the Far East with less than 18 weeks' service. **1957** *B.B.C. Handbk.* 170 British National Servicemen. **1957** C. HUNT *Guide to Communist Jargon* vii. 19 Those who have taken up soldiering as a profession as opposed to National Servicemen, who have not. **1973** D. LEES *Rape of Quiet Town* vii. 113 A number of former national service men who had never heard a shot fired in anger. **1931** *Times Lit. Suppl.* 16 Apr. 296/3 Such is the doctrine, not inaptly named *National Socialism, which by uniting Moscow and Paris in a common anathema has appealed at once to the quiet steady man and to the boisterous patriot. **1933** J. J. BRONOWSKI in *Granta* 19 Apr. 358/2 National Socialism pictures itself as persecuted, not only by the political world but by art, science and philosophy. **1923** *Times* 23 Aug. 9/6 At the conclusion of a *National Socialist meeting last night Herr Hitler's storm troops . . attempted to march through Munich. **1931** *Daily Tel.* 21 May 13/1 The National-Socialists (Hitlerites) are now definitely committed to a Hohenzollern restoration. **1933** J. J. BRONOWSKI in *Granta* 19 Apr. 358/1 The National Socialist revolution in Germany is most deeply founded, has its most bigoted and best organised support in the German universities. **1942** E. BARKER *Reflections on Govt.* xiii. 369 We have here the ultimate roots of the National Socialist doctrines of the Leader and the Folk which he leads and expresses. **1942** L. B. NAMIER *Conflicts* 40 The depression . . everywhere brought new political forces to the surface, violent and brutal—National Socialists and National Radicals. **1967** D. EISENBERG *Re-emergence Fascism* i. 59 The judge . . hit out at Colin Jordan's National Socialist movement. **1973** *Black Panther* 27 Oct. 8/3 On another occasion the National Socialist Party, also known as the 'White People's Party', passed out literature in front of her house pledging to 'get rid of all the niggers'. **1848** BP. WILBERFORCE in *Life* (1881) II. i. 11 A most stormy meeting at the *National Society. **1861** V. LUSHINGTON in *Working Men's Coll. Mag.* 144 The National Society . . planted elementary schools here and there in the land. **1889** G. B. SHAW *London Music 1888–89* (1937) 150 Miss Reimers . . upset even my gravity . . by asking me . . why the splendid, the intellectual, the free English people had no *national theatre. **1901** BEERBOHM *Around Theatres* (1924) I. 245 The offer made (or *not* made) by Mr. Carnegie to endow with us a national theatre has duly revived that periodic cry to which I have alluded. **1928** G. HUGHES *Story of Theatre* xiv. 215 The Burgtheater [in Vienna] . . had been founded in 1741 as a Court Theatre . . and changed in 1776 . . into a National Theatre (in imitation of the Comédie Française). **1961** E. WAUGH *Unconditional Surrender* 306 The foundation stone was solemnly laid for a National Theatre. **1972** *Listener* 18 May 644/3 The new National Theatre rising on the South Bank. Until the coming of the National, the British theatre had survived . . without the alien office of dramaturgs. **1974** *Country Life* 24 Jan. 125 The National has been running successfully for ten years and plays generally to good houses. **1893** *Times* 17 Nov. 9/6 'The *National Trust for Places of Historic Interest or Natural Beauty' is an association which held its first meeting yesterday. **1894** *Spectator* 7 July 12/2 Men who love their glens and their hill-tops . . would far rather see them go to the National Trust than be put up to auction. **1896** O. HILL *Let.* 26 Oct. in C. E. Maurice *Life O. Hill* (1913) x. 538, I suppose you do not happen to know any gentleman likely to do for, and accept, our National Trust secretaryship? **1907** *Hansard Commons* 21 Aug. 758 The following Bills received the Royal Assent:— . . 14. National Trust for Places of Historic Interest or Natural Beauty. **1930** J. S. HUXLEY *Bird-Watching* vi. 115 And he [*sc.* the bird-lover] can help by supporting such bodies as the National Trust and the Royal Society for the Protection of Birds, which are saving wild bits of country from being built over or otherwise developed, or reserving them as actual sanctuaries, inviolate to the birds. **1934** *N. & Q.* 16 June 415/2 East Riddlesden Hall . . has just been publicly handed over to the the National Trust. **1938** D. GARNETT in T. E. Lawrence *Lett.* 873 His cottage at Clouds Hill now belongs to the National Trust. **1958** *Listener* 9 Oct. 556/2 On the preservation of historic buildings many voices must obviously be heard: . . art-historians and archivists, the National Trust. **1971** P. GRESSWELL *Environment* 166 The National Trust . . was founded . . by Octavia Hill, Sir Robert Hunter and Canon Rawnsley.

B. *sb.* †**1.** A representative of a nation. *Obs.*

1653 H. COGAN *Scarlet Gown* 100 The Pope . . did at one and the same time promote both Mazzarino, and Montalto, as declared Nationals, and nominated by France and Spain.

†**2.** One who supports national interests as opposed to those of parties. *Obs. rare.*

1766 *Public Advertiser* 10 Feb. 2/2 A noble Union of . . Nationals in the true Sense of that Word, in contradistinction to any vile Combination of Party. **1768** *Woman of Honor* III. 150 Some truly nationals, men of real worth.

3. A member of a national guard. *rare*$^{-1}$.

1843 BORROW *Bible in Spain* x, The national entered with the passport in his hand.

4. a. *pl.* In recent diplomatic use (after F. *nationaux*): Persons belonging to the same nation; (one's) fellow-countrymen.

1887 *Pall Mall G.* 30 May 1 Each of these Consuls or Ministers has extensive powers over his own nationals. **1894** *Westm. Gaz.* 31 July 2/1 The Chinese Resident . . has a considerable number of his nationals to look after.

b. (See quot. 1904.)

1904 J. WESTLAKE *Internat. Law* I. 3 All the members of a state, whether sovereign, subjects or citizens, are denoted by the convenient name of its nationals. **1929** *Times* 31 Jan., The official thanks of the German Government . . for the rescue by aeroplane of their nationals in Kabul. **1931** *Times* 22 Sept. 7/4 There is no evidence of any substantial export of capital by British nationals. **1953** *Stroud's Judicial Dict.* (ed. 3) III. 1855 In English courts phrases which refer to the national law of a propositus are prima facie to be construed not as referring to the law which the courts of that country would apply in the case of its own nationals domiciled in its own country with regard . . to property in its own country. **1955** *Times* 3 June 6/2 The two Governments have agreed to take measures for the conclusion of a treaty for the purpose of settling questions of citizenship, and with regard to the repatriation of nationals of one contracting party residing in the territory of the other party. **1969** PLANO & OLTON *Internat. Relations Dict.* xi. 266 *Statelessness*, the condition of an individual who is not recognized by any state as one of its nationals.

5. = *Grand National*: see GRAND *a.* 12.

1909 *Westm. Gaz.* 26 Mar. 12/1 A horse that had never run a National. **1931** *Times* 12 Mar. 5/1 Several National horses have been entered at Hurst Park. **1972** L. P. DAVIES *What did I do Tomorrow?* ii. 26 The only time he backed horses was for the Derby or the National.

6. A national as opposed to a local newspaper; usu. *pl.*

1938 C. HUNT *You want to be a Journalist?* iii. 29 It is when staff increase—on county papers, dailies published from the great cities, London nationals—that specialisation develops. **1960** H. L. LAWRENCE *Children of Light* v. 68 Some of the nationals had rushed their own men to Keniston, but a flattering number had wired Johnny for coverage. *a* **1966** M. ALLINGHAM *Cargo of Eagles* (1968) i. 19 She must have sold the idea to the local papers because the nationals picked it up a year or two back. **1966** *Listener* 28 July 129/3 In thirty years' time there could probably be only four nationals left. **1973** J. PORTER *It's Murder with Dover* iv. 36 We'll make the front page of the nationals with this!

national grid. [f. NATIONAL *a.* + GRID.]

1. The grid (sense 8) that interconnects the major power stations and distribution centres in Great Britain; any similar grid in another country. Also *transf.*

1930 *Times* 22 Mar. 19/2 There will be no great rush of new business consequent on the completion of the national 'Grid' system, as was contemplated in some quarters. **1943** [see GRID 8 b]. **1955** [see GRID 8 a]. **1967** *Times* 13 Dec. 4/2 Mr. Wilson had said that comparative calculations were not possible for the gas industry, because there was not yet an equivalent of the national grid.

2. The metric co-ordinate system and reference grid used by the Ordnance Survey and printed on its maps, having a false origin west of the Isles of Scilly and a true origin at 2°W., 49°N.

1938 *Final Rep. Dept. Comm. Ordnance Survey* (Ministry of Agric. & Fisheries) 4 We recommend that a National grid should be super-imposed on all large-scale plans, and on smaller scale maps, to provide one reference system for the maps of the whole of the country. **1952** *Proc. Prehist. Soc.* XVIII. 3 The National Grid position on the 6-inch map Sheet XLIV, N.W. is 832642. **1963** *Atlas of Britain* (Clarendon Press) map 1 The National Grid is used in this Atlas with the sanction of the Director General, Ordnance Survey and of H.M. Stationery Office; the Irish Grid is used with the sanction of the Ordnance Survey of Northern Ireland. **1969** C. B. M. LOCK *Mod. Maps & Atlases* i. 32 The Ordnance Survey maps are now prepared on the Transverse Mercator, which enables the National Grid reference system to be easily operated. **1971** *Nature* 5 Feb. 375/1 A combination of these two surveys showed that before 1900 forty-four species . . occurred in only one or two 10 km squares of the national grid; by 1930 the number was fifty-nine species.

nationalism ('næʃənəlɪz(ə)m). [f. NATIONAL *a.* + -ISM.]

1. *Theol.* The doctrine that certain nations (as contrasted with individuals) are the object of divine election.

1836 G. S. FABER *Prim. Doctr. Election* (1842) 189 The several doctrinal systems, usually denominated Arminianism and Nationalism and Calvinism.

2. Devotion to one's nation; national aspiration; a policy of national independence.

1844 *Fraser's Mag.* XXX. 418/1 Nationalism is another word for egotism. **1853** J. H. NEWMAN *Hist. Sk.* (1873) II. I. iv. 203 Mahometanism is essentially a consecration of the principle of nationalism. **1880** F. G. LEE *Ch. under Q. Eliz.* I. 164 It was only by persecution . . that the new system of nationalism in religion could be maintained.

b. *spec.* The political programme of the Irish Nationalist party.

1885 *Sat. Rev.* 11 Apr. 463/1 It is to them that the portentous development of American-Irish Nationalism is due. **1899** *Daily News* 25 Jan. 4/6 Each of these Councils will become a centre of Nationalism.

3. A form of socialism, based on the nationalizing of all industry.

1892 E. BELLAMY in *N. Amer. Rev.* CLIV. 749 The full programme of Nationalism, involving the entire substitution of public for private conduct of all business, for the equal benefit of all, is not indeed advocated by any considerable number of economists.

4. 'A national idiom or phrase'.

1846 WORCESTER (citing Hamilton).

nationalist ('næʃənəlɪst). [f. as prec. + -IST.]

1. One characterized by national tendencies or sympathies; an adherent or supporter of nationalism; an advocate of national rights, etc.

1715 M. DAVIES *Athen. Brit.* I. Contents, A Low Nationalist of the Calvinistical Establishment. **1716** *Ibid.* II. 335 Mutual upbraiding . ., which appears the more Melancholy because the less Curable; especially amongst our Nationalists and Toleratists. **1873** *Spectator* 23 Aug. 1059/1 Prince Bismarck also observed that concession would encourage the Polish nationalists. **1877** J. F. BRIGHT *Hist. Eng.* (1878) III. 933 Those nationalists who regarded as righteous any act of antagonism to England. **1891** J. RAE *Contemp. Socialism* ii. (ed. 2) 79 The Nationalists have quite recently issued an organ, *The New Nation*, which announces its programme to be [etc.].

b. *spec.* One who advocates the claims of Ireland to be an independent nation.

1869 *Daily News* 20 May, He rejoices in the Bill for the Disestablishment of the Church, . . he thinks it will make Protestants real nationalists. **1893** *Times* 26 Apr. 9/4 The Nationalists, in short, are to call the tune and the people of this country are to pay the piper.

attrib. **1899** *Daily News* 25 Jan. 4/6 The Irish people . . returning Nationalist Town and District Councils.

2. *Theol.* A believer in nationalism.

1846 in WORCESTER (citing *Q. Rev.*).

3. One belonging to a particular nation. *rare*$^{-1}$.

1817 J. EVANS *Excurs. Windsor*, etc. 49 A question was debated, which nationalist of Europe had the greatest ingenuity. . . Heidegger claimed that character for the Swiss.

Hence **nationa'listic** *a.*

1866 VISCT. STRANGFORD *Selection fr. Writ.* (1869) I. 98 She . . seeks to conciliate the nationalistic sympathies and projects of her South-Slavonic or Illyro-Servian populations. **1899** R. H. CHARLES *Eschatology* iii. 84 This popular conception . . was unethical and nationalistic.

nationa'listically, *adv.* [f. NATIONALISTIC *a.*: see -ICALLY.] In a nationalistic manner; on nationalistic lines.

1913 H. W. ROBINSON *Relig. Ideas Old Testament* 32 The redemption is differently conceived and nationalistically applied. **1924** *These Eventful Years* (Encycl. Brit.) II. 126 The nationalist problem is renewing itself in the succession states, which are nationalistically as varied as was Old Austria. **1951** *Current Hist.* Sept. 141/2 The nationalistically minded Japanese might be easily made to believe that all the West has done in Japan in the past is nothing but a plot to use the Japanese for its own purposes.

nationality (næʃə'nælɪtɪ). [f. as NATIONAL *a.* + -ITY: cf. F. *nationalité*.]

1. a. National quality or character.

1691 T. H[ALE] *Acc. New Invent.* 37 The Ingredients employed . . are of Forreign growth; which we make use of not so much for the sake of the Nationality of its Argument [etc.]. **1830** J. WILSON in *Blackw. Mag.* XXVIII. 847 We must again enter our protest against the Nationality of a library conducted on such principles. **1845** GRAVES *Rom. Law* in *Encycl. Metrop.* II. 741/1 Those peculiar institutions which coloured all their nationality. *a* **1854** H. REED *Lect. Eng. Hist.* iv. 121 Ancient British nationality received into itself a Roman nationality.

b. In literature, art, etc., the quality of being distinctively national.

1827 CARLYLE *Misc.* (1857) I. 24 All true nationality vanished from its literature. **1840** *New Monthly Mag.* LIX. 369 That peculiar wildness and eccentricity, or, if we may so term it, nationality, by which the primitive melodies of the Scotch, Welsh, and Irish, are . . distinguished. **1876** LOWELL *Among my Bks.* Ser. II. 129, I have little faith in that quality in literature which is commonly called nationality.

c. With *pl.* A national trait, characteristic, or peculiarity. *rare.*

1797 W. TAYLOR in *Monthly Rev.* XXII. 248 They remember with pleasure those nationalities which civilization is effacing. **1823** *Ibid.* CII. 420 He described our everyday nationalities.

2. Nationalism; attachment to one's country or nation; national feeling.

1772 *Junius Lett.* Pref. (1788) 23 The characteristic prudence, the selfish nationality, the indefatigable smile. **1785** BOSWELL *Tour Hebrides* 11 He could not but see in them that nationality which I should think no liberal minded Scotsman will deny. **1831** *Blackw. Mag.* XXX. 665 Nationality is not patriotism, or it would admire the nationality of other nations. **1858** GLADSTONE *Homer* II. iii. 192 Her strong and profound Greek nationality. **1878** LECKY *Eng. 18th C.* II. vii. 436 A spirit of nationality had arisen.

3. a. The fact of belonging to a particular nation; *spec.* a legal relationship between a state and an individual involving reciprocal rights and duties. Also with reference to the legal device by which ships, aircraft, and companies acquire the protection of the state in which they are registered.

1828 D'ISRAELI *Chas. I*, I. v. 95 [He] had wisely cast off his nationality when it could only occasion pain. **1865** MAFFEI *Brigand Life* II. 139 The safety which his nationality was likely to afford. **1878** MISS BRADDON *Eleanor's Victory* ii. 13 Every article of furniture..bore the impress of its nationality. **1880** W. E. HALL *Internat. Law* II. v. 188 The more important states recognise..that the child of a foreigner ought to be allowed to be himself a foreigner, unless he manifests a wish to assume or retain the nationality of the state in which he has been born. **1893** *Law Rep.* Prob. Div. 209 The ship..was of French nationality. **1907** L. A. ATHERLEY-JONES *Commerce in War* vi. 345 Every merchant vessel is expected to carry on board some official documents vouching for her nationality. **1928** E. M. BORCHARD *Diplomatic Protection of Citizens Abroad* iii. 555 With the rise of the modern state in Europe..nationality became the test of civil and political status. **1961** N. BAR-YAACOV *Dual Nationality* 3 Having wide discretion to formulate their nationality laws according to their own interests, States adopt different methods for acquisition of nationality, the result being that two States may simultaneously confer their nationality on the same individual. **1964** GOULD & KOLB *Dict. Social Sci.* 456/2 The normal way in which nationality is acquired is through birth... Nationality may also be granted to a person who is originally foreign or stateless. This process is known as naturalization.

b. With *pl.* denoting identity or difference of nation among individuals.

1846 H. W. TORRENS *Rem. Milit. Hist.* 50 The confused usage of military terms among the Greeks arising from their differences of dialect and separate nationalities. **1864** DASENT *Jest & Earnest* (1873) I. 140 Curious it was to see how nationalities herded together over their food. **1880** 'VERNON LEE' *Italy* III. iii. 122 The town of Italy where men of all nationalities had most met.

4. Separate or complete existence as a nation; national independence or consolidation.

1832 *Examiner* 488/1 If the nationality of any of the smaller German states were extinguished. **1850** HT. MARTINEAU *Hist. Peace* IV. xiii. (1877) III. 128 The Poles had been fighting—for nationality it is true—but not for national freedom. **1883** FROUDE *Short Stud.* IV. III. 269 So far as force could do it, they annihilated the Jewish nationality.

attrib. **1878** SEELEY *Stein* II. 26 Now he ripens at once into a great nationality statesman.

5. A nation; freq., a people potentially but not actually a nation. Also occas., a racial or ethnic group.

1832 *Examiner* 488/1 It leaves the various existing nationalities of Germany unimpaired. **1856** DASENT *Jest & Earnest* (1873) I. 311 Welded by time and trouble into a distinct nationality. **1874** STUBBS *Const. Hist.* I. iv. 59 The Saxons in Germany were still a pure nationality. **1952** S. SELVON *Brighter Sun* v. 88 Whenever he saw a couple of different nationalities he used to hail out to them, and tell Stella that that was the way to live, especially in Trinidad. *Ibid.*, He used to say that all this business about colour and nationality was balls. **1964** GOULD & KOLB *Dict. Social Sci.* 244/1 In the Soviet Union, *nationalities* is more frequently applied to the diverse national-ethnic units who make up the membership of the Union. **1971** *Times* 17 Dec., 'Nationality', in the sense of citizenship of a certain state, must not be confused with 'nationality' as meaning membership of a certain nation in the sense of race.

6. = NATIONALTY. *rare.*

1830 COLERIDGE *Church & State* 37 The sum total of these heritable portions..I beg leave to name the Propriety; and to call the reserve above mentioned the Nationality.

nationalization (ˌnæʃənəlaɪˈzeɪʃən). [f. next + -ATION.]

1. The action of rendering national in character.

1801 W. TAYLOR in Robberds *Mem.* (1843) I. 383 Does not this forebode the nationalization of liberty-politics at home? **1882** H. VON HOLST *J. C. Calhoun* (1884) 239 The official proclamation of the 'nationalization' of slavery.

2. The action of forming into a nation or nations; the process of becoming a nation.

1813 SIR R. WILSON *Priv. Diary* (1861) I. 274 The Poles are hostile to the Russians as enemies to their freedom and nationalization. **1853** LIEBER *Civ. Liberty* iv. 33 There is a distinct period in the history of our race, which may be aptly called the period of nationalization. **1890** *Times* 15 Dec. 5/4 Count Taaffe's Cabinet will make no further concessions to Bohemian nationalization.

b. Inclusion or absorption into a nation.

1896 *Nation* (N.Y.) 16 July 54/1 The nationalization of the Jew—that is, his absorption by this or that nation.

3. The action of bringing land, property, industries, etc., under the control of the nation.

1874 FAWCETT *Pol. Econ.* II. i. (1876) 107 Nationalization of the land means that all the land in the country should be bought by the State. **1881–3** (*title*) Report of the Land Nationalization Society. **1894** E. BELLAMY in *Forum* (U.S.) Mar. 85 This plan is called Nationalism because it proceeds by the nationalization of industries.

nationalize (ˈnæʃənəlaɪz), *v.* Also -ise. [f. NATIONAL *a.* + -IZE, or ad. F. *nationaliser* (1794 in Hatz.-Darm.).]

1. *trans.* To invest with a national character; to make distinctively national.

1800 *Hist. Eur.* in *Ann. Reg.* 35/2 We wish to nationalize the republic, they to establish only their own party. **1843** *Blackw. Mag.* LIV. 26 'Rule Britannia',..now become a national song... Long before it was nationalized—if one may use such a word—by Englishmen [etc.]. **1851** GALLENGA *Italy* 59 The very government of the Lombardo-Venetian kingdom might be..nationalized. **1870** LOWELL *Among my Bks.* Ser. I. (1873) 226 He took what may be called cosmopolitan traditions,..and nationalized them.

b. To make into a separate nation; to invest with the character of a nation.

1801 F. AMES *Wks.* (1809) 142 New-England..of all colonies that ever were founded the largest, the most assimilated, and, to use the modern jargon, nationalized.

2. To naturalize; to admit into, or make part of, a nation. Also *refl.*

1809 PINKNEY *Trav. France* 41 There are many resident English, who have been nationalized by express edict. **1861** M. PATTISON *Ess.* (1889) I. 32 Only Jutes, Angles, Saxons, and Danes..have succeeded in nationalizing themselves here.

b. *intr.* To become naturalized.

1891 *Sat. Rev.* 4 July 1/2 The curious plan of keeping Russia for the Russians by forcing all foreign 'colonists' to nationalize or quit.

3. To bring under the control of, to convert into the property of, the nation.

1869 *Daily News* 21 Oct., It was 'Bosh' to talk of nationalising the land to starving thousands. **1874** FAWCETT *Pol. Econ.* II. xi. (1876) 299 After the land and the other instruments of production have been nationalised. **1881** BRODRICK *Eng. Land & Landlords* 105 It is a perfectly intelligible proposition that all the land in the kingdom ought to be 'nationalized'.

Hence **ˈnationalized, ˈnationalizing** *ppl. adjs.*

1836 G. S. FABER *Prim. Doctr. Election* (1842) 189 That Neither the Arminian System, nor the Nationalising System, nor the Calvinistic System, exhibits the mind of the sincere Gospel. **1856** MAX MÜLLER *Chips* (1880) II. xvi. 13 An age..exhibiting to us the earliest traces of nationalised language. **1874** FAWCETT *Pol. Econ.* II. xi. (1876) 286 Is not a reduction in rent the chief advantage which the advocates of this nationalising policy hope to secure? **1885** J. ROBSON *Disestablishment* 16 So too..it would be in the Nationalised Church of Scotland.

nationalizer (ˈnæʃənəlaɪzə(r)). [f. prec. + -ER[1].] One who advocates the nationalization of land, etc. Freq. in ***land-nationalizer***.

1883 *Pall Mall G.* 6 Feb. 2/1 Will some of the 'nationalizers'..employ a..real property lawyer to draft a bill for carrying out their purposes? **1883** *Chr. World* 29 Nov. 839 Warred upon by the land nationaliser and socialist.

nationally (ˈnæʃənəlɪ), *adv.* [f. NATIONAL *a.* + -LY[2].] In a national manner or way; as a nation; with regard to the nation as a whole.

1649 *Bounds & Bonds Obed.* 44 There was no change of Government here, till the Covenant was Nationally broke.. by the Scots. **1681** *Whole Duty Nations* 21 That they should have Nationally dedicated themselves to the true Jehovah. **1720** DE FOE *Capt. Singleton* iv. (1840) 68 Take them nationally or personally,..they will behave well. **1791** W. MAXWELL in Boswell *Johnson* (1831) I. 380 He considered the Scotch, nationally, as a crafty designing people. **1824** *Examiner* 53/1 One of the most effective..and nationally honourable State Papers that ever was issued. **1870** ANDERSON *Missions Amer. Bd.* II. xxi. 169 Whether the people of the Sandwich Islands might be represented as nationally Christianized.

Comb. **1822** *New Monthly Mag.* IV. 17 The nationally-charged arrogance of self-opinion.

nationalness (ˈnæʃənəlnɪs). *rare.* [f. as prec. + -NESS.] The character or quality of being national.

1681 *Whole Duty Nations* 22 So far therefore as Nationalness, and Publiqueness agree, so far the thing is undeniable. **1727** in BAILEY, vol. II. **1889** J. M. ROBERTSON *Ess. Crit. Method* 151 Englishmen will hardly think of charging such an artist with deficiency in nationalness.

nationalty (ˈnæʃənəltɪ). [f. as prec. + -TY, after *personalty, realty*.] National property.

1812–29 COLERIDGE in *Lit. Rem.* (1838) III. 119 Their tithes and glebes belong to them as officers and functionaries of the nationalty. **1845** J. MARTINEAU *Ess.* (1891) II. 23 The other constituted a nationalty or inalienable reserve for perpetual income conditional on the performance of certain official services.

nationhood (ˈneɪʃənhʊd). [f. NATION *sb.*[1] + -HOOD.] The state or fact of being a nation.

1850 CARLYLE *Latter-d. Pamph.* i. 23 New elements of polity or nationhood. **1865** LECKY *Ration.* II. 32 A bond of unity that is superior to the divisions of nationhood. **1885** PARNELL in *Times* 2 Sept. 6/3 Our right to nationhood to-day is practically undisputed.

†**ˈnationist.** *Obs. rare*[−1]. [f. as prec. + -IST.] A representative of a nation.

1670 G. H. *Hist. Cardinals* III. III. 312 The Cardinals of the Crowns ought rather to be call'd Nationists than Factionists.

nationless (ˈneɪʃənlɪs), *a. rare.* [f. as prec. + -LESS.] Belonging to no nation.

1819 SHELLEY *Prometh. Unb.* III. iv. 195 Man Equal, unclassed, tribeless, and nationless.

†**naˈtitial.** *Obs. rare*[−1]. [? Error for NATALITIAL.] Nativity, birth.

1612 SYLVESTER tr. *Matthieu's Tropheis Hen. IV* 39 Th' happy planet, which presaged his worth Predominant in his natitial.

native (ˈneɪtɪv), *sb.* Forms: 5 **natif**, 6 **natyve**, 6– **native.** [ad. med.L. *nativus*, sb. use of L. *nātivus* adj. (see next). In later use sometimes directly from the adj. Cf. F. *natif*.]

1. One born in bondage; a born thrall. Now only *Hist.* Cf. NEIF.

c **1450** *Godstow Reg.* (E.E.T.S.) 559 The forsaid bondmen or natifs with all ther catallis sutis or sequelys. **1609** SKENE *Reg. Maj.* 90 b, Some are born bond-men, or natiues of their gudsher, and grandsher, quhom the Lord may challenge to be his naturall natiues. **1651** G. W. tr. *Cowel's Inst.* 8 At this day, the Issue which is begotten by a Free man of a Native, is free. **1706** PHILLIPS (ed. Kersey) s.v. *Nativus*, There being three sorts of Servants, viz. Natives, Bondmen, and Villains. **1878** STUBBS *Const. Hist.* (1896) III. 625 It is obvious that..the native so emancipated laboured under other disqualifications.

2. *Astrol.* **a.** One born under the particular planet or sign mentioned; the subject of a nativity or horoscope.

1509 HAWES *Past. Pleas.* x. (Percy Soc.) 34 Mercury, through his preeminence, Hys natives endeth wyth famous eloquence. **1632** MASSINGER *City Madam* II. ii, Saturn..and Venus..., the disposers of marriage in the radix of the native in feminine figures. **1679** MOXON *Math. Dict.* 95 Nebulous Stars..are found by Experience, being joyn'd with the Luminaries to afflict a Native with blindness or dimness. **1792** SIBLY *Occult Sci.* I. 96 When the moon, or lord of the ascendant, is posited..in any of the Signs we term hot, the native will be manly. **1815** SCOTT *Guy M.* iv, Mars having dignity in the cusp of the twelfth house, threatened captivity or sudden and violent death to the native.

†**b.** *transf.* One born with a particular mark.

1653 R. SANDERS *Physiogn., Moles* 31 A Mole in the lower part of the right Cheek..indicts to the native some kindes of strife.

3. a. One born in a place; one connected with a place by birth, whether subsequently resident there or not. Usu. const. *of*.

Legally, a person is a native of the place or country where the parents have their domicile, which may or may not be the place of actual birth (*N.E.D.*, 1906).

1535 COVERDALE *Isa.* xxiii. 7 Is not that the glorious cite, ..whose natyues dwellinge farre of, commende her so greatly? **1617** MORYSON *Itin.* II. 212 The Army..was encountred and almost distressed by the onely Natives of that Countrie. **1675** *Essex Papers* (Camden) I. 315 Great disputes are likely to arise betweene ye present Inhabitants & auntient Natives of severall of ye Corporacions. *a* **1700** DRYDEN *Death of Amyntas* 77 His passport is his innocence and grace, Well known to all the natives of the place. **1716** POPE *Iliad* VI. 70 Well hast thou known proud Troy's perfidious land, And well her natives merit at thy hand! **1756–7** *Keysler's Trav.* (1760) III. 406 T. Livy, a native of Padua. **1774** GOLDSM. *Nat. Hist.* (1776) II. 218 Those manners, which even a native of Canada can think more barbarous than his own. **1825** LYTTON *Zicci* I. i, He speaks English like a native. **1841** BORROW *Zincali* I. ii. 1. 58 If being born in a country, and being bred there, constitute a right to be considered a native of that country.

fig. **1700** ROWE *Amb. Step-Moth.* v. i, Let Joy the Native of your Soul return. **1703** —— *Fair Penit.* III. i, That Sorrow which..Is the sad Native of Calista's Breast. **1742** YOUNG *Nt. Th.* II. 58 And sport we like the natives of the bough, When vernal suns inspire?

b. Applied disparagingly to local residents belonging to a place.

1800 MRS. HERVEY *Mourtray Fam.* I. 173 The girl..was ..really much superior to the rest of the odious natives in their neighbourhood. **1818** *London Guide & Stranger's Safeguard* 6 The practices of 'shouldering' passengers, on their own account—doing *the natives* out of articles of life, which they bring to town to dispose of—..bring them [*sc.* coachmen] to 'take care of things', for which there is no immediate owner. **1823** 'J. BEE' *Slang* 124 *Natives*, silly people generally; the untravelled population of any town, wrapt up in incipient simplicity are natives. **1975** D. DELMAN *One Man's Murder* ii. 46 The house, Odum Harborage, corrupted to Odum Garborage by irreverent natives, was a notable mishmash even for Long Island.

c. In Australia, a white person born in the country, as distinguished from an immigrant and from an Aboriginal.

Sense 4 also is current in Australia (of the Aborigines).

1861 MRS. MEREDITH *Over Straits* v. 161 Three Sydney natives ('currency' not aboriginal) were in the coach, bound for Melbourne. **1863** R. HENNING *Let.* 21 Sept. (1966) 141 They were natives, and a little colonial, as might be expected. They had just left school in Melbourne. **1886** [see AUSTRALIANA]. **1895** A. B. PATERSON *Man from Snowy River* (1896) 43 They were long and wiry natives from the rugged mountain side. **1966** G. W. TURNER *Eng. Lang. Austral. & N.Z.* iii. 62 Early writers called them *natives* or *Indians*, but *Indians* fell entirely from use, and the word *natives* was required by Europeans born in Australia, who formed an Australian Natives' Association in 1871.

4. a. One of the original or usual inhabitants of a country, as distinguished from strangers or foreigners; now *esp.* one belonging to a non-European race in a country in which Europeans hold political power.

1603 R. JOHNSON *Kingd. & Commw.* 153 He committed no lesse an error in suffering the Natiues to keepe their possessions and to inhabit all their townes. **1652–62** HEYLIN

Cosmogr. iv. (1673) 94 Inhabited by the Natives only, though the Portugals did sometimes endeavour a Plantation in it. **1695** TEMPLE *Hist. Eng.* (1699) 5 The North-East part of Scotland was by the Natives called *Cal Dun.* **1725** DE FOE *Voy. round World* (1840) 2 The stories of their engagements when they have had any scuffle either with natives or European enemies. **1777** ROBERTSON *Hist. Amer.* II. (1778) I. 98 Columbus..continued to interrogate all the natives. **1817** O'HARA *Hist. N.S. Wales* 123 Some convicts, who destroyed the canoe of a young native. **1896** F. C. SELOUS *Sunshine & Storm Rhodesia* i. 5 No one could have recognised..in the quiet, submissive native..the arrogant savage of old times. **1897** MARY KINGSLEY *W. Africa* 74 Her knowledge of the native, his language, his ways of thought, his diseases,..is extraordinary. **1921** G. PAGE *Jill on Ranch* viii. 184 The native is a strange child, and he needs sympathetic dealing... Make a boy laugh and you can do anything with him. **1924** E. M. FORSTER *Passage to India* II. ii. 33 Whether the native swaggers or cringes, there's always something behind every remark he makes. **1931** E. O'NEILL *Mourning becomes Electra* III. ii. 238 The natives dancing naked and innocent without knowledge of sin. **1934** G. B. SHAW *On Rocks* II. 72 *Sir Bemrose*: If a Conservative Prime Minister of England may not take down a heathen native when he forgets himself there is an end of British supremacy. *Sir Arthur*: For Heaven's sake don't call him a native. You are a native. *Sir Bemrose* (*very solemnly*): Of Kent, Arthur: of Kent. Not of Ceylon. **1944** *Living off Land* ii. 43 The corkwood..blossoms are nourishing. The natives chew these.... but..it should be left well alone by the white man. **1948** *Times Lit. Suppl.* 9 Oct. 569/3 'Native' is a good word that may not now be employed without giving deep offence. **1950** M. CHAPPELL *Rhodesian Adventure* xiii. 143 There was nothing here when the pioneers came. Save bushveld and natives and wild animals. **1950** J. C. FURNAS *Anat. Paradise* ii. 24 The meaning of 'Native' can be approximated. It means: Darker. Productive of quaint handicrafts... Greedy for beads..and alcoholic drinks. Suspect of cannibalism. Addicted to drumbeating and lewd dancing. More or less naked. Sporadically treacherous. Probably polygynous and simultaneously promiscuous. Picturesque. Comic when trying to speak English or otherwise ape white ways. **1950** D. LESSING *Grass is Singing* viii. 178 When a white man in Africa by accident looks into the eyes of a native and sees the human being (which it is his chief preoccupation to avoid), his sense of guilt, which he denies, fumes up in resentment and he brings down the whip. **1951** J. MASTERS *Nightrunners Bengal* i. 9 We of the Company's service *live* here all our working lives. We do our work and enjoy ourselves and lord it over the country entirely by the good will of the average native... If you even think of them insultingly, of course they know it and resent it. **1975** C. ALLEN *Plain Tales from Raj* xix. 195 The regimental cook slaughtered a cow... The natives got to know about this and nearly stoned the camp.

b. A coloured person; a Black.

1848 DICKENS *Dombey* x, The Major..went one Saturday growling down to Brighton, with the native behind him.

c. In U.S. and Canada, a North American Indian.

1636 *Public Rec. Colony of Connecticut* (1850) I. 1 None.. shall trade w[i]th the natives or Indians any peece or pistoll or gunn. *a* **1772** J. WOOLMAN *Jrnl.* in *Works* (1774) I. viii. 153 My meditations were on the alterations in the circumstances of the natives..since the coming in of the English. **1846** R. B. SAGE *Scenes Rocky Mts.* xxxiii. 287 Skins furnish to the natives a favorite material for arrow-cases. **1856** R. M. BALLANTYNE *Snowflakes & Sunbeams* vii. 72 This is the trading-store. It is always recognisable, if natives are in the neighbourhood, by the bevy of red men that cluster round it, awaiting the coming of the store-keeper. **1951** R. BULIARD *Inuk* 316 The company nowadays certainly does give help to the natives, in the forms of loans, gifts, and medicine.

d. In phr. ***to astonish the natives*** (orig. *U.S.*), to shock, or otherwise profoundly impress, public opinion.

1807 *Salmagundi* 27 June 233 He was determined to '*astonish the natives a few*'. *Ibid.* 238 Unfortunate Straddle! may thy fate be a warning to all young gentlemen who come out from Birmingham to *astonish the natives*! **1842** *Ainsworth's Mag.* I. 302 At last, having astonished the natives,..he rolled off to bed. **1852** MUNDY *Antipodes* (1857) 104 The brutal drunkenness and reckless debauchery of the Pakehas actually 'astonished the natives'. **1901** M. E. RYAN *That Girl Montana* 96 Much of her afternoon was spent..fashioning a party gown with which to astonish the natives.

e. ***to go native***: see GO *v.* 44 a.

5. a. An animal or plant (†or mineral) indigenous, or peculiar to a country or locality; one not imported or acclimatized.

1690 CHILD *Disc. Trade* Pref. (1698) 29 Our lead and tin, by which we carry on much of those trades, are natives with us. **1774** GOLDSM. *Nat. Hist.* (1776) IV. 38 The marmout is chiefly a native of the Alps. **1799** *Med. Jrnl.* II. 490 To such species as are doubtful natives, a note of interrogation is affixed. **1849** BALFOUR *Man. Bot.* §921 The plants are principally natives of marshy places in New Holland. **1874** LYELL *Elem. Geol.* x. 124 The pine has never been a 'native' of Denmark in historical times.

b. An oyster altogether or partially reared in British waters; now *spec.* applied to those (whether of home or foreign origin) reared in artificial beds, or loosely used to denote an oyster of a superior quality. Also *attrib.*

1818 KITCHINER *Cook's Oracle* (ed. 2) 259 The Milton, or as they are commonly called, the melting Natives do not come in till the beginning of October. **1836–7** DICKENS *Sk. Boz, Mr. J. Dounce*, A newly-opened oyster-shop,..with natives laid one deep in circular marble basins in the windows. **1854** WOODWARD *Mollusca* II. 254 The oysters.. are..removed to artificial grounds, or tanks, where the water is very shallow. They are then called 'natives'. **1879** *Cassell's Techn. Educ.* IV. 154 In the London market oysters are divided into two great classes—'natives' and 'commons'. **1889** A. T. PARK *Eyes Thames* 56 The native beds, not so many years ago, could be had almost for the asking. **1891** *Pall Mall G.* 6 Oct. 2/1 Such a thing as putting seconds on native shells is not entirely unknown.

c. A native cow, horse, etc.

1856 OLMSTED *Slave States* (1861) 6 A few imported Ayrshires and Alderneys, and some small black 'natives'. **1895** A. B. PATERSON *Man fr. Snowy River* (1896) 43 [The horses] were long and wiry natives from the rugged mountain side.

†**6.** *pl.* Fellow-countrymen, compatriots. *Obs.*

1589 WARNER *Alb. Eng.* VI. xxxiii, Henrie..did arriue to right his Natiues wrong. **1632** LITHGOW *Trav.* III. 90 After short acquaintance with his natiues,..he imparted these words. **1655** FULLER *Ch. Hist.* III. xiii. §33 The King (distrusting his Natives) imployed so many French Forrainers in places of power and profit.

7. Native place (or country). Now only *dial.*

1604 R. CAWDREY *Table Alph.*, *Natiue*, Naturall: place where one was borne. **1615** CHAPMAN *Odyss.* IX. 66 Though roofs far richer we far off possess, Yet, from our native, all our more is less. **1820** AMELIA OPIE *Tales of Heart* IV. 328 He asked me some questions about Keswick.., for that's my native, sir. **1828** MOIR *Mansie Wauch* vi, Wearying..to be home again to Lauder, which she said was her native. **1900** *Cornh. Mag.* June 815 When he come back to his native at Yarmouth he knew no one.

8. *ellipt.* **a.** = Native liquor, native language.

1828 SOUTHEY *Ess.* (1832) II. 336 Not as much money left as would..get him a drop of the native at Killala. **1893** STEVENSON *Island Nights' Entertainm.* 70 He turned and spoke to his crew in the native.

b. (See quot.)

1880 *Rep. Comm. Fishing N.S. Wales* 11 At a still greater age the Schnapper..becomes what is known as the 'Native' and 'Rock Native', a solitary and sometimes enormously large fish.

9. *Comb.*, as ***native-built***, ***-fashion***, ***-owned***.

1837 *Lett. fr. Madras* (1843) 132 He sent us, besides, all his own messes, native-fashion. **1863** M. L. WHATELY *Ragged Life Egypt* xiv. 135 The chinks, so numerous in a native-built house. **1895** SWETTENHAM *Malay Sk.* 262 No native-owned boat in the country was white.

native ('neɪtɪv), *a.* Forms: 4, 6 **natyf**, 5 *Sc.* **natyff**, 5–6 **natyfe**, 5 **natif**, 5–6 **natife**, 5 *Sc.*, 6 **natiff**; 6 **natyve**, 5– **native**. [a. F. *natif* (14th c.; OF. also *naif*: see NAÏVE *a.*), or ad. L. *nātīvus* produced by birth, innate, natural, f. *nāt-*, ppl. stem of *nascī* to be born + *-īvus* -IVE.]

I. 1. a. Belonging to, or connected with, a person or thing by nature or natural constitution, in contrast to what is acquired or superadded; *esp.* of qualities which are inherent or innate in the person or thing.

c **1374** CHAUCER *Troylus* I. 102 So angelik was her natyf beute, That lyke thing immortal seemyd she. **1551** ROBINSON tr. *More's Utop.* (1895) 20 Not doubting that you, for your natiue goodnes and gentelnes, will accept in good parte this poore gift. **1581** J. BELL *Haddon's Answ. Osor.* 144 b, The Scriptures..expressing our natures in their most lively and native colours. **1592** J. DAVIES *Immort. Soul* I. ii, A Star, whose Beams do not proceed From any Sun, but from a Native Light. **1613** HEYWOOD *Braz. Age* II. ii, How can I hate,..Or practise ought against my native power? **1660** STANLEY *Hist. Philos.* XI. (1701) 462/2[Atoms] having neither native whiteness, nor blackness,..nor heat, nor cold, nor any other quality. *a* **1680** BUTLER *Rem.* (1759) I. 91 When Puss, wrapt warm in his own native Furs, Dreamt soundly. **1709** ROSCOMMON *Ess. Verse* 194 No cloudy Doubts obscure her Native Light. **1758** S. HAYWARD *Serm.* xvii. 538 How wonderful that the stones break not their native silence. **1782** COWPER *Poet, Oyster, & Sensit. Plant* 6 Ah, hapless wretch! condemned to dwell For ever in my native shell. **1817** J. SCOTT *Paris Revisit.* (ed. 4) 375 Study may be either the sign or the substitute of native feeling. **1854** BREWSTER *More Worlds* x. 166 Every single star, shining by its own native light. **1875** WHITNEY *Life Lang.* ii. 10 A mere native impulse to the exertion of all his native powers.

b. Natural *to* a person or thing.

1533 BELLENDEN *Livy* III. vi. (S.T.S.) I. 268 It was native to him..to persew þe pepill with all humanite & kyndenes he mycht. **1604** SHAKS. *Oth.* II. i. 218 Base men being in Loue, haue then a Nobilitie in their Natures, more then is natiue to them. **1834** DISRAELI *Rev. Epick* I. XLII. 16 To the rose Its fragrance not more native than to states A class thus rising. **1879** M. ARNOLD *Mixed Ess., Irish Cathol.* 116 If there is a thing specially native to religion, it is peace and union.

c. Natural, according to nature; naturally resulting. Now *rare.*

1509 HAWES *Past. Pleas.* XLI. (Percy Soc.) 204, I must nedes dye, it is my native kinde. **1543** *Wills & Inv. N.C.* (Surtees 1835) 121, I gyue and bequeathe to my brother.. fowre poundes by yeare..during his life natiue. *a* **1653** BINNING *Serm.* (1845) 144 O How would it be a pleasant and native thing to walk in his way, as a stone goeth downward. **1677** GALE *Crt. Gentiles* IV. Proem 5 We shal content our selves with this curt, yet apparently more native and distinct distribution of Beings. **1723** WODROW *Corr.* (1843) III. 9 It were hard to say this is a native consequence of any particular set of men's way. **1867** D. DUNCAN *Discourses* 292 To leave us to the native consequences of our folly and impiety.

†**d.** ***native notes***, birth-marks. *Obs. rare*$^{-1}$.

1658 SIR T. BROWNE *Gard. Cyrus* Wks. (Bohn) II. 536 That Augustus had native notes on his body..after the order and number in the stars of Charles wain.

2. a. Left or remaining in a natural state; *esp.* free from, or untouched by, art; unadorned, simple, plain, unaffected.

1560 DAUS tr. *Sleidane's Comm.* 426 The doctrine..is the very natiue and auncient Religion. **1587** GOLDING *De Mornay* xxxiv. (1592) 541 If we haue an eie to the stile, it is natiue, simple, plaine. **1632** MILTON *L'Allegro* 134 If.. sweetest Shakespear..Warble in his native Wood-notes wilde. **1660** DRYDEN *Ep. Sir R. Howard* 5 In your verse a native sweetness dwells, Which shames composure, and its art excels. **1710** STEELE *Tatler* No. 212 ⁋4 She has the greatest Simplicity of Manners of any of her Sex. This makes every Thing look native about her. **1750** JOHNSON *Rambler* No. 166 ⁋1 It has long been observed that native beauty has little power to charm without the ornaments which fortune bestows. **1790** BURKE *Fr. Rev.* 128 We preserve the whole of our feelings still native and entire, unsophisticated by pedantry and infidelity. **1868** MARRIOTT *Vestiar. Chr.* p. xxiv, Sober colours there were, or, as commonly they were called, natural or native colours. **1871** BROWNING *Balaustion* 1899 He shall not say the man was vile Whom he befriended,—native noble heart!

b. Naturally implied or involved; not wrested or forced in any way.

1579 FULKE *Heskins' Parl.* 141 This he dare auouch, to be the natiue and true vnderstanding of this scripture. **1625** GILL *Sacr. Philos.* iv. 61, I hold that this is not the native meaning of this place. **1709** STEELE *Tatler* No. 45 ⁋2 Mere Words,..used only as they serve to betray those who understand them in their native Sense. **1741** W. WILSON *Contin. Def. Ref. Princ. Ch. Scot.* (1769) I. 344, I have drawn such inferences and conclusions from them as I thought just and native. **1875** E. WHITE *Life in Christ* III. xxi. 319 The Septuagint translators..well knew the native meaning of both words.

3. a. Pertaining to, or connected with, one by the fact of one having been born there; that was the place or scene of one's birth. Also const. *to.* ***native country*** occurs frequently in the 16th cent.

1500–20 DUNBAR *Poems* xxii. 24 Kynd natyve nest dois clek bot owlis. **1513** DOUGLAS *Æneis* II. iv. 75 O native cuntre [*Surrey* land], and ryall realme of Troy! **1568** GRAFTON *Chron.* II. 491 He would cause the Scottes..to returne againe into their countrie and natiue region. **1590** SHAKS. *Com. Err.* I. i. 30 Say in briefe the cause Why thou departedst from thy natiue home? **1667** MILTON *P.L.* VI. 226 Disturb, though not destroy, thir happie Native seat. **1671** —— *P.R.* IV. 241 Athens,..Mother of Arts And Eloquence, native to famous wits Or hospitable. **1697** DRYDEN *Virg. Georg.* III. 17 [I shall] With Foreign Spoils adorn my native Place. **1725** POPE *Odyss.* I. 15 At their native realms the Greeks arrived. **1778** MISS BURNEY *Evelina* lxxix, We should first pass a month at my native Berry Hill. **1842** BISCHOFF *Woollen Manuf.* II. 422 The Flemish manufacturers, driven from their native country by the cruelty of the Duke of Alva. **1856** SIR B. BRODIE *Psychol. Inq.* I. i. 2 As boys, we had wandered together through our native woods.

transf. **1833** I. TAYLOR *Fanat.* vi. 167 Some congenial torrid climate—native to abjectness and slavery.

b. Forming the source or origin of a thing or person; original, parent.

1590 GREENE *Orl. Fur.* (1599) 58 All of finest silke, Fetcht from the natiue loomes of labouring wormes. **1596** SPENSER *F.Q.* v. xi. 11 Like fruitlesse braunches, which the hatchets slight Hath pruned from the native tree. **1667** MILTON *P.L.* XI. 463 Is this the way I must return to native dust? **1728** POPE *Dunc.* I. 176 And, lest we err by Wit's wild dancing light, Secure us kindly in our native night. **1813** SHELLEY *Q. Mab* IX. 121 Heaps of broken stone That mingled slowly with their native earth.

4. Belonging to, or natural to, one by reason of the place or country of one's birth, or of the nation to which one belongs.

1509 HAWES *Past. Pleas.* XXXIV. (Percy Soc.) 111 In my natyf language I wyl not opres More of her werke. **1593** SHAKS. *Rich. II*, I. iii. 160 The Language I haue learn'd these forty yeares (My natiue English) now I must forgo. *Ibid.* 173 Thy sentence..robs my tongue from breathing natiue breath. **1638** SIR T. HERBERT *Trav.* (ed. 2) 37 They have a native language of their owne, but the Persian tongue is understood by most. *c* **1700** POPE *Ode Solitude* i, Content to breathe his native air In his own ground. **1780** HARRIS *Philol. Enq.* Wks. (1841) 529 Greek..was still (with a few corruptions) their native language. **1817** SHELLEY *Rev. Islam* I. xix, To the Snake those accents sweet were known His native tongue and hers. **1841** CATLIN *N. Amer. Ind.* (1844) I. 6 Their habits, as we can see them transacted, are native. **1877** M. M. GRANT *Sun-Maid* viii, They were dressed in their native costumes.

Comb. **1876** A. PLUMMER tr. *Döllinger's Hippolytus* II. 87 His name has been metamorphosed in Syria and Egypt into the more native-sounding Abulides.

†**5.** ***native day***, natal day, birthday. *Obs.*

1546 LANGLEY tr. *Pol. Verg. de Invent.* v. i. 99 Which honored the day of consecrating their religions.., callinge it ye natiue daye of their sacred personages. **1566** DRANT *Horace, Sat.* II. ii. F iij b, If he dyd feast his frende at home, or kepe his natiue daye.

6. Belonging or appertaining to one as a possession or right by virtue of one's birth.

1570–6 LAMBARDE *Peramb. Kent* (1826) 453 Whereas all Nobilitie and Gentrie is either Native or Dative. **1593** SHAKS. *3 Hen. VI*, III. iii. 190 Did I put Henry from his Natiue Right? **1660** *Trial Regic.* 29, I am very unwilling to deprive myself of my Native Right. **1681** DRYDEN *Abs. & Achit.* 760 Can People give away, Both for themselves and Sons, their native Sway? **1784** COWPER *Task* v. 436 That man should thus..Abridge him of his just and native rights. **1801** STRUTT *Sports & Past.* Introd. 2 A bold, active, and warlike people, tenacious of their native liberty.

II. †**7.** Born in a state of villeinage. *Obs.*

1432–50 tr. *Higden* (Rolls) VIII. 39 Somme men say this pope was the native man of thabbot of Seynte Alban in Ynglonde. *Ibid.* 457 He scholde make alle men fre.., so that þere scholde not be eny native man after that tyme.

8. a. Connected with one by birth or race; closely related. Also const. †*to* and *with.* Now *rare.*

c **1470** HENRY *Wallace* VIII. 241 Byschope Beik full sodeynly thai se; And Robert Bruce, contrar his natiff men. *Ibid.* x. 169 Thai men, was natyff till Stwart..tuk hardement. **1513** DOUGLAS *Æneis* III. v. 125 Neir he approchit..And his awne native freindis knew in hy. *a* **1578** LINDESAY (Pitscottie) *Chron. Scot.* (S.T.S.) I. 390 His awin natiue cousing and freind. **1602** SHAKS. *Ham.* I. ii. 47 The Head is not more Natiue to the Heart..Then is the Throne of Denmark to thy Father. **1865** SWINBURNE *Atalanta* 504 Old men honourable, Who have..filled with gracious and memorial fame..alien lips and native with their own.

†**b.** = NATURAL *a.* 13. *Obs. rare.*

1567 MAPLET *Gr. Forest* 97 b, So soone as those yong can heare but their owne and Natiue Dams note, they leaue their Stepmother. *c* **1600** *Gentleman in Thracia* in Child *Ballads* VIII. 162 There is but one amongst the foure That is my native sonne.

†**9.** Entitled to a certain position by birth; natural, proper, rightful. *Obs.*

1564 *Reg. Privy Council Scot.* I. 304 The said David is in the rowme of him the auld kyndlie native possesour thairof. *c* **1580** SIDNEY *Ps.* VIII. viii, The fish, of sea the native heire. **1593** SHAKS. *Rich. II*, III. ii. 25 This Earth shall haue a feeling..ere her Natiue King Shall falter vnder foule Rebellious Armes.

10. a. Of metals and other minerals: Occurring naturally in a pure state or uncombined with other substances; also used to describe a mineral occurring in nature, in distinction from the corresponding substance formed artificially. So ***native rock.***

native amalgam: see AMALGAM *sb.* 1.

1695 WOODWARD *Nat. Hist. Earth* (1723) 19 Flint, Native-Vitriol, Spar. **1728** —— *Catal. For. Fossils* 22 Native Sulphur of a lemon color. **1760** WESLEY *Jrnl.* 10 Sept. (1827) III. 16 One end..was native rock. **1796** KIRWAN *Elem. Min.* (ed. 2) II. 156 The existence of Native Iron seems now placed beyond the reach of doubt. **1807** T. THOMSON *Chem.* (ed. 3) II. 531 As it is found native in abundance, it is seldom formed artificially. **1836–41** BRANDE *Chem.* (ed. 5) 953 Native Silver has the general characters of the pure metal. **1874** GARROD & BAXTER *Mat. Med.* 54 Aluminum..does not exist native, but is formed artificially from certain of its compounds.

b. *transf.* Applied to the state or form of such substances.

1753 CHAMBERS *Cycl. Supp.* s.v. *Natrum*, An alkali,.. fermenting very violently..in its native dry state. **1774** GOLDSM. *Nat. Hist.* (1776) I. 74 The variety of substances.. found in the bowels of the earth, in their native state. **1818** W. PHILLIPS *Outl. Min. & Geol.* (ed. 3) 40 Silver occurs in the metallic or native state. **1878** HUXLEY *Physiogr.* 81 In its purest native form [carbon] crystallizes as the diamond.

†**11.** Having a birth or natal origin; coming into existence by being born. *Obs. rare.*

After L. *nātīvus* in Cicero *De Nat. Deorum* I. x. 25.

1655 STANLEY *Hist. Philos.* II. (1701) 61/1 His Opinion.. was, that the Gods are native (having a beginning). **1678** CUDWORTH *Intell. Syst.* 209 A Multitude of such Deities, which yet they conceived to be all (as well as Men) Native and Mortal.

III. 12. a. Born in a particular place or country; belonging to a particular race, district, etc., by birth. In mod. use *spec.* with connotation of non-European (cf. NATIVE *sb.* 4).

c **1470** HENRY *Wallace* VIII. 545 Be caus I am a natyff Scottis man. **1494** FABYAN *Chron.* VI. ccv. 216 They before tyme were sworne to Edmunde.., and also were natyfe Englyssemen. **1560** DAUS tr. *Sleidane's Comm.* 426 b, Straungers being commaunded to departe, & the native countrie men there caste in pryson. **1600** SHAKS. *A.Y.L.* II. i. 23 The poore dapled fooles Being natiue Burgers of this desert City. **1665** BOYLE *Occas. Refl.* v. x. (1848) 335 She is ever a Natural, though no Native, Persian. **1687** A. LOVELL tr. *Thevenot's Trav.* I. 59 The native Turks are honest People, and love honest People. **1716** M. DAVIES *Athen. Brit.* III. *Diss. Drama* 27 England seems to have been always the least concern'd for the Encouragement of poor Native Proselyts to the Protestant Communion. **1782** R. CUMBERLAND *Anecd. Painters* I. 94 Spain at that brilliant æra was in possession of many native painters. **1802** JAMES *Milit. Dict.* s.v., Each regiment of native cavalry and native infantry. **1839** MALCOM *Trav.* (1840) 11/1 Having received endowments from a native gentleman, yielding annually 100,000 rupees. **1884** *Manch. Exam.* 17 May 5/1 The tolls.. were intended to be a protection to the native handicraftsmen in gold and silver.

b. In predicative use or placed after the sb. Also const. †*of* and *to*.

1558 KNOX *First Blast* (Arb.) 33 A man natiue amongest them selues. **1600** SHAKS. *A.Y.L.* III. ii. 356 Are you natiue of this place? **1602** —— *Ham.* IV. vii. 180 Like a creature Natiue, and indued Vnto that Element. **1671** MILTON *P.R.* II. 313 That Prophet bold Native of Thebez wandring here was fed. **1821** SHELLEY *Epipsych.* 426 This land would have remained a solitude But for some pastoral people native there. **1847** TENNYSON *Princ.* VII. 304 No Angel, but a dearer being, all dipt In Angel instincts,..Who look'd all native to her place.

c. ***native son*** *U.S.*, a native of a particular State.

1833 *Southern Patriot* (Charleston, S. Carolina) 27 July 2/6 Col. William Drayton..a native son of Carolina..left our shores. **1850** *Ex. Doc. 31st U.S. Congress 1 Sess. Senate* No. 76. 3 The native sons of the United States living in New Mexico knew their right to equality of privilege. **1864** *Weekly New Mexican* (Santa Fé) 25 Nov. 3 Lieut.-Colonel Chaves..is one of New Mexico's favorite native sons. **1913** *Dialect Notes* IV. 27 You can't get a job in California unless you are a native son. **1916** 'B. M. BOWER' *Phantom Herd* 27 [He] backed out of the way of the Native Son, who sprawled himself over the table corner. **1949** *Sun* (Baltimore) 7 Sept. 12/4 A bare victory in Ohio could not be taken as a decisive popular verdict for Mr. Taft's philosophy because the Taft philosophy had been supplemented by loyalty to a native son and that element could not be counted as a safe factor in general calculations. **1974** *News & Reporter* (Chester, S. Carolina) 22 Apr. 2-A/1 The man is a native son, is old enough and has resided in the state long enough.

13. a. Produced in or belonging to a certain country; of indigenous origin, production, or growth, as opposed to what is foreign or exotic.

1555 EDEN *Decades W. Ind.* 38 Images..very artificiously made of golde... The golde wherof they are made is natiue. **1601** SHAKS. *All's Well* I. iii. 152 'Tis often seene..choise breedes A natiue slip to vs from forraine seedes. **1616** R. C. *Times' Whistle* v. 2197 Tobacco.., Which being far fetcht only doth exceed In vertue all our native hearbes. **1670** R. COKE *Disc. Trade* 1 Trade is twofold, viz. Native, and Forein. *Ibid.* 28 So our Native Commodities are not valuable as if Trade were free. **1817** O'HARA *Hist. N.S. Wales* 242 Of native fruits, a cherry, insipid in comparison of the European sorts, was found. **1845** *Florist's Jrnl.* 143 Even now, when such numbers of our native flowers ought to be in full perfection, they are scarcely to be found. **1894** 'J. S. WINTER' *Red Coats* 118 Some biscuits, a tin of preserved chicken, some native cakes.

b. Of oysters. (See NATIVE *sb.* 5 b.)

1736 *English Oyster Fisheries* (1737) 22 They import none, and yet have, every Winter, very considerable Crops of Laid, as well as Native Oysters. **1855** DALLAS *Syst. Nat. Hist.* I. 428 The 'native' oysters are obtained from artificial oyster banks. **1865** *Pall Mall G.* 5 Dec. 5 It is rather a difficult matter to define what is a native oyster.

c. In names of Australian animals and birds, as ***native bustard, hen, rabbit, turkey.*** Also ***native bear*** = KOALA; ***native cat*** = DASYURE; ***native companion***, the BROLGA, *Megalornis rubicundus*; ***native dog*** = DINGO *sb.*

1820 J. OXLEY *Jrnls. Exped. Australia* 33 That large species of bittern, known on the east-coast by the local name of Native Companions. **1820** W. C. WENTWORTH *Descr. N.S. Wales* 62 The native dog..which is a species of the wolf. **1826** J. ATKINSON *Agric. N.S. Wales* 23 The rat, or native rabbit, has all the habits of the domestic rat of Europe. **1827** P. CUNNINGHAM *N.S. Wales* I. 317 Our *coola* (sloth or native bear) is about the size of an ordinary poodle dog. **1847** LEICHHARDT *Overland Exped.* 260 Several native bustards (*Otis Novæ-Hollandiæ*) were shot. **1848** GOULD *Birds Australia* VI. pl. 4 Australian Bustard;..Native Turkey. *Ibid.* pl. 71 *Tribonyx Mortierii*, Native Hen, of the Colonists. **1863** R. HENNING *Let.* 10 Aug. (1966) 137 It was not rats but a large 'native cat' that had so alarmed John... They are pretty little creatures with soft spotted fur, about the size of a kitten. **1880** MRS. MEREDITH *Tasman. Friends & Foes* 67 The native cat is similar [to the tiger cat], but smaller, and its fur is an ashy-grey. **1896, 1911** Native companion [see BROLGA]. **1911** E. M. CLOWES *On Wallaby* xi. 279 You may yet meet with..a lumbering native bear, like nothing on earth so much as a child's woolly toy, really the most ingratiating creature. Standing about two feet high, and covered with soft, thick fur, it has an odd, blunt, wistful sort of nose. **1916** J. B. COOPER *Coo-oo-ee* xii. 174, I saw for the first time a native bear on the bough of a black butt. **1928** 'BRENT OF BIN BIN' *Up Country* ii. 25 Bert's heelers..were tethered in a number of kennels placed around the fowl-houses as protection against native cats, which could devastate a fowl roost in one attack. **1934** T. WOOD *Cobbers* xvi. 189 Native companions—strange white stalky birds on stilts whose courtship dance is a marvel. **1946** K. TENNANT *Lost Haven* (1968) xiv. 237 The native companions..beating the water with their stumpy wings to frighten the little fish. They seemed to have their legs fastened on backwards at the joints. **1966** G. W. TURNER *Eng. Lang. Austral. & N.Z.* iii. 41 Koalas were more often called native bears in the early years. **1968** *Times* 23 Jan. (Austral. Suppl.) p. xiii/3 He..caught instead a pair of dibblers..believed to be extinct and of importance as a link between the smaller phascogales and the larger native cats.

d. In names of Australian and New Zealand plants, fruits, etc., as ***native borage, box, carrot, cherry, fuchsia, indigo***, etc. Also ***native bread***: see BREAD *sb.* 2 e; ***native bush*** *N.Z.*, woods or forests made up of indigenous trees and shrubs.

1826 Native cherry [see *five corners(s)*]. **1830** R. DAWSON *Pres. State Australia* 411 The shrub which is called the native cherry-tree, appears like a species of cypress. **1847** LEICHHARDT *Overland Exped.* 64 The native carrot..was here withered and in seed. *Ibid.* 124 The native Borage (*Trichodesma zeylanica*). **1860** G. BENNETT *Naturalist in Australia* 372 The *Correa virens*, with its pretty pendulous blossoms (from which it has been named the 'Native Fuchsia'). **1884** A. NILSON *Timber Trees New South Wales* 125 *X[ylomelum] pyriforme.*—Wooden Pear; Native Pear. **1889** J. H. MAIDEN *Useful Native Plants Austral.* 121 'Native Box'..is greedily eaten by sheep. *Ibid.* 286 *Ricinocarpus pinifolius*, Desf., Native Jasmine. This plant yields abundance of seeds, like small castor-oil seeds. They yield an oil. **1891** R. WALLACE *Rural Econ. Austral. & N.Z.* xxii. 294 *Panicum decompositum*, R. Br.—Barley grass, native millet, umbrella grass. Throughout Colonies, except Tasmania. **1898** MORRIS *Austral Eng.* 5/1 Emu A[pple]—*Owenia acidula*, F. v. M.; called also Native Nectarine. **1905** Native nectarine [see *emu-apple*]. **1908** E. J. BANFIELD *Confessions of Beachcomber* I. i. 20 Strong and spicy are the odours..in the jungle, the so-called native ginger, nutmeg ..and many others. **1926** *Trans. N.Z. Inst.* LVI. 662 The word 'native' has been prefixed to almost as many names as the words 'New Zealand'. **1928** 'BRENT OF BIN BIN' *Up Country* iii. 43 Its floor was spread with glowing embers from the bark of the native apple tree, specially suitable for the purpose. **1930** L. G. D. ACLAND *Early Canterbury Runs* vi. 125 The glorious view, native bush and trim gardens make it [*sc.* Peel Forest] one of the most beautiful homesteads in Canterbury. **1933** *Bulletin* (Sydney) 29 Mar. 25/1 Some of the potential plants of these pastures are rib grass, coolah grass..and native wheat grass. *Ibid.* 7 June 25/2 Another ornamental plant is the native jasmine, which grows to about 6 ft. high. This bush is often completely denuded of foliage by stock. **1934** *Ibid.* 15 Aug. 21/4 The thirsty traveller in the western parts of N.S.W. and Queensland welcomes the sight of a native nectarine (*Owenia acidula*) almost as much as a fresh-water spring. **1947** A. VOGT in D. M. Davin *N.Z. Short Stories* (1953) 377 Further back, even here, the hills were thick with native bush. **1959** A. MCLINTOCK *Descr. Atlas N.Z.* 80 Stewart Island..is a popular tourist resort with unspoiled native bush,..and a wealth of birdlife. **1966** W. S. RAMSON *Austral. Eng.* v. 82 In some cases the resemblance to an English species was sufficient for the choice of name, but a qualification was introduced through the use of a particularizer, as, for instance, in..native pear. **1967** A. M. BLOMBERY *Guide Native Austral. Plants* 313 *S[antalum] acuminatum.* Quandong, Native Peach... A shrub or small tree with light greyish-green, narrow, lanceolate leaves and bright-red fruits.

14. Belonging to, used by, characteristic of, the natives of a particular place.

1796 MORSE *Amer. Geog.* I. 471 The native right to half this territory was extinguished by a treaty. **1854** G. H. HAYDON *Austral. Emigrant* 126 *note*, *Carbora*, the native name of an animal of the sloth species. **1891** R. WALLACE *Rural Econ. Austral. & N.Z.* xiv. 215 Mrs. Donnelly is perhaps one of the most able lawyers in relation to native affairs that New Zealand possesses, and..has earned..the reputation of a Maori Portia. **1897** MARY KINGSLEY *W. Africa* 74 Living in the native houses while she built..her present house. **1914** R. FRY *Let.* (1972) II. 378 Are you going to Tunis? If so..he'll give you Arab dinners in a lovely Arab house in the middle of the native quarter. **1950** M. CHAPPELL *Rhodesian Adventure* ix. 101, I believe the original native name for the place where Salisbury stands was 'Harari'. **1961** G. GREENE *In Search of a Character* I. 14 The 'method' here seems to be to drive around the native town until a likely girl is seen. **1975** C. ALLEN *Plain Tales from Raj* i. 25 The native bazaar was..out of bounds..to all European children.

15. Special Combs., as ***Native American***, a North American Indian; also *attrib.* or as *adj.*; ***native location*** *S. Afr.* = LOCATION 5; ***native oven*** (*N.Z.*) = COPPER MAORI; a similar oven in Australia; ***native question***, the question of relations between colonizers and the indigenous population of a country; ***native reserve***, an area of land set aside by a colonial power for the exclusive use of the indigenous population; ***native state, Native State***, during the period of British dominion of India, the term used to designate a state outside British territory which was governed by a native ruler; also called 'Indian State', 'princely state'.

1956 A. HUXLEY *Let.* 20 Oct. (1969) 809 Thank you for your most interesting letter about the Native American churchmen. **1973** *Black Panther* 7 Apr. 4/1 Appearing at the awards in Brando's behalf was the beautiful, gracious, and now famous Native American woman, Sacheen Littlefeather, who, dressed in the traditional garments of her people, read a prepared statement. **1973** *New Society* 19 July 137/1 Services at a Native American Church, a denomination that combines Indian and Christian beliefs. **1974** *Black Panther* 19 Jan. 3/2 In a vain attempt to cover the highly-political nature of the trial, the government has accused the two Native Americans of crimes such as burglary, larceny, and auto theft rather than accuse them of the real charges: of standing up for the dignity and culture of Indian peoples. [**1855** W. C. HOLDEN *Hist. Natal* viii. 176 The plan of government devised was, to preserve the Natives distinct from the whites; and, for this purpose, large tracts of country were set aside, under the designation of 'Locations for the Natives'. On these Locations the Natives were to be collected, and governed by their own laws, through the medium of their own chiefs.] **1866** in *Towards Dict. S. Afr. Eng.* (1971) 51 Crime has considerably increased during the year; which is in a great measure to be attributed to the scarcity of food in the native locations. **1881** *Convention of Pretoria* in J. Nixon *Compl. Story Transvaal* (1884) 348 Article 21, Forthwith, after the taking effect of this Convention, a Native Location Commission will be constituted. **1928** R. L. BUELL *Native Probl. Afr.* I. I. iii. 50 Each South African city has its native location in which the native population must supposedly live, and in which houses are usually rented from the municipality. **1955** *Problems & Tensions in S. Afr.* 374 In a few Native locations there is adequate provision for good schools, health centres, stores and churches. **1832** A. EARLE *Narr. Residence N.Z.* xxviii. 96 On a spot of rising ground, just outside the village, we saw a man preparing a native oven, which is done in the following simple manner:—A hole is made in the ground, and hot stones are put within it, and then all is covered up close. **1834, 1889** [see COPPER MAORI]. **1905** W. B. *Where White Man Treads* 101 (*heading*) The haangi—(native oven). **1911** C. E. W. BEAN *'Dreadnought' of Darling* xxvi. 227 Menindie..swarms with native ovens and other relics of the blacks. **1917** H. W. WILLIAMS *Dict. Maori Lang.* 41/2 *Hāngi*.., native oven, consisting of a circular hole in the ground, in which the food was cooked by heated stones. **1900** (*title*) Native question in South Africa. **1924** E. M. FORSTER *Passage to India* II. ii. 32 Adela, who meditated spending her life in the country, was a more serious matter; it would be tiresome if she started crooked over the native question. **1927** W. PLOMER *I speak of Afr.* 255, I am the only one here who doesn't depend for a living on the native question. **1971** *Oxf. Hist. S. Afr.* II. viii. 403 In 1914 'the Native question' was mentioned only in passing. **1928** R. L. BUELL *Native Probl. Afr.* I. v. 71 All land was simply declared public land,..which alienated it to European settlers after establishing in several cases, notable in Natal, native reserves. **1950** M. CHAPPELL *Rhodesian Adventure* ix. 101 The whole area is a native reserve and looks no different today than it has for centuries. **1953** P. ABRAHAMS *Return to Goli* iv. 106 The result is that nowhere else in Africa is land-hunger as acute as it is in the Union's 'Native Reserves'. **1966** M. M. COLE *S. Afr.* (ed. 2) xlv. 687 The Native Reserves in the Republic are incapable of supporting all the Bantu population in agriculture. **1784** *Act 24 Geo. III* c. 25 §15 Treating or negociating with any of the Native Princes or States in India. [*Ibid.* §35 To negociate or conclude any Treaty of Peace..with any Indian Prince or State.] **1823** J. MALCOLM *Mem. Cent. India* II. xvi. 280 The present condition of our empire in India requires..in the exercise of political control and superintendence over Native States, a school..distinct from other branches of the service. **1883** J. S. COTTON in Cotton & Payne *Colonies & Dependencies* I. iii. 23 The native states are sometimes called feudatory—a convenient term to express their vague relation to the British crown. **1886** KIPLING *Departmental Ditties* (ed. 2) 7 Rustum Beg of Kolazai—slightly backward Native State—Lusted for a C.S.I. **1894** W. LEE-WARNER *Protected Princes India* i. 2 The most cursory examination of the Native states brings to light a confusing variety in their size, their origin, and their development. **1931** P. KENDALL *India & British*

viii. 223 Hyderabad, the largest..of all the Native States, absorbed Golconda centuries ago. **1963** M. A. RAHIM *Ld. Dalhousie's Administration* i. 4 As regards the condition of Indian states, there were many so-called independent native principalities or states, but actually..they were firmly controlled by the British Government.

native-born, *a.* [f. prec. + BORN *ppl. a.*]

†**a.** *Sc.* Having a certain position or status by birth. *Obs.* **b.** Belonging to a particular place or country by birth; sometimes *spec.* applied to persons of immigrant race born in a colony.

1500–20 DUNBAR *Poems* lx. 45 And he is maister natiwe borne, And all his eldaris him beforne. **1524** *Aberdeen Reg.* (1844) I. 109 All begaris excep tham that ar natif borne within this tovne. **1572–3** *Reg. Privy Council Scot.* II. 207 Strangearis and native borne subjectis of the same.

1849 LYELL *2nd Visit U.S.* II. 115 The word creole is used in Louisiana to express a native-born American, whether black or white, descended from old world parents. **1865** J. H. INGRAHAM *Pillar of Fire* (1872) 55 The hieroglyphic form of writing is difficult to be understood, save by a native-born Egyptian. **1894** H. PARRY *Stud. Gt. Composers, Palestrina* 8 The first musical work that was ever published and dedicated to a pope by a native-born Italian.

absol. **1896** KIPLING *Seven Seas, The Native-born.*

natively ('neɪtɪvlɪ), *adv.* [f. NATIVE *a.* + -LY².] In a native manner.

1. †**a.** Naturally, without disguise, plainly, straightforwardly. *Obs.*

a **1564** BECON *Nosegay* Wks. 1564 I. 119 That ye myghte natiuely & vnfayndlye on this sorte loue youre neyghbour. **1626** T. H[AWKINS] tr. *Caussin's Holy Crt.* 110 To represent so natiuely to vs the blindnesse of the great, and rich of this world. **1677** GALE *Crt. Gentiles* IV. 191 To speak natively and distinctly. *Ibid.* 300 This is more natively and clearly laid down in Sacred Philosophie.

b. In the way natural to one; without art or artifice. *rare.*

1639 N. N. tr. *Du Bosq's Compl. Woman* II. 53 In lieu of expressing their thoughts natively, they are troubled and confounded. *Ibid.* 59 There is nothing even or natively done in their behaviours. **1856** EMERSON *Eng. Traits, Manners,* They will let you break all the commandments, if you do it natively, and with spirit.

†**c.** Without forcing or wresting. *Obs.*

1671 [R. MACWARD] *True Nonconf.* 374 Though it arise most natively from the words, and be clearly verifiable. *a* **1732** T. BOSTON *Crook in Lot* (1805) 50 This natively follows on that desire. **1745** WESLEY *Wks.* (1830) I. 496, I often thought since I was favoured with this letter how far it natively and clearly went.

2. Innately, originally, naturally; by virtue of birth, origin, or inherent qualities.

1609 TOURNEUR *Sir F. Vere* 43 Labour increas'd what natively was bred. **1631** R. BYFIELD *Doctr. Sabb.* 79, I cannot tell how any thing should bee evill natively. **1658** SIR T. BROWNE *Gard. Cyrus* Wks. (Bohn) II. 509 How they [spiders] are natively provided with a stock sufficient for such texture. **1710** STEELE *Tatler* No. 211 ¶4 There is something so natively great and good in a Person that is truly devout. **1804** EUGENIA DE ACTON *Tale without Title* III. 211 One of the most natively lovely figures of the sex. **1815** MME. D'ARBLAY *Diary* (1876) IV. lxiv. 307 M. D'Arblay again joined me, revived by his natively martial spirit. **1850** MCCOSH *Div. Govt.* III. i. (1874) 290 Virtue or moral good is not natively known by the mind as an abstract or general idea. **1881** J. CAIRNS in *Chr. World Pulpit* XIX. 315 That which is not natively great cannot be truly or pre-eminently great.

†**b.** As the native language. *Obs. rare*⁻¹.

1612 BREREWOOD *Lang. & Relig.* i. 8 These were the places, where the Greek tongue was natively and vulgarly spoken, either originally or by reason of colonies.

†**c.** In respect of origin; indigenously. *Obs.*

1629 LIGHTFOOT *Misc.* 118, I take two names giuen to Christ..to be natiuely Chaldee words. **1730** A. GORDON *Maffei's Amphith.* 226 The Tuscan Order..is peculiarly and natively our own.

†**3.** By natural structure or growth; not artificially. *Obs.*

1672 in Heath *Grocer's Comp.* (1869) 496 A grass green Mountain natively crowned with a steep rock. **1737** SAVAGE *Public Spirit* 66 Rank above rank here shapely greens ascend, There others natively grotesque depend.

nativeness ('neɪtɪvnɪs). [f. as prec. + -NESS.] The fact or quality of being native; naturalness.

1639 N. N. tr. *Du Bosq's Compl. Woman* II. 53 As a forcednesse displeaseth in the fairest actions, a certain nativenesse takes and pleaseth in the least. *Ibid.* 55. **1727** in BAILEY vol. II. **1817** COLERIDGE *Biog. Lit.* (Bohn) 3 The truth and nativeness both of their thoughts and diction. *a* **1821** KEATS *Sonn.* Wks. (1884) 363 Ocean..never can Subside, if not to dark blue nativeness. **1853** G. JOHNSTON *Nat. Hist. E. Bord.* I. 32 Its nativeness is unquestioned.

nativism ('neɪtɪvɪz(ə)m). [f. as prec. + -ISM: in sense 2 perh. ad. F. *nativisme.*]

1. a. (Chiefly *U.S.*) Prejudice in favour of natives against strangers; the practice or policy of protecting the interests of the native residents against those of immigrants.

1845 *Congress. Globe* 18 Dec. 66 In the City of New York nativism had its origin in the disputes of the Tammany party. **1856** *N. & Q.* 2nd Ser. I. 9/2 In a kind of feud now existing between American-born and foreign-born citizens, the former are said to profess Nativism. **1864** NICOLS *40 Years Amer. Life* II. 90 These necessities destroyed nativism and the political Anti-Catholic party. **1890** S. J. DUNCAN *Social Departure* 230 Graphic fervour, wherein his nativism showed like the cloven foot. **1965** *Guardian* 6 Aug. 5/3 The revived nativism of white, rural, Protestant America. **1968** G. W. STOCKING *Race, Culture & Evolution* xi. 297 This reaction was related to the national outburst of nativism which..was to lead finally in 1923 to the passage of legislation which closed the era of mass immigration by non-'Nordics'.

b. *Anthrop.* (See quot. 1972.)

1964 GOULD & KOLB *Dict. Social Sci.* 458/1 Examples of nativism would include peyotism and cargo cults. Another example is the Ghost Dance of the American Indians. **1972** D. DAVIES *Dict. Anthropol.* 132/1 *Nativism,* the movement of societies back toward a reaffirmation of their native tribal cultures as a reaction when acculturation seems to be threatening their tribal identity and culture.

2. a. *Philos.* The doctrine of innate ideas.

1887 *Mind* XII. 628 The Stoics...he holds, combined the truth that is in sensationalism with the truth that is in nativism. **1901** *Chambers's Encycl.* VIII. 476/1 The opposed views of Nativism and Empiricism.

b. *Psychol.* and *Linguistics.* The doctrine that certain capacities or abilities, esp. those of sense perception, are innate rather than acquired; the theory that in the development of language an inherent connection exists in the mind between sound and sense.

1892 *Monist* II. 316 By Nativism, Marty understands the theory that certain involuntary articulate sounds are associated with certain ideas. **1924** R. M. OGDEN tr. *Koffka's Growth of Mind* i. 1 And even to-day no agreement has been reached between the rival theories of *empiricism* and *nativism,* the first of which emphasizes the influence of environment, and the second the influence of heredity. **1968** D. PRICE-WILLIAMS in J. Clifton *Introd. Cultural Anthropol.* xii. 312/1 Visual illusions have given cross-cultural psychologists a considerable body of data with which to assess the factors of nativism and empiricism in perception. **1970** *Language* XLVI. 139 In the revival of Cartesian philosophical views of language, a number of other moribund doctrines have been brought to spectral life, too: mentalism, nativism (the innate-endowment component in child language studies). **1972** *Encycl. Psychol.* II. 308/1 *Nativism,* the belief that human behavior and particularly human perceptual mechanisms are inborn and determined by genetics, as opposed to the belief that they are the result of learning and experience.

nativist ('neɪtɪvɪst). [f. as prec. + -IST.]

1. *U.S. Pol.* One who favours or advocates a policy of nativism. Also *attrib.*

1864 NICOLS *40 Years Amer. Life* II. 78 The nativist party, with its secret organization. **1885** LALOR tr. *Von Holst's Const. Hist. U.S.* V. ix. 436 Fillmore..was chosen by the Nativists of Philadelphia as their standard-bearer. **1894** *Forum* July 534 [The South] was full of nativist feeling in its best form.

2. a. *Philos.* One who holds the doctrine of innate ideas. Also *attrib.*

1881 *Nation* (N.Y.) XXXII. 191 The Intellectualists and the Sensationalists in vision, or, as Helmholtz prefers to call them, the Empiricists and the Nativists. **1901** *Chambers's Encycl.* VIII. 475/2 The Intuitive or Nativist theory, according to which space is an innate idea.

b. *Psychol.* and *Linguistics.* One who holds the doctrine of innate capacities, or of an inherent connection between sound and meaning in language.

1924 R. M. OGDEN tr. *Koffka's Growth of Mind* iii. §5. 76 To the empiricist the observed development [of fixation] is regarded as a process of learning; while the nativist regards it as a process of maturation. **1930** W. LEOPOLD in J. T. Hatfield et al. *Curme Vol. Ling. Stud.* 106 It might be possible to find..a tie of union even between views as contrasting as those of Wundt and Marty, of nativists and teleologists, in the philosophy of language. **1971** *Jrnl. Gen. Psychol.* LXXXV. 18 The argument of nativists that the phenomenal experience is not found to be as fluid or flexible as would be expected under an empirical approach.

Hence **nati'vistic** *a.*

1880 *Nation* (N.Y.) 22 Apr., The nativistic tendencies of the Whig party. **1881** LE CONTE *Sight* 103 The one is called the nativistic, the other the empiristic theory. **1922** O. JESPERSEN *Lang.* xxi. 415 A closely related theory is the nativistic, nicknamed the *ding-dong,* theory, according to which there is a mystic harmony between sound and sense. **1943** *Amer. Anthropologist* XLV. 230 The term 'nativistic' has been loosely applied to a rather wide range of phenomena... We may define a nativistic movement as, 'Any conscious, organized attempt on the part of a society's members to revive or perpetuate selected aspects of its culture'. **1946** D. MCCARTHY in L. Carmichael *Manual of Child Psychol.* x. 501/2 Sapir..proposes a nativistic theory of phonetic symbolism which has given rise to considerable controversy. **1958** F. M. KEESING *Cultural Anthropol.* xvi. 406 'Nativistic' movements, including the new religious cults spoken of earlier. **1966** M. PEI *Gloss. Ling. Terminol.* 177 *Nativistic theory,* the view that a mystic harmony or connection exists between sound and meaning, and that human speech is the result of an instinct of primitive man. **1968** D. PRICE-WILLIAMS in J. Clifton *Introd. Cultural Anthropol.* xii. 312/1 The results support the Gestalt position and thus the nativistic viewpoint. **1974** *Listener* 7 Mar. 294/1 A nationalist—or as the officials prefer to call it—'nativistic' movement..in the South Pacific.

nativity (nə'tɪvɪtɪ). Forms: (2 **natiuiteð**), 4–5 **natyvyte, -tie,** 4–6 **nativyte, -vite,** (4 **-tee**), 6–7 **nativitie, -tye,** 6– **nativity.** [In ME. a. F. *nativité* (12th c.), ad. L. *nātīvitāt-em*: see NATIVE *a.* and -ITY. The late OE. *nativiteð* represents the older F. form *nativited.*

a **1122** *O.E. Chron.* (Laud MS.) an. 1102 On þisum ȝeare to Natiuiteð wæs se cyng Heanriȝ on Westmynstre.]

1. The birth of Christ, of the Virgin, or of St. John the Baptist.

a **1300** *Cursor M.* 11383 Þis kinges thre þar wai þai tok A tuelmoth ar þe natiuite. *a* **1340** HAMPOLE *Psalter* Cant. 507 Lord þis natiuite of þe maydyn is þi werk. **1382** WYCLIF *Mark* Prol., Mark..tellith not the natiuite of Crist bi fleissche. *c* **1400** MAUNDEV. (Roxb.) xi. 43 Þare schewed þe aungell þe natiuitee of sayn Iohn Baptist. **1450–1530** *Myrr. our Ladye* 212 How men oughte to worshyp her natyuyte in erthe. **1526** *Pilgr. Perf.* (W. de W. 1531) 25 b, To do honour and homage to his grace in his blessed natiuite. **1575–85** ABP. SANDYS *Serm.* (Parker Soc.) 286 At the time of his nativity..there was peace amongst all nations. **1656** VAUGHAN *Thalia Rediv., Nativity,* Poor Galile, thou canst not be The place for His nativity. **1756–7** tr. *Keysler's Trav.* (1760) III. 96 The basso-relievo representing the nativity of Christ. **1844** *Mem. Babylon. P'cess* II. 101 The house..in which St. John the Baptist was born. The place of his nativity is ornamented with magnificent bas reliefs.

b. A picture representing the Nativity.

1644 EVELYN *Diary* 10 Nov., Two famous pieces of Bassano, the one a Vulcan, the other a Nativity! **1876** *Encycl. Brit.* IV. 653/2 Among his..pieces is a Nativity, representing the angels around the infant Christ.

2. The church festival commemorating the birth of Christ, observed on the 25th of December; Christmas. Also, the festivals of the birth of the Virgin, Sept. 8, and of St. John Baptist, June 24.

a **1300** *Cursor M.* 13186 Men mai yeitt se sum sted in france Wod men at his [*sc.* St. John Baptist's] natiuite To kirk be draun. *c* **1380** WYCLIF *Wks.* (1880) 41 And faste þei fro þe feste of alle hawen til þe natyuyte of crist. **1389** in *Eng. Gilds* (1870) 14 Þe sunday aftir þe natiuite of oure lady. **1465** *Mann. & Househ. Exp.* (Roxb.) 302 The Munday next affter our Lady day the Natyvyte. **1495** *Act 11 Hen. VII,* c. 25 §6 At the fest of the Nativyte of oure Lord. **1556** W. TOWERSON in Hakluyt *Voy.* (1589) 104 The 25. day being the day of the natiuitie of Christ. **1642** C. VERNON *Consid. Exch.* 83 Those to bee paid at the Feast of the Nativity of our Lord God. **1659** H. L'ESTRANGE *Alliance Div. Off.* 136 The Nativity of our Lord Jesus Christ was now at hand. **1727–38** CHAMBERS *Cycl.* s.v., When we say absolutely the nativity, it is understood of that of Jesus Christ, or the feast of Christmas. **1883** *Encycl. Brit.* XV. 592/2 The Nativity of Mary..was appointed to be observed by the Synod of Salzburg in 800.

3. Birth, in ordinary contexts.

1382 WYCLIF *Ezek.* xxix. 14, Y shal sette hem to gydre.. in to the loond of her natiuyte. **1390** GOWER *Conf.* III. 77 He which hath the child begete..The time of his nativite.. Awaiteth. *c* **1420** *Pallad. on Husb.* VII. 207 Se where is the kingis natiuite. *c* **1450** *St. Cuthbert* (Surtees) 14 In þe first part sall ȝe se His nation and hes natyuyte. **1535** COVERDALE *Ecclus.* xxiii. 14 Lest thou..wyshe not to haue bene borne, and so curse the daye of thy natiuite. **1590** SHAKS. *Com. Err.* IV. iv. 32, I haue serued him from the houre of my Natiuitie to this instant. **1612** T. TAYLOR *Comm. Titus* iii. 5 Many euen old men,..who know no nativity but one of Adam and Eve. **1672** SIR T. BROWNE *Let. Friend* §5 If it could be made out that such who have easie nativities have commonly hard deaths. **1712** M. HENRY *Reformat. Serm.* Wks. 1853 II. 489/1 Hearty well-wishers to the land of their nativity. **1771** *Antiq. Sarisb.* 235 William Horman had his nativity in Newstreet, Sarum. **1820** SHELLEY *Fiordispina* 14 Which could not be But by dissevering their nativity.

b. *transf.* and *fig.*

1535 COVERDALE *Wisd.* vi. 22 As for wyszdome,..I..wil seke her out from yᵉ begynnynge of the natiuyte. **1590** SHAKS. *Mids. N.* III. ii. 125 Looke when I vow I weepe; and vowes so borne, In their natiuity all truth appeares. **1646** SIR T. BROWNE *Pseud. Ep.* I. vi. (1686) 17 Plagiary had not its Nativity with Printing. **1652** FRENCH *Yorksh. Spa* vi. 56 For the better illustration of this nativity of salts. **1684** T. BURNET *Th. Earth* III. 40 Here you see the birth and nativity of the sea, or of Oceanus, describ'd. **1831** LAMB *Elia* Ser. II. *Newspapers 35 Yrs. Ago,* The jealous waters..reluctant to have the humble spot of their nativity revealed. **1886** RUSKIN *Præterita* I. iv. 124 The native architectural instinct is instantly developed in these,—highly notable for any one who cares to note such nativities.

†**c.** *of one's nativity,* belonging to one by birth, natural. *Obs. rare.*

After *vultus nativitatis* in the Vulgate (Jas. i. 23).

1582 N.T. (Rhem.) *Jas.* i. 23 A man beholding the countenance of his natiuitie in a glasse. **1660** N. INGELO *Bentiv. & Ur.* I. (1682) 121, I see the face of my nativity.

4. Birth considered astrologically; a horoscope.

1390 GOWER *Conf.* I. 55 Bot upon here nativite Such was the constellacion [etc.]. *c* **1391** CHAUCER *Astrol.* II. §4 Yit is the planete *in horoscopo,* be it in natiuite or in eleccioun. **1508** DUNBAR *Poems* vii. 74 Hie furius Mars..Rong in the hevin at thyne natiuite. **1563** *Mirr. Mag., Somerset* vii, A straunge natiuitie in calculation. **1630** *R. Johnson's Kingd. & Commw.* 15 Those who have Mars Lord in their Nativities, become either Souldiers or Trades-men. **1660** PEPYS *Diary* 24 Oct., Mr. Booker..did tell me a great many fooleries which may be done by nativities. **1708** SWIFT *Predict. for* 1708, Wks. 1755 II. I. 150, I have consulted the star of his nativity by my own rules. **1815** SCOTT *Guy M.* iii, I will calculate his nativity according to the rule of the Triplicities. *c* **1850** *Arab. Nts.* (Rtldg.) 448 The king called an assembly of all the astrologers.., and ordered them to calculate the nativity of his child.

5. a. Birth as determining nationality.

1592 WEST *1st Pt. Symbol.* §46 l, Natural capacitie by birth, which euerie liege subject being borne within her Maiesties dominions hath by his natiuitie. **1785** PALEY *Mor. Philos.* (1818) II. 133 The circumstance of nativity, that is of claiming and treating as subjects all those who are born within the confines of their dominions. **1821–30** LD. COCKBURN *Mem.* (1856) 296 He owed this to his Scotch nativity and education. **1870** ANDERSON *Missions Amer. Bd.* II. xx. 161 His Irish nativity, and consequent right to receive British protection.

†**b.** Birth with reference to descent or breeding.

c **1550** H. RHODES *Bk. Nurture* 678 in *Babees Bk.* (1868) 101 A Gentleman should mercy vse to set forth his natiuitye. **1587** GOLDING *De Mornay* xxiv. (1592) 363 Thereby they were certified of their original natiuitie.

†**6.** The condition of being born a serf. *Obs. rare.*

1609 SKENE *Reg. Maj.* 91 The third kinde of nativitie, or bondage. *Ibid.*, Gif he.. flees away fra his maister, or denyes to him his nativitie.

7. Indigenousness.

1871 *Trans. New Zealand Inst.* IV. 238 On the Nativity in New Zealand of *Polygonum aviculare*.

8. *attrib.* and *Comb.*, as ***nativity-caster***, ***-ceremony***, ***-day***, ***-song***, ***-water***; † **nativity-broth**, (?); † **nativity-pie**, ? a Christmas pie.

1584 R. SCOT *Discov. Witchcr.* XI. xxiii. (1886) 172 Who shall obtaine everlasting live by meanes of constellations, as nativitie-casters affirme. **1605** B. JONSON *Volpone* I. i, A precise illuminate brother.. will drop you forth a libel, or a sanctified lie, Betwixt every spoonful of a nativity-pie. **1614** —— *Barth. Fair* I. ii, My mother has had her natiuity-water cast lately by the Cunning men in Cow-lane. **1654** H. L'ESTRANGE *Chas. I* (1655) 156 This Warre was the Epoche, the Nativity day from whence all the series of this Kings troubles are to be compiled. **1665** WITHER *Lord's Prayer* 31 A Complement more Magnificent then the Nativity-Ceremonies, of all other Kings put together. *Ibid.*, A Celestial Army celebrated his Birth, with a Nativity-Song. **1674** T. FLATMAN *Belly God* 107 There is your French Pottage, Nativity broth, Yet that of Fetter lane exceeds them both.

nativize ('neɪtɪvaɪz), *v. Linguistics.* [f. NATIVE *a.* + -IZE.] *trans.* To render native; *spec.* **a.** To adapt (a loan word) to the phonetic structure of the native language. **b.** To develop (a pidgin language) into a creole used as a first language. Hence **'nativized** *ppl. a.*, **,nativi'zation**.

1933 L. BLOOMFIELD *Lang.* xxv. 454 From the completely nativized ['šowfr̩] *chauffeur*, we have the back-formation *to chauffe* [šowf]. **1940** *Proc. Amer. Philos. Soc.* LXXXII. 15 'Scandalous examples of Great Russian chauvinism' have often interfered with what is called the nativization of the Soviet apparatus. **1970** *Language* XLVI. 66 A Nupe speaker will consistently 'nativize' [Cɔ] as [Cʷa] and [Cɛ] as [Cʸa]. *Ibid.*, The position supported by this evidence is that the nativization of foreign sounds is a valid indicator of what rules have been internalized. **1971** I. F. HANCOCK in J. Spencer *Eng. Lang. W. Afr.* 113 When a pidgin supplants a 'full' language, changes must occur... Therefore in becoming *nativised* and thereby *creolised*, it expands its vocabulary, produces more explicit grammatical constructions and becomes more fixed in pronunciation.

N.A.T.O., NATO, Nato ('neɪtəʊ). [Acronym f. the initials of *N*orth *A*tlantic *T*reaty *O*rganization, set up in 1949.] A military alliance of the United States and Canada with certain European nations. So **'Nato-ish** *a.*, supporting N.A.T.O.; **'Natoism**, adherence to N.A.T.O.; **'Natoist**, a supporter of N.A.T.O.

1950 *Newsweek* 14 Aug. 40/3 Nato is the newest synthetic word in the international gobbledygook and stands for the North Atlantic treaty organization. **1962** H. O. BEECHENO *Introd. Business Stud.* i. 5 Britain had also put her military forces under a unified command in NATO (the North Atlantic Treaty Organization). **1965** *Economist* 28 Aug. 770/3 The Socialist People's party has accused Labour of being too capitalist and too Nato-ish. **1965** *New Statesman* 24 Dec. 992/2 De Gaulle will not budge on his slightly neutralist type of Natoism. **1966** *Ibid.* 18 Mar. 366/2 The opposition.. includes a lot of outright Natoists (Mollet and even Mitterrand also support Nato, with reservations). **1975** *Guardian* 5 Dec. 3/1 Britain is interested in buying several of the aircraft provided that other European NATO countries also join in.

natomy, dial. form of ANATOMY.

natour, obs. form of NATURE *sb.*

† **'natre**, anglicized form of NATRON. *Obs. rare.*

1756 P. BROWNE *Jamaica* (1789) 38 The Egyptian Natre, and Tartarian Natre.

natrium ('neɪtrɪəm, 'nætrɪəm). *Chem. rare.* [f. NATR-ON + -IUM.] Sodium.

1842 FRANCIS *Dict. Arts & Sci.*, *Natrium*, the name given by the German chemists to sodium, the metallic base of soda. **1870** GARROD *Mat. Med.* (ed. 3) 131 Sodium.. called also Natrium, is contained in the soda salts, but does not exist native.

natriuresis (,neɪtrɪ-, ,nætrɪ(j)ʊ'riːsɪs). *Med.* [f. NATRI(UM + Gr. οὔρησις urination.] The excretion of abnormally large amounts of sodium in the urine.

1957 H. W. SMITH in *Amer. Jrnl. Med.* XXIII. 625/2 An increase or decrease in sodium excretion will be designated as natriuresis and antinatriuresis. **1974** *Nature* 11 Jan. 109/1 The natriuresis produced by the intra-renal release of kallikrein may be effected by vasodilator and permeability effects on the renal vasculature and tubules.

Hence **natriuretic** (-'ɛtɪk) *a.*, causing or pertaining to natriuresis.

1957 *Amer. Jrnl. Med.* XXIII. 625/1 The natriuretic effects of the infusion of large volumes of saline solution are in part controlled by the absence of natriuresis after the infusion of iso-oncotic albumin. **1974** *Nature* 11 Jan. 109/1 The data on sodium excretion place substance P amongst the most potent natriuretic substances so far described.

natro- ('neɪtrəʊ, 'nætrəʊ-), comb. form of NATRIUM, used in *Min.* to form the names of sodium-containing minerals (as NATROLITE), and also prefixed to existing mineral names to indicate the (often partial) substitution of sodium for some other metal in that mineral, as **natro'alunite**, any of the range of basic sulphates of sodium, potassium, and aluminium, $(Na,K)Al_3(SO_4)_2(OH)_6$, which have the proportion of sodium greater than that of potassium and are found as white hexagonal crystals; *spec.* the sodic end-member of this series; **natro'chalcite** [L. *chalcītes* CHALCITES], a basic hydrated sulphate of sodium and copper, $NaCu_2(SO_4)_2(OH).H_2O$, which is found as emerald-green monoclinic crystals at Chuquicamata in Chile; **natro'davyne** [ad. It. *natrodavyna* (F. Zambonini 1910, in *Atti d. R. Accad. d. Sci. fis. e mat.* XIV. VI. 188)], a silicate and carbonate of aluminium and sodium, found as colourless hexagonal crystals; **natro'jarosite**, a basic sulphate of sodium and iron, $NaFe_3(SO_4)_2(OH)_6$, found as yellow or brown hexagonal crystals; **,natromonte'brasite** [a. F. *natromontebrasite* (F. Gonnard 1913, in *Bull. de la Soc. franç. de Min.* XXXVI. 120)], a basic fluoride and phosphate of sodium, lithium, and aluminium, $(Na,Li)Al(PO_4)(OH,F)$, with more sodium than lithium, which is found as whitish triclinic crystals.

1902 HILLEBRAND & PENFIELD in *Amer. Jrnl. Sci.* CLXIV. 220 The name natroalunite might be employed to designate the two varieties of alunite from Colorado.., where the proportion of the soda to the potash molecule is 7:4. **1937** *Amer. Mineralogist* XXII. 944 Small amounts of finely granular natroalunite have attacked the andalusite ores. **1968** I. KOSTOV *Mineral.* II. 493 Natroalunite is a sodium analogue [of alunite] $NaAl_3(SO_4)_2(OH)_6$. **1969** *Mineral. Abstr.* XX. 146/1 The first occurrence of natroalunite and natrojarosite from Argentina is noted from the area around La Flecha gorge. **1908** PALACHE & WARREN in *Amer. Jrnl. Sci.* CLXXVI. 343 The collection.. was obtained from exhausted copper veins and includes.. natrochalcite (a new mineral). **1944** *Econ. Geol.* XXXIX. 274 The SO_3 concentration is so reduced that chalcanthite, natrochalcite, and krohnkite become unstable and antlerite takes their place. **1968** I. KOSTOV *Mineral.* II. 514 Natrochalcite is monoclinic ($C2/m$), occurring as acute pyramidal green crystals with perfect {001} cleavage. **1913** *Mineral. Mag.* XVI. 367 Natrodavyne... Hexagonal crystals, rich in faces, hitherto referred to nepheline or to davyne. **1963** *Canad. Mineralogist* VII. 632 Dry material of the natrodavyne composition was prepared by mixing α-cristobalite, γ-alumina and Na_2SiO_3 in the correct stoichiometric proportions for the formation of nepheline, and then adding the required weight of anhydrous Na_2CO_3. **1902** HILLEBRAND & PENFIELD in *Amer. Jrnl. Sci.* CLXIV. 219 It has seemed to the writers best to designate the new compounds described in this article as natrojarosite and plumbojarosite, the names signifying their relation to a well known species. **1938** *Amer. Mineralogist* XXIII. 757 At Chuquicamata natrojarosite is associated with chalcanthite, kroehnkite and sulphur. **1969** Natrojarosite [see *natroalunite* above]. **1971** *Norsk Geol. Tidsskrift* LI. 195 Natrojarosite is reported as a secondary mineral from Forvik antimony deposit, Helgeland, North Norway. **1915** *Mineral. Mag.* XVII. 355 Natromontebrasite... To replace the name Natramblygonite or Natronamblygonit of W. T. Schaller.., since the mineral is a hydrofluophosphate rather than a fluophosphate. **1955** *Amer. Mineralogist* XL. 1141 Fremontite.., in which Na:Li = 1·7:1 and OH>F, becomes natromontebrasite and possesses the dubious distinction of having been referred to under three different names within 40 years.

natrolite ('nætrəʊlaɪt, 'neɪtrəʊ-). *Min.* [f. NATRO-N + -LITE; named by Klaproth, 1803.] A hydrous silicate of aluminium and sodium, usually occurring in white, transparent, acicular crystals.

1805 JAMESON *Syst. Min.* II. 541. **1811** SMITHSON in *Phil. Trans.* Cl. 171 The natrolite has been lately met with under a regular crystalline form. **1836** T. THOMSON *Min., Geol.*, etc. I. 317 Perhaps this mineral [mesolite] should.. be considered as a variety of natrolite. **1850** DANA *Geol.* iv. 298 The basalt.. contains minute cavities which are filled, apparently, with natrolite. **1879** RUTLEY *Stud. Rocks* x. 159 A meshwork of little prisms of natrolite, in some instances, almost completely filling the crystal.

natron ('neɪtrən, 'nætrən). [a. F. *natron* (1665), a. Sp. *natron*, ad. Arab. *naṭrūn*, *niṭrūn*, ad. Gr. νίτρον NITRE. Cf. ANATRON.] Native sesquicarbonate of soda, occurring in solution or as a deposit (mixed with other substances) in various parts of the world.

1684 LEIGH in *Phil. Trans.* XIV. 610 The Natron.. is an Alkaly Salt perforated like a Sponge, and of a lixivial tast. **1706** PHILLIPS (ed. Kersey), *Anatron* or *Natron*, a kind of Salt drawn from the Water of the River Nile in Egypt. **1760** *Gentl. Mag.* XXX. 315 The saltness of the dew in that country.. is oweing to the natron,.. which is in plenty on the surface of the earth. **1803** *Med. Jrnl.* IX. 514 The stomachic affections were subdued by natron. **1863** BAKER *Albert N'yanza* i. (1866) I. 64 Found quantities of natron on the marshy ground bordering the river. **1872** —— *Nile Trib.* xvii. 304 The water is impregnated with natron.

b. *attrib.* in **natron lake**, a lake from which natron is obtained.

1821 R. JAMESON *Man. Min.* 6 It abounds.. in the famous natron lakes in Northern Africa. **1876** HARLEY *Mat. Med.* (ed. 6) 149 The natron lakes of Egypt were known to the ancients.

natrophilite (nə'trɒfɪlaɪt). *Chem.* [f. NATRIUM + Gr. φίλ-os friendly + -ITE.] A yellow resinous phosphate of manganese and sodium.

1890 BRUSH & DANA in *Amer. Jrnl. Sci.* Ser. III. XXXIX. 204 Another new member of the triphylite group, a sodium-manganese phosphate, which we shall call natrophilite. *Ibid.* 205–6.

† **natrum**. *Obs. rare.* [a. F. *natrum*, var. of *natron*.] = NATRON.

1748 J. HILL *Hist. Fossils* 387 The Natrum, or Nitrum of the Ancients, is a native Fossile substance. *Ibid.* 389 This native Alkaline Salt, which I have ventured to call the Natrum or true Nitre of the earliest ages. **1795** NICHOLSON *Dict. Chem.* II. 514.

N.A.T.S.O.P.A., NATSOPA, Natsopa (næt'səʊpə). [Acronym f. the initial letters of *Nat*ional *S*ociety of *O*perative *P*rinters and *A*ssistants.] A trade union composed of printing workers; pl., the members of this union.

From 1975 retitled the National Society of Operative Printers, Graphical and Media Personnel.

1917 *Natsopa Jrnl.* May 1/1 Our intentions.. will no doubt go to swell the number with which the road to a certain place is paved, but that does not matter,.. because all Natsopas will go the journey to another place, and will require wings to convey them. **1922** *Times* 18 Feb. 4/1 In the January number of *Natsopa*, the official journal of the society, the executive council gave notice that.. the office of general secretary would be declared vacant. **1926** *Glasgow Herald* 3 May 11 The Natsopas.. at Carmelite House took exception to the leading article. **1935** F. D. KLINGENDER *Condition Clerical Labour Brit.* ii. 48 The following remark made by the secretary of the clerical section of Natsopa. **1958** *Oxford Mail* 6 Aug. 1/1 NATSOPA indicate in a statement that.. the question of craft and non-craft unions [etc.]. **1963** *Times* 11 Feb. 11/2 Severe disruption of the production of the *Daily Mirror* took place last night as a result of unofficial action by some members of the Natsopa union.

natter ('nætə(r)), *v.* [var. of GNATTER *v.*]

1. a. *intr.* To grumble; to fret. *dial.*

1866 E. PEACOCK *Notes to Myrc* 73 She is always a nattering.

b. To chatter, to chat (in an aimless manner). Also with *about*, *away*, *of*, *on*. (Now the usual sense.) *colloq.*

1943 HUNT & PRINGLE *Service Slang* 47 *Natter*, to chide or chatter in an irritatingly aimless fashion. **1949** M. ALLINGHAM *More Work for Undertaker* xxvii. 310 The shares Campion keeps nattering about. **1952** J. CANNAN *Body in Beck* i. 9 No human voices.. nattering of sodomy and of being bumped by Cat's. **1954** C. P. SNOW *New Men* 213 You're saying we ought to find a bogus reason for putting him in the street—just because some old women might natter. **1958** *Sunday Times* 26 Jan. 17/3 They.. nattered away for an hour about nothing. **1959** C. MACINNES *Absolute Beginners* 74 She nattered on. I gave up. 'Well—you win,' I told her. **1972** R. MAUGHAM *Escape from Shadows* iv. 169 Seeing me look like a village idiot when he nattered away at me in Arabic. **1973** *Times* 12 Nov. 10/6 Women who.. natter about discrimination.

2. To gnaw, to nag. *dial.*

1871 E. PEACOCK *Ralf Skirl.* II. 48 It can't hurt me.. let alone a bit o' natterin' pain. **1946** J. B. PRIESTLEY *Bright Day* ix. 274 If you've got summat in you that wants to be let out an' goes on natterin' at you day an' night, then you let go of everything else an' get it out.

So **'nattered** *ppl. a.*, peevish, complaining; hence **'natteredness**; **'natterer**[1]; **nattering** *vbl. sb.* and *ppl. a.*; **'nattery** *a.* = NATTERED *ppl. a.*

1825 J. T. BROCKETT *Gloss. North Country Words* 146 *Nattry*, ill natured, petulant. '*Nattry faced.*' **1829** BROCKETT *N.C. Gloss.* (ed. 2), *Natter*, to scold, to speak in a querulous or peevish manner. **1853** MRS. GASKELL *Ruth* xxix, She believed she grew more 'nattered' as she grew older; but that she was conscious of her 'natteredness' was a new thing. **1859** GEO. ELIOT *A. Bede* I. iv, Lisbeth, whose motherly feeling now got the better of her 'nattering' habit. **1873** J. STANDING *Echoes Lancs. Vale* 17 One o' thoose nattery owd maids 'at con olez tell so mitch better heaw to bring a family o' childer op nor thoose 'at have 'em. **1900** *Eng. Dict. Dial.* II. 657/2 s.v. *Gnatter*, *Lin[colnshire]*. Eh! Miss, she is such a natterer; she is always nattering about. **1923** *Sunday At Home* Mar. 335/2, I 'ate them skinny owd women—always bad tempered and nattery that kind is. **1937** M. ALLINGHAM *Dancers in Mourning* xvii. 217 Her energy, her constant nattering at one. **1942** *Tee Emm* (Air Ministry) II. 64 Your C.O. tears you off a strip for nattering too much over the R/T. **1949** H. PAKINGTON *Young W. Washbourne* 36 It was no longer a dear old pouch, but a nattering, irritating little pouch that twanged upon the strings of his conscience. **1953** E. SIMON *Past Masters* II. vi. 116 I'm sick and tired of all this lily-livered nattering.. behind closed doors. **1956** 'N. SHUTE' *Beyond Black Stump* vii. 207 To kill the nattering of hope that lingered on. **1959** H. HOBSON *Mission House Murder* xviii. 116 'Did this girl talk?' 'Not much.. she wasn't one of the natterers.' **1959** G. MITCHELL *Man who grew Tomatoes* i. 23 Do you hold your tongue, now. Like a nattering old mawther, you are! **1966** J. WAINWRIGHT *Crystallised Carbon Pig* x. 47, I was nattery and on edge.

'natter, *sb.* [f. the vb.] Grumbling, nagging talk; (now esp.) aimless chatter; a chat, a talk.

1866 W. GREGOR *Dial. Banffshire* 119 *Nyatter*, peevish chattering, grumbling. **1943** HUNT & PRINGLE *Service Slang* 47 *Natter party*, a Conference which leads nowhere. **1945** PARTRIDGE *Dict. R.A.F. Slang* 40 *Natter can*, a person—especially a 'Waaf'—prone to talk too much. **1947** *Forum* (Johannesburg) X. I. 23/2 So it is that words like 'interdenominisationalism' and 'polyphiloprogenitive', with which we are wont to sprinkle our normal natter, sound like the mouthings of the village idiot. **1951** *News Chron.* 8 Nov. 6/1 From the swarm he singled out one bird... 'That's Joey, .. he usually comes for a natter when there's nothing else doing.' **1955** 'N. SHUTE' *Requiem for Wren* iii. 57 I've got a natter on with the Americans tomorrow evening. **1959** G. FREEMAN *Jack would be Gent.* v. 94 I'd give anythin' to 'ave a natter with some of them blokes. **1966** 'L. LANE' *ABZ of*

Scouse 74 *Owd natterbag*, a scolding woman. **1967** N. FREELING *Strike Out* 28 The natter of silly women. **1974** E. LEMARCHAND *Buried in Past* vi. 102 We wanted a natter with you... You can fill us in as nobody else can.

natterer[1]: see NATTER *v.*

Natterer[2] ('nætərə(r)). The name of Johann *Natterer* (1787–1843), Austrian naturalist, used in the possessive in **Natterer's bat**, *Myotis nattereri*, a greyish-brown bat with a white underside, found in Europe and Asia. Also *absol.*

1889 J. E. HARTING in *Zoologist* XIII. 245 The present distribution of Natterer's Bat in the British Islands cannot be stated in a few words. **1910** G. E. H. BARRETT-HAMILTON *Hist. Brit. Mammals* I. 178 Natterer's Bat ranges through boreal and temperate Europe and Asia. **1960** *Times* 14 June 14/6 My first encounter with Natterer's bat was a night to remember. *Ibid.*, The most up-to-date bat book today speaks of the Natterer's flight as 'slow and steady'.

natterjack ('nætədʒæk). [Of obscure formation.] A somewhat rare British species of toad (*Bufo calamita*), having a light yellow stripe down the back, and distinguished from the ordinary toad by its superior agility. Also *attrib.* with *toad*.

1769 PENNANT *Brit. Zool.* III. 12 This species.. is found on Putney Common, and also near Revesby Abby, Lincolnshire, where it is called the Natter Jack. **1831** DARWIN in *Life* (1887) I. 187 To Galinghay, to see the wild lily of the valley, and to catch on the heath the rare natter-jack. **1863** *Intell. Observer* Oct. 228 The natterjack is very abundant in South Lancashire in all the ditches in those parts near the coast. **1870** H. A. NICHOLSON *Man. Zool.* (1875) 458 The Natter-jack Toad is the only other British species.

Nattier blue ('nætjeɪ). [f. the name of the Fr. painter Jean-Marc *Nattier* (1685–1766).] A soft shade of blue much used by Nattier and associated *spec.* with his work.

[**1909** *Westm. Gaz.* 4 May 5/3 We have quoted the painter Nattier for the soft shade of blue he used.] **1912** *Queen* 4 May p. xvii, The bonnet is fashioned of Nattier blue satin. **1918** W. J. LOCKE *Rough Road* xxi. 261 His own bedroom with the satinwood furniture and nattier blue hangings. **1923** [see BISQUE[2] 3]. **1928** *Times* 9 May 10/3 A train of Nattier-blue satin and silver lace. **1963** *New Yorker* 1 June 34 She wore Nattier-blue with a collar so high it almost reached her ears. **1969** *Queen* 17–30 Sept. 91/1 Nattier blue silk curtains.

nattily ('nætɪlɪ), *adv.* [f. NATTY *a.* + -LY[2].] In a natty manner; neatly, smartly.

1849 C. BRONTË *Shirley* xv, Putting it gallantly and nattily into his button-hole. **1860** *All Year Round* No. 42. 365 See how nattily the men bind the tubes with fine wire. **1865** LE FANU *Guy Dev.* I. xvii. 225 Lady Alice's nattily-kept gravel inclosure.

nattiness ('nætɪnɪs). [f. as prec. + -NESS.] The quality of being natty; neatness, trimness.

1861 GEO. ELIOT *S. Marner* xi, Everything belonging to Miss Nancy was of delicate purity and nattiness. **1870** HELE *Notes Aldeburgh* 139 Success depends more than anything upon the 'nattiness' with which the boat itself is handled. **1884** *Cassell's Fam. Mag.* Apr. 269/1 The pretty nattiness of the mob-cap and apron.

natting: see NAT *sb.*[1]

nattle ('næt(ə)l), *v. north. dial.* [Imitative.] *intr.* To make a light rattling, crackling, or tapping noise. Hence **'nattling** *vbl. sb.*

1825 BROCKETT *N.C. Gloss.* **1851** GREENWELL *Coal-trade Terms, Northumb. & Durh.* 37. **1855** ROBINSON *Whitby Gloss.* s.v., Hark, how it nattles! **1866** MRS. LYNN LINTON *L. Lorton* II. 9 A ghostly 'nattling' or tapping at the door.

natty ('nætɪ), *a.* (*adv.* and *sb.*) [Of obscure origin; at first app. a slang word.]

1. Neatly smart; spruce, trim; exhibiting dainty tidiness, taste or skill: **a.** of persons.

1785 GROSE *Dict. Vulgar T.*, *Natty lads*, young thieves or pickpockets. **1806** SURR *Winter in Lond.* I. 15 Tommy was what at that period was termed a natty spark of eighteen. **1812** SHELLEY *Juvenilia, Devil's Walk* ii, As natty a beau, As Bond Street ever saw. **1860** MRS. DE WINTON *Valley Hundred Fires* 176 Being exquisitely clean and natty, he luxuriated in clean shirts.

b. of things.

1801 WOLCOT (P. Pindar) *Tears & Smiles* Wks. 1812 V. 74, I recollect.. Full well thy natty bob. **1806** *Simple Narrative* I. 110, I shall keep a smart natty little gig. **1834** M. SCOTT *Cruise Midge* iv. I. 112 An enormously broad-brimmed straw hat, with a black ribbon round it, in rather a natty bow. **1855** THACKERAY *Newcomes* xliv, His uncle used to.. arrange the natty curl on his forehead. **1894** SALA *Things I have seen* II. x. 45 He wore the nattiest little black kid gloves imaginable.

2. quasi-*adv.* Nattily.

1810 *Splendid Follies* II. 111 How she had tied her neck-cloth so natty, was quite a string of perplexities.

3. *absol.* as *sb.* A natty person.

1818 MOORE *Fudge Fam. Paris* viii. 42 As long as.. we Natties May have our full fling at their salmis and pâtés.

Natufian (næ'tuːfɪən). *Archæol.* [f. the name of Wādi an-*Natuf*, seventeen miles north-west of Jerusalem.] Name coined by Prof. D. Garrod for a late Mesolithic culture the type-site of which was discovered by her at Wādi an-Natuf. Also *attrib.*

1932 D. A. E. GARROD in *Jrnl. R. Anthrop. Inst.* LXII. 257 (*heading*) A new mesolithic industry: the Natufian of Palestine. *Ibid.* 261 It was abundantly clear that we were dealing with a microlithic culture that would not fit exactly into any of the pigeon-holes already existing, and I therefore decided to give it a label of its own, adopting the name Natufian from the Wady en-Natuf at Shukba. **1949** [see *food-gatherer* (FOOD *sb.* 8)]. **1960** K. M. KENYON *Archaeol. in Holy Land* ii. 36 The Natufians of Mount Carmel, and of rock-shelters on the eastern and western slopes of the Judaean hills, lived mainly by hunting. **1960** tr. *S. Moscati's Face of Anc. Orient* i. 13 The Natufian civilization brings two principal innovations: the harvesting of wheat and barley, and the beginnings of the domestication of animals. **1970** BRAY & TRUMP *Dict. Archaeol.* 159/1 The shrine at the base of the Tell at Jericho was built during the early Natufian phase and the descendants of the Natufians built the earliest Neolithic town at the site.

'natural, *sb.* [Subst. use of next, in earlier senses after F. *naturel*, L. *nātūrāl-is, -e*, etc.]

I. † 1. A native of a place or country. *Obs.* (very common *c* 1580–1650).

1509 in *Mem. Hen. VII* (Rolls) 436 He schuld send hys commandement unto al the naturalys of the reame of Castyl. **1598** BARRET *Theor. Warres* II. i. 28 Therby do rise.. tumults amongst the naturals of the country. **1615** G. SANDYS *Trav.* 258 The more seuere that these are to the naturals, the greater their repute with the Spaniard. **1657** S. PURCHAS *Pol. Flying-Ins.* 128 The naturals who are acquainted with their manners, presently follow them, to get the honey. **1748** in *Maryland Hist. Mag.* (1911) VI. 229, I.. am become a Natural of the country or country born as some call themselves.

2. One naturally deficient in intellect; a half-witted person. Cf. NATURAL *a.* 14a.

1533 MORE *Debell. Salem* Wks. 934/1 It could never be done more naturally, not thovgh he that wrote it were even a very naturall in dede. *a* **1569** KINGESMYLL *Godly Advise* (1580) 10 If hee bee but meane in that respecte, then yet he is no foole, no naturall. **1623** T. SCOT *Highw. God* 44 Nature cannot bee so blinde as to suffer any but naturals to beleeve this their doctrine. *c* **1680** BEVERIDGE *Serm.* (1729) II. 530 We are still mere naturals, no better than fools and madmen. **1722** STEELE *Consc. Lovers* II. i, I own the Man is not a Natural; he has a very quick Sense, though very slow Understanding. **1777** MME. D'ARBLAY *Early Diary* July, She.. is not quite a natural, that is, not an absolute idiot. **1840** DICKENS *Barn. Rudge* x, The person who'd go Quickest, is a sort of natural, as one may say, sir. **1878** C. GIBBON *For the King* iv, The man shuffled and bowed low, with the vacant grin of a natural.

3. † a. One who is morally in a state of nature. *Obs.* **† b.** A naturalist. *Obs.* **† c.** A mistress. *Obs.* **d.** A poet of nature. *rare.*

1643 TRAPP *Comm. Gen.* i. 24 So it is here with the man that is no more then a meer naturall. But he that is spirituall discerneth all things. *a* **1682** SIR T. BROWNE *Tracts* (1684) 107 By Zoographers and Naturals the same is named *Ispida*. **1688** SHADWELL *Sqr. Alsatia* I, You.. took a pretty wench a Gentleman's natural away by force. *a* **1700** B. E. *Dict. Cant. Crew*, *Natural*, a Mistress, a Wench. *a* **1849** H. COLERIDGE *Ess.* (1851) II. 117 The superiority of Pope to the naturals.

II. † 4. *pl.* **a.** The mental or (rarely) physical endowments of a person; natural gifts or powers of mind (or body). *Obs.* (common in 17th c.).

1526 *Pilgr. Perf.* (W. de W. 1531) 124 Bycause his vnderstandynge and other naturalles be hole in hym. **1586** T. B. *La Primaud. Fr. Acad.* Ep. Ded., The Author thereof was a meere heathen man, and directed onely by his pure Naturals when he wrote it. **1627** SANDERSON *Serm.* I. 264 So much, if he had not been wanting to himself in the use of his naturals, he might have known. **1650** B. *Discolliminium* 46 For my naturalls, I am a proper man, foure foot, twelve inches and an halfe high. **1678** GALE *Crt. Gentiles* IV. III. iv. 144 A person of excellent naturals, and those wel improved by acquired literature.

† b. Natural products. *Obs. rare.*

1599 HAKLUYT *Voy.* II. I. 162 Of them which bee the Naturals of this Realme, and in what part of the Realme they are to be had. **1637** P. VINCENT *Late Battell New Eng.* 19, I speake not of the naturals of the countrey, fish, fowle, &c. which are more than plentifull.

† c. Natural appendages. *Obs. rare*$^{-1}$.

a **1619** FOTHERBY *Atheom.* I. xvi. §1 (1622) 164 Their Temples, their Altars, their Sacrifices, and other such like naturalls of Religion.

† 5. a. *in* one's ***pure naturals*** (after med.L. *in puris naturalibus*): in a purely natural condition, not altered or improved in any way; also, in a perfectly naked state. *Obs.* (common in 17th c.).

1579 J. STUBBES *Gaping Gulf* D iv, Yf they.. remained but in theyr pure naturalles, they would neuer so speake for a faultor prince of Rome. **1607** R. C[AREW] tr. *Estienne's World of Wonders* 58 A Frenchman taken in his pure naturals. **1655** FULLER *Ch. Hist.* IX. v. §8 Exhibiting the inclinations of their Authors in pure Naturalls without any adulterated addition. **1704** NORRIS *Ideal World* II. iii. 257 If we could take them.. in their undress, and see them as they are in their pure naturals. **1737** L. CLARKE *Hist. Bible* (1740) II. XII. 721 He has laid himself open, even in his pure naturals, for the veriest brute.

† b. So (more rarely) ***in*** one's ***naturals***. *Obs.*

1637 P. VINCENT *Late Battell New Eng.* 3 This part (though in its naturals) nourished many natives. **1650** *Bounds Public Obed.* (ed. 2) 26 The Common-wealth were dead, and each man were left in his naturals, to submit of himself. **1704** SWIFT *T. Tub* Bkseller to Rdr., I thought it fairer Dealing to offer the whole Work in its Naturals.

† 6. a. *pl.* Natural things or objects; matters having their basis in the natural world or in the usual course of nature. *Obs.*

1541 R. COPLAND *Guydon's Quest. Chirurg.* A iv b, Than come vnto the naturalles, and after to the vnnaturalles. **1593** G. HARVEY *Pierce's Super.* 193 The abiectest naturalls haue their specificall properties. **1621** BP. MOUNTAGU *Diatribæ* 521 Alway in Naturalls: sometime in Politicalls. **1650** T. VAUGHAN *Anthroposophia* 24 It answers to the Holy Ghost, for amongst Naturalls it is the onely Agent, and Artificer. *a* **1680** J. CORBET *Non-conf. Plea* (1683) 29 As in Naturals, the inferior subordinate causes have no power of acting against the efficacy of the Superior; so in Morals [etc.]. **1705** *Char. Sneaker* in *Harl. Misc.* (Malh.) XI. 29 This is the Aristotelian principle in naturals; but the sneaker adapts it to politicks. **1727–38** CHAMBERS *Cycl.* s.v., These are called naturals, natural things, or things according to nature.. in contradistinction to non-naturals.

b. The genital parts. Also *sing.* [L. *naturalia*.] *Obs.* or *rare.*

1650 BULWER *Anthropomet.* 209 They button up the naturals of Mares. **1922** JOYCE *Ulysses* 396 Any female.. with the desire of fulfilling the functions of her natural.

7. *Mus.* **a.** A note in a natural scale.

1609 J. DOWLAND *Ornithop. Microl.* 81 But set.. a Flat against a Flat, or at least against a naturall. For the Naturals are doubtfull [etc.]. **1818** BUSBY *Gram. Mus.* 224 Any natural, flat, or sharp, proper to the key. **1880** in Grove *Dict. Mus.* II. 52/1 The normal key, which happens.. to begin on C, is constructed of what are called Naturals.

b. The sign ♮ used to cancel a preceding sharp or flat, and give a note its 'natural' value.

1797 *Encycl. Brit.* (ed. 3) XII. 544 This inconvenience may be avoided.. by marking the note *sol* with a natural. **1806** CALLCOTT *Mus. Gram.* v. 57 The Natural must be always considered as representing a Sharp or a Flat. **1838** *Penny Cycl.* X. 302/2 In antient music, before the character of the Natural was introduced, the Flat was employed to reduce any note.. to its natural state. **1880** in Grove *Dict. Mus.* II. 448/1 Naturals do not occur in the signatures of keys, except when it is necessary to cancel all or part of a previous signature.

c. One of the white keys on a pianoforte or similar instrument.

1880 in Grove *Dict. Mus.* II. 53/1 Each natural is covered as far as it is visible with ivory.

† 8. A natural wig. *Obs. rare.*

1724 in *N. & Q.* 3rd Ser. VIII. 307 All sorts of Perukes, as.. Minister's Bobs, Naturalls, Half-Naturals.

9. a. In the card-game of vingt-et-un. (See quots. 1830 and 1897.)

[**1830** 'EIDRAH TREBOR' *Hoyle made Fam.* 78 If 21 is dealt in the first instance, that is, in the first two cards, it is styled a natural vingt-un.] **1849** ALB. SMITH *Pottleton Legacy* (1854) 249 The first natural came in Mr. Flitter's division. **1866** ANNA L. SPENCER *Scenes Sub. Life* 16 Her cards.. she now and then forgot altogether, though excessively pleased when informed that she had had a natural. **1897** FOSTER *Hoyle* 475 The dealer first examines his hand. If he has exactly 21, an Ace and a tenth card, which is called a natural, he shows it at once.

b. (See quot. 1897.) Also in other gambling games, any combination or score that immediately wins the stake. Also *fig.*

1762 GOLDSMITH *Citizen of World* I. 165 He had something in his face gave me as much pleasure as a pair-royal of naturals in my own hand. **1897** FOSTER *Hoyle* 568 *Crap Shooting*, If the total of the two dice on the first throw is seven or eleven, it is called a nick, or natural, and the caster immediately wins the stakes. **1929** E. WALLACE *Red Aces* xi. 110 Somebody would draw a six to these, and the banker would have a 'natural'—which means, I understand, that he would win. **1930** J. LAIT *Big House* 15 Dean Ward Kent arrived at the big house with a 'natural' staring him in the face, for that is what the crap-shooting inmates call a seven-year 'stretch'. **1962** K. ORVIS *Damned & Destroyed* xv. 109 The dice bounced to a natural.

III. † 10. a. Natural disposition, inclination, or character. *Obs.*

1564 in Robertson *Hist. Scot.* (1759) II. App. 17 Of her own natural, her Majesty has a certain inclination to pity the decay of noble houses. **1595** DANIEL *Civ. Wars* IV. xlii, He was not bloody, in his Naturall. **1630** *R. Johnson's Kingd. & Commw.* 188 The same naturall of lightnesse and inconstancie still remaines in the French. *Ibid.* 193 Where you shall see the French naturall, very lively.. described.

† b. Natural form or condition. *Obs.*

1633 J. DONE *Hist. Septuagint* 68 All was most resplendant in their naturall. **1658** EVELYN *Fr. Gard.* (1675) 261 To show you how the fruits of the garden are to be conserved in their naturall. **1684** —— *Mem.* (1857) III. 273 To preserve fruit and flowers in their natural.

11. ***the natural.*** **† a.** The real thing or person; the life. *Obs.*

1589 PUTTENHAM *Eng. Poesie* III. xxv. (Arb.) 310 Painting.. represents the naturall by light colour and shadow in the superficiall or flat. **1659** LEAK *Waterwks.* 31 The Paper was not large enough to draw it so large as the Natural. *a* **1691** SIR D. NORTH in North *Lives* (1826) II. 349, I saw many artificial grots and rocks.., in which the natural of this [petrifaction] was perfectly imitated.

b. That which is natural or according to the ordinary course of things.

1841 MYERS *Cath. Th.* III. §15. 57 To study the Supernatural as the Philosopher studies the Natural. *a* **1854** H. REED *Lect. Brit. Poets* xii. (1857) 275 Blending together the natural and supernatural.

† 12. Native language. *Obs. rare*$^{-1}$.

1665 G. HAVERS *P. della Valle's Trav. E. India* 50 Tartars.. of Samarcand, where the Persian Tongue is the natural of the Country.

13. *colloq.* Short for ***natural life*** (NATURAL *a.* 9b).

1893 G. L. GOWER *Gloss. Surrey Words* 27 *In my natural*, phrase for 'in my life', 'at any time'. **1898** J. D. BRAYSHAW *Slum Silhouettes* 220 Yer never see sich a 'owlin' swell as Cocky was in yer born natural. **1911** L. STONE *Jonah* II. ii. 161, I niver 'eard anythin' like that, in my natural. **1913** C. MACKENZIE *Sinister St.* I. I. iv. 46, I never worked so hard in all my natural. **1925** WODEHOUSE *Carry on, Jeeves!* iii. 59, I didn't want to have England barred to me for the rest of my natural. **1967** J. Porter *Chinks in Curtain* xviii. 185, I couldn't stay like that for the rest of my natural.

14. A person naturally endowed *for* (a role, etc.); one having natural gifts or talents; also, a thing with qualities that make it particularly suitable (*for* some purpose).

1925 *Hearst's International* June 80/2 The fight was what promoters call a 'natural'. **1929** D. Hammett *Red Harvest* xiii. 132 'So you and Noonan are trying to paste his brother's death on me?' 'It doesn't need pasting. It's a natural.' **1930** *Publisher's Weekly* 21 June 2971/2 Mystery fans will devour it; and you can sell it also to anyone who likes a finely written and witty novel. A possible natural. **1933** F. Baldwin *Innocent Bystander* (1935) xiii. 260 But she's a natural... I watched her walk across the stage.. and the audience rose to her. **1939** *Sun* (Baltimore) 2 Jan. 1/8 The Hopkins and Murphy appointments are regarded as 'naturals' for early-session debates. **1946** *Coast to Coast 1945* 125 This is a natural, son. I can pick this one. **1948** F. Brown *Murder can be Fun* (1951) ix. 132 Hell, it was a *natural* for publicity for a writer. **1955** *Observer* 24 July 13/7 The sort of play which should have been a natural for television. **1958** *Times Lit. Suppl.* 15 Aug. 455/1 But the theme of how the Labour Party was born of the Labour Representation Committee is, as the film-makers say, a 'natural'. Poor Party makes good. **1964** *McCall's Sewing* i. 10/2 You're a natural for high fashion. **1966** *Listener* 24 Nov. 780/1 (Advt.), These five talks.. diversified with 64 photos and 8 maps.. make up what will be a 'natural' at Christmas, for young and old. **1971** B. Malamud *Tenants* 154 I'm not a natural. This present play is my last, I've decided. **1975** *Sunday Times* (Colour Suppl.) 23 Feb. 26/4 He was a natural, and gradually began to pick up something of a reputation. **1975** *Times* 25 Feb. 3/6 Railways are a natural for process control and on-line computer systems.

15. *Bullfighting.* A type of pass made with the cape. Also with Spanish pronunc. (natu'ral).

1932 E. Hemingway *Death in Afternoon* xviii. 198 The greatest pass with the muleta, the most dangerous to make.., is the natural. In this the man faces the bull with the muleta held in his left hand, the sword in his right. **1959** V. J. Kehoe *Aficionado!* xiv. 174/1 A natural is always in the direction of the arm that makes it. **1967** McCormick & Mascareñas *Compl. Aficionado* i. 24 A *natural* is a pass; it too may be called a suerte. **1973** *Sat. Rev.* (U.S.) 25 Sept. 29/2 Taking the smaller *muleta*, he ran off several fine *naturales*, bringing the bull tightly round him.

16. *Archæol.* Undisturbed terrain, below the level of cultivation or other working; virgin rock or soil.

1946 R. J. C. Atkinson *Field Archaeol.* 210 *Natural rock or 'natural'*, the undisturbed material upon which the soil lies. **1950** *Notes on Archaeol. Technique* (ed. 3) 13 Many avoidable mistakes have been made through failure to identify the real 'natural' (undisturbed) layer of a site. Before the excavation proper is started, dig a cutting in undisturbed ground... In one half, stop on the 'natural'; in the other dig well into it. The 'natural' can then be studied in plan and section. **1954** M. B. Cookson *Photogr. for Archaeologists* i. 14 A sharp right-angle where the last archaeological layer meets 'natural', balks swept at the end of a day's work, will repay the trouble taken a hundredfold.

17. A hair-style among Blacks in which the hair is not straightened or bleached; *spec.*, an Afro haircut. *U.S.*

1969 *Ebony* Feb. 27 There's a lean young cat wearing a natural who knows where it's at and tells it like it is. **1971** B. Malamud *Tenants* 42 She wore a natural of small silken ringlets, and a plain white mini with purple tights. **1971** *Black Scholar* Apr.–May 17/1 He has a Black is Beautiful bumper sticker on his car; he has a natural and even wears a dashiki to work. **1973** E. Bullins *Theme is Blackness* 150, I love you, baby... I sure dig that sexy natural.

natural ('nætjʊərəl, 'nætʃərəl), *a.* Also 4 -ale, 4–7 -all, 5 -alle. [a. OF. *natural*, or ad. L. *nātūrāl-is*, f. *nātūra* nature *sb.* + -al[1]. The variant OF. form *naturel* was also in use in ME.: see naturel. Most of the leading senses exist in French and Latin.]

I. 1. Of law or justice: Based upon the innate moral feeling of mankind; instinctively felt to be right and fair, though not prescribed by any enactment or formal compact. Esp. in phr. ***natural law***: in political and legal philosophy and theology, doctrines based on the theory that there are certain unchanging laws which pertain to man's nature, which can be discovered by reason, and to which man-made laws should conform; freq. contrasted with positive laws; also (with hyphen) *attrib.*

13.. *Cursor M.* 9449 (Gött.), þe lawis bath he gan for-lete, Bath naturale and positiue. ? *a* **1400** *Creation* 119 in Horstm. *Altengl. Leg.* (1881) 350 In paradys Adam had two lawys.., The naturall & þe posytyfe. The naturall law was skyll & ryȝht. **1538** Starkey *England* I. i. 17 Man, yf he be brought vp in corrupt opynyon, hath no perceyueance of thys natural law. *a* **1614** Donne *Βιαθανατος* (1644) 45 That we be not mislead, with the ambiguity of the word Naturall Law, and the perplex'd variety thereof in Authors. **1651** G. W. tr. *Cowel's Inst.* 2 The naturall Law is that which nature, or rather God, hath instilled into all Creatures. **1688** *Mem. Prince Orange* in Somers *Tracts* (1748) II. 300 Your Highness is not obliged, either by our Laws or natural Justice, to have Witnesses to prove the pretended Prince of Wales to be an Imposture. **1727–38** Chambers *Cycl.* s.v. *Law*, Natural law may be divided into that natural law of men, which.. is called the Law of nature.., and the natural law of countries. **1765** Blackstone *Comm.* I. Introd. 42 Undoubtedly the revealed law is (humanly speaking) of infinitely more authority than what we generally call the natural law. **1845** Jebb in *Encycl. Metrop.* II. 687/1 The term natural law, however, is ambiguous, the same writers frequently using it in different senses. **1883** Sir W. B. Brett in *Law Times Rep.* XLIX. 769/1 Natural justice required that the loss.. should be recouped by the other party. **1899** W. R. Inge *Christian Mysticism* viii. 306 Wordsworth.. shows his affinity with the modern spirit in his firm grasp of natural *law*. **1915** tr. *Aquinas's Summa Theologica* II. I. Question 91. Article 2 This participation of the eternal law in the rational creature is called the natural law. **1934** E. Barker tr. *Gierke's Natural Law Theory of Society* I. III. ii. 111 (*heading*) The natural-law view of the purposes of society and its various groups. **1950** A. Verdross-Drossberg in *Contemp. Pol. Sci.* (Unesco) 598 They are a residue of the ideas of natural law, since the unanimous agreement among civilized nations on a legal principle shows that the latter satisfies the elementary requirements of the legal conscience of mankind. **1951** A. Passerin d'Entrèves (*title*) Natural law: an introduction to legal philosophy. *Ibid.* 15 The belief in natural law, both as a recognition of a law common to humanity and as an assertion of the fundamental rights of man, was.. the distinguishing mark of political thought in Western Europe. **1967** *Encycl. Philos.* V. 451/1 The ideal or ethical law, which is contrasted with positive law.. is regarded by natural-law theorists.. as grounded in something.. more enduring than the mere practical needs of men. **1970** W. E. Volkomer *Passionate Liberal* iii. 64 The immediate reason for Frank's conversion to natural law would appear to lie in the rise of totalitarianism.

2. Constituted by nature; having a basis in the normal constitution of things. **a.** Of periods of time, esp. ***natural day, year*** (see quots.).

c **1391** Chaucer *Astrol.* II. §7 The day natural, þat is to seyn 24 houris. **1558** Warde tr. *Alexis' Secretes* IV. 67 By the space of twoo naturall dayes. **1581** Mulcaster *Positions* xxxii. (1887) 115 The naturall time generally construed is ment by the spring, the summer, the harueſt and the wynter. **1594** Blundevil *Exerc.* III. I. xlviii. (1636) 363 The Astronomers reckon their natural day from noonetide to noonetide. **1679** Moxon *Math. Dict.* 95 *Natural Year*, one Revolution of the Sun by his proper motion, or 365 days and almost 6 hours. **1715** tr. *Gregory's Astron.* (1726) I. 237 A Natural Day is the duration of an entire apparent revolution of the Sun about the Earth. *Ibid.*, The Natural Day is either the Astronomical or Civil. **1727–38** Chambers *Cycl.* s.v. *Year*, Tropical, or Natural Year, is the time which the sun employs in passing through the Zodiac.

b. Of quantities, numbers, measures, etc.

natural logarithm (see hyperbolic *a.* 2 b). ***natural number***, one without fractions; also, an actual number as distinguished from a logarithm. ***natural sine***, etc., one taken in an arc whose radius is 1.

1669 Sturmy *Mariner's Mag.* I. Add. 48, I have joyned the Chord proper to it, which is the Natural Sine of half the Arch doubled. **1743** Emerson *Fluxions* 55 A Circle whose Radius is 1, and natural Tangent [etc.]. **1763** —— *Meth. Increments* 113 To find the product of all natural numbers from 1 to 100. **1816** tr. *Lacroix' Diff. & Int. Calc.* 26 *note*, These logarithms were known under the very improper name of natural or hyperbolic logarithms. **1821** J. Q. Adams in C. Davies *Metric Syst.* III. (1871) 129 As it respects the natural standard it has only been a change from the weight of a kernel of wheat to the length of a kernel of barley. **1864** *Chambers's Encycl.* VI. 172/1 The logarithms.. increased along with their corresponding natural numbers.

c. *Mus.* Of notes, keys, harmony, etc. Also of wind instruments, as ***natural trumpet*** (see quot. 1959).

1727–38 Chambers *Cycl.* s.v., Natural harmony is that produced by the natural and essential chords of the mode. **1797** *Encycl. Brit.* (ed. 3) XII. 544 You may see that there are [here] at the same time both a *sol* natural and a *sol* sharp. **1818** Busby *Gram. Mus.* 30 The natural keys were originally so called in contradistinction to the sharps and flats. *Ibid.* 49 The scales of C major and A minor.. are called natural scales. **1880** in Grove *Dict. Mus.* II. 447/2 The scale of C major.. was called 'the natural scale' because it has no accidentals. **1910** K. Schlesinger *Instruments Mod. Orchestra* I. xviii. 83 The *natural trumpet* in which the length and pitch are varied by means of crooks. **1959** *Collins' Mus. Encycl.* 450/1 *Natural horn, natural trumpet*, a horn or trumpet which is not provided with any method, such a valves, of altering the length of the tube, and can therefore sound no other notes than those of the harmonic series above its fundamental, except as stopped notes. **1966** P. Bate *Trumpet & Trombone* vi. 99 (*heading*) Natural trumpets: medieval to modern.

d. Of sciences, or methods of combination, arrangement, classification, etc.

1630 Wingate (*title*) Arithmetiqve Made easie, In Two Bookes. The former, of Naturall Arithmetique..; The other of Artificiall Arithmetique. **1668** Wilkins *Real Char.* 297 Natural Grammar (which may likewise be stiled Philosophical, Rational, and Universal). **1859** J. R. Greene *Protozoa* Introd. 24 True classification is contradistinguished by the term natural. **1864** Bowen *Logic* v. 141 Natural, or regular, or direct predication they held to be that in which the genus is predicated of the species.

e. *Bot.* Applied spec. to the arrangement of plants originated by Jussieu, in contrast to the sexual system of Linnæus, and to the orders, families, etc. resulting from this division. Also *Zool.*, applied to systems of classification based on the characteristics of the animals concerned, and the groups resulting from a classification of this type.

[**1797** *Encycl. Brit.* (ed. 3) III. 457/2 Linnæus and most other botanists are of opinion, that there is a natural method, or nature's system.] **1803** R. A. Salisbury in *Trans. Linn. Soc.* (1807) VIII. 7 All the Natural Orders. *Ibid.* 15 Melastoma in the Eighth Order perhaps alone constitutes a Natural Family. **1809** R. Brown *ibid.* (1811) X. 15 The Linnæan system of botany.. has.. laid a more solid foundation for the establishment of a natural arrangement. **1830** Lindley *Nat. Syst. Bot.* Introd. 11 The notion of classing species according to the likeness they bear to each other, which is the foundation of the Natural System. **1841** T. R. Jones *Gen. Outl. Animal Kingdom* i. 2 The apparatus of digestion appears to be among the least efficient for the purpose of a natural division [of the animal kingdom]. *Ibid.* 3 The researches of this profound physiologist [*sc.* John Hunter].. did much to approximate a more natural method of classification. **1863** Sowerby *Eng. Bot.* (ed. 3) title-p., English Botany... Third edition.., re-arranged according to the Natural Orders. **1945** *Bull. Amer. Mus. Nat. Hist.* LXXXV. 4/1 It is understood that a 'true' or 'natural' classification has, by intention, quite a different basis and expression. **1970** *Nature* 19 Sept. 1272/2 It is always helpful for students to understand thoroughly the natural orders into which insects are divided.

f. *natural order*, the order apparent in the constitution of matter and operation of forces in nature.

1697 M. Earbery *Answer to Tractatus Theologico Politicus* 18 The one [*sc.* Human Reason] is founded on the Natural Order of things, and therefore subject to those Imperfections, which are common to all the Works of Nature. **1895** F. Thilly tr. *Paulsen's Introd. Philos.* I. ii. 322 The intellectual law of causality is the basis of our belief in the natural order. **1934** *Encycl. Social Sci.* XI. 284/1 The stoics and certain Roman jurists interpreted natural law as that law which conformed to the natural order of the universe. **1941** W. Temple *Citizen & Churchman* v. 83 The 'natural order' by which is meant the consideration of the various departments of life in the light of the essential function of each. **1948** Bergin & Fisch tr. *Vico's New Sci.* §2. 3 The philosophers, contemplating divine providence only through the natural order. **1951** C. C. Gillispie *Genesis & Geol.* vi. 169 Revealed truth, though indispensable to belief, could be apprehended inductively, by inferring a moral order parallel to natural order. **1953** C. E. Raven *Nat. Relig.* i. 2 If grace is radically contrasted with the beauty and truth and goodness of the natural order, then any belief in a real Incarnation is impossible.

g. *natural selection*: see selection 3 b. Hence ***natural selectionist***, a supporter of the theory of natural selection.

1913 G. B. Shaw *Quintessence of Ibsenism Compl.* p. xv, Capitalism, built up by generations of Scotch Rationalists and English Utilitarians, Atheists, Agnostics and Natural-Selectionists.. is proclaimed the bulwark of the Christian churches. **1916** —— *Androcles & Lion* p. lxxi, The efforts of Natural Selectionists.. to reduce evolution to mere automatism.

h. *natural deduction*: in Logic, the name given to a method devised separately in 1934 by G. Gentzen (1935 *Math. Zeitschrift* XXXIX) and S. Jaśkowski (1934 *Studia Logica* I) whereby formal proofs are obtained solely by the application of rules of inference without appeal to axioms.

1950 W. V. Quine *Methods of Logic* (1952) §28. 166 The method set forth in the present pages is of a type known as *natural deduction*, and stems, in its broadest outlines, from Gentzen and Jaśkowski (1934). **1954** I. M. Copi *Symbolic Logic* iv. 119 The methods of proof as far assembled (techniques for 'Natural Deduction', as they are sometimes called) permit the demonstration of all logically true propositions constructed out of truth-functional connectives and the quantification of individual variables. **1966** *Amer. Philos. Q.* III. 27 (*title*) Natural deduction rules for obligation. **1969** *Aristotelian Soc. Suppl. Vol.* XLIII. 53 The expression 'natural deduction' was introduced, I surmise, under the influence partly of the name bestowed on Herbrand's 'theorem of deduction' and partly of the French expression 'la déduction naturelle'. **1973** B. A. Brody *Logic* iii. 103 Two.. methods for showing that inferences are valid. The first, the natural deduction technique, starts from the results of this section.

3. a. *natural magic*. (See note to magic *sb.* 1.)

1477 [see magic *sb.* 1 b]. **1593** G. Harvey *Pierce's Super.* 29 Who such monarches for Phisique.., Palmastry, naturall and supernaturall Magique.. as some of these arrant Impostours? **1602** Shaks. *Ham.* III. ii. 270 Thy naturall Magicke, and dire propertie, On wholsome life, vsurpe immediately. **1633** *Costlie Whore* III. iii. in Bullen *O. Pl.* IV, Naturall Magique you have brought with you, And such an exorcisme in your name. **1831** Brewster *Nat. Magic* i. (1833) 2 The subject of Natural Magic is one of great extent as well as of deep interest. **1841** Lane *Arab. Nts.* I. 69 Natural Magic.. is regarded by most persons of the more enlightened classes.. as altogether a deceptive art.

b. Taking place in conformity with the ordinary course of nature; not unusual, marvellous, or miraculous.

1483 Caxton *Gold. Leg.* 320/2 It was no naturall eclypse. **1595** Shaks. *John* III. iv. 153 No naturall exhalation in the skie.., But they will plucke away his naturall cause, And call them Meteors, prodigies, and signes. **1610** —— *Temp.* v. 227 These are not naturall euents, they strengthen From strange to stranger. **1663** H. Cogan tr. *Pinto's Trav.* 39 It seemed to be rather a miracle than any natural work. **1698** Keill *Exam. Th. Earth* (1734) 37 The Land.. is raised higher than the Sea.. without the help of Natural and Mechanical causes.

c. Having a usual or normal character (†or constitution); not exceptional in any way.

1522 More *De quat. Noviss.* Wks. 101 Abusing yᵉ part & office of a natural man and reasonable creature. **1567** *Gude & Godlie B.* (S.T.S.) 145 We haif in Jesse found the rod, God and man naturall. **1604** E. G[rimstone] *D'Acosta's Hist. Indies* III. ix. 146 We were come into a more convenient and naturall temperature. **1669** Sturmy *Mariner's Mag.* v. xii. 74 The natural or perpendicular motion. **1867** Smyth *Sailor's Word-bk.* 492 *Natural Motion*, a term applied to the descending parabolic curve of a shot or shell in falling.

d. Of death: Happening in the course of nature, as the result of age or disease, as opposed to one brought about by accident, violence, poison, etc. Esp. in phr. ***natural causes***.

1576 Newton *Lemnie's Complex.* (1633) 106 So likewise yong men.. die by naturall death as well as old men doe. **1766** Blackstone *Comm.* II. 121 The grant is usually made 'for the term of a man's natural life'; which can only determine by his natural death. **1796** H. Hunter tr. *St.-Pierre's Stud. Nat.* (1799) III. 350 If there arises the slightest suspicion that his death was not natural, they put his wife to the torture. 1889 A. B. Hicks *Hints to Medical Men concerning Certificates of Death* 6 Deaths which may be due to either natural causes, or to neglect or gross carelessness. *c* 1900 H. A. Jones in M. R. Booth *Eng. Plays of 19th Cent.* (1969) II. 382 When I heard this story was being circulated I thought it would be better to take no notice and let it die a natural death. 1921 A. Christie *Mysterious Affair at Styles* xiii. 292 He strenuously, and quite uselessly, upheld the theory of 'Death from natural causes'. 1970 P. Moyes *Who saw her Die?* viii. 105 The death certificate says 'Natural Causes'. That's the doctor's verdict. 1974 'J. Le Carré' *Tinker, Tailor* xii. 104 Disappeared.. May have died of course. One does *tend* to forget the natural causes. 1975 S. Brett *Cast* xi. 104 Assisting her investigations into a perfectly natural death as if it were murder.

transf. 1837 Lockhart *Scott* (1839) VII. 189 The conversation so far as it tended that way died a natural death.

e. ***natural childbirth***, methods of relaxation and of physical co-operation with the natural process of childbirth, first advocated by G. D. Read in 1933; now applied more generally to childbirth with minimal medical or technological intervention; also *attrib.*

1933 G. D. Read (*title*) Natural childbirth. 1948 H. Heardman (*title*) A way to natural childbirth. 1960 *Guardian* 6 July 5/1 There are still many doctors and hospitals which do little or nothing to teach expectant mothers about the various methods of 'natural childbirth'. 1964 W. Markfield *To Early Grave* (1965) x. 181 Inez, six and a half months gone, was at a natural childbirth class. 1965 W. Lamb *Posture & Gesture* ix. 124 One is the practice of 'natural childbirth', still contentious, but with an organized following. 1971 D. D. Moir *Pain Relief in Labour* ii. 11 The Grantly Dick Read or Natural Childbirth method dates from 1935 and is based on the idea that fear, tension and pain are linked together. 1974 'E. Lathen' *Sweet & Low* vii. 76 It was not easy.. to become an instant swinger after ten years.. of natural childbirth.

4. a. In a state of nature, without spiritual enlightenment; unenlightened, unregenerate.

1526 Tindale *1 Cor.* ii. 14 For the naturall man perceaveth not the thyngs off the sprete off god. —— *Jas.* iii. 15 This wisdom descendeth not from above: but is erthy, and naturall, and divlysshe. 1609 Downam *Chr. Liberty* 36 Let naturall or vnconuerted men apply this to themselues. 1631 Gouge *God's Arrows* iv. §3. 378 Naturall men are as wolves, tigres, devils one to another. 1675 R. Barclay *Apol. Quakers* ii. §1. 19 Many carnal and natural Christians will oppose this Proposition. 1850 Robertson *Serm.* Ser. iii. iv. (1872) 48 The heathen—manifestly natural men—had 'the work of the law written in their hearts'.

b. ***natural religion***. (See quot. 1725.)

1675 Wilkins *Nat. Relig.* 39, I call that Natural Religion, which men might know,.. by the meer principles of Reason, ..without the help of Revelation. 1711 M. Henry *Faith in Christ* Wks. 1853 II. 283/2 The Christian religion.. is consonant to and perfective of natural religion. 1725 Watts *Logic* ii. v. §3 The Things knowable concerning God, and our Duty by the Light of Nature are called natural Religion. 1802 Paley *Nat. Theol.* Ded., The public have now before them the evidences of Natural Religion. *a* 1835 McCulloch *Attributes* (1843) I. 3 This is The Proof from Natural Religion. 1870 J. H. Newman *Gram. Assent* ii. x. 479 Revelation begins when Natural Religion fails.

c. ***natural theology***, theology based upon reasoning from natural facts apart from revelation. Hence ***natural theologian***.

1677 Gale *Crt. Gentiles* iii. 102 The Philosophers,.. assuming a new Divinitie or Religion of their own inventing, called.. Natural Theologie. 1802 Paley *Nat. Theol.* Concl., These points being assured to us by Natural Theology, we may well leave to Revelation the disclosure of many particulars. 1840 Macaulay *Ess., Ranke's Hist.* (1851) I. 129 Enigmas which perplex the natural theologian. 1877 E. R. Conder *Bas. Faith* i. 16 If natural theology be regarded as based on natural religion [etc.].

d. Having only the wisdom given by nature; not educated by study. *rare.*

1791 Newte *Tour Eng. & Scot.* 425 If this had been realized.. the natural man would have outdone the philosopher. *a* 1871 Grote *Eth. Fragm.* v. (1876) 132 The ἀρχαί of the wise man (σόφος) and the natural man (φυσικός) are derived from experience.

5. a. Having a real or physical existence, as opposed to what is spiritual, intellectual, fictitious, etc.

1526 Tindale *1 Cor.* xv. 44 Hit is sowne a naturall body, and ryseth a spretuall body. 1579 Fulke *Heskins' Parl.* 177 If Christes body be a naturall body vpon earth, speaketh he of all naturall bodies of the earth? 1590 Shaks. *Com. Err.* v. 333 Which is the naturall man, And which the spirit? 1618 T. Adams *Wks.* (1862) III. 66 In a natural man at such an affrightment, all the blood runs to the heart. 1691 Hartcliffe *Virtues* 403 They will produce.. Spiritual effects with a power much above what natural Agents can exert. 1710 Berkeley *Princ. Hum. Knowl.* i. §4 That sensible objects have an existence natural or real, distinct from their being perceived. 1712 —— *Pass. Obed.* §14 If from the moral we turn our eyes on the natural world. 1818 Cruise *Digest* (ed. 2) IV. 335 In all feoffments and grants to natural persons.. no word but the word heirs.. will create an estate in fee simple. 1882 *National Bank Act* (U.S.) 8 Associations for carrying on the business of banking.. may be formed by any number of natural persons.

b. Pertaining to, operating or taking place in, the physical (as opposed to the spiritual) world.

1581 J. Bell *Haddon's Answ. Osor.* 141 b, Will, beyng straighted w^{t}in ye same limittes and boundes of naturall causes, hath no power.. to atchieve those spirituall good things. 1639 Rouse *Heav. Univ.* viii. (1702) 103 As in natural marriages two are one flesh. 1872 Liddon *Elem. Relig.* (ed. 2) Pref. 10 'Scientific objectors' to prayer on the ground of a supposed invariability of natural law, are not, generally speaking, Theists at all. 1883 H. Drummond *Nat. Law in Spir. W.* (ed. 2) 5 In its true sense Natural Law predicates nothing of causes.

†**c.** (See quot.) *Obs. rare*$^{-1}$.

1678 Cudworth *Intell. Syst.* 514 The.. Division of Pagan Gods.. into Animal and Natural (by Natural being meant Inanimate) is utterly to be rejected.

6. a. Existing in, or formed by, nature; consisting of objects of this kind; not artificially made, formed, or constructed.

1568 Turner *Natures of Baths* title-p., All sycke persones that can not be healed without the helpe of natural bathes. 1587 Golding *De Mornay* Pref. (1592) 9 Professors of the knowledge of nature and naturall things. 1601 Shaks. *Twel. N.* v. 224 A natural Perspectiue, that is, and is not. 1632 Lithgow *Trav.* vi. 279 We saw also a naturall rocke in the high way. 1668 Evelyn *Diary* 23 July, Divers *glossa petra's* and other natural curiosities found in digging. 1755 B. Martin *Mag. Arts & Sci.* 7 You promised me a regular Account of natural Things, and said we should begin with the Heavens. 1781 Gibbon *Decl. & F.* xix. II. 155 A fertile plain, watered by the natural and artificial channels of the Tigris. *a* 1821 Keats *Hyperion* i. 86 Like natural sculpture in cathedral cavern. 1853 Maurice *Proph. & Kings* xx. 351 To make them acquainted with natural scenery. 1870 Yeats *Nat. Hist. Comm.* 1 In the earth, with its oceans of water and of air, we find those natural resources.

b. Of substances or articles: Not made, manufactured, or obtained by artificial processes. Also sometimes applied to simple products in contrast to those requiring more elaborate preparation. *spec.* in phrs. ***natural foundation*** (see quots. 1906, 1963); ***natural gas*** (orig. *N. Amer.*), inflammable gas occurring underground, consisting chiefly of methane and other simple paraffins and often found associated with petroleum; ***natural glass***, any of various naturally occurring substances which resemble glass in appearance, having solidified too quickly to crystallize.

1600 J. Pory tr. *Leo's Africa* ix. 355 Of pitch there are two kindes, the one being naturall, and taken out of certain stones. 1646 Sir T. Browne *Pseud. Ep.* (1650) 174 There being.. in every thing we eat, a naturall and concealed salt. 1799 G. Smith *Laboratory* I. 5 In some measure like natural camphor. 1825 *Canad. Courant* (Montreal) 17 Dec. 1/5 This is undoubtedly the first attempt which has ever been made to apply natural Gas to so extensive and useful a purpose. 1831 J. Holland *Manuf. Metal* I. 264 That species obtained directly from fused iron, which is termed natural steel. 1835 Sir J. Ross *N.-W. Pass.* xlii. 563 The first natural water we had obtained. 1846 S. F. Smith *Theatr. Apprenticeship* 102 Many of the stores and shops in the village are lighted with natural gas! 1878 Jefferies *Gamekeeper at H.* 134 Just at present 'natural' sticks—that is, those cut from the stem with the bark on—are rather popular. 1887 *Encycl. Brit.* XXIII. 813/2 The use of natural gas for illumination, and even for metallurgical purposes, has lately become a matter of importance... The gas obtained from wells or bore-holes was used for illumination in Fredonia, N.Y., as early as 1821. 1906 H. Y. Margary in G. A. T. Middleton *Mod. Buildings* I. iii. i. 71/1 Natural foundation is the name applied to such as are formed on the soil itself, and it is applicable when the soil is practically incompressible. 1917 *Jrnl. Geol.* XXV. 540 Natural glass is, of course, varied in composition in comparison with the various types of igneous rocks, yet the average obsidian is probably not much more varied than some of the amorphous minerals. 1930 *Economist* 22 Mar. 654/2 Interest is being taken in utilities and oils with natural gas possibilities. 1938 E. G. Warland *Building Construction* i. i. 1 Natural foundation beds should be incompressible or equally yielding over the whole area and not subjected to atmospheric or other influences which may alter its nature or powers to resist the loads to be placed upon them. 1942 *Chem. Abstr.* XXXVI. 6452 (*heading*) Transformation of natural glasses into crystalline rocks by subjection to high gas and water-vapor pressures. 1957 *Ann. Reg. 1956* 76 The Government's proposal for financing the natural gas pipeline from Alberta to Ontario. 1963 *Gloss. Gen. Building Terms* (*B.S.I.*) 18 *Natural foundation*, soil requiring no preparation or other foundation to support a building or structure. 1971 W. Vogel *Struct. & Crystallization Glasses* i. 13 In the earliest times of world history, quartz porphyry in particular, and other extrusive rocks, solidified on rapid chilling as natural glasses, e.g. pitch-stone, perlite, obsidian or pumice. 1972 *Guardian* 17 Feb. 9 People ran from their homes yesterday because of a gas explosion in Elgin Street, Sheffield... The area had been converted to natural gas about six months ago. 1974 *Sat. Rev. World* (U.S.) 2 Nov. 29/1 Calgary, Canada's oil and natural-gas capital.

c. Of things in some way or other connected with persons. Also ***natural wig***, one made of human hair.

1598 Florio, *Neo*, a naturall marke or mole.. vpon the skin. 1599 Shaks. *Hen. V*, iv. ii. 13 Wil you haue them weep our Horses blood? How shall we then behold their naturall teares? 1639 N. N. tr. *Du Bosq's Compl. Wom.* i. C 2 They would consider their naturall beauty much more, if they had not so much borrowed beauty with them. 1708 *Lond. Gaz.* No. 4399/4 The Party wore.. a Suit of black Cloath, and a light brown Natural Wig. 1768 Goldsm. *Good-n. Man* i. i, As her natural face decays, her skill improves in making the artificial one. 1803 *Med. Jrnl.* IX. 193 About 2,500 were afterwards proved to be secure from the Natural Small-Pox. 1863 *Chambers's Encycl.* V. 191/2 The wig, the front, and other imitations of the natural covering of the human head.

d. Of vegetation: Growing of itself; self-sown or planted; not introduced artificially. Also of land: Not cultivated. Esp. in *Forestry*: ***natural regeneration***, the growth of young trees from seed of those already established.

1526 Tindale *Rom.* xi. 24 Yf thou wast cut out of a naturall wilde olive tree. 1657 W. Coles *Adam in Eden* cclix, There groweth up sometimes under the Cistus where it is naturall, a certain Excrescence. 1707 Mortimer *Husb.* (1721) I. 95 It opens the Land, and makes it much more fruitful, especially in natural Grass. 1762 Mills *Syst. Pract. Husb.* I. 151 It was as full of natural white clover.. as any field generally is in twice that time. 1799 J. Robertson *Agric. Perth* 236 There was a considerable tract of natural fir several years ago near Tyndrom. 1828 P. Cunningham *N.S. Wales* (ed. 3) II. 147 The natural lands in this colony have never yet been valued at more than 5*s.* per acre. 1834 *Brit. Husb.* I. 326 Peas, potatoes, and barley, besides natural grass. 1864 Lowell *Fireside Trav.* 108 Orchards, commonly of natural fruit, added to the pleasant home-look. 1902 B. E. Fernow *Econ. Forestry* vii. 167 There is also a choice of producing the new crop by seeds falling from the trees of the old crop, by 'natural regeneration'. 1928 R. S. Troup *Silvicultural Syst.* ii. 11 Natural regeneration.. may be obtained either (1) from seed already on the area, or (2) from seed disseminated from trees outside and usually adjoining it. 1946 *Q. Jrnl. Forestry* XL. 18 A good deal of natural regeneration goes on at Bedgebury and had the seedlings been left.. a Scots Pine forest could have been formed on the whole of the Pinetum area without any trouble. 1964 W. E. Hiley *Forestry Venture* iii. 64 The artificial weeding of natural regeneration, in which the young trees are irregularly scattered, is almost an impossible task.

e. Special collocations: ***natural area*** (see quot. 1964); ***natural break***: see break *sb.*^{1} 8 k; ***natural cement***: a cement obtained by calcining naturally occurring argillaceous limestone; ***natural food*** (see quot. 1972); ***natural language***: any naturally evolved language, as opposed to artificial languages constructed (*a*) for universal or international communications, or (*b*) for formal logical or mathematical purposes; ***natural region***: each of a number of regions of the earth's surface characterized by a certain uniformity and individuality of character (see quots. 1905, 1937); ***natural resources*** (see quot. 1956); ***natural seasoning*** = *air-seasoning* vbl. sb. (air *sb.*^{1} B. 11).

1932 *Amer. Jrnl. Sociol.* XXXVIII. 339 It is more likely that census tracts near the central business districts of Philadelphia would conform more closely to natural areas than in West Philadelphia. 1964 Gould & Kolb *Dict. Social Sci.* 458/2 A *natural area* is a territorial unit whose distinctive characteristics—physical, economic, and cultural—are the result of the unplanned operation of ecological and social processes. 1970 G. A. & A. G. Theodorson *Mod. Dict. Sociol.* 271 *Natural area*, a territorial area with some common, unifying characteristic. The term has been used primarily in human ecology, and usually refers to an area that emerges without planning from the operation of ecological processes. 1882 *Chem. News* 27 Oct. 187/2 (*heading*) Japanese soils—a natural cement. *Ibid.*, The chemist to the Geological Survey Department of the Japanese Government, was led to look for a natural cement. Such cements are formed by mixing burnt lime with substances of volcanic origin, generally tufas. 1921 W. H. Warren *Engin. Construction* II. iii. 38 In America, Rosendale cement is largely used; it is a natural cement, being first found at Rosendale, Ulster County, N.Y. It is slower setting, weaker, and cheaper than Portland cement. 1966 *McGraw-Hill Encycl. Sci. & Technol.* II. 627/1 Natural cement, a naturally occurring argillaceous limestone, calcined and pulverized, is slower-setting and less uniform in quality than portland cement. 1934 H. C. Sherman *Food & Health* xvii. 160 Natural foods,.. nature's wholes of the kinds to which our own bodies have been adjusting themselves throughout our evolutionary history. 1956 I. Orga *Cooking with Yogurt* 8 Yoğurt is a natural food and.. only needs the simplest equipment. 1963 B. T. Hunter *Natural Foods Cookbk.* p. xv, Many thoughtful people are.. seeking out the good old flavors, textures and nutrients of the natural foods their grandparents enjoyed. 1970 U. M. Cavanagh *Cooking & Catering Wholefood Way* 9 The emphasis is on natural whole foods such as stoneground wholewheat flour, brown sugar, natural unpolished rice and honey. 1972 *New York* 8 May 49 *Natural food*.. refers to food after the growing stage; food that is unprocessed, not treated with preservatives, artificial colorings or flavorings... Ideally the rule is 'nothing added, nothing taken away'. [1668 J. Wilkins *Ess. Real Character & Philosophical Lang.* i. i. 2 There is scarce any subject that hath been more thoroughly scanned and debated amongst Learned men, than the Original of Languages and Letters. 'Tis evident enough that no one Language is natural to mankind.] 1774 Ld. Monboddo *Orig. & Progress of Lang.* II. iii. xiii. 445 If we understand the sign, we have in effect the definition of the thing, then is the language truly a philosophical language, and such as must be universal among philosophers... It may also be said to be a *natural* language.. since it follows the order of the human mind in forming the ideas of which language is the expression. 1864 Max Müller *Lect. Sci. Lang.* 2nd Ser. ii. 58 A grammatical framework, too, is wanted before the problem of an artificial language can be considered as solved. In natural languages the grammatical articulation consists either in separate particles or in modifications in the body of a word. 1871 S. P. Andrews *Primary Synopsis Universology & Alwato* vi. 95 The ideas themselves are the most subtle and embarrassing, and *natural* language then exactly *echoes* this embarrassment. As we descend to more *feasible* domains the words will become correspondingly more *feasible.* 1888 H. A. Strong tr. *Paul's Princ. Hist. Lang.* xxiii. 501 The artificial language of a large area has a tendency to become dialectically differentiated.. in much the same degree as the natural language within a particular territory. 1889 *Literary World* 22 June 209/1 The progress of education.. will enable each to divest himself of the crudities of his natural language. 1933 L. Bloomfield *Language* xxviii. 506 The political difficulty of getting any considerable number of people all over the world to study, say, Esperanto, will probably prove so great that some natural language will outstrip it. 1956 J. H. Woodger tr. *Tarski's Logic, Semantics, Metamath.* viii. 267 Philosophers who are not accustomed to use deductive methods.. are inclined to regard all formalized languages with a certain disparagement, because they contrast these 'artificial' constructions with the one natural language—the colloquial language. **1962** U. Weinreich in Householder & Saporta *Probl. Lexicography* 30 Much less can we claim for natural-language lexicography that the definiens should be literally substitutable for the definiendum in normal discourse. **1963** L. Loevinger in H. W. Baade *Jurimetrics* 14 The abstract is recorded in natural language stating the significant index terms. **1970** A. Cameron et al. *Computers & O.E. Concordances* 6 University courses in natural-language programming are now widely available for undergraduates. **1973** M. Dummett *Frege* xiii. 463 A theory of truth which attempts to display the role of the notion of truth..is not a completely separate enterprise from an account of the word 'true' as used within natural language. **1905** J. Herbertson in *Geogr. Jrnl.* XXV. 302 What are the characteristic and distinguishing elements of the areas which we may term natural regions? *Ibid.* 309 We may divide the world up into the following types of natural regions:—1. Polar... 2. The cool temperate regions... 3. The warm temperate regions... 4. (*a*) The west tropical deserts... 5. Lofty tropical or sub-tropical mountains... 6. Equatorial lowlands. *Ibid.*, A natural region should have a certain unity of configuration, climate, and vegetation. **1937** *Geography* XXII. 253 'Natural regions' has been used to cover two distinct types of unit-areas of the earth's surface: (i) those which are marked out as possessing certain common physical characteristics—e.g., a certain kind of structure and surface relief, or a particular kind of climate,—and (ii) those regions which possess a unity based upon any significant geographical characteristics, whether physical, biological or human..as contrasted with areas marked out by boundaries imposed..without reference to any geographical unity of the areas. **1971** *Biol. Conservation* IV. 247 (*heading*) Towards a system for classifying natural regions of the world and their representation by National Parks and Reserves. **1870** Natural resources [see resource 1 b]. **1921** *Daily Colonist* (Victoria, B.C.) 24 Mar. 13/3 We have toasted our natural resources and talked of the wonderful possibilities of the Province. **1956** J. C. Swayne *Conc. Gloss. Geogr. Terms* 100 *Natural resources*, any materials or conditions existing in nature which may be capable of economic exploitation. **1936** R. R. Rivers *How to buy Timber* iii. 15 Small, specially cut pieces of wood (usually Pine) are inserted crossways between each board in order to let in the air, and so season. That method is called 'air-drying', or 'natural seasoning'. It is a slow process. **1966** A. W. Lewis *Gloss. Woodworking Terms* 87 The two main methods of seasoning are natural or air seasoning, and kiln drying or artificial seasoning.

7. a. Closely imitating nature; life-like, exact.

1581 Pettie tr. *Guazzo's Civ. Conv.* i. (1586) 30 b, The most naturall resemblant picture of a Gentleman with two hornes on his forehead. **1585** T. Washington tr. *Nicholay's Voy.* iii. iii. 74 b, Of the Ianissaries going to the warres yee may see the naturall draught by the figure following. **1821** Scott *Kenilw.* vi, How beautiful are these hangings! How natural these paintings, which seem to contend with life! **1851** Ruskin *Stones Ven.* I. App. xxi. 399 By natural representation is here meant as just and perfect an imitation of nature as the technical means of art will allow.

b. Having the ease or simplicity of nature; free from affectation, artificiality, or constraint; simple, unaffected, easy.

1607 Shaks. *Timon* v. i. 88 Thy Verse swels with stuffe so fine and smooth, That thou art euen Naturall in thine Art. **1638** Baker tr. *Balzac's Lett.* (vol. II.) 17 My zeale, which is naturall and honest. **1706** Walsh *Let. to Pope* 20 July, In all the common subjects of Poetry, the thoughts are so obvious (at least if they are natural). **1727–38** Chambers *Cycl.* s.v. *Marotic*, A peculiarly gay, pleasant, yet simple and natural manner of writing. **1774** Goldsm. *Retal.* 101 On the stage he was natural, simple, affecting; 'Twas only that, when he was off, he was acting. **1848** Clough *Amours de Voy.* ii. ix, 'Tis an excellent race..and..E'en under Pope and Priest, a nice and natural people. **1863** Eliz. Sewell *Glimpse of World* 199 Just put all thought of yourself aside and be natural. **1877** W. Bruce *Comm. Revel.* 73 Revealed truth as expressed in natural language.

Comb. **1828** Moore *Mem.* (1854) V. 320 A handsome and natural mannered young fellow.

c. Having the normal form; not disfigured or disguised in any way.

1800 *Med. Jrnl.* IV. 97 Her feet are now as natural and well shaped as any other child's of the same age. **1863** *Chambers's Encycl.* V. 192/1 The people..returning to natural and unpowdered hair.

d. Acting in accordance with one's real character; free from disguise.

1825 J. Neal *Bro. Jonathan* I. 73 At home it is..that we show the natural-man. **1889** *Spectator* 12 Oct., [If he] said to every guest precisely what arose in his mind to say, he would be a more 'natural' man.

e. *U.S.* Wild, savage.

1849 J. P. Kennedy *Swallow Barn* xxxvi, Ned Hazard's a pretty hard horse to ride, too; only look at his eye,—how natural it is!

II. 8. a. Implanted, existing, or present, by nature; inherent in the very constitution of a person or thing; innate; not acquired or assumed.

c **1420** Lydg. *Assembly of Gods* 1622 Now I apply thy naturall reson Vnto my wordys. *c* **1430** —— *Min. Poems* (Percy Soc.) 46 By ther natural hevenly influence. **1447** Bokenham *Seyntys* (Roxb.) 14 In hyr face..of natural yiftys plente was I-now. **1483** in *Lett. Rich. III & Hen. VII* (Rolls) I. 32 Hur naturall kinde and disposicion. **1509** Fisher *Funeral Serm. C'tess Richmond* Wks. (1876) 303 A natural desyre and appetyte to be knytte & ioyned with them agayne. **1551** T. Wilson *Logike* (1580) 10 If either of these twoo would seeke to followe their Naturall aptnesse, it were moste like thei should excell. **1625** N. Carpenter *Geog. Del.* ii. xiv. (1635) 226 Our naturall heat is far more vigorous in Winter then in Summer. **1668** Culpepper & Cole *Barthol. Anat.* i. ix. 18 That it may by Natural Instinct shut up the mouth of the Stomach. **1726** Swift *Gulliver* iii. i, The natural love of life gave me some inward motions of joy. **1777** Sheridan *Sch. Scandal* iii. iii, Wine does but draw forth a man's natural qualities. **1824** Bentham *Bk. Fallacies* Wks. 1843 II. 393/2 He is thus ignorant, if natural talent does not fail him, because he is so idle. **1871** Mozley *Univ. Serm.* v. (1876) 99 The soul has natural feelings and affections for it to feed upon.

b. ***natural parts***, native ability, apart from learning. ? *Obs.*

1655 *Culpepper's Riverius* Printer to Rdr., If they be men of good Natural Parts. *c* **1665** Mrs. Hutchinson *Mem. Col. Hutchinson* (1846) 27 He very well understood his own advantages, natural parts, gifts and acquirements. **1710** [see part *sb.* 12]. **1762–71** H. Walpole *Vertue's Anecd. Paint.* (1786) IV. 125 A rough man, with good natural parts.

c. ***natural right***(*s*), in Western political philosophy, esp. since the 18th century, doctrines derived from concepts of the nature of man and the relationship of the individual to the state whereby certain rights are formulated (see quots.) which the state ought to safeguard.

1689 tr. *B. de Spinoza's Treat. Theol. Pol.* xvi. 343 In Democratical Government, no man so transfers his own Natural Right to another, as for ever after to be excluded from consultation, but only transfers it upon the major part of the Society, of which he still makes one. **1791** T. Paine *Rights of Man* 111 The end of all political associations, is, the preservation of the natural and imprescriptible rights of man; and these rights are liberty, property, security, and resistance of oppression. *Ibid.*, The exercise of the natural rights of every man, has no other limits than those which are necessary to secure to every *other* man the free exercise of the same rights. **1796** *Encycl. Brit.* XVI. 244/1 *Natural* rights are those which a man has to his life, limbs, and liberty; to the produce of his personal labour; to the use, in common with others, of air, light, and water, &c. **1925** A. D. Lindsay *Karl Marx's Capital* iii. 60 The labour theory of value is.., like all theories of natural right, a revolutionary doctrine. *Ibid.* 61 Theories of natural right are always to this extent misleading—that they are statements of ideals which pretend to be statements of fact. **1939** E. Beneš *Democracy* i. 7 The French Revolution became by the declaration of human rights the expression of the whole school of philosophy which for centuries fought for the recognition of the so-called '*natural rights*'—that is, for the innate rights of man, the equality of human beings. **1955** *Philos. Rev.* LXIV. 175, I shall advance the thesis that if there are any moral rights at all, it follows that there is at least one natural right, the equal right of all men to be free. **1971** A. R. Ball *Mod. Pol. & Govt.* vii. 124 The justification for these individual rights was to be found in the theories of natural rights, rights that were beyond the competence of any government interference.

d. ***natural frequency***, the frequency at which a mechanical or electrical system oscillates when not subjected to any external forces.

1908 J. A. Fleming *Elem. Man. Radiotelegr.* i. 33 If.. oscillations are maintained which have a frequency different from the natural frequency of [the] circuit, they are called forced oscillations. **1922** Glazebrook *Dict. Appl. Physics* II. 961/1 If the natural frequency is nearly equal to that of the applied force..we have the phenomenon known as resonance. **1962** F. I. Ordway et al. *Basic Astronautics* ix. 370 Very serious problems arise if the lowest natural frequency of the vehicle approaches the control frequency. **1971** L. T. Agger *Introd. Electr.* xxiv. 435 The resonant frequency..in the present simple case is the same as the natural frequency.

9. a. Normally or essentially connected with, or pertaining to, a person or thing; consonant with the nature or character of the person or thing.

c **1420** Lydg. *Assembly of Gods* 114 He hath me dryuen ayen myn entent And contrary to my course naturall. **1456** Sir G. Haye *Law Arms* (S.T.S.) 75 The thingis that ar corporale in this erde..movis nocht with the moving of it.. bot ȝit have thai othir naturale movementis. **1526** Tindale *Rom.* i. 27 The men lefte the naturall vse of the woman. **1551** Robinson tr. *More's Utop.* ii. (1895) 150 Thyes clookes..be all of one coloure, and that is the naturall colour of the wul. **1579** Langham *Gard. Health* (1633) 1 Acatia..setteth the loose matrix in the naturall place. **1667** Milton *P.L.* x. 740 All from mee..Shall..on mee redound, On mee as on thir natural center light. **1710** Addison *Whig Examiner* No. 5 ¶9 The doctrine has a natural tendency to make a good king a bad one. **1776** J. Adams in *Fam. Lett.* (1876) 148 We have this week lost a very valuable friend..by the smallpox in the natural way. **1815** J. Smith *Panorama Sci. & Art* II. 268 That portion of electricity, which every body is supposed to contain, is called its natural share. **1850** McCosh *Div. Govt.* ii. ii. (1874) 192 The natural recoil of superstition is scepticism. **1885** Sir E. Fry in *Law Rep.* 29 Chanc. Div. 484 The natural inference from the facts.

b. ***natural life***, used chiefly (and now only) with reference to the duration of this.

1483 *Rolls of Parlt.* VI. 238/2 To have and to perceyve yearly the said subsidie of Poundage,..duryng youre Life naturall. **1492** in *Lett. Rich. III & Hen. VII* (Rolls) II. 290 Duryng thayr lifes naturalles. **1555** in Hakluyt *Voy.* (1599) I. 268 To haue and enioy the said office of Gouernour, to him the said Sebastian Cabota during his naturall life. **1568** Grafton *Chron.* II. 701 Till eyther he had lost his awne naturall lyfe, or vtterly..put vnder hys foes. **1766** [see 3 d above]. **1818** Cruise *Digest* (ed. 2) VI. 317 H. Cook devised a messuage to R. Cook for the term only of his natural life. **1836–7** Dickens *Sk. Boz, Our Parish* iv, For the remainder of the old woman's natural life.

c. Naturally pertaining or attached *to* a person or thing; coming easily or spontaneously *to* one. Hence ***to come natural to***, to be a natural action for (one).

1589 Puttenham *Eng. Poesie* iii. v. (Arb.) 160 A certaine contriued forme and qualitie, many times naturall to the writer. **1634** W. Tirwhyt *Balzac's Lett.* 181, I will never believe, that..you will lose those perfections so proper, and naturall unto you. **1678** Cudworth *Intell. Syst.* i. v. 800 If this were most natural to the Humane soul and most perfective of it. **1732** Berkeley *Alciphr.* i. §14 For a thing to be natural..to the mind of man, it must appear originally therein. **1856** Froude *Hist. Eng.* ii. (1858) I. 140 He acted throughout in a manner natural to a timid amiable man. **1881** Jowett *Thucyd.* I. 121 The hope, natural to poverty, that a man though poor, may one day become rich. **1890** *Temple Bar* July 383 It comes quite natural to a poor woman to sit up the night with a sick neighbour.

†**d.** Naturally adapted *for*, or applicable *to*, something. *Obs. rare.*

1603 R. Johnson *Kingd. & Commw.* 12 The gentlenesse of the aire, with the fertilitie of the ground,..is so propitious and naturall for the increase of fruite. *a* **1614** Donne *Βιαθμνατος* (1644) 139 But the most naturall to our present purpose is this. **1639** S. Du Verger tr. *Camus' Admir. Events* A 4 It is a wonder how so many graces and beauties ..increased in him, as in a soyle naturall for eloquence.

e. Naturally arising or resulting from, fully consonant with, the circumstances of the case.

1667 Milton *P.L.* xii. 645 Som natural tears they drop'd, but wip'd them soon. **1678** Dryden *Ess.* (ed. Ker) I. 193, I judged it both natural and probable, that Octavia..would search out Cleopatra to triumph over her. **1750** Johnson *Rambler* No. 25 ¶12 It is natural for those who have raised a reputation..to exalt themselves. **1855** Brewster *Newton* II. xx. 219 It was a very natural wish on the part of physical astronomers. **1891** Helen B. Harris *Apol. Aristides* i. 5 It was natural that defences should be written.

10. a. Standing in a specified relationship to another person or thing by reason of the nature of things or force of circumstances.

1516 *Test. Ebor.* (Surtees) VI. 1 My naturall enemy death. **1816** J. Scott *Vis. Paris* (ed. 5) 185 Justice and establishment have not their natural protectors in that country. **1834** L. Ritchie *Wand. by Seine* 46 In 1440, [Harfleur] again fell into the hands of the 'natural enemies' of France. **1880** L. Stephen *Pope* v. 118 He came forward as the champion of Wit..against its natural antithesis, Dulness.

†**b.** Having a certain relative status by birth; natural-born. *Obs.*

1524 *Act 14 & 15 Hen. VIII*, c. 1 *Preamble*, To brynge the Kynges naturall subiectes from occupacion to idelnes. *a* **1548** Hall *Chron., Hen. VII* 3 b, The Englishe nacion his naturall countrey men. *Ibid.* 116 Suche was the malicious hartburnynge of the Scottes against their naturall lord. **1593** Shaks. *3 Hen. VI*, i. i. 82 Whom should hee follow, but his naturall King? **1615** G. Sandys *Trav.* 15 The Bassa of Aleppo, and naturall Lord of the rich vally of Achillis. **1656** Blount *Glossogr.*, *Naturalize*, to make a natural Subject; to admit into the number of natural Subjects.

†**11.** Native (country or language). *Obs.*

1508 Fisher *7 Penit. Ps.* cii. Wks. (1876) 143 A certayne woman of canane came ferre from her natural countre. *a* **1548** Hall *Chron., Hen. IV* 13 The most pernicious and venemus enemy to..his owne naturall countrey. **1585** T. Washington tr. *Nicholay's Voy.* iv. xxix. 150 The naturall countrie of Castor and Pollux. **1617** Moryson *Itin.* i. 256 All the Candians speaking Italian as well as their naturall Greeke tongue. **1657–61** Heylin *Hist. Ref.* i. ii. §4. 36 The Sclavonians..made suit unto the Pope to have the publick Service in their natural Tongue.

12. a. ***natural spirit***: in *Old Med.*, that one of the three spirits (spirit *sb.* 16) which was held to be produced in the liver and pass thence to the heart (see quots.). Now *Hist.*

1477 Spirit Naturall [see spirit *sb.* 16]. **1533** Elyot *Cast. Helth* (1541) 10 b, Spirit naturall taketh his beginninge of the lyver, and by the vaynes. **1543** Traheron *Vigo's Chirurg.* Interpr. Words *Vital Spirits*, The physitions teache that there ben thre kindes of spirites, animal, vital, and naturall. **1888** *Encycl. Brit.* XXIV. 95/1 The blood-making organ, the liver, separates from the blood subtle vapours, the natural spirits, which, carried to the heart, mix with the air introduced by respiration, and thus form the vital spirits. **1928** C. Singer *Short Hist. Med.* ii. 56 Galen believed that food-substance from the intestines was carried as 'Chyle' by the portal vein to the liver. There it was converted into blood and endowed with a particular pneuma, the Natural Spirit, which bestowed the power of growth and nutrition. *Ibid.* iv. 126 We have already traced the wrecking of the Galenic physiology. With its destruction, the old ideas concerning the three types of spirit, natural, vital, and animal, went by the board. **1945** D. Guthrie *Hist. Med.* v. 77 In the liver the blood, endowed with Natural Spirit, passed to the right ventricle, whence it was distributed to nourish all the tissues and organs, and also to the lungs, in order that impurities might be exhaled.

†**b.** ***natural parts*** or ***places***, the genitals, the privy members. *Obs.*

1569 Androis tr. *Alexis' Secretes* iv. i. 14 To cause the naturall places of women to purge. **1601** Holland *Pliny* II. 181 It is good for the naturall parts of women to sit ouer the decoction of it. **1698** Fryer *Acc. E. India & P.* 111 The strength of their Backs exert themselves into their Natural Parts. *a* **1754** Mead *Wks.* (1775) 480 A flux of blood from the natural parts.

†**c.** ***natural line***: in palmistry (see quots.).

1653 R. Sanders *Physiogn.* 92 The Natural line joyned to the Line of Life, denotes the person exactly studious. **1663** —— *Palmistry* 37 The midle natural line ought to begin at.. the Thenar part of the hand.., and to extend it quite cross the hand.

III. †**13. a.** Of children: Actually begotten by one (in contrast to adopted, etc.), and especially in lawful wedlock; hence freq. = legitimate. *Obs.*

1412–20 Lydg. *Chron. Troy* ii. x, This noble Kynge also Hadde thirty sonnes.., That called were his sonnes naturall. **1503** in *Lett. Rich. III & Hen. VII* (Rolls) I. 195 Ye had..as good mynde towards h[ym] as ye cowd have to your naturall son. **1526** Tindale *1 Tim.* i. 2 Unto Timothe hys naturall Sonne in the fayth. **1556** J. Heywood *Spider & F.* lxvii. 10 What naturall father can se..His naturall childerne in dread quake and start, Without his hart smarting? **1599** *Life More* in Wordsworth *Eccl. Biog.* (1853) II. 122 Not one of his naturall children, yet brought up with his other children. *c* **1611** Chapman *Iliad* xiii. 166 He was lodg'd with Priam, who held dear His natural sons no more than him. **1654** O. SEDGWICK *Funeral Serm.* 17 A Father doth not more love his Natural child, then the faithful Minister doth those whom he hath begotten unto Christ. **1741** T. ROBINSON *Gavelkind* I. ii. 11 By the Law of the Twelve Tables the Descent..was without Distinction of Primogeniture to all the Children, whether Male or Female, natural or adopted.

†**b.** Similarly of other relationships (esp. ***natural father*** or ***brother***) in which there is actual consanguinity or kinship by descent. *Obs.*

c **1400** *Destr. Troy* 6509 þen Synabor..Neghit to þe note,—his naturall brother. **1540** in Ellis *Orig. Lett.* Ser. II. II. 157 Wher it hath pleased Allmyghty Godde to call my naturall father to his fatall end. **1585** T. WASHINGTON tr. *Nicholays Voy.* III. ii. 71 The great Turke being there a natural vncle of the late Rostan. **1611** SHAKS. *Cymb.* III. iii. 107 My selfe..They take for Naturall Father. **1641** HINDE *J. Bruen* lii. 174 If he saw naturall brethren likely to fall out he would..wisely admonish them for peace.

c. In later use denoting a mere blood-kinship not legally recognized; hence, illegitimate, bastard.

1586 FERNE *Blaz. Gentrie* 90 He hath smoothed vp the matter with a fine terme, in calling him a sonne naturall, a prety word. **1632** MASSINGER *Maid of Hon.* I. i, He in the Malta habit Is the natural brother of the King—a by-blow. **1662** J. DAVIES tr. *Mandelslo's Trav.* 112 Mara Ragu..had three sons legitimate, and one natural. **1726** ARBUTHNOT *It cannot rain*, etc., Swift's Wks. 1755 III. I. 133 It has been commonly thought that he is Ulrick's natural brother, because of some resemblance of manners. **1773** JOHNSON in Boswell *Hebrides* (1785) 502 Supposing me to be her son,.. I must have been her natural son. **1817** J. EVANS *Excurs. Windsor* 38 He was never married, but had natural daughters, who enjoyed his property. **1864** BURTON *Scot Abr.* I. iii. 135 To pass off one of his natural children as a legitimate daughter of the house of Castile.

14. a. ***natural fool***: one who is by nature deficient in intelligence; a fool or simpleton by birth. †So ***natural idiot.*** (Cf. NATURAL *sb.* 2.)

c **1430** LYDG. *Min. Poems* (Percy Soc.) 187 'Thou were', quod she, 'a very naturall fole, To suffre me departe'. *c* **1440** *Alph. Tales* 236 Socrates..provid hym bod a wriche & a naturall fule. **1540** *Act 32 Hen. VIII*, c. 46 Ideottes and fooles naturall, now remayning..in his graces custodye. **1590** SIR J. SMYTH *Disc. Weapons* Ded. 10 b, As though their Soldiers had bene either such naturall fooles or children. **1634** EARL CORK *Diary* in *Lismore Papers* Ser. I. (1886) IV. 22 To have the custody of her eldest son.., a naturall Iddeott. *c* **1670** HOBBES *Dial. Com. Laws* (1681) 98 Saying the King was a Natural Fool, and unfit to govern. **1748** CHESTERFIELD *Lett.* (1792) II. cxliv. 14 Which makes those, who do not know him, take him at first for a natural fool. **1825** J. NEAL *Bro. Jonathan* I. 119 Imposed upon by one whom you have thought a natural fool.

b. Having a specified character by nature.

1596 SHAKS. *1 Hen. IV*, II. iv. 542 Thou [art] a naturall Coward, without instinct. **1645** USSHER *Body Divin.* (1647) 45 Was this saving wisdome of God known to the Philosophers and naturall wise men of the world? **1674** *Lond. Gaz.* No. 907/4 A Flea bitten Mare,..a natural pacer. **1713** STEELE *Englishm.* No. 7. 43 A Natural Critick looks upon a Regular as a Dunce. **1776** *New Jersey Arch.* Ser. II. I. 103 A Horse,..a natural pacer, but can trot. **1858** HAWTHORNE *Fr. & It. Note-bks.* II. 85 He..would have made a natural doctor of mighty potency.

†**15. a.** Native to a country; native-born. *Obs.*

a **1533** LD. BERNERS *Gold. Bk. M. Aurel.* (1546) B viij b, Vertue maketh a stranger natural. **1570–6** LAMBARDE *Peramb. Kent* (1826) 193, I wote not how the naturall and auncient inhabitants will beare it. **1582** N. LICHEFIELD tr. *Castanheda's Conq. E. Ind.* I. x. 27 The naturall people of that Countrie are blacke. **1602** WARNER *Alb. Eng.* Epit. 359 Welch-men.., Amongst whom was a succession of Naturall Kings. **1665** J. WEBB *Stone-Heng* (1725) 76 The Romans.. conquered our Britain; reduced the natural Inhabitants from their Barbarism.

†**b.** Freq. with national names, as ***natural Englishmen***, etc. Also of words. *Obs.*

1556 [PONET] (*title*) A shorte treatise of politike power,.. with an Exhortacion to all true naturall Englishemen. **1572** *Reg. Privy Council Scot.* II. 159 Thai ar all..of ane cuntry and naturall Scottismen. **1579** E. K. *Ded. to Spenser's Sheph. Cal.* § 1 Good and naturall English words. **1624** MASSINGER *Renegado* II. iv, Thou an Italian,—Nay, more.. a natural Venetian. **1670–98** LASSELS *Voy. Italy* II. 281 These three castles are guarded by natural Spaniards. **1728** MORGAN *Algiers* I. iii. 49 Twelve Colonies could not do very much towards civilizing a People so prone to Unpoliteness as were the natural Africans.

†**c.** Const. *of* a place. *Obs.*

1574 HELLOWES *Gueuara's Fam. Ep.* (1577) 8 God commaunded that the Kings shoulde be naturall of the Kingdome. **1588** PARKE tr. *Mendoza's Hist. China* 64 Commonly the captaines be naturall of those prouinces. **1622** BACON *Hen. VII* (1876) 201 Till Philip were by continuance in Spain made as natural of Spain.

16. a. Feeling or exhibiting natural kindliness, affection, †or gratitude; having natural feeling. Now *rare.*

1523 FITZHERB. *Husb.* §160 Nature byndeth a man to.. kepe them, or els he is not a naturall man, remembrynge what god hath done for the. *c* **1530** C'TESS SALISBURY in Ellis *Orig. Lett.* Ser. II. II. 107, I pray you to be a good and naturall modre unto hyr. **1589** GREENE *Menaphon* (1616) 66 Doron, to shew himselfe a naturall yong man, gaue her a few kind kisses to comfort her. **1603** SHAKS. *Meas. for M.* III. i. 229 A noble..brother, in his loue toward her, euer most kinde and naturall. **1605** —— *Lear* II. i. 86 Loyall and naturall Boy. **1608** D. T. *Ess. Pol. & Mor.* 10 b, Which are founde in euery well-disposed naturall man. *a* **1640** MASSINGER, etc. *Old Law* II. i, *Ant.* Away, unnatural! *Sim.* ..To be natural at such a time Were a fool's part. **1843** DICKENS *Chr. Carol* iv, A wicked old screw.., why wasn't he natural in his lifetime?

Comb. *a* **1600** HOOKER *Serm. agst. Sorrow* §7 Those men that would gladly haue their friends and brethrens dayes prolonged on earth, (as there is no naturall-hearted man but gladly would).

†**b.** Const. *to* or *towards* a person, etc. *Obs.*

1537 CROMWELL in Merriman *Life & Lett.* (1902) II. 89 If yow wer either naturall towardes your countrey or your famylie, you wolde not thus shame all your kynne. **1561** *Wills & Inv. N.C.* (Surtees 1835) 193 As the said John will haive my blessing, to be naturall to the rest of his brether and sisters. **1611** B. JONSON *Catiline* III. ii, No child can be too natural to his parent.

†**17.** *Sc.* Possessed of natural ability. *Obs. rare.*

a **1578** LINDESAY (Pitscottie) *Chron. Scot.* (S.T.S.) I. 284 The lord Home beand ane wyse and naturall man. *Ibid.* II. 120 Quein regent beand ane vyse and naturall woman.

IV. 18. a. Dealing or concerned with, relating to, nature as an object of study or research; now usual only in ***natural science(s***; hence ***natural-scientific*** adj. †***natural story*** = NATURAL HISTORY.

c **1425** *Orolog. Sapient.* iv. in *Anglia* X. 357/29 þe forseide broþere..lefte þe scoles of natural science and worldely wisdome. **1432–50** tr. *Higden* (Rolls) V. 11 Plinius..made.. xxxvij^{ti} bookes of the story naturalle. **1551** RECORDE *Pathw. Knowl.* Pref., He was a wittie man in naturall knowlege, and obserued well the change of wethers. **1576** FLEMING *Panopl. Epist.* 215 The natural secrets, in the understanding and knowledge of which I haue..beene instructed. **1622** GATAKER *Spir. Watch* (ed. 2) 23 If we may beleeue those that write the naturall story. **1655** STANLEY *Hist. Philos.* I. (1687) 2/1 Thales..first introduc'd Natural and Mathematical Learning into Greece. **1684** *R. Waller's Nat. Exper.* Fly-leaf, The Royal Society for Improving Natural Knowledge. **1707** *Phil. Trans.* XXV. No. 310. 2418 Some Natural Observations made..in Shropshire. **1812** SIR H. DAVY *Chem. Philos.* 5 The School of Aristotle gave a transient attention to the objects of Natural Science. **1840** *Cuvier's Anim. Kingd.* 14 The modes of procedure employed in the three branches of the Natural Sciences. **1890** W. JAMES *Princ. Psychol.* I. vii. 184 It is highly important that this natural-science point of view should be understood at the outset. **1924** R. M. OGDEN tr. *Koffka's Growth of Mind* i. §4. 15 The behaviour of an animal as it takes place is something to be determined as a natural-scientific event. **1944** H. A. HODGES *Wilhelm Dilthey* iii. 49 Natural-science psychology ..takes the mind as a thing among things and studies its processes from a causal point of view. **1949** M. FORTES *Social Struct.* p. xi, Their theme was the comparative study of human society by the methods of the natural sciences. *a* **1963** L. MACNEICE *Astrol.* (1964) viii. 262 He began his huge and gallant undertaking while he was still a natural-sciences student at the University of Geneva. **1970** G. E. EVANS *Where Beards wag All* xx. 231 When he [*sc.* the archaeologist] comes..to the question *Why?*, he is forced to look beyond the natural sciences, and his aids are more likely to come from anthropology, history, geography, [etc.].

b. ***natural philosophy***, the study of natural bodies as such and of the phenomena connected with them; physical science, physics.

1456 SIR G. HAYE *Law Arms* (S.T.S) 75 Be all clerkis of naturale philosophy..it is impossible that the hevin be still bot moving. **1471** [see PHILOSOPHY 3]. **1519** *Interl. Four Elem.* Prol., A few conclusyouns..And poyntes of phylosophy naturall. **1581** MULCASTER *Positions* xxxv. (1887) 129 Naturall Philosophy, the ground mistresse to Physik. **1649** FULLER *Just Man's Funeral* 5 He..was skil'd in natural Philosophie from the Cedar to the Shrub. **1678** HOBBES *Decam.* i. 6 That sublunary Physiques, which is commonly called Natural Philosophy. *a* **1734** NORTH *Life Ld. Keeper North* (1742) 332 He was adept in natural Philosophy and Mechanicks. **1803** WOOD *Mechanics* i. 10 The business of natural philosophy is not to find out what might have been the constitution of nature. **1865** *Chambers's Encycl.* VII. 521/2 Physics..in its narrower sense..is equivalent to Natural Philosophy, which, until of late years, was the term more commonly used in Great Britain.

attrib. **1721** AMHERST *Terræ Fil.* No. 42 (1726) 221 The place appointed for these examinations is the natural-philosophy school (one of the most public places in the university).

c. Given to the study of natural science; esp. ***natural philosopher***, one devoted to, or skilled in, natural philosophy. Also ***natural scientist.***

c **1520** L. ANDREW *Noble Lyfe* a ij, The naturall maister Aristotell saith [etc.]. **1541** R. COPLAND *Guydon's Quest. Chirurg.* C j b, A physycyen and Cyrurgyen ought for to knowe ye complexion of the membres, as natural Phylosophers. **1579** FULKE *Heskins' Parl.* 172 The eternitie of the worlde, which is held by some naturall philosophers. **1629** DONNE *Serm.* xxxi. 307 Naturall men will write of Lands of Pygmies. **1657** TRAPP *Comm. Job* xxxviii. 38 The large Discourses of the natural Philosophers concerning that Subject. **1797** *Encycl. Brit.* (ed. 3) XIV. 653/2 Whether matter is acted on.., or whether it acts of itself.., makes no difference to the natural philosopher. **1888** R. HUNT in *Dict. Nat. Biog.* XIV. 187/1 Davy, Sir Humphry.., natural philosopher, was born at Penzance. **1895** F. THILLY tr. *Paulsen's Introd. Philos.* I. i. 59 Natural scientists..are inclined to pursue the former path. **1951** E. E. EVANS-PRITCHARD *Social Anthropol.* iii. 48 This is not the procedure of natural scientists, which most writers of this persuasion—and that means most English social anthropologists—consider themselves to be. **1975** *Notes & Rec. R. Soc.* XXIX. 193 My first intimation of Johnson's views on natural science and on natural scientists came from the *Life of Milton.*

19. Of wool, cotton, silk, etc.: having a colour characteristic of the natural state when unbleached and undyed. Also ***natural-coloured*** adj. Hence as *sb.* to denote a shade of off-white or creamy beige.

1854 *Morning Post* 7 July 1/5 (Advt.), Aberdeen Linsey Woolseys in granite, heather, and natural wools. *c* **1860** in A. Adburgham *Shops & Shopping* (1964) vii. 74 Vicuna,.. woven in its natural colour,..is admirably adapted for Ladies' Cloaks and Gentlemen's Costumes. **1895** *Montgomery Ward Catal.* 9/3 Dress Linen..in the 'natural' flax color only. *Ibid.* 12/3 Plain Habutai Silk in natural (cream) color only. **1927** T. WOODHOUSE *Artificial Silk* 85 Natural-coloured artificial silk yarns. **1930** *Daily Express* 6 Oct. 9/6 (Advt.), Real Italian hand embroidery on pale cream linen, beautifully worked in blue, gold, rose, or natural. **1941** R. STOUT *Red Threads* i. 6 He must have the natural kasha, the one with nubs, by tomorrow afternoon. **1954** [see ALIZARIN]. **1971** *Vogue* 15 Oct. 144/3 Dress;.. colours: cocoa, blue, natural.

20. ***natural shoulder*** *U.S.* (see quot. 1973). Freq. *attrib.*

1957 *Men's Wear* (N.Y.) 8 Feb. 69/2 Natural shoulders mark the topcoats as well as the suits. **1958** *Ibid.* 21 Feb. 70/2 What is one man's 'Ivy' is another man's 'natural shoulder garment'. **1962** 'I. T. ROSS' *Old Students never Die* i. 13 In a natural-shoulder suit now, instead of a sloppy sweatshirt. **1969** *New Yorker* 11 Oct. 128/1 (Advt.), We don't make outerwear with padding. All our coats are natural shoulder. **1973** *Esquire's Encycl. 20th Cent. Men's Fashions* 670/1 *Natural shoulder.* Term applied to a straight-hanging jacket with medium-width, lightly padded shoulders and a center vent. With this style, favored by university men and others, were worn pleatless, trim-cut trousers.

'natural-born, *a.* [f. prec. + BORN *ppl. a.* Cf. NATIVE-BORN.] Having a specified position or character by birth; used esp. with *subject.*

1583 *Exec. for Treason* (1675) 43 D. Sanders a natural born Subject but an unnatural worn Priest. **1598** W. PHILLIP tr. *Linschoten* (Hakl.) I. 184 The children of Mestiços are of colour and fashion like the naturall borne Countrimen. **1625** in H. L'Estrange *Chas. I.* (1655) 21 Divers of the naturall-born subjects of this Kingdome..do ..claim precedency of the Peers of this Realm. **1709** *Act 7 Anne* c. 5 §3 The Children of all natural-born Subjects, born out of the Ligeance of her Majesty..shall be deemed..to be natural-born Subjects of this Kingdom. **1765** BLACKSTONE *Comm.* I. 370 The prince is always under a constant tie to protect his natural-born subjects. **1833** *Penny Cycl.* I. 338/2 It is not true that every person, born out of the dominion of the crown, is therefore an alien; nor is a person born within them necessarily a natural-born subject. **1876** BANCROFT *Hist. U.S.* VI. xxvi. 27 Every one who first saw the light on the American soil was a natural-born American citizen. **1897** MARY KINGSLEY *W. Africa* 137 The chief being a natural-born idiot, came with two of his head men.

natura'lesque, *a.* and *sb.* [f. NATURAL *a.*]

A. *adj.* Having the characteristics of nature or natural objects.

1880 MRS. COMPTON READE *Brown Hand & White* II. iv. 102 Flung to the lowest depths of despair by the very naturalesque loveliness of Nereide. **1895** *Archæol. Oxon.* VI. 310 The spandrels are filled with foliage, much of which from its naturalesque character is almost unique.

B. *sb.* Imitation of, adherence to, nature.

1888 *Star* 12 Dec. 3/2 Morris..was generally in his designs puzzled between 'naturalesque' and 'conventionalism'.

'natural 'history. [HISTORY *sb.* 5.]

1. A work dealing with the properties of natural objects, plants, or animals; a scientific account *of* any subject written on similar lines.

1567 [see HISTORY *sb.* 5]. **1585** T. WASHINGTON tr. *Nicholay's Voy.* II. x. 43 b, Plinie in his naturall history writeth [etc.]. **1604** E. G[RIMSTONE] *D'Acosta's Hist. Indies* III. i. 117 Every naturall Historie is of it selfe pleasing, and very profitable. **1626** BACON *New Atl.* (1658) 16 That Natural History, which he wrote of all plants. **1693** *Phil. Trans.* XVII. No. 198. 667 [Mr. Bannister] was most likely to have given us a very good Natural History of that place. **1831** RENNIE *Montagu's Ornith. Dict.* p. xxxi, Nobody.. could ever dream of designating any of these [works]..a Natural History. **1855** BAIN *Senses & Int.* II. i. §8 If a Natural History of the human feelings is at all possible.

2. The aggregate of facts relating to the natural objects, etc., *of* a place, or the characteristics *of* a class of persons or things. Also *transf.* the details *of* any subject treated in a similar manner.

Freq. in the titles of works, and so tending to pass into 1.

1593 G. HARVEY *Pierce's Super.* 163 Let him read the naturall histories of the Asse, and the Sheepe, in Aristotle, Pliny, or Gesner. **1677** PLOT (*title*) The Natural History of Oxford-shire, Being an Essay toward the Natural History of England. **1766** SWINTON in *Phil. Trans.* LVII. 111 The natural history of these..insects is sufficiently known. **1797** *Encycl. Brit.* (ed. 3) XIV. 645/1 A short sketch of what may be called the natural history of the physical sciences. **1805** WEAVER tr. *Werner's Fossils* 1 Mineralogy or the natural history of fossils. **1897** MARY KINGSLEY *W. Africa* 621, I.. got a good deal of material for a work on the Natural History of Governors which I do not intend to publish.

3. Originally, the systematic study of all natural objects, animal, vegetable, and mineral; now restricted to the study of animal life, and freq. implying a popular rather than a strictly scientific treatment of the subject.

1662 J. DAVIES tr. *Olearius' Voy. Ambass.* 47 Many other stories were told us..relating more to natural History than Travels. **1682** GREW *Anat. Plants* Pref., Without shewing any purpose of managing this Part of Natural History. **1766** FORDYCE *Serm. Yng. Wm.* (1767) I. vii. 284 Of Natural Philosophy I consider Natural History as a part. **1816** KEATINGE *Trav.* (1817) I. 109 Another incident in natural history..is..Toads eat larks! **1855** KINGSLEY *Glaucus* (1878) 11 It is a question whether Natural History would have ever attained its present honours, had not Geology arisen. **1893** NEWTON *Dict. Birds* p. vii, Persons indifferent to the pleasures of Natural History, except when highly-coloured pictures are presented to them by popular writers.

attrib. **1851** *Lit. Gaz.* 12 July 483/1 The Natural History Section of the British Association. **1877** *Nature* 21 June 137/1 The organisation of natural history museums.

†**b.** In concrete use. (See quot.) *Obs. rare*$^{-1}$.

1749 *Phil. Trans.* XLVI. No. 491. 6 An Account of Glasses..for preserving Pieces of Anatomy or Natural History in spirituous Liquors.

Hence **'natural hi'storian**, a writer or authority on Natural History; **'natural-hi'storical** *a.*, belonging to Natural History.

1665 HOOKE *Microgr.* 27 There are many examples found in Natural Historians, of Springs that do ebb and flow. **1780** J. ADAMS in *Fam. Lett.* (1876) 379 There is a handsome statue of M. Buffon, the great natural historian. **1825** BEDDOES *Let.* in *Poems* (1851) p. xlvii, Blumenbach..is, I fancy, of the first rank as mineralogist, physiologian, geologist, botanist, natural-historian, and physician. *a* **1850** ROSSETTI *Dante & Circ.* II. (1874) 267 Works..whose subjects are genealogical, historical, natural-historical, and even theological. **1884** *Daily News* 28 Aug. 2/2 A natural-historian who told us all about the height of Lundy Island.

naturalism ('nætjʊərəlɪz(ə)m). [f. NATURAL *a.* + -ISM. Cf. F. *naturalisme.*]

1. Action arising from, or based on, natural instincts, without spiritual guidance (†also with *pl.*); a system of morality or religion having a purely natural basis.

a **1641** BP. MOUNTAGU *Acts & Mon.* (1642) 211 Atheists or men..who will admit of nothing but Morality, but Naturalismes, and humane reason. **1753** tr. *Frey's Acc. Moravians* 34 The Naturalism and lawless Priviledges of the first Class. **1866** LIDDON *Bampton Lect.* vi. (1875) 308 Pagans yield to those instincts of creature-worship which mere naturalism is ever prone to indulge. **1884** SYMONDS *Shaks. Predec.* iii. 96 A spirit survived from the old heathen past,..which we may describe as naturalism. **1894** *Thinker* V. 346 A mythological system, with innumerable gods grafted upon the original element of naturalism.

2. *Philos.* A view of the world, and of man's relation to it, in which only the operation of natural (as opposed to supernatural or spiritual) laws and forces is admitted or assumed. Also, the view that moral concepts can be analysed in terms of concepts applicable to natural phenomena.

1750 WARBURTON *Julian* 42 *note*, [Ammianus] being..a religious Theist, and untainted with the Naturalism of Tacitus. **1794** HURD *Life Warburton* 72 Lord Bolingbroke..was of that sect, which, to avoid a more odious name, chuses to distinguish itself by that of Naturalism. **1816** R. HALL *Let.* Wks. 1832 V. 502 Their system is naturalism, not the evangelical system. **1858** SEARS *Athan.* 4 By the word 'Naturalism' we describe a belief in nature alone. **1874** W. WALLACE *Hegel's Logic* §60. 100 Materialism or Naturalism, therefore, is the only consistent and thorough-going system of Empiricism. **1894** J. SETH *Study of Ethical Princ.* III. ii. 398 We are offered..a new version of the 'Ethics of Naturalism', far superior to the old Utilitarian version, superior because so much more scientific. **1903** G. E. MOORE *Principia Ethica* ii. 40, I have thus appropriated the name Naturalism to a particular method of approaching Ethics. **1945** K. R. POPPER *Open Society* I. v. 60 Ethical naturalism..has recently been used for confusing the whole issue by advertising certain reactionary, and allegedly 'natural' rights as 'natural laws'. **1952** R. M. HARE *Lang. Morals* ii. 30 Professor G. E. Moore's celebrated 'refutation of naturalism'. *Ibid.* v. 92 Naturalism in ethics, like attempts to square the circle..will constantly recur so long as there are people who have not understood the fallacy involved. **1967** *Encycl. Philos.* III. 69/1 According to ethical naturalism, moral judgments just state a special subclass of facts about the natural world.

3. A style or method characterized by close adherence to, and faithful representation of, nature or reality: **a.** in literature.

a **1850** ROSSETTI *Dante & Circ.* I. (1874) 21 The earliest prominent example of a naturalism without afterthought in the whole of Italian poetry. **1859** KINGSLEY *Misc.* II. 136 That Naturalism which threatened to end in sheer brutality. **1881** *Daily News* 13 June 4/4 That unnecessarily faithful portrayal of offensive incidents for which M. Zola has found the new name of 'Naturalism'.

b. in art.

1852 MRS. JAMESON *Leg. Madonna* Introd. 37 The mannerism of the Italians, and the naturalism of the Flemish painters. **1853** RUSKIN *Stones Ven.* III. i. §11 The Gothic naturalism advancing gradually from the Byzantine severity. **1884** *Bazaar* 26 Dec. 681/3 Foregrounds of rush and wild flower he paints with extraordinary facility and naturalism.

4. Adherence or attachment to what is natural.

1865 M. ARNOLD *Ess. Crit.* v. 186 Goethe's profound, imperturbable naturalism is absolutely fatal to all routine thinking. **1884** SEELEY in *Contemp. Rev.* Oct. 502 His naturalism, his enjoyment of the world as it is.

naturalist ('nætjʊərəlɪst), *sb.* and *a.* [ad. F. *naturaliste* (1527), = It. and Sp. *naturalista*; or f. NATURAL *a.* + -IST.]

A. *sb.* **1. a.** One who studies natural, in contrast to spiritual, things; one who regards natural causes as a sufficient explanation of the world and its phenomena; an adherent of or believer in, naturalism.

1587 GOLDING *De Mornay* Pref (1592) 9 Against the false naturalists (that is to say professors of the knowledge of nature and naturall things) I wil alledge nature it selfe. **1612** R. CARPENTER *Soul's Sent.* 76 Those blasphemous truth-opposing Heretikes, and Atheisticall naturalists. **1677** GILPIN *Demonol.* (1867) 132 The Naturalists explode Christ and Scriptures at last as unnecessary. **1719** DE FOE *Crusoe* I. (Globe) 191 Let the Naturalists explain these Things [the aspirations of the soul]. **1824** SOUTHEY *Sir T. More* (1831) I. 5 The religious Naturalist in his turn despises the feeble mind of the Socinian. **1864** *Q. Jrnl. Sci.* I. 554 The small semi-educated sect of men calling themselves 'Naturalists', or 'Secularists'. **1952** R. M. HARE *Lang. Morals* v. 92 It is therefore no answer..to claim that a 'naturalist' might if he pleased define 'good' in terms of some characteristics of his choice. **1964** [see CONTEXTUALISM 1].

b. One who follows the light of nature, as contrasted with revelation.

1608 BP. HALL *Epist.* III. iii, Let me but know what action Popery requires of any of hir followers, which a meere Naturalist hath not done, can not do? **1628** FELTHAM *Resolves* II. xcii. 269 For the Manner how God would bee worshipped, no Naturalist could euer find it out, till hee himselfe gaue directions from his sacred Scripture. **1825** COLERIDGE *Aids Refl.* (1848) I. 288, I am here speaking in the assumed character of a mere naturalist, to whom no light of revelation had been vouchsafed.

†**2.** A natural man; one with natural instincts.

1635 J. HAYWARD tr. *Biondi's Banish'd Virg.* 34 Feredo was in one respect a naturalist, desirous of posterity.

3. a. One who studies, or is versed in, natural science; a natural philosopher, a physicist. Now *rare* or *Obs.* (very common in 17th c.).

1587 GREENE *Euphues Cens. Philautus* Wks. (Grosart) VI. 172 Your phisicall reasons bewraies a good naturalist. **1605** TIMME *Quersit.* I. xvii. 89 Diligent physitians or naturalists ..wil put the same to any kind of metall. **1654** WHITLOCK *Zootomia* 227 That Inke hath Poyson in it, the Historian, as well as Naturalist will confesse. **1686** PLOT *Staffordsh.* 8 Because the Lightening first affects the Sense, I give it the precedence, as is usual amongst Naturalists. **1726** SWIFT *Gulliver* III. iii, For the highest clouds cannot rise above two miles, as naturalists agree. **1752** HUME *Ess. & Treat.* (1777) I. 330 All water..remains always at a level. Ask naturalists the reason. **1795** J. HUTTON *Th. Earth* I. 201 Some part of the Theory of the Earth..which will probably give offence to naturalists who have espoused an opposite opinion. **1813** MACKINTOSH *De L'Allemagne* Wks. 1846 II. 537 The naturalist gives no picture of scenery by the most accurate catalogue of mineral and vegetable produce.

b. (In early use only contextual, now specific.) One who is interested in, or makes a special study of, animals or plants. (A less precise term than *zoologist*, *botanist*, etc.)

1600 SUTTON *Disce Mori* vi. (1846) 57 A lion; of whom the naturalist writeth, that he is of such courage [etc.]. **1658** T. WALL *Charact. Enemies Ch.* 30 The great Naturalist observes it of this beast, the Leopard [etc.]. **1733** SWIFT *On Poetry* Wks. 1755 IV. I. 194 So, nat'ralists observe, a flea Hath smaller fleas that on him prey. **1774** GOLDSM. *Nat. Hist.* VII. 27 The sea snail, of which naturalists have..mentioned fifteen kinds. **1808** PIKE *Sources Mississ.* III. 210 This father was a great naturalist, or rather florist; he had large collections of flowers, plants [etc.]. **1859** DARWIN *Orig. Spec.* ii. (1873) 33 Every naturalist knows vaguely what he means when he speaks of a species. **1870** YEATS *Nat. Hist. Comm.* 7 The structure of a bone enables naturalists to build up the animal of which it is a part.

†**4.** One 'natural' to a country; a native. *Obs.*$^{-1}$

1631 HEYWOOD *Eng. Eliz.* (1641) 160 If they aimed at the life of a naturalist, being their..Sovereignes sister.

†**5.** One who lacks technical training. *Obs.*$^{-1}$

1707 SIR W. HOPE *New Method Fencing* (1714) 255 A vigorous and stout ignorant or naturalist, with a swinging irregular pursute, will put any of you from off all your orderly postures of defence.

6. One who aims at reproducing or adhering closely to nature; a representative of naturalism: **a.** in art.

1784 J. BARRY *Lect. Art* iii. (1848) 124 The cavils of the ignorant,—or the Naturalists, as they choose to call themselves. **1856** RUSKIN *Mod. Paint.* III. IV. vi. §2 Others received both good and evil together (thence properly called Naturalists). **1873** PATER *Renaissance* 42 Botticelli lived in a generation of naturalists, and he might have been a naturalist among them.

b. in literature.

1883 LOWELL *Wks.* (1890) VI. 62 Fielding was a naturalist in the sense that he was an instinctive and careful observer. **1888** H. JAMES *Partial Portr.* 124 [Trollope] tells us, on the whole, more about life than the 'naturalists' in our sister republic.

B. *adj.* Naturalistic.

1830 PUSEY *Hist. Enq.* II. 366 Its naturalist tendencies..received their highest power to hurt from corresponding points in the state of theology. **1860** RUSKIN *Mod. Paint.* V. IX. ii. §4 That naturalist art..denied at last the spiritual nature of man. **1893** COLLINGWOOD *Life Ruskin* I. 192 The Naturalist-landscape school, a group of painters who threw overboard the traditions of Turner.

naturalistic (nætjʊərə'lɪstɪk), *a.* [f. prec. + -IC.]

1. a. In accordance with the doctrine of naturalism.

1840 W. H. MILL *Observ.* I. 130 The historical and naturalistic explanations of Paulus and his school. **1858** SEARS *Athan.* 8 Naturalistic tendencies leading to doubts of immortality. **1884** FARRAR in *Contemp. Rev.* Mar. 446 The naturalistic explanation of miracles was exploded finally by Strauss himself.

b. Of the nature of, characterized by, naturalism in various senses. spec. ***naturalistic fallacy*** (see quot. 1903).

1860 MILL *Repr. Govt.* (1861) 9 The supporters of what may be termed the naturalistic theory of politics. **1871** FARRAR *Witn. Hist.* iii. 101 For the old humanistic worship ..it substituted a naturalistic cult. **1891** T. HARDY *Tess* xxvi, Its obvious unreality amid beliefs essentially naturalistic. **1894** J. SETH *Study of Ethical Princ.* III. ii. 398 In spite of his professed impartiality between matter and mind, Spencer does not hesitate to offer such a materialistic or naturalistic interpretation of the moral life. *Ibid.*, A naturalistic scheme of morality, the correlation of the ethical with the physical process. **1903** G. E. MOORE *Principia Ethica* i. 10 Ethics aims at discovering what are those other properties belonging to all things which are good. But far too many philosophers have thought that when they named those other properties they were actually defining good; that these properties, in fact, were simply not 'other', but absolutely and entirely the same with goodness. This view I propose to call the 'naturalistic fallacy'. *Ibid.* vi. 201 The naturalistic fallacy has been quite as commonly committed with regard to beauty as with regard to good: its use has introduced as many errors into Aesthetics as into Ethics. **1934** C. D. BROAD *Five Types Ethical Theory* vii. 257 Those theories which hold that ethical characteristics *can* be analysed without remainder into non-ethical ones may be called..*Naturalistic Theories.* **1936** A. J. AYER *Lang., Truth & Logic* vi. 157 We have already rejected the 'naturalistic' theories which are commonly supposed to provide the only alternative to 'absolutism' in ethics. **1965** *Philos.* XL. 308 The attack on the naturalistic fallacy..has been welcomed.

2. Aiming at a close reproduction of nature; realistic: **a.** in art.

1849 *Fraser's Mag.* XXXIX. 295 They think it a sufficient condemnation of a picture to call it naturalistic. **1862** HAMERTON *Painter's Camp* I. 8 Our modern school of naturalistic landscape painters. **1886** SYMONDS *Renaiss. It., Cath. React.* (1898) VII. xiii. 223 A manner..more naturalistic than that of the Caracci.

b. in literature.

1876 L. STEPHEN *Eng. Th. 18th C.* II. 426 The romantic and the naturalistic school adopted different modes of satisfying the yearning thus excited. **1889** *Harper's Mag.* Nov. 963/1 The perusal of a naturalistic book.

3. Of or belonging to natural history.

1859 G. WILSON *Life E. Forbes* v. (1861) 151 The almost exclusive preference which he showed to the scientific, and especially the naturalistic, over the professional branches of medicine. **1890** *Blackw. Mag.* CXLVII. 149/2 We wish no better guide on a naturalistic ramble.

4. Based on nature; relating to the natural order of things, as opposed to a logical order.

1867 ATWATER *Logic* 53 In a Logical sense, quadrupeds, reptiles, birds, fishes, are species of the genus animal. In the Naturalistic sense, though they include species, they are not themselves species at all.

Hence **natura'listically** *adv.*

1864 *Realm* 2 Mar. 7 His solidly imagined and naturalistically presented groundwork of an autobiography. **1885** J. E. HARRISON *Stud. in Gk. Art* iii. 139 It is usually a natural scene, naturalistically treated.

naturality (nætjʊə'rælɪtɪ). Now *rare.* [a. F. *naturalité* (14th c.), ad. late L. *nātūrālitat-em* (Tertullian): see NATURAL *a.* and -ITY.]

†**1.** Natural character or quality. *Obs.*

a **1533** LD. BERNERS *Gold. Bk. M. Aurel.* Prol. A j b, Contrary in their opinions, as dyuers in their naturalities. *Ibid.* let. x. 131 b, The goddis by their naturalyte and power close vp the furies, and gouerne the steres. **1651** N. BIGGS *New Disp.* ⁋ 174 To arraigne and examine the naturalities of the other universal main pillars of curing. **1659** TORRIANO, *Spécie*, kind.., quality, or naturality.

†**2. a.** A state of nature, as opposed to morality.

1619 SIR J. SEMPIL *Sacrilege Handled* App. 47 They haue even lost the common Principles with Brutish Naturalitie, which..will euen vse a kinde of Commutatiue Iustice, and retribution. **1653** BAXTER *Saints' R.* II. Pref. (1662) 169 As all Morality presupposeth Naturality.

†**b.** Natural unmodified state. *Obs. rare*$^{-1}$.

1649 BULWER *Pathomyot.* II. i. 96 Which expression is seen in its pure naturality in Boyes.

†**3. a.** Naturalness; the fact of being in accordance with nature. *Obs.*

1643 SIR T. BROWNE *Relig. Med.* I. §19 The villany of that Spirit..by demonstrating a naturality in one way, makes us mistrust a miracle in another. **1678** CUDWORTH *Intell. Syst.* Pref., Answering the Objection, against the Naturality of the Idea of God, from the Pagan Polytheism.

†**b.** Closeness to nature. *Obs. rare*$^{-1}$.

1651 G. DANIEL *Let.* Wks. (Grosart) II. 206 You may iudge Draughts sometimes in Cole-Works, to hit the Naturalitie of Lines Studied by finer Pencills.

4. Natural (†modesty,) feeling or conduct. In later use *Sc.*

1628 F. GREVILLE *Life Sidney* x. (1652) 123 Greater resolution..than the naturality, diffidence, and quiet complexion of the Princes then reigning could well bear. **1822** GALT *Sir A. Wylie* xcix, I was vexed when I thought he was dead, and that I should have so little naturality. **1847** MRS CARLYLE *Early Lett.* (1889) 173 To rouse lethargic friends into naturality.

5. An illustration drawn from natural things.

1649 MILTON *Eikon.* xxi. Wks. 1851 III. 484 They..are in his naturalities no better then Spiders. *a* **1849** H. COLERIDGE *Ess.* (1851) II. 41 Any sort of illustrations..are better than stale common-place naturalities, which show no acquaintance with actual nature.

†**6.** The position or rights of a natural-born subject. *Obs. rare.*

1558 *Acts Parlt. Scot.* (1814) II. 507 The maist cristine king of france hes grantit ane lettre of Naturalitie for him and his successouris. **1614** W. BARCLAY *Nepenthes* A 4 b, The Spaniards, who haue giuen it the right of naturalitie in their soyle terme it Tabacco.

†**naturalizant.** *Obs. rare*$^{-1}$. [a. pres. pple. of F. *naturaliser* to NATURALIZE.] A natural citizen or inhabitant.

1653 A. WILSON *Jas. I* 35 We are all fellow-Citizens and Naturalizants of the Heavenly Jerusalem.

naturalization (ˌnætjʊərəlaɪ'zeɪʃən). [f. NATURALIZE *v.* + -ATION; cf. F. *naturalisation.*]

1. The action of admitting an alien to the position and privileges of a native-born subject or citizen; the fact of being so admitted.

1578 *Reg. Privy Council Scot.* II. 693 All respettis, remissionis, tutoreis datives and naturalizationis. **1603** R. JOHNSON *Kingd. & Commw.* 190 Certaine Iesuits.. obtayning the fauour of certaine gouernors, obtained a priuiledge of naturalization. **1622** MALYNES *Anc. Law-Merch.* 442 Those of Flanders.. are not bound to take Letters of Naturalization to dwell in this Kingdome. *a* **1676** HALE *Prim. Orig. Man.* II. x. (1677) 234 Many Scotch.. either by Naturalizations or Transmigrations have increased the Inhabitants of this Island. **1709** STEELE *Tatler* No. 13 ¶4 Our late act of naturalization hath had so great an effect in foreign parts [etc.]. **1769** *Junius Lett.* iv. (1788) 52 Such depopulation can only be repaired.. by some sensible bill of naturalization. *a* **1832** MACKINTOSH *Rev.* 1688, Wks. 1846 II. 49 They resumed the consideration of a bill for the naturalisation of French Protestants. **1867** SMILES *Huguenots Eng.* xviii, (1880) 319 They claimed and obtained letters of naturalisation.

fig. **1795** MASON *Ch. Mus.* II. 120 Our English Cathedral Music has gained.. much from this naturalisation, as it may be called, of Italian Masters.

b. *attrib.*

1711 SWIFT *Examiner* No. 44 Enemies, taking Advantage of the general Naturalization Act, had invited over.. Foreigners of all Religions. **1747** *Gentl. Mag.* 232/2 Tho' the naturalization bill was drop'd, no other was brought in to answer the same good purposes. **1833** *Penny Cycl.* I. 339/1 The most effectual method of naturalizing an alien is by Act of Parliament, called a Naturalization Bill. **1874** BANCROFT *Footpr. Time* xix. 609 A naturalization law was organized.

2. a. The admission or adoption of foreign words, beliefs, arts, practices, etc. into general use or favour.

1747 JOHNSON *Plan Dict.* Wks. 1787 IX. 169 This naturalization is produced.. by admission into common speech, in some metaphorical signification. **1843** *Proc. Philol. Soc.* I. 125 They are also accompanied by many compounds and derivatives, which is commonly regarded as a proof of long naturalization. **1876** L. STEPHEN *Eng. Th. 18th C.* I. ii. 33 The Cartesian philosophy failed to find complete naturalization. **1878** LECKY *Eng. 18th C.* I. iv. 538 The naturalisation of the opera in England.

b. The introduction of plants or animals to places where they are not indigenous, but thrive freely under ordinary conditions.

1859 DARWIN *Orig. Spec.* iv. (1873) 89 The naturalisation of plants through man's agency in foreign lands. **1870** W. ROBINSON (*title*) The Wild Garden, or Our Groves and Shrubberies made beautiful by the Naturalization of Hardy Exotic Plants. **1895** *Oracle Encycl.* I. 528/1 [He] laboured successfully for the naturalisation of British salmon in Colonial waters.

3. The action of making natural.

1897 FAIRBAIRN *Catholicism* (1899) 423 He did not describe the process with Harnack as the Secularization of the Church, or with Sohm as its Naturalization.

naturalize ('nætjʊərəlaɪz), *v.* [ad. F. *naturaliser* (16th c.): see NATURAL *a.* and -IZE, and cf. It. *naturalizzare* (Florio).]

I. 1. *trans.* To admit (an alien) to the position and rights of citizenship; to invest with the privileges of a native-born subject.

1605 VERSTEGAN *Dec. Intell.* viii. (1628) 263 A name of Naturalizing or making the bearer thereof a free Denizen. **1667** SPRAT *Hist. R. Soc.* 64 By their naturalizing Men of all Countries, they have laid the beginnings of many great advantages. **1709** STEELE *Tatler* No. 13 ¶2 All the French Refugees in those dominions [Holland] are to be naturalized. **1753** *Scots Mag.* June 269/1 The King.. had a power to naturalize any foreigner. **1792** J. BARLOW *Constit.* 1791, 37 Many of your citizens have been naturalized. **1837** CARLYLE *Fr. Rev.* III. I. i, We, by act of Assembly, 'naturalise' the chief Foreign Friends of Humanity. **1891** J. WINSOR *Columbus* xx. 479 She.. naturalized his brother Diego to fit him for ecclesiastical preferment.

fig. **1642** FULLER *Holy & Prof. St.* IV. xx. 348 Valour naturalizing a brave spirit through the Universe. *a* **1653** GOUGE *Comm. Heb.* xi. 21 The children of Joseph.. are.. naturalized by Jacob, and made free Denisons of the Church. **1766** CUNNINGHAM *Prol. Merch. Ven.* 18 This Shylock, the Jew,.. Was naturaliz'd oft by your fathers before ye. **1825** LAMB *Elia* Ser. II. *Stage Illusion*, We love in comedy to see an audience naturalised behind the scenes.

absol. **1625** BACON *Ess., Greatness Kingd.* ¶6 They haue not had that vsage, to Naturalize liberally.

b. Const. *into*, *to*. Chiefly in *fig.* uses.

1606 DEKKER *Sev. Sins* VII. (Arb.) 46 Remember.. that your Seruants are your adopted Children, they are naturalized into your bloud. **1622** DONNE *Serm.* cliv. Wks. 1839 VI. 145 Persons.. not naturalized by conversion.. from another religion to this. **1667** WATERHOUSE *Fire Lond.* 107 Whose Credit.. lewred Strangers out of their Countrys to reside in it, and kept them here, and naturalized them to it. **1713** STEELE *Guardian* No. 5 ¶1 My obligations of it are such as might well naturalize me into the interests of it. **1813** CROKER in *Examiner* 22 Feb. 118/2 We naturalized foreign seamen into our service.

2. To introduce or adopt (a word, practice, thing, etc.) into a country or into common use; to put on a level with what is native.

1593 PEELE *Hon. Garter* 42 Harington,.. That hath so purely naturalized Strange words, and made them all free denizens. **1612** SELDEN *Illustr. Drayton's Poly-olb.* i. 40, I have like liberty to naturalize that word [transanimation], as Lipsius had to make it a Roman. *a* **1674** CLARENDON *Hist. Reb.* XI. §161 This Proposition.. seemed to naturalize Rebellion, and to make it current in the Kingdom. **1702** S. PARKER tr. *Cicero's De Finibus* I. 1 When I first attempted to naturalize the Notions and Arguments, which the Grecian Philosophers have. **1756** NUGENT *Montesquieu's Spir. Laws* XXII. xxi, These continual changes.. naturalized usury at Rome. **1801** *Med. Jrnl.* V. 556 To carry back the vaccine virus into his department, with a view to propagate and naturalize it. **1866** ROGERS *Agric. & Prices* I. xxii. 571 The yard was naturalized as an English measure.

fig. **1633** G. HERBERT *Temple, Ch. Porch* lxi, Keep all thy native good, and naturalize All forrain of that name.

3. To introduce (animals or plants) to places where they are not indigenous, but in which they may flourish under the same conditions as those which are native. (Chiefly const. *in*.)

c **1708** (*title*) Canary Birds Naturalized in Utopia. **1711** ADDISON *Spect.* No. 69 ¶5 Our Melons, our Peaches.. are Strangers among us,.. naturalized in our English Gardens. **1763** *Nat. Hist.* in *Ann. Reg.* 68/2 A great variety of African plants have, as it were, been naturalised in the American settlements. **1842** BISCHOFF *Woollen Manuf.* II. 342 An essay on the means and advantages of naturalizing the alpaca in this country. **1845** DARWIN *Voy. Nat.* vi. (1852) 120 No doubt many plants besides the cardoon and fennel are naturalized.

4. *refl.* To become fully settled or established in a place or in new surroundings.

1646 J. HALL *Horæ Vac.* 96 Customs insensibly Naturalize themselves. **1824** SOUTHEY *Sir T. More* (1831) I. 53 An endemic malady.. has naturalized itself among your American brethren. **1827** STEUART *Planter's G.* (1828) 296 From the singular steadfastness of the stem, they soon naturalize themselves to the spot. **1853** J. H. NEWMAN *Hist. Sk.* (1873) II. I. ii. 74 They were brought into it by the Roman Government.., but they never naturalized themselves there.

5. *intr.* To become naturalized; to settle down in a natural manner.

1660 F. BROOKE tr. *Le Blanc's Trav.* 398 Divers of ours being taken, have naturalized amongst them. **1821** JEFFREY *Let. to C. Wilkes* 15 Apr., We do not allow ourselves.. to naturalise in London. **1877** M. M. GRANT *Sun-Maid* viii, How did you get them all to naturalise here?

II. †**6.** *trans.* **a.** To familiarize or accustom (one) *in* or *to* a thing. *Obs. rare.*

1601 SHAKS. *All's Well* I. i. 223, I will returne perfect Courtier, in the which my instruction shall serue to naturalize thee. **1651** HARTLIB *Clavis Apocal.* Ded., An emploiment whereunto.. God hath naturalized my affections.

†**b.** To convert *to* or *into* (something) by custom; to make (a thing) natural or familiar (*to* a person). *Obs. rare.*

1606 WARNER *Alb. Eng.* XVI. ci. 401 Prescription doth naturalize in Court Some Errors to a habit. *a* **1667** SOUTH *Serm.* (1697) I. 30 Custom has naturalized his Labour to him. **1742** YOUNG *Nt. Th.* IX. 41 Conscience, deadened by repeated strokes, Has into manners naturaliz'd our crimes.

7. a. To bring into conformity with nature; to free from conventionality.

1603 FLORIO *Montaigne* III. v. (1632) 491 Were I of the trade I would naturalize Arte, as much as they Artize nature. **1789** SMYTH tr. *Aldrich's Archit.* (1818) 12 Masaccio, the first painter who naturalized the stiff manner of Giotto. **1867** BARRY *Life Sir C. Barry* iv. 127 A style thoroughly naturalized.

b. To reduce to a purely natural basis; to free from the supernatural or miraculous.

1647 M. HUDSON *Div. Right Govt.* II. x. 158 The inward satisfaction of conscience.. is that alone which doth naturalize these supernaturall duties. **1652** *Persuasive* 5 It shall not be the project of this Discourse, either to naturalize, or make invalid the Lines of Princes. **1823** BENTHAM *Not Paul* 305 Willing to contradict the falsity, and thus naturalize the miracle. **1858** SEARS *Athan.* 7 The Divine Being himself is naturalized and brought down to the plane of these conceptions. *a* **1882** T. H. GREEN *Proleg. Ethics* Introd. (1883) 9 To stand in the way of the scientific impulse to naturalise the moral man.

†**8.** *intr.* To adopt methods in conformity with, or indicated by, nature. *Obs. rare*$^{-1}$.

1628 WITHER *Brit. Rememb.* II. 271 Some did a little further nat'rallize, And these unto the Ayre would sacrifize .. pure Frankincense or Myrrhe... They hoped these might purge ill ayres.

9. To pursue the studies of a naturalist.

1787 MME. D'ARBLAY *Diary* 27 Feb., The mountains of Wales, where both had been naturalizing thirteen years ago. **1840** E. FORBES in Wilson & Geikie *Life* ix. (1861) 269 Going to naturalize in the Mediterranean for a couple of years. **1861** WILSON & GEIKIE *Ibid.* 250 Forbes returned to the Isle of Man, where he remained two months, naturalizing, as was his wont.

naturalized ('nætjʊərəlaɪzd), *ppl. a.* [-ED[1].]

1. Of persons: Admitted to the rights or privileges of a native citizen or subject. In looser sense, practically made into a native by residence. **a.** In predicative use. †Also const. *to*.

1559 in Knox *Hist. Ref.* Wks. 1846 I. 440 Frenche men could nott be justlie called strangearis, seeing that thei war naturalized. **1623** tr. *Favine's Theat. Hon.* III. vii. 392 Except they be naturalized, and inhabitants of our owne kingdome. *c* **1677** in Marvell *Growth Popery* 62 The other half, and the whole of the Lading, belonging to Simon Francia, who is naturalized. **1719** DE FOE *Crusoe* I. (Globe) 182, I was.. naturaliz'd to the Place, and to the Manner of Living. **1775** in F. Chase *Hist. Dartmouth Coll.* (1891) I. 332 Mr. Dean.. was early naturalized among the Indians, well understands their customs. **1818** CRUISE *Digest* (ed. 2) III. 339 They must be.. natural-born subjects, or naturalized, or made denizens. **1867** SMILES *Huguenots Eng.* xviii. (1880) 319 Many.. Flemings had no sooner settled.. and become naturalised, than they.. assumed English [names].

transf. and *fig.* **1651** HOBBES *Leviath.* III. xli. 263 The Godly.. as naturalized in that heavenly Kingdome. **1788** SIR J. REYNOLDS *Disc.* xiv. Wks. 1797 I. 305 A mind thrown back two thousand years, and as it were naturalized in antiquity. **1875** BEDFORD *Sailor's Pocket Bk.* v. (ed. 2) 189 It is.. advisable.. that they [chronometers] should be received on board at an earlier period, so that they may become naturalized in their new position.

b. Attributively. (Sometimes qualifying the original, and sometimes the acquired, designation.)

1698 FRYER *Acc. E. India & P.* 69 The Country People and naturalized Portugals live to a good Old Age. **1753** *Scots Mag.* June 270/2 Naturalized Jews claiming the privileges of Englishmen. **1775** WARTON *Hist. Eng. Poetry* I. 112 Spain having learned the art.. from their naturalised guests the Arabians. **1822** J. FLINT *Lett. Amer.* 171 He is a naturalized citizen of the United States, but a native of England. *a* **1859** MACAULAY *Hist. Eng.* xxiv. V. 141 The names of Sir Joseph Williamson.. , a born Englishman, and of Portland, a naturalised Englishman. **1873** SMILES *Huguenots France* II. i. (1881) 313 The disposition of the naturalised Huguenots to adopt names of an English sound.

transf. **1817** KEATS *Lett.* Wks. (1889) III. 74 We sometimes skim into a bed of rushes, and there become naturalized river-folks.

c. Closely attached *to* one. *rare*$^{-1}$.

1809 MALKIN *Gil Blas* XI. ix. ¶6, I am too much naturalized to you on the side of obligation, not to take a permanent interest in all your pleasures and disappointments.

2. Of things, languages, words, practices, etc. (See NATURALIZE *v.* 2.)

1625 in K. Long tr. *Barclay's Argenis* p. iv, Thy Argenis .. by thy paine Is naturalized, and doth in English reigne. **1671** CLARENDON *Dial.* Tracts (1727) 338 Since the Latin hath ceased to be a language,.. the French is almost naturalized through Europe. **1703** T. N. *City & C. Purchaser* 224 The word amongst Artificers is almost naturaliz'd. **1855** MILMAN *Lat. Chr.* XIV. vi. (1864) IX. 213 The native language, or rather the naturalised Latin reasserted its independence. **1878** GLADSTONE *Prim. Homer* 52 Homer never directly assigns to a foreign origin anything that has become naturalised in Greece.

†**b.** Firmly rooted or fixed. *Obs. rare.*

1665 NEEDHAM *Med. Medicinæ* 296 Most mysterious Maladies are naturalised within our Vitals. **1698** NORRIS *Pract. Disc.* (1707) IV. 148 'Tis late, if ever, that we discover out so confirm'd and so Naturalized Mistake.

3. Of animals and plants. (See the vb. 3.)

1796 WITHERING *Brit. Plants* (ed. 3) II. 336 See E. bot. 63, where it is first adopted as a naturalized plant. **1811** *1st Rep. Merino Soc.* 52 This kind cannot be perfectly produced but by naturalized sheep of the pure race. **1859** DARWIN *Orig. Spec.* iv. (1873) 89 These naturalised plants are of a highly diversified nature. **1875** WALLACE in *Encycl. Brit.* I. 84/1 A naturalised animal or plant.. must be able to withstand all the vicissitudes of the seasons in its new home.

4. Affected by naturalism; reduced to the level of natural things; made natural.

1858 SEARS *Athan.* 6 Naturalized faith preserves the scattered dust to be combined anew. *Ibid.* III. vi. 305 Natural men in all ages.. attain only to a belief in a naturalized spirit-world. **1880** in Grove *Dict. Mus.* II. 448/1 A naturalised note is always a white key on the pianoforte or organ, unless it be combined with a sharp or flat.

naturalizer ('nætjʊərəlaɪzə(r)). [f. as prec. + -ER[1].] One who naturalizes.

1826 *Blackw. Mag.* XX. 846 The two-fold character borne by the naturalizer of German novels. **1885** *Athenæum* 17 Oct. 510/1 Upon the naturalizers of this and other noxious species.. we cannot waste much pity.

naturalizing ('nætjʊərəlaɪzɪŋ), *vbl. sb.* [f. as prec. + -ING[1].] The action of the vb. NATURALIZE.

a. In sense 1 of the vb. Also *attrib.*

1636 FEATLY *Clavis Myst.* iv. 45 The naturalizing (if I may so speak) of the Gentiles into the spirituall Common-wealth. **1690** *Lond. Gaz.* No. 2554/4 An Act for the Naturalizing of David le Grand, and others. **1753** *Scots Mag.* Aug. 379/1, I am against this naturalizing bill. **1770** LANGHORNE *Plutarch* (1879) I. 106/1 The wisdom of the law concerning the naturalizing of foreigners.

b. In sense 9 of the vb. Also *attrib.*

1840 E. FORBES in Wilson & Geikie *Life* ix. (1861) 269 It would be the acme of naturalizing happiness. **1860** TRISTRAM *Gt. Sahara* xiii. 231 Naturalizing was a task of some little difficulty, the place being in so unsettled a condition.

So **'naturalizing** *ppl. a.*

1854 E. FORBES in Wilson & Geikie *Life* xv. (1861) 555 We shall turn out a fine set of naturalizing youths by and by. **1865** MOZLEY *Mirac.* (ed. 2) Pref. 11 Here, then, are three naturalizing rationales of miracles.

naturally ('nætjʊərəlɪ), *adv.* Also 6 **-allye**, 6–7 **-allie**. [f. NATURAL *a.* + -LY[2]. The earlier ME. form was NATURELLY.]

I. 1. By natural or inherent instinct, impulse, feeling or tendency.

c **1430** LYDG. *Min. Poems* (Percy Soc.) 79 The lark also ful naturally, Cristes ascencioune.. Commendyd. *c* **1460** FORTESCUE *Abs. & Lim. Mon.* ix. (1885) 128 Manis corage is so noble, þat naturally he aspirith to high thinges. **1538** STARKEY *England* II. i. 159 Euery man naturally ys gyuen to folow plesure, quietnes, and ease. **1560** DAUS tr. *Sleidane's Comm.* 5 b, He whiche is a Germain him selfe wil naturally for the countrie sake.. be helpfull to an other Germaine. **1638** JUNIUS *Paint. Ancients* 212 All of us naturally are too much in love with our owne workes. **1651** HOBBES *Leviath.* II. xvii. 85 Men (who naturally love Liberty, and Dominion over others). **1711** BUDGELL *Spect.* No. 77 ¶1, I have naturally an Aversion to much Speaking. **1766** GOLDSM. *Vic. W.* xix, I naturally hate the face of a tyrant. **1797–1803** FOSTER in *Life & Corr.* (1846) I. xliii. 246 The sympathy which we naturally feel for our kind. **1876** L. STEPHEN *Eng. Th. 18th C.* II. XII. viii. 448 An antiquarian is naturally a conservative.

b. Immediately qualifying an adj. or pple. denoting personal character. (Passing into next.)

1611 SHAKS. *Wint. T.* IV. iv. 732 Though I am not naturally honest, I am so sometimes by chance. **1632** LITHGOW *Trav.* III. 90 They are naturally inclined to singing. *a* **1687** PETTY *Pol. Arith.* Pref. (1690) a 3 b, That many are naturally querulous and envious, is an Evil as old as the World. **1777** WATSON *Philip II* (1839) 437 Philip was not naturally either bold or rash. **1877** E. R. CONDER *Bas. Faith* i. 16 If a youth learn to sing and play easily and with pleasure,.. we say he is naturally musical.

2. In respect of natural constitution, character, or condition.

1526 TINDALE *2 Pet.* ii. 12 As brute beastes naturally made to be taken and destroyed. **1560** DAUS tr. *Sleidane's Comm.* 407 The chiefest castell.. is situated.. upon an hyghe hyll, naturally strong. **1615** W. LAWSON *Country Housew. Gard.* (1626) 5 High grounds are not naturally fat. **1646** SIR T. BROWNE *Pseud. Ep.* IV. x. 201 That Jews stinck naturally,.. is a received opinion. **1683** RAY *Corr.* (1848) 131 Whether the Chondrilla.. have naturally a full or double flower..? **1711** STEELE *Spect.* No. 155 ¶4 A Woman is naturally more helpless than the other Sex. **1766** GOLDSM. *Vic. W.* xix, We have all naturally an equal right to the throne. **1815** ELPHINSTONE *Acc. Caubul* (1842) I. 163 It is naturally fertile, and well watered. **1847** C. BRONTË *J. Eyre* vii, Her face, naturally pale as marble.

3. By natural endowment; by means of, or in virtue of, inherent knowledge or capacity; without special teaching or training. ***to come naturally to*** (one): see NATURAL *a.* 9 c.

1525 LD. BERNERS *Froiss.* II. 312/2 The grayhounde hath this knowledge naturallye, therfore take hym to you. **1551** T. WILSON *Logike* (1580) 2 Euery man can geue a reason naturallie, and without Arte. **1660** F. BROOKE tr. *Le Blanc's Trav.* 100 Some have no religion, yet they hold naturally the immortality of the soul. **1691** HARTCLIFFE *Virtues* 357 For Men have naturally the Notions of good and evil within them. **1710** *Lond. Gaz.* No. 4764/4 [A horse] sets Head and Tail naturally well. **1878** *Scribner's Mag.* XV. 112/2 Statesmanship came so naturally to him. **1889** MRS. RIDDELL *P'cess Sunshine* I. v. 87 It came naturally to him to bear and forbear.

4. Spontaneously; by natural growth, etc.; without the aid of art or cultivation.

1563 HYLL *Art Garden.* (1593) 6 That ground.. which naturally bringeth forth of his own accord, both elms and wilde young springs. **1567** MAPLET *Gr. Forest* 98 A Collar or Chaine naturally wrought like to Sinople or Uermelon. **1617** MORYSON *Itin.* II. 45 The crown of his head was in his latter dayes somthing bald, as the forepart naturally curled. *a* **1661** FULLER *Worthies* (1840) III. 87, I have placed woad.. in this county, because, as I am informed, it groweth naturally therein. **1687** A. LOVELL tr. *Thevenot's Trav.* I. 201 There is naturally upon a Marble Stone, a figure in red Colour of a Virgin on her Knees. **1721** BRADLEY *Philos. Acc. Wks. Nat.* 92 Where Elephants are naturally placed, they are of great Use after they are tamed. **1797** *Encycl. Brit.* (ed. 3) XVIII. 581/1 Where it grows naturally is not known, but it is cultivated in Germany. **1847** C. BRONTË *J. Eyre* vii, Julia's hair curls naturally.

b. Without affectation, with ease.

1840 H. ROGERS *Ess.* (1874) II. v. 259 Some men talk as if to speak naturally were to speak like a natural. **1863** KINGLAKE *Crimea* (1877) II. vi. 55 The Czar called his Empress so naturally by her dear homely title of wife.

II. 5. In accordance with, by the operation of, natural laws or causes.

1456 SIR G. HAYE *Law Arms* (S.T.S.) 78 Sen naturaly thir unresonable bestis has sik contrarietee amang thame. **1509** HAWES *Past. Pleas.* XXXV. (Percy Soc.) 112 Nature made the bodyes above,.. That aboute the worlde naturallye do move. **1546** LANGLEY tr. *Pol. Verg. de Invent.* II. i. 35 We perceive in all kindes of liuing creatures naturally a certaine familiaritie of male and female. **1615** W. LAWSON *Country Housew. Gard.* (1626) A 3 As when good ground naturally brings forth thistles. **1707** FLOYER *Physic. Pulse-Watch* 385 The salt Limpha mixes naturally with the Blood. **1830** R. KNOX *Béclard's Anat.* 301 The muscular actions which take place naturally in the body may be divided into two classes. **1869** TOZER *Highl. Turkey* II. 305 The changes which are naturally wrought by time.

b. In the natural manner; through age or disease as opposed to violence, etc.

1552 LYNDESAY *Monarche* 5136 Thocht sum de Naturally, throuch aige, Fer mo deis raiffand in one raige. **1576** FLEMING *Panopl. Epist.* 199 *marg.*, Tyrants.. verie sildome or neuer are so blessed as to dye naturally. **1660** F. BROOKE tr. *Le Blanc's Trav.* 348 Widows, if their husbands died naturally, marry not again. **1797** MRS. RADCLIFFE *Italian* iii, She did not seem to die naturally.

c. As a natural result or consequence; as might be expected from the circumstances.

1641 J. JACKSON *True Evang. T.* II. 101 To gather that observation, or conclusion, which most naturally buddeth out of it. **1712** ADDISON *Spect.* No. 465 ¶2 Faith and Morality naturally produce each other. **1760–2** GOLDSM. *Cit. W.* xxvii, Poverty naturally begets dependence. **1796** H. HUNTER tr. *St.-Pierre's Stud. Nat.* (1799) II. 5 Those eyes whose balls are blue are naturally the softest. **1849** MACAULAY *Hist. Eng.* ii. I. 182 His situation naturally developes in him.. a peculiar class of abilities. **1892** GARDINER *Stud. Hist. Eng.* 14 He naturally chose the latter alternative.

†**d.** Simply, easily. *Obs. rare*$^{-1}$.

1655 MRQ. WORCESTER *Cent. Invent.* c, A Childs force bringeth up.. an incredible quantity of water.. so naturally, that the work will not be heard even in the next Room.

†**6.** In the natural course of things. *Obs.*

1473 *Rolls of Parlt.* VI. 100/1 Yf the seid Countes were nowe naturally dede. **1495** *Act 11 Hen. VII*, c. 30 §5 If he so longe hadde naturally lyved. **1589** *Act 31 Eliz.* c. 6 §1 As yf the saide person.. then were naturallie deade. **1607** *Statutes in Hist. Wakefield Gram. Sch.* (1892) 60 As tho he were naturallie deade.

†**b.** Normally, regularly. *Obs. rare*$^{-1}$.

1526 *Galway Arch.* in *10th Rep. Hist. MSS. Comm.* App. V. 401 No carpenter nor masson shall not have for his hyre.. but ii.*d.* naturallie every daye, with meate and drincke.

†**7. a.** With *born*. (Cf. NATURAL-BORN *a.*) *Obs.*

1523 *Act 14 & 15 Hen. VIII*, c. 4 §1 Persons being the kinges subiectes naturally borne within this his realme. **1588** PARKE tr. *Mendoza's Hist. China* 383 A man naturally borne in this kingdome.

†**b.** In respect of birthplace or nationality. *Obs.*

a **1533** LD. BERNERS *Gold. Bk. M. Aurel.* I. i. A iv b, This excellent baron was naturally of Rome borne in the mounte Celie. **1615** G. SANDYS *Trav.* 76 About whom there runne fortie Peichi (so called in that they are naturally Persians).

†**8.** By natural generation. *Obs.*

1568 GRAFTON *Chron.* II. 695 He was lineally descended, and naturally procreated of the noble stocke and familie of Lancaster. **1620** T. GRANGER *Div. Logike* 31 So man begetteth man naturallie. **1786** J. ERSKINE *Hist. Redemption* (1812) 90 He was both Legally and Naturally descended from David.

†**9.** Physically, materially. *Obs.*

1546 COVERDALE *Calvin's Sacr.* Pref., Wks. (Parker Soc.) I. 427 The great blindness of them, that knowing.. the immensurable nature of God, would have him really and naturally contained in so small a thing. **1579** FULKE *Heskins' Parl.* 220 The wine is y[t] which was shed out of his side, y[t] is sacramentally, but not naturally. **1597** HOOKER *Eccl. Pol.* v. lv. §5 In that hee is naturally man hee him-selfe is created of God.

10. In a realistic or life-like manner.

a **1568** ASCHAM *Scholem.* II. (Arb.) 155 He doth not expresse the matter liuely and naturally with common speach.., but it is caried and driuen forth artificiallie. **1598** CHAPMAN *Iliad* II. 45 His form did passing naturally Resemble Nestor. **1666** DRYDEN *Pref. Ann. Mirab.* Wks. (Globe) 40 He describes his Dido well and naturally, in the violence of her passions. **1875** JOWETT *Plato* (ed. 2) IV. 122 The character of Antiphon.. is very naturally described.

naturalness (ˈnætjʊərəlnɪs). [-NESS.]

†**1.** Natural instinct, affection, or sympathy. *Obs.*

1553 GRIMALDE *Cicero's Offices* III. (1558) 131 Thys man forgot both godlinesse and naturalnesse that he might obteine the thynge that semed profitable. **1612** DRAYTON *Poly-olb.* ix. 349 Our naturalness therein he greatly did approve. *a* **1665** GOODWIN *Filled w. the Spirit* (1867) 466 There is a kind of naturalness.. between the ear of God and the prayers.. of such a righteous man.

2. The condition or fact of being natural or in accordance with nature.

1660 INGELO *Bentiv. & Ur.* II. (1682) 212 This is no argument against the Immortality of the Soul, or the Naturalness of those Desires which we have of it. **1699** BENTLEY *Phalaris* 140 The very facility and naturalness of every correction will be next to a Demonstration. **1816** COLERIDGE *Lay Serm.* (Bohn) 372 The naturalness of doing as others do. **1873** SPENCER *Stud. Sociol.* vi. (1877) 133 Those connexions.. are not necessary, and often have no particular naturalness.

b. Close resemblance *of* a picture, etc. to the object represented.

1669 A. BROWNE *Ars Pict.* 18 The like Disgrace happened to Zeuxes by the Naturaleness of his Grapes. **1695** DRYDEN *Parall. Poetry & Paint.* Ess. (ed. Ker) II. 123 In the naturalness (if I may so call it) of the eyebrows.

c. The quality of possessing the distinctive features of external nature.

1841 L. HUNT *Seer* II. (1864) 61 Not that he omitted to expatiate on the extreme naturalness of the scene. *a* **1876** HT. MARTINEAU *Autobiog.* (1877) I. 184 Except the vine on its back gable there is not an element of naturalness or poetry about it.

3. The quality of being natural in conduct or bearing; unaffectedness.

1656 W. MONTAGUE *Accompl. Woman* 111 Naturalnesse has so gentle charms, as none resists, because they arise from innocence. **1824** MISS MITFORD *Village* Ser. I. (1863) 85 Her own naturalness of character and simplicity of taste. **1836** T. HOOK *G. Gurney* III. 90 There seemed such a perfect naturalness—if I may use the word—about him. **1872** M. PATTISON *Ess.* (1889) II. 372 He had room in his affections for the naturalness of the Elizabethan writers, and for the artificial epigram of the French school.

b. With reference to thought, language, etc.

1702 ADDISON *Dial. Medals* (1726) 84 The naturalness of the thought, and the beauty of the expression. **1815** W. TAYLOR in *Monthly Rev.* LXXVI. 415 An appropriate talk, a living naturalness, (if we may make such a word,) that give them all a hold on the memory. **1873** HAMERTON *Intell. Life* III. ix. 116 The perfect ease and naturalness of his diction.

†**4.** Genuineness, legitimacy. *Obs. rare*$^{-1}$.

1656 TRAPP *Comm. 2 Cor.* viii. 8 The germanity, the naturalness, legitimateness opposed to bastardliness.

5. One's natural condition or character.

1850 LYNCH *Theoph. Trinal* v. 74 The more hearty and varied our naturalness, the completer do we become. **1893** J. ORR *Chr. View God* v. 205 Sin is the first step of man out of his naturalness.

†ˈ**naturalty.** *Sc. Obs. rare.* [f. NATURAL *a.* + -TY.] = NATURALITY 4.

a **1665** GUTHRIE in *Wodrow Soc. Sel. Biog.* (1847) II. 73 Tho' there be that.. naturalty in us to pity both.

‖**natura naturans** (næˈtjʊərə ˈnætjuːrænz). *Philos.* [L. *nātūra* birth, constitution, etc., f. *nāt-*, pple. stem of *nascī* to be born + med.L. *nāturans* pres. pple.] Nature creating; the essential creative power or act. Also **natura naturata** (-ˈɑːtə), nature created; the natural phenomena and forces in which creation is manifested. Also *transf.* Cf. NATURE *v.*[1] 2.

1605 [see NATURE *v.*[1] 2]. *c* **1818** COLERIDGE *On Poesy & Art* in *Biog. Lit.* (1907) II. 257 If the artist copies the mere nature, the *natura naturata*, what idle rivalry!.. Believe me, you must master the essence, the *natura naturans*, which presupposes a bond between nature in the higher sense and the soul of man. **1855** BAGEHOT in *National Rev.* I. 57 A school of 'common-sense poets',.. who proceed to describe what they see around them, to describe its *natura naturans*, to delineate its *natura naturata*. **1903** R. A. DUFF *Spinoza's Pol. & Ethical Philos.* i. 3 It might be shown that Spinoza did, and could, make no claim to terms such as substance,.. idea, *natura naturans* and *natura naturata*.., nor even to the definitions which he gives of them. **1933** R. TUVE *Seasons and Months* iv. 152 Matfre treats first of the nature and power of God ('natura naturans'), Who has created all 'Natura naturata'. **1950** F. COPLESTON *Hist. Philos.* II. IV. xix. 198 Averroes's.. metaphysical scale reaches from pure matter.. to pure Act, God, as the highest limit, between these limits being the objects composed of potency and act, which form *Natura naturata.* (The phrases of the Latin translation, *Natura naturans* and *Natura naturata*, reappear eventually in the system of Spinoza.) **1958** E. F. J. PAYNE tr. *Schopenhauer's World as Will* II. xvii. 175 Such an *absolute system of physics* as described above, which would leave no room for any *metaphysics*, would make *natura naturata* (created nature) into *natura naturans* (creative nature).

†ˈ**naturant,** *a. Obs. rare*$^{-1}$. [ad. med.L. *nātūrant-em*, pres. pple. of *nātūrāre* to create, give existence or specific nature to (used chiefly in the scholastic phrases *natura naturans* and *natura naturata*): see NATURE *v.* 2.] Creative, generating.

1635 HEYWOOD *Hierarchy* II. 78 Before our Mindes Eyes let us place.. What this great Nature Naturant may be.

†ˈ**naturate,** *a. Obs. rare.* [ad. med.L. *nātūrāt-us*, pa. pple. of *nātūrāre*: see prec.] Created, endowed with a specific nature. Hence †ˈ**naturated** *ppl. a.*; †ˈ**naturately** *adv.*, by creation.

1509 HAWES *Past. Pleas.* XXV. (Percy Soc.) 113 Man upon them hath his dysposycyon, By the naturate power of constellacyon. *Ibid.* XLIV. 216 Nature.. whyche naturynge hath tought Naturately right naturate to make. **1519** *Interl. Four Elem.* in Hazl. *Dodsley* I. 11 He.. hath ordained and created Me here His minister, called Nature Naturate. **1605** TIMMER *Quersit.* I. iii. 9 It resteth that some-what be spoken of nature naturated.

nature (ˈneɪtjʊə(r), ˈneɪtʃə(r)), *sb.* Also 4– 5, 6 *Sc.* natur, 5, 6–7 *Sc.* natour, 6 *Sc.* **nateur, natuir.** [a. F. *nature* (12th c.), ad. L. *nātūra* birth, constitution, character, course of things, etc., f. *nāt-*, ppl. stem of *nascī* to be born. The native English word is KIND *sb.*]

I. 1. a. The essential qualities or properties of a thing; the inherent and inseparable combination of properties essentially pertaining to anything and giving it its fundamental character.

a **1300** *Cursor M.* 22147 O thinges sere þair naturs [he shall cause] turnd to be in sere figurs. **1390** GOWER *Conf.* III. 19 If I schal more seie Upon the nature of the vice. **1456** SIR G. HAYE *Law Arms* (S.T.S.) 20 The bitter herbe is sa felloun bitter of his nature. **1560** DAUS tr. *Sleidane's Comm.* 282 b, Aristotel,.. Plinie, and suche other like, haue wrytten of the nature of Plantes, Herbes, Beastes, Metalles and Precious stones. **1604** E. G[RIMSTONE] *D'Acosta's Hist. Indies* II. i. 82 The knowledge.. depends of the well understanding the nature of the Equinoctiall. *a* **1674** CLARENDON *Surv. Leviath.* (1676) 27 Describing the nature of foul weather. **1711** ADDISON *Spect.* No. 62 ¶5 The Passion of Love in its Nature has been thought to resemble Fire. **1780** BENTHAM *Princ. Legisl.* xvii. §15 This influence will depend upon the nature of the motive. **1832** HT. MARTINEAU *Hill & Valley* ix. 136 You have twice had warning of the fleeting nature of riches. **1878** HUXLEY *Physiogr.* 76 The nature of this absorbed matter may be determined by a simple experiment.

†**b.** Degree (of wrong-doing). *Obs. rare*$^{-1}$.

1642 J. M[ARSH] *Argt. conc. Militia* 22 Delinquents in a high nature against Parliament.

c. Texture as indicative of quality.

1865 J. T. F. TURNER *Slate Quarries* 17 Near the surface it [slate] is softer, looser, and of a red tinge.., but deeper the 'nature' improves.

2. a. The inherent and innate disposition or character of a person (or animal). Also, (one's) ***better nature.***

See also GOOD NATURE, ILL NATURE, and SECOND.

a **1300** *Cursor M.* 21888 Ilk creatur Efter þe state of his natur, Better his maker knaus þan man. **1390** GOWER *Conf.* III. 205 A wolf he was.., The whos nature prively He hadde in his condicion. *c* **1420** LYDG. *Assembly of Gods* 1693 They.. callyd hem goddes.. for the streyngthe & myght of her nature. **1500–20** DUNBAR *Poems* xiv. 42 Sic brallaris and bosteris, degenerat fra thair naturis. **1568** GRAFTON *Chron.* II. 615 The Englishe men (whose natures are not to be faynt hearted, euen at the very ieopardie of death). **1615** G. SANDYS *Trav.* 227 Choosing rather to vndergo all hazards,.. then so long a voyage by sea, to my nature so irksome. **1680** OTWAY *Orphan* II. iv, I must.. Wound his soft Nature, though my own Heart akes for it. **1709** STEELE *Tatler* No. 93 ¶4 Men may change their Climate, but they cannot their Nature. **1781** COWPER *Charity* 153 He.. Puts off his generous nature; and.. puts on the brute. **1833** HT. MARTINEAU *Loom & Lugger* II. ii. 34 My brother has it not in his nature to feel jealousy. **1848** LYTTON *Harold* III. XII. ix. 375 His own better nature which, ere polluted by plotting-craft, and hardened by despotic ire, was magnanimous and heroic, moved and won him. **1860** MOZLEY *Univ. Serm.* vii. (1877) 155 Some persons appear to have a nature richer in good than others. **1919** M. K. BRADBY *Psycho-Anal.* III. x. 129 Any repressed desire which belongs to my undeveloped 'better nature'. **1949** D. SMITH *I capture Castle* xiii. 246 By the time Stephen got home, my better nature had asserted itself and I was terribly worried about his feelings. **1965** M. FRAYN *Tin Men* i. 9 Appeal to their better natures.

b. The general inherent character or disposition of mankind. Also in phr. ***human nature.***

1526 *Pilgr. Perf.* (W. de W. 1531) 140 b, Though ye fall neuer so ofte by impacyency, through yᵉ fraylte of nature. **1551** ROBINSON tr. *More's Utop.* II. (1895) 190 Hereto..our nature is allured and drawen. **1668** DRYDEN *Dram. Poesy* Ess. (ed. Ker) I. 36 A just and lively image of human nature. **1711** STEELE *Spect.* No. 53 ¶7 It was not in Nature to command ones Eyes from this Object. **1768** STERNE *Sent. Journ., Act of Charity*, Nature is shy, and hates to act before spectators. **1835** BROWNING *Paracelsus* IV. 87 One can ne'er keep down Our foolish nature's weakness. **1872** MORLEY *Voltaire* (1886) 3 Human nature, happily for us, ever presses against this system or that.

c. With adjectives, in reference to the different elements of human character.

a **1676** HALE *Prim. Orig. Man.* IV. v. (1677) 332 So much of that in Man that concerns his Animal Nature. **1870** J. H. NEWMAN *Gram. Assent* II. ix. 339 This consciousness, reflection, and action we call our own rational nature. **1878** R. W. DALE *Lect. Preach.* viii. 252 Men have a physical as well as a spiritual nature.

†**d.** Character, capacity; function. *Obs. rare.*

1601 B. JONSON *Ev. Man in Hum.* V. i. 272 (Q.), Which.. I do thus first of all vncase, & appeare in mine owne proper nature, seruant to this gentleman. **1645** *King's Cabinet Opened* in *Sel. Harl. Misc.* (1793) 355 For the French, it was impossible for them to serve her in that nature.

3. a. With *a* and *pl.* An individual character, disposition, etc., considered as a kind of entity in itself; hence, a thing or person of a particular quality or character.

c **1374** CHAUCER *Boeth.* V. pr. ii. (1868) 152 Ne þer ne was neuer no nature of resoun þat it ne hadde liberte of fre wille. **1390** GOWER *Conf.* III. 88 The god commandeth the natures That thei to him obeien alle. *c* **1420** *Pallad. on Husb.* I. 354 Grauellis dolue in iij naturis varye: In red, & hoor, & blak vnvariable. **1533** ELYOT *Cast. Helthe* (1539) 39 b, The natures hotte & moyst, be leste indamaged. **1587** GOLDING *De Mornay* ii. (1592) 22 Making and creating are referred to natures or substances, and all natures and substances are good. *Ibid.*, Euill is neither a nature nor a substance. **1615** CROOKE *Body of Man* 284 In euery Nature there must be a Patient correspondent and answerable to the agent. **1668** TEMPLE *Let.* Wks. 1720 II. 119 There are some Natures in the World who never can proceed sincerely in Business. **1784** COWPER *Task* v. 481 Roughness in the grain Of British natures. **1817** SHELLEY *Rev. Islam* x. vi, So there Strange natures made a brother-hood of ill. **1879** FARRAR *St. Paul* (1883) 172 The unquestioning truthfulness of a sunny nature.

collect. **1667** MILTON *P. L.* v. 834 Dost thou count..all Angelic Nature joined in one, Equal to him begotten Son.

b. *Artillery.* A class or size of guns or shot.

1813 LD. CATHCART in *Examiner* 31 May 342/2 He had an immense quantity of ordnance, of twelve-pounders, and larger natures. **1828** J. M. SPEARMAN *Brit. Gunner* (ed. 2) 130 One Hundred of each Nature of Case-Shot. **1884** *Mil. Engin.* I. II. 61 Lubricators, secured outside for 40-prs., and choked inside the cartridges for lower natures.

4. In various phrases: **a.** *of* (a certain) ***nature.***

In first quot. perhaps in sense of 'origin'.

c **1440** *Generydes* 2656 'We are broderen', quod he, 'of on nature'. *c* **1450** tr. *De Imitatione* II. vii. 47 Thy beloued is of suche nature þat he wol admitte no straunger. **1560** DAUS tr. *Sleidane's Comm.* 204 b, He was a man of verey milde nature. **1588** SHAKS. *L. L. L.* v. ii. 377 Your capacitie Is of that nature, that to your huge stoore, Wise things seeme foolish. **1625** BURGES *Pers. Tithes* 29 Sacriledge, and many other sinnes of a high nature. **1662** STILLINGFL. *Orig. Sacræ* III. iv. §10 Who may in a matter of this nature..be the more credited. **1711** ADDISON *Spect.* No. 1 ¶1 With other Particulars of the like Nature. **1765** BLACKSTONE *Comm.* I. i. 21 A plan of this nature. **1845** M. PATTISON *Ess.* (1889) I. 23 To bring a charge..of such a nature as should fall within this penalty. **1875** JOWETT *Plato* (ed. 2) V. 189 The most barren logical abstraction is of a higher nature than number and figure.

b. *of* or ***in the nature of.***

1597 SHAKS. *2 Hen. IV*, IV. ii. 89 A Peace is of the nature of a Conquest. **1669** R. MONTAGU in *Buccleuch MSS.* (Hist. MSS. Comm.) I. 457 A rich gold campane, which is in the nature of a fringe. **1736** BUTLER *Anal.* Introd., Wks. 1874 I. 1 That the slightest possible presumption is of the nature of a probability, appears from hence. **1749** FIELDING *Tom Jones* Ded., Your desires are to me in the nature of commands. **1817** W. SELWYN *Law Nisi Prius* (ed. 4) II. 1085 A *Quo warranto* being in the nature of a writ of right. **1880** GEIKIE *Phys. Geog.* iv. 217 The earthquake is really of the nature of a wave.

†**c.** Similarly ***in nature of.*** *Obs.*

1614 SELDEN *Titles Hon.* II. iv. 225 The Heriot was, what the Eorle or Thane paid his Lord..in nature of a Relief. **1665** MANLEY *Grotius' Low C. Wars* 497 A Maid, living.. with her Sisters, to whom she was in nature of a Servant.

d. ***in the nature of things, of the case.***

1584 R. SCOT *Discov. Witchcr.* III. xix. (1886) 56 It were follie to staie overlong in the confutation of that, which is not in the nature of things. **1615** CROOKE *Body of Man* 523 There are in the nature of things certaine Sympathies and Antipathies. **1790** PALEY *Horæ Paul.* Rom. ii. 13 It is, in the nature of the case, probable that [etc.]. **1854** MACAULAY *Biog.* (1860) 138 It was not in the nature of things that popularity such as he..enjoyed should be permanent.

e. ***the nature of the beast.***

1678 J. RAY *Coll. Eng. Proverbs* (ed. 2) 77 It's the nature o' th' beast. *c* **1683** J. VERNEY *Let.* in M. M. Verney *Mem.* (1899) IV. vii. 254 I'me very Sorry John my Coachman Should be soe great a Clowne to you..but t'is the nature of the Beast. **1748** RICHARDSON *Clarissa* III. 218, I might as well have preserv'd the first; for I see it is the *nature of the beast.* **1893** KIPLING *Many Inventions* 254 'Twas the nature av the baste to put the comether on the best av thim. **1969** V. GIELGUD *Necessary End* v. 48 Barry Compayne never made bones about..the number of girls that he had 'laid'... Anthea had chosen deliberately to put down such exploits to 'the nature of the beast'.

f. ***nature and nurture, nature-nurture,*** heredity and environment as influences on, or the determinants of, personality (see quot. 1874). Also *attrib.*

[**1610** SHAKS. *Tempest* IV. i. 188 A borne-Deuill, on whose nature Nurture can neuer sticke.] **1874** R. GALTON *Eng. Men of Sci.: their Nature & Nurture* i. 12 The phrase 'nature and nurture' is a convenient jingle of words, for it separates under two distinct heads the innumerable elements of which personality is composed. Nature is all that a man brings with himself into the world; nurture is every influence from without that affects him after his birth. **1914** F. W. MOTT (*title*) Nature and nurture in mental development. *Ibid.* 1 The problem of nature and nurture in mental development is one that has recently acquired importance. **1933** L. HOGBEN (*title*) Nature and nurture. **1946** *Brit. Jrnl. Psychol.* May 159 The particular nature-nurture ratio value, or the physiological or anatomical associations which it possesses. **1952** C. P. BLACKER *Eugenics* 267 Unconscious prejudices can throw the nature-nurture controversy into different perspectives. **1965** R. B. CATTELL *Sci. Analysis of Personality* ii. 50 The nature-nurture ratios are not fixed and immutable laws, but statements which may change with culture patterns and the ranges of racial, genetic difference within the given population. **1972** *Times* 2 Sept. 14/3 The argument between the 'nature' and 'nurture' schools of thought. **1974** *Science* 5 July 20/2 The disagreement about the causation of autism... First, there is the usual nature-nurture controversy.

5. ***by*** (earlier †*of*, †*on*) ***nature,*** in virtue of the very character or essence of the thing or person.

In some cases with suggestion of senses 9 and 11.

c **1430** LYDG. *Min. Poems* (Percy Soc.) 14 For wyne of nature makithe hertes lyghte. **1500–20** DUNBAR *Poems* xlix. 36 Eftir respyt To wirk dispyt Moir appetyt He hes of natour. **1526** TINDALE *Gal.* ii. 15 We which are Jewes by nature and not synners off the gentyls. **1585** T. WASHINGTON tr. *Nicholay's Voy.* IV. xxix. 152 The gulfe Saxonique of nature beset and enuironed with high mountaines. **1615** W. LAWSON *Country Housew. Gard.* (1626) 34 The Oke by nature broad. **1667** MILTON *P. L.* v. 527 He..ordaind thy will By nature free, not over-rul'd by Fate. **1697** DRYDEN *Virg. Georg.* IV. 417 In a Place, by Nature close, they build A narrow Flooring. **1766** GOLDSM. *Vic. W.* i, I was, by nature, an admirer of happy human faces. **1823** BYRON *Juan* XV. lii, Adeline was liberal by nature. **1853** J. H. NEWMAN *Hist. Sk.* (1873) II. I. iii. 116 Asia Minor..was by nature one of the most beautiful..of countries.

II. 6. a. The vital or physical powers *of* man; (a person's) physical strength or constitution (*obs.*); the strength or substance *of* a thing.

c **1250** *Kent. Serm.* in *O.E. Misc.* 35 Þe nature of Man is of greater strengþe and of greater hete ine þo age. **1456** SIR G. HAYE *Law Arms* (S.T.S.) 282 Medicinaris and philosophouris gevis the gold..in medicyne to folk that are debilitez in thair nature. **1508** DUNBAR *Tua Mariit Wemen* 174 He has bene lychour so lang quhill lost is his natur. **1592** WEST *1st Pt. Symbol.* §102 b, Any such corrasiue, sharpe or eager medicine..as the said H. shal think his nature is vnable to suffer. **1886** *Chesh. Gloss.* s.v., Anything which is beginning to deteriorate is said to have lost its nature. **1890** *Nature* 11 Dec. 129 The fungus..as it goes destroys the 'nature' of the wood.

b. With *some, no,* etc. Common in *dial.* use.

1597 BACON *Ess.* Ep. Ded., There mought be as great a vanitie in..withdrawing mens conceites (except they bee of some nature) from the world. **1879** MISS JACKSON *Shropsh. Word-bk.* s.v., [The meat] was 'so overdone, there seemed to be no nature left in it'. **1886** *Chesh. Gloss.* s.v., Land which has become impoverished has no nature in it. **1889** *Reports Provinc.* (E.D.D.), 'Her'd got no natur in her', speaking of a girl who was very weak.

7. †**a.** Semen. *Obs.* **b.** The menses. *Obs.* or *rare.*

c **1386** CHAUCER *Pars. T.* ¶503 Vnkyndely synne, by which man or womman shedeth her nature. **1527** ANDREW *Brunswyke's Distyll. Waters* I vj, Yf a person weneth that his nature wyl fall betwene the flesshe and the skynne. **1575** TURBERV. *Venerie* lxvi. 186 Cut out hir gutte whiche holdeth hir spreame or nature. **1607** TOPSELL *Four-f. Beasts* (1658) 236 The true sign of conception is, when their nature (that is) the fluent humour out of their secrets ceaseth for a moneth, or two, or three. **1922** JOYCE *Ulysses* 373 Frightened she was when her nature came on her first.

†**8.** The female pudendum, esp. that of a mare.

1481 CAXTON *Myrr.* III. xiii. 162 No persone myght haue none, but yf he wente and fette it at the nature of a woman. **1569** R. ANDROSE tr. *Alexis' Secr.* IV. III. 46 Take the nature of a female Hare made into pouder. **1607** TOPSELL *Four-f. Beasts* (1658) 235 Therewithal touch the nature of the mare in her purgation. **1622** T. SCOTT *News fr. Parnassus* 33 If that great Lady had not made a vow of perpetuall chastity and her nature..had not been stytched up. **1750** ELLIS *Mod. Husb.* III. 175 (E.D.S.).

III. 9. a. The inherent dominating power or impulse (in men or animals) by which action or character is determined, directed, or controlled. (Sometimes personified.)

c **1386** CHAUCER *Prol.* 11 And smale fowles maken melodye,..(So priketh hem nature in hir corages). *a* **1450** *Knt. de la Tour* (1868) 4 Alle faders and moders after good nature aught to teche her children to leue alle wrong and euelle waies. **1484** CAXTON *Fables of Æsop* I. vii, No man is chaunged by nature, but of an euyll man maye wel yssue and come a wers than hymself. **1500–20** DUNBAR *Poems* xlvi. 52 To luve eik natur gaif thame inclynnyng. **1551** ROBINSON tr. *More's Utop.* II. (1895) 238 As though nature had not set sufficient loue betwene man and man. **1614** LATHAM *Falconry* (1633) 80 Those phisicall appliments, by which, that skilfull Faulconer (Dame Nature) hath taught her to worke her owne welfare. **1667** MILTON *P. L.* VIII. 506 Nature her self..Wrought in her so, that seeing me, she turn'd. **1729** BUTLER *Serm.* Wks. 1874 II. 22 By nature is often meant no more than some principle in man. **1793** COWPER *Beau's Reply* ii, 'Twas Nature, sir, whose strong behest Impelled me to the deed. **1823** BYRON *Juan* XV. lii, But nature's nature, and has more caprices Than I have time, or will, to take to pieces. **1864** LOWELL *Fireside Trav.* 261 The driving-wheels of all powerful nature are in the back of the head.

b. Contrasted with *grace.*

c **1450** tr. *De Imitatione* III. lix. 138 Nature sekiþ to haue curiose þinges & feire þinges,..but grace delitiþ in simple þinges. **1685** BAXTER *Paraphr. N.T.* Matt. v. 46–8 So far as any thing of God is in them, whether it be Nature or Grace. *a* **1696** P. HENRY in *M. Henry's Wks.* (1853) II. 737/2 Nature is contented with little, grace with less. **1779** J. DUCHÉ *Disc.* (1790) II. I. 14 We must first feel the poverty of nature before we can desire the riches of Grace.

c. ***law of nature:*** (see LAW *sb.*[1] 9 c). ***light of nature:*** (see LIGHT *sb.* 6 b).

d. ***against nature,*** contrary to what nature prompts, unnatural, immoral, vicious. ? *Obs.*

1500–20 DUNBAR *Poems* ix. 90 Off syn als aganis the Haly Spreit,..and syn aganis nateur. **1611** BIBLE *Rom.* i. 26 Euen their women did change the naturall vse into that which is against nature. *a* **1614** DONNE *Βιαθανατος* (1644) 39 Al sinne is very truely said to be against nature... S. Augustine sayes, Every vice, as it is vice, is against nature. **1662** J. DAVIES tr. *Olearius' Voy. Ambass.* 81 They are wholly given up to all licentiousness, even to sins against Nature.

e. Natural feeling or affection. Now *dial.*

1605 SHAKS. *Macb.* I. v. 46 Stop vp th' accesse, and passage to Remorse, That no compunctious visitings of Nature Shake my fell purpose. **1703** POPE *Thebais* 332 Have we not seen..The murd'ring son..Thro' violated nature force his way..? *a* **1718** PENN *Maxims* Wks. 1726 I. 827, I shew little Duty or Nature to my Parents. *a* **1825** FORBY *Voc. E. Anglia* s.v., A simple old woman, as a reason for loving one of her daughters more than the others, said 'she had more nature in her'. **1841** C. H. HARTSHORNE *Salopia Antiqua* 514 There's often more nature in people of that sort, than in..their betters.

f. A natural action or proceeding. *rare.*

1817 CHALMERS *Astron. Disc.* v. (1852) 126 It was nature in the shepherd to leave the ninety and nine of his flock.. alone in the wilderness.

10. a. The inherent power or force by which the physical and mental activities of man are sustained. (Sometimes personified.)

c **1400** MAUNDEV. (1839) xxix. 293 The most part of hem dyen with outen Syknesse, whan nature fayleth hem for elde. **1541** R. COPLAND *Guydon's Quest. Chirurg.* M ij b, For [by blood-letting] nature dyspensed ouer all the body is lyghtned. **1602** SHAKS *Ham.* I. iii. 11 For nature cressant does not grow alone, In thewes and Bulke. **1685** BOYLE *Enq. Notion Nat.* 28 As when Physicians say, that Nature is strong, or weak, or spent. **1742** YOUNG *Nt. Th.* I. 1 Tir'd nature's sweet restorer, balmy sleep! **1836** A. COMBE *Physiol. Digest.* (1842) 238 Nature is more willing to do her part than we are to do ours.

b. The vital functions as requiring to be supported by nourishment.

c **1460** FORTESCUE *Abs. & Lim. Mon.* iii. (1885) 115 Thai bith welthe, and haue all thinges nescessarie to the sustenance of nature. *a* **1658** WALLER *Panegyric to Protector* xiii, Our little world..Of her own growth hath all that nature craves. **1667** MILTON *P.L.* v. 452 When with meats & drinks they had suffic'd Not burd'nd Nature. **1743** BULKELEY & CUMMINS *Voy. S. Seas* 169 We have now nothing but a little water to support Nature. **1807** PIKE *Sources Mississ.* (1810) II. 182, I returned hungry..and had only snow to supply the calls of nature. **1819** SHELLEY *Cenci* II. ii. 16 If you..were reduced at once..To that which nature doth indeed require? **1842** BORROW *Bible in Spain* xl, The prison allowance will not support nature.

c. With reference to other physical requirements.

a **1540** BARNES *Wks.* (1573) 345/2 The night beefore..was hee compelled by nature to goe to the preuy. **1607** TOPSELL *Four-f. Beasts* (1658) 123 His servant..diverted a little out of the way to perform the work of nature. **1701** W. WOTTON *Hist. Rome* 328 He withdrew from the Company to ease Nature. **1747** CHESTERF. *Lett.* cxxxiii. (1792) I. 359 That small portion of [time], which the calls of nature obliged him to pass in the necessary-house.

IV. 11. a. The creative and regulative physical power which is conceived of as operating in the material world and as the immediate cause of all its phenomena. ***balance of nature:*** see BALANCE *sb.* 13 d.

13.. *E.E. Allit. P.* A. 748 Quo formed þe þy fayre fygure? ..þy beaute com neuer of nature. *c* **1400** *Destr. Troy* 4010 Polexena.. was..Alse noble for þe nonest as natur cold deuyse. *c* **1470** HENRY *Wallace* IX. 10 Zepherus..comfort has, be wyrking off natour, All fructuous thing in till the erd. **1526** *Pilgr. Perf.* (W. de W. 1531) 234 b, Of all the membres of the body, nature hath made the eye moost mouable. **1551** T. WILSON *Logike* (1580) 5 This Table sheweth the order of euery substance and kind, as thei are appointed by Nature. **1594** T. B. *La Primaud. Fr. Acad.* II. 557 That common saying, that God and Nature the minister of God doe nothing without cause. **1603** R. JOHNSON *Kingd. & Commw.* 30 All the Ilands which nature hath scatred in these seas. **1697** DRYDEN *Virg. Georg.* III. 231 Where Nature shall provide Green Grass, and fat'ning Clover for their Fare. **1738** SWIFT *Pol. Conversat.* 51 Oh! the wonderful Works of Nature; That a black Hen should have a white Egg! **1774** GOLDSM. *Nat. Hist.* (1776) VI. 260 The weapon with which Nature has armed this animal. **1832** AUSTIN *Jurispr.* (1879) I. v. 213 He attributes the uniformity of succession and coexistence to laws set by nature. **1856** OLMSTED *Slave States* 69 To take advantage of nature's engineering.

b. More or less definitely personified as a female being. (Usu. with capital.)

c **1374** CHAUCER *Ancl. & Arc.* 80 Nature had grete ioy her to beholde. **1412–20** LYDG. *Chron. Troy* I. v, Both two in one So ioyned..By the emperesse that called is Nature. *c* **1450** HOLLAND *Howlat* 32 Thir sauoruss seidis War nurist be dame Natur. **1481** CAXTON *Myrr.* I. xiv. 43 Without nature may nothinge growe, and by her haue alle thinges created lyf. **1545** RAYNOLDE *Birth Mankynde* (1564) 27 Wherefore prudent Lady nature full wisely hath prouided..a continuall course and resort of blood. **1634** SIR T. HERBERT *Trav.* 14 Flowres which only Dame Nature trauels with. **1718** WATTS *Hymn* i, Nature with open volume stands, To spread her Maker's praise abroad. **1784** COWPER *Task* III. 600 Some note of Nature's music from his lips. **1838** *Penny Cycl.* X. 252/2 Nature with her burning sun, her stilled and pent-up wind. **1860** TYNDALL *Glac.* I. xxvii. 205 In the application of her own principles, Nature often transcends the human imagination.

c. Contrasted with medical skill or treatment in the cure of wounds or diseases.

1597 A. M. tr. *Guillemeau's Fr. Chirurg.* 8/2 We recommende such thinges vnto Nature, and followe her instructions. **1658** A. FOX *Würtz' Surg.* I. viii. 33 If Wounds in the dressing be abused..what can be expected, but Natures unwillingness and refractoriness. **1725** N. ROBINSON *Th. Physick* 193 The Physician is Nature's profess'd Servant. **1795** BURKE *Corr.* (1844) IV. 290 Nature, in desperate diseases, frequently does most when she is left entirely to herself.

d. Contrasted with *art*: (see ART *sb.* 2). Also, fidelity or close adherence to nature; naturalness. *from nature*: see FROM *prep.* (*adv.*, *conj.*) 13.

1704 POPE *Disc. Past. Poetry* §8 Theocritus excels all others in nature and simplicity. **1762–71** H. WALPOLE *Vertue's Anecd. Painting* (1786) I. 226 The colouring of the heads clear, and with great nature. **1779–81** JOHNSON *L. P.*, *Pope* Wks. IV. 142 Nature being, in this sense, only the best effect of art. **1826** SCOTT *Woodst.* xxxii, They will do it with more nature and effect, if they believe they are swearing truth.

12. In various phrases:

a. ***against,*** or ***contrary to, nature.***

c **1420** LYDG. *Assembly of Gods* 100 Thys Eolus hath oft, Made me to retourne my course agayn nature. *c* **1440** *Alph. Tales* 157 Nero said vnto þaim; 'Make ye me to be with childe'..And þai answerd agayn & said þat it was not possible, þat was contrarie vnto natur. **1508** KENNEDIE *Flyting w. Dunbar* 305 It war aganis baytht natur and gud ressoun, That Dewlbeiris bairnis were trew. **1526** TINDALE *Rom.* xi. 24 Yf thou waste..graffed contrary to nature in a true olyve tree. **1604** E. G[RIMSTONE] *D'Acosta's Hist. Indies* II. iv. 88 It finally in the time of Summer overfloweth Egypt, which seemeth against nature.

b. ***debt of nature***, etc.: (see DEBT *sb.* 4 b).

c. ***course of nature***: (see COURSE *sb.* 20).

c **1511** *1st Eng. Bk. Amer.* (Arb.) Introd. 34/1 There is nomore than one in all ye cours of nature. **1581** MULCASTER *Positions* vi. (1887) 44 Olde age, which though it come by course, and commaundement of nature [etc.]. **1613** SALKELD *Treat. Angels* 89 A miracle..being out of the common course of nature, beyond or above it, doth cause admiration. *a* **1676** HALE *Prim. Orig. Man.* (1677) 305 Touching the production of Animals,..they are in the ordinary course of Nature of two kinds. **1736** BUTLER *Anal.* I. ii. Wks. 1874 I. 40 The whole course of nature is a present instance of his exercising that government over us. **1771** SMOLLETT *Humph. Cl.* (1815) 219 He cannot be supposed to live much longer, according to the course of nature. **1826** WHATELY *Logic* (1836) 351 According to him, there is no such thing as a Course of Nature.

d. ***law(s) of nature***: (see LAW *sb.*[1] 17).

e. ***in nature***, in the actual basis of things, in real fact.

1605 BACON *Adv. Learn.* II. xxiii. §49 There are in Nature certain Fountains of Justice, whence all ciuile Lawes are derived but as streams. **1667** MILTON *P.L.* VI. 442 [To] equal what between us made the odds, In Nature none. **1672** PETTY *Pol. Anat.* (1691) 61 What other Foundation of Truth it had in Nature, I know not. **1873** HAMERTON *Intell. Life* VIII. ii. 288 There is really, in nature, such a thing as high life.

f. (***one of***) ***nature's gentlemen***: a natural gentleman, a person who is a gentleman by nature. Hence in similar phrases, and in extended use: by temperament.

1841 THACKERAY *Second Funeral of Napoleon* iii. 67 In the matter of gentleman democrats, cry pshaw! Give us one of nature's gentlemen, and hang your aristocrats! *a* **1882** TROLLOPE *Autobiogr.* (1883) I. iii. 53 If I say that a judge should be a gentleman..I am met with a scornful allusion to 'Nature's Gentlemen'. **1898** A. J. MUNBY *Diary* 26 Mar. in D. Hudson *Munby* (1972) 423 A splendid woman, full of rustic health & vigour, & one of Nature's ladies. **1901** G. B. SHAW *Admirable Bashville* II. i. 309 You need not be an idle gentleman. I call you one of Nature's gentlemen. **1929** A. HUXLEY *Let.* 9 May (1969) 311 Now..I can write a letter. It will be a poor return for all yours, because I am not one of nature's letter-writers. **1969** L. DURRELL *Spirit of Place* 19 He was one of nature's lobbyers—a tireless and relentless fellow. **1969** *Times* 15 Nov. 10/4 Nature's gentleman one day Bobby [Charlton] will be remembered as the jewel of them all. **1971** P. O'DONNELL *Impossible Virgin* iii. 67 One of nature's innocents. He couldn't dissemble if he tried. **1973** *Guardian* 18 June 9/6 We all know the kind of women who are just nature's doormats and..put up with anything.

13. a. The material world, or its collective objects and phenomena, esp. those with which man is most directly in contact; freq. the features and products of the earth itself, as contrasted with those of human civilization.

1662 STILLINGFL. *Orig. Sacræ* III. ii. §17 According to the Atomicall principles, no rationall account can be given of those effects which are seen in nature. **1667** MILTON *P.L.* VIII. 153 Such vast room in Nature unpossest By living Soule. **1697** DRYDEN *Virg. Georg.* III. 450 Surveying Nature with too nice a view. **1781** COWPER *Hope* 245 To enjoy cool nature in a country seat. *Ibid.* 740 Unconscious nature,.. Rocks, groves, and streams. **1820** W. IRVING *Sketch Bk.* II. 32 We derive a great portion of our pleasures from the mere beauties of nature. **1840** DICKENS *Barn. Rudge* iv, Nature was not so far removed or hard to get at, as in these days. **1888** BRYCE *Amer. Commw.* III. civ. 497 They lead a solitary life in the midst of a vast nature.

b. In wider sense: (see quots.).

1862 *Edin. Rev.* CXVI. 381 'Nature' is being used in the narrow sense of physical nature... But these selves of ours do belong to 'Nature'. **1873** DAWSON *Earth & Man* xiv. 343 Holding nature to represent the whole cosmos, and to include both the physical and the spiritual.

c. ***in nature***, anywhere; at all. (Used as an intensive with superlatives and negatives.)

1661 WOOD *Life* 3 May, All seniors..did look upon him, as the most impudent fellow in nature. **1673** DRYDEN *Marr. à la Mode* I, With all this, she's the greatest gossip in Nature. **1721** CIBBER *Lady's Last Stake* IV, And what Effect had that? O! none in Nature! **1770** FOOTE *Lame Lover* I. Wks. 1799 II. 63 An engagement that can't in nature be missed. **1848** LOWELL *Biglow P.* Ser. I. ii, It..is one of the curusest things in nater.

d. ***all nature***, everything, everyone, all creation; ***like all nature***, like anything, like blazes. *U.S. colloq.*

1819 *Mass. Spy* 3 Nov. 3/1 Father and I have just returned from the balloon—all nature was there, and more too. **1824** *Woodstock* (Vermont) *Observer* 17 Feb., They said too 'twould shoot like *all nater*, 'Tis singlar what stories they tell. **1825** J. NEAL *Bro. Jonathan* II. 93 Hurra for you—that beats all nater! **1840** C. F. HOFFMAN *Greyslaer* II. III. xiv. 254 The poor critter would have been sucked under, smashed on the rocky bottom, and dragged off like all natur. **1878** MRS. STOWE in *Atlantic Monthly* Oct. 472/2 Cuff would prance round..and seem to think he..had the charge of *all natur'*. **1892** J. C. DUVAL *Early Times in Texas* vi. 82 'Well, I declar, boys,' said he, 'ef this don't beat all natur.'

14. a. ***the*** or ***a state of nature***: (*a*) the moral state natural to man, as opposed to a state of grace; (*b*) the condition of man before the foundation of organized society; (*c*) an uncultivated or undomesticated condition; (*d*) physical nakedness.

a **1667** SOUTH *Serm.* (1697) I. 9 The Difference between a state of Nature, and a state of Grace. **1689** LOCKE *Govt.* II. ii. ¶6 The state of Nature has a Law of Nature to govern it. **1722** WOLLASTON *Relig. Nat.* vii. 152 He who is a member of a society in other respects retains his natural liberty, is still as it were in a state of nature. **1738** SWIFT *Pol. Conversat.* Introd. 58 Quadrille in particular bears some Resemblance to a State of Nature. **1802** C. WILMOT *Let.* 3 Jan. in *Irish Peer* (1920) 23 My first impression was amazement, at beholding the women from 15 to 70 almost in a state of nature. **1817** J. BRADBURY *Trav. Amer.* 326 It will perhaps be found that all countries in a state of nature are liable to this disease. **1833** *Penny Cycl.* I. 184/1 The true civet..is found in a state of nature in most parts of Africa. **1864** PUSEY *Lect. Daniel* ix. 561 It is man's own fault, if..he remain in, or apostatise into, a state of nature. **1970** *Brewer's Dict. Phr. & Fable* (ed. 12) 747/2 *In a state of nature*, nude or naked.

†**b.** ***in nature***, in a natural condition; unmanufactured. *Obs. rare*⁻¹.

1719 W. WOOD *Surv. Trade* 237 Draw-backs upon Goods Exported, in nature as Imported.

c. A malleable state (of iron).

1791 BEDDOES in *Phil. Trans.* LXXXI. 174 It [the pig iron] approaches more and more towards nature [malleable iron]. **1895** PINNOCK *Black Country Ann.* (E.D.D.), My iron's just comin' to natur'.

V. 15. *attrib.* and *Comb.* **a.** Attrib., chiefly in sense 'of, belonging or relating to nature', as ***nature-cure, -folk, -force, -kingdom, -lover, -loving*** (adj.), ***-mystic, -mysticism, -myth, -mythology, -philosophy, poem, poet, poetry, -power, ramble, -religion, -symbol, -symbolism, walk, -worship, -worshipper, -writer, -writing*** (vbl. sb.); **Nature Conservancy**, an organization responsible for the conservation and study of flora and fauna in Britain, which runs nature reserves, research stations, etc.; **nature conservation**, the preservation of wild fauna and flora and the habitat necessary for their continued existence in their native surroundings; **nature-faker** orig. *U.S.*, a person who falsifies reports of natural phenomena, esp. animal behaviour; so **nature-faking** *vbl. sb.* and *ppl. a.*; **nature-god**, one of the powers or phenomena of nature personified as a god; so **nature-being, -deity**; **nature-name**, a toponym embodying an allusion to a natural occurrence or topographical feature; **nature-notes**, comments on natural history; **nature-people**, people in a low or primitive stage of culture; **nature reserve**, a tract of land managed in order to preserve its fauna, flora, physical features, etc.; **nature sanctuary**, an area in which the fauna and flora are protected from any disturbance; **nature-spirit**, a spirit supposed to reside in some natural element or object; **nature strip** *Austral. local* (see quot. 1966); **nature study**, the study of natural objects and phenomena, esp. as a subject taught in schools; an example of this; so (*rare*) **nature-student**; **nature trail**, a path linking features of interest, esp. in relation to local natural history, which are described and interpreted by explanatory notices, printed leaflets, or a guide.

1877 tr. *Tiele's Hist. Relig.* 23 All the spirits which they worship..are *nature-beings of more or less might. **1949** *Times* 12 Feb. 3/4 Mr. Herbert Morrison announced in the House of Commons yesterday that arrangements have been completed for forming a *Nature Conservancy, and that a separate committee will supervise activities in Scotland... The conservancy—'a more convenient title than conservation board'—would be responsible for the whole of Great Britain. *Ibid.* 5/3 The Nature Conservancy is to have a general charge over all matters relating to the native fauna and flora of Britain. **1959** *News Chron.* 4 Dec. 7/6 The Nature Conservancy has had to abandon plans to establish a warden on Dungeness. **1971** O. NORTON *Corpse-Bird Cries* ii. 25 Nature conservancy, or Snowdonia national park, or something. They've laid out a nature trail at Llyn Coedig. **1974** M. BLACKMORE in Warren & Goldsmith *Conservation in Pract.* xxvii. 427 On March 23rd, 1949, it [*sc.* the Government] created the Nature Conservancy by royal charter as a new research council. **1943** *Nature Conservation & Nature Reserves* (Brit. Ecol. Soc.) 7 The whole problem of *nature conservation requires to be viewed against the human or social background. **1948** *Times* 30 Apr. 6/3 Mr. H. Morrison..said that the Government accepted in principle the recommendations..calling for the establishment of a Nature Conservation Board. **1953** *Rep. Nature Conservancy to 1952* 3 Though the Act as a whole does not extend to Scotland, Part III and such other Sections as relate to nature conservation are so extended. **1968** C. BURKE *Elephant across Border* v. 203 You can do more for nature conservation by shocking people..than a whole heap of discussion groups and bird magazines can do. **1974** M. BLACKMORE in Warren & Goldsmith *Conservation in Pract.* xxvii. 423 Nature conservation illustrates the gradual evolution and development of modern attitudes. **1876** LOWELL *Among my Bks.* Ser. II. 249 His system of a *nature-cure, first professed by Dr. Jean Jaques and continued by Cowper. **1906** *Chambers's Jrnl.* 24 Nov. 832/1 At Dr. Lahmann's nature-cure sanatorium,..care is taken to cook vegetables so as to retain the nutritive and soluble salts. **1969** C. WATSON *Flaxborough Crab* xvii. 180 What have I to do with this—this nature cure chicanery? **1875** *Encycl. Brit.* II. 56/2 One of the great *nature-deities, such as Heaven or Sun, is raised to this royal pre-eminence. **1906** *Everybody's Mag.* June 770 (*heading*) Roosevelt on the *nature fakirs. **1909** *Daily Chron.* 8 Dec. 6/4 A President..who never ..'goes for' Congress or nature-fakers or millionaires. **1949** *Natural Hist.* Mar. 131/2 Many nature fakers had obtained free meals..through the gullibility of newspaper reporters. **1921** *Daily Colonist* (Victoria, B.C.) 10 Apr. 17/1, I should be sorry to have Mr. John Burroughs catch me *nature-faking. **1923** KIPLING *Land & Sea Tales* 85 To say that William did not sleep a wink that night would be what has been called 'nature-faking'. **1947** *Sports Afield* Dec. 6/3 It was apparent to me that the writer colored his material, particularly in regard to the nature faking episode. **1927** PEAKE & FLEURE *Peasants & Potters* i. 8 They had settled down into a routine, as had many *nature-folk the world over before European industrialism touched them in the last century. **1876** GLADSTONE *Homeric Synch.* 214 His ideas.. separate so broadly between human beings and the *Nature forces. **1871** TYLOR *Prim. Cult.* (1903) II. 255 The great *Nature-gods are huge in strength and far-reaching in influence. **1865** *Fam. Treas.* 412 In the spiritual kingdom, as in the great *nature-kingdoms. **1902** *Chambers's Jrnl.* July 426/2 Many an angler and *nature-lover is a veritable 'prisoner of Hope'. **1937** *Discovery* Jan. 32/1 The book is a most suitable gift for nature lovers of all ages. **1969** *Islander* (Victoria, B.C.) 31 Aug. 4/1 It is the perfect spot in summertime for lazing on the beach..more than this, it is a nature lover's paradise. **1913** *Eng. Illustr. Mag.* June 254 It is scarcely possible to find a mountain track or woody dell.. which has not fascinated and inspired this *nature-loving poet. **1927** J. S. HUXLEY *Relig. without Revelation* iv. 123 The *nature-mystic. **1958** *Economist* 8 Nov. Suppl. 11/1 Traherne was a visionary possessed of a powerful and discerning mind. To regard him as a lone eccentric or a pre-Romantic Nature-mystic is to under-estimate his stature as a Christian humanist. **1899** W. R. INGE *Christian Mysticism* viii. 302 The true *Nature-Mysticism is prominent in St. Francis of Assisi. **1932** C. WILLIAMS *Eng. Poetic Mind* ii. 13 Wordsworth was..not ever writing a child's primer of Nature-mysticism; he left that to his commentators. **1871** TYLOR *Prim. Cult.* (1903) I. 284 Those most beautiful of poetic fictions, to which may be given the title of *Nature-Myths. **1954** E. E. EVANS-PRITCHARD *Inst. Primitive Society* i. 4 Other anthropologists—if we may include Max Müller and the rest of the nature myth school under this heading—were busy explaining religion in terms of personification of such natural phenomena as sun, sky, and rain. **1895** A. NUTT in *K. Meyer's Voy. Bran* I. 179 During the sway of the organised *nature-mythology. **1960** P. H. REANEY *Orig. Eng. Place-Names* ii. 30 Farnborough 'fern-clad hill', Hertford, 'stag-ford'..were originally *nature-names from which later settlements near-by took their names. **1906** M. CAWEIN (*title*) *Nature-notes and impressions in prose and verse. **1937** *Discovery* Oct. 318 The marvellous journey of Domingo Gonsales..with its ingenious form of aerial transport and its lunar 'nature notes'. **1877** tr. *Tiele's Hist. Relig.* 24 The worship of spirits..and the doctrine of immortality are not developed any further among the Finns than among the *Nature-peoples. **1855** BRIMLEY *Ess.* 23 A sentimental *nature-philosophy and a pantheistical worship. **1905** F. H. SHOOSMITH *'Kingsley' Nature Poetry Books* I (*heading*) The 'Kingsley' *nature poems. **1946** 'G. ORWELL' *Coll. Ess.* (1968) I. 1, I wrote bad and usually unfinished 'nature poems' in the Georgian style. **1906** A. MACKIE *Nature Knowl. Mod. Poetry* v. 55 (*heading*) Wordsworth as a *nature poet. **1925** A. HUXLEY *Along Road* I. 66 A 'nature poet' (the expression is somehow rather horrible, but there is no other). **1938** L. MACNEICE *Mod. Poetry* i. 8 Rooted, as nature-poets should be, in their subject. **1905** F. H. SHOOSMITH (*title*) The 'Kingsley' *nature poetry books for schools. **1936** F. R. LEAVIS *Revaluation* v. 186 'Nature poetry', Victorian or Georgian, pays at the best only an equivocal tribute to his [*sc.* Wordsworth's] greatness. **1865** GLADSTONE *Farew. Addr. Edinb. Univ.* 22 The absorption of Deity into mere *nature-power. **1944** A. THIRKELL *Headmistress* xi. 231 There would be a *Nature Ramble at a good brisk pace in Lord Pomfret's grounds. **1965** 'O. MILLS' *Dusty Death* xi. 121 We used to.. go to one of the cookery classes, or go on a nature ramble. **1877** tr. *Tiele's Hist. Relig.* 6 A description of the so-called *nature-religions..is excluded from our design. **1915** R. LANKESTER *Diversions of Naturalist* ii. 17 A society has been founded for the formation of '*nature-reserves' in the British Islands. **1937** *Handbk. Soc. Promotion of Nature Reserves* 8 Woodwalton Fen, Huntingdonshire. This nature reserve..consists of about 360 acres of primitive fenland, a relic of the once extensive Huntingdonshire fens, and is rich in plant and insect life. **1949** *Act 12 & 13 Geo. VI* c. 97 §15 The expression 'nature reserve' means land managed for the purpose—(*a*) of providing..special opportunities for the study of, and research into, matters relating to the fauna and flora..or (*b*) of preserving flora, fauna or geological or physiographic features of special interest in the area. **1959** *News Chron.* 4 Dec. 7/6 A warden to see that building operations cause as little harm as possible to wild life and plants in what is left of the surrounding nature reserve. **1967** N. FREELING *Strike Out* 39 The sand dunes..have been made into a sort of nature-reserve. **1969** *Times* 3 Mar. 5/8 In a general discussion on establishing nature reserves on farms, the question of unrestricted access and possible vandalism clearly worried some farmers. **1972** *Country Life* 6 Jan. 22/3 Nature-reserve management. **1932** V. E. SHELFORD in *Ecology* XIII. 202 Reports from the Advisory Board and other members of this committee showed them unanimously in favor of *nature sanctuaries to which only persons conducting scientific, artistic or literary work of a serious nature are to be admitted. *Ibid.*, Nature sanctuaries should not be given publicity on account of the desire to visit them created thereby. **1972** *Country Life* 6 Apr. 838/3 Where..a marsh has been reclaimed, one cannot expect back-to-the-wilds compensation in the shape of a nature sanctuary. **1871** TYLOR *Prim. Cult.* (1903) II. 205 Here we must seek to realize to the utmost the definition of the *Nature-Spirits. **1966** BAKER *Austral. Lang.* (ed. 2) xvi. 344 **Nature strip*, a strip of lawn beside the footpath outside Melbourne homes in 'garden suburbs'. **1973** *Listener* 25 Jan. 118/1 The ground in front of the house—what the Australians call a 'nature strip'. **1902** *Pall Mall Mag.* Aug. 485 Few of these *nature-students are men of leisure. **1896** L. C. MIALL (*title*) Round the year. A series of short *nature-studies. **1897** J. H. COMSTOCK (*title*) Insect life: an introduction to nature-study and a guide for teachers, students and others. **1902** *Chambers's Jrnl.* Oct. 683/1 The Nature-study Exhibition which was held at the Botanical Gardens, London, this autumn. **1928** D. PATTON (*title*) Nature study for beginners. **1953** G. BELL *Black Marigolds* i. 19 Bugs got his nature study prize as expected. **1972** J. WILSON *Hide & Seek* ii. 34 Alice taught Mary how to read and how to add up..and they did nature study and learnt about cavemen. **1927** H. CRANE *Let.* 12 Sept. (1965) 305 Pocahontas is the mythological *nature-symbol chosen to represent the physical body of the continent. *Ibid.* 307 The mother who died... Her succession to the nature-symbolism of Pocahontas. **1926** F. E. LUTZ (*title*) *Nature trails. **1927** *58th Ann. Rep. Amer. Mus. Nat. Hist. 1926* 106 Dr. Frank E. Lutz,..has conducted for some time a Station for the Study of Insects, in Harriman State Park, near Tuxedo, N.Y. In connection with this outdoor station, in 1925 he established and developed a Nature Trail in the vicinity. *Ibid.* 107 This Nature Trail has been a wonderful stimulus to the present-day movement toward the emphasis of the outdoor museum and hundreds of nature trails have been made in various parts of the country, and also in foreign countries. **1950** W. HILLCOURT *Field Bk. Nature Activities* 47 The best location for a nature trail is a park, a camp, a grove adjacent to the school grounds. **1963** *Rep. Nature Conservancy* vii. 103 During the [National Nature] Week the Conservancy set up Nature Trails at Castor Hanglands and Studland Heath National Nature Reserves. **1969** M. PUGH *Last Place Left* iv. 23 All the work of..laying out nature trails had been undone. **1974** *Country Life* 14 Mar. 583/3 An excellent nature trail has been laid over this land. **1932** R. LEHMANN *Invitation to Waltz* I. vii. 80 She saw two figures..James and Miss Mivart, returning from their *nature walk. **1964** O. BLAKESTON *Fingers* i. 9 Drilling the catechism class..and giving the children a yearly 'nature walk' as a treat. **1850** R. W. MACKAY *Progress of Intellect* I. iii. 151 The elements of personification, as well as Pantheism, are in all *Nature-worship. **1869** J. MARTINEAU *Ess.* II. 197 The sublime neutrality of our modern nature-worship. **1878** MACLEAR *Celts* ii. 28 Nature-worship, including the adoration of fountains and streams. **1960** C. DAY LEWIS *Buried Day* vii. 147, I took up nature worship now because it was a poetic thing. **1929** A. HUXLEY *Do what you Will* 158 St. Francis is often hailed as the first *nature-worshipper..in Europe since..the Greeks. **1946** BLUNDEN *Shelley* 137 A seer and a nature-worshipper. **1931** —— *Votive Tablets* 259 Some of the..*nature-writers mentioned above. **1969** *Times Lit. Suppl.* 16 Jan. 61/1 Thomas's *nature writing was good of its kind and time.

b. Attrib., passing into adj. = 'natural'; in later use only with reference to natural products, or to land producing these naturally (see Jamieson 1825, s.v.). *Sc.* exc. in ***nature food***.

1568 SKEYNE *The Pest* (1860) 14 Quhilk..testifeis strenthe of nature helth. **1645** RUTHERFORD *Tryal & Tri. Faith* (1845) 178 Blood-bonds, nature-relations are mighty. **1762** BP. FORBES *Jrnl.* (1886) 145 The rapid Spey forms a pleasant Bottom, rich with Corns and nature-Grass. ?**1811** W. AITON *Agric. Surv. Ayrsh.* 291 (Jam.), When they see a field carpeted with rich grasses, or those that grow luxuriant, they say that field produces nature grasses. **1847** E. WALKER *Diary* in C. M. Drury *Elkanah & Mary Walker* (1940) viii. 205 The year has been fruitful in nature food. **1971** *Sunday Express* (Johannesburg) 28 Mar. 5/6 He tended the children himself, using nature foods prescribed by Mr. Peter Dowling, a practising naturopath.

c. Instrumental, as ***nature-favoured***, ***-graced***, ***-hidden***, ***-taught***; objective, as ***nature-drowning***, ***-painting***, ***-shaking***; parasynthetic, as ***nature-hearted***; similative, as ***nature-like***, ***-true***.

1598 SYLVESTER *Du Bartas* II. i. *Eden* 197 The wreakfull *nature-drowning Flood Spar'd not this beauteous place. **1885** *Fortn. Waggonette* 78 Two such *nature-favoured sons of Adam. *a* **1618** SYLVESTER *Maiden's Blush* 73 Joseph.., Whome, *Nature-grac't, the Graces nurtur'd fine In liberall Arts. **1839–48** BAILEY *Festus* xx. 234 Kind *nature-hearted bards. **1891** ATKINSON *Last of Giant-Killers* 224 Such a self-concealing as well as *nature-hidden place. **1530** PALSGR. 319/1 *Naturlyke, *naif, genial, naturel.* **1748** THOMSON *Cast. Indol.* I. lvii, Of the fine stores he nothing would impart, Which or boon nature gave, or *nature-painting art. **1882** GROSART *Spenser's Wks.* III. p. liii, This..widens.. the Nature-painting poetry of our language. **1606** SYLVESTER *Du Bartas* II. iv. I. *Trophies* 674 Whose Hell-raking, *Nature-shaking Spell. **1591** *Ibid.* I. iii. 379 O learned (*Nature-taught) Arithmetician! **1850** MRS. BROWNING *Poems* I. 321 Even like my blossoms, if as *nature-true, Though not as precious.

'nature, *v.*[1] [ad. OF. *naturer* (Godef.), or med.L. *nātūrāre*, f. *nātūra* NATURE *sb.*]

†**1.** *trans.* To invest with a particular nature. *Obs.*

1390 GOWER *Conf.* III. 97 He which natureth every kinde, The myhti god.

2. *intr.* in pres. pple. or ppl. a. *naturing* [after med.L. *natura naturans*]: Creative, and giving to each thing its specific nature. Also in *vbl. sb.* *Obs.* or *rare*.

1509 HAWES *Past. Pleas.* XXXIX. (Percy Soc.) 201 Tyll that dame Nature naturing had made All thinge to grow to theyr fortitude. **1519** *Interl. Four Elem.* in Hazl. *Dodsley* I. 11 The Perfection and First Cause of every thing, I mean that only high Nature naturing. **1605** TIMME *Quersit.* I. ii. 5 Aristotle himselfe..calleth it *naturam naturantem*, naturing nature. **1694** R. BURTHOGGE *Reason* 118 The unwary Expression of some..Theologizing Philosophers, who Denominated God Nature Naturing. **1880** G. M. HOPKINS *Note-bks. & Papers* (1937) 312 The whole function, the naturing, the selving of that nature.

'nature, *v.*[2] *rare.* [f. NATURE *sb.*] *trans.* **a.** To endow with a (new) nature. **b.** To fix in one's nature, to make natural.

1857 J. PULSFORD *Quiet Hours* Ser. I. 39 It is granted to us fallen men, to be born and natured anew, from the Eternal Word. **1890** J. H. STIRLING *Gifford Lect.* v. 89 The patrimonial use and wont, and established manners, so to speak, natured in them.

natured ('neɪtjʊəd), *ppl. a.* [f. NATURE *sb.* + -ED[2].] Having a nature or disposition (of a specified kind).

Chiefly used in compounds, as GOOD-, ILL-NATURED, etc.

1577 [see GOOD-NATURED]. **1589** R. ROBINSON *Gold. Mirr.* (1851) 53 With hounied mouths, yet natur'd like the waspe. **1605** ROWLANDS *Hell's Broke Loose* 27 What is it from the Cocatrice doth passe, But such a natur'd Serpent as him selfe? **1649** BLITHE *Eng. Improv. Impr.* (1653) 36 To all sorts of such natured Lands, thou mayst apply them. **1720** *Humourist* 16 As good a natur'd civil Person as I am, the Spleen is now and then too hard for me. **1836** *Tait's Mag.* III. 163 [Your heart] is natured somewhat after the fashion of the lava that flows from an old mountain. **1879** SPENCER *Data Ethics* xiv. 256 Others, similarly natured, will not permit him in any large measure to do this.

‖**naturel** (natyrɛl), *sb.* [F., sb. use of the adj.: see next.] Natural character or disposition.

1856 EMERSON *Eng. Traits, Result*, The contumacious sharp-tongued energy of English *naturel*. **1870** —— *Soc. & Sol.* vi. 126 What possesses interest for us is the *naturel* of each, his constitutional excellence.

†**naturel**, *a.* *Obs.* Also 4–5 -ell, 5 -ele, -elle, -eel, -ile, -ill. [a. F. *naturel* (12th c.), ad. L. *nātūrāl-is* NATURAL *a.*] = NATURAL *a.*, in various senses. (Common in Chaucer, Gower, and Caxton.)

a **1300** *Cursor M.* 9449 Þe laghes bath he þan for-lete Bath naturel and positif. *c* **1374** CHAUCER *Compl. Mars* 122 A naturel day in derk I let her duel. **1387** TREVISA *Higden* (Rolls) III. 65 Þis naturel philosofer and dyuynour serchede kynde and vertues of þynges. *c* **1400** *Destr. Troy* 6770 All the nobill anon,—þo naturill brether,—Wonderfully wroght with wepyn in hond. *c* **1400** tr. *Secreta Secret., Gov. Lordsh.* 66 To perfitly knowe alle manere of Naturels þinges. **1470–85** MALORY *Arthur* IX. xl. 406 Ye haue done to vs but as a naturel Knyghte ought to doo. **1497** BP. ALCOCK *Mons Perfect.* E ij, Our moost naturell Soueraync lorde Henry the seuenth.

†**'natureless**, *a.* *Obs. rare.* [f. NATURE *sb.* + -LESS.] **a.** Not having a vital nature. **b.** Not in accordance with nature; unnatural.

1548 GESTE *Pr. Masse* B iv, What semblance..is ther betwyxte the natureles bread and wyne, and christes body and bloud? **1644** MILTON *Bucer on Div.* Wks. 1851 IV. 294 Under a bondage not of Gods constraining with a natureles constraint..but laid upon us imperiously.

naturelle (natyrɛl), *a.* and *sb.* [a. Fr. *naturelle* fem. of *naturel* natural. Cf. NATURAL *a.* 19 above.] (Of) a pale pink or beige colour; skin-colour(ed).

1873 *Young Englishwoman* Feb. 78/1 A dark blue marine velvet hat..with black pompom, and long plume naturelle. **1907** *Yesterday's Shopping* (1969) 537/1 Poudre de Riz..in 4 shades (Blanche, Rachel, Naturelle, Rose). **1927–8** *T. Eaton & Co. Catal.* Fall & Winter 367 Pompeian Face Powder..fine and clinging, in White, Rachel, Naturelle or Flesh.

†**naturelly**, *adv.* *Obs.* Also 3 nature(l)liche, 4 naturely. [f. NATUREL *a.* + -LY[2], after OF. *naturelment*.]

1. Naturally; by nature.

c **1250** *Kent. Serm.* in *O.E. Misc.* 30 Þet wyn þat is naturelliche hot ine him-selue. *c* **1374** CHAUCER *Boeth.* V. pr. ii. (1868) 152 Euery þing þat may naturely vsen resoun. *c* **1386** —— *Frankl. T.* 324 Right so the see desireth naturelly To folwen hire. **1413** *Pilgr. Sowle* (Caxton 1483) v. xiv. 107 Euery thyng that werketh naturelly enduceth the fourme of it seluen. **1482** *Monk of Evesham* 59 Wemen..naturelly schuld be more schamfull thenne other.

2. Carnally. *rare*[−1].

1484 CAXTON *Fables of Æsop* VI. iv, Thow arte an inceste & lechour For thow knowest naturelly both thy moder and thy doughter.

†**'naturely**, *a.* *Obs. rare*[−1]. Natural.

c **1511** *1st Eng. Bk. Amer.* (Arb.) 33 They saye yat mans fleyshe is good & naturly to ete rawe.

‖**nature morte** (natyr mɔrt). [Fr.] = STILL LIFE. Also *transf.*

1921 R. FRY *Let.* 14 Dec. (1972) II. 518 He's bought..one superb *nature morte*, and he's two lovely Renoirs. **1923** A. HUXLEY *Antic Hay* xvi. 225 Her face, painted in two tones of red, white, green, blue and black, is the most tasteful of *nature-mortes*. **1938** L. DURRELL *Let.* in *Spirit of Place* (1969) 53 He hasn't painted a stroke..not a bloody *nature-morte* even; and when he admits it he looks rather *nature-morte* himself. **1947** *Horizon* Jan. 17 The fixed elements of cubist nature-morte came to a new life. **1960** *Times* 19 Jan. 13/2 By the religious-minded these *nature morte* passages can be interpreted as a humble hymn to the Creator. **1963** M. MCCARTHY *Group* vi. 123 Pale and lifeless..a veritable *nature morte*. **1970** *Oxf. Compan. Art* 1096/2 Dutch *still-leven*, which..denotes simply a motionless (*still*) aspect of nature (*leven*)...means exactly the same as the French term *nature morte*, which dates from the 18th c.

nature-printing. [Cf. G. *natur(selbst)-druck.*] The method or process of producing a print of a natural object, *esp.* a leaf, by means of the mark made by the object itself, under pressure, on a prepared plate. So **nature-print** *v.* (also in *transf.* use); *sb.*, an impression obtained in this way; **nature-printed** *ppl. a.*

1855 BRADBURY in *Proc. Roy. Inst. Gt. Brit.* II. 106 The Art of Nature-Printing is a method of producing impressions of plants and other natural objects, in a manner so truthful that only a close inspection reveals the fact of their being copies. **1855** T. MOORE (*title*) The Ferns of Great Britain... Nature printed by Henry Bradbury. **1859** JOHNSTONE & CROALL (*title*) Nature-Printed British Seaweeds. **1883** H. DRUMMOND *Nat. Law in Spir. W.* (1884) 259 As if the actual reeds of its native jungle had nature-printed themselves on its hide. **1950** W. BLUNT *Art Botanical Illustr.* xi. 141 Some of these works illustrated by nature printing have considerable charm, especially where the process has been used to record grasses, ferns and delicately formed plants. **1967** CAVE & WAKEMAN *Typographia Naturalis* i. 2 It is appropriate that the earliest description of the original technique of nature printing and the oldest extant nature print should both be by Leonardo da Vinci. *Ibid.* 11 Other nature printed illustrations to books were produced in Germany in the late eighteenth and early nineteenth centuries.

†**'naturer.** *Obs. rare*[−1]. [f. NATURE *v.*[1] + -ER[1].] One who gives a thing its nature.

1587 GOLDING *De Mornay* xiv. (1617) 227 Man can skill to discerne the mortall naturer from the immortall.

†**naturesse.** *Obs.* [a. OF. *naturesse* (Godef.): see NATURE *sb.* and -ESS[2].] Natural affection or feeling; a generous act.

? *a* **1412** LYDGATE *Two Merch.* 771 His herte was meevyd of oolde naturesse To save his freend. **1439** in *Ep. Acad. Oxon.* (1898) I. 184 Your naturesses and benevolence shold enjoy with us of the fortheraunce of the sayde Universite. *c* **1470** HARDING *Chron.* XXXI. vi, With wordes peteous, and mothers naturesse.

†**na'turian.** *Obs.* [f. NATURE *sb.* + -IAN, or ad. obs. F. *naturien* (Godef.).] A student of nature, a natural philosopher; also, a believer in nature as contrasted with divine providence.

1600 W. WATSON *Decacordon* (1602) 358 Amongst Philosophers Aristotle was wise, profound; Plato humane, diuine; Pythagoras hot, precise; and all sound exquisite naturians. *Ibid.* 341. **1621** S. WARD *Life of Faith* 83 Great.. aduantages hath a Christian by virtue of his Faith, aboue any Naturian or Politique by all his reason. **1633** T. ADAMS *Exp. 2 Peter* ii. 5 There is no judgment comes, but naturians will find out other causes for it than God.

So †**na'turien.** *Obs. rare.*

1390 GOWER *Conf.* III. 46 Riht so of the Naturiens Upon the Sterres from above His weie he secheth unto love. *Ibid.* 106 And thus seith the naturien Which is an Astronomien.

naturile, -ill, variants of NATUREL *a.* *Obs.*

naturism ('neɪtjʊərɪz(ə)m). [f. NATURE *sb.* + -ISM, or ad. F. *naturisme.*]

1. Naturalism in regard to religion.

1847 O. BROWNSON *Wks.* V. 531 The rejection of..grace, and the assertion, if the word may be permitted us, of mere naturism. *Ibid.* 534 Infidelity, irreligion, naturism.

2. Nature-worship.

1886 *Encycl. Brit.* XX. 367/1 According to Pfleiderer the original religion must have been a kind of indistinct, chaotic naturism. **1891** tr. *De la Saussaye's Man. Sci. Relig.* xiii. 103 Better with Reville to separate worship of nature (which he calls naturism) from animism.

3. *Med.* The attribution of everything to the workings of nature.

a **1890** DUNGLISON *Med. Dict.*

4. A movement for, or the practice of, communal nudity in private grounds.

1933 *Gymnos* Nov. 18/1 This book..is the first serious attempt to link Nudism with..Naturism, and Feminism. **1961** *Daily Tel.* 30 Oct. 11/2 Delegates..at the annual conference of the British Sun Bathing Association...agreed ..to substitute 'naturism' for 'nudism'. **1973** *Guardian* 28 June 6/1 The Central Council for British Naturism has launched a publicity campaign..[for] official 'naturist beaches'.

naturist ('neɪtjʊərɪst). [f. NATURE *sb.* + -IST; cf. F. *naturiste.*] **1.** An adherent or follower of, or believer in, nature, in various applications. Also *attrib.*

1685 BOYLE *Enq. Notion Nat.* 34 Those that admit and applaud the Vulgar Notion of Nature: whom..I shall hereafter many times call Naturists. **1851** DUNGLISON *Med. Dict.*, *Naturist*, a physician who scrupulously investigates, interprets and follows the indications presented by nature in the treatment of disease. **1892** *Harper's Mag.* LXXXIV. 803/1 Words that must have gone hard sometimes with the 'naturist' he happened to be praising. **1900** *Nation* (N.Y.) 19 July 52/3 Hence, realists, naturalists, and 'naturists', and decadents,..and a host of other ephemeridae. **1950** G. BRENAN *Face of Spain* v. 113 He is a vegetarian and a firm adherent of the Naturist clinic in Malaga, with its theories of opposites and harmonies in foods. **1971** M. MCCARTHY *Birds of America* 184 A naturist diet of fruit and raw vegetables.

2. A practitioner of naturism (sense 4). Also *attrib.*

1929 M. PARMELEE *Nudity in Modern Life* i. 15 We have all heard of so-called 'naturists', who insist that man..should discard everything artificial such as..clothing, books, cooked food, etc. **1930** *Observer* 27 Apr. 12/5 Advocates of the health cure of complete nudity..spent a holiday in a naturist colony on an island in the Seine. **1958** *New Statesman* 15 Mar. 330/3 Nudist clubs ('actually we prefer the word "naturist"') were in violent competition. **1963** *Daily Tel.* 20 Mar. 22/5 The description 'a nudist camp', according to the naturist terminology, is defunct... Instead club members are asked to use the expression 'sun club' or 'naturist club'. **1973** [see NATURISM 4].

natu'ristic, *a. rare.* [f. prec. + -IC.] Pertaining to, or connected with, nature. Hence **natu'ristically** *adv.*, in a way that is suggestive of nature.

1886 *Encycl. Brit.* XX. 366/2 Ethical religions do not exclude the naturistic elements altogether. **1895** *Pall Mall Mag.* Dec. 650/1 If Mrs. Patrick Campbell wants to talk naturally (not to say naturistically) on the stage.

†**na'turity.** *Obs. rare*$^{-1}$. [irreg. f. NATURE + -ITY.] The creative power underlying nature.

1646 SIR T. BROWNE *Pseud. Ep.* 239 Which..cannot be allowed, except we impute that unto the first cause, which we impose not on the second; or what we deny unto nature, we impute unto Naturity it self.

naturize ('neɪtjʊəraɪz), *v. rare.* [f. NATURE *sb.* + -IZE. Cf. NATURE *v.*[1]] *trans.* To invest with a specific nature. Hence **'naturized** *ppl. a.*

1607 J. DAVIES *Summa Totalis* A4*, Which call God, Nature, naturizing all. **1610** B. JONSON *Alch.* II. i, 'Tis the secret Of nature naturiz'd 'gainst all infections. **1880** *Trans. R. Hist. Soc.* VIII. 347 Motion, rest, will, and reason were thus 'naturized nature' (*natura naturata*).

naturopathy (neɪtjʊə'rɒpəθɪ). [f. NATUR(E *sb.* + -O + -PATHY (cf. HYDROPATHY).] A theory of the nature of disease and a system of therapeutic practice founded on the supposition that diseases can be cured by natural agencies.

1901 L. STADEN in *Kneipp Water Cure Monthly* Jan. 30/2 There is no doubt that you can get cured without operation by Naturopathy. **1925** [see KELLGREN]. **1948** [see CULTISH *a.*]. **1971** *Sunday Express* (Johannesburg) 28 Mar. 5/5 Mr. Fell asked the Supreme Court to reverse the magistrate's findings and to accept that naturopathy is a legitimate form of medicine.

Hence **'naturopath**, one who advocates or practises naturopathy; **naturo'pathic** *a.*

1901 *Kneipp Water Cure Monthly* Jan. 30/2 (*heading*) Naturopathic Adviser. *Ibid.* Nov. 311/2 L. Staden, Naturopath. **1928** S. LIEF *Nat. Cure versus Med. Sci.* v. 14 The crux of the naturopathic contention is that the suppression of every acute malady—after the Allopathic procedure—lays the foundation for another acute malady. **1937** *Evening News* 20 Jan. 9/1, I suppose that everybody will admit that we owe the present day benefits of fasting to the teaching of naturopaths. **1960** *Spectator* 28 Oct. 647 A number of naturopathic practitioners. **1973** *Times* 8 May 18/8 The conference of the British Naturopathic and Osteopathic Association. **1973** *Nation Rev.* (Melbourne) 31 Aug.–6 Sept. 1434/5, I do take exception to those people who advocate cures for homosexuality as chiropractor and naturopath.

‖**Naturphilosophie** (na'tuːrfiləsəfiː). Also **natur-philosophie.** [G., f. *natur* nature + *philosophie* philosophy.] The name given to the theory put forward, esp. by Schelling (1775–1854) and other German philosophers, that there is an eternal and unchanging law of nature, proceeding from the Absolute, from which all laws governing natural phenomena and forces derive. Hence **na'turphilosoph, -er**, one who adheres to the theory of Naturphilosophie.

1817 COLERIDGE *Biogr. Lit.* I. ix. 148 In Schelling's '*Natur-Philosophie*',..I first found a genial coincidence with much that I had toiled out for myself. *a* **1834** —— in K. Coburn *Inquiring Spirit* (1951) 118 The Natur-Phil[osophen] are apt to mistake the new-naming of a thing ..for additional insight. *Ibid.* 251 These..are the passages that annoy me in the *Natur-philosophen*! **1846** J. D. MORELL *Hist. View Philos.* II. v. 109 For the method by which Schelling accounts for the three dimensions in space, we refer the reader to a little work containing the Elements of Schelling's Natur-Philosophie. **1892** W. WALLACE tr. *Hegel's Logic* (ed. 2) 430 The formalism of *Naturphilosophie* may teach *e.g.* that understanding is electricity. **1920** A. N. WHITEHEAD *Concept of Nature* ii. 47 A *Natur-philosoph* raises nature to independence, and makes it construct itself, and he never feels, therefore, the necessity of opposing nature as constructed (*i.e.* as experience) to real nature, or of correcting the one by means of the other. **1946** M. R. COHEN *Pref. to Logic* vi. 102 Since the failure of the romantic *Naturphilosophie* to derive infallible knowledge of nature *a priori*,..it has become generally evident that all our factual knowledge..is only probable. **1957** G. S. CARTER *100 Yrs. Evolution* ii. 16 The German abstract or transcendental zoology, usually called Natur-philosophie..owed its origin to Goethe more than to any other biologist. *Ibid.* vi. 70 The theories of the natur-philosophers might have done this. **1965** *Listener* 3 June 833/1 One of the important influences which shaped the intellectual milieu of early Victorian England was German *Naturphilosophie.* **1974** *Sunday Times* (Colour Suppl.) 9 June 52/4 In Germany *naturphilosophie* often coincided with extreme nationalism.

natyf, -yfe, -yff, -yve, obs. ff. NATIVE.

natyvyte, -tie, obs. forms of NATIVITY.

†'**naucify,** *v. Obs.*$^{-0}$ [ad. L. *nauci facĕre* (Plautus), f. *naucum* a trifling thing.] (See quot.)

1656 BLOUNT *Glossogr.*, *Naucifie*, to set nought by, to dis-esteem.

'**naucrar:** see next (quot. 1847).

naucrary ('nɔːkrərɪ). *Greek Antiq.* Also **nauk-**. [ad. Gr. ναυκραρία, f. ναύκραρος (in Hesychius ναύκλαρος), usually supposed to be a var. of ναύκληρος, but the etym. and original meaning are doubtful.] One of the smaller political divisions of the Athenian people.

1836 THIRLWALL *Greece* xi. II. 52 Solon..appears to have laid the foundation of the Attic navy, by charging the forty-eight sections, called *naucraries*, into which the tribes had been divided for financial purposes, each with the equipment of a galley, as well as with the mounting of two horsemen. **1847** GROTE *Greece* III. 71 The Naukrary is a local circumscription, composed of the Naukrars or principal householders (so the etymology seems to indicate). *Ibid.* 72 The forty-eight naukraries are thus a systematic subdivision of the four tribes.

naue, obs. form of NAVY.

naue, have not: see NAVE *v.*

nauen, variant of NAVIN, navy. *Obs.*

†'**naufragate,** *v. Obs. rare*$^{-1}$. [ad. ppl. stem of L. *naufragāre* to suffer shipwreck: see next.] *trans.* To wreck.

1686 CLENCHE *Peter's Suprem.* 123 Peter signifies..a Foundation,..an inexpugnable rock..A Rock able to.. naufragate all the lurid designs of empoisoned Hereticks.

†'**naufrage.** *Obs.* Also 5 **naw-**. [a. F. *naufrage* (1461), ad. L. *naufragium* for **nāvifragium*, f. *nāvi-s* ship + *frag-*, *frangĕre* to break.] Shipwreck: **a.** in figurative uses.

1480 CAXTON *Ovid's Met.* XI. xxi, To gyve her entresignes, by whych she may see appertly the nawfrage and peryll of her husbonde. *c* **1577** BUCHANAN *Let.* Wks. (S.T.S.) 57 Ye being anis escapit the tempestuous stormes and naufrage of mariage. **1628** SIR W. MURE *Fancies Farew.* Wks. (S.T.S.) I. 195 That impetuous streame, Where fynest wits haue frequent naufrage made. **1652** NEEDHAM tr. *Selden's Mare Cl.* 469 To the hazard of their State which hath lately scaped Naufrage. **1715** JANE BARKER *Exilius* (1736) Pref., To avoid such dangerous Naufrages, and fix their Affections where Duty and Merit require.

b. in literal sense. (Chiefly *Law.*)

1623 COCKERAM I, *Naufrage*, shipwracke. **1635** J. HAYWARD tr. *Biondi's Banish'd Virg.* I Thus then being certaine of naufrage. **1681** STAIR *Instit.* I. x. §24. 132 In no case is the borrower oblieged for any Accident, as Death, Naufrage, Burning, unless he hath undertaken that hazard. **1755** MAGENS *Insurances* II. 416 No Abandoning can be made, but in Case of Capture, Naufrage, Bulging, Stranding, Embargo..or an entire loss of the Thing insured.

†'**naufraged,** *ppl. a. Obs. rare.* [ad. F. *naufragé* (14th c.), ad. L. *naufragātus*: see NAUFRAGATE *v.*] Shipwrecked.

1490 CAXTON *Eneydos* xviii. 66 That tyme that thou come firste to me as a man exyled and naufraged. *Ibid.* xx. 72 Naufraged vpon the ryuage of the see.

†**nau'frageous,** *a. Obs. rare*$^{-1}$. [ad. F. *naufrageux*: see NAUFRAGE and -OUS.] In danger of shipwreck.

1694 MOTTEUX *Rabelais* v. (1737) 232 Our State's naufrageous and periclitating.

†'**naufragie.** *Obs. rare.* [ad. L. *naufragium.*] = NAUFRAGE a.

c **1380** WYCLIF *Serm.* Sel. Wks. II. 149 But siþen þes [suffragies] ben nawfragies, wel is him þat bieþ not. *c* **1440** *Gesta Rom.* I. lxv. 293 (Harl. MS.), þerfor seiyth Ierome,.. Penaunce is the secunde table after naufragie.

†'**naufragous,** *a. Obs. rare.* [f. NAUFRAG-E + -OUS: cf. It. *naufragoso.*] Causing shipwreck.

1615 T. ADAMS *Spir. Navig.* 36 It is the most dangerous shipwrack that this naufragous world can give us, the shipwrack of faith. **1656** *Artif. Handsom.* 33 That tempestuous and (oft) naufragous Sea, wherein youth and handsomeneses are commonly tossed.

†'**naufrague.** *Obs. rare.* [ad. Sp. *naufrago*, L. *naufragus.*] A shipwrecked person.

1681 RYCAUT tr. *Gracian's Critick* 4 The grateful Naufrague repeated the expressions of his thanks. *Ibid.* 5.

Naugahyde ('nɔːgəhaɪd). Also (erron.) **naugahide.** [f. *Nauga(tuk*, the name of a town in Connecticut, U.S.A., where rubber is manufactured + *-hyde*, modified form of HIDE *sb.*[1]] The proprietary name of a material consisting of a fabric base coated with a layer of rubber or vinyl resin and finished with a grain like that of leather, which is used in upholstery.

1937 *Official Gaz.* (U.S. Patent Office) 7 Dec. 41/2 United States Rubber Products, Inc... *Naugahyde* for upholstery material, more specifically fabric base which has been treated with rubber and other substances producing artificial leather. **1971** *Flying* Apr. 49/3 He is..a pilot's pilot ..for whom 'cockpit' means not a Naugahyde cell with air-conditioning, but a bucket seat and a parachute. **1973** H. NIELSEN *Severed Key* v. 58 The apartment was..finished in contemporary motel naugahide. **1974** *Anderson* (S. Carolina) *Independent* 22 Apr. 5B/3 (Advt.), Several Console Stereos. Modern sewing machines. One Duncan Phyfe sofa, covered in Red velvet. One 2 piece den set, covered in naugahyde.

nauger, obs. form of AUGER *sb.*[1]

naught (nɔːt), *sb.*, *a.*, and *adv.* Forms: *α.* 1 **náwuht,** 1, 3–4 **-wiht,** (3 **-wihht**), 4 **-wight;** 3–4 **nawit,** (4 **-wete**). *β.* 1 **nawht,** 1–3 **nauht, naht,** (3 **nah**), 2–3 **nacht,** 3–4 **naȝt,** (4 **naght;** 3 **naþt,** 5 **naht**), 4–5 **nauȝt(e,** 4 **nawȝt**), 4– **naught,** (6 **naugh**). *γ.* 1–3 **nawt,** 3, 6 **naut,** 6 **nawtt, nawlt.** [OE. *náwuht, -wiht*, f. *ná* NA *adv.*[1] + *wuht, wiht* WIGHT *sb.*; cf. OFris. *nawet, nauwet, nauet, naut.* In northern ME. texts the full form *nawight* may represent OE. *nánwiht* rather than *náwiht.* For the history of the forms belonging to the OE. variant *nówiht* see NOUGHT.]

A. *sb.* **1.** Nothing, nought. (Now *arch.*)

α. *c* **897** K. ÆLFRED *Gregory's Past. C.* xliv. 328 (Hatton) Me hyngrede, & ȝe me nawuht [*Cotton* nauht] ne sealdun etan. *c* **900** tr. *Bæda's Hist.* II. x. [xiii.] (1890) 134 Eallinga nawiht mæȝenes ne nyttnesse hafað sio æfæstnes. *c* **1000** *Ags. Ps.* (Th.) xiv. 5 Se þe þone awyrȝdan for nawuht hæfð. *a* **1240** *Saules Warde* in *O.E. Hom.* I. 255 Hwet se beo of heardes, ne drede ich nawiht nesches.

β. *c* **888** K. ÆLFRED *Boeth.* iii. §2 Ðis Mod..nauht elles nat butan gnornunga. **971** *Blickl. Hom.* 53 þa halȝan..þe on þyssum life naht ne sohton. *a* **1122** *O.E. Chron.* (Laud MS.) an. 1072 He þær naht ne funde þæs þe him þe bet wære. **1340** *Ayenb.* 131 þanne yefþ him god iuele þet mannes miȝte ne is naȝt and þet he ne may naȝt. *c* **1386** CHAUCER *Prol.* 756 Boold of his speche, and wys and wel ytaught, And of manhood him lakked right naught [*v.rr.* noȝt, nouht]. *c* **1450** *Merlin* 18 Leet my moder be in pese that naht knoweth of that thow puttest on hir. **1535** COVERDALE *2 Macc.* vii. 28 God made them and mans generacion of naught. **1568** GRAFTON *Chron.* II. 113 The Pope had the more hate vnto him, for that he had brought him vp of naught. **1629** MILTON *Hymn Nativ.* XXIV, Naught but profoundest Hell can be his shroud. **1697** DRYDEN *Virg. Georg.* IV. 572 Unconstrain'd he nothing tells for naught. **1738** SWIFT *Pol. Conversat.* 46 You have the old Proverb on your Side, Naught's ne'er in Danger. **1797** COLERIDGE *Christabel* I, Naught was green upon the oak, But moss and rarest mistletoe. **1885–94** R. BRIDGES *Eros & Psyche* July viii, Till seeing nothing lack'd and naught was theirs, Their happiness fell from them unawares.

b. In phr. *to bring*, †*do, come, go to naught.*

c **888** K. ÆLFRED *Boeth.* x, Ne eart þu no eallunga to nauhte ȝedon. *c* **1000** *Ags. Ps.* (Th.) lix. 11 He sona mæȝ ure fynd ȝedon fracoþe to nahte [= cvii. 12 to nawihte]. *a* **1175** *Cott. Hom.* 223 Forði is se man beter..þanne oðre ȝesceafte ..for þan þe hi alle ȝewrðeð to nachte. **1297** R. GLOUC. (Rolls) 9421 Hii asailede þe verste ost & broȝte almest to naȝte. **1535** COVERDALE *2 Esdras* i. 11 In yᵉ east haue I brought two landes and people to naught. **1611** COTGR., *Perir*,..to come to ruine, or to naught. **1668–9** PEPYS *Diary* 6 Mar., He joins with me in his fears that all will go to naught, as matters are now managed.

c. *to set at naught, set naught by*: see SET *v.*[1]

†**d.** *to call* (rarely *to speak*) all to naught, to abuse or decry vehemently. *Obs.*

Originally perh. = *all too naught*, altogether too bad.

1542 UDALL *Erasm. Apoph.* Table, Dionysius would call Aristippus foole and all to naught. **1559–1592** [see ALL *adv.* 12]. **1655** GURNALL *Chr. in Arm.* verse 14. xviii. § 1 (1669) 68/2 His enemies from this take advantage to speak him all to naught. **1705** HICKERINGILL *Priest-cr.* III. Wks. 1716 III. 151 Queen Elizabeth..reigned..above 30 Years after the Pope had call'd her all to naught.

†**e.** *to be naught*, to efface oneself, to keep quiet or withdraw. Usually in imperative. *Obs.*

1593 PEELE *Edw. I* E 2 b, Let go and be naught I say. **1600** SHAKS. *A.Y.L.* I. i. 39 Be better employed, and be naught a while. **1606** CHAPMAN *Gentl. Usher* Plays 1873 I. 289 Kisse her; yfaith you must; get you togither and be naughts awhile, get you together. *a* **1625** FLETCHER *Hum. Lieutenant* v. iii, So, get ye together, and be naught!

†**2.** Wickedness, evil, moral wrong, mischief. *Obs.* (In later use chiefly *to do naught.*)

c **897** K. ÆLFRED *Gregory's Past. C.* xxxv. 241 Ðonne mon onȝiet mid hwelcum stæpum ðæt nawht [L. *nequitia*] wæs ðurhtoȝen. *c* **1000** *Ags. Ps.* (Th.) lviii. 2 ȝenere me fram niþe naht [L. *iniquitatem*] fremmendra.

1560 DAUS tr. *Sleidane's Comm.* 61 The Magistrate doeth naught [L. *inique facit*], but you doe muche worse. **1594** SHAKS. *Rich. III*, I. i. 99, I tell thee Fellow, he that doth naught with her (excepting one) were best to do it secretly alone. **1649** LOVELACE *Poems* 72 Naught [shall] be ignote not so much out of Feare Of being punisht, as offending Her.

1656 SANDERSON *Serm.* (1689) 207 From doing nothing proceed to doing naught.

†b. That which is wrong or faulty in method.

1557 TUSSER *100 Points Husb.* xxxii, All soules that be thursty, bid threshe out for mawlt: well handled and tended, or els thou dost nawlt. 1578 LYTE *Dodoens* 38 Ignorant Apothecaries do dayly use it in steede of the right Cotyledon, wherein they do naught, and commit manifest errour. 1658 A. FOX *Würtz' Surg.* I. ii. 4 Naught will be naught, and never good, though it had been practised a thousand years.

3. With *a* and *pl.*

†a. A thing of no worth or value. *Obs. rare.*

Only in *pl.* adjectival predicate, prob. not derived from the similar OE. use of *náhtas* or *náhtes.*

1548 HALL *Chron., Hen. VIII* 186 The bokes are erronious and naughtes. 1552 LATIMER *Serm. Gosp.* xii. 219 These studies..and such other vayne desires are naughtes and foolishe.

†b. *pl.* Nothing, nought. *Obs. rare.*

1559 *Mirr. Mag., Dk. Suffolk* vii, To which I gaue nigh fiue times fyue assaultes, Tyl at the last they yelded it for naughtes. 1586 KYD *Wks.* (1901) 340 Thy crop of corne is tares auailing naughts.

c. *Arith.* A cipher, a nought.

1649 MILTON *Eikon.* xxvii. Wks. 1851 III. 513 After all thir paines and travell to be dissolv'd, and cast away like so many Naughts in Arithmetick. 1825 M. E. (*title*) Airy Nothings: or Scraps and Naughts, and Odd-cum-Shorts. 1879 MEREDITH *Egoist* xix, 'There is a figure naught', said he.

†d. An evil or wicked thing. (Cf. 2.) *Obs.*$^{-1}$

*a*1639 W. WHATELEY *Prototypes* II. xxix. (1640) 182 Here is revenge, filthinesse and fraud, and a number of naughts put together to make each other worse.

e. (From B. 2.) One who is bad.

1657 TRAPP *Comm. Esther* vii. 7 Unlesse it be *Harang*, that naughtiest of all naughts. 1854 MRS. GASKELL *North & S.* xviii, 'The law expenses would have been more than the hands themselves were worth—a set of ungrateful naughts!' said his mother.

B. *adj.* [Orig. the *sb.* in predicative use.] Freq. in the strengthened form ***stark naught***: see STARK.

1. Of no worth or value; good for nothing; worthless, useless, bad, poor.

*c*888 K. ÆLFRED *Boeth.* xxxvi. §7 Ic secȝe sie unmehtiȝ & eac ealles nauht. *c*1000 ÆLFRIC *Hom.* II. 232 ȝif ic me sylfne wuldriȝe, þonne bið min wuldor naht. *a*1250 *Owl & Night.* (Cott.) 1480 Oþer þe lauerd is wel aht, Oþer aswunde & nis naht. 1393 LANGL. *P. Pl.* C. XVIII. 74 Of muche moneye the metal is ryght naught. 1503 *Act 19 Hen. VII*, c. 6 The said Persons..mix good Metal and bad together, and make it naught. 1551 T. WILSON *Logike* (1580) 3 Logike of it self is good, when Sophistrie on the other side is naught. 1625 PURCHAS *Pilgrims* II. 1715 Their armour and weapons are very naught and weake, as well the one as the other. 1693 EVELYN *De la Quint. Compl. Gard.* II. 2 By Branches that are naught, I mean those that are of false Wood. 1738 SWIFT *Pol. Conversat.* 18 Tom sings well; but his Luck's naught. 1784 COWPER *Ep. J. Hill* 53 The punishment importing this, no doubt, That all was naught within. 1819 BYRON *Let. to Murray* 12 Aug., The poem will be naught. 1832 AUSTIN *Jurispr.* (1879) II. 692 Codes and codification are manifestly naught.

†b. Of no legal value; invalid. *Obs.*

*c*1449 PECOCK *Repr.* IV. iii. 430 And therfore God forbede that ech dede and ech gouernaunce schulde be holde nauȝt and badde. 1540 *Act 32 Hen. VIII*, c. 5 The said pretended mariage, which is of it selfe naught and of no force. 1632 SANDERSON *Serm.* 62 The election is *de jure nulla*, naught and voide. 1660 *Trial Regic.* 53 Your Plea is naught, illegal, and wicked, and ought not to be allowed.

c. Bad in condition or quality; not good for eating or drinking. ? *Obs.*

1588 KYD *Househ. Phil.* Wks. (1901) 271 Things, which.. wold become both hard and naught to eate without some kinde of liquor or conserues. 1609 BIBLE (Douay) *Jer.* xxiv. 3 The good figges, exceeding good, and the naughtie figges exceeding naught: which can not be eaten because they are naught. 1661 PEPYS *Diary* 29 Oct., We..should have been merry, but their wine was so naught..that we were not so. 1720 BP. HUTCHINSON *Witchcraft* xv. (ed. 2) 267 Which after the first taste he refused,..but said it was naught. 1813 C. MARSHALL *Garden.* xvii. (ed. 5) 288 The raspberry is quite naught [1798 very bad] when stale.

†d. Bad or wrong in method. *Obs. rare*$^{-1}$.

1597 MORLEY *Introd. Mus.* 80 It is verie naught, to ascend or descend in that manner.

†2. Morally bad; wicked; naughty. *Obs.*

1536 R. BEERLEY in *Four C. Eng. Lett.* (1880) 35 And mayck me wych am now nawtt to cum unto grace [and] goodnes. 1582 N.T. (Rhem.) *Matt.* vi. 23 But if thine eye be naught: thy whole body shal be darksome. 1603 DRAYTON *Bar. Wars* III. iii, A Man, as subtill, so corrupt and naught. 1656 SANDERSON *Serm.* (1689) 487 Where the Gods are naught, who can imagine the Religion should be good. 1706–7 FARQUHAR *Beaux' Strat.* II. i, Stay, stay, Brother, you shan't get off so; You were very naught last Night. 1740 RICHARDSON *Pamela* II. 253 There was no pleasing her; and I was a Creature, and Wench, and all that was naught.

†b. Immoral, vicious. *Obs.*

1550 ELYOT, *Aquariolus*,..a wyttall, that suffreth his wife to be naught. 1594 LYLY *Moth. Bomb.* I. i, Doest thou imagine thy mistres naught of her bodie? 1617 MIDDLETON & ROWLEY *Fair Quarrel* v. i, I say she is naught... Your intended bride is a whore. 1693 CONGREVE *Old Bach.* III. iv, I'll never see you again, 'cause you'd have me be naught.

†c. Const. *with* (one of the other sex). *Obs.*

1552 LATIMER *Serm. & Rem.* (Parker Soc.) 30 His mistress, perceiving his beauty,..would have him to be naught with her. 1606 HOLLAND *Sueton.* 3 But her afterward hee divorced, suspecting that she had beene naught with P. Clodivs. *a*1641 BP. MOUNTAGU *Acts & Mon.* (1642) 264 That he had, in his absence, been naught with Mariamne. 1699 T. C[OCKMAN] *Tully's Offices* (1706) 305 Upon a false Suspicion, that he had been naught with his Mother-in-law.

†3. Injurious, hurtful; unlucky. *Obs.*

1596 *Edward III*, I. i, In great affairs 'tis naught to use delay. 1620 MELTON *Astrolog.* 46 It is naught for any man to giue a paire of kniues to his sweet heart. 1658 A. FOX *Würtz' Surg.* II. iii. 52 That [diet] which is good for man proveth very naught to a woman.

†4. Lost, ruined. *Obs.*

1607 SHAKS. *Cor.* III. i. 231 Goe, get you to [y]our House; be gone, away, All will be naught else. 1624 FLETCHER *Rule a Wife* v. i, My cause was naught, for 'twas about your honour; And he that wrongs the innocent nere prospers. [1826 SCOTT *Woodst.* iii, All's naught, girl—and our evil days are come at last.]

C. *adv.*

†1. [Orig. the accusative of the *sb.* used adverbially: cf. AUGHT *sb.*^{2} C.] Not. See also NAT *adv.*

α. *c*897 K. ÆLFRED *Gregory's Past. C.* xliii. 314 (Hatton) Ne fæste ȝe ðæs nawuht me. *c*1200 ORMIN 15551 Þær bilæf þe Laferrd..acc nawihht lannge. *a*1225 *Leg. Kath.* 474 For þi þet te lare..ne helpeð nawiht eche lif to habben, ne ȝelpe ich nawiht þrof. *a*1300 *Cursor M.* 654 Yhon tre cum þou nawight to. 13.. *Ibid.* 24626 (Edinb.), Fra me wald þai nawit twin.

β. *c*888 K. ÆLFRED *Boeth.* v. §3 Nu ðu ne þearft þe nauht ondrædan. *c*1000 ÆLFRIC *Hom.* II. 18 Þæt fyr ne derede naht þam ðrim cnihtum. *a*1122 *O.E. Chron.* (Laud MS.) an. 1095 Naht be anan oððe twam. *c*1200 *Vices & Virtues* 35 On ðare oðre woreld and naht hier. *c*1250 *Kent. Serm.* in *O.E. Misc.* 28 Nacht on-lepiliche to day, ac alle þo daies i þo yere. 1297 R. GLOUC. (Rolls) 185 Þe gret evel ne comeþ naȝt þer þat me clupeþ þat holi fur. 1340 *Ayenb.* 103 Ane man of huam me ne kan naȝt his name. 1390 GOWER *Conf.* II. 254 Medea, which foryat him naght, Was redy there.

γ. *c*1175 *Lamb. Hom.* 63 God..ȝife us..þet we ne fallen naut ine sunne. *a*1240 *Sawles Warde* in *O.E. Hom.* I. 257 Þah ha ne trust nawt on hire ahne wepnen.

†2. [From B.] Badly; wrongly. *Obs.*

1549 COVERDALE, etc. *Erasm. Par. Phil.* 8, I rushe not here awaye and there awaye rashely I care not whither, for he loseth his game, that runneth naught. 1552 LATIMER *Serm.* (1562) 139 They that are so vsed to swearing, do very naught. 1625 B. JONSON *Staple of N.* I. Interm. i, How doe's the Play please you? *Censure.* Very scuruily, me thinks, and sufficiently naught.

naught, *v.* [f. prec.] †1. *trans.* To destroy. *Obs.*$^{-1}$

1340 *Ayenb.* 9 Þer by some bronches þet ne byeþ naȝt dyadlich zenne,..and þo me ssell naȝti and wyþdraȝe ase moche ase me may.

2. To bring to naught; to annihilate. Also **'naughting** *vbl. sb.*

1913 E. UNDERHILL *Mystic Way* 137 It is the final disestablishment and 'naughting' of the separate will. 1930 C. WILLIAMS *Poetry at Present* 85 The word death generally suggests a 'naughting' of all that we know. 1958 C. PEPLER *Eng. Relig. Heritage* IV. i. 225 Concentrating only on the outgoing features of simplicity in the naughting of self. 1958 *Times Lit. Suppl.* 10 Oct. 581/3 The Self, the One, in whom a Western mystic..seeks to lose his particular warped and transient self is not Himself naughted, is not naught.

naughtily ('nɔːtɪlɪ), *adv.* [f. NAUGHTY *a.*]

1. †a. Wickedly, viciously. *Obs.*

1552 LATIMER *Serm. & Rem.* (Parker Soc.) 38 They that ..burned their children, they did naughtily. 1577 NORTHBROOKE *Dicing* (1843) 10 They would not liue thus ydlely and naughtily as they do. 1611 COTGR., *Mauvaisement*,..lewdly, naughtily. 1632 LITHGOW *Trav.* x. 434 Their deserts are naught, and the fruite thereof as naughtily spent.

†b. Wrongfully, dishonestly. *Obs. rare.*

1622 FLETCHER *Beggars' Bush* IV. i, How cam'st thou by this mighty sum? If naughtily, I must not take it of thee.

†2. Badly, poorly. *Obs.*

1574 R. SCOT *Hop Gard.* To Rdr., It grieueth me dailye to see tyme yll spent,..good grounde naughtily applyed. 1600 HAKLUYT *Voy.* (1810) III. 509 Maiz and a roll of the same naughtily grinded. 1666 PEPYS *Diary* 26 Dec., Gosnell not singing, but a new wench that sings naughtily. *a*1693 *Urquhart's Rabelais* III. xvii. 137 That straw-thatch'd Cottage, scurvily built, naughtily movabled.

naughtiness ('nɔːtɪnɪs). [f. NAUGHTY *a.*]

1. †a. Wickedness, viciousness, depravity. *Obs.*

1541 WYATT *Def.* Wks. (1861) p. xxxiv, That made me not hold my peace, when I might..improve his naughtiness. 1579 LYLY *Euphues* (Arb.) 152 Neither haue we a short life by Nature, but we make it shorter by naughtynesse. 1646 J. HALL *Horæ Vac.* 119 'Tis..dangerous to cut any naughtinesse before children. 1677 W. HUBBARD *Narrative* 11 He was..forced to acknowledge that it was the naughtiness of his own heart, that put him upon that Rebellion.

b. Waywardness, disobedience.

1740–1 RICHARDSON *Pamela* (1742) 456 There was a sad End of all the Four ungracious Children,..and God punished their Naughtiness. 1833 *Mem. Departed Friend* 55 Not to fret over every little childish fit of naughtiness she has. 1871 M. COLLINS *Mrq. & Merch.* II. iv. 90 What would Miss Pinnock say, if she confessed her naughtiness to her?

c. A naughty act or trait.

1882 SERJT. BALLANTINE *Exper.* xiv. I. 174 Homburg... Its beauties and its naughtinesses have been often described.

†2. The state or condition of being bad, faulty, or defective in some respect. *Obs.*

1550 HARVEL in Froude *Hist. Eng.* (1881) IV. 511 [Huge bales of English goods were lying unsold upon the wharves] through the naughtiness of the making. 1579 FULKE *Refut. Rastel* 740 But to aunswere the naughtinesse of the argument, I say [etc.]. 1600 SURFLET *Countrie Farme* III. xxxiv. 500 Many times..the fruit is spoiled and lost, by the naughtines of the ground. 1658 A. FOX *Würtz' Surg.* III. iii. 225 A Wound that looks well,..yet the Patient..groweth weaker, it intimates the naughtiness of the medicine. 1709–29 V. MANDEY *Syst. Math. Statics* 756 To find out the naughtiness of deceitful Beams.

†**'naughtly**, *adv. Obs.* Also **naughtely**. [f. NAUGHT *a.* + -LY^2.] = NAUGHTILY.

1530 PALSGR. 839/2 Naugthely, *mallement.* 1563 *Mirr. Mag., Glendour* ix, Thus did I for want of better wit, Because my parents naughtly brought me vp. 1575 CHURCHYARD *Chippes* (1817) 134 Before diuers Skotishmen had naughtly discharged certayne shot at him. 1609 BIBLE (Douay) *Susanna* i. 61 They did to them as they had dealt naughtely against their neighbour.

naughty ('nɔːtɪ), *a.* Also 4 **nauȝty**. [f. NAUGHT *sb.* + -Y^1.]

†1. Having or possessing naught; poor, needy.

1377 LANGL. *P. Pl.* B. VI. 226 Alle maner of men..That nedy ben and nauȝty, helpe hem with þi godis. *Ibid.* VII. 72 He wolde ȝiue þat an other, þat were more nedy þan he [*R.* nedyer and nauȝtier].

2. †a. Of persons: Morally bad, wicked. *Obs.*

1529 MORE *Dyaloge* I. Wks. 155/2 Origene..neither was a naughty man nor vnlerned in scripture. *a*1586 SIDNEY *Arcadia* II. (1629) 129 A Prince of great courage and beauty, but fostered vp in bloud by his naughtie father. *a*1677 BARROW *Serm.* Wks. 1716 I. 96 A most vile flagitious man, a sorry and naughty governor as could be. 1699 T. C[OCKMAN] *Tully's Offices* (1706) 257 'Tis a villainous Error of some naughty Men.

absol. *c*1580 SIDNEY *Ps.* XXXVII. xiv, The naughty borrowes, payeng not.

b. Of children: Wayward, disobedient, given to doing wrong. Also playfully applied to older persons in mild reproach or disapproval. Also, ***naughty naughty***: a reprimand used to a child; also used jocularly designating disapproval of something, *spec.* concerning sex.

*a*1633 G. HERBERT *Jacula Prudentum* Wks. (1857) 309 A naughty child is better sick than whole. 1711 SWIFT *Lett.* (1767) III. 147 Go, get you gone, naughty girl, you are well enough. 1778 MME. D'ARBLAY *Diary* Sept. My sweet, naughty Mrs. Thrale looked delighted for me. 1812 H. & J. SMITH *Rej. Addr., Baby's Debut* v, O naughty Nancy Lake, Thus to distress your aunt..! 1865 KINGSLEY *Herew.* xix, They were the naughty young housecarles of his own troop. 1882 *National Police Gaz.* (U.S.) 4 Nov. 10/1 Those naughty naughty parsons up and at it again. 1889 *Sat. Rev.* 23 Feb. 210/2 When a champion of Home Rule behaves like a very naughty child. 1938 I. GOLDBERG *Wonder of Words* viii. 150 To a child..we say, 'Nightie-nightie'. Or, if it has been mischievous, 'Naughty-naughty'. 1940 'G. ORWELL' *Inside Whale* 133 From a mere account of the subject-matter of *Tropic of Cancer* [by Henry Miller] most people would probably assume it to be no more than a bit of naughty-naughty left over from the 'twenties. 1946 —— *Crit. Ess.* 127 The naughty-naughty touches in Dali's autobiography.

†c. Of an animal: Vicious. *Obs. rare*$^{-1}$.

1586 A. DAY *Eng. Secretary* I. (1625) 130 An Ox of mine, being a naughty beast, through the default of mine owne fence, hath goared a Cow of your Worships.

3. a. Of actions, conduct, places, things, etc.: Characterized by moral badness or wickedness; bad, wrong, blameworthy, improper. In mod. use as a term of mild or playful censure (cf. 2 b).

1536 CROMWELL in Merriman *Life & Lett.* (1902) II. 38 Half of that whiche hath ben there rather spoyled from hym by naughty meanes. 1560 DAUS tr. *Sleidane's Comm.* 27 Naughtie and Pestilent bokes should be burned. 1603 SHAKS. *Meas. for M.* II. i. 77 It is a naughty house. 1620 *Form Ordaining Min.* in *Misc. Wodrow Soc.* (1844) 600 This naughtie world. *a*1674 CLARENDON *Surv. Leviath.* (1676) 207 This naughty and impious discourse. 1715 DE FOE *Fam. Instruct.* I. i. (1841) I. 31 I'm sure she would not do a naughty thing. 1740 W. SEWARD *Jrnl.* 3 To prepare us for going abroad into a naughty World. 1792 BURNS *Rights of Woman*, A time, when rough rude man had naughty ways. 1861 FINLAY *Hist. Gk. Rev.* I. I. iii. 74 Euphrosyne..had neglected the study of the lives of the saints, and turned her attention to the naughty reading in the Greek classics. 1871 M. COLLINS *Mrq. & Merch.* II. iv. 90 It was very naughty of her, she felt aware. 1884 *World* 20 Aug. 5/2 Democracy is a naughty word.

Comb. 1581 PETTIE tr. *Guazzo's Civ. Conv.* I. (1586) 28 Certaine naughtie tongued fellowes vnder the maske of modestie saie they will not name him whom they reprehend. *a*1586 SIDNEY *Arcadia* IV. (1629) 432 For the naughty minded wretches.

b. ***the naughty nineties*** (see quot. 1970).

1925 R. LE GALLIENNE *Romantic '90s* iv. 162 'The '90s' are usually spoken of as if they had only one colour: the 'yellow' '90s, or the 'naughty' '90s, or the 'decadent' '90s. 1930 SELLAR & YEATMAN *1066 & All That* lix. 111 Oscar Wilde..was the leader of a set of disgusting old gentlemen called 'the naughty nineties'. 1937 *Jrnl. R. Aeronaut. Soc.* XLI. 128 He is carrying us back into the nineties of last century..(today I note referred to as the 'naughty nineties'!). 1939 *Burlington Mag.* Apr. 200/2 He was essentially a 'naughty 'nineties' figure. 1970 *Brewer's Dict. Phr. & Fable* (rev. ed.) 748/1 *Naughty Nineties, The*, the 1890s in England, when the puritanical Victorian code of behaviour and conduct gave way in certain wealthy and fashionable circles to growing laxity in sexual morals, a growing cult of hedonism, and a more light-hearted approach to life.

†4. a. Bad, inferior, not up to the proper or usual standard or quality. *Obs.* (common *c*1540–1650, in various applications.)

In quot. 1799 used in place of Sc. *nochty*, NOUGHTY.

1526 TINDALE *Wks.* (Parker Soc.) I. 510 As this is a naughty argument, so is the other. 1542–3 *Act 34 & 35 Hen. VIII*, c. 10 §2 Putting the same naughtie ware to sale secretly. 1583 STUBBES *Anat. Abus.* II. (1882) 24 Some put in naughty wool, and cause it to be spun and drawne into a very small thred. 1621 BURTON *Anat. Mel.* III. i. ii (1651) 412 Thou wilt not have bad coin, bad soil, a naughty tree, but all good. 1683 MOXON *Mech. Exerc., Printing* XXIV. ¶19 If he meets with naughty Sheets..as torn, or stain'd, &c. he

Prints them not. *Ibid.* 383 The Compositer will bow the Letter, and pop it into a Waste Box in the Case, where he puts all naughty Letters. **1799** J. ROBERTSON *Agric. Perth* 245 There may happen to be a piece of naughty land,.. whose barren appearance is an eyesore.

Comb. **1577** B. GOOGE *Heresbach's Husb.* IV. (1586) 169 The vnfruitfull and naughtie coloured, and the otherwise faultie, ought cheefely to be fatted.

b. Of articles of food or drink: Of bad quality, in bad condition. Now *rare*.

1535 COVERDALE *Jer.* xxiv. 2 In the other maunds were very naughtie figes, which might not be eaten. **1584** COGAN *Haven Health* lii. (1636) 68 Garlick.. is good for them that travaile.. if they happen to drinke naughty corrupt water. **1639** T. DE GRAY *Compl. Horsem.* 103 Peccant humours.. doe proceed of naughty meat. **1685** J. CHAMBERLAYNE *Coffee, Tea & Choc.* 43, I perceive, that it [tea] is commonly very old and naughty. **1896** A. D. COLERIDGE *Eton in Forties* 209 The bigaroon cherries.. were fraudulent, sour, and naughty throughout.

†**c.** Bad *for* something. *Obs. rare*$^{-1}$.

1573 TUSSER *Husb.* (1878) 120 Ground grauellie, sandie, and mixed with clay, is naughtie for hops.

†**5.** Of weather: Bad, nasty. *Obs. rare.*

1541 WYATT *Def.* Wks. (1861) p. xxiii, Coming in a boat from Aquas-Mortes, both in hazard of the Moors and naughty weather. **1605** SHAKS. *Lear* III. iv. 116 Prithee Nunckle be contented, 'tis a naughtie night to swimme in.

†**6. a.** Bad in respect of health; unhealthy; connected with ill health. *Obs.*

1572 ABP. PARKER *Corr* (Parker Soc.) 412 In better health than I in a naughty body feel. **1578** LYTE *Dodoens* 56 The juyce.. draweth downe from the head phlegmatike and naughtie humors. **1597** GERARDE *Herbal* I. lxxxvi. 138 It heateth the bodie, ingendreth naughtie blood. **1656** RIDGLEY *Pract. Physick* 12 Then followeth a Feaver, and a Troup of most naughty symptoms.

†**b.** Applied to bodily ailments, etc. *Obs.*

1578 LYTE *Dodoens* I. xiii. 21 Butter Burre.. cureth all naughty Vlcers. **1643** J. STEER tr. *Exp. Chyrurg.* iv. 9 They .. do cause a rotten ulcer and naughty Scar. **1657** W. COLES *Adam in Eden* cclxxxiii, Being mixed with Tar it cureth the naughty scurfe of the Head.

†**7.** Unpleasant, disagreeable. *Obs. rare.*

1578 LYTE *Dodoens* II. xxv. 176 Both in their leaves and floures of a naughtie, strong, and unpleasant savour. **1600** SURFLET *Countrie Farme* II. I. 324 Boxe in as much as it is of a naughtie smell,.. is to be left of and not dealt withall.

†**8.** Inherently bad or faulty. *Obs.*

1554 PHILPOT *Exam. & Writ.* (Parker Soc.) 402 As with the good corn naughty cockle and barren weeds do spring together. **1580** BARET *Alv.* H 417 Naughtie poison [*impia venena*] is hid with sweete honie, or Sugar. **1658** A. FOX *Würtz' Surg.* II. xxiii. 142 Touching the Saltpeter.., its naughty humidity is to be taken from it.

9. (For Sc. *nochty.*) Unsubstantial; insignificant.

1696 in Aubrey *Misc.* (1721) 211 A shadowy Substance, or such naughty, and Imperceptible thing, as can.. scarcely be discerned by the Eye. **1806** FORSYTH *Beauties Scotl.* IV. 521 The tenants.. have a very few sheep of an inferior naughty size.

naughty ('nɔːtɪ), *sb.* [f. the adj.]

1. *to do the naughty* (*slang*): to behave in a sexually promiscuous way. Similarly *to go naughty*.

1869 F. HALL in D. Lyndesay *Works* IV. 498 The wealth of the prelates keeps our daughters unwedded. And some of them go naughty. **1902** FARMER & HENLEY *Slang* V. 20/2 Shop and working girls in large towns sometimes say they work for their living, but do the naughty for their clothes. **1937** PARTRIDGE *Dict. Slang* 553/1 *Naughty, do the,* play the whore; to coït (of women only).

2. *Austral.* and *N.Z. colloq.* or *slang.* (An act of) sexual intercourse. Hence as *v. trans.*, to have sexual intercourse with.

1959 D. NILAND *Big Smoke* vii. 169 The woman giggled. .. 'Come on, what about it?' Ocker shook his head, grinning. 'I'd like to oblige, but I can't... It's in me contract, no leaving the job for a naughty.' **1961** PARTRIDGE *Dict. Slang* Suppl. 1195/2 *Naughty, v.*: To coït with... 'He naughties her.' **1962** *Times Lit. Suppl.* 12 Oct. 793/4 Would you please whisper in the ear of the young lady who reviewed *The Stuart Case* in your issue of August 10 that 'to have naughty'.. is throughout the South Seas the polite and strict analogue of 'to have sexual intercourse'. **1963** F. HARDY *Legends from Benson's Valley* 11, I smiled, remembering his oft-repeated remark: 'I get a lot of knock backs but I get a lot of naughties.' **1967** F. SARGESON *Hangover* vii. 55 He read: 'We'll naughty anyone. No, not on your life, not after Coral.' **1969** *Private Eye* 25 Apr. 12 What bloody fun have I had? Eight kiddies and two more on the way and I haven't even negotiated a naughty!

naughty ('nɔːtɪ), *adv.* [f. NAUGHTY *a.*] In a naughty or improper manner.

1898 J. D. BRAYSHAW *Slum Silhouettes* 142 He looked a reg'lar dook. He'd a pair o' lavinder-coloured bell-bottom trowsis, cut werry naughty. **1919** MENCKEN *Amer. Lang.* 228 The child behaved naughty. **1922** JOYCE *Ulysses* 441 Naughty cruel I was.

naughty pack. *Obs.* exc. *dial.* Also 6–7 **naughtipack(e, naughtie-,** etc. [f. NAUGHTY *a.*: cf. PACK *sb.*[1] 4. The adj. is freq. hyphened to, or written as one with, the noun.]

†**1.** A woman of bad character. *Obs.*

1530 PALSGR. 632/1 The counsayle of one naughtypacke [F. *une ribaulde*] may make a wenche to bolde. **1577** tr. *Bullinger's Decades* (1592) 868 Will not all men crie out that shee is a naughtipacke and an adulteresse? **1600** HOLLAND *Livy* XXVI. xii. 592 A Capuan wench.., a naughtie-pack and an harlot. **1638** FORD *Fancies* III. ii, 'Tis scarce possible To distinguish one of these same naughty packs From true and arrant ladies. **1738** SWIFT *Pol. Conversat.* 106, I never heard she was a naughty Pack. **1743** in Howell *State Trials* (1813) XVII. 1159 Until my lord had mentioned she was his wife, he took her to be a naughty pack.

†**2.** A wicked or dissolute man. *Obs.*

1549 COVERDALE, etc. *Erasm. Par. Titus* 28 Wherfore rebuke such naughtypackes earnestly, that they may ones waxe good. **1571** GOLDING *Calvin on Ps.* xii. 9 The naughtipacks or the ofskowrings of men. **1618** *Barnevelt's Apol.* c 3 This base, impudent, and vaine-glorious fellow, this periur'd and adulterous naughty-packe. **1677** W. HUGHES *Man of Sin* III. ii. 31 Monk Ailsi (like a naughty-pack as he was) would never show that respect unto it.

3. *dial.* A naughty child or person.

1828 *Craven Gloss.* **1869** *Lonsdale Gloss.*

naujakasite (naʊjəˈkɑːzaɪt). *Min.* [f. *Naujakasik*, a point on the southern coast of Tunugdliarfik Fiord, Greenland + -ITE[1].] A hydrated silicate of sodium, iron, and aluminium (with substitution by other metals), $(Na,K)_6(Fe^{II},Mn,Ca)(Al,Fe^{III})_4Si_8O_{26}.H_2O$, which is found as white, platy, monoclinic crystals.

1933 O. B. BØGGILD in *Meddelelser om Grønland* XCII. IX. 7 Among the minerals collected by G. Flink on his mineralogical journey in 1897 there is a specimen labelled 'Chorite?' by Flink. The locality is stated to be Naujakasik. .. The specimen containing the naujakasite was probably found loose on the ground. **1960** *Mineral. Abstr.* XIV. 370/2 Naujakasite, formerly only known from a loose boulder, has now been found in situ at Tuperssuatsiaq and the northern part of the Ilímaussaq batholith. **1967** *Meddelelser om Grønland* CLXXXI. VI. 14 Naujakasite alters easily through several stages to analcite.

naukrar(y: see NAUCRAR(Y.

†**naul,** anglicized form of NAULUM. *Obs. rare*$^{-1}$.

1724 STUKELEY *Itin Curiosum* 94 When we had.. paid our naul to the inexorable ferryman.

†**naul(e, naull,** obs. variants of AWL.

1530 TINDALE *Exod.* xxi. 6 Then let his master.. bore his eare thorow with a naule. **1575** *Gamm. Gurton* III. i. 6 Hays lent me here his naull to set the gyb forward. **1607** S. COLLINS *Serm.* (1608) 20 The Naule was vsed.. to bore-through the eare of him [etc.].

naule, obs. form of NAVEL.

†**naulizament.** *Obs. rare.* [ad. med.L. **naulizament-um* (= F. *nolisement*, It. *noleggiamento*), f. *naulizare, -sare, -giare* (= F. *noliser*, †*nauliser*, It. *noleggiare*), f. *naul-um* (see next).] Freighting of a vessel.

1533 in R. G. Marsden *Sel. Pl. Crt. Adm.* (1894) I. 93 Their to dyscharge hur burden accordyng to the fforme of her contracte of naulyzament. *Ibid.* 94 Naulizamentt.

‖**'naulum.** *Obs.* [L. *naulum* (also *naulon*), ad. Gr. ναῦλον (also ναῦλος), f. ναῦς ship.] Passage-money, fare.

1596 NASHE *Saffron Walden* F j b, I hearing the fellow so forlorne.., gaue him his Charons *Naulum* or ferry three half pence. **1636** HEYWOOD *Love's Mistress* V. i, My sop, hast thou thy naulum Ferryman? **1677** T. KIRK in *Thoresby's Corr.* (1832) II. App. 403 At Newsam Ferry we drunk a naulum with Charon.

‖**naumachia** (nɔːˈmeɪkɪə). *Rom. Antiq.* Pl. **-iæ,** †**-ias.** [L. *naumachia*, a. Gr. ναυμαχία, f. ναῦς ship + μάχη fight.]

1. A mimic representation of a sea-fight.

1596 HARINGTON *Metam. Ajax* E iij, All the pastime he & his friends should haue had at a Naumachia or sea-game. **1709** MRS. MANLEY *Secret Mem.* (1720) IV. 272 Those noble Appearances, Naumachias, the Circus, Assemblies! Glories of former Reigns. **1748** H. WALPOLE *Let. to Conway* 6 Oct., The superiority that his firework will have over the Roman naumachia. **1814** SIR R. WILSON *Priv. Diary* (1861) II. 368 An immense oblong building in the interior of which there is space for horse-races and naumachia or sea-fights. **1840** *Penny Cycl.* XVI. 107/2 Claudius exhibited a naumachia on the lake Fucinus.

2. A place specially constructed for the exhibition of mock sea-fights; esp. a building enclosing an artificial piece of water for this purpose.

1617 MORYSON *Itin.* I. 132 Under the Church.. is the Naumachia of Nero, that is a place to represent Navall fights. **1689** EVELYN *Let. to Pepys* 12 Aug., Their famous temples,.. circuses, naumachias, bridges. **1727–38** CHAMBERS *Cycl.* s.v., There were several naumachias at Rome... Nero's naumachia served for the reverse of his medals. **1774** WRAXALL *Tour North. Europe* (1775) 3 The venerable remains of amphitheatres, temples and naumachiae. **1841** W. SPALDING *Italy & It. Isl.* I. 390 After his accession we hear of no more real fights in the naumachiæ.

†**'naumachy.** *Obs.* Also 7 **-ie.** [Anglicized form of prec., or ad. F. *naumachie* (1550).]

1. = NAUMACHIA 1. Also *fig.*

1606 HOLLAND *Sueton.* 17 To set out the Naumachie or naval battaile, there was a place digged for a great poole. *a* **1658** LOVELACE *Luc. Posth.* (1659) 43 And now the Naumachie Begins, Close to the surface. **1681** COTTON *Wonders of Peake* 84 A Pacifick Sea expanded lies A liquid Theater for Naumachies.

2. = NAUMACHIA 2.

1600 HOLLAND *Livy* 1397 In which place before-time likely it is, that Augustus had his Naumachie. **1621** BURTON *Anat. Mel.* II. ii. IV. (1651) 273 The Romans had their feasts, Playes, Naumachies, places for Sea fights.

naumannite ('nɔː-, 'naʊmənaɪt). *Min.* [Named 1845 after Prof. *Naumann.*] (See quot. 1882.)

1849 NICOL *Min.* 471 Naumannite... Easily solvable in concentrated nitric acid. **1882** DANA *Min. & Lith.* (ed. 4) 118 Naumannite, a selenide of silver and lead in iron-black cubes and massive.

†**naundiren,** obs. form of ANDIRON.

1408 *Durham Acc. Roll* in *Eng. Hist. Rev.* XIV. 518 In iii towirens, iii porres alias naundirens.

naunt (nɑːnt). Now *dial.* or *arch.* [var. of AUNT, with *n* transferred from *myn* 'mine': see N 3 b for earlier examples.] Aunt.

1621 FLETCHER *Pilgrim* IV. i, Pr'ythee, keep on thy way, good naunt. **1632** HEYWOOD *2nd Pt. Iron Age* IV. i, If shee doe but take After mine old Naunt Hellen. **1679** DRYDEN *Limberham* I. i, The easiest fool I ever knew, next my naunt of fairies in the Alchemist. **1737–42** SHENSIONE *Schoolmistress* vii, Goody, good woman, gossip, n'aunt,.. Or dame, the sole additions she did hear. **1823** SCOTT *Peveril* xxvi, Naunt and she will soon bend bows on each other.

'nauntle, *v. dial.* [Of obscure origin.] **a.** *trans.* To raise, rear. **b.** *intr.* To rise up, strut.

For other uses, see the *Eng. Dial. Dict.* s.v. *Nantle.*

1820 CLARE *Rur. Life* (ed. 3) 189 The daisy nauntles up its head. **1821** —— *Vill. Minstr.* I. 210 The steeple's taper stretch.., nauntling high and proud.

Hence **'nauntly** *a.*, strutting.

1827 CLARE *Sheph. Cal.* 29 Not far behind them struts the nauntly crow.

†**nau'pegical,** *a. Obs. rare*$^{-1}$. [f. Gr. ναυπηγικ-ός + -AL[1].] Pertaining to ship-building.

1678 CUDWORTH *Intell. Syst.* 155 If the Naupegical Art [*tr.* ἡ ναυπηγική], that is the Art of the Shipwright, were in the Timber it self.

†**naupegy.** *Obs. rare.* [ad. Gr. ναυπηγία, f. ναῦς ship + πηγνύειν to fix.] Ship-building.

1570 J. DEE *Math. Pref.* d iiij b, Three principall, necessary Mechanicall Artes. Namely Howsing, Fortification, and Naupegie.

nauplial ('nɔːplɪəl), *a. Zool.* [f. NAUPLI-US + -AL[1].] Characteristic of a nauplius.

1877 WOODWARD in *Encycl. Brit.* VI. 652/2 The immature Crustacean, in passing through its nauphal and zoëal stages, may moult its skin six or seven times.

naupliar ('nɔːplɪə(r)), *a.* [f. NAUPLI(US + -AR[1].] = NAUPLIAL *a.*

1961 in WEBSTER. **1963** [see COPEPODID *a.*]. **1975** *Sci. Amer.* Mar. 80/2 In some instances there is enough wax in the egg to carry *E*[*uchaeta*] *japonica* through the entire six naupliar stages. **1975** *Nature* 17 Apr. 591/2 The freshwater layer of the lake has been colonised by a calanoid copepod, *Pseudoboeckella* sp. (average concentration recorded 0.5 individuals l^{-1}, including naupliar stages).

'naupliiform, *a. Zool.* [f. NAUPLI-US + -(I)FORM.] Having the form of a nauplius.

1869 W. S. DALLAS tr. *F. Müller's Facts for Darwin* 17 Early Naupliiform stages of the higher Crustacea. **1870** H. A. NICHOLSON *Man. Zool.* (1875) 236 The larvæ are 'Naupliiform', with an ovate unsegmented body.

‖**nauplius** ('nɔːplɪəs). *Zool.* Pl. **nauplii** ('nɔːplɪaɪ). [L. *nauplius* a kind of shellfish, or *Nauplius*, a. Gr. Ναύπλιος, a son of Poseidon.]

†**a.** O. F. Müller's name for a supposed genus of crustaceans. *Obs.* **b.** A larval stage of development in some of the lower crustaceans, characterized by an unsegmented body with a dorsal shield, an unpaired median eye, and three pairs of legs.

1836 *Penny Cycl.* V. 340/2 Some time afterwards.. they acquire another pair of feet; they are then the genus *Nauplius* of the same author [Müller]. **1869** W. S. DALLAS tr. *F. Müller's Facts for Darwin* 62 The Nauplii of the Cirripedia have to undergo several moults whilst in that form. **1877** HUXLEY *Anat. Inv. Anim.* vi. 290 The *Pectostraca*.. leave the egg as a *Nauplius*, provided with three pairs of limb-like appendages.

attrib. **1869** W. S. DALLAS tr. *F. Müller's Facts for Darwin* 84 The Cyclopes of our fresh waters were excluded in the Nauplius-form. *Ibid.* 88 Beneath this Nauplius-skin a very different larva lies ready prepared. **1888** ROLLESTON & JACKSON *Anim. Life* 538 A Nauplius-stage. *Ibid.*, An azygos Nauplius-eye.

nauquayre: see NAQUAIRE.

naure-quare: see NAWER.

Nauruan ('naʊrʊən), *sb.* and *a.* [f. *Nauru*, an island in the western Pacific + -AN.] **A.** *sb.* A native or inhabitant of Nauru. **B.** *adj.* Of or pertaining to Nauru.

1921 R. D. RHONE in *Nat. Geogr. Mag.* Dec. 563/2 The Nauruans have never been cannibals, but they had the reputation of being savage warriors. *Ibid.* 576/1 In the Nauruan legends the coconut.. either owes its eyes and mouth to human ancestry or man owes his eyes and mouth to the coconut. **1925** *Windsor Mag.* Mar. 398/2 A middle-aged Nauruan, clad only in a *ridi*, presents an impressive and ponderous appearance... But.. nothing could be more charming than a Nauruan maiden. **1935** A. F. ELLIS *Ocean Islands & Nauru* v. 41 From time immemorial a special kind of fish has been cultivated by the Nauruans in this lagoon. **1951** L. MASON in O. W. Freeman *Geogr. Pacific* x. 296 About a thousand Nauruans were transferred in 1943 to Truk... A postwar sequel in Nauruan history has to do with its new status as a Trust Territory. **1963** *Austral. Encycl.* VI. 257 In the past most of the Nauruans were skilled fishermen. **1969** *Age* (Melbourne) 24 May 2/4 The Acting Chief Secretary (Mr. Manson) warned yesterday that Victorians taking part in the Nauruan pools could face penalties of up to $100.

ˈnauscopy. *rare*⁻⁰. [ad. F. *nauscopie*, f. Gr. *ναῦ-ς* ship: see -SCOPY.] (See quot.)

1797 *Encycl. Brit.* XII. 776/1 *Nauscopy*, the art of discovering the approach of ships or the neighbourhood of land at a considerable distance. This pretended art was invented by a M. Bottineau..from the year 1782 to 1784. [**1847** in Webster and later Dicts.]

nausea (ˈnɔːʃɪə, ˈnɔːsɪə, ˈnɔːzɪə). [a. L. *nausea*, *nausia*, a. Gr. *ναυσία*, *ναυτία*, f. *ναῦς* ship.]

1. a. A feeling of sickness, with loathing of food and inclination to vomit.

1569 R. ANDROSE tr. *Alexis' Secr.* IV. I. 14 The disease called Nausea. **1590** BARROUGH *Meth. Phisick* (1596) 374 A certaine..disposition to vomit, called of the Latines Nausea. **1693** tr. *Blancard's Phys. Dict.* (ed. 2), *Nausea*, Loathing. **1719** QUINCY *Phys. Dict.* (1722) 41 The most grievous Nausea's and Vomitings. **1763** MACKENZIE in *Phil. Trans.* LIV. 74 This cold fit is soon accompanied with a loathing nausea and desire of vomiting. **1842** COMBE *Digestion* 32 Abstinence was again enforced and tartar emetic given to excite nausea. **1876** BRISTOWE *Th. & Pract. Med.* (1878) 752 Nausea and sickness, again, are frequent symptoms of dyspepsia.

b. Sea-sickness. (The original sense.)

1771 SMOLLETT *Humph. Cl.* 8 Aug., Most of the passengers were seized with a nausea. **1795** *Montford Castle* II. 101 The dispiriting nausea which attends a first voyage. **1861** *All Year Round* 13 July 372 Many of the kidnapped men were in agonies of nausea.

2. *transf.* A strong feeling of disgust, loathing, or aversion.

1619 W. SCLATER *Exp. 1 Thess.* To Rdr., The Nausea of some at home, whom no sermon pleaseth longer then it is in hearing. **1663** J. SPENCER *Prodigies* (1665) 58 That nausea which the tedious repetition of things present and familiar creates in the Soul of man. **1782** COWPER *Flatting Mill* 24 For truth is unwelcome..And unless you adorn it, a nausea follows. **1828** CARLYLE *Misc.* (1857) I. 161 Sated to nausea as we have been with the doctrines of Sentimentality. **1866** CRUMP *Banking* ix. 208 The winds of heaven unable to blow over them without nausea and loathing.

3. That which causes sickness or loathing.

1654 GAYTON *Pleas. Notes* 82 Stifled with the fumes and Nauseæ of his filthy Caldron. **1885** *Harper's Mag.* Mar. 520/2 To escape at once a painful monotony and a nausea of gewgaws.

4. Special Comb.: **nausea gas**, a gas used to induce nausea in people.

1966 *Guardian* 10 May 12/4 US Army planes dropped nearly three and a quarter tons of nausea gas on the suspected jungle headquarters of the Vietcong yesterday. **1970** *Globe & Mail* (Toronto) 28 Sept. 17/1 Soldiers fired nausea gas to drive back a stone-throwing mob..in Belfast.

ˈnauseant, *sb.* and *a. Med.* [ad. L. *nauseant-*, pres. pple. of *nauseāre* to NAUSEATE.]

A. *sb.* A substance which produces nausea.

1846 in WORCESTER. **1851** DUNGLISON *Med. Dict.* s.v., Nauseants are..valuable remedies in diseases of excitement. **1875** H. C. WOOD *Therap.* (1879) 434 As a nauseant the dose is from two to five grains.

B. *adj.* Producing nausea.

1864 *Syd. Soc. Year-bk. Med.* 442 Agents which are.. nauseant and emetic when given in large quantities. **1876** BARTHOLOW *Mat. Med.* (1879) 455 Poke is nauseant and emetic.

†**ˈnauseate**, *sb. Obs. Med.* [ad. L. *nauseāt-um*, neut. pa. pple. of *nauseāre*: see next.] = NAUSEANT *sb.* Also *fig.*

1660 tr. *Paracelsus Archidoxis* I. IV. 57 What need is there of many Writings, to stir up a nauseate, both to our selves and Readers. **1683** TRYON *Way to Health* 544 Certain Syrups, Epidemick Water, and other like Slops, which are all great Nauseates to Nature, even in the Healthiest state.

nauseate (ˈnɔːʃɪeɪt, ˈnɔːsɪeɪt, ˈnɔːzɪeɪt), *v.* Also 7 **nawseate, nautiate.** [f. L. *nauseāt-*, ppl. stem of L. *nauseāre*, f. *nausea*, after Gr. *ναυσιᾶν*, *ναυτιᾶν*.]

1. a. *trans.* To reject (food, etc.) with loathing or a feeling of nausea.

1646 SIR T. BROWNE *Pseud. Ep.* III. xxv. (1686) 137 Many [dishes] are commended..in one age, which are..nauseated in another. **1685** BOYLE *Enq. Notion Nat.* v. 166 'Tis.. profitable for man, that his stomach should nauseate or reject things that have a loathsome taste or smell. *a* **1703** BURKITT *On N.T.* Matt. xiii. 52 Lest the household by always feeding upon the same dish, do nauseate it. **1790** MORRIS in Sparks *Life & Writ.* (1832) II. 46 It is more the taste of the medicine which they nauseate than the quantity of the dose. **1811** A. T. THOMSON *Lond. Disp.* (1818) 119 Many stomachs are apt to nauseate it at that time. **1859** I. TAYLOR *Logic in Theol.* 134 Nauseating the sumptuous dainties of royal banquets.

b. *fig.* To loathe, abhor, feel a strong aversion to (something).

1654 H. L'ESTRANGE *Chas. I* (1655) 3 The Prince began to nauseate the match, and to meditate all honourable evasions. **1699** BURNET *39 Art.* iv. 62 The Herd among the Gentiles.. must have nauseated the Christian Simplicity. **1755** YOUNG *Centaur* vi. Wks. 1757 IV. 250 The grave reader, who nauseates it, sacrifices..the substance of what is right. **1795** MACKNIGHT *Apost. Epist.* (1820) III. 274 The people nauseated the wholesome doctrines of true piety. **1874** PUSEY *Lent. Serm.* 274 Men nauseate..the love of God, because they know it not.

2. To affect with nausea or aversion; to create a loathing in.

1654 EARL MONM. tr. *Bentivoglio's Wars Flanders* 230 Which we thought good to touch upon here only, not to nawseate the Reader. **1692** WASHINGTON tr. *Milton's Def. People* M.'s Wks. 1851 VIII. 194 Which Book will nauseate a great many Readers to death. **1719** DE FOE *Crusoe* II. (Globe) 368 It nauseated their very Stomachs, made them sick when they thought of it. **1774** T. PERCIVAL *Ess.* (1776) III. 144 Lime water often nauseates the patient. **1821–30** LD. COCKBURN *Mem.* ii. (1874) 107 [He] had long nauseated the civil court by his burgh politics. **1875** H. C. WOOD *Therap.* (1879) 456 Castor oil is very repulsive to the palate, so much so as to nauseate..some susceptible individuals.

absol. **1812** *Examiner* 24 Aug. 542/2 A single..drop from the cup of egotism was apt to nauseate. **1875** H. C. WOOD *Therap.* (1879) 54 These are the simple bitters. In overdoses they nauseate.

3. a. *intr.* To become affected with nausea, to feel sick (*at* something).

1640 BP. REYNOLDS *Passions* xxxix, We are apt to nauseate at very good meat, when we know that an ill Cook did dresse it. **1735** POPE *Donne Sat.* IV. 153 As one of Woodward's patients,..I puke, I nauseate. **1740** BAYNARD *Health* (ed. 6) 6 When as your Stomach nauseates and kecks at Smell or Sight of Meats. **1816** SCOTT *Antiq.* xxii, The old-fashioned civility that presses food upon you after you have eaten till you nauseate.

b. *fig.* (Compare 1 b.)

1657 J. SERGEANT *Schism Dispach't* 6 He cannot but hate that in himself, which he nauseates at in another. **1741** WATTS *Improv. Mind* I. xiv. (1801) 111 Do not over-fatigue the spirits..lest the mind be seized with a lassitude, and thereby be tempted to nauseate. **1886** COL. MAURICE *Lett. Donegal* 6 The hard-fisted Orangemen..are beginning to nauseate under this sort of treatment.

Hence **ˈnauseated** *ppl. a.*

1659 *Gentl. Calling* (1696) 163 Forsaking all the unsatisfying nauseated pleasures of Luxury. **1673** *Lady's Calling* I. i. §3 To entertain new scholars only with the cast or nauseated learning of the old.

ˈnauseating, *vbl. sb.* [f. prec. + -ING¹.] The fact of being affected with nausea; an instance of this.

1651 FRENCH *Distill.* v. 144 It..is taken without any nauseating. **1668** CLARENDON *Ess.* Tracts (1727) 90 The very nautiating and aversion that nature hath to surfeits. **1705** STANHOPE *Paraphr.* II. 58 One part of the Body submits..to Nauseatings or Gripings. **1744** BERKELEY *Siris* §12 All unctuous and oily medicines, create a nauseating in the stomach. **1822–34** *Good's Study Med.* (ed. 4) II. 538 Vomiting is here to be preferred to nauseating.

ˈnauseating, *ppl. a.* [f. as prec. + -ING².] That nauseates; sickening.

1645 BP. HALL *Remedy Discontent* 44 To compare it with their own delicate and nauseating superfluities. **1661** K. W. *Conf. Charac.*, *Hording Hagg* (1860) 90 The assefœtida..(by its nauseating odour). **1725** BRADLEY *Fam. Dict.* s.v. *Radish*, They are hard of digestion, causing nauseating eructations. **1809** *Med. Jrnl.* XXI. 119 Administered in nauseating doses. **1865** LIVINGSTONE *Zambesi* xxix. 594 We again allude to the nauseating subject because it is of importance.

Hence **ˈnauseatingly** *adv.*

1883 L. WINGFIELD *Abigel Rowe* I. iv. 72 All birds and trees and cows are nauseatingly alike.

nauseˈation. [f. NAUSEATE *v.*: see -ATION.] The action of nauseating, or the state of being nauseated; sickness.

1628 BP. HALL *Old Relig.* Ded., Let not their palates be humour'd in this wanton nauseation. **1652** —— *Invis. World* I. §9 The angels look upon our natural infirmities.. without any offence or nauseation. **1847** in WEBSTER. **1885** *Science* VI. 154/1 There is no nauseation.

†**ˈnauseative**, *a. Obs.* [ad. med.L. **nauseātīv-us*: see NAUSEATE *v.* and -ATIVE. So obs. F. *nauseatif*, *-ive* (1495).] Inclined to nausea.

1620 VENNER *Via Recta* iii. 48 That flesh which is ouer-fat is hurtfull to the stomacke, by causing a nauseatiue disposition. **1657** B. W. tr. *Bauderon's Expert Phisic.* 111 If the sick bee nauseative, give a vomit.

†**nauseity.** *Obs. rare*⁻¹. [f. NAUSE-OUS + -ITY.] A nauseous medicine.

1683 TRYON *Way to Health* 536 Let no man have Faith.. in such adulterated confused Nauseities.

nauseous (ˈnɔːʃ(ɪ)əs, ˈnɔːsɪəs, ˈnɔːzɪəs), *a.* Also 7 **naus-, nauc-,** 8 **nautious.** [f. NAUSE-A + -OUS, or ad. L. *nauseōs-us* (Pliny); cf. F. *nauséeux*.]

†**1.** Inclined to nausea; fastidious. *Obs. rare.*

1604 R. CAWDREY *Table Alph.* (1613), *Nauseous*, loathing or disposed to vomit. **1651** FRENCH *Distill.* v. 144 It may be given..to children or those that are of a nauseous stomack. **1678** RAY *Prov.* (ed. 2) Pref., I have..so veiled them, that I hope they will not turn the stomach of the most nauseous.

2. a. Causing nausea or squeamishness; in later use also, highly unpleasant to the taste or smell.

1612 WOODALL *Surg. Mate* Wks. (1653) 308 To expel nauseous distempers. **1647** WARD *Simp. Cobler* 27, I have no heart to the voyage, least their nauseous shapes and the Sea, should work too sorely upon my stomach. **1744** BERKELEY *Siris* §1 This method produceth tar-water of a nauseous kind. **1781** COWPER *Hope* 509 The full-gorged savage, at his nauseous feast Spent half the darkness. **1840** DICKENS *Barn. Rudge* vii, Cured by remedies in themselves very nauseous and unpalatable. **1875** HELPS *Soc. Press.* vi. 80, I used to eat the nauseous bits first.

absol. **1793** W. ROBERTS *Looker-on* No. 53 (1794) II. 287 To imitate our fashionable physicians in mixing up together ..the nauseous and the nice.

b. Of tastes or smells: Nasty, unpleasant.

1727 *Philip Quarll* 217 More offensive than the most nautious Odour of an old Sepulchre. **1789** W. BUCHAN *Dom. Med.* (1790) 155 This both improves the medicine, and takes off the nauseous taste. **1828** SIR J. E. SMITH *Eng. Flowers* II. 15 A strong, permanent, nauseous odour, like stale salt-fish. **1868** W. S. O. *Figuier's Ocean World* i. 17 A peculiar flavour, slightly acrid and bitter, and a little nauseous.

3. *fig.* Loathsome, disgusting; highly offensive.

1663 COWLEY *Verses & Ess.* (1669) 21 To those..The good does nauseous or insipid grow. **1697** DRYDEN *Virg. Georg.* Ded., Greatness they said was nauseous, and a Crowd was troublesome. **1751** BUTLER *Serm.* Wks. 1874 II. 337 All affectation of talking piously is quite nauseous. **1771** *Junius Lett.* liv. (1788) 299, I will not insist upon the nauseous detail. **1817** BYRON *Beppo* lxxxvi, A deal of swearing, And nauseous words past mentioning or bearing. **1852** GLADSTONE *Glean.* (1879) IV. 129 A piece of nauseous affectation. **1885** *Manch. Exam.* 30 Mar. 5/2 He had persecuted her..with his nauseous attentions.

ˈnauseously, *adv.* [f. prec. + -LY².] In a nauseous manner; to a nauseous extent, etc. (In *lit.* and *fig.* senses.)

1668 H. MORE *Div. Dial.* II. xviii. (1713) 146 So may the exercise of the Animal Functions or Passions..become very nauseously evil. *a* **1721** SHEFFIELD (Dk. Buckhm.) *Wks.* (1753) I. 97 That silly thing..With which our age so nauseously is cloy'd. **1750** RUTTY in *Phil. Trans.* LI. 470 It is of a subacid taste, and very nauseously vitriolic. **1867** BUSHNELL in *Hours at Home* Nov. 2 This..nauseously absurd way of criticism.

ˈnauseousness. [f. as prec. + -NESS.]

†**1.** A feeling of nausea; squeamishness. *Obs.* (common in 17th c.)

1612 WOODALL *Surg. Mate* Wks. (1653) 306 Accompanied with crude nauseousnesse of the stomach. **1651** J. F[REAKE] *Agrippa's Occ. Philos.* 143 The seeing of any filthy thing causeth nauseousness. **1725** BRADLEY *Fam. Dict.* s.v. *Malt liquor*, Nauseousness at the stomach.

†**b.** *fig.* Also const. *of* (the thing disliked). *Obs.*

1622 MABBE tr. *Aleman's Guzman d'Alf.* II. 9 If thou shalt ..tell me, that..I cause nauciousnesse in this my Discourse. **1673** O. WALKER *Educ.* (1677) 298 To man alone..hath nature given a nauseousness of the present. **1693** SHADWELL *Volunteers* I. i, Affected to nauseousness.

2. The quality of being nauseous.

c **1645** HOWELL *Lett.* (1892) II. 662 They use to stir the humours so violently by their nauseousness. **1687** SETTLE *Refl. Dryden* 6 Which.., besides the nauseousness of the Simile, is no true Position. **1745** P. THOMAS *Jrnl. Anson's Voy.* 148 The Dirt, Nauseousness, and Stench almost every where intolerable. **1821–30** LD. COCKBURN *Mem.* i. (1856) 38 A faint conception of their nauseousness may be formed from the following examples. **1882** 'OUIDA' *Maremma* I. 177 The nauseousness of the atmosphere of the seashore in Maremma.

†**ˈnausiness.** *Obs. rare*⁻⁰. = NAUSEOUSNESS 1.

1598 FLORIO, *Nausea*, nausines,..lothing..of things.

†**ˈnausity.** *Obs. rare.* [f. NAUS-EA + -ITY.]

a. Nauseous procedure. **b.** Nausea.

1654 VILVAIN *Theorem. Theol.* i. 25 'Tis nausity to serv forth twise sod Coleworts. **1685** COTTON tr. *Montaigne* xcvii. (1869) 681 It has in truth given me a kind of nausity to meaner conversations.

Naussie (ˈnɒsɪ, ˈnɒzɪ). *colloq.* [f. N(EW *a.* + AUSSIE *sb.*] = *New Australian* (AUSTRALIAN *sb.* 2 b).

1959 [see AUSTRALIAN *sb.* 2 b]. **1959** BAKER *Drum* 129 *Naussie*, a N(ew) Aussie.

naut, obs. f. NAUGHT; obs. var. NOWT.

nautch (nɔːtʃ), *sb.* Also **nach, nách, nâch, natch.** [a. Urdū (Hindī) *nāch*, Prakrit *nachcha*, Skr. *nṛitya*, dancing, acting, f. *nṛit-* to dance.]

1. An East Indian exhibition of dancing, performed by professional dancing-girls.

α. **1809** BROUGHTON *Lett. Mahratta Camp* xvi. (1892) 142 You Europeans are apt to picture to yourselves a *Nach* as a most attractive spectacle. **1849** EASTWICK *Dry Leaves* 174, I pass over the usual festivities of a native marriage, and the Nách given me by Fazal.

β. *c* **1813** MRS. SHERWOOD *Ayah & Lady* iv. 24, I thought of nothing but..going out to great dinners and nautches. **1862** BEVERIDGE *Hist. India* II. VI. viii. 781 Holkar was said to have had a grand nautch. **1864** TREVELYAN *Compet. Wallah* 126, I could not have believed in the existence of an entertainment so extravagantly dull as a Nautch.

b. A nautch girl.

1872 BROWNING *Fifine* xxxi, The Pariah of the North, the European Nautch!

2. *attrib.* and *Comb.*, as ***nautch dance, dancer, girl, woman.***

1858 W. H. RUSSELL *Diary in India* II. 275, I don't think the *nautch dance calculated to improve their minds. **1879** E. ARNOLD *Lt. Asia* VI. iv, A band of tinselled girls, the *nautch dancers Of Indra's temple. **1809** BROUGHTON *Lett. Mahratta Camp* xi. (1892) 93 Two sets of *Nach girls. **1879** E. ARNOLD *Lt. Asia* I. iv, The nautch girls in their spangled skirts and bells. **1825** HEBER *Journey* (1828) II. 136 The *Nâch women were, as usual, ugly.

Hence **nautch** *v. intr.*, to dance at or as at a nautch. Also **ˈnautching** *vbl. sb.*

1851 R. F. BURTON *Goa* 125 When mere children they are initiated in the mysteries of nautching. **1859** —— *Centr. Afr.* in *Jrnl. Geog. Soc.* XXIX. 266 They will fly to their drums, rush about, jump, and nautch, as if hung on wires.

†**nautheless**, *adv. Obs. rare.* Also **naw-.** [app. f. *naut*, *nawt* NAUGHT.] = NATHELESS.

13.. *E.E. Allit. P.* A. 877 Nauþelez þaȝ hit schowted scharpe. *Ibid.* 950 Of motes two to carpe clene & Ierusalem hyȝt boþe nawþeles.

nauther ('nɔːðə(r)), *pron.* and *conj. Obs.* exc. *dial.* Forms: 1 **nawðer**, 1, 4 **nawþer**, 5, 9 **nawther**, 5 **nawder**; 1 **nauðer** (**-ær**), 4 **nauþer**, 4–5 **nauthir**, (5 **-yr**), 4–5 (9) **nauther**. [OE. *nawðer*, *nauðer* (= OFris. *nauder*), contracted form of *náhwæðer* (OFris. *nahwedder*), f. *ná* NA *adv.*[1] + *hwæðer* WHETHER. See also NATHER, NOTHER, and NOUTHER.]

A. *pron.* Neither (of two persons or things).

c**888** K. ÆLFRED *Boeth.* xvi. §4 Hi ȝecyðað on heora endunge.. þæt hie nauðer ne bioð. *Ibid.* xxix. §3 Swa hwæðer swa hi dydon, ne dohte him ða nawðer. c**1375** *Cursor M.* 5831 (Fairf.), If þai trow nauþer of þa. c**1400** *Destr. Troy* 2837 Nawther company by course hade Kennyng of other. c**1460** *Towneley Myst.* ii. 252 Na, nawder of thise ij will I leife.

B. *conj.* Neither (..nor).

c**888** K. ÆLFRED *Boeth.* xvi. §4 Nawðer ne se wela ne se anweald.. ne beoð to wenanne [etc.]. **971** *Blickl. Hom.* 45 Hi þonne ne mihtan nawþer ne him sylfum, ne þære heorde.. nænige gode beon. **13..** *Cursor M.* 23134 (Edinb.) þat lufe to knaw, þat nauthir.. wil for luf ne au [etc.]. **13..** *Gaw. & Gr. Knt.* 203 Wheþer hade he no helme ne hawbergh nauþer. c**1400** *Destr. Troy* 4329 Nauther law ne belefe lenton hom to. c**1460** *Towneley Myst.* xxvi. 153 To neuen this note nomore vs nedys, nawder euen nor morne. **1828** *Craven Gloss.* **1877** *North-W. Linc. Gloss.* **1883** *Almondbury Gloss.*

nautic ('nɔːtɪk), *a.* and *sb.* Also 7 **nautike**, **-tick**. [ad. F. *nautique* (c 1500) or L. *nautic-us*, ad. Gr. ναυτικός, f. ναύτης sailor, ναῦς ship.]

A. *adj.* Nautical. (Chiefly in poetic or dignified use.) ***nautic mile***: see MILE.

1613 PURCHAS *Pilgrimage* (1864) 46 Cutting off the Mogols Nautike hands in hindring the mutuall Traffike of their Subiects. **1669** GALE *Crt. Gentiles* I. II. vi. 75 Neptune ..was made to be the God of Nautic Science. **1762** FALCONER *To Dk. of York* 201 The incense of a nautic Muse! **1779** FORREST *Voy. N. Guinea* 305 Orators, as well as poets, celebrate the nautic song. **1813** SOUTHEY *Nelson* II. 85 Part of them were drafted into the different regiments, and the remainder formed into a corps, called the nautic legion. **1867** SMYTH *Sailor's Word-bk.* Introd. 10 The most general nautic dishes and refections. **1867** J. B. ROSE tr. *Virgil's Æneid* 122 The nautic clamour echoes on the shores.

B. *sb.* **a.** *pl.* The art or science of navigation.

1793 W. TAYLOR in *Monthly Rev.* XI. 564 After..1600, all the branches of nautics came to be generally studied.

b. A sailor, esp. of the Royal Navy.

1909 *Westm. Gaz.* 3 June 4/2 'Nautics' love the spray of the waves more than they do the dust of the roads. **1943** B. J. HURREN *Eastern Med* vi. 76 A complete reversal of policy was now thrust upon an eager company of flying nautics. **1951** P. BRICKHILL *Dam Busters* xix. 244 A certain.. personality at Bomber Command..when he heard the *Tirpitz* was sunk, [said] 'That's one in the eye for the Nautics!' **1973** *Sunday Tel.* 4 Mar. 38/1 The Army did as they had been done by in the first-half. Now it was the Nautics who were under hideous pressure.

nautical ('nɔːtɪkəl), *a.* Also 6 **nawtical**, 6–7 **nauticall**. [f. prec. + -AL[1].]

1. Pertaining to seamen or to the art of navigation; naval, marine, maritime.

1552– [see below]. **1656** BLOUNT *Glossogr.*, *Nautical*, belonging to ships or Marriners. **1796** H. HUNTER tr. *St.-Pierre's Stud. Nat.* (1799) III. 25 The fifth nautical proof of the elevation of the Poles above the Horizon. **1800** COLQUHOUN *Comm. Thames* Pref., Those..concerned in Navigation and Commerce, and who follow Nautical Pursuits. **1834** M. SCOTT *Cruise Midge* (1859) 325 My nautical enthusiasm fairly got the better of me. **1856** KANE *Arct. Expl.* I. xxvi. 349 As to nautical rules, they do not fit the circumstances.

b. In special applications, as ***nautical almanac***, ***angle***, ***astronomy***, ***card***, ***compass***, ***day***, ***distance***, ***ephemeris***, ***indicator***, ***mile***, ***planisphere***, ***stars***, ***tables***, etc. (see quots. and the various sbs.).

1765 in *Naut. Almanac* (1767) p. i, That it..may be lawful to and for the said Commissioners to cause such *Nautical Almanacks..to be constructed. **1796** HUTTON *Math. Dict.* s.v. *Ephemeris*, The Nautical Almanac,..published in England by the Board of Longitude. **1854** MOSELEY *Astron.* lxxxviii. (ed. 4) 232 The Nautical Almanac for 1835 contained ephemerides of two of them. **1823** CRABB *Technol. Dict.*, *Nautical angle*, an instrument by which a ship's departure, meridional difference, etc. are obtained from inspection. **1867** SMYTH *Sailor's Word-bk.* 492 *Nautical Astronomy*, that part of the celestial science which..relates to the purposes of navigation. **1700** MOXON *Math. Dict.* 103 *Nautical Card*, for Multiplication, Division and Extraction of Roots with much ease. **1552** HULOET B iij b, Anaximander..inuented the *Nauticall..compasse. **1605** CAMDEN *Rem.*, *Impresses* 172 He elegantly shewed by whom he was drawne, which depainted the Nauticall compasse [etc.]. **1668** MOXON *Mech. Dyalling* 8 A Card of the Nautical Compass. **1867** SMYTH *Sailor's Word-bk.* 492 *Nautical Day*. This day commences at noon, twelve hours before the civil day. **1855** OGILVIE *Suppl.* s.v., The rhumb-line intercepted between any two places through which it passes, is called their *nautical distance. **1815** J. SMITH *Panorama Sci. & Art* I. 558 The exact times at which the eclipses of Jupiter's satellites will occur..are given..in the *nautical ephemeris. **1850** OGILVIE, *Nautical indicator*, an instrument for finding the latitude, longitude, and variation of the compass at sea. **1599** E. WRIGHT *Errors Navig.* ii. C 3 To shew by what kinde of proiection..the *nautical planisphere may..be conceiued to bee geometrically made. **1704** J. HARRIS *Lex. Techn.* I, *Nautical Planisphere*, is a Description of the Terrestrial Globe upon a Plane, for the Use of Mariners. **1867** SMYTH *Sailor's Word-bk.* 492 *Nautical Stars*, about 72 of the brightest, which have been selected for determining the latitude or the longitude. *Ibid.*, *Nautical Tables*, those especially computed for resolution of matters dependent on nautical astronomy, and navigation generally.

2. *absol.* A nautical person or writer.

1840 BARHAM *Ingol. Leg.* Ser. I. *Mr. Peter's Story* ix, Sir E. Lytton Bulwer, who brought up the rear of the 'Nauticals'. **1842** *Ibid.* Ser. II. *Dead Drummer* xiii, [He] Began 'spinning' what nauticals term a 'tough yarn'.

Hence **nauti'cality**, the quality of being nautical; **'nautically** *adv.*, in a nautical fashion.

1835 MARRYAT *Jac. Faithf.* xliv, You are very nautically poetical. **1887** THEO. GIFT *Victims* I. i. 5 [Dress] almost Parisian in its dainty nauticality.

nautilian (nɔː'tɪlɪən), *a.* [f. NAUTIL-US + -IAN.] Pertaining to the nautili.

1883 *Proc. Boston* (U.S.) *Soc. Nat. Hist.* 297 The species of this family have the typical nautilian whorls.

nau'tiliform, *a.* [f. NAUTIL-US + -(I)FORM.] Having the form of a nautilus.

1896 *Naturalist* 291 A large nautiliform cephalopod.

nautilite ('nɔːtɪlaɪt). *Palæont.* Also **-ites**. [f. as prec. + -ITE[1].] A fossil nautilus.

1748 *Phil. Trans.* (1750) XLV. 320 A beautiful Nautilites, shewn to the Royal Society by the Rev. Charles Lyttleton. **1794** SULLIVAN *View Nat.* II. 175 Those of the testaceous class, as Nautilites. **1799** KIRWAN *Geol. Ess.* 247 A red argillite, which is secondary; for a petrified nautilite was found in it. **1822** G. YOUNG *Geol. Yorksh. Coast* 255 Polished sections of nautilites or ammonites.

nautiloid ('nɔːtɪlɔɪd), *a.* and *sb.* [-OID.]

A. *adj.* Resembling the nautilus in form.

1847 in WEBSTER. **1851** RICHARDSON *Geol.* (ed. 2) viii. 222 The..structure of their shell, many of which resemble those of the nautiloid molluscs. **1870** H. A. NICHOLSON *Man. Zool.* (1875) 62 In the true nautiloid shell the convolutions of the spiral lie in a single plane.

B. *sb.* A nautiloid mollusc.

1847 in WEBSTER. **1883** *Proc. Boston* (U.S.) *Soc. Nat. Hist.* 297 This is..applicable to all the families of Nautiloids in which the annular lobes appear.

nautilus ('nɔːtɪləs). Pl. **nautili** ('nɔːtɪlaɪ); also **-uses**. [a. L. *nautilus*, ad. Gr. ναυτίλος sailor, nautilus, f. ναύτης seaman, ναῦς ship. Cf. F. *nautile* (16th c.).]

1. The paper or pearly nautilus (see 2), or one of the many fossil species related to the latter.

1601 HOLLAND *Pliny* IX. xxix. I. 250 Of the Calamarie, Cuttles, Polypes, and Boat-fishes called Nautili. **1661** LOVELL *Hist. Anim. & Min.* Isagoge a 7 b, Fishes, which are ..involute, as the Nautilus. **1733** POPE *Ess. Man* III. 178 Learn of the little Nautilus to sail, Spread the thin oar, and catch the driving gale. **1755** *Gentl. Mag.* XXV. 128 The fourth Tribe called Nautiluses. *Ibid.*, The particular species of the Nautilus, as shells, are the paperaceous, the eared, and the umbilical. **1824** W. N. BLANS *Excurs.* 7 The nautili, if in danger of being run over, will, as the sailors term it, capsize. **1860** MAURY *Phys. Geog. Sea* xviii. §740 The tiny little Nautilus, one of the oldest families in the sea. **1893** SIR R. BALL *Story of Sun* 294 Ammonites, which are allied to the nautilus of our present seas.

attrib. **1692** RAY *Disc.* II. iv. (1693) 148 There are no Nautili..comparable in bigness to that Nautilus stone of twenty eight pound found by Mr. Waller. *Ibid.* 150 Mr. Waller..writes, That he..making a search after the *Cornua Ammonis*, found one of the true Nautilus shape. **1746** DA COSTA in *Phil. Trans.* XLIV. 398 A shell related to the Nautilus kind. **1831** SCOTT in Lockhart *Life* (1839) X. 130 A fairy cup made out of a Nautilus shell. **1851** WOODWARD *Mollusca* I. 48 The nautilus shell corresponds to that of the gasteropod.

2. a. ***paper*** (or †***paper-shelled***) ***nautilus***, the argonaut, a small dibranchiate cephalopod, the female of which is protected by a very thin, single-chambered, detached shell, and has webbed dorsal arms which it was formerly believed to use as sails.

1753 CHAMBERS *Cycl. Supp.* s.v., The polypus is by no means to be confounded with the paper-shelled *nautilus*. ?**1792** SHAW *Naturalist's Misc.* III. pl. 101 The Argonaut, or Paper Nautilus. **1854** AGNES CATLOW *Pop. Conchol.* (ed. 2) 28 The curious and beautiful shells of the *Argonauta Argo*, or Paper Nautilus, are found in the seas of warm latitudes. **1870** H. A. NICHOLSON *Man. Zool.* li. (1875) 363 In the former of these [families] there is only the single genus *Argonauta* (the Paper Sailor, or the Paper Nautilus).

b. ***pearly nautilus***, a tetrabranchiate cephalopod (*N. pompilius*) found in the Indian and Pacific Oceans, having a beautiful chambered shell with nacreous septa.

1776 [see PEARLY *a.* 2 b]. c**1800** SHAW *Naturalist's Misc.* XIII. pl. 515 The great pearly Nautilus. **1829** BENNETT in Owen *Pearly Nautilus* (1832) 7 In the evening a Pearly Nautilus..was seen in Marekini Bay. **1870** H. A. NICHOLSON *Man. Zool.* li. (1875) 370 The structure of the shell in the *Ammonitidæ* is exactly that of the Pearly Nautilus.

3. A form of diving-bell. (Knight *Dict. Mech.*)

navaid ('nævеɪd). [f. NAV(IGATIONAL *a.* + AID *sb.*] Any navigational device in an aircraft, ship, etc.

1956 S. ROSENBERG *Systems Analysis Approach to Choice of Long Distance Navaid* (Rome Air Devel. Technical Note 56-279, U.S. Govt. Res. Rep. AD 97714, Aug.) 1 Increased interest has been displayed recently on the need for a single, standard long-distance navigational aid (navaid) capable of meeting the latest..operational objectives. **1960** *Electronics Weekly* 21 Sept. 2 (*heading*) Ocean-based navaid to be tested by US. **1971** *Electronics & Communications Abstr.* XI. 47 An analytical study is presented of a new navaid system designed to assist the navigation of aircraft in remote and low traffic areas by facilitating homing and orbiting on ground beacons. **1971** *Flying* Apr. 53/2 When ranked against the..expenditures proposed for terminal and en-route traffic control (not counting navaids and landing aids), the FSS money looks like a couple of drops they might spill while pouring.

Navajo ('nævəhəʊ), *sb.* and *a.* Also **Nabajo**, **Nabeho**, **Navaho**, **Navajoe**. [f. Sp. *Apaches de Navajó*, f. Tewa *Navahu* large field.]

A. *sb.* **a.** An Athapascan Indian people of Arizona, Utah, and New Mexico; a member of this people. **b.** The Athapascan language of this people. **B.** *adj.* Of, pertaining to, or characteristic of this people.

[**1629** ZÁRATE-SALMERON in *Papers Archaeol. Inst. Amer.* (1892) Amer. Ser. IV. 294 La nacion de los Indios Apaches de Nabajù.] **1780** in *New Mexico Hist. Soc. Publ.* (1918) No. 21, 36 The war cruelly made upon them [*sc.* pueblos] by the Utes and Navajos. **1822** J. FOWLER *Jrnl.* 8 Mar. (1898) 123 The Spanierds Have Sent 700 men against the nabeho Indeans. **1834** A. PIKE *Prose Sk. & Poems* 99 An Indian girl with her Nabajo blanket, her black, with a red border. **1850** [see JICARILLA]. **1873** J. H. BEADLE *Undevel. West* xxv. 524 John H. Van Order acted as interpreter from English into Spanish, and Jesus Alviso from Spanish into Navajo. Nearly all the employes understood a little Navajo, but not enough to interpret. **1907** [see APACHE 1]. **1910** G. W. JAMES *Grand Canyon* iii. 18 Gray Navaho rugs cover the brown floor. **1921** [see APACHE 1]. **1929** D. H. LAWRENCE *Pansies* 39 A Navajo woman, weaving her rug in the pattern of her dream. **1951** see BEAT-UP *sb.* and *a.*]. **1957** P. WORSLEY *Trumpet shall Sound* 243 The Navaho..were one of the few Indian tribes who remained unaffected by the Ghost Dance of 1890. **1972** A. FOWLES *Double Feature* ix. 173, I stared, instead, at a Navajo rug hanging on the wall. It was worked in small black triangles of black and red, worked in a stark zigzag pattern on a cream background. **1973** T. ALLBEURY *Choice of Enemies* xxviii. 155, I can get by quite happily in Navajo. **1975** *Guardian* 21 Jan. 2/6 The more culturally intact tribes such as the Navajos, the nation's largest.

naval ('neɪvəl), *a.* (and *sb.*) Also 7 **navale**, **-all**. [ad. L. *nāvālis*, f. *nāvis* ship: see -AL[1]. Cf. F. *naval*, *-ale* (13–14th c.).]

1. ***naval crown***, etc., the crown or garland given by the Romans to one who had gained a victory, or shown special bravery, in a sea-fight.

1593 PEELE *Edw. I*, A 3 b, Welcome manly followers, That ..on your war drums carry crownes as kings, Crowne Murall, Nauall. **1601** HOLLAND *Pliny* XXII. iii. II. 115 The Navall garlands given to admirals and generals at sea, for obtaining victorie in that kind of service. *Ibid.* Index, Naval chaplets. **1656** BLOUNT *Glossogr.* s.v., The Naval Crown was given to him, who first entred the enemies ship in a Battle at Sea. **1727–38** CHAMBERS *Cycl.* s.v., Though A. Gellius.. says the naval crown was adorned with prows of ships, Lipsius distinguishes two kinds of naval crowns.

2. a. Of or pertaining to, connected with, characteristic of, used in, the navy (†or shipping in general).

1602 DOLMAN *La Primaud. Fr. Acad.* (1618) III. 793 Of the oldest Pines is pitch made, which is called Naual, by reason that it is very good to pitch Ships. **1617** MORYSON *Itin.* I. 54 Our Master, according to the navall discipline, not to put to sea with one anchor, returned backe to the harbour. *Ibid.* 272 Depford, the Navall storehouse. **1665** MANLEY *Grotius' Low C. Wars* 173 The Commands of the Sea was betrayed, by the exhausting the Navall Revenues. *Ibid.* 193 To order and settle all Navall matters. **1710** J. HARRIS *Lex. Techn.* II, *Naval Architecture*. **1756–7** tr. *Keysler's Trav.* (1760) III. 2 One..from the naval ornaments carved on it, is thought to have belonged to a sea-officer. **1796** MORSE *Amer. Geog.* I. 160 At the northern extremity of the Town, is the king's naval yard. **1813** BYRON *Corsair* I. xvii, He.. unfolds his plan..and spreads the chart, And all that speaks and aids the naval art. **1837** W. IRVING *Capt. Bonneville* III. 81 This favoured port combines advantages which..fit it for a grand naval depôt. **1878** BESANT & RICE *Celia's Arb.* ix, A tall and good-looking young sailor, in his naval rig.

b. ***naval stores***, all those articles or materials made use of in shipping or in the navy. Also *spec.* (see quot. 1896).

1678 MARVELL *Growth Popery* 34 It was alleged..That we had not Naval Stores and Ammunition, &c. sufficient for such a Purpose. **1699** DRYDEN *Ep. J. Driden* 148 Be then the naval stores the nation's care. **1753** HANWAY *Trav.* I. VI. lxxxv. 392 The prices this nation might pay for naval stores. **1812** *Examiner* 12 Oct. 648/2 The other, a bombard, laden with naval stores, got aground. **1896** *Pop. Sci. Monthly* Feb. 472 The different resinous products of trade, which go under the name of 'naval stores'.

†**c.** Of the nature of a ship. *Obs. rare*$^{-1}$.

1646 SIR T. BROWNE *Pseud. Ep.* IV. v. 192 The Ark or navall edifice of Noah.

d. ***naval brass***, a type of brass containing about 60 per cent copper, 39 per cent zinc, and one per cent tin, used for bolts and other small fittings of ships.

1881 *Calvert's Mechanics' Almanack 1882* 27 In 1874, an alloy, composed of 62 parts of copper, 37 of spelter, and one of tin, was proposed by Mr. Farquharson... The new alloy is specified for all ships built for the Admiralty, and the details now given may be of service to anyone using naval brass. **1928** S. G. WHEELER *Marine Engin.* II. xvii. 510 Naval brass can be rolled or forged, but unless it can be worked in this way has poor strength when cast. **1964** S. H. AVNER *Introd. Physical Metall.* xii. 353 Leaded naval brass with the addition of 1·75 Pb for improved machinability is used for marine hardware. **1969** D. K. ALLEN *Metall.* xiii. 438/2 Naval brass or Tobin bronze..has increased resistance to salt water spray and is used for condenser plates, welding rod, propeller shafts, and marine hardware.

e. *naval base*, a securely held seaport from which naval operations can be carried out.

1906 F. T. JANE *Heresies of Sea Power* II. ii. 126 These are they who assign the first and second places to the fleet; the shore and the shore forces come but a bad third. The advocates of naval command of naval bases may be found among these. **1941** A. J. MARDER *Brit. Naval Policy 1880–1905* x. 183 England's key position in the Mediterranean, though strongly fortified, could hardly be called a naval base at this time. **1957** P. MACKESY *War in Mediterranean 1803–10* 13 Malta..was the only naval base possessed by England from which the Toulon fleet could be watched and maritime command exercised in the central Mediterranean. **1969** *Islander* (Victoria, B.C.) 9 Nov. 16/2 In the early days Esquimalt was a British naval base, but merchantmen also used the harbor extensively.

f. *naval bank holiday*: (see quot. 1961). *colloq.*

1916 G. FRANKLIN *Naval Digression* vii. 220 We had a typical 'naval bank holiday' on Boxing day—coaling ship. **1948** PARTRIDGE *Dict. Forces' Slang* 124 *Naval bank holiday*, coaling the ship. **1961** —— *Dict. Slang* Suppl. 1195/1 *Naval bank holiday*, a day spent in coaling the ship.

3. a. Fought, gained, sustained, carried out, etc., by means of ships or a navy.

1606 HOLLAND *Sueton.* 17 To set out the Naumachie or naval battaile, there was a place digged for a great poole. **1660** R. COKE *Power & Subj.* 71 Lest..the Seamen should be forgetful and unfitting for naval warfare. **1700** PRIOR *Carm. Sec.* 327 Beaks of ships in naval triumph borne. **1750** BEAWES *Lex. Mercat.* (1752) 244 His Sicilian Expedition, so fatal to his Arms in their naval Conflict with Sir George Byng. **1802** JAMES *Milit. Dict.*, *Naval engagement* implies, in general, either a sea-fight between single ships, or whole fleets of men of war, or gallies, &c. **1849–50** ALISON *Hist. Eur.* VII. xlii. §41. 123 He never again ventured on naval enterprises.

b. Consisting of ships of war.

1617 MORYSON *Itin.* I. 2 The Hamburgers had in vaine attempted by Nauall forces to forbid the arriuall of the English at Stode. **1720** STRYPE *Stow's Surv.* I. I. xxvii. 215 The Naval Strength of this Realm. **1769** BURKE *Late St. Nat.* Wks. 1842 I. 98 What naval force..[is] necessary to keep our marine in a condition commensurate to its great ends. **1836** THIRLWALL *Greece* xv. (1839) II. 259 After the naval armament had coasted the intervening bays. **1887** LD. BRASSEY in T. H. Ward *Reign Q. Vict.* 237 The wide expansion of naval force which has been demanded by the altered circumstances of the times.

c. Distinguished by, resting or based on, the possession of war-ships.

1678 MARVELL *Growth Popery* Wks. (Grosart) IV. 294 So that the two great naval powers of Europe being crushed together, he might remain sole arbitrator of the ocean. **1738** WARBURTON *Div. Legat.* II. iv. Wks. 1788 I. 233 The great advantages of cultivating a naval power. **1813** WELLINGTON in Gurw. *Desp.* (1838) X. 592 Since Great Britain has been a naval power a British army has never been left in such a situation. **1869** RAWLINSON *Anc. Hist.* 78 The naval power of Carthage.

4. a. Of persons: Belonging to, connected with, or serving in, the navy.

1667 PEPYS *Diary* 4 Sept., [Sir W. Coventry] told me that he must now take leave of me as a naval man. **1745** *Observ. conc. Navy* 21 Not only Naval Seamen should have Tickets, but likewise all other Seamen. **1769** FALCONER *Dict. Marine* (1780), *Garde de la marine*, a midshipman, or naval cadet. **1807** *Med. Jrnl.* XVII. 158, I should..be led to conclude he is a naval practitioner. **1839** W. CHAMBERS *Tour Holland* 33/1 Monuments to Dutch naval commanders. **1863** P. BARRY *Dockyard Econ.* 141 Naval Lords of the Admiralty.. have only to talk him over, and he is the servant of those Naval Lords.

b. *naval officer*: (see quots. and OFFICER *sb.* 4).

1769 FALCONER *Dict. Marine* (1780) s.v. *Naval.* **1802** JAMES *Milit. Dict.*, *Naval officers* are admirals, captains, lieutenants, masters, boatswains, midshipmen, gunners, &c. **1846** YOUNG *Naut. Dict.* s.v. *Naval*, The various subjects connected with the duties of naval officers. **1871** DE VERE *Americanisms* 264 Another such office is that of Naval Officer, whose duty it is to receive copies of all manifests and entries in the Custom-House.

c. *(Royal) Naval Reserve*: (see RESERVE *sb.* 2 b).

1863 YOUNG *Naut. Dict.* (ed. 2), *Royal Naval Reserve*, an establishment of volunteers, consisting of able merchant seamen who..agree to serve on board of ships of war in case of need. **1876** HAM *Revenue Vade-m.* 392 Her Majesty may accept offers of persons recommended by the Admiralty to serve as officers of the Royal Naval Reserve. **1885** *Pall Mall G.* 16 June 1/2 These seamen are usually called Royal Naval Reserve men.

d. *naval brigade*, a landing force; a reinforcement force for land troops.

1883 MELTON & OLIPHANT *Cruise of U.S.S. Galena* vii. 80 On several occasions our Naval Brigade was landed upon the breakwater and exercised in marching and counter-marching. **1884** *Naval Encycl.* 510/1 It has been customary in the service to give the name of 'naval brigade' to even a single ship's company, although by rights it refers to a larger organization. **1901** J. BLAKE *How Sailors Fight* xii. 241 Naval brigades took part in the operations with Buller, with Methuen, and with Lord Roberts; but of all it is probable that at the siege of Ladysmith the services rendered were most valuable. **1904** J. S. CORBETT *Eng. in Mediterranean* II. xxiv. 119 The real attack was made from the centre with five battalions of infantry, the naval brigade, and the three troops of British horse. **1937** H. FITCH *My Mis-spent Youth* iii. 14 As a Captain, Beresford had been in charge of the naval brigade during the River War which led up to the battle of Omdurman.

5. *sb. pl.* †**a.** Naval achievements. *Obs. rare*⁻¹.

a **1674** CLARENDON *Life* (1759) II. 507 The Action.. surpassed all that was done in Cromwell's Time, whose Navals were much greater than had ever been in any Age.

b. Naval men. *rare.*

1836 HALIBURTON *Clockm.* Ser. I. xii. (1837) 99, I guess it's natural for you to say so of the buttons of our navals.

navalism (ˈneɪvəlɪz(ə)m). [f. prec. + -ISM.] The domination of naval interests.

1892 *Nation* (N.Y.) 21 Jan. 44/2 Mr. Blaine..co-operated wtih Mr. Tracy in..handing the foreign policy of the Government over to navalism. **1896** *Daily News* 4 Dec. 7/3 His party would not vote a man..for navalism.

navalist (ˈneɪvəlɪst). [f. NAVAL *a.* + -IST.] One who stresses the importance of having a strong navy. Also *attrib.*

1920 *Glasgow Herald* 30 Dec. 6/3 Mr. Daniels's rather flamboyant allusions to the American naval programme would be utilised by our domestic navalists. **1927** *Observer* 20 Mar. 16/4 'Neon'..is a good old-fashioned navalist and an obsolete politician. **1961** A. J. MARDER *From Dreadnought to Scapa Flow* I. 158 The insistence of navalist opinion..that in an era of international strife it was imperative that the private armament firms be kept in efficient condition. **1963** R. A. HOUGH *Hunting of Force Z* iii. 64 Navalists and airmen and their supporting politicians and suppliers bandied about the old dogmas and statistics. *Ibid.* 72 Bombardment from the air, navalists the world over calculated, was no more than another threat to be added to that of the torpedo-boat and submarine.

navally (ˈneɪvəlɪ), *adv.* [f. NAVAL *a.* + -LY².] In a naval manner; from a naval point of view. Also *navally crowned* (see NAVAL *a.* 1).

1816 in J. B. Paul *Ord. Sc. Arms* (1893) 159/2 Or, a lion rampant gu., navally crowned az. **1836** COBDEN *Russia* Pol. Writ. (1878) 120 Russia even at Constantinople would.. commercially and navally speaking be three times as distant as New York from Great Britain. **1898** *Daily News* 8 Aug. 5/5 China cannot compete navally with any of the three Powers either singly or combined.

navarch (ˈneɪvɑːk). *Gr. Antiq. rare.* [ad. Gr. ναύαρχος (L. *nau-*, *navarchus*), f. ναῦς ship + ἀρχός leader.] The commander of a fleet; an admiral.

1828–32 WEBSTER cites MITFORD. **1836** THIRLWALL *Greece* xx. III. 149 Cnemus, the Spartan navarch, or high admiral.

navarchy (ˈneɪvɑːkɪ). [ad. Gr. ναυαρχία (late L. *navarchia*): see prec. and -Y¹.]

†**1.** App. misused for 'ship building'. *Obs.*⁻¹

1648 W. PETTY *Advice to Hartlib* 6 That all Children..be taught some gentile Manufacture, such as are Navarchy and making Modells for building and rigging of Ships.

2. The office of a navarch; the period during which such office is exercised.

1850 GROTE *Greece* II. lxiv. VIII. 187 *note*, The commencement of Lysander's navarchy or year of maritime command appears to me established for this winter.

‖**navarin** (navarɛ̃). [Fr.] A mutton stew made with small onions and potatoes. Also **navarin printanier** (prɛ̃tanje), a navarin made with spring vegetables.

1877 E. S. DALLAS *Kettner's Bk. of Table* 309 Navarin is a stupid word which has arisen from a desire to get rid of the unintelligible and misleading name, Haricot de mouton, without falling back on the vulgar phrase, Ragoût de mouton. It was at first selected with a thought of punning upon the *navet* or turnip, which is so prominent in the Haricot de mouton. **1907** A. ESCOFFIER *Guide Mod. Cookery* xv. 448 Navarin Printanier... Transfer the pieces of mutton ..to another saucepan with..small, new onions..new trimmed carrots..new turnips..new potatoes..fresh peas, and..French beans. **1951** E. DAVID *French Country Cooking* 111 *Navarin Printanier.* This is a ragoût of lamb or mutton to which spring vegetables give special character... As soon as they [*sc.* peas] are cooked the *Navarin* is ready. **1963** *Economist* 30 Nov. 931/2 A basic recipe like *navarin.* **1966** *Vogue* Nov. 154/3 Dishes of the day may be Navarin Printanier, daube of lamb..or Chicken à la King. **1970** SIMON & HOWE *Dict. Gastron.* 275 *Navarin*, the French culinary name for a ragoût of mutton..made either with small onions and potatoes or with different vegetables such as carrots, turnips, new potatoes and green peas in which case *à la printanière* is added to its name.

Navarrese (nævəˈriːz), *sb.* and *a.* Also **Na'varran.** [f. *Navarr(e* a province of northern Spain, formerly a kingdom which included part of south-west France + -ESE.] **A.** *sb.* The people of Navarre; a native or inhabitant of Navarre. **B.** *adj.* Of or pertaining to Navarre.

[**1699** J. STEVENS tr. *Mariana's Gen. Hist. Spain* VIII. iii. 122 At this time the Count of Toulouse, came in with fresh supplies to assist the Navarrois.] **1846** R. FORD *Gatherings from Spain* xiii. 147 The Navarrese drink their Peralta, the Basques their Chacolet. **1855** C. M. YONGE *Lances of Lynwood* xiv. 219 The swarthy Navarrese mountaineer. **1915** C. C. MARTINDALE *In God's Army* I. 122 His servant, Miguel, was a Navarrese of bad character. **1932** E. HEMINGWAY *Death in Afternoon* xii. 125 Navarrese bulls are almost a different race, smaller and usually of a reddish color. **1943** E. A. PEERS *Spain in Eclipse* I. i. 25 The difficult country north of Reinosa had been negotiated by the Navarrans. *Ibid.* ii. 46 Navarran troops entered Barbastro and a rather slower advance began against Lérida. **1956** P. KEMP *Mine were of Trouble* ii. 26 A young Navarrese officer. *Ibid.* iv. 76 Father Vicente, the Company Chaplain, a stern-faced, lean Navarrese.

†**na'vation.** *Obs. rare*⁻¹. [f. L. *nāv-āre* to do zealously, perform diligently, etc. + -ATION.] A contrivance, scheme, plan.

1628 FELTHAM *Resolves* II. xii. 34 Euery good man..must be wise and circumspect, to vaine the sleeke nauations of those that would undoe him.

nave (neɪv), *sb.*¹ Forms: α. 1 **nabæ, nafa, nafu,** 4–5 **nafe,** 4–7 **naue,** (5 **nawe**), 4– **nave.** β. 4 **naf,** 4, 9 **naff,** (9 **knaff**), 5–7 **naffe.** [OE. *nafu* fem., *nafa* masc. = MDu. *nave* (*naef*, *naf*; Du. *naaf*), MLG. *nave*, OHG. *naba*, *napa* (G. *nabe*), ON. *naf-*, *nǫf* (Sw. *naf*, Da. *nav*):—Comm. Teut. *nabō related to Lett. *naba* navel, OPruss. *nabis*, Skr. *nābhi*, *nābha* nave and navel.]

1. a. The central part or block of a wheel, into which the end of the axle-tree is inserted, and from which the spokes radiate; a hub.

α. *c* **725** *Corpus Gloss.* (Hessels) M 256 *Modioli*, habæ [*for* nabæ; *Epinal* nabæ, *Erfurt* nebæ]. *c* **888** K. ÆLFRED *Boeth.* xxxix. §7 þæt hweol hwerfð ymbutan & sio nafu next þære eaxe. *Ibid.*, þa spacan..bioð þeah fæste on ðære nafe, & se nafa on ðære eaxe. **1382** WYCLIF *1 Kings* vii. 33 The spokys, and the felijs, and the naue, alle ȝoten. *c* **1386** CHAUCER *Sompn. T.* 562 Than shal this cherl..sette him on the wheel right of this cart, Upon the nave. *c* **1440** *Promp. Parv.* 351/2 Nave of a qwele, *modius, et modiolus.* *a* **1548** HALL *Chron.*, *Rich. III* 25 b, Blew veluet embroudered with the naues of Cartes burnyng of gold. **1598** CHAPMAN *Iliad* v. 734 The naves, in which the spokes were driven, were all with silver bound. **1679** COCKS *Forest & Fruit-Trees* a 2 Eighty pair of Naves were made out of it. **1720** POPE *Iliad* XXIII. 412 The wheel's round naves appear to brush the goal. *a* **1774** GOLDSM. *Surv. Exp. Philos.* (1776) I. 282 Such as in the nave of a wheel, in the axle of a pulley, and such like. **1803** WELLINGTON in Gurw. *Desp.* (1837) I. 434 Four carriages, for 6 pounders, with brass naves, are preparing. **1838** *Civ. Eng. & Arch. Jrnl.* I. 384/2 The naves of the paddles are of wrought iron. **1877** W. JONES *Finger-ring* 22 The cart-wheels sank up to their naves.

β. **1388–9** *Durham Acc. Rolls* 391 In factura unius par. rotarum cum ij par. de naffs. **1393–4** *Ibid.* 392 Pro rotis, nafs, et alia husbanderia. **1483** *Cath. Angl.* 248/1 A Naffe of a qwele, *meditulium, modiolus.* **1593** R. BARNES *Parthen.* in Arb. *Garner* V. 403 An orient jet which did not move, To Cupid's chariot wheel, made for the naffe, Was fixed. **1653** G. DANIEL *Idyll* iii. 56 Whip vp and downe The grateing Orbes; all in a tracke, t'enflame Their Naffes drye-worne. **1796** W. MARSHALL *Yorksh.* (ed. 2) II. 334. **1824** in *Cumbld. Gloss.* (1899) 221/1 Wheels with naffs (naves), spokes and felloes. **1855** ROBINSON *Whitby Gloss.* **1873–** in north. dial. glossaries (Northumb., Cumb., Yks.).

b. *attrib.* and *Comb.*, as ***nave-band, -box, -deep, -hole, -hoop, -shaped, -stock***; **nave plate** = *hub-cap.*

1388 WYCLIF *1 Kings* vii. 33 The extrees, and the naue stockis [*v.r.* nauelstockis], and the spokis..were ȝotun. **1753** CHAMBERS *Cycl. Supp.* s.v., It is bound at each end with hoops of iron, called the nave-bands. **1802** JAMES *Milit. Dict.*, *Nave-boxes* were formerly made of brass. *Ibid.*, *Nave-hoops* are flat iron rings to bind the nave. **1839** LINDLEY *Bot.* (ed. 3) 454 Nave-shaped. **1867** SMYTH *Sailor's Word-bk.* 493 *Nave-hole*, the hole in the centre of a gun-truck for receiving the end of the axle-tree. **1876** VOYLE & STEVENSON *Milit. Dict.* 269/1 The nave-box is made of gun-metal. **1882** E. ARNOLD *Pearls of Faith* xxiii. (1883) 84 Through foeman's blood nave-deep he drave his wheel. **1962** *Which? Car Suppl.* Apr. 67/1 The Austin A60 has a grease gun, nave plate remover and box spanner. **1968** *Radio Times* 13 June 29/3 A rattle from the tail end [of a car],..sounding..like a loose wheel nut bouncing about inside the nave plate.

†**2.** ? The navel. *Obs. rare*⁻¹.

1605 SHAKS. *Macb.* I. ii. 22 Braue Macbeth..neu'r shooke hands, nor bad farwell to him, Till he vnseam'd him from the Naue to th' Chops.

nave (neɪv), *sb.*² [= Sp. and It. *nave*, ad. L. *nāvem*, acc. of *nāvis* ship: see also NEF.] The main part or body of a church, extending from the inner door to the choir or chancel, and usually separated from the aisle on each side by pillars.

1673 RAY *Journ. Low C.* 261 A double isle on each side of the Nave. **1682** N. O. *Boileau's Lutrin* III. 63 With equal pace the Temples Nave they measure! **1726** AYLIFFE *Parergon* 169 It comprehends the whole Church, viz. the Nave or Body of the Church together with the Chancel. **1791** MRS. RADCLIFFE *Rom. Forest* ii, From this chapel he passed into the nave of the great Church. **1823** BYRON *Island* IV. vii, The fretted pinnacle, the aisle, the nave, Were there. **1859** JEPHSON *Brittany* ii. 15 The massive pillars of the nave have a solemn and grand effect. *a* **1878** SIR G. SCOTT *Lect. Archit.* (1879) I. 52 Let us suppose it applied to the nave of a basilica in place of the timber roof.

attrib. and *Comb.* **1850** INKERSLEY *Styles Archit. France* 311 The windows opened in the nave-aisle walls. **1883** FARRAR in *Pall Mall G.* 27 Dec. 2/2 The nave services of all our great cathedrals are the results of this experiment.

Hence **nave** *v.*, *trans.* to make like a nave.

1820 SHELLEY in Medwin *Convers. Byron* (1824) I. 19 Follow the graceful curve of the palaces on the Lung' Arno till the arch is naved by the massy dungeon-tower.

†**nave,** have not: see NE and HAVE *v.* A. 9. *Obs.*

See also NABBE, NAD, NAS.

c **950** *Lindisf. Gosp.* John iv. 17 Uel ðu cuede þætte nafu [ic] wer. **971** *Blickl. Hom.* 31 He næniȝe mehte wið us nafað. *a* **1000** *Andreas* 311 (Gr.), Nafast þe to frofre..hlafes wiste? *c* **1175** *Lamb. Hom.* 29 Nauest þu nefre milce of heofenlic drihten. *c* **1230** *Hali Meid.* 5 Ha naueð nawt freo of hire seluen. *c* **1330** R. BRUNNE *Chron. Wace* (Rolls) 8223 Y naue no wyt To open þe knottes þat Merlyn knyt. **1362** LANGL. *P. Pl.* A. I. 157 ȝe naue no more merit in masse ne in houres. *c* **1420** *Chron. Vilod.* st. 288 Y naue nouther wytte ny space All here godenesse forto wryte.

nave, obs. f. NAVY, obs. or dial. f. NIEVE, fist.

navee, obs. form of NAVY.

navegar, -gor, obs. (early ME.) ff. AUGER *sb.*¹

navel (ˈneɪv(ə)l), *sb.* Forms: α. 1 **nabula, nafela, navela, nafla,** 3–4 **nauele,** (4 **nav-**), 4–7 **nauel, -ell,** (5–7 **-il, -ill, -yl, -yle, -yll,** 5 **nawelle, -ylle,** etc.),

5–7 navell, (6 -yll, 6–7 -il; 5 nable, 6–7 navle, 7 naple), 5– navel; 4 naule, nawle, 6 nale, 9 *dial.* nawl. β. 3 noule, 4 nouel, 5 nowele, -yl, novyl(l, 9 *Sc.* nuil. [OE. *nafela*, masc. = OFris. *navla*, *naula*, MDu. *navel(e*, *naffel(e*, etc. (Du. *navel*), MLG. *navel*, *naffel*, OHG. *nabalo*, *napalo*, etc. (MHG. *nabele*, G. *nabel*), ON. *nafle* (Sw. *nafle*, *nafvel*, Da. *navle*):—Comm. Teut. **nabalan-*, related to Skr. *nābhīla*, and more obscurely to Gr. *ὀμφαλός*, L. *umbilīcus*, and OIr. *imbliu* (Gael. *imleag*, *iomlag*). The various forms appear to be derivatives of the stem of NAVE *sb.*[1]]

1. a. A rounded depression, with a more or less raised or protuberant centre, situated on the abdomen at the point where the umbilical cord was originally attached; the umbilicus.

α. *c* **725** *Corpus Gloss.* (Hessels) U 243 *Umbilicus*, nabula. *a* **850** *Kentish Glosses* in Wr.-Wülcker 56/15 *Umbilico tuo*, þinum nafelan. *c* **893** K. ÆLFRED *Oros.* IV. i. §5 He ȝenedde under ænue elpent þæt he hiene on þone nafelan ofstang. *c* **1000** *Sax. Leechd.* I. 82 ȝif men innan wyrmas eglen.. nim ðа sylfan wyrte [*sc.* waybread], ȝecnuca, leȝe on þone naflan. *a* **1290** *Pains of Hell* (MS. Digby 86) 104 Þe flod to heere nauele takeþ. *c* **1315** SHOREHAM I. 1197 Me schel þe mannes lenden anelye, Þe nauele of þe femele. **13..** *E.E. Allit. P.* A. 459 Al arn we membrez of ihesu kryst, As heued & arme & legg & naule. **1382** WYCLIF *Prov.* iii. 8 Helthe forsothe shal ben in thi nauele [**1388** nawle]. *c* **1400** MAUNDEV. (Roxb.) vii. 24 It had þe schappe of a man fra þe nauel dunward. **1470–85** MALORY *Arthur* VI. xi. 199 Launcelot.. smote hym on the sholder and clafe hym to the nauel. **1523** FITZHERB. *Husb.* §57 Se the oxe haue a greate codde, and the cowe great nauyll. **1592** J. DAVIES *Immort. Soul* XXXII. xxxv, Children, while within the Womb they live, Feed by the Navil. **1646** SIR T. BROWNE *Pseud. Ep.* 239 The use of the Navell is to continue the infant unto the Mother. **1695** *New Light Chirurg. put out* 37 Run into the Belly about two Inches above the Navel. **1727** A. HAMILTON *New Acc. E. Ind.* I. xxiv. 295 They were all naked above the Navel. **1774** J. BRYANT *Mythol.* I. 245 The Deity was worshipped under the form of a navel. **1805** *Med. Jrnl.* XIV. 361 It likewise reached.. almost to the navel. **1873** LOWELL *Oriental Apol.* v, [He] lifted not His eyes from off his navel's mystic knot.
fig. **1607** SHAKS. *Cor.* III. i. 123 Euen when the Nauell of the State was touch'd, They would not thred the Gates.
transf. **1755** *Gentl. Mag.* XXV. 32 *Navel*,.. an aperture in the base of a shell near the center. **1766** *Compl. Farmer* s.v. *Service-tree*, Roundish berries,.. which have a depressed navel on the top.
β. *c* **1220** *Bestiary* 561 Fro ðe noule niðerward ne is ge [*sc.* the mermaid] no man like. *a* **1400** *Stockh. Medical MS.* i. 175 in *Anglia* XVIII. 299 Bynde it on þe nowele in a clout. *Ibid.* i. 485 Hoot on his nowyl ȝif it be bounde. *c* **1440** *Jacob's Well* 95 þe neþer part of here body fro þe nouyll downward. *Ibid.*, Fro þe novyll vpward. **1860** ROBSON *Song Sol.* vii. 2 Thy nuil is like til a roond goblet.

(*b*) Phr. ***to contemplate*** (or ***regard***) ***one's navel***: to engage in meditation or contemplation; to be complacently parochial or escapist; cf. *navel-contemplation*, etc. (sense 4 below).

1933 E. O'NEILL *Days without End* (1934) I. 21 His letters.. extolled passionless contemplation so passionately that I had a mental view of him regarding his navel frenziedly by the hour and making nothing of it! **1966** *Listener* 24 Nov. 770/1 One sits in a New York traffic jam, contemplating, as it were, the city's navel, and the conclusion is inevitable that death from a combination of congestion and suffocation is not far off. **1975** *Times* 2 June 12/8 Lift our eyes for a moment from the contemplation of our own unlovely navels and look out to where.. our fellow human beings live.

†**b.** The junction of a leaf with a stem. *Obs. rare.*

a **1400** *Stockh. Medical MS.* ii. 761 in *Anglia* XVIII. 326 In euery nowele sche beryth here flowris. **1693** EVELYN *De la Quint. Compl. Gard.* II. 63 From the Navel of every Leaf a Fig will infallibly grow.

†**c.** ***lady's navel***: (see LADY 18 b). *Obs.*

d. *ellipt.* A navel orange (see 4).

1888 *U.S. Dept. Agric. Pomology* 68 These trees.. were called.. the 'Washington' or 'Riverside' Navel, to distinguish the variety from the Australian Navel.

2. a. The centre or central point of a country, sea, forest, etc.

1382 WYCLIF *Judges* ix. 37 The puple fro the nouel of the erthe cometh doun. **1387** TREVISA *Higden* (Rolls) II. 41 Þe þridde ilond.. standeþ.. as it were in þe nauel of þe see. **1481** CAXTON *Godfrey* clxxi. 253 This Cyte standeth as it were in the nauyll of the londe of Byheste. **1571** GOLDING *Calvin on Ps.* lxxiv. 12 Situate as it were in the navle of the world. **1586** J. HOOKER *Hist. Irel.* in *Holinshed* II. 27/1 Some thinke this to be the middle part or nauill of that prouince. **1634** MILTON *Comus* 520 Within the navil of this hideous Wood.. a Sorcerer dwels. **1695** KENNETT *Par. Antiq.* i. 2 Whether any Indigence kept always here in the navel of the land, as Cesar reports. **1746** COLLINS *Ode Liberty* 90 'Midst the green navel of our isle. **1796** MORSE *Amer. Geog.* II. 19 That dreadful vortex, or whirl-pool, called by navigators the navel of the sea. **1834** J. WILSON in *Blackw. Mag.* XXXVI. 17 On the green navel of the lake. **1878** K. OLIPHANT *Old & Mid. Eng.* iii. 212 Derby may be called the philological navel of England.

b. The central or middle point of anything.

1603 B. JONSON *K. Jas.'s Entertain.* Wks. (Rtldg.) 530/2 May thousand branches.. style this land the navel of their peace. **1607** MIDDLETON *Five Gallants* IV. vi, 'Tis now about the navel of the day. **1664** EVELYN tr. *Freart's Archit.* 140 Admitting the light at the top Center or Navil only, without any Lantern. **1895** RIDER HAGGARD *Heart of World* xi, The very navel of this ancient.. civilisation.

†**c.** The middle point of a horse's back. *Obs.* (Cf. NAVEL-GALL.)

1684 *Lond. Gaz.* No. 1937/4 A new sore caused by a Pillion on the navle of his back. **1697** *Ibid.* 3337/4 Having on the Naple of the Back a place that looks as if it was formerly burnt. **1713** *Ibid.* 4880/4 A little swell'd on the Navel with an old Saddle Gall.

†**3.** The nave of a wheel. *Obs. rare.*

Cf. Kilian's *navel van 't rad* i. *nave.*

1388 [see NAVE *sb.*[1] 1 b]. **1535** COVERDALE *1 Kings* vii. 33 Their axeltrees, spokes, nales [**1537** MATTHEW nauelles] & shaftes were all molten. **1624** MASSINGER *Parlt. Love* II. iii, His body be the navel to the wheel In which your rapiers, like so many spokes, Shall meet and fix themselves!

4. *attrib.* and *Comb.*, as ***navel-fibre***, ***-knot***, ***-rupture***, †***-stead***, ***-vein***; ***navel-burst***, ***-high***, ***-like***, ***-shaped*** adjs.; **navel-contemplation** (see sense 1 a (*b*)); so ***navel-contemplator***; **navel-cord** = NAVEL-STRING; **navel-fallen**, a disease in pigeons (see quot.); **navel-gazer** = OMPHALOPSYCHITE; also *transf.* (cf. *navel-contemplator*); so ***navel-gazing*** *vbl. sb.*; **navel-hole** (see quot.); **navel-ill**, a disease in calves and lambs, marked by inflammation about the navel; **navel orange**, a large variety of orange, having a navel-like formation at the top; **navel-point** *Her.* (see quot.); **navel-stone**, a stone that marks a navel (sense 2). See also NAVEL-STRING, -WORT;

1589 J. RIDER *Bibl. Schol.*, That is *navell-burst, *exomphalus*. **1921** D. H. LAWRENCE *Let.* 2 May (1962) II. 650 *Your* Nirvana is too much a one-man show: leads inevitably to *navel-contemplation. **1974** *Times* 27 June 18/3 To fight off the navel-contemplation mood induced by our move of office. **1856** R. A. VAUGHAN *Mystics* (1860) I. 272 They call these devotees *Navel-contemplators. **1922** JOYCE *Ulysses* 385 Our grandam, which we are linked up with by successive anastomosis of *navelcords. **1765** *Treat. Dom. Pigeons* 37 The next distemper is what the fancy calls *navel-fallen; in this case, there is a kind of a bag hanging down near the vent. **1671** GREW *Anat. Plants* I. vii. (1682) 49 From thence.. the *Navel-Fibres shoot. **1952** L. MACNEICE *Ten Burnt Offerings* 37 Crystal-gazers, *navel-gazers. **1963** *Kenyon Rev.* XXV. 549/1 This piece of *navel-gazing also reveals a dangerous and sometimes excessive self-consciousness. **1972** *Publisher's Weekly* 10 July 27/2 David Obst has no monopoly on national navel-gazing. **1663** WOOD *Life* (O.H.S.) I. 479 Railed in with a rayl *navel high. **1828** CARR *Craven Gloss.*, **Navel-Hole*, the hole in the centre of a mill-stone, into which the grain is cast by the hopper. **1834** YOUATT *Cattle* 558 The *navel-ill is a far more serious business than some imagine. **1888** W. WILLIAMS *Pract. Vet. Med.* (ed. 5) 306 From the fact that the umbilicus is often involved in the tumefaction, the disease has been called 'navel-ill'. **1766** *Compl. Farmer* s.v. *Vegetation*, Between the roots and ascending stem, the trunk of the plant is knit by the *navel knot to the flower-leaf. **1849–52** *Todd's Cycl. Anat.* IV. 1013/2 A *navel-like aperture on the anterior surface of the tumour. **1888** *U.S. Dept. Agric., Pomology* 68 The varieties of the *Navel orange, their origin, manner of introduction, etc. *c* **1828** BERRY *Encycl. Herald.* I. *Nombril*, or *Navel Point, is the next below the fesse point, or the very centre of the escocheon. **1698** FRYER *Acc. E. India & P.* 21 Their Children.. are much troubled with the *Navel-Rupture. **1822–34** *Good's Study Med.* (ed. 4) IV. 497 *note*, They are not *navel-shaped, like those of small-pox. *c* **1611** CHAPMAN *Iliad* XXI. 173 Full in the *navel-stead He ripp'd his belly up. **1615** CROOKE *Body of Man* 81 Issuing out at the nauill-stead. **1917** *Encycl. Relig. & Ethics* IX. 492/2 Zeus, wishing to ascertain the exact centre of the earth, sent forth two eagles to fly simultaneously at equal speed from its eastern and western ends. They met at Delphi, and there in Apollo's temple was set up in commemoration the holy *Navel-stone.. to mark earth's central point. **1922** A. E. HOUSMAN *Last Poems* 50 Mute's the midland navel-stone beside the singing fountain. **1634** T. JOHNSON *Parey's Wks.* (1649) 595 The umbilical vein, or *navel-vein, entering into the bodie of the childe.

navel ('neɪv(ə)l), *v. rare.* [f. prec.]

1. In *pa. pple.* Situated in the middle.

1818 BYRON *Ch. Har.* IV. clxxiii, Lo, Nemi! navell'd in the woody hills. **1819** WIFFEN *Aonian Hours* 102 Within the shade a ruined temple stands.., navelled in the pines.

2. *intr.* To come to a centre.

1855 BAILEY *Mystic* 52 Radial avenues of rocks All navelling in the sanctuary divine.

navel- ('neɪv(ə)l). *Naut.* Also 8–9 naval, nave-. [Of obscure origin and meaning, occurring only as the first element in certain combs. There is no obvious connexion with NAVEL *sb.*, and the form *naval* is a late alteration.]

†**a.** ***navel timbers***, the first futtocks. *Obs. rare.*

1626 CAPT. SMITH *Accid. Yng. Seamen* 8 First lay the Keele..; then lay all the Flore timbers... Next your Nauell timbers. **1627** —— *Seaman's Gram.* ii. 2 The Sweepe or Mould of the Foote-hookes and Nauell timbers.

b. ***navel*** or ***nave-line***: (see quots.).

1711 W. SUTHERLAND *Shipbuild. Assist.* 143 Nave-line as big as the Cat-harpings, and as long. **1750** BLANCKLEY *Nav. Expos.* 111 *Naveline* is a Rope reeved through a Block made fast to the middle Rib, and another Block made fast to the Mast-head. **1769** FALCONER *Dict. Marine* (1780), *Nave-line* [**1789** *Naval Line*], a sort of small tackle, depending from the head of the main-mast and fore-mast,.. used to keep the parrel directly opposite to the yard. **1848** G. BIDDLECOMBE *Art of Rigging* 22 Nave-line is a tackle from the masthead to the trusses [etc.]. **1863** A. YOUNG *Naut. Dict.* (ed. 2), *Naval Lines*, a name given to the lines which hold up the truss-pendants parallel to their parts round the centre of a lower yard. **1882** NARES *Seamanship* (ed. 6) 125 The reef or naval line is then middled.

c. ***navel hoods***: (see quots.).

1750 BLANCKLEY *Nav. Expos.* 110 Navel Hoods are large Pieces of Stuff fayd against the Hawse Holes, and fills out to the outer Edge of the Cheeks, to keep the Cable from wearing them. **1769** FALCONER *Dict. Marine* (1780) s.v. *Building*, The navel-hoods [are] fayed on the hawse-holes. **1841** R. H. DANA *Seaman's Man.* 116 *Naval Hoods*, or *Hawse Bolsters*, plank above and below the hawse-holes. *c* **1850** *Rudim. Navig.* (Weale) 135 *Navel hoods*, broad pieces of oak, from 6 to 10 inches thick.. worked afore the hawse-holes on the outside of the ship, and likewise above and below them in those ships which have no cheeks to support a bolster.

d. ***navel pipe***: (see quot.).

1882 NARES *Seamanship* (ed. 6) 4 *Chain or Naval-pipes.*—For leading the cable through, as it passes up from one deck to another, from the chain-lockers.

'navel-gall. ? *Obs.* Also 6 nauyl-, 7 nauill, navil(l, naple, etc. [Cf. NAVEL *sb.* 2 c.] A gall or bruise in the middle of a horse's back.

1523 FITZHERB. *Husb.* §105 Nauylgall is a soraunce, hurte with a saddle, or with a buckle.. in the myddes of the backe. **1600–9** ROWLANDS *Knaue of Clubbes* 44 The Lampasse, crest-fall, withers greife, The nauill-gall. **1631** BRATHWAIT *Whimzies, Postmaster* 120 His Stable is a very shop of all diseases;.. Ringbones, Windgalls, Navelgalls. **1678** *Lond. Gaz.* No. 1348/4 Her navil gaul hath formerly been hurt. **1702** *Ibid.* 3813/4 A lean bay Gelding.., a large Bunch or Navel-Gall on his Back. **1855** W. PERCIVALL *Hippopathology* (ed. 2) I. 199 Saddle-Galls, Navel-Galls, Warbles, Sitfasts.

Hence †**navel-galled** *a.*; †**navel-galling.**

1703 *Lond. Gaz.* No. 3967/4 A strong punch grey Nag,.. a sore Back, being Navelgall'd. **1691** J. WILSON *Belphegor* III. iv, A mere rag of a jade; I wonder thou durst venture on her, for fear of navel-gauling.

navel-hoods *Naut.*: see NAVEL-.

nave-line *Naut.*: see NAVEL-.

navell, obs. variant of NEVEL *v.*

navelled ('neɪv(ə)ld), *a. rare*[−1]. [f. NAVEL *sb.* + -ED[2].] Knobbed; bull's-eyed.

c **1817** HOGG *Tales & Sk.* II. 204 A few panes of thick blue, navelled glass.

'navel-string. [f. NAVEL *sb.*; cf. Du. *navelstreng*, Da. *navlestreng*, Sw. *nafvelsträng*.] The organic structure connecting the fœtus with the placenta; the umbilical cord.

1587 GOLDING *De Mornay* xiv. (1592) 223 As if they should say,.. he cannot liue when he is come out of her womb, if his nauilstrings be cut off. **1634** T. JOHNSON *Parey's Wks.* 604 The navel-string must bee tied with a double thred. **1671** GREW *Anat. Plants* I. vii. (1682) 48 Two slender Fibres, like two Navel-strings. **1754–64** SMELLIE *Midwifery* I. 232 Tie the navel-string about two fingers breadth from the belly of the child. **1822–34** *Good's Study Med.* (ed. 4) IV. 155 The navel-string hangs down below the head. **1846** J. BAXTER *Libr. Pract. Agric.* (ed. 4) II. 269 Inflammation of the navel-string, occurring a few days after a lamb is dropped.

navel-timbers *Naut.*: see NAVEL-.

'navel-wort. [f. NAVEL *sb.*; cf. G. *nabel-wurz*, Da. *navleurt*.] A name given to various plants, esp. *Cotyledon umbilicus* (see PENNYWORT 1).

14.. *Vocab.* in Wr.-Wülcker 567 *Belberici marini*,.. navel wort. *Ibid.* 620 *Vmbilicus*, Nauelworte. **1597** GERARDE *Herbal* II. cxliii. 423 The great Nauelwoort hath round and thicke leaues. *Ibid.* clii. 529 There is a kind of Navel-woorte that groweth in waterie places. **1629** PARKINSON *Parad.* xxxii. 232 Wee doe call them Nauelworts in English rather than Houseleekes. **1671** SALMON *Syn. Med.* III. xxii. 441 Navel wort. That of the water helps the Sciatica, Gout and Kings-evil. **1718** QUINCY *Compl. Disp.* 209 Wall Navel-wort. This is not known of late in Medicine. **1760** J. LEE *Introd. Bot.* App. 320 Navel-wort, Bastard, *Crassula*. *Ibid.*, Navel-wort, Venus's, *Cynoglossum*. *Ibid.*, Navel-wort, Water, *Hydrocotyle*. **1862** ANSTED *Channel Isl.* II. viii. 175 The pretty, round, fresh leaf of the navel-wort (*cotyledon umbilicus*) is seen on every wall. **1865** GOSSE *Land & Sea* (1874) 183 The fleshy coin-like leaves of the pretty navel-wort.

†**naverage**, erron. form of NAUFRAGE.

a **1656** USSHER *Ann.* (1658) 376 Himself coming on shoar.. took up his standing to recover what might be saued out of the naverage.

navet[1]. Now only as Fr. Also 6 nauet(te, naued. [a. F. *navet* (13th c.) ultimately f. L. *nāp-um* (*nāpus*) NAPE *sb.*[3], or F. *navette* (1323) of similar origin. Cf. NAVEW.] A variety of rape (*Brassica napus*), a cruciferous plant with a fleshy fusiform root of a sweet taste. Also *attrib.*

F. *navet* is applied to the esculent, *navette* to the oleiferous, variety of rape. Cotgrave defines *navet* as 'the small Navew gentle, the least (and daintiest) kind of French Navew'.

1530 PALSGR. 247/2 Navet rote, *nauette*. **1548** TURNER *Names Herbs* (E.D.S.) 55, I haue hearde sume cal it in englishe a turnepe, and other some a naued or nauet, it maye be called also longe Rape or nauet gentle. **1583** STOCKER *Civ. Warres Lowe C.* III. 96 b, Bread made of nauettes and of chanure seede. **1600** [see NAPE *sb.*[3]].

1861 MRS. BEETON *Bk. Househ. Managem.* 601 The French Navet.. is a variety of the turnip; but, instead of being globular, has more the shape of the carrot.

†**navet**[2]. *Obs. rare.* Also 5 navitt. [a. F. *navette* (†*navete*, 13th c.; cf. med.L. *naveta*), properly 'little boat', f. L. *nāvis*.] = NAVICULA.

1467 *Will of Dryland* (Somerset Ho.), Thre sensures of siluer with iiij navitte therto. **1540** in V. Green *Worcester* (1796) II. App. p. v, Item a navett with a spone all gylt. **1706** PHILLIPS (ed. Kersey), *Navet*, part of an Incense-pan, or Censer-box.

navette (næˈvɛt). [Fr., lit. = little boat, f. med.L. *naveta*, dim. of *navis* ship. Cf. NAVET[2].] A cut of jewel in the shape of a pointed oval; a jewel cut in such a shape. Also *attrib.* Cf. MARQUISE 4.

1908 H. C. SMITH *Jewellery* 246 Many of the best-known collections contain examples of these 'nef' or 'navette' pendants. **1944** *Times* 21 Mar. 2/2 A flower pendant, the six petals formed of diamond navettes with a single ruby centre. **1945** A. SELWYN *Retail Jeweller's Handbk.* xv. 217 Fancy shapes, such as the three-cornered, the marquise or navette.., the pear-shaped..or pendeloque, make unusual jewels, and are generally suggested by the natural form of the diamond itself. **1949** G. F. H. SMITH *Gemstones* (rev. ed.) xii. 153 The commonest distorted shapes are the marquise or navette..and the pendeloque or drop-form. **1963** *Guardian* 15 Nov. 10/5 The leading trend today in diamond cutting is the navette—shuttle-shape an enormous pendant *navette* diamond. **1967** *Times* 21 Feb. 21/7 (Advt.), A navette-shaped diamond single-stone ring. **1973** *Country Life* 18 Oct. (Suppl.) 71 Sunburst brooch..brilliant baguette and navette diamond set.

navew (ˈneɪvjuː). Now *rare.* Also 6–7 **nauew(e**, 6 **naueu**, 8 **naphew**. [a. F. **naveu*, obs. var. of *naveau* (now only dial.), OF. *navel*, *-iel*:—**nāpellum*, f. L. *nāp-um* (*nāpus*) NAPE *sb.*[3] Cf. NAVET[1].] The rape (*Brassica napus*) or coleseed (*B. campestris*); a plant of this kind.

1533 ELYOT *Cast. Helthe* (1541) 28 b, Navews do not nouryshe so moche as rapes, but they be even as wyndye. **1563** HYLL *Art Garden.* (1593) 144 And the propertie of the place doth change the Nauew into a Rape [= turnip], and the rape contrariwise into a Nauew. **1620** VENNER *Via Recta* vii. 136, I suppose the Nauewe to be a little dryer then the Turnep. **1678** SALMON *Pharm. Lond.* I. vii. 149 Of sweet Navew. The Seed is Alexipharmick. **1733** MILLER *Gard. Dict.* (ed. 2), *Napus*, the Navew or French Turnip. **1796** WITHERING *Brit. Plants* III. 591 *B. Napus*, Wild Navew. **1865** GOSSE *Land & Sea* 7 The navew, loose and sprawling, but bright in hue.

attrib. **1611** FLORIO, *Nauone*, a kind of rape, a Nauew roote. **1658** ROWLAND tr. *Moufet's Theat. Ins.* 1090 They are much delighted with Navew seeds. **1766** *Museum Rust.* VI. 273 Sown in common with rape-seed, or more properly, wild navew-seed.

†**b.** ***navew gentle***, the cultivated variety of rape. *Obs.*

1578 LYTE *Dodoens* 595 Some do also cal it..in English, Nauet, and Nauew gentle. **1607** TOPSELL *Four-f. Beasts* (1658) 102 Likewise Navew-gentil and Oleander, kill the Hart. **1655** MOUFET & BENNET *Health's Improv.* (1746) 322 Navews, especially *Napus Sativus*, called in English Navew Gentle. **1736** AINSWORTH *Lat. Dict.*, *Napus*.., navew [**1783** naphew] gentle, or long rapes.

†**navey.** *Obs.* Also 4–5 **naueye**. [a. ONF. *navey*, *navei* (*c* 1300 in Godef.), = OF. *navoy*, *navoi*:—Lat. type **nāvēt-um*, f. *nāvis* ship.]

a. Ships, shipping. **b.** A navy.

c **1350** *Will. Palerne* 2719 A gret number of naueye to þat hauen longed. **1387** TREVISA *Higden* (Rolls) I. 343 In a naueye of þre score schippes and tweie. *Ibid.* VII. 167 Kyng Edward gedred a strong navey. **1436** *Libel Eng. Policy* in *Pol. Poems* (Rolls) II. 177, I wolde wete why nowe owre navey fayleth. *c* **1460** FORTESCUE *Abs. & Lim. Mon.* vi. (1885) 123 With owt thaym all the kyngs navey shallnot suffice to borde with carrikkes and oþer grete vessailles. **1535** BOORDE *Let.* in *Introd. Knowl.* (1870) 53 A greatt army and navey ys preparyd.

Nav. House, Nav House, *colloq.* name for the Navigation School in H.M. Dockyard, Portsmouth.

1924 'NAUTICUS' *Sea Ways & Wangles* viii. 48 You will then be sent to the Navigation School or 'Nav. House' as it is more familiarly called. This, as you might expect, is situated ashore, near the main gate of Portsmouth Dockyard. *Ibid.* 52 However you are not likely to become Navigator of a flagship until you have been through another course at the 'Nav. House' to qualify you for first class ships. **1948** PARTRIDGE *Dict. Forces' Slang* 124 *Nav House, the*, the R.N. Navigation School, Portsmouth.

navicert (ˈnævɪsɜːt). [f. L. *navis* ship + CERT(IFICATE *sb.*] A consular certificate granted to a neutral ship testifying that her cargo is correctly described in the manifest. Hence as *v. trans.*, to authorize with a navicert.

1923 C. E. FAYLE *Seaborne Trade* II. xx. 304 The 'Navicert System', as it was called, from the code word employed, became, in fact, one of the chief instruments in the prevention of enemy trade. **1939** *Times* 3 Nov. 5/1 Arrangements are approaching completion for introducing the navicert system, which was much used in the last war. **1940** *Times* 21 Mar. 5/5 On Tuesday a vessel came through with no fewer than 200 navicerted items of cargo. **1940** R. W. B. CLARKE *Britain's Blockade* 10 A plan is in operation for issuing compulsory navicerts to all ships coming to Europe and North Africa. **1941** *Ann. Reg. 1940* 7 To make matters easier for neutrals, the 'navicert' system introduced in the last war was being greatly extended. **1941** *Times* 2 Apr. 3/5 After the British Government had agreed to navicert two gift cargoes of flour. **1967** D. L. BUSK *Craft of Diplomacy* ii. 46 During the last war..the British issued what were called 'navicerts'. These guaranteed shippers that 'clean' items of cargo would not be confiscated by the Royal Navy as contraband destined for the enemy.

‖**navicula** (nəˈvɪkjʊlə). *Eccl.* [L., dim. of *nāvis* a ship. Cf. NAVET[2].] An incense-holder in the form of a boat.

1853 J. D. H. DALE *Cerem. Rom. Rite* 8 He..presents the navicula (or incense-boat) to the Master of Ceremonies. **1884** *Nonconf. & Indep.* 14 Feb. 162/2 There was a procession through the new clergy-house, with crosses, candles, thurible and navicula.

navicular (nəˈvɪkjʊlə(r)), *a.* and *sb.* Also 6 **-uler**. [ad. late L. *nāviculāris*: see prec. and -AR. Hence also F. *naviculaire* (16th c., Paré).]

A. *adj.* **1.** ***navicular bone***, the scaphoid bone of the hand (*rare*), or the corresponding bone in the foot lying between the astragalus and cuneiform bones. (Freq. in veterinary works as the seat of a disease in the feet of horses.)

1541 R. COPLAND *Guydon's Quest. Chirurg.* Lj, The bone called Nauyculer, that is a synew concaued on eche syde. **1696** PHILLIPS, *Navicular-Bone*, the third Bone in each Foot in that part of it which immediately succeeds the Leg. **1755** in JOHNSON. **1816** BLAINE *Veter. Art* (ed. 2) 98 The navicular bone would have been too much pressed upon. **1836–9** *Todd's Cycl. Anat.* II. 343/1 The scaphoid or navicular bone is articulated with the three cuneiform. **1870** FLOWER *Osteol. Mamm.* xix. (1876) 309 The navicular bone is interposed between the proximal and distal row on the inner or tibial side of the foot.

b. *Farriery.* Connected with the navicular bone of a horse's foot, esp. ***navicular joint***, ***disease***.

1828 J. TURNER in *Veterinarian* (1829) II. 53 The College Museum..contained but a solitary specimen of the navicular disease. *Ibid.* 58 By articulating with the bone, [it] forms the navicular joint. **1845** SPOONER *Veter. Art* (1851) 86 It is this joint capsule which is the seat of the navicular disease. *Ibid.*, Its posterior and lower surface forms the navicular-joint capsule.

†**2.** Pertaining to, connected with, boats. *Obs.*

1656 in BLOUNT *Glossogr.* *a* **1704** T. BROWN *Thames* Wks. 1720 III. 325 'Rare Game, Master,' cries our Navicular Spokesman. **1721** in BAILEY (and hence in some later Dicts.).

3. Having the form of a (small) boat.

a. Of shrines, etc. Also *transf.* of the deities associated with these.

1774 J. BRYANT *Mythol.* II. 219 The name of this, and of all the navicular shrines was Baris. **1818** G. S. FABER *Horæ Mosaicæ* I. 133 The navicular goddess of Egypt was called Isis. **1819** *Blackw. Mag.* V. 584 We may still behold the figure of that animal standing in that holy navicular coffin.

b. *Bot.* Of the parts of plants.

1806 GALPINE *Brit. Bot.* 23 Glumes navicular, entire. **1845** LINDLEY *Sch. Bot.* iv. (1858) 33 Valves navicular, apterous. **1881** SPENCE in *Jrnl. Bot.* X. 99 With the two lateral lobes complicate into a navicular sheath embracing the stem.

c. *Ent.* Of the bodies or parts of insects.

1826 KIRBY & SP. *Entomol.* IV. xlvi. 268 Navicular,.. when two sides meet and form an angle like the outer bottom of a boat. **1828** STARK *Elem. Nat. Hist.* II. 277 Body navicular, narrowed and pointed at both ends.

4. ***navicular fossa***, (*a*) the depression between the helix and anthelix of the ear; (*b*) the anterior portion of the urethra.

1816 BLAINE *Veter. Art* (ed. 2) 256 When the labia are separated, the internal cavity is called the navicular or scaphoid fossa. **1836–9** *Todd's Cycl. Anat.* II. 550/2. **1849–52** *Ibid.* IV. 1248/2.

B. *ellipt.* passing into *sb.*

1. = Navicular bone (see A. 1).

1816 BLAINE *Veter. Art* (ed. 2) 98 The coronary bone partakes of the form of the pastern,..resting more on the coffin, and less on the navicular than in the front. **1836–9** *Todd's Cycl. Anat.* II. 505/2 The navicular or scaphoid is the largest of the upper row [in the hand]. **1870** FLOWER *Osteol. Mamm.* xix. (1876) 318 The navicular and the external cuneiform are very broad and flat.

2. = Navicular disease (see A. 1 b).

1888 *Pall Mall G.* 4 July 5/2 Not one shows symptoms of navicular by pointing his toes to ease the pain.

naviculoid (nəˈvɪkjʊlɔɪd), *a.* [f. L. *navicula*, dim. of *nāvis* a ship; (in sense 1) adopted as a generic name by J. B. G. M. Bory de St. Vincent in *Dictionnaire classique d'Histoire naturelle* (1827) XI. 472/2: see -OID.] **1.** Of, pertaining to, or resembling a diatom of the genus *Navicula*.

1894 P. T. CLEVE in *Kongelige Svenska Vetenskapsakademien Handlingar* XXVI. II. 10 It is by no means an easy task to construct an artificial key of such numerous and variable forms as the naviculoid diatoms. **1916** G. S. WEST *Algæ* I. 90 In some of the larger naviculoid diatoms the cell-wall is destitute of pores. **1946** *Nature* 26 Oct. 588/1 It was found that the form of the protoplasmic bodies was returning to the naviculoid.

2. = NAVICULAR *a.* 3 b.

1961 R. W. BUTCHER *New Illustr. Brit. Flora* II. 172 Seed ..naviculoid, rugose, black.

†**navie**, obs. variant of NAVET or NAVEW.

1553 EDEN *Treat. New Ind.* (Arb.) 29 The inhabitantes.. vse in ye stede of bread, certayne rotes like vnto nauie rotes. **1555** —— *Decades* (Arb.) 131 The skyn is sumwhat towgher then eyther of nauies or mussheroms. **1575** TURBERV. *Venerie* 151 They lyve and feede upon..all sortes of rootes also unlesse it be rapes and navie rootes.

navie, obs. form of NAVY.

naviˈfauna. *nonce-word.* [f. L. *nāvi-s* ship.] The fauna peculiar to a ship.

1879 MOSELEY *Notes Nat. Challenger* 594 Centipedes of two kinds at least were also amongst the navifauna.

ˈnaviform, *a. rare.* [f. L. *nāvi-s* + -FORM.] Boat-shaped; navicular.

1816 G. S. FABER *Orig. Pagan Idol.* II. 280 The naviform leaf of the Indian fig-tree. **1817** —— *Eight Dissert.* (1845) II. 199 In the sphere, the Moon or Naviform Lunar Crescent was the astronomical representative of the Ark.

navigability (nævɪgəˈbɪlɪtɪ). [f. next + -ITY.] The fact or quality of being navigable.

1846 in WORCESTER. **1865** *Reader* 15 Apr. 415/2 It was said that the navigability of the Thames would be injuriously affected. **1889** *Law Times* LXXXVII. 290/1 This excludes the notion of navigability.

navigable (ˈnævɪgəb(ə)l), *a.* and *sb.* [a. F. *navigable* (14th c.), or ad. L. *nāvigābilis*, f. *nāvigāre*: see NAVIGATE *v.*]

A. *adj.* **1.** Admitting of being navigated, affording passage for ships or boats: **a.** of the sea.

1527 R. THORNE in Hakluyt *Voy.* (1589) 257 To attempt, if our Seas Northwarde be Nauigable to the Pole or no. **1553** EDEN *Treat. New Ind.* (Arb.) 9 Yf the North sea were not nauigable by reason of extreme cold and Ise. **1603** HOLLAND *Plutarch's Mor.* 151 The sea [yieldeth itself] navigable to everie one that will. **1716** POPE *Iliad* VIII. 66 Thence his broad Eye..surveys The Town, and Tents, and navigable Seas.

b. of rivers and other water-ways. (The usual sense). Also const. *for*.

1530 PALSGR. 319/1 Navygable, a water able to be sayled or rowed in, *nauigable*. **1555** EDEN *Decades* (Arb.) 284 They determyned to brynge a nauigable trench vnto the ryuer of Nilus. **1593** NORDEN *Spec. Brit., Cornwall* (1728) 98 The towne seateth nere the nauigable Tamar. **1634–5** BRERETON *Trav.* (Chetham Soc.) 6 A fair navigable river which will carry as great a ship as can sail. **1680** MORDEN *Geog. Rect., Germany* (1685) 120 Here the Danube begins first to be Navigable. **1735** BERKELEY *Querist* §381 The use of slaves in repairing high roads, making rivers navigable. **1776** ADAM SMITH *W.N.* I. iii. I. 24 The plantations have constantly followed either the sea coast or the banks of the navigable rivers. **1835** *Penny Cycl.* III. 176/2 The Avon..is navigable from Stratford for vessels of about 40 tons burden. **1878** HUXLEY *Physiogr.* 3 At Lechlade..the Thames ceases to be navigable.

†**c.** Of passage from one place to another. *Obs.*

1570 J. DEE *Math. Pref.* d iv b, Betwene any two places (in passage Nauigable,) assigned. **1632** LITHGOW *Trav.* II. 60 In this meane while of our nauigable passage, the Captaine.. espied a Saile comming from Sea.

2. a. Of ships: Capable of navigation; fit for sailing; seaworthy. *rare.*

1535 in Ellis *Orig. Lett.* Ser. II. II. 74 His Navy was not navigable thowgh he wold have departid thens. **1627** HAKEWILL *Apol.* (1630) 131 For the better supporting of navigable vessells. **1809** PINKNEY *Trav. France* 31 Two or three ships..sound, and in the best navigable condition.

b. Of balloons and airships: That may be steered; dirigible. Now *Obs.* exc. *Hist.*

1783 in S. STUBELIUS *Balloon* (1960) 151 We have received a prodigious number of letters relative to the aerostatic machine of Mess. de Montgolfier. Some of these propose methods for rendering this machine truly navigable. **1835** *Mechanics' Mag.* 15 Aug. 374/2 This has been the case with steam-carriages, steam-boats, and other machines, and why should a navigable balloon be excepted? **1887** *Nature* 13 Jan. 260/1 Captain Renard has recently sent in to the French Academy an account of his experiments with his so-called navigable balloon, *La France*, at Meudon. **1903** *Edin. Rev.* Apr. 334 The first serious attempt to build a navigable balloon was that of Henry Giffard, in 1852. **1907** *Cornh. Mag.* May 611 We shall not go very far wrong if we say that the limits of speed attainable with navigable balloons are not widely different from those attainable in marine navigation. **1908** H. G. WELLS *War in Air* ii. 41 There were several navigable gas air-ships, not to mention balloons, in the air.

3. Of places: Admitting the approach or passage of vessels; surrounded by water in which a ship can sail. ? *Obs.*

1573 L. LLOYD *Marrow of Hist.* (1653) 53 Mount Athos was made of Xerxes navigable, even unto the sea. **1625** N. CARPENTER *Geog. Del.* II. vii. (1635) 122 An incomparable great iland.., nauigable round about. **1649** *Alcoran* 413 In Navigation we must know, not only what places are Navigable, but also what are not.

†**4.** Nautical. *Obs. rare.*

1597 J. PAYNE *Royal Exch.* 33 In wch. navigable arte I spent the pryme of myne yeres. **1724** WELTON *18 Disc.* 397 The particular engagements which those of the navigable profession lay under.

†**5.** Maritime; naval. *Obs. rare.*

1642 HOWELL *For. Trav.* (Arb.) 60 It will be a wonderfull thing to see what a..huge Navigable power that State is come too. *c* **1645** —— *Lett.* (1650) I. 300 What a mighty navigable power the Hollander is come to.

B. *sb.* A navigable balloon. Cf. DIRIGIBLE *sb.* *Obs.* exc. *Hist.*

1882 W. N. HUTCHINSON in *United Service Mag.* II. 262 This principle of diminishing buoyancy by diminishing bulk is as applicable to the ordinary balloon..as to the navigable, but..the strain on the material..of the navigable ..would be trifling. **1908** H. G. WELLS *War in Air* i. 18 They started ironclads, they started submarines, they started navigables. **1933** —— *Shape of Things to Come* I. §7. 70 That primitive 'navigable' the Zeppelin.

ˈnavigableness. [-NESS.] Navigability.

1720 STRYPE *Stow's Surv.* II. v. xxx. 437/2 Touching the River, and the Navigableness and Fishing thereof. **1805** W. TAYLOR in *Ann. Rev.* III. 14 A commerce co-extensive with the navigableness of the Mississippi. **1865** LIVINGSTONE *Zambesi* ii. 60 To solve the problem of the navigableness of the Kebrabasa.

ˈnavigably, *adv.* [f. NAVIGABLE *a.* + -LY[2].] In a navigable manner. (Webster, 1847.)

†'**navigal**, *a.* *Obs. rare*⁻¹. = NAVIGABLE.
c **1470** HARDING *Chron.* CCXL. (Harl. MS.), The water navigall rynneth thedir for vessels of fourty tonne tight.

†**navigant**, *sb.* *Obs. rare.* [a. F. *navigant*, sb. use of pres. pple. of *naviguer*: see NAVIGATE *v.*] A navigator or voyager.
1527 R. THORNE in Hakluyt *Voy.* (1599) I. 213 Which thing is a great commoditie for the nauigants. **1553** *Ibid.* (1886) III. 19 To be obtained..by humble and heartie praier of the Nauigants. **1594** BLUNDEVIL *Exerc.* v. (1636) 571 This Land is new Guinea, so called of the Navigants and Pilots.

'**navigant**, *a. rare.* [ad. L. *nāvigant-em*, pres. pple. of *nāvigāre*: see next.] Voyaging.
c **1680** in *Pepys' Life, Jrnl.*, etc. (1841) II. 203 The Church of England is worthy of your best services, and..needs them. It has been too long navigant in a valley of tears. **1781** H. WALPOLE *Let. to Cole* 7 July, The church navigant would be an extension of its power.

navigate ('nævɪgeɪt), *v.* Also 7 **navigat**. [f. L. *nāvigāt-*, ppl. stem of *nāvigāre* to sail, sail over, f. *nāvis* ship + *agĕre* to drive, guide, etc.]

1. *intr.* **a.** To go from one place to another in a ship or ships, to sail.
1588 PARKE tr. *Mendoza's Hist. China* 302 They beganne to set sayle to nauigate towardes the port. **1614** SIR R. DUDLEY in *Fortescue Papers* (Camden) 10 Thoughe they maye be able..to navigat to the West Indies. **1705** ARBUTHNOT *Coins*, etc. (1727) 218 The Phoenicians.. navigated into the Ocean by the Straits of Gibraltar, established many Colonies. **1749** CHESTERF. *Lett.* (1792) II. cciii. 272 In the Summer you may navigate as you please. **1821** SOUTHEY *Exped. Orsua* 176 We navigated eleven months, till we reached the mouth of the river.

b. To sail a ship.
1894 *Daily Chron.* 4 Aug. 3/5, I was the only one on board who could navigate.

c. *U.S.* To walk steadily; to keep on one's course.
1843 'J. SLICK' *High Life* (1844) I. vii. 109 It warn't no easy matter tu navigate so as not tu git a second ducking, for every nigger in York seemed to be out a washing winders. **1846** *Spirit of Times* 11 July 234/3 Well, by this time I began to think of navigating. **1881** R. T. COOKE *Somebody's Neighbors* 88 What are you navigating round me for? **1904** *Sun* (N.Y.) 9 Aug. 10 She was so drunk that she could barely navigate. **1908** G. H. LORIMER *Jack Spurlock* 117 While he could navigate successfully..he could only just stuttah. **1930** *Randolph Enterprise* (Elkins, W. Virginia) 13 Feb. 1/1 The fellow was..hardly able to navigate as he was carrying a heavy load of Prohibition poison.

2. *trans.* To sail over, on, or through (the sea, a river, etc.).
1646 SIR T. BROWNE *Pseud. Ep.* 314 The River Oregliana ..hath beene navigated 6000 miles. **1705** ARBUTHNOT *Coins*, etc. (1727) 272 Drusus..was the first who navigated the Northern Ocean. **1791** COWPER *Odyss.* x. 97 Six days we navigated, day and night, The briny flood. **1836** W. IRVING *Astoria* II. 179 To send exploring parties on each side of the river, to ascertain whether it was possible to navigate it further. **1872** YEATS *Techn. Hist. Comm.* 21 The seas were navigated and islands visited by the aid of the earliest canoes.
fig. **1845** STOCQUELER *Hand-bk. Brit. India* (1854) 130 The number of vehicles..which navigate the streets. **1898** *Daily Chron.* 15 Oct. 6/4 Can they navigate the Redistribution shallows?

3. a. To sail, direct, or manage (a ship).
1670 R. COKE *Disc. Trade* 26 Nor must any English man navigate any English built ship..unless she be sailed by ¾ English at least. **1748** *Anson's Voy.* I. iii. (ed. 4) 38 Their great difficulty was to procure a sufficient number of hands to navigate her. **1758** J. BLAKE *Plan Mar. Syst.* 43 Want of hands to navigate his ships. **1813** WELLINGTON in Gurw. *Desp.* (1838) X. 600 The harbour boats at Passages being.. all navigated by women. **1887** MISS BRADDON *Like & Unlike* iii, I know something about navigating a yacht.

b. *transf.* and *fig.*
1901 G. B. SHAW *Capt. Brassbound's Conversion* I. 215 Spiritually a little weatherbeaten, as having to navigate his creed in strange waters crowded with other craft. **1934** DYLAN THOMAS *18 Poems* 12 Sleep navigates the tides of time.

c. *absol.* and *transf.* of a motor vehicle.
1965 I. FLEMING *Man with Golden Gun* v. 67 Mary Goodnight had insisted on coming along, 'to navigate and help with the punctures'. **1967** J. CAIRD *Murder Scholastic* viii. 93 Once they were in the car, David said: 'I'll navigate. Turn left at the school gate'. **1967** L. MEYNELL *Mauve Front Door* ix. 117 We all piled into it [*sc.* the car]. Three of us in the front seat, Ray and Zena behind. Tessa navigated. **1971** 'H. HOWARD' *Million Dollar Snapshot* vii. 108 Zombie tossed me the keys. He said, 'You drive, I'll navigate.'

4. Of vessels: **a.** *intr.* To sail; to ply.
1758 GOLDSM. *Mem. Protestant* (1895) II. 185 Four half Galleys..were to be sent to Antwerp to navigate on the River Scheld. **1795** PHILLIPS *Hist. Inland Nav.* Add. 114 Every boat which shall navigate only between Stainforth Lock and Hangman Hill. **1849–50** ALISON *Hist. Europe* V. xxxiii. §4. 481 The superior power..can..make prize of all neutral vessels navigating to any of its harbours.

b. *trans.* To sail on or over (the sea, etc.).
1858 HAWTHORNE *Fr. & It. Note-bks.* (1872) I. 2 An.. irregular motion, such as the British Channel generally communicates to the craft that navigate it. **1878** MARKHAM *Gt. Frozen Sea* i. 4 Ships destined to navigate the icy seas.

5. *trans.* To convey (goods) by water. Also *intr.* of goods.
1795 PHILLIPS *Hist. Inland Nav.* Add. 6 For all coal navigated between Milton Cross and Kington, six-pence per ton per mile. *Ibid.* 23 Coals, &c. passing this canal, and navigating on the Birmingham canal.

6. a. *trans.* To manage, direct, sail, or fly (a balloon, airship, aeroplane, or the like) in the air. Hence *spec.* to plot and supervise the course of (an aircraft or spacecraft).
1784 *Universal Mag.* LXXIV. p. ii, By imitating the action of..wings, sails, oars, and a rudder, we may be able to navigate a Globe [*sc.* a balloon] in any direction we please. **1877** *Design & Work* III. 603/1 To build it [*sc.* an airship] in England, and navigate it to Zanzibar. **1910** *Blackw. Mag.* July 5/1 The pilot of an aeroplane is almost wholly occupied with navigating his craft. *Ibid.* 13/2 If we can succeed..in building and in navigating a few score of serviceable dirigibles. **1922** *Encycl. Brit.* XXX. 43/1 Not only had the flying-boats on war service to be navigated but the pilot and observer had also to 'navigate' a bomb to its desired target. **1951** *Oxf. Jun. Encycl.* IV. 289/2 Aeroplanes are navigated first by careful planning before the flight, and then by an attempt to keep the course planned throughout the journey. **1958** C. C. ADAMS et al. *Space Flight* xiii. 326 Seven things must be known to properly navigate a ship [*sc.* a spaceship].

b. To travel or fly through (the air).
1901 *Chambers's Jrnl.* Mar. 207/2 Count Zeppelin's airship,..with a row of seventeen balloons inside, for navigating the air, has also pointed cigar-like ends. **1902** *Ibid.* July 479/2 In the meantime his efforts to navigate the air have, as a matter of course, resulted in the inauguration of many rival schemes. **1907** *Cornh. Mag.* May 609 Grotesque and fantastic schemes for navigating the air were put forward. **1927** C. L. M. BROWN *Conquest of Air* 8 Stories of wizards and witches who navigated the upper air with the assistance of tubs and broomsticks.

Hence '**navigated** *ppl. a.*, '**navigating** *vbl. sb.* and *ppl. a.*
1739 C. LABELYE *Short Acc. Piers* 72 Water enough for the working and navigating of Boats. **1751** H. WALPOLE *Lett.* (1846) II. 398 The prospect is as fine as one destitute of a navigated river can be. **1860** MAURY *Phys. Geog. Sea* xv. §624 The best navigated steam-ships do not sail closer than this. **1871** *Daily News* 1 Sept., While professional..critics are discussing whether the special class of navigating officers should be retained or abolished. **1950** M. LASKI in *Contact* May–June 50/2, I must warn you, too, of the danger of letting navigating become an end in itself, of sitting with one's eyes glued to the map until it becomes a substitute for the country outside. **1966** 'E. PETERS' *Piper on Mountain* iii. 51 He enjoyed driving, but to him navigating was a chore. **1971** *Gloss. Electrotechnical, Power Terms* (*B.S.I.*) III. vi. 22 A radar navigating system. **1973** A. ROSS *Dunfermline Affair* 103 Charlie drove, and I did the navigating.

navigation (nævɪ'geɪʃən). [a. F. *navigation* (14th c.), or ad. L. *nāvigātiōn-em*, n. of action f. *nāvigāre* to NAVIGATE.]

1. a. The action of navigating; the action or practice of passing on water, esp. the sea, in ships or other vessels; sailing; †rowing. Also const. *of*.
1533 ELYOT *Cast. Helthe* (1539) 52 Navigation or rowyng nigh to the lande, in a calme water is expedient for them that haue dropsies. **1547** BOORDE *Brev. Health* xxii, I can not away with water, nor waters by nauigacion. **1589** PUTTENHAM *Eng. Poesie* I. xii. (Arb.) 44 The Gentiles prayed ..for safe nauigation to Neptune. **1612** T. TAYLOR *Comm. Titus* iii. 3 The Earth was made for man and beast to liue vpon, the sea for fish and nauigation. **1673** MARVELL *Reh. Transp.* II. Wks. 1776 II. 368 If there were a dead calm always..there would be no navigation. **1724** *Lond. Gaz.* No. 6300/1 The Wind proving contrary.., [she] was forced to return..after about an Hour's Navigation. **1727–46** THOMSON *Summer* 1767 The heaven-conducted prow Of navigation bold, that fearless braves The burning line. **1813** WELLINGTON in Gurw. *Desp.* (1838) XI. 3 From what I have heard of the navigation of the river. **1835** THIRLWALL *Greece* vi. I. 219 The approach of winter put a stop to all ordinary navigation. **1842** *Penny Cycl.* XXIV. 280/2 The navigation of the Thames..is kept up by locks and wears.

b. ***inland navigation***, communication by means of canals and navigable rivers.
1727 DE FOE *Eng. Tradesman* (1732) II. II. iv. 123 Madrid ..has neither Sea-port or Inland Navigation, no Navigable River being near it. **1791** MYLNE *1st Rep. Thames Nav.*, The Thames is..very capable of an improved inland navigation. **1861** *Chambers's Encycl.* II. 551/2 Shewing how canals might be..used for inland navigation, in countries whose surface was irregular.

†**c.** A piece of seamanship. *Obs. rare*⁻¹.
1817 JAS. MILL *Brit. India* II. IV. iii. 101 He returned..by a very able navigation against a contrary monsoon.

d. The action or practice of travelling through the air by means of aircraft; flying. More fully, ***aerial navigation***. ? *Obs.*
1804 [see *aerial navigation* s.v. AERIAL *a.* 5]. **1835** *Mechanics' Mag.* Aug. 290/1 The first experiment of this new system of aërial navigation will be made from London to Paris, and back again. **1870** tr. *F. Marion's Wonderful Balloon Ascents* II. ix. 163 The idea of aerial navigation by means of an apparatus heavier than the atmosphere. **1910** *Blackw. Mag.* July 12/2 The safe navigation of the air. **1920** *Act 10 & 11 Geo. V.* c. 80 §2 Limited to aircraft of any special description, or engaged in any special kind of navigation.

2. a. The art or science of directing the movements of ships on the sea, including more especially the methods of determining a ship's position and course by the principles of geometry and nautical astronomy; seamanship.
1559 W. CUNNINGHAM *Cosmogr. Glasse* 3 They be wryters of Cosmographie, Geographie, Hydrographie, or Nauigation. **1588** GREENE *Pandosto* (1607) 7 Franion.. hauing some small skill in Nauigation, was well acquainted with the Ports. **1642** HOWELL *For. Trav.* (Arb.) 80 The most materiall and usefull parts of the Mathematiques, as the Art of Navigation and Fortification. **1696** WHISTON *Th. Earth* III. (1722) 267 'Tis evident and will be allow'd by Persons skill'd in Navigation. **1726** SWIFT *Gulliver* I. i, My Father now and then sending me small Sums of Money, I laid them out in learning Navigation. **1769** FALCONER *Dict. Marine* (1780) s.v., Every sea-officer is presumed to be furnished with books of navigation. **1836** MARRYAT *Midsh. Easy* xiv, A cruise at sea without knowledge of navigation was a more nervous thing than he had contemplated. **1875** JOWETT *Plato* (ed. 2) III. 215 Safety at sea is the good of navigation.

b. The art or science of directing the movements of aircraft or spacecraft, esp. in regard to a craft's position and course. More fully, ***aerial*** (or ***air***) or ***celestial navigation***.
1922 *Encycl. Brit.* XXX. 14/1 Aerial navigation, as distinct from piloting with the ground in view, developed tardily everywhere, though first in Britain. **1931** *Times* 19 Feb. 17/1 A haze..limited visibility to two miles. Navigation was undoubtedly difficult. **1951** *Oxf. Jun. Encycl.* IV. 291/1 Some methods of navigation employ both radar and radio at the same time... Some of the radar and radio devices..can be used both for the main part of a flight and for the actual landing. **1962** F. I. ORDWAY et al. *Basic Astronautics* ix. 385 (*heading*) Celestial navigation. *Ibid.*, The platform of a celestial navigation system includes an automatic sextant. **1974** *Encycl. Brit. Macropædia* I. 376/2 The flight simulator taught the essentials of air navigation and blind flight to thousands of military pilots during World War II.

c. The action or practice of navigating a motor car (NAVIGATE *v.* 3 c) or other vehicle.
1944 *Return to Attack* (Army Board, N.Z.) 9/1 Battalions and regiments entered the wilderness in battle order and exercised in desert navigation. **1950** [see NAVIGATOR 1 c]. **1973** H. MILLER *Open City* xiii. 148 I'm relying on you for navigation..just keep me on the road.

3. a. A voyage; an expedition or journey by sea or water. Now *rare.*
1527 R. THORNE in Hakluyt *Voy.* (1599) I. 214 In this nauigation..was discouered, that these Islands nothing set by golde. **1553** EDEN *Treat. New Ind.* (Arb.) 7 Such thinges as are spoken of in the nauigacions wherof this boke entreateth. **1599** HAKLUYT *Voy.* II. II. 101 Our nauigation growing so long that it drew neere to seuen moneths. **1632** J. HAYWARD tr. *Biondi's Eromena* 160 Their Navigation was short, and favoured with gentle windes. **1673** *Phil. Trans.* VIII. 6114 Those Countreys that are addicted to long Navigations. a **1715** BURNET *Own Time* IV. (1724) I. 629 The other was a long navigation, and subject to great accidents. **1752** CARTE *Hist. Eng.* III. 560 The Queen..encouraged her subjects to the like adventures and navigations. **1807** SOUTHEY *Espriella's Lett.* II. 172 Our last navigation had ended by transferring us to a coach.

b. *transf.* with reference to fishes.
1822–34 *Good's Study Med.* (ed. 4) IV. 5 Many other marine fishes seek out a fresh-water stream for this purpose; and their navigations are often of very considerable length.

4. *concr.* The means of navigation, vessels collectively; shipping. In later use *U.S.* ? *Obs.*
1605 SHAKS. *Macb.* IV. i. 54 Though the yesty Waues Confound and swallow Nauigation vp. **1748** *Anson's Voy.* III. vii. (ed. 4) 480 The Centurion alone was capable of destroying the whole of the navigation of the port of Canton. **1772** C. HUTTON *Bridges* 86 This will leave more free passage for the water and navigation. **1809** KENDALL *Trav.* I. xxxiii. 321 The word navigation is used in New England for shipping. **1850** SCORESBY *Cheever's Whalem. Adv.* i. (1859) 9 Nearly one-tenth of the navigation of the Union.

†**5. a.** Shipping business; trade or intercourse carried on by sea or water. *Obs.*
1617 MORYSON *Itin.* I. 21 This Navigation is very necessary that the lower Oestreich being fertill, may supply the upper..with wine and corne. **1679** *Establ. Test* 50 Nor will they make any Scruple..to..weaken us..in our Trade and Navigation. **1720** STRYPE *Stow's Surv.* I. I. xxvii. 215/2 The Trade, Navigation, and Naval Strength of this Realm.

†**b.** Export. *Obs. rare*⁻¹.
c **1630** RISDON *Surv. Devon* (1810) 7 Corn we have plentiful.., as well for navigation as for..sustenance.

†**6.** That which one sails on; a passage or course by which one may sail. *Obs. rare.*
1633 G. HERBERT *Temple, Man* vii, Waters united are our navigation; Distinguished, our habitation. **1654** EARL MONM. tr. *Bentivoglio's Wars Flanders* 312 The divulging of a memorable Navigation..which the Hollanders and Zealanders had that year found out.

7. †**a.** A natural inland channel. *Obs.* **b.** A canal or other artificial waterway. Now *dial.*
1720 *Lond. Gaz.* No. 5885/3 A Stock of Money..in the Navigation of Wakefield. **1761** *Ann. Reg.* I. 146 A navigation being compleated from Lynn to Northampton. **1794** WHITWORTH & MYLNE *Rep. Lond. Canal* 6 It is by far the best part of the navigation between London and Lechlade. **1821** SOUTHEY *Exped. Orsua* 89 *note*, There is some obscurity here in Pedro Simon's narrative, as if he were taking Aguirre by some cross navigation. **1861** *Chambers's Encycl.* II. 551/2 *note*, These combinations of drain and canal are commonly called navigations. **1916** A. BENNETT *Lion's Share* i. 7 Probably the largest yacht that have ever threaded that ticklish navigation.

8. *attrib.*, as ***navigation branch***, ***channel***, ***deck***, ***limit***, ***season***; in senses relating mainly to air travel: ***navigation beacon***, ***instrument***, ***log***; **navigation act** or **law**, a legal enactment regulating navigation or shipping; **navigation coal**, steam-coal; **navigation light**, one of a set of lights shown by a ship or aircraft at night; **navigation satellite**, a satellite whose orbit is accurately known and made available, so that observations of its position may be used for navigational purposes; **navigation spade** *dial.* (see quot. and NAVIGATOR 2 b.)
1765 BLACKSTONE *Comm.* I. 405 The navigation-acts. **1867** SMYTH *Sailor's Word-bk.*, *Navigation Acts*, various statutes by which the legislature of Great Britain has in a certain degree restricted the intercourse of foreign vessels with her own ports. **1941** J. MASEFIELD *Nine Days Wonder*

3 In war-time, when the navigation-beacons are extinguished. **1778** *Eng. Gazetteer* (ed. 2) s.v. *Avon*, The river forms an island, the navigation branch going on one side. **1900** *Daily Express* 3 Aug. 5/4 A splendid seam of smokeless navigation coal. **1899** *Westm. Gaz.* 5 Sept. 8/1 She has a navigation deck placed above the promenade deck. **1959** F. D. Adams *Aeronaut. Dict.* 117/1 *Navigation instrument*, an aircraft instrument that indicates, or that is used to ascertain, information relating to the position of an aircraft in flight, or to the direction in which it is flying. **1840** *Penny Cycl.* XVI. 117/1 Navigation laws. **1922** Navigation light [see *landing light*]. **1939** T. L. Stocken *Oncoming Ships* 99/1 Lights..mistaken for navigation lights. **1943** C. D. Lane *Boatman's Manual* x. 355 In addition to the navigation light, the lightship carries a riding light forward. **1951** *Oxf. Jun. Encycl.* IV. 4/1 Small lights attached to the wing tips are navigation lights, similar to those used by ships. **1966** Navigation light [see *collision course*]. **1970** V. Canning *Great Affair* vii. 117 A helicopter..came low over the villa. .. It wasn't showing any navigation lights. **1937** Navigation log [see *air speed* (air *sb.*[1] B. III. 1)]. **1961** *Ann. Reg. 1960* 386 Transit IB (U.S.A.)..Navigation satellite. Not transmitting. **1968** *Listener* 27 June 825/1 On 21 April 1964 the U.S. military authorities launched a navigation satellite. **1891** *Daily News* 28 Oct. 2/8 The navigation season is now nearing its end. **1830** *Cumb. Farm Rep.* 65 in *Lib. Usef. Kn., Husb.* III, The round-mouthed spades used in forming canals, etc., called here navigation spades.

Hence **navi'gational** *a.*

1884 Knight *Dict. Mech.* Suppl. 631/1 Navigational Sounding Machine. **1902** Mahan *Types Naval Officers, Howe* 290 A navigational problem complicated by uncertain winds. **1920** *Act 10 & 11 Geo. V* c.67 §69 Lighthouses, light vessels, buoys, beacons, or other navigational marks. **1930** *Proc. Internat. Illumination Congr. 1931* II. 995 The navigational light on a light-vessel is fitted in a latern which, in the older types, is made in halves bolted together around the mast. **1951** *Oxf. Jun. Encycl.* IV. 291/1 Another radio navigational aid is the radio compass. **1954** *Communications & Electronics* I. 1. 60 The progress of modern aviation is becoming increasingly bound up with developments in communications and navigational aids. **1962** D. Slayton in *Into Orbit* 21 Carpenter..told us what he was doing about navigational aids, although the word 'navigation' was really a misnomer in our case... When you've been..tossed into either a ballistic trajectory or into an orbit, your course is already set. There is nothing you can do to change it. **1966** *Electronics* 3 Oct. 177 Teldix..supply instrumentation, navigational platforms and sensors. **1971** *Gloss. Electrotechnical, Power Terms (B.S.I.)* III. vi. 22 *Navigational radar*, radar equipment installed on a craft as an aid to its navigation. **1973** *Fisheries Fact Sheet* (Environment Canada Fisheries & Marine Service) No. 1. 4/2 Small boats..equipped with..navigational aids and radio.

navigator ('nævɪgeɪtə(r)). Also 7 **-our**. [a. L. *nāvigātor*, agent-n. f. *nāvigāre*: see navigate *v.* and -or. Cf. F. *navigateur* (15th c.).]

1. a. One who navigates; a sailor or seaman, especially one skilled and experienced in the art of navigation; one who conducts explorations by sea.

1590 Greene *Never too late* (1600) 43 He that at euery gust puts to the Lee, shall neuer be good Nauigator. **1625** N. Carpenter *Geog. Del.* I. xi. (1635) 234 Our times haue brought forth the most excellent Nauigators of all ages. *a* **1687** Petty *Pol. Arith.* (1690) 17 Every Seaman of industry and ingenuity, is not only a Navigator, but a Merchant. **1725** De Foe *Voy. round World* (1840) 2 The several navigators whose Voyages round the World have been published. **1776** Gibbon *Decl. & F.* i. I. 17 The enterprising spirit which had prompted the navigators of Tyre. **1829** Marryat *F. Mildmay* iv, I soon became an expert navigator and a good practical seaman. **1860** Maury *Phys. Geog.* xv. §622 When a navigator undertakes a voyage now, he does it with the lights of experience to guide him.

transf. **1803** *Pic Nic* No. 5 (1806) I. 177 Putting it into the hands of our tonish navigators and curricleers.

b. One who navigates an aircraft or spacecraft.

1784 *Universal Mag.* LXXIV. 20/1 But they soon lost sight of our aerial navigators. **1825** in Hone *Every-day Bk.* I. 442 Mr. Graham, another aërial navigator, let off another balloon. **1834, 1915** [see *air navigator* s.v. air *sb.*[1] B. III. 4]. **1929** T. E. Lawrence *Let.* 12 July (1938) 663 The Navigator of the airship will be getting his W/T bearings & time signals all the way, and will plot his course exactly. **1930** *Daily Express* 6 Oct. 3/5 The commander [of the airship] must have known, and the navigator. **1943** [see *air-bomber* (air *sb.*[1] B. III. 3)]. **1951** *Oxf. Jun. Encycl.* IV. 290/2 Once in flight, the navigator's task is continually to 'fix' his position by observations. *Ibid.* 291/2 A pilot or navigator..cannot choose any course he pleases, as his is not the only aircraft in the sky. **1960** F. Gaynor *Dict. Aerospace* 161 *Navigator*, a crew member who plots and directs the movement of a space ship from within the ship.

c. One who navigates a motor vehicle.

1950 M. Laski in *Contact* May–June 26/1 It is..possible to take an extended motor-trip abroad without ever coming into contact with the Art of Navigation... Far better to become an Accomplished Navigator, and be free of all roads everywhere. **1964** W. Markfield *To Early Grave* (1965) vii. 120 A groan went round the car. '—we are a little, little bit *fahrblunged*.' 'Our navigator,' fumed Levine. **1968** M. Carroll *Dead Trouble* ii. 25, I sat in the car, content and lazy. Lisa needed no navigator. She seemed to know just where whe was going. **1971** 'D. Rutherford' *Clear the Fast Lane* 37 Grant would be responsible for everything to do with the car..whilst Ritchie, who would act as his navigator, would be responsible for maps, routes and the latest road information. **1971** M. Tak *Truck Talk* 110 *Navigator*, the co-driver of a two-man operation who reads the road maps while going through unfamiliar towns.

2. a. A labourer employed in the work of excavating and constructing a canal (cf. navigation 7 b), or, in later use, in any similar kind of earthwork. Now usually contracted to navvy.

1775 in Earwaker *Sandbach* (1890) 284 Above forty of the Navigators, now working near Hassal. **1800** *Gentl. Mag.* Dec. 1130/2 Some foundations of buildings were also discovered [in making a canal]..; but Navigators are not very curious in these matters. **1819** Southey in *Q. Rev.* XXI. 396 Seven old navigators (as canal-men are called in the midland counties). **1846** Ld. Stanley in *Croker Papers* (1884) III. 86, I was assured..that the railway navigators.. consume on an average two pounds of meat daily. **1890** Stirling *Gifford Lect.* xiv. 276 What a strong healthy fellow is the navigator on the line.

b. *dial.* (See quot. and *navigation spade*.)

1879 Jefferies *Amateur Poacher* xi. 197 A 'navigator' or draining-tool. This is a narrow spade of specially stout make; the blade..resembles an exaggerated gouge.

Hence †**navigatory** *a.*, nautical. *Obs. rare*$^{-1}$.

1650 Charleton *Paradoxes* 86 A needle..placed at free range in the navigatory Compasse.

†**na'vigerous,** *a. Obs. rare*$^{-0}$. [f. L. *nāviger* navigable + -ous.] 'That will bear a vessell or ship' (Blount *Glossogr.* 1656).

†**navin.** *Sc. Obs.* Forms: 4–5 **nawine, -yn,** 6 **navin(e, -ing, -en.** [var. of navy: the origin of the suffix is obscure.] Shipping, fleet, navy.

1375 Barbour *Bruce* III. 393 Schyr Nele Cambel befor send he, For to get him nawyn and meite. *c* **1375** *Sc. Leg. Saints* xxxviii. (*Adrian*) 603 A gret wynd rase..& scalit his nawine to & fra. *c* **1470** Henry *Wallace* IX. 278 The rede nawyn in to the hawyn thai socht. **1513** Douglas *Æneis* IV. vi. 18 He..bad thai suld..graith his schippis and navine secretly. **1549** *Compl. Scot.* xi. 91 Ane grit nauen of schipis.

†**navire.** *Obs. rare.* In 5 **navir, -ier.** [a. F. *navire* ship.] Ship; shipping.

1442 T. Beckington *Corr.* (Rolls) II. 213 From hens.. went never passage; nor unto this tyme was no maner of navir for to passe inne. **1455** *Rolls of Parlt.* V. 279/1 The kynges Enemies been purveied of grete Armies and Navier.

na-vis, obs. Sc. form of no-wise.

†**'navity.** *Obs. rare*$^{-0}$. [ad. L. (*g*)*nāvit-as*, f. (*g*)*nāvus* busy, active: see -ity.] (See quots.)

1623 Cockeram *Nauitie*, diligence, speed. **1656** Blount *Glossogr.*, *Navitie*, diligence, stirring, quickness.

navvy ('nævɪ), *sb.* Also **navvie**, *pl.* **navies.** [Abbrev. of navigator 2. In north. dial. also used for *navigation* = canal.]

1. A labourer employed in the excavation and construction of earth-works, such as canals, railways, embankments, drains, etc.

1832-4 De Quincey *Cæsars* i. Wks. 1862 IX. 51 If navvies had been wanted in those days. **1839** Lecount *B'ham Railw.* 27 These banditti, known in some parts of England by the name of 'Navies', or 'Navigators', and in others by that of 'Bankers'. **1862** Smiles *Engineers* III. 321 During the railway-making period the navvy wandered about from one public work to another. **1888** Bryce *Amer. Commonw.* III. 408 The navvies of the two companies fought with shovels and pickaxes.

attrib. **1858** R. S. Surtees *Ask Mamma* lxi. 279 The navvie boots that laced his great bulging calves into globes.

2. A machine for excavating earth. Usually called a ***steam navvy***.

1877 *Sci. Amer.* XXXVI. 399 The navvy illustrated is capable of excavating..at the rate of 60 cubic yards per hour. **1884** *Standard* 11 Jan. 3/2 The cranes and mechanical navvy in the excavations.

Hence **'navvy** *v.*, *intr.* to work as a navvy; *trans.* to excavate.

1897 Bartram *People of Clopton* 75, I staarted navvyin' me waay arter 'em—navvyin' an' traampin'. **1897** Mary Kingsley *W. Africa* 138 They are at present..navvying a stiff clay bank.

navy[1] ('neɪvɪ). Forms: 4–5 **nauye, navye,** 4–7 **nauie, navie,** 5–7 **nauy,** 5– **navy;** 4–5 **nauee, navee,** 5–6 **naue, nave.** [a. OF. *navie* fleet:—Romanic **navia*, f. L. *nāvis* ship: see -y[3].]

†**1. a.** (Without article.) Number of ships; ships or shipping. *Obs.*

c **1330** R. Brunne *Chron.* (1810) 24 A duke..aryued on þis lond with fulle grete nauie. *c* **1385** Chaucer *L.G.W.* 960 *Dido*, In libie onethe aryuede he With schepis vij & with no more nauye. *c* **1450** *St. Cuthbert* (Surtees) 4789 In his tyme come ouer þe se A paynyme kyng with grete naue. **1473** Warkw. *Chron.* (Camden) 17 Quene Marget..hade nauy to brynge them to Englonde.

†**b.** ***by navy***, by ship. (Cf. OF. *par navie*.) *Obs.*

c **1400** Maundev. (1839) xxvii. 273 No man may passe that See by Navye, ne be no maner of craft. **1412-20** Lydg. *Chron. Troy* Prol., How they come by lande or by nauy,.. Of this Cornelie maketh no menciowne.

2. a. A fleet; a number of ships collected together, esp. for purposes of war. Now *poet.* and *rhet.*

c **1330** R. Brunne *Chron. Wace* (Rolls) 2152 A gret nauye he dide hym dight. **1382** Wyclif *1 Kings* x. 11 The nauee of Yram, the which bare gold of Oofer. *c* **1450** *Merlin* 378 Gawein made..take shippes and assembled a grete navie. **1483** in Ellis *Orig. Lett.* Ser. II. I. 158 The king shuld have a Navie upon the see, to shewe himself as a king. *a* **1533** Ld. Berners *Gold. Bk. M. Aurel.* (1546) K v, A great nauy of warre, to the numbre of c. and .xxx. ships. *a* **1586** Sidney *Arcadia* ii. (1613) 123 The trayterous Sea began to swell in pride against the afflicted Navie. **1627** Capt. Smith *Seaman's Gram.* xiii. 63 Betweene two Navies they vse often ..to fill old Barkes with pitch, tar [etc.]. **1659** in *England's Conf.* 8 No person shall have..any Command..in any of the Armies or Navyes of England. **1725** Pope *Odyss.* VIII. 550 From the shores the winged navy flies. **1777** Burke *Let. to Rockingham* Wks. IX. 167 We set our faces against great armies..and navies, who have tasted of civil spoil. **1817** Shelley *Rev. Islam* x. iv, The sea shook with their Navies' sound. **1858** Mrs. Oliphant *Laird of Norlaw* I. 279 The masts were in forests, the ships in navies.

†**b.** In phr. ***a navy of ships***, etc. *Obs.*

1390 Gower *Conf.* I. 197 Wher that a gret Navye lay Of Schipes. *c* **1400** Maundev. (Roxb.) xxii. 104 In þe whilk citee es a grete nauee of schippez. **1483** *Cath. Angl.* 249/1 A Navy of schyppis, *classis, navigium.* **1535** Coverdale *Dan.* xi. 40 With a greate nauy of shippes. **1584** Powel *Lloyd's Cambria* 38 Alfred lost a great Nauie of Ships. **1617** Moryson *Itin.* I. 97 The Roman Navie of Gallies.

†**c.** A single ship. *Obs. rare.*

a **1400-50** *Alexander* 3376 If any Naue to it neȝe..þen cleuys it ay to þe clife, carryg & othyre. *c* **1400** *Siege Jerusalem* 58 Nethannys naue a-non on norþ dryueþ.

†**d.** A naval force. *Obs. rare*$^{-1}$.

c **1450** *Merlin* 644 Than was the navie appereiled and entred in to shippes.

3. a. The whole of the ships of war belonging to a nation or ruler considered collectively, with all the organization necessary for their command and maintenance; a regularly organized and maintained naval force. Freq. ***the king's*** (***queen's***) ***navy***, ***Royal Navy***, †***navy royal***.

1540 *Act 32 Hen. VIII*, c. 14 The nauy..is..a great defence and surete of this realme in tyme of warre, as well to offende as defende. **1568** Grafton *Chron.* II. 639 They tooke the principall ships of the kings nauy then lying at the Port. **1592** Moryson *Let.* in *Itin.* (1617) I. 37 What we call warre at sea, and the royall Navy. **1601** R. Johnson *Kingd. & Commw.* (1603) 24 As touching their sea forces (besides the Nauie Royall). **1698** Savery *Navig. Impr.* 8, I shew'd a Draught..to the Lords of the Admiralty... I was referred from them to the Commissioners of the Navy. **1719** W. Wood *Surv. Trade* 55 The Tonnage of our Navy-Royal. **1765** Blackstone *Comm.* I. 408 The executive power, which is limited so properly with regard to the navy. **1769** Falconer *Dict. Marine* (1780) s.v. *Midshipman*, In merchant-ships, or in the royal navy. **1840** *Penny Cycl.* XVI. 117/1 Alfred the Great was the founder of the English navy. **1884** Pae *Eustace* 23 At his own wish he entered the Navy.

b. The officers (and men) serving in, or composing the crews of, the navy.

1648 *Hamilton Papers* (Camden) 188 This is certaine that all the Nauy is discontented and wauering. **1769** Falconer *Dict. Marine* (1780), *Navy* is also the collective body of officers employed in his majesty's sea-service. **1814** *Navy List* 15 List of the Royal Navy. **1845** Stocqueler *Hand-bk. Brit. India* (1854) 59 The Indian navy now consists of 150 officers.

†**4.** The dominion of the sea. *Obs. rare.*

1422 tr. *Secreta Secret., Priv. Priv.* 151 For hym myght not Suffice the brede of the worlde, the nauy of the See, of all to be lorde. **1610** J. Healey tr. *St. Aug. Citie of God* (1620) 157 Ioue got the East, resembling heauen... Neptune had the nauy.

5. *ellipt.* **a.** = *navy blue*. Also *attrib.*

1884 *Chr. World* 17 Jan. 52/1 Brocaded Plush to match in Navy. **1896** *Westm. Gaz.* 2 July 4/3 A green fabric with white foulard figured in navy, and navy ribbon velvet.

b. ? = navy sword.

1777 Wayne in *St. Clair Papers* (1882) I. 388 Lieutenant Henry defended himself with great bravery.., dangerously wounding two of the Indians with his navy.

c. A navy revolver.

1867 *Harper's Mag.* June 131/1 Judge put hand under pillow, drew out 'navy', and fired—*through a looking-glass*! **1875** 'Mark Twain' *Sk. New & Old* 122 She turned on that smirking Spanish fool like a wild cat, and out with a 'navy' and shot him dead in open court. **1931** G. F. Willison *Here they dug Gold* 92 Early boom towns and mining camps generally prefer the Colt 'Navy'(·36). **1968** R. F. Adams *Western Words* (ed. 2) 204 *Navy*, a westerner's term for the Navy Colt revolver.

d. A type of tobacco. Also, cigarette ends, etc., as picked up by tramps.

1872 *Kansas Mag.* 177/1 Another pull at the bottle,..a chaw of navy, and the repast is finished. **1876** G. H. Tripp *Student-Life Harvard* 399 Hawes had smoked 'navy' in it all the year of Sam's probation. **1889** J. W. Riley *Pipes o' Pan* 40, I draw my plug o' navy, and I climb the fence. **1926** *Amer. Speech* I. 652/1 *Navy*, cigar end or 'butts' found on side-walk. **1931** 'D. Stiff' *Milk & Honey Route* 214 *Navy*, butts of cigarettes and cigars. **1934** *Amer. Ballads & Folk Songs* 383 The higher you pitch, the sweeter my navy tastes. **1960** Wentworth & Flexner *Dict. Amer. Slang* 351/2 *Navy*,..a cigar end or butt found on a side walk. Perhaps from 'navy' = a type of chewing tobacco.

e. = navy rum.

1946 J. Irving *Royal Navalese* 121 *Navy*, Service issue; Service ways. Most usually it is a sobriquet for the rum-ration—e.g., 'I'll trade my *Navy* for a turn out of watch!'. **1962** Granville *Dict. Sailors' Slang* 80/1 *Navy, tot of*, measure of Navy rum offered to a guest by one who has saved his ration for some special occasion.

6. *attrib.* and *Comb.*, as ***navy book***, ***debt***, †***fleet***, ***man***, ***revolver***, ***surgeon***, ***wall***, †***washing mill***; articles as supplied to the navy; ***navy biscuit***, ***bread***, ***jacket***, ***-plug***; **navy agent**, one who manages the business affairs of naval officers; also formerly, a disbursing agent in the U.S. navy; **navy bean** = haricot *sb.* 2; **navy bill**, a bill issued by the Admiralty in place of ready-money payment, or drawn by a naval officer on the Admiralty; **navy blue**, a dark blue, the colour of the British naval uniform (also *attrib.*); **Navy Board**, a former title of the Admiralty; **navy bullet**, a bullet used with a navy revolver; **navy catapult** (see quot.); **Navy Cut**, proprietary name of a kind of tobacco; **Navy**

Department *U.S.*, the government department controlling the navy; **Navy League**, a body founded in the 19th-c. with the object of arousing national interest in the Navy; hence ***navy-leaguer***; **Navy List**, an official publication containing a list of the officers of the Navy and other nautical information; **Navy Office**, a former name for the Admiralty building; **navy register** *U.S.* = *Navy List*; **navy stroke**, the style of rowing practised in the navy; **navy-yard**, a government dockyard (now *U.S.*).

1814 *Navy List* 106 List of Licensed *Navy Agents. **1841** MARRYAT *Poacher* xxxvii, [He] was..a navy agent—that is to say, he was a general provider of the officers..of his Majesty's service. **1867** SMYTH *Sailor's Word-bk.* 494 *Navy Agents*, selected mercantile houses,..who manage the affairs of officers' pay, prizes, &c. **1897** *Sears, Roebuck Catal.* 15/3 Beans, small *Navy, hand picked. **1903** A. ADAMS *Log of Cowboy* xii. 77 Our supply of flour and navy beans was running rather low. **1951** *Good Housek. Home Encycl.* 349/2 Haricot Beans (called 'navy beans' in U.S.A.). **1955** W. GADDIS *Recognitions* II. iii. 426 She went out..and left Gwyon staring into a plate of white navy beans. **1972** *Arable Farmer* Feb. 55/2 The navy bean crop must remain a matter for research and speculation for at least a year or two. **1973** *Times* 30 Apr. 9/1 The baked beans that passed over the shelves of Britain's supermarkets..originate in the United States. Navy beans grown in the Michigan area are shipped to Britain..for processing and canning. **1975** *New Society* 3 July 6/1 The Scottish Horticultural Institute are developing plants less susceptible to colder northern conditions; and research is going on into the production of a navy bean (baked bean) which can be grown in this country. **1679–88** *Secr. Serv. Money Chas. & Jas.* (Camden) 28 To compleat 1,477[li] 2[s] on a *Navy bill due to him and owners of the shipp Leister. **1708** *Lond. Gaz.* No. 4496/4 Lost or Mislaid,..two Navy Bills. **1809** R. LANGFORD *Introd. Trade* 130 *Bills navy*, bills issued by the navy board for stores, bearing interest till due and paid. **1867** 'T. LACKLAND' *Homespun* II. 216 The people not only want the Word, but they want it as hard and dry as a *navy biscuit. **1840** MARRYAT *Poor Jack* xxx, [He] was dressed in *navy blue. **1888** *Lady* 25 Oct. 378/2 Wearing a navy-blue serge. **1695** *Lond. Gaz.* No. 3045/4 A Person unknown hath sent a Letter to the *Navy-Board. **1777** J. ADAMS *Wks.* (1854) IX. 464, I had the boldness to make a motion that a navy board should be established at Boston. **1802** JAMES *Milit. Dict.*, *Navy-board*..consists of a lord high admiral, or lords commissioners for executing this office [etc.]. **1758** *M.P.'s Let. on R.N.* 7 Such Payment being requisite to be made..by Clerks possessed of the proper *Navy-Books. **1831** *Constellation* 54/1 Ephraim Treadwell ..has for sale..Pilot and *Navy Bread. **1848** *Rep. Comm. Patents 1847* (U.S.) 374 The 'navy bread' is usually made out of the coarser particles of the meal. **1873** J. MILLER *Life amongst Modocs* 312 Was it possible that this man..could still live with a *navy bullet through his body fired at two feet distance. **1914** C. F. TWENEY *Dict. Naval & Mil. Terms* 161 **Navy Catapult*, a device for launching hydro-aeroplanes from a ship by means of compressed air. **1907** *Yesterday's Shopping* (1969) 67/3 Cigarettes... Virginia... *Navy Cut, mild. **1911** *Trade Marks Jrnl.* 6 Sept. 1309 Player's Navy Cut... Manufactured tobacco. The Imperial Tobacco Company (of Great Britain and Ireland), Limited, ..Bristol. **1959** E. BURGESS *Divided we Fall* vii. 96 Harry was filling his briar with his favourite navy-cut. **1972** 'G. NORTH' *Sgt. Cluff rings True* i. 15 Harrison inhaled contentedly... 'One third navy-cut, two thirds herb mixture.' **1769** BURKE *Late St. Nat.* Wks. II. 49 Only..the exchequer bills, and part of the *navy debt, carried any interest. **1824** *Amer. St. Papers, Naval Affairs* (1860) II. 98 Respecting the concerns of the *Navy Department. **1693** LUTTRELL *Brief Rel.* (1857) III. 53 Most of the seamen..are taken out to serve on board the *navy fleet. **1840** C. MATHEWS *Politicians* II. i. 30 He..had boasted out of doors he could and would save his life with a word as easily as hem-stitch a *navy-jacket! **1864** in *Maryland Hist. Mag.* (1926) XXI. 300 He..had on his navy jacket with bright buttons and pants of the same dark blue. **1898** *Westm. Gaz.* 31 Jan. 4/2 An account..which will stir the blood of *navy-leaguers. **1809** LD. MULGRAVE in G. Rose *Diaries* (1860) II. 357 The senior officers..on the *Navy List. **1818** BYRON *To Murray* v, And then thou hast the 'Navy List'. **1679** PEPYS *Corr.* (1879) V. 301 As old as *Navyman as I am. **1746** W. THOMPSON *R.N. Advoc.* (1757) 38 The..barbarous.. lavishing away the Lives of the poor Navy Men. **1660** PEPYS *Diary* 9 July, To the *Navy-office, where in the afternoon we met and sat. **1758** *M.P.'s Let. on R.N.* 41 Remitting their Wages to themselves there, from the Navy-Office at London. **1799** *Med. Jrnl.* I. 94 A fact, which may be seen by the ship's books in the Navy-office. **1870** T. B. ALDRICH *Story Bad Boy* 245 Between the beer and the soothing fragrance of the *navy-plug, I fell into a pleasanter mood. **1909** 'O. HENRY' *Roads of Destiny* xxi. 357 It seems that the only maritime aid I am to receive from the United States is some navy-plug to chew. **1916** 'TAFFRAIL' *Pincher Martin* xiii. 242 'Care for a bit of navy plug?' He..never dreamt of boarding a trawler without a couple of inches of strong navy plug tobacco in his pocket. **1841** *Southern Lit. Messenger* VII. 4/1 Statistics..furnished by the *Navy Register will show [etc.]. *a***1861** T. WINTHROP *Canoe & Saddle* (1883) iii. 21 This machine..is called a six-shooter, an eight-inch *navy revolver. **1890** 'R. BOLDREWOOD' *Col. Reformer* (1891) 298 A 'navy' revolver hung at each man's belt. **1903** KIPLING *Traffics & Discov.* (1904) 143 Aren't they rowing *Navy-stroke, yonder? *a***1776** JAMES *Diss. Fevers* (1778) 42 For the sake..of the *navy-surgeons, and those committed to their care. **1717** POPE *Iliad* x. 145 [They] prepare to meet us near the *navy-wall. **1799** *Hull Advert.* 15 June 2/4 Mr. Beetham's patent *Navy Washing Mills. **1771** *Ann. Reg., Chron.* 113/1 She had on board some stores..for Halifax *navy-yard. **1828** *Amer. St. Papers, Naval Affairs* (1860) III. (275) On the expediency of establishing a navy yard. **1842** *Knickerbocker* XIX. 107 The General landed at the *navy-yard. **1886** *Harper's Mag.* Sept. 619/1 The fact of establishing a navy-yard. **1936** MENCKEN *Amer. Lang.* (ed. 4) 239 What we call..a navy-yard is a *dock-yard* or *naval-yard*. **1946** E. O'NEILL *Iceman Cometh* I. 75 De booze dey dish out around de Brooklyn Navy Yard.

Hence **'navyless** *a.*, having no navy.

1884 SIR L. GRIFFIN in *Fortn. Rev.* Jan. 55 The too fortunate Yankee, navyless and armyless.

†**navy**², obs. var. of NAVE *sb.*²

1501 in *Letters & Papers Rich. III & Hen. VII* (Rolls) I. 413. App. A, And as for the haulte place, it is devised to be set in the navy and body of the churche.

na-vyis, na-vyse, obs. Sc. ff. NO-WISE.

naw, north. dial. variant of KNOW.

naw, north. dial. and *U.S.* var. of NO *adv.*³

1906 *Dialect Notes* III. 147 Naw sir, we didn't do it. **1930** J. P. BURKE in *Amer. Mercury* Dec. 455/1 Naw, we don't cut hooch any more; we make the bunk with malt. **1949** C. HIMES *Black on Black* (1973) 277 'Naw suh,' Lemuel said. **1959** N. MAILER *Advts. for Myself* (1961) 52 'Does one of you want to go?'.. 'Naw.' **1971** *Black World* June 54/2 Naw, that scene was out. **1973** *New Yorker* 21 Apr. 62/3 'You didn't tear her clothes?' 'Naw, nothing like that.'

‖**nawab** (nə'wɔːb). Also 9 nawaub, -ob, nuwab, -aub. [Urdū *nawwāb*, var. of *nuwwāb*, pl. of *nā'ib* NAIB: cf. NABOB.]

1. A native governor or nobleman in India; = NABOB 1. Now *Hist.*

1758 in Jas. Mill *Brit. India* (1817) III. 276 'My Lord Nawab' answered the Mirza getting up. **1809** VISCT. VALENTIA *Voy. & Trav. India* I. 381, I was surprised that I had heard nothing from the Nawaub of the Carnatic. **1835** BURNES *Trav. Bokhara* (ed. 2) I. 65 He left us..to take.. charge of the Shikarpoor district during the absence of his brother, the Nawab. **1878** *N. Amer. Rev.* CXXVII. 139 Native rajahs and powerful nawobs.

2. A wealthy retired Anglo-Indian; = NABOB 2. Now *arch.*

1825–9 MRS. SHERWOOD *Lady of Manor* III. xix. 136 A certain Nawaub or old Civilian from the East Indies, who was reported to have more rupees than wit. **1878** G. SMITH *J. Wilson* i. (1879) 20 The previous generation had seen.. burghs bought and sold by Anglo-Indian nawabs.

Hence **na'wabship**.

1890 TOUT *Hist. Eng. fr. 1689*, 65 The nawabship of the Karnátik.

na-way(is, -ways, obs. Sc. forms of NO-WAY(S.

nawder, variant of NAUTHER *conj.*

†**nawer**, *adv. Obs.* Forms: 1, 3 **nawer**, 3–4 **naur(e**, 4–5 **nawre**; 4 **nagher(e**. [OE. *náwer*, reduced form of *náhwǽr*: see NA *adv.*¹ and WHERE, and cf. NOWER *adv.*] = NOWHERE.

*c***888** K. ÆLFRED *Boeth.* xviii. §1 Ealle netenu ne notigað nawer neah feorðan dæles þisses eorðan. *c***918** *O.E. Chron.* (Parker MS.) an. 918 Hi ne dorstan þæt land nawer ȝesecan on þa healfe. *c***1205** LAY. 753 Nis nawer nan so wis mon þat me ne mai bi-swiken. **1297** R. GLOUC. (Rolls) 1753 He wolde..delivueri þis lond..þat so fre lond as þis ne ssolde be naur non. *c***1375** *Cursor M.* 4764 (Fairf.), þai miȝt naure finde to by ham brede. **1390** GOWER *Conf.* II. 336 Upon the spring of freisshe welles Sche schop to duelle and nagher elles. *c***1460** *Towneley Myst.* xxvi. 582 In fayth I haue hym soght, Bot nawre he will fond be.

b. In the combs. ***nawer-where, -whither***.

*a***1300** *Cursor M.* 14862 We find writen naur-quar þat vr crist suld be born þar. *c***1375** *Ibid.* 3495 (Fairf.), For-þi was he nawre-quare sent. *Ibid.* 4959 For naure-quidder may we stere, þaire wille be-houis vs suffre here.

nawher(e, obs. ff. NOWHERE.

na-whon: see WHONE *Obs.*

na-wight, -wiht, obs. ff. NAUGHT.

na-wise, obs. Sc. f. NO-WISE.

†**nawle**, obs. form of AWL.

1565 COOPER *Thesaurus*, *Desubulo*, to pearse: properly wyth a nawle or bodken. *a***1619** FOTHERBY *Atheom.* I. xi. §5 (1622) 120 To bore their eares through, with a Nawle.

nawle, obs. f. NAVEL.

nawne, obs. var. *awn*, OWN *a.*

nawnte, obs. var. AUNT.

nawob, var. of NAWAB.

nawt, obs. f. NAUGHT.

nawtheles: see NAUTHELESS.

nawther, var. of NAUTHER, neither.

nawyn, var. of NAVIN *Obs.*

na-wyse, obs. Sc. f. NO-WISE.

Naxalite ('næksəlaɪt). [f. *Naxal(bari* (the name of a place in W. Bengal) + -ITE¹.] A name given in India to supporters of Chinese-type communism (see quot. 1969¹); also *attrib.* Hence **'Naxalism**, Chinese-type communism as practised in parts of India.

1969 *Times* 9 Jan. 9/1 'Naxalites' are in the headlines and seem to be at work in West Bengal, Andhra, Kerala, and half a dozen other states. The name comes from Naxalbari in West Bengal where Indian communists started arming peasants in the spring of 1967. **1969** *Amrita Bazar Patrika* 5 Aug. 5/5 Classes in Calcutta University..could not be held on Monday following a strike call given by the Naxalite-dominated Students' Action Committee. **1970** *Guardian* 2 July 4/4 Three Naxalites were lynched in the Midnapore district of West Bengal after they had killed a school teacher... The first major sign of popular resistance to Naxalite violence. *Ibid.* 4/6 Nepal..is the place where Naxalites and their Chinese mentors meet. **1970** *Guardian Weekly* 26 Dec. 16 The menace of Naxalism, the Maoist movement in West Bengal, may be less virulent than before. **1971** *Illustr. Weekly India* 11 Apr. 33/2 The authorities saw in it an urgent need to stamp out Naxalism before it became too late to do so. **1972** 'E. PETERS' *Death to Landlords!* iii. 58 There are Naxalite bosses who are themselves greedy and tenacious landlords. *Ibid.* v. 88 The Naxalites probably quote the Baghavadgita [*sic*], too. **1974** *Daily Tel.* 18 Mar. 1/6 Four people were killed, one of them a policeman, when Naxalite Communists ambushed a police patrol in a Calcutta suburb yesterday.

Naxian ('næksɪən), *sb.* and *a.* [f. Gr. *Νάξιος*, L. *Naxius* + -IAN.] **A.** *sb.* An inhabitant of Naxos, a Greek island in the Cyclades group, or Naxos, a part of Sicily colonized from the island of Naxos. **B.** *adj.* Of, pertaining to, or characteristic of the island or colony of Naxos. So **Naxiote** *sb.* and *a.*

1601 P. HOLLAND tr. *Pliny's Nat. Hist.* II. XXI. xviii. 101 The Naxian Cypirus hath a quicker sent: the Phœnician Cypirus smelleth but a little. **1797** *Encycl. Brit.* XII. 779/2 The Ionians..in time..possessed the whole island; whence the Naxians are, by Herodotus, called Ionians, and ranked among the Athenian colonies. **1835** MITFORD & DAVENPORT *Hist. Greece* (new ed.) II. i. 4 The expelled Naxians.. consented to guide a Persian army against a Grecian island. **1862** G. GROTE *Hist. Greece* (new ed.) II. II. xxii. 522 The oligarchy of Chalkis..sent out..settlers, Chalkidian and Naxian, who founded the Sicilian Naxos. *Ibid.* V. II. lviii. 169 The Naxians cordially received the armament, which then steered southward along the coast of Sicily to Katana. **1885** J. T. BENT *Cyclades* xiv. 334 The Naxiotes were aghast when they heard that they were to be ruled by a Jew. *Ibid.* 348 This fortress..is..the acropolis of the Naxiote valleys. **1911** *Encycl. Brit.* XIX. 318/1 Four Naxian ships took part in the expedition of Xerxes, but deserted and fought on the Greek side at Salamis in 480. **1913** J. B. BURY *Hist. Greece* (ed. 2) xv. 674 The Naxians were the first Sicilians to welcome the deliverer of Sicily to her shores. **1946** R. CAPELL *Simiomata* I. 33 The Naxian pilot's presence on board was overlooked. *Ibid.* 36 A biggish party of German prisoners has been brought in to join our Naxians. **1968** V. EHRENBERG *From Solon to Socrates* v. 130 The Naxians took to the hills, but a few were taken prisoner. **1972** R. MEIGGS *Athenian Empire* vii. 123 The earlier date will..suit the Naxian evidence better.

naxte, naxty, obs. ff. NASTY.

nay (neɪ), *v. Obs.* exc. *arch.* [a. OF. *neier*, var. *noier*, *nier*:—L. *negāre* (see DENY and RENAY), or, in later use, f. NAY *adv.*]

1. †**a.** To refuse (to do something). *Obs. rare.*

13.. *Gaw. & Gr. Knt.* 1836 He nay[ed] þat he nolde neghe in no wyse, Nauþer golde ne garysoun. **13..** *E.E. Allit. P.* B. 65 An oþer nayed also & nurned þis cawse. *c***1374** CHAUCER *Boeth.* I. met. i. (1868) 4 Wiþ how deef an eere deeþ cruel tourneþ awey fro wrecches and naieþ to closen wepyng eyen. *c***1440** *Generydes* 5248 Now must ye goo Furth in to perse, and this may not be nayde.

†**b.** *trans.* To refuse (a thing) to one. *Obs. rare.*

1440 in *Wars Eng. in France* (Rolls) II. 441 The state of cardinal, which was nayed and denyed hym. *c***1560** ROLLAND *Seven Sages* 286 Gif I had nayit to him battall.

c. To give a refusal to (a person).

*a***1592** GREENE *Shepherd's Ode* 86 The swain did woo; she was nice, Following fashion, nay'd him twice. **1839–48** BAILEY *Festus* xxi. 269 Come, nay me not.

†**2. a.** To deny (a matter). *Obs.*

*c***1400** *Beryn* 2829 It myȝt nat be I-nayid, But Geffrey had ..falsly hem betrayed. *a***1425** *Cursor M.* 19180 (Trin.), We may not nay hit: so is hit kid. *a***1529** SKELTON *Now sing we* 4 The crosses mistry can not be nayd. **1560** ROLLAND *Crt. Venus* II. 719 The quhilk ȝe can not nay.

†**b.** *intr.* (or with *it*). To make denial; to say nay. Hence **'naying** *vbl. sb. Obs. rare.*

1387–8 T. USK *Test. Love* I. vii. (Skeat) I. 7 Yea, quod she, but what if they hadden nayed? Howe woldest thou have maynteyned it? **1657** J. GOODWIN *Triers Tried* 6 [They] refuse to grant the indulgence..but unto such as will..yea it, and nay it, with them from one end of their faith unto the other. **1680** J. C. *Vind. Oaths* (ed. 2) 30 If you will have every thing sinful which is above simple yea-ing and naying.

nay (neɪ), *adv.*¹ and *sb.* Forms: 2 **nei**, 3 **næi**, 2–4 **nai**, (3 **naȝȝ**), 4–6 (9) **naye**, 6 **naie**, **na**, 3– **nay**. [a. ON. *nei* (Sw. and Da. *nej*), f. *ne* NE + *ei* ever = OE. *á*: cf. NA *adv.*¹ and *adv.*²]

A. *adv.* **1. a.** A word used to express negation, dissent, denial, or refusal, in answer to some statement, question, command, etc. Now *arch.* or *dial.*

In older usage *nay* (like *yea*) was usually employed when the preceding statement, etc., had no negative word in it; when a negative was expressed, the usual answer was *no* (or *yes*). This distinction is clearly stated by Sir T. More in his *Confutation of Tindale* Wks. (1557) 448/1.

*c***1175** *Lamb. Hom.* 27 He..weneð þat hit wulle him helpen. Nei, soðliche, nawiht. *c***1200** ORMIN 10658 [John] seȝȝde: naȝȝ, lef Laferrd, naȝȝ, Ne darr i þe nohht fullhtnenn. *c***1250** *Owl & Night.* 464 Hwanne myn erende is ido, Scholde ich bileue? Nay; hwar to? *c***1315** SHOREHAM VII. 670 ȝef we þer-of ete, We scholde deye... Nay, quaþ þe fend, ac ȝe ne scholde. **1362** LANGL. *P. Pl.* A. VI. 47 'Ye, leue Pers', quod this palmers... 'Nai, bi the peril of my soule', quod Pers. *c* **1420** Lydg. *Assembly of Gods* 151 'Nay in dede', they seyde, 'we kepe noon in store'. **1470–85** Malory *Arthur* I. iii–v. 41 Found ye ony kny3tes..seid sir ector. Nay said Arthur. **1553** T. Wilson *Rhet.* (1580) 211 Shall I goe to her? Naie I will not. **1593** G. Harvey *Pierce's Super.* 154 Ganging weeke? Na, a ganging day, I' trow, is a large allowance. **1642** Fuller *Holy & Prof. St.* v. xii. 406 When Jesuites unto us answer Nay, They do not English speak, 't is Greek they say. **1819** Shelley *Prometh. Unb.* III. iv. 95 Nay, mother, while my sister trims her lamp, 'Tis hard I should go darkling. **1840** Barham *Ingol. Leg.* Ser. I. *Lay St. Nicholas* ii, Now naye, in sooth it may hardly be. **1898** *Westm. Gaz.* 10 Jan. 2/1 The channel..between the Scylla of Aye and the Charybdis of Nay.

b. Doubled for the sake of emphasis.

c **1200** *Vices & Virtues* 9 Ne sweri3eð, naiðer ne be heuene ne be ierðe ne bie nan oðer ðing, bute ia, ia, næi, nai. *a* **1300** *Cursor M.* 3729 'Was þou not at me right now?'..'I?' he said, 'nai, nai, goddote'. *c* **1386** Chaucer *Wife's T.* 242 'Amended?' quod this knight, 'allas! nay, nay!' **1470–85** Malory *Arthur* I. vi. 42 Nay nay..I was neuer your fader. **1528** Roy *Rede me* (Arb.) 61 Thynkest that with theym it is scant, Naye naye man, I the warant. **1828** Scott *F.M. Perth* xxix, 'What, turn glover at last, Conachar?' said Simon; ..'Nay, nay, your hand was not framed for that'. **1841** Lane *Arab. Nts.* I. 84 The Efreet exclaimed, Nay, Nay!—to which the fisherman answered, Yea.

c. In proverbs and phrases.

to nick (one) *nay* or *with nay*: see nick *v.*

1562 J. Heywood *Prov. & Epigr.* (1867) 130 He that will not when he may, When he would he shall haue nay. **1573** Baret *Alv.* s.v. *Flatter*, To praise to the intent to get fauer, to hold vp one with yea and nay. **1637** Rutherford *Lett.* cxxxviii. (1862) I. 330 With whom Scribes and Pharisees were at yea and nay and sharp contradiction. **1827** Coleridge *Improvisatore, Answ.* 17 Then came a restless state, 'twixt yea and nay.

d. Occas. used as an introductory word, without any direct negation.

c **1460** *Play Sacram.* 586 *Master Brundyche.* I haue gyven hyr a drynke made full well..*Colle.* Nay than she ys fulle saue. **1610** B. Jonson *Alch.* II. iii, Well said, father! Nay, if he take you in hand, sir, [etc.]

2. *to say nay*: **a.** To make denial, prohibition, or refusal (*to* a thing or person).

c **1320** *Sir Tristr.* 624 A ring he rau3t him tite; þe porter seyd nou3t nay. *c* **1369** Chaucer *Dethe Blaunche* 1243 This was the grete Of hir answere. She sayde nay Alle outerly. *c* **1450** *St. Cuthbert* (Surtees) 4230 Some bad þe bolnyng cutt away, Some þai saide þarto nay. **1500** in Leadam *Star Chamb. Cases* (Selden Soc.) 110 They wold reteyne theym wo so euer wold sey nay. *a* **1542** Wyatt in *Tottel's Misc.* (Arb.) 63 Fortune semed at the last, That to her promise she said nay. **1771** Lady A. Lindsay *Auld Robin Gray*, My heart it said nay. **1779** J. Lovell in *J. Adams' Wks.* (1854) IX. 481 Could I say nay to Deane..?

b. To deny or refuse (one); to forbid, prohibit. Also, to refuse (a thing) *to* one.

1390 Gower *Conf.* I. 281, I..preie hire of som good ansuere:..Sche seieth me nay. *c* **1489** Caxton *Sonnes of Aymon* xix. 433 Noo thing shall be sayd nay to you. **1535** Coverdale *1 Kings* xx. 7 He sent vnto me..for sylver & golde, & I haue not sayde him naye. **1560** Daus tr. *Sleidane's Comm.* 94 b, The Ambassadours of the Cities,..requyryng a Copye, were sayde naye. **1648** Crashaw *Poems* (1858) 208 What dangers can there be dare say me nay? **1692** R. L'Estrange *Fables* xxxi, The Fox made Several Excuses,.. but the Stork..would not be said Nay. **1709** Steele *Tatler* No. 105 ⁋3 He would not say her nay in any Thing. **1842** Tennyson *Will Waterproof* 92 Long and largely we carouse As who shall say me nay. **1878** Bosw. Smith *Carthage* 299 On he went through Latium.., no one daring to say him nay, till he pitched his camp upon the Arno.

†**c.** To express dissent or contradiction. *Obs.*

c **1325** *Song of Yesterday* 171 in *E.E.P.* (1862) 137 Sum men seiþ þat deþ is a þef..And .i. say nay. *c* **1386** Chaucer *Can. Yeom. Prol. & T.* 786 Mighte no man saye nay But that they were as hem oughte be. **1480** Caxton *Chron. Eng.* ccxliv. 305 He was examyned of certayne poyntes that were put vpon hym and he sayd not nay. **1568** Grafton *Chron.* II. 772, I say not nay, but that it were very conuenient.

†**3. a.** *without nay*, beyond doubt or dispute, assuredly, certainly. *Obs.*

a **1300** *Cursor M.* 1283 Seth went him forth wit-outen nai To paradis. ? *a* **1400** *Arthur* 401 þat name wyþoute nay Hyt bereþ 3ut in-to þis day. *c* **1480** Henryson *Mor. Fab., Lion & Mouse* 51 My natall land is Rome withouttin nay. **1509** Barclay *Shyp of Folys* (1570) 237 Vnder foote of fooles without nay, Philosophie lieth oppressed. **1563** Man *Musculus' Commonpl.* 31 We do al declare without nay..that this law is wryten within us.

†**b.** So *without any* (or *all*) *nay*. (Cf. B. 2.)

c **1460** *Play Sacram.* 93 In all maner of londis w^t^out ony naye My merchandyse renneth. **1563** Man *Musculus' Commonpl.* 286 We be without any naye..sealed up unto the fayth of the holye Trinitie. **1581** Marbeck *Bk. of Notes* 759 Without al nay (sayth Musculus) it conteyneth the prophesie of the proud King of Babylon. **1621** Bp. Montagu *Diatribæ* 156 Without all nay, the Church of England is of his minde.

†**4. a.** In elliptical uses, sometimes passing into the sense of 'not'. *Obs.*

a **1300** *Cursor M.* 10441 Ne wat þou noght, it semes nai, Quat a fest it es to dai? **1362** Langl. *P. Pl.* A. viii. 135 Bote Catoun construweþ hit nay An[d] Canonistres boþe. **1428** in *Surtees Misc.* (1890) 2 Had noght Thomas Bracebrygg counseld hym nay and lettid hym. **1480** *Robt. Devyll* 860 in Hazl. *E.P.P.* I. 252 Robert poynted as naye; And woulde have them to beare the bed awaye. **1525** Ld. Berners *Froiss.* II. 378 Every thyng consydred they thought it best naye.

†**b.** *or nay*, or not, or no. *Obs.*

a **1300** *Cursor M.* 8432 He sal be king, qua wil or nai. *Ibid.* 13451, I dar noght sai quere þis was þat ilk or nai. **1526** *Pilgr. Perf.* (W. de W. 1531) 20 b, Demaunded of hym..whether he was in purgatory or nay. **1583** Rich *Phylotus* (1835) 20 Let me aske you this question, dooe you knowe my father, or naie. **1709** J. Johnson *Clergym. Vade M.* II. p. lx, By any other means to force and drive People, whether they will or nay, into Compliance.

5. a. Used to introduce a more correct, precise, or emphatic statement than the one first made.

1585–6 Earle Leicester *Corr.* (Camden) 380 We haue but a litle monie, only so much, na, skant so much, as shall bringe vs together. **1634** Ford *Perk. Warbeck* I. i, What folly, nay, what madness 'twere to lift A finger up. **1662** Stillingfl. *Orig. Sacræ* III. ii. §14 Nay, Epicurus himself takes away any center of that motion of Atoms. **1711** Addison *Spect.* No. 93 ⁋2 Several Hours of the Day hang upon our Hands, nay we wish away whole Years. **1778** Miss Burney *Evelina* ii, I have weighty, nay unanswerable reasons. **1817** Jas. Mill *Brit. India* II. v. vii. 623 The terms of this agreement, the gentlemen..arraigned as inadequate, nay humiliating. **1849** Macaulay *Hist. Eng.* v. I. 598 He would see Bristol burned down, he said, nay, he would burn it down himself, rather than [etc.]. **1884** tr. *Lotze's Metaph.* 262 Nay if we go further and make the provisional admission that [etc.]

b. *nay even.* (More emphatic than *even* alone.)

1709 Stanhope *Paraphr.* IV. 4 Can the Jews in particular pretend Ignorance Nay even of this Dispensation..? **1868** Miss Yonge *Cameos* Ser. I. xxiii. 171 Such alliances as might obtain a still wider power for them; nay, even the kingdom of France. **1884** J. Gilmour *Mongols* xvii. 205 He is surprised to find that a..teacher of Christianity may kill vermin, eat flesh, nay even marry a wife.

B. *sb.* **1.** An utterance of the word 'nay'; a negative reply or vote (*U.S.*); a denial, refusal, or prohibition.

13.. *Cursor M.* 19773 (Edinb.), Petir nickid þaim na nai. **13..** *Cristene-mon & Jew* (Vernon MS.) 125 Oþer a nay, or a 3a? Soone tel þou me swa! **1509** Hawes *Past. Pleas.* xvi. (Percy Soc.) 65 A nay of you myght cause my herte to breke. **1562** J. Heywood *Prov. & Epigr.* (1867) 29 Ye maie..mend three naies with one yee. **1583** Stocker *Civ. Warres Lowe C.* III. 75 For the tenth penny which the Duke woulde haue no nay of. **1613** Radcliffe *Lett.* 26 Mar. (T.), There is a faire bedde there also, which she determineth to sell, and would have you to have the first nay of it. **1643** Trapp *Comm. Gen.* xxxii. 26 He would have no nay at Gods hands. **1774** in *Vermont Hist. Soc. Coll.* (1870) I. 8 Passed in the affirmative—all yeas, no nays. **1807** J. Turner *Let.* 23 Jan. in J. Steele *Papers* (1924) II. 492 A Bill has passed the H.R. repealing the duty on salt with only 5 nays. **1812** Jefferson *Writ.* (1830) IV. 178 It is a notification to the factionaries that their nay is the yea of truth. **1844** Mrs. Browning *Lost Bower* x, A straight walk, unadvised by The least mischief worth a nay. **1871** *Trans. Illinois Agric. Soc.* VIII. 5 Mr. Dalton demanded the yeas and nays. **1896** *Omaha Bee* 18 Feb. 3/5 The members had taken the alarm and numerous 'nays' came back in response to the roll call.

†**2.** *it* (*this, that, there*) *is no nay*: **a.** = 'It cannot be denied'. Also simply *no nay*. *Obs.*

c **1386** Chaucer *Clerk's T.* 1083 This world is nat so strong, it is no nay, As it hath been in olde tymes yore. *c* **1400** *Gamelyn* 429, I wot wel for sothe that this is no nay. *c* **1420** *Pallad. on Husb.* II. 38 For no nay is That snaylis rather latte hem for to growe. *c* **1475** *Rauf Coil3ear* 691 Heir is Ryaltie, ..With all nobilnes anournit, and that is na nay. **1526** Skelton *Magnyf.* 2457 Without fayle, syr, that is no nay. ? **1554** Coverdale *Hope of Faithful* Pref., The Lord, no nay, shall grant our request. **1627** W. Sclater *Exp. 2 Thess.* (1629) 141 No nay, but Rome must be the Church, against which the gates of hell preuaile not.

†**b.** = 'No refusal was possible'. *Obs. rare*$^{-1}$.

a **1643** W. Browne (T.), There was no nay, but I must in.

†**nay**, *adv.*[2] *Obs.* [f. ne + ay *adv.*] Never.

c **1430** *Pilgr. Lyf Manhode* II. cix. (1869) 116 But nay of his song he ne rouhte. *a* **1547** Surrey *Poems, Descr. Restless State* 184 Thus shall my heart nay part her fro. **1575** Gascoigne *Fruits of War* ccv, I beare it well in minde And shall it nay forget whiles lyfe doth last.

†**nay**, variant of na *conj.*[2] than. *Obs.*

1533 Gau *Richt Vay* 94 Ramember that thy marcie and grace is..greittar nay al our sinnis. *Ibid.* 103.

nay, obs. Sc. variant of *na*, no *a.*

nayad, nayaunt, obs. ff. naiad, naiant.

‖**naya paisa** ('naɪjə 'paɪsə). Pl. **naye paise.** [Hindi, = new pice.] A unit of currency in India, equal to 1/100 rupee.

1956 *India: Reference Ann.* (Ministry of Information, Govt. India) xi. 127 The Indian rupee..will be divided into 100 units, each unit being called *naya paisa*. **1957** *Times* 2 Apr. 10/6 India's new decimal coinage was introduced today [*sc.* 1 Apr.]... All business transactions will now be calculated in rupees and *naye paise*, 'new coins', of the value of one hundredth of a rupee. **1957** *Whitaker's Almanack 1958* 974/1 An issue of 600m. coins of one, two, five, and 10 *naye paise* denominations was begun. **1963** *Times* 30 Jan. 12/7 King Edward rupees and everything since even to *naya paisa*. **1969** H. R. F. Keating *Inspector Ghote plays Joker* viii. 114 He plonked down fifteen naye paise, asked if he could use the phone. **1972** 'E. Peters' *Death to Landlords!* xi. 158 At the cost of a few *naye paise* they acquired three satisfied business contacts.

Nayar, var. Nair.

naybe, obs. form of naib.

nayborly, obs. form of neighbourly.

†**nayct**, var. ME. *eiht* property: see aught *sb.*[1]

c **1310** in *Rel. Ant.* I. 146 Hi sal gef the of my nayct.

†**nayed**, *a. Obs. rare*$^{-0}$. (See quot.)

1688 Holme *Armoury* III. xvii. (Roxb.) 119/1 He beareth Argent a Forked club Azure... This is termed also a Giants forked or Nayed club.

naygheing, naying, obs. ff. neighing.

naygue, obs. f. naik.

naying *vbl. sb.*: see nay *v.*

nayl(e, obs. f. nail *sb.* and *v.*

nayled, obs. f. nealed.

†'**nayless**, *a. Obs. rare*$^{-1}$. [f. nay *sb.* + -less.] Accepting no refusal.

a **1618** Sylvester *Maiden's Blush* 991 Like a nay-lesse wooer, Holding his cloak, shee puls him hard unto her.

nayne, obs. Sc. form of none.

nayque, obs. form of naik.

nayre, obs. variant of heir, Nair.

nay-say, *sb.* Also **naysay.** [f. nay *adv.* + say *sb.*] Refusal, denial.

1631 R. H. *Arraigum. Whole Creature* v. 39 Hee will have no nay say. *a* **1666** Blair *Autobiog.* vi. (1848) 84 They would take no naysay. **1721** Ramsay *Ode to the Ph—* xiii. (1877) II. 144 Nineteen nay says are ha'f a grant. **1762** Sterne *Let. to Mrs. Sterne* 14 June, Whoever buys the fifth and sixth volumes of Shandy's must have the nay-say of the seventh and eighth. **1816** Scott *Bl. Dwarf* v, That..depends entirely on the manner in which the nay-says are said. **1857** Sir F. Palgrave *Norm. & Eng.* II. 44 Not Cromwell's faltering nay-say, nor Cæsar's affected disdain.

So **nay-say** *v.*, to refuse (one). *dial.* and *arch.* More freq. in dial. forms *na-* or *nae-say*.

1773 Fergusson *Election* ix. Poet. Wks. (1800) 138 The foul ane durst him na-say. *a* **1800** *James Hadley* vii. in Child *Ballads* IV. 371/1 If it should be my hole estate, Naesaid, naesaid, it shall not be. **1864** Latto *Tam. Bodkin* xv, The evidence..was ower strong an' conclusive to be nae said. **1890** Morris *Glittering Plain* xix, He naysaid them because he was fain of his work.

nay-sayer. [Cf. next.] A refuser; one who votes against something.

1721 Kelly *Scot. Prov.* 21 A sturdy Beggar should have a stout Naysayer. **1939** Joyce *Finnegans Wake* 108 Naysayers we know. **1961** C. MacInnes *England, Half English* 47 In this decade we witness the second Children's Crusade, armed with strength and booty, against all 'squares', all adult nay-sayers. **1962** *Times* 5 Apr. 7/3 Mephistopheles the eternal nay-sayer. **1970** *New Statesman* 12 June 835/2 Food scientists should try to be 'nay-sayers against profit curves'. **1972** *Guardian* 28 Nov. 12/6 The Republican Party began the Nixon years as an unrepresentative minority of nay-sayers. **1974** *Publishers Weekly* 5 Aug. 57/3 Further to refute the nay-sayers, he cites poll after poll in which Americans say they are happy despite their feelings that all is not well with the country.

nay-saying. [f. nay *adv.* + saying *vbl. sb.*] Denial, contradiction.

1535 Coverdale *Heb.* vii. 7 Now is it so without all nay-sayenge that the lesse receaueth blessynge of ye greater. **1542** Udall *Erasm. Apoph.* 272 A straunge facion of puttyng awaye feare, not by naye saiyng, ne [etc]. **1952** B. Wolfe *Limbo* (1953) iv. 222 His mind brimming with..the necessity for some nay-saying gesture against EMSIAC. **1972** *Jrnl. Social Psychol.* LXXXVI. 220 Subjects who obtained scores of 0, 1, and 11, 12 were dropped from the analysis as representing extremes of yeasaying or naysaying.

naysch, obs. f. nesh *a.*

nayssant, obs. f. naissant.

nayt(e, varr. of nait *v.*[1] and *v.*[2]

naytheless(e, obs. ff. natheless.

naythir, obs. Sc. f. neither.

naytly, var. of naitly.

'**nayward.** *rare*$^{-1}$. [f. nay *sb.* + -ward.] *to the nay-ward*, towards denial or disbelief.

1611 Shaks. *Wint. T.* II. i. 64 Ile be sworne you would beleeue my saying, How e're you leane to th' Nay-ward.

nayword[1] ('neɪwɜːd). Also 7 **ay-.** [Of obscure formation; there is no obvious connexion with either nay or ay.]

1. A watchword or catchword. *rare.*

1598 Shaks. *Merry W.* II. ii. 131 In any case haue a nay-word, that you may know one anothers minde. *Ibid.* v. ii. 5 We haue a nay-word, how to know one another. I come to her in white, and cry Mum; she cries Budget. **1828** Mrs. Bray *Protestant* viii. (1884) 73 A rosary. A priest's treasury—his fortune, his nayword, his mask, through the mumming of this goodly farce, called the world. **1837** Gen. P. Thompson *Exerc.* (1842) IV. 285 A persuasion that the first of the sounds 'Victoria Regina' was the proper nay-word for gentlemen to know when to take off their hats.

2. A byword, a proverb. ? *Obs.*

1601 Shaks. *Twel. N.* II. iii. 146 If I do not gull him into an ayword, and make him a common recreation. **1664** Cotton *Scarron.* 14 And with a Gibing kind of Nayword, Quoth he [etc.]. *a* **1700** B. E. *Dict. Cant. Crew* s.v. *Taudry*, It grew into a Nay-word, upon any thing very Gawdy. **1777** *Gentl. Mag.* XLVII. 321 A Nayword..is a common expression for a by-word and is probably a crasis of an Aye-word.

nayword[2]. *rare*$^{-1}$. [f. nay *adv.*[1]] Refusal.

1898 *Blackw. Mag.* Apr. 565 There will be no hasty nay-word from me.

nazal, obs. form of nasal *sb.*

‖**nazar** ('næzɑː(r)), **nuzzer** ('nʌzə(r)). Also 8 nuzr, *pl.* nuzzies, 9 nuz(z)ur, nazur. [Urdū

(Pers., Arab.) *nazr* gift, f. Arab. *nazara* he vowed.] In India, a present made by an inferior to a superior.

1776 *Trial Joseph Fowke*, etc. 3/1 You have given.. 15,000 rupees in nuzzies to the Governor. **1785** H. T. COLEBROOKE in *Life* (1873) 16 Presents of ceremony, called nuzzers, were to many a great portion of their subsistence. **1828** J. B. FRASER *Kuzzilbash* I. ix. 119 A young Eersanee whelp as an offering—as a nuzzer from my servant to his master's daughter. **1855** H. H. WILSON *Gloss. Judicial & Revenue Terms* 373/2 *Nazr, nazar, najar*,.. a present, an offering, especially one from an inferior to a superior, to a holy man, or to a prince [etc.]. **1857** SIR F. PALGRAVE *Norm. & Eng.* II. 617 Notwithstanding this nuzur, Otho decided in favour of France. **1870** KAYE *Hist. Sepoy War* II. App. 662, I.. presented my nuzzur to his Majesty to accept. **1885** G. C. WHITWORTH *Anglo-Indian Dict.* 225/2 *Nazar*,.. a present, an offering; especially one made by an inferior on his presentation to a superior. **1922** *Glasgow Herald* 11 Feb. 10 Twelve Nobles, each offering 'Nazar', or the symbolic tribute of gold. **1934** E. L. TOTTENHAM *Highness of Hindostan* iv. 110 The deputations from the various States were presenting their gifts—the *poshaks* and *nazars*—of valuable cloth and plate. **1956** K. FITZE *Twilight of Maharajas* ii. 41 All Durbaris made their act of homage and obeisance, accompanied by the presentation of coins, known as *nazar*, which.. found their way in due course to the Palace treasury. **1973** M. BENCE-JONES *Palaces of Raj* x. 169 The civilians offering *nazars* of a few repees laid on a white handkerchief.

So **nuzze'rana**. [Urdū *nazrānah*.]

1788 BURKE *Sp. agst. W. Hastings* Wks. XIII. 432 The Nuzzer or Nuzzeranah, which is a tribute of acknowledgement from an inferiour to a superiour. **1858** J. B. NORTON *Topics* 85 The native state.. also took its occasional nuzzerana... Nuzzerana is not required, because it is not included in our regular system.

'Nazarate. *rare*$^{-1}$. = NAZARITESHIP.

1833 *Bagster's Treasury Bible* Num. vi, His subjection to God through all the peculiarities of his Nazarate.

nazardly: see NAZZARD.

Nazarean (næzə'riːən). [ad. F. *Nazaréen* or f. L. *Nazarē-us*, var. of *Nazaræ-us*, ad. Gr. Ναζωραῖος: cf. next.] = NAZARENE *sb.* 2.

1577 HANMER *Anc. Eccl. Hist., Chron.* (1585) 558 The Nazareans were such as vsed no liuing creatures. **1727–38** CHAMBERS *Cycl.* s.v., S. Epiphanius tells us, the Nazareans were the same with the Jews in everything relating to the doctrine and ceremonies of the Old Testament. **1797** *Encycl. Brit.* (ed. 3) XII. 781/2 These Nazareans preserved this first gospel in its primitive purity. **1874** J. H. BLUNT *Dict. Sects.*

Nazarene (næzə'riːn), *a.* and *sb.* Also 3–4 -en, 5 -yen. [ad. L. *Nazarēn-us*, ad. Gr. Ναζαρηνός (Mark i. 24), f. Ναζαρέτ Nazareth.]

A. *adj.* **1.** Of or belonging to Nazareth. *rare.*

c **1275** *Passion our Lord* 183 in *O.E. Misc.* 42 He to heom seyde, hwam ye seche here? Heo hym onswerede, ihesum nazaren. *a* **1300** *Cursor M.* 19622, I hatt iesus nazaren. **1855** BROWNING *Ep. Karshish* 100 That he was dead and then restored to life By a Nazarene physician.

2. a. Belonging to the sect of the Nazarenes.

1689 tr. *Simon's Crit. Hist. N.T.* 51 These Nazarene Sectaries. *a* **1724** J. JONES *Meth. N.T.* (1726) I. 387 Having never seen the Nazarene Gospel, for ought he knew, it might be the very same with that of the Ebionites. **1765** MACLAINE tr. *Mosheim's Eccl. Hist.* (1768) I. 174 *note*, He.. alledges that the Ebionites had only made some small additions to the old Nazarene system.

b. Of or pertaining to, or characteristic of, the Church of the Nazarene (sense B. 3 b).

1910 *New Schaff-Herzog Encycl. Relig. Knowl.* VIII. 453/2 As official organs of the church the *Nazarene Messenger*, Los Angeles, Cal.,.. and the *Holiness Evangel*, Pilot Point, Tex., are recognized. **1958** M. ARGYLE *Relig. Behaviour* iv. 33 Many of these sects—the Pentecostal, Holiness, Nazarene churches and others—have increased enormously in proportion to their size during this period [*sc.* 1926–1953]. **1968** [see C.O. (C III. 3)]. **1968** *War Resistance* II. xxiv. 26 The Nazarene Church is a plain building with simple furniture. *Ibid.* 28 Many do leave for USA, Canada or Australia where there are Nazarene Communities.

†**3.** (See quot.) *Obs. rare*$^{-0}$.

1796 *Grose's Dict. Vulgar T.* (ed. 3), *Nazarene Foretop*, the foretop of a wig made in imitation of Christ's head of hair, as represented by the painters and sculptors.

4. Of, pertaining to, or characteristic of the school of artists called Nazarenes. Cf. B. 4 below.

1950 *Chambers's Encycl.* XIV. 380/1 In many respects Wackenroder was a forerunner of the Nazarene school of painters. **1952** W. GAUNT *Victorian Olympus* i. 29 The master was found in the Nazarene painter, Jacob Eduard von Steinle. **1959** *Listener* 29 Jan. 217/3 The Bayreuth *Parsifal* has escaped from the old-fashioned 'Nazarene' presentation only to fall into a kind of fashionable 'grimness'. **1965** *Ibid.* 9 Sept. 382/2 For a short time after settling in London in 1846, Brown painted in the Nazarene style. **1970** T. HILTON *Pre-Raphaelites* i. 20 *Wycliffe*, with its light, flat tones and dispersed composition, looks very like a Nazarene painting.

B. *sb.* **1. a.** A native of Nazareth.

1611 BIBLE *Matt.* ii. 23 He shalbe called a Nazarene. **1797** *Encycl. Brit.* (ed. 3) XII. 781/1 We find no particular place in the prophets in which it is said that the Messiah should be called a Nazarene. **1881** A. O'SHAUGHNESSY *Songs of Worker* 11 Great folk no whit ashamed now to beseech That Nazarene to come and be their king.

b. A follower of Jesus of Nazareth; a Christian. (So called esp. by Jews and Muslims.)

1382 WYCLIF *Acts* xxiv. 5 Auctour of seducioun of the secte of Nazarens. **1481** CAXTON *Godfrey* lxxxv, 134 Thenne was establysshed that they shold be called crysten men of crist; ffor byfore they were called nazaryens. **1685** BAXTER *Paraphr. N.T.* Acts xxiv. 5 Calling the Christians Nazarenes in scorn. **1704** J. PITTS *Acc. Moham.* iv. 24, I never saw a Nazarene (i.e. a Christian) before. **1813** BYRON *Giaour* xxxv, The very name of Nazarene Was wormwood to his Paynim spleen. **1889** HUXLEY *Sci. & Chr. Trad.* (1895) 301 On the whole.. the Nazarenes were but little troubled for the first twenty years of their existence.

2. *pl.* An early Jewish Christian sect, allied to the Ebionites.

1689 tr. *Simon's Crit. Hist. N.T.* 51 Epiphanius.. observes.., that these ancient Nazarenes.. were descended from the Primitive Christians of the same Name. *a* **1724** J. JONES *Meth. N.T.* (1726) I. 385 The Nazarenes.. differ'd only from the Jews, in that they profess'd the Name of Christ [etc.]. **1765** MACLAINE tr. *Mosheim's Eccl. Hist.* (1768) I. 173 This body of judaizing Christians.. was afterwards divided into two sects.. distinguished by the names of Nazarenes and Ebionites. **1840** *Penny Cycl.* XVI. 125/1 The early fathers do not appear to have regarded the Nazarenes as heretics. **1876** L. STEPHEN *Eng. Th. 18th C.* I. III. ii. 103 The doctrine afterwards maintained by Priestley that the Jewish sects, the Nazarenes and Ebionites.. were the genuine Christians.

3. a. A member of a sect of Christian reformers in Hungary.

1886 W. J. TUCKER *E. Europe* 155 No Nazarene may take up a weapon to attack his brother-man, not even in self-defence.

b. A member of the Church of the Nazarene, a Protestant sect formed at the beginning of the 20th cent.

1898 P. F. BRESEE in T. L. Smith *Called unto Holiness* (1962) v. 121 It is now somewhat more than two years since .. the Nazarenes, putting the old things behind them, went out to follow in the footsteps of Him whose name they bear. **1962** K. S. LATOURETTE *Christianity in Revolutionary Age* V. i. 14 On the Pacific coast denominations of recent American origin loomed larger... the Four-Square Gospel, the Pentecostals, the Churches of God, and the Nazarenes. **1962** T. L. SMITH *Called unto Holiness* iv. 75 Men of the Green Mountain State have been significant leaders among New England Nazarenes. **1968** *War Resistance* II. xxiv. 26 According to a report in the mid-20's there were 12–15,000 Nazarenes in Yugoslavia.

4. A name given to members of a group of German artists called the Brotherhood of St. Luke, founded in 1809, who aimed to restore to art the religious quality founded in mediæval painting; cf. PRE-RAPHAELITE *sb.*; = NAZARITE[1] 3. Sometimes in pl. **Nazarener**. Also *transf.*, of a style of musical composition.

1889 ARMSTRONG & GRAVES *Bryan's Dict. Painters & Engravers* (rev. ed.) II. 460/1 Schadow.. went.. to Rome, and joined the 'Nazarenes'. **1911** *Encycl. Brit.* X. 375/1 The group of artists who styled themselves *Nazarener*. **1928** E. WAUGH *Rossetti* ii. 29 Nazarene, Florentine, and Crusader fused into one shadowy figure, glowing and distorted. **1942** *Archit. Rev.* XCI. 29 (*caption*) There is nothing elegant in this interior except for the reredos by William Dyce, the 'Nazarene' amongst English Early-Victorian painters. **1947** A. EINSTEIN *Mus. Romantic Era* xii. 161 The 'Nazarenes' of church music were replaced by the 'Caecilians'. *Ibid.*, Nazarene-like church music. **1965** *Listener* 9 Sept. 382/2 He.. had come under various influences, including that of the Nazarenes,.. a group of German artists who had founded a 'pre' Pre-Raphaelite movement.. in the eighteen-tens. **1973** *Country Life* 20 Sept. 779/2 One of his [*sc.* William Dyce's] Nazarene-type paintings.

Nazarenism ('næzəriːnɪz(ə)m). [f. NAZARENE *a.* and *sb.*] **1.** The principles or doctrines of early Christianity.

1892 T. H. HUXLEY *Let.* in J. S. Huxley *Ess. Pop. Sci.* (1926) 161, I have a great respect for the Nazarenism of Jesus—very little for later 'Christianity'. **1923** *Expository Times* Nov. 73/2 Here.. the story of Jesus ends, and the story of Nazarenism begins.

2. The characteristics or artistic principles of the Nazarene school of artists.

1895 E. DOWSON et al. tr. *Muther's Hist. Modern Painting* I. vi. 229 It was of no avail to him [*sc.* Phiip Veit] that he mingled with his Nazarenism a certain air of the world. **1947** A. EINSTEIN *Mus. Romantic Era* iv. 36 The Protestant church turned back to Bach..; the Catholic went back still further, to Palestrina and his time, in whose style it fostered a new musical Nazarenism, comparable to the Pre-Raphaelitism of the English school of painters. **1960** R. H. BOOTHROYD tr. *Novotny's Painting & Sculpture Europe 1780–1880* vi. 69 In the strange mixture of styles pervading his paintings of saints there appear a kind of return to the beginnings of Nazarene and Romantic principles and a breaking down of the narrow confines of academic Nazarenism reminiscent even of Blake.

†**'Nazarism.** *Obs. rare*$^{-1}$. = NAZARITISM.

1638 MEDE *Diatribæ* ii. Wks. (1672) 7 The Law given Numbers 6. concerning the Vow of Nazarisme.

†**Nazaritan.** *Obs. rare.* [f. next + -AN.] A Christian.

1625 PURCHAS *Pilgrims* IX. vi. II. 1482 The.. Corrector of the things of all the Nations of the Nazaritanes. **1632** LITHGOW *Trav.* 192 The most part of the inhabited villages [of Libanus] are Christians, called Amaronites, or Nostranes, *quasi* Nazaritans, and are governed by their owne Patriarke.

Nazarite[1] ('næzəraɪt). Also 6 -ete. [f. L. *Nazar-æus* (see NAZAREAN) + -ITE[1].]

1. A native or inhabitant of Nazareth.

1535 COVERDALE *Matt.* ii. 23 He shalbe called a Nazarite. **1596** SHAKS. *Merch. V.* I. iii. 35 The habitation which your Prophet the Nazarite coniured the diuell into. **1685** BAXTER *Paraphr. N.T.* Matt. ii. 23 The Jews called Christ a Nazarite, from that place of his dwelling. **1903** H. BLACK *Work* i. 10 The Jews sneered at the Nazarite and the Nazarites sneered at the Carpenter.

†**b.** = NAZARENE *sb.* 1 b. *Obs. rare.*

1535 COVERDALE *Acts* xxiv. 5 A maynteyner of the secte of the Nazaretes. **1656** BLOUNT *Glossogr.* s.v., The Disciples were first called Nazarites.. from Jesus of Nazareth.

†**2.** = NAZARENE *sb.* 2. *Obs. rare*$^{-0}$.

1661 BLOUNT *Glossogr.* (ed. 2), *Nazarite*,.. also certain Heretics so called.

3. = NAZARENE *sb.* 4.

1880 J. B. ATKINSON *Schools of Mod. Art in Germany* ii. 11 Enemies in the opposite camp nicknamed the new saints 'Nazarites' and 'Pre-Raphaelites'. **1882** J. B. ATKINSON *Overbeck* iii. 74 The type is ascetic and æsthetic after the pre-Raphaelite pattern affected by the Nazarites.

Nazarite[2] ('næzəraɪt). Also 9 nazirite. [f. L. *Nazar-æus* (cf. prec.), repr. Hebr. *nāzīr*, f. *nāzar* to separate or consecrate oneself, to refrain from anything.] The name given among the Hebrews to one who had taken certain vows of abstinence (see Numbers vi.).

In the Wyclif Bible the earlier version uses the form *Nazare*, the later *Nazarei* or *-ey*. Coverdale has *Nazaree* in Judges xiii. 5, 7.

1560 BIBLE (Genev.) *Num.* vi. 2 When a man or woman doeth separate them selues to vowe a vowe of a Nazarite. *c* **1585** R. BROWNE *Answ. Cartwright* 64 To drinke wine.. was a pollution both of the Nazarites and Priestes. **1671** MILTON *Samson* 1386 Nothing to do.. that may dishonour Our Law, or stain my vow of Nazarite. **1706** A. BEDFORD *Temple Mus.* iv. 78 Samuel was.. a Nazarite (which consisted only in a Vow of Abstinence). **1797** *Encycl. Brit.* (ed. 3) XII. 781/2 The priest or some other shaved the head of the Nazarite at the door of the tabernacle. **1831** E. BURTON *Eccl. Hist.* viii. 248 There were always persons in Jerusalem.. who took upon them the vow of a Nazarite. **1882** FARRAR *Early Chr.* I. 520 There are traces in Scripture that the Nazarites were regarded with peculiar pride.

attrib. **1593** NASHE *Christ's T.* 23 With Nazarite-tresses, to my Crosse will I bind her crossing frowardness and contaminations. **18..** *Bible Helps* (Bagster) 88/2 Various interpretations have been given of the Nazarite vow.

Hence **'Nazariteship; Naza'ritic** *a.*; **'Nazaritish** *a.*; **'Nazaritism.**

1611 BIBLE *Num.* vi. 4 All the days of his separation [*marg.* *Nazariteship] shall he eat nothing that is made of the vine. **1650** TRAPP *Comm. Num.* vi. 14 He must come with his sin-offering.. before he could be released of his Nazarite-ship. **1738** CRUDEN *Concord.* s.v. *Nazarite*, When the time of their Nazaritship was accomplished. **1797** *Encycl. Brit.* (ed. 3) XII. 781/2 They began again the whole ceremony of their consecration and Nazariteship. **1864** WEBSTER, **Nazaritic*, pertaining to a Nazarite, or to Nazarites. **1874** H. R. REYNOLDS *John Baptist* iii. §2. 161 Those who had put themselves for different periods under the Nazaritic vow. **1675** BROOKS *Gold. Key* Wks. 1867 V. 295 God's departing from him when he lost his *Nazaritish hair by Delilah. **1854** J. BRUCE *Biog. Samson* i. 15 The Nazaritish vow had preceded the birth of both. **1692** J. EDWARDS *Inq. Remark. Texts N.T.* 47 The law of *Nazaritism concerning long and uncut hair. *c* **1762** D. JENNINGS *Jewish Antiq.* (1808) I. 422 The institution of Nazaritism was no doubt partly religious. **1882** FARRAR *Early Chr.* I. 520 The Nazaritism of St. James is a circumstance of great moment in the explanation of his life and character.

naze (neɪz). Also 8 nase. [app. inferred from place-names such as *the Naze* in Essex or that at the southern extremity of Norway (*Lindesnæs*).] A promontory or headland, a ness.

1774 T. WEST *Antiq. Furness* 93 Furness being a kind of peninsula, or nase or ness of land, as its name imports. **1826** EWING *Geog.* (ed. 7) 23 *note*, Naze, ness, and mull, are also used to signify remarkable portions of land stretching out into the water. **1837** MACDOUGALL tr. *Graah's E. Coast Greenland* 24 Hiding.. the whole actual shore, except here and there some inconsiderable naze.

Nazi ('nɑːtsɪ, 'nɑːzɪ), *sb.* and *a.* [repr. pronunc. of *Nati-* in G. *Nationalsozialist.*] **A.** *sb.* A member of the National Socialist (Workers') Party in Germany, led by Adolf Hitler from 1920 and in power from 1933–45; a member of a similar organization; a person who believes in the aims of Nazism or similar doctrines and in the methods necessary to achieve them. Also *Comb.* So **'Naziphil(e**, a person sympathetic to the ideology of Nazism.

1930 *Times* 19 Sept. 10/1 Herr Hitler, the leader of the victorious National-Socialists (Nazis), has very carefully refrained from saying anything. **1931** W. LEWIS *Hitler* 57 The Democrats.. have not been able to deal with the Nazi because of his Mastery of the Street. **1934** D. TEILHET *Talking Sparrow Murders* xiv. 202 The police are Nazi-controlled even in Heidelberg. **1938** *Sun* (Baltimore) 6 Sept. 1/3 The center of Santiago was kept in turmoil after Chilean Nazis.. seized the National University. **1939** *Ann. Reg. 1938* 195 Added a number of minor Naziphile persons to the Cabinet. *Ibid.* 234 The chief change made by the new Premier in the Cabinet was to replace Dr. Homan, a strong Naziphil, with Count Paul Teleki. **1942** W. S. CHURCHILL *End of Beginning* (1943) 222 The horde of divisions provided by Finland, Rumania, Hungary, and others of the Nazi-ridden or Fascist-ridden states. **1946** *R.A.F. Jrnl.* May 169 Lancasters.. carried the war from one end of Nazi-controlled Europe to the other. **1956** A. H. COMPTON *Atomic Quest* i. 7 The Nazis saw in the atomic bomb the possibility of a new weapon of decisive importance. **1967** D. EISENBERG *Re-emergence of Fascism* iii. 127 The American Nazi and his uniformed 'storm-troopers' have frequently demonstrated outside the White House against racial integration in the South. **1974** *Times* 21 May 1/3 Mr Begin described Arab terrorists as 'the new Nazis' who made children their targets..adding: 'We must arm the population to fight these Nazis.'

B. *adj.* Of, pertaining to, or connected with the National Socialist Party in Germany or a political organization with similar aims, beliefs, or methods elsewhere. So **'Nazi-ish** *a.*

1930 *Times* 16 Sept. 16 (*caption*) Herr Hitler, the leader of the National Socialists, speaking at the last big Nazi election meeting. **1935** C. ISHERWOOD *Mr. Norris changes Trains* vii. 105 The local Nazi storm-troop. **1939** W. S. CHURCHILL *Into Battle* (1941) 108 There is the Nazi-Fascist ideology, and the Communist ideology. **1939** 'N. BLAKE' *Smiler with Knife* x. 154 There's nothing Nazi-ish about it... No talk of labour camps and so on. **1949** KOESTLER *Promise & Fulfilment* I. v. 54 To put the callous policy of the Mandatory Power on a par with the barbarity of Hitlerism, as the Jewish terrorists did in their slogan of the 'Nazi-British', is..unjust and stupid. **1967** W. SOYINKA *Kongi's Harvest* 64 The carpenters end with a march down-stage with stiff mallet-wielding arms pistoning up in the Nazi salute. **1973** *Guardian* 29 Mar. 16/4 'Nazi' has become an indiscriminate political cliché applied to insensitive bureaucrats, Americans in Vietnam, IRA Provos, British paras in Ulster, Black September, Zionists, *et al.* **1974** R. THOMAS *Porkchoppers* xviii. 162 'You mean Peter Majury?' '*Jawohl*,' Gayan said and made a Nazi salute.

Nazidom ('nɑːtsɪdəm, 'nɑːzɪ-). [f. prec. + -DOM.] The concepts and institutions of the Nazis.

1933 *Time* 20 Nov. 19/3 To make sure of a real 'intellectual eruption' last week—an utter blasting of Nazidom's foes—the Chancellor and his chief henchmen have been shouting themselves hoarse. **1935** *Times* 25 June 15/3 Professor Karl Barth..has been finally dismissed by the German Minister of Education. Into the details of his dispute with Nazidom there is no need to enter. **1941** *Ann. Reg. 1940* 387 Do not think that Hitler's Nazidom is going to be easily overthrown. **1947** A. L. ROWSE *End of Epoch* xv. 181 The threat to ourselves and the rest of Europe involved by Nazidom. **1971** D. E. WESTLAKE *I gave at the Office* (1972) 179 The story of his escape from Nazidom took slightly longer than a dental appointment.

Nazify ('nɑːtsɪfaɪ, 'nɑːzɪ-), *v.* Also **nazify**. [f. as prec. + -FY.] *trans.* To cause or force to adopt Nazism or similar doctrines. Hence **Nazifi'cation**; **'Nazifying** *vbl. sb.*; **'Nazified** *ppl. a.*

1933 *Times* 7 June 13/3 Dr. Dollfuss..is resisting..the combined efforts of the German and Austrian Nazis to nazify Austria. **1933** *Christian Cent.* 20 Sept. 1164 (*heading*) Nazification of German Protestantism continues. **1934** *Times Lit. Suppl.* 26 July 524/2 It may, of course, be said that the process of 'Nazifying' has not had time to achieve its full results. **1934** *Sun* (Baltimore) 24 Sept. 8/2 Such events do not augur well for the future of the 'unified', *i.e.*, Nazified, Evangelical Church of Germany. **1939** *Ann. Reg. 1938* 199 Preparations for the plebiscite..fully occupied the party and the nazified administration during the preceding weeks. **1941** *Ibid. 1940* 229 Their policy of..nazifying the population gradually. **1961** R. SETH *How Resistance Worked* vi. 67 Throughout 1941 he issued a number of laws by which he intended to nazify Norway. **1972** C. SHORT *Naked Skier* xvi. 79 This Nazified policeman was on the side of the Countess and against us. **1973** E. OSERS tr. *Waldheim's Austrian Example* iii. 45 At first the new regime made a point of cultivating public opinion, but as the process of Nazification spread to all spheres of public life less and less attention was paid to it.

‖**nazir** ('nɑːzɪr). Also 7 **-ar, -er.** [a. Pers. or Urdū (from Arab.) *nāẓir* superintendent, inspector, etc. f. *naẓar* sight, vision.] The title of various officials in Muslim countries; a native official in Anglo-Indian courts.

1678 J. PHILLIPS *Tavernier's Trav.* I. I. 42 The King advanc'd him to the Office of Nazar, or Grand Master of the House. **1687** A. LOVELL tr. *Thevenot's Trav.* II. 97 He commanded the Nazer..to be exposed naked to the Sun; and the Nazer is one of the chief Officers of that Court. **1797** *Encycl. Brit.* (ed 3) XII. 782/1 In this sense Joseph was the Nazir of the court of Pharaoh. **1840** J. B. FRASER *Koordistan* I. ii. 30 He addressed..his *Nâzir*, or steward, and told him to go to certain of his guests. **1878** GRANT *Hist. India* I. lxxxi. 431/1 The rajah had few privileges beyond those of the Nàzirs, or nobles.

Nazirite, variant of NAZARITE[2].

Nazism ('nɑːtsɪz(ə)m). Also **Naziism, Nazi-ism.** [f. NAZI *sb.* and *a.* + -ISM.] The political doctrines evolved and implemented by Adolf Hitler and his followers, esp. those relating to racial superiority, the all-powerful state, and the cult of the leader. So **'Nazist, Na'zistic** *adjs.*

1934 *Times* 28 Feb. 14/3 Finally it is urged that the disinterested support given by Italy to Nazism should counsel higher respect on her part for Italian foreign policy. *Ibid.* 16 Mar. 20/4 A clever essay on the cultural aims of Nazi-ism. **1938** *Ann. Reg. 1937* 171 Chancellor Schuschnigg rejected the Italian suggestion that he should introduce a representative of Naziism into the Austrian Government. **1938** *Times* 17 Mar. 15/5 In Belgium there is already a semi-Nazist party of Germanic nationality looking for help abroad. **1938** *New Statesman* 25 June 1053/2 Quite recently ..a new Nazistic party called the Christian Nationalist Socialist Front has been formed. **1940** A. HUXLEY *Let.* 24 Apr. (1969) 453 The doctrines of Nazism, Communism, nationalism..are..manifestly idiotic. **1957** J. S. HUXLEY *Relig. without Revelation* (rev. ed.) iii. 63 Nazism was inherently self-destructive because of its claim to world domination by a small group. **1971** *Nature* 16 July 205/2 Feelings about the scientific community's relationship to Naziism. **1973** *Guardian* 29 Mar. 16/4 Nazism was the ultimate degradation of mankind, singular even in the history of vileness.

nazold. Also 9 *dial.* **nazzald, nazzle.** [Of obscure origin: cf. NAZZARD.] A silly or weak-minded person.

1607 WALKINGTON *Opt. Glass* 83, I know some selfe-conceited nazold, and some jaundice-fac'd idiot; that uses to deprave and detract from mens worthines. **18..** (see *Eng. Dial. Dict.* s.v. *Azzald*).

'nazy, *a. slang* or *dial.* Also 9 **nazzy.** [Cf. NASE *a.*] Drunken.

a **1700** B. E. *Dict. Cant. Crew*, *Nazie*, drunken. **1855** ROBINSON *Whitby Gloss.*, *Nazzy*, stupified, intoxicated.

'nazzard. *Obs.* exc. *dial.* [Of obscure origin: cf. NAZOLD.] An insignificant or feeble person.

1619 H. HUTTON *Follie's Anat.* (Percy Soc.) 36 Women by nature doe a nazzard spight, Because he's a light-horse-man and wants weight. **1882** in *E.D.D.* s.v. *Azzard.*

Hence **'nazzardly** *a.*, poor, ill-thriven.

1675 COTTON *Scoffer Scoft* 68 Such a nazardly Pigwiggin, A little Hang-strings in a Biggin.

N'Dama (n'dɑːmə). Also **N'dama, Ndama.** [Native name.] A West African breed of cattle, usually fawn or light red in colour and bearing lyre-shaped horns; an animal belonging to this breed. Also *attrib.*

1938 J. L. STEWART in *Vet. Rec.* 9 Oct. 1291/2 The present day N'Dama is almost identical with the Longhorn of the ancient Egyptian drawings. *Ibid.* 1292/1 The N'Dama cattle until a few years ago were found in the Fouta Djalon mountains of French Guinea but have now spread over a large part of West Africa as this breed is especially good for stock improvement. **1952** *Ann. Trop. Med. & Parasitol.* XLVI. 128 The N'damas were born and bred at the Nigerian Agricultural Department's farm at Ilorin. **1956** *Nature* 21 Jan. 132/2 The West African N'Dama breed of cattle shows a remarkable tolerance to trypanosomiasis. **1973** *Guardian* 20 June 12/3 The Zebu cattle of Senegambia ..[are] less resistant than the tougher Ndama breed.

Ndebele (ndə'biːliː). [Native name, f. *n-* sing. prefix + *Tebele.*] The name of a Zulu people branches of which are found in Zimbabwe and in the Transvaal; also a member of this people; (also **Sin-debele**), the language of this people.

The Zimbabwean Ndebele are better known as the Matabele (*ma* = pl. prefix).

1913 J. O'NEIL (*title*) A grammar of the Sindebele dialect of Zulu. **1919** [see MATABELE]. **1930** C. G. SELIGMAN *Races Afr.* viii. 187 The Zulu-Xosa, chiefly in the coastal region south and east of Drakenberg Mountains,..include..the Amandebele (Matabele) of Matabeleland. **1937** A. W. HOERNLÉ in I. Schapera *Bantu-Speaking Tribes S. Afr.* iv. 86 Among the Southern Transvaal Ndebele, each..clan has a special species of animal..which may not be named or eaten or used by the members of that clan... The Rhodesian Ndebele..have introduced a new hierarchy of rank resulting from their conquest of indigenous tribes in their new homes. **1951** P. ABRAHAMS *Wild Conquest* 175 'This one brought the news.' 'An Ndabele?' 'No, a Barolong.' **1971** *Rand Daily Mail* 27 Mar. 6/2 Our Zululand and Ndebele beadwork..has always been regarded as the best in the world. **1973** *Drum* (Johannesburg) 8 Jan. 18/3 My mother language is Shona and I can speak English and Ndebele.

‖**Ndugu** (n'duːguː). [Swahili, = relative, brother.] A general form of address in Tanzania.

1973 *Black World* May 47 San Francisco Afrikans (brothers) Afrikan Afrikans (*ndugu*) West Indian Afrikans (Hey man). **1974** *Sunday Tel.* 16 June 36/3 A [Tanzanian] Government directive says that mister, honourable, excellency and all other honorifics will be replaced by the Swahili word *ndugu*, which means brother. **1974** *Daily News* (Tanzania) 13 Sept. 3/1 One of the passengers Ndugu Mohamed Ismaili had this to say: 'We have a transport problem about buses going to Lindi.' *Ibid.* 3/4 'Ndugu' (to trained nurse) 'you're going to work in the ward for four hours today.'

†**ne,** *sb. Obs. rare*$^{-1}$. [ad. OF. **nie*, acc. of *nies*:—L. *nepos*: see NEPHEW.] A nephew.

1387 TREVISA *Higden* (Rolls) II. 273 His successour and ne was Octauianus Augustus.

†**ne,** *v. Sc. Obs. rare*$^{-1}$. [ad. OF. *neer*, var. of *neier*, *nier*: see DENY *v.*] To deny.

c **1400** *Sc. Trojan War* (Horstm.) I. 578 It syt no cristyne mane [to] Ne, gode of myght baith may & kane [etc.].

ne (niː), *adv.* and *conj.*[1] Now only *arch.* Also 1 **ni,** 4–5 **ny.** [OE. *ne*, *ni* = OFris. and OS. *ne*, *ni* (MDu. *ne*), OHG. *ni* (*ne*), ON. *né* (for *ne*), Goth. *ni* = Lith. *nè*, OSl. *ne-*, L. *ne-* (in *nefās*, *nequeo*, etc.), Skr. *na*, related by ablaut to Goth. *nē*, Lat. *nē*, Gr. *νη-*, Skr. *nā*.]

A. *adv.* = NOT. **1.** As simple negative.

c **725** *Corpus Gloss.* (Hessels) N 199 *Numquid*, ne huru is. *c* **825** *Vesp. Psalter* iii. 7 Ne ondredu ic ðusend folces ymsellendes me. *a* **900** *Leiden Riddle* 3 in *O.E. Texts* 150 Ni uuat ic mec biuorth[n]æ wullan fliusum. **971** *Blickl. Hom.* 7 Ne ondræd þu þe, Maria. *c* **1000** ÆLFRIC *Gen.* iii. 1 Hwi forbead god eow, þæt, ȝe ne æton of ælcum treowe. *a* **1122** *O.E. Chron.* (Laud MS.) an. 1086 Hwam ne mæȝ earmian swylcere tide? *a* **1225** *Leg. Kath.* 1390 Hwi ne hihe we for to beon i-fulhet. *a* **1250** *Owl & Night.* 47 West thu that ich ne cunne singe..? *c* **1320** *Sir Tristr.* 1749 Þan doute we for no þing þat we ne may han our wille. *c* **1375** *Sc. Leg. Saints* xxx. (*Theodora*) 73 He trawalyt sa þat he ne mycht rest nycht na day. *a* **1450** *Knt. de la Tour* 39 The lady..asked whi he ne wolde with her speke. **1485** CAXTON *Chas. Gt.* 39, I ne entende but onely to reduce thauncient ryme in to prose. **1559** *Mirr. Mag.*, *Cambridge* iii, He ne had, nor could encrease his line. *a* **1592** GREENE *Looking-gl.* Wks. (Rtldg.) 144/2 Twenty thousand infants that ne wot The right hand from the left. **1812** BYRON *Ch. Har.* I. ii, A youth Who ne in virtue's ways did take delight.

†**b.** In the conditional clauses ***ne were, ne had ..been***, were it not, had it not been (for). Also with omission of verb. *Obs.*

c **1050** *O.E. Chron.* (MS. D.) an. 943 He hy ȝewyldan meahte, nære þæt hi on niht ut ne æt burston of þære byriȝ. **13..** *Sir Beues* (A.) 2005 Ne wer is douȝter Iosiane, Sertes, ich wolde ben is bane! **1375** BARBOUR *Bruce* II. 424 He.. haid till erd gane fullyly, Ne war he hynt him by his sted. *c* **1482** in *Cal. Proc. Chanc. Q. Eliz.* (1830) II. Pref. 64 The same Thomas..was in grete juperdie of life, ne only the grace of God. **1494** FABYAN *Chron.* VI. ccxii. 228 Alfrede shulde haue holpen me, ne hadde erle Goodwyn ben. **1513** DOUGLAS *Æneis* XI. xvii. 97 Ne war, as than, the rosy Phebus red Hys wery stedis had dowkyt our the hed.

†**c.** ***ne-for-thi***, nevertheless. *Obs. rare.*

a **1300** *Cursor M.* 11621 Maria and ioseph ne for-þi For the child war ful dreri. **13..** *Ibid.* 7628 (Gött.), Bot saule he dred him ne for-þi.

†**2. a.** With another negative following. *Obs.*

Also occas. doubled, esp. when combined with the verb.

971 *Blickl. Hom.* 13 Ne herede heo hine no mid wordum anum, ac mid ealre heortan. *c* **1000** *Ags. Gosp.* Matt. xxv. 43 Ic wæs cuma and ȝe me ne in ne ȝelaðodun. **1154** *O.E. Chron.* (Laud MS.) an. 1137 Þe erthe ne bar nan corn. *c* **1200** *Trin. Coll. Hom.* 21 He ne hadde him selue nane. *c* **1275** *Passion our Lord* 17 in *O.E. Misc.* 37 Ne þerfþ þer non adrede. *c* **1380** WYCLIFF *Serm.* Sel. Wks. II. 306 Lo, ne ben not al þes þat speken of þe cuntre of Galile? **1411** *Rolls of Parlt.* III. 650/2 He knoweth wel that..he ne hath noght born hym as he sholde hav doon. **1485** CAXTON *Chas. Gt.* 95 Ne doubte ye not for I shal rendre you anone al hole.

†**b.** With another negative preceding. *Obs.*

971 *Blickl. Hom.* 21 Þæt leoht on nanre tide ne ablinneþ. **1154** *O.E. Chron.* (Laud MS.) an. 1140 Hi nan helpe ne hæfden of þe kinge. *a* **1250** *Owl & Night.* 905 Þu neauer ne singst in Irlonde. **1297** R. GLOUC. (Rolls) 4493 Vor þer nas vnneþe non Prynce in al þe world, þat ne moste be þere. **1450–1530** *Myrr. our Ladye* 2 Ye wote well that no man ne may well shewe the worthynes..therof. **1480** CAXTON *Chron. Eng.* xxii. 20 It was not long after that brenne ne come ageyne with a grete nauye.

†**3. a.** As *n-* in combination with a verb. *Obs.*

Even in OE. *ne* was reduced to *n-* before certain common words, as in *ná*, *nán*, *næfre*, *næniȝ* and the verbal forms *nabban*, *neom*, *nys*, *næs*, *nyllan*, *nytan*, etc. In ME. various parts of the verbs *be*, *have*, *will*, and *wit* occur frequently with this prefixed *n-* (for illustrations see NABBE, NAD, NAVE; NAM, NAS, NIS; NILL, NOTE, etc.), and the same phenomenon is not unusual with other verbs.

c **1200** *Moral Ode* 102 (Trin. Coll. MS.), Þeih we hes ne niseien hie waren ure iferen. *c* **1275** *Passion our Lord* 611 in *O.E. Misc.* 54 Yet heo hit nyleuede þe more ne þe lesse. *c* **1330** R. BRUNNE *Chron. Wace* (Rolls) 6576 Þeym nauaillede mast ne roþer. **1390** GOWER *Conf.* II. 40 That time schal noght overpasse, That I naproche hir ladihede. *c* **1407** LYDG. *Reson & Sens.* 5553 They nentende nyght nor day But vnto merthe. **1425** *Rolls of Parlt.* IV. 267/2 My Lord Mareschall naleyeth no possession nor continuance hadde.

†**b.** Suffixed (as *-n*) to the preceding word. *Obs.*

a **1300** *Cursor M.* 17223 Quin suld i, iesu, do þi will? **13..** *Ibid.* 1108 (Gött.), His dede..had euer ben hid, warn iesu him-self had it kid. **13..** *Ibid.* 23362 (Edinb.), Þain sal wit naþing of site. *c* **1375** *Ibid.* 6130 (Fairf.), Was na hous..attyn þer was dedemon in liggande.

B. *conj.*

1. = NOR. **a.** Following a negative clause, or a word with negative force. ***ne..ne*** (sometimes) = neither..nor. Now only *arch.*

In ME. occas. prefixed to the following word, as in A. 3 a.

c **825** *Vesp. Psalter* v. 6 Ne eardað neh ðe awerȝed ne ðorhwuniað ða unrehtwisan [etc.]. *a* **900** *Leiden Riddle* 5 in *O.E. Texts* 151 Uundnae me ni biað ueflæ, ni ic uarp hefæ. **971** *Blickl. Hom.* 25 Nis þær æniȝ sar gemeted, ne adl, ne ece. **1154** *O.E. Chron.* (Laud MS.) an. 1137, I ne can ne i ne mai tellen alle þe wunder ne alle þe pines. *c* **1205** LAY. 10260 Ne bi-læfde he..suster ne broðer Ne quene ne næh cun. *c* **1275** *Passion our Lord* 3 in *O.E. Misc.* 37 Nis hit nouht of karlemeyne ne of þe Duzeper. *c* **1330** R. BRUNNE *Chron. Wace* (Rolls) 9906 Þey nadde neyþer drede naffray. *c* **1380** WYCLIFF *Serm.* Sel. Wks. I. 41 Neiþir in noumbre ne in cloþing, ne in mete ne in housynge. **1426** AUDELAY *Poems* 1 Thai schuld never be schamyd ne chent, ne lost here lyfe, ne lond, ne rent. *c* **1500** *Melusine* 28 He ne wyst where he was, ne whither he went. **1537** CRANMER *Let.* in *Misc. Writ.* (Parker Soc.) II. 336 He cannot in that diocese be accepted ne allowed. **1581** MARBECK *Bk. of Notes* 666 They ne could ne would help the afflicted. **1600** HOLLAND *Livy* XLV. XXXV. 1225 No doubt was made at all of the triumph of Anicius, ne yet of Octavius. *a* **1648** LD. HERBERT *Hen. VIII* (1683) 257 They could not, ne did say that they had. **1742** SHENSTONE *Schoolmistr.* (ed. 1) viii, Ne did she e'er complain, ne deem it rough. **1798** COLERIDGE *Anc. Mar.* III. iii, Ne could we laugh, ne wail.

†**b.** Used with a negative following. *Obs.*

1154 [see above]. *c* **1386** CHAUCER *Knt.'s T.* 488 Arcite is exiled.., Ne nevere mo he schal his lady see. *c* **1420** *Chron. Vilod.* 1723 He myȝt not challange þat heritage, Ny nomore ryȝt hadde þerto. **1452** *Anc. Cal. Rec. Dublin* (1889) I. 275 Ne they shulde not go in to the contre to byge corne.

†**c.** With omission of preceding negative (sometimes expressed in what follows). *Obs.*

a **1300** *Cursor M.* 4146 For man þat liuand es, ne wijf, Ne sal he scappus wit þe lijf. *c* **1330** R. BRUNNE *Chron. Wace* (Rolls) 14995 Swilk men..þat dide ne seide to noman ille. *c* **1386** CHAUCER *Knt.'s T.* 767 Love ne lordschipe Wol not, his thonkes, have no felaschipe. **1435** MISYN *Fire of Love* 1 The whilk boke in sentence ne substance I þink to chaunge. **1484** in *Surtees Misc.* (1890) 42 Thay ne noon of theim were nevere privey to ye sealing. **1542** UDALL *Erasm. Apoph.* 21 They would receive ne take not a scholare without a great fee. **1618** *Kalender of Sheph.* xxxv, Thus orison riseth ne resconceth. Meridian also riseth not ne resconseth.

†**d.** = Nor, and.. not, neither. *Obs. rare.*

1590 SPENSER *F.Q.* III. iv. 56 That doest all thinges deface, ne lettest see The beautie of his worke. **1599** HAKLUYT *Voy.* II. II. 76 These boates are so many that it seemeth wonderfull, ne serue they for other then to take small fish.

†**2.** = OR. *Obs. rare.*

c **1500** *Melusine* 144 The moost strong and fell folke that euer I sawe ne herde speke of. **1548** CRANMER in Strype *Eccl. Mem.* (1721) II. App. AA. 97 There be but few matters more necessary ne more expedyent for kynges.. to loke upon.

† **ne**, *conj.*², variant of NA *conj.*² than. *Obs.*

c **1400** *Sc. Trojan War* (Horstm.) I. 399 That nane was wisser vndre the hewene Ne Medea ine hyr dais. **1508** DUNBAR *Tua Mariit Wemen* 377 3ing lusty gallandis, that I held more in daynte,.. Ne him that dressit me so dink.

ne, obs. f. NEIGH, NIGH.

ne', ne (nɛ), colloq. shortening of NEVER *adv.*

1934 J. D. CARR *Eight of Swords* ii. 28 His daughter and my son—hurrumph, ne' mind. **1949** C. HIMES *Black on Black* (1973) 277 Ne you mind.

nea, north. and Sc. var. of NO.

nead(e, neadle, neady, obs. ff. NEED, NEEDLE, NEEDY.

neaf(ful), obs. ff. NIEVE(FUL).

† **neagues, neakes**, variants of *nigs* in *God's nigs*: see GOD 14 b. *Obs. rare.*

1602 MARSTON *Ant. & Mel.* III. ii, Gods neakes, they would have shone like my mystresse browe. *Ibid.* IV. i, Gods neakes, proude elfe,.. give the Duke reverence. **1619** FLETCHER, etc. *Knt. Malta* v. i, I'll.. goe up and downe drinking small beere and swearing 'odds neagues.

neakit, obs. Sc. form of NAKED *a.*

† **neal**, *a. Obs.* In 6 neall, 7 neale(d). [repr. OE. *néol, níol*, var. *neowol, niwol* deep, profound.] Of water: Deep. Also *neal(ed) to* (see quots.).

1574 W. BOURNE *Regiment for Sea* xxii. (1577) 61 Those be neall or deepe harde unto the sandes or daungers. **1626** CAPT. SMITH *Accid. Yng. Seamen* 30 Come to an Anchor vnder the Ley of the weather shore, the Ley shore, nealed too, looke to your stoppers. **1627** —— *Seaman's Gram.* ix. 44 If it be Nealed to, that is, deepe water close aboord the shore. **1644** MAINWAYRING *Sea-Man's Dict.*, *Neale-too.* [Also in PHILLIPS (1658) and CHAMBERS *Cycl. Supp.* (1753).]

neal (niːl), *v. Obs.* exc. *dial.* Also 6–7 nele, 7 neil(l)e, neale, 9 neeal, nale. [Aphetic form of ANNEAL *v.*]

1. *trans.* To fire or bake (earthenware, etc.), esp. so as to glaze it. = ANNEAL *v.* 2. ? *Obs.*

1538 [implied in NEALED *ppl. a.*]. **1601** HOLLAND *Pliny* I. 425 The wine-vessels.. must be nealed with pitch, presently vpon the rising of the dog-star. **1615** G. SANDYS *Trav.* 31 Divers.. make the particles of clay, gilt, and coloured before they be neiled by the fire. **1683** PETTUS *Fleta Min.* I. (1686) 9 Plaster it all over the inside of the Furnace, let it dry well.. that it may be neald. **1799** G. SMITH *Laboratory* I. 9 Blood stone, which has been nealed and beaten to a.. powder.

b. *fig.* To burn. Also with *into.*

1673 O. WALKER *Educ.* 209 Yet are they not to be neglected, but to be neal'd into youth, that they may not through defect of them, miscarry in their age. **1829** HOGG *Shepherd's Cal.* ii, Till that hard and cruel heart o' yours be nealed to an izle.

2. To temper, to soften or toughen (metal or glass), by the action of fire or heat, *esp.* by a process of heating and slow cooling. = ANNEAL *v.* 4.

1558 PHAER *Æneid* VII. U iij b, Swordes and glaiues in furneis neale they tough. **1611** MARKHAM *Countr. Content.* I. x. (1668) 56 Strong wier.., being nealed and allaid in the fire, you may bend and bow at your pleasure. **1665** HOOKE *Microgr.* 42 By a leisurely heating and cooling, the parts are nealed into another posture. **1685** BOYLE *Effects of Motion* viii. 93 A Glass that seemed to have been well-baked or nealed (as they call it). **1745** *Phil. Trans.* XLIII. 506 Those Drops or *Lachrymæ* of Glass, which, instead of being nealed, had been immediately quenched in Water. **1763** W. LEWIS *Phil. Comm. Arts* 5 The wire is softened and made pliable by nealing or heating it on live coals. **1881** *I. Wight Gloss.*, *Neeal*, to temper by fire. **1894** *S.E. Worc. Gloss.*, *Nale*, to anneal; to soften or toughen iron.

† **3.** *intr.* To undergo the process of annealing.

c **1626** MEVEREL *Answ. Bacon Touching Metals* B.'s Wks. 1857 III. 817 Reduction is chiefly effected by fire, wherein if they stand and nele, the imperfect metals vapour away. **1684** BOYLE *Porousn. Anim. & Solid Bod.* viii. 137 We laid this Glass.. warily upon a few Quick-coals, and having suffered it to neal awhile [etc.].

nealed, *ppl. a.* [f. prec. + -ED¹.] Annealed; having undergone the process of annealing.

1538 LELAND *Itin.* (1769) VI. 72 Pottes exceeding finely nelyd and florishid. **1576** BAKER *Jewell of Health* 193 b, Poure a fourth parte of it into a newe and stronge nealed potte. **1615** CROOKE *Body of Man* 110 On the inside [they are] lined with slime, and as it were nealed like earthen pots. **1658** A. FOX *Würtz' Surg.* I. iv. 13 The stenching of blood must be effected onely with nealed Irons and other burning meanes. **1684** R. WALLER *Nat. Exper.* 111 A Leaden Plummet being fastened to a nealed Brass-Wire. *a* **1734** NORTH *Exam.* I. ii. §46 (1740) 52 The Patent for the Invention of nealed Cannon.

neal-fire. *nonce-wd.* Annealing fire.

1813 HOGG *Queen's Wake, Young Kennedy* iii, His soul was the neal-fire, inhaled from his den.

nealie ('niːlɪ). *Austral.* Also **nelia.** [Etym. unknown.] = *needle-bush* (*b*) (NEEDLE *sb.* 14).

1889 [see *needle-bush* s.v. NEEDLE *sb.* 14]. **1933** *Bulletin* (Sydney) 15 Nov. 21/4 Two miles farther on.. was a mile-wide stretch of nelia scrub. **1936** I. L. IDRIESS *Cattle King* xxxviii. 326 Where had all the mulga gone, the whitewood, and acacias, and turpentine bush, the black oak and nelia, and bullocky bush, the thick shrub life that had carpeted this country when he rode through here a boy? **1965** [see *needle-bush* s.v. NEEDLE *sb.* 14].

nealing ('niːlɪŋ), *vbl. sb.* (and *ppl. a.*) [f. NEAL *v.*] The action of the verb, in various senses; the process of annealing or tempering.

1622 MALYNES *Anc. Law-Merch.* 284 By the working, hammering, often nealing and blaunching, which alwaies in base moneys is verie great. **1678** *Phil. Trans.* XII. 955 Neither was it altogether free from Copper; because, upon Nealing, it always turned black on the surface. **1727–38** CHAMBERS *Cycl.*, *Nealing of glass* is the baking of glass, to dry, harden, and give it the due consistence, after it has been blown. **1799** G. SMITH *Laboratory* I. 71 Heat soon restores its ductility, which is termed nealing or annealing. **1839** URE *Dict. Arts* 47 *Annealing* or *Nealing*, a process by which glass is rendered less frangible, and metals.. are again rendered malleable.

b. *attrib.* or *ppl. a.*

1644 DIGBY *Nat. Bodies* viii. (1658) 69 To let it [glass] cool by degrees in such relentings of fire, as they call their nealing heats. **1666** BOYLE *Orig. Formes & Qual.* 169 To deprive it of its spring it needs the violent agitation of a nealing fire. **1722** DE FOE *Col. Jack* (1840) 8 We got into the ash-holes, and nealing-arches in the glass-house. **1745** *Phil. Trans.* XLIII. 508 Set to cool gradually in what is called the nealing Furnace.

neam(e, variants of EME (see N 3 b).

1589 *Pappe w. Hatchet* (1844) 25 The babie comes in with Nunka, Neame, and Dad. *a* **1652** BROME *Queenes Exch.* III. Wks. 1873 III. 501 *King.* Pull the fool off me. *Jeff.* O but they shall not, neam, 'tis more than they can do. **1684–** in dialect use (Warw., Staff., Derby, Yks., Lancs), chiefly *my neam* (see *Eng. Dial. Dict.*).

neamble, obs. form of NIMBLE *a.*

nean(e, north. dial. forms of NONE.

Neanderthal (nɪ'ændətɑːl). Also **Neandertal.** The name of a valley near Düsseldorf in western Germany, used *attrib.* in **Neanderthal man, skull**, etc., to designate the Middle Palæolithic fossil hominid *Homo neanderthalensis*, first identified from a skull found there in 1856, and also known from other remains in Europe, Africa, and Asia. Also *absol.*, *fig.* (with reference to appearance), and as *adj.*

1861 G. BUSK tr. D. Schaaffhausen in *Nat. Hist. Rev.* Apr. 167 The considerations which have led us to compare the Neanderthal cranium with those of the most ancient races are still further confirmed by the discovery.. of skulls exhibiting a yet closer correspondence with it. **1863** T. H. HUXLEY *Evidence Man's Place in Nature* iii. 142 The posterior lobe of the brain of the Neanderthal man must have been as much flattened as I suspected it to be. In truth, the Neanderthal cranium has most extraordinary characters. **1864** *Q. Jrnl. Sci.* I. 88 It is my intention to confine myself to the consideration of the Neanderthal fossil with reference to its place in Nature. *Ibid.* 90 The Neanderthal skull is of an elongated oval form. **1899** A. H. KEANE *Man Past & Present* 9 Certain skulls from South Australia seem cast in almost the same mould as the Neanderthal. **1922** *Encycl. Brit.* XXX. 145/2 Neanderthal man is now revealed as an uncouth race with an enormous flattened head, very prominent eye-brow ridges and a coarse face. **1923** A. L. KROEBER *Anthropol.* ii. 24 Neandertal man was short. *Ibid.* xv. 472 Whenever the origin of a people remains obscure, be they Neandertals, Alpines, Sumerians,.. or what not, some one propounds the convenient hypothesis of deriving them from this vast interior land [*sc.* central Asia]. **1928** *Weekly Dispatch* 13 May 12/3 The pictures which show modern influence are even more unpleasant than the streaky bacon sunsets.. or the most realistic neanderthal clergymen which otherwise decorate the walls. **1939** 'N. BLAKE' *Smiler with Knife* iii. 57 You know what the other side says—.. 'Woman's place is in the kitchen'—all the rest of that Neanderthal tommyrot. **1966** E. PALMER *Plains of Camdeboo* vii. 117 Neanderthal Man lived here in Southern Africa. **1966** M. WOODHOUSE *Tree Frog* xii. 86 A fourteen-stone Neanderthal with a sub-machine gun appeared. **1970** *Guardian* 9 July 10/4 The Neanderthal men of the military and industrial establishments. **1971** *Observer* 23 May 24/6 Neanderthal grunts over the cornflakes.. were the best most husbands could manage. **1973** B. J. WILLIAMS *Evolution & Human Origins* xi. 176/2 In the material that follows I shall use the term Neandertal *sensu lato*, that is, in the broad sense. The term will designate the early stages of the within-species evolution of *Homo sapiens*. *Ibid.* 185/2 In 1958 part of a Neandertal skull was recovered from a cave at Ma-pa, southern Kwangtung. **1973** A. PRICE *October Men* xi. 164 He is a creature from the Dark Ages, a man of violence. A Neanderthal. **1973** D. RAMSAY *Deadly Discretion* 97 How about your pal Ivan? Does he have sensitive feelings under that Neanderthal exterior?

Hence **Ne'ander,thaler**, a Neanderthal man; **Neander'thalian** *a.* and *sb.*; **Neander'thalic** *a.* (in quot. *fig.*).

1913 *Science Progress* VIII. 278 The Neandertaler differed from *Homo sapiens* in having an extremely receding forehead, with enormously developed brow-ridges. **1920** H. G. WELLS *Outl. Hist.* I. ix. 51/2 The Tasmanians were not racially Neanderthalers. *Ibid.* x. 58/2 The tremendous advance they [*sc.* later Palæolithic men] display upon their Neanderthalian predecessors. **1920** H. REINHEIMER *Symbiosis* III. i. 205 Some of them, e.g., the Neanderthalians, reached the stage of the savage beast, marked by chronic acromegaly. **1955** *Sci. News Let.* 19 Feb. 122/2 With succeeding generations Neanderthalers became adapted physically to withstand the cold. **1967** *Boston Sunday Herald* 26 Mar. I. 29/3 Neanderthalic sadists forced near-dead men to run when they scarcely had the strength to put one foot ahead of another. **1971** *Times* 11 Feb. 14/7 He pointed out that Neanderthalers, living as they did in the ice age, might easily have suffered from a deficiency in vitamin D.

Neanderthaloid (nɪ,ændə'tɑːlɔɪd), *a.* (*sb.*) [f. NEANDERTHAL + -OID.] Having the characteristics of the fossil hominid found at Neanderthal in Rhenish Prussia in 1856.

1887 W. H. FLOWER in *Jrnl. Anthrop. Inst.* XVI. 377 A type which has received the name 'Neanderthaloid'. **1890** HUXLEY in *19th Cent.* Nov. 776 Skulls do approach the Neanderthaloid type, among both the brunet and the blond long-head races. **1971** *Nature* 23 Apr. 489/2 Although Swanscombe had long been considered closely affiliated with modern *Homo sapiens* the multivariate analysis indicated a closer resemblance to the neanderthaloids.

neanic (niː'ænɪk), *a. Zool.* [f. Gk. νεανικ-ός youthful.] Designating the early stages of the growth of an animal, esp. the pupal stage of an insect.

1892 BUCHMAN & BATHER in *Zool. Anzeiger* XV. 421 Hyatt... Neologic. Here proposed.. Neanic. Literary equivalent.. Adolescent. *Ibid.* 430 Neanic. During this stage specific characters and all other morphological features present in the adult, appear and undergo development. **1903** *Amer. Naturalist* XXXVII. 519 At this stage [in the growth of *Sycotypus canaliculatus*], the early neanic, the lines of growth are well marked and of nearly equal strength with the revolving lines, the two together giving the shell surface a reticulated appearance. **1906** J. B. SMITH *Explanation Terms Entomol.* 87 Neanic: referring to the pupal stage. **1938** *Nature* 20 Aug. 341/1 It is helpful to distinguish between the very early, or embryonic, stages of development and the later, or neanic stages, during which the young gradually assumes the characteristics of the adult. *Ibid.* 10 Sept. 461/1 In the neanic phase the organism exhibits a combination of less stable characters. **1971** F. E. EAMES *Davies's Tertiary Faunas* (ed. 2) I. i. 90 Neanic. Youthful stage in ontogeny.

neanthropic (niːæn'θrɒpɪk), *a.* Also **neoanthropic**, and with capital initial. [f. NEO- + ANTHROPIC *a.*] Of, pertaining to, or designating the single extant species of man as distinguished from extinct forms known from their fossil remains.

Quot. 1916 may represent an independent coinage.

1894 J. W. DAWSON *Meeting-Place Geol. & Hist.* i. 17 The modern, or anthropic [period], is.. divisible into two sections—the early modern, or palanthropic, sometimes called quaternary, or post-glacial, and which may coincide with the antediluvian period of human history; and the neanthropic, extending onward to the present time. [*Note*] I have preferred.. to call the earlier races of men palaeocosmic and the later neocosmic,.. while the periods to which they belong are respectively the Palanthropic and Neanthropic. **1916** G. E. SMITH *Primitive Man* 18 Thus the new spirit of man and modern man himself are revealed in the Upper Palaeolithic period. This Neoanthropic phase, as I have called it, thus begins in the Aurignacian period. **1939** MCCOWN & KEITH *Stone Age Mt. Carmel* II. xxii. 362 In Neanderthal skulls the great wing and the orbital plate of the malar tend to be wide; in Neanthropic skulls they tend to be narrow. **1959** J. D. CLARK *Prehist. S. Afr.* iv. 77 The 'neanthropic' or modern (*Homo sapiens*) form of man. **1973** B. J. WILLIAMS *Evolution & Human Origins* xi. 175/1 The neanthropic (new man) line included fossils that were more or less modern throughout time.

neap (niːp), *sb.*¹ *north. dial.* and *U.S.* Also 6, 9 nepe, 7 neep, nape. [perh. of Scand. origin: cf. Norw. dial. *neip* a forked pole, a wooden stay (Aasen), Icel. *neip* the space between two fingers.]

1. The pole or tongue of a cart. (Now *U.S.*) Also *attrib.* in †*nepe-yoke.*

1553 *Inventory* in *Midl. Counties Hist. Collector* (1855) I. 233 Itm iij waynes, iij dongcarts.. iij nepe yoks. **1659** HOOLE *Comenius' Vis. World* (1672) 173 The parts of a Wagon are, the Neep (or draught-tree) [etc.]. **1877** C. D. WARNER *Being a Boy* i, When I rode on the neap of the cart, and drove the oxen. **1884** *Harper's Mag.* Sept. 613/1 They had.. perched themselves on a cart neap.

2. (See quots.)

1691 RAY *N.C. Words* (ed. 2) 51 A *Nape* or *Neap*; a piece of Wood, that hath two or three feet, with which they bear up the fore-part of a laded Wain. **1876** *Mid-Yorksh. Gloss.*, *Neap*,.. a three-legged rest, constructed of natural branches, and used to support the shaft of a vehicle.

neap (niːp), *a.* and *sb.*² Forms: 1 nép-, 5–8 neep, (6 -e), 6–8 nepe, (6 nep, neb, 7 nape), 7–8 neipe, (8 niepe, nip), 6– neap, (6–7 -e). [OE. *nép* in *népflód*, of obscure etym. and meaning, otherwise found only in *Exod.* 469 in the phrase *forðganges nép*, app. = 'without power of advancing'. Da. *niptid* is prob. from English.]

1. ***neap tide***, a tide occurring shortly after the first and third quarters of the moon, in which the high-water level stands at its lowest point. †Orig. ***neap-flood***, and occas. with other sbs. as *stream*. Also *neap rise* (see quot.); *neap season*, the time of neap tide.

c **725** *Corpus Gloss.* (Hessels) Int. 196 *Ledo*, nep flod. *c* **850** *O.E. Martyrol.* 40 Se fylleðflod bið nemned on leden *malina*, & se nepflod *ledo*. *c* **1050** *Suppl. Ælfric's Gloss.* in Wr.-Wülcker 182 *Ledona*, nepflod *vel* ebba.

1479 in *Eng. Gilds* (1870) 425 That they leue resonable stuff upon the bak fro spryng to sprynġ, to serue the pouere people..in the neep sesons. *a* **1548** HALL *Chron., Hen. VIII* 131 Thre horsemen..whiche wel knewe the hauen of Calice, came at a nepe tide. **1561** EDEN *Arte Navig.* II. xviii, Whiche the Mariners call nepe tydes, lowe ebbes, lowe waters, dead waters, or lowe fluddes. **1622** HAWKINS *Voy. S. Sea* (1847) 155 Our shippe..in the neap streames comming a-ground in the sterne. **1694** *Lond. Gaz.* No. 3025/3 The great Ships..wanted Water to come over the Flatts..by reason of the Neep Tides. **1720** STRYPE *Stow's Surv.* (1754) I. I. vi. 34/2 The Tides were then at the Neapest. **1794** SULLIVAN *View Nat.* I. 390 The spring tides will be greater ..and the neap tides on that account will be less. **1860** *All Year Round* No. 69. 449 The tides are weak, or neap; the oscillation of the sea is less. **1870** PROCTOR *Other Worlds* iii. 73 We have tides ranging between the highest spring tides.. and the lowest neap tides. **1888** *Encycl. Brit.* XXIII. 369/2 The height between high-water mark at neap tide and mean low-water mark at spring tide is called the neap rise.

fig. **1645** QUARLES *Sol. Recant.* XII. 73 When ebbing bloods neap tides shall strike thy lims With trembling Palsies. **1875** TENNYSON *Q. Mary* I. v, The realm is poor, The exchequer at neap-tide [*ed.* 1, neap-ebb].

2. *absol.* as *sb.* A neap tide.

1584 in J. J. Cartwright *Chapt. Hist. Yorks* (1872) 268 We say that there ryseth at the sprynge 18 foott water, and at the nepe eleaven foot water. **1661** J. CHILDREY *Brit. Baconica* 91 So do the Neaps too after the Quarters. **1679** SALMON *Horæ Math.* IV. xvii. 405 The Neaps and lowest Tides at her.. quarters. **1727–38** CHAMBERS *Cycl.* s.v., The lowest of the neap is four days before the full or change—on which occasion the seamen say, that it is deep neep. **1776** COOK in *Phil. Trans.* LXVI. 448 During the neep, the tide was very inconsiderable. **1849** H. MILLER *Footpr. Creat.* xiii. (1874) 233 A zone still less deeply covered by water, and which even the lower neaps expose. **1875** BEDFORD *Sailor's Pocket Bk.* v. (ed. 2) 146 For both springs and neaps give the height of high water.

b. In phr. *dead neap*: see DEAD *a.* 27.

1589 GREENE *Tullie's Love* C 3 The lowest ebbe may haue his flow, and the deaddest neape his full tide. **1627** HAKEWILL *Apol.* (1630) 131 High springs and dead Neapes. *a* **1641** [see DEAD *a.* 27]. **1751** *Anc. St. Navig. Lyn*, etc. 24 Ships of considerable Burden could..come up to the Townside at Low-water, and even at dead Niepe. **1882** *White's Lincolnsh. Direct.* 750 Ships of over 500 tons register can come to Sutton Bridge at dead neap.

neap (niːp), *v.* Forms: 7 nepe, 8 neep, neip, 8– neap. [f. NEAP *sb.*[2]]

1. *intr.* **a.** Of tides: To become lower, to tend towards the neap. Also *pass.*

1652–62 HEYLIN *Cosmogr.* Introd. (1682) 23 From the first quarter to the full it [the sea] is said to spring: from the full to the last quarter it is said to nepe. **1854** G. B. RICHARDSON *Univ. Code* v. (ed. 12) 3270 The tides are neaped. **1866** *Even. Star* 24 Mar., The tides are now neaping.

b. To reach the highest point of neap tide.

1805 *Chron.* in *Ann. Reg.* 410/2 At 40 minutes past 2 the tide had neaped and fell above 3 inches.

2. *to be neaped*: of a vessel (see quots.).

1704 J. HARRIS *Lex. Techn.* I. s.v. *Neipe*, When a Ship wants Water, so that she cannot get out of a Harbour, off from the Ground, or out of the Dock, the Seamen say she is Neiped. **1769** FALCONER *Dict. Marine* (1780), *Neaped*, the situation of a ship which is left aground on the heighth of a spring-tide. **1835** SIR J. ROSS *Narr. 2nd Voy.* xxxiii. 467 The tides were now diminishing, while we could not run the risk of being neaped in this manner. **1865** *Pall Mall G.* 21 Nov. 6 Owing to a sudden change in the river.., the *Mooltan* is neaped, and cannot leave here until the 14th inst. **1891** *Law Times* XC. 248/2 Inasmuch as she could load 'always afloat' in the dock, she was not entitled to leave it in order to avoid being neaped.

b. *trans.* with personal agent. *rare*⁻¹.

1770 in Hawkesworth *Voy.* (1773) III. 559, I hauled her bow close ashore; but kept her stern afloat, because I was afraid of neiping her.

neapil, neaple, obs. forms of NIPPLE.

neapkyn, obs. Sc. form of NAPKIN.

†**'neapness.** *Obs. rare*⁻¹. [f. NEAP *a.* + -NESS.] The condition of being at the neap.

1720 STRYPE *Stow's Surv.* (1754) I. I. vi. 33/2 The Tides were very slack and in a manner at the very Neapness.

Neapolitan (niːə'pɒlɪtən), *a.* and *sb.* Also 6–7 Neo-. [ad. L. *Neāpolītān-us*, f. *Neāpolītēs* (see -ITE), f. *Neāpolis* (Gr. Νεάπολις, new town), Naples.]

A. *adj.* **a.** Belonging or native to, distinctive or characteristic of, connected with, Naples.

1596 SHAKS. *Merch. V.* I. ii. 43 First there is the Neopolitane Prince. **1617** MORYSON *Itin* III. 133 English Coursers, bred of the Neapolitan Horses and English Mares. **1664** EVELYN *Kal. Hort.* (1729) 234 Medlars. The Great Dutch, Neopolitan and One without Stones. **1705** ADDISON *Italy* 203 The Lybian Port is but the Neapolitan Bay in little. **1797** MRS. RADCLIFFE *Italian* xii, The strangers of distinction, dressed in the splendid Neapolitan habit. **1830** LYELL *Princ. Geol.* I. vi. (1837) I. 141 Recent shells procured..from the Neapolitan seas. **1862** BURGON *Lett. fr. Rome* xxii. 276 There seemed in fact a marked change of race on getting into the Neapolitan States.

b. In special uses. †*Neapolitan disease* (also euphem., *consolation*, *favour*), a form of syphilis (cf. NAPLES 1 a). *Neapolitan ice*, a block of ice cream made in layers of different colours and flavours; also *transf.* and *fig.* *Neapolitan maple* (see quots.). *Neapolitan ointment*, a mercurial ointment used for syphilis. †*Neapolitan scab* = N. disease. *Neapolitan sixth* (see quots). *Neapolitan system* (see quots.). *Neapolitan violet*, a double sweet-scented variety of viola. *Neapolitan yellow*, Naples yellow.

a **1704** T. BROWN *Lett. to Gent. & Ladies* Wks. 1709 III. II. 47 Had'st thou administered a little *Neapolitan Consolation to thy Hibernian. **1656** BLOUNT *Glossogr.*, *Neopolitan disease. *a* **1704** T. BROWN *Pleasant Lett. to Gent.* Wks. 1709 III. II. 7 That which we call the Neapolitan Disease. **1777** ROBERTSON *America* (1783) II. 76 This distemper..has been sometimes called the Neapolitan and sometimes the French disease. **1592** GREENE *Conny Catch.* Wks. (Grosart) X. 44 They..find nothing but a *Neapolitan fauour for their labour. **1895** 'M. RONALD' *Century Cook Bk.* xxii. 498 **Neapolitan ice-cream*. This cream is molded in brick form in three layers of different flavors and colors. **1911** *Daily Colonist* (Victoria, B.C.) 26 Apr. 7/1 (Advt.), Ice Cream Bricks, Neapolitan, Vanilla, Strawberry, Pineapple, [etc.]. **1933** A. HUXLEY *Let.* 29 Apr. (1969) 369 Mexico was ..very curious. Such a strange Neapolitan ice, with its layers of Indian, mestizo, white. **1954** —— *Let.* 25 Oct. (1969) 714 We have to think of the mind in terms of a stratified Neapolitan ice, with a peculiar flavour of consciousness at each level. **1969** R. & D. DE SOLA *Dict. Cooking* 158/1 *Neapolitan ice cream*, ice-cream brick containing several flavors arranged in contrasting color layers, usually chocolate, vanilla, and strawberry. **1833** *Penny Cycl.* I. 77/1 *Acer obtusatum*, the *Neapolitan maple. **1882** *Garden* 18 Nov. 459/2 The Neapolitan Maple, with its reddish purple branches, is a handsome tree. **1753** CHAMBERS *Cycl. Supp* s.v., *Neapolitan ointment..is a mixture of quicksilver, and other things into an ointment. **1899** *Allbutt's Syst. Med.* VIII. 469 He has several times seen E. iris to follow a friction with Neapolitan ointment. **1671** H. M. tr. *Erasm. Colloq.* 531 The New Leprosie, which some..do call the *Neapolitan scab. **1871** STAINER *Harmony* xii. §138 A chord consisting of the sub-dominant and its minor third and minor sixth is used in the major or minor mode. It is called the *Neapolitan Sixth. **1889** E. PROUT *Harmony* (ed. 10) xii. §276 The first inversion of this chord is generally known as the 'Neapolitan sixth', a name for which it is difficult to give a satisfactory reason. **1959** REESE & DORMER *Bridge Player's Dict.* 151 **Neapolitan System*,..one of the principal Italian systems, played by Forquet and Siniscalco and others. It is one-club system, with a series of artificial responses. **1962** *Listener* 22 Nov. 886/2 West, playing the Neapolitan system, opened Two Diamonds. **1964** *Official Encycl. Bridge* 374/2 *Neapolitan*, a system..played in many World Championship events by a group of Neapolitan players. **1836** LOUDON *Encycl. Plants* 187 *Viola odorata* is a favorite flower... The double purple and the *Neapolitan are the most esteemed varieties. **1843** *Penny Cycl.* XXVI. 344/1 Some of them have double flowers, which is the case in the variety known as the Neapolitan violet. **1891** THORPE *Dict. Applied Chem.* II. 692/2 *Neapolitan Yellow.

B. *sb.* **a.** An inhabitant or native of the kingdom or city of Naples.

1412–20 LYDG. *Chron. Troy* I. (MS. Digby 230) lf. 34 Cecile,..To wiche ful many Neapolitans longith this day. **1593** SHAKS. *2 Hen. VI*, v. i. 117 A blood-bespotted Neopolitan, Out-cast of Naples. **1610** —— *Temp.* II. ii. 117 O Stephano, two Neapolitanes scap'd. **1670** G. H. *Hist. Cardinals* I. I. 8 The poor Neapolitan..was not slow to take his leave. **1756–7** tr. *Keysler's Trav.* (1760) II. 227 Cardinal Gieronimo Casanata, a Neapolitan. **1822** W. ROBINSON in J. A. Heraud *Life Midshipm.* v. (1837) 81 Genoese, French, Sards, and Neapolitans. **1862** BURGON *Lett. fr. Rome* xxii. 278 Two Neapolitans..soon entered into conversation with me.

†**b.** (See quot.) *Obs. rare*⁻¹.

1597 MORLEY *Introd. Mus.* 180 The Neapolitans or *Canzone a la Napolitana*, different from them [*sc.* canzonets] in nothing sauing in name.

†**c.** The Neapolitan disease. *Obs. rare*⁻¹.

1631 T. POWELL *Tom of All Trades* 28 Their best benefactor [is] the Neapolitan.

d. A dialect or language of Naples.

1598 FLORIO *Worlde of Wordes* Epistle Dedicatorie, How shall we, naie how may we ayme at the Venetian, at the Romane, at the Lombard, at the Neapolitane, at so manie, and so much differing Dialects, and Idiomes, as be vsed and spoken in Italie, besides the Florentine? **1901** M. CARMICHAEL *In Tuscany* 99 Had Dante been born not at Florence but in Venice and written in Venetian, had Petrarch been born not at Arezzo but in Naples and written in Neapolitan, there would have been two classical languages in Italy today. **1936** G. F.-H. & J. BERKELEY *Italy in Making* II. xviii. 276 As a general rule he spoke French or Neapolitan, not Italian. **1973** A. PRICE *October Men* xi. 157 The man's Italian was..faultless... There was even..the hint of Neapolitan in it.

near (nɪə(r)), *adv.*[1] (and *prep.*) *Obs.* exc. *dial.* Forms: 1 néar, néor, nér, níor, nýr, 3–4 neor, ner, nier, 4–5 neer, 4–7 nere, (7 neere), 5–6 *Sc.* neir, 6– near. [OE. *néar*, etc., comparative of *néah* NIGH *adv.*, = OFris, *nîar*, *nîer*, *nyer*, etc., OS. *nâhor* (MDu. *naer*), MLG. (*nâger*), *nâer*, *nâr*, OHG. *nâhor* (MHG. *nâher*, *nâr*, G. *näher*, ON. *nǽr* (see NEAR *adv.*[2]), Goth. *nêhwis*. Cf. NAR *a.* and *adv.*]

I. In purely adverbial (or prepositional) use.

†**1.** With verbs of motion. Nearer or closer (to a place, point, or person). Freq. governing a noun in the dative. *Obs.*

Beowulf 745 Forð near ætstop, nam þa mid handa..rinc on ræste. *c* **888** K. ÆLFRED *Boeth.* iii. §1 Ða eode se Wisdom near..minum hreowsiendum ȝeþohte. **971** *Blickl. Hom.* 179 Gang me near hider. *c* **1205** LAY. 8884 þæne kæisere he eode neor. **1297** R. GLOUC. (Rolls) 4920 + 132 Cadwal.. Aryuede bysyde toteneys [and] come somdel ner. *c* **1400** *Rom. Rose* 2442 But ofte thou faylest of thy desyre, Er thou maiest come her any nere. **1533** J. HEYWOOD *Mery Play* 653 Stand styll, drab, I say, and come no nere. **1596** *Edw. III*, I. ii, Pardon me,..I will come no near.

†**b.** *near and near*, nearer and nearer. *Obs.*

13.. *K. Alis.* 599 He schal wende of londe feor..and comen neor and neor. *c* **1380** *Sir Ferumb.* 350 þe knyȝt him neȝeþ ner & ner. **1470–85** MALORY *Arthur* VI. vii. 193 Euer as they came nere and nere, syre launcelot thouȝt he shold knowe hym. *a* **1557** *Diurn. Occurr.* 45 Then the rest fled, and the Scottis drew neir and neir. *c* **1611** CHAPMAN *Iliad* xxiii. 206 Still creeping near and near the heap.

c. *Naut.* in *no near!* (or *near!*), a command to the helmsman to come no closer to the wind.

c **1450** *Pilgrims' Sea-voy.* 29 Go to the helm!..no nere! **1627** CAPT. SMITH *Seaman's Gram.* ix. 37 No neere, ease the Helme, or beare vp, is to let her fall to Lee-ward. **1669** STURMY *Mariner's Mag.* I. ii. 18 No near, keep her full. **1710** *Pol. Ballads* (1860) II. 80 Avast, cried out the Admiral, No-near, you rogues, no-near. **1769** FALCONER *Dict. Marine* (1780) s.v. *No nearer*, It is often abbreviated into *no near*, and sometimes into *near*; and is generally applied when the sails shake in the wind. **1841** DANA *Seaman's Man.* 116 'Near!' the order to the helmsman when he is too near the wind. **1867** SMYTH *Sailor's Word-bk.*

†**2.** At a nearer distance, with a less interval.

a **1000** in Cockayne *Narrat.* (1861) 22 Mid þy ic þa wolde near ȝeseon. **1297** R. GLOUC. (Rolls) 4549 þe traytour..fley atte laste To cornwaile.., he ne dorste no ner abyde. **1375** BARBOUR *Bruce* XVI. 258 The king and all that with him war Raid..neir to-giddir than ere did thai. *c* **1380** WYCLIF *Wks.* (1880) 409 Men wolen not be euene wiþ crist ne go bifore hym..but sue crist neer or ferrere.

†**b.** In phrases equivalent in meaning to *far and near* (see NEAR *adv.*[2] 1 b), but properly meaning 'farther (off) and nearer (at hand)'. *Obs.*

a **1000** *Instit. Polity* in Thorpe *Laws* II. 332 Hit ȝebyreð eow þa ȝe me ȝearwe beon, swa fyr swa nyr. *c* **1175** *Lamb. Hom.* 137 Hereword to habbene & beon iwurðeȝede fir & neor [= *Trin. Hom.* 157 fer & ner]. *a* **1250** *Owl & Night.* 923 East & west, feor & neor, I do wel faire mi meoster. *c* **1290** *S. Eng. Leg.* I. 21/72 Men speken muche of his guodnesse, wel wide feor and ner.

†**c.** More closely or intimately. *Obs. rare.*

c **1200** ORMIN 15688 þatt lott off menn..þatt was till Crist ȝet ner bitahht þan hise posstless wærenn. **1572** *Satir. Poems Reform.* xxxviii. 18 I[n] greis neir to Ganȝelon nor grit Charlie Mane.

II. In predicative use after the subst. verb. (Freq. with dative or *to*.)

3. Nearer in space or time; nearer at hand.

c **850** *O.E. Martyrol.* 44 Swa he bið þære sunnan near swa bið his leoht læsse. *c* **1000** ÆLFRIC *Hom.* II. 370 Swa near ende þyssere worulde swa mare ehtnys þæs deofles. *c* **1200** ORMIN 15235 [The] oþerr [bench] wass abufen þatt & summ del ner þa waȝhe. *a* **1250** *Owl & Night.* 1260 Nis heom þer fore harem no þe ner. **1303** R. BRUNNE *Handl. Synne* 9243 þe nere þe cherche, þe fyrþer fro God. **1382** WYCLIF *Rom.* xiii. 11 Sothli now oure heelthe is neer, than whanne we bileueden. **1398** TREVISA *Barth. De P.R.* VIII. ii, þe nere euerich bemy lyne is to oþer lynes..the more strong he is. **1562** J. HEYWOOD *Prov. & Epigr.* (1867) 17 The nere to the churche, the ferther from God.

†**4.** Nearer in kinship or relationship. *Obs.*

831 *Charter* in *O.E. Texts* 445 Nis Eðelmode eniȝ meȝhond neor ðes cynees ðanne Eadwald. **1340** *Ayenb.* 234 Vor manie þer byeþ þet more byeþ nier god þanne manye maydines. *c* **1380** WYCLIF *Sel. Wks.* III. 69 Watir is neer hevene in kynde þan is erþe. *a* **1450** *Knt. de la Tour* (1868) 18 Y saide, she was bothe good and faire, but she shulde be to me no nere than she was. **1523** LD. BERNERS *Froiss.* I. xxxii. 46 That the duke of Brabant wold be redy for his part, sayeng, yᵗ he was nere than they. **1605** SHAKS. *Macb.* II. iii. 146 The neere in blood, the neerer bloody.

5. Nearer to one's end or purpose. Only in negative and interrogative clauses, esp. *never the near* (common 1560–1625). Now only *dial.*

1362 LANGL. *P. Pl.* A. XI. 250 ȝet am I neuere the ner.. To wyte what is Do wel. *c* **1386** CHAUCER *Can. Yeom. Prol. & T.* 168 With this chanoun I duelled have seven yer, And of his science am I never the ner. *a* **1533** FRITH *Answ. More* (1548) K 2 b, Then is he neuer the nere hys purpose, but much the further from it. **1558** G. CAVENDISH *Poems* (1825) II. 97 For all my conquests and my royal powers,..what ame I the nere? **1624** BP. MOUNTAGU *Gagg* 54 He may call his heart out..and not the neere. **1657** R. LIGON *Barbadoes* (1673) 121 If it be not under lock and key, they are never the neer. **1854** MISS BAKER *Northampton Gloss.* s.v. *Nivver*, I've worked all day, and am nivver the near.

b. With impersonal subject.

c **1590** GREENE *Fr. Bacon* vi, You're early up, pray God it be the near. *a* **1592** —— *Jas. IV* 80 There I kept a great house with smal cheer, but all was nere the neere. **1811** *Ora & Juliet* IV. 93 As for staying with them there French rascals, it was never the near. **1886** ELWORTHY *W. Som. Word-bk.* s.v. What's the near to tell up such stuff's that?

near (nɪə(r)), *adv.*[2] (and *prep.*) Forms: 2–6 ner, 4–7 nere, neer(e; *north.* and *Sc.* neir, (5 neyre, 7 neire); 6 nyer, 7 nier; 6–7 neare, 6– near. [a. ON. *nǽr* (Da. *nær*, Sw. *när*), properly the comparative of *ná-* = OE. *néah* NIGH, but also used as a positive: cf. NAR *adv.*

The transition from the comparative to the positive sense in ON. probably originated in such expressions as *koma* or *ganga nær* 'to come *or* go nearer' (to a person or place), which readily passes into the sense of going absolutely 'close' or 'near'. The positive sense having thus attached itself to the word, *nær* could be employed with other verbs than those of motion, as *standa* or *vera* (to be). A similar development has taken place in MDu. *naer* near (whence mod. Du. *naar*, to, for, after, etc.). Even in English some difference is felt in the sense of *near* according as it goes with a verb of motion or not, and in predicative use after the verb *to be* (expressed or implied) the adverbial sense tends to pass into a purely adjectival one.

ON. *nær* (like OE. *néar*) might be used either absolutely or governing a noun in the dative case. Both usages were adopted in ME., and a further construction introduced by the use of *to* before the noun. When the noun directly depends on *near*, this acquires practically the force of a preposition, but differs from real prepositions in having comparative and superlative forms.]

I. Used absolutely (without *to* or dependent sb.).

* *Denoting proximity.*

1. a. To, within, or at, a short distance; to, or in, close proximity.

c **1250** *Gen. & Ex.* 2611 Egipte wimmen comen ner. **1352** Minot in *Pol. Poems* (Rolls) I. 67 When he herd.. That king Edward was nere tharby. *c* **1386** Chaucer *Sqr.'s Prol.* 1 Squier, come ner, if it youre wille be. *c* **1470** Henry *Wallace* ix. 272 He gaiff commaund na schip suld ner apper. **1508** Dunbar *Tua Mariit Wemen* 161 To speik..I sall nought spar; ther is no spy neir. **1568** Grafton *Chron.* II. 698 Two of the chiefest Aldermen..earnestly admonished him..to come not one foote nerer. **1596** Spenser *F.Q.* vi. vi. 19 The salvage man did take his steede And in some stable neare did set him up to feede. **1642** H. More *Song of Soul* ii. ii. ii. iii, Things near seem further off; farst off, the nearst at hand. **1697** Dryden *Virg. Past.* i. 35 Like Shrubs, when lofty Cypresses are near. **1726** Leoni *Alberti's Archit.* I. 16/1 They ought..not..to stand nearer or more remote than Use and Necessity requires. **1794** Mrs. Radcliffe *Myst. Udolpho* xviii, Now they come nearer. **1807** Crabbe *Par. Reg.* i. 379 Where noisy sparrows, perched on penthouse near. **1855** Tennyson *Maud* i. xviii. viii, I have climb'd nearer out of lonely Hell. **1876** T. Hardy *Ethelberta* (1890) 347 Come away there:..what need have ye for going so near?

Phr. **1610** B. Jonson *Alch.* iii. v, Though to Fortvne neere be her petticote, Yet, neerer is her smock. **1890** Caine *Bondman* ii. x, Near is my shirt, but nearer is my skin!

fig. **1852** Mrs. Stowe *Uncle Tom's C.* xxvi. 249 'Did Miss Eva say she felt more unwell than usual to night?' 'No; but she telled me this morning she was coming nearer'.

b. ***far and near***: (see far *adv.* 1 b, and cf. near *adv.*[1] 2 b). [So MDu. *verre ende naer*.]

a **1300** *Cursor M.* 3521 Bath on fer and ner [*v.r.* nere] he soght. *c* **1375** *Sc. Leg. Saints* xix. (*Christopher*) 152 Crystofore..passyt one fere and neyre, sekand cryst. *c* **1430** [see far *adv.* 1 b]. **1560** Daus tr. *Sleidane's Comm.* 16 b, The Church of Christe was spreade abroade farre and nere. **1638** Baker tr. *Balzac's Lett.* (vol. III.) 86 The happiness which I have from you..spreads itself both farre and neere. *a* **1704–97** [see far *adv.* 1 b].

c. In phrases ***near at hand***, †***-away***.

13.. *Cursor M.* 15709 (Gött.), He es comand nere at hand. **1530** Palsgr. 821/1 Nere at hande, *bien pres.* *a* **1586** Sidney *Arcadia* (1622) 96 She drew thither neare-away. **1670–98** Lassels *Voy. Italy* II. 25, I once saw it near at hand. **1820** [see hand *sb.* 25 b]. **1891** *Daily News* 31 Oct. 2/8 Near at hand parcels are being sold in considerable quantities.

d. *Naut.* Close to the wind. (Cf. *adv.*[1] 1 c.)

1634 Sir T. Herbert *Trav.* 25 The ship could lie no neerer then South-east. **1669** Sturmy *Mariner's Mag.* i. ii. 17 Keep her as near as she will lie. **1769** Falconer *Dict. Marine* (1780), *No Nearer!* the command given..to the helmsman, to steer the ship no nigher to..the wind than the sails will operate. **1846** Young *Naut. Dict.* 218.

e. ***so near and yet so far***: describing a person who or thing which is unattainable despite its apparent proximity.

1755 W. Hay tr. *Martial's Sel. Epigrams* i. 15 In the whole town no soul can be So near, and yet so far from me. **1850** Tennyson *In Mem.* xcv. 145 He seems so near and yet so far. **1863** 'Ouida' *Held in Bondage* I. i. 25 The long sunny future that stretched before us in dim golden haze,—so near and yet so far from our young longing eyes. **1863** *Harper's Mag.* Dec. 93/2 Thou art so near, and yet so far! **1920** R. Macaulay *Potterism* i. i. 8 In June and July 1914 the conversation turned largely and tediously on militant suffragists, Irish rebels, and strikers... It was a curious age, so near and yet so far, when the ordered frame of things was still unbroken, and violence a child's dream. **1939** Joyce *Finnegans Wake* 213 I've lost it!.. So near and yet so far! **1962** E. Cleaver in A. Dundes *Mother Wit* (1973) 12/1 The actual conditions to which they aspired were..all around them, as it were 'so near and yet so far'.

2. a. Of time: Close at hand.

13.. *Cursor M.* 18023 (Gött.), Þe time es nu comand nere. *c* **1375** *Sc. Leg. Saints* i. (*Petrus*) 328 As linus sais, his dede wes nere. **1415** Sir T. Grey in *43rd Rep. Dep. Kpr. Rec.* 584 Skrop said þer was but iij. wais, þe tyme was so nere. **1535** Coverdale *Rom.* xiii. 11 For now is oure saluacion nearer, then whan we beleued. **1560** Daus tr. *Sleidane's Comm.* 232 Thende of his lyfe drewe nere. *c* **1600** Shaks. *Sonn.* cxl, Testie sick-men, when their deaths be neere. **1724** Ramsay *Vision* xvi, How neir's that happie tyme? **1816** J. Wilson *City of Plague* i. ii. 114, I trust my hour is near. **1866** Mrs. Carlyle *Lett.* III. 312 My heart failed me as the time drew near. **1875** Jowett *Plato* (ed. 2) I. 497 Now the hour of sunset was near.

b. ***near upon***, close upon a particular time.

1681 tr. *Belon's Myst. Physick* 4 A Physitian at Bruxells, did near-upon that time write against the use of that Remedy. **1814** Cary *Dante, Par.* xxi. 115 Near upon my close Of mortal life. **1880** Meredith *Tragic Com.* xv, Near upon morning he roused with his tender fit strong on him.

3. Closely connected with one by kinship or intimacy; esp. ***near akin*** or ***of kin*** (see akin *adv.* and kin *sb.*[1] 8 b). Also ***near and dear*** (cf. 13).

14.. in *Tundale's Vis.* (1843) 102 His son schall..hys place to occupye Or ellis won that wer ner next of alye. **1491** *Act 7 Hen. VII*, c. 22 *Preamble*, They be ner of kyn. *a* **1533** Ld. Berners *Huon* xliv. 147 How nere akyn art thou to the admyrall..? **1568** Grafton *Chron.* II. 420 He was so neere of the bloud of king Richard. **1621** Hakewill *David's Vow* 265 Though he were..never so neare and deare,..away hee must. **1687** A. Lovell tr. *Thevenot's Trav.* i. 55 The Turks never Marry their Kinswomen, if they be nearer than eight Generations inclusively. **1767–8** [see kin *sb.* 8 b]. **1826** in Hone *Every-day Bk.* II. 1155 In company with one 'near and dear'. **1855** Macaulay *Hist. Eng.* xii. III. 230 Many of them near in blood and affection to the defenders of Londonderry. **1878** [see akin A. 2].

4. In elliptical uses. †**a.** ***to drive*** (one) ***near***, to force into some strait or extremity. *Obs.*

1594 Marlowe & Nashe *Dido* i. i, See, what strange arts necessity finds out! How near, my sweet Æneas, art thou driven!

†**b.** ***the nearer***, closer to one's end or purpose. (Cf. near *adv.*[1] 5.) *Obs.*

1594 Hooker *Eccl. Pol.* iv. xiii. §8 We are not a whit the nearer for that they have hitherto said. **1630** *R. Johnson's Kingd. & Commw.* 88 A hungry belly may call for more meat, and be never the nearer.

c. ***to lie near***, to be natural or reasonable.

1846 Trench *Mirac.* xv. (1862) 257 It lies near to suppose that he was there, returning thanks for the signal mercy.

** *Denoting approximation in degree or amount.*

5. Within a (very) little, all but, almost. (Freq. intensified by *very*, †*well*, or †*full*. Now usually expressed by nearly.)

a. In general use, esp. with pa. pples. or verbs to denote that an action is all but completed or accomplished.

c **1200** Ormin 9638 All þe Judewisshe follc Well ner wass all forrworrpenn. *Ibid.* 15517. *a* **1300** *Cursor M.* 4760 Þan iacob and his suns warn For defaut wel ner forfarn. **1377** Langl. *P. Pl.* B. vi. 180 He bette hem so bothe, he barste nere here guttes. *c* **1430** *Syr Tryam.* 1568 Thy gode dayes are nere done, Thy power ys nere paste! **1470–85** Malory *Arthur* iii. xiii. 116 Her arme was sore brysed and nere she swouned for payne. **1559** Aylmer *Harborowe* I 3 b, I mighte neare gather an equall authoritie betwixte the wife and the husbande. **1595** Daniel *Civ. Wars* v. viii, If what we do shall perish neere as soone as it is donne. **1662** *Irish Act 14 & 15 Chas. II*, c. 2 §31 That that near ruined kingdom will be restored to peace and plenty. **1696** Whiston *Th. Earth* iii. (1722) 246 They appear to have been pretty near of an Age. **1733** Tull *Horse-Hoeing Husb.* iii. 26 One would serve to keep Plants fix'd and steady, very near, if not quite as well as the other. **1770** Foote *Lame Lover* iii. Wks. 1799 II. 91 The knight is..very near drunk. **1836** Haliburton *Clockm.* Ser. i. xii. 99 It's near about the prettiest sight I know of. **1851** Maclagan *Poems* 65 The laft near comes doon. **1891** Barrie *Little Minister* iii, He prays near like one giving orders.

b. With terms of number, quantity, extent, etc. †Also *ellipt.* = nearly all.

a **1300** *Cursor M.* 3155 He welk þat fell ner dais thre. *c* **1375** *Sc. Leg. Saints* xxii. (*Laurence*) 165, I spendyt hafe nere al þe tresoure, þat þu me gafe. *c* **1400** Maundev. (Roxb.) v. 14 Fra Rodes to Cypre es nere v[c] myle. *c* **1470** Henry *Wallace* i. 208 A sone he had ner xx[ty] ȝer of age. **1523** Ld. Berners *Froiss.* I. ccvii. 246 His men were ner slayne or taken, but fewe that were saued. *a* **1553** Udall *Royster D.* i. ii. (Arb.) 16 Hir Thousande pounde.. Is muche neere about two hundred and fiftie. **1604** E. G[rimstone] *D'Acosta's Hist. Indies* i. ii. 5, I have sayled neere 70 degrees from North to South. **1673** Ray *Journ. Low C.* 8 At near an hundred foot depth they met with a Bed or Floor of Sand. **1719** De Foe *Crusoe* i. (Globe) 231 It cost us near a Fortnight's Time. **1796** C. Marshall *Garden.* xiv. (1813) 201 There should be near four feet distance between each set of plants. **1876** Gladstone *Homeric Synch.* 21 The discussion..has continued for near a century.

c. So ***near upon*** (chiefly as in b).

1658–9 *Burton's Diary* (1828) III. 335 They did near upon represent half the property of the nation. **1706** Hearne *Collect.* (O.H.S.) I. 222 He said near upon as big as Mr. Dodwell's Book. **1829** Landor *Imag. Conv., Lucian & Timotheus* Wks. 1853 II. 18/1, I am near upon eighty years of age. **1865** *Athenæum* No. 1944. 121/3 Near upon thirty servants.

6. With negatives: (Not) by a great deal or a long way, (not) anything like, (not) nearly. Usu. followed by *so*.

1447 Bokenham *Seyntys* (Roxb.) 3 The forme of procedyng artificyal Is in no wyse ner poetycal. **1638** Junius *Paint. Ancients* 120 He is nothing neere so much delighted. **1669** R. Montagu in *Buccleuch MSS.* (Hist. MSS. Comm.) I. 465 The King gave me fifteen hundred pound.., which did not near serve. **1734** tr. *Rollin's Anc. Hist.* (1827) II. ii. 5 His army was not near so numerous as when he left Spain. **1827** Southey *Penins. War* II. 14 They are not near so fine a people now as they were then.

7. Closely, in various senses, esp. in respect of pressure or touching, of resemblance, connexion, scrutiny, etc. (See quots.) Now *rare*.

a. **1456** Sir G. Haye *Law Arms* (S.T.S.) 204 His inymyes..pressit him sa nere that outhir him behufit to be slayne or ellis to leve the barne. *c* **1470** *Gol. & Gaw.* 1177 It tuichis myne honour sa neir. *a* **1533** Ld. Berners *Huon* lxvi. 227 He that hath besynes that toucheth hym nere ought not to slepe. **1590** Spenser *F.Q.* ii. ii. 23 But he..suffred not their blowes to byte him nere. **1619** W. Sclater *Exp. 2 Thess.* (1629) 254 In this, which toucheth neerest clamourous plaintiues. **1647** Clarendon *Hist. Reb.* i. §42 His Majesty had another Exception against the Duke, which touched him as near. **1710** *Lond. Gaz.* No. 4674/8 The near Foot before pared very near towards the Heel.

b. **1526** *Pilgr. Perf.* (W. de W. 1531) 27 No religyon is founded hytherto y[e] so nere representeth y[t] primityue chirche of Chryst. **1586** A. Day *Eng. Secretary* i. (1625) 21 We will see how neere in writing they concurre. **1660** F. Brooke tr. *Le Blanc's Trav.* 46 Elephants..are animals approaching very near to reason. **1726** Shelvocke *Voy. round World* 401 They are in shape and bigness the nearest like our green grasshoppers. **1756** Burke *Subl. & B.* i. xv, The nearer it [tragedy] approaches the reality,..the more perfect is its power.

c. **1560** Daus tr. *Sleidane's Comm.* 254 b, He is allied so nere that he may haply claime som ryght. **1591** Shaks. *1 Hen. VI*, v. i. 17 The Earle of Arminacke, neere knit to Charles. **1671** Milton *P.R.* i. 400 Long since with wo Nearer acquainted.

d. **1560** Daus tr. *Sleidane's Comm.* 17 Thinges, which beynge nerer looked to, conteyne ofte tymes great errours. **1673** Marvell *Corr.* Wks. (Grosart) II. 412 If it be thought fit to enter nearer and further into the matter.

8. In phr. ***as near as*** (one can, etc.). Esp. in colloq. phrases: (***as***) ***near as dammit*** (or ***damn-it***), ***as near as makes no difference*** (or ***matter***), extremely near; virtually.

1538 Starkey *England* ii. i. 145 We wyl take nature for our exampul, and, as nere as we can, folow hyr steppys. **1615** W. Lawson *Country Housew. Gard.* (1626) 27 A plaine without a knot, or as neere as you can without a knot. **1635** R. N. tr. *Camden's Hist. Eliz.* i. 16, I will..take such a husband as neere as may be. **1680** Moxon *Mech. Exerc.* (1703) 209 Work that Molding as near as you can with the Hook. **1894** G. F. Northall *Folk-Phrases* 9 As near as damn it. As near as fourpence to a groat. As near as two ha' pennies for a penny. **1897** Conrad *Nigger of Narcissus* iv. 91 You were as near hanging as damn-it tonight. **1911** A. Bennett *Hilda Lessways* v. i. 338 That first night..I was as near as dammit to letting out the whole thing and chancing it. **1931** [see dammit]. **1937** D. L. Sayers *Busman's Honeymoon* viii. 171 You left here some time after 6.10 by that clock, which was right as near as makes no difference. **1961** [see dammit]. **1961** I. Jefferies *It Wasn't Me!* iv. 54 They near as dammit showed interest. **1970** P. Moyes *Who saw her Die?* xiv. 183 Funny, isn't it, Miss Threep ending up in the hospital with Billing? Well, not *with* him, of course, but as near as makes no matter.

†**9.** Narrowly, only by a little. *Obs. rare.*

1590 Greene *Orl. Fur.* (1599) 17 The Foxe is scapte:..I mist him neere, t'was time for him to trudge. **1592** Marlowe *Massacre Paris* i. vii, See where my soldier shot him through the arm; He miss'd him near. **1819** W. Tennant *Papistry Storm'd* (1827) 67 Acquentin' him.. How near he 'scap't frae bein' stabbit.

*** *Denoting manner.*

10. Thriftily; parsimoniously, meanly.

a **1625** Fletcher *Woman's Prize* iii. i, If thou canst love so neer [as] to keep thy making, Yet thou wilt lose thy language. **1723** De Foe *Col. Jack* (1840) 58, I had lived so near and so close that in a whole year I had not spent the 15*s.* which I had saved. **1871** *Routledge's Ev. Boy's Ann.* 240, I and my wife may have to live a little nearer for the next month or two.

11. With the legs close together.

1710 *Lond. Gaz.* No. 4785/4 Goes near before. **1737** Bracken *Farriery Impr.* (1757) II. 40 A Horse that goes wide before, and near behind. *Ibid.* 63 He should stand pretty wide behind, and near before.

II. Followed by *to* (†or *unto*).

12. a. Close *to* a place, thing, or person, in respect of space, or *to* a point in time.

c **1250** *Gen. & Ex.* 1395 Laban cam to ðat welle ner. *a* **1300** *Cursor M.* 12647 Ai to iesu was cummen neir Vn-to þe eild of thritte yeir. **1509** Hawes *Past. Pleas.* iii. (Percy Soc.) 15, I..sawe a craggy roche Farre in the west, neare to the element. *a* **1548** Hall *Chron.*, *Rich. III* 49 b, The custome..nere to ye see is..on every hill or high place to erect a beckon. **1600** J. Pory tr. *Leo's Africa* iii. 171 Neere vnto the said plaine are diuers woods and forrests. *a* **1628** Preston *Breastpl. Faith* (1630) 107 The neerer we draw to God in this life, the more pleasure we have. **1700** Dryden *Pal. & Arc.* i. 609 To Theseus' person he was ever near. *a* **1774** Harte *Eulogius* 19 Whether they nearer lived to the blest times [etc.]. **1816** Byron *Siege Corinth* iii, Nearest to the wall..Was Alp, the Adrian renegade! **1852** Mrs. Stowe *Uncle Tom's C.* xix. 199 Eva had come gradually nearer and nearer to her father. **1868** Lockyer *Elem. Astron.* iii. §16 (1879) 89 As the Moon's orbit is elliptical, she is sometimes nearer to us than at others.

fig. **1710** Berkeley *Princ. Hum. Knowl.* i. §6 Some truths there are so near and obvious to the mind that [etc.].

†**b.** ***to come*** or ***go near to***, to touch closely. *Obs.*

1600 Holland *Livy* xlii. xiv. 1123 In this last speech he came neere unto the LL. of the Senat, and touched them to the quick. **1692** L'Estrange *Josephus, Antiq.* iv. viii. (1733) 92 Nothing went nearer to them than the Memory of their Outrages against Moses in the Desart.

13. Closely related *to* one by kinship or some other connexion, esp. in ***near and dear***.

c **1450** *St. Cuthbert* (Surtees) 7510 He was þe first seculere þat was bischop to cuthbert nere. **1548** Udall, etc. *Erasm. Par. Matt.* xii. 57 He is moste neere and moste deere vnto me. **1630** *R. Johnson's Kingd. & Commw.* 61 In this dangerous age, since every man is neerest, and onely neere unto himselfe. **1660** Gauden *Brownrig* 241 Our inward garment, that should be nearer and dearer to us than our skins. **1711** Addison *Spect.* No. 126 ¶2 With the Hazard of all that is near and dear to us. **1746** Eliza Heywood *Female Spect.* No. 22 (1748) IV. 197 Those persons so near and dear to him. **1875** Jowett *Plato* (ed. 2) III. 347 They are all of one opinion about what is near and dear to them.

14. Close *to* something in respect of resemblance or correspondence.

1548 Udall *Erasm. Par. Luke* x. 93 b, He came verai nere to man, bothe seeyng and beeyng seen. **1601** J. Manningham in Ingleby *Shaks. Cent. Praise* (1879) 45 Most like and neere to that in Italian called Inganni. **1651** Hobbes *Leviath.* i. viii. 38 Which is very neere to direct Atheisme. **1751** Chatham *Lett. Nephew* i. 2, I have..altered the..lines, in order to bring them nearer to the Latin. **1758** *Handmaid to Arts* 382 The hollow parts must be covered with a colour the nearest in appearance to gold. **1820** *Examiner* No. 654. 686/1 She comes near again to the excellence of her first performance. **1868** Browning *Ring & Bk.* vi. 88 Fool that's near To knave. **1895** North in *Law Times Rep.* LXXIII. 23/1 The case which comes nearest to this of those I have seen.

15. a. ***to go near to*** (with inf.): to be on the point of, almost to succeed in (doing something).

1593 Shaks. *2 Hen. VI*, i. ii. 102 If you take not heed, you shall goe neere To call them both a payre of craftie Knaues.

1660 SHARROCK *Vegetables* 16 If a sharp spring chance to follow it may goe near to spoile all..the seed. 1699 LUTTRELL *Brief Rel.* (1857) IV. 482 It's thought that about 8 of the members will goe near to be expelled. 1742 RICHARDSON *Pamela* III. 223 Such another Example.. would go near..to ruin the Devils Kingdom in Bedfordshire. 1781 EARL MALMESBURY *Diaries & Corr.* I. 405 She goes near to think herself infallible. 1858 MASSON *Milton* I. 602 The panegyrics themselves went near to prove it. 1889 F. BARRETT *Under Strange Mask* II. xii. 34 It would go near to break her heart.

b. Const. with gerund. (Also *come near to.*)

1862 GLADSTONE *Glean.* (1879) I. 1 They droop and come near to dying. 1890 *Temple Bar* June 282 This final stroke went near to overcoming her.

III. Governing a sb. (passing into *prep.*).

16. a. Close to, within a short distance of (a place, thing or person) in space.

a 1300 *Cursor M.* 3348 Sco..rade til þai come ner þe stedd. 13.. *E.E. Allit. P.* A. 404 Meke am I..alle þat wonez hym nere. *c* 1400 *Destr. Troy* 8075 The derf kyng Diamede drughe the lady ner. *c* 1475 *Rauf Coilȝear* 91 Into sic talk fell thay Quhill thay war neir hame. 1577 B. GOOGE *Heresbach's Husb.* II. (1586) 94 The Almonde is graffed not neere the top of the stocke, but about the middest. 1631 JORDEN *Nat. Bathes* iii. (1669) 22 Although neer the Coasts it be depressed and lower than the Shore. 1682 T. FLATMAN *Heraclitus Ridens* No. 52 (1713) II. 76, I have seen many a lusty Cur troubled..when they have come near the Gallows. 1711 STEELE *Spect.* No. 49 ¶2 Our Coffee-house is near one of the Inns of Court. 1776 *Trial of Nundocomar* 47/1, I who am a Bramin will not go near a Mussulman that is dead. 1839 G. BIRD *Nat. Philos.* 209 Those portions of the atmosphere nearest the earth. 1863 GEO. ELIOT *Romola* xx, He lost no time in speaking as soon as she came near him. *fig.* 1592 LYLY *Gallathea* III. i, I thinke we came neere you when wee saide you loued. 1620 MIDDLETON *Chaste Maid* I. i, You'le steale away some Mans Daughter; am I nere you? 1685 BAXTER *Paraphr. N.T.* Matt. xi. 11 John..being nearest the Kingdom of the Messiah. *a* 1704 LOCKE (J.), He is not one jot nearer the end of such addition than at first setting out. 1889 BARRIE *Window in Thrums* xx, If you would cease to dislike a man, try to get nearer his heart.

b. *to lie, come* or *go near* (one, the heart, etc.), to touch or affect deeply. Now *rare.*

c 1420 *Sir Amadace* (Camden) xxvii, To serue the pore folke he was fulle fayne, For thay lay his hert nere. 1591 SHAKS. *Two Gent.* IV. iii. 19 No griefe did euer come so neere thy heart. 1611–12 in *Crt. & Times Jas. I* (1848) I. 162 This went so near him, that it drove him into these diseases. 1722 DE FOE *Plague* (1754) 133 Private Safety lay so near them, that they had no Room to pity the Distress of others. 1849 AYTOUN *Poems, Heart of Bruce* vi, There is a freit lies near my soul, I fain would tell to thee.

17. a. Close upon or to (a point in time).

13.. *Cursor M.* 1393 (Gött.), It sal be nere þe worldes end. 1470–85 MALORY *Arthur* II. xiii. 115 So that ye wille lodge with me, for it is nere nyghte. 1662 STILLINGFL. *Orig. Sacræ* II. i. §4 Persons who have lived nearest those times when the things were done. 1711 ADDISON *Spect.* No. 127 ¶6 Walking abroad when she was so near her Time. 1833 HT. MARTINEAU *Brooke Farm* ii. 18 Setting out the table for dinner; for it was near one o'clock. 1850 TENNYSON *In Mem.* civ, The time draws near the birth of Christ.

b. Close upon, almost at (a state or condition).

1635 A. STAFFORD *Fem. Glory* (1869) 60 The House of David..was neere utter extinction. 1661 BOYLE *Spring of Air* To Rdr., Which is really so near a readiness, that part of it has lain at the Press these six months. 1780 H. WALPOLE *Let. to Sir D. Dalrymple* 11 Dec., He..took much notice of me when I was near man. 1823 F. CLISSOLD *Ascent Mt. Blanc* 22 The sun being now near his setting. 1902 J. BUCHAN *Watcher by Threshold* 142 The hope was near fulfilment.

c. With gerund. Close to (*doing* something).

1762–71 H. WALPOLE *Vertue's Anecd. Painting* (1782) I. vii. 218 The comeliness of whose person was very near raising him to that throne. 1825 *New Monthly Mag.* XIV. 205, I must have gone very near convincing him. 1877 *Scribner's Mag.* XV. 259/1 One instance came very near having a serious result. 1895 *Bookman* Oct. 23/1 He was perilously near showing his whole hand to the other side.

†18. Closely related to, intimate with (one). *Obs.*

c 1470 HENRY *Wallace* v. 919 Off kyn he was, and Wallace modyr ner. 1597 SHAKS. *2 Hen. IV*, v. i. 81, I would humour his men, with the imputation of beeing neere their Mayster. 1660 T. HALL *Funebr. Flor.* G2 Under Heavens Cope, There's none as I so near the Pope.

19. Close to (a thing or person) in point of similarity or achievement.

1585 T. WASHINGTON tr. *Nicholay's Voy.* IV. x. 122b, The people..are of complection neerer the blacke then white. 1632 LITHGOW *Trav.* IX. 387 Their language..is nearer the Latine, then the Italian. 1687 A. LOVELL tr. *Thevenot's Trav.* d b, There are but few in the Western Parts who come near him in that. 1815 W. H. IRELAND *Scribbleomania* 250 Those..Approximate nearest the Great Judge of all. 1845 M. PATTISON *Ess.* (1889) I. 8 Which of the more recent historians..have come near them in the vigour and truth which they threw into that history?

IV. In combs.

20. a. In the sense of 'closely' or 'close at hand', as ***near-acquainted, -adjoining, -bordering, -coming, -fighting, -following, -guessed, -resembling, -smiling, -stored, -threatening, -touching, -ushering.***

1639 FULLER *Holy War* I. xiii. (1647) 21 Denmark and Norway *near-acquainted with the Arctick Pole. 1625 K. LONG tr. *Barclay's Argenis* I. viii. 21 The King..walked in a *neere-adjoyning valley. 1630 DRAYTON *Moses* Wks. 1753 IV. 1604 The *near-bord'ring envious Amalek. 1600 FAIRFAX *Tasso* I. lxvi, Each soldier, longing for *neere comming glorie. 1598 CHAPMAN *Iliad* II. 529 The bold *near-fighting men, who did in Phæneus live. 1625 K. LONG tr. *Barclay's Argenis* II. iv. 75 Prodigies, by which the *neere-following miseries were affirmed. 1683 MOXON *Mech. Exerc., Printing* xxiv. ¶7 That with a *near-guess'd strength in the tossing it up it may just Stand. 1739 G. OGLE *Gualtherus & Griselda* 96 The lovely Maid and *near-resembling Boy. 1820 KEATS *Lamia* I. 125 Swift was seen.. the guarded nymph *near-smiling on the green. 1729 SAVAGE *Wanderer* II. 27 Tho' dress, *near-stor'd, its vanity supplies. *a* 1586 SIDNEY *Arcadia* (1622) 295 The vnpitifulnesse of his owne *near-threatning death. 1615 *Marr. & Wiving* vii. in *Harl. Misc.* (Malh.) III. 267 These blood *near-touching witcheries and inducements. 1634 MILTON *Comus* 279 Could that divide you from *near-ushering guides?

†b. ***near-coloured,*** of much the same colour. *Obs.*

1606 in Nichols *Progr. Jas. I* (1828) II. 67 Themselves not farre unlike, and their horses neere-couloured and suited.

c. *Sc.* ***near-(be)going*** or ***-(be)gawn,*** niggardly. [So Da. *nærgaaende.*] Also ***near-goingness.***

a 1774 FERGUSSON *Poems* (1789) II. 105 A niggard, near-gawn elf. *Ibid.* 158 A hard, near-be-gawn miser. 1821 GALT *Ann. Parish* vii. 76 The near-begoing Major and his sister. 1854 H. MILLER *Sch. & Schm.* (1858) 238 After a' his near-goingness wi' them. 1900 S. MACMANUS in *Century Mag.* Feb. 607/2 Without..bein' either niggardly or near-goin'.

21. Prefixed to adjs. in the sense 'almost, nearly, approximately' as ***near-great, -perfect, †-sinking, †-wretched,*** and to sbs. in the sense 'something that is nearly the same as, or is a substitute for, the thing specified'; 'artificial'; *spec.* **near-beer** orig. *U.S.*, a beverage resembling beer; beer with a very low alcoholic content; also *attrib.*; **near-print** (see quot. 1943); **near-seal** *N. Amer.*, any fur treated and dyed to resemble sealskin; **near-silk,** artificial silk. Also **†near-isle,** a peninsula; **†nearlike** *adv.*

1928 *Daily Express* 27 Apr. 12/4 The aspirant painters.. drink near-absinthe instead of beer. 1909 *N.Y. Even. Post* (Semi-Weekly ed.) 23 Aug. 2 The refusal of the Cities Commission to prohibit the sale of imitation beer, commonly known as 'near beer'. 1921 *Daily Colonist* (Victoria, B.C.) 27 Mar. 7/5 The thirty-six near-beer bars in operation here at present pay into the city treasury a total of $5,400 a year in the form of licence fees. 1963 *Times* 14 Feb. 4/7 A hostess in a Soho near-beer club told a jury..that.. customers were charged 15s. for two soft drinks made from blackcurrant juice. 1952 *Manch. Guardian Weekly* 4 Sept. 3 Add the near-certainty of Massachusetts. 1822 W. SEWALL *Diary* 27 Sept. (1930) 89, I am much troubled with a bowel complaint. This must have been caused by drinking freely of near cider. 1973 L. SNELLING *Heresy* I. i. 11 Andover, Yale, fine athlete..captained the Yale crew, near-effortless Phi Beta key, et cetera. 1926 *Ladies' Home Jrnl.* Apr. 24 The decision was based on..two broken engagements, one near-engagement..and several flirtations. 1949 KOESTLER *Promise & Fulfilment* II. ii. 218 Each of them means a cherished near-escape story to some member of the commune. 1973 C. BONINGTON *Next Horizon* xix. 261 Twenty-four hours later the shock of my near-escape really hit me, and manifested itself mainly in a sense of horror at letting down my family. 1942 *Daily Tel.* 22 May 5/3 If the harvest collection should break down through a failure of fuel supplies, then near-famine conditions..may not be far away. 1938 *New Statesman* 3 Dec. 904/2 He must now embrace..not merely those propertied groups which are reliably republican, but near-Fascists of the Flandin type as well. 1926 *Scribner's Mag.* Sept. 34/2 (Advt.), Some more piquant revelations of the great and near-great in English and Continental Society. 1855 W. WHITMAN *Leaves of Grass* 37 The laughing-gull..laughs her near-human laugh. 1943 *Times* (Weekly ed.) 10 Feb. 5 A British army pitch-forked on to Mars would first smile at and then discover near-human characteristics in any local inhabitants that might appear. 1964 M. CRITCHLEY *Developmental Dyslexia* xiv. 81 Many of them..become items within the community of illiterates or near-illiterates. 1625 LISLE *Du Bartas' Noe* 124 There lies higher a neere-isle, betwixt Cuba and Mexico. 1598 FLORIO, *Quasi*, almost,..veri-neere,.. neerelike. 1955 KOESTLER *Trail of Dinosaur* 253 The trouble with all near-miracles..is the unpredictability of their timing. 1957 C. S. LEWIS *Let.* 6 Mar. (1966) 275, I married ..a very sick, save by near-miracle, a dying woman. 1949 KOESTLER *Promise & Fulfilment* III. i. 391 Transport cooperatives which have..a near-monopoly of cross-country bus services. 1964 *Oceanogr. & Marine Biol.* II. 326 A temperature of 25° C represents near-optimum conditions. 1939 *Ann. Reg. 1938* 261 The condition of the inhabitants was one of near-panic after this merciless destruction. 1956 *Nature* 4 Feb. 239/2 Carbons in which neighbouring ordered regions lie in near-parallel orientation. 1963 C. R. COWELL et al. *Inlays, Crowns & Bridges* ii. 5 The principle of 'near parallelism'—that is, opposing walls must be nearly parallel with only enough divergence to make withdrawal of the pattern or impression possible. 1962 Near-perfect [see ATTITUDE 2c]. 1934 DYLAN THOMAS *Let.* 9 May (1966) 124 You've brought 'conventional' poetry..to a point of near-perfection. 1943 E. H. THOMPSON *A.L.A. Gloss. Library Terms* 106/2 *Processed*, reproduced by duplicating processes other than ordinary printing, as by mimeograph, mulitgraph, rotoprint, multilith, etc. Also called *Near-print.* 1956 WILSON & TAUBER *University Library* 7 Journals, government documents, near-print, newspapers, manuscripts..have to be secured on an unprecedented scale. 1969 *N.Z. National Bibliogr.* II. p. viii, The growing volume of mimeographed and near-print editions has presented particular difficulty. 1949 *Word Study* Apr. 2/2 Cat..gut. Near rhyme..is the most generally accepted name. 1912 J. H. MOORE *Ethics & Educ.* 109 That state of near-savagery when any low-browed irresponsible..is allowed to go out and shoot to death everything that has the breath of life in it. 1902 G. H. LORIMER *Lett. Merchant* 184 He leads the nag out..and examines every hair of his hide, as if he expected to find it near-seal. 1906–7 *T. Eaton & Co. Catal.* Fall & Winter 4/1 Near Seal Jacket, made of finest quality skins, closely resembling real seal in appearance. 1919 MENCKEN *Amer. Lang.* 159 Many characteristic Americanisms of the sort to stagger lexicographers—for example, *near-silk*—have come from the Jews. 1937 D. CANFIELD *Fables for Parents* (1938) 251 Nude-coloured, near-silk stockings with a run down one leg. 1625 K. LONG tr. *Barclay's Argenis* I. i. 3 Whom..The now neere-sinking Mariner invokes. 1911 E. FERBER *Dawn O'Hara* iii. 34 Assuming a near-smile, she entered the room. 1950 KOESTLER et al. *God that Failed* 63 The next five years were for me years of near-starvation. 1962 W. NOWOTTNY *Lang. Poets Use* vii. 169 The treachery of near-synonyms which can slant meaning in a new direction. *Ibid.* 168 Ambiguities (drawn variously from near-synonymity and from rhetorical repetitions involving syntactical similarity). 1910 *Century Mag.* Apr. 891 Clothes and the Man. A near-true story. By Edith Rickert. 1951 S. SPENDER *World within World* iii. 138 These writers wrote with a near-unanimity, surprising when one considers that most of them were strangers to one another. 1964 *Language* XL. 206 Many of these 'near-universals' involve structural relationships. 1930 *Cambridge Daily News* 25 Sept. 3/2 Never having worn even near-wool within rubbing distance of my skin. 1611 B. JONSON *Catiline* III. ii, O neere-wretched Rome, When both thy Senate and thy gods doe Sleepe.

near (nɪə(r)), *a.* Forms: 4–5 ner, 5–6 nere, 6–7 neere, (7 neer; 6 *Sc.* neir, 7 neire), neare, 7– near. [f. NEAR *adv.*[2]]

1. Closely related by blood or kinship.

13.. *Cursor M.* 20068 (Gött.), Sant iohan þat was his sibe ner kines-man. 1375 BARBOUR *Bruce* I. 54 He thair king suld be That wes in alsner degre. 1470–85 MALORY *Arthur* III. xii. 114 [He] sayd she was his cosyn nere. 1560 DAUS tr. *Sleidane's Comm.* 471b, It shall styre up fyre also amonges the nere of bloud. 1611 BIBLE *Lev.* xviii. 17 They are her neere kinsewomen. 1651 HOBBES *Leviath.* II. xix. 101 A man receives..the most honour from the greatnesse of his neerest kindred. 1711 ADDISON *Spect.* No. 23 ¶1 To raise Uneasiness among near Relations. 1760 T. HUTCHINSON *Hist. Mass.* ii. 258 A near kinswoman of Sir William Bird. 1840 ARNOLD *Hist. Rome* II. xxxi. 218 The sons or near relations of the most influential members of the senate. 1867 TENNYSON *Victim* i, Were it our nearest, Were it our dearest, ..We give you his life.

2. a. Of persons: Closely attached to, very intimate or familiar with, another. Freq. in phr. ***nearest and dearest***; also *absol.* as *sb.*, one's closest and most beloved relatives or friends.

1523 CROMWELL in Merriman *Life & Lett.* (1902) I. 35 By the mowthe of hys most nere and cheffest Counsaylour. 1576 FLEMING *Panopl. Epist.* 22 Your neere friends and familiar companions. 1596 SHAKES. *1 Hen. IV* III. ii. 123 Why, Harry, doe I tell thee of my Foes, Which art my neer'st and dearest Enemie? 1610 J. CHAMBERLAIN *Let.* 23 Jan. (1939) I. 296 The neerest and deerest frends he hath know not what to guesse of this humor. 1629 WADSWORTH *Pilgr.* vi. 51 Hee had a brother a neere retainer to his Highnesse of Wales. 1654 LOVEDAY tr. *Calprenède's Cleopatra* II. 124 The nearest and dearest friends I had. 1822 T. CREEVEY *Let.* 23 Dec. in *Creevey Papers* (1963) xi. 186 Brougham arrived here on Saturday, on his way—or rather *out* of his way—to his nearest and dearest. 1839 DICKENS *Let.* 21 Jan. (1965) I. 493 For those who are nearest and dearest to me I can realise little more than a genteel subsistence. 1887 BOWEN *Virg. Æneid* II. 85, I was his comrade near and companion. 1926 F. M. FORD *Man could stand Up* I. ii. 38 Look how you let in your nearest and dearest—those who have to sympathise with you. 1959 J. BURKE *Echo of Barbara* ix. 92 One never does know much about one's nearest and dearest. 1975 'C. AIRD' *Slight Mourning* iv. 42 It's always family or friends who do you in. .. Nearest and dearest, that's who it'll be.

b. Of friendship, etc.: Close, intimate, familiar.

1560 DAUS tr. *Sleidane's Comm.* 249b, For a nerer frendship, the lady Elenore..was promised freely to my eldest sonne. *c* 1616 FLETCHER & MASS. *Thierry & Theod.* II. i, Princely Son; And in this, worthy of a near[er] name. 1652 NEEDHAM *Selden's Mare Cl.* Ep. Ded. 16 All overtures of Amitie and nearest alliance. 1702 ROWE *Tamerl.* I. i, A Slave, of near Attendance on his Person.

3. With reference to animals or vehicles: Left (as opposed to *far, off,* or right).

This use is based on the fact that horses and cattle are commonly mounted, led, or approached, from the left side, which is consequently the one *near* to the person dealing with them. It is possible that the adj. here had originally a comparative force (from NEAR *adv.*[1]).

a. of parts of animals, esp. horses.

1559 *Will J. Hilde* (Somerset Ho.), A filly..with a white nere foote behinde. 1578 in W. H. Turner *Select. Rec. Oxford* (1880) 396 One grey..mare,..the neare ie walled. 1610 GUILLIM *Heraldry* III. xxvi. (1611) 184 A Horse.. spanceled on both legs of the nearer side. 1641 BEST *Farm. Bks.* (Surtees) 12 To runne the edge of the botte downe the neare liske. 1707 *Lond. Gaz.* No. 4325/4 A Nanberry on the inside of the near Leg. 1766 *Compl. Farmer* s.v. *Walk*, Just as he is setting down his far fore-foot, he lifts up his near hind-foot. 1844 H. STEPHENS *Bk. Farm* II. 456 We are accustomed to approach all the larger domesticated animals by what we call the near side—that is, the animal's left side. 1884 E. L. ANDERSON *Mod. Horsemanship* I. ii. 7 To mount without stirrups the rider should stand facing the near shoulder of the horse.

b. of horses in a team, cart-wheels, etc.

c 1611 CHAPMAN *Iliad* xxiii. 325 Thy near horse..yet.. gave thy skill the prize. 1756 [F. GREVILLE] *Maxims, Char.*, etc. 22 The poor boy..whipped up the off instead of the near horse. 1764 [see OFF *a.* 2]. 1840 DICKENS *Barn. Rudge* lix, One..who sat postilion-wise upon the near horse. 1842 *Act 5 & 6 Vict.* c. 79 §17 The track of the left or near wheel. 1890 'R. BOLDREWOOD' *Col. Reformer* (1891) 188 The near leader dashed round the back of the coach.

Comb. a 1840 in J. Buel *Farmer's Comp.* 129 In this operation, the left-hand or near-side horse walks on the ground not yet ploughed. 1889 H. F. WOOD *Rue Caïn* iv, The carman was patching up the near-side wheels.

c. Of a motor vehicle; usu. in ***near side*** (freq. *attrib.*).

In countries where one drives on the right, the 'near' side is the righthand side.

1926 *Times* 6 May 3/7 The defendant.. went to the rear of the car and attempted to rip open the near side wheel with a knife. **1927** [see *dip-stick* s.v. DIP *sb.* 11]. **1959** *Times* 15 Dec. 13/5 The windscreen wipers were so arranged that the nearside blade flicked rain from the offside blade across the driver's line of vision. **1973** 'H. HOWARD' *Highway to Murder* i. 12 It felt like they'd got a flat on the nearside front wheel.

4. a. Close at hand; not distant. ***near space***: space in the immediate vicinity of the earth; inner space.

1565 STAPLETON tr. *Bede's Hist. Ch. Eng.* 68 For that was the next nere water, which he could conueniently use for baptism. **1600** J. PORY tr. *Leo's Africa* Introd. 27 Wilde Negros, who.. utterly misliked their so neere neighbourhood. **1667** MILTON *P.L.* I. 192 Satan talking to his neerest Mate. **1709** BERKELEY *Th. Vision* §16 When we look at a near object with both eyes. **1752** GERSAINT *Catal. Rembrandt's Etch.* 115 On the Near-Ground, at the Bottom of the Print is a Globe. **1820** KEATS *Ode to Nightingale* 76 Thy plaintive anthem fades Past the near meadows. **1833** HT. MARTINEAU *Loom & Lugger* II. ii. 19 Those whose near residence tempted to an acquaintance. **1865** DICKENS *Mut. Fr.* I. xiv, I'll find the nearest of our men to come and take charge of him. **1962** *New Statesman* 24 Aug. 219/1 The Russians 'have been busily preoccupied with the near-space environment and have ably demonstrated their.. de-orbiting accuracies'. **1967** *Economist* 20 May 791/3 The practical uses of 'near-space' in weather observation and in geological surveys of the earth.

Comb. **1641** BEST *Farm. Bks.* (Surtees) 9 To have a care that they bee not too neare-stoned, or eare-marked. **1834** M. SCOTT *Cruise Midge* (1859) 479 The outline indeed [was] dangerously distinct and near like.

b. ***near point***: (see quots.). ***near work***, work involving proximity of the eye to the object.

1876 BERNSTEIN *Five Senses* 70 This point, which is at a distance from the eye of about 4 or 5 inches, is called the near-point of the eye. **1880** *Sat. Rev.* 15 May 637/2 For every eye there is a point within which clear vision is no longer possible without optical assistance; and this.. is called the near-point. **1895** SWANZY *Diseases Eye* (ed. 5) iv. 89 The use of the eyes for near work without spectacles when the condition.. requires them.

c. With reference to time. ***near-term***, used *attrib.* = *short-term*; occurring in or pertaining to the near future; opp. LONG-TERM *a.*

1849 MACAULAY *Hist. Eng.* v. I. 617 The near prospect of reward animated the zeal of the troops. **1885** *Manch. Exam.* 15 May 5/7 A thing of the near future. **1958** *Listener* 18 Sept. 407/1 To turn to Australia. There the near-term position is much more comfortable, unemployment is less than two per cent. **1965** H. I. ANSOFF *Corporate Strategy* (1968) iv. 50 If the profitability picture urgently needs a near-term boost, a more modest goal.. will be acceptable. **1971** *Flying* Apr. S1/2 This.. certainly does not suggest near-term improvement.

d. ***nearest neighbour***, the member of a series or array nearest to that being considered; freq. *attrib.* (usu. with hyphen).

1937 *Jrnl. Appl. Physics* VIII. 654/1 In a liquid the number of nearest neighbors and the interatomic distances are roughly the same as in the crystalline material. **1945** A. F. WELLS *Structural Inorg. Chem.* iii. 110 In each of these close-packed arrangements, cubic and hexagonal, each atom has twelve equidistant nearest neighbours, six in its own plane and three in each adjacent layer. **1961** *Jrnl. Biol. Chem.* CCXXXVI. 864 (*heading*) Frequencies of nearest neighbor base sequences in deoxyribonucleic acid. **1972** *Computers & Humanities* VII. 40 The statistical analysis of pattern in such horizontal distributions is another area to which some attention is now being given, with nearest-neighbour analysis the most frequently adopted method.

e. ***near money***, a deposit, bond, etc., that can easily be converted into ready money.

1948 G. CROWTHER *Outl. Money* (rev. ed.) ii. 65 Bank deposits, in those circumstances, might be something very close to money, but still not quite within the definition. They would be 'near-money'. *Ibid.* 66 We have already come across another example of 'near-money' in the form of the Bill of Exchange. **1968** *Economist* 23 Nov. 83/1 Ottawa itself is relying on a $2 billion 'near-money' savings bond issue at 6¾ per cent to meet its current excessive needs.

5. Of a road: Short, direct. (Chiefly in *compar.* and *superl.* See also CUT *sb.*[1] 15.)

1579 SPENSER *Sheph. Cal.* July 96 Yet nearer wayes I knowe. **1662** HICKERINGILL *Apol. Distressed Innoc.* Wks. 1716 I. 292 By pretending.. a nearer cut than going up to Hierusalem. **1702** ADDISON *Dial. Medals* I. (1726) 17 It is a pity indeed there is not a nearer way of coming at it. **1801** tr. *Gabrielli's Myst. Husb.* II. 116, I presume.. the road we came is a nearer cut. **1885** *Act 48 & 49 Vict.* c. 54 §14 Within four miles of one another by the nearest road.

6. a. Close, narrow, in various applications.

1548 UDALL, etc. *Erasm. Par. Matt.* i. 3 b, In this nere & narowe poynt betwene seruitute & libertie. **1568** GRAFTON *Chron.* II. 9 He then had a neerer eye to the Lordes.. and kept them a little strayter. **1662** J. DAVIES tr. *Mandelslo's Trav.* 146 Having weighed one parcel, so as they may have a near guess at the rest. **1685** DRYDEN *Sylvæ* Pref., Ess. (ed. Ker) I. 256 The nearest, the most poetical.. of any translation of the Æneids. **1856** WHYTE MELVILLE *K. Coventry* i, It was a near race. **1860** RUSSELL *Diary India* II. 396 Long chases and near escapes.

b. ***near miss***, a shot that only just misses a target; also *transf.* and *fig.*; ***near thing***, something barely effected; a narrow escape.

1751 FIELDING *Amelia* IV. xi. ii. 123 You certainly know.. how hard Colonel Trompington is run at your Town, in the Election of a Mayor; they tell me it will be a very near Thing, unless you join us. **1894** SOMERVILLE & 'ROSS' *Real Charlotte* II. xxiii. 120 'That was a near thing,' remarked Mr. Hawkins complacently, as a slight grating sound told that they had grazed one of these smooth-backed monsters. **1930** W. GIBSON *Hazards* 8 A near thing! But he caught the plane: 'twas well He did not miss it. **1940** *Life* 9 Sept. 120/2 The other was a near miss amidships. **1940** *Illustr. London News* 28 Dec. 829/2 They came back with direct hits on a mine-sweeper and a supply ship, and a near miss on a destroyer to their credit. **1957** F. HOYLE *Black Cloud* i. 17 You mean, Dave, that there's no chance of the cloud missing the solar system, of it being a near-miss, let us say? **1957** *Listener* 21 Nov. 853/2 For those children who are near-misses as well as for those who make the grade. **1964** D. VARADAY *Gara-Yaka* xxi. 190 When one moving coil lashed over the crocodile's head, Mulembe snapped at it with spiky-toothed jaws which almost bit through... It was a near thing for the snake. **1967** G. F. FIENNES *I tried to run a Railway* iv. 38 It had a lot of bomb damage to repair from a near miss whose crater was still unfilled. **1972** 'E. LATHEN' *The Longer the Thread* xiv. 129 The taxi-drive.. was.. marked by enough near-misses to put from his mind any thoughts but survival. **1973** *Guardian* 7 Mar. 2/1 French and Scandinavian pilots.. had reported 11 'near misses' over France to their airlines since Friday.

7. Closely affecting or touching one.

1605 SHAKS. *Macb.* III. i. 118 Euery minute of his being thrusts Against my neer'st of Life. **1642** J. M[ARSH] *Argt. conc. Militia* 2 It is a more neare and immediate offence against the King. **1701** NORRIS *Ideal World* I. vi. 378 It was of nearer consequence to Archimedes. **1775** JOHNSON *Tax. no Tyr.* 9 Eagerness for the nearest good.

8. Niggardly, stingy, mean.

1616 R. CARPENTER *Christ's Larumbell* 49 Cold comfort, a neere hand, a needy reward. *a* **1656** HALES *Gold. Rem.* III. (1673) 20 A near and hard and trucking chapman shall never buy good flesh. **1712** STEELE *Spect.* No. 402 ¶4, I always thought he lived in a near Manner. **1753** MRS. DELANY *Life & Corr.* (1861) III. 208 A good-natured man, but reckoned near. **1824** MRS. SHERWOOD *Waste Not* I. 11 She is mighty near, and there is but one fire and candle between them. **1874** T. HARDY *Far fr. Mad. Crowd* xlix, Some were beginning to consider Oak a near man.

near (nɪə(r)), *v.* Also 6 (8) nere, 6 *Sc.* neire, 6–7 neere, 7 neare. [f. NEAR *adv.*[2] or *a.*]

1. *intr.* To draw or come near, to approach (in place or time).

1513 DOUGLAS *Æneis* XII. xii. 147 The swipir Tuscan hund assais And nerys fast. **1582** STANYHURST *Æneis* III. (Arb.) 86 Wee sayle bye Ceraunia swiftly. Wheare.. a cantel of Italye neereth. **1613** HEYWOOD *Braz. Age* II. ii, Their sports I'le neere to marre. **1798** COLERIDGE *Anc. Mar.* III. ii, Still it ner'd and ner'd. **1844** MRS. BROWNING *Poems* II. 242 Nay, keep smiling, little child, Ere the sorrow neareth. **1860** PUSEY *Min. Proph.* 379 As the time of the birth of our Lord neared.

2. *trans.* To draw near to, to approach (a person, place, etc.). †Also, to be near.

1610 HEYWOOD *Gold. Age* I. i, Keep off, I charge thee neere me not. **1637** —— *Royal King* II. ii, Give up your Key Vnto that Lord that neares you. **1748** *Anson's Voy.* II. v. 177 We must by this means unavoidably near her. **1808** SCOTT *Marm.* II. xi, Soon as they neared his turrets strong. **1874** T. N. HARPER *Peace through Truth* Ser. II. I. 90 The quotation.. does not even near the point in debate.

3. To bring near to (one). *rare*$^{-1}$.

1849 RUSKIN *Sev. Lamps* vi. §10. 171 [To] separate man from man, and near him to his Maker.

Hence **'nearing** *ppl. a.*

1863 W. LANCASTER *Praeterita* 44, I feign some nearing issue.., On which I wait. **1871** MORLEY *Condorcet* in *Crit. Misc.* Ser. I. (1878) 49 The nearing dawn after a long night.

nearabout ('nɪərəbaʊt), *adv.* Also near about, nearabouts, near 'bout. [f. NEAR *adv.*[2] + ABOUT *adv.* and *prep.*, ABOUTS *adv.* and *prep.*] †**a.** In this vicinity; nearby. *Obs.* **b.** *dial.* Nearly, almost; approximately.

c **1400** MAUNDEV. (Roxb.) vi. 20 þe fairest maydens of þe cuntree nere aboute. **1634** SIR T. HERBERT *Trav.* 133 Neere abouts was that great and terrible combat. [**1702** *Rec. Early Hist. Boston* (1882) VIII. 20 The front of the Old house.. is neer abt Eleven foot from the street.] **1708** *Ibid.* 81 The mouth of the Said creek bears Neer about North East from ye Knowl of Trees. **1834** W. A. CARUTHERS *Kentuckian in N.Y.* II. 206 Yes, I believe everybody's married, near-abouts, as far as I can learn. *a* **1878** AINSLIE *Land Burns* (1892) 357 A towmond nearabout has run. **1907** A. QUILLER-COUCH *Major Vigoureux* xxii. 251 The tide bein' nearabouts on the top of the flood. **1928** 'M. CHAPMAN' *Happy Mountain* iii. 25 All the fields were nearabout flat. **1938** M. K. RAWLINGS *Yearling* i. 9 'I near about give you out, son,' he said. **1941** J. FAULKNER *Men Working* i. 19 We can make twelve bales of cotton, near 'bout, every year.

near by, *adv.*, *prep.*, and *a.* Also near-by, nearby, and 5 (9) *Sc.* ner, 5–6 nere, 6 *Sc.* neir. [NEAR *adv.*[2] and BY *adv.*]

A. *adv.* **1.** Close by, close at hand.

c **1375** *Sc. Leg. Saints* v. (*John*) 101 Sancte Iohne, þat þan erand had ner by, and herd quhat wes done. *c* **1470** HENRY *Wallace* I. 378 Ridand thar come, ner by quhar Wallace was, The lorde Persye. *a* **1533** LD. BERNERS *Huon* lviii. 197 Galaffer was nere by, and herd what Huon sayd. **1728** P. WALKER *Life Peden* Pref. (1827) 30 The Preaching was near-by, for we heard the Psalms sweetly sung. **1868** MORRIS *Earthly Par.* I. 145 Nearby is my asses' stall. **1888** E. L. WILSON in *Century Mag.* July 328/1 The ruins of an old temple near by bear the cartouches of Rameses II. **1931** *News Chron.* 25 Aug., There had been feverish activity at the Trade Union Congress office nearby. **1965** E. GOWERS *Fowler's Mod. Eng. Usage* (ed. 2) 382/1 *Near by* has been long established as an adverb, and there is no good reason for those who draft police notices to prefer *in the vicinity*.

2. Nearly, almost; thereabouts. Chiefly *Sc.*

1456 SIR G. HAYE *Law Arms* (S.T.S.) 169 [He] distroyit and slew nereby all the kingis of the warld. **1509** in *Mem. Hen. VII* (Rolls) 439 Hyt ys nere by an hole yere that a servant of hys hathe byn yn themperows corte. **1558** KENNEDY *Compend. Tract.* in *Wodrow Soc. Misc.* (1844) 166 Neirby ane thousand ȝeir or Augustine was borne. **1596** DALRYMPLE tr. *Leslie's Hist. Scot.* v. 262 Al passage of Treffik.. Was neirby cuttit away fra Britannie. **1815** SCOTT *Guy M.* xlv, After a trot o' sixty mile, or near by.

B. *prep.* **1.** Close to (a place, etc.). Now *dial.*

1456 SIR G. HAYE *Law Arms* (S.T.S.) 43 The citee of Hostrye.. is nereby Rome. **1814** NICHOLSON *Country Lass* iii, Near by the poet's houseless head. **1889** *N.W. Linc. Gloss.* s.v., He lives near by th' Calvin capil.

†**2.** *Sc.* Nearly in accordance with. *Obs.* *rare*$^{-1}$.

1535 STEWART *Cron. Scot.* I. 231 Judges he maid neirby the vse of Rome.

C. *adj.* Close at hand, neighbouring; not far off.

1858 G. MACDONALD *Phantastes* vii. (1878) 120 The cows in a near-by field were eating. **1862** *Independent* (N.Y.) 1 May (Cent.), The near-by trade and Western dealers are buying moderately. **1878** *N. Amer. Rev.* CXXVII. 361 Great problems in the near-by future. **1887** *Times* 31 Aug. 4/3 Many people.. are housed.. in near-by towns [U.S.]. **1939** JOYCE *Finnegans Wake* 448 Take a good longing gaze into any nearby shopwindow. **1954** *Manch. Guardian Weekly* 26 Aug. 4 He went to the near-by police station. **1973** *Times* 24 May 27/3 There was a slackening interest in nearby metal.

Nearctic (niː'ɑːktɪk), *a.* *Zool.* [f. Gr. νέ-ος NEO- + ARCTIC *a.*] Comprising, or pertaining to, the temperate and arctic parts of N. America, in respect of the distribution of birds, etc.

1858 SCLATER in *Proc. Linn. Soc.*, *Zool.* II. 136 The northern, or Nearctic region, extending down the centre of the table-land of Mexico. **1877** LE CONTE *Elem. Geol.* IV. (1879) 161 The Nearctic [region] has been subdivided into four provinces. **1882** *American* V. 188 The opinion already expressed, that the 'Nearctic' fauna.. could not be considered as a fauna. **1893** NEWTON *Dict. Birds* 329 The total of peculiar and characteristic Nearctic genera being.. 51.

neare, obs. form of NE'ER.

Near East. [NEAR *a.* 4, EAST *sb.*] A region comprising the countries of the eastern Mediterranean, sometimes also including those of the Balkan peninsula, south-west Asia, or north Africa. (Also ***Nearer East.***) Also *attrib.* Cf. FAR EAST, MIDDLE EAST.

[**1869** *Wesleyan-Methodist Mag.* (Sixpenny ed.) July 312 (*heading*) Peeps at the Near East [*i.e.* Spitalfields in London].] **1891** J. L. KIPLING *Beast & Man in India* iv. 84 There was once a time when in the nearer East.. he [*sc.* the ass] was held in high honour. **1898** W. MILLER (*title*) Travels and politics in the Near East. **1902** D. G. HOGARTH (*title*) The Nearer East. **1909** [see MIDDLE EASTERN *a.*]. **1910** *Chambers's Jrnl.* Dec. 800/1 In the Near East the keynote of cookery is disguise. The Turk brings his oriental love of mystery with him to the dinner-table. **1912** *Review of Reviews* July 70/1 (*heading*) The Near East problem. **1920** *Sat. Rev.* 16 Oct. 320 He took very little notice of Balkan intrigues, because the Near East was not his business. **1923** E. WHARTON *Son at Front* 10 Poor little circumscribed Paul Dastrey, whose utmost adventure had been.. an occasional six weeks in the Near East. **1936** *Discovery* Sept. 264/1 The Wellcome Archaeological Expedition to the Near East. **1959** *Listener* 1 Jan. 31/2 Interest in the lands and peoples of the nearer east. **1973** 'D. JORDAN' *Nile Green* xliv. 283 Sue.. told the Near East Desk, who.. sent a cable to the Cairo Embassy.

Hence **Near-'Easterly** *adv.*, **Near-'Eastern** *a.*, **Near-'Easterner**.

1906 *Q. Rev.* Jan. 284 Lord Salisbury and his successor have.. skilfully withdrawn England from the Near-Eastern entanglements. **1909** *Ibid.* Apr. 654 (*heading*) The Near Eastern question. **1909** *Daily Chron.* 25 Aug. 3/6 Near-Easterly. Bosnia and Herzegovina have figured recently in European politics. **1925** A. J. TOYNBEE *Survey Internat. Affairs 1920–23* I. 3 They appear.. to have refrained from interfering in any way regarding Near Eastern affairs. **1951** E. PAUL *Springtime in Paris* ii. 24 There were a few North Americans, hordes of English, many South Americans, and a few Near-Easterners. *Ibid.* xii. 215 Helen Hatounian put an Armenian record on the gramophone... The afternoon stillness.. was rent with the shrill voice of a near-eastern soprano. **1959** *Listener* 15 Jan. 145/2 His predilection for the interval of the augmented second (of the near-Eastern scale).

near hand, *adv.*, *prep.*, and *a.* Now only *Sc.* and *dial.* Also near-hand, nearhand; nerand, 6 *Sc.* neirand. [NEAR *adv.*[2] and HAND *sb.*]

A. *adv.* **1.** Close at hand, close by.

a **1300** *Cursor M.* 2844 Al þe land þat our a-boute þam lai ner hand. **1375** BARBOUR *Bruce* XVI. 538 Men of the cost of Yngland, That duelt on Hummyr or neirhand. *c* **1450** *St. Cuthbert* (Surtees) 2221 A larger house was made nere-hande. **1535** STEWART *Cron. Scot.* I. 13 Of nychtbour men that duelt than neirand by. **1582** N. LICHEFIELD tr. *Castanheda's Conq. E. Ind.* 157 *note*, They met with spices better cheap, and nerer hand then at Grangalor. **1635** SWAN *Spec. M.* (1670) 103 Which.. makes the black seem to be far off, and the white near hand. **1653** HOLCROFT *Procopius, Vandal Wars* II. 31 Uliaris.. fled into the Church of a Village near hand. **1795** *Montford Castle* II. 146 One ran before to a cottage, near hand, to order a bed. **1858** MRS. CARLYLE *Lett.* II. 373 There is no other place nearer hand where I could get any good.

b. Close *to* a place or person.

1375 BARBOUR *Bruce* IX. 129 Till the Slevach thai com neirhand. *c* **1450** *St. Cuthbert* (Surtees) 1999 As he.. nere-hande to þe house leend. **1645** RUTHERFORD *Tryal & Tri. Faith* (1845) 62 It is good to border with Christ, and to be near-hand to him. **1836** HALIBURTON *Clockm.* Ser. I. xii. (1837) 106 A lady that had a plantation near hand to hisn.

†**c.** At close quarters; closely. *Obs. rare.*

a **1548** HALL *Chron., Edw. IV* 218 This battaill was fought so nere hande, that kyng Edwarde was constrained to fight his awne person. **1670** LASSELS *Voy. Italy* II. 45, I arrived at the great terras..and there saw the thirteen statues of our Saviour and the twelve Apostles near hand, which seem below little taller than the statue of our tallest men.

†**d.** *to go near hand*: To be economical. *Obs.*⁻¹

a **1626** ANDREWES *Serm.* Wks. 1843 V. 546 This is that that makes the devil so good a husband and thrifty, and to go near hand.

2. Nearly, almost. (Common *c* 1300–1600.)

13.. *Cursor M.* 989 (Gött.), Adam was put vte nerehand nakid. **1377** LANGL. *P. Pl.* B. XIII. 1, I awaked there-with witles nerehande. **14..** *Sir Beues* (O.) 3560 He had Beuys nerehande slayne. *c* **1471** FORTESCUE *Wks.* (1869) 468 Lords and Officers, had nerehand as many matters of their own.. as had the Kyng. **1530** PALSGR. 718/1 He syghed tyll his herte dyd nerehande bruste. **1600** HOLLAND *Livy* XXVIII. v. 671 He destroid all the standing corne, which now was neere-hand ripe. **1677** CARY *Chronol.* 267 This makes near hand a Years difference. **1730** RAMSAY *Fables, Two Cats & Ch.* 42 Thus he went on, Till baith the haves were near-hand done. **1785** BURNS *Death & Dr. Hornbook* xiii, Sax thousand years are near hand fled. **1818** SCOTT *Rob Roy* xxix, His race is near-hand run. **1865** G. MACDONALD *A. Forbes* xii, We're a' keepit in..and nearhan' hungert.

B. *prep.* Near to, close to (a place, person, point of time, or action).

a **1300** *Cursor M.* 758 Þe nedder nerhand hir gun draw. *c* **1340** HAMPOLE *Psalter* lxx. 12 God is nerehand his lufers. **1418** *E.E. Wills* (1882) 43 Nerhande holichyrche. *a* **1450** *Le Morte Arth.* 2898 Whan it was nyghed nere hand none. **1500–20** DUNBAR *Poems* xcii. 79, I say nocht, schir, ȝow to repreif; Bot doutles, I ga rycht neir hand it. **1577–8** *Reg. Privy Council Scot.* II. 666 The said Alexander..wes not present at the doing thairof nor neir hand the samyn. **1633** RUTHERFORD *Lett.* xxix. (1862) I. 104 Your winter-night is near spent, it is near hand the dawning. **1792** *New Year's Morning* 13 (E.D.D.), They filled it near han' the brim. **1868** G. MACDONALD *R. Falconer* xxiii, We war near-han' the hoose. **1877** *N.W. Linc. Gloss.* s.v., Don't thou go near-hand Ned.

C. *adj.* Near. (See also *Eng. Dial. Dict.*)

1835 CLARE *Rustic Muse* 158 The near-hand stubble-field ..Showed the dimmed blaze of poppies.

So †**near hands** *adv.*, almost. *Obs. rare*⁻¹.

c **1460** *Towneley Myst.* xiii. 11 In fayth we are nere handys outt of the doore.

'nearish, *a.* [f. NEAR *a.*] Somewhat near.

1853 G. J. CAYLEY *Las Alforjas* I. 141, I had a nearish escape—look at the rim of my hat. **1881** 'RITA' *My Lady Coquette* xxxix, He had a nearish shave of his life.

near-legged, *a. rare*⁻¹. [f. NEAR *adv.*² II.] Going near with the (fore) legs.

1596 SHAKS. *Tam. Shr.* III. ii. 57 His horse..Waid in the backe, and shoulder-shotten, neere leg'd before.

nearly ('nɪəlɪ), *adv.* Also 6–7 ner(e)ly, neer(e)ly, 6 -li(e. [f. NEAR *a.* + -LY².]

1. With close inspection or scrutiny; carefully, narrowly. Now *rare*.

1540 MORYSINE *Vives' Introd. Wysd.* B vj, If a man woll more nerelyer behold this thinge. **1604** E. G[RIMSTONE] *D'Acosta's Hist. Indies* II. xi. 106 Whoso woulde neerely consider the causes and generall reasons before mentioned. **1669** in Sturmy *Mariner's Mag.* a 4 b, If you neerly mark him, and his End. **1751** JOHNSON *Rambler* No. 155 ¶4 If its operation be nearly examined. **1797** BURKE *Regic. Peace* iii. (1892) 209 Inspect the thing more nearly. **1825** SCOTT *Talism.* xvi, His liveries, his cognizance, his feats of arms.. were nearly watched.

†**b.** With close attention or great care. *Obs.*

1554–9 *Songs & Ball. Phil. & Mary* (Roxb.) 4 He shall.. the fyne flowr from the bran nerly syfft. *a* **1693** *Urquhart's Rabelais* III. xl. 332 Narrowly, precisely, and nearly garbelled.

c. Parsimoniously; frugally. *rare*.

1592 GREENE *Conny Catch.* 9 Hauing some xx. markes in his purse, long in gathering, and neerelie kept. **1673** RAY *Journ. Low C.* 396 They had rather live nearly than take much pains.

2. With close kinship, relationship, or connexion; in close intimacy.

1561 T. NORTON *Calvin's Inst.* I. 11 Vs, whom it pleased him more nereli and more familiarly to draw together to himself. **1646** MAYNE *Serm. Unity* 27 The most united, happyest, neerliest allyed people in the world. **1689** POPPLE tr. *Locke's 1st Let. Toleration* L.'s Wks. 1727 I. 240 Which things are nearlier related to the Government of the Magistrate than the other. **1753** JOHNSON *Adventurer* No. 84 ¶2 To be nearly acquainted with the people of different countries can happen to very few. **1845** TRENCH *Huls. Lect.* Ser. I. i. 1 Discourses which should more or less nearly have to do with the..vindicating that Truth. **1874** CARPENTER *Ment. Phys.* I. iv. (1879) 167 A lady nearly connected with the writer.

3. In a special degree or manner; particularly.

1562 J. HEYWOOD *Prov. & Epigr.* (1867) 177 Spide in a freende it toucheth him neerely. **1605** SHAKS. *Lear* I. i. 287 It is not little I haue to say, Of what most neerely appertaines to vs both. **1642** CHAS. I *Answ. 19 Propos.* 24 Those Treaties in which We are neerlyest concerned. **1729** SWIFT *Let. to Pope* 31 Oct., This..I only mention, because it so nearly touches myself. **1788** PRIESTLEY *Lect. Hist., Ess. Educ.* p. xxxi, Every man is nearly interested in the conduct of his superiors. **1833** HT. MARTINEAU *Brooke Farm* i. 5 A piece of news which nearly concerned the interests of our village.

4. At, within, or from, a short distance; closely in respect of place or position.

1577 B. GOOGE *Heresbach's Husb.* IV. (1586) 174 b, And neighbour like their houses nearely stand. **1605** SHAKS. *Macb.* IV. ii. 67, I doubt some danger do's approach you neerely. **1630** *R. Johnson's Kingd. & Commw.* 39 The Sea, ..a Soveraigne..bulwarke to that Nation that is neerliest situated unto it. **1773–83** HOOLE *Orl. Fur.* VI. 417 When now more nearly to the walls he drew,..He left the plain and beaten path. **1827** SOUTHEY *Penins. War* II. 769 Three days elapsed before the invaders again approached the works of the allies so nearly. **1853** FELTON *Fam. Lett.* x. (1865) 95, I was well pleased with such an opportunity of seeing him more nearly.

fig. **1620** T. GRANGER *Div. Logike* 49 The former doth more neerely, or immediately cause the effect. *a* **1731** ATTERBURY (J.), They are diligent to observe whatever may nearly or remotely blemish it.

†**b.** Closely (upon one): straitly. *Obs.*

1568 GRAFTON *Chron.* II. 98 They pursuyng the French men, in their flight did so nerely folow them into their holde [etc.]. **1587** R. HOVENDEN in *Collect.* (O.H.S.) I. 221 Expences..which pinch us very neerlye. **1627** MAY *Lucan* IX. (1631) 129 Neerely hugging woe She feedes on teares.

5. Closely in respect of agreement or similarity.

1594 O. B. *Quest. Profit. Concern.* 7 That which shall neereliest agree with that I said before. **1638** JUNIUS *Paint. Ancients* 343 Making a new difference between two neerely resembling brothers. **1656** SANDERSON *Serm.* (1689) 377 He is best pleased with those that nearliest resemble him. **1863** LYELL *Antiq. Man* 10 The age of iron corresponded more nearly with that of the beech tree. **1875** JOWETT *Plato* (ed. 2) I. 183 The *Euthydemus* is..that in which he approaches most nearly to the comic poet.

6. With close approximation or near approach (to some state or condition, etc.).

1606 SHAKS. *Ant. & Cl.* II. ii. 91 As neerely as I may, Ile play the penitent to you. *a* **1615** DONNE *Ess.* (1651) 95 God, which cannot be known by his own Name, may nearlyest by the names and prosperity of his. **1827** KEBLE *Chr. Y., Morning* xvi, To live more nearly as we pray. **1855** MACAULAY *Hist. Eng.* xvi. III. 718 As nearly prime minister as any English subject could be under a prince of William's character.

b. Within a (very) little; almost, all but.

1683 SALMON *Doron Med.* I. 92 Made neerly stiff enough. *Ibid.* 107 Till the Water is neerly consumed. **1750** JOHNSON *Rambler* No. 4 ¶2 This kind of writing..is to be conducted nearly by the rules of comic poetry. **1766** GOLDSM. *Vic. W.* xviii, I languished here for nearly three weeks. **1800** FOSTER in *Life & Corr.* (1846) I. 125 Years nearly lost to my own happiness. **1823** F. CLISSOLD *Ascent Mt. Blanc* 21 It was nearly six o'clock. **1875** JOWETT *Plato* (ed. 2) I. 54, I..was very nearly making a blunder.

c. *not..nearly*, nothing like.

1811 COLERIDGE in Southey *Life Andrew Bell* (1844) II. 646, I have not received nearly one-half of the subscriptions. **1884** M. MACKENZIE *Dis. Throat & Nose* II. 261, I do not employ irrigation nearly so frequently as formerly.

'nearmost, *a.* [f. NEAR *a.*] Nearest.

1570 LEVINS *Manip.* 176/15 Nermost, *proximus.* **1876** *Mid-Yorksh. Gloss.* s.v. *Nearder*, When contact in person is implied, then the superlatives are *Nearmost* [etc.]. **1913** E. H. BARKER *Wayfaring in France* 468 It is almost a shriek when the wind strikes the nearmost crests [of trees]. **1952** *Times Lit. Suppl.* 7 Mar. 168/4 You are my nearmost, you who have travelled the farthest.

nearness ('nɪənɪs). Also 5–6 nerenes(se, 6–7 nearenesse, neere- neer-. [f. NEAR *a.* + -NESS.] The state, fact, or quality of being near.

1. Close kinship or relationship.

1444 *Reg. Mag. Sig.* (1882) 63/2 For naturale affection [and] nerness of kyn and blude. **1539** CROMWELL in Merriman *Life & Lett.* (1902) II. 187 The mater cannot be concluded without the Bishop of Romes despensacion for nerenes of blod. **1605** VERSTEGAN *Dec. Intell.* ii. (1628) 29 Betweene that and this, here is no neerenesse of affinitie at all. **1660** SHARROCK *Vegetables* 66 To tell what neernesse in every kind is enough, is matter of great art. **1732** BERKELEY *Alciphr.* v. §17 No regard being had to merit..or nearness of blood. **1786** BURKE *Art. agst. W. Hastings* Wks. 1842 II. 131/2 From proximity of situation and nearness of connexion, [he] was likely to have any intelligence concerning his female relations from the best authority. *a* **1859** MACAULAY *Hist. Eng.* xxiii. V. 99 If nearness of blood alone were to be regarded. **1878** J. P. HOPPS *Rel. & Mor. Lect.* xix. 61 His nearness to God as a son was a nearness we also might enjoy.

b. Close intimacy or friendship.

1593 SHAKS. *Rich. II*, II. ii. 127 Besides our neerenesse to the King in loue, Is neere the hate of those loue not the King. **1647–8** COTTERELL *Davila's Hist. France* (1678) 9 The king received him into the same nearness as before. **1681–6** J. SCOTT *Chr. Life* (1747) III. 105 In that Nearness and Intimacy, he could not but have a most perfect Knowledge of him. **1703** ROWE *Ulyss.* I. i, He still has held him In more especial Nearness to his Heart. **1871** PALGRAVE *Lyr. Poems* 73 But has love with knowledge grown, does nearness bind more nearly?

2. Proximity in space. Also *fig.*

1560 DAUS tr. *Sleidane's Comm.* 399 b, This countrie was linked unto them in great amitie,..for the nerenes therof. **1635** SWAN *Spec. M.* (1670) 37 The nearness to it, gives motion, heat, and lightness. **1756** BURKE *Subl. & B.* IV. iii, In proportion to the nearness of the cause, and the weakness of the subject. **1815** J. SMITH *Panorama Sci. & Art* II. 771 Their nearness to each other must be increased or diminished according to..the shade required. **1850** TENNYSON *In Mem.* cxvii, That out of distance might ensue Desire of nearness. **1887** RUSKIN *Præterita* II. 264 The house itself had every good in it, except nearness to a stream.

3. Close resemblance or similarity.

1577 B. GOOGE *Heresbach's Husb.* III. (1586) 152 Hogs flesh..hath such a nearenesse and agrement with our bodies. **1624** BEDELL *Lett.* i. 39 The neernesse of my name to one Master William Bidulph. **1681** *Whole Duty Nations* 14 United by nearness of Manners, Customs, and Disposition. **1864** PUSEY *Lect. Daniel* (1876) 131 Media was allied to Persia..by nearness of language.

b. Close approximation (to accuracy).

1669 STURMY *Mariner's Mag.* v. xii. 73 To come to a necessary nearness at first, [is] far surer than by uncertain guessing. **1838** DE MORGAN *Ess. Probab.* 178 Pointing out, with great nearness, the law which regulates the mortality of large masses of people.

4. Parsimony, niggardliness; frugality.

1584 LODGE *Alarum agst. Usurers* (Shaks. Soc.) 77 Some terme it thriftinesse, some neernesse, but in plaine tearmes, it is usurie. **1601** R. JOHNSON *Kingd. & Commw.* (1603) 238 He being so percimonious and sparing in his expences, that from this his nearenesse [etc.]. **1677** *Govt. Venice* 188 The Greeks..eat Fish for Luxury, whereas the Venetian does it for Nearness. **1856** in Thornbury *Turner* (1862) II. 180 It was..the nearness that is capable of life-long self-sacrifice.

†**5.** Importance, consequence. *Obs. rare*⁻¹.

1679 *Establ. Test* 2 In a Concern of so common and universal Nearness.

nearshore ('nɪəʃɔə(r)), *a.* [NEAR *a.* + SHORE *sb.*¹] Situated or occurring (relatively) close to a shore; pertaining to or involving the study of such a zone.

1896 B. WILLIS in *U.S. Geol. Survey Geol. Folio* XXXIII. 2/2 This formation..represents the near-shore, muddier sediment of those times. **1936** *Rep. Comm. Sedimentation* (Nat. Research Council) 3 The main subjects that are contemplated are (1) relation of oceanography to sedimentation, including both physical and biological oceanography, (2) pelagic deposits, (3) inland sea deposits, (4) near-shore deposits, [etc.]. **1957** *Gloss. Geol.* (Amer. Geol. Inst.) 196/1 *Nearshore zone*, in beach terminology an indefinite zone extending seaward from the shore line somewhat beyond the breaker zone. It defines the area of nearshore currents. **1966** R. W. FAIRBRIDGE *Encycl. Oceanogr.* 614/1 Nearshore oceanography may be taken to include the study of all aspects of the area lying between the backshore zone and the outer edge of the continental shelf. **1973** *Nature* 6 Apr. 393/1 The Galana Boi beds..range from coarse-grained fluvial deposits to fine-grained near-shore lacustrine silts. **1974** *Ibid.* 15 Feb. 452/1 Deposition in a shallow, nearshore marine environment.

near-sighted, *a.* [f. NEAR *a.* + SIGHT *sb.* Cf. Icel. *nærsýnn*, Da. *nærsynet*, Sw. *närsynt*.]

1. Having distinct vision only of near objects; unable to see clearly at a distance; short-sighted.

1686 *Lond. Gaz.* No. 2103/4 He is about 17 years old,.. near sighted. **1723** *Pres. St. Russia* II. 63 Being lame, near-sighted, pitted with the Small-Pox. **1775** MME. D'ARBLAY *Early Diary* 3 Apr., He is so near-sighted, that he peers in every body's face a minute or two before he knows them. **1833** J. RENNIE *Alph. Angling* 17 The form of the eye in fishes proves that they are all very near-sighted. **1890** F. W. ROBINSON *Very Strange Fam.* 146 Lewis..peered at me in his old near-sighted way.

fig. **1856** R. A. VAUGHAN *Mystics* (1860) II. 42 He had a near-sighted mind. **1864** DASENT *Jest & Earnest* (1873) II. 41 Let our philology..rather be near-sighted than far-fetched. **1877** MORLEY *Crit. Misc.* Ser. II. 349 Learn not to be near-sighted in history.

2. Close, careful.

1828 MOIR *Mansie Wauch* vi, I found myself..well instructed in the tailoring trade, to which I had paid a near-sighted attention.

Hence **near-'sightedness**.

1811 *Malone's Boswell* I. 360 Alluding, no doubt, to his nearsightedness. **1822–34** *Good's Study Med.* (ed. 4) III. 155 He was informed that nearsightedness was almost unknown among them. **1884** E. P. ROE *Nat. Ser. Story* ix, The result of near-sightedness.

near-'sightedly, *adv.* [f. NEAR-SIGHTED *a.* + -LY².] In a near-sighted manner.

1909 *Daily Chron.* 11 Oct. 7/1 Dr. Shuttleworth blinked near-sightedly throughout the time he was in the witness box. **1971** B. MALAMUD *Tenants* 209 With furrowed brows he reads the marriage contract over and over, then nearsightedly reads it again.

nease, obs. variant of NESE, nose.

neashness, obs. form of NESHNESS.

neast(e, dial. variants of *neist*, NEXT.

neast(ling, obs. forms of NEST(LING.

neat (niːt), *sb.* Forms: 1 néat (næt, 2 niatt), 1, 3–4 net, 3–6 neet, 3–7 nete (4 nett, 5 nette, 6 neette, neyte), 6–7 neate, 6– neat. [OE. *néat* neut. = OFris. *nât*, *naet*, OS. **nôt* (MDu. *noot*), OHG. *nôz* (obs. or dial. Germ. *nosz*, *nos*), ON. *naut* NOWT (Norw. *naut*, Sw. *nöt*, Da. *nöd*):—OTeut. **nautoᵐ*, f. *naut-* ablaut-variant of *neut-* to enjoy or possess, OE. *néotan*: cf. NAIT *sb.* and *v.*¹]

1. *sing.* An animal of the ox-kind; an ox or bullock, a cow or heifer. Now *rare*.

c **825** *Vesp. Psalter* lxxii. 23 Swe swe neat ȝeworden ic eam. *c* **897** K. ÆLFRED *Gregory's Past C.* xiv. 80 Ða breost ðæs neates. *c* **1250** *Gen. & Ex.* 940 A net, and a got, and a sep. **1377** LANGL. *P. Pl.* B. XIX. 261 Iohan most gentil of alle, The prys nete of Piers plow. *c* **1400** *Ywaine & Gaw.* 252 His hevyd..was als grete Als of a rowncy or a nete. *c* **1440** *Promp. Parv.* 354/2 Neet, beest, *bos*. **1573** TUSSER *Husb.* (1878) 77 [He] may well kill a neate and sheepe of his owne. *a* **1661** FULLER *Worthies* (1840) III. 203 In the concave of a horse or neat's footing. **1669** WORLIDGE *Syst. Agric.* (1681) 329 *Neat*, a Heifer, or any of the kind of Beeves. **1895** MORRIS in Mackail *Life* (1899) II. 318 A savage Bull.., he was a gallant-looking neat.

2. a. (†*pl.* or) *collect.* Cattle. *neat leather* (= NEAT'S LEATHER).

c **825** *Vesp. Psalter* xxxv. 7 Men & neat hale ðu does dryhten. *c* **1000** *Boeth. Metr.* xx. 249 Se þas foldan ȝesceop, & hi ȝefylde þa..neata cynnum. *c* **1131** *O.E. Chron.* (Laud MS.) an. 1131 Micel orfcwalm..on næt & on swin. *c* **1205** LAY. 369 Children & hinen þa ure nete sculen ȝemen. *c* **1250**

Gen. & Ex. 3712 Ðe lond is god, ful of erf and of netes brod. *a* **1300** *Cursor M.* 3019 His fadir slow bath schep and net. *c* **1380** WYCLIF *Wks.* (1880) 172 Prestis also . . bien schep and neet. **1461** *Paston Lett.* II. 55 He . . toke there xxxvj. heede of nete. **1535** *Goodly Primer, Matins* Ps. viii, As flockes of sheep, all herds of neat. **1573** TUSSER *Husb.* (1878) 110 Be suer thy neat haue water and meat. **1611** SHAKS. *Wint. T.* I. ii. 125 The Steere, the Heyefer, and the Calfe, Are all call'd Neat. **1698** FRYER *Acc. E. India & P.* 329 Their Neat, though small are sleek and well-liking. **1707** MORTIMER *Husb.* (J.), Set it in rich mould, with neats dung and lime. **1802** W. FORSYTH *Fruit Trees* xxiii. (1824) 331 Rotten neats-dung is the best dressing that you can give it. **1867** MORRIS *Jason* I. 241 The herdsmen drave Full oft to Cheiron woolly sheep, and neat.

Comb. *c* **1440** *Promp. Parv.* 354/2 Neet Dryvare, *armentarius.* **1776** in *New Hampsh. Hist. Soc. Coll.* (1889) IX. 263 Mens Neat Leather Shoes of the best common sort. **1894** ATKINSON *Old Whitby* 21 The unromantic homeliness of the neat-stalls.

b. Used appositively, in ***neat beast, -beef, cattle, stock.***

1624 in *Essex Inst. Hist. Coll.* (1914) L. 235 All my Cattell nowe upon the farme . . as neat bests, horse bests, and swine. **1727** *Rec. Smithtown, N.Y.* (1898) 82 It is agreed on that the pounder shall have for pounding a horse four pence, for a net best four pence. **1755** in S. M. HAMILTON *Lett. to Washington* (1898) I. 135 Not under twelve shillings and sixpence per Hundred Neet Beef. **1619** *Jrnl. House of Burgesses, Gen. Assembly Virginia* (1915) 13 No man without leave from the Governour shall kill any Neat cattle whatsoever. **1648** *Archives of Maryland* (1887) IV. 390 Certaine neate-cattle to the number of 27. **1677** W. HUBBARD *Narrative* 60 Two hundred sheep and fifty head of Neat Cattle. **1753** *Scots Mag.* Nov. 540/2 Drawn by oxen or neat cattle. **1805** R. W. DICKSON *Pract. Agric.* I. 378 Sheep, horses, and even every kind of neat cattle. **1872** YEATS *Growth Comm.* 339 Neat cattle were sent to France in large numbers. **1850** *Rep. Comm. Patents: Agric. 1849* (U.S. Dept. Agric.) 94 It is estimated that there are in this country . . fifteen thousand two hundred and eighty five neat stock. **1869** *Rep. Comm. Agric. 1868* (U.S. Dept. Agric.) 427 The present winter (1868) he feeds forty-three head of neat stock, equivalent to thirty-four mature animals. **1882** *Rep. Maine Board Agric.* XVI. 265 The way is to fence off such a piece, and allow no neat stock or horses to run in it at any time.

neat (niːt), *a.* and *adv.* Also 6–7 **neate, nete.** [ad. AF. *neit, net,* F. *net* = Prov. *net, ned,* Sp. *neto,* It. *netto,* for **net'do*:—L. *nitid-um* (cf. Pg. *nedeo*), f. *nitēre* to shine.]

In 17th c. examples the precise sense intended is not always clear.

A. *adj.* **I.** **†1. a.** Clean; free from dirt or impurities. Also const. *from. Obs.*

1542 UDALL *Erasm. Apoph.* (1877) 62 His mainor place being in euery corner verie neat and clene. **1579** TOMSON *Calvin's Serm. Tim.* 244/2 [They] must shewe them selues neate and cleane from the faultes which S. Paule condemneth here. **1626** BACON *Sylva* §46 Mince the two Capons... Put them into a large neat Boulter. **1632** LITHGOW *Trav.* v. 184 Linnen cloth, that will not burne being cast into the fire, but serveth to make it neate and white.

†b. Denoting freedom from disease. *Obs. rare*$^{-1}$.

1615 G. SANDYS *Trav.* 226 Euery ship had a neat Patent to shew that those places from whence they came were free from the infection.

†2. Clear, bright. *Obs.*

1591 SPENSER *Virg. Gnat* 119 Fresh springing wells, as christall neate. **1668** CULPEPPER & COLE *Barthol. Anat.* III. xi. 154 A Membrane . . wherewith it is covered, and shines with a neat color. **1687** A. LOVELL tr. *Thevenot's Trav.* I. 133 This stone is very hard, looks like a kind of Porphyrie, and is very neat when polished. **1797** *Encycl. Brit.* (ed. 3) VII. 764/1 The sand . . was peculiarly adapted to the making of glass, as being neat and glittering.

3. a. Of liquors: Pure, unadulterated; *spec.* not mixed with water, undiluted.

1579 LYLY *Euphues* (Arb.) 191 The Wine that runneth on the lees, is not therefore to be accompted neate bicause it was drawne of the same peece. **1649** ROBERTS *Clavis Bibl.* 80 Thou didst drink wine both pure and neate. **1686** tr. *Chardin's Trav. Persia* 124 She saw me mix water with my wine, . . she and her women drank it neat. **1712** STEELE *Spect.* No. 264 ⁋5 The Hogsheads of Neat Port came safe. **1762** LLOYD *Poet Wks.* (1774) II. 6 Will you pour out to English swine, Neat as imported, old Greek wine? **1815** *Chron.* in *Ann. Reg.* 68 Accustomed to drink neat spirits. **1851** MAYHEW *Lond. Labour* I. 359/2, I was obliged to drink rum; it wouldn't ha done to ha drunk the water neat. **1876** BESANT & RICE *Gold. Butterfly* i, I should take a small glass of brandy neat.

fig. **1860** O. W. HOLMES *Prof. Breakf.-t.* vi, A remark . . is not . . to be taken 'neat', but watered with the ideas of common sense. **1887** *Brit. Weekly* 5 Aug. 219/2 They could take the truth neat, so to speak.

b. So of other substances. *rare.*

1651 R. CHILD in *Hartlib's Legacy* (1655) 53 If one take pure neat Honey, and ingeniously clarifie and scum and boyl it. **1660** F. BROOKE tr. *Le Blanc's Trav.* 385 Grains of gold, absolute gold, pure and neat. **1885** W. L. CARPENTER *Soap & Candles* 174 The soap . . may . . be put in the 'neat' state direct into the cooling-boxes.

†c. Of a language: Pure. *Obs. rare*$^{-1}$.

1686 tr. *Chardin's Trav. Persia* 378 They speak Persian, more or less neat, as the people are more or less at a distance from Shiras.

d. ***neat cement***: a mortar made from cement and water only, without the addition of sand.

1932 T. CORKHILL *Conc. Building Encycl.* 142 *Neat,* a term applied to cement mortar without sand. **1947** J. C. RICH *Materials & Methods Sculpture* xi. 328 Neat cement is a mixture of cement and water. It is not recommended for sculptural use save as a retouching medium. **1964** H. F. W. TAYLOR *Chem. of Cements* I. 2 Mechanical or physical determinations, such as strength tests, are usually made with an aggregate present, as determinations of this type on neat cement pastes can give misleading results.

4. a. Free from any reductions; clear, net.

1599 HAKLUYT *Voy.* II. 200, 600,000 ducates of golde neat and free of all charges. **1670** PETTUS *Fodinæ Reg.* 19 Paying the King the eighth part neat. **1685** SIR W. PETTY *Will* p. vii, I have of neat profits out of the lands . . 1100*l.* per ann. **1714** STEELE *Lover* No. 24 (1727) 142 The Brother's Estate . . when cleared would not be a neat Thousand a Year. **1747** W. HORSLEY *Fool* (1748) II. 150 The Commander has . . Two-Eighths of the neat Produce of every Prize. *a* **1790** ADAM SMITH *W.N.* I. ix. (1869) I. 101 It is this surplus only which is neat or clear profit. **1817** JAS. MILL *Brit. India* II. v. iv. 457 He offered to give a neat sum, to cover all expenses. **1887** *Daily News* 28 June 2/5 Sheep trade improved and prices higher, especially for prime neat weights.

†b. Unbroken, complete. *Obs. rare*$^{-1}$.

1715 *Lond. Gaz.* No. 5360/9 All the . . French Wines are neat and entire parcels.

c. Exact, precise. Now *dial.*

1682 SCARLETT *Exchanges* 58 If the Endorser cannot meet with a Remitter, for the Neat and precise Sum. **1755** MAGENS *Insurances* I. 69 This is the sum whereon the Repartition ought to be made; all the particular Goods bearing their neat Proportion. **1875** PARISH *Sussex Dict.*, 'Tis ten rod neat, no more and no less. **1894** 'IAN MACLAREN' *Brier Bush* 201 It cam tae the hundred neat.

II. **†5. a.** Of persons: Inclined to refinement or elegance; finely or elegantly dressed; trim or smart in apparel. *Obs.*

1546 HEYWOOD *Proverbs* (1874) 140 Like one of fond fancie so fine and so neate, That would have better bread than is made of wheate. **1579** LYLY *Euphues* (Arb.) 118 Be not curious to curle thy haire, nor carefull to be neat in thine apparel. **1609** B. JONSON *Sil. Wom.* I. i, Still to be neat, still to be drest, As you were going to a feast. **1655** VAUGHAN *Silex Scint.* II. *Providence* iii. (1858) 167, I, like flowers, shall still go neat As if I knew no month but May.

†b. Of dress: Elegant, trim. *Obs. rare.*

1634 SIR T. HERBERT *Trav.* 191 Deckt in neat attire. **1695** KENNETT *Paroch. Antiq.* Gloss. s.v. *Garba,* A neat or handsome garb.

†6. Of women: Trim, smart. *Obs.*

Possibly with more or less implication of sense 5.

1559 *Mirr. Mag., Dk. Clarence* xliv, Matched with a mayden nete. **1607** TOPSELL *Four-f. Beasts* (1658) 354 This your neat Bride is one of the *Empusæ* called *Lamiæ.* **1656** R. FLETCHER tr. *Martial* v. ii, Ye Matrons, Boyes, and Virgins neat, To you my Page I dedicate.

7. Characterized by elegance of form or arrangement, with freedom from all unnecessary additions or embellishments; of agreeable but simple appearance; nicely made or proportioned.

In early use the handsomeness of the thing appears to be the more prominent idea.

a. of towns, buildings, etc.

1549–62 STERNHOLD & H. *Ps.* cxxii. 3 O thou Jerusalem full faire; . . much like a Citie neat. **1601** B. JONSON *Poetaster* III. i, Here's a most neate fine street, is't not? **1630** M. GODWYN tr. *Bp. Hereford's Ann. Eng.* (1675) 65 Hampton Court, the neatest pile of all the King's houses. *a* **1661** FULLER *Worthies* (1840) I. 112 Many neat houses and pleasant seats there be in this county. **1717** BERKELEY *Jrnl. Tour Italy* Wks. 1871 IV. 522 The gardens are neat, spacious, and kept in good order. **1773** JOHNSON *Let. to Mrs. Thrale* 25 Aug., We lay at Montrose, a neat place. **1806** *Gazetteer Scotl.* 302/1 A neat and commodious mansion-house. **1865** DICKENS *Mut. Fr.* I. xv, It was made neater by there really being two halls in the house.

b. in general use.

1576 FLEMING *Panopl. Epist.* 393 When I thinke vpon thy neate proportion. **1601** R. CHESTER *Love's Mart., Compl.* (1876) 6 Her Feete . . Are neat and litle to delight the eye. **1669** STURMY *Mariner's Mag.* II. ii. 53 You must have . . Sets of Steel Letters . ., with a neat Hammer to use with them. **1710** HEARNE *Collect.* (O.H.S.) III. 43 Mr. Aubrey . . writ a neat Hand. **1781** COWPER *Conversat.* 239 In a focus round and neat, Let all your rays of information meet. **1833** J. HOLLAND *Manuf. Metal* II. 244 An agate style, ground and polished to a smooth neat point. **1858** MRS. CARLYLE *Lett.* II. 393 What our livery-stable keepers call a neat fly. **1888** MISS BRADDON *Fatal Three* I. ii, The furniture was neat.

absol. **1871** LOWELL *Pope* Prose Wks. 1890 IV. 48 It seems to me that Pope had a sense of the neat rather than of the beautiful.

c. *spec.* of wool: (see quot.).

1884 W. S. B. MCLAREN *Spinning* 19 Fine [wool] from the shoulders; neat, from the middle of the sides and back.

d. Semi-proverbial phr. ***neat (but) not gaudy*** and variants. Also *absol.* and *fig.*

[**1602**: see GAUDY *a.*[2] 3.] **1700** S. WESLEY *Epistle to Friend concerning Poetry* 5 Style is the Dress of Thought; a modest Dress, Neat, but not gaudy, will true Critics please. **1806** C. LAMB *Let.* 26 June (1935) II. 14 A little thin, flowery border round, neat, not gaudy. **1838** RUSKIN in *Archit. Mag.* Nov. 484 That admiration of the 'neat but not gaudy', which is commonly reported to have influenced the devil when he painted his tail pea-green. **1849** THACKERAY *Pendennis* I. xiii. 116 'You seem to like my dressing-gown, sir,' he said to Mr. Tatham. 'A pretty thing, isn't it? Neat, but not in the least gaudy.' **1887** *Lippincott's Mag.* July 116, I have sent, I say, just such manuscript as editors call for, fair, clean, written on one side, not with a pencil, but with a good gold pen, stamps enclosed for return if declined; the whole thing 'neat, but not gaudy, as the monkey said' on the memorable occasion 'when he painted his tail sky-blue'. **1892** *Society* 6 Aug. 757/1 Tennyson when in a rage is neat and not gaudy. **1974** L. DEIGHTON *Spy Story* xxi. 222 If Toliver complains to the Home Secretary you say it was the C.I.A. doing it. Neat, but not gaudy.

8. a. Of language or style: Well selected or expressed; *esp.* brief, clear, and to the point; cleverly or smartly put or phrased.

1586 A. DAY *Eng. Secretary* I. (1625) 2 Aptnesse of words and sentences respecting that they be neate and choicely picked. **1621** in *Crt. & Times of Jas. I* (1848) II. 277, I have heard extraordinary commendation made of a neat speech by one Pym. **1687** EVELYN *Diary* 27 Feb., A very quaint neate discourse of moral righteousnesse. **1706** HEARNE *Collect.* (O.H.S.) I. 165 A neat Answer made to his Paper. **1784** COWPER *Task* III. 278 Though the stile be neat, The method clear, the argument exact. **1830** MACAULAY *Let.* in Trevelyan *Life* (1876) I. 196 A clear and neat statement of the points in controversy. **1865** TYLOR *Early Hist. Man.* i. 11, I am not sure that the simpler Hottentot version is not the neater of the two.

b. Of preparations, esp. in cookery: Dainty, elegant, tasteful.

1611 SHAKS. *Cymb.* IV. ii. 48 *Arui.* How Angell-like he sings? *Gui.* But his neate Cookerie? **1634** SIR T. HERBERT *Trav.* 51 A very neat and curious Banquet. **1668–9** PEPYS *Diary* 26 Feb., Had a mighty neat dish of custards and tarts. *a* **1682** SIR T. BROWNE *Misc. Tracts* (1684) 10 The Camphyre that we use is a neat preparation of the same. **1731** BOLINGBROKE in *Swift's Lett.* (1766) II. 127 You keep servants and horses, and frequently give little neat dinners. **1799** UNDERWOOD *Diseases Children* (ed. 4) I. 55 A few grains of magnesia . . forms a much neater medicine. **1844** H. STEPHENS *Bk. Farm* II. 248 The male [fowls] making the best roast, and the female the neatest boil.

c. Cleverly contrived or executed; involving special accuracy or precision.

1598 MARSTON *Sco. Villanie* x. Hiij b, The Orbes celestiall Will daunce Kemps Iigge. They'le revel with neate iumps. **1625** MASSINGER *New Way* v. i, Was it not a rare trick . . to make the deed nothing? I can do twenty neater. **1675** A. BROWNE *App. Art Limning* 10 Rather make choice of a good Free and Bold Following of Nature, then to affect an extreme Neat way. **1846** GREENER *Sci. Gunnery* 150 The neatest part of the process consists in the joining of the points of the two rods. **1855** MACAULAY *Hist. Eng.* xi. III. 90 A neater specimen of legislative workmanship. **1865** DICKENS *Mut. Fr.* I. iv, This was a neat and happy turn to give the subject.

9. a. Of persons (and animals): Inclined to cleanliness or tidiness.

1577 tr. *Bullinger's Decades* (1592) 154 Let euery young man be neate, not nastie. **1596** SHAKS. *1 Hen. IV,* II. iv. 502 Wherein is he . . neat and cleanly, but to carue a Capon, and eat it? **1617** MORYSON *Itin.* II. 46 He was very neat, loving clenlinesse both in apparrell and diet. **1670** BROOKS *Wks.* (1867) VI. 441 The neatest person may sometimes slip into a slough. **1758** JOHNSON *Idler* No. 16 ⁋2 He was remarkably neat in his dress. **1802** PALEY *Nat. Theol.* xv. (1817) 132 Inhabiting dirt, it is, of all animals, the neatest. **1885** MISS BRADDON *Wyllard's Weird* I. i. 14 He was neat and methodical in all small matters. **1898** *Cable* 9 Apr. 231/1 A neat farmer is easily distinguished by his fences.

transf. **1650** BULWER *Anthropomet.* 121 Finding one haire in a platter of meat, they will not touch it... So strict are they in their neat Superstition.

b. Exhibiting skill and precision in action or expression.

1612 SELDEN *Illustr. Drayton's Poly-olb.* iv. 215 Your more neat judgements . . rather make it symbolicall than truely proper. *a* **1623** FLETCHER *Wife for Month* I. ii, *Men.* To be a villain is no such rude matter. *Cam.* No, if he be a neat one. **1684** tr. *Agrippa's Van. Arts* liv. 148 In Discourse, the Italians are grave, . . the Spaniards neat, . . the French quick and ready. **1806** WOLCOT (P. Pindar) *Tristia* Wks. 1812 V. 337 You paint so sweetly Love's alarms The neat Historian of their charms.

10. Put or kept in good order, tidy.

1596 SHAKS. *Tam. Shr.* IV. i. 117 Now my spruce companions, is all readie, and all things neate? **1718** LADY M. W. MONTAGU *Let. to C'tess Bristol* 10 Apr., The exchanges are all noble buildings . . and kept wonderfully neat. **1745** *De Foe's Eng. Tradesman* I. xxxi. 311 A tradesman's books should always be kept clean and neat. **1794** MRS. RADCLIFFE *Myst. Udolpho* v, They met with simple but neat accommodation. **1865** MISS YONGE *Clever Woman* I. 296 The hair and dress, though always neat, and still as simply arranged as possible. **1884** F. M. CRAWFORD *Rom. Singer* I. 14 Everything is very neat about him and very quiet.

11. a. *slang.* In ironical use: Rare, fine.

1827 T. CREEVEY in *C. Papers* (1904) II. 138 So much for my new friend! Is he not a neat one? **1828** *Ibid.* 186 His wife seems to have been quite as neat an article as his sister.

b. *colloq.* Excellent, desirable, attractive.

1934 J. T. FARRELL *Calico Shoes* 54 A girl in a two-piece bathing suit without brassière walked by them. 'Oh, baby, you can make me so happy!' Don sing-songed. 'Neat!' Jack appraised. **1942** BERREY & VAN DEN BARK *Amer. Thes. Slang* §29/4 Excellent; first-rate . . . neat. **1947** *Sat. Rev.* (U.S.) 10 May 26/1 Each of these adjoining rooms has a radio in it, which they find 'neat' and I don't. **1972** D. WESTHEIMER *Over Edge* (1974) i. 10 'I could drive you on into Idyllwild if you want. . .' 'That would be neat.' **1974** *Washington Post* 24 Feb. H. 13/5 I've passed up some neat dinner invitations.

12. *Comb.,* as ***neat-faced, -fingered, -footed, -limbed***; also NEAT-HANDED.

1641 MILTON *Animadv.* Wks. 1851 III. 200 Doubtlesse the neat finger'd Artist will answer yes. **1747** *Mem. Nutrebian Crt.* II. 252 The neat-limbed Nugmeg suckling the infant. **1823** LAMB *Elia* Ser. II. *Old Margate Hoy,* Thy neat-fingered practice in the culinary vocation. **1844** LD. HOUGHTON *Palm Leaves* 109 That bright-eyed and neat-limbed boy. **1870** BRYANT *Iliad* I. IX. 293 For the sake Of his neat-footed bride. **1876** GEO. ELIOT *Dan. Der.* xlii, The pale, neat-faced copying clerk.

B. *adv.* **a.** Neatly.

1665 HOOKE *Microgr.* 195 Its head was much bigger and neater shap'd. **1755** J. SHEBBEARE *Lydia* (1769) II. 53 She was dressed extremely neat, without show or ostentation. **1784** COWPER *Task* III. 423 The rest . . he disposes neat At measured distances. **1822** J. PLATTS *Bk. Curiosities* 752 To lay their colour or ink neater on the paper. **1840** DICKENS *Old C. Shop* xiv, I think I could do it neater than you.

b. *Comb.,* as ***neat-bound, -cut, -dressed, -polished.***

1729 SAVAGE *Wanderer* v. 43 Neat polish'd mansions rise in prospect gay. **1757** DYER *Fleece* III. Poems (1761) 138 The neat-dress'd housewives..Come tripping on. **1782** PENNANT *Journ. Chest. to Lond.* 127 Moxhull hall, the neat-dressed seat of Mr. Hacket. **1822** LAMB *Elia* Ser. II. *Thoughts on Books*, To be strong-backed and neat-bound is the desideratum of a volume. *a* **1852** MOORE *Case of Libel* x, A cloven hoof, Through a neat-cut Hoby smoking out.

neat, *v.* Now *rare* or *Obs.* [f. prec.]

1. *trans.* (and *intr.*) To make neat; †to clean. **1574** HELLOWES *Gueuara's Fam. Ep.* (1577) 356 It shall be more expedient, to neate and purge the snuffers, than to snuffe the candels. ? **1579** MONTGOMERIE *Misc. Poems* xlviii. 101 Our bottismen our geir perfytlie neits. **1581** MULCASTER *Positions* xl. (1887) 231 The houres before learning..are to be bestowed, vpon either neating of the bodie, or solacing of the minde. *a* **1658** DURHAM *Exp. Revelation* vi. (1680) 32 A girdle..was used for neating the long robe. **1736** PEGGE *Alph. Kenticisms* s.v., 'She neats about', i.e. she goes about the house, making things neat and clean.

2. *trans.* To clear, net (a sum). **1788** W. MARSHALL *Yorksh.* I. 246 It would have neated only 2*d* a foot. **1803** *Trans. Soc. Arts* XXI. 120 These have ..neated fully eighteen pounds ten shillings an acre.

neate, obs. form of NEAT *sb.*

neaten ('ni:t(ə)n), *v.* [-EN[5].] To make neat. Often const. *up*. **1898** *Sun* 23 Apr. 4/1 The neck is neatened with a collar-band and tabbed collar. **1942** BERREY & VAN DEN BARK *Amer. Thes. Slang* §4/4 Arrange; Put in order; Clean up ..*neaten up*. **1954** *Daily Progress* (Charlottesville, Virginia) 11 Mar. 10/1 (*heading*) Shrubs and fences neaten up yards. **1970** 'H. PENTECOST' *Plague of Violence* (1972) II. ii. 92 If the killers had tried to neaten up the room after a struggle, they couldn't have put everything back in place just as it had been. **1972** *Daily Tel.* 27 May 9/7 Finally, pulling and weaving neatens the whole nest.

†'**neatery.** *Obs.* [f. NEAT *sb.* + -ERY.] A place for cattle. **1647** HAWARD *Crown Rev.* 30 The Neatery... Seven Yeomen Purveyor of Oxen, Mutton, Veale, Lambe, &c.

neath (ni:θ), *prep. dial.* and *poet.* Also **'neath.** [Aphetic for ANEATH.] Beneath. **1787** TAYLOR *Poems* 25 (E.D.D.), Grannie's crown fu' weil he claw'd, An' 'neath her kirtle. **1824** MACTAGGART *Gallovid. Encycl.* 352 Tykes wad bask..neath the auld arm-chair. **1871** PALGRAVE *Lyr. Poems* 54 Had I seen 'neath a face of mercy Hell's particular malice mask'd. **1887** P. MCNEILL *Blawearie* 177 One of the pair caught him by the feet, the other neath the armpits.

neat-handed, *a.* [NEAT *a.*] Having a neat or deft manner of handling things; dexterous. **1632** MILTON *L'Allegro* 86 Their savory dinner..Which the neat-handed Phillis dresses. **1832** HT. MARTINEAU *Homes Abroad* i. 4 A neat-handed dairy-maid. **1845** *Peter Parley's Ann.* VI. 195 Bracelets for the neatest-handed of her nymphs. **1877** MRS. FORRESTER *Mignon.* I. 5 Neat-handed Phillis and a coadjutor served tea and coffee.

Hence **neat-'handedness.** **1839** URE *Dict. Arts* 218 The French with all their ingenuity and neat-handedness. **1865** *Cornh. Mag.* Nov. 533 The French doctor had praised her skill and neat-handedness.

neather, obs. Sc. f. NEITHER, obs. f. NETHER.

neatherd ('ni:thɜ:d). Also 4–5 **neet-**, 4, 6 **net-**, 6 **nete-**. [f. NEAT *sb.* + HERD *sb.*[2]] One who has the care of neat cattle, a cowherd. **1382** WYCLIF *Amos* vii. 14 Y am not a prophete,..but a neet heerde Y am. **1390** GOWER *Conf.* II. 161 The loresman of the Schepherdes, And ek of hem that ben netherdes. *c* **1440** *Promp. Parv.* 354/2 Neet Hyrde, *bubulcus*. *a* **1540** BARNES *Wks.* (1573) 190/1 Hee..went to the kinges Neteherdes house, and there desired lodginge. **1577–87** HOLINSHED *Chron.* III. 1045/1 The sheepe will obeie the shepheard, and the neat be ruled by the neatheard. **1603** R. JOHNSON *Kingd. & Commw.* 233 Vpon the mountains dwell neat-herds and sheapheards. **1668** H. MORE *Div. Dial.* III. xxix. (1713) 253 More like to the blowing of a Neatherd's or Swineherd's Horn than to the sound of a Trumpet. **1725** BRADLEY *Fam. Dict.* s.v. *Scabbed heels*, If the Disease returns,..apply the Neatherds Ointment. **1761** HUME *Hist. Eng.* I. ii. 44 A neatherd, who had been entrusted with the care of some of his cows. **1823** SCOTT *Quentin D.* xxxv, A bull..compelled by the neat-herd from the road which he wishes to go. **1878** ADDY *Mem. Beauchief Abbey* 53 *note*, These may have been..huts for the neatherds.

fig. **1581** MARBECK *Bk. of Notes* 842 The Pope, who is his Neatheard heere vpon earth.

Hence **'neatherdess**, a female neatherd. **1648** HERRICK *Hesper.*, *Neatherds*, Hark how can I now expresse My love unto my Neatherdesse. **1885** A. DOBSON *Sign of Lyre* 203 Whither away, fair Neat-herdess?

'neathmost, *a. Sc.* Also **neith-, neth-**. [f. NEATH + -MOST; cf. NETHEMEST.] Lowest. **1790** MORISON *Poems* 27 (E.D.D.), Garter height the neith'most clout Is banged wi' awfu force. **1850** BLACKIE *Æschylus* I. 93 How? Thou who sittest on the neathmost bench, Speak'st thus to me? **1871** W. ALEXANDER *Johnny Gibb* xiv. 106 The vera nethmost shall o' the lamp's dry.

'neat-house. Also **neats'**. [f. NEAT *sb.* Cf. Da. dial. *nöds* for *nödhus*.]

1. A house or shed in which cattle are kept. *c* **1440** *Promp. Parv.* 354/2 Neet howse, *boscar*. **1600** SURFLET *Countrie Farme* IV. iii. 634 The best and purest dung that you can find in your neathouse. **1615** MANWOOD *Lawes Forest* xxiv. 242 Any Swine-house, Neat-house, or Sheepe-house. **1806** BLOOMFIELD *Wild Flowers* 43 Sue round the Neathouse squalling ran. **1825** *Let it alone*, etc. in *Houlston Tracts* (Brit. Mus.) I. xiv. 5, I must not put off.. building a neat-house.

2. A locality near Chelsea Bridge, where there was a celebrated market-garden. Also *pl.* **1632** MASSINGER *City Madam* III. i, The neat-house for musk-melons, and the gardens Where we traffic for asparagus. **1663** *Clarke Papers* (Camden) IV. 305 In a garden by the neats' howse. **1696** *Lond. Gaz.* No. 3162/4 A Messuage and 14 Acres of Garden ground at the Neathouses, Westminster. **1721** BRADLEY *Philos. Acc. Wks. Nat.* 184 The first, which are Kitchen Gardens,..are those at the Neat-Houses near Tuttle-fields, Westminster. **1761** *Lond. & Environs* V. 24. **1804** EARL LAUDERDALE *Public Wealth* iii. 132 *note*, The produce of the soil at the Neat-houses before mentioned.

attrib. **1727** S. SWITZER *Pract. Gard.* Pref. 11 The practice of our Neathouse-men and Gardiners.

neatify ('ni:tɪfaɪ), *v.* Now *rare* or *Obs.* Also 6 **netify**, 7 **-fie.** [f. NEAT *a.* + -(I)FY.] *trans.* To make neat, to purify. Hence **'neatifying.** **1601** HOLLAND *Pliny* II. 11 With Wines delaied, neatified, and guelded, as it were, by passing thorow an Ipocras bag. *c* **1611** CHAPMAN *Iliad* II. *Comm.* 34 That which he addeth is onelie the worke of a woman, to netifie and polish. **1684** BAXTER *One Thing Nec.* Pract. Wks. 1830 X. 424 Did Christ or his apostles spend their time..neatifying their bodies, or such like? **1826** POLWHELE *Trad. & Recoll.* I. v. 161 The internal decoration, or rather neatifying of the Church, was at length accomplished.

†'**neatish**, *a. Obs. rare*[−1]. In 3 **netisse.** [f. NEAT *sb.* + -ISH[1].] Resembling cattle. *c* **1200** *Trin. Coll. Hom.* 37 þe shepisse and þe netisse men beð under cristes þralshipe.

†**neat-land.** *Obs. rare*[−0]. [For OE. *ʒenéat-land*: see GENEAT.] (See quot.) **1672** BLOUNT *Law Dict.*, Neatland, land let or granted out to the Yeomanry.

neatly ('ni:tlɪ), *adv.* [f. NEAT *a.* + -LY[2].] In a neat manner or style.

1. So as to present a neat appearance; in a nicely finished way. **1577** B. GOOGE *Heresbach's Husb.* IV. (1586) 187 If their woorkmanship bee neately, and equally wrought. **1660** F. BROOKE tr. *Le Blanc's Trav.* 75 They wear..pumps very neatly made. **1712–4** POPE *Rape Lock* II. 38 Twelve vast French Romances, neatly gilt. **1784** COWPER *Task* II. 587 There closely braced And neatly fitted, it..binds the shoulders flat. **1819** SHELLEY *Peter Bell 3rd* VII. viii, A genteel drive..With sifted gravel neatly laid. **1860** MRS. CARLYLE *Lett.* III. 61 My clothes folded neatly up.

2. With neatness or tidiness (in dress, etc.). **1581** PETTIE tr. *Guazzo's Civ. Conv.* III. (1586) 172 b, Neither take we anie great care to be serued honourablie, neatelie, and reuerentlie. **1601** SHAKS. *All's Well* IV. iii. 168, I will neuer trust a man againe, for keeping his sword cleane, nor..wearing his apparrell neatly. **1656** STANLEY *Hist. Philos.* IV. (1701) 235/1 Seeing a young man very neatly dress'd. **1735** BERKELEY *Querist* §60 Whether there be any instance of a state wherein the people, living neatly and plentifully, did not aspire to wealth?

3. With brevity, clearness, and point. **1570** *Marriage Wit & Sci.* II. iii. in Hazl. *Dodsley* II. 346 Ah flattering quean, how neatly she can talk! **1585** T. WASHINGTON tr. *Nicholay's Voy.* Ep. Ded., In a matter nothing doubtfull to vse needlesse proofes, as Tullie neatly saith. **1638** JUNIUS *Paint. Ancients* 54 Simonides expounded this point somewhat neatlier. **1664** POWER *Exp. Philos.* I. 10 How neatly Sir Theodore Mayhern delivers his Observation of this Animal. **1724** WEBSTED *Wks.* (1787) 378 Of Hyperboles..those are the best which are the neatliest couched. **1884** *Manch. Exam.* 24 Nov. 6/1 It may be doubted whether a ticklish point was ever put more neatly.

4. Cleverly, dexterously. **1603** KNOLLES *Hist. Turks* (1638) 252 To haue a boy.. neatly placed behind him vnder his large robes. **1665** MANLEY *Grotius' Low C. Wars* 341 Averring, that he onely counterfeited a face of modesty, the more neatly to hide the cruelty of his heart. **1698** FRYER *Acc. E. India & P.* 88 A notable Skirmish..wherein they were neatly intrapp'd. **1860** MOTLEY *Netherl.* ix. (1868) II. 35 The plan was neatly carried out. **1890** BAKER *Wild Beasts* I. 131 You naturally wish to kill your animal neatly.

5. *Comb.*, as *neatly-finished*, *-made*, etc. **1599** B. JONSON *Cynthia's Rev.*.. IV. v, I am the neatlyest-made gallant i' the companie. **1681** CHETHAM *Angler's Vade-m.* xxxvii. §2 (1689) 233 The very best and neatliest spun Hemp yarn. **1836–9** DICKENS *Sk. Boz, Parish* vii, There was a neatly-written bill in the parlour window. **1859** W. COLLINS *Q. of Hearts* ii, Little neatly-gloved hands. **1860** GEO. ELIOT *Mill on Fl.* II. ii, With the neatliest finished border.

neatness ('ni:tnɪs). [f. NEAT *a.* + -NESS.]

1. The quality or condition of being neat, in various applications of the adj. **1555** EDEN *Decades* 138 It was so named for the neatenesse and bewtifulnes therof. **1593** NORDEN *Spec. Brit.*, *Cornwall* (1728) 63 Ther is not a towne..more comendable for neatnes of buyldinges. **1638** JUNIUS *Paint. Ancients* 120 There is a wonderfull great difference between pure neatnesse and curious affectation. **1682** NORRIS *Hierocles* 97 Too much Neatness will slide into Luxury and softness. **1741** RICHARDSON *Pamela* II. 359, I was much pleas'd with the Neatness of the Good Woman. **1774** GOLDSM. *Nat. Hist.* (1776) VII. 171 There is much geometrical neatness in the disposal of the serpent's scales. *c* **1850** *Arab. Nts.* (Rtldg.) 584 She had even neglected that neatness and cleanliness so becoming to persons of her sex. **1867** A. DUNCAN *Mem. W. Duncan* 28 It was quite a model in respect of order and neatness and freeness from weeds.

pl. **1834** H. MILLER *Scenes & Leg.* xx, She retained a few of the mechanical neatnesses of her earlier years. **1859** MEREDITH *R. Feverel* xlii, Looking to their neatnesses.

b. In reference to language or style. **1548** PATTEN *Exped. Scotl.* Pref. a v, For the neatnes of making and fynenes of sense. **1576** FLEMING tr. *Caius' Dogs* To Rdr., The elegantnes and neatnesse of his Latine phrase. *c* **1645** HOWELL *Lett.* (1650) I. 407, I find..such a gallantry and neatness in your lines, that you may give the law of lettering to all the world. **1685** COTTON tr. *Montaigne* (1711) I. xxxix. 354 Neatness of stile is no manly Ornament. **1824** I. MURRAY *Eng. Gram.* (ed. 5) I. 313 There is a peculiar neatness in the sentence beginning with the conjunctive form of a verb. **1859** HELPS *Friends in C.* Ser. II. II. xii. 311 Neither does neatness of expression affect us much.

2. Dexterity, smartness. **1862** STANLEY *Jew. Ch.* (1877) I. xvi. 313 The neatness with which the Philistine watchmen are outdone.

neatnik ('ni:tnɪk). *slang* (chiefly *U.S.*). [Modelled on BEATNIK.] One who is neat in his personal habits, as opposed to a BEATNIK. **1959** *N.Y. Times* 30 Aug. 67/1 The beatniks and the neatniks had at each other this week. **1960** *Ibid.* 3 Jan. 48 (Advt.), Seeing how you're a Neatnik, you'll be buying things like soap and ties and stuff from now on. **1961** *Britannica Bk. of Year* 537/1 The reaction of one section of beatniks to the appearance of others produced first *Washed Beatnik* and then *Neatnik*. **1962** *Amer. Speech* XXXVII. 146 *Neatnik*..one who is neat in his personal habits. **1969** *Sears Catal.* Spring/Summer 16 A new look in Rally-back Jeans that can be worn by Neatniks of any age.

†'**neatress.** *Obs.* [irreg. f. NEAT *sb.* + *-ress* as in *actress*, etc.] A female neatherd. **1586** WARNER *Alb. Eng.* IV. xx. (1612) 96 The Neatresse, longing for the rest, Did egge him on to tell [etc.]. **1621** LADY M. WROTH *Urania* 485 She was a Neatresse, and in truth an neate one.

neat's foot. [f. NEAT *sb.*] The foot of an ox, used as an article of food. [**1589** ? LYLY *Pappe w. Hatchet* B iv, Why shuld I feare him that walkes on his neats-feete?] **1595** *Eng. Tripe-wife* (1881) 149 Thy tripes were yong, thy neates feete fat and faire. **1620** VENNER *Via Recta* iii. 70 The feete of a Bullocke or Heifer, which we commonly call Neats feete. **1652** FRENCH *Yorksh. Spa* xiii. 101, I forbid all flesh that is very salt, and fat, Bacon, Pork, Neats-feet, Tripes. **1720** STRYPE *Stow's Surv.* I. II. v. 89/2 Such as sell Tripe, Neats Feet, Sheep's Trotters, &c. **1846** MRS. BIRCH *Mrs. Rundell's Dom. Cookery* 108 Boil a pair of neat's feet very tender. **1862** DRAPER *Intell. Devel. Europe* v. (1865) 111 His death was in consequence of devouring a neat's foot raw.

b. *attrib.* in **neat's-foot oil** († *neat-foot*, *neat's-feet*), an oil obtained from the feet of neat cattle. **1579** LANGHAM *Gard. Health* (1633) 445 Three spoonfull of Neatefoot oyle. *c* **1720** W. GIBSON *Farrier's Dispens.* xiv. (1734) 273 It has a proportion of Neets-feet oil in it's composition. **1787** HUNTER in *Phil. Trans.* LXXVII. 389 Either hard fat or marrow, or fluid fat called Neat's-foot oil. **1825** J. NICHOLSON *Operat. Mechanic* 734 The neatsfoot oil prevents the varnish from being sticky. **1875** *Ure's Dict. Arts* III. 450 The feet of oxen..yield, when boiled with water, a peculiar fatty matter, which is known under the name of neat's foot oil.

neat's leather. [f. NEAT *sb.*] Leather made of the hides of neat cattle. **1530** PALSGR. 248/1 Neates ledder, *cordovayn*. **1558** WARDE tr. *Alexis' Secr.* (1568) 88 If you wil die Nettes leather or Spanishe skinnes. **1601** SHAKS. *Jul. C.* I. i. 29 As proper men as euer trod vpon Neats Leather. **1664** BUTLER *Hud.* II. i. 224 Some have been..kicked until they can feel whether A Shoe be Spanish or Neat's Leather. **1794** W. FELTON *Carriages* (1801) I. 215 The best leather is the Ox hide, called Neat's leather. **1821** SCOTT *Kenilw.* viii, Exchanging a sheath of neat's leather for one of flesh and blood.

attrib. **1675** HOBBES *Odyssey* (1677) 113 A tough and strong neats-leather sack. **1701** *Lond. Gaz.* No. 3694/4 A strong Neats-leather Saddle and Bridle.

neat's tongue. [f. NEAT *sb.*] An ox-tongue, used as an article of food. **1596** SHAKS. *Merch. V.* I. i. 112 Silence is onely commendable In a neats tongue dri'd. **1626** BACON *Sylva* §350 Smoake preserveth Flesh; As we see in Bacon and Neats-Tongues. **1676** D'URFEY *Mme. Fickle* II. i, Bid him get a Bottle of Claret, and a Neat's Tongue ready. **1747–96** MRS. GLASSE *Cookery* xviii. 289 Take a neat's tongue and boil it till tender. **1820** SCOTT *Abbot* xix, The remains of a cold capon and a neat's tongue. **1846** MRS. BIRCH *Mrs. Rundell's Dom. Cookery* 80 Some people like neat's tongues cured with the root.

neauer, neaver, obs. forms of NEVER.

neave, obs. form of NIEVE.

neavil, variant of NEVEL *v. dial.*

†'**neaving.** *Obs.* (See quot. and NEWING.) **1669** WORLIDGE *Syst. Agric.* Dict. Rust., *Neaving* Yeast or Barm. [Hence in Phillips (1706) and Bailey.]

neay, obs. form of NEIGH *v.*

neb (nɛb), *sb.* Now chiefly *north.* and *Sc.* Also 1, 5–7 **nebb**, 2–7 **nebbe.** [OE. *nębb* (:—**nefj-*) neut. = ON. *nef* (stem *nefj-*; Norw. *nev*, *næv*, Sw. *näf*) neut., related to MDu. *nebbe* fem. and masc. (Du. *nebbe*, *neb* fem.), MLG. *nebbe* fem. (hence Da. *næb* neut., Sw. *näbb*, Norw. *nebb* masc.). It is not clear whether the root **naf-* is the same as that of NAVE *sb.*[1]]

I. 1. a. The beak or bill of a bird. Also *transf.* *c* **725** *Corpus Gloss.* (Hessels) R 204 *Rostrum*, neb uel scipes caeli [*Epinal* celae]. *a* **1000** *Phœnix* 299 Sindon þa fiþru hwit ..& þæt nebb lixeð swa glæs oþþe ʒim. *c* **1375** *Sc. Leg. Saints* xxviii. (*Margaret*) 598 þane com a dou of hewin fleand,..& in þe neb brocht a cron. *c* **1400** MAUNDEV. (Roxb.) viii. 31 Ilk ane of þam bringes in þaire nebbe..a braunche of olyue. c1450 Holland *Howlat* 57 My neb is netherit as a nok, I am bot ane Owle. 1535 Coverdale *Gen.* viii. 11 She had broken of a leaf of an olyue tre, & bare it in hir nebb. 1567 Golding *Ovid's Met.* viii. (1593) 199 Diana.. Makes wings to stretch along their sides, and horned nebs to stand Upon their mouthes. 1641 Best *Farm. Bks.* (Surtees) 123 The right side of the nebbe [of a swan]. 1745 tr. *Egede's Descr. Greenland* vi. 80 Fishes..with long Nebs or Bills like Birds. a1813 A. Wilson *Disconsolate Wren* Poet. Wks. (1846) 98 Through the glen we took our flight, And soon my neb I filled. 1831 Jas. Wilson *Let.* in J. Hamilton *Mem.* iv. (1859) 135 The mother..sits with her neb generally open. 1885 W. K. Parker *Mammalian Descent* ii. 45 The thin horny layer still shows the 'neb' for breaking the egg-shells.

fig. 1721 Kelly *Scot. Prov.* 390 You may dight your Neb and flie up... You have ruined and undone your Business, and now you may give over. 1828 Moir *Mansie Wauch* ii. 25 Imagining that nothing remained for them, but to dight their nebs and flee up. 1830 Galt *Lawrie T.* v. ix. (1849) 235 If he were to throw a sheep's eye at you, and ye had a neb in your heart to pick it up.

b. The mouth (of a person).

1611 Shaks. *Wint. T.* i. ii. 183 How she holds vp the Neb, the Byll to him! 1640 Brome *Sparagus Gard.* iii. ix, How kindly he kisses her! and how feately she holds up the neb to him! 1867 Waugh *Home Life* vii. 62 A little, light-haired lass, holding up her rosy neb to the soup-master. 1894 Crockett *Raiders* 391 Then Rab would come oot, dichting his neb frae the byre.

2. The nose; the snout of an animal.

c1000 *Laws Ælfred* in Thorpe *Laws* I. 94 ʒif mon oðrum þæt neb of aslea, ʒebete him mid lx scill. a1100 *Voc.* in Wr.-Wülcker 290 *Nasu*, nosu... *Internasum*, neb. a1529 Skelton *Sp. Parrot* 418 The nebbis of a lyon they make to trete and trembyll. 1583 Golding *Calvin on Deut.* cc. 1245 He will not deceiue vs in his promises, nor holde vs downe with our nebbes in the Water as they say. 1737 Ramsay *Sc. Prov.* (1750) 114 Ye breed of Saughton swine, your neb's ne'er out of an ill turn. 1793 T. Scott *Three Auld Men* Poems 323 The snell frost-win' made nebs an' een To rin right sair. 1834 M. Scott *Cruise Midge* (1863) 177 Your eyes are blinded..and your neb peeled like an ill scraped radish. 1893 Kipling *Many Invent.* 233 He..laid his finger to his nose—his dishonourable, carnelian neb.

3. a. The point or nib of a pen (or pencil).

1599 Middleton *Micro-cynicon* Wks. (Bullen) VIII. 114 My pen's two nebs shall turn into a fork. 1610 Holland *Camden's Brit.* i. 517 He had sharpned the neb of his pen against the Popes authority. a1661 Fuller *Worthies, Hereford* ii. (1662) 36, I have so worne out the Neb of my Pen in my Church-History. 1688 Holme *Armoury* iii. xv. (Roxb.) 20/2 In the pen there is the nick or slip or slit, called the neb. 1798 Crawford *Poems* 48 (E.D.D.), The words just at the pen-neb hung. 1825 J. Wilson *Noct. Ambr.* Wks. 1855 I. 11 With the neb of my keelivine pen.

b. Any projecting part or point; a peak, tip, toe, spout, etc.; the extremity of anything ending in a point or narrowed part.

1611 Cotgr., *Penneton d'un clef*, the bit, or neb of a key. 1626 Bacon *Sylva* i. §14 Take a Glasse with a Belly and a long Nebb. 1673 Ray *Journ. Low C.* 456 They melt the wax again..and run it..through the neb of a tin pot into water. 1698 *Providence Rec.* (1894) VI. 211 A stubb sithe with sneaths, nebbs and Rings. 1797 *Encycl. Brit.* (ed. 3) II. 590/2 Raise or depress the tube of the level by twisting the neb of the screw. 1807 Vancouver *Agric. Devon* (1813) 117 The light Dorset swing-plough..has a well-curved iron breast, one foot ten inches long from the neb to the end of the wrest. 1825 *Ann. Reg.* 268* Improvements in producing ..a neb or slot in the roller..used in the printing of calico. 1881 Butterworth *Cotton* 62 Each line of rollers ought to be movable by separate stand slides and cap nebs. 1893 R. L. Stevenson *Catriona* xi. 116, I couldna see the nebs of my ten fingers.

†**c.** The embryo or radicle of a seed. *Obs. rare.*

1646 Sir T. Browne *Pseud. Ep.* iii. xxvii. (1686) 146 To destroy the little nebbe or principle of germination. 1660 Sharrock *Vegetables* 36 All seeds that I know have within their covers actually a Neb, which answers to a roote.

d. 'The pole of an ox-cart' (E.D.D.); ***neb ox***, a draught ox.

1710 *New Hampsh. Probate Rec.* (1907) I. 650 All my household goods and four Cows, and a yoak of neb Oxen.. to be for her own proper use. 1865 'G. Hamilton' *Skirmishes* ii. 7 Men left their oxen standing by the nebs.

II. †**4. a.** The face. *Obs.*

c897 K. Ælfred *Gregory's Past. C.* v. 42 Ðonne hræce hio him on ðæt neb foran. c1000 Ælfric *Hom.* II. 102 Se ðe awent his neb fram clypiȝendum ðearfan. c1175 *Lamb. Hom.* 43 Alle heore teres beoð berninde gleden glidende ouer heore aȝene nebbe. a1225 *Ancr. R.* 98 Scheau to me þi leoue neb & ti lufsume leor. c1290 *S. Eng. Leg.* I. 468/203 Op heo stod with wordes bolde, With briȝt neb and glade chere. 13.. *Guy Warw.* (A.) lxxv. 7 Wiþ a long berd his neb was growe. a1400–50 *Alexander* 3940 Of sum þai nyppid fra þe nebb þe nose be þe eȝen.

†**b.** ***neb to*** or ***with neb***, face to face. *Obs.*

c1175 *Lamb. Hom.* 61 Cristes wille bo us bitwon, neb wið neb for him to son. c1230 *Hali Meid.* 17 Secheð erst upon hire, nebbe to nebbe. c1330 *Florice & Bl.* 615 He..find thar twai neb to neb, Neb to neb an mouth to mouth.

Hence **neb** *v.*, (*a*) *intr.* to kiss or bill; (*b*) *trans.* to adapt the point of (a pen) for writing.

1609 Armin *Maids of More-Cl.* (1880) 90 Shall not busse knight, shall not neb? a1819 in Hogg *Jacobite Relics* I. 241 These two drakes may neb, go hand in hand. 1880 Gordon *Chron. Keith* 69 (E.D.D.), Caught nebbing the pen on the desk, and not on the thumb.

nebbed (nɛbd), *a.* Also nebed, neb'd, *Sc.* nebbit. [f. neb *sb.* + -ed².] Having a neb, esp. of a specified kind, as ***black-, blue-, red-, sharp-nebbed***, and esp. ***long-nebbed*** (see long *a.*¹ 18).

?17.. in Herd *Scot. Songs* (1776) II. 143 My daddie left me gear enough,..A nebbed staff [etc.]. 1720 [see long *a.*¹ 18]. 1808 R. Anderson *Cumbld. Ball.* 79 Blue-nebb'd Wat. 1824 Mactaggart *Gallovid. Encycl.* 29 The mavis and the yellow-nebed blackburd. 1871 S. S. Jones *Northumbld.* 204 (E.D.D.), No long neb'd shoes or bootes. 1882 Strathesk *Blinkbonny* 148 A brood o' chickens, lang-leggit, sharp-nebbit things.

‖**nebbich** ('nɛbɪç), *sb.* and *a.* Also **nebbish, nebbishe, nebbisher, nebish.** [Yiddish.] A nobody, a nonentity. As *adj.*, innocuous, ineffectual, luckless, hapless, etc. Also as *int.*, an expression of commiseration, dismay, etc.

1892 I. Zangwill *Childr. Ghetto* I. 46 '*Achi nebbich*, poor little thing!' cried Mrs. Kosminski, who was in a tender mood. 1907 —— *Ghetto Comedies* 205 '*Nebbich*, the poor little children!' cried Natalya, horrified. 1959 A. Wesker *Chicken Soup with Barley* iii. i, in *New Eng. Dramatists* I. 222 It's ach a nebish Harry now. It's not easy for him... Other men get ill but they fight. 1960 *Commentary* June 530/1 The *nebbish*, the cynic, the sophisticate. *Ibid.* 539/1 The sad *nebbishe* Podolsky is the owner of the building. 1960 F. Raphael *Limits of Love* i. i. 11 Your daughter ends up by ..marrying a good for nothing, nebbisher nobody. 1962 B. Abrahams tr. *Life Glückel of Hameln* i. 4 All the pleasures and riches he, *nebbich*, was denied here. 1968 *Times* 6 Apr. 21 The central character is so nebbish he has not even a name. 1969 *Atlantic Monthly* Sept. 57 Paranoid psychopaths who, after nebbish lives, suddenly feel themselves invulnerable in the certain wooing of sweet death. 1973 *Jewish Chron.* 9 Feb. 5/1 The kings [in this Jewish chess-set] are dead, long live the nebbishes (the deprived, signifying the decline of royal power). 1975 *New Yorker* 3 Feb. 77/2 Mr. Antonacci is both antic and affecting as the jumpy, craven *nebbish* Honey Boy, and John Bottoms is superb in several roles.

‖**Nebbiolo** (nɛbiː'əʊləʊ), *sb.* and *a.* Also Nebiolo. [It.] A black grape of northern Italy; the red table wine made from this grape. Also *attrib.* or as *adj.*

1833 C. Redding *Hist. Mod. Wines* ix. 246 At Asti, the plants called *Passaretta* and *Malvasia Nebiolo* produce *vins de liqueur*, with the smell of the raspberry. 1875 [see Barolo]. 1957 *Encycl. Brit.* XXIII. 664/2 Good honest red drinking wine comes from northern Italy, usually marketed under vine names (Nebiolo, Grignolino, Freisa, Barbera). 1958 A. L. Simon *Dict. Wines* 117/2 *Nebbiolo*, one of the best black grapes grown in the North of Italy for the making of red table wines. Many of the wines made from Nebbiolo grapes are sold as *Nebbiolo* wines. 1959 W. James *Word-Bk. Wine* 132 *Nebbiolo*. The vine of this name produces some of the best red wines of northern Italy. 1970 Simon & Howe *Dict. Gastron.* 275/2 *Nebbiolo*, a black grape grown in Piedmont and Lombardy and used to make red table wines. Among these are Barolo and Barbaresco, two of Italy's best-known wines. 1970 *Sat. Rev.* (U.S.) 12 Sept. 69/1 In Piedmont and Lombardy they have harvested the Nebbiolo grapes (a variety named because it ripens late in the autumnal *nebbia*, or mist). 1970 *House & Garden* May 138/3 Nebbiolo is a red wine named after the most aristocratic of the Piedmont grape varieties.

‖'**nebbuk, 'nebek.** Also nebeck, nebk. [Arab. *nebq, nebeq, nebiq*, the fruit of the lote-tree, or the tree itself.] A thorny shrub of the genus *Zizyphus*, common in Palestine. Also *attrib.* with *tree*.

1850 W. Irving *Mahomet* I. 107 Here grew..the nebecktree producing the lotus. 1850 Gosse *Sacred Streams* (1878) 189 The groves of plane-trees and nebeks that line its banks. 1891 E. Arnold *Lt. of World* ii. 48 Where knot-grass with its spikes,..and nebbuk-thorns Bind..the marble wrecks.

‖**nebel** ('niːbəl). [Heb. *nebel* or *nēbel*: see nable.] A Hebrew instrument of music, usually supposed to have been a kind of harp.

1753 Chambers *Cycl. Supp.*, *Nebel*, in the Jewish antiquities, a kind of musical instrument. 1845 *Kitto's Cycl. Bibl. Lit.* II. 372 The *nebel* was an instrument of a principal species, the name of which was applied to the whole genus. 1864 Engel *Mus. Anc. Nat.* 281 Some writers on Hebrew music consider the *nebel* to have been a kind of dulcimer. 1879 Stainer *Music of Bible* 24 Certain writers..have believed the *nebel* to be of that simple form of harps, describing a mere Δ shape.

Hence '**nebelist**, a player on the nebel.

1845 *Kitto's Cycl. Bibl. Lit.* II. 371 Asaph..was only the overseer of the nebelists.

‖**nebelwerfer** ('neːbəlvɛrfər, -wɜːfə(r)). [G., f. *nebel* mist, fog, haze + *werfer* thrower, mortar, f. *werfen* to throw.] A German six-barrelled rocket mortar. Also *attrib.*

1943 *Hutchinson's Pict. Hist. War* 4 Aug.–26 Oct. 191 These German gunners have certainly chosen a well-concealed position in which to hide their nebelwerfer (fog-thrower) battery. 1946 C. Wilmot in R. W. Zandvoort et al. *Wartime Eng.* (1957) 163 The nebelwerfers—those many-barrelled mortars that put down the rocket-propelled bombs with the high wailing sobbing note. 1948 A. M. Taylor *Lang. World War II* (rev. ed.) 136 *Nebelwerfer*, a German rocket thrower similar to the Russian Katyusha. 1961 W. Vaughan-Thomas *Anzio* vi. 112 The Scots Guards captured a German officer who had driven into their lines while looking for sites for the unpleasant *Nebelwerfers*, or six-barrel mortars.

nebenkern ('neːbənkɛrn). *Cytology.* Pl. **-kerne.** [a. G. *nebenkern* (O. Bütschli 1871, in *Zeitschr. f. wissensch. Zool.* XXI. 527), f. *neben* near + *kern* kernel, nucleus.] Any of various cytoplasmic structures associated with or resembling the nucleus (see quots.).

1898 *Jrnl. R. Microsc. Soc.* 624 (*heading*) 'Nebenkern' in spermatogenesis of Pulmonata. 1901 G. N. Calkins *Protozoa* i. 14 He [*sc.* Bütschli] held..that in addition to the macronucleus there is a second and a smaller nucleus in Infusoria, and to this he gave the name *Nebenkern* or micronucleus ('76). 1917 *Q. Jrnl. Microsc. Sci.* LXII. 416, I have been unable to find any body in the spermatid formed from 'spindle fibres' or 'yolk granules', and I do not intend to use the term 'nebenkern', which has been, and still is, used without discrimination for almost any granule or body in a cell. For example, Hegner..lately draws attention to the 'granules of Blochmann' in the wasp and two ants, which have also been called 'nebenkerne', quite regardless of whether or no they are of the same nature as the original 'nebenkern' of Bütschli. 1928 E. L. Opie in E. V. Cowdry *Special Cytol.* I. ix. 246 The name 'nebenkern' or 'paranucleus' has been given to structures situated within the cytoplasm [of the pancreatic acinous cell] and staining like nuclear material... Other chromatin-like bodies designated 'nebenkerne' are spherical and have an even contour. 1958 *Internat. Rev. Cytol.* VII. 223 In other invertebrates..the mitochondrial *nebenkern* is transformed into a spiral wrapping that extends for the greater part of the length of the sperm tail. 1962 D. W. Bishop *Spermatozoan Motility* 157 In insects, gastropods, and other invertebrates the conspicuous *nebenkern* formed during spermiogenesis arises by fusion of mitochondria. 1965 E. N. Willmer *Cells & Tissues in Culture* II. xi. 531 The round or oval nucleus of the hair-cell [in the organ of Corti] occupies the third quarter of the cell. The infranuclear part contains a small number of mitochondria and a group of granular cisternae. Occasionally, the granular cisternae might be arranged in a circular fashion forming a 'Nebenkern' which recalls the so-called Retzius Body.

†**neber**, variant of eber, manifest. *Obs.*

a1300 *Cursor M.* 13041 Sco cried and mad ful mikel dole, Als sco þat was a neber fole.

neble, obs. form of nipple.

neb-mark, *sb.* [f. neb *sb.*] A mark of ownership on the beak of a swan. Hence **neb-mark** *v.*

1641 Best *Farm. Bks.* (Surtees) 123 The kinges swanner hayth all the markes, both nebbe-markes and foote-markes, sette downe in his booke. *Ibid.*, If wee doe not intende to nebbe-marke them..then wee putte them up to feedinge soe soone as they come hoame.

‖**neb-neb.** [? African.] (See quots.)

1839 Ure *Dict. Arts* 82 The rind or shell which surrounds the fruit of the *mimosa cineraria*..comes from the East Indies, as also from Senegal, under the name of Neb-neb. 1875 *Encycl. Brit.* I. 68/2 The pods of *Acacia nilotica*, under the name of neb-neb, are used by tanners.

neborate, variant of neighboured. *Obs.*

Nebraskan (nɪ'bræskən), *a.* and *sb.* [f. *Nebraska*, name of a state in the central U.S. + -an.] **A.** *adj.* **1.** Of, pertaining to, or from Nebraska.

1875 E. A. Curley *Nebraska* xxii. 289 The Mormon fields, irrigated as they are, are much smaller than those of Nebraskan farmers. 1884 *N.Y. Weekly Tribune* 2 Apr. 10/4 The advantages which the Nebraskan Mennonites secure by co-operative purchasing of their implements, machinery, and supplies of all kinds, are manifestly..great. 1933 Blunden & Norman *We'll shift our Ground* 155 Some thesis writer, Nebraskan or Wisconsinese. 1973 S. Dobyns *Man of Little Evils* (1974) x. 96 The story concerned a Nebraskan couple who had been..robbed.

2. *Geol.* Of, pertaining to, or designating the first Pleistocene glaciation in North America, now generally identified with the Günz glaciation in the Alps. Also *absol.*, the Nebraskan glaciation or the deposits it produced.

1909 B. Shimek in *Bull. Geol. Soc. Amer.* XX. 408 The tough, impervious, bluish-black fill which has been known as the sub-Aftonian or pre-Kansan drift in Iowa, is here so well developed, reaching an exposed thickness of more than 15 feet.., that it can no longer be regarded as merely a remnant, but should rank with other well developed drift sheets... This leaves it without a name, and in view of this fact, and of the wide distribution of this formation, the name *Nebraskan* is proposed for it... The name Nebraskan was suggested to the writer by Professor Calvin. 1930 *Science* 22 Aug. 194/1 The Nebraskan is probably a million years old. 1934, 1957 [see Illinoian *sb.* and *a.* B]. 1966 *Science* 11 Nov. 771/3 The Early Pleistocene record in Nebraska is at present interpreted as indicating two stadial advances of the continental glacier during Nebraskan time and three stadial advances during Kansan time. 1970 [see Günz].

B. *sb.* A native or inhabitant of Nebraska.

1888 [see Minnesotan]. 1900 *Congress. Rec.* 27 Jan. 1241/2 He aided in the nomination of Mr. Bryan for President, and was an enthusiastic supporter of the brilliant Nebraskan. 1948 *Time* 26 Apr. 13/2 Ohioans seemed as friendly to him as Nebraskans. 1969 I. Kemp *Brit. G.I. in Vietnam* iii. 49 The medic, 'Jake' Jacobs..was a pale, thin Nebraskan, recently married.

‖**nebris** ('nɛbrɪs). *Archæol.* [L. *nebris*, a. Gr. νεβρίς fawn-skin, f. νεβρός fawn.] A fawn-skin, worn by Dionysus and his votaries.

1776 J. Bryant *Mythol.* III. 196 They also at their sacrifices wore the nebris, or spotted skin, like the Bacchanalians in the west. 1850 Leitch tr. *C.O. Müller's Anc. Art* §127 (ed. 2) 100 A beautiful youth crowned with ivy, engirt with a nebris, resting his lyre on the thyrsus. 1872 Ruskin *Eagle's N.* §225 The nebris of Dionusos and leopard-skin of the priests of Egypt relate to astronomy.

†**nebshaft.** *Obs.* In 3–4 -schaft, 3 -scheft, 4 -sseft. [f. neb *sb.* + *-shaft*, repr. OE. *-sceaft*, f. the root of *sciępan*, to shape.]

1. Countenance, face.

a1225 *St. Marher.* 4 Nim ȝeme of þi ȝuheðe, ant of þi semli schape, ant of þi schene nebschaft. a1225 *Ancr. R.* 94 ȝe schulen habben, þer uppe, þe brihte sihðe of Godes nebscheft. *a* **1400** *Minor Poems fr. Vernon MS.* 127/259 Blessed beo, ladi, thi brihte neb-schaft.

2. Likeness, image.

1340 *Ayenb.* 265 Do we to worke godes nebsseft ine ssrifte and ine zalmes.

neb-tide, var. *nep-*, *neap-tide*: see NEAP *a.*

Nebuchadnezzar (nɛbjuːkəd'nɛzə(r)). [So called in allusion to *Nebuchadnezzar* King of Babylon, d. 562 B.C.] A very large wine-bottle (see quots.).

1913 A. HUXLEY *Let.* 11 Nov. (1969) 55 Fireworks ensue, then (children dismissed) supper and afterwards, the most magnificent Nebuchadnezzars, and finally a good form of blind man's buff. **1962** [see BALTHAZAR]. **1967** *Punch* 27 Sept. 484/3 In the thirtieth of fifty-one chapters, Patrick Forbes lists the eleven different sizes of champagne bottle, from the quarter-bottle to the Nebuchadnezzar, eighty times as big. **1967** A. LICHINE *Encycl. Wines* 317/2 Since wine ages more slowly in large bottles, there are many magnums and double magnums in the Lafite cellars, as well as Imperials, which hold eight bottles, and Nebuchadnezzars (ten bottles). **1970** SIMON & HOWE *Dict. Gastron.* 80/2 *Nebuchadnezzar*, 20 bottles.

‖**nebula** ('nɛbjʊlə). Pl. nebulæ (-iː). [L. *nebula* mist, vapour, related to Gr. νεφέλη, OHG. *nebul* (G. *nebel*).]

1. a. A film upon, or covering, the eye; *spec.* a clouded speck or spot on the cornea causing defective vision.

1661 LOVELL *Hist. Anim. & Min.* Isagoge b 5 The Raie hath a long and rough taile, the eye is covered with a nebula. **1719** QUINCY *Phys. Dict.* (1722), *Nebula*..is figuratively applied to Appearances..in the human Body, as to Films upon the Eyes. **1836–9** *Todd's Cycl. Anat.* II. 177/2 Slight opacities, or *nebulæ*, as they are called, if confined to the conjunctival covering of the cornea. **1844** H. STEPHENS *Bk. Farm* II. 229 Farm-horses..being liable to accidents, the effects of inflammation,—nebulæ, or specks,—do sometimes occur. **1895** SWANZY *Diseases Eye* (ed. 5) 150 The opacity..is called a nebula.

b. A cloudy or flocculent appearance.

1805 S. WESTON *Werneria* 70 Quartz is distinguishable from glass by the nebulæ, or appearance of clouds in its transparency. **1846** DAY tr. *Simon's Anim. Chem.* II. 184 When the temperature is sufficiently elevated, the coagulation begins to occur in the form of small white nebulæ.

2. *fig.* A misty or obscure affair. *rare*⁻¹.

a **1734** NORTH *Exam.* II. iv. §147 (1740) 310 He, that could pass over the Items of the Grand Plot without Notice, will not amuse the Reader with these *Nebulæ*.

3. *Astron.* An indistinct cloud-like cluster of distant stars, or a luminous patch of supposed gaseous or stellar matter lying beyond the limits of the solar system. In mod. use the term is applied to (*a*) a cloud of gas or dust situated within the interstellar space of a galaxy (usu. our own) and appearing as either a bright or a dark cloud (according to whether or not there are stars present to make it luminous); (*b*) a galaxy (usu. one other than our own).

1727–38 CHAMBERS *Cycl.* s.v. *Stars*, Nebulous stars, being such as only appear faintly, in clusters, in the form of little lucid nebulæ or clouds. **1781** *Gentl. Mag.* LI. 526 This..nebula was discovered March 23, 1779. **1802** HERSCHEL in *Phil. Trans.* XCII. 499 A stellar nebula..may be a real cluster of stars. *Ibid.* 523 It is of a middle species, between the planetary nebulæ and nebulous stars. **1841** BREWSTER *Mart. Sci.* ii. 31 Upon directing his telescope to nebulæ and clusters of stars. **1873** DAWSON *Earth & Man* i. 8 The spectroscope has.. shown that some nebulæ are actually gaseous. **1924** H. DINGLE *Mod. Astrophysics* xvi. 302 A dark nebula is really dark, and not merely too faint for its light to be seen on account of its great distance from us. **1930** R. H. BAKER *Astron.* xi. 465 Frequently a 'nebula' turned out to be a star-cluster, thereby encouraging the opinion, in former times, that all nebulae are really clusters of stars. *Ibid.*, Modern investigations have shown that nebulae, as distinguished from ordinary star-clusters, fall into two classes having entirely different characteristics, namely, the galactic nebulae and the extra-galactic nebulae. **1963** B. & J. LOVELL *Discovering Universe* ix. 114 The Milky Way system is typical of many extra-galactic spiral nebulae, and very much akin to M31 in Andromeda. **1968** P. MOORE *Sky at Night* II. xxxii. 232 With other nebulæ, there are no convenient stars—and so the nebulæ cannot be seen directly, but betray themselves because they blot out the light of the stars beyond... Mention should also be made of the nebulæ which shine by pure reflection. Such is the nebula in the Pleiades. *Ibid.* 235 The old term of 'spiral nebula' has become obsolete, to be replaced by 'spiral galaxy'; a proper nebula is gaseous, and belongs to the Galaxy in which we live. **1971** D. W. SCIAMA *Mod. Cosmol.* iii. 39 In this way he [*sc.* E. P. Hubble] obtained a distance of 800,000 light-years for the Andromeda nebula, and similar values for other spiral nebulae. Now that these nebulae are well established as stellar systems outside our own, we shall henceforth call them galaxies. **1974** F. W. COLE *Fund. Astron.* xiii. 358/1 The Orion nebula is 1600 LY distant and about 30 LY in diameter. In our galaxy, other emission nebulae of the same type are about the same size. Vastly larger emission nebulae are known outside our galaxy; an excellent example is in M33, a spiral galaxy in Triangulum.

b. *transf.* and *fig.*

1817 J. ADAMS *Wks.* (1856) X. 245 Hutchinson and all his nebula of stars and satellites. **1856** MISS MULOCK *J. Halifax* xii, The world of existence to him seemed to have lazily melted down into a mere nebula. **1880** DISRAELI *Endym.* xxix, The present was too hard for him, and his future was only a chaotic nebula.

c. *attrib.*, as ***nebula hypothesis***, ***line***, ***photography***, etc. Also in *pl.* as ***nebulæ spectrum***.

1877 *Nature* XVI. 401/2 The brightest line of the nebulæ spectrum. *Ibid.* 414/1 If we accept the bright line..to be veritably the chief nebula line. *a* **1891** *Anthony's Photogr. Bull.* IV. 363 His primary object was to use it for nebula photography. **1892** A. TAYLOR in *Photogr. Ann.* II. 116 The central nucleus..demanded by Laplace's nebula hypothesis.

4. Fog, mist.

1894 W. C. LEY *Cloudland* 33 The spherules of water which constitute nebula vary greatly in diameter. *Ibid.* 35 Nebula must not..be regarded as in all cases a very local phenomenon.

nebular ('nɛbjʊlə(r)), *a.* *Astron.* [f. prec. + -AR¹: cf. F. *nébulaire*.]

1. ***nebular hypothesis*** or ***theory***, the theory, propounded by Kant and elaborated by Herschel and Laplace, which supposes a nebula to be the first state of the solar and stellar systems.

1837 WHEWELL *Hist. Induct. Sci.* (1857) II. 229 The Nebular Hypothesis, which has been propounded by Laplace. **1871** TYNDALL *Fragm. Sci.* (1879) II. x. 211, I hold the nebular theory, as it was held by Kant. **1877** LOCKYER in *Nature* XVI. 414/1 The nebular hypothesis..remains untouched by these observations.

2. Consisting of, concerned with, or relating to a nebula, or to nebulæ.

1856 PAGE *Adv. Text-bk. Geol.* ii. 21 Such hypotheses, then, as nebular condensation. **1878** NEWCOMB *Pop. Astron.* IV. ii. 480 On each side of the galactic and stellar region we have a nebular region. **1892** A. TAYLOR in *Photogr. Ann.* II. 117 Nebular, lunar, and planetary photography.

†**'nebulate**, *v.* *Obs.* *rare*⁻¹. [f. the ppl. stem of med.L. *nebulāre* to cloud: cf. NEBULA 1 b.] *intr.* To become cloudy or turbid.

1753 N. TORRIANO *Gangr. Sore Throat* 118 The Water nebulated, and tended to deposit a laudable Hypostasis.

'nebulated, *ppl. a.* *rare.* [cf. prec.]

†**1.** *Her.* = NEBULÉ 1. *Obs.*

1486 *Bk. St. Albans, Her.* d iij b, Ther is also a partyng of ij. colowris clowdit or nebulatit. *Ibid.* d iiij b, Off armys partyt aft the long way clowdy or nebulatyd.

2. Clouded, dimmed.

1874 COUES *Birds of N.W.* 608 On the head and neck the light rufous decidedly predominates, and seems indistinctly but thickly nebulated with dusky.

nebule¹ ('nɛbjuːl). [Anglicized f. NEBULA.]

1. A cloud; a mist or fog. Also *fig.*

c **1420** LYDG. *Commend. Our Lady* 53 O..Light withoute nebule, shyning in thy spere.

1869 BLACKMORE *Lorna D.* iii, The Baroness will not touch unless a nebule be formed outside the glass. **1877** —— *Cripps* (1887) 175 Nebules of logic, dialectic fogs, and thunderstorms of enthymem.

2. *Astron.* A nebula. Also *fig.*

1830 W. TAYLOR *Hist. Surv. Germ. Poetry* I. 179 The nebule of returning culture in Germany first became visible to the naked eye at Zurich and Leipzig. **1837** GOODRICH *Sun, Moon & Stars* xxxii. (ed. 2) 185 Small luminous spots, of a cloudy appearance, which we thence call *nebulæ* or *nebules*.

nebule² ('nɛbjuːl). *Arch.* [app. a misapprehension of NEBULÉ.] A moulding of a wavy or serpentine form (see next).

1823 P. NICHOLSON *Pract. Build.* 589 Nebule; a zigzag ornament, but without angles, frequently found in the remains of Saxon architecture. **1836** H. G. KNIGHT *Archit. Tour Normandy* 199 The most common mouldings are the billet,..hatchet, nebule, star, rope.

attrib. **1848** B. WEBB *Cont. Ecclesiol.* 45 The nave and aisles and west transept have a nebule corbel-tabling. **1875** KNIGHT *Dict. Mech.* 1515/2 *Nebule-molding*.

transf. **1849** ROCK *Ch. of Fathers* II. 251 *note*, The stocking is of silver tissue, worked with gold birds..and a peculiar ornament—a nebule, white and blue, with yellow rays shooting from its edge.

nebulé ('nɛbjuːleɪ), **nebuly** ('nɛbjuːlɪ), *a.* Also 7 -ee, 9 -ée. [a. F. *nébulé*, ad. med.L. *nebulāt-us*: see NEBULATE *v.*]

1. *Her.* Of a wavy or serpentine form, like the edges given to conventional representations of clouds; represented in the form of a cloud.

a **1550** in Baring-Gould & Twigge *W. Armory* (1898) 5 Blount: Barry nebule or and sables. **1562** LEIGH *Armorie* 135 He beareth party per Pale, Nebule Ermines and Ermin. **1610** GUILLIM *Heraldry* II. iii. (1660) 54 Of these [lines] some are Nebulee. **1661** BLOUNT *Glossogr.* (ed. 2) s.v., Nebule of six pieces, Or and Sable is the Blounts Arms. **1725** *Lond. Gaz.* 6363/3 The Coat a Fess Nebule between six Flowers-de-Lis. **1838** *Penny Cycl.* XII. 141/2 Of crooked lines there are eight recognised by English heralds, namely:—1. Engrailed... 5. Nebuly. **1864** BOUTELL *Her. Hist. & Pop.* xv. (ed. 3) 217 Two bendlets nebulée sa. **1893** CUSSANS *Heraldry* (ed. 4) 47 The lines by which a shield is divided..may assume any of the following forms: Engrailed... Nebulé.

2. *Arch.* Of mouldings: (see NEBULE²).

1842 GWILT *Archit.* 1008 *Nebuly Moulding*, an ornament in Norman architecture, whose edge forms an undulating or wavy line. **1861** NEALE *Notes Dalmatia* vi. 99 A nebuly moulding running round the cornice.

nebu'liferous, *a.* *rare*⁻⁰. [f. NEBULA + -IFEROUS.] 'Having nebulous spots, as the *Vorticella nebulifera*' (Mayne 1856).

'nebulist. *rare.* [f. NEBULA + -IST.]

1. An artist whose work is marked by indistinctness of outline.

1836 *New Monthly Mag.* XLVII. 99 We would rather not have been told..that our celebrated landscape-painter is too much a nebulist.

2. One who maintains the nebular hypothesis.

1890 *Cent. Dict.* cites PAGE.

ne'bulium. [f. NEBUL-A + -IUM: orig. called *nebulum*.] An element distinguished by a green line it was held to produce in the spectrum of gaseous nebulæ, but not otherwise evidenced.

It is now considered that no such element exists, the lines formerly attributed to it having been identified with those produced by known elements.

1898 SIR W. CROOKES *Addr. Brit. Assoc.* 19 Still awaiting discovery by the fortunate spectroscopist are the unknown celestial elements Aurorium..and Nebulum. **1899** *Atlantic Monthly* Apr. 469 It is an impressive fact that hydrogen and nebulium are the only elements recognized in the nebulae. **1937** J. W. T. SPINKS tr. *Herzberg's Atomic Spectra & Atomic Struct.* iv. 157 Bowen..first showed that the nebulium lines, which had been observed in the spectra of many cosmic nebulae but were long a complete mystery, were to be explained as forbidden transitions between the deep terms of O^+ (^4S, ^2D, ^2P), O^{++} (^3P, ^1D, ^1S), and N^+ (^3P, ^1D, ^1S). **1940** *Astrophysical Jrnl.* XCII. 408 The free electrons, liberated from hydrogen by photoionization, may excite the 'nebulium' lines by inelastic impact. **1965** PHILLIPS & WILLIAMS *Inorg. Chem.* I. ii. 43 Transitions between these states in atomic spectra are also 'forbidden', but they have been observed for the isoelectronic N^+ and O^{2+} ions in the spectra of cosmic nebulae (so called nebulium lines). **1973** L. OSTER *Mod. Astron.* xiii. 205 For a long time, in fact until 1928, the origin of some of the strongest lines was unclear, and, in desperation, they were ascribed by some astronomers to a hypothetical element called nebulium.

nebulization (nɛbjʊlaɪ'zeɪʃən). *Med.* [f. NEBULIZ(E *v.* + -ATION.] **a.** The conversion of a liquid into a mist or spray. **b.** Medical treatment using a nebulizer.

1906 *Index-Catal. Library Surg.-General's Office, U.S. Army* 2nd Ser. XI. 366/1 (*heading*) Nebulizers and nebulization. **1949** *Dis. Chest* XVI. 410 The technique designed..by us is based on nebulization of the surface anesthetic solution. **1968** *Jrnl. Asthma Res.* V. 253 Each child was subjected to 15 minutes of nebulization, three times daily. **1969** *Daily Tel.* 25 June 15/5 You can have different products incorporated into your nebulisation shower: products to help ease pregnancy scarring, correct dry or greasy skin, [etc.].

nebulize ('nɛbjʊlaɪz), *v.* *rare.* [f. NEBULA.]

1. *trans.* To reduce to a mist or spray. Hence **'nebulized** *ppl. a.*, **'nebulizing** *vbl. sb.*

1872 COHEN *Dis. Throat* 24 The nebulized spray of a solution of tannin. **1915** WRIGHT & SMITH *Text-bk. Dis. Nose & Throat* i. 58 There are a number of mechanical devices for nebulizing medicated solutions, which have a certain amount of value in tracheal and bronchial affectations. **1944** *Proc. Soc. Exper. Biol. & Med.* LVII. 257/1 The nebulizing unit..consists of a container and a metal atomizer. **1949** *Dis. Chest* XVI. 412 Oxygen or air may be used to nebulize the solution. **1958** *Ann. Allergy* XVI. 628 The liquid is disrupted by the air jet in the nebulizing area and forms an aerosol. *Ibid.* 631 The DeVilbiss No. 40 model nebulizes about twice as much water as the Vaponefrin model. **1973** *Amer. Rev. Respiratory Dis.* CVIII. 511/2 The small deposition of ^{99m}Tc in the lungs in these normal subjects even during slow, deep breathing raises serious doubts that effects claimed for aerosol therapy are related to nebulized fluid.

2. *intr.* To become nebulous or indefinite. *rare.*

1891 *Inquirer* 26 Sept. 624/2 We know the faculty of the human mind to..trim and nebulize in its statements concerning religious belief.

nebulizer ('nɛbjʊlaɪzə(r)). [f. prec. + -ER¹.] An instrument for converting a liquid into a fine spray, esp. for medical purposes.

1874 ROOSA *Dis. Ear* 301 One of the nebulizers that are now so largely employed in the treatment of the throat. **1898** *Allbutt's Syst. Med.* V. 82 The finest sub-division is obtained—as in Oppenheimer's 'nebuliser'—by combining strong pressure with smallness of orifice.

,nebulo-cha'otic, *a.* *nonce-wd.* [f. NEBULA.] Hazily confused.

1881 G. MACDONALD *Mary Marston* I. x. 178 The altogether nebulochaotic condition of her mind.

†**'nebulon.** *Obs.* *rare*⁻¹. [a. obs. F. *nebulon* (Cotgr.), or ad. L. *nebulōn-*, *nebulo*.] A worthless fellow.

1578 SIDNEY *May Lady* in *Arcadia* (1605) 574 Why, you brute Nebulons,..cannot [you] yet tell how to edefie an argument?

nebulose (nɛbjʊ'ləʊs), *a.* [ad. L. *nebulōs-us*, f. *nebula*: see NEBULA and -OSE.]

1. †**a.** Resembling a cloud or mist; inclined to be foggy or misty. *Obs. rare.*

c **1420** *Pallad. on Husb.* IX. 114 Yf smoke ascende Al faaty, weet, and cloudy nebulose. *Ibid.* XII. 21 Sad lond wol the bene Indwelle, and hatith nebulose and lene.

b. *fig.* Cloudy, misty, indistinct.

1799 in *Spirit Pub. Jrnls.* II. 322 The nebulose or obumbratory style. **1855** *Fraser's Mag.* LI. 548 Illustrious professor of nebulose hypotheses and nonsense.

c. Clouded; cloud-like in appearance.

1826 KIRBY & SP. *Entomol.* IV. xlvi. 288 *Nebulose*, painted with colour irregularly darker and lighter, so as to exhibit some resemblance of clouds. **1849–52** *Todd's Cycl. Anat.* IV. 1221/2 There then appears on the surface of the vitellus a nebulose spot of pale yellow.

†**2.** (See quot. and cf. *nebulé*.) *Obs. rare*$^{-0}$.

1704 J. HARRIS *Lex. Techn.* I, *Nebulose*, a Term in Heraldry, when the out-line of any Bordure, Ordinary, &c. is..something of the Figure of Clouds.

3. Of the nature of nebulæ. *rare*$^{-1}$.

1714 DERHAM *Astro-Theol.* (1769) 7 The last thing I shall mention is the Nebulose, which are those glaring whitish appearances, seen with our telescopes.

nebulosity (nɛbjʊˈlɒsɪtɪ). [a. F. *nébulosité* or ad. late L. *nebulōsitāt-em*; see next and -ITY.]

1. Nebulous or indistinctly luminous appearance; a faintly luminous patch or mass.

1761 *Phil. Trans.* LII. 398 Mr. Hirst..affirms, that such nebulosity was seen by them. **1789** HERSCHEL *ibid.* LXXIX. 221 It is among these that we find the largest assemblages of stars, and most diffusive nebulosities. **1802** *Ibid.* XCII. 499 The great milky nebulosity of Orion. **1837** GORING & PRITCHARD *Microgr.* 105 A slight fog of the diffused kind.., or a penumbra or nebulosity encircling numerous points. **1878** NEWCOMB *Pop. Astron.* III. v. 380 A very faint nebulosity, about 3′ in diameter.

b. Nebulous state or form; matter in a nebulous condition.

1833 HERSCHEL *Astron.* xii. 407 A phænomenon which seems to indicate the existence of some slight degree of nebulosity about the sun itself. **1865** BRISTOW tr. *Figuier's World bef. Deluge* xix. (1869) 464 We have seen the globe floating in space in a state of gaseous nebulosity. **1898** *Pop. Sci. Monthly* LIII. 410 The molecules of which the primitive nebulosity of the universe was composed.

fig. **1881** T. HARDY *Laodicean* III. i, He had been a mere nebulosity whom she had never distinctly outlined.

2. Cloudiness; indistinctness.

1809 JEBB *Corr. w. Knox* (1834) I. 522 Eternal misconceptions, misrepresentations, nebulosities and logomachies. **1848** *Jrnl. R. Agric. Soc.* IX. II. 326 Delicate appreciation of degrees of nebulosity. **1876** *Trans. Vict. Inst.* 30 That dim nebulosity in which they are too often enveloped.

nebulous (ˈnɛbjʊləs), *a.* Also 4 -us. [ad. L. *nebulōs-us*, f. *nebula*: see NEBULA and -OUS, and cf. F. *nébuleux* (1509).]

1. Cloudy, foggy, misty, dank. *rare.*

c **1386** *Almanack* (1812) 8 A thyk tyme, þat es for to say nebulus and cloudy. **1597** LOWE *Chirurg.* (1634) 40 Evill Ayre..is that which is..nebulous and commeth from stinking breaths. **1656** BLOUNT *Glossogr.*, *Nebulosous* [**1658** Phillips, *Nebulous*], cloudy, misty, foggy; full of clouds.

2. *Astron.* **a.** ***nebulous star***, a small cluster of indistinct stars, or a star which is surrounded by a luminous haze.

1679 MOXON *Math. Dict.* 95 Nebulous..Stars, are certain Fixed Stars of a dull, pale, and obscurish Light. **1682** SIR T. BROWNE *Chr. Mor.* III. §24 Like lacteous or nebulous stars, little taken notice of, or dim in their generations. **1727–38** CHAMBERS *Cycl.* s.v. *Stars*, Those not reduced to classes or magnitudes are called nebulous stars. **1775** *Chron.* in *Ann. Reg.* 116/2 A meteor, representing a nebulous star, appeared just above the moon. **1801** *Encycl. Brit.* Suppl. II. 297/1 Through a moderate telescope, these nebulous stars plainly appear to be congeries or clusters of several little stars. **1854** BREWSTER *More Worlds* xi. 173 Nebulous stars, or luminous points, surrounded with an immense visible atmosphere. **1892** A. TAYLOR in *Photogr. Ann.* II. 116 Mr. Roberts in a photograph of this region..has failed to find any nebulosity or nebulous star.

b. Of the nature of a nebula or nebulæ; consisting of, abounding in, nebulæ.

1784 HERSCHEL in *Phil. Trans.* LXXIV. 438 The interior construction of the heavens, and its various nebulous and sidereal strata. **1826** GOOD *Bk. Nat.* (1834) I. 101 The nebulosity will be broken into different nebulæ, or smaller nebulous clouds. **1853** KANE *Grinnell Exp.* xxxv. (1856) 318 A floating, waving band of nebulous illumination. **1876** P. E. CHASE in *Philos. Mag.* Ser. v. I. 316 The position of Saturn.., its low density, and its nebulous rings.

Comb. **1869** DUNKIN *Midn. Sky* 136 A small nebulous-looking object in the Crab's body.

c. = NEBULAR *a.* 1. *rare*$^{-1}$.

1860 LD. LYTTON *Lucile* II. ii. §1. 134 Some mention Of the nebulous theory demands your attention; And so on.

3. Cloud-like; resembling a cloud or clouds.

1805 WEAVER tr. *Werner's Fossils* 71 Nebulous—Large and irregular spots, forming with the ground colour mixed colours, resembling clouds. **1838** *Economy of Vegetation* 155 Some lichens..display concentric circles, and others exhibit nebulous images. **1857** LONGF. *Sandalphon* viii, Sandalphon the angel, expanding His pinions in nebulous bars.

b. *fig.* Hazy, vague, indistinct, formless.

1831 CARLYLE *Sart. Res.* II. ix, Nebulous disquisitions on Religion. **1860** MOTLEY *Netherl.* (1868) I. 24 The new-risen republic remained for a season nebulous. **1872** BLACK *Adv. Phaeton* xi. 150 A sort of nebulous faith in the Crown and Constitution.

4. Clouded in colour; turbid.

1820 W. SCORESBY *Acc. Arctic Reg.* I. 177 A little of this snow, dissolved in a wine glass, appeared perfectly nebulous. **1869** G. LAWSON *Dis. Eye* (1874) 37 There are two forms of superficial ulcers of the cornea: the nebulous and the transparent ulcer.

Hence ˈ**nebulously** *adv.*

1882 BERESF. HOPE *Brandreths* III. xlii. 147 The ladies were nebulously suspecting a coming match.

ˈ**nebulousness.** [-NESS.] The state of being nebulous; cloudiness, mistiness. Also *fig.*

1653 GAUDEN *Hierasp.* 525 Many spots in the brightest Moones, and much nebulousnesse in the fairest Stars. **1727** in BAILEY, vol. II. **1878** T. HARDY *Ret. Native* IV. iii, Her outdoor attire..always had a sort of nebulousness about it, devoid of harsh edges anywhere.

nebuly: see NEBULÉ.

†**nebus**, *v. Obs. rare*$^{-1}$. (See quot.)

1712 ARBUTHNOT *J. Bull* IV. Pref., Let not Posterity a thousand years hence look for truth in the voluminous annals of Pedants... If they do, let me tell them they will be nebused! [*Note in ed.* 1727. Another cant word, signifying deceiv'd.]

nebylle, obs. form of NIBBLE.

nec, obs. form of NECK.

†**neˈcation.** *Obs. rare*$^{-0}$. [ad. L. **necātiōnem*, f. *necāre* to kill.] 'A killing' (Bailey 1721).

necclygency, obs. form of NEGLIGENCY.

nece, var. NESE, nose; obs. form of NIECE.

†**neˈcess**, *sb. Obs. rare*$^{-1}$. [a. L. *necesse*: cf. next.] Necessity.

a **1460** *Play Sacram.* 772 Thow woldyst preve thy powr me to oppresse, but now I consydre thy necesse.

†**neˈcess**, *a. Obs. rare.* Also 5 **nesesse**. [a. L. *necesse* neut. adj.] Necessary.

1456 SIR G. HAYE *Law Arms* (S.T.S.) 89 Quhat thingis may ger move bataill necesse. *c* **1460** *Macro Plays* II. 442 Be in þe worlde! vse thyngis nesesse!

†**neˈcess**, *v. Obs. rare*$^{-1}$. [ad. late L. *necessāre* to render necessary, f. *necesse*: see prec.] *trans.* To compel.

c **1374** CHAUCER *Boeth.* III. met. ix. (1868) 87 Ne forein causes necesseden þe neuer to compoune werke of floterynge mater.

†**necessaire**, *a. Obs. rare.* [a. F. *nécessaire* (13th c.), ad. L. *necessārius*.] Necessary.

c **1374** CHAUCER *Troylus* IV. 1021 Al seme it not ther-by That prescience put falling necessaire To thing to come. **1390** GOWER *Conf.* III. 135 Which is a thing full necessaire To contrepeise the balance.

‖**nécessaire** (nesesɛr), *sb.* Also **necessaire**. [Fr. (see NECESSAIRE *a.*).] A small case, sometimes ornamental, for small articles, as pencils, scissors, tweezers, articles of cosmetics, etc.

1800 E. HERVEY *Mourtray Family* III. ix. 177 A chance of his travelling *necessaire*, and all the apparatus of his toilet, being burned. **1854** THACKERAY *Newcomes* I. xxviii. 266 Gousset empty, tiroirs empty, nécessaire parted for Strasbourg! **1876** GEO. ELIOT *Dan. Der.* I. I. ii. 29 Gwendolen..thrust necklace, cambric..and all into her *nécessaire*. **1960** *Times* 16 Feb. 20/7 An old English gold and agate necessaire. **1967** V. NABOKOV *Speak, Memory* (rev. ed.) xiii. 253 The handful of jewels which Natasha, a farsighted old chambermaid,..had swept off a dresser into a *nécessaire*. **1973** *Times* 11 Dec. 18/5 A George III gold and enamel *nécessaire* attributed to James Cox.

necessar (ˈnɛsɛsər), *a.* and *sb. Sc.* Forms: 5–6 **necessare**, 5–6 **necessair**, (6 **-e**), 6 **necesser**, **necesare**, **neccessare**, 6–7, 9 **necessar**. [ad. L. *necessār-ius* NECESSARY.] **A.** *adj.* Necessary.

c **1375** *Sc. Leg. Saints* xxvii. (*Machor*) 691 Bukis, þat ware necessare to hyme to prech godis lare. **1456** SIR G. HAYE *Law Arms* (S.T.S.) 67 It is necessair that ane be as prince, and all the lave be obeysant till it. **1533** GAU *Richt Vay* 32 Ye licht of grace is necesser to scheyne in the..blyndnes of natur. **1561** WINȜET *First Tract.* Wks. (S.T.S.) I. 5 The trew Word of God necessar to al manis saluation. **1633** W. STRUTHER *True Happiness* 23 The necessity is great, because it is about this greatest necessar one thing. **1656** in *Boyd's Zion's Flowers* (1855) App. 35/1 Necessar materialls..to the buildings. *c* **1714** in Maidment *Ballads* (1844) 69 All things are provided that necessar be. **1821** LIDDLE *Poems* 50 (E.D.D.), Adversity is necessar If it's not too severe. **1882** G. MACDONALD *Castle Warlock* xxix, Some said he had sellt himself, but I'm thinkin' it was na necessar'.

B. *sb.* in *pl.* Necessaries. Now *rare* or *Obs.*

1596 DALRYMPLE tr. *Leslie's Hist. Scot.* X. 419 A gret sum of siluer, als vtheris necesares to sustein the weiris. **1632** LITHGOW *Trav.* VI. 269 Each furnisher..giueth warning to his friends, to come receiue their necessars. **1699** R. SINCLAIR in *Leisure Hour* (1883) 205/1 Item for keeping of the house in fresh meat and other necessars. **1725** in Peterkin *Notes* (1822) 221 The carpenter having neglected to take some necessars with him for the boat's reparation.

necessarian (nɛsɪˈsɛərɪən), *sb.* and *a.* [f. NECESSAR-Y + -IAN; cf. F. *nécessarien* sb.] A believer in necessity; a necessitarian.

1777 PRIESTLEY *Doctr. Philos. Necessity* 111, I cannot, as a necessarian, hate any man. **1790** CATH. GRAHAM *Lett. Educ.* 464 The free-willers agree with the necessarians in the opinion, that the mind perceives the difference of things. **1822** HAZLITT *Table-t.* Ser. II. iv. (1869) 87 The precise knowledge of antecedents and consequents makes men practical as well as philosophical Necessarians. **1872** LITTLEDALE in *Contemp. Rev.* XX. 445 Here is the dilemma for Necessarians who plead God's changelessness.

b. *attrib.* or as *adj.*

1795 W. TAYLOR in *Monthly Rev.* XVIII. 127 Being fostered by the necessarian philosophy, it is likely to become a prevailing passion. **1831** BLAKEY *Free-will* Pref. 10 One of those epitomes of the necessarian hypothesis. **1878** MORLEY *Diderot* II. 199 The establishment in men's minds of a Necessarian theory.

neceˈssarianism. [f. prec. + -ISM.] = NECESSITARIANISM.

1840 HARE *Vict. Faith* 45 Such a doctrine..implies the barest rankest necessarianism. **1886** A. WEIR *Hist. Basis Mod. Europe* (1889) 498 His materialism and necessarianism ..resulted from his observations on man's 'frame'.

necessarily (ˈnɛsɪsərɪlɪ, nɛsɪˈsɛrɪlɪ), *adv.* [-LY^{2}.]

1. (Senses now merged in 3.)

†**a.** By force of necessity; unavoidably. *Obs.*

1488–9 *Act 4 Hen. VII*, c. 1 By which Commyssions.. meny greate hurtes and inconvenyences..were necessarily redressed. *a* **1540** BARNES *Wks.* (1573) 315/1 These things no man is able to make indifferent, but they must neede bee necessarily done. **1607** *Statutes* in *Hist. Wakefield Gram. Sch.* (1892) 72 Their tymes of being abrode necessarilie may be drawne to other times of the yeare. **1663** H. COGAN tr. *Pinto's Trav.* lx. 246 He was necessarily to be assistant at this funeral pomp. **1710** PRIDEAUX *Orig. Tithes* iii. 143 The Tithes which were necessarily due.

†**b.** As a necessary aid or concomitant; indispensably. *Obs.*

1526 *Pilgr. Perf.* (W. de W. 1531) 152 Of all vertues mercy is moost necessaryly requyred to this myserable worlde. **1577** M. HANMER *Anc. Eccl. Hist.* 66 All thinges necessarily required for the execution. **1627** in Rushw. *Hist. Coll.* (1659) I. 476 There never was a time in which this duty was more necessarily required. **1748** HARTLEY *Observ. Man* II. ii. §27. 140 Animal Diet..requires Art and Preparation necessarily.

†**c.** By a necessary connexion. *Obs. rare.*

1551 T. WILSON *Logike* (1580) 34 Neither is the consequent good, when woordes that agree not necessarily are ioyned together. **1655** T. BROWN in Hartlib *Ref. Commw. Bees* 5 Of such a fashion, as doth naturally and necessarily agree with..this design.

†**d.** In accordance with a necessary law or operative principle. *Obs.*

1664 H. MORE *Myst. Iniq.* 215 By necessarily determining what is more naturally left loose to play of itself. **1705** STANHOPE *Paraphr.* I. 43 Moral persuasions cannot act mechanically and necessarily. **1748** HARTLEY *Observ. Man* I. iv. Concl. 504 The Moral Sense is generated necessarily and mechanically.

2. As a necessary result or consequence.

1509 FISHER *Funeral Serm. C'tess Richmond* Wks. (1876) 307 It must necessaryly folowe, that..her soule is in that ioyous lyfe. **1599** SHAKS. *Much Ado* II. iii. 201 If hee doe feare God, a must necessarilie keepe peace. **1655** STANLEY *Hist. Philos.* II. (1701) 63/2 It follows necessarily, that they be made of things that are. **1710** STEELE *Tatler* No. 201 ¶7 If the Actor is well possessed of the Nature of his Part, a proper Action will necessarily follow. *a* **1790** ADAM SMITH *W.N.* I. v. (1869) I. 31 The mere possession of that fortune does not necessarily convey to him either [civil or military power]. **1825** MᶜCULLOCH *Pol. Econ.* I. 29 These opinions necessarily led to the celebrated doctrine of the Balance of Trade. **1862** SPENCER *First Princ.* I. ii. §11 (1875) 35 If the non-existence of space is absolutely inconceivable, then, necessarily, its creation is absolutely inconceivable.

3. Of necessity; inevitably.

1562 *Act 5 Eliz.* c. 4 §15 The Plenty or Scarcity of the Time and other Circumstances necessarily to be considered. **1612** T. TAYLOR *Comm. Titus* i. 6 He expoundeth the same precept necessarily to be meant litterally. **1682** NORRIS *Hierocles* 9 All which is necessarily verified in an intelligent and purifi'd nature. *c* **1775** BURKE *Addr. Colonists N. Amer.* Wks. IX. 204 A very large proportion of the wealth and power of every Empire must necessarily be thrown upon the presiding State. **1840** DICKENS *Barn. Rudge* ii, In handing up the lantern, the man necessarily cast its rays full on the speaker's face. **1896** *Law Times* C. 552/1 In quality of probative force direct evidence necessarily has an inherent advantage.

necessariness (ˈnɛsɪsərɪnɪs). Now *rare.* [f. as prec. + -NESS.] The fact or quality of being necessary; indispensability, necessity.

1551 T. WILSON *Logike* (1580) 38 b, The necessarinesse of this place. **1584** LODGE *Alarum* (Shaks. Soc.) 68 They conclude..that their necessarinesse in this world makes them unnecessary for God. **1622** MALYNES *Anc. Law-Merch.* 468 Which sheweth the necessarinesse of the Office of Prior and Consulls. **1679** PEPYS *Let. to Dk. York* 6 May, Some opinion they have of the necessaryness of my service to them. **1818** BENTHAM *Ch. Eng.* Pref. 24 Their necessariness to salvation. **1829** —— *Justice & Cod. Petit.*, *Abr. Petit. Justice* 6 The supposed necessariness..of these same instruments.

†**necessarious**, *a. Obs. rare.* [f. as NECESSARY + -OUS.] Necessary.

c **1386** CHAUCER *Melib.* ¶287 In so gret..a neede it hadde be necessarious mo counseilours and more deliberacioun to performe youre emprise. **14..** *Gesta Rom.* xxxvi. 140 (Cambr. MS.), Also that thou norissh my grehoundys, as it is necessarious for hem.

ˈ**necessarly**, *adv. Sc.* ? *Obs.* [f. NECESSAR *a.* + -LY^{2}.] Necessarily.

1566 *Reg. Privy Council Scot.* I. 446 Quhilk..necessarlie mon be careit and transportit. **1609** SKENE *Reg. Maj.* To Rdr. A iv b, These reasons..proves necessarlie, that all the statuts..were authentick. **1639** DRUMM. OF HAWTH. *Hist. Jas. IV* Wks. (1711) 66 What comes from Heaven he should bear necessarly.

necessary (ˈnɛsɪsərɪ), *a.* and *sb.* Forms: 4–7 **necessarie** (5 **-ari**, 6 **-arye**, **nessarre**, **nessesary**, 7 **nesesary**), 4– **necessary**. [ad. L. *necessārius*, f. *necesse* needful: see -ARY. Cf. It. *necessario*, Sp. *necesario*, F. *nécessaire* (13th c.). See also NECESSAIRE *a.*, NECESSAR *a.* In early use the pl. form of the adj. sometimes occurs.]

A. *adj.*

I. 1. a. Indispensable, requisite, essential, needful; that cannot be done without. Also const. *to* or *for* (a person or thing) and with *inf.* Phr. ***necessary evil.***

In 16th and early 17th c. use freq. approaching the sense of 'useful' without being absolutely indispensable.

1382 WYCLIF *Eccl.* xxxix. 31 The bygynnyng of necessarie thing to the lif of men. **1387-8** T. USK *Test. Love* III. iii. (Skeat) l. 42 Bicause this mater is good and necessary to declare. *a* **1400-50** *Alexander* 125 þen takis to him tresour.. And oþire necessari notis as nedis to his craftis. **1462** *Paston Lett.* II. 16 Remembryng divers maters..necessary for the wele of his sowle. **1523** FITZHERB. *Husb.* §1 Than is the ploughe the most necessaryest instrumente that an husbande can occupy. **1547** W. BALDWIN *Treat. Morall Phylosophie* III. xv. sig. O5ᵛ A woman is a necessary euyll. **1583** GOLDING *Calvin on Deut.* cxxvi. 775 Were there no greater and necessarier things to speak of than young birdes? **1617** MORYSON *Itin.* I. 174, I prepared all things necessary for my journey. *c* **1645** HOWELL *Lett.* (1650) I. 329 They advance trade wheresoever they come,..and so are permitted as necessary evils. **1671** MILTON *Samson* 90 Since light so necessary is to life. **1704** SWIFT *T. Tub* ii, Obedience was absolutely necessary, and yet Shoulder-Knots appeared extremely requisite. **1750** JOHNSON *Rambler* No. 24 ¶2 What more can be necessary to the regulation of life..? **1765** JOHNSON in Shakes. *Plays* I. Pref. p. lxix, Notes are often necessary, but they are necessary evils. **1776** T. PAINE *Common Sense* 1 Society in every state is a blessing, but Government even in its best state is but a necessary evil; in its worst state an intolerable one. **1815** C'TESS GRANVILLE *Let.* 18 July (1894) I. 54 The humiliation of now having him is great, but he is reasonable about it and thinks it a necessary evil. **1832** HT. MARTINEAU *Life in Wilds* iv. 47 Food is the most necessary of all things. **1863** *Country Gentleman* 16 Apr. 254/3 The manuring of the vines is regarded as 'a necessary evil'. **1875** JOWETT *Plato* (ed. 2) IV. 12 Change and alternation are necessary for the mind as well as for the body. **1927** E. O'NEILL *Marco Millions* I. iv. 51 Don't waste pity. Her kind are necessary evils.

b. ***it is necessary that*** or with *inf.* Also *ellipt.* with omission of the complement.

c **1386** CHAUCER *Manciple's Prol.* 95 It is necessarie..good drink we with us carie. *c* **1460** FORTESCUE *Abs. & Lim. Mon.* iv. (1885) 118 Trewly it is veray necessarie that thay be alwey grete. *a* **1533** LD. BERNERS *Huon* lxxxiv. 264 It is not necessarye to requyre me of this. **1582** N. LICHEFIELD tr. *Castanheda's Conq. E. Ind.* I. lxv. 133 We fought in open fielde, where it was necessarie there should be many. **1649** BP. REYNOLDS *Hosea* vi. 91 It is necessarie for us to draw nigh unto God. *a* **1699** LADY HALKETT *Autobiog.* (Camden) 2 Wch. I have by mee to produce if itt were nesesary. **1747** WESLEY *Prim. Physick* (1762) p. xvii, It was necessary to have a variety. **1776** *Trial of Nundocomar* 27/2 Is it necessary that such a writing as this be confirmed by witness? **1841** LANE *Arab. Nts.* I. 86 When he had continued this exercise as long as was necessary.

†**c.** Commodious, convenient. *Obs. rare.*

1540-1 ELYOT *Image Gov.* 40 b, He caused..the houses to be not onely clensed, but also made more ornate and necessary. **1547-8** in E. Green *Somerset Chantries* (1888) 25 The same Scolehowse..no doubte is [the] most bewtyfull and most necessarie place of all that shire.

d. ***necessary condition*** = CONDITION *sb.* 4; cf. *sufficient condition.*

1817 COLERIDGE *Biog. Lit.* I. ix. 136, I began to ask myself; is a system of philosophy..possible? If possible, what are its necessary conditions? **1859** MILL *On Liberty* i. 9 The consent of the community..was made a necessary condition to some of the more important acts of the governing power. **1949** A. PAP *Elem. Analytic Philos.* x. 212 If a sufficient condition is complex—as it almost invariably is—then it may consist in a conjunction of necessary conditions. **1965** E. J. LEMMON *Beginning Logic* i. 28 Whenever it is the case that only if *P* then *Q*, *P* is a necessary condition for *Q*.

2. Of persons, esp. servants: Rendering (certain) necessary or useful services; in later use only ***necessary woman*** (now *arch.*).

1425 *Rolls of Parlt.* IV. 306/1 Clerks necessaries beyng in ye service of ye Prince. **1501** in *Letters Rich. III. & Hen. VII* (Rolls) I. App. A. VII, That no persone.., except he be a necessary officier, ride befor out of the company of the said princesse. **1599** NASHE *Lenten Stuffe* (1871) 60 Those that be his stewards, or necessariest men about him. **1607** SHAKS. *Cor.* II. i. 91 You are well vnderstood to bee a perfecter gyber for the Table, then a necessary Bencher in the Capitoll. **1679-88** *Secr. Serv. Money Chas. & Jas.* (Camden) 194 Late necessary woman to King Charles the Second. **1711** SWIFT *Jrnl. to Stella* 9 Nov., I want a necessary woman strangely; I am as helpless as an elephant. **1719** DE FOE *Crusoe* II. (Globe) 325 A most necessary handy Fellow as could be desir'd. **1762** *Chron.* in *Ann. Reg.* 98/2 Attendants on..the prince of Wales,..Wet nurse,..Dry nurse,..Necessary woman. **1899** *Tit-Bits* 1 Apr. 10/2 The most interesting member of all the [Queen's] kitchen staff is, perhaps, the 'necessary woman'.

3. ***necessary house***, a privy. So ***necessary place, stool, vault.*** Now *dial.*

1609 N. FIELD *Woman is Weathercock* IV. i, She shew'd me to a necessarie vault. **1611** —— *Amends for Ladies* II. iv, I met her in the necessary house. **1667** PRIMATT *City & C. Build.* 93 The digging of Vaults for the Necessary-house. **1697** *C'tess D Aunoy's Trav.* (1706) 232 There being no necessary places in their Houses. **1761** NICHOLLS in *Phil. Trans.* LII. 267 He appeared to have just come from his necessary-stool. **1789** BRAND *Newcastle* I. 176 In the wall of the western front have been several necessary-houses. **1828** BENTHAM *Mem. & Corr.* Wks. 1843 X. 582 Written pleadings are of no more use in a court than they would be in a necessary-house.

4. Of actions: Requiring or needful to be done.

1601 SHAKS. *Jul. C.* II. i. 178 This shall make Our purpose Necessary, and not Enuious. **1655** S. ASHE *Funeral Serm. Gataker* 49 Constant retirement..made the choice..a necessary act of prudence. **1716** JEFFERY *Pref. Sir T. Browne's Chr. Mor.*, Where an Oversight had made the Addition or Transposition of some words necessary. **1771** *Junius Lett.* lxiv. (1788) 336 In this sense the levy of ship-money..was not necessary. **1819** SHELLEY *Cenci* III. ii. 8 Still doubting if that deed Be just which is most necessary. **1858** GREENER *Gunnery* 156 We never saw it done,..but the Doctor decribes it as a necessary proceeding.

II. 5. a. Inevitably determined or fixed by predestination or the operation of natural laws; happening or existing by an inherent necessity.

c **1374** CHAUCER *Boeth.* v. pr. iv. (1868) 164 þilke þinges þat ne han non endes and bytidynges necessaryes. **1387-8** T. USK *Test. Love* III. iv. (Skeat) l. 40 God than..al these thinges, as they arne spontanye or necessarie, seeth. **1597** SHAKS. *2 Hen. IV*, III. i. 87 By the necessarie forme of this, King Richard might create a perfect guesse. **1621** BURTON *Anat. Mel.* II. ii. III. (1651) 258 Columbus did not find out America by chance:..it was contingent to him, but necessary to God. *a* **1676** HALE *Prim. Orig. Man.* (1677) 37 Otherwise we must of necessity make all successes in the World purely natural and necessary. **1720** WATERLAND *Eight Serm.* Pref. 20 We are not indeed to expect the Word *necessary existence* (a School Term, and none of the most proper). **1784** COWPER *Task* II. 192 Of causes, how they work By necessary laws their sure effects. **1826** WHATELY *Logic* 290 It is 'mathematically Necessary' that two sides of a triangle should be greater than the third. **1875** E. WHITE *Life in Christ* III. xxiii. (1878) 339 The identification..of the Necessary Being with the vanishing phantasmal shadow.

b. Of mental concepts or processes: Inevitably resulting from the constitution of things or of the mind itself.

1551 T. WILSON *Logike* (1580) 31 b, The other called infallible reasons, or rather necessarie argumentes, must by all reason be euermore true. **1628** T. SPENCER *Logick* 157 A necessary axiome, is when it is alwayes true, and cannot be false. **1656** STANLEY *Hist. Philos.* v. (1701) 180/1 Syllogism [is divided] into the Apodeictick, which concerneth necessary ratiocination [etc.]. **1705** STANHOPE *Paraphr.* II. 264 The Connexion..is not so close and necessary, as will warrant us from the Former certainly to infer the Latter. **1856** FERRIER *Inst. Metaph.* 20 A necessary truth or law of reason is a truth the opposite of which is inconceivable. **1878** J. COOK *Transcendentalism* i. 19 The ideas of space and time are called in philosophy necessary ideas.

c. Inevitably determined or produced by a previous condition of things.

1860 WESTCOTT *Introd. Study Gosp.* i. (ed. 5) 78 Active speculation followed as a necessary result. **1872** J. L. SANFORD *Estim. Eng. Kings* 336 He was quite as incapable..of perceiving its necessary issues.

6. Of actions: **a.** Determined by force of nature or circumstances.

1387-8 T. USK *Test. Love* III. iv. (Skeat) l. 27 If a man wol sinne, it is necessarye him to sinne. **1706** STANHOPE *Paraphr.* III. 529 The first Motions of Anger seem to be mechanical and necessary. **1855** ABP. THOMSON *Laws Th.* §122 The necessary action, where all the motives are on one side.

b. Enforced by another; compulsory.

1655 FULLER *Ch. Hist.* IX. vi. §51 In the following words, he taketh away all necessary Oaths (and leaveth none but voluntary). **1677** W. HUGHES *Man of Sin* II. vii. 115 Such Penance, were it voluntary, deserveth greatly to be admired at; but when 'tis necessary, and upon a Prince, is worthy of utmost detestation.

7. Of agents: **a.** Impelled by the natural force of circumstances upon the will; having no independent volition.

1690 LOCKE *Hum. Und.* II. xxi. §13 Agents that have no Thought, no Volition at all, are in every thing necessary Agents. **1774** WESLEY *Wks.* (1872) X. 462 They all agree, that man is not a free but a necessary agent. **1871** R. H. HUTTON *Ess.* (1877) I. 53 That a necessary being should give birth to a being with any amount, however limited, of moral freedom.

b. Compelled by practical necessity, or by some law or regulation.

1724 SWIFT *Drapier's Lett.* iii. Wks. 1751 VIII. 337 The Necessary Receivers [of Wood's halfpence] will be Losers of two Thirds in their Salaries or Pay. *a* **1768** ERSKINE *Inst. Sc. Law* (1773) 146 Servants are..either necessary or voluntary. Those may be called necessary whom the law obliges to work. **1880** MUIRHEAD *Gaius* II. 153 A necessary heir is a slave instituted with gift of freedom; so called because in every case, whether he will or not, he straightway on the testator's death becomes free and heir. **1893** FOWLER *Hist. C.C.C.* (O.H.S.) 42 The 'necessary regents' among the Masters, that is, those Masters of Arts who had not yet completed two years from the date of that degree.

III. †**8.** [After L. use.] Closely related or connected; intimate. *Obs. rare.*

1382 WYCLIF *Job* vi. 13 There is not helpe to me in me; also my necessarie men [L. *necessarii*] wenten awei fro me. **1655** STANLEY *Hist. Philos.* III. (1701) 81/2 Such as seek after Sordid Gain, and neglect their necessary Friends.

B. *sb.*

1. That which is indispensable; an essential or requisite: **a.** in *pl.*

a **1340** HAMPOLE *Psalter* xxxiii. 9 God..hight til his lufers þaire necessaris. **1377** LANGL. *P. Pl.* B. xx. 248 ȝe shal haue bred and clothes, And other necessaries i-nowe. **1415** *E.E. Wills* (1882) 23, I woll that..my wyfe haue all the necessaries. **1489** CAXTON *Faytes of A.* I. xii. 31 Shot and all other deffensable necessaryes. **1523** FITZHERB. *Husb.* §19 To cary wodde and other necessaryes. **1592** GREENE *Conny Catch* III. 28 He came vp to London to prouide himselfe of such necessaries as the Cuntry is not vsually stored withall. **1663** GERBIER *Counsel* 25 The materials, and all necessarys as they are brought in. **1711** STEELE *Spect.* No. 114 ¶5 The Care of Superfluities is a Vice no less extravagant, than the Neglect of Necessaries. **1788** PRIESTLEY *Lect. Hist.* III. xv. 124 The articles of their expence must be the necessaries of life. **1818** CRUISE *Digest* (ed. 2) VI. 345 If a man devises lands..to provide his children with necessaries. **1875** JOWETT *Plato* (ed. 2) III. 348 The money to buy the necessaries of their household.

b. in *sing.*

1516 *Galway Arch.* in *10th Rep. Hist. MSS. Comm.* App. V. 397 No man..shall not lende galley, botte, nor barque.., nor no furnitors or necessary to them appertayninge. **1663** GERBIER *Counsel* e 3 b, From the least that lives to the greatest Building is a main necessary. **1682** MRS. BEHN *City Heiress* II. i, That damn'd Necessary call'd Ready Money. **1724** SWIFT *Drapier's Lett.* i, Your Bread and Clothing, and every common Necessary of Life. **1771** MME. D'ARBLAY *Early Diary* (1889) I. 135 She denied herself every necessary. **1833** HT. MARTINEAU *Loom & Lugger* I. iv. 60 A foreign article, be it a necessary or a luxury. **1884** *American* VII. 339 The cost of this necessary [salt] since the duty was imposed upon it.

c. *attrib.*, as ***necessaries-man***, one who supplies necessaries to a vessel to enable her to continue the voyage; ***necessary money*** (see quot. 1867).

1866 *Law Rep., Adm. & Eccl.* I. 305 A necessaries-man has until institution of suit no claim upon a Vessel. **1867** SMYTH *Sailor's Word-bk.* 495 *Necessary Money*..formerly allowed to pursers for the coals, wood, turnery-ware, candles, and other necessaries provided by them.

†**2.** A near friend or kinsman. *Obs. rare*⁻¹.

1382 WYCLIF *2 Macc.* iv. 3 By summe necessaries (or niȝ freendis) of Symount man-sleayngus weren don.

†**3. a.** *pl.* Necessary expenses. *Obs. rare*⁻¹.

c **1449** PECOCK *Repr.* III. xi. 347 Her endewing so myche schranke..that it was aftirward ouer litle to supporte her necessaries.

†**b.** A necessary action. *Obs. rare.*

1596 HARINGTON *Metam. Ajax* D 5 b, There is no obscenitie..in words concerning our necessaries: but now for the place where these necessaries are to be done.

4. A necessary house. (See A. 3.)

1756 *Connoisseur* No. 120 ¶6 The Connoisseurs in Architecture, who build..necessaries according to Palladio. **1805** R. W. DICKSON *Pract. Agric.* I. 223 Strewing them in the bottoms of poultry and pigeon houses, dung heaps, and necessaries. **1844** H. STEPHENS *Bk. Farm* II. 412 A necessary might easily be constructed in connection with the liquid manure tank. **1877-** in various dial. glossaries.

5. With *the.* **a.** That which is needful; *spec.* the necessary funds or money.

1772 C. HUTTON *Bridges* 84 To make the convenient give place to the necessary when their interests are opposite. **1897** *Daily News* 6 Sept. 3/6 A fund..for the purpose of providing the 'necessary' in order to bring test cases.

b. That which is necessarily determined.

1809-10 COLERIDGE *Friend* (1865) 97 So far as..we possess the ideas of the necessary and the universal.

necesser, obs form of NECESSAR *a. Sc.*

†**ne'cessiated**, *ppl. a. Obs.* [erron. for *necessitated.*] **a.** Necessitous. **b.** Necessitated *to* do something.

1727 *Philip Quarll* 182 Necessiated and destitute. **1738** [G. SMITH] *Cur. Relat.* II. 410 They train'd up such persons as they knew were necessiated, yet of a daring and resolute Spirit. **1741** WARBURTON *Div. Legat.* II. 352 Necessiated to comply with the Passions of the People.

necessism ('nɛsɪsɪz(ə)m). [f. L. *necess-e* (see NECESSARY) + -ISM.] Necessitarianism.

1872 LITTLEDALE in *Contemp. Rev.* XX. 433 To Necessism there are some fatal objections. **1892** HOULT *Dial. Effic. Prayer* 79 But this is sheer necessism!

So '**necessist** *sb.* and *a.*, necessitarian.

1873 W. G. WARD *Ess. Philos. Theism* (1884) I. 149 He has here assumed very solid ground against necessists. *Ibid.* 177 He takes refuge in a..reproduction of that very necessist theory, which he so energetically repudiates.

†**ne'cessitable,** *a. Obs. rare*⁻¹. [See NECESSITATE *v.* and -ABLE.] Subject to necessity.

1673 O. WALKER *Educ.* 210 Those Instruments..not inanimate or necessitable, but spontaneous and free.

necessitarian (nɪˌsɛsɪ'tɛərɪən), *sb.* and *a.* [f. NECESSITY + *-arian*: cf. NECESSARIAN.] **a.** One who maintains that all human action is necessarily determined by the law of causation, as opposed to one who believes in the doctrine of free will.

1796 F. A. NITSCH *Gen. View Kant's Princ. concerning Man* 17 The Necessitarians..make a considerable party in the philosophic world. **1798** COWPER *Let. to Lady Hesketh* 8 Dec., He is a wretch indeed who is a necessitarian by experience. *a* **1806** HORSLEY (L.), These necessitarians maintain the certain influence of moral motives as the.. means whereby human actions..are brought into the continued chain of causes and effects. **1817** COLERIDGE *Biog. Lit.* (Bohn) 135 Hume, Priestley, and the French fatalists or necessitarians. **1855** MANSEL *Lett., Lect.*, etc. (1873) 145 The Necessitarian..concludes that I am a determined effect. **1874** W. WALLACE *Hegel's Logic* §52. 93 This experience in consciousness is at once met by all that the Necessitarian produces from contrary experience. **1912** KIPLING *Songs from Books* (1913) 154 (*title*) The necessitarian. **1952** C. P. BLACKER *Eugenics* 267 Unconscious prejudices can throw the Nature-Nurture controversy into different perspectives. Those who believe in predestination as an article of religion have a necessitarian bias which might incline them to over-estimate the role of heredity. **1956** E. H. HUTTEN *Lang. Mod. Physics* vi. 212 Ever since Hume the necessitarian interpretation [of determinism] has been rejected. **1966** M. R. D. FOOT *SOE in France* viii. 183 By one of those accidents that baffle the necessitarians, the only sentry awake at the moment of the drop was a newcomer who did not know where the alarm telephone was.

b. *attrib.* or as *adj.*

1810 BENTHAM *Packing* (1821) 185 According to this learned gentlman's necessitarian theory. **1825** COLERIDGE *Aids Refl.* (1848) I. 120 It was in strict consistency, therefore, that these writers supported the Necessitarian scheme. **1872** CALDERWOOD *Handbk. Mor. Philos.* (1878) 194 The necessitarian doctrine in denying freedom of will, does not altogether refuse a place to freedom.

necessi'tarianism. [f. prec. + -ISM.] The theory or doctrine that action is necessarily determined by antecedent causes.

1854 FROUDE *Short Stud., Spinoza* (1867) II. 43 The fallacy of all common arguments against necessitarianism lies in the assumption that it leaves no room for self-direction. **1885** R. H. HUTTON in *Contemp. Rev.* Mar. 376 Whose crude rationalistic necessitarianism.. reconciled him to a confident expectation of annihilation.

ne'cessitate, *pa. pple.* Now *rare.* [ad. med.L. *necessitāt-us*: see next.] Necessitated.

1640 *Remonstr. Pres. Troubles Est. Scot.* 24 Albeit we be not diffident of God's assistance whensoever we shall be necessitate to our own defence. *a* **1699** LADY HALKETT *Autobiog.* (Camden) 60 Beeing necesitate to leave London. **1710** W. BLACK in W. S. Perry *Hist. Coll. Amer. Col. Ch.* I. 186, I shall be necessitate to return for Great Britain. **1839-52** BAILEY *Festus* 397 They are necessitate in kind, As change in nature, or as shade to light.

necessitate (nɪ'sɛsɪteɪt), *v.* Also 7 *Sc.* **necessitat.** [f. ppl. stem of med.L. *necessitāre*, f. *necessitas* NECESSITY: cf. It. *necessitare*, Sp. *necesitar*, F. *nécessiter* (14th c.).]

1. *trans.* To bring (a person) under some necessity; to compel, oblige, or force. (Chiefly in *passive.*) **a.** Const. with *inf.* (Very common in 17th and 18th c.; now chiefly Amer. or Sc.)

1628 LE GRYS *Barclay's Argenis* 290 Not necessitated to holde out till the ruine of his party. **1646** H. LAWRENCE *Comm. Angells* 72 For hee may necessitate a man to feele temptation, but not to consent to it. **1697** DAMPIER *Voy.* I. 272 He had no mind to this Voyage; but was necessitated to engage in it or starve. **1736** BUTLER *Anal.* I. iii. 50 He has directed and necessitated us to preserve our Lives by Food. **1779** J. MOORE *View Soc. Fr.* (1789) I. xxxi. 271 Each boy is necessitated to decide and act for himself. **1834** MARRYAT *P. Simple* (1863) 305 If any one, by doing wrong, necessitated another to do wrong to circumvent him. **1854** EMERSON *Lett. & Soc. Aims* i. (1875) 22 All that is wondrous in Swedenborg is.. his extraordinary perception; that he was necessitated so to see.

b. Const. *to*, †*in*, †*into*. Now *rare* (freq. in 17th c.).

1628 EARLE *Microcosm., Poor Man* (Arb.) 101 No man is necessitated to more ill, yet no mans ill is lesse excus'd. **1631** LD. DORCHESTER in *Lismore Papers* (1888) Ser. II. III. 177 Ordinances might be raysed to necessitate the Irish in a more industrious course of life. *a* **1661** FULLER *Worthies* (1840) III. 2 Deer are daily diminished in England, since the gentry are necessitated into thrift. **1700** C. NESSE *Antid. Armin.* (1827) 103 Man.. in a.. state of creation.. had free-will either to good or evil, but was necessitated to neither. **1888** PATER in *Pall Mall G.* 25 Aug. 1/2 Necessitated by weak health to the regularity and the quiet of a monk.

c. Without const. Now *rare.*

1640 in Rushw. *Hist. Coll.* III. (1692) I. 97 Some Occasions of his own necessitating him. *a* **1666** SPURSTOWE *Spir. Chym.* (1668) 7 God is no way necessitated, or limited by the disposition.. of the matter. **1700** DRYDEN *Pal. & Arc.* II. 221 They.. by foresight necessitate the will. **1869** J. MARTINEAU *Ess.* II. 279 Causation [is] a power necessitating but not necessitated.

absol. **1654** OWEN *Saints' Perseverance* Wks. 1853 XI. 446 Where one necessitates and another only persuades, they cannot be said to cooperate.

2. To render necessary; *esp.* to demand, require, or involve as a necessary condition, accompaniment, or result.

1628 WITHER *Brit. Rememb.* II. 977 Or thinke, because our sinne he doth permit That therefore he necessitateth it. **1655** FULLER *Ch. Hist.* III. i. §11 As if.. the elevation of the one necessitated the depression of the other. **1700** C. NESSE *Antid. Armin.* (1827) 31 Such a decree.. without any obligation to necessitate the passing thereof. **1726** POPE *Odyss.* Postscr. V. 301 This renders his Poems more animated, but.. necessitates the frequent use of a lower style. **1843** LYTTON *Last Bar.* I. v, They necessitated a still more various knowledge. **1873** M. ARNOLD *Lit. & Dogma* Pref. 13 A string of other unverifiable assumptions.. such as the received theology necessitates.

†**3.** To reduce (a person) to want or necessity. Also *refl.* *Obs.*

1641 EARL MONM. tr. *Biondi's Civil Wars* IV. 67 They there made Forts and Trenches for their owne safties, and to necessitate the besieged. **1649** *Alcoran* 22 The father and mother shall not necessitate themselves for their children.

†**b.** In *pass.* Also const. *in*, *for*. *Obs.*

1647 LILLY *Chr. Astrol.* cxiv. 553 The Native shall attain a very great Estate,.. and be necessitated in nothing. **1684** *Contempl. St. Man* II. ii. (1699) 148 That he was not Poor who wanted, but he who was necessitated. **1700** TYRRELL *Hist. Eng.* II. 973 The King.. being necessitated for Money.

Hence **ne'cessitating** *vbl. sb.*

1649 C. WALKER *Hist. Independ.* II. 78 The necessitating of the Prince to cast himself into the Arms of forreign Popish Princes.

necessitated (nɪ'sɛsɪteɪtɪd), *ppl. a.* [-ED[1].]

1. Rendered necessary or unavoidable; necessarily fixed, determined, or appointed. Now *rare* (common in 17th c.).

a **1635** NAUNTON *Fragm. Reg.* (Arb.) 18 With very many pressing reasons, and as the state of her Kingdome then stood,.. necessitated Arguments. **1650** BOYLE *Wks.* (1772) I. p. xlvi, The necessitated fault of returning.. so short and so hasty an answer. **1676** *Doctrine of Devils* 83 To the (necessitated) injustice of the judicial proceedings. **1790** PENNANT *London* (1813) 282 The necessitated use of bad and unwholesome diet. **1893** [see NECESSITATING *ppl. a.*].

absol. **1898** MEREDITH *Odes Fr. Hist.* 22 To weld the nation in a name of dread, The Necessitated came.

†**2.** Of persons or their condition: Reduced to necessity or want. *Obs.*

1646 J. BENBRIGGE *Vsura Accom.* 9 These poore and necessitated borrowers. **1656** DUCHESS OF NEWCASTLE *True Relation* in *Life* (1886) 306 His loyalty is proved.. by his necessitated condition. **1706** J. SERGEANT *Acc. Chapter Bp. Chalcedon* (1853) 117 Relief for superannuated or other necessitated priests. **1781** R. KING *Mod. Lond. Spy* 79 [He] put a piece of gold into his necessitated friend's hand. **1857** A. & M. WARD *Husband in Utah* xvii. 194 Mrs. Farrow informed me of several sisters, who having inherited money from Eastern quarters, were immediately assailed by the necessitated priest.

Hence **ne'cessitatedly** *adv.*, in a necessitated manner; necessarily.

1864 WHEDON *Freedom of Will* I. ii. 37 Is he at liberty to be controlled by it necessitatedly, as the nine-pin is by its predecessor?

ne'cessitater. *rare*[−1]. [f. NECESSITATE *v.* + -ER[1].] One who necessitates.

1654 VILVAIN *Theorem Theol.* ii. 71 b, For the Necessitater is Commander.., but the Wil a servil instrument.

ne'cessitating, *ppl. a.* [f. as prec. + -ING[2].] That necessitates or compels.

1652 GAULE *Magastrom.* 2 Magesterial, fatale, necessitating Signes. **1704** M. HENRY *Nat. Schism* Wks. 1853 II. 254 They prophesied by a necessitating and irresistible impulse. **1739-56** DODDRIDGE *Fam. Expositor* clxx. (1799) II. 419 In consequence of his volition, without any necessitating agency. **1825** COLERIDGE *Aids Refl.* (1848) I. 248, I now proceed.. from the necessitating occasion of the Christian dispensation to Christianity itself. **1893** FAIRBAIRN *Chr. Mod. Theol.* I. viii. §4. 171 Necessitating action on the one side and necessitated on the other.

Hence **ne'cessitatingly** *adv.*

1654 OWEN *Saints' Perseverance* Wks. 1853 XI. 445 It impresseth the will.. persuadingly, not ravishingly or necessitatingly. *a* **1665** J. GOODWIN *Filled w. the Spirit* (1867) 256 To work, either compulsively or necessitatingly, upon the hearts and wills of men.

necessitation (nɪsɛsɪ'teɪʃən). [f. NECESSITATE *v.*: see -ATION.] The action of necessitating, of rendering necessary or subjecting to necessity; the result of this.

1652 GAULE *Magastrom.* 154 Now, what fatation or fatall necessitation to man, among all these? **1654** OWEN *Saints' Perseverance* Wks. 1853 XI. 194 God's working in them.. is very far from any compulsion or necessitation. *a* **1703** BURKITT *On N.T.* John xi. 44 Souls go not to heaven by necessitation, as the fire naturally and necessarily ascends upwards. **1807** W. TAYLOR in *Ann. Rev.* V. 182/2 In human conduct.. there is much of necessitation; that is of behaviour resulting from local transient circumstance. **1856** DOVE *Logic Chr. Faith* v. i. §2. 266 Conceding no compromise.. to a necessitation of nature. **1886** MOMERIE *Personality* 132 Our necessitation is.. compatible with a certain ability to control the forces of nature.

ne'cessitative, *a.* [f. NECESSITATE *v.* + -IVE.] Tending to necessitate.

1864 WHEDON *Freedom of Will* I. ii. 37 To subject the Will to a previous necessitative causation which is itself necessitated, is the annihilation of alternativity.

ne'cessitator. [f. NECESSITATE *v.* + -OR.] = NECESSITATER.

1904 HARDY *Dynasts* I. VI. iii. 118 O Great Necessitator, heed us now!.. Quicken the issue as Thou knowest how.

†**necessite,** *v.* *Obs.* [? ad. F. *nécessiter*: see NECESSITATE *v.*] *trans.* To necessitate.

1600 SIR W. CORNWALLIS *Ess.* viii. F 4 The earth stands necessited because it cannot go. **1630** B. JONSON *New Inn* IV. iii, Who were he now necessited to beg, Would ask an alms, like Conde Olivares. **1644** MAXWELL *Prerog. Chr. Kings* Ep. Ded. 12 The love and zeale which have necessited me to take recourse to Your Honours patrocine.

Hence **necessited** *ppl. a.*; **necessiting** *vbl. sb.*

a **1615** DONNE *Ess.* (1651) 178 That must either imply a necessiting therof from God, or else Pelagianisme. **1635** NABBES *Hannibal & Scipio* III. ii, All From a necessited and innate temperance Would be as you are.

†**ne'cessitied,** *ppl. a.* *Obs.* *rare*[−1]. [? error for prec.] Brought into necessity.

1601 SHAKS. *All's Well* v. iii. 85, I bad her if her fortunes euer stoode Necessitied to helpe, that by this token I would releeue her.

†**ne'cessitively,** *adv.* *Obs.* *rare*[−1]. [irreg. f. NECESSITE *v.*] By or of necessity.

1647 J. LILBURNE *Jonah's Cry* 10 Cost it what it will, I valew it not, being necessitively compelled.. to remove every stone that lyes in my way.

necessitous (nɪ'sɛsɪtəs), *a.* [ad. F. *nécessiteux*, or f. NECESSIT-Y + -OUS.]

1. Placed or living in a condition of necessity or poverty; having little or nothing to support oneself by; poor, needy; hard-up.

1611 COTGR., *Necessiteux*, necessitous, needie, poore, indigent. **1660** JER. TAYLOR *Duct. Dubit.* III. v. rule 3 §5 The necessitous father may put the duty actually upon the son. **1727** A. HAMILTON *New Acc. E. Ind.* I. iv. 39 He exhausts all his Revenues, and is always necessitous. **1780** BURKE *Œcon. Reform* Wks. III. 252 It holds out a shadow of present gain to a greedy and necessitous publick. **1826** DISRAELI *Viv. Grey* III. ii, The wants of their necessitous neighbours. **1877** MISS YONGE *Cameos* Ser. III. iii. 22 His niggardly or necessitous master had only advanced one thousand francs.

absol. **1693** *Humours Town* 95 What they can in any way screw out of the necessitous. **1742** CHESTERF. *Lett.* (1792) II. clxiii. 90 The ambitious hoped for kingdoms; the greedy and the necessitous for plunder. **1786** HORSLEY *Serm.* (1816) III. 103 It may be proper that the law should do something for the protection of the necessitous. **1866** FELTON *Anc. & Mod. Gr.* I. II. xi. 482 The very wealthy.. on the one hand, and, on the other, the necessitous.

†**b.** In need *of* a thing. *Obs.* *rare*[−1].

1650 GENTILIS *Consid.* 213 The German Legions cry up Vitellius for Emperour, they see him necessitous of money.

†**c.** Standing in need of aid. *Obs.* *rare.*

1711 M. HENRY *Forgiv. Sin* Wks. 1853 II. 318/2 Our natures are necessitous, and continually depending upon the divine providence. **1754** EDWARDS *Freed. Will* IV viii. (1762) 251 Being more sinful, and so more miserable and necessitous than others.

2. Characterized by necessity or poverty.

1639 MASSINGER *Unnat. Combat* Dedic., Divers whose Necessitous fortunes made it [poetry] their profession. **1654** *Nicholas Papers* (Camden) II. 75 He.. was in a most necessitus condicion. **1726** SHELVOCKE *Voy. round World* 417 By means of our necessitous misfortunes. **1791** COWPER *Iliad* XVI. 1021 That I may turn from them that evil hour Necessitous. **1885** *Act 48 & 49 Vict.* c. 40 *Preamble*, Relations of the said testator.. in necessitous circumstances.

†**b.** Caused by want or necessity. *Obs.* *rare*[−1].

1716 M. DAVIES *Athen. Brit.* II. 341 The incurring of necessitous Debts, by reason of the Penurious straighteness of his Fortune.

†**3.** Enforced, obligatory. *Obs.* *rare*[−1].

1631 MASSINGER *Emperor East* IV. iv, If sick with the excess of heat or cold, Caused by necessitous labour.

†**4.** Necessary, requisite. Also const. *for*. *Obs.* (In quot. 1742 attributed to an illiterate speaker.)

1742 FIELDING *J. Andrews* I. iii, [Mrs. Slipslop] proceeded: 'And why is Latin more necessitous for a footman than a gentleman?' **1793** J. WILLIAMS *Calm Exam.* 59 Drawing the line of necessitous propriety between what the people require, and their leaders would enforce.

Hence **ne'cessitously** *adv.*; **ne'cessitousness.**

1637 HEYWOOD *Lond. Spec.* Wks. 1874 IV. 307 One thing more is necessitously to be added. *a* **1668** DAVENANT *Fair Favorite* Wks. (1673) 96 Patience, which Before was but necessitously kind, is grown Most willingly devout. **1682** SIR T. BROWNE *Chr. Mor.* (1716) 6 Though sometimes necessitousness be dumb,.. yet true Charity is sagacious. **1776** PAINE *Com. Sense* 10 Tho' avarice will preserve a man from being necessitously poor.

necessitude (nɪ'sɛsɪtju:d). Now *rare.* [ad. L. *necessitūdo*, f. *necesse* necessary: see -TUDE.]

†**1.** A relation or connexion between persons. *Obs.*

1612 T. TAYLOR *Comm. Titus* i. 7 There are many necessitudes and occasions between the Minister and people. **1649** JER. TAYLOR *Gt. Exemp.* Ad Sect. ix. §1 Breaking.. the great relations and necessitudes of the world. **1653** —— *Serm. for Year* I. iii. 34 Between Parents and their children there is so great a necessitude.

†**b.** The connexion of one thing *with* another.

1637 MEDE *Wks.* (1672) 869 Fundamental Truths, measured by the necessitude they have with those Acts which are required to Salvation.

†**2.** A necessity *of* something. *Obs.* *rare*[−1].

1677 GALE *Crt. Gentiles* IV. 140 Radicated [evil] customes produce a necessitude of sin and servitude.

3. Need, necessity. *rare*[−1].

1839 J. ROGERS *Antipapopr.* xi. §3. 267 All their moral merit, they require for their own, their private, their individual necessitude.

necessitudi'narian, *a.* *rare*[−1]. [f. stem of L. *necessitūdo* (see prec.).] Necessitarian.

1834 *New Monthly Mag.* XLI. 358 [He] advocates necessitudinarian doctrines with the warmth of an enthusiast.

†**necessi'tudinary,** *a.* *Obs.* *rare*[−0]. [f. as prec. + -ARY[1].] 'Belonging to Friendship, Relation, &c.' (Bailey 1721).

necessity (nɪ'sɛsɪtɪ), *sb.* Forms: 4-6 **necessite,** (5 **nessesite**), 5-6 **necessitee, -yte(e,** (5 **-ytie**), 6-7 **necessitie, -itye,** 6- **necessity.** [a. F. *necessité* (12th c.), ad. L. *necessitāt-em*, f. *necesse* needful, necessary: see -ITY.]

I. †**1. a.** The fact of being inevitably fixed or determined. *Obs.*

c **1374** CHAUCER *Troylus* IV. 1012 Whether that the prescience of God is The certaine cause of the necessite Of things that to comen be. **1387-8** T. USK *Test. Love* III. iii. (Skeat) l. 16 Liberte of arbitrement, thorow whiche thou belevest many thinges to be without necessite. **1534** MORE *Treat. Passion* Wks. 1286/1 Not onely the necessitye of temporal deathe. **1568** GRAFTON *Chron.* II. 619 The necessitie of destinie cannot by any mans deuise, be eyther letted or interrupted.

†**b.** The constraining power *of* something. *Obs.*

1529 MORE *Dyaloge* IV. Wks. 261/2 Those that wrechedly lai al the weyght and blame of our sinne to the necessite and constraynt of goddes ordinaunce. **1533** BELLENDEN *Livy* I. xvii. (S.T.S.) I. 93 ȝit he could nocht brek be witt and engyne of man þe necessite and violence of fortoun.

2. a. Constraint or compulsion having its basis in the natural constitution of things; *esp.* such constraint conceived as a law prevailing throughout the material universe and within the sphere of human action.

1423 JAS. I *Kingis Q.* cxlvi, So that the diuersitee Off thaire wirking suld cause necessitee. **1590** SPENSER *F.Q.* I. v. 25 Who can turne the stream of destinee, Or breake the chayne of strong necessitee? **1603** HOLLAND *Plutarch's Mor.* 816 Thales saith, that Necessitie is most potent and forcible, for it is that which ruleth the whole world. **1667** MILTON *P.L.* v. 258 He..ordaind thy will By nature free, not overrul'd by Fate Inextricable, or strict necessity. **1754** EDWARDS *Freed. Will* I. iii. (1762) 13 The common Notion of Necessity and Impossibility implies something that frustrates Endeavour or Desire. **1803** MALTHUS *Popul.* I. i. (1806) I. 3 Necessity, that imperious, all-pervading law of nature. **1884** F. TEMPLE *Relig. & Sci.* iii. (1885) 84 When we turn from abstract arguments to facts, the doctrine of necessity is unquestionably unproven.

b. With defining terms, as *absolute*, *conditional*, *logical*, *moral*, *natural*, *philosophical*, *physical*.

1587 GOLDING *De Mornay* ix. (1592) 131 Of the necessitie that is conditional, and not of the necessitie that is absolute as they terme it. **1620** T. GRANGER *Div. Logike* 36 Euen God effecting by absolute necessitie [etc.]. **1697** tr. *Burgersdicius' Logic* I. 60 By natural necessity we understand not only that by which inanimate things act, as plants [etc.]. *a* **1740** WATERLAND *Diss. Argument* Wks. 1823 IV. 432 Connection of mental or verbal propositions..makes up the idea of logical necessity. Connection of end and means makes up the idea of moral necessity. Connection of causes and effects is physical..necessity. **1777** PRIESTLEY *Philos. Necess.* Pref. 26 Mr. Hobbes was the first who understood..the proper doctrine of philosophical necessity. **1840** *Penny Cycl.* XVI. 127/2 Physical necessity has its origin in the established order and laws of the material universe. **1862** SPENCER *First Princ.* II. iv. §53 (1875) 174 The consciousness of logical necessity.

3. a. The constraining power of circumstances; a condition or state of things compelling to a certain course of action. (Sometimes with implication of sense 10.)

1382 WYCLIF *Wisd.* xix. 4 Ther ladde them to that ende wrthi necessite. **1390** GOWER *Conf.* III. 157 To helpe..his oghne lond Behoveth every man his hond To sette upon necessite. **1509** FISHER *Funeral Serm. C'tess Richmond* Wks. (1876) 296 Compelled by necessyte to seche helpe & socoure in theyr cause. **1560** DAUS tr. *Sleidane's Comm.* 108 Necessitie requyred to make all the power againste hym that myght be gathered. **1617** MORYSON *Itin.* I. 218, I would rather admit (if necessitie require) any figurative speech. **1665** SIR T. HERBERT *Trav.* (1677) 26 They are justly suspected, and seldome traffiqued with, but in case of necessity. **1690** LOCKE *Hum. Und.* II. xxi. §9. 118 Every one pities him, as acting by Necessity and Constraint. **1735** BOLINGBROKE *On Parties* 100 Necessity and Self-Preservation are the great Laws of Nature. **1781** BURKE *Corr.* (1844) II. 423, I know the rigour of political necessity; but I see here, as little of necessity..as of propriety. **1824** MACKINTOSH *Sp. Ho. Comm.* Wks. 1846 III. 407 Its introduction can be justified only by necessity; its continuance requires precisely the same justification of necessity. **1867** SMYTH *Sailor's Word-bk.* 495 If a ship be compelled by necessity to change the order of the places to which she is insured.

b. *work of necessity*, something which cannot possibly or naturally be left undone.

a **1600** W. PERKINS *Wks.* (1617) II. 110 Workes..of present necessity..such as cannot be done before or after the Sabbath. **1647** [see MERCY *sb.* 7]. **1684** SPELMAN *Law Terms* 67 For saving that which otherwise would perish: A work of Necessity. **1824** [see MERCY *sb.* 7].

4. *of necessity*: **a.** Necessarily, inevitably, unavoidably.

1387–8 T. USK *Test. Love* III. ii. (Skeat) l. 125 And of necessite of suche justice..was free choice..graunted to resonable creatures. **1390** GOWER *Conf.* III. 142 Of verray necessite The Philosophre him hath betake Fyf pointz. *c* **1440** *Generydes* 2552 Thenne of necessite They them withdrewe. **1526** *Pilgr. Perf.* (W. de W. 1531) 13 We must all dye of necessite for original synne. **1577** B. GOOGE *Heresbach's Husb.* IV. (1586) 168 At such time as the ground is covered with snowe,..you must of necessitie helpe them with a little meat. **1611** BIBLE *Luke* xxiii. 17 Of necessitie hee must release one vnto them at the Feast. **1662** STILLINGFL. *Orig. Sacræ* III. iv. §5 For supposing a production of the world, several things must of necessity be supposed in it. **1756** BURKE *Subl. & B.* Introd., Wks. I. 105 A little attention will convince us that this must of necessity be the case. **1814** CARY *Dante, Par.* IV. 10 Of necessity It happen'd. **1866** HERSCHEL *Fam. Lect. Sci.* 209 Those [stars] to which every observer of necessity resorts to test the stability of his instruments.

†**b.** Necessary, indispensable. *Obs. rare.*

a **1533** LD. BERNERS *Huon* lviii. 202 It is of necessyte that ye goo to kynge Iuoryn..and pray hym to haue mercy of you. **1581** FULKE in *Confer.* II. (1584) M iij b, It is not of necessitie by Christes commandement.

5. In phrases and proverbs.

c **1386** CHAUCER *Knt.'s T.* 2184 Than is it wisdom..To maken vertu of necessite. *c* **1420** *Pallad. on Husb.* I. 176 Necessite nath neuere halyday. *a* **1555** [see LAW *sb.*[1] 3 a]. **1581** PETTIE tr. *Guazzo's Civ. Conv.* I. (1586) 5 Therefore wee must force our will,..whereof followeth a vertue of necessitie. **1614–16** R. C. *Times' Whistle* IV. 1379 Signior Necessity, that hath no law. **1658** R. FRANCK *North. Mem.* (1694) 44 Art imitates Nature, and Necessity is the Mother of Invention. *a* **1708** BEVERIDGE *Thes. Theol.* (1711) III. 59 By patience you make a vertue of necessity. **1758** J. BLAKE *Plan Mar. Syst.* 60 Necessity has no law. **1837** MARRYAT *Perc. Keene* xxi, One must always make a virtue of necessity. **1885** *Times* (weekly ed.) 17 Apr. 9/1 Necessity is the mother of inventions. **1897** *Pall Mall Mag.* June 228 It may seem cool, but necessity has no law.

†**6. a.** A necessary piece of business; a necessary act. *Obs.* (Cf. NEED *sb.* 12.)

c **1450** *Merlin* 64 He toke leve, and yede thourgh the courte in his othir necessitees. *c* **1532** DU WES *Introd. Fr.* in *Palsgr.* 1037 In all her necessities and busenes. **1613** SHAKS. *Hen. VIII*, v. i. 2 These should be houres for necessities, Not for delights. **1662** J. DAVIES tr. *Mandelslo's Trav.* 268 They never do their necessities, but they lay a stick cross a pit, upon which they sit for their greater ease. **1676** HALE *Contempl.* I. *Gt. Audit* 85 That is not a Necessity which may be forborn to be done..until the Morrow.

†**b.** Necessary duty. *Obs. rare.*

1546 *Mem. Ripon* (Surtees) III. 17 In the sayde Church the necessitie is to pray and to ayde dyvyne service. **1546** *Yorksh. Chantry Surv.* (Surtees) II. 213 The necessitie thereof is to do dyvine servyce.

†**c.** Something unavoidable. *Obs. rare.*

1597 SHAKS. *2 Hen. IV*, III. i. 92 Are these things then Necessities? Then let vs meete them like Necessities. **1611** —— *Wint. T.* IV. iv. 38 One of these two must be necessities, Which then will speake.

7. a. An unavoidable compulsion or obligation *of* doing something. Also with *inf.* Now *rare.*

1630 PRYNNE *Anti-Armin.* 123 Who haue a necessity of sinning since his fall. **1686** tr. *Chardin's Trav. Persia* 182 There was a necessity for us to let our Horses rest. **1727** DE FOE *Syst. Magic* I. iv. (1840) 99 Bringing them to a necessity of laying it aside, before they had carried it on too far. **1747** WESLEY *Prim. Physick* (1762) p. xxv, Honest Men are under no Necessity of touching them. **1817** JAS. MILL *Brit. India* II. v. v. 498 It was in such distress for want of provisions, as to find a necessity of applying to the Bengal Government for aid.

b. An imperative need *for* or †*of* something.

1673 *True Worship* 27 If any argue..a necessity of a Sermon; he must..conclude [etc.]. **1707** FREIND *Peterborow's Cond. Sp.* 185 God be praised we are not in a Necessity of a Victory. **1751** JOHNSON *Rambler* No. 170 ¶10 He..compelled me to repose on him as my only support, and produced a necessity of private conversation. **1785** *Liberal Amer.* II. 99 She thinks there will be a necessity for it. **1817** JAS. MILL *Brit. India* II. v. viii. 678 The strongest necessity existed for rendering the resources of the country available to its defence. **1875** WHITNEY *Life Lang.* iii. 40 They were..recent additions to the language. The introduction of Christianity had created a necessity for them.

8. The fact of being indispensable; the indispensableness *of* some act or thing.

1597 HOOKER *Eccl. Pol.* v. l. §3 Vpon their force their necessitie dependeth. **1707** ADDISON *Pres. St. War* Misc. Wks. 1766 III. 271 We see the necessity of an augmentation if we intend to bring the enemy to reason. **1751** JOHNSON *Rambler* No. 170 ¶9, I had seen mankind enough to know the necessity of outward cheerfulness. **1813** WELLINGTON in Gurw. *Desp.* (1838) XI. 22 If you will point out to them the necessity of adopting some measures to subsist their armies. **1835** I. TAYLOR *Spir. Despot.* III. 66 Whatever may enhance our ideas of the necessity and sovereignty of divine grace. **1891** *Speaker* 2 May 532/2 Modern Socialists..have not overlooked the necessity of protecting individual freedom.

II. 9. †**a.** What is necessarily required; necessaries. *Obs.*

1375 BARBOUR *Bruce* VI. 29 His men fra him sua scalit war, Till purchess thame necessite. *c* **1400** *Rom. Rose* 6740 Thanne may he begge til that he Have geten his necessite. *c* **1440** *Gesta Rom* II. xciv. 424 (Addit. MS.), Man was not made to so grete superfluyte, but to necessite of nature. **1483** CAXTON *Gold. Leg.* 381 b/2 He had the poure peple wryton by name..for to gyue to theym theyr necessyte. **1650** T. B[AYLEY] *Worcester's Apoph.* 37 You have the prittiest peece of necessity yonder, at the side Table.

b. An indispensable or necessary thing.

1481 CAXTON *Godfrey* clvi. 231 For to..bye theyr necessytees at the shippes. **1563** SHUTE *Archit.* B iij, Many other necessities therunto belonging. **1799** E. DU BOIS *Piece Family Biog.* I. 19 Sufficient for many things more than the necessities of life. **1842** MISS MITFORD in L'Estrange *Life* (1870) III. ix. 154 Trees and fresh air are necessities to my constitution. **1876** E. MELLOR *Priesthood* ii. 65 That which rendered the gospel a necessity.

10. a. The condition of being in difficulties or straits, esp. through lack of means; want, poverty.

c **1475** *Partenay* 3818 Off me shall ye haue both ayde and comfort In all your nedes of necessite. **1514** BARCLAY *Cyt. & Uplondyshm.* (Percy Soc.) 5 Wynter declareth harde nede & poverte, Than men it feleth whiche have necessyte. **1550** COVERDALE *Spir. Perle* xi. Wks. (Parker Soc.) I. 128 When he was in extreme anguish and necessity, he made his humble prayer. **1605** SHAKS. *Lear* II. iv. 214 Necessities sharpe pinch. **1639** S. DU VERGER tr. *Camus' Admir. Events* 7 This came in good time to keepe this poore family from necessity. **1728** MORGAN *Algiers* II. ii. 231 As those People had a very indifferent Harvest, they underwent great Necessity. **1768** in *Priv. Lett. Ld. Malmesbury* (1870) I. 166 The people are labouring under the greatest necessity, garden-stuff and bread..being raised in price one third.

b. With possessive pron. or genitive.

1447 BOKENHAM *Seyntys* (Roxb.) 37 Al that longyth to thy necessyte Shal be provydyd by God and me. *c* **1511** *1st Eng. Bk. Amer.* (Arb.) Introd. 32/1 We shall gyue theym gold & syluer to th[e]yr necessitie. **1596** SHAKS. *Merch. V.* I. iii. 157 You shall not seale to such a bond for me, Ile rather dwell in my necessitie. **1617** MORYSON *Itin.* II. 153 The necessity of the Spanish forces already in Ireland being more then was expected. **1651** HOBBES *Leviath.* II. xx. 106 They will not ask whether his necessity be a sufficient title. **1859** HAWTHORNE *Marb. Faun* v, All of whom find such..saloons ..as their necessity can pay for.

c. Bad, illicit spirit.

1796 MARSHALL *West of Eng.* I. 236 [The liquor] is drank in a recent state, under the appropriate name of 'necessity'. **1886** ELWORTHY *W. Som. Word-bk.* s.v. *Still-waters*, I too have often tasted 'necessity', as it was sometimes called.

11. A situation of hardship or difficulty; a pressing need or want. (Chiefly in *pl.*)

c **1450** tr. *De Imitatione* III. l. 120 Seldom is founden a trusty frende, þat is perseuerant in all þe necessites of his frende. **1494** FABYAN *Chron.* 7 Comforte to suche as calle To the for helpe in eche necessyte. **1526** *Pilgr. Perf.* (W. de W. 1531) 152 This mortall lyfe, whiche for synne is full of necessytees and myseryes. **1585** T. WASHINGTON tr. *Nicholay's Voy.* II. xviii. 51 b, To succour and supply the instant necessities which might happen. **1611** BIBLE *Transl. Pref.* ¶4 Whereby all our necessities may be prouided for. **1667** J. CORBET *Disc. Relig. Eng.* 24 Many of them live in Necessities, and most of them upon the kindness of others. **1704** HEARNE *Duct. Hist.* (1714) I. 410 He attended little to his Art and wrought at it only so far as Necessities obliged him. **1775** *Hist. Eur.* in *Ann. Reg.* 59/2 The necessities of the mother country. **1794** COLERIDGE *Relig. Musings* 218 Their keen necessities To ceaseless action goading human thought. **1876** MOZLEY *Univ. Serm.* xv. (ed. 2) 261 We must aim at a habit of gratitude, which has no relation to present necessities.

†**12.** Want *of* a thing. *Obs.*

c **1460** FORTESCUE *Abs. & Lim. Mon.* iii. (1885) 114 For gret necessite wich the French kynge hade of goode. **1558** in Strype *Ann. Ref.* (1824) I. App. iv. 396 By this means..her majesty's necessity of money may be..relieved. **1675** EARL ESSEX *Lett.* (1770) 352 Several of the foot companies in Ireland are in great necessity of clothing. **1754** SHEBBEARE *Matrimony* (1766) I. 173 You..are in Necessity of many things.

†**13.** A bond or tie *between* persons. *Obs. rare*$^{-1}$.

1595 in Spottiswood *Hist. Ch. Scot.* VI. (1677) 411 The necessity between Prince and subject is reciproque.

14. *attrib.* **necessity-operator** *Logic*, a word or symbol signifying that the proposition to which it attaches is a necessary truth.

1957 A. N. PRIOR *Time & Modality* 57 Church's necessity-operator is not an operator of this sort. **1968** HUGHES & CRESSWELL *Introd. Modal Logic* ii. 24 We shall call *L* the necessity operator. **1973** M. J. CRESSWELL *Logics & Lang.* ii. 32 The simplest is the necessity operator, or as Dana Scott calls it, the universal necessity operator.

Hence **ne'cessity** *v.*, to necessitate. *rare*$^{-1}$.

1827 I. TAYLOR *Trans. Anc. Bks.* xii. (1875) 132 One climate..necessities a much greater degree of permanency in the habits of the people than another.

nech(e, obs. Sc. variants of NIGH *v.*

neche, obs. form of NESH.

necht, obs. Sc. variant of NIGH *v.*

nechyr, obs. form of NEIGHER, to neigh. *Sc.*

†**'necial,** *a.* *Obs.*$^{-1}$ [ad. L. type **neciālis*, f. *nex*, *necis* death + *-ālis* -AL[1].] Funeral, sepulchral.

1606 BIRNIE *Kirk-Buriall* (1833) 23 Mens nuptial festivities ar ofttimes exceeded by their necial folies in making their burials..a mont to show worldly glory.

neck (nɛk), *sb.*[1] Forms: α. 1 **hnecca**, 4–6 **nekke**, 4–7 **nek**, (5–6 **neke**, 6 **neeke**), 3–7 **necke**, 4– **neck**. β. 4 **nycke**, **nhicke**, **nihcke**; **nak**. [OE. *hnecca* wk. masc. = OFris. *hnecka*, *necke*, MDu. *necke* (Du. *nek*), MHG. *nacke* (G. *nacken*), ON. *hnakki* (Da. *nakke*, Sw. *nacke*); a strong masc. form appears in MDu. *nac*, *nack-*, OHG. *hnacch*, *(h)nach* (MHG. *nac*). The word has app. no cognates outside of the Teutonic languages. In OE. it is comparatively rare, the more general sense of 'neck' being expressed by the words *heals* HALS and *swíra* SWIRE. It is not clear how the ME. variants *nicke* and *nak* are related to *nekke*.]

I. 1. a. The back part of that portion of the body lying between the head and shoulders; also, by extension, the whole of this portion, the narrow part below or behind the head.

The wider sense is now the usual one, the original meaning being commonly expressed by *the back*, or *the nape, of the neck* (see NAPE *sb.*[1] 1 b).

α. *c* **897** K. ÆLFRED *Gregory's Past. C.* xix. 142 Wa ðæm þe willað under ælcne elnboȝan lecȝean pyle & bolster under ælcne hneccan. *c* **1000** ÆLFRIC *Deut.* xxviii. 35 þæt þu næbbe nan þing hales fram þam fotwolmum oð þone hneccan [L. *ad verticem*]. *a* **1225** *St. Marher.* 12 þis milde meiden..sette hire fote uppon his ruhe necke. *c* **1290** *S. Eng. Leg.* I. 37/117 Ane Rop he dude a-boute is necke. *c* **1330** R. BRUNNE *Chron. Wace* (Rolls) 13031 Beof by þe nekke Petron hent. **1390** GOWER *Conf.* I. 99 Hire Necke is schort, hir schuldres courbe. *c* **1475** *Rauf Coilȝear* 123 He tyt the King be the nek, twa part in tene. **1559** *Mirr. Mag.*, *Dk. Suffolk* xxv, My necke in two he smoat. **1600** J. PORY tr. *Leo's Africa* 20 Sometimes they lay their legs acrosse vpon the camels neck. **1667** MILTON *P.L.* VII. 438 The Swan with Arched neck Between her white wings. **1711** STEELE *Spect.* No. 76 ¶3 He would..make two Fellows who hated, embrace and fall upon each other's Neck. **1774** GOLDSM. *Nat. Hist.* (1776) V. 283 The green parakeet, with a red neck. *a* **1821** KEATS *Hyperion* III. 132 His golden tresses famed Kept undulation round his eager neck. **1897** H. O. FORBES *Hand-bk. Primates* I. 171 The Orangs are..heavy in build, with the head set on a very thick neck.

β. *a* **1300** *K. Horn* (Harl. MS.) 1328 Hue comen in wel sone..Y-armed swiþ þicke From fote to þe nycke. **1340** *Ayenb.* 216 þe fole wyfmen þet guoþ mid stondinde nihcke ase hert ine launde. **1382** WYCLIF *Gen.* xxvii. 16 She forcoueride the nakid of the nak [1388 necke].

†**b.** As the part of the body on which burdens or other articles are carried. *Obs.*

a **1225** *Ancr. R.* 322 Ich chulle..trussen al þi schendfulnesse o þine owune necke. *a* **1300** *Cursor M.* 5523 Apon þer neckes sal þai bere Hott wit stan and wit morter. **1340** *Ayenb.* 138 Huet ssel þe ilke paye þat naȝt ne heþ bote þane nhicke y-carked mid zenne. *c* **1386** CHAUCER *Monk's T.* 120 He..bar the heven on his nekke longe. *c* **1450** LOVELICH *Grail* xlv. 434 The Enemy hym there took vpe Anon In hys Nekke. **1561** NORTON & SACK. *Gorboduc* i. Dumb Show, Of whom the first bare in his necke a Fagot of smal stickes.

c. The cervical vertebræ. Chiefly in phr. *to break the neck.*

a **1250** *Owl & Night.* 122 Werp hit vt myd þe vyrste, þet his nekke him toberste. **1297** R. GLOUC. (Rolls) 7709 Richard, is o neueu, brec þere is nekke. **1387** TREVISA *Higden* (Rolls) VII. 21 þat nyse abbot werþe wood,..and brak his nekke and deide. **1470–85** MALORY *Arthur* x. li. 496 One of them his neck was nyghe broken in tweyn. **1562** J.

Heywood *Prov. & Epigr.* (1867) 33 In that house..A man shall as soone breake his necke as his fast. **1600** Shaks. *A.Y.L.* i. i. 153, I had as liefe thou didst breake his necke as his finger. **1643** [see 5 b]. **1712** Steele *Spect.* No. 474 ⁋2 The President must necessarily have broken his Neck. **1803** *Med. Jrnl.* IX. 406 Turning it round, whereby the neck was dislocated. **1893** Earl Dunmore *Pamirs* I. 67 One and all rode like demons, without the slightest regard for the safety of their own necks.

†**d.** Inexactly used for 'head'. *Obs. rare.*

1560 Daus tr. *Sleidane's Comm.* 431 She..offered to the hangeman her necke to be striken of. **1611** Bible *Deut.* xxi. 4 The Elders..shall strike off the heifers necke there. **1647** Hexham s.v., To chop or cutt off ones Necke.

e. Phrases. ***to get (catch, take) it in the neck***: to be hard hit (by something); to be severely reprimanded or punished. Conversely, ***to give it in the neck***: to assault or reprimand (someone) severely.

1882 *National Police Gaz.* 25 Nov. 3/3 An 'Artless' Young Girl Gives it to Her 'in the Neck', as the Sports Say. **1887** [see dub *sb.*[6]]. **1903** A. Adams *Log of Cowboy* xi. 175 Old Nat will get it in the neck this time, if that old girl dallies with him as she did with us. **1908** H. G. Wells *War in Air* ii. 58 They'll get it in the neck in real earnest one of these days, if they ain't precious careful. **1914** D. O. Barnett *Let.* 31 Dec. (1915) 30 You probably don't know what a village looks like when it has caught it in the neck. **1923** Wodehouse *Inimitable Jeeves* iii. 30 Something always comes along to give it you in the neck at the very moment when you're feeling most braced about things in general. **1927** F. Niven *Wild Honey* iii. 21 If you sit..facing ahead, that's called 'punching the breeze'. If you sit..looking back, it's called 'taking it in the neck'. **1928** 'Sapper' *Female of Species* x. 169 I'd never forgive myself if one of you took it in the neck. *a* **1930** D. H. Lawrence *Phoenix II* (1968) 259 Give it the blue-bottles [*sc.* policemen] in the neck! **1955** *Times* 11 July 12/7 Do they belong to an unlucky generation that has got it in the neck before the law can catch up with the swift development of civilian aviation, and insist upon silenced airliners? **1973** *Guardian* 18 June 10/2 It's the poor old vicar who gets it most in the neck... He runs the risk of losing the best-kept-village competition because..the churchyard is looking its shaggiest. **1974** *Times* 12 Dec. 14/4 Giscard..apparently caught it in the neck from his continental colleagues.

2. a. The skin from the neck of an animal. *rare*[−1].

1552 *Act 5 & 6 Edw. VI*, c. 15 §3 Every Girdler..may..sell..Necks, Wombs and Shreds of tanned Leather.

b. The flesh of the neck of an animal, esp. of beef or mutton.

1603 Dekker & Chettle *Grissil* (Shaks. Soc.) 9 Eight to a neck of mutton—is not that your commons? **1632** Massinger *City Madam* i. i, His family fed on roots and livers, And necks of beef on Sundays. **1753** *Scots Mag.* Apr. 191/1 A neck, a loin, or leg of veal. **1813** *Examiner* 31 May 351/2 He..should like to have a neck of mutton. **1861** Mrs. Beeton *Bk. Househ. Managem.* xxv. 328 The Sheep..Fore quarter: No. 3, the shoulder; 4 and 5 the neck.

c. That part of a garment which covers, or lies next to, the neck.

1530 Palsgr. 247/2 Necke of a cappe, *rebras dung bonnet*. **1577–87** Holinshed *Chron.* III. 921/1 His pillion of fine scarlet, with a necke set in the inner side with blacke veluet. **1687** A. Lovell tr. *Thevenot's Trav.* ii. 91 Their shirts have no necks but onely a hem like Womens Smocks. **1752** Berkeley *Th. Tar-water* Wks. 1871 III. 500 Unbuttoning the neck and wristbands of his shirt. *c* **1817** Hogg *Tales & Sk.* III. 158 With a scarlet neck in his coat. **1866** [see low *a.* 1 c].

d. In Racing, ***to win by a neck***, i.e. by the length of the horse's neck. Also *fig.* So ***a neck***, such a distance separating two horses at the end of a race. Also of greyhounds.

1823 'J. Bee' *Slang* 94 Won by..indeed 'a neck'. **1865** 'Mark Twain' *Sk. New & Old* (1875) 32 She'd always fetch up at the stand just about a neck ahead. **1873** J. Blackwood *Let.* 7 June in Geo. Eliot *Lett.* (1956) V. 421 There was a grand [golf] match...my man the young champion Tom Morris came in winner by a neck. **1886** [see head *sb.*[1] 1 c]. **1930** *Daily Express* 6 Oct. 17/6 Three-quarters of a length; neck. Beggarman fourth. **1931** T. R. G. Lyell *Slang* 544 The worst of it is that I only lost by a neck; the other fellow beat me by three marks! **1975** *Times* 21 July 7/4 If Juliette Marny had not cocked her head..a few strides from the post Piggott thought the margin of success would have been half a length rather than a neck.

e. *N.Z.* The wool shorn from the neck of a sheep.

1950 *N.Z. Jrnl. Agric.* Oct. 311 (*caption*) Frames hinged to a wall [in the shearing shed] can be very useful to support a wool pack for bellies, necks, etc.

II. 3. In various figurative or allusive expressions: **a.** Implying subjugation (or deliverance).

Usu. in connexion with the fig. use of yoke.

1382 Wyclif *Jer.* xxx. 8 Y shal to-brose his 3oc fro thi necke. **1388** —— *Acts* xv. 10 To putte a 3ok on the necke of the disciplis. *a* **1400** *Chron. R. Glouc.* (Rolls) 2804 þe saxons nekken vnder is fet to trede. **1591** Shaks. *1 Hen. VI*, ii. iii. 64 These are his..armes, and strength, With which he yoaketh your rebellious Neckes. **1601** —— *Twel. N.* ii. v. 206 Wilt thou set thy foot o' my necke? **1649** Owen *Serm.* Wks. 1851 IX. 217 Our necks are yet kept from the yoke of lawless lust. **1847** Tennyson *Princ.* ii. 127 To..Disyoke their necks from custom. *Ibid.* vi. 150 See, your foot is on our necks, We vanquish'd.

b. Implying submission, resistance, or obstinacy. Also implying insolent speech or presumptuous behaviour, esp. in phr. ***to have a neck***.

c **1386** Chaucer *Clerk's T.* 57 Boweth your nekke under that blisful yok Of soverayntee. *c* **1400** *Rule St. Benet* (Prose) 38 [She may not] þe life of þe reule fle, ne caste it fra hir nek. **1535** Coverdale *2 Kings* xvii. 14 They..herdened their neckes, acordinge to the hardneck of their fathers. **1593** Shaks. *Rich. II*, iii. i. 19 My selfe..haue stoopt my neck vnder your iniuries. **1671** Milton *P.R.* iv. 418 Sturdiest Oaks Bow'd thir Stiff necks. **1757** Burke *Abridgm. Eng. Hist.* iii. iv, The barbarians..had at length submitted their necks to the Gospel. **1893–4** R. O. Heslop *Northumb. Words* II. 494 *Neck*, forwardness, impudence. 'What a neck ye hev efter aa'!' **1933** *Punch* 25 Jan. 108/3 I'm afraid I was so overcome by his barefaced 'neck' that it never occurred to me to call him back. **1935** G. Heyer *Death in Stocks* iii. 34 He'd had the infernal neck to say I wasn't going to marry the man. **1942** L. A. G. Strong *Unpractised Heart* xii. 77 And then you have the sheer neck, the bloody effrontery to say you think there's more in life than I do. **1960** J. Symons *Progress of a Crime* v. 34 If that doesn't beat anything for hard neck.

†**c.** Denoting the setting-on of an assailant, the imposition of some burden, or the laying of a charge, upon a person. *Obs.* (freq. in 16th c. use).

1536 *St. Papers Hen. VIII*, II. 356 They princypally delyte to put oon of us Inglishmen in an others necke. **1551** Robinson tr. *More's Utop.* i. (1895) 103 The wyckednes and folysshenes of others shalbe imputed to hym, and layde in hys necke. **1596** Spenser *State Irel.* Wks. (Globe) 664/1 The countrey [n]ever should dare to mutinie, having still the souldiours on theyr necke. **1604** Shaks. *Oth.* v. ii. 170 You haue done well, That men must lay their Murthers on your necke.

d. With allusion to hanging or beheading.

1496 *Fysshynge w. Angle* (1883) 36 Theuys & brybours..whyche are punysshed for theyr euyll dedes by the necke. **1599** Shaks. *Hen. V*, iv. viii. 45 Let his Neck answere for it, if there is any Marshall Law in the World. **1646** *Hamilton Papers* (Camden) 118 To this litle purpose hath the King's commands put his necke to a new hazard. **1685** Evelyn *Diary* 24 Dec., West, who..had reveal'd the accomplices to save his owne neck. **1809** Malkin *Gil Blas* ii. vii. ⁋27 [I] rejoiced at getting my neck out of an halter.

e. In miscellaneous uses. ***to speak (talk) through (the back of) one's neck***: to use extravagant or inaccurate words or language; ***to stick*** (or ***put***) ***one's neck out***: to expose oneself to danger, reprisal, criticism, etc.; ***up to the neck***: fully concerned or deeply implicated in (a transaction, freq. illegal); also *ellipt.*, occupied without intermission; ***to breathe down (someone's) neck***: to be close behind (someone); to keep a close or oppressive watch upon; ***dead from the neck up***: see dead *a.* 32 h.

1388 Wyclif *Gen.* xlv. 14 And whanne he hadde biclippid, and hadde feld [*other MSS.* falle] in to the necke of Beniamyn, his brother, he wepte, the while also Benjamin wepte in lijk maner on the necke of Joseph. *c* **1489** [see long *a.*[1] 1 c]. **1535** Coverdale *Neh.* iii. 5 Their greate men put not their neckes to yᵉ seruyce of their lorde. **1579** Tomson *Calvin's Serm. Tim.* 261/1 God layeth the bridle in their neckes as it were. **1611** Bible *Gen.* xlv. 14 And he fel vpon his brother Beniamins necke, and wept: and Beniamin wept vpon his necke. **1599**, **1676** [see heel *sb.*[2] 24 b]. **1738** Swift *Polite Conv.* i. 47 If ever I hang, it shall be about a fair Lady's Neck. **1797** Mrs. M. Robinson *Walsingham* II. 173 The constable of the night, making a long neck to examine the bribe. **1856** Lever *Martins of Cro' M.* 288 You'll go from this place to the Lodge, where you'll be fed 'to the neck'. **1862** Carlyle *Fredk. Gt.* xii. ix. (1872) IV. 196 The vacant edifices..are filled to the neck with meal and corn. **1896** [see oafish *a.*]. **1899** E. W. Hornung *Amat. Cracksman* 199 'Don't talk through yer neck,' snarled the convict. 'Talk out straight, curse you!' **1903** A. H. Lewis *Boss* 174 Still I must say you went in up to your neck on sparks and voylets. **1907** *Strand Mag.* June 672/1 We are not slow to tell them they are 'talking through the back of their neck'. **1909** R. Brooke *Let.* 3 Nov. (1968) 192 Your offer is splendid and noble. I fall upon your neck. **1912** Kipling *Songs from Books* (1913) 153 So back I go to my job again, Not..quite so ready to sob again On any neck that's around. **1923** Conrad *Rover* xii. 203 It's the very spot for hatching treacheries. One feels steeped in them up to the neck. **1923** *Pall Mall Gaz.* 13 Apr. 3/3 Anybody who gets up in this House and talks about universal peace knows he is talking through the back of his neck. **1926** *Univ. Mag.* (Univ. Va.) Oct. 16/2 Absolutely original slang at the University of Virginia includes..*to stick one's neck out*. **1933** *New Republic* 22 Nov. 45/2 Instead, there is a general disposition now to regard him as a fat-headed fellow..who 'put his neck out' and got what he deserved. **1935** *Planning* III. xlix. 2 Opinion in administration and in industry, among people who are up to the neck in current problems, is far more advanced than opinion among some of those who occupy comfortably detached positions. **1936** R. Chandler in *Black Mask* June 31/2 You sure stick your neck out all the time. **1941** Wodehouse *Berlin Broadcasts* in *Performing Flea* (1961) i. 266 Algy didn't know a thing about it and was almost certainly talking through the back of his neck. **1946** K. Tennant *Lost Haven* (1947) vii. 97 There were big black moths in the wardrobe; not to mention a beastly big mountain breathing down the back of your neck. **1950** H. Hastings *Seagulls Over Sorrento* in *Plays of Year* IV. 64 We've stuck our necks out—we're looking for trouble, see? **1955** R. Frost *Small Hotel* in *Ibid.* XIII. 189 I'll be out of here on my neck as soon as they've got what they want out of me in this court business. **1955** A. L. Rowse *Expansion Eliz. Eng.* ii. 64 Three mayors..were up to their neck in the trade. *Ibid.* viii. 302 The conclusion she [*sc.* Elizabeth] drew from that was not to put out her neck again. **1957** A. Huxley *Let.* 18 Jan. (1969) 816 Selznick is up to his neck in his forthcoming..film and probably won't be able to read the piece for some days. **1959** *Listener* 5 Mar. 414/1 It was likely that he would be thrown out on his neck very quickly. **1959** *Times* 19 May 5/5 Because Kent were always breathing down their necks, Hampshire could never really establish themselves. **1961** *Debates Senate Canada* 5 July 1021/1 So I shall try not to stick my neck out on the legal aspect too much; although, as I say, even from a legal standpoint it does seem rather simple to me. **1961** A. Wilson *Old Men at Zoo* iii. 162 But you shouldn't worry. You can never do the best work that way. Of course with Falcon and Sanderson round your neck, I'm not surprised. **1965** J. Porter *Dover Two* xi. 141 MacGregor rushed..away, delighted to be able to pursue his own line of investigation and..not to have Dover breathing down his neck all the time. **1971** 'F. Clifford' *Blind Side* iv. ii. 157 'I haven't seen him for a couple of days. .. He's been up to his neck.' 'Who with?' 'Same man.' **1971** A. Price *Alamut Ambush* xiii. 157 You don't have to stick your neck out, David—I'll stick mine out. And it'll be a pleasure! **1973** J. Fleming *You won't let me Finish* ix. 79 You're in it up to the neck whether you like it or not. **1973** *Times* 27 Feb. 14/4 He..unfortunately began a sentence 'If I disagree with my local party..' whereupon a heckler added loudly 'You'll be out on your neck.' *Ibid.* 24 Apr. 11/7 Shakespeare..gives the troupe a chance to try something new without the Academie breathing down its neck.

4. ***in, on,*** or ***upon the neck of***: on the top of, immediately upon or after; esp. (***one***) ***in*** or ***on the neck of another***. Now only *dial.* (very common in 16–17th c.).

1525 Ld. Berners *Froiss.* II. clx. [clvi.] 442 One tayle coude nat be payde but yᵗ another was redy on ye necke therof. **1545** Ascham *Toxoph.* i. (Arb.) 56 Heaping othes upon othes, one in a nothers necke. **1577** tr. *Bullinger's Decades* (1592) 50 Vpon the necke of this againe, he argueth this. **1605** Willet *Hexapla Gen.* 357 One temptation folloed in the neck of an other. **1683** Temple *Mem.* Wks. 1720 I. 376 This Offer coming upon the Neck of the Parliament's Advice to his Majesty. **1700** Dryden *Fables* Pref., Ess. (ed. Ker) II. 256 A dozen more of such expressions, poured on the neck of one another. **1877** *N.W. Linc. Gloss.* s.v., One bad job alus falls on th' neck of another.

5. ***to break the neck of***: †**a.** To destroy, finish, bring to an end. *Obs.*

1576 Fleming *Panopl. Epist.* 32 These foule mischeefs which haue almoste broken the necke of the Common wealth. **1624** Jas. I *Declar.* in Rushw. *Hist. Coll.* (1659) I. 140 Though I have broken the Necks of three Parliaments.

b. To counteract or annul the chief force or main effect of; to finish the main part of.

1643 *Plain English* 9 The neck of this designe will scarce be broken, till the necks of some of the..authors..be. **1674** R. Godfrey *Inj. & Ab. Physic* 131 The Doctor..gave him Medicines to fortifie his Stomach, and break the neck of the Fever. *a* **1734** North *Lives* (1742) I. 201 To break the Neck of those wicked Delays used there. **1755** Johnson s.v., To break the neck of an affair; to hinder any thing being done; or, to do more than half. **1837** Lockhart *Scott* (1869) II. xiv. 263 He had done enough (in his own language) 'to break the neck of the day's work'. **1886** Mrs. Lynn Linton *Paston Carew* xlii, The neck of the winter was broken, and the day was bright and clear.

6. †**a.** ***neck over head***, headlong. *Obs. rare*[−1].

1579 Tomson *Calvin's Serm. Tim.* 247/1 Matters goe so necke ouer head, and men crye out, All is naught.

b. ***neck and heels***, = neck and crop. Now *dial.*

a **1734** North *Exam.* (1740) 72 The Liberty of the Subject is brought in Neck and Heels, as they say. **1778** Miss Burney *Evelina* xxv, To take and pull him neck and heels out. **1818** M. G. Lewis *Jrnl. W. Ind.* (1834) 137 The first thing that we now did was to turn him out of the sick-house, neck and heels. **1890** *Glouc. Gloss.* s.v., If there be another 'lection, they'll be obligated to go out neck and heels.

c. ***neck and crop***, bodily, completely, altogether. Also *attrib.*

1816 in Hone *Every-day Bk.* (1825) I. 461 Explain the terms..neck and crop—bang up—and—prime. **1833** M. Scott *Tom Cringle* xvi, Chuck them neck and crop..down a dark staircase. **1865** Dickens *Mut. Fr.* i. xv, We're going in neck and crop for fashion. **1932** Kipling *Limits & Renewals* 398 That does not excuse the neck-and-crop abruptness..of..our expulsion. **1963** A. Ross *Australia 63* v. 110 Titmus,..trying to force an in-swinger away, was bowled neck and crop. **1967** [see decolonization].

7. ***to tie*** (or †***lay***) ***neck and heels***, to confine or bind securely.

1643 Chillenden *Inhumanity King's Prison-kpr.* 2 He swore he would lay me neck and heels in Irons. **1678** Butler *Hud.* iii. ii. 1092 Insolences, That to your own imperious wills Laid Law and Gospel neck and heels. **1701** Cibber *Love makes Man* iv. ii. Take this Fool, let him be gagg'd, ty'd Neck and Heels, and lock'd into a Garret.

8. ***neck or nothing*** (occas. ***nought***), a phrase expressing determination and readiness to venture everything or to take all risks.

1715 M. Davies *Athen. Brit.* I. 321 Worth venturing Neck or Nothing for. **1738** Swift *Pol. Conversat.* 99 Neck or nothing; come down, or I'll fetch you down. **1782** Cowper *Gilpin* 89 Away went Gilpin, neck or nought. **1810** Clarke *Trav. Russia* 333 She rides, to use the language of English sportsmen, 'neck or nothing'. **1836–7** Dickens *Sk. Boz, Scenes* vii, Cabs are all very well in cases of expedition, when it's a matter of neck or nothing. **1895** W. C. Hazlitt *4 Generations* II. 357, I launched my scheme neck or naught.

b. *attrib.* of persons or actions: Headlong, reckless.

1814 Scott *Let. to Morritt* 30 Apr. in *Lockhart*, A neck-or-nothing London bookseller. **1835** W. Irving *Tour Prairies* 235 Crashing along with neck-or-nothing fury, where it would have been madness to follow him. **1840** Dickens *Barn. Rudge* xxxv, Three great neck-or-nothing chaps, that could keep on running over us.

9. ***neck and neck***, of horses, etc.: Keeping abreast, neither falling behind nor getting ahead of each other. Also freq. in fig. use.

1799 *Sporting Mag.* XIII. 309/1 In this way, neck and neck, whipping and spurring, all the speed of the horses, and all the skill of the jockies exerted, they rode up to the ending post. **1835** Dickens *Let.* 2 May (1965) I. 58 We came in literally neck and neck. **1837** T. Hook *Jack Brag* iii, They ..entered the winning-field nearly neck-and-neck. **1890** 'R. Boldrewood' *Col. Reformer* (1891) 222 Having forced an immense black bullock out of the camp, [he] was racing neck-and-neck with him. **1901** *Chambers's Jrnl.* June 361/2 There a horse fell or staggered, and was instantly recovered. Now we were a few yards ahead, again neck-and-neck with the 'Quicksilver'; and so we raced on until we approached the old bridge at Bow.

fig. c **1812** CROKER in *C. Papers* (1884) I. 40 In the House of Commons.. where the parties were, if I may use the expression, neck and neck. **1877** GREEN *Lett.* (1901) 456 To keep neck and neck with the printers.. would be a daily pressure. **1926** P. GUEDALLA *Palmerston* vii. 320 The republicans, the Orleans princes.., and the President might soon be running neck and neck. **1955** *Times* 23 June 9/4 Production ran neck-and-neck in the studios, but the second version.. reached the public screen last.

b. *attrib.* Close, near.

1828 M. R. MITFORD *Our Village* III. 204 The strength and luck of the parties were so well balanced, that it produced quite a neck-and-neck race, won only by two notches. **1859** FARRAR *J. Home* xxxi, Our lots in life, since at Harton we ran a neck and neck race, have been widely different. **1871** M. COLLINS *Mrq. & Merch.* II. iii. 71 It's late in the day, and a neck and neck thing. **1952** E. F. DAVIES *Illyrian Venture* v. 84 Nicholls and I had a race across the plain, with a neck-and-neck finish.

c. As *sb.* Exact coincidence.

1858 DE QUINCEY *Secr. Societies* Wks. VII. 245 The birth and the death.. synchronise by a metaphysical nicety of neck-and-neck.

10. ***neck-to-knees***: (see quot. 1941). Also ***neck-to-knee*** attrib. *Austral.*

1941 BAKER *Dict. Austral. Slang* 49 *Neck-to-knees*, bathing costumes covering the body from the neck to half-way down the thigh. **1965** G. MCINNES *Road to Gundagai* xiv. 261 Refusing to wear the regulation 'neck-to-knee' bathing togs.

III. In transferred uses, applied to such parts of things as have some resemblance to the neck.

11. a. The narrow part *of* some passage, cavity, or vessel, *esp.* the part of a bottle next the mouth.

c **1400** *Lanfranc's Cirurg.* 175 Þe necke of þe maris is fleischi,.. & in þe necke of þe maris ben veynes. **1460–70** *Bk. Quintessence* 5 Putte it into a glas clepid amphora, with a long necke. **1611** COTGR., *Goulet*,.. the mouth, or necke of a Violl, Bottle, or other long, and narrow-neckt vessell. **1660** BOYLE *New Exp. Phys. Mech.* 12 The glass neck of the Receiver.. was thrust into this Cement. **1710** J. CLARKE tr. *Rohault's Nat. Philos.* (1729) I. xxii. 145 A Bottle.. which has a very streight Neck. **1797** M. BAILLIE *Morb. Anat.* (1807) 293 The portion which is most frequently inflamed is that near the neck of the bladder. **1844** *Jrnl. R. Agric. Soc.* V. I. 9 These necks, as they are termed, to the main drain or leaders are cut into the open ditch. **1897** *Allbutt's Syst. Med.* IV. 438 It is here that a narrowing exists which has been called the upper neck of the ureter.

b. A pass between hills or mountains; the narrow part *of* a mountain pass.

1707 *Lond. Gaz.* No. 4359/2 Monsieur Medavi.. was to advance towards the Neck of the Mountains at Ceurs. **1850** R. G. CUMMING *Hunter's Life S. Afr.* (1856) I. 122 Their vast legions continued streaming through the neck in the hills in one unbroken phalanx. **1890** L. C. D'OYLE *Notches* 133 They went by way of the pass, and as they entered the 'neck' the wind was blowing hard.

c. A narrow channel or inlet; the narrow part *of* a sound, etc.

1719 DE FOE *Crusoe* I. 59, I.. found a Neck or Inlet of Water between me and the Boat. **1736** WESLEY *Wks.* (1872) I. 39 As we were crossing the neck of St. Helena's Sound. **1894** HALL CAINE *Manxman* v. iii. 288 The neck of the harbour was narrow.

d. *Fortif.* The narrow part *of* a bastion or embrasure.

1668 *Lond. Gaz.* No. 252/4 One Bastion onely being reserved upon the Petition of the Jesuites, whose Church is situated upon the neck of it. **1669** STAYNRED *Fortif.* 8 You may as you see occasion widen the Necks of the Gorges. **1859** F. A. GRIFFITHS *Artil. Man.* (1862) 248 The neck of the embrazure is the inward, or narrowest part of it.

12. a. A narrow piece of land with water on each side; an isthmus or narrow promontory.

1555 EDEN *Decades* 352 Vppon the innermoste necke to the landewarde is a tufte of trees. **1601** HOLLAND *Pliny* I. 73 From whence proceedeth and beareth forth the necke or cape of Peloponnesus. **1677** W. HUBBARD *Narrative* 13 Mount-Hope, Pocasset and several other Necks of the best land in the Colony. **1767** *Hull Navig. Act* 1061 In case the said Commissioners shall become possessed of any necks of land. **1831** SIR J. SINCLAIR *Corr.* II. 220 They are planning canals.. to let small vessels through, across a neck of land. **1872** BLACK *Adv. Phaeton* xviii. 247 The long neck of land lying between.. the Dee and the Mersey.

b. A narrow stretch of wood, ice, etc. ***neck of the woods*** (orig. *U.S.*), a settlement in wooded country; a small or remotely situated community; a district, neighbourhood, or region. Also ***neck of timber***, and *ellipt.*

1780 YOUNG *Tour Irel.* I. 266 You see three other necks of wood,.. generally giving a deep shade. **1839** *Spirit of Times* 15 June 175/2 In this neck of the woods. **1857** DUFFERIN *Lett. High Lat.* (ed. 3) 296 The little schooner.. pushed her way through the intervening neck of ice. **1871** S. DE VERE *Americanisms* 178 He will.. find his neighborhood designated as a neck of the woods, that being the name applied to any settlement made in the well-wooded parts of the South-west especially. **1874** [see BEATENEST *a.*]. **1931** 'GREY OWL' *Men of Last Frontier* 15 A man may be soaking wet, half-frozen, hungry, and tired, landed on some inhospitable neck of the woods, vowing that a man is a fool to so abuse himself. **1955** M. GILBERT *Sky High* vi. 76 They don't come to live in this particular neck of the woods. **1967** *Listener* 19 Oct. 501 Some jerk has applied for a job as the new Cyril Connolly. Perhaps you would look him over, he lives in your neck of the woods. **1973** R. D. SYMONS *Where Wagon Led* I. vi. 95 Lee said there were springs about two miles up, and any cattle in what he called 'this neck of the woods' would probably be there. **1973** J. WAINWRIGHT *Devil you Don't* 21 In this neck, I say what. I also say when.

c. *Geol.* (See quot. 1876.)

1876 A. H. GREEN *Phys. Geol.* 246 The columns of cooled lava which fill up an old volcanic chimney are known as Necks. **1882** GEIKIE *Text-bk. Geol.* IV. 558 Necks of agglomerate and fine tuff abound among the.. volcanic regions of Scotland.

13. a. A narrow or constricted part in any implement, instrument, or other manufactured article; a connecting part between two portions of a thing.

For various technical applications see Knight *Dict. Mech.*

1598 HAKLUYT *Voy.* I. 62 Some of them vpon the necke of their launce haue an hooke. **1607** TOPSELL *Four-f. Beasts* (1658) 370 Acmon signifieth an Eagle, or else an Instrument with a short neck. **1683** MOXON *Mech. Exerc., Printing* 385 So much of the Punch as is Sunk into the Matrice is called the Neck. **1733** TULL *Horse-Hoeing Husb.* xxi. (Dubl.) 304 Its [the share's] under Side at c, which is its Neck, should be a little hollow from the Ground. **1799** G. SMITH *Laboratory* I. 7 The necks of rockets may be formed in various ways. **1825** J. NICHOLSON *Operat. Mechanic* 366 The bearings on which the necks.. of the spindle are supported. **1867** SMYTH *Sailor's Word-bk.* 495 *Neck*, the elbow or part connecting the blade and socket of a bayonet. **1876** PREECE & SIVEWRIGHT *Telegraphy* 35 A copper wire.. is attached to a neck cast in the zinc plate.

b. The part of a violin, or similar musical instrument, connecting the head and the body.

1611 COTGR., *Manche*,.. the necke of a musicall Instrument. **1662** PLAYFORD *Skill Mus.* II. (1674) 93 Seven Frets on the Neck of the Viol. **1727–38** CHAMBERS *Cycl.* s.v. *Lute*, The lute consists of four principal parts: the table; the body..; the neck,.. and the head or cross. **1811** BUSBY *Dict. Music* (ed. 3) s.v. *Viol*, The frets with which the neck was furnished. **1879** STAINER *Music of Bible* 28 The 'necks',.. twice or three times the length of the body or resonance-box.

c. *Arch.* The lower part of a capital, lying immediately above the astragal terminating the shaft of the column.

1727–38 CHAMBERS *Cycl.* s.v. *Capital*, The gorge, or neck, terminates in an astragal, or fillet, belonging to the fust, or shaft. *Ibid.*, In the Trajan column there is no neck. **1837** *Penny Cycl.* VII. 384/1 Beneath this baluster and [above] the astragal surmounting the top of the shaft of the column is the neck of the capital. **1850** LEITCH tr. *C. O. Müller's Anc. Art* §80 (ed. 2) 46 The columns.. have a contracted neck.

d. In cannon, (*a*) the narrow part connecting the cascabel with the breech; (*b*) the part immediately behind the swell of the muzzle.

(*a*) **1753** CHAMBERS *Cycl. Supp.* **1797** *Encycl. Brit.* (ed. 3) VIII. 230/2 Diameter of the button [= cascabel]... Diameter of its neck. **1867** SMYTH *Sailor's Word-bk.* 495.

(*b*) **1753** CHAMBERS *Cycl. Supp.* s.v., Neck of a gun is that part between the muzzle mouldings, and the Cornish ring. c **1860** H. STUART *Seaman's Catech.* 5 Name the mouldings, &c. Neck—notch—chock [etc.]. **1876** VOYLE & STEVENSON *Milit. Dict.* 270/1.

14. *Bot.* **a.** A neck-like part. Applied *spec.* to certain parts in plants (see quots.).

1672–3 GREW *Anat. Roots* i. §15 The saide Buds.. are at length formed into so many Necks, of three.. or more Inches long. **1823** CRABB *Technol. Dict.*, *Neck*, the upper part of the tube in a corolla of one petal. **1832** LINDLEY *Introd. Bot.* 188 The *cauliculus* or neck [in the embryo]. **1849** BALFOUR *Man. Bot.* §119 The part where the stem and root unite is the collum or neck. **1852** HENSLOW *Dict. Bot. Terms* 113 *Neck*,.. the point at which the limb separates from the sheathing petiole of certain leaves. **1875** BENNETT & DYER tr. *Sachs' Bot.* 290 This piece of the envelope.. De Bary calls the Neck.

b. Excessive elongation of stem or stalk.

1882 *Garden* 5 Aug. 114/3 Instead of Onions of monstrous size we want varieties.. that will not.. run into 'neck'.

15. *Anat.* **a.** Of a tooth: (see quot. 1732).

1732 MONRO *Anat. Bones* (ed. 2) 165 At the Place where the Base [of the tooth] ends, and the Roots begin, there is generally a small circular Depression, which some call the Neck or Collar. **1797** *Encycl. Brit.* (ed. 3) I. 684/2. **1822–34** *Good's Study Med.* (ed. 4) I. 65 The gums are detached from their respective necks. **1885** BURDETT *Helps to Health* iii. 72 The chief causes of decay in the teeth are an accumulation of tartar about their necks [etc.].

b. A constricted part in certain bones.

1726 MONRO *Anat. Bones* 231 The Neck of the *Femur* must have struck upon them. **1847–9** *Todd's Cycl. Anat.* IV. 573/1 A slight constriction, the neck of the scapula. *Ibid.* 1026/1 The head of the rib is supported by a narrow round part,.. the neck. **1881** MIVART *Cat* 77 The piece of bone which.. supports the condyle is termed the neck.

IV. 16. *attrib.* and *Comb.* **a.** Intended for placing or wearing on or round the neck, as ***neck-bond***, ***-bow***, ***-buckle***, ***-chain***, ***-cross***, ***-gear***, ***-guard***, ***-gyve***, ***-habit***, ***-iron***, ***-ribbon***, ***-ring***, ***-rope***, ***-ruff***, ***-scarf***, ***-shawl***, ***-snaffle***, ***-stock(s)***, ***-strap***, ***-swing***, ***-wear***, ***-yoke***. **b.** Lying on or in the neck, as ***neck-feather***, ***-fin***, ***-furrow***, ***-hackles***, ***-joint***, ***-lappet***, ***-pit***, ***-skin***, ***-wool***. **c.** Miscellaneous, as ***neck-fixings***, ***-hold***, ***-opening***, ***-part***, ***-plate***; ***neck-stroke***. **d.** Objective, as ***neck-cracking***; ***neck-comforter***, ***-warmer***; † ***neck-venturer***. **e.** With adjs., as ***neck-deep***, ***-fast***, ***-high***, ***-like***, ***-stiff***, ***-strong***; also ***neck-twined***.

1864 BURTON *Scot Abr.* I. i. 9 These were *neck-bonds, of which two or three men had enough to bear one. **1607** J. CARPENTER *Plaine Mans Plough* 222 Their soules, which are as the *neck-bowes of this yoke. **1767** in *Essex Inst. Hist. Coll.* (1917) LIII. 298, 7 pair silver Sleeve Buttons, together with *Neck-Buckles, etc. **1648** GAGE *West Ind.* xii. 56 She will be in fashion with her *Neck-chain and Bracelets of Pearls. **1835** *Court Mag.* VI. p. xiii/1 Neck-chain of enamelled gold. **1858** *Zoologist* XVI. 5858 Little children call their warm *neck-comforters by the name of 'pussies'. c **1613** MIDDLETON *No Wit like Woman's* I. iii, I'll not die guilty of a lover's *neck-cracking. **1849** ROCK *Ch. of Fathers* II. vi. 178 The *neck-cross.. of St. Elphege is particularly noticed. a **1814** *Gonzanga* II. i. in *New Brit. Theatre* III. 113 To.. tell her I'm *neck-deep in love. **1876** A. ARNOLD in *Contemp. Rev.* June 27 Fixing them neck-deep in cylinders of brickwork. **1722** RAMSAY *Three Bonnets* III. 143 Put in slav'ry *neck-fast. **1849** D. J. BROWNE *Amer. Poultry Yd.* (1855) 22 *Neck feathers with dark edges. **1726** G. ROBERTS *4 Years' Voy.* 111, I.. jamm'd the Noose close, before the *Neck Fins were got through. **1864** ATKINSON *Stanton Grange* 80 A.. trial of the toughness of their *neck-fixings. **1872** NICHOLSON *Palaeont.* 161 A third groove, which is termed the '*neck-furrow'. **1888** *Judge* (U.S.) 29 Sept. 401/1 *Neck-gear will, as always, cause the torture of dudes and dukes. **1890** HARDY *Melancholy Hussar* ii, in *Three Notable Stories* 167 His head would probably have been bent.. but for his stiff neck-gear. **1912** W. OWEN *Let* 3 Apr. (1967) 127 In Church with a neck-gear such as Wordsworth wore. **1869** BOUTELL *Arms & Armour* iii. 45 The prevailing arrangement is for the prolonged crest to be carried from the visor to the *neck-guard. **1573** *Nottingham Rec.* IV. 152 A boulte for the *neckegyves. **1656** HEYLIN *Surv. France* 24 [The stole] is a *neck habit.. made much after the manner of a tippet. **1872** DARWIN *Emotions* iv. 97 Two cocks,.. preparing to fight, with erected *neck-hackles. **1660** BONDE *Scut. Reg.* 16 Yet foodfull Tellus.. *Neck-high advanceth her all-bearing head. **1723** DK. WHARTON *True Briton* No. 58 II. 503 Immerging Neck-high in Ordure. **1905** *Daily Chron.* 23 Feb. 3/5 By means of a peculiar '*neck-hold' he can render his man unconscious. **1864** ANNE MANNING *Interrupted Wedding* i. 3 Hung with handcuffs, leg-chains and *neck-iron. **1647** WARD *Simp. Cobler* 65 When a kingdome is broken just in the *neck joynt. **1849** J. A. CARLYLE tr. *Dante's Inf.* xxx, Fixed its tusks on his neck-joint. **1851** WOODWARD *Mollusca* I. 34 In the plant-eating sea-snails.. one of the '*neck-lappets' is sometimes curled up. **1847–9** *Todd's Cycl. Anat.* IV. 13/1 Its body is unprovided with a *neck-like prolongation. **1822–34** *Good's Study Med.* (ed. 4) IV. 502 A commodious box with a *neck-opening for his head. **1894** *Season* X. 113/1 The.. neck-opening filled in with shirt-front. **1623** MIDDLETON *More Dissemblers* IV. ii, The ruin Of your *neck-part, or some nine years' imprisonment. c **1400** *Lanfranc's Cirurg.* 41 Vndir þe arme holis & in þe *necke pitt. **1674** N. FAIRFAX *Bulk & Selv.* 122 The aforesaid thread of sand.. posting through the *neck-plate of the hour-glass. **1852** A. CARY *Clovernook* 97 She selected a white muslin which she thought would do if she only had a new *neck-ribbon. **1883** *Century Mag.* Aug. 572/2 Partly to rescue the rest of her raiment from the shower which had ruined her neck-ribbon. **1841** LANE *Arab. Nts.* I. 118 Sometimes to Emeers [were given] *neck-rings, or collars. **1868** G. STEPHENS *Runic Mon.* II. 572 This Runic ornament is apparently a neck-ring. **1777** *Horae Subsecivae* (MS.) 302 **Neck-rope*, a wooden bow to come round the neck of a bullock, and fastned above to a small beam, by which bullocks are fastned with a cord or rope in the linney. **1822** J. FOWLER *Jrnl.* 18 June (1898) 159 In the evening the Indeans [s]tole all the neck Roaps of our Horses. **1611** COTGR., *Collerette de femme*, a small *necke-ruffe. **1895** *Daily News* 6 Dec. 6/5 Neck ruffs made of violets. **1859** LANG *Wand. India* 7 The bonnet is bought; likewise a *neck-scarf. **1892** E. REEVES *Homeward Bound* 247 Having red and gold neck-scarves. **1870** DICKENS *E. Drood* xi, He took off his greatcoat and *neck-shawl. **1769** MRS. RAFFALD *Eng. Housekpr.* (1778) 54 When they are half roasted, cut the *neck-skin. **1885** A. CAMPBELL *Rec. Argyll* 256 A purse made of neck-skin of a sea-bird. **1697** BRADLEY *Houghton's Husb.* (1727) III. 234 Both snaffles and bits, such as the wheel and jointed-snaffle, the *neck-snaffle [etc.]. **1570** LEVINS *Manip.* 117/37 *Neckstiff, *peruicax*. **1681** T. FLATMAN *Heraclitus Ridens* No. 8 (1713) I. 47 He should.. have the Honour to attend him to the *Neck-Stocks. **1732** *Acc. Workhouses* 10 Hats, caps, neckstocks, coats. **1844** H. STEPHENS *Bk. Farm* II. 693 The cheek-reins.. which pass below the *neck-strap of the martingale. c **1489** CAXTON *Blanchardyn* v. 24 The knyght.. gaaf him þe *necstroke of knighthode. c **1530** LD. BERNERS *Arth. Lyt. Bryt.* (1814) 422 He didde giue them the neck strokes of knighthode. a **1618** SYLVESTER *Wks.* (Grosart) II. 339 Our neck the *neck-strong Bull doth sway. **1822–34** *Good's Study Med.* (ed. 4) III. 246 Steel crutches, spiked-collars, *neck-swings. a **1881** ROSSETTI *House of Life* c, O'er the book of Nature mixed their breath With *neck-twined arms. **1617** MORYSON *Itin.* I. 21 He that rides on the horse neerest the Barke, is called Wage-halse, that is, *Necke venturer. **1852** C. W. H[OSKINS] *Talpa* 129 The mouth that had spoken dropped into the *neck-warmer again. **1879** WEBSTER Suppl. 1569/1 **Neck-wear*, a collective term for cravats and collars. (*Colloq.*) **1887** *Harper's Mag.* May 947/2 He waited at the corner of the block,.. affecting an interest in the neckwear of a furnisher's window. **1910** *Westm. Gaz.* 15 Apr. 4/1 Similar good results have followed upon the use of looser neck-wear. **1924** *Barnsley Brit. Drapery Stores Sale Catal.*, Lace, embroideries and neckwear. **1959** *Sears, Roebuck Catal.* Spring & Summer 145/2 Neckwear... Collar and Cuff set. .. Nylon Dickey. **1726** AYLIFFE *Parergon* [507] *Neck-Wool shorn from the Neck of the Sheep. **1886** C. SCOTT *Sheep-farming* 138 The other twists a rope out of the neck-wool. **1688** HOLME *Armoury* III. xxi. (Roxb.) 253/2 Carrying water.. by a *neck-yoke, which compasseth a mans neck, and so lyeth on both shoulders. **1891** C. ROBERTS *Adrift Amer.* 200 Picking up an old buggy neck yoke, I laid him out with it.

17. Special combs.: **neck-about**, **-barrow** (see quots.); **neck-canal** *Bot.*, in ferns and bryophytes, a central channel in the neck of the archegonium, made up of **neck canal cells**; **neck-cell** *Bot.*, a cell forming (part of) the neck in the archegonium of ferns or bryophytes; **neck-defeat**, a defeat by a neck in racing (so ***neck-victory***); **neck-fillet**, in cannon, a fillet on the breech, next to the neck of the cascabel; † **neck-herring**, a blow on the neck; † **neck-hoop**, the hoop round the neck of a cask; **neck-lock**, (*a*) in a wig, a sausage-curl (see also quot. 1966); (*b*) in *Judo*, a form of strangle-hold; **neck-mould(ing)** *Archit.*, a moulding on the neck of a capital; **neck-oil** *slang*, alcoholic drink, chiefly beer; † **neck-question**, a test question, one endangering one's neck; **neck-rein** *v.* (see quot. 1946); also as *sb.*; so **neck-reining** *vbl. sb.*; **neck-roll**, (*a*) in *Gymnastics*, a swing of the body backwards to rest on the back of the neck; (*b*) (see quot. 1966); †**neck-stamper** (see quot.); †**neck-stropiat**, of spurs, damaged at the neck; **neck-towel**, a small towel (formerly carried on the neck by attendants at table) for wiping dishes (now *dial.*); **neck-twines** (see quot.); **neck-twister** *U.S. slang*, a kind of drink; **neck-word**, a word on which one's neck depends (cf. *neck-verse*). See also NECK-BAND, -BONE, etc.

1674 RAY *N.C. Words* 35 A *Neckabout: any womans neck linnen. Sheffield. **1825** BROCKETT *N.C. Gloss.*, *Neck-about*, a woman's neck-handkerchief. **1847** HALLIWELL, **Neck-barrow*, a..shrine on which relics or images were carried.. in processions. **1887** W. HILLHOUSE tr. *Strasburger's Handbk. Pract. Bot.* xxv. 275 The neck [of the archegonium] is traversed by the *neck-canal, which is composed of a series of neck canal-cells, the walls between which are dissolved, and the disorganized contents of the four neck canal-cells are thus fused into a connected string. **1938** G. M. SMITH *Cryptogamic Bot.* II. ii. 17 During the course of development of the neck, the primary canal cell divides to form four neck canal cells. **1957** *New Biol.* XXII. 116 In effecting fertilization the spermatozoid has to traverse a lengthy 'neck-canal', a distance perhaps 200 times its own length. **1965** BELL & COOMBE tr. *Strasburger's Textbk. Bot.* 524 The ventral and neck canal cells may be regarded as gametes which have become functionless. **1877** HUXLEY & MARTIN *Elem. Biol.* 69 A large nucleated granular basal cell, with two or three smaller granular cells (*neck-cells) above it. **1938** G. M. SMITH *Cryptogamic Bot.* II. ii. 16 Marchantiales typically have six rows of *neck cells. **1886** *Pall Mall G.* 9 Nov. 11/1 He suffered a *neck defeat..in the Newmarket Handicap. **1859** F. A. GRIFFITHS *Artil. Man.* (1862) Plate 50 *Neck Fillet. **1876** VOYLE & STEVENSON *Milit. Dict.* 270/1 That portion of metal..contained between the neck fillet and the button astragal. *c* **1470** HENRYSON *Mor. Fab.* IX. (*Wolf & Fox*) xx, Thus can the cadgear say, 'Abyde, and thow ane *nekhering sall haif'. *Ibid.* xxxi, Euer vpoun the nekhering he thinkis. **1483** *Cath. Angl.* 251/2 A Nekherynge; *colaphus*. **1641** S. SMITH *Herring Buss Trade* 26 Between the third hoope and the *necke-hoope. **1761** W. HOGARTH *Works* (1833) II. facing p. 177 Triglyph membretta or *necklock. **1906** MIYAKE & TANI *Game of Ju-Jitsu* ix. 59 L may make direct opposition to the neck-lock in several ways. **1925** KELLY & SCHWABE *Historic Costume* vi. 201 The twisted central neck-lock is a survival of the late seventeenth century dildo. **1962** E. G. BARTLETT *Judo & Self-Defence* 56 The Single Wing Necklock.. Stranglehold.., pass your left hand under his left armpit and up behind his head, so as to press his head forward. **1966** J. S. COX *Illustr. Dict. Hairdressing* 169/1 *Neck lock*, the vertical curl at the neck of a barrister's wig. **1851** TURNER *Dom. Archit.* II. ii. 45 The capitals consist only of an abacus and *neck-mould. **1836** PARKER *Gloss. Archit.* (1850) I. 324 **Neck-Moulding*, the ring-like moulding which separates the capital from the shaft. **1860** HOTTEN *Dict. Slang* (ed. 2) 179 *Neck*, to swallow. **Neck-oil*, drink of any kind. **1880** C. H. POOLE *Attempt towards Gloss. Words Stafford* 16/2 *Neck-oil*, ale. A word I once heard at Walsall. **1919** H. JENKINS *John Dene of Toronto* i. 27 They'd be attacked all along the three thousand miles route, and would go down like neck-oil on a permit night. **1936** F. RICHARDS *Old Soldier Sahib* iv. 75 He inquired if we were fond of a drop of 'neck-oil', which like 'purge' was a nickname for beer. **1970** *Private Eye* 2 Jan. 12 A chance encounter..leads Barry to consume a lot of nice neck-oil. **1655** FULLER *Ch. Hist.* VIII. xvi. II. §26 This *neck-question ..the most dull and duncicall Commissioner was able to aske. **1935** H. D. CHAMBERLIN *Riding & Schooling Horses* iv. 153 'Bearing' or '*Neck Rein'. The right hand is carried just over the crest of the neck, and acts towards the left front. **1940** W. FAWCETT *Young Horseman* xii. 151 'Neck reining'. .. Here the horse is taught with voice, hand and heel to turn away from the side on which he feels the rein against his neck. *Ibid.*, It is very handy to have a horse which is trained to 'neck rein'. **1946** M. C. SELF *Horseman's Encycl.* 288 Neck reining a horse is turning him by use of the indirect rein. That is, in turning to the left the reins are carried to the left with no backward pull nor any direct pull on the left rein; the right rein, coming against the neck, gives the signal for the turn. **1953** G. BROOKE *Introd. Riding* vii. 76 What in polo language is called 'neck-reining', e.g. when turning or diverging to the right, while applying the left leg, the hand is carried over to the right. **1959** E. COLLIER *Three against Wilderness* ii. 23, I..neck reined the gelding northward. **1920** *Royal Navy Handbk. Physical & Recreational Training* v. 180 'Tricks of Ground Work'... *Neck roll (backwards) to Long-arm Balance. Back Handspring, [etc.]. *a* **1935** T. E. LAWRENCE *Mint* (1955) II. xii. 133 Hand-springs and neck-rolls. **1946** G. MILLAR *Horned Pigeon* xiii. 177 Instead of hitting something very solid,..I found myself doing neck rolls down a granite chip embankment. **1966** J. S. COX *Illustr. Dict. Hairdressing* 169/1 *Neck roll*, (1) The ends of the natural hair worn in a roll at the nape. (2) A postiche worn at the nape. Also called neck piece. **1676** COLES, **Neck-stamper*, a pot-boy. *a* **1700** B. E. *Dict. Cant. Crew.* **1632** LITHGOW *Trav.* IX. 395 The French man hangeth in the stirrop, at the full reach of his great toe.., pricking his horse with *neck-stropiat spurres. **1494** in *Househ. Ord.* (1790) 111 The King's carver and sewer and the Queene's to beare their *necke towels. **1877** *N.W. Linc. Gloss.*, *Neck towel*, a small cloth used for drying crockery. **1875** KNIGHT *Dict. Mech.* 1516/1 **Neck-twines*, in fancy weaving, small strings by which the mails are connected with the compass-board. **1859** CORNWALLIS *New World* I. 300 Cold punch, gum ticklers, and *neck twisters, drinks of Yankee concoction. **1650** FULLER *Pisgah* II. ii. §20 Shiboleth is their *neck-word..; lisping of their tongues was a certain Symptome of their death.

†**neck**, *sb.*[2] *Obs.* [Of obscure origin.] In *Chess*, a move to cover check.

a **1547** SURREY in *Tottel's Misc.* (Arb.) 21 Although I had a check, To geue the mate is hard, For I haue found a neck To kepe my men in gard. **1570** FOXE *A. & M.* (ed. 2) 24/1 So would..Woulsey haue don, had not the kyng geuen him a necke to his mate by time. **1614** SAUL *Chesseplaye* 21 Through all the colours of the field in such wise may he check, And also when occasion serves relieve the king with neck.

neck, *sb.*[3] [Of obscure origin.] In South-western counties, the last handful or sheaf of corn cut at harvest-time. (Cf. KIRN-BABY, MELL *sb.*[4])

1688 HOLME *Armoury* III. 73/2 Cutting the Neck, is the last handful of standing Corn, which when it is cut down, the Reapers give a shout, and fall to Eating and Drinking. [Hence in Phillips (1706) and Bailey.] **1826** in Hone *Every-day Bk.* (1827) II. 1170 After the wheat is all cut, on most farms in the north of Devon, the harvest people have a custom of 'crying the neck'. *Ibid.* 1172 'The neck' is generally hung up in the farm house. **1848** MRS. PASCOE *Neck Cutting* 45 Round around first bind the neck Next with flowers and ribbons deck. **1899** 'Q.' (QUILLER-COUCH) *Ship of Stars* xv. 143 Taffy was staring at a 'neck' of corn elaborately plaited which hung above the mantle shelf.

neck, obs. var. KNACK *sb.*[2] and NICK *sb.*

neck (nɛk), *v.*[1] Now only *techn.* or *dial.* [f. NECK *sb.*[1] Cf. Du. *nekken* to kill.]

1. a. *trans.* To strike on the neck, esp. so as to stun or kill; to behead; to pull the neck of (a fowl).

c **1450** [implied in NECKING *vbl. sb.* 1]. **1653** CHISENHALE *Cath. Hist.* Ep. Ded., As if the Protestant Religion were neckt in the Sparring blowes. **1707** J. STEVENS tr. *Quevedo's Com. Wks.* (1709) 164 They would have neck'd me as they do Rabbets to kill them. *c* **1712** in *Whig & Tory* iii. 33 Like thy bold Sires in Forty-Eight, Who neck'd their Prince, a worthy Fate! **1820** KEATS *Cap & Bells* xxii, The next [hour] shall see him in my grasp, And the next after that shall see him neck'd. **1879** MISS JACKSON *Shropsh. Word-bk.*, *Neck*, to kill fowls by pulling their necks out, or rabbits by giving them a blow on the back of the neck.

b. In *pass.* and *intr.* (See quots.)

1828 *Craven Gloss.* s.v. *Necked*, Growing corn is said to be necked when the straw is so weakened by the rain or wind, that the ears hang down, or are broken off. **1863** YOUNG *Naut. Dict.* (ed. 2), Tree-nails are said to be necked where they are found to be cracked, nipped, or bent at their necks between the outside skin and the timbers of a vessel. **1877** *N.W. Linc. Gloss.*, Barley is said to neck when the heads fall off by being too ripe before it is cut.

2. *slang.* To drink, to swallow.

1514 BARCLAY *Cyt. & Uplondyshm.* (Percy Soc.) 26 She couthe well..necke a mesure, her smyrkynge gan her sale: She made ten shylynge of one barell of ale! **1860** [see *neck-oil* (NECK *sb.*[1] 17)]. **1889** E. PEACOCK *Gloss. Words Manley & Corringham, Lincolnshire* (ed. 2) 366 He neck'd a good share o' beer that neet o' th' jewbilee. **1899** C. ROOK *Hooligan Nights* i. 13 He wasn't selling 'is meat over-quick, 'cos 'alf the time he was necking four-ale in the pub 'cross the way. **1929** J. MASEFIELD *Hawbucks* 135, I do wish..you'd chuck necking Scotch the way you do.

3. To make or clear the neck of (a drain). Also with *in*.

1844 *Jrnl. R. Agric. Soc.* V. I. 9 When the drainer arrives at one of the drains that enter the leader, he commences upon it by necking it in. **1846** *Ibid.* VII. I. 53 The workman as he proceeds in his main necks each common ditch as he comes to it.

4. a. *trans.* To clasp (a member of the opposite sex) round the neck; to fondle. **b.** *intr.* To engage in holding and fondling, or to embrace and caress, a member of the opposite sex.

1825 [implied in NECKING *vbl. sb.* 2]. **1842** ALLNUTT *Diary* (MS.) 10 Newcastle... I came rather suddenly upon a man who unceremoniously put his arm round a young lady, and..said..'I was only a-necking on her a little bit, Sir.' **1877** G. FRASER *Wigtown & Whithorn* 272 When sufficiently near him, she necked her supposed partner, greeting him with the following affectionate salute. **1890** J. SERVICE *Thir Notandums* xi. 82 I'm muckle mista'en if I haena seen him neckin' wi' the said Betty. **1924** P. MARKS *Plastic Age* xiv. 149 Some of those janes certainly could neck, and they were ready for it any time. **1932** E. WAUGH *Black Mischief* v. 179 It's pretty dim for me, floundering about half the day,..while you neck with the chap who's cut me out. **1935** WODEHOUSE *Blandings Castle* xii. 296 Do you know who that is that this necker is necking?.. My girl. No less. **1940** J. O'HARA *Pal Joey* 59, I was even surprised I could neck her at all. **1950** G. BARKER *True Confession* iv. 24 That this rapscallion Was necking with his legal bride. **1970** G. GREER *Female Eunuch* 181 The best behaved teenager necks. **1974** 'J. LE CARRÉ' *Tinker, Tailor* xiii. 115 A loving couple necking in the back of a Rover.

5. To fasten *to* or *together* by means of ropes put around the neck. *U.S.*

1857 D. E. E. BRAMAN *Information Texas* iv. 73 The usual practice of farmers whenever they want work oxen, is to.. neck together, with ropes, as many pair of..steers as they desire. **1923** J. H. COOK *50 Yrs. on Old Frontier* 21 Each of them had to be 'necked' to a gentle one, to be led for a time. **1930** J. F. DOBIE *Coronado's Children* iii. 102 Every animal in the pen had been roped and led in necked to an old brindle ox. **1933** J. V. ALLEN *Cowboy Lore* I. 9 *Necking*, in range terminology... On the range an unruly cow or one with roving proclivities will often be necked or tied to a more tractable animal.

6. *intr.* To undergo a local reduction in width when subjected to tension. Usu. with *down*.

1938 J. NEWTON *Introd. Metall.* iv. 105 The contraction begins to concentrate at some one point on the bar, [and] the piece begins to 'neck down'. **1942** *Industr. & Engin. Chem.* Jan. 56/2 During drawing each filament 'necks down' and takes a smaller diameter. **1964** *Mod. Textiles Mag.* Jan. 67/2 When an undrawn nylon filament is stretched beyond its elastic limit, it suddenly (and irreversibly) 'necks down' to a fraction of its original diameter. **1965** P. I. VINCENT in P. D. Ritchie *Physics of Plastics* ii. 84 It may also happen that a specimen does not neck at low speeds because there is not sufficient strain softening.

†**neck**, *v.*[2] *Obs. rare.* [f. NECK *sb.*[2]] *trans.* and *intr.* To cover check in chess.

a **1585** MONTGOMERIE *Cherrie & Slae* 215, I gat sik chek, Quhilk I micht nocht remuif nor nek, Bot eyther stail or mait. *a* **1618** SYLVESTER *Mathieu's Mem. Mort.* viii. Wks. (Grosart) II. 223 This [piece] leaps, that limps, this checks, that necks, that mates.

neck, obs. variant of NICK *v.*

†**neckatee.** *Obs. rare.* [Obscurely f. NECK *sb.*[1]] A lady's neckerchief.

1752 FIELDING *Covent Gard. Jrnl.* No. 37 The manteel.. again was succeeded by the pelorine; the pelorine by the neckatee; the neckatee by the capuchine. **1825** BROCKETT *N.C. Gloss.*, *Neck-about*, a woman's neck-handkerchief—a neckatee.

ˈ**neck-band.** [f. NECK *sb.*[1] Cf. Sw. *nackband* cap-string.]

1. a. A band for the neck of an animal.

1446 *Wills & Inv. N.C.* (Surtees, 1835) 95, j shole ligat' cum ferro, et xv nekbandez. **1535** COVERDALE *Judg.* viii. 26 The neckbandes of their Camels. *a* **1842** A. CUNNINGHAM in *Milton's Wks.* (1853) 562 A neck-band of the red berries of the same tree was a full security of the wearer.

b. A band worn round the neck by a person.

1530 PALSGR. 247/2 Necbande, *gorgias*. Necbande for a woman, *gorgerette*. **1535** COVERDALE *Song Sol.* i. 10 A neck bande of golde wil we make yᵉ with syluer bottons. **1611** COTGR., *Collerette de femme*, a small necke-ruffe, neckercher, or neck-band, (worne by women).

2. The part of a garment encircling the neck.

1591 PERCIVALL *Sp. Dict.*, *Cabeçon de camiça*, the necke bande of a shirt. **1705** *Lond. Gaz.* No. 4161/4 A new blue Shirt, with a little piece of old blue at the Neck-band. **1884** *Girl's Own Mag.* Jan. 201/1 The neckbands of all dresses are made very wide.

ˈ**neck-beef.** [f. NECK *sb.*[1]] Beef from the necks of cattle, which is of inferior quality. Hence *transf.* of anything inferior or cheap.

1662 PETTY *Taxes* 86 A little bread and cheese,..neck beef, and inwards twice a week. **1687** SEDLEY *Bellamira* IV. i, She is very pretty, and as cheap as neck-beef. **1707** CIBBER *Double Gallant* IV. Wks. 1777 III. 59 If I had the feeding of you, I'd bring you in a fortnight to neck-beef. **1772** FOOTE *Nabob* II. Wks. 1799 II. 311 Dog-cheap; neck-beef; a penny loaf for a halfpenny! **1802-12** BENTHAM *Ration. Judic. Evid.* (1827) IV. 438 As neck-beef and sticking-pieces are provided by the butcher for those who cannot come up to the price of ribs and sirloins.

ˈ**neck-bone.** Also 4 **nek bon, nekke boon**, etc. [f. NECK *sb.*[1] Cf. MDu. *nacbeen* (Du. *nekbeen*), Da. *nakkeben* (Norw. *-bein*), Sw. *nackben*.] The bone (†or nape) of the neck; a cervical vertebra.

c **1320** *Sir Tristr.* 1480 Tristrem rauȝt his brain And brak his nek bon. *c* **1386** CHAUCER *Man of Law's T.* 571 A hand him smoot upon the nekke-boon. *c* **1400** *Ywaine & Gaw.* 3257 Sir Ywain with his brand was boun, And strake his nek-bane right in sonder. **1565** COOPER *Thesaurus*, *Astragalus*... In Homere, it is taken for the neckebone, where it ioygneth to the backebone. **1632** SHERWOOD, The neck-bone, *l'os du gaujon*. **1675** HOBBES *Odyssey* (1677) 126 So to the earth he headlong fell, And broke his neck-bone. **1711** ADDISON *Spect.* No. 32 ¶2 Alexander the Great wore his Head a little over the left Shoulder; and then not a Soul stirred out 'till he had adjusted his Neck-bone. **1791** BURNS *Tam o' Shanter* 92 Past the birks and meikle stane, Whare drunken Chairlie brak's neck-bane. **1831** YOUATT *Horse* 154 It is the base of the column of neck-bones.

ˈ**neck-break**, *adv.* and *sb.* [Cf. BREAK-NECK.]

A. *adv.* In a break-neck or headlong manner. In dial. use also as *adj.*: see *Eng. Dial. Dict.*

1631 R. H. *Arraignm. Whole Creature* xv. §2. 256 Ventring neck-breake, (as Goates in Winter, that climbe for Ivie) over Pales, and Walles. **1705** HICKERINGILL *Priest-cr.* III. Wks. 1716 III. 162 That they may ride them Neck-break to both their Destructions here and hereafter. **1877** *Holderness Gloss.*, *Neck-brek, -brake*,..impetuously, at dangerous speed.

†**B.** *sb. Sc.* = BREAK-NECK *sb.*

a **1665** W. GUTHRIE *Serm.* 14 (Jam.), Folks poring over much on the tentation is their neck-break and their snare. **1709** BRUCE *Serm.* in Kirkton *Hist. Ch. Scot.* (1817) 274 Beware of Scripture, for you may be your own neck-break.

So **neck-breaking** *vbl. sb.* and *ppl. a.*

1650 FULLER *Pisgah* II. ix. §19 Soon after happned..Eli's heart-breaking with the news, neck-breaking with his fall. **1810** *Sporting Mag.* XXXVI. 166 The Baronet begged leave to decline the neck-breaking experiment. **1852** R. S. SURTEES *Sponge's Sp. Tour* (1893) 39 Fox-hunting.., though exciting and exhilarating, does not..present such conveniences for neck-breaking as people..imagine.

ˈ**neckcloth.** [f. NECK *sb.*[1]] A cloth worn round the neck; a cravat, neckerchief. Now *rare.*

1639 *Knaresb. Wills* (Surtees) II. 167 One linen apron and one neck cloth. **1699-1700** in Hedges *Diary* (Hakl. Soc.) III. 62, I made a tryall of making some neck cloths here. **1721** AMHERST *Terræ Fil.* No. 13 (1726) 63 His man..puffs out his neck-cloth with as smart an air as Mr. Anybody. **1784** KIPPIS *Biog. Brit.* III. Corr. & Add. s.v. *Betterton*, His countenance..turned..as pale as his neckcloth. *a* **1839** PRAED *Poems* (1864) II. 65 In his neckcloth's studied fold Sat Fashion. **1888** MRS. H. WARD *R. Elsmere* xvii, He wore an old-fashioned neckcloth.

b. *transf.* The hangman's rope.

1836 F. MAHONY *Rel. Father Prout* II. 115 'Hould your tongue in that matter', says he; 'For the neckcloth I don't care a button'.

Hence **'neckclothed** (-klɒθt, -ɔː-) *a.*, provided with, wearing, a neckcloth.

1833 LYTTON *Godolphin* vii, In the panoply of neckclothed silence. **1864** *Mattie, a Stray* I. 133 White neckclothed servility struggled..for the distinction of waiting on her.

'neck-collar. Now *arch.* [f. NECK *sb.*[1]] A collar. Also *transf.*

1530 PALSGR. 247/2 Neccoller for a woman, *gorgias.* **1546** *Test. Ebor.* (Surtees) VI. 245 One neccoller wroght withe golde. **1549** *Rutland MSS.* (1905) IV. 570 Nekcollers for horse drought, xliij. **1821** SCOTT *Pirate* xxxi, Are you avised what death he died of?..for I have heard that it was of a tight neck-collar—a hempen fever, or the like. **1865** J. H. INGRAHAM *Pillar of Fire* (1872) 326 Many of the prisoners were confined to a long iron bar, by neck-collars.

necked (nɛkt), *a.* [f. NECK *sb.*[1]]

1. Having a neck *like* something specified.

1486 *Bk. St. Albans* F iv b, A Grehounde shulde be heded like a Snake, and necked like a Drake. *a* **1529** SKELTON *E. Rummyng* 519 She was nothynge plesant; Necked lyke an olyfant. **1601** HOLLAND *Pliny* I. 205 The one is called of the Æthyopians, the Nabis, necked like an horse. **1824** MISS MITFORD *Village* Ser. I. (1863) 128 A model of grace and symmetry, necked and crested like an Arabian.

2. In *Combs.*, as *long-*, *narrow-*, *short-*, *stiff-necked*, etc. (see the first element).

3. Having a neck.

1841 E. NEWMAN *Hist. Insects* IV. v. 260 Necked capricorn-beetles, or Lepturites. **1864** GOSSE in *Gd. Words* Dec. 891/2 Necked Barnacles, so long believed..to be legitimately descended from..a certain species of goose. **1956** R. J. C. ATKINSON *Stonehenge* v. 154 Two main groups of population, distinguished by the forms of their pottery as the Bell-Beaker and Necked-Beaker cultures. *Ibid.*, The Necked-Beaker culture..is an indigenous development in England. **1967** *Antiquaries Jrnl.* XLVII. 174 The latter comprised sherds of two pots—part of the body of a probable rusticated beaker and part of the base of a beaker of indeterminate type—probably a necked variety. **1972** *Sci. Amer.* Dec. 54/3 The Taslan process feeds a filament into a rapidly moving airstream at the necked region of a nozzle.

4. [perh. f. NECK *v.*[1] 6.] Reduced in width as a result of having been subjected to tension.

1959 C. E. BIRCHENALL *Physical Metall.* vi. 136 A_f is the cross-sectional area in the necked region. **1964** R. E. REED-HILL *Physical Metall. Princ.* xviii. 555 Fracture begins at the center of the necked region on a plane that is macroscopically normal to the applied tensile-stress axis.

neckenger: see NECKINGER.

Necker[1] ('nɛkə(r)). [The name of Louis Albert *Necker* (1786–1861), Swiss naturalist and mineralogist, who described the phenomenon in 1832 (*Phil. Mag.* I. 329).] ***Necker('s) cube***: a line drawing of a transparent cube in which parallel sides are drawn with the same length, so that one seems to look successively down at the top and up at the bottom as the perspective reverses.

1901 E. B. TITCHENER *Exper. Psychol.* I. II. ix. 309 The Instructor should have a few prepared as large wall-diagrams:..Schröder's stair-figure, Necker's cube,..the. Müller-Lyer figure. **1938** R. S. WOODWORTH *Exper. Psychol.* xxv. 628 Many line drawings readily suggest three dimensions and are called figures of ambiguous or reversible perspective. The Necker cube and the Schröder staircase are the best known. **1966** R. L. GREGORY *Eye & Brain* xiii. 231 Certain figures..are ambiguously seen in depth, for example the Necker cube. **1975** *Sci. Amer.* Jan. 8/1 Rubin's well-known vase, Schröder's stairs and Necker's cube did almost certainly provide the seed of inspiration for M. C. Escher's work on the regular subdivision of the plane.

necker[2] ('nɛkə(r)). [f. NECK *v.*[1] 4 + -ER[1].] One who indulges in caresses and fondling.

1923 MENCKEN *Amer. Lang.* (ed. 3) 373 *Necker*, one given to cheek-to-cheek dancing. **1925** H. L. FOSTER *Trop. Tramp with Tourists* xvi. 300 Listen, you would-be necker! **1935** [see NECK *v.*[1] 4]. **1947** I. BROWN *Say the Word* 81 But they [*sc.* young gentlemen] are not known, I think, as neckers. **1966** 'D. SHANNON' *With a Vengeance* (1968) i. 15 Well, it's a body... Found about half an hour ago... By, I gather, a couple of neckers.

neckercher ('nɛkətʃə(r)). Now *dial.* [var. of next: cf. *handkercher* and KERCHER.] = next.

1467 *Mann. & Househ. Exp.* (Roxb.) 390 My mastyr paid for nekchers for my lady, x. s. *a* **1548** HALL *Chron., Hen. VIII* 216 Euery mantle had lettice about y[e] necke like a neckercher. **1598** B. JONSON *Ev. Man in Hum.* III. vi, My wife ha's pawn'd her neckerchers for cleane bands for him. **1611** COTGR., *Collerette de femme*, a small necke-ruffe, neckercher, or neck-band. **1662** *Stat. Irel.* (1765) II. 460 Neckerchers of Flanders making. **1888** 'Q.' (QUILLER COUCH) *Troy Town* iv, Him wi' the red neckercher.

neckerchief ('nɛkətʃɪf). Also 4 **necke couercheue**, 6 **kerchef**; 4 **neckercheue**, **-chiff**, 5 **nekkyrchefe**, **-erchyff**. [f. NECK *sb.*[1] + KERCHIEF.] A kerchief worn about the neck.

1382 WYCLIF *Isa.* iii. 23 Pynnes, and sheweres, and necke couercheues [*v.r.* neckercheuys] , and filetes. **1483** *Cath. Angl.* 251/1 A Nekkyrchefe, *anaboladium.* **1495** *Nottingham Rec.* III. 36 Unius nekkerchyff, pretii iiij d. *c* **1532** DU WES *Introd. Fr.* in *Palsgr.* 907 The necke kerchef, *la colerette.* **1611** in Heath *Grocers' Comp.* (1869) 92 That none should wear..any band, neckerchief, gorget, or stomacher, but only plain. **1679** *Hist. Jetzer* 37 A Quoif and Neckerchief, and other Accoutrements to dress him up like a Countrey-woman. **1786** MME. D'ARBLAY *Diary & Lett.* (1842) III. 28 Giving the gown before the hoop, and the fan before the neck-kerchief. **1824** MISS MITFORD *Village* Ser. I. (1863) 39 Trying to relieve his sufferings by the removal of his neckerchief. **1881** BESANT & RICE *Chapl. of Fleet* I. iv, She ..pulled down the ends of her neckerchief.

So **neck-'handkerchief.**

1642 *Archives of Maryland* (1887) IV. 95, 9 plaine neck-cloths and 5 plaine neckhandkercheifes. **1712** STEELE *Spect.* No. 478 ¶ 12 To buy Cravats or Neck-Handkerchiefs. **1740** RICHARDSON *Pamela* I. 223 So what will I do, but strip off my upper Petticoat, and throw it into the Pond, with my Neck-handkerchief. **1817–18** COBBETT *Resid. U.S.* (1822) 16 Stockings..and a waistcoat and neck-handkerchief. **1853** READE *Chr. Johnstone* 226 Their neck-handkerchiefs and hair were wet with spray.

neckful ('nɛkfʊl). *colloq.* [f. NECK *sb.*[1] + -FUL 2.] As much (punishment, vituperation, etc.) as one can endure; cf. phr. ***to get*** (or ***catch, take***) ***it in the neck*** (NECK *sb.*[1] 1 e). So **'neckfull** *a.*, full up to the neck; cf. NECK *v.*[1] 2.

1920 R. GRAVES *Country Sentiment* 71 On pay-day nights, neck-full with beer, Old soldiers stumbling homeward here. **1950** W. HAMMOND *Cricketers' School* ii. 30 There was plenty of time..to give them a neckful of their own medicine.

'neck-hole. [f. NECK *sb.*[1] + HOLE *sb.* Cf. Norw. dial. *nakke-hola* in sense 1.]

1. *dial.* The hollow in the back of the neck; the space between the back of the neck and the collar.

c **1340** *Nominale sive Verbale* (Skeat) 10 Fossolet, nekke-hole. *c* **1400** *Destr. Troy* 13889 He nolpit on with his Neue in the necke hole, þat the bon alto brast. *c* **1475** *Pict. Voc.* in Wr.-Wülcker 748 *Hec fontinella*, the nekhole. **1592** in *Vicary's Anat.* (1888) App. ix. 228 Two [veins] in the neke holes shall thowe fynde. **1874** WAUGH *Chimney Corner* (1879) 27 Yo met set potitos in her neck-hole. **1892** MRS. H. WARD *David Grieve* I. viii, I'll put soom o' that watter down yor neckhole.

2. The hole through the neck of an hour-glass.

1674 N. FAIRFAX *Bulk & Selv.* 121 What a long thread of sand passes the neck-hole of an hour-glass.

3. An opening for the neck.

1886 CORBETT *Fall of Asgard* I. 250 He drew on his glittering hauberk. When his head emerged again through the neck-hole, he went on [speaking].

necking ('nɛkɪŋ), *sb.* [f. NECK *sb.*[1] + -ING[1].]

1. a. *Arch.* The part of a column lying between the capital and the shaft. Cf. NECK *sb.*[1] 13 c.

1804 *Europ. Mag.* XLV. 8/2 Under the necking in the brick-work are made crosses formed like the letter T. **1831** *Fraser's Mag.* IV. 281 The moulding that divides the necking from the shaft. **1880** *Archæol. Cant.* XIII. 38 The pattern occurs on the necking of a shaft.

b. *Naut.* (See quot.)

c **1850** *Rudim. Navig.* (Weale) 135 *Necking*, a small neat moulding at the foot of the taffrail over the lights.

2. A neck-like stem or stalk.

1831 T. HOPE *Ess. Origin Man* II. 110 These neckings remain so flexible that..the pressure from the air above weighs them down.

3. necking-cord: in a draw-loom (see quot. 1910).

1910 L. HOOPER *Hand-Loom Weaving* 328 *Necking cords*, cords joining pulley cords and leashes in a monture. **1958** A. HINDSON *Designer's Drawloom* II. 26 The doubled part of the cord stretching from top to bottom of the Simple frame is known as the Simple cord and the divided sections from the top of the Simple frame to where they meet the cords from the shafts as the Necking cords.

4. *Archæol.* A circlet around a projection (as the boss of a shield).

1946 *Antiquity* XX. 24 A decorative necking of tinned bronze connects the boss with its wide ornamental border.

'necking, *ppl. a. rare.* [f. NECK *v.*[1] 1.] Falling on the neck; stunning.

1681 T. FLATMAN *Heraclitus Ridens* No. 31 (1713) I. 204 This Scottish Parliament has given the Whigs a Necking blow. *a* **1734** NORTH *Exam.* (1740) 220 The Plot had a fatal necking Stroke at that Execution.

necking ('nɛkɪŋ), *vbl. sb.* [f. NECK *v.*[1] + -ING[1].]

1. Striking on the neck (see NECK *v.*[1] 1).

c **1450** *Mirour Saluacioun* 3237 The buffets, reproves, neckings, blasphemes, derisionne.

2. Embracing and caressing a member of the opposite sex (see NECK *v.*[1] 4). Also *attrib.*

1825 A. CRAWFURD *Tales my Grandmother* I. 138 Let's see nae mair o' Peter Wallett's neckin' an' touslin' here. **1922** *Dialect Notes* V. 148 *Necking*, dancing with cheeks together, also known as 'parking'. **1923** *Cosmopolitan* Nov. 72/3 The necking parties in dark nooks about the deck at night. **1928** *Daily Tel.* 4 Sept. 7/5 High school children..whose favourite pastime is 'necking' in motor-cars in dark roads with the lights turned off. **1930** *Punch* 26 Mar. 341/3 *Necking-Control.* The Ministry of Transport is now building a chain of illuminated posts... Red means 'stop', amber 'get ready to love' and green 'go'.—*Indian Paper.* **1938** E. BOWEN *Death of Heart* II. vi. 278 A spot of necking with Daphne. **1958** *Times Lit. Suppl.* 15 Aug. p. x/3 For the active young non-reader, sport, cars, dancing and necking are the prime immediacies. **1971** *Petticoat* 24 July 39/5 In necking and/or petting, a boy may ask his partner to 'make love to him'.

3. Also **necking down.** A local reduction in width occurring when a sample is subjected to tension.

1957 *Textile Terms & Definitions* (Textile Inst.) (ed. 3) 67 *Necking*, the sudden reduction in diameter occurring on stretching an undrawn filament. **1959** C. E. BIRCHENALL *Physical Metall.* vi. 145 The fcc [*sc.* face-centred cubic] metals, like copper and aluminium, undergo duplex slip and necking without a distinct fracture stage. **1966** *McGraw-Hill Encycl. Sci. & Technol.* VIII. 270/2 Even the tension test, which is in general the most satisfactory, gives some difficulty because of the instability that leads to necking down. **1974** COLANGELO & HEISER *Analysis Metall. Failures* ii. 15 When failure occurs, the necking leads to a variety of fracture surfaces, depending on the material's ductility.

neckinger ('nɛkɪndʒə(r)). Now *dial.* Also 6 **-enger.** [Corrupt form of NECKERCHER.] A neckerchief.

1598 DELONEY *Jacke Newb.* ix. 107 His wife..would not ..turne her head aside for feare of hurting the set of her neckenger. *a* **1825** FORBY *Voc. E. Anglia*, *Neckinger*, a cravat or any other covering for the neck. **1866–** in Yorksh. glossaries.

neck-kerchief, obs. variant of NECKERCHIEF.

necklace ('nɛklɪs), *sb.* Also 7 **nycklease**, **necles**, **necklasse.** [f. NECK *sb.*[1] + LACE *sb.*]

1. An ornament of precious stones or precious metal, beads, etc. worn round the neck.

c **1590** MARLOWE *Faustus* vi, Next, like a necklace, I hang about her neck. **1600** SURFLET *Countrie Farme* I. xii. 62 You must put about your necke a necklace of Iaspar stone. **1673** RAY *Journ. Low C.* 5 This Chain is round in form of a Bracelet, Neck-lace, or Wheel-band. **1762–71** H. WALPOLE *Vertue's Anecd. Paint.* (1786) V. 127 Instead of the garland she has a necklace in her hand. **1814** JANE AUSTEN *Mansf. Park* II. 182 Being requested to chuse from among several gold chains and necklaces. **1877** A. B. EDWARDS *Up Nile* xiii. 350 The necklaces consist of onyx, carnelian, bone, silver, and coloured glass beads.

†**b.** A lace or ribbon for the neck; a neck-tie.

1697 DAMPIER *Voy.* (1729) II. I. 43 They have Band-strings or Necklaces fastened to their Hats; which coming under their Chins are there tied. **1740** RICHARDSON *Pamela* I. 50 Then I bought of a Pedlar..two Yards of black Ribband for my Shift Sleeves, and to serve as a Necklace.

2. *transf.* A noose or halter.

a **1616** BEAUM. & FL. *Bonduca* II. iii, What are these fellows? what's the crime committed, That they wear necklaces? *a* **1625** FLETCHER *Bloody Brother* III. ii, You peaching rogue, that provided us With these necklaces.

b. *S. Afr.* (Freq. with definite article). A tyre soaked or filled with petrol, placed round the victim's neck and shoulders, and set alight, as a form of lynching or unofficial execution. Freq. *attrib.*, as ***necklace murder***, etc.

1985 *Washington Post* 12 Aug. A9/2 A group of young blacks caught him and pulled him to the ground. As he lay there they smashed rocks into his skull and body. Then came the 'necklace' burning. **1985** *Grocott's Mail* (Grahamstown, S. Afr.) 1 Oct. 3 Notes put under doors threatening occupants with 'the necklace' should they buy from white shops. **1986** *Times* 22 Apr. 7/7 Four more blacks ..have been killed in 'necklace' murders..in South African townships. **1987** *Daily Tel.* 28 May 10/4 Setting fire to tyre 'necklaces' is a method of execution used by blacks to execute informers.

3. *Naut.* **a.** A chain or strop round a mast.

1860 H. STUART *Seaman's Catech.* 55 Necklaces are rove round the heel of the mainmast. **1882** NARES *Seamanship* (ed. 6) 33 The necklace..goes round the mast-head immediately on top of the trestletrees and crosstrees.

b. A ring of wads placed round a gun.

1867 SMYTH *Sailor's Word-bk.* 495.

4. *attrib.* and *Comb.*, as ***necklace-collar***, ***-maker***; ***necklace-like***, ***-shaped*** adjs.

1769 *Public Advertiser* 14 Mar. 2/2 A Parcel of Beads, Bugles, &c., the Property of Mrs. Smith, Necklace-Maker. **1835** LINDLEY *Introd. Bot.* (1839) 450 *Necklace-shaped*.., cylindrical or terete, and contracted at regular intervals. **1849** BALFOUR *Man. Bot.* §398 The hairs are beautifully coloured, and moniliform..or necklace-like. **1865** J. H. INGRAHAM *Pillar of Fire* (1872) 189 The chief standard-bearer is distinguished by a gold necklace-collar.

b. Special combs., as **necklace-moss**, the lichen *Usnea barbata*; **necklace-poplar**, the cottonwood or Carolina poplar, bearing racemes of pods which resemble strings of beads; †**necklace-snake** (see quot. 1753); **necklace-tree** (see quot. 1866); **necklace-wood** (see quot. 1883).

1753 CHAMBERS *Cycl. Supp.* App. s.v. *Snake*, Necklace-Snake, the English name of the *natrix torquata* of zoologists. **1758** *Phil. Trans.* L. 664 The long beaded *usnea*, or necklace moss, enters into the like œconomical uses in Virginia. **1846–50** A. WOOD *Class-bk. Bot.* 507 *Populus monilifera*, Necklace Poplar. **1866** *Treas. Bot.* 823/1 *Ormosia dasycarpa* is the West Indian Bead-tree or Necklace-tree, the seeds of which..are roundish, beautifully polished, and of a bright scarlet colour. **1883** MOLONEY *W. African Fisheries* (Fish. Exhib. Publ.) 34 The poison residing in the stems of the Barbasco or Necklace wood (*Jacquinia armillaris*, Linn.).

necklace ('nɛklɪs), *v.* [f. prec.]

1. *trans.* and *intr.* To form into a necklace.

1702 PETIVER in *Phil. Trans.* XXIII. 1251 The Roots..are fibrous, to which lower adhere others as it were Necklaced and Strung. **1893** *Jrnl. R. Agric. Soc.* Dec. 709 The sheaves shewed a slight tendency to necklace—i.e. to hang together by the heads.

2. *trans.* To encircle or surround with, or as with, a necklace.

1763 GRAINGER *Sugar Cane* IV. 6 Quick papaw, whose top is necklac'd round With numerous rows of party-colour'd fruit. **1817** COLERIDGE *Satyrane's Lett.* ii. 215 A church.. necklaced near the top with a round of large gilt balls. **1893** *National Observer* 24 June 144/2 He necklaced a certain Dutch captain with sausages.

b. *S. Afr.* To lynch or kill by means of the necklace (sense 2 b).

1986 *Guardian* 16 Apr. 6/6 Their first statement on the discovery of 32 charred bodies suggested that the victims had been 'necklaced'. **1986** *Sunday Tel.* 7 Sept. 2/7 Last year, he [*sc.* Bishop Tutu] did shoulder his way through a crowd to save the life of a man who was about to be 'necklaced'. **1987** *Sunday Tel.* 28 June 9/5 According to the British-born scholar, Dr Tom Lodge, the first person to be necklaced was Mr T B Kinkini, a town councillor in the Eastern Cape township of Kwanobuhle.

Hence (or from the sb.) **'necklaced** *a.*; **'necklacing** *vbl. sb.*

1731 FIELDING *Covent Gard. Trag.* II. vi, Ten thousand load of timber shall embrace Thy necklaced neck. *a* **1794** SIR W. JONES (T.), The hooded and the necklaced snake. **1968** G. JONES *Hist. Vikings* IV. i. 322 Frey was a god of fruitfulness and sexuality. His necklaced sister was his genial counterpart. **1986** *Washington Post* 18 Feb. A16/2 The policeman had been prepared for 'necklacing' by being doused with gasoline and having a rubber tire placed around his neck. **1986** *Times* 22 Apr. 7/7 The man's 'necklaced' body was found in a primary school toilet.

†**neckland.** *Obs.* [f. NECK *sb.*[1]] A neck or narrow strip of land.

1598 HAKLUYT *Voy.* I. 572 Streights, bayes, harboroughs, necklands, creekes. **1627** HAKEWILL *Apol.* I. iii. §2. 32 The Promontories and necklands which butt into the sea, what are they but solide creekes.

neckless ('nɛklɪs), *a.* [f. NECK *sb.*[1] + -LESS.] Having no neck.

1610 HEALEY *St. Aug. Citie of God* XVI. viii. (1620) 548 Those monstrous men..such as are necklesse, with the face of a man in their breasts. **1812** W. TENNANT *Anster F.* II. xxxvi, Neckless coats brush'd smooth and clean. **1833** LONGF. *Outre-Mer* Prose Wks. 1886 I. 87 Among broken crucibles, and neckless retorts. **1841** E. NEWMAN *Hist. Insects* IV. v. 260 Neckless capricorn-beetles.

necklet ('nɛklɪt). [f. NECK *sb.*[1] + -LET.]

1. An ornament for wearing round the neck. **1865** *Morn. Star* 23 May, The Prince and Princess presented their god-daughter with a necklet. **1884** J. HAWTHORNE *Pr. Saroni's Wife* v. 27 Her only ornaments were the necklet and bracelets of chased silver.

b. A small fur protector for the neck. **1896** *Daily News* 3 Oct. 6/5 The sable necklet is to be as much worn as ever this winter, the whole animal being used to form it.

2. A collar or belt for the neck. **1865** M. MACKENZIE *Use Laryngoscope* (1871) 108 The necklet which the patient wears, and to which one chain of the battery is attached.

'neck-line. [NECK *sb.*[1]] †**1.** = NECK *sb.*[1] 11 d. *Obs.*

1672 J. LACY tr. *Tacquett's Mil. Archit.* 34 Look in the Table for the Neck line, you'll find it to be 169,706. feet. **1810** C. JAMES *New Mil. Dict.* (ed. 3) II, *Neck-line*, an old term in fortification, signifying the gorge.

2. The shape of the neck of a garment; the line of the top of a woman's garment at the front of the neck.

1904 A. K. SMITH *Cutting Out* xxviii. 217 Construction lines... The lower line is the 'waist' line and the upper line the 'neck' line. **1923** [see BATEAU 2]. **1958** *Times* 5 Dec. 14/4 The bride..wore a gown of ivory-tinted satin with a square neckline. **1964** *McCall's Sewing* viii. 116/2 Neckline fits smoothly without pulling or gaping. **1974** *Country Life* 17 Jan. 106 Sweater with a sweetheart neckline... Spotted pullover..with a fashionable square neckline.

3. (See quot. 1966.)

1931 G. A. FOAN *Art & Craft of Hairdressing* iii. 136/1 Note the flat top, ragged crown, high neck line, and straight side-pieces. **1966** J. S. COX *Illustr. Dict. Hairdressing* 102/2 *Neckline*, (1) That part of the neck where the hair growth begins... (2) The outline at the neck of a cut head of hair. **1972** L. PALLADINO *Princ. & Pract. Hairdressing* viii. 113 Necklines may be curved, straight, pointed, or graduated high or low.

4. *Archæol.* An ornamental line around the neck of a vessel.

1937 *Antiquity* XI. 394 They show minor differences, additional necklines and bosses on the smaller vessel.

'neck-piece. [f. NECK *sb.*[1]]

1. The collar, or the part next the neck, of a garment.

1611 COTGR., *Collet*,..the necke-peece of any garment. **1653** URQUHART *Rabelais* I. ix. 45 A foxes taile should be fastened to the neck-piece [F. *collet*] of..every one that [etc.]. **1713** ADDISON *Guard.* No. 100 ⁋1 A certain female ornament by some called a Tucker, and by others the Neck-piece, being a slip of fine linnen or muslin that used to run ..round the uppermost verge of the women's stays. **1787** BEATTIE *Scoticisms* 61 The neck-piece of a coat is in Scotland called the neck, and in England the cape. **1862** *Eng. Wom. Dom. Mag.*, The neck-piece is perfectly plain.

b. A piece of armour, cloth, etc., covering or protecting the neck.

1823 CRABB *Technol. Dict.*, *Neck-Piece*, a piece formerly used to cover the breast of an officer or soldier. **1896** *Harper's Mag.* Apr. 728/2 A worsted hood..with a neck-piece that fitted about the chin.

2. †**a.** The neck. *Obs. rare.*

1605 MARSTON *Dutch Courtezan* III. iii, God bless thy neck-piece, and foutra! **1648** FANSHAWE *Il Pastor Fido* 77 To try all whether's stronger And faster on, thy neckpiece or My arm.

b. Of meat: The part of the carcass between the shoulder and the head.

c **1818** *Yng. Woman's Comp.* 22 The butcher should take out the kernels in the neck-pieces. **1844** H. STEPHENS *Bk. Farm* II. 99 The neck-piece..is partly laid bare by the removal of the shoulder.

'necktie. [f. NECK *sb.*[1]] **a.** A narrow band of woven or knitted material placed round the neck and tied in front, a common item of modern dress.

1838 *Workwoman's Guide* 80 Some-times the neck-tie is of a dark-coloured silk in the middle with two coloured ends. **1861** HUGHES *Tom Brown at Oxf.* xiv, Blake had great difficulty in adjusting his necktie before the glass. **1866** *Sat. Rev.* 21 Apr. 466/1 The gentleman in a white neck-tie.

b. *attrib.*, *spec.* in **necktie-party**, a lynching or hanging. *slang* (orig. and chiefly *U.S.*).

1871 *Harper's Mag.* Nov. 949/2 Mr. Jim Clemenston, equine abductor, was..made the victim of a neck-tie sociable. **1882** in *Nat. Geogr. Mag.* (1929) Aug. 247 If Found within the Limits of this City after Ten O'Clock p.m. this Night, you will be Invited to attend a Grand Neck-tie Party. **1893** *Spectator* 7 Oct. 463 A lynching is gracefully described as a neck-tie party. **1932** 'S. WOOD' *Shades Prison House* xxii. 340 An investigation brought to light the remains of the woman and her children, and Mr. Burrows was now booked to play lead at a neck-tie party, shortly to be convened. He walked to and fro with the death guards. **1967** N. LUCAS *C.I.D.* x. 157 Oh well—if you have a necktie party, it's a quick way to go. Better than being killed by an atom bomb. **1973** *Listener* 4 Jan. 10/3 A drunk or a loud-mouth could wind up like a rustler—the victim of a neck-tie party.

Hence **'necktieless** *a.*, wearing no necktie.

1890 S. J. DUNCAN *Soc. Departure* 25 A necktie-less, heavy-coated, high-booted young man.

'neck-vein. [f. NECK *sb.*[1]] A large vein in the neck (esp. of a horse).

1647 HEXHAM (1660), A Necke-veine, *een-Hals-ader.* **1707** MORTIMER *Husb.* (1721) I. 236 If it lie in the Maw.., let Blood in the Neck-Vein. **1766** *Complete Farmer* s.v. *Gripes*, It is more eligible to take it from the neck-vein. **1844** H. STEPHENS *Bk. Farm* II. 164 If the shoulder-point..is covered,..it..indicates a well-filled neck-vein.

'neck-verse, [f. NECK *sb.*[1]] A Latin verse printed in black-letter (usually the beginning of the fifty-first psalm) formerly set before one claiming benefit of clergy (see CLERGY 6), by reading which he might save his neck. Now only *Hist.*

a **1450** *Mankind* (Brandl) 506 Lett ws conne well owur neke verse, þat we haue not a choke. **1528** TINDALE *Obed. Chr. Man* (1550) 81 b, They have a sanctuary for yᵉ, to save yᵉ, yee and a necverse, if thou canst but rede a litle latenli. **1578** WHETSTONE *Promos & Cass.* IV. iv, It behoues me to be secret, or else my neck verse cun. **1607** HIERON *Wks.* I. 223 It is not good to put it vpon the psalme of *Miserere*, and the neck-verse, for sometime he prooues no clarke. **1681** OTWAY *Soldier's Fort.* II. i, The Rogue can't write his Name, nor read his Neck-Verse, if he had occasion. **1735** SAVAGE *Progr. Divine* 14 Four years, thro' foggy ale, yet made him see, Just his neck-verse to read, and take degree. **1805** SCOTT *Last Minstr.* I. xxiv, Letter nor line know I never a one, Wer't my neck-verse at Hairibee. **1872** SHIPLEY *Gloss. Eccl. Terms* 338 A deputy of the bishop..appointed to give malefactors their neck-verses, and judge whether they read or not.

†**b.** In phr. *to put* (or *bring*) *to the neck-verse.* Also in *fig.* use. *Obs.*

1567 GOLDING *Ovid's Met.* VI. (1593) 127 She purposed to put the Lydian maid Arachne to her neck-verse. **1619** in *Crt. & Times Jas. I* (1848) II. 151 He..dissuaded earnestly from the enterprise, as that which was like enough..to bring them all to the neck-verse. **1623** MABBE tr. *Aleman's Guzman d' Alf.* II. 105, I swear I will put him to his Necke-verse, and see how well or ill he will come off.

†**c.** In *transf.* or *fig.* uses. *Obs.*

1615 BRATHWAIT *Strappado* (1878) 113 Her humour is my neck-verse, which to sort I cannot, if I should be hanged for't. **1655** FULLER *Ch. Hist.* IV. i. §20 These words, bread and cheese, were their neck-verse or Shibboleth, to distinguish them. *a* **1659** BP. BROWNRIG *Serm.* (1674) I. xxxviii. 473 He looks upon the Scripture..as the very Neck-verse of his Condemnation.

'neckweed. [f. NECK *sb.*[1]]

†**1.** The plant hemp (with ref. to the use of hempen rope for hanging persons). Also *attrib.*

1562 [see GALLOW-GRASS]. **1588** *Marprel. Epist.* (Arb.) 17 A cawdell of Hempseed, and a playster of neckweed. **1611** in *Coryat's Crudities* L 2 b, The neck-weed-gallow-grasses sapling plant. **1620** J. TAYLOR (Water P.) *Praise Hempseed* Wks. (1630) III. 66/2 Some call it Neck-weed, for it hath a tricke To cure the necke that's troubled with the crick. **1681** T. FLATMAN *Heraclitus Ridens* No. 4 (1713) I. 23 Have a care your Tutors do not give you some of the *Salad de Gascon*, which we call Neck-weed [*printed*-week], for it is apt to make a Man laugh but on one side of his Mouth.

2. *U.S.* (See quots.)

1846–50 A. WOOD *Class-bk. Bot.* 406 *Veronica Agrestis.* Neckweed. Field Speedwell. **1860** W. DARLINGTON *Amer. Weeds*, etc. 227 *Veronica peregrina*,..Foreign Veronica. Purslane Speedwell. Neckweed. *Ibid.*, It was at one time supposed to possess medicinal virtues in scrofulous affections—which acquired for it the name of 'Neckweed'.

neclect, neclekk, obs. forms of NEGLECT *v.*

necles, obs. form of NECKLACE *sb.*

necligence, -ent, obs. ff. NEGLIGENCE, etc.

necro- (nɛkrəʊ), sometimes **necr-**, combining form of Gr. νεκρός dead body or person, occurring in various compounds either of Gr. origin, as *necrolatry*, *necromancy*, *necropolis*, or of more modern formation, as *necrobiosis*, *necroscopy*, etc. (see below); also **necrobaci'llosis** (pl. **-'oses**) *Path.* [BACILL(US + -OSIS], any of several conditions in animals, esp. domestic animals, and occas. in humans, characterized by diffuse or localized necrotic lesions caused by the bacterium *Sphærophorus necrophorus* (also called *Bacteroides funduliformis*, etc.); **necrodialo'gistical** *a.*, consisting of dialogues of the dead (*nonce-wd.*); **necro'genic** *a.*, arising from, produced by, contact with dead bodies; **ne'crogenous** *a.*, growing on dead or dying tissues or organs (Mayne 1856); **necro'morphous** *a.*, of coleopterous pupæ, motionless like a dead body; **necro'philia, ne'crophily** = *necrophilism*; hence **necro'philic, necrophi'listic** *adjs.*; **'necrophile, necro'philiac, ne'crophilist** *sbs.*, one who is morbidly attracted to corpses; also *attrib.* and *fig.*; **ne'crophilism,** a morbid fancy for the dead, or for contact with dead bodies; **ne'crophilous** *a.*, (*a*) of fungi or beetles, living on dead substances or carrion; (*b*) of, pertaining to, or resembling necrophilism; also *fig.*; **'necrophobe,** one who has a horror of death or of dead bodies; **necro'phobia, -'phoby,** a horror of death or of dead bodies (Craig 1849); **necro'phobic** *a.*, of the nature of necrophobia (Mayne 1856); **'necrophore,** a burying-beetle, one belonging to the genus *Necrophorus*; so **ne'crophorous** *a.*, belonging to this genus (*Cent. Dict.* 1890); **necro'tomic(al)** *a.*, of or pertaining to necrotomy (Mayne 1856); **ne'crotomist,** a dissector of dead bodies (Craig 1849); **ne'crotomy,** the dissection of dead bodies (*ibid.*); the excision of dead bone or tissue; **'necrotype,** a type formerly existing in a region and now extinct; hence **necro'typic** *a.*

Necr(o)- is also used in a number of other scientific terms, as ***necræmia, necrencephalus, necronarcema***, etc.: see Mayne *Expos. Lex.* and the *Syd. Soc. Lex.* Virginia Woolf preferred to Græcize to *nekro-*.

1907 *Ann. Rep. Bureau Animal Industry, U.S. Dept. Agric. 1905* 18 The presence of only one of the morbid conditions noted may be the starting point of an enzootic outbreak of necrobacillosis. **1933** R. A. KELSER *Man. Vet. Bacteriol.* (ed. 2) xxvii. 284 *Actinomyces necrophorus* is the etiological factor of a variety of 'necrobacilloses' among domestic animals. It is the cause of gangrenous dermatitis of equines, 'foot-rot' and 'lip-and-leg' ulceration of sheep. **1961** M. HYNES *Med. Bacteriol.* (ed. 7) xii. 172 *F[usiformis] necrophorus* (*Bacteroides funduliformis*) causes calf diphtheria and other animal diseases. In man it is the cause of various infections grouped together as necrobacillosis. **1715** M. DAVIES *Athen. Brit.* I. Pref. 23 Such Infernal Pamphlets were Lucian's Dialogues of old; and the Ingenious Mr. Brown's Parallels, of the same Necrodialogistical kind. **1899** *Allbutt's Syst. Med.* VIII. 788 The sore putting on all the character of the 'necrogenic wart'. **1892** C. G. CHADDOCK tr. *Krafft-Ebing's Psychopathia Sexualis* iii. 67 Following the preceding horrible group of perversions..come naturally the necrophiles. **1895** tr. *Ferri's Crim. Sociol.* 28 Again there are the necrophiles, like Sergeant Bertrand. **1932** V. WOOLF *Let. to Young Poet* 20 The large and highly respectable society of nekrophils.. who..are even now intoning the sacred and comfortable words, Keats is dead, Shelley is dead, Byron is dead. **1937** M. HIRSCHFELD *Sexual Anomalies* xxiii. 510 The mentally weak necrophile imagines that it is possible to inflict pain on the corpse. *Ibid.*, The necrophile act is..a frenzied intensification of the aggressive and destructive impulse. **1892** C. G. CHADDOCK tr. *Krafft-Ebing's Psychopathia Sexualis* iii. 68 The impulse to indulge in acts of necrophilia. **1926** W. MCDOUGALL *Outl. Abnormal Psychol.* viii. 164 He [*sc.* Ferenczi] assumes that coprophilia and necrophilia are normal components of the sex instinct. **1946** 'G. ORWELL' *Crit. Ess.* 122 [Dali's] most notable characteristic is his necrophilia. **1949** J. RODKER tr. *Bonaparte's Life & Works E. A. Poe* I. xii. 45 The necrophilia of this poet whom death alone inspired, and who was to cast so terrible, though irresistible, a spell on mankind. **1967** D. PINNER *Ritual* x. 105 He keeps corpses in here for amateur necrophilia. **1959** *20th Cent.* Dec. 426 In ghoulism the necrophiliac traffic is one way as it were. **1962** *John o' London's* 14 June 583/3 Lazarus..is trotted out..presumably for the benefit of any necrophiliacs in the audience. **1969** C. ALLEN *Textbk. Psychosexual Disorders* (ed. 2) xi. 256 Necrophiliacs are very rare, some are insane and inaccessible, and infrequently consult the psychiatrist. **1974** *Country Life* 23 May 1269/1 The sadistic and even necrophiliac horrors of the Symbolists. **1926** J. I. SUTTIE tr. *Ferenczi's Further Contrib. Theory & Technique Psycho-Anal.* 279 A necrophilic dream was due to anxiety in regard to coitus. **1940** H. ELLIS *My Life* ix. 373 She symbolised it [*sc.* this special problem].., making her hero..a fisherman with a kind of necrophilic attraction to corpses. **1955** J. STRACHEY et al. tr. *Freud's Compl. Psychol. Works* X. 278 A necrophilic phantasy which he once had consciously. **1864** *Chambers's Encycl.* VI. 695 The most extraordinary exhibition of necrophilism. **1932** V. WOOLF *Let. to Young Poet* 5, I replied after all these years to that elderly nekrophilist—Nonsense. **1949** J. RODKER tr. *Bonaparte's Life & Works E. A. Poe* I. v. 37 The lost and always sought for mother with whom his [*sc.* Poe's] necrophilist soul forever longed to unite. **1950** *John o' London's* 7 July 411/4 There they go, a grubby procession of blasphemers, perverts, lechers, necrophilists and drunkards. **1924** C. GRAY *Survey Contemporary Mus.* 185 The general public has taken to its great soft heart the necrophilistic ardours of the *Valse Triste.* **1932** V. WOOLF *Let. to Young Poet* 28, I, at any rate, refuse to be nekrophilus. **1956** 'M. INNES' *Old Hall, New Hall* I. v. 51, I don't think he was positively necrophilous. **1967** G. GREENE *May we borrow your Husband?* 12, I think she wants something more nubile and less necrophilous. **1971** R. E. WITT *Isis in Graeco-Roman World* iii. 37 Horus, Harsiesis ('Har, Son of Aset'), had been miraculously conceived by Isis in a necrophilous union. **1974** *Time* 7 Jan. 60/2 Chilling psycho-biographies of Sadists Stalin and Himmler, and the necrophilous Adolf Hitler. **1897** tr. *T. Ribot's Psychol. of Emotions* 257, I pass over the extreme cases, those of necrophily, or of sexual erethism. **1905** H. ELLIS *Stud. Psychol. Sex* IV. iii. 188 Necrophily, or sexual attraction for corpses,..may perhaps be regarded as a kind of perverted sadism. **1927** *Observer* 8 May 6/4 His circumstances and his griefs, and his disease fostered his necrophily. **1932** V. WOOLF *Let. to Young Poet* 20 Nekrophily induces slumber. **1939** T. S. ELIOT *Family Reunion* I. ii. 62 Let your necrophily Feed upon that carcase. **1962** *Times* 4 May 20/6 The phœnix rebirth of Toscanini's N.B.C. Orchestra which continued, after the maestro's death, to give Toscanini performances until it became plain to all that photographic reproduction from memory is..a variety of necrophily. **1973** Necrophobe [see HYPOCHONDRIAC *sb.* 1]. **1833** DUNGLISON *Dict. Med. Sci.* II. 72 *Necrophobia*... This symptom occurs in patients where the disease is not mortal; as in hypochondriasis. **1936** R. FLEMING *News from Tartary* v. i. 189 Since Greys hated anything dead, I gave the goose to her. But necrophobia was rife that morning. **1965** *New Statesman* 30 Apr. 684 (*heading*) Necrophobia. **1898** P. MANSON *Trop. Dis.* xxvi. 421 Necrotomy for bone disease may sometimes have to be performed. **1883** GILL in *Smithsonian Rep.* 460 It is quite improbable that any of the American Melaniiform mollusks are necrotypes of Africa.

‖**necrobiosis** (nɛkrəʊbaɪˈəʊsɪs). *Path.* [mod.L., f. NECRO- + Gr. βίος life: see -OSIS. Cf. F. *nécrobiose.*] The process of decay or death in tissues of the body; the gradual degeneration and death of a part through suspended or imperfect nutrition; an instance of this.

1880 A. FLINT *Princ. Med.* II. v. iii. 717 The majority of cases of softening are..the result of suspended nutrition (necrobiosis). **1897** *Allbutt's Syst. Med.* III. 517 A circumscribed loss of substance of one or more coats of the stomach by a process which appears to be a necrobiosis.

necrobiotic (nɛkrəʊbaɪˈɒtɪk), *a. Path.* [f. as prec. + -OTIC. Cf. F. *nécrobiotique.*] Of, pertaining to, or characterized by necrobiosis.

1875 PAYNE *Jones' & Siev. Pathol. Anat.* 399 A hæmorrhagic block passes through a series of necrobiotic changes ending with absorption. **1899** *Allbutt's Syst. Med.* VII. 272 Necrobiotic softenings, conditioned by non-irritative vascular occlusion.

necrographer (nɛˈkrɒgrəfə(r)). [-GRAPHER.] One who writes an obituary notice; a necrologist.

1862 THACKERAY *Philip* xxi, Those obituary notices to which noblemen of eminence must submit from the mysterious necrographer engaged by that paper. **1866** *London Rev.* 30 June 721/1 His necrographer does not take the trouble of burying him.

necrolatry (nɛˈkrɒlətrɪ). [ad. eccl. Gr. νεκρολατρεία worship of the dead, f. νεκρός NECRO- + λατρεία worship.] Worship of, or excessive reverence displayed towards, the dead.

1826 G. S. FABER *Sacr. Calend. Prophecy* (1844) II. 291 The members of that Church alone can be suspected of idolatry and necrolatry. **1842** —— *Prov. Lett.* (1844) II. 59 Curious specimens of the Necrolatry of the fourth century. **1882** LYALL *Asiat. Stud.* 18 The process by which other.. ideas of supernaturalism may..have developed out of this universal necrolatry.

necroˈlogic, *a.* ? *Obs. rare.* [f. NECROLOG-Y + -IC. Cf. F. *nécrologique.*] = next.

1796 W. TAYLOR in *Monthly Rev.* XXI. 497 The necrologic table of the men of letters or artists whom Rome could muster. **1804** —— in *Crit. Rev.* III. 559 The remarkable deaths..continue to be recorded in this necrologic almanac.

necrological (nɛkrəʊˈlɒdʒɪkəl), *a.* [f. as prec. + -ICAL.] Belonging to necrology; obituary.

1828-32 in WEBSTER. **1845** *Proc. Amer. Philos. Soc.* IV. 196 A necrological notice of Judge Story. **1856** W. H. SMYTH *Catal. Coins Dk. Northumbld.* 244 The truth of history has been greatly corrupted by necrological laudatory essays. **1880** *Daily Tel.* 7 Oct., The task of compiling a necrological account..was obviously a very easy one.

Hence **necroˈlogically** *adv.*, with reference to necrology, in the fashion of an obituary notice.

1802 SOUTHEY *Lett.* (1856) I. 203 The gentleman..that will one day execute me biographically or rather necrologically dissect me. **1900** R. BUCHANAN in *Contemp. Rev.* Feb. 223 This, by the by, is a little necrologically mixed.

necrologist (nɛˈkrɒlədʒɪst). [f. NECROLOG-Y + -IST.] One who writes an obituary notice.

1803 *Naval Chron.* X. 177 The necrologist has every previous collection before him. **1894** *Review Current Hist.* (Buffalo, N.Y.) IV. 967 An attempt to describe..might almost be spared his immediate necrologist.

necrologue (ˈnɛkrəʊlɒg). [f. NECRO- + -LOGUE.] An obituary notice.

1884 *Standard* 27 Oct. 5/4 An extremely warm necrologue of the deceased Duke. **1891** *Athenæum* 11 July 61/2 Both the necrologues and the reviews were originally printed in these columns.

necrology (nɛˈkrɒlədʒɪ). [See NECRO- and -LOGY. In sense 1, ad. med.L. *necrologium*, repr. Gr. *νεκρολόγιον (cf. MARTYROLOGY): hence also F. *nécrologe.* Cf. F. *nécrologie* in senses 2 and 3.]

1. An ecclesiastical or monastic register containing entries of the deaths of persons connected with, or commemorated by, the church, monastery, etc.

1727-38 CHAMBERS *Cycl.* **1817** FOSBROKE *Brit. Monachism* xxxvi. (ed. 2) 305 They were entered in the Necrology, selected from thence on the day of their decease, and.. suitable prayers said. **1846** MASKELL *Mon. Rit.* I. p. cxlix, The Martyrology must not be confounded with a volume.. which more properly was the Necrology.

b. A list of persons who have died within a certain time; a death-roll.

1854 *Tait's Mag.* XXI. 16 The necrology of the period in question does not contain in its registers the names of many great men. **1879** *Athenæum* 6 Dec. 731 Very heavy is this year's necrology in the Royal Society.

2. An obituary notice.

1799 SOUTHEY in Robberds *Mem. W. Taylor* (1843) I. 294 If this be worth mentioning in your necrology. **1812** B. FIELD in *Examiner* 9 Nov. 715/1 To the Memory of Daniel Parker, Esq...upon reading his Necrology.

3. The history of the dead.

1830 GALT *Lawrie T.* III. iv, It is believed by those to whom I was formerly known, that I exist no longer. My story belongs to necrology.

necromance. *Obs.* exc. *arch.* Forms: 4 nigromaunce, 4-5 -mance, 5 nygramance, 9 negromance. [a. OF. *nigromance, nigra-*, etc. (12th c.): see NECROMANCY.] Necromancy.

a **1300** *Cursor M.* 22112 (Edinb.), Of enchanteors, Of nigromance and of guglurs. **1390** GOWER *Conf.* III. 45 With Nigromance he wole assaile To make his incantacioun. *c* **1400** *Beryn* 2772 The wich been so perfite of Nygramance. **1483** *Cath. Angl.* 255/1 Nigromance, *nigromancia.* **1836** *For. Q. Rev.* XVII. 102 He came from Toledo hence, Where he had learned negromance.

necromancer (ˈnɛkrəʊmænsə(r)). Forms: α. 4-6 nygro-, (5 nygra-); 4-7 (9) nigro-, (5-6 nigra-); 6-8 negro-. β. 6- necro-, (6 nicro-). Also 4-5 -mauncer(e, 5 -mancere, -ciere, 5-7 -mancier; 4-6 -manser, 4 -sere, 5 -sier, -syer, *Sc.* -sour, 6 -sir. [a. OF. *nigromansere*: see NECROMANCY and -ER[1].]

1. One who practises necromancy; one who claims to carry on communication with the dead; more generally, a wizard, magician, wonder-worker, conjurer.

Quot. 1970 involves a pun on 'Negro'.

α. **13..** *Cursor M.* 22112 (Gött.), Noris him sal enchanturs, Of nigromancers and of iugelurs. **1375** BARBOUR *Bruce* IV. 242 The erll Ferrandis moder was Ane nygramansour. **1432-50** tr. *Higden* (Rolls) VI. 19 Machometus, þe fals prophete and nigromancier, deceyvede the Agarenys in thys maner. *c* **1489** CAXTON *Sonnes of Aymon* xi. 277 He was the subtillest nygramancer that ever was in the worlde. *a* **1540** BARNES *Wks.* (1573) 331/2 Gregory the seuenth, which was..a great nygromancer, and very familyar with the deuill. **1580** LYLY *Euphues* (Arb.) 444 It may bee, thought I, that in this Island..some odd Nigromancer did inhabit, who would shewe me Fayries. **1658** tr. *Bergerac's Satyr. Char.* xii. 46, I teach the Negromancers to destroy their Enemies. **1710** *Pict. of Malice* 11 The Print is..a Talisman (bequeath'd..by a.. Negromancer). **1829** W. IRVING *Granada* (1850) 342 The Moorish nigromancer stood beside him. **1922** E. R. EDDISON *Worm Ouroboros* xxxi. 388 Yet was it apparent to one so deeply learned in nigromancy and secrets astronomical that this thing was fatal. **1970** I. REED in A. Chapman *New Black Voices* (1972) 329 He who meddles w/ nigro-mancers courts his demise.

β. *a* **1548** HALL *Chron., Edw. IV* 211 Her frendes on the other side, said..her iorney [was] empeched by Sorcerers and Necromanciers. **1579** FULKE *Refut. Rastel* 728 Marcus an heretique and Necromanser, made that by enchantment, there should appeare very bloud in the chalice. **1634** MILTON *Comus* 649 You may Boldly assault the necromancers hall. **1681** H. MORE in *Glanvill's Sadducismus* I. Postscr. (1726) 19 Necromancers; that is, those that..do raise the Ghosts of the deceased to consult with. **1709** SWIFT *Vind. Bickerstaff* Wks. 1751 IV. 223 The General who was forced to kill his Enemies twice over, whom a Necromancer had raised to life. **1796** BP. WATSON *Apol. Bible* vi. 55 There were false prophets, witches, necromancers..among the Jews. **1857** HUGHES *Tom Brown* I. iii, The young necromancer declared that the same wonder would appear in all the rooms in turn. *a* **1873** LYTTON *Pausanias* III. i, Does it need the Necromancer to convince us that the soul does not perish when the breath leaves the lips?

appos. **1854** CDL. WISEMAN *Fabiola* II. vii, She promised to prevent the nightly excursions of her necromancer slave.

2. A silver or pewter dish with closely fitting lid and wide rim (see quots.).

1747 H. GLASSE *Art of Cookery* ii. 51 Take a large Pewter or Silver Dish, made like a deep Soop Dish, with an Edge about an Inch deep on the inside, on which the Lid fixes (with a Handle at top) so fast that you may lift it up full, by that Handle without falling; this Dish is called a Necromancer. **1784** S. MACIVER *Cookery & Pastry* (ed. 4) iii. 56 A necromancer is a flat white-iron pan with two handles, and a lid that checks in very close. *Ibid.* 57 Send it to the table in the necromancer. **1967** *Canad. Antiques Collector* Apr. 16/2 An interesting if rather odd relative of the chafing dish. It was called a 'necromancer' and was made of silver or pewter and fashioned like a deep soup dish with a well-fitting-lid and with a wide rim. When filled with thinly sliced meat, the container was hung by the rim between two chairs. Heat was applied by burning fifteen spills of brown paper.

†**necromancien.** *Obs.* Forms: 4 negre-, negro-, nigromancien, nygromancyene, 5 nygromancien, 6 nigromancian. [a. OF. *negro-, nigromancien*, f. *negro-, nigromancie*, NECROMANCY.] A necromancer.

1303 R. BRUNNE *Handl. Synne* 8154 þat sheweþ well seynt Cypryene, He was a nygromancyene. *c* **1386** CHAUCER *Pars. T.* ¶529 (Harl. MS.), As doon these false enchantours or nigromanciens in bacines ful of water. **1430-40** LYDG. *Bochas* I. iv. (MS. Bodl. 263) 20 Where philisophres & Nygromanciens Gan first tabounde. **1509** BARCLAY *Shyp of Folys* (1570) 198 Nigromancians, and false witches also Are of this sort folowing like offence.

necromancing (ˈnɛkrəʊmænsɪŋ), *vbl. sb.* [f. NECROMANC-ER + -ING[1].] The art or practice of necromancy. So **ˈnecromancing** *ppl. a.*

1853 DE QUINCEY *Autob. Sk.* vi. Wks. I. 173 The mighty necromancing witch. **1883** J. MACKENZIE *Day-dawn Dark places* 65 The chief season of praying and necromancing begins when they have sown their corn.

necromancy (ˈnɛkrəʊmænsɪ). Forms: α. 4-6 nygro-, 4-7 nigro-, 5-7 negro-; 4 nygre-, nigre-, 5 negre-; 4-6 nygra-, 4 nigra-. β. 6 nycro-, nicro-, 6- necro-. Also 4 -maunci, 4-5 -mauncy(e; 4-6 -mancye, -manci, 4-7 -mancie; 4-5 -mansi, 6 -sie, 4-6 -mansy(e, 5 -monseye. [a. OF. *nygromancie* (more commonly *-mance*: see NECROMANCE) = Sp. *nigromancia*, It. *nigro-, negromanzia*, med.L. *nigromantia* (1212 in Du Cange), an alteration, by association with L. *niger, nigr-*, black (cf. BLACK ART), of L. *necromantia*, ad. Gr. νεκρομαντεία, f. νεκρο- NECRO- + μαντεία divination, prophecy. From *c* 1550 the form *necro-* has been restored after Gr., as in F. *nécromancie.*

In *Merlin* (*c* 1450) pp. 375 and 508 the form *egramauncye* occurs; for an archaic 19th c. example see EGROMANCY. This dropping of the *n* appears also in the OF. form *igromancie.*]

1. The pretended art of revealing future events, etc., by means of communication with the dead; more generally, magic, enchantment, conjuration.

α. *a* **1300** *Cursor M.* 22112 Norijs him sal enchaunters, O nigramanci and o jugulors. **1362** LANGL. *P. Pl.* A. XI. 158 Nigromancye and perimancie the pouke to rise maketh. *c* **1420** LYDG. *Assembly of Gods* 867 Nygromansy, Geomansy, Magyk and Glotony. **1496** *Dives & Paup.* (W. de W.) I. xxxvi. 77/2 He forbedeth..nygromancye, that is wytchecrafte done by deed bodyes. *c* **1530** LD. BERNERS *Arth. Lyt. Bryt.* (1814) 43 A passage of the bred of a spere length made by nygramancye. **1594** ? GREENE *Selimus* Wks. (Grosart) XIV. 257 He may by diuellish Negromancie Procure my death. **1627** DRAYTON *Agincourt*, etc. 118 This Pallace standeth in the Ayre, By Nigromancie placed there. **1660** R. COKE *Power & Subj.* 161 We do forbid feigned Will-worship, Negromancy, Divinations, Witchcrafts. **1862** S. LUCAS *Secularia* 121 Nigromancy took its place among the regular callings.

β. **1522** SKELTON *Why not to Court* 693 It was by nycromansy, By carectes and coniuracyon. **1555** EDEN *Decades* 298 The great citie of Cambalu was in maner destroyed by necromancie. **1610** B. JONSON *Alch.* I. iii, I would know..Which way I should make my dore, by necromancie. **1672** MARVELL *Reh. Transp.* I. 73 You by your Necromancy have disturb'd him, and rais'd his Ghost. **1726** SWIFT *Gulliver* III. vii, By his Skill in Necromancy he hath a Power of calling whom he pleaseth from the Dead. **1774** WARTON *Hist. Eng. Poetry* I. Diss. i. 59 Jarl, a magician of Saxland, exhibits his feats of necromancy before Charlemagne. **1819** G. S. FABER *Dispensations* (1823) II. 94 One of the prohibited modes of divining was by necromancy. **1864** BURTON *Scot Abr.* II. i. 60 A world of wandering theories..taken from necromancy, and all the imaginative sciences.

transf. **1665** BOYLE *Occas. Refl., Disc. Occas. Medit.* II. ii, To be able, by an innocent kind of Necromancy, to consult the dead. **1827** HARE *Guesses* (1859) 174 Much of this world's wisdom is still acquired by necromancy,—by consulting the oracular dead. **1852** MRS. STOWE *Uncle Tom's C.* xxxv, A dread, unhallowed necromancy of evil.

b. With *a* and *pl.*

1550 BALE *Apol.* 20 b, Neuer had the sothsayers of Egypte ..more subtile pointes of conueyaunce, wyth all their incantacious and necromancies. **1585** T. WASHINGTON tr. *Nicholay's Voy.* IV. xix. 134 All..sorts of southsayings and Nicromancies. **1612** DRAYTON *Poly-olb.* iv. 338 Her to the rocke hee brought In which hee oft before his Nigromancies wrought. **1831** BREWSTER *Nat. Magic* iv. (1833) 68 An account of a modern necromancy, which has been left us by the celebrated Benvenuto Cellini. *a* **1849** J. C. MANGAN *Poems* (1859) 79 Love, with all his necromancies, fled.

2. Applied, after Gr. and L. use, to the part of the Odyssey describing Ulysses' visit to Hades.

1601 HOLLAND *Pliny* II. 548 The Necromancie of the Poët Homer. This picture Nicias held at so high a price, that [etc.]. **1850** MURE *Lit. Greece* II. x. §5 Nowhere, perhaps, does the contrast between the Ulysses of Homer and the Ulysses of the later fable..appear in a more prominent light than in the 'Necromancy'.

necroˈmaneous, *a. rare*$^{-1}$. [irreg. f. prec. + -EOUS.] Necromantic.

1801 tr. *Gabrielli's Mysterious Husb.* II. 21 The priest, who by a necromaneous assistance, persuaded himself he had attained the Papal dignity.

†**necromant.** *Obs.* In 7 nigro-, 7-8 negromant. [ad. It. *negromante*, = Sp. *nigromante*, obs. F. *négromant* (mod.F. *nécro-*), ad. Gr. νεκρόμαντις, f. νεκρο- NECRO- + μάντις diviner: see NECROMANCY.] A necromancer.

1598 FLORIO, *Emetren*, a precious stone..vsed of Nigromants. *a* **1626** MORYSON *Itin.* IV. (1903) 268 Scotus an Italian, calling himselfe an Astrologer,..but by others reputed a Negromant. **1755** T. H. CROKER *Orl. Fur.* III. lxvi, You could not stand against this negromant. **1887** A. LANG *Myth, Ritual & Relig.* I. 105 The power of..Sorcerers and Necromants.

necromantic (nɛkrəʊˈmæntɪk), *a.* and *sb.* Also 6-7 nigro-, negro-; 6 nekro-, 7 nicro-. [ad. late L.

necromanticus or med.L. *negro-*: see prec. and -MANTIC. Cf. obs. F. *nigromantique*, Sp. *nigro-*, It. *negromantico*.]

A. *adj.* **1.** Of persons: Given to the practice of necromancy.

1574 HELLOWES *Gueuara's Fam. Ep.* (1577) 33 A Nekromantike priest did aduertise him, that hee should not dismay. **1621** BURTON *Anat. Mel.* III. ii. III. v. (1651) 500 Wenches could not sleep in their beds for Necromantick Friers. **1737** WHISTON *Josephus, Antiq.* VI. xiv. §2 This sort of necromantic women, who bring up the souls of the dead. **1821** SCOTT *Pirate* xx, Had she really seen and conversed with a necromantic dwarf [etc.].

2. Of, belonging to, or used in necromancy or magic; performed by necromancy.

c **1590** GREENE *Fr. Bacon* i, It must be nigromanticke spels, And charmes of Art that must inchaine her loue. **1638** SIR T. HERBERT *Trav.* (ed. 2) 232 Nicromantic studies are much applauded, as profound. **1664** BUTLER *Hud.* II. iii. 95 Oh! that I cou'd.. find,.. by necromantick art, How far the dest'nies take my part! **1754** CATESBY *Nat. Hist. Carolina* II. p. xiv, By such necromantic delusions.. these crafty doctors .. raise their own credit. **1782-3** W. F. MARTYN *Geog. Mag.* I. 687 Their bodies marked with necromantic figures. **1813** SCOTT *Trierm.* II. xxvii, Till, in necromantic night, Gyneth vanish'd from their sight. **1878** SPURGEON *Treas. Dav.* Ps. cvi. 28 Perhaps they assisted in necromantic rites which were intended to open a correspondence with departed spirits.

b. *transf.* Magical, wonderful.

1630 J. TAYLOR (Water P.) *Navy Land Ships* Wks. I. 93/1 What Necromanticke spells are Rut, Vault, Slot, Pores, and Entryes. *c* **1645** HOWELL *Lett.* v. 28 O powrfull Negromantic eyes. **1849** RUSKIN *Sev. Lamps* ii. §12. 39 To give a delightful sense of a kind of necromantic power in the architect. **1883** *Knowledge* 15 June 357/1 The planets.. whose mysterious portals we.. are seeking to enter this night with necromantic art.

B. *sb.* †**1.** A necromancer. *Obs.*

1574 HELLOWES *Gueuara's Fam. Ep.* (1577) 142 Perchaunce thou art a Nekromantike, and hast enchaunted him. **1609** SIR E. HOBY *Let. to T. H[iggons]* 97 Had not Syluester been a Necromanticke.. and Marcellinus an open Idolater. **1652** GAULE *Magastrom.* 221 By the stone called elitropia (or, as the nigromanticks) the Babylonian gemme.

2. *pl.* Conjuring tricks. *rare*$^{-1}$.

1742 YOUNG *Nt. Th.* VIII. 346 Two state-rooks,.. With all the necromantics of their art, Playing the game of faces on each other.

†**necromantical**, *a. Obs.* Also 6 nigro-, 7 negro-. [f. prec. + -AL[1].] Necromantic.

1590 FORMAN *Diary* (Halliw.) 21 At Al-hallontyd I entred the cirkell for nigromanticall spells. **1603** HEYDON *Jud. Astrol.* xii. 309 These Negromanticall Images, fathered vpon Albertus. **1651** *Raleigh's Ghost* 180 The like Negromantical evocation to be made by Scipio, is read in Silvius. *a* **1682** SIR T. BROWNE *Tracts* (1683) 177 That he principally affected Poetry.. seems plain from his necromantical Prophecies.

Hence **necromantically** *adv.*

a **1646** J. GREGORY *Posthuma, Assyr. Monarch.* (1650) 199 After som diabolical Exorcisms, Necromantically performed, the head shall proue vocal. **1963** *Times* 1 May 13/6 Voodoo.. is seen as a religion of fear in which people become like animals, being possessed by demons and necromantically meddling with the spirits of the dead. **1965** *New Statesman* 12 Nov. 749/1 The most marvellous, necromantically speaking, is probably the title piece, where a boy learns the hazards of magic.

necromantist. *rare.* [f. as next + -IST.] A necromancer.

a **1608** DEE *Relat. Spir.* I. (1659) 247 A bankrupt Alchimist, a Conjurer, and Necromantist. **1910** *Daily Chron.* 8 Apr. 4/4 A sheaf of conjectures.. which have been drawn from the various necromantists.

†**necromanty.** *Obs. rare.* In 6-7 -tie. [ad. L. *necromantīa*.] = NECROMANCY.

1560 DAUS tr. *Sleidane's Comm.* 340 Is it not a great shame, that thou shouldest wholy depend upon Astrology and Necromantie? **1601** HOLLAND *Pliny* II. Table, Necromantie of Homer painted by Nicias. **1677** GALE *Crt. Gentiles* III. 68 Divinations.. from dead persons, which they called νεκρομαντεια, Necromantie.

ˈ**necronite.** *Min.* [f. NECRO- + -(N)ITE.] A variety of orthoclase, giving out a fetid smell when broken or struck.

1819 HAYDEN in *Amer. Jrnl. Sci.* (1820) I. 306 Necronite .. occurs, for the most part, in isolated masses in the blocks or slabs, both in an amorphous and crystallized state. *c* **1830** *Encycl. Metrop.* (1845) VI. 509/1 Necronite.. appears from its cleavage, hardness, and some other characters to be felspar. **1861** BRISTOW *Gloss. Min.* 256/2. **1885** RAMSAY *Min.* (ed. 3) 280.

neˈcrophagan. *Zool. rare*$^{-0}$. [Cf. next and -AN.] A necrophagous beetle.

1842 BRANDE *Dict. Sci.*, etc., *Necrophagans*, the name of a family of Clavicorn beetles, comprehending those which feed on dead and decomposing animal substances. [Hence in Ogilvie *Suppl.* (1855) and later Dicts.]

necrophagous (nɛˈkrɒfəgəs), *a. Zool.* [ad. Gr. νεκροφάγος: see NECRO- and -PHAGOUS. Cf. F. *nécrophage*.] Feeding on dead bodies or carrion.

1835 KIRBY *Hab. & Inst. Anim.* II. xvi. 70 Necrophagous animals, or those which devour dead ones, or any other putrescent substances. **1845** DARWIN *Voy. Nat.* iii. (1879) 56 Their vulture-like, necrophagous habits are very evident to any one. **1899** *19th Century* June 943 A part is at once assimilated by necrophagous creatures.

necropolis (nɛˈkrɒpəʊlɪs). Also nekro-. [a. Gr. νεκρόπολις city of the dead, cemetery, f. νεκρός corpse + πόλις city.] A cemetery; freq. used as the name of large cemeteries in or near cities.

1819 SOUTHEY in *Q. Rev.* XXI. 381 To rid the city of its burial places, and establish a necropolis without the walls. **1831** J. STRANG *Necropolis Glasguensis* Pref. 6 Argument for the establishment in this neighbourhood of a Necropolis. **1870-4** J. THOMSON *City Dreadf. Nt.* I. viii, In some necropolis you find Perchance one mourner to a thousand dead.

fig. **1831** CARLYLE *Sart. Res.* III. vii, How shall we domesticate ourselves in this spectral Necropolis, or rather City both of the Dead and of the Unborn?

attrib. **1854** CDL. WISEMAN *Fabiola* II. i, It was not a cemetery or necropolis company.., but rather a pious and recognised confraternity.

b. An old or prehistoric burying-place.

1850 GROTE *Greece* II. lix. (1862) V. 213 Extensive catacombs yet remain to mark the length of time during which this ancient Nekropolis served its purpose. **1874** GREEN *Short Hist.* i. §1. 9 Hill and hill-slope were the necropolis of a vanished race.

c. *pl.* in various forms.

Necropoles may possibly be intended as pl. of *necropole*, after F. *nécropole*; there is, however, no example of such a form in the singular.

1864 *Chambers's Encycl.* VI. 695 The most remarkable necropolises are that of Thebes, [etc.]. **1874** LADY HERBERT tr. *Hübner's Ramble* II. vii. (1878) 380 Save these two necropoli, I have seen all the most celebrated monuments of Japan. **1885** *Century Mag.* XXXI. 2 The necropoleis of Lycian Myra. **1885** *Pall Mall G.* 13 June 4/2 Mr. Richter's researches into the early necropoles of Cyprus.

Hence **necroˈpolitan** *a.*, of or belonging to a necropolis.

1892 *Spectator* 23 Jan. 115 That singular necropolitan peerage, the death-list of the *Times*. **1914** C. MACKENZIE *Sinister St.* II. IV. v. 965 Always in contrast with these necropolitan streets, these masks of human dwellings, were Michael's own thoughts thronged with fancies of himself and Lily. **1916** A. HUXLEY *Burning Wheel* 48 The necropolitan ground. **1931** A. GIBBS *New Crusade* 78 The long arm of coincidence was in his case the long arm of the law, white sleeved, and it was raised against the further progress of her vehicle to allow a large necropolitan car to come swinging serenely from the Embankment to the left over Westminster Bridge. **1960** *Times Lit. Suppl.* 20 May p. xi/2 The curiously necropolitan conventions of the worst comic strips.

necropsy (nɛˈkrɒpsɪ), *sb. Surg.* [ad. Gr. type *νεκροψία, f. νεκρός corpse + ὄψις sight. Cf. F. *nécropsie*.]

1. A post-mortem examination, an autopsy.

1856 MAYNE *Expos. Lex.* **1860** TANNER *Pregnancy* vii. 288 At the necropsy the corpus luteum was found in the right ovary. **1880** MACKENZIE *Dis. Throat & Nose* I. 99 At the necropsy of a case.. ulcers were found on the lateral walls of the pharynx.

2. Surgical investigation of a dead body.

1881 *Nature* No. 615. 347 It was pathological anatomy which replaced mysticism by realism, speculation by necropsy. **1891** *Cycl. Temp. & Prohib.* 628/1 Necropsy reveals either an empty heart or black fluid.

necropsy (ˈnɛkrɒpsɪ, nɛˈkrɒpsɪ), *v.* [f. the sb.] *trans.* To perform a necropsy on. So **neˈcropsied** *ppl. a.*

1927 *Arch. Path.* III. 985 It is of interest to compare in some detail the death rates at ages in the necropsied population as a whole, with the life table death rates of a general population, and with that portion of the necropsied population which had some malignant tumor at death. **1958** *Amer. Jrnl. Path.* XXXIV. 863 Kidneys from an unselected series of 200 necropsied patients were sectioned and stained by a modification of the Bowie technique. **1966** *Internat. Encycl. Vet. Med.* II. 964 In 7 per cent. of 52 severely affected pigs necropsied there was inflammation or ulceration of the stomach wall. **1971** *Nature* 16 Apr. 460/2 All surviving animals were killed and necropsied after 60 weeks.

necroscopic (nɛkrəʊˈskɒpɪk), *a. Surg.* [f. NECROSCOP-Y + -IC.] Of or belonging to necroscopy or post-mortem examinations.

1843 R. J. GRAVES *Syst. Clin. Med.* xxii. 267 An opinion which was borne out by the necroscopic phenomena. **1869** *Athenæum* 9 Oct. 464/2 A necroscopic room in which will be received all cases of doubtful death. **1895** *Forum* (U.S.) Sept. 37 The necroscopic characteristics which assimilate the European criminal to the Mongolian.. type.

Hence **necroˈscopical** *a.*

1855 in OGILVIE *Suppl.* **1859** SEMPLE *Diphtheria* 110 The results of my first observations have been confirmed by new necroscopical researches.

necroscopy (nɛˈkrɒskəpɪ). *Surg.* [ad. Gr. type *νεκροσκοπία, f. νεκρός corpse + σκοπεῖν to look, examine. Cf. F. *nécroscopie*.] The examination of bodies after death.

1842 PRICHARD in Abdy *Water Cure* 173 We know sufficiently from necroscopy, that the results of inflammatory action take place. **1847** tr. *Feuchtersleben's Med. Psychol.* 259 These are the.. more constant results of psychiatric necroscopy. **1893** W. R. GOWER *Man. Dis. Nerv. Syst.* (ed. 2) II. 325 *note*, The Pathological Society received the curiosities of Metropolitan necroscopy.

necrose (nɛˈkrəʊs, ˈnɛkrəʊs), *v. Path.* [f. NECROS-IS. Cf. F. *nécroser*.] *intr.* To mortify; to become affected with necrosis.

1873 F. T. ROBERTS *Handbk. Med.* 283 The cartilages often necrose. **1898** P. MANSON *Trop. Diseases* xxxvii. 563 Lymph which subsequently and rapidly necroses.

Hence **necrosing** *ppl. a.*

1897 *Allbutt's Syst. Med.* IV. 708 The somewhat hypothetical 'necrosing ethmoidites'. *Ibid.* V. 969 Producing inflammatory or necrosing changes in the tissues.

necrosed (nɛˈkrəʊst, ˈnɛkrəʊst), *ppl. a. Path.* [f. NECROS-IS + -ED, perh. after F. *nécrosé*.] Mortified, affected by necrosis.

1830 R. KNOX *Béclard's Anat.* 273 The specimen of necrosed scapula in the museum of Charenton. **1849-52** *Todd's Cycl. Anat.* IV. 939/2 The portion of necrosed bone .. was removed many years before. **1876** *Trans. Clinical Soc.* IX. 180 The entire shaft is denuded of periosteum and necrosed.

‖**necrosis** (nɛˈkrəʊsɪs). [mod.L., a. Gr. νέκρωσις deadness, f. νεκροῦν to kill, mortify, f. νεκρός corpse: see -OSIS.]

1. *Path.* The death of a circumscribed piece of tissue; mortification, esp. of the bones.

1665 NEEDHAM *Med. Medicinæ* 410 Which congeled portions cause a Necrosis or inward Mortification. **1693** tr. *Blancard's Phys., Dict.* (ed. 2), *Necrosis*, a black and blue Mark in any part. **1706** PHILLIPS (ed. Kersey), *Necrosis*... In Surgery, a perfect Mortification of the soft and hard Parts of the Body. **1799** *Med. Jrnl.* II. 382 Mr. Russell, who published, in 1794, a Practical Essay on Necrosis. **1805** *Ibid.* XIV. 300 At the first sight I suspected it to be a Necrosis. **1830** R. KNOX *Béclard's Anat.* 236 The repairing of bones when divided or affected with necrosis. **1876** BRISTOWE *Th. & Pract. Med.* (1878) 369 Cases in which the cartilages are in a state of necrosis.

b. *attrib.* and *Comb.*, as ***necrosis-producing*** adj.; **necrosis forceps**, an instrument for removing portions of diseased bone (Knight, 1884).

1891 *Daily News* 16 Jan. 2/4 Wherever tubercle bacilli.. have already impregnated their surroundings with the necrosis-producing substance.

2. *Bot.* (See quots.)

1866 *Treas. Bot.* 780/1 *Necrosis*. Canker. A drying and dying of the branch of a tree, beginning with the bark and eating gradually inwards. **1901** H. M. WARD *Disease in Plants* xxvi. 240 Necrosis.—This is a general term for cases where the tissues gradually turn brown or black in patches which die and dry up... Necrosis is often due to frost. **1951** L. L. PYENSON *Elem. Plant Protection* xvi. 302 Necrosis. The browning and death of tissues is a characteristic effect of some viruses. *Ibid.* 303 Internal symptoms may show a necrosis of the phloem. **1958** *U.S. Dept. Agric. Yearbk.* 1957 763/1 Necrosis. Death associated with discoloration and dehydration of all or parts of plant ograns, such as leaves.

†**3.** (See quot. and Coloss. iii. 5.) *Obs. rare*$^{-0}$.

1706 PHILLIPS (ed. Kersey), *Necrosis*, (in Divinity) a mortifying of corrupt Affections.

†**necrosy.** *Obs. rare.* [Anglicized f. NECROSIS.] Necrosis.

1657 TOMLINSON *Renou's Disp.* 113 They bring to the parts a certain necrosy or mortification.

necrotic (nɛˈkrɒtɪk), *a. Path.* [f. Gr. νεκροῦν (see NECROSIS) + -OTIC.] In a state of necrosis; characterized by, exhibiting necrosis.

1876 tr. *Wagner's Gen. Pathol.* 203 After 4 or 5 days of ligation the tongue becomes necrotic. **1897** *Allbutt's Syst. Med.* III. 340 The necrotic process extending from within outwards.

necrotiˈzation. *Path.* [-ATION.] The process of bringing tissue into a state of necrosis.

1859 *Chamb. Jrnl.* XI. 205 Kussmaul has tried some curious experiments on what he calls the necrotisation of limbs, by injection of chloroform. **1891** *Daily News* 27 Apr. 5/3 We now only hear of tuberculin as 'an agent that can.. hasten the necrotisation of tubercle'.

necrotize (ˈnɛkrəʊtaɪz), *v. Path.* [f. NECROT-IC + -IZE.] *intr.* To become affected with necrosis.

1873 T. H. GREEN *Introd. Pathol.* (ed. 2) 15 The extension of the necrotizing process to the surface.

ˈ**necrotizing,** *ppl. a.* [f. NECROTIZE *v.* + -ING[2].]

a. Undergoing or becoming affected with necrosis.

1899 *Allbutt's Syst. Med.* VIII. 715 The peculiar lesions ..might be described as necrotising chillblains. **1966** [see GRANULOMATOSIS].

b. Causing necrosis.

1901 *Ann. Rep. Bureau Animal Industry, U.S. Dept. Agric.* 1900 276 Dorset and de Schweinitz described the isolation of a necrotizing acid which they obtained from tuberculous cultures. **1957** SMITH & JONES *Vet. Path.* xxiv. 831 Each of these latter infections produces a minimum of exudate, but their toxins are no less deadly and the latter two are also necrotizing. Many streptococci also produce necrotizing (lytic) toxins.

nectar (ˈnɛktə(r)). Also 6 -er. [a. L. *nectar*, a. Gr. νέκταρ, of obscure origin.]

1. *Class. Myth.* The drink of the gods.

Sometimes incorrectly applied to the food of the gods: see AMBROSIA 2.

1555 EDEN *Decades* To Rdr. (Arb.) 49 The sweete ambrosia and nectar wherwith the goddes are fedde. **1579** SPENSER *Sheph. Cal.* Nov. 195 There lives shee with the blessed Gods in blisse, There drincks she Nectar with Ambrosia mixt. **1616** R. C. *Times' Whistle* v. 1913 He esteemes the nectar of the goddes.. to come short.. Of this delicious iuice. **1684** T. BURNET *The. Earth* I. 190 They would never have seen seven.. hundred years go over their heads, though they had been nourisht with nectar and ambrosia. *c* **1718** PRIOR *Mercury & Cupid* 21 We'll take one cooling cup of nectar. **1819** SHELLEY *Prometh. Unb.* III. i. 30 Drink! be the nectar circling through your veins The soul of joy. **1873** HAMERTON *Intell. Life* I. iii. 21 Not the nectar of the gods..were worth the dash of a wave upon the beach. *fig.* **1557** GRIMALDE in *Tottel's Misc.* (Arb.) 104 Woords, sweeter than the sugar sweet, with heauenly nectar drest. **1601** B. JONSON *Poetaster* v. i, Knowledge is the nectar, that keepes sweet A perfect soule. **1657** H. PINNELL *Philos. Ref.* 215 That..they may..drink of the everlasting Ambrosian Nectar of Eternity. **1758** JOHNSON *Idler* No. 32 ¶9 All.. implore from Nature's hand the nectar of oblivion. **1784** COWPER *Task* VI. 244 He inspires Their balmy odours,.. And bathes their eyes with nectar.

b. *fig.* (cf. AMBROSIA 5).

1592 SHAKS. *Ven. & Ad.* 572 Had she then gave over, Such nectar from his lips she had not suck'd. **1631** MASSINGER *Emperor East* II, May I taste then The nectar of her lip?

2. *transf.* **a.** Any delicious wine or other drink.

1583 STUBBES *Anat. Abus.* M iv b, The Nippitatum, this Huf-cap (as they call it) and this nectar of lyfe. **1638** BAKER tr. *Balzac's Lett.* (vol. II.) 200 These fellowes..call the worst wine they drink Nectar. **1662** H. STUBBE (*title*) The Indian Nectar, or a Discourse concerning Chocolate. **1718** OZELL tr. *Tournefort's Voy.* I. 283 In making Nectar, so called even to this day, they make use of another kind of grape. **1775** R. CHANDLER *Trav. Greece* (1825) II. 3 It lay opposite to the rugged tract called Arvisia, once famous for its nectar. **1800** MOORE *Anacreon* xxxviii, Grasp the bowl; in nectar sinking, Man of sorrow, drown thy thinking! **1863** MARY HOWITT tr. *F. Bremer's Greece* I. vii. 246 The Malvasia wine is an earthly nectar.

b. The sweet fluid or honey produced by plants, esp. as collected by bees.

1609 BUTLER *Fem. Mon.* i. (1623) B iij, Whereas they gather with the one Nectar, with the other Ambrosia. **1657** PURCHAS *Pol. Flying-Ins.* I. xv. 94 Thyme, which onely yeeldeth Nectar. **1697** DRYDEN *Virg. Georg.* IV. 240 Sweet Honey some condense,..The rest, in Cells apart, the liquid Nectar shut. **1742** YOUNG *Nt. Th.* II. 463 As bees mixt Nectar draw from fragrant flow'rs. **1796** C. MARSHALL *Garden.* ii. (1813) 22 From flowers we eventually gratify the palate by a valuable nectar. **1859** DARWIN *Orig. Spec.* iv. (1873) 74 The bees, which had flown from tree to tree in search of nectar. **1875** BENNETT & DYER tr. *Sachs' Bot.* 472 Insects..searching for the nectar.

†**c.** (See quot.) *Obs. rare*$^{-0}$.

1693 tr. *Blancard's Phys. Dict.* (ed. 2), *Necta[r]*..with Physicians..signifies rather a Medicinal Drink, but with a most delicious colour, taste and smell. [Hence in Phillips (1696) and some later Dicts.]

3. *attrib.*, as ***nectar cup, dew, epistle, -flood, fountain, love, stream***; (sense 2 b) ***nectar-chamber, -gland***; **nectar-bird**, a honey-sucker or sunbird belonging to the *Nectariniidæ*; **nectar-guides, -marks,** or **-spots**, coloured marks or spots on certain plants, supposed to indicate the point at which the nectar is secreted (*Syd. Soc. Lex.* 1892).

1842 *Penny Cycl.* XXIII. 284/2 The difference between the two structures is softened down by the intervention of the *nectar-birds. **1865** DK. ARGYLL in *Gd. Words* Mar. 231 Some of these have *nectar-chambers of most curious plan. **1847** EMERSON *Poems, To Rhea*, Who drinks of Cupid's *nectar cup Loveth downward, and not up. **1798** SOTHEBY tr. *Wieland's Oberon* (1826) I. 118 Scarce his tongue..Had from the goblet suck'd the *nectar dew. **1622** PEACHAM *Compl. Gent.* x. (1634) 92 What can be..more sweete than that *nectar Epistle of his? **1610** G. FLETCHER *Christ's Vict.* I, To allay With dropping *nectar floods, the furie of their way. *a***1618** RALEIGH *Rem.* (1644) 256 Over the silver Mountains, Where springs the *Nectar Fountains. **1883** *Evang. Mag.* July 310 This is the *nectar-gland, and it, with its scale, is called the Nectary. *a***1649** DRUMM. OF HAWTH. *Poems* Wks. (1711) 23/1 So in the sweetness of his *nectar love..Sowr is far better. **1602** MARSTON *Ant. & Mel.* v. Wks. 1856 I. 67 On *Nectar streams of your sweete ayres, to flote.

b. *Comb.*, as ***nectar-breathing, -dropping, -like, -loving, -secreting, -seeking, -spouting, -streaming, -tongued***.

1597 *Pilgr. Parnass.* IV. 386 One touch of her sweete *nectar-breathinge mouth. **1619** DRAYTON *Wks.* (1753) IV. 1280 Where..myrrhe-breathing zephyr..Gently distills his *nectar-dropping showers. **1647** H. MORE *Cupid's Conflict* lxviii, Thy Nectar-dropping Muse, thy sugar'd song. **1839–52** BAILEY *Festus* 490 Intwined about with nectar-dropping flowers. **1598** FLORIO, *Nettareo*,..sweet, pleasant, *Nectar-like. **1897** *Jrnl. R. Agric. Soc.* Dec. 663 *Nectar-loving insects. **1880** BESSEY *Botany* §531 Provided with *nectar-secreting glands. **1835** W. IRVING *Tour Prairies* 63 A very paradise for the *nectar-seeking bee. **1601** WEEVER *Mirr. Mart.* (Roxb.) 233 By Elysiums *Nectar-spouting fountaines. **1745** WARTON *Pleas. Melanch.* 292 Though Venus..With her on *nectar-streaming fruitage feast. **1596** FITZ-GEFFREY *Sir F. Drake* (1881) 78 *Nectar-tongu'd Sydney, Englands Mars, and Muse.

nec'tareal, *a. rare.* [-AL¹.] = next.

1652 CRASHAW *Carmen Deo Nostro* Wks. (1904) 197 In.. Thy Nectareall Fragrancy..there meetes An universall Synod of All sweets. **1658** ROWLAND tr. *Moufet's Theat. Ins.* 907 First of all we will treat of Honey, that immortal, nectareal, pleasant, wholsome juice. **1809** E. S. BARRETT *Setting Sun* III. 39 A bottle of nectareal champaigne.

nectarean (nɛk'tɛərɪən), *a.* [f. L. *nectare-us* (see NECTAREOUS) + -AN.] Of the nature of, or resembling, nectar.

1624 BURTON *Anat. Mel.* III. ii. III. (ed. 2) 418 Shee will adventure all her estate..for a Nectarean, a balsome kisse alone. **1651** STANLEY *Poems* 68 The vernal violets Nectarean juice. **1695** BLACKMORE *Pr. Arth.* I. 406 Ambrosial Food, and rich Nectarean Wine. **1813** *Sporting Mag.* XLII. 218 Like Homer's Gods quite muzz'd in oceans, Or the pure nectarean potions. **1857** B. W. PROCTER *Dram. Scenes*, etc. 401 Where the streams Of Poesy refine the brain With sweet thoughts nectarean.

nectared ('nɛktəd), *a.* [f. NECTAR + -ED².] Filled, flavoured, or impregnated with nectar; deliciously sweet or fragrant. (*lit.* and *fig.*)

*c***1595** SOUTHWELL *St. Peter's Complaint* 15 You Nectar'd Aumbryes of soule feeding meates. *c***1614** SIR W. MURE *Dido & Æneas* I. 461 Her sweet ambrosiall breath and nect'red hair. **1634** MILTON *Comus* 476 A perpetual feast of nectar'd sweets. **1715** POPE *Iliad* I. 769 Each to his lips applied the nectar'd urn. **1772** SIR W. JONES *Laura* 79 Ye radiant tresses! and thou, nectar'd smile! **1850** MRS. HAWTHORNE in *N. Hawthorne & Wife* (1885) I. 375 The children have lived upon the blue nectared air all winter. **1888** E. C. THOMAS *Bury's Philobiblon* (1902) 3 They are repelled violently from the nectared cup of philosophy.

†**'nectarel**, *adv. Obs. rare*$^{-1}$. [irreg. f. NECTAR.] Like nectar; fragrant.

1648 HERRICK *Hesper., To his Mistresses* 18 For your breaths too, let them smell Ambrosia-like, or Nectarell.

nectareous (nɛk'tɛərɪəs), *a.* [ad. L. *nectareus*, ad. Gr. νεκτάρεος, f. νέκταρ NECTAR: see -EOUS.] Of the nature of, consisting of, or resembling nectar.

1708 J. PHILIPS *Cyder* I. 32 Chear'd with her nectareous juice. **1725** POPE *Odyss.* XIV. 94 Luscious as the Bees nectareous dew. **1769** SIR W. JONES *Palace Fortune* Poems (1777) 17 From her smooth cheek nectareous dew he sips. **1832** *Fraser's Mag.* V. 120 They abandoned all..for the nectareous delicacies of Edinburgh ale. **1866** ROSE *Virg., Ecl. & Georg.* 132 With nectareous wine Libating thrice.

Hence **nec'tareously** *adv.*; **nec'tareousness**.

1847 in WEBSTER. **1858** HAWTHORNE *Fr. & It. Note-bks.* I. 149, I remembered the nectareousness of the new cider.

nec'tarial, *a. rare.* [f. NECTARY + -AL¹.] Of the nature of a nectary.

1808 ROXBURGH in *Asiat. Researches* VIII. 500 Pistil, germ conical..downy, surrounded with a downy nectarial ring.

nec'tarian, *a. rare.* [f. NECTAR + -IAN.] Nectarean.

1658 J. JONES *Ovid's Ibis* 2nd Ded., On Parnasse Hill rose the Nectarian Font. **1708** GAY *Wine* 138 Choicest Nectarian juice Crown'd largest Bowles. **1845** HIRST *Com. Mammoth*, etc. 39 Jewelled o'er With diamonds of nectarian dew. **1853** MOODIE *Life Clearings* 17 The impatient doctor grasped the nectarian draught.

nectaried ('nɛktərɪd), *a.* [f. NECTARY.] Of flowers or plants: Provided with nectaries.

1890 in *Cent. Dict.*

nectariferous (nɛktə'rɪfərəs), *a. Bot.* [See -FEROUS.] Bearing or producing nectar.

1760 J. LEE *Introd. Bot.* II. xxix. (1765) 145 The Adonis had been join'd to the Ranunculus, but was parted from it again, on observing that it wanted the nectariferous Pore. **1816** KIRBY & SP. *Entomol.* xxiii. (1818) II. 369 When they unfold their long tongue, and wipe its sweets from any nectariferous flower. **1882** G. ALLEN *Colours of Flowers* ii. 56 With separate petals,..and with a nectariferous cavity at their base.

nectarine ('nɛktərɪn, -iːn), *sb.*¹ Forms: α. 7 nectarya (?), nectaren, -orin(e, 8 -arin, -arne, 7– nectarine. β. nectrine, 7–8 -tron. [app. a subst. use of next.] A variety of the common peach, differing from this in having a thinner and downless skin and a firmer pulp. ***native nectarine***, the native quince or emu-apple of Australia.

α. **1616** SURFL. & MARKH. *Countrey Farme* III. i. 335 The principall fruit trees which delight to be planted against a wall are peaches, abricots, nectaryas [*sic*], all sorts of sweet plumbs. **1664** EVELYN *Kal. Hort.* (1729) 195 Now also plant Peaches and Nectarines. **1676** ETHEREDGE *Man of Mode* v. i, A strange desire I had To eat some fresh Nectaren's. **1685** TEMPLE *Ess., Gardening* Wks. 1720 I. 183 The only good Nectorins are the Murry and the French. **1712** ARBUTHNOT *J. Bull* III. ii, John had his golden Pippens, Peaches and Nectarnes. *a***1763** SHENSTONE *Ess.* Wks. 1765 II. 17 On an earwig that crept into a nectarin. **1802** W. FORSYTH *Fruit Trees* iii. (1824) 66, I have often heard of Peaches and Nectarines growing on the same tree. **1855** DELAMER *Kitch. Gard.* (1861) 157 Although the peach is so common in France, the nectarine..is rarer even than in England. **1889** MAIDEN *Usef. Nat. Pl.* 49.

attrib. and *Comb.* **1763** MILLS *Syst. Pract. Husb.* IV. 249 Nectarine trees generally produce their fruit..upon the young wood of the preceding year. **1854** M. HARLAND *Alone* xxxi, Black eyes, nectarine bloom and pouting rosy lips. **1856** OLMSTED *Slave States* 639 Of a warmer brown, and a more nectarine-like texture of skin.

β. **1657** AUSTEN *Fruit Trees* I. 57, I shall joyne the Nectrine with the Aprecock although another kind of fruit. **1686** PLOT *Staffordsh.* 227 Where there are now growing..7 sorts of Nectrons and Peaches. **1715** *Lond. Gaz.* No. 5360/9 Good Peaches, Nectrons and Apricock Trees.

nectarine ('nɛktərɪn), *a.* and *sb.*² [f. NECTAR + -INE¹.]

A. *adj.* Of the nature of, sweet as, nectar.

1611 COTGR., *Nectarin*, Nectarine, of Nectar, diuinely sweet, as Nectar. **1633** J. DONE *Hist. Septuagint* 13 To taste and relish those most nectarine..and excellent things. **1668** H. MORE *Div. Dial.* II. xviii. (1713) 144 The roscid Lips and nectarine Kisses of thy silver-faced Cynthia! **1854** F. TENNYSON in *Fraser's Mag.* L. 646 He drank up The precious drops, bright, dewy, nectarine.

†**B.** *sb.* A nectarean draught. *Obs. rare*$^{-1}$.

1628 BURTON *Anat. Mel.* III. ii. v. iii. (ed. 3) 509 [It is] to no purpose to prescribe Narcoticks, Cordials, Nectarines, potions, Homers Nepenthes, or Helena's Bole.

nec'tarious, *a. rare.* [-IOUS] Nectareous.

1771 SMOLLETT *Humph. Cl.* III. 4 My dairy flows with nectarious tides of milk and cream. **1791** W. ENFIELD *Hist. Philos.* II. ii. 53 He [*sc.* Apuleius]..drank freely of..the nectarious but unfathomable deep of philosophy. **1841** ORDERSON *Creoleana* iii. 29 The nectarious sweets distilled from the..charms of this..fair one. **1867** J. B. ROSE tr. *Virgil's Æneid* 16 Some ease the fragrant load Of food nectarious.

‖**nectarium** (nɛk'tɛərɪəm). *Bot.* Also 8 **-eum**. Pl. nectaria. [mod.L.] = NECTARY 2.

1753 CHAMBERS *Cycl. Supp.*, *Nectarium*, among botanists, ..a part of the corolla, sometimes, though more rarely the whole. **1774** GOLDSM. *Nat. Hist.* (1776) VIII. 75 As for the honey, it is extracted from that part of the flower called the nectareum. **1792** M. RIDDELL *Voy. Madeira* 58 The honied essences lodged in the nectaria of flowers. **1813** SIR H. DAVY *Agric. Chem.* iii. (1814) 145 Saccharine matter is found in the nectarium of flowers. **1851–9** BRODERIP in *Man. Sci. Enq.* 399 Liquefied honey..might be placed in a little reservoir on the site of the nectarium.

nectarivorous (nɛktə'rɪvərəs), *a.* [f. L. *nectar* (Gk. νέκταρ) nectar + -I- + *vor-us* devouring + -OUS, after CARNIVOROUS *a.*, etc.] Of birds or insects: feeding on the nectar of flowers.

1898 *Ann. Rep. Board of Regents Smithsonian Inst. 1896* 421 The nectarivorous insects localize their action upon these nectaries.

'nectarize, *v. rare.* [f. NECTAR + -IZE.] *trans.* To sweeten. Hence **'nectarized** *ppl. a.*

1592 G. HARVEY *Four Lett.* Sonn. viii, Gently assemble Delicacies all, And sweetely nectarize this bitter gall. **1593** NASHE *Christ's T.* Wks. (Grosart) IV. 170 The nectarized *Aqua celestis* of water-mingled blood, sluced from Christ's side. **1623** COCKERAM I, *Nectariz'd*, sweetned.

nectarous ('nɛktərəs), *a.* [f. NECTAR + -OUS.] Resembling nectar.

1667 MILTON *P.L.* v. 306 Thirst Of nectarous draughts. *Ibid.* VI. 332 From the gash A stream of Nectarous humor issuing flow'd. **1816** KEITH *Phys. Bot.* I. 183 The fluid secreted is nectarous. **1878** J. THOMSON *Plenip. Key* 24 A nectarous food, a most ambrosial balm.

nectary ('nɛktərɪ). [f. NECTAR, or ad. mod.L. *nectarium*: see -ARY.]

†**1.** *fig.* ? A nectareous fluid. *Obs. rare*$^{-1}$.

1598 F. ROUS *Thule* T 3, Her folded eyes, Drowning themselues in their owne Nectaries.

2. *Bot.* The organ or part of a flower or plant which secretes honey.

1759 B. STILLINGFLEET *Misc. Tracts* Introd. (1762) 31 The part of the flower that contains honey is called The nectary. **1796** WITHERING *Brit. Plants* (ed. 3) I. 3 The tube of the blossom serves the purpose of a Nectary in many flowers, as in the Honey-suckle. **1811** A. T. THOMSON *Lond. Disp.* (1818) 227 The corolla consists of six..petals, enclosing a tuberculated bristled nectary. **1856** R. A. VAUGHAN *Mystics* II. 324 Some pierced the nectaries of the flowers with their fine bills. **1874** COUES *Birds N.W.* 269 An arrangement which..facilitates the extraction of honey from the nectaries of flowers.

3. *Ent.* A wart-like tube on the body of an aphis, from which 'honey-dew' is exuded.

1890 in *Cent. Dict.* **1898** PACKARD *Text-bk. Entom.* 365 Busgen..observed that on reaching the air the drops issuing from the 'nectary' or 'honey' tube stiffened almost instantly into a wax-like mass.

nectiferous, irreg. var. of NECTARIFEROUS.

1830 LINDLEY *Nat. Syst. Bot.* 7 In Ranunculus itself, which has a nectiferous gland at the base of the petals. **1873** E. SMITH *Foods* 264 Honey is found usually at the base of the petal of the flower, and in the nectiferous glands.

necting: see NETTING.

nectocalycine (nɛktə'kælɪsaɪn), *a. Zool.* [See next and CALYCINE.] Of the nature of, resembling or pertaining to, a nectocalyx.

1859 HUXLEY *Oceanic Hydrozoa* 15 These nectocalycine canals are lined by a continuation of the endoderm. **1861** J. R. GREENE *Man. Anim. Kingd., Cœlent.* 37 A continuation of the endoderm lines the 'nectocalycine canals'. **1888** ROLLESTON & JACKSON *Anim. Life* 773 *note*, The nectocalycine section of the coenosarc.

nectocalyx (nɛktə'keɪlɪks). *Zool.* Pl. **-calyces**. [mod.L., f. Gr. νηκτός swimming (f. νήχειν to swim) + CALYX.] The swimming-bell which forms the natatory organ in many hydrozoans.

1859 HUXLEY *Oceanic Hydrozoa* 15 The presence of the valvular membrane at once distinguishes a nectocalyx from an umbrella. **1888** ROLLESTON & JACKSON *Anim. Life* 773 A furrow or canal formed at the side of the distal nectocalyx.

So **'nectosac**, the interior of a nectocalyx (also called ***nectocyst***); **'nectosome**, the upper portion of a siphonophore, bearing the natatory organs; **'nectostem**, the axis of a series of nectocalyces.

1859 HUXLEY *Oceanic Hydrozoa* 15 The cavity of the cup, which, with its muscular wall, may be termed the nectosac. **1870** H. A. NICHOLSON *Man. Zool.* 85 The interior of the nectocalyx is often called the 'nectosac'. **1888** *Stand. Nat. Hist.* I. 99 Just below the float on the nectostem there is a small cluster of minute buds in which can be found nectocalices of all sizes. **1898** SEDGWICK *Text-bk. Zool.* I. 139 The nectosome, to which the swimming organs (nectocalyces and pneumatophores) are attached.

necton, var. NEKTON.

'nectopod. *Zool.* [f. as NECTOCALYX + -POD.] A foot used as a swimming organ.
1896 tr. *Boas' Text-bk. Zool.* 195 The short thorax is provided with laminate nectopods like the limbs of the Phyllopoda, though there are only four to six pairs.

nectorin(e, -trine, -tron, obs. ff. NECTARINE.

†**necyomancy, -manty.** *Obs. rare*$^{-0}$. [ad. L. *necyomantīa*, Gr. νεκυομαντεία.] (See quots.)
1623 COCKERAM I, *Necyomantie*, diuination by calling vp damned spirits. **1656** BLOUNT *Glossogr.*, *Necyomancie*, the same with Necromancy.

ned[1] (nɛd). *Sc. slang.* [? f. *Ned*, a familiar abbrev. of the name *Edward*; cf. TEDDY BOY.] Hooligan, thug, petty criminal. Also used as a general term of disapprobation.
1959 *Times* 18 Dec. 5/3 He can..give gloriously funny imitations of Glasgow charwomen, tram drivers, and neds. **1964** B. GASTON *Drifting Death* iv. 57 Lomax..was a tuppeny-ha'penny little ned, not even attached to one of the big mobs. **1968** H. C. RAE *Few Small Bones* II. i. 71 Even the bloody neds from the newspapers were getting critical with their wisecracks. **1969** B. KNOX *Tallyman* ii. 21 Millside had the worst pockets of unemployed and unemployable,..and some of the toughest hooligan 'neds' in the city [*sc.* Glasgow]. **1971** —— *To kill a Witch* i. 10 Most were neds, the city's [*sc.* Glasgow's] verbal shorthand for petty thugs, second-rate criminals and professional layabouts. **1973** P. MALLOCH *Kickback* xvi. 100 He was a ned. You could always spot them. There was something about them that no trained policeman would ever miss.

Ned[2] (nɛd). Short for NEDDY 3.
1961 *Guardian* 19 Dec. 14/1 His National Economic Development Council (or 'Ned', as it is ominously being called). **1963** *Ann. Reg. 1962* 3 The National Economic Development Council (already familiarly known as Ned or even Neddy). **1964** *New Society* 23 Jan. 23/2 Each little Ned ..is going to have a highly individual character, according to the wishes of the industry involved.

ned, obs. form of NEED *sb.* and *v.*

†**nedde**, had not: see NE and HAVE *v.* A. 9.
c **1200** *Trin. Coll. Hom.* 69 For þat hie nedden here synnes er bet. *a* **1300** *Vox & Wolf* 99 in Hazl. *E.P.P.* I. 61 This ilke shome neddi nouthe, Nedde lust i-ben of mine mouthe. *c* **1315** SHOREHAM VII. 877 Elles nedde hyt be no senne. **1362** LANGL. *P. Pl.* A. v. 4 Me was wo..That I nedde sadloker i-slept and i-seȝe more.

nedder, variant of NITHER *v.*

nedder, -ir, -re, obs. ff. ADDER, NETHER.

neddy ('nɛdɪ). [dim. of *Ned*, a familiar abbrev. of the name *Edward*: see -Y[4].]
1. a. A donkey.
a **1790** POTTER *Dict. Cant* (1795), *Neddy*, a jackass. **1794** WOLCOT (P. Pindar) *Rowland for Oliver* Wks. 1816 II. 119 Thou think'st thyself on Pegasus so steady; But, Peter, thou art mounted on a Neddy. **1858** MISS YONGE *Christmas Mummers* 5 There is old Harry Spinner's grey donkey..and Mrs. Brown's handsome Neddy. **1894** BARING-GOULD *Kitty Alone* III. 19 The neddy is in the stable here, and there is his cart.
transf. **1866** BLACKMORE *Cradock Nowell* lvii. (1883) 400 A beautiful schooner of the true American rig, which made such lagging neddies of our yachts a few years since.
b. A fool, a simpleton.
1823 'J. BEE' *Slang* 124 *Neddy*—sometimes 'ass-neger', other names for jackass—the living emblem of patience and long suffering. **1853** THACKERAY *Newcomes* (1854) I. i. 4 All types of all characters march through all fables:..victims and bullies; dupes and knaves; long-eared Neddies, giving themselves leonine airs. **1854** A. E. BAKER *Gloss. Northamptonshire Words* II. 49 What a neddy you must be, to do that! **1963** L. DEIGHTON *Horse under Water* xlix. 212 'I'm sorry,' he said, 'you must think I'm a terrible neddie.'
c. *Austral. slang.* A horse, esp. a racehorse.
1900 [see BAG *sb.* 18 c(*a*)]. **1918** B. CRONIN *Coastlanders* 74 A hot cinder lit on my neddie's rump. **1965** W. DICK *Bunch of Ratbags* 40 My old man was backing the neddies as usual.
2. *Cant.* A life-preserver.
1864 *Cornh. Mag.* VI. 647 The weapon is generally a 'neddy' or life-preserver. **1879** *Macm. Mag.* XL. 503/1 We shall want..the stick (crow-bar), and bring a Neddie (life-preserver) with you.
3. [Properly a different word.] *colloq.* name for the *N*ational *E*conomic *D*evelopment Council. Also, one of its sub-committees. Also *attrib.*
1962 *Engineering* 1 June 729/2 Since poor Neddy was formed everyone seems to be jumping on to his band wagon. **1963** *Times* 11 June 6/6 The great significance of Neddy is that it is the first time in this country that a concerted effort has been made by the Government, management and the unions to set the country moving on a course which can be steadily sustained. **1964** *Financial Times* 8 Sept., We shall deal with them [*sc.* problems]..most of all through N.E.D.C., which we shall retain, and the regional and industrial Neddies. **1966** *Times* 14 May 17/6 Two little neddies are due to meet, wool on Tuesday and mechanical engineering on Thursday. **1968** W. DAVIS *Three Years Hard Labour* I. iv. 50 The so-called 'Little Neddies'. These were Councils for individual industries, designed to bridge the gap between Whitehall and industry. **1968** *Times* 18 Apr. 21/7 A Neddy-sponsored questionnaire sent out to 2,000 firms in the wool trade, is the first phase of a £80,000 survey designed to establish the competitiveness of the British wool textile industry. **1969** *Times* 30 Apr. 25/4 New chairman for building Neddy... A new chairman for the building and civil engineering economic development committees has been found.

neddy, neddyr, obs. ff. NEEDY, ADDER.

nede, obs. form of NEED, NEEDY, GNEDE *a.*

nedel(l, -ill(e, etc., obs. forms of NEEDLE.

ned(e)les, -lich, -ling(is, -ly, etc., obs. ff. NEEDLESS, etc.

neder, obs. form of ADDER, NEITHER, NETHER.

‖**Nederlands** ('ne:dəlants). *S. Afr.* [Afrikaans, ad. Du. *Nederlandsch.*] The Dutch language.
1926 *Spectator* 21 Aug. 278/2 Africaans resembles, in vocabulary, the Dutch of the seventeenth and early eighteenth centuries almost more than modern Nederlands does. **1959** *Cape Times* 8 June 8/5 Nederlands is an old and highly-developed language with a wide literature.

nedes, obs. form of NEEDS.

nedi, nedy, -ness, obs. forms of NEEDY, -NESS.

Ned Kelly (nɛd 'kɛlɪ). *Austral.* The name of the most famous Australian bush-ranger (1857–1880), used allusively to designate one of reckless courage or unscrupulous business dealings. *colloq.* See also GAME *a.*[1] 2.
1941 BAKER *Dict. Austral. Slang* 41 *Kelly, Ned*, any person of buccaneering business habits. **1945** 'R. RENE' *Mo's Memoirs* 24 He was game as Ned Kelly, and he'd ride anything. **1953** D. CUSACK *Southern Steel* 41 Is that kid game? Game as Ned Kelly. **1953** R. BRADDON in I. Bevan *Sunburnt Country* 129 Such a feat of bluff is known to Australians as a 'Ned Kelly'... It is phrases such as 'do a Ned Kelly' that lend so much verve and colour to the Australian serviceman's vocabulary. **1958** H. D. WILLIAMSON *Sunlit Plain* 90 In fact, to pay him his due compliment, he was as game as Ned Kelly. **1965** J. O'GRADY *Aussie English* 62 Included in this Ned Kelly category are.. characters who overcharge for mediocre work and services, and the bloke who sells you a second-hand, guaranteed, 'every bit as good as new..' vehicle, which falls to pieces in the first hundred miles. *Ibid.*, To say that a man is 'as game as Ned Kelly', on the other hand, is to praise him highly. It means that he..is brave to the point of recklessness in the face of any odds. **1966** D. CRICK *Period of Adjustment* 66 'Are you game?' 'As Ned Kelly.' **1973** *Guardian* 19 Mar. 7/7 Sporty boys now..peer out of the windowed skull of the full-face [crash] helmet dubbed Ned Kelly. **1974** *Courier-Mail* (Brisbane) 20 Aug. 12/5 Mr. Bizzell said the council offered him £740 for 74 perches of land, including a 33 perch block he had levelled... 'They are just Ned Kellys,' he said. 'They certainly won't put it back on the market without making a handsome profit.'
2. Rhyming slang for 'belly'.
1945 BAKER *Austral. Lang.* xv. 271 Here are a few examples of undisguised rhyme that seem to be Australian: ..*Port Melbourne Pier*, an ear; *Ned Kelly*, the belly. **1960** J. FRANKLYN *Dict. Rhyming Slang* 100/1 *Ned Kelly*, belly. **1970** *Private Eye* 27 Mar. 16 If I don't get a drop of hard stuff up me old Ned Kelly there's a good chance I might chunder in the channel.

nedyl(le, nedyr(e, obs. ff. NEEDLE, ADDER.

nedyrcopp, obs. form of ATTERCOP.
c **1475** *Pict. Voc.* in Wr.-Wülcker 766 *Hec aranea*, a nedyrcopp.

‖**née** (ne), *a.* [Fr., fem. of pa. pple. of *naître* to be born.] Born: placed before a married woman's maiden name.
1758 M. W. MONTAGU *Let.* 27 Nov. (1967) III. 192 The advantage of being casually admitted in the train of Madame de B., *née O.* **1831** M. EDGEWORTH *Let.* 30 Apr. (1971) 529 This Abroad & at Home is by Mrs. Eaton née Waldy. **1848** THACKERAY *Van. Fair* xlviii. 429 The interview between Rebecca Crawley, née Sharp, and her Imperial Master. **1919** T. S. ELIOT *Sweeney Among Nightingales* in *Poems*, Rachel née Rabinovitch Tears at the grapes with murderous paws. **1955** *Times* 2 July 8/7 He married, after divorce proceedings, Mary Barrie (*née* Ansell), by whom he was, himself, subsequently divorced. **1973** *Times* 3 Nov. 16/6 Mrs Fanny Harwood, nee Fanny Pain..was born in 1889.

nee, obs. form of NEIGH *v.*

neece, neech, obs. forms of NIECE, NICHE.

neechee, var. NITCHIE.

need (ni:d), *sb.* Forms: α. 1 néad, 2 neat. β. 1–4 néod, 1–5 neode, 2 neoð, neot; 2–5 node, 3 nod, noede. γ. 1–2 níed, 3 nyede; 1 nýd, 1, 3–4 nud, 5 nude. δ. 1–5 ned, 1–6 nede, 4– need, 4–7 neede, (6 neade, 5 neethe, 6 nide); 4–7 *Sc.* neid, 4–6 neide, (4, 6 neyd). [A Common Teutonic word, of which the normal representative in OE. is the form *níed* (*nýd, néd*) = OFris. *nêd, nâth*, OS. *nôd* (MDu. *nood-, noot*, Du. *nood*), OHG. *nôt* (MHG. *nôt*, G. *noth, not*), ON. *nauð, neyð* (Sw. and Da. *nöd*), Goth. *nauþs*, fem. *i*-stem:—OTeut. **nauđi-*, **nauþi-* related to OPruss. *nauti-n* need.
Both in form and gender, however, the word exhibits curious variations in OE. The forms *níed, nýd, néd* would be normal as representatives of a fem. *i*-stem, but in cases where the gender can be distinguished they usually appear as neuters. A form without umlaut also occurs (*néad*: cf. the ON. *nauð*), which appears to have been feminine. The very common form *néod*, which is distinctly fem., is difficult to account for; if not an independent ablaut-variant, its vowel has probably been influenced by the frequent word *néod* desire, earnestness, pleasure, etc.]

I. †**1.** Violence, force, constraint, or compulsion, exercised by or upon persons. *Obs.*
Beowulf 2454 þonne se an hafað þurh deaðes nyd dæda ȝefondad. *c* **825** *Vesp. Psalter* xxxvii. 13 Ned [L. *vim*] dydun ða sohton sawle mine. *c* **888** K. ÆLFRED *Oros.* II. iv. §9 Hiere anweald is ma hreosende for ealddome þonne of æniȝes cyninges niede. *c* **1000** *Ags. Gosp.* Matt. xi. 12 Heofena rice þolað nead, & strece nimað þæt. *a* **1300** *Cursor M.* 7694 Childer of his aun sede Suld be for-driuen vte wit nede [*Gött.* for nede]. *c* **1375** *Sc. Leg. Saints* xxxi. (*Eugenia*) 388 Scho was nere quhen þe monk assalȝeit sa hyr laydy þar for ned to ta.

†**2.** ***for, of,*** or ***on need***, of or by necessity, unavoidably. *Obs.* (in later use chiefly *Sc.*)
c **900** tr. *Bæda's Hist.* II. xx. 148 His sunu for neade..to Pendan þæm cyninge ȝebeaȝ . *Ibid.* IV. xxv. 350 Seo þearlwisnis..him ærest of nede becwom. *a* **1122** *O.E. Chron.* (Laud MS.) an. 1016 Ða forlet he his herȝunga..& beah þa for nede. *c* **1375** *Sc. Leg. Saints* i. (*Peter*) 654 Quha had ben þar, of ned his hart suld have ben sar. *c* **1470** *Gol. & Gaw.* 332 Yow worthis on neid For to assege yone castel. ? *a* **1550** *Freiris Berwik* 97 in *Dunbar's Poems* (1893) 288 Thairfoir of verry neid we mon byd still. **1567** *Gude & Godlie B.* (S.T.S.) 89 The peple follow man, on neid, Thir prelatis.

3. a. Necessity arising from the facts or circumstances of the case. Chiefly in phr. ***if*** (etc.) ***need require, if need be*** (or ***were***).
c **900** tr. *Bæda's Hist.* I. xxvii. 86 þa symbelnesse to mærsienne mæssesonges, ȝif þæt ned abædeþ. *c* **1200** *Trin. Coll. Hom.* 215 Swo hoh [= ought] ech chirche socne don þenne hie nede sen. *a* **1300** *Cursor M.* 14913 Fast it neghes to þe nede For his to suffur passion. **1389** in *Eng. Gilds* (1870) 8 That he haue þo torches redy to brynge hym withe to cherche ȝif nede be. **1390** GOWER *Conf.* I. 117 Thou, which art withoute nede For lawe of londe in such a drede. **14..** *Gesta Rom.* xxxiii. 128 (Harl. MS.), I wolde for his love shede my blode, yf nede wer. **1503** in *Surtees Misc.* (1890) 30 For reparacioncz, when neide requierethe. **1568** GRAFTON *Chron.* II. 242 Archers to comfort them that were most wearie, if neede were. **1600** J. PORY tr. *Leo's Africa* v. 254 To the end he might finde safe refuge when neede required. **1640** BROME *Sparagus Gard.* II. iii, Learne to shift for myselfe in time and need be. *a* **1687** PETTY *Pol. Arith.* viii. (1691) 105 There may be about six Millions.., which (if need require) might actually Labour. **1747** WESLEY *Prim. Physick* (1762) 32 Repeat this if Need be. **1808** SCOTT *Marm.* II. iv, To hold A chapter,..And if need were to doom to death.
b. In later use with ***there is*** expressed or implied. (Only with qualifying word as ***what, little, no,*** etc.)
a **1600** HOOKER *Eccl. Pol.* VIII. vi. §11 What need was there that they should bargain with the cardinal? **1624** in *Capt. Smith's Wks.* (Arb.) 408 Little neede there was and lesse reason, the ship should stay. **1667** MILTON *P.L.* VIII. 420 No need that thou Shouldst propagat, already infinite. **1724** SWIFT *Drapier's Lett.* iii. Wks. 1751 VIII. 312 But what need is there of disputing. **1845** F. E. PAGET *Tales Village Childr.* Ser. II. 40 There was no need of you to confess it.

†**4. a. *need is,*** or ***it is need***, it is necessary or needful ***that*** or ***to*** (with inf.). Also with adjs. as ***great need***, etc. *Obs.*
c **950** *Lindisf. Gosp.* Matt. xviii. 7 Ned *vel* ðarflic is..þæt hia cyme ondspyrniso. *c* **1000** ÆLFRIC *Hom.* I. 516 Neod is þæt æswicunga cumon. *c* **1175** *Lamb. Hom.* 9 Hit is muchel neot þet we þonkien ure drihten. *a* **1225** *Ancr. R.* 110 Hit is neod forte habben þe betere warde. *a* **1300** *Cursor M.* 19589 [To] do penance ned es i-nogh. *Ibid.* 20225 Now is ned þat i haf o þe deuil na drede. *c* **1380** WYCLIF *Serm.* Sel. Wks. I. 18 If no man hadde partid from God bi synne, it hadde be noo nede to make siche feestis. *c* **1450** HOLLAND *Howlat* 33 All thar names to nevyn as now it nocht neid is. **1556** *Aurelio & Isab.* (1608) G vj, It is neade unto hus to abyde overcommen. **1676** HALE *Contempl.* I. 351 The best of men are visited with them, and it is but need they should.
†**b.** With dat. of the person concerned. *Obs.*
c **975** *Rushw. Gosp.* John xvi. 30 Ne ned is ðe þæte hwelc ðec ȝifregne. *c* **1055** *Byrhtferth's Handboc* in *Anglia* VIII. 317 Me ys neod þæt ic menge þæt lyden amang þissum englisce. *c* **1175** *Lamb. Hom.* 37 Ne reccheð crist nane leasunge ne him nis na neoð. *c* **1220** *Bestiary* 181 Newe ðe fordi so ðe neddre doð; It is te ned. *a* **1300** *Cursor M.* 10852 Es þe na nede to be radd.

5. In predicative use: Necessary, needful. In early use also with adjs. Now *rare*.
In some cases (as *c* 1386) an elliptic use of 4 a.
c **1000** ÆLFRIC *Hom.* II. 590 þæt man underfo mare þonne his lichaman neod sy. *c* **1175** *Lamb. Hom.* 11 Muchel is us þenne neod..sod scrift. *a* **1225** *Ancr. R.* 180 To þe uttre temptaciun is neod pacience... To þe inre is neod wisdom & gostlich strencðe. *c* **1290** *St. Brandan* 578 in *S. Eng. Leg.* I. 235 þe ston..In one weiȝe ich hyne fond þare non neode nas no ston. *c* **1386** CHAUCER *Pars. T.* ¶855 Crist loved holy chirche..so wel that he deyed for it; so schulde a man for his wyf, if it were neede. *c* **1400** MAUNDEV. (1839) xxvii. 270 In the yle of Cathay, men fynden alle maner thing that is nede to man. **1450–80** tr. *Secreta Secret.* 12 It is a precious and an honurabille thing to a kyng forto..speke but litille but if it be nede. **1535** CRANMER *Let.* in *Misc. Writ.* (Parker Soc.) II. 311 Whose labours and endeavours were never more need to be had. **1849** TRENCH *Sacr. Lat. Poetry* Pref. 6 Some Reformed Churches..have..made themselves much poorer than was need.

6. a. *to have need to*, to be under a necessity *to* do something, to require *to*. †Also with omission of *to*, and with *that*.
c **950** *Lindisf. Gosp.* Matt. xiv. 16 Nabbas ned..þæt hia ȝegæ. *c* **1000** *Ags. Gosp.* ibid., Nabbað hi neode to farenne. *c* **1375** *Cursor M.* 19589 (Fairf.), þou has nede to do penance I-nogh. *c* **1380** WYCLIF *Serm.* Sel. Wks. II. 224 Al Cristene men han nede to knowe bileve of þe gospel. **1413** *Pilgr. Sowle* (Caxton 1483) v. xi. 103 Nede hadde he none to wesshen hym selue. **1456** *Paston Lett.* I. 375 Ye have nede fare fayre with hym, for he ys full daungerouse. **1594** *1st Pt.*

Contention (1843) 50 *George*... They have bene up this two daies. *Nicke*. Then they had more need to go to bed now. **1611** Shaks. *Cymb.* ii. iii. 67 We shall haue neede T'employ you towards this Romane. **1850** O. Winslow *Inner Life* ii. 55 The best of saints have need to be warned against the worst of sins.

b. In pret. ***had need to***, would require *to*, ought *to*. (Common in 16–17th c.)

c **1380** Wyclif *Serm.* Sel. Wks. I. 26 þei ben worse than frentikes, and so þei hadden nede to be chastised til þis passion were fro hem. **1472** *Paston Lett.* III. 34 And ye purpose to bargayn with hym, ye had nede to hye yow. **1548** Udall *Erasm. Par. Luke* ix. 85 b, Therunto had we nede to haue a good summe of money. **1620** E. Blount *Horæ Subs.* 456 Women, as the weaker vessels, had need to be very careful. **1675** Cotton *Scoffer Scoft* Wks. (1725) 252 He who to determine is Of such a tickle-point as this, Had need to have his Wits about him. **1843** Carlyle *Past & Pr.* iii. xii, The Unseen Powers had need to watch over such a man. **1879** Geo. Eliot *Theo. Such* 129 If the bad-tempered man wants to apologize, he had need to do it on a large public scale.

c. So with omission of *to*.

In sentences of this form *need* tends to lose its distinct substantival character and to become only a modifying element attached to the verb.

1461 *Paston Lett.* II. 13 Ye had nede send a man byfore, ..that no thing be to seke. *c* **1580** G. Harvey *Letter-bk.* (Camden) 175 It had neede be a high point of pollicie that should rob Master Machiavel of his pollicie. **1607–12** Bacon *Ess., Seditions* (Arb.) 390 Sheapardes of people had neede knowe the Kalenders of Tempestes in State. **1681** Hickeringill *Sin Man-catching* Wks. 1716 I. 191 They had need be Men of Cunning and Ability that can swear thorow-stitch and cleverly. **1753** L. M. tr. *Du Bosc's Accomplished Woman* II. 80 Morality had need employ its strongest reasonings. **1834** Beckford *Italy* II. 233 The Portuguese had need have the stomachs of ostriches. **1863** Cowden Clarke *Shaks. Char.* i. 19 Men had need bear 'charmed lives'.

7. a. Imperative call or demand for the presence, possession, etc., *of* something. †Also const. *to*.

a **908** in Birch *Cart. Sax.* II. 280 þenne þæs nud bið, his men beon gearuwe ʒe to ripe ʒe to huntoðe. *c* **1000** Ælfric *Hom.* I. 140 Nis Gode nan neod ure æhta. *c* **1300** *St. Brandan* 573 In a wei ich him fond ligge, there no neod nas to ston. *a* **1300** *Cursor M.* 16280 O wijtnes es na nede. **1667** Milton *P.L.* ix. 311 Stronger, if need were Of outward strength. **1766** Fordyce *Serm. Yng. Wm.* II. ix. 91 Who does not see the need of Piety? **1802** *Med. Jrnl.* VIII. 142 They were never in danger of losing any; and therefore there was no need of the new discovery. **1874** Green *Short Hist.* iv. § 5. 200 The crisis had taught the need of further securities against the royal power.

b. In phr. ***to have need of*** (*†to, †unto*) the thing required.

c **1200** Ormin 7373 Alle þa þatt hafenn ned off hellpe. *Ibid.* 11582 He wass mann..þatt haffde ned to fode. *c* **1250** *Lutel Soth Serm.* 12 in *O.E. Misc.* 186 To ʒiuernesse and prude none neode he nedde. *c* **1320** *Sir Tristr.* 1722 þer of hadde sche no nede. **1387** Trevisa *Higden* (Rolls) III. 445 What nede hast þou to riches? **1426** Lydg. *De Guil. Pilgr.* 815 Thow shalt me call in dede, Whan thow hast on-to me nede. **1484** Caxton *Fables of Poge* i, His hows..had grete nede of reparacion. **1523** Fitzherb. *Husb.* §24 The teth wyll fall out whan he hath moost nede to them. **1611** Bible *Transl. Pref.* ¶3 A wastefull Prince, that had neede of a Guardian. **1671** Milton *P.R.* ii. 253 Nature hath need of what she asks. **1753** L. M. tr. *Du Bosc's Accompl. Woman* I. 25 Innocence itself hath as much need of a mask or veil as the Face. **1849** Macaulay *Hist. Eng.* ii. I. 156 Was he to be ranked with men who had no need of the royal clemency? **1853** J. H. Newman *Hist. Sk.* (1873) II. i. i. 6 The Tartars ..have in their wars no need of any commissariat at all.

†c. Const. with direct object: To need, require. *Obs.*

c **1375** *Cursor M.* 12929 (Fairf.), þorou kinde of his manhede þat fode of body has ay nede. **1557** North *Gueuara's Diall Pr.* i. xxxviii. (1568) 56 To kepe himselfe only from one evyl man, he had nede both hands, feete, and frends. **1667** Milton *P.L.* ii. 413 Here he had need All circumspection. **1671** —— *Samson* 1107 Thou hast need much washing to be toucht.

8. ***to have need***, to be in straits or in want. (Also *ellipt.* for 7 b.) Now *rare* or *Obs.*

c **950** *Lindisf. Gosp.* Mark ii. 25 Huæt dyde David ða ned hæfde & hyngerde. *c* **1200** *Vices & Virtues* 11 We sculen bliðeliche ʒiuen and leanen, wið uten erðliche mede, alle ðe niede habbeð. *c* **1380** Wyclif *Sel. Wks.* III. 411 If he willefuly begge, and haves no nede, he is a schrewid begger, reproved of God. *c* **1460** Fortescue *Abs. & Lim. Mon.* iv. (1885) 116 It is a synne to gyve no mete, drynke, clothynge or other almes to hem that haue nede. *c* **1530** R. Hilles *Common-pl. Bk.* (1858) 140 He that hath nede must blowe at the cole. **1671** Milton *P.R.* ii. 318 They all had need, I as thou seest have none.

9. a. A condition of affairs placing one in difficulty or distress; a time of difficulty, straits, or trouble; exigency, emergency.

c **1000** Ælfric *Exod.* xv. 25 þa clypode Moises to drihtne and sæde him þæs folces neode. *c* **1205** Lay. 435 þa lette he ..bi-ʒeoten wepnen & mete: Muchel wes þa neode. **1297** R. Glouc. (Rolls) 1763 þe king basian hii bitraiede in is nede [*v.r.* nude]. *c* **1330** R. Brunne *Chron.* (1810) 23 Priue help of þe Scottes he had at his nede. **1377** Langl. *P. Pl.* B. xi. 28 þow shalt fynde fortune þe faille at þi moste nede. *a* **1450** *Le Morte Arth.* 1706 And hym ned by-stode, Many a lande wolde with hym holde. *c* **1489** Caxton *Sonnes of Aymon* xii. 286 At the nede the frende is knowen. *c* **1530** Ld. Berners *Arth. Lyt. Bryt.* (1814) 322 Whan nede is, than a frende is proued. **1596** Dalrymple tr. *Leslie's Hist. Scot.* vii. 17 He could, in tyme of neid, ather stap a trane or mak a trayne. **1633** G. Herbert *Temple, Collar* 31 He that forbears To suit and serve his need, Deserves his load. **1684** Bunyan *Pilgr.* ii 66, I thank you for lending me a hand at my need. **1726** Watts *Logic* (ed. 2) ii. iii. iii. §4 And these Judgments.. should be treasur'd up in the Mind, that we might have Recourse to them in Hours of Need. **1826** Scott *Woodstock* iii, A short passage.., secured at time of need by two oaken doors. **1856** Froude *Hist. Eng.* I. v. 399 He fell back upon his Italian cunning, and it did not fail him in his need. **1864** Browning *Jas. Lee's Wife* ii. iii, God help you, sailors, at your need!

b. In phr. ***at*** (also ***†to***) ***need***.

c **1200** Ormin 12245 ʒiff þu wære rædiʒ till To nittenn itt att nede Onn alle þa þatt haffdenn ned [etc.]. *c* **1205** Lay. 529 Brutus hefede gode Cnihtes to neode. **13..** *K. Alis.* 2406 That scholden come, on fresche steden, Heom to socoure at most nede. **1390** Gower *Conf.* I. 338 Wher-of they token hem to rede, And soghten frendes ate nede. *c* **1420** *Anturs of Arth.* xliii, Als he stode by his stede, þat was so goode at nede. *c* **1470** Henry *Wallace* ii. 55 He drew a suerd at helpit him at neide. **1567** *Gude & Godlie B.* (S.T.S.) 107 He sall deliuer the at neid. **1667** Milton *P.L.* ix. 260 Where each To other speedie aide might lend at need. **1805** Scott *Last Minstr.* i. xxii, Sir William of Deloraine, good at need. **1873** Browning *Red Cott. Nt.-cap* iv. 241 This power you hold for profit of myself And all the world at need.

†c. ***with need***, with difficulty; not easily or readily. *Obs. rare.*

1422 tr. *Secreta Secret., Priv. Priv.* 152 The doloure is to me so stronge, that wyth nede y may my breth wyth-drawe. *Ibid.* 180 Any officere that he had makyd with nethe he chaungyd but yf hit were for opyn falsnys.

10. a. A condition marked by the lack or want of some necessary thing, or requiring some extraneous aid or addition.

c **1000** Ælfric *Hom.* II. 340 Ne lufode he woruldlice æhta for his neode ana, ac to dælenne eallum wædliendum. *c* **1050** *O.E. Chron.* (MS. C.) an. 1043 Eadsiʒe arcebisceop..hine wel lærde & to his aʒenre neode & ealles folces wel manude. *c* **1175** *Lamb. Hom.* 75 Ne na Mon nah him solue wernen, þenne Mon him for node þer to bide. *c* **1200** *Trin. Coll. Hom.* 215 þanne prest specð inne chirche of chirche nede. *c* **1300** *Harrow. of Hell* 38 Tho Jhesu hevide shed ys blod For oure neode upon the rod. **1387** Trevisa *Higden* (Rolls) III. 471 ʒif þurst and honger of golde come of kyndeliche nede. **1480** Caxton *Chron. Eng.* ccxxiv. 229 Ther folowed..honger, scarcite, meschyef, and nede of money. **1482** *Monk of Evesham* (Arb.) 88 They that vsyn scarsly to her nede the godys that they haue. **1577** *St. Aug. Manual* (Longman) 1 Thou Lorde..alwayes gathering, but not for any neede. **1667** Milton *P.L.* v. 629 We have also our Eevning and our Morn,..for change delectable, not need. **1863** Geo. Eliot *Romola* xxvii, The great need of her heart compelled her to strangle..every rising impulse of suspicion.

b. A state of want or destitution; lack of the means of subsistence or of necessary articles; extreme poverty or indigence.

c **1200** *Trin. Coll. Hom.* 217 Nes riche non nod, ac wrecches habben michele. *a* **1225** *Leg. Kath.* 2428 Hwen se ha hit eauer doð in neode & in nowcin. *a* **1300** *Cursor M.* 21873 Hunger and qualm, and neede i-nogh In erth sal rise for mans wogh. **1387** Trevisa *Higden* (Rolls) VI. 47 ʒeveþ wyn to hem..þat þey mowe drynke and forʒete here sorwe and her nede. *c* **1400** *Apol. Loll.* 107 If ned, or pouert of þe place, axe þat þei be occupied to gedre frutis. **1526** *Pilgr. Perf.* (W. de W. 1531) 19 b, So you sholde be mercyfull to your poor neyghbour in his nede. **1592** Shaks. *Rom. & Jul.* v. i. 70 Famine is in thy cheekes; Need and opression starueth in thy eyes. **1697** Dryden *Virg. Georg.* i. 203 Jove ..Remov'd from Humane reach the chearful Fire..That studious Need might useful Arts explore. **1774** Goldsm. *Nat. Hist.* (1776) II. 129 These, from often being in need, and as often receiving an accidental supply, pass their lives between surfeiting and repining. **1847** B. Thorpe *Yule-tide Stories* (1888) 72 They therefore lived in great poverty, and as is but too often the case, when need crept in, love walked out.

c. *Psychol.* A state of physiological or psychological want that consciously or subconsciously motivates behaviour towards its satisfaction.

1929 J. B. Miner tr. *Piéron's Princ. Exper. Psychol.* iii. 54 These instincts are generally designated by a special name.. which expresses in a measure the imperious character of the tendencies; we say that they are needs. **1935** K. Koffka *Princ. Gestalt Psychol.* viii. 329 But needs are..states of tension which persist until they are relieved. **1936** *Jrnl. Psychol.* III. 27 Two commonly used terms for a motivational process are *drive* and *need*, and, since I cannot see that one is to be preferred to the other, I shall..use them interchangeably. Need is a concept to account for certain objective and subjective facts. **1961** F. H. Sanford *Psychol.* viii. 200/2 The need for achievement, referred to in the literature and in the following paragraphs as *n ach*. **1964** L. J. Bischof *Interpreting Personality Theories* ii. 146 In studying the need structure of man, Murray found that he required criteria in order to establish that a need existed.

11. In proverbial phrases.

1377 Langl. *P. Pl.* B. xx. 10 Nede ne hath no lawe, ne neure shal falle in dette. *c* **1440** *Jacob's Well* 206 ʒif þei mowe noʒt getyn here lyiflode be none of þise maners forseyde, þanne nede hath no lawe. **1480** *Robt. Devyll* 39 Alacke, thought Robert, nede hath no cure. *c* **1530** R. Hilles *Common-pl. Bk.* (1858) 140 Nede makyth the old wyffe to trotte. **1562** J. Heywood *Prov. & Epigr.* (1867) 20 Neede hath no lawe, neede maketh his hither iet. **1655** *Nicholas Papers* (Camden) II. 233 Need makes trott, but contempt makes vs run on the Pikes rather then moulder away. **1712** Steele *Spec.* No. 509 ¶6, I think, a Speculation upon..It is Need that makes the old Wife trot, would be very useful to the World.

II. †12. a. A matter requiring action to be taken; something falling necessarily to be done; a piece of necessary business. In later use chiefly *pl.* Also ***good need***, good service. *Obs.*

c **900** tr. *Bæda's Hist.* iii. iii. [v.] (1890) 160 Ne he on horses hricge cuman wolde, nemne hwilc mare nyd abædde. *c* **1000** Ælfric *Saints' Lives* vi. 290 Siððan nolde maurus of ðam mynstre faran for nanre neode. *a* **1122** *O.E. Chron.* (Laud MS.) an. 675 Ouðer for lauerdes neode..ouðer for hwilces sinnes oðer neod, he ne muge þær comen. *a* **1250** *Owl & Night.* 388 [They] doth bi niʒte gode noede. **1297** R. Glouc. (Rolls) 8324 þe Cristene ost..hopede do gode nede, ac bote lute worþ it nas. *c* **1330** R. Brunne *Chron. Wace* (Rolls) 12563 þe messegers þat wente þo nedes, Horsed þem on gode stedes. *c* **1400** *Destr. Troy* 11519 þat erend for to wend With hym-seluyn, for-sothe, on þe same nedis. **1508** Dunbar *Tua Mariit Wemen* 467, I have ane secrete serwand .. That me supportis of sic nedis.

†b. Chiefly *pl.* One's errands or business. *Obs.*

c **1000** Ælfric *Hom.* I. 290 He wolde gan embe his neode forð. *c* **1205** Lay. 29452 þa wes hit..þat þe pape wolde wenden..an one of his neoden. *a* **1300** *Cursor M.* 24827 Quen all his nedis wele war dun þai dightid him his scipping son. **1387** Trevisa *Higden* (Rolls) I. 375 Owen..dwelled al his lyf tyme afterward in þe nedes of þe abbay of Ludensis. *c* **1400** *Rule St. Benet* (Prose) 12 Lokys þat ye do wel, þat yure angel may do yure nedis to god. **1483** Caxton *Gold. Leg.* 442 b/1 In his nedes or besynesse to werke trewely and wel. ?*a* **1550** *Freiris Berwik* 463 in *Dunbar's Poems* (1893) 300, I wait nocht gif ʒe ma ay cum hidder Quhen that we want our neidis sic as this.

c. Offices of nature. Now *dial.*

1297 R. Glouc. (Rolls) 6338 þe king þer to com..is nede uor to do, þe luþer þef..smot him þoru þe fondement. **1573** Baret *Alv.* s.v. *Priuie*, He is gone to the priuie or to doe his needes. **1621** Burton *Anat. Mel.* iii. iii. ii. i. (1676) 370/2 She shall not go forth of his sight, so much as to do her needs.

13. A particular point or respect in which some necessity or want is present or is felt.

c **1000** Ælfric *Hom.* I. 272 Ealle ure neoda, æʒðer ʒe gastlice ʒe lichamlice, ðæron sind belocene. *c* **1300** *Beket* 97 As hit were at a Parlement for Neodes of the londe. **1450–80** tr. *Secreta Secret.* 5 Y haue hastid me and ordeynyd me to make a book for the, the which shalle conteyne alle thi nedes. **1603** Shaks. *Meas. for M.* iii. ii. 151 The very streame of his life..must, vppon a warranted neede, giue him a better proclamation. *a* **1716** Blackall *Wks.* (1723) I. 543 We ought to be content if we have now so much as will serve our present Needs. **1795–1814** Wordsw. *Excurs.* iii. 796, I.. promptly seized All that Abstraction furnished for my needs. **1874** Symonds *Sk. Italy & Greece* (1898) I. i. 3 Improved arts of life had freed men from servile subjection to daily needs.

†14. a. ***at a need***, in an emergency or crisis.

a **1122** *O.E. Chron.* (Laud MS.) an. 1101 Hi sume æft æt þære neode abruðon, & fram þam cynge ʒecyrdon. *c* **1330** R. Brunne *Chron.* (1810) 35 He was boþe gode & wys..& right vnderstandyng, to help at alle nedis. **1375** Barbour *Bruce* ii. 231 He had thar, at that ned, Full feill that war douchty off deid. *c* **1420** Lydg. *Assembly of Gods* 755 Wherfore hit behoueth to helpe at thys nede. *c* **1489** Caxton *Sonnes of Aymon* ix. 222 Bayarde, whiche shall maye bere vs all four at a nede.

†b. So ***in a need***. *Obs.*

c **1250** *Kent. Serm.* in *O.E Misc.* 32 þet se þet sucurede hem ine þa peril;..us sucuri in ure niedes. **1340** Hampole *Pr. Consc.* 3614 þai may in þat nede Be boght fra payn thurgh almusdede. *a* **1400–50** *Alexander* 2518 Alexander.. Naytis him-selfe in ilke nede & so his name rysis. *c* **1450** *Merlin* 678 In many a nede he hadde hym socoured.

†c. ***for a need***, in an emergency, at a pinch.

1562 Turner *Herbal* iii. (1568) 25 He maye for a nede occupye this herbe. *c* **1585** R. Browne *Answ. Cartwright* 47 For a neede, reading ministers may bee in the Church in steade of preaching ministers. **1647** Ward *Simp. Cobler* 8 He..will for a need hang God's Bible at the Devills girdle.

15. *attrib.* and *Comb.*, as ***need-achievement, condition, -disposition, pattern, -push; needs analysis, test***; †**need-(be)stead** *a.*, in difficulty or danger; †**need-doer**, trader; †**need-doing**, trading, traffic; †**need-gates** *adv.*, of necessity; **need-rooted** *a.*, fixed by necessity; †**need-sweat**, sweat of distress.

Attributive and other combs. of *níed-, nýd-*, etc., are numerous in OE. See also Du Cange s.v. *Nydbedripes*.

1971 F. H. Farley in H. J. Eysenck *Readings in Extraversion-Introversion* III. xlv. 406 The personality variables of anxiety and need-achievement were considered. **1456** Sir. G. Haye *Law Arms* (S.T.S.) 251 And thai war nede bestad of lyfing..I wald counsale that thai war refreschit with bathe mete and drink. **1960** N. Maier in Kaplan & Wapner *Perspectives Psychol. Theory* 153 Like all need conditions, social needs select goal-oriented behaviors. **1951** Parsons & Shils *Toward Gen. Theory Action* i. i. 18 The child's development of a 'personality'..is to be viewed as the establishment of a relatively specific, definite, and consistent system of need-dispositions. **1958** D. Emmett *Function, Purpose & Powers* 30 From the point of view of any given actor in the system it is both a mode of the fulfilment of his own need-dispositions and a condition of 'optimizing' the reactions of other significant actors. **1382** Wyclif *Isa.* xxiii. 8 Tirun..whos nededoeres princes, his marchaunders noble men of the erthe. *Ibid.* 18 His nede doyngus and his meedus shuln ben halewid to the Lord. *c* **1375** *Cursor M.* 2450 (Fairf.), þaire fee nedegates most þai flitt. **1947** G. Murphy *Personality* iii. xvi. 395 It would seem that mood or need patterns can intensify and enrich the world of images. *Ibid.* 992/1 *Need pattern*, total organization of the needs of the organism. **1951** Parsons & Shils *Toward Gen. Theory Action* iii. iii. 308 Identification does involve..locomotion away from some other region of valenced activity because of the stronger need-push to get to the region of love and approval. **1850** Lynch *Theoph. Trinal* xii. 233 Need-rooted here on earth we are. **1969** J. Argenti *Managem. Techniques* 175 Needs analysis, then, consists of systematically examining the requirements of each job and comparing these with the skills of the incumbent of, or an applicant for, the job. *c* **1450** *St. Cuthbert* (Surtees) 5492 He was anes nede-stad in þe se. **1932** *Ann. Reg. 1931* i. iv. 102 By the regulations issued by the Ministry of Labour in October, the task of applying the 'needs test' to applicants for transitional benefit had been left to the Public Assistance Committees. **1940** *Economist* 29 June 1106/2 The chief objection is..that it introduces another needs test. It is now possible that in the same household there will be a means test for an unemployed member..and a means test for pensions of war. *a* **1225** *Ancr. R.* 110 So ful of anguise was þet ilke ned swot þet com of his licome.

†**need**, *v.*[1] *Obs.* Forms: 1 níedan, nídan, nýdan, nédan, 2 néoden, 2–5 néde(n), 4 neede. [OE. *níẹdan* etc., f. *néad* NEED *sb.*, = OFris. *nêda*, OS. *nôdian*, MDu. and MLG. *nôden* (Du. *nooden*), OHG. *nôtjan*, *nôten* (G. *nöten*, *nöthen*), ON. *neyða* (Sw. *nöda*, Da. *nöde*), Goth. *nauþjan*. OE. had also the form *néadian* in the same sense.]

1. *trans.* To exercise constraint or compulsion upon (one).

*c*825 *Vesp. Hymn* vii. 41 Hie in hatheortnisse neddun mec. *c*888 K. ÆLFRED *Boeth.* xvi. §1 ȝ if..hwelce mus wære hlaford ofer oðre mys..& nedde hie æfter gafole. *c*950 *Lindisf. Gosp.* Luke xxiv. 29 [Hia] nedon hine, cuoeðendo, 'wuna usiȝ mið'. *c*1175 *Lamb. Hom.* 15 Hit is riht þet me us nede and isegge þet sceamie. *c*1220 *Bestiary* 216 Neded ðe ðe deuel nogt. 1496 *Dives & Paup.* (W. de W.) I. xix. 53/1 His..werkes be not neded ne arted by the planetes.

2. To constrain, compel, or force *to* a thing.

*c*888 K. ÆLFRED *Boeth.* xli. §4 Ac he us ne ned no þy hraðor to þam þæt we nede scylen good don. 971 *Blickl. Hom.* 213 Þa nyddon hine hys yldran toðæm þæt he sceolde ..wæpnum onfon. *a*1122 *O.E. Chron.* (Laud MS.) an. 1114 Þa neodde he him to þam biscoprice of Hrofeceastre. *a*1300 *Cursor M.* 27992 If þou..nedd þe euer þar-till at force womman agayn hir will. *c*1380 WYCLIF *Wks.* (1880) 265 Holy writt old & newe & cristis lif..neden hem to mekenesse & wilful traueile. *a*1400–50 *Alexander* 1819 The saȝes of ȝour soueravn..Nedis me to slike notis as I had neuer etlid.

b. Const. with *inf.* (Freq. in Wyclif.)

*c*1000 ÆLFRIC *Hom.* II. 376 Far nu ȝeond weȝas & heȝas, & nyd hi inn to farenne. *c*1200 *Trin. Coll. Hom.* 179 ȝif he net him to ȝiuene, þat beoð strengðe and refloc. *a*1225 *Ancr. R.* 72 Þeonne is hit ined aȝein uor to climben upward. *a*1300 *Cursor M.* 16596 Him þai can to nede At tak þe tan end o þe tre. *c*1380 WYCLIF *Sel. Wks.* III. 358 Aftir þat þis prelat ordeyneþ ben sugettis nedid for to do. *c*1449 PECOCK *Repr.* III. vii. 320 Tho..whiche were nedid..forto lyue in thilk maner.

need (niːd), *v.*[2] Forms: 1 néodian, 3–5 neoden, neden, (5 -yn), 3–6 nede, 4–7 neede, (5–7 *Sc.* neid, 5 neyd, 6 neade, 7 nead, nied), 4– need. [OE. *néodian* (rare), f. *néod* NEED *sb.* Cf. MHG. *nôten*, G. (dial.) *nothen*, *nöthen*, in the same senses.]

The irregular form *need* in the 3rd pers. sing. of the present tense (in place of *needs* or *needeth*) becomes fairly common in the 16th c., and is now usual in the forms of expression mentioned in the note to sense 8.]

I. *intr.* †**1. a.** *it needs*, it is needful or necessary. Usu. const. with *that* or inf., and sometimes with *it* omitted. *Obs.*

*c*960 ÆTHELWOLD *Rule St. Benet* (Schröer) 89 On cealdum eardum neodað, þæt þæs reafes mare sy. *a*1225 *Ancr. R.* 20 Ȝe muwen siggen Preciosa biuoren & efter vhtsong anon ȝif hit so neodeð. 13.. *K. Alis.* 6525 Hit nedeth nothyng to wond. Hit is a best founde in boke. *c*1375 *Sc. Leg. Saints* x. (*Matthew*) 211 It nedyt þat he suld mak a tempil. *c*1440 *Generydes* 2893 It nedeth not to make all this arraye. *c*1489 CAXTON *Sonnes of Aymon* vii. 167 Of Rowlande nedeth not to speke. 1503 *Waterf. Arch.* in *10th Rep. Hist. MSS. Comm.* App. V. 324 The owners of all suche nettis shall repaire them when it nedith. 1575–85 ABP. SANDYS *Serm.* (Parker Soc.) 357 To seek out many expositions of these words, it shall not need. 1634 CANNE *Necess. Separ.* 24, I could produce many others of them,.. but it needs not. 1765 H. WALPOLE *Otranto* v, 'It needs not' ..'the horrors of these days..corroborate thy evidence'.

†**b.** *what needs..?* what need is there (*to* do something)? *Obs.*

1377 LANGL. *P. Pl.* B. XVII. 30 What neded it thanne a newe lawe to bigynne..? *c*1470 *Gol. & Gaw.* 506 'Quhat nedis', said Spinagrus, 'sic notis to nevin?' 1551 RECORDE *Pathw. Knowl.* Ep. King, What needeth to alledge one sentence of him? 1641 MILTON *Reform.* ii. 69 Seeke onely Vertue, not to extend your Limits; for what needs?

c. *needs not*, it is not necessary to. *rare.*

1865 W. G. PALGRAVE *Arabia* I. 112 Needs not say how lovely are the summer evenings. *Ibid.* 451.

2. a. *there needs*, there is need for (some thing or person); there requires or is requisite.

1440 *Paston Lett.* I. 39, I hope there shall nede no gret trete be twyxe hym. 1539 CRANMER *Let.* in *Misc. Writ.* (Parker Soc.) II. 393, I know your lordship's discretion is such that there need no such monition in this behalf. 1594 SHAKS. *Rich. III*, III. vii. 104 There needes no such Apologie. 1613 PURCHAS *Pilgrimage* I. iv. 15 There needeth some Herald to shew the true petigree. *a*1687 PETTY *Pol. Arith.* ix. (1691) 111 There needs but one Million to pay the said Rents. 1813 SHELLEY *Q. Mab* III. 79 There needeth not the hell that bigots frame. 1879 SPENCER *Data Eth.* viii. §50. 135 There needs great subordination to men who command.

†**b.** *what needs..?* what need is there for (something)? *Obs.*

*c*1386 CHAUCER *Man of Law's T.* 134 What needeth gretter dilatacioun? *c*1470 HENRY *Wallace* III. 28 Lord Persye said; 'Quhat nedis wordis mor?' 1560 DAUS tr. *Sleidane's Comm.* 110 b, What shoulde this obligation nede? 1592 SHAKS. *Ven. & Ad.* 250 Struck dead at first, what needs a second striking? 1662 STILLINGFL. *Orig. Sacræ* II. iii. §7 Was this a duty before these miracles, or no? if it was, what need miracles to confirm it?

c. *it needs*, it requires.

1839 *Times* 19 Oct., It needed not, nevertheless, the published correspondence of such a hero to convince us. 1853 M. ARNOLD *Scholar Gypsy* v, It needs heaven-sent moments for this skill.

3. Of things: To be needful or necessary.

1526 *Pilgr. Perf.* (W. de W. 1531) 163 That he forme & pronounce euery lettre & syllable..with more diligence than nedeth. 1545 ASCHAM *Toxophilus* II. (Arb.) 139 Stoppynge of heades..wyth leade..shall not nede now. 1610 DAY *Festivals* iii. (1615) 63 That in this place..are meant the Dead, is a Note perhaps that needes not. 1663 GERBIER *Counsel* 25 Waste no more than needs in Slabs. 1687 DRYDEN *Hind & P.* III. 468 But little learning needs in noble blood. 1846 BROWNING *Soul's Trag.* I. 22 Lest you, even more than needs, embitter Our parting.

II. †**4. a.** To be needful or necessary *to* a person, or (more usually) *to* some end or purpose. *Obs.*

*a*1225 *Ancr. R.* 414 Non ancre ne ouh forto nimen bute gnedeliche þet hire to neodeð. 1375 BARBOUR *Bruce* III. 692 Thai..maid redy..all that nedyt to schipfar. 1393 LANGL. *P. Pl.* C. VI. 20 Eny oþer kyns craft þat to þe comune nedeþ. 1470–85 MALORY *Arthur* VIII. iv. 278 He hadde al thynge that to hym neded. 1496 *Fysshynge w. Angle* (1883) 11 It shall be also fyne a tawney colour as nedyth to our purpoos.

†**b.** With dative of person. *Obs.*

1362 LANGL. *P. Pl.* A. XI. 187 Seken out þe seke & sende hem þat hem nediþ. *a*1400 HYLTON *Scala Perf.* (W. de W. 1494) I. xxiv, He knoweth wel ynough what the nedeth. *c*1485 *Digby Myst.* (1882) v. 664 We haue that nedith vs, so thryve I. 1597 BP. HALL *Sat.*, *Defiance to Envie* 25 Needs me then hope, or doth me need mis-dread. 1691 *Andros Tracts* (1869) II. 248 What need us so many Instances abroad?

†**5.** Impersonally: **a.** To be necessary for (one) *to* do something. *Obs.*

1377 LANGL. *P. Pl.* B. XI. 282 Þanne nedeth nouȝte ȝow to take syluer for masses þat ȝe syngen. *c*1400 *Destr. Troy* 11309 Hit nedis vs another way now for to laite. *c*1450 *Mirour Saluacioun* 939 Me nedes fro hire presence withdrawe me priuely. *a*1533 LD. BERNERS *Huon* lxxxi. 242 It nede not you to demaunde for ye are lyke to knowe it to soone. 1590 SPENSER *F.Q.* I. i. 26 Now needeth him no lenger labour spend.

†**b.** So *what need(s)..?* why should (one)?

*c*1375 *Sc. Leg. Saints* xxxviii. (*Adrian*) 197 Quhat ned þe to begyne þe thing þat þu mycht nocht bring til ending? *c*1386 CHAUCER *Sompn. T.* 292 What nedith yow, Thomas, to make strif? 1535 COVERDALE *Eccl.* ii. 15 What nedeth me then to laboure eny more for wyszdome? 1550 LATIMER *Last Serm. bef. Edw. VI*, Wks. (Parker Soc.) I. 244 What should need me to give a penny to have my bills warranted? 1597 BP. HALL *Sat.* II. ii. 30 What needes me care for any bookish skill?

†**c.** (*it*) *needs one*, one has need (of something). Also const. *of* and *that*. *Obs.*

1362 LANGL. *P. Pl.* A. XI. 50 Þat lord..þat þus parteþ with þe pore A parcel whon him neodeþ. 1390 GOWER *Conf.* I. 272 The nedeth of non other leche. *c*1420 *Pallad. on Husb.* I. 261 Yf thee nede In londis salt that treen or graynys growe. *c*1489 CAXTON *Sonnes of Aymon* xxii. 490, I can well aske brede whan me nedeth. 1508 DUNBAR *Tua Mariit Wemen* 264 And quhen it nedis ȝow, onone, note baith ther stranthis.

III. †**6.** To have need *of* (also *to*) a thing. *Obs.*

*c*1200 ORMIN 6161 Fremmde menn, þat nedenn to þin hellpe. *a*1450 *Fysshynge w. Angle* (1883) 1 He schall make iij thynges hys medicens or leches and he schall neuer neyd to mo. *a*1533 LD. BERNERS *Huon* ci. 329 Yf ye nede of ony ayde, take my horne and blowe it. 1598 GRENEWEY *Tacitus, Ann.* XIV. xii. (1622) 213 If at any time the common-wealth should nede of counsell.

7. a. *trans.* To stand in need of, to require (some thing or person).

1382 WYCLIF *Gen.* xxxiii. 15 This oon oonliche Y nede, that Y fynde grace in thi siȝt. *c*1400 *Apol. Loll.* 81 Men nedyn euer þe counseil of God, to led hem in al þingis. *c*1475 *Rauf Coilȝear* 546, I neid nane airar myne erand nor none of the day. 1530 PALSGR. 643/2 It is veryly the thyng that we nede. *Ibid.*, And shall we nede an habyt or a cope. 1568 GRAFTON *Chron.* II. 768, I trust, quod he, we shall not neede it. *a*1628 PRESTON *New Covt.* (1634) 68 There is nothing that you neede, nothing that you want, but it shall be supplyed. 1667 MILTON *P.L.* IV. 617 Other Creatures all day long Rove idle unimploid, and less need rest. 1741–2 GRAY *Agrip.* 2 The message needs no comment. 1837 DICKENS *Pickw.* vii, Pickwick needed no second invitation. 1871 FREEMAN *Norm. Conq.* (1876) IV. xx. 604 Such a deed needed a worse man than was needed for any of William's earlier deeds.

(*b*) *spec.* In colloq. phrases implying that something is completely unnecessary or unwanted, as ***who needs it?*** [tr. Yiddish *ver darf es?*]; ***to need (something) like a hole in the head***: see HOLE *sb.* 11. orig. *U.S.*

1951, etc. [see HOLE *sb.* 11]. 1960 *Mademoiselle* Jan. 34/2 Popular idiom deals best with racial prejudice: 'Who needs it?' 1960 *N.Y. Post* 24 Feb. 56/5 Who needs them? 1962 *Sat. Even. Post* 31 Mar. 70 (*heading*) Good news—who needs it? 1963 *TV Times* 11 Jan. 8 It was so easy to say: 'Education? Who needs it?' 1968 *Melody Maker* 23 Nov. 11/3 They envision themselves wearing berets..and crawling about the rubble, throwing Molotov cocktails. 'But who needs Che Guevara? It's not like that.' 1968 M. WOODHOUSE *Rock Baby* xvii. 164 A twenty-two-year-old bomb disposal expert? I needed a twenty-two-year-old bomb disposal expert like I needed four more thumbs and a teen-age brain surgeon. 1973 R. HAYES *Hungarian Game* xxxi. 185, I needed a cat like I needed a nervous breakdown. 1974 *New Yorker* 17 June 92 True, he's one damn hell of a fine human being. But who needs him?

b. *intr.* To be in need or want.

1382 WYCLIF *Ecclus.* xl. 29 Betere is to dyen, than to neden. 1387–8 T. USK *Test. Love* II. v. (Skeat) l. 16 Thou nedest in richesse, whiche nede thou shuldest not have, if thou hem wantest. 1671 MILTON *P.R.* II. 251 If Nature need not, Or God support Nature without repast Though needing. 1801 ELIZ. HELME *St. Marg. Cave* IV. 283 Money was sent him..to distribute among such of his poor neighbours as needed. 1857 HEAVYSEGE *Saul* (1869) 153 How poor thou art to him who truly needs.

8. a. To be under a necessity or obligation *to* do something.

In modern usage the *to* is expressed except when the clause has the forms *it* (*he, I*, etc.) *need not*, (*why*) *need* (*it*, etc.)?, or is virtually equivalent to one of these.

*c*1380 WYCLIF *Sel. Wks.* III. 348 More þan he nediþ for to have. *c*1400 *Sowdone Bab.* 3216 Be ye togeder as breth[e]rn both! No man ye nedith to drede. *c*1460 *Towneley Myst.* xii. 163 Ye nede not to care if ye folow my sawe. *a*1533 LD. BERNERS *Huon* lxi. 212 Ye nede not to speke of any golde or syluer. 1579 FULKE *Heskins' Parl.* 333 This is as plaine as neede to be. *a*1667 JER. TAYLOR *Serm.* (1673) 54 Though Christ knew it, and therefore needed not to ask. 1732 POPE *Ess. Man* II. 218 Vice..to be hated, needs but to be seen. 1771 T. HULL *Sir W. Harrington* (1797) II. 9 My stooping need not to have disturbed you. 1827 SOUTHEY *Penins. War* II. 630 He needed not to have undertaken an arduous march of 260 miles. 1842 R. I. WILBERFORCE *Rutilius & Lucius* 116 They need to be taught ..how vain are those objects. 1873 BROWNING *Red Cott. Nt.-cap* II. 24 Man worked here Once on a time; here needs again to work.

b. With omission of *to*.

Now regular in the cases mentioned in the note above, otherwise rare.

*c*1470 HENRY *Wallace* VII. 414 The woman..Cawkit ilk ȝett, that thai neid nocht gang by. 1538 BALE *Thre Lawes* 1629 Hys selfe may do that, he nede commaunde non other. 1576 FLEMING *Panopl. Epist.* 325 You neede not doubt of their vncerteintie. 1654–66 EARL ORRERY *Parthen.* (1676) 688, I hope I shall not need employ them to win another. *a*1687 PETTY *Pol. Arith.* vii. (1691) 103 A Man needs spend but a twentieth part less. 1728 R. MORRIS *Ess. Anc. Archit.* 90 How prejudicial such Proceedings are..need not be defin'd. 1761 HUME *Hist. Eng.* III. liii. 154 This incident.. needed be no surprise to him. 1818 BENTHAM *Ch. Eng.*, *Catech. Exam.* 389 The office might need be revived. 1855 TENNYSON *Maud* II. ii. ix, Who knows..Whether I need have fled? 1875 JOWETT *Plato* (ed. 2) V. 370, I need hardly ask again.

c. With omission of complementary infinitive.

1577–87 HOLINSHED *Chron.* III. 917/1 Doubting that thing, that in good faith yee need not. 1665 BOYLE *Occas. Refl.* II. iii. 197 We are often more unhappy than we need. 1710 STEELE *Tatler* No. 137 ¶1 Some use Ten Times more Words than they need.

Hence '**needed** *ppl. a.*, required.

1887 *Pall Mall G.* 1 Dec. 11/1 It is to be hoped that a needed lesson will not lose force. 1891 *Daily News* 31 Oct. 6/3 When rich men..are appealed to for needed help.

†**need**, *adv.* *Obs.* Forms: 1 níede, nýde, (3) néade, néode, 1–5 nede, 4 ned, 5–6 *Sc.* neid, (5 neyd), 5–7 need, (7 neede). [OE. *níẹde*, *néade*, etc., orig. the instrumental case of *níẹd*, *néad*, NEED *sb.*] Of necessity, necessarily, etc. (Usually with *shall* or *must*: cf. NEEDS *adv.*)

*c*893 K. ÆLFRED *Oros.* v. ii. §7 Ic sceal eac niede þara moneȝena ȝewinna ȝeswiȝian. 971 *Blickl. Hom.* 49 Þis sceal se mæssepreost nede bebeodan. *c*1000 ÆLFRIC *Gen.* xliii. 11 ȝif ȝe néade swa don sceolon, doð swa ȝe wyllon. *a*1122 *O.E. Chron.* (Laud MS.) an. 1006 Man nyde moste þam [here] gafol ȝyldan. *c*1205 LAY. 1052 Heo mot nede beien þe mon þe ibunden bið. 1297 R. GLOUC. (Rolls) 787 He bileuede as he nede moste vorþ mid one kniȝte. *c*1320 *Cast. Love* 572 Then most it nede be,..That Goddys sone shuld mon be come. *c*1380 WYCLIF *Serm.* Sel. Wks. I. 222 As þe first mut nede be good, so þe toþer mut nede be yvel. *c*1450 *Merlin* 611 Seth yow be-hove nede for to go. 1500–20 DUNBAR *Poems* xxx. 12 Cleith the thairin, for weir it thow most neid. 1614 DAY *Festivals* xi. (1615) 307 She must need be above an Hundred. 1631 HEYLIN *St. George* 72 His good Horse Arundell, from whence the ancient Castel of that name, must neede be call'd so. 1732 DE FOE *Eng. Tradesman* I. Suppl. 446 Perhaps they are in hurry enough, or indeed too much for any more concern than need must.

b. With *will* or *would*: see NEEDS *adv.*

1641 J. TRAPPE *Theol. Theol.* 347 Yet they will need be the only Musulmans, that is, right Beleevers. 1654 DOROTHY OSBORNE *Lett.* (1888) 246 Jane would need make me some for them and myself.

need-be. *rare.* [f. NEED *v.*[2] + BE *v.*] An essential or necessary reason; a necessity.

1728 P. WALKER *Life Peden* (1827) 118 He afterwards saw a remarkable Providence in it, and a Need-be for it. 1791 MRS. UNWIN in Southey *Cowper* (1836) III. 55 There is no doubt but that there is a need-be for the manifold temptations to which they are exposed. 1838 TUPPER *Proverb. Philos.* (1852) 22 Were there not a need-be of wisdom, nothing would be as it is.

need'cessity. *dial.* [Alteration of NECESSITY, after NEED *sb.*] Necessity, need.

1818 SCOTT *Hrt. Midl.* xxi, 'Is this necessary?' said Jeanie. ..'A matter of absolute needcessity', said Saddletree. 1839 W. CARLETON *Fardorougha* ii, There's no needcessity for blowin' it about to every one I meet. 1871 DE VERE *Americanisms* 619 Needcessity, a corruption of necessity, is continually heard in the South and often so written.

needeles(se, obs. forms of NEEDLESS *a.*

needely, variant of NEEDLY *adv.* *Obs.*

'**needer.** [f. NEED *v.*[2] + -ER[1].] One who needs.

1553 GRIMALDE *Cicero's Offices* II. (1558) 102 What is more prayseworthy..than eloquence: either for the admiration of the hearers or the hope of the needers. 1601 SIR W. CORNWALLIS *Ess.* II. xxx. (1631) 50 Loving them that they have neede of, but never loving the needers of them. 1641 HINDE *J. Bruen* lvi. 188 Hee sent into the towne to such persons as were the greatest needers. *a*1860 H. H. WILSON *Ess. & Lect.* (1862) I. 349 Glorification of the cherisher of all things, and the needer of none.

'**needfire.** Also 6 *Sc.* neidfyre, 6- fire, (7 ned-). [f. NEED *sb.* + FIRE, prob. repr. an OE. *níẹdfýr* = OS. *nôdfŷr*, MLG. *nôtvûr* (LG. *nood-*, *naadfür*), MHG. *nôtviur* (G. *nothfeuer*), in sense 2: cf. Da. *nödild*, Sw. dial. *nödeld*, Norw. dial. *nau(d)eld* in the same sense.]

†**1.** *Sc.* Spontaneous combustion. Only in phr. *to take need fire*. *Obs.*

1535 STEWART *Cron. Scot.* II. 424 That tyme his stalf, in presens of thame all, It tuik neidfyre richt thair into his hand. **1536** BELLENDEN *Cron. Scot.* (1821) II. 162 His staf tuk neid-fire, and micht not be slokinnit.
fig. **1669** R. FLEMING *Fulfilling of Script.* (1801) I. 69 Ere ever they were aware they had taken life and needfire with a word.

2. Fire obtained from dry wood by means of violent friction, formerly credited with various magical or prophylactic virtues, esp. as a means of curing disease among cattle.

1633 PRYNNE *1st Pt. Histrio-m.* 21 Sacrilegious fires, called Nedfire or Bonefires, with all other Heathenish Obseruations, and Ceremonies. **1644** *Presb. Bk. Strathbogie* (Spalding Club) 51 It was regraited by Mr. Robert Watsone that ther vas neid fyre raysed vithin his parochin..for the curing of cattell. **1812** J. HENDERSON *Agric. Survey Caithness* xiv. 200 In those days [*c* 1785] when the stock of any considerable farmer was seized with the murrain, he would send for one of the charm doctors to superintend the raising of a need-fire. **1825** BROCKETT *N.C. Gloss.* **1864** *Chambers's Encycl.* VI. 695/2 In various parts of the Scottish Highlands, the raising of needfire was practised not long ago. **1893** ELWORTHY *Evil Eye* 64 It was usual to drive cattle through the needfire as a preservative against disease.

3. A beacon or bonfire. (? Due to Scott.)

1805 SCOTT *Last Minstr.* III. xxix, The ready page with hurried hand Awaked the need-fire's slumbering brand. **1844** RICHARDSON *Historian's Table-bk., Leg. Div.* II. 15 The far distant need-fire or beacon light proclaimed the approach of foes. **1865** MISS YONGE *Dove in Eagle's Nest* vi, Each..article of rubbish that had been in reserve for the needfire.

†**need-force.** *Sc. Obs.* [f. NEED *sb.* + FORCE *sb.*] (*on*) ***need force***, perforce, on compulsion, of necessity.

1456 SIR G. HAYE *Law Arms* (S.T.S.) 165 [He] behovit for his honour on nede force to geve him bataill. *Ibid.* 177 Hame agayne behufis him gang on nede fors. **1549** *Compl. Scot.* vi. 67 Quhar for on neid forse, i vas constrenȝeit to be his sodiour. **1636** RUTHERFORD *Lett.* lxxi. (1862) I. 185 Their synagogue will need-force to cast me out.

needful (ˈniːdfʊl), *a.* (and *sb.*) Forms: 2–4 néod-, 2 níed-, (4 nud-), 3–6 ned-, (5 nedde-), 4–6 nede-, *Sc.* neid(e-, 4–7 neede-, (6 nyd-, nide-, nead-), 4, 6– need-. Also 3–5 -fol, 4–7 -full(e, (5 -ffull). [f. NEED *sb.* + -FUL.]

1. Of persons: Needy, necessitous. Now *rare*.

a. Used absolutely. (Chiefly as *pl.*)

a **1175** *Cott. Hom.* 217 Heo is..mancenne hiht and hope, richtwisen strenhcþe, and niedfulle frouer. *c* **1200** *Trin. Coll. Hom.* 9 Gief þe nedfulle, help þe hauelease. **13..** *Cursor M.* 103 (Gött.), Lady scho is of ledes all,..To nedefull neist on to call. *c* **1386** CHAUCER *Pars. T.* ⁋958 If þou may not visite þe needful wiþ þy persone; visite by þy message. *c* **1440** *Jacob's Well* 252 Tyl þou forȝyue þine enemyis, & haue pyte on þe nedefull. *c* **1510** BARCLAY *Mirr. Gd. Manners* (1570) Dij, If he haue plentie of riches and treasour He parteth it abrode to nedefull with honour. **1535** COVERDALE *Ecclus.* xxxiv. 21 The bred of the nedefull is the life of the poore.

b. In attributive or predicative use.

a **1300** *Cursor M.* 12852 A nedful wreche here am i hidd. **1387** *E.E. Wills* (1882) 1 Y be-quethe x.s. to the most nedful men. *c* **1450** MYRC *Festial* (E.E.T.S.) 15 He departyd his good yn þre partyes; on to wydows..; anoþyr to þo þat wern pore and nedfull. **1523** *Test. Ebor.* (Surtees) V. 166 The most nedfull poore people in the said townnes. **1586** T. B. *La Primaud. Fr. Acad.* (1589) 305 After he understood that the saide Nicanor was a needfull fellow..he sent him a rich present. **1631** BRATHWAIT *Whimzies, Exchange-man* 38 Our nicer Dames bestow that upon trifles, which might support a needfull family. **1822** GALT *Provost* xxx, [To] distribute it in the winter to needful families.

2. a. Of circumstances, occasions, etc.: Characterized by need, necessity, or straits. Now *rare*.

c **1250** *Gen. & Ex.* 2130 And .vij. oðere [years] sulen after ben, Sori and nedful men sulen is sen. *c* **1440** *Generydes* 60 [He] his goodis is redy to purvaye For good people in euery nedefull case. *c* **1480** *Childe of Bristowe* 153 in Hazl. *E.P.P.* I. 116 Thu so sone failest me at my nedeful day. **1540** BIBLE (Cranmer) *Ps.* x. 1 Why..hydest [thou] thy face in that neadefull tyme of trouble? **1585–6** EARL LEICESTER *Corr.* (Camden) 190 To recommend to your lordships the nedefull estate of the captains and souldiers here. **1814** WORDSW. *White Doe* III. 267 A Cause, which on a needful day Would breed us thousands brave as they.

†**b.** Standing in need *of* something, also *ellipt.*; requiring *to* do something. *Obs.*

1432 *Rolls of Parlt.* IV. 405/1 A place..full nedefull of grete reparation. **1561** T. HOBY tr. *Castiglione's Courtyer* I. (1577) Dj b, A manne woulde weene hee were more meete to teache, than needefull to learne. **1606** *N. Riding Rec.* I. 52 The highway to be amended and repayred in all places needfull.

3. a. Requisite, necessary, indispensable. Also const. *to* or *for* the person or thing concerned.

a **1340** HAMPOLE *Psalter* iv. 8 Whet, wyne, and oile..are mast nedful til mannys oise. **1362** LANGL. *P. Pl.* A. I. 21 Heore nomes beth neodful and nempnen hem I thenke. **1452** in Gross *Gild Merch.* (1890) II. 66 Statutes nedffull & profytabille for þe sayd bretherhed. **1545** BRINKLOW *Compl.* xxiv. (1874) 62 We myght doo any nedeful busynesse vpon the Sunday. **1583** GOLDING *Calvin on Deut.* xxxix. 232 Yet is that lesson needfuller than the former. **1612** WOODALL *Surg. Mate* Wks. (1653) 29 It is a needful Emplaster in the Surgeons Chest. **1697** DRYDEN *Virg. Georg.* III. 480 The Fleece..Is dearly sold; but not for needful use. **1742** YOUNG *Nt. Th.* IX. 483 The winter is as needful as the spring. **1808** SCOTT *Marm.* I. xxii, [He is] The needfulest among us all When time hangs heavy in the hall. **1868** E. EDWARDS *Ralegh* I. iii. 38 Stern retaliation of this sort was probably seen to be needful.

b. With complementary infin. clause. Now *rare*.

c **1340** HAMPOLE *Prose Tr.* 22 Occupacion and besynes of the worlde which ar nedefulle to vsen. **1377** LANGL. *P. Pl.* B. XIX. 20 Ergo is no name..so nedeful to nempne by nyȝte ne by daye. **1560** DAUS tr. *Sleidane's Comm.* 111 They wold take further advisement, what were than nedeful to be done. **1582** N. LICHEFIELD tr. *Castanheda's Conq. E. Ind.* I. iii. 8 b, Other things also which were necessarye and needfull to be looked unto.

c. ***it is needful that*** or ***to*** (with inf.).

1340 HAMPOLE *Pr. Consc.* 3168 Nedeful it es, þat sorow war als mykel and na les For ilka syn. *a* **1400** *Pistill of Susan* 266 Hit is nedful nou þi names to nempne. **1500–20** DUNBAR *Poems* xv. 26 Nocht neidfull is men sowld be dum. **1593** SHAKS. *3 Hen. VI*, IV. vi. 53 It is more then needfull Forthwith that Edward be pronounced a Traytor. **1657** SPARROW *Bk. Com. Prayer* (1661) 33 Needful it is that the Church should call upon us for this duty. **1796** H. HUNTER tr. *St.-Pierre's Stud. Nat.* (1799) III. 680 But is it needful to recur to authority when we have that of Nature? **1848** W. H. BARTLETT *Egypt to Pal.* xiii. (1879) 295 It is needful to be cautious.

4. a. ***the needful***, what is necessary or requisite. Esp. in phr. ***to do the needful***.

1709 STEELE *Tatler* No. 78 ⁋7 If you want any further Particulars..let me know, and *per* first will advise the needful. **1710** J. LOVETT *Let.* 1 Apr. in M. M. Verney *Verney Lett.* (1930) I. xii. 210 Waiting on proper persons and doing the needful in all places. **1771** FOOTE *Maid of B.* II. Wks. 1799 II. 224 *Lady Cath.*... Prepare the minister and aw the rest of the tackle...*Flint*... I will straight set about getting the needful. **1822** M. EDGEWORTH *Let.* 27 Jan. (1971) 338, I resolved to write..only 3 or 4 lines just to say the needful. **1831** SCOTT *Jrnl.* 24 Apr. (1946) 164 Young Clarkson had already done the needful—that is had bled & blisterd severely, and placed me on a very restrictd diet.

b. *colloq.* The necessary funds; money, cash.

1774 FOOTE *Cozeners* III. Wks. 1799 II. 187 *Mrs. Air*... You have the needful? *Air.* All but five hundred pounds. **1794** WASHINGTON in *Bulletin N.Y. Publ. Lib.* I. 209 As you had acknowledged the receipt of the needful for purchasing the Buck Wh[eat]. **1822** SCOTT in Lockhart *Life* (1837) V. 236, I will send the *needful* when you apprise me of the amount total. **1855** C. BRONTE *Professor* vi, To live I must have 'the needful', which I can only get by working. **1891** *Daily News* 28 Oct. 5/7 A few friends supply the needful, which is about a hundred a year.

5. *sb.* A necessary thing.

1856 MRS. H. O. CONANT *Eng. Bible Transl.* ii. (1881) 14 Should the worthy friends..replenish his empty wallet with such needfuls as they could spare. **1865** MRS. WHITNEY *Gayworthys* II. 127 Landy came over early with..a parcel —Say's dress for the Sunday and other needfuls.

needfully (ˈniːdfʊlɪ), *adv.* Now *rare*. [f. prec. + -LY².] Necessarily, upon compulsion or constraint; urgently, pressingly.

a **1340** HAMPOLE *Psalter* ix. 22 Nedfully þou suffirs vs to be angird & tribled. *c* **1374** CHAUCER *Troylus* IV. 976 (1004) For nedfully by-houeth it not to be That þilke þinges fallen in certayn That ben purueyed. **1456** SIR G. HAYE *Law Arms* (S.T.S.) 148 [He] hapnyt to be nedefully send for to cum and se his awin place for grete caus. **1541** PAYNELL *Catiline* xlv. 71 To retourne ageyne, where I lefte, whan I nedefully spake of Cæsar. **1573** TUSSER *Husb.* (1878) 17 To keepe no more but needfullie, and count excesse vnsauerie. **1616** B. JONSON *Epigr.* xciv, [They] must needfully, though few, Be of the best. **1646** CRASHAW *Poems* (1858) 162 He [shall] more needfully and nobly prove The nations' terror now. **1861** *Macm. Mag.* IV. 135/1 The presence of one evil action.. does not always or needfully make the whole piece of action ugly.

ˈ**needfulness.** [f. as prec. + -NESS.]

1. The state or quality of being needful; the fact of something being needful; necessity.

a **1425** *Cursor M.* 19553 (Trin.), May no mon..Conferme but bisshopes honde. Þis nedefulnes phelip wist. **1553** T. WILSON *Rhet.* (1580) 89 The hearers maie bothe knowe the nature of praier, and the nedefulnesse of praier. **1578** BANISTER *Hist. Man* v. 71 Makyng the stomach to feele the needefulnes of meate and drinke. **1674** N. FAIRFAX *Bulk & Selv.* 59 Because [it is] needful for God to dwell in, and such needfulness cannot be spoken of nothing. **1748** G. WHITE *Serm.* (MS.), How should we ever be made sensible of the needfulness of the Love..of God? **1856** MISS YONGE *Daisy Chain* I. xxiii, More fully aware than her father of the needfulness of the lady's-maid. **1885** *Spectator* 30 May 415/1 He..appreciates..the occasional needfulness of war.

†**2.** A condition of need; a strait. *Obs. rare.*

a **1340** HAMPOLE *Psalter* ix. 22 Þou despisis in nedfulneses, in tribulacyon. *a* **1400** *Prymer* (1891) 80 Of myn needfulnesses delyuere me.

So †ˈ**needfulty**. *Obs. rare*⁻¹.

1382 WYCLIF *Ps.* ix. 22 [x. 1] Wherto, Lord, wentist thou awei along? Thou despisist in nedfultees, in tribulacioun.

†ˈ**Needham.** *Obs.* Also 6 needam, 7 needom(e. Properly the name of a small town (Needham Market) near Ipswich in Suffolk, used punningly with allusion to NEED *sb.*; hence, need, poverty, beggary.

1573 TUSSER *Husb.* (1878) 188 Toiling much and spoiling more..Soone sets thine host at needams shore, to craue the beggers bone. **1592** GREENE *Upst. Courtier* Dj, Such yoong youths, when the Broker hath blest them with saint Needams cross, fall then to priuy lifts and cosenages. **1616** T. ADAMS *Soul's Sickness* Wks. (1629) 466 Idlenesse is the coach to bring a man to Needome, Prodigality the post-horse. *a* **1661** FULLER *Worthies, Suffolk* III. (1662) 56 They are said to be in the high way to Needham who do hasten to poverty.

needie, obs. form of NEEDY *a.*

†ˈ**needihood.** *Obs. rare*⁻¹. In 7 needy-. [f. NEEDY *a.* + -HOOD.] Neediness.

1648 HERRICK *Hesper., Beggar to Mab*, Floure of fuz-balls, that's too good For a man in needy-hood.

needil, obs. form of NEEDLE.

†ˈ**needily,** *adv. Obs. rare.* [f. NEEDY *a.* + -LY².]

a. Necessarily. **b.** In a needy fashion.

1577–87 HOLINSHED *Chron.* III. 506/2 It followeth, that needilie [*Fabyan* nedely] great inconuenience must fall to that people, that a child is ruler and gouernour of. **1579** TWYNE *Phisicke agst. Fortune* II. cxx. 324 Which both the shortnesse of lyfe, and swyftnesse of tyme,..needily constrayneth to be so. **1642** MILTON *Apol. Smect.* Wks. 1851 III. 305 If I should make my selfe so poore, as to sollicite needily any such kinde of rich hopes as this Fortuneteller dreams of.

ˈ**neediness.** [f. NEEDY *a.* + -NESS.] The state or condition of being needy; poverty, want, indigence.

1382 WYCLIF *Lev.* xxvi. 16 Y shal visyte ȝow swiftly in nedynes, and in brennynge. *a* **1440** *Found. St. Bartholomew's* (E.E.T.S.) 54 From howe grete ricches with sodeyne case I am come yn nedynes. **1534** MORE *Comf. agst. Trib.* III. Wks. 1234/1 Hee lyued here in needynesse and pouertye all hys lyfe. **1565** GOLDING *Ovid's Met.* To Rdr., Of health and sicknesse, life and death, of needinesse and wealth. **1603** HOLLAND *Plutarch's Mor.* 210 That penurie and needinesse of the soule. **1827** SOUTHEY *Penins. War* II. 476 These measures proved the neediness of the intrusive government. **1883** *Fortn. Rev.* 1 Sept. 347 It is not from neediness, nor yet from niggardliness.

ˈ**needing,** *vbl. sb.* [f. NEED *v.*² + -ING¹.]

†**1.** An occasion or time of need. *Obs. rare*.

a **1300** *E.E. Psalter* ix. 10 He..made is Laverd..Helper in nedinges. *a* **1340** HAMPOLE *Psalter* xxiv. 18 For þi delyuerd me lord of my nedynges.

†**2.** A necessary act. *Obs. rare*⁻¹.

c **1475** *Mankind* 776 in *Macro Plays* 29, I am doynge of my nedynges; be ware how ȝe schott!

3. The fact of being in need; (a) need or want.

1500–20 DUNBAR *Poems* ix. 124, I synnit als in reif and in oppressioun,..but rewth of peure folkis neiding. *c* **1600** SHAKS. *Sonn.* cxviii, To be diseased ere that there was true needing. **1674** N. FAIRFAX *Bulk & Selv.* 147 We see then the soul can do after the needings of its own kind. **1821** CLARE *Vill. Minstr.* II. 117 The daily needings want's worst shifts require.

ˈ**needing,** *ppl. a.* [f. NEED *v.*² + -ING².] That needs; poor, indigent. Also *transf.*

1569 J. SANFORD tr. *Agrippa's Van. Artes* 7 The Latine Gramer is so poore and needinge and bounde to the Greek literature. **1642** ROGERS *Naaman* 133 But a poore needing soule so sees Christ offered. **1898** BP. MOULE *Colossian Stud.* vii. 139 We, in Him, derive that Fulness into our needing Souls.

†ˈ**needings,** *adv. Obs. rare.* [repr. OE. *néadinga, -unga, níedinga*, f. *néad, níed* NEED *sb.*] Of necessity.

a **1300** *Cursor M.* 2450 Þair fee nedings þai most flit. *Ibid.* 5926 O þis watur..Wa was þam þat it nedings dranc.

needisly: see NEEDSLY *adv. Obs.*

needle (ˈniːd(ə)l), *sb.* Forms: α. 1–2 **nǽdl, nédl,** (1 **naeðl, nethl, netl**), 3–6 **nedle,** 4–5 **nedel,** (5 **-ele**), 4–6 **nedill,** (5 **-il, -ille, -yl, -ylle,** 6 **-yll**), 5–6 **nedell, nydel,** (5 **nydle**), 6 **neidil, neadle;** 5–6 **needell,** 6–7 **needel,** (6 **-il**), 6– **needle.** β. 3–7 **neld(e,** 4 **neelde,** 6–9 **neeld,** 6 **neilde,** 8 **ne(e)ald,** 9 **nield, nild;** 6, 9 **neele,** 9 **neel, neal, nill, nail.** [OE. *nǽdl* fem. = OFris. *nedle, nidle,* OS. *nâdla, nâthla,* MLG. *nâtel,* OHG. *nâdela, nâdla, nâdal* (MHG. *nâdele, nâdel,* G. *nadel*), ON. *nál* (for **náþl*; Sw. *nål*, Da. *naal*), Goth. *nêþla*:—pre-Teut. **nētlā*, f. the root **nē-* to sew, which appears in OHG. *nâian* (G. *nähen*), MDu. *nayen* (Du. *naaien*), and prob. in L. *nēre* to spin, Gr. νῆσις spinning, νῆμα thread. The ME. metathetic form *neld(e* has parallels in OFris. *nelde*, MDu. *naelde* (Du. *naala*), OHG. *nalda* (MHG. *nalde*): forms representing it are still common in northern and western dialects.]

I. 1. a. An instrument used in sewing, usually a small and slender piece of polished steel having a fine point at one end and at the other a hole or eye (see EYE *sb.* 20 a) through which the thread is passed.

naked, or ***sharp, as a needle***: see the adjs. ***pins and needles***: see PIN *sb.* 3 d.

α. *c* **725** *Corpus Gloss.* (Hessels) A 160 *Acus*, netl. *Ibid.* P 421 *Pictus acu*, mið nethle [*Ep.* naeðlæ, *Erf.* nedlæ] asiowid. *a* **1000** *Soul & Body* 120 ȝifer hatte se wyrm, þam þe ȝeaflas beoð nædle scearpran. *a* **1000** *Colloq. Abp. Ælfric* in Wr.-Wülcker 99/17 Hwanon fiscere ancgel oþþe sceowyrhton æl oþþe seamere nædl? *c* **1200** ORMIN 6341 Wiþþutenn cnif & shæþe & camb & nedle. ? *a* **1366** CHAUCER *Rom. Rose* 97 A sylvre nedle forth I drogh Out of an aguiler queynt. *c* **1400** *Lanfranc's Cirurg.* 36 Haue a nedle þre cornerid..& þe lippis of þe wounde schal be sowid togideris. **1484** CAXTON *Æsop* III. i, [The shepherd] with a nydle subtylly drewe oute of his foote the thorne. **1523** FITZHERB. *Husb.* §142 [Have] thimble, nedle, threde,..leste that thy gurthe breake. **1584** R. SCOT *Discov. Witchcr.* XII. vii. (1886) 182 She sticketh also needels fine In livers, whereby men doo pine. **1653** WALTON *Angler* v. 111 With a needle or pin divide the wing into two. **1712** STEELE *Spect.* No. 430 ⁋1 With a Needle and Thread thriftily mending his Stockings. **1751** JOHNSON

Rambler No. 85 ¶12 A knot of misses busy at their needles. **1835** Sir J. Ross *Narr. 2nd Voy.* xxxvii. 515 Presenting the women with a needle each. **1865** Lubbock *Preh. Times* xii. 407 For needles they use bones either of birds or fishes. *fig.* **1678** *Yng. Man's Call.* 156 This [sin] is..that needle, that too surely draws a thread of divine vengeance after it. **1860** Reade *Cloister & H.* lxxv, Catherine ran infinite pins and needles of speech into them. **1872** Black *Adv. Phaeton* xx. 279 Sticking another needle in her mental image of that poor monarch.

β. *a* **1225** *Ancr. R.* 152 A sopare, þet ne bereð buten sope & nelden. *a* **1300** *Estorie del Euangelie* 358 (Vernon MS.) in *Engl. Stud.* VIII. 258 þat mayde won hire bred Wiþ hire nelde and hire þred. **1387** Trevisa *Higden* (Rolls) VIII. 249 That childe was..prikkede thro alle the body with nalles, neldes, and pynnes. **1432–50** tr. *Higden* (Rolls) I. 225 They made a subtile hoole vnder hit with a nelde. *a* **1557** Mrs. M. Basset tr. *More's Treat. Passion* M.'s Wks. 1365 Yf a man do but with a neldes point pricke them in yᵉ eye. **1575** *Gamm. Gurton* I. iv. 5 My fayre, longe, strayght neele, that was myne onely treasure! **1600** Fairfax *Tasso* xx. xcv, For thee fit weapons weare Thy neeld and spindle. **1701** J. White *Cy. Man's Conductor* 127/2 *Neald*, Needle. The *ea* sounded as in yea. **1775** Watson *Hist. Halifax* Vocab. 543 *Neeld*, a Needle. **1814** *Monthly Mag.* XXXVIII. 127 Needle, *neel.* **1825** Jennings *Obs. Dial. W. Eng.* 166 Whitechapel nills all sizes. **1848–** in many dial. glossaries (usually in form *neeld*).

†**b.** As an object of trifling importance or value; hence, a particle. *Obs.*

a **1225** *Ancr. R.* 400 Alle þeos þingis somed, aȝean mine bode, ne beoð nout wurð a nelde. *c* **1330** *Arth. & Merl.* 4012 (Kölbing), þo he þe stede was opon, He ȝaue a nedel of his fon. *c* **1400** *Plowman's Tale* in *Pol. Poems* (Rolls) I. 327 Soche willers witte is not worth a nelde. *c* **1460** *Towneley Myst.* ii. 123 When all mens corn was fayre in feld Then was myne not worth a neld. *Ibid.* xiii. 233, I ete not an nedyll Thys moneth and more.

c. Phr. ***to look for***, or ***seek, a needle in a meadow, haystack, bottle*** (***truss*** or ***bundle***) ***of hay***, to attempt an extremely difficult, impossible, or foolish task.

c **1530** More *Answ. Frith* Wks. 837/2 To seke out one lyne in all hys bookes wer to go looke a nedle in a medow. **1592** [see bottle *sb.*³ 1]. **1690** W. Walker *Idiomat. Anglo-Lat.* (1695) Pref., A labour much like that of seeking a needle in a Bottle of Hay. **1711** E. Ward *Vulgus Brit.* viii. 95 Seeking we may say, A Needle in a Truss of Hay. **1742** Gray *Lett.* (1900) I. 105 A coach that seem'd to have lost its way, by looking for a needle in a bottle of hay. **1855** Kingsley *Westw. Ho!* xxx, But it's ill looking for a needle in a haystack. [**1875** Lowell *Spenser* Prose Wks. 1890 IV. 268 These thin needles of wit buried in unwieldy haystacks of verse.]

d. ***needle's eye***, denoting a minute opening or space, chiefly in echoes of Matt. xix. 24, etc.

Direct citations of the N.T. passages are frequent. The rendering *the eye of a needle* goes back to Tindale (1526).

a **1530** T. Lupset *Compendious Treat. Dyenge Well* (1534) 35 For as harde a thynge it is to plucke through the smale nedels eie a greatte caboull rope, as to brynge a ryche man in at heuens wycket. **1579** Gosson *Sch. Abuse* (Arb.) 27 Euerie one of them may..daunce the wilde Morice in a Needles eye. **1593** Shaks. *Rich. II*, v. v. 17 It is as hard to come, as for a Camell To thred the posterne of a Needles eye. **1622** Fitz-Geffrey *Elisha* 46 He had learned also how to make the Camell passe through the needles eye, namely by casting off the bunch on the back. **1668** Davenant *Man's the Master* I. i, The invisible rogue threaded a lane as narrow as a needle's eye. **1872** Besant & Rice *Ready-Money Mortiboy* III. xiii. 234 A single-hearted..rich man, for whom the needle's eye is as easy to pass, as for the poorest pauper. **1925** A. Huxley *Those Barren Leaves* I. i. 11 Those roaring lions at Lady Trunion's..had no hope of passing through the needle's eye. **1929** H. W. Nevinson *The English* vi. 43 They are well fitted to carry on the traditions of Victorian vulgarity, and to prove yet again that no camel will ever get through the needle's eye. **1940** V. W. Brooks *New England* xx. 414 People solemnly chewed their food very fine and slowly to be slender enough to pass through the eye of the needle. **1957** F. R. Scott (*title*) Eye of the needle.

e. *transf.* A needlewoman. *rare.*

1834 Beckford *Italy* II. 83 Sister Francisca Salesia..is acknowledged to be one of the first needles in Christendom. **1855** Dickens *Dorrit* II. xvii, There was no favour in half-a-crown a day to such a needle as herself.

2. a. A piece of magnetized steel (orig. a needle in sense 1) used as an indicator of direction (in later use as a part of the compass), or in connexion with magnetic or electric apparatus such as the telegraph. Also *ellipt.* = needle telegraph.

1375 Barbour *Bruce* v. 23 Thai wist nocht quhar thai wer, For thai na nedill had na stane. **1436** *Libel Eng. Policy* in *Pol. Poems* (Rolls) II. 191 Men have practised by nedle and by stone Thider-wardes wythine a lytel whylle. **1475** *Bk. Noblesse* (Roxb.) 58 Yet the eldist man..seethe to the nedille for to gide the ship to alle costis. **1555** Eden *Decades* Contents (Arb.) 45 Who fyrst founde the nedle of the compass and the vse thereof. **1625** N. Carpenter *Geog. Del.* I. iii. (1635) 66 At Guinea the magneticall needle inclines to the East. **1665** Glanvill *Scepsis Sci.* xiv. 78 As is the trembling Needle, till it find its beloved North. **1774** M. Mackenzie *Maritime Surv.* 16 They will be less affected by any Inaccuracy in the Bearing by the Needle. **1837** Wheatstone & Cooke in *Repert. Pat. Invent.* (1839) XI. 9 Whenever the needle does so point upwards and downwards, it denotes that it is quiescent. **1867** Smyth *Sailor's Word-bk.* 462 After an action at sea, the needles are often found to be useless, until re-magnetized. **1876** Preece & Sivewright *Telegraphy* 96 The Needle is specially adapted for railway purposes and for linking together several towns on one wire.

fig. **1679** *Establ. Test* 2, I do not pretend..to meddle with the Needle and Compass of the Publique Bottom. *a* **1700** Ken *Hymnotheo* Poet. Wks. 1721 III. 335 The Needle turn'd from God, to point at ill.

b. A small strip of gold or silver of known or standard fineness used with a touchstone in testing the purity of other pieces of those metals.

1469 in *Archaeol.* (1806) XV. 173 That ii gode stones and good nedeles for to touche be alwey ther redie..to make assaie of gold. **1753** Chambers *Cycl. Supp.* s.v. *Touch-Needles*, You will be able to determine..what allay it is of, by the mark of the Needle. **1763** W. Lewis *Phil. Comm. Arts* 119 Oblong pieces, called needles,..kept in readiness..as standards of comparison. **1825** J. Nicholson *Operat. Mechanic* 766 Assayers make a comparison upon a touch-stone, between it and certain needles composed of gold and silver,..which are called Proof Needles.

c. (See quots.)

1589 Rider *Bibl. Schol.* 989 A needle, or tongue of a ballance or beame, *examen.* **1616–61** Holyday *Persius* (1673) 301 The parts of the balance... The Needle (or Tongue) that arises from the middle of the beam [etc.]. **1789** M. Madan tr. *Persius* (1795) 8 *note*, The tongue, needle, or beam of a balance. **1856** *Orr's Circle Sci., Mech. Phil.* 107 A needle is usually fixed to the beam.., which points vertically upwards or downwards when the beam is in a horizontal position.

d. A slender, usu. pointed, indicator on a dial or other measuring instrument, *spec.* on a speedometer.

1928 Kipling *Limits & Renewals* (1932) 60 She preferred cars to her own feet... Her place was at his left elbow, nose touching his sleeve, until the needle reached fifty. **1937** D. L. Sayers *Busman's Honeymoon* xiv. 244 He let the needle drop back to twenty-five and they dawdled on through the lanes. **1958** 'Castle' & 'Hailey' *Flight into Danger* ii. 31 The altimeter needle on the winking instrument panel steadily registered a climb of five hundred feet a minute. **1962** J. Glenn in *Into Orbit* 42 The periscope..gives you an horizon-to-horizon view of the earth below so you can check your actual attitude against the needles. **1973** 'S. Harvester' *Corner of Playground* II. v. 118 He drove faster, watching the needle flick up to a hundred.

3. a. A pointed instrument used in engraving or etching.

1662 Evelyn *Chalcogr.* (1769) 22 The use both of the point, needle, and etching in aquafortis. **1727–38** Chambers *Cycl.* s.v. *Engraving*, The design..is traced through on the copper, with a point or needle. *c* **1790** Imison *Sch. Arts* II. 32 The principal instruments for etching are needles, oil-stone [etc.]. **1837** *Penny Cycl.* IX. 441/2 Etching-points or needles are nearly similar in appearance to sewing-needles, but fixed into handles four or five inches long.

b. *Surg.* A long slender pointed instrument used in operations; the sharply pointed end of a hypodermic or other syringe; a pointed electrode used in surgical electrolysis.

1727–38 Chambers *Cycl.* s.v. *Cataract*, Turning the needle round, they twist the cataract about its point. **1803** *Med. Jrnl.* X. 566 If the anterior part of the capsula remain, ..the needle is retracted from the lens. **1846** Brittan tr. *Malgaigne's Man. Oper. Surg.* 309 A silver or golden needle about three inches long... The oculist holds this needle as a pen. **1895** *Arnold & Sons' Catal. Surg. Instr.* 267 Syringe, Laryngeal,..with needles for injecting the Larynx hypodermically. **1899** *Allbutt's Syst. Med.* VIII. 828 The positive needle should be held in position and the negative needle passed in various directions through the nævoid tissue.

(*b*) *spec.* A hypodermic needle used to inject drugs; the use of, or addiction to, injected drugs, esp. in phr. ***on the needle***, engaged in, or addicted to, injecting drugs; also *rarely*, a morphine-addict; a dose of a drug for injection. *slang* (orig. *U.S.*).

1929 M. A. Gill *Underworld Slang* (s.v. *don't*), *Don't break the needle*, don't use all the dope. **1936** L. Duncan *Over Wall* i. 21, I saw and became familiar with the hopheads or cokes—the cocaine addicts on the snow; the needles or hypes—morphine users. **1943** *N.Y. Times* 9 May II. 5/6 He's got a band that don't need a five o'clock needle like some other bands. **1953** W. Burroughs *Junkie* (1972) x. 94 'You've been hooking that spot so much it's about to get infected,' he said, pointing to a needle welt. **1955** W. Gaddis *Recognitions* I. v. 196 I've heard about her... On the needle. A schiz. **1957** C. MacInnes *City of Spades* II. iv. 102 He's using all his dope allowance now... You know who put him on the needle and supplied him? **1968** R. Jeffries *Traitor's Crime* i. 8 'When d'you get your fixes?' asked Elwick. 'In—in the evenings.' 'How much?' 'Fifteen bob a needle.' **1973** *Listener* 6 Sept. 306/1 Middle Britain thinks..one puff on the joint leads to the needle.

c. In breech-loading fire-arms, a slender steel pin by the impact of which the cartridge is ignited.

1853 Ure *Dict. Arts* (ed. 4) I. 727 On pulling the trigger, the interior needle, from which the musquet takes its name, is darted forward..and thus effects the ignition. **1876** Voyle & Stevenson *Milit. Dict.* 270/1 The spiral spring.. forces the needle into the cartridge and fires the piece.

d. A thin pointed or tapering rod used to secure fine adjustment in closing apertures, as in valves.

1884 Knight *Dict. Mech.* Suppl. 632/2 In order to regulate the supply of oil [from a needle lubricator], a metallic feed-rod (needle) passes through the tube, and rests upon the shaft to be lubricated. **1909** *Chambers's Jrnl.* Nov. 698/1 The gas-regulator can be adjusted to the fiftieth part of an inch, with dead centralisation of the needle. **1927** G. W. C. Kaye *High Vacua* iv. 52 The needle readily beds itself into its seating, and very little pressure is needed to close the valve completely. **1965** C. M. Van Atta *Vacuum Sci. & Engin.* viii. 328 The principal feature of the design [of the needle valve] is the slowly tapering needle fitting snugly into a carefully reamed conical seat.

e. The small pointed jewel or piece of metal, wood, etc., which rests in the groove of a gramophone record when it is being played and communicates the undulations to the pick-up or diaphragm; also, a similar device used to cut the groove; = stylus 2.

1902 *Encycl. Brit.* XXXI. 679/2 The marker..instead of being a stiff needle coming from the centre of the membrane or glass plate, is now a lever. **1930** A. B. Wood *Textbk. Sound* 438 The vibrations of the diaphragm cause a needle to cut grooves on the surface of a prepared cylinder or disc. **1949** Frayne & Wolfe *Elem. Sound Recording* xiii. 240 Motion of the needle can be utilized to apply a force to a piezoelectric crystal and thus generate a voltage. **1957** *Records & Recording* Nov. 20/1 These grooves..must be tracked with absolute accuracy by the pickup needle—nowadays it is more usually called a stylus. **1973** D. Ramsay *Deadly Discretion* 190 The concerto came to an end. The needle began to click against the ungrooved portion of the record.

4. a. A knitting or netting pin.

1719 D'Urfey *Pills* (1872) V. 282 She let her Iv'ry Needle fall. **1753** Chambers *Cycl. Suppl.* s.v. *Net*, All the tools necessary to it are wooden needles, of which there should be several of different sizes. **1797** *Encycl. Brit.* (ed. 3) XVII. 805/1 The method of knitting stockings by wires or needles. **1843** *Penny Cycl.* XXVII. 180/1 In the process of knitting.. polished steel needles or wires are used to link threads together into a series of loops.

b. One of a set of parallel pieces of wire forming part of the mechanism of a stocking-frame or of the Jacquard loom.

1839 Ure *Dict. Arts* 660 There must be as many endless cords in this frame as needles in the weaving-loom. **1843** *Penny Cycl.* XXVII. 178/2 Each bar or needle is a lever by which certain warp-threads are governed.

5. a. A metal pin or rod used as a fixing.

1837 *Civil Eng. & Arch. Jrnl.* I. 6/1 Long iron needles pass through holes in the strips of saw-plate, and pin them to the ground.

b. *Mining.* (See quot. 1883.)

1839 *Penny Cycl.* XV. 241/2 The charge having been firmly rammed down with clay..the wire or 'needle' is withdrawn. **1883** Gresley *Gloss. Coal-mining* 173 *Needle*, a sharp-pointed copper or brass rod with which a small hole is made through the stemming to the cartridge in blasting operations.

II. 6. a. A pillar or obelisk, usually with fanciful attribution to some historical person.

1387 Trevisa *Higden* (Rolls) IV. 211 Iulius his piler þat now pylgryms clepeþ Seynt Petres nedle. **1615** G. Sandys *Trav.* 114 An Hieroglyphicall Obelisk of Theban marble.. called Pharos Needle. **1660** F. Brooke tr. *Le Blanc's Trav.* 278 There is yet left a kind of Obeliske or Needle. *a* **1693** Huntingdon in Ray's *Travels* (1693) II. 153 The Franks call them Aguglia's, the English particularly Cleopatra's Needles. **1842** Gwilt *Archit.* 1009 s.v. *Obelisk*, Two obelisks, one at Alexandria, vulgarly called Cleopatra's Needle.

†**b.** (See quot. 1617.) *Obs. rare.*

1617 Moryson *Itin.* III. 143 Rippen had a most flourishing Monastery, where was the most famous needle of the Archbishop Wilfred. It was a narrow hole, by which the chastity of women was tried. **1650** T. Fuller *Pisgah* III. iii. §17. 323 We.. account the threading of Saint Wilfride's needle as a conceit..to have as much gravity and truth therein.

7. A sharp-pointed mass of rock; *esp.* in *pl.* as the name of those to the west of the Isle of Wight, or those which form the summits of many Swiss mountains.

c **1400** *Anc. Pet.* 9425 (Public Rec. Office), La terre deuaunt les nedeles del Isle de Wight. **1594** Nashe *Terrors of Night* Wks. (Grosart) III. 263 A fortunate blessed Iland, nere those pinacle rocks called the Needles. **1706** Phillips (ed. Kersey), The *Needles*, certain Shelves in the Sea, about the Isle of Wight. **1721** *New Gen. Atlas* 146 On the Platform of the Mountain there is a natural Pyramid, whence it was called a needle. **1775** C. & F. Davy tr. *Bourrit's Journ. Glaciers* (1776) 67 The chain..is composed of masses of rocks, which terminate in pikes, or spires called the Needles. **1820** Mariana Starke *Trav. Cont.* ii. 66 The *Mer de Glace* ..on its margin rise pyramidical rocks, called Needles. **1852** Mitchell *Rev. Bachelor* 279 Far behind them..Mont Blanc and the Needles of Chamouni.

8. A beam or post of wood, *esp.* one used as a temporary support for a wall during underpinning.

1471 *Acc. Bodmin Ch.* (Camden) 25 Cariage of neldis for scafelys. **1512–13** *Rec. Nottingham* (1889) IV. 452 Item for a tree, the hewyng and sawyng in neldes v.*s.* **1587** Fleming *Contn. Holinshed* III. 1541/1 What prouision of stuffe should be made..of timber,..needels, keies, beetels. **1684** I. Mather *Remark. Provid.* (1856) 5 b, A violent flash, or rather flame of lightning, which brake and shivered one of the needles of the katted or wooden chimney. **1842** Gwilt *Archit.* 1008 *Needle*, an horizontal piece of timber serving as a temporary support to some superincumbent weight. **1867** *Guardian* 24 Dec. 1383/1 One of the 'needles'—upright pieces of timber supporting the keystone of the arch—slipped from under. **1889** *Whitby Gaz.* 5 Apr. 3/7 If a plank had been placed between the needles, the stone could not have fallen upon plaintiff.

9. a. A common wild plant (*Scandix pecten*), also called *Adam's, beggar's, shepherd's needle*, etc.

1793 *Trans. Soc. Arts* XI. 52 Unaccountably foul with catlock, needles, &c. **1851** *Jrnl. R. Agric. Soc.* XII. II. 348 Weeds are very troublesome, especially the wild oat, buttercup, and 'needle'. **1877** *N.W. Linc. Gloss.*, *Needles*, a weed, with sharp needle-like seed-pods, which grows among corn.

b. The name of a fish. (Cf. needle-fish.) *rare.*

1589 Rider *Bibl. Schol.* 1722 Nedelis, a kind of fish, *belone.* **1603** Owen *Pembrokeshire* (1892) I. 123 The Erle or needle whose fynes growe forward contrarie to the nature of all fishe.

c. Some kind of shell. *rare*$^{-1}$.

1713 Petiver *Aquat. Anim. Amboinæ* 3/2 *Strombus*.. Curl girdled Needle.

10. *Chem.* and *Min.* A crystal or spicule resembling a needle in shape.

1712 tr. *Pomet's Hist. Drugs* I. 184 Benjamin being very full of volatile Particles.., the Flowers ascend in little Needles very white. 1758 Reid tr. *Macquer's Chym.* I. 215 Pyrites.. being broken present a number of shining needles, all radiating, as it were, from a center. 1800 tr. *Lagrange's Chem.* II. 128 You will obtain a salt under the form of small needles. 1855 Kingsley *Glaucus* (1878) 87 A twisted wisp of strong flexible flint needles. 1880 Collins in *Mineral. Mag.* IV. 104 Some of these 'needles' [of needle-tin] are extremely fine.

11. One of the sharp slender leaves of the fir and pine trees.

1798 *Trans. Soc. Arts* XVI. 357 Its needles are longer and darker than those of the famous Weymouth Pine. 1845 *Zoologist* III. 901 A pine tree.. stripped of its leaves, or needles, as the Germans more aptly term them. 1883 Jefferies *Nat. near Lond.* 159 His golden crest distinctly seen among the dark green needles of the fir.

12. *slang.* †**a.** A sharper. *Obs.*

a 1790 Potter *New Dict. Cant, Needle*, a sharp fellow, a sharper, a cheat. 1821 Egan *Life in London* 138 (Farmer), Among the needles at the West end of the town.

b. *the needle*, a fit of irritation or nervousness. Also (sometimes without *the*), anger, bad temper, enmity; esp. *to get the needle*, to become angry or upset, to lose one's temper.

1874 Hotten *Slang Dict.* 235 To 'cop the needle' is to become vexed or annoyed. 1884 [see bird *sb.* 5b]. 1887 *Punch* 30 July 45 It give 'im the needle.. being left in the lurch this way. 1890 Barrère & Leland *Dict. Slang* II. 84/2 It gives a man the needle when he hasn't got a bob, To see his pals come round and wish him joy. *Ibid.*, To get the needle is to feel very nervous and funky. 1900 G. Swift *Somerley* 83 But when the final gun has gone and you are 'off', nervousness, 'needle', everything goes. 1923 *Daily Mail* 1 Aug. 8/2 It may be, of course, that there was too much 'needle' (to employ a boxing term which means bad spirit) about this contest. 1929 H. A. Vachell *Virgin* viii. 141 The silly ass got the needle, 'cos she asked for the ring. 1959 *Times* 8 June 3/1 Perhaps it was this very lack of needle, this air of unreality in the late evening of Saturday.. that failed to see Davies home to a victory. 1967 *Time* 22 Dec. 48 A needle from [Bob] Hope becomes an emblem instead of a scar. 1970 G. F. Newman *Sir, You Bastard* v. 130 He's got the needle with you. You've got to go very careful.

III. 13. *attrib.* and *Comb.* **a.** Objective, and obj. genitive, as ***needle-grinder***, ***-grinding***, ***-maker***, ***-making***, ***-monger***, ***-pointer***, ***-polisher***, ***-seller***.

c 1836 *Encycl. Metrop.* (1845) VIII. 672/2 A back elevation of a *needle-grinder's wheel. *Ibid.*, The injurious effect of needle grinding upon the health of the individuals. 1611 Cotgr., *Esguillier*, a *needle-maker. 1723 *Lond. Gaz.* No. 6134/4 John Lowe,.. Needle-maker. *c* 1836 *Encycl. Metrop.* (1845) VIII. 673/1 Measures to be taken by the larger needle-makers themselves. *Ibid.* 671/1 *Needle-making, old process. 1872 Yeats *Techn. Hist. Comm.* 343 In England needle-making has become a staple trade. 1837 Wheelwright tr. *Aristophanes* I. 13 The *needlemonger too with Pamphilus. 1835 Ure *Philos. Manuf.* 402 The Sheffield dry-grinders and *needle-pointers. 1898 *Allbutt's Syst. Med.* V. 159 Flint-workers, *needle-polishers,.. supply the largest contingent of pulmonary diseases. 1848 Hickie tr. *Aristophanes* (Bohn) II. 692 And will not the *Needle-seller [suffer] along with Pamphilus?

b. Instrumental, as ***needle-made***, ***-painted***, ***-run***, ***-scarred***, ***-worked*** adjs.; also ***needle-hole***, ***-puncture***, ***-puncturing***.

1847 *Nat. Encycl.* I. 851 A very minute *needle-hole made in the centre of it. 1883 *Cassell's Fam. Mag.* July 500/2 The lacet point is a *needle-made lace. 1598 Chapman *Iliad* III. 386 The *needle-painted lace, with which his helm was tied Beneath his chin. 1910 *Westm. Gaz.* 2 Feb. 5/4 An exhibition of needle-painted wild flowers of South Africa was opened yesterday. 1899 *Allbutt's Syst. Med.* VIII. 847 Cancerous deposits may form at the sites of the *needle punctures. 1822–34 *Good's Study Med.* (ed. 4) III. 268 Advantage has sometimes been derived from *needle-puncturing. 1894 *Westm. Gaz.* 31 May 3/3 The mingling of *needle-run.. lace and broad white satin ribbon. 1854 Whyte Melville *Gen. Bounce* ix, Holding up her *needle-scarred hands to the bystanders. 1856 Dickens in *Househ. Words* XXXIV. 130/2 Of rich oak carvings and quaint *needleworked tapestry there was none.

c. Similative, as ***needle-form***, ***-formed***, ***-like***, ***-nosed***, ***-shaped***, ***-sharp***, ***-tailed*** adjs.; also ***needle-foliage***, ***-leaf***, ***-rock***, ***-spire***.

1898 Cath. Phillimore *Dante at Ravenna* 152 Through their *needle foliage passes a sweet murmur. 1807 T. Thomson *Chem.* (ed. 3) II. 623 It may, however, be obtained in small *needleform crystals. *Ibid.* 289 Some of them lance-shaped, others *needle-formed. 1856 Miss Yonge *Daisy Chain* II. xxii. (1879) 600 The dark path, bestrewn with brown slippery *needle-leaves. 1672 Josselyn *New Eng. Rarities* 7 They feed upon Honey, which they suck out of Blossoms.. with their *Needle-like Bills. 1797 *Encycl. Brit.* (ed. 3) XI. 440/2 The smoothness and needle-like figure of the particles. 1847–9 *Todd's Cycl. Anat.* IV. 66/2 In the shape of simple needle-like crystals. 1955 *Sci. News Let.* 26 Mar. 196/2 An eight-foot-tall, *needle-nosed rocket. 1973 *Times* 4 June 1/3 The crash came at the end of the last of three passes the needle-nosed plane made to show off its qualities. 1867 Smyth *Sailor's Word-bk.* 495 In California many of the *needle rocks are of volcanic origin. 1786 Aiken tr. *Beaumé's Man. Chem.* 94 The liquor .. furnishes *needle-shaped crystals. 1863 A. C. Ramsay *Phys. Geog.* 22 Needle-shaped masses of rocks. 1923 J. Galsworthy *Captures* 161 That fellow was *needle-sharp, though not always correct in his conclusions. 1973 *Times* 5 Oct. (Safety Suppl.) p. i/3 Everything depends on needle-sharp reflexes. 1864 *Daily Tel.* 23 Sept., Its tall brick cathedral, with the two *needle-spires. 1801 Latham *Syn. Birds* Suppl. II. 259 *Needle-tailed Sw[allow].

d. Attributive, as ***needle-factory***, ***-hand***, ***-housewifery***, ***-job***, ***-toil***, ***-trade***, ***-wire***.

1747 in *Chester Misc.* (1750) 247 Jacintha employ'd in Needle-housewifry. 1822 Lamb *Elia* Ser. II. *Thoughts on Bks.*, The milliner.. after her long day's needle-toil. 1836 *Going to Service* xi. 122 Several little needle jobs. 1839 Ure *Dict. Arts* 879 The first operation.. of the needle factory. 1862 *Catal. Internat. Exhib., Brit.* II. No. 6449 The early history of the needle-trade. *Ibid.*, The distance between the two eyes in each needle-wire. 1899 *Allbutt's Syst. Med.* VIII. 14 Cases of break-down in the needle-hand of tailors and seamstresses.

14. Special combs., as **needle-alphabet** (*nonce-wd.*), one in which stitches are substituted for letters according to a pre-arranged code; **needle-and-pin**, rhyming slang for gin *sb.*[2]; **needle-and-thread**, rhyming slang for 'bread'; **needle-bath**, a form of shower-bath with a very fine and strong spray; **needle-beam**, a transverse beam in the flooring of a bridge (Knight, 1875); **needle bearing**, a bearing using needle rollers; **needle beer** *U.S. slang* (see quot. 1928); **needle board** (see quots.); **needle-bolt**, the bolt which carries the needle in a needle-gun; **needle-book**, a needle-case resembling a small book; **needle-bug** (see quot.); **needle-bush** *Austral.*, (*a*) either of two shrubs or small trees of the genus *Hakea*, *H. leucoptera* or *H. vittata*, of the family Proteaceæ; (*b*) the nealie or nelia, *Acacia rigens*, of the family Leguminosæ; **needle-cast**, a fungus disease of conifers, causing the leaves to go brown and drop off; **needle-chervil** = needle 9 a; **needle contest** = *needle match*; **needlecord**, a finely ribbed cut-pile fabric; **needle-craft**, the art of using the needle for sewing or embroidering; **needle-dial**, a dial bearing a needle in an electrical apparatus; **needle-felt, needlefelt** = *needle-loom* (*b*); **needle fight** = *needle match*; **needle-file** [cf. G. *nadelfeil*], a fine round file used by jewellers (Knight, 1875); †**needle-fodder**, a needle-case; **needle-furze** or **-gorse**, *Genista anglica*; **needle game** = *needle match*; **needle gap** *Electr.*, a pair of needle-shaped electrodes placed in line, between which an electric discharge can take place when the potential difference between them exceeds a value dependent on the size of the gap; **needle gate**, a dam or sluice consisting of several thin spars which are placed vertically one after the other into a frame; **needle-girder** (cf. *needle-beam* above); **needle-grass**, a species of grass (*Aristida oligantha*), common in the south-western U.S.; **needle greenweed** = *needle-furze*; †**needle-house** [cf. Da. *naalehus*, Sw. *nålhus*], a needle-case; **needle ice**, ice formed into thin needle-like crystals just beneath the soil surface and often pushing up through it; **needle iron-ore** or **iron-stone**, a variety of hydrate of iron; **needle-jerker**, (*slang*) a tailor; **needle-lace**, lace made with the needle, as opposed to bobbin-lace; **needle-loom, needleloom**, (*a*) (see quot. *a* 1877); also *attrib.*; (*b*) carpeting made of felt attached to a base of rubber, hessian, or other material; **needle lubricator, oiler**, a form of lubricator in which the supply of lubricant is controlled by a needle fitted in the supply tube and resting on the shaft to be lubricated; **needle manganese** (see quot.); **needle mark**, a mark made by a hypodermic injection; **needle match**, a match or contest that arouses much interest and excitement; a crucial or keenly fought match; a contest in which the contestants have a grudge against each other; a dispute; **needle-musket**, one fired by means of a needle; **needle-ore** (see quots.); **needle paper**, a stout black paper orig. used for wrapping up needles; **needle-rifle** (cf. *needle-musket*); **needle roller**, a roller in the form of a long, thin, sometimes tapered cylinder, used in roller bearings; freq. *attrib.*; **needle scar**, a scar made by a hypodermic injection; †**needle-screw**, ? a very fine screw; **needle-shell** (see quots.); **needle shower, spray**, a shower-bath of strong fine jets of water; also *fig.*; †**needle-shuttle**, a shuttle resembling a large needle; †**needle-spar**, aragonite; **needle-spitter** (*nonce-wd.*), one who uses sharp language; **needle-syringe**, a sharp-pointed hypodermic syringe; **needle-telegraph**, a telegraph in which the needle is employed as an indicator; **needle-threader**, a device for threading needles; **needle-timber, -tin** (see quots.); **needle time**, an agreed time during which gramophone records are allowed to be broadcast; **needle track** = *needle mark*; **needle-tree**, a tree bearing needles, as the pine or fir; **needle-urchin** (see quot.); **needle valve**, a valve which works by means of a narrow pointed rod fitting into a conical seating and is operated either automatically or by a screw; **needle-weaving** (see quots.); **needle-weed** = needle 9 a; **needle-whin**, = *needle-furze*; **needle-wood** = *needle-bush* (*a*); also *attrib.*; **needle-worm** [G. *nadelwurm*, Du. *naaldworm*], a small worm parasitic in horses; **needle zeolite**, natrolite.

Also in a number of other technical combs., as ***needle-bar***, ***-forceps***, ***-loom***, ***-valve***; ***needle-bearer***, ***-holder***, etc. (see Knight *Dict. Mech.*).

1655 Mrq. Worcester *Cent. Invent.* Index, *A Needle-alphabet. 1937 Partridge *Dict. Slang* 555/2 **Needle and pin*, gin. 1973 J. Leasor *Host of Extras* vi. 118 You owe him some needle and pin—gin. 1859 Hotten *Dict. Slang* 144 **Needle and thread*, bread. 1935 A. J. Pollock *Underworld Speaks* 80/1 *Needle and thread*, bread. 1887 *Brit. Med. Jrnl.* 11 June 1291/2 There are reclining baths;.. *needle-baths; local baths; and special baths. 1930 *Automotive Industries* LXIII. 869/1 The *needle bearing offers particular advantages for certain applications in high speed engines, as on crankpins. 1946 L. E. O. Charlton *R. Air Force July 1943 to Sept. 1944* 154 (*caption*) Bomber Command launched an attack on a needle-bearing factory.. in France. 1972 R. C. Gunther *Lubrication* xiii. 408 Needle bearings are suited for slow speeds, or for oscillating and intermittent motion which permits the rollers to return to their required position upon load relief. 1928 *Flynn's* 14 Apr. 29/2 On the same spot you can get your *needle beer—near beer shot with alki or ether. 1936 J. Dos Passos *Big Money* 81 He.. had a session with the helpwanted columns over some glasses of needle beer. 1879 T. R. Ashenhurst *Pract. Treat. Weaving & Designing Textile Fabrics* 63 The pressure thus bestowed upon the crosswires keeps them in position through the *needle-board. 1889 *Cent. Dict.*, *Needle-board*, in the Jacquard loom, a perforated board or plate through which the points of the needles presented to the cards pass, and the perforations of which act as guides for the needles when the latter are actuated by the cards. The needle-board holds all the needles in proper relation with the prism or cylinder to which the cards are attached, and with the perforations in the cards. 1961 Webster, *Needle board*, a board covered with very short fine wires that is used for pressing pile fabrics. 1868 *Rep. Govt. U.S. Munitions War* 24 The catch *h* is drawn down sufficiently to allow the *needle-bolt shoulder *a* to pass over it. 1693 *Lond. Gaz.* No. 2905/4 A little Silk Bag, with a *Needle-Book and a little Key in it. 1858 Mrs. Gatty *Aunt Judy's Tales* (1859) 75 The needle-book that he'd bought for me in his hand. 1896 Lydekker *Royal Nat. Hist.* VI. 191 *Limnobates stagnorum*.. is remarkable for its elongated slender body, whence its name of *needle bug or water gnat. 1889 Maiden *Usef. Native Pl.* 34 *Hakea leucoptera*,.. '*Needle-bush', 'Pin-bush'. *Ibid.* 314 *Acacia rigens*,.. 'Nealie', or 'Needle Bush'. 1909 A. E. Mack *Bush Calendar* 4 All through the bush the needlebush showed white blossoms amongst its spiky leaves. 1944 *Living off Land* iii. 47 One of the main water supplies of the aborigines came from tree roots, principally those of the mallee, the needle-bush. *Ibid.* 48 The needlebush, a dark green shrub with sharp-pointed needles in place of leaves. 1965 *Austral. Encycl.* VI. 266/2 Needlewood or Needlebush, popular names for *Hakea leucoptera* and *H. vittata*, dry-country shrubs or small trees possessing rigid acicular leaves. *Ibid.*, The so-called 'nealie', *Acacia rigens*, is sometimes referred to as needle-bush, because of its long terete phyllodes. 1895 W. R. Fisher *Schlich's Man. Forestry* IV. 408 This sudden shedding of pine needles is the characteristic of the disease so widely spread in Germany, and termed *Schütte*, or *needle-cast. 1964 W. E. Hiley *Forestry Venture* iv. 81 We are inclined to associate the trouble with a needle-cast fungus (*Phaeocryptopus gaumannii*). 1578 Lyte *Dodoens* 615 This herbe is called.. in Englishe, Shepheardes Needel, wilde Cheruel, and *Needel Cheruill. 1922 *Daily Mail* 22 Nov. 11 There is also a '*needle' contest, recently arranged, between two stable-lads. 1963 *Times* 15 Jan. 9/4 And then what about that 'needle' contest, the University match? 1959 *Manch. Guardian* 26 June 5/3 A *needlecord in a dove-like grey was excellent for slacks or jackets. 1973 'D. Halliday' *Dolly & Starry Bird* xvi. 236 Charles had on a needlecord shirt with a flower pattern. 1382 Wyclif *Ex.* xxxix. 28 The girdil forsothe of bijs foldun aȝen, iacynct, purpur and reed clooth, twynned with *nedle craft. 1846 B. Barton *Select.* (1849) 41 A piece of sempstress-ship or needle-craft, forming the forepart of a waistcoat. 1868 *Rep. Govt. U.S. Munitions War* 241 A short circuit is thus made with a *needle-dial. 1957 *Textile Terms & Definitions* (Textile Inst.) (ed. 3) 67 **Needle felt*, felt produced by the needleloom process. 1927 *Daily News* 25 May 8/1 England's native champion.. went down in a *needle fight with Samuel Robinson, an experienced golfer. 1970 *Globe & Mail* (Toronto) 28 Sept. 21/2 In soccer there is a word for a tense match, it is called a needle game and this one fitted into that category. 1382 Wyclif *Isa.* iii. 20 Combys, and ribanes,.. and oynement boxes [*altered from* *nedle foddris]. 1650–1738 *Needle Furze [see furze 2]. 1785 Martyn *Rousseau's Bot.* xxv. (1794) 352 Needle Furze or Petty-Whin, which you will find wild on heaths. 1916 C. C. Garrard *Electr. Switch & Controlling Gear* viii. 563 One source of uncertainty can be removed if needles are used for the measuring gap, in which case the result obtained is termed the 'equivalent *needle gap'. 1927 *Ibid.* (ed. 3) viii. 641 Let us assume that this [line] is protected by a needle gap with a breakdown voltage.. of 66,000 volts. 1962 *Newnes Conc. Encycl. Electr. Engin.* 701/2 Needle gaps have been used for measuring voltages of a few kilovolts as they have larger, and therefore more convenient, spacings than sphere gaps at these low voltages. 1909 H. M. Wilson *Irrigation Engin.* (ed. 6) 230 Simple flash-board or *needle gates should be used only where the pressure upon them is low. 1898 *Daily News* 18 Nov. 2/1 '*Needle' girders were then 'threaded' crosswise over the main girders. 1893 Turner in *Annals Andersonian Nat. Soc.* 2 On the drier banks.. the *needlegorse (*Genista anglica*) is not quite unknown. 1885 H. C. McCook *Tenants Old Farm* 341 A sort of grass known as ant-rice, or *needle-grass. 1796 Withering *Brit. Plants* (ed. 3) III. 625 *Genista anglica*, *Needle Greenweed. *c* 1425 *Voc.* in Wr.-Wülcker 659 *Hec acuaria*, *nedylhows. 1483 *Cath. Angl.* 250/2 A Nedylle howse, *acuarium*. 1547 Salesbury *Welsh Dict.*, *Nildws*, a nedle ouse. 1918 *Engineering-News Record* 7 Feb. 262/2 The ice columns, or '*needle ice', formed on bare clayey soils are familiar to most people living in regions where the nights are cold enough for heavy frosts. **1939** H. H. BENNETT *Soil Conservation* xii. 284 Where there is sufficient soil moisture, a freeze will produce layers of needle ice, or spew frost, which will lift the overlying soil and vegetation as much as several inches. **1968** R. W. FAIRBRIDGE *Encycl. Geomorphol.* 381 Such 'needle ice' is sometimes called pipkrake. **1885** A. RAMSAY *Min.* (ed. 3) 178 *Needle-iron Ore; Onegite; Ferric Monohydrate. **1807** *Sporting Mag.* XVII. 19 His galligaskins have been made by the same *needle-jerker. **1891** *Daily News* 13 Nov. 5/5 There is Irish lace of all kinds, and some of the *needle lace is really exquisite. *a* **1877** KNIGHT *Dict. Mech.* II. 1519/1 **Needle-loom*, one in which the weft is carried by a needle instead of a shuttle. The usual form of loom for narrow wares, such as ribbons, tapes, bindings, etc. **1956** *Good Housek. Home Encycl.* (ed. 4) 92/2 Needleloom carpetings have a rubber or plastic back. **1957** *Textile Terms & Definitions* (Textile Inst.) (ed. 3) 68 The needleloom process is essentially a method of attaching a lap or batt..of loose fibrous material to a base, e.g. fabric, paper, rubber and/or plastic materials. **1957** *Observer* 20 Oct. 10/2 Almost all the new *tufted* carpets (which have, to a large extent, superseded the rubber-backed felt called *needleloom*) are made almost entirely of rayon. **1969** A. J. HALL *Stand. Handbk. Textiles* (ed. 7) iii. 161 For the manufacture of needle-loom carpets a machine is used which comprises rows of vertical needles. **1884** KNIGHT *Dict. Mech.* Suppl. 632/2 *Needle lubricator. **1887** D. A. LOW *Introd. Machine Drawing & Design* vii. 32 In the block illustrated the journal is lubricated by a needle lubricator. **1876** PREECE & SIVEWRIGHT *Telegraphy* 26 The binoxide of manganese which is used is of the form known as *needle manganese. **1949** N. MARSH *Swing, Brother, Swing* ix. 206 He hasn't been long on the injection method... Curtis had a look for needle-marks and didn't find many. **1971** 'D. SHANNON' *Murder with Love* (1972) iv. 69, I doubt very much whether he's really hooked... No needle marks on him. **1923** *Daily Mail* 16 Jan. 9 There will be a '*needle' match in Sheffield if Barnsley beat Swindon and visit the Wednesday. **1952** L. A. G. STRONG *Darling Tom* xvii. 136 (*headline*) Needle match. Family quarrel will be fought out at Olympia. **1962** *Listener* 1 Nov. 732/3 More enjoyable was an off-beat needle match between Hans Keller, who held that Gershwin was a neglected genius, and Deryck Cooke, who didn't. **1965** D. FRANCIS *For Kicks* iii. 41, I..watched Paddy and one of Granger's lads engage in a needle match of dominoes. **1898** *Edin. Rev.* Apr. 350 The so-called *needle-musket of the Prussians. **1810** *Nicholson's Jrnl.* XXVII. 236 The *Needle-ore has been considered..an auriferous ore of Nickel. **1836** T. THOMSON *Min., Geol.*, etc. I. 596 Needle ore of Bismuth..was first described and analyzed by Karsten and John. **1875** *Ure's Dict. Arts* (ed. 7) III. 412 *Needle-ore* or Aciculite. A native sulphide of bismuth, copper, and lead, in acicular crystals, found in Siberia. **1909** *Westm. Gaz.* 3 Apr. 14/2 If *needle-paper of the required kind is not available a very excellent substitute can be prepared by placing good stout paper in a solution of gelatine and glycerine to which has been added some good strong black colouring. **1973** *Sci. Amer.* May 118/1 Black needle paper and white typewriter bond differ by about a factor of 15 in reflectance all across the spectrum. **1866** *Chambers's Encycl.* VIII. 259/2 The Prussians, meanwhile, had armed their troops with the *needle-rifle. **1935** *Jrnl. R. Aeronaut. Soc.* XXXIX. 470 The crankshaft was mounted on roller bearings, and the connecting rod big ends were mounted on *needle rollers in split housings. **1951** *Engineering* 26 Oct. 533/1 An open propeller shaft provided with Hardy Spicer needle-roller joints transmits the drive to the rear axle. **1959** R. R. SLAYMAKER *Mech. Design & Analysis* II. xv. 299 Loose needle rollers are now universally used throughout the automotive industry to serve as bearings in planetary gear systems. **1974** 'A. HAIG' *Peruvian Printout* 37 A rubber-wheeled trolley which glided on needle roller bearings. **1962** K. ORVIS *Damned & Destroyed* vii. 52, I made a mental note of the *needle-scar item. **1655** MRQ. WORCESTER *Cent. Inv.* (1663) §81 The head being opened with a *Needle-scrue drawing a Spring towards them. **1752** HILL *Hist. Anim.* 134 The slender Turbo, with ventricose spires, and a small rounded mouth. The *Needle-shell. **1863** J. G. WOOD *Nat. Hist.* III. 380 The Spotted Needle-shell, or Spotted Auger, derives its name from the long and sharply pointed form of the shell. **1935** A. J. CRONIN *Stars look Down* I. xix. 183 After that a *needle shower and a hard rub down. **1973** 'H. HOWARD' *Highway to Murder* iii. 34 Ten minutes under a needle-shower washed the clammy heat out of me. **1974** E. MCGIRR *Murderous Journey* 6, I..shivered under a cold needle shower. **1699** L. WAFER *Voy.* 86 The Men make Arrow-Heads of this Wood; the Women *Needle-Shuttles to weave their Cotton. **1967** *Freedomways* VII. 153 A scattered *needle-spray of unrelated, often ephemeral, facts and events which confuse the readers more than they inform them. **1970** H. MCLEAVE *Question of Negligence* (1973) vii. 54 In the shower room he..focussed the needle spray on his head and body. **1836** T. THOMSON *Min., Geol.*, etc. I. 117 Arragonite, igloite, flos ferri, *needle spar. **1805** *Sporting Mag.* XXV. 315 My landlady—a perfect *needle-spitter. **1894** *Daily News* 15 Jan. 3/2 This is inserted beneath the skin of the stomach by means of a small *needle-syringe. **1849** NOAD *Electricity* (ed. 3) 375 The telegraph here patented they call their *needle telegraph. **1860** G. PRESCOTT *Electr. Telegr.* 100 The essential part of the needle telegraph is the multiplier. **1889** *Cent. Dict.*, **Needle-threader*, a device for passing a thread through the eye of a needle. **1964** *McCall's Sewing* v. 66/1 If you have an eyesight problem, or just find threading needles a chore, use a needle threader. **1802-3** tr. *Pallas's Trav.* (1812) I. 36 *Needle-timber, that is, resinous-trees, or such as have acuminated leaves. **1962** *Sunday Express* 30 Dec. 1/6 '*Needle time'—the number of hours given to records. **1970** *B.B.C. Handbk.* 223 An agreement with *Phonographic Performance Ltd.* provides for the right to broadcast commercial gramophone records 'live', the B.B.C.'s various radio and television services being allocated fixed periods of 'needle time' in return for an annual lump sum payment. **1880** J. H. COLLINS in *Mineral. Mag.* (1882) IV. 7 F. Becke regards Wood Tin as an extreme form of the well known acicular crystals sometimes spoken of as '*Needle Tin'. **1959** A. K. LANG in H. Q. Masur *Murder Most Foul* (1973) 69 The kid had been a user; they'd know that from the gear in her purse and the *needle-tracks in her arm. **1973** J. MARTIN *95 File* 80 He checked her arms but found no needle tracks. **1849** OTTÉ tr. *Humboldt's Cosmos* II. 455 In the *needle-tree we have the greatest contraction of the leaf vessels. **1868** G. STEPHENS *Runic Mon.* I. 209 The stuff could scarcely be of birch, or of any other leaf-tree, but rather of a needle-tree. **1713** PETIVER *Aq. Anim. Amb.* 1/2 *Echinus setosus*..*Needle-Urchin. **1903** *Sci. Amer. Suppl.* 24 Jan. 59/2 The inventor's idea, in designing the vaporizer, was to do away with the *needle-valve usually employed for controlling the flow of gasoline. **1925** N. E. ODELL in E. F. Norton *Fight for Everest 1924* 362 The pressure gauge was connected close to the mouths of the cylinders on the back [of the breathing apparatus], and the rate of flow regulated by a needle-valve close beside it. **1971** *Sci. Amer.* Sept. 222/3 All gases are admitted through needle valves to a manifold that connects to the laser. **1932** D. C. MINTER *Mod. Needlecraft* 16/1 *Needleweaving is a form of embroidery worked on the threads of the material when the threads in the opposite direction (i.e. either the warp or the weft) have been withdrawn. **1967** E. SHORT *Embroidery & Fabric Collage* ii. 48 *Needleweaving*. This is a variation of drawn thread work which could be used effectively on accessories such as handbags and belts. **1787** W. MARSHALL *Norf.* (1795) Gloss., *Needleweed, *Scandix pecten Veneris*, shepherd's needle. **1890** *Daily News* 8 Sept. 3/1 Though there is plenty of *needle-whin in places, its green spines are too tender to goad the hides of horses much. **1911** C. E. W. BEAN '*Dreadnought' of Darling* xv. 141 The pretty grey *needle-wood. **1936** F. CLUNE *Roaming round Darling* xxv. 286 Plenty of mulga, needlewood, belah, budda, and broad leaf-box. **1941** I. L. IDRIESS *Great Boomerang* i. 1 Upon a needlewood-tree a crow waited. *Ibid.* iii. 22 It [*sc.* the gold] lay by a needlewood bush. **1959** A. UPFIELD *Bony & Black Virgin* xiii. 111 He sat in the shade of the needlewood tree, or rather its trunk, for the narrow leaves give but scant shelter. **1766** *Compl. Farmer*, *Ascarides*, small worms common in horses, resembling needles... They are often called *needle-worms by the farriers. **1831** YOUATT *Horse* 210 A smaller, darker coloured worm, called the needle worm or *ascaris*, inhabits the large intestines. **1805** S. WESTON *Werneria* 95 Scapolite is not solvable in nitric acid, ..in..which it differs from the *needle-zeolite. **1836** T. THOMSON *Min., Geol.*, etc. I. 314 Thomsonite.., needle zeolite of Werner in part.

needle ('niːd(ə)l), *v.* [f. the sb. Cf. G. *nadeln*, *nädeln*, to sew or fix with needles.]

1. *trans.* **a.** To sew or pierce with (or as with) a needle. Also with *up*.

a **1715** BURNET *Own Time* II. (1724) I. 270 Coventry had his nose so well needled up, that the scar was scarce to be discerned. **1827** H. COLERIDGE in *Blackw. Mag.* XXII. 43 She who gives her tawny skin to be needled and flowered as if it were an insensible garment. **1835** HOGG in *Fraser's Mag.* XI. 359 The pangs of terror now needled his soul. **1879** *St. George's Hosp. Rep.* IX. 483 The youngest had both lenses needled at the close of the year.

b. *slang.* (See quot. 1812.) Also in recent use, to annoy or irritate; also, to goad; to provoke into anger.

1812 J. H. VAUX *Flash Dict.* s.v., To needle a person is to haggle with him in making a bargain, and if possible take advantage of him. **1881** G. R. SIMS *Dagonet Ballads* 77 There, he's off! the young warmint, he's needled; whenever I talks about work He puts on his cap and he hooks it. **1898** G. B. SHAW *Our Theatres in Nineties* (1932) III. 358 Old Indian women get 'fairly needled' at the spectacle of their houses and crops being burnt. **1941** *Time* 7 Apr. 22/3 Some 20 Manhattan reporters gave the Ambassador a going-over for 50 minutes... He did not let it appear that he knew he was being needled. **1958** J. WAIN *Contenders* 154 It was that bit about forgetting his business worries that needled Ned. **1959** M. PUGH *Chancer* 177 He was needling me, needling me this night, and I wouldn't provoke. **1972** D. HASTON *In High Places* ii. 36 Once again we'd needled each other into a state of open warfare.

c. To penetrate; to pierce or thread (one's way); to pass (a thing) through like a needle; to underpin with needle-beams, etc.

c **1820** HOGG *Connel of Dee* xxxiii, He rainbowed the hawthorn, He needled the brake. **1866** HERSCHEL *Fam. Lect. Sci.* 159 The particles of one species of gas or vapor struggle to interpenetrate or needle, as it were, their way among those of every other. **1877** G. FRASER *Wigtown* 231 (E.D.D.), He used adroitly to needle a stick backwards and forwards between his legs. **1901** *J. Black's Carp. & Build., Scaffolding* 52 The walls..may be needled under the superimposed brickwork.

2. *intr.* **a.** To form acicular crystals. **b.** To pass through, or in and out, like a needle. **c.** To use the needle, to sew.

1828-32 WEBSTER, *Needle*, to shoot in crystalization into the form of needles. **1835** D. WEBSTER *Rhymes* 24 (E.D.D.), Sae nimbly, They needled grumphy's legs between. **1861** THACKERAY *Four Georges* iii. (1862) 161 Groups of women in..tight bodies and full skirts, needling away.

3. *U.S. slang.* (See quots.) Also '**needled** *ppl. a.* (cf. *needle beer*, NEEDLE *sb.* 14).

1929 *Amer. Speech* IV. 387 Many Kansans..buy the ordinary non-alcoholic near-beer, and add a little alcohol to each bottle. The resulting mixture is called..*needled beer*. **1929** HOSTETTER & BEESLEY *It's a Racket!* 233 *Needle*, to inject alcohol or ether into any liquid, such as beer, to make it stimulating. **1930** *Amer. Mercury* Dec. 456/2 *Needle*, to make near-beer intoxicating by injecting ether or alcohol. 'This beer knocks you for a loop. It's needled with ether.' **1931** D. RUNYON *Guys & Dolls* (1932) iv. 79 It is sleeping so sound that I am commencing to figure that Butch must give it some of the needled beer he is feeding us.

'**needle-case.** [NEEDLE *sb.* 1.] A case in which needles are kept.

c **1440** *Promp. Parv.* 352/1 Nedyl case, *acuarius*. **1597** A. M. tr. *Guillemeau's Fr. Chirurg.* lf. xvi b/2 The Needle-case, wherin we may sticke thredede Needles. **1686** *Lond. Gaz.* No. 2173/4 A Silver Needle-Case with Open Work. **1706** *Ibid.* No. 4234/5 Two Scisser Cases and a Needle Case, both of Silver. **1827** in Hone *Every-day Bk.* II. 189 A needle-case, a spectacle-case. **1875** KNIGHT *Dict. Mech.* s.v.

needled ('niːd(ə)ld), *a.* [f. NEEDLE *sb.* or *v.*] Having a needle in it; done with the needle; pointed or shaped like a needle, etc.

1646 SIR T. BROWNE *Pseud. Ep.* 61 The same..may be observed in a needled sphere of corke. **1738** H. BROOKE *Tasso* II. 355 Each important toil of female hearts, The tricking ornament, and needled arts. **1786** AIKEN tr. *Beaumé's Man. Chem.* 147 The solution of tin in the marine acid, set to evaporate, yields needled crystals. **1839-52** BAILEY *Festus* 339 Like The needled angle of a high church spire. **1868** NETTLESHIP *Ess. Browning* i. 38 The fairy needled moss.

'**needledom.** [-DOM.] The 'world' of sewing.

1847 *Bachelor of Albany* (1854) 74 The most industrious embroiderer in Needledom.

'**needle-fish.** [NEEDLE *sb.* 1. Cf. G. *nadelfisch*, Du. *naaldvisch*, Da. *naale-*, Sw. *nålfisk*.] A name given to various fishes; esp. the pipe-fish or gar-fish.

1601 HOLLAND *Pliny* I. 266 The Horne-beakes or Needle-fishes. **1666** J. DAVIES *Hist. Caribby Isles* 100 There is a Fish without scales, four foot or thereabouts in length, called the Needle-Fish. **1683-4** ROBINSON in *Phil. Trans.* XXIX. 479 A Species of Sea Pike, a-kin to the Needle-Fishes. **1752** HILL *Hist. Anim.* 203 The Syngnathus, with the middle of the body hexangular, and the tail pinnated. The Needle-fish. **1796** STEDMAN *Surinam* II. xxiii. 172 A kind of needle-fish..was found here in great abundance. **1863** BATES *Nat. Amazon* ix. (1864) 279 Little troops of needle-fish, eel-like animals with excessively long and slender toothed jaws. **1880-4** F. DAY *Brit. Fishes* II. 148 *Belone vulgaris*,..horn-fish, needle-fish or long-nose.

'**needleful.** [NEEDLE *sb.* 1.] The amount of thread which can be conveniently used at one time with a needle.

1611 COTGR., *Esguillée*, a needlefull of. **1810** *Splendid Follies* II. 124, I must beg a needleful of thread to tie up my nose. **1880** *Plain Hints Needlework* 59 You have at once ready half-yard needlefuls.

'**needle-gun.** [NEEDLE *sb.* 3 c.] A gun in which the cartridge is exploded by the impact of a needle. Also *attrib.*

1865 J. E. F. SKINNER *Danish Heroism* 206 Loading his needle-gun like fury. **1868** *Rep. Govt. U.S. Munitions War* 18 The fulminate of the needle-gun cartridge was at one time believed to be kept a secret. **1879** *Cassell's Techn. Educ.* IV. 272 The needle-gun is not at all a satisfactory arm, considered..as a breech-loader.

'**needleman.** [NEEDLE *sb.* 1.]

1. A man who works with the needle, esp. a tailor.

1823 SYD. SMITH *Wks.* (1867) II. 24 The nefarious needle-man writes home, that he is as comfortable as a finger in a thimble. **1839** URE *Dict. Arts* 1239 The open thimble being employed by tailors, upholsterers, and, generally speaking, by needle-men. **1876** L. STEPHEN *Eng. Th. 18th C.* I. 458 The 'rebellious needleman' [Paine] was an incendiary.

2. (Spelt as two words, or hyphenated.) A drug-addict, esp. one who is addicted to injecting drugs. *U.S. slang.*

1925 *Flynn's* 11 July 128/1 So surely was Howard a needle man—that is, a hopeless drug addict. **1955** [see HYPE *sb.*[1]].

'**needle-point.** [NEEDLE *sb.* 1.]

1. The point of a needle; also *transf.*

a **1700** B. E. *Dict. Cant. Crew*, *Needle-point*, a Sharper. *c* **1836** *Encycl. Metrop.* (1845) VIII. 672/2 The dust thrown off from the needlepoints and from the grindstone. **1879** *St. George's Hosp. Rep.* IX. 502 To thrust the needle-points through..the centre of the opacity. **1888** *Pall Mall G.* 23 Aug. 5/2 Spires, domes, and needle-points of dolomite. **1889** *Ibid.* 5 Sept. 1/3 'Needle point' is the name of the most pointed shoe. **1929** *Radio Times* 8 Nov. 444/2 The needle-armature is so light that the needle point actually *feels* its way along the record groove. **1949** B. SEMEONOFF *Record Collecting* v. 22 The term 'tracking' refers to the path traced by the needle-point as it travels inward towards the centre of a record.

2. Point-lace made with the needle. Also *attrib.*

1865 F. B. PALLISER *Hist. Lace* iii. 28 Lace is divided into point and pillow. The first is made by the needle on a parchment pattern, and termed needle point. **1882** *Encycl. Brit.* XIV. 189/2 A technical peculiarity in making needlepoint lace is that a single thread and needle are alone used to form the pattern. **1893** *Westm. Gaz.* 2 Mar. 4/1 When next time we buy a Vandyke collar of Irish lace..or ..a flounce of needle-point. **1902** JOURDAIN & DRYDEN *Palliser's Hist. Lace* (rev. ed.) xiii. 195'Needle point' is the name by which point d'Alençon was alone known in England during the last century. **1967** E. SHORT *Embroidery & Fabric Collage* ii. 39 Cut work..later developed into needlepoint lace. *Ibid.*, This delicate embroidery with its contrasts of cut work, eyelets, fine needlepoint fillings, [etc.].

'**needle-pointed,** *a.* [NEEDLE *sb.* 1.] Having a point like that of a needle. Chiefly *fig.*

1599 T. M[OUFET] *Silkwormes* 73 With needle-pointed tongue The Flies have bor'd a passage through their clewes. **1635** QUARLES *Embl.*, *Farewell* i, He whose gentle palmes Thy needle-pointed sinnes have naild. **1768-74** TUCKER *Lt. Nat.* (1834) I. 541 Philology!..lend me thy needle-pointed pencil, that I may trace out the hair-breadth differences of language. **1851** MAYNE REID *Scalp Hunt.* xxxv. 270 The next opening brought in view sharp needle-pointed peaks.

needler ('niːdlə(r)). Also 4 **neldere**, 4-6 **nedeler**. [f. NEEDLE *sb.* + -ER[1]. Cf. MLG. *nâteler*, MHG.

nâdelære (G. *nadler*).] A needle-maker; also *transf.* (see quot. 1829).

1362 LANGL. *P. Pl.* A. v. 161 Hikke the hakeney mon and Hogge the neldere [B. v. 318 Hughe the nedeler]. *c* **1515** *Cocke Lorell's B.* 9 Pynners, nedelers, and glasyers. **1688** HOLME *Armoury* III. 387/1 *Needler's Punch*...With this tool the Eye of the Needle is made. **1720** STRYPE *Stow's Surv.* II. v. xv. 241/1 Pinners and Needlers. **1829** BROCKETT *N.C. Gloss* (ed. 2), *Needler*, a keen, active, thrifty person—a niggard. **1881** DUFFIELD *Don Quixote* I. 209 Three needlers from the square of Cordova.

needless ('niːdlɪs), *a.* Forms: 3 neodeles, 4 ned(de)les, -lez, 4–6 nedeles, (6 -lesse), 6–7 need(e)lesse, (6 -les, neadeles), 6– needless. [f. NEED *sb.* + -LESS. Cf. MDu. *nodeloos* (Du. *noodeloos*), MHG. *nôtlôs* (G. *nothlos*).]

†**1.** In quasi-adverbial use: Without any compulsion or necessity; needlessly. *Obs.*

a **1225** *Leg. Kath.* 1023 Monnes unmihte þet he neodeles nom upon him seoluen. *Ibid.* 1176. *c* **1290** *Beket* 1630 in *S.E. Leg.* I. 153 'Beth stille', he seide, 'ȝe makiez deol neodeles nouþe ech-on.' *a* **1300** *Cursor M.* 28460 Neddeles oft bot for glotri Stulth o mete and drink did i. *c* **1380** WYCLIF *Wks.* (1880) 51 þei gon ydel fro contre to contre..beggynge nedles of pore men. **1475** *Rolls of Parlt.* VI. 136/1 For..fere of deth theruppon folowyng, which he must nedles have entred in if he had appered.

2. Not needed or wanted; unnecessary, useless, uncalled for. (Common from *c* 1570.) Freq. in phr. (*it is*) ***needless to say*** (or *add*), often used parenthetically.

a **1300** *Cursor M.* 1141 For þi nedeles wickedhede, þou sal lede euer þi lijf in nede. *c* **1380** WYCLIF *Sel. Wks.* III. 274 Freris þat..robben þe pore peple bi stronge beggynge and nedles. **1475** *Bk. Noblesse* (Roxb.) 72 Many nedeles officers ..reignyng and ruling over theym. **1530** PALSGR. 643/2 It is nedelesse to speake of the price. **1588** J. UDALL *Demonstr. Discipline* (Arb.) 21 That office which is needles in the church is also vnlawful. **1612** WOODALL *Surg. Mate* Wks. (1653) 21, I have seen men lamed by the needless use of caustick medicines. **1667** MILTON *P.L.* VII. 494 Thou.. gav'st them Names, Needless to thee repeated. **1727** DE FOE *Syst. Magic* I. ii. (1840) 38 The search after their names would be..needless. **1770** A. YOUNG *Six Months' Tour North of Eng.* I. 185 It is almost needless to add upon the course of crops in question, that the turnips ought..to be fed off the land by sheep. **1770** BARETTI *Journey London to Genoa* I. xx. 148 It is needless to say that thousands and thousands have migrated to other places. **1780** BENTHAM *Princ. Legisl.* xii. §22 It is needless to multiply examples any further. **1826** *Kaleidoscope* 31 Jan. 247/3 The Squire was hard hit by this nonchalance, and (as the newspapers say), 'it is needless to add', acted upon Sheridan's suggestion. **1855** MACAULAY *Hist. Eng.* xix. IV. 280 The message was needless. **1880** SPURGEON *Ploughm. Pict.* 117 Beware of evil questions which raise needless doubts. **1885** RIDER HAGGARD *K. Solomon's Mines* vi. 88 That night we covered nearly five-and-twenty miles, but, needless to say, found no more water. **1902** R. J. MECREDY in A. C. Harmsworth *Motors* vii. 122 Needless to say, the shoulder F is thereby raised. **1930** *Sunday Times* 12 Oct. 5/5 Needless to say, such a visitor is immensely impressed and at once enrols for the Pelman Course in the particular language in which he is interested.

†**3.** Having no want; not in need or want. *Obs.*

1380 *Lay Folks Catech.* (Lamb. MS.) 666 þey don here almes more to þe nedles þan to þe verry nedy. **1390** GOWER *Conf.* I. 152 Erthe is the most nedeles, And most men helpe it natheles. **1600** SHAKS. *A.Y.L.* II. i. 46 First, for his weeping into the needlesse streame. **1668** R. STEELE *Husbandm. Calling* v. (1672) 94 He considers that it's safer to relieve nine needless beggars, than to turn away one needy one.

needlessly ('niːdlɪslɪ), *adv.* [f. prec. + -LY[2].] In a needless or unnecessary manner; without necessity.

1388 PURVEY *Prol. Bible* x, Thei sweren custumably, nedelesly, and ofte unavisily and fals. **1628** WITHER *Brit. Rememb.* v. 322 They did but needlesly their fictions borrow To set it forth. **1651** HOBBES *Leviath.* III. xlii. 272 They have needlessely cast away their lives. **1710** BERKELEY *Princ. Hum. Knowl.* I. §22, I am afraid..I am needlessly prolix in handling this subject. **1784** COWPER *Task* VI. 563 The man Who needlessly sets foot upon a worm. **1816** J. WILSON *City of Plague* II. i. 21 We often..Needlessly wept when they were in their joy. **1859** BUCKLE in Huth *Life* (1880) II. 6, I do not see why I should needlessly charge myself with inaccuracy.

needlessness ('niːdlɪsnɪs). [f. as prec. + -NESS.] The fact of being needless; unnecessariness.

1607 *Schol. Disc. agst. Antichr.* I. iii. 126 [134] He will wipe this suspition of a needlessnes away, and so will proue it needfull. **1699** R. L'ESTRANGE *Erasm. Colloq.* (1725) 16 To convince the World of the vanity and needlessness of invocating saints. **1775** DE LOLME *Eng. Constit.* Advt. (1784) 18 The needlessness of an armed force to support itself by. **1894** *Chicago Advance* 22 Nov. 254/2 Speaking of the needlessness of the Sunday paper.

'**needlestone.** *Min.* [ad. G. *nadelstein.*] A name formerly given to various minerals having needle-like crystals, as natrolite and scolecite.

1820 BROOKE in *Annals Philos.* XVI. 193, I shall call the Auvergne variety, Mesotype; that from Iceland and Ferro, Needlestone. **1836** T. THOMSON *Min., Geol.*, etc. I. 318 Most of the needlestones found in the amygdaloidal rocks in Scotland belong to it likewise. **1843** J. E. PORTLOCK *Geol.* 220 Implanted tufts of radiating crystals of needle-stone frequently occur. **1885** RAMSAY *Mineral.* (ed. 3) 296.

'**needlewoman.** [NEEDLE *sb.* I.] A woman who works with the needle; a sempstress.

1611 MIDDLETON & DEKKER *Roaring Girl* I. i, You are busied with a needle-woman. *a* **1667** JER. TAYLOR *Suppl. Serm. for Year* (1678) 104 She was a good needle-woman and a good huswife. **1776** *Carlisle Mag.* 7 Sept. 143 She endeavoured to procure employment as a needle-woman. **1863** W. PHILLIPS *Speeches* ii. 31 The crowded and starved ranks of the needlewomen. **1879** MEREDITH *Egoist* xiv, As a rule authoresses are not needlewomen.

'**needlework.** Also 6 neilde-. [f. NEEDLE *sb.* I. Cf. G. *nadelwerk*, Du. *naaldenwerk.*]

1. Work done with the needle; sewing, embroidery, or fancy work.

1382 WYCLIF *Exod.* xxvi. 1 Ten curteyns..dyuersid with nedle werk, thow shalt make. **1466–7** *Abingdon Rolls* (Camden) 134, ij paroll' de nedylworke. **1534** in Peacock *Eng. Ch. Furniture* (1866) 194 Enclosid in a purse of neilde werk. **1555** EDEN *Decades* 103 A fair sherte wrought with needle woorke. **1615** *Band, Ruffe, & Cuffe* (Halliwell) 11, I scorn to make anything of thee, Band, but needle-worke. **1697** DRYDEN *Æneid* XI. 1142 With Flowers of Needlework distinguished o're. **1753** HOGARTH *Anal. Beauty* xii. 97 There is a sort of needle-work called Irish-stitch. **1784** COWPER *Task* I. 34 A splendid cover..of tapestry richly wrought..or needlework sublime. **1848** LYTTON *Harold* I. i, The industry of the women decorated wall and furniture with needlework and hangings. **1865** DICKENS *Mut. Fr.* I. iii, A girl sat engaged in needlework.

attrib. **1686** tr. *Chardin's Trav. Persia* 262 Embroider'd Handkerchers, Toylets, Needlework Night-Caps.

†**b.** *pl.* Different pieces or kinds of this work.

1585 T. WASHINGTON tr. *Nicholay's Voy.* IV. xiv. 128 Making of diuers faire needleworks vpon cloth. **1621** BURTON *Anat. Mel.* II. ii. IV. (1651) 286 Women..have curious needle-works, Cut-works, spinning. **1673** *Lady's Call.* II. i. §9 Writing, needle-works, languages, music, or the like. **1748** RICHARDSON *Clarissa* (1811) VIII. 336 Her skill in almost all sorts of fine needle-works.

2. Wooden frame-work in house-building. *rare.*

1686 PLOT *Staffordsh.* 173 Plaister for floors, seelings, and the walls of Needle-work houses. **1849** WEALE *Dict. Terms.*

So '**needleworker**, a worker with the needle.

1611 BIBLE *Exod.* xxxvi. 37 *marg.*, The work of a needle-worker, or embroiderer. **1753** HOGARTH *Anal. Beauty* xii. 97 The nicest needle-workers are taught to weave it into every flower and leaf. **1865** *Chr. Remembrancer* Apr. 347 More fixity of purpose than the lower class of needle-workers are equal to. **1898** *Woman's Signal* 23 June 387/1 Governesses, needleworkers, or secretaries.

'**needle-wrought**, *a.* Also 6 neeld-. [f. NEEDLE *sb.*] Worked or ornamented with the needle; embroidered.

1562 PHAER *Æneid* IX. Ccjb, The worthy son of Arceus duke Gay needlewrought in cloke. **1582** STANYHURST *Æneis* I. (Arb.) 40 On neeld wroght carpets theese guestes were al vsshered aptly. **1643** LIGHTFOOT *Glean. Ex.* 52 A needle-wrought girdle. **1692** WASHINGTON tr. *Milton's Def. People Eng.* M.'s Wks. 1738 I. 533 You describe no true Britains, but painted ones, or rather Needle-wrought Men instead of them.

†'**needling**, *sb.* *Obs.* *rare*$^{-1}$. [f. NEED *sb.* + -LING[1] I.] A needy person.

1608 SYLVESTER *Du Bartas* II. iv. III. *Schism* 467 Sure, a good turn shall never guerdon want; A Gift to Needlings is not given, but lent.

needling ('niːdlɪŋ), *vbl. sb.* [f. NEEDLE *v.*]

1. a. (See quot. 1854.) **b.** The operation of inserting needle-beams; the method of doing this.

1854 MISS BAKER *Gloss. Northampt.*, *Needling*, a builder's term for perpendicular studding, to part off the acute angle of a roof. *c* **1880** *Architect. Soc. Dict.* s.v., One of the most important examples of needling was that performed at Bayeux cathedral. **1901** *J. Black's Carp. & Build.*, *Scaffolding* 48 Fig. 3..gives needling of bottom shore and strutting to top and second rakers.

2. a. The action or process of using a needle of any kind; work done with a needle.

1878 SALA in *Gentl. Mag.* May 565 The last [engraving] being at least three parts of machine work to one of free-handed needling.

b. *spec.* An operation performed on the eye with a surgical needle.

1879 *St. George's Hosp. Rep.* IX. 483 Cataracts..dealt with by needling, suction, and a..capsular operation.

c. The action of annoying, irritating, or goading (see NEEDLE *v.* 1 b). Also as *ppl. a.*

1941 *Sun* (Baltimore) 10 Jan. 12/7 The word 'needling'.. is being used more and more frequently in the sense of using sharp bits of persuasion to bring a person to adopt a desired course. **1945** *Ibid.* 17 Feb. 7/3 P.K.W...was plainly irked by some sharp needling of his group. **1956** W. H. WHYTE *Organization Man* (1957) 246 It was Keefer, with his clever mind, his needling of authority, who led the ordinary people ..astray. **1958** *Spectator* 10 Jan. 33/1 Their needling and often impertinent questions. **1959** *Times Lit. Suppl.* 27 Nov. 698/5 She undergoes, still buoyant, the familiar needlings of interrogation. **1962** *Listener* 7 June 999/1 When the next careful, needling letter arrived from Samuel, the black temper broke loose again. **1971** C. BONINGTON *Annapurna South Face* xi. 128 '..Anyway, if you want to go out in front on this trip, you'd better prove you can keep going.' This kind of needling was the ideal treatment for Mick. **1973** *Islander* (Victoria, B.C.) 28 Oct. 2/1 He was the great complainer of his time, and..Victoria became a better place because of his needling.

†'**needling**, *adv.* *Obs.* Forms: 1 néadlunga, nýdlinga, 3 nedlunge, 3–4 -linge, 4 -ling, -lyng, nedelynge. [See NEED *sb.* and -LING[2], and cf. next.]

1. Forcibly; by force.

c **1000** ÆLFRIC *St. Basil's Admon.* ix. (1849) 52 Maneȝa.. beoð benæmede neadlunga hyra aȝenes. *c* **1000** *Penit. Egbert* in Thorpe *Laws* II. 186 ȝif hwa..mæden nydinga [*v.r.* nydlinga] nimð. *c* **1200** *Trin. Coll. Hom.* 199 [The adder] criepeð nedlinge þureh nerewe hole, and bileueð hire hude baften hire.

2. Necessarily.

a **1225** *Ancr. R.* 190 Nedlunge ȝe moten underuongen me. *c* **1375** *Sc. Leg. Saints* l. (*Catherine*) 126 All ydolis of stok & stane mone nedling rot, & wast, & wane. *c* **1380** *Lay Folks Catech.* (Lamb. MS.) 100 þese askyngys most nedelynge be fulfyllyd.

'**needlings**, *adv.* *Obs.* (exc. *north. dial.*) Forms: 4–6 ned-, nede-, (5 nedy-), 5–6 *Sc.* neid-, 6 neyd- (also with -linges, -is, -lynges, -is, etc.); 5 nedelonges. [f. NEED *sb.* + *-lings*: see prec. and -LING[2].] Necessarily; of necessity.

13.. *Cursor M.* 2450 (Gött.), þair bestis nedlinges most þai flitt. *c* **1380** WYCLIF *Serm.* Sel. Wks. I. 61 Mannis spirit ..mut nedelingis do what ony of þes vertues doiþ. *c* **1420** *Sir Amadace* (Camden) xii, Nedelonges most I sitte him by,.. For he wasse my wedutte fere. *c* **1450** LOVELICH *Merlin* 2372 Nedylynges thedyr moste He go. **1513** DOUGLAS *Æneis* x. viii. 76 Ane schort..terme is set Of lyfe, quhen all most neydlyngis pay that det.

needly ('niːdlɪ), *a.* *rare.* [f. NEEDLE *sb.* + -Y[1].] Resembling a needle or needles.

1671 MARTEN *Voy. Spitzbergen* in *Acc. Sev. Late Voy.* II. (1694) 52 The needly Snow is generated by Westerly and Southerly Winds. **1869** BLACKMORE *Lorna D.* (1891) 132 His..small quick eyes, and black needly beard.

†'**needly**, *adv.*[1] *Obs.* Forms: 1 néodlíce, 3 neod(e)liche, 4–5 ne(e)dely. [OE. *néodlíce* (= OS. *niudlîko*), f. *néod* desire, eagerness.] Zealously, carefully; earnestly.

c **900** tr. *Bæda's Hist.* II. xiii, Næniȝ þinra þeȝna neodlicor ..hine sylfne underþeodde. *c* **1000** *Sax. Leechd.* II. 262 Rudan ȝeseoð on ele oððe on wine..smire þa sidan mid þy neodlice. *c* **1205** LAY. 15594 Heo arisen up & eoden neor & neodeliche ȝerden of þissere uncuðe talen. **1340–70** *Alisaunder* 748 A rink [she] sendes Anon too Nectanabus & needely hym praies, þat he cofly comme too carpen her tyll. ?*c* **1475** *Sqr. lowe Degre* 293 He bethought hym nedely, Every daye,..How he myght venged be On that lady.

†'**needly**, *adv.*[2] *Obs.* Forms: 4 nedlych(e, -like, 4–5 ned(e)lich(e; 4–5 nedly, 4–6 nedely, (4 -li), 6 neeedely, need(y)lie, -lye, 6–7 needly. [f. NEED *sb.* + -LY[2]. Cf. MDu. *nodelike*, MLG. *nôtliken*, MHG. *nôt-*, *nœtlîche.*] Necessarily; of necessity.

1303 R. BRUNNE *Handl. Synne* 12399 Alle þo þat sey 'hem behoueþ nedely', þey acoupe God of here folye. *c* **1330** —— *Chron. Wace* (Rolls) 8040 Nedlike at þe y mot wyse how, Who þan gat þy sone Merlyne. *c* **1380** WYCLIF *Serm.* Sel. Wks. II. 342 Ech sufficience of man mut nedeli be ȝovun of God. **1432–50** tr. *Higden* (Rolls) VII. 259 He muste nedely obbey the writynge of the pope. **1477** EARL RIVERS (Caxton) *Dictes* 22 Slouthe nor delay not that thou must nedely execute. **1515** BARCLAY *Egloges* I. (1570) Biij, Of a trene vesell then must thou nedely drinke. **1596** LODGE *Marg. Amer.* 38 A grove, thorow which the new married couple should needly passe. **1647** TRAPP *Comm. Rev.* xiii. 7 The Jesuites will still needly have the Roman Church to be the Catholike Church.

needment ('niːdmənt). [f. NEED *sb.* or *v.*]

1. *pl.* Things needed, necessaries; *esp.* personal requisites carried as luggage.

1590 SPENSER *F.Q.* I. i. 6 A dwarfe..wearied with bearing of her bag Of needments at his backe. *a* **1641** BP. MOUNTAGU *Acts & Mon.* (1642) 426 To provide apparell and other needments for them. **1748** THOMSON *Cast. Indol.* II. vi, There, up to earn the needments of the day, he found dame Poverty. **1847** WORDSW. in Chr. Wordsw. *Mem.* (1851) I. 14 Carrying each his needments tied up in a pocket handkerchief. **1862** SALA *Ship Chandler* i, Longport supplied the colonial isles and the plantations with all their needments.

2. *pl.* Needs, requirements. Now *Sc. rare.*

1603 H. CROSSE *Vertues Commw.* (1878) 94 A man should ..impart the benefite to the needments and necessitie of other. **1613** PURCHAS *Pilgrimage* VI. x. 515 They haue not left the people sufficient for their needments. **1871** GILMOUR *Pen-Folk* (1873) 39 If I am set in judgment on the needments of others.

†**need-nail**, *sb.* *Sc.* *Obs.* *rare*$^{-1}$. [ad. LG. *neednagel* (G. *nietnagel*, Sw. *nitnagel*, Da. *netnagle*), f. (M)LG. *neden* to clinch = MDu. *nieden*, OHG. *hniotan* (G. *nieten*; Sw. *nita*, Da. *nitte*), ON. *hnjóða* (Norw. *njoda*, *noda*, Sw. *nåda*).] A clinched nail. In quot. *fig.*

a **1732** T. BOSTON *Crook in Lot* (1745) 111 Who will not humble themselves..will find their obstinacy a need-nail, that will keep their misery ever fast on them.

†**need-nail**, *v.* *Sc.* *Obs.* [prob. ad. LG. **neednagelen*: see prec.] *trans.* To secure firmly by means of clinched nails. (See also quot. 1808.)

1563 WINȜET *Four Scoir Thre Quest.* Wks. (S.T.S.) I. 139 Wtheris..hes in thare imaginatioun cloisit vp, slotit, and neidnalit the samin ȝettis of our hæretage. **1580** *Reg. Privy Council Scot.* III. 337 Quhill he neid naillit and lockit the duris thairof. **1659** A. HAY *Diary* (S.H.S.) 44, I vieued also the yairds and caused neednaile the dors. **1689** in *Lauder & Lauderdale* vii. (1902) 76 Lady Lauderdale..caused neidnail all the Church doors and windows. **1808** JAMIESON s.v., A window is said to be neidnail'd, when it is so fixed with nails in the inside, that the sash cannot be lifted up. This is an improper sense.

need-not (ˈniːdnɒt). [f. NEED *v.* + NOT.] An unnecessary thing.

1650 FULLER *Pisgah* I. iii. 8 Such glittering need-nots to humane happinesse. **1809** MALKIN *Gil Blas* VII. xvi. ¶12, I have not laid out the veriest trifle in need-nots. **1859** W. H. GREGORY *Egypt* II. 204 Purchasing the necessaries..and the many need-nots which one considers so indispensable, and so soon flings away.

Needom(e, variants of NEEDHAM *Obs.*

needs (niːdz), *adv.* Forms: 1 nýdes, 1–6 nedes, 4 neodes, 4–5 nedez, 4–6 nedis, 4–7 needes, 5 neds, needis, 5–6 nedys, 7 *Sc.* neids, 4– needs. [OE. *nýdes, nédes*: see NEED *sb.* and -S¹.] Of necessity, necessarily.

a. In general use. Now *rare.*

In 14–15th c. frequently used with *behove.*

a **1000** *Laws Ælfred* xiii, Se þe hine þonne nedes ofsloȝe, oððe unwillum. *c* **1131** *O.E. Chron.* (Laud MS.) an. 1131 Hi scolden nedes. **13..** *Cursor M.* 5869 (Gött.), Fra þat time nedis had þai, Do tua iornays apon a day. *a* **1352** MINOT *Poems* (ed. Hall) ix. 28 At þe Neuil cros nedes bud þam knele. **1393** LANGL. *P. Pl.* C. XIII. 215 [Thou] art so loth to leue that leue shalt needs. *c* **1449** PECOCK *Repr.* I. ii. 9 Perceuyng whanne an argument procedith into his conclusioun needis. **1624** BP. MOUNTAGU *Gagg* 49 [We] claim and prove a succession and therefore needes a visibilitie from the time of the apostles. **1870** ROSSETTI *Poems, Burden Nineveh* xv, And needs were years and lustres flown Ere strength of man could vanquish thee.

b. In clauses containing *must.*

c **1374** CHAUCER *Boeth.* III. pr. xii. (1868) 106 Nedes the wordes moten ben cosynes to þo þinges of whiche þei speken. *c* **1440** *Jacob's Well* 261 Nedys I, & my wyif, & my chylderyn..muste lyve. **1470–85** MALORY *Arthur* VIII. i. 273 Depe draughtes of deth toke her, that nedes she must dye. **1583** T. WATSON *Poems* (Arb.) 60 But needes perforce I must become content To mealt in minde. **1642** ROGERS *Naaman* 346 It must be needs a very reproveable evill which causeth such a fulsomenesse. **1782** COWPER *Gilpin* 89 Stooping down as needs he must Who cannot sit upright.

c. Directly following the vb., in *must needs.*

13.. *Guy Warw.* (A.) 3668 So miche folk þer was y-slawe ..He most nedes opon men go. *c* **1380** WYCLIF *Serm.* Sel. Wks. I. 218 Þes þingis moten nedis be, but ȝit is not anoon ende. *c* **1449** PECOCK *Repr.* II. iii. 149 The argument now maad muste needis haue his entent. **1529** WOLSEY in *Four C. Eng. Lett.* (1880) 10 Thes thyngs consyderyd..must nedys make me yn agony. **1641** J. JACKSON *True Evang. T.* II. 129, I must needs begin with Ignatius. *a* **1688** CUDWORTH *Immut. Mor.* (1731) 113 The Soul must needs have the same Passions. **1741** MIDDLETON *Cicero* (1742) I. ii. 126 If every thing must needs be committed to Pompey. **1822** W. IRVING *Braceb. Hall* II. 374 The Squire must needs have something of the old ceremonies observed on the occasion. **1875** HELPS *Ess., Dom. Rule* 37 A man thinks that he must needs understand those whom he sees daily.

Prov. *c* **1420** LYDG. *Assembly of Gods* 21 He must nedys go that the deuell dryves. **1532** [see DRIVE *v.* 1 b]. **1601** SHAKS. *All's Well* I. iii. 31. **1638** SANDERSON *Serm.* (1681) II. 95.

d. So *needs must.* Freq. as an elliptic phrase, esp. after *than* or *if.* With the proverbial uses cf. sense c.

1390 GOWER *Conf.* I. 291 For it is seid thus overal, That nedes mot that nede schal. **1447** BOKENHAM *Seyntys* (Roxb.) 38 For than he nedys must yeve credence. **1550** CROWLEY *Epigr.* 88 Nedes must we have places for vitayls to be solde. **1604** E. GRIMSTONE *Hist. Siege Ostend* 195 We beleeue them no more then needs must. **1667** MILTON *P.L.* IV. 412 Needs must the Power That made us..Be infinitly good. **1734** BERKELEY *Lett.* Wks. 1871 IV. 218, I shall stay no longer in Dublin than needs must. **1782** COWPER *Gilpin* 188 My head is twice as big as yours, They therefore needs must fit. **1821** SCOTT *Kenilw.* xvi, I..would have no more of these follies than needs must. **1871** BROWNING *Balaustion* 2287 She shall go, if needs must.

Prov. **1523** SKELTON *Garl. Laurel* 1434 Nedes must he rin that the deuyll dryuith. **1613** PURCHAS *Pilgrimage* I. xv. 71 Needs must they goe whom the diuell driueth. *a* **1659** [see DRIVE *v.* 1 b]. **1835** SOUTHEY *Doctor* III. lxxxiii. 77 'Needs must go when the Devil drives', says the proverb: but the Devil shall never drive me. **1838** DICKENS *Nich. Nick.* v, Needs must, when somebody drives. **1853** T. C. HALIBURTON *Sam Slick's Wise Saws* I. xiii. 267 'Needs must when the devil drives, so here goes,' and off he went for the water. **1886** [see DRIVE *v.* 1 b]. **1898** J. ARCH *Story of Life* xvi. 379 Needs must when illness drives. **1916** E. WALLACE *Clue of Twisted Candle* (1918) xi. 133 But needs must when the devil drives, as the saying goes. **1956** G. DURRELL *My Family* xiv. 189, I think we had better have a cab. An extravagance, of course, but needs must where the devil drives, eh?

e. *will* or *would needs,* implying determination or fixity of purpose. Now *arch.*

1387 TREVISA *Higden* (Rolls) V. 143 And ȝif ȝe willeþ nedes stryve, abydeth þe dome of God Almyȝty. **1534** MORE *Treat. Passion* Wks. 1274/1 She bi the diuels entisement wold nedes knowe euyll to. **1610** SHAKS. *Temp.* I. ii. 108 He needes will be Absolute Millaine. **1662** J. DAVIES tr. *Olearius' Voy. Ambass.* 36, I would needs..go and see the town of Wisby. **1768** STERNE *Sent. Journ., Passport (Versailles* i.), The master of my hotel..will needs have it.. that I should be sent to the Bastile. **1828** SCOTT *F.M. Perth* xxx, Vulcan..would needs wed Venus, and our Chronicles tell us what came of it.

Hence ˈ**needs-be** *sb.*, necessity.

1881 A. W. MOMERIE *Orig. Evil* 31 Peter could discover no needs-be in the humiliation and death of Christ. **1894** *Westm. Gaz.* 27 Nov. 2/2 A penetrating insight into the needs-be of a finely touched nature.

† **needs cost,** *adv. Obs.* [f. prec. + COST *sb.*¹ 1.] Necessarily, of necessity.

c **1385** CHAUCER *L.G.W.* 2697 *Hypermnestra,* Nedis cost this thyng muste haue an ende. *c* **1449** PECOCK *Repr.* III. iv. 301 Therfore needis cost it muste be grauntid, that Crist [etc.]. **1513** MOORE *Rich. III* (1883) 49 If we should, nedes cost, fall in perill one way or other.

† ˈ**needsly,** *adv. Obs.* Forms: 4–5 nedesly, 5 nedysly, needisli, -ly, 6 needesly, (7 -lie), 6–7 needsly. [f. as prec. + -LY².] Necessarily, of necessity. (Usually with *must.*)

c **1449** PECOCK *Repr.* II. xiv. 192 The..vsing of this thing is not necessarie (that is to seie, is not needisly to be had). **1495** *Trevisa's Barth. De P.R.* XIX. vi. (W. de W.) 864 Thenne must the coloure nedesly be meane. **1593** G. HARVEY *Pierce's Super.* 139, I never longed to fight it out with flat strokes, untill I must needesly needes. **1612** DRAYTON *Poly-olb.* vii. 243 By no meanes she could hold, but needsly she must showe Her liking. **1656** J. TRAPP *Comm. Heb.* ii. 15 Death..must needsly therefore be terrible to those whose lives and hopes end together.

needsome (ˈniːdsəm), *a. rare.* [f. NEED *sb.* + -SOME.] † a. Necessary. *Obs.*⁻¹ b. Needy.

c **1650** *Don Bellianis* 49 So many needsome advertisements I presume to tell you. **1870** VERNEY *Lettice Lisle* 305 I'm a needsome woman now, without e'er a one o' 'um.

need-to-know (ˌniːdtəˈnəʊ). [NEED *v.*² 8.] Used, freq. *attrib.*, to denote a principle or practice, esp. in counter-espionage, whereby people are kept ignorant of things which they do not need to know.

1954 *Amer. Documentation* V. 120 In most security controlled report systems, the dissemination of information is regulated by 'need-to-know' or 'compartmentalization' principles. **1956** W. A. HEFLIN *U.S. Air Force Dict.* 342/2 *Need-to-know,* n. A criterion used in security procedures that requires a person requesting classified information to establish his need to know such information in terms of his mission. **1966** J. BINGHAM *Double Agent* ix. 137 Mr. Ryan had then hastily told him to keep that to himself. Nothing further had been said. Mr. List had been naturally dismayed at this gross breach of the need-to-know principle. **1969** A. MARIN *Rise with Wind* i. 7 You will notice that there are some gaps in the Clay material. Part of the information is..strictly on a 'need to know' basis. **1970** K. BENTON *Sole Agent* xviii. 193 There is the rule about need-to-know. They won't *need* to know the details of your contacts with MI5. **1971** D. BAGLEY *Freedom Trap* vi. 127 They worked on the 'need to know' principle, and an escapee didn't need to know how he escaped—just that he had done so. **1975** *Observer* 12 Jan. 1/1 The CIA has instructed the companies to limit all knowledge of the exercise to the spymaster's traditional 'need-to-know' criterion. **1975** N. LUARD *Robespierre Serial* iv. 27 There was no need for Carswell to be filled in on all the ramifications... On the strict need-to-know basis they simply didn't concern him.

† **needways,** *adv. north.* and *Sc. Obs.* [f. NEED *sb.* + -WAYS.] By or because of necessity.

a **1300** *Cursor M.* 5869 Fra þat tide ned-wais suld þai Do tua dais werkes on a dai. *Ibid.* 8712 Nede-wais it most tuix þam be part. **1375** BARBOUR *Bruce* v. 242 Schir, neidwais I will wend, And tak auentur that god will giff.

So † **needway** *adv. Sc. Obs.*

1375 BARBOUR *Bruce* XIX. 156 The behufis neid-way..To this thing heir say thine aviss. *c* **1375** *Sc. Leg. Saints* xxxii. (*Justin*) 8 He man fle nedway magre his.

needy (ˈniːdɪ), *a.* Forms: 2–4 neodi, 3–4 neody, 3–5 nedi, 4 needi, 4–5 nede, 4–6 nedy, 5 neddy, nedye, nedie, neady, *Sc.* neidy, 6–7 needie, 6– needy. [f. NEED *sb.* + -Y¹. Cf. MDu. *nodich* (Du. *noodig*), OHG. *nôtag, nôteg* (MHG. *nôtic, noetic,* G. *nöthig*), ON. *nauðigr* (Sw. and Da. *nödig*).]

1. Of persons, etc.: Poor, indigent, necessitous. a. Used absolutely. (Chiefly as *pl.*)

c **1175** *Lamb. Hom.* 135 Delen heo þet euric neodi ðe heo biseceð sum þing þer of afo. *a* **1300** *Cursor M.* 103 Lauedi scho es o leuedis all.., To nedi neghest on to call. **1362** LANGL. *P. Pl.* A. VII. 14 The neodi and the nakede, nym ȝeeme hou thei liggen. *a* **1450** MYRC 1591 To þe nedy ȝeue þow large. **1560** DAUS tr. *Sleidane's Comm.* 47 b, What time the pore and nedye are releved. **1633** BP. HALL *Occas. Medit.* §138, I am sure I want no lesse then the neediest. **1764** GOLDSM. *Trav.* 307 At gold's superior charms all freedom flies; The needy sell it, and the rich man buys. **1801** *Med. Jrnl.* V. 528 Not only to accommodate the poor and the needy, but to advance the public good. **1864** PUSEY *Lect. Daniel* (1876) 483 The sons of the needy.

b. In attributive or predicative use.

1297 R. GLOUC. (Rolls) 6780 Reufol he was to nedi men, of is almes large & fre. **1362** LANGL. *P. Pl.* A. VIII. 51 The pore That is innocent and neodi and no mon hath apeyret. **1439** *E.E. Wills* (1882) 130 To x of the nedyest parys-chirches yn the Cuntre by sidys. *c* **1510** MORE *Picus* Wks. 6/1 [To] releue the necessitie and misery of poore nedie people. **1576** GASCOIGNE *Steele Gl.* (Arb.) 59 But fewe regard their needy neighbours lacke. **1611** B. JONSON *Catiline* III. iii, With the old needie troops that follow'd Sylla. **1738** POPE *Epil. Sat.* II. 44 Have you less pity for the needy Cheat, The poor and friendless Villain, than the Great? **1829** J. W. CROKER in *C. Papers* 21 Aug. (1884) II. 23 Our papers are now very poorly done, by needy adventurers. **1878** LECKY *Eng. in 18th C.* I. ii. 246 For the education of his needy fellow-citizens.

transf. **1630** R. *Johnson's Kingd. & Commw.* 626 In some places it is admirable fruitfull, in other places very barren and needy. **1868** LYNCH *Rivulet* CXLVIII. ii, The sky is in its working dress, And needy earth befriends.

† c. In need *of* a thing. *Obs. rare.*

1597 HOWSON *Serm.* 31 We..are..needy of all things but hunger and feare. **1601** R. JOHNSON *Kingd. & Commw.* 111 They agaíne are needie of the waxe, honie [etc.]..which are brought thither from Prussia.

2. Of circumstances, etc.: Characterized by poverty or need.

1574 R. COX in Ellis *Orig. Lett.* Ser. III. IV. 17 In this nedy and beggerly tyme. **1592** SHAKS. *Rom. & Jul.* v. i. 42 In his needie shop a Tortoyrs hung. **1638** JUNIUS *Paint. Ancients* 29 Our poor and needy life. **1674** TEMPLE *Misc., To C'tess Essex* (1680) 173 We bring into the world with us a poor needy uncertain life.

b. Of search: Close, anxious.

1867 G. MACDONALD *Poems* 19 That neediest search will not avail To find a refuge here.

† 3. Under a necessity *to* do something. *Obs.*⁻¹

c **1400** LOVE *Bonavent. Mirr.* ix. (B.N.C. MS.) lf. 29 As the childe Jesu were a pure man and not god, nedy to kepe the obseruance of the lawe.

† 4. Needful, necessary. *Obs.*

1487 *Act 3 Hen. VII*, c. 11 §1 Fullers..that shuld lyve and obtayne their nedy sustentacion by meane of drapery. *a* **1535** *Frere & Boye* 45 (W. de W.), Therto soone I assent, For that me thynketh moost nedy. **1608** SHAKS. *Per.* I. iv. 95 These our ships..Are stored with corn to make your needy bread.

needyhood: see NEEDIHOOD.

needylie, var. of NEEDLY *adv.*² *Obs.*

neef, var. of NIEVE.

neeger, var. of NEGER.

neeȝh, obs. f. NIGH.

neejee, var. NITCHIE.

† **neel,** obs. form of ANIL.

1583 J. NEWBERY in Hakluyt *Voy.* (1589) 209 Neel the churle, 70 ducats.

Néel (ˈneɪəl). The name of Louis Eugène Félix *Néel* (b. 1904), French physicist, used *attrib.* to designate certain phenomena connected with his work on magnetism, as **Néel point** or **temperature,** the transition temperature for an antiferromagnetic or ferrimagnetic substance, above which it is paramagnetic (analogous to the Curie point for ferromagnetics); **Néel spike,** a sharply pointed triangular domain extending from a small hole or inclusion in a magnetic substance diagonally in relation to the field direction in the surrounding area; **Néel wall,** a type of domain boundary that Néel predicted should occur in thin layers of magnetic material, in which the rotation of the field direction in passing from one side of the wall to the other occurs in the plane of the film.

1949 *Rev. Mod. Physics* XXI. 572/2 Measurement of the ratio of length to width of the Néel domains offers a possible experimental method for determining..the surface energy density of a Bloch wall. **1951** *Jrnl. de Physique et le Radium* XII. 311 (*heading*) Néel 'spikes' around holes in a crystal surface. **1952** *Physica* XVIII. 714 In warming the salt through the region of the Néel temperature a continuous but rapid change occurs from a state in which the spins of the Cu^{++} ions are highly ordered to a state of comparative disorder. **1960** *Jrnl. Appl. Physics* XXXI. 303S/1 The smooth parts of the wall at the thin and thick ends of the film have to be interpreted as pure Néel and Bloch walls, respectively. **1963** J. S. SMART in Rado & Suhl *Magnetism* III. ii. 66 The Néel point..of a ferrimagnet or an antiferromagnet can be determined in a number of different ways, of which magnetic susceptibility is probably the most common and specific heat measurements one of the most accurate. **1966** CAREY & ISAAC *Magn. Domains* ii. 24 Néel walls become energetically more favourable than Bloch walls for thin films. *Ibid.* 28 In films of thickness less than about 200 Å no cross-tie walls occur but normal Néel walls are observed. *Ibid.* viii. 142 Consideration of the magnetostatic energy associated with large inclusions in iron crystals led Néel to predict the existence of closure domains ..now termed Néel spikes. **1973** *Physical Rev.* B. VII. 287 (*heading*) Heat-capacity measurements on manganese dibromide tetrahydrate near its Néel temperature.

† **neele,** obs. form of EEL *sb.*

14.. in Wr.-Wülcker 625 *Anguilla,* neele.

neel-gaw, obs. form of NYLGHAU.

neem (niːm). Also neemb, nim(b. [a. Hindī *nīm,* Skr. *nimba.*] a. An East Indian tree; the margosa. Also *neem-tree.*

1824 HEBER *Jrnl.* 1 Oct., A grove of neem-trees. **1846** [see MARGOSA]. **1876** *Cornh. Mag.* Sept. 320 There was Beena.. standing apart under a *nim* tree. **1885** E. ARNOLD *Secret of Death* Introd. 3 Bright with fragrant blossoms, borne By neem and baubul. **1911** J. FRAZER *Golden Bough: Magic Art* (ed. 3) I. v. 293 In order to procure rain people of low caste in the Central Provinces of India will tie a frog to a rod covered with green leaves and branches of the *nîm* tree. **1937** *N. & Q.* 8 May 338/1 The 'nimb' was used by Terence Mulvaney to make 'a thundering big poultice av neem leaves ..'. The Indian sais (or groom) still uses the neem leaf as a poultice for galls. **1949** H. W. FLOREY et al. *Antibiotics* I. xiv. 586 The nim tree (*Melia azadirachta, M. indica*) has been cultivated throughout India on account of its medicinal properties. **1969** T. H. EVERETT *Living Trees of World* 210/2 The neem or nim tree..common in India and Ceylon, is greatly valued for its bitter, antiseptic resin, which is used in medicines, soaps, lotions and toothpaste. *Ibid.* 211/1 The neem tree is a graceful evergreen, up to 50 feet tall; it thrives in dry climates. Its pinnate leaves have an odd number of curved, pointed, toothed, shiny leaflets. The numerous small, fragrant white flowers occur in loose panicles.. followed by small yellow berries. **1971** R. RUSSELL tr. *Ahmad's Shore & Wave* i. 9 There were only tracks on

Gipsies' Hill, winding their way through the trees of.. bitter-leaved neem among rocks.

b. *attrib.* with *oil*, *bloom*, etc.

1856 *Orr's Circ. Sci., Pract. Chem.* 453 A solid fat called Neem oil, or *Vaypum unnay*, is obtained from the ripe fruit of the margosa tree. **1879** E. ARNOLD *Lt. Asia* IV. iii, When the foot fell as though it trod on piles Of neem-blooms.

neemly, obs. form of NIMBLY *adv.*

neen, north. dial. form of NINE.

neencephalon (niːɛn'sɛfəlɒn). *Anat.* [a. G. *neencephalon* (L. Edinger *Vorlesungen über den Bau der nervösen Zentralorgane des Menschen und der Tiere* (ed. 7, 1908) II. xvi. 242): see NEO-1 e and ENCEPHALON.] The phylogenetically younger part of the brain, comprising the cerebral cortex and related structures. So **neence'phalic** *a.*

1917 *Jrnl. Compar. Neurol.* XXVIII. 216 The emergence of the true cortex (neencephalon, or suprasegmental apparatus of the brain). *Ibid.* 217 Here the picture is uncomplicated by the great neencephalic systems. **1948** *Brit. Jrnl. Psychol.* XXXIX. 71 The infant is born without mental life... Only gradually does the neëncephalon exert its influence. **1972** *Encycl. Psychol.* II. 310/2 *Neencephalon*, the 'new brain' or 'harmonious prolongation' lying above the 'old brain' or paleencephalon. A fairly pure neencephalic area of the brain is the six-layer cerebral cortex (isocortex) in mammals... Under narcosis or the influence of alcohol the neencephalic systems are the first to cease to operate.

neentishe: see ANIENTISE *v.*

neep (niːp). Forms: 1 *nǽp*, 1, 4–5 nep, 4–7 nepe, 5–6 neppe, *Sc.* neip, 5– neep, (9 neap). [OE. *nǽp*, ad. L. *nāpus* NAPE *sb.*³ ON. *næpa* (still in mod. Norw. and Icel.) was prob. adopted from English.]

1. A turnip. Also *attrib.*

The usual name in all Sc. dialects, and current in Northumberland and some southern counties.

c **725** *Corpus Gloss.* (Hessels) N 40 *Napis*, naep. *c* **1000** *Sax. Leechd.* II. 214 Healde hine þonne.. wiþ pisan, & beana, & næpas. **13..** *S.E. Leg.* (MS. Bodl. 779) in Herrig *Archiv* LXXXII. 335/68 Al his lyf to penaunce þis goodman haþ I-dyȝt; xv. nepus he et ech day. *c* **1340** *Nominale* (Skeat) 236 Man in the ȝerde pullith nepus. *c* **1420** *Pallad. on Husb.* IX. 29 Now rape and neep in places drie is sowe. *c* **1470** HENRYSON *Mor. Fab.* x. (*Fox & Wolf*) xxiv, Quhite as ane neip, and round als as ane seill. **1502** ARNOLDE *Chron.* (1811) 171 Porettis, tame nepis, and parcely, and other erbis off medecyn. **1544** PHAER *Regim. Life* (1553) I iv, Nepes also and rapes and radyshe.. maye bee well inoughe permitted. **1674** BLOUNT *Glossogr.* (ed. 4), *Nepe*, a turnip or navew. The word is still retein'd in Herefordshire. **1724** RAMSAY *Tea-t. Misc.* (1733) II. 167 As round as a Neep come todlen hame. **1826** J. WILSON *Noct. Ambr.* Wks. 1855 I. 207 Juicy neeps that melt in the mooth o' their ain accord. **1871** C. GIBBON *Lack of Gold* xviii, The laddies paraded the village with neep-lanterns. **1887** P. MᶜNEILL *Blawearie* 112 You might as well send a hungry stirk into a field among neeps, and expect it not to eat.

†**2.** *wild neep*, (see quots. and NEP *sb.*²). Also *English neep* (?). *Obs.*

c **1000** ÆLFRIC *Gloss.* in Wr.-Wülcker 135 *Napa siluatica*, sperewyrt, *vel* wilde næp. *Ibid.* 136 *Diptamnus, vel bibulcos*, wilde næp. *c* **1000** *Sax. Leechd.* III. 12 To wensealfe nim.. hræmnes fot, ængliscne næp & finul. *a* **1387** *Sinon. Barthol.* (Anecd. Oxon.) 13 *Brionia*, wilde nepe. *c* **1440** *Promp. Parv.* 353/1 Nepe, herbe, *coloquintida, cucurbita.*

neep, neer, obs. forms of NEAP, NEAR.

neer (nɪə(r)). Now *dial.* Forms: 4–5, 9 nere, 5–6, 9 neer, 6, 9 neir(e, 9 niere; 6 neare, 8–9 near, (8 inear, 9 ear). [ME. *nēre*, perh. repr. an OE. **néora* or **néore* = MDu. *niere* fem. (*nire, nyre*, Du. *nier*), MLG. *nêre*, OHG. *nioro, niero* masc. (G. *niere* fem.), ON. *nýra* neut. (Norw. *nyra, nyre*, Da. *nyre*; Sw. *njure* masc.), of uncertain origin.] A kidney.

In common dial. use in the northern, north-midland, and eastern counties; the Suffolk *nire, nyre* is prob. from ON.

a **1300** *E.E. Psalter* lxxii. 21 Mi neres ere torned for vnquert. *c* **1375** *Sc. Leg. Saints* xxii. (*Laurence*) 12 It brakis þe stane, þat man in bledyr ore nere has tane. *c* **1420** *Liber Cocorum* (1862) 52 þe hert of schepe, þe nere þou take. *c* **1440** *Promp. Parv.* 353/1 Neere of a beest, *ren.* **1535** COVERDALE *Isa.* xxxiv. 6 With the fatnesse of neeres of the wethers. **1549** *Compl. Scot.* vi. 67 Tansay, that is gude to purge the neiris. **1595** DUNCAN *App. Etymol.* (E.D.S.) 73 *Ren*, the neire. **1788** W. MARSHALL *Yorksh.* II. 337 *In-ear*, or *Near*, the kidney. **1828** CARR *Craven Gloss.* **1841** HAMILTON *Nugæ Lit.* 348 Will you eat a part of the niere? **1868** G. MACDONALD *R. Falconer* I. 41, I would like a dish o' your chits and nears.

b. *attrib.*, as *neer-creesh, -end, -fat, -strings.*

1444 *Aberdeen Regr.* (1844) I. 11 That na fleshowar.. tak oute of ony mutonne the neris or the nerecress. **1824** MACTAGGART *Gallovid. Encycl.* s.v. *Neers, Neer-strings*, those strings which are connected with the kidneys. **1877** *N.W. Linc. Gloss* s.v., The near-end of a loin of veal is the part next the kidneys. **1886** *S.W. Linc. Gloss., Near-fat*, the fat round the kidneys in a sheep, pig, or other animal.

ne'er (nɛə(r)), *adv.* Forms: 3–6 ner, 4–7 nere, 6–8 *Sc.* neir, 6 neare, 7 ne'r, neer(e, 7–8 ne're, 6– ne'er. [Contracted form of NEVER, as *e'er* for *ever*.]

1. Never. Chiefly *poetic.*

c **1205** LAY. 30205 He wolde aȝein wenden heom to his folke.. and ner [*c* **1275** neuere] æft a-ȝen teon. *c* **1320** *Cast. Love* 427 Nere nowther speketh him good. **1387–8** T. USK *Test. Love* I. vi. (Skeat) l. 89, I nere desyred wrathe of the people ne indignacion of the worthy. *c* **1420** *Chron. Vilod.* 3089 In þe ȝere of grace.. A thousonde euene and ner on mo. **1500–20** DUNBAR *Poems* xxxv. 21 Thy trublit gaist sall neir moir be degest. **1589** R. HARVEY *Pl. Perc.* (1590) 25 Thou gettest such praise, As neer decaies. *a* **1631** DONNE *Poems* (1650) 57 So these extreames shall ne'r their office doe. **1680** OTWAY *Orphan* v. vii, *Mon.* We ne're must meet again... *Cast.* Ne're meet again? *Mon.* No, never. **1738** SWIFT *Pol. Conversat.* 46 You have the old Proverb on your Side, Naught's ne'er in Danger. **1795** BURNS *Dumfries Volunteers* i, We'll ne'er permit a foreign foe On British ground to rally. **1829** A. HALLAM in Lockhart *Scott* (1839) IX. 332 Those dogs that from him ne'er would rove.

†**b.** *I wot ne'er*, I know not. *Obs.*

c **1380** WYCLIF *Serm.* Sel. Wks. II. 93 þei seiden to him, Where is he? And he seide, Y woot nere. *c* **1400** MAUNDEV. (1839) xx. 219 Where [= whether] it be by Craft or be Nygromancye, I wot nere. *c* **1475** *Partenay* 5702 Wherfor it gan do, certes wote I nere. **1513** MORE *Rich. III*, Wks. 39/1, I wote nere whither any preachers woordes ought more to moue you. **1589** R. HARVEY *Pl. Perc.* (1590) 5 Nay I wot neere, but it hath left behind it a wale in my throate.

c. *Sc.* Used euphem. in place of *deil*, devil.

1814 SCOTT *Wav.* lviii, The ne'er be in me, sir, if I think you're safe. **1816** —— *Antiq.* ix, I was at the search..; but ne'er-be-licket could they find that was to their purpose.

2. *ne'er the less* = NEVERTHELESS.

a **1300** *Cursor M.* 21247 Bot ner-þe-less for his liuelade, o biscop siþen he tok þe hade. *c* **1374** CHAUCER *Compl. Mars* 130 But ner the lesse, for al his heuy armure, He foloweth her. **1447** BOKENHAM *Seyntys* (Roxb.) 33 Nertheles vertu of necessyte I wyl make. **1542** UDALL *Erasm. Apoph.* 168 b, Nerethelesse many princes there bee, whiche.. abuse the good menne. **1621** QUARLES *Div. Poems, Esther* Argt. viii, Yet be thy iust Petition ne'rthelesse Entirely granted. **1822** BYRON *Werner* I. i. 684 Ne'er the less I must have three.

†**b.** So *ne'er the later* or *latter*. *Obs.*

1382 WYCLIF *Prov.* xxiii. 3 If ner the latere thou haue power in to thi soule. *c* **1400** *Beryn* 3120 Ner the lattir He held it nat al foly that Geffrey did clatir.

3. *Comb.* as *ne'er-changing, -dying, -ending*; *ne'er-seen, -sufficed, -touched.*

1594 SHAKS. *Rich. III*, II. ii. 46 His new Kingdome of nere-changing night. **1606** —— *Ant. & Cl.* III. xii. 31 Want will periure The ne're touch'd Vestall. **1612** J. DAVIES *Muse's Sacrifice* Wks. (Grosart) II. 83 Like a ne'er-suffized Graue. **1647** STAPYLTON *Juvenal* 226 The white sow.. That for her thirty ne're-seen paps was fam'd. **1693** CONGREVE in *Dryden's Juvenal* xi. (1697) 280 Arms, which to Man ne'er-dying Fame afford. *a* **1704** T. BROWN *Satire Woman* Wks. 1730 I. 56 A veng'ance of ne'er-ending harms.

b. *ne'er-be-good, -do-good* = NE'ER-DO-WELL. So †*ne'er-thrift.*

c **1440** *York Myst.* xxxiii. 266 þou nerthrift [*printed* -thrist] of Nazareth, now neuend is þi name. **1675** COTTON *Burlesque upon B.* Wks. (1725) 210 'Tis that Nere-be-good, thy Son, Has made me do what I have done. *a* **1814** *Intrigues of a Day* v. i. in *New Brit. Theatre* I. 168 A couple of as arrant ne'er-be-goods as ever cheated a poor poet. **1814** SCOTT *Wav.* xxx, D'ye hear what the.. young gentleman says, ye drunken ne'er-do-good?

ne'er, var. NEW-YEAR. *Sc.*

ne'er a, *adj. phr.* Forms: 5–6 nere a, 7 ne're a, ne'r a, 8– ne'er a; 8 *dial.* narrow a, 9 ner a, nar a, narra, norra, etc. See also NARY. [f. prec. + *a adj.*² 1 c.] Never a, not a, no.

In common Eng. dial. use: for forms see *Eng. Dial. Dict.*

c **1420** *Pallad. on Husb.* I. 622 Ryght nere a del. *Ibid.* VI. 154 Vche oon so from other That nere a sister touche nere a brother. *c* **1530** *Crt. of Love* 1197 Me thoughte, he loved her nere a dele. **1599** B. JONSON *Ev. Man out of Hum.* II. i, There's ne're a Gentleman i' the countrey has the like humors for the Hobby-horse as I haue. **1620** QUARLES *Pentelogia* ii, Could Sinners finde out ne're a one, More fit than Thee, for them to spit upon? **1749** FIELDING *Tom Jones* VIII. ii, There is narrow a one of all those officer fellows but looks upon himself to be as good as arrow a Squire of 500 l. a-year. **1786** BURNS *Farmer's Salut.* ix, At Brooses thou had ne'er a fellow. **1786** —— *Twa Dogs* 184 The ne'er a bit they're ill to poor folk. **1816** SCOTT *Old Mort.* i, They are ne'er a hair better than them that [etc.]. **1859** THACKERAY *Virgin.* xxii, Ne'er a one of them has ever whispered her pretty little secrets to me.

ne'er-do-well, *sb.* and *a.* Also *north.* and *Sc.* -weel. [Cf. NE'ER *adv.* 3 b.

The word being of northern and Sc. origin, the form *-weel* is freq. employed even by southern writers.]

A. *sb.* One who never does, and is never likely to do, well; a good-for-nothing, worthless, disreputable person.

1737 RAMSAY *Sc. Prov.* (1750) 87 Some ha'e a hantla fauts, ye are only a ne'er-do-well. **1837** DICKENS *Pickw.* xlviii, Only some drunken ne'er-do-weel finding his way home. **1845** ALB. SMITH *Fort. Scatterg. Fam.* v, I went to sea,—the refuge of all the ne'er-do-wells. **1893** LELAND *Mem.* II. 76 A literary ne'er-do-weel, destined never to achieve fortune.

B. *adj.* Never doing any good; good-for-nothing, worthless.

a **1773** FERGUSSON *Hallow Fair* Wks. (1800) 109 Ne'er-do-weel horse coupers. **1818** SCOTT *Hrt. Midl.* xviii, Our auld ne'er-do-weel deevil's-buckie o' a mither. **1857** MRS. GASKELL *C. Bronte* ii. I. 17 One of those ne'er-do-well lads who seem to have a kind of magnetic power for misfortunes. **1872** JEAFFRESON *Brides & Bridals* I. ix. 132 A saucy, tippling, ne'er-do-well fellow.

Hence **ne'er-do-wellish** *a.*; **ne'er-do-wellism.**

1890 JEAN MIDDLEMASS *Two False Moves* I. xiii. 199 Only the rowdyish and ne'er-do-weelish. **1891** *Pall Mall G.* 5 Aug. 3/1 Drunkenness, ne'er-do-wellism [etc.].

neere, -ness, neerhand, obs. ff. NEAR, etc.

nees, obs. form of NESE, nose; NIECE.

neese, variant of NEEZE *v.*, NESE, nose.

neest, variant of *neist* NEXT; obs. form of NEST.

neet, obs. f. NEAT *sb.*, NET, NIT; dial. f. NIGHT.

neethur, -yr, obs. forms of NEITHER.

neeve, variant of NIEVE, fist.

neewe, obs. form of NEW.

neeyng, obs. form of NEIGHING.

neeze (niːz), *v.* Now *north. dial.* and *Sc.* Forms: 4–6 nese, 6 niese, *Sc.* neys, nyse, 6–9 neese, (7 nees), 6– neeze. [ME. *nēsen*, prob. ad. ON. *hnjósa* (Norw. *njosa, nysa*, Sw. *nysa*, Da. *nyse*) = OHG. *niosan* (G. *niesen*), MLG. *nêsen, neysen*, MDu. *niesen* (Du. *niezen*), prob. of imitative origin: cf. FNESE, SNEEZE.] To sneeze.

c **1340** *Nominale* (Skeat) 172 Man cowith and nesith. **1432–50** tr. *Higden* (Rolls) V. 389 A man nesynge. **1486** *Bk. St. Albans* c vij, When ye se yowre hawke Nesyng and Castyng wat thorogh her Nostrellis. **1544** PHAER *Regim. Life* (1553) A viij b, Ye must put in the nose of the pacient, pouder of pellitory of Spain.. to make him to nese. **1586** COGAN *Haven Health* xxviii. (1636) 48 By eating of Mustard ..we are straightway.. provoked to neese. **1665** SPENCER *Vulg. Proph.* 96 When any one neezed they would venerate the noise as a kind of expression of the Deity inshrined in the head. **1725** BRADLEY *Fam. Dict.* s.v. *Neesing*, A Horse, whose Head being stopp'd.. so that he cannot neeze. **1788** W. MARSHALL *Yorksh.* II. 343. **1825** BROCKETT *N.C. Gloss.* **1849–** in northern dial. glossaries (also Chesh. and Shropsh.). **1870** J. NICHOLSON *Idylls* 64 A waff frae the door gars her 'neeze.

Hence **neeze** *sb.*, a sneeze. *rare.*

1656 S. HOLLAND *Zara* (1719) 54 Circumgyring about his Weasand, [it] inforced him to a manly Neese. **1866** in *Banffsh. Gloss.* **1899** in *Cumbld. Gloss.*

†**neeze-wort.** *Obs.* Also 6–7 nese-, (6 niese-, nise-), neese-. [ad. G. *nies(e)-wurz(el* or Du. *nieswortel* (also *nieskruid*): see NEEZE *v.* and WORT.] A former book-name of HELLEBORE.

1548 TURNER *Names Herbs* (E.D.S.) 79 Veratrum.. maye be called in englishe Nesewurte. *Ibid.* 80 The herbe.. which hath bene hytherto taken for blacke Nisewurt, or Veratrum nigrum. **1578** LYTE *Dodoens* 347 This kinde of Hellebor is called.. in English White Hellebor, Neseworte, and Lingwort. **1601** R. CHESTER *Love's Martyr* (1878) 93 First of the Nesewort, it doth driue away, And poysoneth troublesome Mice. **1629** PARKINSON *Parad.* lxxxii. 346 White Ellebor, Neesewort or Neesing roote, because the powder of the roote is vsed to procure neesing. **1668** WILKINS *Real Char.* II. iv. 78.

neezing ('niːzɪŋ), *vbl. sb.* Forms: 4, 6 nesing, (5 -ynge, 6 -yng, -inge), 6 nysynge, -ing, nies-, nising, 6–7 neesing, (6 -yng, kn-), neezing. [f. NEEZE *v.*: cf. MDu. *niesinge*, MHG. *niesunge*.] Sneezing; a sneeze.

1382 WYCLIF *Job* xli. 9 His nesing [is] shynyng of fyr, and his eȝen as eȝelidis of morutid. **1432–50** tr. *Higden* (Rolls) V. 389 A mervellous pestilence folowede.., peresche ynge moche peple in yoskenge or nesynge. **1530** PALSGR. 247/2 Nesyng with the nose, *esternuement.* **1543** TRAHERON *Vigo's Chirurg.* IV. 148 Nysynge also, provoked by arte, is convenient in thys case. **1578** LYTE *Dodoens* 194 The same roote.. put into the nose causeth Sternutation or niesing. **1609** B. JONSON *Sil. Wom.* IV. i, The spitting, the coughing, the laughter, the neesing. **1663** J. SPENCER *Prodigies* (1665) 61 That.. usage of praying for a Person upon neezing. **1676** *Gentleman's Jockey* 286 There be two other excellent helps for sick Horses, as Frictions and Neesings.

fig. **1647** H. MORE *Exorcismus* Wks. (Grosart) 178 You summer neezings.. That fill the air with a quick fading fire.

attrib. **1622** S. WARD *Woe to Drunkards* (1627) 45 An Epidemicall disease, such as the.. Neezing sicknesse.

†**b.** *Combs.* **neezing powder**, a powder used to cause sneezing, esp. that prepared from hellebore [cf. Du. *niespoeder*, G. *nies(e)pulver*]; **neezing root** or **wort** = NEEZE-WORT. *Obs.*

1544 PHAER *Regim. Life* (1560) S v, After that cause hym to nese.. with a litle pellitory of spain, or *nesing pouder. **1607** TOPSELL *Four-f. Beasts* (1658) 84 A neesing powder made of the gall of a black cat. *a* **1657** R. LOVEDAY *Lett.* (1663) 22 The neezing-powder I take constantly, but have much adoe to perswade it to make me neeze. **1597** A. M. tr. *Guillemeau's Fr. Chirurg.* 43/1 Little pellets.. of the blacke *neesinge roote. **1599** —— tr. *Gabelhouer's Bk. Physicke* 11/2 Whyte neesing roote. **1629** [see NEEZE-WORT]. **1591** PERCIVALL *Sp. Dict.*, *Yerva de ballestero*, *neesing-woorte, bearefoote, *Helleborus.* **1602** FULBECKE *1st. Pt. Parall.* 12 So neesingwort doth cure phrensie or madnesse.

‖**nef** (nɛf). Also 8–9 neff. [F. *nef* ship, etc.:—L. *nāvem*: cf. NAVE *sb.*²]

†**1.** The nave of a church. Also *attrib.* *Obs.*

1687 A. LOVELL tr. *Thevenot's Trav.* I. 187 The Church is very spacious, the Nef or Body of it is round. **1705** ADDISON *Italy* (1766) 55 The long nef consists of a row of five cupolas. **1775** JOHNSON in *Boswell* 5 Nov., We saw the cathedral... The choir splendid... The Neff very high and grand.

2. (See quots.)

1834 MAR. EDGEWORTH *Helen* II. 192 Every officer of the household making reverential obeisance as they passed to the *Nef*,—the *Nef* being.. a piece of gilt plate in the shape of the hull of a ship in which the napkins for the king's table are kept. **1862** WRIGHT *Dom. Mann. & Sent. Eng. Mid. Ages* 163 Of these ornaments, one of the most remarkable was the nef or ship—a vessel generally of silver which contained the salt-cellar, towel, &c., of the prince or great lord.

3. An incense-boat. Cf. NAVET^{2}.
1867 LADY HERBERT *Impress. Spain* (1868) 208 In the sacristy was..a nacre *nef* and some fine heads of saints.

nef, obs. form of NEIF.

†**nefand**, *a. Obs.* Also 5 nephande. [a. OF. *neph-*, *neff-*, *nefande*, or ad. L. *nefand-us*: see next.] = NEFANDOUS.
1490 CAXTON *Eneydos* vi. 26 Ye grete, horribyle, nephande, & detestable cryme. *Ibid.* vii. 32 The nephande deth of hir sayd somtyme husbond. **1616** SHELDON *Mirac. Ch. Rome* 198 Knowing what nefand abominations are practised.

nefandous (nɪˈfændəs), *a.* [f. L. *nefand-us*, f. *ne-* not + *fandus* 'to be spoken', gerundive of *fārī* to speak: see -OUS.] Not to be spoken of; unmentionable; abominable, atrocious.
1640 HOWELL *Dodona's Gr.* (1645) 150 There was a complication of many nefandous crimes. **1702** C. MATHER *Magn. Chr.* VI. vii. (1852) 449 Sometimes he..belch'd out most nefandous blasphemies against the God of heaven. **1780** J. HOWIE *Faithful Contend.* Pref. 8 That wicked and nefandous act of Parliament. **1826** SOUTHEY *Vind. Eccl. Angl.* 108 That spirit of nefandous impiety with which it was ..carried on by the Monastic Orders. **1827** SIR H. TAYLOR *Isaac Comnenus* v. vi, 'Tis a foul offence, A most nefandous error.
Hence **neˈfandousness** (Bailey vol. II, 1727).

nefarious (nɪˈfɛərɪəs), *a.* [f. L. *nefārius*, f. *nefas* wrong, impiety: see -OUS.] Wicked, iniquitous, villainous.
1604 R. CAWDREY *Table Alph.* (1613), *Nefarious*, wicked, detestable. **1660** F. BROOKE tr. *Le Blanc's Trav.* 244 A man once observed to be nefarious, is hated and avoyded by all men. **1726** AYLIFFE *Parergon* 107 But the most nefarious kind of Bastards are they whom the Law stiles Incestuous Bastards. **1790** BURKE *Fr. Rev.* Wks. V. 261 Those who, for the same nefarious purposes, have perverted every other part of learning. **1830** GEN. P. THOMPSON *Exerc.* (1842) I. 245 There wants a collection of dying speeches of nefarious governments. **1866** LIVINGSTONE *Last Jrnls.* (1873) I. i. 6 Lending their flag to slaving dhows, so that it covers that nefarious traffic.
Hence **neˈfariously** *adv.*, in a nefarious manner; **neˈfariousness** (Bailey vol. II, 1727).
1599 NASHE *Lenten Stuffe* Wks. (Grosart) V. 284 Nefariously..prophaning & penetrating our holy fathers nostrils. **1659** J. OWEN *Integr. Heb. & Grk. Text* Wks. 1853 XVI. 413 They have wickedly and nefariously corrupted the text. **1695** *Pol. Ballads* (1860) II. 50 The Bar, the Pulpit, and the Press Nefariously combine To cry up an usurped pow'r. **1827** SCOTT *Napoleon* xxiv, It was nefariously unjust.

nefast (nɪˈfɑːst, -æ-), *a. rare.* [ad. L. *nefast-us*, f. *nefas*: cf. prec. and F. *néfaste*.] Nefarious.
1849 LYTTON *Caxtons* xlvi, If you really take for truth and life monsters so nefast and flagitious. **1887** R. L. STEVENSON *Let.* Oct. (1899) II. 71 In good case and spirits, as I am now, after a most nefast experience of despondency before I left.
So **neˈfastous** *a.* (Bailey vol. II, 1727).

nefe, obs. f. NIEVE, fist; var. NEVE, nephew.

nefedyevite (nɛfɛˈdjɛvaɪt). *Min.* Also †**nefediewite, nefedievite.** [ad. Russ. *nefed'evit* (P. Puzyrevsky 1872, in *Zapiski imperat. S.-Peterburgsk. mineral. Obshch.* VII. 15, f. the name of V. V. *Nefed'ev*, 19th-cent. Russian mineralogist: see -ITE^{1}.] A white or pinkish aluminosilicate of magnesium and calcium belonging to the clay family and similar to montmorillonite.
1873 *Jrnl. Chem. Soc.* XXVI. 1210 Nefediewite; a new mineral... This amorphous mineral, very much like lithomarge, occurs, together with fluorspar, in the limestone of Nertschinsk. **1938** *Mineral. Abstr.* VII. 104 Greenish-grey unctuous clay interbedded among Cretaceous limestones, the bulk of which consists of a fibrous crystalline aggregate..and in composition..corresponds to nefedievite. **1961** *Doklady Earth Sci.* CXXXV. 1296/1 In view of the great structural similarity between true montmorillonite and nefedyevite, doubling of the unit cell along the *c* axis can be expected.

nefen, var. of NEVEN *v.*

nefere, obs. f. NEVER.

neff(e, obs. ff. NIEVE, fist.

neffel, obs. f. NEVEL *v.*

neffew(e, obs. ff. NEPHEW.

neffow, dial. var. NIEVEFUL.

nefre, obs. f. NEVER.

†**nefresie.** *Obs. rare*$^{-1}$. [a. OF. *nefresie*, ad. med.L. *nefresis* for *nephrītis*.] = NEPHRITIS.
1590 BARROUGH *Meth. Physick* VII. xvii. (1639) 406 A particular bath, which is applyed for paines of the Nefresie.

nefretick, obs. form of NEPHRITIC.

†**nefte.** *Obs.* [a. Russ. *neft'* or Pers. *neft*: see NAPHTHA.] Naphtha.
1598 HAKLUYT *Voy.* I. 400 This oyle is blacke, and is called Nefte. **1662** J. DAVIES tr. *Olearius' Voy. Ambass.* 402 We saw..above thirty sources of Nefte, which is a kind of Medicinal Oil. **1698** J. CRULL *Muscovy* 48 Whole Rivulets of an Oily substance, by them call'd Nefte.

neg (nɛg), colloq. abbrev. of *negative* or *negatively*, esp. = NEGATIVE *sb.* 8.
1874 W. H. JACKSON *Diaries* (1959) 275 While Bob was saddling and packing up, I made a couple of negs. **1909** *Cent. Dict.* Suppl., *Neg.* An abbreviation (*a*) of *negative*; (*b*) of *negatively*. **1948** M. ALLINGHAM *More Work for Undertaker* xv. 185, I told you it was like a neg. Black shadows and everything else a sort of chilly grey. **1959** H. HAMILTON *Answer in Negative* i. 8 You don't want to keep negs in the same place as pix..because there's always a risk of fire. **1971** *Hi-Fi Sound* Feb. 71/1 It is not always so difficult to identify 'pos. and neg.' but long practice has made it a habit with me to tie a knot in each negative connection. **1972** *Amat. Photographer* 12 Jan. 29 The resultant negs had a remarkable degree of density.

neg, obs. form of NAG *sb.*^{1}, NIGH *a.*

†**negan(n)epant.** *Obs.* Also **negani-**. [Of obscure etym.] Some kind of East Indian piece-goods imported in the 18th cent.
1725 *Lond. Gaz.* No. 6388/2 The following Goods, viz... Negannepants, Tapseils,..Perpetts, Welch Plains. **1757** tr. *Guyon's Hist. East Indies* II. 145, 560 neganepants. **1788** CLARKSON *Impolicy Slave Trade* 104 In the second class may be reckoned..Chelloes, Nicamees, Neganipants.

†**ˈnegant.** *Obs. rare.* [f. L. *negant-*, *negans*, pres. pple. of *negāre* to NEGATE.] One who denies; a negative proposition.
c **1560** W. KINGSMILL in Strype *Cranmer* (E.H.S.) II. 38 The affirmants..were almost treble so many as were the negants. **1654** Z. COKE *Logick* 116 The fight of Propositions both in quality and quantity, as is between an universal affirmant, and a particular negant.

negar: see NEGER.

negardchepe, negarship, obs. ff. NIGGARDSHIP.

negarde, obs. f. NIGGARD.

negardy, -tie, var. NIGGARDY.

negate (nɪˈgeɪt), *v.* [f. *negāt-*, ppl. stem of L. *negāre* to deny.] **a.** *trans.* To deny, negative; to deny the existence of; to destroy, nullify, render ineffective. (Freq. in recent use.)
[**1623** COCKERAM II, To Deny, *negate*.] **1837** *Fraser's Mag.* XV. 723 Understanding..establishes its quality as a real object, by negating the board on which it is drawn. **1874** *Contemp. Rev.* XXIII. 405 When the lower life asserts itself against the higher, the higher may consciously negate it. **1891** H. JONES *Browning* 207 Evolution not only postulates unity.., but it also negates all differences.
absol. **1835** *Fraser's Mag.* XI. 642 Whatever negates is something, else no negation were possible.
b. *Gram.* To render negative in sense.
1930 W. EMPSON *Seven Types of Ambiguity* vii. 269 *Not* may negate *going* or *weeping*. That the ear expects *did go* may mean that all nature wept for Polonius. **1961** R. B. LONG *Sentence & its Parts* iv. 105 Even the words that commonly negate clauses do not always do so. **1972** R. QUIRK et al. *Gram. Contemp. Eng.* 382 *Not* here functions as a predeterminer in the italicized noun phrase; but it has the effect of negating the whole clause.
Hence **neˈgated** *ppl. a.*, **neˈgatedness, neˈgating** *ppl. a.*
1876 F. H. BRADLEY *Eth. Stud.* 118 Real pain is the feeling of the negatedness of the self. *Ibid.*, Where pain comes from the negated function. **1885** W. C. COUPLAND *Spir. Goethe's Faust* ii. 53 One of..a negating class of..beings.

negater (nɪˈgeɪtə(r)). *Computers.* Also **negator.** [f. NEGAT(E *v.* + -ER^{1}. Cf. NEGATOR.] = INVERTER 2 c.
1962 *Gloss. Terms Automatic Data Processing* (*B.S.I.*) 60 Negater. **1963** *New Scientist* 14 Nov. 387/3 The system employs a 'negator' element—a logical element which reverses, for example, the polarity of the voltage, or the direction of the magnetic flux. **1971** J. H. SMITH *Digital Logic* iv. 65 The British standard gives little guidance to the use of a digital buffer amplifier and the reader is recommended to use a single input NOR symbol as an inverting buffer (this is defined as a negater) and the amplifier symbol for the non-inverting buffer.

negatif(e, obs. forms of NEGATIVE.

negation (nɪˈgeɪʃən). [a. F. *négation* (12th c.), or ad. L. *negātiōn-em*, n. of action f. *negāre* to say no, deny. Cf. It. *negazione*, Sp. *negacion*.]
1. a. The action of denying or of making a statement involving the use of 'no', 'not', 'never', etc. Also const. *of*. (Sometimes passing into 2.)
1530 PALSGR. Introd. 41 In negation they use one of these thre wordes, *pas*, *point* or *mye*. **1550** BALE *Apol.* 23 b, But I founde therin no answere appoynted to be made..neyther by affyrmacion nor yet negacion. **1634** BP. HALL *Contempl.*, *N.T.* IV. xvii, Not by way of negation, as if nothing were necessary but this; but by way of comparison. **1654** BRAMHALL *Just Vind.* vi. (1661) 159 Our Negation is only of humane controverted additions. **1713** BERKELEY *Hylas & Phil.* II. Wks. 1871 I. 315, I superadd to this general idea the negation of all those particular things, qualities, or ideas. **1790** R. MERRY *Laurel of Liberty* (ed. 2) 13 O! better were it, ever to be lost In black Negation's sea. **1851** GLADSTONE *Glean.* (1879) IV. 7 This is the negation of God erected into a system of Government. **1875** H. JAMES *R. Hudson* (1879) III. 76 She made a gesture of negation.

b. An instance of this; a negative statement, doctrine, etc.; a refusal or contradiction; a denial *of* something.
1576 FLEMING *Panopl. Epist.* 111 Some things there be which of custome I shake off, with a manifest negation. **1606** SHAKS. *Tr. & Cr.* v. ii. 127 Why my negation hath no taste of madnesse. **1675** R. BARCLAY *Apol. Quakers* v. §25. 183 Is a bare Negation sufficient to overturn the strength of a positive Assertion? **1726–31** TINDAL *Rapin's Hist. Eng.* (1743) VII. XVII. 127 To judge whether more credit were to be given to her bare negation than to their affirmation. **1797** BURKE *Let. Aff. Irel.* Wks. IX. 465 Our difference is only a negation of certain tenets of theirs. **1817** COLERIDGE *Biog. Lit.* (Bohn) 164 Negations involve impediments not less formidable than sophistication. **1866** ROGERS *Agric. & Prices* I. iv. 70 Villenage..implied a negation of all rights in land and chattels.
c. As a term of Logic, opp. to AFFIRMATION 3. As a logical operation in *Computing*: = INVERSION 2 k. Also **negation-sign,** the sign or symbol used to indicate negation.
1570 BILLINGSLEY *Euclid* I. vii. 17 In this proposition the conclusion is a negation. **1588** FRAUNCE *Lawiers Log.* II. i. 88 A negation dooth but deprive and take away. **1620** T. GRANGER *Div. Logike* 105 The one is a thing being, the other a negation of the being thereof. **1725** WATTS *Logic* I. ii. §6 A negation is the absence of that which does not naturally belong to the thing we are speaking of. **1788** REID *Aristotle's Logic* i. §4. 14 Negation is the enunciation of one thing from another. **1864** BOWEN *Logic* v. 136 Negation is only the affirmation of difference or exclusion. **1948** MCKINSEY & TARSKI in *Jrnl. Symbolic Logic* XIII. 1 As regards constants, they are three in number: the negation sign, the conjunction sign, and the possibility sign. **1949** E. C. BERKELEY *Giant Brains* iii. 34 The simplest computing operation is negation. **1955** A. N. PRIOR *Formal Logic* III. ii. 253 We regard..his negation-sign as meaning impossibility. **1959** E. M. MCCORMICK *Digital Computer Primer* v. 64 The NOT logical operation (negation) results in an output which is opposite to its single input. **1962** T. C. BARTEE et al. *Theory & Design Digital Machines* iii. 23 Some authors refer to *x'* as *not x* or as the negation of *x* corresponding to our complement of *x*. **1965** HUGHES & LONDEY *Elem. Formal Logic* x. 67 We used the Law of Double Negation to insert a pair of negation signs. **1969** F. M. HALL *Introd. Abstr. Algebra* II. xi. 313 The negation, or complement, of *A*, written *A'*, is the statement 'it is false that *A*', or briefly 'not *A*'.
2. The absence or opposite of something which is actual, positive, or affirmative.
1642 H. MORE *Song of Soul* II. iii. III. xviii, Rash man that dost inferre negation From thy dead eare, or non-experience. **1651** C. CARTWRIGHT *Cert. Relig.* I. 223 Not to will a mans salvation, is properly no act, but rather a negation of an act. **1673** KERSEY *Algebra* I. i. (1725) 6 This character—is a sign of Negation. *a* **1754** FIELDING *Remedy of Affliction* Wks. 1775 IX. 258 Death is nothing more than the negation of life. **1837** GORING & PRITCHARD *Microgr.* 79 Some compound of black (which implies a negation of colour). **1871** TYNDALL *Fragm. Sci.* (1879) I. xxi. 492 Death in this case would be simply the sudden negation of life.
3. A negative or unreal thing, a nonentity; a thing whose essence consists in the absence of something positive.
1707 *Curios. in Husb. & Gard.* Pref. 5 Meer Negations, and simple Privations, as Death, Ignorance, Blindness, and the like. **1821** LAMB *Elia* Ser. I. *Old Benchers*, Next to him was old Barton—a jolly negation. **1893** HUXLEY *Evolution & Eth.* ii. 65 Though reduced to a hypostatized negation, Brahma was not to be trusted.
Hence **neˈgational** *a.*, negative, using or involving negation.
1865 D. W. THOMPSON *Odds & Ends* iii. 6 We can but imperfectly describe the conditions of its actuality by negational terms. **1882** C. E. TURNER in *Macm. Mag.* Apr. 484/1 Bazaroff..should profess exclusively negational and abolitionary doctrines.

negationist (nɪˈgeɪʃənɪst). [f. prec. + -IST.] One who uses negation; esp. one who merely denies accepted beliefs without advancing anything positive in their place.
1856 DOVE *Logic Chr. Faith* 423 The German Negationist who makes thought the all. **1882** BAIN *J. S. Mill* 140 In everything characteristic of the creed of Christendom he was a thorough-going negationist.

ˈnegatism. *rare*$^{-1}$. Negativism.
1885 *American* IX. 297 She has Goethe's detestation of antagonism and negatism.

negatival (nɛgəˈtaɪvəl), *a.* [f. NEGATIVE *sb.* + -AL.] Negative; negativistic; characterized by negation.
1936 J. J. COHEN *Psychotherapy* ii. 7 Psychophonism, or mental logography, is a word which I have coined to distinguish a psychotherapeutic system of negatival auto-suggestion from all rival systems which, all, start from an entirely wrong foundation, this in their being all alike positival in their psychology. **1966** J. E. BUSE in C. E. Bazell *In Memory of J. R. Firth* 56 Phrases are classed as..negatival if they commence with a negative.

negative (ˈnɛgətɪv), *sb.* Also 4 -ife, -yfe. [f. next, or a. F. *négative* (13th c.).]
I. † 1. a. A negative command, a prohibition.
c **1380** WYCLIF *Sel. Wks.* III. 234 O if God so scharply biddes þese negatifes.., who are more heretikes þen þese þat done hit ageynes hym? **1581** W. CHARKE in *Confer.* IV. (1584) Ee iv b, The text Deut. 6. hath the negatiue, Thou shalt serue no strange gods.
b. A negative statement or proposition; a negative mode of stating anything.
1567 JEWEL *Def. Apol.* v. xv. §1. 579 By a like Negative Chrysostome saithe,..'This tree neither..Paule planted.., nor God encreased'. **1581** W. CHARKE in *Confer.* IV. (1584)

Eej b, Your affirmatiue is contrarie to the holy Ghostes.. negatiue, Not of workes. 1628 T. Spencer Logick 177 The first, is an vniversall affirmatiue. The third, is a particular negatiue. 1658 Bramhall Consecr. Bps. vii. 155 First to accuse us of Forgery, and then to put us to prove a Negative. 1736 Gray Let. in Poems (1775) 7 Almost all the employment of my hours may be best explained by negatives. 1771 Junius, Lett. xliv. (1788) 252 I am not bound to prove a negative. 1856 R. A. Vaughan Mystics (1860) I. 12 Almost all we are in a position to say, concerning spiritual influence, consists of negatives. 1876 Tait Rec. Adv. Phys. Sci. iii. (ed. 2) 69 The consequent establishment of a definite and scientifically useful negative.

c. A negative reply or answer; †a denial or refusal. ***negative pregnant***: see PREGNANT.

1571 Campion Hist. Irel. ii. ix. (1633) 113 Who was the messenger? where are the letters? convince my negative. 1634 W. Wood New Eng. Prosp. (1865) 61 A false asseveration usually winneth more beleefe than two verifying negatives can resettle. 1748 Richardson Clarissa (1811) I. ii. 12 Such-like consenting negatives. 1784 Cowper Ep. J. Hill 22 Dreading a negative, and overawed Lest he should trespass. 1802 Playfair Illustr. Hutton. The. 516 Appearances that give the most direct negative to the Neptunian system. 1891 T. Hardy Tess liii, He asked his father if she had applied for any money during his absence. His father returned a negative.

d. Used quasi-*advb.*, orig. in radio communication, = NO *adv.*[3] *colloq.*

Quot. 1946 perhaps illustrates sense 2 a of the adj.

[1946 J. Irving Royal Navalese 121 Orders for a Church Parade 'Dress for Officers No. 3, negative swords'.] 1955 Amer. Speech XXX. 118 Negative.., I refuse; I disagree; no (in answer to a question). (For reasons of clarity, any negative expression is expressed over the radio as negative. ..) 1961 E. Waugh Unconditional Surrender I. i. 29 'Any result of my application for the return of my typist?' 'Negative,' said Mr Oates. 1972 C. Kearey Last Plane from Uli vii. 81 'Any snags, Captain?' 'Negative, she's running like a clock.' 1972 P. Cleife Slick & Dead ix. 69, I shook my head. 'Negative,' I said.

2. A negative word or particle; a negative term.

?a1580 in Lyly's Wks. (1902) III. 462 In womens mouthes in case of loue no, no negatiue will proue. 1601 Shaks. Twel. N. v. i. 24 If your foure negatiues make your two affirmatiues, why then the worse for my friends. 1641 W. Cartwright Lady-Errant I. ii, Because two Negatives make an Affirmative. 1711 J. Greenwood Eng. Gram. 160 Two Negatives, or two Adverbs of Denying do in English affirm. 1827 Gentl. Mag. XCVII. I. 498 Double negatives were commonly used to strengthen the negation in the time of Shakespeare. 1844 Dickens Mart. Chuz. xi, The remark was rendered somewhat obscure..by reason..of a redundancy of negatives. 1870 Jevons Elem. Logic iii. 22 Negatives signify the absence of the same qualities.

3. a. The right to refuse consent to a proposed measure; a right of veto. Now *rare* or *Obs.*

1613 Purchas Pilgrimage v. xv. 445 The meanest person amongst them hauing a Negatiue in all their consultations. 1672 Petty Pol. Anat. (1691) 36 The Parliament..have a Negative upon any Law that the Lord Lieutenant and Councel shall offer to the King. 1765 Blackstone Comm. I. 156 We may apply to the royal negative..what Cicero observes of the negative of the Roman tribunes. 1796 Morse Amer. Geog. I. 505 Each branch of the legislature has a negative upon the other.

†b. A negative or adverse vote. *Obs.*

1654 Clarke Papers (Camden) III. 11 The most part of the last weeke was spent about the qualifications of Electors.. and many negatives passed upon them. 1683 Temple Mem. Wks. 1720 I. 462 The House of Commons pass'd another Negative upon the Debate for Money. 1708 Kennett in Ellis Orig. Lett. Ser. ii. IV. 256 A Majority of the Aldermen ..put a negative upon the motion for printing his sermon. 1743 Pitt in Almon Anecd. (1792) I. v. 131 If we put a negative upon this question, it may awaken our ministers out of their deceitful dream.

4. ***the negative***: **a.** The side, position, or aspect of a question, which is opposed to the affirmative or positive.

1579 W. Wilkinson Confut. Fam. Love 5 b, Our Papistes, which can not abide an Argument drawen from the Negative. 1614 Raleigh Hist. World ii. (1634) 486 Whether Nebonassar were an Astrologer or no, I cannot tell; it is hard to mainteine the negative. 1656 Earl Monm. tr. Boccalini's Advts. fr. Parnass. 356 The Negative to this was often broacht, and disputed. 1754 Edwards Freed. Will i. i. 3 The Positive and the Negative are set before the Mind for it's Choice, and it chuses the Negative. 1865 C. J. Vaughan Plain Words vi. (1866) 99 Let the negative have its positive.

†b. The capacity of refusal. *Obs. rare*⁻¹.

1632 J. Hayward tr. Biondi's Eromena 94 Full little was he as yet aware of that the negative might have place in a courteous Lady.

5. ***in the negative***: **†a.** In the face *of*, in opposition to, something. *Obs. rare*⁻¹.

1598 Manwood Lawes Forest xxiii. §3 (1615) 219 Although that this Statute of Charta de Foresta were made in the negatiue of the Law and vsage that was before.

†b. On the negative side of a question. *Obs.*

1634 Rainbow Labour (1635) 7 In the Negative, the inconvenience of the Obiect must deterre us. 1646 Sir T. Browne Pseud. Ep. i. vii. (1686) 20 A Testimony is of no illation in the Negative. 1697 Dampier Voy. round World (1699) 485 After all, I will not be peremptory in the Negative.

c. On the side of, in favour of, or with the effect of, rejecting a proposal or suggestion.

1650 R. Stapylton Strada's Low C. Wars v. 109 It was carried by most voices in the negative. 1654 Nicholas Papers (Camden) II. 84 There were 120 for the affirmative..and 150 in the negative that it should not be determyned. 1711 Fingall MSS. in 10th Rep. Hist. MSS. Comm. App. V. 144 The majority of votes carryed it in the negative. 1750 Beawes Lex Mercat. (1752) 53 It was resolved in the Negative. 1803 Wellington in Gurw. Desp. (1837) II. 321 If that should be determined in the negative.

d. With denial or negation; negatively; of a negative character.

1648 Nethersole Proj. for Peace 6 To the three first I should make a short Answer in the Affirmative, to the fourth in the Negative. 1746 H. Walpole Lett. (1846) II. 137 They unanimously answered in the negative. 1756 Burke Vind. Nat. Soc. Wks. I. 65 The grave doctor answers me in the affirmative; the reverent sergeant replies in the negative. 1871 H. Ainsworth Tower Hill i. iv, Cromwell replied in the negative. 1875 Scrivener Lect. Text N. Test. 7 The answer might well be looked for in the negative.

†6. a. One who takes the negative side. *Obs.*

1649 Bounds Publ. Obed. (1650) 10 Nothing ought in this case to be concluded against the negatives, though fewer in number. 1673 Essex Papers (Camden) I. 160 After great contest, there were no other Negatives but these two.

†b. A negative heretic (see quot.). *Obs. rare.*

1731 Chandler tr. Limborch's Hist. Inquis. II. 295 Such as have confessed their Heresy, and are impenitent, and Negatives, viz. such who are convicted by a sufficient number of witnesses, and yet deny their Crime.

II. 7. a. The opposite or negation *of* something. *rare.*

1387–8 T. Usk Test. Love iii. ii. (Skeat) l. 92 Badde is nothing els but absence or negative of good, as derkenesse is absence or negative of light. 1882 Spurgeon Treas. Dav. Ps. cxix. 19 As the one prays to see, the other deprecates the negative of seeing.

b. A negative quality or characteristic.

1647 Clarendon Hist. Reb. ii. §25 Which good qualifications were allayed by another negative, he did love nobody else. 1770 Junius Lett. xxxvi. (1788) 196 You have now added the last negative to your character.

c. *Alg.* A negative quantity.

1706 W. Jones Syn. Palmar. Matheseos 35 To Add a Negative, is to take away a Positive. 1753 Chambers Cycl. Supp. s.v. Negative sign, The square root of a negative implies an imaginary quantity.

d. One devoid *of* some quality. *rare*⁻¹.

1813 Examiner 1 Feb. 73/2 Those negatives of feeling and thought who..call themselves people of fashion.

e. *Austral.* A shaft yielding no gold.

1864 J. Rogers New Rush, Miner's Melody 56 So we'll laugh at all negatives And on high our anchor cast.

8. a. *Photogr.* A print made on specially prepared glass or other transparent substance by the direct action of light, in which the lights and shadows of nature are reversed, and from which positive prints are made.

1853 W. H. T. Photogr. Manip. (ed. 2) 14 Fifth operation. Fixing the negative. 1859 Jephson & Reeve Brittany 88 We were only making what were called negatives on glass. 1867 Brothers in G. F. Chambers Astron. 698 From the small negative a positive on glass must be made.

fig. 1892 Stevenson & L. Osbourne Wrecker x. 162 A negative of a street scene..rose in my memory with not a feature blurred.

attrib. 1875 Knight Dict. Mech. 1521/1 Negative-bath, the bath-holder..used to contain the nitrate of silver solution. 1884 Ibid. Suppl. 632/2 Negative Rack, a frame for holding glass negatives to drip. 1889 Anthony's Photogr. Bull. II. 24 A large negative closet off the studio.

b. A mould for, or reverse impression of, a piece of sculpture or the like. Cf. next, sense 11 a.

1911 A. Toft Modelling & Sculpture x. 195 The mould or negative is next coated with a preparation of plumbago or black-lead, and placed in a bath where the metal is deposited into it. 1947 J. C. Rich Materials & Methods Sculpture i. 18 The 'negative' is the term applied to the hollow containing form or mold into which the positive, temporarily plastic casting material is poured. Ibid. v. 95 If a plaster negative is fashioned over an earth-clay model, the original should not be too dry. 1961 J. Challinor Dict. Geol. 134/1 Negative, a fossil in the form of an impression. 1973 D. Cowley Working with Clay & Plaster 81 (caption) Plaster negative taken from a positive plaster cast.

c. A disc similar to a gramophone record but having ridges in place of grooves.

1918 H. Seymour Reproduction of Sound 17 In 1900 he applied the vacuous deposit system in electrolysis to the production of record negatives. 1931 A. Nadell Projecting Sound Pict. xiv. 240 This metal plate..constitutes a 'negative' with which any number of 'positive' records may be stamped. 1974 Encycl. Brit. Macropædia XVII. 52/1 Berliner did not, however, contemplate using this etched master as the record to be played; rather, a negative was made from the master by electroforming.

9. The negative plate or metal in a voltaic battery.

1884 Knight Dict. Mech. Suppl. 368 Negative depolarized by jet of steam. Ibid. 369 Negative rotated by a crank.

negative (ˈnɛgətɪv), *a.* Also 5 -yff, 6 -yfe, -yve. [ad. F. *negatif, -ive*, (13th c.), or late L. *negātīv-us*: see NEGATE *v.* and -IVE.]

I. †1. Of persons: Making denial of something. *Obs. rare.*

c1400 Beryn 2268 And he had mysseyd onys, or els I-seyd nay,..then he had been negatyff. Ibid. 2606 To ȝew that were negatyff, the lawe wold graunte anoon. 1611 Shaks. Wint. T. i. ii. 274 If thou wilt confesse, or else be impudently negatiue, To haue nor Eyes nor Eares nor Thought. 1736 Chandler Hist. Persec. 208 Negative hereticks are such, who being..convicted of some heresy before an Inquisitor, yet will not confess it.

2. a. Expressing, conveying, or implying negation or denial. ***negative flag*** (see quots.).

1509 Hawes Past. Pleas. xxxiv. (Percy Soc.) 110 By the comyn wytte to be affyrmatyve Or by decernynge to be negatyve. 1571 Golding Calvin on Ps. vii. 5 So must the negatyve woord (not) bee supplyed. 1579 Fulke Heskins' Parl. 89 Hee did..beate doune the proclaymers negatiue argumentes. 1649 Nicholas Papers (Camden) I. 146 There are two negative conclusions which seeme necessary. 1670 Clarendon Dial. Tracts (1727) 333, I long to see a good negative Catechism of religion. 1791 Burke App. Whigs Wks. VI. 186 Their negative declaration obliges me to have recourse to the books which contain positive doctrines. 1803 J. Marshall Const. Opin. (1839) 22 Affirmative words are often..negative of other objects than those affirmed. 1850 Grote Greece ii. lxviii. (1862) VI. 138 It is by Plato that the negative and indirect vein of Sokratês has been worked out. 1891 Ld. Coleridge in Law Times Rep. LXV. 581/1 The negative statement that the 6 Geo. 4, c. 129, is not now on this subject the governing statute. 1909 Daily Chron. 18 Aug. 7/5 If it is hoisted superior to the flag called the Negative flag, it signifies that the man is drowned. 1916 'Taffrail' Carry On! 24 If the 'Negative flag', white with five black crosses, had been displayed, he would have known that the worst had happened, and that a life had been lost. 1948 R. de Kerchove Internat. Maritime Dict. 487/1 Negative flag, a single-letter signal consisting of letter 'N' of the International Code of signals. Means 'No'.

b. *spec.* in *Logic*, of propositions, etc., or names.

1551 T. Wilson Logike (1580) 24 If one of the Propositions be particular, or negatiue, the conclusion is particular, or negatiue. 1628 T. Spencer Logick 92 In this Chapter..wee must handle negatiue contraries. 1651 Hobbes Leviath. i. iv. 16 Names, called Negative; which are notes to signifie that a word is not the name of the thing in question. 1690 Locke Hum. Und. ii. viii. §5 We have negative Names, which stand not directly for positive Ideas, but for their Absence, such as Insipid, Silence, Nihil, etc. 1725 Watts Logic iii. i, The Foundations of all negative Conclusions. 1846 Mill Logic i. ii. §6 Negative names are employed whenever we have occasion to speak collectively of all things other than some thing or class of things. 1870 Jevons Elem. Logic vii. 63 A negative proposition..asserts a difference or discrepancy.

3. a. Of commands, statutes, etc.: Prohibitory.

1526 Pilgr. Perf. (W. de W. 1531) 238 b, All the commaundementes of the seconde table, that be negatyue. 1596 Bacon Max. & Use Com. Law ii. (1635) 14 But the Statute of Mag. Char. Cap. ii. 5 is negative against it. a1711 Ken Divine Love Wks. (1838) 261 Keep my love watchful.., that in thy negative precepts I may continually resist evil. 1765 Blackstone Comm. I. i. 137 A few negative statutes, whereby abuses, perversions, or delays of justice..are restrained.

b. Expressing refusal to do something; refusing consent to a proposal or motion.

1535 Stewart Cron. Scot. II. 592 Malcolme..Wald nocht consent,..And gaif to him ane ansuer negatiue. 1576 Fleming Panopl. Epist. 194 They..yealded to his request, notwithstanding my negatiue voyce. 1621 T. Williamson tr. Goulart's Wise Vieillard 56 Hee gaue his negatiue voyce and crossed the treatie of a dishonourable peace. 1681 H. Nevile Plato Rediv. 125 But for this point of the Negative Vote, it is possible [etc.].

c. Able to impose a veto. Now *rare.*

1648–9 Eikon Bas. vi. (1662) 20 Denying me any power of a Negative voice as King. 1712 Addison Spect. No. 287 ¶5, I do not find that the Consuls had ever a Negative Voice in the passing of a Law. 1775 De Lolme Eng. Const. ii. xvii. (1784) 263 To make use, even once, of its negative voice.

d. quasi-*adv.* Negatively, on the negative side.

1868 Maidment Bk. Sc. Pasquils 238 This cherub..swore negative.., much to the astonishment of Fountainhall. 1897 Daily News 7 May 3/2 Twenty-five of the Senators voting negative are free silver advocates.

†4. Opposed (*to* a measure). *Obs. rare.*

1642 Sir E. Dering Sp. on Relig. xvi. 71, I am so fixed negative. Ibid. 88 That I may as negative to this bill, be poasted up [etc.].

II. 5. Characterized by the absence, instead of the presence, of distinguishing features; devoid of, or lacking in, distinctly positive attributes.

In very common use in the 19th century.

1565 T. Stapleton Fortr. Faith 103*, I will not labour to recite euery particular of their negatiue religion. 1642 in Clarendon Hist. Reb. v. §49 His discharge was but negative. 1647 Clarendon ibid. ii. §25 A man who..was thought to be made choice of only for his negative qualities. 1662 Stillingfl. Orig. Sacræ iii. i. §5 How ever positive we apprehend it, yet we alwaies apprehend it in a negative way. 1702 Eng. Theophrastus 249 No better than a negative traitor to his country. 1788 Priestley in Phil. Trans. LXXIX. 15 The positive evidence of actually finding a substance is always more conclusive than the negative one, of not finding it. 1801 Fuseli in Lect. Paint. ii. (1848) 383 He contented himself with a negative colour. 1838 W. Bell Dict. Law Scot. 769 The negative prescription..not only presumes the debt to have been extinguished [etc.]. 1873 Spencer Stud. Sociol. x. 259 These negative causes of dissatisfaction are joined with the positive cause indicated.

6. a. In *Algebra*, denoting quantities which are to be subtracted from other quantities, or which are taken as indicating a subtraction from zero; marked by the sign − .

1673 Kersey Algebra I. 269 A negative Root (which Cartesius calls a false Root) expresseth a Quantity whose Denomination is opposite to an affirmative, as −5 or −20. 1727–38 Chambers Cycl. s.v. Quantity, Negative or privative quantities are those less than nothing. 1753 Ibid., Supp. s.v., Negative powers arise from the division of any power of a quantity, by a greater power of the same quantity. 1768 Horsefall in Phil. Trans. LVIII. 101, $d + 9 = 1$ cannot be; because d would be negative. 1798 Hutton Course Math. (1807) II. 282 The fluxion of any negative integer power of a variable quantity. 1842 Gwilt Archit. §611 We immediately perceive that those powers are negative whose exponents are odd numbers. 1885 Watson & Burbury Math. The. Electr. & Magn. I. 25 Every possible spherical harmonic function of negative integral degree.

b. ***negative sign***, the sign − used to mark a negative quantity. Also applied to a sign used in the Sanskrit alphabet (see quot. 1851).

1704 J. HARRIS *Lex. Techn.* I, *Negative Quantities* in Algebra, are such as have before them the Negative Sign. **1743** EMERSON *Fluxions* 164 The negative Sign only shews that the Curvature increases. **1823** MITCHELL *Dict. Math. & Phys. Sci.*, *Negative index*, of a logarithm, are those which are affected with a negative sign. **1851** *Proc. Philol. Soc.* V. 86 When the word closes with a consonant, there is a peculiar negative sign to be affixed to the consonant to show that no vowel follows.

7. a. Applied to that form of electricity which is produced by friction upon resin, wax, gutta-percha or similar substances, as distinguished from that produced by rubbed glass, which is called *positive*.

1755 B. MARTIN *Mag. Arts & Sci.* 322 What they had observed of positive and negative Electricity. **1770** PRIESTLEY in *Phil. Trans.* LX. 194, I could not find that either positive or negative electricity was communicated to the insulated tube. **1860** G. PRESCOTT *Electr. Telegr.* 11 The one of the fluids we call positive, or vitreous electricity; the other, negative, or resinous. **1873** F. JENKIN *Electr. & Magn.* i. §8 It is found invariably that equal quantities of positive and negative electricity are produced.

transf. **1755** B. MARTIN *Mag. Arts & Sci.* 303 This positive and negative Doctrine of Electricity.

b. Characterized by the presence or production of negative electricity. ***negative booster***, a booster used to lower the potential of the station end of a negative feeder to below earth potential; ***negative feeder***, a wire which connects the rails forming the negative connection for an electric traction vehicle to the bus-bars at a substation.

1799 *Med. Jrnl.* I. 55 Electricity..produces this effect particularly by what is called the negative bath. **1837** WHEWELL *Hist. Induct. Sci.* (1857) III. 137 An alkali was separated on the negative plates. **1860** G. PRESCOTT *Electr. Telegr.* 22 These extremities are termed poles; the former the negative, and the latter the positive pole of the pile. **1873** F. JENKIN *Electr. & Magn.* xxii. §3 These currents may be either positive or negative; that is to say, they may be sent from the copper or zinc pole of the battery. **1890** *Proc. R. Soc.* XLVII. 543 How far the positive charges in the polarising layer and the negative charges projected away from the kathode are *alone* sufficient to account for the whole current, cannot be decided at present. **1902** Negative electron [see ELECTRON[2] 1 a]. **1909** P. DAWSON *Electr. Traction on Railways* xv. 475 The negative booster consists simply of a rotating machine driven at a constant speed by an independent motor. *Ibid.* 476 The booster is usually designed so that the E.M.F. produced in the armature is sufficient to cancel out the loss of voltage in the negative feeder. **1932** R. RAWLINSON in E. Molloy *Pract. Electr. Engin.* V. 1598/2 The negative booster is so connected as to reduce the station end of the negative feeder to below earth potential. **1933** *Discovery* Mar. 69/1 The negative electron, the massless unit charge of electricity, was isolated first in the Cavendish Laboratory by Sir J. J. Thomson in 1897. **1956** *Ann. Reg. 1955* 402 The bevatron, at Berkeley, made possible the discovery of a new atomic particle—the negative proton. **1974** *Encycl. Brit. Macropædia* VI. 666/1 The magnitude of the negative charge *e* was obviously of basic importance and a scale parameter for the whole of atomic physics.

c. Chemically opposed *to* something.

1882 *Rep. to Ho. Repr. Prec. Met. U.S.* 611 Iron is also negative to gold under this condition.

d. ***negative glow***, the luminous region in a discharge tube between the Crookes dark space and the Faraday dark space.

1890 *Proc. R. Soc.* XLVII. 557 This is the dark interval separating the positive part of the discharge from the negative glow. **1939** H. J. REICH *Theory & Applic. Electron Tubes* xi. 369 The brightness of the negative glow decreases toward the anode, and the glow gradually merges into another relatively dark region, the Faraday dark space. **1971** J. F. WAYMOUTH *Electr. Discharge Lamps* iv. 71 In the negative glow, the rate of ion production required to supply a cathode ion current of 10% of the total may be many times what it is in the positive column.

8. a. Reckoned in an opposite direction to the positive; falling on the other side of the point from which the positive is measured.

1802–12 BENTHAM *Ration. Judic. Evid.* (1827) IV. 61 Separated from argument, the value of such opinion will not simply be nothing, but negative. **1817** COLERIDGE *Biog. Lit.* (Bohn) 141 The subtraction will be the same, whether we call the capital negative debt, or the debt negative capital. **1831** BREWSTER *Optics* xvii. 147 The axis is called..in the second case a negative axis of double refraction. *c* **1865** J. WYLDE in *Circ. Sci.* I. 79/2 The optic axes are respectively positive and negative when the extraordinary ray is bent either to or from the geometrical axis of the crystal. **1893** SIR R. BALL *Story of Sun* 170 If the Sun's axis lie to the right.. then the position angle is regarded as negative.

b. Proceeding or tending in an opposite direction to that regarded as positive.

1831 BREWSTER *Optics* xxv. 215 The double refraction is negative in relation to the axes to which the doubly refracted ray is perpendicular. **1875** BENNETT & DYER tr. *Sachs' Bot.* 677 Both positive and negative heliotropism. **1879** *Cassell's Techn. Educ.* IV. 313/1 Spherical aberration of a negative character.

c. Misc. special collocations: ***negative capability*** (see quot. 1817); now also used (in the light of Keats's other observations on the nature of the creative artist) for EMPATHY; ***negative catalysis*** (Chem.) = INHIBITION 3 b; ***negative catalyst*** = INHIBITOR 2 c; ***negative eugenics***, an attempt to prevent the birth of children to persons considered unfit to be parents; cf. DYSGENIC *a.*; ***negative feedback***, feedback that tends to diminish or counteract the process giving rise to it; ***negative g*** or ***G***, (a force resulting from) the deceleration of a vehicle, esp. an aircraft or spacecraft; ***negative growth***, the cessation or reversal of growth, esp. in lower animals, in response to starvation or other unfavourable conditions; ***negative income tax***, a scheme whereby low-paid workers receive a government subsidy to raise their pay to subsistence level; also ***negative tax***; ***negative (phase) sequence*** (Electr. Engin.), a three-phase system in which the voltages or currents in each phase reach their maxima in the opposite order (i.e. red—blue—yellow) from the positive sequence; ***negative resistance***, (the property of) a device in which an increase in the potential difference between its terminals causes a drop in the current flowing through it; ***negative transfer***, habits or methods learned for one task which interfere with or transfer negatively to the learning of a subsequent task; cf. TRANSFER *sb.* 3, POSITIVE *a.* 8; ***negative transference***, the transfer or imputing to a doctor of feelings of hostility, or of resistance and constraint, that may be aroused in the patient through fear of giving expression to his repressed emotions; also, the transferring to a relationship of negative emotions which persist from a previous relationship or experience; cf. TRANSFERENCE 1, POSITIVE *a.* 8.

1817 KEATS *Let.* *c* 21 Dec. (1958) I. 193, I had not a dispute but a disquisition, with Dilke, on various subjects; several things dovetailed in my mind, & at once it struck me, what quality went to form a Man of Achievement especially in Literature & which Shakespeare possessed so enormously —I mean *Negative Capability*, that is when man is capable of being in uncertainties, Mysteries, doubts without any irritable reaching after fact & reason—Coleridge, for instance, would let go by a fine isolated verisimilitude caught from the Penetralium of mystery, from being incapable of remaining content with half knowledge. **1964** S. BARNET et al. *Dict. Literary Terms* 97 Negative capability is sometimes identified with empathy, sometimes with objectivity. **1975** *Studies in Eng. Lit.: Eng. Number* (Tokyo) 167 The poem is representative of the poet [*sc.* Wallace Stevens] in that it is a poem of 'Negative Capability', his basic mental attitude. **1904** *Jrnl. Chem. Soc.* LXXXVI. ii. 113 The simultaneous effect of a positive catalyst (copper sulphate) and a negative catalyst (mannitol or stannic chloride) has been studied, and the experiments support the view that negative catalysis consists in a counteracting of the effect of positive catalysis. **1940** GLASSTONE *Text-bk. Physical Chem.* xiii. 1121 Negative catalysis in gas reactions is probably also to be ascribed to the breaking of reaction chains. **1966** *McGraw-Hill Encycl. Sci. & Technol.* II. 546/2 Such substances, formerly called negative catalysts, are now known to be consumed in the process... Accordingly such materials are not true catalysts. **1968** M. M. JONES *Ligand Reactivity & Catalysis* i. 10 Negative catalysis resulting from the removal of catalytically active metals by a chelating agent, for example, the inhibition of hemoglobin by carbon monoxide. **1908** F. GALTON in *Nature* 22 Oct. 645/2 Little or nothing will be said relating to what has been well termed by Dr. Saleeby 'negative' eugenics, namely,..hindering the marriages and the production of offspring by the exceptionally unfit. **1914** C. W. SALEEBY *Progress Eugenics* i. 20 It is no less necessary to discourage parenthood among defective individuals, and to this, with Galton's approval, I gave the name of negative eugenics, calling his own scheme positive eugenics. **1931** J. S. HUXLEY *What dare I Think?* iii. 93 Negative eugenics is concerned with preventing degeneration. **1974** J. R. BAKER *Race* iv. 57 He [*sc.* Madison Grant] was harsh in his schemes for negative eugenics... He favoured the forcible sterilization of criminals, diseased and insane persons, and 'worthless race-types', and the enactment of laws against race-mixture. **1934** H. S. BLACK in *Bell Syst. Techn. Jrnl.* XIII. 5, $1/(1-\mu\beta)$ will be used as a quantitative measure of the effect of feedback and the feedback referred to as positive feedback or negative feedback according as the absolute value of $1/(1-\mu\beta)$ is greater or less than unity. Positive feedback increases the gain of the amplifier; negative feedback reduces it. **1956** *Science* 11 May 848/1 (*heading*) Evidence for a negative-feedback mechanism in the biosynthesis of isoleucine. **1966** 'A. HALL' *9th Directive* x. 97, I put in fifty or sixty shots,.. gradually allowing the negative feedback data to correct the aim. **1967** M. ARGYLE *Psychol. Interpersonal Behaviour* iii. 62 Such unstable sequences are known as cases of 'positive feedback' (unstable vicious circles) and can be contrasted with self-correcting 'negative feedback', which is also a common feature of social performance. **1952** R. L. CHRISTY in White & Benson *Physics & Med. Upper Atmosphere* 510 Certain unusual attitudes of the aircraft in which irregular accelerations, including negative g, are encountered. **1955** *Aeroplane* 25 Nov. 794/1 The need for a negative-g stressing case for civil aircraft was questioned. **1962** J. GLENN in *Into Orbit* 71 We also made runs to simulate the forces of deceleration, or negative Gs. **1932** J. S. HUXLEY *Probl. Relative Growth* iii. 87 Here [*sc.* in the shore crab Ocypoda] the low point of growth, or 'negative growth-centre', is also in the merus. **1957** G. E. HUTCHINSON *Treat. Limnol.* I. iii. 217 The life of such lower organisms as are capable of negative growth may be greatly prolonged. **1964** A. E. NEEDHAM *Growth Process in Animals* iii. 29 In the lower animals negative growth or degrowth is commonly reversible, sometimes to a remarkable degree. It is a normal response to starvation and to some other conditions. **1967** *Yale Law Jrnl.* Nov. 1 (*title*) Is a negative income tax practical? **1969** *Daily Tel.* 17 Jan. 27/1 The use of 'negative income tax', by which low-wage earners receive a PAYE handout. **1973** *Guardian* 30 Mar. 6/4 The Government's proposed tax credit system—the 'negative income tax' proposed in a Green Paper last year. **1930** M. G. MALTI *Electr. Circuit Analysis* xv. 244 We shall call a negative phase sequence such a sequence of the phases that phase 1 leads phase 3 by 120° and leads phase 2 by 240°. **1896** FRITH & RODGERS in *Phil. Mag.* XLII. 410 [Prof. Ayrton concluded that if an attempt were made to measure the resistance of the arc by altering the P.D. between the carbons and finding the corresponding alteration of current produced, the resistance found by taking this ratio must be *negative*.] *Ibid.*, All these experiments..lead to the conclusion that the arc has a *negative* resistance. **1932** W. L. EVERITT *Communication Engin.* xviii. 479 A negative resistance can be used in a circuit to counteract the effect of positive resistance and so cause a combination of inductance and capacitance to oscillate. **1942** C. L. AMICK *Fluorescent Lighting Manual* ii. 21 The 'negative-resistance' characteristic of fluorescent lamps means that the voltage drop across the lamp decreases as the arc current goes up. **1974** G. J. ANGERBAUER *Electronics for Mod. Communications* xvi. 319 This negative-resistance effect depends upon secondary emission from the plate. **1973** J. R. NEUENSWANDER *Mod. Power Syst.* ix. 175 The revolving field..rotates *with* the rotor while the negative-sequence armature currents..set up a revolving field rotating at the same speed but in opposite direction to the rotor. **1963** M. S. GORDON *Econ. Welfare Policies* vi. 117 A few economists, appalled at the piecemeal character of our approach to welfare policies, have espoused the so-called 'negative tax' proposal. **1921** F. N. FREEMAN *Exper. Educ.* ii. 47 There is strong negative transfer from Set 2 to Set 3. **1933** M. VITELES *Industr. Psychol.* III. xx. 427 The study of transfer effect has indicated that under certain conditions the practice of similar tasks may induce a negative transfer or interference with the acquisition of skill. **1938** R. S. WOODWORTH *Exper. Psychol.* viii. 176 When an act is carried over but impedes the learning of a second act we obviously have positive transfer and a negative transfer effect. **1950** O. MOWRER *Learning Theory & Personality Dynamics* vii. 193 If 'reinforcement' learning were alone operative, the initial 'mistraining' given to the experimental-group subjects should have produced negative transfer. **1966** J. T. & K. W. SPENCE in C. D. Spielberger *Anxiety & Behavior* 303 An investigation..that involved a type of negative transfer design. **1916** C. E. LONG tr. *Jung's Coll. Papers Analytical Psychol.* ix. 270 If it is a 'negative' transference, you can see nothing but violent resistances which sometimes veil themselves in seemingly critical or sceptical dress. **1924** J. RIVIERE et al. tr. *Freud's Coll. Papers* II. xxviii. 319 One is forced to distinguish 'positive' transference from 'negative' transference, the transference of affectionate feeling from that of hostile feeling and to deal separately with the two varieties of the transference to the physician. **1954** R. W. PICKFORD *Analysis of Obsessional* i. 20 A technique for manipulating the positive and negative transferences to the patient's advantage. **1960** L. PINCUS *Marriage* ii. 91 The distress, pain and aggression of a negative transference. **1964** ZALEZNIK & MOMENT *Dynamics Interpersonal Behavior* viii. 268 The negative transference reactions where the individual experiences hatred toward a person in the present because of a past relationship. **1968** A. J. MANDELL in J. Marmor *Mod. Psychoanal.* xi. 283 Side reactions may begin to take the place of verbalized negative transference.

9. a. ***negative crystal***, (*a*) a crystal in which the index of refraction is greater for the ordinary than the extraordinary ray; (*b*) a crystalliform cavity in a mineral mass.

1831 BREWSTER *Optics* xxii. 196 Those produced by the positive crystals..though to the eye they differ in no respect from those of negative crystals, yet they possess different properties. **1882** GEIKIE *Text-bk. Geol.* 96 Such a space defined by crystallographic contours is a negative crystal.

b. ***negative eye-piece***: (see quot. 1867).

1831 BREWSTER *Optics* xliii. 361 This eyepiece is called the negative eyepiece. **1867** G. F. CHAMBERS *Astron.* 617 A negative eye-piece consists..of 2 plano-convex lenses, the convex sides of both being..turned towards the object-glass. **1875** KNIGHT *Dict. Mech.* 1521/1 The Huyghenian, or negative eye-piece..is the usual combination of lenses at the eye-end of a telescope or microscope.

10. a. *Photogr.* Characterized by a reversal of the lights and shadows of the actual object, scene, etc.

1840 HERSCHEL in *Proc. Roy. Soc.* IV. 206 In order to avoid circumlocution the author employs the terms positive and negative to express respectively pictures in which the lights and shades are the same as in nature..and in which they are opposite. **1841** FOX TALBOT *Spec. Patent* No. 8842. 5 The portrait..is a negative one, and from this a positive copy may be obtained. **1853** *Fam. Herald* 3 Dec. 510/1 Having obtained negative pictures on both glass and paper. **1867** BROTHERS in G. F. Chambers *Astron.* 698 The negative or positive copy having been placed the wrong way.

fig. **1858** O. W. HOLMES *Aut. Breakf.-t.* xi. 109 Books are the negative pictures of thought.

b. ***negative after-image***, an after-image of complementary colour or brightness to that of the original impression.

1899 L. HILL *Man. Human Physiol.* xxxv. 439 Look steadfastly at a piece of white paper placed on a sheet of black paper, and then look up at a dark wall. You will now see a black spot on a whitish ground. This is a negative after-image... Look steadfastly now at a piece of red paper; a negative after-image appears on looking at the ceiling. This image will not be red, but of the complementary colour greenish blue. **1967** D. A. SCHREUDER in J. B. de Boer *Public Lighting* iv. 167 Complete adaptation [to the luminance of the field of vision] requires a certain length of time. The slowest, and hence in practice the most important process is the disappearance of the negative after-images.

11. a. Of, pertaining to, or designating a mould or reverse impression. Cf. NEGATIVE *sb.* 8 b.

1911 G. H. WILSON *Man. Dental Prosthetics* ii. 55 An impression is a negative likeness of an object or part taken in a plastic material, from which a cast or positive likeness may be produced. **1939** M. HOFFMAN *Sculpture Inside & Out* xii. 214 While working, it is useful to squeeze the wax often against the negative mold, thereby verifying just what the effect will be. **1940** J. OSBORNE *Dental Mech.* i. 1 The technique necessary for the accurate construction of a model, or positive likeness of the patient's mouth, from an impression or negative likeness. **1947** J. C. RICH *Materials & Methods Sculpture* v. 90 Negative molds are of two varieties: those that are flexible and those that are rigid. *Ibid.*

96 Agar-base negative mixtures are a recent casting development. *Ibid.* 122 Wax is rarely used as a negative material in sculpture. **1966** D. Z. MEILACH *Creating with Plaster* iv. 58/2 Grease the negative mold very well with a separating medium. **1975** *N.Y. Times* 29 Nov. 19/2 The work, unusual for a cast bronze in that it has a negative impression on the back corresponding to the subject on the front, was apparently designed that way so castings could easily be made from it.

b. Having the character of a negative (NEGATIVE *sb.* 8 c).

1949 FRAYNE & WOLFE *Elem. Sound Recording* xiv. 264 A negative matrix or 'stamper' must be made from the original record. **1974** *Encycl. Brit. Macropædia* XVII. 54/1 To make copies of the recording, dies must be made the surface of which is a negative replica of the master-record surface.

12. *Theol.* = APOPHATIC *a.*

1956, 1961 [see APOPHATIC *a.*]. **1964** C. S. LEWIS *Discarded Image* iv. 70 It is the 'negative Theology' of those who take in a more rigid sense, and emphasise more persistently than others, the incomprehensibility of God.

III. 13. Comb.: **negative-going**, increasing in magnitude in the direction of negative polarity; becoming less positive or more negative; **negative-positive** *a.*, pertaining to or designating a photographic process, device, etc., employing or producing both negative and positive film, or employing negative film to produce a positive image, or vice versa.

1957 Negative-going [see *positive-going* adj. s.v. POSITIVE *a.* 16]. **1959** J. M. PETTIT *Electronic Switching* v. 136 The plate waveforms in Fig. 5–15 are square waves, except for the negative-going spikes and the exponential rise. **1969** J. J. SPARKES *Transistor Switching* v. 121 The logic inputs.. predetermine the direction the circuit will tend to switch next time a negative-going voltage step (from *ECC* to zero) is applied to the pulse inputs. **1936** C. E. K. MEES *Photogr.* 212/1 Negative-positive process, cine film. **1938** G. H. Sewell *Amateur Film-Making* ii. 12 The 'negative-positive' method consists of recording the negative image on one piece of film, and 'printing off' the positive image on to another piece of material in the manner described above. **1958** *Newnes Compl. Amat. Photogr.* 3 The next step [after daguerreotype], technically, was the development by Fox Talbot of a negative-positive process... Light-sensitive paper was the negative, reversed on to a second sheet of sensitised paper for the positive. *Ibid.* v. 85 Negative-positive films are designed to produce colour negatives, from which colour prints can be made. **1967** E. CHAMBERS *Photolitho-Offset* x. 145 The line positive is made on 'lith' film from the negative-positive combination.

negative ('nɛgətɪv), *v.* [f. prec.]

1. *trans.* **a.** *U.S.* To reject (a person proposed for some office).

1706 [see *negatived* below]. **1720** S. SEWALL *Diary* 26 May, The Govr. consented to the Choice of the Councillours, having Negativ'd Col. Byfield and Dr. Clarke. **1760** T. HUTCHINSON *Hist. Mass.* i. (1765) 10 Disputes.. caused him to insist upon his right of negativing the speaker. **1876** BANCROFT *Hist. U.S.* IV. xxv. 6 Negativing six of the ablest 'friends of the people' in the board.

b. *U.S.* To veto (a bill, law, etc.).

1749 *Col. Rec. Connect.* (1876) IX. 453 It would.. invest the Governor.. with a power to negative all acts that should be passed in our Assembly. **1834** D. WEBSTER *Sp. in Senate* 18 Mar. 12 We passed a bill for such a recharter, through both Houses, two years ago, but it was negatived by the President. **1876** BANCROFT *Hist. U.S.* II. III. i. 18 (Funk), Madison struggled to confer on the national legislature the right to negative at its discretion any state law whatever.

2. To reject, set aside (a proposal, suggestion, motion, etc.); to refuse to accept or entertain.

1778 EARL MALMESBURY *Diaries & Corr.* I. 194 Having.. obtained.. the outlines of a treaty, the negativing it.. would not carry with it [etc.]. **1812** *Examiner* 11 May 297/1 The Resolutions.. were negatived without a division. **1861** MRS. H. WOOD *East Lynne* I. ix. 120 Something was said about a fly, but Miss Carlyle negatived it. **1879** E. K. BATES *Egypt. Bonds* I. vii. 140 O'Grady negatives the idea so decidedly that there is no appeal.

b. To refuse to countenance (a claim, etc.).

1788 J. POWELL *Devises* (1827) II. 89 Claim of the heir negatived in Noel *v.* Lord Henley. **1833** COLERIDGE *Table-t.* 16 Aug., Taxation.. implies compact, and negatives any right to plunder.

3. To disprove; to show to be false.

1790 PALEY *Horæ Paul.* i. 6 By ancient testimony.. they are negatived and excluded. **1836–41** BRANDE *Chem.* (ed. 5) 158 The inference.. is negatived, in regard to mercury at least, by substituting that metal for the cold water. **1853** KANE *Grinnell Exp.* xlii. (1856) 381 All our reasonings seemed to be negatived by the results. **1885** *Law Times Rep.* LII. 625/1 A plaintiff.. must also negative contributory negligence in himself.

b. To deny, contradict.

1812 *Examiner* 7 Sept. 570/2 An affidavit.. negativing the keeping.. any horse.. by Mr. Weddall. **1884** *Law Times Rep.* L. 177/2 An affidavit categorically negativing the statements in the libel.

4. To render ineffective, neutralize.

1837 MISS PARDOE *City of Sultan* (1855) 225 The next eruption may lay waste his lands, and negative his labour. **1882** *Daily Tel.* 16 Sept. (Cassell), The wash.. was happily negatived by the inert hull of the.. barge.

5. To take a negative photograph of. *nonce-use.*

1894 SALA *London up to Date* ii. 17, I doubt whether any male creature.. would care much about being focussed, negatived, and positived in that apparel.

Hence **'negatived** *ppl. a.*, **'negativing** *vbl. sb.* and *ppl. a.*

1706 S. SEWALL *Diary* 6 June, Instead of the Negativ'd were chosen B. Brown [etc.]. **1776** in F. Chase *Hist. Dartmouth Coll.* (1891) I. 657 A negativing body over those that form the laws. **1777** MME. D'ARBLAY *Early Diary* (1889) II. 194 He had persisted.. I could never have consented, however pained by perpetual negativing. **1809** W. IRVING *Knickerb.* (1861) 256 Your weighty men, though slow to devise, being always great at 'negativing'. **1895** ZANGWILL *Master* 430 He saw her as in her later guise, stern, sorrowful, negativing.

negatively ('nɛgətɪvlɪ), *adv.* [f. NEGATIVE *a.* + -LY².] In a negative manner.

1. By way of negation or denial; in the negative; on the negative side.

c **1559** R. HALL *Life Fisher* in *F.'s Wks.* (E.E.T.S.) II. p. lxiii, Being againe negatively answered by the counsell of the queenes side, all seemed to rest vpon proof. **1570** BILLINGSLEY *Euclid* I. vii. 17 The mathematicall artes.. for the most part vse to conclude affirmatiuely, and not negatiuely. **1620** VENNER *Via Recta* iii. 46 Now to the question. I answer negatiuely. **1642** FULLER *Holy & Prof. St.* III. xvii. 195 We will describe Contentment first negatively. **1674** tr. *Scheffer's Lapland* vi. 15 Negatively we may pass sentence and conclude they were not Swedes. **1749** FIELDING *Tom Jones* Ded., Negatively, at least, I may be allowed to say [etc.]. **1794** BURKE *Sp. agst. W. Hastings* Wks. XV. 420 He has told you here indeed negatively, that he did not know [etc.]. **1812** LD. ELLENBOROUGH in *Examiner* 28 Dec. 832/2 The annuity did not appear, negatively, in the Prince's household accounts. **1845** STODDART *Gram.* in *Encycl. Metrop.* I. 169/1 It is.. negatively asserted that virtue cannot be hurt. **1866** ROGERS *Agric. & Prices* I. iv. 84, I can confirm this statement negatively, for I have seen no trace of personal servitude in the numerous accounts.

b. In a manner indicating refusal.

1804 EUGENIA DE ACTON *Tale without Title* II. 166 Telling her she looked so negatively at that period, that he would not then attend to her decision.

†**2.** With incapacity of being the opposite. *Obs.*

1622 R. HARRIS *God's Goodness* 17 Preserving or conserving Mercy in the first sense is Negatiuely endlesse, that is, vncapable of end. **1670** R. COKE *Disc. Trade* Ded., A man negatively blind, cannot be made to perceive things which are only visible.

3. With negative electricity.

1747 FRANKLIN *Wks.* (1840) V. 186 Hence have arisen some new terms among us; we say B is electrized positively; A, negatively. **1787** CAVALLO in *Phil. Trans.* LXXVIII. 14 This plate A being now electrified negatively. **1833** *Penny Cycl.* I. 412/1 When mercury is negatively electrified in a solution of ammonia. **1849** NOAD *Electricity* (ed. 3) 133 The phial.. would.. be charged negatively. **1881** MAXWELL *Electr. & Magn.* I. 48 A negatively electrified particle.

4. In a negative manner or direction.

1789 WARING in *Phil. Trans.* LXXIX. 175 The preceding co-efficients.. are to be taken negatively or affirmatively, as *s* is an even or an odd number. **1832** MACGILLIVRAY *Trav. & Res. Humboldt* ii. 37 The visibility of mountains which are only negatively perceived. **1862** SIR B. BRODIE *Psychol. Inq.* II. iii. 95 The opium-taker is only negatively mischievous to society. **1876** PREECE & SIVEWRIGHT *Telegr.* 41 The N poles will all be 'negatively rotated', or moved to the right.

'negativeness. [f. as prec. + -NESS.] The fact or quality of being negative; negativity.

1827 HARE *Guesses* (1859) 314 Self-conceit.. delights in negativeness, far more than in anything positive and real. **1876** GEO. ELIOT *Dan. Der.* i, There was a certain uniform negativeness of expression which had the effect of a mask.

negativism ('nɛgətɪvɪz(ə)m). [f. as prec. + -ISM.]

1. The doctrines of a negationist; doctrine characterized by denial.

1824 in *Mem. F. Perthes* (1856) II. xx. 295 The superlative of positivism is a bedlamite: of negativism a cipher. **1865** *Athenæum* No. 1949. 312/3 The negativism which Comte calls positivism. **1872** MORLEY *Voltaire* 208 The inundation of Europe by the literature of negativism and repudiation.

2. *Psychol.* Resistance to attempts to impose a change of activity or posture, characteristic of various neuropsychiatric disorders.

1892 D. H. TUKE *Dict. Psychol. Med.* II. 724/2 As soon as we attempt to produce passive movements of any part of the patient's body, we meet almost always with a powerful resistance; the groups of muscles antagonistic to the attempted movement commence to contract energetically—this has been termed the symptom of negativism. **1902** A. R. DEFENDORF *Clin. Psychiatry* 63 Negativism consists in the reaction to stimuli which are [*sic*] the reverse of the normal reaction. **1916** A. A. BRILL tr. *Freud's Wit & its Relation to Unconscious* III. vi. 278 This.. behavior of antagonistic relationships is probably not without value for the understanding of the symptom of negativism in neurotics and in the insane. **1947** G. MURPHY *Personality* II. ix. 218 Negativism appears.. at *any* period in which the external interference is insufficient to redirect behavior but is sufficient to necessitate an extra effort in continuing one's own activities. **1969** *Sci. Jrnl.* June 72/2 The patient continued to maintain his negativism and said 'I don't know'. **1971** *Publishers' Weekly* 30 Aug. 209/3 Solutions to the problems of fear, tension, guilt, loneliness, and negativism.

'negativist. [-IST.] = NEGATIONIST. Also *attrib.* or as *adj.*

1873 L. STEPHEN *Ess. Freethinking* 190 A positivist, or a negativist, or a materialist. *a* **1876** M. COLLINS *Th. in Garden* (1880) I. 271 The atheists and negativists of the day fondly fancy.. they would produce a perfect civilisation. **1927** J. S. HUXLEY *Relig. without Revelation* i. 52 They have .. rejected the whole ground of divinity.., and so been forced into a negativist attitude, compelled to satisfy their natural and normal religious needs in other ways and other spheres. **1958** W. STARK *Sociol. of Knowl.* 317 The main representatives of this doctrine which.. we wish to label the *negativist* theory, are.. Nietzsche and.. Pareto.

negativistic (ˌnɛgətɪ'vɪstɪk), *a.* [f. NEGATIV(ISM + -ISTIC.] Of, pertaining to, or characterized by negativism.

1902 A. R. DEFENDORF *Clin. Psychiatry* 64 The negativistic patient shows great equanimity, he seldom defends himself.. but merely resists. **1916** C. E. LONG tr. *Jung's Coll. Papers Analytical Psychol.* vi. 200 Disposing causes of negativistic phenomena are: the *ambitendency* by which every impulse is accompanied by its opposite. **1930** E. & F. JENSEN tr. *Adler's Educ. Children* xii. 213 If an adolescent shows himself very negativistic in regard to the other sex, we will find, if we trace back his life, that he was probably a fighting child. **1957** M. MILLAR *Soft Talkers* 186, I do hope your negativistic attitude towards me personally won't interfere with your better judgement. **1970** H. MCLEAVE *Question of Negligence* (1973) x. 84 The negativistic attitude of Fairchild, the ministry sneak with the almost psychotic habit of saying no to everything.

negativity (nɛgə'tɪvɪtɪ). [f. as NEGATIVE *a.* + -ITY.] The fact or quality of being negative.

1854 GEO. ELIOT tr. *Feuerbach's Essence Christianity* ii. 42 It is true that thus, negativity, as the speculative philosophers express themselves—*nothing* is the cause of the world. **1860** in WORCESTER (citing *Eclectic Review*). **1865** GROTE *Plato* I. i. 31 The negativity or destructive interference of the universal process. **1882** *Nature* 12 Jan. 258 Sudden negativity of under surface. **1899** J. CAIRD *Fundam. Ideas Chr.* II. ix. 13 That universal negativity or nothingness which pertains to all finite agents alike. **1953** R. LEHMANN *Echoing Grove* 41 Had decided to my own satisfaction what it meant, in psychological terms: not tension, not active boredom—simply negativity. **1956** D. GASCOYNE *Night Thoughts* 17 The Tyrant Negativity has usurped power. **1975** *Times* 24 Oct. 3/3 Rabies virus was not found in a man who died of the disease after intensive vaccine treatment... 'The negativity of the finding.. was perhaps the light at the end of the tunnel.'

negativo-, combining form of NEGATIVE *a.*, in ***negativo-affirmative, -positive.***

1726 COLSON in *Phil. Trans.* XXXIV. 162 Common Numbers may be reduced to negativo-affirmative Numbers a great variety of Ways. **1899** *Month* Dec. 614 We get the idea by a negativo-positive process: or, to speak more exactly, the idea is a negativo-positive one.

negaton ('nɛgətɒn). *Physics.* [f. NEGAT(IVE *a.* + -ON¹.] = NEGATRON 2.

1928 H. D. HUBBARD *Explanatory Key to Periodic Chart of Atoms* 20 The positive atom of electricity, the 'proton' is 1845 times heavier than the negative. (Since 'electron' is ambiguous, the term 'positon' is suggested as more explicit, and 'negaton' would avoid ambiguity as the corresponding name for the negative electron.) **1938** *Encycl. Brit. Bk. of Year* 404/1 The prediction of the possibility under certain conditions of the materialization of radiation quanta into a positon and a negaton. **1955** O. KLEIN in W. Pauli *Niels Bohr* 115 Assuming.. that there are no negaton-positon interaction terms. **1955** R. D. EVANS *Atomic Nucleus* xviii. 569 The Sixth General Assembly of the International Union of Pure and Applied Physics (Amsterdam, July 8 to 10, 1948) unanimously recommended the use of the terms *positon* and *negaton* as a means of distinguishing between positive and negative electrons. However, common usage, as seen in the periodical literature, still tends to retain the 'r'.

negator (nɪ'geɪtə(r)). [a. L. *negātor*, agent-n. f. *negāre*: see NEGATE *v.*]

1. One who denies; *spec.* a member of a sect of Russian anarchists.

1805 in *Spirit Pub. Jrnls.* VIII. 241 The grand inflictor and grand negator—one who in doing or denying stands nearly unmatched. **1888** *Science* XI. 178 One such [sect] calls itself the 'Negators', and its members keep themselves aloof from all men.

2. A word expressing negation; = NEGATIVE *sb.* 2.

1961 R. B. LONG *Sentence & its Parts* iv. 100 *Not* is by no means the only adjunct with negator force... Negative subjects and negative complements can serve as negators. **1966** G. N. LEECH *Eng. in Advertising* xviii. 159 The universal negators *no*, *never*, etc. **1973** *Archivum Linguisticum* IV. 14 Of these auxiliaries, only one negator /no/ can occur independently. **1974** L. TODD *Pidgins & Creoles* iii. 34 In the 1830 examples the negator occurs in the same position as in the pidgins and creoles we have examined.

3. See NEGATER.

negatory ('nɛgətərɪ), *a.* Also 6 7 -orie. [ad. F. *négatoire* or late L. *negātōri-us*: see NEGATE *v.* and -ORY.] Of the nature of negation.

1580 HOLLYBAND *Treas. Fr. Tong. Negatoire, vne action negatoire*, a negatorie action. **1611** COTGR., *Negatoire*, negatorie, inficiatorie, negatiue, denying. [Hence in Blount, Phillips, and Bailey.] **1827** CARLYLE *Germ. Rom.* III. 86, I on the morrow must overcloud her arrival.. by my negatory intelligence. **1850** THACKERAY *Let.* in *Westm. Gaz.* (1902) 10 July 4/3 A negatory nod of his honest.. old head. **1877** MORLEY *Crit. Misc.* Ser. II. 362 Mere aggressive and negatory criticism.

negatron ('nɛgətrɒn). [f. NEGA(TIVE *a.* + -TRON.] **1.** *Electronics.* A kind of valve that exhibits negative resistance, having two anodes (one either side of the cathode) and a control electrode between the cathode and one of the anodes.

1919 J. SCOTT-TAGGART *Brit. Pat. 166,260* 17 Sept., The present invention relates to an electron discharge device, hereinafter to be termed a negatron, which is capable of being used as a negative resistance. **1964** J. GROSZKOWSKI *Frequency of Self-Oscillations* iii. 70 The negatron belongs to the voltage-controlled negative resistors.

2. *Physics.* The ordinary, i.e. negatively charged, electron (as distinct from the positron). Cf. NEGATON.

1934 C. D. ANDERSON et al. in *Physical Rev.* XLV. 353/1 To remove the ambiguity in the definition of the term 'electron'..the terms 'negatron' and 'positron' are here used. **1955** R. D. EVANS *Atomic Nucleus* xviii. 576 Consider the collision of an incident negatron..with an atomic electron. **1961** G. R. CHOPPIN *Exper. Nucl. Chem.* vii. 100 When the gamma energy is greater than 1·02 MeV, a certain probability exists for the creation of a negatron..and a positron. **1971** STERN & LEWIS *X-Rays* iii. 47 Triplet production can occur when the photon interacts with an electron and not with a nucleus. Three particles result, the original electron as well as the positron and negatron pair.

negatyfe, etc., obs. forms of NEGATIVE.

†**nege**, *v. Obs. rare*$^{-1}$. [ad. L. *negāre*: cf. *renege*, RENEGUE *v.*] *trans.* To deny.

1624 BP. MOUNTAGU *Gagg* 147 False Christians..That neged as necessary unto salvation, workes, and observing of the law.

negebure, obs. form of NEIGHBOUR.

negentropy (nɛ'gɛntrəpɪ). [f. NEG(ATIVE *a.* + ENTROPY.] Negative entropy, as a measure of order or information.

1950 L. BRILLOUIN in *Amer. Scientist* XXXVIII. 594/1 Every observation in the laboratory..is made at the expense of a certain amount of negative entropy (abbreviation: negentropy), taken away from the surroundings. **1956** —— *Sci. & Information Theory* p. xii, We prove that information must be considered as a negative term in the entropy of a system; in short, information is negentropy. *Ibid.* ix. 117 An isolated system contains negentropy if it reveals a possibility for doing mechanical or electrical work. **1958** *Archivum Linguisticum* X. 137 The calculation of redundancy, by the method taken over from information theory, requires the three terms 'negentropy', 'relative negentropy' and redundancy. **1966** S. BEER *Decision & Control* ix. 188 Hence the energy transferred through the system is exactly balanced by the information flowing the opposite way; to speak of a change in entropy is *ipso facto* to speak of an equivalent change in negentropy. **1970** H. C. SHANDS *Semiotic Approaches to Psychiatry* xxiii. 386 Knowing systems lose information as physical systems gain entropy. The continuous input of 'negentropy'..is required to maintain balance in either context. **1971** *Sci. Amer.* Sept. 183/2 Taking commonly accepted average values for the temperatures of the sun and the earth, the 1·6 × 10^{15} megawatt-hours of energy radiated to outer space carries with it the capability for an entropy decrease, or 'negentropy flux', of 3·2 × 10^{22} joules per degree K. per year, or 10^{38} bits per second.

neger ('ni:gə(r)). Now *north. dial.* and *Sc.* Forms: 6–7 (9) **neager**, 6 (9) **neeger**, 7 **negar**, 7, 9 **negre**, 9 **negur**, 7– **neger**. [ad. F. *nègre*, ad. Sp. *negro* NEGRO. So Du., G., Da., Sw. *neger*.]

1. A Negro, esp. in disparaging use.

1587 *MS. Robert Leng* (Brit. Mus.), There were also in her 400 neegers, whome they had taken to make slaves. **1599** MINSHEU s.v. *Caçuéla*, Vpon Moores or Neagers, and on other malefactors. **1624** CAPT. SMITH *Virginia* IV. 126 A dutch man of warre that sold vs twenty Negars. **1686** in *Annals of Albany* (1850) II. 91 The court have ordered ye said neger Hercules to be whipt throw ye towne. **1729** GAY *Polly* III. Wks. (1772) 197, I don't see..why we should be commanded by a Neger. **1794** MRS. A. M. BENNETT *Ellen* I. 17 She was sure the strangers were negers. **1829** B. HALL *Trav. N. Amer.* II. 77 Entering into social intercourse with a 'negur.'

attrib. and *Comb.* **1657** R. LIGON *Barbadoes* 51 The outward medicine is a thing they call Negre-oyle, and 'tis made in Barbary. **1683** TRYON *Way to Health* 461 Sporting themselves with negre nosed Dogs. **1689** *Lond. Gaz.* No. 2501/4 A Neager Boy, about 14 years old. **1831** TRELAWNY *Adv. Younger Son* II. 96 As to poor negur man, I saw his carcase to-day.

2. (See quot.)

1848 *Jrnl. R. Agric. Soc.* IX. II. 565 These aphides have their enemies in the..ladybird, and its progeny the neger.

Hence †'**negerous** *a.*, barbarous. '**negery** [ad. Du. *negerij*], a Negro village or compound.

1609 HEYWOOD *Brit. Troy* VII. lxxix, Which to prevent the Negerous Lady takes The young Absyrtes. **1814** W. BROWN *Hist. Propag. Chr.* App. (1823) 708, In some of the negerys the people had still retained their idols.

negh, obs. form of EYE *sb.*

negh, neȝ, obs. forms of NIGH *a.* and *adv.*

negh(e, obs. forms of NIGH *v.*

neghe, obs. form of NINE.

negh(e)bur, obs. forms of NEIGHBOUR.

neghnesse, obs. form of NIGHNESS.

neght, obs. form of NIGHT.

neȝt: see NET *a.*²

negh(t)som: see NIGHSOME *a. Obs.*

neglect (nɪ'glɛkt), *sb.* [ad. L. *neglect-us* (rare), f. the ppl. stem *neglect-*: see next.]

1. The fact of disregarding, slighting, or paying no attention to, a person, etc.; the fact or condition of being treated in this way; †an instance of this, a slight.

1588 SHAKS. *L.L.L.* III. 204 It is a plague That Cupid will impose for my neglect Of his almighty..might. **1600** —— *A.Y.L.* v. iv. 188 The Duke hath put on a Religious life, And throwne into neglect the pompous Court. **1665** BOYLE *Occas. Refl.* 179 Unable to make him think himself happy, as long as he could not neglect a Captives neglect of him. **1670** R. MONTAGU in *Buccleuch MSS.* (Hist. MSS. Comm.) I. 466 He complained [of]..several neglects on M[onsieu]r['s] part towards him. **1711** PRIOR *Henry & Emma* 616 Rescue my poor remains from vile neglect. **1797** BURKE *Corr.* (1844) IV. 435 Neglect, contumely, and insult, were never the ways of keeping friends.

b. Disregard *of*, or with respect to, something; †indifference.

1597 HOOKER *Eccl. Pol.* v. lvii. §1 How easily neglect and careless regard of so heauenly mysteries may follow. **1709** STEELE *Tatler* No. 51 ⁋1 Orlando..also had a Neglect whether Things became him or not. *a* **1715** BURNET *Own Time* III. (1724) I. 512 Tho' the Duke sent the offer of pardon to them..it was refused with great neglect. **1862** SPENCER *First Princ.* I. iv. §26 (1875) 90 Assuming that consciousness contains nothing but limits and conditions; to the entire neglect of that which is limited and conditioned.

2. Want of attention to what ought to be done; the fact of leaving something undone or unattended to; negligence. Also const *of*.

1591 SHAKS. *Two Gent.* v. iv. 90 My master charg'd me to deliuer a ring to Madam Siluia: which (out of my neglect) was neuer done. **1634** MILTON *Comus* 510 Without blame, Or our neglect, we lost her as we came. **1683** TEMPLE *Mem.* Wks. 1720 I. 459 This he made good, dying with Neglect upon a Fit of the Gout. **1784** COWPER *Task* II. 456 This..offends me more Than in a churchman slovenly neglect And rustic coarseness would. **1802** JAMES *Milit. Dict.* s.v., Officers or soldiers convicted of neglect of duty, are punishable at the discretion of a court martial. **1821–2** SHELLEY *Chas. I*, II. 76 Our royal forests, Whose limits, from neglect, have been o'ergrown. **1881** JOWETT *Thucyd.* I. 91 Everybody fancies that his own neglect will do no harm.

b. An instance of negligence; an omission or oversight. Now *rare*.

1638 JUNIUS *Paint. Ancients* 316 The neglects committed in the disposition, are discovered by the lightsomenesse of the things themselves. **1698** [R. FERGUSON] *View Eccles.* 34 It would be matter of Enquiring how he came in and by what neglects he escapes being cast out. **1736** BUTLER *Anal.* I. ii. 39 Neglects from Inconsiderateness, want of Attention,..are often attended with Consequences..as dreadful as any active Misbehaviour. **1845** STOCQUELER *Handbk. Brit. India* (1854) 340 A province..gradually recovering from the effects of Mahratta ravages and neglects.

c. *in neglect of*, in default of. *rare*$^{-1}$.

1807 ROBINSON *Archæol. Græca* I. ix. 41 They forfeited double the sum, to be paid by themselves or their sureties; and, in neglect of this, they and their sureties were imprisoned.

d. (See quot.)

1867 SMYTH *Sailor's Word-bk.* 495 *Neglect*, a charge not exceeding £3, from the wages of a seaman, in the Complete Book, for any part of the ship's stores lost overboard, or damaged, from his gross carelessness.

†**ne'glect**, *pa. pple.* and *ppl. a. Obs.* [ad. L. *neglect-us*, pa. pple. of *neglegĕre*: see next.]

1. Neglected.

1530 TINDALE *Answ. More* Wks. (1573) 276/2 And then because it should not be neglect or left undone, an higher officer..came about..at tymes conuenient. **1561** DAUS tr. *Bullinger on Apoc.* Pref. (1573) 7 The Romane Empire..laye neglecte without an Emperoure. **1586** ? BRYSKETT *Thestylis* 96 Her haire hung lose, neglect, about her shoulders twaine. **1724** RAMSAY *Wyfe of Auchtermuchty* iv, Therefore let naithing be neglect [*rime* break].

2. Negligent. *rare*.

1603 FLORIO *Montaigne* I. xxv. 83 It represents a kinde of ..neglect carelesnesse of arte. **1620** tr. *Boccaccio's Decam.* 84 b, The man..knew nothing hereof, and therefore was the more neglect and carelesse.

neglect (nɪ'glɛkt), *v.* Also 6 neg-, necg-, neclecte, 6–7 neclect, (6 *Sc.* -leck, -lekk), 6– *Sc.* negleck, (6 -lec, -lek). [f. L. *neglect-*, ppl. stem of *neglegĕre*, *-ligĕre* (also *nec-*), f. *neg-* not + *legĕre* to pick up.]

1. *trans.* To disregard; to pay little or no respect or attention to; to slight, leave unnoticed.

1529 MORE *Dyaloge* IV. Wks. 257/2 Fastyng, prayer, & such other thynges, he taught them to neglecte and set at nought as vayne & vnfrutefull ceremonies. **1581** RICH *Farew.* (1846) 160 She would never neclect that care and regarde to her honoure which all women ought to have. **1638** JUNIUS *Paint. Ancients* 37 Every one hath within his own brest a certaine law of nature, the which he may not neglect. **1667** MILTON *P.L.* III. 200 This my long sufferance..They who neglect and scorn, shall never taste. **1712** LADY M. W. MONTAGU *Let. to W. Montagu* 9 or 11 Dec., If his kindness is sincere, 'tis too valuable to be neglected. **1781** COWPER *Charity* 36 Some nobler minds a law respect, That none shall with impunity neglect. **1855** MACAULAY *Hist. Eng.* xix. IV. 354 That noble discourse had been neglected by the generation to which it was addressed. **1868** TENNYSON *Spiteful Let.* 6 O little bard, is your lot so hard, If men neglect your pages?

†**b.** To leave out, omit, discard. *Obs. rare*$^{-1}$.

1603 OWEN *Pembrokeshire* (1892) I. 77 In all new buildinges these vaultes are altogether neclected.

2. To fail to bestow proper attention or care upon; to leave unattended to or uncared for.

1538 STARKEY *England* I. ii. 27 Yf men knew certaynly what ys the true commyn wele.., they wold not so..neclecte hyt. **1560** DAUS tr. *Sleidane's Comm.* 272 b, All these thinges neglected. **1615** G. SANDYS *Trav.* 216 A leuell naturally fertil, but now neglected. **1668** R. STEELE *Husbandm. Calling* x. (1672) 272 The Philosopher could say, he had rather neglect his means, than his mind. **1756** BURKE *Subl. & B.* Pref., Whilst the mind is intent on the general scheme of things, some particular parts must be neglected. **1784** COWPER *Task* III. 368, I seek to improve, At least neglect not..The mind He gave me. **1819** SHELLEY *Cenci* IV. iv. 120 Heaven doth interpose to do What ye neglect. **1875** JOWETT *Plato* (ed. 2) I. 73 Their own education..has been neglected.

b. With personal object.

1556 OLDE *Antichrist* 4 b, Neclecting them that he hathe taken charge of. **1685** BAXTER *Paraphr. N.T.* Matt. vi. 26 God that made you better than they, will not neglect you. **1771** *Junius Lett.* xlix. (1788) 267 You did not neglect the magistrate while you flattered the man. **1842** MISS MITFORD in L'Estrange *Life* III. ix. 137, I must so far neglect my dear father as to gain time for writing what may support us.

3. To fail to perform, render, discharge (a duty), or take (a precaution).

1533 BELLENDEN *Livy* I. xiii. (S.T.S.) I. 73 þe rite and cerymonis of divine religioun was neclectit. **1548** *Galway Arch.* in *10th Rep. Hist. MSS. Comm.* App. V. 412 The said officers so neceglectinge ther deuties to paye and forfait xx. li. **1667** MILTON *P.L.* III. 738 In Heav'n, Where honour due and reverence none neglects. *a* **1694** J. MASON *Sel. Rem.* iv. (1828) 97 If others neglect their duty to you, be sure that you perform yours to them. **1819** SHELLEY *Cenci* v. ii. 103 That ..I should have neglected So trivial a precaution. **1896** *Law Times Rep.* LXXIII. 615/1 There was evidence that Judges habitually performed this duty, though he sometimes neglected it.

4. a. With *inf.* To omit through carelessness, to fail through negligence, *to* do something.

1548 *Galway Arch.* in *10th Rep. Hist. MSS. Comm.* App. V. 412 If the officers neglecte to put the same person to execucion. **1563** WINȜET *Four Scoir Thre Quest.* Wks. (S.T.S.) I. 90 Qvhy neclect ȝe to ministrat this haly sacrament to the seik? **1617** MORYSON *Itin.* I. 95 They have neglected to preserve it. **1736** BUTLER *Anal.* I. ii. Wks. 1874 I. 42 Which consequences they for the most part neglect to consider..beforehand. **1786** BURKE *Sp. agst. W. Hastings* Wks. XII. 208 The said Hastings..did neglect to write a formal letter to Lieutenant Anderson. **1819** SHELLEY *Cenci* III. i. 183 If they neglect To punish crime.

b. To omit *doing* something.

1710 STEELE *Tatler* No. 203 ⁋1, I did not neglect spending a considerable Time in the Crowd. **1729** BUTLER *Serm.* Wks. 1874 II. 128 It is not uncommon for persons..entirely to neglect looking into the state of their affairs.

†**5.** To cause (something) to be neglected. *Obs.*

1594 SHAKS. *Rich. III*, III. iv. 25, I trust, My absence doth neglect no great designe. *c* **1620** FLETCHER & MASS. *Lit. Fr. Lawyer* III. ii, His fighting has neglected all our business.

Hence **ne'glecting** *vbl. sb.* and *ppl. a.*

1552 HULOET, Neglecting, or little regard. **1611** BIBLE *Col.* ii. 23 In will-worship and humilitie, and neglecting of the body. **1625** BACON *Ess., Revenge* (Arb.) 502 Perfidious or Neglecting Friends. **1646** JENKYN *Remora* 9 By neglecting of his worship. **1782** COWPER *Names of little Note* 6 Those twinkling tiny lustres..Drop one by one from Fame's neglecting hand. **1888** A. T. PIERSON *Evang. Wk.* 243 The neglected and neglecting masses of our city population.

ne'glectable, *a.* [f. prec. + -ABLE.] That may be neglected or disregarded; negligible.

1884 *Proc. Roy. Soc.* XXXVIII. 42 Subsequent experiments proved that all of these are practically neglectable. **1898** *Daily News* 13 Dec. 4/5 The dangerous doctrine that Great Britain was a neglectable quantity.

neglected (nɪ'glɛktɪd), *ppl. a.* [f. NEGLECT *v.* + -ED¹.] Not attended to or cared for; not treated with proper attention; disregarded.

1600 SHAKS. *A.Y.L.* III. ii. 394 A beard neglected, which you haue not. **1634** MILTON *Comus* 743 Like a neglected rose It withers on the stalk. **1705** STANHOPE *Paraphr.* II. 208 All the neglected Opportunities of Amendment. **1781** COWPER *Table-t.* 546 Neglected talents rust into decay. **1819** SHELLEY *Cenci* IV. i. 54 Where evil thoughts Shall grow like weeds on a neglected tomb. **1872** MORLEY *Voltaire* (1886) 10 The too neglected list of good causes lost.

Comb. **1866** GEO. ELIOT *Felix Holt* i, He was not a neglected-looking old man.

Hence **ne'glectedly** *adv.*; **ne'glectedness**.

1659 HAMMOND *On Ps.* cii. 9 Make them look sadly and neglectedly. **1660** S. FORD *Loyal Subj. Exult.* 21 In warre all things are cloathed with a dismall neglectedness. **1825** *New Monthly Mag.* XIII. 141 Not leaving thee neglectedly Like things forgotten. **1865** G. MACDONALD *A. Forbes* xiv, Seeing ..a girl so neglectedly attired. **1887** ABP. BENSON in *Life* (1899) II. 139 The peace and stillness and happy neglectedness, so to speak, over all.

neglecter (nɪ'glɛktə(r)). Also 6 **necg-**, *Sc.* **-ar.** [f. NEGLECT *v.* + -ER¹.] One who neglects.

1580 LUPTON *Sivquila* 74 The neglecters thereof shall dwell in Hell wyth the Divell. **1597** J. PAYNE *Royal Exch.* 27 All misspenders, abusers and voluntarie necglecters of the tyme. **1630** *R. Johnson's Kingd. & Commw.* 103 You shall finde him a meere neglecter of us. **1697** G. BURGHOPE *Disc. Relig. Assemb.* 5 My business is..with the absenters and neglecters of the Divine Service. **1753** RICHARDSON in Mrs. Barbauld *Life* (1804) VI. 241 To make his neglecters..feel the importance of his talents. **1820** SCOTT *Monast.* xiii, The chase..made Halbert a frequent neglecter of hours. **1887** *Spectator* 2 Apr. 463/2 There was more to be said for the Ritualists than for the neglecters of ritual.

neglectful (nɪ'glɛktfʊl), *a.* [f. NEGLECT *sb.* + -FUL.] Characterized by neglect or inattention; heedless, careless.

1644 BULWER *Chirol.* 121 The same neglectfull carriage of his Hand. **1682** *News fr. France* 35 To free themselves from the guilt of a neglectful silence. **1729** T. COOKE *Tales*, etc. 205, I shall first shew in what even our best Writers..have been neglectful. **1788** *Gentl. Mag.* LVIII. 481 It cannot but appear grossly neglectful. **1817** Jas. Mill *Brit. India* II. v. iv. 422 A government at once insatiable and neglectful. **1872** E. Peacock *Mabel Heron* I. 24 Did you ever see anything in such a neglectful condition?

b. Const. *of*, or *to* with inf.

1624 Massinger *Renegado* I. iii, I must grant Myself neglectful of all you have taught me. **1648** Milton *Observ. Peace Ormond* Wks. 1851 IV. 555 In neither of those wayes neglectfull of our just defence. **1795** Southey *Joan of Arc* v. 285 Nor were our chieftains..neglectful to implore That heavenly aid. **1856** Merivale *Rom. Emp.* xxxviii. (1865) IV. 344 Varus was not so neglectful of his own security.

Hence **ne'glectfully** *adv.*; **ne'glectfulness**.

1646 Earl Monm. tr. *Biondi's Civil Wars* vi. 31 A great many Gentlemen, who talked neglectfully of Edward. **1693** J. Edwards *Author. O. & N. Test.* 329 The looseness and neglectfulness of the stile. **1805** Nelson 29 Aug. in Nicolas *Disp.* (1846) VII. 22 The omission of their delivery wilfully or neglectfully. **1882** Farrar *Early Chr.* I. 448 *note*, In this neglectfulness he saw the dangerous germ of apostasy.

neglecting: see neglect *v.*

†**ne'glectingly**, *adv. Obs.* [f. neglecting *ppl. a.* + -ly².] Negligently, neglectfully.

1596 Shaks. *1 Hen. IV*, I. iii. 52, I then..Answer'd (neglectingly) I know not what. **1616** Beaum. & Fl. *Scornful Lady* iv. i, See how neglectingly he passes by me.

†**ne'glection**. *Obs.* [ad. L. *neglectiōn-em*: see neglect *v.* and -ion¹.] Negligence, neglect.

1591 Shaks. *1 Hen. VI*, iv. iii. 49 Sleeping neglection doth betray to losse. **1608** —— *Per.* iii. iii. 20 If neglection Should therein make me vile. **1628** Feltham *Resolves* ii. xxxi. 98 Who would haue beleeued, that one neglection of his counsell would haue truss'd vp Achitophel in a voluntarie Halter.

neglective (nɪ'glɛktɪv), *a.* Now *rare* or *Obs.* [f. neglect *v.* + -ive.] Neglectful, inattentive. (Very common in 17th c.)

1611 Speed *Hist. Gt. Brit.* ix. xxiv. (1623) 1179 Shee often seemed somewhat too remisse and neglectiue in the care of her selfe. **1628** Feltham *Resolves* ii. lxxxviii. 254 A carelesse freenesse, and a kind of neglectiue easinesse. **1670** Brooks *Wks.* (1867) VI. 55 How remiss, how neglective were many in their families. **1715** *Wodrow Corr.* (1843) II. 33 The Synod found their own Presbytery neglective. **1827** *Lincoln Cabinet* 44 While they were thus as enterprising, as Lincoln was neglective.

b. Const. *of*. (Also freq. in 17th c.)

*c***1611** Chapman *Iliad* xiv. 356 No one neglective was Of Hector's safety. **1661** H. D. *Disc. Liturgies* 8 So wofully neglective of their duty. *a***1684** Leighton *Serm.* Wks. (1868) 405 God seems neglective of his people.

Hence **ne'glectively** *adv.*; †**ne'glectiveness**. *Obs.*

1609 Daniel *Civ. Wars* viii. xlvi, And then, neglectively, Nothing at all [he offers]. **1621** Lady M. Wroth *Urania* 362 Her haire..cast into a delightfull neglectiuenes. *Ibid.* 393 Her hayre..shee onely kept cleane, and neglectiuely wore it. **1646** Jenkyn *Remora* 8 Sinfull neglectiveness of the worship of God. **1876** Robinson *Mid.-Yorksh. Gloss.*, *Mislook*, to overlook, neglectively.

†**ne'glectly**, *adv. Obs. rare*⁻¹. [f. neglect *ppl. a.* + -ly².] Negligently.

1594 Kyd *Cornelia* v. 427 Let your haire that wont be wreath'd in tresses, Now hang neglectly.

neglector (nɪ'glɛktə(r)). [a. late L. *neglector*: see neglect *v.* and -or.] = neglecter.

*a***1619** Hieron *Wks.* I. 451 There was a peremptorie commandement that the neglector of them should bee cut off. **1645** in Ellis *Orig. Lett.* Ser. iii. IV. 239 Upon paine of plundering the neglectors thereof. **1822** *Examiner* 353/2 The cold-hearted neglectors of complaints and sufferings. *a***1848** W. A. Butler *Serm.* (1849) I. xx. 363 The confession of this tremendous truth among its neglectors.

‖**négligé** (neglіʒe, 'nɛglɪʒeɪ). Also **negligee**, **negligée**. [F., pa. pple. of *négliger* to neglect.] Informal or unceremonious attire as worn by women when not in complete toilette. Cf. negligee.

1835 *Court Mag.* VI. p. ii/2 Those for elegant *negligé* are of velvet, with satin linings and trimmings. **1865** Ouida *Strathmore* I. vii. 113 No toilette was so becoming as the azure négligé of softest Indian texture. **1890** *Athenæum* 4 Oct. 457/3 Lydie Vaillant comes in most compromising *negligé* from the chamber of Paul Astier. **1908** R. W. Chambers *Firing Line* xviii. 313 Cecile, in distractingly pretty negligee, waved him audacious adieu from her window. **1945** S. Lewis *Cass Timberlane* (1946) xliii. 308 Jinny weaved in, much too pretty in her négligé.

attrib. **1859** L. Oliphant *China & Japan* II. v. 113 The women wore a sort of jacket above their skirt, which was however constructed upon a rather *negligé* principle. **1913** E. M. Forster *Let.* 1 Jan. in *Hill of Devi* (1953) 24 Her dress was on the negligée side, but she had not been intending to receive. **1917** 'Taffrail' *Sub* iv. 99 The members of the mess had purchased pictures, most of them of beautiful ladies in rather négligé raiment. **1954** A. Gardiner *Theory of Proper Names* (ed. 2) p. v, The bulk of this book is an exact reprint of a..booklet published..in 1940. Doubtless owing to the circumstances of the times, but possibly also to the original publication's somewhat négligé apparel, this passed almost unnoticed.

negligeable ('nɛglɪdʒəb(ə)l), *a.* [a. F. *négligeable*, f. *négliger* to neglect.] Negligible.

1882 G. H. Darwin in *Nature* 16 Feb. 361 It appears that the amount of this acceleration may not be entirely negligeable. **1889** *Sat. Rev.* 23 Mar. 361/1 Scherer's criticism was never a negligeable quantity.

negligee. Also 8–9 **-gée**, 8 **neglejay**. [ad. F. *négligé*: see négligé. The current pron. in sense 1 was app. (nɛglɪ'dʒiː).]

1. a. A kind of loose gown worn by women in the 18th century. Also, an informal garment worn by men in the 18th century. *Obs.* exc. *Hist.*

1756 *Connoisseur* No. 134 (1774) IV. 231, I saw several Negligees, with furbelowed aprons. **1764** T. Brydges *Homer Travest.* (1797) I. 315 Then bid them lay upon her knee The richest satin negligee. **1776** R. Graves *Euphrosyne* (1776) I. 194 Such as now-a-days one sees, In gauze and lace and negligées. **1795** tr. *C. P. Moritz's Trav.* 87 In the morning, it is usual to walk out in a sort of negligèe [*sic*], or morning-dress, your hair not dressed, but merely rolled up in rollers, and in a frock and boots. **1823** R. Chambers *Trad. Edinb.* (1847) 193 The negligee was a gown projecting in loose and ample folds from the back.

b. *negligee shirt* (N. Amer.), a soft-fronted shirt worn by men.

1895 *Montgomery Ward Catal.* 278/3 Men's negligee shirts. **1921** *Daily Colonist* (Victoria, B.C.) 19 Oct. 7/2 (Advt.), Men, if you want the best shirt..buy..these well made Cambric Negligee Shirts, in neat stripes.

c. *transf.* A shroud. *U.S.*

1927 *Amer. Mercury* May 33/1 The corpse is not a corpse nor does it wear a shroud. It is the body, or the remains;.. and the garment in which it is wrapped, when there is one aside from ordinary clothing, is a negligée. **1963** J. Mitford *Amer. Way of Death* i. 26 Florence Gowns Inc... exhibited their line of 'streetwear type garments and negligees'..at a recent convention of the National Funeral Directors Association.

2. A necklace formed of irregular beads.

1841 Mrs. Mozley *Fairy Bower* xlv. 336 My uncle had given her a very handsome long *negligée*, of Venetian beads. **1858** Simmonds *Dict. Trade*, *Negligee*, a long necklace, usually of coral.

3. A woman's dressing-gown, usu. made of flimsy, semi-transparent fabric trimmed with ruffles, lace, etc.

1930 M. Story *Individuality & Clothes* iii. 311 *The negligée*, this garment for intimate occasions may be..silky, lacy, colorful, and dainty. **1942** H. Pepin *Mod. Pattern Design* x. 219/1 The boudoir negligée is not to be confused with the ' hostess gown'. **1952** S. Kauffmann *Philanderer* (1953) i. 12 She shrugged and walked lazily over to the kitchenette, her filmy negligée heightening the illusion that she floated. **1960** A. Clarke *Later Poems* (1961) 80 Rosalind, in a négligée, Began to sketch me as I lay Naked. **1967** B. Patten *Little Johnny's Confession* 51 A thousand negligées, pyjamas, nightgowns.

negligence ('nɛglɪdʒəns). Forms: 4–6 **neclyg-**, (4 **necc-**, 6 **necke-**), **neclig-**, (4 **necc-**), 6 **necleg-**; 4 **necglig-**, **-lyg-**, 5 **necglig-**; 4–6 **neglyg-**, 4– **negligence**. Also 4–6 **-ens**, 4 **-ense**. [a. OF. *negligence* (12th c.), or ad. L. *neg-*, *necligentia*, *-legentia*, f. *neglegĕre* etc. to neglect.]

1. Want of attention to what ought to be done or looked after; carelessness with regard to one's duty or business; lack of necessary or ordinary care in doing something.

*a***1340** Hampole *Psalter* xlix. 8 We take not his saghe wiþ necgligens, bot wiþ besynes. *c***1380** Wyclif *Serm.* Sel. Wks. I. 96 Bi..necligence of prelatis is mannis lawe medlid wiþ Goddis lawe. *c***1420** Lydg. *Assembly of Gods* 1626 By hys owne neglygence takyn prysonere. **1483** Caxton *Cato* F vij b, Lucan sayth that alle delayeng and neglygence oughte to be sette a parte. **1530** Palsgr. 181, I impute that to the neglygence or rather ignorance of the printers. **1577** tr. *Bullinger's Decades* (1592) 153 It is abhominable to see the negligence of maisters in teaching their schollers. **1617** Moryson *Itin.* i. 115 The Haven of this City..by negligence is growne of no use. **1676** Temple *Let.* Wks. 1720 II. 410, I believe, it may have been only Negligence. **1736** Butler *Anal.* i. iv. Wks. 1874, I. 80 By their own negligence and folly in their temporal affairs. **1784** Cowper *Task* ii. 800 Those whose negligence or sloth Exposed their inexperience to the snare. **1834** Ht. Martineau *Demerara* iv. 55 Robert was slightly punished for negligence. **1884** Ld. Esher in *Law Times Rep.* LXXIII. 616/2 *note*, The deceased was also guilty of negligence or of want of reasonable care contributing to the accident.

†**b.** Neglect *of* something. *Obs.*

*c***1340** Hampole *Prose Tr.* 28 In als mekill als þou will noghte tente to thaym for neclygence of þi-selfe. **1482** *Monk of Evesham* (Arb.) 78 The..peynys that thes thre ware in, was for the neglygens of soulys the whiche they had cure of. **1638** Rawley tr. *Bacon's Life & Death* (1650) 11 To finde out a Rule..is very difficult, by reason of the negligence of observations. **1729** Butler *Serm.* Wks. 1874 II. 16 There is a manifest negligence in men of their real happiness.

c. Disregard (of a thing or person); neglect.

1602 Shaks. *Ham.* iv. v. 134 Both the worlds I giue to negligence, Let come what comes. **1778** Miss Burney *Evelina* lxviii, It was impossible for negligence to be more pointed, than that of Lord Merton to me.

2. An instance of inattention or carelessness; a negligent act, omission, or feature.

*c***1385** Chaucer *L.G.W.* 537 A ful grete necgligence Was yt to the..That thou forgate hire in thi songe to sette. **1509** *Bury Wills* (Camden) 108 Prayng my ordinary to excuse my conscyens for alle necclygencys. **1526** *Pilgr. Perf.* (W. de. W. 1531) 133 b, O, how they wyll wayle and wepe theyr negligences. *a***1800** Blair (Ogilvie), Remarking his beauties,..I must also point out his negligences and defects. **1865** C. J. Vaughan *Plain Words* xi. (1866) 199, I speak not of those daily negligences which belong to another subject.

3. A careless indifference, as in appearance or costume, or in literary or artistic style; in later use esp. with suggestion of an agreeable absence of artificiality or restraint.

*c***1430** *Stans Puer ad Mensam* 33 (Lamb. MS.) Drinke not bridelid for haste ne necligence. *c***1440** *Partonope* 2772 Grete negligence Was neuer founden in his persone. **1665** Boyle *Occas. Refl.* Pref. (1848) 10 Most of the following Papers, being written for my own private Amusement, a good deal of Negligence in them may appear..pardonable. *a***1680** Butler *Rem.* (1759) I. 149 T'affect the purest Negligences In Gestures, Gaits, and Miens. **1711** Addison *Spect.* No. 119 ⁋2 Nothing is so modish as an agreeable Negligence. **1741** Middleton *Cicero* II. x. 445 The coldness and negligence with which it is drawn. **1843** Whittier *Ego* 12 Hence my pen unfettered moves In freedom which the heart approves, The negligence which friendship loves.

So '**negligency**. *rare.*

1800 Wellesley in Owen *Desp.* (1877) 653 The loss sustained by their negligencies or errors. **1841–4** Emerson *Ess.* Ser. i. ix. (1876) 235 The negligency of that trust which carries God with it.

negligent ('nɛglɪdʒənt), *a.* and *sb.* Forms: 4–6 **neclig-**, 5–6 **neclyg-**, 4 **necglig-**, 6 **neglyg-**, 4– **negligent**. [a. OF. *negligent* (13th c.), or ad. L. *negligent-*, *negligens*, pres. pple. of *neglegĕre* to neglect.]

A. *adj.* **1. a.** Of persons: Inattentive to duty; not attending to, or doing, what ought to be done; neglectful. Also const. *of*.

*c***1380** Wyclif *Sel. Wks.* III. 312 O worldly prest necligent and unkunnynge. *c***1450** tr. *De Imitatione* i. xxv. 37 The negligent religiose & þe leuke haþ tribulacion. **1485** Caxton *Chas. Gt.* 22 Yf the kyng be neclygent the peple wote not what to doo. **1551** Crowley *Pleas. & Pain* 155, I found you negligent in fedynge my family. **1581** Mulcaster *Positions* xxxix. (1887) 192 To better him if he be negligent, to be like him if he be diligent. **1651** Hobbes *Leviath.* i. xv. 79 The most part are too busie in getting food, and the rest too negligent to understand. **1675** Evelyn *Diary* 22 Mar., He was very negligent himselfe, and rather so of his person. **1706** E. Ward *Wooden World Diss.* (1708) 103 He's nothing of a Soldier (Thanks to his negligent Officers). **1784** Cowper *Task* iii. 276 The proud, uncandid, insincere, Or negligent inquirer. **1879** Cable *Old Creole Days* v. (1883) 144 He was a great student and rather negligent of his business.

absol. **1726** Leoni *Alberti's Archit.* II. 99/1 Faults which the negligent and unadvised easily fall into.

b. Heedless, careless, indifferent. *rare.*

*c***1440** *Alph. Tales* 416 He, negligent of þe said perels,.. wold hafe þis drope of honye. **1709** Steele *Tatler* No. 61 ⁋4 They carry it so far, as to be negligent, whether they offend or not.

2. a. Of actions, conduct, etc.: Characterized by, or displaying, negligence or carelessness.

1500–20 Dunbar *Poems* ix. 118 Fals vane gloir and deidis negligent. **1538** Starkey *England* i. i. 14 Theyr maner of lyfyng, wych they, by negligente incontynence, suffur to be corrupt. **1591** Shaks. *1 Hen. VI*, iv. ii. 44 O negligent and heedlesse Discipline. **1617** Moryson *Itin.* i. 278, I will confess my negligent omission in noting the rates of my exchanges. **1678** Moxon *Mech. Exerc.* iv. 73 You might with a negligent, or unlucky knock with the Mallet, drive the edge..under the work. **1705** Stanhope *Paraphr.* I. 12 A sordid or negligent Temper. **1781** Johnson in *Boswell*, Does it not suppose, that the former judgement was temerarious or negligent? **1805** Scott *Last Minstr.* i. x, All loose her negligent attire, All loose her golden hair. **1852** Mrs. Stowe *Uncle Tom's C.* xxxiii, The person..with a haughty, negligent air, delivered her basket.

b. Due to negligence. *rare.*

1606 Shaks. *Ant. & Cl.* iii. vi. 81 Till we perceiu'd both how you were wrong led, And we in negligent danger. **1660** Young *Vade Mecum* (ed. 6) 95 Negligent Escape, is where one is arrested, and afterward escapes against the will of him that arrested him. **1843–56** Bouvier *Law Dict.* (ed. 6) s.v., For a negligent escape, the sheriff or keeper of the prison is liable to punishmnent in a criminal case.

3. quasi-*adv.* Negligently. *rare*⁻¹.

1738 Wesley *Hymn, My drowsy Powers* ii, Yet we who have a Heav'n t'obtain How negligent we live!

B. *sb.* **1.** A negligent person.

1616 W. Sclater *Serm.* 18, I know not whether I may say Recusants or Negligents. **1638** —— *Serm. Experimentall* 129 Taxed here are..Negligents in this duty. **1853** Whewell *Grotius* II. 192 It often happens in agents or negligents of the secondary order. **1892** *Star* 14 Dec. 2/5 [A] congenial company of negligents.

2. A type of wig worn in the 18th century.

1753 in F. W. Fairholt *Costume in England* (1885) II. 320 The pigeon's wing, the comet, the cauliflower,..the rose, the crutch, the negligent, the chancellor, [etc.]. **1762** Goldsmith *Life R. Nash* 74 *Nash*..had seen flaxen bobs succeeded by majors, which in their turn gave way to negligents. **1971** J. Woodforde *Strange Story False Hair* vii. 46 *Men's—eighteenth century*..Negligent.

negligently ('nɛglɪdʒəntlɪ), *adv.* Forms: 4 **necglig-**, 5 **neclig-**, 6 **nec(t)lyg-**, 5–6 **neglyg-**, 6– **negligently**. [f. prec. + -ly².] In a negligent manner; carelessly, heedlessly; slightingly.

1382 Wyclif *Ezra* iv. 22 Seeth, lest necgligentli this be fulfild. **1439** *E.E. Wills* (1882) 113 Tithes..necligently foryeten. **1482** *Monk of Evesham* (Arb.) 65 Perauenture he neglygently kepte hys ordre. **1530** Palsgr. 363 There is no graunt made lyberally, if it be demaunded neglygently. **1560** Daus tr. *Sleidane's Comm.* 370 They wrote the safe-conduite with a few wordes, and very negligentlye. **1617** Moryson *Itin.* To Rdr., Flowers..carelessly and negligently bound together. **1666** Pepys *Diary* 6 Aug., I wondered at the reason of my being received so negligently. **1711** Steele *Spect.* No. 152 ⁋3 A Gentleman who had the Rein of his Horse negligently under his Arm. **1781** Cowper *Expost.* 695 A spot Not quickly found, if negligently sought. **1838** Dickens *Nich. Nick.* xxii, Graceful and grotesque thrown negligently side by side. **1885** *Law Times Rep.* LIII. 325/2 The defendant..negligently and unskilfully navigated and managed the said vessel.

negligible (ˈnɛglɪdʒɪb(ə)l), *a.* [f. L. *neglig-ĕre* to neglect + -IBLE. Cf. F. *négligible* (rare).] Capable of being neglected or disregarded.

1829 HERSCHEL *Ess.* (1857) 541 Within very negligible limits of error. **1879** THOMSON & TAIT *Nat. Phil.* I. I. §431 When their difference is too large to be negligible. **1895** *Nation* (N.Y.) 22 Aug. 137/3 Admitting such a thing as negligible quantities in a work of art.

Hence ˈ**negligibly** *adv.*

Also, in recent use, ***negligibleness*** and ***negligibility***.

1888 *Philos. Mag.* XXVI. 160 The work wasted..is negligibly small compared with the work done.

†**neˈgoce.** *Obs. rare.* [ad. L. *negōti-um*: cf. F. *négoce.*] Intercourse, commerce.

1697 BENTLEY *Phal.* 46 Could not that perpetual negoce and converse with Dorians bring his mouth..to speak a little broader? **1699** *Ibid.* (ed. 2) Pref. 85 Negoce, Putid, and Idiom..were in Print, before I us'd them.

So †**neˈgocy.** *Obs. rare*$^{-1}$.

1603 HOLLAND *Plutarch's Mor.* 1329 For to make it [deity] intermeddle in the negocies and affaires of men.

negociall, -ant, -ate: see NEGOTIAL, etc.

‖**négociant** (negɔsjɑ̃). [Fr., = merchant, used *ellipt.* for *négociant des vins.*] A wine merchant.

1910 'SAKI' *Reginald in Russia* 104 The little Lemberg *négociant* plucked up heart. **1961** W. E. MASSEE *Wines & Spirits* 51 A shipper who owns vineyards in one town but ships from another must put the word *négociant* on the label. **1970** *House & Garden* May 38/3 The principal *négociants* of Burgundy are very hospitable to properly introduced visitors who have a serious interest in wine. **1974** *Harpers & Queen* Sept. 73/1 It's a good thing for a young man to have the M[aster of] W[ine]... Continental *négociants* and growers now recognise and respect it.

negon, variant of NIGON, niggard. *Obs.*

Negoos, variant of NEGUS[1].

negotiability (nɪgəʊʃ(ɪ)əˈbɪlɪtɪ). [See next and -ITY. Cf. F. *négociabilité.*] The quality of being negotiable.

1828–32 in WEBSTER. **1856** H. BROOME *Comment. Comm. Law* 11 The negotiability of bills of exchange. **1885** *Law Times* LXXVIII. 378/2 Negotiability..is a good consideration for the relinquishment of the residue of the debt.

negotiable (nɪˈgəʊʃ(ɪ)əb(ə)l), *a.* [f. NEGOTI-ATE *v.* + -ABLE, or ad. F. *négociable* (1688).]

1. Of bills, drafts, cheques, etc.: Capable of being negotiated; transferable or assignable in the course of business from one person to another.

1758 *Monthly Rev.* 132 Bills of Exchange..negotiable at Hispaniola. **1772** FOOTE *Nabob* II. Wks. 1799 II. 304 A masquerade ticket is more negotiable there than a note from the bank. **1809** R. LANGFORD *Introd. Trade* 20 Negotiable bills under five pounds. **1848** MILL *Pol. Econ.* III. xxiii. §1 (1876) 386 The quoted prices of the funds and other negotiable securities. **1879** LUBBOCK in *19th Cent.* Nov. 793 These Assyrian drafts were negotiable, but from the nature of things could not pass by endorsement.

†**2.** Capable of being negotiated with. *Obs. rare.*

1794 BURKE *Corr.* (1844) IV. 218 It is not said..what state of things in France may be said to put her in a condition negotiable or not negotiable.

3. Admitting of being crossed, ascended, etc.

1880 *Daily Tel.* 25 Oct., The riders remain behind, for the wall from the road is hardly negotiable. **1895** A. G. BRADLEY *Wolfe* xi. 183 That this [path] was negotiable was very evident, from the white gleam..of tents which proclaimed the presence of an outpost at its summit.

†**neˈgotial,** *a. Obs. rare.* [ad. L. *negōtiāl-is* (see Quintilian III. vi. 58, etc.), f. *negōtium.*] Relating to facts without consideration of persons.

c **1530** L. COX *Rhet.* (1899) 79 This state is negociall or iuridicall, whiche conteyneth the ryght or wronge of the dede. *Ibid.* 80 State negociall absolute is whan the thynge.. is absolutely defended to be laufully done.

negotiant (nɪˈgəʊʃ(ɪ)ənt). Also 8–9 **negociant.** [f. L. *negōtiant-*, ppl. stem of *negōtiāre* (see next), or ad. F. *négociant*, It. *negoziante.*] One who negotiates or carries on negotiations; an agent, representative; †a merchant or trader.

1611 FLORIO, *Negotiante*,..a negotiant. *a* **1618** RALEIGH *Arts Empire* xxv. (1658) 88 Ambassadors, Negotiants, and generally all other Ministers. *a* **1665** SIR K. DIGBY *Priv. Mem.* (1827) 298 You having been the only negotiant in a long treaty..between..the old King and me. **1768–74** TUCKER *Lt. Nat.* (1834) II. 542 In sympathizing with the criminal, the debtor, the necessitous, and the negotiant, we do well. **1802** MRS. E. PARSONS *Myst. Visit* III. 98 Near a week passed without seeing any persons but negociants and bankers. **1863** *Life in South* II. 65 If I must enter a College it might as well be in Alabama or Mississippi, in both of which States there were negotiants. **1884** *St. James's Gaz.* 28 Mar. 11/1 His more compliant colleague, the Solicitor-General, taking his place as negotiant.

negotiate (nɪˈgəʊʃɪeɪt), *v.* Also 7–8 **negociate, -at.** [f. ppl. stem of L. *negōtiāre*, f. *negōtium*, f. *neg-* not + *ōtium* ease, quiet.]

1. *intr.* **a.** To hold communication or conference (*with* another) for the purpose of arranging some matter by mutual agreement; to discuss a matter with a view to some settlement or compromise.

1599 SHAKS. *Much Ado* II. i. 185 Let euerie eye negotiate for it selfe, And trust no Agent. **1601** R. JOHNSON *Kingd. & Commw.* (1603) 150 The Secretaries themselues commonly can neither write, nor answere ambassadors..when they negotiat. **1671** WOODHEAD *St. Teresa* I. xv. 93 Let the will then..know, that she is not to negotiate with God by strength of Arme. **1783** JUSTAMOND tr. *Raynal's Hist. Indies* VI. 215 The ministry negotiated, bribed and threatened. **1840** THIRLWALL *Greece* VII. 289 She was now reduced to utter despair, and sent to negotiate with the conqueror. **1856** KANE *Arct. Expl.* II. x. 103, I have authorized Hans to negotiate..for four of these, even as a loan. **1861** BUCKLE *Civiliz.* (1873) III. ii. 80 Both parties were now willing to negotiate with the view of gaining time.

†**b.** To do business or trade; to traffic. *Obs.*

1601 HOLLAND *Pliny* I. 117 Our Romanes were forced to prouide..interpreters, when they would negotiate and traffick with the people. **1645** EVELYN *Diary* June (Venice), Jews, Turks, Armenians,..negotiating in this famous Emporium. **1759** JOHNSON *Rasselas* xxxvi[i], It is difficult to negociate where neither will trust.

2. *trans.* **a.** To deal with, manage, or conduct (a matter, affair, etc., requiring some skill or consideration).

1619 DRAYTON *Bar. Wars* III. xxxi, That weightie Bus'nesse to negotiate, They must find One of speciall worth and trust. **1639** FULLER *Holy War* I. viii. (1840) 12 Our Saviour himself appointed him his legate with a commission to negotiate the Christian cause. **1703** MAUNDRELL *Journ. Jerus.* (1732) 9 To negotiate this affair we sent a Turk. **1765** WILKES *Corr.* (1805) II. 215, I leave you..to negociate all these matters. **1807** SOUTHEY *Espriella's Lett.* III. 313 They negotiate with the utmost anxiety the amours of their cows and sheep.

b. To arrange for, obtain, bring about (something) by means of negotiation.

1721 DE FOE *Mem. Cavalier* (1840) 193 That treaty..was negotiating. **1754** H. WALPOLE *World* No. 102 III. 284 Our country squires made treaties about their game, and ladies negociated the meeting of their lap-dogs. **1794** S. WILLIAMS *Vermont* 264 Send a flag into Canada, to negociate their release or exchange. **1838** PRESCOTT *Ferd. & Is.* (1846) II. xvii. 129 It was impossible..to negotiate a sale of their effects. **1853** J. H. NEWMAN *Hist. Sk.* (1873) II. I. i. 25 He ..sent ambassadors to negotiate an equal alliance with the Chinese Empire.

c. To set right by negotiation. *rare*$^{-1}$.

1776 PAINE *Com. Sense* (1791) 44 A republican government, by being formed on more natural principles, would negociate the mistake.

3. a. To transfer or assign (a bill, etc.) to another in return for some equivalent in value; to convert into cash or notes; to obtain or give value for (bills, cheques, etc.) in money.

1682 SCARLETT *Exchanges* 54 None can negotiate or redraw a Bill of Exchange, except it be made payable to his order who must negotiate it. **1711** *Lond. Gaz.* No. 4823/3 We cannot..perceive that any such Bills are Negotiating. **1777** COWPER *Let.* 11 Dec., I am obliged to you..for the thirty pounds, which I hope I shall be able to negociate here. **1833** HT. MARTINEAU *Vanderput & S.* iii. 49 Every bill drawn upon Amsterdam, or negotiated here. **1856** LEVER *Martins of Cro'M.* 355 When I paid it by these securities, you pledged yourself not to negotiate them. **1868** ROGERS *Pol. Econ.* xv. (1876) 208 The merchant..imports goods, and gives bills to such countries as receive and negotiate bills.

b. To deal with, carry out, as a business or monetary transaction.

1809 R. LANGFORD *Introd. Trade* 55 The dividend warrants of the Stock negotiated by N. M. Rothschild. **1875** STUBBS *Const. Hist.* xvii. II. 534 'Utter destruction' had been the common fate of those who..had negotiated the king's loans.

4. a. (Orig. *Hunting.*) To clear (a hedge or fence); to succeed in crossing, getting over, round, or through (an obstacle, etc.) by skill or dexterity.

1862 WHYTE MELVILLE *Ins. Bar* i, The first fence I negotiated most successfully. **1866** *Daily Tel.* 25 Oct., A stiff bit of timber which his neighbours..were chesting or declining to negotiate. **1882** *Bazaar Exch. & M.* 15 Feb. 174 No sweeping curve is required to negotiate a corner, as the machine may be swung round directly. **1909** *Q. Rev.* Oct. 492 Some rival..had 'negotiated'—this we believe to be the sporting phrase—the same 150 miles in forty-seven hours. **1922** H. TITUS *Timber* xvi. 151 Pelly negotiated the *cuspidor* safely. **1973** E. LEMARCHAND *Let or Hindrance* xiii. 157 Toye negotiated the narrow entry, and they arrived in a small enclosed space in which several cars were already parked.

b. To succeed in dealing with in the way desired; to get the better of.

1888 *Pall Mall G.* 14 Nov. 5/2 The difficulty of simultaneously negotiating creatures whose divergent natures demand..widely different tactics.

Hence **neˈgotiated** *ppl. a.* (†engaged, busy); **neˈgotiating** *vbl. sb.* and *ppl. a.*

1604 DEKKER *Honest Wh.* I. Wks. 1873 II. 17 Where's.. thy Maister? Faith signior, hee's a little negotiated; he'l appeare presently. **1622** BACON *Hen. VII* 21 Certaine it is, shee was a busie negotiating woman. **1659** *Gentl. Calling* ix. §5. 452 This surely is enough to excite men to a diligent negotiating with those talents they have received. **1713** SWIFT *Hist. Last Sess.* Wks. 1758 IX. 223 This low Talent in Business the Cardinal..used in contempt to call a spirit of Negotiating. **1870** *Daily News* 5 Dec., Some negotiating was going on. **1890** 'R. BOLDREWOOD' *Col. Reformer* (1891) 253 The easily negotiated drafts of fat cattle.

negotiation (nɪgəʊʃɪˈeɪʃən). Also 6–9 **negoci-.** [ad. L. *negōtiātiōn-em*, noun of action f. *negōtiāre*: see prec. and -ATION. Cf. F. *négociation* (14th c., Oresme).]

1. †**a.** A matter of private occupation or business; a business transaction. *Obs.*

c **1580** G. HARVEY *Letter-bk.* (Camden) 142 If any negotiation requires advizements, None more than matrimony. *c* **1645** HOWELL *Lett.* (1650) II. 37 Falling into infirmities as he follows his worldly negotiations. **1685** PETTY *Will* p. iii, Exhorting them to improve the same [estate] by no worse negociations. *a* **1704** T. BROWN *Praise Poverty* Wks. 1730 I. 102 There is no need of money in any negotiation with me.

transf. **1662** MORE *Philos. Writ.* Pref. Gen. (1712) 9 Which though Aristotle mainly appropriates to external Affairs, I must..transfer also to the Negotiations of the Mind.

†**b.** Trading, traffic. *Obs.*

1601 HOLLAND *Pliny* I. 109 The towne..is now decayed ..and the traffique and negotiation in all affaires turned from thence. **1622** MALYNES *Anc. Law-Merch.* 2 The vse of trusting, exchanging, and trading;..both for fishing and negotiation. **1669** GALE *Crt. Gentiles* I. I. viii. 42 The Phenicians..possessed themselves of the sea coasts, the better to carry on their negotiation.

†**c.** Occupation, exercise. *Obs. rare*$^{-1}$.

1628 FELTHAM *Resolves* II. xlviii. 141 How bright does the Soule grow with use and negotiation!

2. A process or course of treaty with another (or others) to obtain or bring about some result, esp. in affairs of state. Freq. in *pl.*

1579 FENTON *Guicciard.* Ep. Ded., The high negociations and emploiments which he managed long time vnder great Princes. **1606** SHAKS. *Tr. & Cr.* III. iii. 24 Their negotiations all must slacke, Wanting his mannage. **1647** CLARENDON *Hist. Reb.* I. §104 He was sent..to treat about the restitution of the Palatinate: in which Negociation he behaved himself with great Prudence. **1709** STEELE *Tatler* No. 105 ⁋2 During the Negotiation for his Enlargement, I had an Opportunity of acquainting myself with his History. **1769** ROBERTSON *Chas. V*, VI. Wks. 1813 VI. 85 The pope continued his negociations for convoking a general council. **1828** D'ISRAELI *Chas. I*, I. iv. 90 The long negociation of a political marriage was terminated by a war. **1877** FROUDE *Short Stud.* (1883) IV. I. ii. 18 The archbishop..employed him afterwards in the most confidential negotiations.

3. The action or business of negotiating or making terms with others.

1614 RALEIGH *Hist. World* III. (1634) 112 Supposing, that by his great skill in subtile negotiation he should.. circumvent the Greeks. **1779** JOHNSON *Wks.* IV. 546 Finding negociation thus ineffectual. **1798** WELLINGTON in Gurw. *Desp.* (1837) I. 6 The established channels of peaceable negotiation. **1836** THIRLWALL *Greece* xxv. III. 365 Phæax possessed talents well suited for negotiation. **1845** S. AUSTIN *Ranke's Hist. Ref.* II. 253 To appoint time and place for an interview for the purpose of negotiation.

b. With possessive pronouns. Now *rare* or *Obs.*

1597 R. CECIL in Ellis *Orig. Lett.* Ser. I. III. 43 His negotiation tendeth to a proposition of peace. **1603** KNOLLES *Hist. Turks* (1638) 62 These Embassadors had at length brought their negotiation to..good passe. **1695** CONGREVE *Love for L.* I. ii, Sir, if you don't like my negotiation, will you be pleased to answer these yourself? **1748** RICHARDSON *Clarissa* (1811) V. 101 Frustrate not Captain Tomlinson's negociation. **1781** GIBBON *Decl. & F.* xix. II. 152 The progress of their negociation was opposed and defeated.

4. The action of getting over or round some obstacle by skilful manœuvring.

1885 *Sat. Rev.* 28 Nov. 706 Courses which required what in some curious way has come to be called 'negotiation'. **1898** *St. James's Gaz.* 15 Nov. 6/1 They were said to attempt the negotiation of impossible obstacles, to their own imminent risk.

negotiator (nɪˈgəʊʃɪeɪtə(r)). Also 6–8 **negoci-.** [a. L. *negōtiātor*, agent-n. f. *negōtiāre* to NEGOTIATE. Cf. F. *négociateur* (14th c., Oresme).]

†**1.** A trader, a business man. *Obs.*

1598 FLORIO, *Facendiere*,..a dealer in business affaires, a negociator, an agent, a dealer. **1602** WARNER *Alb. Eng.* XII. lxx. 294 Yeat still to gratefull eares may those Negotiators sound. **1623** MABBE tr. *Aleman's Guzman d'Alf.* I. III. v. 209 Those great Dealers and Negociators of Genoa.

2. One who carries on negotiations.

1610 in Birch *Crt. & Times Jas. I* (1848) I. 120 The same diligence may be expected of a new negociator. **1637–50** ROW *Hist. Kirk* (Wodrow Soc.) 149 That Bruce is a negotiator in Spaine with the King, and in the Low Countreys with the Duke of Parme. **1702** *Eng. Theophrastus* 132 The dislike we commonly have of negotiators (or arbitrators) arises from their being generally apt to sacrifice all the interest of their friends. **1742** BLAIR *Grave* 497 Here lie abash'd The great negotiators of the earth. **1791** MACKINTOSH *Vind. Gallicæ* Wks. 1846 III. 62 The lawyers of Boston, and the planters of Virginia, were transformed into ministers and negociators. **1849** MACAULAY *Hist. Eng.* ii. I. 254 Negotiator and courtier as he was, he never learned the art of..concealing his emotions. **1884** COURTHOPE *Addison* viii. 146 The alleged sacrifice of British interests through the incompetence or corruption of the negotiators.

fig. **1654** WHITLOCK *Zootomia* 319 Hee of any deserveth it, among the Negociatours for Destruction.

3. One who negotiates bills, loans, etc.

1682 SCARLETT *Exchanges* 55 The Redrawer or the Negotiator of a Bill, does not make a new Bill, but endorseth the old. **1809** R. LANGFORD *Introd. Trade* 16 There are other persons occasionally concerned in a Bill of Exchange, such as the Seller or Negotiator. **1861** M. PATTISON *Ess.* (1889) I. 42 The Germans began to supplant the Jews and Lombards as negotiators of loans to the Crown.

neˈgotiatory, *a. rare*$^{-1}$. [f. as NEGOTIATE *v.* + -ORY[2].] Pertaining to negotiation.

1727 in BAILEY, Vol. II. **1763** in *C. Gist's Jrnls.* (1893) 196 Before I wold attempt to undertake ye Negocieatory Maters with a Number of Indian Nations.

negotiatress (nɪ'gəʊʃətrɪs). [See next and -ESS.] A female negotiator.

1827 CARLYLE *Germ. Rom.* I. 31 By means of a negotiatress, whom he had gained, [he] had it offered to the mother for a cheap price. **1897** OUIDA *Massarenes* xxxvii, The percentage received by the fair negotiatress of the sale.

negotiatrix (nɪ'gəʊʃ(ɪ)ətrɪks). [a. late L. *negōtiātrix*, fem. agent-n. f. *negōtiāre* to NEGOTIATE.] A female negotiator.

1624 T. SCOTT *Votivæ Angliæ* D j b, It is a Castilian policie, to make the Archdutchesse a Negotiatrixe in..all Treaties. **1809** MAR. EDGEWORTH *Manœuvring* xv, Our fair negociatrix prepared to show the usual degree of gratitude. **1852** MISS MITFORD in L'Estrange *Life* (1870) III. xiii. 242 A most elegant young woman,..of course the negotiatrix of the forgeries.

†**negoti'osity.** *Obs. rare.* [f. L. *negōtiōs-us* (see next) + -ITY.] Constant occupation in affairs.

1678 CUDWORTH *Intell. Syst.* 81 Such infinite negotiosity would be absolutely inconsistent with a happy state.

†**ne'gotious,** *a. Obs. rare.* [ad. L. *negōtiōsus*, f. *negōtium*: see -OUS.] Involving, or given to, occupation or business.

1603 FLORIO *Montaigne* III. ix. 580 Let them not looke for any cumbersome negotious and carefull matter. **1642** ROGERS *Naaman* 128 What is so negotious and eagerly busie, as an usurping Absalon? *Ibid.* 309 Some servants..are very nimble and negotious. **1656** BLOUNT *Glossogr.*

Hence †**ne'gotiousness.** *Obs. rare*$^{-1}$.

1642 ROGERS *Naaman* 606 God needs not our negotiousnesse, or double diligence, to bring his matters to passe.

†**negre,** *a. Obs. rare*$^{-1}$. In 5 neyger. [a. OF. *negre, nigre* (Godef.).] Black.

14.. in *Househ. Ord.* (1790) 440 Sause blaunk for Capons sothen... Sause neyger for Hennes or Capons.

negremancien: see NECROMANCIEN.

Negress ('niːgrɪs). [ad. F. *négresse*: see NEGRO and -ESS.] A female Negro.

In recent years felt by some to have 'racist' connotations.

1786 tr. *Beckford's Vathek* (1868) 31 The Princess remained in the company of her negresses. **1799** HOME in *Phil. Trans.* LXXXIX. 163 The most remarkable instance of this kind, that has come to my knowledge, was a Negress. **1817** T. L. PEACOCK *Melincourt* I. 71 His gentleness and sweet temper winning the hearts of the negro and negress. **1891** C. ROBERTS *Adrift Amer.* 101 A fine strapping young negress came out of the house. **1970** J. UPDIKE *Bech: a Book* 113 'In *Travel Light*, for example, you keep calling Roxanne a Negress.' 'But she was one.' He added, 'I loved Roxanne.' 'The fact is, the word has distinctly racist overtones.' **1974** *Times Lit. Suppl.* 21 June 671/1 Blacks all over the world find the term 'Negress' offensive. What is wrong with saying 'a Black woman'?

transf. **1801** WOLCOT (P. Pindar) *Tears & Smiles* Wks. 1812 V. 58 Now Negress Night came solemn down. **1920** E. SITWELL *Wooden Pegasus* 92 The negress Night, within her house of glass Watched the processions pass.

Negri ('neɪgriː). *Path.* The name of Adelchi *Negri* (1876–1912), Italian physician, used *attrib.* (and formerly in the possessive) to designate eosinophil cytoplasmic inclusion bodies (first described by him in 1903) found in the neurons of the brains of human beings and animals infected with rabies, the demonstration of which provides the most certain diagnosis of that disease.

1904 *Brit. Med. Jrnl.*, *Epitome of Current Med. Lit.* 30 Apr. 72/2 (*heading*) The minute structure of Negri's bodies. **1905** *Jrnl. Amer. Med. Assoc.* 2 Sept. 744/1 It is just as possible that the Negri bodies are the result of the infection as that they are the cause of rabies. **1906** *Jrnl. R. Microsc. Soc.* 626 (*heading*) Demonstrating Negri's corpuscles. **1952** [see CHROMATOID *a.*]. **1970** *Sci. Jrnl.* Apr. 38/1 Diagnosis of rabies by the recognition of Negri bodies in the brain of an affected animal..requires the animal to be dead. **1974** PASSMORE & ROBSON *Compan. Med. Stud.* III. xii. 96/2 Smears and tissue sections should be searched for Negri bodies which stain pink with polychrome stains.

negrification (ˌniːgrɪfɪ'keɪʃən). Also Negrification. [f. NEGRO on model of words in *-fication*, as *pacification*. Cf. NIGRIFICATION.] The action or fact of making Negro in character; placing under the control of Blacks. So '**Negrify** *v. trans.*

1929 *Nation* (N.Y.) 9 Jan. 56 At the beginning of 1928 it seemed as if an end would be made to the slave traffic and the 'negrification' of Cuba, when the Government decided to restrict the output of sugar to 4,000,000 tons per year. **1961** *Spectator* 9 June 835 Through the ceremony the negroes 'negrify' themselves. **1962** *Economist* 7 Apr. 28/2 Some young Belgian technicians have complained of the effects of 'negrification'. **1966** P. GREEN tr. *Escarpit's Novel Computer* vi. 76 Suppose..you were asked to join a revolt..to save the Western world from materialism and Arabo-Marxist negrification. **1972** *Daily Tel.* 7 Mar. 11/4 'Black' in Trinidad means black... Hence the need for 'Negrification' of public and private employment.

Negrillo (nɪ'grɪləʊ). [a. Sp. *negrillo*, dim. of *negro* NEGRO.] **a.** A little Negro. **b.** One of a race of dwarf Negro people living in Central and Southern Africa.

1853 THACKERAY *Let.* 19 Mar., A little negrillo of five years old. **1866** LAING *Prehist. Rem. Caithn.* 8 The extreme of the elongated type is the Southern Savage—the Negro, Negrillo, and Australian. **1899** *Q. Rev.* July 271 The belief that all Negritos and all Negrillos belong to one or other of two primitive races.

†**Negrine**, *sb. Obs. rare*$^{-1}$. [f. NEGRO + -INE^{3}.] A female Negro; = NEGRESS.

1703 DAMPIER *Voy.* III. I. 81 Lying..promiscuously with their Negrines and other She-slaves.

Negrine ('niːgraɪn), *a. rare.* [f. NEGRO + -INE^{1}.] Resembling that of Negroes.

1857 *Zoologist* XV. 5491 The Portuguese, who, living within the tropics, have blackened to a negrine dye.

†'**Negrish,** *a. Obs. rare*$^{-1}$. [f. NEGRO + -ISH^{1}.] Used by the Negroes.

1735 J. ATKINS *Voy. Guinea* 149 *Mattan*, the Negrish Word for a pair of Bellows.

negritic (niː'grɪtɪk), *a.* Also **Negritic.** [f. NEGRO + -ITIC. Cf. NIGRITIC *a.*] Of or pertaining to Negroes or Black peoples; nigritic.

1878 C. KEARY *Dawn of Hist.* 220 The reader may consult an interesting paper by Professor Huxley..for some further views concerning the extension of the Negritic family. **1926** *Contemp. Rev.* Apr. 529 The one class that had kept itself pure from negritic intermixture. **1947** E. HOOTON in H. Gladwin *Men out of Asia* p. xi, I am fairly sure that the earliest arrivals here were non-Mongoloids carrying archaic White strains ('Australoids', if you like) probably mixed with Negritic elements. **1950** *Cold Spring Harbor Symposia on Quantitative Biol.* XV. 260/1 Using the living Andamanese as a basis for reference, the negritic migrants may be characterized as of very short stature, dark skin color, woolly hair form, moderate round-headedness, low nasal relief, and a very short and narrow face.

negritize ('niːgrɪtaɪz), *v.* Also **Negritize.** [Irreg. f. NEGRO or NEGRIT(IC *a.* + -IZE.] *trans.* To make Negro or nigritic in character or appearance.

1901 *Ann. Rep. Board of Regents Smithsonian Inst. 1899* 513 Not one fact is in evidence from which we may conclude that a single neighbouring people known to us has been Negritized. **1930** C. G. SELIGMAN *Races Afr.* v. 112 The less negritized type are of a slight, rather graceful build.

Negrito (nɪ'griːtəʊ). [a. Sp. *negrito*, dim. of *negro* NEGRO.] A member of a diminutive Negroid race existing in the Malayo-Polynesian region; esp. one of the Aëtas in the Philippine Islands.

1814 J. MAVER tr. *Martinez de Zuñiga's Hist. View Philippine Islands* I. p. xii, It is generally allowed that the language spoken by the Papuans..and Negritos of the Philippines, and adjacent islands, is totally different from the Malayan. **1840** *Penny Cycl.* XVIII. 88/1 The Negritos were probably the aborigines of the islands. **1865** LUBBOCK *Preh. Times* xiii. (1869) 440 The Islands of the Pacific contain two very distinct races of men—the Negrito and the Polynesian. **1898** F. T. BULLEN in *Nat. Rev.* Aug. 857 The Negritos..are a diminutive black race with woolly hair, and undoubtedly of Papuan origin. **1928** *Times Lit. Suppl.* 9 Feb. 90/4 The Negritoes..live at a primitive level, using wind-breaks and not houses. **1958** J. SLIMMING *Temiar Jungle* ii. 22 Originally much of this part of the Nenggiri was Negrito country. **1965** C. SHUTTLEWORTH *Malayan Safari* i. 16 Negritoes—a small negroid people with crinkly hair. **1969** *Age* (Melbourne) 24 May 12/5 Mr. Robinson..takes it for granted that two 'waves' of Negritos, the Kartans and the Tartangans, preceded the Aborigines to Australia. **1972** *Guardian* 22 Sept. 9/3 At the top of the mud bank was a tiny village of palm shelters, just high enough to sit in and here I met the Negritos, the oldest inhabitants of Malaysia, a short, negroid nomadic group.

b. In attributive or predicative use.

1843 LATHAM in *Proc. Philol. Soc.* I. 37 The Languages of the Papuan or Negrito race. *Ibid.*, The Samangs of the interior are Negrito. **1864** *Chambers's Encycl.* VI. 698/2 A description of a Negrito native of Erromango.

Negritude ('niːgrɪtjuːd). Also with small initial and in Fr. form **Négritude.** [a. F. *négritude* NIGRITUDE.] The quality or characteristic of being a Negro; affirmation of the value of Black or African culture, identity, etc.

1950 *French Rev.* XXIII. 383 Their [*sc.* pre-1939–45-war young French Colonial Negro authors'] writing would be different, so different that only a new term could describe it; hence they invented the word: *négritude*. **1960** *Guardian* 29 July 4/2 The deeper cultural manifestations of colonialism. The best of this..kind of analysis seems..to be coming from those who have been colonised themselves—in Africa ..from 'Présence Africaine's' explorations of *négritude*. **1960** *Observer* 20 Nov. 7/1 A movement for what French Pan-Africanists call 'Negritude'—the recognition of the Negro personality in world civilisation. **1961** *Ibid.* 29 Oct. 13/7 Senghor has been one of the leading prophets of *Négritude*, a literary and philosophical movement which expresses in an almost mystical way the African identity over against Western materialism. **1962** *Times Lit. Suppl.* 10 Aug. 596/4 The recent African Writers Conference..was significant for its hostility to négritude. **1963** *Internat. Year Bk.* 274/1 Aimé Césaire, a Martinique poet, invented the term, 'négritude', to describe the poetry that he and Haitians Jacques Roumain and Léon Laleau, and Léon Damas from Guiana were attempting to write. The word referred to the elevating of Africa as a place toward which all people of Negro blood aspired spiritually, but this Africa was not so much a geographical location as a condition of the mind. **1965** *Time* 27 Aug. 19 The whole-hearted attempt by other Negroes to emphasize their Negroid features and hair texture shows their pride in their 'negritude'—a word currently in fashion in Negro communities. **1966** *New Statesman* 18 Nov. 730/1 Negritude is the least characteristic thing about Senator-elect Edward Brooke... On election night..Walter Cronkite told..television listeners that Brooke was 'five-fourths White'. **1969** N. HARE in A. Chapman *New Black Voices* (1972) 435 The debate was kicked off by leading Negritude theoretician, Leopold Senghor. *Ibid.* 436 Negritude..permitted an escape into excessive glorification of the past and the traditional..so that one found difficulty in incorporating the techniques of the present and the future or in turning them effectively against the oppressor. **1971** *Black Scholar* Apr.–May 8 The laws and order of this nation are contrary to the black man's nature, contrary to our Negritude. **1972** M. RIOFRANCAS in J. Pinkham tr. *Césaire's Discourse on Colonialism* 72 (*tr. interview*) How did you come to develop the concept of Negritude? A [imé] C[ésaire]. I have a feeling that it was something of a collective creation. I used the term first, that's true... It was really a resistance to the policy of assimilation. **1975** *Times Lit. Suppl.* 7 Mar. 247/2 (Advt.), Negritude has been defined by Senghor as 'the sum of the cultural values of the black world as they are expressed in the life, the institutions, and the works of black men'.

Negro ('niːgrəʊ). Also 7–8 **negroe**, 8– **negro.** [a. Sp. or Pg. *negro*:—L. *nigrum, niger* black: cf. NIGRO. Hence also F. *nègre*: see NEGER and NIGGER.]

I. 1. An individual (esp. a male) belonging to the African race of mankind, which is distinguished by a black skin, black tightly-curled hair, and a nose flatter and lips thicker and more protruding than is common amongst white Europeans. In the nineteenth and twentieth centuries also applied (now somewhat less frequently because of the increasing use of the word *Black*) to individuals of African ancestry born in or resident in the United States or in other English-speaking countries. (Now customarily written with a capital initial.) Cf. NEW NEGRO, NIGGER *sb.*

1555 EDEN *Decades* 239 They are not accustomed to eate such meates as doo the Ethiopians or Negros. **1580** FRAMPTON *Dial. Yron & Steele* 149 In all Ginea the blacke people called Negros doe use for money..certayne little snayles. **1613** PURCHAS *Pilgrimage* v. xvi. 450 There is amongst them an Iland of Negro's inhabited with blacke people. **1677** W. HUBBARD *Narrative* 99 His design being strangely discovered by a Negroe. **1716** S. SEWALL *Diary* 22 June, I essay'd..to prevent Indians and Negros being Rated with Horses and Hogs. **1782** PRIESTLEY *Corrupt. Chr.* II. IX. 212 His coat of mail made his skin as black as a negroe. **1837** HT. MARTINEAU *Soc. Amer.* II. 120 No mean testimony to the intellectual and moral capabilities of negroes. **1864** C. GEIKIE *Life in Woods* xxii. (1874) 349 As he came near, I saw he was a negro. **1876** tr. *O. Peschel's Races of Man* 464 Narrow and more or less high skulls are prevalent among the negroes. **1906** *Harper's Weekly* 2 June 763/2 Professor Booker T. Washington, being politely interrogated..as to whether negroes ought to be called 'negroes' or 'members of the colored race' has replied that it has long been his own practice to write and speak of members of his race as negroes, and when using the term 'negro' as a race designation, to employ the capital 'N'. **1911** E. C. SEMPLE *Influences Geogr. Environment* ii. 38 It is generally conceded by scientists that pigment is a protective device of nature. The Negro's skin is comparatively insensitive to a sun heat that blisters a white man. **1930** *N.Y. Times* 7 Mar. 22/5 (*heading*) 'Negro' with a capital 'N'... Major Robert R. Moton..has written..that his people universally wish to see the word 'Negro' capitalized... In our 'style book' 'Negro' is now added to the list of words to be capitalized. It is not merely a typographical change; it is an act in recognition of racial self-respect. **1938** F. BOAS *Gen. Anthropol.* iii. 104 In a strict sense a race must be defined as a group of common origin and of stable type. In this sense extreme forms like the Australians, Negroes, Mongolians, and Europeans may be described as races because each has certain characteristics which set them off from other groups, and which are strictly hereditary. **1965** S. S. SMITH *Ess. Causes of Variety of Complexion & Figure* p. lvi, It remains hazardous..to offer summary findings as to skeletal differences between whites and negroes. **1970** R. D. ABRAHAMS *Positively Black* ii. 33 By espousing the term 'black' for themselves, they are also arguing implicitly that 'Negro' is a status term imposed by whites to underline the white's sense of the place of blacks in the American system. **1970** C. MAJOR *Dict. Afro-Amer. Slang* 84 *Negro*, another way of calling [a] person an *Uncle Tom*. **1971** *Black Scholar* Jan. 53/2 His protagonist, a white-skinned Negro..decides to leave the black race. *Ibid.* Apr.–May 9 The United States of America has..deprived me and my brothers and sisters, the 30 to 60 million so-called Negroes, better known as Asiatic Black people, of life, liberty, and the pursuit of happiness. **1973** *Black World* May 37/2 Upon spotting the Afro-American, the Ghanaians shouted out, 'Hey, Negro!' The other..retorted angrily, 'I'm a Black Man, not a Negro. Don't call me Negro.'

†**b.** *to wash a Negro*, to attempt an impossible task. *Obs. rare.*

1611 MIDDLETON & DEKKER *Roaring Girl* I. i. D.'s Wks. 1873 III. 147, I wash a Negro, Loosing both paines and cost. *a* **1677** BARROW *Serm.* (1686) III. 42 Therefore was he put to water dry sticks, and to wash Negros; that is,..to reform a most perverse and stubborn generation.

c. *transf.* in various uses (see quots.).

1666 J. DAVIES *Hist. Caribby Isles* 100 Also a kind of fish called Negroes or Sea-Devils, which are large and have a black scale. **1698** FRYER *Acc. E. India & P.* 53 The out-ward Skin was a perfect Negro, the Bones also being as black as Jet. **1797** *Encycl. Brit.* (ed. 3) VI. 432/1 A white kidney-bean..; black negroe of the same; scarlet of the same. **1816** KIRBY & SP. *Entomol.* xvii. (1818) II. 82 The sanguine ants at length rush upon the negroes [black ants]. **1855** MORTON

Cycl. Agric. II. 120 *Negroes* and *Niggers*, provincial names of the caterpillars of the turnip saw-fly.

d. The English spoken by American Blacks. Also in *Combs.* with a language name, as ***Negro-English***, ***-French***, etc.

1704 S. KNIGHT *Jrnl.* (1825) 38 You speak negro to him. I'le ask him. **1808** T. ASHE *Trav. Amer.* 79 The husband.. had lived long enough in Virginia to pick up some Negro-English. **1819** R. L. MASON *Narr. in Pioneer West* (1915) 56 Negro-French is the common language of this town. **1862** 'E. KIRKE' *Among Pines* 132 Not to weary the reader with a long repetition of negro-English, I will tell in brief what I gleaned from an hour's conversation with the two blacks. **1884** *Trans. Amer. Philol. Assoc.* XVI. App. 32 Such parasynetic forms as *sparrer-grass* for *asparagus*.. are common enough in Negro. **1932** W. L. GRAFF *Lang.* 436 As a result of European trade a number of creolized trade languages have developed along the Atlantic Coast. They are chiefly Negro-Portuguese, Negro-English, and Negro-French. **1964** *Language* XL. 291 Sranan (also known as.. Surinam Negro-English). **1971** J. SPENCER *Eng. Lang. W. Afr.* 9 A pidginised form of Portuguese (often referred to as Negro-Portuguese).

2. *Comb.* (chiefly objective) as ***Negro-baiting*** vbl. sb. and ppl. a., ***Negro-auction***, ***-breaker***, ***-breaking***, ***-dealer***, ***-driver***, ***-driving***, ***equality***, ***-hate***, ***-holder***, ***-hunter***, ***-monger***, ***-owned*** adj., ***question***, ***-rank*** adj., ***slavery***, ***-stale*** adj., ***-stealer***, ***-stealing***, ***-trader***, ***-whipping***, ***-white*** adj., ***-worship***.

1856 OLMSTED *Slave States* 31 This must not be taken as an indication that *negro auctions are not of frequent occurrence. **1949** *Sat. Rev. Lit.* (U.S.) 24 Sept. 6 Something about *Negro-baiting in the South. **1951** KOESTLER *Age of Longing* x. 183 You are a Negro-baiting, half-civilised nation. **1845** F. DOUGLASS *Narr. Life F. Douglass* x. 73 Mr. Covey enjoyed the most unbounded reputation for being a first-rate overseer and *negro-breaker. **1855** —— *My Bondage & my Freedom* xv. 216 His proficiency in the art of *negro breaking. **1799** *Hull Advertiser* 7 Sept. 4/1 He took him to one of the *negro-dealers, who.. advanced eighty pounds. **1856** OLMSTED *Slave States* 30 The negro-dealers had confidential servants always in attendance. **1771** SMOLLETT *Humph. Cl.* (1815) 67, I have known a *negro-driver, from Jamaica, pay.. sixty-five guineas. **1781** J. MOORE *View Soc. It.* (1795) II. 3 The unrelenting frown of a negro-driver. **1857** GEN. P. THOMPSON *Audi Alt.* (1858) I. xvi. 55 These must be old negro-drivers. **1826** SCOTT *Diary* in *Lockhart* (1839) VIII. 223 The true *negro-driving principle of self-interest. **1856** *Illinois State Register* (Springfield) 26 June 3/3 The cry for *negro equality is on their lips. **1905** N. DAVIS *Northerner* 52 You think I might be nice to Mr. Falls, negro equality and all? **1862** *N.Y. Tribune* 21 Apr., Southern *negro-hate, being based on Slavery, is kept within bounds; that of the North, being mainly a hypocrisy or imitation, is affected & exaggerated to caricature. **1780** J. JONES *Lett.* (1889) 47 The *negro holders in general already clamour against the project. **1817** COBBETT *Wks.* XXXII. 90 The Deputies.. of the Negro-holders, of the Sugar-growers [etc.]. **1857** GEN. P. THOMPSON *Audi Alt.* (1858) I. xvi. 55 We are to be overwhelmed with an avalanche of *negro-hunters. **1741** T. JONES *Let.* 1 July in *Colonial Rec. Georgia* (1906) IV. 678 This exposes them to the Envy and Hatred of our *Negro-Mongers. **1879** SIR G. CAMPBELL *White & Black* 154 The *negro-owned lands are not now much increasing. **1832** *Reg. Deb. Congress U.S.* 2 Apr. 2348 The South must be threatened with the *negro question. **1949** *Time* 31 Oct. 84/3 The South gradually transformed 'the Negro-question' into a fanatical folk bias, coloring its segregated religion, its sex attitudes, its every moment in life. **1942** *Negro-rank [see *Negro-stale* adj. below]. **1831** M. HOLLEY *Texas* (1833) 87 The question of *negro slavery.. is one of great importance. **1942** W. FAULKNER *Go Down, Moses* 199 It all seemed to stand there about them, intact and complete and visible in the drafty, damp, heatless, *negro-stale negro-rank sorry room. **1827** *Western Monthly Rev.* I. 69 It will be the refuge of *Negro-stealers and the Elysium of rogues. **1819** *Niles' Reg.* XVI. 160/1 Sentence of death has been pronounced on a fellow in North Carolina, for *negro stealing. **1732** in *Rhode Island Hist. Soc. Coll.* (1923) XVI. 108, 4 *Negro Traders then on board. **1873** 'MARK TWAIN' & WARNER *Gilded Age* VII. 78 The Hawkins hearts had been torn to see Uncle Dan'l and his wife pass from the auction-block into the hands of a negro trader. **1845** YOUATT *Dog* v. 113 You.. find that your dogs do not want this unmerciful *negro-whipping. **1956** J. C. FURNAS *Goodbye to Uncle Tom* II. 70 Our town then had the largest *Negro-white ratio in the North. **1961** *Times* 2 Dec. 11/5 Eight Negroes, mostly of mixed Negro-white descent. **1861** *Illustr. Lond. News* 17 Aug. 152/2 The damnable heresy of '*negro-worship'.

b. Negro's head, the Ivory Palm.

1670 EVELYN *Sylva* (ed. 2) 3 Descended immediately from the Genius of the Soyls.., and (as the Negros-Heads in the Barbados) even without Seeds. **1846** LINDLEY *Veget. Kingd.* 138 The natives of Columbia call it Tagua, or Cabeza de Negro (Negro's head), in allusion, we presume, to the figure of the nut.

†**c.** (See quot.) *Obs. rare*$^{-0}$.

1796 *Grose's Dict. Vulg. Tongue*, *Negroes Heads*, brown loaves delivered to the ships in ordinary.

II. *attrib.* (passing into *adj.*).

3. With names of persons: Belonging to the race of Negroes; black-skinned. Also ***Negro minstrel*** (see quots. 1864 and 1871).

1594 CAREW *Huarte's Exam. Mens Wits* 316 A negro woman. **1625** PURCHAS *Pilgrims* II. 978, I departed.. with two Negro Boyes that I had. **1665** HOOKE *Microgr.* 207 Negro Women.. bringing forth.. tawny hided Mulattos. **1686** *Lond. Gaz.* No. 2177/4 A black Negro Man about 30 years of age. **1719** DE FOE *Crusoe* I. (Globe) 37, I bought me a Negro Slave. **1761** *Chron.* in *Ann. Reg.* 145 A negroe man .. attacked a negroe wench.. and would have killed a negroe boy. **1799** HOME in *Phil. Trans.* LXXXIX. 163 The Negro women of the Mandingo and Ibbo nations. **1837** HT. MARTINEAU *Soc. Amer.* II. 142 Does it never enter the heads of negro husbands and fathers to retaliate? **1855** C. E. DE LONG in *Calif. Hist. Soc. Q.* (1929) VIII. 346 A negro minstrel performance at home went to it and took some girls. **1858** ELIZ. TWINING *Short Lect. Plants* i. 10 The negro women working in the hot cotton plantations. **1864** *Chambers's Encycl.* VI. 699/1 In most cases the members of the negro minstrel troupes are only negroes in name, with faces and hands blackened. **1871** DE VERE *Americanisms* 116 The Negro-minstrel is the artist who blackens his face, adopts the black man's manner and instrument, and recites his field and plantation songs. **1884** *Century Mag.* Mar. 688/1 At that time the negro-minstrel was not a black-faced singer of sentimental songs but a man who sang and jumped Jim Crow.. and other genuine plantation songs. **1915** *Scribner's Mag.* June 754 Time was when the Negro-minstrels held possession of three or four theatres in the single city of New York. **1970** *Oxf. Compan. Mus.* (ed. 10) 675/1 Towards the end of the nineteenth century Negro Minstrels were a feature of every considerable British coast resort.

b. *transf.* of insects.

1816 KIRBY & SP. *Entomol.* xvii. (1818) II. 85 Thirty of the rufescent ants.. with the addition of several negro pupæ. **1864** *Athenæum* 10 Dec. 788 A remarkable negro variety of *Abraxas grossulariata*.

4. Consisting or composed of Negroes.

1652 TATHAM in *Brome's Joviall Crew* B.'s Wks. 1873 III. 348 Ingratefull Negro-kinde. **1842** PRICHARD *Nat. Hist. Man* 350 The Pelagian Negro races have been supposed to reach eastward as far as.. the Fejee Islands. **1849–52** *Todd's Cycl. Anat.* IV. 1353/2 The languages of the Negro nations. **1879** FROUDE *Cæsar* iv. 33 The Negro tribes have never extended north of the Sahara.

5. Inhabited or occupied by Negroes.

1720 DE FOE *Capt. Singleton* v. (1840) 88 We met with a little negro town. **1734** *New York Gaz.* 18–25 Mar. 1/1 Thomas L——d keeps at some Miles distance from his dwelling House, Negro-Quarters (as they are called). **1796** MORSE *Amer. Geog.* II. 628 The European nations.. [have] encouraged in the Negroe countries, wars, rapine,.. and murder. **1813** E. GERRY JR. *Diary* 26 June (1927) 144 Mr. Carrol has 1000 slaves, whose huts, called negro quarters, constitute a small town around the mansion. **1841** LANE *Arab. Nts.* I. 62 The slaves of the Arabs are mostly from Abyssinia and the Negro countries. **1849–52** *Todd's Cycl. Anat.* IV. 1352/2 Here the true Negro area.. is exceedingly small. **1913** W. P. EATON *Barn Doors & Byways* 167 The old foundation stones show that the house was once one hundred and ten feet long, with a gigantic kitchen and outstanding negro quarters.

6. Of or belonging to, connected with, characteristic of, etc., a Negro or Negroes. Spec. of any art form: associated with or characteristic of Negroes. Of clothes, fabrics, etc.: designed to be worn or used by Negroes.

1661 HICKERINGILL *Jamaica* 31 The inclosed shell [of the cocoa-nut], whose Negro-skull is not easily broke. **1732** *South Carolina Gaz.* 1 Apr., He had on.. blue Negro Boots. *Ibid.* 30 Sept. 4/2 Just imported, white and blue Negro Cloth. **1740** W. SEWARD *Jrnl.* 2 Subscriptions for a Negroe School in Pensilvania. **1769**, etc. Negro cloth, see sense 7]. **1786** *Maryland Jrnl.* 26 Sept., Fine and coarse broadcloths; coatings; Negro cottons. *a* **1818** M. G. LEWIS *Jrnl. W. Ind.* (1834) 64 The hermitage-like appearance of the negro buildings. *Ibid.* 330 To be found in almost every negro garden throughout the island. **1818** *Amer. Beacon* (Norfolk, Va.) 19 Dec. 1/4 Negro cotton. 10 Bales just received. **1841** *Picayune* (New Orleans) 3 Mar. 3 Negro Blankets, in store and for sale. **1844** J. COWELL *30 Yrs. among Players* 66 [Blakeley] was the first to introduce negro singing on the American stage. **1847** F. A. KEMBLE *Let.* Dec. in *Rec. Later Life* (1882) III. 279 Do you remember that delightful Negro song, the 'Invitation to Hayti'? **1849–52** *Todd's Cycl. Anat.* IV. 1352/2 The true Negro type of conformation. *Ibid.*, The proper Negro character. **1855** A. M. MURRAY *Lett.* (1856) 395 This morning we have had some negro music. **1864** *Chambers's Encycl.* VI. 699/1 The sentiment of.. these negro melodies. *Ibid.*, This negro minstrelsy now comprehends a large variety of songs. **1867** SMYTH *Sailor's Word-bk.* 32 Some of the larger square-sterned negro-boats are also thus designated. **1912** *Chambers's Jrnl.* Jan. 23/1 Negro songs have always been popular among us, and deservedly so. **1925** W. S. BRAITHWAITE in A. Locke *New Negro* 39 It was the stirring year of 1917 that heard the first real masterful accent in Negro poetry. **1936** A. LOCKE *Negro & his Mus.* i. 1 Negro music is the closest approach America has to a folk music, and so Negro music is almost as important for the musical culture of America as it is for the spiritual life of the Negro. *Ibid.* ii. 15 The Negro dance has the feature, characteristic of Russian, Polish and other Slavic folk-dances, of sudden changes of the pace and daring climaxes of tempo. **1960** A. E. KEEP tr. *Leuzinger's Afr.* (1962) I. i. 13 Negro art attracts and enthrals us by its emotional vigour and clarity of form. *Ibid.* vi. 52 Is negro art primitive? No—if the word 'primitive' is understood to mean something crude, barbaric and contemptible. Yes—if by 'primitive' we mean something honourable, as the term is applied, for instance, to the Fauvists in European painting. **1963** *Times Lit. Suppl.* 18 Jan. 43/2 The rock 'n roll and Negro-jazz rhythms of his American cycle of poems. **1970** R. D. ABRAHAMS *Positively Black* ii. 51 Distrust of even one's closest friends is a constant theme of Negro life and Negro fictions.

7. In special uses, as **Negro ant**, a blackish ant; **Negro bat**, a European and Asiatic bat (*Vesperugo maurus*) of a black or sooty-brown colour; **Negro cachexy** (see quot.); **Negro cloth**, cloth intended to be worn by negroes; **Negro coffee**, the seeds of *Cassia occidentalis*; **Negro corn** (see quot.); **Negro dog**, a dog used in hunting runaway negro slaves; **Negro felt** (cf. *Negro cloth*); **Negro fish, fly, fowl** (see quots.); **Negro lethargy** (see LETHARGY *sb.* 1); **Negro monkey**, a black monkey of the Malay Peninsula, Java, etc. (*Semnopithecus maurus*), also called the *Negro langur*; **Negro oil** (see quot.); **Negro peach** (see PEACH *sb.*[1] 3 a); **Negro pepper** (see PEPPER *sb.* 3); **Negro pot** (?); **Negro Renaissance** (see quot. 1973); **Negro spiritual**, an American Negro religious song; **Negro State**, any of the Southern States of America in which slavery was legal; **Negro tamarin**, a tamarin monkey (*Midas ursulas*) of the lower Amazon; **Negro yam**, the West India yam, *Dioscorea sativa* (also called ***Negro-country yam***).

1816 KIRBY & SP. *Entomol.* xvii. (1818) II. 97, I observed the little *negro ant (*F. fusca*) engaged in the same employment upon an elder. **1855** OGILVIE *Suppl.*, **Negro-cachexy*, a propensity for eating dirt, peculiar to the natives of the West Indies and Africa. **1769** *Boston Chron.* 7–10 Aug. 250/2 *Negro cloth, commonly called white and coloured plains. **1856** OLMSTED *Slave States* 27 Many.. wore clothing of coarse gray 'negro-cloth', that appeared as if made by contract. **1887** MOLONEY *Forestry W. Afr.* 330 *Negro Coffee, *L'herbe puante*. Fedigose seeds of Tette. **1858** SIMMONDS *Dict. Trade*, **Negro-corn*, a West Indian name for the Turkish millet or dhurra. **1856** OLMSTED *Slave States* 161, I have since seen a pack of *negro-dogs, chained in couples... They were all of a breed, and in appearance between a Scotch stag-hound and a fox-hound. **1857** GEN. P. THOMPSON *Audi Alt.* (1858) I. xvi. 55 Sending for packs of negro dogs from New Orleans. **1846** McCULLOCH *Acc. Brit. Empire* (1854) I. 763 Wool felts.. have now materially decreased, the article termed '*negro felts' being almost extinct. **1734** MORTIMER in *Phil. Trans.* XXXVIII. 316 *Perca marina puncticulata*. The *Negro Fish. **1855** OGILVIE *Suppl.*, **Negro fly*, the *Psila rosæ* , a dipterous insect, so named from its shining black colour. It is also called the *carrot-fly*. **1835–6** *Todd's Cycl. Anat.* I. 270/1 The Silk or *Negro-fowl of the Cape de Verd Islands (*Gallus Morio*, Temminck). **1849** D. J. BROWNE *Amer. Poultry Yd.* (1855) 81 The 'silky' and 'negro' fowls,.. with skin, combs, and bones which are black. **1888** *Syd. Soc. Lex.*, *Negro lethargy. **1898** P. MANSON *Trop. Diseases* xvi. 251 Negro lethargy, or the sleeping sickness of the Congo. **1830** *Edinb. Encycl.* XIII. 401/1 *Negro Monkey. Long-tailed, blackish, with.. blackish beard. **1753** CHAMBERS *Cycl. Supp.* App., **Negro-oil*, a name by which the palma of botanists is sometimes called. **1849** CRAIG s.v., **Negro* or *Ethiopean pepper*, the plant Unona Æthiopica. *a* **1818** M. G. LEWIS *Jrnl. W. Ind.* (1834) 307 They boiled a *negro-pot for him, but he was too ill to swallow a morsel. **1925** A. LOCKE *New Negro* p. xi, We speak of the offerings of this book.. as culled from the first fruits of the *Negro Renaissance. **1952** B. ULANOV *Hist. Jazz in Amer.* (1958) x. 103 The Negro poets who won such a large audience for their work, good, bad, and indifferent, in the intense days of the so-called Negro Renaissance. **1964** J. H. CLARKE *Harlem* 16 The stock market collapse of 1929 marked.. the end of the period known as the Negro Renaissance. **1973** BASKIN & RUNES *Dict. Black Culture* 324 *Negro Renaissance*, a creative outpouring in art, music, and literature in the 1920's, giving expression to the discontent of the Negro... Writers of the twenties displayed considerable talent.. in developing Negro themes in a highly personal way. **1867** *Atlantic Monthly* June 685/1, I had for many years heard of this class of songs under the name of '*Negro Spirituals'. **1928** *Observer* 22 July 21/1 As important.. is their singing of negro spirituals and 'work songs'. **1949** *Oregonian* (Portland) 10 Aug. 8/4 He found time to write books on his hobbies, on alligators and on Negro spirituals. **1970** *Oxf. Compan. Mus.* (ed. 10) 1064/2 The words of Negro spirituals are for the most part adaptations of passages from the Bible. **1780** in *Essex Inst. Hist. Coll.* (1877) XIII. 220 You did not carry home contemptible Ideas enough of the *negro States or of this great Braggadocio. **1809** *Deb. Congress U.S.* 20 Jan. (1853) 1152 The Potomac the boundary—the Negro states by themselves! **1881** *Proc. Zool. Soc.* 1003 *Negro Tamarins. **1896** H. O. FORBES *Hand-bk. Primates* II. 149 In Para, the Negro Tamarin is often seen in a tame state. **1696** H. SLOANE *Catal. Plantarum Jamaica* 219 *Negro Country Yam. **1707** —— *Voy. Jamaica* I. 140 Negro Country Yams. This has a great Root a Foot broad... They being cut into pieces and boiled or rosted are eaten by Negros, Slaves, or Europeans, instead of Bread. **1756** P. BROWNE *Civil & Nat. Hist. Jamaica* 359 The Negro Yam... The Yam. Both these plants are cultivated for food, the roots, which grow very large, being mealy and easy of digestion. **1814** J. LUNAN *Hortus Jamaicensis* II. 308 This [sc. *Dioscorea sativa*] is commonly called negro yam. **1864** A. H. R. GRISEBACH *Flora Brit. W. Indian Islands* 789/2 Yams, Negro country: *Dioscorea alata*. **1892** *Syd. Soc. Lex.*, *Negro yam. **1953** *Caribbean Q.* II. IV. 32 *Dioscorea sativa* the so-called negro-yam, may have been indigenous, for it.. sometimes grows wild; but more probably the wild specimens were originally escapes from cultivation. **1971** *Jamaican Weekly Gleaner* 3 Nov. 34/3 (Advt.), Negro yams, yellow yams, sweet potatoes.

Hence '**Negrocide**, the killing of a Negro. '**Negrodom**, the region or community of Negroes. '**Negrofy** *v. trans.*, to make into, or as black as, a Negro. '**Negrohood**, Negro race or stock. '**Negroish** *a.*, characteristic of the Negro. '**Negroite**, a Negrophil. '**Negroized** *a.*, given over to the Negroes. **Ne'grolatry**, excessive admiration of the Negro. '**Negrolet**, '**Negroling**, a little Negro. **Negro'mania**, extravagant Negrophilism; hence **Negro'maniac**.

1852 MUNDY *Antipodes* v. (1855) 109 It must have been considered a case of justifiable *negrocide. **1847** *Congress. Globe* 13 Feb. App. 376/1 Our measures have given all that wide region to the empire of *negrodom. **1862** HAWTHORNE in Bridge *Pers. Recollect.* (1893) 173, I ought to thank you for a shaded map of negrodom, which you sent me a little while ago. **1864** NICHOLS *40 Years Amer. Life* I. 248 All Negrodom has put on its wonderful attire of finery. **1942** Z. N. HURSTON in A. Dundes *Mother Wit* (1973) 31/2 Neither the top nor the bottom of Negrodom. *Ibid.* 32/1 A flight away from Negrodom. *a* **1790** B. FRANKLIN *Autobiogr.* in *Writings* (1905) I. 391 Finding he was likely to be *negrofied himself, he.. grew tir'd of the contest. **1799** SOUTHEY *Nondescripts* iii, If no kindly cloud will parasol me,.. I shall be negrofied. **1863** RUSSELL *Diary North & S.* I. 190 The small settlement of *negro-hood, which is separated from our house by a wooden palisade. **1789** J. MORSE *Amer. Geogr.* 65 The children, by being brought up, and constantly associating with the negroes..contract a *negroish kind of accent and dialect. **1861** *Temple Bar* II. 201 The sentimental songs had nothing peculiarly negroish about them. **1851** J. Campbell *Negromania* 543 The *Negroites have been ignominiously driven from their strongholds. **1888** *Voice* (N.Y.) 23 Aug., The only party that stands between the people and a *negroized government. **1862** Russell in *Times* 29 Jan., The Conservative masses, which lie between *negrolatry or niggerworship and Secession. **1873** Leland *Egypt. Sketch Bk.* 230 There came up a small jet-black *negrolet, eight years of age. **1886** R. F. Burton *Arab. Nts.* (abr. ed.) I. 71 O my darling! O my *negroling! **1851** J. Campbell (*title*) *Negro-mania. **1864** R. F. Burton *Dahome* II. 180, I foresee the..hard compulsory labour which the *negro-maniac will have brought upon his African protégé.

Negro-head. Also negrohead.

†**1.** A nest of tree-ants. *Obs. rare*$^{-1}$.

1781 Smeathman in *Phil. Trans.* LXXI. 161 *note*, The colour of these nests..is black, from which, and their irregular surface and orbicular shape, they have been called Negro Heads by our first writers on the Carribbee Islands.

2. A strong plug tobacco of a black colour.

1839 'J. Fume' *Paper on Tobacco* 116 A few iron nerved smokers occasionally take a pipe of negrohead. **1851** *Catal. Gt. Exhib.* I. 203 Cavendish, negro head, and other forms of tobacco. **1861** Dickens *Gt. Expect.* xl, A handful of loose tobacco of the kind that is called Negro-head.

attrib. **1809** 'D. Knickerbocker' *Hist. N.Y.* II. vi. ii. 88 He..thrust a prodigious quid of negro head tobacco into his left cheek. **1858** Simmonds *Dict. Trade, Negrohead-tobacco*, tobacco softened with molasses or syrup and pressed into cakes, generally called Cavendish. **1892** W. Pike *Barren Ground* 29 The Hudson's Bay negrohead tobacco.

3. An inferior quality of india-rubber.

1881 *Encycl. Brit.* XIII. 836/2 The scrapings from the tree..are mixed with the residues of the collecting pots.., and are made up into large rounded balls, which form the inferior commercial quality called 'negrohead.' **1896** *Daily News* 4 Apr. 2/1 The proportions of 'fine' and 'negrohead' rubbers depend on the appliances and care of the collectors.

4. ***Negrohead beech***, the Australian evergreen or myrtle beech, *Fagus Cunninghamii*.

1889 Maiden *Usef. Native Pl.* 534 Negro-head Beech..is a hard richly-coloured furniture wood, and the warty protuberances on the trunk..afford a most beautiful figure.

5. = niggerhead 2.

1910 F. Wood-Jones *Coral & Atolls* xxiv. 284 There are many enormous 'negro heads' upon the windward barrier flats of the Southern islands of the Cocos-Keeling atoll. **1943** Baker *Dict. Austral. Slang* (ed. 3) 54 *Nigger-head*, an anthill-like peak of coral showing above water. Also called 'negro-head'. **1963** D. W. & E. E. Humphries tr. *Termier's Erosion & Sedimentation* xiii. 280 Reefs are broken into blocks, the large mushroom-shaped fragments are thrown up onto the beaches, where they form 'negro-heads'.

Negroid ('ni:grɔɪd), *a.* and *sb.* [f. Negro.]

A. *adj.* Of a Negro type; resembling or having some of the characteristic features of Negroes.

1859 R. F. Burton *Centr. Afr.* in *Jrnl. Geog. Soc.* XXIX. 196 They are usually of a dark sepia brown..with negroid features. **1877** Dawson *Orig. World* xiii. 272 Flattened lips, and certain negroid peculiarities in his limbs. **1893** Selous *Trav. S.E. Africa* 342 A type of man which is Asiatic or Semitic rather than negroid.

B. *sb.* A person of a Negro type.

1859 R. F. Burton *Centr. Afr.* in *Jrnl. Geog. Soc.* XXIX. 115 Free negroids from Zanzibar island or coast. **1882** Sala *Amer. Revis.* (1885) 172 At Wormley's..the negro and negroid were seen at their very best.

Hence **Ne'groidal** *a.*

1878 H. M. Stanley *Dark Cont.* I. v. 113 Though they were truly negroidal in hair and colour. **1881** Cable *Mme. Delphine* ii. 5 Comely Ethiopians culled out of the less negroidal types of African live goods.

Negroism ('ni:grəʊɪz(ə)m). [f. Negro + -ism.]

1. Advancement of Negro interests or rights.

1847 *Congress. Globe* 29th Congress 2 Sess. App. 323/2 He..thanked God that he voted against that Wilmot proviso. It smelt rank of negroism. **1851** J. Campbell *Negro-mania* 549 Who dare say anything in favor of Negroism after having read them? **1861** *Sat. Rev.* 4 May 454 Originated the idea of 'free negroism' and started a crusade in favour of inferior races. **1935** Z. N. Hurston *Mules & Men* (1970) 17 When I pitched headforemost into the world I landed in the crib of negroism. **1970** D. Caute *Fanon* vi. 80 The vague, cosmic cults of Negroism and Arabism.

2. A Negro pronunciation, expression, or idiom.

1859 Bartlett *Dict. Amer.* (ed. 2) p. viii, The term 'Americanisms'..may then be said to include the following classes of words:..8. Negroisms. **1864** *Spectator* 27 Feb. 238/2 'Hyur' for 'here'..is..a negroism. **1876** Douse *Grimm's L.* 66 The Americanism 'this child', or the negroism 'dis nigger'. **1930** G. B. Johnson in B. A. Botkin *Treas. S. Folklore* (1949) iv. iii. 697 *Ax*, ask. Not a Negroism, but a usage which was once good English.

Negroization (,ni:grəʊaɪ'zeɪʃən). [f. Negro + -ization.] A making or becoming Negro in character.

1898 A. J. Butler tr. *Ratzel's Hist. Mankind* III. 258 From them Rohlfs expects an ever-increasing 'negroisation' of the Libyan oasis.

'Negroland. [f. Negro + land.] The land or region (in Africa) inhabited by Negroes; the Southern States of the U.S.A. (*rare*).

1756 J. Wesley *Works* (1872) IX. 209 Either in Negroland or round the Cape of Good Hope. **1764** Goldsm. *Hist. Eng. in Lett.* (1772) I. 187 The princes on the coast of Negroland. **1802–12** Bentham *Ration. Judic. Evid.* (1827) III. 302 In Negroland, witchcraft is even now the most common of all crimes. **1836** F. A. Kemble *Let.* 5 Oct. in *Rec. Later Life* (1882) I. 66 The nearest town to this estate, Brunswick, is..a wretched hole, where I am assured it will be impossible to obtain a decent lodging for me... The owner will go..without us, on his expedition to Negroland. **1842** Prichard *Nat. Hist. Man* 316 The destitute savages who occupy the insulated hamlets of central Negroland. **1901** *Daily Chron.* 12 Aug. 7/5 Nothing, they declare, will place the white man in lasting possession of Negroland. **1931** *Times Lit. Suppl.* 26 Feb. 145/1 Africa south of the Sahara is by no means coterminous with negroland.

'Negroloid, *a. rare*$^{-1}$. [irreg. f. Negro, perh. after *Mongoloid*.] Negroid.

1842 *Proc. Amer. Philos. Soc.* II. 240 Negroloid crania.

negromancer, -mancie, etc., obs. ff. necromancer, -cy.

Negroness ('ni:grəʊnɪs). [f. Negro + -ness.] Negro qualities and characteristics in the aggregate.

1946 *Sat. Rev. Lit.* (U.S.) 29 June 42 The native suffixes *-hood*, *-ness*, and *-wright* have given us *Hottentot-hood* and *sahib-hood*; *at-easeness*, *Negroness*, and *tasklessness*; and *filmwright*. **1958** J. Kerouac *Subterraneans* 31 The old eccentric lady not any more conscious of her *Negroness*. **1965** *Times Lit. Suppl.* 25 Nov. 1047/5 He had to confront being 'Baldwin' without atrophying into an idol, and his method is to transcend enforced initial Negroness, even to avoid being 'a Negro writer', or any 'Negro' trap. **1971** G. S. Holt in T. Kochman *Rappin' & Stylin' Out* (1972) 155 So identifying someone as 'Jew' or 'Negro' devastates the category of Negroness or Jewishness more so than saying Negro *writer*, Jewish *doctor*. **1973** *Black World* Mar. 19 Bakara asks: 'Where is the Negro-ness of a literature written in imitation of the meanest of social intelligences to be found in American culture, *i.e.*, the white middle class?'

‖**negroni** (ne'groni, nɪ'grəʊni:). Also **negrone**. [It.] A drink made from gin, vermouth, and Campari; a glass of this.

1950 E. Hemingway *Across River* vi. 34 They were drinking *negronis*, a combination of two sweet vermouths and seltzer water. **1952** P. Bonner *SPQR* (1953) xx. 174, I called the barman for a *negrone*. **1960** I. Fleming *For your Eyes Only* v. 146 Bond nodded. 'A Negroni. With Gordon's, please.' **1960** B. Marshall *Divided Lady* ii. vi. 129 Before I had finished my third *negrone*. **1972** J. D. Buchanan *Professional* xvi. 158 Summoning the waiter he ordered a Negroni.

Negrophil ('ni:grəʊfɪl). Also **-phile**. [f. Negro + -phil or a. F. *négrophile*.] A friend of the Negroes; one who favours the advancement of Negro interests or rights.

1803 *Edin. Rev.* III. 82 Colonists who have been ruined by the revolution of the '*negrophiles*'. **1858** Macaulay in Trevelyan *Life* (1883) I. 24 *note*, The nigger driver and the negrophile are two odious things to me. **1868** W. R. Greg *Lit. & Soc. Judgm.* 447 An enthusiastic abolitionist and negrophile. **1889** *Sat. Rev.* 18 May 620/1 Like the work of all negrophils, it is sometimes wanting in criticism. **1934** R. Campbell *Broken Record* iii. 58 Pringle obtained and asserted the freedom of the Press... He had a negrophile bias and misrepresented much. **1936** H. Preece in A. Dundes *Mother Wit* (1973) 36/2 Our indictments of the professional Negrophiles need not even be so personal. **1958** *Times Lit. Suppl.* 10 Jan. 21/1 Many of the first explorers had an objectivity and sympathy with the indigenous people which would startle a modern negrophile.

Negrophilism (nɪ'grɒfɪlɪz(ə)m). [f. as Negrophil + -ism.] Fondness for the Negro; zealous advocacy of Negro rights.

1846 *Congress. Globe* 18 May 838/1 The gentleman from Ohio.., the advocate of *negro-philism*. **1859** *Harper's Mag.* Oct. 694/2 If negrophilism seeks to substitute the Chinaman or the Indiaman for the African, it will neglect all the lessons of experience. **1860** A. B. Longstreet in *U.S. Ann. Treas. Rep.* 475 A man..of more negrophilism than brains. **1865** *Sat. Rev.* 14 Jan. 61/2 You have got nigger-on-the-brain; you are carried away with this everlasting negrophilism. **1876** R. F. Burton *Gorilla L.* II. 237 The year 1816 was the Augustan age of outrageous negrophilism. **1889** Farmer *Americanisms* 386/2 *Negro-philism*, the anti-slavery movement.

Negrophilist (nɪ'grɒfɪlɪst). [f. as prec. + -ist.] A lover or friend of the Negro.

1842 S. Ward in *Longfellow's Life* (1891) I. 449 When the Eastern negrophilists are prepared to pay a tax, they will have a right to dispose of the property of their Southern brethren. **1899** *Pop. Sci. Monthly* LV. 178 The most infatuated negrophilist.

Negrophilistic (,ni:grəʊfɪ'lɪstɪk), *a. rare.* [f. Negrophil + -istic.] Having Negrophil characteristics.

1899 *Leisure Hour* Dec. 168/2 The Colonists have always despised the volume [Thomas Pringle's South African poems] because of the Negrophilistic character of some of the pieces therein.

Negrophobe ('ni:grəʊfəʊb). [f. Negro + -phobe.] One who has a violent aversion to or hatred of Negroes.

1900 *Spectator* 15 Sept. 329/2 Negrophiles may be..wiser as well as better men than negrophobes. **1962** C. L. Barnhart in Householder & Saporta *Probl. Lexicogr.* 179 A vulgar, offensive term of contempt, as used by Negrophobes. **1974** *Guardian* 23 Jan. 12/2 Edward Long, historian, statistician and so-called absentee sinecurist and negrophobe.

Negrophobia (ni:grəʊ'fəʊbɪə). [f. Negro + -phobia.] Intense dislike of the Negro.

1819 *Niles' Reg.* XVI. Suppl. 173/2 The gentleman from Kentucky..has charged us..with being under the influence of *negrophobia*. **1833** *Westm. Rev.* Oct. 374 The mark of cast blood, the *Negrophobia*, shows itself in three cases out of four. **1859** N. P. Willis *Convalescent* 173 His hatred of colored people amounted to a negrophobia. **1863** W. Phillips *Speeches* 528 The North had a second element, negrophobia. **1898** T. J. Morgan *Negro in Amer.* vi. 125 It would not be fair to say that they are hated, that there exists well-defined Negrophobia among us. **1945** Mencken *Amer. Lang.* Suppl. I. 408 Whenever a new suffix appears in the United States, it is put to use. An example is..*-phobia*, borrowed from the psychiatrists, and made to do heavy duty in a multitude of nouns designating violent aversions *e.g.*,..*negrophobia*..with attendant adjectives in *-phobic*.

Hence **Negro'phobiac** *a.*; **Ne'grophobist**.

1867 *Morn. Star* 21 Feb., It is the mere bunkum of the negrophobiac. **1878** H. M. Stanley *Dark Cont.* I. ix. 195, I am aware that there are negrophobists who may attribute this conduct of Mtesa to..duplicity.

Ne'grotic, *a. rare*$^{-1}$. [f. Negro, on anal. of forms in *-otic*.] Of or pertaining to the Negro.

1876 R. F. Burton *Gorilla L.* I. 34 Nothing negrotic now astonishes us.

‖**Negus**[1] ('ni:gəs). Now *Hist.* Also 6–7 (9) **neguz**, 9 **negoos**. [Amharic *negus* or *n'gus* kinged, king.] The title of the supreme ruler of Abyssinia.

1594 Blundevil *Exerc.* v. xi. (1636) 554 Of his own subjects, he is called Acegue, and Neguz of the Abassines. **1613** Purchas *Pilgrimage* vii. i. 549 The Great Neguz his titles comprehend thus much [etc.]. **1664** Butler *Hud.* ii. i. 239 The Negus when some mighty lord Or potentate's to be restor'd [etc.]. **1667** Milton *P.L.* xi. 397 Th' Empire of Negus to his utmost Port. **1805** Southey in C. C. Southey *Life* (1849) II. 314 The king, or, to give him his proper title, the Neguz. **1865** *Lit. Churchman* 25 Mar. 124/2 That strange compound of intelligence and savagery the Negus Theodore II. **1888** *Times* (weekly ed.) 6 Apr. 13/1 The Negus..is not much more than a semi-barbarous Prince.

negus[2] ('ni:gəs). [From the name of the inventor, Colonel Francis *Negus* (died 1732).] A mixture of wine (esp. port or sherry) and hot water, sweetened with sugar and flavoured.

1743 in *Etoniana* iv. (1865) 70 Warming a little negus. **1753** H. Walpole *Let.* 4 Aug., He desired the water might be warm..; Montagu understood the dialect, and ordered a negus. **1783** S. Chapman in *Med. Comm.* I. 285 He was directed to drink..a little weak red wine negus. **1831** T. L. Peacock *Crotchet Castle* xii, He wiled away the evening with making a bottle of sherry into negus. **1874** L. Stephen *Hours in Library* I. 373 The difference between the stiffest of nautical grogs and the negus provided by thoughtful parents for a child's evening party.

attrib. **1848** B. D. Walsh *Aristoph.* 292 *note*, Socrates then..Filches the negus-ladle.

neh(e, obs. forms of nigh *adv.* and *v.*

nehebor, -bur, obs. forms of neighbour.

†**nehleche,** *v. Obs.* Forms: 1 **néa(h)lǽcan, néolécan, -lican,** 2–3 **neh(t)-, neih-,** 3 **ney(h)lechen;** 2–3 **neih-, neolachen,** 3 **nechleache.** [OE. *néa(h)lǽcan*, f. *néah* nigh *adv.* + *-lǽcan*, a common verbal suffix related to *lácan* to move, play. In OE. the pa. t. is *-lǽhte*, *-léhte*, *-lécte*; in ME. it appears as *-læhte*, *-le(c)hte*, *-leþte*, *-leyhte* and *-lechede*.] *intr.* To approach, or draw near (*to* or *toward* a place or person).

c **900** tr. *Bæda's Hist.* i. xiv. [xxv.] (1890) 60 Heo ferdon & nealehton to ðære ceastre. *c* **950** *Lindisf. Gosp.* Matt. xxvi. 46 Heono neoleces seðe me seleð. **971** *Blickl. Hom.* 39 Nu nealæceþ þæt we sceolan..ure wæstmas ȝesamnian. *c* **1175** *Lamb. Hom.* 3 þe helend nehlechede to-ward ierusalem. *a* **1225** *Ancr. R.* 60 Heo schekeð hire spere, & nehlecheð upon hire. *c* **1275** *Wom. Samaria* 6 in *O.E. Misc.* 84 He neyleyhte to one bureh þat hatte samarie.

Hence †**nehleching, -ung,** approach. *Obs.*

c **960** Æthelwold *Rule St. Benet* (Schröer) 135 þridde cyn is ansetlena, þe..na[n]ra manna nealæcynge na underfoþ. *c* **1000** Ælfric *Hom* I. 88 Ðaða he ȝefredde his deaðes nealæcunge. *a* **1225** *Ancr. R.* 196 Ine wildernesse beoð alle wilde bestes, & nulleð nout iðolien monnes neihlechunge.

Nehru ('nɛəru:). [f. the name of Jawaharlal *Nehru* (1889–1964), first Prime Minister of independent India from 1947 to 1964.] A garment of the style often worn by Nehru, consisting of a long narrow jacket with a high, stand-up collar. Usually *attrib.*, as ***Nehru coat, collar, jacket, suit***, etc.

1967 *N.Y. Times* 24 May 46 Variations on the narrow 'Nehru' jacket with the stand-up collar continue. **1967** *Time* 25 Aug. 38 There came the groom,..wearing baggy trousers, a white, Nehru-collar tunic with red trim and cowboy boots. **1968** *N.Y. Times* 6 June 50, I wouldn't wear Nehrus or those damn beads either. **1968** *Punch* 24 July 107/2 In, says an informed source, are 'the Nehru coat and the Nehru suit'. Gandhi's turn next? **1969** C. F. Burke *God is Beautiful, Man* (1970) 47 A new chain to wear with his turtle neck sweater and Nehru jacket. **1971** 'G. Black' *Time for Pirates* ii. 33 The man is tall for a Chinese and very thin. He wears a white Nehru jacket over black cotton jeans. **1973** *Caribbean Contact* Feb. 9/4 The Ambassador for the People's Republic of China stands in a corner with the interpreter, wearing a black, Nehru-style shirt.

nei, obs. f. NAY, NIGH.

neibour, Sc. f. NEIGHBOUR.

neice, obs. f. NIECE.

neichtbour, obs. Sc. f. NEIGHBOUR.

neid, obs. Sc. f. NEED.

neider, obs. f. NEITHER.

neidlingis, -lings, -lyngis, Sc. varr. NEEDLINGS *adv. Obs.*

neidy, obs. Sc. f. NEEDY *a.*

neieȝbor, obs. f. NEIGHBOUR.

neies, obs. var. of NESE, nose.

neif (niːf). Now only *Hist.* Forms: α. 6–8 **neife**, (7 **neiffe**), 7– **neif**, 9 **neyf**; 6 **nef**. β. 6–7 **niefe**, (6 **nyef(e, nyeffe**), 8 **nief**. γ. 7, 9 **naif**. [a. AF. (*c* 1300) *neyf, neif, nief* = earlier *nayf, naif*:—L. *nātīvum*: see NAÏF and NAIVE *a.*]

1. One born in a state of bondage or serfdom (cf. NATIVE *sb.* 1); sometimes *spec.* a female serf, a bondwoman.

α. **1547** *Act 1 Edw. VI*, c. 3 §17 Persons, to whom any such Ward, Bondman, or Neife shall apperteine. **1610** W. FOLKINGHAM *Art of Survey* IV. ii. 82 Villaines & Neifes, which are alwayes saide to be Regardant to a Manour. *c* **1630** RISDON *Surv. Devon* §206 (1810) 215 In which manor were bond men, anciently called Villains, and the women Neifs. *c* **1780** SIR W. JONES *Wks.* VII. 10 A lord in feudal times might have been convicted of murder for killing his villain or his neife. **1818** HALLAM *Mid. Ages* (1872) I. 201 Bracton.. holds that the spurious issue of a neif, though by a free father, should be a villein. **1872** C. INNES *Lect. Scot. Legal Antiq.* ii. 50, I cannot pretend to distinguish with any accuracy the bondman from the neyf.

β. **1532** *Dial. on Laws Eng.* II. xliii. 107 If a woman be a nyef, and she maryeth a free man. **1582** STANYHURST *Æneid* III. (Arb.) 81 Me his nyefe to his seruant Helenus ful firmelye betroathed. **1628** COKE *On Litt.* 122 A woman which is Villein, is called a Niefe. **1641** *Termes de la Ley* 263 In a writ *de Libertate probanda* may be put as many Niefes as the plaintife will.

γ. **1679** BLOUNT *Anc. Tenures* 143 Every naif or she villain that took a husband.. paid marchet, for redemption of her blood. **1865** NICHOLS *Britton* I. 195 *note*, The annotator in MS. N distinguishes between naifs, villains, and serfs.

†**2.** *writ of neif*: (see NEIFTY). *Obs.*

1625 SIR H. FINCH *Law* (1636) 259 In a mort dancestor cosinage, ayell, entry, and Writ of Niefe, from Henrie the thirds Coronation. **1651** tr. *Kitchin's Jurisd.* (1657) 328 If the Plaintiff in a writ of (Neife) be non-suited [etc.].

neif(e, obs. forms of NIEVE, fist.

neifful, variant of NIEVEFUL.

ˈ**neifty.** *rare.* Also 7 **niefty**, 9 **naifty**. [a. AF. *neifté*: see NEIF and -TY.] *writ of neifty*, a writ by which a lord claimed a person as his neif.

1641 *Termes de la Ley* 263 In a writ of Niefty may not be put more Niefes than two onely. **1771** in Howell *State Trials* (1814) XX. 42 The only writ in the law for the recovery of a villein is.. always called the.. writ of Neifty. **1865** NICHOLS *Britton* I. 195 Free men.. convicted as villains by plea under our writ of Naifty.

neigh (neɪ), *sb.* Also 6 *Sc.* **ne**. [f. next.] The natural cry or call uttered by a horse.

1513 DOUGLAS *Æneis* XI. x. 24 He sprentis furth, and full provd walxis he, Heich strekand vp his hed with mony a ne. **1599** SHAKS. *Hen. V*, III. vii. 29 It is the Prince of Palfrayes, his Neigh is like the bidding of a Monarch. **1635–56** COWLEY *Davideis* IV. 707 Here with sharp Neighs the warlike Horses sound. **1781** COWPER *Charity* 177 Responsive to the distant neigh, he neighs. **1821** SCOTT *Kenilw.* vii, The neigh of horses and the baying of hounds were heard. **1879** BEERBOHM *Patagonia* v. 65 At our approach he gave a faint neigh of satisfaction.

neigh (neɪ), *v.* Forms: α. 1 **(h)nǽȝan**, 3–6 **neye(n)**, 4 **nay-**, **neȝ-**, **neiȝ-**, 4–5 **neyȝ-**, **neyh-**, 4–6 **neyghe**, (4 **nayghe**), 4– **neigh**, (7 **neay**). β. 4–6 **nye**, 5 **nyȝe**, 6 **nie**. γ. 5–6 *north.* and *Sc.* **ne(e**. [OE. *hnǽȝan* = MDu. *neyen* (Flem. and Du. dial. *neijen*), MHG. *nêgen*, of imitative origin: cf. also OS. *(to)hnechian*; MDu. *nijgen, nighen, nien, nyen*, MLG. *nigen, nihen*, MHG. *nyhen*. The vbl. sb. also appears in early OE. as *hnæggiung*, app. parallel to ON. *gneggia* (Sw. *gnägga*, Da. *gnegge*), Icel. *hneggja*, Norw. *(k)neggja*. Other imitative forms are NEIGHER, NICHER, and NICKER.]

1. *intr.* Of a horse: To utter its characteristic sound or cry.

α. *c* **1000** ÆLFRIC *Gram.* xxx. (Z.) 192 *Hinnio*, ic hnæȝe. *Ibid.* 129 *Equus hinnit*, hors hnæȝð [*v.r.* næȝþ]. **1297** R. GLOUC. (Rolls) 9417 Þe hors neyde & lepte þat it was gret fere. **13..** *K. Alis.* 1872 Mony stede [there was] loude neyghyng. **1387** TREVISA *Higden* (Rolls) III. 403 Bucefal þe hors.. neyhede as it were þe rorynge of leons. *c* **1400** *Laud Troy Bk.* 7729 As he were a hors, he neyes and ondes. **1470–85** MALORY *Arthur* VI. iii. 186 They herde by them a grete hors grymly neye. **1530** PALSGR. 643/2 It is a comfortable thyng to here a horse neye whan he is on his journaye. **1601** SHAKS. *Jul. C.* II. ii. 23 The noise of Battell hurtled in the Ayre; Horsses do neigh, and dying men did grone. **1663** BUTLER *Hud.* I. ii. 138 As once in Persia, 'tis said Kings were proclaimed by a horse that neighed. **1735** SOMERVILLE *Chase* II. 92 My Courser hears their Voice,.. neighing he paws the ground. **1829** LYTTON *Devereux* III. ii, I heard my horse neighing beneath the window. **1865** MAX MÜLLER *Chips* (1880) I. vi. 130 The horse of Darius neighed first.

β. **13..** *Guy Warw.* (A.) 1336 Þe stedes nyen, and togider whine. *c* **1400** MAUNDEV. (Roxb.) xxxiii. 149 Þe meres herez þaire foolez nye. **1530** PALSGR. 644/1, I nye, as a horse dothe. **1570** LEVINS *Manip.* 102/2 To Nie as an horse.

γ. *c* **1400** *Destr. Troy* 7727 He neyt as a nagge, at his nose thrilles. **1483** *Cath. Angl.* 249/2 To Nee as a horse, *hinnire*. **1513** DOUGLAS *Æneis* XI. xvii. 94 The dynnyng of thar hors feit eik hard he,.. and thar stedis ne. **1549** *Compl. Scot.* vi. 39 Baytht horse & meyris did fast nee, & the folis nechyr.

transf. **1382** WYCLIF *Isa.* x. 30 Neȝe with thi vois, thou doȝter of Galyn. —— *Jer.* v. 8 Eche to the wif of his neȝhebore neyȝede. **1530** PALSGR. 664/1 Thou nyest for an other otes, wiche we expresse by.. 'thou lokest after deed mens shoes',.. is an adage in the frenche tonge. *a* **1616** BEAUM. & FL. *Wit without M.* IV. i, The he your wisdom play'd withal,.. neigh'd at his nakedness, And made his cold and poverty your pastime. **1676** *North's Plutarch, Add. Lives* 81 He divorced her (say some) for her barrenness, but the effect declared that he neigh'd after others. **1781** COWPER *Expost.* 39 Adultery neighing at his neighbour's door.

2. *trans.* To utter in neighing, or with a sound like neighing.

1623 MASSINGER *Bondman* IV. ii, The noble horse.. Neighed courage to his rider. **1642** MILTON *Apol. Smect.* Wks. 1851 III. 292 Who.. could neigh out the remembrance of his old conversation among the Viraginian trollops. **1789** CHARLOTTE SMITH *Ethelinde* (1814) IV. 146 D'ye think one might neigh out civilities to this female Nimrod?

neiȝ, obs. variant of *ey*, EGG.

neighborite (ˈneɪbəraɪt). *Min.* [f. the name of Frank *Neighbor* (see quot. 1961) + -ITE¹.] A fluoride of sodium and magnesium, $NaMgF_3$, which occurs as colourless orthorhombic crystals, isostructural with perovskite.

1961 E. C. T. CHAO et al. in *Amer. Mineralogist* XLVI. 379 The mineral is named 'neighborite' in grateful acknowledgement of the continued friendly interest and helpfulness of Mr. Frank Neighbor, District Geologist of the Sun Oil Co. at Salt Lake City. *Ibid.* 380 Neighborite was first found as clusters of pink and brown rounded grains in a dark brown to grayish black dolomitic oil shale of the Green River formation of South Ouray, Utah. **1967** *Doklady Earth Sci.* CLXXIV. 140/1 In the USSR neighborite was detected in alkalic metasomatite developed in the Western Urals from porphyry tuff and argillaceous carbonate sediments of Proterozoic age. **1971** *Amer. Mineralogist* LVI. 1520 Neighborite is synthesised from NaF and MgF_2 via a eutectic solidification process in which the product is a two-phase mixture of NaF and $NaMgF_3$.

neighbour (ˈneɪbə(r)), *sb.* Forms: α. 1–3 **néahȝe-**, 1–2 **néahhe**, 1–3 **nehȝe-**, (3 **nehgi-**); 1–2 **nehhe-**, **nehe-**, (1 **neche-**, 3 **nehte-**, 4–5 *Sc.* **neth-**); 3 **nege-**, 3–6 **negh(e-**, 4–5 **neȝ(e-**, **neght(e-**, 5 **neȝt-**; 2 **neihi-**, 3–4 **neiȝ(e-**, 4 **neieȝ-**, 4– **neigh-**, (4 **neighe-**, **neight-**, **neihe-**, 5 **neihȝe-**, 6 **neig-**, *Sc.* **neicht-**); 4–5 **neyh(e-**, (4 **neyhȝe-**, **neyȝ-**), 4–6 **neygh(e-**, 5–6 **neyg-**, 1 **nýhȝe-**, 3 **nijhge-**, 5–6 *Sc.* **nicht-**; 4–7 *Sc.* **nycht-**, 5 **nygh(e-**, 6 *Sc.* **nych-**. 1–6 **-bur(e**, 3–7 **-bore**, 4–7 **-boure-**, (4 **-boer**, 4–6 *Sc.* **-bowr**, 5 **-borgh**, **-burgh**), 3– (now *U.S.*) **-bor**, 4– **-bour**. β. 4 **neybor**, (5 **-bour**, 5–6 **-bowre**); 4 **nyebore**, 6 *Sc.* **nibour**, (9 **-ber**), 6 **ne-**, 7 **neibour**, (8–9 **-bor**, 9 **-ber**), 8–9 **nee-bor**, (9 **-bour**, **-ber**, **-bir**), 9 **nebber**; 5 **neypur**, 8– **neiper**, 8 **ni-**, 9 **neepour**. [OE. *néahȝebúr, néahhe-*, etc. (f. *néah* NIGH *a.* + *ȝebúr*: see BOOR) = MDu. *nagebuer, -buy(e)r, -boer*, OHG. *nâhgibûr* and *-bûro* (MHG. *nâchgebûr, -bûre*); also OS. *nâbûr*, MDu. *nabuer, -bur, -ber*, MLG. *nabur, -ber, neber*, etc., MHG. *nâchbûr* (G. *nachbar*); cf. ON. *nábúe, -búi* (Sw. and Da. *nabo*).]

1. One who lives near or next to another; one who occupies a near or adjoining house, one of a number of persons living close to each other, esp. in the same street or village.

c **897** K. ÆLFRED *Gregory's Past. C.* xliv. 322 Ne laða ðærto ..ðine cuðan, ne ðine weleȝan neahȝeburas. *c* **950** *Lindisf. Gosp.* Luke i. 65 Aworden wæs ondo ofer alle neheburas hiora. *c* **1000** in Assmann *Ags. Hom.* (1889) XVI. 268 Alle hyre nehheburas, æȝðer ȝe weresȝe wyf, swyðe weopon. *c* **1055** *Byrhtferth's Handboc* in *Anglia* VIII. 322 Þon nyme he hys neahȝebur þe him ȝehendost sy. *c* **1200** *Trin. Coll. Hom.* 83 Hie gon to chirche.. for to biregen nehebores speche. **1297** R. GLOUC. (Rolls) 11143 To driue and to gaderi þuder god of neiȝebores aboute. **1382** WYCLIF *2 Kings* iv. 3 Aske by borwynge of alle thi neyȝbours. *c* **1470** HENRY *Wallace* v. 1012 With thaim thow was a nychtbour off this toun. *a* **1500** in C. Trice-Martin *Chanc. Proc. 15th C.* (1904) 5 Your suppliaunt sent into London for his neighburghs whiche took him to bayle. **1589** R. HARVEY *Plain Perc.* (1590) 10 It wil.. set the next neighbors medowes all on a floate. **1650** HUBBERT *Pill Formality* 137 Their tears.. pierce the hearts of their pittying neighbors. **1699** DRYDEN *Ep. J. Driden* 7 Contending neighbours come, From your award to wait their final doom. **1744** BERKELEY *Siris* §72, I live in a remote corner, among poor neighbours. **1790** GOUV. MORRIS in Sparks *Life & Writ.* (1832) II. 25 Near neighbors are seldom good ones. **1847** H. MILLER *First Impr. Eng.* xx. (1857) 357 Neighbours of a class that in Scotland would be on the most intimate terms. **1871** FREEMAN *Norm. Conq.* (1876) IV. xvii. 55 The Norman landowner held his lands on the same tenure.. as his English neighbour.

Proverbs. **13..** *Minor Poems fr. Vernon MS.* 527/83 Bettre is a neiȝebore neiȝe Then a brothur fer fro thin eiȝe. **1387–8** T. USK *Test. Love* II. ix. (Skeat) l. 144 An olde proverbe aleged by many wyse:— 'Whan bale is greetest, than is bote a nye-bore.' *c* **1450** *Merlin* 434 Men seyn an olde sawe, who hath a goode neighbour hath goode morowe. *c* **1530** LD. BERNERS *Arth. Lyt. Bryt.* (1814) 464 It is oftentymes sayd, he yᵗ hath an yl neyghbour hath oftentymes an yll mornynge. **1539** TAVERNER *Erasm. Prov.* (1552) 49 Our Englysh prouerbe, which speketh in this wyse. A nere neyghbour is better than a farre frende. **1594** *Mirr. Policy* (1599) O iij, The common Prouerbe saith, That who so hath a good neighbor, hath a good morrow.

b. In echoes of Biblical passages (as Luke x. 27) inculcating men's duties towards each other, or in similar contexts. Hence sometimes taken in a widely extended sense.

In OE. versions expressed by *níehsta*, etc.; see NEXT.

a **1300** *Ten Commandm.* 33 in *E.E.P.* (1862) 16 Loue þi neiȝbore as þine owe bodi: non oþer þou him wil. **1340** HAMPOLE *Pr. Consc.* 5860 Yhit sal men yhelde acount.. of ilka neghebur, þat men fals to help and to socur. *c* **1386** CHAUCER *Pars. T.* ¶442 In the name of thy neighebour thou schalt understonde the name of thy brother. **1426** AUDELAY *Poems* 9 ȝif thou love thi neȝtboure. **1500–20** DUNBAR *Poems* ix. 109 Preysing my self, and evill my nichtbouris deming. **1570** T. NORTON tr. *Nowel's Catech.* (1853) 138 The name of neighbour containeth.. also those whom we know not, yea, and our enemies. **1729** BUTLER *Serm.* Wks. II. 140 The.. rivalship is between self-love and the love of our neighbour. **1841** TRENCH *Parables* xvii. (1877) 328 Who is a neighbour, he who shows love, or he who shows it not? **1844** LINGARD *Anglo-Sax. Ch.* (1858) II. xi. 170 The worship of God and the sanctification of his neighbour.

c. As a form of address. Now only *dial.*

? *a* **1500** *Chester Pl.* (E.E.T.S.) xiii. 82 Neighbour, if I the truth should say. **1599** SHAKS. *Much Ado* III. iii. 7 Giue them their charge, neighbour Dogbery. **1607** —— *Cor.* I. i. 63 Why Masters, my good Friends, mine honest Neighbours, will you vndo your selues? **1779** COWPER *Yearly Distress* 50 Come, neighbours, we must wag. **1873** in Ellis *E.E. Pronunc.* v. (1889) 7* Well, neighbour, you and he may both laugh at this news of mine.

†**d.** *good neighbours*, the fairies. *Sc. Obs.*

a **1585** MONTGOMERIE *Flyting* 275 in Jas. I. *Ess. Poesie* (Arb.) 68 In the hinder end of haruest vpon Alhallow ene, Quhen our gude nichtbors rydis. **1588** [see GOOD *a.* 2 d]. **1615** *Orkney Witch Trial* in *Maitl. Cl. Misc.* II. 167 The fary folk callit of hir our guid nichbouris.

2. a. (Chiefly *pl.*) One who dwells in an adjoining or not far distant town, district, or land. Also applied to the rulers of adjacent countries.

971 *Blickl. Hom.* 201 Neapolite ða heora nehȝeburas.. on hæðnum þeawum dwelȝende wæron. *a* **1122** *O.E. Chron.* (Laud MS.) an. 1117 Eall þis ȝear wunode se cyng.. on Normandiȝ for þes cyninges unsehte of France & his oðra nehhebura. *c* **1330** R. BRUNNE *Chron. Wace* (Rolls) 5941 From o stede til oþer he hasted; To ney neyghebours, & ferþer fro, Til alle he dide skaþe & wo. **1375** BARBOUR *Bruce* I. 87 Thai trowyt that he, as gud nychtbur, And as freyndsome compositur, Wald hawe iugyt in lawte. *c* **1400** *Destr. Troy* 12959 He was neghbur full negh to þe noble yle, There Agamynon the gode gouernaunce hade. **1533** BELLENDEN *Livy* I. xi. (S.T.S.) I. 66 We faucht nocht alanerlie with oure Inemyis, bot als with.. oure nychtbouris [*v.r.* nebouris] and freyndis. **1560** DAUS tr. *Sleidane's Comm.* 399 b, Nowe that he possesseth Lorayne, he shall be their nere neighbour. **1596** DALRYMPLE tr. *Leslie's Hist. Scot.* I. 97 In speiche thay differ noᵗ far frome thair nyᵗbouris the Inglise men. **1667** SPRAT *Hist. R. Soc.* 65 This has rous'd all our neighbors to fix their eies upon England. **1674** BREVINT *Saul at Endor* 239 Being worth one thousand Years [indulgence] to the Romans, two thousand to remoter Neighbours. **1827** J. F. COOPER *Prairie* I. xv. 220 Those States, of which he had been an ignorant neighbour half his life. **1858** CARLYLE *Fredk. Gt.* VI. ii. (1872) II. 143 A difficult huff of quarrel.. had fallen-out with his neighbour of Saxony.

b. A person or thing which is in close proximity to another; one who stands or sits near or next to another on some occasion.

1567 MAPLET *Gr. Forest* 9 b, For infection of rustie.. Mineralles being nigh neighbour to them. **1593** SHAKS. *Lucr.* 1416 One man's hand lean'd on another's head, His nose being shadow'd by his neighbour's ear. **1697** DRYDEN *Virg. Georg.* IV. 66 Nor place them.. where the Yeugh their pois'nous Neighbour grows. **1738** WESLEY *Ps.* CXLVII. v, Cedars, Neighbours to the Sky. **1820** SHELLEY *Sensit. Pl.* I. 67 Each one was interpenetrated With the light and the odour its neighbour shed. **1880** DISRAELI *Endym.* xxxviii, 'Lady Montfort looks well to-night', said the neighbor of Myra.

fig. **1577** B. GOOGE *Heresbach's Husb.* II. (1586) 60 b, Oignon, the next neighbour to the Leeke. **1594** SHAKS. *Rich. III*, IV. ii. 43 The deepe reuoluing wittie Buckingham No more shall be the neighbor to my counsailes.

c. *Sc.* A thing which makes a pair with another; a fellow, 'marrow'.

1820 [implied in NEIGHBOURLESS]. **1887** SERVICE *Life Dr. Duguid* 213 The stockins werna neebors. **1896** SETOUN *R. Urquhart* xxvii, I mind o' her gettin' the neighbour made to it in Edinburgh.

3. In predicative use. In *Sc.* used in *pl.*

1528 PAYNELL *Salerne's Regim.* F iij, Sklender and white wyne is vniuersally neighbour to water. **1596** DALRYMPLE tr. *Leslie's Hist. Scot.* Prol. 47 Nichtbouris to thame is Buquhane. **1871** W. ALEXANDER *Johnny Gibb* xv, I ance was neepours wi' a chap 't could 'a deen that.

4. In *attrib.* use, passing into *adj.* Living or situated near or close to some other person or thing. **a.** With names of persons. Now *rare.*

1530 PALSGR. 247/2 Neighbour woman, *uoisine*. **1535** STEWART *Cron. Scot.* II. 272 The nychbour men that duelt into that steid, Tha schew to him that Convallus wes deid. **1611** SHAKS. *Cymb.* I. i. 150 Our Neighbour-Shepheard's Sonne. **1687** T. BROWN *Saints in Uproar* Wks. 1730 I. 82, I can dive into a millstone as far as any of my neighbour princes. **1712** ARBUTHNOT *J. Bull* I. vii, His neighbour tradesmen began to shun his company. **1785** FORBES *Ulysses* 27 (E.D.D.), I dinna like to tell ill tales Upo' my neiper man. **1853** WATSON *Poems* 42 (E.D.D.), The lasses.. Ay botherin' at their neibor chiels.

b. Of peoples, countries, cities, etc. (Very common *c* 1580–1700.)

1579 SPENSER *Sheph. Cal.* Jan. 50, I longed the neighbour towne to see. **1587** GOLDING *De Mornay* ix. (1592) 136 Many euen of our Neighbour nations. **1616** R. C. *Times' Whistle* IV. 1594 In a neighbour land he died. **1668** SPRAT *Life Cowley* C.'s Wks. 1710 I. P. xiii, Many great Revolutions, which..disturb'd the Peace of all our Neighbour-States. **1719** W. WOODS *Surv. Trade* 366 The Proportion they severally bear..in our Neighbour Nations. **1797** GODWIN *Enquirer* I. xi. 97 Treat the neighbour-state as a conquered province. **1869** F. W. NEWMAN *Misc.* 288 In Rome I see a power which..drove out every neighbour people.

c. Of things, places, buildings, etc.

1579 SPENSER *Sheph. Cal.* June 52 Whose Echo made the neyghbour groues to ring. **1602** SHAKS. *Ham.* III. iv. 212 Ile lugge the Guts into the Neighbor roome. **1662** J. CHANDLER *Van Helmont's Oriat.* 121 Lights of Heaven, which do suit themselves to the motion of the nearest, or Neighbour-lights. **1696** WHISTON *The. Earth* (1722) 13 The Moon, our attending and Neighbour Planet. **1784** COWPER *Task* III. 665 Some..catch the neighbour shrub With clasping tendrils. **1842** TENNYSON *Gardener's Dau.* 86 The steer.. Leaning his horns into the neighbour field, And lowing to his fellows. **1876** GLADSTONE *Glean.* (1879) II. 332 Saint John's, the neighbour college to Macaulay's justly loved and honoured Trinity.

d. With abstract sbs. Now *rare*.

1593 SHAKS. *Rich. II*, I. i. 119 Such neighbour-neerenesse to our sacred blood, Should nothing priuiledge him. **1643** [ANGIER] *Lanc. Vall. Achor* 11 That their lent assistance might be loosed for home and neighbour defence. **1678** DRYDEN *All for Love* Pref., To Christen an Imperfection by the Name of some neighbour Virtue.

†**e.** = Neighbourly. *Obs. rare.*

1619 W. SCLATER *Exp. 1 Thess.* (1630) 155 Perhaps also neighbour offices of kindnesse and mercy sometimes passe from them.

5. *Comb.*, as ***neighbour-stained***. *rare.*

1592 SHAKS. *Rom. & Jul.* I. i. 89 Prophaners of this Neighbor-stained Steele.

neighbour (ˈneɪbə(r)), *v.* [f. prec.]

I. *intr.* **1.** Of persons: To live near or close *to* a person, place, etc.; to border *upon*. Also freq. with *near*. Now *rare*.

1586 A. DAY *Eng. Secretary* I. (1625) 130 A certaine poore man,..neighbouring neere unto one worshipful and of great account. **1615** DAY *Festivals* xii. 349 Let us, Beloved, beare affection..unto such as Neighbour at any time neere unto us. **1657** EARL MONM. tr. *Paruta's Pol. Disc.* 81 Their own Soldiers, and..their Associates, who did all neighbor neer upon them. **1805** SOUTHEY *Madoc in Azt.* i, Oh no! we neighbour nearer to the Sun.

2. Of things or places: To lie near or close (*to* or *upon* something else); to be contiguous *with*.

1592 SHAKS. *Ven. & Ad.* 259 A copse that neighbours by. **1610** HOLLAND *Camden's Brit.* I. 268 Neighbouring hereunto is Odiam, glorious in these daies. **1668** CULPEPPER & COLE *Barthol. Anat.* I. 1 The upper part..is termed Hypochondrium, neighbouring upon the lower gristles of the Ribs. **1821** CLARE *Vill. Minstr.* II. 97 Neighbouring nigh, one lonely elder-tree Is all that's left. **1850** BLACKIE *Æschylus* II. 51 The peaks That neighbour with the stars.

b. To come near *to*, almost amount *to*, something. *rare*$^{-1}$.

1631 MASSINGER *Believe as You List* v. ii, To have faith in him Neighbours to treason.

3. With *it*. To associate like neighbours. *rare.*

1586 BRIGHT *Melanch.* xii. 58 Neither that diverse [things] will so neighbour it together, as to dwell in one indiuiduall subiect. **1828–32** WEBSTER s.v., To neighbor it, in colloquial language, to cultivate friendly intercourse by mutual visits.

4. To be on neighbourly terms, to associate in a friendly way, *with* others. Also *transf.*

1820 SCOTT *Abbot* xxvi, The electuary..neighboured ill with the two spoonfuls of pease-porridge and the kirnmilk. **1862** BORROW *Wales* III. 79 The Welsh won't neighbour with them, or have anything to do with them, except now and then in the way of business. **1879** TOURGEE *Fool's Err.* xvi. 83 The few country-people who 'neighbored with them', as it is termed there, comprised their only society.

b. *dial.* To go visiting or gossiping among neighbours.

1854– in dial. glossaries (Lanc., Yks., Leic., Warw., etc.).

II. *trans.* **5.** To adjoin, touch, border upon, lie next or close to.

Very common *c* 1600–1660, and freq. in 19th c.

a **1586** SIDNEY *Arcadia* (1622) 333 As they were walking alongst a Gallerie, they heard from a Chamber neighbouring the side of it, a dolorous sound. **1630** *R. Johnson's Kingd. & Commw.* 591 The principall Citie is called Paquin, neighbouring Tartary. *a* **1661** FULLER *Worthies*, *Bucks* I. (1662) 132 Those that in the same earth neighbour thee. **1798** COWPER *Let. to Lady Hesketh* 13 Oct., It neighbours nearly, and as nearly resembles, the scenery of Catfield. **1822** LAMB *Elia* Ser. I. *Compl. Decay Beggars*, He seemed.. to suck in fresh vigour from the soil which he neighboured. **1873** BROWNING *Red Cott. Nt.-cap* II. 308 One whose father's house upon the Quai Neighboured the very house. **1893** *Nat. Observer* 25 Nov. 41/1 The years that neighboured their departure.

b. To come near to, to approach.

1859 MEREDITH *R. Feverel* viii, I can pretty nigh neighbour it with a guess. **1891** —— *One of our Conq.* xxxv, He neighboured sagacity when he pointed that interrogation relating to Nesta's precociousness.

c. To be neighbour to (one).

1872 E. J. IRVING *Lays* 228 (E.D.D.), Twa lads that I neiboured lang syne. **1892** LUMSDEN *Sheep-head* 212 Will you neighbour us in the smoking-room?

6. In *pa. pple.* **a.** ***neighboured by*** or ***with***, having (some person or thing) as near neighbour or close at hand.

a **1586** SIDNEY *Astr. & Stella* Sonn. xxix, Like some weak Lords neighbord by mightie Kings. **1615** G. SANDYS *Trav.* (1637) 22 The hot water bathes, heretofore adorned, and neighboured with magnificent building. **1670** MILTON *Hist. Eng.* v. Wks. (1847) 537/2 The Danes..not liking perhaps to be neighboured with strong towns. **1836** R. A. VAUGHAN *Mystics* (1860) II. VIII. vii. 79 Such passages..are preludes or interludes neighboured by heavy monologue. *a* **1873** LYTTON *Ken. Chillingly* II. viii, Provided they be neighboured by water.

b. Brought or placed near *to* some person or thing; situated close together.

1594 CAREW *Huarte's Exam. Wits* v. (1596) 54 These ventricles..are so vnited and nere neighboured, that neither ..can be distinguished. **1605** SHAKS. *Lear* I. i. 121 The barbarous Scythian..shall to my bosome Be as well neighbour'd. **1760–72** H. BROOKE *Fool of Qual.* (1809) IV. 127 That..my dust may be neighboured to your precious dust. **1803** GODWIN *Chaucer* II. xlvi. 400 To contemplate this ancient baron neighboured to a throne. **1820** KEATS *Lamia* I. 240 So neighbour'd to him, and yet so unseen She stood.

7. (Cf. prec.) **a.** To bring near *to* something. **b.** To place in conjunction *with* something.

a **1662** HEYLIN *Laud* (1668) 60 The Reversion of a Prebend in that Church; which..neighbour'd him to the Court. **1791** COWPER *Odyss.* xv. 590 But Jove Hath neighbour'd all thy evil with this good.

Hence **ˈneighbouring** *vbl. sb.*

1651 G. W. tr. *Cowel's Inst.* 31 The building together, and neighbouring of houses, by which means we have our Cities, Borroughs, and Villiages. **1886** *S.W. Linc. Gloss.*, I was never one for so much neighbouring and newsing.

†**ˈneighbourage.** *Obs. rare.* [f. NEIGHBOUR *sb.* + -AGE.] The collective surroundings and outside conveniences of a plot of land.

1610 W. FOLKINGHAM *Art of Survey* II. ii. 49 Respicient Situation hath dependance vpon Boundage and Neighbourage. *Ibid.* iii. 51 In Neighbourage it is not impertinent to particularize, how the Plot is accommodated for Tillage, Meddow, Pasture, &c. **1688** HOLME *Armoury* III. 139/1 Neighbourage is the shewing how the Plot is accomodated with Wood, Water, Fewel [etc.].

†**ˈneighboured,** *sb. Obs.* [f. NEIGHBOUR *sb.* + -RED.] = NEIGHBOURHOOD.

c **1175** *Lamb. Hom.* 137 Swulche monne ðe he for scome wernen ne mei for neȝeburredde. *c* **1200** *Trin. Coll. Hom.* 83 Hie giuen here elmesse noht for godes luue ac for neheboreden, oðer for kinraden. *c* **1440** *Promp. Parv.* 352/2 Neyborede, *proximitas, vicinitas.* **1556** in *Archæol. Jrnl.* (1874) XXXI. 70 To beare us true amytie and to use good neighbored towards us. **1575** *Rec. Elgin* (New Spald. Cl.) I. 150 Katherein Ros..wes decernit to keip neborat in schawing masleach.

ˈneighboured, *ppl. a.* [f. NEIGHBOUR *sb.* or *v.* + -ED.] Provided with (a certain kind of) neighbours or surroundings.

1562 J. HEYWOOD *Prov. & Epigr.* (1867) 99 Few more commodious reason sees, Than is this one commoditee, Quietly neighboured to be. **1598** BACON *Ess.* Ep. Ded., I doe nowe like some that haue an Orcharde ill neighbored, that gather their fruit before it is ripe, to preuent stealing. *a* **1641** BP. MOUNTAGU *Acts & Mon.* (1642) 315 Syria was ill-neighboured, continually pillaged by Arabian theeves and robbers. **1829** *Examiner* 741/2 The low and gloomy but beautifully neighboured castle of Chillon.

ˈneighbourer. *rare*$^{-1}$. [f. NEIGHBOUR *v.*] One who neighbours, a neighbour.

1612 DRAYTON *Poly-olb.* i. 265 A neighbourer of this Nymphes, as high in Fortune's grace.

ˈneighbouress. *rare.* [f. NEIGHBOUR *sb.* + -ESS.] A female neighbour.

1388 WYCLIF *Exod.* iii. 22 A womman schal axe of hir neiȝboresse and of her hoosteesse siluerne vesselis and goldun. **1535** COVERDALE *Jer.* ix. 20 That euery one maye teach hir neghbouresse to make lamentacion. **1849** THACKERAY *Gt. & Lit. Dinners* Wks. 1902 VI. 655 You may chance to get near a pleasant neighbour and neighbouress.

ˈneighbourhead. Now *rare.* [f. NEIGHBOUR *sb.* + -HEAD.] = next.

c **1425** *Eng. Conq. Irel.* 30 The men of Watterford..waren I-ware that thay y-hadden such neghborhede ful loth. **1499** *Exch. Rolls Scotl.* XI. 395 That the balye hald foure balye courtis..for..reforming of plants of nychtbourhed and uthiris. **1560** DAUS tr. *Sleidane's Comm.* 399 b, He..wyll do nothing against the maner of neighbourhead. **1596** DALRYMPLE tr. *Leslie's Hist. Scot.* x. 345 True nychtbourheid, constitute weil and maid betueine the Inglis and Scotis bordiris. **1884** G. MACDONALD *Unspoken Serm.* 220 It is the humanity that originates the claim of neighbourhead.

neighbourhood (ˈneɪbəhʊd). [f. NEIGHBOUR *sb.* + -HOOD.]

1. a. Friendly relations between neighbours; neighbourly feeling or conduct.

c **1449** PECOCK *Repr.* v. v. 512 To bere him anentis his fadir and modir more and other wise than the hiȝest degre of neiȝborehode askith. **1503** in *Surtees Misc.* (1890) 3c Accordyng to olde neghburode and gude custome. **1551** T. WILSON *Logike* (1580) 17 b, We see muche neighbourhoode, and good will to helpe the needie. **1592** WARNER *Alb. Eng.* IX. liii. (1602) 239 Exiling hence wel-neere all Troth, meet Sports, and Neighbourhood. **1650** JER. TAYLOR *Holy Living* i. §1. (1727) 7 Works of nature, recreation, charity, friendliness and neighbourhood. **1708** SWIFT *Sent. Ch. Eng. Man* Wks. 1755 II. I. 79 All the laws of charity, neighbourhood, alliance, and hospitality. **1796** BURKE *Regic. Peace* i. (1892) 82 There is a Law of Neighbourhood which does not leave a man perfect master on his own ground. **1842** CAMPBELL *Pilgrim of Glencoe* 139 He stood With neighbours on kind terms of neighbourhood. **1853–7** HAWTHORNE *Eng. Note-bks.* (1879) I. 136 A more efficient sense of neighbourhood than exists among ourselves.

b. Esp. in phr. ***good neighbourhood*** (†also in early use ***evil*** or ***ill neighbourhood***).

1574 HELLOWES *Gueuara's Fam. Ep.* (1577) 126 The Duke of Sogorbe and the Monkes..did vse euill neighbourhoode. **1594** T. B. *La Primaud. Fr. Acad.* II. Ep. Rdr. a 6 What a notable lesson of good neighbourhood. **1604** E. G[RIMSTONE] *D'Acosta's Hist. Indies* VII. viii. 515 They practised against the Mexicaines their neighbours, all the ill neighbourhood they could. **1640** BROME *Sparagus Gard.* I. iv, Whose hatred I would not lose for all the good neighborhood in the Parish. **1711** ADDISON *Spect.* No. 131 ¶8 The Country is not a Place for a Person of my Temper, who does not love Jollity, and what they call Good-Neighbourhood. **1768–74** TUCKER *Lt. Nat.* (1834) II. 305 A pattern for any who desire to fulfil the duties of good neighbourhood. **1825** E. HEWLETT *Cottage Comf.* xv. 218 Good neighbourhood does not require persons to waste their own and each other's time in idle gossipping. **1894** *Times* 6 Oct. 7/3 Such a departure from the rules of good neighbourhood..might well be left unnoticed.

2. a. The quality, condition, or fact of being neighbours or lying near to something; nearness.

1567 MAPLET *Gr. Forest* 11 The Jacinct is blew, and of nigh neighborhoode with the Saphire. **1570–6** LAMBARDE *Peramb. Kent* (1826) 147 To these also may be added for neighbourhoode sake..the Monasterie of white Chanons. **1615** H. CROOKE *Body of Man* 156 Where..with most ease, because of the neighbour-hoode of the heart.., the blood might be altred. **1652** NEEDHAM tr. *Selden's Mare Cl.* 35 Both by reason of their neighborhood, and the frequent convers of the Israelits among them. **1728** MORGAN *Algiers* I. iv. 279 The Turks whose Neighbourhood to Sicily, &c. he liked not. **1752** HUME *Ess. & Treat.* (1777) I. 222 The neighbourhood of the sun inflames the imagination of men. **1835** LYTTON *Rienzi* x. ix, Then the prison and the palace were in awful neighbourhood. **1871** FREEMAN *Norm. Conq.* (1876) IV. xvii. 73 The South..was through its neighbourhood and intercourse with Gaul somewhat less savage.

†**b.** Situation in respect of surroundings. *Obs.*$^{-1}$

1668 CULPEPPER & COLE *Barthol. Anat.* II. ix. 117 The Vena arteriosa..is just like the Aorta in substance, largeness, neighbourhood, and Valves.

3. a. The vicinity, or near situation, *of* something.

1577 B. GOOGE *Heresbach's Husb.* I. (1586) 9 Some..who can not shunne the neighbourhood of the Riuer or the Sea. *c* **1630** MILTON *Passion* 52 The gentle neighbourhood of grove and spring Would soon unboosom all their Echoes milde. **1708** SWIFT *Sacram. Test* Wks. 1755 II. I. 127, I have done all in my power..to preserve two or three English fellows in their neighbourhood. **1745** POCOCKE *Descr. East* II. 242 Cutting off so many Greek villages in the neighbourhood of that city. **1813** WELLINGTON in Gurw. *Desp.* (1838) XI. 23 To strengthen our position in front and in the neighbour-hood of Irun. **1875** MANNING *Mission H. Ghost* xi. 305 When two flames are brought into the neighbourhood of each other they draw to each other.

transf. **1654** JER. TAYLOR *Real Pres.* 237 This comparison ..is odious up to the neighbourhood and similitude of a great impiety. **1894** NEWTON *Dict. Birds* 764 The curious genus *Mesites* of Madagascar, which has been referred..to the neighbourhood of the Rails.

b. ***in the neighbourhood of***, somewhere about.

1857 in Bartlett *Dict. Amer.* s.v., The Catholic clergy of this city have purchased in the neighborhood of forty acres of land. **1893** *Times* (weekly ed.) 15 Dec. 1000/2 The rate of exchange with India has been maintained in the neighbourhood of 16*d*.

c. *Math.* (i) The set of points whose distance from a given point is less than, or is less than or equal to, some non-zero, usu. small, value (see also quot. 1921).

1891 G. L. CATHCART tr. *Harnack's Introd. Study Elem. Differential & Integral Calculus* I. v. 26 We have attained the conception of the Region or Neighbourhood of a point. By it we mean an arbitrarily small but still always finite interval at both sides of the value *x*. **1921** H. S. CARSLAW *Introd. Theory Fourier's Series & Integrals* (ed. 2) iii. 52 Sometimes the neighbourhood is meant to include the point $x = a$ itself. In this case it is defined by $|x - a| \leq h$. **1939** M. H. A. NEWMAN *Elem. Topology of Plane Sets of Points* ii. 20 If *a* is a point of a space with the metric ρ, and ϵ any positive number, the set of all points, *x*, satisfying $\rho(x, a) < \epsilon$ is called a spherical neighbourhood, and more particularly an ϵ-neighbourhood of *a*. **1956** E. M. PATTERSON *Topology* ii. 22 A convenient way of describing continuity is to introduce the idea of neighbourhood... The set of points whose coordinates *x* satisfy $|x - x_0| < \epsilon$ is called the ϵ-neighbourhood of x_0; it consists of all points whose distance from x_0 is less than ϵ. **1971** M. GEMIGNANI *Introd. Real Analysis* iii. 32 We denote the *p*-neighborhood of *a* by $N(a, p)$. (Thus, $N(a, p)$ consists of all real numbers within distance *p* of *a*.) *Ibid.*, Not only is every *p*-neighborhood an open interval, but every open interval is a *p*-neighborhood.

(ii) Any open set containing a given point or non-empty set; also, any set containing such an open set.

1934 C. C. KRIEGER tr. *Sierpiński's Introd. Gen. Topology* ii. 33 We shall understand by a neighbourhood of an element *a* any open set containing *a*. **1946** E. LEHMER tr. *Pontrjagin's Topological Groups* ii. 28 We shall give a method of defining a topological space by means of neighborhoods rather than by means of the operation of closure. This method is rather important and is often used as the foundation of the axiomatic treatment of the concept of a topological space. **1964** W. J. PERVIN *Found. Gen. Topology* iii. 45 A set is open iff it is a neighborhood of each of its points. **1967** I. ADLER *New Look at Geom.* xii. 372 The sets that belong to this special class of subsets in a topological space are called the open sets of the space or the neighborhoods of the space. **1968** S. MORAN tr. *H. Schubert's Topology* 86 An open set is a neighbourhood of every one of its subsets.

4. a. Resort or haunt of persons near one; company; neighbours.

1596 SPENSER *F.Q.* VI. v. 34 A little Hermitage there lay, Far from all neighbourhood. *a* **1716** BLACKALL *Wks.* (1723) I. 97 A Member of a.. Corporation, consisting of his Neighbourhood, and Acquaintance. **1800** KNOX & JEBB *Corr.* I. 3 Immediate neighbourhood I have none, save one family. **1854** H. MILLER *Sch. & Schm.* xvi. (1857) 366 They had been known, each in his own circle of neighbourhood.

†**b.** A place lying near to one. *Obs. rare*$^{-1}$.

1634 MILTON *Comus* 314, I know.. every bosky bourn from side to side, My daily walks and ancient neighbourhood.

5. a. A community; a certain number of people who live close together.

1625 BACON *Ess., Friendship* (Arb.) 165 In a great Towne .. there is not that Fellowship.. which is in lesse Neighbourhoods. **1711** STEELE *Spect.* No. 49 ⁋3 Those little Communities which we express by the Word Neighbourhoods. **1774** G. WHITE *Selborne* xl, [Whitethroats] are shy and wild in breeding-time, avoiding neighbourhoods, and haunting lonely lanes. **1809–10** COLERIDGE *Friend* (1865) 126 Men remain in the domestic state and form neighbourhoods, but not governments. *a* **1882** EMERSON in Hinsdale *Garfield & Educ.* II. 413 The banian of the forest, yielding shade and fruit to wide neighbourhoods of men.

b. A (religious) society of neighbours.

1883 *Century Mag.* Oct. 856/2 This movement led to the establishment of a neighborhood of Friends in the streets leading from Chatham Square.

6. a. The people living near to a certain place or within a certain range.

1686 tr. *Chardin's Trav. Persia* 73 The Commanders of this Fortress make always Leagues with the Neighborhood. **1766** GOLDSM. *Vic. W.* iv, The whole neighbourhood came out to meet their minister. **1802** MRS. E. PARSONS *Myst. Visit* III. 204 The neighbourhood had scandalized [her].

b. A district or portion of a town or country, freq. considered in reference to the character or circumstances of its inhabitants.

1697 DRYDEN *Virg. Past.* I. 15 The raging Sword and wastful Fire Destroy the wretched Neighbourhood around. **1778** PENNANT *Tour Wales* (1883) I. 24 The several sorts of founderies in the neighborhood. **1813** WELLINGTON in Gurw. *Desp.* (1838) XI. 60 All the camps in this neighbourhood quite quiet. **1838** DICKENS *O. Twist* xv, Darkness had set in; it was a low neighbourhood. **1880** DISRAELI *Endym.* lvii, The back slums of his ferocious neighbourhood.

c. In urban planning and development, a small sector of a larger inhabited area with an integrated community provided with its own shops and other facilities.

1951 *Social Aspects Town Devel. Plan* (Univ. Liverpool, Social Sci. Dept.) ii. 25 It must be emphasised that the essence of a Neighbourhood from the point of view of the planner and sociologist alike, is the opportunity it provides for people to meet together, to share the burdens of daily life, and to co-operate in an endeavour to overcome their common problems. **1961** *Listener* 2 Nov. 702/2 People are beginning.. to insist that their local authorities give proper consideration to all those aspects of life which make a neighbourhood different from an estate. **1961** *Observer* 3 Dec. 23/3 The principle, so depressingly practised in the first batch of British new towns, of grouping low-density housing in so-called neighbourhoods, punctuated by random acres of open space and served by small shopping centres. **1973** *Country Life* 6 Dec. 1952/1 One of London's greatest attractions is.. its village-like localities. In planning jargon these are called neighbourhoods or.. environmental areas.

7. *attrib.*, as ***neighbourhood bookie, bookstore, centre, council, grocery, market, meeting, park, party, road, school, shop, shopping centre, store, unit, -war***; **neighbourhood friendly** *U.S. colloq.*, a well-known local shop, a neighbourhood shop; **neighbourhood watch** orig. *U.S.*, (a programme of) systematic vigilance by citizens in order to combat crime in their neighbourhood; freq. *attrib.*

1971 *Black Scholar* June 6/1 A man of some kind is usually around. He may be a boyfriend, an uncle or just the neighborhood bookie. **1973** *N.Y. Law Jrnl.* 17 Apr., Each appellant managed a large neighborhood bookstore. **1961** *Listener* 28 Sept. 470/3 The idea that a neighbourhood centre was a sort of rag-bag where you put all the social functions if you could not find anywhere else to put them. **1973** *Guardian* 24 Dec. 13/6 The idea of neighbourhood councils or 'community councils' or 'urban parish councils' is based on the simple proposition that there is no urban equivalent of the rural parish council and that there should be. **1970** J. HANSEN *Fadeout* (1972) xx. 167 But those envelopes were there. Nine of them. The kind you buy at your neighbourhood friendly. In packs of a dozen. **1966** B. H. DEAL *Fancy's Knell* v. 67 The supermarkets had killed the neighborhood grocery. **1938** *Richmond* (Va.) *News-Leader* 28 Sept. 1/3 The rush of tobacco to market has operated greatly to the advantage of the smaller towns of the belt. Leaf that once was sold in the big centers of North Carolina and Virginia is overflowing into the neighborhood markets. **1823** S. HUNTINGTON in *Mem.* 348 The neighbourhood meeting for this quarter of the city. **1961** L. MUMFORD *City in Hist.* xvi. 502 The neighborhood park, conceived either as a Greenbelt around the neighborhood, .. or as a ribbon of internal green. **1972** *Village Voice* (N.Y.) 1 June 16/3 Proceeds of the fair will help the association purchase two vacant lots to be developed into a neighborhood park. **1869** MRS. WHITNEY *We Girls* xi. (1874) 244, I daresay Mrs. Pennington will have her neighbourhood parties again. **1835** W. G. SIMMS *Partisan* II. xxviii. 266 A small track—a common wagon or neighborhood road—wound into the forest. **1843** 'R. CARLTON' *New Purchase* i. 89 Notice here, a neighborhood road does not imply necessarily much proximity of neighbours. **1842** *Southern Lit. Messenger* VIII. 65/1 As this was what is called a 'neighborhood school', the pupils necessarily came from a great distance. **1967** *New Yorker* 31 May 88/2 School integration and the preservation of neighborhood schools have been white-collar movements. **1973** *Times* 19 Apr. 18/1 The tendency for neighbourhood schools to develop on class lines. **1966** B. H. DEAL *Fancy's Knell* v. 67 The shopping centers had killed the neighborhood shops. **1968** *Guardian* 26 Mar. 9/3 Her customers.. used to shop in the West End, but are thankful to find a first-rate fashion shop nearer home. The success of such 'neighbourhood shops'.. is an interesting trend. **1961** *Listener* 28 Sept. 471/1 Strong neighbourhood shopping centres. **1949** E. S. GARDNER in *Argosy* Apr. 108/3 In that district of small neighbourhood stores, he's in a position to keep irregular hours. **1974** *Amer. Speech* 1971 XLVI. 76 *Grocery store*,.. neighborhood store. **1943** *Archit. Rev.* XCIII. 91/1 Five such residential units make up into one neighbourhood unit of approximately a thousand families. **1953** P. C. BERG *Dict. New Words* 114/1 *Neighbourhood unit*, one of the residential areas in a planned town, containing about 10,000 inhabitants, complete with schools, shops, and a community centre of its own. **1961** E. A. POWDRILL *Vocab. Land Planning* iii. 40 It is by now a fundamental concept of town and country planning that the rehabilitation of existing towns and the building of new towns should be based on the 'neighbourhood unit' principle. **1966** *Listener* 19 May 729/3 It was interesting to discover how much Patrick Abercrombie's neighbourhood-unit concept.. had influenced Moscow planners. **1888** H. C. LEA *Hist. Inquis.* I. 60 Torn with unceasing and savage neighbourhood-war. **1972** *National Sheriff* Aug.–Sept. 9 Materials and related techniques designed to encourage local citizens to be alert to and the circumstances which may prevent as well as indicate a burglary or larceny [*sic*], and to take appropriate actions are being developed... The program will be known as the *National Neighborhood Watch Program*. **1977** *Crime Prevention Bk. for Senior Citizens* (Midwest Research Inst.) ii. 30 If or when you decide to establish a 'neighborhood watch', call a group of neighbors together, not to be merely sociable, but to agree to keep an eye on each other's property and on the neighborhood in general. **1983** *Daily Tel.* 6 Apr. 19/3 Scotland Yard, impressed by the success of America's 'neighbourhood watch' citizen crime prevention projects, sent two officers on a fortnight's study tour of US cities. **1986** *New Socialist* Sept. 5/1 Neighbourhood watch schemes are catching on fast. In January a Home Office minister said 8,000 schemes were in operation.

b. Attrib. phr. ***the, your,*** etc., ***friendly neighbourhood***, applied to a well-known and popular local person or thing; also *ironical. colloq.*

1955 W. GADDIS *Recognitions* II. ii. 366 Just tell Mummy to ask about *Cuff* next time she visits her friendly neighborhood druggist. **1968** *Peace News* 25 Oct. 7 (*heading*) Your friendly neighbourhood senior detective officer. **1971** *Guardian* 4 June 5/5 Their friendly neighbourhood stockbroker gave his talents free. **1973** 'R. MACLEOD' *Nest of Vultures* vii. 154, I feel like I've just made a date with the friendly neighbourhood vampire. **1974** *Times* 22 Mar. 21/4 (*heading*) Your friendly neighbourhood fuel cell.

'neighbouring, *ppl. a.* [f. NEIGHBOUR *v.* + -ING^2.] That neighbours, in various senses of the vb.; lying or living near, adjacent.

1601 SHAKS. *All's Well* IV. i. 18 He hath a smacke of all neighbouring Languages. **1641** H. THORNDIKE *Govt. Churches* 66 They were made in due time by the heads of neighbouring Churches. **1712** J. JAMES tr. *Le Blond's Gardening* 2 Paris and Versailles, whose Neighbouring Parts contain so many Wonders of this Nature. **1770** BURKE *Pres. Discont.* Wks. II. 308 The scheme of bringing our court to a resemblance to the neighbouring monarchies. **1838** DICKENS *Nich. Nick.* ix, Miss Squeers had been spending a few days with a neighbouring friend. **1863** GEO. ELIOT *Romola* xxxvi, He stood and watched the scene from behind a neighbouring bush.

neighbouring, *vbl. sb.*: see NEIGHBOUR *v.*

neighbourize ('neɪbəraɪz), *v. rare.* [f. NEIGHBOUR *sb.* + -IZE.] *intr.* To associate with others as neighbours; to act in a neighbourly fashion.

1899 G. B. BURGIN *Bread of Tears* I. ii. 43 We thought we'd just neighbourise, and happen in to hear what it says.

'neighbourless, *a.* [f. NEIGHBOUR *sb.* + -LESS.] Without a neighbour; solitary.

1562 J. HEYWOOD *Prov. & Epigr.* (1867) 100 For this neighbourlie quietnesse, Thou art the neighbour neighbourlesse. **1820** *Blackw. Mag.* May 163/1 The quean's as single yet as a neighbourless stocking. **1846** PROWETT *Prometh. Bound* 14 Lone dweller by a neighbourless ravine. **1892** J. S. FLETCHER *When Chas. was King* 4 Some homestead.. so far from a village that its occupants are entirely neighbourless.

'neighbour-like, *a.* and *adv.* [f. as prec. + -LIKE.] **a.** *adv.* In a neighbourly fashion. **b.** *adj.* Neighbourly, friendly, kindly. (In later use chiefly *Sc.*)

1499 *Exch. Rolls Scotl.* XI. 395 Ane sufficient tenant and nychtbour.. abill to keip the said steid nychtbourlike. *c* **1572** GASCOIGNE *Fruites Warre* cxxxvii, Three dayes wee fought, as long as water serued, And came to ancor neyghbourlike yfeere. **1602** *2nd Pt. Return fr. Parnass.* III. iii. 1290 A dunce I see is a neighbourlike brute beast, a man may liue by him. **1674** *Ch. & Court of Rome* 6 The Neighbour-like Terms of the old *Regulæ Patrum*. **1790** D. MORISON *Poems* 157 (E.D.D.), To gar our bed look hale and neighbour-like. **1815** SCOTT *Guy M.* xliv, He'll be glad to carry me through, and be neighbour-like. **1827** MISS SEDGWICK *H. Leslie* (1872) II. 158 Kindness and neighbour-like conduct.

'neighbourliness. [f. next + -NESS.] The condition, quality or fact of being neighbourly; friendliness, kindly feeling.

1662 PEPYS *Diary* 5 Nov., There was not the neighbourliness between her and my wife that was fit to be. **1685** H. MORE *Refl. Baxter* Pref. A 3 Neighbourliness and Good-nature washes them out of the remembrance of both. **1816** COLERIDGE *Lay Serm.* (Bohn) 340 It is the science of.. philanthropy without neighbourliness. **1879** *Spectator* 7 June 719 He has tried to make out how far neighbourliness, as amongst ants of the same nest, really goes.

neighbourly ('neɪbəlɪ), *a.* [f. NEIGHBOUR *sb.* + -LY^1.]

1. Characteristic of, or befitting, a neighbour or neighbours; friendly, kindly.

1558 *Reg. Gild Co. Chr. York* 305 *note*, A good occasion of .. renewyng of amytie and neighburghly love one with an other. **1596** SHAKS. *Merch. V.* I. ii. 85 He hath a neighbourly charitie in him. **1658** *Whole Duty Man* xvii. §1 By any neighbourly and friendly office. **1727** SWIFT *What passed in London* Wks. 1755 III. I. 182 He in a very neighbourly manner admonished me. **1791** BURKE *Hints for Mem.* Wks. VII. 5 His majesty's benevolent and neighbourly offers. **1884** SIR J. W. CHITTY in *Law Rep.* 27 Chanc. Div. 629 He considered it was not a neighbourly thing to press for payment.

b. Friendly but not cordial.

1599 SANDYS *Europæ Spec.* (1632) 154 As their States, so their loves and his are but neighbourly. *a* **1628** PRESTON *Mt. Ebal* (1638) 39 It must be onely with a neighbourly and civill, but not with a conjugall.. love.

2. Of persons: Inclined to act as neighbours; situated as neighbours.

1612 T. TAYLOR *Comm. Titus* i. 8 Who thinke it Christianitie enough to be harmlesse, ciuill, or neighbourly men. **1628** WITHER *Brit. Rememb.* II. 513 Scarce one man would be so neighbourly, To helpe his brother in this malady. **1778** MISS BURNEY *Evelina* xl, Our lodgings were in Holborn, that we might be near his house, and neighbourly. **1822** SCOTT *Nigel* xxiii, In Alsatia, look ye, a man must be neighbourly and companionable. **1886** A. E. B. SOULBY in *Law Times* LXXXI. 446/2 Farmers as a rule are neighbourly and forbearing.

'neighbourly, *adv.* ? *Obs.* [f. as prec. + -LY^2.] After the manner of neighbours; in a friendly or kindly fashion.

1525 in *Vicary's Anat.* (1888) App. iii. 169 The housholders.. be neybourly drynkyng to-gethers.. In Ioyous maner. **1578** T. N. tr. *Conq. W. India* 3 Who friendly and neighbourly graunted his desire. **1654** E. JOHNSON *Wonder-wrkg. Provid.* 194 It would joyn all the Towns in the same neighbourly together. **1690** MACKENZIE *Siege London-Derry* 53/1 Whilst they behave themselves peaceably and neighbourly amongst us.

'neighbourship. [f. as prec. + -SHIP.]

1. The state or fact of being a neighbour; nearness, propinquity. Also *pl.*

1456 SIR G. HAYE *Law Arms* (S.T.S.) 101 Nychtbourschip till evill folk gerris oft tymes the gude tak scathe. **1523** FITZHERB. *Surv.* 5 b, Commen per cause vicynage .s. neyghbourshepe. **1599** T. M[OUFET] *Silkwormes* 9 This neighbourship was formost steppe to loue. **1798** JOANNA BAILLIE *Count Basil* v. i, Rest.. each.. in a hallow'd neighbourship with those, Who when alive his social converse shar'd. **1838** *Tait's Mag.* V. 113 The uneasy accommodations, foul air, and unsatisfactory neighbourships of a public theatre. **1891** *Tablet* 29 Aug. 327 The accidental neighbourship of grains of sand upon the shore.

2. Neighbourly relations or intercourse; *esp.* in phr. ***good*** (***bad, ill***) ***neighbourship***.

1796 MORSE *Amer. Geog.* II. 64 Since Denmark has no further hope of recovering its lost provinces, its true interest is a good neighbourship. **1857** TOULMIN SMITH *Parish* 177 Every bond of mutual sympathy or of wholesome neighbourship. **1858** CARLYLE *Fredk. Gt.* v. v. I. 588 These violences and acts of ill-neighbourship. **1889** *Sat. Rev.* 2 Mar. 237/2 To keep their tendencies to bad-neighbourship in check.

neighe, obs. form of NIGH *v.*

neigher ('neɪə(r)), *sb.*^{1} [f. NEIGH *v.* + -ER^1.] One that, or that which, neighs; a horse.

1649 LOVELACE *Poems* 101 Amadis, Sir Guy and Topaz With his fleet Neigher shall keep no-pace. **1865** TYLOR *Early Hist. Man.* iv. 63 The horse is the neigher.

neigher ('nixər), *sb.*^{2} *Sc.* [f. next.] A neigh; *transf.* a loud laugh.

1830 GALT *Lawrie T.* IV. iii, A sudden recollection.. would.. cause his sob to change into a most irreverent neigher.

neigher ('nixər), *v. Sc.* Also 6 **nechyr**, 9 **neicher**. [Imitative: cf. NICHER and NICKER.] *intr.* To neigh; also *transf.* to laugh loudly.

1549 *Compl. Scot.* vi. 39 Baytht horse & meyris did fast nee, & the folis nechyr. **1722** RAMSAY *Three Bonnets* III. 2 His lang whip gae cracks Upon his neighering coursers' backs. **1812** W. TENNANT *Papistry Storm'd* (1827) 60 The very naig that he bestrides Seems neicherin' too for joy.

1826 GALT *Last of Lairds* vii, I could but look in her cleer een and neigher like Willie Gouk.

neighing ('neɪɪŋ), *vbl. sb.* [f. NEIGH *v.* + -ING[1].] The action, on the part of a horse, of uttering its characteristic sound. Also *transf.*

c **725** *Corpus Gloss.* (Hessels) H 124 *Hinnitus*, hnaeggiung. *c* **1000** ÆLFRIC *Gram.* i. (Z.) 4 Hryðera ȝehlow and horsa hnæȝung. **13..** *K. Alis.* 2091 There was gret naygheing of stede. **1382** WYCLIF *Jer.* xiii. 27 And aperede thi shen-shepe, thi vouteries, and thi neȝingus. **1412–20** LYDG. *Chron. Troy* III. xxii, The..furious neyhing of many bastard stede. **1481** CAXTON *Godfrey* cv. 161 Ther was so grete noyse ..& so terryble neyhyng of horses. *a* **1543** HALL *Chron., Edw. IV* 217 b, What for neighyng of horses and talkyng of menne, none..could that night take any rest or quietnes. **1620** T. GRANGER *Div. Logike* 33 The neying of an horse caused Darius..to be made King. **1697** DRYDEN *Virg. Georg.* III. 150 And with shrill Neighings fill'd the Neighbouring Plain. **1736** SHERIDAN in *Swift's Lett.* (1768) IV. 165 The noise of guns, the neighing of the horses. **1859** TENNYSON *Elaine* 298 The strong neighings of the wild white Horse.

neighing ('neɪɪŋ), *ppl. a.* [f. NEIGH *v.* + -ING[2].] That neighs; uttering a neigh.

1382 WYCLIF *Jer.* viii. 16 Fro the vois of his neiȝende fiȝteres to-stirid is alle the lond. **1596** SHAKS. *Tam. Shr.* I. ii. 207 Haue I not..heard Loud larums, neighing steeds, and trumpets clangue? **1609** B. JONSON *Sil. Wom.* IV. iii, What a neighing hobby-horse is this. **1697** DRYDEN *Æneid* VIII. 5 The sprightly trumpet, from afar..Had rous'd the neighing steeds to scour the fields. **1706** PHILLIPS (ed. Kersey), *Neighing-Bird*, a little Bird that imitates the Neighing of a Horse. **1810** CLARKE *Trav. Russia* (1839) 76/1 The flower of the Cossack army, in most sumptuous dresses, curbing their foaming and neighing steeds. *a* **1821** KEATS *Hyperion* I. 184 Neighing steeds were heard, Not heard before by Gods or wondering men.

†**neight**, obs. form of AIT.

1766 *Award Inclos. Comm. Lenchwick & Norton*, The osier neights in the river Avon.

neighther, obs. f. NEITHER.

neih, obs. f. NIGH *a.* and *adv.*

neihȝebor, obs. f. NEIGHBOUR.

neihleche, var. of NEHLECHE *Obs.*

neil, obs. f. NAIL, NEAL.

Neil Robertson stretcher (ˌniːl 'rɒbətsən). [App. f. a proper name.] (See quots. 1941, 1967.)

1941 N. HAMMER *Warwick & Tunstall's First Aid* (ed. 18) xviii. 242 The Neil Robertson stretcher (the hammock stretcher) is made of split bamboo sewn onto stout canvas, on the principle of Gooch splinting. It surrounds and encloses the patient completely and rigidly. **1959** *Times* 16 Mar. (Port of London Suppl.) p. xvi/3 All boats carry a Neil Robertson stretcher designed to remove casualties from such awkward places as the hold or engine room of a ship. **1967** J. WAINWRIGHT *Worms must Wait* lxii. 154 The 'Neil-Robertson' stretcher was a contraption of stout canvas, bamboo, leather straps, buckles and rope. Its purpose was (to quote the book of words) 'to lift casualties in any position through small hatches, man-holes, sewer ventilators and for lowering from heights'. **1974** P. MCCUTCHAN *Call for S. Shard* xiv. 134 Tuball and his plastered leg safely strapped into a Neil Robertson stretcher with his crutches attached.

‖**neinei** ('neːneː). *N.Z.* Also **nene**. [Maori.] A New Zealand shrub or small tree of the genus *Dracophyllum*, esp. *D. latifolium*, of the family Epacridaceæ, distinguished by clusters of long, narrow leaves; also called *grass-tree*.

1858 S. P. SMITH in N. M. Taylor *Early Travellers N.Z.* (1959) 355 Some of us..found what was to us quite a new kind of tree, called *Nei nei.* **1879** J. VON HAAST *Geol. Provinces Canterbury & Westland, N.Z.* 78 An undescribed, superb, tree-like *Dracophyllum*..began to appear here... The natives call it Nene. **1882** W. D. HAY *Brighter Britain!* II. 197 The Neinei..is but a small tree. **1949** P. BUCK *Coming of Maori* (1950) II. x. 262 The wood [of this flute] is *neinei.* **1966** *Encycl. N.Z.* I. 498/2 Some of the larger-leaved species [of *Dracophyllum*] like nei-nei or *D. latifolium* are true forest plants.

neip, obs. f. NEAP; var. of NEEP.

neipce, obs. f. NIECE.

neiphew, obs. f. NEPHEW.

neipkynne, obs. Sc. f. NAPKIN *sb.*

neir, obs. f. or var. of NEAR, NEER, NE'ER.

neir(h)and, obs. ff. NEARHAND.

neis(e, neiss, obs. varr. NESE, nose.

neisch(e, etc., obs. ff. NESH *a.*

neischede: see NESHHEAD.

neist, obs. f. NEST; obs. or dial. f. NEXT.

neith, obs. f. NEATH.

neither ('niːðə(r), 'naɪðə(r)), *adv.* (*conj.*) and *a.* (*pron.*) Forms: α. 2 **naiðer**, 5 **nayther**, 6 *Sc.* **naythir**; 4 **neyþur**, 4–5 **-der**, 5- **-þer**, **-þir**, **thir**, **-thyr**, **-dyr**, 5–7 **-ther**; 5 **neider**, **neiþir**, 3–5 **neiþer**, 5- **neither**. β. 4 **nethir**, (5 **-yr**), 4–5 **neþer**, 6–7 **nether**, (6 **-ar**, **neder**); 5 **neethur**, **-yr**. γ. 5–6, 7 *Sc.* **nather**, 6 *Sc.* **naþir**, **nathir**, **neather**. δ. 6–7 **nither**. [Early ME. *naiðer*, *neyþer*, etc., alterations of NA(U)THER, NO(U)THER, on analogy of EITHER (q.v. for etym. and pron.).

The Sc. forms *nather*, *nathir*, may be survivals of the older NATHER, but are placed here on the ground that *ather*, *athir* are the normal Sc. forms of EITHER.]

A. *adv.* (*conj.*) **1.** Introducing the mention of alternatives or different things, about each of which a negative statement is made.

The regular position of *neither* is immediately before the first of the alternative expressions, but it is frequently placed earlier in the sentence.

†**a.** ***neither..ne.*** *Obs.*

In early use *ne* is also inserted after *neither*.

c **1200** *Vices & Virtues* 9 Ne sweriȝeð, naiðer ne be heuene ne be ierðe. *a* **1300** *Cursor M.* 1660 Sal neþer liue ne fouul ne best. **13..** *Ibid.* 6941 (Gött.), His hali wandis..greu neyder less ne mare, Bot euer befor as þai ware. *c* **1380** WYCLIF *Wks.* (1880) 343 To him is þis thanke propur, & neyþur to pope ne confessour. **1413** *Pilgr. Sowle* (Caxton 1483) v. xiv. 109 The sone dependeth of the fader..neither latter ne rather than the fader. **1496** *Fysshynge w. Angle* (1883) 10 You shall not put therto neyther coporose ne vertgrees. **1526** *Pilgr. Perf.* (W. de W. 1531) 2 b, Spared no labours neyther by see ne yet by lande.

b. ***neither..nor.***

Phr. ***neither here nor there***: see HERE *adv.* 12.

α. **13..** *Cursor M.* 5857 (Gött.), Neyder i knou him þat ȝe say, Nor i ne wil lat þe folk away. *c* **1460** *Pol. Rel. & L. Poems* (1866) 164 Thowe canst me neyder thank nor pleasse. *c* **1485** *Digby Myst.* (1882) I. 198 Of me thu shalt neyther haue ffee nor aduauntage. *a* **1548** HALL *Chron., Edw. IV* 242 b, That gain once gotten.., neither othe holdeth, nor frendship continueth. **1594** O. B. *Quest. Profit. Concern.* L 2 b, Neither God nor nature giues this value vnto all. **1630** W. BEDELL in *Ussher's Lett.* (1686) 454 This Protestation having neither Latin, nor Law, nor Common Sence. **1690** LOCKE *Govt.* I. ix. (Rtldg.) 103 Adam..being neither monarch, nor his imaginary monarchy hereditable. **1728** RAMSAY *Step-daughter* ii, She neither has lawtith nor shame. **1746** HERVEY *Medit.* (1818) 259 Neither care disturbs their sleep, nor passion inflames their breast. **1784** COWPER *Task* v. 90 Neither grub nor root nor earth-nut now Repays their labour more. **1849** MACAULAY *Hist. Eng.* v. I. 555 Quarter was to be neither taken nor given. **1879** M. ARNOLD *Mixed Ess., Irish Cathol.* 120 There are neither fairies nor gnomes.

β. **1535** COVERDALE *Tobit* v. 2 Nether doth he knowe me, ner I him. **1549** RIDLEY *Let.* in Potts *Liber Cantabr.* (1855) 245, I am assuredly persuaded that it is neder the Kinge's Majesties nor your Graces pleasor. **1622** *Dunbar's Poems* lxxix. 4 Left is nether corce nor cunȝie. **1673** SCROGGS in *Hatton Corr.* (Camden) 112, I choose the rather to write when I have nether business nor newes.

γ. *c* **1560** A. SCOTT *Poems* (S.T.S.) iii. 23 Tho' naþir hairt nor mynd consentis. **1572** *Satir. Poems Reform.* xxxv. 52 Yit wer thay nather sauld nor slaine. **1611** SIR W. MURE *Misc. Poems* Wks. (S.T.S.) I. 11 Nather prayers could prevaile nor wisses.

c. With another negative, usually preceding. Now *rare*.

1470–85 MALORY *Arthur* xx. xii. 818 That neyder you my lord kynge Arthur nor you syre Gawayne come not in to the felde. **1535** COVERDALE *Josh.* viii. 20 They had no place to flie vnto, nether hither ner thither. **1568** GRAFTON *Chron.* II. 42 Dauid king of Scottes..spoyled the Countrie,..not sparing neyther man woman nor chylde. **1606** BRYSKETT *Civ. Life* 32 Not tying himselfe absolutely to follow neither Plato nor Aristotle. **1678** CUDWORTH *Intell. Syst.* 494 No part neither of Nature, nor of the World, is to Homer Godless. **1827** SOUTHEY *Penins. War* II. 131 There was now no respite neither by day nor night for this devoted city. *a* **1849** H. COLERIDGE *Ess.* (1851) II. 277 Christianity abrogated no duty..neither for Jew nor Gentile.

d. With two sing. subjects and pl. verb.

1759 JOHNSON *Idler* No. 44 ¶3 Neither search nor labour are necessary. **1777** COWPER *Wks.* (1837) XV. 37 Neither the Duke of Bedford nor Lord Sussex have cut yet. **1826** SOUTHEY *Vind Eccl. Angl.* 478 Neither the Law nor the Gospel were introduced with such appalling miracles. **1874** RUSKIN *Fors Clav.* xliii. 139 Neither painting nor fighting feed men.

e. ***neither..or.***

1530 TINDALE *Answ. More* (Parker Soc.) 64 The outward place neither helpeth or hindereth. **1566** *Pasquine in a Traunce* 111 That..we neyther tourne asyde to the right or left hande. **1621** LADY M. WROTH *Urania* 416 A..woman, neither walking, running, or staying. **1671** MILTON *P.R.* I. 268 Yet, neither thus disheartn'd or dismay'd, The time prefixt I waited. **1719** DE FOE *Crusoe* II. (Globe) 478, I can neither tell how many we kill'd, or how many we wounded. **1786** MRS. A. M. BENNETT *Juvenile Indiscr.* I. 70 Engaging to spare neither trouble or expence. **1830** W. TAYLOR *Hist. Surv. Germ. Poetry* III. 26 These modern antiques neither supply the interest of classical or of German poetry. **1874** DASENT *Tales fr. Fjeld* 204 Wasn't it true that he neither knew anything or could do anything?

†**f.** ***neither..neither*** (or ***nother***). *Obs.*

a **1539** in *Archaeol.* XLVII. 54 Nither at the christening nother at the confirmacion. **1568** GRAFTON *Chron.* II. 102 We..intend so to proceed in this matter, neither enclynyng on the right hande, neyther yet on the left. **1620** VENNER *Via Recta* viii. 176 Neither alwaies, neither to euery one, neither of euery sort.

†**g.** Irregularly followed by *and* or *but*. *Obs.*

1598 GRENEWEY *Tacitus, Ann.* IV. xvi. (1622) 115 They neither gaue courage to the fearfull, but carried away them-selues with like fear, ran al away for company. *Ibid.* XI. vii. 148, I will neither vtter any thing falsely, and am ashamed to tell the truth. **1673** MARVELL *Reh. Transp.* II. 200 He that chuses a just weight does neither find himself the weaker.., and reaches the length he aim'd at. **1678** BUNYAN *Pilgr.* I. (1862) 121 That neither thou, but especially I, am not made myself this example.

2. = Nor, nor yet; and not, also not. Now used only when the alternatives are expressed in clauses or sentences.

1462 *Anc. Cal. Rec. Dublin* (1889) I. 313 No bowcher nayther bowcher ys man, neethyr no nothyr man. **1513–14** *Act 5 Hen. VIII*, c. 17 §2 That no persone that is taxed for landes..be sett or taxed for his godes..neither econtrarye. **1560** DAUS tr. *Sleidane's Comm.* 25 b, He said it was a matter newly invented, neyther used in former time. **1615** W. BEDWELL *Arab. Trudg., Sarraceni*..are those people which otherwise..were called..Arabians. Neither were they so named of Sara, Abrahams wife. **1662** STILLINGFL. *Orig. Sacræ* III. ii. §7 Wee cannot then, neither ought we to determine any thing concerning the particular waies of Gods bounty. **1719** DE FOE *Crusoe* I. (Globe) 120 But that there was no help for; neither was my Time so much Loss to me. **1784** COWPER *Task* III. 217 Such powers I boast not —neither can I rest A silent witness of the head-long rage. **1875** JOWETT *Plato* (ed. 2) I. 300 If there are no teachers, neither are there disciples?

3. a. Used to strengthen a preceding negative: = Either.

1551 T. WILSON *Logike* (1580) 81 It is euen so, and yet not true neither, that [etc.]. **1591** SHAKS. *Two Gent.* II. iii. 18 Nay that cannot bee so neyther. **1638** BAKER tr. *Balzac's Lett.* (vol. II) 103 Yet desire I not neither to tire my hands with writing continually to no profit. **1668** ETHEREDGE *She Wou'd if She Cou'd* III. i, Now I have thought better on 't, that is not absolutely necessary neither. **1712** STEELE *Spect.* No. 423 ¶2 Expressions of Rapture and Adoration will not move her neither. **1753** RICHARDSON *Grandison* (1781) I. xxxvii. 264 Perhaps I may not make it in form neither. **1790** BURKE *Fr. Rev.* Wks. V. 436, I would not exclude alteration neither. **1844** DISRAELI *Coningsby* IV. ix, There were no books neither. **1871** MEREDITH *H. Richmond* lv, Lady Edbury would never see Roy-Richmond after that, nor the old lord neither.

b. Without preceding negative, or not in direct connexion with one.

1590 SHAKS. *Com. Err.* v. i. 94 *Ad.* Then let your seruants bring my husband forth. *Ab.* Neither: he tooke this place for sanctuary. **1630** *R. Johnson's Kingd. & Commw.* 596 The Inhabitants cannot travell but with a licence, and with that neither, but for a prefixed season. **1742** RICHARDSON *Pamela* III. 272, I can more freely speak my Mind upon the Occasion, though I am but a poor Casuist neither. **1909** L. M. MONTGOMERY *Anne of Avonlea* x. 98 'Davy declares he never saw her since I left.' 'Neither I did,' avowed Davy. **1926** J. BLACK *You can't Win* xiii. 165 'I wouldn't plead guilty to anything if I were you,' I advised him. 'Me, neither,' said his partner. **1973** R. BUSBY *Pattern of Violence* iv. 61 'Can you place either of them?' The young detective shook his head. 'Me neither.'

B. *adj.* **1.** Not the one or the other.

Also formerly ***neither nother***: see NOTHER.

c **1400** *Lanfranc's Cirurg.* 143 Þat þei moun not wagge to neiþir side aboute þe sowynge. **1560** DAUS tr. *Sleidane's Comm.* 236 b, I should have but small thanke of neyther partie. **1602** SHAKS. *Ham.* v. ii. 312 Nothing neither way. **1697** DRYDEN *Virg. Georg.* III. 53 But neither Shoar his Conquest shall confine. **1850** THACKERAY *Pendennis* xvii, Neither one of us was particularly eager about rushing into that near smoking Babylon.

2. *absol.* as *pron.* Also const. *of*.

Also formerly ***never neither*** (1449); ***neither other*** (1529); ***neither nother*** (see NOTHER), or following another negative.

c **1250** *Gen. & Ex.* 1276 Ðor ben he boðen feren pliȝt ðat here neiðer sal don oðer un-riȝt. *c* **1449** PECOCK *Repr.* I. iii. 14 Sithen to neuer neither thei han sufficient euydence. **1529** MORE *Dyaloge* I. Wks. 163/2 What if neyther other.. were likely to be trewe, but semed bothe twayne impossible. **1567** J. SANFORD *Epictetus* 27 We haue not any thing written of neither of them. **1609** BIBLE (Douay) *Deut.* xxiv. *comm.*, For no cause neither of them can marie againe, so long as the other liveth. **1667** MILTON *P.L.* IX. 1188 Thus they in mutual accusation spent The fruitless hours, but neither self-condemning. **1759** JOHNSON *Rasselas* xxviii. [xxix], Neither can forbear to wish for the absence of the other. **1870** E. PEACOCK *Ralf Skirl.* III. 191 Neither of his visitors saw him. **1886** R. C. MOBERLY *Probl. & Princ.* x. (1904) 314 They are co-ordinate,..they neither override the other.

†**b.** ***neither of both, of either.*** *Obs.*

1537 in Ellis *Orig. Lett.* Ser. III. III. 148 Prosperity and.. adversite, for nedyr off both doth tary, but brevely over-passe. **1588** SHAKS. *L.L.L.* v. ii. 459 *Qu.* Will you haue me, or your Pearle againe? *Ber.* Neither of either, I remit both twaine. **1600** HOLLAND *Livy* x. xxxvi. 377 But neither of both had any stomacke to fight. **1633** ROWLEY *Match at Midn.* in Dodsley *O. Pl.* (1780) VII. 405 Troth, neither of either, so let him understand.

c. Not any one (of more than two).

1644 [H. PARKER] *Jus Populi* 14 Our adversaries boast of three Conquests in this Island, and yet neither of them all was just or totall. **1678** CUDWORTH *Intell. Syst.* 164 Matter, Form, and Accidents; neither of which can be the Aristotelick Nature. **1796** SOUTHEY *Let.* in *Life* (1849) I. 263 He at last fixed upon a leg of mutton, soles and oyster sauce, and toasted cheese—to the no small amusement of those who knew he could get neither. **1846** GROVE *Corr. Phys. Forces* (1855) 15 Heat, light, electricity, magnetism,..are all correlatives,..neither, taken abstractedly, can be said to be the essential cause of the others.

d. With plural verb.

1611 SHAKS. *Cymb.* IV. ii. 253 Thersites body is as good as Aiax, When neyther are aliue. **1648** HEYLIN *Relat. & Observ.* I. 142 b, Neither of which are able to read any one Record in those Offices. **1700** DRYDEN *Pref. Fables* Ess. (ed. Ker) II. 254 Both writ with wonderful facility and clearness; neither were great inventors. **1741** C'TESS HARTFORD *Corr.* (1805) II. 245 Neither of your letters mention these disagreeable circumstances. **1781** G. WAKEFIELD in *Mem.* (1804) I. 461 Neither of us are the proper judges. **1859** F. W. NEWMAN *Phases of Faith* 184 Neither of them declare themselves eyewitnesses of Christ's resurrection. **1875**

RUSKIN *Fors Clav.* li. 62 What at present I believe neither of us know.

neither, obs. f. NETHER *a.*

neithless, var. of NETHELESS.

neiuind, obs. var. NINTH.

neive, var. of NIEVE, fist.

neiven, var. NEVEN *v. Obs.*

neiver, var. of NIFFER, to exchange.

neiwat, var. of NIGHWHAT.

‖**nek.** *S. African.* [Du. *nek* NECK.] A neck or saddle between two hills.

1834 PRINGLE *African Sketches* vi. 223 They had to travel along the narrow ridge (nek) in order to reach the opposite highland. **1883** T. F. CARTER *Narrative Boer War* viii. 161 The flat which lies between the camp and the Nek. *Ibid.*, The high road which runs through the Nek.

nek, obs. form of NECK.

†**nekard, neker.** *Obs. rare*$^{-1}$. [Of obscure origin.] App., an insignificant person.

Both form and sense are against identity with *niggard*.

a **1400–50** *Alexander* 1742 Slike a nekard [*v.r.* neker] as þi-selfe, a noȝt of all othire, Is bot a madding to mell with mare þan him-seluen.

neke, obs. form of NECK *sb.*, NICK *v.*

†**neked.** *Obs. rare.* Also **nykid.** [Perh. a. ON. *nekkvat*, something, somewhat.] A little, a small amount.

13.. *Gaw. & Gr. Knt.* 1062 Of þat ilk nwȝere bot neked now wontez. *Ibid.* 1805 Bot to dele yow for drurye, þat dawed bot neked. *a* **1400–50** *Alexander* 3935 All at was bitten of þa best was at a brunt dede, Bot ȝit þai noyed bot a nykid to nane þat was ermed.

neke name, obs. f. NICKNAME.

nekoite ('nɛkəʊaɪt). *Min.* [anagram of OKENITE.] A triclinic form of the hydrated calcium silicate $Ca_3Si_6O_{15}.6H_2O$ found at Crestmore, California, which differs from the okenite of other localities in its optical and X-ray properties.

1956 GARD & TAYLOR in *Mineral. Mag.* XXXI. 20 The Crestmore material must be regarded as a new species. Because of the likeness to okenite, the anagram *nekoite* is suggested. **1962** *Ibid.* XXXIII. 70 Nekoite was discovered at Crestmore, California, by Eakle (1917), who identified it as okenite. **1971** *Acta Crystallogr.* B.XXVII. 473/2 When fibre bundles of nekoite are heated to temperatures between 200 and 250°C water is lost reversibly, the apparent limiting water content of the crystal from the 'immediate weight-loss' curve corresponding to the composition $3CaO.6SiO_2.3H_2O$.

nekro-: see NECRO-.

nekton ('nɛktən). *Zool.* Also **necton.** [ad. G. *necton, nekton* (E. Haeckel 1890, in *Jenaische Zeitschr. Naturw.* XXV. 251, 252), f. Gr. *νεκτόν*, neut. of *νεκτός* swimming, f. *νεῖν* to swim.] A collective name for aquatic animals that are able to swim and move about independently. Cf. BENTHOS, PLANKTON. So **nek'tonic** *a.*

1893 G. W. FIELD tr. *Haeckel's Planktonic Stud.* in *Rep. U.S. Comm. Fisheries 1889–91* 580 We must distinguish the actively swimming nekton from the passively drifting plankton. **1895** *Natural Sci.* July 31 The Plankton, Nekton, and Benthos form three well-marked communities of organisms. **1903** *Amer. Geologist* XXXI. 211 It has been asserted..that slowly creeping organisms preceded the planktonic and nektonic forms. **1909** *Chambers's Jrnl.* Dec. 784/1 The Nekton are those animals which are capable of vigorous swimming movements, and are able to migrate freely from one part of the sea to another. **1923** *Nature* 17 Mar. 374/2 The author concludes that the kerogen has arisen from 'nectons and kelps' which have 'been repeatedly buried by ash and detritus from submarine volcanoes'. **1923** *Glasgow Herald* 17 Nov. 4/2 The animals of the sea are sometimes divided into the Nekton and the Plankton, the swimmers and the drifters. **1956** *Nature* 25 Feb. 375/2 Only one nektonic species apart from *Thyrsites* itself has been found to occur in Bass Strait at the time of year in question. **1969** *Austral. Law Jrnl.* XLIII. 430 The traditional biological classification of fish and fish like creatures into drifters or plankton, swimmers or necton, and the bottom dwellers or benthos. *Ibid.*, The nectonic species of fish are divided into demersal and pelagic. **1974** LUCAS & CRITCH *Life in Oceans* ii. 25 The nekton comprises all those animals, such as squid, cuttlefish, fishes, seals and whales, which are able to swim more or less powerfully and which are therefore independent of water movements for transport. **1975** *Nature* 17 Apr. 591/2 The stomachs of the fish contained the remains of nektonic, planktonic and benthic organisms.

‖**nekulturny** (neɪkʊl'tʊrnɪ), *sb.* and *a.* Also **nekulturniiy.** [Russ. *nekul'turnyĭ* uncivilized.]

A. *sb.* One who is by Russian standards considered unenlightened, a boor. **B.** *adj.* Not having cultured manners, boorish. Cf. KULTURNY.

1959 I. R. LEVINE *Real Russia* xxiv. 347 It is *nekulturny* for a man..to put feet up on a desk, to cross legs, or to keep hands in trouser pockets. **1960** W. MILLER *Russians as People* vi. 139 To accuse someone of being 'uncultured' (*nekulturny*) is not a light matter... It may signify that you do not clean your teeth, that you never read a book, or that you are pushing rudely or giving way to a coarse expression of opinion. **1962** J. WADE *Running Sand* xiii. 166 To dance so close to a woman was uncultured, *nekulturny*, a sign of western decadence. **1965** *New Statesman* 16 July 71/3 What bothers Washington is that the President is so determinedly *nekulturniiy.* **1967** J. FORES *Desirable Dictator* iv. 97 We are not gangsters, Mr. C.I.A. We leave that kind of *nekulturny* behaviour to the West.

neld(e, obs. ff. NEEDLE.

nele, obs. f. EEL *sb.*, NILL *v.*

neli, obs. f. NIGHLY.

nelia, var. NEALIE.

†**neling**, obs. variant of ANELING, anointing.

1567–8 in Swayne *Sarum Churchw. Acc.* (1896) 110 Two lytell Clothys that holdeth the neling box. *Ibid.*, The nelinge box of led.

nell, obs. form of ELL.

nelle, var. of NILL *v.*

nelly[1] ('nɛlɪ). [Of uncertain origin; perh. as next.] A large sea-bird (*Ossifraga gigantea*) belonging to the petrel group.

1823 J. WEDDELL *Voy.* 59 The bird next in size found here is called by sailors a Nelly. It is of the peterel kind. **1845** DARWIN *Voy. Nat.* xiii. (1873) 289 The largest kind of petrel, *Procellaria gigantea*, or nelly. **1895** *Pall Mall G.* 16 Dec. 2/2 Arctic raven and fox..are ten thousand times worse than nelly or albatross.

nelly[2] ('nɛlɪ). Also **Nelly, Nellie.** [A fem. Christian name, familiar form of Helen or Eleanor.] **1.** Slang phr. ***not on your Nelly*** [f. rhyming slang *Nelly Duff* = *puff* = breath of life], 'not on your life' (see LIFE *sb.* 3 d), not likely.

1941 *New Statesman* 30 Aug. 218/3 *Not on your Nelly Duff*,..not likely. **1961** *John o' London's* 14 Dec. 663/1 You might have thought Mr. Samuel Bronston would have rested... Not, as they say, on your nelly. **1961** PARTRIDGE *Adventuring among Words* xi. 55 The trouble begins when part, usually the latter part, of the rhyming phrase is omitted, as so often it is, as in..'not on your *Nellie*' for '... Nellie Duff!' = 'not on your *puff*' = 'not on your life' or 'most certainly not' or, less politely, 'like hell, I will!'. **1966** *Times* 15 May 9 That would mean me investing in another man's career. Not on your Nelly! **1968** *Manch. Guardian Weekly* 11 Apr. 15/1 So the Liberals dropped Acton and Dudley and concentrated on Warwick and Leamington? Not on your Nellie! **1972** *Times* 24 June 11/4 Ooh, no, not on your nelly, ah, fearless Francis! **1974** *Globe & Mail* (Toronto) 21 Sept. 35/2, I appear to be giving away most of the plot? Not on your nelly. That's only the beginning.

2. A cheap wine. *Austral. slang.*

1945 BAKER *Austral. Lang.* ix. 166 Here is a group of indigenous terms used to describe cheap wines: *Africa speaks,..nelly, nelly's death* [etc.]. **1952** A. G. MITCHELL in *Chambers's Shorter Eng. Dict.* Suppl., *Nelly*,..(*slang*) cheap wine.—phr. *on the nelly*, given to drinking cheap wine.

3. A weak-spirited or silly person; a homosexual. Also as quasi-adj., of feminine appearance, effeminate. Cf. NICE-NELLYISM.

1961 *Sunday Times* 17 Sept. 41/4 [Henry] Livings's latest work, 'Sacred Nit'... This same play, now called 'Big Soft Nellie', opens at the Oxford Playhouse. **1962** *Sunday Times* 29 Apr. 12/4 See, what you've got to do is get on the same wavelength as the nellies who write in. **1967** 'T. WELLS' *Dead by Light of Moon* (1968) iv. 45 You don't suppose it could have anything to do with that Strangler business, do you? Not that I'm a nervous Nelly type. **1970** K. PLATT *Pushbutton Butterfly* (1971) xvi. 182 He..puffed daintily on a long cigarette as he watched the nellies cruising to the 'tearoom'. **1971** *Psychiatry* XXXIV. 187/2 Some guy came up to me and tried to take me for some money, and I knew it, and he said, 'You know, you're very nellie.' **1972** B. RODGERS *Queens' Vernacular* 141 *Nelly*..outrageously effeminate; coy, silly. **1973** C. WITTMAN in P. Brown *Radical Psychol.* xix. 459 There is a tendency among 'homophile' groups to deplore gays who play visible roles—the queens and the nellies.

4. Slang phr. ***sitting next to*** (or ***by, with***) ***Nelly***, learning an occupation on the job by observing how others do it.

1963 J. U. FRASER *Psychol.* (ed. 2) xiv. 173 Observation of a skilled operator (often characterized as 'sitting next to Nellie'). **1966** *Guardian* 30 July 6/5 The generous 'General Trainees Scheme' which allows them to spend up to two years in different departments [of the BBC]—'sitting with Nellie', is the union phrase. **1972** *Listener* 10 Aug. 180/2 Journalists are the casual labourers of the intellectual world. .. Most training still consists of sitting next to Nellie. **1975** *New Society* 17 July 130/1 It was then made compulsory for doctors from overseas to 'sit by Nellie' for a month. Immigrant doctors had to complete satisfactorily a month's supervision under a consultant supervisor.

Nelson ('nɛlsən).

1. *Wrestling.* [App. f. a proper name.] The name of a class of holds in which one or both arms are passed under the opponent's from behind and the hand(s) applied to his neck; often with words prefixed to indicate the precise form of the hold, as ***double nelson, half nelson,*** (***three-***) ***quarter nelson.*** Also *fig.*

1889 W. ARMSTRONG *Wrestling* 233 Probably the most dangerous move in Lancashire and Cornwall and Devon wrestling..is what is called the 'Double Nelson'. **1893** *Lippincott's Mag.* Feb. 211 Among the many holds the Nelson is the most popular one with wrestlers, while the half-Nelson and half-walch-lock are next in order. **1897** [see *hammer-lock* (HAMMER *sb.* 7)]. **1900** A. E. T. WATSON *Young Sportsman* 644 The principal chips associated with catch as catch can wrestling are the double Nelson, the half Nelson, the heave, the Lancashire lock, the flying mare and the three-quarter Nelson. **1930** P. MACDONALD *Link* ix. 168 They lose Dinwater—or lose half the Nelson they've got on him, so immediately they switch on to you.

2. The name of Admiral Lord *Nelson* (1758–1805) used *attrib.* in **Nelson cake** (see quot. 1966); **Nelson eye**, a blind eye: usu. *transf.* and *fig.* (cf. EYE *sb.*[1] 5 e); **Nelson knife**, a combined knife and fork for the use of a one-armed person; **Nelson's blood**, Navy rum; **Nelson touch**, a stroke, action, or manner characteristic of Nelson.

1909 *Daily Chron.* 16 Dec. 4/7 The Nelson cake consists of two thin pieces of reputed pastry, with a dark agglomeration between them of currants and sweet mush. **1966** F. SHAW et al. *Lern Yerself Scouse* 42 *Nelson cake*, a cake made from compressed, broken biscuits, pastry remnants etc. with dried fruit added: the whole soaked in syrup or burnt sugar and stacked in great piles. **1965** *New Society* 7 Jan. 12/3 The police made no attempt to arrest him. The State simply turns a Nelson eye to his presence. **1970** B. TURNER *Another Little Death* xxiv. 149 It's often possible for the police to turn a Nelson eye to misdemeanours confessed to them if they can catch a blackmailer by doing so. **1973** J. LEASOR *Mandarin Gold* i. 13 He makes most out of opium. Turning a Nelson eye to a trade he should be stamping out. **1902** *Chambers's Jrnl.* 4 Oct. 692/2 The mention of knife *and* fork attached to the one wrist is at first slightly puzzling; but probably the combination was what is called the 'Nelson knife', after its most distinguished user. The handle is like that of an ordinary table-knife; but the end of the blade, instead of being rounded off in the ordinary way, turns up at a right angle in its own plane, and is divided into four fork-prongs. **1974** *Times* 27 Nov. 17/6 A 'Nelson' knife..has a curved blade..and also teeth at the end of the blade... Nelson knives are a Government issue to those..who have lost an arm but they can also be purchased. **1925** FRASER & GIBBONS *Soldier & Sailor Words* 166 *Nelson's Blood*, rum. Old Navy, and probably derived from the old story of the sailors on board the *Victory* tapping the cask in which Nelson's body was brought home and drinking the spirits. **1968** *Telegraph* (Brisbane) 26 June 45 To preserve Nelson's body it was placed in the ship's rum ration—that's why rum is now often referred to as 'Nelson's blood'. **1970** A. DRAPER *Swansong for Rare Bird* ix. 76 After all the Nelson's blood he'd stashed away the night before, I was surprised to see Gorgeous already there. **1805** LD. NELSON *Let.* 25 Sept. in C. Oman *Nelson* (1947) xix. 607, I am anxious to join the fleet, for it would add to my grief if any other man was to give them the Nelson touch, which *we* say is warranted never to fail. *Ibid.* 1 Oct. 609 When I came to explain to them the '*Nelson touch*', it was like an electric shock. **1898** H. NEWBOLT *Island Race* 26 But cared greatly to serve God and the king, And keep the Nelson touch. **1963** *Economist* 12 Jan. 90/1 There was a 'Nelson touch' about the bloodless occupation of Jadotville. **1968** B. TURNER *Sex Trap* xiii. 116 A little of the old Nelson touch is a big help in getting on with other departments. **1971** D. CORY *Sunburst* i. 20 Only the British, in Intelligence matters, retain the Nelson touch. *What's Fedora doing in Spain?*.. Up goes the old telescope. *Fedora? I see no Fedora.*

Nelsonian (nɛl'səʊnɪən), *a.* [f. NELSON 2 + -IAN.] Belonging to the time of Nelson; pertaining to, characteristic of, or relating to Nelson. Hence **Nelsoni'ana**, a collection of papers, relics, etc., relating to Nelson.

1909 *Daily Chron.* 24 Feb. 3/5 A volume of Nelsoniana, which realised £145. **1913** *Q. Rev.* Apr. 461 We have only to go back to the eighties to find ships..with their..guns still mounted on the Nelsonian trucks worked by hand-spikes. **1931** *Times Lit. Suppl.* 17 Sept. 699/4 The Nelsonian mannerisms of words, dress and movements. **1958** *Listener* 2 Oct. 519/1 This valuable addition to Nelsoniana is the hundredth volume published by the Navy Records Society. **1969** *Sunday Times* 2 Nov. 8/7 Every editor knows how to turn a Nelsonian eye on a lack of O and A levels if he has a promising journalist before him. **1971** B. CALLISON *Plague of Sailors* iv. 134 It was conceivable that Their Lords of the Admiralty might have been prepared to turn a Nelsonian blind eye to H.M. Ships shooting up the odd foreign cargo boat.

Nelsonic (nɛl'sɒnɪk), *a.* [f. NELSON 2 + -IC.] Pertaining to, relating to, or characteristic of Nelson.

1846 R. FORD *Gatherings from Spain* xvi. 188 They are ill-bred enough, in spite of the Montpensier marriage, and the Nelsonic achievements of Monsieur de Joinville, to consider the words as synonymes. **1909** *Daily Chron.* 13 Sept. 3/3 These Nelsonic qualities in Wolfe do not..come out very clearly in the letters. **1922** *Q. Rev.* Apr. 361 Orders of this nature..are always dangerous in the absence of the Nelsonic spirit. **1972** V. GIELGUD *Black Sambo Affair* xxviii. 220 Various persons at the airports were given the hint to turn the Nelsonic blind eye.

nelt(ou: see NILL *v.*

nelumbi'aceous, *a. Bot. rare*$^{-0}$. [See def.] Of or belonging to the order *Nelumbiaceæ*, or Water Beans, represented by the different species of Nelumbium. So **nelum'boneous** *a.*

1856 MAYNE *Expos. Lex.*

‖**nelumbium** (nɪˈlʌmbɪəm). *Bot.* [mod.L. (A. L. de Jussieu *Genera Plantarum* (1789) 68), f. Singhalese *nelumbu* or *nelum*.] An aquatic plant of the genus *Nelumbo*, belonging to the family Nymphæaceæ, formerly called *Nelumbium*, and including the East Indian or sacred lotus, *N. nucifera*, which has white or pink flowers, and the American lotus, *N. pentapetala*, which has fragrant yellow flowers.

1806 *Curtis's Bot. Mag.* XXIII. 903 The Nelumbium is no longer found in Egypt. **1853** *Harper's Mag.* Nov. 751/2 The broad prairies..are also diversified by lakes, their surfaces shaded from the hot sun by the broad-leafed nelumbium. **1857** A. GRAY *First Less. Bot.* (1866) 59 The common Watershield, the Nelumbium, and the White Water-lily..exhibit this sort of leaf. **1882** *Garden* 11 Nov. 421/1, I am somewhat interested in Nelumbiums. **1886** *Standard* 8 May 3/4 The [seed of] Nelumbium has been known to grow after a hundred years. **1916** L. H. BAILEY *Stand. Cycl. Hort.* IV. 2117/1 Nelumbiums are bold plants, suitable for large ponds. **1951** *Dict. Gardening* (R. Hort. Soc.) III. 1359/1 The Nelumbiums need rich soil.

nelumbo (nɪˈlʌmbəʊ). [mod.L. (M. Adanson *Familles des Plantes* (1763) I. 73); see NELUMBIUM.] = NELUMBIUM.

1794 E. DARWIN *Botanic Garden* (ed. 4) II. 169 With sweet loquacity Nelumbo sails, Shouts to his shores, and parleys with his gales. *Ibid.*, Linneus [*sic*], who has enlisted all our senses into the service of botany, has observed this rattling of the Nelumbo. **1804** J. E. SMITH *Exotic Botany* I. 61 A carved horn of a rhinoceros, sent to Linnæus from China,.. is now before me... The whole inverted base of the horn is carved into an elegant leaf of *Nelumbo*, rising from the water. **1818** C. ABEL *Narr. Journey in China* v. 103 Fields of *Nelumbo* rearing high its glossy leaves and gorgeous flowers ..spread at our feet. **1850** S. F. COOPER *Rural Hours* 275 It is chiefly in our western waters that the Nelumbo is found. **1884** tr. *A. de Candolle's Orig. Cultivated Plants* II. i. 75 The nelumbo of Indian origin has ceased to grow in Egypt. **1916** L. H. BAILEY *Stand. Cycl. Hort.* IV. 2117/1 American Lotus, or Nelumbo... A bold and useful plant for colonizing. **1961** F. PERRY *Water Gardening* (ed. 2) vii. 75 Nelumbos are reproduced by means of long creeping rootstocks. *Ibid.* 76 [In India] the stranger is presented with fruit and flowers laid in a simple basket fashioned from Nelumbo leaves.

nem, variant of NEMN *v.*, to name.

nemaline (ˈnɛməlaɪn), *a. Min. rare.* [irreg. f. Gr. νῆμα thread.] Having the form of threads.

1835 SHEPARD *Min.* s.v. *Nemalite*, Nemaline atelene Picrosmine.

nemalite (ˈnɛməlaɪt). *Min.* [f. Gr. νῆμα thread + -LITE: named by Nuttall, 1821.] A fibrous variety of Brucite.

1821 NUTTALL *Amer. Jrnl. Sci.* Oct. 19 Nemalite.. possesses the usual silky lustre and flexible fibrous texture [of amianthus] and is commonly of a pale blue colour. **1861** BRISTOW *Gloss. Min.* 256/2. **1882** DANA *Min.* (ed. 4) 204 The fibrous variety [of Brucite] has been called nemalite..; it occurs at Hoboken.

nemasperm (ˈnɛməspɜːm). *rare*$^{-1}$. [f. Gr. νῆμα thread + SPERM *sb.*] = SPERMATOZOON.

1922 JOYCE *Ulysses* 411 Must we accept the view of Empedocles of Trinacria that the right ovary..is responsible for the birth of males or are the too long neglected spermatozoa or nemasperms the differentiating factors.

nemathece (ˈnɛməθiːs). *Bot.* = NEMATHECIUM.

1889 BENNETT & MURRAY *Handbk. Cryptog. Bot.* 202 The cystocarps are enclosed in nematheces.

nemathecial (nɛməˈθiːʃ(ɪ)al), *a. Bot.* [f. next.] Of or belonging to the nemathecium.

1890 in *Cent. Dict.* **1899** DARBISHIRE in *Annals Bot.* XIII. 261 At first as a rule these nemathecial bodies are formed only on one side of the flattened spermaphore. *Ibid.* 262 Outer cells of nemathecial filaments.

‖**nemathecium** (nɛməˈθiːʃ(ɪ)əm). *Bot.* Pl. -ia. [mod.L. (Agardh), f. Gr. νῆμα thread + θήκη box, chest, sheath, etc.] A warty protuberance developed in some of the florideous algæ, usually containing tetraspores.

1830 GREVILLE *Algæ Brit.* 131 Dark red masses.. composed entirely of vertical moniliform filaments (nemathecia of Agardh). *Ibid.* 136 The nemathecia are very beautiful under the microscope. **1841** HARVEY *Man. Brit. Algæ* 78 Nemathecia also frequently occur on the frondlets. **1899** DARBISHIRE in *Annals Bot.* XIII. 262 The extramatrical filaments gradually form the nemathecium of the parasite.

Comb. **1846-51** HARVEY *Phycologia Brit.* III. (Syn. 198), Mr. Dillwyn was..the first to notice the nemathecia-fructification.

nemathelminth (nɛməˈθɛlmɪnθ). *Zool.* [f. Gr. νήματ-, νῆμα thread + ἑλμινθ-, ἕλμινς worm.] A thread-worm or round-worm; one of that class of worms which includes the nematodes and related forms. Hence **ˌnemathelˈminthic** *a.*

1890 in *Cent. Dict.* **1896** SHIPLEY in *Cambridge Nat. Hist.* II. vi. 124 In no Nemathelminth is there any closed vascular system, nor are special respiratory organs developed.

nematic (nɛˈmætɪk), *a. Physical Chem.* [ad. F. *nématique* (G. Friedel 1922, in *Ann. de Physique* XVIII. 227), f. Gr. νῆμα, νήματ- thread: see -IC.] Applied to (the state of) a mesophase in which the molecules all have the same orientation but are not arranged in well-defined planes (as they are in a smectic phase). Also as *sb.*, a nematic substance.

1923 *Chem. Abstr.* XVII. 3267 A complete treatise upon the types and properties of matter existent between the true amorphous and cryst. states. The condition formerly designated as liquid crystals or anisotropic liquids is divided into 2 classifications: smectic.., and nematic. **1940** S. GLASSTONE *Text-bk. Physical Chem.* vii. 505 Nematic liquids are closer to true anisotropic liquids than are the smectic phases. **1971** *Physics Bull.* June 357/2 One of Marconi's exhibits at this year's Physics Exhibition demonstrated the effective use of organic nematic liquid crystals for visual display purposes. **1972** *Sci. Amer.* Mar. 39/1 (Advt.), We hereby announce the commercial availability of a multicomponent nematic that might suffice to call off some chemists. **1974** *Nature* 25 Jan. 178/3 Nuclear magnetic resonance spectra of molecules oriented in themotropic and lyotropic nematics.

nematicide (ˈnɛmət-, nɛˈmætɪsaɪd). [irreg. f. Gr. νῆμα, νήματ- thread + -CIDE.] = *nematocide* s.v. NEMATO-.

1933 [see NEMATOLOGY]. **1952** *Nature* 8 Mar. 420/2 Work has already been published..on the value of chlorphenol as a nematicide. **1960** *Jrnl. R. Horticultural Soc.* LXXXV. II. 54 Trial of various nematicides has shown that treatment with methyl bromide gives a yield almost double that of the control plots. **1972** P. SIVAPALAN in J. M. Webster *Economic Nematology* xiii. 308 In order to improve the trend of the decline in yield in the tea fields infested with *Pratylenchus loosi*, the field is..treated with suitable nematicides.

Hence **nematiˈcidal** *a.* = *nematocidal* adj. s.v. NEMATO-.

1950 *Helminthol. Abstr.* XVI. 122 Ethylene dibromide is highly nematicidal since 0·1 c.c. will eradicate nematodes from a gallon of soil. **1973** C. A. ANDERSON in G. Zweig *Analyt. Methods for Pesticides* VII. x. 253 Dasanit® exhibits both insecticidal and nematicidal activity.

nemato- (ˈnɛmətəʊ), combining form of Gr. νῆμα, νήματος thread, used in a number of scientific terms, as **ˈnematoblast**, *Biol.* a blastema which develops into a spermatozoon. **ˌnematoˈcalycine** *a.*, pertaining to, of the nature of, a nematocalyx. **ˈnematoˈcalyx**, *Zool.* a calyx containing nematocysts, occurring in some *Hydromedusæ*. **ˌnematoˈceratous** *a.*, *Entom.* having filiform antennæ (Mayne 1856); so **nemaˈtocerous** *a.* **ˈnematocide**, a substance or preparation employed to kill nematode worms. **nematoˈcidal** *a.*, characteristic of a nematocide. **ˈnematogen**, *Biol.* [ad. Fr. *nématogène* (E. van Beneden 1876, in *Bull. Acad. R. Belgique* 2 Sér. XLI. 1195)], in Dicyemids, the form which produces a filiform embryo; hence **ˌnematoˈgenic**, **nemaˈtogenous** *adjs.* **ˈnematognath**, *Zool.* a fish of the sub-order *Nematognathi*; a catfish; also **ˌnematoˈgnathous** *a.* **ˌnematoˈneurous**, **-ˈneurose** *a.*, *Zool.* of or pertaining to the *Nematoneura*, Owen's name for a division of *Radiata* 'in which nervous filaments are always distinctly traceable'. †**ˈnematopode**, *Zool.* a cirriped; also **nemaˈtopodous** *a.* (Mayne 1856). **ˌnematoˈthec(i)ous** *a.*, *Bot.* of or belonging to a filamentous family of gymnocarpous mushrooms (Mayne 1856). **ˌnematoˈzooid**, *Zool.* one of the stinging filaments of a siphonophore considered as a zooid.

1886 *Encycl. Brit.* (ed. 9) XX. 413/1 A central cavity.. from which the tails of the incipient spermatozoa or '*nematoblasts' project into the lumen of the duct. **1943** *Phytopathology* XXXIII. 1174 The *nematocidal effect of chloropicrin was tested in the field against the root-knot nematode, *Heterodera marioni*. **1973** *Biol. Abstr.* LVI. 6884/2 Nematocidal activity, similar to that of trichothecin, was detected in mycelial extracts and volatile substances of *Arthrobotrys*, a predacious fungus. **1898** *Daily News* 4 Aug. 2/1 That the..antiseptic remedy thymol will be of service as a *nematocide. **1888** ROLLESTON & JACKSON *Anim. Life* 815 The first-named [a monogenic Dicyemid] produces only vermiform embryoes, and is hence a primary *Nematogen. **1896** *Cambridge Nat. Hist.* II. 94 Other individuals which produce a more elongated larva..are called Nematogens. **1899** *Zoologischer Anzeiger* XXII. 171 The mother of vermiform embryos is called a *nematogen, the mother of infusoriform embryos a rhombogen. **1972** *Sci. Amer.* Dec. 98/2 Two different wormlike stages of the Mesozoa have been described: 'nematogens' were reported to produce nematogens and 'rhombogens', whereas rhombogens were reported to produce infusoriform dispersal larvae and occasionally to both produce larvae and revert to the nematogen stage. Observations on laboratory populations of Mesozoa make this distinction untenable. **1885** GEDDES in *Encycl. Brit.* XVIII. 259/1 The embryos are of two kinds, *nematogenic or vermiform, and rhombogenic or infusiform. **1877** HUXLEY *Anat. Inv. Anim.* xi. 654 The *nematogenous Dicyema gives rise by an agamogenetic process to new Dicyemas. **1888** ROLLESTON & JACKSON *Anim. Life* 817 The Nematogenous individual varies somewhat in shape. **1835-6** OWEN in *Todd's Cycl. Anat.* I. 47/2 The difference in the condition of the digestive system between the Acrite and *Nematoneurous classes is still more striking. **1839-47** T. R. JONES *ibid.* III. 535/1 The Bryozoa ..belong to the Nematoneurose type. **1837** *Penny Cycl.* VII. 202/1 [The] Cirrhopodes of Cuvier,..*Nematopodes of De Blainville.

nematocyst (ˈnɛmətəsɪst). *Zool.* [f. NEMATO- + CYST.] A small cell in the external layer of jelly-fishes and other cœlenterates, containing a thread capable of being ejected and of producing a stinging sensation; a lasso-cell or thread-cell.

1875 HUXLEY in *Encycl. Brit.* I. 129/1 The Actinozoa agree with the Hydrozoa..in possessing thread cells, or nematocysts. **1877** —— *Anat. Inv. Anim.* iii. 124 In its most perfect form, a nematocyst is an elastic thick-walled sac, coiled up in the interior of which is a long filament, often serrated or provided with spines. **1888** ROLLESTON & JACKSON *Anim. Life* 781 The tentacles especially are provided with nematocysts of two sizes.

nematode (ˈnɛmətəʊd), *a.* and *sb.* [See NEMATO- and -ODE¹, and cf. NEMATOID.]

A. *adj.* **1.** Of worms: Pertaining to the class *Nematoda* or *Nematoidea*, comprising those of a slender cylindrical or thread-like form (chiefly parasitic in animals or plants), such as the common round-worm, maw-worm, Guinea-worm, etc.

1861 HULME tr. *Moquin-Tandon* II. VII. i. 339 The embryos of the nematode worms may pass the winter in a sort of torpid state. **1876** *Beneden's Anim. Parasites* Introd. 26 The greater part..have not lived long in captivity, before nematode and cestode worms completely disappear.

2. [Partly *attrib.* uses of the sb.] Of or pertaining to, resembling or characteristic of, worms of this class.

1866 *Standard* 19 Feb., We now proceed to look our foe in the face—if, indeed, the nematode nuisance possesses any face. **1889** GEDDES & THOMSON *Evol. Sex* 17 They become parasitic, and lose both activity and nematode form. **1897** *Allbutt's Syst. Med.* II. 1032 An embryo of the usual nematode character.

B. *sb.* A nematode worm.

1865 T. S. COBBOLD in *Pop. Sci. Rev.* IV. 163 In various plants I have..noticed free nematodes within their parenchyma. **1876** *Beneden's Anim. Parasites* 155 A nematode which I observed under very singular circumstances. **1888** ROLLESTON & JACKSON *Anim. Life* 684 Three stages..have been distinguished in the growth of a Nematode after hatching.

Comb. **1898** SEDGWICK *Text-bk. Zool.* I. vii. 291 A.. vermiform body carrying a small Nematode-like worm.

nematodiriasis (ˌnɛmətəʊdɪˈraɪəsɪs). [f. NEMATODIR(US + -IASIS.] A disease of young lambs caused by the larvæ of nematodes of the genus *Nematodirus* and characterized by diarrhœa, loss of weight, and dehydration.

1957 FRASER & STAMP *Sheep Husbandry & Diseases* (ed. 3) x. 384 This disease for which the rather ugly word 'nematodiriasis' might be used is characterised by its sudden and dramatic appearance in low-ground flocks during late May and early June. **1967** *New Scientist* 13 July 63/3 Nematodiriasis, a worm-caused disease of young lambs. **1971** *Farmers Weekly* 19 Mar. 66 (Advt.), Frantin Paste halts the scours associated with nematodiriasis and other worm infestations in unweaned lambs.

nematodirus (ˌnɛmətəʊˈdaɪrəs). [mod.L. (B. H. Ransom 1907, in *U.S. Dept. Agric. Bur. Anim. Ind.* No. 116. 4), f. NEMATO(DE *a.* and *sb.* + Gr. δειρή neck.] A parasitic nematode worm of the genus so called, belonging to the family Trichostrongylidæ, which is found in the intestine of many mammals and causes disease in young lambs. Also *attrib.*

1915 *Parasitology* VIII. 146 The *Nematodirus* larvae are able to withstand complete desiccation. **1934** *Jrnl. Agric. Sci.* XXIV. 207 *Nematodirus* larvae can regain the surface after being turned in by the plough. **1956** *Vet. Rec.* 21 July 471 (*title*) Some observations on Nematodirus Disease in Northumberland and Durham. **1957** FRASER & STAMP *Sheep Husbandry & Diseases* (ed. 3) x. 384 Until recently the worm nematodirus was thought to be relatively harmless to sheep. *Ibid.* 385 Nematodirus worms may be present in large numbers. **1960** *Farmer & Stockbreeder* 9 Feb. 64/3 Border farmers..who have never seen nematodirus and who have long ceased to drench for worms. **1963** *Times* 20 May 16/5 Forecasts could now be made of conditions likely to induce..fluke and nematodirus infections.

nematoid (ˈnɛmətɔɪd), *a.* and *sb.* [Cf. NEMATODE and -OID.]

A. *adj.* = NEMATODE *a.*

1836-9 OWEN in *Todd's Cycl. Anat.* II. 134/2 A close affinity to the Nematoid type. **1836-9** T. R. JONES *ibid.* II. 407/2 Some of the Nematoid worms..propagate by spontaneous division. **1877** HUXLEY *Anat. Inv. Anim.* xii. 680 The lowest known term of the Arthrozoic series is a Nematoid worm. **1882** *Pall Mall G.* 26 July 4/2 The intestines of the many diseased birds..contain nematoid entozoa.

B. *sb.* = NEMATODE *sb.*

1870 ROLLESTON *Forms Anim. Life*, The ventral surface of the parasitic Nematoids. **1880** BASTIAN *Brain* v. 86.

Hence **nemaˈtoidean**. (Craig 1849.)

nematology (nɛməˈtɒlədʒɪ). [f. NEMAT(ODE *a.* and *sb.* + -OLOGY.] The study of nematodes. So **nematoˈlogical** *a.*, of or pertaining to this study; **nemaˈtologist**, a person making such a study.

1926 C. W. STILES in Yorke & Mapleston *Nematode Parasites of Vertebrates* p. v, A few genera..were of some slight interest in human and veterinary medicine, but this fact played a distinctly secondary *rôle* in nematological studies... Zenker..and others, pointed out the far-reaching medical and economic bearings of nematology. **1933** T. GOODEY *Plant Parasitic Nematodes* i. 2 In the United States of America these small forms are often called 'nemas'; a word introduced by the late Dr. N. A. Cobb together with several cognate terms such as nematology, nematologist, nematized, and nematicide, &c. **1960** *Times* 7 July 3/6 Research appointments in..plant nematology. **1961** G. THORNE *Princ. Nematology* p. ix, The writer is indebted to the..U.S. Department of Agriculture, for the opportunity to work on nematological problems in many parts of the United States. **1963** *New Scientist* 5 Sept. 490/1 The comparative effectiveness of four nematicides..has recently been under investigation by the Nematology Department at Rothamsted Experimental Station. **1971** *Nature* 15 Jan. p. xvii (Advt.), A nematologist is required to work in some aspects of the biology of *Trichodorus* species. **1974** *Ibid.* 19 Apr. 715/3, I commend this book to all thoughtful nematologists, plant pathologists and ecologists.

nematophore ('nɛmətəfɔə(r)). *Zool.* Also **-phor.** [f. NEMATO- + -PHORE.] A special cup-shaped process of the cœnosarc in certain hydrozoans, having nematocysts at the extremity.

1859 HUXLEY *Oceanic Hydrozoa* (Ray Soc.) 11 These nematophores..are cæcal processes of the cœnosarc. **1861** J. R. GREENE *Man. Anim. Kingd., Cœlent.* 34 The nematophores probably serve as organs of offence. They are most numerous in the genus *Plumularia.* **1898** SEDGWICK *Text-bk. Zool.* I. 126 Nematophores are probably nutritive, catching food as an Amœba does.

Comb. **1871** ALLMAN *Gymnoblastic Hydroids* (Ray Soc.) I. 28 The nematophore-bearing genera. *Ibid.* 115 The contents of the nematophore-sheaths.

Hence **nema'tophorous** *a.*, of the nature of a nematophore.

1878 BELL *Gegenbaur's Comp. Anat.* 102 Among the Siphonophora all the medusiform persons want the marginal filaments..; as for example, in the nematophorous enlargements of the protective persons.

nembie ('nɛmbɪ). Also **nebbie, nemish, nemmie, nimby.** *U.S. colloq.* contractions of NEMBUTAL.

1950 [see *goof ball*]. **1953** W. BURROUGHS *Junkie* (1972) ii. 23 This night Herman was knocked out on 'nembies' and his head kept falling down onto the bar. *Ibid.* iv. 40 Next day I was worse and could not get out of bed. So I stayed in bed taking nembies at intervals. *Ibid.* 158 *Nembies, Goof Balls, Yellow Jackets*... Nembutal capsules. **1969** R. R. LINGEMAN *Drugs from A to Z* 182 Nembutal... Slang names: nebbies, nemmies, nemish, yellow jackets. **1971** E. E. LANDY *Underground Dict.* 139 Nembutal... Nemish, nemmie, nimby.

nemble, obs. form of NIMBLE.

Nembutal ('nɛmbju:tæl). Also **nembutal.** [f. *Na*, chemical symbol for sodium (f. NA(TRIUM) + initial letters of the elements of 5-*e*thyl-5-(1-*m*ethyl*but*yl) barbiturate, chemical name of the compound + *-al* (as in *Veronal, barbital*).] A proprietary name of pentobarbitone sodium, a short-acting barbiturate used as a hypnotic and an anticonvulsant. Also, a capsule of Nembutal.

[**1930** *Anaesthesia & Analgesia* IX. 215/2 Sodium ethyl 1-methyl butyl barbiturate (sodium embutal).] **1930** *Druggists Circular* Dec. 73/2 Nembutal, '844', a new pre-anesthetic sedative and hypnotic,..described as being effective in allaying the apprehension and fear of patients about to undergo an operation. **1931** *Lancet* 10 Jan. 74/1 (*heading*) Nembutal as a basal hypnotic in general anæsthesia. **1931** *Official Gaz.* (U.S. Patent Off.) 21 Apr. 560/1 Nembutal. For hypnotic sedative anesthetic compound. **1936** *Discovery* July 206/2 Another modern method of lessening nervous apprehension is to give the patient a sleeping draught the night before, and then in the morning, sometime before the operation, he is given a capsule of Nembutal or Pronocton. **1937** *Trade Marks Jrnl.* 15 Dec. 1474/1 Nembutal... Medicated preparations for use as hypnotics and sedatives. Abbott Laboratories Limited.., Montreal. **1953** W. BURROUGHS *Junkie* (1972) xiii. 128, I drank it all with two nembutals and slept several hours. *Ibid.* 158 Nembutal is a barbiturate used by junkies 'to take the edge off' when they can't get junk. **1959** N. MARSH *Singing in Shrouds* ix. 183 I've given her a nembutal. She's asleep in bed. **1962** A. PIRIE *Lens Metabolism Rel. Cataract* 429 Rabbit lenses were obtained from the laboratory stock of Dutch rabbits killed by overdose of Nembutal. **1971** J. WRIGHT *Coll. Poems* 274 This was the dream that woke me From nembutal sleep into the pains of grief.

nembutalized (nɛm'bju:təlaɪzd), *ppl. a. Vet.* [f. NEMBUTAL + -IZ(E + -ED[1].] Anæsthetized with Nembutal.

1940 *Amer. Jrnl. Physiol.* CXXIX. 55 Two of the nembutalized dogs included in group II..were adrenalectomized. **1972** *Brain Res.* XXXVI. 350 Presynaptic inhibition in nembutalized cats.

nem. con., an abbreviation of the L. phrase *nemine contradicente* '(with) no one contradicting'.

The full form has been in common use since at least the middle of the 17th c.; rarely abbrev. to *nemine con.*

1588 R. HOVENDEN in *Collect.* (O.H.S.) I. 232 The Coll. flatly denied to grant the Lease (*nem. con.*). **1772** *Town & Country Mag.* 19 Preparations were ordered, *nem. con.*, for the decisive day. **1822** BYRON *Let. to Moore* 1 Mar., I thought that you had always been allowed to be a poet..—a bad one, to be sure.., but still always a poet, *nem. con.* **1866** *Routledge's Mag.* July 394 A resolution was now passed, *nem. con.*, not to land on Monk's Island.

So **nem. diss.,** abbrev. of *nemine dissentiente.*

1791 *Hist. Eur.* in *Ann. Reg.* 37/2 The lord chancellor put the question..when it was declared that the contents had it *nem. diss.* **1870** *Brewer's Dict. Phr. & Fable* 610/1 *Nem. diss.*, without a dissentient voice. (Latin, *nem'inĕ dissent'ientĕ.*) **1945** R. HARGREAVES *Enemy at Gate* 123 The thanks of both Houses were duly agreed *nem. diss.*

†**neme,** obs. variant of EME, uncle.

c **1450** *Nominale* (Harl. MS. 1002) lf. 143 *Patrius*, a neme. **1696** PHILLIPS (ed. 5), *Neme*, (Old English) signifying Uncle; used by those of Staffordshire.

neme, variant of NIM *v.*

Nemean (nɪ'mi:ən, 'ni:mɪən), *a.* Also 7 -ian, 7–9 -æan. [f. L. *Nemeæus, Nemæus, Nemēus*, ad. Gr. Νεμεαῖος, Νέμειος, Νέμεος, etc., f. Νεμέα, the name of a wooded district near Argos in Greece.] Of or belonging to Nemea.

1. ***Nemean lion***, a lion said to have been killed by Hercules at Nemea.

1588 SHAKS. *L.L.L.* IV. i. 90 Thus dost thou heare the Nemean Lion roare. **1602** —— *Ham.* I. iv. 83 As hardy as the Nemian Lions nerue. **1649** OGILBY *Virg. Georg.* III. (1684) 94 *note*, As he went to kill the Nemæan Lion. **1830** *Tales of Classics* II. 156 Having covered the pile with the skin of the Nemæan Lion. **1845** BROWNING *Glove* 164 Had our brute been Nemean [*rime* plebeian].

2. ***Nemean games*** or ***festival*** [Gr. Νέμεα, Νέμεια], one of the great Greek festivals, held at Nemea in the second and fourth years of each Olympiad.

1656 BLOUNT *Glossogr.* **1663** BUTLER *Hud.* I. i. 682 For authors do affirm it came From Isthmian or Nemæan game. **1776** BURNEY *Hist. Mus.* (1789) I. iv. 396. **1844** THIRLWALL *Greece* VIII. 277 At the Nemean festival.., being a second time General, he exhibited his phalanx. **1864** *Chambers's Encycl.* VI. 704/2 We have eleven odes by Pindar in honour of victors in the Nemean Games.

Nemedian (nɪ'mi:dɪən). [f. *Nemed*, name of a legendary invader of Ireland + -IAN.] One of the followers or descendants of Nemed of Scythia, who settled in Ireland, and who were later driven out by the Fomorians.

1876 *Encycl. Brit.* V. 299/2 We find four successive colonies mentioned in the following order:—*Nemedians, Firbolgs, Tuatha Dé Danann*, and *Milesians.* The *Nemedians* are said to have occupied the country during only two hundred years..owing to..their final overthrow, by a people..called Fomorians. **1898** [see FOMORIAN]. **1911** *Encycl. Brit.* XIV. 757/2 After undergoing great hardship the Nemedians succeeded in destroying the fortress..but the Fomorians received reinforcements... Of the Nemedians only thirty warriors escaped. **1950** *Funk's Stand. Dict. Folklore* II. 788/1 *Nemedians*, an early people who invaded Ireland; descendants of Nemed, son of Agnoman of Scythia; the third group to land in Ireland, following next after Partholan and his people. **1971** *It* 2–16 June 24/1 The Partholyans, Nemedians..are all remembered as being of semi-human stock.

†**nemel,** ? obs. variant of ENAMEL *sb.*

a **1400–50** *Alexander* 3671 Sum was smeth smaragdyns & oþire small gemmes, And new nychometis nemellus endentid.

†'**nemel,** *v. Obs.* [app. an alteration of NEMN *v.*] *trans.* To name.

c **1250** *Gen. & Ex.* 3533 God hem bad bodes maniȝe on.. And nemeld it beseel, And two oðere to maken it wel. **14..** *Pol. Rel. & L. Poems* (1866) 23 þat [non] raton dwelle in þe place þat her namis were nemeled in. **1447** BOKENHAM *Seyntys* (Roxb.) 250 How darst thou..Hym nemelyn ageyn in my presence.

nemel, -ly, obs. forms of NIMBLE, -LY.

nemen, var. f. NEMN *v.* (Also occas. miswritten for *neuen* NEVEN *v.*)

nemertean (nɪ'mɜ:tɪən), *sb.* and *a.* [f. mod.L. *Nemertes* (Cuvier), a. Gr. Νημερτής the name of a sea-nymph.]

A. *sb.* = NEMERTINE *sb.*

1861 T. R. JONES *Anim. Kingd.* vii. 156 The male Nemerteans present phenomena very similar to those just described as occurring in the female. **1880** H. A. NICHOLSON *Man. Zool.* xxiv. (ed. 6) 242 The Nemerteans..make a near approach to the dendrocœlous Planarians. **1888** ROLLESTON & JACKSON *Anim. Life* 641 The larger Nemerteans feed on fixed tubicolous Chaetopoda.

B. *adj.* = NEMERTINE *a.*

1873 M^cINTOSH *Brit. Annelids* (Ray Soc.) I. p. xii, The former did much to place Nemertean anatomy on a proper basis. **1888** ROLLESTON & JACKSON *Anim. Life* 814 This species is found in saccules..between the body-walls and digestive tract of its Nemertean host.

nemertian (nɪ'mɜ:tɪən), *a.* and *sb.* [f. as prec. + -IAN.] = NEMERTEAN.

1861 T. R. JONES *Anim. Kingd.* vii. 150 They may be divided into two families, the Planariæ and the Nemertian Worms. **1874** DARWIN *Desc. Man* ix. (ed. 2) 264 Even the Nemertians..vie in beauty..with any other group in the invertebrate series. **1876** *Beneden's Anim. Parasites* 46 Among the nemertians, we may allude to the *Anoplodium parasita.*

ne'mertid. [f. as prec. + -ID.] A nemertean form. Also *attrib.* or as *adj.*

1870 HUXLEY in Nicholson *Man. Zool.* 150 Eventually it ..detaches itself from the *Pilidium* as a Nemertid. **1877** —— *Anat. Inv. Anim.* xi. 651 The production of the Nemertid larva within its *pilidium.*

nemertine (nɪ'mɜ:taɪn), *sb.* and *a.* [f. mod.L. *Nemert-es* (see NEMERTEAN) + -INE.]

A. *adj.* Belonging to the class of flat-worms (chiefly marine) known as *Nemertina, Nemertida*, or *Nemertea*, usually characterized by an elongated, very contractile body, and often brilliantly coloured.

1851 T. WILLIAMS in *Phil. Trans.* (1852) CLXII. 620 As the Nemertine Annelida differ from all the other orders of their class. **1875** MOSELEY in *Ann. & Mag. Nat. Hist.* XV. 168 In other respects *Pelagonemertes* is thoroughly Nemertine in structure. **1896** KIRKALDY & POLLARD tr. *Boas' Zool.* 155 Invagination of the skin, from which a great part of the final Nemertine body arises.

B. *sb.* A flat-worm of the class *Nemertina*; a ribbon-worm.

1875 MOSELEY in *Ann. & Mag. Nat. Hist.* XV. 167 The outer surface of the body of the Nemertine is covered with a hyaline, very thin integument. **1896** KIRKALDY & POLLARD tr. *Boas' Zool.* 153 The Nemertines are, as a rule, elongate, often even ribbon-like, animals of considerable size.

nemesia (nə'mi:ʒ(ɪ)ə). [mod.L. (E. P. Ventenat *Jardin de la Malmaison* (1803) 41), f. Gr. νεμέσιον a name used by Dioscurides for a similar plant.] An annual or perennial herb of the genus so called, native to southern Africa, belonging to the family Scrophulariaceæ, and usually bearing racemes of flowers of various colours.

1815 F. PURSH *Donn's Hortus Cantabrigiensis* (ed. 8) 196 Nemesia, [English name] Nemesia. Germander-leav. [*sic*]. **1829** J. C. LOUDON *Encycl. Plants* 526 Nemesia, Vent[enat. English name] Nemesia...fœtid...horned. **1838** *Edwards's Bot. Reg.* XXIV. 39 (*heading*) Many-flowered Nemesia. **1892** *Gardeners' Chron.* 3 Sept. 269/3 There are many plants that vary to the extent of two or three colours in a wild state, but it is exceedingly rare to find them indulging in such wholesale variation as this Nemesia does. I have seen sixteen varieties of colour. **1927** *Observer* 20 Mar. 24/3 Modern florists and men of science..have made a rainbow out of a single colour (as in the nemesia). **1949** L. G. GREEN *In Land of Afternoon* v. 72 Hybrid gladioli, nemesias, even the Hottentot fig, were all startling novelties. **1970** C. LLOYD *Well-Tempered Garden* ii. 97 There is a freshness about a display of nemesias.

nemesis ('nɛmɪsɪs). Also **Nemesis.** [a. Gr. νέμεσις (f. νέμειν to give what is due), righteous indignation, just resentment, also personified as 'the goddess of Retribution, who brings down all immoderate good fortune, checks the presumption that attends it,..and is the punisher of extraordinary crimes'.]

1. The goddess of retribution or vengeance; hence, one who avenges or punishes.

1576 GASCOIGNE *Philomene* (Arb.) 114 She calles on Nemesis.., The Goddesse of al iust reuenge. **1591** SHAKS. *1 Hen. VI*, IV. vii. 78 Is Talbot slaine, the Frenchmens only Scourge, Your Kingdomes terror, and blacke Nemesis? **1642** H. MORE *Song of Soul* III. II. xiii, Thus sensuall souls do find their righteous doom which Nemesis inflicts. **1818** BYRON *Ch. Har.* IV. cxxxii, Thou, who never yet of human wrong Left the unbalanced scale, great Nemesis! **1867** EMERSON *Nemesis*, In spite of Virtue and the Muse, Nemesis will have her dues.

2. Retributive justice; an instance of this.

divine Nemesis (sometimes personified as in sense 1) is common in the 17th cent.

1597 BACON *Coulers Good & Evill* Ess. (Arb.) 149 Expecting..that Nemesis and retribution will take holde of the authours of our hurt. *a* **1652** J. SMITH *Sel. Disc.* v. 161 It must..find a severe Nemesis arising out of its guilty conscience. **1664** H. MORE *Myst. Iniq.* xix. 72 Penalties inflicted by that Nemesis that is interwoven in the very Law of Nature thus transgressed. *Ibid. Apol.* 530 Intangling themselves in those unavoidable trains of the Divine Nemesis. **1733** W. CRAWFORD *Infidelity* (1836) 164 Guilt naturally produces a fear of the divine Nemesis. **1859** BUCKNILL *Psychol. Shaks.* 21 It is a pathological Nemesis of guilt. **1867** JEBB *Sophocles' Electra* Introd. 8 The nemesis which overtook Clytaemnestra.

nemesism ('nɛmɪsɪz(ə)m). *Psychol.* [f. NEMES(IS + -ISM.] Feelings of frustration turned inward and expressed by aggression directed against the self. So **neme'sistic** *a.*, of or connected with nemesism.

1938 S. ROSENZWEIG in H. A. Murray *Explorations in Personality* vi. 588 The psycho-analyst might appropriately call the turning of aggression upon the individual's own self 'nemesism' from the name of the Greek goddess of vengeance. Nemesism could then be thought of as the counterpart of narcism. **1945** J. C. FLÜGEL *Man, Morals & Society* vii. 78 We propose here to adopt Rosenzweig's suggestion and to use the term 'nemesism' as an alternative and technical term for 'aggression turned against the self'. *Ibid.* 87 The channel for the discharge of the children's aggressiveness towards the natural outer objects being blocked, there may be no alternative for them but to become nemesistic and intropunitive. *Ibid.* xi. 143 This nemesistic urge. **1946** [see INTROJECTION 3 a]. **1968** P. MCKELLAR *Experience & Behav.* ix. 248 Nemesism is a term coined by Flügel.

‖**nemine contradicente** (ˈnɛmɪniː ˌkɒntrədɪˈtʃɛntiː). See NEM. CON. Also **nemine con.**

1662 J. DAVIES tr. *A. Olearius's Voyages & Travels of Ambassadors* III. 77 Where, *nemine contradicente*, it was declar'd. **1718** VANBRUGH *Let.* 7 Aug. in *Athenæum* 30 Aug. (1890) 290/2 Amongst many material things in our conversation it was Nemine Contradicente agreed, That your Grace had writ a most Tyrannical letter. **1762** *Monthly Review* XXV. 363 The very vote that should be passed in our favour, would, in all likelihood, be a new grievance; as we should possibly see the honest English resolution, dated, *Die Mercurii, Feb.* 10mo, and concluded with a *Nemine Contradicente.* **1766** H. BROOKE *Fool of Qual.* II. x. 145 They concluded, *nemine con.* to get as speedily as they might from the ministers of darkness. **1962** *Listener* 10 May 798/2 The decision, although not strictly unanimous, can be described as *nemine contradicente.* **1966** *Rep. Comm. Inquiry Univ. Oxf.* I. 316 A special resolution.. shall be published.. and shall be deemed to have been approved *nemine contradicente.*

nemish, nemmie: see NEMBIE.

nemly, obs. form of NIMBLY.

nemmind, nemmine (ˈnɛmaɪn(d), nɛˈmaɪn(d)), representation of a colloq. pronunciation of *never mind*. Chiefly *U.S.*

1914 *Dialect Notes* IV. 77 *Nemmind!*.. Contraction of *never mind!* **1935** R. BASS in A. Dundes *Mother Wit* (1973) 389 Nemmine dat. **1960** N. HILLIARD *Maori Girl* III. ix. 241 'You better not do that. They might put you in jail.' 'Nemmine. I get all the baby things, that's all I'm worried about.'

†**nemn**, *v. Obs.* Forms: α. 1–3 **nemnan**, 3 **nemnen**, 3–4 **nemne**, 4 **nemny**. β. 3–6 **nempne**, (3–4 **-pnen**), 4 **nempe (nymphe)**, 6 *pa. pple.* **nempt**, 7 **nemp'd**. γ. 1–4 *pa. t.* **nemde**, 3 *pa. pple.* **i-nemd**; 3–4 **nemmen**, 4–5 **nem(m)yn**, (5 **nemon**), 4– 6 **nemme, nem**. [OE. *nemnan* = OFris. *namna, namne*, OS. *nemnian*, MDu. *nennen* (usu. in forms *nande, genant*), MLG. *nennen* (rare), OHG. *nemnan, nemman, nennen* (G. *nennen*), ON. *nefna, nemna* (Sw. *nämna*, Da. *nævne*), Goth. *namnjan*, f. the stem ***namn-**: see NAME *sb.*] *trans.* To name; to call (by some name); to mention.

α. *c* **888** K. ÆLFRED *Boeth.* xxxvii. §4 Ne meaht þu hine na mid ryhte nemnan man ac neat. *c* **950** *Lindisf. Gosp.* Mark vii. 26 Wæs þæt wif hæðen ðæs cynnes is nemned syrophoenissa. *c* **1000** *Sax. Leechd.* I. 222 Ðas wyrt man.. lilium nemneþ. *c* **1175** *Lamb. Hom.* 123 Þe mon þe bið efter criste selue cristene mon inemned. *c* **1250** *Gen. & Ex.* 82 Ðes frenkis men o france moal, it nemnen 'un iur natural'. *a* **1272** *Luue Ron* 161 in *O.E. Misc.* 98 Þis ilke ston þat ich þe nemne Mayden-hod icleoped is. *c* **1330** R. BRUNNE *Chron. Wace* (Rolls) 7357 When þe kyng herde hym nemne a God, He asked þenne how þey trowd. **1382** WYCLIF *Isa.* lxii. 2 A newe name, that the mouth of the Lord nemnede. **1408** *E.E. Wills* (1882) 15 For hys labour more than he ys nemnyd a-fore the date of thys.

β. *a* **1225** *Ancr. R.* 158 Þeos þet ich habbe inempned her weren of þen olde lawe. *c* **1320** *Cast. Love* 299 Good is to nempnen hem for-þi. *c* **1380** *Sir Ferumb.* 3196 Gy of Borgoyne he is þer.. And oþer þat buþ noȝt nempned her. *c* **1430** *Hymns Virgin* (1867) 40 Þou schalt þinke ioie to heere þe name of ihesu be nempned. **1483** CAXTON *Gold. Leg.* 118 b/2 Thou art not worthy to nempne so.. swete a name. **1559** *Mirr. Mag.* (1563) Fij, Than had my father.. Of laufull barnes, me and one only other, Nempt Dauy Rothsay. **1590** SPENSER *F.Q.* III. x. 29 Much disdeigning to be so misdempt, Or a war-monger to be basely nempt. [*a* **1643** W. CARTWRIGHT *Ordinary* in Dodsley *O. Pl.* (1780) X. 236 That were transmued into birds, nemp'd pyes.]

γ. *c* **888** K. ÆLFRED *Boeth.* xxxvii. §1 Hi hi underþiodað eallum þam unþeawum þe ic þe ær nemde. **971** *Blickl. Hom.* 13 Heo sylf hie þeowen nemde. *c* **1200** *Trin. Coll. Hom.* 39 Ðese fower mannisshe þe ich er inemd habbe. *Ibid.* 143 Hali boc nemmeð þes woreld sæ. *a* **1225** *Ancr. R.* 292 Nem ofte Jesu. *c* **1275** *Passion our Lord* 577 in *O.E. Misc.* 53 Iesus þo nemde marie. **13..** *E.E. Allit. P.* A. 997 As þise stonez in writ con nemme, I knew þe name after his tale. *c* **1380** WYCLIF *Wks.* (1880) 465 An accident, þe which þey kunnen not nemyn to men. *c* **1400** *Destr. Troy* 153 An aunter in an yle þat I nem shall. *c* **1470** *Gol. & Gaw.* 664 Schir Bedwar to schir Bantellas.. That baith war nemmyt in neid. **1508** DUNBAR *Tua Maritt Wemen* 117 Quhen I heir nemmyt his name, than mak I nyne crocis. **1562–3** *Reg. Privy Council Scot.* I. 234 The saidis partiis.. hes nemmit Maister George Buchquhannane.

Hence †**ˈnemning** *vbl. sb. Obs. rare.*

a **1225** *Ancr. R.* 290 Nim anon þene rod stef, mid nemmunge iðine muðe. **1382** WYCLIF *Eccl.* xxiii. 10 The nemnyng [*v.r.* nemyng] forsothe of God be not continyuel in thi mouth.

nemo (ˈniːməʊ). *U.S.* [Etym. unknown.] (See quots.)

1937 *Printers Ink Monthly* May 39/3 *Nemo*, any program originating outside of the broadcasting studios. A collection of 'remote'. **1942** BERREY & VAN DEN BARK *Amer. Thes. Slang* §619/2 A program originating outside the studio and transmitted to the studio for broadcasting... Nemo. **1950** CHESTER & GARRISON *Radio & Television* 527 *Nemo*, a remote, a program originating away from the studio. **1960** O. SKILBECK *ABC of Film & T.V.* 89 *Nemo* (American), a telecast from location: an outside broadcast. **1961** H. B. JACOBSON *Mass Communications Dict.* 222 *Nemo*, a program originating outside of the station's studios.

neˈmoceran, *a.* and *sb. Ent.* [f. as next + -AN.] **a.** *adj.* = next. **b.** *sb.* An insect belonging to the *Nemocera.*

1890 in *Cent. Dict.*

nemocerous (nɪˈmɒsərəs), *a. Entom.* [f. mod.L. *Nemocera* (Latreille), irreg. f. Gr. νῆμα thread + κέρας horn.] Belonging to the *Nemocera*, a family of dipterous insects with thread-like antennæ, comprising the midges, gnats, crane-flies, etc.; nematocerous.

1856 in MAYNE *Expos. Lex.* **1883** DALLAS in *Cassell's Nat. Hist.* VI. 82 This last family of the Nemocerous Diptera includes a number of fly-like species.

ˈnemocyst, variant of NEMATOCYST.

1878 BELL *Gegenbaur's Comp. Anat.* 103 The urticating capsules (nemocysts) are special differentiations of the epithelial elements, which are found in all the Acalephæ.

nemoˈglossate, *a. Ent.* [f. mod.L. *Nemoglossatus* (Latreille), f. Gr. νῆμα thread + γλῶσσα tongue.] Having a filiform tongue. So **nemoˈglossatous** *a.*

1856 in MAYNE *Expos. Lex.* **1890** in *Cent. Dict.*

ˈnemolite. *rare*$^{-0}$. [f. Gr. νέμος (see next) + -LITE.] 'An arborized stone'.

1828–32 WEBSTER (citing *Dict. Nat. Hist.*).

‖**Nemophila** (nɪˈmɒfɪlə). *Bot.* Also *erron.* **-phyla, -phylla.** [mod.L., f. Gr. νέμος wooded pasture, glade + φίλος loving.] A genus of ornamental herbaceous annuals (N.O. *Hydrophyllaceæ*), of N. American origin, of which the chief variety, *N. insignis*, has showy blue flowers with a white centre; a plant of this genus.

1838 *Penny Cycl.* XII. 401/1 Many of the species, especially those of the genera Nemophila and Eutoca, are beautiful objects. **1858** GLENNY *Gard. Every-day Bk.* 43/2 By hardy annuals we mean those that want no nursing.., [as] Nemophylla, Eschscholtzia, Coreopsis, Sweet Pea, Lupin. **1882** *Standard* 9 Oct. 5/3 Indian cress, the sweet pea, and nemophila, redeem the dingy walls.. from their.. repulsiveness. **1890** BARING-GOULD *Grettir* i. 17 The blue of the nemophyla or forget-me-not.

neˈmophilist. *rare*$^{-1}$. [See prec. and -IST.] One who is fond of the woods; a forest-lover. So **neˈmophilous** *a.*, fond of, or frequenting, woods; **neˈmophily**, love of, fondness for, woods.

1860 *Atlantic Monthly* Jan. 26 Not as a naturalist in close patient study... but as a nemophilist, taking simple delight in mere observation. *Ibid.* 29, I say, in the full faith of the creed of Nemophily,—Get into the woods!

nemoral (ˈnɛmərəl), *a. rare.* [ad. L. *nemorāl-is*, f. *nemor-, nemus* grove.] Of or pertaining to, living in, frequenting, groves or woods.

1656 BLOUNT *Glossogr.* **1657** TOMLINSON *Renou's Disp.* 524 All of them require nemoral snails. **1845** MACGILLIVRAY *T. Brown's Conchol. Text-bk.* 224 *Nemoral*, of or belonging to a wood. **1881** tr. *J. Verne's Tigers & Traitors* v. 87 Lions do not figure in great numbers among the nemoral beasts of India.

nemoˈrivagant, *a. rare*$^{-0}$. [f. L. *nemorivag-us* (Catullus).] 'Wandering in the wood' (Blount *Glossogr.* 1656). So **nemoˈrivagous** *a.* (Bailey 1721).

nemoˈrose, *a. rare*$^{-0}$. [ad. L. *nemorōs-us*: see NEMORAL and -OSE.] 'Full of woods or groves' (Bailey 1721); 'growing in groves' (*Treas. Bot.* 1866). Hence **nemoˈrosity**, 'fullness of woods, woodiness' (Bailey 1721).

nemorous (ˈnɛmərəs), *a. rare.* [ad. L. *nemorōs-us*: cf. prec. and -OUS.] (See quots.)

1623 COCKERAM I, *Nemorous*, woody. **1656** BLOUNT *Glossogr.*, *Nemorous*, full of Woods, Groves or Trees, shadowed and dark with Trees. **1679** EVELYN *Sylva* (ed. 3) 256 Paradise it self was but a kind of Nemorous Temple, or Sacred Grove, planted by God himself.

†**nemot**, obs. form of EMMET.

c **1375** *Sc. Leg. Saints* iv. (*James*) 137 Na mycht haff we to grewe.. a nemot, quhare þat þu restis þi corse.

nemp(t: see NEMN *v.*, NIM *v.*

nemyl(l, obs. forms of NIMBLE *a.*

†**nen**, *conj.*[1], obs. var. NE, nor. (Cf. NYN.)

c **1430** LYDG. *Min. Poems* (Percy Soc.) 41 He brak no covenaunt nen condicioun. *Ibid.* 44 That ye your lif ne shorte nen yt appeyr.

†**nen, non**, *conj.*[2] [Cf. NA, NE, *conj.*[2]] Than.

c **1420** *Chron. Vilod.* 1584 Hurre was leuer to hir mayteynesse and masse.. Nen to be duchas. *Ibid.* 1724 Þey sayden þat he.. nomore ryȝt hadde þerto by ony lawe Non hadde he þat nas not of þat lynage.

nenadkevichite (nɛˈnædkəvɪtʃaɪt). *Min.* [ad. Russ. *nenadkevichit* (Kuzʹmenko & Kazakova 1955, in *Doklady̆ Akad. Nauk SSSR* C. 1159), f. the name of K. A. *Nenadkevich* (b. 1880), Russian mineralogist: see -ITE[1].] A hydrated silicate of sodium, calcium, niobium, and titanium, $(Na,Ca)(Nb,Ti)Si_2O_7.2H_2O$, which is found as pale yellow orthorhombic crystals.

1955 *Mineral. Abstr.* XII. 569 (*heading*) Nenadkevichite —a new mineral. **1965** *Doklady Acad. Sci. U.S.S.R. Earth Sci. Sect.* CLX. 118/1 Among the natrolite and feldspar are .. large (to 10 cm and more) dull flakes of nenadkevichite of a pale to pinkish yellow color. **1972** *Mineral. Abstr.* XXIII. 225/2 Localities are described representing the alkalic complex of Augusta County [Virginia]... Associated with the alkalic rocks are nenadkevichite, astrophyllite, and bastnäsite.

nenadkevite (nɛˈnædkəvaɪt). *Min.* [ad. Russ. *nenadkevit*, f. as prec.] Any member of a range of isomorphous, basic, hydrated silicates of uranium(IV), uranium(VI), magnesium, calcium, thorium, and lead.

1955 *1st Internat. Conf. Peaceful Uses Atomic Energy: U.S.S.R. Sci. & Techn. Exhibition* (Eng. ed.) 7 Of interest in the second group of silicates containing tetra- and hexavalent uranium is the new mineral species nenadkevite. .. This mineral is deposited from hydrothermal solutions in the form of veins. **1960** *Mineral. Abstr.* XIV. 401/1 Rarer uranium deposits include those in which the ore mineral is the silicate nenadkevite.

†**nend(e**, obs. forms of END *sb.*

c **1320** *Sir Tristr.* 3287 Þai hadde wounders ille At þe nende. *a* **1400–50** *Alexander* 4860 Of þis way.. sone worthis him a nende. **1420** in *Surtees Misc.* (1890) 17 Als wele at the ta nende als at the other. *c* **1440** *Alph. Tales* 470 Þe clerk went at all þis werld had bene at a nend.

‖**nene** (ˈneɪneɪ). Also **néné**. [Hawaiian.] = *Hawaiian goose* (HAWAIIAN *a.* and *sb.* II).

1902 H. W. HENSHAW *Birds of Hawaiian Islands* 103 Upon the island of Hawaii the haunts of the nene.. are the uplands. **1915** [see *Hawaiian goose*]. **1945** *Condor* XLVII. 34 Direct influences were brought to bear upon the Nene by white men directly and indirectly through altered environment. **1958** [see *Hawaiian goose*]. **1962** *Punch* 1 Aug. 177/3 Various animals whose survival is in question, with the accent on big game rather than.. the Hawaiian *ne-ne.* **1972** *Shooting Times & Country Mag.* 1 July 19/2 The Wildfowl Trust established the principle with the Ne-ne or Hawaiian goose. **1975** *Nat. Geographic* Mar. 411/1 A beautiful, unique species of goose called the nene (nay-nay) was being brought back from near extinction here.

nene, var. NEINEI.

Nenets (ˈnɛnɛts). Pl. **Nentsi, Nentsy.** [a. Russ. *Nénets*, pl. *Néntsy.*] A Samodian (formerly Samoyedic) people inhabiting the far north-east of Europe and the north of Siberia; a member of this people; their language.

[**1886** *Encycl. Brit.* XXI. 251/1 The names assumed by the Samoyedes themselves are Hazovo and Nyänyäz.] **1944** GREGORY & SHAVE *U.S.S.R.* iv. 162 Occupying territory lying roughly between that of the Palæo-Asiatic groups and the groups of Finnish origin are the peoples commonly known in the past as the Samoyedes, although now more correctly named Nentsi and Ostyak Samoyedes. *Ibid.* viii. 286 The.. Nentsi are nomadic tent dwellers. **1954** PEI & GAYNOR *Dict. Ling.* 189 Samoyedic.. consists of Samoyed, called *Nenets* by the speakers themselves (with various local dialects), Yurak, Kamassin and Tagvy. **1957** *Encycl. Brit.* XX. 598/1 The earliest known inhabitants of Siberia were the Finno-Ugrian Nentsy. **1962** *Amer. Speech* XXXVII. 68 The phonemic systems of five languages of the Samoyed subgroup (Nenets, Nganasan, Enets, Sel'Kup, Kamas). **1967** D. S. PARLETT *Short Dict. Lang.* 107 The Northern language [of Samoyedic] has three dialects: Yurak (Nenets) with Taiga and Tundra variants, Yenisei (Enets) and Tavgi (Nganasan). **1968** S. P. DUNN tr. *Diószegi's Pop. Beliefs & Folklore Trad. Siberia* 123 An 'Enetsized' Nenets called Yar. **1968** *Encycl. Brit.* XVI. 210/2 The Nenets people, a Finno-Ugrian group formerly known as the Samoyed, make their living chiefly by reindeer herding. **1972** *Language* XLVIII. 206 Soviet scholars usually distinguish three languages: Nenets ('Yurak Samoyed'), Enets.. and Nganasan.

†**nent(es, nentis**, obs. aphetic forms of ANENT(S. Also mod. north. dial. **nenst.**

a **1300** *Cursor M.* 25246 In þis ilk clause we prai For all es nentes domes-dai. *Ibid.* 27406 Lufand he be nent godd and man. *c* **1380** WYCLIF *Serm.* Sel. Wks. I. 75 As nentis godhede, Crist was not made. **1829** BROCKETT *N.C. Gloss.* (ed. 2) s.v., The cash was paid nenst his year's rent.

nente, nenteyn, nenty, obs. ff. NINTH, NINETEEN, NINETY.

nenuphar (ˈnɛnjuːfɑː(r)). Also 6–8 **-far**, 6 **-farre**, 7 **-fer** (and *erron.* **nune-, nemi-, nem-**). [a. med.L. *nenuphar, -far* (It. and Sp. *nenufar*, F. *nénufar*), ad. Arab.-Pers. *nīnūfar, nīlūfar*, Pers. also *nīlūfal, -pal*, ad. Skr. *nīlôtpala* blue lotus, f. *nīl* blue + *utpala* lotus, water-lily.]

1. A water-lily, esp. the common white or yellow species. In early use freq. in ***oil, syrup, water of nenuphar.***

1533 ELYOT *Cast. Helth* (1534) 76 Syrope of violettes, nemipher, or the wine of sweet pomegranates. **1563** T. GALE *Antidotarie* I. viii. 5 Among compoundes these are in vse, butter, oile of roses, Violettes, Nenuphar, Popye. **1621** BURTON *Anat. Mel.* II. v. 1. vi. (1651) 397 To refrigerate the face, by washing it often with Rose, Violet, Nenuphar, Lettuce, Lovage waters and the like. **1612** PEACHAM *Gentl. Exerc.* III. 162 Of Flowers you haue Roses, Gilliflowers, Violets, Nenuphar, Lilly. **1725** BRADLEY *Fam. Dict.* s.v.

Syrup, Syrup of Nenuphar, or Water-Lilly. **1759** tr. *Adanson's Voy. Senegal* in Pinkerton *Voy.* (1814) XVI. 631 The leaves of the *nenufar*, or water-lilly. **1832** Lyell *Princ. Geol.* II. vi. 98 On these green isles of the Mississippi,..the pistia and nenuphar display their yellow flowers. **1858** O. W. Holmes *Aut. Breakf.-t.* x. (1891) 250 The stream with.. clustering nenuphars Sprinkling its mirrored blue like golden-chaliced stars! **1874** A. O'Shaughnessy *Music & Moonlight* 14 Here and there great lakes of nenuphar And lustrous lotos glimmered.

†**b.** ***petty nenuphar***, applied by Turner (apparently) to the Marsh Marigold. *Obs.*

1548 Turner *Names Herbs* (E.D.S.) 26 It groweth in watery middowes with a leafe like a water Rose, wherefore it may be called also Petie nunefar [*sic*].

2. *Ent.* (See quot.) *rare*$^{-1}$.

1852 T. W. Harris *Insects New Eng.* 66 A small beetle of the weevil tribe, called *Rhynchænus Nenuphar*, the Nenuphar or plum-weevil.

neo- ('niːəʊ), combining form of Gr. *νέος*, new (as in *νεόγαμος* newly married, *νεογενής* newborn), common in recent use as a prefix to adjs. and sbs.

1. a. In combs. denoting a new or modern form of some doctrine, belief, practice, language, etc., or designating those who advocate, adopt, or use it, as ***neo-American*** adj., ***-Anglican***, ***-Anglicanism***, ***-Aramaic*** adj., ***-Aristotelian*** adj. and sb., ***-Aristotelianism***, ***-Babylonian*** adj., ***-barbarism***, ***-baroque*** adj., ***-behaviourism***, ***-behaviourist***, ***-istic*** adjs., ***-Bloomfieldian*** adj., ***-Buddhist*** adj. and sb., ***-Buddhistic*** adj., ***-Calvinism***, ***-capitalism***, ***-capitalist*** adj., ***-Catholic*** adj. and sb., ***-Catholicism***, ***-Christian*** adj. and sb., ***-Christianity***, etc., ***-Confucian*** adj., ***-Confucianism***, ***-conservatism***, ***-conservative*** adj. and sb., ***-critic***, ***-critical*** adj., ***-criticist***, ***-Dada***, ***-Dadaism***, ***-Darwinian*** adj. and sb., ***-Darwinism***, ***-Darwinist***, ***-Dixieland*** adj., ***-Edwardian*** adj., ***-Elizabethan*** adj. and sb., ***-expressionism***, ***-expressionist*** adj. and sb., ***-Fascism***, ***-Fascismo***, ***-Fascist*** adj. and sb., ***-feminist***, ***-Firthian*** adj. and sb., ***-Freudian*** adj. and sb., ***-Freudianism***, ***-Gaullism***, ***-Gaullist*** adj. and sb., ***-Georgian*** adj. and sb., ***-Georgianism***, ***-German***, ***-Gothicism***, ***-Hegelian*** adj and sb., ***-Hegelianism***, ***-Hittite*** adj. and sb., ***-Humboldtian*** adj. and sb., ***-imperial*** adj., ***-imperialism***, ***-imperialist***, ***-isolationism***, ***-isolationist*** adj. and sb., ***-Kantian*** (adj.), ***-Kantism***, ***-Keynesian*** adj. and sb., ***-Keynesianism***, ***-Lamarckian*** sb., ***-Lamarckism***, ***-liberal*** adj., ***-Maoist*** adj., ***-Marxism***, ***-Marxist*** adj. and sb., ***-modal*** adj., ***-modalism***, ***-modality***, ***-nationalism***, ***-Nazi*** adj. and sb., ***-Nazism***, ***-Nietzschean*** adj., ***-Norman*** adj., ***-orthodox*** adj., ***-orthodoxy***, ***-paganism***, ***-Palladian*** adj., ***-Pentecostal*** adj. and sb., ***-Pentecostalism***, ***-Pentecostalist*** sb. and adj., ***-populism***, ***-positivism***, ***-positivist*** adj. and sb., ***-primitivism***, ***-Pythagorean*** (sb.), ***-realism***, ***-realist*** adj. and sb., ***-realistic*** adj., ***-revisionist*** adj. and sb., ***-rococo*** adj., ***-Romantic*** (sb.), ***-scholastic*** adj. and sb., ***-scholasticism***, ***-slave***, ***-slaver***, ***-slavery***, ***-Stalinism***, ***-Stalinist*** adj. and sb., ***-symbolist*** adj. and sb., ***theosophical*** adj., ***-Thomism***, ***-Thomist*** adj. and sb., ***-Tory***, ***-Toryism***, ***-traditionalism***, ***-Tudor*** adj., ***-Victorian*** adj. and sb., ***-vitalism***, ***-vitalist*** adj. and sb., ***-vitalistic*** adj.

The number of such formations is practically unlimited, and only some of the more prominent or typical are illustrated here. Similar forms are also current in French (as *néo-catholique*, *-chrétien*, *-grec*, *-latin*, etc.) and the other Romance languages.

1904 *Amer. Naturalist* XXXVIII. 682 The *Neo-American nomenclature is adopted—with synonymic citation where the generic name is unfamiliar to the ordinary reader. **1970** I. Reed in A. Chapman *New Black Voices* (1972) 334 So sez d neoamerican hoodoo Church of free spirits. **1894** L. Tollemache in *Jrnl. Educ.* 1 Feb. 126 Matthew Arnold was a good *Neo-Anglican. **1859** Kingsley *Yeast* (ed. 4) Pref. 10, I have said, that *Neo-Anglicanism has proved a failure, as seventeenth-century Anglicanism did. **1948** D. Diringer *Alphabet* 289 The east-Syrian or *neo-Aramaic dialect. **1931** *Times Lit. Suppl.* 16 July 561/1 The attempt to apply the *neo-Aristotlean [*sic*] rules was..doomed to failure. **1947** *College English* VIII. 403 We should not leave the new critics without notice of the neo-Aristotelians who do not accept fellowship with the new critics, nor with the neo-Thomists. **1953** R. S. Crane *Languages of Criticism* 149 It is not a question of..looking upon ourselves, in any exclusive sense, as forming an 'Aristotelian' or 'Neo-Aristotelian' school. **1962** W. S. Scott *Five Approaches of Lit. Criticism* 183 He also arraigns the 'Neo-Aristotelians' for going outside the poem—not to history, psychology, or morality, but to a theory of the genre. **1952** R. S. Crane *Critics & Criticism* 2 A particular philosophic dogma the nature of which has been defined.. as Aristotelianism or *neo-Aristotelianism. **1915** L. W. King *Hist. Babylonia* II. 278 Nebuchadnezzar..established the *Neo-Babylonian empire on a firm basis. **1931** *Times Lit. Suppl.* 31 Dec. 1054/1 Reliefs in glazed brick of the neo-Babylonian revival. **1892** Mahaffy *Rambles & Stud.* 15 *Neo-barbarism means the occurrence in later times of the manners and customs which generally mark very old and primitive times. **1966** *Daily Tel.* 9 Nov. 17/3 'The Rake's Progress'..is either one of the most enigmatic or the most straight forward, according to the view you take of its neo-rococo or *neo-baroque idiom. **1970** *Canadian Antiques Collector* June 10/1 His execution of neo-baroque designs to some degree anticipates the Victorian penchant for period revivals. **1967** *Philos. Rev.* LXXVI. 97 The stimulus-response (S-R) theories of *neo-behaviorism. **1964** *Listener* 14 May 785/2 Watsonian Behaviourism is..the foundation on which the..*neo-Behaviourist systems of Professor Guthrie, Clark Hull, and Skinner were built. **1952** *Mind* LXI. 349 In *The Concept of Mind* Professor Gilbert Ryle has presented us with a *neo-behaviouristic theory. **1964** *Language* XL. 265 Weinreich rejects..the hard-boiled *neo-Bloomfieldian behaviorism of such philosophers as Carnap and Quine. **1891** *Literary World* 17 Apr. 357/1 The extracts we have given serve to show the dogmatic assertiveness of the *Neo-Buddhist philosophy. **1972** *Times of India* 28 Nov. 11/3 A majority of them come from the Scheduled Castes. Many say they are neo-Buddhists. **1896** A. H. Keane *Ethnology* xiii. 346 There is something similar in the *Neo-Buddhistic teachings. **1854** J. Guthrie in *Evang. Union Worthies* (1883) 322 Calvinism and *Neo-Calvinism. **1968** *Economist* 20 July 25/3 By *neocapitalism they mean the new type of industrial economy dominated by the very large industries. *Ibid.*, An educational system which they look upon as the instrument of '*neocapitalist' oppression. **1842** Mill *Let.* 10 Jan. in *Wks.* (1963) XIII. 497 Our *neo-Catholic school at [Oxf]ord. **1867–71** Froude *Short Stud.* II. 145 The Neo-Catholics of our own day. **1956** K. Clark *Nude* viii. 333 The neo-Catholic doctrines of his [*sc.* Rouault's] friend Leon Bloy, by which in the lukewarm, materialistic society of 1900, absolute degradation came closer to redemption than worldly compromise. **1876** E. Mellor *Priesthood* viii. 393 The *Neo-Catholicism of the Church of England. **1882** Seeley *Nat. Relig.* 116 The *Neochristian.., if he is not provoked by argument, gradually forgets his crotchet. **1910** Wyndham Lewis *Lett.* (1963) 44 He [*sc.* Masefield] makes Pompey a sort of Tolstoyan or neo-Christian hero. **1882** Seeley *Nat. Relig.* 115 A *Neochristianism must inevitably arise. **1860** F. Harrison in *Westm. Rev.* Oct. 293 *Neo-Christianity. **1864** Pusey *Lect. Daniel* Pref. 27 Some-where between Genesis and Revelation, but probably, according to the neo-Christianity, to the exclusion of both. **1948** *Mind* LVII. 535 Dr. Fung..does not, like many Chinese and most Occidental expositors, make Confucius teach medieval *Neo-Confucian doctrine. *Ibid.*, Fung continues Chinese traditions by attempting to bring up to date medieval *Neo-Confucianism. **1960** *Encounter* Nov. 78/1 If anything can render *neo-conservatism intellectually respectable, it is writing of this kind. **1964** K. Winetrout in I. L. Horowitz *New Sociology* 151 They can turn to Russell Kirk and his fellow *neo-conservatives. **1971** *Time* 23 Aug. 31 Judaism and Christianity have always placed primacy in man. Now this primacy is being attacked by what I call the neoconservative ecological approach to life. **1865** W. Kay *Crisis Hupfeld.* 3 The philology of the *neo-critics is.. conjectural and arbitrary. **1960** *Times Lit. Suppl.* 3 June 357/2 Though it may be short on *neo-critical know-how, it will provide valuable ammunition for the literary gamesman. **1925** *Neo-criticist [see empirio-critical *a.*]. **1962** *Times* 8 Mar. 16/7 The *neo-dada work of which Rauschenberg's 'combine-paintings' (i.e. collages) are the only example here. **1966** *Times* 16 July 7 Perhaps a change in the air encouraged..the recent revival of surrealism and *neo-Dadaism. **1895** G. J. Romanes *Darwin* II. iii. 61 The *Neo-Darwinian doctrine of the absolute non-inheritance of acquired characters. *Ibid.* 10 The Neo-Darwinians strain the teachings of Darwin. **1902** J. M. Baldwin *Development & Evol.* 135 The possible truth of either of the current doctrines of heredity, called *Neo-Darwinism and Neo-Lamarckism respectively. **1970** *Observer* (Colour Suppl.) 15 Feb. 18/1 All that neo-Darwinism does at present, the critics say, is to pronounce that 'what survives, survives'. **1895** G. J. Romanes *Darwin* II. 28, I am not a *Neo-Darwinist, and so have no desire to make 'natural selection' synonymous with 'natural causation'. **1972** *Listener* 3 Aug. 138/2 You have said one or two things which would be regarded by neo-Darwinists as treasonable. **1955** L. Feather *Encycl. Jazz* vii. 235 The conventional *neo-Dixieland jazz of the Eddie Condon variety. **1867** Pearson *Hist. Eng.* I. 80 There is other evidence for *Neo-Druidism, as it may be termed. **1947** 'N. Blake' *Minute for Murder* iv. 84 The hair brushed up from the back in the *neo-Edwardian manner. **1878** *N. Amer. Rev.* CXXVII. 495 A *Neo-Egyptian style came into vogue. **1909** *Westm. Gaz.* 7 Aug. 7/1 Mr. Figgis is enlightened enough to be a *neo-Elizabethan. **1924** R. Graves *Mock Beggar Hall* 29 Don't cramp my neo-Elizabethan manner. **1958** *Listener* 3 July 23/3 Conditions would exist that would justify a renewal of the nexus between Church and State; there might be a sort of neo-Elizabethan settlement. **1962** *Guardian* 20 Feb. 5/2 An antiquated system more in keeping with Victoria than with neo-Elizabethan England. **1961** *Neo-Expressionism [see Neo-Liberty]. **1955** P. Heron *Changing Forms of Art* 171 The occasional gaunt landscapes by young French *neo-expressionists such as Bernard Buffet or Raymond Guerrier. **1968** *N.Y. Times* 20 Jan. 25 Landscape and other subjects are handled by Miss Rosenberger as a series of neoexpressionist clichés. **1946** *Commonweal* (N.Y.) 1 Feb. 398/2 (*title*) *Neo-fascism: Italian sample. **1973** *Guardian* 20 June 14 As neofascism under the leadership of Giorgio Almirante makes new gains, suspicions and fears are once again rife in Italy. **1928** *Observer* 29 Jan. 17/1 Herein lies an incident of neo-Fascismo which has no controversial element. **1944** *Birmingham* (Alabama) *News* 28 June 8/5 The Germans had dissolved the *Neofascist movement in Northern Italy. **1944** H. McCloy *Panic* 143 She—or rather he—is a neo-Fascist and Nazi sympathizer. **1972** *Guardian* 17 Feb. 2/5 Seven people are now in Milan prison in connection with recent neo-Fascist activities. **1969** *Harper's Mag.* Nov. 28 'Are you still against abortion?' Ellen Willis asks, alluding to a position I had once taken which gave me, for a time, some small notoriety among the rest of the *neo-feminists. **1964** R. H. Robins *Gen. Linguistics* p. xix, Several of the principles taught by [J. R.] Firth..are continued in the work of those who are coming to be known as '*neo-Firthians'. **1964** *Language* XL. 305 The term 'neo-Firthian linguistics' may be suggested to characterize the recent work of M. A. K. Halliday, R. M. Dixon, and others. **1948** L. Schneider *Freudian Psychol. & Veblen's Social Theory* v. 166 Some of the work of the *neo-Freudians.. suggests that the strain in Freud above referred to has not quite been eliminated. *Ibid.* 173 This lacuna in neo-Freudian literature is..quite evident in Fromm's *Escape From Freedom.* **1959** Neo-Freudian [see biologistic *a.*]. **1958** W. J. H. Sprott *Human Groups* iv. 64 The '*neo-Freudianism' of Karen Horney. **1958** *Spectator* 6 June 720/2 A *neo-Gaullism that has little to do with anything he [*sc.* General de Gaulle] has sought to represent. **1958** *Ibid.* 30 May 677/1 All the *neo-Gaullists who have been utilised by M. Soustelle to create the situation in which the General [*sc.* de Gaulle] is invited to act as supreme arbitrator. **1958** *Times* 19 Dec. 8/1 The innovation was proposed by the leader of the neo-Gaullist Union for the New Republic. **1915** *Truth* 24 Mar. 459/2 Essentially early nineteenth century in character, he was hopelessly out of his element in this *neo-Georgian era. **1923** Hardy *Coll. Poems* (ed. 2) 525 The launching of a volume of this kind in neo-Georgian days by one who began writing in mid-Victorian, and has published nothing to speak of for some years, may seem to call for a few words of excuse or explanation. **1923** W. Deeping *Secret Sanctuary* xix. 195 The Jinkses with their drink-philosophy, their blatant motor-bike, their stout insensitiveness, were Neo-Georgians. **1933** *Archit. Rev.* LXXIV. 130/2 The Kirkgate and the Briggate..cast off their Georgian glory and assumed the Jacobean,..the Perpendicular and the neo-Georgian, in Leeds phorpres brick and stone and terra-cotta. **1955** J. Betjeman in R. S. Thomas *Song at Year's Turning* 12 The 'wain and stook' pastoral poetry of the neo-Georgians. **1970** *English Studies* LI. 270 The insipidly 'pleasant' strain which..became a conditioned reflex in the 'neo-Georgian' ripplings of the Squire-Turner-Freeman school. **1940** *Scrutiny* IX. 289 The 'simplicity' of Auden's later manner merges into *neo-Georgianism. **1940** *Tablet* 4 May 421/1 This is the feat attempted only by the *neo-Germans of the two Great Wars. **1892** *Nation* (N.Y.) 15 Dec. 447/1 The New Gallery is not even true to the *neo-Gothic School, who were its first supporters. **1964** *Daily Tel.* 3 Feb. 12 It savours of all the *neo-Gothicism of Sir Walter Scott. **1885** W. James *Let.* 13 Aug. (1920) I. 254 Why don't you have a special '*Neo-Hegelian Department' in 'Mind',..which educated readers skip? **1928** *London Aphrodite* Aug. 6 This analysis is carried on so as to involve anyone at all who admits Time as a philosophic symbol, whether he be an academic neo-Hegelian like Bosanquet, or an intelligent one like Croce. **1917** *Encycl. Relig. & Ethics* IX. 300/2 *Neo-Hegelianism is a title which has been given to that current of thought inspired by Hegel and the idealists of Germany which began to make itself felt in British and American philosophy in the third quarter of the 19th century. **1971** *Jrnl. Gen. Psychol.* Apr. 253 Philosophical tendencies have also influenced the practice of psychology in the course of the nineteenth century: in particular neo-Kantianism, neo-Hegelianism, [etc.]. **1869** Tozer *Highl. Turkey* II. 116 *Neo-Hellenic, as the regenerated language of modern Greece is called to distinguish it from the vulgar Romaic. **1879** Symonds *Sk. Italy & Greece* 79 A genuine instance of what we may call the *Neohellenism of the Renaissance. **1925** J. B. Bury et al. *Cambr. Anc. Hist.* III. p. vii, Dr Hogarth..discusses the successors of the Hittites, and the history and art of the *Neo-Hittite states of North Syria. **1952** O. R. Gurney *Hittites* i. 40 The language and the religion of these 'Neo-Hittite' inscriptions are not those of the Hittites of Hattusas. **1964** G. Roux *Anc. Iraq* xvii. 223 We reach, in the extreme north of Syria, the realm of the people called 'Hieroglyphic Hittites' or, more simply, 'Neo-Hittites'. *Ibid.* 224 It is important to emphasize that there was no break in the transmission of Hittite culture in those regions, and that the term 'Neo-Hittite' is no more than a convenient appellation. *Ibid.* xviii. 245 The Neo-Hittite and Aramaean princes whom Ashurnasirpal had caught by surprise had had time to strengthen themselves. **1952** H. Basilius in J. A. Fishman *Readings Sociol. of Lang.* (1968) 447 (*title*) *Neo-Humboldtian ethno-linguistics. *Ibid.* 458 The basic point of departure for the Neo-Humboldtians is always Wilhelm von Humboldt's idea that language is simply 'the human being approaching the objective idea'. **1962** *Language* XXXVIII. 319 Karl-Otto Apel provides an excellent illustration of the interconvertibility of Neo-Humboldtian and Existentialist terminology. **1968** *N.Y. Times* 17 Mar. IV. 12 This analysis could embrace not just *neoimperial China and neoimperial Russia. **1962** *Listener* 5 Apr. 583/2 It does..make sense to regard this *neo-imperialism of the left as an extension of its traditional Little Englanderism. **1971** *Yearbk. World Affairs* XXV. 136 Neo-imperialism is more broadly defined to include the creation and maintenance of an economic sphere of influence by one or more developed countries embracing one or more countries at a very much lower state of economic development. **1967** *Atlantic Monthly* Jan. 55, I believe that, in fact, we are in danger of seeing the isolationists of the 1920s and 1930s replaced by the *neoimperialists, who somehow imagine that the United States has a mandate to impose an American solution the world around. **1952** *Britannica Bk. of Year* 666/2 **Neo-isolationism*, an isolationism in which military preparedness plays a part. **1971** *Atlantic Monthly* Jan. 4 Disillusionment about the Indochina War and preoccupation with domestic ills will bring on neoisolationism in the United States. **1950** *N.Y. Times* 30 Dec. 12/1 The *neo-isolationists..propose to retreat to the Western hemisphere, with some outlying bases. **1967** *Listener* 21 Dec. 813/1 People who think we ought not to be in Asia are neo-isolationists. **1971** *Atlantic Monthly* Jan. 4 This month's magazine offers a considerable dose of anti-neoisolationist nourishment: two articles on Egypt and the Middle East situation, reports on Berlin, Canada, and China policy; as well as a lighthearted exercise in the ways of England. **1895** Zangwill *Master* III. ii. 300 The excesses of the *Neo-Japanese school. *a* **1881** A. Barratt *Phys. Metempiric* iv. (1883) 40 Like the *Neo-Kantians. **1886** S. H. Hodgson *Let.* 23 Nov. in R. B. Perry *Tht. & Char. W. James* (1935) I. 640 Bradley's *Logic*.. belongs to that Neo-Kantian line of thought from which, except as mental gymnastic, I hope nothing. **1958** W. Stark *Sociology of Knowledge* p. x, Heinrich Rickert was a member of the neo-Kantian school. **1888** *Pall Mall G.* 6 Aug. 11/1 The *Neo-Kantianism of English and French contemporaries. **1904** W. James *Ess. Rad. Emp.* (1912) i. 5 If *neo-Kantism has expelled earlier forms of dualism, we shall have expelled all forms if we are able to expel neo-Kantism in its turn. **1959** *Encounter* Jan. 52/1 *Neo-Keynesian models. **1968** *Time* 25 Oct. 31 [Senator Hubert H.] Humphrey pledges to continue neo-Keynesian policies that have helped stimulate the nation to $7\frac{1}{2}$ years of unprecedented growth in jobs, wages and production. **1970** *Times* 7 Sept. 19 It was also recognized that monetary policy could be effectively exploited for purposes of stabilization policy, and this position is accepted by Neo-Keynesians and monetarists alike. **1965** *Times Lit. Suppl.* 25 Nov. 1039/3 It was only towards the end of his life that the *neo-Keynesianism of his professional advisers prevailed. **1884** Packard in *Stand. Nat. Hist.* I. p. liii, In the United States a number of naturalists have advocated what may be called *neo-Lamarckian views of evolution. **1899** J. A. Thomson *Sci. of Life* xvi. 228 The *Neo-Lamarckians have added breadth and subtlety to Lamarckism. **1910** *Contemp. Rev.* Jan. 107 This important factor of direct action, which has been brought so much into prominence by the Neo-Lamarckians. **1884** Packard in *Stand. Nat. Hist.* I. p. liv, We believe in a modified and greatly extended Lamarckianism, or what may be called *neo-Lamarckianism. **1902** *Neo-Lamarckism [see *neo-Darwinism* above]. **1966** *Economist* 14 May p. xii/3 The restrictive view of the common market as a strictly *neo-liberal free trade affair would win the day. **1876** Fairbairn in *Contemp. Rev.* June 139 *Neo-Lutheranism..became more and more intolerant. **1970** *Times* 21 Feb. 7 If a *neo-Maoist China is to take shape after the cultural revolution and the ninth congress one can say that it is still very murky and that its institutional life is not in sight yet. **1960** *Twentieth Cent.* May 438 A younger [generation]..is being tempted by very strange gods, including a depressing *neo-Marxism. **1974** M. B. Brown *Econ. of Imperialism* iii. 69 The manifest failure of capitalism to develop industrialization equally throughout the whole world..has raised problems for Marxist analysis which have been the special concern of neo-Marxism. **1986** *N.Y. Times* 31 Aug. vii. 19/1 This new scholarship owes much to European neo-Marxism. **1971** *Times Lit. Suppl.* 31 Dec. 1621/5 The *neo-Marxist dialectic according to which all institutions and even doctrines are frozen forms of..the ever-flowing, ever-creative, human praxis. **1978** *Dædalus* Fall 101 British student militants were regarded by their German or Parisian counterparts as extraordinarily ignorant of neo-Marxist theory. **1983** *Financial Times* 4 May i. 19 The agreement of the Right-wing Press and neo-Marxists that British management has hacked and clawed its way [etc.]. **1881** *Standard* 7 Feb., To Carlyle above all men in England we owe it that *Neo-materialism is not atheistic. *a* **1878** Sir G. Scott *Lect. Archit.* (1879) II. 229 Our revived and redeveloped *Neo-mediæval style. **1959** D. Cooke *Lang. Mus.* ii. 76 The austere nature of modal and *neo-modal music. **1930** *Music & Lett.* XI. i. 62 Polytonality or atonality on the one hand, and *neo-modalism on the other, must set the bounds of our next enquiry. **1958** *Times* 6 June 4/4 The neo-modalism of Vaughan Williams nor the neo-primitivism of Carl Orff. **1947** *Penguin Music Mag.* Sept. 11 They needed a stronger purgative, needed a new instrument—*neo-modality, atonality, polytonality, quarter-tonality. **1896** H. R. Haweis *Dead Pulpit* i. 5 The *neo-Mystic Broad Church prophet. **1899** W. R. Inge *Chr. Mysticism* vii. 262 The so-called *neo-mystical school of modern France. **1968** *N.Y. Times* 11 May 13 Signs that 'middle-class radicalism and *neo-nationalism' were growing in West Germany. **1950** *Neo-Nazi [see *neo-Nazism* below]. **1952** *Time* 9 June 30 Threateningly resurgent neo-Nazis. **1952** *Harper's Mag.* Dec. 33/1 Fissures are appearing in Communist and neo-Nazi parties. **1973** D. Bagley *Tightrope Men* xxv. 172 Who the hell cares what happens to a lot of neo-Nazis? **1974** *Washington Post* 18 Jan. A29/5 The facade of the Euram Building looks almost neo-Nazi. **1950** *Britannica Bk. of Year* 739/2 **Neo-Nazism*, a rightist movement designed to revive former nazi principles and beliefs (1947; neo-Nazi, 1938). **1966** *Daily Tel.* 15 Aug. 17/8 Deep concern about an increase in neo-Nazism and other forms of bigotry was expressed at the end of the International Conference on Jewish-Christian Co-operation. **1974** *Times* 22 Oct. 5/1 National Front members..have been embarrassed..by Mr Tyndall's vulnerability to the charge of neo-Nazism. **1920** E. Pound *H.S. Mauberley* 25 Mildness, amid the *neo-Nietzschean clatter. **1958** *Listener* 19 June 1025/3 The neo-Nietzschean oracles of Colin Wilson. **1960** J. Betjeman *Summoned by Bells* v. 46 St. Andrew's first, with *neo-Norman apse. **1958** *New Statesman* 6 Sept. 296/2 Serious *neo-orthodox theologians regard the Billy Grahams and Norman Vincent Peales with revulsion. **1952** *Britannica Bk. of Year* 666/2 **Neo-orthodoxy*, certain new interpretations, especially on original sin, the righteousness of God, and the Bible as a source of revealed religious truth to which man must respond in every situation by a decision involving obedience or disobedience. **1876** L. Stephen *Eng. Th. 18th C.* II. 437 The 'man of feeling'..would in these days be a ritualist or a *neopagan. **1877** Symonds *Renaiss. It.* iv. 193 The neopagan impulse of the classical revival. **1880** J. McCarthy *Hist. Own Times* IV. 542 Pre-Raphaelitism..has got mixed up with æstheticism, *neo-paganism, and other such fantasies. **1888** Palgrave in *19th Cent.* Sept. 346 To classicalise, to *neopaganise, his native and natural Teutonic genius. **1940** *Burlington Mag.* Sept. 79/2 The *Neo-palladian architecture in England from the twenties of the eighteenth century onwards. **1864** Pusey *Lect. Daniel* viii. 541 So is *neo-Parsism doing at this day. **1647** Trapp *Comm. 2 Tim.* iii. 17 In our controversies against Antichristians, Antinomists, *Neopelagians. **1963** R. T. Hitt in *Eternity* July 11/2 The present *neo-Pentecostal movement does not include some of the extravagances and excesses of the earlier more revivalistic type of Pentecostalism. **1966** J. T. Nichol *Pentecostalism* xii. 241 Doubtless scores of 'neo-Pentecostals' are intellectually or experientially acquainted with charismatic phenomena like speaking in tongues. **1981** *N.Y. Times* 10 May i. 26/3 Two kinds of independent churches predominate. One is a byproduct of the neo-Pentecostal or charismatic revival. **1963** R. T. Hitt in *Eternity* July 10/1 One of the most amazing religious movements of the day is the sudden sweep of Pentecostalism into the main line denominations of U.S. Protestantism. Not following the patterns of the older Pentecostalism, it might better be described as *neo-Pentecostalism. **1978** C. E. Hummel *Fire in Fireplace* iv. 43 During the late 1950s a Neo-Pentecostalism began to flow in mainline Protestant churches. **1976** *Time* 26 Apr. 42/2 Like other *Neo-Pentecostalists, Stapleton believes in miraculous physical healings, but has played down her own involvement in them. **1977** *Washington Post* 6 May D20/1 Haughey,..a member of the neo-Pentecostalist charismatic movement.., cautioned healing enthusiasts. **1878** *N. Amer. Rev.* CXXVII. 495 A *Neo-Phoenician style was also attempted. **1972** *Newsweek* 27 Mar. 3 Once dismissed as a racist demagogue, Alabama Gov. George Wallace brings a quirky but potent *neopopulism to 1972 Presidential politics—as witnessed by his triumph in the Florida Democratic primary. **1975** *Times Lit. Suppl.* 31 Jan. 116/5 In small, localized communities, the tyranny of social control and of majority pressures can be all the more dangerous, as the neopopulism of Mid-Western small towns and the American South amply illustrates. **1935** *Mind* XLIV. 540 (*title*) Some metaphysical assumptions and problems of *neo-positivism. **1963** R. Carnap in P. A. Schilpp *Philos. of R. Carnap* 866 Since Lenin's book against Mach's philosophy, no author in the Soviet Union has dared to discuss neo-positivism with sympathy. **1935** *Mind* XLIV. 540 *Neo-positivists who define the class of possible operations by reference to *future* acts of verification can do so only by assigning some metaphysical status to time. **1964** *English Studies* XLV. Suppl. 109 Present-day British philosophers of the analytical or neo-positivist schools have therefore one criterion, namely the contribution to positive knowledge. **1927** *Observer* 24 Apr. 14/4 Post-impressionism, Expressionism, *Neo-primitivism. **1971** *Times Lit. Suppl.* 31 Dec. 1622/1 He would have denounced their neo-primitivism, the Rousseauian belief that poverty and roughness are closer to nature than austerity and civilized habits, and therefore more authentic and morally pure. **1884** *Manch. Exam.* 30 June 5/3 The mischievous misrepresentations of the *neo-protectionist and 'fair' trader. **1863** *Sat. Rev.* 12 Dec. 763/2 The Nought was known in the *Neo-Pythagorean schools. **1891** *Chambers's Encycl.* VII. 436/2 *Neopythagoreans may be divided into two groups. **1865** tr. *Strauss' New Life Jesus* I. i. xxx. 249 The artificially invented systems of *Neopythagoreanism and Neoplatonism. **1891** *Edin. Rev.* July 218 The function of *Neo-Quakerism. **1916** *Mind* XXV. 314 The theory of *neo-realism that colours, shapes and sounds must be accepted at their face value whatever the difficulties. **1955** *Times* 4 July 12/3 The earnest talker on films, the *cinéaste*, finds his brother in the balletomane and his cousin in the first-nighter..and his conversation is full of words like montage, neo-realism, and audio-visual correspondence. **1917** A. S. Pringle-Pattison *Idea of God* x. 191 The opening years of the twentieth century have been marked..by a strong attack on the fundamental tenet of Mentalism on the part of thinkers who call themselves Realists or *Neo-Realists. **1931** G. F. Stout *Mind & Matter* 171 The Neo-Realist holds that when we see a star the star itself becomes in one aspect of its being an immediate content of our actual sense-experience. **1940** *Mind* XLIX. 122 The 'neo-realist' positions of Russell, Alexander, and Whitehead. **1974** *Times* 11 Dec. 14/4 *Downpour*, a gentle neo-realist study of the difficulties of a young teacher. **1955** *Times* 26 May 13/3 The *neo-realistic Italian cinema has made English audiences familiar with the poverty and crime that flourish in the back streets of Italian cities. **1970** *Times* 26 Feb. 6 One of the Maoists' main targets is the Marxist Communist Party, branded by Peking as *neo-revisionist to distinguish it from the pro-Moscow Communist Party. **1970** *Guardian Weekly* 18 July 5 The Indian Marxists have often been denounced by Radio Peking as 'neo-revisionists'. **1926** A. Huxley *Two or Three Graces* 76 That sham *dix-huitième* language, those *neo-rococo sentiments. **1891** *Ch. Times* 28 Aug. 822/4 Whether married in the Anglo-Catholic or the *Neo-Roman Church. **1875** Stedman *Vict. Poets* 361 This master of the *Neo-Romantic school. **1899** Beerbohm *More* 95 The Neo-Romantics, the dalliers with pretty sentiment, would paint admirable sign-boards. **1947** A. Einstein *Music in Romantic Era* xv. 221 That crude, scribbling materialism with which the French neo-Romantics amuse themselves. **1882** *Athenæum* 27 May 660/1 The *neo-romanticism of the nineteenth [century]. **1915** *London Q. Rev.* Jan. 49 The '*Neo-scholastic' movement would have attracted no attention outside Catholic circles, had it not been for the literary activity of the Louvain professors. **1930** *Times Lit. Suppl.* 26 June 524/4 It is true that there are certain neo-Scholastics and certain naturalists who divide into neo-Realists and critical Realists influenced both by William James and Mr. Bertrand Russell. **1915** *London Q. Rev.* Jan. 46 It is strange that a movement with so much verve as '*Neo-scholasticism' has attracted so little attention in Britain. **1934** C. S. Lewis *Let.* 7 June (1966) 157 Beware of people who are at present running what they call 'neo-scholasticism' as a fad. **1970** G. Jackson *Let.* 4 Apr. in *Soledad Brother* (1971) 211 Part of the credo of the *neoslave, the latter-day slave,..is to shuffle away from any situation that becomes too difficult. *Ibid.* 214 The *neoslaver destroyed the uneconomic plantation, and built upon its ruins a factory. **1965** —— *Let.* 30 Mar. in *Soledad Brother* (1971) 70 Our people react in different ways to this *neoslavery. **1969** *Guardian* 30 Sept. 12/2 Those who are allowed to speak to the [Czech] nation speak with the accents of *neo-Stalinism. **1974** *Times* 27 May 4/2 The [Yugoslav] climate changed and the attacks began to centre on neo-Stalinism. **1960** *Guardian* 28 July 9/6 The *neo-Stalinists..are now prepared to make their stand known in public. *Ibid.* 9/7 This is also the neo-Stalinist view in China. **1973** A. Mann *Tiara* i. 3 Things are beginning to simmer again in Moscow, and the neo-Stalinists or hard-liners..have recovered a good deal of influence. **1930** *Times Educ. Suppl.* 3 May 197/2 The schools or coteries of the last few decades—the symbolists, neo-classicists, *neo-symbolists, synthetists..and so forth. **1960** *Guardian* 19 Aug. 4/5 How to combine the neo-symbolist image..with the language of rational discourse. **1907** W. de Morgan *Alice-For-Short* viii. 75 A *neo-theosophical reincarnationism without so much as a single Himalayan Brother to back you up! **1964** P. F. Anson *Bishops at Large* ix. 367 He [*sc.* Steiner] founded his own neo-theosophical body. **1915** *London Q. Rev.* Jan. 51 Neo-scholasticism is essentially '*Neo-Thomism'. **1968** P. B. Austin *On being Swedish* xxiii. 168 Neo-Thomism is also making its voice heard. **1928** H. Crane *Let.* 17 Apr. (1965) 323 This method is reversed—as with the *neo-Thomists. *c* **1928** R. Fry *Lett.* (1972) II. 632 He [*sc.* Herbert Read]'s one of this neo-Thomist lot with a whole bag of metaphysical nostrums on his back. **1947** Neo-Thomist [see *neo-Aristotelian* adj. and sb. above]. **1945** 'G. Orwell' *England Your England* (1953) 56 All *Neo-Tories are anti-Russian, but sometimes the main emphasis is anti-American. *Ibid.*, The real motive force of *Neo-Toryism..is the desire not to recognise that British power and influence have declined. **1962** *Economist* 19 May 674/1 *Neo-traditionalism was now so strong that Buganda became its own political 'party'. **1932** Auden *Orators* iii. 103 In the *neo-Tudor club-house the captains frown. **1960** J. Betjeman *Summoned by Bells* vi. 57 And not far off the neo-Tudor shops. *a* **1866** J. Grote *Exam. Utilit. Phil.* i. (1870) 15 His *neo-utilitarianism, as I have called it. **1929** Galsworthy *Modern Comedy* p. x, Such subsidiary *neo-Victorians as the self-righteous Mr. Danby. **1959** Neo-Victorian [see Betjeman]. **1902** *Encycl. Brit.* XXXI. 712/2 These efforts..by their unfortunate designations of Vitalism and *Neo-vitalism give rise to entirely false conceptions. **1899** J. A. Thomson *Sci. of Life* 9 The rise of a school of '*neovitalists', who have helped to save the science from self-conceit by their emphasis on the partial nature of all physiological analysis. **1920** A. S. Pringle-Pattison *Idea of God* (ed. 2) p. vi, I have added some detailed criticism of recent neo-vitalist statements from which I wish to dissociate myself. **1966** C. G. Hempel *Philos. of Nat. Sci.* vi. 72 All that the neovitalist doctrine enables us to do is to make the *post factum* pronouncement. **1902** *Encycl. Brit.* XXXI. 712/2 All the so-called *neo-vitalistic efforts..have nothing to do with the older vitalism.

b. In the designations of certain forms of chemical substances (so named when newly discovered), as ***neoparaffin***; **neo-ars'phenamine**, a bicyclic arsenic compound, $H_2NC_6H_3(OH)As{:}As(OH)C_6H_3NHCH(_2 SO_2Na$, which is a derivative of arsphenamine and is a toxic yellow powder formerly much used in the treatment of syphilis; **neohe'speridin** [a. G. *neohesperidin* (Kolle & Gloppe 1936, in *Pharmazeut. Zentralhalle* LXXVII. 425)], a bitter compound, $C_{28}H_{34}O_{15}$, which is a glycoside of a flavone and is found in Seville oranges; **neo'salvarsan** [a. G. *neosalvarsan* (E. Schreiber 1912, in *München. med. Wochenschr.* 23 Apr. 905/1)] = ***neoarsphenamine*** above; **neo'stigmine** [physo)-stigmine], the aromatic quaternary ammonium ion $(CH_3)_2N{\cdot}CO{\cdot}O{\cdot}C_6H_4N^+ (CH_3)_3$ or its bromide or methylsulphate salts, which are white crystalline compounds used in treating myasthenia gravis and other muscular complaints.

1876 W. Odling in *Philos. Mag.* XXV. 217 Isomerism does or may occur..among neo acids with one another. **1918** *Public Health Rep.* (U.S.) XXXIII. 1003 Previous to the year 1914, all of the arsphenamine (salvarsan) and neo-arsphenamine (neosalvarsan) on the market was manufactured by a single German firm. **1951** A. Grollman *Pharmacol. & Therap.* xxx. 698 Neoarsphenamine is easier to prepare and administer than arsphenamine; causes fewer reactions; and is less irritant to the tissues. **1969** *Radiation Res.* XXXIX. 579 Neoarsphenamine, a sulfhydryl-binding agent, sensitizes hypoxic suspensions of *E. coli*..to irradiation. **1936** *Chem. Abstr.* XXX. 6509 The new glucoside '244', for which the name *neohesperidin* is suggested, is split on hydrolysis in 2 phases in accordance with the following scheme. **1962** *Anal. Biochem.* IV. 110 The isolation and identification of neohesperidin, a 7-rhamnoglucoside of hesperetin..from a commercially produced grapefruit flavonoid preparation containing mostly naringin. **1970** Neohesperidin [see Naringin]. **1876** W. Odling in *Philos. Mag.* XXV. 206 The subclass typified by the hydrocarbon $C(CH_3)_4$ may be conveniently designated as that of neo- or latest paraffins. **1876** *Encycl. Brit.* V. 557-8. **1881** Roscoe & Schorlemmer *Chem.* III. i. 136 *Neoparaffins.* In these compounds one atom of carbon is connected with four other carbon atoms. **1912** *Chem. Abstr.* VI. 2111 Neo-salvarsan is more easily sol. than salvarsan, thus simplifying this part of the salvarsan therapy and preventing the effects produced by NaOH. It is more easily tolerated than salvarsan; intestinal disturbances and collapse are nearly entirely absent. **1932** Schamberg & Wright *Treatment of Syphilis* x. 159 The product known as '914' or 'neosalvarsan' (neoarsphenamine) possessed the very desirable property of being more freely soluble in water and being neutral in reaction. **1970** Passmore & Robson *Compan. Med. Stud.* II. xx. 2/1 Salvarsan tended to be toxic and was soon replaced by a less toxic compound called neosalvarsan, which was universally employed until it was superseded by penicillin in 1945. **1943** *Proc. Soc. Exper. Biol. & Med.* LIV. 254/1 Oral administration of 0·2 mg/kg of neostigmine bromide to mice reduces mortality in severe anoxia but larger doses are not prophylactic. **1951** A. Grollman *Pharmacol. & Therap.* xiii. 253 Neostigmine, like physostigmine, exerts its action by inactivating cholinesterase. **1973** *Exper. Eye Res.* XV. 35 The increase in blood flow in the ciliary processes may be due to a direct effect on the muscarinic receptor of neostigmine, which is a quaternary compound, but it may also be due to an ability of neostigmine to release acetylcholine from the nerve terminals besides protecting it.

Spec. (after *neoparaffin*: see above), denoting compounds and radicals in which one carbon atom is linked to four others, as ***neohexane***, ***neohexyl***; **neo'pentane**, an isomer, $C(CH_3)_4$, of pentane which is an easily condensable gas and which is found in small amounts in petroleum; **neo'pentyl**, the radical $(CH_3)_3C{\cdot}CH_2-$ derived from neopentane.

1876 *Phil. Mag.* I. 207 (*caption*) Neohexane. **1942** V. J. Clancey *Chem. & Aeroplane* iv. 64 Neo-hexane, with an octane value of 94, has been produced for use in blending with normal aviation fuels. **1957** G. I. Brown *Introd. Org. Chem.* vi. 83 Ethylene and iso-butane react..at 500°C and 250 atmospheres to form neo-hexane. **1968** R. O. C. Norman *Princ. Org. Synth.* viii. 263 The simplest example of an efficient alkylation is the preparation of neohexyl chloride..from t-butyl chloride and ethylene. **1876** W. Odling in *Philos. Mag.* XXV. 209 Isopentane and neopentane. **1938** *Encycl. Brit. Bk. of Year* 145/1 The highly symmetrical neopentane molecule. **1966** *McGraw-Hill Encycl. Sci. & Technol.* I. 249/1 Two alkanes, neopentane (dimethylpropane) and neohexane (2,2-dimethylbutane) are named unambiguously by using the prefix 'neo'. **1876** *Phil. Mag.* I. 209 The paraffin- or alcohol-monad radicals propyl, butyl, isobutyl, pentyl, isopentyl or amyl, and neopentyl, &c. **1933** *Jrnl. Amer. Chem. Soc.* LV. 3803 Because of the importance of the neopentyl system in rearrangements the preparation and properties of the parent hydrocarbons have been studied. **1969** A. NICA *Theory & Pract. Lubrication Syst.* vi. 168 The neopentyl polyol esters were used in gas turbine engines when the temperatures..prohibited the utilisation of diesters.

c. In geological terms (opposed to *palæo-*) denoting the later or more recent portion of a period, as ***Neo-cambrian, -carboniferous, -devonian***, etc.

1888 HATCH in Teall *Petrogr.* 442 Rosenbusch.. subdivides the group of volcanic rocks into paleovolcanic and neo-volcanic. **1894** H. S. WILLIAMS in *Jrnl. Geol.* II. 155 Neosilurian. *Ibid.* 158 It began at the beginning of the Neodevonian. **1897** *Bull. U.S. Geol. Surv.* No. 87. 57 Carboniferous and Permian Brachiopoda, Neo-carboniferous.

d. In terms denoting scientists who study recent, in contrast to ancient, forms of plants, animals, etc., as ***neo-botanist, -zoologist***.

1889 NICHOLSON & LYDEKKER *Palæont.* I. 5 The domain of the neozoologist or the neobotanist.

e. In anatomical terms designating parts of the brain which are considered to be of relatively recent development phylogenetically, as NEENCEPHALON, NEOCEREBELLUM, NEOCORTEX, NEOPALLIUM, NEOSTRIATUM, NEOTHALAMUS. Cf. PALÆO-, PALEO- b.

2. In misc. combs., as **neo'arctic** *a.* = NEARCTIC. **'neoblast** *Zool.* [-BLAST], any of the specialized cells in annelid worms by the division of which a lost portion of the body can be regenerated; **neo'blastic** *a.*, of the nature of a new growth. **neo'catechu** (see quot.). **'neocene** *a.*, *Geol.* = *neogene*. **neo'chrysolite**, *Min.* a variety of chrysolite. **neo'cosmic** *a.* (see PALÆOCOSMIC). **neo'crinoid**, *Zool.* a crinoid of later than palæozoic date. † **'neoctese** [Gr. κτῆσις acquisition], *Min.* (see quot.). **neo'cyanite**, *Min.* an uncertain mineral found in the fumeroles of Vesuvius. **'neodox** *a.*, holding new views. **'neodoxy**, a new doctrine or view. **neo'embryo**, *Zool.* a metazoan embryo at the stage before it develops any special characters to indicate to what group it belongs; hence **neoembry'onic** *a.* **neogæan, -gean** (niːə'dʒiːən) *a.*, of or pertaining to the New World or western hemisphere. **'neogam** [ad. Gr. νεόγαμος], a newly-married person (*nonce-wd.*); so † **ne'ogamist** (Blount 1656). **neogene** ('niːədʒiːn) *a.*, *Geol.* belonging to the later Tertiary (Miocene and Pliocene). **neo'genesis**, chiefly in scientific use: the formation of something new; the renewed formation of something formed previously. **neoge'netic** *a.*, *Biol.* of atavism, denoting that the abnormal part does not appear as a germ in the embryo. **'neograph** *a.* (see quot.). **neo'graphic** *a.*, of the nature of, pertaining to, a new system of writing or spelling. **'neography**, a new system or method of writing. **Neo-'Grec** [F. *grec* Greek], a modern style of architecture based on classical Greek architecture. **neo'morphism**, the process of change into a new form. **neomor'phosis** *Biol.*, a type of regeneration (see quot.); **neo'natal** *a.*, *Med.* relating to newly-born children. **neo'natally** *adv.*, soon after birth. **neonto'logical** *a.*, pertaining or belonging to neontology. **neon'tologist**, a student of neontology. **neon'tology**, the zoology or study of extant animals. **neo'phobia**, fear or dislike of what is new. **neo'phobic** *a.*, fearing or disliking what is new. **'neoplase**, *Min.* an obsolete name for botryogen. **neo'tantalite** *Min.* [ad. F. *néotantalite* (P. Termier 1902, in *Bull. de la Soc. franç. de Minéral.* XXV. 37)], a mineral found as yellow octahedra in Allier, France, that was formerly thought to be a tantalate and niobate of iron, manganese, and sodium but is now thought to be an impure microlite. **neo'teinia, -'tenia** [Gr. τείνειν to keep], *Biol.* the retention of juvenile conditions in an individual (esp. a termite) capable of reproduction; hence **neo'teinic** *a.* **neo'tenin** *Ent.* [*neoten(ia)* = *juvenile hormone* s.v. JUVENILE *a.* 4. **neo'tesite**, *Min.* a hydrous silicate of manganese.

1868 LYELL *Princ. Geol.* (ed. 10) II. 473 Two of the great zoological regions..the *Neoarctic and Neotropical. **1891** H. RANDOLPH in *Zoologischer Anzeiger* XIV. 154 The new mesoderm is formed in great part from specialized cells in the region of the peritonaeal epithelium of the ventral longitudinal muscles, on each side of the ventral nerve cord between it and the ventral row of setae. These cells, which I propose to call *neoblasts, are distinguishable from the cells of the peritonaeum by their great size and by the presence of a cell body. **1930** *Jrnl. Linn. Soc.* XXXVII. 186 The cells concerned in the phagocytosis and replacement of tissues are derived from neoblasts in the ventral body-wall. **1972** *Jrnl. Morphol.* CXXXVII. 217/2 The confusion between peritoneal cells, so-called neoblasts, and oocytes in polychaetes has a considerable historical basis. **1854** R. D. THOMSON *Cycl. Chem.* 379/1 *Neocatechu consists of tannin 32·2, gallic acid 35·, colouring matter 18·8, fibre, &c. 12·. **1895** DANA *Man. Geol.* (ed. 4) 880 The Miocene and Pliocene are sometimes united under the name *Neocene. **1897** *Amer. Microsc. Jrnl.* Mar. 91 The same forms are to be found in the Neocene of California. **1892** DANA *Syst. Min.* (ed. 6) 455 *Neo-chrysolite... In small, black crystalline plates. **1882** CARPENTER in *Proc. Zool. Soc.* 734 The presence of three radials is such an absolutely constant character in all the five-rayed *Neocrinoids. **1854** DANA *Syst. Min.* (ed. 4) II. 419 The *Neoctese, from Brazil, is shown..to be identical with Scorodite. **1892** *Ibid.* (ed. 6) 562 *Neocyanite... In very minute monoclinic crystals.. colour blue. **1897** *Daily Chron.* 2 Sept. 4/6 The views of the *neodox Israelites. **1896** *Daily News* 3 Aug. 5 A shapeless and ever varying fancy, which I venture to describe as *neodoxy. **1887** HYATT in *Proc. Boston* (U.S.) *Soc. Nat. Hist.* 398 *Neoembryos are..so similar that they may be considered as indicating a common ancestor for the entire Animal Kingdom. **1862** ALFORD in *Life* (1873) 357 At Lucerne our *neogams met us. **1857** SCLATER in *Proc. Linn. Soc., Zool.* II. 134 The most really characteristic region of *Neogean Ornithology. **1878** LAWRENCE tr. *Cotta's Rocks Class.* 261 A Miocene or *Neogene deposit of clay in the Vienna basin. **1903** *Ibis* III. 15 But the opposite hypothesis, that we have in this singular small Owl a case of *neogenesis —i.e. the *ex-abrupto* formation of a new type with sufficient differential characters to constitute, if maintained, a new species,—can, I believe, be upheld. The term neogenesis was first used to explain this sudden origin of new forms from old-established species, if I am not mistaken, by my friend and colleague Prof. Paolo Mantegazza, many years ago; it has been since used, more or less in the same sense, by the late Prof. Cope and by others. **1946** *Nature* 10 Aug. 202/1 The situation is essentially different in coma, in the sense that although neogenesis of sugar occurs (high blood sugar during fast) storage of glycogen in the liver is no longer possible. **1959** *Ann. N.Y. Acad. Sci.* LXXXIII. 507 (*heading*) Neogenesis of human hair follicles. **1972** *Gloss. Geol.* (Amer. Geol. Inst.) 477/1 *Neogenesis*, the formation of new minerals, as by diagenesis or metamorphism. **1882** GARSON & GADOW tr. *Gegenbaur's Jrnl. Anat.* XVI. 622 The first form we propose to call 'Palæogenetic', the second '*Neogenetic' atavism. **1886** SUTTON in *Proc. Zool. Soc.* 551 My object is to shew..that Neogenetic Atavism has no existence. **1892** *Nation* (N.Y.) 23 June 474/1 The illustrations are reproduced from remarkably clear photographs by the *neograph process. **1825** (*title*) Enchiridion..by the author of the *Neographic Alphabet. *a* **1876** M. COLLINS *Th. in Garden* (1880) I. 150 *Favour* was spelt in the American fashion—*favor*. This *neographic tendency is based on ignorance. **1810** *Gentl. Mag.* LXXX. I. 136 A new system called *neography, by which the publisher..has attempted to simplify..all the various modes of writing. **1931** C. H. REILLY in W. Rose *Outl. Mod. Knowl.* 989 The next stage, generally called the *Neo Grec, was probably due to the indirect influence of the Gothic revivalists. **1939** *Archit. Rev.* LXXXV. 52/3 No better background could be imagined for the parade ground manoeuvrings of redcoated guards than these stern, unadorned neo-grec façades. **1888** GADOW in *Nature* XXXIX. 151/2 Still greater is the difficulty when the *neomorphism..takes place in the next following metamere. **1901** T. H. MORGAN *Regeneration* i. 24 In one case [of heteromorphosis] the new part is not only different from the part removed, but is also an organ that belongs to a different part of the body (or it may be unlike any organ of the body). This we may call '*neomorphosis'. **1902** *Brit. Med. Jrnl.* 22 Mar. 721/1 Chapters on antenatal in relation to postnatal and *neonatal pathology. **1945** *Ann. Amer. Acad. Political & Social Sci.* CCXXXVII. 140 Puerperal fatality increases sharply when the infant is either stillborn or dies *neonatally. **1974** *Nature* 7 June 564/2 No significant increase in tumour incidence has been observed in either neonatally thymectomised..mice or congenitally athymic.. mice. **1896** *Nat. Sci.* Dec. 355 Systems founded on *neontological evidence only have had their day. **1889** *Nature* XXXIX. 364/2 The *neontologist, if we may venture to call anyone by that name. *Ibid.* 364/1 The division of zoology into palæontology and *neontology..is, no doubt, logically defensible. **1886** *Pop. Sci. Monthly* XXIX. 782 In the student, curiosity takes the place of *neophobia. **1895** *Westm. Gaz.* 3 Dec. 1/3 He is particularly subject to neophobia. **1925** *Glasgow Herald* 20 June 4 The greeting extended to the steamship was quite as *neophobic. **1971** W. HANLEY *Blue Dreams* iii. 22 Her unfailingly neophobic response to those attempts. **1854** R. D. THOMPSON *Cycl. Chem.* 379/1 *Neoplase, a synonyme of red sulphate of iron, and also of arsenide of nickel. **1903** *Mineral. Mag.* XIII. 374 *Neotantalite... Minute, regular octahedra resembling pyrochlore, in kaolin from dép. Allier, France. **1932** *Mineral. Abstr.* V. 185 The several minerals (..microlite, neotantalite, atopite, [etc.]..) of this group [*sc.* pyrochlore-romeite]..crystallize as small octahedra and have the same type of crystal-structure. **1973** *Ibid.* XXIV. 282/1 'Neotantalite' is a microlite $A_2B_2O_6(OH,F)$ with large deficiences in the *A* ions which may be Ba, Pb, U, or Ca. Microprobe analyses show that the Fe and Mn included in the first description..are impurities. **1894** *Proc. Entom. Soc.* 14 Mar. p. vii, What Grassi calls *neoteinic queens, that is fertile females, that in some portions of the development of the body still retain the immature condition. **1896** *Nature* LIII. 323/2 Pædogenesis..is an extreme form of the more general phenomenon of *neotenia. **1954** V. B. WIGGLESWORTH *Physiol. Insect Metamorphosis* iv. 56 The 'inhibitory hormone'..has..been called for preference the 'juvenile hormone'. If a Greek term is preferred it might be called '*neotenin'. **1966** tr. *V.J.A. Novák's Insect Hormones* 79 (*heading*) The juvenile hormone (neotenin), JH (= inhibitory hormone, Wigglesworth, 1935; = status quo hormone, Williams, 1952; = das Larvalhormon, Weber, 1954). **1968** *New Scientist* 16 May 354/1 In larval insects, moulting and metamorphosis are controlled by two hormones produced by epithelial endocrine glands:.. neotenin from the corpora allata controls the change towards the adult form. **1892** DANA *Syst. Min.* (ed. 6) 705 Klipsteinite is another hydrated manganese silicate... See also..epigenite or *neotesite.

neoanthropic, var. NEANTHROPIC *a.*

neocerebellum (niːəusɛrɪ'bɛləm). *Anat.* [mod.L., f. NEO- 1 e + CEREBELLUM.] The phylogenetically youngest portion of the cerebellum, comprising mainly its lateral lobes ('hemispheres').

1925 W. H. F. ADDISON tr. *Villiger's Brain & Spinal Cord* (ed. 3) 80 The hemispheres constitute the neocerebellum, and the vermis and flocculus constitute the palaeocerebellum. **1954** JANSEN & BRODAL *Aspects Cerebellar Anat.* vi. 384 We may appropriately close this discussion by commenting briefly on the much debated concepts paleocerebellum, comprising the vermis and the flocculus, and neocerebellum, comprising the cerebellar hemispheres... From the point of view of gross morphology these concepts may appear well founded. On the basis of fiber connections, however, a paleocerebellum and a neocerebellum *sensu strictiori* are not distinguishable. **1974** *Encycl. Brit. Macropædia* XII. 990/2 This new part of the cerebellum, or neocerebellum, coordinates skilled movements initiated at cortical levels.

So **neocere'bellar** *a.*, of or pertaining to the neocerebellum.

1914 *Jrnl. Nerv. & Mental Dis.* XLI. 540 (*heading*) Neocerebellar hemiatrophy. **1948** A. BRODAL *Neurol. Anat.* v. 126 The neo-cerebellar syndrome. Here homolateral hypotonia and atactic movements, asynergic and clumsy, appear, and when the dentate nucleus is involved tremor also develops. **1958** *Jrnl. Neurophysiol.* XXI. 3 Stimulation of some neocerebellar areas, however, resulted in equilibratory changes.

neo-'classic, -'classical, *a.* [NEO-.] Of, pertaining to, or characteristic of a style of art, architecture, music, literature, etc., that is based on or influenced by classical style or by a style that has become established as 'classical'; *spec.* of such a style in 18th-century literature, late-18th-century art and architecture, or 20th-century music.

1877 *Contemp. Rev.* Feb. 360 The imagination of the men of Spenser's time was affected by his use of the neo-classical mythology of the Renaissance. **1881** *Athenæum* 19 Feb. 270/2 The neo-classic, if not the Italian, mood of design. **1882** PITMAN *Mission Life Greece* 42 The written [modern Greek] is a form of the ancient, called neo-classical. **1923** C. GRAY *Contingencies* (1947) ii. 65 We find throughout almost all the work of Brahms..the perpetual striving after the ideal of a grandiose, neo-classic art. **1927** *P.M.L.A.* Mar. 237 This linguistic attitude, expressing itself in grammars of arbitrary rules, seems to be but another manifestation and *survival* of that tendency called the neo-classic creed of literary criticism. **1933** *Archit. Rev.* LXXIV. 79/2 Many is the ill-built block of London flats whose internal planning has been sacrificed for some ponderous neo-classical façade. **1934** C. LAMBERT *Music Ho!* II. 101 Stravinsky's neo-classical period,..apart from the adoption of eighteenth-century forms and titles, is chiefly noticeable for its attempt to create melody by synthetic means. **1944** *Burlington Mag.* Apr. 97/1 A fully developed neo-classic sculptor. **1964** J. SUMMERSON *Classical Lang. Archit.* v. 37/1 The Panthéon is the first major building which can be called neo-classical —'neo-classical' being the expression which has come to be used for architecture which..tends towards the rational simplification advocated by Cordemoy and Laugier and.. seeks to present the orders with the utmost antiquarian fidelity. **1966** *English Studies* XLVII. 150 In the period up to the Civil War the neo-classic Happy Husbandman becomes the neo-Stoic Contemplator of the world. **1974** *Times Lit. Suppl.* 15 Mar. 259/4 Throughout the book—as for example in the emphasis on jobs rather than on the ownership of capital as a key determinant in occupational mobility—the authors assume the validity of neo-classical economics as taught in the United States.

Hence **neo-'classicism**, neo-classic style or principles; **neo-'classicist**, a follower or exponent of neo-classic style or principles.

1893 *Times* 6 May 17/2 A man must be a scholar before he can make neo-classicism even tolerable in art. **1930** *Times Educ. Suppl.* 3 May 197/2 The schools or coteries of the last few decades—the symbolists, neo-classicists, neo-symbolists, [etc.]. **1934** C. LAMBERT *Music Ho!* II. 73 *Pulcinella*..marks the beginning of the movement sometimes dignified with the name of neo-classicism. *Ibid.* IV. 245 It may seem contradictory to condemn composers like Honegger for basing their work on the contemporary scene after complaining that the neo-classicists are so out of touch with contemporary life. **1943** *Philological Q.* XXII. 143 The fairy tales about 'neo-classicism' and 'romanticism' in the eighteenth century which have so long been allowed to come between us and the direct appreciation of eighteenth-century texts. **1944** *Burlington Mag.* Apr. 97/2 He..gives no hint of any sympathy with the principles of the Neo-Classicists. **1947** *Penguin Music Mag.* Sept. 24 Both men [*sc.* Schumann and Mendelssohn] turned to a sort of neo-classicism before they had done. **1965** *Times Lit. Suppl.* 25 Nov. 1063/2 The 'lower order' was one which allowed Gay his particularly delicate critical assimilation of the vulgar writers and the 'trivial' moderns, while himself remaining, in theory at least, in the camp of the neo-classicists. **1972** *Listener* 21 Sept. 361/3 What was then called the 'True Style' which we now tend to call Neo-Classicism.

ˌneo-co'lonialism. [f. NEO- + COLONIALISM.] The acquisition or retention of influence over other countries, esp. one's former colonies, often by economic or political measures. So **ˌneo-co'lonial** *a.* and *sb.*; **ˌneo-co'lonialist** *a.* and *sb.*; **ˌneo-coˌloniali'zation**; **ˌneo-co'lonialized, ˌneo-'colonized** *adjs.*

1961 *New Statesman* 20 Jan. 82/1 The most dangerous type of colonialism is neo-colonialism. **1961** *New Left Rev.* July–Aug. 12/1 One of the effects of EEC is therefore to deepen the split between independent and neo-colonial Africa. **1961** *Economist* 16 Dec. 1113/2 Casuistry worthy of the most devious neo-colonialist. **1963** *Ann. Reg. 1962* 98 Accepting the Indonesian Communist Party's definition of 'Malaysia' as a 'neo-colonialist' device. **1964** K. NKRUMAH *Consciencism* v. 111 Just as a liberated territory can be produced by the application of D (na > pa), so a neo-colonized territory can be produced by the application of D (pa > na). **1965** —— *Neo-colonialism: the Last Stage of Imperialism* p. ix, In place of colonialism as the main instrument of imperialism we have today neo-colonialism. The essence of neo-colonialism is that the State which is subject to it is, in theory, independent and has all the outward trappings of international sovereignty. In reality its economic system and thus its political policy is directed from outside. **1966** *Economist* 26 Mar. 1226/1 Libya is not nearly so neo-colonialised as a country like Algeria with its government-to-government oil and development agreements with France. **1967** *N.Y. Times* 5 July 12 The 'neocolonials' (the Belgians) and the 'imperialists' (the Americans). **1969** *Listener* 3 July 12/2 You'll always have people moving from a stage of neo-colonialisation back to capitalism. **1971** *Black Scholar* Apr.–May 9 The black people in the United States..are de facto neocolonial subjects. **1972** *Sci. Amer.* Apr. 19/3 Strong elements of neocolonialism persist in the economic relations of the rich and poor countries. **1973** J. REX *Discovering Sociology* ix. 109 The inhabitants of the former British and French empires..addressed themselves to the twin tasks of dealing with their own poverty and fighting neo-colonialism. **1973** *Times* 1 Jan. 14/4 One of the black speakers..mentioned Europe in passing as a 'massive neo-colonialist conspiracy to castrate black men everywhere'.

Neocomian (niːəʊˈkəʊmɪən), *a.* and *sb. Geol.* [ad. F. *Néocomien* (Thurmann, 1832), f. *Neocomi-um* (f. Gr. νέος new + κώμη village), latinized form of *Neuchâtel*.]

1. Of or belonging to the series of lower cretaceous rocks found at Neuchâtel in Switzerland.

1843 R. A. C. AUSTEN in *Proc. Geol. Soc.* IV. I. 170 Argillaceous (Neocomian of Leymerie and D'Orbigny). **1863** LYELL *Antiq. Man* xvi. 335 The lower cretaceous or neocomian beds were deposited conformably on the oolitic. **1891** *Edin. Rev.* July 177 The neocomian sandstone in the Lebanon.

b. Characterized by the formation of the Neocomian rocks; belonging to the period at which these were formed.

1882 W. J. HARRISON *Geol. Counties Eng.* 76 Neocomian or Lower Cretaceous Period. **1888** PRESTWICH *Geol.* II. 266 Strata of..Neocomian age. *Ibid.*, The early Neocomian Sea spread over a great part of central and southern Europe.

2. *absol.* as *sb.* The Neocomian series or period.

1888 PRESTWICH *Geol.* II. 267 At the close of the Lower Neocomian. **1897** F. R. C. REED *Handbk. Geol. Cambr.* 48 It is not believed to include any part of the Neocomian of D'Orbigny.

neocorate (niːˈɒkərət). [f. L. *neōcor-us*, ad. Gr. νεωκόρος the custodian of a temple: see -ATE[1], and cf. F. *néocorat*.] The office or dignity of having the custody or charge of a temple, as a distinction assumed by, or granted to, Asiatic cities under the Roman Empire.

1850 LEITCH tr. *C. O. Müller's Anc. Art* §405 (ed. 2) 544 Cities which have the neocorate of a temple, usually hold an idol or the temple in the hand. **1889** W. M. RAMSAY in *Class. Rev.* 175 The neocorate—which was granted by formal decree of the Roman Senate to certain cities of Asia—related to local cults of Emperors and imperial families.

neocortex (niːəʊˈkɔːtɛks). *Anat.* Also (with hyphen) **neo-cortex**. [mod.L., f. NEO- I e + CORTEX.] The phylogenetically youngest portion of the cerebral cortex, which is co-extensive with the neopallium.

1909 C. U. A. KAPPERS in *Arch. Neurol. & Psychiatry* IV. 162 Just as in the pallium there can be distinguished three territories according to the connections which they exhibit, so the cortical structures occurring in them should be distinguished, according to the same principle, into a palæo-cortex, archi-cortex and neo-cortex. **1947** H. C. ELLIOTT *Textbk. Nerv. Syst.* vii. 87/1 This first, or paleocortex..is soon overshadowed by the development of a general, or neocortex. **1948** [see NEOPALLIUM]. **1964** J. Z. YOUNG *Model of Brain* xiv. 234 Although it is notoriously dangerous to try to speak of the locality of 'engrams' in a mammal, there can be little doubt that they reside largely in the neocortex. **1972** T. W. JENKINS *Functional Mammalian Neuroanat.* xvi. 250/2 The area of the canine neocortex is 84·2 per cent of the entire hemispheric area. **1972** *Science* 19 May 804/1 We have used the development of the neocortex..as an index of generation length in extinct taxa.

Hence **neoˈcortical** *a.*, of or pertaining to the neocortex.

1909 *Arch. Neurol. & Psychiatry* IV. 163 The upper part of the lateral cortex layer has certainly already a neo-cortical character. **1971** *Nature* 11 June 397/1 All rats were killed 4 h later and the RNA was extracted from hippocarpal, thalamic and medial neocortical tissue. **1971** *Daily Colonist* (Victoria, B.C.) 7 Oct. 5/1 There are other species like ourselves who through evolutionary quirk if not neocortical ascendancy lack biological commands to insure reasonable populations.

neod(e, obs. forms of NEED *sb.*

neodamode (niːˈɒdəməʊd). *Gr. Antiq.* [ad. Gr. νεοδᾱμώδης, f. νέος new + δᾶμος, δῆμος people.] Among the ancient Spartans, an enfranchised Helot. Chiefly *attrib.*

1808 MITFORD *Greece* xix. §1. II. 403 Three hundred only of those called neodamodes, newly-admitted citizens, were granted for the service. **1838** THIRLWALL *Greece* xxxix. V. 97 A Spartan who was posted near it..with a garrison of neodamode troops. **1852** GROTE *Greece* II. lxxiii. (1862) VI. 422 The cavalry being assigned to Xenoclês, the Neodamode hoplites to Skythês.

neod(e)liche, variants of NEEDLY *adv. Obs.*

neodes, obs. form of NEEDS.

†**ˈneodful**, *a. Obs. rare.* [OE. *néodful*, f. *néod* zeal, etc.] Earnest, eager.

a **1000** *Juliana* 720 in *Exeter Bk.* 284 Bidde ic monne ȝehwone..þæt he mec neodful bi noman minum ȝemyne. *a* **1225** *Ancr. R.* 400 Þus neodful he was..to ontenden his luue in his leoues heorte.

neodi, neody, obs. forms of NEEDY *a.*

neodymium (niːəʊˈdɪmɪəm). *Chem.* [mod.L., f. G. *neodym* (C. A. von Welsbach 1885, in *Monatshefte f. Chem.* VI. 490), f. *neo-* NEO- + *di)dym* DIDYMIUM: see -IUM.] A metallic element that is a typical member of the lanthanide series, forms red compounds in which it has a valency of three (some of the salts being used for colouring glass and for glazes), and can also have a valency of two or four. Atomic number 60; symbol Nd.

1885 *Jrnl. Chem. Soc.* XLVIII. II. 1113 By repeated crystallisation of a mixture of the double nitrates of lanthanum and didymium with ammonium, the lanthanum salt was obtained pure, whilst the didymium salt separated into the salts of two new elements, neodymium and praseodymium. **1923** *Glasgow Herald* 16 Feb. 11 Number 61 is a rare-earth metal in the midst of that troop of strange elements with stranger names found chiefly in Scandinavian minerals; its neighbours are neodymium and samarium. **1971** *Sci. Amer.* June 20/3 At present solid-state ruby and neodymium-glass laser materials are used to obtain the highest peak-power output in pulsed operation. **1974** *Encycl. Brit. Micropædia* VII. 253/2 Of the rare earths, only cerium and yttrium are more plentiful than neodymium.

neofe, obs. form of NIEVE.

neoglacial (niːəʊˈgleɪsɪəl, -ˈgleɪʃəl), *a.* Also **Neo-**. [f. NEO- + GLACIAL *a.*] Of or pertaining to a neoglaciation; also *absol.*, a neoglacial period.

1960 *Amer. Jrnl. Sci.* CCLVIII. 325 Some Neoglacial ice bodies are judged to have attained a length of nearly two miles. **1970** *Sci. Amer.* June 103/3 In 1794, George Vancouver observed the position of ice in Glacier Bay. At that time glaciers in southern Alaska had begun to retreat from a maximum neoglacial position attained earlier in the 18th century. **1974** *Nature* 20/27 Dec. 680/1 During the Neoglacial, the three major advance phases of alpine and polar glaciers around 4,590–5,260, 2,100–2,940 and 40–460 yr b.p. were exactly contemporaneous with the three major post-Wisconsin volcanic phases..in New Zealand, Japan and southern South America.

neoglaciation (ˌniːəʊgleɪsɪˈeɪʃən). Also **Neo-**. [f. NEO- + GLACIATION.] A minor, short-lived increase in glaciation following the major glacial retreat at the end of the Ice Age.

Though freq. attributed to F. E. Matthes, the term appears not to have been used by him in print.

1951 J. H. MOSS *Early Man in Eden Valley* v. 62 In the Sierra Nevada, Matthes (1939) has described a similar set of small, very fresh moraines fronting the existing glaciers... They contrast sharply with the older moraines slightly farther down the valley. Matthes suggested the name Neoglaciation for the minor glacial pulsation represented by these moraines, and pointed out that it probably postdates the so-called Climatic Optimum. **1954** *Jrnl. Geol.* LIV. 340/1 Most of the moraines described in the literature which have been correlated with the Neoglaciation are close to, or in contact with, existing ice masses and are devoid of all vegetation. **1970** *Sci. Amer.* June 102 Historical records of the latest glacier fluctuations during neoglaciation are available from many alpine regions.

ˌneo-graˈmmarian, ˌneograˈmmarian. [f. NEO- + GRAMMARIAN.] A member of the JUNGGRAMMATIKER. Also as *adj.*

1885 *Encycl. Brit.* XVIII. 782/2 This younger school (often branded with the name of Neo-Grammarians, 'Junggrammatiker', by its opponents real and imaginary) is marked by certain distinct tendencies. **1933** L. BLOOMFIELD *Lang.* xx. 354 The neo-grammarian insists..that his hypothesis..sorts out the resemblances that are due to factors other than phonetic change. *Ibid.* 355 The opponents of the neo-grammarian hypothesis claim that resemblances which do not fit into recognized types of phonetic correspondence may be due merely to sporadic occurrence or deviation or non-occurrence of sound-change. **1947** E. STURTEVANT *Introd. Linguistic Sci.* vii. 70 In the 1870's a number of scholars announced..that phonetic laws have no exceptions. The earliest declaration ..seems to have been made by August Leskien in 1876, but the discovery really belonged to a group, who, from that time to this, have been called the neo-grammarians (*Junggrammatiker*). **1965** *Language* XLI. 188 Mention of the neogrammarians..can elicit so much emotional noise that no one can hear what you are saying. **1972** *Ibid.* XLVIII. 437 The subsequent section illustrates..the Neogrammarian position. *Ibid.*, Arens refers to Saussure's association with the Neogrammarians.

ˌneo-imˈpressionism. Freq. with capital initials. [ad. F. *néo-impressionnisme*, f. NEO- + IMPRESSIONISM.] A movement or style in art, originated by the French painter Georges Seurat (1859–91), and characterized by a systematic use of divisionism. Cf. POINTILLISM. So **ˌneo-imˈpressionist** *a.* and *sb.*

[**1886** F. FÉNÉON in *L'Art Moderne* 19 Sept. 302/1 La vérité est que la méthode néo-impressionniste exige une exceptionnelle délicatesse d'œil.] **1892** *Mag. of Art* p. xxxv/1 Though neo-impressionism has, indeed, asserted itself in the exhibitions of the Twenty, symbolism and realism also hold their own. *Ibid.*, M. Camille Pissaro, a neo-impressionist in his pictures, betrays Japanese influence in his woodcuts. **1901** *Sat. Rev.* 23 Feb. 240/1 Impressionism in France had..passed through the phases of luminism, vibration, pointillisme, independence and neo-impressionism, all comparatively short-lived extreme phases. **1903** *Studio* XXIX. 112/1 Coteries of artists..have ..tried to 'go one better', the most formidable and temporarily successful being that of the 'Néo-Impressionists'. **1908** R. FRY *Let.* Mar. (1972) I. 299 These neo-Impressionists follow straight upon the heels of the true Impressionists. **1914** A. J. EDDY *Cubists & Post-Impressionism* (1915) 27 Neo-Impressionism was the logical outcome of Impressionism. It was simply the attempt to paint light in still more scientific fashion, by the use of the primary colors laid on in fine points in such a manner that at the proper distance the points fuse and produce the tone desired. **1938** *Burlington Mag.* June 289/2 A confirmed disciple of the neo-impressionists. **1944** *Ibid.* Apr. 104/1 A history of the whole Neo-Impressionist movement. **1968** *Michelin Guide N.Y. City* 37 Adepts of Neo-Impressionism, like Seurat. **1972** *Country Life* 23 Nov. 1369/2 These artists' [*sc.* Futurists'] neo-Impressionist brushwork and Expressionist colour is invariably awful. **1975** *Physics Bull.* Feb. 59/2 Our start is the beginning of the 20th century, taking for granted the legacy of Leonardo Da Vinci, photography and the effects of the theories of colour on the neoimpressionists.

ˌneo-ˈLatin. Also **Neo-Latin.** [f. NEO- + LATIN *sb.*] **a.** = ROMANCE *sb.* 1. **b.** Latin in use since the end of the Renaissance. Also *attrib.* or as *adj.* Hence **ˌneo-ˈLatinist**, a writer of neo-Latin.

1850 *Gentl. Mag.* CXX. I. 143 The Neo-Latin or French dialect of the intruders. **1880–1** L. BONAPARTE in *Trans. Philol. Soc.* I. App. iii. *47 That the Latin neuter gender.. has almost disappeared from the greater number of the Neo-Latin dialects. **1946** H. JACOB *On Choice of Common Lang.* 16 Idiom Neutral is considered a neo-Latin rather than an autonomic system. **1951** [see COPULATIVE *a.* 1]. **1964** *Archivum Linguisticum* XVI. 4 The author's uniquely panoramic view of the neo-Latin languages. **1965** J. LAWLOR in J. Gibb *Light on C. S. Lewis* 79 Lewis consistently turned his neo-Latin authors into sixteenth-century English. **1966** *English Studies* XLVII. 150 Miss Røstvig stresses the importance of the hitherto neglected neo-Latinist Casimir Sarbiewski. **1970** B. M. H. STRANG *Hist. English* 130 These learned written sources, usually referred to as *Neo-Latin*, are not confined to the donation of whole words. *Ibid.*, The following suffixes come from Neo-Latin.

Neo-ˈLiberty. Also **Neoliberty.** [f. NEO- + LIBERTY *sb.*] A movement or style in architecture originating in Italy, a revival of *art nouveau*.

1959 *Archit. Rev.* CXXV. 232/2 Paolo Portoghesi seems to have been the first to call the style of the Retreat by the apt term 'Neoliberty' as late as the end of 1958. **1961** *Listener* 16 Feb. 300/1 There is Neo-Liberty in Italy, there is quite a lot of Neo-Gaudí, and there is Neo-Expressionism.

neo-ˈlinguist. Also **neolinguist.** [f. NEO- + LINGUIST.] A member of a school of linguistics which arose in opposition to the neo-grammarians, rejecting the claim that phonetic laws have no exception, and maintaining that linguistic change results from individual innovation. So **neo-linˈguistic** *a.*; **neo-linˈguistics** *sb. pl.*

[**1925** M. BARTOLI (*title*) Introduzione alla neolinguistica.] **1937** J. ORR tr. *Iordan's Introd. Romance Linguistics* i. 29 Here..is..the source of the misunderstanding between the neo-linguists..and the Italian neo-grammarians of to-day, with regard to their attitude towards Ascoli. *Ibid.* iii. 273 The so-called Neo-linguistic School, whose tenets..are little more than a somewhat hard-and-fast formulation of certain of Gilliéron's ideas. **1944** *Jrnl. Amer. Oriental Soc.* LXIV. 177 The *areal* theory of linguistics..has been developed and brought into a system by the Italian neolinguistic school. **1946** *Language* XXII. 273 Bartoli's 'Neo-Linguistics' has both a negative and a positive side. **1953** J. H. GREENBERG in A. L. Kroeber *Anthropology Today* 265/1 The reconstructions of the neo-linguistic school are not generally accepted by other scholars. **1972** *Language* XLVIII. 439 The Neo-Humboldtians in Germany and the Neolinguists in Italy.

neolite (ˈniːəʊlaɪt). *Min.* [See NEO- and -LITE: named by Scheerer, 1847.] Hydrous silicate of aluminium and magnesium.

1854 DANA *Syst. Min.* (ed. 4) II. 278 Neolite is a recent formation produced in mines at Arendal and Eisenach, through the agency of infiltrating waters that have passed over rocks containing magnesia. **1875** DAWSON *Dawn of Life* v. 118 *Neolite*, an alumino-magnesian silicate related to loganite and chlorite in composition. **1892** DANA *Syst. Min.* (ed. 6) 708 *Neolite*... In silky fibers stellately grouped.. colour green.

neolith (ˈniːəʊlɪθ). *Archæol.* [See next.]

1. A person belonging to the later stone age.

1882 G. Allen in *Knowledge* No. 17. 352 The neoliths were unacquainted with the use of metal, but they employed weapons and implements of stone,.. carefully ground and polished. **1883** *Pall Mall G.* 3 Oct. 2/1 The tall Saxon did not.. oust the shorter Celt or neolith.

2. A weapon or implement of the later stone age.

1882 *Jrnl. Anthropol. Inst.* XI. 136 *note*, As a connecting link between neoliths and palæoliths.. is a large series of quartz arrow-heads. **1894** *Nat. Sci.* Apr. 266 The usual neoliths on the surface.

3. *attrib.* Neolithic.

1882 *Jrnl. Anthropol. Inst.* XI. 136 It was found associated with other neolith weapons.

neolithic (niːəʊˈlɪθɪk), *a. Archæol.* [f. Gr. νέος new (see NEO-) + λίθος stone. Hence F. *néolithique*.] Of or belonging to the later stone age, characterized by the use of ground or polished stone implements and weapons.

1865 Lubbock *Preh. Times* i. 3 The later or polished Stone age; a period characterized by beautiful weapons and instruments made of flint and other kinds of stone... This we may call the 'Neolithic' period. **1874** Dawkins *Cave Hunt.* vi. 189 This ancient neolithic race of men. **1880** —— *Early Man in Brit.* i. 5 The lower Neolithic civilisation, characterised by the use of polished stone.

neolocal (niːəʊˈləʊkəl), *a. Anthrop.* [f. NEO- + LOCAL *a.*] Denoting a place of residence chosen by a newly-married couple which is independent of parental or family ties. Hence **neoˈlocally** *adv.*

1949 G. P. Murdock *Soc. Structure* i. 16 When a newly wedded couple, as in our own society, establishes a domicile independent of the location of the parental home of either partner.. residence may be called neolocal. **1958** F. M. Keesing *Cultural Anthrop.* x. 264 The married couple may.., as in the modern urban society, set up a home apart from the parents of both: neolocal (new-place). **1967** J. Deetz *Invitation to Archaeology* 95 We Americans reside *neolocally*, apart from both parents. **1973** *Times Lit. Suppl.* 6 July 774/5 Many young married couples must live 'neolocally': that is, away from the extended family households characteristic of other kinds of area.

neologian (niːəʊˈləʊdʒɪən), *a.* and *sb.* [f. NEOLOGY + -AN.]

A. *adj.* **1.** Inclined towards, or imbued with, theological neologism.

1833 R. Pinkerton *Russia* 144 The.. neologian literati and clergy of Germany. **1865** *Daily Tel.* 12 Apr. 6 Bavaria is the head-quarters of a neologian school. **1884** D. Hunter tr. *Reuss's Hist. Canon* xvi. 305 This truth.. has never been to the taste of scholars, orthodox or neologian.

2. Of the nature of, marked by, neologism.

1831 Macaulay in Napier *Sel. Corr.* (1879) 119 The neologian article about German divinity. **1851** Bp. Wilberforce *Let.* in *Life* (1881) II. iii. 109, I am not blind to the threatening evils of Neologian teaching.

B. *sb.* One who introduces or adopts new (rationalistic) views in theology; a neologist.

1846 *Brit. Quart. Rev.* III. 143 The argument.. will furnish some further employment to the critical powers of the Neologian. *a* **1857** R. A. Vaughan *Essays & Rem.* (1858) I. 50 The heathen philosophy of the Rationalist and the Neologian. **1875** Jowett *Plato* (ed. 2) I. 316 He thinks you are a neologian.

Hence **neoˈlogianism**, neologian views.

1846 Worcester cites *Eclectic Rev.* **1869** *Contemp. Rev.* XII. 274 He had himself passed through every phase of opinion.., except.. Romanism and neologianism.

neoˈlogic, *a. rare.* [See next.] = NEOLOGICAL.

1797 W. Taylor in *Monthly Rev.* XXIII. 486 Those neologic opinions which appear to require further elucidation. **1828-32** in Webster.

neological (niːəʊˈlɒdʒɪkəl), *a.* [ad. F. *néologique* (1726): see NEOLOGY and -ICAL.]

1. Dealing with, characterized by, new words or phrases. *rare.*

1754 Chesterfield *World* No. 101 ¶11 A genteel neological dictionary, containing those polite.. words and phrases, commonly used.. by the *beau monde*. **1774** *Chesterfield's Lett.* (1792) III. ccxxxvii. 83 The affected, the refined, the neological, or new and fashionable style, are at present too much in vogue at Paris.

2. Of the nature of, characterized by, neologism in theological views or doctrines.

1827 *Eclectic Rev.* July 26 Disgusted.. by the Neological infidelity of Protestant clergymen. **1841** D'Israeli *Amen. Lit.* (1867) 718 Some German systems, stripped of their deep neological disguise, have borrowed from Cudworth. **1870** Anderson *Missions Amer. Bd.* III. vi. 82 The advocates of the neological system.

Hence **neoˈlogically** *adv.* (Webster 1847.)

neologism (niːˈɒlədʒɪz(ə)m). [ad. F. *néologisme* (1735): see NEOLOGY and -ISM.]

1. a. The use of, or the practice of using, new words; innovation in language.

1800 W. Taylor in *Monthly Mag.* X. 318 Quaintness, the unavoidable companion of neologism, is.. hostile to grace. **1858** De Quincey *Language* Wks. IX. 76 Neologism, in revolutionary times, is not an infirmity of caprice. **1895** Saintsbury *Ess. Eng. Lit.* Ser. II. 34 Not.. alarmed at an appearance of neologism now and then.

b. A new word or expression.

1803 *Edin. Rev.* II. 104 Scotticisms, neologisms.. dance through each page. **1841** D'Israeli *Amen. Lit.* (1867) 361 Since that day neologisms have fertilised the barrenness of our Saxon. **1875** Maine *Hist. Inst.* ii. 52 The class which, to use a modern neologism, 'formulates' the ideas [etc.].

c. *Psychol.* An invented or concocted word or word-sound without recognizable meaning, freq. interpolated in otherwise correct sentences, and used by persons in a variety of neuropsychiatric disorders.

1905 A. J. Rosanoff tr. *Rogues de Fursac's Man. Psychiatry* ii. 46 Neologisms the meaning of which may remain absolutely enigmatical to the patient himself. *Ibid.* viii. 200 Neologisms are frequent in the period of dementia. **1906** J. H. Macdonald tr. *Bianchi's Textbk. Psychiatry* III. xiii. 680 In the typical form [of mania].. neologisms and symbols are found in great number. **1932** Cannon & Hayes *Princ. & Pract. of Psychiatry* 378 The verbal repetition of these 'new' words—neologisms or senseless words invented by himself. **1960** R. F. C. Hull tr. *Jung's Coll. Wks.* III. i. 25 Word-formations, which are so bizarre that they immediately bring to mind the neologisms of dementia praecox. **1969** W. Mayer-Gross et al. *Clin. Psychiatry* (ed. 3) v. 286 Other patients refer the origin of neologisms to hallucinatory experiences.

2. Tendency to, adoption of, novel (rationalistic) views in theology or matters of religion.

1827 *Eclectic Rev.* July 15 Neologism, a system which is not confined to Germany, but has been zealously fostered in other countries. **1851** Bp. Wilberforce *Let.* in *Life* (1881) II. iii. 108, I have seen for twenty-six years that Neologism was the peril which was before the English Church. **1865** *Guardian* 19 Apr. 401/2 However despicable.. the temper of modern neologism may be.

Hence **neoloˈgismal** *a.*

1836 *New Monthly Mag.* XLVIII. 455 The neologismal appellatives, 'tiger', and 'tigerism'.

neologist (niːˈɒlədʒɪst). [= F. *néologiste*: see NEOLOGY and -IST.]

1. One who invents or uses new words or forms; one who makes innovations in language.

1785 Trusler *Mod. Times* I. 135 He called himself a nealogist [*sic*], or a former of new words. **1814** D'Israeli *Quarrels Auth.* (1867) 481 The vicious neologist, who debases the purity of English diction by affecting new words or phrases. **1827** *Westm. Rev.* VIII. 395 We have an interesting anecdote.. inserted in the language of Gravina, as a hint to neologists.

2. One who adopts neologism in theology or religious matters; a rationalist.

1827 *Eclectic Rev.* July 3 They go under the denominations of Rationalists, Neologists, and Anti-supernaturalists. **1833** J. H. Newman *Arians* I. iv. (1876) 104 The Neologists of the present day deny that the miracles took place in the manner related in the sacred record. **1875** Merivale *Gen. Hist. Rome* li. (1877) 404 In vain had Rome attempted.. to ward off the attacks of the foreign neologists by pretending to interpret her own mythology and ritual. *attrib.* **1827** *Eclectic Rev.* July 17 Sentiments which will.. separate him from the Neologist divines. **1830** Pusey *Let.* in Liddon *Life* (1893) I. x. 242 The Neologist.. solution of miracles. **1864** —— *Lect. Daniel* (1876) 185 Neologist interpreters do not hesitate to admit this.

Hence **neoloˈgistic, neoloˈgistical** *adjs.*

1827 *Eclectic Rev.* July 18 The most false and dangerous notions.. lie at the basis of the Neologistic theory. **1935** *Mind* XLIV. 524 Philosophers who have absorbed a glut of new systems of logistic during the last decade.. must face the invention of yet another neologistic language with something like dismay. **1936** *Theology* XXXII. 73 The Catholic is quite sure that there is a God, and that in no neologistic sense.

neologiˈzation. *rare*⁻⁰. [f. next + -ATION.] The action of neologizing.

1846 Worcester cites Jefferson.

neologize (niːˈɒlədʒaɪz), *v.* [See NEOLOGY and -IZE.]

1. *intr.* To use new words or phrases; to make linguistic innovations.

1846 Worcester cites Jefferson. **1858** De Quincey *The. Grk. Trag.* Wks. IX. 56 At every step of the introvolution (to neologise a little in a case justifying a neologism). **1895** *Westm. Gaz.* 25 Nov. 4/2 Prone to take strange liberties with the language, and to neologise.

2. To introduce or accept new theological doctrines.

a **1882** Tulloch (Ogilvie), Dr. Candlish lived to neologize on his own account.

ˈneologous, *a. rare*⁻¹. [See next and -OUS.] Of the nature of neology.

1812 W. Taylor in *Monthly Rev.* LXVII. 465 The neologous omniscience of a German student.

neology (niːˈɒlədʒɪ). [ad. F. *néologie* (1762), f. *néo-* NEO- + *-logie*, Gr. -λογία: see -LOGY.]

1. The use of new terms. = NEOLOGISM 1.

1797 *Monthly Mag.* III. 417 Disfigured by neology, corruption, and barbarous modes of speech. **1812** Sir H. Davy *Chem. Philos.* Advt., Innovation will be censured.. and neology a constant reproach. **1870** M. Williams *Fuel of Sun* 38 He.. advocates the continued use of the term, in order to avoid neology.

b. A new word or term. = NEOLOGISM 1 b.

1846 Grove *Corr. Phys. Forces* 45, I cannot avoid this without a neology, which I have not the presumption to introduce. **1877** *Reg. Privy Council Scot.* I. Introd. 44 Neologies and corruptions of all kinds crept into the text.

2. Novel views in theology. = NEOLOGISM 2.

1834 Sir W. Hamilton *Discuss.* (1852) 506 The dangerous neology so deprecated in the German divines. **1848** Kingsley *Yeast* vi, He had been taught to scent German neology in everything, as some folks are taught to scent Jesuitry.

ˌneo-Malˈthusian, *a.* and *sb.* Also **Neo-Malthusian**. [f. NEO- + MALTHUSIAN *a.* and *sb.*] **A.** *adj.* Of or pertaining to the belief that the size of population should be controlled, *spec.* by the use of contraceptives. **B.** *sb.* An advocate of birth control or the limitation of population. So **ˌneo-Malˈthusianism**.

1885 J. Bonar *Malthus* I. i. 24 The questions associated in our own times with Neo-Malthusianism. **1901** J. A. Godfrey *Sci. Sex* II. vi. 253 The main points to be proved by the Neo-malthusian are, therefore, that it is advisable for society to have some means of checking the increase of population in advance, and that the means now at hand are both harmless and effective. **1910** G. B. Shaw *Brieux: a Preface* 31 Just about forty years ago the propaganda of Neo-Malthusianism changed the bearing of children from an involuntary condition of marriage to a voluntary one. *Ibid.*, The expectation of the Neo-Malthusians that the regulation of births in our families would give the fewer children born a better chance of survival.. has no doubt been fulfilled in some cases. **1911** Havelock Ellis *Stud. Psychol. Sex* VI. xii. 594 James Mill was the pioneer in advocating Neo-Malthusian methods. **1934** A. Huxley *Beyond Mexique Bay* 255 You cannot teach primitive Indians to practise the Neo-Malthusian techniques and expect them to remain primitive Indians. **1934** H. G. Wells *Experiment in Autobiogr.* II. vii. 436 The spreading knowledge of birth-control,—Neo-Malthusianism was our name for it in those days—seemed to justify my contention that love was now to be taken more lightly than it had been in the past. **1962** *Punch* 3 Jan. 52/1 Some neo-Malthusians have been heard to suggest that the bomb is Nature's Way.. of checking.. the.. over-spawning of our species. **1967** *Listener* 20 July 94/2 Mr Eversley.. dispelled any doubt in the minds of those listeners who felt guilty about having '*two* children and a motor-car'—apparently anti-social luxuries in the neo-Malthusian wave.

ˌNeo-Melaˈnesian. [f. NEO- + MELANESIAN *sb.*] (See quots.)

1961 Webster, *Neo-melanesian*, an English-based pidgin language used in New Guinea and the Solomon islands. **1962** *Listener* 20 Sept. 418/2 This word 'neo-Melanesian' is an indication of the changed status that pidgin English has in south-east Asia. The name is given to the pidgin that is spoken particularly in places like New Guinea, and a translation of the Bible has appeared in neo-Melanesian; grammars of neo-Melanesian and a dictionary of neo-Melanesian have appeared. **1972** W. B. Lockwood *Panorama Indo-European Lang.* 120 An important language used in the South Seas, technically known as Neo-Melanesian, but more popularly as Beach-la-Mar... Beach-la-Mar came to denote the Pidgin English spoken between East Australian and Melanesian tripang fishermen... Neo-Melanesian is.. of obvious political importance. **1973** *Sunday Times* (Colour Suppl.) 10 June 42/2 Pidgin is taught as a subject at Brisbane University and is referred to by some American scholars as 'Neo-Melanesian'.

neomen, ME. variant of *nimen* NIM *v.*

‖**neomenia** (niːəʊˈmiːnɪə). [eccl. L. *neomēnia*, a. Gr. νεομηνία (Attic νουμηνία), f. νέος new NEO- + μήνη moon.] In Greek and Jewish antiq., the time of the new moon, the beginning of the lunar month; also, the festival held at that time.

1398 Trevisa *Barth. De P.R.* ix. xxvii. (Bodl. MS.), þis feste þat hatte neomenia.. was swiþe hiȝe and holy. **1534** More *Treat. Passion* Wks. 1308/1 Amonge the Jewes Neomenia the fyrste daye of the new mone nexte after the Equynoctiall *in vere*.. is the fyrste daye of the yere. **1655** Stanley *Hist. Philos.* III. (1701) 75/1 The Neomenia of Hecatombæon did.. never precede the Solstice. **1727-38** Chambers *Cycl.* s.v., Some say, the Jews reckoned two kinds of *Neomenia*, or new moons. **1876** Birch *Rede Lect. Egypt* 26 The battle of Megiddo, fought.. in the neomenia of that month. **1888** tr. *Renan's Hist. Israel* I. 86 It will become the clarion of the neomenia and the trumpet of judgment.

So †**neomeny**. *Obs.* [Cf. F. *néoménie*.]

1382 Wyclif *Col.* ii. 16 In part of feeste day, or neomenye, or of sabotis. **1388** —— *Isa.* i. 13 Y schal not suffre neomenye, and sabat and othere feestis. *c* **1449** Pecock *Repr.* v. i. 481. **1569** J. Sanford tr. *Agrippa's Van. Artes* 84 b, Neomenies, (that is, the times of the newe Moone) perpetuall.

neomorph (ˈniːəʊmɔːf). [f. NEO- + -MORPH.]

1. *Biol.* An anatomical structure or feature that is of recent origin phylogenetically.

1886 W. N. Parker tr. *Wiedersheim's Elem. Compar. Anat. Vertebrates* 33 It is uncertain whether the dermal skeleton present in Armadillos.. is to be derived directly from that of Reptiles, or whether it is to be considered as formed independently, that is, as a new acquisition or 'neomorph' (Gadow).

2. *Genetics.* A mutant allele which effects a different character from that effected by the wild-type allele.

1932 H. J. Muller in *Proc. Sixth Internat. Congress Genetics* I. 245 Somewhat different from the negatively acting, competing mutant genes, or antimorphs, is the class which I am provisionally terming 'neomorphs'. A good example is the dominant mutant, Hairy wing, near the left end of the X chromosome. **1946** *Nature* 12 Oct. 520/1 Among spontaneous mutations which are known to occur at this locus some would be expected to be neomorphs. **1967** *Evolution* XXI. 850 (*heading*) Latent neomorphs and the evolution of dominance.

Hence **neoˈmorphic** *a.*, of, pertaining to, or being a neomorph (in either sense).

1903 *Rep. Brit. Assoc. Advancement of Sci.* 1902 631 Madagascar has yielded a Physa (*P. lamellata*) with a neomorphic gill, a character shared by species of Planorbis (*P. corneus* and *P. marginatus*). **1922** W. GARSTANG in *Jrnl. Linnean Soc.: Zool.* XXXV. 99, I propose in future to use *palæogenetic* and *neogenetic* when referring to ontogenetic processes, and *palæomorphic* and *neomorphic* when contrasting primitive and modified types of structure. **1932** H. J. MULLER in *Proc. Sixth Internat. Congress Genetics* I. 245 (*heading*) Neomorphic mutations. **1940** G. R. DE BEER *Embryos & Ancestors* xiv. 89 A palaeomorphic character may of course..have made its first appearance in early stages of ontogeny. Conversely, characters of more recent origin, to which Garstang applies the term neomorphic, may have originated in terminal ontogenetic or adult stages. **1966** E. A. CARLSON *Gene* xiii. 113 In this neomorphic class, Muller placed Bar eyes.

neomycin (niːəʊˈmaɪsɪn). *Pharm.* [f. NEO- + -MYCIN.] An antibiotic that is a mixture of two stereoisomers produced by a selected strain of *Streptomyces fradiæ*, is active against many strains of Gram-positive and Gram-negative bacteria, and is used (as the sulphate) in lotions and injections for treating a wide variety of infections and orally as an intestinal antiseptic; also, either of the two constituent isomers (*neomycin B* and *C*) or an inactive degradation product of them (*neomycin A*).

1949 WAKSMAN & LECHEVALIER in *Science* 25 Mar. 305/2 In search for new compounds, particular attention was paid to those that would be effective against streptomycin-resistant bacteria, notably against the streptomycin-resistant strains of *M[ycobacterium] tuberculosis*. The discovery of such an agent, designated as neomycin, is reported here. **1949** R. L. PECK et al. in *Jrnl. Amer. Chem. Soc.* LXXI. 2590/2 Evidence has been obtained that the neomycin activity is due to more than one chemical entity; hence one may define it as a 'neomycin-complex'. The substance isolated as described herein, has been designated neomycin A. **1960** M. E. FLOREY *Clinical Applications of Antibiotics* IV. v. 140 Neomycin..was expected to replace streptomycin since it was much less liable to induce resistance in pathogenic organisms. **1963** *Lancet* 19 Jan. 161/2 The infant [*sc.* a *Salmonella heidelberg* excretor] was treated with neomycin, and thereafter all specimens were negative. **1970** PASSMORE & ROBSON *Compan. Med. Stud.* II. xx. 30/1 Neomycin and kanamycin reduce ventilation during general anaesthesia by a neuromuscular blocking action. **1974** M. C. GERALD *Pharmacol.* iii. 45 The antibiotic neomycin is used to sterilize the gastrointestinal tract prior to abdominal surgery.

neon (ˈniːɒn). [Gr. νέον neut. of νέος new.]

1. *Chem.* One of the inert or noble gases, which is present in low concentration in the earth's atmosphere and is used at low pressure in discharge tubes, where it emits an orange-red glow. Atomic number 10; symbol Ne.

1898 SIR W. RAMSAY & TRAVERS in *Proc. Roy. Soc.* 438 The density of this gas, which we propose to name 'neon' (new) was next determined. **1905** *Chem. News* 5 May 204/1 A fair quantity of the mixture of neon and helium was prepared by liquefying air. **1935** *Industr. & Engin. Chem.* Jan. 116/1 Neon is characterized by its high electrical conductivity and light-emissive powers when an electrical current is discharged through it. **1966** *McGraw-Hill Encycl. Sci. & Technol.* IX. 36/1 Neon is used as the current-carrying agent in lightning arrestors; virtually no current is carried at voltages below the breakdown potential of the neon, but when lightning strikes, the neon is ionized and allows the current to flow to ground. **1966** COTTON & WILKINSON *Adv. Inorg. Chem.* (ed. 2) xxiii. 598 Helium, neon and argon have so far not been brought into chemical combination..and it seems unlikely that they are capable of reaction.

2. A neon lamp or tube; neon lighting. Also *fig.*

1934 S. GOLD *Neon* 18 Whilst the customer may want his name expressed in neon and surrounded by a border, it is up to the sign-man to supply it with 'finish'. **1957** J. BRAINE *Room at Top* vi. 54 Too clean and well-lighted. They'll be installing neons soon. **1958** *Spectator* 30 May 687/3 The dialogue [of a play] is stuffed as full of metaphors as a copywriter's prose and Tony Richardson's production sets up each phrase in neon. **1969** A. GLYN *Dragon Variation* v. 162 To the left it was the glare of the rest of the Strip, the great river of neon, the jazziest in the world. **1974** R. BUTLER *Buffalo Hook* iii. 26 The neons were flashing over the plushy restaurants.

3. *attrib.* and *Comb.*, as *neon advertisement, glow, lighting, strip, wilderness, world*; *neon-blazing, -bright, -coupled, -filled, -lighted, -lit* adjs.

1972 D. HASTON *In High Places* iv. 57 There was a neon advertisement by the entrance. **1962** K. ORVIS *Damned & Destroyed* xxvii. 206 The city's wide, neon-blazing Sunset Strip. **1958** *Spectator* 25 July 133/3 A neon-bright café. **1946** *Nature* 21 Sept. 414/1 The rectified signal from the second detector was amplified by a neon-coupled two-stage D.C. amplifier. **1935** MILLER & FINK *Neon Signs* iii. 37 (*caption*) Relative light energy from a neon-filled tube. **1966** *McGraw-Hill Encycl. Sci. & Technol.* IX. 36/1 A very small wattage produces visible light in neon-filled glow lamps. **1935** MILLER & FINK *Neon Signs* iii. 37 Why is it, then, that the neon glow has such a powerful effect? **1945** A. HUXLEY *Time must have Stop* xxx. 276 The neon glow from those technological New Jerusalems beyond the horizons of the next revolution. **1936** C. ROUSE *Old Towns* i. 21 Inside, a neon-lighted glass sign directs you to 'Ye olde Beamed Tudor Cocktail Bar'. **1954** *Encounter* Feb. 37/2 It begins, in the West, with the neon-lighted brilliance of the Kurfürstendamm. **1913** *Trans. Illum. Engin. Soc.* (U.S.) 371 (*heading*) Neon lighting. **1933** *Times* 5 Dec. (Electricity Supply Number) p. xxiii/7 Neon lighting can be seen in almost every town of any size in the country. **1958** *Times Lit. Suppl.* 31 Jan. 63/2 His wrath is only excited by the Subtopia, the neon lighting, the petrol fumes, the 'soulless concrete' of our time. **1954** Neon-lit [see ASPIRIN]. **1958** *Spectator* 14 Feb. 197/1 The actress, the best-selling author, or the famous film star who..remain tragically single, trapped in their own accursed, neon-lit achievement. **1972** R. BUSBY *Reasonable Man* iii. 24 They left the car outside the store and went..into the brash, neon-lit interior. **1939** 'J. STRUTHER' *Mrs. Miniver* 243 This part of the town was almost unrecognizable—a street of angular lettering and neon strips. **1973** 'H. HOWARD' *Highway to Murder* xiii. 149 Over the dressing chest a neon strip shone down on jars and bottles. **1953** *Encounter* Nov. 8/1 The neon wilderness of noise and music, fun and sin, boredom and high, desperate spirits. **1959** *Listener* 10 Dec. 1048/3 The American neon-wilderness. **1959** *New Statesman* 28 Feb. 302/3 Living in a neon-world of semi-legality, its leadership organises conferences and 'stay-at-homes' as if keeping the government informed about its intentions was a rule in the revolutionary game.

b. Special Comb.: **neon fish** = *neon tetra*; **neon lamp, light**, a lamp in which an electric discharge is passed through neon (giving an orange-red coloured light) or a mixture of neon with other gases (giving other colours); **neon sign**, a sign incorporating a neon light (usu. a neon tube), and often serving as an advertisement on a building; **neon tetra**, a small characin, *Hyphessobrycon innesi*, native to the Amazon, and remarkable for its colouring, which is dark green and white with a shining blue-green stripe; **neon tube**, a neon light in the form of a tube.

1938 L. MACNEICE *Zoo* 182 The tiniest fish here are the neon fish. **1911** *Chem. Abstr.* V. 1024 In contradistinction to the Hg vapor lamp the neon lamp's light is rich in red rays. **1931** *B.B.C. Year-bk.* 447/1 A special type of neon lamp is now used in television receivers to convert the electrical impulses back into light impulses, dependent for its action on a linear relation between light response and applied electrical potential and on an absence of time-lag. **1940** L. MACNEICE *Last Ditch* 15 And the neon-lamps of London Stain the canals of night. **1966** AINSWORTH & ROBINSON in Hewitt & Vause *Lamps & Lighting* xix. 309 Neon lamps using the positive column as the light source do exist however, the conventional 'neon lamps' used in advertising displays being of this type. **1913** *Trans. Illum. Engin. Soc.* (U.S.) 376 The neon light is physiologically excellent on account of its dull luminescence. **1931** H. G. WELLS *Work, Wealth & Happiness of Mankind* (1932) v. 211 This Neon light has great penetrating power in a fog. **1958** J. BETJEMAN *Coll. Poems* 231 So up I rose and went along To that old village alehouse where In neon lights is written 'Bear'. **1972** J. POTTER *Going West* 38 'Aloha', the airport tower announced in neon lights... Aloha meant welcome. **1927** *Advertising & Selling* 28 Dec. 34/3 Neon signs overcome the handicap of high first cost by lowered current consumption. **1934** *Times* 19 Feb. 13/5 In two of our quiet residential streets flaring neon signs have been put up to announce that the houses on which they are placed are hotels. **1958** J. BETJEMAN *Coll. Poems* 232 The neon sign's a work of art and visible for miles. **1973** *Black World* Mar. 62 Pulsating rock music seemed to control the flashing neon signs. **1936** W. T. INNES in *Aquarium* V. 82/2 The recent feat of bringing some wonderful new Characins, Neon Tetras (*Hyphessobrycon innesi* Myers), from Germany to the Shedd Aquarium in Chicago..in less than 60 hours. *Ibid.* 135/2 Regarding the Neon fishes... Four of these fishes were dead when the airship arrived... The red coloring from the fishes had made bright red blotches on the paper. *Ibid.* 136/2 The very good descriptive popular name for the fish, 'Neon Tetra' or 'Neontet' was originated by M. Lepaut, of Paris... The name is so fitting that Mr. Lew Willumsen, on seeing the new importation, independently hit upon the same name for them. **1952** D. GOHM *Tropical Fish* 100 The Neon Tetra is generally regarded as the most beautiful of all aquarium fish. **1962** *Listener* 22 Nov. 852/2 One [*sc.* tropical fish] which seemed to be lit up by a greenish blue light running from his head to his tail—this was a neon tetra. **1971** *Ceylon Observer Mag. Ed.* (Colombo) 19 Sept. 2/6 (Advt.), Goldfish, Angelfish, Neontetras. **1904** *Electr. World & Engin.* XLII. 583/2 The wavelength of the oscillator's vibration can..be measured by isolating a complete wave on the helix by means of a sliding earthed saddle using a neon tube as indicator. **1936** *Discovery* Nov. 364/2 The manufacture, erection, and maintenance of all neon tubes for advertising and display purposes. **1945** R. C. WALKER *Electronic Equipment & Accessories* xi. 211 Fig. 187 shows an application of the neon tube as a voltage stabiliser in a valve-rectifier circuit. **1962** A. NISBETT *Technique Sound Studio* 272 Stroboscopes work best with neon tubes.

neonate (ˈniːəʊneɪt). *Med.* [f. NEO- + L. *nāt-us* born.] A recently born individual; *spec.* an infant less than four weeks old. Also *attrib.* or as *adj.*

1932 M. B. McGRAW in *Child Development* III. 292/1 Most 'partunates'[1] display a decidedly helpless response to the force of gravity. [*Note*] [1] A term indicating infants who are just born... It covers about the first fifteen or thirty minutes of life since it includes the time during and immediately following parturition. When the umbilical cord is dressed and the baby is taken to the maternity nursery, then he becomes a 'neonate'. **1936** *Q. Rev. Biol.* XI. 70 (*heading*) Problems in the classification of neonate activities. **1951** L. CARMICHAEL in S. S. Stevens *Handbk. Exper. Psychol.* viii. 289/1 The fetus shows most of the specific patterns of response that can be elicited in the neonate. **1962** *Lancet* 12 May 1026/2 Neonates are capable of withstanding quite profound hypothermia for a short period of time. **1967** *Nature* 10 June 1099/2 The dentate gyrus is considerably more mature in the neonate guinea-pig than in the rat. **1973** *Jrnl. Genetic Psychol.* CXXII. 320 The overall body proportions of the typical neonate, 2-year-old, 6-year-old, [etc.].

neonatology (niːəʊneɪˈtɒlədʒɪ). *Med.* [f. prec. + -OLOGY.] The branch of medicine concerned with the disorders and problems of recently born infants. Hence **neonaˈtologist**, an expert or specialist in neonatology.

1960 A. J. SCHAFFER *Diseases of Newborn* 1/1 We trust we shall be forgiven for coining the words 'neonatology' and 'neonatologist'. We do not recall ever having seen them in print. The one designates the art and science of diagnosis and treatment of disorders of the newborn infant, and the other the physician whose primary concern lies in this specialty. *Ibid.* p. vi/1 The situation of the pediatrician practising neonatology differs but little qualitatively from his everyday posture with respect to older infants and children. **1967** *Obstetrics & Gynecol.* XXX. 890 The obstetric trainee would assume the role of a pediatric resident in the field of neonatology. **1972** *Daily Colonist* (Victoria, B.C.) 3 Aug. 26/5 The intensive care unit.. combines the disciplines of both fetology and neonatology. **1975** *Sci. Amer.* Jan. 51 (Advt.), Most neonatologists contend that many of these tragedies can be prevented by specially-trained perinatal medical teams using intensive care techniques.

neoned (ˈniːɒnd), *a.* [f. NEON + -ED[2].] Illuminated by neon lighting.

1945 *Tomorrow* Mar. 46 The shadow went, he hardly noticed that he was already moving again toward the neoned glare. **1968** *Punch* 29 May 778/3 We..came upon an imperfectly neoned structure which might have passed for a church hall. **1973** J. WAINWRIGHT *Devil you Don't* 34 The neoned entrance to the *Roll-a-Ball Arcade*.

ˈneonism. *rare*$^{-0}$. [irreg. f. Gr. νέον (see NEON) new + -ISM.] Neologism.

1846 WORCESTER cites HUNTER.

neonomian (niːəʊˈnəʊmɪən), *sb.* and *a.* [f. Gr. νέος NEO- + νόμος law, after ANTINOMIAN.] **a.** *sb.* One who maintains that the Gospel is a new law entirely supplanting the old or Mosaic law. **b.** *adj.* Pertaining to the assertion of a new law.

1692 CHAUNCY *Neonomianism Unmasked* Ep. Ded., One that Asserts the Old Law is abolished..but pleads for a New Law, and Justification by the Works of it, and there-fore is a Neonomian. *Ibid.* A iv, Some of the Paradoxes contained in the Neonomian Scheme. **1693** G. FIRMIN *Rev. Mr. Davis's Vind.* ii. 20 Whither Mr. Crisp, and Mr. Davis, will charge me there-fore to be a Neonomian, I cannot tell. **1882–3** SCHAFF *Encycl. Relig. Knowl.* II. 1417 Antinomian error and Neonomian heresy. *Ibid.*, Every effort was made by the Neonomians to prevent the settlement of ministers holding the Marrow doctrines.

Hence **neoˈnomianism**. (See quot. 1882–3.)

1692 CHAUNCY (*title*) Neonomianism Unmask'd: or, The Ancient Gospel pleaded, against the other, called a New Law or Gospel. **1882–3** SCHAFF *Encycl. Relig. Knowl.* II. 1622 Neonomianism.., a term..applied to the views of Dr. Daniel Williams and his adherents because they defined and construed Christianity as a 'new law'.

neopallium (niːəʊˈpælɪəm). *Anat.* Also (with hyphen) **neo-pallium**. Pl. **-pallia**. [mod.L., f. NEO- 1 e + PALLIUM.] The phylogenetically youngest portion of the pallium of the brain, which appears first among the more advanced reptiles and which among the mammals has become the largest part of the brain. Cf. NEOCORTEX.

1901 G. E. SMITH in *Jrnl. Anat. & Physiol.* XXXV. 431 It is only one of the three histological formations which constitute the true pallium; and, as it is the latest of these to reach the height of its development, we may call it the 'new pallium' or..'neopallium', in contradistinction to the 'old pallium' of the Sauropsida and earlier Vertebrata, which is *chiefly* formed of the other two pallial areas. **1907** *Arch. Neurol.* III. 51 Maps have been obtained of these neopallia which are fairly full. *Ibid.* 52 The term neopallium is employed throughout in the sense suggested by Elliot Smith to indicate the variable area intercalated between the 'basal pallium' or pyriform lobe and the marginal pallium, or hippocampus. **1922** *Glasgow Herald* 23 Dec. 4/2 When our ancestors, with their free hands, their enlarged cerebral cortex or neopallium, and their capacity for co-operative action, had resources sufficient to enable them to stand up to Carnivores.., they left the trees and became once more terrestrial. **1948** A. BRODAL *Neurol. Anat.* x. 323 With the development of the neopallium or neo-cortex, the two more primitive areas are finally pushed medially, and in man are found entirely on the medial aspect of the hemisphere. **1973** *Gray's Anat.* (ed. 35) vii. 921/1 In the course of evolution visual, auditory and other conduction paths have been transferred, through the thalamus, to the pallium of the cerebral hemispheres... Consequently, each cerebral hemisphere enlarges as a result of the formation of an additional region, the neopallium.

Hence **neoˈpallial** *a.*, of or pertaining to the neopallium.

1907 *Arch. Neurol.* III. 112 This appears to be the lowest grade of conscious neopallial association—*i.e.*, of psychic function. **1921** TILNEY & RILEY *Form & Functions Central Nervous Syst.* xlii. 772 (*heading*) Neopallial projection system. **1953** G. A. G. MITCHELL *Anat. Autonomic Nerv. Syst.* v. 66 This neopallial responsibility for autonomic activities is shared by subcortical centres in the hypothalamus. **1962** E. C. CROSBY et al. *Correl. Anat. Nerv. Syst.* vii. 411/1 Neopallial cortex makes up the major portion of the cerebral cortex in man.

neophilia (niːəˈfɪlɪə). [f. NEO- + -PHILIA.] Love for, or great interest in, what is new; a love of novelty. So **neoˈphiliac**, a person characterized by neophilia; also **neoˈphili(a)c** *a.*; **neˈophily**.

1932 B. MALINOWSKI in R. F. Fortune *Sorcerers of Dobu* p. xxvii, Terminological neophily..is a habit to which I have always been hostile. **1966** R. & D. MORRIS *Men & Apes* vii. 217 There is a perpetual struggle going on inside the brain, between the fear of the new (neophobia) and the love of the new (neophilia). The neophobic urges keep the animal out of danger, while the neophilic urges prevent him from becoming too set in his ways. **1969** C. BOOKER (*title*) The neophiliacs. **1971** R. PETRIE *Thorne in Flesh* xi. 142 From where Thorne had sat, without neophiliac needs, he had seen.. not spangles but sweating flesh. **1972** *Daily Tel.* 2 Aug. 2/2 The exaltation of novelty (neophilia) had been turned into a cult. *Ibid.*, Neophiliacs suffer from a collective fantasy which leads them to describe every change as inevitable and an improvement on what preceded it.

neophron (ˈniːəʊfrɒn). [L. *Neophron* (a. Gr. νεόφρων), the name of a man transformed into a vulture in the *Metamorphoses* of Antoninus Liberalis: adopted as a generic name by Savigny.] The white Egyptian vulture, or a vulture belonging to the same genus.

1833 SELBY *Illustr. Brit. Ornith.* (ed. 2) 4 Egyptian Neophron. **1840** *Cuvier's Anim. Kingd.* 165 The Neophrons ..have a long and slender beak. *Ibid.* 166 The White Neophron. **1848** *Zoologist* VI. 1959 A tame neophron, kept at the public slaughter-house at Malaga.

neophyte (ˈniːəʊfaɪt). Also 6–7 (9) **-phite**. [= F. *néophyte* (†*neofite*, 14th c.), ad. eccl. L. *neophytus*, ad. Gr. νεόφυτος (1 Tim. iii. 6), lit. 'newly planted', f. νέος NEO- + φυτόν plant, φυτεύειν to plant.

Not in general use before the 19th c. Its employment in the Rheims N.T., though defended by the translators, was objected to by their contemporaries:—

1582 N. T. (Rhem.) Pref. to Rdr. ciij, If Proselyte be a received word in the English bibles, .. why may not we be bold to say, Neophyte? **1583** FULKE *Def. Tr. Script.* iii. (1843) 207 Except you would coin such ridiculous inkhorn terms, as you do in the New Testament, *azymes, prepuce, neophyte*.. and such like. *a* **1603** T. CARTWRIGHT *Confut. Rhem. N.T.* Pref. (1618) 35 Neophyte, to a bare Englishman is nothing at all, no more then *depositum, exinanited, exhaust*.]

1. a. A new convert; one newly admitted to a church or religious body. Used chiefly with ref. to the primitive Christian, or the Roman Catholic, Church; in the latter also applied to a newly ordained priest, or to a novice of a religious order.

a **1550** *Image Hypocr.* II. in *Skelton's Wks.* (1843) II. 423/2 Of these neophites, And pevishe proselites, Springe vpp ipocrites. **1582** N.T. (Rhem.) 1 Tim. iii. 6 Not a neophyte: lest being puffed up with pride, he fall into the judgment of the devil. **1610** DONNE *Pseudo-martyr* 341 What opinion was held of our Bishoppe Grosthead.. a late Neophite of your Church hath obserued. *a* **1661** FULLER *Worthies, Durham* I. (1662) 293 S. Paul forbidding such a Neophyte or Novice admission into that Office. **1760** T. HUTCHINSON *Hist. Mass.* iii. (1765) 264 To secure his neophytes or converts to the interest of his sovereign. **1834** LYTTON *Pompeii* IV. iv, The face of the old man was as balm to the excited spirit of the neophyte. **1876** FARRAR *Marlb. Serm.* iii. 23 Nor in the inexperienced neophyte.. do we expect the vision of the mystic.

†**b.** In predicative use as adj. *Obs. rare*⁻¹.

1600 HAKLUYT *Voy.* (1811) IV. 559 Being Neophyte (that is) newly come to the fayth, and not yet confirmed in our religion.

2. One who is new to a subject; a beginner, tyro, novice.

1599 B. JONSON *Ev. Man out of Hum.* v. iv, Away, neophite, do as I bid thee, bring my dear George to me. **1601** —— *Poetaster* I. ii, He tells thee true, my noble Neophyte. **1648** GAGE *West Ind.* xii. 66 Better observations then myself (who am but a Neophyte) am able to deduct. **1826** SCOTT *Woodst.* ix, It was almost ludicrous to see how often the hand of the neophyte directed itself naturally to a large black leathern jack. **1841** D'ISRAELI *Amen. Lit.* (1867) 116 These editors assuredly have scared away many a neophyte in our vernacular literature. **1874** COOKE *Fungi* 1 Such an encounter usually perplexes the neophyte at first.

attrib. **1599** B. JONSON *Cynthia's Rev.* III. i, It is with your young grammaticall courtier, as with your neophyte-player. **1860** ADLER *Prov. Poet.* xv. 310 The neophyte warrior was required to take an oath.. dictated by the Church. **1883** STEVENSON *Silverado Sq.* 44 A certain neophite and girlish trepidation.

3. *Bot.* A plant found in an area in which it has not been recorded before.

1916 B. D. JACKSON *Gloss. Bot. Terms* (ed. 3) 248/1 Neophyte.. a newly introduced plant (Rikli). **1970** *Watsonia* VIII. 157 Besides these three widespread neophytes, some other exotic taxa occur as ornamentals in gardens and parks.

Hence **ˈneophytic, ˈneophytish** *adjs.*; also **ˈneophytism**, the condition of a neophyte.

1862 *Temple Bar* IV. 476, I might plead my neophytism as an excuse. **1886** *Pall Mall G.* 6 Sept. 3/1 Rushing to this conclusion with.. neophytic ardour. **1897** *Daily News* 7 July 7/3 Every limb of the law, however neophytish he might be.

neopilina (niːəʊpɪˈlaɪnə). [mod.L. (H. Lemche 1957, in *Nature* 23 Feb. 414/1), f. NEO- + *Pilina*, name of a similar fossil genus of molluscs.] A primitive, deep-sea mollusc of the monotypic genus so called, belonging to the order Monoplacophora.

1957 H. LEMCHE in *Nature* 23 Feb. 416/1 It would seem probable.. that one of the main food-sources of *Neopilina* is radiolarians. **1959** *Listener* 12 Feb. 300/2 The recent discovery of *Neopilina*.. is scientifically quite as important as that of the coelacanth. **1968** A. S. ROMER *Procession of Life* v. 101 Belief as to the primitive nature of these little ancient molluscs was abundantly confirmed by the discovery by a Danish oceanographic vessel a few years ago of specimens of a modern descendant of *Pilina*, living in deep oceanic waters off the west coast of South America; American exploration has resulted in further finds of this small mollusc, appropriately named *Neopilina*... Little *Neopilina* has aroused little public interest, but scientifically it is far more important than *Latimeria*... *Neopilina* sheds much light on the origin of a whole animal phylum. **1973** P. TASCH *Paleobiol. Invertebrates* viii. 325/2 *Neopilina* is segmented (that is, has internal metamerism) in a way similar to that of annelid worms and arthropods.

neoplasia (niːəʊˈpleɪzɪə). *Biol.* and *Med.* [f. NEO- + Gr. πλάσις formation: see -IA¹.] The formation of neoplasms; the state or condition of having neoplastic growth.

1890 C. P. MITCHELL *Philosophy Tumour-Dis.* i. 7 (*heading*) Explanation of the self-dependence of tumours: neoplasia identified with genesis in the Protozoa. **1926** *Glasgow Herald* 22 May 7/2 No one who had made a broad study of neoplasia of all varieties could support either of those theses. **1947** *Radiology* XLIX. 358/2 The late effects resulting from exposure to penetrating radiations.. consisted of generalized atrophy and neoplasia of hemopoietic organs. **1962** *New Scientist* 12 Apr. 48/2 These processes do resemble in certain respects neoplasia. **1970** *Nature* 18 Apr. 290/1 The general belief in clinical circles is that bladder tumours are.. produced as the result of chemical constituents in the urine which act on the urinary epithelium and produce neoplasia.

neoplasm (ˈniːəʊplæz(ə)m). *Path.* [f. NEO- + Gr. πλάσμα formation: cf. F. *néoplasme*.] A new growth or formation of tissue in some part of the body; a tumour.

1864 W. T. FOX *Skin Dis.* 67 Hypertrophies. Atrophies. Neoplasms. **1876** GROSS *Dis. Bladder*, etc. 136 Papillary fibroma, or villous growth, is by far the most frequent of the fibrous neoplasms. **1896** *Allbutt's Syst. Med.* I. 113 *note*, Neoplasms as a class.. not improbably develop as a consequence of some irritation.

So **neoˈplasma** (*pl.* **-plasmata**).

1876 tr. *Wagner's Gen. Pathol.* 355 Growths, neoplasmata, are, histologically speaking, homœoplastic or heteroplastic. **1876** DUHRING *Dis. Skin* 46 They are.. produced in great part by the cellular neoplasmata.

neoplastic (niːəʊˈplæstɪk), *a.*¹ *Path.* [Cf. prec. and PLASTIC.] Pertaining to, of the nature of, a neoplasm.

1890 in *Cent. Dict.* **1896** *Allbutt's Syst. Med.* I. 113 *note*, There is evidence.. favouring this relationship between inflammation and neoplastic growth. **1899** *Ibid.* VI. 222 A neoplastic tuberculous mass.

ˌneo-ˈplasticism. Freq. with capital initials. [ad. F. *néoplasticisme*, f. NEO- + PLASTICISM.]

A movement or style in art originated by the Dutch painter Piet Mondrian (1872–1944), characterized by the use of primary colours and abstract forms. So **neoˈplastic** *a.*²; **neoplaˈstician; neoˈplasticist** *a.*

[**1920** P. MONDRIAN (*title*) Le Néo-plasticisme.] **1933** *Gallery of Living Art Catal.: A.E. Gallatin Coll.* (N.Y.), Mondrian, the neo-plastician. **1934** J. J. SWEENEY *Plastic Redirections in 20th Cent. Painting* 40 Piet Mondrian, member of the Dutch 'de Stijl' group and founder of the Neoplastic school, can.. be taken as a producer of .. 'abstractions'... Yet, Mondrian has said, 'It is a great error to envisage a Neoplastic work as a total abstraction from life.' *Ibid.* 69 Such groups as the Purists, the Neo-plasticians, and the Constructivists. **1935** *Art Digest* 15 Jan. 9/1 The Gallery of Living Art at New York University.. has reopened after redecoration... In the rearrangement, emphasis has been placed on the work of the Cubists and on Constructivism and Neo-plasticism. **1936** A. H. BARR in *Cubism & Abstract Art* (N.Y. Mus. Mod. Art) 140 (*heading*) Abstract art in Holland: *de Stijl* and Neo-Plasticism. *Ibid.* 144 This project is clearly a three-dimensional projection of a Neo-Plasticist painting. **1970** *Oxf. Compan. Art* 770/2 Neo-plasticism.. was distinguished from Cubism in that it did not make use of figurative elements even as a starting-point for abstraction.

Neoplatonic (niːəʊpləˈtɒnɪk), *a.* [f. NEO- + PLATONIC *a.*] **A.** *adj.* Of or pertaining to Neoplatonism or the Neoplatonists. **B.** *sb.* = NEOPLATONIST.

1836–7 SIR W. HAMILTON *Metaph.* vi. (1859) I. 107 The Neoplatonic system, of which the last great representative is Proclus. **1840** E. COX tr. *Döllinger's Hist. Church* i. 71 The Neoplatonics endeavoured, therefore, to unite the different systems of philosophy, especially the Pythagorean, Platonic, and Aristotelean, in one body with the principles of oriental learning. **1877** LECKY *Europ. Mor.* (ed. 3) I. 335 The Pythagorean and Neoplatonic schools revived the feeling of religious reverence, inculcated humility. **1879** *Dublin Rev.* Apr. 524 On the Catholic side no theologian has followed Scotus Erigena: his system may be called an offspring of the Neoplatonics.

Hence **neoplaˈtonically** *adv.*

1886 *Encycl. Brit.* XXI. 429/2 The Neoplatonically conceived *Fons Vitæ* of the Jew Gebirol.

Neoplatoˈnician, *a.* and *sb. rare.* [f. as NEOPLATONIC *a.* + -IAN, or ad. F. *néo-platonicien*.] **a.** *adj.* Neoplatonic. **b.** *sb.* A Neoplatonist.

1831 *Fraser's Mag.* IV. 54 The Neo-platonician doctrines emanated from this school. **1842** BRANDE *Dict. Sci.*, etc., Neoplatonicians, or Neoplatonists.

Neoplatonism (niːəʊˈpleɪtənɪz(ə)m). [f. NEO- + PLATONISM: cf. F. *néo-platonisme*.] A philosophical and religious system, chiefly consisting of a mixture of Platonic ideas with Oriental mysticism, which originated at Alexandria in the 3rd century, and is especially represented in the writings of Plotinus, Porphyry, and Proclus.

1845 LEWES *Hist. Philos.* II. 192 In losing Julian, Neo-Platonism lost its power, political and religious. **1869** LECKY *Europ. Mor.* (1877) I. 325 Neoplatonism and the philosophies that were allied to it were fundamentally pantheistic.

Neoplatonist (niːəʊˈpleɪtənɪst). [f. NEO- + PLATONIST.] One of the originators or adherents of Neoplatonism.

1837 WHEWELL *Hist. Induct. Sci.* IV. iii. I. 284 Ammonius Saccas.. is looked upon as the beginner of the Neoplatonists. **1853** KINGSLEY *Hypatia* Pref. 7 The great Neo-Platonists were.. persons of the most rigid and ascetic virtue. **1882** FARRAR *Early Chr.* I. 263 The dislike of the body.. which was afterwards so strongly felt by the Neoplatonists.

attrib. **1856** R. A. VAUGHAN *Mystics* (1860) II. XIII. i. 252 The ultra-Neoplatonist rodomontade he utters in praise of mathematics. **1869** LECKY *Europ. Mor.* I. 356 The Pythagorean and Neoplatonist [*ed.* 3 Neoplatonic] schools.

Neopolitan, obs. form of NEAPOLITAN.

neoprene (ˈniːəʊpriːn). [f. NEO- + *-prene*, after ISOPRENE, CHLOROPRENE.] Any of various synthetic rubbers made by polymerizing chloroprene (2-chloro-1,3-butadiene, CH_2:CCl·CH:CH_2) and useful for their resistance to oil, heat, and weathering and their higher strength than natural rubber.

1937 *Du Pont Mag.* Feb. 16/3 As of December 15th the name *Neoprene* has been adopted to describe our chloroprene rubber formerly sold under the trade-mark 'DuPrene'. **1939** *Jrnl. R. Aeronaut. Soc.* XLIII. 150 In the matter of fuel tank construction, there are just about as many welded tanks as riveted tanks, the latter using duprene or neoprene as a leak preventative. **1950** *Archit. Rev.* CVIII. 411 Exterior butt joints are sealed with a flexible neoprene tube which is compressed when the panels are bolted together. **1957** H. L. FISHER *Chem. Natural & Synthetic Rubbers* ix. 101 The neoprenes are available in several types of latexes. **1959** *Observer* 27 Sept. 4/3 Diving-suits, made out of 'expanded neoprene' (a kind of foamed rubber), are now coming on the market. **1959** J. P. MUNN in M. Morton *Introd. Rubber Technol.* xiii. 339 Neoprene Type KNR is a soft, chemically plasticizable type, suitable for the production of cement, paints, and in spreading compounds. **1969** *New Scientist* 28 Aug. 430/3 The pyrotechnical compound is ignited by applying a soldering iron or propane gas flame to a small ignition hole. The heat makes the neoprene gasket expand to form a continuous seal. **1974** 'J. GRAHAM' *Bloody Passage* i. 24, I took down a neoprene wetsuit in black and pulled it on.

neore, were not: see NERE *Obs.*

neosa, variant of NEOZA.

neose, obs. variant of NESE, nose.

neossine (niːˈɒsaɪn). [f. Gr. νεοσσ-ός a young bird + -INE⁵.] The substance of which the edible birds' nests of the East are made, being a mucus secreted by the salivary glands of a genus of swifts (*Collocalia*). Hence **neˈossidine**.

1849 tr. *Mulder's Chem. Veg. & Anim. Physiol.* 241 The mucus from the œsophagus of the swallows, which in India build their edible nests of it... The pure mucous matter, which I called neossine, consists of [etc.]. **1894** MORLEY & MUIR *Watts' Dict. Chem.* IV. 342/2 It.. is chiefly composed of a hyalogen (*neossine*), which yields as its hyalin, *neossidine*.

neoˈssology. *Ornith.* [f. as prec. + -LOGY.] That part of ornithology which deals with the hatching and rearing of the young.

1864 NEWTON in *Zool. Record* (1865) I. 61.

neˈossoptile. *Ornith.* [f. as prec. + πτίλον a down-feather.] One of the soft feathers of a newly-hatched bird, as contrasted with those of a mature type (*teleoptiles*).

1893 GADOW in Newton *Dict. Birds* 243 Soft feathers.. possessing several characters which make it advisable to distinguish them by the name of 'Neossoptiles'.

neostriatum (niːəʊstraɪˈeɪtəm). *Anat.* [mod.L., f. NEO- 1 e + STRIATUM.] The phylogenetically younger portion of the corpus striatum, consisting essentially of the caudate nucleus and the putamen.

1909 *Arch. Neurol. & Psychiatry* IV. 163 As the nucl. med. thal. (and also the nucl. rotund.) receive trigeminal fillet-fibres, it results that the first neocortical tactile region is one of oral sensibility (just as the first neostriatum). **1929** *Physiol. Abstr.* XIV. 398 (*heading*) Morphogenesis of neo- and palæostriatum in man. **1972** T. W. JENKINS *Functional Mammalian Neuroanat.* xvi. 237/1 Functionally the neostriatum (caudate nucleus and putamen) differs from the paleostriatum (globus pallidus). **1974** *Nature* 1 Feb. 284/1 Brains from other animals prepared similarly were dissected into neostriatum, nucleus accumbens, [etc.].

Hence **neostriˈatal** *a.*, of or pertaining to the neostriatum.

1936 C. U. A. KAPPERS et al. *Compar. Anat. Nervous Syst. Vertebr.* II. ix. 1475 It.. forms a hypopallial (or neostriatal) area. **1958** L. HAUSMAN *Clin. Neuroanat.* xxxiii. 287 (*heading*) The efferent neostriatal connections.

Neo-Synephrine (niːəʊsɪˈnɛfrɪn, -iːn). *Pharm.* Also **neo-synephrin(e, neosynephrine.** [f. NEO- + *synephrine* (f. SYN- + EPIN)EPHRINE.] A proprietary name for phenylephrine.

1934 *Jrnl. Amer. Med. Assoc.* 16 June 2024/1 Neo-synephrin hydrochloride is a vasoconstrictor which is active when administered orally. **1937** *Amer. Jrnl. Ophthalmol.* XX. 176/2 In ophthalmoscopy neo-synephrine has the properties of other epinephrines. It produces mydriasis as quickly, as fully, and as safely as any mydriatic. **1950** *Trade Marks Jrnl.* 2 Aug. 711/1 Neo-Synephrine... Vasoconstrictors and antispasmodics being pharmaceutical preparations. Winthrop-Stearns, Inc...City and State of New York, United States of America; manufacturing chemists. **1972** *Obstetr. & Gynecol.* XL. 23/1 The nonsuture technic using a neosynephrine injection procedure for hemostasis..is recommended. **1974** M. C. GERALD *Pharmacol.* vi. 109 Drugs such as..phenylephrine (Neo-Synephrine) activate the adrenergic receptor directly.

neotechnic (niːəʊˈtɛknɪk), *a.* [f. NEO- + Gr. τεχνικ-ός (see TECHNIC *a.* and *sb.*).] Denoting, or belonging to, the most recent stage of industrial development. Hence **neoˈtechnics**, neotechnic technology.

1915 P. GEDDES *Cities in Evolution* iv. 64 Simply substituting *-technic* for *-lithic*, we may distinguish the earlier and ruder elements of the Industrial Age as Paleotechnic, the newer and still often incipient elements disengaging themselves from these as Neotechnic. **1927** Neotechnics [see *geotechnics* (GEO-)]. **1934** [see EOTECHNIC *a.*]. **1963** *Punch* 21 Aug. 284/1 The forms, symbolism and idiom of neotechnics. **1967** *Punch* 27 Sept. 451/1 The country would be rejigged to meet the challenge of the neotechnic revolution.

neotene (ˈniːəʊtiːn). *rare*⁻¹. [Cf. next.] A species (or member of a species) in which the period of immaturity is indefinitely prolonged.

1959 AUDEN *Homage to Clio* (1960) 25 The neotene who marches Upright and can subtract.

neoteny (niːˈɒtənɪ). *Zool.* [ad. G. *neotenie* (J. C. E. Kollman 1884, in *Verh. Naturf. Ges. Basel* VII. 391), f. Gr. νέος young + τείνειν to extend.] **a.** The retention of juvenile characteristics in adult life. **b.** The possession of sexual maturity by an animal still in its larval stage. Cf. *neoteinia*, *-tenia* (NEO- 2).

1901 H. GADOW in *Cambr. Nat. Hist.* VIII. iii. 65 These cases of neoteny are therefore instances of more or less complete retardation, or of the retention of partially larval conditions. **1920** *Conquest* Apr. 278/2 Neoteny..here means the abnormal time-extension of youthful characters. **1932** J. S. HUXLEY *Probl. Relative Growth* vii. 237 It is clear that changes in rate-genes could as easily lead to the opposite of recapitulation as to recapitulation. Many examples of neoteny would fall under this head. **1962** D. NICHOLS *Echinoderms* xiv. 178 An interesting embryological phenomenon known as neoteny, in which, by the acceleration of development of the gonads, an animal becomes sexually mature while still retaining the larval body form. **1965** *New Scientist* 14 Jan. 86/1 The retention of the puppy characteristic (neoteny) of floppy ears. **1971** J. Z. YOUNG *Introd. Study Man* xxxiv. 479 Such a change, technically called neoteny (or paedomorphosis), has in fact occurred often in the course of the evolution of diverse animals.

Hence **neoˈtenic**, **neˈotenous** *adjs.*, **neˈotenously** *adv.*

1901 H. GADOW in *Cambr. Nat. Hist.* VIII. iii. 64 Not unfrequently typical neotenic and overgrown specimens occur side by side with others which have completed their metamorphosis. **1930** G. R. DE BEER *Embryol. & Evol.* 27 Some animals have become permanently committed to this neotenous state. **1932** J. S. HUXLEY *Probl. Relative Growth* ii. 67 Workers [*sc.* termites] have been derived from soldiers by a suppression of their final development into the normal big-jawed type—..in fact, they are neotenic. **1957** *New Biol.* XXIII. 103 Animals which breed as juveniles or larvae are described as 'neotenous'. **1963** R. P. DALES *Annelids* iii. 72 The fusiform typhloscolecids..were possibly derived neotenously from phyllodocid stock. **1965** B. E. FREEMAN tr. *Vandel's Biospeleology* xiv. 233 All the troglobious urodeles are neotenous. They do not undergo metamorphosis and thus retain their larval characters throughout life.

neoteric (niːəʊˈtɛrɪk), *a.* and *sb.* Also 7 neoterique, 6–8 neoterick (7 -e). [a. late L. *neōtericus* adj. and sb., ad. Gr. νεωτερικός, f. νεώτερος, compar. of νέος new.]

A. *adj.* Recent, new, modern:

a. of things, esp. beliefs, practices, or the like.

1596 NASHE *Saffron Walden* Wks. (Grosart) III. 18 My fancie as touching those Neoterick tongues thou professest. **1652** URQUHART *Jewel* Wks. (1834) 218 Declining from that Neoterick faith..as he waxed in experience of the world. **1676** *Phil. Trans.* II. Ded., The same hand puts a stop to the Neoteric Notions of Chymists. **1716** M. DAVIES *Athen. Brit.* II. 340 The Title of this Neoterick Tract against Judiciary Astrology. **1816** W. TAYLOR in *Monthly Rev.* LXXXI. 118 The neoteric jargon of scholastic terms which he introduced. **1838** PUSEY *Let.* in Liddon *Life* (1893) II. xxi. 65, I said it must be said somehow 'Catholic and primitive truth' as opposed to 'Neoteric'. **1879** MEREDITH *Egoist* xviii, The neoteric fashion of spending a honeymoon on the railway.

b. of persons, esp. of authors.

1611 CORYAT *Crudities* Ep. Rdr., Celebrated partly by the ancient Roman historiographers and partly by other neotericke travellers. **1637** BASTWICK *Litany* II. 21 Both ancient and neoterick Expositors. **1678** CUDWORTH *Intell. Syst.* 4 That very Fate that is maintained by some Neoterick Christians. **1716** M. DAVIES *Athen. Brit.* III. 2 Most of the Neoterick Popish Writers. **1822–34** *Good's Study Med.* (ed. 4) III. 146 This species, the nyctalopia of neoteric authors, ..is said to be endemic in Poland. *a* **1876** M. COLLINS *Th. in Garden* (1880) II. 283 Such are the wise sayings of our neoteric sages.

B. *sb.* **1.** A modern; esp. a modern writer or author. (Very common in 17th c.)

1598 MERES *Palladis Tamia* 280 As these Neoterickes.. haue obtained renown. **1609** SIR E. HOBY *Let. to T. H[iggons]* 49 Is it possible, that that holy man should..come to be taxed by an obscure Neoterique of malignitie? **1686** GOAD *Celest. Bodies* II. i. 122 All the great Neotericks have espoused the Copernican [system]. **1728** POPE *Dunc.*, *M. Scriblerus* Wks. (Globe) 363 Such severe indispensable rules as are laid on all Neoterics, a strict imitation of the Ancients. **1833** LAMB *Elia* Ser. II. *Productions Mod. Art*, A landscape of a justly admired neoteric.

2. *pl.* The study of modern things.

1857 A. LEIGHTON *Wilson's Tales Borders* I. 52 She was no antiquary.., being rather given to neoterics.

neoˈterical, *a. arch.* [-AL¹.] = NEOTERIC *a.*

1588 J. HARVEY *Disc. Probl.* 34 Sundrie as well ancient, as neotericall interpreters. *a* **1625** BOYS *Wks.* (1629) 3 The petition in the judgements of neotericall authors hath six branches. **1650** HOWELL *Lett.* III. 19 Whosoever cryeth it down for a new neotericall opinion [etc.]. **1941** E. R. EDDISON *Fish Dinner* (1972) xvi. 266 For the more mockery, let it arise from the sea: a very neoterical Anadyomene.

neˈoterism. [ad. Gr. νεωτερισμός, f. νεωτερίζειν, to make innovations: cf. NEOTERIC.] The use of new words or phrases; a new term or expression. So **neˈoterist**; **neoteˈristic** *a.*; **neˈoterize** *v.*

1873 F. HALL *Mod. Eng.* 19 Neoterisms we must have.. to the end of time. *Ibid.* 150 If purism is ridiculous, neoterism..may easily become nauseating. *Ibid.* 164 Neoteristic canons. *Ibid.* 192 Among writers of the first class, none are wild neoterists. *Ibid.* 193 Popularity..or even celebrity is no guarantee of skill in neoterizing.

neothalamus (niːəʊˈθæləməs). *Anat.* [mod.L. (L. Edinger *Vorlesungen über den Bau der nervösen Zentralorgane des Menschen und der Tiere* (ed. 7, 1908) II. xv. 234), f. NEO- 1 e + THALAMUS.] The phylogenetically younger portion of the thalamus, which includes its lateral part.

1917 *Jrnl. Compar. Neurol.* XXVIII. 217 These parts of the thalamus..are termed by Edinger the neothalamus by reason of their functional relationship with the neopallium. **1921** TILNEY & RILEY *Form & Functions Central Nerv. Syst.* xxxi. 567 The neothalamus is an addition to the pars thalamica appearing in mammals only. **1973** *Gray's Anat.* (ed. 35) 893/1 The anterior and medial part of the thalamus, together with some of the smaller groups of nuclei, are often regarded as phylogenetically the older regions, and designated paleothalamus in contrast with the lateral part or neothalamus, which reaches its greatest development in anthropoid apes and man.

So **neoˈthalamic** *a.*, of or pertaining to the neothalamus.

1909 *Arch. Neurol. & Psychiatry* IV. 163 The upper part of the lateral cortex layer has certainly already a neo-cortical character, as is proved by the fact that a certain amount of fibres, originating in a neo-thalamic nucleus of the fillet.., end in it. **1936** C. U. A. KAPPERS et al. *Compar. Anat. Nervous Syst. Vertebr.* II. ix. 1481 Here for the first time there are projection fibers from neothalamic centers.

neoþeles, neoþemest: see NETHELESS, -MEST.

neotocite (niːəʊˈtəʊkaɪt) *Min.* Also †neotokite. [ad. G. *neotokit* (N. Nordenskiöld *Verzeichn. d. in Finland gefund. Min.* (1852) (Dana)), f. Gr. νεότοκ-ος new-born, recent (f. νέος new + τόκος offspring, childbirth) + G. *-it* -ITE¹.] A hydrated silicate of manganese and iron, approximately $Mn_2Fe_2Si_4O_{12}.6H_2O$, which is found as black amorphous masses.

1854 DANA *Syst. Min.* (ed. 4) II. 169 A related mineral [to Stratopeite] has been called Neotokite. **1861** BRISTOW *Gloss. Min.* 257/1 Neotokite. Probably an altered form of Rhodonite allied to Stratopeite. **1882** DANA *Min.* (ed. 4) 316 Neotocite (Stratopeite) and Wittingite are results of the alteration of rhodonite, and contain manganese. **1921** *Jrnl. Washington Acad. Sci.* XI. 27 Some specimens of the bementite rock are cut by thin veinlets of dark brown to black amorphous neotocite. **1932** *Amer. Mineralogist* XVII. 18 Areas of neotocite, several centimeters across are characterized by glistening black color and conchoidal fracture. **1968** I. KOSTOV *Mineralogy* 351 The amorphous silicate of manganese known as neotocite, occurring as black, opal- or coal-like masses is found as a weathering product of rhodonite and as a volcanogenic-sedimentary mineral.

neoˈtropic, *a.* [Cf. next.] = NEOTROPICAL.

1877 LE CONTE *Elem. Geol.* (1879) 161 Neotropic [region], including Central and South America.

neoˈtropical, *a.* [f. NEO- + TROPICAL *a.*] Including, belonging to, or characteristic of, Tropical and South America as a zoogeographical region.

1858 SCLATER in *Proc. Linn. Soc., Zool.* II. 134 They are all quite foreign to Neotropical (Tropical American) Ornithology. *Ibid.* 143 Neotropical or South-American Region. **1877** COUES *Fur-Bearing Anim.* i. 18 The extension of neotropical types over the nearctic region. **1881** *Nature* XXIV. 209/2 In Ungulates, like the rest of the neotropical regions, the Argentine territory is poor.

†**neotsum**, *a. Obs. rare*⁻¹. [? f. OE. *néotan* to enjoy, have good of.] ? Profitable, thriving.

c **1205** LAY. 343 Heore nutene neotsume weren.

neottious (niːˈɒtɪəs), *a. Bot.* [f. mod.L. *Neottia* (Linnæus), ad. Gr. νεοττιά, νεοσσιά a nest.] Characteristic of the Bird's-nest Orchid; resembling a bird's nest.

1850 HOOKER & ARNOTT *Brit. Flora* 418 That [genus] which contains the *Nidus-Avis*, the only one having the neottious root.

neotype (ˈniːəʊtaɪp). [f. NEO- + TYPE.]

1. *Min.* A variety of calcite containing barytes.

1854 DANA *Syst. Min.* (ed. 4) II. 438 A variety [of calcite] contains barytes and has been named neotype by Breithaupt.

2. *Taxonomy.* [a. F. *néotype* (A. E. M. Cossman *Essais de Paléoécologie Comparée* (1896) II. 2 and (1904) VI. 9), f. NEO- + TYPE *sb.*¹ 8.] A specimen designated as a type, in the absence of any other type material.

1905 C. SCHUCHERT in *Bull. U.S. Nat. Mus.* No. 53. 13 The term is here used as redefined by Cossman in 1904..as follows: Neotype for the specimen afterwards taken as the type of a species when the original type has been destroyed. **1961** G. G. SIMPSON *Princ. Animal Taxonomy* i. 32 Neotype: a substitute for a type that has been lost or (in some usages) is otherwise inadequate for the type role. (Neotypes have not hitherto been recognized in the Rules, but there are proposals to incorporate them therein.) **1966** *Internat. Code Bot. Nomenclature* ii. 19 A neotype is a specimen or other element selected to serve as nomenclatural type as long as all of the material on which the name of the taxon was based is missing.

neowe, -nesse, obs. ff. NEW, NEWNESS.

‖**neoza** (niːˈəʊzə). Also **neosia, neosa, nioza.** [Bhutanese *neoza, neosa.*] ***neoza pine***, a Himalayan pine (*Pinus Gerardiana*), the cones of which contain edible seeds (***neoza seeds***).

1840 *Penny Cycl.* XVIII. 172/1 The Neoza Pine... A native of the coldest forests of the Himalayas, and chiefly occupying..the Tartarian side of those mountains. **1866** *Treas. Bot.* 893/1 *P. Gerardiana*, the Neosa Pine of the Himalayas, affording the Neosa or Chilgoza seeds sold as food in the bazaars of Upper India. **1886** A. H. CHURCH *Food Grains Ind.* 177 The neosia or edible pine is a moderate-sized conifer found in the arid parts of the North-West and Punjab Himálaya... The seeds are collected and stored for use. *Ibid.*, Compostion of Neosia-kernels.

Neozoic (niːəʊˈzəʊɪk), *a. Geol.* [f. NEO-, after PALÆOZOIC.]

1. Belonging to the later period of geological history; post-palæozoic (comprising both Mesozoic and Cainozoic).

1854 E. FORBES in *Q. Jrnl. Geol. Soc.* X. p. lxxix, Both the palæozoic and the after—I must coin a word—neozoic mollusca. **1854** MURCHISON *Siluria* xviii. 469 In the Vertebrata, the main direction of development of generic ideas, is, he [Forbes] admits, towards the newer or Neozoic pole. **1888** FORD *Catal. Foss. Ceph.* Introd. 6 The Palæozoic epoch was of much longer duration than the Neozoic.

2. = CAINOZOIC.

1873 DAWSON *Earth & Man* x. 235 The term Neozoic was proposed by Edward Forbes for the Mesozoic and Cainozoic combined; but I use it here as a more euphonious and accurate term for the Cainozoic alone. *Ibid.* 239 Tertiary or Neozoic Time.

nep, *sb.*¹ *Obs.* exc. *dial.* Also 5–7 **neppe.** *β.* 6–7 **nepe.** See also NIP *sb.*² [var. of NEPT, ad. med.L. *nepta*, L. *nepeta* (Celsius and Pliny). Cf. Du. *neppe.*] = CATMINT (*Nepeta cataria*), CATNIP.

a. c **1420** *Liber Cocorum* (1862) 48 With persoley, sauge, ysope, saveray, A litel nep. **1486** *Bk. St. Albans* b vij b, Ye shall take an herbe that is called neppe. **1530** PALSGR. 247/2 Neppe, an herbe, *herbe de chat.* **1561** HOLLYBUSH *Hom. Apoth.* 18 He that hath a feruent cough, let him take Neppe, that cattes delite in. **1601** HOLLAND *Pliny* II. 23 Wild Mint, Nep, Endiue, and Peniroial. **1648** BP. HALL *Select Th.* §51 The dog when he is stomach-sick can go right to his proper grass; the cat to her nep. **1756** WATSON in *Phil. Trans.* XLIX. 837 Nep, or Cat-mint. On dry banks about hedges. **1797** *Encycl. Brit.* XIII. 6/1 There are 14 species; the most remarkable is the cataria, common nep, or catmint. **1802** RANKEN *Hist. France* II. IV. ii. 292 He treats of sage, rue,.. ambrosia, nep, radish, the rose.

β. **1548** TURNER *Names Herbs* (E.D.S.) 22 The thyrde kynde is called in latin Nepeta, in english Nepe. **1591** PERCIVALL *Sp. Dict.*, *Nebeda*, nepes, *Nepeta.* **1698** FRYER *Acc. E. India & P.* 307 Here grow also the Black Horehound, Spurge, Catminth or Nepe, Liverwort.

†**nep**, *sb.*² *Obs.* Also 6 neppe. [var. of NEEP, prob. through absence of stress in the comb., which is OE. (*wildnǽp*).] ***wild nep***, Bryony.

c **1450** *Alphita* (Anecd. Oxon.) 5/2 Vitis alba, brionia idem. *gall.* navet, *angl.* wildnep. *Ibid.* 26/2 Brionia.., cucurbita agrestis..*gall.* brione *uel* naue sauuage, *anglice* wildenep. **1545** RAYNOLD *Byrth Mankynde* R ij, Take..of wyld neppe dried the leues. **1597** J. KING *On Jonas* (1618) 612 Some called it Bryonia, bryony or wilde nep. **1615** MARKHAM *Eng. Housew.* II. i. (1668) 32 The root of the wild Nep, which is like Woodbine.

nep, *sb.*³ *U.S.* [Of obscure origin.] A small lump or knot upon cotton-fibres, either due to

irregular growth or produced during such processes as ginning.
1881 J. BUTTERWORTH *Cotton* 23 When the saw-gin is run too quickly the tendency is to whip or string the Cotton, and thus produce neps. **1881** F. H. BOWMAN *Structure of Cotton Fibre* 27 In artificially produced neps the cluster consists of fragments of broken fibre while in the natural neps the short fibres are comparatively whole and unbroken.

N.E.P., NEP, Nep[4] (nɛp). [f. the initial letters of *New Economic Policy*.] A programme initiated in the Soviet Union in 1921 for the revival of the wage system and private ownership in industry. Hence **'nepman, NEP-man**, one engaged in this programme.
[**1922** *Communist Rev.* June 107/2 The basic task of 'Nepa' (New Economic Policy),..is to establish a close connection between the socialist economy..and the economy of the peasant masses.] **1924** *Glasgow Herald* 2 Jan. 7 The wholesale arrest of thousands of persons, including many 'Nepmen' supporters of the new economic policy. **1927** *19th Cent.* Nov. 655 In 1921 the economic catastrophe threatened to bury under its ruins even the Soviet Government. It was then that Lenin proclaimed the New Economic Policy or 'N.E.P.' This 'Nep' was nothing else than a whole series of concessions to life—it was the victory of life over the deadly system inaugurated by the Soviet Government. **1929** *Daily Tel.* 22 Jan. 10/7 The Nep..is continually reasserting itself, in spite of the persecution and restrictions under which the Nepmen suffer. **1949** E. POUND *Pisan Cantos* lxxiv. 25 But in Russia they bungled and did not apparently Grasp the idea of work-certificate And started the N.E.P. with disaster And the immolation of men to machinery. **1951** KOESTLER *Age of Longing* vi. 98 There were rich and poor again; though the rich were now called NEP-men. **1961** C. COCKBURN *View from West* ix. 127 The British upper middle classes..richer and happier than ever—the great NEP-men of the 1950s. **1971** W. H. MCNEILL in A. Bullock *20th Cent.* 48/1 Extreme economic disruption even compelled Lenin to abandon Communist principles to the extent of allowing limited private trading (NEP or New Economic Policy, 1921). **1973** *Times Lit. Suppl.* 3 Aug. 910/3 The wickedness, real or alleged, of Nepmen became a favourite theme of official propaganda.

nep, *v. U.S.* [Cf. prec.] *trans.* To form knots on (cotton-fibre), esp. during ginning.
1875 *Ure's Dict. Arts* I. 961 The rough teeth of the saws do not use the fibre gently enough, but cut and 'nep' or knot it.

nep, variant of NAP *sb.*[1] cup. *Obs.*

nep, obs. variant of NEAP *a.*

Nepalese (nɛpɔː'liːz), *a.* and *sb.* Also **Nepaulese**. [f. *Nepal*, name of a country on the north-eastern frontier of India + -ESE.] **A.** *adj.* Of, pertaining to, or connected with Nepal. **B.** *sb.* A native or inhabitant of Nepal; these people collectively. Also, the language of this people.
The form ***Nepali*** (*a.* and *sb.*) also occurs, esp. as the name of the language of the Nepalese.
[**1811** W. KIRKPATRICK *Acct. Nepaul* vii. 207 The Nepaulians most commonly barter it for the rock salt and borax of Tibet.] **1819** F. HAMILTON *Acct. Nepal* I. i. 39 The following account of the Nepalese, or rather Newar, architecture, I have taken from papers communicated by Colonel Crawford. The Nepalese possess a great advantage in having an excellent clay for making bricks and tiles. **1848** J. D. HOOKER in L. Huxley *Life J. D. Hooker* (1918) I. xiii. 251 The Sikkim Rajah, whose territories were once the prey of the Nepalese. *Ibid.* 263 Accepting the invitation of Major Thoresby, the Nepaulese Resident. **1884** *Encycl. Brit.* XVII. 343/1 In all matters of domestic policy the Nepalese brook no interference. **1885** G. C. WHITWORTH *Anglo-Indian Dict.* 226/2 *Nepáli*, an inhabitant of Nepal or an emigrant from that country. The principal Nepáli tribes are the Gurkhás, the Gurungs, the Newárs and Limbus, the Kirátis, the Bhutiás, the Lepchás. Also the name of the language of the country, which is a dialect of Hindi. **1908** T. G. TUCKER *Introd. Nat. Hist. Lang.* 187 *Gujarāti*, *Sindhi*, *Punjābi*, *Kashmīri*, and *Nepāli* in the regions which their names imply. **1911** *Encycl. Brit.* XX. 453/1 Khas-kurā,..passes under various names. The English generally call it Nēpālī or Naipālī (i.e. the language of Nepal), which is a misnomer, for it is not the principal form of speech of that country. **1920** *Mission News* June 45/2 He has translated..the whole of the Bible into his own Nepali language. **1927** *Chambers's Jrnl.* June 370/1 The bungalow..remained in charge of a Nepali. **1931** *Times* 16 Mar. 22/5 Nepalese bronzes and brass work. **1961** *Listener* 10 Aug. 211/1, I had once known Nepali almost as well as I know English. **1964** R. PERRY *World of Tiger* iv. 52 The Nepalese stockmen were only too well aware of this habit. **1969** *Sunday Tel.* 12 Jan. 7/3 Many of the hippies..left Nepal..in 1968. The Nepalese didn't like them. **1971** C. BONINGTON *Annapurna South Face* i. 13 He spoke fluent Nepali. *Ibid.* iii. 40 The Internal Departures office, an open shed crammed with Nepalis and hippies. **1973** *Times* 14 Apr. (Nepal Suppl.) p. ii/2 It was only after the unification of the country under the royal house of Gorkha that Nepali became the *lingua franca* of the whole of Nepal. *Ibid.* p. ii/3 Traditionally Nepali Hindus are extremely conservative.

nepe, obs. form of NEAP, NEEP, NEP.

ne'penth. *Bot. rare.* [Anglicized f. NEPENTHES.] A plant of the genus *Nepenthes*.
1846 LINDLEY *Veg. Kingd.* 288 In which case Nepenths and Birthworts will be brought into contact.

‖**nepenthe** (nɪ'pɛnθiː). [Alteration of NEPENTHES.]
1. A drink or drug supposed to bring forgetfulness of trouble or grief. = NEPENTHES 1.
1596 SPENSER *F.Q.* IV. iii. 42 In her other hand a cup she hild, The which was with Nepenthe to the brim upfild. ?*c* **1600** *Distr. Emperor* I. i. in Bullen *O. Pl.* (1884) III. 171 From thys lypp Puerer Nepenthe flowes. **1630** BRATHWAIT *Eng. Gentlem.* (1641) 100 Those who are ever carousing in the cup of Nepenthe, steeping their senses in the Lethe of forgetfulness. **1738** POPE *Epil. Sat.* I. 98 Lull'd with the sweet Nepenthe of a Court. **1754** CHESTERFIELD *World* No. 92 ¶6 Gallons of the Nepenthe would be lost upon him. The more he drinks, the duller he grows. *a* **1822** SHELLEY *Triumph Life* 359 In her right hand she bore a crystal glass, Mantling with bright Nepenthe. **1898** T. WATTS DUNTON *Coming of Love* 45 [They] prated of some nepenthe..To quell his love as by a magic potion.
b. *Med.* A drug possessing sedative properties.
1681 tr. *Willis' Rem. Med. Wks.* Vocab., *Nepenthe*, a drink to drive away melancholy. **1727-38** CHAMBERS *Cycl.*, *Nepenthe*, in pharmacy, is a name given to a kind of opiate. **1898** *Allbutt's Syst. Med.* V. 775 Dr. Cheadle speaks highly of nepenthe for children.
2. The plant supposed to supply the drug.
1623 COCKERAM III, *Nepenthe*, an hearb which being steeped and dranke in wine, expelleth sadnesse. **1649** JER. TAYLOR *Gt. Exemp.* III. Disc. xviii. 115 The Moly or Nepenthe of Pliny. **1819** SHELLEY *Prometh. Unb.* II. iv. 61 Folded Elysian flowers, Nepenthe, Moly, Amaranth.
Hence **ne'penthean** *a.*
1892 AGNES CLERKE *Fam. Stud. Homer* viii. 229 The proposal of Telemachus to retire to rest shortly after the nepenthean cup has gone round.

‖**nepenthes** (nɪ'pɛnθiːz). [L. *nēpenthes* (Pliny), a. Gr. νηπενθές (*Odyss.* iv. 221, qualifying φάρμακον), neut. of νηπενθής, f. νη- not (see NE) + πένθος grief.]
1. A drug of Egyptian origin mentioned in the Odyssey as capable of banishing grief or trouble from the mind; hence, any drug or potion having, or conceived as having, the same power; also, occas. the plant or herb supposed to yield the drug.
1580 LYLY *Euphues* (Arb.) 425 Where is..that herbe Nepenthes that procureth all delights? **1586** SIR E. HOBY *Cognet's Pol. Disc. Truth* xix. 81 The drougg which Homer called Nepenthes, which he said was able to keep one from smelling yll sauors. **1619** *Pasquil's Palm* (1877) 154 It is the true Nepenthes, Which makes a sad man frolike. **1653** BAXTER *Peace of Consc.* Pref., There is so much Opium in these Mountebanks Nepenthes, or Antidote of Rest. **1699** EVELYN *Acetaria* 14 Some will have it [Bugloss] the Nepenthes of Homer. **1739** *Gentl. Mag.* IX. 477 As the Herb Nepenthes gives Joy and Spirits. **1850** LEITCH tr. *C. O. Müller's Anc. Art* §115. 84 In it the Greeks beheld Zeus face to face; to see it was a nepenthes. **1884** *Conf. Hachish Eater* 112, I have found it [hachish] to be a nepenthes, a sweet bringer of delicious oblivion.
2. A genus of plants (chiefly East Indian) in which the leaves have the form of pitchers; the Pitcher-plant.
1747 *Gentl. Mag.* XXVII. 452 The most remarkable instance of evacuations of this kind..is in the Nepenthes. **1839** LINDLEY *Introd. Bot.* (ed. 3) 141 The singular form of leaf in..Nepenthes, which has been called a pitcher. **1857** DARWIN in *Life & Lett.* (1887) II. 97 If Nepenthes consisted of one or two species..then I should have expected it to have been very variable. **1882** *Garden* 1 Apr. 214/3 The moisture-laden atmosphere required by the Nepenthes.
b. A plant belonging to this genus.
1882 *Garden* 5 Aug. 121/3 No collection of Stove plants ought to be without at least one Nepenthes.

neper (niː-, 'neɪpə(r)). Also †**napier**. [f. *Neperus*, Latinized form of the name of John *Napier* (or *Neper*) (see NAPIER'S BONES).] A unit used in comparing the power levels in two communication circuits or the intensities of two sounds: their difference in nepers is equal to half the natural logarithm of their ratio.
1924 K. S. JOHNSON *Transmission Circuits for Telephonic Communication* vii. 46 The transformer loss (expressed in napiers). **1929** [see BEL]. **1931** [see *decineper* (DECI- 1)]. **1954** *Electronic Engin.* XXVI. 91 The short line with which we are concerned in this article is defined as one for which the overall attenuation coefficient is small, say not greater than 0·2 neper, although the line may be several wavelengths long. **1972** J. M. TAYLOR tr. *Meyer & Neumann's Physical & Appl. Acoustics* i. 11 One neper corresponds to 8·69 dB.

nepeta (nə'piːtə). [L. *nepeta* catmint, perh. f. *Nepeta* ancient name of Nepi, a town in central Italy, adopted as the name of a genus by Linnæus (*Genera Plantarum* (1737) 170) and earlier botanists.] An annual or perennial herbaceous plant of the genus so called, belonging to the family Labiatæ; = CATMINT.
1915 H. H. THOMAS *Bk. Hardy Flowers* 304 Some of the Nepetas are little more than weeds, though a few kinds are attractive. **1939** R. E. CLARKSON *Magic Gardens* ii. 21 If you like, the gray santolina (but only for wide edgings), the nepetas, French thyme. **1961** *Times* 28 Jan. 9/3 Interplanted with the nepeta were daffodils. **1975** *Country Life* 6 Mar. 561/2 Blue anchusas..rising from misty blue nepeta.

nepevewe, obs. form of NEPHEW.

nephalism ('niːfəlɪz(ə)m). *rare.* [ad. late Gr. νηφαλισμός (Suidas), f. νηφάλιος sober. Cf. F. *néphalisme*.] Total abstinence from intoxicating liquors, teetotalism.
1861 J. MILLER (*title*) Nephalism, the True Temperance of Scripture, Science, and Experience. **1889** *Lancet* 6 Apr. 702 Some figures had been extracted from a report on Intemperance.., and had been misunderstood as implying that nephalism was more fatal than tippling.
So **'nephalist**, a teetotaller.
1861 J. MILLER *Nephalism* 16 The Nephalist..possesses a comparative immunity from contagious diseases.

nephanalysis (nɛfə'nælɪsɪs). *Meteorol.* Pl. **-ses**. [f. Gr. νέφ-ος cloud + ANALYSIS.] An analysis of the amounts and kinds of cloud present over an area; *esp.* a chart showing this in symbolic form.
1945 F. A. BERRY et al. *Handbk. Meteorol.* XI. 882 Synoptic studies of clouds (nephanalysis) indicate the possibility of a visual weather analysis based on cloud observations. *Ibid.* 905 Observations plotted on maps for nephanalysis include clouds, weather, [etc.]. **1961** *N.Y. Times* 21 Sept. 31/5 Meanwhile the meteorologists were translating the cloud pictures into diagrammatic meteorological charts, known as 'nephanalyses'. **1965** *Q. Jrnl. R. Meteorol. Soc.* XCI. 526 The latest Tiros 9 weather satellite is on a polar orbit and facsimile nephanalyses are received twice daily at Bracknell for an area close to or covering the British Isles. **1973** BARRY & PERRY *Synoptic Climatology* ii. 52 With the NIMBUS and ESSA satellites, global coverage is now available on a daily basis and nephanalyses are prepared from the photography.

nephande, obs. form of NEFAND *a.*

nephelauxetic (nɛfəlɔːk'sɛtɪk), *a. Physical Chem.* [f. Gr. νεφέλ-η cloud + αὐξητικ-ός AUXETIC *a.*] Causing an expansion of the *d*-electron cloud of a central atom, i.e. a decrease in the inter-electron repulsion parameter; ***nephelauxetic series***, a series of ligands arranged in order of their nephelauxetic effects.
1958 SCHÄFFER & JØRGENSEN in *Jrnl. Inorg. & Nuclear Chem.* VIII. 147 We shall propose to call this series the nephelauxetic (cloud expanding) series, as it corresponds to a development of the *d* shell in the region of the ligands. The neo-greek word was constructed by Professor Kaj Barr from the University of Copenhagen. **1965** *Molecular Physics* X. 7 The red shift of the ligand field bands in metal complexes with respect to the free ions has been explained..as being due to the nephelauxetic effect. **1966** PHILLIPS & WILLIAMS *Inorg. Chem.* II. xxviii. 402 The nephelauxetic (cloud-expanding) series.., it is suggested, represents the spread of the electron away from its parent nucleus on increase of covalent character in the binding of a given cation. **1973** *Chem. Soc. Rev.* II. 177 The *cis*-influence of ligands increases in accordance with their position in the nephelauxetic series.

nephelescope ('nɛfəlɪskəʊp). [f. Gr. νεφέλη cloud + -SCOPE.] (See quots.)
1841 *Proc. Amer. Philos. Soc.* II. 128 Mr. Espy exhibited an instrument.., which he calls the Nephelescope, intended to show the changes induced in the temperature of the air by its greater or less rarefaction. **1862** *Catal. Internat. Exhib., Brit.* II. No. 2851 Nephelescope, for viewing the upper strata of clouds.

nepheliad (nɛ'fiːlɪəd). *rare.* [f. Gr. νεφέλ-η + -IAD, on the analogy of *naiad*, *dryad*, etc.] A cloud-nymph.
1818 L. HUNT *Foliage, The Nymphs* p. xxxi, Ho! We are the Nepheliads, we, Who bring the clouds from the great sea. **1821** *Blackw. Mag.* X. 268 The pretty Nepheliads were dispatched to their own quarters.

nepheline ('nɛfəlɪn). *Min.* Also **-in**, *erron.* **nephiline**. [a. F. *néphéline* (Haüy, 1800), f. Gr. νεφέλη cloud, because its fragments are rendered cloudy by immersion in nitric acid.] A double silicate of aluminium and sodium, occurring chiefly in volcanic deposits in Italy. **nepheline-syenite** [ad. G. *nephelin-syenit* (H. Rosenbusch *Mikrosk. Petrogr.* (1877) II. 203)], a rare plutonic rock which resembles syenite in containing alkali feldspars such as orthoclase as essential minerals and usu. dark ferromagnesian minerals also (commonly amphibole or pyroxene), but differs in containing nepheline as an additional essential mineral, in being rich in soda but always lacking quartz, and in the frequent occurrence of rare minerals as accessories.
1814 J. BLACK tr. *Berzelius' Min.* 45 Nephelin. **1852** TH. ROSS tr. *Humboldt's Trav.* I. ii. 51 We could discover neither nepheline, leucite, nor feldspar. **1877** *Nature* XV. 384/1 Mineralogists have often been troubled to distinguish with certainty between apatite and nephelin. **1892** F. H. HATCH *Text-bk. Petrol.* (ed. 2) vi. 143 The syenites and diorites are plutonic granitoid rocks, less acid than granite, and consequently containing little or no free silica. They may be divided into—Syenites. Nepheline-syenites. Diorites. **1938** A. JOHANNSEN *Descr. Petrogr. Ign. Rocks* IV. 78 The nepheline-syenites are generally gray rocks with a greasy luster, usually moderately dark... Yellows, reds, and blues are not unknown. **1967** M. J. COE *Ecol. Alpine Zone Mt. Kenya* 11 The lava cooled slowly and produced a material that is highly crystalline. These rocks are called nepheline-syenite and contain large Felspar crystals up to 3 cm long as well as smaller nepheline crystals.
attrib. **1863** DANA *Man. Geol.* 89 *Nephelinite*, nephelin dolerite. **1882** GEIKIE *Text-bk. Geol.* II. 150 Nepheline

Rocks. **1888** TEALL *Brit. Petrogr.* 360 The olivine-bearing rocks [of Nephelinite] are termed nepheline-basalts.

Hence **nephe'linic** *a.* (Cassell, 1886.)

'nephelinite. *Min.* [f. prec. + -ITE.] (See quots.) Hence **nepheli'nitic** *a.*, containing or characteristic of nephelinite.

1863 DANA *Man. Geol.* 89 *Nephelinite*,..a crystalline granular volcanic rock consisting of nepheline and augite with some magnetic iron. **1888** TEALL *Brit. Petrog.* 360 Nephelinite..is applied to rocks in which nepheline takes the place of felspar. **1909** J. P. IDDINGS *Igneous Rocks* I. II. ii. 386 Rocks rich in feldspar have a trachytic texture; those rich in nephelite have a nephelinitic texture. **1944** C. PALACHE et al. *Dana's Syst. Min.* (ed. 7) I. 733 Pegmatites of the contact zone of the nephelinitic intrusive of the Chibina tundra, Kola. **1974** *Nature* 8 Feb. 354/1 An older series of basaltic-trachytic shield volcanoes, together with smaller nephelinitic centres.

nephelinization (nɛfəlɪnaɪ'zeɪʃən). *Petrol.* [f. NEPHELIN(E + -IZATION.] The alteration of a rock to one in which nepheline is an essential constituent.

1943 *Science* 26 Mar. 286/2 It is believed that the nephelinization is post-folding, since the flow marble contains fragments of all rocks except those containing nepheline. **1969** *Bull. Brit. Mus.* (*Nat. Hist.*) *Mineral.* II. 214 The nepheline syenites and ijolites are capable of desilicating the enclosing rock envelope—nephelinization. *Ibid.*, The nephelinization at Tundulu has been shown..to be related to the main ring-dyke of foyaite.., while at Dorowa the nephelinized fenite..surrounds a body of foyaite and ijolite.

So **'nephelinized, 'nephelinizing** *ppl. adjs.*

1943 *Science* 26 Mar. 286/2 (*heading*) The nephelinized paragneisses of the Bancroft region, Ontario. **1946** *Jrnl. Geol.* LIV. 167/2 The nephelinizing solutions..carried.. soda and alumina, with quantities of volatiles, including H_2O, Cl, P, and others. **1959** W. W. MOORHOUSE *Study Rocks in Thin Section* xv. 311 The nephelinized gneisses include a wide variety of melanocratic to leucocratic rocks. **1969** Nephelinized [see above].

'nephelite. *Min.* [-ITE.] = NEPHELINE.

1868 DANA *Min* (ed. 5) 328 Nephelite occurs both in ancient and modern volcanic rocks.

nephelo-, combining form of Gr. *νεφέλη*, used in a few scientific terms, as **ˌnephelo'dometer** (see quot.). **nephe'lognosy**, a systematic practice of observing the clouds. **nephe'lolater** (see quot.). **nephelo'logical** *a.*, relative to clouds or cloudiness. **nephe'lology**, the scientific study of clouds (*Syd. Soc. Lex.* 1892). **nephe'lometer**, (*a*) an instrument to register the comparative cloudiness of the sky; (*b*) any of various instruments by which the turbidity of a suspension, culture, etc., can be measured or compared with a standard by means of the light scattered (at right angles) by it. **nephelo'metric** *a.*, relating to the process of estimating the degree of cloudiness in a fluid (*Syd. Soc. Lex.*) or to nephelometry. **nephelo'metrically** *adv.*, by nephelometry; **nephe'lometry** *Chem.*, the technique of quantitative analysis using a nephelometer. **ˌnephelo'rometer** (see quot.). **'nepheloˌsphere**, a cloudy envelope surrounding a planet or other heavenly body.

1875 KNIGHT *Dict. Mech.* 1521/2 **Nephelodometer*, an instrument for ascertaining the distances of the clouds. **1816** BENTHAM *Chrestom.* Wks. 1843 VIII. 27/2 Of late years, *Nephelognosy..has become a candidate for existence. **1895** *Pop. Sci. Monthly* Sept. 645 All men in all lands are *nephelolaters or cloud admirers. **1881** *Arctic Cruise Corwin* 14 The *nephe[lo]logical state of the atmosphere. **1884** *Amer. Meteorol. Jrnl.* I. 4 It bears about the same relations to the *nephelometer which we should have, that the sun-dial bears to the clock. **1895** T. W. RICHARDS in *Proc. Amer. Acad. Arts & Sci.* XXX. 385 Since the opalescence was so faint that one could only with difficulty see it at all under ordinary conditions, a piece of apparatus, which may be named a 'nephelometer' (*νεφελη*, a cloud), was devised for detecting it. **1906** MCFARLAND & L'ENGLE in *Medicine* (Detroit) XII. 249/1 It occurred to us that uniformity in the number of bacteria..could be secured with reasonable accuracy by some means of measuring and standardizing the turbidity of the fluid containing them. We therefore devised a simple instrument, for which we suggest the name *nephelometer*.., by which it became easy to secure any desired degree of turbidity. **1936** F. D. & C. T. SNELL *Colorimetric Methods of Anal.* viii. 91 In the usual nephelometer the opaque tubes with clear glass bottoms used in colorimetry have been replaced with clear glass tubes with opaque bottoms. **1969** *Atmospheric Environment* III. 561 The multi-wavelength adaptation of the integrating nephelometer makes possible the local measurement of the wavelength dependence of the extinction coefficient due to scatter of atmospheric air. **1974** *Times-Herald-Record* (Middletown, N.Y.) 12 May, (*caption*) Researchers set up a light scattering instrument called an integrating nephelometer atop Mount Beacon. The tests were part of an air-pollution study. **1905** *Jrnl. Amer. Chem. Soc.* XXVII. 485 The application of these observations to the *nephelometric analysis of a very dilute silver chloride solution is obvious. **1929** P. A. KOBER in J. H. Yoe *Photometric Chem. Anal.* II. vi. 71 Precipitants for the production of nephelometric suspensions are as varied as the substances precipitated. **1971** P. R. HESSE *Textbk. Soil Chem. Anal.* xii. 314 The only difference between turbidimetric and nephelometric measurement of sulphate is in the measurement of the final turbidity. **1905** *Jrnl. Amer. Chem. Soc.* XXVII. 507 When in a day or two the precipitate had settled and the mother-liquor had become clear the latter was examined *nephelometrically. **1971** P. R. HESSE *Textbk. Soil Chem. Anal.* xvi. 423 Silver is extracted from soil by acid digestion and is classically determined nephelometrically as the chloride. **1876** T. P. BLUNT in *Chem. News* 7 Jan. 7/2 It would appear that the usefulness of colorimetry, and also of judgment by turbidity, which may provisionally be termed '*nephelometry', might be widely extended. **1906** *Amer. Chem. Jrnl.* XXXV. 113 In order to save the time of those attempting nephelometry, the precautions for several typical cases are here collected. **1929** J. H. YOE *Photometric Chem. Anal.* II. iii. 18 When colorimetry or nephelometry is used at all, in routine analytical work or in research problems, it is apt to be used almost continuously. **1966** *McGraw-Hill Encycl. Sci. & Technol.* IX. 40/1 The advantage of nephelometry [over turbidimetry] is its greater sensitivity, accuracy, and precision in the determination of small amounts of turbidity. **1875** KNIGHT *Dict. Mech.* 1521/2 **Nephelorometer*, an instrument for ascertaining the speed and direction of motion of the clouds. **1889** WINCHELL *World-life* 543 It [water mist] gathers into a vaporous envelope, constituting a true atmosphere or *nephelosphere.

'nepheloid, *a.* [f. Gr. *νεφέλ-η* + -OID.] **1.** Of urine: Cloudy, nebulous. (Cassell 1886.) *rare*$^{-0}$.

2. Of the ocean: chiefly in ***nepheloid layer***, a layer about a kilometre thick in the deep water of the western North Atlantic and elsewhere that is turbid owing to suspended mineral matter.

1965 EWING & THORNDIKE in *Science* 12 Mar. 1291/1 Strong background haze in some of our ocean bottom photographs has been difficult to explain by any cause other than clouded (nepheloid) water. *Ibid.* 1291/2 The degree to which the water is nepheloid. *Ibid.* 1291/3 A sample of 200 liters obtained from the nepheloid layer was found..to contain some organisms and about 0·50 g of suspended lutite. **1972** ETTREIM & EWING in A. L. Gordon *Stud. Physical Oceanogr.* II. 123 The turbulence associated with the vigorous bottom currents of the western North Atlantic maintains a nepheloid layer with an average thickness of one kilometer. **1974** *Nature* 6 Sept. 43/2 The thickness of this nepheloid layer is several orders of magnitude greater than the characteristic thickness of the turbulent Ekman layer at the ocean floor.

nephew ('nɛvjuː, 'nɛfjuː). Forms: *α.* 3–5 **neueu(e**, 3–6 **neuew**; 4–6 **nevewe**, 4, 6 **neveu**, (4 **-oeu**, 5 **-ue**); 4 **neweu**, (5 **-ewe**); 5 **nepveu**, **-vew**, 6 **-evewe**, **-heu(e**, **-hue**; **neffewe**, **-ue**; 5– **nephew**, (7 **neiphew**). *β.* 4 **neuu**, **-ou**, **-ow**; 4–6 **nevow**, (4 **-ou**, 5 **-oue**). *γ.* 4–9 *Sc.* **nevo**, 5 **neuo**, **newo**, **nepho**, 6 **nepuo**. *δ.* 4– *Sc.* **nevoy**, 6 **newoy**, **nepvoy**, 7 **nephoy**. *ϵ.* 6 **neuie**, **-ye**, 6–7 **nevie**, 6, 9 *dial.* **nevy**, 9 *dial.* **nevey**, **neffi**. [a. OF. *neveu* (ONF. also *nevu*, *nevou*, *nevo*) = Prov. *nebot*, It. *nepote*, *nipote*:—L. *nepōtem*, acc. of *nepos*, grandson, nephew, descendant, related to OE. *nefa*: see NEVE.]

1. A brother's or sister's son; also, by extension, the son of a brother- or sister-in-law.

α. **1297** R. GLOUC. (Rolls) 4508 Þo was þe king arþure vol of sorwe & sore,..Ac to awreke him of is luþer neueu, his herte bar alre best. *c* **1350** *Will. Palerne* 5098 Glad he was þat his neweu so nobul was wox. **1387** TREVISA *Higden* (Rolls) IV. 111 He wente into Egipt..forto see his suster and his nevewes. **1454** *Paston Lett.* I. 298 To take possession and saison, in the name and to the use of our ful worshipful nepveu, th'erl of Warrewic. *c* **1489** CAXTON *Blanchardyn* xx. 63 Blanchardyn..ranne vpon Corbodas, that neuewe was to kynge Alymodes. **1523** LD. BERNERS *Froiss.* I. 599 Use yourselfe to him as good uncles shulde do to their nephewes. *a* **1586** SIDNEY *Arcadia* (1613) 169 Euardes..had three Nephewes, sonnes to a sister of his. **1621** BP. MOUNTAGU *Diatribæ* 120 As Plinius the elder was wont to say unto his nephew. **1655** STANLEY *Hist. Philos.* I. (1701) 41/2 He reposed his Head in the Bosom of his Sisters Son;..the Court dismist, he was found dead in his Nephew's Bosom. **1722** DE FOE *Relig. Courtsh.* I. iii. (1840) 79 What kind of a lady has my nephew got? **1749** FIELDING *Tom Jones* XVIII. ix, 'Mr. Jones your nephew, sir!'.. 'He is indeed..my own sister's son.' **1828** SCOTT *F.M. Perth* xxiii, The interview between the uncle and nephew being thus concluded, the Prince retired. **1867** LADY HERBERT *Cradle L.* viii. 207 It was here that Abraham encamped with his nephew Lot.

β. *a* **1300** *Cursor M.* 20551 Mi moder was ful wa for me, And sua was hir neuu iohan. *c* **1320** *Sir Tristr.* 737 He kist tristrem ful skete And for his nevou toke. **1468** *Paston Lett.* II. 329 Wilbeloved nevoue, I recomaunde me to yow. **1508** DUNBAR *Flyting* 529 Nero thy nevow, Golyas thy grantsire.

γ. **1375** BARBOUR *Bruce* XVI. 44 And specialy the erll Thomass Of Murreff, that his nevo was. *c* **1470** HENRY *Wallace* II. 431 Welcum, neuo, welcum deir sone to me. **1533** BELLENDEN *Livy* III. xiv. (S.T.S.) I. 301 C. Claudius.. began to speik to his said nevo, erare in maner of prayer þan ony displesere. **1558** KENNEDY *Compend. Tractive* in *Wodrow Misc.* (1844) I. 97 To my derrest and best beluiffit Nepuo, Gilbert, Maister of Cassilis. **1678** ANNE KEITH in Kirkton *Ch. Hist.* (1817) 357, I have written to your nevo the tresorer of Edin. **1844** W. CROSS *Disruption* i. (E.D.D.), To tell me that my nevo is comin' doun the burn-side.

δ. **1509** *Test. Ebor.* (Surtees) V. 5 My son Hugh Hulley, and Sir Thomas Pilley my newoy. **1562** TURNER *Bathes* Ded., Duke of Summerset, and Protector of his Nepvoy King Edward the Sixt. *a* **1578** LINDESAY (Pitscottie) *Chron. Scot.* (S.T.S.) I. 107 Dawid Lyndsay..quhois nevoy, sone to Johnne his brother [etc.]. **1816** SCOTT *Old Mort.* vi, Haud your peace, Alison! I was speaking to my nevoy. **1839** MOIR *Mansie Wauch* (ed. 2) xxvii. 359 A leather-cap, edged with rabbit-fur, for her little nevoy.

ϵ. **1530** *Test. Ebor.* (Surtees) V. 285 To John Bradford, my nevy. **1555** EDEN *Decades* 40 Aries Pinzonus his neuie by his brothers syde. **1607** in *Antiquary* XXXII. 242 To Symon hallyday, my nevie. **1840** HOOD *Up Rhine* 4 Nunky, Nevy and Watch go on as usual. [**1848** DICKENS *Dombey* xxxii, Poor nevyless old Sol.] **1858–61** RAMSAY *Remin.* v. (1870) 117, I am real glad to find my nevy has made so good a choice.

b. Euphemistically applied to the illegitimate son of an ecclesiastic.

1587 HARRISON *England* II. ii. (1877) 48 For nephues might say in those daies; 'Father, shall I call you uncle?' And vncles also; 'Son, I must call thee nephue.' **1617** MORYSON *Itin.* I. 104 The chiefe of these banished men was the Nephew (so they call Church-mens bastards) of the Cardinall Caietano. *a* **1848** RUXTON *Life in Far West* (1849) 218 They were probably his nieces and nephews—a class of relations often possessed in numbers by priests and monks. **1873** DIXON *Two Queens* I. III. ii. 125 More papal 'nephews' had been stalled and mitred in the English Church.

c. ***nephew-in-law***, the husband of a brother's or sister's daughter. ***nephew-elect***, one who is intended to have this relationship.

1834 *Tait's Mag.* I. 381/2 It was not his fault that I, your nephew-elect, am not a Northamptonshire Squire. **1838** DICKENS *Nich. Nick.* xv, The company added their entreaties to those of his nephew-in-law. **1870** MISS BRIDGMAN *R. Lynne* II. x. 199 The..youth who purposes being my nephew-in-law.

†**2.** A brother's or sister's daughter; a niece.

1494 FABYAN *Chron.* V. xcvii. 71 The beaute and great vertue of Clotildis, neuewe to Cundebald. **1535** STEWART *Cron. Scot.* II. 712 To my nevoy Matildis, that hes richt Till all Ingland intill hir faderis sicht, I haif maid homage. **1585** T. WASHINGTON tr. *Nicholay's Voy.* IV. xxxii. 155 The Athenians were wont to marry the brother with the sister, but not the Vncle with the nephew.

†**3.** A grandson. *Obs.* (Common in 17th c.)

α. **1297** R. GLOUC. (Rolls) 7709 Richard is o neueu brec þere is nekke þer to. *c* **1384** CHAUCER *H. Fame* II. 109 That thou..Hast served so ententtyfly Hys blynde nevewe Cupido. **1387** TREVISA *Higden* (Rolls) IV. 91 Scipio Nasica, þe greet Scipio þat heet Affricanus his nevewe. *a* **1533** LD. BERNERS *Gold. Bk. M. Aurel.* (1546) Ccij, Ye had your nevewes, sonnes of your chyldren, maryed. **1591** SPENSER *Ruines of Rome* viii, Vertuous nephewes..Striving in power their grandfathers to passe. **1632** HOLLAND *Cyrupædia* V. v. 115 Naturall children and nephewes [*marg.*, childrens children, as we say unproperly, Grand-children]. **1656** TRAPP *Exp. 2 Tim.* i. 5 The grandmothers also..love their nephews better than their own immediate children. **1699** BENTLEY *Phalaris* 43 Among the ancient Greeks the name of the Grandfather was commonly given to the Nephew.

γ. *δ.* **1513** DOUGLAS *Æneis* IV. iv. 86 The ȝong Ascanyus, Nevo to King Dardane and to Venus. **1579** *Reg. Privy Council Scot.* III. 140 He..as nevoy and air be progres of umqquhile Andro Wod.., his guidsire. **1609** SKENE *Reg. Maj.* 34 Gif ane man deceis, haueand ane after-borne sonne, and ane Nephoy of his first-begotten sonne [etc.].

†**b.** *transf.* (after L. use). A prodigal. *Obs.*$^{-1}$.

1532 MORE *Confut. Tindale* Wks. 638/1 Whyther the olde holy doctours and saynctes..be better to be beleued.., or els these yong new naughty nephewes.

†**4.** A descendant; one of remote or unspecified degree of descent; a successor. *Obs.*

1387 TREVISA *Higden* (Rolls) V. 263 Engistus and Horsus ..were Woden his nevewes [L. *abnepotes*]. **1549** COVERDALE *Erasm. Par. Rom.* xi. 30b, The Jewes..yf they this do not, then are they not his [Abraham's] neuewes. **1597** J. KING *On Jonas* (1618) 135 Thy childrens children & nephews to com. **1647** TRAPP *Comm. 2 Cor.* v. 10 On that day Adam shall see all his nephews together. **1676** GLANVILL *Seasonable Reflect.* 189 All the ancient Sages, with their Sons, and Nephews to the latest Posterity.

†**5.** A figure in geomancy. *Obs. rare.*

1591 SPARRY tr. *Cattan's Geomancie* 9 Nowe resteth it to declare the making of the Nephews, with their qualities.

†**6.** A secondary shoot. *Obs. rare*$^{-1}$.

1745 tr. *Columella's Husb.* IV. vi, From that place from which you have taken away the nephew or secondary twig [L. *nepotem*], it presently pours forth another.

Hence **'nephewship**, the state or position of a nephew; †nepotism.

1647 HEXHAM, *Neefschap*, nephewship. **1669** *Hist. Pope's Nephews* II. (1673) 80 If Nephewship ever did good in Rome, 'twas in the time of Pius the Fifth. **1857** BORROW *Rom. Rye* ii, People..who..are disposed..to swallow the reality of the nephewship of Camillo Astalli. **1885** *Harper's Mag.* Apr. 787/1 This good sonship and good nephewship.

nephograph: see PHOTONEPHOGRAPH.

nephology (nɛ'fɒlədʒɪ). [f. Gr. *νέφο-ς* cloud + -LOGY.] The study of the clouds. Hence **nepho'logical** *a.* Also **ne'phologist**.

1890 in *Cent. Dict.* **1894** W. C. LEY *Cloudland* 201 The fact that there is also a science of Nephology, nascent though this science may be. **1894** *Academy* 29 Dec. 560/1 Plain people..settle questions of weather for themselves, and the most advanced nephologists can do little more.

nephometer (nɛ'fɒmɪtə(r)). [ad. F. *néphomètre* (L. Besson 1906, in *Annuaire de la Soc. météorol. de France* LIV. 241), Gr. *νέφ-ος* cloud + -OMETER.] = *nephelometer* s.v. NEPHELO-.

1910 J. MOORE *Meteorol.* (ed. 2) xvii. 218 Spherical Mirror Nephometer.—This instrument..permits the cloud-percentage (nebulosity) to be measured without any fear of an error in the number of the tenths. The description of, and the method of using, this new nephometer have been given by the inventor, M. L. Besson. **1959** R. E. HUSCHKE *Gloss. Meteorol.* 388 *Nephometer* (also called *nephelometer*), a general term for instruments designed to measure the amount of cloudiness.

nephoscope ('nɛfəʊskəʊp). [f. Gr. *νέφο-ς* cloud + -SCOPE.] An instrument used to determine the altitude of clouds and the velocity and direction of their movement.

1881 *Nature* 17 Mar. 458 A full description of the nephoscope will be found in the *Zeitschrift der Oesterreich. Ges. für Meteorologie*..vol. ii. p. 337. **1889** *Times* 21 Mar. 3/3 Several new barometers, anemometers, nephoscopes, &c.

‖**nephralgia** (nɛ'frældʒɪə). *Path.* [mod.L., f. Gr. νεφρ-ός kidney + -αλγία, f. ἄλγος pain.] Pain in, or neuralgia of, the kidneys.

1800 *Med. Jrnl.* III. 109 Nephralgia. **1874** Van Buren & Keyes *Dis. Genit. Org.* 353 The main causes of nephralgia are very acid urine, kidney-stone [etc.]. **1897** *Allbutt's Syst. Med.* III. 482 Nephralgia is perhaps the commonest of the abdominal neuroses.

Hence **ne'phralgic** *a.*

1811 *Monthly Rev.* LXIV. 17 In 1800 he was attacked by a violent nephralgic complaint. **1892** *Syd. Soc. Lex.* s.v., *Nephralgic crisis*, the paroxysmal pain of locomotor ataxy which is felt in the loins.

nephrectomize (nɛ'frɛktəmaɪz), *v. Surg.* [f. next + -ize.] *trans.* To subject to the operation of nephrectomy. So **ne'phrectomized** *ppl. a.*, deprived of a kidney by surgery.

1900 *Lancet* 5 May 1299/2 The animals previously nephrectomised lived longer when kidney juice was injected into them. **1949** Florey & Jennings in H. W. Florey et al. *Antibiotics* II. xl. 1286 The slopes of the curves showing the disappearance of the two penicillins from the plasma were roughly parallel for both normal and nephrectomized dogs. **1953** Nephrectomized [see *hypokalæmic* adj. s.v. hypo- II]. **1972** *Science* 9 June 1146/3 Rats..either had their ureters ligated or were bilaterally nephrectomized.

nephrectomy (nɛ'frɛktəmɪ). *Surg.* [f. Gr. νεφρ-ός kidney + ἐκτομή excision.] Excision or removal of the kidney.

1880 A. E. Barker in *Medico-Chirurg. Trans.* LXIII. 181 *note*, The term 'nephrectomy' is employed..as distinct from 'nephrotomy', or simple incision into the kidney. **1897** *Allbutt's Syst. Med.* IV. 315 The..most marked effects are seen after partial bilateral nephrectomy.

nephretic, obs. form of nephritic.

nephric ('nɛfrɪk), *a.* [f. Gr. νεφρ-ός + -ic.] Related to, or connected with, an excretory organ or kidney.

1887 *Amer. Naturalist* XXI. 589 The advantage of converting the nephric groove into the nephric duct.

nephridial (nɛ'frɪdɪəl), *a. Zool.* [f. nephridium + -al[1].] Pertaining or relating to a nephridium.

1888 Rolleston & Jackson *Anim. Life* 462 The walls of the nephridial and viscero-pericardial sacs. *Ibid.* 463 The nephridial epithelium..is..longitudinally striated.

nephridiopore (nɛ'frɪdɪəʊpɔə(r)). [f. nephridium + pore *sb.*[1]] The excretory opening of a nephridium.

1888 F. E. Beddard in *Q. Jrnl. Microsc. Sci.* XXVIII. 397 There are more than one pair of nephridiopores in each segment of the body. **1946** *Nature* 9 Nov. 665/2 Overton observed an initial loss of weight on handling the worm, and attributed this to the expulsion of fluid through the nephridiopores. **1963** R. P. Dales *Annelids* v. 98 The fluid which issues from the nephridiopores of an earthworm does not have the same composition as the coelomic fluid.

nephridiostome (nɛ'frɪdɪəʊstəʊm). [f. nephridium + *-stome*, ad. stoma.] = *nephrostome* s.v. nephro-.

1902 *Encycl. Brit.* XXXIII. 882/2 The Hesionidæ have compound organs, serving both as excretory and as genital ducts, formed by the grafting of the coelomostome on to the nephridiostome. **1963** R. P. Dales *Annelids* i. 29 In many other polychaetes..and in oligochaetes and leeches, an open funnel or nephridiostome is formed.

nephridium (nɛ'frɪdɪəm). *Zool.* Pl. **nephridia.** [mod.L. (Ray Lankester), ad. Gr. *νεφρίδιον, dim. of νεφρ-ός; cf. *gonidium*, etc.] A primitive excretory organ in the lower invertebrates, analogous in function to the kidney, but also, in some forms of Mollusca, used in reproduction.

1877 Ray Lankester in *Q. Jrnl. Microscop. Sci.* XVII. 428 The Nephridia or segmental organs of the Entozoa. **1883** Balfour *Ibid.* XXIII. 244 It will be convenient to commence with one of the hinder nephridia.

nephrite ('nɛfraɪt). *Min.* [a. Gr. *nephrit* (Werner 1780), f. Gr. νεφρ-ός, in allusion to its supposed efficacy in kidney disease: cf. jade *sb.*[2]] The mineral jade.

1794 Kirwan *Elem. Min.* I. 171 Jade. Nephrit of Werner. **1816** P. Cleaveland *Min.* 272 Nephrite does not receive a brilliant polish. **1865** Lubbock *Preh. Times* 132 Flint was sometimes used, and nephrite, or jade, in a few cases. **1879** Rutley *Stud. Rocks* x. 131 Nephrite or jade is in part a tough compact fine-grained tremolite.

nephritic (nɛ'frɪtɪk), *a.*[1] and *sb.* Also 6–7 -ick, 6 nefreticke, 7 nephretic(k. [ad. late L. *nephrīticus* (Celsius), ad. Gr. νεφρῖτικός, f. νεφρῖτις nephritis. Cf. F. *néphrétique* (†*nephritique*, OF. *nefretique*).]

A. *adj.* **1.** Of pains, diseases, etc.: Affecting, having their seat or origin in, the kidneys; renal.

1580 *Well of Woman Hill, Aberdeen* A iij b, It cuiris Nephritick dolouris baith of Neiris and Bladder. **1590** Barrough *Meth. Physick* vii. xvii. (1639) 406 When we would in the Nefreticke disease, have the pores and passages of the body enlarged [etc.]. **1650** Baxter *Saints' R.* iii. iv. (1662) 345 Epileptick, Arthritick, Nephritick pains. **1725** Bradley *Fam. Dict.* s.v. *Vomiting*, This Medicine is also good against the Nephritick Cholick. **1781** J. T. Dillon *Trav. Spain* 160 A remedy for a nephritic complaint. **1822–34** *Good's Study Med.* (ed. 4) IV. 396 She was never known to have had a nephritic symptom till just before her death. **1859** R. F. Burton *Centr. Afr.* in *Jrnl. Geog. Soc.* XXIX. 389 Chronic nephritic disease, and rheumatism.

2. Of medicines or remedies: Operating on, helping to cure affections of, the kidneys. ? *Obs.*

1657 Tomlinson *Renou's Disp.* 10 The..strengthening Medicament is that which..conserves some part of our Body, as..Nephritick to the reins. **1684** tr. *Bonet's Merc. Compit.* iii. 60 This is a noble and royal Nephritick liquor. **1710** *Brit. Apollo* No. 41. 2/1 Garlick is..Nephritick. **1799** *Med. Jrnl.* II. 291 The best manner of making the nephritic alkaline waters.

†**b.** ***nephritic wood***, a wood of which the infusion (***nephritic tincture***) was formerly used as a remedy in diseases of the kidneys. *Obs.*

In earlier accounts said to come from 'New Spain' and to be the *coatli* of Hernandez; but in later use also applied to the wood of the Horse-radish Tree (*Moringa pterygosperma*).

1661 Boyle *Contn. New Exp.* ii. (1682) 140, I tried the same experiment, with the infusion of Nephritick-wood. **1684–5** —— *Min. Waters* 86 To destroy the blewness of the Nephritic Tincture. **1718** Quincy *Compl. Disp.* 156 Nephritick Wood. This is brought to us from New Spain; it is from a Tree reckon'd of the Ash-kind. The Wood is hard and colour'd almost like Saunders. **1753** Chambers *Cycl. Supp.* s.v. *Transmutation*, The change of colour of a decoction of the nephritic wood, according to the different lights it was viewed in. **1797** *Encycl. Brit.* (ed. 3) VIII. 176/2 The wood [of moringa] dyes a beautiful blue colour. It is the *lignum nephriticum*, or nephritic wood, of the dispensatories.

c. ***nephritic stone***, jade, nephrite. ? *Obs.*

1666 H. Stubbe *Mirac. Conformist* 10 The Nephritick and Eagle-stones..whose operation is certain and undeniable. *Ibid.* 13 The Nephritic-stone drives out gravel. **1777** G. Forster *Voy. round World* I. 161 A piece of green nephritic stone, or *jadde.* **1811** Pinkerton *Petral.* I. 346 The nephritic stone was supposed, when only worn, to cure diseases of the reins, or the lumbago.

3. Of persons: Affected with pain or disease of the kidneys. Also *absol.*

1656 Blount *Glossogr.*, *Nephritick*, that is troubled with a pain in the Reins of the back. **1702** Floyer *Hot & Cold Bath.* i. iv. (1709) 92 He advises the Nephritick to place their Backs against the Stream of the River. **1806** *Med. Jrnl.* XV. 36 The drops..have given great relief to many nephritic patients. **1834** *Cycl. Pract. Med.* III. 165/1 The infusion of its leaves has often given decided relief to nephritic patients.

†**B.** *sb.* A medicine for the kidneys. *Obs.*

1661 Lovell *Hist. Anim. & Min.* 453. **1671** Salmon *Syn. Med.* iii. xv. 358 Renals or Nephreticks, are such Medicines as are dedicated to the Reines and Bladder. **1694** —— *Bate's Dispens.* (1713) 215/1 A most admirable Nephritick.

ne'phritic, *a.*[2] *rare*[−1]. [f. nephrite + -ic.] Of the nature of, related to, nephrite.

1806 *Gazetteer Scotl.* (ed. 2) 248 Marble,..nephritic asbestos, violet-coloured quartz, and porphyry.

†**ne'phritical**, *a. Obs.* [Cf. nephritic *a.*[1] and -al[1].] Nephritic, in various senses.

a. **1639** Wotton *Let.* in *Reliq.* (1672) 481 Troubled with certain Nephritical fits. **1663** Boyle *Usef. Exp. Nat. Philos.* ii. ii. 104 Patients, who were wont frequently to have recourse to him in their nephritical distempers. **1702** Young in *Phil. Trans.* XXIII. 1582 Hypocondriacal Pains, and sometimes Nephritical.

b. **1661** Lovell *Anim. & Min.* 453 Nephritical wood.

c. **1684** tr. *Bonet's Merc. Compit.* f. 5 A certain Physician thinking him Nephritical, gave him many things against the Stone.

nephritis (nɛ'fraɪtɪs). *Path.* [ad. late L. *nephrītis* (Isidore), a. Gr. νεφρῖτις, f. νεφρός kidney.] Inflammation of the kidneys.

1580 Blundevil *Horsemanship* iv. 44 b, The inflamation of the kidnies, which is called of them Nephritis. **1661** Lovell *Hist. Anim. & Min.* 381 The inflammation of the reines, or nephritis, is a swelling of the same [etc.]. **1747** tr. *Astruc's Fevers* 154 Hepatitis, nephritis, dysentery. **1797** *Encycl. Brit.* (ed. 3) XI. 175/2 The nephritis has the same symptoms in common with other inflammations. **1849–52** *Todd's Cycl. Anat.* IV. 1291/2 In arthritic nephritis the quantity of the uric acid crystals is sometimes extremely great. **1878** T. Bryant *Pract. Surg.* (1879) II. 49 Nephritis may occur as a consequence of local injury, or as an attack upon a chronically diseased organ.

nephro- ('nɛfrəʊ), comb. form of Gr. νεφρός kidney, employed in a number of scientific terms, as **'nephroblast**, one of the cells from which nephridia are developed (*Syd. Soc. Lex.* 1892). **,nephrocalci'nosis**, deposition of concretions of calcium compounds in the kidneys. †**nephroca'thartic** *a.*, serving to cleanse the kidneys. **'nephrocele**, hernia of the kidney (Craig, 1849). **nephro'colic**, renal colic (*ibid.*). **'nephrocyte** *Zool.* [ad. G. *nephrocyt* (A. Korotneff 1894, in *Mitt. Zool. Stat. Neapel* XI. 344)], a cell in insects which stores or excretes waste products. **nephro'dinic** *a.*, of molluscs, discharging the genital products by means of nephridia. **nephro'gastric** *a.*, relating to the kidneys and stomach (*Syd. Soc. Lex.*). **nephro'genic** *a.*, arising in the kidneys (*ibid.*). **nephro'gonaduct**, a nephridium which serves as a gonaduct. **ne'phrography**, the scientific description of the kidneys (Dunglison, 1842). **nephroli'thiasis**, disease caused by the presence of renal calculi. **nephro'lithic** *a.*, pertaining to calculi in the kidney. **nephroli'thotomy**, the removal by incision of a renal calculus. **ne'phrologist**, one skilled in nephrology. **ne'phrology**, the scientific study of the kidneys and their diseases (Dunglison, 1842). **nephro'mixium** (pl. **-mixia**) *Zool.* [Gr. μίξις mingling], in certain polychaetes, an organ formed by the fusion of the coelomoduct and the nephridium. **ne'phropathy**, disease of the kidneys; hence **nephro'pathic** *a.* **'nephropexy** *Surg.* [Gr. πῆξις fixing], the operation of securing an abnormally movable kidney. **nephro'plegy**, paralysis of the kidney (Mayne, 1856). **nephro'ptosis**, falling of the kidney. **nephropye'litis**, inflammation of the parenchyma of the kidney and adjacent parts. **nephropy'osis**, suppuration of the kidney (Mayne, 1856). **nephro'rrhagia**, hæmorrhage from the kidney. **ne'phrorrhaphy**, the operation of fixing a movable kidney by sewing. **nephroscle'rosis**, thickening and hardening of the walls of the blood vessels of the kidney, which is often associated with hypertension and can lead to renal failure. **ne'phrostoma, 'nephrostome**, a funnel-shaped ciliated aperture in a primitive kidney. **ne'phrostomy** *Surg.* [ad. F. *néphrostomie* (Guyon & Albarran 1898, in *Rev. de Chir.* XVIII. 1052), f. Gr. στόμα mouth], the operation of making an opening from the surface of the body directly into the pelvis of the kidney. **'nephrotome** *Zool.* [ad. G. *nephrotom* (J. W. van Wijhe 1889, in *Arch. f. mikrosk. Anat.* XXXIII. 465): see -tome], a block of tissue at the edge of a somite, giving rise to the excretory organs. **nephro'toxic** *a.*, having a toxic effect on the kidneys; so **,nephroto'xicity**, the property or effect of being nephrotoxic. **'nephrotoxin**, (*a*) a nephrotoxic antibody produced by injecting kidney tissue into an animal; (*b*) any nephrotoxic substance. **nephro'typhoid**, a form of nephritis. **nephro'zymose**, a compound ferment occurring in urine.

Similar forms are employed in French, as *néphrocèle, -graphie, -lithiase, -lithique, -logie, -pyose, -rrhagie*, etc.

1934 F. Albright et al. in *Amer. Jrnl. Med. Sci.* CLXXVII. 60 The initial disturbance, however, is not an inflammation, but presumably a deposition of calcium. Therefore, the term chronic *nephro-calcinosis would seem preferable. **1951** A. C. Allen *Kidney* xi. 366/2 Parenchymal nephrocalcinosis rarely interferes with renal function to any significant degree. **1974** Passmore & Robson *Compan. Med. Stud.* III. xxiii. 51/1 In nephrocalcinosis calcium is deposited in the basement of renal tubules in cortex and medulla, in tubular lumina and in small foci in the interstitial tissue. **1661** Lovell *Hist. Anim. & Min.* 454 *Nephrocathartick [syrup] of Joubertus. **1895** *Jrnl. R. Microsc. Soc.* 165 He [*sc.* Korotneff] finds colossal cells, whose possible function is suggested in the title '*nephrocytes'. **1932** Borradaile & Potts *Invertebrata* xiv. 390 Nitrogenous end products are found in the nephrocytes (cells found commonly associated with the fat body and the pericardium [of insects]). **1969** R. F. Chapman *Insects* xxv. 494 Nephrocytes, or pericardial cells, are cells occurring singly or in groups in various parts of the body. They may be very large, as in dipterous larvae, or small and numerous and usually they contain more than one nucleus. **1883** Lankester in *Encycl. Brit.* XVI. 682 The Porodinic group [of Cœlomate animals] is divisible into *Nephrodinic and Idiodinic, in the former the nephridium serving as a pore. *Ibid.*, The genital ducts of the Idiodinic forms may be called Idiogonaducts, as distinguished from *nephrogonaducts of nephrodinic forms. **1842** Dunglison, *Nephrolithiasis. **1880** A. Flint *Princ. Med.* (ed. 2) 906 The treatment of nephro-lithiasis..will depend on the nature of the concretions. **1842** Dunglison *Med. Dict.*, *Nephrolithic. .. This epithet has been applied to ischuria, occasioned by calculi formed in the kidneys. **1849** Craig, *Nephrolithotomy. **1883** Holmes & Hulke *Syst. Surg.* (ed. 3) III. 179 Nephro-lithotomy: designating incisions expressly intended not only to expose a portion of the kidney, but to remove a stone therefrom. **1897** *Allbutt's Syst. Med.* IV. 444 When anuria supervenes.. nephrolithotomy is indicated. **1900** E. S. Goodrich in *Q. Jrnl. Microsc. Sci.* XLIII. 742 The ordinary wide-mouthed segmental organs of the Polychæta, formed by the fusion of the nephridium with the genital funnel, may be called *Nephromixia... Kindly suggested to me by Professor E. Ray Lankester. **1900** E. R. Lankester *Treat. Zool.* II. ii. 37 The composite organ thus formed may be termed a 'nephromixium' or 'nephromix', in reference to its hybrid composition. **1932** Borradaile & Potts *Invertebrata* ix. 229 Nephromixia may take on the functions of coelomoducts where these do not exist independently. **1963** R. P. Dales *Annelids* i. 30 In other polychaetes the coelomoducts may be grafted on to the stem of the nephridium to form a nephromixium, which may be used both as a genital and as an excretory duct. **1917** Dorland *Med. Dict.* (ed. 9) 655/1 *Nephropathic. **1973** *Nature* 3 Aug. 289/2 In the nephropathic form of cystinosis, patients appear normal at birth. **1916** *Nephropathy [see nephrosis b]. **1956** Root & White *Diabetes Mellitus* xv. 189 Diabetic nephropathy is commonly first indicated by recurring edema, persistent albuminuria and in many cases an increase in the plasma lipids. **1968** A. Walsh tr. *J. Hamburger's Nephrology* I. xvi. 529/1 Even in the group of nephropathies of toxic origin, mercury poisoning takes second place..after carbon tetrachloride. **1897** *Jrnl. Amer. Med. Assoc.* 11 Dec. 1190/1 *Nephropexy is a legitimate and established procedure in all cases in which it can be established that the kidney is not only displaced, but is at the same time the direct cause of the manifold symptoms which such a condition may and often will produce. **1932** Ball & Evans *Dis. of Kidney* xiii. 394 Nephropexy has proved a sufficient method of treatment of mild degrees of hydronephrosis associated with excessive mobility of the kidney. **1968** Nephropexy [see FIXATION 3 c]. **1892** *Syd. Soc. Lex.*, **Nephroptosis.* **1897** *Allbutt's Syst. Med.* IV. 341 The condition of mobility has been named Nephroptosis. **1876** tr. *Wagner's Gen. Pathol.* 107 Cases of hæmorrhagic *Nephro-pyelitis in various acute diseases. **1885** W. ROBERTS *Urin. & Renal Dis.* III. xiv. (ed. 4) 681 A much less dangerous operation, *nephroraphy, in which the kidney is stitched to the posterior abdominal walls. **1894** *Lancet* 3 Nov. 1035 The woman was referred..for nephrorrhaphy, as the case was considered to be one of movable kidney. **1890** BILLINGS *Med. Dict.* II. 199/2 *Nephrosclerosis. **1926** H. ELWYN *Nephritis* xvi. 280 Arteriosclerosis of the kidney with its end stage of primary contracted kidney was classified under the term nephrosclerosis. **1951** A. C. ALLEN *Kidney* xiii. 397/1 The color of the kidneys with malignant nephrosclerosis is brownish or greyish red. **1966** *McGraw-Hill Encycl. Sci. & Technol.* VII. 343/2 Nephrosclerosis is only part of a generalized disorder of arteries. **1878** BELL *Gegenbaur's Comp. Anat.* 605 The rudimentary ducts are always provided with functionally active *nephrostomata. **1888** ROLLESTON & JACKSON *Anim. Life* 204 Each organ consists of a ciliated funnel or *nephrostome. **1900** KEEN & DACOSTA *Amer. Yr.-bk. Med. & Surg.* II. 184 MM. Guyon and T. Albarran discussed the subject of nephrotomy at the French Surgical Congress of 1898. They restrict the term nephrotomy to the making of an incision into the kidney; but when the pelvis of the kidney is opened through the kidney-substance, and the wound is kept open and a fistula is formed, they call the operation *nephrostomy. *Ibid.*, Nephrostomy is employed, in the first place, to relieve renal retention, septic or aseptic. **1932** *Jrnl. Amer. Med. Assoc.* 8 Oct. 1229/2 Nephrostomy on only one side makes the care of the urinary drainage apparatus much easier. **1967** S. TAYLOR et al. *Short Textbk. Surg.* xxv. 357 If the patient is too ill for a major operation nephrostomy or drainage of the kidney only may be possible, with secondary nephrectomy later, a very difficult operation. **1895** GADOW & ABBOTT in *Phil. Trans. R. Soc.* B. CLXXXVI. 166 Concerning the segmentally arranged mesodermal products (omitting *nephrotomes and gonotomes) the following subdivision is adhered to. **1949** A. S. ROMER *Vertebrate Body* xii. 378 In our embryological story we noted that in every trunk segment the mesoderm includes, on either side, a nephric region, often segmentally distinct as a nephrotome, a small discrete block of tissue interposed between somite and lateral plate. **1974** M. HILDEBRAND *Analysis of Vertebrate Structure* xiii. 308 Relatively few nephrotomes are incorporated [in the pronephros]. **1902** VAUGHAN & NOVY *Cellular Toxins* (ed. 4) vii. 144 The blood of animals in which one ureter has remained tied for some time becomes laden with a *nephrotoxic substance. **1937** Nephrotoxic [see *nephrotoxin* below]. **1973** *Jrnl. Pharmacol. & Exper. Ther.* CLXXXVI. 593/1 Administration of the nephrotoxic agent uranyl nitrate to rats specifically stimulated organic base accumulation by renal cortical slices. **1961** *Lancet* 22 July 179/1 The new preparation..appeared..to be devoid of ..*nephrotoxicity. **1970** PASSMORE & ROBSON *Compan. Med. Stud.* II. xxxii. 4/2 Mercury poisoning is the oldest and best understood type of nephrotoxicity. **1902** *Jrnl. Chem. Soc.* LXXXIV. II. 443 Repeated injections into the rabbit..of kidney cells from the dog..provoke the appearance in the rabbit's blood of a substance, *nephrotoxin, which is most harmful to the kidney cells of the dog. **1937** *Jrnl. Exper. Med.* LXV. 564 The nephrotoxic effect induced by anti-kidney serum is dependent upon a relatively organ specific antibody, nephrotoxin. **1961** A. G. WHITE *Clin. Disturbances of Renal Function* v. 153 Among the nephrotoxins encountered most frequently in clinical practice is carbon tetrachloride. **1970** R. C. MUEHRCKE in F. W. Sunderman *Lab. Diagnosis Kidney Dis.* xxxvii. 444/1 Other nephrotoxins such as sulfonamides produce their adverse pathopharmacological effects through a hypersensitivity reaction. **1896** *Allbutt's Syst. Med.* I. 812 Symptoms of acute nephritis (*nephrotyphoid).

nephroid ('nɛfrɔɪd), *a.* [f. Gr. νεφρό-ς + -OID: cf. Gr. νεφροειδής, νεφρώδης.] Kidney-shaped.

1849 in CRAIG. **1882** OGILVIE s.v., A nephroid fruit; a nephroid cancer.

So †**ne'phroideous** *a. Obs. rare*⁻¹.

1677 GREW *Anat. Seeds* i. §5 Other [seeds] are Nephroideous, or as it were Hemispherick.

nephron ('nɛfrɒn). *Anat.* [a. G. *nephron* (H. Braus *Anat. d. Menschen* (1924) II. 351), f. Gr. νεφρός kidney.] Each of the numerous filtration units in the kidney, which consist of a tube divided (in higher forms) into a glomerulus, a proximal convoluted tubule, a loop of Henle, a distal convoluted tubule and a collecting tubule, and through which the glomerular filtrate passes, undergoing selective reabsorption and emerging as urine.

1932 *Anat. Record* CIV. 185 The nephron of the sculpin was nevertheless compared with that of the toadfish. **1937** *Amer. Jrnl. Anat.* LXI. 21 (*heading*) Observations upon the structure of the nephron in the common eel. **1965** *New Scientist* 24 June 868/2 A human kidney contains approximately one million units called nephrons, each consisting of a thin tube about 20 to 50 micrometres wide and 50 millimetres long. **1974** PASSMORE & ROBSON *Compan. Med. Stud.* III. xxii. 11/1 Such surviving nephrons would be in a state of continuous osmotic diuresis. **1975** A. DILLARD *Pilgrim at Tinker Creek* viii. 133 The nephron..is a filtering structure which produces urine and reabsorbs nutrients.

nephrops ('nɛfrɒps). [mod.L. (W. E. Leach 1816, in *Trans. Linn. Soc.* XI. 344), f. NEPHR(O- + Gr. ὤψ eye.] = *Dublin (Bay) prawn* (DUBLIN); = *Norway lobster* (s.v. NORWAY¹).

[**1830** *Edin. Encycl.* VII. 398/2 This last [sc. *Astacus Norvegicus*] is considered as a distinct genus by Mr. Leach, under the name of Nephrops, from the kidney shaped eye.] **1961** *New Statesman* 23 June 1000/3 She is fishing off Barra, both seine-netting and after nephrops (scampi), a new and at present a paying type of fishery. **1971** *Nature* 29 Jan. 299/1 *Nephrops* tends to stay hidden away during the day, coming out during the night.

nephrosis (nɛ'frəʊsɪs). *Path.* Pl. -oses. [f. NEPHR(O- + -OSIS.] †**a.** (See quot.) *Obs.* exc. as in b.

1900 DORLAND *Med. Dict.* 428/1 *Nephrosis*, any disease of the kidney.

b. [a. G. *nephrose* (F. Müller 1905, in *Verhandl. d. Deut. Path. Ges.* IX. 65).] A syndrome characterized by œdema, albuminuria, a fall in the plasma albumin, and usu. an increase in the blood cholesterol, formerly attributed to degeneration of the renal tubules but now known to arise from increased permeability to protein of the glomerular capillary basement membranes.

1916 L. F. BARKER *Monogr. Med.* III. 954 (*heading*) Toxic degenerative tubular nephropathies without marked glomerular involvement (the so-called nephroses). **1926** H. ELWYN *Nephritis* v. 74 Tubular degenerations occurring in the course of other diseases, when presenting definite renal symptoms, may be similarly designated by the term nephrosis of the particular disease in which they occur. **1929** *Amer. Jrnl. Path.* V. 619 Lipoid nephrosis is to be regarded as a form of glomerulonephritis in which the glomeruli are damaged but their capillaries are only partially obstructed. **1946** E. T. BELL *Renal Dis.* vi. 217 The tubular atrophy in lipoid nephrosis is due to disuse and anemia. **1973** J. BROD *Kidney* xix. 405/1 Unlike glomerulonephritis pure nephrosis is encountered mostly in children under 5 years of age.

nephrotic (nɛ'frɒtɪk), *a. Path.* [f. prec.: see -OTIC.] Of, associated with, or suffering from nephrosis.

1928 *Amer. Jrnl. Path.* IV. 633 Every case of glomerulonephritis has a certain nephrotic element. **1940** *Jrnl. Clin. Invest.* XIX. 317/1 The albumin was much reduced in plasma, but unlike a nephrotic serum with a similar diminution of albumin, the globulin increase was most striking in the γ-fraction. **1954** *Amer. Jrnl. Physiol.* CLXXVIII. 329/2 The results demonstrated either an unchanged or a diminished hepatic synthesis of cholesterol by the nephrotic rat. **1966** *McGraw-Hill Encycl. Sci. & Technol.* III. 141/2 An example of edema formation secondary to a decrease in the colloid osmotic pressure of the plasma proteins is nephrotic edema.

b. ***nephrotic syndrome*** = NEPHROSIS b.

1939 *Arch. Internal Med.* LXIII. 646 Throughout the last fifteen months of the patient's illness all the cardinal signs of the nephrotic syndrome were repeatedly found. **1961** *Lancet* 5 Aug. 290/2 Specimens were obtained from..2 [patients] with the nephrotic syndrome. **1974** PASSMORE & ROBSON *Compan. Med. Stud.* III. xxii. 30/2 In the case of toxic or allergic nephrotic syndrome the offending agent should be removed.

nephrotomi'zation. *Surg. rare*⁻¹. [Cf. next and -ATION.] The operation of nephrotomy.

1825 FOSBROOKE *Obs. Kidneys* 132 It occurs to me that Nephrot[om]ization was formerly tried in this country.

ne'phrotomize, *v. Surg.* [Cf. next and -IZE.] *trans.* To perform nephrotomy upon. Hence **ne'phrotomized** *ppl. a.*

1825 FOSBROOKE *Obs. Kidneys* 132 Five ounces of blood from a dog nephrotomised afforded more than twenty grains of urea. **1876** tr. *Wagner's Gen. Pathol.* 572 The quantity of water in the brain of nephrotomized animals.

nephrotomy (nɛ'frɒtəmɪ). *Surg.* [ad. mod.L. *nephrotomia*, f. Gr. νεφρό-ς kidney + -τομία, τομή cutting. Cf. F. *néphrotomie*.] Incision of the kidney, esp. for renal calculus.

1696 *Phil. Trans.* XIX. 333 Nephrotomy, restraining its Signification to Cutting into the Kidney for the Stone, is an Operation which hath been hitherto so little practised [etc.]. **1767** GOOCH *Treat. Wounds* I. 415 The celebrated Professor ..performed the operation of Nephrotomy, with success. **1836** J. M. GULLY *Magendie's Formul.* (ed. 2) 160 When nephrotomy had been performed. **1874** VAN BUREN & KEYES *Dis. Genit. Org.* 369 Where the abscess is renal, it becomes a question of true nephrotomy.

nephsystem ('nɛfsɪstɪm). *Meteorol.* [f. Gr. νέφ-ος cloud + SYSTEM.] (See quot. 1959.)

1945 F. A. BERRY et al. *Handbk. Meteorol.* XI. 903 Cloud forms and cloud species over large areas form synoptic entities (called nephsystems) usually surrounded by fair-weather areas of clear sky, cumulus humilis, or cirriform clouds. **1959** R. E. HUSCHKE *Gloss. Meteorol.* 113 *Cloud system* (or *nephsystem*), an array of clouds and precipitation associated with a cyclonic-scale feature of atmospheric circulation. **1974** E. C. BARRETT *Climatol. from Satellites* iv. 116 Especially heavy and prolonged rain may be expected from major nephsystems within the meteorological tropics.

nephta, obs. form of NAPHTHA.

nephue, obs. form of NEPHEW.

nepionic (ni:pɪ'ɒnɪk), *a. Zool.* [f. Gr. νήπιος child + *-onic* as in *embryonic*.] Larval; in an early stage of development.

1889 A. HYATT in *Smithsonian Contrib. Knowledge* XXVI. II. 9 The first larval or næpionic stage of a Nautiloid was, therefore, represented by the apex of the conch in that order. **1893** —— in *Proc. Boston Soc. Nat. Hist.* XXVI. 94 Larval or young: nepionic. Here first used as a substitute for 'næpionic'. **1898** A. S. PACKARD *Text-bk. Ent.* 706 As regards the organization of larval (nepionic) as compared with imaginal forms, the nymphs and larvæ of insects are, with the exception of many Diptera, nearly as perfectly developed as the adult. **1903** *Amer. Naturalist* XXXVII. 517 The nepionic stage of shell growth begins with the second whorl.

‖**nepitella** (nɛpɪ'tɛlə). [It.] = CALAMINT.

1926 D. H. LAWRENCE *Sun* iv. 13 The paths were all grown high with grass and flowers and nepitella.

‖**ne plus ultra** (ni: plʌs 'ʌltrə). Also 7–8 **ne plus.** [L. '(let there) not (be) more (sailing) beyond', alleged to have been inscribed on the Pillars of Hercules. In French the phrase has the forms *nec* and *non-plus-ultra*.]

1. A command to go no further; a prohibition of further advance or action; also, an impassable obstacle or limitation.

c **1661** *Argyle's Last Will* in *Harl. Misc.* (1746) VIII. 27/1 That Bound-mark of Presbytery, its *ne plus Ultra*, Hitherto shall you go and no further. **1664** J. WORTHINGTON *Life Mede* in *M's Wks.* (1672) p. xiii, To look upon their Resolves as if they were Hercules's Pillars with a *Nè plus ultrà* upon them. *c* **1730** BURT *Lett. N. Scotl.* (1818) I. 293 He may wander into a bog to impassable bourns or rocks, and every *ne plus ultra* oblige him to change his course. **1786** HAN. MORE *Bas Bleu* 131 Her fancy of no limits dreams, No ne plus ultra bounds her schemes.

attrib. **1845** FORD *Hand-bk. Spain* I. 340 The *ne plus ultra* land and sea marks of jealous Phœnician monopoly.

2. The utmost limit to which one can go or has gone; the furthest point reached or capable of being reached.

1638 SANDERSON *Serm.* II. 120 Here then we have our bounds set us; our *ne plus ultra*; beyond which if we pass, we transgress. **1665** SIR T. HERBERT *Trav.* (1677) 254 Historians some fix his *Ne plus* at the River Indus; others at the River Ganges. **1751** ELIZA HEYWOOD *Betsy Thoughtless* II. 227 Mr. Munden often found himself at his ne plus ultra, but was not in the least disconcerted at it. **1776** MICKLE tr. *Camoen's Lusiad* Introd. 27 Cape Nam, as its name intimates, was then the *Ne plus ultra* of European navigation. **1805** EUGENIA DE ACTON *Nuns of Desert* II. 182 It might be supposed that the gentry of Ivy Tower would now have found themselves at their ne plus ultra. **1835** SIR J. ROSS *Narr. 2nd Voy.* xxix. 418 Victory point; being the 'ne plus ultra' of our labour.

b. *esp.* The point of highest attainment; the highest point or pitch *of* some quality, etc.; the acme or final culmination.

1696 D'URFEY *3rd Pt. Don Quix.* Ep. Ded., Whilst I with Pride fix my Fame at its *Ne plus ultra*. **1707** J. STEVENS tr. *Quevedo's Com. Wks.* (1709) 145 He was the superlative Degree of Avarice, and he was the very Neplus of Want. **1736** LD. CHESTERFIELD *Misc. Wks.* (1777) I. 2 This example should hinder one from thinking any thing brought to its *ne plus ultra* of perfection. **1760–72** H. BROOKE *Foot of Qual.* (1792) II. 81 The populace..have arrived to their *ne plus ultra* of insolence. **1823** SCOTT *Let. to Terry* 14 Feb. in *Lockhart*, It may be called the *ne plus ultra* of bell-ringing. **1893** *Nation* (N.Y.) 29 June 469/2 The people of Leinster.. do not vaunt Dublin as the ne-plus-ultra of cities.

attrib. **1823** BYRON *Age of Bronze* xi, The all-prolific land Of *ne plus ultra* ultras. **1830** MARRYAT *King's Own* xlviii, By ..ne-plus-ultra corkscrews.

†**3.** As *pl.* Unsurpassable persons. *Obs. rare*⁻¹.

1672 CLARENDON *Ess.* Tracts (1727) 237 Since men have looked upon the ancients as fallible writers, and not as upon those *Ne plus ultra*, that could not be exceeded.

nepman, NEP-man: see N.E.P. (as main entry).

†**'nepos.** *Obs. rare.* [a. L. *nepos*.] = NEPOTE.

1535 STEWART *Cron. Scot.* I. 130 Nepos als he wes till Drustus King. *Ibid.* II. 374 This ȝoung Alpyne, quhilk wes his nepos neir.

nepotal ('nɛpətəl), *a.* [f. L. *nepōt-*, *nepos* nephew + -AL¹: cf. late L. *nepōtālis* prodigal.] Of the nature of, belonging or pertaining to, a nephew or nephews.

1837 LYTTON *E. Maltrav.* VII. i, Provided Mrs. T. did not supersede the nepotal parasite by indigenous olive-branches. **1845** *Blackw. Mag.* LVII. 47 The Vladikas are appointed by the emperor in nepotal succession from the family of Petrovitch. **1862** MISS MULOCK *Mistress & Maid* xxiv, His proper nepotal corner in Hilary's heart.

†**nepo'tation.** *Obs. rare*⁻⁰. [f. L. *nepōtāt-*, ppl. stem of *nepōtāri* to squander, be prodigal.] 'Wasting or riotousness' (Blount *Glossogr.* 1656).

nepote ('ni:pəʊt). *Sc.* Now *rare.* [ad. L. *nepōt-*, stem of *nepos*: see NEPHEW.]

†**1.** A grandson. *Obs. rare.*

1533 BELLENDEN *Livy* I. xiii. (S.T.S.) I. 73 This Ancus was nepote to Numa pompilius, gottin on his dochter. **1536** —— *Cron. Scot.* (1821) I. 19 We ar faderis, ye, our sonnis; your sonnis ar our nepotis.

2. A nephew.

1533 BELLENDEN *Livy* III. xix. (S.T.S.) II. 26 Þe pride of his nepote [L. *fratris filii*] Appius Claudius. **1569** *Reg. Privy Council Scot.* II. 2/2 Nepote and heyre to the Erll of Montroise. **1889** R. BRYDALL *Art in Scotl.* ix. 158 Any other than a nepote of the Holy Father.

ne'potian. *rare.* [= F. *Népotien* (Littré), f. L. *Nepōt-*, stem of *Nepos*: see def.] A follower of Nepos, an Egyptian bishop of the 3rd cent., who held views similar to those of the millenarians.

1641 R. BROOKE *Eng. Episc.* II. vi. 89 Novatians, Sabellians, Nepotians,..have troubled the Church from time to time.

nepotic (nɪˈpɒtɪk), *a.* [f. L. *nepōt-*, *nepos* nephew + -IC.] **a.** Inclined to, of the nature of, nepotism. **b.** Holding the position of a nephew.
1847 *Fraser's Mag.* XXXVI. 715 The nepotic dispenser of patronage. **1854** MILMAN *Lat. Chr.* VII. vi. (1864) IV. 203 To set bounds.. to the personal or nepotic ambition of the ruling pontiff. **1873** *St. Paul's Mag.* 19 Jan., Regarding this nepotic youngster with amazement.

nepotious (nɪˈpəʊʃ(ɪ)əs), *a. rare*⁻¹. [f. as prec. + -IOUS.] Excessively fond of one's nephews.
1834 SOUTHEY *Doctor* x. (1848) 29 We may use the epithet nepotious for those [uncles] who carry this fondness to the extent of doting.

nepotism (ˈnɛpətɪz(ə)m). [ad. F. *népotisme* (1653) or It. *nepotismo*, f. *nepote* nephew: see -ISM.]
†**1.** The advantages, or opportunities for advancement, pertaining to a pope's nephew. *Obs.*
1662 J. BARGRAVE *Pope Alex. VII* (1867) 95 The Pope's only nephew.. married her, quitting his Cardinal's cap and nepotism.
2. The practice, on the part of the Popes or other ecclesiastics (and hence of other persons), of showing special favour to nephews or other relatives in conferring offices; unfair preferment of nephews or relatives to other qualified persons.
1670 G. H. *Hist. Cardinals* II. I. 116 Ministers that by the favour of the Nepotisme, do revive.. a new Neronisme of Tyranny. **1688** *Answ. Talon's Plea* 10 His great aversion from all kind of Pride; the freest from Nepotism of any. **1705** ADDISON *Italy* 184 It is to this Humour of Nepotism that Rome owes its present Splendor. **1740** RICHARDSON *Pamela* (1824) I. xxxii. 320 His holiness declared against nepotism. **1791** BURKE *Th. French Aff.* Wks. 1842 I. 569/2 The spirit of nepotism prevails there nearly as strong as ever. **1836** E. HOWARD *R. Reefer* xxxviii. The nepotism of the treasurer of the navy. **1876** FREEMAN *Norm. Conq.* V. xxii. 44 This nepotism of the Bishop who made a maintenance for his kinsfolk out of the estates of the Church.
b. Fondness for one's nephews.
1818 LADY MORGAN *Autobiog.* (1859) 9, I am sure that nepotism is an organic affection in single and childless women; it is a maternal instinct gone astray.

nepotist (ˈnɛpətɪst). [Cf. prec. and -IST.] One given to nepotism.
1837 SYD. SMITH *Wks.* (1850) 608 To be accused of Nepotism by Nepotists, who were praising themselves indirectly by the accusation. **1898** G. SMITH *Twelve Ind. Statesmen* x. 276 The Marquess of Dalhousie was no nepotist.
Hence **nepoˈtistical, nepoˈtistic** *adjs.*
1886 SYMONDS *Renaiss. It., Cath. React.* (1898) I. ii. 68 It was the last.. and the most brilliant display of nepotistical ambition in a Pope. **1936** *Fortune* Jan. 133 Mr. Aldrich's sudden elevation, whereas it may have been dramatic, was certainly not nepotistic. **1949** KOESTLER *Promise & Fulfilment* II. v. 296 The one-time pioneers have, as so often happens, developed into a somewhat nepotistic coterie of the ancients. **1955** W. GADDIS *Recognitions* II. i. 305 The Viareggio, a small Italian bar of nepotistic honesty before it was discovered by exotics.

neppe, obs. variant of NEP *sb.*¹, catmint.

nepperkin, dial. variant of NIPPERKIN.

†**nept(e.** *Obs.* [OE. *nepte*, ad. L. *nepeta*. Cf. MDu. *nepte*, *nipte*, G. *nepte(n*, *nept*.] = NEP *sb.*¹
c **1000** *Sax. Leechd.* I. 208 þas wyrte man nepitam on [leden] & oþrum naman nepte nemneþ. *Ibid.* III. 72 Neptan sæd & wuduhrofan sæd. *a* **1400-50** *Stockholm Med. MS.* 209 Nepte or cattys mynte, *nepta*. *c* **1440** *Promp. Parv.* 353/1 Nepte, herbe, *nepta*. **1523** SKELTON *Garl. Laurel* 982 The columbyne, the nepte, The ieloffer well set. **1600** SURFLET *Countrie Farme* II. xlix. 320 Cats mint or nept is a kind of calamint.

neptha, obs. form of NAPHTHA.

Neptune (ˈnɛptju:n). [a. F. *Neptune*, or ad. L. *Neptūn-us*.]
1. a. In Roman religion and mythology, the god of the sea, corresponding to the Greek *Poseidon*; also *transf.* the sea or ocean.
c **1385** CHAUCER *L.G.W.* 2421 *Phyllis*, The se.. possith hym now vp now doun Til neptune hath of hym compassioun. **1564** *Brief Exam.* Bivb, Wyne was consecrated vnto Bacchus,.. Water vnto Neptune. **1590** SHAKS. *Mids. N.* II. i. 126 Full often hath she.. sat with me on Neptunes yellow sands. **1634** MILTON *Comus* 18 Neptune besides the sway Of every salt Flood, and each ebbing Stream [etc.]. **1747** *Scheme Equip. Men of War* 23 Their Tide of Learning,.. whilst under the Influence of Neptune, is always Ebb. **1820** SHELLEY *Hymn Merc.* xxxi, The sacred wood, Which.. echoes the voice of Neptune. **1873** J. GEIKIE *Gt. Ice Age* xvii. 231 Neptune, when imprisoned in such deep, narrow ocean valleys, is powerless.
b. The sailor impersonating the sea-god in the ceremony observed in crossing the Line.
1815 *Chron.* in *Ann. Reg.* 104 At the usual ceremony of passing the Line,.. Buonaparte made a present to old Neptune of one hundred Napoleons.
2. *Neptune's cup* (or *goblet*): **a.** A species of coral (see quot. 1855).
1839 MALCOM *Trav.* (1840) 28/1 One of these curious productions, a species of alcyonium, called 'Neptune's cup'. **1855** DALLAS *Syst. Nat. Hist.* I. 239 The *Alcyonium poculum*, or Neptune's cup, which is found upon the coral reefs in the eastern Archipelago. **1885** LADY BRASSEY *The Trades* 312 There were grey sponges.. in shape not unlike coral Neptune's cups.
b. A kind of sponge (*Thalassema neptuni*).
1863 WOOD *Illustr. Nat. Hist.* III. 770 The extraordinary object which is called by the appropriate name of Neptune's cup is one of the most magnificent.. of the sponge tribe. **1867** SMYTH *Sailor's Word-bk.* 496 *Neptune's Goblets*, the large cup-shaped sponges found in the eastern seas.
3. The second most remote planet of the solar system, discovered by Galle in 1846, and lying beyond Uranus. (A more distant planet, PLUTO¹, was discovered in 1930.)
1846 *Astron. Obs. Radcliffe Observ.* (1848) 284 Observed Right Ascensions and North Polar distances of the Planet Neptune. **1868** LOCKYER *Guillemin's Heavens* (ed. 3) 267 The density of the matter of which Neptune consists.
4. (See quots.)
1861 DU CHAILLU *Equat. Afr.* viii. 90 The 'neptune'—a plate of yellow copper, which has long been one of the standard articles of trade imported hither by the merchants. **1867** SMYTH *Sailor's Word-bk.* 496 *Neptunes*, large brass pans used in the Bight of Biafra for obtaining salt.

nepˈtunean, *a. rare*⁻¹. = next.
1852 TH. ROSS tr. *Humboldt's Trav.* I. i. 36 A mountain.. celebrated on account of the disputes of volcanean and neptunean geologists.

Neptunian (nɛpˈtju:nɪən), *a.* and *sb.* [f. L. *Neptūni-us*, f. *Neptūnus* Neptune + -AN. Cf. F. *neptunien*.]
A. *adj.* **1.** Pertaining to the sea-god Neptune, or to the sea. *rare.*
1656 BLOUNT *Glossogr.* **1848** G. B. CHEEVER *Wand. Pilgrim* xxxiii. 204 A social Neptunian pic-nic of this sort.
2. *Geol.* Resulting from, produced by, the action of water. (Opposed to *volcanic* or *plutonic*.)
1794 KIRWAN *Elem. Min.* I. 425 Mountains of Neptunian origin are distinguished by their materials. **1805** *West's Antiq. Furness* 374 The progress of this neptunian process is very curious. **1857** DUFFERIN *Lett. High Lat.* 194 Layers of trap, alternating with Neptunian beds.
b. Based upon the view that certain geological formations are due to the action of water.
1802 *Edin. Rev.* I. 206 A destruction of the primitive mountains.. is deducible from the Neptunian.. hypothesis.
3. Of or belonging to the planet Neptune.
a **1849** POE *Mellonta Tauta* Wks. 1864 IV. 299 A fine view of the five Neptunian asteroids. **1885** AGNES CLERKE *Pop. Hist. Astron.* 114 No further Neptunian or Uranian satellites can be perceived.
B. *sb.* **1.** = NEPTUNIST 2.
1799 *Charac.* in *Ann. Reg.* 329/2 In general he was a Neptunian, that is to say he attributed the changes the earth has undergone to the operation of water. **1822** CLEAVELAND *Min. & Geol.* (ed. 2) II. 723 Neptunians and Vulcanists.
2. An inhabitant of the planet Neptune.
1870 PROCTOR *Other Worlds* 173 The Neptunians would be wholly unable to see Uranus.
Hence **Nepˈtunianism**, belief in, or advocacy of, the Neptunian hypothesis.
1830 LYELL *Princ. Geol.* I. 69 By a singular coincidence, neptunianism and orthodoxy were now associated in the same creed.

Neptunism (ˈnɛptjunɪz(ə)m). *Geol.* [f. NEPTUN(E + -ISM.] = NEPTUNIANISM.
1905 A. GEIKIE *Founders of Geol.* (ed. 2) viii. 257 Powerful as an advocate for the Vulcanist doctrines in opposition to the prevailing Neptunism of his time, he wrote some excellent monographs on the geology of different parts of Italy. **1951** C. C. GILLISPIE *Genesis & Geol.* ii. 46 The appeal of Neptunism is easier to understand than its acceptability. **1953** S. F. MASON *Hist. Sci.* xxxiii. 321 In the period 1790–1830.. the Vulcanist view became associated with the theory that rock strata had gradually evolved, and Neptunism with the theory that the strata were formed suddenly and catastrophically. **1966** *Mercian Geol.* I. 291 The geological concepts Plutonism and Neptunism have, until recently, been thought to belong more properly to the igneous and sedimentary environments respectively.

Neptunist (ˈnɛptjunɪst). [f. NEPTUNE + -IST.]
†**1.** A nautical person. *Obs. rare.*
1593 G. HARVEY *Pierce's Super.* Wks. (Grosart) II. 290 Let.. fine Dædalist, skilful Neptunist, maruelous Vulcanist.. be respected [etc.]. **1597** A. M. tr. *Guillemeau's Fr. Chirurg.* *iv, The Neptunist, of windes, of stormes, and of tempest,.. can talke best.
2. An asserter of the Neptunian or aqueous origin of certain geological formations.
1802 *Edin. Rev.* I. 201 Its author cannot be considered either as a Vulcanist purely, or a Neptunist. **1830** LYELL *Princ. Geol.* I. 346 The confidence with which the contending Neptunists and Vulcanists in the last century dogmatized on the igneous or aqueous origin of certain rocks. **1856** PAGE *Adv. Text-bk. Geol.* 65 The Wernerians or Neptunists contended strenuously for the aqueous origin of all the old rock-formations.
attrib. or as *adj.* **1863** SPENCER *Ess.* II. 60 This Neptunist hypothesis.. was quite untenable if analyzed. **1905** A. GEIKIE *Founders of Geol.* (ed. 2) viii. 262 He would have run some risk of being regarded as having gone over to the Neptunist camp. **1951** C. C. GILLISPIE *Genesis & Geol.* ii. 44 The Neptunist synthesis explained stratification by postulating that all rock formations had been precipitated from an aqueous solution and suspension. **1965** M. SMITH *Essent. Mod. Geol.* vi. 101 Considerable controversy existed in the eighteenth century until the Vulcanists, led by Nicholas Desmarest, finally overcame the opposition of the Neptunists.

neptunite (ˈnɛptju:naɪt). *Min.* [ad. Sw. *neptunit* (G. Flink (at the suggestion of N. O. Holst) 1893, in *Geol. Förening i Stockholm Förhandl.* XV. 196): see NEPTUNE and -ITE¹. (So called because of its occurrence with ÆGIRITE, Ægir being the Scandinavian god of the sea.)] A silicate of sodium, potassium, iron, manganese, and titanium, $(NA,K)_2(Fe^{II},Mn)TiSi_4O_{12}$, which is found as black monoclinic crystals.
1895 *Mineral. Mag.* XI. 100 Owing to the close similarity of the crystal angles to those of sphene, neptunite is placed in the titanite group. **1926** *Mineral. Abstr.* III. 102 Neptunite has been found at eight spots in the Kola peninsula. **1950** *Mineral. Mag.* XXIX. 27 The main point of interest in the new material is the presence here and there of the rare mineral neptunite in the syenite, a mineral previously unknown in the British Isles. **1966** *Doklady Acad. Sci. U.S.S.R.* (*Earth Sci. Sect.*) CLXVI. 121/2 The pyroxenic structure of neptunite is typically apparent from the endless zigzag baroque columns, in which Ti and Mn octahedra connected by common edges alternate in pairs.

neptunium (nɛpˈtju:nɪəm). *Chem.* [mod.L., f. NEPTUN(E + -IUM.] †**1.** [coined in G. (R. Hermann 1877, in *Jrnl. f. prakt. Chem.* XV. 105).] A supposed element similar to tantalum found in a sample of tantalite from Haddam, Connecticut, U.S.A. *Obs.*
1877 *Jrnl. Chem. Soc.* XXXII. 167 Neptunium is distinguished from tantalum by the fact that its fluoride forms an easily soluble double salt with potassium fluoride. **1877** *Potter's Amer. Monthly* Sept. 238/2 Hermann calls it neptunium.
2. An artificially produced transuranic element (traces of which have subsequently been found in nature) which is a silvery metal and whose longest-lived isotope has a half-life of about 2¼ million years. Atomic number 93; symbol Np.
The word does not occur in the article by McMillan and Abelson (*Physical Rev.* (1940) LVII. 1185) in which they announced the discovery of the element, though McMillan is often said to be the coiner (e.g. quot. 1945; cf. also *Jrnl. Amer. Chem. Soc.* (1948) LXX. 1128 (an abridgement of a secret report of 1942)).
1941 *Sci. News Let.* 30 Aug. 135/1 The uranium outpost was passed some years ago by Prof. Enrico Fermi.. with his discovery of the radioactive element No. 93, now called neptunium. **1945** *Chem. & Engin. News* 10 Dec. 2190/3 Element 93 was given the name neptunium by McMillan after Neptune, the planet immediately beyond Uranus, which gives its name to uranium. **1946** *Electronic Engin.* XVIII. 88 On bombarding the 238 isotope of uranium with a neutron of resonant energy value, a new isotope of uranium.. is formed. This isotope is unstable.. and emits one electron to become a new element.. called neptunium. **1950** M. LOWRY *Let.* 6 Mar. (1967) 200 Oddly enough I put neptunium in but abandoned it for niobium... I just took the elements out of the dictionary. **1968** *New Scientist* 23 May 410/2 Neptunium-237 is an important isotope because it is the precursor of plutonium-238. **1974** *Encycl. Brit. Micropædia* VII. 261/3 Neptunium is chemically reactive and similar to uranium with oxidation states from + 3 to + 6.

nepuo, -veu, -vew, -voy, obs. ff. NEPHEW.

†**ˈnequient**, *a. Obs. rare*⁻⁰. [f. pres. pple. of L. *nequīre* to be unable.] 'Not being able, disable' (Blount *Glossogr.* 1656).

†**ner**, *conj. Obs.* Also 5–6 **nere**, 6 **nar**. [var. of NOR, perh. after NE: but cf. OFris. *ner*.] Nor.
c **1420** *Avow. Arth.* xli, Ther schalle no mon do nere say, That schalle greue the. *c* **1450** tr. *De Imitatione* I. iii. 4 No man wiþouten him undirstondiþ ner demeþ rightwesly. *a* **1500** in C. Trice-Martin *Chanc. Proc. 15th C.* (1904) 2 Youre besecher never receyved of hym ner of none other to his use the value of xij. d. **1538** *Anc. Cal. Rec. Dublin* (1889) I. 503 To by nar sell wythe any man.

ner, in *ner nother*: see NOTHER.

ner, obs. var. NAR and NEAR *a.* and *adv.*

neral (ˈnɪəræl). *Chem.* [f. NER(OL + AL(DEHYDE.] A colourless oily aldehyde, $C_{10}H_{16}O$, which is the *cis* form of citral (CITRAL b) and gives nerol on reduction.
1939 [see CITRAL]. **1953** [see GERANIAL]. **1973** *Zoon* Suppl. I. 56 The main components of the secretion [of four species of *Prosopis*] have been identified as the two isomers of citral, geranial.. and neral.

neram (nɛˈrɑ:m). [Malay.] A large evergreen tree, *Dipterocarpus oblongifolius*, of the family Dipterocarpaceæ. Also *attrib.*
1927 F. W. FOXWORTHY *Commercial Timber Trees of Malay Peninsula* 41 *D[ipterocarpus] oblongifolius*.. is known as Neram and is not used commercially. **1940** E. J. H. CORNER *Wayside Trees of Malaya* I. 211 The *Neram* is the big tree that arches over the rocky rivers in the eastern and northern states of Malaya. **1965** R. MCKIE *Company of Animals* i. 24 Neram trees, with trunks that weigh many tons and sprawling root systems.. reached thirty degrees from the jungle banks to meet above the centre of the stream.

nerand, obs. f. ERRAND, NEARHAND.

nercotical, obs. form of NARCOTICAL.

nerd (nɜ:d). *slang* (chiefly *U.S.*). Also **nurd**. [Of uncertain origin: sometimes taken as a euphemistic alteration of *turd* (see, for example, D. L. Gold in *Comments in Etymol.* (1983) XII. 27), though perh. simply derived from the children's book character cited in quot. 1950.] An insignificant or contemptible person, one who is conventional, affected, or studious; a 'square', a 'swot'.

[**1950** 'Dr. Seuss' *If I ran Zoo* 49 And then, just to show them, I'll sail to Ka-Troo And Bring Back an It-Kutch, a Preep and a Proo, a Nerkle, a Nerd, and a Seersucker, too!] **1957** *Sunday Mail* (Glasgow) 10 Feb. 11 *Nerd*—a square. **1968–70** *Current Slang* (Univ. S. Dakota) III–IV. 88 *Nurd*, someone with objectionable habits or traits; an affected person... An uninteresting person, a 'dud'. **1971** *Observer* 23 May 36/3 Nerds are people who don't live meaningful lives. **1979** *Tucson Mag.* Feb. 21/2 Graffitti... Possibly the world's largest depository of nerd art. **1980** *Internat. Herald Tribune* 21 July 16/1 At MIT, 'nerd' is spelled 'gnurd'... Gnurds study all the time because they like to. **1983** *Truck & Bus Transportation* July 129/1 When loose-brained nurds crack up the top arrangements of a man o' my calibre, I got no union t' thump them nurds with. **1984** *Guardian* 17 June 21/2 His..rage..is directed at the whole of American society for its bland, tasteless, pretentious, illiterate 'nerd-pack' mentality. **1986** M. Howard *Expensive Habits* 107 He feels..like a total nerd in his gentleman's coat with the velvet collar.

Hence '**nerdy** *a.*, characteristic of a 'nerd'.

1978 *N.Y. Times* 25 Jan. D18 (Advt.), The nerdiest nerds on TV are really smart cookies. **1979** *New Yorker* 19 Feb. 92 The nurdier clients want foil... 'If the potatoes are in foil, that's gourmet.' **1982** *Guardian* 26 Oct. 8/8 She goes for a really tubular type of dude, the kind of hot babe with a cute butt who isn't all hairy and gross but isn't any nerdy zod either. **1987** *N.Y. Times Mag.* 31 May 46/3 Our wives.. agreed that we had been pretty nerdy back then.

†**nere**, *a. Obs. rare*$^{-1}$. [a. OF. *ner*, *neir*, var. *noir*:—L. *nigr-um*.] Black.

13.. *Coer de L.* 6526 A robe i-furryd with blaun and nere.

†**nere**, were not: see NE and BE *v*. A. 6–7.

c **1000** Ælfric in Assmann *Ags. Hom.* (1889) ii. 124 Ðas halȝan næron næfre mid wifum besmitene. *c* **1175** *Lamb. Hom.* 97 Hi neren aferede of nane licamliche pinunge. *c* **1205** Lay. 538 þa Grickes neoren noht warre. *Ibid.* 1118 Leode nere þar nane. *a* **1300** *Seven Sins* 27 in *E.E.P.* (1862) 19 He nold þat aliue nere none so riche as he were. **13..** *E.E. Allit. P.* B. 21 Nif he nere scoymus & skyg..Hit were a meruayl. *c* **1374** Chaucer *Compl. Mars* 35 Commaundynge him that neuere in her seruise He ner so bolde. *c* **1425** *Seven Sag.* (P.) 2058 None ther nas, That thay nere al at on. **1503** Hawes *Examp. Virt.* x. 4 Vnto your grace fayne wolde I go Ner lettynge of this water blo. **1600** Fairfax *Tasso* xii. lxxxi, He trembled so, that nere his squires beside To hold him vp, he had sunke downe.

†**nere**, obs. form of EAR.

1483 *Cath. Angl.* 252/2 A Nere, *auris*.

nere, variant of NEER, kidney.

nere, ne're, obs. variants of NE'ER, never.

'**Neread**. *rare*. Also 6 pl. **Nereiades**. [Erron. form of NEREID, after *dryad*, *oread*, etc.] A Nereid; a mermaid.

1555 Eden *Decades* 12 The fayre nimphes or fayeres of the sea (cauled Nereiades). **1656** Blount *Glossogr.*, *Neread*, a Maremaid, or Fish, like a beautiful Woman down to the Girdle, and the rest like a Fish.

attrib. **1860** C. Sangster *Hesperus*, etc. 145 Verdurous headlands looking down On Neread shapes.

nerehand(e, -hond(e, obs. ff. NEARHAND.

Nereid ('nɪərɪːɪd). [ad. L. *Nērēid-*, *Nērēïs*, a. Gr. Νηρηΐς, Νηρεΐς, f. Νηρεύς the name of an ancient sea-god.]

1. *Myth.* A daughter of Nereus; a sea-nymph.

1680 Oldham *Pastoral Earl Rochester* 1, Now does that lovely Nereid.. The Sea, and all her fellow Nymphs forsake. **1720** Pope *Iliad* xviii. 45 The circling Nereids with their mistress weep. **1776** Pennant *Brit. Zool.* I. 213 These birds were equally favourites with Thetis as with the Nereids. **1819** Shelley *Prometh. Unb.* iii. ii. 44 Behold the Nereids under the green sea. **1869** Tozer *Highl. Turkey* II. 309 The beauty of the Nereids is proverbial. **1885–94** R. Bridges *Eros. & Psyche* Mar. 27 The Nereids all, who live among the caves.

attrib. **1767** Fawkes *Theocritus* vii. 76 Halcyons,.. Most lov'd and honour'd by the Nereid train. **1847** *Gentl. Mag.* CXVII. i. 173 This structure..may be styled the Nereid monument.

transf. **1781** Cowper *Retirem.* 537 Nereids or Dryads, as the fashion leads, Now in the floods, now panting in the meads. **1876** Geo. Eliot *Dan. Der.* i, The Nereid in sea-green robes and silver ornaments..was Gwendolen Harleth.

2. *Zool.* An errant annelid of the family *Nereidæ*, having an elongated body composed of a large number of similar rings, with rudimentary branchiæ; a sea-centipede.

1840 *Penny Cycl.* XVI. 147/1 The Nereids are widely spread, and some of the species are found in most seas. **1845** T. R. Jones *Nat. Hist. Anim.* I. 334 The nereids, as might be expected from their activity and erratic habits, are carnivorous animals. **1876** *Beneden's Anim. Parasites* 24 This annelid is a long worm, like all the nereids.

attrib. **1885** Lady Brassey *The Trades* 316 A large Nereid worm, about six or seven inches long.

nere'idean. *Zool. rare*. [f. mod.L. *Nereideæ* (Savigny), f. L. *Nēreid-*, NEREID: see -EAN.] A nereid or similar marine annelid.

1835 Kirby *Hab. & Inst. Anim.* I. xii. 333 His first Order he denominates Nereideans. *Ibid.* II. xvii. 128 The approach which many of the Nereideans of Savigny make to the Myriapod Condylopes. **1842** Brande *Dict. Sci.*, etc.

‖**Nereides** (nɪ'riːɪdiːz, 'nɪərɪːɪdiːz), *sb. pl.* [L. *Nereïdes*, Gr. Νηρηΐδες, Νηρεΐδες, pl. of Νηρηΐς, Νηρεΐς: see NEREID.] Nereids.

1390 Gower *Conf.* II. 172 The Greks..such a name upon hem leiden, Nereides that thei ben hote. **1579–80** North *Plutarch*, *Antonius* (1612) 923 Apparelled like the Nimphes Nereides (which are the Myrmaides of the waters). **1601** Holland *Pliny* II. 567 The Sea-nymphs or Meere-maides also called Nereides. **1656** Blount *Glossogr.*, *Nereides* are also taken for Nymphs, or Fairies of the Water.

nere'idian, *sb.* and *a. Zool. rare*. [f. NEREID + -IAN.] **a.** *sb.* A nereidean or nereidous annelid. **b.** *adj.* = next.

1860 in Worcester. **1890** in *Cent. Dict.*

ne'reidous, *a. Zool.* [f. as prec. + -OUS.] Resembling a nereid; belonging to the *Nereidæ*.

1839 Darwin *Voy. Nat.* xiii. 305 Crawling nereidous animals of a multitude of forms. **1845** *Ibid.* (ed. 2) xx. 465 Nereidous worms, which perforate every block of dead coral.

‖**nereis** ('nɪərɪːɪs). *Zool.* [L.; see NEREID. Formerly used as a name for several unrelated marine forms of animal life.]

†**1.** A medusid. *Obs. rare.*

1752 J. Hill *Hist. Anim.* 92 The body of the Nereis is of a cylindric figure; and the tentacula are four in number, but two of them are usually very short, often scarce perceptible. **1770** Pennant *Brit. Zool.* IV. 38 Nereis Noctilucous. These are the animals that illuminate the sea, like glow-worms. **1797** *Encycl. Brit.* (ed. 3) XIII. 8/1 The..noctilucous nereis, which inhabits almost every sea. **1813** Bingley *Zool.* III. 424 The night-shining nereis.

2. The typical genus of the *Nereidæ*; the sea-centipede (see NEREID 2).

1797 *Encycl. Brit.* (ed. 3) XIII. 8/2 *Nereis gigantæa*, or giant nereis... The three rows of small tufts..serve this nereis instead of feet. **1839–47** *Todd's Cycl. Anat.* III. 538/2 In the *Nereis*, *Aphrodite*, and other erratic worms. **1845** T. R. Jones *Nat. Hist. Anim.* I. 334 The mouth of the dead Nereis appears to be a simple opening, quite destitute of teeth. **1883** *Harper's Mag.* Jan. 184/1 The nereis, with opal tints and gleams of pearl,..resplendent with light.

†**nereon**, obs. variant of NERIUM.

1661 Lovell *Hist. Anim. & Min.* 115 They are hurt by aconite, nereon, prickwood,..and scorching fennel.

†**nerf**, *sb. Obs. rare.* Also **nerfe**, **nerff**. [a. OF. *nerf*:—L. *nerv-um*: see NERVE *sb.*] A sinew.

c **1374** Chaucer *Troylus* ii. 642 His sheld..In which men mightyn meny an arwe fynd, That thrilled hath both horn, nerfe, and rynd. *c* **1400** *Lanfranc's Cirurg.* 29 þat þat is maad of þis nerf [*v.r.* nerff] and þis ligament is clepid a corde; þe which þat meueþ þe lymes to þe wille of þe soule.

nerf (nɜːf), *v. slang* (orig. *U.S.*). [Origin unknown.] *intr.* In drag-racing, to bump another car. Hence '**nerf-bar**, '**nerfing-bar**, a bumper fitted to a car used in drag-racing.

1953 Berrey & Van den Bark *Amer. Thes. Slang* (1954) §728/1 *Nerfing*, bumping another car out of the way. **1955** *Hot Rod Mag.* May 28 The nerf bar itself is mounted in a 'slip tube' that is welded permanently to the reworked bumper irons. **1960** Wentworth & Flexner *Dict. Amer. Slang* 352/2 The nerfing bar that supports the bumper on most cars. **1962** *Punch* 17 Oct. 561/1 A custom-built nerfing bar (bumper). **1969** R. E. Jennings *Automotive Dict.* 158/1 *Nerf bar*: see 'Nerfing Bar'. *Nerfing bar*, small, lightweight, vertical bumpers normally used on race cars, hot rods, and custom cars. *Ibid.*, *Nerf*, to bump, shove, or push a car during a racing event with another racer. Nerfing is very popular on short tracks.

nerhand(e, -honde, obs. ff. NEARHAND.

nerine (nɪ'raɪniː). *Bot.* Also **nerina**. [mod.L. (W. Herbert 1820, in *Curtis's Bot. Mag.* XLVII. 2124), f. L. *Nērīnē* (Virg. *Ecl.* vii. 37), Gr. νηρηΐς a water nymph; see NEREID.] A South African bulbous plant of the genus so called, belonging to the family Amaryllidaceæ and including *Nerine bowdenii*, widely cultivated for its autumn-blooming pink flowers, and the Guernsey lily, *Nerine sarniensis*. Also *attrib.*

1820 *Curtis's Bot. Mag.* XLVII. 2124 Rose-coloured Nerine... Nerine is probably confined to South Africa. **1837** W. Herbert *Amaryllidaceæ* 285, I have no hesitation in saying that it is a Nerine. **1886** G. Nicholson *Dict. Gardening* II. 446/2 When in flower, Nerines are amongst the most beautiful of greenhouse bulbous plants. **1923** *Chambers's Jrnl.* Dec. 786/2 The scarlet or rose-red nerine (the Japanese spider lily) appeared next. **1929** *Amateur Gardening* 3 Aug. 292/3 Nerines, or Guernsey lilies, are attractive flowering bulbs. **1949** L. G. Green *In Land of Afternoon* v. 69 They [*sc.* lilies growing on the Guernsey coast] were identified as the nerinas of the Table Mountain ledges. **1955** K. A. Thompson *Great House* iv. 116 A Nerine lily glistening like rose-crystal. **1961** *Amateur Gardening* 14 Oct. 19/3 Nerines are often looked upon as bulbs to grow in favoured gardens. **1974** R. L. Fox *Variations on Garden* 165, I prefer its [*sc.* the amaryllis's] cousin, the Nerine or Guernsey lily.

‖**Nerita** (nɪ'raɪtə). *Zool.* Pl. **Neritæ**, also **-as**. [L. *nērīta*, ad. Gr. νηρίτης, νηρείτης sea-mussel, f. Νηρεύς: see NEREID.] A genus of gasteropod molluscs; a mollusc belonging to this genus.

The name was widely applied by Linnæus, but was subsequently restricted to a group typical of the family *Neritidæ*, having a thick globular shell with a small spire and semilunate aperture.

1748 J. Hill *Hist. Fossils* 648 The *Neritæ* are not unfrequent in many parts of England. **1845** W. Macgillivray *Conchol. Text-bk.* 58 The Shore Nerita. *Ibid.* 98 The Bloody-Tooth Nerita. **1859–63** J. G. Wood *Nat. Hist.* III. 388 The Neritas are all inhabitants of the warmer seas.

nerite ('nɪəraɪt). *Zool.* Also **nerit**. [ad. L. *nērīta* NERITA.] = prec.

α. **1708** *Phil. Trans.* XXVI. 79 The Nerite, or Fossil Sea Snail. **1752** J. Hill *Hist. Anim.* 127 The black, red-streaked, and spotted Nerite. **1755** *Gentl. Mag.* XXV. 248 A very fine Nerite. **1802–3** tr. *Pallas's Trav.* (1812) I. 523 The Yelanatsh forms deep marshes..and produces the small variegated nerite before mentioned. **1851** Woodward *Mollusca* I. 13 The bivalve may close, and the operculated nerite retire into his home. **1872** Nicholson *Palæont.* II. xxi. 255 The true Nerites are inhabitants of warm seas.

attrib. **1823** Buckland *Reliq. Diluv.* 89 Both rods and rings, as well as the nerite shells, were stained superficially with red.

β. **1713** Petiver *Aquat. Anim. Amb.* 2/2 Red Nerit. **1835** Kirby *Hab. & Inst. Anim.* I. ix. 274 Upon a comparison of them with the nerit, the snail, or the periwinkle. **1843** *Penny Cycl.* XXV. 383/2 The Nerits are very widely spread in warm climates.

neritic (nɪ'rɪtɪk), *a.* [a. G. *neritisch* (E. Haeckel 1890, in *Jenaische Zeitschr. Naturw.* XXV. 253), perh. f. NERIT(A + -IC.] Of, pertaining to, or inhabiting the region of water bordering coasts, down to a depth of a hundred fathoms.

1891 Murray & Renard *Rep. Deep-Sea Deposits* iv. 251 The organisms living in mid-ocean in the great oceanic currents are quite different from those in the surface waters near land, and Haeckel proposes to designate the former oceanic Plankton, and the latter neritic Plankton. **1909** [see *holoplankton* (HOLO-)]. **1913** J. Murray *Ocean* vii. 136 The neritic area surrounds all continents and islands. **1926** [see *bathyal* adj.]. **1957** *Sci. News* XLIII. 71 Certain environments, such as the neritic zone of the ocean, are much more commonly represented in the fossil record than others. **1967** *New Scientist* 16 Mar. 546/2 Marine fish from the 'neritic' zone between the low-water mark and the edge of the continental shelf. **1974** Lucas & Critch *Life in Oceans* i. 24 The pelagic division is divided into the region inshore of the continental edge, known as the 'neritic province', and the remainder, called the 'oceanic province'.

ne'ritidan. *Zool. rare.* [f. *Neritid-æ* (see NERITA) + -AN.] A mollusc of the family *Neritidæ*.

1835 Kirby *Hab. & Inst. Anim.* I. ix. 274 Passing from this by one of the chambered-limpets, it will lead him to the neritidans, or top-shells.

'**neritine**. *Zool.* [ad. mod.L. *Neritina*: see NERITA and -INE.] A mollusc of the genus *Neritina* (family *Neritidæ*).

1843 *Penny Cycl.* XXV. 383/1 The crowned Neritines. **1874** Wood *Nat. Hist.* 639 Several allied shells are inhabitants of the fresh instead of the salt waters, and are known as Neritines.

‖**nerium** ('nɪərɪəm). *Bot.* [L., ad. Gr. νήριον, oleander.] A plant of the genus *Nerium*, belonging to the dog's-bane family, esp. *N. oleander*, the common Oleander.

1882 *Garden* 18 Mar. 186/2 Small plants of Neriums are most useful.

nerka ('nɜːkə). Also 8 **nar-**, **naerka**, 9 **nerker**. [Evidently a native name, but the precise source is obscure.] A common salmon (*Oncorhynchus nerka*) of Alaska and Kamtchatka.

1764 J. Grieve *Hist. Kamtschatka* 150 Another species of fish is called muikisi and is about the bigness of the narka. **1784** Pennant *Arctic Zool.* Introd. 125 The Naerka is another species called by the Russians Krasnoya ryba. **1888** Goode *Amer. Fish* 481 The Nerka or Blue-back Salmon.. known as the 'Red fish' to the English speaking inhabitants of Alaska and Kamtchatka. **1898** F. T. Bullen *Cruise of Cachalot* xv. 185 One kind known as the 'nerker' was far better flavoured than any of the others.

nerly, obs. form of NEARLY.

Nernst (nɛːrnst, nɜːnst). [Name of Walther Hermann *Nernst* (1864–1941), German physical chemist.] **a.** Used *attrib.* to designate an electric incandescent lamp invented by Nernst in which an unenclosed rod or wire consisting of a mixture of rare earths and other metallic oxides (as magnesia or zirconia) is made hot and luminous by the passage of an electric current (after being first brought to a conducting state by heating), and which is used esp. as a source of infra-red radiation.

1899 *Chambers's Jrnl.* 25 Mar. 269/2 For some time there have been rumours of an electric lamp on an entirely new principle, and..the contrivance was recently exhibited at the Society of Arts, London. It is known as the Nernst incandescent electric lamp, and its chief peculiarity is that it employs a rod of refractory earth in place of the usual carbon filament, and that this material is not enclosed in a glass exhausted of air. **1912** W. S. Franklin *Electric Lighting* v. 134 There are five important kinds of glow lamps as follows: ... (*e*) The Nernst lamp in which the glower is a small rod of porcelain-like material. **1950** L. J. Brady in M. G. Mellon *Analytical Absorption Spectrosc.* viii. 444 One serious objection to the Nernst glower is the frequent mechanical failure of the source due to the poor bonding of the platinum leads to the element itself. **1962** R. E. Dodd

Chem. Spectrosc. i. 16 For use in the infra-red region, mainly beyond 2μ, the hot body takes the form of a rod of semi-conducting lanthanon oxides, a Nernst glower. *Ibid.* 17 The Nernst filament is only suitable for the near infra-red and visible.

b. Used *attrib.* with reference to a thermo-magnetic effect investigated by Nernst, in which a temperature gradient in a metal subject to a magnetic field at right angles to the gradient gives rise to an e.m.f. in a direction at right angles to both.

1901 M. G. LLOYD in *Amer. Jrnl. Sci.* CLXII. 57 It has already been proposed† to call the galvano-magnetic temperature-difference, the thermo-magnetic temperature-difference, and the thermo-magnetic potential-difference by the respective names, Ettingshausen effect, Leduc effect and Nernst effect. [*Note*] †Thesis: The Transversal Thermo-magnetic Effect in Bismuth, M. G. Lloyd, Philadelphia, 1900; Beiblätter, 24, p. 1014. **1911** *Physical Rev.* XXXIII. 300 Both the Hall electromotive force and the Nernst electromotive force seem to be proportional to the intensity of magnetization in the plate rather than to the magnetic field. **1960** E. H. PUTLEY *Hall Effect & Related Phenomena* ii. 27 In the Nernst effect, electrons attempting to diffuse down a temperature gradient are deflected by a magnetic field but a transverse electric field is set up to balance out the Lorentz force. *Ibid.* 28 The units for the Nernst coefficient are cm² sec⁻¹ (°K)⁻¹ or m² sec⁻¹ (°K)⁻¹.

c. Used *attrib.* and in the possessive to designate a theorem in thermodynamics enunciated by Nernst: the change in entropy accompanying a chemical reaction between pure crystalline solids tends to zero as the temperature at which it occurs tends to absolute zero. (Also called the third law of thermodynamics, esp. in more generalized formulations.)

1913 J. R. PARTINGTON *Text-bk. Thermodynamics* xvii. 484 The required information is furnished by a hypothesis put forward in 1906 by W. Nernst, and usually called by German writers 'das Nernstsche Wärmetheorem'. We can refer to it without ambiguity as Nernst's Theorem. **1928** J. K. ROBERTS *Heat & Thermodynamics* xviii. 354 Such a wide range of reactions is considered that we are certainly justified in regarding the Nernst Heat Theorem as being established as a first approximation. *Ibid.* 355 If the Nernst Theorem as originally stated should prove to be only a first approximation, the theorem does not on that account become less important. **1971** G. SOCRATES *Thermodynamics & Statistical Mech.* vii. 139 An alternative statement of Nernst's heat theorem is: It is impossible to reduce the temperature of any system to absolute zero in a finite number of operations.

Neroic (nɪˈrəʊɪk), *a.* [f. *Nero*: see NERONIAN *a.*] = NERONIC.

1887 *Temple Bar* Mar. 436 It is a flaming picture of almost Neroic brutality.

nerol (ˈnɪərɒl). *Chem.* [a. G. *nerol* (Hesse & Zeitschel 1902, in *Jrnl. f. prakt. Chem.* LXVI. 498): see NEROLI and -OL.] An oily unsaturated primary alcohol, $C_{10}H_{18}O$, which is present in neroli and some other essential oils and is used in perfumery, having a fragrance similar to but finer than that of geraniol, with which it is stereoisomeric.

1903 *Jrnl. Chem. Soc.* LXXXIV. I. 189 Nerol, $C_{10}H_{18}O$, is an oil which boils at 225–227° under 765 mm. pressure.. and is distinguished from geraniol by its odour of roses. **1949** E. GUENTHER *Essent. Oils* II. 174 Nerol and its acetic ester have been found in several volatile oils, for instance, in oil of helichrysum (30–50 per cent), neroli, bigarade, petitgrain, rose, linaloe, lavender, bergamot, Ceylon citronella, etc. **1949** T. F. WEST et al. *Synthetic Perfumes* iii. 19 Nerol is a superior odorant [to geraniol] in exquisite rose compositions as it provides them with that velvety blossom top-note of freshly cut dark-red roses. **1974** *Jrnl. Chem. Soc.: Perkin Trans. I* 1637 Treatment of geraniol or nerol with fluorosulphonic acid at low temperatures gave good.. yields of a novel iridoid ether.

neroli (ˈnɪərəlɪ). Also 7–8 **neroly.** [F. *néroli*, It. *neroli*, from the name of an Italian princess to whom its discovery is attributed.] An essential oil distilled from the flowers of the bitter orange. Also *neroli oil, oil of neroli.*

1676 SHADWELL *Virtuoso* 111, I have.. Neroly, Tuberose, Jessimine, and Marshal. **1706** PHILLIPS (ed. Kersey), *Neroly*, a sort of Perfume. **1727–38** CHAMBERS *Cycl.* s.v. *Orange*, There are various oils drawn from oranges; the oil of neroli is the produce of the flowers by distillation. **1839** URE *Dict. Arts* 885 In distilling water from neroli, an aroma is obtained different from that of the orange-flower. **1849** BALFOUR *Man. Bot.* §796 The Bitter or Seville Orange, from the flowers of which an essential oil, called Neroli-oil, is procured. **1870** J. POWER *Handy Bk. about Bks.* iii. 46 Musk, with one or two drops of oil of Neroli,.. will give a powerful odour.

Neronian (nɪˈrəʊnɪən), *a.* [ad. L. *Nerōniān-us*, f. the name of C. Claudius *Nero*, Roman Emperor 54–68 A.D.]

1. Characteristic of, resembling that (or those) of, Nero; exhibiting the tyranny, cruelty, or moral depravity of Nero.

1598 FLORIO, *Neronarie*, cruell, Neronian cruelties. **1606** *Proc. agst. Late Traitors* 370 Inforced.. by this late more than Neronian attempt of endangering both their soules and bodies. **1637** GILLESPIE *Eng. Pop. Cerem.* III. viii. 195 A certaine Amphibian brood, sprung out of the stem of Neronian tyranny. **1678** LEE *Alexander* Ep. Ded. (1776) 4 An age, whose business is senseless riot, Neronian gambols, and ridiculous debauchery. **1778** HAMILTON *Wks.* (1886) VII. 543, I abhor such Neronian maxims. **1870** ANDERSON *Missions Amer. Bd.* III. iv. 58 The very horrible Neronian doctrine, 'that it is our duty to destroy heretics'.

2. Of or pertaining to, connected with, the emperor Nero or his times.

1650 B. *Discolliminium* 20 Paul had a good intention.., so had the Neronian, Arrian, and Marian Butchers. **1802** GIFFORD tr. *Juvenal* viii. 108 The youth, whom Rumour brands as vain, And swelling—full of his Neronian strain. **1864** *Nat. Rev.* 339 If it were necessary to speak of the extent of the Neronian persecution, we should refer to Tertullian. **1880** MUIRHEAD *Ulpian* xxiv. §11 It is confirmed by the Neronian senatusconsult. **1882** HALL CAINE *Recoll. Rossetti* 102 Defending (in sport) the vices of Neronian Rome.

b. *spec.* (See quots.)

1672 *Phil. Trans.* VII. 5106 It hath been observed to be dangerous, to have a vein opened at once in both arms, or leggs, which is here called a Neronian Venæ-section. **1892** *Syd. Soc. Lex.* s.v., *Neronian phlebotomy*, venesection when more than one vein is opened in the same day; so called because.. Seneca was thus bled to death under Nero.

Neronic (nɪˈrɒnɪk), *a.* [f. *Nerōn-*, stem of *Nero* (see prec.) + -IC.] Neronian.

1901 *Contemp. Rev.* Jan. 19, I saw some horrible instances of this rapid growth of this Neronic cruelty. **1902** J. DENNEY *Death of Christ* v. 246 The martyrs in the Neronic persecution.

ˈNeronism. *rare*⁻¹. [f. as prec. + -ISM.] A system of government resembling that of Nero.

1670 G. H. *Hist. Cardinals* II. I. 116 Ministers that by the favour of the Nepotisme, do revive as a man may say a new Neronisme of Tyranny.

ˈNeronist. *rare*⁻¹. [f. as prec. + -IST.] One who imitates the depravity of Nero.

1593 G. HARVEY *Pierce's Super.* Wks. (Grosart) II. 91 Phy on.. impure Ganimedes, Hermaphrodits, Neronists, Messalinists [etc.].

Neronize (ˈnɪərənaɪz), *v.* [f. as prec. + -IZE.] *trans.* **a.** To stigmatize as resembling Nero. **b.** To deprave on the model of Nero. **c.** To tyrannize over like Nero.

1673 MARVELL *Reh. Transp.* II. 179 You muster up all Christian Princes to Neronize and Caligulize them. **1675** J. SMITH *Chr. Relig. App.* I. 46 Poppæa.. had so much Debauchery in her, as to Neronize Nero himself. **1889** *Voice* (N.Y.) 7 Mar., Grant was a 'drunken tyrant', who was about to Neronize the capital.

nerr(e, obs. variants of NAR *a.*, nearer.

nerre, variant of ARR, scar. *Obs.*

nerrer, nearer: see NAR *a.*

nerrest, nerst, nearest: see NAR *a.*

nert, art not: see NE and BE *v.* A. I. 2.

‖**nerte.** *rare*⁻¹. [F. *nerte*, ad. Pr. *nerto*, app. an alteration of *mirto*.] Myrtle.

1585 T. WASHINGTON tr. *Nicholay's Voy.* 3 b, The Ilande.. is low.. full of Nerte, lentisque, and Lysardes.

nerteˈrology. *rare*⁻¹. [f. Gr. νέρτερος lower, inferior, νέρτεροι the dead, + -OLOGY.] Learning relating to the dead or the shades.

1800 W. TAYLOR in *Monthly Mag.* VIII. 598 Works.. of nerterology.. and of witchcraft.

nerthrift, neverthrift: see NE'ER *adv.* 3 b.

nerts (nɜːts), repr. a colloq. or euphemistic pronunc. of *nuts* (NUT *sb.*¹ 7 e).

1932 *Amer. Speech* VII. 334 (Johns Hopkins jargon) Nerts—exclamation of incredulity or disgust. (Nuts?) **1932** *Sun* (Baltimore) 28 Sept. 10/6 The first couple of months are devoted to getting the right title, suggestions running all the way from 'Alors, Mes Enfants' to 'Nerts'. **1933** M. ALLINGHAM *Sweet Danger* xviii. 222 'Life's very beautiful, isn't it?' 'Speaking as a soul not yet mated, nerts,' said Amanda. **1937** HEMINGWAY *To have & have Not* III. vii. 128 Oh, nerts to you. **1937** B. HOWARD in *New Statesman* 9 Jan. 52/1 Heaven knows that no little word of mine can possibly be heard above the deepening hosannas, but all the same, I shall say it, and it is Nerts. Nerts to everybody, all round, except the authoress. **1948** D. BALLANTYNE *Cunninghams* II. xiii. 222 Nerts, you did your part bringing them into the world.

†**ˈnerval**, *sb. Obs.* Forms: 4 **nerwall**, 5 **-al**, 6 **nervall(e**, **nervell**, 7 **nerval**. [ad. med.L. *nervāle* (Heinrich *M.E. Medizinb.* 159), neut. of *nervālis*, f. L. *nerv-us* NERVE *sb.*] Healing ointment for the sinews.

a **1400** *Stockholm Med. MS.* 702 in *Anglia* XVIII. 313 Ewene with oþer in porsion all He goth to þe nerwall, And.. is good to euery salwe. *a* **1500** *M.E. Medizinb.* (Heinrich) 159 Her is a makyng of an oyntment þat men callen neruale ant it [is] pris oyntment for synnews. [Cf. Halliwell, s.v.] **1577** B. GOOGE *Heresbach's Husb.* iii. (1586) 134 b, Take Nerualle and Hony, boyled togeather.. and annoynt al the sayde places. **1577–87** HOLINSHED *Chron.* III. 1031/1 That he should annoint the other [horses] with neruall, as if they had beene lamed with trauell. **1607** TOPSELL *Four-f. Beasts* (1658) 315 If the Horse be.. hurt in the hip,.. take of the Oyl de-bay,.. of Nerval, of Swines grease.

b. With *a* and *pl.*

1587 MASCALL *Govt. Cattle, Horses* (1627) 134 Take two penny weight of Uerdigrese, with a Smiths neruall. **1597** LOWE *Chirurg.* (1634) 259 For Paralysie.. you shall use fomentations, nervals,.. and lineaments.

nerval (ˈnɜːvəl), *a.* [a. F. *nerval* (16th c.), or ad. L. *nervālis*: see NERVE *sb.* and -AL¹.] Of, relating to, or affecting the nerves; neural.

1636 DAVENANT *Platonick Lovers* II, Whether the nervall Conjugations be But seven. **1702** BAYNARD in Floyer *Hot & Cold Bath.* II. (1709) 216 A Daughter cur'd in a Nerval Case, where there was Aphonia. **1706** PHILLIPS (ed. Kersey), *Nerval Bones*, the Bones of the hinder part of the Head. **1884** GRANVILLE in *Brit. Med. Jrnl.* 7 June 1084 Sometimes.. the nerval or primary nerve-stage.. of fever is prolonged.

nervate (ˈnɜːvət), *a. Bot.* [f. NERVE *sb.* + -ATE².] Of leaves: Having nerves or veins.

1866 *Treas. Bot.* 786/1 *Nervate*, having several ribs.

So **ˈnervated**, *ppl. a.*

1802–3 tr. *Pallas's Trav.* (1812) I. 149, I observed a particular kind of Astragalus,.. with nervated leaves.

†**ˈnervate**, *v. Obs.* [f. L. type **nervāt-*, ppl. stem of **nervāre*, f. *nervus* NERVE *sb.*] *trans.* To nerve, support, strengthen.

1682 D'URFEY *Butler's Ghost* 64 And what if Learn'd Doctoro has, To nervate and support the Cause, Rais'd doubts and fears. *a* **1737** M. GREEN *On Barclay's Apol.* 75 His art.. nervates so the good design, That King Agrippa's case is mine. **1786–92** J. WILLIAMS (A. Pasquin) *Childr. Thespis* (ed. 13) 213 His bolts cannot nervate thy somnific slaves.

nervation (nɜːˈveɪʃən). [ad. L. type **nervātiōn-em*, f. **nervāre*: see prec. Cf. F. *nervation*.]

†**1.** (See quot.) *Obs. rare*⁻⁰.

1721 BAILEY, *Nervation*, a joining together, a strengthening as it were by Sinews.

2. *Bot.* The disposition of the fibro-vascular bundles in the blades of leaves, etc.

1849 BALFOUR *Man. Bot.* §141 The distribution of the veins has been called Venation, sometimes Nervation. **1854** HOOKER *Himal. Jrnls.* I. i. 8 The outlines of the fronds of ferns and their nervation. **1884** BOWER & SCOTT *De Bary's Phaner.* 168 Those vessels.. which traverse the nervation of the leaf.

3. The action of the nerves.

1851 J. W. HADDOCK (*title*) Somnolism and Psycheism; or, the Science of the Soul, and the Phenomena of Nervation, as Revealed in Vital Magnetism.

So **ˈnervature.**

1866 DK. ARGYLL *Reign of Law* iv. 195 In the mantis the tracery.. is drawn in imitation of the nervature of a leaf.

nerve (nɜːv), *sb.* Also 6–7 **nerue**, 7 **nerv.** [ad. L. *nerv-us* sinew, tendon, bow-string, etc., app. related to the synonymous Gr. νεῦρον, which in later use (Galen, etc.) also has the mod. sense of 'nerve'. Hence also It. *nervo*, Sp. *nervio*, F. *nerf*; the latter is represented in ME.: see NERF *sb.*]

I. 1. a. A sinew or tendon. In later use only *poet.* or in phr. ***to strain every nerve***, to make the utmost (physical) exertion.

1538 STARKEY *England* II. i. 158 Thys ordur, vnyte, and concord, wherby the partys of thys body are, as hyt were, wyth senewys and neruys knyt togyddur. *c* **1605** DRAYTON *Odes* xiii. 30 Vp whose steepe side who swerues, It behoues t'haue strong Nerues. **1671** MILTON *Samson* 1646 This utter'd, straining all his nerves, he bow'd. **1697** DRYDEN *Virg. Georg.* III. 297 Before his tender Joints with Nerves are knit. **1736** GRAY *Statius* ii. 7 He.. Brac'd all his nerves, and every sinew strung. **1784** COWPER *Task* III. 90 He that sold His country, or was slack when she required His every nerve in action and at stretch. **1818** SHELLEY *Julian* 425 Like some maniac monk, I had torn out The nerves of manhood by their bleeding root. **1871** L. STEPHEN *Playgr. Eur.* (1894) viii. 184 We strained every nerve to reach the top.

fig. **1780** JEFFERSON *Corr.* Wks. 1859 I. 251 We shall exert every nerve to assist you. **1860** SMILES *Self Help* 164 Lawrence and Montgomery.. strained every nerve to keep their own province in perfect order.

†**b.** [After L. use.] The penis. *Obs. rare.*

1662 J. BARGRAVE *Pope Alex. VII* (1867) 138 Receiving so many blows a day with a bull's nerve until he was beaten to death. **1693** DRYDEN *Juvenal* x. 262 The limber Nerve, in vain provok'd to rise. **1693** —— *Persius* iv. (1699) 462.

2. *fig.* **a.** in *pl.* Those things, parts, or elements, which constitute the main strength or vigour *of* something.

1603 SHAKS. *Meas. for M.* I. iv. 53 Those that know the very Nerues of State. **1638** SIR T. HERBERT *Trav.* (ed. 2) 86 Not that he wanted (the nerves of war) mony. **1683** *Argt. for Union* 20 They have the Nerves of worldly Power, that is, banks of Money. **1776** GIBBON *Decl. & F.* xvi. I. 564 Prosperity had relaxed the nerves of discipline. **1832** AUSTIN *Jurispr.* (1879) I. 301 Good laws well administered are.. the nerves of the common weal.

b. *sing.* in same sense. Also applied to persons.

1606 SHAKS. *Tr. & Cr.* I. iii. 55 Agamemnon, Thou great Commander, Nerue, and Bone of Greece. **1682** DRYDEN & LEE *Dk. Guise* II. ii, Ordnance, munition, and the nerve of war, Sound infantry. **1726** CAVALLIER *Mem.* I. 109 Money, which is the Nerve and Sinew of War. **1878** BOSW. SMITH *Carthage* 341 Hannibal had been the nerve and soul of the war. **1894** ILLINGWORTH *Personality* iii. 65 Morality, which is the very nerve of personality.

c. *pl.* without const. Resources. *rare*⁻¹.

1643 PRYNNE *Sov. Power Parl.* II. 2 His Revenues; (the Nerves with which he should support this unnaturall civill warre).

3. a. Strength, vigour, energy.

1605 CHAPMAN, etc. *Eastw. Hoe* III. i, Braue Gossip, all that I can do To my best Nerue, is wholy at your seruice. **1659** MILTON *Civ. Power* Wks. 1851 V. 336 Having herin the scripture so copious and so plane, we have all that can be properly calld true strength and nerve. **1671** —— *Samson* 638 He led me on to mightiest deeds Above the nerve of mortal arm. **1760–2** GOLDSM. *Cit. W.* lxxii, Not.. too near extreme wealth to slacken the nerve of labour. **1841** CATLIN *N. Amer. Ind.* lvi. (1844) II. 207 Nerve was given liberally to our paddles. **1874** STUBBS *Const. Hist.* ix. (1897) I. 269 The Normans..added nerve and force to the system with which they identified themselves.

b. *transf.* Texture (of wool).

1839 URE *Dict. Arts* 144 Too long a continuance of the wool in the yolk water, hurts its quality very much... It is said then to have lost its nerve.

c. Of cork: (see quot.).

1878 *Encycl. Brit.* VI. 402/1 In the heating operation the surface is charred, and thereby the pores are closed up, and what is termed 'nerve' is given to the material.

4. a. A sinew or tendon extracted from the body of an animal, esp. as used for some purpose.

1674 tr. *Scheffer's Lapland* 100 Pine or Deale boards, not fasten'd with nails, but sew'd together..commonly with Rain-deers nerves. **1802** *Brookes' Gazetteer* (ed. 12) s.v. *Lapland*, They prepare the nerves of the raindeer in such a manner as to make them serve for thread. **1865** TYLOR *Early Hist. Man.* 130 They would throw nerves or sinews into the fire.

b. *poet.* [After L. use.] A bow-string.

1719 YOUNG *Busiris* I. i, When a Persian arm Can thus with vigour its reluctance bend, And to the nerve its stubborn force subdue. **1791** COWPER *Iliad* VIII. 371 Teucer had newly fitted to the nerve An arrow keen. **1818** KEATS *Endym.* IV. 411 He tries the nerve of Phoebus' golden bow. *fig.* **1781** COWPER *Table-T.* 623 Then like a bow long forced into a curve, The mind, released from too constrained a nerve, Flew to its first position.

c. (See quot. and Du Cange, s.v. *Nervus.*)

1854 WISEMAN *Fabiola* II. xxi, Let this Lucianus be kept in the nerve (stocks) with his feet stretched to the fifth hole.

†5. *Sc.* A narrow band or strap of material used to ornament a garment. *Obs. rare*$^{-1}$.

After French use: cf. NERVE *v.* 1.

1531 *Acc. Ld. H. Treas. Scotl.* (1905) VI. 20 For xv elnis blak satyn..to be ane goune cuttit out with tway nervis of the selff.

6. a. *Bot.* One of the ribs or fibres of vascular matter extending through the parenchyma of a leaf; esp. the midrib.

1585 HIGINS tr. *Junius' Nomencl.* 113 *Neruus.* The nerue, sinew or string of a leafe, as in plantaine. **1607** TOPSELL *Four-f. Beasts* (1658) 474 There is an herb..the nerve whereof in the middle is red. **1671** MARTEN in *Acc. Sev. Late Voy.* II. (1694) 68 Through the middle of it run two black Stroaks or Nerves to the Stalk. **1712** tr. *Pomet's Hist. Drugs* I. 180 The Leaves are smal and fine, growing by Couples on each Side of a Nerve or Rib. **1796** WITHERING *Brit. Plants* (ed. 3) III. 794 The nerve or keel does not extend to the extremity of the leaves. **1835** LINDLEY *Introd. Bot.* (1839) 129 If other veins similar to the midrib pass from the base to the apex of a leaf, such veins have been named nerves. **1863** M. J. BERKELEY *Brit. Mosses* iii. 14 There is one central nerve of variable length and thickness, occasionally projecting far beyond the tip of the leaf.

b. *Ent.* = NERVURE.

1833 LYELL *Princ. Geol.* III. 277 The nerves of the wings in almost all the Diptera, are perfectly distinct.

7. *Arch.* (See quots.)

A French sense, perh. never in actual English use.

1727–38 CHAMBERS *Cycl.* s.v., Nerves, in architecture, denote the mouldings of projecting arches of vaults. **1823** P. NICHOLSON *Pract. Build.* 589 *Nerves*, the mouldings of the groined ribs of Gothic vaults. **1850** PARKER *Gloss. Archit.* (ed. 5) 325 *Nerves*, a term sometimes applied to the ribs and mouldings on the surface of a vault, but it is not technical.

II. 8. a. A fibre or bundle of fibres arising from the brain, spinal cord, or other ganglionic organ, capable of stimulation by various means, and serving to convey impulses (esp. of sensation or motion) between the brain, etc., and some other part of the body.

1606 SHAKS. *Ant. & Cl.* IV. viii. 21 Yet ha we A Braine that nourishes our Nerues. **1626** BACON *Sylva* §400 An Eye..thrust forth, so as it hanged a pretty distance by the Visuall Nerve. **1656** tr. *Hobbes' Elem. Philos.* (1839) 392 Certain spirits and membranes, which..involve the brain and all the nerves. **1704** F. FULLER *Med. Gymn.* (1711) 25 Cutting off a Nerve always causes the wasting of the Part to which that Nerve leads. **1744** BERKELEY *Siris* §102 As the nerves are instruments of sensation, it follows that spasms in the nerves may produce all symptoms. **1800** *Med. Jrnl.* IV. 340 Fallopius was the first who distinguished this nerve from the proper nerve of the voice. **1868** SPENCER *Princ. Psychol.* (1872) I. II. iii. 207 A nerve is a thread of unstable nitrogenous substance..along which..there runs a wave of molecular change. **1873** MIVART *Elem. Anat.* 399 The spinal nerves arise in pairs from opposite sides of the spinal marrow.

b. In non-scientific use, with reference to feeling, courage, etc. Phr. ***to live on one's nerves***: to lead an emotionally exhausting life.

1601 B. JONSON *Poetaster* Introd., Light, I salute thee, but with wounded nerues. **1742** POPE *Dunc.* IV. 56 Chromatic tortures soon shall..Break all their nerves, and fritter all their sense. **1764** GOLDSM. *Trav.* 220 Those powers that..Catch every nerve, and vibrate through the frame. **1802** MAR. EDGEWORTH *Angelina* iv, Not the fittest companion in the world for a person of your ladyship's nerves. **1842** TENNYSON *Walking to Mail* 95 What know we of the secret of a man? His nerves were wrong. **1879** BROWNING *Martin Relph* 56 We soldiers need nerves of steel! **1927** *Daily Tel.* 1 Nov. 7 The correspondence about the dramatic version of 'The Secret Agent'..is almost interminable. One sees that Conrad lived on his nerves, as the French say, and that he took a secret delight in parading his petty cares. **1932** AUDEN *Orators* I. 16 Dare-devils of the soul, living dangerously upon their nerves.

c. *transf.* and *fig.*

1681–6 J. SCOTT *Chr. Life* (1747) III. 280 The political Nerves and Arteries, by which their several Parts..are united to one another. **1781** COWPER *Table-T.* 487 The Muse..pours a sensibility divine Along the nerve of every feeling line. **1856** STANLEY *Sinai & Pal.* ii. (1858) 126 The nerves of the faith of Israel were not unstrung. **1898** H. H. FURNESS *Pref. Winter's Tale* 13 In feeling the pulse of that public he had as a guide the most sensitive of nerves: the pocket.

d. *pl.* A disordered nervous system; nervousness.

Quots. ?1792 and 1839 perhaps belong in sense 8b.

?**1792** I. PIGOT *Let.* in A. Leslie *Mrs. Fitzherbert* (1960) ix. 87 She says her spirits are so damped and her nerves so bad, she must go out to..soothe her mind by change of scene and country. **1839** DICKENS *Let.* 5 Mar. (1965) I. 519 Recovering from an attack 'on the Nerves'. **1890** *Spectator* 5 Apr., As to his dying of 'nerves', that is a story sure to be circulated about anybody whose life it is necessary to guard. **1892** M. NORTH *Recoll. Happy Life* I. 107 That tree..always gave me a fit of nerves. **1914** G. W. YOUNG *From Trenches* vii. 143 The control of the population is admirable in its restraint. We have no 'nerves' here yet. **1920** H. CRANE *Let.* 23 Nov. (1965) 46 I'm sorry to know you are having such an ordeal of 'nerves'. **1948** A. CHRISTIE *Taken at Flood* I. i. 20 The poor girl was blitzed and had shock from blast... She's a mass of nerves.

e. Phr. ***to get on one's nerves***: to (begin to) affect one with irritation, impatience, fear, or the like.

1903 'C. E. MERRIMAN' *Lett. from Son to his Self-Made Father* vi. 75 I've worried a lot since you went away. The business seems to have got on my nerves. **1908** H. G. WELLS *War in Air* iv. 125 This flying gets on one's nerves. *Ibid.* v. 174 All this looking down and floating over things and smashing up people, it's getting on my nerves. **1910** *Chambers's Jrnl.* Mar. 155/2 Sometimes I hate this accursed country... It gets on one's nerves at times. **1920** B. C. CRONIN *Timber Wolves* ii. 34 Hotel hogs, I call 'em. Come in and jolly a chap as if they owned the whole joke. Gets on your nerves when you've been out of your bed all night. **1941** A. L. ROWSE *Tudor Cornwall* xi. 276 The siege..got on people's nerves. **1959** T. S. ELIOT *Elder Statesman* III. 99, I remember, when I came home for the holidays How it used to get on my nerves, when I saw you Always sitting there with your nose in a book. **1972** J. WILSON *Hide & Seek* vii. 118 Alice and I are really close, even if we do get on each other's nerves sometimes.

f. ***war of nerves***: the use of hostile or subversive propaganda to undermine morale and cause confusion and uncertainty; psychological warfare.

1940 *Ann. Reg. 1939* 81 The British public..did not allow the 'war of nerves' organised by the Nazi Government to interfere in the least with its August holiday. **1953** E. SIMON *Past Masters* IV. ii. 223 War of nerves... Best thing to do is take no notice. **1974** P. WRIGHT *Lang. Brit. Industry* ii. 26 Recent threats of conflicts have produced, e.g., *cold war* and *war of nerves*.

9. a. Nervous fibre.

1839–47 *Todd's Cycl. Anat.* III. 596/1 The influence which nerve exerts upon muscle to provoke it to contraction. **1877** HUXLEY & MARTIN *Elem. Biol.* 257 Tease out a bit of fresh nerve in..sodic chloride.

fig. **1778** MISS BURNEY *Evelina* lxiv, 'Your Ladyship's constitution..is infinitely delicate'. 'Indeed it is... I am nerve all over!' **1855** PRESCOTT *Philip II*, I. (1857) 79 Paul seemed to be always in a state of nervous tension. 'He is all nerve', the Venetian minister..writes of him.

b. An attack or fit of nervousness.

1815 JANE AUSTEN *Emma* xi, She..had many fears and many nerves.

10. a. Courage or coolness in exciting or dangerous circumstances; boldness, assurance.

1809 W. IRVING *Knickerb.* IV. ii. (1820) 365 He..spoke forth like a man of nerve and vigor. **1826** DISRAELI *Viv. Grey* II. xiii, You have nerve enough, you know, for anything. **1852** TENNYSON *Ode Wellington* 37 O iron nerve to true occasion true! **1873** BLACK *Pr. Thule* xxvii. 456 Do you think you have nerve to cut this hook out of my finger?

b. *colloq.* Audacity, impudence, cheek. Esp. in phr. ***to have a nerve*** or ***to have the nerve to***.

1887 *Lantern* (New Orleans) 6 Aug. 3/3 Oh, this is a nerve, sure. **1890** BARRÈRE & LELAND *Dict. Slang* II. 84/2 *Nerve* (Eton), impudence. *a* **1911** D. G. PHILLIPS *Susan Lenox* (1917) I. xx. 352 More money!.. You *have* got a nerve!—when factories are shutting down everywhere. **1921** *Daily Colonist* (Victoria, B.C.) 5 Apr. 4/2 No one had the nerve to claim this should be done, because it would have been laughed out of court immediately. **1925** WODEHOUSE *Sam the Sudden* xxv. 219 'You mean to tell me that you had the—the nerve—the insolence—.' He gulped. **1929** [see HONESTLY *adv.* 2b]. **1930** V. SACKVILLE-WEST *Edwardians* vi. 220 The cabby exclaimed that the young toff had a nerve and no mistake. **1942** *Q. Jrnl. Speech* Feb. 6/2 In low brow programs..we note..'you've got a nerve'. **1975** S. BRETT *Cast* xiii. 136 Joanne Menzies looked at him coolly. 'You've got a nerve.'

11. *attrib.* and *Comb.* **a.** Attributive, as ***nerve-ache, -action, -branch, -bulb, -bundle, -chain, -channel, -end, -network, -pill, -test, -tester, -tip, -world***, etc.

The number of such combs., esp. in recent medical works, is very great; only some of the earlier or more prominent examples are illustrated here.

1822–34 *Good's Study Med.* (ed. 4) III. 217 *Nerve-ache of the face. **1889** MIVART *Truth* 266 The other *nerve-actions, which are not felt. **1877** M. FOSTER *Physiol.* III. i. 344 The sensory nerves..can readily be traced in the mixed *nerve-branches. **1888** ROLLESTON & JACKSON *Anim. Life* 678 The granular mass..is probably a sensory *nerve-bulb. **1876** BRISTOWE *Th. & Pract. Med.* (1878) 279 The connective tissue of the *nerve-bundles. **1888** ROLLESTON & JACKSON *Anim. Life* 505 A ventral sinus..lodging the *nerve-chain. **1902** *Chambers's Jrnl.* 15 Feb. 166/1 Muscular repose means that the muscles are relaxed and the *nerve-channels free. **1951** J. M. FRASER *Psychol.* ii. 13 A message..will be sent along a nerve-channel to the brain. **1879** *St. George's Hosp. Rep.* IX. 781 Those who study *nerve diseases. **1884** tr. *Lotze's Metaph.* 456 Producing effects in the same *nerve-element. **1874** GARROD & BAXTER *Mat. Med.* 182 It is doubtful whether it affects the motor *nerve-ends. **1953** R. LEHMANN *Echoing Grove* 159 In the silence Dinah's nerve ends crept, contracted, listening for the guns, the sirens. **1969** *Listener* 22 May 733/3 In Debussy's case this led to Impressionism, which lived at the nerve ends. **1888** ROLLESTON & JACKSON *Anim. Life* 498 The antennæ lodge peculiar *nerve-endings. **1855** *Q. Rev.* XCVI. 110 There is already a mind to attend to the *nerve excitation. **1879** HARLAN *Eyesight* ii. 19 The internal..layer is composed of delicate *nerve-fibrils. **1839–47** *Todd's Cycl. Anat.* III. 594/1 The *nerve filaments are simply placed in juxta-position. **1870** ROLLESTON *Anim. Life* 132 The chain of *nerve ganglia. **1878** J. FISKE in *N. Amer. Rev.* CXXVI. 33 The causation of consciousness by *nerve-matter. *Ibid.* 36 The *nerve-motion, in disappearing, is simply distributed into other nerve-motions. **1947** *Mind* LVI. 57 In the nervous system the 'variables' are mostly impulse-frequencies at various points in the *nerve-network. **1972** *Sci. Amer.* Feb. 88/2 The major part of the sympathetic nerve network stimulates the secretion of norepinephrine. **1907** *Yesterday's Shopping* (1969) 505/1 Carter's little liver pills... *Nerve pills. **1975** M. CRICHTON *Great Train Robbery* xiii. 78 He was forced to down two Carter's Little Nerve Pills and some tincture of opium for his pain. **1879** CALDERWOOD *Mind & Br.* iii. 41 A network of controlling fibres, known as a *nerve-plexus. **1877** HUXLEY & MARTIN *Elem. Biol.* 241 Divide the *nerve-roots of the spinal cord. **1839–47** *Todd's Cycl. Anat.* III. 593/1 Bound together by fibrous membrane, the *nerve-sheath. **1884** J. TAIT *Mind in Matter* (1892) 123 The unit of sensation is a *nerve-shock. **1876** BERNSTEIN *Five Senses* 23 In the healed scar the *nerve-stems are often irritated. **1876** *Trans. Clinical Soc.* IX. 101 Something like the '*nerve-storm' of migraine swept the medulla oblongata. **1888** ROLLESTON & JACKSON *Anim. Life* 568 The..radial vessels lie beneath the corresponding *nerve structures. **1839–47** *Todd's Cycl. Anat.* III. 596/1 We have no evidence of any mingling of the true *nerve-substance with the sarcous elements. **1872** HUMPHRY *Myology* 7 The arrangement does not interfere with the *nerve-supply. **1909** *Westm. Gaz.* 29 May 8/3 (*heading*) A zoological *nerve-test. **1894** *Strand* Feb. 119/1 A visit to this place is the finest and most complete *nerve-tester in the world! **1890** W. JAMES *Princ. Psychol.* I. vi. 150 This must be because the number of sensations from the elementary *nerve-tips affected was too small. **1936** F. R. LEAVIS *Revaluation* v. 184 The sentiments and attitudes of the patriotic and Anglican Wordsworth..are external, general and conventional; their quality is that of the medium they are proffered in, which is..not felt into from within as something at the nerve-tips, but handled from outside. **1868** SPENCER *Princ. Psychol.* (1872) I. I. i. 12 Were it the sole function of *nerve-tissue to originate motion. **1839–47** *Todd's Cycl. Anat.* III. 647/2 A very interesting form of *nerve-vesicle. **1878** *N. Amer. Rev.* CXXVI. 35 Heat-waves, light-waves, *nerve-waves, etc. **1890** *Nerve-world [see *mind-world*].

b. Objective, as ***nerve-cutting, -destroying, -dissolving, -irritating, -lacerating, -racking, -rending, -shaking, -shattering, -stretching, -testing, -trying, -wracking; nerve-wrackingly*** adv.; instrumental, as ***nerve-drawn, -racked, -ridden, -shaken, -shattered, -worn, -wracked***.

1831 YOUATT *Horse* 110 The operation of neurotomy, or *nerve-cutting. **1874** J. W. LONG *Amer. Wild-fowl* 31 They must consequently have greater bone-smashing and *nerve-destroying effects. **1842** TENNYSON *Vis. Sin* 44 The *nerve-dissolving melody Flutter'd headlong from the sky. **1937** V. WOOLF *Years* 388 A queer face; knit up; *nerve-drawn; fixed. **1887** HISSEY *Holiday on Road* 162 The sounds are rather peace-giving than *nerve-irritating. **1911** W. OWEN *Let.* 17 Sept. (1967) 83 The *nerve-lacerating speech of the pompous vigilator. **1933** A. N. WHITEHEAD *Adventures of Ideas* xvi. 245 A red-irritation is prevalent among *nerve-racked people and among bulls. **1812** SHELLEY *Let.* 27 Dec. (1964) I. 347 My removal from your *nerve racking & spirit quelling metropolis. **1908** *Westm. Gaz.* 22 Feb. 2/3 The nerve-racking work of the telephone-girls. **1909** *Chambers's Jrnl.* Mar. 205/2 In all the large towns in Britain there is also far too much nerve-racking, unnecessary noise. **1973** *Times* 30 June 13/5 My own King Charles's head is the use of 'nerve-wracking' for 'nerve-racking'. **1897** *Month* Oct. 374 The next *nerve-rending sound which might occur. **1892** E. LAWLESS *Grania* II. 7 He..seemed to be even more *nerve-ridden than usual. **1930** R. MACAULAY *Staying with Relations* xxi. 313 Adrian..had already shown himself a husband too impatient and too nerve-ridden to endure for long so much irrational excitement at his side. **1939** D. CECIL *Young Melbourne* vi. 150 He [sc. Byron] was a raw, nerve-ridden boy of genius. **1818** SCOTT *Hrt. Midl.* xiii, Men whose spirits..are *nerve-shaken, timorous, and unenterprising. **1820** KEATS *Let.* ? Feb. (1958) II. 262 The medicine I am at present taking..is of a *nerve-shaking nature. **1897** MARY KINGSLEY *W. Africa* 192 During breakfast their conduct is nerve-shaking. **1933** J. CARY *Amer. Visitor* vii. 88 Uli shrank away from the white men and uttered another nerve-shaking yell. **1929** *Observer* 17 Nov. 11/3 Jean Jacques Bernard's interesting play..about a *nerve-shattered and unreasonably jealous husband. **1975** C. DENNIS *Somebody just grabbed Annie!* 195 Close-up of a nerve-shattered Ilima. **1909** *Westm. Gaz.* 28 Sept. 4/2 The work of the engine-driver and fireman is..by no means of the *nerve-shattering description that some would have us believe. **1973** *Nation Rev.* (Melbourne) 31 Aug. 1464/3 Marasco's nerve-shattering novel *Burnt offerings*. **1879** *St. George's Hosp. Rep.* IX. 332 This case..was treated by *nerve-stretching. **1973** D. FRANCIS *Slay-Ride* vii. 80 A *nerve-testing isolation. **1853** R. S. SURTEES *Sponge's Sp. Tour* (1893) 175 The more *nerve trying noise of a floundering stumble over a heap of stones. **1792** J. BYNG *Torrington Diaries* (1936) III. 5, I will not accord to the unnatural hours. *Nerve-worn, and with reason, I must..take the field. **1922** D. H. LAWRENCE *Let.* 15 May (1932) 547 In many ways it [sc. Australia] is older: more nerve-worn. **1911** E. POUND *Canzoni* 46 How our modernity, *Nerve-wracked and broken, turns Against time's way. **1925** Nerve-wracked [see GONE *ppl. a.* 3b]. **1909** *Daily Chron.* 9 Feb. 5/1 Despite his *nerve-wracking experience, he had the courage to endeavour to return to search for him. **1973** *Guardian* 28 June 11/1 The worst thing is getting a call in the middle of the night saying that the windows of my husband's business have been blown in again... It's nerve wracking sitting here. **1963** A. Ross *Australia 63* i. 42 The handsome and the hazardous were jostling *nerve-wrackingly together.

12. Special combs., as **nerve block, blocking,** inactivation of the nerve supplying a particular area of the body, esp. by use of a local anæsthetic; **nerve-canal, -cavity,** the pulp-cavity of a tooth; **nerve cell,** one of the cells composing the cellular element of nervous tissue; also *attrib.*; **nerve-centre,** a group of ganglion-cells closely connected with one another and associated in performing some function; also *fig.*; **nerve-collar** = *nerve-ring*; **nerve-cord,** a cord of nervous tissue; **nerve current,** a signal propagated along a nerve; a series of nerve impulses; **nerve-deafness,** deafness due to disorder of the acoustic nerve; **nerve-doctor,** a specialist in the treatment of nervous diseases; **nerve-fibre,** the fibrous matter composing the nervous system, or one of the thread-like units of this; **nerve-force,** the force supposed to be liberated in nerve-cells; **nerve gas,** any poisonous gas or vapour that has a weakening or paralysing effect on the nervous system, esp. for use in warfare; also *fig.*; **nerve-glue,** neuroglia; **nerve impulse,** a wave of excitation in a nerve fibre accompanied by a brief, temporary change in electrical potential, motion of which constitutes transmission of a stimulus along the fibre; **nerve-instruments,** dentists' instruments for extracting or destroying a nerve, or for cleaning out the nerve-cavity (Knight, 1875); **nerve-knot,** a ganglion; also *fig.*; **nerve-needle,** (*a*) an æsthesiometer; (*b*) a dental instrument (see the quot. for *nerve-canal*); **nerve net,** a diffuse network of neurones found in cœlenterates, echinoderms, and other organisms which conducts excitations in all directions from the area stimulated; †**nerve-oil,** an oil for strained sinews (*obs.*); **nerve-paste,** a paste used to kill the nerve of a tooth; **nerve-path,** a route (assumed to be inborn or developed through use) by which a specific sensory stimulus or motor response is propagated through the nervous system; **nerve-patient,** a patient suffering from a nervous disorder; **nerve physiology** = *neurophysiology* s.v. NEURO-; so ***nerve-physiologist***; **nerve-plate,** a disk-like termination of a nerve; **nerve-ring,** the nerve-cords and ganglia forming a ring round the œsophagus in worms and other animals; **nerve-route** = *nerve-path* above; **nerve-sick** *a.*, suffering from nervous illness; **nerve-specialist** = *nerve-doctor* above; **nerve-track,** 'the collective nerve-fibres which run through parts of the central nervous system to a distant collection of ganglion-cells' (*Syd. Soc. Lex.* 1892); so **nerve-tract**; **nerve-trunk,** a main stem or chief nerve; **nerve-tube** = *nerve-fibre*; so **nerve-tubule**; **nerve-tunic,** an investiture of nervous tissue; **nerve-twig,** one of the ultimate ramifications of a nerve; **nerve war** = *war of nerves* (sense 8 f); also *joc.*; **nerve-winged** *a.*, having wings marked with nerves.

1923 *Jrnl. Amer. Med. Assoc.* 29 Sept. 1079/1 (*heading*) The value of sacral *nerve block anesthesia in obstetrics. **1941** *Brit. Jrnl. Psychol.* July 69 The simplest explanation of the blindness [due to pressure] is that the stoppage of circulation produces retinal anoxia and nerve-block, probably in the ganglionic layers. **1970** W. H. Parker *Health & Dis. in Farm Animals* viii. 94 Dehorning is the removal of horns already in existence on older cattle, essentially a veterinarian's job involving nerve block anaesthesia. **1906** J. M. Patton *Anaesthesia & Anaesthetics* (ed. 2) xvii. 208 Bodine sees no reason why all major surgery should not be done by Corning's *nerve-blocking method of injecting directly into the nerves supplying the limb. **1972** *Jrnl. Pharmacol. & Exper. Ther.* CLXXXII. 442/1 The nerve blocking action of the insecticide, allethrin, is unique in the sense that it is highly dependent on temperature. **1875** Knight *Dict. Mech.* 1521/2 *Nerve-needle*, a tool used for broaching out the *nerve-canal. *Ibid.* s.v. *Nerve Instruments*, Instruments for excavating and filling *nerve-cavities. **1858** G. H. Lewes *Let.* 19 July in G. S. Haight *Geo. Eliot Lett.* (1954) II. 469 It was so very amusing to find myself thinking of '*nerve cells' amid the grand mountains, and of physiological processes on the shores of a lake. **1873** A. Flint *Physiol. Man* i. 18 The nerve-cells..are the only parts capable..of generating..the nerve-force. **1877** Huxley & Martin *Elem. Biol.* 259 The nerve-cell layer. **1868** Spencer *Princ. Psychol.* (1872) I. i. vi. 109 The *nerve-centre which is the seat of the sensation. **1888** Bryce *Amer. Commw.* ci. III. 418 Wall Street is the great nerve centre of all American business. **1910** *Blackw. Mag.* July 9/2 The nerve centres of London, such as the General Post Office, the Telephone Exchanges, the Bank of England,..the Railway Termini, and so on. **1930** Nerve-centre [see *control room*]. **1939** *War Illustr.* 29 Dec. 526 The superstructure is the nerve centre of the ship from which she is navigated and her gunfire controlled. **1942** D. Jenkins *Nature of Catholicity* ii. 48 This brings us to the doctrine of Reformation according to the Word of God which is the nerve-centre of the Reformed doctrine of the Church. **1959** *Daily Tel.* 30 Nov. 19/3 A 'nerve centre' opens to-day opposite Victoria Station for cross-Channel steamer car traffic. **1971** 'D. Halliday' *Dolly & Doctor Bird* v. 71, I was being dragged..through the nerve-centre [*sc.* Miami] of the Sunshine State. **1888** Rolleston & Jackson *Anim. Life* 119 The buccal mass, the *nerve-collar and the columellar muscles. **1877** Huxley & Martin *Elem. Biol.* 150 Tease out a bit of..fresh *nerve-cord in water. **1879** *Mind* IV. 317 All feeling whatever..seems to depend for its physical condition not on simple discharge of *nerve-currents, but on their discharge under arrest, impediment or resistance. **1951** J. M. Fraser *Psychol.* ii. 13 These cells..send a nerve-current along the olfactory nerve to the brain. **1899** *Allbutt's Syst. Med.* VI. 805 Symptoms of *Nerve deafness. **1892** W. James *Coll. Ess. & Rev.* (1920) 327 The men who care little or nothing for ultimate rationality, the biologists, *nerve-doctors, and psychical researchers. **1839–47** *Todd's Cycl. Anat.* III. 592/1 Remak and others describe three distinct parts in the *nerve fibre. **1855** Bain *Senses & Int.* I. ii. §23 The conducting power of nerve fibre. **1872** Huxley *Physiol.* 212 Every fraction of a tone..is represented by its separate nerve-fibre. **1851** Carpenter *Man. Phys.* (ed. 2) 38 The *nerve-force..must be accounted..as the highest of all the forms of vital force. **1877** E. R. Conder *Bas. Faith* ii. 83 When the nerve force ceases to act, all manifestation of the presence of mind ceases. **1940** *Sun* (Baltimore) 13 May 1/5 A specialist in nervous diseases and a chemist..said tonight that a '*nerve gas', reported possibly used by the Nazis..was 'entirely within the range of possibility'. **1960** Koestler *Lotus & Robot* II. xii. 274 Once a balm for self-inflicted bruises, it [*sc.* Zen Buddhism] has become a kind of moral nerve-gas. **1962** L. Deighton *Ipcress File* xxi. 141 They won't be using kids' stuff like this bomb. It will be area saturation with suitable nerve gases. **1968** *Observer* 16 June 9/1 The nerve gases are liquids which are most lethal when inhaled as fine droplets, but can also be absorbed through the skin. **1975** *Times* 6 Jan. 1/2 MPs are to question ministers about a report that the formula for a lethal nerve gas has been taken off the secret list. **1879** Calderwood *Mind & Br.* ii. 25 The cells are packed together in a glutinous substance, which Virchow has named *nerve-glue. **1900** *Nature* 26 July 291/1 The futility of those hypotheses which would explain the passage of the *nerve-impulse as a mere propagated polarisation. **1927** Haldane & Huxley *Animal Biol.* v. 123 (*caption*) Diagram to illustrate the course of nerve-impulses concerned in a spinal reflex. **1966** *McGraw-Hill Encycl. Sci. & Technol.* IX. 52/2 The rate of conduction of nerve impulses varies in proportion to the diameter of the nerve fiber. **1971** J. Z. Young *Introd. Study Man* ii. 28 This is best known for nerve cells, whose signals the nerve impulses (action potentials) are propagated by serial breakdown of the charged surface membrane, allowing sodium to enter and potassium to leave. **1834** *Penny Cycl.* II. 232/1 The nervous system of the arachnida is ganglionic, consisting of *nerve-knots (*ganglia*). **1886** T. Hardy *Mayor Casterbr.* I. 113 Casterbridge was..but the pole, focus, or nerve-knot of the surrounding country life. **1904** C. S. Sherrington in *Nature* 8 Sept. 460/1 We can distinguish two main types of [nervous] system according to the mode of union of the conductors.—(i.) the *nerve-net system, such as met in Medusa and in the walls of viscera, and (ii.) the synaptic system, such as the cerebro-spinal system of Arthropods and Vertebrates. **1942** O. Larsell *Anat. Nervous System* i. 3 The older view of the nerve net as a conduction apparatus for diffusing nerve impulses by protoplasmic continuity of the nerve cell processes has largely yielded to the conception of a synaptic system, even in coelenterates. **1968** D. W. Wood *Princ. Animal Physiol.* x. 214 The nerve nets found in phyla other than the Coelenterata are mostly peripheral to a more organized central nervous system. **1607** Topsell *Four-f. Beasts* (1658) 277 Anoint his body all over with *Nerve oil. **1890** W. James *Princ. Psychol.* I. xi. 458 A downward *nerve-path is thus kept constantly open during concentrated thought. **1926** J. S. Huxley *Essays in Popular Science* vi. 65 The secretions of ovaries pick out and bring into action the nerve-paths appropriate to females, those of testes the paths appropriate to males. **1968** *Biol. Abstr.* XLIX. 2670/1 (*heading*) Age changes of the optic nerve path. **1909** *Chambers's Jrnl.* Dec. 818/1 Every medical practitioner..obtains an increasing number of *nerve-patients year after year. **1890** W. James *Princ. Psychol.* I. i. 5 In still another way the psychologist is forced to be something of a *nerve-physiologist. **1860** *Rep. Brit. Assoc. Adv. Sci. 1859* II. 166 (*heading*) Necessity of a reform in *nerve-physiology. **1890** W. James *Princ. Psychol.* I. ii. 23 The conception of *all* action as conforming to this type [*sc.* reflex] is the fundamental conception of modern nerve-physiology. **1927** J. S. Huxley *Relig. without Revelation* iv. 135 How, precisely, these experiences are generated, psychology and nerve-physiology must learn and tell us. **1888** *Encycl. Brit.* XXIV. 187/1 Strands connecting dorsal *nerve-plate with outer wall of collar. **1878** Bell *Gegenbaur's Comp. Anat.* 110 It is clear that they represent sensory organs from their intimate connection with the *nerve-ring. **1890** A. Hill tr. *H. Obersteiner's Anat. Central Nerv. Organs* 162 One must be very careful in assigning an object to *nerve-routes, especially when they exceed an internode..in length. **1933** A. N. Whitehead *Adventures of Ideas* xiv. 276 Also incipient sense-percepta may be forming themselves in the nerve-routes. **1929** W. Faulkner *Sartoris* III. 173 His thin, *nerve-sick face clouded over with a fine cold distaste. **1930** R. Macaulay *Staying with Relations* xv. 219 Poor child, to be born of quarrelling, nerve-sick parents into a home of strife. **1889** *Nerve-specialist [see SPECIALIST 1]. **1920** A. J. Cummings in 'W.N.P. Barbellion' *Last Diary* p. xxx, I persuaded him..to see a first-class nerve specialist. **1877** M. Foster *Physiol.* III. i. 344 When the anterior roots are cut, the motor nerves alone degenerate, and can be similarly diagnosed in a mixed *nerve-tract. **1851** Carpenter *Man. Phys.* (ed. 2) 463 If all the *nerve-trunks supplying the organ on one side be divided. **1893** Eccles *Sciatica* 69 Inflammation of the nerve-trunk or its branches. **1839–47** *Todd's Cycl. Anat.* III. 592/1 It is evident that the contained matter of the *nerve-tube is extremely soft. **1879** *St. George's Hosp. Rep.* IX. 803 The nerve-tubes of the white matter were natural. **1893** Eccles *Sciatica* 31 Where there is a change in the *nerve-tubules themselves. **1888** *Encycl. Brit.* XXIV. 184/1 An elongate animal, with a plexiform *nerve-tunic. **1899** *Allbutt's Syst. Med.* VIII. 20 If we find..the *nerve-twigs of the limb affected. **1941** *Argus* (Melbourne) *Week-End Mag.* 15 Nov. 1/4 **Nerve war*, grousing or complaining to get things done. **1942** *Ann. Reg. 1941* 212 The firm stand..against Japanese blackmail, cajolery, threats, and 'nerve-war'. **1943** *Daily Tel.* 26 Aug. 6 Berliners are really panicky... Channel steamer has reached a climax which I never thought possible. **1946** F. Williams *Press, Parliament & People* iii. 61 They [*sc.* the Germans]..convinced themselves that the message had been put out deliberately as part of a clever piece of nerve war to mislead them and try to make their defence forces jumpy. **1884** *Leisure Hour* Dec. 742/1 The well-marked, *nerve-winged, solitary ant-lion.

nerve (nɜːv), *v.* Also 6 **nerue, nerf.** [In sense 1, ad. F. *nerver* (Godef. *Compl.*); otherwise from the sb.]

†**1.** *trans. Sc.* To ornament with threads or narrow bands of some material. *Obs. rare.*

1501 Douglas *Pal. Hon.* I. xlvii, Mony entrappit steid with silkis seir, Mony pattrell neruit with gold I tald. **1532** *Acc. Ld. H. Treas. Scot.* (1905) VI. 24 For foure elnis blak taffateis to nerve and geit them [*sc.* hose]. **1532** *Id.* in Pitcairn *Crim. Trials* I. 276* Ane pair of hoise... Item, for ij elnis taffate, to draw þame and nerf þame.

2. To give strength or vigour to (the arm, etc.).

a **1749** A. Hill (T.), Thou, last, Tremendous goddess, nerve this lifted arm! **1791** E. Darwin *Bot. Gard.* I. 105 The mingling currents..Nerve the strong arm, and tinge the blushing cheek. *a* **1810** Shelley *M. Nicholson Fragm.* 3 How long will horror nerve this frame of clay? **1870** Bryant *Iliad* II. xv. 104 He nerved their limbs With vigor ever new. *fig.* **1856** Emerson *Eng. Traits, Literature*, A good writer..makes haste to chasten and nerve his period by English monosyllables. **1887** Bowden *Virg. Æneid* IV. 452 Further to nerve her purpose to leave this world of the sun.

3. To imbue with courage, to embolden.

1810 Scott *Lady of L.* V. xiv, The word..nerves my heart, it steels my sword. **1849** Grote *Greece* II. xxxix. (1862) III. 414 We find thus the Athenians nerved up to the pitch of resistance. **1877** Black *Green Past.* iii, A murmur of indignant repudiation nerved him to a further effort.

absol. **1842** Lytton *Zanoni* I. iii, So much that warmed, and animated, and nerved. **1890** Lowell *To C. F. Bradford*, Bracing essences that nerve To wait, to dare, to strive.

b. *refl.* (also with *mind*, etc.).

1821 Byron *Two Fosc.* I. i, He hath nerved himself, And now defies them. **1829** Lytton *Devereux* I. iii, I think you have been now some years nerving your mind to the exertion. **1887** R. N. Carey *Uncle Max* xxvii. 212 His expression..was that of a man who was nerving himself to bear some great trouble.

†**4.** *intr.* To show signs of nervousness. *Obs.*$^{-1}$.

1801 tr. *Gabrielli's Myst. Husb.* II. 197 Bless me, how dark it is! you ought to have had lamps! Come, child, how you nerve!

nerved (nɜːvd), *ppl. a.* [f. NERVE *sb.* + -ED^2.]

1. *Bot.* Of leaves: Having a nerve or nerves; ribbed. Also in combs., as ***one-, five-nerved.***

1800 *Asiatic Ann. Reg.* 264/1 Leaves..entire, one nerved, smooth, veinless. **1835** Lindley *Introd. Bot.* (1839) 129 A leaf with such an arrangement of its veins has been called a nerved leaf. **1874** Garrod & Baxter *Mat. Med.* 226 The leaf..minutely crenated five-nerved.

b. *Her.* (See quot.)

c **1828** Berry *Encycl. Her.* I, *Nerved*..is said of leaves and plants, the fibres of which are borne of a different tincture. **1868** Cussans *Her.* (1893) 104.

2. In *Comb.* Having nerves of a specified kind, as ***full-, strong-, weak-nerved.***

nerveless (ˈnɜːvlɪs), *a.* [f. NERVE *sb.* + -LESS.]

1. Wanting in nerve, incapable of effort, weak, inert. **a.** Of persons, their wills, etc.

1742 Pope *Dunc.* IV. 41 There sunk Thalia, nerveless, cold, and dead. **1796** Morse *Amer. Geog.* I. 687 Other concurrent causes have rendered them corrupt and nerveless. **1858** Merivale *Rom. Emp.* lvi. (1865) VII. 69 As an old soldier he despised the nerveless mob of the streets. **1885** *L'pool Daily Post* 7 Mar. 4/6 A nerveless diplomatist who has only to be menaced and he will yield.

b. Of the body or its parts.

1744 Akenside *Pleas. Imag.* I. 519 His keen tempestuous arm Hung nerveless. **1792** S. Rogers *Pleas. Mem.* II. 53 His high heroic spirit bleeds, And from his nerveless frame indignantly recedes. *a* **1821** Keats *Hyperion* I. 18 His old right hand lay nerveless, listless, dead, Unsceptred. **1878** B. Taylor *Deukalion* I. v. 43 He seems to slumber, head on nerveless knees.

2. Of actions, conditions, etc.: Characterized by lack of vigour or energy.

1735 Thomson *Liberty* III. 448 Sad o'er all, profound dejection sat, And nerveless fear. **1851** Ruskin *Stones Ven.* (1874) I. i. 15 Sinking into nerveless rest.., incapable of advance or change. **1888** Mrs. Spender *Kept Secret* III. viii. 136 A spiritless and nerveless life had been his.

b. Of style in writing, drawing, etc.

1763 Warburton *Doct. Grace* I. ix, The Western Eloquence..appeared nerveless and effeminate. **1822** *Blackw. Mag.* XII. 719/1 Lord Byron retains the same nerveless and pointless kind of blank verse. **1899** *Daily News* 20 Feb. 8/4 His nerveless drawing, his awkwardness in the grouping.

3. a. *Bot.* and *Ent.* Having no nervures.

1796 Withering *Brit. Plants* (ed. 3) III. 881 Leaves nerveless, cloven, points acute. **1841** E. Newman *Insects* IV. vi. 271 The fore and hind wings are alike,..generally nerveless. **1870** Hooker *Stud. Flora* 329 *Euphorbia paralias*: ..leaves..nerveless.

b. *Anat.* and *Zool.* Having no nerves.

1862 *Syd. Soc. Year-bk.* 18 The nerveless spots of the..muscle. **1880** Bastian *Brain* 9 The nerveless Amœba.

Hence **ˈnervelessly** *adv.*

1850 Hawthorne *Scarlet L.* xxiii, A man..that tottered on his path so nervelessly. **1894** Mrs. Dyan *Man's Keeping* (1899) 339 Her hand..fell nervelessly to her side.

ˈnervelessness. [f. prec. + -NESS.] A nerveless condition; want of nerve.

1857 R. TOMES *Amer. in Japan* vi. 130 He sank into a state of nervelessness and emaciation painful to look upon. **1888** *Times* 25 Sept. 9/3 He has been exonerated by them from.. gross stolidity and nervelessness.

ˈnervelet. *rare.* [f. NERVE *sb.* + -LET.] †**a.** A tendril. *Obs.* **b.** A little nerve.

1648 HERRICK *Hesper., The Vine*, Her Belly, Buttocks, and her Waste, By my soft nerv'lits were embrac'd. **1894** GOSSE *In Russet & Silver* 20 Every nervelet that upbraids Takes comfort from the pangs that pass.

nerver (ˈnɜːvə(r)). [f. NERVE *sb.* or *v.* + -ER[1].] Something, esp. a drink, that gives one 'nerve' or courage.

1886 BAUMANN *Londinismen* 117/2 *Nerver*, eins für den Durst, Magenlikör. **1889** *St. James's Gaz.* 10 Aug. 3/2 His dose.. possibly contains cardamums, hydrocyanic acid, and tincture of capsicum; a capital 'nerver' in its way. **1895** 'G. MORTIMER' *Like Stars that Fall* iii. 33 You'll pull through all right. I'll give you a nerver of pale sherry and a drop of brandy before you go on.

ˈnervid, *a. rare.* [f. NERVE *sb.* + -ID.] Nervous, strong.

1813 T. BUSBY *Lucretius* v. 1183 What earth spontaneous gave,.. Careless they took, and propt their nervid powers. *Ibid.* 1549 Whose limbs so nervid not to quake, when roll The pealing thunders?

nerviˈfolious, *a. rare*[−1]. [f. L. *nerv-us* NERVE + *folium* leaf. Cf. F. *nervifolié*.] Having nerved leaves.

a **1682** SIR T. BROWNE *Misc. Tracts* (1683) 21 The learned Bauhinus hath not placed it in the Classis of Lilies, but nervifolious Plants.

nervily (ˈnɜːvɪlɪ), *adv.* [f. NERVY *a.*: see -LY[2].] In a nervy manner; boldly; agitatedly.

1911 [see CLASSISM]. **1928** *Daily Express* 15 June 9/4 The blue eyes were not as serene as he would like to have seen them. The professor's grey ones roved nervily from side to side. **1957** M. SPARK *Comforters* iii. 63 Caroline jogged round nervily as the door opened.

nervine (ˈnɜːvaɪn), *a.* and *sb. Med.* [ad. mod.L. *nervīnus* relating to the sinews or nerves (in late L. 'made of sinews'): cf. F. *nervin*, It. and Sp. *nervino*.]

A. *adj.* †**1.** Used for the sinews. *Obs. rare*[−1].

1661 LOVELL *Hist. Anim. & Min.* 423 [Rickets are cured by] balsam of Tolu, the nervine ointment, aregon, and martiat.

2. Having the quality of acting on the nerves, so as to restore them to a normal state; relieving disorders of the nervous system.

1718 QUINCY *Compl. Disp.* 93 This.. enters almost into all the nervine compositions of the Shops. **1822–34** *Good's Study Med.* (ed. 4) III. 446 The warm nervine stimulants as musk, camphor, valerian. **1897** *Allbutt's Syst. Med.* II. 883 One of those nervine agents which all people civilized or uncivilized.. discover to soothe the nervous system.

B. *sb.* **1.** A medicine that acts upon and strengthens or soothes the nerves; a nerve-tonic.

1730 STUART in *Phil. Trans.* XXXVI. 361 Other Medicines taken from the common Class of Nervines. **1777** LIGHTFOOT *Flora Scot.* I. 85 The roots are esteem'd an excellent nervine. **1866** WARING *Trop. Res.* 222 The use of tonics.. of that class termed nervines of which nux vomica is the best.

fig. **1803** BEDDOES *Hygëia* IX. 113, I know not if stories.. would not prove excellent nervines and anodynes.

2. A greasy preparation used in massage.

1887 D. MAGUIRE *Art Massage* ii. (ed. 4) 35 A masseur can use.. balsam of opodeldoc, nervine, and fierveranti.

ˈnerviness. [f. NERVY *a.* + -NESS.]

1. Sinewiness. *rare*[−0].

1611 FLORIO, *Neruosita*, sinewinesse, neruinesse.

2. The state or character of being nervous (sense 9) or nervy (sense 5).

1921 *Glasgow Herald* 15 June 8 The home men had only to shake off their 'nerviness' to reduce the Australian bowling to trundling of good class. **1924** J. SUTHERLAND *Circle of Stars* xxiii. 232 At every footstep he started... Indeed he was so unlike himself that even Barbara commented upon his nerviness. **1975** J. RATHBONE *Kill Cure* I. i. 16 Bury, she supposed, was all right, but there was a nerviness about him that she did not quite like.

nerving (ˈnɜːvɪŋ). *Bot.* [f. NERVE *sb.* + -ING[1].] A nerve or rib of a leaf.

1861 S. THOMSON *Wild Fl.* III. (ed. 4) 215 Many of the glumes and paleæ of the grass flowers are marked by nervings or ribs.

nervism (ˈnɜːvɪz(ə)m). [f. NERVE *sb.* + -ISM.]

1. Nerve-force.

1836–9 *Todd's Cycl. Anat.* II. 94/2 Is the agent discharged by the fish.. identical with common nervism? *Ibid.* 95/2 Theories which make nervism identical with electricity.

2. Nervous excitement.

1887 SMILES *Life & Labour* 67 An altogether abnormal state of nervism and exaltation.

nervo- (also †nerveo-), combining form of L. *nervus* NERVE, as in †**nervo-electric** *a.* = *neuro-electric* adj. s.v. NEURO-; so **nervo-electricity; nervo-muscular** *a.*, concerned with both nerves and muscles; **nervo-sanˈguineous** *a.*, of a nervous and sanguine temperament; **nervo-ˈvital** *a.*, concerned with the nervous and vital functions.

[**1792** A. GALVANI *De Viribus Electricitatis in Motu Musculari* IV. 48 Nerveo-electrici fluidi excursum per musculum ad nervum illum esse.] **1860** A. C. GARRATT *Electro-Physiol. & Electro-Therapeutics* iv. 216 (*heading*) Effects of heat and cold on the *nervo-electric batteries. *Ibid.* vi. 349 May not the brain be thus incessantly charged, says Dr. Watson, if indeed it be.. 'an electric pile constantly in action', discharging itself by the nerves at brief intervals, 'when the tension of the nervo-electricity, developed, reaches a certain point'? **1822** GOOD *Study Med.* IV. 659 The learned Pereboom.. has divided palsy.. into three species; a nervous, muscular and *nerveo-muscular. **1862** SPENCER *First Princ.* II. xvii. §143 (1875) 391 The visible nervo-muscular actions. **1897** *Allbutt's Syst. Med.* III. 493 The nervo-muscular machinery seems to be poisoned by the toxins in the blood. **1884** *Harper's Mag.* Aug. 440/2 Ultra-susceptible and *nervo-sanguineous subjects. *c* **1850** in *Cosmopolitan* (1896) XX. 370/1 He will displace some of the *nervo-vital fluid from the passive brain and deposit it in his own instead.

nervose (nəˈvəʊs), *a.* [ad. L. *nervōs-us* sinewy, vigorous, etc.: see NERVE *sb.* and -OSE.]

†**1.** Affecting the sinews. *Obs. rare*[−1].

c **1400** *Lanfranc's Cirurg.* 99 (Add. MS.), The crampe ys a sekenesse cordouse, oþere ellys nervose.

†**2.** Vigorous, energetic. *Obs. rare*[−1].

1667 *H. More's Div. Dial.* (1713) p. vi, The nervose prosecution of the main Subject of these Dialogues.

3. †**a.** Consisting of, having the nature of, nerves.

1673 RAY *Journ. Low C.* 144 The vapour of Quicksilver doth principally affect the brain and nervose parts. **1725** N. ROBINSON *Th. Physick* 46 Two Kinds of Fibres,.. the one Nervose, and exquisitely quick of Sensation.

b. Pertaining to, characteristic of, the nerves; strengthening or stimulating the nerves.

1880 *Cope's Tobacco Pl.* 539/2 The grown man, in the full exercise of all the nervose functions, can use the nervose aliments with a prudent moderation.

4. *Bot.* Of leaves: Nerved.

1753 CHAMBERS *Cycl. Supp.* s.v. *Leaf, Nervose Leaf*, one whose vessels are simple, and extend themselves parallely from the base toward the summit, without any ramifications. **1760** MILLER *Introd. Bot.* (1775) p. xxx, A nervose leaf.. is one that has single veins [etc.]. **1866** *Treas. Bot.* 786/1.

b. *Ent.* Having nervures.

1819 SAMOUELLE *Entomol. Compend.* 219 Elytra coriaceous, nervose, decussating each other.

Hence †**nerˈvosely** *adv.*, strongly, vigorously.

1678 GALE *Crt. Gentiles* IV. III. 113 Aquinas has copiosely and nervosely defended our hypothesis.

ˈnervosism. [a. F. *nervosisme*: see prec. and -ISM.] A state of nervous disorder.

1884 L. BRACHET *Aix-les-bains* I. 94 Nervosism may be engendered by rheumatic.. diathesis.

nervosity (nəˈvɒsɪtɪ). [ad. L. *nervōsitas* strength: see NERVOSE *a.* and -ITY. Cf. F. *nervosité* (Cotgr.).]

†**1.** Strength. *Obs. rare.*

1611 COTGR., *Nervosité*, neruositie, sinewie strength. **1681** H. MORE *Exp. Dan.* Pref. 17 His Expositions are.. devoid of that strength and nervosity he shews in other things.

2. The state or quality of being nervous; nervousness.

1787 HAWKINS *Life Johnson* 385 How far nervosity.. will excuse a conduct so opposite to.. philanthropy. **1821** *New Monthly Mag.* II. 530 A poor cracked creature, the miserable victim of nervosity. **1884** *Pall Mall G.* 11 Aug. 4/1 Andrieux's.. nervosity is betrayed.. in the husky and tremulous tones of his usually clear voice.

b. A fit of nervousness.

1791 I. MILNER in *Life* vi. (1842) 70 [Working] amuses, and it tends to lessen nervosities, and to dull pain.

3. *Bot.* The fact of being nerved (*Cent. Dict.*).

nervous (ˈnɜːvəs), *a.* Also 7 -vouse, 8 narvous. [ad. L. *nervōs-us*: see NERVOSE *a.* and -OUS. Cf. It., Sp., Pg. *nervoso*, F. *nerveux*.]

†**1.** Affecting the sinews. *Obs. rare*[−1].

c **1400** *Lanfranc's Cirurg.* 99 (Ashm. MS.), Þe crampe is a sijknes cordous eiþer neruous, in þe which.. þe senewis weren drawen to her bigynnynge.

2. Sinewy, muscular; vigorous, strong. **a.** Of parts of the body. Now *rare.*

1413 *Pilgr. Sowle* (Caxton 1483) IV. xxxii. 81 These armes ben neruous, that is to seyn wel frett with senewes. **1653** R. SANDERS *Physiogn.* 248 The arms strong and nervous, having the veins conspicuous. **1677** SIR T. HERBERT *Trav.* (ed. 3) 26 The body of this fish is.. narrow towards the tail, which is nervous. **1720** POPE *Iliad* XXII. 497 The nervous ankles bor'd, his feet he bound With thongs. **1763** SIR W. JONES *Caissa* Poems, etc. (1777) 136 Nervous limbs, where youthful ardour glow'd. *c* **1842** M. J. HIGGINS *Ess.* (1875) p. xviii, By a judicious application of his nervous tail to some prominent branch.

b. Of animals or persons. Now *rare.*

1616 J. LANE *Contn. Sqr.'s Tale* XI. 305 His nervous horse of sorrell shininge hyde. **1756** TOLDERVY *Hist. 2 Orphans* IV. 186 The nervous reaper had levelled the golden field. **1762–9** FALCONER *Shipwr.* I. 716 The nervous crew their sweeping oars extend. **1829** I. TAYLOR *Enthus.* viii. 202 The busy, nervous, and frigid people of the north. **1844** EMERSON *Lect., Yng. Amer.* Wks. (Bohn) II. 296 The nervous, rocky West is intruding a new and continental element into the national mind.

c. Of strength, energy, courage, etc. Also, ***nervous tension*** (with admixture of sense 7).

1828 SCOTT *F.M. Perth* ii, The nervous strength and weight of one of the muscular armourer's [hands]. **1849** THOREAU *Week Concord Riv.* 338 They.. handled their paddles unskilfully, but with nervous energy and determination. **1870** FROUDE *Hist. Eng.* XI. 491 The nervous courage which could face death without flinching. **1933** *Burlington Mag.* Feb. 54/1 Everywhere the nervous tension is relaxed, the rhythms are less vital and less consistent. **1936** *Discovery* Nov. 357/2 His nervous tension is surely not lessened if precautions are taken against his actually watching the operation [on himself]. **1951** M. MCLUHAN *Mech. Bride* (1967) 33/1 Books on how to relax would seem just about to cancel out books on how to build up nervous tension for success drive. **1953** J. S. HUXLEY *Evolution in Action* iv. 91 Behaviour is always the result of a flow of something—what many psychologists and most laymen call nervous energy. Unfortunately, the physiologists are driven to say 'excitation', because *energy* is another word the physicists have taken over from ordinary speech and given a restricted scientific meaning. Perhaps the term 'neurergy' would serve.

3. a. Of writings, arguments, etc.: Vigorous, powerful, forcible; free from weakness and diffuseness.

1637 MEDE *Wks.* (1672) 847 A nervous, close and well-composed Discourse. **1691** T. H[ALE] *New Invent.* p. xlii, The Author hath in so nervous a Manner given.. Directions. **1727** GAY *Fables* I. xxviii, When envy reads the nervous lines, She frets. **1780** COWPER *Let.* 2 July, Whatever is short should be nervous, masculine, and compact. **1828** CARLYLE *Misc.* (1857) I. 197 Mr. Lockhart's own writing is generally so good, so clear, direct and nervous. **1896** F. HARRISON in *19th Cent.* June 981 The nervous and learned works of his more glowing autumn.

b. So of speakers and writers.

1775 T. SHERIDAN *Art Reading* 140 The plain nervous orator will no longer gain attention. **1867** H. KINGSLEY *Silcote of S.* I. 225 Miss Brontë? A good and nervous tho' coarse describer of a narrow landscape.

†**4. a.** Sinewy, tendinous. *Obs.*

1541 R. COPLAND *Guydon's Quest. Chirurg.* D iv, It is a neruous or synewy substaunce. **1615** CROOKE *Body of Man* 777 In the originall this Muscle is broade.. & Neruous. **1661** LOVELL *Hist. Anim. & Min.* 77 Some eate the flesh which is very nervouse. **1726** LEONI *Alberti's Archit.* I. 25/2 The Oak, being hard, close, and nervous, and of the smallest Pores. **1747–96** MRS. GLASSE *Cookery* v. 81 Roast a piece of fillet of veal, cut off the skin and nervous parts.

†**b.** Resembling a sinew in texture; strong. *Obs.*

1601 HOLLAND *Pliny* II. 3 The thred it selfe that they make of their Flax.. is.. neruous also and strong. **1655** tr. *Sorel's Com. Hist. Francion* VII. 9 Which of all thy strings is the hardest to tune?.. It is that which is the biggest and most nervous of all. **1762** FALCONER *To Dk. York* 225 To wake the lyre.. And tune to war the nervous string.

†**c.** Strung with sinews. *Obs. rare*[−1].

1718 ROWE tr. *Lucan* III. 689 From nervous Cross-Bows whistling Arrows fly.

†**5.** *Bot.* Of leaves: Nerved, nervose. *Obs.*

1668 WILKINS *Real Char.* II. iv. 78 Herbs of nervous leaves. **1707** SLOANE *Jamaica* (1725) II. 52 Seven or more ribs.. going through the leaf with some transverse ones, making the leaf very nervous. **1776** J. LEE *Introd. Bot.* 385 *Nervosum*, nervous, with Nerves extended from the Base to the Apex.

6. Full of nerves.

1659 PEARSON *Creed* (1741) 189 The dilaceration of those nervous parts created a most sharp and dolorous sensation. **1727** DE FOE *Eng. Tradesman* vi. (1841) I. 44 As they lessen his stock, so they wound him in the tenderest and most nervous part. **1756** BURKE *Subl. & B.* IV. ix, The retina, or last nervous part of the eye. **1855** BAIN *Senses & Int.* II. ii. §2 The retina, or the nervous coat of the eye.

7. a. Of or belonging to the nerves. ***nervous system***, the complex of nerves and nerve-centres.

1665 *Phil. Trans.* I. 75 Whether there be a Nervous and Nutritious Juice? **1740** CHEYNE *Regimen* 168 Accidents that injure the arterial and nervous system. *Ibid.* 306 The extreme Tenuity of.. nervous Fibre. **1830** R. KNOX *Béclard's Anat.* 226 A very ancient opinion.. attributed to the pericranium the origin of all the nervous membranes. **1848** CARPENTER *Anim. Phys.* 56 The brain and spinal cord are termed the nervous centres. **1874** —— *Ment. Phys.* I. ii. (1879) 53 Irritating.. the cut extremity of the nervous cord.

b. Affecting the nerves; characterized by a disordered state of the nerves. ***nervous breakdown***: see BREAK-DOWN 1 c. Freq. as ***nervous exhaustion, nervous fever, nervous headache.***

1734 CHEYNE (*title*) On Nervous Diseases. **1768** WESLEY *Jrnl.* 4 Jan. (1827) III. 302 It is the most efficacious medicine in nervous disorders. **1787** H. MORE *Let.* June (1925) 120 A very tedious nervous headache has made me less than ever qualified to traffic with you. **1807** A. PUTNAM in *Danvers Hist. Soc. Coll.* (1917) V. 57 Mr. David Tapley is very sick with the nervous fever. **1813** L. HUNT in *Examiner* 22 Feb. 113/2 It was a disorder of what is called the nervous species... A nervous consumption was apprehended. **1857** J. A. SYMONDS *Let.* 16 Nov. (1967) I. 125, I must.. not work much these trials since yesterday I had the same sort of nervous headache. **1869** CLARIDGE *Cold Water Cure* 195 A severe nervous fever ensued. **1899** *Allbutt's Syst. Med.* VIII. 415 In all nervous cases the determination of the dose is a matter of experiment. **1924** H. CRANE *Let.* 23 Sept. (1965) 190 The sneezing and nervous fever.. begin to subside. **1927** 'R. CROMPTON' *William—in Trouble* viii. 207 He's suffering from *nervous exhaustion.* **1973** E. BERCKMAN *Victorian Album* 142 The thought of any considerable threat to her happiness.. is always enough to give me a nervous headache.

c. Pertaining or relating to, occupied with, the nerves.

1804 *Gentl. Mag.* LXXIV. I. 219 You have an unequivocal proof of nervous sympathy. **1848** MILL *Pol. Econ.* I. i. §1 (1876) 15 Labour is.. either muscular or nervous. **1877** M. FOSTER *Physiol.* III. i. 342 The foundation of modern nervous physiology.

Comb. **1858** *Proc. Amer. Philos. Soc.* VI. 291 The electrical nervous-muscular sensibility of man.

8. Of medicines: Acting upon the nerves or nervous system; curative of nervous disorders.

1718 QUINCY *Compl. Disp.* 76 Nervous Simples.. may be extended to take in all those Parts of the Materia Medica by which the Nerves are affected. **1790** *Med. Comm.* II. 489, I ordered.. a cordial or nervous medicine to be taken. **1844** LADY G. FULLERTON *Ellen Middleton* II. xv. 169 She gave me a nervous draught.

9. Of persons: Suffering from disorder of the nerves; also, excitable, easily agitated, timid. Also, ***nervous wreck*** (*colloq.*).

1740 CHEYNE *Regimen* Pref. 1 The.. Consumptive, or Nervous Valetudinarian-low-livers. **1763** *Brit. Mag.* Aug. 406/1 The ladies were too narvous to venture further than the entrance of the cavern. **1783** JOHNSON *Let. to Mrs. Thrale* 24 Nov., A tender, irritable, and as it is not very properly called, a nervous constitution. **1812** J. W. CROKER in *C. Papers* (1884) I. 39 A disposition naturally anxious and nervous. **1865** TROLLOPE *Belton Est.* xi. 126 He was at that moment so nervous that he had cut himself slightly through the trembling of his hand. **1897** *Allbutt's Syst. Med.* VIII. 296, I usually found the stock on both sides to be a highly 'nervous' one. **1899** [see WRECK *sb.*[1] 7 b]. **1906** W. JAMES *Let.* 9 May (1920) II. 251, I didn't hear one pathetic word uttered at the scene of disaster, though of course the crop of 'nervous wrecks' is very likely to come in a month or so. **1932** H. CRANE *Let.* 22 Apr. (1965) 412 It certainly has about made a nervous wreck of me. **1936** J. BUCHAN *Island of Sheep* I. vi. 110 He started at every noise. He was the very model of a nervous wreck.

Comb. **1842** COMBE *Digestion* 303 An energetic or excitable temperament, such as the bilious or nervous-bilious. **1846** LONGF. in *Life* (1891) II. 35 Let us be calm and happy, rather than excitable and nervous-minded.

10. Of feelings or actions: Characterized or accompanied by agitation of the nerves.

1797 JANE AUSTEN *Sense & Sens.* xxix, With all the eagerness of the most nervous irritability. **1844** LADY G. FULLERTON *Ellen Middleton* II. xi. 64 With a nervous attempt at a laugh. **1871** DIXON *Tower* III. i. 7 Nervous terror often makes men bold.

11. Agitating to the nerves; exciting.

1775 CRABBE *Inebriety* Wks. 1834 II. 300 The gentle fair on nervous tea relies. **1834** R. H. FROUDE *Rem.* (1838) I. 359 Really I never saw such a nervous sight. **1843** RUSKIN *Mod. Paint.* I. II. i. §18 (1846) 337 It is a very nervous thing for an ignorant artist.

nervously ('nɜːvəslɪ), *adv.* [f. prec. + -LY[2].]

1. With strength or vigour; forcibly.

1641 J. JACKSON *True Evang. T.* II. 156 S. Augustine nervously takes from them that glorious wreath. **1709** STRYPE *Ann. Ref.* I. xlviii. 483 The Writer undertook to weigh and examine the Grounds and Reasons distinctly,.. which he doth nervously. **1756** W. DODD *Fasting* (ed. 2) 12 The true ground of fasting is very fully discovered and nervously expressed. **1800** *Naval Chron.* IV. 227 The authors.. have been.. nervously concise. **1884** LAURIE *Comenius* (1887) 105 Let all things be taught from the foundation, briefly and nervously.

2. With weakness or agitation of the nerves; in a nervous or excited manner.

1838 LYTTON *Alice* I. iii, Evelyn spoke quickly and nervously, and with quivering lips. **1858** FROUDE *Hist. Eng.* III. xvii. 462 Cromwell.. was waiting nervously at Greenwich for the result of the experiment. **1876** HARDY *Ethelberta* (1890) 336 He paused a few moments nervously.

nervousness ('nɜːvəsnɪs). [f. as prec. + -NESS.] The state or quality of being nervous.

1. Strength, vigour, force.

1727 BAILEY, vol. II, *Nervousness*, fulness of nerves [etc.]. **1756–82** J. WARTON *Ess. Pope* II. ix. 106 If there had been epithets joined with the other substantives, it would have weakened the nervousness of the sentence. **1795** SEWARD *Anecd.* II. 57 His Sermons have great energy of thinking, and a nervousness of language. **1839** HALLAM *Hist. Lit.* II. v. §94 Sometimes we find a spirit and nervousness of strength and sentiment worthy of his name. **1895** SALA in *Daily Tel.* 15 May, His artistic perception has gained.. in strength and nervousness of grasp.

2. Weakness of nerves.

1798 CHARLOTTE SMITH *Yng. Philos.* I. 22 She was led away in a fit of extreme nervousness. **1813** *Examiner* 17 May 317/2 The present luxurious age is remarkable for it's nervousness. **1843** SIR C. SCUDAMORE *Med. Visit Gräfenberg* 55 So distressing a state of nervousness, that.. he became painfully confused. **1878** LECKY *Eng. in 18th C.* II. viii. 440 His faults sprang.. from extreme feebleness, inconstancy, and nervousness.

nervule ('nɜːvjʊl). *Ent.* [a. F. *nervule*, or ad. L. *nervulus*, dim. of *nervus* NERVE.] A small nervure.

1889 *Athenæum* 12 Oct. 491/1 A dense mass of scales crowded together on each side of the nervules. **1897** W. F. KIRBY in Mary Kingsley *W. Africa* 725 Anterior wings with three bullæ—.. one on the recurrent nervule, and the third on the cross-nervule running upwards from the extremity of the internal nervule.

'nervulet. [f. as prec. + -ET[1].] = NERVULE.

1826 KIRBY & SP. *Entomol.* xlvi. IV. 340 *Nervulet.* A little nervure diverging obliquely from the costal into the disk of the wing towards the apex.

nervuration (nɜːvjuː'reɪʃən). [f. NERVURE + -ATION.] = NEURATION.

1899 D. SHARP in *Cambr. Nat. Hist.* VI. v. 319 In the aberrant moths of the genus Costina the nervuration is unusually complex.

nervure ('nɜːvjʊə(r)). [a. F. *nervure*, f. L. *nervus* NERVE: see -URE.]

1. *Ent.* One of the slender hollow tubes forming the framework of the wings of insects.

1816 KIRBY & SP. *Entomol.* xxiii. (1818) II. 347 The nervures are a kind of hollow tube.. which take their origin in the trunk. **1846** DANA *Zooph.* (1848) 155 The ridges of the surface constituting its nervures. **1877** HUXLEY *Anat. Inv. Anim.* vii. 399 The wing is strengthened by radiating thickenings, or nervures, united by delicate transverse ridges.

2. *Bot.* A principal vein of a leaf.

1842 BRANDE *Dict. Sci.* etc. **1848** LINDLEY *Introd. Bot.* (ed. 4) I. 263 In order to obviate the inconvenience of using the word nerve, the term nervure is now often substituted. **1861** H. MACMILLAN *Footn. Page Nat.* 49 What is called the nervure in the membraneous or leafy species, is nothing more than the stalk itself.

nervy ('nɜːvɪ), *a.* [f. NERVE *sb.* + -Y[1].]

1. Vigorous, sinewy, full of strength.

1607 SHAKS. *Cor.* II. i. 177 Death, that darke Spirit, in's neruie Arme doth lye. **1671** SALMON *Syn. Med.* III. xvi. 361 The musculous and nervy parts of the body. **1818** KEATS *Endym.* I. 174 Between His nervy knees there lay a boar-spear keen. **1871** R. ELLIS tr. *Catullus* lxiii. 83 On a nervy neck be tossing that uneasy tawny mane.

transf. **1633** WILSON in *Donne's Poems* 399 Thy nimble Satyres too, and every straine (With nervy strength) that issued from thy brain.

2. a. Courageous, full of nerve.

1882 J. WALKER *Jaunt to Auld Reekie* 221 His prentice laddie, A nervy chiel. **1893** C. KING *Foes in Amb.* 46 He was one of the nerviest men in the whole troop.

b. Cool, confident, impudent. *U.S. colloq.*

1896 ADE *Artie* viii. 75, I just received your nervy letter. **1897** FLANDRAU *Harvard Episodes* 89 'Well, I call it pretty nervy', grumbled Sears. **1904** E. ROBINS *Magnetic North* II. 118 Feeling that it is a little 'nervy'.. to walk into another man's house uninvited. **1948** *Pauls Valley* (Okla.) *Daily Democrat* 2 May 4 Wouldn't it be rather nervy to ask her help?

3. Jerky, sudden.

1884 CABLE *Dr. Sevier* xxviii, The nervy, unmusical waking cry of the mocking-bird. **1885** —— in *Century Mag.* Apr. 918/2 The movements were quick, short, nervy.

4. Requiring nerve.

1897 *Outing* (U.S.) XXX. 481/2 It takes nerve, and lots of it, to play polo. It's the nerviest game played.

5. Having one's nerves disordered; easily excitable, 'jumpy'; = NERVOUS *a.* 9.

1891 R. T. COOKE *Huckleberries gathered f. New England Hills* 319, I expect I be sort o' nervy, what with takin' a journey and the thought o' seein' Melindy. **1906** *Sat. Rev.* 3 Mar. 254 They are very 'nervy' in Russia. **1916** *Daily Mail* 21 Sept. 7 (Advt.), When you are weak, anæmic, 'nervy', run-down, [etc.]. **1923** W. DEEPING *Secret Sanctuary* viii. 77 You can explain that your brother was shell-shocked, and that he is still a bit nervy. **1932** A. CHRISTIE *Peril at End House* iii. 40, I have been worried to death. Everybody's been telling me I'm nervy. **1973** J. BURROWS *Like Evening Gone* v. 63 Greta was grey as paper and peevish and nervy.

†**nes**, variant of NAS, was not. *Obs.*

c **1175** *Lamb. Hom.* 43 Elmesȝeorn nes heo nefre. *a* **1225** *Ancr. R.* 404 Neuer er nu nes ich ful pined. *a* **1300** *Thrush & Night.* 44 in Hazl. *E.P.P.* I. 52 In the world nes non so crafti mon. *c* **1320** *Sir Tristr.* 2215 Sore him greued his vene, As it no wonder nes.

†**nes**, variant of NIS, is not. *Obs.*

c **1400** MAUNDEV. (Roxb.) ix. 35 Men may noȝt make þe pitte.. so depe.. þat it nes at þe ȝere end full agayne.

nes, variant of NESE, nose.

Nescafé ('nɛskæfeɪ). The proprietary name of a brand of instant coffee; a drink made of Nescafé. Also *colloq.* abbrev. **Nes**; [cf. CAFF] **Nescaff.**

1946 *Trade Marks Jrnl.* 4 Sept. 475/2 Nescafé... Preparations of coffee in powder form. Nestlé's Milk Products Limited,.. London,.. Manufacturers. **1959** [see ABLUTE *v.*]. **1962** A. LEJEUNE *Duel in Shadows* xi. 156 'Only Nescaff, I'm afraid,' said Fiona Stewart-Long. **1966** *Observer* 19 June 29/5 Silk shantung dress in Nescafé brown. **1966** *New Statesman* 24 June 939/3 Maurice Ronet as a devil-may-care sadist, and George Segal in Nescafé as an old Algerian buddy. **1968** H. READE *Comeback for Stark* xii. 175 Sure you won't have a cup of nes? I prefer it to anything except the real bottled yellow. Take it cold in the summer. **1968** *Listener* 18 Apr. 515/1 How many spoonfuls of Nescafé did the Chancellor of the Exchequer have in his elevenses that vital morning? **1970** J. FLEMING *Young Man, I think you're Dying* ii. 33, I could make you a cuppa hot Nescaff, eh? How about it? **1971** 'P. HOBSON' *Three Graces* viii. 54 Downstairs for a cup of Nes. **1975** N. FREELING *What are Bugles blowing For?* iv. 17 We'll have some coffee —or to be accurate, Nes. *Ibid.* v. 21 La Touche seemed to be waking up... Shock wearing off, or the stimulus of Nescafé.

Nescaupick, var. NASKAPI *a.* and *sb.*

nesch(e, obs. forms of NESH.

nescience ('nɛʃ(ɪ)əns, 'niːʃ(ɪ)əns). [ad. late L. *nescientia*, f. *nesciens*: see next.] Absence or lack of knowledge, ignorance.

1612 WOODALL *Surg. Mate* Pref., Wks. (1653) 19, I can yet adde many more needfull particulars, which the Author hath in his nescience omitted. **1653** JER. TAYLOR *Serm. for Year* I. viii. 92, I need not instance in the ignorance and involuntary nescience of men. **1715** A. A. SYKES *Innoc. Error* 26 If his salvation is not at stake by reason of his nescience. *a* **1761** HUGGINS in Boswell *Johnson* an. 1780, I will militate no longer against his nescience. **1831** CARLYLE *Sart. Res.* III. iv, The miserable fraction of Science which united Mankind, in a wide Universe of Nescience, has acquired. **1883** H. DRUMMOND *Nat. Law in Spir. W.* (ed. 2) 160 These touching, and too sincere confessions of universal nescience.

b. An instance of this. *rare.*

a **1625** BOYS *Wks.* (1629) 306 According to these distinctions every nescience is not a sinne. **1652–62** HEYLIN *Cosmogr.* App. (1682) 157 The knowledge of them so imperfect as comes near a Nescience.

c. Const. *of* a thing.

1637 JACKSON *Serm. Jer. xxvi.* 19 Wks. 1844 VI. 93 Not out of a nescience of this rule. **1691** E. TAYLOR *Behmen's Theos. Philos.* 107 A Nescience or Oblivion of Divine Tranquility. *a* **1734** NORTH *Lives* (1826) III. 351 Brutes have an advantage over human kind.. in their nescience of evils to come. **1856** FERRIER *Inst. Metaph.* 414 A nescience of that which it would contradict the nature of all intelligence to know. **1875** MANNING *Mission H. Ghost* i. 6 There was in Adam a nescience of many things.

nescient ('nɛʃ(ɪ)ənt, 'niːʃ(ɪ)ənt), *a.* and *sb.* [ad. L. *nescient-em*, pres. pple. of *nescīre* to be ignorant, f. *ne* not and *scīre* to know.]

A. *adj.* Ignorant. Chiefly const. *of.*

1626 JACKSON *Creed* VIII. xii. 118 Infinite knowledge.. can neither be ignorant or nescient of anything. **1678** CUDWORTH *Intell. Syst.* I. iv. 198 Such a nature, as.. is notwithstanding nescient of what it doth. *Ibid.* v. 899 A Blind and Nescient.. Nature. **1881** PALGRAVE *Visions Eng.* 158 They 'neath their feet tread nescient pride and fear. **1884** RUSKIN *Fors Clav.* xcv. 257 Only scientific of their.. pasture, peacefully nescient of all beyond.

b. Agnostic; asserting man's necessary ignorance of the ultimate constitution of the universe.

1876 J. MARTINEAU *Ess. & Addr.* (1891) IV. 242 A modern *savant*, whether of the Nescient or the Omniscient school.

B. *sb.* An agnostic.

1872 W. G. WARD *Ess. Philos. Theism* (1884) I. 63 A far larger number, of whom Professor Huxley may be taken as representative, are 'nescients'. **1878** MORLEY *Diderot* II. 212 The most eager Nescient or Denier to be found in the ranks of the assailants of theology in our own day.

†**'nescious**, *a. Obs. rare.* [ad. L. *nescius* ignorant, f. *nescīre*: see NESCIENT.] Ignorant.

1633 T. ADAMS *Exp. 2 Peter* iii. 5 He begins with the dunces, those.. inscious, nescious, conscious, wilful ignorants. **1683** J. GADBURY in *Wharton's Wks.* Pref., So regardless and nescious are they of the very Principles that lead to a just Discovery of this.. Knowledge.

nescock: see *nest-cock*, NEST *sb.* 8.

nese, *sb.* Now only *Sc.* Forms: α. 2–4 **neose**. β. 3–5 **nese**; 3, 6 **nease**, 4 **neise, neyse, neies**, 4–5 **nes**, 5 **nees(e, nece**; *Sc.* 5 **neys**, 6, 9 **neis**, 8 **neese**, 8–9 **niz**, 9 **nizz, nis(e.** [Early ME. *neose, nese*, perh. = MDu. and MLG. *nese* (hence Da. *næse*, Sw. *näsa*): the relationship to NASE and NOSE is obscure.] The nose.

α. *c* **1175** *Lamb. Hom.* 127 Ure neose and ure muð and ure earan. *c* **1205** LAY. 22845 þa wifmen þa ȝe maȝen ifinden.. kerueð of hir neose. *a* **1310** in Wright *Lyric P.* ix. 34 Hire neose ys set as hit wel semeth. *a* **1400** *Minor Poems fr. Vernon MS.* 19/18 To ofte ichaue.. With neose i-smullet.

β. *c* **1175** *Lamb. Hom.* 23 His fet and his hondan and his muð and his nesa. *c* **1220** *Bestiary* 3 [If the lion] man hunten here, Oðer ðurg his nese smel Smake ðat he negge. *a* **1240** *Sawles Warde* in *O.E. Hom.* I. 251 Eiðer curseð oðer & fret of þe oðres earen & te nease alswa. *c* **1300** *Havelok* 2450 Hise nese went un-to þe crice. *c* **1330** R. BRUNNE *Chron.* (1810) 166 His nese & his ine he carfe at misauentoure. *c* **1400** MAUNDEV. (Roxb.) xxxi. 139 Oute of his mouthe and his neese commez.. fyre. *c* **1440** *Alph. Tales* 152 As he kissid hym, he bate of his fadur nece. **1500–20** DUNBAR *Poems* xiii. 16 Sum with his fallow rownis him to pleis That wald for invy byt of his neis. **1580** HAY *Demandes* in *Cath. Tract.* (S.T.S.) 64 Of the wourd ye mak ane neis of walx, thrawing it to quhat.. absurditie ye list. **1590** BRUCE *Serm. Sacr.* P 8 It will.. conjoine thee with God, and make all thine actions to smell weill in his nease. **1718** RAMSAY *Christ's Kirk Gr.* III. xxi, [He] brak the brig o' 's neese. **1798** CRAWFORD *Poems* 86 (E.D.D.), The clout wi' whilk ane dights his niz. *a* **1800** *Rob Roy* xii. in Child *Ballads* IV. 247 Ilka ane that did him wrang, He beat him on the neis. **1884** GRANT *Lays & Leg.* 44 Here her Tammie.. Lies wi' broken niz an' neck.

†**b.** *Sc.* A ness or headland. *Obs. rare.*

1497 *Aberdeen Reg.* (1844) I. 61 It was.. ordanit that ij kelis one the tovnis aventouris be brocht to the neyss. **1513** DOUGLAS *Æneis* VI. viii. 58 Than I.. Doun at the neis Rethe, by the costis law, A voyd tumb raisit.

c. *Comb.* **nese-bit** *Sc.* (see quot. 1808); †**nese-blood**, the plant milfoil or yarrow; †**nese-end**, the tip of the nose; †**neselong** *adv.*, face downwards; **nese-wise** *a.*, *Sc.* clever, sagacious [cf. Da. *næsvis*, Sw. *näsvis*, impertinent].

a **1400** *Stockholm Med. MS.* 202 Millefoly or neseblod or ȝarwe. *c* **1400** *Sir Beues* (S.) 649 He leide him neslong [*v.r.* noselyng] to þe grounde. *c* **1425** *Voc.* in Wr.-Wülcker 634 *Hic purulus*, a nesehende. **1483** *Cath. Angl.* 253/1 A Nese ende, *pirula.* **1790** SHIRREFS *Poems* 138 Ye're a' nis-wise; but, ere ye sleep.. Ye'll maybe see [etc.]. **1808** JAMIESON, *Nisbit*, the iron that passes across the nose of a horse, and joins the branks together.

Hence †**nese** *v. trans.*, to scent, smell. *Obs.*[−1]

1637 B. JONSON *Sad Shepherd* II. i, Allbe he know her, As doth the vauting hart his venting hind, Hee nere fra' hence sall neis her i' the wind To his first liking.

nese, obs. form of NEEZE *v.*; NIECE.

†**nesebek.** *Obs. rare.* Also 4 **nyse-.** [Of obscure origin.] The name of a dish in mediæval cookery.

c **1390** *Form of Cury* (1780) 77 Nysebek. Take þe þridde part of sowre Dokks and flour þerto and bete it togeder [etc.]. *c* **1430** *Two Cookery-bks.* I. 45 Nese Bekys. Take Fygys & grynd hem wel [etc.].

nesesary, obs. form of NECESSARY.

†**nesethirl.** *Obs.* Forms: 3 **neose-þurle, neosturle;** 4 **nesethirle,** 5 **-thyrl(e, -tyrlle, nesthyrylle,** 6 *Sc.* **neis-, ney(i)sthyrl;** 4 **nees-,** 5 **nes(e)-, neasethrill, nesthryll.** [ME., f. *neose* NESE + *thürl* THIRL: cf. OE. *næsþyrel* and *nosþyrel* NOSTRIL *sb.*] A nostril.

c **1250** *Death* 235 in *O.E. Misc.* 182 Of his neose þurles [*v.r.* neosturles] cumeð þe rede leie. *a* **1340** HAMPOLE *Psalter* cxiii. 14 Nesethirles þai hafe & þai sall noght smell. **1382** WYCLIF *2 Sam.* xxii. 9 Smook stiede vp fro the neesthrillis of hym. *c* **1440** *Alph. Tales* 51 þis angell.. stoppyd his nease-thrillis. **1513** DOUGLAS *Æneis* VII. v. 201 At thair neis thyrlis the fyir fast swermand out.

nesewort, variant of NEEZEWORT *Obs.*

nesh (nɛʃ), *a.* (and *adv.*) Now *dial.* Forms: *α.* 1 **hnesce, (hnysce, hnisce; nesc, næsc),** 2 **nexce, neche,** 3-5 **nesche, nesshe,** 4 **ness(s)e,** 4-5 **nessche,** 5-6 **neshe;** 4-5 **nesch, ness(h,** 5- **nesh.** *β.* 3 **neys(se,** 4- 5 **neische, -sshe, neysshe,** (5 **-ssche, neyshe),** 4 **neisch, -ssh,** 5 **neysch(e, naysch(e,** 9 *dial.* **naish,** *U.S. dial.* **nish.** *γ.* 5 **nassh(e,** 6 *Sc.* **nasche,** 7, 9 **nash,** 8 **gnash.** [OE. *hnesce*, = Du. (16th c.) *nesch, nisch* soft (of eggs), damp, sodden, foolish, Goth. *hnasqus* soft, tender; the ultimate etym. is unknown.]

1. a. Soft in texture or consistency; yielding easily to pressure or force; in later use esp. tender, succulent, juicy.

α. *c* **888** K. ÆLFRED *Boeth.* xxxiii. §5 þæt hnesce & flowende wæter. *c* **950** *Lindisf. Gosp.* Matt. xi. 8 Mið hnescum [*Rushw.* næscum] ȝerelum ȝescirped. *c* **1000** *Sax. Leechd.* I. 96 Ðeos wyrt.. bið hnesceum leafum. *Ibid.* III. 134 Syle hym etan hnesce æȝere. *c* **1200** ORMIN 995 Smeredd wel wiþþ elesæw & makedd fatt & nesshe. *a* **1225** *Ancr. R.* 134 Nest is herd.. wiðuten, & wiðinnen nesche & softe. *c* **1290** *S. Eng. Leg.* I. 75/141 þe staf wende into þe marbreston, ase it were in nesche sonde. **1340** HAMPOLE *Pr. Consc.* 614 Mar filthe es nane, hard ne nesshe, þan es þat comes fra a mans flesshe. *c* **1400** tr. *Secreta Secret., Gov. Lordsh.* 73 Eyren.. nesshe to be suppyd. *c* **1460** J. RUSSELL *Bk. Nurture* 986 Lett hym go to bed, but looke it be soote & nesche. **1546** PHAER *Bk. Childr.* (1553) R v, The sinues of a child be verye neshe and tender. **1579** LANGHAM *Gard. Health* (1633) 529 Bake it hard, and apply it till it wax nesh. **1788** CROWE *Lewesdon Hill* 30 The darker fir, light ash, and the nesh tops Of the young hazel. **1802** FOSBROOKE *Econ. Monastic Life* I. vii, Their feathery leaves where nesh Acacias spread. *a* **1834** R. SURTEES in G. Taylor *Mem.* (Surtees) 301 The nesh hazles, bending in the blast. **1844** W. BARNES *Poems Rur. Life* Gloss. s.v., This meat is nesh. **1883-** in various dialects (chiefly of grass or meat, but also of coal, steel, etc.). **1915** R. C. THOMPSON *Pilgr. Scrip* 71 The road from the bridge is like an English lane with blackberry hedgerows.. and a nesh track for a morning gallop.

Comb. **1864** W. BARNES in *Macm. Mag.* Oct. 477 The nesh-bleäded grass, By the young apple-trees.

β. *c* **1300** *Havelok* 217 The blod ran of his fleys, þat tendre was, and swiþe neys. **1387** TREVISA *Higden* (Rolls) IV. 429 Harde þinges beeþ bettre wiþstonde wiþ nesche [*v.r.* naysche] þinges þan with hard. *c* **1430** LYDG. *Min. Poems* (Percy Soc.) 195 Fyr.. Makith hard thyng neisshe and.. Neisshe thyng hard. **1893** [see *γ*].

Comb. **1460-70** *Bk. Quintessence* II. 23 Fleisch of a cok, neysch soden and sotilly brayed.

γ. **1495** *Trevisa's Barth. De P.R.* XIX. liii. 894 Certen moysture cometh at endes of certeyne wode.., as Colophonia and Nassh pitche. **1686** PLOT *Staffordsh.* 148 The coal of the upper wallings being generally nasher; i.e. softer and more friable. *a* **1722** LISLE *Husbandry* (1757) 250 The first spring-grass, which was luscious and gnash. **1893** *Wilts. Gloss., Nash, Naish,*.. tender and juicy: applied to lettuce.

†**b.** *transf.* Not harsh or violent. *Obs. rare.*

a **1225** *Ancr. R.* 192 ȝe muwen more dreden þe nesche dole þene þe herde of þeos fondunges. **1422** tr. *Secreta Secret., Priv. Priv.* 231 A nesh brekynge and Plesaunte voice tokenyth a.. wel y-manerit man. *c* **1440** *Partonope* 6063 That in Armys me shall teche Thought my stroke be hard of nasshe.

c. Damp, moist, wet. *rare.*

1387 TREVISA *Higden* (Rolls) I. 333 þe lond is nesche, reyny, and wyndy. **1573** TWYNE *Æneid* X. Ee j b, Whan by nighttime nesh som blasing star All bloodred sanguine shewes.

2. a. Slack, negligent; lacking in energy or diligence.

c **897** K. ÆLFRED tr. *Gregory's Past.* C. lx. 453 Swa he ðone hnescan ðafettere on recceleste ne ȝebrenge. *a* **1225** *Ancr. R.* 272 Hwon Recabes sunen.. ivindeð so unwakere & so nesche ȝeteward. *c* **1290** *Beket* 1589 in *S. Eng. Leg.* I. 152 For þat þe bischopus bifore me weren to nesche.. þe stude-fastore i mot beo. **1382** WYCLIF *Prov.* xviii. 9 Who is nesshe [*v.r.* neisch] and dissolut in his werk. **1879** MISS JACKSON *Shropsh. Word-bk.* s.v., 'Er's a nesh piece, 'er dunna do above 'afe a day's work.

b. Timid; wanting in courage; faint-hearted.

1382 WYCLIF *Jer.* li. 46 Lest par auenture waxe nesshe [*v.r.* neische] ȝoure herte, and ȝee drede the heering. **1422** tr. *Secreta Secret., Priv. Priv.* 139 Doghty men and hardy hit makyth lyke women, neshe and feynte. *Ibid.* 226 Tho.. bene nesse of corage an lyke to women. **1841** HAMILTON *Nugæ Lit.* 354 *Nesh* is applied to a cowardly, undecided person.

†**3. a.** Tender, mild, gentle, kind; inclined to pity, mercy, or other tender feelings. *Obs.*

c **897** K. ÆLFRED tr. *Gregory's Past. C.* xvii. 126 Sie ðær eac lufu, næs ðeah to hnesce. **971** *Blickl. Hom.* 99 Drihten næfre ne forsyhþ þa eaþmodan heortan ne þa hnescestan. *c* **1175** *Lamb. Hom.* 159 Hit melt of þe neche horte swa deð þe snaw to-ȝeines þe sunne. *a* **1225** *Ancr. R.* 334 ȝif þu.. holdest God to nesche uorto awreken sunne. **1340** *Ayenb.* 153 Riȝtuolnesse is.. þet me deþ be dome riȝtuol and trewe, ne to nesssse ne to hard. **1382** WYCLIF *Prov.* xv. 1 A nesshe answere brekith wrathe; an hard woord rereth woodnesse. **1470-85** MALORY *Arthur* XIII. xx. 641 Neuer woldest thow be maade neysshe nor by water nor by fyre. *c* **1530** *Crt. of Love* 1092 It semeth for love his harte is tender nessh.

†**b.** Easily yielding to temptation; inclined to lust or wantonness. *Obs.*

c **1000** ÆLFRIC *Hom.* II. 220 Hnesce on mode to flæsclicum lustum. *a* **1250** *Owl & Night.* 1387 Wymmon is of neysse [*v.r.* nesche] fleysse, & fleysses lustes is strong to queysse. *a* **1300** *Cursor M.* 8986 Man for to fall in filth o fless, Thoru forme kind þat es sa nesse. **1382** WYCLIF *1 Cor.* vi. 10 Nether auouters, neither neische, neither lecchours of men.

4. a. Tender, delicate, weak; unable to endure fatigue or exposure; susceptible to cold.

The most prevalent sense in mod. dialect use.

α. *c* **1000** ÆLFRIC *Gen.* xxxiii. 13 Ic hæbbe hnesce litlingas.. mid me. *c* **1450** *Cov. Myst.* (Shaks. Soc.) 32 Oure hap was hard, our wytt was nesche. **1553** T. WILSON *Rhet.* (1580) 37 We are all so weake of witte.. and our bodie so neshe, that it looketh euer to be cherished. **1583** STUBBES *Anat. Abus.* I. (1879) 54 This pampering of our bodies makes them weker, tenderer and nesher, than otherwyse they would be. **1607** TOPSELL *Four-f. Beasts* (1658) 294 If the Horse be nesh and tender, and so wax lean without any apparent grief. **1639** T. DE GRAY *Expert Farrier* 59 These.. are naturally slow, dull, heavy, and nesh or wash of their flesh. **1789** MARSHALL *Rur. Econ. Glouc.* I. 330 *Nesh*; the common term, for tender or washy, as spoken of a cow or horse. **1839-52** BAILEY *Festus* 334 He.. let All rigour do its worst, which only served To harden him, though nothing nesh at first. **1887** HALL CAINE *Deemster* vi, Their own little room.., where no fire burned lest they should grow 'nesh'.

β. **1925** *Dialect Notes* V. 237 *Nish*.., delicate. **1963** *Amer. Speech* XXXVIII. 299 [Newfoundland] *Nish, adj.* (1) Tender. (2) Easily injured. **1964** L. E. F. ENGLISH *Historic Newfoundland* 31 *Nish*, tender, easily injured.

γ. **1665-6** *Phil. Trans.* I. 318 If he be (as the Phrase is among Horse-masters) a Nash or Wash-Horse. **1674** RAY *N.C. Words* 34 *Nash*: Washy, tender, weak, puling. **1825** BROCKETT *N.C. Gloss.* **1860** GEO. ELIOT *Mill on Fl.* iv, They're nash things, them lop-eared rabbits.

b. Dainty, fastidious, squeamish.

1839- in various dialects (see *Eng. Dial. Dict.*). **1848** A. B. EVANS *Leicestersh. Words, Naish*, or *Nash*,.. is also used for dainty. 'A naish feeder' is said of a horse.

†**5.** *absol.* (usually in conjunction with *hard.*)

a. That which is soft; soft ground; also *pl.* of persons (quot. *c* 1330). *Obs.*

a **1000** in Thorpe *Laws* II. 264 Æȝhwæt hnesces oððe heardes, wætes oððe driges. *a* **1000** *Sal. & Sat.* 286 (Gr.) Him on hand gæð heardes & hnesces. *c* **1330** *Arth. & Merl.* 8166 (Kölbing), He hadde wonder of his pruesse, þat so leyd doun hard & nesse. *c* **1450** *St. Cuthbert* (Surtees) 1413 Hongyr and calde it semed him aylde, Als he [had] gane thurgh harde and nesche. **1460-70** in C. Innes *Sketches Early Sc. Hist.* (1861) 506 Ascendand up.. betwix the hard & the naysch ewyn sowth owr to the burn. **1584** *Reg. Mag. Sig.* 23 Dec., Keipand betuix the nasche and the hard north and northeist.

†**b.** Mild or gentle treatment. *Obs.*

c **1200** ORMIN 3734 Mann mihhte himm fon & pinenn Wiþþ hat & kald, wiþþ nesshe & harrd. *a* **1225** *Ancr. R.* 352 þe deade nis nan more.. of herd þen of nesche, vor he ne iueleð nouðer. **13..** *E.E. Allit. P.* A. 606 Queþer-so-euer he dele nesch oþer harde. *c* **1375** *xi. Pains of Hell* 166 in *O.E. Misc.* 227 þei soffred harde and noþing nessche. **1417** in Rymer *Fœdera* (1709) IX. 435/1 Thys two, my Lordys wylle abyde harde and nesche all weyes.

†**c.** *in nesh and hard*, etc., under all or any circumstances. *Obs.*

c **1200** ORMIN 14828 To wurrþenn herrsumm till þin Godd Inn harrd, i nesshe, & æfre. *c* **1330** *Arth. & Merl.* 2961 (Kölbing), In Nesse, in hard.., In al stedes þou him avowe. **1390** GOWER *Conf.* II. 284 Lihtere is to fle the flint Than gete of him in hard or neisshe Only the value of a reysshe.

†**d.** So *for nesh or hard*, etc. *Obs.*

c **1330** R. BRUNNE *Chron.* (1810) 228 A letter þis fole tok, bad him for nessh or hard þeron suld no man loke. *c* **1400** *Laud Troy Bk.* 17454 Holde we to-gedur for hard or nesche. *c* **1420** *Liber Cocorum* (1862) 33 Feyre hony do into hit.. Too fyngurs thyke for harde or nesshe. *a* **1460** *Lybeaus Disc.* 1573 No kniȝht for nesche ne hard,.. Ne geteþ her non ostell.

†**6.** *adv.* Softly, gently, tenderly. *Obs. rare.*

1297 R. GLOUC. (Rolls) 8964 þis gode mold.. wess þe meseles vet.. & wipede is nessce afterward. **13..** *Seuyn Sag.* (W.) 732 Hit had of thre norices keping;.. The child was keped tendre an nessche.

nesh (nɛʃ), *v.* Now *dial.* Forms: 1 **hnescian, hnexian,** 3-5 **neschen,** (5 **-yn,** 4 **neischen, naisschen), nesshen,** (4 **nhessen, ness-, neyss-),** 9 *dial.* **nesh, naish.** [OE. *hnescian*, f. *hnesce* NESH *a.* Cf. mod.Flem. *neschen* to wet.]

†**1.** *intr.* To become soft. *Obs.*

c **897** K. ÆLFRED tr. *Gregory's Past. C.* xxxvii. 271 Se hearda stan.. hnescað onȝean ðæt liðe blod. *c* **1000** *Sax. Leechd.* II. 202 Hnescað se swile sone & ȝeberstеþ innan. *c* **1290** *S. Eng. Leg.* I. 331/286 Huy nescheden ase doth wex aȝein þe fuyre. **1398** TREVISA *Barth. De P.R.* XVII. clxvi. (Bodl. MS.), Thyse treen brenneþ nouȝt in fire noþer naisscheþ in water. *a* **1400** *Relig. Pieces fr. Thornton MS.* (1867) 31 Now es na herte sa herde þat it na moghte nesche.

†**2.** *trans.* To make soft. *Obs.*

c **1000** ÆLFRIC *Gram.* (Z.) 191 *Mollio*, ic hnexiȝe. *a* **1100** *Eadwine's Canterb. Ps.* liv. 22 Hy hnescodon spreca here ofer ele. *c* **1200** ORMIN 1549 þu brekesst wel þin corn & grindesst itt & nesshesst. *a* **1300** *E.E. Psalter* liv. 22 Nesched als oyle his saghs bene. **1340** *Ayenb.* 94 God þe uader, huanne he nhesseþ þe herte and makeþ zuete and tretable. *c* **1380** WYCLIF *Sel. Wks.* III. 68 Iys and leed.. ben neischid aȝein by hoot. **1422** tr. *Secreta Secret., Priv. Priv.* 190 Loue of women.. nesshyth a manes herte. **1471** RIPLEY *Comp. Alch.* in Ashm. (1652) 113 Nesh not your Wombe by drinking ymmoderatly.

3. *dial.* with *it.* To turn faint-hearted; to draw back; to 'funk' it.

1881- in dialect glossaries, etc. (Yks., Chesh., Derby, Staff., Leic.).

Hence **'neshing** *vbl. sb.*

1398 TREVISA *Barth. De P.R.* XIX. clxvii. (1495) 907 The vertue of nesshynge nouryssheth by heete and by moysture.

†**'neshhead.** *Obs. rare.* [f. NESH *a.* + -HEAD. Cf. Du. and Flem. *neschheid.*] Softness.

c **1440** *Jacob's Well* 238 In valeys.. [are] moysture.., softhed & neschhed. **1460-70** *Bk. Quintessence* 7 þanne mars schal take algate þe neischede and þe softnes of saturne.

'neshly, *adv.* Now *dial.* [f. NESH *a.* + -LY².] Softly, gently.

c **897** K. ÆLFRED tr. *Gregory's Past. C.* xxi. 159 He his hieremonna yfelu to hnesclice forberan ne sceal. *Ibid.* xliii. 313 Ðonne he his wambe sua hnesclice olecð. *c* **1400** *Chron. R. Glouc.* (Rolls) 8964 (MS. B), þys gode Mold.. wess þe mysseles vet.. And wypede ys nesselyche. **1422** tr. *Secreta Secret., Priv. Priv.* 242 Noght vpon harde erthe ne Pament, but vpon erthe nesshly y-st[r]awet or russhet. **1875** *Whitby Gloss., Neshly*, noiselessly.

'neshness. [f. NESH *a.* + -NESS.] Softness, weakness; †lack of courage.

c **897** K. ÆLFRED *Gregory's Past. C.* xxi. 159 Ðære tidernesse & ðære hnescnesse ures flæsces we beoð underðiedde. *c* **950** *Lindisf. Gosp.* Matt. xi. 8 Ðone monno mið hnescnisum ȝewoded [L. *hominem mollibus vestitum*]. *c* **1000** *Sax. Leechd.* I. 324 Wið innoðes astyrunge, ȝenim þyses wæstmes hnescnysse innewearde. **1387** TREVISA *Higden* (Rolls) VIII. 287 Som men seide þat þat myshap fel for neschenesse of Englisch men. *c* **1400** *Lanfranc's Cirurg.* 29 þe senewe haþ .ij. oþere defautis: neischenesse and liȝtnesse. **1496** *Dives & Paup.* (W. de W.) x. vi. 380/1 The Iacke.. by his softenesse & nesshenesse softeth & feynteth all strokes that cometh there ayenst. **1553** T. WILSON *Rhet.* 7b, To be borne a woman declares weakenes of spirite, neshenes of body, and fikilnesse of mynde. **1587** MASCALL *Govt. Cattle, Sheepe* (1627) 225 When any Sheep by running out or neashnes of his dung, doe ray and defile his taile. **1610** MARKHAM *Masterp.* I. li. 106 There is also another consumption.. which proceedeth from neshnesse, tendernesse, freenesse of spirit. **1874** HARDY *Far fr. Mad. Crowd* xli, I should be inclined to think it was from general neshness of constitution.

nesing, obs. form of NEEZING.

Nesite ('nɛsaɪt). Also **Nesian, Nesitic.** [f. Hittite *našili*, *nešumnili*, f. *Nešaš* name of an ancient Hittite city in Asia Minor (identified by B. Hrozný 1929, in *Archiv orientální* (Prague) I. 273-99) + -ITE¹.] **a.** A name given to the official language used in Hittite documents, suggested as an alternative to KANESIAN. **b.** A member of the Hittite people who used this language.

The meaning of *našili* and *nešumnili* in Hittite texts has been disputed, but the view of Hrozný (above, and 1931, in *Journal Asiatique* CCXVIII. 318-19) is now generally accepted, that the words relate to the former Hittite capital Nešaš (or Nesa) and designate the Indo-European Hittite aristocracy and its language (see also quot. 1954).

[**1920** A. H. SAYCE in *Jrnl. Royal Asiatic Soc.* 605 Literary Hittite is once called 'Luvian', *Lûi-li*, 'in Luvian', taking the place of the more usual *nâsi-li.* **1921** M. BLOOMFIELD in *Jrnl. Amer. Oriental Soc.* XLI. 197 The supposedly I. E. Hittite [in the Boghazköi inscriptions] seems, according to both authors [*sc.* Forrer and Hrozný], to be well entitled to the name Kanesian, named after the city of Kaneš. But this latter designation is never indicated by an ethnical adjective. .. Instead there occurs, more frequently than the mention of Kaneš, the ethnical designation Nāšili, which Forrer takes to be the same as Kanesian. **1929** B. HROZNÝ in *Archiv orientální* (Prague) I. 296 Les Nêsites sont donc en effet les fondateurs du grand empire hittite... La langue hittite doit donc être nommée.. la langue nésite.] **1933** E. H. STURTEVANT *Compar. Gram. Hittite Lang.* i. 28 Hrozný.. may be correct in thinking that the word *Nesumnili*.. refers to official Hittite and therefore in calling the latter Nesite. **1949** F. O. STEIN tr. *L. Matouš's Bedřich Hrozný* 26 Later, in a paper published in Volume I of '*Archiv orientální*' (Oriental Archives).., Hrozný shewed that the Indo-European Hittites originally called themselves *Nesites*, from their ancient city *Neshash*, and that therefore their language should more correctly be called *Nesitic*, and not Hittite, as had always been taken for granted. **1954** O. R. GURNEY *Hittites* (ed. 2) 122 While Hrozný adopted the name 'Nésite' (i.e., the language of the city Nesa), Forrer preferred 'Kanisisch' (i.e., the language of Kanesh). It is now generally agreed that 'Nésite' or 'Nesian' (derived from the Hittite adverb *našili* or *nešumnili*) is indeed the true name of the language. **1959** *Chambers's Encycl.* VII. 155/1 The language.. was seen to be mainly Indo-European in structure and vocabulary. In the Hittite texts it is sometimes called the speech of Nesas, and has therefore been termed Nesite. **1964** G. ROUX *Ancient Iraq* xiv. 191 The Luwians.. settled to the west of Cilicia, along the coast,.. and the so-called Nesites in Cappadocia... Centuries later, those Nesite-speaking invaders conquered the centre of the Anatolian plateau. **1972** W. B. LOCKWOOD *Panorama Indo-Europ. Lang.* xiv. 262 The terms used are *nasili* (or *nisili*) and *nesumnili* meaning respectively 'in the language of Nesa' and 'in the language of those of Nesa', and Hittite has since occasionally been called Nesite.

nesk(h)i, varr. NASKHI *sb. pl.*

‖**nespola** ('nɛspələ). [It.] = MEDLAR.

1883 LADY MONKSWELL *Jrnl.* 29 Apr. in *Victorian Diarist* (1944) 104 On the entrance terrace were lemon trees in pots, trees of magnolia (not in flower) & nespola. **1920** D. H. LAWRENCE *Let.* 7 May (1932) 504 Nespoli look like apricots, and taste a bit like them—but they're pear-shaped. They're a sort of medlar. **1922** *Blackw. Mag.* Feb. 157/2 Florindo threw a number of nespole with deadly accuracy.

nesquehonite (nɛskwiː'həʊnaɪt). *Min.* [f. *Nesquehon-ing* (see quot. 1890) + -ITE[1].] Magnesium carbonate trihydrate, $MgCO_3.3H_2O$, found as colourless monoclinic crystals.

1890 GENTH & PENFIELD in *Amer. Jrnl. Sci.* CXXXIX. 122 The clear crystals..proved on examination to be a new mineral, having the composition $MgCO_3.3H_2O$, to which we have given the name Nesquehonite, after the locality where the mineral was found, the Nesquehoning Mine being one of the best known in Pennsylvania. **1934** *Mineral. Abstr.* V. 431 Galleries in the Cogne magnetite mine in serpentine rocks, at an elevation of 2500 metres in the Piedmontese Alps, have a constant temperature of 4°C., and this has favoured the formation of lansfordite..and nesquehonite. **1957** G. E. HUTCHINSON *Treat. Limnol.* I. x. 665 At ordinary temperatures the carbonate that precipitates when saturation is reached at from 10^{-3} to 10^{-1} atm. of CO_2 is $MgCO_3.3H_2O$, or nesquehonite. **1971** *Contrib. Mineral. & Petrol.* XXXIII. 88 The 'cauliflower' crusts mainly consist of hydromagnesite and/or nesquehonite with traces of monohydrocalcite and calcite.

ness (nɛs), *sb.* Forms: 1 næs(s-), ness-, 5 nasse, naisse, (4) 6–7 nesse, (6 nes, nesch), 6– ness. [OE. *næs* (*nes*) masc. = ON. *nes* (Sw. *näs*, Da. *næs*) neut., LG. *nesse* fem., related to OE. *nasu* nose NASE: cf. NESE *sb.* 2. In ME. app. retained only in place-names, from which the later use is probably derived. The normal representative of the OE. form would be *nass* (cf. *glæs* glass, *græs* grass); *ness* may be due either to the unstressed position in place-names, to dialect variation, or to Scand. influence.] A promontory, headland, or cape.

Beowulf 1912 Hie ʒeata clifu onʒitan meahton, cuþe næssas. *Ibid.* 2805 Se scel..heah hlifian on Hrones næsse. **956** in Birch *Cartul. Saxon.* III. 149 Of þam wylle be ʒemære on scearpannesse. *a* **1000** *Andreas* 1710 (Gr.) Hie ða ʒebrohton æt brimes næsse..wiʒan unslawne. [*c* **1050** *O.E. Chron.* (MS. C) an. 1049 þa oðre foron on East Seaxon to Eadolfes næsse. *c* **1330** R. BRUNNE *Chron. Wace* (Rolls) 2805 Ilk del in-tyl Katenesse Held Brenne of Belyn, more ne lesse.] **14..** *Sailing Directions* (Hakl. Soc.) 12 Yif ye go oute of Orwell waynys to the Naisse ye must go south-west fro the Nasse to the merkis of the spetis. **1491** *Rolls of Parlt.* VI. 441/2 Within the Nasse and Haven of Orford. **1535** STEWART *Cron. Scot.* I. 38 All fra ane nes lyis far within the se. **1538** LELAND *Itin.* (1769) VII. 143 Running ynto a Poynt yt standeth as an Arme, a Foreland, or a Nesse. **1587** GOLDING *De Mornay* viii. (1592) 108 That great Nesse which conteyneth both Brasilie and Perow. **1618** BOLTON *Florus* (1636) 314 The points or nesses of the Ambracian Bay. **1674** N. FAIRFAX *Bulk & Selv.* 68 When we first make a Ness at Land too, it seems more a Ness than when we are less off at Sea. **1851** WOODWARD *Mollusca* I. iii. 13 The myriads of small shells which the sea heaps up in every sheltered 'ness'. **1868** MORRIS *Earthly Par.* (1870) I. Prol. 55 We stood Somewhat off shore to fetch about a ness. **1896** KIPLING *Seven Seas, Coastwise Lights* ii, From reef and rock and skerry—over headland, ness, and voe.

Hence †**ness** *v. intr.*, to form a ness. *Obs.*[−1]

1538 LELAND *Itin.* (1769) VII. 143 The Marsch Land beginneth to nesse and arme yn to the Se.

-ness, *suffix*, representing OE. *-nes(s)*, *-nis(s)*, *-nys(s)*, fem. (inflected, and later also in nom., *-nesse*, etc.) = OFris. *-nesse*, *-nisse*, OS. *-nesse*, *-nessi*, *-nissi*, *-nussi* (also *-nissea*, *-nussea*; MDu. *-nesse*, *-nisse*, Du. *-nis*), OHG. *-nessi*, *-nassi*, *-nissi* (also *-nissa*; MHG. *-nisse*, G. *-niss*), Goth. *-nassus*; the *-n* is originally part of the stem, the real suffix being *-assus*, formed from weak verbs in *-atjan*. The variations in the vowel of the West Germanic forms have not been satisfactorily explained.

In middle and early modern English the initial of the suffix is occasionally omitted when preceded by another *n*, as in *brownesse* brownness, *clenesse* cleanness, *kenesse* keenness, *meanesse* meanness, etc. (cf. note to FINESSE).

2. In OE. *-nes* is the suffix most usually attached to adjectives and past participles to form substantives expressing a state or condition, as *biternes*, *deorcnes*, *heardnes*, *ábolʒennes*, *forþryccednes*, etc. A large number of these survive in middle and modern English, and new formations of the same type have been continually made in all periods of the language, it being possible to add the suffix to any adjective or participle, whatever its form or origin may be. Formations from compound adjectives are also common, as *selfconceitedness*, *kindheartedness*, *square-toedness*, *water-tightness*, *tonguetiedness*, etc.; and even from adjectival phrases, such as *used-upness*, *get-at-ableness*, *up-to-dateness*, *à-la-modeness*, *little-boyishness*; few of the latter, however, are in established or serious use, and most of them are of recent introduction. This is also the case with formations on pronouns, adverbs, etc., as *I-ness*, *me-ness*, *whatness*; *whyness*, *withoutness*, *nowness*, *everydayness*, etc. The following are examples of some of the more exceptional uses of the suffix by writers of the 19th century.

1804 COLERIDGE in *Lit. Rem.* (1836) II. 414 The exclusive Sir-Thomas-Brown-ness of all the fancies. **1853** GEO. ELIOT in Cross *Life* (1885) I. 319 Dislike-to-getting-up-in-the-morningness. **1859** SALA *Gas-light & D.* iv. 43 An irreproachable state of clean-shirtedness, navy blue-broadclothedness and chimney-pot-hattedness. **1891** BAX *Outlooks New Standp.* iii. 199 All nowness is the form of I-ness. *Ibid.* 201 The *in-itselfness* which Kant saw behind the sense-impression. **1893** MORRIS & BAX *Socialism* iii. 58 The this-worldliness..of barbarian society.

b. Used absolutely in *pl.*

1775 S. J. PRATT *Liberal Opin.* lxxxv. (1783) III. 135 The shrewdness, acuteness, ..and all other nesses that promised the man of wealth. **1888** LOWELL in *Century Mag.* Feb. 515/2 Cheerfulness, kindliness, cleverness and contentedness, and all the other good nesses.

3. Uses of the suffix somewhat varying from those mentioned above occur in a few words, such as FORCENESS, MILKNESS, WILDERNESS, WITNESS.

nessberry ('nɛsbɛrɪ). [f. the name of Helge *Ness* (d. 1928), American horticulturist + BERRY *sb.*[1]] A variety of *Rubus*, produced by crossing a dewberry and a raspberry, introduced by Helge Ness in 1921.

1925 H. NESS in *Bull. Texas Agric. Exper. Stat.* No. 326. 19 This new fruit has been named the Nessberry by the authorities of the College. *Ibid.*, The Nessberry is of an excessively strong growth, some of its branches attaining a length of 10 to 15 feet in a single season. **1948** J. S. SHOEMAKER *Small Fruit Culture* (ed. 2) iii. 232 Nessberry.. has a delightful flavor and thrives well in East Texas, but it proved unpopular because of poor picking quality and difficulty in propagation. **1952** *New Biol.* XIII. 46 Among the newer crops which have arisen by allopolyploidy..the most notable are the various berries related to blackberry and raspberry... Two typical examples are the nessberry and loganberry. **1972** BROOKS & OLMO *Register of New Fruit & Nut Varieties* 164 Nessberry... Fruit: larger than Logan; size variable; hemispherical; skin deep to blood red.

nessche, nesshe, obs. ff. NESH *a.* and *v.*

nesse, obs. form of NESE, NESH *a.*, NESS.

Nesselrode ('nɛsəlrəʊd). The name of Karl R. *Nesselrode* (1780–1862), Russian statesman, used *attrib.* in ***Nesselrode pie***, ***pudding***, etc., an iced dessert made with chestnuts, cream, preserved fruits, etc., and freq. flavoured with rum. Also ellipt. ***Nesselrode***.

1845 E. ACTON *Mod. Cookery* xx. 441 *Nesselrode Cream*,.. Chestnuts..sugar..isinglass..cream..vanilla [etc]. *Ibid.* 461 Nesselrode pudding. We give Monsieur Carême's own receipt..as it originated with him. **1877** E. S. DALLAS *Kettner's Bk. of Table* 311 (*heading*) Nesselrode pudding was invented..by Mony, cook to the famous Count Nesselrode. **1894** E. SKUSE *Compl. Confectioner* 155 Nesselrode or Ice Pudding. Prepare a custard of one pint of cream, [etc.]. **1952** S. J. PERELMAN *Ill-Tempered Clavichord* (1953) 12, I wouldn't bolt that Nesselrode if I were you. **1965** *Harper's Bazaar* Nov. 136/2 Make a Nesselrode pudding such as Françoise made for Monsieur de Norpois the first time he went to dine with the Prousts. **1972** *New Yorker* 15 Apr. 35/2 Toward the back of the shop are two refrigerated cases —one for birthday cakes, the other for ice-cream cakes and for desserts composed of perishable whipped cream, such as Nesselrode pie.

nessesary, obs. form of NECESSARY.

†**nesset, -itt**, ? corrupt forms of NEST *sb.* 2 c.

1614–5 in Willis & Clark *Cambridge* (1886) II. 488 Item to Thorpe about the nessetes pictures and Armes... Item to John Symes..for 3 tunn of Freestone vsed about the Nessitts.

Nessie ('nɛsɪ). *colloq.* Also **Nessy**. [f. *Ness* (see below) + -IE or -Y[6].] A name for a monster or monsters supposedly inhabiting Loch Ness in northern Scotland. Cf. LOCH NESS.

1945 *Sun* (Baltimore) 25 June 2 'Nessie', the unidentified Loch Ness monster which used to disport itself in those Scottish waters before the war..has reappeared, according to several women residents. **1960** in T. Dinsdale *Loch Ness Monster* (1961) v. 76 According to substantiated reports, Nessie was seen a number of times last spring..and a few times in the autumn. **1968** *New Scientist* 26 Dec. 729/1 The trouble with Nessie was that she became an immediate newspaper sensation. **1971** *Ibid.* 10 June 641/2 Nessy has lost her mythical charm and has become the target of serious-minded technocrats. **1974** *People's Jrnl.* (Inverness & Northern Counties ed.) 29 June 2/6 They sighted Nessie as they returned from a delivery at Inverfarigaig. **1975** *Nature* 11 Dec. 467/3 Should the Nessies wish to breathe quite frequently, they would not be detected easily if the nostrils were at the topmost point to break surface.

nessle cock, obs. variant of NESTLE-COCK.

Nessler ('nɛslə(r)). *Chem.* The name of Julius *Nessler* (1827–1905), German agricultural chemist, used *attrib.* and in the possessive with reference to a delicate test for ammonia he devised; as **Nessler('s) reagent** or **solution**, an alkaline solution of potassium mercuric iodide, which gives a yellow or brown colour or precipitate when added to an aqueous solution containing ammonia; **Nessler('s) tube**, a glass cylinder marked with a line indicating a certain volume and depth, used in nesslerization and other colorimetric procedures.

1865 *Jrnl. Chem. Soc.* XVIII. 125 The distillate is divided into two equal portions; one of these is submitted to Nessler's test for ammonia. **1868** *Ibid.* XXI. 87 Mr. Chapman..recommends that the ammonia determination should be made by the application of Nessler's solution directly to the water. *Ibid.*, Waters containing chalk in solution become turbid on the addition of the Nessler test. **1873** *Chem. News* 11 July 13/2 The time required for the development of the Nessler colour. *Ibid.*, One sample of Nessler reagent gives its maximum of colour almost immediately, and another takes a quarter of an hour or an hour. **1913** CUMMING & KAY *Text-bk. Quantit. Chem. Anal.* IV. 156 Measure into a 100 c.c. Nessler tube a portion of the solution containing from 0·1 to 3 mgrm. of iron. **1946** *Thorpe's Dict. Appl. Chem.* (ed. 4) VII. 579/1 The action of ammonia on an alkaline solution of potassium mercuri-iodide..is the basis of the Nessler test for ammonia. **1963** SKOOG & WEST *Fund. Analytical Chem.* xxviii. 656 In its simplest form, colorimetry consists of visual matching of the color of the solutions of the substance with a set of standards. For such a procedure flat-bottomed tubes called Nessler tubes are frequently employed. **1970** Nessler's reagent [see NESSLERIZATION].

nesslerize ('nɛsləraɪz), *v.* *Chem.* Also **Nesslerize.** [f. the name NESSLER + -IZE.] *trans.* To treat with Nessler's reagent in order to test for the presence of ammonia; also, to test for (ammonia) by this means. Also *absol.* So **nessleri'zation**; **'nesslerized** *ppl. a.*, **'nesslerizing** *vbl. sb.*

1873 *Chem. News* 11 July 13/2 Whether the Nesslerising takes a couple of minutes, or whether it takes an hour, is a matter of vital importance to those persons who are working the ammonia process of water analysis. **1881** *Nature* XXIII. 403 Converted into ammonia, which is estimated by nesslerising. **1884** *Jrnl. Amer. Chem. Soc.* VI. 122 Such a tube was found..to be unsuitable for comparison with the color of Nesslerized liquids. **1890** *Amer. Chem. Jrnl.* XII. 426 Standards and distillates are made ready for nesslerisation during the day, and all stand on the same table overnight. In the morning they are nesslerised and compared. **1916** *Jrnl. Biol. Chem.* XXVI. 473 It was hoped that it would be possible to Nesslerize directly the ammonia produced by the destructive digestion of the urine. *Ibid.* 475 This sediment does not interfere with the Nesslerization of the ammonia, but it must be removed before the color comparison is made. *Ibid.* 481 It is better when working in urine to dilute the final Nesslerized solution to 200 cc. instead of to 100 cc. **1956** *Jrnl. Lab. & Clin. Med.* XLVII. 645 In one the clot is dried and weighed to the nearest microgram; in the other it is nesslerized and assayed colorimetrically. *Ibid.* 646 If a microbalance is not available, the fibrin may be estimated by digesting it in sulfuric acid and hydrogen peroxide, nesslerizing, and determining the color density. **1964** *Oceanogr. & Marine Biol.* II. 148 They determine ammonia in the digest by Nesslerization. **1970** *Nature* 12 Sept. 1136/2 L-Glutaminase and L-asparaginase assays were performed..as previously described except that the colour formed by nesslerization of ammonia was measured 1–3 min after addition of Nessler's reagent.

Nessus ('nɛsəs). Name of the centaur slain by Hercules and in whose blood was soaked the tunic which consumed Hercules with fire, used allusively in ***Nessus robe***, ***Nessus shirt***, ***shirt of Nessus*** of any destructive or expurgatory force or influence.

1606 SHAKES. *Ant. & Cl.* IV. xii. 43 The shirt of Nessus is vpon me. **1835** CARLYLE *Lett. to his Wife* (1953) 108 It is now almost my sole rule of life: to clear myself of Cants and formulas, as of poisonous Nessus' shirts. **1905** S. J. WEYMAN *Starvecrow Farm* xxxii. 297 Remorse is the very shirt of Nessus. It is of all mental pains the worst. **1924** R. GRAVES *Mock Beggar Hall* 10 The Nessus-robe that beauties wear, Burning away their beauty. **1931** *Times Lit. Suppl.* 5 Mar. 162/2 The Nessus-robe of vice clings festering about him. **1957** E. SITWELL *Coll. Poems* 414 Then the heart that was the Burning-Bush May change to a Nessus-robe of flame. **1961** M. WEST *Daughter of Silence* iv. 116 Accept the guilt, know yourself for what you are, wear the knowledge like a Nessus shirt on your own back and bear the pricks and the poison with as much dignity as you can muster.

Nessy, var. NESSIE.

nest (nɛst), *sb.* Also 1 **nestþ**, **nestð**, 2 **nyst**, 3–5 **neste**, 4, 6 **neeste**, 6–7 **neast**. [OE. *nest* neut. = MDu. (and Du.), OHG. (and G.) *nest* (hence obs. Da. *nest*, MSw. *näste*, *nesta*), related to OIr. *net* (mod. *nead*; W. *nyth*), L. *nīdus*, Skr. *nīḍá-*:—**nizdo-*, f. the roots *ni-* down (see NETHER) and *sed-* to sit.]

1. a. The structure made, or the place selected, by a bird, in which to lay and incubate its eggs, and which serves as a shelter for its unfledged young. (Cf. BIRD'S NEST 1.)

c **950** *Lindisf. Gosp.* Matt. viii. 20 Foxas holas habbas & fleʒende heofnes nestas *vel* nesto. *a* **1000** *Phœnix* 215 þonne on swole byrneð þurh fyres feng fuʒel mid neste. *c* **1220** *Bestiary* 801 In hole of ston ʒe [*sc.* the dove] makeð hire nest. **1297** R. GLOUC. *Chron.* (Rolls) 3670 In ech roche þer is In tyme of ʒere an ernes nest, þat hii bredeþ inne. *c* **1330** R. BRUNNE *Chron. Wace* (Rolls) 10202 In þo roches foules reste, & ernes brede, & make þer neste. **1377** LANGL. *P. Pl.* B. XI. 336 Briddes I bihelde that in buskes made nestes. *a* **1400–50** *Alexander* 506 þen come þar-in a litell brid.., And þar it nestild in a noke as it a nest were. **1484** CAXTON *Fables of Æsop* I. xiii, The egle and his yonge were in theyr nest. **1508** DUNBAR *Gold. Targe* 6 Glading the mery foulis in thair nest. **1593** SHAKS. *2 Hen. VI*, III. ii. 191 Who finds the

Partridge in the Puttocks Nest, But may imagine how the Bird was dead? **1678** VAUGHAN *Thalia Rediv., Bee*, Birds, from the shades of night releast Look round about, then quit the neast. **1697** DRYDEN *Virg. Georg.* IV. 744 The Mother Nightingale..Whose Nest some prying Churl had found. **1774** GOLDSM. *Nat. Hist.* (1776) I. 244 On these..are sometimes found, not only earth, but nests with birds eggs. **1822** BYRON *Heaven & Earth* I. ii, He hovers nightly, Like a dove round and round its pillaged nest. **1879** BEERBOHM *Patagonia* iv. 53, I found the nest to be of the roughest description, being simply a hole scooped in the ground.

b. In proverbial phrases. (Cf. FEATHER *v.* 5.)

a **1250** *Owl & Night.* 100 Dahet habbe that ilke best That fuleth his owe nest. *c* **1350** *Will. Palerne* 83 þan fond he nest & no neiȝ, for nouȝt nas þer leued. *c* **1400** *Gamelyn* 610 Tho fond þe sherreue nyst, but none eye. *c* **1440** CAPGRAVE *Life St. Kath.* v. 1594 It is neyther wurshipful ne honest On-to mankeende to fule soo his nest. **1509** BARCLAY *Ship of Folys* (1570) 65 It is a lewde birde that fileth his own neste. **1599** BRETON *Praise Vertuous Ladies* (Grosart) 57/2 The proverbe sayes, 'That it is an evill birde, will file its owne nest'. **1624** BP. HALL *Rem. Wks.* (1660) 7 Were it not for..profaneness, these men would be dull, and (as we say) dead on the nest. **1676** *North's Plutarch, Addit. Lives* 77 By this means the Spaniards found nothing in the Nest. **1823** [see FILE *v.*[2] 1 b].

c. A place or structure used by animals or insects as an abode or lair, or in which their eggs, spawn, or young are deposited.

c **1386** CHAUCER *Prioress' T.* 107 The serpent Sathanas, That hath in Jewes hert his waspis nest. *c* **1400** *Rom. Rose* 6504 It is but foly to entremete, To seke in houndes nest fat-mete. **1593** SHAKS. *2 Hen. VI*, III. ii. 86 Fore-warning winde Did seeme to say, seeke not a Scorpions Nest. **1611** —— *Wint. T.* IV. iv. 814 Hee has a Sonne: who shall be..set on the head of a Waspes Nest. **1697** DRYDEN *Virg. Georg.* III. 667 A Snake..Leaving his Nest, and his imperfect Young. **1741** *Compl. Fam.-Piece* II. i. 303 The Does [of rabbits] prevent them by stopping or covering their Stocks or Nests with Earth or Gravel. **1774** GOLDSM. *Nat. Hist.* (1776) IV. 77 They [dormice] inhabit woods or very thick hedges, forming their nests in the hollow of some tree. **1818** KIRBY & SPENCE *Entomol.* xvi. II. 60 Which sent most of the ants in a fright to the nest. **1835** KIRBY *Hab. & Inst. Animals* II. xxi. 384 Fishes..sometimes..prepare regular nests for their young. **1899** *19th Cent.* Sept. 400 Spring floods..wash out the nests [of salmon] by wholesale.

d. A malformation on a tree, so called from its outward resemblance to a bird's nest.

1887 W. PHILLIPS *Brit. Discomycetes* 404 Producing 'nests', or 'witches' besoms', on birch.

2. a. A place in which a person (or personified thing) finds rest or has residence; a lodging, shelter, home, bed, etc., esp. of a secluded or comfortable nature; a snug retreat.

a **1000** *Phœnix* 553 [from *Job* xxix. 18] Ic in minum neste neobed ceose, hæle hrawerig. *a* **1225** *Ancr. R.* 134 þeos [ancren] in swuche neste muwen habben herde reste. *Ibid.* 136 Wiðine þine heorte, þet is Godes nest. *c* **1375** *Cursor M.* 22556 (Fairf.), Lorde quere salle we þan rest, quen we mai naure-quere finde a nest. **1382** WYCLIF *Hab.* ii. 9 Woo to hym that gadrith euyl coueitise to his hous, that his nest be in heeȝ. **1423** JAS. I *Kingis Q.* clxxiii, That place that thou cam fro, Quhich is thy first and verray proper nest. **1562** J. HEYWOOD *Prov. & Epigr.* (1867) 45 Husbande, I would we were in our nest. **1596** SPENSER *F.Q.* IV. v. 32 A little cottage, like some poore man's nest. **1726** *Penn's Wks.* I. *Life* 194 How to raise to your selues a great Name and Estate to exalt your Nests. **1784** COWPER *Task* I. 227, I called the low-roofed lodge the Peasant's Nest. **1822** SHELLEY *To Jane, Recollection* 11 The lightest wind was in its nest, The tempest in its home. **1865** *Times* 30 Aug., In one of the third-floor rooms of my hotel,..a nest of unspotted tidiness.

b. A place in which a thing is lodged or deposited.

1589 COOPER *Admon.* 22 The excessive buildings and needelesse nestes of mens treasures. **1605** BACON *Adv. Learn.* II. x. §5 To obserue, what cauities, nestes and receptacles the humors doe finde in the parts. **1697** EVELYN *Numism.* vii. 251 Taking them [medals] out of their respective Nests and Localities. **1842** L. HUNT *Palfrey* iv. 15 Their drowsy noses droop'd alway To meet the beard's attractive nest.

†**c.** A niche. *Obs. rare*[−1].

Prob. a mistranslation of F. *niche*, after the vb. *nicher* to nest. See also NESSET.

1640–1 *Wood's Life* (O.H.S.) IV. 57 To Mr. Jackson for makeing the nest of the king's picture in the Librarie, 6*li.*

d. *Mil.* An emplaced group of machine-guns.

1914 E. A. POWELL *Fighting in Flanders* v. 120 Other wagons..contained 'nests' of nine machine-guns. **1949** 'G. ORWELL' *Nineteen Eighty-Four* I. 8 A maze of barbed-wire entanglements, steel doors and hidden machine-gun nests. **1959** R. POSTGATE *Every Man is God* xviii. 157 The Germans come out of the machine-gun nest holding up their hands.

3. a. A place in which persons of a certain class (*esp.* thieves, robbers, or pirates) have their usual residence or resort.

c **1386** CHAUCER *Sompn. Prol.* 27 Lat the frere see Wher is the nest of freres in this place! **1500–20** DUNBAR *Poems* lxxxii. 43 Ȝour burgh of beggeris is ane nest. **1568** GRAFTON *Chron.* II. 741 The king of Englande woulde not haue suffered the French kyng to haue buylded such a couert nest so nere his towne of Calice. **1617** MORYSON *Itin.* II. 272 He had razed Hen. Ovington's Castle, and Mac Hughes Iland, which both had been neasts and starting holes for theeves. **1648** GAGE *West Ind.* 159 That Church of Rome is a wide and spatious nest. **1747** COOKE in Hanway *Trav.* (1762) I. IV. lvi. 260 This is said to have been formerly a nest of robbers. **1776** GIBBON *Decl. & F.* x. I. 285 The western and mountainous part of Cilicia, formerly the nest of those daring pyrates. **1842** BORROW *Bible in Sp.* xxiv, Were the friars still in their nest above there. **1869** FREEMAN *Norm. Conq.* (1875) III. xii. 125 The hill-fortress became a mere nest of robbers.

b. A place or quarter in which some state of things, quality, etc. (esp. of a bad kind), is fostered or is prevalent; a haunt *of* crime, vice, etc.

1576 GASCOIGNE *Steele Gl.* (Arb.) 60 Gold, which is..The neast of strife, and nourice of debate. **1592** SHAKS. *Rom. & Jul.* v. iii. 151, I heare some noyse Lady, come from that nest Of death, contagion, and vnnaturall sleepe. **1642** ROGERS *Naaman* 35 Scarce one in a long time gastred out of his neast of forme or profanenesse. **1879** FARRAR *St. Paul* (1883) 130 Damascus, he had heard, was now the worst nest of this hateful delusion. **1899** F. T. BULLEN *Way Navy* 75 The ship is a very nest of rumours.

4. a. A number of birds, insects, or other animals, occupying the same nest or habitation; a brood, swarm, colony.

c **1470** *Hors, Shepe & G.* (Caxton 1479, Roxb. repr.) 29 An erthe of foxes: a neste of rabettis. **1562** J. HEYWOOD *Prov. & Epigr.* (1867) 54 There is a nest of chickens. **1589** *Pasquil's Ret.* D iv, They swell at him with enuie like a nest of foule Toades. **1642** C. VERNON *Consid. Exch.* 88 Men will be wary how they..provoke a nest of waspes. **1727–8** POPE *Let. to Swift* 23 Mar., How much that nest of Hornets are my regard, will easily appear to you. **1760** STILES in *Phil. Trans.* LII. 42 The undulating motion of a nest of caterpillars, when climbing the trunk of some vegetable. **1818** KIRBY & SPENCE *Entomol.* xvi. II. 62 A nest of ants..discovered a closet..in which conserves were kept. **1881** CABLE *Mme. Delphine* ii. 6 Like a nest of yellow kittens.

b. A number or collection of people, esp. of the same class or frequenting a common resort.

1589 ? LYLY *Pappe w. Hatchet* C ij, It was one of your neast, that writt this for a loue letter. **1652** CRASHAW *Carmen Deo* Wks. (1904) 275 Asham'd that our world, now, can show Nests of new Seraphims here below. **1695** LUTTRELL *Brief Rel.* (1857) III. 531 This week a whole nest of clippers were discovered by one Smith in hopes to gett a pardon. **1721** AMHERST *Terræ Fil.* No. 20 (1726) 101 Should I call the whole university of Oxford a nest of fools. **1778** GEO. III in T. Hutchinson *Diary* II. 217 They [the Americans] are a sad nest. **1864** BURTON *Scot Abr.* II. i. 94 A little nest of Covenanting refugee clergy.

5. a. An accumulation or collection of similar objects; also *fig.* of immaterial things.

1642 FULLER *Holy & Prof. St.* v. v. 373 People found out a nest of miracles in her education. **1666** G. ALSOP *Mary Land* (1869) 107 A most horrid neast of condemned Evils. **1703** *Let. in Pepys' Diary* (1893) I. p. 1, There was found in his left kidney a nest of no less than seven stones. **1845** TALFOURD *Vac. Rambles* I. 135 A small nest of low bushes. **1856** KANE *Arct. Expl.* II. xv. 161 Making..for a nest of broken hummocks. **1874** DEUTSCH *Rem.* 192 Perfect nests of arguments..stolen from the mediæval successors of those same Rabbis.

b. A number of buildings, or of narrow streets, lying in close proximity to one another.

1796 COMBE *Boydell's Thames* II. 165 Durham House was become a nest of wharfs and warehouses. **1861** T. A. TROLLOPE *La Beata* II. xvi. 157 They entered the nest of little quiet streets. **1875** HELPS *Soc. Press.* ii. 16 A little London boy, born and bred in some hideous nest of alleys.

6. a. A set or series of similar objects, *esp.* of such as are contained in the same receptacle, or are so made that each smaller one is enclosed in, or fits into, that which is next in size to it.

nest of goblets was common in the 16th c., and ***nest of drawers*** in the first half of the 18th.

1524 *Test. Ebor.* (Surtees) V. 190 My nest of my goblettes. **1540** *Act 32 Hen. VIII*, c. 14 Item for euery nest of compters, xviii. s. **1583** *Rates of Customs* C iv b, Hampers the nest containing three iijs. iiij*d.* **1609** B. JONSON *Sil. Wom.* IV. i, Hee has got on his whole nest of night-caps. **1658** OSBORN *Adv. Son* Wks. (1673) 231 They are all contained within the compass of a just proportion (like a nest of boxes). **1686** PLOT *Staffordsh.* 335 Turned one within another, like a nest of Crucibles or Boxes. **1704** *Lond. Gaz.* No. 4060/5 One Nest of Drawers. **1785** R. CUMBERLAND *Observer* No. 50 ¶2 He has now gone pretty nearly through my whole nest of shelves. **1807** R. SOUTHEY *Lett. from England* I. 155 Here is also a nest of tables for the ladies, consisting of four, one less than another, and each fitting into the one above it. **1834** SOUTHEY *Doctor* II. 22 The public is like a nest of patent coffins.., one within another. **1849** ALB. SMITH *Pottleton Legacy* (1854) 37 There are nests of flower-pots, rakes, water-pots. **1863** TYNDALL *Heat* v. §184 (1870) 148 Here is a nest of watch glasses. **1924** R. KEABLE *Recompence* iv. 76 A delightful nest of occasional tables. **1973** J. LEASOR *Host of Extras* i. 17 A nest of spanners and some lengths of wire that might come in useful in starting an engine. **1975** *Country Life* 20 Feb. Suppl. 32d/2 A rare nest of five rosewood 'quartetto' tables..English, circa 1820.

b. A connected series of cogwheels or pulleys.

1875 KNIGHT *Dict. Mech.* 1521/2.

7. a. *Min.* An isolated deposit of a mineral or metal occurring in the midst of other formations.

1725 T. THOMAS in *Portland Papers* (Hist. MSS. Comm.) VI. 120 Near his house has been discovered..a considerable silver mine, or, as they call it, a nest of silver. **1796** KIRWAN *Elem. Min.* (ed. 2) I. 188 Generally found in nests or veins of rocks. **1833** LYELL *Princ. Geol.* III. 371 The secondary rocks..contain nests and small veins of..iron and copper pyrites. **1875** DAWSON *Dawn Life* ii. 13 Strata often diversified with veins and nests of crystalline minerals.

b. *Path.* A group of epithelial cells.

1871 T. H. GREEN *Introd. Pathol.* 177 These masses are the 'concentric globes', or 'epithelial nests', which are so characteristic of epithelioma. **1884** M. MACKENZIE *Dis. Throat & Nose* II. 413 The microscopic characters of lupus are..infiltration of the integument with small cells arranged in 'nests' [etc.].

8. *attrib.* and *Comb.*, as ***nest-burrow, -door, -factory, -hole, -mate, -material, -part, -place, -plumage, -relief, -room, -scrape, -site, -tree; nest-builder, -maker, -robber, -wright; nest-building, -composing, -keeping, -making, -raiding, -taking; nest-deserted;*** †**nest-cock, -cockle, -frame** (see quots.); †**nest-gut** (?); **nest-spring, -sugar** (see quots.).

1883 *Harper's Mag.* Dec. 100/2 Nearly all the sun-fishes are *nest-builders. **1894** *Outing* (U.S.) XXIII. 380/2 This is the home of the *nest-building tree ants. **1895** *Daily News* 19 Dec. 2/3 A lesson from the magpie on the art of nest-building. **1948** *British Birds* XLI. 341 During our short stay we saw no trace of *nest burrows of the Great Shearwater. **1961** G. DURRELL *Whispering Land* ii. 55 Once the parent bird [*sc.* a penguin] reached the edge of the colony it had run the gauntlet of several thousand youngsters before it reached its own nest-burrow and babies. **1674** BLOUNT *Glossogr.* (ed. 4), *Nescock* or **Nestcock*, one that never was from home, a Fondling or Wanton. **1611** COTGR., *Closcuau*, the Nestling, or *Nest-cockle; the last-hatched bird in a neast. **1601** CHESTER *Love's Mart.* clxxxii, The artificiale *nest-composing Swallow. **1856** MRS. BROWNING *Aur. Leigh* I. 43 As restless as a *nest-deserted bird. **1818** KEATS *Endym.* I. 733 Within the space Of a swallow's *nest-door. **1908** *Westm. Gaz.* 19 Aug. 5/3 The Hungarian Government go so far as to pay large sums of money in subsidies to artificial *nest factories, these nests being fixed in the forests by the thousand and regularly looked after. **1683** MOXON *Mech. Exerc., Printing* ii. ¶1 *Nest-Frames to..hold the Cases that may lye out of present use. *a* **1653** G. DANIEL *Idyll* iv. 30 We're indeed soe Dull In the *Nest-Gutt, wee Crye fasting and full. **1893** G. D. LESLIE *Lett. Marco* xxxviii. 256 The sand-martins' *nest-holes. **1851** *Zoologist* IX. 3123 Capturing flies among the gay petals for his *nest-keeping partner. **1611** COTGR., *Annicheur*, a nestler; a *nest-maker. **1864–5** J. G. WOOD *Homes without H.* xxvii. (1868) 514 When in a state of liberty..it is an admirable nest-maker. **1817** RAFFLES *Java* I. 51 The materials commonly employed in *nest-making. **1863** ATKINSON *Stanton Grange* (1864) 10 A favourite place, well suited for nest-making. **1913** G. STRATTON-PORTER *Laddie* v. 146 If a young bird failed to get the bite it wanted, it sometimes grabbed one of its *nestmates by the bill..and tried to swallow it whole. **1941** J. S. HUXLEY *Uniqueness of Man* x. 214 The nestling cuckoo..does not know why he is murdering his fellow nest-mates. **1923** —— *Essays of Biologist* iii. 121 We invariably find the seizing of *nest-material in the beak as a part of courtship. **1953** N. TINBERGEN *Herring Gull's World* vii. 68 We often wondered how another gull knew whether a grass-pulling gull was in an aggressive mood or merely collecting nest-material. **1794** *Rigging & Seamanship* I. 164 Close up between the *nest part and jaw of the block. **1879** E. ARNOLD *Lt. Asia* 15 Wild swans..voyaging..To their *nest-places. **1854** *Zoologist* XII. 4267 Describing the *nest plumage from a dark specimen. **1937** *British Birds* XXXI. 205 The evidence for *nest raiding is so scanty as to lead to the conclusion that it is not a usual habit. **1953** D. A. BANNERMAN *Birds Brit. Isles* I. 15 It is in the early morning ..that the crow carries out most of its nest-raiding. **1923** J. S. HUXLEY *Essays of Biologist* iii. 112 After the eggs [of the Louisiana Heron] are laid both sexes brood, and there is a *nest-relief four times in every twenty-four hours. **1953** N. TINBERGEN *Herring Gull's World* xvi. 136 The variation in the behaviour of the birds at nest-relief is primarily due to variations in the intensity of the incubation urge. **1893** *Scribner's Mag.* June 769/1 He is a *nest-robber at times, and a field-robber always. **1886** P. ROBINSON *Teetotum Trees* 159 Turtle-doves recompense us by their beauty for our trifling concession of *nest room. **1953** N. TINBERGEN *Herring Gull's World* ii. 11 When the birds of a pair make a *nest-scrape together..they make a queer rhythmical sound. **1964** *Oxf. Bk. Birds* 48/1 The nest scrape [of the kestrel] may be in a hollow tree. **1930** J. S. HUXLEY *Bird-Watching* iii. 53 Each breeding pair occupies and defends against intrusion a considerable area around its *nest-site. **1964** A. L. THOMSON *New Dict. Birds* 531/1 Summer migrants may select a nest site and begin building on the same day. **1884** KNIGHT *Dict. Mech.* Suppl. 633/1 **Nest Spring*, a spiral spring of several concentric coils. **1890** ROSCOE & SCHORLEMMER *Treat. Chem.* III. 641 *Trehala manna*, which is obtained from the nest of a coleopterous insect;..in Persia it is known as *nest-sugar. **1894** *Daily News* 8 Dec. 5/4 The former Act..did not forbid *nest-taking or egg-stealing in general. **1768** PENNANT *Brit. Zool.* (1776) I. 191 After the breeding season rooks forsake their *nest-trees. *a* **1793** G. WHITE *Selborne, On the Weather*, The cawing rook..haunts her tall nest-trees. **1674** N. FAIRFAX *Bulk & Selv.* 152 Apprenticeship to the craft of a *Nestwright.

nest (nɛst), *v.* Also 3 **næstien**, 7 **neast.** [ME. *nest(i)en* (= MDu. and MLG. *nesten*), f. NEST *sb.*, in place of OE. *nist(i)an*, = MDu. and OHG. (also mod.G.) *nisten*, with umlaut of the stem-vowel.

c **825** *Vesp. Psalter* ciii. 17 Ðer spearwan nistað. *c* **1000** *Ags. Ps.* (Spelman) ciii. 18 þær sperwan nistiað.]

1. a. *intr.* Of birds, etc.: To make or have a nest or abode in a particular place. †Also, to resort to the nest, to survive (quot. *a* 1300).

c **1205** LAY. 21753 [There] is a clude hæh and strong. þer næstieð arnes & oðere græte uoȝeles. *a* **1225** *Ancr. R.* 132 þeos..beoð eorð briddes, & nesteð o þer eorðe. *a* **1300** *Vox & Wolf* 48 in Hazl. *E.P.P.* I. 59 Thou hauest that ilke ounder the splen; Thou nestes neuere daies ten. **1570** LEVINS *Manip.* 92/4 To Nest, *nidulari.* **1587** HARMAR tr. *Beza* 279 This poore doue,..did shee not nest, and as it were hide her head in secret holes? **1650** FULLER *Pisgah* II. xiii. 285 Wild Bees, not civilized in hives, but nesting on the ground. **1680** OTWAY *Orphan* IV, Let's find some place where adders nest in winter. **1773** G. WHITE in *Phil. Trans.* LXIV. 200, I have..seen them nesting in the Borough. *a* **1806** H. K. WHITE *Poems* (1837) 127 Where nests the raven, sits the toad. **1827** POLLOK *Course T.* VIII, A thousand snakes..Nest there. **1873** G. C. DAVIES *Mount. & Mere* xviii. 157 The unsavoury smelling hole..where the same pair of kingfishers nested year after year.

b. To engage in nest-building.

1774 G. WHITE in *Phil. Trans.* LXV. 265 They begin nesting about the middle of May. **1863** [WHEELWRIGHT] *Spring Lapl.* 51, I observed a sparrow with a straw in his beak, evidently nesting.

2. a. To settle or lodge as in a nest.

1591 SPENSER *Teares Muses* 389 Sweete Love..spotles, as at first he sprong Out of th' Almighties bosome, where he nests. **1633** P. FLETCHER *Purple Isl.* XII. lxxxvi, Where better could her love then here have nested? **1655** H. VAUGHAN *Silex Scint.* I. *Dressing* ii, These dark confusions that within me nest. **1700** C. DAVENANT *Disc. Grants* iii. 109 The Flemings who had nested here in hopes of Booty. **1742** YOUNG *Nt. Th.* II. 219 To..join anew Eternity his sire; In his immutability to nest. **1876** GEO. ELIOT *Dan. Der.* lviii, This sort of passion had nested in the sweet-natured, strong Rex.

†**b.** To sit down to ease oneself. *Obs. rare*[−1].
1670 *Mod. Acc. Scot.* in *Harl. Misc.* (1745) VI. 123 The most Mannerly step but to the Door, and nest upon the Stairs.

c. *U.S. colloq.* To squat. (Cf. NESTER 2.)
1918 C. E. MULFORD *Man from Bar-20* xi. 114 Not satisfied with nestin' on a man's range, you had to start a little herd.

†**3.** *refl.* **a.** Of persons: To repose or rest, to domicile or settle, (oneself) in a place. *Obs.* (freq. in 17th c.)
a **1300** *Cursor M.* 22556 Quar sal we þan rest Quen nan sal wite quar þam to nest. *a* **1425** *Ibid.* 9873 (Trin.), God þat wolde so him nest, In clene stud þen most he rest. **1573** TUSSER *Husb.* (1878) 27 Let wood and water request thee, In good corne soile to nest thee. **1588** in Arb. *Garner* III. 37 What meaneth Love to nest him in the..eyes..Of my mistress? **1652–62** HEYLIN *Cosmogr.* IV. (1682) 37 A Rabble of Pirats nest themselves in Salla. **1705** HICKERINGILL *Priest-cr.* IV. (1721) 214 Some nest themselves, like Wasps, only to buz about and sting.

†**b.** *transf.* of things. *Obs.*
1607 *Schol. Disc. agst. Antichr.* I. iii. 151 The fift hipocrisie..neasteth it self in the affections of the heart. **1641** MILTON *Ch. Govt.* I. iii. 12 Such a ministery establish't in the Gospell, as..nests it selfe in worldly honours.

4. In *pa. pple.* **a.** Settled, established, comfortably placed, in or as in a nest.
1599 HAKLUYT *Voy.* II. 132 The Masters and mariners..being then nested in their owne homes. **1628** FELTHAM *Resolves* II. l. 147 If we considered detraction to be..nested onely in deficient minds. **1673** TEMPLE *Obs. United Prov.* Wks. 1720 I. 61 The Flock of People that for some time had been nested there. **1754** FIELDING *Voy. Lisbon* Wks. 1784 X. 205 The wind had been long nested, as it were, in the south west. **1834** MEDWIN *Angler in Wales* I. 155 The side hills are well wooded, and nested among them are some delightful country-houses. **1883** E. ARNOLD *Ind. Idylls* 241 There perched A thousand crows,..Some nested, some on branchlets, deep asleep.

b. Packed one inside another; *transf.* of abstract entities: cf. NEST *sb.* 6 and NESTED *ppl. a.* 2. Also *intr.* for *pass.*, to admit of nesting.
1870 *Eng. Mech.* 4 Mar. 596/3 [Crucibles] are sold one in the other, and are then called 'nested'. **1879** *Cassell's Techn. Educ.* IV. 63/1 Glazed boxes round and square..are supplied 'nested', consecutively of various depths. **1925** N. E. ODELL in E. F. Norton *Fight for Everest 1924* 362 Two saucepans that nest into one another. **1961** D. V. HUNTSBERGER *Elem. Statist. Inference* ix. 230 Situations of this sort, where every classification is nested within the next larger one, are called nested or hierarch[ic]al classifications. **1967** KLERER & KORN *Digital Computer User's Handbk.* I. i. 16 Groups of loops need not be strictly nested and may have parts which are done in parallel or parts which are done in series. **1968** J. LYONS *Introd. Theoret. Linguistics* vi. 233 In subordinative constructions one modifier may be recursively 'nested' within another. **1970** P. M. SHERMAN *Techn. Computer Programming* iii. 43 In many problems one loop is nested within another one. This occurs when a loop contains a box with a repetitious process that itself can be drawn as a loop.

c. Used as a nest, or for making nests *in*.
1844 CHEEVER *On Bunyan's Pilgr.* iv. (1847) 108 Leaves nested with worms and overcurled. **1883** STEVENSON *Silverado Sq.* (1886) 42 Chestnuts..nested in by song birds.

5. *intr.* To go bird's-nesting.
1876 BP. HANNINGTON in *Life* x. (1887) 146, I nested in the Bishop's garden, and round the belfry tower for swifts' eggs.

6. *trans.* To provide with a nesting-place.
1896 WOOLLEY in *Advance* (Chicago) 305 Better be a vine and cling to some grand old pile..and nest its bats and owls.

nest, obs. form of NEXT.

'nestage. [f. NEST *sb.*] Nesting; nests.
1865 T. TATE in *Proc. Berw. Nat. Club* 223 Want of room for nestage.

nestalik, nestaliq, varr. NASTALIK.

†**nestarm**, app. for *erstarm*: see ARSE *sb.* 3.
c **1475** *Pict. Voc.* in Wr.-Wülcker 751 *Hoc intestinum, hic colus*, nestarme.

nest-box. [f. NEST *sb.* + BOX *sb.*[2]]
1. A box containing others of graduated sizes packed in a nest.
1660 *Act 12 Chas. II*, c. 4 *Schedule* s.v. *Boxes*, Nest boxes, the groce, containing twelve dozen nests. **1812** J. SMYTH *Pract. of Customs* (1821) *49 Nest boxes.—The gross to contain 12 dozen Nests, each Nest 8 Boxes. *Ibid.*, 1 Case, containing..2½ Gross of Nest Boxes.

2. A box provided for a domestic fowl or other bird to make its nest in.
1849 D. J. BROWNE *Amer. Poultry Yd.* (1855) 88 Every poultry house..should be provided with nest boxes. **1893** *Burpee's Farm Ann.* 64 These gourds are useful for many household purposes, such as..nest-boxes, soap and salt dishes. **1946** *Q. Jrnl. Forestry* XL. 83 The habit of maintaining a territory also leads to birds being well scattered over the area, and as a consequence nest boxes should not be too close together. **1963** *Times* 8 June 12/7 Your Correspondent recalls a horrid stench from a nest-box after seven or eight young great tits had flown. **1971** *Country Life* 2 Sept. 541/1 Many bird-lovers put up two or three nest-boxes in their gardens.

neste, obs. f. of NEXT; var. NIST *v. Obs.*

'nested, *ppl. a.* [f. NEST *v.* + -ED[1].]
1. That is settled in, or provided with, a nest.
1729 SAVAGE *Wanderer* IV. 67 The chatt'ring swallows leave their nested care. **1807** WORDSW. *White Doe* VII. 187 They, like a nested pair, reposed. **1876** E. HOPKINS *Rose Turquand* I. xix. 277 The tender tweet! tweet! of the nested birds in the ivy.

2. Such that each item or constituent contains or is contained within another similar item in a hierarchical arrangement. **a.** Of concrete objects (cf. NEST *v.* 4 b).
1921 *Glasgow Herald* 1 June 7 Two or three 'nested' dishes, the biggest one large enough to take two plates side by side. **1969** 'S. TROY' *Swift to its Close* vi. 81 A little man carrying three nested chairs brushed past. **1972** *Sci. Amer.* Apr. 32/1 The magnetic field in the compressor is supplied by a nested set of copper coils.

b. Of abstract entities.
1959 E. L. LEHMANN *Testing Statistical Hypotheses* vii. 290 (*heading*) Nested classifications. **1963** ERVIN & MILLER in J. A. Fishman *Readings Sociol. of Lang.* (1968) 80 Preliminary evidence suggests that nesting is learned early. .. It is difficult to assess the evidence, however, because nested constructions are usually delineated by markers which are largely lacking in the early grammatical systems. **1965** N. CHOMSKY *Aspects of Theory of Syntax* i. 12 The phrases *A* and *B* form a nested construction if *A* falls totally within *B*, with some nonnull element to its left within *B* and some nonnull element to its right within *B*. **1967** [see NESTING *vbl. sb.* 2]. **1968** J. F. HART et al. *Computer Approximations* iv. 68 Consider a polynomial given in the conventional power form $P_n(x) = \sum_{i=0}^{n} a_i x^i$. It can be written in nested form $P_n(x) = [\ldots(a_n x + a_{n-1})x + \ldots + a_1]x + a_0$. **1970** P. M. SHERMAN *Techn. Computer Programming* iii. 43 Some flowcharts contain three or more nested loops. **1973** A. M. COHEN et al. *Numerical Anal.* ii. 21 The computation of a polynomial function is usually done by means of 'nested multiplication'. **1973** *Computers & Humanities* VII. 226 Procedures for handling nested loops and subscripted variables.

'nest-egg, *sb.* [f. NEST *sb.* + EGG *sb.*]
1. a. An egg, natural or artificial, left in a nest to induce the bird to continue to lay in the same place, after the other eggs have been abstracted.
1611 COTGR., *Nicheul*, a neast-egge. **1614** MARKHAM *Cheap. Husb.* (1623) 139 You shall gather your Egges vp once a day, and leaue in the nest but the nest-Egge, and no more. **1844** H. STEPHENS *Bk. Farm* III. 1197 A nest-egg should be left in every nest. **1859** *All Year Round* No. 32. 125 If you want to make a farm-yard profitable,..keep no roosters and allow no nest-eggs. **1939–40** *Army & Navy Stores Catal.* 989/2 Poultry nest eggs. **1973** *Country Life* 18 Oct. 1129/3 What happened to the old-fashioned nest-egg, the white pot egg one could once..buy to ensure that hens would lay where they were supposed to lay?

b. In figurative context.
1606 *Proc. agst. late Traitors* 207 [You] endeavoured your best and uttermost to broose the very neast-egge of this royale and his flying ayerie. *a* **1673** G. SWINNOCK in Spurgeon *Treas. David* Ps. cxix. 104 A hypocrite ever leaves the devil some nest-egg to sit upon.

2. Something displayed, or serving, as an inducement or decoy.
1678 BUTLER *Hud.* III. iii. 625 Books and money laid for shew, Like nest-eggs to make clients lay. **1709** *Brit. Apollo* No. 56. 2/1 Lay Guineas carelesly on your Table for Nest-Eggs. **1796** WASHINGTON *Lett.* Writ. 1892 XIII. 227, I should view the residence of the Commissioners..as a nest egg (pardon the expression) which will attract others. **1834** *Tait's Mag.* I. 421/1 Ye must try for grand names, sir, for nest-eggs to begin with. **1884** SHARMAN *Hist. Swearing* i. 7 It was by the aid of such simple nest-eggs as these that the men managed to establish reputations.

3. a. A sum of money laid or set by as a reserve.
a **1700** B. E. *Dict. Cant. Crew* s.v. *Egge*, *To leave a Nest-egg*, to have alwaies a Reserve to come again. **1758** J. BLAKE *Plan Mar. Syst.* 68 The..payments will constitute a bank, or nest egg. **1825** SCOTT 15 Oct. in *Fam. Lett.* (1894) II. xxiii. 359 You might..lay by the balance, which..will make a tolerable nest-egg. **1860** GEN. P. THOMPSON *Audi Alt.* clxi. III. 175 They preserved a nest-egg in the shape of a duty of 8 per cent. on low stuffs. **1876** RUSKIN *Fors Clav.* VI. 249 A nice little nest-egg of five hundred pounds in the bank.
attrib. **1852** R. S. SURTEES *Sponge's Sp. Tour* xxxii. 194 The Mangeysterne hounds wanted that great ingredient of prosperity, a large nest-egg subscriber.

b. Something kept in reserve.
1837 BROWNING *Strafford* II. i, But, brother, where's your word for Strafford's other nest-egg, the Scots war? **1862** BP. WILBERFORCE in *Life* (1882) III. ii. 70, I and others kept the Church as his nest-egg when he became a Whig, till it was almost addled.

4. A sum of money serving as a nucleus for the acquisition of more.
1822 GALT *Provost* xxxvii, The laird made him his man of business, and, in a manner, gave him a nest egg. **1857** SMILES *Stephenson* (1859) 51 The first guinea which he had saved..had proved the nest-egg of future guineas. **1968** J. R. ACKERLEY *My Father & Myself* 41 This nest-egg towards the cost of the farm. **1975** *Radio Times* 24 Apr. 12 (Advt.), Williams & Glyn's Nest Egg is a regular savings plan.

nestel, obs. form of NESTLE.

'nester. [f. NEST *v.* + -ER[1].]
1. A bird that is building, or has built, a nest.
1887 *Ibis* 95 It [sc. *Cisticola cursitans*] is both an early and late nester. **1895** *Daily News* 20 Apr. 9/1 The preservers of our Heronry..noted a falling off in the number of nesters.

2. *N. Amer.* An opprobrious term for a person who settles permanently in a cattle-grazing region as a farmer, homesteader, etc. (Cf. NEST *v.* 2 c.)
1880 *Ft. Griffin* (Tex.) *Echo* 3 Jan., [A sheep man is] a tramp, an ingrate, a 'Nester', and a liar. **1907** C. E. MULFORD *Bar-20* xix. 192 Ain't th' Panhandle full of nesters (farmers)? **1918** —— *Man from Bar-20* iii. 27 He had found the ruins of a burned homestead..and he guessed that it had been used by 'nesters'. **1970** *Alberta Hist. Rev.* Summer 9/2 The one small cloud on this otherwise sunny horizon was the would-be farmer, or as he was more inhospitably known to the cattlemen—the 'sodbuster' or 'nester'. **1973** R. D. SYMONS *Where Wagon Led* p. xx, You plant a garden and someone'll see it an' we'll have nesters.

'nestful. [f. NEST *sb.* + -FUL.] The quantity (of eggs or young) that a nest can contain.
1598 FLORIO, *Nidiata*, a nestfull, a couie. **1611** COTGR., *Nyaie*, an Airie, or neastful of. **1842** MRS. BROWNING *Grk. Chr. Poets* (1863) 100 The swallows had time to hatch two nestfulls in a chimney. **1885** FORBES *Nat. Wand. E. Archip.* 72, I stumbled on a nestful of six fledglings.

nesthande, obs. variant of NEXTHAND.

'nesting, *vbl. sb.* [f. NEST *v.* + -ING[1].]
1. a. The action, or manner, of constructing a nest or nests.
1767 G. WHITE *Selborne* xii, From the colour, shape, size, and manner of nesting, I make no doubt..the species is nondescript. **1864–5** WOOD *Homes without H.* xxxi. (1868) 623 The bird is gregarious in its nesting, the rocky ledges being crowded with the rude nests. **1874** COUES *Birds N.W.* 50 An..account of the nesting and eggs of this species.

b. *attrib.*, as ***nesting-burrow**, **-call**, **-cover**, **-ground**, **-habit**, **-hole**, **-place**, **-season**, **-site**, **-song**, **-station**, **-territory**, **-time**, **-tree***; **nesting-box** = NEST-BOX 2. Also *fig.*
1873 *Young Englishwoman* May 225/1 The space beneath the *nesting-boxes should be partitioned from the rest of the cage. **1895** W. SCHLICH *Man. Forestry* IV. ii. 148 The wooden nesting-boxes..are made out of half-inch boards, and tarred. **1933** H. NICOLSON *Diary* 5 Jan. (1966) 131 Up Broadway and Madison to the hotel. Nesting-boxes. **1938** *Brit. Birds* XXXI. 331 Noticing..a Blue Tit..entering about dusk a nesting box..I began watching. **1970** *New Yorker* 8 Aug. 56/3 We're building nesting boxes and doing everything else we can think of to encourage the kestrels. **1937** *Brit. Birds* XXX. 237 On Rona the thrift-grown banks ..are riddled with *nesting burrows of Leach's Petrels. **1959** VAN TYNE & BERGER *Fundamentals of Ornithology* x. 277 The Turquoise-browed Motmot..may dig nesting burrows over 5 feet long. **1924** J. A. THOMSON *Sci. Old & New* xxi. 116 The selection is marked by the bird's remaining near the chosen spot and giving the *nesting-call to the mate. **1936** *Brit. Birds* XXIX. 28 Elstree reservoir.. is about 80 acres in extent with relatively little suitable *nesting-cover for the Great Crested Grebe. **1921** *Daily Colonist* (Victoria, B.C.) 27 Oct. 10/3 The purchasing of suitable marsh and swamp lands to furnish *nesting grounds for the birds in the North. **1961** O. L. AUSTIN *Birds of World* (1962) 38/2 They [*sc.* diving petrels]..are nocturnal on the nesting grounds. **1936** *Brit. Birds* XXX. 98 The average size of the broods of the Swallow..and other questions connected with their *nesting-habits..bring the enquiry to a close. **1964** *Oxf. Bk. Birds* 102/2 They [*sc.* rock doves] build on ledges in caves and crevices and have..nesting habits like other doves. **1936** *Brit. Birds* XXIX. 379 The height above ground of the *nesting-hole varies according to the choice there is of decayed wood. **1961** O. L. AUSTIN *Birds of World* (1962) 173/2 Guatemalans have always claimed that the Quetzal selects a nesting hole with two entrances... Recent studies have shown this to be pure legend. **1611** FLORIO, *Nidamento*, a *nesting-place. **1774** G. WHITE in *Phil. Trans.* LXV. 270 They are fearless while haunting their nesting places. **1861** L. L. NOBLE *Icebergs* 180 As wild-looking as the nesting-place of sea-fowl. **1879** JEFFERIES *Wild Life in S. Co.* 338 In the *nesting season snakes are the terror of those birds that build in low bushes. **1888** *Zoologist* XIII. 18 Not finally deciding on a *nesting-site until May 17th. **1879** E. ARNOLD *Lt. Asia* I. xiii, All the jungle laughed with *nesting-songs. **1882** *Proc. Berw. Nat. Club* IX. 506 They..cling to their *nesting stations. **1923** J. S. HUXLEY *Ess. Biologist* vii. 291 The sense of being a trespasser so often shown by a bird that has ventured upon the *nesting-territory of another. **1959** VAN TYNE & BERGER *Fundamentals of Ornithology* x. 268 Small nesting territories of colonial and some non-colonial birds—a small area round the actual nest. **1974** *Country Life* 14 Feb. 285/3 Fulmars.. lay claim to sites, even when there is frost... Ravens, too, patrol a nesting territory. **1600** SURFLET *Countrie Farme* VII. xx. 836 The heron-shewes haunting the same in *nesting time, would forsake it. **1883** *Harper's Mag.* Dec. 101/1 In the warm weeks of June come the sterner duties, the nesting-time. **1935** *Brit. Birds* XXVIII. 347 Return to *nesting-trees.—First seen on February 18th.

2. (The making of) a nested arrangement (see NESTED *ppl. a.* 2).
1957 D. D. MCCRACKEN *Digital Computer Programming* xvii. 207 The truncated series is factored: $e^x = 1 + x/1! + x^2/2! + x^3/3! + x^4/4! + x^5/5! + x^6/6! = 1 + x[1 + \frac{1}{2}x[1 + \frac{1}{3}x[1 + \frac{1}{4}x[1 + \frac{1}{5}x[1 + \frac{1}{6}x]]]]]$. The factored series is then evaluated 'from the inside out', which is also called nesting. **1958** C. F. HOCKETT *Course in Mod. Linguistics* xxi. 189 The presence of certain attributive constructions in the nesting precludes the occurrence of certain others at a more inclusive level: we can say *this fresh milk*, but not *fresh this milk*. **1963** [see NESTED *ppl. a.* 2 b]. **1965** *Language* XLI. 71 Internal layering and multiple nesting characterize many syntagmemes. **1966** Y. BAR-HILLEL in *Automatic Transl. of Lang.* (NATO Summer School, Venice 1962) 11 The same degree of nesting is also assigned to the terminal expression as analysed by this tree. **1967** KLERER & KORN *Digital Computer User's Handbk.* I. iii. 75 Another technique to reduce operations is by nesting when increasing powers of a variable are to be calculated. For example, the expression $AX^3 + BX^2 + CX + D$ may be written in nested form as $((B + Ax)x + C)x + D$ which requires less arithmetic.

1972 Hartmann & Stork *Dict. of Lang. & Linguistics* 150/2 *Nesting*, the embedding of a phrase or clause within an endocentric phrase to modify its head word.

'nesting, *ppl. a.* [f. as prec. + -ING[2].]

1. Making or occupying a nest.

1658 Rowland tr. *Moufet's Theat. Ins.* 930 The Bombylus, greatest of the nesting Insects, is bigger than either of the Sirens. **1797** Holcroft tr. *Stolberg's Trav.* (ed. 2) III. lxxxviii. 467 There is a wall, which has cavities for nesting doves. **1851** Mrs. Browning *Casa Guidi Wind.* 29 Insecure, The nesting swallows fly off. **1895** *Atlantic Monthly* July 63 The nesting-bird was one of the group.

2. Of a table, chair, etc.: that forms part of a set of similar articles which can be fitted into one another (cf. NEST *sb.* 6).

Passing into the *vbl. sb.*

1934 H. Read *Art & Industry* II. 89 Another chair designed by Alvar Aalto. The plywood process combined with tubular steel to make nesting-chairs. **1934** A. Woollcott *While Rome Burns* 29 He [*sc.* Harpo, a French poodle] was gracious, for instance, toward Erich Maria Remarque, a dachshund who fitted under him like a nesting table. **1958** J. Cannan *And be a Villain* iii. 57 In the meagre lounge, half-heartedly modernized with nesting chairs and formica-topped tables. **1959** N. Mailer *Advts. for Myself* (1961) 436 Hand-worked nesting tables. **1961** G. Millerson *Technique Telev. Production* viii. 150 (*caption*) Nesting sets may be placed one within the other, the inner one being struck to reveal the outer. **1969** *Guardian* 26 Sept. 11/7 Nesting tables..5 gns. each or £15. 10s. per set of three. **1970** *Washington Post* 30 Sept. B8/5 (Advt.), Front-zipped cotton luggage... Six nesting sizes. **1975** *Harpers & Queen* May 145/2 Gladstone bags in woven rush; 3 nesting sizes.

nestle ('nɛs(ə)l), *v.*[1] [OE. *nestlian* = MDu. (mod.Du.) and MLG. *nestelen*; cf. OE. *nistl(i)an*, *nystlan* = late MHG. *nisteln*.

c **1000** *Ags. Ps.* (Thorpe) lxxxiii. 3 Turtle nistlað, þær heo afedeð fuȝelas ȝeonge. *Ibid.* ciii. 16 On þam..spearwan nystlað (*Cant. Ps.* nistliæþ).]

I. *intr.* **1.** Of birds: To make or have a nest, esp. *in* a place. = NEST *v.* I. Also *fig.*

c **1000** *Lamb. Psalter* ciii. 16 Ðar spearwan nestliaþ. *c* **1275** Lay. 21753 A chlud swiþe strong, þar nestleþ hearnes and oþer grete foȝeles. *a* **1300** *E.E. Psalter* ciii. 17 þar sal sparwes be nestland. **1382** Wyclif *Jer.* xxii. 22 Thou shalt be confoundyd,..that sittist in Liban, and nestlist in cedris. *c* **1440** *Promp. Parv.* 354/1 Nestlyn, *nidifico.* **1545** Joye *Exp. Dan.* iv. 48b, The birdes nested in hir branches. **1587** Golding *De Mornay* xiv. (1617) 233 Euery of them in their kind, do all liue, nestle, and sing after one sort. **1600** Surflet *Countrie Farme* vii. liii. 885 They nestle thrice a yeere, that is to say, in May, Iune, and August. **1629** H. Burton *Truth's Triumph* 328 Let such vncleane birds neuer nestle or roost in Christian nurceries. **1769** Pennant *Brit. Zool.* III. 20 It will prey on young birds, whether on such as nestle on the ground [etc.]. **1855** W. S. Dallas *Syst. Nat. Hist.* II. 259 They nestle in rocks and holes of trees, and lay five or six eggs.

b. To lodge or settle as in a nest.

a **1400–50** *Alexander* 506 þar it nestild in a noke as it a nest were. **1692** R. L'Estrange *Fables* ccccxxxix, A Cock was got into a Stable, and there was he Nestling in the Straw among the Horses. **1751** *Narr. of H.M.S. Wager* 100 When they [penguins] breed,..they nestle three or four together in a Hole. **1851** Kingsley *Sonn.* Poems (1878) 222 Nightingales who nestle side by side. **1853** —— *Hypatia* xii, The warblings of the tropic birds which nestled among the branches.

c. Of other living things.

1705 Addison *Italy* Wks. 1721 II. 163 The floor is strowed..with several kinds of plants, amongst which the Snails nestle all the winter. *a* **1738** Swift *South Sea* 95 The Monsters nestle in the Deep, To seize you in your passing by. **1881** Tyndall *Floating Matter Air* 161 It was no uncommon thing to see from ten to twenty monads nestling and quivering in this 'moss'.

†**2.** To take up one's abode, to settle or squat, in a place. *Obs.*

1406 Hoccleve *La Male Regle* 288 Lest fauel yow fro wele tryce, No lenger souffre hir nestlen in your ere. **1555** W. Watreman *Fardle Facions* II. ix. 190 Thei nestled first vpon the floude Araxis. **1610** Holland *Camden's Brit.* I. 672 Some out of Ireland, entred in by stealth into this Isle also, and nestled there. *a* **1656** Ussher *Ann.* vi. (1658) 304 Menander was coming on with a great army, which would not suffer him to nestle in Cappadocia. **1797** Burke *Corr.* (1844) IV. 422 If they can nestle in the country for any time ..they cannot fail of profiting of the discontents.

3. Of persons: To settle down as in a nest, or in a snug or comfortable manner. (Freq. with implication of affection, as in next.)

1687 A. Lovell tr. *Thevenot's Trav.* I. 30 The Turks.. think it strange that the Francks suffer their Hair to grow; for they say that the Devil nestles in it. **1821** Joanna Baillie *Metr. Leg., Lady G. Baillie* xxxii, With her in mimick war they wrestle, Beneath her twisted robe they nestle. **1832** Ht. Martineau *Ireland* 119 Begging by day, and nestling wherever they could find a hole by night. **1840** Dickens *Barn. Rudge* lxxi, She nestled..in Emma Haredale's bosom. **1883** J. Hawthorne in *Harper's Mag.* Nov. 935/1 She nestled luxuriously among the cushions.

b. To draw or press *close*, or near, *to* a thing or person, esp. in an affectionate manner.

1709 Steele *Tatler* No. 9 ¶3 Here Parisatis heard her Niece nestle closer to the Key-hole. **1838** Lytton *Alice* I. ii, She drew a stool to her mother's feet,..nestling to her and clasping her hand. **1863** Jeaffreson *Sir Everard's Dau.* 176 Nestling closer to him in the dark corner.

4. Of things or qualities: To lie half-hidden or embedded in some place or thing.

1788 Burke *Impeachm. W. Hastings* Wks. XIII. 17 It is feared, that partiality may lurk and nestle in the abuse of our forms of proceeding. **1849** Robertson *Serm.* Ser. I. xi. (1866) 193 The beauty of the lily nestling in the grass. **1863** Cowden Clarke *Shaks. Char.* ii. 36 His cheerful morality nestles in his heart, and inspires his actions.

b. Of dwellings, etc.: To lie in a snug or sheltered manner in some situation.

1842 J. B. Fraser *Allee Neemroo* II. 320 Numerous villages..nestled in sheltered nooks among the ravines. **1850** B. Taylor *Eldorado* I. 3 The country-houses of planters..nestling in orange groves. **1884** J. Colborne *Hicks Pasha* 69 Large groves of palm trees, among which nestled small hamlets.

II. 5. a. *refl.* To settle or establish (oneself) in a place. Also with *into*. Now *rare*.

1547 J. Harrison *Exhort. Scottes* d viij, These men.. nesteled themselfes in the nighte of that ignoraunt worlde. **1577–87** Holinshed *Chron.* I. 72/1 The Picts..came and nestled themselues in Louthian. **1621** Burton *Anat. Mel.* III. iv. I. v. (1651) 681 The Socinians, that now nestle themselves about Crakowe and Rakowe in Poland. **1642** Rogers *Naaman* Table, The Creature..nestles it selfe in her ease and welfare. *a* **1716** South *Serm.* (1823) III. 106 They have seen perjury and murder nestle themselves into a throne. **1826** *Gen. Hist.* in *Ann. Reg.* 101/2 A gentleman.. who had nestled himself in an English borough.

b. *trans.* To push *in*, to press, rest, or settle (one's head, etc.) in a snug or affectionate manner.

c **1696** Prior *Love Disarmed* 7 He found a downy bed And nestled in his little head. **1798** Mme. D'Arblay *Let.* Mar., He only nestled his little head in my neck. **1886** *Tip Cat* xix. 261 Letty, quite contented, nestled her face against Tip Cat's sleeve and dozed. **1894** Crockett *Raiders* (ed. 3) 266 She walked very close to me, as though she would nestle her shoulder against mine.

6. To place in, or as in, a nest; to set in a secure place; †to tend, nurse.

a **1548** Hall *Chron., Hen. VI* 185 King Henry and his faction nesteled and strengthend him and his alyes in the North regions. *c* **1611** Chapman *Iliad* xxiii. 687 This Ithacus so highly is indeared To this Minerua that..She, like his mother, nestles him. **1822** W. Irving *Braceb. Hall* (1890) 148 He..had nestled her as an eagle does its young among the rocky heights of the Sierra Morena. **1876** Geo. Eliot *Dan. Der.* xxxv, The words had nestled their venomous life within her.

b. To provide with a nesting-place.

1644 Evelyn *Diary* 17 Oct., Trees..which serve to nestle and pearch all sorts of birds. **1838** Eliza Cook *Land of Birth* iii, Where the citron-tree nestles the soft humming-bird. **1863** Cowden Clarke *Shaks. Char.* xvi. 402 Her first speech is one of those pleasant jests that nestle a gentle philosophy beneath their light wording.

c. In *pa. pple.* Nested; settled or placed as in a nest. Also with *in*, *away*.

1582 Stanyhurst *Æneis* III. (Arb.) 77 Where foule bird foggye Celæno And Harpy is nestled. *c* **1595** Southwell *St. Peter's Compl.* 38 My life was nestled In the summe of happinesse. **1649** G. Daniel *Trinarch., Hen. IV*, xxxviii, In Danae's Cage Wee Nestled happy are. **1824** Miss Mitford *Village* Ser. I. (1863) 80 There are lambs amongst them.. nestled in by their mothers. **1860** Pusey *Min. Proph.* 235 So nestled was Petra in its rocks, that [etc.]. **1883** *Harper's Mag.* Mar. 533/1 Little clusters of..trees..told where the little villages were nestled away.

Hence **'nestled** *ppl. a.*

1868 Sill *Poems* 63 Odorous airs, with blessing filled From nestled blossoms round my grave.

'nestle, *v.*[2] Now only *dial.* [Of obscure origin: identity with prec. is not clear.] *intr.* To be uneasy or restless; to fidget; to move or bustle about; to trifle. Hence **'nestling** *vbl. sb.*[2]

a **1700** B. E. *Dict. Cant. Crew* s.v., *What a nestling you keep*, how restless and uneasy you are. **1704** Steele *Lying Lover* III. i, Did you mind how she nestled and fumed inwardly to see your Ladyship look so well. **1706** Phillips (ed. Kersey), s.v., To *Nestle about*, to move here and there. **1796** Marshall *Yorksh.* (ed. 2) II. 335 To *Nessle*, or *Nestle*, to fidget. **1828** in *Craven Gloss.* **1853–** in dial. glossaries (Lanc., Yks., Linc.; Hants, Surr., Suss.).

nestle-chick. = NESTLE-COCK.

1932 R. Macaulay *They were Defeated* I. 32, I couldn't spare her—my last nestle-chick, and the best. **1937** —— *I would be Private* 36 It was to have been her..nestle-chick.

nestle-cock. Now only *dial.* Also 7 nessle-. [f. NESTLE *v.*[1] + COCK *sb.*[1]: cf. *nest-cock*, *-cockle*, s.v. NEST *sb.* 8.] The last-hatched bird, or weakling of a brood; hence, a mother's pet; a spoilt or delicate child or youth.

1626 Middleton *Anything for Quiet Life* IV. ii, My mother was wont to call me your nestle-cock, and I love you as well as she did. **1640** Nabbes *Bride* Prol., A play Wherein a nesslecock, or youth o'th' towne..'s a gallant growne. *a* **1661** Fuller *Worthies, London* (1662) II. 196 One coaks'd or cocker'd, made a wanton or a Nestle-cock of, delicately bred and brought up. *a* **1791** in Pegge *Derbicisms* (E.D.S.) 48. **1864–83** in Lanc. and Yks. glossaries.

nestler ('nɛslə(r)). [f. NESTLE *v.*[1] + -ER[1]; cf. G. *nist(e)ler*.] A nesting bird; a nestling; also *transf.* a little child.

1611 Cotgr., *Annicheur*, a nestler; a nest-maker. **1655** Moufet & Bennet *Health's Improv.* (1746) 183 Cuckows Flesh, whilst it is a Nestler, is by Perot highly extolled. **1827** Atherstone *Tomorrow* 149 What 'tis he sings to the soft nestler there. **1866** Alger *Solit. Nat. & Man* II. 43 The mother..missing..the darling nestler.

nestle-tripe. Now only *dial.* Also 7 -trett. [f. as *nestle-cock* with obscure second element; mod. dialects also have the form *nestle-bird*, *-bub*, *-draff*, *-draft*, *-dris*: see the *Eng. Dial. Dict.*] = NESTLING *sb.* 2.

1616 J. Lane *Contn. Sqr.'s T.* v. 76, I, that am his eldest and first borne, shall have the nesteltrett sett mee beforne. *Ibid.* 139 Shees but the nesteltrett. **1823** *New Monthly Mag.* VII. 235 The little nestle-tripe we hoisted out of the brine. **1823** *Ibid.* VIII. 497 The nestletripe of the sons.

'nest-like, *a.* [f. NEST *sb.* + -LIKE.] Resembling a nest.

a **1793** G. White *Selborne, Invitation*, Where nods in air the pensile, nest-like bower. **1816** Kirby & Sp. *Entomol.* xxi. (1818) II. 262, I once found it..in the nest-like umbel of the wild carrot. **1864** Tennyson *En. Ard.* 59 He..made a home For Annie, neat and nestlike.

nestling ('nɛstlɪŋ, 'nɛslɪŋ), *sb.* [ME. *nestling*, f. NEST *sb.* + -LING[1], or NESTLE *v.*[1] + -ING[3], = MDu. *nestlinc*, Du. *-ling*, G. *nest-*, *nist(e)ling*.]

1. A young bird which is not yet old enough to leave the nest.

1399 *Pol. Poems* (Rolls) I. 395 The nedy nestlingis, whan they the note herde of the hende egle. **1611** Cotgr., *Niais*, a neastling. *a* **1700** B. E. *Dict. Cant. Crew*, *Nestlings*, Canary-Birds, brought up by hand. **1773** G. White *Selborne* xxxviii, These small weak birds, some of which were nestlings twelve days ago. **1801** Southey *Thalaba* v. iv, The mother-bird had moved not, But cowering o'er her nestlings, Sate. **1859** Darwin *Orig. Spec.* iii. 62 We forget how largely these songsters,..or their nestlings, are destroyed by birds and beasts of prey.

transf. *a* **1693** *Urquhart's Rabelais* III. xxxviii. 317 Nestling, ninny and youngling fool. **1860** Reade *Cloister & H.* xxxviii, 'Here is something hard lurking in this soft nest. Come forth, I say, little nestling!'.. It was a gold ring.

2. The youngest child of a family.

1572 *Wills & Inv. N.C.* (Surtees 1835) 388 Bartye Andersonne..was the nestlynge of all her doughters childre. **1597** Hall *Sat.* II. ii. 43 Second brothers, and poor nestlings Whom more injurious Nature later brings Into the naked world. **1853** J. Raine *Richmond Wills* (Surtees) 160 *note*, His mother could give but a scanty portion to the nestling of her family.

3. *attrib.* with *bird*, *cuckoo*, *nightingale*, etc.

1772 Barrington in *Phil. Trans.* LXII. 325, I have taken four young ones from a hen skylark, and placed in their room five nestling nightingales. **1804** Bingley *Anim. Biog.* (1813) I. 26 The attempt of a nestling bird to sing, may be compared with the imperfect endeavour of a child to talk. **1860** *All Year Round* No. 63. 295 The nestling cuckoo ungratefully ejects his legitimate foster-brethren out of the family nest. **1889** A. R. Wallace *Darwinism* 26 The destruction commences, and is probably most severe, with nestling birds.

nestling ('nɛslɪŋ), *vbl. sb.*[1] [f. NESTLE *v.*[1] + -ING[1]; cf. MDu. *nestelinge*, G. *nistelung*.]

1. The action of the vb. in various senses.

c **1440** *Promp. Parv.* 354/1 Nestelynge, *nidificacio.* **1557** Tusser *Husb.* 41 Nestling of verlettes..Make[s] many a rich man, to shet vp his doores. **1625** Bacon *Ess., Gardens* (Arb.) 564 That the Birds may haue more Scope, and Natural Nestling. **1774** Goldsm. *Nat. Hist.* (1862) II. 10 Previous.. to laying, the work of nestling becomes the common care. **1816** L. Hunt *Rimini* III. 409 Places of nestling green, for poets made.

†**2.** A place of settling. *Obs. rare*[−1].

1605 Bacon *Adv. Learn.* II. x. §5 The secresies of the Passages, and the Seats or nestling of the humours.

3. *Comb.* as *nestling-place*.

1824 W. Irving *T. Trav.* I. 268 This little nestling place of her childhood. **1854** H. Miller *Sch. & Schm.* (1858) 296 A tall inaccessible precipice..had furnished a secure nestling-place to a pair of ravens.

nestling, *vbl. sb.*[2]: see NESTLE *v.*[2]

'nestling, *ppl. a.* [f. NESTLE *v.*[1] + -ING[2].] That nestles, in various senses of the verb.

1839 Longf. *Voices of Night* Prel. viii, When nestling buds unfold their wings. **1846** Dickens *Battle of Life* i, In the nestling town among the trees. **1863** Geo. Eliot *Romola* Introd., The rosy warmth of nestling children.

Nestor ('nɛstə(r)). [a. Gr. *Νέστωρ*.] The name of a Homeric hero famous for his age and wisdom, applied allusively to, or used as a designation of, an old man.

1588 Shaks. *L.L.L.* IV. iii. 169 To see..Nestor play at push-pin with the boyes. **1614** R. Tailor *Hog hath lost Pearl* IV. in Dodsley *O. Pl.* (1780) VI. 429 What, weep'st thou, aged Nestor? Take comfort, man. **1656** Blount *Glossogr.* s.v., We take it proverbially when we use Nestor for a man of great age. **1727** Gay *Fables* I. xliii, Thus spoke the Nestor of the plain. **1817** J. Bradbury *Trav. Amer.* 120 Some aged Nestors tottered along with the crowd. **1883** *Harper's Mag.* May 860/2 This Nestor of art is not forgotten by his old associates.

Comb. **1591** Shaks. *1 Hen. VI*, II. v. 6 These grey Locks, the Pursuiuants of death, Nestor-like aged, in an Age of Care.

Hence **Ne'storian** *a.*[1] *rare*[−1].

1605 Timme *Quersit.* I. xvii. 92 It will suffice..to prolong our dayes to Nestorian yeares.

Nestorian (nɛ'stɔərɪən), *sb.* and *a.*[2] [ad. L. *Nestoriān-us*, f. *Nestori-us*: see next.]

A. *sb.* An adherent or follower of Nestorius; one who accepts or professes Nestorianism.

c **1449** Pecock *Repr.* v. iii. 500 The sect of Nestorianys. **1579** Fulke *Confut. Sanders* 552 Anastasius was a fauourer of Nestorians. **1612** Brerewood *Lang. & Relig.* xix. 175 The Nestorians in the north part of Mesopotamia. **1681** Baxter *Acc. Sherlock* iv. 190 The Christians, called Nestorians,..are exceeding numerous in a great part of the East. **1797** *Encycl. Brit.* (ed. 3) XIII. 11/2 The see of

Seleucia, which the patriarch of the Nestorians has always filled. **1840** *Penny Cycl.* XVI. 155/1 The Nestorians at one time spread into Persia. **1880** *Expositor* XI. 458 The Nestorians appealed to Theodore in support of their doctrine.

B. *adj.* **1.** Of persons: Accepting, professing, or adhering to, Nestorianism.

1565 JEWEL *Repl. Harding* To Rdr., The Nestorian heretics. **1602** T. FITZHERBERT *Apol.* 37 Being a magician, and a nestorian heretyk. **1665** SIR T. HERBERT *Trav.* (1677) 32 The Epithete we give, more probably belongs to another Nestorian Prince. **1765** tr. *Mosheim's Eccl. Hist.* (1833) 471 The great Nestorian pontiffs.. look with a hostile eye on this little patriarch. **1863** *Chr. Work* Dec. 644 The people among whom the Nestorian Christians are groaning.

2. Pertaining to, connected with, Nestorius or the Nestorians; of the nature of Nestorianism.

1680 BAXTER *Cath. Commun.* (1684) 14 The Nestorian Liturgy is one of the.. best that I find recorded. **1724** WATERLAND *Crit. Hist. Athan. Creed* vii. 108 They also condemn'd the Nestorian tenets. **1797** *Encycl. Brit.* (ed. 3) XIII. 11/2 One of the chief promoters of the Nestorian cause was Barsumas. **1840** *Penny Cycl.* XVI. 155/1 This doctrine.. was the origin of the Nestorian schism. **1880** *Expositor* XI. 456 His writings were thought to countenance the Nestorian heresy.

So †**Nestorine.** *Obs. rare*$^{-1}$.

c **1400** *Three Kings Cologne* 132 þe heretikes of þis yle, þe wich be cleped Nestorynes, take but litil kepe of his body.

Ne'storianism. *Theol.* [f. NESTORIAN + -ISM.] The doctrine of Nestorius, patriarch of Constantinople (appointed in 428), by which Christ is asserted to have had distinct human and divine persons.

1612 BREREWOOD *Lang. & Relig.* xix. 172 Cosrhoes.. inforced all the Christians of the Persian empire to Nestorianism. **1659** PEARSON *Creed* II. 256 He ejected him .. under the pretence of Nestorianisme. **1727–38** CHAMBERS *Cycl.* s.v. *Nestorians*, The Chaldee Christians, who still profess Nestorianism. **1866–7** BARING-GOULD *Myths Mid. Ages* (1894) 48 The report which reached Europe of the wonderful successes of Nestorianism in the East. **1884** *Catholic Dict.* (1897) 658/1 The writings of Theodore of Mopsuestia prepared the way for Nestorianism.

Ne'storianize, *v.* [f. as prec. + -IZE.] *intr.* To hold Nestorianism. Hence **Ne'storianizer.**

1888 *Guardian* 18 Apr. 570/3 Theodore of Mopsuestia, .. a Nestorianizer before Nestorius. **1895** EDWARDS in *Expositor* Oct. 247 Nestorianizing tendencies in Eustathius.

Ne'storiously, *adv. rare*$^{-1}$. [f. NESTOR.] After the manner of Nestor.

1620 T. GRANGER *Div. Logike* 318 Because hee did it *Strategicos*, that is, Imperatoriously, or Nestoriously.

'Nestorize, *v. rare.* [f. NESTOR.] *trans.* To fill (one) with the idea of being as wise as Nestor.

1612 J. DAVIES *Wks.* (Grosart) II. 89 Fauour and base flatt'ry Fooles haue spild; for with them both, we Fooles doe Nestorize.

net (nɛt), *sb.*¹ Forms: 1–6 nett, (1 hnett, 2 nyt), 3 neth, 5 nete, neett, 4–6 nette, (3–7 *pl.* nettes), 1– net. [Common Teut.: OE. *net(t* neut. = OS. *net*, MDu. *net* (*nette*; Du. *net*), MLG. *nette*, OHG. *nezzi, nezi* (MHG. *nezze, netze*, G. *netz*), ON. *net* (Da. *net*, Sw. *nät*), Goth. *nati*. The existence of an ON. *nót*, large net, appears to imply an ablaut-stem *nat-, nōt-*, the original sense of which is obscure.]

1. a. An open-work fabric made of twine or strong cord, forming meshes of a suitable size, used for the capture of fish, birds, or other living things.

Freq. also with defining terms, denoting the purpose or form of the net, or the method of using it, as *bag-, beach-, cast(ing)-, dip-, dredge-, drift-, fishing-, trawl-net*, etc.; *herring-, mackerel-, rabbit-, sparrow-net*, etc.

c **888** K. ÆLFRED *Boeth.* xxxii. §3 Hwæðer ȝe nu settan eower nett on þa hehstan dune, þonne ȝe fiscian willað? *c* **950** *Lindisf. Gosp.* Matt. iv. 18 [Peter and Andrew] ȝesendon hnett in sæ. *c* **1000** ÆLFRIC *Colloq.* in Wr.-Wülcker 92 Ne canst þu huntian buton mid nettum? *c* **1200** *Trin. Coll. Hom.* 209 Alse hunte drieð deor to grune oðer to nette. *a* **1225** *Ancr. R.* 334 þer beoð his nettes, & þer beoð his greahundes .. igedered togederes. *c* **1300** *Havelok* 752 Mani god fish þer-inne he tok, Boþe with neth, and with hok. *c* **1330** R. BRUNNE *Chron. Wace* (Rolls) 14679 þe Payens wyþowte leide nettes & lynes, & sparewes toke. **1390** GOWER *Conf.* II. 83 Jadahel, as seith the bok, Ferst made Net and fisshes tok. *c* **1440** *Promp. Parv.* 354/2 Nett, to take wythe fysche, *rete*. **1530** PALSGR. 248/1 Net to catche byrdes with, *tonnelle*. **1597** MIDDLETON *Wisd. Solomon* iv. 12 The fisher lays his bait, fowler his net. **1660** N. INGELO *Bentiv. & Ur.* I. (1682) 6 [The fish] swam voluntarily every day into their Nets. **1697** DRYDEN *Virg. Past.* III. 117, I hold the Nets, while you pursue the Prey. **1774** GOLDSM. *Nat. Hist.* (1776) V. 302 By watching the seasons when our small birds begin to migrate .. and by taking them with nets in their passage. **1832** G. R. PORTER *Porcelain & Gl.* 6 The men employed in fishing.. frequently drew up in their nets some coarse.. earthen vessels. **1853** READE *Chr. Johnstone* 159 These nets are tied to one another, and paid out at the stern of the boat.

b. *fig.* A means of catching or securing a person; *esp.* a moral or mental snare, trap, or entanglement.

c **825** *Vesp. Psalter* cxl. 10 Fallað in nette his synfulle. *c* **1200** ORMIN 13474 To lacchenn himm wiþþ spelless nett To brinngenn himm to criste. *c* **1375** *Sc. Leg. Saints* xxxiv. (*Pelagia*) 183, I haf bene dissaweful nete, þat þe feynde sere sawlis has gert gete. **1426** LYDG. *De Guil. Pilgr.* 15192 It ys ful hard a man tescape.. Fro my nettys off tresoun. **1500–20** DUNBAR *Poems* xlvi. 102, I counsall every man, that he With lufe nocht in the feindis net be tone. **1576** FLEMING *Panopl. Epist.* 213 Many haue beene so insnared & intangled (as it were) in nettes of doubtfull reasons. *a* **1628** F. GREVIL *Poems* I. (1633) 38 Nets of opinion to entangle spirits. **1671** MILTON *P.R.* II. 162 Skill'd to.. draw Hearts after them tangl'd in Amorous Nets. **1738** *Keill's Anim. Oecon.* Pref. (ed. 4) 24 Nature.. will not suffer herself to be taken by Nets spun out of the Brain. **1780** COWPER *Progr. Err.* 313 Caught in a delicate soft silken net By some lewd earl. **1814** BYRON *Lara* I. xix, Vain was the struggle in that mental net. **1888** STEVENSON *Black Arrow* IV. vi, Not only was the town.. a mere net of peril for their lives.

c. *transf.* A spider's web.

c **1000** *Ags. Ps.* (Th.) xxxviii. 12 He.. wyrð swa tedre swa swa gange-wifran nett. *Ibid.* lxxxix. 10. *c* **1220** *Bestiary* 479 Ðanne renneð ȝe [the spider] rapelike.. nimeð anon to ðe net. **1483** CAXTON *Gold. Leg.* 274 b/2 Spyders takyng flyes by the nettes of theyr copwebbes. [**1513** DOUGLAS *Æneis* XII. Prol. 171 Full byssely Aragne wevand was, To knit hyr nettis.] **1658** ROWLAND tr. *Moufet's Theat. Ins.* 1070 In Autumn amongst small Rose-boughs it extendeth an artificiall Net. **1727–38** CHAMBERS *Cycl.* s.v. *Web*, Attending nearly to a spider weaving a net. **1753** *Ibid. Supp.* s.v. *Spider*, The hazel spider.. spins very large nets. **1840** *Cuvier's Anim. Kingd.* 461 It constructs its net with loose and irregular meshes.

d. In proverbs and phrases.

1523– [see FISH *sb.*¹ 1 c]. **1535** STEWART *Cron. Scot.* II. 451 Tha socht the fische rycht far befoir the net. **1562** J. HEYWOOD *Prov. & Epigr.* (1867) 167 It is yll fyshyng before the net.

2. a. An open fabric of mesh-work (as in sense 1, or of other materials), used for such purposes as covering, protecting, confining, holding, etc. *spec.* in Games and Sports: a piece of netting used as part of the equipment for the game; esp. *Cricket*, the netting used to divide off practice wickets; hence in *pl.*, a name for such a wicket. Also, the safety net used by acrobats.

a **1000** *Cædmon's Exod.* 74 (Gr.), þær haliȝ god.. bælce oferbrædde byrnendne heofon, halȝan nette hatwendne lyft. *c* **1050** *Voc.* in Wr.-Wülcker 373 *Conopio*, nette, fleoȝryfte. **1382** WYCLIF *1 Kings* vii. 17 Seuen litil nettis.. in the toon heed couerynge, and seuen lytil nettis in the tothir heed couerynge. **1577** B. GOOGE *Heresbach's Husb.* III. (1586) 141 b, The shepeheard carrieth with him his Hardelles and his nets and other necessaries. **1613** PURCHAS *Pilgrimage* (1614) 836 They lie in Nets or Beddes hanging above the ground.. to avoide hurtfull creatures. **1632** SHERWOOD s.v., A net of wire (set afore glass windowes), *araigne*. **1721** [see *cabbage-net* s.v. CABBAGE *sb.*¹ 5]. **1784** COWPER *Task* IV. 263 Weaving nets for bird-alluring fruit. **1824** LOUDON *Encycl. Gard.* (ed. 2) §2210 Protecting by nets is effected by throwing either straw, hay, bass, hempen, or woollen nets over standard trees. **1845** 'N. FELIX' *Felix on Bat* I. I. 7 The way to secure much practice.. is to procure a large net, about twenty yards long and six feet in height, [etc.]. **1856** 'STONEHENGE' *Brit. Rural Sports* 502 A low net divides this [tennis] court into two equal spaces. **1884** E. M. BUTLER in F. Gale *Life R. Grimston* (1885) xii. 191 In the evenings he would stand behind the nets when the eleven were practising, and coach them very thoroughly. **1889** *Pauline* VIII. 24 Their wickets at the nets were as a rule very poor. **1899** *Captain* II. 127/1 The most difficult shot for a goal-keeper to stop is a low one that crosses him into the corner of the net.. Beware lest.. you shoot outside the net. **1903** G. B. SHAW *Man & Superman* IV. 144 There is no tennis net nor set of croquet hoops. **1905** A. BENNETT *Tales of Five Towns* II. 250 We should.. flash past each other in mid-flight ..and soar to opposite platforms again, amid frenzied applause. There were no nets. **1915** W. S. MAUGHAM *Of Human Bondage* xvii. 67 They practised at nets in the summer. **1937** [see HOOP *sb.*¹ 8 c]. **1947** *Sun* (Baltimore) 8 Nov. 12/2 Although Friends took the ball on several long runs down the field, the Bryn Mawr defense was too effective to be penetrated and Goalie Jo Nelson found little to do in the nets. **1955** *Times* 6 July 3/6 With his left side heavily plastered he batted in the nets before the Yorkshire game resumed. **1958** [see GRAFT *v.*³]. **1958** J. BETJEMAN *Coll. Poems* 50, I adore you, Pam, you great big mountainous sports girl, Whizzing them over the net. **1960** N. STREATFEILD *Look at Circus* iv. 80 In any properly run circus under the trapezes or high tight-rope act a net is stretched. **1961** J. S. SALAK *Dict. Amer. Sports* 295 *Net* (ice hockey), the goal. **1965** *Men's Hockey* ('Know the Game' Series) 6 Nets are attached to the goal-posts, cross bar and ground behind the goal. Goal-boards.. are placed at the foot of the goal-nets. **1967** C. B. MILLS *B. Mills Circus* viii. 109 Fritzi Bartoni.. did one very difficult trick in which she fell forward from a trapeze and caught herself by her heels on the cross bar and she had been doing this without a net. **1975** *Times* 4 Dec. 10/1 Their goal-keeper.. rolled out a ball that rebounded.. to Summerill who sent Hart away to run the ball into an empty net.

b. *to dance* (or *march*) *in a net*, to act with practically no disguise or concealment, while expecting to escape notice; in later use, to do something undetected. Now only *arch.*

1583 FULKE *Def. Tr. Script.* vi. (1843) 242 Now you haue gotten a fine net to dance naked in, that no ignorant blind buzzard can see you. **1592** KYD *Sp. Trag.* IV. iv. 118 Whose reconciled sonne Marcht in a net, and thought himselfe vnseene. **1679** DRYDEN *Limberham* II. i, I have danced in a net before my father,.. retired to my chamber undiscovered. **1822** SCOTT *Nigel* xxiii, You must not think to dance in a net before old Jack Hildebrod.

c. *Lawn Tennis.* = LET *sb.*¹ 2. *colloq.*

1904 J. P. PARET et al. *Lawn Tennis* 344 *Net*,.. also (same as 'let'), a ball that touches the net and goes into the proper court. **1929** D. MACKAIL *How Amusing!* 450 Clampson served a let. They actually—yes, in the twentieth century and the Centre Court—they distinctly called it a 'net'.

3. a. A piece of fine mesh-work used as a part of dress, as a veil, or as a means of confining the hair (cf. HAIR-NET).

1483 RICH. III in Drake *Eboracum* I. iv. (1736) 117 Two short Gowns.., the one with Drippis and the other with Netts. **1599** T. M[OUFET] *Silkwormes* 68 Arachne that doth tinsels forme, And nets, and lawnes. **1617** MORYSON *Itin.* III. 173 They weare nets and black vailes, covering therewith their faces. **1813** SCOTT *Trierm.* III. xxxviii, Her dark locks dishevell'd flow From net of pearl. **1878** *Encycl. Brit.* VI. 470/2 The hair is usually.. inclosed in a net or cowl.

b. A kind of machine-made lace composed of small meshes. Also *attrib.*

1832 [see BOBBIN-NET]. **1844** G. DODD *Textile Manuf.* vii. 213 In some of these establishments various kinds of net and lace.. are made. **1862** MRS. H. WOOD *Channings* xvii, Her mob-cap was of spotted net. **1897** *Westm. Gaz.* 4 Feb. 3/3 Three deep flounces on a fine net foundation.

4. a. Something resembling a net; a number of lines, veins, fibres, etc., arranged like the threads of a net; a reticulation or network.

1594 BLUNDEVIL *Exerc.* VI. Introd. (1636) 604 In the said Net are certaine Circles, which are Parallels to the foresaid Finitor. **1615** CROOKE *Body of Man* 466 That place where the wonderfull Net is made by those soporarie Arteries. **1845** *Encycl. Metrop.* VII. 183/2 The soft inner layers were distinguished by the name of mucous body or Malpighian net. **1884** BOWER & SCOTT *De Bary's Phaner.* 433 The nets of laticiferous tubes of the stem.

b. *Crystall.* (See quots.)

1855 *Orr's Circle Sci., Crystallogr.* 297 A drawing of the faces of a solid, arranged so that the model may be folded up from a single piece of pasteboard, is called a net. **1862** J. B. JORDAN *Const. Models Crystallogr.* 1 The term net.. has been given to a series of geometrical figures drawn on a plane, representing the faces of a crystal.

c. A network; *spec.* (*a*) a network of spies; (*b*) a broadcasting network.

1919 J. BUCHAN *Mr. Standfast* iii. 63 By the middle of 1915 most [enemy spies].. had been gathered in. But there remained loose ends, and.. somebody was very busy combining these ends into a net. **1952** *Brewer's Dict. Phr. & Fable* (rev. ed.) 644/2 *On the Old Boy net*, to arrange something through a friend (originally, someone known at school) instead of through the usual channels. **1959** *Listener* 22 Oct. 668/2 Television programmes are to be exchanged among the East European countries and the Soviet Union. .. A coaxial cable is already being laid on the Soviet-Polish section of the net. **1961** H. B. JACOBSON *Mass Communications Dict.* 222 *Net*, abbreviation for radio network, which is merely a group of stations joined by wires to release a given program simultaneously. **1966** 'H. TALBOT' *Catch me Traitor* i. 14, D.I. 6 was probably short of yet another carefully built up net in the East German People's Republic. **1966** *Electronics* 17 Oct. 129 Capt. D. A. Jones.. cautioned that 'our national security could be affected by the dissemination of data by these geodetic nets'. **1967** M. CHILDS *Taint of Innocence* (1968) ii. 97 She's got her own net going in that nest of vipers and I'd stake a lot on it. **1969** J. ELLIOT *Duel* I. i. 25, I had a regular weekly spot on a national net—thirty-six in a year. **1969** A. MARIN *Rise with Wind* xiv. 168 Whenever a net was surfaced.. the word went around the *intelligence community*. **1971** C. BONINGTON *Annapurna South Face* iii. 33 He eventually got an agreement that the set in Katmandu should be kept in the Nepalese Army headquarters so that they would have control of the wireless net. **1972** 'W. HAGGARD' *Protectors* iv. 42 Shay was after the gold, on information received through the usual net.

5. *attrib.* and *Comb.* **a.** attrib. in various uses, as ***net-basin, -cord, -fisher(man), -fishing, -frame, game, -man, -mesh, -pole, shot, -trade, -trap, -twine***; 'made of net', as ***net cap, comforter, garter, -pocket, purse***; **b.** objective or obj. genitive, as ***net-bearer, -braider, -caster, -cutter, -making, -monger, -owner, -worker***; **c.** similative, as ***net-fashion, -like, -traceried, -veined, -wise*** adv.; **d.** special combs., as **net-bag,** (*a*) the pocket of a bag-net; (*b*) a bag made of net; **net-ball,** (orig. an American) game in which a ball is thrown into a large pocket-net attached to a high pole; **net-cord,** the cord passing along and supporting the top of a net, esp. a tennis net; so **net-cord (stroke),** in lawn tennis, a stroke which hits the net cord but still crosses the net; **net curtain,** a curtain made of net, usu. now fixed permanently across windows to ensure privacy; hence **net-curtained** *a.*; †**net-danced** (see 2 b); **net-drifter,** earlier term for *net-layer*; also *attrib.*; **net-fern,** a fern of the genus *Gleichenia*; **net-fish,** (*a*) a basket-fish; (*b*) fish taken with the net; *v. intr.*, to fish with a net; **net-layer,** a vessel which lays anti-submarine nets; hence **net-laying** *vbl. sb.*; **net-masonry,** a form of masonry in which the joints resemble the meshes of a net; **netminder** = *goal-tender* (GOAL *sb.* 6); **net-passing,** a form of needlework; **net-pin,** a pin used in net-making; **net-player** *Lawn Tennis* and *Badminton*, a player who advances close to the net; hence **net play; net-practice,** cricket practice at the nets; **net-roper,** *dial.* the man in charge of a net-rope; **net-sinker** or **-weight,** a weight used to sink a net in fishing. Also NETMAKER, -WORK.

1598 J. FLORIO *Worlde of Wordes* 61/1 *Carnero, Carniéro*, a *net-bag to carie meat in, a hawking bag. **1727** *Philip Quarll* (1816) 27 Finding a fowl in the net-bag. **1834** M. SCOTT *Cruise Midge* (1859) 244 Taking half a dozen wild sea fowl's eggs out of the net bag that he usually wore his hair in. **1934** *Discovery* Sept. 261/1 In those days the wild fowler had not learnt the trick of curving the pipes, and so had to trust to frightening the duck into the net bag, or some such contraption. **1951** COLYER & HAMMOND *Flies Brit. Isles* 324 This instrument can often be used under conditions where a net-bag is liable to be torn, e.g. on thorn or bramble. **1970**

New Yorker 28 Nov. 51/1 On the third bed lay a bulging net bag. 1900 *Daily News* 29 May 6/3 An American game called '*Net Ball' was played last evening at the Alhambra. 1883 in Goode *Fish. Indust. U.S.A.* 76 (Fish. Exhib. Publ.), Turning them from their course into *net basins which were placed there. 1647 R. Stapylton *Juvenal* 31 A retiarius, or *net-bearer, so named from a kind of floate net, which he carryed in his hand. c1440 *Promp. Parv.* 354/2 *Neet Breydare, *reciarius*. 1599 Nashe *Lenten Stuffe* 17 Netbrayders, or those that haue no cloathes .. but what they earne .. by brayding of nets. 1835 Mrs. Carlyle *Lett.* I. 51, I notice she puts on a certain *net cap. 1586 J. Hooker *Hist. Irel.* in *Holinshed* II. 27/1 The *net-caster hauing ouerthrowne the swordplaier. 1834 *Tait's Mag.* I. 59/1 A green and white *net-comforter was twisted round its chin. 1844 H. Stephens *Bk. Farm* II. 72 Stakes to .. be 3 inches above the *net-cord. 1887 *Boy's Own Paper* 3 Sept. 778/1 If you are tall enough, take it before it descends to the level of the net-cord. 1904 J. P. Paret et al. *Lawn Tennis* 345 Net-cord stroke. 1959 *Times* 1 Sept. 3/3 It was the third game when twice MacKay got away with net cords. 1961 F. C. Avis *Sportsman's Gloss.* 258 *Net cord stroke*, one that causes the ball to contact the net, the ball afterwards going into the proper court. 1931 M. Allingham *Look to Lady* xxii. 224 There was a thin *net curtain over the windows, but the light inside rendered it transparent. 1935 A. Fremantle tr. *Wynne Diaries* I. i. 2 The Curé of Berkheim's house is very pretty. There is in it a sofa and net curtains which he himself has made. 1967 E. Short *Embroidery & Fabric Collage* iii. 83 On net curtains, permanently in place across a window, designs of a more pictorial type would be quite suitable. 1972 J. Mann *Mrs Knox's Profession* x. 78 The local style was for picture windows, sometimes *net curtained. 1973 C. Egleton *Seven Days to Killing* xviii. 188 The net-curtained window. 1899 *Daily News* 27 July 7/2 If any *net cutter is found which will effectually pierce these new nets, .. the torpedo net will be doomed. 1602 Warner *Alb. Eng.* xiii. lxxix. 327 Nor shall be said the *Net-danc't fals of diuers wish't more trew. 1919 R. Bacon *Dover Patrol 1915–17* I. vi. 157 The procedure of the mine-*net drifters was simple. As each division arrived at its mark-buoy, the rear boats proceeded to shoot their nets, and, after steaming a definite time interval, each succeeding pair stopped and shot their nets to complete the line. *Ibid.*, In addition to the above, the 10th, 11th, and 12th Divisions of net-drifters anchored parallel to the West Hinder and shot their nets. 1923 E. K. Chatterton *Auxiliary Patrol* iii. 41 Net-drifter bases were quickly established also at Peterhead .. and Larne. 1925 *Home Waters* (Naval Staff Monogr., Historical, XIII.) iv. vii. 126 By the beginning of March [1915] the term 'Net Drifter Flotillas' was in use to designate units of drifters working indicator nets, or other anti-submarine devices. 1521 *Rutland MSS.* (Hist. MSS. Comm.) IV. 264 To make engynes and calteroppes, *nette fashion for the warre. 1671 Winthorp in *Phil. Trans.* VI. 2223 Until a fitter English name be found for it, why may it not be called .. a Basket-Fish, or a *Net Fish, or a Purs-net-Fish? 1891 *Chambers's Encycl.* VIII. 256/1 He may be arrested if he is *net-fishing, but not if he is fishing in another way. 1677 in *Ray's Corr.* (1848) 128 If the *net-fishers would open any considerable number. 1894 *Westm. Gaz.* 25 Sept. 2/1 The net-fishers did not .. make enough to pay for their licences. 1883 Shea *Newfoundl. Fish.* 12 (Fish. Exhib. Publ.), *Net fishing is more regular and satisfactory. 1968 J. Arnold *Shell Book of Country Crafts* 228 As no new licences are being granted, net fishing on the upper stretch of the river will die out. 1824 Loudon *Encycl. Gard.* (ed. 2) §2210 Placing it over tender flowers .. by means of *net frames. 1961 F. C. Avis *Sportsman's Gloss.* 259 **Net game*, that kind of play taking place in the vicinity of the net, and thus the opposite of base line game. a1613 Overbury *A Wife*, etc. (1638) 180 From ever having leisure to weare *net-Garters. 1930 *Economist* 8 Mar. 513/1 Five submarines, one submarine depôt ship, two sloops and one *netlayer. 1957 *Observer* 1 Dec. 1/1 H.M.S. Protector, a converted net-layer. 1923 E. K. Chatterton *Auxiliary Patrol* xv. 229 One hundred and two ships were secretly assembled, and the actual operation of *net-laying was carried out in an hour and a half. 1615 Crooke *Body of Man* 81 Which .. doe forme a *Net-like complication. 1698 Petiver in *Phil. Trans.* XX. 327 With the Canes split they make their Net-like Seats. 1796 Withering *Brit. Plants* (ed. 3) IV. 52 Disposed .. over the whole surface in a chain-like or net-like manner. 1844 H. Stephens *Bk. Farm* II. 72 All the instruments required in this sort of *net-making. 1847 C. Lanman *Summer in Wilderness* xxvi. 160 A false movement of the *net-man will cause the canoe to be swamped. 1883 *Pall Mall Gaz.* 9 Mar. 4/1 Tons of fish .. are carted away by this means by the net men. 1915 [see *cross-court* adj. s.v. cross- B]. 1934 R. Graves *Claudius the God* xxx. 518 He was disarmed and a net-man was standing over him with his trident raised. 1611 Cotgr., *Macque*, a Lozenge, or *Net-mash. 1706 Phillips (ed. Kersey), **Net-Masonry*, a particular sort of muring, or walling. 1727–38 Chambers *Cycl.* s.v. *Masonry*, Net-masonry, called by Vitruvius, *reticulatum*, from its resemblance of the mashes of a net. 1847 A. Smeaton *Builder's Man.* 107 Net masonry. .. Where the stones are squared and placed upon one of the angles, their joints thus forming a net-like appearance. 1942 Berrey & Van den Bark *Amer. Thes. Slang* §662/2 **Net minder*, .. a goalkeeper. 1961 J. S. Salak *Dict. Amer. Sports* 296 *Net minder* (ice hockey), the goaltender. 1968 *Globe & Mail* (Toronto) 15 Jan. 19/1 Eddie Shack spoiled Montreal net-minder Rogatien Vachon's chance for a shutout when he scored. 1973 *Cleveland* (Ohio) *Plain Dealer* 6 Apr. 10-C/1 Cheevers has come on strong to maintain his reputation as one of the best netminders in hockey. 1630 J. Taylor (Water P.) *Jacke-a-Lent* Wks. i. 117/2 Lent might gape for Gudgeons, .. were it not for these *Netmongers. 1901 *Chambers's Jrnl.* Sept. 585/1 The estuary limits .. have been fixed more in the interests of *net-owners than in those of the salmon. 1901 Day & Buckle *Art in Needlewk.* ix. (ed. 2) 86 *Net Passing .. is not very differently worked from [lace buttonholing]. a1652 Brome *Queen* iv. i, But I have other Arts: .. The Wheel, the Frame, the *Net-pin .. are most familiar with me. 1961 J. S. Salak *Dict. Amer. Sports* 296 **Net play* (badminton), the player returning the bird from a position close to the net. 1919 S. Lenglen *Lawn Tennis for Girls* 53 The *net player .. has a free hand at the net. 1930 *Amer. Speech* VI. 118 California's net players. 1902 *Chambers's Jrnl.* Jan. 48/2 The younger man .. swung the captive ashore in the *net-pocket. 1813 *Sporting Mag.* XLII. 4 By this means manage his *net-poles with greater ease. 1899 *Captain* I. 378/2 *Net practice is good in moderation, but nothing is so good as practice games. 1975 *Country Life* 19 June 1625/3, I waited to greet the Australians for their first net practice. 1840 Mrs. Gaugain *Lady's Assist.* 169 Very pretty long Grecian *net purse for a lady. 1892 P. H. Emerson *Son of Fens* 58 The master, mate, hawse-man, wheelman, *net-roper, and me lived aft in the cabin. 1961 J. S. Salak *Dict. Amer. Sports* 296 In mixed doubles the lady is usually responsible for the *net shots. 1865 Tylor *Early Hist. Man.* viii. 192 The natural *net-sinkers, formed of chalk flints. 1896 J. F. Hodgson in *Durh. Arch. Trans.* IV. 113 The four-light *net-traceried east window. 1845 *Encycl. Metrop.* VIII. 741/2 Statistical view of the *net trade. 1768 Barrington in Pennant *Brit. Zool.* II. App. iv. 560 They are caught in a *net trap. 1844 H. Stephens *Bk. Farm* II. 36 The shepherd should always be provided with *net-twine. 1861 Bentley *Man. Bot.* 427 Leaves *net-veined, deciduous. 1865 Lubbock *Preh. Times* 81 Many of .. the stones employed as *net-weights would there be lost. 1577 B. Googe *Heresbach's Husb.* ii. 71 You must place them .. eyther Checkerwyse or *Netwyse. 1727–38 Chambers *Cycl.* s.v. *Mail*, Coat of Mail is a piece of defensive armour, made of iron wire interwoven net-wise. 1869 Farrar *Fam. Speech* iv. (1873) 118 Nature connects organic bodies netwise rather than by organic links. 1658 Rowland *Moufet's Theat. Ins.* 1070 Amongst the *Net-workers I saw one the greatest of all.

net, *sb.*² Now *rare*. Also 6 nett. [OE. *nette* fem. = OFris. *nette*, *nitte*, OS. *netti*, OHG. *nezzi*, *nezi*, ON. *netja* (Sw. dial. *nätja*, MDa. *nædhæ*), a derivative of net *sb.*¹] The omentum or caul; the mesentery.

c725 *Corpus Gloss.* (Hessels) O 147 *Oligia*, nettae. a1100 *Voc.* in Wr.-Wülcker 293 *Disceptum i. reticulum*, nette. *Ibid.* 459 *Oligia*, nette. 1535 Coverdale *Exod.* xxix. 13 Thou shalt take all the fat that coureth the bowels and the nett vpon the leuer. 1597 A. M. tr. *Guillemeau's Fr. Chirurg.* 16/1 In such woundes the guttes and the net come to sincke out. 1648 Hexham ii. s.v. *Net*, The Net or the Cawle of the bowels or entrailes. 1722 Chamberlayne in *Phil. Trans.* XXXII. 97 The Hind-Quarter of a sucking Lamb, over which was spread what we call the Net, or Caul. 1737 Bracken *Farriery Impr.* (1756) I. 9 The Mesentery or Net (as it is called in other Creatures besides Men). 1808 in Jamieson. 1828 in *Craven Gloss.* 1844 H. Stephens *Bk. Farm* II. 93 The space between the intestines and lumbar region or loin [is] gradually filled up by the net and kidney fat.

net, *sb.*³ *dial.* [f. net *v.*³] A wash or rinse.

1703 Thoresby *Let. Ray* (E.D.S.), *Net*, to wash clothes, give them a net. 1841 Hamilton *Nugæ Lit.* 356 *Net*, or *netting*, a fresh water in scouring any thing.

net (nɛt), *a.* Also 6 nette, 6– nett. [a. F. *net*, *nette* (see neat *a.*), whence also Du. and Da. *net*, G. *nett*, Sw. *nätt*.]

1. †**a.** Of persons: Trim, smart, or elegant, esp. in dress. *Obs. rare.*

13.. *Guy Warw.* (A.) 4084 Þer miȝt men se þat Gij was wel net. 1542 Udall *Erasm. Apoph.* (1877) 32 To soche a minion feloe as Agatho is, I maie go trim, nette, and well beseen. 1562 Bulleyn *Bulwark, Sicke men* 69 Whiche Heathen are bothe comely, cleane, worldly wise, valiaunte, nette and fine.

b. Of things: Neat, smart. *rare.*

1637 Cleveland *Elegy on B. Jonson* 114 When thou in Company wert met, Thy Meat took Notes, and thy Discourse was Net. 1819 Shelley *Peter Bell 3rd* ii. iii, A thief, who cometh in the night, With whole boots and net pantaloons.

†**2. a.** Clean, free from filth, etc.; bright, clear. *Obs.*

1481 Caxton *Myrr.* i. i. 6 Tofore the soueraуn creatour whiche is clere net and pure. 1528 Paynell *Salerne's Regim.* Dij, He shulde eate no maner of meates, without his stomake be net, and purged of all yll humours. 1579 Tomson *Calvin's Serm. Tim.* 615/2 He is pure and net from all filthinesse, and pollution. 1590 Spenser *F.Q.* iii. xii. 20 Her brest all naked, as nett yvory. 1596 *Ibid.* vi. ix. 45 The priest with naked armes full net. 1609 Bible (Douay) *Prov.* v. 3 The lippes of an harlot are as a hony combe distilling, and her throte netter [Vulg. *nitidius*] then oyle.

b. Pure, unadulterated, unmixed. *rare.*

1713 *Guardian* No. 132 Advt., A Vault .. for the sale of Net Natural French Wine. 1765 *Universal Mag.* XXXVII. 320/2 Refined sugar in the loaf, .. being net, that is to say, of one uniform whiteness throughout. 1839 *Civil Eng. & Arch. Jrnl.* II. 107/1 This account he believes to be correct, except that nett cement was used instead of mortar.

3. a. Of amounts: Free from, or not subject to, any deduction; remaining after all necessary deductions have been made. Also as *sb.*

1520 J. Dorne in *Collect.* (O.H.S.) I. 97 Suma is net 12*li.* 18*s.* 6*d.* 1588 J. Mellis *Briefe Instr.* Bij b, The remaine is the net rest, substance or capitall of the owner. 1666–7 Pepys *Diary* 21 Jan., The net profits of which .. will amount to 3000*l.* 1702 S. Sewall *Diary* 30 Dec., Weight One Hundred One Half One Quarter wanting 3 pounds, i.e. 193 pounds, Net. 1768–74 Tucker *Lt. Nat.* (1834) I. 190 The net income of real pleasures they will yield upon the balance. 1825 McCulloch *Pol. Econ.* ii. iv. 186 It would give its owner the same .. net profit. 1840 *Civil Eng. & Arch. Jrnl.* III. 89/2 The 'net effective power', or available power of an engine. 1844 H. H. Wilson *Brit. India* III. 368 A pension proportioned to the nett revenue. 1878 Huxley *Physiogr.* 186 The net result showed a permanent elevation. 1910 *Gt. Central Railway Rep.* 11 Feb. 7 Deducting from our receipts .. our expenses of £1,488,474, we have a net of £796,956. 1961 H. B. Jacobson *Mass Communications Dict.* 222 *Net*, the amount paid to the advertising medium by the advertising agency after deducting the agency commission. 1969 *N.Y. Rev. Books* 2 Jan. 6/4 Its net after taxes .. after allowing for sales of assets, .. was only $9million.

b. Sold at, based upon, net prices. *spec.* in phr. ***net book***, a book sold at the net price; ***Net Book Agreement***, the formal arrangement between publishers and booksellers, binding the latter not to sell below the net price; also, an agreement between publishers and public libraries to adhere to a set discount; ***net (and) net***, used to indicate that the price of a book so marked cannot be subject to any discount whatever; ***net system***, the system laid down in the Net Book Agreement for the sale of net books.

1890 *Bookseller* 6 Mar. 244/2 With the hearty co-operation of the retail trade, the *net* system could easily be introduced. 1893 *Athenæum* 1 Apr. 410/3 Over 71,000 copies of net books. 1894 *Daily News* 3 Nov. 6/4 If a book .. sold at 12s., becomes under the net system 10s. net. 1911 *Encycl. Brit.* XXII. 630/1 The Booksellers' Association signed an agreement to charge the full published price for every net book. *Ibid.* 630/2 The net system was gradually introduced, net books and discount books being issued side by side. *Ibid.* 631/2 In 1901 the net system, as adopted in Great Britain, was partially introduced into America. 1938 L. M. Harrod *Librarians' Gloss.* 105 *Net book agreement*, an agreement drawn up in 1929 .. between the Publishers' Association, the Booksellers' Association, and the Library Association, enabling rate-supported libraries and other libraries .. to receive a discount of 10 per cent on all new books purchased. 1939 M. Plant *Eng. Bk. Trade* xx. 441 Net books were to come, but not in that way. It was Frederick Macmillan who was to take the lead. He wrote to the *Bookseller* in 1890 suggesting the publication of net books. 1952 *Bookseller* 5 Jan. 27 This list is .. published .. at quarterly intervals .. with Classified List, May 6/-net net. 1959 L. M. Harrod *Librarians' Gloss.* (ed. 2) 187 *Net book*, one which .. may be sold to a signatory to the agreement at a recognized discount. 1960 G. A. Glaister *Glossary of Book* 274/2 The 1901 Net Book Agreement, now replaced, was based on the right of the Publishers Association to act on behalf of its publisher members in ensuring that the conditions of supply of net books were observed. *Ibid.* 275/2 *Net net*, an indication that a book so marked or described must be sold at the full published price, and that the publisher will not allow any discount to the book trade... Confined almost exclusively to reference works published at the lowest possible sum for the benefit of the trade. 1961 M. C. Turner *Bookman's Gloss.* (ed. 4) 113 When an English book carries no trade discount, it is sometimes called a 'net net' book. 1963 Kenneison & Spilman *Dict. Printing* 133 *Net net*, term indicating that a book will not be sold to the book trade at any discount. 1972 C. Bingley *Business Bk. Publishing* iv. 135 The validity of the British Net Book Agreement does not extend beyond the U.K.

c. ***net reproduction rate***: a reproduction rate representing the average number of girls born to each woman of a population who can be expected to reach their mothers' age at the time of birth, calculated from the average fertility rates and death rates of each age-group during the period considered.

1928 R. R. Kuczynski *Balance Births & Deaths* I. iii. 46 The net reproduction rate, as we may call it, was 1·435. 1952 C. P. Blacker *Eugenics* viii. 170 Gross and net reproduction rates have been published for France since 1806. 1972 *Nature* 7 Apr. 270/1 In a population which is just barely reproducing itself, the Net Reproduction Rate should, of course, be 1·0. 1973 *Sci. Amer.* Apr. 19/1 Under conditions of high mortality the difference between the net reproduction rate and the gross reproduction rate is large.

d. ***net worth*** (see quot. 1930).

1930 *Economist* 17 May 1108/2 'Net worth' (that is, the stockholders' equity, made up of preferred and common stock outstanding, surplus account and undivided profits, taken at the beginning of the fiscal year). 1955 *Times* 13 July 13/1 Some estimates .. have now been made .. of the net worth of consumers. 1964 Gould & Kolb *Dict. Social Sci.* 465/2 The expression *net worth* is becoming obsolete. The British now frequently use the expression *total equity*.

e. ***net national product*** (see quot. 1964 and *national product*, national *a.* 5).

1945 S. Kuznets *National Product in Wartime* i. ii. 13 Net national product consists of (a) flow of goods to consumers, (b) net nonwar Capital formation, (c) net war output, i.e., net additions to the inventory of war goods. 1945 S. E. Harris *Inflation & American Economy* i. 31 (*table*) Output rises. The percentage rise of 1939–43: .. Net national product. 1962 *Listener* 25 Oct. 679/1 The proportion of the net national product going to property and enterprise .. has fallen relative to that going to wages and salaries. 1964 Gould & Kolb *Dict. Social Sci.* 453/2 In defining national product, .. one has a choice about whether or not to subtract from the total an allowance for the depreciation of capital goods that occurs during the period... If one does make such a subtraction, the results are called *net* national product... Net national product measures the value of goods and services produced, *after setting aside* whatever is required to maintain the stock of capital goods as it was at the beginning of the period.

4. *Comb.*, as ***net-priced*** adj.

1909 *Daily Chron.* 16 July 3/2 In his new net-priced series. 1973 *Writers' & Artists' Year Bk.* 218 They agree to sell their net-priced books to booksellers.

net (nɛt), *v.*¹ [f. net *sb.*¹ Cf. ON. *netja*, Swed. *nätja*, Da. *nette*, G. *netzen*.]

1. *trans.* **a.** To cover with, or as with, a net. To fasten *down* with a net.

1593 Nashe *Christ's T.* (1613) 146 Your morn-like cristall countenances shall be netted ouer .. with crawling venemous wormes. 1758 Reid tr. *Macquer's Chym.* I. 263 The inside of the ballon begins to be netted over with a volatile salt of a singular nature. 1800 Miss Edgeworth *Belinda* xxi, To leave his favourite tree .. after .. netting it to keep off the birds. 1850 Tennyson *In Mem.* ii, Thy fibres net the dreamless head. 1857 Dufferin *Lett. High Lat.* (ed. 3) 196 The level sea, like a pale blue disc netted in silver lace. 1909 H. G. Wells *Tono-Bungay* iii. iii. 363 Practically I contracted my sausage gas-bag by netting it down.

b. To hem *in*, close *round*, as with a net.

1607 TOPSELL *Four-f. Beasts* (1658) 156 They..with their tails net in and entangle his legs and feet. **1833** MRS. BROWNING *Prometh. Bound* Poems 1850 I. 143 He is netted round with chains. **1877** TENNYSON *Harold* II. ii, How dense a fold of danger nets him round.

c. To enclose, pen in, by means of nets.

1847 *Jrnl. R. Agric. Soc.* VIII. II. 431 Where larger breadths of turnips are sown, the wedder lambs are netted upon them in October. **1886** C. SCOTT *Sheep-farming* 95 A break, in size suitable to the number of sheep, should be netted or hurdled off. *Ibid.*, After that they may be netted on where the turnips grow.

2. a. *fig.* To take, catch, or capture, as with a net; to sweep *in* in this manner. Hence in *colloq.* or *slang* use, to acquire (cf. LAND *v.* 3 b).

1801 SOUTHEY *Lett.* (1856) I. 166 Losing the chance of netting you at Oswestry, I have been in hopes of hearing from you. **1863** BARRY *Dockyard Econ.* 177 French navy seamen, netted in as they are from stagnant and unknown fishing hamlets. **1880** MEREDITH *Tragic Com.* ii, One or two of Plutarch's touches..had netted her fancy. **1900** ADE *Fables in Slang* 178 The Management of the Bazaar was pleased to learn that the Sixty-cent Vase had Netted over Seven Hundred Dollars. **1912** GALSWORTHY *Inn of Tranquility* 126 The dusk is falling... Some stars are already netted in the branches of the pines. **1936** H. L. MENCKEN *Amer. Lang.* (ed. 4) v. 199 The favorite verbs of the newspaper copy-desk are those of three letters, *e.g.*, *to air*,.. *to net.* **1975** *Publishers Weekly* 10 Feb. 52/3 Miss Read begins her summer holiday with a mishap, a fall that nets her a broken arm and an injured ankle.

b. To take (fish, birds, etc.) with a net or nets.

1868 *Daily News* 15 July, The fishermen..were netting large takes of mackerel. **1870** YEATS *Nat. Hist. Comm.* 58 Shrimps are netted on most shallow shores. **1883** *Eng. Illustr. Mag.* Nov. 69/2 Netting the ruffs and reeves in the summer time.

c. To fish (a river, etc.) with a net; to set or use nets in.

1843 JAMES *Forest Days* vii, There is somebody netting the stream. **1885** R. BUCHANAN *Annan Water* iii, The body had been discovered by some salmon fishers when netting the river.

3. a. *intr.* To make nets or network; to occupy oneself with netting.

Formerly used esp. of making small fancy-work articles, such as purses: cf. NETTING *vbl. sb.* 1 b.

1674 N. FAIRFAX *Bulk & Selv.* 152 The Spider drives on the great business of catching flies, by netting in corners within doors. **1789** ANNA SEWARD *Lett.* (1811) II. 314, I often..see you..sitting netting in your parlour. **1866** MRS. GASKELL *Wives & Dau.* li, She was netting away as if nothing unusual had occurred.

b. *trans.* To make (a thing) by the process of producing network; to work up as a net.

1789 in *A. C. Bower's Diaries & Corr.* (1903) 58 The purse..was very pretty and monstrously well net. *a* **1845** HOOD *I'm not a single Man* iv, I had more purses netted then Than I could hope to fill. **1883** in N. Okoshi *Fisheries Japan* 33 (Fish. Exhib. Publ.), There will remain 384 meshes, which, being netted again [etc.].

c. *refl.* To form into a net.

1889 RANDOLPH *New Eve* I. vii. 251 Circumstances had netted themselves round him with meshes of steel.

4. *trans.* and *absol.* In ball games in which a net is employed: to send (a ball) into the net.

1906 *Peel City Guardian* 10 Mar. 8/3 It seemed as if they meant to force the custodian into the net, not net the ball. **1907** *Ibid.* 26 Oct. 5/2 A rush in the goal resulted in Cain netting. **1927** *Daily Express* 20 Apr. 13/2 Scriven netted for Birmingham in the first five minutes. *Ibid.* 22 June 2/2 Raymond, striving for extra speed, netted and outed a succession of returns. **1942** BERREY & VAN DEN BARK *Amer. Thes. Slang* §648/5 *Score*,..net, net a goal. **1970** *Times* 1 Oct. 10/4 Reading gained ground at the expense of Bradford City, Williams netting the only goal. **1972** D. DELMAN *Sudden Death* (1973) vi. 169 A shocking bounce on a shoddy return, and I net what I should have put away. **1975** *Football Echo* (Liverpool) 12 Apr. 14/3 Winsford knocked up their 100th Cheshire League goal of the season when Haughton netted their second goal.

net (nɛt), *v.*[2] [f. NET *a.* 3.]

1. *trans.* To gain as a net sum or as clear profit; to succeed in clearing (a certain sum).

1758 J. ADAMS *Diary* Wks. 1850 II. 44 He retails sugar [etc.]..to save these articles in his family, and net a few shillings profit. **1765** *Museum Rust.* IV. 201, I..could never yet find that two pounds per cow could be netted per annum. **1815** W. H. IRELAND *Scribbleomania* 141 The spells, whereby publishers sweated For profit, first paying those hundreds Ann netted. **1862** L. WEEDON *Syst. Husb.* 7 If by the new plan..he can net a full profit of £4 per acre.

2. To bring in or yield as a profit or net sum.

1786 MACKENZIE *Lounger* No. 78 ¶4 The estate indeed..was considerably increased in its rent; 'but..it nets nothing'. **1833** W. IRVING in *Life & Lett.* (1866) III. 58 We had a benefit here,..which netted nearly four thousand dollars. **1893** KATE SANBORN *Truthf. Wom. S. California* 131 These berries..netted an average of about eight cents per pound.

b. To amount to. *rare*[−1].

1800 *Hull Advertiser* 16 Aug. 3/1 His share of prize-money has netted..ten thousand pounds currency per month.

net, *v.*[3] Now *dial.* [ad. OF. *nettir*, f. *net* NET *a.*; cf. F. *nettoyer.*] *trans.* To clean, to wash; to rinse *out* (clothes); †to rid *of.*

1536 *Rem. Sedition* 12 b, Even so, neyther the bodye [can be cleansed], without the mynde be firste netted. *Ibid.* 23 He hath netted his realme of ydle vacabundes. **1634–5** BRERETON *Trav.* (Chetham Soc.) 106 They..trample it with their feet (never vouchsafing a hand to nett or wash it withal). **1703** THORESBY *Let. Ray* (E.D.S.), *Net*, to wash clothes, give them a net. **1862** C. C. ROBINSON *Dial. Leeds* 373 After linen has been washed it generally has to undergo the 'netting-out' process.

†**nete**, for *ne wite* to know not. *Obs. rare.*

c **1160** *Hatton Gosp.* Matt. vi. 3 Nete þin wynstre hwæt do þin swiðre. *c* **1315** SHOREHAM I. 1839 Wanne þou weneþ þe oþer be hol, And weddeþ þane syke Netinde.

nete, obs. form of NEAT *sb.*

netel(l)e, obs. forms of NETTLE *sb.*[1] and *v.*

†**'neten.** *Obs.* [OE. *néten* (also *níeten*, *nýten*, etc.), f. *néat* NEAT *sb.*] An animal, esp. of the ox or horse kind.

c **825** *Vesp. Psalter* viii. 8 All ðu underdeodes under fotum his, scep & oxan..& netenu foldes. *c* **888** K. ÆLFRED *Boeth.* xxxi. §1 Hwi nele he cweðan eac þæt ða netenu seon ȝesæleȝu. *c* **1000** *Sax. Leechd.* I. 326 Sum fyþerfette nyten is, þæt we nemnað..broc on englisc. *c* **1175** *Lamb. Hom.* 129 Alle þa deor and alle þe nutenu þe on eorðe weren. *c* **1200** *Vices & Virtues* 151 Hie lokeden wel ðat ðe tail ware on auriche netene.

'netful. [f. NET *sb.*[1]] The fill of a net.

1855 BROWNING *Popularity* v, A fisher..A netful brought to land. **1898** *Pall Mall Mag.* June 219 A netful of the..oysters.

†**neth**, hath not: cf. NAVE *v.*

c **1315** SHOREHAM I. 182 He þat bilefeþ hit nauȝt Riȝt wyt neþ of blisse.

neth, -ar, obs. forms of NET, NEITHER.

netheard, -heerd, -herd, obs. ff. NEATHERD.

netheist ('niːθiːɪst). [f. L. *ne-*, *nē-* or Gr. νη- + THEIST.] An atheist.

1855 *Chamb. Jrnl.* III. 307 The missionaries are met..by propagandists of another kind—by Netheists, Theists, Setheists, and Pantheists. **1862** *Westm. Rev.* Jan. 86 Several other names, such as Cosmists, Netheists, and Rational Utilitarians, that the party has tried at different times.

†**netheless**, *adv. Obs.* Forms: 2–3 neoðe-, neoþe-, neðeles, 4 neþ(e)les, -lesse, 4–6 netheles, (4 -less, -lees), 6 -lesse, 7 ne(i)thlesse. [f. NE, etc.: cf. NA- and NOTHELESS.] Nevertheless.

c **1175** *Lamb. Hom.* 137 Neoðeles he heom sulleð. *c* **1200** *Trin. Coll. Hom.* 79 He makeð lete of þoleburdnesse and neðeles ne haueð non. *c* **1250** *Gen. & Ex.* 3853 At ðe laste neðeles, Eft ne come sone to cades. *c* **1330** R. BRUNNE *Chron. Wace* 9855 Netheles þey were at meschef. **1382** WYCLIF *Luke* xii. 31 Nethelees seke ȝe first the kyngdom of God. *c* **1400** *Apol. Loll.* 13 Neþles it is not iust as to soþfastnes. **1480** CAXTON *Chron. Eng.* cxxxi. 110 And netheles..he wold not mysdone hym. **1549** COVERDALE, etc. *Erasm. Par. Rom.* Argt., They fell nethelesse into all kyndes of mischief. **1579** E. K. *Ded. to Spenser's Sheph. Cal.* §3 Nethelesse, let them..feede on theyr owne folly. **1611** SPEED *Hist. Gt. Brit.* IX. xviii. §49. 704 The thing..that all the world wist was true, and that neithlesse euery man laughed at.

†**nethemest**, *a. Obs.* Forms: 1 nyðe-, niðe-, nioð-, 1–2, 4 neoþe-, 2–4 neþe-, 3 nythe-, 4 nyþe-; 1 -mæsta, -mesta, -mysta, 2–4 -mest(e, 4 -mast(e. [OE. *niþemest*, etc., f. the stem *niþ-* under: see NETHER and -MOST.] Lowest, undermost, furthest down.

c **888** K. ÆLFRED *Boeth.* vii. §3 Þa niðemystan ic ȝebringe æt þæm hehstan, & þa hehstan æt ðæm niðemæstan. **971** *Blickl. Hom.* 185 Swa swiþe he biþ bedyped on þa neoþemestan helle witu. *c* **1175** *Lamb. Hom.* 117 He bið eft i-niþered on þan neoþemeste pinan. *c* **1200** *Trin. Coll. Hom.* 219 Þe uuemeste bou is sib þe neþemeste rote. *c* **1290** *S. Eng. Leg.* I. 287/332 Ase he sat on þis laddre lowe, on þe neþemeste roungue. **13..** *Ipotis* 390 (Vernon MS.) in Horstm. *Altengl. Leg.* (1881) 345 In to þe neoþemaste put of helle. *c* **1380** *Sir Ferumb.* 3257 Þe heȝeste hiȝt mangurel, þe middel hiȝt launcepre, þe nyþemest was callid hagefray. *a* **1425** *Cursor M.* 9926 (Trin.), Hit..ȝyueþ to þe neþemast [*v.r.* -mest] liȝt.

†**'nethen**, *adv. Obs.* [OE. *neoðan*, *-on*, etc.: see BENEATH *adv.*] Below; from below.

c **888** K. ÆLFRED *Boeth.* xxxiii. §5 On ælcere stowe he is hire emnneah, ȝe ufan ȝe neoðon. **971** *Blickl. Hom.* 211 Þæt wæter wæs sweart under þæm clife neoðan. *c* **1000** ÆLFRIC *Hom.* II. 258 Ða tobærst þæs temples wahryft, fram ðære fyrste ufan oð ða flor neoðan. *c* **1200** *Trin. Coll. Hom.* 105 Ech idel..and iuel [giue cumeð] neðen uppard.

nether ('nɛðə(r)), *a.* Forms: 1 nioðerra, niðera, nyðera, 3 nyþere; 1 neoþ(e)ra, 3 neoþere; 4 nethere, 4–5 neþer, (5 -ire), 5–6 nethir, (5 -yr, *Sc.* nathir), neder, (6 -ur, *Sc.* neddir); 4 nei-, neyþer, 6 neyther, 7 neither, 6–7 neather; 5– nether. [Common Teut.: OE. *neoþera*, *niþera*, etc., = OFris. *nithere*, *nedere*, OS. *nithiri* (MDu. *neder*, Du. *neder-* in combs.), MLG. *neder*, *nedder*, OHG. *nidari*, *-eri*, *-iri* (MHG. *nidere*, *nider*, G. *nieder*), ON. *neðri* (Sw. and Da. *nedre*), f. *niþer(e*, NETHER *adv.*[2] or [3]. See also NETHERER and NETHEREST.] Lower, under (in contrast to *higher*, *over*, or *upper*).

1. With partitive terms, esp. *part* or *end*. †Also (in OE.) *absol.* in *pl.*

c **825** *Vesp. Psalter* cxxxviii. 15 In ðæm nioðerum eorðan. **971** *Blickl. Hom.* 239 Gangað on þas niðeran dælas þisse ceastre. **1375** BARBOUR *Bruce* x. 21 The nethir half [of the way] wes perelouss. **1382** WYCLIF *Ecclus.* xxiv. 45, I shal persen alle the nethere partis of the erthe. *c* **1400** *Destr. Troy* 3076 Fingurs full small, With nailes at the neþer endes as a nepe white. *c* **1440** *Promp. Parv.* 355/2 Nethyr part of a thynge, *inferior.* **1525** *Tale of Basyn* 40 in Hazl. *E.P.P.* III. 45 When the baly was full, [he would] lye downe and wynke, And rest his neder ende. **1570** BILLINGSLEY *Euclid* XI. xxix. 341 Lines..which ioyne together the angles of the vpper and nether bases. **1604** E. G[RIMSTONE] *D' Acosta's Hist. Indies* II. xii. 108 Experience dooth teach vs, that the middle region of the ayre is colder than the neather. **1697** DRYDEN *Virg. Past.* VI. 108 A beautous Maid above, but Magick Arts With barking Dogs deformed her neather parts. **1798** COLERIDGE *Anc. Mar.* III. xiv, With one bright star Within the nether tip. **1826** SCOTT *Woodst.* iii, At the nether end of the hall, a huge..chimney-piece projected. **1860** MAURY *Phys. Geog.* (Low) xi. §519 Upon the nether side of the cloud-ring.

2. With terms denoting locality, esp. the proper names of countries, districts, hamlets or farms, etc.

Now usually expressed by *Lower* or *Low*, but retained in various districts in local place-names, or the names of streets (as *Nethergate*), etc. in towns.

Nether Dutch and ***Nether German*** have occas. been used in English in place of the usual *Low* (†*Dutch* or) *German*.

c **888** K. ÆLFRED *Boeth.* v. §1 Ne onscuniȝe ic no þæs neoþeran & þæs unclænan stowe. **1387** TREVISA *Higden* (Rolls) I. 127 In þe west side of þe neþer Galilea toward þe grete see. *c* **1425** WYNTOUN *Cron.* I. xiii. 1198 Þir lyis in Neþir Sithia. *Ibid.* 1227 In þat Neþir Germany All Northtwaye is. **1513** DOUGLAS *Æneis* VIII. iii. 124 Thai wester partis..Quhilkis ar bedeit wyth the neder se. **1560** BIBLE (Genev.) *1 Kings* ix. 17 Salomon buylt Gezer and Beth-horon the nether. **1596** DALRYMPLE tr. *Leslie's Hist. Scot.* Prol. 17 Vuir Clydisdale..as lykwyse nathir Cludisdale. **1629** RUTHERFORD *Lett.* v. (1862) I. 47 While we are lodged here, we..must be content to remove from one corner of our Lord's nether house to another. **1697** DRYDEN *Virg. Georg.* I. 442 The rising rivers float the nether ground. **1745** POCOCKE *Descr. East* II. ii. 202 We were now in the nether principality of the kingdom of Naples.

†**b.** ***Nether House***, the House of Commons. *Obs.*

App. current only in the reign of Henry VIII.

1536 CROMWELL in Merriman *Life & Lett.* (1902) II. 47 Suche Actes as haue been in this session of that parliament passed the nether and higher houses. **1577–87** HOLINSHED *Chron.* III. 911/1 When the commons were assembled in the nether house, they began to commune of their griefes. **1640** YORKE *Union Hon.* 47 Certaine Lords of the upper house of parliament, came into the nether. **1687** *Assur. Abb. Lands* 180 After which the Speaker with the Commons departed to the Nether House.

3. Of lip or jaw. Now commonly expressed by *lower* or *under*.

c **1000** ÆLFRIC *Gloss.* in Wr.-Wülcker 157 *Labrum*, niðera lippe. *c* **1050** *Voc.* ibid. 264 Neoþera welor. *c* **1300** *St. Margarete* 160 He..gan his ouere cheoke ouer hire heued do & his nyþere cheoke byneþe at hire ho. *c* **1320** *Sir Tristr.* 1468 His neþer chauel he smot doun. **1387** TREVISA *Higden* (Rolls) II. 173 Tantalus stondeþ alway in a water vp anon to þe ouer brerde of þe neþer lippe. **1548** VICARY *Anat.* 40, xij Muscles..moue the nether Iawe. **1648** GAGE *West Ind.* 77, Pieces of gold..hanging upon their nether lips. **1657** TRAPP *Comm. Job* v. 9 Who can give a naturall reason of the strength of the neather-chap? **1843** LYTTON *Last Bar.* III. v, An uneasy gnawing of the nether lip. **1857–61** BUCKLE *Civiliz.* (1869) II. viii. 469 A nether jaw protruding so hideously that his teeth could never meet.

b. Of the legs or their clothing. Also in ***nether man*** (common in recent use) or ***person***.

1522 SKELTON *Why not to Court* 1197 Lest he..make hym lame of his neder limmes. **1667** MILTON *P.L.* II. 784 All my nether shape thus grew Transform'd. **1835** J. P. KENNEDY *Horse Shoe R.* xvi, His nether person was rendered conspicuous by a pair of dingy small-clothes. **1836** MARRYAT *Japhet* i, Long before the old porter could pull his legs through his nether garments. **1846** MRS. GORE *Eng. Char.* (1852) 151 We found a still idler fellow..warming his nether-man on the hearth-rug.

c. *absol.* in *pl.* Lower limbs or parts. *rare*[−1].

1822 T. MITCHELL *Aristoph.* II. 175 With a cloak duly tuck'd round their nethers.

4. In general use, of things. Now only *literary*.

†***nether glove***, a greave. †***nether vert*** (see quot. 1598).

a **1225** *Ancr. R.* 332 Þe neoþere [stone] þet lið stille..bitocneð ferlac..; þe vuere ston bitocneð hope. **1387** TREVISA *Higden* (Rolls) II. 185 Þe planetes and þe neyþer wolkons moeueþ out of þe west in to þe est. *a* **1400–50** *Alexander* 4959 Nymes of ȝour nethirgloue & nakens ȝoure leggis. *c* **1425** *Craft Nombrynge* (E.E.T.S.) 6 Write þe first figure of þe hyer nombur euene vndir the first figure of þe nether nombur. **1470–85** MALORY *Arthur* VIII. xiv. 294 Syr Tristram bebled both the ouer shete and the nether. **1523** FITZHERB. *Husb.* §5 The bodye of the wayne.., the nether rathes, the ouer rathes. **1598** MANWOOD *Lawes Forest* vi. 34 Neather vert, is that which the Lawiers do call South Boys, and that is properly all manner of vnder-wood, and all Bushes, Thornes, Gorse, and the like. **1615** G. SANDYS *Trav.* 14 The skirts flow loosely fringed below; the upper shorter then the neather. **1667** MILTON *P.L.* I. 346 'Twixt upper, nether, and surrounding Fires. *a* **1718** PARNELL *Night-Piece on Death*, Thro' their ranks in silver pride The nether crescent seems to glide. **1850** KINGSLEY *Alt. Locke* xxxviii, The nether fires of doubt glaring through. **1866** HOWELLS *Venet. Life* ii. 20 All my nether-spirit, so to speak, was dulled and jaded.

b. ***nether millstone*** (or ***stone***). Now only in fig. or allusive use.

1560 BIBLE (Genev.) *Job* xli. 14 His heart is as strong as a stone, and as hard as the nether milstone. **1647** N. BACON *Disc. Govt. Eng.* I. xxxix. (1739) 59 The Defendant's Arms (which were accounted as the Nether-milstone, or stock of maintenance). **1760–72** H. BROOKE *Fool of Qual.* (1809) III. 3 The nether millstone of my heart began to dissolve. **1869** BROWNING *Ring & Bk.* x. 1110 He shall make the sword To match that piece of netherstone his heart. **1877** BLACK *Green Past.* xxviii, I believe you have a heart as hard as the nether millstone.

†**c.** ***nether clerk***, under-clerk. *Obs. rare*[−1].

1567 *Reg. Privy Council Scot.* I. 614 Maister James Makgill of Rankelour, Nethir Clerk of Register.

5. Denoting the earth or things upon it, in contrast to heaven or the upper regions. (Usually with *this*.)

1590 SPENSER *F.Q.* II. vii. 49 This darksom neather world her light Doth dim. **1605** SHAKS. *Lear* IV. ii. 79 This shewes you are aboue, You Iustices, that these our neather crimes So speedily can venge. **1760** FAWKES tr. *Anacreon, Ode* iii. 2 The sable Night had spread around This nether World a Gloom profound. **1786** S. ROGERS *Ode Superstit.* III. ii, To aspire Beyond this nether sphere. **1832** CARLYLE *Misc.* (1857) III. 68 Thus do Men and Sheep play their parts in this Nether Earth. **1857** BUCKLE *Civiliz.* I. xi. 645 The intellect of man in this nether world.

6. Denoting what lies, or is imagined as lying, beneath the earth; esp. ***nether world*** or ***regions***.

[*c* **825** *Vesp. Psalter* lxxxvii. 7 Settun mec in seaðe ðæm nioðerran in ðeostrum. **971** *Blickl. Hom.* 89 Þu ȝeneredest mine saule of þære neoþeran helle.]

1638 BROME *Antipodes* I. vi, No Isle nor Angle in that Neather world, But I have made discovery of. **1697** DRYDEN *Æneid* III. 497 Must pass the Stygian Lake and view the neather Skies. **1720** GAY *Poems* (1745) I. 172 When dread Jove the son of Phœbus hurl'd..to the nether world. **1817** SHELLEY *Rev. Islam* I. xxx, The hell, His reign and dwelling beneath nether skies. **1830** LYELL *Princ. Geol.* I. 397 The great reservoirs of melted matter..in the nether regions. **1877** L. MORRIS *Epic Hades* I. 10 A cauldron fired With the fires of nether hell.

Comb. **1828** CARLYLE *Misc.* (1857) I. 127 In this way can the nether-world Scapin sport with the perplexed beauty. **1869** TOZER *Highl. Turkey* II. 300 Besides this nether-world character.

b. ***nether-formed*** adj. = HYPOGENE.

1833 [see HYPOGENE]. **1862** ANSTED *Channel Isl.* II. x. 248 It is where the old, hard, nether-formed rocks frowningly appear above the water.

† **ˈnether**, *adv.*[1] *Obs.* Forms: 1 **nioðor, niðor, nyðor, neoðor, -er,** 2 **neðer.** [A comparative form based on the stem *niþ-*: see next.] Lower, lower down.

Beowulf 2699 Þæt he þone niðgæst nioðor hwene sloh. *c* **888** K. ÆLFRED *Boeth.* xxxiii. §5 Sio eorþe..is nioðor þonne æniȝ oðru ȝesceaft buton þam rodore. *c* **1000** ÆLFRIC *Saint's Lives* i. 58 Þelæs þe þæt mod sy neoðer þonne se lichoma. *c* **1200** *Trin. Coll. Hom.* 103 He beð neðer þanne he er was.

† **ˈnether**, *adv.*[2] *Obs.* Forms: 1–3 **niþer, niðer;** 1 **nyþer, nyðer,** (3 **nuðer**); 2–3 **neoðer,** (3 **neouðer**); 2–3 **neðer,** (3 **nedðer**); 5 **nether.** [OE. *niþer* = OFris. *nither-*, *nider-*, OS. *nidar* (MDu. and Du. *neder*), MLG. *neder*, *nedder*, OHG. *nidar*, *nider* (G. *nieder*), ON. *niðr* (MSw. *nidher*, Sw. *ner*, *ned*; MDa. *nedher*, Da. *ned*), repr. an OTeut. **niþar* = Skr. *nitarām*, f. *ni-*, down, with comparative suffix.] Down, downwards.

Beowulf 1360 Ðær fyrȝenstream under næssa ȝenipu niþer ȝewiteð. *c* **888** K. ÆLFRED *Boeth.* xli. §6 Þæt tacnað Þæt he sceal ma þencan up þonne nyðer. **971** *Blickl. Hom.* 101 Þæt flæsc afulað, & wyrmum awealleþ, & neþer afloweþ. *a* **1122** *O.E. Chron.* (Laud MS.) an. 1012 Sloh hine þa an heora ..þet he mid þam dynte niðer asah. *c* **1200** *Trin. Coll. Hom.* 111 He ferde fro þe fader, for þat he com neðer to helle. *c* **1250** *Gen. & Ex.* 370 Niðful neddre, loð an liðer, sal gliden on hise brest neðer. *c* **1450** tr. *De Imitatione* II. xii. 57 Turne thiself aboue [turne þiself nether].

Comb. *c* **960** ÆTHELWOLD *Rule St. Benet* (Schröer) 23 Æȝðer ȝe upstiȝende englas ȝe niþerstiȝende. *Ibid.* Se upstiȝe and se niþerstiȝe. *c* **1000** *Sax. Leechd.* III. 246 Hi ȝefyllað twa tida mid hyra upgange oððe nyþergange. *c* **1200** *Trin. Coll. Hom.* 111 Erest he steg neoðer..: of neoðerstienge specð dauid on þe salm boc.

† **ˈnether**, *adv.*[3] *Obs.* In 1 **niðere, niþre,** 3 **neoðere;** also in comb. 1–3 **niðer-,** 3 **nyþer-, neoþer-.** [f. prec. = MDu. *ned(e)re*, OHG. *nidaro* (MHG. *nidere*), ON. *niðri* (MSw. *nidhre*, Sw. *nere*; MDa. *nedre*, Da. *nede*).] Down, low down.

c **888** K. ÆLFRED *Boeth.* xxxix. §13 Þæt leohte fyr..up ȝewit, & sio hefiȝe eorðe sit þær niðere. *a* **900** CYNEWULF *Crist* 1466 Læȝ min flæschoma in foldan bigrafen, niþre ȝehyded. *c* **1205** LAY. 1982 Þa Englisce ouercomen þe Brutuns & brouhten heom þer neoðere.

b. In *Comb.* = NETHER *a.*

c **1000** *Ags. Ps.* (Thorpe) cxxxviii. 13 Þeh min lichama.. on niðer-dælum eorðan wuniȝe. *c* **1200** *Trin. Coll. Hom.* 173 Hie turneð..fram þe dome to helle to þe niðer wunienge. *c* **1290** *St. Brandan* 527 in *S.E. Leg.* I. 234 To is chin tilde þe neoþer [*v.r.* niþer] ende.

nether, var. of NITHER *v.*; obs. f. NEITHER.

net-herd, obs. form of NEATHERD.

† **ˈnetherer.** *Obs. rare.* [f. NETHER *a.* + -ER[3].] **a.** The lower parts. **b.** An inferior.

a **1340** HAMPOLE *Psalter* cxxxviii. 14 My substaunce in neþerere of erth. *c* **1449** PECOCK *Repr.* Prol. 1 Correccioun.. which longith oonli to the ouerer anentis his netherer, and not to the netherer anentis his ouerer.

† **ˈnetherest,** *a. Obs.* [A superlative formed on NETHER *a.*; cf. OFris. *nithereste*, *nedereste*, MDu. *nederste*, OHG. *nidirôsto* (MHG. *nidereste*), MSw. *nidherst(a*, MDa. *ne(d)erste* (Sw. and Da. *nederst*).] Lowest, undermost. Also *absol.*

a **1300** *E.E. Psalter* cxxxviii. 15 Þou made..þe staþelnes of me In netherest of erthe to be. *c* **1374** CHAUCER *Boeth.* I. pr. i. (1868) 5 In þe neþerest[e] hem or bordure of þese cloþes. **1417** in *Surtees Misc.* (1890) 12 Un to the netherest stake safe ane. *c* **1440** *Jacob's Well* 281 False cristene men schul be nethirest in helle. **1558** GRIMALDE *Cicero's Offices* Pref., This learning teacheth, so much to graunt the vital part and the netherest.

† **nethering**, var. *eddering*: see EDDER.

1688 HOLME *Armoury* II. 86/1 A Nethering is a twig or stick bent about Stakes and Poles by which fences and hedges are made secure.

ˈNetherlander. [ad. Du. *Nederlander* (G. *Niederländer*), f. *Nederland*: see -ER[1].] An inhabitant or native of the Netherlands or Holland (formerly including Flanders or Belgium).

1610 HOLLAND *Camden's Brit.* I. 475 Verily much beholden it is to the Netherlanders [*Note.* Or Dutchmen of the Low countries.] **1638** SIR R. COTTON *Abstr. Rec. Tower* 5 William de Ipre, Earle of Kent, a Netherlander. **1876** BANCROFT *Hist. U.S.* II. xxii. 25 Manned by a mixed crew of Netherlanders and Englishmen. **1880** W. NEWTON *Serm. Boys & Girls* (1881) 332 The great leader of the Netherlanders.

ˈNetherlandian, *a. rare.* [f. as prec. + -IAN.] = NETHERLANDISH *a.*

1600 W. WATSON *Decacordon* (1602) 209 An alien prince, Spanyard or Burgundian, Netherlandian or the like. **1902** B. KIDD *Western Civiliz.* ix. 297 The Swabian peasants and the Netherlandian burghers.

ˈNetherˌlandic, *a.* [f. *Netherland* + -IC.] = NETHERLANDISH *a.*

1902 *Encycl. Brit.* XXXI. 294/1 Wienecke is interesting for the sake of his early Netherlandic manner. **1972** E. KRISPYN in A. Dixon tr. *Boon's Chapel Road* p. i, Louis Paul Boon, born in 1912, is one of the most interesting and controversial contemporary prose writers in the Netherlandic area. *Ibid.* p. ii, The medieval Netherlandic story of Reynard the Fox. **1973** *Mod. Lang. Assoc. Newsletter* Mar. 1 There are Provencal and Netherlandic groups, but with the exception of 'Chinese Language and Literature', which presently has provisional status, there are no groups in Oriental or African languages or literatures. **1975** *Times Lit. Suppl.* 28 Nov. 1429/1 There is also one [series of books] of international studies and translations, including a Dutch (or, as the publishers call it, Netherlandic) section.

ˈNetherlandish, *a.* and *sb.* [ad. Du. *Nederlandsch*, (G. *Niederländisch*), or f. *Netherland* + -ISH[1].]

a. *adj.* Of or pertaining to the Netherlands.

1600 J. PORY tr. *Leo's Africa* II. 61 Fower and twentie elles of Portugall or Neatherlandish cloth. **1680** *Relig. Dutch* iv. 39 All the Cities of this Netherlandish Country are full of these Mennonites. **1839** W. CHAMBERS *Tour Holland* 41/1 The coats of arms of the old Netherlandish nobility. **1875** WHITNEY *Life Lang.* x. 181 Two important cultivated tongues, the Netherlandish and the English.

b. *sb.* The language of the Netherlands; Dutch.

1890 *Chambers's Encycl.* V. 744/2 The origin of new Netherlandish or Dutch is to be found with the *Rederijkers*. **1944** *Britannica Bk. of Year* (U.S.) 759/1 Languages: Spanish, English, French and Netherlandish. **1954** *Word* X. Apr. 91 He [*sc.* Geschiere] admits that lg. *amo* ('orge hâtive,' barley) may come from German; or may come from Netherlandish. What he does not add explicitly is that lg. *amo* may have a fourfold source: German plus Netherlandish plus limbourgeois plus eupenois. **1974** *N.Y. Times* 3 Feb. 14 The great majority, especially the educated and young, do not call the language they speak 'Vlaams', or Flemish; they call it 'Nederlands', meaning Dutch, or Netherlandish.

† **netherless**, contracted f. NETHERTHELESS.

c **1400** *Three Kings Cologne* 34 Neþirles sume bokes seiȝe þat in þe same day þat god was bore, were manye sunnes seiȝe. **1464** *Rolls of Parlt.* V. 511/2 Yet netherles, of their mere and extreme malice [etc.]. **1498** *Promp. Parv.* 353/2 (MS. S.) Neythirlesse, *nichilominus*.

ˈnetherling. *nonce-wd.* [f. NETHER *a.* + -LING[1].] *pl.* Nether garments.

1852 DICKENS in *Househ. Words* V. 565/1 The plain young woman darning the poet's netherlings.

ˈnethermore, *a.* (*sb.*) and *adv.* Also 4–5 **neþer-, neder-,** 5–6 **nethirmare,** 6 **nethermair.** [f. NETHER *a.* + -MORE: cf. MSw. *nidhirmeer*, MDa. *nedhermere*.]

A. *adj.* Nether, lower, inferior. Now *rare*.

1382 WYCLIF *Deut.* xxiv. 6 Thow shalt not taak..the nethermore and ouermore grynstoon. **1382** —— *Judg.* xx. 36 Whanne thei hadden seen hem self to be the nethermore, thei begunne to flee. *c* **1400** MAUNDEV. (Roxb.) xvi. 72 Liby þe neþermare begynnez at þe Spaynisch see. **1601** HOLLAND *Pliny* II. 257 The nethermore [root], which also is the bigger. **1610** HOLLAND *Camden's Brit.* I. 337 The upper part of the Church, and..the nethermore. **1867** LONGF. tr. *Dante, Inf.* III. 41 The heavens expelled them; Nor them the nethermore abyss receives.

† **B.** *sb.* The lower parts. *Obs. rare*$^{-1}$.

1382 WYCLIF *Ps.* cxxxviii. 15 My substaunce is in the nethermoris [*v.r.* -more] of the erthe.

† **C.** *adv.* Lower or further down. *Obs.*

c **1480** HENRYSON *Orph. & Eur.* 260 Nethirmare he went, as ye heir sall. **1513** DOUGLAS *Æneis* VI. v. *Heading*, Tyl hellis fluids Enee socht nether mair. **1565** GOLDING *Cæsar* V. (1567) 116 Thone corner..is toward the East: and thother nethermore is towarde the South.

ˈnethermost, *a.* Also 4 **-mast,** 5 **-mest, nethur-, nethern-,** 6 **neathermost.** [f. as prec. + -MOST.] Lowest, undermost, furthest down.

a **1300** *Cursor M.* 357 Þe neþermast es watur and erth. *Ibid.* 9248 Þat was þe nethermast step. *c* **1400** *Destr. Troy* 3084 Hir corse [was] comly.., As nobly to þe nethur-most as nature cold shape. *c* **1468** in *Archaeol.* (1846) XXXI. 334 The nethernmost part of the said candelstikes. **1535** M. COVERDALE *Ps.* lxxxvi. 13 Thou hast delyuered my soule from yᵉ nethermost hell. **1578** LYTE *Dodoens* 340 The first and neathermost leaves are like the litle leaves of Plantayne. **1635** J. HAYWARD tr. *Biondi's Banish'd Virg.* 216 The fairest of them..were on the nether-most of the staires. **1669** WORLIDGE *Syst. Agric.* (1681) 196 You may take the most remote Box..and place it the nethermost. **1715** LEONI *Palladio's Archit.* (1742) II. 11 The middle of the upmost Wall ought to be perpendicular with the middle of the nethermost. **1814** CARY *Dante, Inf.* XXIV. 37 Toward the mouth Inclining of the nethermost abyss. **1866** J. H. NEWMAN *Gerontius* i. 8 From the nethermost fire..Thy servant deliver.

ˈnetherstock. *Obs.* exc. *Hist.* Also 6–7 **neather-,** 6 **neither-.** [f. NETHER *a.* + STOCK.] A stocking.

1565–6 *Roy. Proclam. Apparel* 12 Feb., Any maner of sylke netherstockes of Hosen. **1592** GREENE *Upst. Courtier* in *Harl. Misc.* (Malh.) II. 220 A plaine pair of cloth-breeches..of white kersie.., the nether-stocke of the same. **1607–8** *Knaresb. Wills* (Surtees) II. 2 My best over hoose and my best netherstockes. **1671** H. M. tr. *Erasm. Colloq.* 436 Neither did they commonly wear breeches without netherstocks or slops.

1821 SCOTT *Kenilw.* xix, A dispute upon the preference due to the Spanish nether-stock over the black Gascoigne hose. **1863** SALA *Captain Dangerous* I. vi. 170 A plain black shag gown untrimmed, with camlet netherstocks.

transf. **1605** SHAKS. *Lear* II. iv. 11 When a man [is] ouer-lustie at legs, then he weares wodden nether-stocks.

So † **nether-stocking.** *Obs. rare*$^{-1}$.

1591 FLORIO *2nd Fruites* 7 Foure payre of breeches, fiue of nether-stockins.

† **nethertheless,** variant of NEVERTHELESS.

c **1440** *Promp. Parv.* 353/2 Nethyrtheles, *nichilominus*. *c* **1450** *Merlin* 43 Netherdeles, thei knewe wele ther cowde no man have seide thise wordes but it hadde a be Merlin.

† **ˈnetherty.** *Obs. rare.* In 5 **-te.** [f. NETHER *a.* + -TY.] Inferiority.

c **1449** PECOCK *Repr.* IV. i. 416 In the clergie ben dyuerse statis and degrees of ouerte and netherte. *Ibid.* ii. 425 Poul ..vsid in that ouerte upon hem, and not netherte as being vndir hem.

ˈnetherward(s, *adv.* Now *rare.* Forms: 1 **niþerweardes, nyþerwerd, -wyrd;** 3 **niðer-, neþer-, noþer-,** 4–5 **nethire-,** 4– **netherward(s.** [f. NETHER *adv.*[2] + -WARD(S).] Downwards. Also (in form *netherward*) as *adj.*

c **975** *Rushw. Gosp.* Matt. viii. 32 Unȝerece..eode all siu suner..niþer-weardes in sae. *c* **1000** ÆLFRIC *Gram.* (Z.) 238 *Deorsum versum*, nyðerwerd. *a* **1100** in Napier *O.E. Glosses* i. 3968 *In præceps*, nyþerwyrd. *c* **1220** *Bestiary* 561 Fro ðe noule niðerward ne is ȝe [= the mermaid] no man like. *a* **1250** *Owl & Night.* 144 Þeos vle.. heold hire eyen neþerward [*v.r.* noþerward]. *a* **1400–50** *Alexander* 5048 Moves ȝow to þe nethire-ward. *c* **1400** *Destr. Troy* 7717 Fro the Nauell netherward he was an able horse. *c* **1630** RISDON *Surv. Devon* §215 (1810) 224 Netherward to Great Lynd. **1656** RIDGLEY *Pract. Physick* 293 Chafe him from above nether-wards. **1865–6** W. WHITMAN *When Lilacs last in Door-Yard Bloom'd* 6, I watch'd where you pass'd and was lost in the netherward black of the night. **1878** HARDY *Ret. Native* I. vii. 149 But celestial imperiousness, love, wrath, and fervour had proved to be somewhat thrown away on netherward Egdon. **1894** DU MAURIER *Trilby* i, Clad in the grey overcoat of a French infantry soldier, continued netherwards by a short striped petticoat.

netherworld (ˈnɛðəwɜːld). [f. NETHER *a.* 6 + WORLD *sb.*] = UNDERWORLD 4.

1930 *Sat. Evening Post* 26 July 145/1 Who could possibly deny his skill in the affairs of the netherworld? **1955** P. HERON *Changing Forms of Art* 106 It seems in itself a symbol of the artist, and particularly of his work in recent years: for it is a sort of ambassador of the Dark, of the vast netherworld which psychologists call the Unconscious. **1973** *Daily Tel.* 5 Apr. 15/2 When to admit a new word is always a problem, but President Nixon has made it with 'netherworld' ('the netherworld of deceit, subversion and espionage'). **1975** *Times Lit. Suppl.* 13 June 679/1 Occasionally he even descended from Baltimore into this netherworld of benighted yokels and hillbillies.

† **netheward,** *a. Obs.* [OE. *niðe-*, *nyðe-*, *neoþoweard*, etc.; cf. NETHEMEST.] Downward.

a **1000** *Phœnix* 299 Se hals [is] grene nioþoweard & ufeweard. *c* **1000** ÆLFRIC *Hom.* II. 452 Fram his hnolle ufewerdan oð his ilas neoðewerde. *c* **1200** *Trin. Coll. Hom.* 165 On þe steire of fiftene stoples, fro neþewarde to uue-warde.

nethir, obs. f. NEITHER.

nethlesse, var. of NETHELESS *Obs.*

nethring: see NITHER *v.*

nethtebure, obs. f. NEIGHBOUR.

nethyr, obs. f. NEITHER.

netifie, -fy, obs. ff. NEATIFY.

netinde, unwitting: see NETE *v.*

netle, obs. f. NETTLE.

netling, obs. f. NETTLING.

†'**netly**, *adv. Obs. rare*$^{-1}$. [f. NET *a.* + -LY^2.] Neatly, smartly.

1577–87 HOLINSHED *Chron.* III. 802/2 These first entred the field, in taking by and turning their horses, netlie and freshlie.

'**netmaker.** [f. NET *sb.*^{1}] A maker of nets.

1380 in Rogers *Oxford City Docum.* (1891) 10 De Marrabilla Terre Netmaker xij *d.* **1411** *Close Roll 12 Hen. IV* (dorso), John Mannyng, netmaker. **1483** *Cath. Angl.* 253/2 A Nette maker, *cassiarius*. *c* **1515** *Cocke Lorell's B.* 11 Nette makers, and harlote takers. **1595–6** *Observ. Fishdaies* 1 Ropemakers, Net-makers, Saile-makers. **1654** WHITLOCK *Zootomia* 416 To be a Net-maker (in Chrysostomes sense) is better than to be a Throne-maker. **1771** SMEATON in *Phil. Trans.* LXI. 204 That particular kind called by net makers flaxen three threads laid. **1884** KNIGHT *Dict. Mech.* Suppl. 633/2 *Netmaker's Knife.*

'**netsman.** [f. NET *sb.*^{1}] One who uses a net.

1867 F. FRANCIS *Angling* i. (1880) 13 The netsman should never dash at the fish. **1887** D. C. MURRAY & HERMAN *Traveller Returns* iv. 52 The netsmen bore long nets of stout bark rope and thong. **1937** H. POPE *St. Augustine of Hippo* vi. 245 One of the netsmen has just been bitten by a crab. **1962** *Punch* 21 Feb. 328/2 Who but a lunatic or a salmon netsman would be astir? **1973** *Nature* 27 July 232/1 Many were caught by netsmen off other neighbouring salmon rivers. **1975** *Times Lit. Suppl.* 7 Mar. 258/5 The salmon netsmen of the east coast of Scotland were the first to complain of the damage done by seals.

‖**netsuke** ('nɛtsuːkeɪ). Also -ké. [Japanese.] A small piece of ivory, wood, or other material, carved or otherwise decorated, worn by the Japanese as a bob or button on the cord by which articles are suspended from the girdle.

1883 *Century Mag.* Sept. 743 Come in here a moment, please, and see my new netsukes. **1888** *Art Jrnl.* Dec. 374 The mark which distinguishes a netsuké from an okimono.. is the presence of two small holes, usually in the back, which admit of a cord being strung through them.

nett(e, obs. forms of NEAT *sb.*

'**nettable**, *a.* [f. NET *v.*] Capable of being netted.

1820 *Blackw. Mag.* VII. 140 It was the annual custom.. to sweep the nettable parts of the Coquet to a large extent.

'**netted**, *ppl. a.* [f. NET *sb.*^{1} or *v.*^{1}]

1. Covered with, or as with, a net.

1577 B. GOOGE *Heresbach's Husb.* IV. (1586) 169 b, The windowes.. hauing a hole of sufficient widenesse ouer against them, well netted and tunnelled. **1833** SIR F. B. HEAD *Bubbles fr. Brunnen* 310 The graves were netted over with brambles. **1860** EMERSON *Cond. Life, Wealth* Wks. (Bohn) II. 347 How did North America get netted with iron rails? **1895** *Atlantic Monthly* Mar. 425 The snow, barred and netted by shadows.

2. Made of net or network.

1710 *Lond. Gaz.* No. 4672/4 Supposed to have robbed.. his Master of a Silver netted Purse. **1785** MISS FIELDING *Ophelia* II. i, Like gold through a netted purse. **1812** BYRON *Ch. Har.* II. xviii, The well-reeved guns, the netted canopy. **1866** (*title*) Abridgments of the Specifications relating to Lace and other Looped and Netted Fabrics. **1870** ROCK *Text. Fabr.* v. (1876) 39 Rich textiles so figured in gold were denominated 'de fundato', or netted.

b. Arranged like, or forming a, network.

1805 SOUTHEY *Madoc in Azt.* xv, On the strong corselet and the netted mail. **1855** TENNYSON *Brook* 176, I make the netted sunbeam dance Against my sandy shallows. **1884** BOWER & SCOTT *De Bary's Phaner.* 229 At those points where the spiral or netted fibres separate.

Comb. **1825** *Greenhouse Comp.* II. 44 *Ciconium reticulatum*, netted-veined Ciconium. **1857** A. GRAY *First Less. Bot.* (1866) 56 Netted-veined leaves belong to plants which have a pair of seed-leaves or cotyledons.

3. *Bot.* Having veins, fibres, etc., arranged like network; covered with a network of lines, etc.

1847 W. E. STEELE *Field Bot.* 164 Seeds indefinite; testa loose, netted. **1849** BALFOUR *Man. Bot.* §143 Reticulated or netted leaves, in which there is an angular net-work of vessels. **1882** *Garden* 11 Mar. 170/3 The deep crimson of the interior of the bells being finely netted and veined.

b. In names of plants, etc.: (see quots.).

1854 *Encycl. Brit.* (ed. 8) V. 181/1 *Anona reticulata* [yields] the netted Custard-apple. **1857** MISS PRATT *Flower. Pl.* V. 229 The plant is sometimes called Netted Crocus. **1882** *Garden* 4 Mar. 139/3 The Netted Iris (*I. reticulata*) is in full bloom.

4. Caught in a net.

1856 MRS. BROWNING *Aur. Leigh* II. (1898) 81 Need you tremble and pant Like a netted lioness? **1867** JEAN INGELOW *Story of Doom* VII. 19 As in the toils A netted bird.

nettel, obs. form of NETTLE.

'**netter.** [f. NET *v.*^{1} + -ER^1.]

1. A netmaker. *rare*$^{-1}$.

1481–90 *Howard Househ. Bks.* (Roxb.) 192 My Lord rekened with his netter, and he had sent home to Stoke a dragge of viij. fadom.

2. One who uses a net. Also *fig.*

1591 LYLY *Wks.* (1902) I. 427 Here be the Netters, these be they that.. will draw a whole pond for the market. **1838** J. E. TYLER *Mem. Hen. V*, II. 56 He was called the Netter from the expertness.. with which he caught.. his antagonists in argument. **1873** G. C. DAVIES *Mount. & Mere* xi. 86 A gang of netters sweeping the stream.

3. *U.S. colloq.* A lawn-tennis player.

1932 *Sun* (Baltimore) 6 Sept. 14/1 (*heading*) Coast netter stops invader. Stoefen injects drama into Forest Hills meet defeating Japanese. **1974** *Anderson* (S. Carolina) *Independent* 23 Apr. 6A/3 The Anderson College netters took an 8–1 win over Gainesville here Monday but the AC No. 1 doubles team of Rajiv Kapur and Elango Ranganathan dropped its first match after 18 straight wins.

'**netting**, *sb.*^{1} *dial.* [Prob. f. NET *v.*^{3}, although this is not recorded till much later; but cf. also the synonymous MLG. *nette* (MDa. *nættæ*, MSw. *nätte*, *näcte*, *necte*; G. *netze*), f. *nat* wet.] Urine, *esp.* as used for washing with.

c **1375** *Sc. Leg. Saints* xliv. (*Lucy*) 275 þane ves it tald þe presydent þat wischcrafte.. vith nettyng [*printed* nect-; L. *lotium*] mocht be lousit sone. þane gert he caste on hire.. Of netting [*printed* nect-] a gret quantyte. *c* **1475** *Pict. Voc.* in Wr.-Wülcker 794 *Hoc locium*, ley and nettyng. **1557** *Court Leet Rec. Manchester* (1884) I. 40 Any undecente or noysome thinge as.. Nettinge or Fylthe. **1691** RAY *N.C. Words* (ed. 2) 52 *Netting*, Chamber-Lee, Urin. **1796** PEGGE *Derbicisms* (E.D.S.) 48 'Old netting', old urine; so called from neat or net, as being us'd in washing. **1828–** in dial. glossaries (Durham, Yks., Lanc., Linc., Leic.). **1886** *S.W. Linc. Gloss.* s.v., She killed her two swaarms of bees; she poured netting on the hives.

'**netting**, *sb.*^{2} [f. NET *sb.*^{1} or *v.*^{1} + -ING^1.]

1. *Naut.* A coarse network of small ropes used now or formerly for various purposes, as to prevent boarding, keep off splinters or falling spars, stow hammocks or sails in, etc.

1567 G. FENNER in Hakluyt *Voy.* (1589) 149 They had prepared their false nettings. **1582** N. LICHEFIELD tr. *Castanheda's Conq. E. Ind.* I. xxviii. 71 Seruing in trimming the sayles, and others the nettings and foretop sayles. **1626** CAPT. SMITH *Accid. Yng. Seamen* 14 A grating, netting or false decke for your close fights. **1673** DRYDEN *Amboyna* III. i, Up with your Fights and your Nettings prepare. **1748** *Anson's Voy.* III. viii. 379 The mats, with which the galeon had stuffed her netting, took fire. **1794** *Rigging & Seamanship* I. 170 Quarter-deck netting is stopped over the officers heads, to prevent any thing falling thereon, in time of action. **1837** MARRYAT *Dog Fiend* x, The men.. came up with their hammocks.., which they put into the nettings. **1867** LATHAM *Black & White* 116 A steamer just arrived had.. her nettings frozen into a solid wall.

b. *attrib.* as †*netting-deck*, *-sail*.

1626 CAPT. SMITH *Accid. Yng. Seamen* 17 A drift sayle, a crosiack, a netting sayle. **1627** —— *Seaman's Gram.* vii. 32 A Netting saile is.. a saile laid ouer the Netting, which is small ropes from the top of the fore castle to the Poope. **1745** P. THOMAS *Jrnl. Anson's Voy.* 289 A Netting-Deck very well fitted over her Main-Deck, to hinder Boarding.

2. Nets or network used for various purposes.

1846 T. BAXTER *Libr. Pract. Agric.* I. 141 It will be needful to cover the beds.. with netting to keep off the birds. **1863** TREVELYAN *Compet. Wallah* (1866) 27 In the netting overhead are plentiful stores of bottles of milk. **1883** WALSH *Irish Fisheries* 7 (Fish. Exhib. Publ.), Over 1200 miles of netting for the fleet;.. the largest amount of netting in use in the world.. at any one fishery.

'**netting**, *vbl. sb.* [f. NET *v.*^{1} + -ING^1.]

1. a. The process of making a net.

1785 E. SHERIDAN *Jrnl.* 20 June (1960) ii. 58, I called at the toyshop and desired my purchases to be properly pack'd.. —there is a box for you to put your netting in while you work it and to keep it in when you are idle, with lock and key. **1872** YEATS *Techn. Hist. Comm.* 279 Netting is a mode of entwining the thread so that each mesh is fastened with a knot. **1883** *Standard* 26 June 3/3 Its process consists in the looping of a thread, after the manner of netting, into circles.

b. *attrib.* as ***netting-box***, *-case*, *-cotton*, *-needle*, *-pin*, *-weight*, etc.

1801 MAR. EDGEWORTH *Gd. Fr. Governess* (1831) 178 There was a pretty little netting-box upon the table. **1790** F. BURNEY *Diary* Jan. (1905) IV. xlii. 348 The air of common employment was such, that.. everything of that sort was spread about..—workboxes, netting-cases, etc. etc.! *a* **1817** JANE AUSTEN *Northanger Abbey* (1818) II. x. 194 Assured of Isabella's having matched some fine netting-cotton. **1865** MRS. GASKELL *Wives & Daughters* (1866) II. xviii. 185 The netting-cotton she was using kept continually snapping.. from the jerks of her nervous hands. **1875** KNIGHT *Dict. Mech.* 1523/1 Netting-machine. *a* **1817** JANE AUSTEN *Persuasion* (1818) III. xi. 234 He fashioned new netting-needles and pins with improvements. **1832** in A. Adburgham *Shops & Shopping* (1964) iv. 38 Knitting, netting and mending needles. **1847** C. BRONTË *Jane Eyre* II. ii. 44, I try to concentrate my attention on these netting-needles, on the meshes of the purse I am forming. **1854** DICKENS *Hard T.* I. xi, Mrs. Sparsit, easily ambling along with her netting-needles. **1918** N. DUNCAN *Battles Royal* 6 It is said of our people that they are born with a netting needle in their hand and an ax by the side of their cradle. **1942** [see *battle-twig*]. **1973** W. ELMER *Terminol. Fishing* iv. 256 Two instruments are used for braiding or mending nets, the *netting-needle*, on which a certain amount of twine is wound, and the *spool*. **1808** HAN. MORE *Cœlebs* xxii. I. 324, I have known a lady.. search for her netting-pin, in the midst of Cato's soliloquy. **1813** MAR. EDGEWORTH *Harry & Lucy* I. 260 It.. was intended to be used as a netting weight.

2. The action, or right, of fishing with a net or nets; an occasion of fishing with a net.

1875 F. T. BUCKLAND *Log-Bk.* 158 Not a single one was seen or heard of during the whole of the netting. **1884** *Times* (weekly ed.) 26 Sept. 13/3 Till about twenty years ago the netting was in the hands of the Rev. Mr. Eyre.

nettle ('nɛt(ə)l), *sb.*^{1} Forms: 1 netele, (netel), 1–5 netle, 5 netel(le, netyl(le; 4–5 nettille, 4–6 -yll, 5 -yle, 5–6 -ylle, 6 -yl, -ill, -ell, 5–6 (8) nettel, 3– nettle. [Common Teut.: OE. *netele*, *netle* (and *netel*) fem. = Fris. *nettel*, MDu. *net(e)le*, *netel* (Du. *netel*), MLG. *net(t)ele*, OHG. *nez(z)ila*, *-ela* (MHG. *nezzele*, *-el*, G. *nessel*), MDa. *næt(h)-*, *nædlæ*, *nedle* (Da. *nelde*, *nælde*), MSw. *netla*, *nätla* (Sw. dial. *nättla*), and *netsla*, *nesla* (Sw. *nässla*, *nässel-*), Norw. *netla*, *nesla*, etc., Icel. *netla*:—OTeut. **natilōn-*, a derivative (see -LE 1) from a stem **nat-* which appears in the synonymous OHG. *nazza*, and in various Scand. forms, as Sw. dial. *nata*, *näta*, Norw. dial. *nata*, *neta*, *not(a)*, etc., the relationship of which to each other is obsure.]

1. a. A plant of the genus *Urtica*, of which the commoner species (*U. dioica*, the Common or Great Nettle, and *U. urens*, the Small Nettle) grow profusely on waste ground, waysides, etc., and are noted for the stinging property of the leaf-hairs.

The Greek, Italian, or Roman Nettle is *U. pilulifera*. With distinctive epithets the name of *nettle* is also given to a number of plants belonging to other genera, as *blind*, *dea-*, *dead*, *deaf*, *red*, *white nettle*; *bee-*, *hedge-*, *hemp-*, *wood-nettle*, which are treated under the first element or as main words.

c **725** *Corpus Gloss.* 2168 in *O.E. Texts* 107 *Urticeta*, netlan. *c* **1000** *Sax. Leechd.* I. 310 Ðenim þysse wyrte seaw, þe man urticam, & oðrum naman netele nemneð. *Ibid.* II. 68 Smale netelan. *Ibid.* 86 þa greatan netlan. *a* **1250** *Owl & Night.* 593 Among þe wede, among the netle, þu syttest & singst. **1303** R. BRUNNE *Handl. Synne* 7514 With-oute hys celle þornes wore And netles grewe, þat byten sore. **1387** TREVISA *Higden* (Rolls) VI. 461 As þe netle groweþ somtyme next þe rose. *c* **1400** MAUNDEV. (Roxb.) xiv. 65 Humbloks and nettles and swilk oþer wedes. **1481** CAXTON *Reynard* 86, I haue nothyng but thystles and nettles. **1563** *Mirr. Mag., Jane Shore* iii, In groping flowers wyth Nettels stong we are. **1578** LYTE *Dodoens* 129 The first kind is now called.. in English Greek or Romayne Nettel. **1631** E. JORDAN *Nat. Bathes* xi. (1669) 84 The heat of the Sun is no more apt to breed a Nettle than a Dock. **1693** EVELYN *De la Quint. Compl. Gard.* I. 18 Thistles, Nettles, and a Thousand other Plants of no Use to us. *a* **1732** GAY *Poems* (1745) I. 167 Elder's early bud With nettle's tender shoots, to cleanse the blood. **1810** CRABBE *Borough* xviii. 296 At the wall's base the fiery nettle springs. **1849** BALFOUR *Man. Bot.* §1022 The young shoots of the common nettle are sometimes used like spinach or greens. **1890** *Knowledge* 1 Dec. 274/2 The common nettle occurs in two forms; the male plant which produces the pollen is quite distinct from that which bears the seeds.

transf. and *fig.* **1596** SHAKS. *1 Hen. IV*, II. iii. 10 Out of this Nettle, Danger; we plucke this Flower, Safety. **1836** *Gentl. Mag.* V. 221 When he did apply the rod, it was generally formed of nettles. **1841–4** EMERSON *Ess., Friendship* Wks. (Bohn) I. 88 Better be a nettle in the side of your friend than his echo. **1870** LOWELL *Study Wind.* 39 Those driving nettles of frost that sting the cheeks.

b. The Sea-nettle. (Cf. RED NETTLE 2.) *rare*$^{-1}$.

1601 HOLLAND *Pliny* II. 444 The sea fish called a Nettle.

c. = NETTLE-TREE 2.

1889 J. H. MAIDEN *Usef. Native Plants* 192 *Laportea gigas* ..'Giant Nettle'. The poisonous fluid secreted from the foliage is very powerful.

2. In phrases, etc.: **a.** ***nettle in, dock out***, see DOCK *sb.*^{1} 3. **b.** (See quot. *a* 1700.) **c.** ***on nettles***, in fidgets, uneasy, excited.

1592 GREENE *Upst. Courtier* B 3, All these women that you heare brawling.. and skolding thus, have seuerally pist on this bush of nettles. *a* **1700** B. E. *Dict. Cant. Crew* s.v. *Nettled, He has pist upon a Nettle*, he is very uneasy or much out of Humor. **1828** *Craven Gloss.* s.v., 'Thou's p——d of a nettle this morning', said of a waspish, ill-tempered person. **1892** STEVENSON *Across Plains* i. 56 Some of them were on nettles till they learned your name was Dickson.

d. ***to cast (throw) one's frock*** (or ***cassock***) ***to the nettles*** [= Fr. *jeter le froc aux orties*], to renounce the clerical life; also *transf. rare.*

1916 W. J. LOCKE *Wonderful Year* xviii. 255 Now, indeed, he had burned his boats, thrown his cap over the windmills, cast his frock to the nettles. **1918** —— *Rough Road* vi. 58 Young parsons.. threw their cassocks to the nettles and put on the full.. panoply of war.

3. *ellipt.* A nettle-tap moth (see 4 b). *rare*$^{-1}$.

1819 SAMOUELLE *Etymol. Compend.* 385 *Tortrix urticana.* The barred Nettle.

4. *attrib.* and *Comb.* **a.** Simple attrib., etc., as ***nettle-bed***, *-blossom*, *-bush*, *-field*, *-juice*, *-leaf*, *-plant*, *-root*, *-seed*, *-stalk*, *-stem*, *-sting*, *-top*; in sense 'made with nettles', as ***nettle-beer***, *-broth*, *-kale*, *-porridge*, †*-pottage*, *-tea*; ***nettle-leaved***, *-like*, *-rough*, *-stung* adjs.; †***nettle-sting*** vb. (hence *-stinging*).

1894 R. KERR *Pioneering in Morocco* 205 Such commotion about a *nettlebed. **1864** *Chambers's Encycl.* VI. 726/1 The stalks and leaves of nettles are employed.. for the manufacture of a light kind of beer, called *Nettle beer. **1910** A. BENNETT *Clayhanger* I. xii. 103, I won't have them apprentices drinking!.. Mrs. Nixon'll give 'em some nettle-beer if they fancy it. **1953** *Word for Word* (Whitbread & Co.) 12/2 *Nettle beer*, brewed from nettles as opposed to barley. **1868** RUSKIN *Pol. Econ. Art.* Add. 194 The beautiful circlet of the white *nettle blossom. **1825** JAMIESON, **Nettle-broth*, broth made of nettles, as a substitute for greens. **14..** *Nom.* in Wr.-Wülcker 711 *Hoc urticetum*, a *netyl-bushe. **1919** *Chambers's Jrnl.* May 298/2 In the boggy regions.. people have begun to cultivate *nettle-fields. **1965** G. B. SCHALLER *Year of Gorilla* vii. 171 The guard and I cut a narrow trail through the stands of lobelias and nettle fields. **1747** WESLEY *Prim. Physick* (1762) 35 Take an ounce of *Nettle juice. **1846** LINDLEY *Veget. Kingd.* 261 The causticity of Nettle juice is owing to the presence of bicarbonate of ammonia. **1859** BROCKIE in J. Watson *Bards of Border* 195 The laich herd's hoose, Where I suppit *nettle kail. **1884** *Chamb. Jrnl.* 8 Mar. 147/1 The common stinging nettle.. in Scotland is occasionally used for making a kind of soup termed nettle kail. **1677** HORNECK *Gt. Law Consid.* ii. (1704) 18 Who would suspect such things as needles, or sharp transparent pikes in a *nettleleaf? **1789** J. PILKINGTON *View. Derbysh.* I. 351 *Nettle-leaved Bellflower, Great Throatwort, or Canterbury Bells. **1828** SIR J. E. SMITH *Eng. Flow.* II. 11 Nettle-leaved Goosefoot. **1777** PENNANT *Brit. Zool.* IV. 49

Many species on being handled affect with a *nettle-like burning. **1764** *Museum Rust.* II. 159 The fibres of the *nettle plant. **1660-1** PEPYS *Diary* 25 Feb., There we did eat some *nettle porridge. **1776** T. PERCIVAL *Ess.* (1776) III. 258 The children breakfasted of *nettle-pottage, that is, oatmeal gruel with fresh nettles boiled in it. **1747** WESLEY *Prim. Physick* (1762) 36 Chew *Nettle root. **1850** MRS. BROWNING *Poems* I. 337 The thought I called a flower, grew *nettle-rough. *c* **1440** *Promp. Parv.* 355/1 *Nettyl-seede, *gnydisperma*. **1601** HOLLAND *Pliny* II. 121 As touching Nettle seed, Nicander affirms, That it is a very counterpoison against Hemlock. **1643** J. STEER tr. *Exp. Chyrurg.* iii. 7 A sharpe and pricking pain, like as though the skin were rubbed with Nettle-seed. **1684** RAY *Phil. Lett.* (1718) 175, I wish I had Assurance..that those Sorts of Linen..are made of *Nettle-Stalks. **1766** *Museum Rust.* VI. 429 Making cloth of Hop Binds and Nettle Stalks. **1891** T. HARDY *Tess* liv, The pale and blasted *nettle-stems of the preceding year. **1822-34** *Good's Study Med.* (ed. 4) II. 337 Florid, itching, *nettle-sting wheals. **1898** *Westm. Gaz.* 30 Sept. 4/1 The dock-leaf..is useful as a remedy for nettle-sting. **1598** E. GUILPIN *Skial.* (1878) 40, I applaud my selfe For *nettle-stinging thus this fayery elfe. **1666** W. BOGHURST *Loimogr.* (1894) 93 Little red superficiall pimples in clusters like nettle stinging. **1891** C. JAMES *Rom. Rigmarole* 102 The leaf of the common dock I have found efficacious, if applied..to *nettle-stung legs. **1758** WESLEY *Wks.* (1872) XII. 203 *Nettle-tea..would do you more good than any other. **1843** *Penny Cycl.* XXVI. 62/2 'Nettle-tea' is a popular remedy for many diseases. **1797** *Encycl. Brit.* (ed. 3) XVIII. 693/2 *Nettle-tops in the spring are often boiled and eaten by the common people. **1836-48** B. D. WALSH *Aristoph., Knights* I. iii, Like those who're fond of nettle-tops.

b. Special combs.: **nettle battery**, one of the stinging organs of a hydrozoon; **nettle-bird** = *nettle-creeper*; **nettle-blight**, *Æcidium urticæ*, a parasitic plant common on nettles (Ogilvie *Suppl.* 1855); **nettle-bulb** (see quot.); **nettle butterfly**, *Vanessa urticæ*, whose larvæ feed on nettles; **nettle cell**, a stinging cell; †**nettle cheese** (see quots.); **nettle-creeper**, a name applied to the Whitethroat (*Sylvia cinerea*), and the Golden Warbler (*Sylvia hortensis*) from their nesting in hedge-bottoms among nettles; **nettle-docken**, the common dock, which is used to relieve nettle-stings; **nettle-earnest** *Sc.*, downright earnest; **nettle-fever**, urticaria (*Cent. Dict.* 1890); **nettle-fish**, a stinging jelly-fish (*ibid.*); **nettle-geranium**, *Coleus fruticosus*; **nettle-grub**, a stinging caterpillar injurious to the tea-plant (*Stand. Dict.* 1895); **nettle-hemp** = *hemp-nettle* s.v. HEMP *sb.* 5; **nettle-lichen**, a skin disease (see LICHEN *sb.* 3); **nettle-monger**, (*a*) the Reed Sparrow or Reed Bunting; (*b*) the Whitethroat; (*c*) the Blackcap; **nettle-spring** *dial.*, nettle-rash; **nettle-tap (moth)**, a moth which frequents nettle-beds; **nettle-thread**, one of the stinging hairs of acalephs (*Cent. Dict.* 1890); **nettle-tom** *dial.*, the White-throat; **nettle-weed** *U.S.*, a plant of the nettle family; **nettle-whip** (see quot.); **nettle-wort**, (*a*) a spurgewort of the genus *Acalypha*; (*b*) a plant of the nettle family; **nettle-yarn**, the prepared fibre of nettles.

1888 ROLLESTON & JACKSON *Anim. Life* 770 Cnidoblasts, from which new '*nettle batteries' are derived in growth. **1854** MISS BAKER *Northampton Gloss.* Add. II. 415 *Nettle-bird, the white-throat. **1888** ROLLESTON & JACKSON *Anim. Life* 783 Some Rhizostome genera also possess '*nettle-bulbs', stalked processes with or without a terminal opening. **1802** BINGLEY *Anim. Biog.* (1813) III. 211 The *Nettle tortoise-shell butterfly. **1826** KIRBY & SP. *Entomol.* xxix. III. 101 The eggs of..the nettle butterfly..when laid in summer are hatched in a few days. **1902** R. W. CHAMBERS *Maids of Paradise* xiii. 222 The scarlet-banded nettle-butterflies flitted and hovered. **1870** NICHOLSON *Zool.* 109 The '*nettle cells' or 'cnidæ' of the *Cœlenterata*. **1896** tr. *Boas' Text-bk. Zool.* 107 Numerous 'batteries' of nettle cells. **1615** MARKHAM *Eng. Housew.* II. iv. 118 A very dainty *nettle Cheese, which is the finest summer Cheese which can be eaten... You shall lay [the curd] vpon fresh nettles and couer it all ouer with the same. **1694** *Ladies' Dict.* 155/1 Cheese, of which there are two kinds, Morning-Milk-Cheese, Nettle Cheese. **1817** T. FORSTER *Nat. Hist. Swallows* (ed. 6) 79 *Sylvia atricapilla*, Black-cap, Haychat, *Nettlecreeper, or Nettlemonger. **1845** *Encycl. Metrop.* XXV. 364/2 The White Throat..is seen..among weeds and nettles, whence one of its provincial names is the Nettle Creeper. **1891** MISS DOWIE *Girl in Karp.* 234 The common *nettle-docken, the stuff that no creature will eat. **1818** HOGG *Brownie of Bodsbeck* xiii, Ane canna speak a word but it is taen in *nettle-earnest. **1860** PIESSE *Lab. Chem. Wonders* 67 Two very luxuriant *nettle-geraniums. **1597-1744** [*Nettle-hemp: see HEMP *sb.* 5]. **1822-34** *Good's Study Med.* (ed. 4) IV. 432 The Urticose or *Nettle Lichen is, perhaps, the most distressing form of all the varieties. **1712** MORTIMER *Northampt.* 428 The Reed Sparrow..is found upon Willows and Bushes by our Brook-sides, as also upon Bunches of Nettles; and is therefore called the *Nettlemonger by some. **1831** RENNIE *Montagu's Ornith. Dict.* 42 The provincial names of Mock-nightingale, Nettle-creeper, Nettle-monger. **1819** SAMOUELLE *Entomol. Compend.* 364 *Tortrix lutosa*. The early *Nettle-tap. *Ibid.* 442 *Tortrix Oxyacanthæ*. The Autumn Nettle-tap. **1845** *Encycl. Metrop.* XXIV. 597/1 Flitting with a very peculiar flight over the tops of nettles, and thence termed Nettle-taps. **1830** in W. Cobbett *Rur. Rides* (1885) II. 320 The sweet and soft voice of the white-throat or *nettle-tom. **1843** 'R. CARLTON' *New Purchase* I. xix. 159 They gathered a peculiar species of nettle, (called there *nettle-weed,) which they succeeded in dressing like flax. **1867** 'T. LACKLAND' *Homespun* I. 18 Their blackened skeletons..overgrown with nettleweeds and long grasses. **1888** ROLLESTON & JACKSON *Anim. Life* 783 '*Nettle-whips'..are elongated funnel-shaped openings,..beset with digitelli. **1834** *Miller's Dict. Gard.* 46 *Acalypha*.., *Nettle Wort. **1846** LINDLEY *Veget. Kingd.* 261 Nettleworts will then be easily known from Morads and Hempworts, which have a hooked embryo. **1885** J. S. STALLYBRASS tr. *Hehn's Wand. Plants & Anim.* 469 The Germans also made nets of *nettle-yarn.

'nettle, *sb.*[2] [f. NETTLE *v.*] A state of uneasiness or impatience.

1723 DK. WHARTON *True Briton* No. 60 II. 516 Trebellius, you may be sure somewhat upon the Nettle, addresses himself to the Favourite. **1792** M. CUTLER in *Life*, etc. (1888) I. 487 Congress..are extremely tedious in their debates..and, at the same time, all in a nettle to rise and adjourn.

'nettle, *sb.*[3], variant of *knettle*, KNITTLE.

1841 DANA *Seaman's Man.* 43 Take two parts of different yarns and twist them up taut into nettles... Lay half the nettles down [etc.]. **1875** BEDFORD *Sailor's Pocket Bk.* x. (ed. 2) 360 Nettle stuff.

nettle ('nɛt(ə)l), *v.* Forms: 5 nettil, nettyl(le, 5-7 netle, 6 nettel(l, nettyll, 6- nettle. [f. NETTLE *sb.*[1] Cf. MDu. *netelen* (Du. *nettelen*), G. *nesseln*.]

1. *trans.* To beat or sting (a person or animal) with nettles.

c **1440** *Promp. Parv.* 355/1 Netlyn, *urtico*. **1483** *Cath. Angl.* 253/2 To Nettylle, *vrticare*. **1530** PALSGR. 644/1, I nettyll, *je ourtie*. If a horse be well nettelled under the tayle he wyll kycke jolyly. **1596** SHAKS. *1 Hen. IV*, I. iii. 240, I am whipt & scourg'd with rods, Netled, and stung with Pismires. **1616** SURFL. & MARKH. *Country Farme* I. xv. 71 To nettle him with the strongest and most stinging Nettles that you can get. **1670** RAY in *Phil. Trans.* V. 2064 Ants, if they get into peoples clothes,..will cause a smart and tingling, as if they were netled. **1882** R. HOLLAND in *N. & Q.* 6th Ser. VI. 54 It is customary in Cheshire to punish those who do not wear a sprig of oak by nettling them.

b. *refl.* To get (oneself, one's hands, etc.) stung by nettles.

1719 D'URFEY *Pills* II. 284 Like Boy that had nettl'd his Breech. **1869** W. CORY *Lett. & Jrnls.* (1897) 267, I worked hard at lighting a fire, nettling my hands in gathering fuel. **1902** BARNES-GRUNDY *Thames Camp* 111 I nettled myself badly.

c. (Also *absol.*) To sting as a nettle does.

1858 LEWES *Sea-side Stud.* 149 If the capsules are the nettling organs, why do they not nettle in those parts where they are most abundant? **1879** S. LANIER *Poems* (1884) 92 A flower That clung with pain and stung with power, Yea, nettled me, body and mind.

2. To irritate, vex, provoke, pique.

1562 J. HEYWOOD *Prov. & Epigr.* (1867) 82 She nettled him. **1568** GRAFTON *Chron.* II. 683 The Erle of Warwicke..toke many riche ships of the Duke of Burgoyns countries, (which sore netteled the Duke). **1601** B. JONSON *Poetaster* I. ii, I know this nettles you now, but answere me. **1668** DRYDEN *Even. Love* I. ii, She has nettled me; would I could be revenged on her! **1722** DE FOE *Col. Jack* (1840) 211 This last discourse nettled me. **1761** MRS. F. SHERIDAN *Sidney Bidulph* II. 319 This foolish woman's behaviour nettled me extremely. **1814** I. D'ISRAELI *Quarrels Auth.* (1867) 308 A ridiculous story..nettled Pope more than the keener remonstrances. **1859** MASSON *Milton* I. 618 Cottington would now and then nettle his Grace by a jibe.

absol. **1726** SWIFT *To Lady* Wks. 1751 XIV. 229 But with Raillery to nettle, Sets your Thoughts upon their Mettle.

b. In *pa. pple.* Irritated, vexed, provoked, annoyed. Const. *at*, *by*, *with*, etc.

a **1400-50** *Alexander* 737 Now is ser Nicollas anoyed & nettild with ire, As wrath as a waspe. *c* **1460** *Towneley Myst.* xxx. 169 She that is most meke..can rase vp a reke if she be well nettyld. *a* **1548** HALL *Chron., Hen. IV* 19 He beyng netteled with these uncurteous..prickes & thornes. **1579** FENTON *Guicciard.* VIII. (1599) 310 Cæsar being netled by so many infamies..received. **1618** BOLTON *Florus* (1636) 267 Cæsar, throughly nettled at the newes, resolved [etc.]. **1672** MARVELL *Corr.* Wks. (Grosart) II. 410 Sir Philip..knew not so much and is well netled. **1724** DE FOE *Mem. Cavalier* (1840) 171 Essex, nettled to be both beaten in fight, and outdone in conduct, decamps. **1782** MISS BURNEY *Cecilia* II. iv, The haughty Baronet, extremely nettled, forced his way on. **1838** DICKENS *Nich. Nick.* xiii, Not a little nettled to observe that they were enjoying the scene from a snug corner. **1853** KINGSLEY *Hypatia* xxvii, A little nettled by her contemptuous tone.

c. *intr.* To become irritated or annoyed. *rare.* Also ***nettle up*** (dial.).

1810 *Splendid Follies* II. 31 Milford..began to nettle at the fidgets of his visitor. **1875** WAUGH *Owd Cronies* ii, Sally blushed and nettled up.

3. To prick or stir up; to incite, rouse.

a **1592** GREENE *George a Greene* Wks. (Rtldg.) 257/2 There are few fellows in our parish so nettled with love as I have been of late. **1650** R. STAPYLTON *Strada's Low C. Wars* IX. 46 His Souldiers, that were..nettled with the example and danger of their General. **1841** CATLIN *N. Amer. Ind.* (1844) II. iii. 150 He rode and nettled his prancing steed in front of my door.

4. To make sharp, to intensify. *rare*$^{-1}$.

1821 CLARE *Vill. Minstr.* II. 4 Delays so lingering dampt her joys, And expectation nettled woe.

'nettle-cloth. [f. NETTLE *sb.*[1] Cf. Du. *neteldoek* (Da. *netteldug*, Sw. *nätteldu*k), G. *nesseltuch*.]

a. Cloth made of nettle-fibres. **b.** Cotton cloth, calico. (See also quot. 1858.)

1539 *Will of E. Carleton* (Somerset Ho.), My best rayle of Nettyll cloth. **1598** FLORIO, *Ortichino*, a kinde of cloth we call calico or nettle cloth, or the rootes to make it. **1599** HAKLUYT *Voy.* II. I. 230 Cloth of herbes, which is a kinde of silke which groweth amongst the woods without any labour of man. *marg.* This cloth we call Nettle cloth. **1626** BACON *Sylva* §614 Nettles, (whereof they make Nettle-Cloth). **1858** SIMMONDS *Dict. Trade*, *Nettle-cloth*, a new German material, consisting of a very thick tissued cotton, which is japanned and prepared as a substitute for leather, particularly for the peaks of caps, waistbelts, &c. **1884** *Chamb. Jrnl.* 8 Mar. 147/1 At Dresden, Herr F. C. Seidel has recently established a manufactory for nettle-cloth.

nettled ('nɛt(ə)ld), *ppl. a.* [f. NETTLE *sb.*[1] or *v.*]

1. Irritated, angry. (Cf. the vb. 2 b.)

1582 STANYHURST *Poems* (Arb.) 138 They be fresh forging toe the netled Palias an armoure. **1585** FETHERSTONE tr. *Calvin on Acts* xxiii. 521 Paul meant..with this excuse to mollifie their nettled minds. **1888** *Sat. Rev.* 20 Oct. 466/2 Her own rather nettled defence..of the hideous rhymes which she affected.

2. Stung by nettles. (Cf. the vb. 1.)

1671 H. CROUCH *Welch Trav.* 369 in Hazl. *E.P.P.* IV. 343 He sate him down Upon a bed of nettles there..His nettled flesh did smart.

3. Full of nettles. Also in *Comb.*, as ***well-nettled***.

1830 *Blackw. Mag.* XXVIII. 631 Buried in some nettled nook of the kirkyard. **1834** *Tait's Mag.* I. 732/2 He lies in a well-nettled corner of St. George's burying-ground.

†**'nettlefy**, *v.* = NETTLE *v.* 1 (*nonce-wd.*).

1602 DEKKER *Satirom.* L 4 You shall bee a Poet, though not Lawrefyed, yet Nettlefyed.

'nettler. [f. NETTLE *v.* + -ER[1].] One who nettles, stings, or irritates.

1611 COTGR., *Ortieur*, a nettler. **1641** MILTON *Animadv.* Wks. 1851 III. 191 These are the nettlers, these are the blabbing Bookes that tell, though not halfe your fellows feats.

nettle-rash. [f. NETTLE *sb.*[1] + RASH *sb.*[3]] An exanthematous eruption on the skin, appearing in patches like those produced by the sting of a nettle; essera, urticaria.

1740 C'TESS HARTFORD in *Corr. w. C'tess Pomfret* (1805) II. 157, I then..found I had got what the doctor at Windsor calls a nettle-rash. **1799** UNDERWOOD *Diseases Children* I. 93 The Essera, or Nettle-rash, is attended perhaps, with the slightest of all fevers. **1818-20** E. THOMPSON tr. *Cullen's Nosol. Method.* (ed. 3) 326 Nettle Rash is not contagious. **1867** PRINCESS ALICE *Mem.* (1884) 172 Laid up with the most awful nettle-rash all over face and body. **1884** M. MACKENZIE *Dis. Throat & Nose* II. 309 In some patients hay fever is accompanied by nettle rash.

attrib. **1803** *Med. Jrnl.* X. 481 Observations on the Nettle-Rash Fever.

nettlesome ('nɛt(ə)lsəm), *a.* [f. NETTLE *sb.*[1] or *v.* + -SOME.] Easily nettled, irritable.

1766 *Life of Quin* iv. (repr.) 24 He was a native of Wales, and was not the least nettlesome of his countrymen. **1828** *Blackw. Mag.* XXIV. 22 He..gets, if not mettlesome,..very nettlesome indeed. **1888** *Argosy* Oct. 307 There is something highly attractive to that nettlesome insect [a wasp] in the folds of a surplice.

'nettle-tree.

1. A tree of the genus *Celtis*, belonging to the natural order *Ulmaceæ*, esp. *C. australis*, the European, and *C. occidentalis*, the N. American species.

1548 TURNER *Names Herbs* (E.D.S.) 24 It hath a leafe lyke a Nettel, therfore it may be called in englishe Nettel tree or Lote tree. **1611** COTGR., *Algisié*, the Lote, or Nettle tree. **1693** *Phil. Trans.* XVIII. 620 An elegant sort of Christophoriana,..called Nettle-Tree by those of Barbados. **1741** J. MARTYN *Virg. Georg.* II. 84 *note*, The nettle tree, the fruit of which is far from that delicacy which is ascribed to the Lotus of the ancients. **1817** BRADBURY *Trav. Amer.* 16 The cotton wood, elm, mulberry, and nettle trees suffered the most. **1832** *Planting* 106 in *Lib. Usef. Kn., Husb.* III, The wood of the European nettle-tree is considered to be one of the hardest. **1849** BALFOUR *Man. Bot* §1022 *Celtis*, the Nettle-tree, or Sugar-berry, has a sweet drupaceous fruit. **1866** *Treas. Bot.* 245/2 The North American Nettle-tree..differs from the European species in having longer leaves.

2. An Australian tree of the genus *Laportea*, esp. the Giant Nettle (*L. gigas*) and Small-leaved Nettle (*L. photiniphylla*).

1849 J. P. TOWNSEND *Rambles in N.S. Wales* 34 In the scrubs is found a tree, commonly called 'the nettle tree' (*Urtica gigas*). **1852** MUNDY *Antipodes* (1857) 198 The *Urtica gigas* or stinging nettle tree... It may be forty feet high, and the stem nine or ten feet round.

nettling ('nɛtlɪŋ), *vbl. sb.*[1] [f. NETTLE *v.* + -ING[1].] The application of nettles to the skin.

c **1440** *Promp. Parv.* 355/1 Netlynge, *urticacio*. **1611** COTGR., *Empoule*, a little wheale,..such as comes after netling. **1664** POWER *Exp. Philos.* I. 51 You may..see the Causes, as well as you have formerly felt the Effects, of their Netling. **1884** *Folk-Lore Jrnl.* II. 382 This nettling business is only performed up to midday.

'nettling, *vbl. sb.*[2] [f. NETTLE *sb.*[3]] **a.** The process of joining two ropes by spinning or twisting their loosened ends together. **b.** The action or practice of tying yarns in pairs to keep them from entangling.

1875 KNIGHT *Dict. Mech.* 1523/2.

'nettling, *ppl. a.* [f. NETTLE *v.* + -ING[2].]

1. Irritating, provoking.

1652 KIRKMAN *Clerio & Lozia* 100 Stinging words and netling speeches. **1702** C. MATHER *Magn. Chr.* VII. iii. (1852) 514 This disposition in Mr. Cotton was very nettling to the sectaries. *c* **1769** *Junius Lett.* ix. (L.), This latter was a nettling occurrence.

2. Stinging.

1858 Lewes *Sea-side Stud.* 149 If the capsules are the nettling organs. **1890** *Cent. Dict.*, *Lasso cell*, a nettling cell.

nettly (ˈnɛtlɪ), *a.* [f. nettle *sb.*[1] + -y[1]. Cf. Du. *netelig.*]

1. Overgrown with nettles.

c **1825** Beddoes *Poems* (1851) 177 The common wild.. Dimpled twice with nettly graves. **1870** Miss Broughton *Red as Rose* 284 These drenched, nettly charnels.

2. Irritable.

1825 Jamieson *Suppl.* **1854** S. Thomson *Wild Fl.* 260 Even the most nettly of the human species seem to have some friend or other. **1888** G. M. Fenn *Man with Shadow* II. xxii. 263 I'm not cross, old fellow—only nettly.

†ˈ**netty**, *a.*[1] *Obs. rare*$^{-1}$. [f. net *a.* + -y[1].] Neat, natty.

1573 Tusser *Husb.* (1878) 159 How prettie, how fine and how nettie, Good huswife should iettie.

netty (ˈnɛtɪ), *a.*[2] Now *rare.* [f. net *sb.*[1] + -y[1].] Net-like; netted, made of net.

a **1628** F. Grevil *Cælica* lii, Yet Venus choose with Mars the netty bed. **1658** Sir T. Browne *Gard. Cyrus* iii. 55 In the netty fibres of the veines and vessels of life. **1891** *Daily News* 9 Feb. 6/3 An ascending salmon.. is caught in a netty cul-de-sac.

ˈ**network**, *sb.* [f. net *sb.*[1] + work *sb.* Cf. Du. *netwerk*, G. *netzwerk*, Da. *netværk*, Sw. *nätverk.*]

1. Work in which threads, wires, or similar materials, are arranged in the fashion of a net; *esp.* a light fabric made of netted threads.

1560 Bible (Genev.) *Exod.* xxvii. 4 Thou shalt make vnto it a grate like networke of brasse. **1575** in J. W. Clay *Clifford Fam.* (1906) 35, I do give to my said aunte one suyte of networke. **1695** Wood *Will* in *Life* (O.H.S.) III. 503 All the network, that I am now possess'd of, and which was formerly left me by my mother. **1712** Addison *Spect.* No. 275 ¶5 Ribbons, Lace and Embroidery, wrought together in a most curious Piece of Network. **1781** E. Darwin *Bot. Gard., Econ. Veget.* iii. 556 So shoot the Spider-broods at breezy dawn, Their glittering net-work o'er the autumnal lawn. **1849** James *Woodman* ix, A light coif of network confined.. the rich glossy curling hair. **1881** *Truth* 19 May 686/2 The train was of cerise satin and gold network.

transf. **1816** Shelley *Alastor* 446 The woven leaves Make net-work of the dark blue light of day. **1837** Whewell *Hist. Induct. Sci.* (1857) I. 135 A sort of band of net-work running round the middle of the sky.

2. a. (With *a* and *pl.*) A piece of work having the form or construction of a net; a collection or arrangement (of some thing or things) resembling a net.

1590 Spenser *Muiopot.* 368 With this so curious networke [a spider's web] to compare. **1611** Bible *Isa.* xix. 9 They that weaue net-works shall be confounded. **1748** *Anson's Voy.* iii. viii. 380 The galeon.. was.. provided against boarding ..by a strong net-work of two inch rope. **1814** *Chron.* in *Ann. Reg.* 70/1 The fastening which secures the net-work and the valve at the top of the Balloon. **1849** Willmott *Jrnl. Summer-time* 19 July, A paper network is where a fire ought to be. **1881** *Truth* 19 May 686/2 The bodice is covered with a network of pearls.

b. *transf.* Of structures in animals or plants.

1658 Sir T. Browne *Gard. Cyrus* iii. 55 This Reticulate or Net-work was also considerable in the inward parts of man. *a* **1729** Blackmore (J.), This curious and wonderful net-work of veins. **1783** Justamond tr. *Raynal's Hist. Ind.* V. 188 A mucous substance, which forms a kind of network between the epidermis and the skin. **1830** R. Knox *Béclard's Anat.* 214 Net-works which form in a great measure the serous.. membranes. **1884** Bower & Scott *De Bary's Phaner.* 250 After entering the skin they pass over into a network of bundles.

c. A complex collection or system *of* rivers, canals, railways, or the like. Also without *of.*

1839 Thirlwall *Greece* xlvii. VI. 110 The island, or net-work of islands, formed by the Danube. **1857** Livingstone *Trav.* x. 199 The flat prairies between the net-work of waters. **1869** *Bradshaw's Railway Manual* XXI. 346 The Antwerp and Rotterdam, in conjunction with the East Belgian and the Sambre and Meuse, is now worked under the title of the Great Central Belgian. The network thus constituted comprises 310 miles. *Ibid.* 348 The concessions accorded by a new convention.. may be said to constitute a seventh great French network. *Ibid.* 366 The guarantee of interest given by the State on the new network capital. **1871** Freeman *Hist. Ess.* Ser. i. viii. 233 The Northmen.. had surrounded their whole camp with a net-work of trenches. **1890** A. Hill tr. *Obersteiner's Anat. Cent. Nervous Organs* 161 The richer the network of rails the more numerous are the connections, the 'tracts' between the two chief termini. **1937** *Discovery* May 163/2 Few people realise how vast is the network of airlines which now links up the United States with Central and South America. **1950** *Britannica Bk. of Year* 682/2 *Network*, any system of related but not necessarily interconnected units; *e.g.*, a network of naval bases. **1966** G. F. Allen *British Rail after Beeching* viii. 243 Each Region drafted a scheme to.. thin out its depots to a network sited so that they could be economically served by feeder services direct from a yard handling long-distance trains.

d. *fig.* An interconnected chain or system of immaterial things. Also *attrib.* Also, a representation of interconnected events, processes, etc., used in the study of work efficiency. Hence **networking** *sb.*

1816 Coleridge *Lay Serm.* (Bohn) 373 The arterial or nerve-like net-work of property. **1856** Emerson *Eng. Traits, Ability* Wks. (Bohn) II. 43 Their law is a network of fictions. **1876** Freeman *Norm. Conq.* V. xxiv. 381 A network of feudal tenures is thus spread over the whole land. **1959** S. Beer *Cybernetics & Management* xi. 95 Each of the dots in the network represents some binary situation. **1964** K. G. Lockyer *Introd. Critical Path Analysis* i. 4 This could then be simplified to the diagram (now known as a network). **1964** A. Battersby *Network Analysis* ii. 13 It is not the purpose of this book to discuss such methods of charting in detail.. but rather to point out why their inadequacies have made necessary a new method of charting: arrow diagrams, otherwise known as networks. **1966** S. Beer *Decision & Control* ix. 191 Naturally, the critical path through a converging network can be discovered under any criterion or balance of criteria. **1966** *Economist* 3 Dec. 1042/2 If one wanted to work out what was involved in doing something, an engineer would use a bar chart. (The 'hard way' in our charts showing the networking of a cup of tea.) **1967** S. Woodgate in Wills & Yearsley *Handbk. Management Technol.* v. 73 Network planning techniques first came into general use in 1957. *Ibid.* 74 Since 1957 hundreds of variations of network planning systems have proliferated and many of these variations have perished while undergoing the supreme test of operational effectiveness. *Ibid.* 98 *Network*, a schematic representation of events and activities which shows their inter-relationships. **1968** *Listener* 4 July 13/2 They propose.. a 'network' system which would allow variety and versatility to be developed. **1970** O. Dopping *Computers & Data Processing* xxii. 345 Network planning helps to reveal all the possibilities for parallel operations, identify critical activities, and follow up the job... A network is built up of the different *activities* which constitute the project. **1970** *Canadian Jrnl. Linguistics* XV. 103 Once we express a grammar in terms of a relational network, intermediate symbols become completely superfluous. *Ibid.* 108 One can organize types of grammar in a two-by-two table. There are rewrite grammars and network grammars.

e. A system of cables for the distribution of electricity to consumers; *spec.* one in which interconnections are such that each consumer is supplied by more than one route; hence, any system of interconnected electrical conductors or components, sometimes including a source of e.m.f., that provides more than one path for the current between any two points.

1883 *Jrnl. Soc. Telegr.-Engineers & Electricians* XII. 551 (*heading*) On a method of calculating the total horsepower expended in a network of conductors (such, for instance, as a system of street mains). **1914** J. W. Meares *Electr. Engin. in India* iii. 47 The terms 'network' and 'distributor' are also applied to any system of distributing mains. **1930** Dannatt & Dalgleish *Electr. Power Transmission & Interconnection* v. 110 Any network can be divided into conducting polygons or meshes. **1940** *Proc. IRE* XXVIII. 415/1 Figs. 3 and 4 represent mathematically identical networks, even though they refer to physically different systems. **1962** *Newnes Conc. Encycl. Electr. Engin.* 201/1 Distribution systems can be classified into the following basic categories: (*a*) Radial system. (*b*) Ring system: (i) h.v. feeders ring. (ii) l.v. distribution ring. (*c*) Network system. **1966** *McGraw-Hill Encycl. Sci. & Technol.* IX. 72/1 A network may be solved when it is possible to set up a number of independent equations equal to the number of unknown quantities.

f. A broadcasting system, consisting of a series of transmitters capable of being linked together to carry the same programme; also, in a more general sense: a nation-wide broadcasting company; the broadcasting companies as a whole. Also *attrib.*

1914 W. A. Du Puy *Uncle Sam's Modern Miracles* 170 This great network of stations may not merely hurl forth its messages. **1933** *B.B.C. Year Bk.* 37 In step with the gradual nationalisation of the network, local autonomy has declined. **1941** *B.B.C. Gloss. of Broadcasting Terms* 20 *Network cue*, cue consisting of a standardized phrase which constitutes a signal for the performance of technical operations at switching centres and transmitting stations forming part of a network. **1956** *Newsweek* 7 May 59 On its three wholly owned TV stations, exclusive of network operations, CBS reported a total net investment as of Dec. 31, 1953, of $3.322.023. **1957** *Listener* 21 Nov. 853/3 His hour-by-hour account of what the networks were saying. **1961** *Washington Post* 17 Feb. A14 The Columbia Broadcasting System's handling of its excellent TV show 'The Spy Next Door' on Wednesday night at 10 is a good illustration of what is amiss with network television. **1966** *Publ. Amer. Dial. Soc.* xlii. 46 A Southern rustic's imitation of 'network' pronunciation. **1969** *New Statesman* 11 Apr. 506/1 If there were 100 commercial stations.. on the air all day they would either have to negotiate.. or have back-up programmes from some central concern— virtually a network outfit. **1970** *New Yorker* 28 Feb. 29/2 The more general avoidance of controversial issues which has been noticeable among politicians and on the networks and in the press. **1972** *Daily Tel.* 14 Aug. 7/6 The plans for Radios 1 and 2 are designed to put the networks into an impregnable position when the commercial companies start. **1972** *Sci. Amer.* Sept. 117/1 The radio and television broadcasting networks provide the people of the world with on-the-spot news reports, entertainment and educational programs through a billion radio and television receivers. **1972** J. L. Dillard *Black English* vi. 261 Many a preacher of this type [*sc.* 'storefront'] presents a better performance on Sunday than is ever to be seen on network television.

g. A structure proposed for glass in which the non-oxygen atoms (usu. silicon) are joined together in a three-dimensional array by oxygen atoms.

1932 W. H. Zachariasen in *Jrnl. Amer. Chem. Soc.* LIV. 3842 As in crystals, the atoms in glasses must form extended three dimensional networks. **1947** *Jrnl. Soc. Glass Technol.* XXXI. 117 A quantitative factor may be deduced which is ..an indication of the extent to which these atoms may be expected to take part in the glass network. **1971** *Oxidation of Metals & Alloys* (Amer. Soc. for Metals) 42 Oxides of the form.. M_2O_3 can form a network if the oxygens form triangles around each metal atom.

h. An interconnected group of people; an organization. Also *attrib.*

1947 *Science News* IV. 37 He [*sc.* the habitual criminal].. is matching his brain and slender resources against all the might of a vast police network with infinite resource. **1954** [see girl *sb.* 2a]. **1957** E. Bott *Family & Social Network* iii. 62 Intermediate degrees of conjugal role-segregation and network-connectedness. *Ibid.* 92 Although the networks of husband and wife are distinct, it is very likely, even at the time of marriage, that there will be over-lapping between them. **1960** *Analog Science Fact/Fiction* Dec. 68/1 As long as they're allowed to think they haven't been spotted, they may lead the way to other spies or spy net-works. **1960** L. Pincus *Marriage* i. 15 Supports and satisfactions.. normally provided by participation in.. social and kinship networks are sought, and often not found, within the resources of marriage. **1972** *Daily Tel.* 19 June 2/1, I was paid.. about £500 for infiltrating the IRA network in London. **1973** *Times* 15 Aug. 21/7 'Multinational organizations are becoming increasingly integrated..', especially in the case of 'network' companies having subsidiaries in many countries. **1974** 'J. Le Carré' *Tinker, Tailor* xxii. 196 Moscow.. was busy denouncing him for blowing the San Francisco network.

3. Used as a name for plants (see quots.).

1841 *Penny Cycl.* XXI. 156/2 The *Dictyoleæ*, or sea-net-works,.. are characterised by the beautifully reticulated texture of the integument. **1897** *Jrnl. R. Agric. Soc.* Dec. 617 One [water-weed] known locally as network or silkwort, on account of its thread-like stems.

4. *attrib.* or as *adj.* Made of network; arranged in the fashion of network.

1601 Holland *Pliny* xix. i. II. 3 The net-worke Habergeon or Curet of Amasis. **1658** Sir T. Browne (*title*) The Garden of Cyrus, or the Quincunciall, Lozenge, or Net-work Plantations of the Ancients. **1747** Johnson (*title*) To Miss.. on her giving the Authour a Gold and Silk Net-work Purse, of her own weaving. **1796** Withering *Brit. Plants* (ed. 3) I. 390 Seeds entangled in.. network membranes. **1898** *Daily News* 19 Oct. 5/7 One of the network racks of a first-class compartment.

†**b.** *fig.* Complicated, involved. *Obs. rare*$^{-1}$.

1675 Baxter *Cath. Theol.* ii. i. 255 You will have more solid.. truth.. than.. such Writers do teach you in their learned Net-work treatises.

5. *attrib.* and *Comb.*, as **network analyser**, an assembly of inductors, capacitors, and resistors used to model an electrical network and facilitate its analysis; **network analysis**, (*a*) *Electr.*, calculation of the currents flowing in the various meshes of a network; (*b*) *Work Study* (see quot. 1968; cf. sense 2d above); **network former**, (a substance containing) an atom which can become part of the network of a glass; so **network-forming** *a.*; **network modifier**, (a substance containing) a metal ion which can occupy an interstice in the network of a glass; so **network-modifying** *a.*; **network structure** *Metallurgy*, the structure of an alloy in which one component forms a continuous network around the grains of the other component; **network theorem**, any of various theorems about the currents and voltages in an electrical network that can be used to determine their values in any particular case.

1930 H. L. Hazen et al. in *Trans. Amer. Inst. Electr. Engin.* XLIX. 1102/1 The following paper deals with an improved form of network-computing device... The Network Analyzer, as this device is called, is installed in the Electrical Engineering Research Laboratory. **1945** *Physical Rev.* LXVII. 48/1 The tests reported here.. indicate that it is practical to use for this purpose [*sc.* determining eigenvalues and eigenfunctions of the Schrödinger equation] existing a.c. network analyzers. **1974** *Encycl. Brit. Macropædia* VI. 625/2 Since World War II, digital computers have largely replaced network analyzers. **1930** *Trans. Amer. Inst. Electr. Engin.* XLIX. 1102/1 Several types of experimental computing devices or miniature systems for network analysis have been developed. **1945** H. W. Bode *Network Analysis & Feedback Amplifier Design* xvi. 360 Expressions having the mathematical form of a reflection coefficient appear frequently in network analysis. **1962** *Operations Res.* X. 728 Network analysis—also known as PERT (program evaluation and review technique), PEP (program evaluation procedure), CPM (critical-path method), CPS (critical path scheduling), and arrow diagramming—for the planning and control of research and industrial projects and programs has been the subject of many published articles. **1966** *Economist* 3 Dec. 1043/1 The Post Office Savings Bank has made massive use of network analysis to control its move to Glasgow. **1968** *Gloss. Terms Project Network Analysis (B.S.I.)* 5 *Project network analysis*, a group of techniques for presenting information to assist the planning and controlling of projects. The information, usually represented by a network, includes the sequence and logical interrelationships of all project activities. **1969** *Power System Protection* (Electr. Council) I. iii. 201 Network analysis by manual computation may involve a very considerable amount of labour. **1973** A. Parrish *Mech. Engineers' Ref. Bk.* xx. 73 Network analysis is a general term which is used to embrace a whole series of similar planning methods dealing with project control. **1947** *Jrnl. Soc. Glass Technol.* XXXI. 114 For some years it has been customary to classify the various constituents of glass into network formers, such as SiO_2 and B_2O_3; intermediates..; and modifiers. **1966** C. R. Tottle *Sci. Engin. Materials* iii. 83 Aluminium occurs in the natural glass obsidian, as a network former, in the proportion of one aluminium to five silicon ions, with sodium and potassium to modify the network. **1950** Kirk & Othmer *Encycl. Chem. Technol.* V. 723 Oxygen ratio is defined as the total number of oxygen ions to the total number of network-forming ions. **1971** Fehlner & Mott in *Oxidation of Metals & Alloys* (Amer. Soc. for Metals) 43 Ionic transport by anions is expected in network-forming oxides. **1961** *Progress Ceramic Sci.* I. 7

Systematic measurement of elastic properties of glasses, containing various proportions of the single network former SiO_2, and a single univalent network modifier, would be of great value in assessing the role of the network former in determining theoretical strength. **1971** *Materials & Technol.* II. vi. 335 Aluminium, when in tetrahedral coordination.. is undoubtedly a network former, and when in octahedral configuration it is a network modifier. **1950** KIRK & OTHMER *Encycl. Chem. Technol.* V. 732 The 'holes' between these tetrahedral groups are considered to be occupied by the network-modifying ions. **1966** C. R. TOTTLE *Sci. Engin. Materials* iii. 83 Healing glass containing metallic ions that are network-modifying tends to move them into positions that are network-forming and so varies the colour. **1939** E. C. ROLLASON *Metall. for Engin.* vii. 101 If sufficient time is allowed for the diffusion phenomena all the ferrite is precipitated, whilst the pearlite occupies the centre forming a network structure. **1940** E. J. TEICHERT *Ferrous Metallurgy* III. xiv. 317 Slow cooling will induce the Widmanstatten and rapid cooling will promote the network structure. **1965** A. D. MERRIMAN *Concise Encycl. Metall.* 594 When the structure of an alloy is such that one constituent occurs partly or completely surrounding the crystals of another constituent, then the appearance of an etched section taken across the grains shows as a network structure. **1930** DANNATT & DALGLEISH *Electr. Power Transmission & Interconnection* vii. 220 (*heading*) Network theorems. **1966** *McGraw-Hill Encycl. Sci. & Technol.* IX. 75/2 In the solution of specific problems, much time can often be saved by making use of special methods or relations, known as network theorems.

network ('nɛtwɜːk), *v.* [f. the sb.] **a.** To cover with a network.

1887 *Courier-Jrnl.* (Louisville, Kentucky) 24 Jan. 8/1 It is only a question of time when railroads will net-work the Pan-handle. **1914** *Cycl. Amer. Govt.* III. 139/1 Whole regions are networked, and one can go by trolley car from the Atlantic to the Middle West. **1928** E. WRIGHT *Great Horn Spoon* xviii. 217 Gourds and several varieties of squashes networked the compound with their vines.

b. To broadcast simultaneously over a network of radio or television stations.

1940 [implied in *networking* vbl. sb. below]. **1952** *Sun* (Baltimore) 12 Feb. 14/3 Matthews beat Murphy in a bout networked out of Madison Square Garden. **1957** *Times* 28 Aug. (Radio & Television Suppl.) p. iii/3 This practice of networking the major items will continue. **1958** *Observer* 21 Sept. 16/6 The first sample of *This Wonderful World* to be networked in England came up to high expectation. **1968** *Times* 13 Nov. 1 (Advt.), Early in 1969 Thames Television are networking twelve one hour documentaries about one man. **1973** *Times* 8 Jan. 3/2 His series on the castles of Wales is being networked.

c. To link (computers) together to make possible one or more of several functions, as the transfer of data, the sharing of processing capability or workloads, and accessibility from many locations.

1972 [implied at NETWORKING *vbl. sb.* below]. **1982** *Which Computer?* June 64/1, 16-bit systems.. capable of supporting up to 16 processors which can be networked together to allow up to 256 simultaneous users. **1983** *Austral. Microcomputer Mag.* Sept. 51/1 Personal computers will be heavily networked. **1984** E. P. DEGARMO et al. *Materials & Processes in Manuf.* (ed. 6) xxxviii. 942 The microcomputers of the CNC machine tools are networked together. **1985** *Personal Computer World* Feb. 5 (Advt.), We specialise in networking your IBM PC's and Apricots together using manufacturers' related products.

Hence **'networked** *ppl. a.*; **'networking** *vbl. sb.* and *ppl. a.*

1940 PORTERFIELD & REYNOLDS *We present Television* iv. 149 Television, now that a practicable means of networking has been developed, has been supplied with the final implement necessary for the creation of what will eventually be a nation-wide service. **1956** *Newsweek* 7 May 59 The television networking business is a complicated and delicate business. **1962** *Rep. Comm. Broadcasting 1960* 159 in *Parl. Papers 1961–2* (Cmnd. 1753) IX. 259 They must.. use an old recorded networked programme. **1968** *Listener* 8 Aug. 187/1 The new companies.. operate within a networking system still dominated by Granada, ATV and Thames. **1970** *New Statesman* 4 Sept. 281/3 A small [television] company can rely on getting full networking for just about four programmes a year... This figure of about four hours' worth of fully networked television time ought to be placed beside.. the fact that STV is obliged.. to do nine hours' output of its own every week. **1971** *Writing for B.B.C.* 65 Scotland contributes to all the networked series described under the 'Drama' heading... Plays intended for networking.. should not be so Scottish that they cannot be readily understood by listeners in the other parts of the British Isles. **1972** *Computers & Humanities* VII. 96 The potential contribution of computer networking to research and education. **1974** *Telecommunications* VIII. 37/2 The markets for both stand-alone computers and networked computers will grow. **1978** *New Scientist* 7 Sept. 669 Networking also means that particular jobs can be run on special machines rather than many machines handling all types of jobs which is inefficient. *Ibid.* It would be sensible to build networked systems enabling expensive machines to serve a large number of users. **1982** *Financial Times* 18 Jan. (Survey: Computers) p. ix/4 The future trend in computing is towards networked systems, which will link together a wide variety of information-processing equipment. **1985** *Personal Computer World* Feb. 192/2 Local area networking involves the transmission of data.. between participating nodes on the network. **1985** *Acorn User* Feb. 21/3 Meadnet is a low-cost networking system which allows up to 16 BBC micros to share disc drives and printer.

netyl(le, obs. forms of NETTLE *sb.*[1]

neu, obs. f. NEW.

Neuchâtel (nøʃatɛl). The name of a town and a canton in western Switzerland, used *attrib.* or *absol.* to designate the white wine, or the less common red one, made there.

1903 S. WEYMAN *Long Night* i. 8 The landlord.. vanished, to return.. with four tall glasses and a flask of Neuchatel. **1967** A. LICHINE *Encycl. Wines & Spirits* 516/1 The Neuchâtel white wines, grown in a chalky soil, are light and sprightly. *Ibid.* 516/2 Neuchâtel is the most widely exported wine of Switzerland. **1969** N. DENNY tr. *Veraldi's Spies of Good Intent* viii. 114 My brother's a wine-grower and he keeps the best of his Neutchatel [*sic*] for me.

neuck, dial. f. NOOK.

neue, var. NEVE; obs. f. NEW *a.*, NIEVE *sb.*

neueling: see NEVELING.

neuen, var. NEVEN *v.*

neuent, obs. var. NINTH.

neuer(e, obs. ff. NEVER.

‖**Neue Sachlichkeit** ('nɔɪə 'zaxlɪçkaɪt). [G., 'new objectivity'.] A movement in the fine arts, music, and literature, which developed in Germany during the 1920s and was characterized by realism and a deliberate rejection of romantic attitudes.

1929 G. F. HARTLAUB *Let.* 8 July in *Arts* (1931) XVII. 237 The expression *Neue Sachlichkeit* was in fact coined by me in the year 1924. A year later came the Mannheim exhibition which bore the same name. The expression ought really to apply as a label to the new realism bearing a socialistic flavor. **1938** C. FULLMAN tr. *Thoene's Modern German Art* 87 The new group.. wanted super-concrete precision; after the elimination of objects, journalistic reporting of time and place. This was the starting-point for German *vérisme*, the 'Neue Sachlichkeit', and the art of such men as Max Beckmann, Otto Dix, George Grosz and their like. **1950** B. S. MYERS *Modern Art in Making* xix. 351 There appeared a movement since classified as *Neue Sachlichkeit*, or New Objectivity, begun in 1920 by Otto Dix and George Grosz. **1954** *Grove's Dict. Mus.* VI. 53/1 *Neue Sachlichkeit*.., a term that came into fashion in Germany between the two world wars. It describes a tendency in some composers of that time to write music entirely detached from sentiment and free from any pictorial suggestion. **1959** J. WILLETT *Theatre of Bertolt Brecht* vii. 194 A deliberately impersonal quality marks much of the art of that time [*sc.* the late 1920s], as the words 'Neue Sachlichkeit' themselves imply. **1964** *Listener* 17 Sept. 445/1 After its first performance in 1923..[Hindemith's] *Marienleben* was hailed as a shining example of *Neue Sachlichkeit*, a new matter-of-fact contrapuntal style then emerging, which represented a conscious reaction against the hyper-romantic attitude prevalent earlier this century. **1970** *Oxf. Compan. Art* 772/2 *Neue Sachlichkeit*, a movement in German art and literature that arose in the mid 1920s. It represented a sharp reaction against experimental and idealistic art of any sort. .. Artists strove for an 'honest objectivity' (Sachlichkeit), depicting with matter-of-fact literalness their everyday experience.

neueu(e, -ew(e, obs. ff. NEPHEW.

†**neuf**[1]. *Her. Obs. rare.* [a. OF. *neuf*, var. of *neu*, *nou* (later *noud*, mod. *nœud*):—L. *nod-um*, *nodus* knot.] A sword-knot.

1562 LEIGH *Armorie* 160 b, He beareth Gueules iii arming Swordes argent, hiltes and pomills Or, the neufes Sable. **1586** FERNE *Blaz. Gentrie* 222 Two swordes trauersed barre-wayes, Argent: hilts, pomels and neufes, Or. **1688** HOLME *Armoury* III. xviii. (Roxb.) 125/2 Parts and appurtenances belonging to a sword and belt... The Neufes.

†**neuf**[2], erron. form of *neaf*, NIEVE, fist.

1601 B. JONSON *Poetaster* III. iv, Reach mee thy neufe. Do'st heare? **1625** ROWLEY, etc. *Witch Edmonton* III. i, Oh, sweet ningle, thy neufe once again.

Neufchâtel (nøʃatɛl). The name of a small town in Normandy, NE. of Rouen, used *attrib.* or *absol.* to designate the soft, white cheese originally made there.

c **1865** E. C. GASKELL *Let.* 6 Oct. (1966) 778 Lunch.. chocolate, cold meat, bread & butter Neufchatel Cheese & grapes. **1902** [see BONDON]. **1951** *Good Housek. Home Encycl.* 568/2 *Neufchâtel Cheese*, a soft whole-milk cheese prepared in Normandy and other parts of France. **1966** P. V. PRICE *France: Food & Wine Guide* 283 *Neufchâtel*, the name of the best cheese produced in the Pays de Bray. It may be eaten when it has only been kept for a few days, in which case it is creamy, soft and mild..; if allowed to ferment and ripen it.. is fairly strong.

†**neuft,** obs. variant of NEWT.

Cf. *ewftes* in Spenser *F.Q.* v. x. 23.

1601 B. JONSON *Poetaster* IV. iii, Sting him my little neufts: I'le give you instructions. **1614** —— *Barth. Fair* II. iii, What? thou'lt poyson mee with a neuft in a bottle of Ale, will't thou?

neuie, obs. var. NEPHEW.

neuin, var. of NEVEN *v.*

neuir, obs. f. NEVER.

neuis, obs. pl. of NIEVE, fist.

neuk, Sc. f. NOOK.

†**ne ultra,** obs. variant of NE PLUS ULTRA.

1646 G. DANIEL *Poems* (Grossart) I. 102 As though another Hercules had plac'd Witt's great *Ne vltra*, never to be pass'd. **1676** GLANVILL *Ess. Philos. & Relig.* III. 1 It is presumed that their Books are the *Ne Ultra's* of Learning.

neulyngis, obs. form of NEWLINGS *adv.*

‖**neuma** ('njuːmə). *Mus.* Pl. 'neumata, 'neumæ. [med.L.] = NEUME.

1776 HAWKINS *Hist. Music* I. 345 Neuma.. signifies an aggregation of as many sounds as may be uttered in one single respiration. **1782** BURNEY *Hist. Music* II. 172 The Neuma or recapitulation of a chant at the end of an anthem. **1848** MÜLLER tr. *Kiesewetter's Hist. Mus.* 281 In choral chants by Neuma is understood a melodious phrase at the end of verse. *Ibid.* 380 The Neumata, in which the oldest Chant-books of the Latin Church now extant are noted, consist of points, little hooks, strokes, and flourishes, in different shapes and directions. **1880** *Grove's Dict. Mus.* II. 468/1 The Neumæ did.. shew at a glance the general conformation of the Melody they were supposed to illustrate. **1886** ROCKSTRO *Hist. Music* 31 Every Neuma placed upon the red line was understood to represent the note F.

attrib. **1879** RITTER *Hist. Music* (1880) 33 The oldest neumæ manuscripts do not reach farther back than the end of the 8th century.

Neumann ('nɔɪman). The name of Johann G. *Neumann*, 19th-cent. Austrian geologist (?), used *attrib.* to designate narrow bands, lines, or lamellæ parallel to crystallographic planes which are seen in α-iron (ferrite) subjected to a sudden shock, and are usu. attributed to twinning (investigated by Neumann *c* 1848).

1886 *Proc. Amer. Acad. Arts & Sci.* XXI. 498 On different sections of meteorites Widmanstättian figures and Neumann lines can be exhibited in every gradation, from the broadest bands to the finest markings. **1914** *Jrnl. Soc. Chem. Industry* 15 Aug. 791/2 The Neumann lamellæ occurring in any given grain are parallel to not more than 6 planes corresponding to the crystalline orientation of the grain itself. **1922** *Chem. Abstr.* XVI. 3845 (*heading*) Neumann bands as evidence of action of explosives upon metal. **1946** *Jrnl. Iron & Steel Inst.* CLIV. 129P/1 The Neumann band is primarily a shearing or faulting movement operating along the pre-existent planar disjunctions of the mosaic structure, and.. as a secondary operation twinning may be completed, as is known to be possible in ferrite. **1966** C. R. TOTTLE *Sci. Engin. Materials* iii. 64 In alpha iron (b.c.c.) impact loading at room temperature can produce shear twins, called Neumann bands (which are found, incidentally, in metallic meteorites).

neu'matic, *a. Mus.* [ad. med.L. *neumatic-us*, f. *neuma*: see NEUMA.] Of the nature of neumes.

1890 in *Cent. Dict.* **1897** *Dublin Rev.* Oct. 335 The great difficulty which the uncertainty of the neumatic signs presented in rendering the chant.

'neumatize, *v. Mus. rare*[−1]. [ad. med.L. *neumatizāre*.] *trans.* To provide with neumes.

1776 HAWKINS *Hist. Mus.* I. 345 He dictated or pointed, and actually neumatized the muscial cantus both to the antiphonary and gradual.

neume, neum (njuːm). *Mus.* Also 5 **newme, nevme.** [a. F. *neume* (14th c.), ad. med.L. *neuma*, *neupma* (neut. and fem.), NEUMA, ad. Gr. πνεῦμα breath: see PNEUM, PNEUMA.]

1. In plainsong, a prolonged phrase or group of notes sung to a single syllable, esp. at the end of a melody.

c **1440** *Promp. Parv.* 354/1 Newme of a songe [*H.* nevme], *neupma*. **1879** HELMORE *Plainsong* i. 3 Neumes, *i.e.* certain rhythmical expansions of the melodies, occur on the stronger accents of the poetry. **1884** *Catholic Dict.* (1897) 720/1 Sometimes these *neumes* or breathings are hung to the last syllable. *Ibid.* 721/2 The descending series of short notes, called passing notes, which bind together the different limbs of the prolonged breathings or *neumes*.

2. One of a set of signs employed in the earliest plainsong notation to indicate the melody.

1843–5 WESTWOOD *Palæogr. Sacra* s.v. *Lombardic MSS.*, Here the simple neume consists of short oblong dash; but sometimes it is merely a round dot. **1874** CHAPPELL *Hist. Mus.* I. 382 Neumes did not originally designate any definite notes or pitch, because musical intervals were not required in recitation. **1897** *Dublin Rev.* Oct. 334 From the eighth to the eleventh centuries the chant was noted by means of certain signs called neums. *Ibid.* 339 The chant is written in neum-accents.

Hence **'neumic** *a.*, neumatic. (*Cent. Dict.* 1890.)

neuo(u, neuow, obs. forms of NEPHEW.

neur-, var. of NEURO-, employed before vowels (and *h*), as in **neurady'namia**, nervous debility, neurasthenia; **neurady'namic** *a.*, of or pertaining to, of the nature of, suffering from, neurasthenia (Mayne 1856). **neu'ranal** *a.*, pertaining to the neural system together with the anus or outlet. **neurar'thropathy**, disease of the joints in which the nerves are affected. **neu'raxial** *a.*, pertaining to the neuraxis. **neu'raxis**, the nervous axis of the body; the brain and spinal column. **neu'raxon**, a process given off from a cell-body (neuron). **neu'rectasy**, stretching of a nerve. **neurhyp'nology** (see NEURYPNOLOGY). **neur'hypnotist**, one who practises neurypnology.

Also in various other pathological or anatomical terms, as *neuragmia*, *-arteria*, *-ataxia*, *-ectopy*, *-empodism*, etc.: see Mayne *Expos. Lex.* and the *Syd. Soc. Lex.*

1888 *Encycl. Brit.* XXIV. 184/1 A current of water which escaped by the *neuranal canal (as in larval *Amphioxus*).

1897 *Allbutt's Syst. Med.* III. 73 The word *neur-arthropathy conveniently represents this class of arthritic cases. **1889** *Buck's Handbk. Med. Sci.* VIII. 108 The impossibility of determining the exact limits of these two *neuraxial regions. **1899** *Allbutt's Syst. Med.* VI. 512 The.. unaltered continuity of the primitive fibrils of the *neuraxon across the 'cell body'. **1883** J. MARSHALL (*title*) On Nerve-Stretching or *Neurectasy for the Relief of Pain. *a* **1876** M. COLLINS *Pen Sketches* (1879) II. 182 That peculiar idiosyncrasy which gives us our mediums, and mesmerists, and *neurhypnotists.

'neurad, *adv.* [f. NEUR-AL + *-ad*: see DEXTRAD.] Towards the neural axis or aspect of the body. (Opposed to *hæmad*).

1890 in *Cent. Dict.*

neural ('njʊərəl), *a.* [f. Gr. νεῦρ-ον nerve + -AL[1].]

1. *Anat.* Pertaining or relating to, connected with, the nerves; *spec.* pertaining to the cerebrospinal or central nervous system of vertebrates (as opposed to *hæmal*). Freq. in ***neural arch, canal, cavity, spine, tube***, etc.

1839–47 T. R. JONES in *Todd's Cycl. Anat.* III. 825/2 The caudal vertebræ of the Fish.. have the neurapophyses and neural spine as well as the hæmapophyses and hæmal spine. **1849** H. MILLER *Footpr. Creat.* viii. (1874) 147 The bodies of the vertebræ, with their neural and hæmal processes. **1888** ROLLESTON & JACKSON *Anim. Life* 438 The tube represents an aperture left when the neural plate folds over in development to form the neural tube.

b. Situated on, or inclining to, that side of the body in which the central nervous axis lies.

1861 J. R. GREENE *Man. Anim. Kingd., Cœlent.* 18 There is no distinction between neural and hæmal regions. **1870** ROLLESTON *Anim. Life* p. xxxi, In Invertebrata the motor organs are developed upon the neural aspect of their bodies.

2. *Phys.* Relating to, or occurring in, the nerves as organs which convey sensation or impulse.

1864 SPENCER *Princ. Biol.* 50 Neural discharges that follow the direct incidence of external forces. **1899** *Allbutt's Syst. Med.* VI. 492 The more elaborate the dendritic expansions, the more elaborate the psychic or neural activity.

3. *Path.* Involving or affecting the nerve-tissues or nervous system; nervous.

1883 *Harper's Mag.* Nov. 901/2 The eminent authority on neural disorders. **1897** *Allbutt's Syst. Med.* III. 73 Neural arthritis comprises all joint diseases which are the sequel of central or peripheral nerve-lesions.

neuralgia (njʊ'rældʒɪə). *Path.* [a. mod.L. *neuralgia*, f. Gr. νεῦρον nerve + ἄλγος pain. Cf. F. *névralgie* (1801).] An affection of one or more nerves (esp. of the head or face), causing pain which is usually of an intermittent but frequently intense character; an instance of this, a neuralgic pain.

1822–34 *Good's Study Med.* (ed. 4) III. 217 The term neuralgia has of late been employed by various nosologists to express this group of diseases. **1840** *Penny Cycl.* XVI. 164/2 Neuralgia.. may be called a modern disease, as the first distinct description of it that we possess is that published by André, a surgeon of Versailles, in 1756. **1873** MISS BROUGHTON *Nancy* III. 80 Mother's neuralgia is very bad, and she is sadly in want of change. **1884** H. M. JONES *Health of Senses* v. 132 The neuro-mimetic, with.. fits, neuralgias, aches in every part of the body.

attrib. **1897** *Allbutt's Syst. Med.* IV. 762 The sensory throat neuroses of the climacteric period.. may be classed under two headings, 'paræsthesia' and 'neuralgia' cases.

Hence **neu'ralgiac**, one affected by, or suffering from, neuralgia.

1897 *Allbutt's Syst. Med.* III. 482 The risk of permitting any of these abdominal neuralgiacs themselves to get hold of opium in any of its forms.

neuralgic (njʊ'rældʒɪk), *a.* *Path.* [f. prec. + -IC. Cf. F. *névralgique* (1801).] Of the nature of, characterized or caused by, affected with, neuralgia.

1834 *Cycl. Pract. Med.* III. 167/2 The absence of heat, swelling, redness.. make it merit the epithet neuralgic. **1861** DICKENS *Lett.* (1880) II. 142 Neuralgic pains in the face have troubled me a good deal. **1875** H. C. WOOD *Therap.* (1879) 42 In simple neuralgic gastric pain.. bismuth is often of great service.

neurally ('njʊərəlɪ), *adv.* [f. NEURAL *a.* + -LY[2].]

a. By a nerve or nerves.

1902 W. JAMES *Var. Relig. Exper.* p. vii, All states of mind are neurally conditioned. **1974** *Nature* 13 Dec. 591/2 Neurally-evoked responses.

b. As regards one's 'nerves'.

1936 L. C. DOUGLAS *White Banners* vi. 141 He was too far spent, neurally, to offer any resistance.

neuraminic (njʊərə'mɪnɪk), *a.* *Chem.* [tr. G. *neuraminsäure* neuraminic acid (E. Klenk 1941, in *Zeitschr. f. physiol. Chem.* CCLXVIII. 51): see NEUR-, AMINE and -IC.] ***neuraminic acid***: a crystalline carboxylic acid, $HOOC{\cdot}CO{\cdot}CH_2{\cdot}CHOH{\cdot}CHNH_2{\cdot}(CHOH)_3{\cdot}CH_2OH$ (or a cyclic form of this), acyl derivatives of which are the sialic acids.

1942 *Chem. Abstr.* XXXVI. 3204 (*heading*) Neuraminic acid, the cleavage product of a new brain lipoid. **1956** *Nature* 17 Mar. 524/2 Klenk *et al.* have also investigated the amount of ganglioside in human brain by determining the content of neuraminic acid. **1966** *McGraw-Hill Encycl. Sci. & Technol.* II. 12/1 Neuraminic acid, an important constituent of carbohydrate-protein complexes of animal cells and tissues, has been reported in polymeric form in cultures of *Escherichia coli.*

Hence **neu'raminate**, a salt or ester of neuraminic acid.

1970 R. W. MCGILVERY *Biochemistry* xxiv. 585 Part of the neuraminates contain an additional 4-O-acetyl group.

neuraminidase (njʊərə'mɪnɪdeɪz, -s). *Biochem.* [f. NEURAMIN(IC *a.* + -ID[4] + -ASE.] (See quot. 1957.)

1957 A. GOTTSCHALK in *Biochim. & Biophys. Acta* XXIII. 646 We propose the name 'neuraminidase' for the enzyme and define its action as the hydrolytic cleavage of the glycosidic bond joining the keto group of neuraminic acid to D-galactose or D-galactosamine and possibly to other sugars. **1960** —— in P. D. Boyer et al. *Enzymes* (ed. 2) IV. xxvii. 472 The wide distribution of neuraminidase among microorganisms inhabiting the respiratory and intestinal tracts would suggest that the enzyme has been evolved as a vital mechanism to guard the microbe against solitary confinement in a coating of host mucin. *Ibid.* 473 Neuraminidase has not been met in animal tissues. It is not a metabolic enzyme but a tool to facilitate accommodation of a parasite or symbiont within its host. **1970** *New Scientist* 8 Jan. 51/1 Influenza viruses possess another surface protein, the enzyme neuraminidase. *Ibid.* 31 Dec. 608/3 The enzyme neuraminidase, injected into mice as a post-coital contraceptive, seemed to be the most effective base for a 'morning-after pill' of any yet tried.

neurapophysial (ˌnjʊəræpəʊ'fɪzɪəl), *a.* *Anat.* [f. next + -AL[1].] Relating, belonging to, or forming, the neurapophyses.

1856 in MAYNE *Expos. Lex.* **1870** ROLLESTON *Anim. Life* 11 The neurapophysial processes.

neurapophysis (njʊrə'pɒfɪsɪs). *Anat.* Pl. **-physes** (-fɪsiːz). [f. NEUR- + APOPHYSIS.]

1. (Chiefly in *pl.*) One or other of the two processes of a vertebra which form the neural arch.

1839–47 *Todd's Cycl. Anat.* III. 824/2 Two superior laminæ.. to protect the great nervous cord.., which Professor Owen proposes to call Neurapophyses. **1870** H. A. NICHOLSON *Man. Zool.* (1875) 388 Two bony arches which are called the 'neural arches' or 'neurapophyses', because they form with the body.. the 'neural canal'.

2. The spinous process arising from the junction of the bony elements which compose the neural arch; the neural spine.

1870 H. A. NICHOLSON *Man. Zool.* (1875) 695 Neurapophysis. The 'spinous process' of a vertebra, or the process formed at the point of junction of the neural arches. **1881** MIVART *Cat* 35 This is the spinous process, neural spine, or neurapophysis.

neurasthenia (njʊəræs'θiːnɪə). *Path.* [f. as prec. + ASTHENIA.] An atonic condition of the nervous system; functional nervous weakness; nervous debility.

1856 in MAYNE *Expos. Lex.* **1879** BEARD (*title*) The Nature and Diagnosis of Neurasthenia. **1899** *Allbutt's Syst. Med.* VIII. 135 Neurasthenia is indeed often the product of stresses upon the function of the mind. **1922** J. RIVIERE tr. *Freud's Introd. Lectures on Psycho-Anal.* xxiv. 325 We distinguish three pure forms of actual neurosis: neurasthenia, anxiety-neurosis and hypochondria. Even this classification has been disputed. The terms are certainly all in use, but their connotation is vague and unsettled. **1926** J. I. SUTTIE tr. *Ferenczi's Further Contrib. Theory & Technique Psycho-Anal.* ii. 35 The obsessional neuroses are nowadays mostly ranked among the 'neurasthenias'. **1965** ROSEN & GREGORY *Abnormal Psychol.* xii. 250/1 Neurasthenia is observed with such frequency in housewives who are bored and feel neglected by their husbands that it has often been called 'housewives' neurosis'. **1968** C. RYCROFT *Crit. Dict. Psychoanal.* 96 *Neurasthenia*, obsolescent medical and psychiatric term for a state of excessive fatiguability and lack of vigour. **1974** M. SAINSBURY *Key to Psychiatry* xiv. 234 Much disagreement is in evidence through the years regarding the status of neurasthenia as a nosological entity.

neurastheniac (njʊəræs'θiːnɪæk). *rare.* [f. NEURASTHENIA: see -AC.] = NEURASTHENIC *sb.*

1904 *Lancet* 18 June 1737/2 The 'neurastheniacs' that present themselves at the clinic for diseases of the nervous system.

neurasthenic (njʊəræs'θɛnɪk), *a.* and *sb.* *Path.* [f. as NEURASTHENIA + -IC.]

A. *adj.* Caused by, affected with, symptomatic or characteristic of, neurasthenia.

1876 tr. *von Ziemssen's Cycl. Med.* XI. 141 A form of headache which I shall take the liberty of calling *neurasthenic headache.* **1881** *Med. Temp. Jrnl.* XLVII. 163 The neurasthenic.. condition is first recognised by lassitude. **1899** *Allbutt's Syst. Med.* VIII. 135 Neurasthenic persons would.. escape even medical recognition.

B. *sb.* A person who suffers from neurasthenia.

1884 DOWSE *Brain & Nerves* 26 No class of people are more anxious about the future than neurasthenics. **1899** *Allbutt's Syst. Med.* VII. 897 A state that may find expression in the fibrillary trembling of neurasthenics.

Hence **neuras'thenical** *a.*; **neuras'thenically** *adv.*

1890 in *Cent. Dict.* **1899** *Brit. Med. Jrnl.* No. 2001. 72 Investigations carried out.. upon healthy and neurasthenical individuals.

neu'rastheny. *rare*[−0]. Neurasthenia.

1849 in CRAIG. **1856** in MAYNE *Expos. Lex.*

neuration (njʊ'reɪʃən). [irreg. f. NEUR- + -ATION, after NERVATION.] The arrangement or distribution of the nervures or veins, esp. in the wings of insects, or the leaves of plants.

1826 KIRBY & SP. *Entomol.* xxxv. III. 610 The circumstance that most strikingly distinguishes tegmina from elytra is their neuration or veining. **1846** DANA *Zooph.* (1848) 271 The neuration of a leaf. **1859** DARWIN *Orig. Spec.* v. (1873) 124 In certain genera the neuration differs in the different species. **1889** A. R. WALLACE *Darwinism* 241 The very distinct neuration of the wings.. can be easily seen.

neure, obs. form of NEVER.

'neurectome. *Surg.* [cf. NEURECTOMY and *hysterotome.*] 'A narrow-bladed instrument used to divide and excise a portion of nerve' (*Syd. Soc. Lex.* 1892).

neurec'tomic. *a.* [f. next. + -IC.] 'Of or belonging to neurectomy' (Mayne *Expos. Lex.* 1856).

neurectomy (njʊ'rɛktəmɪ). *Surg.* [f. NEUR- + Gr. ἐκτομή: see -TOMY.] The operation of excising a nerve or a portion of a nerve.

1856 in MAYNE *Expos. Lex.* **1880** FLINT *Princ. & Pract. Med.* 799 Carnochan was the first to perform neurectomy beyond the spheno-palatine ganglion for the relief of persistent neuralgia. **1887** *Brit. Med. Jrnl.* 11 June 1280/2 Neurectomy promises to be of greater value in the painful affections of the head and face.

neurenteric (njʊərɛn'tɛrɪk), *a.* *Anat.* [f. NEUR- + ENTERIC.] Connected with the nervous and intestinal systems. ***neurenteric canal***, A prolongation of the neural canal behind the notochord into the archenteron in some vertebrate embryos.

1884 HYATT in *Proc. Boston Soc. Nat. Hist.* XXIII. 119 The presence of a fore neurenteric canal may be assumed. **1888** ROLLESTON & JACKSON *Anim. Life* 335 A post-anal section of the archenteron in Vertebrata which communicates by a neur-enteric canal with the neural tube.

'neuric, *a.* *rare.* [f. Gr. νεῦρ-ον + -IC: cf. next.] Of or pertaining to a nerve or the nerves.

1857 in MAYNE *Expos. Lex.* **1886** *Proc. Soc. Psych. Res.* Oct. 173 Dr. Baréty.. has attempted to show that actual 'neuric rays' are emitted by eyes and fingers.

'neurical, *a.* *rare*[−0]. [f. Gr. νευρικ-ός.]

1623 COCKERAM I, *Newricall*, gowtie.

neuricity (njʊ'rɪsɪtɪ). [f. as NEURIC *a.* + -ITY.] The special form of activity peculiar to the nerves; nerve-force.

1866 OWEN *Anat. Vertebr.* I. 318 Neuricity is convertible into myonicity and into other forms of polar force.

neuridine ('njʊərɪdaɪn). *Chem.* Also **-in.** [f. Gr. νεῦρ-ον (see NEURO-) + -ID + -INE.] A non-poisonous ptomaine of a gelatinous nature, chiefly occurring as a product of putrefaction.

1887 A. M. BROWN *Anim. Alkaloids* 34 Neuridine $C^5H^{11}N^2$.—This base is one of the most constant products of the putrefaction of albumenoid substance. **1897** *Allbutt's Syst. Med.* II. 788 From decomposed beef and horse-flesh Brieger separated several alkaloids—neuridine, neurine, choline, and one apparently identical with muscarine.

neurilemma (njʊərɪ'lɛmə). *Anat.* Also **neurilema** (njʊəraɪ'liːmə), **-elema**; (sense c) **neurolemma.** [Orig. f. Gr. νεῦρ-ον nerve + εἴλημα covering, involucrum; subsequently taken as f. Gr. λέμμα husk, skin (correctly reformed *neurolemma*). Cf. F. *névrilème* (Bichat, 1801).]

a. The delicate membranous outer sheath which invests and protects a nerve (now usually called *epineurium*). **b.** The sheath of a nerve-funiculus, the perineurium.

Senses a, b are now *rare* or *Obs.*

α. **1830** R. KNOX *Béclard's Anat.* 357 These filaments, as they penetrate into the ganglia, leave off their neurilema. **1846** BRITTAN tr. *Malgaigne's Man. Oper. Surg.* 285 The optic nerve, with the neurelema of which it appears to become continuous. **1856–8** W. CLARK *Van der Hoeven's Zool.* I. 11 The nerve-stems and the bundles of which they consist, are surrounded with coats of conjunctive tissue, called neurilema.

β. **1825** GOOD *Study Med.* (ed. 2) IV. 24 Solid fibres or capillaments of a particular kind, the *neurilemma* of Bichat. **1851** CARPENTER *Man. Phys.* (ed. 2) 224 When the neurilemma has been removed, and the trunk has been separated into its component fasciculi. **1888** ROLLESTON & JACKSON *Anim. Life* 212 The giant fibres are separated from the nerve-cord by the inner neurilemma.

attrib. **1889** *Allbutt's Syst. Med.* VI. 626 If the nucleus of the segmental neurilemma cell remain perfectly healthy. *Ibid.* 643 Leucocytes enter the neurilemma sheath.

c. The thin outer sheath that is seen with the light microscope surrounding the axon (and the myelin sheath, if present) of an individual peripheral nerve fibre; also called *sheath of Schwann.* (The usual sense.)

1852 DANA *Crust.* II. 1333 The nerves.. are flat, fibrous cords, enclosed within a membranous envelope or neurolemma. **1874** A. E. J. BARKER *tr. Frey's Histol. & Histochem. of Man* 307 The existence of an envelope on the nervous tube [*sc.* fibre] is easily inferred... This neurilemma may be seen not infrequently as [etc.]. *Ibid.* 317 The nerves of the brain and spinal cord.. become clothed with a delicate envelope at their exit from the nervous centres. This covering receives another addition from the *dura mater* of connective-tissue bundles in its passage through the latter, and..constitutes what was formerly known as 'neurilemma', but which we will designate from henceforth 'perineurium'. **1890** *Gray's Anat.* (ed. 12) 42 The tubular sheath of the funiculi, called the neurilemma or perineurium. **1892** E. A. SCHÄFER *Essent. Histol.* (ed. 3) xviii. 83 Outside the medullary sheath is a delicate but tough homogeneous membrane, the primitive sheath or nucleated sheath of Schwann... The primitive sheath is also known as the neurolemma. **1930** MAXIMOW & BLOOM *Text-bk. Histol.* xii. 251 Some European writers, like Cajal, apply the term 'neurilemma' to the epineurium and not to the sheath of Schwann of the individual fibers. **1966** WRIGHT & SYMMERS *Systemic Path.* II. xxxiv. 1252/1 Neurolemmomas arise from the cells of the neurolemma, or nerve sheath. It is believed that the cell of origin is the Schwann cell. **1968** BLOOM & FAWCETT *Textbk. Histol.* (ed. 9) xii. 321/1 The myelin is actually part of the Schwann cell, consisting of spirally wrapped layers of its surface membrane... The outer membrane..and the protein-polysaccharide boundary layer on its outer aspect were resolved with the light microscope as a single layer, which has traditionally been called the neurilemma.

Hence **neuri'lemmal** *a.* (now the usual adj.); also **neurile'm(m)atic** *a.* [F. *névrilématique*]; **neuri'lem(m)atous** *a.*

1836–9 *Todd's Cycl. Anat.* II. 534/2 The expansion and interlacing of the neurilemmatic sheaths. **1839–47** *Ibid.* III. 776/1 The plaiting must be considered..independent of neurilematous investment. **1875** PAYNE *Jones & Siev. Path. Anat.* 310 The neurilemmatous sheath is the part mainly affected in inflammation. **1903** *Rep. Brit. Assoc. Adv. Sci. 1902* 782 From the microscopic study of the distal portions of divided nerve-trunks we arrived at the conclusion that the activity of the neurilemmal cells has some relation to the development of the new nerve-fibres. **1937** E. E. HEWER *Text-bk. Histol.* 96 Within the central nervous system there is no neurilemmal sheath. **1954** T. L. PEELE *Neuroanat. Basis Clin. Neurol.* i. 13/2 The neurolemmal sheath of the spinal nerves, and of those cranial nerves possessing it, terminates (or begins) a short distance from spinal cord or brain stem. **1973** H. M. RÁLIŠ et al. *Techniques Neurohistol.* i. 19 The neurilemmal sheath plays an important role in the nutrition and protection of nerve fibres.

neurilemoma, neurilemmoma (njʊərɪlɛˈməʊmə). *Path.* Also **neuro-**. [f. NEURILEM(A, NEURILEMM(A + -OMA.] A tumour formed by proliferation of the neurilemma.

1935 A. P. STOUT in *Amer. Jrnl. Cancer* XXIV. 752 Therefore it seemed advisable to take this phrase 'nerve sheath tumor'..and to construct from it a new name for the neoplasm. After consultation with Dr. G. F. Laidlaw and Dr. F. H. Vizetelly, editor of the *New Standard Dictionary*, the word 'neurilemoma' has been constructed and it is proposed to use this term for the tumor under discussion. *Ibid.* 753 Neurilemomas can be found sometimes in cases of von Recklinghausen's disease. **1948** J. M. BEATTIE et al. *Text-bk. Path.* (ed. 5) II. xxix. 1310 On the supposition that this word is derived from the Greek words *νεῦρον, neuron*, a nerve-fibre.., *λέμμα*, lemma, a skin or sheath..we ventured to alter the spelling of Dr. Purdy Stout's term 'neurilemoma' to 'neurilemmoma'... Dr. Purdy Stout..has persuaded us of the error of our ways... It is a pleasure..to take this opportunity of altering our spelling of the word back to..'neurilemoma'—though we are still in some doubt as to whether..it might not with propriety take the form 'Neurolemoma'. **1948** R. A. WILLIS *Path. Tumours* liv. 828 Masson's and Stout's names 'Schwannoma' and 'neurilemmoma', and Mallory and Penfield's name 'perineural fibroblastoma', express the two opposing views regarding the histogenesis of this distinctive nerve-sheath tumour. **1954** ACKERMAN & DEL REGATO *Cancer* (ed. 2) vii. 202 Neurilemomas [*ed.* 1 (1947): neurilemmomas] have also been reported to arise in the nasal fossa. **1962** *Lancet* 29 Dec. 1354/2 The pre-operative diagnosis rested between a neurilemmoma of the posterior tibial nerve and compression of the nerve by the retinaculum. **1966** Neurolemmoma [see NEURILEMA].

neurility (njʊˈrɪlɪtɪ). [f. NEUR- + -ILITY. Cf. F. *neurilité*.] The power of a nerve to convey or transmit impulse or sensation.

1860 LEWES *Physiol. Com. Life* II. 19 Neurility simply means the property which the nerve-fibre has, when stimulated, of exciting contraction in a muscle, secretion in a gland, and sensation in a ganglionic centre. **1879** N. SMYTH *Old Faiths in New Lights* vii. (1882) 300 *note*, So long as sensibility and neurility..cannot be shown to be necessarily related and convertible.

neurine (ˈnjʊəraɪn), *sb.* and *a.* Also neurin. [f. NEUR- + -INE. Cf. F. *neurine, névrine*.]

A. *sb.* **1.** *Anat.* Nerve substance or tissue; the matter contained in the nerve-tubes.

1839–47 *Todd's Cycl. Anat.* III. 593/2 It contains the elements of the true nervous tissue or neurine. **1854** OWEN in *Orr's Circ. Sci., Org. Nat.* I. 161 Tubular tracts are formed, some of which become filled with 'neurine', or nervous matter. **1870** MAUDSLEY *Body & Mind* 56 The vesicular neurine has increased in quantity and in quality.

2. *Chem.* **a.** A poisonous alkaloid or ptomaine, derived from putrefying flesh, etc.; choline. **b.** An alkaloid produced with the former, and differing very slightly from it in chemical composition, but possessing more actively poisonous properties.

1869 *Syd. Soc. Year-bk. Med.* 16 A basic substance.. which he [Liebreich] has termed neurine... By slightly modifying this method neurine has been artificially formed. **1880** J. W. LEGG *Bile* 52 By boiling with baryta water, lecithin is decomposed into neurin or cholin. **1899** *Allbutt's Syst. Med.* VI. 496 An effect also produced by snake venom, as well as by neurine and choline.

B. *adj.* Of or relating to the nerves.

1870 J. SCOFFERN *Stray Leaves Sci.* 446 When he began his neurine enquiries the prevalent belief..was [etc.].

neurinoma (njʊərɪˈnəʊmə). *Path.* Pl. **-omas, -omata.** [mod.L. (J. Verocay 1910, in *Beitr. z. path. Anat. u. z. allgem. Path.* XLVIII. 65), f. NEUR- + INO- + -OMA.] = NEURILEMOMA, NEURILEMMOMA.

1913 in STEDMAN *Med. Dict.* (ed. 2) 600/1. **1917** H. CUSHING *Tumors of Nervus Acusticus* vii. 195 Though the term 'fibrosarcoma' predominates, other terms, which have been met with in cases which appear to be unquestionably acoustic tumors, are as follows: steatoma of the older writers,..neurinoma (Verocay), fibroblastoma (Borst). **1928** W. G. MACCALLUM *Text-Bk. Path.* (ed. 4) liv. 966 Such neurinomata occur only in peripheral nerves in which there are the sheath cells of Schwann. Of this character is the so-called acusticus tumor which is a neurinoma (formerly called neurofibroma). **1932** W. PENFIELD *Cytol. & Cellular Path. Nervous Syst.* III. xix. 968 These tumors contain long slender fibers of even caliber which tend to be arranged in parallel sheaves. Verocay (1910) considered these fibers to be nerve fibers and the type cell to be the sheath of Schwann cell... He therefore suggested the term neurinoma, meaning nerve fiber tumor. **1935** *Amer. Jrnl. Cancer* XXIV. 751 It is proposed..to limit the discussion to that specific encapsulated tumor composed of highly differentiated tissues which is so characteristic of the nerve sheath within which it develops... Neurinoma is the term most widely used,..but there is the insuperable objection to it that it means 'nerve fiber tumor'. Whatever else..all authorities are convinced that this is not a nerve fiber tumor but a nerve sheath tumor. **1948** A. BRODAL *Neurological Anat.* vii. 240 Likewise it may happen that patients affected with a neurinoma of the VIIIth nerve tell a story of their sufferings starting with a pain situated deep in the ear. **1961** R. D. BAKER *Essent. Path.* xx. 554 Neurinomas (neurilemmomas) of the skin are rare.

'neurism. *rare.* [f. NEUR- + -ISM.]

1. Nerve-force; neuricity.

1871 COPE *Origin of Fittest* v. (1887) 205 The Vital Forces are (nerve-force) Neurism, (growth-force) Bathmism, and (thought-force) Phrenism.

2. 'The hypothesis according to which all the phenomena of the living body are due to the action of a nervous fluid' (*Syd. Soc. Lex.* 1892).

neuristor (njʊˈrɪstə(r)). *Electronics.* [f. NEUR- + *-istor*, as in *resistor, transistor*.] Any device that is effectively a transmission line along which a signal will travel without attenuation (generally with a supply of energy along its length).

1960 H. C. CRANE in *IRE Trans. Electronic Computers* IX. 370/1 A novel device and its properties have been hypothesized and possible digital systems employing it are briefly outlined in this note. The device, termed Neuristor, may be used to synthesize all digital logic functions... A neuristor may be visualized as a one-dimensional channel along which signals may flow. A signal propagates along the channel in the form of a discharge... A discharge signal has the following properties: 1) attenuationless propagation, 2) uniform velocity of propagation, 3) a refractory period. These characteristics are somewhat similar to the gross properties of transmission of discharge pulses by neurons in the nervous system—hence the name neuristor. **1963** *New Scientist* 7 Feb. 285/1 The concept of devices called 'neuristors', which behave like the axon or connection process of the neuron in the brain, is exciting to medical workers. **1965** *Electronics Lett.* I. 134/1 In most cases, neuristors which can propagate pulses have been considered, but one which can only propagate a discharge has also been studied. **1972** *Nuclear Instruments & Methods* CIV. 593 (*heading*) On the possibility of using superconducting neuristor line as particle detector.

neurite (ˈnjʊəraɪt). *Anat.* [f. NEUR- + *-ite*, after DENDRITE 3.] An axon or dendrite (formerly, an axon only).

1894 P. A. FISH in *Jrnl. Compar. Neurol.* IV. 173 For the axis-cylinder process the term neurite is proposed and for the other processes of the cells, retain the word dendrites. **1898** *Jrnl. R. Microsc. Soc.* 64 Nerve-cells with a long neurite (Purkinje's cells). **1924** R. M. OGDEN tr. *Koffka's Growth of Mind* ii. 53 At its end this neurite divides into a fine net-work. **1956** *Nature* 28 Jan. 185/2 Individual nerve cell bodies and a part of their neurites 100–200μ long were dissected out by micromanipulation. **1973** *Gray's Anat.* (ed. 35) vii. 750/1 The neurites..may be divided into those which conduct broadly towards the cell body..and another one which may branch more or less profusely, and conducts away from the cell body.

neuritic (njʊˈrɪtɪk), *a.* (and *sb.*) [ad. Gr. type **νευριτικ-ός*, f. *νεῦρον* nerve: see -ITIC, and cf. F. *névritique* (1762).]

†**1.** Good for the nerves. *Obs. rare*⁻¹.

1725 BRADLEY *Fam. Dict.*, *Marjoram*..is vulnerary, Cephalick, Hysterick, Neuritick, and proper to expel wind.

†**b.** *sb.* (See quot.) *Obs. rare*⁻⁰.

1727–38 CHAMBERS *Cycl.*, *Neuritics*, or *nervines*,.. remedies proper for diseases of the nerves and nervous parts.

2. *Path.* Relating to, of the nature of, neuritis.

1857 in MAYNE *Expos. Lex.* **1887** *Brit. Med. Jrnl.* 1 Jan. 9/2 The main objections which have been advanced against the neuritic theory. **1899** *Allbutt's Syst. Med.* VIII. 751 Pompholyx is generally regarded as a neuritic inflammation or vaso-motor neurosis.

neuritis (njʊˈraɪtɪs). *Path.* [a. Gr. type **νευρῖτις*, f. *νεῦρον* nerve: see -ITIS.] Inflammation of a nerve or nerves.

1840 *Penny Cycl.* XVI. 166/2 In neuritis we shall find the usual attendants of inflammation. **1880** FLINT *Princ. & Pract. Med.* 781 In acute neuritis the nerves are swollen, reddened, and more succulent than normal. **1899** *Allbutt's Syst. Med.* VI. 44, I have seen instances of neuritis and perhaps of neuralgia of the cardiac nerves in diphtheria.

neuro- (ˈnjʊərəʊ), combining form of Gr. *νεῦρον* nerve, used in a number of scientific terms, chiefly *Anat.* and *Path.*, as **neuroa'natomy**, the anatomy of the nervous system; hence **ˌneuroana'tomical** *a.*, **neuroa'natomist**; **neurobi'ology**, the branch of biology which deals with nervous tissue; hence **ˌneurobio'logical** *a.*, **neurobi'ologist**; **ˌneurobio'taxis** *Biol.* [BIO- + TAXIS], a tendency of nerve cells, in the course both of development and of evolution, to remain close to their source of stimulation by migrating; so **ˌneurobio'tactic** *a.*; **'neuroblast**, an embryonic nucleated cell from which the nerve-fibres originate; hence **neuro'blastic** *a.*; **neurobla'stoma** (pl. **-omas, -omata**) *Med.* [-OMA], a tumour composed of neuroblasts; *spec.* a malignant tumour composed of small cells with darkly staining nuclei and little cytoplasm, which is common in infants and usually appears in the adrenal gland; **neuro-'central** *a.*, connected with the centrum and neural arch of a vertebra, esp. in *neurocentral suture*; **neuro-'centrum**, one of the parts forming the neuro-central arch; **neuro'chemistry**, (the study of) the chemical composition and processes of nervous tissue; hence **neuro'chemical** *a.*, **-'chemist**; **'neurochord**, a set of tubular fibres on the dorsal aspect of the ventral nerve-cord in annulates and crustaceans; **ˌneurocircu'latory** *a. Med.*, of or pertaining to the nervous system and the circulatory system jointly; chiefly in *neurocirculatory asthenia* = *irritable heart* s.v. IRRITABLE *a.* 2 b; **neuro'clonic** *a.*, characterized by nervous spasms; **'neurocœle** (-siːl), the central cavity of the cerebrospinal system; hence **neuro'cœlian** *a.*; **neuro'cranium** *Anat.* = CRANIUM 1 a; **'neurocrine** (-kraɪn) *a. Physiol.* [a. F. *neurocrine* (Masson & Berger 1923, in *Compt. Rend.* CLXXVI. 1750), after *olocrine* holocrine, *endocrine* endocrine, etc.], secreting or secreted directly into nervous tissue; **'neurocyte** [-CYTE], a neurone, a nerve cell; hence **neurocy'toma** (pl. **-omas, -omata**) *Med.* [-OMA], a tumour composed of nerve cells; **neuro-'dendron** (see quot.); **neuro'dermal** *a.*, pertaining to the epiblast; **ˌneuroderma'titis** (pl. **-dermatitides**) *Path.* [ad. F. *névrodermite* (Brocq & Jacquet 1891, in *Ann. de Dermatol. et de Syphiligraphie* II. 98)], lichen simplex chronicus or atopic dermatitis, esp. when aggravated by a nervous disorder; also more widely, = next; **ˌneuroderma'tosis** (pl. **-oses**) *Path.*, any skin disorder that is nervous or psychosomatic in nature; **neuro-e'ffector** *a. Physiol.*, pertaining to or composed of both a nerve and an effector; also as *sb.*, a neuro-effector system; **neuroe'lectric** *a.*, of or pertaining to the electrical phenomena and properties of the nervous system; cf. *nervoelectric* adj. s.v. NERVO-; also **neuroe'lectrical** *a.* (*rare*), **-elec'tricity**; **neuroembry'ologist**, a specialist or expert in neuroembryology; **neuroembry'ology**, the science which deals with the development of the nervous system in embryos; hence **ˌneuroembryo'logic** (chiefly *U.S.*), **-'logical** *adjs.*; **neuro'endocrine** *a.*, involving both nervous and endocrine participation; **ˌneuroendocri'nology**, the study of the interactions between the nervous system and the endocrine system; hence **ˌneuro-endocrino'logical** *a.*, **-endocri'nologist**; **neuro-en'teric** *a.* = NEURENTERIC; **neuro-epi'dermal** *a.*, pertaining to the nerves together with the epidermis (*Syd. Soc. Lex.*); **neuroepi'thelial** *a.*, pertaining to the nerves together with the epithelium; **neuro'fibril, -'fibrilla**, any of the fibrils visible within the body of a nerve cell using light microscopy; hence **neuro'fibrillar, -'fibrillary** *adjs.*; **neurofi'broma** (see quot.); **neuro'filament**, a long filamentary structure, typically about 100 ångströms in diameter, visible in the cytoplasm of neurones under electron microscopy; **neuro'glandular** *a.*, involving or possessing both glandular and nervous tissue or functions; **neuro'hæmal** (*U.S.* **-hemal**) *a.*, designating any of the organs, esp. among insects, which are composed of a group of nerve endings closely associated with the vascular system and are believed to have a neurosecretory function; **neurohi'stologist**, an expert or specialist in neurohistology; **neurohi'stology**, the histology of the nervous system or of nervous tissue; so ˌ**neurohisto'logic** (chiefly *U.S.*), **-'logical** *adjs.*; **neurohyp'nology** = NEURYPNOLOGY; so **neurohyp'notic** *a.*, **-'hypnotism**; ˌ**neuro-inter'mediate** *a. Anat.*, used to designate the posterior lobe (pars nervosa) of the neurohypophysis together with the adjacent pars intermedia (which is usu. regarded as part of the adenohypophysis); **neuro'keratin**, a substance closely resembling keratin, found in certain nerve-tissues; **neuro'kinin** *Med.*, a kinin reported to have been obtained from subcutaneous fluid in the scalp during attacks of migraine; **'neurokyme** *Psychol.* [ad. G. *neurokym* (O. Vogt 1895, in *Zeitschr. f. Hypnotismus* III. 300), f. Gr. κῦμ-α wave] (see quot. 1908); **neurolin'guistic** *a.*, of or connected with the application of neurology to linguistic research; so **neuro'linguist**, an expert or specialist in neurolinguistics; **neurolin'guistics** *sb. pl.* (const. as *sing.*), neurological linguistics; **'neuromere**, a part or segment of the nervous system; hence **neu'romerous** *a.*, characterized by a segmented nervous system; **neurometa'physical** *a.*, characterized by a metaphysical view or treatment of nervous phenomena; **neu'rometer**, a means of measuring the strength of the nerves; **neuromi'mesis**, a form of neurosis characterized by imitative actions or pathological conditions; neurotic imitation of disease; hence **neuromi'metic** *a.* and *sb.*; **neuro'muscular** *a.*, relating or belonging to both nerve(s) and muscle(s); having characteristics of both nervous and muscular tissue; being or pertaining to a junction between a nerve fibre and a muscle fibre; **neuro'myal**, **-'myic** *adjs.* [MYO-] = prec.; **neuromy'ology**, the classification of muscles with reference to the nerves; **neuromyo'sitis**, an affection of both nerve and muscle; **'neuronym**, the scientific name of a muscle; **neuropa'ralysis**, paralysis due to some affection of the nerves; so **neuropara'lytic** *a.*; ˌ**neuropharma'cology**, the study of the action of drugs on the nervous system; hence ˌ**neuropharmaco'logic** (chiefly *U.S.*), **-'logical** *adjs.*, ˌ**neuropharmaco'logically** *adv.*, ˌ**neuropharma'cologist**; **neurophysin** (-'faɪsɪn) *Biochem.* [ad F. *neurophysine* (J. Chauvet et al. 1960, in *Biochim. & Biophys. Acta* XXXVIII. 266), f. *neuro(hypo)physe* NEUROHYPOPHYSIS], any of a group of proteins which are found in the neurohypophysis in complexes with oxytocin and vasopressin and are believed to act as carriers for these hormones during their passage from the hypothalamus; **neurophysio'logic** *a.* (chiefly *U.S.*), neurophysiological; **neurophysio'logically** *adv.*, with respect to neurophysiology; **neuro-physi'ologist**, an expert or specialist in neurophysiology; **neurophysi'ology**, the physiology of the nervous system; hence **neurophysio'logical** *a.*; **'neuroplasm**, the cytoplasm of a neurone; occas. applied to that of the cell body, as distinguished from AXOPLASM; hence **neuro'plasmic** *a.*; **'neuropore**, an exterior orifice in the neural canal of some embryos; **neuro'psychic** *a.*, pertaining to the nervous and psychic functions; **neuropsycho'logical** *a.*, dealing with psychology in relation to the nerves; so **neuropsy'chologist**; **neuro-psycho'pathic** *a.*, pertaining to diseased states of the nervous and mental functions; **neuropsy'chosis** *Psychol.*, a neurotic condition in which certain features characteristic of a psychosis can be recognized; **neuroradi'ologist**, a specialist or expert in neuroradiology; **neuroradi'ology** *Med.*, radiology of the central nervous system; hence ˌ**neuroradio'logic** (chiefly *U.S.*), **-'logical** *adjs.*; **neuroreti'nitis**, combined inflammation of the optic nerve and retina; **'neuroscience**, any of the sciences (as neuro-chemistry or psychology) which deal with the nervous system or mental phenomena; such sciences collectively; hence **neuro-'scientist**, a specialist in a neuroscience; **neurose'cretion**, (*a*) the process of secretion by a (specially adapted) nerve cell; (*b*) the substance secreted in this process; so **neurose'cretory** *a.*, performing, produced by, or pertaining to neurosecretion; **neurose'mantic** *a.*, of or connected with a neurological approach to semantics; **neuro'sensory**, pertaining to or involving both nervous and sensory properties; *spec.* applied to a sensory nerve cell, esp. one in which the cell body (usu. situated in epithelium) is the receptor and has a single process by which impulses are transmitted to a ganglionic neurone or an effector organ; **'neurosur-geon**, one who practises neurosurgery; **neuro'surgery**, surgery of the nervous system; hence **neuro'surgical** *a.*; **neuro'syphilis** *Path.*, syphilis involving the central nervous system; hence ˌ**neurosyphi'litic** *a.* (also as *sb.*, a neurosyphilitic person); **neuro'tendinous** *a.*, of or pertaining to a nerve fibre and a tendon, esp. the termination of a nerve in a tendon; **neuro'tonic**, a medicine used to brace the nerves (Ogilvie 1882); **neuro'toxic**, *a.*, acting poisonously upon the nerves; so **neuro'toxical** *a.* (Mayne 1857); **neuroto'xicity**, (*a*) toxicity towards the nerves; (*b*) poisoning by a neurotoxin; **neuro'toxin**, a substance having a poisonous effect on the nerves; **neuro'tubule**, a microtubule of a neurone; **neuro'vascular** *a.*, having both a nervous and vascular character; **neuro'virulence**, virulence towards the nervous system.

A large number of similar compounds, the currency of many of which is doubtful, are given in Mayne's *Expos. Lex.* and the *Syd. Soc. Lex.*

1904 *Biol. Bull.* VI. 90 These facts point toward either a specialization or a modification in function which is of interest because of its bearing upon certain *neuro-anatomical facts. **1971** H. A. WHITAKER in W. O. Dingwall *Survey of Linguistic Science* 148 It is plausible.. that there is a universal neuroanatomical substrate for the language system. **1931** H. L. HOLLINGWORTH *Abnormal Psychol.* iv. 68 This condition would be difficult to understand if it were not that the *neuro-anatomist had mapped out the course of the various sensory pathways in the spinal cord. **1963** *Zeitschr. für Zellforschung* LX. 815 The basis of the neuron doctrine was established by the work of a few eminent neuro-anatomists. **1974** *Nature* 6 Sept. 83/1 For the neuroanatomists of the nineteenth century, the cerebellum was a source of fascination. **1900** DORLAND *Med. Dict.* 441/1 *Neuro-anatomy. **1913** *Official Publ. Cornell Univ.* IV. XVI, Strauss, Israel. A.B., M.D., Instructor in Neuro-Anatomy, 1911. **1931** H. L. HOLLINGWORTH *Abnormal Psychol.* iv. 77 We may illustrate the 'fictional' or hypothetical notion of explanation also in the field of neuro-anatomy. **1971** *Sci. Amer.* May 89/3 In view of the basic neuro-anatomy of the visual system, this means that the visual effects must have been the result of neuronal activity in the brain rather than in the eye itself. **1959** *Internat. Rev. Neurobiol.* I. p. vii, Progress in *neurobiological research must maintain a delicate balance between the fascination of basic explanation of clinical and physiological phenomena by means of chemical and physical concepts on the one hand and the pressing needs for the development of new and effective treatments of disease on the other. **1971** *Nature* 5 Mar. 25/1 The neurobiological approach to mental health. **1957** H. READ *Tenth Muse* xiii. 110 If one reads a *neurobiologist such as J. R. Smithies one has the feeling, perhaps deceptive, that the problems discussed by Professor Ayer are being discussed more realistically. **1971** J. Z. YOUNG *Introd. Study Man* p. vii, What the neurobiologist finds out about the brain must surely be relevant to fundamental views of the nature of all this knowledge. **1906** *Index-Catal. Library Surg.-General's Office, U.S. Army* 2nd Ser. XI. 622/1 (*heading*) *Neurobiology. **1960** *Times* 22 Sept. 4/2 Researches cover neurobiology—such as 'eye movements and optogyral illusion'. **1972** *Sci. Amer.* Sept. 51/1 Thus neurobiology has now shown why it is human—and all too human—to hold Euclidean geometry and its non-intersecting co-planar parallel lines to be a self-evident truth. Non-Euclidean geometries of convex or concave surfaces, although our brain is evidently capable of conceiving them, are more alien to our built-in spatial-perception processes. **1908** C. U. A. KAPPERS in *Jrnl. Physiol.* XXXVII. 143 Another feature of the autonomic system might find its explanation in the *neurobiotactic influence of the axon stimulation. **1948** A. BRODAL *Neurological Anat.* vii. 192 The neurobiotactic influences (Kappers) of which the above-mentioned fact is an example, are also revealed in other morphological features. **1908** C. U. A. KAPPERS in *Jrnl. Physiol.* XXXVII. 140 Referring for further details concerning these phenomena of *neurobiotaxis to my former papers on this subject, I only wish to state here that.. it is obvious that the motor cells migrate in the direction whence they get the greatest quantity of stimuli. **1961** P. GLEES *Exper. Neurol.* vi. 168 In accordance with his hypothesis of neurobiotaxis.. Kappers (1920) believes that the dendrites grow from the cell towards the source of their afferent stimuli. **1892** *Syd. Soc. Lex.*, **Neuroblast*, the pear-shaped cells which arise by a process of mitosis from the germinal cells of the early embryo. **1897** *19th Cent.* July 25 The embryonal nerve-cell (neuroblast) will be simply an oval sac. **1910** J. H. WRIGHT in *Jrnl. Exper. Med.* XII. 556 The essential cells of the tumor are considered to be more or less undifferentiated nerve cells or neurocytes or neuroblasts, and hence the names neurocytoma and *neuroblastoma. **1925** *Arch. Neurol. & Psychiatry* (Chicago) XIV. 193 In our Brigham Hospital records.. many of them have in the past been designated neurocytomas or neuroblastomas. **1948** R. GREENE *Pract. Endocrinol.* iv. 128 The neuroblastomata are highly malignant tumours. **1974** *Nature* 17 May 224/1 The C1300 mouse neuroblastoma has been useful for studies of the differentiation and trophic interactions of nerve cells. **1870** ROLLESTON *Anim. Life* p. lxii, The *neurocentral suture is usually absent. **1873** MIVART *Elem. Anat.* 61 The line of junction of the lateral pieces with the central pieces is termed the neuro-central suture. **1884** HYATT in *Proc. Boston Soc. Nat. Hist.* XXIII. 121 The distribution and formation of the *neurocentra.. in the vertebræ of the Permian Rhachitomi. **1949** KOESTLER *Insight & Outlook* v. 68 Their *neurochemical substratum [*sc.* that of our emotional impulses] cannot be worked off in overt activities. **1963** *Lancet* 12 Jan. 79/1 If their effect on the brain could be evaluated, understanding of the neurochemical changes in depression might follow. **1972** *Sci. Amer.* Nov. 28/3 The hypothesis proposed that hypothalamic control of the secretory activity of the anterior pituitary could be neurochemical. **1958** *Neurology* VIII. (Suppl. 1) 27/2 Many investigators using such methods would not consider themselves *neurochemists, but they certainly contribute to the growing body of neurochemical data. **1971** *Nature* 22 Mar. 130/3 Undoubtedly, it [*sc.* myelin] now has the added attraction to neurochemists that it can be obtained in bulk from the mammalian nervous system. **1955** *Neuropharmacology* I. 11 There are enough problems and enough possibilities for an entire science in the field of '*neuro-chemistry' or/and 'neuro-pharmacology'. **1969** *Nature* 11 Oct. 118/2 A significant development in neurochemistry has been the finding that thiol groups and disulphides are involved in the functioning and activity of neurones. **1888** ROLLESTON & JACKSON *Anim. Life.* 212 The apparatus is hence termed '*Neurochord' by Vejdovsky.., who compares it physiologically with the noto-chord of Chordata. *Ibid.* 598 The so-called 'giant-fibres' or 'neurochord' are found in nearly all Oligochæta. **1918** 'T. LEWIS' [*i.e.* B. S. Oppenheimer et al.: see *Jrnl. Amer. Med. Assoc.* (1918) 21 Sept. 994] in *Military Surgeon* XLII. 410 An appreciable number of soldiers present a well-defined symptom-complex, in which certain nervous and circulatory symptoms are associated with an increased susceptibility to fatigue. The descriptive name of *Neuro-Circulatory Asthenia ('N.C.A.') is suggested for this syndrome in preference to Disordered Action of the Heart ('D.A.H.'). **1953** R. A. MCFARLAND *Human Factors in Air Transportation* vi. 305 The effect of smoking on neurocirculatory efficiency.. may be of particular importance to the airman since this test is often used to appraise fitness. **1971** Neurocirculatory [see *irritable heart* (IRRITABLE *a.* 2 b)]. **1899** *Allbutt's Syst. Med.* VII. 898 The *neuroclonic state of the neurons of the spinal cord may appear subsequently. **1889** *Buck's Handbk. Med. Sci.* VIII. 110 The entire neuraxis is a tube, a subcylindrical mass inclosing a cavity. This cavity is the *neurocœle. **1907** W. N. PARKER tr. *Wiedersheim's Compar. Anat. Vertebrates* (ed. 3) 75 The portion of the skull which is situated along the main axis in continuation of the vertebral column and which encloses the brain, is known as the brain-case or cranium (*neurocranium). **1942** GROVE & NEWELL *Animal Biol.* xv. 257 Other cartilage is laid down at the sides and above the brain until it becomes enclosed in a cartilaginous box, the brain box or neurocranium. **1972** *Nature* 24 Mar. 143/2 A sulcus on the outer face of the neurocranium in front of the supposed foramen for the vagus nerve is interpreted as the lateral occipital fissure. **1925** *Physiol. Abstr.* IX. 544 The secretion of these '*neurocrine' glands acts directly on the nerves. **1947** *Phil. Trans. R. Soc.* B. CCXXXII. 394 The relationship of the pars distalis of the pituitary and the possible neurocrine secretion by the hypothalamic nuclei to the water balance of the body are still debatable points. **1962** *Science Survey* III. 264 There exist equally interesting relationships between odours and animal behaviour on a different and perhaps more profound level.. which are very likely mediated by the vegetative nervous system and the neurocrine and other endocrine glands. **1890** BILLINGS *Med. Dict.* II. 209/1 **Neurocyte*, nerve-cell. **1894** P. A. FISH in *Jrnl. Compar. Neurol.* IV. 174 For the equivalent of a nerve unit including the nerve cell with all its processes to the uttermost filament, the term neurocyte is suggested. It has not been possible to trace the word to its originator. It is in use in the French language and is included in the dictionary of the New Sydenham Society and Gould's New Medical Dictionary with the simple definition; a nerve cell. **1932** W. PENFIELD *Cytol. & Cellular Path. Nervous Syst.* III. xviii. 941 Between the neurocytes are numerous smaller cells. **1910**, **1925** *Neurocytoma [see *neuroblastoma* above]. **1948** R. GREENE *Pract. Endocrinol.* iv. 127 The most malignant tumours are the neuroblastomata or neurocytomata. **1966** WRIGHT & SYMMERS *Systemic Path.* II. xxxiv. 1246/1 A ganglioneuroma (neurocytoma) of the brain is a slowly growing tumour composed of neurons. **1899** *Allbutt's Syst. Med.* VI. 490 From the cell-body, or from a protoplasmic extension of the cell (*neuro-dendron) the nerve process or axon is given off. **1877** E. R. LANKESTER in *Jrnl. Microsc. Sci.* XVII. 430 [The] epiblast and the musculo-skeletal portion of the mesoblast—or.. *neurodermal and myoskeletal moieties. **1896** *Amer. Year-bk. Med. & Surg.* 715 (*heading*) Vitiligo, lichen ruber planus, and chronic circumscribed *neurodermatitis. **1935** Neurodermatitis [see *neurodermatosis* below]. **1947** *N.Y. State Jrnl. Med.* XLVII. 1889/2 MacKenna and others have suggested that the neurodermatitides may have a corresponding symbolic meaning. **1954** *Bull. Muscogee County Med. Soc.* Aug. 9 A large list of diseases has been included under the term 'psychosomatic',.. it includes.. certain skin diseases—notably the so-called neurodermatitides. **1974** PASSMORE & ROBSON *Compan. Med. Stud.* III. xxxi. 13/1 The condition [*sc.* lichen simplex chronicus] is sometimes referred to as neurodermatitis because it is most frequently encountered in obsessional and anxious individuals. **1909** *Cent. Dict.* Suppl., *Neurodermatosis. **1911** M. MORRIS *Dis. Skin* (ed. 5) iv. 54 (*heading*) Neuroses of the skin. Classification of neuro-dermatoses. **1935** *Jrnl. Amer. Med. Assoc.* 5 Oct. 1099/1 A group of eighty patients presenting typical clinical examples of the neurodermatoses.. was selected.., with diagnoses as follows: neuro-dermatitis (dry type), nineteen; pruritus ani or vulvae, five; neurodermatitis (exudative type), twenty-eight; dyshidrosis, four; [etc.]. **1941** S. H. KRAINES *Therapy of Neuroses & Psychoses* xiv. 313 Clearing up of these neurodermatoses is more difficult than removal of many other emotionally conditioned physical symptoms. **1961** *Lancet* 12 Aug. 369/1 MacKenna very artistically described neurodermatosis when he stated that 'in some cases the skin is an organ of stress which bears the brunt of nervous agitation, acting as the canvas on which the perturbation of the mind is painted.' **1935** *Q. Rev. Biol.* X. 335/2 According to the data available, the following is the sequence of functionally related events which probably occur in the electrical excitation of a *neuro-effector system. **1937** CANNON & ROSENBLUETH *Autonomic Neuro-Effector Systems* p. viii, Previous researches on autonomic neuro-effectors and the occurrences at their synapses. **1973** *European Jrnl. Clin. Pharmacol.* VI. 92/1 Further investigations are possible.. of the possible role of these [neuronal] pools in the control of NA exchanges at the level of the sympathetic neuro-effector junction. **1973** *Science* 16 Feb. 693/2 (*heading*) Neuroeffectors controlling mucus release by the leech. **1849** G. Bird *Lect. Electr. & Galvanism* i. 24 The *neuro-electric theory of Galvani. *Ibid.* 25 Valli.. believed the neuro-electric fluid to be secreted by the capillary arteries supplying the nerves. **1956** L. S. Frishkopf in *Technical Rep. Res. Lab. Electronics Mass. Inst. Technol.* No. 307 (*title*) A probability approach to certain neuroelectric phenomena. **1965** *Math. in Biol. & Med.* (Med. Res. Council) iv. 131 Modern electrophysiological techniques permit the recording of several types of neuroelectric potentials, and the patterns of voltage-versus-time traces provide the electrophysiologist's basic data. **1974** *Nature* 15 Feb. 481/1 An exactly similar method is widely used in studying EEG visual evoked responses and other neuroelectric phenomena. **1914** *Practitioner* June 838 The immediate cause of an epileptic attack is a *neuro-electrical brain storm. *Ibid.* 831 The chemical generation of nerve force (*neuro-electricity) in the human body. *Ibid.* 832 The grey matter of the brain must be the site of generation of this neuro-electricity. **1933** *Science* 18 Aug. 132/1 A notable beginning was made in *neuro-embryologic study of behavior. **1950** Hamburger & Levi-Montalcini in P. Weiss *Genetic Neurol.* 129 The *in vitro* culture of nerve cells made important contributions to the solution of *neuro-embryological problems. **1970** D. Bodian in F. O. Schmitt *Neurosciences: 2nd Study Program* xiii. 139/2 The considerable insight gained in recent times through analysis of neuroembryological processes. **1950** Hamburger & Levi-Montalcini in P. Weiss *Genetic Neurol.* 141 The *neuroembryologist is largely concerned with the further elaboration of these elementary patterns of the early neural tube. **1970** M. V. Edds in F. O. Schmitt *Neuro-sciences: 2nd Study Program* v. 51/2 The roster of experimental neuroembryologists active since Harrison opened the field early in the century includes some of the most able developmental biologists. **1933** *Science* 18 Aug. 137/1 The whole subject of *neuro-embryology of higher vertebrates should be reexamined. **1950** Hamburger & Levi-Montalcini in P. Weiss *Genetic Neurol.* 131 The material used in experimental neuroembryology has been confined largely to teleosts, amphibians, and the chick embryo. **1974** *Nature* 22 Mar. p. xi/1 (Advt.), By combining the facts of neurophysiology, neuroembryology, and behaviour, a new theory is built up. **1922** P. Fridenberg in L. F. Barker et al. *Endocrinol. & Metabolism* II. 769 (*heading*) *Neuro-endocrin control of intra-ocular tension. **1944** Neuro-endocrine [see hypothalamico-hypophysial *a.*]. **1959** T. Lidz in S. Arieti *Amer. Handbk. Psychiatry* I. xxxii. 650/1 The hypothalamus.. is now understood to form a critical juncture in a circular feedback system that mediates and regulates neural impulses concerned with emotions and neuro-endocrine activity. **1973** *Folia Biol.* (Cracow) XXI. 329 It has been suggested that alterations in the.. secretory pattern of the neuroendocrine components are due to the action of stress. **1963** *Annales d'Endocrinol.* XXIV. 198 (*heading*) Introduction to the *neuro-endocrinological study of the pineal gland. **1974** *Nature* 17 May 213/1 Recent neuroendocrinological findings of most of the leading laboratories in Europe were discussed informally. **1969** *Britannica Yearbk. of Sci. & Future 1968* 389 These organic compounds, which were thought to act as chemical mediators (neurohumors) at synaptic junctions.. were of interest to *neuroendocrinologists. **1922** P. Fridenberg in L. F. Barker et al. *Endocrinol. & Metabolism* II. 757 (*heading*) Ophthalmic *neuro-endocrinology. **1961** *Lancet* 19 Aug. 442/2 In 1952 he was appointed senior lecturer in experimental neuroendocrinology at the Institute of Psychiatry. **1967** E. Bajusz (*title*) An introduction to clinical neuroendocrinology. **1893** Tuckey tr. *Hatschek's Amphioxus* 69 The *neuro-enteric canal which is generally typical in the development of the vertebrate animals. **1898** *Jrnl. R. Microsc. Soc.* 64 The general conception [of Prof. Apáthy] may be briefly stated. The nerve-cell is analogous to the muscle-cell, producing conducting substance (primitive fibrils, *neurofibrils), as the muscle-cell produces contractile substance (myofibrils). **1970** A. Peters et al. *Fine Struct. Nervous Syst.* iv. 62/2 The precise correlation between the classical neurofibrils of silver preparations and the structures seen in electron micrographs remains uncertain. **1973** Neurofibril [see *neurofibrillary* adj. below]. **1902** *Jrnl. Nerv. & Mental Dis.* XXIX. 435 (*heading*) The *neuro-fibrillae in nerve cells and nerve fibers of the retina. **1963** R. P. Dales *Annelids* vii. 138 Hess suggested that the irregularly shaped refractory body directed the light on to a dense reticulum of neurofibrillae which joined to form the basal nerve fibre. **1902** *Jrnl. R. Microsc. Soc.* 542 (*heading*) *Neurofibrillar theory. **1949** Neurofibrillar [see *neurofibrillary* adj. below]. **1971** *Jrnl. Compar. Neurol.* CXLIII. 395/2 Neurofibrillar boutons appear following section of the axons. **1902** *Jrnl. Nerv. & Mental Dis.* XXIX. 435 The author concludes.. that a *neuro-fibrillary structure of nerve cells and their processes.. is abundantly proven. **1949** B. W. Lichtenstein *Textbk. Neuropath.* iv. 46 Neurofibrillary abnormalities occur in a variety of disease states. The normal configuration of the neurofibrillar apparatus is well seen in preparations impregnated with silver according to Bielschowsky's method. **1973** H. M. Rális et al. *Techniques Neurohistol.* iv. 89 Methods for neurofibrils may also be used to demonstrate.. the neurofibrillary tangles which are found in certain pathological conditions. **1892** *Syd. Soc. Lex.*, **Neurofibroma*, a fibroma arising from the neurilemma of a nerve. **1899** *Allbutt's Syst. Med.* VI. 635 Multiple neurofibroma. **1955** Palay & Palade in *Jrnl. Biophysical & Biochem. Cytol.* I. 78 *Neurofilaments.—Fine, long threads, 60 to 100A in diameter and of indefinite length, traverse the cytoplasmic matrix [of the neuron] between masses of Nissl substance and other organelles. **1965** *Progress Brain Res.* XIV. 57 Electron microscopical studies have shown that the neurofibrils of light microscopists are made up of fine, long, apparently non-branching structures approximately 100 Å in diameter. These are the neurofilaments. **1968** G. A. Horridge *Interneurons* i. 11 Throughout the animal kingdom.. many axons and dendrites of nerve cells have tubules in the axoplasm; others, such as the squid giant axon, have neurofilaments that are thinner and less obviously tubular. **1969, 1970** Neurofilament [see *neurotubule* below]. **1909** *Cent. Dict.* Suppl., **Neuroglandular*, having the characteristics of sensory and glandular organs: as, the neuroglandular pit of some *Nemertini*. **1941** *Jrnl. Compar. Neurol.* LXXIV. 106 Neuroglandular cells are described in three species of cockroaches... The main center of neurosecretory activity is found to be the suboesophageal ganglion. **1943** H. Read *Education through Art* 26 Temperament.. is closely connected with the neuro-glandular system and the relations of the cortex to the sub-cortex. **1964** J. Z. Young *Model of Brain* xviii. 296 There must be some common principle involved to produce these similar neuroglandular arrangements in completely independent phyla. **1953** Carlisle & Knowles in *Nature* 29 Aug. 405/1 It seems preferable to call these organs by some purely topographical name which does not denote any function, actual or supposed. The adjective '*neurohæmal' seems to us to be the most appropriate topographical name denoting the common feature of these organs. The organs may thus be referred to collectively as neurohæmal organs, while the adjective may be combined with any of the pre-existing names for these various organs, as, for example, 'the post-commissural neurohæmal organ' and 'dorsal neurohæmal lamella'. **1967** C. A. G. Wiersma *Invertebr. Nervous Systems* x. 125 (*heading*) Correlation of propagated action potentials and release of neurosecretory material in a neurohemal organ. **1973** *Nature* 12 Oct. 288/2 Thus another useful criterion for the definition of a neurosecretory neurone—that it ends in a neurohaemal organ—loses its generality. **1957** *A.M.A. Arch. Path.* LXIII. 3/2 Histologic analysis of these alterations does not require special *neurohistologic methods. **1940** *Jrnl. Anat.* LXXIV. 413 (*heading*) Observations on the *neurohistological basis of cutaneous pain. **1973** H. M. Rális et al. *Techniques Neurohistol.* iv. 82 (*heading*) Neurohistological staining methods. **1901** *Buck's Handbk. Med. Sci.* (ed. 2) II. 336/1 Until further knowledge has been gained it is safer for the *neuro-histologist to work with the various methods [etc.]. **1968** Clarke & O'Malley *Human Brain & Spinal Cord* ii. 87 Two opposing groups of neurohistologists arose. On the one hand were those who believed that the nerve cells and their processes.. constituted independent units in contiguity with other units but not in continuity... Their opponents.. considered the cells and fibres to be in direct continuity with one another by way of a network to which the fibres contributed. **1897** *N.Y. Med. Jrnl.* 15 May 652/2 The most important contributions of Golgi in the domain of *neuro-histology consisted in (1) the invention of the silver method of staining; (2) the recognition within the central regions of cells of different types..; and (3) the discovery of lateral branches from the axis-cylinder process. **1940** *Jrnl. Anat.* LXXIV. 426 The neuro-histology of this area establishes that in the human skin pain is subserved by fine nerve fibres bearing free nerve endings. **1973** H. M. Rális et al. *Techniques Neurohistol.* v. 146 This final chapter.. mentions histochemical methods used in neurohistology as well as some applications of autoradiography in the study of nerve tissue. **1842** *Fraser's Mag.* XXVI. 375 Mr. Braid having failed in obtaining a hearing for his curious discoveries in Mesmerism, or *neurohypnology, as he calls it. **1843** Braid *Neurypnol.* 7 In respect to the *Neuro-Hypnotic state. **1842** —— in *Trans. Brit. Assoc.* 29 June, Practical Essay on the Curative Agency of *Neuro-Hypnotism. **1926** G. R. de Beer *Compar. Anat. Pituitary Body* ii. 28 The anterior lobe consists only of the pars anterior, but the posterior lobe, which always contains the partes intermedia and nervosa, may or may not also be associated with the pars tuberalis, since many authors fail to distinguish between the latter and the pars intermedia. In order to avoid ambiguity the term **neuro-intermediate lobe* may be used to include the pars nervosa and the pars intermedia, since they are always in the closest morphological association. **1965** Lee & Knowles *Animal Hormones* ii. 28 In fishes the pituitary gland is conveniently divided into three portions... Closely associated with the posterior portion of the adenohypophysis (pars intermedia), and extending into it, is the pars nervosa; the term neuro-intermediate lobe is often applied to this region. **1973** *Nature* 28 Sept. 207/2 Pituitary control of sebaceous gland activity has generally been assumed to be a function of the anterior lobe. The possibility that the neurointermediate (NI) lobe is involved was first suggested when we found that its removal led to a decrease in sebum secretion. **1883** Klein *Elem. Histol.* §140 Its own hyaline more or less elastic sheath, composed of *neurokeratin. **1960** L. F. Chapman et al. in *Trans. Assoc. Amer. Physicians* LXXIII. 263 Specimens collected from the head during the headache attacks contained a substance that could be distinguished from serotonin,.. acetylcholine and histamine... The heat stabilized substance had many of the properties of bradykinin, Kallidin, or 'plasma kinin'... This polypeptide has been labeled '*neurokinin' and has been found.. to be released during neuronal excitation. **1969** J. Pearce *Migraine* vii. 39 More recently the polypeptides and kinins have been examined more critically, because of the claims of isolation of neurokinin from the scalp tissue fluid in migraine attacks. **1908** W. McDougall in *Brain* XXXI. 247 This distinction between chemically stored or potential nervous energy and the liberated active nervous energy is, I feel sure, one of the first importance for neurological speculation... Oscar Vogt.. has proposed to mark it by calling the freed nervous energy '*neurokyme'... I adopt Vogt's term. **1926** —— *Outl. Abnormal Psychol.* v. 104 All mental activity involves the discharge of neurokyme from the sensory to the motor side of the brain. **1944** W. Brown *Psychol. & Psychotherapy* (ed. 5) v. 57 McDougall regards the passage of nervous energy (neurokyme) across the synapses of the cerebral cortex as the physical correlate of the psychical process. **1961** *Studies in Linguistics* XV. 70 Ideally, the *neurolinguist would have thorough training in scientific linguistics and in neuroanatomy and neurophysiology. **1936** *Neuro-linguistic [see *neurosemantic* adj. below]. **1961** *Studies in Linguistics* XV. 70 Neurolinguistic work has certainly been carried out under other names, by people who work with aphasia, by neurosurgeons and neurologists, [etc.]. **1970** J. Laver in J. Lyons *New Horizons in Linguistics* iii. 61 The healthy adult brain is not itself accessible to neurolinguistic experiment. There is thus no possibility of directly observing the neural mechanisms involved in constructing a neurolinguistic program. **1961** E. C. Trager in *Studies in Linguistics* XV. 70 *Neurolinguistics is the term proposed here for a field of interdisciplinary scientific study which does not as yet have a formal existence. Its subject matter is the relationship between the human nervous system and language. **1970** J. Laver in J. Lyons *New Horizons in Linguistics* iii. 61 In neurolinguistics the subdisciplinary boundary between phonetics and linguistics, which has always been of doubtful validity, is largely disappearing. **1973** *Tuscaloosa* (Ala.) *News* 10 Apr. 5/4 She is interested in neurolinguistics and studies of aphasia. **1975** *Canad. Jrnl. Linguistics* XX. 94 *A Study in Neurolinguistics* is perhaps the first publication in the form of a monograph in the field of 'language and the brain' with the term 'neurolinguistics' in its title. **1866** Owen *Anat. Vertebr.* I. 203, I would suggest.. *neuromere. **1897** *Nat. Sci.* Feb. 114 That.. branch of morphology which deals with the nerve-segments of the head (cerebral neuromeres). **1851** tr. *Unzer & Prochaska's Nervous Syst.* (Syd. Soc.) Introd. 1 He showed an early inclination to *neuro-metaphysical studies. **1818** Southey *Let.* 5 Dec. in *Life* (1850) IV. 327 The nitrous oxyde approaches nearer to the notion of a *neurometer than anything which perhaps could be devised. **1899** *Allbutt's Syst. Med.* VIII. 88 '*Neuro-mimesis' lays too much stress on the resemblances .. between the symptoms of hysteria and of other diseases. **1884** H. M. Jones *Health of Senses* v. 132 The *neuromimetic, with curved spine, pain in joints,.. aches in every part of the body. **1864** *Jrnl. Mental Sci.* X. 37 There appears to be a *neuro-muscular, as well as a purely mental retentiveness. **1877** Huxley *Anat. Inv. Anim.* 63 Kleinenberg terms those neuro-muscular elements. **1892** J. A. Thomson *Outl. Zool.* iii. 36 In some Cœlenterates it is possible that some of the external cells combine contractile, nervous, and even other functions. Under this impression many call them 'neuro-muscular'. **1896** *Allbutt's Syst. Med.* I. 159 The development and activity of the neuro-muscular system. **1904** *Jrnl. Physiol.* XXX. 494 If our conception of this neuro-muscular junctional tissue is correct the name nerve-ending is obviously a misnomer. **1937** *Physiol. Rev.* XVII. 538 It may be concluded that synapses and neuro-muscular junctions are essentially similar, there being close contact but not protoplasmic continuity. **1948** *Federation Proc.* VII. 452/1 The fundamental change which accounts for the neuromuscular block produced by curare itself is a decrease in the end-plate potential. **1950** J. H. Burn *Lect. Notes Pharmacol.* (ed. 2) 14 Neostigmine restores neuromuscular transmission. **1963** R. P. Dales *Annelids* vi. 119 The failure to respond is not due to failure of the giant fibre itself, but to the relay or to the neuromuscular junction. **1926** *Physiol. Rev.* VI. 564 Comparable data on muscle and the *neuromyal junction. **1965** *Jrnl. Pharmacol. & Exper. Therap.* CXLVII. 350 (*heading*) Pharmacological actions of oxamides and hydroxyanalinium compounds at frog neuromyal junction. **1839–47** *Todd's Cycl. Anat.* III. 30/1 An argument in favour of the theory of *neuromyic action. *a* **1890** Coues & Shute in *N.Y. Med. Record* XXXII. 93 (Cent.), Neurology is the key to myology, and a *neuro-myology is practicable. **1899** *Allbutt's Syst. Med.* VI. 463 *Neuro-myositis, in which the primary lesion is nervous. **1897** Wilder in *Nature* 7 Jan. 224 The *neuronyms adopted by the Anatomische Gesellschaft in 1895. **1875** H. Walton *Dis. Eye* 907 *Neuroparalytic corneitis. **1878** T. Bryant *Pract. Surg.* I. 317 Cases of neuro-paralytic ophthalmia. **1913** *Jrnl. Pharmacol. & Exper. Therap.* V. 107 We now approach the subject of the susceptibility of the central heat-regulating mechanism to more specific *neuro-pharmacologic influences. **1973** *Folia Biol.* (Cracow) XXI. 331 The CAH-positive cells of the brain in the cockroach undergo most of the alterations.. after the administration of various types of neuropharmacologic agents. **1959** *Jrnl. Pharmacol. & Exper. Therap.* CXXVI. 312/1 Thioridazine hydrochloride.. and chlorpromazine hydrochloride.. have been examined for *neuropharmacological properties in mice and rats. **1971** *New Scientist* 9 Dec. 119 These various poisons have proved novel tools in neuro-pharmacological research, especially in elucidating the mechanism of nervous conduction. **1971** *Nature* 24 Sept. 285/2 Other *neuropharmacologically-active or serotonin-related drugs were also tested. **1966** *Sci. News Let.* 1 Jan. 6 Rats.. given the compound.. retained what they had learned longer, Dr. N. P. Plotnikoff, an Abbott *neuro-pharmacologist, reported. **1973** *Nature* 14 Dec. p. xvi/1 (Advt.), We seek a Technician to join a team of neuro-pharmacologists. **1955** *Neuropharmacology [see *neurochemistry* above]. **1973** *Nature* 28 Sept. p. xx/3 (Advt.), General experience of either neurochemistry, neurophysiology, or neuropharmacology is essential. **1960** *Biochim. & Biophys. Acta* XXXVIII. 266 From sheep posterior hypophysis a complex was obtained containing 90% of the oxytocic and vasopressic activity of the gland. The complex is an association of oxytocine and vasopressine with a protein, *neurophysine [*sic*: *Eng. summary of article in Fr.*]. **1970** *Biochem. Jrnl.* CXVI. 908/2 The neurophysins of the pig form a group of proteins of different electrophoretic mobilities but all possessing the capacity to bind oxytocin and [8-lysine]-vasopressin. **1973** *Nature* 2 Mar. 63/1 This system is characterized immunochemically by the neurophysins, the specific carrier-proteins for vasopressin and oxytocin. **1937** *Surgery* I. 132 The vast literature on recent *neurophysiologic research. **1972** *Science* 12 May 607/1 Any changes in the action potentials of trained motor units.. must reflect neurophysiologic changes of the single neuron supplying the motor unit. **1862** *Syd. Soc. Year-bk. Med.* 43 *Neuro-physiological Inquiries. **1962** C. L. Buxton *Study of Psychophysical Methods for Relief Childbirth Pain* vii. 60 Attempts were made also to explain *neurophysiologically how it might be possible for fear and tension to increase the pain and length of labor. **1971** *Jrnl. Gen. Psychol.* LXXXIV. 141 In the early experimentation, there was no way to isolate a channel neurophysiologically. **1949** Koestler *Insight & Outlook* iv. 44 The demonstration or refutation by the *neuro-physiologist of the existence of corresponding mechanisms in the central nervous system. **1966** I. Asimov *Fantastic Voyage* i. 17 The extension of the technique could be of great importance to the neuro-physiologist. **1973** *Sci. Amer.* July 96/3 Between 1900 and 1920 Charles S. Sherrington, the foremost neuro-physiologist of the time, applied the technique of electrical stimulation to study how the cerebrum controlled movement. **1868** Spencer *Princ. Psychol.* (1872) I. I. vii. 142 The truths of *Neuro-physiology.. set down in the foregoing chapters. [**1892** *Syd. Soc. Lex.*, *Neuroplasma*, Kupffer's term for a fluid which he supposed to lie between the fibrils of the cylinder-axis of a nerve.] **1894** Gould *Dict. Med.* 869/1 *Neuroplasm. **1896** E. L. Billstein tr. *Stöhr's Text-bk. Histol.* II. i. 81 Each fibrilla [of the axon] represents a special conducting path and is cemented to neighboring fibrillae by a small amount of finely-granular interstitial substance—neuroplasm. **1960** L. Picken *Organization of Cells* vii. 291 In the light of electron microscope studies.. it is likely that the axoplasm differs from the neuroplasm rather in the relative abundance and orientation of the various components.. than in absolute composition. **1970** *Nature* 5 Sept. 1006/2 It is generally believed that neuroplasm is constantly synthesized in the cell body and moves as a gel down the axon (and probably also along the dendrites). **1909** *Cent. Dict.* Suppl., *Neuro-plasmic. **1965** *Acta Neuropath.* IV. 33 Neuroplasmic swellings were found within dendrites. **1970** P. A. Weiss in F. O. Schmitt *Neurosciences: 2nd Study Program* lxxiii. 840 (*heading*) Neuronal dynamics and neuroplasmic flow. **1884** Hyatt in *Proc. Boston Soc. Nat. Hist.* XXIII. 119 The homology of the fore and hind *neuropores with the fore and hind openings of the actinostome. **1893** Tuckey tr. *Hatschek's Amphioxus* 177 Transverse section through the anterior part of the neuropore. **1891** D. Wilson *Right Hand* 186 The centres of the *neuro-psychic factors of language. **1851** tr. *Unzer & Prochaska's Nervous Syst.* (Syd. Soc.) Introd. 2 The *neuro-psychological essays.. are frequently referred to in the present work. *Ibid.* 6 There was.. another *neuro-psychologist, whose name is less known in England. **1900** Dorland *Med. Dict.* 442/2 **Neuropsychosis*, nervous disease complicated with mental disorder. **1918** A. A. Brill tr. *Freud's Totem & Taboo* iii. 158 The system formation is most ingenious in delusional states (paranoia) and dominates the clinical picture, but it also must not be overlooked in other forms of neuropsychoses. **1924** J. Riviere et al. tr. *Freud's Coll. Papers* I. 59 (*heading*) The defence of neuropsychoses. **1936** A. Myerson in *Amer. Jrnl. Psychiatry* XCIII. 281, I formally introduce the concept of the neuropsychosis. The neuropsychosis comes into being by an intensification of the symptomatology of the neuroses. **1964** Taveras & Wood *Diagnostic Neuroradiol.* 2 The use of gamma rays from radioactive isotopes for scanning, and the use of heat waves in thermography,.. are being incorporated in *neuroradiologic clinical practice. **1962** *Brit. Jrnl. Radiol.* XXXV. 501/1 Problems of *neuroradiological nomenclature and the radiographic projections were discussed. **1955** *Brit. Jrnl. Surg.* XLIII 8/1 A very high proportion of successful angiograms justifies a wider trial. Even if it may not be equally successful in other hands I believe that it will become an important part of the armamentarium of *neuroradiologist and neurosurgeon. **1961** *Lancet* 30 Sept. 746/1 Dr. J. L. G. Thomson, the neuroradiologist in Bristol, and all of the neurosurgical team are now performing about 700 angiographies a year. **1938** Wakeley & Orley (*title*) A textbook of *neuro-radiology. **1964** Taveras & Wood *Diagnostic Neuroradiol.* 1 During the last fifteen years, angiography has arrived at its appropriate place of importance in diagnostic neuroradiology. **1878** A. M. Hamilton *Nerv. Dis.* 187 Loss of vision complete, *neuroretinitis of both eyes. **1899** *Allbutt's Syst. Med.* VI. 707 The occurrence of attacks of neuro-retinitis in gouty subjects. **1963** (*title of periodical*) *Neurosciences research program bulletin. **1964** *New Scientist* 10 Sept. 643/1 Man's search for the physical basis of mental processes has evolved a number of disparate neurosciences. Some of these, such as neurology, neuroanatomy, neurophysiology, neurochemistry, neuropathology, and psychology, have advanced to the status of mature sciences. **1970** *Nature* 5 Sept. 1006/1 During the past few years neuroscience, comprising the sciences of brain and behaviour, has been differentiating, integrating, regrouping. **1974** *Times Lit. Suppl.* 18 Oct. 1151/3 It will transform the established neuro-sciences until they become increasingly able to comprehend the problems of behaviour, possibly even of mind. **1967** R. B. Livingston in G. C. Quarton et al. *Neurosciences: Study Program* 500/1 *Neuro-scientists are drawn to this field..by a desire to learn more about ourselves as human beings. **1974** *Nature* 1 Mar. p. v/1 (Advt.), This new book by the well-known neuroscientist Elliot S. Valenstein. **1941** *Jrnl. Compar. Neurol.* LXXIV. 93 *Neurosecretion is present in both vertebrates and invertebrates. **1961** *Biol. Abstr.* XXXVI. 1201/1 (*heading*) Neurosecretions in the insect. **1963** R. P. Dales *Annelids* viii. 166 Neurosecretion may be of major importance in the co-ordination of the annelid body. **1968** *New Scientist* 16 May 355/1 It is quite possible that neurosecretions are the 'oldest' hormones in the animal kingdom. **1973** *Proc. Indian Acad. Sci.* B. LXXVII. 148 Involvement of neurosecretion in some of the physiological activities of this scorpion will be reported here. **1940** *Nature* 17 Feb. 264/1 (*heading*) *Neurosecretory cells in the ganglia of Lepidoptera. **1956** *Ibid.* 17 Mar. 532/1 In the cockroach, activity rhythms may have a neurosecretory basis. **1963** R. P. Dales *Annelids* viii. 166 In *Nephthys* the cells in the blood greatly increase and take up neurosecretory material from the back of the brain during posterior regeneration following amputation. **1968** H. O. Hofer in G. H. Bourne *Struct. & Function of Nervous Tissue* I. xi. 471 The neurosecretory substances act as hormones, long-range and long-acting; and they are not directly transmitted, but are released in a circulating body fluid as acting agents. **1936** A. Korzybski in *Amer. Jrnl. Psychiatry* XCIII. 29 By using the term *evaluation* as a fundamental term, we bridge methodologically and linguistically the exact sciences with other sciences, psychiatry included. We gain thereby powerful neuro-linguistic and *neuro-semantic direct methods for education and psychotherapy. **1946** S. A. Hayakawa in W. S. Knickerbocker *Twentieth Century English* 47 In accounting for human behavior it postulates the 'neuro-semantic environment'—the environment, that is, of dogmas, beliefs, creeds, knowledge, and superstitions to which we react as the result of our training—as a fundamental and inescapable part of our total environment. **1929** C. U. A. Kappers *Evolution Nervous Syst. Invertebr., Vertebr. & Man* 3 The different forms of nervous conductors are three: the *neuro-sensory cell, which generally retains its place in an epithelial layer, the primitive or asynaptic ganglion cell and the polarized or synaptic neurone, both of which are nearly always located under the epithelium. **1940** O. Lowenstein *Parker & Haswell's Text-bk. Zool.* (ed. 6) I. i. 36 The photosensitive cells in the retina of the vertebrate eye and the olfactory receptor cells situated in the epithelium coating of the vertebrate nose have the structure of neuro-sensory cells. **1946** L. A. White in W. S. Knickerbocker *Twentieth Century Eng.* 93 The animal hearing them understands them..by virtue of his own inborn neuro-sensory equipment. **1962** D. Nichols *Echinoderms* iii. 43 Besides the general scattering of neurosensory cells over the asteroid body, there are five light-sensitive optic cushions, one at the base of each terminal tentacle. **1974** *Sci. Amer.* Nov. 14/3 Reader in neurosensory physiology. **1925** *Arch. Neurol. & Psychiatry* (Chicago) XIV. 192 It.. is important, more especially for the *neurosurgeon..that his clinical experiences should be correlated with a more detailed classification of the gliomas than is customary. **1972** *Oxford Times* 26 May 6/7 Mr R. Gye, consultant neurosurgeon, explained the many uses to which the blanket could be put. **1904** *Alienist & Neurologist* XXV. 404 (*heading*) *Neurosurgery. Trigeminal neuralgia treated by intraneural injections of osmic acid. **1937** *Surgery* I. 132 With the later days of Victor Horsley in England and the early days of Harvey Cushing in America, neurosurgery may truly be said to have been born. **1966** *Lancet* 24 Dec. 1400/1 A speciality like neuro-surgery requires an extra year's training. **1932** *Glasgow Med. Jrnl.* CXVIII. 137 (*heading*) The work of a *neuro-surgical clinic. **1955** A. Huxley *Let.* 25 Sept. (1969) 767 Penfield says, absence of evidence, in the present state of neurosurgical knowledge, proves nothing. **1974** *Nature* 13 Dec. 582/2 Recordings of unit activity during neurosurgical operations have demonstrated neuronal activity in cortex and subcortical structures. [**1877** *Med. Times & Gaz.* 10 Nov. 511/1 Nerve-syphilis appears to affect with preference those persons in whom there is the neuropathic constitution.] **1878** *Boston Med. & Surgical Jrnl.* XCVIII. 278 *Neuro-Syphilis.—As nervous diseases of syphilitic origin are more amenable to treatment than the corresponding idiopathic ones, a correct diagnosis may at times be sufficient to save a life otherwise lost. **1915** *Ibid.* CLXXIII. 996/1 (*heading*) The significance of changes in cellular content of cerebrospinal fluid in neurosyphilis. **1946** *Nature* 17 Aug. 243/2 Penicillin sodium in saline solution is effective to a greater or lesser degree in all aspects of neurosyphilis studied. **1974** Passmore & Robson *Compan. Med. Stud.* III. xiii. 6/1 In all forms of neurosyphilis the results of treatment depend on the number of neurones already destroyed. **1877** *Med. Times & Gaz.* 10 Nov. 511/1 *Neuro-syphilitic affections belong generally to the later portions of the secondary stage, or to the tertiary period of the complaint. **1918** *Jrnl. Amer. Med. Assoc.* 28 Sept. 1023/2 We can..control the majority of the early infections of the [cerebrospinal] fluid and greatly limit the number of neurosyphilitics in the future. **1921** *Ibid.* 2 July 3/2 In eight of the twenty-one neurosyphilitic partners the type of neurosyphilis was the same as in the original patient. **1954** D. Nabarro *Congenital Syphilis* viii. 282 Unless neurosyphilis is actively sought by routine C.S.F. investigations upon patients, many neurosyphilitics will be overlooked. **1972** *Afr. Jrnl. Med. Sci.* III. 195 Cases.. diagnosed as neurosyphilitic on clinical grounds should be given the benefit of adequate penicillin therapy. **1901** *Gray's Anat.* (ed. 15) [52] (*heading*) Organ of Golgi (*neuro-tendinous spindle) from the human tendo Achillis. **1920** S. W. Ranson *Anat. Nervous Syst.* v. 72 Somewhat analogous structures [to the neuromuscular end organs] are the neurotendinous end organs or tendon spindles where myelinated nerve-fibers end in relation to specialized tendon fasciculi. **1962** E. C. Crosby et al. *Correlative Anat. Nervous Syst.* ii. 87/2 The dendritic endings may be of neuromuscular or neurotendinous type (that is, muscle spindles or tendon spindles). **1904** *Brit. Med. Jrnl.* No. 2280. 574 A strongly *neurotoxic poison such as cobra venom. **1949** *Jrnl. Compar. Neurol.* XCI. 339 Only such procedures as bear specifically on the comparative *neurotoxicity of this drug for various animals will be set forth here. **1959** *Arch. Internat. de Pharmacodynamie et de Thérapie* CXXII. 98 Rats on a diet deficient in pyridoxine developed signs of neurotoxicity when administered IDPN. **1968** W. C. Bowman et al. *Textbk. Pharmacol.* xxviii. 722 All of the potent compounds which cause neurotoxicity are inhibitors of butyryl cholinesterase. **1971** *Nature* 20 Aug. 525/2 Between them the two proteins manifest ferocious neurotoxicity. **1902** *Brit. Med. Jrnl.* No. 2154. 920 Enriquet and Sicard [deal] with *neurotoxin. **1948** De Robertis & Schmitt in *Jrnl. Cellular & Compar. Physiol.* XXXI. 3 Although unequivocal proof of the structure of the fibers cannot yet be given, the available evidence is consistent with the view that they are tubular, possessing a thin wall of relatively high electron density and a core of low density. To facilitate description they will be called '*neurotubules'. **1969** *Nature* 15 Nov. 710/1 The chief axoplasmic components, extending beyond the neurone cell body, are neurofilaments and neurotubules. **1970** P. A. Weiss in F. O. Schmitt *Neurosciences: 2nd Study Program* lxxiii. 845/2 In contrast to the straight neurotubules, the neurofilaments, 70–100 Ångström units in diameter, show a more wavy course. **1888** Rolleston & Jackson *Anim. Life* 570 An aboral stem, generally jointed and containing a *neuro-vascular apparatus. **1899** *Allbutt's Syst. Med.* VIII. 609 A certain disposition to nutritive disturbance, or even neuro-vascular tension. **1961** *Lancet* 23 Sept. 717/2 The Cox strains..exhibit a much higher level of monkey *neurovirulence. **1973** *Nature* 26 Jan. 248/2 The vaccine was used on a limited scale but was withdrawn after Dick had claimed that he had detected a reversion to neurovirulence.

neuroepithelial (ˌnjʊərəʊɛpɪˈθiːlɪəl), *a.* *Histology.* Also **neuro-epithelial**. [f. neuro- + epitheli(um + -al.] **a.** Of or pertaining to neuroepithelium (sense a); applied *spec.* to an epithelial nerve cell that is a sensory receptor.

1889 McKendrick & Stoehr *Text-bk. Physiol.* II. xi. i. 448 In certain medusæ, the transition between a neuro-epithelial cell and a ganglionic or nerve cell may be traced. **1907** G. A. Piersol *Human Anat.* 1463 The inner lamella [of the retina] may be subdivided..into the neuro-epithelial and the cerebral layers. **1952** Habel & Biberstein tr. *Trautmann & Fiebiger's Fund. Histology Domestic Animals* iii. 32 The neuroepithelial cells occur in taste buds, the olfactory epithelium, the cristae and maculae staticae, the organ of Corti, and the retina. **1966** T. S. & C. R. Leeson *Histology* xiv. 267/2 The neuroepithelial taste cells are distributed between the supporting cells and number only 4 to 16 in each taste bud. **1974** P. Constantinides *Functional Electronic Histology* vi. 81/2 (*heading*) Neuro-epithelial synapses.

b. Composed of or derived from neuroepithelium (sense b).

1948 R. A. Willis *Path. Tumours* lii. 818 While it is possible that the tumours containing undoubted embryonic neuro-epithelial tissue..were indeed pure embryonic neuro-epithelial growths, this remains uncertain. **1949** B. W. Lichtenstein *Textbk. Neuropath.* iv. 47 One generally recognizes two varieties of interstitial tissue in the fully developed nervous system—the neuroglia of neuro-epithelial origin and the microglia or mesenchymal origin. **1971** J. Minckler *Path. Nervous Syst.* II. clvii. 2111/1 Very primitive tumors occasionally occur in peripheral nerves which are regarded as neuroepithelial.

neuroepithelium (ˌnjʊərəʊɛpɪˈθiːlɪəm). *Histology.* Also **neuro-epithelium**. [mod.L., f. neuro- + epithelium, as tr. G. *neuroepithel* (G. Schwalbe in Graefe & Saemisch *Handb. d. ges. Augenheilkunde* (1874) I. 358).] **a.** The sensory epithelium in organs of special sense, such as the eye or the nose.

1885 W. Stirling tr. *Landois's Text-bk. Human Physiol.* II. 960 The layer of rods and cones or neuro-epithelium of Schwalbe. **1899** F. H. Gerrish *Text-bk. Anat.* 43 Sensory epithelium, or neuro-epithelium cells, are found in close relation with the filamentous terminals of the nerves devoted to taste, smell, hearing, and sight. **1929** S. Duke-Elder *Recent Adv. Ophthalm.* (ed. 2) iii. 104 As the primary optic vesicle invaginates, two layers are formed... The inner layer shows two well-differentiated regions: a marginal layer.., and deep to this the cells proper of the primitive neuro-epithelium. **1943** Fischer & Wolfson *Inner Ear* x. 319 There was a circular fold of neuro-epithelium segmenting the utricle. **1952** Habel & Biberstein tr. *Trautmann & Fiebiger's Fund. Histol. Domestic Animals* ii. 32 (*heading*) Sensory epithelium (neuro-epithelium).

b. Embryonic ectoderm that develops into nervous tissue.

1889 *Nature* 10 Jan. 260/2 The epithelium of this ciliated groove..is the only part of the primary central cylinder which is ciliated, and which does not form ganglion elements, and hence it is the only part which is not neuro-epithelium. **1940** S. A. K. Wilson *Neurol.* II. lxxii. 1176 In the epiblast of the embryo there appears a medullary tube lined by primitive neuroepithelium. **1958** R. A. Willis *Borderland Embryol. & Path.* iii. 115 This undifferentiated prospective nervous tissue, from which neurones, neuroglia and ependyma will all arise, is neuro-epithelium. **1971** —— in J. Minckler *Path. Nervous Syst.* II. cxlvi. 1938/2 Malignant teratomas in adults..may contain nervous tissue at all stages of development, from early neuroepithelium to its fully differentiated derivatives.

neurofibromatosis (ˌnjʊərəʊfaɪbrəʊməˈtəʊsɪs). *Path.* [f. *neurofibromat-* (taken as stem of *neurofibroma*, s.v. neuro-) + -osis.] Any condition characterized by multiple neurofibromas; *spec.* a condition in which multiple (often very numerous) palpable neurofibromas occur on the peripheral nerves (also called *von Recklinghausen's disease*).

1896 *Brit. Med. Jrnl.* 10 Oct. 1024/1 (*heading*) On neuro-fibromatosis and tumours relating to nerves. **1899** *Lancet* 29 July 271/2 The nature of Recklinghausen's disease or, as it has sometimes been called, generalised neuro-fibromatosis. **1900** A. Thomson (*title*) On neuroma and neuro-fibromatosis. **1966** Wright & Symmers *Systemic Path.* II. xxxiv. 1236/1 The rare condition that is sometimes referred to as central neuro-fibromatosis, or Wishart's disease, may occur in association with neurofibromatosis of the peripheral nerves (von Recklinghausen's disease), or it may exist without the latter. **1973** *Daily Colonist* (Victoria, B.C.) 4 Oct. 2/3 A rare condition called neurofibromatosis is featured by multiple bumps.

neurogenesis (njʊərəʊˈdʒɛnɪsɪs). *Biol.* [f. neuro- + -genesis.] The development of nervous tissue.

1900 in Dorland *Med. Dict.* **1908** *Jrnl. R. Microsc. Soc.* 27 Arguments based on embryonic neurogenesis. **1928** R. M. May tr. *Ramón y Cajal's Degeneration & Regeneration Nervous Syst.* I. xvi. 381 The ideas of Harrison..are perfectly applicable to normal neurogenesis as well as to nervous regeneration. **1967** M. V. Edds in G. C. Quarton et al. *Neurosciences: a Study Program* 232/1 Faced with the limitations imposed by working with the embryo, investigators of neurogenesis have often turned to older organisms with the fortunate capacity of regenerating amputated nerve fibers.

neurogenetic (njʊərəʊdʒəˈnɛtɪk), *a.* [f. neuro- + -genetic.] = neurogenic *a.* 2.

1889 *Jrnl. R. Microsc. Soc.* 494 The primordial cells of the embryonic brain are therefore neurogenetic, giving rise to the special nerve-cells. **1928** R. M. May tr. *Ramón y Cajal's Degeneration & Regeneration Nervous Syst.* I. xvi. 383 In the neurogenetic process the following factors come into play.

neurogenic (njʊərəˈdʒɛnɪk), *a.* [f. neuro- + -genic.] **1. a.** Of a theory: implying or assuming control (esp. of the heart-beat) by the nervous system.

1901 *Buck's Handbk. Med. Sci.* (ed. 2) III. 111/1 The neurogenic theory is based on the following considerations: Muscular tissue.. depends upon its motor-nerve impulses to set it into action. **1922** C. P. Howard in L. F. Barker *Endocrinol. & Metabolism* I. 313 Biedl has come to the conclusion that the neurogenic theory was based upon inconclusive experiments.

b. Caused or controlled by (a disorder of) the nervous system.

1904 [see *myogenic* adj. s.v. myo-]. **1949** Koestler *Insight & Outlook* v. 69 They [*sc.* digestive disorders] could be called neurogenic rather than psychogenic. **1961** *Lancet* 19 Aug. 409/1 The book..ends with a detailed account of the surgical treatment of neurogenic disorders of the entire urogenital tract. **1974** *Nature* 8 Mar. 106/3 In the singing katydids..relatively high rates of sound pulses..are controlled by synchronous, or neurogenic, muscles in which each contraction is initiated by a nerve impulse.

c. ***neurogenic bladder***, abnormal functioning of the bladder owing to disturbances of nervous control.

1930 *Urologic & Cutaneous Rev.* XXXIV 541/2 (*heading*) Treatment of the neurogenic bladder with the slow sinusoidal current. **1952** P. A. HERBUT *Urological Path.* I. iii. 323 In neurogenic bladder the sphincteric mechanism ceases to exist as an efficient functioning structure and the detrusor mechanism dictates the behavior of the bladder. **1966** WRIGHT & SYMMERS *Systemic Path.* I. xxv. 782/1 The neurogenic bladder is in effect a functional obstruction of the urinary tract.

2. Of or pertaining to neurogenesis; giving rise to nervous tissue.

1915 J. A. NELSON *Embryol. of Honey Bee* viii. 127 The neurogenic area..comprises two longitudinal thickenings, the primitive swellings..which are separated by a median furrow. **1928** R. M. MAY tr. *Ramón y Cajal's Degeneration & Regeneration Nervous Syst.* I. xvi. 381 Some of the neurogenic factors mentioned by Harrison seem to us highly doubtful. **1941** JOHANNSEN & BUTT *Embryol. of Insects & Myriapods* xv. 242 A thin layer of elongated cells, the neurilemma, probably arising from the outlying ganglion cells, covers the neurogenic tissue dorsally.

Hence **neuro'genically** *adv.*, by the nervous system or by nerves.

1960 *Arch. Neurol.* III. 229/1 The result is a sterile inflammatory reaction, neurogenically induced. **1967** *Jrnl. Pharmacol. & Exper. Therap.* CLV. 37/2 Phentolamine blocked with equal facility..the norepinephrine- and neurogenically evoked constriction. **1971** *Nature* 28 May 264/2 Increased sensitivity at the receptor level could play a role in enhancement of neurogenically mediated responses.

neuroglia (njʊ'rɒglɪə). *Anat.* [f. NEURO- + late Gr. γλία glue; named by Virchow.] The delicate connective tissue found in the great nerve-centres, and in the retina; the reticular or sustentacular tissue.

1873 T. H. GREEN *Introd. Pathol.* (ed. 2) 121 Round-celled sarcoma growing from the neuroglia or connective tissue of nerve. **1888** ROLLESTON & JACKSON *Anim. Life* 52 A mass of neuroglia or *substantia reticularis* lies immediately dorsal to the central canal.

attrib. **1897** *Allbutt's Syst. Med.* II. 699 The small neuroglia corpuscles or cells. **1899** *Ibid.* VII. 172 A thick cluster of neuroglia fibres.

Hence **neu'rogliac, -ial, -iar, -ic** *adjs.*

1890 in *Cent. Dict.* **1892** in *Syd. Soc. Lex.* **1899** *Allbutt's Syst. Med.* VII. 33 The excess of neuroglial connective tissue... The neuroglial cells with radiating processes.

neurogram ('njʊərəʊgræm). [f. NEURO- + -GRAM.] An enduring structural change postulated as being produced in the nervous system by experience and as being the physiological basis of memory.

1914 M. PRINCE *Unconscious* v. 131, I have been in the habit of using the term *neurograms* to characterize these brain records... Richard Semon..has adopted the term Engramm with much the same signification that I have given to Neurogram. **1921** M. GARNETT *Educ. & World Citizenship* v. 42 Examples of neural dispositions, or neurograms, are furnished by the functional systems of nervous arcs. **1939** —— *Knowledge & Character* iv. 54 The same neurones and systems of neurones may form part of several different neurograms.

neurography (njʊ'rɒgrəfɪ). [ad. mod.L. *neurographia* (Vieussens, 1684): see NEURO- and -GRAPHY. Hence also F. *névrographie*.]

1. Scientific description of the nerves; descriptive neurology.

1727-38 CHAMBERS *Cycl.* s.v. *Neurology*, Neurology seems to be of less extent than neurography. **1875** SIR W. TURNER in *Encycl. Brit.* I. 813/2 The publication of his great work on neurography in 1684.

2. Neuration.

1880 RUSKIN *Notes on Prout & Hunt* 15 In the articulation of the fly's legs, or the neurography of the bee's wings.

3. A name proposed for: all the neurograms of an individual, considered collectively.

1921 M. GARNETT *Educ. & World Citizenship* v. 63 In the course of life's experience, then, an individual's neurography—if we may so describe all his neurograms, however distributed and arranged—tends to become organised into interest-systems. **1939** —— *Knowl. & Character* xi. 215 That our neurographies do tend to correspond to the realm of facts..is so important that we must insist further upon it.

neurohormone (njʊərəʊ'hɔːməʊn). *Physiol.* [f. NEURO- + HORMONE.] Any hormone or neurotransmitter released by the nervous system.

1941 A. GROLLMAN *Essent. Endocrinol.* i. 2 This definition [of true hormones] excludes the..neurohormones,..for these are..local in their effects or are transported by diffusion. **1955** J. H. WELSH in Pincus & Thimann *Hormones* III. iii. 99 In this chapter an attempt will be made to see what all neurons have in common with respect to production, transport, storage, and release of regulator substances. It is proposed that the term 'neurohormone' be used to designate these substances. We may well continue to speak of 'neurohumors' and of 'neurosecretory materials', but it appears highly desirable to have an exclusive term, and 'neurohormone', previously used in this sense without precise definition,..seems highly appropriate. *Ibid.*, The term neurohormone..may be defined as an organic compound produced by neurons and released at their endings to act as a chemical messenger or hormone, either locally or at a distance. **1965** J. POLLITT *Depression and its Treatment* iv. 53 Monoamines are neurohormones regarded as essential for normal activity of the brain, and the two substances of this group playing particularly important roles in mood regulation, are serotonin..and noradrenalin. **1972** *Sci. Amer.* Nov. 28/3 The hypothesis that pituitary function is controlled by neurohormones originating in the hypothalamus was soon well established. **1974** *Nature* 15 Mar. 238/1 Many hormones, including noradrenaline, the neurohormone of the sympathetic nervous system.

So **neurohor'monal** *a.*, involving both the nervous system and the endocrine system; of or pertaining to a neurohormone.

1949 KOESTLER *Insight & Outlook* v. 69 Digestive disorders..may be explained in direct neurohormonal terms. *Ibid.* viii. 127 The neurohormonal excitation may persist for a while like the duffed-down pain. **1962** *Science Survey* III. 266 The neuro-hormonal chain of events leading to the olfactory pregnancy block has to some extent been explored. **1965** LEE & KNOWLES *Animal Hormones* ii. 32 The ejection of milk at suckling..is a neurohormonal reflex. **1974** *Sci. Amer.* Sept. 8/3 What magic gives Grinspoon and Singer the power to know that a behavioral condition..is not due to, say, a neurohormonal deficiency?

neurohumoral (njʊərəʊ'hjuːmərəl), *a. Physiol.* [a. F. *neuro-humoral* (H. Fredericq 1927, in *Compt. Rend. des Séances de la Soc. de Biol.* XCVII. (Réunion plénière) 3), f. *neuro-* NEURO- + *humoral* HUMORAL *a.*] Of, involving, or being a neurohumour. Cf. HUMORAL *a.* 1 a.

1929 P. BARD in C. Murchison *Foundations Exper. Psychol.* xii. 449 (*heading*) The neuro-humoral basis of emotional reactions. **1947** *Jrnl. Endocrinol.* V. 136 The possibility of a neurohumoral transmission of stimuli has been tentatively suggested on many occasions. **1966** G. B. KOELLE in Rodahl & Issekutz *Nerve as Tissue* 291 The neurohumoral theory is most consistent with the known facts concerning transmission at the vast majority of synaptic and neuro-effector junctions. **1971** *Nature* 31 Dec. 570/1 Neurohumoral agents from the hypothalamus were discharged into the portal vessels for transmission to the anterior lobe of the pituitary to affect the secretion of hormones.

neurohumour ('njʊərəʊhjuːmə(r)). *Physiol.* Also (*U.S.*) **-humor.** [f. NEURO- + HUMOUR, HUMOR *sb.* Cf. next.] A neurohormone, esp. a transmitter.

1933 *Proc. Soc. Exper. Biol. & Med.* XXX. 556 That this stripe should be dark is due to the fact that the severance of the nerve fibers excites the discharge of an expanding neurohumor whereby the melanophores are made to enlarge and thus to darken the skin. **1948** *Special Publ. N.Y. Acad. Sci.* IV. 292 Fries..has obtained considerable evidence pointing to the conclusion that xanthophores are also doubly innervated and believes that neurohumors are involved. **1959** J. H. WELSH in A. Gorbman *Compar. Endocrinol.* 123 Although it is convenient to refer to the products of ordinary neurons as neurohumors and to those of neurosecretory cells as neurosecretory substances, their common role as regulatory agents must be recognized. **1971** *Compar. Biochem. & Physiol.* XXXVIII. A.239 The neurohumor, serotonin, has been shown to be functionally involved in hibernation in the ground squirrel.

neurohypophysial (ˌnjʊərəʊhaɪpəʊ'fɪzɪəl), *a. Med.* Also **-physeal** (-'fɪzɪəl, -fɪ'siːəl). [f. next after HYPOPHYSIAL *a.*

In sense a, f. NEURO- + HYPOPHYS(IS + -AL.]

a. Pertaining to the neural tube and the hypophysis (in the embryo). ? *Obs.*

1893 *Q. Jrnl. Microsc. Sci.* XXXV. 301 The process of constriction by which the tube, or, as it may at once be called, the neuro-hypophysial canal, comes to be entirely separated from the cerebral vesicle has therefore now commenced. *Ibid.* 306 The hypophysis and the ganglion.. have been gradually differentiating themselves from the common neuro-hypophysial tube. **1929** *Ibid.* LXXII. 79 The whole of the adult nervous system [in Ascidians] is a new development proliferated from a minute remnant of the embryonic neural canal. The region in which this proliferation takes place is usually included in the neurohypophysial canal.

b. Of or pertaining to the neurohypophysis.

1934 *Physiol. Abstr.* XIX. 481 (*heading*) The central effect on blood pressure of the neurohypophyseal circulation hormone. **1939** *Res. Publ. Assoc. Res. Nerv. & Mental Dis.* XX. 444 There is some question..that the antidiuretic substance in the urine is of neurohypophysial origin. **1963** MONTGOMERY & WELBOURN *Clin. Endocrinol.* viii. 336 Any condition which damages the integrity of the neurohypophyseal system causes diabetes insipidus. **1973** C. EZRIN et al. *Systematic Endocrinol.* iii. 21/2 Recovery follows because damage to the supraoptic neurohypophyseal tract is mild enough to be reversible. **1973** *Nature* 12 Oct. 287/2 This also means that the rat now has two neurohypophysial hormones and two neurophysins.

neurohypophysis (njʊərəʊhaɪ'pɒfɪsɪs). *Med.* [f. NEURO- + HYPOPHYSIS.] The portion of the hypophysis that develops from the embryonic brain, comprising the posterior lobe and usually the infundibulum and median eminence, and differing from the adenohypophysis in having little glandular activity and in being richly supplied with nerve fibres, which originate in the hypothalamus (being the means by which the latter exercises its control of the hormonal activity of the anterior lobe) and release the hormones oxytocin and vasopressin following their production in the hypothalamus.

1912 H. CUSHING *Pituitary Body & its Disorders* I. 2 The tip becomes thickened into the infundibular body (neurohypophysis, or pars nervosa). *Ibid.* 3 The neuro-hypophysis itself is connected with the tuber cinereum by a stalk which varies in length in different species. **1939** *Res. Publ. Assoc. Res. Nerv. & Mental Dis.* XX. 24 It is convenient to regard the neurohypophysis as being divisible into two major divisions, namely, the neural lobe and the neural stalk. **1954** L. C. MARTIN *Clin. Endocrinol.* (ed. 2) i. 2 The neural division or neuro-hypophysis consists of the pars nervosa or infundibular process, the pituitary stalk or infundibular stem, and the median eminence of the tuber cinereum. **1968** A. VAN TIENHOVEN *Reproductive Physiol. Vertebr.* viii. 249/1 Some of the hypothalamic hormones, e.g. oxytocin and vasopressin, are stored in the neurohypophysis. **1968** PASSMORE & ROBSON *Compan. Med. Stud.* I. xxv. 15/2 The neurohypophysis is a point of contact between neurological and hormonal control mechanisms. **1972** *Sci. Amer.* Nov. 24/3 This double organ..is the pituitary gland, or hypophysis. The part that migrated from the brain is the posterior lobe, or neurohypophysis; the part that migrated from the pharynx is the anterior lobe, or adenohypophysis.

'neuroid, *a.* and *sb.* [Cf. NEURO- and -OID.]

a. *adj.* Resembling a nerve or nervous substance (Mayne 1857). **b.** *sb.* One of the two elements of a neural arch; a neurapophysis.

1887 *Amer. Naturalist* Oct. 945 The two elements composing the neural arch ought to be called the 'neuroids'.

neuroleptic (njʊərəʊ'lɛptɪk), *a.* (*sb.*) *Pharm.* [ad. F. *neuroleptique* (Delay & Deniker 1955, in *Bull. de l'Acad. Nat. de Méd.* CXXXIX. 145), after *psycholeptique* PSYCHOLEPTIC *a.*] Able to reduce nervous tension; tranquillizing; also as *sb.*, a neuroleptic drug; a tranquillizer.

1958 *Science* 10 Jan. 59/1 Other [*sc.* terms for psychopharmacologic drugs] are *ataraxic*.., and *neuroleptic* and *neuroplegic*, indicating diminutions in the intensity of nerve functions. **1959** *Jrnl. Clin. & Exper. Psychopath.* XIX. 286 We believe..the higher dosage of neuroleptics, combination of neuroleptics with other medications, or combinations of neuroleptics is frequently responsible for the unfavorable reactions. **1965** J. POLLITT *Depression & its Treatment* v. 67 This drug [*sb.* chlorpromazine] is neuroleptic, producing Parkinsonism. **1968** *New Scientist* 21 Nov. 417/1 Schizophrenics treated over long periods with neuroleptics have sometimes shown symptoms typical of endogenous depression. **1971** *Nature* 26 Nov. 224/2 All patients remained on their previous neuroleptic medication throughout the study. **1972** *Encycl. Psychol.* II. 310/2 After acute application in healthy subjects, even in low doses, neuroleptics only seldom induce motor relaxation and emotional stabilization.

neurolite ('njʊərəlaɪt). *Min.* [f. NEURO- + -LITE.] A variety of pinite with fibrous texture.

1836 T. THOMSON *Min., Geol.*, etc. I. 355 The constitution of neurolite is 5 atoms quatersilicate of alumina [etc.]. **1850** DAUBENY *Atom. The.* xii. (ed. 2) 411 The former combinations are called hydrosilicates... Example: Neurolite. **1896** CHESTER *Dict. Min.* 188 *Neurolite*,..a pinite-like mineral of a wax-yellow color, occurring in a large belt at Stanstead, Quebec.

neurological (njʊərəʊ'lɒdʒɪkəl), *a.* [f. NEURO- + -LOGICAL.] Relating or belonging to, connected with, interested in, neurology.

1832 J. THOMSON *Life Cullen* I. 442 The Neurological inquiries and speculations of these Authors. **1845** *Encycl. Metrop.* VII. 157/2 Neurological physiology was thus advancing, though but slowly. **1883** ROMANES *Ment. Evol. Anim.* iii. 38 The most fundamental of neurological principles—reflex action.

neurologically (njʊərəʊ'lɒdʒɪkəlɪ), *adv.* [f. NEUROLOGICAL *a.* + -LY².] From a neurological point of view; as regards neurology.

1936 *Acta Med. Scand.* LXXXVIII. 479 Nothing neurologically abnormal was found. **1971** *New Scientist* 5 Aug. 335/1 Psychiatric disorders in neurologically handicapped children. **1974** *Sci. Amer.* July 106/1 Neurologically speaking, brains whose organization was essentially human were already in existence some three million years ago.

neurologist (njʊ'rɒlədʒɪst). [f. NEURO- + -LOGIST.] One interested or versed in neurology.

1832 J. THOMSON *Life Cullen* I. 443 The Neurologists, whom he terms the Solidists. **1841-44** EMERSON *Ess., Nom. & Real.* Wks. (Bohn) I. 251 The..new allegations of phrenologists and neurologists are of ideal use. **1878** A. M. HAMILTON *Nerv. Dis.* 113 Acute cerebral anæmia..comes within the province of the surgeon rather than within that of the neurologist.

neurology (njʊ'rɒlədʒɪ). [ad. mod.L. *neurologia*, ad. mod.Gr. νευρολογία (Willis 1664): see NEURO- and -LOGY. Cf. F. *névrologie*.] The scientific study or knowledge of the anatomy, functions, and diseases of the nerves and the nervous system; †the nervous system, or its operation.

1681 WILLIS *Rem. Med. Wks.* Vocab., *Neurologie*, the doctrine of the nerves. *a* **1706** EVELYN *Hist. Relig.* (1850) I. 54 The soul, as seated more conspicuously in the brain, does, by the originated neurology, give intercourse to the animal spirits. **1796** SOUTHEY *Lett. fr. Spain* (1799) 477 The three exercises for the Professor of Anatomy..shall be upon Myology, Neurology, and Splanchnology. **1830** R. KNOX *Béclard's Anat.* 327 To consider..its principal parts, referring for the detail to particular neurology. **1878** A. M. HAMILTON *Nerv. Dis.* 93 The literature of neurology is replete with examples of so-called atheotosis.

b. A scientific account of the nerves.

1704 J. HARRIS *Lex. Techn.* I, *Neurology*, is an accurate Description of, or Discourse on, the Nerves of an Human Body. **1727–38** CHAMBERS *Cycl.* s.v., Willis has given a fine neurology in his *Anatome Cerebri.* **1801** *Med. Jrnl.* V. 531 To the latter editions.. he added a Neurology, or Anatomy of the Nerves.

neuroma (njʊˈrəʊmə). *Path.* Pl. **-mata.** [ad. Gr. type *νεύρωμα, f. νεῦρον nerve.] A swelling or tumour growing upon a nerve or in nerve-tissue.

1839–47 *Todd's Cycl. Anat.* III. 720 G/2 Certain gangliform tumours are formed upon nerves, to which the term neuroma has been applied. **1873** T. H. GREEN *Introd. Pathol.* (ed. 2) 128 True neuromata, however—*i.e.*, new formations of nerve-tissue—are amongst the rarest forms of new formations. **1887** *Brit. Med. Jrnl.* 15 Jan. 113/1 He had removed a neuroma from the wrist.

Hence **neuˈromatous** *a.*, of the nature of, resembling, a neuroma.

1857 in MAYNE *Expos. Lex.* **1875** H. WALTON *Dis. Eye* 139 It is unlike a neuromatous tumour, which is a fibrous tumour imbedded in the sheath of a nerve.

neuromast (ˈnjʊərəʊmɑːst, -æ-). *Zool.* [f. NEURO- + Gr. μαστ-ός breast.] An organ of sensory perception forming part of the lateral line system of fishes and larval or aquatic amphibians.

1912 J. S. KINGSLEY *Compar. Anat. Vertebrates* 167 Distally the fibres terminate in peculiar collections of sense cells known as sense hillocks or neuromasts occurring in the inner ear and in the lateral line organs of the ichthyopsida. **1937** *Proc. R. Soc.* B. CXXIII. 474 The distinction between pit organs and canal neuromasts is purely conjectural. **1957** O. LOWENSTEIN in M. E. Brown *Physiol. Fishes* II. ii. 156 Fundamentally the end-organs of the lateral line system consist of groups of secondary sensory cells called neuromasts. **1962** K. F. LAGLER et al. *Ichthyology* iii. 105 Each ampulla contains sensory nerve endings (neuromast cells) in a gelatinous terminal cup. **1974** M. HILDEBRAND *Analysis Vertebr. Struct.* xvi. 395 The lateral line system.. is present in fishes and in both larval and aquatic adult amphibians. It consists of thousands of microscopic organs called neuromasts.

neuromotor (ˈnjʊərəʊməʊtə(r)), *a.* [f. NEURO- + MOTOR *sb.* and *a.*] Pertaining to or involving both the nervous system and motor activities; applied *spec.* to a system of minute ectoplasmic fibrils connecting some of the cirri to the motorium in some ciliate protozoa.

1914 [see MOTORIUM 2]. **1940** L. H. HYMAN *Invertebrates* I. iii. 169 It is probable that at least some of the fibrils of the neuromotor system are conductile and serve to coordinate ciliary activities..; but others are presumably of a supporting nature. **1959** W. ANDREW *Textbk. Compar. Histology* xiv. 539 The neuromotor system of Stylonichia appears to be very similar to that of Oxytricha... Some authors have ascribed a neuromotor function to certain fibrils connected to the basal granules of flagellates. **1966** *New Scientist* 3 Nov. 242/1 These neuromotor fibres have since been generally accepted as indicating the presence of an elementary intracellular 'nervous system'. **1966** *Amer. Speech* XLI. 226 Speech production by control of vocal tract configuration changes treats.. phonemic distinction in terms of neuromotor commands. **1971** *Language* XLVII. 51 We have now reached the stage where automatic phonetic and phonological rules take over, converting the sequences of segments into actual neuro-motor commands to the muscles in the articulation of the utterance.

‖**neuron, neurone** (ˈnjʊərɒn, -rəʊn). *Anat.* and *Biol.* [a. Gr. νεῦρον sinew, cord, nerve.]

1. The cerebro-spinal axis; the spinal cord and brain.

1884 WILDER in *N.Y. Med. Jrnl.* 2 Aug. 114.

2. A process of a nerve-cell. *Obs.*

1893 [see DENDRON]. **1896** *Allbutt's Syst. Med.* I. 181 Golgi has shewn that every nerve-cell possesses one process, the 'neuron' which becomes the axis cylinder process of a nerve. **1897** *Med. Chron.* VII. 234 We notice that Mr. Schäfer uses the word 'neuron' in a somewhat different sense from that applied to it by Waldeyer, who used it—and we believe that in his sense it is extensively, if not universally, used—to denote a nerve cell with all its processes. Mr. Schäfer uses it to designate the axis-cylinder process of a nerve cell. **1930** HARTRIDGE & HAYNES *Histol.* 114 Nerve processes are of two kinds, long and short. The long are called axons, axis cylinders,.. and neurons.

3. A nerve-cell with its appendages. [a. G. *neuron* (W. Waldeyer 1891, in *Berliner klin. Wochenschr.* 13 July 691/1).]

The spellings *neuron* (ˈnjʊərɒn) and *neurone* (ˈnjʊərəʊn) are both still widely current.

1891 *Brain* XIV. 569 [*Abstr. of Waldeyer*, 1891] Thus a nerve element, a nerve entity, or 'neuron', as I propose to call it, consists.. of the following pieces:—(*a*) a nerve cell, (*b*) the nerve process, (*c*) its collaterals, and (*d*) the end-branching. **1896** PR. KROPOTKIN in *19th Cent.* Aug. 258 The microscopical units of which the nervous system is built up—the so-called 'neurons', whose protoplasmic ramifications intimately penetrate into the tissues. **1896** L. F. BARKER in *Johns Hopkins Hosp. Bull.* VII. 201/1 Van Gehuchten has adopted Waldeyer's word, spelling it in French 'le neurone', and French writers generally employ it. The leading investigators in Spain and Italy have also adopted the same term... The question arises, how is Waldeyer's form to be anglicized? Would it be justifiable to bring it into English through the French and to spell it *neurone*, pronounced neurōne, or could it be brought into English directly from the Greek and be so spelled and pronounced? **1899** MACPHERSON *Mental Affections* 83 Each neuron is a distinct, separate and independent organic unit, composed of a cell body containing a nucleus and nucleolus and of several processes. **1904** E. B. TITCHENER tr. *Wundt's Physiol. Psychol.* I. vi. 326 This spatial connexion may.. consist either in the immediate proximity of neurones lying upon the same side of the brain, or in the union of distant areas by association fibres. **1939** W. E. LE GROS CLARK *Tissues of Body* xii. 294 Within the central nervous system impulses are conducted from one part to another along a chain of neurones. **1950** A. HUXLEY *Themes & Variations* i. 94 The gulf between thought.. and.. neurones and electric charges is just as wide as that which in Biran's day divided thought from fluids and fibres. **1964** *New Scientist* 10 Sept. 643/1 The brain is estimated to contain ten thousand million nerve cells (neurons) and ten times as many glial cells. **1971** J. Z. YOUNG *Introd. Study Man* xxii. 296 Neurons are probably lost steadily in the later decades of life. **1973** H. M. RÁLIŠ et al. *Techniques Neurohistol.* i. 16 The nerve cell can make contact with a large number of other neurones through the multiple branches of dendrites.

4. Special Comb: **neuron(e theory**, the theory (now generally accepted) that the nervous system is composed of individual cells which, though effectively in contact with one another, are structurally distinct units all derived from a single neuroblast in the embryo.

1897 *Cincinnati Lancet-Clinic* LXXVIII. 565/1 (*heading*) The histological basis of the neuron theory. **1939** W. E. LE GROS CLARK *Tissues of Body* xii. 320 At one time the neurone theory excited considerable controversy, and even to-day some anatomists question its validity. **1972** M. L. BARR *Human Nervous Syst.* ii. 9/1 The Neuron Theory, as opposed to the view that nerve cells form a continuous reticulum, was advanced by His on the basis of embryological studies, by Forel on the basis of the response of nerve cells to injury, and by Ramón y Cajal from his observations with silver staining methods... Wholly convincing evidence in support of the Neuron Theory had to await the introduction of electron microscopy.

Hence **neuˈronic** *a.* (now a less common word than NEURONAL *a.*).

1899 *Allbutt's Syst. Med.* VI. 490 Diagram illustrating the Neuronic System. **1906** *Athenæum* 1 Sept. 246/2 The controversy on the neuronic theory still continues. **1931** *Brit. Jrnl. Psychol.* XXII. 141 If there be some such automatic regulating device in the neuronic mechanism, we must assume that it is in operation in the intact animal. **1964** S. DUKE-ELDER *Parsons' Dis. Eye* (ed. 14) xxii. 334 The disease is a primary lipid neuronic degeneration of the whole of the central nervous system.

neuronal (njʊˈrəʊnəl), *a.* [f. NEURON, NEURONE + -AL[1].] Of or pertaining to a neurone or neurones.

1901 *Brit. Med. Jrnl.* 29 June 1610/2 (*heading*) Changes in the neuronal centres in beri-beric neuritis. **1946** *Nature* 9 Nov. 647/2 Nachmansohn deals with the theory (his own) that acetylcholine is released at the neuronal surface during the passage of an impulse. **1953** *Brit. Jrnl. Psychol.* XLIV. 304 The final verification of an explanatory hypothesis in psychology will not come from its direct identification in terms of neuronal systems. **1971** CHIN-WU KIM in W. O. Dingwall *Survey of Linguistic Sci.* 32 Lenneberg.. is of the opinion that the orders of neuronal firings are adjusted so as to achieve a temporal coincidence at the neuro-muscular juncture. **1974** [see NEURONOPHAGIA].

Hence **neuˈronally** *adv.*, by a neurone or neurones.

1960 *Exper. Neurol.* II. 364 (*heading*) Effects of various drugs on activity of the neuronally isolated cerebral cortex. **1975** *Nature* 6 Feb. 448/1 The contractile responses are neuronally mediated.

neurone: see NEURON 3.

neuronophagia (ˌnjʊərɒnəˈfeɪdʒɪə). *Med.* Also anglicized as **-phagy**. [f. NEURON, NEURONE + -O + Gr. -φαγία eating (*sb.*).] The destruction of neurones by phagocytes.

1911 STEDMAN *Med. Dict.* 584/1 Neuronophagia, neuronophagy. **1932** M. BIELSCHOWSKY in W. Penfield *Cytol. & Cellular Path. Nervous Syst.* I. iv. 153 The neuroglia cells not only multiply, but some of them invade the marginal hollows and vacuoles. This process is included under the rather ill-chosen name of neuronophagia. **1958** J. G. GREENFIELD et al. *Neuropath.* ii. 62 Neuronophagy is specially common in all forms of encephalomyelitis which affect the grey matter. **1974** PASSMORE & ROBSON *Compan. Med. Stud.* III. xxxiv. 128/2 The occurrence of perivascular lymphocytic cuffing may distract attention from the more subtle isolated neuronal necrosis, each dead cell being surrounded by a ring of satellite phagocytes (neuronophagia).

neuropath (ˈnjʊərəpæθ). [f. NEURO- + Gr. -παθής, f. πάθος suffering.]

1. A person having an abnormal nervous sensibility; one subject to, or affected by, nervous disease.

1890 *Q. Rev.* CLXXI. 245 The Paris practitioners hold that susceptible persons are always to some extent neuropaths. **1897** *Allbutt's Syst. Med.* II. 865 The unstable condition of brain matter.. is hereditary in the neuropath, and in the offspring of drunkards.

2. a. One who attributes diseases in general to the nervous system (*Cent. Dict.* 1890).

b. A neuropathist.

1896 *Voice* (N.Y.) 6 Feb. 5/5 This expert neuropath having recently made a professional visit to the United States.

neuropathic (njʊərəʊˈpæθɪk), *a.* [f. as prec. + -IC. Cf. f. *névropathique*.] Relating to, caused or distinguished by nervous disease or functional weakness of the nervous system.

1857 in MAYNE *Expos. Lex.* **1880** FLINT *Princ. & Pract. Med.* 770 A neuropathic paralysis depends on some cause which.. prevents the action of volition. **1897** *Allbutt's Syst. Med.* III. 85 All rheumatoid atrophy represents a neuropathic or myopathic disturbance of nutrition.

So **neuroˈpathical** *a.*; **neuroˈpathically** *adv.*

1892 *Monist* II. 273 A decidedly neuropathical character.

neuˈropathist. [Cf. prec. and -IST.] One who makes a special study of nervous diseases.

1864 W. T. FOX *Skin Dis.* 13 That the middle course of humoralist and neuropathist is the tenable one. **1899** *Westm. Gaz.* 7 Apr. 8/2 The celebrated neuropathist.. ordered it to be treated with systematic electrisation.

neuropathologic (ˌnjʊərəʊpæθəʊˈlɒdʒɪk), *a.* Chiefly *U.S.* [f. NEUROPATHOLOG(Y + -IC.] = NEUROPATHOLOGICAL *a.*

1950 *Veterinary Bull.* XX. 278 The neuropathologic diagnosis of hog cholera. **1973** *Neurology* XXIII. 561/1 Neuropathologic studies of 10 cases of Huntington's disease are known to us.

neuropathoˈlogical, *a.* [f. NEURO- + PATHOLOGICAL *a.*] Relating to, concerned with, neuropathology.

1875 PAYNE *Jones & Siev. Pathol. Anat.* 56 It is impossible to deny the neuro-pathological theory. **1897** *Daily News* 6 Sept. 5/3 A scholarship in neuro-pathological sanitary science.

neuropathologist (njʊərəʊpəˈθɒlədʒɪst). Also **neuro-pathologist.** [f. NEUROPATHOLOG(Y + -IST.] = NEUROPATHIST.

1876 VAN DUYN & SEGUIN tr. *Wagner's Man. Gen. Path.* I. 5 Physicians have distinguished themselves as humoralists or solidists. Among solidists the neuropathologists and cellular pathologists must be separately designated. **1903** *Proc. Soc. Psychical Res.* XVIII. 23 Conservatives in anthropologic science will immediately say that Myers used the concept of the 'subliminal' far too broadly, and that the only safe demarcation of the term is that of the neuro-pathologists. **1932** M. BIELSCHOWSKY in W. Penfield *Cytol. & Cellular Path. Nervous Syst.* I. iv. 147 In his method of study the neuropathologist must amalgamate investigation of localization together with investigation of the pathological process. **1973** *Neurology* XXIII. 561/1 The striking clinical disparity between the manifestations of Huntington's chorea in children and those in adults is a challenge to the physiologist and neuropathologist.

neuropaˈthology. [f. NEURO- + PATHOLOGY.]

1. The study of nervous diseases and their treatment; the pathology of the nervous system.

1853 tr. *Romberg's Man. Nerv. Dis.* (Syd. Soc.) II. l. 402 In no other department of neuropathology is the absence of critical judgement so much felt as in the doctrine of cerebral affections. **1897** *Allbutt's Syst. Med.* II. 479 A disease which is.. of considerable interest to the student of neuro-pathology.

2. The view that disease originates from disturbance of the nervous system.

1892 *Syd. Soc. Lex.*

neuropathy (njʊˈrɒpəθɪ). [f. NEURO- + -PATHY.] Nervous disease; a case of this.

1857 in MAYNE *Expos. Lex.* **1895** *Pop. Sci. Monthly* July 388 Marriages which have been charged with being an important factor in the genesis of neuropathy. **1899** *Allbutt's Syst. Med.* VII. 834 This observer.. relegates that form to the category of neuropathies.

neuropil (ˈnjʊərəʊpɪl). *Neurology.* Also neuropile (-paɪl). [prob. a shortening of next: cf. PILE *sb.*[5]] **a.** A network of interwoven unmyelinated nerve fibres and their branches and synapses; hence, esp. in organisms with simple nervous systems, a structure composed of, or a region in which is concentrated, such a network. **b.** *rare.* An ultimate branch of a nerve fibre.

1899 L. F. BARKER *Nervous System* xxiii. 271 This investigator.. isolated the neuropil of the second antenna of Carcinus—in other words, he removed the ganglion cells of the neurones supplying the antenna, but left their processes and side branches. **1900** tr. A. Bethe in J. Loeb *Compar. Physiol. Brain* iii. 45 It was easy to decide this question by separating the ganglion-cells with their axis-cylinder process from the motor neurons without injuring the neuropiles. **1934** *Jrnl. Compar. Neurol.* LIX. 95 In some parts of the [amphibian] brain much branched and contorted unmyelinated axons form a dense entanglement which is termed neuropil. **1941** JOHANNSEN & BUTT *Embryol. Insects & Myriapods* ii. 21 The neuropile (Punctsubstanz, fibrillar substance, nerve fibers) develops in the ganglia in the older stages. **1953** *Nature* 29 Aug. 405/1 The neurohæmal organs of the heart ligaments [in higher Crustacea] are.. neuropiles. **1964** R. M. & J. W. FOX *Introd. Compar. Entomol.* vi. 179 A ganglion.. has a central mass of medullary tissue (neuropile) consisting of the intermixed axons and dendrons of motor and internuncial neurons and the terminal arborizations of sensory dendrons. **1974** *Sci. Amer.* Jan. 41/1 In addition to the major branches running through roots and connectives there are many such processes within the neuropil, the region in the center of the ganglion where synaptic connections are made. **1974** *Nature* 4 Oct. 428/1 The ganglia.. have a central fibrous neuropile containing most of the synapses.

†**neuropilema** (njʊərəʊpaɪˈliːmə). *Obs.* Also **neuropilem.** [ad. G. *neuropilem* (W. His 1890, in *Arch. f. Entwickelungsges.* (*Anat. Abth.*) Suppl.

113), f. Gr. νεῦρο-ν nerve + πίλημα felt.] = NEUROPIL a.

1891 *Brain* XIV. 568 Nerve-felt, neuro-pilema, *His.* **1900** A. HILL tr. *Obersteiner's Anat. Cent. Nervous Organs* (ed. 2) iii. 156 The last and finest ramifications of the cell-processes, collaterals and arborescent systems alike, are closely interwoven in the grey substance, forming not so much a network as a felt-work, the neuropilema or neurospongium. **1900** *Jrnl. Nerv. & Mental Dis.* XXVII. 476 He [*sc.* Waldeyer] acknowledges that his ideas of the mode of conduction are based on the view that no anastomosing nerve networks occur, but only a nerve feltwork (neuropilema, His). **1902** BALDWIN *Dict. Philos. & Psychol.* II. 175/2 *Neuropilem*, a meshwork of nervous arborizations forming a system of intercommunication between various neurocytes. **1929** C. U. A. KAPPERS *Evolution Nervous Syst. Invertebr., Vertebr. & Man* 43 In the higher Molluscs..they are arranged peripherally to the neuropilema as in Annelids.

neuropod ('njʊərəpɒd). *Zool.* [f. NEURO- + -POD.] An annulose or invertebrate animal, in which the limbs or motor organs are on the neural aspect of the body.

1856 GOODSIR in *Edinb. New Philos. Jrnl.* (1857) V. 121, I employ, as morphological designations, the term Neuropod ..for an Annulose, and Hæmapod..for a Vertebrate animal. **1870** ROLLESTON *Anim. Life* 168 Vertebrata may be spoken of as 'Hæmapods', in contradistinction to Invertebrata which are 'Neuropods'.

neuro'podial, *a. Zool.* [f. next: see -AL[1].] Relating or belonging to a neuropodium.

1877 HUXLEY *Anat. Inv. Anim.* v. 229 The neuropodial is very much longer than the notopodial aciculum. **1888** ROLLESTON & JACKSON *Anim. Life* 595 There is usually a dorsal or notopodial cirrus, and a ventral or neuropodial.

neuropodium (njʊərəʊ'pəʊdɪəm). *Zool.* [mod.L., f. NEURO- + Gr. πόδιον, dim. of πούς a foot.] The lower, ventral, or neural branch of a parapodium.

1870 H. A. NICHOLSON *Zool.* 161 A lower process, termed the 'neuropodium' or 'ventral oar'. **1877** HUXLEY *Anat. Inv. Anim.* v. 229 The notopodium and the neuropodium carry each a single, sharp, style-like aciculum. **1888** ROLLESTON & JACKSON *Anim. Life* 594 The parapodia of *Polychæta* are.. either simple..or divided..into a dorsal notopodium and a ventral neuropodium.

neu'ropodous, *a. Zool.* [Cf. NEUROPOD.] Having the limbs on the neural aspect of the body.

1870 ROLLESTON *Anim. Life* Index, Neuropodous character of Invertebrata.

neuropsychiatry (njʊərəʊsaɪ'kaɪətrɪ). *Med.* [f. NEURO- + PSYCHIATRY.] Psychiatry which relates mental or emotional disturbance to disordered brain function; neurology and psychiatry as a single discipline.

1918 M. W. BROWN (*title*) Neuropsychiatry and the war. **1945** *Times* 11 Jan. 2/4 Smith was examined by Major Thomas March, chief of the section of neuropsychiatry at a United States service hospital. **1955** *Psychiatric Q.* XXIX. 392 The brain has been enthroned once again as the organ of thought, and a new era of neuropsychiatry is about to unfold. **1971** *New Scientist* 5 Aug. 335/1 This careful and scholarly investigation is of great help to the understanding of this difficult aspect of neuropsychiatry; it also..stresses the necessity of close cooperation between paediatricians, neurologists, and psychologists.

So ,**neuropsychi'atric** *a.*; **neuropsy'chiatrist,** an expert or specialist in neuropsychiatry.

1918 M. W. BROWN *Neuropsychiatry & the War* 113 A plea..for the establishment also of medico-legal centers to collaborate with the medical and neuro-psychiatric centers. **1922** *N.Y. State Jrnl. Med.* XXII. 512/2 The neuropsychiatrist..has to deal with the structure and functions in health and in disease of the most highly organized part of man, namely the multi-neuronic integrate known as the nervous system. **1952** *Sun* (Baltimore) 28 Feb. 11/3 The neuropsychiatrist conducts his interviews in an office apart from the hospital buildings. **1953** *A.M.A. Arch. Neurol. & Psychiatry* LXX. 428 (*heading*) Neuropsychiatric aspects of infantile eczema. **1971** *New Scientist* 5 Aug. 335/1 For anyone who has struggled with the diagnosis of mild conditions in psychologically affected children *A Neuropsychiatric Study in Childhood* comes as very welcome help.

neuropsychology (njʊərəʊsaɪ'kɒlədʒɪ). *Med.* [f. NEURO- + PSYCHOLOGY.] The field of study concerned with the relationship between behaviour and the mind on the one hand, and the nervous system, esp. the brain, on the other; neurological psychology.

1893 DUNGLISON *Dict. Med. Sci.* (ed. 21) 751/1 *Neuropsychology*, neurology including psychology. **1955** *Sci. Amer.* 72/2 Neuropsychology is Lashley's specialty, and ..its studies of cerebral function and neurological structure have been conducted under his personal direction. **1963** *Neuropsychologia* I. 1 Under the term 'neuropsychology', we have in mind a particular area of neurology of common interest to neurologists, psychiatrists, psychologists, and neurophysiologists. This interest is focused mainly..on the cerebral cortex. Among topics of particular concern to us are disorders of language, perception and action. **1964** R. L. ISAACSON *Basic Readings Neuropsychol.* p. vii, Since the work of Lashley, neuropsychology has become a major branch of physiological psychology. **1973** *Daily Tel.* 23 Aug. 7/1 A high degree of specialisation by each of man's 'two brains'—the cerebral hemispheres—have [*sic*] been shown by recent work in neuro-psychology.

So ,**neuropsycho'logical** *a.*; **neuropsy'chologist,** an expert or specialist in neuropsychology.

The mod. use appears to be independent of quots. 1851, where the meaning is rather less specific.

1851 T. LAYCOCK tr. *Unzer's Princ. Physiol.* p. ii, The neuro-psychological essays he inserted in it are frequently referred to in the present work. *Ibid.* p. vi, Sylvius.. followed Descartes, while Willis was influenced..by the doctrines of Paracelsus. There was, however, yet another neuro-psychologist. **1949** D. O. HEBB (*title*) Organization of behavior: a neuropsychological theory. **1970** *Sci. Amer.* Mar. 67/3 Of the various lesions in the second block of the brain those in the tertiary zones are particularly interesting to us as neuropsychologists. *Ibid.* 72/3 The neuropsychological approach provides a valuable means of dissecting mental processes as well as diagnosing illness. **1973** B. HAIGH tr. *Luria's Working Brain* 12 The author.. attempts to fit the facts obtained by neuropsychological studies of individual brain systems into their appropriate place in the grand design of psychological science. **1974** *Nature* 31 May 495/1 Thus was born the 'frontal lobe syndrome', the study of which in modern times owes much to the Russian neuro-psychologist Alexander Luria.

neu'ropter. *rare. Ent.* [f. next.] A neuropterous insect.

1828-32 WEBSTER s.v., The neuropters are an order of insects having four membranous, transparent, naked wings. **1873** DAWSON *Earth & Man* vi. 137 Any modern Neuropter, a group of insects remarkable even in the present world for their large and complex organs of vision.

‖**Neuroptera** (njʊ'rɒptərə), *sb. pl. Ent.* [mod.L., f. NEURO- + Gr. πτέρον wing.] An order of insects, having four naked membranous transparent wings, with reticulate neuration.

1752 J. HILL *Hist. Anim.* 69 *Tetraptera.* Insects having four wings. Class the Third, *Neuroptera.* Those which have membranaceous wings, with nerves and veins disposed in a reticulated form in them. **1797** *Encycl. Brit.* (ed. 3) IX. 253/1 The fourth class of insects (*neuroptera*) may be killed with spirit of wine. **1816** KIRBY & SP. *Entomol.* iii. (1818) I. 67 Neuroptera consisting of Dragon-flies, Ant-lions, Ephemeræ, &c. **1840** *Cuvier's Anim. Kingd.* 573 In the Neuroptera these wings have their surface furnished with a very fine net-work. **1870** H. A. NICHOLSON *Man. Zool.* (1875) 302 The earliest known insects..consist of the remains of Neuroptera.

Hence **neu'ropteral** *a.*, neuropterous (Webster 1828-32). **neu'ropteran,** a neuropterous insect. **neu'ropterist,** a student of the Neuroptera. **neu'ropteroid** *a.*, resembling the Neuroptera. **neuroptero'logical** *a.*, pertaining to **neuropte'rology,** the scientific study of neuropterous insects (Mayne 1857).

1842 BRANDE *Dict. Sci.*, etc., **Neuropteran.* **1895** *Science Gossip* Apr. 49 An important article..especially to *neuropterists. **1897** *Naturalist* 115 All our present-day British neuropterists and trichopterists. **1889** NICHOLSON & LYDEKKER *Palæont.* I. 594 The *Neuropteroid section.. includes a number of Palæozoic insects.

neu'ropterous, *a. Ent.* [f. prec. + -OUS.] Belonging or relating to, consisting or representative of, the Neuroptera.

1802 BINGLEY *Anim. Biog.* (1813) I. 48 Neuropterous insects..have four membranaceous, transparent, naked wings. **1835** KIRBY *Hab. & Inst. Animals* II. xx. 351, I am speaking here of the Neuropterous Order. **1867** F. FRANCIS *Angling* vi. (1880) 239 Neuropterous flies of the genus Perlidæ.

neurosal (njʊ'rəʊsəl), *a. Path.* [f. NEUROSIS + -AL[1].] Having the character of a neurosis; arising from a nervous disorder.

1884 *Contemp. Rev.* May 684 Gouty neuralgia is the monitor..with those persons of a neurosal diathesis. **1898** *Allbutt's Syst. Med.* V. 824 Not only does it..cut short a neurosal paroxysm of dyspnœa or restlessness [etc.].

neurose (njʊ'rəʊs), *a.* [ad. L. type **neurōs-us*: see NEURO- and -OSE.]

1. *Ent.* Having other than marginal nervures.

1826 KIRBY & SP. *Entomol.* xlvi. IV. 340 Neurose (*Neurosæ*). Wings that have nervures besides the marginal ones.

2. *Path.* Neurotic.

1886 *American* XII. 287.

neurosis (njʊ'rəʊsɪs). Pl. **neuroses.** [ad. Gr. type *νεύρωσις, f. νεῦρον nerve: see -OSIS.]

1. *Path.* A functional derangement arising from disorders of the nervous system, esp. such as are unaccompanied by organic change in the structures of the body; a nervous disease.

1776-84 W. CULLEN *First Lines Pract. Physic* §1091, I propose to comprehend, under the title of Neuroses, all those preternatural affections of sense or motion which are without pyrexia, as a part of the primary disease. **1797** *Encycl. Brit.* (ed. 3) XI. 96/2. **1822-34** *Good's Study Med.* (ed. 4) I. 167 *note*, He considers it [lead colic] to be a neurosis. **1845** *Encycl. Metrop.* VII. 527/1 The diseases of function..embrace the neuroses, hæmorrhages, and dropsies. **1874** MAUDSLEY *Mental Dis.* i. 32 Families in which insanity, epilepsy, or some other neurosis exists. **1899** *Allbutt's Syst. Med.* VIII. 296 For two or three preceding generations such neurotic stocks had intermarried, and so accentuated the neuroses present.

2. *Psychol.* A change in the nerve-cells of the brain prior to, and resulting in, psychic activity.

1871 HUXLEY in *Contemp. Rev.* Nov. 462 As it is very necessary to keep up a clear distinction between these two processes, let the one be called neurosis, and the other psychosis. **1882** ROMANES in *Nature* No. 641. 335 Some intimate association between neurosis and psychosis being thus accepted as a fact by the hypothesis of automatism.

neuro'skeletal, *a. Anat.* [f. NEURO- + SKELETAL *a.*] Belonging or pertaining to the neuroskeleton.

1854 OWEN in *Orr's Circle Sci., Org. Nat.* I. 171 Outlines of the chief developments of the dermoskeleton..are added to the neuroskeletal archetype. *Ibid.* 180 The neuroskeletal bones are arranged in four segments.

neuro'skeleton. *Anat.* [f. NEURO- + SKELETON.] The bones connected with, and serving as a protection for, the cerebro-spinal axis and the nervous system; the endoskeleton.

1844 GOODSIR in *Trans. Roy. Soc. Edinb.* XV. 250 Anatomical description of the *Amphioxus.* Neuro-skeleton. **1854** OWEN in *Orr's Circle Sci., Org. Nat.* I. 168 The main part of the skeleton..consists of the neuroskeleton... The parts of the neuroskeleton are arranged in a series of segments. **1880** GÜNTHER *Study of Fishes* 85.

†**neurospast.** *Obs.* [ad. Gr. νευρόσπαστ-ον, neut. of νευρόσπαστος, f. νεῦρον sinew + σπᾶν to draw.] A figure or puppet moved by strings.

1642 CUDWORTH *Serm. 1 John ii.* 3, 4 (1676) 64 They that are acted only by an outward Love are but like Neurospasts, or those little Puppets that skip nimbly up and down. **1660** INGELO *Bentiv. & Ur.* I. (1682) 91 [He] denied God power to make any other sort of creatures besides Neurospasts.

Hence †**neurospastic** *a. Obs. rare*$^{-1}$.

a **1706** EVELYN *Hist. Relig.* (1850) II. 281 To these [images] with subtile wires and neurospastic springs, they give..various motions of head, and eyes.

neurotic (njʊ'rɒtɪk), *sb.* [See next.]

1. *Med.* A drug having a marked effect, esp. of a bracing kind, upon the nervous system.

1661 LOVELL *Hist. Anim. & Min.* 335 It's cured..by alexipharmicks, roborants, neuroticks, and fitt diet. **1694** SALMON *Bate's Dispens.* (1713) 586/1 It is a famous Cephalick, Neurotick, Stomachick, Cardiack and Uterine. **1716** M. DAVIES *Athen. Brit.* II. 356 [Infuse] Rose-Water [upon it] for an Hypnotick or a Neurotick. **1869** J. HARLEY (*title*) The old Vegetable Neurotics.., their physiological action and therapeutical use.

2. *Path.* 'A disease having its seat in the nerves' (Webster 1847).

3. A neurotic person.

1896 *Allbutt's Syst. Med.* I. 475 They may be made into 'blue-stockings' or neurotics, or both together. **1897** *Ibid.* II. 851 The offspring of drunkards or neurotics.

neurotic (njʊ'rɒtɪk), *a.* [ad. Gr. type *νευρωτικός, f. νεῦρον nerve: see -OTIC.]

1. Acting upon, or stimulating, the nerves.

1775 in ASH, and in later Dicts.

2. Of the nature of, marked or characterized by, neurosis or nervous disorder.

1873 F. T. ROBERTS *Handbk. Med.* 531 Angina pectoris is supposed to be a neurotic affection. **1887** *Brit. Med. Jrnl.* 29 Jan. 205/1 Those neurotic ailments which have hitherto taxed the skill and care of physicians.

3. a. Of persons: Affected by, suffering from, neurosis; having disordered nerves.

1887 *Buck's Handbk. Med. Sci.* V. 162 The neurotic woman is sensitive, zealous, managing. **1897** *Allbutt's Syst. Med.* II. 888 The cause of morphinism in persons not more neurotic than the rest of us. **1899** *Ibid.* VIII. 180 It is probable that in the neurotic the nervous system is more likely to be disturbed by general diseases.

b. Characteristic of a neurosis or a neurotic. Also *fig.*

1918 A. A. BRILL tr. *Freud's Totem & Taboo* iii. 143 Neurotics live in a special world in which..only the 'neurotic standard of currency' counts. **1948** L. MACNEICE *Holes in Sky* 31 The taut-necked donkey's neurotic-asthmatic-erotic lamenting. **1972** *Newsweek* 10 Jan. 3/1 The Nixon Administration has blundered again—having become enslaved by its neurotic emphasis on seeking re-election in '72 at all costs. **1975** M. BABSON *There must be Some Mistake* xix. 161 My husband simply disappears..and I was foolish enough to get upset about it. Neurotic of me, wasn't it?

neurotically (njʊ'rɒtɪkəlɪ), *adv.* [f. NEUROTIC *a.* + -AL + -LY[2].] In a neurotic manner; as the result of a nervous disorder. Also *fig.*

1890 W. JAMES *Princ. Psychol.* II. xxviii. 685 In many cases..the parental alcoholics are themselves degenerates neurotically. **1919** M. K. BRADBY *Psycho-Anal.* 78 Many.. thrust their qualms into the unconscious and become neurotically deaf, blind or what not. **1924** R. GRAVES *Mock Beggar Hall* 21 A row of post-war villas, neurotically built, Standing each at different curious angles to the road. **1961** C. WILLOCK *Death in Covert* iii. 69 He had a dark, keen, neurotically intelligent face. **1972** *Daily Tel.* 20 Apr. 10/6 Christopher Dowson, who slides into a house-party uninvited.., yearns neurotically after an unchanging situation.

neuroticism (njʊ'rɒtɪsɪz(ə)m). [f. NEUROTIC *a.* + -ISM.] The condition or state of being neurotic; a tendency towards neurosis; esp. as a factor showing liability to neurosis included in certain types of personality assessment.

1900 *Daily Chron.* 5 June 4/5 The holiday season has been darkened by the reports of suicides which suggest..the neuroticism of Paris. **1902** W. JAMES *Var. Relig. Exper.* i. 25, I think that I may let the matter of religion and neuroticism drop. **1922** *Glasgow Herald* 5 Oct. 5 The brilliant neuroticism of recent novels. **1952** H. J. EYSENCK *Sci. Study of Personality* ii. 58 We have extracted a general factor of 'neuroticism' from the intercorrelations of fifteen tests for normal and neurotic groups separately. **1957** P. LAFITTE *Person in Psychol.* iii. 34 Neuroticism and psychoticism are defined with scrupulous statistical care in terms of factorial scores..: but neither is directly related to ordinary behaviour. **1959** *Times Lit. Suppl.* 31 July 445/1 Mr. Johnston is subtle and satisfying when he shows them needling one another into neuroticism. **1973** *Jrnl. Genetic Psychol.* CXXII. 197 Iranian female subjects had scored higher than their male counterparts on neuroticism but lower on both extraversion and psychoticism.

'neurotome. *rare*—⁰. [f. NEURO-: cf. NEURECTOME.] 'A long and very narrow scalpel, having two edges' (Dunglison 1855).

neuro'tomical, *a. rare*—⁰. [f. NEUROTOMY.] 'Pertaining to the anatomy or dissection of nerves' (Webster 1828–32; hence in later Dicts.).

neu'rotomist. [See next and -IST.] One who practises or studies neurotomy. Also *fig.*, a dissector of feelings or emotions.

1726 BAILEY (ed. 3), *Neurotomist*, an Anatomist who dissects human Bodies on account of the Nerves. **1775** ASH, *Neurotomist*, one skilled in dissections of the nerves. **1866** OWEN *Anat. Vertebr.* I. 203 Sclerotomists, neurotomists, lithotomists and other classes of operating surgeons. **1898** *Westm. Gaz.* 13 May 3/1 As a neurotomist and student of temperament she is not convincing.

neurotomy (njʊˈrɒtəmɪ). *Surg.* [ad. mod.L. *neurotomia*: see NEURO- and -TOMY.] The section of a nerve, for the purpose of producing sensory paralysis. (See also early quots.)

1704 J. HARRIS *Lex. Techn.* I, *Neurotomy*, is an Anatomical Section of the Nerves..; and sometimes also a pricking of the Nerves by unskilful Bleeding. **1755** JOHNSON *Neurotomy*, the anatomy of the nerves. **1831** YOUATT *Horse* 110 These are the fibres which we divide in the operation of neurotomy or nerve-cutting. **1860** *Syd. Soc. Year-bk. Med.* 179 On Facial Neuralgia, and its Cure by Neurotomy. **1887** *Brit. Med. Jrnl.* 15 Jan. 112/2 The rules which had been gained by studying the effects of neurotomy in horses.

'neurotrans,mitter. *Physiol.* [f. NEURO- + TRANSMITTER.] A substance which is released at the end of a nerve fibre by the arrival of a nerve impulse and, by diffusing across the synapse or junction, effects the transfer of the impulse to another nerve fibre, a muscle fibre, or some other receptor.

1961 *Lancet* 2 Sept. 530/1 In these sections appears much of the most recent work on the metabolic as well as the neurotransmitter actions of these amines. **1965** LEE & KNOWLES *Animal Hormones* ix. 123 Acetylcholine is also released in the ganglia of the autonomic nerves and at the endings of the parasympathetic nerves, acting as a neurotransmitter substance. **1971** *New Scientist* 17 June 669/1 The neurotransmitter serotonin stimulates salivation in the salivary gland of the housefly. **1974** *Sci. Amer.* June 59/1 Neurotransmitters make the heart beat faster or slower and make muscles contract or relax. They cause glands to synthesize hormone-producing enzymes or to secrete hormones.

So **neurotrans'mission**, the transmission of nerve impulses.

1961 *Harvey Lect.* LV. 43 (*heading*) Neurotransmission in the adrenergic nervous system. **1973** *Nature* 15 June 426/1 Reviews on biochemical aspects of neurotransmission.

neurotrophic (njʊərəʊˈtrəʊfɪk, -ˈtrɒfɪk), *a.* [f. NEURO- + -TROPHIC.] Of or pertaining to the control of cells exerted by nervous tissue, esp. in relation to cellular nutrition.

1887 T. W. MILLS in *Med. Record* 22 Oct. 529/2, I propose..to substitute for mechanical explanations as applied to cardiac pathology, neuro-trophic ones. **1899** *Allbutt's Syst. Med.* VI. 545 Neurotrophic affections of bones and joints. **1935** *Amer. Jrnl. Cancer* XXIV. 416 Every epithelial cell is normally under constant neurotrophic control. **1970** *Nature* 28 Feb. 824 (*heading*) Neurotrophic control of protein synthesis in the regenerating limb of the newt, *Triturus. Ibid.*, We have examined the chemical nature of the neurotrophic action in a system which is clearly nerve-dependent, the regenerating salamander limb.

neurotropic (njʊərəʊˈtrəʊpɪk, -ˈtrɒpɪk), *a.* [f. NEURO- + -TROPIC.] **1.** *Path.* Tending to attack or affect the nervous system preferentially.

1903 *Buck's Handbk. Med. Sci.* (ed. 2) VI. 270/2 Thus the poisons which have at the same time neurotropic and lipotropic effects..will have a much more marked influence upon the nervous system in an emaciated animal than in one which is very fat. **1922** *Med. Jrnl. Australia* II. 261/2 Vaccinia is the least neurotropic, while poliomyelitis is the most exclusively neurotropic. **1933** *Amer. Jrnl. Cancer* XIX. 648 Thus the tumor employed is not neurotropic. **1939** *Lancet* 4 Mar. 497/1 (*heading*) A neurotropic strain of human influenza virus. **1961** R. D. BAKER *Essent. Path.* viii. 136 Venoms of snakes are hemolytic or neurotropic. **1973** *Nature* 26 Jan. 247/1 The MV strain of [poliomyelitis] virus ..was then shown to be so adapted to monkey brain passage and so neurotropic that it would no longer grow in cells from other organs.

2. *Anat.* Of or pertaining to the control or regulation of nerves, esp. in relation to their growth and regeneration.

1912 *Jrnl. Nerv. & Mental Dis.* XXXIX. 774 Is the comparative incapacity of the nervous system to regenerate due to some incapacity of the mechanical obstacles, absence of preestablished routes, or to some peculiar defect in the Schwann cells, the chief if not the only elaborators of neurotrophic [*sic*] material? **1928** R. M. MAY tr. *Ramón y Cajal's Degeneration & Regeneration Nervous Syst.* I. 374 Several neurotropic currents may act simultaneously on the same cone of growth. *Ibid.*, This fact bears out the view that the neurotropic material is an enzyme segregated by the living cells, instead of a product of the decomposition or disintegration of the nervous tissue. **1968** A. F. W. HUGHES *Aspects Neural Ontogeny* i. 33 For Ramon y Cajal the association of a regenerating fibre with the bands of Büngner was an instance of neurotropic attraction. **1968** S. SUNDERLAND *Nerves & Nerve Injuries* xxxii. 405 Whether or not the tissues of the distal stump exert a neurotropic influence on the regenerating process..is still unsettled.

neurotropism (njʊərəʊˈtrəʊpɪz(ə)m, njʊəˈrɒtrəpɪz(ə)m). [ad. Gr. *neurotropismus* (J. Forssman 1900, in *Beiträge z. path. Anat. u. z. allgem. Path.* XXVII. 408): see NEUROTROPIC *a.* and -ISM.] **1.** *Anat.* The supposed attraction (or repulsion) exerted by one mass of nervous (or other) tissue upon another mass of nervous tissue which is in the process of growing or regenerating.

1905 GOULD *Dict. New Med. Terms* 380/1 *Neurotropism*, the attraction or repulsion exercised upon regenerating nerve-fibers. A substance is said to have positive neurotropism when these regenerating nerve fibers have a tendency to grow toward and into it. **1912** *Jrnl. Nerv. & Mental Dis.* XXXIX. 774 (*heading*) Influence of neurotropism on regeneration. **1955** B. H. WILLIER et al. *Analysis of Devel.* VII. i. 356/2 Such 'distance action', commonly referred to as 'neurotropism' and assumed to be a form of either galvanotropism or chemotropism, has been invoked to explain oriented nerve growth in the embryo.., as well as during later nerve regeneration. **1968** A. F. W. HUGHES *Aspects Neural Ontogeny* i. 34 The two principles which have been proposed as forces which direct the growing nerve fibre, the 'contact-guidance' of Weiss.., and the neurotropism of Ramon y Cajal, both rest on inference from the behaviour of growing fibres under various circumstances, and at present on nothing more.

2. *Path.* The tendency of a virus or other pathological agent to attack the nervous system preferentially.

1911 STEDMAN *Med. Dict.* 585/2 *Neurotropism*, the attraction of certain pathogenic microorganisms, poisons, and nutritive substances, toward the nerve-centers. **1925** *Jrnl. Exper. Med.* XLII. 523 His theories of dermotropism and neurotropism of viruses. **1933** *Amer. Jrnl. Cancer* XIX. 647 (*heading*) Neurotropism of neoplasms in the mouse. **1940** *Nature* 2 Nov. 596/1 A curious characteristic of the yellow fever virus..is its manifestation of two types of virulence, namely, 'viscerotropism', meaning that it attacks such viscera as the liver, kidneys and heart, and 'neurotropism', meaning that it damages the nervous system. **1959** *New Scientist* 19 Mar. 620/1 Sabin himself admits that there is some return of virulence—neurotropism he calls it, the power to cause paralysis.

neurula (ˈnjʊərələ). *Embryol.* Pl. **neurulæ**. [mod.L., f. NEUR- + *-ula*, as in BLASTULA, GASTRULA.] An embryo at the time when it is developing a neural tube from the neural plate. So **neuru'lation**, the formation of a neurula.

1888 *Amer. Naturalist* XXII. 470 The neurulation is normal. **1909** *Cent. Dict.* Suppl., Neurula. **1926** J. S. HUXLEY *Essays Popular Sci.* xviii. 259 The late gastrula or neurula is bisected as a whole. **1973** *Nature* 2 Mar. 55/2 In amphibian neurulae following initial removal of much of the totipotent blastula, abnormally few cells create a whole pattern. *Ibid.* 56/2 Gastrulation and neurulation movements are unaffected by mitomycin C.

neurypnology (njʊərɪpˈnɒlədʒɪ). [f. NEUR- + HYPNOLOGY.] That branch of science which deals with the phenomena of hypnotism.

1843 BRAID (*title*) Neurypnology; or, The Rationale of Nervous Sleep considered in relation with Animal Magnetism. **1846** G. MOORE *Power of Soul over Body* (ed. 3) 161 Assuming all that is related of..neurypnology to be true. **1887** *Daily News* 1 Apr. 5/2 Dr. Charcot, the famous Parisian Professor who, with Dr. Braid, has told us so much about the science of neurypnology, or nerve sleep.

Hence **neurypno'logical** *a.*, having a hypnotic basis. **neuryp'nologist**, a student of neurypnology (Worcester 1846).

1893 *Athenæum* 21 Oct. 550 The neurypnological novel has many forms.

neuston (ˈnjuːstɒn). [a. G. *neuston* (E. Naumann 1917, in *Biol. Zentralbl.* XXXVII. 99), f. Gr. νευστόν neuter of νευστός swimming, f. νεῖν to swim, after *plankton*.] A collective term for minute organisms inhabiting the surface layer of fresh water. Also *attrib.*

1928 K. E. CARPENTER *Life in Inland Waters* ii. 35 Neuston.—This term, applied..especially to minute forms, such as bacteria and Protista, which float against the surface-film, may be extended to include all types especially associated with the film. **1939** *Nature* 28 Jan. 139/1 It [*sc.* the book under review] divides the plankton into plankton proper and the so-called 'neuston'—a term new to us—which means the organisms the peculiar province of which is the surface-film. **1957** G. E. HUTCHINSON *Treat. Limnol.* I. vi. 418 The organisms may be associated with the surface film and the resultant coloration should then be termed *neuston color* rather than section color. **1968** *New Scientist* 26 Sept. 669/2 Neuston are the organisms which live in the surface layer of [*sic*] film of water. **1974** A. MAYR-HARTING tr. *Rheinheimer's Aquatic Microbiology* iii. 31 In the neuston—that is, the living community which develops during calm weather on the surface of lakes at the water-air interface—a characteristic microflora develops. **1974** *Nature* 4 Jan. 30/2 Thirty-seven surface tows were made with a neuston net to collect particulate pollutants quantitatively.

Neustrian (ˈnjuːstrɪən), *sb.* and *a.* [f. med.L. *Neustria* + -AN.] **A.** *sb.* A native or inhabitant of Neustria, the western part of the Frankish empire in the Merovingian period. **B.** *adj.* Of or pertaining to Neustria or its inhabitants.

1794 W. BECKFORD *Hist. France* I. vi. 104 The Austrasians ..assisted by the Neustrians..drove him from the throne, and raised Childeric..to the sovereignty. **1874** [see AUSTRASIAN *a.* and *sb.*]. **1918** A. HASSALL *France Mediaeval & Modern* i. 6 In spite of the efforts of Ebroin, the Neustrian Mayor,..the tendency of Austrasia and Burgundy towards independence was too strong to be resisted. **1924** *Public Opinion* 27 June 618/2 The descendants of the Neustrian Franks now garrison the conquered Rhineland. **1927** O. M. DALTON *Gregory of Tours's Hist. of Franks* I. II. ii. 165 We are told that Charles addressed his Neustrians in 'Roman'. *Ibid.* 168 The Neustrian army of Charles was harangued in the Latin vulgar tongue. **1951** B. & R. NORTH tr. *Martin's Making of France* iv. 37 Aquitanians fought with Neustrians, and Austrasians with Burgundians in battles in which the unity of Roman Gaul was undone. **1968** *Encycl. Brit.* XVI. 302/1 In the later Merovingian period the names Neustria and Francia were used interchangeably by Neustrian writers to designate the kingdom of which they were subjects, thus betraying their conviction that Neustria formed the heart and core of the Frankish lands. **1975** F. HEER *Charlemagne & his World* i. 16 After Ebroin was murdered..Pepin defeated the Neustrians in battle. He crushed Neustria as an independent state by confiscating the lands of the great Neustrian magnates and rewarding his own followers with them.

neut, obs. form of NEWT.

neuter (ˈnjuːtə(r)), *a.* and *sb.* Also 5–6 **neutre**, 6 **nuter**, 6–7 **newter**. [a. F. *neutre* (14th c.) or L. *neuter* neither, f. *ne* not (see NE) + *uter* either (of two).]

A. *adj.* **1.** *Gram.* **a.** Of gender: Neither masculine nor feminine. Hence also, in later use, of parts of speech, etc.

1398 TREVISA *Barth. De P.R.* XIX. cxxviii. (1495) 933 *Cathinum*..is better sayde in the neutre gender than in the Mascul. **1530** PALSGR. Introd. 24 A latin nowne of the newter gender. **1579** FULKE *Heskins' Parl.* 101 *Aliud* in the Neuter gender put absolutely. *a* **1637** B. JONSON *Eng. Gram.* I. x, The neuter, or feigned gender: whose notion conceives neither sex. **1694** SALMON *Bate's Dispens.* (1713) 323/1 We used it as a Neutral, putting the adjective in the Neuter Gender. **1727–38** CHAMBERS *Cycl.* s.v., In English, and other modern tongues, there is no such thing as neuter nouns. **1838** *Penny Cycl.* XI. 111/1 In the age of Shakspeare the only form for the neuter genitive was *his*. **1894** W. M. LINDSAY *Latin Lang.* 369 The confusion of masculine and neuter O-stems.

absol. **1612** BRINSLEY *Lud. Lit.* 128 In wordes of three terminations..the third is the Neuter. **1654** WARREN *Unbelievers* 105 φυράματος in the Neuter. **1838** *Penny Cycl.* XI. 110/1 The neuter is employed to denote that the notion of gender is not entertained. **1896** TOYNBEE *Hist. French Gram.* 177 This suppression of the neuter..was brought about in two ways.

b. Of verbs: Neither active nor passive; intransitive.

1530 PALSGR. 107 Verbes personnalles, besydes actives, as neuters. **1668** WILKINS *Real Char.* III. i. 303 That part of speech, which..is stiled a Verb (whether Neuter, Active or Passive). **1696** PHILLIPS (ed. 5) s.v. *Verb*, The Verb Neuter, which..hath such a kind of Active Signification, as is not capable of a Passive, as *Curro*, I run. **1740** J. CLARKE *Educ. Youth* (ed. 3) 99 To teach them the Difference betwixt a Neuter and a Transitive Verb. **1824** L. MURRAY *Eng. Gram.* (ed. 5) I. 107 A Verb Neuter expresses neither action nor passion, but being. **1845** STODDART *Gram.* in *Encycl. Metrop.* I. 48/1 The neuter verb supposes an action terminating with the agent.

transf. **1658** OWEN *Temptation* i. 16 Though temptation seemes to be of a more active importance,..in the Scripture it is commonly taken in a neuter sense.

c. ***neuter passive***, having the character both of a neuter and a passive verb. Also *fig.*

In Latin grammar applied to those neuter verbs in which the perfect tense has a passive form (as *audeo, ausus sum*), in French grammar to those which form their perfect tense with *être*.

1530 PALSGR. 107 The Latins have many other sortes of verbes personnalles,..as neuters, deponentes, commons, neutre passives and suche other. **1647** TRAPP *Comm. Rev.* iii. 115 Such are our..neuter-passive Christians. **1650** —— *Num.* xxiii. 2 God abhors these luke-warme neuter-passives. **1755** JOHNSON *Gram.* b4/1 There is another manner of conjugating neuter verbs, which, when it is used, may not improperly denote them neuter passives.

2. Taking neither one side nor the other; not declaring oneself on, or rendering assistance to, either side: **a.** of rulers, states, etc., in relation to others, esp. in time of war; also of the towns, ships, etc., of such states. Cf. NEUTRAL *a.*

1525 LD. BERNERS *Froiss.* II. clx. [clvi.] 441 The Kynge of Aragon, and his father before hym was as neuter. **1560** DAUS tr. *Sleidane's Comm.* 427 It was a neuter town indifferent to both. **1614** RALEIGH *Hist. World* II. (1634) 417 An opinion, that the Trojans..sought for succour from David, and that hee stayed neuter in that warre. **1693** *Mem. Count Teckely* I. 74 When they had taken the Count of Serin, and knew that the Turks continued neuter. **1755** *Mem. Capt. P. Drake* I. xiv. 117 The Ship he was in (though neuter) was boarded by a French Privateer. **1771** GOLDSM. *Hist. Eng.* IV. 363 He supposed that the Russians would at least continue neuter. **1827** SOUTHEY *Penins. War* I. 582 The port would be considered neuter. **1859** JEPHSON *Brittany* xiv. 225 In the wars of Blois and Montfort the citizens flattered themselves that they could remain neuter.

b. Of individuals in relation to any matter where difference of opinion or conduct exists or is possible.

1713 STEELE *Guard.* No. 1 ⁋3 As to these matters I shall be impartial, though I cannot be neuter. **1769** BURKE *Corr.* (1844) I. 176 When it came to the question, eleven were for it, only three against. One was neuter. **1802–12** BENTHAM *Ration. Judic. Evid.* (1827) V. 457 In some instances, interest would really be neuter. **1886** *Act 49 Vict.* c. 22 §4 An answer stating whether the person so served assents, dissents, or is neuter in respect of taking such land.

c. In phr. ***to stand neuter.***

a **1548** HALL *Chron., Hen. VII* 11 b, Helpe hym, or elles stand neuter betwene both parties. **1642** FULLER *Holy & Prof. St.* v. ii. 362 The sword of the Magistrate cannot stand neuter. **1699** BENTLEY *Phal.* xii. 343 Cicero himself..seems to stand Neuter, and pronounces on no side. **1721** DE FOE *Mem. Cavalier* (1840) 214 Had the Scots stood neuter. *a* **1774** GOLDSM. *Hist. Greece* I. 308 Those who had stood neuter took this occasion to declare against them. **1863** KINGLAKE *Crimea* (1876) I. xiv. 221 His conscience being used to stand neuter in these mental conflicts.

3. Belonging to neither of two specified or usual categories.

a **1591** H. SMITH *Wks.* (1867) II. 444 Thou art not God, neither art thou man, but neuter, mixed of both! **1660** STANLEY *Hist. Philos.* XII. (1701) 497/2 Dialectick is the Science of things True, False and Neuter. **1668** CULPEPPER & COLE *Barthol. Anat.* Man. IV. i. 336 Obscure (which others cal neuter or doubtful Articulation). **1890** *Athenæum* 4 Jan. 24/1 Their samisens..were marked on the neck for a neuter third in one part of the octave... The Japanese pentatonic scale..would be minor were it not for the one indeterminate third.

4. a. *Bot.* Having neither pistils or stamens; neither male nor female; asexual.

1785 MARTYN *Rousseau's Bot.* x. (1794) 101 The fourth of these I call neuter floscules. **1849** BALFOUR *Man. Bot.* 344 Florets of the disk hemaphrodite, those of the ray neuter. **1870** HOOKER *Stud. Flora* 185 Ray-flowers female or neuter.

b. *Ent.* Sexually undeveloped, sterile.

1816 KIRBY & SP. *Entomol.* xvii. (1818) II 50 That the neuter ants..are imperfectly organized females appears from the following observation. **1859** DARWIN *Orig. Spec.* vii. 239 Considering how few neuter-insects out of Europe have been examined.

B. *sb.* **1.** *Gram.* **a.** A neuter verb.

1530 PALSGR. Introd. 34 All suche verbes as be used in the latin tong, lyke neuters or deponentes. **1535** JOYE *Apol. Tindale* (Arb.) 9 Tindale..turneth..the verb passiue into a neuter. **1611** COTGR. *Brief Direct.* 4/2 Newters, whose Preterperfect tense is formed by *je suis.* **1727–38** CHAMBERS *Cycl.* s.v. *Verb,* Others..form their compound parts by the auxiliary *to be*;..These are called *neuters passive.* **1751** HARRIS *Hermes* I. ix. 178 Even those Verbs, called Actives, ..can drop their subsequent Accusative, and assume the Form of Neuters. **1843** *Proc. Philol. Soc.* I. 100 In both languages most of the verbs belonging to this conjugation are passives or neuters.

b. A neuter noun or adjective.

1611 BRINSLEY *Pos. Parts* (1669) 105 Give your Rule for Neuters wanting the singular. **1668** WILKINS *Real Char.* III. i. 303 Adjectives, which are also distinguishable into Neuters Active, Passive. **1755** JOHNSON *Gram.* b/1 *He* and *his* having formerly been applied to neuters in the place now supplied by *it* and *its.* **1838** *Penny Cycl.* XI. 110/1 This third class [of nouns] are called somewhat incorrectly neuters. **1896** TOYNBEE *Hist. French Gram.* 177 As a rule Latin neuters singular..became masculine in French.

2. A neutral thing. *rare.*

1522 SKELTON *Why not to Court* 902 Your cupboard that was Is turned to glasse. From gold to pewter Or els to a newter. **1547** BOORDE *Brev. Health* cxci. 67 b, I do saye al inflacions and appostumacions be nuters, for they may be as well exteryal as interial. **1574** WHITGIFT *Def. Answ.* ii. Wks. 1851 I. 252 There be other some traditions which we may call neuters.

3. One who holds himself neutral; one who takes neither side in a dispute or controversy, or favours neither of two opposed views.

1556 J. HEYWOOD *Spider & F.* lxiii. 15 These indiffrentes (or newters) that part most take, That strongest is. **1600** W. WATSON *Decacordon* (1602) 21 Thus thinke worldlings to haue a good excuse to hold out, and so be of neither side, but be as neuters or impersonals. **1646** J. WHITAKER *Uzziah* 16 He was loved of his friends, feared by his enemies, honoured by the neuters. **1699** BENTLEY *Phal.* 293 Must we stand dubious and neuters between both? **1761** HUME *Hist. Eng.* II. xxxi. 203 A certain creed was embraced by each party; few neuters were to be found. **1814** BYRON *Lara* II. viii, Which knows no neuter, owns but foes or friends. **1885** E. GOSSE *Shaks. to Pope* (1893) 86 To use his influence to collect the neuters into a body strong enough to paralyse the extreme party.

†**b.** Of rulers, states, etc. (Cf. A. 2a and NEUTRAL *sb.* 1) *Obs.*

1560 DAUS tr. *Sleidane's Comm.* 209 The Duke of Lorayne ..had long syns couenaunted with them both, that he myght be a newter. **1636** E. DACRES tr. *Machiavel's Disc. Livy* II. 328 Their agents that were with the King, agreed with him, to stand neuters. **1665** *Surv. Aff. Netherl.* 182 The first are either shut up by neuters, or blocked by Enemies. **1747** in *Col. Rec. Pennsylv.* V. 146 They all stood Neuters except the French Praying Indians.

4. a. *Ent.* A sexually undeveloped female insect; a mature worker.

1797 *Encycl. Brit.* (ed. 3) VII. 348/2 The neuters or working ants which have no sexual characteristics. **1816** KIRBY & SP. *Entomol.* xvii. (1818) II. 33 These neuters are quite unlike those in the Hymenoptera perfect societies. **1877** HUXLEY *Anat. Inv. Anim.* 31 It depends on the nutriment supplied to the female larva of a bee whether it shall become a neuter or a sexually perfect female.

b. A castrated animal.

1900 *Daily News* 10 Jan. 6/5 A finer assembly of Blues, Siamese, Manx, and Long-haired neuters..it would be difficult to secure.

Hence **ˈneuter** *v. trans.*, to castrate. **ˈneuterdom,** the state of being (sexually) neuter. **ˈneuterlike** *a.*, neutral. **ˈneuterly** *adv.*, in a neuter sense. **ˈneuterness,** the fact of being (grammatically) neuter.

1556 J. HEYWOOD *Spider & F.* lxiii. 96 That we all maie ..cut of clerelie All vnkindnesse of newterlike indiffrencie. **1774** BARCLAY *Eng. Dict.*, To *Emaciate*... Neuterly, to grow lean. **1894** DAVIDSON *Hebr. Syntax* 2 When 3 p. pr. is used neuterly for it. **1893** A. KENEALY *Dr. Janet* 136 With the bugbear of neuterdom before her eyes. **1899** *Amer. Jrnl. Philol.* XX. 246 The neuterness of the uncompounded neuter verbal. **1903** F. SIMPSON *Bk. Cat* xxi. 237 A cat should be kept on low plain diet..before being neutered.

†**neuth,** *prep.* and *adv. Sc. Obs. rare.* [Obscurely related to OE. *neoðan* NETHEN.] Beneath.

1375 BARBOUR *Bruce* XI. 538 Beneth the Park [sa] can thai fair, Quhill neuth the kirk, in-till a rout. *c* **1425** WYNTOUN *Cron.* v. x. 3594 (Royal MS.), At þe nauil it was a mas, And outhe and neuthe [*v.r.* neythe] dyuysyd it was.

neutral (ˈnjuːtrəl), *a.* and *sb.* Also 6–7 **newtrall,** 7 **neuterall.** [a. obs. F. *neutral* (1536 in Godef.), or ad. L. *neutrāl-is* (of gender, Quintilian): see NEUTER and -AL[1].] **A.** *adj.*

1. a. Of rulers, states, etc.: Not assisting, or actively taking the side of, either party in the case of a war or disagreement between other states; remaining inactive in relation to the belligerent powers.

1549 *Compl. Scot.* xi. 88 He professit himself to be neutral bot ȝit he furnest the empriour vitht sex thousand fut men. **1600** EDMONDS *Observ. Cæsar's Comm.* 101 Such other Commonweales, as before that time had remained newtrall. **1618** BOLTON *Florus* (1636) 11 Being sent as aydes..they turned neuterall in battell for their owne advantage. **1709** *Lond. Gaz.* No. 4548/2 The Ships of Neutral Nations shall only be seized. *a* **1781** WATSON *Philip III* (1839) 13 The Spanish general, who..had seized on the towns of neutral powers. **1842** BRANDE *Dict. Sci.*, etc. s.v. *Neutrality,* A neutral nation has the right of furnishing to either of the contending parties all supplies which do not fall within the description of contraband of war. **1881** JOWETT *Thucyd.* I. 142 If you prefer to be neutral..receive both sides in peace, but neither for the purposes of war.

b. Belonging to a power which remains inactive during hostilities; exempted or excluded from the sphere of warlike operations.

1711 *Lond. Gaz.* No. 4989/3 The entire Cargo of a Neutral Ship. **1777** WATSON *Philip II,* III. (1793) I. 296 Some merchants whom he had sent..under neutral colours to procure intelligence. **1817** W. SELWYN *Law Nisi Prius* (ed. 4) II. 928 An insurance effected by him on goods to be delivered at a neutral or friendly port. **1855** BRIGHT *Sp., Russia* 7 June (1876) 257 With regard to making the Black Sea a neutral Sea. **1878** LUBBOCK *Addr. Pol. & Educ.* vii. 129 Neutral goods..are not liable to capture under enemy's flag.

2. a. Taking neither side in a dispute, disagreement, or difference of opinions; not inclining toward either party, view, etc.; assisting neither of two contending parties or persons.

1551 *Reg. Privy Council Scot.* I. 116 That the said Provest be chosin be newtrall personis havand regard to the commoun weill of the said burghe. **1603** B. JONSON *Sejanus* I. i, Is he Drusian or Germanican? Or ours? or neutrall? **1650** STAPYLTON *Strada's Low C. Wars* v. 100 The multitude thus storming, the Lords neutrall or wavering. **1746** SMOLLETT *Reproof* 197 While sagely neutral sits thy silent friend, Alike averse to censure or commend. **1760** JOHNSON *Idler* No. 100 ⁋3 My resolution was, to keep my passions neutral, and to marry only in compliance with my reason. **1827** COOPER *Prairie* I. vii. 108 [He] had evidently persuaded himself that it was his duty to be strictly neutral. **1876** MOZLEY *Univ. Serm.* x. (ed. 2) 208 They discard a middle and neutral relation as lukewarm.

b. Belonging to neither party or side.

1564–5 *Reg. Privy Council Scot.* I. 316 Ordaining the officiar to..collect the saidis teindis, to stak the samyn in neutrall places. **1857–61** BUCKLE *Civiliz.* (1869) II. v. 233 The neutral ground of physical science. **1873** HAMERTON *Intell. Life* VIII. i. 277 The largest and best minds..arrive at a sort of neutral region.

c. ***neutral corner***: (see quot. 1954).

1952 *Amateur Boxing* ('Know the Game' Series) 29 When a boxer is 'down', his opponent must immediately retire to the farther neutral corner where he shall remain until ordered to resume boxing by the Referee. **1954** F. C. AVIS *Boxing Reference Dict.* 89 *Neutral Corners,* the two corners of the ring not occupied, between the rounds, by the boxers and their seconds.

3. a. Comprised under, or belonging to, neither of two specified or implied categories; occupying a middle position with regard to two extremes.

1567 *Reg. Privy Council Scot.* I. 583 Ane newtrall and indifferent way. **1592** DAVIES *Immort. Soul* xx. ii, Some Things good, and some Things ill do seem, And neutral some, in her fantastick Eye. **1609** DOULAND *Ornith. Microl.* 13 Certain Songs, which do ascend as an Authenticall, and descend as a Plagall, and those are called Neutrall, or mixt Songs. **1675** BAXTER *Cath. Theol.* I. II. 114 Some..deny Adam to have been Holy, and suppose him only Innocent, and Neutral. **1759** WILSON in *Phil. Trans.* LI. 334 The second cause, which electrified both sides *plus* when the stone was in an intermediate (or, as Æpinus calls it, neutral) state, between the two extremes. **1845** *Encycl. Metrop.* IV. 522 Crystals at once attractive, repulsive, and neutral. **1855** BAIN *Senses & Int.* II. i. §20 The greater number..are indifferent or neutral, as respects our enjoyments.

b. Having no strongly marked characteristics or features; undefined, indefinite, vague.

1805 FOSTER *Ess.* IV. iii. II. 150 That uncoloured neutral vehicle of expression..which may be called the language of generality. **1876** GEO. ELIOT *Dan. Der.* iii, Miss Merry was elderly and altogether neutral in expression. *Ibid.* xli, Dissatisfied with his neutral life.

c. Having no decided colour; of a bluish or greyish appearance; esp. ***neutral colour*** or ***tint*** (see also quot. 1911). Also ***neutral orange*** (see quots. 1934 and 1969).

1821 CRAIG *Lect. Drawing,* etc. v. 267 The most remote distance becomes a mass of neutral colour. **1835** G. FIELD *Chromatography* xx. 178 Several mixed pigments of the class of gray colours are sold under the name of Payne's gray, neutral tint, &c. **1858** HAWTHORNE *Fr. & It. Note-bks.* I. 297 The pillars and walls of this Duomo are of a uniform, brownish, neutral tint. **1869** T. W. SALTER *Field's Chromatogr.* (new ed.) xi. 253 Neutral orange or Penley's Neutral Orange, is a permanent compound pigment composed of yellow ochre and the russet-marrone known as brown madder. **1879** HARLAN *Eyesight* vii. 97 The best glasses, in daylight at least, are the..neutral gray. **1911** M. TOCH *Materials for Permanent Painting* xiv. 145 Neutral tint ..is a complex mixture of ultramarine, sienna, lamp black or ochre and lamp black, and..is an excellent color which is perfectly permanent. *Ibid.*, Neutral orange..has many of the characteristics of mars orange, but sometimes is made by mixing a brilliant yellow, free from lead, with a bright oxide of iron. **1924** F. W. WEBER *Artists' Pigments* 98 Payne's Gray, like Neutral Tint, is prepared by various color manufacturers. **1934** H. HILER *Notes on Technique Painting* ii. 113 Neutral orange, Penley's orange, a mixture of cadmium yellow with Venetian red. It is only used in water colour. **1969** R. MAYER *Dict. Art Terms & Techniques* 262/1 *Neutral orange,* a prepared artists' color made of mixed pigments. The best grades would contain cadmium orange or deep cadmium yellow and light red.

Comb. **1860** TYNDALL *Glac.* I. xiv. 94 The dense neutral-tint masses crept along the sides of the mountains. **1869** G. LAWSON *Dis. Eye* (1874) 28 The neutral-tint glasses are far more efficient in affording relief from glare than those of a cobalt-blue colour.

d. Of sounds: Indistinct, indefinite, obscure.

1874 SAYCE *Compar. Philol.* vi. 247 The farther back we push our phonological researches, the greater becomes the number of neutral sounds.

e. *Phonetics.* Of the central, usu. unstressed, vowel sounds [ə] and [ɨ], produced with the tongue in a rest position and having indefinite quality.

1891 L. SOAMES *Introd. Phonetics* I. iii. 50 The obscure vowel 'a' in attend.., sometimes called the *natural* or the *neutral vowel.* **1948** J. R. FIRTH *Papers in Ling. 1934–51* (1957) ix. 131 The weak, neutral, or 'minimal' vowel... The term neutral suits it in English, since it is in fact neutral to the phonematic system of vowels in southern English. **1956** D. ABERCROMBIE *Problems & Principles* iii. 33 The ubiquitous English 'neutral' vowel ə. **1965** W. S. ALLEN *Vox Latina* 4 The so-called 'neutral' vowel of standard southern British English, as at the end of *sofa.* **1972** R. A. PALMATIER *Gloss. Eng. Transformational Gram.* 103 *Neutral vowel,*..the mid central vowel 'schwa' [ə]—or the high central vowel 'barred i' [ɨ]—to which insufficiently stressed vowels are reduced.

f. *Philos.* Belonging neither to the mental nor to the physical; esp. as ***neutral monism,*** the theory that there is but one substance of existence of which mind and matter are varying arrangements. So ***neutral monist.***

1904 W. JAMES in *Jrnl. Philos., Psychol. & Sci. Methods* 1 Sept. 487 Matter we know, and thought we know, and conscious content we know, but neutral and simple 'pure experience' is something we know not at all. **1912** R. B. PERRY *Present Philos. Tendencies* II. iv. 79 It is evident that Mach's view can only mean a reduction of both the physical and the mental order to a manifold of neutral elements. **1914** B. RUSSELL in *Monist* XXIV. Apr. 161 'Neutral monism' —as opposed to idealistic monism and materialistic monism. *Ibid.* 171 Neutral monists..infer that the mental and the physical are composed of the same 'stuff'. **1920** S. ALEXANDER *Space, Time & Deity* II. III. viii. 216 Nor are we free to suppose that there is a neutral non-mental world containing illusions amongst other neutral objects, neither mental nor physical. **1925** C. D. BROAD *Mind & its Place in Nature* iii. 133 It might be so on a Double-Aspect theory, or on a theory of Neutral Monism. **1944** J. E. BOODIN in P. A. Schilpp *Philos. B. Russell* xv. 495 It seems to me that Russell's neutral monism is an illusion. Our sensory awareness—'sensation' as Russell calls it—is real. But it is not identical with a mathematical equation. **1973** A. QUINTON *Nature of Things* III. 237 There is the kind of phenomenalistic or neutral monist theory intimated by Hume and Mill. *Ibid.* xi. 318 Minds, for the neutral monist, are literally composed of impressions.

4. a. *Chem.* Having the properties neither of an acid nor of a base; not distinguished by either acid or alkaline reaction.

1661 BOYLE *Exper. & Notes* II. iv, I was wont to give them a negative appellation, and call each of them the neutral or adiaphorous spirit of the body that affords it. **1727–38** CHAMBERS *Cycl., Neutral Salts,* among chemists, are a sort of intermediate salts between acids and alkalies; partaking of the nature of both. **1797** *Encycl. Brit.* (ed. 3) IV. 398/2 The liquor will neither have the properties of an acid nor an alkali, but will be what is called neutral. **1838** T. THOMSON *Chem. Org. Bodies* 106 The solution is neutral. **1875** *Ure's Dict. Arts* (ed. 7) III. 844 Natural or neutral fats and oils, chemically considered, are really salts.

b. *Optics.* Having or indicating none of the phenomena of polarization.

1813 BREWSTER *New Philos. Instr.* IV. iv. 336 The horizontal and vertical lines.. drawn upon the plate of mica, may be called the neutral axes of the mica. **1845** *Encycl. Metrop.* IV. 565 Every point in a certain line.. will therefore be in a neutral state as to polarization, and, of course, appear black.

c. *Electr.* Neither positive nor negative. Also ***neutral temperature***, that at which no current is produced by two metals arranged to exhibit thermoelectric force; ***neutral point*** (see quot. 1892).

1837 BREWSTER *Magnet.* 363 The decomposition of the neutral fluid will begin immediately. **1860** G. PRESCOTT *Electr. Telegr.* 15 The quantity of neutral fluid which a body contains cannot be determined. **1885** WATSON & BURBURY *Math. The. Electr. & Magn.* I. 241 In an iron and copper couple this neutral temperature is, according to Sir W. Thomson, about 280°C. **1892** G. F. BARKER *Physics* 731 The point of temperature at which a given pair of metals have the same thermo-electric power.. is called the neutral point.

d. *Mech.* Lying at the point where the forces of extension and compression meet and are in equilibrium.

1845 *Encycl. Metrop.* III. 60/2 An isosceles triangle, having its vertex in the neutral axis. **1869** SIR E. REED *Shipbuild.* v. 80 The score in the centre plate is cut very near the neutral axis of the girder.

e. Of equilibrium: (see quot. 1879).

1865 *Intell. Observ.* No. 47. 344 Equilibrium stable, unstable, and neutral. **1879** THOMSON & TAIT *Nat. Phil.* I. I. §291 If a material system, under the influence of internal and applied forces, varying according to some definite law, is balanced by them in any position in which it may be placed, its equilibrium is said to be neutral.

f. Electr. Engin. ***neutral point***, the point in an electrical system which has the same potential that the junction of equal resistances would have if they were connected at their other ends to the lines making up the system; (see also sense 4 c); ***neutral wire***, a wire connected to a neutral point (and usu. also to earth).

1896 R. ROBB *Electr. Wiring* iii. 44 The taps are taken off from the neutral wire and either of the other two in such a way that the loads on the two sides of the system will balance as nearly as possible. **1907** J. F. C. SNELL *Distribution Electr. Energy* 19 A usual practice is to require the middle of the star, or neutral point, to be earthed. **1930** *Engineering* 7 Mar. 321/3 The necessary apparatus for earthing the neutral point of a three-phase system. **1962** *Newnes Conc. Encycl. Electr. Engin.* 543/1 If no neutral point on a system is earthed and one of the line conductors becomes accidentally earthed, the other two line conductors will immediately assume line voltage to earth and the neutral will assume the line-to-neutral voltage. **1972** SMITH & HOSIE *Basic Electr. Engin. Sci.* ix. 238 The current in the neutral wire of a balanced 3-ph[ase], 4-wire star-connected system is zero and the conductor may be omitted.

g. ***neutral-density*** (Photogr.): applied to a filter that absorbs light of all wavelengths to the same extent and so causes no change in its colour.

1938 K. HENNEY *Color Photogr.* iii. 58 By the use of a neutral-density filter of the proper transmission, in addition to the colored separation filters, it is possible to lengthen the exposure of the green and the red filters. **1962** M. L. HASELGROVE *Photographers' Dict.* 151 Mainly used in sensitometry and color work, a neutral density filter is sometimes resorted to in black and white photography when the camera is loaded with a film of very high speed. **1965** M. J. LANGFORD *Basic Photogr.* xi. 195 Other, colourless, filters include neutral density (grey) filters for reducing image brightness without affecting colour reproduction.

5. Asexual; having no sexual characteristics.

a. *Ent.* Sexually abortive or undeveloped.

1747 GOULD *Eng. Ants* 35 The Queen Ant lays three different Sorts of Eggs, the Male, Female, and Neutral. **1802** PALEY *Nat. Theol.* xviii. (1817) 151 The grub is nurtured neither by the father nor the mother, but by the neutral bee.

b. *Bot.* Having neither pistils nor stamens.

1796 WITHERING *Brit. Plants* (ed. 3) I. 323 Floret. Tubular,.. Neutral, containing neither stamens nor pistil. **1846–50** A. WOOD *Class-bk. Bot.* 311 Where the flowers.. of the ray or margin are pistillate or neutral.

c. Belonging to the class of eunuchs.

1820 BYRON *Juan* v. xxvi, Just now a black old neutral personage Of the third sex stept up.

6. Denoting various classes of dyes. **a.** Applied to various basic azine dyes: ***neutral blue***, a brown crystalline compound, $C_{24}H_{20}N_3Cl$, which dyes cotton a dull blue but has poor fastness; ***neutral red***, a dark green crystalline compound, $C_{15}H_{16}N_4.HCl$, which forms a red solution in water or alcohol and is used as an acid-base indicator and for staining granules and vacuoles in living cells; ***neutral violet***, a dark green crystalline compound, $C_{22}H_{24}N_6.HCl$, which is occasionally used as a biological stain or an indicator.

1889 *Cent. Dict.* s.v. *blue*, Neutral blue. **1890** THORPE *Dict. Appl. Chem.* I. 229/2 The commercial product [*sc.* toluene red], which contains a certain amount of impurities, is sold under the name of 'neutral red'... A similar product is.. sold under the name of 'neutral violet'. **1905** CAIN & THORPE *Synthetic Dyestuffs* xviii. 133 The only other Eurhodine of importance is Neutral violet.., prepared by the oxidation of a mixture of *p*-amidodimethylaniline and *m*-phenylenediamine. *Ibid.* 140 Neutral blue.. and its derivatives, Basle blue B.. and Azine green GB.. are important tannin cotton dyes. **1914** *Chem. Abstr.* VIII. 723 (*heading*) Neutral red as indicator in determination of the alkalinity of the serum. **1930** *Stain Technol.* V. 133 Dyes employed in the vital staining are:.. neutral red, neutral violet, fuchsin, [etc.]. **1950** *Proc. Linn. Soc.* CLXII. 69 He [*sc.* the French cytologist Paiat] saw there no net: on the contrary, he saw separate spheres, and these he called neutral red vacuoles, because he was accustomed to colour them in the living cell with neutral red. **1952** K. VENKATARAMAN *Chem. Synthetic Dyes* II. xxv. 768 A further distinction has been made between Rosindulines.. and *iso*Rosindulines, such as Neutral Blue,.. in which the auxochrome is in the benzene part of the naphthophenazine nucleus. **1967** *Oceanogr. & Marine Biol.* V. 364 She ascertained the region of epithelial elongation using Neutral Red marks. **1971** E. GURR *Synthetic Dyes* 110 Neutral violet is only occasionally used as a biological stain.

b. Applied to textile dyes which can be used directly in an approximately neutral dye-bath. So ***neutral-dyeing*** ppl. adj.

1892 COLLIN & RICHARDSON tr. *Nietzki's Chem. Org. Dyestuffs* 14 The salts of certain azosulphonic acids may be termed neutral dyestuffs. They may be directly fixed on vegetable fibres. **1920** J. M. MATTHEWS *Application of Dyestuffs* v. 156 A separate group of dyestuffs is frequently made of the eosin or phthalein dyes. This group includes certain of both the acid and basic dyes, which.. might be termed 'neutral' dyes... They are applied in neutral or slightly acid bath, and are largely used for the dyeing of silk. **1955** A. J. HALL *Handbk. Textile Dyeing & Printing* iii. 49 Acid wool dyes are sometimes divided into two groups, *viz.* acid dyeing and neutral dyeing. **1955** H. E. WOODWARD in H. A. Lubs *Chem. of Synthetic Dyes & Pigments* iii. 151 Many neutral-dyeing dyes are aggregated more than level-dyeing acid dyes. **1962** [see sense A. 6 c below].

c. *Histology.* [Introduced in this sense by P. Ehrlich 1880, in *Zeitschr. f. klin. Med.* I. 557.] Applied to biological stains or dyes precipitated on mixing an acid dye and a basic dye.

1893 *N.Y. Med. Jrnl.* LVII. 2/2 Other granules react only to basic, or still others only to neutral colors. **1925** H. J. CONN *Biol. Stains* viii. 86 Compound dyes of this sort are sometimes referred to as neutral dyes or neutral stains. This terminology, of course, does not indicate that they are neutral in reaction any more than do the corresponding terms acid and basic dyes. A dye chemist, in fact, uses the term neutral dye in an entirely different sense. **1958** J. R. BAKER *Princ. Biol. Microtechnique* xiv. 263 The granules of polymorphonuclear leucocytes are coloured by both the components of the neutral dye, and that is why Ehrlich called them 'neutrophil'. He regarded the specific dyeing of these granules as an important property of the neutral dyes, not to be obtained without their use. **1962** E. GURR *Staining Animal Tissues* 31 Neutral 'dyes' should not be confused with 'neutral' or compound stains. The latter are formed by chemical union between a basic and an acid dye.

B. *sb.* **1. a.** One who remains neutral between two parties or sides; a subject of a neutral state, etc.

c **1449** PECOCK *Repr.* I. xvi. 87 Summe of ȝou ben clepid Doctour-mongers, and summe ben clepid Opinioun-holders, and summe ben Neutralis. **1581** J. BELL *Haddon's Answ. Osor.* 289 They that tooke part with neither of them, were called Newtralles. **1601** LD. MOUNTJOY *Let.* in Moryson *Itin.* (1617) II. 173 The whole Province either is joyned with them, or stand neutrals. **1627** HAKEWILL *Apol.* IV. ii. 286 Such as are Neutralls, who may labour with the one side and with the other to compound the quarrell. **1756** *Boston News-Letter* 22 Jan. 2/2 The French Inhabitants of Nova-Scotia, commonly call'd Neutrals. **1777** J. ADAMS in *Fam. Lett.* (1876) 323 In politics they are a breed of mongrels or neutrals. **1807–8** SYD. SMITH *P. Plymley's Lett.* Wks. 1859 II. 182/1 There should be a free entry of neutrals into the enemy's ports. **1877** BROCKETT *Cross & Cr.* 26 The powers of Western Europe were either allies of Turkey or neutrals.

b. A neutral vessel.

1805 *Spirit Public Jrnls.* IX. 378 Come my lads, let's run down that merchantman; let's overhaul that neutral.

†2. A neuter word. *Obs. rare*$^{-1}$.

1694 SALMON *Bate's Dispens.* (1713) 323/1 Here it signifies neither Male nor Female, but a Neutral thing without Life, and therefore we used it as a Neutral.

3. A neutral salt.

1822–34 *Good's Study Med.* (ed. 4) II. 396 It can then be taken in larger quantity, and need not interfere with ammoniacal neutrals.

4. *Electr.* A neutral point or conductor (cf. A. 4 f above).

1900 *Jrnl. Inst. Electr. Engin.* XXIX. 538 Each of these boards receives from the main generator board five cables, a pair of 'outers' for lighting, a similar pair for power, and a common neutral. **1930** H. P. SEELYE *Electr. Distribution Engin.* vi. 98 On many systems, the neutral of the primary circuit, whether or not it is brought out as a four-wire circuit, is grounded at the substation. **1973** [see LIVE *a.* 4].

5. = *Idiom Neutral* (s.v. IDIOM 5). Also *attrib.*

1907 W. J. CLARK *Internat. Lang.* II. v. 99 Members of the academy.. carry on their business by means of circulars, drawn up, of course, in Neutral. **1922** A. L. GUÉRARD *Short Hist. Internat. Lang. Movement* II. vi. 137 International words were selected.. and were altered only in order to conform to Neutral spelling. **1928** O. JESPERSEN *Internat. Lang.* I. 49 Occidental... It forms in that respect a continuation of Neutral and especially of Rosenberger's Reform-Neutral. **1947** H. JACOB *Planned Auxiliary Language* ii. 45 The most favoured systems [based on ethnic languages] were Esperanto, Neutral, Novlatin, and Universal.

6. A position of the driving and driven parts in a gear mechanism in which no power is transmitted. Also *fig.*

1912 G. HARRIS et al. *Audel's Answers on Automobiles* 442 With clutch still disengaged, the transmission lever is moved from neutral to first speed position. **1925** *Morris Owner* Jan. 1154/1 Don't lose your head and start the car in gear. Take things quietly, put the lever in neutral, [etc.]. **1926** 'J. J. CONNINGTON' *Death at Swaythling Court* xiii. 250 The Colonel slipped his gear into neutral. **1958** *Spectator* 22 Aug. 251/2 A time-waster filling the hours when the brain is in neutral. **1962** J. BRAINE *Life at Top* xix. 222 She turned the ignition key; the car jerked forward convulsively, then stopped. 'Put it in neutral, first.' **1971** R. DENTRY *Encounter at Kharmel* iii. 42 Pepper threw the gear stick into neutral, applied the handbrake firmly, switched off. **1973** 'D. JORDAN' *Nile Green* xxxv. 174 Sue's face went into neutral. **1975** T. ALLBEURY *Special Collection* xix. 132 The Special Collection [Operation] has been put into neutral by the Presidium.

neutralism (ˈnjuːtrəlɪz(ə)m). [f. prec. + -ISM.] Maintenance of neutrality; *spec.* a policy of maintaining neutrality and attempting conciliation in conflicts between major world powers.

1579 W. WILKINSON *Confut. Familye of Love* 39 b, Our owne Newtralisme, and Lukwarmenes shall.. vtterly condemne vs. **1861** M. ARNOLD *Pop. Educ. France* 221 Their neutralism will be at an end, denominationalism will have made them prisoners. **1951** *Here & Now* (N.Z.) May 5/1 The second feature of French opinion which seems important today is.. the anxiety to keep out of future wars and is summed up in the term 'neutralism'. **1955** *Times* 6 July 11/3 Russia might take a favourable view of some at least of Japan's requests in order to stimulate Japanese 'neutralism' and the adoption of a foreign policy less friendly to the western Powers. **1958** *Listener* 27 Nov. 864/2 The interests of the Arabs require the political neutralization of their countries. This should mean genuine neutrality, and not neutralism; that is, exacerbating and exploiting the rivalries of the great powers, for immediate political advantage. **1959** *Times* 26 Oct. 11/2 Neutralism differs from neutrality in that it is an attitude of mind in time of peace rather than a legal status in time of war. **1963** M. BRECHER *New States of Asia* iv. 112 *Neutralism* has in common with non-alignment an expressed desire to remain aloof from bloc conflict. But neutralism goes much further, for it involves a positive attitude towards bloc conflicts. A neutralist state assumes an obligation to help reduce tensions between blocs with a view to maintaining peace or bringing about peace, and more particularly to prevent the outbreak of war.

neutralist (ˈnjuːtrəlɪst). Also 7 neuter-. [f. as prec. + -IST.] One who maintains a neutral attitude (in early use *spec.* in matters of religion). Also rarely as *adj.* (quot. 1810).

1623 T. SCOTT *Highw. God* 58 The prophane Naturalist and Neuteralist, who is of all religions, or no religion. *a* **1665** J. GOODWIN *Filled w. the Spirit* (1867) 359 Absolute neutralists in all manner of tenets and opinions in matters of religion. **1713** *Humble Plead. Gd. Old Way* App. 9 Malignants, Episcopalians, Neutralists, with many professed (tho' unsound) Presbyterians. **1797** *Hist.* in *Ann. Reg.* 166/1 The neutralists were at pains to explain.. their principles. **1810** THIRLWALL *Lett.* (1881) I. 7, I am at present, therefore, neutralist. **1833** LYTTON *Godolphin* lv, The silent neutralist soon became regarded.. as the secret foe. **1915** *Morning Post* 1 Feb. 8/6 A meeting of neutralists, held here to-day, was broken up by Republicans, who shouted 'Long live the war!' **1920** *Glasgow Herald* 26 May 9/2 The Neutralist elements.. hate the very idea of celebrating Italy's entrance into the war. **1957** *Economist* 28 Dec. 1114/2 They have been supported by perhaps an equal number of pacifists, near-pacifists and neutralists. **1963** *Ann. Reg. 1962* 351 The congress called for the withdrawal of American influence from South Vietnam and the formation of a neutralist Government there. **1975** *Nature* 6 Feb. 482/2 Neutralists, however, are delighted to find that this molecule of a living fossil underwent changes at least as rapidly as the homologous molecules in highly-evolved species.

neutralistic (njuːtrəˈlɪstɪk), *a.* [f. NEUTRAL *a.* + -ISTIC.] Characterized by a neutral attitude.

1949 *Mind* LVIII. 57 The element in, for example, a sensation of blue.. will be susceptible to Mr. Gallie's neutralistic analysis.

neutrality (njuːˈtrælɪtɪ). Also 5–7 newtral(l)-. [ad. F. *neutralité* (14th c.), or med.L. *neutrālitas*, f. *neutrālis* NEUTRAL *a.*: see -ITY.]

1. (With *the*.) The neutral party in any dispute or difference of opinion; the neutral powers during a war (†also *pl.*). Now only *Hist.*

1480 CAXTON *Chron. Eng.* ccxlix, The threfold governance in the chirche, that is to wete, of Eugenye, of the counseyll, and of the neutralyte. **1599** HAYWARD *1st Pt. Hen. IV* 25 The Archbishop of Canterbury, and certaine others of the neutrality,.. perswaded the king to come to a treaty with the lordes. **1711** *Lond. Gaz.* No. 4933/1 The Troops of the Neutrality, that were in Silesia, are separated. **1781** COWPER *Lett.* Wks. 1837 XV. 73 And as to the neutralities, I really think the Russian virago an impertinent puss for meddling with us. **1827** SCOTT *Napoleon* IV. 253 The association of the Northern States in 1780, known by the name of the armed Neutrality.

2. a. A neutral attitude between contending parties or powers; abstention from taking any part in a war between other states.

1494 FABYAN *Chron.* VII. 612 Some countres vphelde that one [pope], and some that other, so that there were allowyd none of theym both, and that was called the newtralytie. **1571** *Reg. Privy Council Scot.* II. 88 Thinking be thair newtralitie and baklying to be welcum to quhatsumevir party beis victour. **1601** LD. MOUNTJOY *Let.* in Moryson *Itin.* (1617) II. 143 No better then neutralitie is to be expected from those that are best affected. **1672** R. MONTAGU in *Buccleuch MSS.* (Hist. MSS. Comm.) I. 517 The ill answers this Court has received from Spain to their proposition of a neutrality. **1710** *Lond. Gaz.* No. 4669/4 The Neutrality which is to be observed by the Northern Crowns. **1831** SIR J. SINCLAIR *Corr.* II. 222 What.. the country would prefer, is a war between France and England, and the advantages of a lucrative neutrality. **1874** GREEN *Short Hist.*

vii. §6. 405 England set aside the balanced neutrality of Elizabeth.

b. The state or condition of being on neither side or inclined neither way; absence of decided views, feeling, or expression; indifference.

1561 DAUS tr. *Bullinger on Apoc.* (1573) 58b, The lothsomenes which God conceaueth of this newtralitie or warmnes. **1600** E. BLOUNT tr. *Conestaggio* A2 Those Readers that can iudge of the truth of a historie and the newtrallitie of the writer. **1665** GLANVILL *Scepsis Sci.* i. 15 The grey heads of Reverend Antiquity have been content to sit down here in profest Neutrality. **1751** JOHNSON *Rambler* No. 89 ¶9 That no part of life be spent in a state of neutrality or indifference. **1788** GIBBON *Decl. & F.* xlvii. IV. 573 On a subject which engrossed the thoughts..of men, it was difficult to preserve an exact neutrality. **1871** GEO. ELIOT *Middlem.* xxiii, [He] looked before him with as complete a neutrality as if he had been a portrait by a great master.

c. The neutral character *of* a place during a war.

1745 P. THOMAS *Jrnl. Anson's Voy.* 297 Why the Neutrality of their Ports should be violated. **1808** WELLINGTON in Gurw. *Desp.* (1837) IV. 205 The Russian Admiral..would claim the neutrality of the port of Lisbon. **1833** M. SCOTT *Tom Cringle* xix, He will never venture to infract the neutrality of the waters surely.

3. a. An intermediate state or condition, not clearly one thing or another.

1570 J. DEE *Math. Pref.* ivb, A meruaylous newtralitie haue these thinges Mathematicall, and also a straunge participation betwene thinges supernaturall..and thynges naturall. *a***1631** DONNE *Anat. World* Poems (1633) 238 Physitians say that wee, At best, enjoy but a neutralitie. **1743** H. WALPOLE *Corr.* (ed. 3) I. lx. 229, I wish I could make as long a letter for you, but we are in a neutrality of news. **1843** J. MARTINEAU *Chr. Life* (1867) 154 A striking neutrality of treatment.

b. *Chem.* The fact or state of being neutral.

1880 CLEMINSHAW *Wurtz' Atomic The.* 13 The..well-known fact of the permanence of neutrality in the double decomposition of two neutral salts. **1882** TYNDALL in *Longm. Mag.* I. 36 Its behaviour..approaches that of elementary bodies. May it not help to explain their neutrality?

4. a. The fact of being of the neuter gender.

1659 PEARSON *Creed* II. 271 The plurality of the verb, and the neutrality of the noun, with the distinction of their persons, speak a perfect identity of their essence. **1883** J. S. STALLYBRASS tr. *Grimm's Teutonic Mythol.* II. 883 Out of the Goth. fairguni's neutrality unfolded themselves both a male *Fiörgynn* and a female *Fiörgyn*.

b. The condition of belonging to neither sex.

1823 BYRON *Juan* VI. cxvii, The trouble that they [*sc.* women] gave, their immorality, which made him daily bless his own neutrality.

neutralization (njuːtrəlaɪˈzeɪʃən). [f. next + -ATION. Cf. F. *neutralisation* (1797).]

1. The action of neutralizing by means of something having an opposite nature or effect; an instance of this: **a.** *Chem.* and *Electr.*

1808 DAVY in *Phil. Trans.* XCIX. 101 A species of neutralization, by the oxide or inflammable body. **1827** FARADAY *Chem. Manip.* xii. 274 Neutralizations are best effected with the assistance of heat. **1860** G. PRESCOTT *Electr. Telegr.* 16 The neutralization of the two contrary electricities..may take place according to different modes. **1881** *Rep. Brit. Assoc.* 574 The neutralisation of a particular quantity of a given acid.

b. In general use.

1817 COLERIDGE *Biog. Lit.* I. ii. 45 This is one instance among many of deception, by the telling the half of a fact, and omitting the other half, when it is from their mutual counteraction and neutralization, that the *whole* truth arises. **1856** DOVE *Logic Chr. Faith* I. ii. §2. 84 The cause of the neutralization or compensation of equal opposing force. **1866** AITKEN *Pract. Med.* II. 35 The principle of cure..which has been called the method of neutralization. **1885** AGNES CLERKE *Pop. Hist. Astron.* 52 The point of neutralisation of opposing tendencies.

c. *Ophthalm.* Combination of a lens with one or more of known power, as a means of finding its power.

1897 J. THORINGTON *Retinoscopy* iv. 34 This movement, at such a point in neutralization, may give a hint as to the presence of astigmatism. **1946** DICKINSON & HALL *Contact Lenses* vii. 82 The lenses should be checked for accuracy of focus and curve. In the absence of a refractionometer, neutralization may be employed. **1974** JALIE & WRAY *Pract. Ophthalmic Lenses* 5 The measurement of the focal power of lenses can be done in many ways. Two main methods are used for ophthalmic lenses: (1) Neutralization. (2) Vertex power measuring instruments.

d. *Electronics.* The cancellation of internal feedback in an amplifier, etc. (see NEUTRALIZE *v.* 3c).

1923 *Wireless World* 21 Apr. 69/2 Neutralisation is secured provided coils L and L_1 are correctly coupled. **1943** F. E. TERMAN *Radio Engineers' Handbk.* v. 469 Cross neutralization is used with push-pull amplifiers... It can be thought of as a form of neutrodyne that takes advantage of the fact that the voltages on the two sides of a push-pull amplifier are of opposite polarity, thus giving the phase relations required for neutralizing. **1961** GRAY & GRAHAM *Radio Transmitters* iii. 64 Many systems of neutralization are based on forming a balanced bridge with the tube grid-to-plate capacity forming one of the arms of the bridge. **1962** SIMPSON & RICHARDS *Physical Princ. Junction Transistors* vii. 132 It is possible to determine the elements of an external feedback circuit which will accomplish the required neutralization. Since the transistor is thereby made into a one-way device, in which an input signal can influence the output but the reverse is not true, the compensation process is often called 'unilateralization'. **1968** [see NEUTRALIZE *v.* 3c].

2. The action of making neutral in time of war.

1870 *Echo* 14 Nov., Russia had..declared that the neutralisation of the Black Sea was unsupportable. **1885** *Manch. Exam.* 27 Feb. 5/3 The neutralisation of the Congo basin.

3. *Linguistics.* The levelling out of certain phonemic or morphemic distinctions in particular contexts.

1942 C. F. HOCKETT in *Language* XVIII. 10 Any talk of neutralization or cancellation or archiphonemes confuses the facts without adding anything. **1947** K. L. PIKE *Phonemics* 243/2 *Neutralization of oppositions*, the occurrence in some environment of a segment phonetically similar to and mutually exclusive with two other contrasting segments. **1949** A. MARTINET *Phonology as Functional Phonetics* 7 Care should be taken not to mistake the non-appearance of a phoneme in a given position with a neutralization. **1962** *Amer. Speech* XXXVII. 69 Review of extant phonemic analyses of Modern Icelandic..and proposal of a third solution hinging on the Prague concept of neutralization. **1964** E. PALMER tr. *Martinet's Elem. General Linguistics* iii. 69 Where an archiphoneme is manifested there is said to be neutralization. **1968** *Language* XLIV. 475, I understand neutralization to mean the lack of consonance between form contrasts and function contrasts in all parts of a single linguistic sub-system. **1972** HARTMANN & STORK *Dict. Lang. & Ling.* 151 *Neutralisation*, the cancelling of a phonemic opposition in certain positions. **1973** *Word 1970* XXVI. 102 Morphological neutralization occurs in such examples as *alemães* and *alemãs* (both pronounced [the same]).

neutralize (ˈnjuːtrəlaɪz), *v.* [ad. F. *neutralizer* (1611), or med.L. *neutrālisāre* (Du Cange): see NEUTRAL *a.* and -IZE.]

†**1.** *intr.* To remain neutral. *Obs.* *rare*$^{-1}$.

*a***1665** J. GOODWIN *Filled w. the Spirit* (1867) 337 Whether it be better and safer to neutralise between these two opinions, and hang in suspense?

2. *trans.* **a.** *Chem.* To render neutral. Also *refl.*

1759 COLEBROOKE in *Phil. Trans.* LI. 51, I neutralized Spanish White, by fermenting it with vinegar. **1816** FARADAY *Exp. Researches* i. 2 The solution was..neutralized by sulphuric acid, and precipitated. **1836–41** BRANDE *Chem.* (ed. 5) 639 The alkali in the basin is now to be neutralized with the acid in the tube. **1883** *Hardwich's Photogr. Chem.* (ed. Taylor) 180 Nitric Acid added to such a Bath neutralizes itself and displaces Acetic Acid.

b. *Electr.* To make void of electricity; to render electrically inert.

1837 BREWSTER *Magnet.* 122 If we carry the needle, when perfectly neutralized, round the sphere. **1860** G. PRESCOTT *Electr. Telegr.* 16 The contrary electricities may be neutralized..by means of an insulated conductor. **1885** WATSON & BURBURY *Math. The. Electr. & Magn.* I. 93 If the enclosed system, together with the distribution on the inner surface, were..allowed to..neutralise each other.

3. a. To counterbalance; to render ineffective or void; to destroy by an opposite force or effect.

1795 BURKE *Regic. Peace* iv. Wks. IX. 13 Regicide neutralizes all the acrimony of that power, and renders it safe and social. **1820** HAZLITT *Lect. Dram. Lit.* 11 The very nature of our academic institutions..neutralizes a taste for the productions of native genius. **1875** OUSELEY *Mus. Form* ii. 18 Thus one irregularity of construction in this case neutralises the effect of the other.

b. *Ophthalm.* To annul the refractive power of (a lens) by combination with one or more other lenses (of known power).

1902 TAYLOR & BAXTER *Key to Sight Testing* xxxvi. 243 A deep convex, if it could be made infinitely thin, would practically neutralize a concave of the same power. **1962** L. S. SASIENI *Optical Dispensing* (ed. 2) xv. 354 When plastic lenses have to be neutralized, the trial lenses should on no account be allowed to touch the outer surface. **1974** JALIE & WRAY *Pract. Ophthalmic Lenses* 8 It may be necessary for unknown lenses of high focal power to be neutralized by a combination of two neutralizing lenses.

c. *Electronics.* To cancel internal feedback in (an amplifier stage, valve, or transistor), esp. that due to interelectrode capacitance, by providing an additional external feedback voltage of equal magnitude but opposite phase.

1924 MOYER & WOSTREL *Pract. Radio* viii. 123 The adjustment of each neutralizing capacity is made by tuning to the radio current of some transmitting station, turning out the filament of the vacuum tube to be neutralized..and adjusting the capacity until all the sounds in the telephone receiver disappear. **1948** A. L. ALBERT *Radio Fund.* ix. 367 Triodes used in radio-frequency amplifiers must be neutralized, otherwise feedback from the plate to the grid through the interelectrode capacitance may cause oscillations. **1962** SIMPSON & RICHARDS *Physical Princ. Junction Transistors* vii. 132 We now consider a general determination of the circuit constants required to neutralize a *CB* or *CE* amplifying stage. **1968** ROMANOWITZ & PUCKETT *Introd. Electronics* x. 410 Push-pull circuits operating at high frequencies also require neutralization. They may be neutralized by a criss-cross connection of two capacitors, one from each tube plate, to the end of the input parallel circuit that is connected to the grid of the other tube.

4. To exempt or exclude (a place) from the sphere of warlike operations.

1856 in McCarthy *Own Times* xxviii. (1887) I. 417 The Black Sea is neutralised. **1883** *Manch. Guard.* 15 Oct. 5/4 Such an Egypt..would..be neutralised under a general European guarantee.

5. In motor rallying, to exempt (a section of the course) from having to be covered at a set average speed, so that that section has no effect on the result of a race.

1902 *Encycl. Brit.* XXXI. 13/2 Deducting the Swiss portion of the route (which was neutralized), the distance was 615 miles. **1903** *Sci. Amer. Suppl.* 20 June 22958 A number of different villages were neutralized, and the chauffeurs were given from 5 to 25 minutes to make the passage. **1971** P. BROWNING *Rally Manual* vi. 54 My immediate reaction was to neutralize the frontier crossing—that is to say..disregard the time taken to pass between the two officials. **1972** H. S. VILLARD *Great Road Races 1894–1914* vi. 115 The Taunus Circuit took in eight neutralized control areas..and was eighty-seven miles in length.

Hence ˈ**neutralized** *ppl. a.*

1766 CAVENDISH in *Phil. Trans.* LVII. 100 There is still a good deal of earth remaining in it in a neutralized state. **1796** KIRWAN *Elem. Min.* (ed. 2) I. 484 The neutralized solution should then be divided into two equal portions. **1881** TYNDALL *Floating Matter of Air* 230 To send me a supply of neutralized urine. **1899** CAGNEY tr. *Jaksch's Clin. Diagn.* ii. (ed. 4) 107, 3 parts sheep's serum, one part neutralized veal bouillon.

ˈ**neutralizer.** [f. prec. + -ER[1].]

†**1.** One who adopts a neutral attitude. *Obs.*

1628 H. BURTON *Israel's Fast* Ded. 10 A third sort of Achans are Neutralizers. **1629** —— *Babel no Bethel* 64 We should have fewer Neutralizers.

2. One who, or that which, neutralizes something.

1843 *Blackw. Mag.* LIV. 53 Accrediting them as neutralizers of regular armies to an enormous amount. **1869** BROWNING *Ring & Bk.* VII. 1596 The neutralizer of all good and truth. **1879** *Cassell's Techn. Educ.* IV. 175/2 Plaster of Paris is a still more powerful neutraliser of heat.

ˈ**neutralizing,** *vbl. sb.* [f. as prec. + -ING[1].] The action of NEUTRALIZE *v.* Formerly also the fact of remaining neutral.

1642 BRIDGE *Serm. Norfolk Volunteers* 10 Want of courage and neutralizing in a Magistrate is worse then in others. **1657** REEVE *God's Plea* 175 Let not the Country man..blush at your neutralizing. **1902** TAYLOR & BAXTER *Key to Sight Testing* xxiii. 148 The lenses used for testing should not be used for neutralizing. **1962** L. S. SASIENI *Optical Dispensing* (ed. 2) xv. 355 The usual practice in neutralising is to hold the neutralising lens against the front surface of the spectacle lens and with the front surface towards the observer.

ˈ**neutralizing,** *ppl. a.* [f. as prec. + -ING[2].]

†**1.** Inclined to be neutral. *Obs.* *rare*$^{-1}$.

1643 BURROUGHES *Exp. Hosea* ii. (1652) 186, I had a neutralizing spirit, I looked which way the wind blew.

2. Rendering neutral, in various senses.

1784 WATT in *Phil. Trans.* LXXIV. 420 It acted the part of a neutralizing acid. **1849** NOAD *Electricity* (ed. 3) 369 The neutralizing needle in his instrument is attached to the principal one. **1853** W. GREGORY *Inorg. Chem.* (ed. 3) 131 The composition of which may vary..without affecting the neutralising power. **1870** *Standard* 16 Nov., We may consent to a modification of the neutralising clauses of the treaty in her favour.

neutrally (ˈnjuːtrəlɪ), *adv.* [f. NEUTRAL *a.* + -LY[2].] In a neutral manner or sense.

1571 GOLDING *Calvin on Ps.* xx. 7 It is no new thing among the Hebrewes for woordes to be put newtrally which properly are transitive. **1585–6** EARL LEICESTER *Corr.* (Camden) 141 Some other places, also, that lyved newtraly before. **1632** LITHGOW *Trav.* VI. 243 Not much condemning, neither absolutely qualifying them, but shall (as it were) neutrally nominate..those places. **1837** ARNOLD *Let.* in Stanley *Life* (1844) II. viii. 96 It was then impossible to give even physical instruction neutrally. **1884** *Manch. Exam.* 24 Nov. 4/6 What may be conveniently, because neutrally, described as a 'transaction'.

ˈ**neutralness.** *rare*$^{-1}$. [f. as prec. + -NESS.] The condition of being of no gender.

1865 J. GROTE *Explor. Philos.* I. 50 Grammatical gender, as compared with the notion of actual sex and of neutralness or absence of personality.

neutral-tinted, *a.* [See NEUTRAL *a.* 3c.] Of a neutral tint; not brightly or clearly coloured.

1879 F. W. ROBINSON *Coward Consc.* II. i, Hers had been a neutral-tinted existence. **1882** J. HAWTHORNE *Fort. Fool* I. xxxi, The sober, neutral-tinted world. **1893** SIR R. BALL *Story of Sun* 211 Through a neutral-tinted dark glass.

neutretto (njuːˈtrɛtəʊ). *Nuclear Physics.* [f. NEUTR(INO + It. *-etto*, dim. suffix (see -ET).]

†**a.** A neutral pion. *Obs.* **b.** A neutral particle having low rest-mass. *rare.*

1938 ARLEY & HEITLER in *Nature* 23 July 159/1 Neutrons would have a much smaller penetrating power and there is no process known by which neutrinos could produce heavy electrons in sufficiently large numbers. We therefore think that we have to deal in these experiments with the neutral counterpart of the heavy electron, for which we propose the name neutretto. *Ibid.*, A neutretto (denoted by Y°) can be transformed into a heavy electron, $Y^{\pm}$, during a collision with a proton (*P*) or neutron (*N*) and vice versa: $Y^{\circ} + N \rightleftharpoons P + Y^{-}$ or $Y^{\circ} + P \rightleftharpoons N + Y^{+}$. **1939** *Physical Rev.* LV. 24 These non-ionizing particles must be much more penetrating than photons. This high penetrating power suggests their identification with the neutrettos (neutral particles having mass and other properties similar to the barytron) postulated by Heitler. **1947** *Sci. News* IV. 123 A neutral meson is also expected to appear; the romantic name Neutretto is ready waiting for it. **1948** *Rev. Mod. Physics* XX. 550/1 If the neutral particle is a neutrino, the electron energy should be almost exactly one-half the rest energy of the meson, i.e., 50 Mev. If the neutral particle is considerably heavier than an electron (neutretto) the energy of the decay electron should be correspondingly smaller. **1952** R. E. MARSHAK *Meson Physics* vi. 208 If one is willing to consider the possibility of a new neutral decay particle of small rest mass (we shall call it a neutretto and denote it by μ°), then an alternative decay scheme would be $\mu^{\pm} \rightarrow e^{\pm} + \nu + \mu^{\circ}$. **1963** *New Scientist* 1 Aug. 255 The terms 'electron neutrino' and 'muon neutrino' respectively for 'neutrino' and 'neutretto' are probably more common at present in distinguishing these two particles.

neutricion, obs. form of NUTRITION.

neutrino (njuːˈtriːnəʊ). *Nuclear Physics.* [a. It. *neutrino* (E. Fermi 1933, in *La Ricerca sci.* II. 491), f. *neutro* NEUTER *a.* and *sb.*, neutral + *-ino*, dim. suffix.] Either of two stable, uncharged leptons (associated respectively with the electron and the muon) which have zero or negligible mass and an extremely low probability of interaction with matter; also, the antiparticle of either of these, one of which is produced (along with an electron and a proton) in the beta decay of a neutron.

1934 *Sci. Abstr.* A. XXXVII. 383 A quantitative theory of the emission of β-rays is explained. This admits the existence of the 'neutrino', a new particle proposed by Pauli having no electric charge and mass of the order of magnitude of that of the electron or less. **1938** *Ann. Reg. 1937* 354 The neutrino was generally accepted as a useful working hypothesis, but at least one attempt was made to show that the beta-ray spectrum could be explained without assuming its existence. **1948** *Sci. News* VI. 79 Beta decay is very slow compared to the times taken by other nuclear reactions, and one must, therefore, expect the reverse process, i.e., the capture of a neutrino, also to be very rare. On the Fermi theory, a neutrino could indeed go very many times across the interior of the earth and still have practically no chance of hitting anything. **1956** *Time* 2 July 46/3 For 20 years nuclear physicists have used neutrinos (small, uncharged particles) in their calculations... But no known apparatus has ever detected neutrinos... Last week from the Atomic Energy Commission came big news. Neutrinos do exist. **1958** *New Scientist* 25 Dec. 1567/1 Pauli produced the sorely needed explanation for the variability of the energy of beta-particles thrown out by radioactive materials. He postulated the simultaneous emission of a ghost particle which caried away part of the energy but which had no charge and virtually no mass and so was not observable directly. The neutrino.. has been fully vindicated and now occupies a position of great importance in contemporary theory. **1962** *Physical Rev. Lett.* IX. 36/1 The neutrinos we have used produce μ mesons but do not produce electrons, and hence are very likely different from the neutrinos involved in β decay. *Ibid.* 42/2 The most plausible explanation for the absence of electron showers.. is then that $\nu_\mu \neq \nu_e$; i.e., that there are at least two types of neutrinos. This also resolves the problem raised by the forbiddenness of the $\mu^+ \rightarrow e^+ + \gamma$ decay. **1968** M. S. Livingstone *Particle Physics* iv. 74 The muon decays into an electron and two neutrinos: $\mu^- \rightarrow e^- + \bar{\nu}_e + \nu_\mu$. **1969** *Times* 20 Feb. 17/5 Neutrinos are emitted as by-products in a great many nuclear reactions. **1974** *McGraw-Hill Yearbk. Sci. & Technol.* 306/1 The neutrino is the only known particle that has only weak interactions. Thus, the neutrino is a unique tool in the study of the weak forces, since the interactions are free of the effects of the strong and the electromagnetic interactions, which are many orders of magnitude stronger. **1974** *Sci. Amer.* Dec. 115/1 At proton accelerators muon neutrinos are produced about 100 times more copiously than electron neutrinos.

†ˈ**neutrize**, *v.* *Obs.* *rare*$^{-1}$. [f. NEUTER *a.* + -IZE.] *intr.* To stay neutral.

1609 Heywood *Lucrece* Wks. 1874 V. 192, I can.. fret with Horatius Cocles, be mad like my selfe, or neutrize with Collatine.

neutro-, combining form of NEUTER *a.*, occurring in a few words, such as **neutroloˈgistic** *a.* (see quot. 1824); **neutroˈpassive** *a.*, neuter passive; **neutroˈpenia** *Med.* [-PENIA], the presence of an abnormally low concentration of neutrophils in the blood; hence **neutroˈpenic** *a.*, suffering from neutropenia; ˈ**neutrophil(e** *a.* [a. G. *neutrophil* (P. Ehrlich 1880, in *Zeitschr. f. klin. Med.* I. 558)], that can be stained with neutral dyes (NEUTRAL *a.* and *sb.* A. 6c); not strongly stained by acid or basic dyes; also as *sb.*, a neutrophil cell; so **neutroˈphilic** *a.*, neutrophil; of or pertaining to neutrophil cells; **neuˈtrophilous** *a.*

1824 J. Gilchrist *Etym. Interpreter* 77 Mr. Bentham again divides the first division into eulogistic and dyslogistic, and thence denominates the unimpassioned class *neutrologistic. **1530** Palsgr. Introd. 35 As for verbes *neutropassyves, I fynde none in all the tong saufe onely *je nays*. **1706** Phillips (ed. Kersey), *Neutro-passive Verbs*, verbs Neuter that have their Preterperfect Tense form'd out of a Passive Participle: as *Gaudeo, gavisus sum* [etc.]. **1931** *Arch. Otolaryngol.* XIII. 864 The term agranulocytosis has come into the literature because of its brevity. The name is not strictly correct... At present, the name applied by Tuerk, 'malignant *neutropenia', seems to be more appropriate. **1973** *Acta Haematol.* L. 223 Neutropenia early in haemodialysis is probably due to the return into the circulation of leucocytes damaged by the first contact with the dialyzing surface. **1961** Webster, *Neutropenic. **1963** *Federation Proc.* XXII. 671/1 (*heading*) Potentiation of arthus reactivity in neutropenic rabbits. **1973** *Jrnl. Infectious Dis.* CXXVIII. 248 Both normal and neutropenic mice were treated with gentamicin. **1890** *Cent. Dict.*, *Neutrophile. **1893** *N.Y. Med. Jrnl.* LVII. 3/2 The neutrophile granules of the polynuclear cells are not stained by this solution. **1897** *Allbutt's Syst. Med.* IV. 578 These leucocytes are often called 'neutrophiles'. **1899** Cagney tr. *Jaksch's Clin. Diagn.* i. (ed. 4) 37 Neutrophil granules stain best with neutral dyes, *i.e.* those composed of a coloured base and an acid. **1954** Neutrophil [see DRUMSTICK 2e]. **1973** *Daily Tel.* 2 Oct. 19/2 Neutrophil cells in a healthy person are usually six per cent. of the total number of white blood cells. *Ibid.*, A medical expert said last night: 'An increase of neutrophils to 12 per cent. in a two-year-old is a thoroughly satisfactory reaction to an ear infection.' **1893** *N.Y. Med. Jrnl.* LVII. 4/2 The uninuclear leucocyte does not show *neutrophilic granulations. **1962** Luntz & Wright in A. Pirie *Lens Metabolism Rel. Cataract* 321 Group A... These show mainly neutrophilic infiltration. **1900** *Pop. Sci. Monthly* Jan. 380 The most abundant.. are those called the polynuclear, *neutrophilous leucocytes.

neutrodyne (ˈnjuːtrəʊdaɪn). *Radio.* [f. NEUTRO- (taken as repr. *neutralize, -ization*) + -DYNE.] A type of high-frequency valve amplifier in which neutralization was first employed to prevent oscillation throughout a range of frequencies. Freq. *attrib.*

1923 *Wireless World* 21 Apr. 68/2 Professor L. A. Hazeltine has designed receivers in which the valve capacity coupling is neutralised. The capacity coupling is neutralised with the aid of fixed condensers, and the receivers are called by him 'Neutrodyne' receivers. **1924** *Mod. Wireless* II. 590/2 In the receivers to be described here, a fixed coupling is used between the anode coil and the neutrodyne coil. **1924** Moyer & Wostrel *Pract. Radio* viii. 124 The neutrodyne works best on an antenna but may be used on a loop. **1936** R. S. Glasgow *Princ. Radio Engin.* ix. 256 The neutrodyne circuit was used quite extensively in broadcast receiving sets prior to the general introduction of screen-grid tubes in 1929. **1943** [see NEUTRALIZATION 1d]. **1964** Ghirardi & Dines *Radio & Television Receiver Circuitry* (rev. ed.) iii. 79 A modification of the famous Hazeltine 'neutrodyne' circuit is perhaps the most widely used in commercial receivers that employ triodes.

Hence ˈ**neutrodyning** *vbl. sb.* and *ppl. a.*, neutralizing (see NEUTRALIZE *v.* 3c).

1924 *Mod. Wireless* II. 590/3 The reaction is controlled entirely by this neutrodyning condenser. **1926** R. W. Hutchinson *Wireless* 217 Several methods have been devised for the control of this oscillation; neutrodyning, as it is termed, is one of the best. **1943** C. L. Boltz *Basic Radio* xiv. 226 This [instability] was decreased by using condensers to provide negative feed-back to nullify the positive feed-back. These were called neutralizing condensers, and the process was one of neutralization or neutrodyning.

neutron (ˈnjuːtrɒn). *Physics.* [f. NEUTRAL *a.* and *sb.* + -ON[1].] An electrically uncharged sub-atomic particle whose mass (939·6 MeV) is very slightly greater than that of the proton, which can decay into a proton, an electron, and an antineutrino (as in beta decay), and which is a constituent (with the proton) of all atomic nuclei except that of the common isotope of hydrogen; it is now usu. regarded as a particular state of a nucleon.

Before its discovery in 1932 it was conceived as a close association of a proton and an electron. Rutherford (who communicated Glasson's 1921 paper to the Royal Society) discusses this concept in a paper of 1920 cited by Glasson, but without using the word *neutron*. Harkins (of Chicago) seems to have coined the term independently. (The use in quot. 1899 is unrelated to the current use.)

[**1899** W. Sutherland in *Phil. Mag.* 5th Ser. XLVII. 273 If the electrons are distributed through the æther, we must suppose that in æther showing no electric charge each negative electron is united with a positive electron to form the analogue of a material molecule, which might conveniently be called a neutron.] **1921** W. D. Harkins in *Ibid.* 6th Ser. XLII. 309 Any complex atom has a mass and weight 0·76 per cent. less than the hydrogen atoms (neutrons) from which it may be assumed to be built. *Ibid.* 315 The term neutron represents one proton plus one electron. **1921** J. L. Glasson in *Ibid.* 597 In the ordinary atom of hydrogen we have a single electron separated from the nucleus by a distance of the order of 10^{-8} cm. It is here contemplated that a more intimate union of the two is possible... Such a particle, to which the name neutron has been given by Prof. Rutherford, would have novel and important properties. It would, for instance, greatly simplify our ideas as to how the nuclei of the heavy elements are built up. **1930** E. Rutherford et al. *Radiations from Radio-Active Substances* xvii. 523 The existence of a neutron, i.e. a close combination of a proton and electron, has been suggested. **1932** J. Chadwick in *Nature* 27 Feb. 312/1 (*heading*) Possible existence of a neutron. *Ibid.*, These results.. are very difficult to explain on the assumption that the radiation from beryllium is a quantum radiation, if energy and momentum are to be conserved in the collisions. The difficulties disappear, however, if it be assumed that the radiation consists of particles of mass 1 and charge 0, or neutrons. The capture of the α-particle by the Be^9 nucleus may be supposed to result in the formation of a C^{12} nucleus and the emission of the neutron. **1938** R. W. Lawson tr. *Hevesy & Paneth's Man. Radioactivity* (ed. 2) ix. 94 We must regard these protons and neutrons as the ultimate constituents of the nuclei, and consider the α-particle as a kind of 'molecule' of the 'nuclear atoms' possessing especial stability, and arising from the union of 2 protons and 2 neutrons. **1950** Glasstone *Sourcebk. Atomic Energy* xi. 287 One of the most striking arguments for the wave-particle duality of matter.. has been provided by the diffraction of neutrons. **1951** S. Dushman *Fund. Atomic Physics* xiii. 227 The U-235 nucleus, in splitting, emits high-speed neutrons which may produce fission in other U-235 nuclei, thus initiating a chain reaction. **1968** M. S. Livingstone *Particle Physics* ii. 25 The nucleus could now be conceived as a closely packed assemblage of protons and neutrons, with the atomic charge number Z given by the number of protons and the atomic weight number A by the total of protons and neutrons. **1972** *Physics Bull.* June 349/1 Although it is comforting and often convenient to consider the proton and neutron as elementary particles with no internal substructure, they are in fact particles in a state of continual change... The neutron divides its time between being a neutron and a composite proton-negative pion system, while remaining electrically neutral. **1973** A. J. MacLeod *Instrumental Methods Food Analysis* vii. 684 Isotopes of an element possess different numbers of neutrons in their nuclei, but are otherwise identical.

2. *attrib.* and *Comb.*, as ***neutron absorption***, ***bombardment***, ***flux***; ***neutron-absorbing*** adj.; **neutron activation**, the process of making a substance radioactive by irradiating it with neutrons; freq. *attrib.*, esp. in ***neutron activation analysis***, activation analysis in which this is employed; **neutron bomb**, a bomb that would produce large numbers of neutrons but little blast, and would consequently be harmful to life but not destructive of property; **neutron capture**, the absorption of a neutron by an atomic nucleus; **neutron chopper**, a device for converting a continuous beam of neutrons into a pulsed beam by passing it through a rotating slotted disc or cylinder; **neutron diffraction**, diffraction of a beam of neutrons; **neutron excess**, the excess of the number of neutrons in an atomic nucleus over the number of protons; **neutron number**, the mass number of a nucleus minus its atomic number, taken as being the number of neutrons it contains; **neutron radiography**, radiography in which the radiation employed is a beam of neutrons; **neutron star** *Astr.*, a hypothetical extremely dense kind of star composed predominantly of closely packed neutrons, which is believed to have a mass similar to that of the sun but a diameter of only a few kilometres; cf. PULSAR; **neutron therapy**, radio-therapy in which the radiation employed is a beam of neutrons.

1947 *Physical Rev.* LXXII. 16 Introduction of a neutron-absorbing substance into a pile decreases the reactivity. **1964** M. Gowing *Britain & Atomic Energy* 29 The Paris group also worked out the idea of controlling the reaction by introducing neutron-absorbing material to limit the multiplication of neutrons. **1947** *Physical Rev.* LXXII. 16 (*heading*) Method for measuring neutron-absorption cross sections by the effect on the reactivity of a chain-reacting pile. **1951** *Analyst* LXXVI. 644 (*heading*) The estimation of tantalum in mixtures by neutron activation analysis. **1960** *Nature* 16 Jan. 196/2 (*heading*) Neutron activation analysis of ancient Roman potsherds. **1965** D. Gibbons in Lenihan & Thomson *Activation Analysis* x. 68 Phosphorus and barium can be determined, rapidly and non-destructively, in lubricating oil in the range 0·01–1% and 0·05–2% using 14 MeV neutron activation and γ-ray spectrometry. **1966** *Encycl. Industr. Chem. Analysis* I. 52 With the high neutron flux of a nuclear reactor, neutron activation analysis (NAA) provides the most sensitive means of detection of low concentrations known today for most of the elements of the periodic system. A typical limit of detection is about one part per billion (ppb) in a 1-g sample. **1973** A. J. MacLeod *Instrumental Methods Food Analysis* vii. 695 Of the three methods described for separation and analysis of the products of neutron activation, gamma ray spectrometry is by far the most common. **1960** *Congress. Rec.* 12 May 10138/3 Although there have been a few fragmentary references to the neutron bomb in the press, I was told.. that the matter was classified. **1962** L. Deighton *Ipcress File* xxiv. 155, I guessed that it was a neutron bomb that they were about to explode. **1967** *New Scientist* 14 Sept. 534/1 Whenever the possibility of a neutron bomb was discussed in the late 'fifties and early 'sixties it was with particular reference to the military interest in the application of tactical nuclear firepower in a controlled and highly selective fashion. **1937** G. Gamow *Struct. Atomic Nuclei* x. 193 These phenomena (of induced activity by neutron bombardment) were observed by Fermi for many very heavy elements also. **1964** M. Gowing *Britain & Atomic Energy* ii. 55 It was known that in some nuclei fission occurred spontaneously, without neutron bombardment. **1945** H. D. Smyth *Gen. Acct. Devel. Atomic Energy Mil. Purposes* i. 17 [By 1940] neutron-capture cross-sections had been measured. **1959** *Listener* 19 Nov. 872/1 At slow or 'thermal' speeds neutron capture by nuclei of Uranium 238 is less important. **1966** Phillips & Williams *Inorg. Chem.* II. xxxv. 635 Neutron-capture efficiencies are usually measured in terms of nuclear cross-sections, for which the whimsical unit the 'barn' has been devised. **1950** Glasstone *Sourcebk. Atomic Energy* xi. 306/2 Three main techniques have been developed for making measurements with neutrons of specific energies; these are the time-of-flight velocity selector..; the mechanical selector, sometimes referred to colloquially as a 'neutron chopper'..; and the crystal spectrometer. **1971** *New Scientist* 8 July 72/1 Another rotating component developed at Harwell has been the so-called 'neutron chopper'... When it rotates, the beam is chopped into pulses of neutrons of the same energy level. **1949** *Physical Rev.* LXXVI. 1256/2 (*heading*) Detection of antiferromagnetism by neutron diffraction. **1973** J. Yarwood *Atomic & Nuclear Physics* xiii. 381 Whereas X-ray diffraction cannot readily lead to a knowledge of the positions of hydrogen atoms in a crystal because the scattering is dependent on the number of orbital electrons.., neutrons are strongly scattered by hydrogen nuclei. The technique of neutron diffraction therefore supplements that of X-ray diffraction. **1955** R. D. Evans *Atomic Nucleus* iii. 99 $(N-Z)$ is called.. the 'neutron excess'. **1947** *Science* 9 May 491/1 Facilities will include.. another pile with 100 times the neutron flux of the first. **1971** *Engineering* Apr. 34/2 The neutron flux reaching the sample is in excess of 10^7 neutrons cm^{-2} sec^{-1}. **1955** R. D. Evans *Atomic Nucleus* iii. 99 Nuclei having the same neutron number are isotones. **1973** *McGraw-Hill Yearbk. Sci. & Technol.* 181/1 Theoretical calculations.. have shown that the same r-process which synthesizes the actinides.. may also synthesize the predicted superheavy elements with atomic number $Z \sim 114$ and neutron number $N \sim 184$. **1948** H. Kallmann in *Research* I. 254/1 The first successful experiments in neutron radiography are due to the author and his collaborator E. Kuhn, who in the years 1935–39 developed and partly tried out the fundamental methods of neutron radiography. **1962** *Sci. Amer.* Nov. 107/2 Neutron radiography has become practical with the advent of nuclear reactors and particle accelerators, which can provide a source of neutrons of the required intensity. **1971** *Engineering* Apr. 37/1 An advantage of using neutron radiography is the possibility of detecting small amounts of low density materials, within sections of high density materials such as lead or steel. **1934** BAADE & ZWICKY in *Physical Rev.* XLV. 138/2 We advance the view that supernovae represent the transitions from ordinary stars into neutron stars, which in their final stages consist of extremely closely packed neutrons. **1968** *New Scientist* 16 May 331/1 Neutron stars, if they exist, could have densities as much as ten million times higher even than a white dwarf. **1970** B. LOVELL in *Times* 19 Aug. 9/7 It is now generally accepted that the pulsars are the remnants of stars which have collapsed to form neutron stars. **1974** *Nature* 13 Sept. 99/3 The neutron star represents the most extreme density of matter in the observable Universe (greater densities lead to unobservable black hole matter). **1947** *Radiology* XLVIII. 431/1 (*heading*) Possible progress in the radiotherapy of cancer (neutron therapy, Joliot therapy, alpha therapy, beta therapy..). **1974** *Nature* 25 Jan. 173/1 Because of Hammersmith Hospital's success in the use of neutron therapy for the treatment of cancer a second British hospital is to be supplied with a compact cyclotron. *Ibid.*, The effectiveness of neutron therapy depends on the ability of the neutrons to destroy cancer cells even in the absence of oxygen.

neutronic (njuːˈtrɒnɪk), *a. Physics.* [f. prec. + -IC.] Of, pertaining to, or employing neutrons.
1934 [see ISOMER 2]. **1952** *Proc. Nat. Acad. Sci.* XXXVIII. 450 Particles which are heavy in the sense used here may be said to have unit neutronic charge. The neutronic charge should play the same role for the conservation law of heavy particles as the electric charge plays in the conservation law of electric charges. **1955** *Sci. News Let.* 28 May 349/1 Drs. Fermi and Szilard originally filed application for a patent on the 'neutronic reactor', on Dec. 19, 1944. **1958** *Times* 2 Jan. 2/4 Neutronic calculations on the steady state performance of thermal reactors. **1971** *Nature* 26 Nov. 217/2 If the reflecting box is expanding, all enclosed quantal systems will be decaying and emitting quanta of [*printed* on] all sorts of electromagnetic, electronic, neutronic and so on, waves.

ˌneutro-ˈsaline, *a. Chem.* That possesses the properties of a neutral salt. Also *absol.*
1751 STACK in *Phil. Trans.* XLVII. 270 Being put on the fire, it evaporated.., and left..a frothy neutro-saline sediment. **1806** DAVY *ibid.* XCVII. 19 The smallest proportion of neutrosaline matter seemed to be acted on with energy. **1839** URE *Dict. Arts* 1142 These acids.. combine with the bases, in definite proportions, to form compounds analogous to the neutro-saline.

neuu, neuy(e, obs. ff. NEPHEW.

neuyn, var. NEVEN *v. Obs.*

neuyr, obs. f. NEVER.

nev, obs. Sc. f. NEW *a.*

nevadite (nɪˈvɑːdaɪt). *Min.* [f. *Nevada*, one of the United States + -ITE[1].] A variety of rhyolite, having a resemblance to granite.
1883 *Amer. Jrnl. Sci.* XXVI. 231 Baron von Richthofen.. mentions the locality as a typical one for a variety of rhyolite which he named nevadite. **1884** *Ibid.* XXVII. 462 Both nevadite and liparite possess the porphyritic structure. **1888** TEALL *Brit. Petrogr.* 75 The typical nevadites, however, are not granitic, but trachytic in texture.

†**neve**[1]. *Obs.* Forms: 1 nefa, 2 neafa, nefe, 2–5 neue, 4 newe, 4–6 neve, 6 nevve, nephe. [OE. *nefa* = OFris. *neva*, OS. *nevo* (MDu. *neve, neef*, Du. *neef*), MLG. *neve*, OHG. *nevo, nefo* (MHG. *neve, nefe*, G. *neffe*), ON. *nefi*:—OTeut. **nebon-*, related to L. *nepōt-, nepos* grandson, Gr. *νέποδες* (pl.), offspring, Skr. *napāt-, napt-* descendant, grandson: cf. NEPHEW.]
1. A nephew.
Beowulf 2206 Hearde hildefrecan..niða ȝenæȝdan nefan Hererices. *c* **900** *O.E. Chron.* (Parker MS.) an. 670 Hloþhere feng to biscepdome ofer Wesseaxan, Æȝelbryhtes biscopes nefa. *a* **1122** *Ibid.* (Laud MS.) an. 1114 Þone ærcediæcne Iohan þes arcebiscopes neafe. **1154** *Ibid.* an. 1137 Þar he nam..hise neues. *c* **1250** *Gen. & Ex.* 724 He toc him loth on sunes stede; He was hise neve. **13..** *Guy Warw.* (A.) 1418 Hougoun, þat was þe doukes neve Otoun. *c* **1350** *Will. Palerne* 3418 Þe stiward had a newe but of ȝong age. *c* **1440** *Jacob's Well* 96, I louyd my neve as wel as ony of my kyn. **1516** *Test. Ebor.* (Surtees) VI. 1 To Walter Percehay my neve xx s. *c* **1540** *Plumpton Corr.* (Camden) 238 You required me to helpe Tho. Compton, your nephe, to some honiest ocopation.
2. A grandson.
c **1440** *Promp. Parv.* 355/1 Neve, sonys sone, *nepos*. **1534** TINDALE *1 Tim.* v. 4 If eny widdowes have children or neves [**1525** neveus].
3. A spendthrift. *rare*[−1].
c **1440** *Promp. Parv.* 355/1 Neve, neuerthryfte, or wastour.

†**neve**[2]. *Obs. rare*[−1]. [a. obs. F. *neve*, or ad. L. *næv-us* NÆVUS.] A mark on the skin.
1624 BURTON *Anat. Mel.* III. ii. v. iii. (ed. 2) 442 Frechons, haires, warts, neues, inequalities.

neve, obs. form of NIEVE.

‖**névé** (neve). [mod.F., ad. Alpine dial. *nevé*:—Romanic type **nivāt-um*, f. L. *niv-, nix* snow: cf. late L. *nivātus* cooled with snow.]
1. The crystalline or granular snow on the upper part of a glacier, which has not yet been compressed into ice; = FIRN.
1843 J. D. FORBES *Travels through Alps of Savoy* 31 The part of a glacier covered with perpetual snow is what I understand to be meant by the term *névé* in the writings of the modern glacialists, although that term is vaguely defined. **1853** KANE *Grinnell Exp.* xlviii. (1856) 450 The change of the Arctic snows into *névé* or firn. **1856** —— *Arct. Expl.* I. 336, I found grains of *neve* larger than a walnut. **1871** L. STEPHEN *Playgr. Eur.* (1894) v. 118 The steep slopes of névé above us..bulged out into huge overhanging masses.
attrib. **1873** J. GEIKIE *Gt. Ice Age* (1894) 545 The névé-fields under the Schneestock. **1897** *Outing* (U.S.) XXIX. 339/1 The inland ice, beyond the glacier's 'névé' basin.
2. A field or bed of frozen snow.
1884 *Academy* 23 Aug. 113/2 His descriptions certainly point to nevés and frozen snow-beds rather than to glaciers in the exact sense. **1892** LUBBOCK *Beauties Nature* vii, If.. we trace one of the Swiss rivers to its source we shall generally find that it begins in a snowfield or névé.

†**nevede**, had not: see NE and HAVE *v.*
a **1300** *Vox & Wolf* 98 in Hazl. *E.P.P.* I. 61 Ȝef ich neuede to muchel i-ete, This ilke shome neddi nouthe.

ˈ**nevel**, *sb. Sc.* Also 6 -ell, 7 newell, 8 nevvel. [f. NEVEL *v.*] A blow with the fist.
15.. *Christ's Kirk* vii, They partit manly with a nevell. **1602** in *J. Mill's Diary* (1889) 187 James Brown hes giffin Hendrie Waltersoun ane newell. **1715** RAMSAY *Christ's Kirk* II. iii, Wi' nevels I'm amaist fawn faint. **1739** A. NICOL *Nature without Art*, Some wi' Nevvels had sair snouts. **1819** TENNANT *Papistry Storm'd* (1827) 154 Was naething gain but knocks and nevels. **1846** tr. *Drummond's Muckomachy* 17 (E.D.D.), Gave his cheeks some dainty nevels.

nevel (ˈnɛv(ə)l), *v. Sc.* and *north. dial.* Forms: 6 neffel, 7 nauell, 9 knevel, neavil, nevil, 8– nevel. [f. *neve* NIEVE, fist + *-el*, -LE 3; perh. directly from Scand., cf. Norw. dial. *nevla* to knead (Ross).] *trans.* To beat with the fists; to pound or pummel. Hence ˈ**nevelling** *vbl. sb.*
a **1572** KNOX *Hist. Ref.* Wks. 1846 I. 146 Frome schouldering, thei go to buffetis, and from dry blawes, by neffis and neffelling. **1603** *Philotus* cxxxiv, Thow sall beir me a beuell, For with my Neiues I sall the nauell. **1684** MERITON *Yorksh. Dialogue* 603 She'l Nawpe and Nevel them with-out a Cause. **1791** J. LEARMONT *Poems* 337 [He] nevell'd me sae sair, That for a week I could nae draw my breath. **1815** SCOTT *Guy M.* xxiv, Twa landloupers..got me down and knevelled me sair aneuch. **1855** ROBINSON *Whitby Gloss.*, *Neavill'd* or *Nevilled*, pummelled with the fist. 'A good nevilling'. [Also in later northern glossaries.]

nevel, variant of NIVEL *sb.* and *v. Obs.*

†ˈ**neveling**, *adv. Obs. rare.* [f. OE. *nifol*, var. of *neowol* prone, prostrate + -LING[2].] Face downwards.
1387 TREVISA *Higden* (Rolls) II. 193 Dede wommen kareyns..ligge neuelynge and dounriȝt. *Ibid.* III. 401 Þere þou liest nevelynge, and schuldest telle after þese þynges of hevene.

†ˈ**neven**, *v. Obs.* Forms: 4 neiuen, neyuen, 4–5 neuyn, 5–6 nevyn, (4, 6 -yne), 4–6 neuin, nevin, neuen, (4–5 -ene), neven, (4–5 -ene); 4–5 nefen; 4 newine, 5 -yn(e. [a. ON. *nefna* (Da. *nævne*), also *nemna* (Sw. *nämna*), f. *nafn, namn*: see NAME *sb.* and NEMN *v.*
The form *nemen(e* is occas. found in MSS. where the rime-word shows that *neven* is intended.]
1. *trans.* To give as a name to (a person or thing).
a **1300** *Cursor M.* 4980 Þai war breþer elleuen at ham, Þai neuend me þe yongeist nam. **13..** *Gaw. & Gr. Knt.* 10 Þat burȝe he biges vpon fyrst, & neuenes hit his aune nome. *a* **1400–50** *Alexander* 619 And so him neuyned was þe name of his next frendis Alexsandire þe athill. *Ibid.* 1119 He.. comandis þaim swyþe..to make a cite, And neuens it his awen name.
b. To call (a thing) by a certain name.
a **1400–50** *Alexander* 2119 Scamandra þe skyr flode þe scripture it neue[n]s. **1412–20** LYDG. *Chron. Troy* III. xxvii, I note in sothe what I may it neuene, Outher a dreme or veryly a sweuene.
2. To name (a person, etc.), to mention by name.
a **1300** *Cursor M.* 2327 Þis abram þat ȝee her me neuen. *c* **1330** R. BRUNNE *Chron. Wace* (Rolls) 8012 Þy fader canstow nought neuen. *c* **1384** CHAUCER *H. Fame* III. 348 By hym stonden other seuene Wise and worthy for to neuene. *c* **1430** LYDG. *Min. Poems* (Percy Soc.) 214 Alle constellaciouns that any man can neven. *c* **1475** *Pol. Poems* (Rolls) II. 284 Many moo londes that I can not nevene. **1513** DOUGLAS *Æneis* VII. v. 60 The maist souerane realme,.. That..man can nevin.
b. To appoint, nominate (a person) to a position.
1442 *Rolls of Parlt.* V. 60/1 Collectours therto to be nevend. *Ibid.* 60/2 Capitayns as by the Kyng shall be nevend.
3. To mention, speak of, give an account of.
a **1300** *Cursor M.* 4056 Ioseph he sagh a night in sueuen, Þe quilk es worþie for to neuen. *c* **1330** R. BRUNNE *Chron.* (1810) 20 Þe date of Criste to neuen þus fele were gon. *c* **1400** tr. *Secreta Secret., Gov. Lordsh.* 102 Þe vertuz & þe maners þat y shall neuen þe. *c* **1460** *Towneley Myst.* iii. 12 Fulle meruelus to neuen yit was ther vnkyndnes. **1509** HAWES *Past. Pleas.* III. (Percy Soc.) 19 A great gyaunt..To marveylous nowe for me to neven. *a* **1529** SKELTON *Col. Cloute* 826 He dare not well neuen What they do in heuen.
b. With clause as object.
c **1386** CHAUCER *Can. Yeom. Prol. & T.* 920 Syn that God ..Ne wol not that the philosophres nevene, How that a man schal come unto this stoon. *a* **1400–50** *Alexander* 318 How he is merkid & made is mervaile to neuyn. *Ibid.* 1105, I sall þe neuen sen þou me now prays, þou sall be drechid of a drinke.
c. To tell (a story, the truth).
c **1350** *Will. Palerne* 2453 Whan it was so neiȝ niȝt, to neuen þe soþe, þe werwolf wist wel [etc.]. *a* **1400–50** *Alexander* 5306 Se þi-selfe a sampill þat I þe sothe neuyn. *c* **1430** *Syr Tryam.* 6 Of a story y wylle begynne, That gracyus ys to nevyne.
d. With *as, than*, etc.
a **1300** *Cursor M.* 2743 Þe word es wers þan man mai neuen. **13..** *Ibid.* 2085 (Gött), For he liued leleli as I ȝou neuen, He ssittes wid mighti godd in heuen. *c* **1450** HOLLAND *Howlat* 716 Thair notis anone, gif I richt newyne, War of Mary the myld. *c* **1485** *Digby Myst.* (1882) III. 315 Gold perteynyng to þe sonne, as astronomers nevyn. **1513** DOUGLAS *Æneis* III. ii. 144 A deidlie ȝeir, fer wers than I can nevin, Fell on our membris.
4. With cognate object: To utter, mention (the name of a person or thing).
a **1300** *Cursor M.* 8913 For sco had neuend crist nam, ..þai heued þat womman. **13..** *E.E. Allit. P.* B. 410 Noe þat ofte neuened þe name of oure lorde. *c* **1400** MAUNDEV. (Roxb.) xxv. 116 Þan saise þe steward of þe courte þat lord and þat lorde, and neuens þaire names. *c* **1450** HOLLAND *Howlat* 33 Bot all thar names to nevyn as now it nocht neid is. **1500–20** DUNBAR *Poems* lxxxv. 60 Thy name I sall ay nevyne.
5. *intr.* To tell or make mention *of* a person or thing.
a **1330** *Roland & V.* 157 For þi herodes lete me sle, þer of y the neuen. **13..** *Cursor M.* 3116* (Gött.), Of ysaac nou wil i neuen. *a* **1400–50** *Alexander* 4881 Of þe noblay to neuen it neyd any cristen. *c* **1470** HENRY *Wallace* VI. 196 Quhar gret dulle is,..Newyn off it is bot ekyng off payne.
b. To say, speak.
c **1400** *Song of Roland* 1048 Then answerd olyuer with a ruffull steuyn, Angry in hert thus gan he nevyn.
Hence †ˈ**nevening** *vbl. sb.*
a **1300** *K. Horn* (Camb. MS.) 220 Þanne hym spak þe gode king, 'Wel bruc þu þi neuening'.

never (ˈnɛvə(r)), *adv.* Forms: 1–3 næfre, (1 -ræ, -ra), 2–3 nefre, 3–4 nefere, (3 nafre, næfer, neofer); 3 næ u(e)re, nau(e)re, (-ære, -er), neaure, -uer, neou(u)ere, 4 nouer; 4 neure, 4–5 neuere, (5 -ire), 4–7 neuer, (4 neyuer), 5–6 neuir, (5 -yr); 3 newere, 3, 6–7 newir, 6–7 newer; 4 nev(e)re, 4–6 nevir, 7 *Sc.* neaver, 4– never. See also NE'ER. [OE. *næfre*, f. *ne* NE + *æfre* EVER.]
I. 1. a. At no time, on no occasion.
In former use (down to 17th c.) frequently accompanied by other negatives, esp. *ne, no*, or *none*.
Beowulf 247 Næfre ic maran ȝeseah eorla ofer eorþan. *c* **888** K. ÆLFRED *Boeth.* v. § 1 Of ðære næfre nan, buta he self wolde, ne wearð adrifen. *c* **950** *Lindisf. Gosp.* Matt. vii. 23 Næfra [*Rushw.* næfræ] ic cuðe iuih. **971** *Blickl. Hom.* 39 Þonne ne hingreþ us næfre on ecnesse. *a* **1100** *Gerefa* in *Anglia* IX. 260 Ne læte he næfre his hyrmen hyne oferwealdan. **1154** *O.E. Chron.* (Laud MS.) an. 1137 Ne uuæren næure nan martyrs swa pined alse hi wæron. *c* **1200** *Trin. Coll. Hom.* 33 Ne wot no man hwat blisse is þe naure wowe ne bod. *c* **1275** *Passion our Lord* 56 in *O.E. Misc.* 39 Swich leche bi-vore hym ne com her neuer non. *c* **1315** SHOREHAM III. 161 Þou ne myȝt hytte nefere do. **1390** GOWER *Conf.* I. 26 A newe [world] schal beginne, Fro which a man schal nevere twinne. *c* **1450** LOVELICH *Grail* xxvii. 44 Ȝit wolde he neuere to his God Offensse. **1470–85** MALORY *Arthur* IV. i. 119 To swere that he shold neuer do none enchauntement vpon her. **1525** LD. BERNERS *Froiss.* II. 133 They wolde answere and saye, they trusted that sholde neuer be. **1560** DAUS tr. *Sleidane's Comm.* 442 b, Therfore thought they now, or els never, y[t] God was on theyr side. **1632** LITHGOW *Trav.* VII. 327 Serpent like,..That bowes the Grasse, but neuer makes no path. **1697** DRYDEN *Virg. Georg.* III. 448 Time is lost, which never will renew. **1727** GAY *Begg. Op.* I. viii, Then or never is the time to make her fortune. **1782** MISS BURNEY *Cecilia* V. vii, Is this lady-like tyranny then never to end? **1808** SCOTT *Marm.* III. xix, A braver never drew a sword; A wiser never. **1872** LEVER *Ld. Kilgobbin* xxi, I certainly shall never be rebuked for my becomingness.
Prov. **1862** TROLLOPE *Orley F.* II. x. 77 Never is a long word. **1904** *Q. Rev.* July 152 Never, it is rightly said, is a long day.
b. With addition of limiting word, as ***after***, ***before*** (†*afore*, †*tofore*), †*eft*, †*ere*, ***since*** (†*sithen*), ***yet***. Also †***never-te***, never yet.
Beowulf 583 Breca næfre ȝit..swa deorlice dæd ȝefremede. *c* **900** *O.E. Chron.* (Parker MS.) an. 409 Næfre siþan Romane ne ricsodon on Bretone. *c* **1200** ORMIN 750 Ȝet wass ȝho swa bifundenn, þatt ȝho..Ne mihhte nærfær tæmenn. *c* **1250** *Kent. Serm.* in *O.E. Misc.* 35 Þat hi ne hedden neuer-te i-heed prophete ne apostle. **1297** R. GLOUC. (Rolls) 6836 Neuereft hii of denemarch hiderward ne come. **1340** *Ayenb.* 99 Zuyche wenep hit wel conne..þet neuerte ne couþe bote þe rynde wyþoute. **1377** LANGL. *P. Pl.* B. XVI. 216 Widwe with-oute wedloke was neure ȝete yseye. *c* **1420** *Anturs of Arth.* xxxi, Siche glee Seȝhe he neuyr are. *c* **1500** *Melusine* 360 Sayeng þat neuer tofore they herd of suche a thing. **1582** N. LICHEFIELD tr. *Castanheda's Conq. E. Ind.* I. ii. 4 Pedro..never after returned into Portingale. **1600** J. PORY tr. *Leo's Africa* IX. 336 Neuer did any man as yet see where Nilus taketh his originall. **1667** MILTON *P.L.* IX. 504 Never since of Serpent kind Lovelier. **1766** GOLDSM. *Vic. W.* xv, I never yet found one instance of their existence. **1860** TYNDALL *Glac.* II. xxiv. 354, I believe the fact was never before observed.
c. Repeated for the sake of emphasis.
1605 SHAKS. *Lear* V. iii. 308. **1681–6** J. SCOTT *Chr. Life* (1747) III. 546 They are safe arrived into each others Arms, never, never to be parted more. **1768** BEATTIE *Minstr.* I. xxix, From the prayer of Want,..O never, never turn away thine ear! **1777** PITT in Almon *Anecd.* (1792) III. xliv. 167 If I were an American..I never would lay down my arms —never—never—never. **1809–10** COLERIDGE *Friend* (1865) 127 To be found..in the realities of Heaven, but never, never, in creatures of flesh and blood.
d. In emphatic denial, or as an expression of surprise.
1836–7 DICKENS *Sk. Boz, Our Parish* vi, Could such things be tolerated in a Christian land? Never! **1848** THACKERAY *Van. Fair* i, This almost caused Jemima to faint with terror. 'Well, I never',—said she. **1896** A. MORRISON *Child of Jago* xii. 120 'I never,' protested Dicky stoutly. **1926** A. BENNETT *Lord Raingo* II. lxxi. 322 She faintly

annoyed him by her ingenuous exclamations: Oh my! Well, I never! Well I never did! *a* **1930** D. H. LAWRENCE *Phoenix II* (1968) 21 'I never, I never!!' he declared, more emphatically. **1939** L. M. MONTGOMERY *Anne of Ingleside* xxv. 171 'I've an idea Bruno has gone back there.' 'Six miles? He'd never!' said Jem. **1950** [see INJUN b]. **1972** N. MARSH *Tied up in Tinsel* ii. 49 'A booby-trap.' 'I never!' Mervyn burst out. 'My God.. I swear I never.' **1974** N. BENTLEY *Inside Information* xv. 151 'There's a fellow.. got a gun—a pistol.' 'Never!'

e. With suppression of the personal pronoun as subject.

1874 HARDY *Far from Madding Crowd* I. vi. 76 Never heard the man's name in my life. **1968** *Listener* 7 Nov. 610/2 He said: 'Never heard of it.'

2. a. Not at all, in no way. In later use chiefly with imperatives, esp. ***never (you) fear*** or ***mind***; ***to make*** (or ***pay***) ***no nevermind*** (U.S.), to make no difference; to pay no attention.

In some cases the temporal sense is not completely effaced.

1362 LANGL. *P. Pl.* A. Prol. 12 A Meruelous sweuene, þat I was in a Wildernesse wuste I neuer where. *a* **1450** *Knt. de la Tour* (1868) 79 He.. asked what that was. And his wiff saide she wost neuer. *c* **1500** *Melusine* 297 He was ryght dolaunt.. and coude neuer hold hys tonge, but he said [etc.]. *c* **1590** MARLOWE *Faustus* Wks. (Rtldg.) 124/2 'Sblood, I am never able to endure these torments. **1605** SHAKS. *Macb.* III. iv. 56 Neuer shake Thy goary lockes at me. **1774** FOOTE *Cozeners* III. Wks. 1799 II. 182, I take care, Missy, never you fear. **1795** tr. *C. P. Moritz's Trav.* 261, I do not recollect to have heard any expression repeated oftener than this *never mind it!* A porter.. fell down, and cut his head.. 'O, never mind it!' said an Englishman who happened to be passing by. **1825** BENTHAM *Offic. Apt. Maximized, Indications* (1839) 42 Never you mind that; your business is to make sure of the fees. **1849** G. E. JEWSBURY *Sel. Lett. to Jane Welsh Carlyle* (1892) 344 Dear child, the solution will come to you, never fear. **1875** JOWETT *Plato* (ed. 2) I. 25 Give your opinion.., never minding whether Critias or Socrates is the person refuted. **1935** H. DAVIS *Honey in Horn* xvi. 264 That ain't no nevermínds to me, though. **1946** MEZZROW & WOLFE *Really the Blues* (1957) xii. 225 He pays it no nevermind. **1968** *Guardian* 27 Dec. 8/1 We still have to adapt to Prime Ministers and Presidents, never mind astronauts, who have the essential quality of ordinariness. **1971** B. MALAMUD *Tenants* 177 Those are old books of his he wrote long ago, says Willie. Both been published. Then it makes no nevermind if we burn them.

b. ***never any*** or ***one***, no one, none at all.

c **1205** LAY. 2593 Nefde he næfer enne of alle his monnen. *a* **1225** *Leg. Kath.* 1261 Cwich ne cweð þer neuer an. **13..** *E.E. Allit. P.* A. 864 Vchonez blysse is breme & beste, & neuer onez honour ȝet neuer-þe-les. *c* **1400** *Gamelyn* 582 We have foomen atte gate and frendes neuer oon. *c* **1430** *Pilgr. Lyf Manhode* II. cxxii. (1869) 121 And j were wel disclosed ..j shulde of neueroon be preysed. **1500–20** DUNBAR *Poems* lii. 6 In malice spaik I newir ane woord. **1555** in Strype *Eccl. Mem.* (1721) III. App. xliv. 125 Another thing much do I mervail at, that never one priest.. did venture his life. **1669** STURMY *Mariner's Mag.* a, Never any man living, in his writing, could please the phansie of all men.

†**c.** ***never kins***, no kind of. ***never where***, nowhere. ***never neither***, neither. *Obs.*

a **1300** *Cursor M.* 18856 Thris he wep.., bot we find neuer quar he logh. *c* **1300** *Havelok* 2690 Godrich.. also leun fares þat neuere kines best ne spares. *c* **1400** MAUNDEV. (Roxb.) vii. 26 It growes newer whare bot þare. **1449** PECOCK *Repressor* I. x. 53 Neuer neither of the ij textis. *Ibid.* II. xx. 273 Neuer neither of hem is contrarie to other of hem.

3. a. never a, not a, no.. at all. Cf. NE'ER A. †*never a deal*, not a bit, not in the least: see ADEAL and DEAL *sb.*[1] 5 b. So ***never a whit***: see WHIT.

c **1250** *Gen. & Ex.* 230 It ne wrocte him neuere a del. *c* **1300** *Havelok* 2685 On þe feld was neuere a polk þat it ne stod of blod so ful. **13..** *Guy Warw.* (A.) 737 Now atrow þe better neuer a del. *c* **1386** CHAUCER *Nonne Prestes T.* 336, I hem defye, I love hem never a del. *c* **1440** *Generydes* 3703 Of your waye ye shall fayle neuer a dele. *c* **1489** CAXTON *Sonnes of Aymon* iii. 102 There was never a myle but that they iusted togyder. **1542** UDALL *Erasm. Apoph.* 99 He had never a drye threde about hym. **1581** RICH *Farew.* (1846) 220 She had never a gowne to putte on her backe but of a stale cutte. **1632** LITHGOW *Trav.* III. 101 There were seuenteen boats cast away.., and neuer a man saued. **1666** EVELYN *Mem.* (1857) III. 178, I must beg a copy of those papers.., having never a duplicate by me. **1722** DE FOE *Col. Jack* (1840) 39 You have never a shirt on. **1756** NUGENT *Gr. Tour, Italy* III 141 They have never an university, but an academy of wits. **1861** A. LEIGHTON *Trad. Sc. Life* Ser. II. 153 Though the never a M'Pherson was connected with her. **1864** DASENT *Jest & Earnest* (1873) II. 263 He still said never a word about the treasure.

b. ***never a one***, not (a single) one.

1523 [COVERDALE] *Old God & New* (1534) A, Neuer a one of the pyllers of the chyrche.. nede to be a shamed of it. **1579** FULKE *Heskins' Parl.* 132 Fiue hundreth propositions, that are false, and yet neuer a one expressely denied. **1645** T. HILL *Olive Branch* (1648) 16 There is never a one of you but hath a Publique Place. **1692** S. PATRICK *Answ. Touchstone* 33 Near a dozen places; in never a one of which there is any mention.. of Tradition. **1733** TULL *Horse-hoeing Husb.* 128 They have seen it produce six Crops in six Years.., and never a one of them fail.

c. ***never say die*** (see quot. *a* 1865); also *attrib.*

a **1865** SMYTH *Sailor's Word-Bk.* (1867) 497 *Never say die*, an expressive phrase, meaning do not despair, there is hope yet. **1971** *Scope* (S. Afr.) 19 Mar. 10/2 Israel is a land that lives by the maxim: 'Never say die.' **1974** *Country Life* 5 Dec. 1717/2 The mental stamina, and the never-say-die spirit.

4. never so, in conditional clauses, denoting an unlimited degree or amount. (Cf. EVER 9 b.)

a **1122** *O.E. Chron.* (Laud MS.) an. 1086 Nan man ne dorste slean oðerne man, næfde he næfre swa mycel yfel ȝedon. *c* **1175** *Lamb. Hom.* 35 Ne beo he nefre swa riche, forð he scal þenne is dei cumeð. *a* **1250** *Owl & Night.* 345 Ne beo þe song neuer so murie [etc.]. *c* **1300** *Havelok* 80 Were he neure knicth so strong [etc.]. *c* **1380** WYCLIF *Wks.* (1880) 321 Betere.. þen preyere of any ordre.., blabere þei neuere so meche wiþ lippis. *c* **1400** MAUNDEV. (Roxb.) xxxiii. 151 A man may noȝt here anoþer, crie he neuer so hie. **1486** *Bk. St. Albans* a iv b, Though thow pike the flesh neuer so clene, yet thow shalte fynde thredes ther in. **1535** COVERDALE *Ps.* xcix. 1 He sytteth upon the Cherubins, be the earth neuer so vnquiete. **1589** PUTTENHAM *Eng. Poesie* III. xxiv. (Arb.) 296 He neuer once changed his countenance.., though the sight were neuer so full of ruth. **1611** BIBLE *Transl. Pref.* ¶4 Sufficient for a whole host, be it neuer so great. **1691** RAY *Creation* I. (1714) 18 Tho the Trees grow never so irregularly. **1711** ADDISON *Spect.* No. 120 ¶15 When the Birth appears of never so different a Bird, [the hen] will cherish it for her own. *a* **1774** GOLDSM. *Hist. Greece* I. 342 Some vigorous effort, though it carried never so much danger, ought to be made. *a* **1806** C. J. FOX *Reign Jas. II* (1808) 204 Let him be weighed never so scrupulously,.. he will not be found.. wanting. **1885** SWINBURNE *Misc.* (1886) 298 Were the critic never so much in the wrong, the author will have contrived to put him.. in the right.

5. a. never the, followed by a comparative: None the, not at all the (better, etc.). ***never the near***: see NEAR *adv.*[1] 5.

13.. *Cursor M.* 23162 (Gött.), Bot for ȝou was i neuer þe bett. **1377** LANGL. *P. Pl.* B. IX. 78 More bilongeth.. þan nempnyng of a name and he neuere þe wiser. **1508** FISHER *7 Penit. Ps.* li. Wks. (1876) 132 But Achab was neuer the better. *c* **1550** BALE *K. Johan* (Camden) 58 The Lord.. call them to grace, and faver them never the worsse. **1628** HOBBES *Thucyd.* (1822) 105 In the end never the nearer to the victory. **1705** STANHOPE *Paraphr.* II. 332 The Condition of the Receiver is.. never the better. **1768** GRAY in *Corr. w. Nicholls* (1843) 73, I am never the wiser, nor the more able to account for Temple's letter. **1802–12** BENTHAM *Ration. Judic. Evid.* (1827) I. 602 *note*, The conviction of the criminal.. would be never the nearer. **1886** POLLOCK *Oxford Lect.* iv. (1890) 108 He who is in these ways.. a better man will be never the worse lawyer.

b. ***never the less, nevertheless***, no less, not in any way less, by no means less. Now *rare* or *Obs.* exc. as in NEVERTHELESS *adv.*

13.. *E.E. Allit. P.* A. 864 Neuer onez honour [is] ȝet neuer-þe-les. *c* **1374** CHAUCER *Anel. & Arc.* 236 For to love him Alweye never the lesse. *a* **1400–50** *Alexander* 4228 And ȝour lare of a leke suld neuire þe les worth. **1526** TINDALE *2 Cor.* viii. 15 He that gaddered lytell had neverthelesse. **1549** EDW. VI in Strype *Eccl. Mem.* (1721) II. I. xxv. 213 He [the king] thought good to require him [the bishop] and nevertheless to charge him [etc.]. **1601** DENT *Pathw. Heaven* 390 When she arriseth she loueth it neuerthelesse, but dandles it. **1609** BIBLE (Douay) *Num.* xi. *comm.*, That they might have so much helpe of grace as pleased God, and Moyses have nevertheless. **1642** ROGERS *Naaman* 173 Let us make never the lesse of it, nor be discouraged.

c. So ***never the more, neverthemore***.

a **1400–50** *Alexander* 322 If he be þus diȝt drede þe neuer þe more. **1483** CAXTON *Gold. Leg.* 248/2 Whan ony was made Cezar neuerthemore he was Augustus ne emperour. **1526** TINDALE *2 Cor.* viii. 15 He that gaddered moche had never the more aboundance. **1571** GOLDING *Calvin on Ps.* xl. 6 David sinking under the burthen, ceased neverthemore to mount up. **1606** BRYSKETT *Civ. Life* 37 His law, though it be milder then the other, was neuerthemore allowable.

II. 6. In attributive phrases: **a.** With *enough* (or *too much*), followed by a pa. pple.

1604 HIERON *Wks.* I. 530 The neuer-enough reuerenced exercise of preaching. **1623** ROWLANDSON *God's Bless.* 21 O the never too much admired goodnesse of the Lord. **1710** BERKELEY *Princ. Hum. Knowl.* I. §146 The never-enough-admired laws of pain and pleasure.

b. With *enough* (or *too much*) and *to be*, followed by a pa. pple.

1624 QUARLES *Sion's Elegies* Pref., This ancient, most true, and never enough to be lamented Desolation. **1657** W. RAND tr. *Gassendi's Life Peiresc* I. 67 That never to be enough praised Arch-bishop. **1670** EACHARD *Cont. Clergy* 50 The never-to-be-commended-enough Licosthenes. **1752** A. MURPHY *Gray's Inn Jrnl.* No. 11 The never enough to be admired Art of Humbugging. **1802** *Noble Wanderers* I. 205 That never to be sufficiently regretted step of leaving my house. *a* **1834** COLERIDGE *Notes & Lect.* (1849) I. 49 The never to be too much valued advantage of the theatre. **1873** RUSKIN *Fors Clav.* xxxvi. 6 The never to be enough damned guilt of men.

c. With *to be*, esp. ***never to be forgotten***.

1607 COLLINS *Serm.* (1618) 85 A long desired, and neuer to be disannulled conformitie. **1657** W. RAND tr. *Gassendi's Life Peiresc* I. 46 That never to be forgotten man is gone away. **1688** *Lond. Gaz.* No. 2381/1 A never-to-be-shaken Loyalty to Your Majesty. **1709** SACHEVERELL *Serm.* 5 Nov. 5 This Never-to-be-forgotten Festival. **1747** *Mem. Nutrebian Crt.* I. 166 By your often-vowed, never-to-be-changed love. **1807** SOUTHEY *Ess.* (1832) II. 284 That never-to-be-forgotten massacre of the Protestants. *a* **1849** H. COLERIDGE *Ess.* (1851) I. 94 The product of his never-to-be-seen acres. **1887** FRITH *Autobiog.* I. xi. 137 We had.. on one never-to-be-forgotten occasion, a speech from Turner. **1917** E. WALLACE *Just Men of Cordova* ii. 32 One never-to-be-forgotten occasion. **1925** R. GRAVES *Welchman's Hose* 59 In the compilation Of their Grand Dictionnaire de la Langue Française, The full, the final, never-to-be-gainsaid. **1935** L. MACNEICE *Poems* 56 That never-to-be-touched Vision is your mistress.

d. In various phrases.

1806 *Simple Narrative* II. 48 You are such a puritanical never-do-amiss lady. **1837** S. R. MAITLAND *Six Lett. on Fox's A. & M.* 42 This 'never mind' school of history. **1841** S. C. HALL *Ireland* I. 186 That's a never-my-care sort.. as ever I met with.

7. *Comb.* **a.** With pa. pples., as ***never-adone, -broken, -come, -conquered, -contented, -contracted, -daunted, -dreamt, -dried, -ended, -erased, -glutted, -lost, -quelled, -rebuked, -satisfied, -tarnished, -tracked***, etc.

1716 M. DAVIES *Athen. Brit.* II. To Rdr. 11 The *never-adone Physicking and Taking of Fees. **1817** COLERIDGE *Biog. Lit.* II. xv. 16 A series and *never broken chain of imagery. **1873** J. R. LOWELL *Cathedral* in *Poetical Wks.* 452/1 Never-broken secrecies of sky. **1892** W. B. YEATS *Let.* Nov. (1954) 218 The ever-coming *never-come light of that ideal peace and freedom. **1631** WEEVER *Anc. Funeral Mon.* 104 That *neuer-conquered Nation of Scotland. **1951** L. MACNEICE tr. *Goethe's Faust* 235 Now even my army, I fear, must needs Obey the conquering, never-conquered woman. **1845** POE *Fairy-land* in *Raven & Other Poems* 86 Those butterflies, Of Earth, who seek the skies, And so come down again (*Never-contented things!). *a* **1656** BP. HALL *Rev. Unrevealed* § 11 That old and *never-contracted distinction of the Church Militant and Triumphant. **1590** GREENE *Orl. Fur.* Wks. (Rtldg.) 109 Hadst thou.. [the] *never-daunted thoughts of Hercules. **1951** L. MACNEICE tr. *Goethe's Faust* 302 Make to *this* good soul concession—Only once misled by pleasure To a *never-dreamt transgression. **1607** HIERON *Wks.* I. 198 It shall be in their bowels as a *neuer-dryed fountaine. **1855** D. G. ROSSETTI *Let.* 25 Nov. (1965) I. 282 One of his *neverended stories was about an anonymous letter. **1859** TENNYSON *Last Tourn.* 581 Here in the never-ended afternoon. **1855** W. WHITMAN *Leaves of Grass* 83, I see your rounded *never-erased flow, I see neath the rims of your haggard and mean disguises. **1613** PURCHAS *Pilgrimage* (1614) 828 His *neuer-filled mouth. **1594** ? GREENE *Selimus* 2493 Beating the *never-foiled Tonombey. **1843** J. R. LOWELL *Prometheus* in *U.S. Mag. & Democratic Rev.* Aug. 149 The bitter peak, This *never-glutted vulture, and these chains. **1600** *1st Pt. Sir J. Oldcastle* IV. ii, Oh *never-heard-of, base ingratitude! **1641** MILTON *Animadv.* Wks. 1851 III. 198 O new and never-heard of Supererogative. **1850** TENNYSON *In Mem.* lxxxiv, I see their unborn faces shine Beside the *never-lighted fire. **1957** A. MILLER *Coll. Plays* (1958) iv. 27 His terror springs from his *never-lost awareness of time and place. **1607** SHAKS. *Cor.* V. i. 35 If you refuse your ayde In this so *neuer-needed helpe. **1802–12** BENTHAM *Ration. Judic. Evid.* (1827) IV. 581 One *never-omitted portion of scandal. **1859** CORNWALLIS *New World* I. 130 The never-omitted tin pot for making their tea. **1860** W. WHITMAN *Leaves of Grass* 368 Those with a *never-quell'd audacity. **1950** D. GASCOYNE *Vagrant* 12 The serene, robust air as of *never-rebuked gaiety. **1873** HOWELLS *Chance Acquaint.* i. (1883) 12 A *never-relinquished, never-fulfilled purpose. **1562** PILKINGTON *Expos. Abdyas* 65 The.. harde-hearted *never satisfied horsleches, the lawers. **1625** K. LONG tr. *Barclay's Argenis* IV. vii. 159 He, whose never-satisfied maw Devoures poore people. **1940** C. DAY LEWIS tr. *Virgil's Georgics* I. 16 That crop.. Will answer at last the prayers of the *never-satisfied Farmer. **1642** H. MORE *Song of Soul* II. iii. II. xii, On *never-shaken pillars of Æternitie. **1860** PUSEY *Min. Proph.* 175 The long *never-shorn hair. **1631** WEEVER *Anc. Funeral Mon.* 460 The terrible *neuer-tamed Scot. **1944** AUDEN *For Time Being* iii. 29 Present to the speculative eye an ever-shining, *never-tarnished proof of her amazing unheard-of power to combine and happily contrast. **1848** J. R. LOWELL *Growth of Legend* in *Poems* 2nd Ser. 71 The lake's frore Sahara of *never-tracked white. **1818** BYRON *Ch. Har.* IV. lxxiii, I have seen the soaring Jungfrau rear Her *never-trodden snow. **1742** SHENSTONE *Song* viii. Wks. 1777 I. 156 Let their very changes prove The *never-vary'd force of love. **1812** BYRON *Ch. Har.* II. xxxvii, Her *never-wean'd, though not her favour'd child. **1603** KNOLLES *Hist. Turks* (1638) 304 Vsing therin such expedition and *neuer-wearied patience. **1622** DRAYTON *Poly-olb.* xxiv. 116 This justly named Saint, this never-wearied man.

b. With pres. pples., as ***never-agreeing, -blushing, -changing, -diminishing, -ebbing, -eldering, -erring, -hastening, -intermitting, -lifting, -moving, -pardoning, -rejecting, -sinking, -stopping***, etc. Also NEVER-CEASING, -DYING, -ENDING, -FADING, -FAILING.

1613 DRUMM. OF HAWTH. *Cypress Grove* Wks. (1711) 118 The *never agreeing bodies of the elemental brethren. **1728** POPE *Dunc.* III. 231 His *never-blushing head he turn'd aside. *c* **1615** SIR W. MURE *Sonn.* iii. Wks. (S.T.S.) I. 49 Can any crosse.. Mak me to chaunge my *neuer chaunging mynd? **1685** DRYDEN *Lucretius* III. Misc. II. 77 That never changing state which all must keep. **1811** W. R. SPENCER *Poems* 44 Where never-changing Spring Rules all the halcyon year. **1898** 'MARK TWAIN' *Man that Corrupted Hadleyburg* (1900) 326 The war of epithets crashes along with *never-diminishing energy for a couple of hours. **1866** J. G. WHITTIER *Our Master* in *Tent on Beach* (1867) 143 Immortal Love, forever full, Forever flowing free, Forever shared, forever whole, A *never-ebbing sea! **1876** G. M. HOPKINS *Wreck of Deutschland* xviii, in *Poems* (1967) 57 Tears; such a melting, a madrigal start! *Never-eldering revel and river of youth, What can it be, this glee? **1679** MARG. MASON *Tickler Tickled* 4 By the Affirmative of *never-erring Scripture it self. **1697** CONGREVE *Wks.* (1730) III. 262 Our never-erring Pilot. **1821–2** SHELLEY *Chas. I*, II. 479 Stamped on the heart by never-erring love. **1867** A. BARRY *Sir C. Barry* x. 323 Its *never-flagging interest to him. **1950** W. DE LA MARE *Inward Companion* 13 With *never-hastening feet Time pursues the Infinite. **1864** MUNRO *Lucretius* I. 2 Vanquished by the *never-healing wound of love. **1594** DRAYTON *Idea* xxvi, Yet hope draws on my *never-hoping care. **1849** J. S. MILL in *Westm. Rev.* LI. 34 The immense majority are condemned.. to a life of never-ending, *never-intermitting toil. **1589** *Marprel. Epit.* F j b, Thus M.D. to his *neuerlasting fame, hath.. translated the greeke word *presbyteros*. **1885** W. B. YEATS *Island of Statues* I. iii, in *Dublin Univ. Rev.* May 84/1 Where their sinewy might is strung In the *never-lifting dark. **1613** DRUMM. OF HAWTH. *Cypress Grove* Wks. (1711) 117 Two so loving friends and *never-loathing lovers. **1860** GOSSE *Rom. Nat. Hist.* 51 Covered with deep, *never-melting snow. **1913** J. MASEFIELD *Daffodil Fields* 24 The stars did house Their lights like lamps upon those *never-moving boughs. **1863** I. WILLIAMS *Baptistery* I. xiv. (1874) 178 Upon them clos'd the *never-opening grave! **1923** R. GRAVES *Whipperginny* 54 This *never-pardoning life we live May earn God's blackest punishment. **1593** SHAKS. *Rich. II*, V. v. 109 That hand shall burne in *neuer-quenching fire. **1849** J. R. LOWELL *Day in June* in *National Anti-Slavery Standard* 8 Mar. 162/1 O *never-rejecting roof of blue. **1727–46** THOMSON *Summer* 726 The *never-resting race of men. **1851** G. BIRD *Urin. Deposits* (ed. 3) 98 The heart, a never-resting muscle. **1742** YOUNG *Nt. Th.* IX. 2285 Sun of the soul! her *never-setting sun! **1825** PRAED *Portrait* ii, Like never-setting stars. **1849** THOREAU *Week Concord Riv.* 244 The unwearied, *never sinking shore. **1697** CONGREVE *Mourn. Bride* III. vi, Drink bitter draughts with *never-slaking thirst. **1661** *Don Juan Lamberto* F 4, This wall was to be guarded by *never-sleeping Dragons. **1680** OTWAY *Caius Marius* I. i, Never-sleeping Care. **1848** DICKENS *Dombey* xxiii, A frown upon its *never-smiling face. **1590** T. WATSON *Poems* (Arb.) 173 Whose *neuerstooping quill can best set forth such things of state. **1931** R. GRAVES *To Whom Else?* 9 What drew the legs along Was the *never-stopping, And the senseless frightening Fate of being legs. **1871** PALGRAVE *Lyr. Poems* 78 Who treads The road with *never-swerving strength. **1835** BROWNING *Paracelsus* IV. 145 Their pet nest and their *never-tiring home. **1885** J. K. JEROME *On the Stage* 84 A quiet, never-tiring persistence. *a* **1649** DRUMM. OF HAWTH. *Poems* Wks. (1711) 31/1 The *never twinkling, ever wandring lights. **1814** WORDSW. *Excursion* V. 747 Of *never-varying motion. **1863** I. WILLIAMS *Baptistery* I. i. (1874) 7 Sabbath of Sabbaths, *never-waning rest. *c* **1600** COSOWARTH in Farr *S.P. Eliz.* (1845) II. 407 Thou hast clothed my soule with *never-weering gladnes. **1609** HOLLAND *Amm. Marcell.* 361 The *never-winking eye of Iustice. **1656** COWLEY *Pindar. Odes, Nemeæan* ix, Through the thick Groves of *never-withering Light. **1707** WATTS *Hymn, 'There is a land of pure delight'* ii, There ever-lasting spring abides And never-with'ring flowers.

c. With adjs., as ***never-anxious, -certain, -constant, -quiet***, etc.

1889 W. B. YEATS *Wanderings of Oisin* I. 5 And always *never-anxious sleep. **1594** DRAYTON *Idea* xxvi, My *never-certain joy breeds ever-certain fears. *a* **1627** SIR J. BEAUMONT *Bosworth F.*, etc. (1629) 85 The *neuer-constant Moone. **1596** SPENSER *Hymn Heav. Love* 126 In bonds.. Of *never-dead yet ever-dying paine. **1694** F. BRAGGE *Disc. Parables* viii. 296 The *never-deficient grace of that good God. **1561** DAUS tr. *Bullinger on Apoc.* (1573) 209 b, A ioyfull, and *neuerloth-some fulnes. **1913** J. MASEFIELD *Daffodil Fields* 2 The *never-quiet joy of dancing daffodils. **1637** MILTON *Lycidas* 2 Ye Myrtles brown, with Ivy *never-sear. **1701** CONGREVE *Wks.* (1730) III. 252 A never ceasing, *never silent Choir. **1714** MANDEVILLE *Fab. Bees* (1723) 283 The fickle Breath of *never Stable Fortune. **1812** BYRON *Ch. Har.* I. l, The stationed bands, the *never-vacant watch.

8. Misc. combs., as †**never-being**, non-existence; **never-do-well**, a ne'er-do-well; **never-fail**, (*a*) a person who never fails (one); (*b*) an Australian grass, *Eragrostis setifolia*, used as pasture in areas of low rainfall; †**never-mass**, a date which never comes; **never-mention-ems**, unmentionables, trousers; **never-ready**, one who is never ready; **never-strike**, one who will not yield; **never-sweat**, an idle or lazy person; †**never-thrift**, a ne'er-do-well, a waster; †**never-thriving**, a thriftless pack; **never-was**, a person who has never been great, distinguished, useful, or the like; also **never-waser, -wozzer**.

1633 (*title*) The Progeny of Catholicks and Protestants, whereby.. is proved the lineal Descent of Catholicks.. and the *never-being of Protestants. **1856** B. W. PROCTER *Barber's Shop* xiv. (1883) 118 He was one of those *never-do-wells who lean persistently upon others. **1850** H. C. WATSON *Camp-Fires of Revolution* 188 Morgan's one of the *never-fails. **1936** F. CLUNE *Roaming round Darling* xiii. 114 He has a marvellous collection of native grasses, nardoo, Mitchell, neverfail, and a dozen others. **1964** *Austral. Encycl.* IV. 367/1 *E*[*ragrostis*] *setifolia* ('never-fail') is a drought resistant species of the inland. **1967** *Coast to Coast 1965–66* 191, I had been riding through.. the high grained heads of the grasses, the spinifex and the neverfail. *c* **1550** *Thersites* in Hazl. *Dodsley* I. 429 That shall be at *Nevermass, Which never shall be, nor never was. **1631** R. H. *Arraignm. Whole Creature* xiv. §2. 244 As our Country Phrase is, when Hens make Holy-water, at new-Nevermasse. **1856** T. TAYLOR in *Kingsley's Lett. & Life* (1877) I. 496 Socks, boots, and *never-mention-ems, Mrs. Owen still has dried for us. **1862** TROLLOPE *Orley F.* xlii, They are not the least happy of mankind, these *never-readies. **1855** KINGSLEY *Westw. Ho!* xvi, Yeo.. returned with Drew and a score of old *never-strikes. **1851** MAYHEW *Lond. Labour* I. 419 Flare up, my *never-sweats. *c* **1440** *Promp. Parv.* 355/1 Neve, *neuerthryfte, or wastour. **1520** WHITINTON *Vulg.* (1527) 39 b, It is more pleasure for a mayster to se foure suche neuer thryftes go out of his schole, than se one to come into it. **1486** *Bk. St. Albans* f vij, A *Neuer-thriuyng of Iogoleris. **1911** J. C. LINCOLN *Cap'n Warren's Wards* xv. 238 One of 'em's a used-to-be, and the other's a *never-was. **1923** 'B. M. BOWER' *Parowan Bonanza* i. 14 'Nope, I'm a never-was,' Bill retorted shamelessly. **1938** L. MACNEICE *I crossed Minch* I. iii. 36 You ninny you, you automaton, You Never-Was, you As-Good-As-Gone! **1891** *Sportsman* 1 Apr. 2/6 He is one of the 'has beens' or else one of the '*never wasers', as Dan Rice, the circus man, always called ambitious counterfeits. **1915** A. S. NEILL *Dominie's Log* xiv. 155 The average married woman is a 'has been' in thought, while not a few are 'never wasers'. **1931** WODEHOUSE *Big Money* viii. 176 It's always been half-way between a may-be and a never-waser. **1974** *Economist* 9 Nov. 6/1 With respect, it is silly, on the strength of a typical remark of some anonymous Brussels diplomat, no doubt a strong advocate of the absurd procedure rules of the council of ministers, to describe them as 'has beens' or 'never wasers'. **1929** *Neverwozzer [see HAS-BEEN *sb.*].

9. a. ***Never Never*** (***Land*** or ***Country***), in Australia, the unpopulated northern part of Queensland; the desert country of the interior.

Variously taken as implying that one may never return from it, or will never wish to go back to it. According to F. Cooper *Wild Adventures* (1857) 68 the phrase is really a corruption of the Comderoi *nievah vahs* signifying 'unoccupied land', but the explanation is not regarded as certain. (Morris.)

1882 A. J. BOYD *Old Colonials* 202 My soliloquy ends with the inquiry, 'What on earth is to be done in this wretched Never-never country?' **1884** A. W. STIRLING (*title*) The Never Never Land: a Ride in North Queensland. **1887** *Cassell's Picturesque Austral.* I. 279 In very sparsely-populated country such as the district of Queensland, known as the 'Never Never Country'. **1890** 'R. BOLDREWOOD' *Colonial Reformer* 174 But here it seems to be the Never-Never country, and no mistake. **1900** H. LAWSON *On Track* 81, I rode back that way five years later, from the Never Never. **1916** J. B. COOPER *Coo-oo-ee* iii. 39 He had not forgotten the palship that is often made between men tramping along the bush distances that cover the sunburnt tracks to the Never-Never. **1942** C. BARRETT *On Wallaby* iii. 43 Tim.. owned a copper show in the Never Never country near the West Australian border. **1963** V. B. CRANLEY *27,000 Miles through Australia* v. 34 It was far beyond Yuendumu along the great desert traverse.. back in the Never-Never, as they call those wastes. **1969** 'A. GARVE' *Boomerang* ii. 71 His intention was to enjoy this trip.. not to 'do a perish' in the Never-Never.

b. ***Never*(*-Never*) *Land***, an imaginary, illusory, or Utopian place; freq. with allusion to the ideal country in J. M. Barrie's *Peter Pan* (see quots. 1904 and 1908).

1900 *N.Y. Dramatic Mirror* 3 Nov. 16/1 At Wallack's on Tuesday evening Sarah Cowell Le Moyne supplemented The Greatest Thing in the World with the initial performance of The Moment of Death; or, The Never, Never Land, a drama in one act and three scenes, by Israel Zangwill. **1904** J. M. BARRIE *Peter Pan* (1928) I. 34 *Wendy.* Where do you live now? *Peter.* With the lost boys... They are the children who fall out of their prams when the nurse is looking the other way. If they are not claimed in seven days they are sent far away to the Never Land. **1907** *Canadian Mag.* XXIX. 135/1 But instead of the unreal *never-never-land*.. the scene is dear old England. **1908** J. M. BARRIE *When Wendy grew Up* (1957) 17 Do they ever wish they were back in the Never Never Land? *Ibid.* 28 The dear Never Never Land. **1938** AUDEN & ISHERWOOD *On Frontier* I. i. 24 Dream of your never-never land, where the parks are covered with naked cow-like women, quite free. **1938** L. MACNEICE *Mod. Poetry* v. 80 William Morris.. looking wanly.. back to a medieval Never-Never Land. **1958** *Spectator* 8 Aug. 203/1 It was no longer the real India they wanted to escape to; it was the Never-Never Land of the East. **1961** *Times* 1 Nov. 13/1 This commercial never-never land. **1968** MRS. L. B. JOHNSON *White House Diary* 4 Apr. (1970) 647, I was back at the White House by 3 o'clock from my brief visit to that beautiful never-never land—Mrs. Merriweather Post's home. **1971** *Nature* 30 July 287/1 The result is that the report of the committee under Sir Frederick Dainton on the reorganization of civil research,.. has disappeared into never-never land. **1975** *Times* 16 Oct. 13/8 Sending the hero and heroine at the end into an azure never-land that is clearly some distance from both Dorset and London.

c. ***never-never*** adj., *colloq.* (or *joc.*), denoting a system of paying for articles by periodic instalments over an extended period; = *hire-purchase*; also *ellipt.* as *sb.*, and as ***never***.

1926 E. WALLACE *More Educated Evans* ii. 39 Her uncle.. drove a taxi which he.. had purchased on the 'never never' system. You pay £80 down and more than you can afford for the rest of your life. **1939** 'N. SHUTE' *What Happened to Corbetts* viii. 261 We could have the radiogram.... Even if we had to put it on the Never-Never. **1957** F. KING *Man on Rock* i. 7, I can't even afford to pay the never-never on a wireless. **1960** *News Chron.* 29 Apr. 6 Twenty per cent is a small deposit for hire purchase, and the most reputable 'never-never' firms have been asking that. **1967** M. PROCTER *Exercise Hoodwink* iii. 21 'I'm getting it on the never. Anybody can do that.' 'Not a new Rover.' **1973** J. WILSON *Truth or Dare* ii. 24 They've still not paid off their mortgage, you know, and I wouldn't mind betting that Rover of theirs is on the never-never.

d. ***never-never*** adj., unrealistic, unrealizable, imaginary. Also applied to a person who says 'never, never'.

1928 D. H. LAWRENCE *Lady Chatterley* xiv. 243 'So when you did get a woman who wanted you.. you got a bit too much of a good thing.' 'Ay! Seems so! Yet even then I'd rather have her than the never-never ones.' **1950** [see CLOUD-CUCKOO-LAND]. **1952** DYLAN THOMAS *Let.* 21 Nov. (1966) 384 A day's life in a small town in a never-never Wales. **1955** *Bull. Atomic Sci.* Jan. 36/2 Norman Thomas, who had the courage to deplore our never-never attitude to the recognition of Red China, did so with an acute sense of his own isolation. **1956** H. GOLD *Man who was not with It* (1965) xiii. 113 She predicted the never-never happiness of others. **1958** *Sunday Times* 16 Nov. 21/7 The atmosphere of some never-never hotel is certainly caught.

10. Colloq. phrases: ***never a dull moment!***: see MOMENT *sb.* 1 c; ***never again!***, a phrase expressing emphatic refusal to repeat an experience, etc.

1873 HARDY *Pair of Blue Eyes* II. iv. 51 Thank you. But never again. **1901** ADE *Forty Modern Fables* 161 And everybody said, 'Never Again.' **1915** T. F. A. SMITH *Soul of Germany* 298 The oft-quoted phrase is applicable to the case: Never again!

never ('nɛvə(r)), *sb. Naut. slang.* [f. the adv.] In phr. ***to do a never***: to shirk; to loaf.

1946 J. IRVING *Royal Navalese* 121 *Never, to do a*, to dodge work. **1948** PARTRIDGE *Dict. Forces' Slang* 124 *Doing a never* means—in the Navy—shirking work. **1961** F. H. BURGESS *Dict. Sailing* 74 *Doing a Never*, loafing on a job.

never-ceasing, *a.* [NEVER 7 b.] Unceasing, ceaseless; constant, continual.

c **1602** F. DAVISON in Farr *S.P. Eliz.* (1845) II. 326, I thine aid importune With neuer-ceasing cries. **1670** *Devout Commun.* (1688) 172 Multiplied with a never-ceasing numeration. **1738** WESLEY *Ps.* VI. iv, With never-ceasing Moans I languish for Relief. **1826** MILMAN *A. Boleyn* (1827) 33 The full organ's never-ceasing sound. **1878** HUXLEY *Physiogr.* 129 There is a never-ceasing transference of solid matter from the land to the ocean.

Hence **never-ceasingly** *adv.*

1869 J. HAIG *Symbolism* i. 1 The thoughts of each are necessarily, or never-ceasingly, confined to himself alone.

never-dying, *a.* [NEVER 7 b.] Undying; immortal.

1596 SHAKS. *1 Hen. IV*, III. ii. 106 What neuer-dying Honor hath he got? **1633** FORD *'Tis Pity* III. vi, Many thousand.. sorts Of never-dying deaths. **1647** TRAPP *Comm. Mark* ix. 49 Those bad humours in us that breed the never-dying worm. **1728** R. MORRIS *Ess. Anc. Archit.* 66 From never-dying Corinth it first arose. **1781** COWPER *Charity* 593 That sight imparts a never-dying flame. **1873** E. BRENNAN *Witch of Nemi* 22 Wedded to a never-dying strife.

never-ending, *a.* [NEVER 7 b.] Unending, endless, everlasting, perpetual.

1667 MILTON *P.L.* II. 221 The never-ending flight Of future days. **1713** BERKELEY *Guardian* No. 55 ¶7 The expectation of never-ending happiness. **1768–74** TUCKER *Lt. Nat.* (1834) I. 648 All [have] become obnoxious to her never-ending severity. **1848** R. I. WILBERFORCE *Doctr. Incarnation* v. (1852) 144 A mere Brahminical dream of never-ending forgetfulness. **1881** BESANT & RICE *Chapl. of Fleet* I. viii, Day and night there was a never-ending riot.

never-fading, *a.* [NEVER 7 b.] Unfading, fadeless, ever fresh or new.

1621 BURTON *Anat. Mel.* III. ii. III. iii. (1624) 448 Virginity is.. a neuer-fading flowre. **1690** TEMPLE *Ess. Heroic Virtue* Wks. 1720 I. 228 This Crown of never-fading Laurel. **1727** GAY *Fables* I. xlv, Might I supply that envy'd place With never-fading love! **1760–72** H. BROOKE *Fool of Qual.* (1809) III. 5 A garland.. of never-fading flowers. **1827** G. HIGGINS *Celtic Druids* 214 Clothed with never-fading vestures. **1916** BLUNDEN *Pastorals* 32 Nor where the never-fading rainbow plays.

never-failing, *a.* [NEVER 7 b.] Unfailing.

1622 FLETCHER *Sea-Voy.* III. i, The never-failing purchase Of lordships and of honours! **1670** EACHARD *Cont. Clergy* 92 The never-failing hen has unhappily forsaken her wonted nest. **1709** STEELE *Tatler* No. 47 ¶3 A never-failing Medicine for the Spleen. **1770** GOLDSM. *Des. Vill.* 11 The never-failing brook, the busy mill. **1836–7** DICKENS *Sk. Boz, Tales* x, Wrapt in profound reveries on this never-failing theme. **1878** HUXLEY *Physiogr.* 27 A never-failing source of supply to the shallow wells.

Hence **never-failingly** *adv.*

1709 *Brit. Apollo* No. 44. 2/2 A Cure, Speedy,.. Never-failingly sure.

†**neverlat(t)er**, var. of NEVER THE LAT(T)ER.

c **1400** *Chron. Eng.* (Caxton) ccxxvi. 232 Neuerlater he.. come by nyght to the tour of london. *Ibid.* ccxxix. 241 The castel neuerlatter was saued.

†**neverless**, obs. variant of NEVERTHELESS.

a **1300** *Cursor M.* 11207 Ihesu crist hir barn sco bar,.. and maiden neuer less. *c* **1330** R. BRUNNE *Chron.* (1810) 97 Þe parties were fulle stark, neuerlesse þorgh praiere [etc.]. ? *c* **1400** *Ser. J. Mandeville & Gt. Souden* 43 in Hazl. *E.P.P.* I. 156 Neverlesse we knaw they salle be above. **1450** *Paston Lett.* I. 111 Never lese I trest not to her promese. **1525** LD. BERNERS *Froiss.* II. clxxxvi. [clxxxii.] 568 Suche as loued hym nat, thought neuerlesse [etc.].

†**nevermo**, obs. variant of NEVERMORE.

c **1129** *O.E. Chron.* (Laud MS.) an. 1129 Se.. nefra ma nan clepunge þær to na hafde mare. *c* **1250** *Prov. Alfred* 220 in *O.E. Misc.* 116 His wit ne agoþ hym neuer-mo. **1390** GOWER *Conf.* II. 77 He schal be riched so, That it mai faile neveremo. *c* **1440** *Rom. Rose* 6641 In such maner care, That konne wynne hem nevermo.

nevermore, *adv.* (*sb.*) Also α. 3 **nauere mare**, 4–5 **neuer-mar**, 4–6 **-mare**, 6 **-mair**. β. 3–4 **neuer(e)-mor**, etc. [f. NEVER *adv.* + MORE *adv.*]

A. *adv.* Never again, at no future time.

α. *c* **1205** LAY. 26845 Ne scalt þu nauere mare þi lif þenne lede. *Ibid.* 32236 Næuere seoððen mære kinges neoren here. *a* **1300** *Cursor M.* 484 He ne has merci neuer-mare. *Ibid.* 10055 þe welle o grace.. þat fines neuermar to rin. **1375** BARBOUR *Bruce* I. 166 The tothir.. swar That he suld have it neuir-mar. *c* **1375** *Sc. Leg. Saints* xxvii. (*Machor*) 1374 Forsuth þe lewe sall I neuirmare. **1508** DUNBAR *Gold. Targe* 222, I saw hir nevir mare. **1567** *Gude & Godlie B.* (S.T.S.) 15 They salbe saif, and neuer mair shall dee.

β. *c* **1220** *Bestiary* 618 Ðoȝ he ðre hundred ȝer.. wuneden her, bigeten he neuermor non. *c* **1250** *Gen. & Ex.* 1240 Wende ȝhe it coueren neuere mor. *c* **1325** *Chron. Eng.* 570 in Ritson *Metr. Rom.* II. 294 Neuermore he nolde come.. In the bed. **1390** GOWER *Conf.* I. 203 This sorghfull king was so bestad, That he schal nevermor be glad. ? **1507** *Comunyc.* (W. de W.) c iij, And than to lyue and neuermore dye. **1581** RICH *Farew.* (1846) 208, I will never more contende with thee duryng life. **1634** MILTON *Comus* 559 Silence.. wish't she might.. be never more Still to be so displac't. **1671** —— *P.R.* IV. 610 He never more henceforth will dare set foot In Paradise. *a* **1859** DE QUINCEY *Posth. Wks.* (1891) I. 261 Nevermore will it be excited by mere court intrigue. **1871–74** J. THOMSON *City Dreadf. Nt.* XVI. vii, This chance recurreth never, nevermore.

B. as *sb.*

1951 KOESTLER *Age of Longing* II. v. 257 The evermore of desire and the nevermore of satiety. **1952** R. CAMPBELL tr. *Baudelaire's Poems* 50 It's by such charms the Never-more Intoxicates us in the Now.

‖**Nevers** (nɛvɛr). The name of a city in central France, used freq. *attrib.* to describe a type of deep blue-ground faience in the style of Italian majolica, made there from the latter part of the 16th century to the 18th.

1863 W. CHAFFERS *Marks Pott. & Porc.* 93 *Nevers*, fine Faïence, in the Italian style, decorated in colours, sometimes like Faenza ware; also in blue *en grisaille*, as well as in a deep blue ground of enamel with splashes or spots of white. **1900** F. LITCHFIELD *Pott. & Porc.* vii. 219 Specimens of Nevers are difficult to identify, owing to the similarity of their characteristics to those of the Rouen and other similar faiences. **1960** H. HAYWARD *Antique Coll.* 198/1 *Nevers faience*, the chief Nevers pottery was founded early in the 17th cent. by Italian potters... Nevers glass. **1960** R. G.

HAGGAR *Conc. Encycl. Cont. Pott. & Porc.* 68/1 Nevers faience decorated with pseudo-oriental or oriental motifs in white, or white, yellow and orange. **1971** L. A. BOGER *Dict. World Pott. & Porc.* 241/2 The so-called Bleu Persan or Décor Persan was introduced during the second half of the 17th century and is probably the most important Nevers creation. **1972** *Times* 21 June 16/4 A charming seventeenth-century Nevers glass picture depicting Diana surprised by Actaeon.

†**never the lat(t)er**, *adv.* *Obs.* Also 5-6 **neuerthelat(t)er.** [See NEVER 5 and LATER *adv.*, LATTER *adv.*] = NEVERTHELESS.

α. *c* **1330** *Spec. Guy Warw.* 832 He weneþ wasshe him wid þat water, And he is foul neuere þe later. **1387-8** T. USK *Test. Love* I. i. (Skeat) l. 19 Never-the-later yet hertly.. have mynde on thy servaunt. *c* **1450** tr. *De Imitatione* II. ix. 51 Neverþelater amonge þese he dispeiriþ not. **1531** TINDALE *Exp. 1 John* (1537) 88 Neuerthelater it were some-what yet yf [etc.]. **1571** GOLDING *Calvin on Ps.* iii. 9 Never-thelater I have folowed that which is plainest. **1609** HOLLAND *Amm. Marcell.* 207 Never the later.. [he] endevoured earnestly to prepare all things. **1652** W. SCLATER *Civ. Magistracy* (1653) 28, I must therefore, never the later, condemn you, being convicted.

β. **1340** HAMPOLE *Pr. Consc.* 3650 Bot never-þe-latter.. Yhit may he helpe þe saules þus. *c* **1400** MAUNDEV. (Roxb.) xvii. 76 If all he ware a paynymme, neuer þe latter he serued Godd full deuoutely. **1483** CAXTON *Gold. Leg.* 420b/1 Neuerthelatter he shal not haue the vyctorye of me. *a* **1550** *Image Hypocr.* IV. 245 in *Skelton's Wks.* (1843) II. 442/1 Nowe never the latter I intend to clatter. **1587** GOLDING *De Mornay* xiii. (1617) 197 They which haue flatly denied the Creation, haue neuer the latter granted the Prouidence.

ˌ**neverthe'less**, *adv.* [See NEVER 5 (and 5 b) and LESS *adv.* Earlier equivalents are NA-, NE-, and NOTHELESS.] Notwithstanding; none the less.

a **1300** *Cursor M.* 79 Scho es.. Moder and maiden neuer þe lesse. *c* **1330** R. BRUNNE *Chron.* (1810) 61 Neuerþeles to William he ȝeld him wele his bone. *c* **1380** WYCLIF *Sel. Wks.* III. 430 Neverþelees spek we of apostasye of prests. *c* **1420** LYDG. *Assembly of Gods* 1018 Neuerthelese they seyde they wold endure tho shoures. **1484** CAXTON *Fables of Alfonce* iv, The woman wold haue resysted, Neuertheles in thende she was content. **1512** in Willis & Clark *Cambridge* (1886) I. 609 Neuerthelasse hyt is agreed and couenaunted betwyn the said [etc.]. **1577** B. GOOGE *Heresbach's Husb.* II. (1586) 57b, It may be sowed neuerthelesse.. at any time of the sommer. *a* **1610** HEALEY *Cebes* (1636) 155 Then wee benefit by his reading neuerthelesse. **1696** WHISTON *The. Earth* (1722) 4 The Reader will never the less embrace the Conclusions. **1774** GOLDSM. *Nat. Hist.* (1776) II. 323 Nevertheless.. they generally lead a life of famine and fatigue. **1841** BORROW *Zincali* II. ii. III. 54 The Gitanos.. have nevertheless found admirers in Spain. **1875** JOWETT *Plato* (ed. 2) I. 169 They, knowing them to be evil, nevertheless indulge in them.

neves ('nɛvɪs). *Back-slang.* Also **nevis.** [Reversed form of 'seven'.] Seven years' hard labour.

1901 FARMER & HENLEY *Slang* V. 31/2 *Nevis*,.. Seven... Nevis-stretch = seven year's hard. **1958** F. NORMAN *Bang to Rights* 22 Your f——ing lucky, I'm doing a bleeding neves.

†'**nevet**, variant of *evet* EFT *sb.*[1] (Cf. NEWT.)

1565 COOPER *Thesaurus*, *Lacerta*, a lisarde: a neuet. **1593** NASHE *Christ's T.* 33b, Grashopper, Worme, Neuette or Cancker. *a* **1601** J. HOOKER in Polwhele *Devon* (1797) I. 124 We have.. the snake, the sloworme, and the nevet.

neveu, -ewe, nevie, obs. forms of NEPHEW.

nevie-: see NIEVIE.

nevil, var. NEVEL *v. dial.*

nevin, var. NEVEN *v. Obs.*

nevir, obs. f. NEVER.

nevo, nevoeu, obs. ff. NEPHEW.

†**ne'vosity.** *Obs. rare*—[0]. [ad. med. or mod.L. *nævōsitas*, f. *nævōsus*: see NÆVUS.] (See quot.)

1656 BLOUNT *Glossogr.*, *Nevosity*, speckedness, fulness of moles or freckles.

nevou(e, -ow, -oy, variants of NEPHEW.

nevre, obs. form of NEVER.

nevue, nevy, variants of NEPHEW.

nevus, var. NÆVUS.

nevve, var. NEVE *sb.*[1] *Obs.*

nevvy, nevy, colloq. abbrevs. of NEPHEW.

1847 DICKENS *Dombey* (1848) xv. 149 'He might die a little sooner for the loss of—' 'Of his Nevy,' interposed the Captain. **1903** WODEHOUSE *Tales of St. Austin's* 138 Yes, prarper good runner, his nevvy. **1940** M. MARPLES *Public School Slang* 133 Nunky and nevvy, uncle and nephew, are quoted by Wrench's WB as current before 1901 at Winchester; they are certainly now obsolete. **1959** E. POUND *Thrones* civ. 91 Sammy's nevvy got the gold out of the palace bed-room.

nevyanskite (nɛ'vjænskaɪt). *Min.* Also †**newjanskite.** [ad. G. *newjanskit* (W. Haidinger *Handbuch der bestimm. Min.* (1845) 558), f. *Newjansk* Nevyansk, a city in Russia: see -ITE[1].] A variety of iridosmine containing about 35 to 50 per cent of osmium.

1854 J. D. DANA *Syst. Min.* (ed. 4) II. vi. 20 At a high temperature.. Newjanskite is not decomposed and does not give an osmium odor. **1938** *Mineral. Abstr.* VII. 162 Ruthenium-bearing nevyanskite was found in alluvial deposits associated with serpentine of the Great Laba river, northern Caucasus. **1963** *Mineral. Mag.* XXXIII. 714 Iridosmine for the hexagonal phase (with Nevyanskite and Sysertskite as varieties) and Osmiridium for the cubic phase.

†**nevyn.** *Obs. rare.* Also 5 **newyne.** [Of obscure origin.] App. some precious stone.

1393 *Will of Brauncepeth* (Somerset Ho.), Vnum monile de auro cum tribus neuynys super illud positis et cum tribus scutis. *a* **1440** *Sir Degrev.* 630 All of pall work fyn With miche and nevyn [*Lincoln MS.* Cowchid with newyne].

nevyn(e, varr. NEVEN *v. Obs.*

†**new**, *sb.*[1] *Obs. rare.* [For *nue*, *nuy*, aphetic form of *anuy* ANNOY *sb.*] Trouble, sorrow.

c **1440** *York Myst.* xlv. 144 All þat are in newe or in nede. *Ibid.* xlvii. 96 Thy tyme is paste of all þi care,.. Of newe schall þou witte neuere more.

new (njuː), *a.* and *sb.*[2] Forms: 1-3 niwe, (1 niue, 3 nywe, niewe), 1 niowe, 1-3 neowe, (3 neouwe), 1-7 newe, (3 neuwe, 5 neewe), 4 nu(we), nwe, 5 now(e, 4-6 neu, (5 nev), 4- new. [Common Teut.: OE. *níwe*, *níowe*, *néowe* = OFris. *nŷ*, *nî*, MDu. *nieuwe*, *nuwe*, *nie*, OS. *niwi*, *nigi*, OHG. *niuwi*, *niuui* (MHG. *niuwe*, *niwe*, *niu*, G. *neu*), ON. *nýr* (Sw. and Da. *ny*), Goth. *niujis*:—OTeut. **neujoz*, from the common Aryan stem **neu(j)-*, which appears in Gr. *νέος* (Ionic *νεῖος*), Lith. *naũjas*, Skr. *návyas* and *navas*, Lat. *novus*, OSl. *novŭ* (Russ. *novȳĭ*), OIr. *nūe* (Ir. and Gael. *nuadh*).] **A.** *adj.*

I. 1. a. Not existing before; now made, or brought into existence, for the first time.

c **825** *Vesp. Psalter* xxxii. 3 Singað him song neowne. *a* **1000** *Exod.* 362 Niwe flodas Noe oferlað.. mid his þrim sunum. *a* **1000** *Phœnix* 431 He ȝetimbreð tanum & wyrtum ..eardwic niwe, nest on bearwe. *c* **1000** ÆLFRIC *Gloss.* in Wr.-Wülcker 150/36 *Constructio*, niwe timbrung. *c* **1205** LAY. 2675 þa ferde þe king.. & ane neowe burh makede. **1297** R. GLOUC. (Rolls) 5494 Nywe abbeys he made vaste þe gode aþelston. **1377** LANGL. *P. Pl.* B. xx. 255 God.. nempned names newe and noumbred þe sterres. **1382** WYCLIF *1 Sam.* vi. 7 Nowe thanne takith, and makith a newe weyn. **1520** *Calisto & Melib.* Cj b, Well mother, to morow is a new day. **1575-85** ABP. SANDYS *Serm.* (Parker Soc.) 66 They should remember that their religion is as new as false. **1611** BIBLE *Transl. Pref.* ¶6 Aquila fell in hand with a new Translation. **1697** DRYDEN *Virg. Georg.* III. 460 Pleas'd I am ..the way to new Discov'ries make. **1774** GOLDSM. *Nat. Hist.* (1776) VIII. 18 A new crop of hair grows between the old skin and the new. **1852** M. ARNOLD *Empedocles* Poet. Wks. (1890) 449 So each new man strikes root into a far foretime. **1876** DUHRING *Dis. Skin* 404 Diseases, which.. consist pathologically of a new growth in the skin. **1891** *Law Rep., Weekly Notes* 78/2 The lessor was desirous of pulling the house down and building a new one on its site.

b. Of a kind now first invented or introduced; novel.

13.. *E.E. Allit. P.* B. 1354 In notyng of nwe metes & of nice gettes. **1611** W. GODDARD *Satir. Dial.* Ej b, Newe-fashiond cloathes I loue to weare, Newe tires, newe ruffes. **1673** *S'too him Bayes* 9 He would imagine it was a sluice, or some newer kind of engine. **1784** COWPER *Task* I. 43 A lattice-work that braced The new machine, and it became a Chair. **1818** J. C. HOBHOUSE *Hist. Illustr.* (ed. 2) 402 He composed a sort of drama, altogether new, which he called a melo-tragedy.

2. Not previously known; now known for the first time: **a.** of things spoken or heard.

Beowulf 2898 Lyt swiȝode niwra spella. *c* **900** tr. *Bæda's Hist.* I. xxv. (Schipper) 54/1 Fæȝere word þis syndon.., ac forðon hi niwe synðon & uncuðe [etc.]. *a* **1000** in *Narrat. Angl. Conscr.* (1861) 3 Ðas niwan spel ic ðe ealle in cartan awrite. *c* **1205** LAY. 26194 He talde þan kinge neouwe tiðende. *c* **1250** *Gen. & Ex.* 1286 Ðo herde abraham steuene fro gode, Newe tiding. *c* **1400** MAUNDEV. (1839) xxxi. 314 Men seyn alle weys, that newe thynges and newe tydynges ben plesant to here. **1638** BAKER tr. *Balzac's Lett.* (vol. II.) 30 Your part is not.. to bring it forth as a New Matter. **1667** MILTON *P.L.* v. 855 Strange point and new! Doctrin which we would know whence learnt. **1687** NORRIS *Coll. Misc.* 150 How absurd.. that venerable non-sense should be prefer'd before new-sense. **1751** R. PALTOCK *P. Wilkins* xliii, Another went on, till we had heard ten of them, and in every one something new. **1781** COWPER *Conversat.* 237 Tell not as new what everybody knows. **1821** SHELLEY *Hellas* 592 Prophesyings horrible and new Are heard among the crowd.

(*b*) ***a new one*** (*spec.* an anecdote or a joke; also, a circumstance not previously encountered). Usu. const. *on* (a person). orig. *U.S.*

1887 *Lantern* (New Orleans) 17 Dec. 2/3 Isn't this a new one on you, Messrs. Police? **1900** ADE *Fables in Slang* 74 The Pew-Holders didn't even admit among themselves that the Preacher had rung in some New Ones. **1930** D. L. SAYERS *Strong Poison* xx. 256 'I warn you.. that you still have to establish evidence as to means and opportunity.' 'I know that. Tell us a new one.' **1931** T. H. DEY *Leaves from Bookmaker's Bk.* iii. 72 Charles Austin, Wilkie Bard and Ernie Lotinga too, are excellent private raconteurs and George Robey has always got a 'new one'. **1939** C. ISHERWOOD *Goodbye to Berlin* 72 That's a new one on me... I never suspected the boy of having a mind at all. **1940** J. CARY *Charley is My Darling* xv. 77 Ginger reflects a moment and says then: 'It's a new one on me', meaning that he has not yet broken the law. **1952** 'M. INNES' *Private View* iii. 45 He said there was blood pouring through his ceiling. That was a new one on the station sergeant. **1971** 'A. GILBERT' *Tenant for Tomb* vi. 93 Her brother?.. That's a new one on me.

b. Of feelings, experiences, events, etc.

a **900** CYNEWULF *Elene* 869 Hæfdon neowne ȝefean mærðum ȝemeted. **971** *Blickl. Hom.* 135 Him ne wæs nænig earfoþe þæt lichomlice ȝedal on ȝære neowan wyrde. *c* **1330** R. BRUNNE *Chron.* (1810) 66 His falshed brouht vs sorowe alle newe. *c* **1368** CHAUCER *Compl. Pite* 29 Yet encreseth me this wonder newe. *a* **1400-50** *Alexander* 1240 Neȝis þam a-nothire note as new as þe first. *c* **1470** *Gol. & Gaw.* 501, I suld fynd thame new notis for this ix yeir. **1551** RECORDE *Pathw. Knowl.* Ep. King, Thei again shal haue new and new causes to pray for your maiestie. **1671** MILTON *P.R.* I. 334 Where ought we hear, and curious are to hear, What happ'ns new. **1732** LEDIARD *Sethos* II. IX. 306 The successes of war are not new. **1781** COWPER *Table-T.* 734 'Twere new indeed to see a bard all fire. **1876** J. PARKER *Paracl.* II. xviii. 295 Opposition is nothing new as applied to Christain faith. **1899** J. SMITH *Chr. Charac.* 196 The new religious consciousness of acceptance and union with God.

Comb. **1844** H. STEPHENS *Bk. Farm* I. 34 Such new-like occurrences.

c. Of countries, etc., now first discovered.

c **1511** *1st Eng. Bk. Amer.* (Arb.) Introd. 27 Of the newe landes.. founde by the messengers of the kynge of portyngale. **1610** SHAKS. *Temp.* v. i. 184 *Mir.* O braue new world That has such people in't. *Pro.* 'Tis new to thee. **1667** MILTON *P.L.* I. 290 To descry new Lands, Rivers or Mountains in her spotty Globe. **1725** DE FOE *Voy. round World* (1840) 280 What signifies.. the people of Spain seeking new countries? **1879** MORLEY *Burke* 21 In East and West new lands were being brought under the dominion of Great Britain.

d. Of things or persons.

1626 BACON *Sylva* §477 So you may have great Varietie of New Fruits, and Flowers yet unknowne. **1697** BURGHOPE *Disc. Relig. Assemb.* 181 New things only are able to awake us. *a* **1734** NORTH *Lives* (1826) III. 145 This new kind of Arithmetic, which he had never heard of before. **1781** COWPER *Conversat.* 531 The new acquaintance soon became a guest. **1840** DICKENS *Old C. Shop* i, We were going quite a new road.

e. Strange, unfamiliar (*to* one).

1595 SHAKS. *John* III. i. 305 Alacke, how new Is husband in my mouth. **1638** JUNIUS *Paint. Ancients* 25 Nothing in such a case could be new unto him. **1667** MILTON *P.L.* III. 613 Here matter new to gaze the Devil met Undazl'd. ? **1710** LADY M. W. MONTAGU *Lett., to Mrs. Hewet* (1887) I. 28 We go next week into Wiltshire, which will be quite a new world to us. **1784** COWPER *Task* IV. 710 New to my taste, his Paradise surpassed [etc.]. **1855** MACAULAY *Hist. Eng.* xxi. IV. 545 To English shopkeepers and farmers military extortion was happily quite new. **1859** TENNYSON *Geraint* 808 She could cast aside A splendour dear to women, new to her, And therefore dearer.

3. a. Coming as a resumption or repetition of some previous act or thing; starting afresh.

Beowulf 1789 þa wæs eft swa ær.. fæȝere ȝereorded niowan stefne. *c* **1000** *Cædmon's Gen.* 1555 Ða Noe ongan niwan stefne mid hleomaȝum ham staðelian. *c* **1205** LAY. 27494 Heo.. neouwe ueht [*c* **1275** neuwe fiht] bi-gunnen narewe iþrungen. *a* **1300** *Cursor M.* 1592 For-þi in forme of iugement He thoght a neu wengaunce to sent. **1340** *Ayenb.* 107 þet is a newe cristninge. *c* **1386** CHAUCER *Frankl. T.* 287 Tho come hir othere freendes many oon, And.. sodeinly bigonne revel newe. **1508** DUNBAR *Flyting* 297 Ȝit of new tressone, I can tell the tailis. **1560** DAUS tr. *Sleidane's Comm.* 91 Thus was he brought agayne in to a newe hope of a concorde. **1607** SHAKS. *Cor.* III. i. 1 Tullus Auffidius then had made new head. **1674** MILTON *P.L.* (ed. 2) XII. 5 The Archangel paus'd.. ; Then with transition sweet new Speech resumes. **1818** CRUISE *Digest* (ed. 2) III. 471 Upon a motion for a new trial, it was urged [etc.]. **1872** RAYMOND *Statist. Mines* 209 The quartz-mining enterprises.. took a new start.

b. Fresh, further, additional.

1576 FLEMING *Panopl. Epist.* 17, I had rather cut off all old acquaintance with him,.. then to seeke after newe friendship. **1580-1** *Reg. Privy Council Scot.* III. 362 He obtenit confirmatioun of his said pensioun.., with supplement of new gift and dispositioun thairof. **1667** MILTON *P.L.* III. 468 [They] still with vain designe New Babels, had they wherewithall, would build. **1759** GOLDSM. *Bee* No. 2 Wks. (Globe) 366/1 The most calamitous events ..can bring no new affliction. **1796** H. HUNTER tr. *St.-Pierre's Stud. Nat.* (1799) III. 4 This perception adds a new degree of probability. **1849** MACAULAY *Hist. Eng.* v. I. 531 If he gave no new cause of displeasure. *Ibid.* 580 Commissions were issued for the levying of new regiments.

c. Restored after demolition, decay, disappearance, etc.

c **1000-** [see NEW MOON 1]. **1056-66** *Inscr. at Kirkdale Ch.* (Yorks), He hit let macan newan from grvnde. *c* **1375** *Cursor M.* 23399 (Fairf.), Squa has our lorde be-fore vs hi3t þat he sal new our bodis make. **1377** LANGL. *P. Pl.* B. XVIII. 43 To fordone it on o day, and in thre dayes after Edefye it eft newe. **1483** *Cath. Angl.* 254/1 To make Newe, *novare*. *c* **1600** SHAKS. *Sonn.* lxxvi, As the Sun is daily new and old. **1697** DRYDEN *Virg. Georg.* III. 476 Till the new Ram receives th' exalted Sun. **1859** TENNYSON *Geraint* 70 The new sun Beat thro' the blindless casement of the room.

4. a. Other than the former or old; different from that previously existing, known, or used. Also †***new and new.*** ***new breed***: see BREED *sb.* 2 c; ***new order***, a new regime or government; *spec.* (cf. G. *die neue Ordnung*), Hitler's plan for the reconstitution of the States of Europe on the basis of a National-Socialist regime; ***new technology***: esp. (a) technology that radically alters the way something is produced or performed, often involving computers. Of a coinage: replacing a former monetary unit, e.g. ***new franc***, ***new penny***.

c **950** *Lindisf. Gosp.* Mark i. 27 Huælc lar [is] ðius.. niua [*c* **1000** Hwæt is þeos niwe lar]. *Ibid.* John xiii. 34 Bebod niua ic selo iuh. *c* **1000** ÆLFRIC *Hom.* I. 96 þu bist ȝeciȝed niwum naman. *c* **1205** LAY. 30701 Heo scupten heore lauerde ænne nome neowe. *a* **1300** *Cursor M.* 1975 A couenand neu ic hight to þe. **1382** WYCLIF *2 Cor.* v. 17 Oolde thingis han passid, and lo! alle thingis ben maad newe. **1526** *Pilgr. Perf.* (W. de W. 1531) 150b, He shall haue a newe knowlege in his soule by grace. **1577-87** HOLINSHED *Chron.* I. 21/2 He must turne the leafe, and take out a new lesson. **1617** MORYSON *Itin.* I. 271 From the Citie Armstat.. we had a new measure of oates called Hembd. **1644** DIGBY *Nat. Bodies* v. §1. 33

The sides of it be ioyned successiuely to new and new partes of the rare body that giueth way vnto it. **1667** MILTON *P.L.* v. 676 New Laws thou seest impos'd. **1781** COWPER *Conversat.* 724 Partakers of a new ethereal birth. **1835** THIRLWALL *Greece* I. 97 The Messenian legends of a new race of settlers. **1842** New order [see ORDER *sb.* 16]. **1849** MACAULAY *Hist. Eng.* iii. I. 411 It was then that Ray made a new classification of birds and fishes. **1884** F. TEMPLE *Relat. Relig. & Sci.* v. (1885) 147 The New Testament contains not only a new morality, it contains also a new account of human nature. **1917** KIPLING *Divers. Creatures* (1917) 333 He and his friends had helped the world a step nearer the Truth, the Dawn, and the New Order. **1936** *Discovery* Sept. 295/1 The higher motives of a new order. **1940** *Times* (Weekly ed.) 27 Nov. 16 Every effort of the Quisling Government to induce the Norwegian people to believe that the 'new order' in Norway means the real liberation of the people and the erection of a new and happier Norway, freed from party strife and class distinctions, seems to have fallen on very deaf ears. **1941**, **1944** New order [see CO-PROSPERITY SPHERE]. **1944** G. B. SHAW *Everybody's Political What's What?* viii. 67 There is much talk at present of a New Order to follow the war. **1960** *Whitaker's Almanack 1961* 864/2 The *New Franc*, worth 100 old francs, came into use on Jan. 1, 1960, in metropolitan France and Algeria. **1964** M. MCLUHAN *Understanding Media* I. vii. 65 The ability of the artist to sidestep the bully blow of new technology..is age-old. **1966** J. G. BURKE *New Technol. & Human Values* p. iii, This interaction between basic science—that is, pure research—and applied science.. is what I have termed the new technology. **1966** *New Statesman* 16 Dec. 896/3 The government has opted for a pound divided into 100 'new pennies'. **1966** H. YOXALL *Fashion of Life* xxiv. 221 A *menu gastronomique* at twenty-five new francs. **1969** *Times* 21 July p. i/3 In 1971 our coins will be ½p, 1p, 2p, 5p, 10p, and 50p, each new penny equalling 2·4 of our present pennies. **1970** A. TOFFLER *Future Shock* xix. 380 We frequently apply new technology stupidly and selfishly. **1971** 'J. FRASER' *Death in Pheasant's Eye* xxvi. 163 Game bird soup at twenty new pence a helping. **1972** D. LEES *Zodiac* 47 I've won twenty-five thousand new francs—it's a fortune. **1973** *Listener* 22 Feb. 258/3 If the Nazis considered it worth their while to be so subtle in their propaganda, surely we should be at least as discerning in our exposure of the New Order. **1981** M. H. ASTON in Lewis & Tagg *Computers in Educ.* 385 New technologies in both broadcast and P.T.T. networking systems offer an opportunity for authorities to provide a useful service..in the provision of educational software. **1984** *Guardian* 22 Oct. 2/2 National NUJ and NGA officers are to meet on Wednesday in an attempt to agree a joint approach to the introduction of new technology in the provincial press. **1986** *Sunday Tel.* (Colour Suppl.) 31 Aug. 15/2 Let us suppose that the new technology will relieve us of the drudgery and oppression of tedious and repetitive tasks. What will we do then with our time?

b. Of persons occupying a certain position or relationship. ***new bug*** (slang), a new boy. Cf. BUG *sb.*² 3 c. Also (rare) ***new tick***. Cf. NEW BOY, NEW GIRL.

c **1000** ÆLFRIC *Exod.* i. 8 Ðemang þam aras niwe cing ofer Egipta land. *c* **1200** ORMIN 7149 Þatt Kalldisskenn genge, Þatt cumenn wass inntill hiss land An new king forr to sekenn. *a* **1225** *Leg. Kath.* 2137 Mi neowe leofmon, þe ich on wið luue leue. **1297** R. GLOUC. *Chron.* (Rolls) 7496 Þus, lo, þe englisse folc..come to a nywe louerd, þat more in riȝte was. *c* **1386** CHAUCER *Clerk's T.* 785 Of your newe wyf, god ..graunte yow wele. *c* **1400** *Solomon's Bk. Wisdom* 36 Þine olde frende þat þou fonded haste bileue þou for no newe. **1563** WINȜET tr. *Vincent. Lirin.* Wks. (S.T.S.) II. 12 The peple..entering vnhappelie to be refreschit in the cumpanie of thir neu techearis. **1590** SHAKS. *Mids. N.* I. i. 219 To seeke new friends and strange companions. **1630** CAPT. SMITH *Wks.* (Arb.) 953 New Lords, new lawes. **1665** PEPYS *Diary* 19 June, After dinner, to my little new goldsmith's. **1784** COWPER *Task* II. 110 The sylvan scene..finds out A new possessor, and survives the change. **1863** GEO. ELIOT *Romola* ix, She had beforehand felt an inward shrinking from a new guide. **1900** FARMER *Public School Word-Bk.* 139 *New-bug*, a new boy. **1934** 'G. ORWELL' *Burmese Days* v. 79 New-tick Flory does look rum. **1936**, **1960** New bug [see BUG *sb.*² 3 c]. **1971** 'M. INNES' *Awkward Lie* v. 90 It mayn't be too bad an idea for the new bugs.

c. Of places: Different from that previously inhabited or frequented.

1387 TREVISA *Higden* (Rolls) III. 287 What profiȝteþ newe lond þere þe fliȝt fleeþ nouȝt [thee]? **1594** SHAKS. *Rich. III*, II. ii. 46 That our swift-winged Soules may..follow him, To his new Kingdome. **1637** MILTON *Lycidas* 193 To morrow to fresh Woods, and Pastures new. **1667** —— *P.L.* IV. 184 A prowling Wolfe, Whom hunger drives to seek new haunt for prey. **1819** SHELLEY *Cenci* v. i. 89 'Tis easy..for a country new..To change the honours of abandoned Rome.

d. Morally or spiritually changed.

1533 GAU *Richt Vay* 31 Faith..quhilk renwis the hart and makis ane nev man. **1552** *Bk. Com. Prayer, Communion*, Ye that do..intend to lead a new life following the Commandments of God. **1593** G. HARVEY *New Letter* Wks. (Grosart) I. 274 If vnfaynedly he hath stripped-of the snakes skinne, and put-on the new man. **1677** LADY CHAWORTH in *12th Rep. Hist. MSS. Comm.* App. V. 43 The D[uchess] of Portsmouth..they say will lead a new lyfe. *a* **1770** JORTIN *Serm.* (1771) VII. i. 19 Christians upon their repentance become new creatures.

†**e.** Inclined to change or novelty. *Obs. rare*⁻¹.

1500–20 DUNBAR *Poems* xlv. 13 Scho is so new of acquentance, The auld gais fra remembrance.

f. ***new thing*** (freq. with capital initials): something avant-garde or innovative; *spec.* a type of experimental jazz music of the 1960s dispensing with the normal harmonic and rhythmic framework. Also *attrib.* Hence ***new thinger***. *slang* (orig. *U.S.*).

1928 [see MUCKER *v.*² b]. **1962** *Down Beat* 12 Apr. 20 Coltrane's cohort Eric Dolphy, a member of that group of musicians who play what has been dubbed the 'new thing'. **1966** *New Statesman* 25 Mar. 438/3 'Pure feeling, pure expression, pure movement' (I quote from *Change/1*, an extended manifesto of the New Thingers). **1966** *New Yorker* 1 Oct. 214 The newest rock'n'roll groups are tuning in on the new thing. *Ibid.* 217 Charles Lloyd..wears new-thing clothes (an Army officer's jacket, tinted glasses, and bell-bottom trousers). **1967** *Melody Maker* 28 Jan. 15 Near the end, Dolphy had adopted a determinedly 'new thing' attitude, becoming more and more anarchistic in his playing, especially on alto. **1970** C. MAJOR *Dict. Afro-Amer. Slang* 84 *New thing* , in jazz, an aggressive and original attitude and feeling..; in black writing, the 'new thing' trend is best indicated through..*The New Black Poetry*.

5. Used with *the* to distinguish the thing spoken of from something old, or already existing, of the same kind: **a.** Of institutions, practices, methods, etc., with implication of some change in the nature or character of these. ***the New Humanism***, in the U.S., a school of cultural thought based on the pragmatic philosophy of Dewey and others and emphasizing man's superiority to the natural order through the use of his reason; so ***New Humanist***, a proponent of the New Humanism; ***the New Journalism*** (orig. *U.S.*), a style of journalism that developed during the 1960s, characterized by the use of subjective and fictional elements so as to elicit an emotional response from the reader; also without *the* and *attrib.*; hence ***New Journalist***, a practitioner of this style of journalism; ***the New Kingdom***, a name given collectively to the Eighteenth, Nineteenth, and Twentieth Dynasties, which ruled Egypt from the sixteenth to the eleventh centuries B.C.; ***the new mathematics***, a system of teaching mathematics to younger children in which an emphasis is laid on investigation and discovery on their part and topics are included that are not in the traditional school curriculum (as set theory, symbolic logic, and number systems); usu. abbreviated to ***the new maths*** (U.S. ***math***); also without *the*; ***the new psychology***, a term denoting new and major fields of psychological investigation, such as experimental psychology in the 19th century and esp. those theories in the 20th century that recognize the irrational and unconscious motivations of human behaviour.

In a number of cases this use of *the new* has given rise to phrases with a special meaning or application; for examples see *Church, connexion, husbandry, jet* sb.², *law, learning, light, model, police, style, Testament, woman, world. new journalism* in quot. 1960 refers to 'interpretative journalism'. In later editions of his book Hohenberg uses the term in the sense defined.

c **900** tr. *Bæda's Hist.* II. iv. (Schipper) 127 Þære niwan cyricean, þe of Anȝelcynne ȝesomnad wæs. *c* **950** *Lindisf. Gosp.* Matt. xxvi. 28 Ðis is forðon blod min ðære niua ȝewitnessæ. **971** *Blickl. Hom.* 163 Se godspellere wæs fæstnung æȝþer ȝe þære ealdan æ ȝe þære niwan. *c* **1175** *Lamb. Hom.* 85 Þet boð þa twa laȝen þe alde and þe nowe. *c* **1200** ORMIN 15159 All Godess lare off eȝȝþerr boc, Off þalde & off þe newe. *a* **1300** *Cursor M.* 12887 Þe ald testament hir-wit nu slakes, And sua þe neu bigining takes. **1303** R. BRUNNE *Handl. Synne* 3212 Þey..haunte alle þe newe gyse. **1390** GOWER *Conf.* III. 6 Wher as I moste daunce and singe The hovedance and carolinge, Or forto go the newefot. **1523** [COVERDALE] (*title*) A Worke entytled of ye Olde God and the Newe, of the old faythe and the newe, of the olde doctryne and ye newe. **1590** SIR J. SMYTH *Disc. Weapons* 33 b, According to the newe fashion. **1731** TULL *Horse-Hoeing Husb.* (1733) xix. 263 Of Differences between the Old and the New Husbandry. **1799** *Med. Jrnl.* II. 214 The new inoculation was immediately introduced in London. **1833** J. HOLLAND *Manuf. Metal* II. 12 The latter, indeed, frequently became..victims to the new system. **1849** GROTE *Greece* II. lxvii. VIII. 450 The gradual transition of..the Old Comedy into the Middle and New Comedy. **1898** SIR E. MONSON in *Times* 7 Dec. 5/1 We had not [then] heard so much of what is called the 'new diplomacy'. **1899** W. JAMES *Talks to Teachers* ii. 20 In the light of some of the expectations that are abroad concerning the 'new psychology', it is instructive to read the unusually candid confession of its founder Wundt. **1920** A. G. TANSLEY (*title*) The new psychology. *Ibid.* i. 9 Before we consider the developments of the New Psychology we must first glance at the causes of this failure of the older psychology... Not very many years ago the subject-matter of psychology was almost entirely limited to what is called the 'content of consciousness'. **1928** N. FOERSTER *Amer. Criticism* v. 236 A better way to consider the reconstruction proposed by the new humanism would be to examine its fundamental assumption. **1928** C. DAWSON *Age of Gods* viii. 173 The Late Minoan [corresponds] to the New Kingdom [in Egypt]. **1930** *Proc. Brit. Acad.* XVI. 414 The 'new psychology' with its perhaps exaggerated stress on the hidden roots of our conscious convictions and purposes in the depths of our unconscious mind, had not yet brought all reasoning into suspicion of being merely the 'rationalization' of irrational impulses. **1930** C. H. GRATTAN *Critique of Humanism* 6 In attacking the New Humanism, then, I am not casting aspersions upon the attitude which more than any other will lead to the good life. **1930** K. BURKE in *Ibid.* 169 The men whom the New Humanists in America recognize as their colleagues in France are advocates of Catholicism. **1942** S. R. K. GLANVILLE *Legacy of Egypt* 105 His tomb..bore witness to a period when the art of the New Kingdom had..reached its highest point. **1957** *Antiquity & Survival* II. 122/1 One of the raids carried out by one of the New Kingdom Pharaohs along the Palestinian coast. **1958** *Time* 3 Feb. 48/2 (*heading*) The new mathematics. **1958** I. ADLER (*title*) The new mathematics. [*In the text referred to as* modern mathematics.] [**1960** J. HOHENBERG *Professional Journalist* xxiii. 322 The new journalism not only seeks to explain as well as to inform; it even dares to teach, to measure, to evaluate.] **1960** *Math. Teaching* July 21 The self-styled Public Relations Officer for the New Mathematics..declared himself the herald of New Mathematics. **1961** A. H. GARDINER *Egypt of the Pharaohs* iii. 40 It is a matter of some surprise that the much less pleasing sand-stone should have supplanted it [*sc.* limestone] from the New Kingdom (*c.* 1500 B.C.) onwards. **1963** J. S. BRUNER in Z. P. Dienes *Exper. Study of Math.-Learning* p. xii, In recent years there has been much misguided debate about the introduction of 'the new mathematics' into the schools. **1965** R. WELLEK *Hist. Mod. Criticism* IV. 59 His theory of commonplaces..is practically the same as that of the American new humanists. **1966** MEYER & HANLON (*title*) Fun with the new math. **1967** *Punch* 8 Mar. 332/1 If we realised..how much the New Maths derived from a foreign professor attending to the babbling of infants.. our suspicions would be even deeper and darker. **1969** *Antioch Rev.* Spring 24 Such truth doesn't belong to the new journalism; the mode is too uniformly blackish and self-accusatory. **1970** T. WOLFE in *Writer's Digest* Jan. 32/2 New Journalism is the use by people writing nonfiction of techniques which heretofore had been thought of as confined to the novel or to the short story. **1970** in *Ibid.* 33/2, I don't think Tom Wolfe started as a New Journalist; I don't think Gay Talese started as a New Journalist. I think they started as marvelously original writers. **1971** R. A. PARKER in J. R. Harris *Legacy of Egypt* (ed. 2) i. 22 A papyrus known as the Turin Canon..listed the kings of Egypt from the earliest dynasties down to the end of the Hyksos period, that is just prior to the New Kingdom. **1972** *Village Voice* (N.Y.) 1 June 22/3, I read several thousand words of the New Journalism's praise of itself. **1973** *Sci. Amer.* Apr. 101/1 The triumph of the 'new math' in the elementary schools of America during the past decade. **1973** H. WHITNEY in E. Choat *Preschool & Primary Math.* 9 After centuries with little change in the mathematics curriculum in schools, we find ourselves in an era of 'new maths', typified by the acquisition of concepts. **1976** *National Observer* (U.S.) 1 May 5/2 It was pretty awful stuff,.. representative..of a lot of 'new' journalism these days. **1977** *Rolling Stone* 7 Apr. 87/2 Thomas' new-journalism prose is often so slick as to give the impression he's told you all you need to know. **1984** *Christian Science Monitor* 4 Dec. 48/1 The new journalism..is no longer new. **1986** *Ibid.* 9 May 23/3 Write your novel and *call* it a memoir. What with historians writing like novelists and novelists writing like historians—and New Journalists writing like both—who can tell the difference?

b. Of things, places, or persons.

c **893** K. ÆLFRED *Oros.* IV. vi. 176 Com Hasterbal se niwa cyning of Cartainum. **971** *Blickl. Hom.* 163 Se niwa eorendel [wæs] Sanctus Iohannes. **1154** *O.E. Chron.* (Laud MS.) an. 1137 Martin abbot..brohte heom into þe neuuæ mynstre on S. Petres mæsse dæi. **1362** LANGL. *P. Pl.* A. v. 171 Clement þe Cobelere caste of his cloke, And atte newe Feire he leyde hire to sulle. *c* **1400** *Chron. R. Glouc.* (Rolls) 9220 (MS. B), Þe king..ladde him to þe newe worc, to a uayr castel & god. *c* **1470** *Gregory's Chron.* (Camden) 223 That fals Duke of Somersett .. stale owte of Walys .. towarde the Newecastelle. *c* **1489** CAXTON *Sonnes of Aymon* iii. 89 Whan the newe tyme shall be come. **1568** GRAFTON *Chron.* II. 167 In this yere was..ended the newe worke of the Church of Westminster, to the ende of the Quire. **1596** SHAKS. *1 Hen. IV*, II. i. 3 Charles waine is ouer the new Chimney. **1679** BEDLOE *Popish Plot* Ep. a j b, To fire the Water-Houses, and get the New River-Water stopt, if they can. **1774** GOLDSM. *Nat. Hist.* (1776) VII. 272 The remainder of the old aliment will be seen mixing with the new. **1826** in E. H. Barker *Parriana* (1828) I. 380 It was at the time when the new jail was being built. **1848** R. I. WILBERFORCE *Doctr. Incarnation* iii. (1852) 48 The new Adam was..the type and pattern of the renewed..creation.

(*b*) ***new entry***: a recruit; *collect.*, persons who have recently qualified or become eligible to do something. Also *transf.* and *attrib.*

1919 W. LANG *Sea Lawyer's Log* 5 Approaching him with diffidence our spokesman modestly announced us as 'new entries'—the Navy does not deal in 'recruits'. **1958** *Listener* 20 Nov. 812/1 If the electoral behaviour of the new entry [of voters] differs from that of those who have joined the great majority, there will be a swing one way or the other in consequence. **1962** *Economist* 18 Aug. 623/3 Competition seems to have prevented prices from ever going near their new-entry ceiling.

c. In names of cities or countries. (Without *the.*)

1500–20 DUNBAR *Poems* lxxxviii. 10 Citie that some tyme cleped was New Troy. **1535** COVERDALE *Rev.* xxi. 2 I Ihon sawe that holy cite newe Ierusalem come downe from God out of heauen. **1604** E. G[RIMSTONE] *D'Acosta's Hist. Indies* VII. ii. 498 Where now they have discovered a kingdome they call New Mexico. **1687** A. LOVELL tr. *Bergerac's Com. Hist.* 8 It was in New-France. **1719** W. WOOD *Surv. Trade* 280 They cannot Trade into the.. South West Coast of New-Spain. **1761** *Charac.* in *Ann. Reg.* 10/1 There are a greater number of noblesse in New France than in all the other colonies put together. **1833** *Penny Cycl.* I. 438/1 These concussions, which are very common about New Madrid, are felt..from New Orleans to the mouth of the Missouri.

d. In names of inhabitants of countries, provinces, etc. whose names include the word *New*. Cf. NEW ENGLANDER, NEWFOUNDLANDER, NEW MEXICAN, NEW ZEALANDER.

1874 C. M. YONGE *Life J. C. Patteson* I. viii. 214 The little New Caledonian remained at Taurarua. **1890** W. A. FOSTER in R. Reid *Canadian Style* (1973) ii. 40 All we need is a sentiment which shall make us feel not as Ontarions or Quebeckers, Nova Scotians or New Brunswickers, but as Canadians proud of our country as a whole. **1911** *Encycl. Brit.* XIX. 469/1 Many New Caledonians having black skins and woolly hair with Polynesian superiority of limb. **1957** *Ibid.* XVI. 696/2 The new-comers spoke languages of the Austronesian..family, which were in time adopted by most of the coastal New Guineans. **1973** *Country Life* 13 Sept. 745/1 Shell jewellery still valued for its magical powers by the New Guineans.

II. 6. a. Of recent origin or growth; that has not as yet existed long; †young. Also, of events or points in time: Recent, not long ago. Also used of colour names.

*c*825 *Vesp. Psalter* lxviii. 32 Licað gode ofer caelf niowe. *c*888 K. ÆLFRED *Boeth.* xxv., Ʒif.. heo blodes onbiriʒð, heo forʒit sona hire niwan taman. *c*1000 *Sax. Leechd.* II. 292 Ʒenim þone neowran wyrttruman, delf up. *c*1290 *St. Michael* 451 in *S.E. Leg.* I. 312 Ase man may bi þe Mone i-seo, þe ȝwyle heo is neowe riȝt. 13.. *Guy Warw.* (A.) 739 Bot on þatow [hast] newe dobing & art cleped kniȝt wiþ-outen lesing. ?*a*1366 CHAUCER *Rom. Rose* 856 She semede lyk a rose newe Of colour. *a*1400–50 *Alexander* 1460 For he had nite him a nerand noȝt bot o new time. 1507 *Justes May & June* 31 in Hazl. *E.P.P.* II. 122 At the felde ende was pyght.. A pauyllyon on the grasse fresshe and nue. 1523 LD. BERNERS *Froiss.* I. 587 Howe is it thus, in oure newe knyght-hode, that [etc.]? 1611 SHAKS. *Cymb.* II. iii. 46 The Exile of her Minion is too new, She hath not yet forgot him. 1785 PHILLIPS *Treat. Inland Nav.* 25 Rival Nations, especially the new States of America. 1845 T. MILNER *Gallery Nat.* 642 The new red sand stone and carboniferous systems in Leicestershire. 1865 TYLOR *Early Hist. Man.* 17 The two-handed or French alphabet, generally used in England, is of newer date. 1897 *Sears, Roebuck Catal.* 360/3 Colors for Artists... Neutral Tint, New Blue, Olive Lake. *Ibid.* 361/1 Water Colors... Dark Green, New Rose, Flesh, New Violet. 1927 [see DAWN *sb.* 1 b]. 1948 F. A. STAPLES *Watercolor Painting* iv. 49 *New Blue*, bright blue transparent.

b. Of articles of food or drink: Freshly made, produced, or grown; not yet old or stale; belonging to the fresh crop or growth.

*c*950 *Lindisf. Gosp.* Matt. ix. 17 Ne sendas win niwe in byttum aldum. 1362 LANGL. *P. Pl.* A. VII. 287 Til hit to heruest hiȝede þat newe corn com to chepynge. *a*1400 *Pistill of Susan* 99 With wardons winlich and walshe notes newe. *c*1440 *Promp. Parv.* 360/2 Nwe ale, *celia*. *c*1560 A. SCOTT *Poems* (S.T.S.) v. 31 Butter, new cheis, and beir in May. 1590 SHAKS. *Mids. N.* IV. i. 40, I haue a venturous Fairy, That shall.. fetch thee new Nuts. 1667 MILTON *P.L.* IX. 1008 As with new Wine intoxicated both They swim in mirth. *a*1756 ELIZA HEYWOOD *New Present* (1771) 133 Lay these into a stewpan with some new-milk. 1819 SHELLEY *Cyclops* 188 Is The new cheese pressed into the bulrush baskets? 1884 E. P. ROE in *Harper's Mag.* Aug. 452/2 New potatoes, dug for the first time that day.

c. Recently made; not yet used or worn; still unimpaired by use.

*c*950 *Lindisf. Gosp.* Matt. xxvii. 60 [He] sette ðæt in byrȝenne his niwe. *Ibid.* Luke v. 36 Ne aeniȝ þæt esceapa from woedo niuue onsendeð on ȝewedo ald. *c*1205 LAY. 7394 þeos [scipen] weoren al neowe stronge & wel itreowe. *a*1300 *Cursor M.* 20214 A neu smock scho did hir on. 1382 WYCLIF *Judg.* xvi. 11 If I were boundun with newe coordis, the whiche weren not ȝit in werk, I shal be feble. *c*1462 *Wright's Chaste Wife* 117 Felowe, where hadyst þou þis hatte That ys so feyre and newe? 1538– [see BROOM *sb.* 3]. 1655 FULLER *Ch. Hist.* II. v. §39 Though they swept clean at the first, as new Besomes. 1703 MOXON *Mech. Exerc.* 242 They choose the newest, to wit, that which is newly drawn out of the Kiln. 1775 JOHNSON *Let. to Mrs. Thrale* 22 May, The key is the newest of those two that have the wards channelled. 1837 DICKENS *Pickw.* xiv, A large bare-looking room, the furniture of which had no doubt been better when it was newer.

d. Now first used for some purpose.

1666 H. STUBBE *Mirac. Conformist* 19 The Brewers either pover the same or new in again to fill up the Barrel. 1693 EVELYN *De la Quint. Compl. Gard.* I. 27 [By] New Earth.. I mean Earth never having seen the Sun... It is certain that this New Soil possesses.. all the first Salt, which was given it at.. the Creation.

e. Recently inhabited or settled.

1817 J. BRADBURY *Trav. Amer.* 331 In the early settlements.. of new country, its progress in improvements is slow. 1823 J. F. COOPER *Pioneers* viii, It was a term in common use throughout the new parts of the state. 1871 DE VERE *Americanisms* 176 If he.. must go to what is called New Lands, he has to be careful in his selection.

f. Recently formed; *spec.* (see quot. 1958): said of deposits of ice or snow, esp. in polar regions.

1860 *Jrnl. R. Dublin Soc.* Jan. 374, I have before stated that we were frozen in on the 7th of September, 1857; the new ice then forming around us was of specific gravity 1·0235 (30°). 1918 FINCH & HAWKS *Water in Nature* vi. 126 Nansen has given us particulars of thickness attained by the ice of the Polar seas... 'This formation of new ice on the underside was owing to the layer of fresh water which, by reason of the surface thaw on the ice, now floated above the cold, salt water.' 1935 *Handbk. Weather, Currents & Ice, for Seamen* (Meteorol. Office) vii. 102 Between the Arctic Pack and the fast ice is a moving belt consisting partly of new ice and partly of broken ice from the pack and from the fast ice. 1958 ARMSTRONG & ROBERTS *Illustr. Ice Gloss.* 94 *New snow*, a recent snow deposit in which the original form of the ice crystals can be recognized; usually the daily new snowfall, measured in the morning. 1966 T. ARMSTRONG et al. *Illustr. Gloss. Snow & Ice* 28 *New ice*, a general term for floating ice recently formed. It includes frazil ice, grease ice, slush, shuga, ice rind, milas and pancake ice.

7. Having or retaining the qualities of a fresh or recent thing; showing no sign of decline or decay. In later use esp. *ever new*.

*c*1220 *Bestiary* 76 Ðer he wurdeð heil & sund, & cumeð ut al newe. *c*1250 *Hymn to Virgin* in *Trin. Coll. Hom.* App. 257 þi loue is euer iliche neowe. *a*1300 CURSOR M. 16557 þis tre.. þai fand.. als neu and fress als it on stouen ware. *c*1330 R. BRUNNE *Chron. Wace* (Rolls) 8688 Ʒour mercy schal hem be newe. 1496 *Fysshynge w. Angle* (1883) 32 As longe as they ben quycke & newe they ben fyne. 1610 SHAKS. *Temp.* II. ii. 28 A very ancient and fish-like smell; a kind of not of the newest poore-Iohn. 1626 BACON *Sylva* (J.), Men, after long emaciating diets, wax plump, fat, and almost new. 1667 MILTON *P.L.* v. 19 Heav'ns last best gift, my ever new delight. 1711 POPE *Temp. Fame* 51 These ever new, nor subject to decays, Spread, and grow brighter. 1781 COWPER *Charity* 326 All.. to pursue Still prompt him, with a pleasure always new. 1877 M. ARNOLD *Switzerland, Parting*, To thee only God granted A heart ever new.

8. a. Having but recently come into a certain state, position, or relationship. Cf. *New Australian* (AUSTRALIAN *sb.* 2 b).

new chum: see CHUM *sb.*[1]

*c*900 tr. *Bæda's Hist.* III. xxii. (Schipper) 295 Swa swiþe swa þa niwan cristenan ða ȝyt hit niman mihton. 1387 TREVISA *Higden* (Rolls) VII. 263 As he þat was a newe man.. and knewe nouȝt þe customs and þe usages of Engelond. 1422 tr. *Secreta Secret., Priv. Priv.* 180 So is hit.. of new officers, that like ben to newe hungri flies. *c*1489 CAXTON *Sonnes of Aymon* ii. 65 So departed the newe knyghtes. *a*1533 LD. BERNERS *Huon* lxii. 217 The new brydes lay togyther in grete pleasure all that nyght. 1590 SIR J. SMYTH *Disc. Weapons* 47 b, The shot of them.. scare newe soldiers and nouices of warre. 1665 J. WEBB *Stone-Heng* (1725) 63 The Evidence of our Claim shall be well attested, not by New-men, but such as.. speak of their own Knowledge. 1714 MANDEVILLE *Fable Bees* (1723) 314 If such a New-Beginner has but a little Pride.. he is soon mortify'd in the Vestry. 1807 SOUTHEY *Lett. from England* II. xxix. 27 The heretical sects in this country... form a curious list! Arminians, Socinians, Baxterians, Presbyterians, New Americans, Sabellians, [etc.]. 1849 MACAULAY *Hist. Eng.* vi. II. 20 James's parliament contained a most unusual proportion of new members. *a*1860 ALB. SMITH *Med. Student* (1861) 14 The new man does not enter much into society. 1907 H. A. KENNEDY (*title*) New Canada and the New Canadians. 1919 *Ladies' Home Jrnl.* Sept. 35 The New Americans. 1939 J. M. GIBBON *Canadian Mosaic* ix. 231 Anthology of verse written by New Canadians. 1940 *Chatelaine* Jan. 40/1 Native-born and new Canadians work together for the nation's good. 1965 *Listener* 10 June 860/2 The idealist who saw his vision of the New Man shattered by harsh reality. 1970 *Guardian* 14 Apr. 11/5 The machines.. are obviously the New Men, the ultimate revolutionaries. 1970 *Toronto Daily Star* 24 Sept. 7/6 If New Canadians prefer to learn English from Eaton's or Simpson's catalogue, there must be something wrong?

b. Const. *to* a thing.

1697 DRYDEN *Virg. Georg.* IV. 30 New to the Pleasures of their native Spring. 1725 POPE *Odyss.* IV. 861 Twelve young mules.. New to the plough, unpractis'd in the trace. 1853 'C. BEDE' *Verdant Green* xi, Mr. Verdant Green was quite new to round bowling. 1884 *Times* (weekly ed.) 10 Oct. 3/3 The Government was new to office.

c. Fresh *from* some place, state, or operation.

1700 DRYDEN *To Duchess of Ormond* 102 Nor dare we trust so soft a messenger, New from her sickness, to that northern air. 1833 TENNYSON *Dream Fair Wom.* 60 Branches fledged with clearest green, New from its silken sheath. 1896 *Pall Mall Mag.* Nov. 316 It was a Thursday and I was new from the razor.

d. spec. ***new rich***: in recent use, common as a translation of the French *nouveaux riches*, persons who have recently acquired wealth. Also as *adj.* Hence ***new poor***, recently impoverished persons; ***new money***, a fortune recently acquired, funds recently raised; so by metonymy, the new rich.

1886 *Harper's Mag.* Oct. 795/2 There are.. the sons of the 'new rich' who are like men drunk with new wine. 1920 *Punch* 6 Oct. 279 *Exhausted War Profiteer*. 'Deer forests for the 'idle rich' be blowed! The 'new poor' can 'ave 'em for me.' 1923 'B. M. BOWER' *Parowan Bonanza* xiii. 157 You've never seen *me* look New-rich, have you, Bill? 1926 A. BENNETT *Lord Raingo* I. xxxv. 165 He had demonstrated publicly.. that he belonged to the type of the new rich. 1942 H. C. BAILEY *Dead Man's Shoes* x. 46 Not a drop of fizz for you. I am the new poor and proud of the title. 1958 *New Statesman* 23 Aug. 222/2 How typical is his new-rich business man, seen leaving an elaborate Tudoresque house.. who seemed genuinely to feel no animosity either towards the class to which his father, a jobbing gardener, had belonged or towards the class in which, economically at least, he now finds himself. 1961 'W. HAGGARD' *Arena* iii. 25 They had most of the new money: all the new men used them, the takeover boys, the property men. 1967 M. PROCTER *Exercise Hoodwink* xvii. 119 He moves with a pricey crowd, though I wouldn't call 'em classy. Small business people. New money. 1969 *Triumph* (U.S.) Mar. 25/1 The new poor, the misplaced workers, who are a by-product of our technology. 1970 *Daily Tel.* 2 June 20/3 'New money' raised in the United Kingdom during May by the issue of marketable securities was £32 million. 1973 R. LUDLUM *Matlock Paper* xvi. 139 The blooded first families.. migrated just a little west to avoid the new rich. 1975 *Daily Tel.* 30 Aug. 13/4 The amount of new money raised in August at £120·1 million was the lowest since last January.

9. That has just recently risen to distinction or notice; not belonging to a noted family.

1611 B. JONSON *Catiline* III. i, A new man, as I am styled in Rome, Whom you have dignified. 1670 G. H. *Hist. Cardinals* II. II. 156 Lorenzo Raggi.. is descended of a new Family in Genoa. 1709 SWIFT *Adv. Relig.* Wks. 1755 II. I. 106 Nine in ten.. are younger brothers, or new men. 1741 MIDDLETON *Cicero* (1742) I. i. 4 A New Man, not that his Family was new or ignoble. 1849 MACAULAY *Hist. Eng.* i. I. 38 There were new men who bore the highest titles. 1890 *Spectator* 25 Jan., A family that is really 'new' is generally delighted to be mistaken for an old family. 1903 MRS. H. WARD *Lady Rose's Daughter* xiv. 230 He was a good deal of a politician, himself a 'new man', and on the side of 'new men'. 1936 M. MITCHELL *Gone with Wind* iii. 52 Gerald was a 'new man', despite his nearly ten years' residence. 1943 D. W. BROGAN *English People* iii. 81 Lord Reading was the first Marquess of Reading, a 'new man'. 1962 *Spectator* 30 Mar. 392 It strikes fear, not into the manual worker so much as into the hearts of the new men.

III. 10. *Comb.* **a.** ***new-old***, both new and old through revival, repair, or imitation. Also, †***new-new***, very new.

1592 G. HARVEY *Four Lett.* iv. Wks. (Grosart) I. 233 Our new-new writers, the Loadstones of the Presse. 1662 STILLINGFL. *Orig. Sacræ* I. vi. §5 Thus Annius puts a good face on his new-old Authors. 1798 CHARLOTTE SMITH *Yng. Philos.* II. 34 Hopes were given my father that Lord and Lady Daventry would.. stay a fortnight with him at his new-old castle. 1824 MISS MITFORD *Village* Ser. I. (1863) 229 The same pot.. with which he furbished up our new-old pony-chaise. 1876 GEO. ELIOT *Dan. Der.* xxxv, As for most of your new-old building [etc.]. 1926 D. H. LAWRENCE *Plumed Serpent* xvii. 279 They seized upon the new-old thrill, with a certain fear, and joy, and relief. 1932 H. CRANE *Let.* 31 Mar. (1965) 405 An environment not half so strange and distractingly new-old curious as this. 1961 *Guardian* 14 June 10/6 These new-old problems that face our daughters.

b. With substantives, forming attributive compounds, as ***new-charter man***, etc. ***new-face*** = *modern-face(d)* adjs. (MODERN *a.* 2 g); ***new time***: in the Stock Exchange: of dealings, having the settlement postponed to the next settling-day; of prices, quoted for the next settling-day before the previous settlement is completed; also in more general contexts; ***new wheat disease***: a pyelonephritis affecting young poultry, possibly caused by a virus; also called *blue comb (disease)* (BLUE *a.* 13) or *pullet disease* (PULLET 3).

Some of these expressions also occur in non-*attrib.* contexts.

1684 LUTTRELL *Brief Rel.* (1857) I. 307 A contest between the old charter men and the *new charter men. 1900 H. HART *Cent. Typogr.* 120 These are the first examples of what are called nowadays '*new-face' types. 1683 MOXON *Mech. Exerc., Printing* 37 There are two sorts of Presses in use, viz. the old fashion and the *new fashion. 1729 SWIFT *Direct. Serv., Footman* Wks. 1751 XIV. 45 Learn all the new-fashion Words. 1899 S. BUTLER *Shaks. Sonn.* 97 A sub-didactic, *new-leaf, good-resolution tone. 1898 *Allbutt's Syst. Med.* V. 756 Bouillaud classified pericardial friction sounds as grazing, *new leather sound, and grating. 1685 DRYDEN *Theocritus* i. Misc. II. 358 A dainty Kid, and a large *New-milk Cheese. *a*1910 'MARK TWAIN' *Autobiogr.* (1924) I. 198 Any other old-time or *new-time palace on the continent of Europe. 1912 *Century Mag.* Jan. 476 Open Letters... On the New-time Negro. 1922 New-time [see CARRY-OVER]. 1927 *Daily Express* 27 Sept. 101/1 The price for 'new time' was about 15s. 6d., compared with a making up price of 14s. *Ibid.* 10/3 The 'new time' price at one time touched the new record of 4½. 1964 *Financial Times* 25 Feb. 17/1 First Dealings... 'New time' dealings may take place two business days earlier. 1887 *Pall Mall G.* 1 Jan. 2/1 All naval Powers have provided their ships with.. *new-type guns. 1950 *New wheat disease [see *blue comb (disease)* s.v. BLUE *a.* 13]. 1957 L. ROBINSON *Mod. Poultry Husbandry* (ed. 4) xx. 677 Since outbreaks usually occur in late summer and autumn, the disease has been called 'New Wheat disease'. There is no evidence, however, that new wheat is responsible. 1847 TENNYSON *Princ.* IV. 466 Clamour grew As of a *new-world Babel. 1866 HOWELLS *Venet. Life* xi. 169, I doubt if even these would save them from the new-world pigs. 1886 W. J. TUCKER *E. Europe* 141 Hair-brained, new-world notions of independence.

c. In derivatives of the type ***new-æraist***, ***new-birthite***, ***new-schoolish***, etc.

1872 BAGEHOT *Physics & Pol.* (1876) 193 *New æraists, who want their new æra started forthwith. 1810 COLERIDGE in *Lit. Rem.* (1839) IV. 342 The very term by which the German *New-Birthites express it is enough to give one goose-flesh. 1844 T. PARKER in Weiss *Life & Corr.* I. 244 Here they concoct one of the best journals in Germany. It is Hegelian and *new-schoolish of course. 1838 JACKSON tr. *Krummacher's Elisha* ix. 201 Many other things are *New Testamental and remind us of the Gospel. 1851 LOWELL *Lett.* I. 212 Genoa,—a very fit place for us. *New-Worlders to land at. 1893 PATMORE *Religio Poetæ* 206 Perhaps the unkindest hit in her book is that in which she laughs at the *New-Worldling.

d. ***new style***: in Chronology, see STYLE *sb.* 27; gen., forming attributive compounds.

1914 'I. HAY' *Lighter Side School Life* vii. 193 The new-style parent breaks right away from tradition—kicks over the traces, in fact. 1937 B. H. L. HART *Europe in Arms* iii. 26 These new-style formations were not shown to the foreign officers and military publicists. 1961 *Times* 18 May 19/4 The new-style Arab. 1965 *New Statesman* 7 May 707/2 Such a department, like the rest of a new-style Transport House, would have to have a long-term career structure.

B. *absol.* or as *sb.*

1. That which is new.

*c*888 K. ÆLFRED *Boeth.* vii. §2 Wenst þu þæt hit hwæt niwes sie..? *a*900 WÆRFERTH tr. *Gregory's Dial.* 4 Ʒelamp þe aht niwes [*v.r.* æniȝ þing niwes]? *c*1000 *Ags. Gosp.* Luke v. 36 Elles þæt niwe slit, & se niwa scyp ne hylpð þam eal-dan. *c*1250 *Gen. & Ex.* 250 Ðis dai was forð in reste wrogt, Ilc kinde newes ear was brog[t]. 13.. *Gaw. & Gr. Knt.* 1407 [They agreed] hor cheuysaunce to chaunge, What newez so þay nome, at naȝt quen þay metten.

1601 WEEVER *Mirr. Mart.* A 3 b, Man's memorie, with new, forgets the old; One tale is good, untill anothers told. 1819 SHELLEY *Peter Bell 3rd* v. ii, All things he seemed to understand, Of old or new. 1875 WHITNEY *Life Lang.* 266 The actual creation of the new in speech is.. very rare. 1881 JOWETT *Thucyd.* I. 45 As in the arts, so also in politics, the new must always prevail over the old.

b. A new thing. *rare.*

*c*1470 HARDING *Chron.* LXXXVIII. xi, We wyll not chaunge for your doctrine ne lore, There shall no newe emong vs been abused. 1887 MEREDITH *Ballads & P.* 147 An unborn New, To make the plagues afflicting us things past.

2. ***the new of the moon***, the time at which the moon is new (see NEW MOON). Now *rare.*

1398 TREVISA *Barth. De P.R.* v. lviii. (Bodl. MS.), Greete scarsete þerof in þe new of þe mone. 1523 FITZHERB. *Husb.* §68 Whether it were gette in the newe of the mone or in the olde of the mone. 1572 BOSSEWELL *Armorie* II. 48 Apes.. are merye, and reioice at the newe of the moone. 1610 MARKHAM *Masterp.* II. civ. 388 Shooe him in the new of the moone. 1682 *Riders Brit. Merlin* Jan., Set all kind of.. Fruit-trees in the New of the Moon. 1728 PEMBERTON *Newton's Philos.* 200 The moon would be neare the earth at the new and full, than in the quarters. 1805 in Kittredge *Old*

Farmer's Almanack (1904) 313 Apple trees..should be set out in the new of the moon.

†**3. a.** *for, of* or *on the new*, anew, afresh. *Obs.*

c **1395** *Plowman's T.* 926 Gaye gownes, That mot be shape for the newe. **1399** LANGL. *Rich. Redeles* III. 161 Yt was y-sent sone to shape of the newe. **1450** *Paston Lett.* I. 172, I pray you that the said maters may be called uppon of the new. **1535** COVERDALE *2 Sam.* xxiv. 1 The Lorde was wrothfully displeased of yᵉ new agaynst Israel.

†**b.** *on the new*, something novel. *Obs. rare*⁻¹.

c **1485** *Digby Plays* (1882) I. 338 Thu make me a knyght, that were on the newe!

4. of new. †**a.** Of late, recently; newly. *Obs.*

1375 BARBOUR *Bruce* XIV. 92 The castell wele wes stuffit then Of-new with wittale and vith men. *c* **1386** CHAUCER *Clerk's T.* 882 Ther can no man..ben half so trewe As wommen been, but it be falle of-newe. *c* **1470** HENRY *Wallace* VIII. 585 The men he tuk, that come till hym off new, Gydys to be. **1579** FENTON *Guicciard.* 736 Regiments of Italians leavyed of newe. **1609** SKENE *Reg. Maj.* I. 118b, Qvha is made of new the Kings Burges..sall sweare to be..trew to the King. **1669** R. MONTAGU in *Buccleuch MSS.* (Hist. MSS. Comm.) I. 444 The Suisses..are of new strictlier engaged, and more in the French interest than ever. **1728** [see ANEW *adv.* 3].

b. Afresh, over again. Now *rare*.

Also rarely *on new*: see ANEW *adv.* 1 γ.

1413 *Pilgr. Sowle* (Caxton) I. xvi. (1859) 17 Here ne may ther none aduocate be procured of newe. **1490** CAXTON *Eneydos* lv. 151 The chyeff capytaynes..beganne the medle and the crye of newe. **1542** UDALL *Erasm. Apoph.* 67 By this meanes thei wer reconciled of newe. **1651** tr. *De-las-Coveras' Don Fenise* 270 He was much satisfied, and of new obliged to love me. *a* **1715** BURNET *Own Time* I. (1724) I. 6 Lasting feuds and animosities, which upon every turn are apt to ferment and to break out of new. **1752** J. LOUTHIAN *Form of Process* (ed. 2) 79 A Warrant obtained for imprisoning him of new. **1827** SCOTT *Napoleon* lxix, His attention was of new summoned. **1865** [see ANEW *adv.* 1 α].

†**c.** By new arrangement, appointment, etc.; with some change or alteration. *Obs.*

c **1400** *Rom. Rose* 5169 Either must I love or hate. And if I hate men of newe [etc.]. **1485** *Rolls of Parlt.* VI. 304/1 Suche Assignements as oure said Soveraine Lord shall of newe make and appointe. **1523** LD. BERNERS *Froiss.* I. clxi. 197 This ordynaunce they had made of newe, that the frenchmen knewe nat of. *c* **1543–82** [see ANEW *adv.* 4]. **1658** W. BURTON *Itin. Anton.* 164 Then it was of new called Augusta.

†**d.** Shortly, soon. *Obs. rare*⁻¹.

c **1500** *Lancelot* 955 [G]if me leif to ga To the assemble, wich sal be of new.

5. A naval cadet during his first term in a training-ship.

1909 J. R. WARE *Passing Eng.* 181/2 *New* (*Britannia training ship*), fresh arrival, last addition. Used in the plural. **1914** 'BARTIMEUS' *Naval Occasions* ix. 63 The path of the 'New' in those days was by no means strewn with roses. **1953** J. MASEFIELD *Conway* (rev. ed.) IV. 224 The 'News' very rarely ventured into the upper room. **1962** GRANVILLE *Dict. Sailors' Slang* 81/1 *New!*, HMS *Britannia's* equivalent of the public school's 'Fag!'

†**new**, *v. Obs.* Forms: 1–2 niwian, (1 neowian), 3 niwe; 4–6 newe, (4 neu, 5 neewe, nwyn, *Sc.* nev), 5–6 new. [OE. *níwian*, f. *níwe* NEW *a.*, = MDu. *nuwen* (Du. *-nieuwen*), OS. *niwian* (*nigean*), MLG. *nygen*, OHG. *niwôn* (MHG. *niuwen*, *niwen*, G. *-neuen*), ON. (*endr*)*nýja*, Goth. (*ana*)*niujan*.]

1. *trans.* To renew, to make new.

Common in 14–15th c. in a variety of contexts.

a **900** CYNEWULF *Elene* 940 (Gr.), Ne þearft ðu swa swiðe ..sar niwiᵹan & sæce ræran. *c* **1000** *Sax. Leechd.* I. 192 Swa þæt ðu þeah æᵹhwylce dæᵹ þone drenc niwie. *a* **1122** *O.E. Chron.* (Laud MS.) an. 1064 He niwade þær Cnutes laᵹe. *c* **1220** *Bestiary* 55 Kiðen i wille ðe ernes kinde,..wu he neweð his ȝuðhede. *a* **1300** *Cursor M.* 23399 He sal neu vr bodis slike, þai sal be till his aun like. *c* **1380** WYCLIF *Sel. Wks.* I. 49 Al þe chirche of men and aungels is newid bi þe Incarnacioun. *a* **1450** MYRC 642 Thow moste chawnge þyn oyle also þat þey mowe be newed bo. **1503** in *Trans. Roy. Hist. Soc.* (1902) 153 The seyd Walter newed a pond of his. *a* **1555** HUTCHINSON *Three Serm.* ii. Wks. (Parker Soc.) 251 The sacraments also be newed and changed.

refl. *c* **1220** *Bestiary* 123 Neddre is te name: ðus he him neweð.

2. *intr.* To become new again, renew itself.

a **1300** *Cursor M.* 20356 Now me neus al mi wa. **13..** *Propr. Sanct.* (Vernon MS.) in Herrig *Archiv* LXXXI. 83/2 But greine of whete in eorþe dye, hit schal not newe. *c* **1400** tr. *Secreta Secret., Gov. Lordsh.* 73 Veyr ys hoot and moyst, ..And þerynne newys þe blood. *a* **1500** *Chaucer's Dreme* C.'s Wks. (1561) 242 Euery day her beautie newed.

b. Used of the yearly renewal of produce or increase of stock.

a **1400** *Minor Poems fr. Vernon MS.* xxxvii. 524 [Let a man] of al þat neweþ him be ȝere do his tiþinge. *c* **1460** *Towneley Myst.* vi. 57 Of all that newes me rightwys tend shall I gif the. **1496** *Festial* (W. de W.) Sentence General, Tythes..of al maner bestis that are newyng. *Ibid.*, Of hay also often as it newes.

c. To fall (constantly) to (one).

1399 LANGL. *Rich. Redeles* IV. 6 Ne for-feyturis fele þat felle in his daies, Ne þe nownagis þat newed him euere.

Hence †**newed** *ppl. a. Obs. rare.*

a **1440** *Found. St. Bartholomew's* (E.E.T.S.) 31 Of them that runne to religione with an ynwarde newydde deuocyone.

new (njuː), *adv.* Forms: 1 niwe, 3–6 newe, (5 neewe), 4 neu, 5– new. [OE. *níwe*, f. the adj.]

†**I.** In ordinary adverbial uses. Now *Obs.*

1. Newly, recently, lately.

971 *Blickl. Hom.* 247 Forþon þe we niwe syndon to þissum ᵹeleafan ᵹedon. **1307** *Elegy Edw. I*, i, Herkneth to my song, Of duel that Deth hath diht us newe. *c* **1386** CHAUCER *Merch. T.* 582 His berd..sharp as brere, For he was shave al newe in his manere. *c* **1440** *Alph. Tales* 202 He saw a pope at hight Benett, att wold new be dede. *c* **1470** HENRY *Wallace* VI. 134 'Quhy, schir', he said, 'come yhe nocht new our se?' **1562** HEYWOOD *Prov. & Epigr.* (1874) 92 A man from a fever recovered new His greedy appetite could not eschew. **1595** SHAKS. *John* III. i. 233 Euen before this truce, but new before.

2. a. Anew, afresh, over again.

1297 R. GLOUC. (Rolls) 3029 Gode lawes þat were aleyd, nywe he let make. *a* **1300** *Cursor M.* 26921 Sin þis sinn was neuer forgiuen, nedinges most it neu be scriuen. *c* **1385** CHAUCER *L.G.W.* Prol. 103 My bisy goost, that thursteth alwey newe To seen this flour. *c* **1430** *Pol. Rel. & L. Poems* (1903) 195 þou haste slayn þi lord, And euery day þou woundist me newe. *c* **1470** HENRY *Wallace* XI. 1224 His fatell hour I will nocht fenȝe new. **1523** FITZHERB. *Husb.* §126 They must nedes be dryuen newe and hardened agayne. **1599** SHAKS. *Hen. V*, IV. i. 311, I Richards body haue interred new. **1615** BEDWELL *Moham. Impost.* I. §18 This statute was commanded new againe.

b. *new and new*, ever anew, over and over.

c **1374** CHAUCER *Troylus* III. 116 Pandare weep..And poked ever his nece newe and newe. *c* **1430** *Syr Gener.* (Roxb.) 638 Hir sorow encresed new and new. *a* **1529** SKELTON *P. Sparowe* 896 She floryssheth new and new In bewte and vertew. *a* **1542** WYATT *Poet. Wks.* (1858) 191 Chastisings..that new and new begin With thousand fears the heart to strain and bind.

II. Preceding, and closely connected (in later use hyphened) with, the qualified word.

3. With pa. pples. used attributively, in the sense of 'Newly, recently, freshly'.

Common only after 1550, and esp. after Shakespeare, who has about a score of examples, as *new-crowned*, *-dated*, *-delivered*, *-enkindled*, *-healed*, etc. In later use the number of such combs. is practically unlimited; a large collection from various writers is given in Jodrell's dictionary. Those which have most frequently been employed will be found here in their alphabetical places as main words.

In OE. a few combs. of this type appear with the bare adj. stem *níw-*, *niᵹ-*, *ní-*, as *níwtyrwyd* new-tarred, *ní*(*w*)*cealct* new-chalked, *niᵹbacen*, new-baked; with these compare the numerous ON. forms in *ný-*, as *nýfundiun*, *-gefinn*, *-tekinn*, etc.

a. With the pa. pples. of trans. verbs, as ***new-accepted***, ***-adopted***, ***-baked***, ***-bought***, ***-crowned***, ***-cut***, ***-dated***, ***-dropped***, ***-engendered***, ***-fulfilled***, ***-gnarled***, ***nurtured***, ***-scored***, ***-skeined***, ***-washed***, etc.

c **1375** *Sc. Leg. Saints* xl. (*Ninian*) 406 Caile & leikis faire ..cummyne of nev sawine seide. **1501** DOUGLAS *Pal. Hon.* Prol. vii, The purgit air with new engendrit heit. **1515** BARCLAY *Egloges* IV, Suche other newe forged Muses nine. **1570** T. NORTON tr. *Nowel's Catech.* (1853) 114 Other-wise we should daily forge ourselves new-feigned religions. **1620** VENNER *Via Recta* vii. 115 The ripe and new-gathered Mulberries. **1684** T. BURNET *The. Earth* I. 263 When he came to act upon this new-erected stage. **1726** POPE *Odyss.* XVII. 66 My new-accepted guest I haste to find. **1775** S. J. PRATT *Liberal Opin.* xxvii. (1783) I. 177 Discovering a fat new-shorn pate. **1793** W. BLAKE *Visions Daughters Albion* in *Compl. Writings* (1972) 191 The new wash'd lamb ting'd with the village smoke, & the bright swan. **1800** WORDSW. *Brothers* 358 He had gone forth among the new-dropped lambs. **1821** BYRON *Don Juan* V. clvi. 289 The new-bought virgin, made her blush and shake. **1825** J. NICHOLSON *Operat. Mechanic* 766 A mixture of new-slaked lime with beer. **1851** H. MELVILLE *Whale* xi, Illuminated by the flame of the new-lit lamp. **1865** G. M. HOPKINS *Poems* (1967) 21 New-dated from the terms that reappear, More sweet-familiar grows my love to thee. **1877** —— *Ibid.* 68, I hear the lark ascend, His rash-fresh re-winded new-skeinèd score In crisps of curl off wild winch whirl. **1889** W. B. YEATS *Wanderings of Oisin* III. 35 Whiter than new-washed fleece. **1897** MARY KINGSLEY *W. Africa* 32 You can't want new-dug graves daily. **1909** KIPLING *Actions & Reactions* 51 Over their heads in the branches Of their new-bought ancient trees. **1913** —— *Songs from Books* 43 My new-cut ashlar takes the light. **1918** E. SITWELL *Clown's Houses* 14 In new-washed air. **1922** JOYCE *Ulysses* 155 Steam of newbaked jampuffs. **1934** E. BLUNDEN *Choice or Chance* 37 Yet one I knew who most of all seemed sent Among earth's flowers for new-fulfilled content. **1935** W. EMPSON *Poems* 27 With plump or splash on the new-nurtured field To Reason's arm they proper homage yield. **1942** *R.A.F. Jrnl.* 3 Oct. 7 The wheels kicking up a frenzied cloud of new-cut grass. **1943** L. B. LYON *Evening in Stepney* 20 A script of blackening girders, New-scored by old despair. **1948** E. POUND *Pisan Cantos* (1949) lxxx. 107 Nor is the white bud Time's inquisitor Probing to know if its new-gnarled root Twists from York's head or belly of Lancaster. *a* **1963** C. S. LEWIS *Poems* (1964) 69 A seminal breeze from the far side Calls to their new-crowned race.

b. With the pa. pples. of intrans. verbs, as ***new-awakened***, ***-bloomed***, ***-calved***, ***-departed***, ***-flown***, ***-kerned***, ***-landed***, etc. Also †***new-***(***up***)***start***.

a **1548** HALL *Chron., Edw. IV*, 192 The husbandman ought first to tast of the new growen frute. **1570** FOXE *A. & M.* (ed. 2) 17/2 The lyke..reason of late renued by a certayne newe start Englysh Clarke. **1618** *Barnevelt's Apol.* Ded. A 2 The tottering and extreme ruine of the new vpstart Arminians. *a* **1649** DRUMM. OF HAWTH. *Poems* Wks. (1711) 2 The locks of amber Of new bloom'd sicamores. *a* **1700** KEN *Hymnotheo* Poet. Wks. 1721 III. 44 Bright Gabriel new-departed Souls collects. **1775** G. WHITE *Selborne* xliii, To make sad havock..among the new-flown swallows. **1785** BURNS *2nd Ep. to J. Lapraik* i, Whyle new-ca'd kye rowte at the stake. **1819** SHELLEY *Prometh. Unb.* II. i. 148 The white dew on the new-bladed grass. **1846** PROWETT *Prometh. Bound* 42 To cower beneath These new-grown gods. **1851** H. MELVILLE *Moby Dick* I. xxiii. 169 One Bulkington was spoken of, a new-landed mariner, encountered in New Bedford. **1884** T. SPEEDY *Sport Highl.* vii. 80 Clean, new-run sea-trout are often caught..with small fly. **1908** HARDY *Dynasts* III. VII. ii. 486 The peaceful produce of the grange, ..new-kerned apples, hairy gooseberries green. **1918** E. SITWELL *Clown's Houses* 7 The new-awakened flower-strange hair.

4. Similarly with pa. pples. (and some adjs.) used predicatively, or placed after the noun, as ***new-awakened***, ***-crushed***, ***-desired***, etc.

Shakespeare has about a dozen examples of this use: as *new-adopted*, *-begot*, *-burned*, etc.

a **1340** HAMPOLE *Psalter* Cant. 516 Sere errours..new broght vp thorgh entysynge of þe deuyll. *c* **1375** *Sc. Leg. Saints* xlix. (*Thecla*) 302 þane fand scho thamyrum nev ded. *c* **1386** CHAUCER *Clerk's Prol.* 3 Ye ryde as coy and stille, as dooth a mayde Were newe spoused. *c* **1400** MAUNDEV. (Roxb.) xxxi. 140 þai ware..so fresch as þai had bene euen new deed. *c* **1440** *Alph. Tales* 77 He broght þaim owder a swyne or a schepe new slayn. **1480** *Bury Wills* (Camden) 65 The colage of preestes newe bildid within the town of Bury. **1581** PETTIE tr. *Guazzo's Civ. Conv.* I. (1586) 1b, He.. found him at the table, but new dined. **1588** J. UDALL *Diotrephes* (Arb.) 31 He is but newe gone out of the gate. **1600** FAIRFAX *Tasso* XX. xlvi, Like a man new-turn'd to marble stone. **1663** GERBIER *Counsel* 28 Stone..new taken out of the Quarry. **1684** T. BURNET *The. Earth* I. 289 Every hypothesis that is new-propos'd and untri'd. *a* **1711** KEN *Hymnarium* Wks. 1721 II. 117 Allotting Mansions ev'ry Day, For all new-stript of Clay. **1742** YOUNG *Nt. Th.* IX. 1301 As new-awak'd, I lift A more enlighten'd eye. **1791** COWPER *Iliad* II. 53 His fleecy vest New-woven he put on. **1817** KEATS *I stood tiptoe* 8 The clouds were pure and white as flocks new shorn. **1859** TENNYSON *Geraint & Enid* 862 As sullen as a beast new-caged. **1870** BRYANT *Iliad* II. xv. 101 The horse-hair crest New-tinged with purple. **1878** O. WILDE *Ravenna* 13 Thou hast not drunk this wine From grapes new-crushed. **1917** D. H. LAWRENCE *Look! We have come Through!* 131 Now here was I, new-awakened. **1959** BLUNDEN *Hong Kong House*, Except when they, of one tree tired Into another new-desired Over the lawn and scattered playthings chose to glide.

5. a. With pa. pples. used predicatively in the sense of 'Anew, afresh'.

Common in, and after, Shakespeare. Cotgrave uses such forms to render a number of French pa. pples. in *re-*, as '*reaplani*, new-levelled'.

a **1300** *Cursor M.* 20215 Quen scho was schod and neu clad, To ihesu crist a bone scho badde. ?**1370** *Robt. Cicyle* 54 Thy crowne schalle be newe schorne. **1470–85** MALORY *Arthur* XIII. xvii. 636 Syr Percyuale..knewe hym not, for he was newe desguysed. **1485** *Rutland Papers* (Camden) 23 The King, thus unaraied,..shalbe by the said Chamberlayn new arraied. *a* **1533** LD. BERNERS *Huon* xxxvi. 113 A M. horses let to be new shode. **1581** J. BELL *Haddon's Answ. Osor.* 415 Such..must be newskowred in the Popes Purgatory. **1587** GOLDING *De Mornay* xvii. (1592) 274 To be as it were newfurbished, to scoure of the great Rust. **1641** SIR E. DERING *Sp. on Relig.* xi. 38 That was revised, and new senced by us. **1663** HEATH *Flagellum* (1672) 112 The same day..he was new proclaimed. **1706** POPE *Let. to Wycherley* 10 Apr., Some [verses]..I have entirely new express'd. **1733** P. LINDSAY *Interest Scot.* 195 They put a-shore their Nets to be repair'd and new-barkt. **1802–12** BENTHAM *Ration. Judic. Evid.* (1827) II. 351 The bill..comes back to be new tinkered up by the same hand. **1847** MRS. CARLYLE *Lett.* I. 394 When the parlour is new-papered. **1859** LD. LYTTON *Wanderer* (ed. 2) 180 The streets are new-peopled: the morning is bright.

b. Placed after a noun or pronoun.

[**1590** SPENSER *F.Q.* I. vi. 44 Then backe to fight againe, new breathed and entire.] **1593** SHAKS. *Rich. II*, II. i. 31 Me thinkes I am a Prophet new inspir'd. **1636** MASSINGER *Bashful Lover* v. i, Here he comes, With his officers, new-rigged. *a* **1661** FULLER *Worthies* (1840) II. 412 So many houses daily, new-dipt, assume to themselves new names. **1705** ADDISON *Italy* Wks. 1721 II. 11 A St. Bartholomew, new-flead, with his skin hanging over his shoulders. **1767** S. PATERSON *Another Trav.* I. 288 The self-same picture, new modified. **1796** BURNEY *Mem. Metastasio* II. 91 You will receive four of my first dramas, new written. **1827** KEBLE *Chr. Y., Burial Dead*, Then cheerly to your work again With hearts new-brac'd and set. **1897** W. WATSON in *Westm. Gaz.* 16 July 3/1 Behold him Rise, new-fanged.

6. a. With active forms of transitive verbs, in the same sense.

Also freq. in Cotgrave to render French verbs in *re-*.

1442 *Rolls of Parlt.* V. 44/1 And ther with..newe edifie and bilde anothir Brigge. **1570** *Norton & Sackville's Gorboduc* Printer to Rdr., They..haue..new apparelled, trimmed and attired her. **1590** SPENSER *F.Q.* I. ii. 17 Streams of purple bloud new die the verdant fields. **1633** FORD *Broken H.* V. iii, Thus I new-marry him, whose wife I am. **1666** PEPYS *Diary* 13 June, She had new-whitened the house all below stairs. **1713** STEELE *Guard.* No. 84 ¶2 They will new-plait and adjust your neckcloth. **1745** P. THOMAS *Jrnl. Anson's Voy.* 299 The Commodore..sent Assistance to get her off and new-moor her. **1771** FOOTE *Maid of B.* I. Wks. 1799 II. 213 To scour and new-line the coachman and footman's old frocks. **1803** *Edin. Rev.* II. 36 The whole nation exerting itself to new-floor the Government-house. **1833** N. ARNOTT *Physics* (ed. 5) II. 119 Separating, combining, and new-modifying them to serve to him most useful purposes. *a* **1861** MRS. BROWNING *Void in Law* vii, He thinks that..he'll new-stamp the ore?

b. With active forms of intransitive verbs, as ***new-dapple***, ***new-nestle***.

a **1885** G. M. HOPKINS *Poems* (1967) 193 As sure as what is most sure, sure as that spring primroses Shall new-dapple next year. *a* **1889** —— *Ibid.* 185 Say it is ásh-boughs: whether on a December day and furled Fast ór they in clammyish lashtender combs creep Apart wide and new-nestle at heaven most high.

7. a. With pres. pples. of intransitive verbs used attributively, as ***new-appearing***, ***-bleeding***, ***-breaking***, ***-budding***, ***-dawning***, etc. Also *new-emergent*.

1594 SHAKS. *Rich. III*, IV. iv. 10 My vnblowed Flowres, new appearing sweets. **1597** —— *Lover's Compl.* 153 Experience for me many bulwarks builded Of proofs new-bleeding. **1610** DONNE *Pseudo-martyr* 327 Not vpon new emergent matter, but vpon better knowledge of the former.

1669 DRYDEN *Tyrannic Love* IV. i, We slide on the back of a new-falling star. **1726** POPE *Odyss.* XIX. 703 Down her pale cheek new-streaming sorrow flows. **1817** BYRON *Manfred* II. ii, On the swift whirl of the new-breaking wave. **1820** J. TRUMBULL *Poetical Wks.* II. 108 Prove to the world in these new-dawning skies, What genius kindles and what arts arise. *a* **1861** CLOUGH *London Idyll* 37 Odours of new-budding rose. **1895** *Outing* (U.S.) XXVI. 443/1 Patches of the new-starting rushes.

b. With pres. pples. of intransitive verbs that are const. with predicative adverbs, as ***new-looking, -seeming***.

1905 J. JOYCE *Let.* c 12 Oct. (1966) II. 121 A good new-looking..suit. **1928** D. H. LAWRENCE *Lady Chatterley* xv. 276 The man's face, that was smooth and new-looking with love. **1951** S. SPENDER *World within World* 87 Rain-drops.. through the sun..would gleam with a new-seeming whiteness. **1969** *Sears Catal.* Spring/Summer 15 Enamel colors oven-baked to stay new-looking longer.

8. With verbal sbs. *rare*.

1484 *Churchw. Acc. Wigtoft, Linc.* (Nichols 1797) 78 Paide for neweshotyng of the grete bell claper. **1611** COTGR., *Reedification*, a..reedifying, new-building. **1700** C. NESSE *Antid. Armin.* (1827) 106 If conversion be a new-begetting ..then fallen man hath no free-will.

New A'cademy. Also new Academy. [ACADEMY 2.] A name given to schools of philosophy founded in Athens by the successors of Plato as Heads of the Academy and developing some of its principles, *spec.* (*a*) that founded by Arcesilaus (316/15–242/1 B.C.) in the third century B.C. (now more usually called *Middle Academy*); (*b*) (more usually) that founded in the second century B.C. by Carneades of Cyrene (214/13–129/8 B.C.) and developing the mainly sceptical philosophy of Arcesilaus. Also *attrib.* So **New Aca'demic** *sb.* and *a.*

1659 T. STANLEY tr. *Sextus Empiricus's Pyrr. Hyp.* in *Hist. Philos.* III. IV. 33 Those of the new Academy, though they say all things are incomprehensible, differ from the Scepticks... Now the new Academicks, before Phantasie which is simply credible, preferre that which is credible and circumcurrent. **1702** S. PARKER tr. *Cicero's De Finibus* v. 280 For all that, I'll venture to dissuade you from following the new Academicks, and bespeak you in behalf of the Old ones. **1744** W. GUTHRIE tr. *Cicero's Morals* p. v, It was by Sincerity alone that the New Academy could hope to recommend that Moderation which was their peculiar Distinction. *Ibid.*, Thus, The New Academic, by admitting a Degree of Comprehension, preserv'd a Principle of Agency. *Ibid.* 321 This they call'd the new Academy, tho' it appears to me to be the old one, at least we may look upon Plato to have been of the old. **1853** C. D. YONGE tr. *Cicero's Academic Questions* p. xxix, *Arcesilaus*, or *Arcesilas*, flourished about B.C. 280... On the death of Crantor he succeeded to the chair of the Academy, in the doctrines of which he made so many innovations that he is called the founder of the New Academy. **1856** W. A. BUTLER *Lect. on Hist. of Ancient Philosophy* II. IV. i. 318 The sceptical side of Platonism represented by the New Academy, the doctrinal by the Neo-platonists. **1874** J. S. REID *Cicero's Academica* p. lvi, Cicero..merely attaches Philo's name to those general New Academic doctrines which had been so brilliantly supported by the pupil of Clitomachus in his earlier days. **1902** BALDWIN *Dict. Philos. & Psychol.* II. 496/2 The New Academy, under Philo of Larissa (about 100 B.C.) and Antiochus, turned to dogmatism and eclecticism. **1946** F. C. COPLESTON *Hist. Philos.* I. xxxviii. 414 The founder of the Third or New Academy was Carneades of Cyrene. **1967** P. MERLAN in *Cambr. Hist. Later Greek & Early Medieval Philos.* 61 Plutarch even has kind words for the scepticism of the New Academy.

newalty, variant of NEWELTY *Obs.*

Newar (niː'wɑː(r)). A member of one of the castes of Nepal, of Mongol or partly Mongol origin. Also *attrib.* So **Ne'wari**, a language of partly Tibetan origin spoken by the Newars.

1811 [see MAGAR[2]]. **1819** F. HAMILTON *Acct. Kingdom Nepal* I. i. 49 They afterwards settled in the valley of Nepal, and are the people now called Newars. **1877** [see BAEL, BEL]. **1877** D. WRIGHT *Hist. Nepal* App. vii. 306 (*heading*) Newārī songs. **1893** A. L. WADDELL in *Indian Antiquary* XXII. 292 The Nêwârs are the aborigines of Nêpâl Proper, that is, of the valley in which the present capital Khâtmândû stands. *Ibid.* 293 The original name of this section of the Pâl country, which contained the home of the Nêwârs, seems to have been *Nê*, while the people were hence called by the Hindus *Nêwâr*, or '*Inhabitants of Nê*'. **1911** FRAZER *Golden Bough: Magic Art* (ed. 3) I. v. 294 The Newars..worship the frog. **1928** P. LANDON *Nepal* II. App. xvi. 236 He was buried in the little Christian cemetery with an inscription in two languages, Latin and Newari. **1971** J. PEMBLE *Invasion of Nepal* i. 6 Jaya Yaksha Malla..patronized native letters and raised Newari to the status of an official language. **1972** W. B. LOCKWOOD *Panorama Indo-European Lang.* 208 Spoken in 1952–4 by close on 400,000 persons in Nepal, Newari is the only Himalayan language of the Tibeto-Burman group to have developed a considerable literature. The Newars have evolved a high degree of material culture. **1973** *Times* 14 Apr. (Nepal Suppl.) p. ii/5 The three towns of Katmandu, Patan and Bhadgaon are the creation of Newars. **1974** M. PEISSEL *Great Himalayan Passage* xiv. 206 The Newars do not like anyone to die in their houses, so they turn the dying outside on mats. *Ibid.*, All the windows of traditional Newar houses have to be entirely closed by wooden lattices, as these are believed to stop evil spirits entering.

Newark ('njuːək, 'nuːək). The name of a city in New Jersey, U.S.A., used *attrib.* or in *Comb.* in various special collocations (see quots.).

1787 in T. F. De Voe *Market Book* (1862) I. 181 (New) *Jersey*, a Burlington ham and Newark cyder. **1804** A. F. M. WILLICH *Domestic Encycl.* III. 111/1 *Newark Pippin*... It is said to have been imported from France. **1858** S. P. AVERY *Harp of Thousand Strings* 289 A well-known sporting character of the city had made a bet that he would drive his 'Newark waggon' (a light carriage with two horses) the whole length of Broadway. **1870** R. TOMES *Bazaar Bk. Decorum* 136 He will be sure to detect the Newark cider in your Champagne bottle. **1910** A. E. BOSTWICK *Amer. Public Library* 45 In the type of two-card system known as the 'Newark' system.., an additional record of the date is made on a flap attached to the inside of the book. **1961** T. LANDAU *Encycl. Librarianship* (ed. 2) 261/1 *Newark charging system*, the method of recording book loans which is most widely used in America.

New Art, new art. = *art nouveau* (ART *sb.* VI. f).

1903 W. B. YEATS *Let.* 14 May in *Florence Farr, Shaw, Yeats* (1946) 38, I have had a letter from the editor of the 'Daily News' asking permission to interview me on the Theatre and the New Art. **1906** M. H. BAILLIE-SCOTT *Houses & Gardens* i. 13 A bizarre striving after originality and eccentricity of design,..posing as the 'new art'. **1909** *Cottage Furniture* (Heal & Son) 1 The 'new art' overmantel smothered in rococo photograph frames. **1909** H. G. WELLS *Tono-Bungay* III. i. 266 Beautiful jam-pots! Get one of those new art chaps to design all the things they make ugly now. **1912** L. WEAVER *House & its Equipment* 35 The superficial clevernesses of the New Art movement. **1914** C. MACKENZIE *Sinister Street* II. III. vi. 617 New Art flower vases. **1938** G. GREENE *Brighton Rock* I. iii. 46 He touched a little buzzer, the New Art doors opened. **1969** J. GLOAG *Short Dict. Furniture* (ed. 2) 469 New Art was characterized by the free use of naturalistic motifs: chairs, tables, cabinets and bedsteads were contorted by writhing plants, exuberant blossoms, and intricate arabesques, while surfaces were punctuated by inserted patches of hammered copper and coloured enamel, and pierced by heart-shaped apertures.

new ball. *Cricket.* A previously unused ball, such as is brought into use at the beginning of an innings or after a prescribed number of overs; freq. used *attrib.* (with hyphen) of an opening bowler or of the type of bowling (usu. fast) in which the new ball is employed. Also *fig.*

1956 R. ALSTON *Test Commentary* 12 The most devastating pair of new-ball bowlers in the world. **1960** J. FINGLETON *Four Chukkas to Australia* vi. 65 We saw a magnificent piece of new-ball bowling. **1963** *Times Lit. Suppl.* 18 Jan. 27/3 One has the impression [in reading a novel] of waiting for the new ball to become available. **1971** *Times* 15 Feb. 8/1 Edrich and Luckhurst..batted with the greatest of ease against some modest new-ball bowling. **1975** *Cricketer* May 23/2 It was the finest display of new-ball bowling I ever saw.

'new-bear, *a. dial.* Also 7, 9 new-bare, 9 -bay'd. [ad. ON. **nýbær* (MDa. and mod. Norw. *nybær*; Icel. *nýbæra*, *-bæringr* sb.), f. *ný-* new + *-bær* (cf. ON. *síð-* and *snemmbær*), f. *bera* to BEAR.] Of a cow: That has newly calved.

1615 MARKHAM *Eng. Housew.* 106 Those Kine are said to be deepest of milke, which are new bare; that is, which haue but lately calued. **1856** THOMPSON *Hist. Boston* 716. **1877** *N.W. Linc. Gloss.*, *New-bay'd-cow*, a cow which has very recently had a calf. **1886** *S.W. Linc. Gloss.* s.v., 'Two newbear cows, two rearing calves'; or 'New-bare cow, two reared calves'.

newberyite ('njuːbərɪaɪt). *Min.* [ad. G. *newberyit* (G. vom Rath (at the suggestion of G. Ulrich) 1879, in *Sitzungsber. der niederrhein. Ges. in Bonn* XXXVI. 8), f. the name of J. Cosmo *Newbery* (19th-cent. Australian mineralogist) + *-it* -ITE[1].] A hydrated magnesium acid phosphate, $MgH(PO_4).3H_2O$, which is found as colourless orthorhombic crystals.

1879 *Mineral. Mag.* III. 108 Newberyite... Found at Skipton Caves, Victoria, with Hannayite. **1928** *Amer. Mineralogist* XIII. 397 (*heading*) Newberyite and other phosphates from Ascension Island. **1957** *Mineral. Mag.* XIII. 190 Newberyite, together with pyrrhotine and vivianite, was found in cracks of mammoth tusk buried in clay. **1966** *Amer. Mineralogist* LI. 1764 Subsequent submergence and removal of the source of ammonia permitted the replacement of struvite by newberyite in a subaqueous environment.

new-blown, *ppl. a.* [NEW *adv.* 3.]

1. Of flowers: Just come into bloom; newly opened. Also *fig.*

a **1667** COWLEY (J.), All in that new-blown age which does inspire Warmth in themselves. *a* **1706** OTWAY *Ovid's Ep. Phædra* 142 Who would not pluck the new-blown blushing Rose? **1740** J. MILLER *Mahomet* I. ii, Converting the sweet Flow'r of new blown Hope To deadly Night-Shade. **1795–1814** WORDSW. *Excurs.* IV. 497 A bee That..thither soars, to feed On new-blown heath. **1809** MALKIN *Gil Blas* XII. vi. ¶5, I put my new-blown honours in my pocket.

2. Of bubbles: Just blown.

1747 JOHNSON *Prol. at Opening Theatre Royal*, Hard is his lot, that here by Fortune plac'd Must..chase the new-blown bubbles of the day.

new-born, *ppl. a.* Also newborn, new born. [NEW *adv.* 3: cf. MDu. *nie(u)boren*, OHG. *niwiboran* (MHG. *niuwe-*, *niuborn*), ON. *nýborinn*.]

1. a. Just born; newly brought forth.

a **1300** *Cursor M.* 1342 A new born barn lay in þe croppe. *c* **1460** *Towneley Myst.* xiv. 292 He shall neuer haue myght to me, That new borne lad. **1535** COVERDALE *Matt.* ii. 2 Where is the new borne kynge of the Iues? **1570** GOOGE *Kirchmeyer's Papal Kingdom* IV. (1880) 45 The crying noise of Iupiter new borne. **1629** MILTON *Hymn Nativ.* xi, Harping in loud and solemn quire,..to Heav'ns new-born Heir. **1697** DRYDEN *Virg. Georg.* II. 501 The Nurse-ling spare, Nor exercise thy Rage on new-born Life. **1764** BURN *Poor Laws* 228 A Chinese, according to their laws, may cast his new born child into the river. **1801** *Med. Jrnl.* V. 479 The new-born animal staggers in walking and standing. **1886** A. WINCHELL *Walks Geol. Field* 316 The mother-fowl calls her new-born chicks.

b. *transf.* and *fig.* in various senses.

a **1586** SIDNEY (J.), To give the new-born letters both to death and burial. *a* **1650** CRASHAW (J.), He saw heav'n blossom with a new-born light. **1781** COWPER *Hope* 170 Nothing else can nourish and secure His newborn virtues. **1827** KEBLE *Chr. Y.*, *Monday in Easter Week*, The new-born rill Just trickling from its mossy bed. **1878** HUXLEY *Physiogr.* 136 When rain fell upon this new-born land.

2. Born anew: *fig.* regenerated. Also *absol.*

c **1375** *Sc. Leg. Saints* xxxii. (*Justin*) 614 [He] mad hyme þane as to cryst a now-borne mane. **1590** SPENSER *F.Q.* I. xi. 34 So new this new-borne knight to battell new did rise. **1593** SHAKS. *Lucrece* 1190 My shame so dead, mine honour is new-born. **1620** QUARLES *Feast of Wormes* (1638) 34 Once more the voice..Came downe from heaven to Jonah new born man, To re-baptized Jonah. **1726** POPE *Odyss.* XX. 296 These aged nerves with new-born vigour strung. **1768** WESLEY *Jrnl.* 5 May (1827) III. 310 The number of the new-born is increased.

3. *absol.* as *sb.* A new-born individual; chiefly in ***the new-born*** (usu. with pl. or collective sense).

1879 A. JACOBI in A. H. Buck *Treat. Hygiene & Public Health* I. I. 75 Landau's essay on 'The Melæna of the New-Born, with Notices on the Obliteration of the Fœtal Blood-Vessels', proves that..but little attention has been paid to the subject. **1907** *Jrnl. Amer. Med. Assoc.* 31 Aug. 775/1 Occurences of vaginal hemorrhage of the new-born are.. rare. **1929** R. HURWITZ tr. *Bernfeld's Psychol. of Infant* 2 The new-born is not capable of maintaining life for itself. **1937** *Amer. Jrnl. Dis. Child.* LIV. 1215 Tetany of the new-born..may occur at any time during the neo-natal period. **1968** PASSMORE & ROBSON *Compan. Med. Stud.* I. xxxix. 6/2 The distribution and amount of brown fat in the newborn varies among different species. **1974** *Nature* 6 Dec. 514/3 A doubtful study..indicating that newborns can orient visually to a voice source in space.

new boy. Also new-boy, newboy. [NEW *a.* 8.] A schoolboy during his first term(s) at a school, esp. one at a preparatory school or English public school. Also *transf.*, a (young) man newly come into a given set of circumstances. Cf. NEW *a.* 4b, NEW GIRL.

1847 DICKENS *Dombey* (1848) xli. 410 Here is the table upon which he sat forlorn and strange, the 'new boy' of the school. **1847** *Punch* 25 Dec. 255 (*caption*) Here's a New Boy, Johnny Russell. Now you see that nobody bullies him. **1905** R. BROOKE *Let.* 12 Mar. (1968) 18 Such brave souls can be content with the admiration of one another, and of the new boys. **1935** H. NICOLSON *Diary* 21 Nov. (1966) 229 He says the rather dramatic circumstances of my election may arouse some jealousy in that old hen the H. of C. I must do the new-boy for six months at least. **1948** PARTRIDGE *Dict. Forces' Slang* 124 *New boy*, a new member of a ship's ward-room. **1953** A. HUXLEY *Let.* 5 Apr. (1969) 667 He had been part of my Order of Things for almost fifty years, ever since we first met as newboys at our preparatory school in the autumn of 1903. **1970** E. PACE *Saberlegs* (1971) x. 87 He was a new boy here, a novice 'philanthropoid', as people in the foundation business called themselves. **1973** *Washington Post* 13 Jan. A. 22/2 Neither the anxious war critic Mr. Hughes nor the cautious new boy Mr. Clements was familiar with the unequivocal policy statement..made.. just two years ago. **1974** 'J. LE CARRÉ' *Tinker, Tailor* i. 10 Roach was a new boy... Thursgood's was his second prep school.

new-broached, *ppl. a.* [NEW *adv.* 3.] Newly opened up, brought forth, etc.

1547, **1612** [see BROACHED *ppl. a.* 2]. **1645** QUARLES *Sol. Recant.* IV. 34 They shall..leave a Tang Vpon thy new-broach'd Honor. *a* **1700** CREECH *Lucretius* (1715) Pref., The very Arguments..are revived afresh, and alledg'd to justifie new-broach'd Opinions.

new-broke(n, *ppl. a.* [NEW *adv.* 3.] Newly broken (also with *-up*, *-in*).

1660 SHARROCK *Vegetables* 21 The flax seed is sowen upon new broken ground. **1707** MORTIMER *Husb.* (1721) I. 128 They commonly sow..If new-broke-up Ground, two Bushels and a Peck. **1765** *Museum Rust.* IV. xl. 178 Burnet will not do in new-broke-up land. **1844** H. STEPHENS *Bk. Farm* II. 217, I groomed a new-broke-in blood filly for four months.

new broom. [In allusion to the prov. *new brooms sweep clean* (SWEEP *v.* 13b).] One newly appointed to a position who vigorously makes changes in personnel or procedures; one who effects fundamental or numerous alterations. Also (with hyphen) *attrib.* and as *v. trans.* and *intr.*

[**1776** G. COLMAN (*title*) New brooms! An occasional prelude. *Ibid.* 15, I am glad he is gone. *Catcall.* Glad! *Phelim.* To be sure I am glad. *New Brooms*, you know.] **1855** [see BROOM *sb.* 3b]. **1925** [see CLEAN *v.* 6c]. *a* **1930** D. H. LAWRENCE *Phoenix II* (1968) 114 The Reverend Mr. Flewitt is newly arrived on the circuit, and wants to sweep the chapel very clean of sin, being a new broom. **1938** *Ann. Reg.* *1937* 93 The War Ministry, where Mr. Hore-Belisha was proving himself a veritable 'new broom'. **1951** N. MARSH *Opening Night* v. 114 Our little stranger..seems to be new-brooming away. **1963** *Economist* 10 Aug. 496/3 Lord Hill of Luton, new-brooming his way through the Independent Television Authority. *Ibid.* 7 Sept. 809/1 The new government's new-broom mentality. **1969** *Listener* 14 Aug. 205/1 This seems to me exactly what is happening at the BBC, new brooms bustling about tidying up, rationalising and sorting out on very ill-thought-out principles.

'newbuilding. [tr. Da. *nybygning* new building, new ship: NEW *adv.* 8.] A newly constructed ship; the construction of ships.

1948 *N.Y. Maritime Register* 12 May 3/2 The newbuildings include a number of large fast cargo liners. **1957** *Times* 19 Dec. 16/6 It is the intention of that company to arrange a time charter on its newbuilding. **1968** *Marine West* Mar.–Apr. 2 The extra thick plates and oversize scantlings once used in tanker new buildings. **1968** *Marine Digest* 13 July 23 There is a steady trickle these days of newbuilding contracts for sale.

new-built, *ppl. a.* [NEW *adv.* 3.] Freshly or recently built; rebuilt. Also *fig.*

1596 SHAKS. *Tam. Shr.* v. ii. 118 Her new built vertue and obedience. **1597** WARNER *Alb. Eng., Æneidos* 330 In a new-built Fortresse. **1630** DRAYTON *Noah's Flood* 96 Hauing sented out Noah's new-built Arke. **1715** LEONI *Palladio's Archit.* (1742) II. 100 Warming their new-built Houses. **1827** G. HIGGINS *Celtic Druids* 44 Their grand and new-built city. **1856** KINGSLEY *Heroes, Argonauts* v. 133 What is this new-built town?

'newcal(d, *ppl. a. Sc.* and *north. dial.* Also 8 nuckle, 9 neucle(d, newkeld, etc. [For *new-calved* (see NEW *adv.* 3 b), or perh. ad. ON. **nýkelfd*.] Of a cow: That has newly calved.

1719 RAMSAY *Richy & Sandy* 72 Nuckle kye stand rowting in the loans. **1725** —— *Gentle Sheph.* III. iii, My faulds contain twice fifteen forrow nowt, As mony newcal in my byres rowt. **1801** W. BEATTIE *Fruits of Time Parings* (1873) 67 (E.D.D.), A new-cal' cow to fill my byre. **1829** BROCKETT *N.C. Gloss.* (ed. 2), *Newcal-cow*, a cow newly calved. [Also in recent northern glossaries: see *Eng. Dial. Dict.*]

new-cast, *v.* [NEW *adv.* 6.] *trans.* To recast; to form or mould anew. Also *refl.*

1650 R. STAPYLTON *Strada's Low C. Wars* II. 40 He had a wit that could easily new-cast it self into any mould. **1691** T. H[ALE] *Acc. New Invent.* 97 All's returned again to be new Cast. **1753** *World* No. 10. 59 To prepare and new-cast the established rhimes for public use. **1789** *Hist. Eur.* in *Ann. Reg.* 81/2 To proceed in a different way; first to new-cast the office and then to declare the officer.

So **new-cast** *ppl. a.*

1642 SIR T. BROWNE *Relig. Med.* I. §1, I am of that reformed new-cast Religion. **1785** BURKE *Nabob of Arcot's Debts* Wks. IV. 277 The only fund left.. for a new-cast peace establishment.

Newcastle[1] ('nju:kɑ:s(ə)l, -æ-; also with main stress on second syllable). [Name of a city (in full *Newcastle upon Tyne*) in the north of England.] **1.** Phr. ***to carry coals to Newcastle***: see COAL *sb.* 13.

2. Used *attrib.* in various special collocations: **Newcastle brown**, a strong brown ale; **Newcastle disease**, an infectious, often fatal, virus disease of poultry, first recorded in Britain near Newcastle in 1927 and characterized by lethargy followed by paralysis and difficulty in breathing; also called *fowl pest*; **Newcastle glass**, a type of colour-free glass manufactured in Newcastle; also *ellipt.*; **Newcastle pottery**, a type of coarse pottery manufactured around Newcastle.

1972 J. WAINWRIGHT *Requiem for Loser* ii. 43 A beer?.. There's a can o' Newcastle Brown in the fridge. **1973** 'J. PATRICK' *Glasgow Gang Observed* iii. 29 Pints of lager, heavy beer and bottles of Newcastle Brown were ordered. **1927** T. M. DOYLE in *Jrnl. Compar. Path. & Therapeutics* XL. 144 In order to facilitate description we propose to refer to it [*sc.* a virus disease of fowls] as 'Newcastle disease'. **1938** *Poultry Keepers' Year Book* v. 178 Newcastle Disease is notifiable to the Ministry of Agriculture... Recognisable by dribbling from beak and sudden death of many birds at the same time. **1955** *Sci. News Let.* 21 May 326/3 Newcastle disease virus, cause of a frequently fatal epidemic in poultry.. can also cause eye inflammation in humans. **1968** *New Scientist* 5 Dec. 561/1 The infection—the dreaded Newcastle disease—is normally so lethal to chickens that a strict quarantine is imposed on imported poultry. **1972** *Daily Colonist* (Victoria, B.C.) 9 Jan. 35/5 Vaccination of hens against Newcastle disease is being urged by the B.C. Poultry Commissioner. **1767** in *Sc. Nat. Dict.* (1968) VII. 17/1 All the windows to be glazed with Newcastle crown glass, bedded and back-pottied, and all hung with paces. **1779** COWPER *Let.* 26 May in *Corr.* (1904) I. 153, I shall be obliged.. if you will inquire at a glass-manufacturer's how he sells his Newcastle glass, such as is used for frames and hothouses. **1883** J. W. MOLLETT *Illustr. Dict. Art & Archæol.* 225/1 *Newcastle glass*, a crown glass, held the best for windows from 1728 to 1830... It was of an ash colour,.. and frequently warped. **1923** H. J. POWELL *Glass-Making in Pottery* vii. 93 In later years John Tyzack's warehouse for Newcastle glass near the Old Swan Stairs was well known. In 1691 Newcastle cut window-glass was sold at 13s. per 100 feet. **1965** P. M. HUBBARD *Hive of Glass* i. 9 It was..[a] quite faultless Newcastle light baluster.. ten inches high, the rounded perfect bowl perched on a breathless series of knobs. **1972** *Country Life* 28 Dec. 1783/2 The great rarities in this sale were two Dutch engraved Newcastle glasses of the mid-18th century. **1874** L. W. *Eng. Pott. & Porc.* 40 The principal marks on Sunderland and Newcastle pottery are (stamped in the clay or printed in transfer). **1971** R. C. BELL *Tyneside Pottery* II. 95/2 The Willett Collection in the Brighton Museum contains two rare earthenware mugs marked 'Newcastle Pottery'.

Newcastle[2]. The title of Henry Pelham-Clinton, fifth Duke of *Newcastle*-under-Lyne (1811–64), used as the name of a classical scholarship at Eton College, established by him in 1829. Also *attrib.*

1832 *Eton College Mag.* 25 June 7 It was on the second of April.. that we went up for the last Newcastle scholarship. **1845** J. PATTESON *Let.* in C. M. Yonge *Life J. C. Patteson* (1874) I. ii. 46 Do not distress yourself about this unfortunate failure as to the Newcastle. **1875** H. C. MAXWELL-LYTE *Hist. Eton College* xix. 369 One Newcastle Scholar is elected annually after a competitive examination open to Oppidans and Collegers alike. **1879** C. M. YONGE *Magnum Bonum* II. xxiv. 484 But you did like Eton so, and you were going to get the Newcastle and the Prince Consort's Prize. **1884** E. W. HAMILTON *Diary* 5 Nov. (1972) II. 725 Dined at Dilke's—Chamberlain, Sir L. Playfair, Lord Advocate, L. Lawson, Romer, and Kennedy (the Newcastle Scholar of my day). **1922** S. LESLIE *Oppidan* vii. 83, I would rather get the Newcastle than make a century at Lord's. **1953** H. NICOLSON *Diary* 3 Jan. (1968) 236, I feel as if I had got a fourth prize in scripture when I should have liked the Newcastle. **1959** *Chambers's Encycl.* V. 422/1 The classical tradition in Eton education, strengthened by the institution of the Newcastle scholarship in 1829, remains strong to-day. **1975** *Times* 18 Oct. 7/5 My [*sc.* Harold Macmillan's] brother Daniel had won the Newcastle at Eton.

new-coin, *v.* [NEW *adv.* 6.] To coin afresh.

1700 CONGREVE *Way of World* IV, While it passes current with me, that you endeavour not to new Coin it. **1804** *Europ. Mag.* XLV. 94 *note*, He.. new-coined their words, and so made them his own.

new-coined, *ppl. a.* [NEW *adv.* 3.] Freshly coined; newly made or invented.

1598 SYLVESTER *Du Bartas* II. ii. II. 489 Wits.. doe new coyn'd words inhance With current freedome. **1624** BEDELL *Lett.* ix. 120 Whose new-coyned faith.. came in peecemeale. **1684** E. CHAMBERLAYNE *Pres. St. Eng.* I. (ed. 15) 217 To scatter new-coyned two-pences in the.. places where the King passes. **1785** REID *Intell. Powers* II. x. 287 His style is disagreeable, being full of new-coined words. **1817** COLERIDGE *Biog. Lit.* (Bohn) 214 If the reader will pardon an uncouth and new-coined word.

new-come, *ppl. a.* and *sb.* [NEW *adv.* 3 b.]

A. *ppl. a.* Newly arrived; but lately come.

c **950** *Lindisf. Gosp.* Matt. x. 14 *marg.*, Biscope is forboden þæt he onfoe niwe cumenum preost & to ȝehælȝenne ferunga. *c* **1205** LAY. 8562 Cassibellaune lette.. cuðen his kempen þa tiðende neowe cumene. **13..** *Gaw. & Gr. Knt.* 60 Wyle nw ȝer was so ȝep þat hit was nwe cummen. *a* **1350** *St. Barth.* 69 in Horstm. *Altengl. Leg.* (1881) 119 A new-cumen schrew, A lurdan þat hat Bertelmew. *c* **1440** *Promp. Parv.* 89 Come-lynge, newcum man or woman. **1535** LYNDESAY *Satyre* 2426 Quhair traist ȝe I sall find ȝon new-cumde King? **1590** MARLOWE *Edw. II*, I. i, The sight of London.. Is as Elysium to a new-come soul. **1633** FORD *'Tis Pity* II. vi, A fellow with a broad beard (they say he is a new-come doctor). **1681** HICKERINGILL *Sin Man-catching* Wks. 1716 I. 179 A New-Mode, lately Invented, and new come over from beyond Seas. **1712** E. COOKE *Voy. S. Sea* 405 The six new-come Nations liv'd friendly together. **1785** BURNS *Brigs of Ayr* 87 It chanced his new-come neebor took his e'e. **1808** SCOTT *Marm.* v. vi, While burghers, with important face, Described each new-come lord. **1873** LELAND *Egypt. Sketch Bk.* 35 They don't object to speak the language before their new-come companions.

B. *sb.* A new or recent arrival; a novice.

1577 B. GOOGE *Heresbach's Husb.* II. (1586) 106 b, The Plane tree is but a stranger, and a newe come to Italie. **1586** FERNE *Blaz. Gentrie* I. 18 Is it reason that a new-come should disturbe him from so auncient a possession? **1633** FORD *Broken H.* II. i, Fear not, I am no new-come to 't. **1821** EGAN *Life Lond.* I. 300 There were some New-comes. [*note*, The name given to any new faces discovered among the usual visitants.] **1867** SMYTH *Sailor's Word-bk.* 497 *Newcome*, an officer commencing his career. Any stranger or fresh hand newly arrived.

So **new-comeling.** *rare.*

1577, 1815 [see COMELING].

'new-,comer. Also new comer, newcomer. [f. NEW and COMER, after NEW-COME *ppl. a.*] One who has newly come to a place; a new arrival. Also used of things.

1592 GREENE *Groat's W. Wit* (New Shaks. Soc.) 31 For other new commers, I leaue them to the mercie of these painted monsters. **1637** SIR H. BLOUNT *Voy. Levant* 61 A new Commer aprehends them with a judgement fresh and sincere. **1717** BERKELEY *Jrnl. Tour Italy* Wks. 1871 IV. 519 To produce a good effect on the eye of a new-comer. **1783** HERSCHEL in *Phil. Trans.* LXXIII. 259 Several of them strongly suspected to be new-comers. **1832** HT. MARTINEAU *Weal & Woe* i. 8 He.. went to new comers in preference to old neighbours. **1882** BESANT *Revolt of Man* xii. (1883) 288 Drill was renewed, and the new-comers taught the first elements of marching. **1886** W. B. YEATS *Mosada* III. 8 Yonder a leaf Of apple blossom circles in the gloom, Floating from yon barred window. New-comer, Thou'rt welcome. **1930** *New Statesman* 27 Dec. 357/2 The Gum-trees or Eucalypts are new-comers to California. **1966** *B.B.C. Handbk.* 23 A new-comer to many schools is 'radio-vision'.

So †**new-coming.** *Obs. rare*$^{-1}$.

1387 TREVISA *Higden* (Rolls) VII. 33 It were a wrecched schame þat a newe comynge [L. *novus advena*] schulde putte olde londesmen out of here place.

New Commonwealth. [COMMONWEALTH 4 c.] *collect.* Those countries which have achieved self-government within the British Commonwealth since 1945, opp. the old Dominions; also used *attrib.* of persons from (or whose parents came from) such countries; a genteelism for persons considered 'non-white'.

1960 *New Commonwealth* Oct. 626/3 The Rt. Hon. Ian Macleod, M.P., Secretary of State for the Colonies, will be the guest-of-honour at the next New Commonwealth luncheon, to be held at Claridges. **1964** *Listener* 6 Feb. 219/1 A respected voice from the new Commonwealth, that of Professor Rajan of the Indian School of International Studies, declared that [etc.]. **1964** S. A. DE SMITH *New Commonwealth & its Constitutions* iv. 137 In a new Commonwealth country there is a presumption against leaving the power of appointment exclusively in the hands of the executive. **1970** *Guardian* 10 Mar. 7/3 The number of 'new' Commonwealth immigrants admitted during the whole year fell by very nearly one-third. **1973** *Times* 4 Oct. 4/7 About 547,000 people whose parents were born in the New Commonwealth live in Greater London. **1975** *Times* 28 Feb. 3/2 The total New Commonwealth population in Britain. **1976** *Times* 27 Jan. 4/3 The total number of births [in Britain] to New Commonwealth and Pakistan mothers fell.

new-create, *v.* [NEW *adv.* 5, 6.] *trans.* To create anew.

1604 SHAKS. *Oth.* IV. i. 287 Or did the Letters.. new-create his fault? *a* **1680** BUTLER *Rem.* (1759) I. 7 When her Orb was new created. **1720** WELTON *Suffer. Son of God* II. xxvii. 720 To.. new-create the Worst of Infidels into thy faithful Servants. **1748** THOMSON *Cast. Indol.* II. lx, To high discovery.. that new creates The face of earth. **1800** COLERIDGE *Lett.* (1895) 322 Every hour new-creates him. **1870** EMERSON *Soc. & Solit.* iii. 42 Language.. is not new-created by the poet for his own ends. *a* **1930** D. H. LAWRENCE *Last Poems* (1932) 77 Then I have been dipped again in God, and new-created. **1952** R. CAMPBELL tr. *St. John of the Cross's Poems* 25 And have been new-created There where your mother first was violated.

Hence **new-creating** *ppl. a.*

1850 MRS. BROWNING *Poems* II. 274 Prayer that would Commend thee to the new-creating God.

new-created, *ppl. a.* [NEW *adv.* 3.] Newly made or brought into existence.

1656 in *Burton's Diary* (1828) I. 280 A charter confirmed, makes it not a new-created charter. *a* **1711** KEN *Psyche* Poet. Wks. 1721 IV. 290 While I possess'd Of new-created Eve the Breast. **1782** V. KNOX *Ess.* xx. (1819) I. 122 The true origin of this new-created want. **1813** SHELLEY *Q. Mab* III. 185 A new created sense within his soul. **1863** H. COX *Instit.* I. vii. 74 An unlimited number of new-created lords.

New Criticism, new criticism. [NEW *a.* 5.] An approach to the analysis of literary texts, associated spec. with American critics who subscribed to the procedures outlined by John Crowe Ransom (see quots. 1941), which concentrates on the linguistic organization of a text with particular emphasis on irony, ambiguity, paradox, etc. So **New Critic; New Critical** *a.*

1941 J. C. RANSOM (*title*) The new criticism. *Ibid.* p. vii, He [*sc.* R. P. Blackmur] is nevertheless a 'new' critic in the sense of this book. *Ibid.* i. 3 Discussion of the new criticism must start with Mr. Richards. **1948** *Poetry* LXXIII. 153 The Father of the New Criticism is probably I. A. Richards. **1948** [see CONCRETE *a.* and *sb.* A. 4 b]. **1951** R. P. BLACKMUR in *Hudson Rev.* III. iv. 501 The one thing the 'new critics' shared was skill in analysis. **1952** M. MCCARTHY *Groves of Academe* (1953) x. 212 The true attitude of Eliot, he suspected, was manifest in his disciples, who in all their voluminous New Criticism had given Joyce scarcely a word of exegesis. **1955** J. WAIN *Interpretations* 215 Poetic difficulty.. is not identical with grammatical difficulty.. nor is the 'New Critic'.. simply the old note-maker writ large. **1956** A. WILSON *Anglo-Saxon Att.* I. iii. 59 Hardy was back from New York with some frightfully funny stories about the New Criticism boys. **1960–1** M. SPILKA in *Modern Fiction Studies* VI. iv. 285 The concept of the author is conspicuous, in New Critical thought, by its absence. **1963** P. WEST *Mod. Novel* III. ii. 291 Robert Penn Warren.. one of the old New Critics. **1969** *Encycl. Brit.* VI. 781/2 In 1941 John Crowe Ransom coined the term 'new criticism' for what is in certain essential respects a return to the Renaissance rhetorician's principle that a poem is an arrangement of words, to be apprehended in their interaction. **1973** *Observer* 8 Apr. 37/5 The so-called New Critics in America made a great deal of their capacity to submit poems or prose-passages to detailed, word-by-word analysis. **1973** *College English* XXXIV. 573 The pattern is the same as he moves from one caricature of a 'New Critical' assumption to the next.

†**new-cut,** *sb. Obs.* [f. NEW *a.* + CUT *sb.*[2]] An old card-game.

1594–5 *Gesta Grayorum* in Nichols *Progr. Q. Eliz.* (1823) III. 301 Losses by shipwreck upon certain rocks of hazard,.. the sands of bowle-allies, the shelf of new-cut, the gulf of myne and gill [etc.]. **1600** J. LANE *Tom Tel-troth* 119 New-cut at Cards brings some to beggarie. **1607** HEYWOOD *Wom. killed w. Kindn.* E 2 b, *Fran.* You are best at New-cut, wife; you'l play at that. *Wend.* If you play at new-cut, I'me soonest hitter of any here, for a wager. **1663** TUKE *Adv.* 5 *Hours* IV. i, They are deeply engag'd At New Cut, and will not leave their Game.

New Dealish, *a. U.S.* Of, pertaining to or supporting a 'new deal': see DEAL *sb.*[2] 4 d. Hence **New Dealing, New Dealism.**

1934 *Sun* (Baltimore) 23 Oct. 1/2 In many sections Republican candidates have gone New Dealish. **1936** *Rocky Mt. News* (Denver, Colorado) 7 May 10/3 Two towers of progressive strength, more 'New Dealish' than most Democrats, will be lost to the administration in the next Congress. **1939** in *Amer. Speech* (1941) XVI. 309/1 New Dealism.. is nothing but the American form of Communism. **1962** R. B. FULLER *Epic Poem on Industrialization* 21 Lugubrious New Dealing Of a mixed pack Of bright new cards And dirty old ones. **1965** *Punch* 27 Oct. 593/1 Somehow President Johnson has managed to inject his countrymen with a new, and better, shot of New Dealism. **1965** *New Statesman* 29 Oct. 634/3 By that time Mr Johnson may have done all the New Dealing he thinks necessary. **1973** *New Yorker* 13 Jan. 56/2 Melvin Laird.. saved everyone's dignity by declaring that the name—Family Security System—sounded 'too New Dealish'.

new-devised, *ppl. a.* [NEW *adv.* 3.] Newly or lately contrived or invented.

1588 SHAKS. *L.L.L.* I. ii. 66, I would.. ransome him to any French Courtier for a new deuis'd curtsie. **1637** C. DOW *Answ. H. Burton* 159 Any new-devised formes of praier. **1795** SEWARD *Anecd.* I. 147 He was.. carried away with an affection of their new-devised discipline.

Newdigate ('nju:dɪgət). The name of Sir Roger *Newdigate* (1719–1806), M.P. for Oxford University, used *attrib.* and *absol.* to designate an English verse prize founded by him at Oxford University in 1805, or the poetry associated with this prize.

1852 *Prospective Rev.* VIII. 523 These [*sc.* the mechanical parts of rhythm and metre] any industrious person will find in any collection of the Newdegate forms [ed. 1965 Newdigate poems]. **1856** C. M. YONGE *Daisy Chain* II. v. 383 You should try for the Newdigate Prize. *Ibid.* viii. 414, I am not going to have the Newdigate prizeman shown as brother to a scare-crow. **1860** J. A. SYMONDS *Let.* 15 June (1967) I. 245, I am so glad you are pleased about the Newdigate. **1929** LD. BIRKENHEAD *Hundred Best Eng. Ess.* 386 He subsequently entered Christ Church, Oxford, and won the Newdigate Prize. **1931** 'G. TREVOR' *Murder at School* i. 12 So far he seemed to have done nothing in life except win the Newdigate. **1969** G. SMITH in A. Huxley *Lett.* 11, 1915... His Byronic poem on Glastonbury fails to gain the Newdigate Prize. **1975** *Times* 25 Aug. 5/7 John Buchan.. won the Newdigate and was President of the Union.

new-discovered, *ppl. a.* [NEW *adv.* 3.] Lately found or made known.

1654 DOROTHY OSBORNE *Lett.* (1888) 277 The new discovered plot against the Protector. **1690** LOCKE *Hum. Und.* III. x. §32 In a new-discovered Country. **1776** DA COSTA *Elem. Conchol.* v. 107 A new-discovered species, genus, or family. **1816** KIRBY & SP. *Entomol.* xxvii. (1818) II. 520 They had resolved upon an emigration to this new-discovered country.

new-dress, *v.* [NEW *adv.* 5, 6.] *trans.* To dress afresh; to put a new dressing on. Also *absol.*

1611 COTGR., *Raccoustré*,.. new dressed or trimmed vp. **1700** WATTS *Horæ Lyr.*, *Mourning Piece*, The wishing Muse new-dresses the fair garden. **1741** LADY POMFRET *Lett.* (1805) III. 110, I returned home to new dress. **1795** WASHINGTON *Lett.* Writ. 1892 XIII. 84 By the time it is revised and new dressed [etc.]. **1871** R. ELLIS tr. *Catullus* lxv. 16 A verse I tender of ancient Battiades, new-drest.

newe, var. NEVE *Obs.*; obs. f. NIEVE.

newed, *ppl. a.*: see NEW *v.*

newel[1] ('nju:əl). Forms: 4–5 **nowell**, (7 **noel**), 7–8 **nuel**, (7 **nuell**), **newell**, (9 **-ill**, **-al**), 7– **newel**. [a. OF. *nouel*, *noel*, *noal* (later *noiel*, *noial*, mod.F. *noyau*), kernel, stone, newel, etc. = Prov. *nogalh*:—Rom. **nucale*, f. L. *nuc-*, *nux* nut.]

1. *Arch.* The pillar forming the centre from which the steps of a winding stair radiate; †one of the stones forming such a pillar.

Also called *solid newel* in contrast to b.

1365 in Brayley & Britton *Houses Parlt.* (1836) 188 [Fifteen stones of Reygate, for the work called] nowells, [bought for the same stair-case]. **1416–17** in Willis & Clark *Cambridge* (1886) II. 442, Pro x nowelles pro gradibus xv[s]. **1611** COTGR., *Noyau*, the Nuell or spindle of a winding staire. **1655** MRQ. WORCESTER *Cent. Invent.* §48 A scrued Ascent, instead of Stairs,.. with Back-stairs within the Noell of it. **1679** MOXON *Mech. Exerc.* 170 *Newel*, the upright Post that a pair of Winding-stairs are turned about. **1711** W. SUTHERLAND *Shipbuild. Assist.* 65 A pair of winding Stairs, having a Nuel in the Center. *a* **1734** NORTH *Lives* (1826) III. 207, I could go round between the columns and the newel. **1823** P. NICHOLSON *Pract. Build.* 184 When the ends of the steps terminate upon a vertical prism or pillar, the prism or pillar is called a newal. **1870** F. R. WILSON *Ch. Lindisf.* 59 The steps ascend round an oblong newell.

transf. **1683** *Weekly Memorial* 64 The spiral blade of the Cochlea is fastened on the one side to its Nuel.

b. *open* or *hollow newel*, a central open space or well in a winding stair.

1625 BACON *Ess.*, *Building* (Arb.) 550 The Staires.. to the vpper Roomes, let them bee upon a Faire open Newell. **1720** STRYPE *Stow's Surv.* (1754) I. II. ix. 501/2 To the Stairs having an open Newel, there is a rail of Iron. **1727–38** CHAMBERS *Cycl.* s.v. *Stair*, The one winding round a solid, the other round an open newel. **1842** GWILT *Archit.* 1008 Where the steps are pinned into the wall, and there is no central pillar, the staircase is said to have an open newel. **1851** *Dict. Archit.* IV. 68 *Hollow Newel*, a name often given as well as 'open newel', to an open well-hole staircase.

2. The post at the head or foot of a stair supporting the hand-rail.

1833 LOUDON *Encycl. Archit.* 125 Deal turned newels (posts firmly framed to which the handrail is fixed) and moulded handrail. **1858** *Skyring's Builders' Prices* 55 Square framed newill... Inch square bar ballusters. **1878** W. W. FENN *Blindman's Holiday* II. 46 The carved oak balustrade, the newels, and the polished flooring.

b. In ships: (see quot.).

c **1850** *Rudim. Navig.* (Weale) 135 *Newell*, an upright piece of timber to receive the tenon of the rails that lead from the breast-work to the gangway.

3. 'A cylindrical pillar terminating the wingwall of a bridge'.

1882 in OGILVIE and later Dicts.

4. *attrib.*, as *newel-post*, *-stair(s)*, *-staircase*, *-step*.

1798 HUTTON *Course Math.* (1828) II. 86 Take the.. girt over its end till it meet the top of the *newel-post. **1881** OAKEY *Building Home* 71 To attain decorative effects in newel-posts and balusters. **1667** PRIMATT *City & C. Build.* 66 A pair of open *Newel-Stairs (which are Stairs with a well or light coming from the top). **1851** TURNER *Dom. Archit.* II. iii. 81 Internal communication by a newel stair at one angle of the building. **1859** JEPHSON *Brittany* v. 55 We next ascended the broad *newel staircase. **1883** SIR W. H. COPE *Bramshill* 64 A newel staircase ascending to the attics. **1883** *Archæol. Cant.* XV. 256 Some broken stone *newel-steps which were found close by.

†**newel**[2]. *Obs. rare.* Also 6–7 **-ell**. [var. of NOVEL, after NEW *a.*] A novelty; news.

c **1475** *Songs & Carols 15th C.* (Warton Club) 64 Syns that Eve was procreat.. Cowd not such newels in this lond be inventyd. **1579** SPENSER *Sheph. Cal.* May 276 He was so enamored with the newell, That nought he deemed deare for the jewell. *a* **1618** J. DAVIES *Eglogues* Wks. (Grosart) II. 20 O! how my heart's ioy-rapt, as I had cought A Princedome to my share, of thilk newell.

newelled ('nju:əld), *a.* [f. NEWEL[1] + -ED[2].] Having a newel. Also *solid-* or *open-newelled*.

1677 PLOT *Oxfordsh.* 268 This stair-case seems to be a composition of 4 half-pace-open-newel'd stair-cases. **1727–38** CHAMBERS *Cycl.* s.v. *Stair*, Solid and open newelled fliers and winders. **1865** DIRCKS *Life Mrq. Worcester* 445 Such stairs are said to be neweled. **1884** C. ROGERS *Soc. Life Scot.* I. ii. 44 A circular newelled staircase within the walls.

†'**newelry.** *Obs. rare*[−1]. [var. of NOVELRY: cf. next.] A novelty.

1575 LANEHAM *Let.* (1871) 47 Olld hags, az fond of nuellries, az yoong girls that had neuer seen Court afore.

newelty ('nju:əltɪ). Now *dial.* Forms: 5 **nwelte**, 6 **nueltie**; 5 **newelte**, 6–7 **neweltie**, (6 **-tee**, **-tye**), 7, 9 **newalty**, 6– **newelty**. [ad. OF. *nov-*, *nouveleté*, etc. (mod. F. *nouveauté*) NOVELTY, after NEW *a.*]

1. Novelty, newness.

c **1410** *Sir Cleges* 214 Loo dame! here ys newelte! **1509** BARCLAY *Shyp of Folys* (1874) I. 17 The neweltye of the name was more plesant unto the first actour. **1532** MORE *Confut. Tindale* Wks. 397/2 After a little vse thereof, the pleasure of the neweltie passed. **1570** FOXE *A. & M.* (ed. 2) 783/2 Accusing the true doctrine of the word of God, for neweltie. **1748** RICHARDSON *Clarissa* (1768) I. 23 He had heard [that] *newelty*, that was the man's word, was every-thing with him. **1886** ELWORTHY *W. Som. Word-bk.*

2. A novelty; a new thing.

1435 MISYN *Fire of Love* 95 Not seand kynde qwhat be-semys, bot qwhat.. vayne nwelte þe feynd.. may vp brynge. *c* **1500** *For to serve a Lord* in *Babees Bk.* (1868) 373 Cheryes, pepyns, and such neweltees as the tyme of the yere requereth. **1549** COVERDALE, etc. *Erasm. Par. Thess.* 4 You must not thinke it any neweltie, though these thinges happen. **1617** COLLINS *Def. Bp. Ely* I. iv. 181 One Grauius .. brought it first from Rome, and set it out as a neweltie. **1683** MRS. BEHN *Young King* v. iii, My wife loves Newalties abominationly, and I must tell her something about the King. **1854** MISS BAKER *Northampt. Gloss.* s.v., I aint had a bit of pig-meat so long, it's quite a newalty.

†**3.** Used as *adj.* Novel, new. *Obs. rare*[−1].

1590 FENNE *Frutes* To Rdr., I assure thee that the Cates themselves be as daintie and neweltie as the best.

†'**newen**, *adv. Obs.* Forms: 1 **níwan(e**, **néowan**, 3 **neow-**, **neaw-**, **newene**, **ne(o)uwen**, **newenn**. [OE. *níwan(e*, f. *níwe* NEW *a.*]

1. Newly, quite recently.

c **888** K. ÆLFRED *Boeth.* xxxix. §3 Se weas ȝeworden niwane. *c* **893** —— *Oros.* II. vi. 86 þone ænne consul þe hie þa niwan ȝeset hæfdon. **971** *Blickl. Hom.* 177 Nu niwan ȝelamp þæt ic me sylf onfand [etc.]. *c* **1000** ÆLFRIC *Deut.* xxiv. 5 þonne man niwan wif nymð. *c* **1200** ORMIN 13221 He þe Laferrd Iesu Crist þa newenn haffde fundenn. *c* **1205** LAY. 3591 Buten he beo neowene icume. *Ibid.* 20683 Ænne castel.. þe wes neouwen [*c* **1275** newene] iworht.

2. Shortly, soon. *rare.*

c **1200** ORMIN 715 To kiþenn to þe follc þatt Crist þa shollde cumenn newenn.

Hence †'**newenly** *adv.*, shortly, soon. *Obs.*[−1]

c **1205** LAY. 13320 Heo habbeoð me itald.. þat þe king of Norewæiȝe neowenliche wule hider uaren.

New England. [See NEW ENGLANDER.]

a. Used to denote a form of U.S. speech characteristic of New England, and *attrib.* of persons, produce, etc., native to New England; of mentality, idiom, etc., marked by the characteristics of New England.

1638 J. UNDERHILL in *Mass. Hist. Soc. Coll.* (1837) 3rd. Ser. VI. 5 Let the clamor be quenched.., that New England men usurp over their wives. **1655** *Deeds Suffolk County, Mass.* (1883) II. 166 Thirty quintalls he reciued.. was New England fish. **1709** W. BYRD *Secret Diary* (1941) 13 Parson Ware sent to me for a pint of canary, he being sick of the gripes with the New England rum. **1715** S. SEWALL *Diary* (1882) III. 56 Gave Mr. Short's daughter a New-England shilling. **1787** M. CUTLER in Parker & Cutler *Life M. Cutler* (1888) I. 195 [You are] acquainted with the institution of a Company in the New England States by the name of the Ohio Company. **1839** *Southern Lit. Messenger* V. 112/2 Noah Webster.. will ere long succeed in giving us a New England tongue which shall not be intelligible in Britain. **1842** DICKENS *Let.* 29 Apr. (1974) III. 217 A New England Poet buzzed about me on the Ohio, like a gigantic Bee. **1845** J. F. COOPER *Chainbearer* II. xiv. 466 The supercilious feeling of the New Englandman can very easily be traced to his origin in the mother country. **1850** W. C. FOWLER *Eng. Gram.* II. iii. 92 To pass over the local peculiarities of smaller districts, there are certain generic dialectal differences which characterize, 1. New England. 2. The Southern States. 3. The Western States. **1905** R. FRY *Let.* Jan. (1972) I. 228 The Philadelphia Quakeress.. said 'You know I can't bear it because I've got a New England conscience.' **1917** T. S. ELIOT *Prufrock* 34 The barren New England hills. **1934** WEBSTER p. xlviii/1, Another variety of short *o* is the 'New England short *o*'. This is acoustically intermediate between *ō* (*nōte*) and *ŭ* (*nŭt*), being practically an *ŭ* sounded with rounded lips. **1935** A. C. BAUGH *Hist. Eng. Lang.* 446 In the English language spoken in America three major dialects can be distinguished: New England, Southern, and General American. **1951** *Language* XXVII. 425 The division into Northern, Midland, and Southern (instead of the older New England, General American, and Southern) does not come as a shock. **1952** S. KAUFFMAN *Philanderer* (1953) iii. 33 They had just been graduated from a small New England college. **1975** *Daily Colonist* (Victoria, B.C.) 26 Oct. 30/8 New England peachblow [glass] is made in one layer shading from red to white. **1975** P. ORGAN *House on Cheyne Walk* v. 31 We could stand a little New England uprightness here. One tires of the bohemian life.

b. In special collocations, as **New England aster**, a large Michaelmas daisy, *Aster novæangliæ*; **New England boiled dinner**, a *boiled dinner*, esp. one including corned beef; **New England mayflower**, a prostrate, evergreen shrub, *Epigæa repens*, belonging to the family Ericaceæ, native to the eastern half of North America, and better known as trailing arbutus; **New England theology**, a movement in American Congregationalism, also affecting other American Protestant bodies, which repudiated much Calvinist doctrine.

1814 J. BIGELOW *Florula Bostoniensis* 199 *Aster Novæ Angliæ*. New England aster... A tall, and very beautiful plant. Stem three feet high, brown, very hairy. **1931** W. N. CLUTE *Common Names of Plants* 140 The New England aster (*Aster Nova* [sic] *Angliæ*), which lingers long in the fields and fence corners, is further distinguished as last-rose-of-summer. **1968** PETERSON & MCKENNY *Field Guide to Wildflowers Northeastern & Northcentral N. Amer.* 356 New England Aster. *Aster novæ-angliæ*. Our most showy wild aster, deeper violet than the others; rarely rose-colored. **1936** F. M. FARMER *Boston Cooking-School Cook Bk.* (new ed.) 277 New England boiled dinner. Served warm, unpressed corned beef with cabbage, beets, turnips, carrots, and potatoes. **1975** *Times Lit. Suppl.* 20 June 703/2 We have a New England boiled dinner as well as pot-au-feu. **1855** *Harvard Mag.* I. 232 Most admired of our spring flowers is the Ground Laurel, *Epigæa repens*, commonly called Trailing Arbutus, or New England Mayflower. **1952** A. G. L. HELLYER *Sanders' Encycl. Gardening* (ed. 22) 178 *Epigæa* ..*repens*, 'American Ground Laurel', 'New England Mayflower', 'Trailing Arbutus', white, fragrant. **1899** G. N. BOARDMAN (*title*) A history of New England theology. **1967** D. T. KAUFFMAN *Dict. Religious Terms* 329/1 *New England theology*, term for the movement in New England in the latter part of the eighteenth century and the first half of the nineteenth century to tie Calvinism to human reason and experience.

New 'Englander. [f. *New England* (so named by Captain John Smith in 1616) + -ER[1].] An inhabitant or native of New England, a part of the United States of America, comprising the six north-eastern states.

1637 HEYLIN *Antid. Lincoln.* iii. 12 Not a New-Englander of them all, could have done it better. **1681** T. FLATMAN *Heraclitus Ridens* No. 13 (1713) I. 88 For the New Englanders,.. it is no matter what Religion he be of. **1768** C. BEATTY *Tour* 109 Such have been the endeavours of the New Englanders. **1825** J. NEAL *Bro. Jonathan* I. 13 This was the character of a New Englander half a century ago. **1883** *Harper's Mag.* Feb. 420/1 The carrying trade was entirely monopolized by New-Englanders.

So **New-'Englandish** *a.*, characteristic or typical of New England (hence ***New-Englandishness***). **New-'Englandism**, (*a*) the tone or tendency characteristic of New England life or sentiment; (*b*) an idiom or mode of expression characteristic of New Englanders. **New-'Englandize** *v.*, to imbue with a New England character. **New-'Englandy** *a.*, suggestive of New England.

1831 *Boston Transcript* 7 Sept. 2/3 Mr Pickering, however, thinks *hub* a New-Englandism only. **1861** F. G. TUCKERMAN in *N. Hawthorne & Wife* (1885) II. 275 For the book.. I claim little, but that it is New Englandy (I hope). **1858** H. W. BEECHER *Life Th.* (1859) 27 New Englandism is but another word for Puritanism in the Independent sense. **1863** N. HAWTHORNE *Our Old Home* (1883) I. 35 A respectable-looking woman,.. decidedly New-Englandish in figure and manners. **1887** *Chicago Advance* 17 Mar. 169/3 This grand work of New-Englandizing that Southeasternmost State of the Union. **1896** *Ibid.* 9 Jan. 51/1 There is a still more striking New Englandishness in the people themselves. **1948** MENCKEN *Amer. Lang.* Suppl. II. 198 Dr. R-M. S. Heffner, who was born in 1892 at Bellefontaine, in the west central part of the State [*sc.* Ohio], testifies that New Englandisms were common there in his boyhood.

New 'English, *a.* [f. *New England*, after ENGLISH.] Of or pertaining to New England.

1634 E. WINSLOW in Morton *New Engl. Canaan* (1883) 84 Two of the arrantest knaves that ever trod on New English shore. **1647** WARD *Simp. Cobler* 53 It is.. as empty as a New-English purse. **1713** S. SEWALL *Diary* 16 Sept., An August Speech, Shewing the Validity and Antiquity of New English Ordinations. **1870** LOWELL *Among my Bks.* Ser. I. (1873) 234 All their unconscious training by eye and ear, were New English wholly.

†**b.** *absol.* as *pl.* The inhabitants of New England. *Obs.*

1643 TRAPP *Comm. Gen.* iv. 23 A certaine Indian comming into a house of the New-English. **1647** WARD *Simp. Cobler* 3 Such as have given or taken any unfriendly reports of us New-English, should do well to recollect themselves.

newer, obs. variant of EWER, NEVER.

newerds eve, newermes: see NEW YEAR.

neweu, -ewe, -eye, obs. forms of NEPHEW.

new-fallen, *a.* [NEW *adv.* 3. Cf. ON. *nýfallinn* (Sw. *nyfallen*).]

1. Newly or recently fallen.

1592 SHAKS. *Ven. & Ad.* 354 As apt as new-fall'n snow takes any dint. **1621** QUARLES *Div. Poems, Esther* (1638) 91 Here lies a new-falne ranke and there a sheave. **1738** GRAY *Tasso* 14 A vestment unadorn'd though white as new-fal'n snows. **1847** TENNYSON *Princ.* VI. 119 Like a new-fall'n meteor on the grass. **1887** MORRIS *Odyss.* XI. 194 Down on the leaves new-fallen. **1926** J. FERGUSSON in *Oxford Poetry* 23 Like a shield New-fallen on a stricken field.

†**2.** Newly fallen to one. *Obs. rare.*

1596 SHAKS. *1 Hen. IV*, V. i. 44 You swore to vs,..That you did..claime no further, then your new-falne right. **1600** —— *A.Y.L.* V. iv. 182 Meane time, forget this new-falne dignitie, And fall into our Rusticke Reuelrie.

3. Newly dropped; new-born.

1684 CARYLL in *Dryden's Misc., Virgil's Ecl.* 3 This poor Mother of a new-fall'n Pair. **1714** GAY *Sheph. Week, Monday* 16, I love thee more by half, Than..cows the new-fall'n calf. *a* **1763** SHENSTONE *Progr. Taste* II. 24 He wink'd at many a gross design The new-fall'n calf might countermine.

newfangle (njuːˈfæŋg(ə)l), *a.* and *sb.* Now *dial.* Forms: 4–5 newe-, 4– new-; 4 -fongel, 4–5 -fangel, 4–6 -fangil, (5 -ille, -yl(le, 6 -ill), 6– -fangle. [ME. *newefangel*, f. *newe-* NEW *a.* + *-fangel*, repr. OE. **fangol* 'inclined to take', from the stem *fang-* (infin. *fón*) to take. Cf. MDu. *nievingel(heit)*.]

A. *adj.* **1.** = NEWFANGLED 1.

c **1386** CHAUCER *Sqr.'s T.* 610 So newefangel been they of hire mete, And louen nouelrie of propre kynde. **1390** GOWER *Conf.* II. 273 Every newe love quemeth To him which newefongel is. *c* **1400** *26 Pol. Poems* 56 We ben newe fangyl, vnstable in dede. **1470–85** MALORY *Arthur* XXI. ii. 841 The moost party..helde with sire mordred, the peple were soo newe fangle. **1513** DOUGLAS *Æneis* XIII. vi. 141 The lusty matronis newfangill of sik thyng. **1583** BABINGTON *Commandm.* (1590) 274 He would not haue them new-fangle, wanton, and phantasticall in their appearell. *a* **1649** DRUMM. OF HAWTH. *Hist. Jas. I*, Wks. (1711) 9 The English ..with new guises daily resorted hither, and turned new-fangle the court. **1724** RAMSAY *Tea-t. Misc.* (1733) I. 36 A Paris edition of new-fangle Sany. *a* **1773** FERGUSSON *Wks.* (1800) 114 Newfangle grown wi' new got form, You soar aboon your mither worm. **1826** D. ANDERSON *Poems* 8 (E.D.D.), Nor are they to incomes newfangle, Until acquainted wi' their character.

2. = NEWFANGLED 2.

1578 in *Priv. Prayers* (1851) 465 So fond are we Englishmen of strange and foreign things, so greedy of new-fangle novelties. **1614** JACKSON *Creed* III. 179 Neglecting new-fangle tricks or flashes of extemporary wit. **1655** GURNALL *Chr. in Arm.* verse 14. iii. (1669) 15/2 He..that vainly covets novelties, and listens after every new-fangle opinion. **1720** RAMSAY *Concl.* 3 Ye're [a book] newfangle to be seen, In gilded Turkey clad, and clean.

B. *sb.* A new thing or fashion; a novelty.

c **1520** *Treat. Galaunt* (1860) 16 So hath the newe fangles our welth obscured. **1581** RICH *Farew.* (1846) 224 Men, that are busied with new fangles at the least once a daie. **1603** FLORIO *Montaigne* I. xxvii. (1632) 96 The changes, innovations, newfangles, and hurly burlies of his time. **1897** J. WRIGHT *Sc. Life* 75 Like mony new-fangles, ye're brisk, New Year!

Hence **newˈfangle** *v.*, to make newfangled.

1530 PALSGR. 644/1, I newefangyll. *c* **1600** SHAKS. *Sonn.* xci, Some glory..in their garments, though new-fangled ill. **1641** MILTON *Prel. Episc.* 21 Not hereby to controule, and new fangle the Scripture. **1861** *Temple Bar* II. 539 He will new-fangle all our old-fashioned schemes.

newfangled (njuːˈfæŋg(ə)ld), *a.* Also 6 -fangulyd, -phangled. [f. NEWFANGLE *a.*]

1. Very fond of novelty or of new things; unduly ready to take up new fashions or ideas; easily carried away by whatever is new.

a **1470** TIPTOFT *Cæsar* ii. (1530) 12 He was man new fanglyd and ambicious. *c* **1496** *Serm. Episc. Puer.* (W. de W.) b iij, Boyes of fyfty yere of age are as newe fangled as ony yonge men be. **1547** BOORDE *Introd. Knowl.* iii. (1870) 132, I am not new fangled, nor neuer wyll be. **1583** STUBBES *Anat. Abus.* II. (1882) 74 Diuers new phangled felows sprong vp of late, as the Brownists. *a* **1659** BP. BROWNRIG *Serm.* (1674) I. xi. 155 Imputations..cast upon these new fangled Christians. **1732** LEDIARD *Sethos* II. VII. 103 Make these new-fangled prisoners stand upright. **1792** GOUV. MORRIS in Sparks *Life & Writ.* (1832) II. 163 How much dependence is to be placed on these new-fangled statesmen? **1867** TROLLOPE *Chron. Barset* I. xvi. 142 When his time came to be made a bishop, he was not sufficiently new-fangled; and so he got passed by.

†**b.** Const. *of* or *with*. *Obs.*

1670 MARVELL *Corr.* Wks. (Grosart) II. 351 All the French curiosityes and trinkets, of which our people are so new-fangled. **1785** in *A. C. Bower's Diaries & Corr.* (1903) 23 So excessively am I new-fangled with my present.

2. New-fashioned, novel. (Used in depreciation.)

a **1533** FRITH *Disput. Purgat.* (1829) 123 Let us see and examine more of this new-fangled philosophy. **1579** G. HARVEY *Letter-bk.* (Camden) 68 Me thinkes I see the bite yᵉ lipp, At queinte newfanglid vanities. **1598** BARCKLEY *Felic. Man* III. (1603) 254 Gorgeous apparell and new fangled fashions. **1648** GATAKER *Myst. Cloudes* 2 Endeavouring to draw Disciples after them, by broaching of new-fangled fancies. **1726** LEONI *Designs* Pref. 1 New-fangled Proportions which give pain to the sight. **1789** BELSHAM *Ess.* II. xl. 496 A new-fangled and mystical state-oratory. **1830** CUNNINGHAM *Brit. Paint.* II. 11 To flaunt about, after the deliriums and new-fangled whims of fashionable people. **1876** FREEMAN *Norm. Conq.* V. xxiv. 440 Those new-fangled sources of income which arose out of the new-fangled feudal tenures.

Hence **newˈfangledism**, fondness for novelty; **newˈfangledly** *adv.*, in a newfangled manner.

1882 OGILVIE. **1883** J. MARTIN *Reminisc. Old Haddington* 42 She had a great dislike to 'newfangledism'.

newˈfangledness. [f. prec. + -NESS.] The fact or state of being newfangled or new-fashioned; novelty, innovation.

1549 CHALONER *Erasm. on Folly* F iv, The superstición of the Chaldees, and idle newfanglednesse of the Grekes. **1575** *Brieff Disc. Troub. Franckford* (1846) 37 So sore charged with newfangledness and singularitie. **1608** HIERON *Wks.* I. 724/2 How easilie am I ouer-caried with this humour of newfanglednesse. *a* **1693** *Urquhart's Rabelais* III. vii. 63 The Novelty and new-fangledness thereof..I dislike. **1823** *Spirit Public Jrnls.* 523 But this is the age of anomaly and newfangledness. **1877** G. FRASER *Wigtown* 361 So averse was he to titles and 'newfangledness', as he used to call it.

newˈfanglement. [f. NEWFANGLE *a.* + -MENT.] Novelty; a novel thing.

1798 LD. PLUNKET in *Edin. Rev.* (1899) Jan. 176 The novelty and newfanglement of revolutionary clubs and committees having worn off. **1895** J. S. FLETCHER *Wapentake* 155 The old gentleman must ha' turned in his grave to see all these here new-fanglements.

newˈfangleness. Now *rare* or *Obs.* Also 4–6 -fangel-, -fangil-, (4 -ul-, 5 -yl-), etc. [f. NEWFANGLE *a.* + -NESS.] = NEWFANGLEDNESS.

c **1374** CHAUCER *Anel. & Arc.* 141 This Fals Arcite of his nuwefangulnesse..Tooke lasse deyntee of hir stedfastnesse. *c* **1403** LYDG. *Temple Glas* 103 If þe spirit of nvfangilnes In any wise ȝoure hertis would assaile. *a* **1460** *How Wise Man taught Son* 51 in Hazl. *E.P.P.* I. 171 Lat [no] newefangylnes the plese Oftyn to remewe nor to flyt. **1533–4** *Act 25 Hen. VIII*, c. 12 Other the kinges subiectes.., inclined to new-fangilnes, haue spoken with the same Elizabeth. **1604** T. WRIGHT *Passions* IV. ii. §6. 137 This newfanglenesse proceedeth from an inconstant mind. **1658** tr. *Ussher's Ann.* VI. 262 The old luxury of the Persians and the new fanglenes of the Macedons. **1725** RAMSAY *Gentle Sheph.* I. ii, Soon as your newfangleness is gane, He'll look upon you as his tether-stake.

†**newˈfanglist.** *Obs. rare.* [f. as prec. + -IST.] One given to novelties.

1604 TOOKER *Fabrique Ch.* 90 The private spirits of these new-fanglists. **1607** *Schol. Disc. agst. Antichr.* II. ix. 120 We are Newfanglistes, hating antiquitie and delighting in noveltie.

†**newˈfangly,** *adv. Obs. rare.* [f. as prec. + -LY².] In a newfangled manner.

1529 MORE *Dyaloge* III. Wks. 213/2 Diuers yonge scolers such as thei founde..newfangly minded.

new-fashioned, *ppl. a.* [NEW *adv.* 3.] Made after a new fashion; of a new type or of recent invention.

1611 W. GODDARD *Satir. Dial.* E j b, Newe-fashiond cloathes I loue to weare. **1679** *Establ. Test* 43 What tongue is able to express..the new fashion'd garments of cruelty? **1712** ADDISON *Spect.* No. 271 ¶4 He had not given a decisive Opinion upon the new-fashioned Hoods. **1768–74** TUCKER *Lt. Nat.* (1834) I. 560 When she..teazes papa for money to buy a new-fashioned silk. **1806** SURR *Winter in Lond.* I. 150 He hates every thing about that new-fashioned lord. **1872** FREEMAN *Gen. Sk. Europ. Hist.* xvi. §2 (1874) 327 Departments, called in a new-fashioned way after rivers and mountains.

Newfie (ˈnjuːfɪ, ˈnuːfɪ). *colloq.* [Hypocoristic, f. NEWFOUNDLAND, NEWFOUNDLANDER: see -IE.] Newfoundland; a Newfoundlander. Also *attrib.* or as *adj.*

1942 BERREY & VAN DEN BARK *Amer. Thes. Slang* §49/4 Newfie, New Foundland [*sic*]. *Ibid.* §385/5 Newfie, Newfier, a Newfoundlander. **1945** W. H. PUGSLEY *Saints, Sinners & Ordinary Seamen* 81 This certainly is a change after those winters off Sydney and Newfie. **1958** *In Flight* (Montreal) Summer 8/1 Cod fishing has..long been synonymous with Newfoundland, but today the canny 'Newfies' are no longer putting all their economic eggs in one basket. **1963** R. I. McDAVID *Mencken's Amer. Lang.* 166 Colonial days, when rum was actually the chief tipple of American dipsomaniacs. .. It still is in Newfoundland, where screech or Newfie screech designates the cheapest grade. **1965** *Globe & Mail* (Toronto) 29 Jan. 7/6 Nobody in Newfie..underestimates Joey Smallwood's abilities as a propagandist. *Ibid.* 7 Dec. 6/4, I described a rail trip (on the famous Newfie Bullet) through the great dead heart of the island-province. **1971** S. E. MORISON *European Discovery Amer.: Northern Voy.* vi. 180 The rocky surface of eastern Newfoundland is full of small depressions..; swarms of mosquitoes breed therein and make life miserable for all but most hardened 'Newfies'. **1972** *Evening Telegram* (St. John's, Newfoundland) 24 June 10/4 It was Newfie entertainment at its best.

new-fledged, *ppl. a.* [NEW *adv.* 3.] Newly furnished with feathers. Also *fig.*

1682 OTWAY *Venice Preserved* II. ii, Those Lazy Owls, who..Sit only watchful with their heavy Wings To cuff down new fledg'd Virtues. **1770** GOLDSM. *Des. Vill.* 168 As a bird each fond endearment tries To tempt its new-fledged offspring to the skies. **1807** WORDSW. *Ode Intim. Immort.* 142 With new-fledged hope still fluttering in his breast. **1817** SHELLEY *Rev. Islam* V. Song i, Swift and strong As new-fledged Eagles. **1881** SHAIRP *Asp. Poetry* xi. 334 The fresh gleam of new-fledged leaves in spring.

new-form, *v.* [NEW *adv.* 6.] *trans.* To form or shape anew.

1610 SHAKS. *Temp.* I. ii. 83 Thy false vncle..new created The creatures that were mine,..Or els new form'd 'em. **1675** OWEN *Serm.* Wks. 1851 IX. 317 Christ takes the Church and goes to new-form it and fashion it more for the glory of God. **1720** WELTON *Suffer. Son of God* I. iii. 56 Do thou regulate and new-form my Desires. **1778** MISS BURNEY *Evelina* lxxv, You shall new-form, new-model me.

new-formed, *ppl. a.* [NEW *adv.* 3.] Newly formed; formed anew.

1647 COTTRELL *Davila's Hist. Fr.* I. 26 Until such time as the foundation of their new formed Government were setled. **1665** BRATHWAIT *Comment Two Tales* 196 The Bridegroom joyes in his new-formed Bride. **1777** POTTER *Æschylus* (1779) I. 202 Pressing on His hurried step to learn their new-form'd measures. **1836** BUCKLAND *Geol. & Min.* I. 505 To take first possession of new-formed land.

new-found, *a.* [NEW *adv.* 3.] Newly found or invented; recently discovered.

c **1496** *Serm. Episc. Puer.* (W. de W.) b iij, [We take] paynted gyrdels of Spaynardes, newe founde hattes of Romayns. **1579** FULKE *Confut. Sanders* 551 The conuersion of the Infidels..is a newe found argument. **1634–5** BRERETON *Trav.* (Chetham Soc.) 60 A couple of these perspectives, which shew the new-found motion of the stars about Jupiter. **1670** SIR J. VAUGHAN in *Phenix* (1721) I. 415 Which were a strange new-found Conclusion. **1749** FIELDING *Tom Jones* XVIII. x, Wished him heartily joy of his new-found uncle. **1781** COWPER *Expost.* 6 Can..art confer A new-found luxury not seen in her? **1856** KINGSLEY *Heroes, Theseus* ii. 189 Ægeus his new-found father. **1865** J. H. INGRAHAM *Pillar of Fire* (1872) 303 They are the first to hail the new-found calf-god.

b. Of lands, islands, etc., esp. with reference to America or certain parts of it; hence *Newfoundland* as the proper name of a large island at the mouth of the St. Lawrence.

1509 BARCLAY *Shyp of Folys* (1874) II. 25 Apuly, Afryke, and the newe fonde londe. **1527** R. THORNE in Hakluyt *Voy.* (1589) 253 They should come to the New founde islandes that wee discouered. **1588** T. HARIOT (*title*) A Briefe and True Report of the New Found Land of Virginia. **1626** SIR W. VAUGHAN *Golden Fleece* title-p., The Southernmost part of the Island commonly called the Newfoundland. **1668** H. MORE *Div. Dial.* III. xxxiv. (1713) 270 The Salvation of them of the New-found World upon Earth, I mean those of America. **1777** ROBERTSON *Hist. Amer.* (1783) I. 137 Various opinions and conjectures were formed concerning the new-found countries. **1807** J. BARLOW *Columb.* I. 6 Who sway'd a moment..Iberia's sceptre on the new found shore.

Newˈfoundland. a. The name of the island (see prec. b) used attributively, esp. in *Newfoundland dog*, a large breed of dog, noted for its sagacity, good temper, strength, and swimming powers. *Newfoundland fish*, codfish.

1611 [see next 1]. **1617** MORYSON *Itin.* III. 134 Great quantity of Hearrings, and new found land Fish dried. **1720** DE FOE *Capt. Singleton* xi. (1840) 195 We found..some Newfoundland fish. **1773** M. RISHTON *Let.* 25 Apr. in F. Burney *Early Diary* (1889) I. 204 We intend getting a very large Newfoundland dog before we leave this place. **1779** W. COXE *Sketches of Swisserland* v. 49 How we contrived to arrange ourselves, our servants, a large Newfoundland dog, and the baggage, in so narrow a compass. **1824** *Goldsmith's Nat. Hist.* II. 9 It is not certain whether the Newfoundland Dog be a distinct breed. **1838** LYTTON *Alice* I. i, A splendid dog of the Newfoundland breed. **1876** DAVIS *Polaris Exp.* ii. 48 The ship..took on board caplins and six Newfoundland dogs.

b. *ellipt.* A Newfoundland dog.

1827 DISRAELI *Vivian Grey* V. VII. v. 29 They were instantly saluted by an immense Newfoundland. **1845** YOUATT *Dog* 52 The Newfoundland is a spaniel of large size. **1864** TENNYSON *Aylmer's F.* 125 He..Would care no more for Leolin's walking with her Than for his old Newfoundland's.

Newˈfoundlander. [Cf. prec. and -ER¹.]

1. A native or inhabitant of Newfoundland.

1611 COTGR., *Terreneufviers*, New-found-landers, new-found-landmen. **1817–18** COBBETT *Resid. U.S.* (1822) 154 With as much fury as the Newfoundlanders attack people who speak against the Pope. **1885** *Athenæum* 5 Sept. 301/2 The principal question which agitates the Newfoundlanders relates to the French claims.

2. A ship belonging to Newfoundland.

1801 *Naval Chron.* VI. 512 Four Newfoundlanders.. went plump ashore.

3. A Newfoundland dog.

1806 *Spirit Public Jrnls.* IX. 311 Two terriers,..a Newfoundlander, and a fine tan-yard dog. **1856** KANE *Arct. Expl.* I. xi. 126, I take four of our best Newfoundlanders, now well broken, in our lightest sledge.

new-front, *v.* [NEW *adv.* 6.] *trans.* To put a new front on.

1748 RICHARDSON *Clarissa* (1811) III. 245 The house where he had lodgings was new-fronting. **1811** W. TAYLOR in *Monthly Rev.* LXVI. 471 He new-fronted some churches in the same style. **1851** MAYHEW *Lond. Labour* I. 369/1 The Wellingtons are to be new-fronted.

New Frontier. [cf. FRONTIER *sb.* 4 b.] A new approach to reform and social betterment; *spec.* the name given to a programme of social improvement advocated by J. F. Kennedy, President of the U.S. from 1961 to 1963. Hence **New Frontiersman, new frontiersman,** a proponent of this programme.

1934 H. A. WALLACE (*title*) The new frontier. **1960** J. F. KENNEDY in *N.Y. Times* 16 July 1/8 The New Frontier of which I speak is not a set of promises—it is a set of challenges. **1962** *Listener* 21 June 1057/2 Even the most ardent new frontiersman..would agree that Mr McCormack was probably not exaggerating. **1963** *Guardian* 22 Feb. 11/4 The energy and sophistication of the New Frontiersmen. **1964** *New Statesman* 10 Apr. 574/1 Baulked of any hope of keeping up with the new frontiersmen of science, it is determined to keep tabs on the new backwoodsmen of architecture. **1969** C. Booker *Neophiliacs* vii. 162 Kennedy's New Frontier America. **1973** R. Thomas *If you can't be Good* (1974) ii. 14 The doctoral thesis I had been researching when summoned to the New Frontier.

new-furnish, *v.* [New *adv.* 6.] *trans.* To refurnish.

1611 Cotgr., *Regarnir*, to regarnish, to new-furnish. **1713** *Guardian* No. 91 ¶ 10 We therefore new furnished the Room in all Respects proportionably to us. **1806** Surr *Winter in Lond.* II. 80 You must new furnish your wardrobe.

† **newgar,** obs. form of auger *sb.*[1]

14.. *Childh. Jesus* 408 in Horstm. *Altengl. Leg.* (1878) 117 He plucked hym out Euen at a newgarus hole.

Newgate ('nju:geɪt). The name of a celebrated London prison (pulled down in 1902–3), used attrib. as ***Newgate fashion, term, wretch***; also **Newgate bird**, a gaol-bird; **Newgate Calendar**, a publication (first issued in 1773) containing accounts of prisoners in Newgate; **Newgate frill** or **fringe**, a fringe of beard worn under the chin; **Newgate hornpipe**, a hanging; **Newgate knocker**, a lock of hair twisted back from the temple towards the ear, worn by costermongers, etc.; **Newgate novel**, a picaresque novel of the second quarter of the nineteenth century; so ***Newgate novelist, Newgate school***.

1596 Shaks. *1 Hen. IV*, iii. iii. 105 *Fal.* Must we all march? *Bard.* Yea, two and two, Newgate fashion. **1600** S. Nicholson *Acolastus* (1876) 15 When naught but Newgate tearmes can store yͤ tongue. **1607** Dekker & Wilkins *Jests* D.'s Wks. (Grosart) II. 343 Our Newgate-Bird..spreading his Dragon-like wings..beheld a thousand Synnes. **1677** Otway *Cheats of Scapin* i. i, Newgate-bird, rogue, villain. **1722** De Foe *Col. Jack* (1840) 166 Every Newgate wretch.. has here a fair opportunity. **1757** Wesley *Wks.* (1872) IX. 233 What are they who steer by this rule better than a company of Newgate-birds? **1829** W. Maginn in Partridge *Dict. Slang* (1937) 558/1 Toeing a Newgate hornpipe. **1836** *Wilson's Tales Borders* II. 5/1 That extraordinary record of human vice and suffering, 'The Newgate Calendar'. **1851** Mayhew *Lond. Labour* I. 36/2 As for the hair, they say it ought to be long in front, and done in 'figure-six' curls, or twisted back to the ear 'Newgate-knocker style'. **1854** C. Knight *Old Printer & Modern Press* vi. 281 The host of penny Newgate novels..may continue to be sold; but, as far as we can trace, there are no novelties in this once popular literature of the gallows. **1865** Dickens *Mut. Fr.* i. xiv, I also felt that I had committed every crime in the Newgate Calendar. **1885** *Cornh. Mag.* Sept. 259 Some of them beardless, others with a fringe of hair around their faces, such as the English call a Newgate frill. **1896** Georgiana M. Stisted *True Life R. F. Burton* xi. 266 A man with a Newgate fringe, clad in grey homespun garments. **1959** *Brno Studies in English* I. 104 The 'Newgate novelists' of the 'thirties (Edward Bulwer, W. H. Ainsworth, and Charles Whitehead) represent a literary school, which is generally called 'the Newgate School' or 'Bulwer's school'. **1963** K. Hollingsworth *Newgate Novel 1830–47* i. 14 A series of novels having criminals as prominent characters aroused widespread attention. Contemptuous critics at the time called them Newgate fiction, and later writers have grouped them under the label of the Newgate novel. **1965** S. Marcus *Dickens: from Pickwick to Dombey* ii. 67 In *Catherine*.. Thackeray..identified Dickens with the Newgate novelists. **1970** G. M. Fraser *Royal Flash* 188 And then it would be the Newgate hornpipe for Flashy, with the whole damned crew of Sons of the Volsungs hauling on the rope. **1971** R. L. Wolff *Strange Stories* i. 24 The vogue of the 'Newgate' novel—as the new genre was called after the famous prison, where some of the most affecting scenes usually took place, and after the Newgate Calendar of crime—ran fast and furious.

Hence '**Newgated** *pa. pple.*, put into Newgate; **Newga'teer**, a Newgate prisoner; '**Newgatory** *a.*, belonging to Newgate (with pun on *nugatory*).

1678 *Narr. Proc. Old Bayly* 4 An old Newgateer..was convicted for stealing Silver spoons. *a* **1734** North *Exam.* (1740) 258 Soon after this, he was taken up and Newgated. *a* **1845** Hood *To Mrs. Fry* xiii, But I don't like your Newgatory teaching. **1877** Ruskin *Fors Clav.* lxxxii. 297 The modern philanthropist of the Newgatory school.

new girl. [New *a.* 8.] A schoolgirl during her first term(s) at a school, esp. one at an English boarding-school; also *transf.*, a (young) woman newly come into a given set of circumstances. Also (with hyphen) *attrib.* or as *adj.* Cf. new boy.

1853 Mrs. Gaskell *Ruth* I. i. 16 Most new girls get impatient at first; but it goes off. **1924** D. Moore *Fen's First Term* v. 59 A dozen people charged hospitably at the new girl with biscuits and milk. **1936** M. Kennedy *Together & Apart* i. 130 New girls are always sort of freaks. **1951** N. Mitford *Blessing* i. viii. 93 She was a new girl, she must watch her step. **1968** 'R. Llewellyn' *End of Rug* (1969) xix. 151, I went from school to school... I was rather new-girl at times, of course. A little lonely.

new ground. [Ground *sb.* 16.] **a.** Ground which has been cleared and cultivated only recently. *U.S. local.* **b.** A part of a goldfield unexploited until recently. *Austral.* (Cf. *to break* (*new*) *ground* s.v. ground *sb.* 11 b.)

1624 J. Smith *Gen. Hist. Virginia* iv. 126 We haue ordinarily foure or fiue [barrels of produce an acre], but of new ground six, seuen, and eight. **1771** in *Maryland Hist. Mag.* (1919) XIV. 134 Our new ground tob[acc]o here has been housed 3 or 4 days past. **1862** *Burrangong* (New South Wales) *Courier* 13 Aug. 2/3 The rush to the Three Mile Diggings..is..going ahead in a most satisfactory manner, and a large extent of new ground has lately been taken up. **1868** *Mining Surveyors & Registrars' Rep.* (Victoria, Dept. Mines) Sept. 36 At Barkly some new ground has been opened south of the main lead. **1915** *Dialect Notes* IV. 186 *New-ground*, virgin land prepared for cultivation. **1937** *Shenandoah* (Va.) *Nature Jrnl.* I. iii. 11/1 Each year the acre and half of rough rocky mountain and perhaps a little 'new ground' patch were tilled by hand. **1949** H. Hornsby *Lonesome Valley* 44 The next time he looked back Chester's place was like a newground that had been burned over. **1953** *Amer. Speech* XXVIII. 251 [Bedford Co., Pa.] *New ground.* .. Pronounced with a heavily accented *new* and as if it were a single word, *newground*. 'There are lots of teaberries this year out on John Bussard's new ground.' In general use.

New Hall. The name of a site at Shelton, Staffordshire, used to designate china and porcelain produced there.

1829 S. Shaw *Hist. Staffordshire Pott.* viii. 201 The partners..settled the manufactory at the New Hall, Shelton ..; on which account the Porcelain had the appellation of *New Hall China*. **1896** E. A. Downman *Eng. Pott. & Porc.* (new ed.) 132 As no distinguishing mark was used before 1820, New Hall porcelain is difficult to identify. **1969** [see Bristol 2 b].

† **new head.** *Obs. rare.* [f. new *a.* + -head: cf. MDu. *niewheit* (Du. *nieuwheid*), MLG. *nye-*, G. *neuheit*, Da. *nyhed*, Sw. *nyhet*.] Newness.

a **1340** Hampole *Psalter* xlii. 4 þat gladis my ȝouthed, þat is, newhed of my saule in grace. *Ibid.* lxviii. 36 þe figure of þis newhed. *c* **1400** Hylton *Scala Perf.* (W. de W. 1494) ii. xxxi, But be ye refourmed in newehede of felyng.

newie ('nju:i:). *colloq.* Also **newy.** [f. new *a.* + -ie.] **a.** Something new, as a new joke, story, or suggestion. **b.** A person without previous experience in professional entertainment. **c.** A song recently issued on a gramophone record. **d.** = new ball.

1947 *Amer. Speech* XXII. 157 On the 'Can You Top This?' radio show of November 16, 1946, one of the principal characters said, 'Here's a *new-y*.' His reference was to a joke. **1951** Cusack & James *Come in Spinner* 495 'Yeah! I seem to have heard your propositions before.' Kim leaned over and took the bottle from her. 'Put that down and listen to me. You haven't heard this one, this is a newy.' **1961** A. Berkman *Singers' Gloss. Show Business* 61 *Newies* (Var.), novices; neophytes. **1966** *Melody Maker* 26 Nov. 2 Dave Dee's newie 'Save Me' has an 'African sound with cowbells'. **1971** *West Indian Weekly* 12 Nov. 14/4 The Staples Singers are turning out some incredible soul discs of which their newie, 'Respect Yourself', is a classic in the message song genre. **1972** *Shout* Mar., When this newie turned up..I snatched up a copy. **1975** *Saturday Night* (Toronto) July/Aug. 29/1 Mostly, synectics involves sticking big pieces of paper up around the walls, writing down every bright remark that anyone comes up with, and then winnowing these down to a few golden newies. **1975** *Daily Tel.* 6 Sept. 14/5 But did I say 'ball?' How old-fashioned can one get? 'Ah, the new cherry,' mutters Trevor Bailey with nostalgia in his voice. 'It's the newie,' exclaims Brian Johnston.

newine, Sc. var. neven *v.*, to name. *Obs.*

'**newing,** *vbl. sb.* [f. new *v.* + -ing[1].]

† **1.** The action of renewing or making new. *Obs.*

c **1375** *Sc. Leg. Saints* xxxvii. (*Vincent*) 81 He wald nocht þai de suld sa, but newing of gret payne. **1387** Trevisa *Higden* (Rolls) III. 117 He sigh visiouns and siȝtes of þe newynge of þe temple. **1456** Sir G. Haye *Law Arms* (S.T.S.) 3 To mak some newing of thing till enforme ȝour ȝouthede of mony syndry knaulagis. *a* **1500** in Arnolde *Chron.* (1811) 42 The grauntis yeftis confirmacions newyng and ordinauncis aboue sayd.

† **b.** A new growth or product. *Obs. rare.*

1547 Boorde *Introd. Knowl.* ii. (1870) 127 They wyl sell there lams..and theyr corne the whyche is not sowen, and all other newynges, a yere before that they be sure of any newynge.

2. A new thing, a novelty; *pl.* news, something new. Now *dial.*

Chiefly surviving in the N. of Ireland in the pl. form, also written *newins, newans*, and *newance*.

c **1410** *Sir Cleges* 372 He seyd, 'I thanke Cryst Iesu; Thys is a fayre neweynge.' **1562** Q. Kennedy *Ressoning w. J. Knox* ✠ iij b, That was na newingis in this cuntrie. *Ibid.* D ij, Apperanlie that sould be na newingis to yow. **1633** Rutherford *Lett.* xxix. (1862) I. 104 Strokes were not newings to Him, and neither are they to you. **1875** Knox *Hist. Down* 49 Newance. **1880** *Antrim & Down Gloss.* s.v. *New-ans*, It's new-ans to see you down so early.

'**newing,** *sb. dial.* (See quot. and neaving.)

1674 Ray *S. & E.C. Words* 73 *Newing*, yeast or Barm. Ess[ex]. [Hence in Coles (1676), Bailey (1721), Ainsworth (1736), etc.] **1863** Jephson in *Trans. Arch. Soc. Essex* II. 186 *Newin*, yeast.

new-invented, *ppl. a.* [New *adv.* 3.] Recently invented or devised.

1573 L. Lloyd *Marrow of Hist.* (1653) 280 Those new invented torments which they made for others. **1676** Worlidge *Cider* title-p., Description of the new-invented Ingeno or Mill. **1723–4** Dk. Wharton *True Briton* No. 65 II. 552 This new-invented Piece of Law-Artifice. **1791** Boswell *Johnson* I. 324 A new-invented machine which went without horses. **1818** Bentham *Ch. Eng.* Introd. 53 In the new-invented system of instruction.

newir, obs. Sc. form of never.

newish ('nju:ɪʃ), *a.* [f. new *a.* + -ish[1].] Somewhat new.

1570 Levins *Manip.* 145/26 Newish, *recentulus.* **1626** Bacon *Sylva* §46 It drinketh not newish at all. **1824** A. Headley in J. Raine *Mem. J. Hodgson* (1858) II. 27, I like everything about the place but the newish church. **1866** Carlyle *Remin.* (1881) I. 282 We ascended..[a] narrow newish wooden staircase.

† **newity,** obs. form of annuity.

1559 *Richmond Wills* (Surtees) 131 Boitht with hys newytie and his chylds portion. *Ibid.* 132 In consyderation of his newytie geyvyne to hym by my faither.

New Jersey. The name of one of the eastern states of the United States, used *attrib.* in the names of plants native to the region, as **New Jersey pine** = *Jersey pine* (Jersey[2]); **New Jersey tea** = *Jersey tea* (Jersey[2]).

1759 [see *Jersey tea* (Jersey[2])]. **1785** H. Marshall *Arbustrum Americanum* 27 American Ceanothus, or New-Jersey Tea-tree,..is a low shrub, growing common in most parts of North America. **1818** W. P. C. Barton *Compendium Floræ Philadelphicæ* II. 183 *P[inus] inops*... New Jersey Pine. Scrub Pine. Pitch Pine. A low straggly, and very common species particularly in Jersey. **1832** D. J. Browne *Sylva Amer.* 234 New Jersey Pine. **1877** *Rep. Vermont Board Agric.* IV. 159 Riley recommends persons..to plant a small patch of New Jersey Tea (*Ceanothus*)..as a decoy near the strawberry bed. **1941** R. S. Walker *Lookout* 59 The New Jersey tea or redroot..grows profusely on the summit as well as on both sides of the mountain. **1958** G. A. Petrides *Field Guide to Trees & Shrubs* 139 New Jersey Tea, *Ceanothus americanus* L... A low shrub. Leaves egg-shaped to triangular... Flowers white in dense heads.

newk(e, obs. forms of nook.

new-laid, *ppl. a.* [New *a.* 3.] Of eggs: Newly or freshly laid.

1528 Paynell *Salerne's Regim.* F j b, Dyuers nouryshynge meates. The fyrst are newe layde egges. **1563** Hyll *Art Garden* (1593) 101 Against the dropsie, take a new laid Eg. **1687** A. Lovell tr. *Thevenot's Trav.* i. 39 Lovely Virgins.. as white as new-lay'd Eggs. **1706** E. Ward *Wooden World Diss.* (1708) 63 There's no Bolus to him comparable to a new-laid Egg. **1782** Cowper *Fable* 2 Her new-laid eggs she fondly pressed. **1881** Besant & Rice *Chapl. of Fleet* i. v, Like fresh butter and new-laid eggs.

† '**Newland.** *Obs.* [f. the name of Abraham *Newland*, chief cashier of the Bank of England from 1782 to 1807.] A Bank of England note.

1801 *Sporting Mag.* XVII. 243 The cash was likewise composed of paper commonly called young Newlands. **1823** Syd. Smith *Wks.* (1859) II. 21/2 Forth from his bill-case this votary of Plutus drew his nitid Newlands.

new-land. [New *a.* + land *sb.*[1]]

† **1.** ***New-land fish***, Newfoundland fish. *Obs.*

[**1550–1600** *Customs Duties* (Brit. Mus. Addit. MS. 25097), Fishe of Newland the c. .xxxs.] **1580** R. Hitchcock *Politic Plat* c ij, They shalbe sette out to fishe for Codd and Lyng.., or els to Newfounde lande, for Newlande fishe. **1591** Percivall *Sp. Dict.*, *Bacalaos*, a kinde of newlande fish.

2. *new-land hay*: (see quot.).

1894 *Northumbld. Gloss.*, *New-land-hay*, clover hay. Hay from a new-sown pasture.

New Left, new left. [Phr. coined by C. Wright Mills (1916–62), American political sociologist.] The name of a movement originated by young radicals opposed to the philosophy of the 'old' liberal society; now applied to many movements of protest. Also *attrib.* Hence **New Lefter, New Lefty**, a supporter of radical policies; **New Leftish** *a.*, **New Leftist** *a.* and *sb.*

1960 *New Left Rev.* Jan.–Feb. 1 Our hope is that people in the New Left will feel, with a special urgency, the poverty of ideas in the Labour Movement. *Ibid.* Mar.–Apr. 70/2 The 'anarchism' of young New Lefters. *Ibid.* Sept.–Oct. 15/2 Stop the new-leftist dogs from yapping. **1960** New Lefty [see hobohemia]. **1961** *New Left Rev.* Jan.–Feb. 51/1 What can..be called 'new left' student opinion. **1966** *Economist* 3 Sept. 887/1 The phrase 'new left' is applied to all sorts of protesters in the United States, to Provos in Amsterdam, to dissatisfied intellectuals in eastern Europe. **1967** *Philosophy* XLII. 287 The emphasis is rather New-Leftish and Gramscian. **1967** *Time* 28 Apr. 15 The New Leftists have a mystical faith in the purity and wisdom of the poor, 'uncorrupted' by the Establishment. **1968** *Listener* 3 Oct. 442/1 The would-be Monday Clubber and the New Lefter will both shut up when they hear of the accident in the Headrow. **1971** *Daily Tel.* 18 Nov. 15/3 Berkeley City Council—first and only city government in America to represent the 'New Left'—has passed an astonishing resolution..to offer asylum to military deserters. **1973** *Times Lit. Suppl.* 23 Nov. 1422/5 Whose sympathies are clearly more towards the New Left than towards bureaucratic communism. **1975** *Listener* 13 Feb. 209/1 All over Europe in the Sixties you could see a proliferation of political sects—Marxists, Trotskyists, Maoists, Castroists. .. This New Left..was, above all, a manifestation of youth.

new light. [Light *sb.* 6 d.] **1. a.** Novel religious views or doctrines (see light *sb.* 6 d).

1650–1785 [see light *sb.* 6 d]. **1806** T. G. Fessenden *Democracy Unveiled* ii. 181 Altho' not bless'd with second sight, Divine inflation, or new light.

b. Any of the religious sects or doctrines of the 'New Lights'.

1750 J. Birket *Voy. N. Amer.* (1916) 4 There is two Presbyterian meeting houses here, one of the Newlight, and one of the old. **1819** J. G. Lockhart *Peter's Lett. to his Kinsfolk* III. lxii. 100 The Old Light Antiburghers enjoy the ministrations of..Dr. McCrie... The New Light..are ruled *in spiritualibus* by Dr. Jamieson. **1850** W. H. Foote *Sk. Virginia* 373 In his discourse he..read a hue and cry, for the arrest of 'the new light'. **1874** [see light *sb.* 6 d]. **1943** J. Macleod *Scottish Theology* 229 As a term, New Light came especially to be used in connection with the change that took place in the thinking of the Seceders towards the end of the 18th century.

2. A person holding 'new lights' or novel (religious) doctrines; a revivalist; a member of any of various schisms from several Protestant churches in Scotland and N. Amer. during the eighteenth and nineteenth centuries.

a **1734** R. Wodrow *Analecta* (1842) II. 169 You have brought in a stranger, one of the neu-lights, among us. **1743** J. Hempstead *Diary* 30 Mar. (1901) 407 All come to settle the disorders that are subsisting among those called New Lights which follow Mr Davenport. **1750** J. Birket *Voy. N. Amer.* (1916) 22 There is Nineteen different places of Worship in the Town (to wit) thirteen of the Independents Presbyterians & newlights &Ca. **1796** Grose *Dict. Vulgar T.* (ed. 3) *New Light*, one of the new light; a methodist. **1807** R. McNemar *Kentucky Revival* 29 These..taught as an important truth, that the will of God, was made manifest to each individual..by an inward light... Hence they received the name of 'New-Lights'. **1828** J. McGregor *Sk. Maritime Colonies Brit. Amer.* II. 465 Let us leave abstract points of Christian doctrine to theological disputants, and the raving of *new lights*. **1847** R. Davidson *Hist. Presbyterian Church in Kentucky* 219 In the Great Revival, Mr. Stone was conspicuous..[in] the subsequent formation of societies, known under the various names of New Lights, Christians, Arians, Marshallites, and Stoneites. **1872** [see hickory 4 a]. **1888** J. M. Barrie *Auld Licht Idylls* iii. 60 The congregation..had split, and as the New Lights (now the U.P.'s) were in the majority, the Old Lights..had to retire to the community. **1949** *William & Mary Q.* Jan. 43 The New Brunswick group, the 'new lights', wished to give eloquence in preaching precedence over formal knowledge. **1959** *Chambers's Encycl.* XII. 309/1 The original seceders.. formed themselves into a body independent of the state church in 1733. The new group of separatists were divided in 1747 by the anti-Jacobite burgess oath into burghers and anti-burghers. Subsequently each of these bodies split into Old and New Lights (1799 and 1806 respectively).

b. *transf.* = Campbellite 2.

1877 *Bull. U.S. Nat. Museum* No. 9. 21 *Pomoxys annularis*... Throughout Kentucky it is known as the 'New Light', and sometimes as 'Campbellite'. **1884** [see Campbellite 2].

3. *attrib.* or as *adj.* **a.** Belonging to or holding the views of the 'New Lights'.

1732 Swift *Advantages repealing Sacramental Test* 10 The Quarrel between Old and New Light-Men, is managed with more Rage and Rancour, than any other Dispute. **1742** J. Hempstead *Diary* 20 Dec. (1901) 402, 2 of them Newlight Exhorters begun their meeting. **1744** [see light *sb.* 6 d]. **1793** 'T. Thrum' *Look before ye Loup* 3, I took the advice of a *newlight* neighbour upo' this knotty point. **1807** R. McNemar *Kentucky Revival* 46 Taking what is called the *New-light* doctrine, as the rudiments of divine truth, they proceeded to consider the nature of justification, reconciliation to God, etc. **1837** W. Jenkins *Ohio Gazetteer* 373 There are in this country..eight christian (or newlight) ..and five dunkard churches. **1874** [see light *sb.* 6 d]. **1883** P. Schaff *Relig. Encycl.* II. 1634/2 [New England divines] announced a few principles, which were called 'New-Light Divinity', or 'New Divinity'. **1949** *Canad. Hist. Rev.* Mar. 75 Henry Alline, the New Light evangelist, was shattering the less sedate Dissenting congregations of the Nova Scotian out-ports.

b. *transf.* Novel, newfangled.

1831 J. N. Catron *Let.* 1 May in N. N. Scott *Mem. H. L. White* (1856) xii. 249 A union of N. Light Federalists with Kentucky republicans..cannot last. **1833** J. B. Wyeth *Oregon* 4 What the *new-light* doctrine of Phrenology calls the disposition bump of *Inhabitiveness*. **1839** *Spirit of Times* 26 Oct. 399/3 *Abbreviations*... We heard of this 'new light system' being carried so far as to be adopted by a lady.

Hence **New Lightism**, new-light doctrines.

1755 in *Essex Inst. Hist. Coll.* (1916) LII. 78 He seems a grave, close heavy Man, not given to talk & deeply immerged in New Lightism. **1857** P. Cartwright *Autobiogr.* 32 B. W. Stone stuck to his New Lightism.

'newlings, *adv. Sc.* Also 8–9 -lins. [f. new *a.* + -lings: cf. OE. *néowlinga* anew; MDu. *nieweling(e, -lings*, MLG. *nîlinge(s*, MHG. *niuwelingen, newe-, neuling(e)s*.]

1. Newly, recently; †immediately.

1375 Barbour *Bruce* xiv. 86 Newlyngis at thair ariwyng, In playne ficht thai discomfit thar Thar fais. *c* **1475** *Rauf Coilȝear* 962 Sic tythingis come..That the Marschell of France was newlingis deid. **1513** Douglas *Æneis* ix. x. 14 His breist and hart That newlingis of the kynryk was a part. **1785** in Shirrefs *Poems* (1790) 318 A cripple chiel,..just but newlins frae the school. **1880** J. E. Watt *Poet. Sketches* 10 The pat's but newlins on the fire.

†**2.** Afresh, anew. *Obs.*

c **1500** *Lancelot* 36 The scharp assay and ek the Inwart peine Of dowblit wo me neulyngis can constrein. **1522–3** *Burgh Rec. Edinb.* (1869) I. 214 And thairfore desyrit the samyne newlingis againe to be granted.

new look. [look *sb.* 2 f.] **1.** (Freq. with capital initials.) A style of women's clothes introduced in Paris by Christian Dior in 1947, characterized esp. by skirts longer and fuller than those previously worn. Also applied to more recent new styles.

1947 *Time* 15 Sept. 87 What was going on [in fashion]? The search for the 'New Look'. What was the New Look? No one knew precisely. **1948** *Economist* 14 Feb. 285/2 Clothing in styles which the New Look has superseded. **1949** *Ann. Reg. 1948* 59 The 'new look' had swept the great cities. **1957** *Daily Mail* 25 Oct. 10/2 When Christian Dior launched the New Look in 1947 it met with an enthusiasm which amounted to hysteria. **1958** *Spectator* 8 Aug. 187/1 The [fashion] trade now bitterly resents St. Laurent's new look.

2. In wider use: a change in policy or procedure; a renovated or up-to-date presentation or appearance. Also (with hyphen) *attrib.*

1948 *Melody Maker* 3 Apr. 3/3 (*heading*) The 'New Look' in jazz has come to stay. **1952** *Economist* 27 Sept. 765/2 (*heading*) Czech trade unions reorganized... The 'new look' given to, and by, the trade union officials at once brought them into conflict with the rank and file of the movement. **1952** *Science News Let.* 25 Oct. 258/1 A 'New Look' for veterans with smashed noses due to war-time injuries is being developed. **1955** *Ann. Reg. 1954* 169 On January 12 the Secretary of State, Mr. Dulles, announced what came to be called the 'New Look' policy. **1956** E. J. Ruppelt *Report on Unidentified Flying Objects* 85 In early 1949 the term 'new look' was well known. The new look in women's fashions was the lower hem-lines, in automobiles it was longer lines. In UFO circles the new look was cuss 'em. **1958** J. Cannan *And be a Villain* iii. 61 How different life looked now, and how strange that the begetter of this New Look was..the depraved and disgraced Jonathan. **1959** *News Chron.* 2 Nov. 5/1 The new-look colours and markings which are to be on all B.E.A. airliners. **1960** *Guardian* 28 Apr. 6/6 The 'new look' which..the Glasgow business man who now runs the Tourist Board, is giving to tourist centres. **1966** *Melody Maker* 15 Oct. 19 A slightly new-look Johnny Parker band restored to full vigour. **1974** S. Gulliver *Vulcan Bulletins* 107 It's the new-look Libyan justice. Or rather, it's medieval but recently revived.

Hence **new-'lookish** *a.*

1950 *Christian Sci. Monitor* 20 Feb. 10/1 Visitors recently returned from Moscow report that it is the most New Lookish of any Russian city.

newly ('nju:lɪ), *adv.* Forms: 1 niwlice, 3 neowe-, 4 new(e)liche, 3 newelike; 4 newli, neuli, -ly, 5 nvly, nulye, nyowely, 4–6 newelie, (5 -li), 4– newly, 6–7 newlie. [f. new *a.* + -ly²: cf. MDu. *niewelike, -lijc*, MLG. *ni(g)elik(en*, MHG. *niuwelîch(e, niulîch(e*, G. *neulich*, ON. *nýliga* (Da. *nylig*, Sw. *nyligen*).]

1. a. Very recently or lately; within a very little time (before that spoken of).

Now rare except as in b and c; formerly sometimes with present tense.

c **893** K. Ælfred *Oros.* iv. x. 202 Romane hæfdon þa niwlice ʒesett þæt [etc.]. *Ibid.* vi. iv. 260 Hio þa wæs niwlice cristen. *c* **1000** Ælfric *Hom.* II. 494 Her cumað to eow niwlice tweʒen Ebreisce men. *a* **1225** *Ancr. R.* 218 Hwonne a mon haueð neoweliche wif iled hom, he nimeð ȝeme..of hire maneres. *c* **1250** *Gen. & Ex.* 293 Newelike he was of erðe wrogt, And to ðat mirie blisse brogt. *c* **1330** R. Brunne *Chron.* (1810) 67 Harald was comand, neuly was mad kyng. *c* **1400** Maundev. (1839) xxviii. 284 That myghte not ben, to myn avys, that so manye scholde have entred so newely. **1490** Caxton *Eneydos* xi. 41 This man..neweli hither comyn to soiourne in our countreys. **1523** Ld. Berners *Froiss.* I. cclv. 378 The towne of Breure, the which was newely before turned frenche. **1602** Middleton *Phœnix* I. i. 141, I heard newly Of sudden travel which his grace intends. **1641** Evelyn *Diary* 8 Oct., The Infante Cardinal..being dead but newly. **1699** Bentley *Phal.* 95 Did he not newly say [etc.]. **1738** Wesley *Ps.* lxxx. ix, A generous and right noble Vine When newly out of Egypt brought. **1866** Howells *Venet. Life* 29 [I] being newly from a land where everything..was in good repair.

b. With pa. pples. used predicatively.

a **1300** *Cursor M.* 3653 Þou sal sai þou ert esau, Fra þe forest newli comen. *c* **1374** Chaucer *Boeth.* iv. met. iii. (1868) 122 Þat oþer of hem is newliche chaunged in to a wolf. *c* **1400** Maundev. (1839) xxviii. 284 But that might not ben .., ne so manye newely slayn, with outen stynkynge. **1422** tr. *Secreta Secret., Priv. Priv.* 193 This ordir ys not nyowely maket. *a* **1533** Ld. Berners *Huon* xlvi. 155 Than he..toke leue of his cosyn that was newly maryed. **1581** Mulcaster *Positions* xxxiii. (1887) 120 Such as be newly recouered from sicknes. **1657** Sparrow *Bk. Com. Prayer* (1661) 22 Our Saviour's rule given to him that was newly cured..by him. **1676** Etheredge *Man of Mode* i. i, A Ladies head newly dress'd for a Ball. **1711** Addison *Spect.* No. 45 ¶6 A Woman of Quality..newly returned from France. **1784** Cowper *Task* iii. 750 A transient guest, newly arrived, And soon to be supplanted. **1818** Shelley *Rosal. & Helen* 800 Like some bright spirit newly born. **1886** *Act 49 & 50 Vict.* c. 54 §1 Any hop ground..newly cultivated as such after the passing of this Act.

c. In *attrib.* combs. (now hyphened).

These are especially common in the 19th and 20th cents.

1560 Daus tr. *Sleidane's Comm.* 21 He wrote an Epistle to the newlye created Emperoure. **1590** Spenser *F.Q.* i. xi. 34 His newly-budded pineons to assay. **1615** Chapman *Odyss.* xii. 137 A newly kitn'd kitlings cries. **1659** Pearson *Creed* (1839) 443 The ancient, but newly-revived heresy of the Arians. **1690** Locke *Ess. Hum. Understanding* III. x. §32 He that, in a newly-discovered country, shall see several sorts of animals and vegetables, unknown to him before, may have as true ideas of them, as of a horse or stag. **1711** Shaftesb. *Charac.* (1737) II. 336 With your newly-espous'd system. **1740** Richardson *Pamela* (1824) I. xx. 267 To have confirmed the poor woman in her newly-assumed penitence. **1807** Wordsw. *Ode Intim. Immort.* 92 Shaped by himself with newly-learned art. **1826** Kirby & Sp. *Entomol.* xxix. III. 57 In the newly-hatched caterpillar. **1831** Mill *Let.* 22 Oct. (1910) I. 19 They have formed a plan for a new colony,..on the coast of Southern Australia, near the place where the newly discovered navigable river discharges itself into the sea. **1834** —— in *Monthly Repos.* VIII. 163 The many are..likely to make a most dangerous use of their newly-acquired power. **1848** S. M. Gray *Let.* 11 Apr. in M. Lutyens *Ruskins & Grays* (1972) xi. 107 Many compliments [were] paid to the newly married couple. **1857** Dufferin *Lett. High Lat.* (ed. 3) 170 A newly-stripped bullock's hide. **1890** 'R. Boldrewood' *Col. Reformer* (1891) 135 This newly-discovered fairyland. **1937** *Burlington Mag.* Apr. 173/2 Prince of a newly-constituted State. **1968** R. A. Lyttleton *Myst. Solar Syst.* v. 166 It endows the newly-formed comets with orbits that are almost parabolic. **1974** J. Wainwright *Evidence I shall Give* viii. 35 Lennox was bringing the newly-arrived Sugden up to date on the murder.

d. newly-wed, newlywed, a person newly married.

1918 *Cosmopolitan* Feb. 90/2 It seemed that a Newly-wed can live on Marmalade for about three months. **1932** Auden *Orators* iii. 103 To-day may mean division for the newly-weds. **1935** *Discovery* Mar. 91/1 Generation upon generation of newly-weds are tempted to 'come and live in leafy ——'. **1938** J. I. Rodale *King's English on Horseback* 146/1 Newlyweds. First-nighters. **1959** G. Freeman *Jack would be Gentleman* viii. 163 'Quite the blissful newly-weds, aren't we?'..'Well, we are newly-weds.' **1973** *Guardian* 12 Mar. 9/6 The advertisement..was one of a series which featured a newly-wed, an insurance man and a saleslady.

†**2. a.** Within a little (from now); soon. *Obs.*

c **1330** *Arth. & Merl.* 4648 (Kölbing), ȝe schullen haue neweliche Hors & armes & alle þing. **1387** Trevisa *Higden* (Rolls) VII. 237 Now sire eorle, þu holdest Engelond, þu schalt riȝt newliche [L. *in proximo*] be kyng.

†**b.** Immediately or soon (after a particular time); quickly. *Obs.*

c **1330** *Arth. & Merl.* 1984 (Kölbing), A chapman..seyd of Merlin openliche, He wald him telle neweliche. **1375** Barbour *Bruce* v. 122 Sic hansell to the folk gaf he,..Newly at his ariwyng. *a* **1400–50** *Alexander* 4740 Newly eftir þe none or nere þare-abowte. *c* **1530** Ld. Berners *Arth. Lyt. Bryt.* (1814) 54 Yf I should mary me so newly, I should be greatly blamed.

3. Anew, afresh.

c **1000** *Ags. Ps.* (Thorpe) cxliii. 10 Ic niwlice niwne cantic þam godan Gode gleawne singe.

c **1375** *Sc. Leg. Saints* xiii. (*Mark*) 169 þane one þe morne ..þai drew hyme newly thru þe towne. *c* **1400** Love *Bonavent. Mirr.* (B.N.C. MS.) lf. 116 þan bigan þey alle newely to wepe. **1530** Palsgr. 839/2 Newly, *de nouueau*. **1568** Grafton *Chron.* II. 663 The lawes of the realme, in part he reformed, and in part he newely augmented. *a* **1648** Ld. Herbert *Hen. VIII* (1683) 371 Our King having gotten York-house..did newly enlarge and beautify it. **1673** Owen *Sacram. Disc.* Wks. 1851 IX. 56 He is as it were (so the word is) newly sacrificed. **1876** Davis *Polaris Exp.* i. 29 She was newly planked inside and out. **1880** Swinburne *Stud. Shaks.* 182 We have but the eternal..figures of jealousy and innocence newly vamped and veneered.

4. In a new fashion or manner.

1553 T. Wilson *Rhet.* (1580) 137 That mirth is more worthe, which is moued by a worde newlie spoken, then if a long tale should pleasauntly bee tolde. **1562** J. Heywood *Prov. & Epigr.* (1867) 216 Talke or walke oldly or newly. **1812** Sir H. Davy *Chem. Philos.* 184 Instances in which these elements are newly arranged, and in which their transfer and changes produce very important phænomena. **1885** Chitty in *Law Times Rep.* LIII. 80/2 Not merely in a new word, but in a word newly or fancifully applied.

new-made, *ppl. a.* [new *adv.* 3.] Recently or freshly made.

c **1400** *Laud Troy Bk.* 6231 That saw an hardy newe-made knyȝt. *c* **1470** Henryson *Mor. Fab.* iv. (*Fox's Confess.*) xx, He..of that new-maid salmond eit enewch. **1500–20** Dunbar *Poems* xxxiii. 53 He come hame a new maid channoun. **1595** Shaks. *John* i. i. 187 New made honor doth forget mens names. **1634** Milton *Comus* 472 Sitting by a new made grave. **1684** T. Burnet *The. Earth* ii. 132 As if new-made matter, like new clothes,..had a better gloss. **1717** Rowe *Epil. Mrs. Centlivre's Cruel Gift*, Was that a Present for a new-made Widow? **1818** Keats *Endym.* iv. 102 Sweet as a musk-rose upon new-made hay. **1886** A. Winchell *Walks Geol. Field* 52 The soil..torn from our new-made road.

b. Of the tide: (see make *v.* 72).

1808 Forsyth *Beauties Scotl.* V. 33 The flood-tide.. according as it is new made, half run, or approaching to still water.

new-make, *v.* [new *adv.* 6.] *trans.* To make again or anew.

1617 Hieron *Wks.* II. 205 The great worke of new making a mans heart. **1649** Milton *Eikon.* 57 The King can no more reject a Law than he can new make a Law. **1714** Derham *Astro-Theol.* (1769) 11 When my hand was in, I new-made some part of it. **1790** J. Adams *Wks.* (1854) IX. 567 It would give me pleasure..to correct or new-make the whole work. **1835** *Gentl. Mag.* i. 376 He new-made the light.

Hence **new-making** *vbl. sb.*

1495 *Naval Acc. Hen. VII* (1896) 274 In Newmaking of takle and apparell. **1580** R. Hitchcock *Politic Plat* c j b, Euerie shippe..shall paie tenne shillynges (towardes the newe makyng of euery shippe so wanting). **1633** Earl Manch. *Al Mondo* (1636) 94 Our bodies..are not cast off by death, but put to new making.

Newmania (nju:'meɪnɪə). [f. the name of J. H. *Newman* (see Newmanism) + -ia¹, punning on mania.] Enthusiastic support for Newmanism. Also *attrib.* Also **Newmanic** (nju:'mænɪk) *a.*, pertaining to or characteristic of J. H. Newman or his views.

1838 J. Romilly *Diary* 9 Dec. (1967) 158 A very objectionable sermon..as faulty as the 'Newmania' sect at Oxford. **1849** F. D. Maurice *Let.* 9 Mar. in J. F. Maurice *F. D. Maurice* (1884) I. xxv. 518 Froude's hero..adopted the Newmanic theory. He gave God credit for being a tyrant. **1900** W. Tuckwell *Reminisc. of Oxford* ii. 17 Men who formed in Oxford what was known as the Noetic school .., provoking by their political and ecclesiastical liberalism the great revolt of the Newmania. **1958** *Spectator* 7 Feb. 167/3 The Newmania [in Oxford] was succeeded by the Railway Mania.

Newmanism ('nju:mənɪz(ə)m). [f. the name of J. H. *Newman* (1801–90) + -ism.] The views on theological and ecclesiastical matters put forward by Newman while a member of the Anglican Church; the principles involved in Newman's teaching.

1838 Arnold in Stanley *Life* (1844) II. 126 This restless love of paradox, is, I believe, one of the main causes of the growth of Newmanism. **1841** Stanley in *Life* (1894) I. 302 The debatable points of Newmanism and Evangelicalism. **1893** Liddon *Life Pusey* II. xxiv. 139 The principles reasserted by the Oxford writers had been before denounced by their Latitudinarian opponents as Newmanism.

Newmanite ('nju:mənait). [f. as prec. + -ITE.] A follower or adherent of Newman.

1837 ARNOLD in Stanley *Life* (1844) II. 89 My strong condemnations of Tories and Newmanites. **1837** LD. HOUGHTON in T. W. Reid *Life* (1891) I. 196 It is, perhaps, the confessorship of the Newmanites which makes them so interesting. **1884** ORNSBY *Mem. J. R. Hope-Scott* I. 267 The Tractarians soon began to divide off into the Moderates of various shades, and the Newmanites.

b. *attrib.* or as *adj.*

1838 ARNOLD in Stanley *Life* viii. (1844) II. 113 All the Newmanite language about baptism might be..used by the Jews..about circumcision. **1841** *Ibid.* ix. 250 The clergy are becoming more and more Newmanite.

'**Newmanize**, *v. rare.* [f. as prec. + -IZE.]

1. *intr.* To incline to, or adopt, Newmanism.

1836 MAURICE in *Life* (1884) I. xiii. 204, I believe I shall perforce Newmanise, protesting, however, against his doctrine all the time.

2. To follow the principles of (Homeric) translation advocated by F. W. Newman.

1861 M. ARNOLD *On transl. Homer* 86 We should say, *He Newmanises*, and his diction would offend us. **1886** *Athenæum* 10 Apr. 483/1 Mr. Way, in fact, is a little inclined to 'Newmanize'... Pure English of the simple sort is amply sufficient for the translating of Homer.

Newman-Keuls (ˌnju:mən'kœls). *Statistics.* The names of D. *Newman* (of the Dept. of Statistics, University College, London) and M. *Keuls* (of the Institute of Horticultural Plant Breeding, Wageningen, Holland), used *attrib.* to designate a test they devised for assessing the significance of differences between the means of different sets of observations, using the ranges of the sets contributing to the means.

1955 D. B. DUNCAN in *Biometrics* XI. 26 The Newman-Keuls Test. A test proposed by Newman..in 1939 and again by Keuls..in 1952 succeeds very simply in raising all of the low protection levels of the multiple *t* test. This test is equivalent to a multiple *t* test preceded by several preliminary range tests. **1962** B. J. WINER *Statistical Princ. Exper. Design* iii. 85 The level of significance for the Newman-Keuls procedure is considered individually with respect to each test. **1970** *Jrnl. General Psychol.* LXXXII. 159 The Newman Keuls test..was run on the means for the different diagnostic classes.., with results indicating significantly more cartoon enjoyment for normals than for the neurotic and sociopathic *Ss.* No other differences reached significance.

Newmarket (nju:'mɑ:kɪt, 'nju:ˌmɑ:kɪt). The name of a town (situated east of Cambridge) famous for its horse-races, used *attrib.* or *ellipt.* in several applications.

1. *attrib.*, as ***Newmarket boot, condition, cut, tail***; also **Newmarket coat**, a close-fitting coat for men, originally worn for riding, or an outdoor coat of a similar style for women; **Newmarket greyhound**, a greyhound of a special breed (see quot. 1856).

1685 *Lond. Gaz.* No. 2041/4 One light Gray Gelding with a long Newmarket Tail. **1698** *Ibid.* No. 3360/4 A long bushy Tail cut after the New-Market Cut. **1709** *Brit. Apollo* No. 19. 3/2 To reduce his Corpus..Unto a New-Market Condition. **1714** *Lond. Gaz.* No. 5252/4 Both Heels white behind, and a New-Market Tayle. **1837** B. WEBSTER *My Young Wife & my Old Umbrella* in *Acting National Drama* I. 7 Green Newmarket cut coat. **1854** DICKENS *Hard T.* I. vi, He was dressed in a Newmarket coat and tight-fitting trousers. **1856** 'STONEHENGE' *Brit. Rural Sports* 163/1 The Newmarket greyhound..is a racing-like, speedy animal, yet possessed of as much stoutness as possible. **1933** J. BUCHAN *Prince of Captivity* II. iv. 248 She had been gardening..and wore Newmarket boots. **1958** *Times* 6 Oct. 13/1 The foot which would be warm and practical with sheepskin or Newmarket boots.

2. *ellipt.* A Newmarket coat.

1843 MRS. ROMER *Rhone, Darro*, etc., I. 288 His travelling cap was exchanged for a fashionable white hat; his frock-coat for a Newmarket. **1883** MISS BRADDON *Phant. Fort.* xxxvi, A brown velvet Newmarket, which completely covered her short satin gown.

3. a. A card-game in which the main object is to play the same cards as certain duplicates which are exhibited.

1840 DICKENS *Old C. Shop* xxxvi, Going the odd man or plain Newmarket for fruit, ginger-beer [etc.]. **1887** *All Year Round* 5 Feb. 66 Pope Joan has survived to the present day in the modified form of 'Newmarket'.

b. (See quot.)

1894 MASKELYNE *Sharps & Flats* 250 Yankee-grab or Newmarket..is played with three dice, and the object in view is to get nearest to an aggregate of eighteen pips.

new-married, *ppl. a.* [NEW *adv.* 3.] Newly married.

c **1540** COVERDALE *Ord. Ch. Denmark* Wks. (Parker Soc.) I. 481 To call these new-married folks unto holy wedlock. **1599** SHAKS. *Hen. V*, v. ii. 190 Like a new-married Wife about her Husbands Necke. *a* **1649** DRUMM. OF HAWTH. *Poems* Wks. (1711) 26 All-bearing earth, like a new married queen, Her beauties hightens. **1711** ADDISON *Spect.* No. 15. ¶4 Talk of a new married Couple, and you will immediately hear whether they keep their Coach and six. **1771** *Chron.* in *Ann. Reg.* 160/2 The Duke of Cumberland and his new-married Dutchess. **1824** MISS MITFORD *Village* Ser. I. (1863) 240 He foretold all happiness to the new-married pair. **1860** MRS. CARLYLE *Lett.* III. 21 There were four young new-married ladies.

newme, variant of NEUME.

New Mexican, *a.* and *sb.* [f. *New Mexico*, one of the United States.] **a.** *adj.* Of or belonging to New Mexico. **b.** *sb.* A native or inhabitant of New Mexico.

1834 A. PIKE *Sketches* 137 To an American, the first sight of these New Mexican villages is novel and singular. *Ibid.* 170 Even the New Mexicans call him a great rascal. **1893** C. F. LUMMIS *Land of Poco Tiempo* 294 Twenty miles south of the New Mexican hamlet of Manzano..is..the pueblo of Abó. **1940** E. FERGUSSON *Our Southwest* 228 Few families are so completely urbanized as not to have a little ranch somewhere, and New Mexicans care for their own as long as they can.

new-minted, *ppl. a.* [NEW *adv.* 3.] Newly coined or formed. Also **new-mint** *v.*

1593 NASHE *Christ's T.* (1613) 2 New mint my mind to the likeness of thy lowlines. **1598** MARSTON *Sco. Villanie* To iudiciall Perusers, Some of his new-minted Epithets, (as Reall, Intrinsecate, Delphicke). **1643** TRAPP *Comm. Gen.* xli. 25 Novellists, that can abide to hear nothing but what is new-minted. **1713** *Guardian* No. 149 ¶19 Horace advises, that all new minted Words should have a Greek derivation. **1781** COWPER *Charity* 513 When Scandal has new-minted an old lie,.. 'Tis called a Satire.

new-model, *v.* [NEW *adv.* 6.] *trans.* To remodel; to rearrange in a new way.

c **1665** MRS. HUTCHINSON *Mem. Col. Hutchinson* (1846) 231 Those in the parliament..devised to new-model the army. **1714** R. FIDDES *Pract. Disc.* II. 193 The design of whose religion is to new-model human nature. **1769** ROBERTSON *Chas. V*, v. Wks. 1813 V. 439 Twelve persons were elected to new-model the constitution of the republic. **1818** SCOTT *Hrt. Midl.* viii, He new-modelled his troops, and more especially those immediately about his person. **1878** SHERMAN in *N. Amer. Rev.* CXXVI. 200 That at the commencement of hostilities there should be nothing either to new-model or to create.

Hence **new-modelling, new-modeller.**

1673 [R. Leigh] *Transp. Reh.* 146 The new modelling of a state is somewhat beyond the oeconomy of a school. **1748** *Anson's Voy.* I. v. 48 To what causes the late new modelling of this settlement is owing. *a* **1806** C. J. FOX *Reign Jas. II* (1808) 153 From the new-modelling of the corporations. **1831** CARLYLE in *Westm. Rev.* XV. 43 Their successive redactors and new-modellers. **1899** BALDOCK *Cromwell as Soldier* 206 The new modelling or reorganization of its army.

† **new-modelize**, *v. Obs.* [NEW *adv.* 6.] = NEW-MODEL *v.* Hence † **new-modelizing** *vbl. sb.*

1645 *City Alarum* 26 We have new modelized our army, and ought to new modelize our excise. **1671** tr. *Palafox's Conquest China* v. 98 Victory had now new Modeliz'd his Conscience. **1716** M. DAVIES *Athen. Brit.* II. 158 Asserius's Life of King Ælfrid..was new-modeliz'd into English by.. Spelman. **1727** BROWNE WILLIS *Cathedrals* I. 33 He had his diocese entirely to new modelize.

new-modelled, *ppl. a.* [NEW *adv.* 3.] Newly modelled; put into a new form.

1654 WHITLOCK *Zootomia* 196 Beleiving and Knowing doth so share the all of some new model'd Christians. **1711** G. HICKES *Two Treat. Chr. Priesth.* (1847) II. 389 The book itself was opposite..to many new-modelled churches. **1757** DYER *Fleece* II. Poems (1761) 114 What nation did not seek, Of thy new modell'd wool, the curious webs? **1813** *Metrical Remarks* 10 The new-modelled Baron was acquainted with no other building. **1827** HALLAM *Const. Hist.* (1876) II. x. 219 In the new-modelled army of 1645.

new moon. [NEW *a.* 3c + MOON *sb.*[1]]

1. The moon when first seen as a slender crescent shortly after its conjunction with the sun.

c **1000** *Sax. Leechd.* III. 242 We cweðað þonne niwne monan æfter menniscum ʒewunan, ac he is æfre se ylca. *c* **1055** *Byrhtferth's Handboc* in *Anglia* VIII. 309 Swa byð se niwa mona bradra gesewen. **1508** DUNBAR *Tua Mariit Wemen* 432 As the new mone, all pale, oppressit with change, Kythis quhilis her cleir face. **1598** W. PHILLIP tr. *Linschoten's Voy.* (1864) 187 They pray likewise to the New Moone,..and salute her with great Deuotion. **1634** SIR T. HERBERT *Trav.* 86 At the appearing of euery new Moone, they goe out to worship it. **1687** A. LOVELL tr. *Thevenot's Trav.* I. 44 They look out at Night for the new Moon. **17..** *Sir Patrick Spens* vi, I saw the new moone..Wi' the auld moone in hir arme. *a* **1742** STUKELY in J. Smith *Panor. Sci. & Art* (1815) I. 614 The [eclipsed] sun looked very sharp like a new moon. **1851** MEREDITH *Love in the Valley* iv, Earth to her is young as the slip of the new moon.

2. The time when the new moon appears; also *Astron.* the time at which the moon is in conjunction with the sun. **b.** The festival celebrated by the ancient Hebrews at the time of the new moon (cf. NEOMENIA).

c **1000** *Saxon Leechd.* III. 243 þis ʒelimpð seldon & næfre buton on niwum monan. *c* **1200** *Vices & Virtues* 27 Oðer [to think] newe mone betere ðan æld-mone in to newe huse te wænden. **1382** WYCLIF *1 Esdras* viii. 6 In the newe mone of the fifte moneth. **1382** —— *Isa.* i. 13 The newe moone, and sabot, and othere festus. *c* **1440** *Promp. Parv.* 360/2 Nwe mone, *neomenia*. **1535** COVERDALE *2 Chron.* xxxi. 3 The burntofferynges of the Sabbath and of the new-mone and of the feastes. *a* **1649** DRUMM. OF HAWTH. *Poems* Wks. (1711) 27 To thee give place The old new-moons, with all festival days. **1682** *Riders Brit. Merlin* Oct., Sow Wheat and Rie about the New Moon. **1727–38** CHAMBERS *Cycl.* s.v. *Moon*, Before the new moon the horns were turned westward. **1797** *Encycl. Brit.* (ed. 3) II. 522/1 Having completed her course ..she disappears; and we say it is new moon. **1864** *Chambers's Encycl.* VI. 556/2 A few hours after 'new moon', the moon appears a little to the east of the sun as a thin crescent.

new-mould, *v.* [NEW *adv.* 6.] *trans.* To mould or form anew.

1650 BAXTER *Saints' R.* III. v. §4 It changeth his opinion, ..but it never melted and new molded his heart. **1695** WOODWARD *Nat. Hist. Earth* II. (1723) 105 Its prime Errand was to Re-form and New-mold the Earth. **1738** WESLEY *Hymn*, '*When shall thy lovely Face*' viii, Jesus..New-moulds our Limbs of cumb'rous Clay. **1784** R. BAGE *Barham Downs* II. 286 This affliction may in some measure new mould her. **1827** HALLAM *Const. Hist.* (1876) I. i. 37 The more wily courtiers..deemed it less obnoxious to violate than to new-mould the constitution.

new-mown, *ppl. a.* [NEW *adv.* 3 and 4.] Freshly cut, just mown. ***new-mown hay***: also as the name of a scent.

1470–85 MALORY *Arthur* VII. xi. 228 There was a fayre medowe that semed newe mowen. *c* **1586** C'TESS PEMBROKE *Ps.* LXXII. ii. As showres thrown On meades new mown. **1725** RAMSAY *Gentle Sheph.* II. ii, Sweeter than gowany glens or new-mawn hay. **1789** J. PILKINGTON *View Derbysh.* I. 327 This..is said by Linnæus to occasion the smell of new mown hay. **1876** J. SAUNDERS *Lion in Path* i, The scent of the new-mown hay comes through the..windows. **1890–1** *T. Eaton & Co. Catal.* Fall & Winter 42/2 Jockey club, new-mown hay, lily of the valley, 25 c. per bottle. **1926–7** *Army & Navy Stores Catal.* 490/2 Perfumes..Lilas Blanc, New Mown Hay, Oeillet Blanc. **1971** *Guardian* 17 Aug. 7/2 Their new Meadowsong fragrance range..based on..newmown hay, honeysuckle, clover.

new-name, *v.* [NEW *adv.* 6.] *trans.* To name anew; to give a new name to. Also **new-named** *ppl. a.*; **new-namer.**

1589 PUTTENHAM *Eng. Poesie* III. xvii. (Arb.) 192 Onomatopeia, or the New namer. **1621** BP. MOUNTAGU *Diatribæ* 343 New-name it thus, The poore mans Tithe at home, and at Ierusalem. **1622** DRAYTON *Poly-olb.* xix. 357 Hawkins..Vpon that new-nam'd Spaine, and Guinny sought his prize. **1643** TRAPP *Comm. Gen.* xxvi. 33 Isaac therefore new names it. **1793** ANNA SEWARD *Lett.* (1811) III. 244 That consciousness would tempt me to new-name her book. *c* **1800** R. CUMBERLAND *John de Lancaster* (1809) II. 64 The giant son of Neptune, who entailed the trident of his father on his new-named Albion to all posterity.

New Negro, new negro. *U.S.* **a.** During the period of slavery, a Negro brought from Africa to the New World. **b.** An artist belonging to the ***New Negro Movement***, the efflorescence of Negro writing, etc., during the 1920s. **c.** A Negro claiming equal status with a white American.

1701 C. WOLLEY *Two Years' Jrnl. N.-Y.* 32 In Barbados new Negro's (*i.e.* such as cannot speak English) are bought for twelve or fourteen pound a head. **1732** *Calendar State Papers Amer. & W. Indies* (1939) 55 Except proof were made that they were all new negroes and not been above 6 months in America. **1860** S. MORDECAI *Virginia* 350, I do not speak of the New Negroes, as the imported Africans were called, but of their descendants. **1922** A. P. RANDOLPH in A. Dundes *Mother Wit* (1973) 400/1 It does not occur to the Old South that there is a 'New Negro'; that the 'Uncle Toms' are passing. **1925** A. LOCKE in *Survey* (N.Y.) Graphic No., 1 Mar. 632/1 The Negro is being carefully studied, not just talked about and discussed. In arts and letters, instead of being wholly caricatured, he is being seriously portrayed and painted. To all of this the New Negro is keenly responsive as an augury of a new democracy in American culture. **1953** S. A. BROWN in A. Dundes *Mother Wit* (1973) 40/1 We go then to what is called the New Negro Movement. *Ibid.* 43/2 She wouldn't let anybody kick her around (something like the New Negro). **1963** in J. H. Clarke *Harlem* (1964) 40 For a racial dilemma in Negro art, a racial solution was necessary. This came in the mid-twenties from the inspiration of the New Negro Movement with its crusade of folk expression in all of the arts. *Ibid.* 49 Many of the New Negroes were unwilling victims of an inverted racialistic nationalism,..priding themselves that they could sing, paint and write as well as their white-skinned patrons.

newness ('nju:nɪs). Forms: 1 néow-, níwnys, níownes, 4–6 newnes, 4, 6 neunes, 6 newenes(se, 7– newness. [f. NEW *a.* + -NESS.] The state, fact, or quality of being new, in various applications of the adj.

c **900** tr. *Bæda's Hist.* I. vii. (1890) 40 Mid þa neownysse swa moniʒra heofonlicra wundra. *c* **1000** *Saxon Leechd.* II. 240 þæt seo niownes þara metta mæʒe him gode beon. *a* **1300** *Cursor M.* 26924 Quils þat neunes es in wonde es plaster nan mai mak it sond. *a* **1340** HAMPOLE *Psalter* Prol. 4 To conforme men..til crist in newnes of lyf. **1483** *Cath. Angl.* 254/2 A Newnes, *nouitas*. **1526** *Pilgr. Perf.* (W. de W. 1531) 211 [To] ryse from synne, and walke in a newnes of lyfe. *a* **1568** ASCHAM *Scholem.* II. (Arb.) 156 Neyther oldnes nor newnesse of words maketh the greatest difference betwixt Salust and Tullie. *a* **1613** OVERBURY *A Wife*, etc. (1638) 251 She will desire him for newnesse and variety. **1674** BREVINT *Saul at Endor* 240 Either to blind or to countenance the Newness of their Indulgences. **1729** LAW *Serious C.* xxiii. (1732) 471 It will give you such a newness of mind. **1796** H. HUNTER tr. *St.-Pierre's Stud. Nat.* (1799) II. 176 This reflection..evidently demonstrates the newness of the World. **1813** SHELLEY *Q. Mab* VI. 153 The babe, In the dim newness of its being. **1876** LOWELL *Among my Bks.* Ser. II. 243 The same startle of newness and beauty that pleased our youth.

b. With *a* and *pl. rare.*

1690 DRYDEN *Don Sebastian* Pref., Some newnesses of English, translated from the Beauties of Modern Tongues. **1760–72** H. BROOKE *Fool of Qual.* (1809) IV. 69 She became as it were a newness of ever-rising delight. **1850** LYNCH *Theoph. Trinal* ix. 154 Many such marriages must there be before all the newnesses will be born that mankind requires.

c. ***the Newness***, New England transcendentalism.

1865 LOWELL *Thoreau* Prose Wks. 1890 I. 363 There was a much nearer metaphysical relation .. between Carlyle and the Apostles of the Newness, as they were called in New England, than has been commonly supposed. *c* **1870** R. CARTER in *Century Mag.* (1889) Nov. 129 Next to Brook Farm, Concord was the chief resort of the disciples of the 'Newness'.

Newnhamite (ˈnjuːnəmaɪt). [f. *Newnham* (see below) + -ITE[1].] One who is, or has been, a student at Newnham College, one of the Cambridge colleges for women.

1896 [see GIRTONIAN]. **1907** R. BROOKE *Let.* 28 Nov. (1968) 115 Most of the committee are Newnhamites, strange wild people. **1913** J. VAIZEY *College Girl* xx. 282, I am proud to be a Newnhamite. **1936** M. V. HUGHES *London Girl of Eighties* vi. 119 Miss Rogers, a large and genial Newnhamite.

newo(y, obs. forms of NEPHEW.

New Orleans (njuː ɔːˈliːənz, -ɔːˈliːnz). The name of a city in SE. Louisiana, giving its name to various commercial and natural products; used *spec.* to designate a style of jazz which originated there.

1807 C. SCHULTZ *Travels* (1810) I. 132 Kentucky and New-Orleans boats from one dollar to one and a half a foot. **1849** G. G. FOSTER *N.Y. in Slices* 82 The grocery-keeper .. buys a barrel of common New Orleans molasses at twenty-five cents per gallon. [**1905** (*title of tune composed by Jelly Roll Morton*) New Orleans Blues. **1922** (*name of jazz band*) New Orleans Rhythm Kings.] **1935** *Swing Music* July 120/1 The expressions 'Chicago Style', 'New Orleans Style' were certainly invented by the American musicians, and not at all by European hot fans. **1938** D. BAKER *Young Man with Horn* I. v. 42 Jeff's band .. had two styles of playing, known to the present trade as Memphis style and New Orleans style. *Ibid.* 43 Memphis style is sometimes called 'take your turn', and New Orleans has everybody in at the same time. **1952** B. WOLFE *Limbo* (1953) II. ix. 102 Program of jazz recordings. .. Maybe New Orleans had come back .. to a world it .. belonged to. **1955** R. BLESH *Shining Trumpets* (ed. 3) iii. 58 They prophesy New Orleans jazz as clearly as they recall Africa. **1958** OSBORNE & CREIGHTON *Epitaph G. Dillon* I. 14 Do you mind if we do without New Orleans just for the moment? **1965** G. MELLY *Owning-Up* xi. 128 What the revivalists thought of as 'New Orleans Jazz' was the music of Armstrong, Morton and Oliver—New Orleans musicians but based on, and recorded in, Chicago, during the Prohibition era. What the traditionalists meant by New Orleans Jazz .. was the music played by musicians who had never left the city. **1973** J. DRUMMOND *Bang! Bang! You're Dead!* xiii. 34 One of the early New Orleans rags.

new-raised, *ppl. a.* [NEW *adv.* 3.]

1. Of troops: Recently enlisted; newly formed.

1667 MARVELL *Corr.* Wks. (Grosart) II. 213 To disband all the new-raised land forces. **1748** *Anson's Voy.* I. i. 12 New-raised marines who had never been at sea before. **1769** GOLDSM. *Hist. Rome* II. 428 The fourth legion, which consisted of new raised soldiers. **1816** A. C. HUTCHISON *Pract. Obs. Surg.* (1826) 309 An annual fluctuation of 30,000 new-raised men to supply the deficiencies.

2. Newly erected, elevated, reared, etc.

1697 POTTER *Antiq. Greece* I. ii. (1715) 7 In his new rais'd kingdom. **1735** J. PRICE *Stone-Br. Thames* 7 The new-rais'd Centers. **1777** POTTER *Æschylus* (1779) I. 15 This new-rais'd ruler of the gods. **1896** KIPLING *Seven Seas* 80 Where the new-raised tropic city sweats and roars. **1896** *Daily News* 24 Nov. 8/5 With numbers vastly increased by the addition of these new-raised broods.

New Realism, new realism. *Philos.* Chiefly *U.S.* Doctrines of Realism as revived at the beginning of the twentieth century to refute certain tenets of Idealism, emphasizing the existence of objects in the external world independently of the way they are subjectively experienced. (For the contemporary movement in Britain, cf. REALISM I c.) So **New Realist** *sb.* and *a.*, an adherent or advocate of, pertaining to, New Realism.

1906 J. S. MACKENZIE in *Mind* XV. 308 (*heading*) The New Realism and the Old Idealism. *Ibid.*, Some of the leading supporters of the new Realism (especially Mr. Moore and Mr. Russell) connect it with an extremely nominalistic type of Logic. **1920** W. R. SORLEY *Hist. Eng. Philos.* xii. 297 Forms of what is called the new realism seem to have been started independently in the United States and in this country. **1929** C. I. LEWIS *Mind & World-Order* ii. 39 Immediacy is thus emphasized .. by the American new-realists. **1947** *Mind* LVI. 290 As everyone knows, the revolt against Idealism, initiated chiefly by Moore and Russell in this country and by the New Realist group in the United States, proved quite prodigiously successful. **1966** F. COPLESTON *Hist. Philos.* VIII. v. xvii. 387 The new realists were at any rate agreed on the truth of a basic tenet.., 'things known are not products of the knowing relation nor essentially dependent for their existence or behaviour upon that relation'.

newricall, obs. variant of NEURICAL.

New Right. orig. *U.S.* [After NEW LEFT, NEW LEFT.] The name given to a political movement that arose in response to the challenge of the New Left, characterized by rejection of all forms of socialism, emphasis on traditional, conservative values with regard to the law, morality, and social consciousness, or (esp. in the U.S.) by libertarian, esp. free-market policies, and a desire to improve the public image of conservatism; the supporters of this movement.

1966 *Time* 11 Nov. 90/3 The paper that claims to have discovered the New Left has recently discovered a New Right, rebelling against the upper-class gentility of Bill Buckley. **1970** *Guardian Weekly* 12 Dec. 7/3, I belong to the New Right in Japan .. and I agree with the New Left .. that what the Japanese were taught after the war about American peace and democracy was not true. **1979** *London Rev. Bks.* 25 Oct. 17/2 Is not this a paradigm of the policy of levelling-down which the New Right professes to abhor? **1985** S. LOWRY *Young Fogey Handbk.* v. 50 It is both paradoxical and predictable that Cambridge should have spawned a breed of thinkers, talkers and poseurs commonly .. known as the intellectuals of the New Right.

Hence **New ˈRightist** *sb.* and *a.*

1977 *Nation* (U.S.) 5 Mar. 258 Those such as [Howard] Phillips who call themselves 'New Rightists' regard the free exchange of ideas as intolerable. **1978** *U.S. News & World Rep.* 23 Jan. 25/3 Some New Rightists .. see the Republican Party as 'elitist'. **1981** *Time* 14 Sept. 25/3 All of Helms' proposals may be overshadowed by more politic New Rightist initiatives. **1985** S. LOWRY *Young Fogey Handbk.* v. 51 A conventional Conservative vicar hurries to dismiss the New Rightists as 'irrelevant—idiots who like dressing up and poncing about in wing collars'.

new-risen, *ppl. a.* [NEW *adv.* 3 and 4.] Newly, just lately, risen.

1591 SHAKS. *1 Hen. VI*, I. iv. 102 A holy Prophetesse new risen vp. **1596** —— *Tam. Shr.* IV. i. 189 As one new-risen from a dreame. **1650** BAXTER *Saints' R.* I. vii. §1 Our new-risen Lord. **1667** MILTON *P.L.* I. 594 The Sun new ris'n Looks through the Horizontal misty Air. **1760–72** H. BROOKE *Fool of Qual.* (1809) IV. 158 A new-risen phœnix. **1860** FORSTER *Gr. Remonstr.* 98 Eager to be shone upon by the new-risen sun.

†**ˈnewry.** *Obs.* [ad. Malay *nūrī*.] = LORY.

In early 17th c. translations from foreign languages the forms *nori* and *noyra* occur: see Yule & Burnell *Anglo-Ind. Gloss.* 398 and C. P. G. Scott *Malayan Words* 84–5.

1698 J. FRYER *Acc. E. India & P.* 116 Here were .. Cockatoos and Newries from Bantam, as also a Cassawar that digests Iron. **1698** in Wheeler *Madras in Old. Time* (1861) I. 333 Brought ashore from the 'Resolution' .. a newry and four yards of broadcloth for a present for the Havildar.

news (njuːz), *sb.* (*pl.*) Forms: 4–7 **newes**, (5 **-esse**), 5–6 **newys**, *Sc.* **newis**, (5 **nevis**), 6 **neu(e)s**, 7 **niewse**, 6–7 **nues**, (6 **nuze**, 7 **nuse**), 6– **news**. [pl. of NEW *a.*, after OF. *noveles*, *nuveles* (mod.F. *nouvelles*), or med.L. *nova*, pl. of *novum* a new thing.

The synonymous Du. *nieuws* probably originated in the expressions *wat nieuws*, *iet(s) nieuws*, in which the form is genitive singular (cf. NEW *a.* B 1), but the evidence is against a similar origin for the English word.]

†**1.** New things; novelties. *Obs. rare.*

Neus in *Cursor M.* 26768 (Cott.) is evidently a scribal error for *treus*.

1382 WYCLIF *Ecclus.* xxiv. 35 The which fulfilleth, as Fison, wisdam; and as Tigris in the daȝes of newes [L. *novorum*]. **1551** ROBINSON *More's Utop.* (1895) 7 Not for a vayne and curious desiere to see newes. **1565** T. STAPLETON *Fortr. Faith* 109* Differences .. betwene the auncient faith of England and the vpstert newes of protestants.

2. a. Tidings; the report or account of recent events or occurrences, brought or coming to one as new information; new occurrences as a subject of report or talk.

In common use only after 1500.

1423 JAS. I *Kingis Q.* clxxix, I bring the newis glad, that blisfull ben. *c* **1485** *Digby Myst.* (1882) II. 431 Yet of late I haue hard of no newys. **1523** LD. BERNERS *Froiss.* I. cccci. 794 He was right pensyue and sore troubled with those newes. **1581** RICH *Farew.* (1846) 58 These newes were sodainly spred throughout the citie of Cherona. **1621** LADY M. WROTH *Urania* 412 Calling his Lords .. about him, to whom hee deliuered these glad newes. **1685** DRYDEN *Thren. August.* 19 The amazing news of Charles at once were spread. **1717** LADY M. W. MONTAGU *Let. to Pope* 17 June, The great gulf between you and me cools all news that come hither. **1776** JEKYLL *Corr.* (1894) 64 The ill news of your health are still worse than my late suspense. **1821** SHELLEY *Ess. & Lett.* (1852) II. 228 There are bad news from Palermo. **1855** MACAULAY *Hist. Eng.* xviii. IV. 214 The Dutch ministers regularly reported all the Scotch news to their government. **1868** VISCT. STRANGFORD *Select.* II. 265 Courier-borne news .. can reach England as quickly by way of Peshawur.

b. Construed as *sing.*

1566 *Pasquine in Traunce* 36, I hearde speak of it, when yͤ newes therof was brought to Pope Iulie the seconde. **1625** B. JONSON *Staple of N.* I. v, When Newes is printed, It leaues Sir to be Newes. **1664** H. MORE *Myst. Iniq.* 339 Of such a division .. there is no News nor Example in Antiquity. **1711** M. HENRY *Hope & Fear Balanced* Wks. 1853 II. 313/1 The stocks are as the news is. **1784** COWPER *Task* VI. 660 When .. the news was fresh. **1828** SCOTT *F.M. Perth* xxvii, Was there any news in the country? **1897** MARY KINGSLEY *W. Africa* 351 The next news was that I was in the water.

c. In proverbial expressions.

1574 HELLOWES *Gueuara's Fam. Ep.* (1577) 58 Euil newes neuer come too late. **1616** JAMES I *Let.* 13 May in A. J. Kempe *Loseley Manuscripts* (1835) 403 No newis is better then evill newis. *c* **1645** HOWELL *Lett.* II. xviii, I am of the Italians mind that said, *Nulla nuova, buona nuova*, no news, good news. **1685** DRYDEN *Thren. August.* 49 Ill News is wing'd with Fate, and flies apace. **1821** SCOTT *Kenilw.* xi, The truth of two old proverbs, namely, that Ill news fly fast [etc.]. **1850** F. E. SMEDLEY *Frank Fairlegh* x. 101 Arguing .. (on the 'no-news being good-news' system) that I should have heard again if anything had gone wrong, I dismissed the subject from my mind. **1916** 'TAFFRAIL' *Pincher Martin* xviii. 336 They could not bring themselves to believe that 'no news was good news'. **1941** A. HUXLEY *Let.* 27 Nov. (1969) 473 Matthew never writes; but we interpret no news as good news.

†**d.** ***no news***, no novelty, nothing new. *Obs.*

1557 N. T. (Genev.) *1 Pet.* i. *heading*, Saluation in Christ is no newes, but a thynge prophecied of olde. **1618** BP. HALL *Serm.* Wks. 1837 V. 112 The poor and proud is the wise-man's monster, but the proud and rich are no news. **1659** HAMMOND *On Ps.* cvii. 43 'Tis no news to pass from the singular to the plural number, without varying the subject.

e. ***that*** (or ***it***) ***is news to me***: I did not know that. *colloq.*

1898 S. WEYMAN *Castle Inn* xvi. 159 For the rest, which this gentleman says, about who she is and her claim .. it is news to me. **1919** D. ASHFORD *Young Visiters* viii. 69 Ethel he said blushing a deep red I always wished to marry you some fine day. This is news to me cried Ethel still peevish. **1943** J. B. PRIESTLEY *Daylight on Saturday* xii. 76 If you've had any trouble with your husband, I'm sorry, but it's news to me. **1968** S. B. HOUGH *Sweet Sister Seduced* xv. 79, I had thought we were in tune with one another ... that my reactions were her reactions. It was news to me, as she told me in round phrases, that in fact they weren't. **1974** M. Z. LEWIN *Enemies Within* xxxiv. 154 'I'm going to Chicago shortly.' News to me. But not a bad idea.

f. ***bad news***, used to designate something or someone unpleasant, unlucky, or undesirable (see quots.). *colloq.*

For the literal use cf. quot. 1821 s.v. 2 a above.

1926 MAINES & GRANT *Wise-Crack Dict.* 5/2 *Bad news*, piece of pasteboard handed by the waiter after a meal. **1929** M. A. GILL *Underworld Slang*, *Bad news*, shot gun. **1930** *Amer. Mercury* Dec. 454/1 *Bad news*, trouble. 'Sucker, stay out of me district! It's bad news if you don't.' **1935** A. J. POLLOCK *Underworld Speaks* 120/1 *The bad news*, the bill (check) in a restaurant, speakeasy or night club. **1942** BERREY & VAN DEN BARK *Amer. Thes. Slang* §256/1 *Difficulty, trouble* .., bad news. **1963** I. FLEMING *On H.M. Secret Service* i. 13 Their waiter .. had simply put them in the category of 'bad news' and hoped they would soon be on their way. **1964** *Amer. Speech* XXXIX. 189 *Bad news*, 'a poor social evening, a wasted night'. **1968** 'J. WELCOME' *Hell is where you find It* iv. 67 'Where is she?' I said.. . 'Listen, I don't know. She's bad news, that one. **1973** ' E. MCBAIN' *Let's hear It* v. 69 Bikies had begun drifting into the area, sporting their leather jackets and their swastikas... The bikies were bad news. **1973** H. MILLER *Open City* xviii. 197 Any kind of witness would be bad news on a job with such a tight specification. **1974** D. GRAY *Dead Give Away* iii. 31 Milly these days was plain bad news. Her fascination had evaporated.

g. A person, place, etc., regarded as a topic of discussion or note.

1912 KIPLING *Diversity of Creatures* (1917) 192 The great Baron Reuter himself .. flashed that letter in full to the front, back, and both wings of this scene of our labours. For Huckley was News. **1946** E. WAUGH *When Going was Good* v. 260 Abyssinia was News. Everyone with any claims to African experience was cashing in. **1965** *Listener* 23 Sept. 452/2 The reading boom .. has made poets news, and it has made them think about being news. **1974** V. GIELGUD *In Such a Night* vii. 58, I am not what is commonly called 'news'. But .. my wife is 'news' in the biggest possible way.

†**3.** A piece or item of news. *Obs.*

1574 HELLOWES *Gueuara's Fam. Ep.* (1577) 2 A case so graue, a newes so new, a victorie so seldome hearde of. **1641** EARL MONM. tr. *Biondi's Civil Wars* v. 157 At that same time there came two important nuses. *a* **1652** BROME *Eng. Moor* I. ii, Durst thou hear a news Whose mirth will hazard cracking of a rib?

†**4.** A news messenger. *Obs. rare*$^{-1}$.

1665 PEPYS *Diary* 31 July, In the mean time there coming a News thither with his horse to go over [etc.].

5. a. The newspaper(s); a newspaper. Now *rare.*

1738 SWIFT *Pol. Conversat.* 183 You know his House was burnt down to the Ground. Yes; it was in the News. **1782** COWPER *Names of little Note* 10 When a child .. Has burnt to tinder a stale last-year's news. **1785** CRABBE *Newspaper* 26 A daily swarm .. Come flying forth, and mortals call them News: For these, unread, the noblest volumes lie. **1886** ELWORTHY *W. Som. Word-bk.* s.v., To read out the war 'pon the news.

b. *Printing.* (See quot.)

1887 SOUTHWARD *Pract. Print.* (ed. 3) 716 'Writings', 'Printings', and 'News', are kinds [of paper] whose names show the purposes for which they are made.

c. A television or radio programme in which the news is announced and sometimes discussed; a newsreel. Also *attrib.*

1923 *Radio Times* 28 Sept. 9/1 10.0. —— Time signal, general news bulletin. Broadcast to all stations, followed by London News and Weather Report. **1925** *Daily Herald* 23 June 4/3 To hear the news from your favourite announcer is like buying your favourite newspaper. **1932** G. GREENE *Stamboul Train* II. i. 66 Janet Pardoe said that she wanted to see the news and they both stayed [in the cinema]. **1939** T. S. ELIOT *Family Reunion* II. i. 97 And now it is nearly time for the news We must listen to the weather report And the international catastrophes. **1940** 'G. ORWELL' in *World Rev.* (1950) June 21, I went to the pub to hear the 9 o'clock news. **1947** AUDEN *Age of Anxiety* (1948) I. 17 Now the news. Night raids on Five cities. **1953** M. LASKI *Victorian Chaise Longue* 64 It was that programme just before the news. **1968** 'D. RUTHERFORD' *Skin for Skin* iv. 95 Crisp .. glanced at his watch. 'Five minutes till news time... Can you look after her while I listen to the news?' **1972** D. DELMAN *Sudden Death* (1973) iv. 121 It was news time so .. I turned on the TV. **1973** J. DRUMMOND *Bang! Bang! You're Dead!* xxxvi. 126 The ginger-headed Crabbe was watching the nine o'clock news.

6. ***attrib.*** and ***Comb.*** **a.** With agent-nouns, as ***news-bearer***, ***-bringer***, ***-dealer***, ***-gatherer***, etc.

1611 COTGR., *Rapporte-nouvelle*, a *newes-bearer, or tale-carrier. **1895** *Atlantic Monthly* Mar. 357 Citizens who had flocked as near as possible to the newsbearer. **1639** W. C. *Italian Convert* xxviii. 213 So this *newes bringer had his passe-port to be packing. **1857** HOLLAND *Bay Path* xxiv. 278

Each of the news-bringers was surrounded with his little knot of auditors. **1673** O. WALKER *Educ.* ix. 77 Breeders of all petit factions, *news-brokers. **1612** DAVIES *Why Ireland*, etc. (1747) 178 These *Newes-Carriers did..many times raise troubles. **1788** *New London Mag.* title-p., Sold by all Booksellers, Stationers, and News-Carriers. **1808** ELEANOR SLEATH *Bristol Heiress* V. 335 The Viscountess..lived and died in the profession of a news-carrier. **1827** in Hone *Every-day Bk.* II. 1276 Those *newscriers are spoken of in the past sense. **1861** *Chicago Tribune* 15 Apr., We..are now prepared to furnish *News Dealers and Booksellers with Every Paper, Periodical and Book. **1868** G. DUFF *Pol. Surv.* 47, I wish the news-dealers at Athens would be more scrupulous in their assertions. **1966** R. ELLISON in A. Chapman *New Black Voices* (1972) 407 One newsdealer in Harlem. **1712** ADDISON *Spect.* No. 439 ¶2 They have *News-gatherers and Intelligencers distributed into their several..Quarters. **1824** MISS MITFORD *Village* Ser. I. (1803) 187 By far the best news-gatherer of the country side. **1963** *Punch* 20 Feb. 273/1 He is a seer rather than an exclusive news-gatherer. **1971** *Guardian* 20 Dec. 11/1 The Guardian's specialist correspondents are not only newsgatherers but also distinguished commentators. **1598** SYLVESTER *Du Bartas* II. i. II. 283 Poor Woman..Light, credulous, *news-lover. **1849** *Southey's Common-pl. Bk.* Ser. II. 412 Indian *News-Messengers. **1759** (*title*) *News-Readers Pocket-Book. *a* **1817** T. DWIGHT *Trav. New Eng.*, etc. (1821) II. 63 A..means of gratifying the curiosity of news-readers. **1858** T. GUTHRIE *Christ Inher. of Saints* (1860) 207 News such as these *news-seekers had never dreamed of. **1696** *View Crt. St. Germain* in *Sel. Harl. Misc.* (1793) 556 This gentleman..was his weekly *news-sender, and project-drawer. *a* **1586** SIDNEY *Arcadia* (1622) 419 Thinking his life onely reserued to be bound to be the vnhappy *newes-teller. **1612** DAVIES *Why Ireland*, etc. 214 It was made pænall..to entertaine any of their Minstrels, Rimers, or Newes-tellers.

b. Miscellaneous combs., as ***news-crammed***; ***news-gathering***, ***-making***, ***-seeking***, ***-telling***, ***-thirsting***; ***news black-out***, ***-board***, ***bulletin***, ***conference***, ***-day***, ***editor***, ***feature***, ***film***, ***item***, ***magazine***, ***-master***, ***-matter***, ***media***, ***-office***, ***-page***, ***-print***, ***-scribe***, ***-shop***, ***story***, ***summary***, ***value***, ***-whoop***; ***news-greedy*** adj.

1944 *Sun* (Baltimore) 17 Aug. 1/6 The whole sector east of the Falaise bottleneck was under an Allied *news blackout. **1945** [see BLACK-OUT 2]. **1974** HAWKEY & BINGHAM *Wild Card* xxiii. 192 To reduce the risk of panic..a news blackout was requested. **1922** JOYCE *Ulysses* 116 A stately figure entered between the *newsboards. *Ibid.* 218 He passed Grogan's the tobacconist against which newsboards leaned. **1915** (*title*) *News Bulletin (Aero Club Amer.). **1923** [see sense 5c above]. **1925** News bulletin (see BULLETIN 2b]. **1973** C. EGLETON *Seven Days to Killing* xx. 211 Julyan sat..listening to the transistor radio... The music faded to give way to the news bulletin. **1966** 'G. BLACK' *You want to die, Johnny?* i. 11 At a *news conference in Los Angeles..Lil had said to television cameras..: 'Boots and I think God is a drag.' **1972** *N.Y. Times* 3 Nov. 1/1 The Prime Minister's announcement at a televised news conference was a rejection of demands..that the Liberal Prime Minister resign. **1600** SHAKS. *A.Y.L.* I. ii. 101 Then shal we be *newes-cram'd. **1746** BERKELEY *Lett.* Wks. 1871 IV. 305 Regret..which was on the following *news-day increased upon hearing the fate of your niece. *a* **1883** G. W. BAGBY *Old Virginia Gentleman* (1910) 190 Pollard he declared was 'the best *news editor in the whole South'. **1931** *Daily Express* 16 Oct. 11/3 Before I die, I wish to see the countenance of my own news editor when I stand before him admitting a similar circumstance. **1951** *Oxf. Jun. Encycl.* IV. 300/2 The news editor also receives a great deal of information from Government departments. **1974** *Times* 16 Nov. 15/5 The issue at the *Kentish Times* is..whether six journalists styled 'district editors'..are in fact the editors of newspapers... Each..works under the direction of the news editor of the *Kentish Times*. **1912** *International* (N.Y.) Apr. 79/1 It is wonderful what a variety of cultured subjects are concentrated in the Gould article—economics..and heart interest '*news feature' as the daily papers would say. **1973** 'S. HARVESTER' *Corner of Playground* II. i. 81 She loved news-features about herself. **1940** J. REITH *Diary* 16 Jan. (1975) v. 238 Very bothered about a *news film..in which Hore-Belisha was cheered and Gort received in silence. **1941** E. NIGGEMAN *Let.* 2 Jan. in H. Nicolson *Diaries & Lett.* (1967) 136, I also went to a News film and saw the film of London's fire. **1965** *B.B.C. Handbk.* 65 The BBC's own newsfilm cameramen. **1974** *Times* 9 Dec. 13/2 Producers of television..want..access to Parliament for the making of news film on the big occasions. **1918** W. G. BLEYER *Profession of Journalism* 27 The Allied governments abroad and our courts at home have struck a hard blow at the Hearst *news-gathering concern. *Ibid.* 114 The Associated Press is the child of the first effort at cooperative news-gathering ever made. **1966** *B.B.C. Handbk.* 52 General news-gathering facilities have been enlarged. **1972** H. EVANS *Newsman's English* i. 1 This news-gathering is a prodigious if familiar achievement. *a* **1618** SYLVESTER *Wks.* (Grosart) II. 63 So it also fares with our *news-greedie eare. **1844** *Knickerbocker* XXIV. 179 *News-items, matters of information, actual discoveries. **1930–1** G. ADE *Let.* Dec.–Jan. (1973) 149 Here are some news items which have not been printed but which come from pretty reliable sources. **1938** News-item [see *cover design* s.v. COVER *sb.*[1] 8]. **1958** *New Statesman* 20 Dec. 871/1 The second intrusive news-item concerns the budget. **1923** (*title*) Time, the weekly *news-magazine. **1953** *Encounter* Nov. 5/1 He shifted to the weekly news-magazine, *Der Spiegel*. **1968** *Listener* 4 Apr. 442/3 His job was to compile the early morning news magazine which I shall present at ten past seven. **1858** GEN. P. THOMPSON *Audi Alt.* I. lxi. 237 Not as a piece of gossip or *news-making. **1624** B. JONSON *Neptune's Triumph* Wks. 1641 II. 111 Grave Mr. Ambler, *Newes-master of Poules. **1923** O. G. VILLARD *Some Newspapers & Newspapermen* 88 His rivals and critics accuse him..of going to the very edge of the salacious in some of his *news-matter and fiction. **1959** *Times* 14 Jan. 12/5 The setting and make-up of newsmatter. **1962** *Amer. Speech* XXXVII. 44 The *news media in Moscow relayed to the American press the sensational story of Gagarin's space flight. **1972** J. MANN *Mrs. Knox's Profession* xiv. 105 The news media had got on to the story very quickly. **1973** *Sat. Rev. Soc.* (U.S.) May 69/3 Survey results can be disseminated through the news media. **1625** B. JONSON *Staple of N.* I. vi, Giue your worship ioy O' your new place, your Emissary-ship, I' the *Newes office. **1808** SCOTT *Marm.* v. Introd. 21 When wrinkled *news-page, thrice conn'd o'er, Beguiles the dreary hour no more. **1843** *Knickerbocker* XXII. 283 The *news-prints kept their works and worth before the public eye. **1897** 'SARAH TYTLER' *Lady Jean's Son* 244 That the letters and news-prints might be greedily read. **1791–1823** D'ISRAELI *Cur. Lit.* (1866) 341/2 All the race of *news-scribes. **1843** JAMES *Forest Days* (1847) 171 A somewhat timid and *news-seeking gentleman. **1688** *Lond. Gaz.* No. 2375/2 The Man being..hang'd before his own *News-shop. **1932** *News story [see MONEY *sb.* 6b]. **1974** M. G. EBERHART *Danger Money* (1975) xiii. 136 She can't stop the news stories but perhaps she can soften them. **1941** *B.B.C. Gloss. Broadcasting Terms* 20 *News summary: (1) Brief statement of salient news items, broadcast at a fixed time. (2) Brief statement of principal news items, broadcast as a preface in a news bulletin. **1973** A. MACVICAR *Painted Doll Affair* ii. 33, I turned on the dashboard radio... The pop music was interrupted by a news summary. **1611** COTGR., *Nonciation*, a..*newes telling. **1600** *Look About You* in Hazl. *Dodsley* VII. 393 In the hollow of *news-thirsting ears. **1906** J. LONDON *Let.* 8 Apr. (1966) 198 But what I did propose to you was 'events of large *news-value'. **1926** T. BEER *Mauve Decade* 172 He had no 'news value'—Julian Ralph invented the phrase in 1892 although it would be long before it became sacred. **1941** [see EPHEMERAL *a.*] . **1960** G. BUTLER *Death lives Next Door* vii. 149 Ezra could see at once that he had news value. **1972** P. BLACK *Biggest Aspidistra* III. viii. 229 Lord Hill..justified the occasional trivialisation as better than some academic selection of news values. **1775** ADAIR *Amer. Ind.* 301 To call them, by sounding the *news-whoop, as soon as he arrived at camp.

c. Special combs., as **news agency**, (*a*) a business that sells newspapers and periodicals; (*b*) a business organization that collects and supplies news to subscribing newspapers, broadcasters, etc.; **news-agent**, a regular dealer in newspapers and periodicals; **news-bell** *dial.*, a singing in the ears supposed to portend news; **news-boat**, a boat which puts out to passing vessels to receive and communicate news; **news break**, a newsworthy item (see also quot. 1969); **news butch(er)** *U.S. colloq.* [BUTCHER *sb.* 3b], a seller of newspapers, sweets, etc., on a train; **news cinema**, a cinema which shows a succession of short films, cartoons, and newsreels; **news desk**, the department of a newspaper office responsible for collecting and reporting the news; **news-dick** *literary nonce-wd.*, a news-hawk, a news-hound; **news flash** (see FLASH *sb.*[2] 1d); **news-girl**, a girl who sells newspapers; **news-hawk, -hound** *colloq.* (orig. *U.S.*), a newspaper reporter; **news peg**, a news story that forms the basis of an editorial, interview, cartoon, etc.; **newsprint**, cheap paper made from mechanical and chemical wood-pulp, and used chiefly for newspapers (see also 6b); also **news-printing** *vbl. sb.*; **news-reader**, a person who reads the news on radio or television (see also 6a); hence **news-reading** *vbl. sb.*; **newsreel, news reel**, a short cinema film dealing with news and current affairs; also *attrib.*; **news room**, (*a*) a reading-room specially set apart for newspapers; (*b*) the office in a newspaper, radio, or television station, etc., where the news is processed; **news-sheet**, a printed sheet containing the news, a simple form of newspaper; **news-stand**, a stand or stall for the sale of newspapers; **news theatre** = *news cinema*; **news ticker**, a telegraphic recording instrument which automatically prints the news on to a tape; **newsvendor**, a newspaper seller; **news-work**, the class of composition or printing employed in ordinary newspapers.

1873 F. HUDSON *Journalism* 521 *News agencies..branched out and extended into colossal news companies as a..necessity of the age. **1883** *Encycl. Brit.* XX. 405/2 The demand for such reporting had led, on the passing of the telegraphs into the hands of the state, to the formation of news agencies which undertook to supply the provincial newspapers. **1887** *Postal Laws* (U.S.) 147 In admitting second-class publications sent from a news agency, postmasters will observe the following [rules]. **1890** [see BURGLAR *v.*]. **1933** J. BUCHAN *Prince of Captivity* III. ii. 291 A statement to an international news agency. **1959** *New Statesman* 25 Apr. 564/3 Chancellor is a brilliant journalistic administrator who deserves a very large part of the credit for the wartime and post-war recovery of that famous world news-agency, but he has had no previous experience in actual magazine or newspaper publication. **1974** J. BANNING *How I fooled the World* iv. 23 One difference..between working for a newspaper and working for a news agency was that a news agency correspondent is much more vulnerable. **1851** MAYHEW *Lond Labour* I. 291/2 The regular price at a *news-agent's shop being 5*d.* **1879** *Print. Trades Jrnl.* XXIX. 43 Charged by your news-agent one shilling for a single number. **1876** T. HARDY *Far fr. Mad. Crowd* viii, I've had the *news-bell ringing in my left ear quite bad enough for a murder. **1830** *Boston Transcript* 1 Sept. 2/2 The *news-boat, T. H. Smith, belonging to the Associated Morning Papers, boarded the packet ship Caledonia,..25 miles outside Sandy Hook, and before she was boarded by any other news-boat. **1833–5** ELIZA LESLIE *That Gentleman* in *Casquet Lit.* V. 25/1 We were visited by a news-boat. **1860** *Merc. Mar. Mag.* VII. 347 Steamers bound West..will be boarded by the News-boat, and their advices telegraphed to all parts of America. **1954** D. DODGE *Lights of Skaro* vi. 218 Filing coverage on one of the *news breaks of our time. **1959** J. THURBER *Years with Ross* v. 80 Newsbreaks, those garbled..items from American journals..which conveniently fill out..*New Yorker* columns. **1969** *New Yorker* 11 Oct. 43/1 We've just received a letter..enclosing three newsbreaks (those little items we print at the bottom of the page) for our consideration. **1930** A. HENDERSON *Contemporary Immortals* 54 In connection with his profession as '*news butch' or seller of newspapers, candy and the like, he established a printing press and a small laboratory upon the train. **1894** *Daily Ardmoreite* (Ardmore, Okla.) 1 Jan. 3/1 Ben R. Wheeler, an old time and popular *news butcher on the Santa Fe..is in the city. **1930** J. DOS PASSOS *42nd Parallel* 294 He got a concession as news-butcher on the daily train. **1947** L. M. BEEBE *Mixed Train Daily* 85 The news butcher..still carries as stock in trade the immortal volume of senescent anecdotes, Thomas W. Jackson's *On a Slow Train Through Arkansas*. **1935** *Punch* 14 Aug. 192/1 Trousers go wrong the moment you move in them. The *news-cinemas and photographs in the papers tell you that. **1965** M. STEWART *Airs above Ground* i. 16 There was an hour to Angy's train and we wanted somewhere to sit, so we went to the news cinema. **1950** *Kemsley Man. Journalism* I. 67 Touch must constantly be kept with the picture *news desk which controls the photographers. **1962** A. LEJEUNE *Duel in Shadows* i. 11 The staff of the Night News Desk could be seen in their usual state of harassment. **1973** *Times* 21 Sept. 5/3 He asked to be put through to the news desk. **1974** *New Society* 7 Feb. 308/1 Wrote for British newspapers through more than three decades of lack of interest on London foreign newsdesks. *a* **1953** DYLAN THOMAS *Quite Early One Morning* (1954) 80 Two typewriter Thomas the ace *news-dick. **1904, 1938** *News flash [see FLASH *sb.*[2] 1d]. **1972** J. WILSON *Hide & Seek* vi. 111 He was in control now. News-flashes couldn't scare him. **1974** E. AMBLER *Dr. Frigo* I. 56 There was a television news flash. The announcer didn't get your father's name quite right. **1868** *Putnam's Mag.* Apr. 518/1 A few years ago, a *news-girl was as rare a sight as a Dodo. **1870** *Scribner's Monthly* I. 115 Old and young are enlisted in the street-vending service from the grey-haired grandsire..to the tiny news-girl. **1937** B. BOARD (*title*) Newsgirl in Palestine. **1931** *Amer. Speech* VI. 283 **Newshawk*.., used for 'reporter'. **1935** [see *big time* (BIG *a.* B2)]. **1940** *Illustr. London News* CXCVI. 544/1 News-hawks reading the tape-machines in New York and California. **1970** E. K. WALKER in W. King *Black Short Story Anthol.* (1972) 54 Bull, flanked by his sergeant, the newshawk, and his cameramen, walked to the ambulance. **1974** N. FREELING *Dressing of Diamond* 17 Just ringing the police..is equivalent to inviting the newshawks. They'll be here in half an hour. **1918** *Hatchet* 7 Apr. 48/2 'Got what all figured out,' queried the *news hound eagerly. **1926** *Time* 12 July 22/3 In a jazzed age no news hound delved through the reference 'morgue' of his paper to turn up the great story. **1936** E. AMBLER *Dark Frontier* x. 163 'What have you been doing with yourself?' 'Trying to be a good newshound.' **1973** 'S. HARVESTER' *Corner of Playground* I. iv. 41 You newshounds never spare yourselves once you've gotten latched onto a story. **1974** H. MACINNES *Climb to Lost World* ii. 35 Our trip was getting more like Conan Doyle's Lost World expedition every day, and I was obviously being cast as Ed Malone of the *Daily Gazette*. 'That stalwart news-hound of the cleft sticks', as Neil put it. **1960** *20th Cent.* Apr. 357 These jousts don't seem to need a *news peg. **1960** *New Statesman* 15 Oct. 556/2 The BBC's interview programme *Face to Face*..subjects selected public figures to sustained personal questioning before the cameras—without necessarily any particular topical news-peg. **1909** *Westm. Gaz.* 3 June 2/2 The duty of 5 dollars a ton on *news-print. **1935** *Geogr. Jrnl.* LXXXVI. 354 A large mill on the Wirral which manufactures newsprint. **1967** KARCH & BUBER *Offset Processes* xi. 485 Newsprint.., (Use) Newspaper, hand-bills, posters. **1974** *Publishers Weekly* 18 Feb. 44/2 Newsprint remains a headache for most paperback publishers [in Britain] and one was shocked recently to find himself quoted a price almost twice what he usually pays. **1937** *Tablet* 2 Oct. 436/2 The growth of large newspaper combines makes competition increasingly difficult, because the large proprietors are in fact deeply interested in the allied industries like the manufacture of *news printing. **1925** *Daily Herald* 23 June 4/3 Instead of receiving a shock at a national calamity, the *news reader breaks it to you in a calm and quiet voice. **1959** P. MCCUTCHAN *Storm South* i. 6, I hadn't realized it was News-time... I heard the news-reader's voice coming over. **1973** *Times* 15 Jan. 14/8 Mr William Alexander Moyes, the former BBC news reader and announcer, has been found dead at his flat. **1975** J. WOOD *North Kill* xii. 181 A BBC news-reader was announcing the details. **1951** in M. McLuhan *Mech. Bride* (1967) 8/3 The Editors of *Time* hope to give..a clearer picture of the world of news-gathering, news-writing, and *news-reading. **1971** T. F. MITCHELL in *Archivum Linguisticum* II. 38 Although the implication of spoken utterance is less assured for some written functions than others, nevertheless rehearsals.., newsreading, lecturing and public address, though not 'colloquial' language, illustrate speech with the implication of writing and vice versa. **1916** *Wells Fargo Messenger* V. 39/3 Some companies issue their *news reels twice a week. **1928** *Manch. Guardian Weekly* 26 Oct. 335/1 There are four motion picture newsreel cameramen, and four 'still' photographers. **1934** *B.B.C. Year-Bk.* 60 There has been another development of this new service by 'special correspondent' in the five-minute topical talk which in turn has now been extended to the 'News Reel'. **1944** L. MACNEICE *Christopher Columbus* 15 The radio play..is competing with the Soviet art-cinema rather than with Hollywood or the standardised news-reel. **1949** *Radio Times* 15 July 15/2 Radio Newsreel, a summary of events of the past week. **1973** 'D. JORDAN' *Nile Green* xliii. 218 We were safe..bowling across the desert like old newsreels of the Eighth Army chasing Rommel into the sea. **1817** *Morning Chron.* 25 Apr. (Jod.), Every circulating library and *newsroom throughout the kingdom. **1836** *Penny Cycl.* V. 238/1 There are two subscription libraries and two news-rooms. **1929** C. N. WARREN *News Reporting* i. 2 Ed Markham, reporter, entered the *Times* local news room, ready to start his work for the day. **1959** *Times* 5 May 13/5 The news-room scoop is almost a thing of the past—an exciting aspect of newspaper life remembered only by the journalist whose career began in the heady Fleet Street days before the war. **1973** *Scotsman* 13 Feb. 15/6 (Advt.), The Scotsman Publications Limited require a newsroom typist.

.. You will be typing our news stories as phoned in live by 'The Scotsman' reporters. **1841** W. SPALDING *Italy & It. Isl.* III. 81 Literature in all its branches, from philosophical treatises to magazines and *news-sheets. **1872** E. EGGLESTON *Hoosier Schoolm.* viii. 77 You can buy trap-doors.. dirt-cheap at the next *news-stand. **1894** S. FISKE *Holiday Stories* (1900) 141, I advised him.. to buy or rent a news stand in some hotel. **1926** G. ADE *Let.* 29 Nov. (1973) 116 You.. finally met out west the news-stand girl who had been your friend. **1932** E. WILSON *Devil take Hindmost* iii. 19 Communist publications, sold openly on news-stands. **1973** 'J. ASHFORD' *Double Run* vi. 42 Ryan crossed the main hall of Charing Cross station to the Smith news-stand in the centre. **1973** *Philadelphia Inquirer* (Today Suppl.) 14 Oct. 7/2 The Digest.. has lowered its newsstand price a dime. **1933** J. B. PRIESTLEY *Wonder Hero* iii. 95 He paid his shilling and entered one of the little *News Theatres. **1961** S. CHAPLIN *Day of Sardine* ii. 54 We nipped into the News Theatre one night and saw one of these Barbecue affairs, in colour. **1974** E. LEMARCHAND *Buried in Past* ix. 152 Enquiries at steak houses and news theatres in the Tottenham Court Road area. **1902** *News ticker [see TICKER^2 b]. **1933** BALMER & WYLIE *When Worlds Collide* v. 46 The news-ticker carried, as additional information, only the effect of the announcement on the markets in Europe. **1967** MRS. L. B. JOHNSON *White House Diary* 1 Aug. (1970) 550 It was 11 when we got back.. and Lyndon wanted me to go into his office with him to take that last look at the news ticker. **1834** *Gentl. Mag.* CIV. I. 101 A public meeting of the *Newsvenders of the metropolis. **1860** W. COLLINS *Wom. White* III. i, The ground floor.. is occupied by a small newsvendor's shop. **1820** *Rep. Comm. Working on Newspapers* in E. Howe *London Compositor* (1947) xv. 378 The Committee commenced their labours by tracing the Regulations for *News Work back to a certain period. **1890** W. J. GORDON *Foundry* 217 Illustrated work differs from ordinary newswork in one important particular. **1971** *Library* XXVI. 302 If we can trust the 'oral testimony' reported in 1820, long galleys were in use in newswork as early as 1770.

news (nju:z), *v.* Now *dial.* [f. the sb.]
1. *trans.* To tell or spread as news.
1650 R. STAPYLTON *Strada's Low C. Wars* IX. 45 This being newsed about the Town, many afterwards shunned the occasion of meeting with the Prince. **1875** PARISH *Sussex Gloss.* s.v., It was newsed about. **1895** *E. Anglian Gloss.* s.v., It was newsed at market yesterday.
2. *intr.* To tell news; to gossip.
1871 W. ALEXANDER *Johnny Gibb* (1873) 188 Topics to keep himself and his cronies 'newsin' for several days. **1886** *S.W. Linc. Gloss.* s.v., There's a deal of newsing goes on in that row.

†**'news-book.** *Obs.* A small newspaper.
In common use from about 1650 to 1700.
1652 HEYLIN *Cosmogr.* To Rdr. A 5 The situation and affairs of each Town of War.. which are presented to him in the Weekly Newsbooks. **1680** LUTTRELL *Brief Rel.* (1857) I. 44 For suppressing the printing and publishing unlicens'd news books and pamphlets of news. **1719** D'URFEY *Pills* IV. 326 It is in the News-book put, There's nothing can be truer.

'news-boy. A boy who sells newspapers in the streets, or delivers them at houses.
1764 in O. E. Winslow *Amer. Broadside Verse* (1930) 205 The news-boy's christmas and new-year's verses. **1812** COMBE *Picturesque* XXIII, Deafen'd by a news-boy's din. **1860** THACKERAY *Round. Papers, Late Gt. Vict.* (1876) 34 A news-boy had stopped in his walk, and was reading aloud the journal which it was his duty to deliver. **1879** E. K. BATES *Egypt. Bonds* II. viii. 188 The news-boys are plying their morning trade with harsh, piercing shrieks. **1939** T. S. ELIOT *Family Reunion* I. i. 43 The hidden shall be exposed and the newsboy shall shout in the street.

'newscast, *sb.* [Modelled on BROADCAST *sb.* 2.] A broadcast of the news on radio or television. Also as *vb.* So **'newscaster,** (*a*) a person who reads out the news on radio or television; (*b*) (see quot. 1966); **'newscasting** *vbl. sb.*
1930 *Observer* 28 Sept. 21 Graham MacNamee, the news-caster of our American newspaper newsreel, takes the part of an unseen dramatist. **1934** M. WESEEN *Dict. Amer. Slang* XII. 169 *Newscast*, to broadcast news by radio; a radio report of news. **1943** *Amer. Speech* XVIII. 147 The *-cast* of *broadcast* long since cast loose to attach itself in *newscast*. **1956** *Ann. Reg.* 1955 358 I.T.A. news was planned, intentionally, as something different from the traditional, wholly dignified, and impartial B.B.C. news, and was given instead from a personal angle, from less orthodox sources, by a skilful team of 'newscasters'. **1958** *New Statesman* 26 July 106/2 ITN one evening played martial music.. during the newscasting between shots. **1966** *Times* 8 Mar. 4/5 An electric newscaster is to be erected in Piccadilly Circus. A newscaster was one of three illuminated signs for the Circus approved by the Minister.. last month... Headline news bulletins, containing up-to-the-minute news from all over the world, will be flashed direct from the Press Association. Interspersed with the news bulletins will be advertising 'commercials' in four colours. **1970** *Toronto Daily Star* 24 Sept. 30/4 When the CBC hits it lucky, nobody can beat its newscasts. **1972** J. WAINWRIGHT *Requiem for Loser* viii. 171 He, too, momentarily disbelieved the B.B.C. newscaster... The wireless set continued to broadcast the news item. A lot of people listened to the newscast. **1972** 'G. BLACK' *Bitter Tea* (1973) xi. 180 The American style of newscasting, a breathless outpouring of words. **1973** *Daily Tel.* (Colour Suppl.) 9 Mar. 21/4 We've always had great success using newscasters for our appeals, and we prefer to use them, to make it a current affairs thing. The BBC don't see it our way, quite. **1973** *Daily Tel.* 3 Dec. 14/2 The first business to become a victim, presumably unintentionally, of the Government's ban on outdoor illuminated display advertising is Newscaster Publicity, which runs the newscaster on the outside of the Swiss Centre in Leicester Square.

new school. a. An advanced or liberal faction of a party or organization, *spec.* applied to the section of the Presbyterian Church of the United States which was separated from the rest of that Church between 1838 and 1869. Chiefly *attrib.*
1806 T. FESSENDEN *Democracy Unveiled* I. 113 That were not justice in arrears, These New School folks would lack their ears. **1816** *Emigrant's Guide* 17 Local politicians assume various appellations, such as New School and Old School Democrats, Snyderites, Clintonians, and many others, mostly derived from the name or principles of some popular demagogue. **1837** W. JENKINS *Ohio Gaz.* 317 The public buildings consist of.. two presbyterian churches, one of the old, and one of the new school. **1837** J. M. PECK *Gaz. Illinois* (ed. 2) I. 72 McDonough College.. is identified with the interests of the 'old school' Presbyterians, as the Illinois College at Jacksonville is with the 'New School' Presbyterians. **1872** R. G. MCCLELLAN *Golden State* 406 The Old and New School Presbyterians have.. 2,600 members and 3,500 Sunday-scholars. **1884** P. SCHAFF *Relig. Encycl.* III. 2306/1 The 'New-Haven Theology'.. was one of the most influential of the types of so-called 'New School Divinity'. **1959** *Chambers's Encycl.* XI. 184/1 The controversies of the old country were reflected in the colony, for instance, in the divisions of the Philadelphian presbyterians into the Old and New sides or schools. **1961** K. S. LATOURETTE *Christianity in Revolutionary Age* III. 87 The congregations which had sprung up from the Plan of Union, the 'New School' Presbyterians, were made up mainly of New Englanders and their descendants. **1967** D. T. KAUFFMAN *Dict. Relig. Terms* 329/2 *New School*, term for that part of American Presbyterianism in mid-nineteenth century which favored liberal positions in theology, church government, and social issues such as slavery.
b. *transf.*
1837 *Southern Lit. Messenger* III. 107 As I once read medicine.. under a disciple of the 'new school' (vulgarly called steam doctors). **1838** J. F. COOPER *Eve Effingham* II. iii. 84 But they evidently inclined to the opinion that the new school of pews was far better than the old. **1974** *Times* 18 Apr. 19/6 We conclude that the New School are mistaken in relying on some 'black box' stability in the relationships between the various sectoral balances.

new-set, *v.* [NEW *adv.* 6.] *trans.* To set afresh or in a new fashion.
1611 COTGR., *Regoldronné*,.. new set, or starched, as a ruffe. **1719** YOUNG *Revenge* I. i, Bid physicians talk our veins to temper, And with an argument new-set a pulse. **1792** A. YOUNG *Trav. France* 255 A rehearsal of *l'Olympiade*, new-set by a young composer. **1796** BURNEY *Mem. Metastasio* I. 293 The operas which he entirely new sets.
b. *esp.* To re-set (jewels) in a new style. Also *fig.*
1709 MRS. MANLEY *Secret Mem.* (1720) II. 121 Pawning her Diamond-Necklace, upon pretence of having it new-set. **1790** MME. D'ARBLAY *Diary* (1842) V. 143 Our usual Windsor life, which I shall not undertake to new-set for your inspection. The old setting will amply suffice.
So **new-set** *ppl. a.* Also ***new-set-up***, recently established.
a **1553** UDALL *Roister D.* II. i, Now that my maister is new set on wowyng. **1607** MIDDLETON *Fam. Love* IV. iii, I am.. of the spick and span new-set-up company of porters. *a* **1732** GAY *Araminta* Wks. 1775 II. 120 Her new-set jewels round her robe are plac'd.

'newsful, *a. rare.* [f. NEWS *sb.* + -FUL.] Full of tidings.
1639 G. DANIEL *Ecclus.* xxvi. 111 The Newes-full Host to order soe his waies He may be Iustified in what he Says. **1732** FIELDING *Cov. Gard. Trag.* II. x, Oh! Leathersides, what means this newsful look!

newsie ('nju:zɪ). Chiefly *U.S.* and *Austral. colloq.* Also **newsy.** [f. NEWS *sb.* (*pl.*) + -IE, -Y^6.] = NEWS-BOY.
1875 *North Alabamian* (Tuscaloosa, Ala.) 1 July 3/2 A newsboy on the M. and C. road was cruelly beating a dog which had jumped on the train, when its owner suddenly appeared at the car door, knocked 'newsy' off and commenced to pay him in his own coin. **1889** *Kansas City Times & Star* 12 Jan., Nearly 900 'newsies' applied for licenses and badges. **1904** *N.Y. Times* 16 July 7 He approached the 'newsy' and offered to buy a paper. **1916** C. SANDBURG *Chicago Poems* 42 The newsies are pitching pennies. **1953** BAKER *Australia Speaks* iv. 105 *Newsie*, a paper seller. **1962** *John o' London's* 4 Jan. 7/2 To be polite the newsie took a couple of swigs of it. **1962** J. ONSLOW *Bowler-Hatted Cowboy* i. 10 One early morning as the 'newsy' passed my berth, I leant out to ask him quietly for some fruit. **1969** 'E. LATHEN' *Murder to Go* (1970) xvi. 161 The newsie in the lobby.

newsily ('nju:zɪlɪ), *adv.* [f. NEWSY *a.* + -LY^2.] In a newsy manner or style.
1949 'N. R. NASH' *Young & Fair* 17 Have a nice summer? *Patty* (Newsily): Oh, fine. We got here in August. **1967** *Listener* 3 Aug. 136/3 Twenty years ago it [*sc.* a newspaper] was laid out rather newsily too.

'newsiness. [f. NEWSY *a.* + -NESS.] The quality or character of being full of news.
1892 *Lond. & Prov. Music Trades Rev.* 15 Nov. 33/3 Reading it for its brightness and its general newsiness. **1898** W. R. NICOLL in *Brit. Weekly* 18 Aug. 301/2 Its strength lies in its newsiness and in its moderation.

'newsless, *a.* [f. NEWS *sb.* + -LESS.] Destitute or devoid of news.
1746 H. WALPOLE *Lett.* clxix. (1833) II. 191 We are in such a news-less situation, that I have been some time too without writing to you. **1754** *Ibid.* (1846) III. 83, I am as newsless as in the dead of summer. **1865** *Daily Tel.* 13 Apr. 5 The disappointed and newsless Briton. **1881** *Blackw. Mag.* CXXX. 270 His adventures were like a page from the 'Arabian Nights' after the soldier's newsless life.
Hence **'newslessness.**
1864 SALA in *Daily Tel.* 3 Sept., The earlier pangs of news-lessness [being] assuaged.

'news-letter. A letter specially written to communicate the news of the day, common in the later part of the 17th and beginning of the 18th century; also, a printed account of the news (sometimes with a blank space left for private additions). Also, a periodical sent or handed out to subscribers, members of an organization, etc.
1674 *Essex Papers* (Camden) I. 216 The last week's Packett brought over a News Lettre, wch hath bin dispersed through all ye country & read at severall coffee houses in this Citty. **1711** *Lond. Gaz.* No. 4803/2 The common News Letters from Paris will not yet own the raising of the Siege of Gironne. **1724** SWIFT *Drapier's Lett.* ii. Wks. 1751 VIII. 288 In your News-Letter of the first Instant there is a Paragraph.. relating to Wood's Half-pence. **1849** MACAULAY *Hist. Eng.* iii. I. 390 People who lived at a distance.. could be kept regularly informed of what was passing there only by means of newsletters. **1880** 'GEO. ELIOT' *Let.* 19 Sept. (1956) VII. 325 Your 'news-letter' was very welcome, and I was especially glad to know that Gertrude tries to keep up her health by little devices of change. **1893** JESSOPP *Stud. Recluse* vii. 249 The newsletters of the 17th century did the work of the newspapers now. **1914** *Writer's Mag.* Jan. 313/2 Some of the journals take daily news letters. **1936** *Time* 29 June 26/2 He runs a publishing house with offices in Chicago and Philadelphia, keeps his friends informed in periodic news-letters which he calls 'Rainbow-Graphs'. **1961** 'E. LATHEN' *Banking on Death* (1962) xi. 91 Martin seems to be a persistent reader of stock market newsletters. **1972** *Physics Bull.* Sept. 562/2 The purpose of the new Group will be.. to circulate newsletters to Group members and to promote the general advancement and dissemination of knowledge in the field of neutron scattering.

'news-man. Also **newsman.**
1. A bearer or collector of news; a news-writer. Also, a newspaper reporter, a journalist.
1596 SPENSER *F.Q.* v. vi. 11 Cease, thou bad newes-man! .. The rest my selfe too readily can spell. **1650** R. STAPYLTON *Strada's Low C. Wars* I. 3, I dare promise to produce more Cabinet counsels, then all the Civill and military news-men. **1693** ECHARD (*title*) The Gazetteer's, or Newsman's Interpreter. **1775** SHERIDAN *Rivals* Prol., No newsman from our session is dismiss'd. **1833** T. HOOK *Love & Pride, Snowdon* viii, Having volunteered his labours as an amateur court newsman. **1878** *Hatton Corr.* (Camden) Pref. 3 Of the two principal news-men, Charles Hatton writes with some humour. **1953** *Manch. Guardian Weekly* 7 May 2. **1958** *Church Times* 24 Jan. 4/3 None the less, the theatre critic or the theatre newsman, each with his seat in the stalls on most nights in the year, must sit through many weary hours. **1968** *Globe & Mail* (Toronto) 17 Feb. 7/5 Some newsmen were concerned about Mr. Trudeau's talk of a government information service. **1970** N. ARMSTRONG et al. *First on Moon* iii. 64 Deke Slayton went outside to tell newsmen, standing in the glare of television camera lights, that the crew would soon be out. **1973** *Nature* 2 Feb. 300/1 A high-ranking newsman from the BBC. **1974** *Anderson* (S. Carolina) *Independent* 23 Apr. 3B/3 The Envoy Towers was evacuated and among its dazed occupants a newsman counted three dozen persons, children included, bleeding from head and body cuts sustained when windows blew in.
2. A man who sells or delivers newspapers.
1796 CHARLOTTE SMITH *Marchmont* IV. 31 A paper.. carried round every Saturday by an itinerant newsman. **1848** DICKENS *Dombey* xv, Railway journals in the windows of its newsmen. **1885** *Manch. Exam.* 26 Jan. 5/4 The news-men.. selling the latest editions at double price or more.

'newsmonger. One who collects and retails news.
1596 SHAKS. *1 Hen. IV*, III. ii. 25 By smiling Pick-thankes and base Newes-mongers. **1654** WHITLOCK *Zootomia* 302 The Complementall visitant Athenian, Newes-monger, and Amorous Trifler. **1692** BENTLEY *Boyle Lect.* iv. 109 Cardan and other News-mongers from the skies. **1724** SWIFT *Drapier's Lett.* iv. Wks. 1751 VIII. 343 Wood prescribes to the Newsmongers in London what they are to write. **1793** MME. D'ARBLAY *Let.* 22 Feb., We hear no news here,.. and see no newspapers, and not an English newsmonger. **1824** MISS MITFORD *Village* Ser. I. (1863) 227 She is a gentle newsmonger, and turns her scandal on the sunny side. **1884** COURTHOPE *Addison* v. 82 Towards the end of the sixteenth century newsmongers began to issue little pamphlets.
Hence **'newsmongering;** also **'newsmongery.**
1592 NASHE *Four Lett. Confut.* H 4, That.. which a scrutinie.. hath concluded to be viler than newesmungrie. **1822** HAZLITT *Table-t.* Ser. II. iv. 61 The mechanical operations of the spirit of newsmongering.

†**'newsome.** *Obs. rare*$^{-1}$. [f. NEW *sb.*^{1}] Noisome; grievous.
c **1440** *York Myst.* xxx. 183 Schall I trauayle þus tymely þis tyde?.. Slyke note is newsome to neven.

newspaper ('nju:zpeɪpə(r)), *sb.* [f. NEWS *sb.* Cf. Du. *nieuwspapier.*] **1. a.** A printed, now usually daily or weekly, publication containing the news, commonly with the addition of advertisements and other matters of interest.
1670 in *Westm. Gaz.* (1900) 12 Sept. 2/3, I wanted ye newes paper for Monday last past. **1688** in Ellis *Orig. Lett.* Ser. II. IV. 130 Any foreign or domestic Newspapers besides the printed Gazette. **1730** BERKELEY *Lett.* Wks. 1871 IV. 185 The newspapers of last February mentioned Dr. Clayton's being made bishop. **1789** *Bath Jrnl.* 27 July Advt., The Act inflicts a penalty of Ten Pounds on persons letting out News-papers to read for hire. **1833** HT. MARTINEAU *Loom & Lugger* II. i. 14 To throw down among the crowd the newspaper containing the advertisements. **1864** BOWEN *Logic* x. 346 The ordinary dialect of the market, the parlor, and the newspaper.
b. *attrib.* and *Comb.*, as ***newspaper account, advertisement, advertising, agent, article, boy, carrier, chase, clipping, column, controversy, correspondence, corresponding, correspond-***

ent, critic, cutting, directory, editor, hack, kiosk, letter, man, office, owner, paragraph, postage, press, printing, proprietor, reader, reporter, round, seller, selling, stand, syndicate, woman, wrapper.

1851 D. B. Woods *Sixteen Months at Gold Diggings* 199 Divesting the *newspaper accounts from California of certain expressions bordering rather too much upon the hyperbolic order, they amount to the fact that the outcrops of certain veins [of goldbearing quartz] have been removed. **1936** *Discovery* Dec. 384/2 It was not until February, 1626, that the first *newspaper advertisement appeared. *Ibid.*, The next step was *newspaper advertising. **1874** 'G. Hamilton' *Twelve Miles* ii. 30 The religious *newspaper-agents bore into your house like worms of the dust. **1832** J. S. Mill in *Tait's Edin. Mag.* II. 343 Books are run through with no less rapidity, and scarcely leave a more durable impression than a *newspaper article. **1858** *Missouri Democrat* 23 Oct. 2/2, I have not seen the letter, and but very few of the newspaper articles on the subject. **1972** D. Wainwright *Journalism made Simple* iv. 109 A magazine article needs an attractive and if possible startling opening sentence, like a good newspaper article. **1848** Dickens *Dombey* iv, The *newspaper boy in the oil-skin cap. **1920** M. Beer *Hist. Brit. Socialism* II. iv. xiii. 249 He played the part of a newspaper-boy. **1974** P. Lovesey *Invitation to Dynamite Party* iii. 32 Newspaper-boys..bawled their wares. **1851** C. Cist *Sk. Cincinnati in 1851* 50 Occupations... Newspaper publishers, 9; *Newspaper carriers, 23. **1926** *Daily Colonist* (Victoria, B.C.) 9 Jan. 14/3 With the neck broken and a deep gash in the head, the body of William Merchant, fourteen-year-old newspaper carrier, was found last night. **1888** Jacobi *Printers' Vocab.*, **Newspaper chases*, specially made chases to allow of the pages being laid closely together on the machine. **1906** W. Churchill *Coniston* ii. xi. 374 She had brought a note from her father... Two *newspaper clippings fell out of it. **1958** C. Watson *Coffin scarcely Used* iv. 33, I am here now instead of concocting a mysterious message from newspaper clippings. **1974** J. Banning *How I fooled World* iv. 23 Rosemary was putting teleprinter and newspaper clippings into the filing cabinet. **1843** M. Fuller *Summer on Lakes* (1844) vi. 185 Has ever Art found..a richer theme..sketched carelessly in the *newspaper column of to-day? **1860** W. G. Clark *Vac. Tour* 65 The *newspaper controversies and the theatre-riots of Naples. **1868** 'Mark Twain' *Lett. to Publishers* (1967) 14, I have cut my *newspaper correspondence down a good deal. **1868** Holme Lee *B. Godfrey* xxvi, [He] had vagabondised..over Europe as a *newspaper correspondent. **1868** 'Mark Twain' *Lett. to Publishers* (1967) 15 If you can stand an advance, I wish you would, and relieve me of this *newspaper corresponding until July. **1859** B. Bodichon *Let.* 28 June in Geo. Eliot *Lett.* (1954) III. 103 The book could not have succeeded if it had been known as hers; *every *newspaper critic would have written against it* (!!!). **1907** *Yesterday's Shopping* (1969) 436D Albums for *Newspaper Cuttings. **1886** 'Mark Twain' *Lett. to Publishers* (1967) 206 Please take a glance..at your *Newspaper Directory and tell me the aggregate number of dailies in the U.S., big cities and all. **1785** *Daily Universal Register* 1 Jan. 4/1 A *Newspaper Editor..should rest himself on truth and facts. **1837** H. Martineau *Society in America* I. i. iii. 151 The majority of newspaper editors made themselves parties to the act, by refusing, from fear, to reprobate it. **1972** C. Wintour *Pressures on Press* i. 6 It is essential for newspaper editors to be concerned with accuracy. **1821** Shelley *Hellas* Pref., The display of *newspaper erudition to which I have been reduced. **1885** *Newspaper-hack [see cipherer 2]. **1894** E. L. Shuman *Steps into Journalism* 65 One of the most prolific newspaper hacks in Chicago once remarked that he did not consider a man..a reporter unless he could make good made up of anything. **1792** W. Roberts *Looker-on* No. 28 (1794) 397 Such like inanities of *news-paper history. **1791** Burke *App. Whigs* Wks. VI. 74 *Newspaper intelligence ought always to be received with some degree of caution. **1975** N. Luard *Robespierre Serial* xvii. 151 Carswell..stopped at a *newspaper kiosk. **1868** 'Mark Twain' *Lett. to Publishers* (1967) 15 In order to give to the book the amount of attention it really requires I shall have to cut loose from everything but one, and sometimes two, *newspaper letters a week. **1806** Surr *Winter in Lond.* II. 70 The *newspaper-man was of course gratified. **1883** F. M. Crawford *Mr. Isaacs* vi. 105 A Yankee newspaper man. **1954** G. Kersh in D. Knight *100 Yrs. Sci. Fiction* (1969) iv. 217 I'm a war correspondent, and newspaperman, so I have the right to ask impertinent questions. **1966** *Listener* 21 July 79/1 For newspapermen throughout the world Washington has always been the Mecca of journalism. **1972** J. Mosedale *Football* v. 71 Newspapermen..confessed they could not look on him objectively. **1834** J. S. Mill in *Monthly Repos.* VIII. 173 The priest of the nineteenth century..sets up his pulpit in a *newspaper office. **1915** R. Fry *Let.* 27 Aug. (1972) II. 390 Those who encounter the enemy in the newspaper offices are the most bloodthirsty. **1966** Harris & Spark *Pract. Newspaper Reporting* iii. 34 Different newspaper offices mean different things when they refer to 'district reporting'. **1975** A. Fraser *Whistler's Lane* x. 159 I'll take the bus into Clitheroe..that's where the nearest newspaper office is. I want to look up the files. **1959** *Chambers's Encycl.* IX. 845/2 The fears of journalists in Britain that similar systems of chain newspapers, all propagating the views of one *newspaper owner, might have ill effects both on the journalistic profession and on the newspapers. **1961** A. Clarke *Later Poems* 92 The leader of the Dublin capitalists was William Martin Murphy, a newspaper owner and ruthless clericalist. **1798** *Deb. Congress U.S.* 5 July (1851) 2107 The gentleman from Connecticut..had communicated to the House..a number of *newspaper paragraphs. **1800** *Asiatic Ann. Reg.* ii. 146/1 The suspicions..were nothing but idle rumours and newspaper paragraphs. **1768–74** Tucker *Lt. Nat.* (1834) II. 170, I should think, to use the *newspaper phrase, the thing merited confirmation. **1812** *Niles' Reg.* I. 361/1, I..admit your publication to be a newspaper and to be rated at *Newspaper Postage. **1829** J. S. Mill *Let.* 7 Nov. in *Wks.* (1963) XII. 38 You know in how low a state the *newspaper press of this country is. **1837** H. Martineau *Society in America* I. i. iii. 75 Of all newspaper presses, I never heard any one deny that the American is the worst. **1840** *Penny Cycl.* XVI. 194/1 The two principal persons..concerned in the newspaper press. **1959** *Chambers's Encycl.* IX. 843/1 In America only the periodical press is national and therefore has priority for advertising purposes over the newspaper press. **1824** J. Johnson *Typographia* II. 651 (*heading*) *Newspaper printing offices. **1847** H. Howe *Hist. Coll. Ohio* 241 Kenton..now contains..1 newspaper printing office. **1974** *Encycl. Brit. Macropædia* XV. 243/1 The practice resulted in considerable overmanning in newspaper printing departments. **1885** *List of Subscribers, Brighton* (S. of Eng. Telephone Co.) 14 Printers and *Newspaper Proprietors. **1933** J. Buchan *Prince of Captivity* i. iv. 114 Falconet was..a newspaper proprietor on a large scale. **1974** *Encycl. Brit. Macropædia* XV. 243/2 Many of Scripps' methods were adopted by his rivals and by newspaper proprietors in other countries. **1935** *Discovery* Aug. 244/1 To the average *newspaper-reader, Mongol is but a generic term. **1959** *Chambers's Encycl.* IX. 842/2 The steadily growing body of potential newspaper readers which increased educational facilities had brought into being. **1834** *Tait's Mag.* I. 735/1 To the uttermost ends of the *newspaper-reading earth. **1813** *Theatrical Inquisitor* II. 213 Newspaper critics and *reporters..have had a prodigious addition to their necessary employments. **1910** 'O. Henry' *Strictly Business* 87 The newspaper reporters dug out of their trunks the old broad-brimmed hats and leather belts. **1963** L. E. & B. Ryan *So you want to go into Journalism* i. 27 Newspaper reporters make modest salaries. **1948** C. Day Lewis *Otterbury Incident* iv. 48, I was a bit late, the *newspaper-round taking longer than I expected. **1973** J. Wayne *Brown Bread & Butter* x. 183 Was she eating breakfast, wasn't the newspaper round too much? **1927** C. Parsons in *Oxford Poetry* 24 Beneath me in the windy stir *Newspaper-sellers advertise The death of a philosopher By unintelligible cries. **1974** *Country Life* 28 Nov. 1656/3, I had a word..with a newspaper seller outside the building. **1957** J. Kerouac *On Road* (1958) 58 The little midget *newspaper-selling woman. **1857** W. Collins *Dead Secret* iii. i, The *newspaper-slip..contained the paragraph from the *Times*. **1893** W. K. Post *Harvard Stories* 31 At a *news-paper stand he bought all the picture papers. **1889** W. D. Howells *Hazard of New Fortunes* II. 120, I told 'em I hadn't much practice with Go-devils in the *newspaper syndicate business. **1891** 'Mark Twain' *Lett. to Publishers* (1967) 275 McCluny..the manager of the newspaper syndicate. **1885** *Times* (weekly ed.) 22 May 7/2 Left King's Cross at 5 o'clock in the morning by the *newspaper train. **1849** Sir F. B. Head *Stokers & Pokers* iii. (1851) 41 The *newspaper-vendors..are indolently reclining at their stalls. **1881** H. James *Portr. Lady* xxxviii, He really must object to that *newspaper woman. **1925** F. Scott Fitzgerald *Great Gatsby* vi. 120 Ella Kaye, the newspaper woman. **1954** D. Dodge *Lights of Skaro* ii. 55 She was a very good newspaperwoman, and not too scrupulous. **1971** B. Graham *Spy Trap* i. 13 Christ! A bloody newspaper woman! He told her everything! **1873** *Brit. Postal Guide* 1 Jan. 21 Every Head Postmaster is required to keep, for sale to the public..*newspaper wrappers bearing an impressed halfpenny stamp, and Post Cards. **1926–7** *Army & Navy Stores Catal.* 363/2 *Newspaper wrappers.* Size $12\frac{1}{4} \times 4\frac{3}{4}$ in., plain, gummed. **1813** Creevey in *Examiner* 24 May 336/1 Prohibited to *newspaper-writers.

c. newspaper English, the style of English used in newspapers; journalese; **newspaper stamp**, a stamp tax imposed on newspapers between 1711 and 1855.

1888 *Harper's Mag.* May 962/2 The phrase 'newspaper English' has come to have a significance which is not flattering to newspapers. **1942** P. G. Perrin *Writer's Guide & Index* 606 Good newspaper English is simply informal English applied to the daily recording of affairs. It is a style written to be read rapidly and by the eye—tricks of sound outside the headlines are out of place. **1947** Partridge *Usage & Abusage* 38/2 *Betrothal* [for 'engagement'] and *betrothed* are current in American newspaper-English. **1835** J. S. Mill in *London Rev.* I. 513 It was understood..that the ministry intended to take off the newspaper stamps. **1956** J. E. Gerald *British Press under Govt. Econ. Controls* i. 5 The newspaper stamp duty..was allowed to lapse in 1855.

2. *Underworld slang.* (See quots.)

1926 Maines & Grant *Wise-Crack Dict.* 11/2 *Newspaper*, crook's term for thirty days in jail. **1931** G. Irwin *Amer. Tramp & Underworld Slang* 134 *Newspaper*, a thirty days' gaol sentence. **1949** Partridge *Dict. Underworld* 467/2 *Newspaper*, a thirty-days jail sentence... The time it takes an illiterate to read one.

Hence (chiefly *nonce-words*) **newspape'racious** *a.*, of the kind usual in newspapers. **'newspaperdom**, the world or sphere of newspapers. **'newspapered** *ppl. a.*, brought by, provided with, a newspaper. **newspape'rese**, the language or style usual in newspapers. **newspa'perial** *a.*, of or belonging to newspapers. **newspa'perically** *adv.*, in the newspapers. **'newspapering**, journalism. **'newspaperish** *a.*, somewhat in newspaper style. **'newspaperishly** *adv.*, in a newspaper manner. **'newspaperism**, the characteristic features or style of newspapers; a newspaper phrase or expression. **'newspaperist** (see quot.). **'newspaperized** *ppl. a.*, adapted to, affected by, the usual style of newspapers. **'newspaperling**, a small newspaper. **'newspaperly** *adv.*, as regards the newspapers. **'newspapery** *a.*, in newspaper style; given to reading newspapers. **newspa'porial** (*U.S.*) *sb.*, an item from a newspaper; *adj.*, of or belonging to newspapers; **newspa'porialist**, a newspaper writer.

1843 *Fraser's Mag.* XXVII. 76 Critiques, both epistolary and *newspaperacious. **1882** *Daily News* 7 Oct. 5/7 Ludgate is in the heart of *Newspaperdom. **1933** *Times Lit. Suppl.* 30 Mar. 223/4 *Shooting the Bull*..is a tongue-in-the-cheek march through newspaperdom. **1946** *Sun* (Baltimore) 9 May 12/3 [A] new era of independent journalism in country newspaperdom. **1703** De Foe *Trueborn Eng.* Pref. (ed. 2) 4 The Publisher of this has been *News-papered into Goal already for it. **1855** Dickens in *Household Words* 29 Sept. 193/1 Every house was shut up and newspapered. **1926** W. W. Bishop *Backs of Books* 229 We are the most newspapered and magazined nation on earth, I suppose. **1973** E. Williams *Emlyn* i. 7, I saw my two brothers sitting at the table neatly newspapered to save the cloth. **1889** *Sat. Rev.* 30 Nov. 612/2 His picture..may have something of '*newspaperese' about it. **1868** *Lond. Rev.* 12 Dec. 638/1 Sensationalism..is, in the main, a '*newspaperial' product, as the name itself is newspaperial. **1768–74** Tucker *Lt. Nat.* (1834) I. 475 The vast Pacific Ocean, commonly, yea vulgarly, not to say *news-papericaly,..called..the South-sea. **1862** Thackeray *Philip* vii I've tried schoolmastering, bear-leading, *newspapering. **1911** E. Ferber *Dawn O'Hara* iii. 29, I would fall to thinking of those years of newspapering—of the thrills of them, and the ills of them. **1968** L. J. Braun *Cat who turned on & Off* (1969) i. 11 Interviewing artists, interior decorators and Japanese flower arrangers was not Qwilleran's idea of newspapering. **1971** *Daily Colonist* (Victoria, B.C.) 26 Sept. 2/1, I care because newspapering is my business—make that my life, not business. **1825** M. Wilmot *Let.* 26 Sept. (1935) 225 And so ends my story, which is a stupid *newspaperish sort of thing, tho' it was exceedingly interesting and amusing and pretty to look at at the time. **1892** *Academy* 10 Feb. 120/1 Some of these essays are a little too newspaperish. **1929** A. Noyes *Return of Scare-Crow* iv. 54, I know that it's all very noble and distinguished and broad-minded and generally newspaperish. **1858** Sir R. Christison *Let.* in *Life* (1886) II. iii. 22 Though not inclined to retort *newspaperishly, I would [etc.]. **1838** *Fraser's Mag.* XVII. 315 They have upon them the undeniable sin of *newspaperism. **1900** *Edin. Rev.* Jan. 77 Colloquialisms, Americanisms, or what may be called newspaperisms. **1830** *Fraser's Mag.* I. 721 You make no mistake in calling a man a *newspaperist who talks much about newspapers. **1831** *Ibid.* III. 605 To give a *newspaperized report of the proceedings. **1890** *Harper's Mag.* Apr. 807/2 The ordinary more or less newspaperized English of our day. *a* **1842** Maginn in A. A. Watts *Life Watts* (1884) II. 175 Head nurse of a hospital of rickety *newspaperlings. **1816** Polidori *Let.* in Smiles *Mem. J. Murray* (1891) I. xv. 364 Some pleasant accidents..is all we have to keep us *news-paperly alive. **1864** *Realm* 6 Apr. 8 Desiring to be in tone and language..as little *newspapery as a newspaper may be. **1890** *Catholic Househ.* 11 Jan. 9 The modern Londoner is..newspapery. **1787** *Mass. Centinel* 18 July 4/1 English *Newspaporials. **1794** *Columbian Centinel* (Boston) 14 May 2/4 Newspaporial rule of three. **1853** in A. E. Lee *Hist. Columbus* (Ohio) (1892) I. 474 In this day of newspaporial dearth, anything above the mud level will create a sensation. **1871** *Vermont. Hist. Gazetteer* II. 721/1 One of the Editors of the 'New York World'—the popular *newspaporialist.

newspaper ('nju:zpeɪpə(r)), *v. U.S. rare.* [f. the sb.] To work on a newspaper, to do newspaper work. Cf. newspapering *vbl. sb.*

1943 *Time* 8 Mar. 64 He had newspapered in Hawaii. **1959** *Time* (Atlantic ed.) 6 July 11 Who newspapered in Chicago.

'newspaperland. [f. newspaper + land *sb.*] = newspaperdom.

1910 *Daily Chron.* 22 Mar. 8/2 As he is one of those who sit in the high places of newspaperland his voice is an authority that must not be overlooked. **1931** G. B. Shaw in *Ellen Terry & Bernard Shaw* 338 In newspaperland a slander is interesting news, always welcomed by news-editors. **1931** T. H. Pear *Voice & Personality* ii. 20 In newspaper-land, too, persons in danger when sleeping, escape in 'night attire'.

'newspaperless, *a.* [f. newspaper + -less.] Without a newspaper.

c **1889** 'Mark Twain' *Speeches* (1923) 152 This was a newspaperless globe. **1909** *Westm. Gaz.* 10 Aug. 7/2 Newspaperless Sweden... No newspapers..are published here this morning. **1920** *Glasgow Herald* 1 Sept. 6 The demand for a distantly printed issue imported into Liverpool was a revelation of the eagerness with which a newspaperless public will snatch at anything conveying a semblance of the news of the day.

Newspeak ('nju:spi:k). Also **newspeak.** [f. new *a.* + speak *v.*] The name of the artificial language used for official communications in G. Orwell's novel *Nineteen Eighty-Four*, freq. applied to any corrupt form of English, *spec.* the propagandist and ambiguous language of some politicians, broadcasters, etc. Also *attrib.*

1949 'G. Orwell' *Nineteen Eighty-Four* i. 51 Syme was a philologist, a specialist in Newspeak. Indeed, he was one of the enormous team of experts now engaged in compiling the Eleventh Edition of the Newspeak Dictionary. *Ibid.* ii. 133 Do you know the Newspeak word *goodthinkful*? *Ibid.* App. 299 Newspeak was the official language of Oceania and had been devised to meet the ideological needs of Ingsoc, or English Socialism. In the year 1984 there was not as yet anyone who used Newspeak as his sole means of communication, either in speech or writing. **1950** A. A. Roback *Personality in Theory & Practice* i. 27, I do not think it necessary to resort to 'Newspeak' in order to write scientifically. **1959** *New Statesman* 2 May 602/2 This cynical 'newspeak' naming of Nationalist legislation has, in recent months, been matched by a remarkable change in the language used by their press and politicians. **1961** Y. Olsson *On Syntax Eng. Verb* vi. 148 Even George Orwell's progressive Newspeak still preserves a few 'clumsy remnants of a bygone past'. **1963** *Guardian* 8 Mar. 10/6 Mr John Snagge, Head of Presentation at the BBC, is asking applicants for jobs as announcers to read aloud the 'Guardian's' leading article about 'newspeak', a method of speech, said by the writer to have become common among broadcasters, in which fullstops are put in the middle of sentences. **1966** *Punch* 27 July 140/1 Accusing the Prime Minister of 'the same old excuses', it [*sc.* the *Daily Telegraph*] labelled 'redeployment' as 'new-speak', which would be 'victimisation of the workers' in any but a Labour Government. **1972** *Guardian* 17 Feb. 14/5 The Orwellian

Newspeak style. **1972** *Times Lit. Suppl.* 11 Aug. 935/2 The new party line, directed this time against 'rootless cosmopolitans'—newspeak for Jews. **1975** *Ibid.* 31 Jan. 115/4 A Khrushchevian panache which still makes a refreshing contrast with the computerized newspeak that passes for political discourse among many of his successors.

new-sprung, *ppl. a.* [NEW *adv.* 3.] Newly sprung into existence; lately sprung up.

1592 SHAKS. *Ven. & Ad.* 1171 She bows her head, the new-sprung flower to smell. **1622** MASSINGER & DEKKER *Virg. Mart.* I. i, We dare dispute against this new-sprung sect. **1667** DRYDEN *Dram. Poesie* Ess. (ed. Ker) I. 64 Every new-sprung passion, and turn of it, is a part of the action. **1728–46** THOMSON *Spring* 606 In the freshening shade Of new-sprung leaves. **1790** BURKE *Fr. Rev.* 111 Not being illuminated by a single ray of this new-sprung modern light. **1853** LYNCH *Self-Improv.* iv. 102 Words will sometimes flow suddenly like new-sprung fountains.

newst, var. NOUST.

newsworthy (ˈnjuːzwɜːðɪ), *a.* [f. NEWS *sb.* (*pl.*) + WORTHY *a.*] Of sufficient interest to the general public to warrant mention in the news. Also **ˈnewsworthily** *adv.*; **ˈnewsworthiness**.

1932 *Time* 15 Feb. 4/2 *Time* is grateful for support and criticism of its policy, and repeats its promise to cause the minimum of offense in respect to newsworthy oaths. **1936** L. C. DOUGLAS *White Banners* v. 88 The manner of the taciturn chemist's departure had doubled the insurance his widow would have received in the event of his having died less newsworthily. **1940** *Harper's Mag.* Nov. 588a The Nazi offensive..is, judging from our newspapers, apparently the only newsworthy topic on Latin America. **1951** L. Z. HOBSON *Celebrity* (1953) x. 145 They were finding his speech a shade less newsworthy than they were supposed to. **1957** *Observer* 29 Sept. 10/7 His lot is harder than Mr. Colvin's, if not so newsworthy. **1960** 'M. CRONIN' *Begin with Gun* vii. 82 A celebrated French *modiste* who had become eminently newsworthy..had consented to be interviewed. **1961** *Guardian* 22 Mar. 10/4 Publicity-conscious people..make 'newsworthiness' a determinant of their actions. **1967** G. PLAYFAIR *Prodigy* vii. 167 His newsworthiness had dwindled. **1969** *Listener* 24 July 113/2 Not that by living life more newsworthily one could hope to provide more than the raw material. **1970** G. F. NEWMAN *Sir, You Bastard* iii. 89 They might get a lot of newsworthy items, but no exclusives. **1972** M. WILLIAMS *Inside Number 10* xiv. 345 While the general public will know the names of the political heads of the more newsworthy ministries, there is rarely any knowledge of the names of the permanent features of the departments, the Civil Service heads. **1973** *Guardian* 13 Apr. 11/2 The newsworthiness of the [Black Panther] movement.

ˈnews-writer. One who writes up the news for the information of others; *esp.* in early use, a writer of news-letters.

1700 T. BROWN tr. *Fresny's Amusem.* iv. Wks. 1709 III. 46 Like our common News-writers, [they] steal from one-another. **1724** SWIFT *Drapier's Lett.* iv. Wks. 1751 VIII. 348 As Wood has taught the London News-writer to express it. **1794** BURKE *Impeachm. W. Hastings* Wks. XVI. 54 Who in fact is this Hoolas Roi whom they represent..to be nothing but a news writer? **1810** JEFFERSON *Writ.* (1830) IV. 152, I have indulged freer views on this question, on your assurances..that they will not get into the hands of news-writers. **1849** MACAULAY *Hist. Eng.* iii. I. 390 The newswriter rambled from coffee room to coffee room, collecting reports. **1879** *Spectator* 13 Sept. 1148 The infallible oriental sign of brewing trouble..was apparent to the native news-writers.

newsy (ˈnjuːzɪ), *a.* [f. NEWS + -Y[1].] **1.** Full of news; given to retailing news.

1832 JEKYLL *Corr.* ix. (1894) 304 *Mille graces* for a newsy letter. **1886** FENN *Master Cerem.* I. xxvi. 248 She looks pretty shabby now, a newsy, gossiping old hag.

2. Likely to create news.

1959 *Vogue* Nov. 83 A newsy new car, the red sleek Daimler. **1971** *Daily Tel.* 28 July 11 Tweed sprouts all over the collection, best in separates such as..the ponchos worn over slim skirts or (far more newsy) skin-tight tweed trousers.

newsy, var. NEWSIE.

newt (njuːt). Forms: 5–6 **neute**, 5–7 **newte**, 6–7 **nute**; 5 **newtt**, 6–7 **neut**, 6– **newt.** [For *ewt* (with *n-* from *an*: see N 3), var. of *evet* EFT *sb.*[1] The change of *v* to *w* is unusual, and the intermediate form *euft* NEUFT is also difficult to explain.] A small tailed amphibian (*Triton*), allied to the salamander, of which two or three species are common in Britain; an eft or ask.

c **1420** *Pallad. on Husb.* III. 865 For rotyng of the crop the galle is boote To towche hem with of neutes grene [L. *lacertæ viridis*]. *c* **1440** *Promp. Parv.* 355/2 Newte, or ewte, wyrme, *lacertus*. **1530** PALSGR. 248/1 Newte a worme, *lisarde*. **1584** R. SCOT *Discov. Witchcr.* XIII. viii. (1886) 246 Our newt is..like to the lizzard in shape. **1627** MAY *Lucan* IX. 826 The water-spoyling Newte, the dart-like Snakes. **1699** GARTH *Dispens.* 79 Where hateful Nutes and painted Lizzards sleep. **1761** STERNE *Tr. Shandy* IV. xxvii, A Newt, or an Asker, or some such detested reptile. **1774** GOLDSM. *Nat. Hist.* (1776) VII. 113 Though the Newt may be looked upon in this contemptible light. **1818** SHELLEY *Marenghi* xix, He had tamed every newt and snake and toad. **1870** H. A. NICHOLSON *Man. Zool.* (1875) 454 The Water-salamanders or Newts are distinguished from the terrestrial forms by being furnished with a compressed fish-like tail, and by being strictly oviparous.

Comb. **1891** *Daily News* 14 Sept. 5/4 A small newt-like creature from North America, which is known as the spotted eft.

new-take. [NEW *a.* + TAKE *sb.*] On Dartmoor, a piece of moorland newly enclosed and cultivated. Also *attrib.*

1889 PAGE *Explor. Dartmoor* ii. 25 Portions of the Moor are frequently granted by the Duchy to persons willing to farm them. These are known as 'newtakes'. **1899** BARING GOULD *Furze Bloom* 18 Tonks..said he would finish his new-take wall by himself.

newter, obs. form of NEUTER.

New Thought, new thought. [THOUGHT[1] I.] A theory of the nature of disease, a system of therapeutic practice, and a religious sect believing in these, founded on principles formulated by Phineas P. Quimby of Portland, Maine, U.S.A. Hence **New Thoughter**, one who holds and practises 'new thought'; a member of the sect following the principles of Quimby. Also *transf.*

1887 W. H. HOLCOMBE *Condensed Thoughts Christian Sci.* (ed. 6) 45 New thought always excites combat in the mind with the old thought, which refuses to retire. **1899** H. W. DRESSER *Voices of Freedom* ii. 22 The term 'New Thought', now the accepted appellation of a doctrine which has differentiated itself from..mental science..and become the representative teaching of those who..are not worshippers of personality, are not bound to certain books, but remain independent. *Ibid.* 23 The New Thought..is both a philosophy of life and conduct and a mode of healing. **1902** W. JAMES *Var. Relig. Exper.* iv. 94 A current..has recently poured over America..to which..I will give the title of the 'Mind-cure movement'. There are various sects of this 'New Thought', to use another of the names by which it calls itself. **1907** —— in *American Mag.* Nov. 58/2 To relax, to say to ourselves (with the 'new thoughters') 'Peace! be still!' is sometimes a great achievement of inner work. *a* **1910** —— *Some Probl. Philos.* (1911) i. 18 Compare Prentice Mulford and others of the 'new thought' type. **1937** D. CANFIELD *Fables for Parents* 128 Being a Congregationalist and not a Christian Scientist or a New Thoughter. **1942** A. HUXLEY *Let.* 30 Dec. (1969) 485 The strengthening and extension of such religions as Christian Science, Theosophy, New Thought, 'I Am', in which the stress is wholly on powers, personal advantages and future time. **1949** *Sun* (Baltimore) 7 Sept. 12/4 Loss of that strength would weaken the old-line men as against the groping 'new-thoughters' in the party. **1967** D. T. KAUFFMAN *Dict. Relig. Terms* 330/1 *New Thought*, American religious movement,..emphasizing 'the divinity of man and his infinite possibilities..'. Groups are now found in many parts of the world.

Newton (ˈnjuːtən). [Name of Sir Isaac *Newton*: see NEWTONIAN *a.* and *sb.*] **1.** ***Newton's rings***: a set of concentric circular fringes seen surrounding the point of contact when a convex lens is placed on a plane surface (or on another lens), which join points where the intervening thin layer of air has the same thickness and are caused by interference between light reflected from its upper and lower surfaces. When used *attrib.* also *sing.*

[**1807** *Phil. Trans. R. Soc.* XCVII. 180 (*heading*) Experiments for investigating the cause of the coloured concentric rings, discovered by Sir Isaac Newton, between two object-glasses laid upon one another. **1809** *Ibid.* XCIX. 299 In order completely to account for the Newtonian rings.] **1835** *Phil Mag.* VII. 363 In examining Newton's rings I was induced to place a convex lens..between two surfaces of plate-glass, in order to effect the superposition of the rings. **1904** A. SCHUSTER *Introd. Theory of Optics* iv. 72 The colours observed in Newton's rings are the colours of thin films, the film being the layer of air included between the lens and the plate. **1969** S. G. & H. LIPSON *Optical Physics* xii. 382 Lens surfaces can be tested to a high degree of accuracy by forming Newton's rings with a known surface. *Ibid.* 383 Coefficients of thermal expansion of quite small crystals can be measured by counting the fringes that pass through the centre of a Newton's ring system as the crystal is heated.

2. (Written **newton.**) The unit of force in the metre-kilogramme-second system (now incorporated in the S.I.): the force that would give a mass of one kilogramme an acceleration of one metre per second per second; 100,000 dynes (approximately the weight of 102 grammes or 3·6 oz.). Abbrev. N.

1904 D. ROBERTSON in *Electrician* 22 Apr. 25/1 The writer suggests that the name 'Newton' be given to the unit of force (10^5 dynes). **1919** *Nature* 4 Sept. 13/2 A fourth matter.. which was discussed was the proposal to adopt in future legislation for metric countries the M.K.S. system of units. .. On this system the unit of force is the 'Newton'. **1935** HARTSHORN & VIGOUREUX in *Ibid.* 7 Sept. 397/2 In the M.K.S. system..no name has yet been assigned to the unit of force... G. Giorgi has provisionally used the word 'vis'. .. We venture to suggest that 'newton' would be more appropriate. **1942** H. HOWE *Introd. Physics* iv. 57 The awkwardly large numbers in Ex. 2 would have been avoided had mks units been used; the answer would have been $F =$ 300 newtons. **1962** CORSON & LORRAIN *Introd. Electromagnetic Fields* ii. 29 In these units Coulomb's law is written as $\mathbf{F}_{ab} = (1/4\pi\epsilon_0)\,(Q_aQ_b/r^2)/\mathbf{r}_1$, where the force **F** is measured in newtons; the charges Q_a and Q_b, in coulombs ..; and the distance r, in meters. **1970** *Daily Tel.* 14 May 18 In the SI the force is measured not in kilogrammes, but in newtons—spelt with a small 'n' but abbreviated with a large one, 'N'. One newton (reinforcing the legend) is roughly the pull of gravity on one apple.

Newtonian (njuːˈtəʊnɪən), *a.* and *sb.* [f. the name of Sir Isaac *Newton* (1642–1727) + -IAN.]

A. *adj.* **1.** Devised, discovered, or suggested, by Newton; pertaining to, or arising from, the theory of the universe propounded by Newton.

1713 DERHAM *Phys.-Theol.* II. v. (1754) 52 The Pressure of the Atmosphere, and the Newtonian Attraction. **1778** [W. MARSHALL] *Minutes Agric., Observ.* 146 The Philosophy of the Weather may happily be rendered as obvious as the Newtonian Principles. **1830** LYELL *Princ. Geol.* I. iii. I. 40 For which reason they objected to the Newtonian theory of gravitation. *a* **1866** J. GROTE *Exam. Utilit. Phil.* xxi. (1870) 343 The grand simplicity of the Newtonian discoveries.

2. Resembling, characteristic of, accepting the views of, Newton.

1742 YOUNG *Nt. Th.* (1751) 338 Ye searching, ye Newtonian angels! tell, Where your great Master's orb? **1762–9** FALCONER *Shipwr.* I. 827 Borne on Newtonian wing, through air she flies. **1823** *Gentl. Mag.* XCIII. I. 628 From these data the Newtonian philosophers have drawn conclusions [etc.]. **1871** MORLEY *Condorcet* in *Crit. Misc.* Ser. I. (1878) 87 Men of Newtonian capacity.

3. Of telescopes, their parts, etc.: Of the kind devised by Newton.

1761 DUNN in *Phil. Trans.* LII. 184 A Newtonian reflecting telescope, six feet in length. **1794** G. ADAMS *Nat. & Exp. Philos.* II. xxii. 471 A reflecting telescope was produced to the world of the Newtonian construction. **1831** BREWSTER *Optics* xlii. 353 The Newtonian telescope, which may be regarded as an improvement upon the Gregorian one. **1872** PROCTOR *Ess. Astron.* i. 4 An excellent Newtonian reflector.

B. *sb.* **1.** A follower of Newton; one who accepts the Newtonian system.

1741 tr. *D'Argens' Chinese Lett.* xvii. 117 The Newtonian having said, That Descartes was an Ignoramus, the Disciple of that Philosopher reply'd in a Passion, You lie. **1813** SHELLEY *Q. Mab* Notes, Poet. Wks. (1891) 52/2 The consistent Newtonian is necessarily an atheist. **1833** *Tracts for Times* No. 11. 5 The knowledge of which does not bind us to be Newtonians, or Aristotelians.

2. A Newtonian telescope or reflector.

1877 G. F. CHAMBERS *Astron.* (ed. 3) 661 Awkwardness of reflectors (that is to say Newtonians, which virtually are the only ones in use).

Hence **Newˈtonianism**, the Newtonian system.

1890 *Athenæum* 19 July 92/2 [Mercier] declared Newtonianism to be the 'most absurd scientific extravagance that has ever issued from the human imagination'.

Newtonically (njuːˈtɒnɪkəlɪ), *adv. rare.* [f. the name of Sir Isaac *Newton* (see NEWTONIAN *a.* and *sb.*) + -ICALLY.] In the manner of Sir Isaac Newton.

1869 J. S. MILL *Let.* 30 Jan. (1910) II. xii. 181 In regard to the Darwinian hypothesis,..Darwin has found (to speak Newtonically) a *vera causa*. **1953** K. BRITTON *John Stuart Mill* v. 182 His [*sc.* Mill's] preference for a mechanical view of forces..arises in part from his insistence upon 'speaking Newtonically' in opposition to the Baconian language of Macaulay and the empiricists.

ˈNewtonist. [Cf. NEWTONIAN *a.* and *sb.*] A Newtonian.

1741 tr. *D'Argens' Chinese Lett.* xvii. 117, I was t'other Day at the hearing of a smart Dispute between a Cartesian and a Newtonist.

ˈnewtonite. *Min.* [Named (1891) from its locality, *Newton* County, Arkansas.] A hydrous silicate of aluminium.

1891 *Amer. Jrnl. Sci.* XLII. 13 Newtonite is a pure white, soft, compact, homogeneous substance.

New Town, new town. A planned urban area designed to ease the congestion of a nearby large city, usu. one with special provision for housing, employment, and amenities for a delimited population. Also *transf.* Also *attrib.*, as ***New Town blues***, despondency or anxiety suffered by a person resident in a New Town. Hence **New Towner; New-Townish** *a.*

1918 (*title*) New towns after the war. **1946** *Hansard Commons* 17 Apr. 2710 *New Towns Bill* 'to provide for the creation of new towns by means of development corporations, and for purposes connected therewith' presented by Mr. Silkin. **1948** 'J. TEY' *Franchise Affair* xxiii. 266 The little house on the outer rim of the 'new' town. **1958** *Engineering* 21 Feb. 227/1 Suburban railway peak problems could be eased by more New Towns. **1958** *Spectator* 8 Aug. 191/1 An immense new-town bicycle shed. **1958** *Listener* 23 Oct. 655/2 His analysis of the Hellenistic 'new town', Priene. **1959** *Manch. Guardian* 6 Aug. 4/2 The new-town voters. **1960** *News Chron.* 2 July 3/5 He was born in St. Pancras, London, and is now a Hemel Hempstead new towner. **1962** *Britannica Bk. of Year* 546/1 In Great Britain a topical term was New Town Blues, used to describe the dissatisfied, discontented condition of people from large cities who found the recreational amenities of the new towns inadequate. **1962** *Harper's Bazaar* Aug. 58/1 Castries, the capital..is entirely modern and rather New-Townish. **1964** *Daily Tel.* 4 Feb. 14/2 The new environment, though brighter, cleaner and more commodious, is said to lack the social attraction of the old. Hence the so-called complaint of the 'new town blues'. **1965** *Economist* 6 Nov. p. x/2 New towners also pay rates at the level set by the local authorities in whose territory they lie. **1970** *Americana Ann.* 176 The high hopes that 'new towns'..could provide a solution to congestion, high population densities, and the erosion of public services have collapsed. **1971** P. GRESSWELL *Environment* 174 A visit to one or more of the new towns is essential to anyone interested in architecture and environment. **1973** *Guardian* 30 May 7/1 The fears of the old-towners are certainly understandable. The population has declined... Runcorn new town has been growing. **1975** *Ibid.* 20 Jan. 15 Milton Keynes..is the latest (possibly the final?) refinement of new town theory.

Newtown ('nju:taʊn). Also **Newton**. The name of a town on Long Island in New York state, used *attrib.* or *absol.* to designate two varieties of dessert apple first introduced there, the **Newtown pippin** and the **Newtown Spitzenburg**. So **'Newtowner**, a Newtown apple.

1760 G. WASHINGTON *Diary* 30 Mar. (1925) I. 147 Grafted 10 of the New Town Pippin from Collo. **1770** in *Maryland Historical Mag.* (1918) XIII. 69 Things sent by the wagon 4 Barrills of Apples Russetins, Golden Pippins, Newtown Pippins & Pairmains. **1785** G. WASHINGTON *Diary* 12 Nov. (1925) II. 435 Received two New Town and 2 Golden Pippin trees. **1803** A. F. M. WILLICH *Domestic Encycl.* (Amer. ed.) III. 110 Newton Pippin. *Ibid.* IV. 182/2 The New-town Pippin, or New-York Rennet, a noble American apple. **1817** W. COXE *View of Cultivation of Fruit Trees* 126 Newton Spitzemberg [*sic*]. This apple is in some parts of this State [*sc.* Pennsylvania] called the English, or Burlington Spitzemberg: it was brought from Newton on Long-Island. **1840** *N.Y. Mirror* 4 Apr. 327/2 Dealers in Newton pippins and maple candy tell you..they can't afford their accommodations so low as they can be afforded in Chatham and Church streets. **1846** J. F. COOPER *Ravensnest* I. i. 27 Their *poire beurrée*, here at Paris..will not compare with the Newtowners we grow at Satanstoe. **1860** R. HOGG *Fruit Manual* 18 Newtown Pippin, D. — Medium sized, roundish, rather irregular, and obscurely ribbed... Requires a wall in this country. December to April. **1863** *Rep. Comm. Agric. 1862* (U.S. Dept. Agric.) 168 Newtown Spitzenberg... A very hardy tree; good bearer; fruit of superior quality; keeps and bears transportation well. **1877** E. S. DALLAS *Kettner's Bk. of Table* 34 Newtown Pippin... Named after Newtown, Long Island. This apple is imported from America. *Ibid.* 36 Kitchen Apples... Newtown Spitzemberg [*sic*]... Named by William Cobbett 'the matchless'. **1913** J. LONDON *Valley of Moon* 364 Every year he goes to England, and he takes a hundred carloads of yellow Newton pippins with him. **1925** B. D. DRAIN *Essent. Systematic Pomology* v. 78 Newtown Spitzenburg Group. Medium size, round-oblate, red-striped, high quality. **1953** BROOKS & HESSE *Western Fruit Gardening* 97 Yellow Newtown is most widely grown in the coastal districts... The fruit is medium to large, roundish to flattened, green to yellow.

newtral(ity, obs. forms of NEUTRAL(ITY.

new-vamp, *v.* [NEW *adv.* 6.] *trans.* To vamp up afresh; to furbish up anew.

1640 T. D. (*title*) The Knave in Grain New Vampt: a witty Comedy. **1702** *Eng. Theophrastus* 16 A Play, writ by an ancient celebrated author, new-vampt and furbish'd up. **1783** COLMAN *Prose on Sev. Occas.* (1787) III. 239 Let us new-vamp the Box, new-lay the Stage. **1817** HAZLITT *Pol. Ess.* (1818) 308 Such is the old doctrine of Divine Right new-vamped up under the style and title of Legitimacy.

So **new-vamped** *ppl. a.*

1675 COTTON *Scoffer Scoft* A 3 This Antick new-vaump't Wit. **1707** *Reflex. upon Ridicule* II. 212 New-vamped Trades-women. **1763** *Brit. Mag.* IV. 604 Now new-vampt silks the mercer's window shews.

new-waked, *ppl. a.* [NEW *adv.* 3 and 4.] Newly awakened.

1674 MILTON *P.L.* VIII. 4 He..stood fixt to hear; Then as new wak't thus gratefully repli'd. **1685** BOWLES *Compl. Ariadna* in *Dryden's Misc.* II. 380 New wak'd..she flew To the dire Shoar. **1791** MRS. RADCLIFFE *Rom. Forest* v, The carols of new-waked birds saluted her as she passed. **1824** MISS FERRIER *Inher.* xxvii, A fat, sour, new-waked-looking creature, sucking its finger.

new wave. Also **New Wave**.

1. = NOUVELLE VAGUE. Also (with hyphen) *attrib.*

1960 *News Chron.* 19 July 6/8 A 'new wave' is emerging here [in Spain], too, with an up-to-date philosophy. *Ibid.* 6 Aug. 6/7 Cy Grant will sing 'Carnival' from the French new-wave movie. **1960** *Guardian* 15 Oct. 5/2 The Italian neo-realists..and..the Frenchmen of the 'New Wave' have all been pursuing the same course. **1961** *Sunday Times* 12 Feb. 11/8 Blanchflower is the very crest of the New Wave among professional footballers. **1962** *Spectator* 23 Feb. 242/1 Her central situation concerns a new-wave actress. **1967** *Economist* 18 Mar. 1008/2 The new-wave nationalists have not bothered to think out what sort of nationalism they want. **1972** *Newsweek* 10 Jan. 22/1 As New York's new-wave mayor in 1966, he had portrayed himself as a reform insurgent battling the city's 'power brokers'. **1975** *Times Lit. Suppl.* 21 Nov. 1374/2 The defining characteristic of the New Wave, and its ambiguous legacy to all films made since 1958–61, was selfconsciousness... The New Wave brought the film director to the public's immediate attention as a potential cultural hero.

2. *spec.* A style of rock music, popular in the late 1970s, that was originally associated with punk rock (see PUNK ROCK), but later developed its own, more restrained character.

1976 *Listener* 23 Dec. 847/2 The Pistols are..the best known of the 'new-wave', or 'punk-rock' groups. **1977** [see PUNK ROCK]. **1977** *Time Out* 17 June 9/2 If New Wave means anything at all as a description, it means, says Petty, 'young bands playing again. For a long time the young bands were just joining the old bands.' **1979** *N.Y. Times* 13 Aug. C16/3 Punk soon turned to new wave, which especially in the United States meant a more deliberately clever, even arty approach to rock minimalism. **1980** *Washington Post Mag.* 18 May 28/5 The first bands I heard referred to as New Wave were Englishmen Elvis Costello and Joe Jackson and the Police. **1984** *Listener* 24 May 8/3 The general lack of success British companies had with punk and New Wave music in America was only in part a result of the differing musical tastes of the two countries.

Hence **new waver**, a performer or follower of new wave music; **new wavish** *a.*

1977 *Sounds* 9 July 38/4 (Advt.), New wave band Penetration, the premier new wavers in the North-East. **1982** *Washington Post* 10 June D10/6 Anderson is a borderline New Waver who looks as though she has been out in the rain upside down. **1963** *Punch* 20 Feb. 285/1 Perhaps she's New Wavish enough to scorn love. **1974** *Publishers Weekly* 25 Nov. 47/1 Malzberg is rather on the New Wavish side, writing 'speculative' rather than straight science fiction.

'new-wed, *a.* and *sb. arch.* [NEW *adv.* 3.]

A. *adj.* Recently married. **B.** *sb.* = *newly-wed* (NEWLY *adv.* 1 d).

1886 KIPLING *Departmental Ditties* (ed. 2) 21 Jones had left his new-wed bride to keep his house in order. **1893** W. B. YEATS *Celtic Twilight* 94 The new-born or the new-wed moves henceforth in the bloodless land of Faery.

new woman, etc.: see WOMAN *sb.* 1 i.

New World, new world. [WORLD *sb.* 11.] Used *attrib.* to designate phenomena characteristic of, or territories pertaining to, the western hemisphere. Hence **New-Worlder, New-Worldling**, a native or inhabitant of the western hemisphere; **newworldward** *adv.*, towards the western hemisphere.

[**1823** BYRON *Don Juan* IX. xxxix. 24 How the new worldlings of the then new east.] *a* **1855** C. BRONTË *Professor* (1857) II. xviii. 7 Some natural and graphic touches disclosed to the reader the scene of virgin forest and great, New-World river—barren of sail and flag. **1863** H. W. BATES *Naturalist on Amazons* II. v. 324 All the New World genera of apes..are represented in the Amazon regions. **1867** O. W. HOLMES *Guardian Angel* 216 There is a double proportion of oxygen in the New-World air. **1876** H. MELVILLE *Clarel* I. II. xxvi. 256 Oh, that a New-Worlder should talk so! **1901** *Munsey's Mag.* XXIV. 530/1 These and other causes have acted and reacted to bring about, in this new world metropolis,..a crowding together of the poor. **1930** *Tablet* 24 May 686/1 Old Worldlings in Europe..the New-Worldlings of the U.S.A. **1935** E. E. CUMMINGS *Let.* 29 Jan. (1969) 134 Delighted to learn that you're casting your anchor and blowing newworldward!!!!! **1944** *Amer. Fern Jrnl.* XXXIV. 69 (*heading*) The New World species of *Azolla*. **1951** in M. McLuhan *Mech. Bride* (1967) 77/2 A new-world man towering free and confident in an untroubled generation. **1957** P. J. DARLINGTON *Zoogeography* vi. 346 Whether one of them [*sc.* a primitive primate] reached South America and evolved the New World monkeys..is unknown. *Ibid.* 390 Erethizontidae, New World porcupines. **1965** *New Statesman* 24 Sept. 435/1 Great Victorian relics, long since peeled of their paint, electric-light bulbs and courteous service—especially toward dollar-bearing New Worlders. These are some recent experiences of myself and a pair of Montreal acquaintances. **1968** *Times* 15 Nov. 8/7 The New World monkeys, or Ceboidea, include such species as the marmosets and the howler monkeys. **1970** *Nature* 24 Oct. 382/1 In Jamaica the fifth instar larvae of the New World hawkmoth, *Erinnyis ello*, exhibit four basic colours.

newy, var. NEWIE.

new-yeaned, *ppl. a.* [NEW *adv.* 3.] Newly born or dropped.

1567 GOLDING *Ovid's Met.* VII. 85 The bleating of a new yeand Lambe. **1598** SYLVESTER *Du Bartas* II. i. I. *Eden* 5/3 Their bodies..Of new-yeand Lambs have full the form and guise. **1649** OGILBY *Virg. Bucolicks* VII. 17 Phyllis..might at home Shut up my new-yean'd Lambs. *a* **1711** KEN *Sion* Poet. Wks. 1721 IV. 322 The new-yean'd Lambs he'll in his Bosom lay. **1849** C. BRONTE *Shirley* II. xi. 263 Some little new-yeaned lambs.

new year. Also **new-year, New year, Newyear**; 4 nw(e) ȝer(e; *Sc.* 6, 9 **newer-**, 8 **nur-**, **ne'er-**. [f. NEW *a.* + YEAR[1]. Cf. MDu. *niewejaer*, *nie(u)jaer* (Du. *nieuwjaar*), MLG. *niejâr*, G. *neujahr*, Icel. *nýjár*, Sw. *nyår*, Da. *nytaar*.]

1. a. The coming year; the year about to begin or just beginning; the commencement of another year; the first few days of a year. ***to see the new year in***: see YEAR 7.

c **1200** [see 3 below]. **13..** *Gaw. & Gr. Knt.* 284 Hit is ȝol & nwe ȝer. *a* **1400** *Relig. Pieces fr. Thornton MS.* 63 One þe aughtene day of thi byrthe here That þe firste day es of þe newe ȝere. **1500–20** DUNBAR *Poems* lxxx. 12 God giue the guid prosperitie..In hansell of this guid new ȝeir. **1602** *2nd Pt. Ret. fr. Parnass.* v. i. 2003 At this good time of Newyeare he will be liberall. **1641** HOWELL *Vote* in *Lett.* (1650) II, Then let me somthing bring May hansell the New-Year to Charles my King. **1786** BURNS *Farmer's Salut.* i, A Guid New-year I wish you, Maggie. **1831** SCOTT *Diary* 1 Jan. in *Lockhart*, I cannot say the world opens pleasantly for me this New year. **1864** *Chambers's Encycl.* VI. 739/1 Complimentary visits, and mutual wishes for a Happy New Year.

†**b.** *ellipt.* A new-year address. *Obs. rare*[−1].

1595 COPLEY *Wits, Fits, & Fancies* 68 A scholler presented a gratulatorie new yeer unto Sir Thomas Moore in prose.

c. *Sc.* New-year cheer. (Cf. quot. 1897 in 2.)

2. *attrib.* as ***New-year day, mass, ode***, etc. ***New-year('s) honours list***: see *honour(s) list* (HONOUR *sb.* 10).

? *a* **1400** *Morte Arth.* 78 On the newȝere daye, at þe none evyne. **1456** *Paston Lett.* I. 368 The god chiere that the persons ye wote off had here uppon New Yeer Day. **1588** KING *Canisius* in *Cath. Tract.* (S.T.S.) 175 Newermes quhilk is the circumcision of Christ vnder Augustus. **1728** POPE *Dunc.* I. 44 New-year Odes, and all the Grub-street race. **1786** BURNS (*title*) The auld farmer's New-year-morning salutation to his auld mare. **1788** PICKEN *Poems* 14 To glad their sauls wi' Nurday cheer. **1897** WRIGHT *Sc. Life* 15, I am again visiting my grannie to get my 'ne'erday', which meant..a daud of shortbread and currant-bun and a bawbee.

3. a. ***New-year's day***, the first day of the year. Also (*N. Amer.*) with ellipsis of *day*.

Cf. MDu. *nie(u)jaersdach* (Du. *nieuwjaarsdag*), G. *neujahrstag*, Icel. *nýjársdagr*, Sw. *nyårsdag*, Da. *nytaarsdag*.

c **1200** ORMIN 4230 þatt daȝȝ iss New ȝeress daȝȝ Mang Engleþeode nemmnedd. **13..** *Gaw. & Gr. Knt.* 1968 To dele, on nw ȝerez day, þe dome of my wyrdes. **1470–85** MALORY *Arthur* I. iii–v. 41 Vpon newe yeersday the barons lete maake a Iustes and a tournement. **1531** in *Vicary's Anat.* (1888) App. ii. 102 Rewardes geuen on Sonday, Newe-yeres day at Grenewiche, as hathe ben accustomde. **1568** GRAFTON *Chron.* II. 955 This yere Henrie..was borne at Richemond vpon Neweyers daye. **1625** GODWIN *Moses & Aaron* III. (1641) 121 According to their civill Computation it was their first moneth, so that this feast may be termed their New-yeares day. **1701** C. WOLLEY *Jrnl. New York* (1860) 57 The English observed one anniversary custom,.. a neighbourly commerce of presents every New-Years day. **1783** BLAGDEN in *Phil. Trans.* LXXIII. 391 The following new-year's day it was sunk to—56° at eight in the morning. **1845** *Knickerbocker* XXV. 128 Stay away on New-Year's and you stay away all the year. **1852** R. S. SURTEES *Sponge's Sp. Tour* lxv. 363 New-Year's Day is generally a bright, bitter, sunshiny day. **1909** *Springfield* (Mass.) *Weekly Republ.* 4 Nov. 1 The general elections are not now expected until after New Year's. **1952** J. REANEY in R. Weaver *Canad. Short Stories* (1960) 383 The Christmas holidays were haunted for me by my fear of what would happen when I went back there after New Year's. **1975** F. DECKER in S. Terkel *Working* IV. 190 She's just lucky he's home Christmas and New Year's.

fig. **1635–56** COWLEY *Davideis* II. 230 Whether by this in mystick Type we see The New-Year's Day of great Eternity.

b. So ***New-year's eve*** or ***even*** (see EVE *sb.*[1] 2), ***morn, morrow, tide***.

13.. *Gaw. & Gr. Knt.* 453 To be ȝederly ȝolden on nw ȝeres morn. *Ibid.* 1669 þer þay dronken & dalten..on nwe ȝerez euen. **1482** CAXTON *Chron. Eng.* ccxlix. 319 And on newyers euen after they take harflete. *a* **1500** *Pol. Rel. & L. Poems* (1866) 66 Iuellis pricious..to sende you, my Souerein, þis newe yeres morowe. **1556** *Chron. Gr. Friars* (Camden) 57 Item at Newyeeres tyde after was put downe the qwyne of the testornes. **1625** MASSINGER *New Way* IV. ii, Thy wife brought me, Last new year's tide, a couple of fat turkeys. **1840** *Penny Cycl.* XVI. 177/1 Gifts at new-year's-tide formed a charge of no small amount in the privy-purse expenses of royalty. **1864** *Chamb. Encycl.* VI. 739/1 The night of New-Year's Eve, 'St. Sylvester's Eve'.

4. a. ***New-year's gift***, a gift made to another on, or for, New-year's day.

Cf. Du. *nieuwjaarsgift*, G. *neujahrsgabe*, etc.

1530 PALSGR. 248/1 Newe yeres gyfte, *estrayne*. *a* **1568** ASCHAM *Scholem.* Pref. (Arb.) 21, I thought to præpare some litle treatise for a New yeares gift that Christmas. **1665** SIR T. HERBERT *Trav.* (1677) 314 To send him yearly the value of twenty thousand Crowns as a New-years-gift. **1699** BENTLEY *Phal.* Pref. 118 He might..make the Book his worthy New-years-gift to the Scholars of his House. **1777** BRAND *Pop. Antiq.* xvi. 187 The Sending of Presents, which are termed New Year's Gifts. **1840** *Penny Cycl.* XVI. 177/1 An order of Tiberius, forbidding the giving or demanding of new-year's-gifts.

b. A popular name for the Winter Aconite.

1856 DELAMER *Fl. Gard.* 51 Aconite (Winter)..is commonly known as 'The New Year's Gift'.

newyn(e, variants of NEVEN *v. Obs.*

New York (nju: 'jɔːk, nu: 'jɔːk). The name of a city and state in the United States used *attrib.* in various special collocations (see quots.).

1714 S. SEWALL *Diary* 14 Apr. in *Mass Hist. Soc. Coll.* (1879) 5th Ser. VI. 440, I had my New York Biscuit to eat. **1771** T. PENNANT *Synopsis Quadrupeds* 367 New York Bat with a head shaped like that of a mouse. **1842** J. E. DEKAY *Zool. N.Y.* I. 140 Index, New York Weasel. **1843** J. TORREY *Flora State of New-York* II. 497 *Aspidium Noveboracense*... New-York Shield-fern. Moist woods and thickets. **1862** *Amer. Ann. Cycl. 1861* 307/2 The highest, lowest, and average quotations..at the New York Stock Exchange for the stocks most largely dealt in. **1892** *Scribner's Mag.* Sept. 386/1 A fellow-pupil dictated to him Latin and Greek, and he printed the text in New York point. **1901** C. MOHR *Plant Life Alabama* 316 *Dryopteris noveboracensis*... New York Shield Fern... Alleghenian and Carolinian areas. **1943** H. W. SHIMER *Origin & Significance Plant Names* 47 New York fern, Dryopteris noveboracensis. **1955** R. BLESH *Shining Trumpets* (ed. 3) xii. 275 New York jazz, even at its best, was inept. **1956** B. COBB *Field Guide to Ferns* 50 The Marsh Ferns, the Massachusetts Ferns, and the New York Fern have upright, narrow, oblong leaves... These five species of the genus *Thelypteris* have been moved from one genus to another... Elsewhere they are classified in the genus *Dryopteris*. **1974** *Guardian* 23 Jan. 4/7 The poultry industry ..called in a slim blonde to wheel to the platform a 30-lb New York dressed turkey—New York dressed being a dying species.

New 'Yorker. [-ER[1].] A inhabitant or native of the state or city of New York. Also *attrib.*, pertaining to or characteristic of the magazine *The New Yorker* (founded 1925).

1756 WASHINGTON *Lett.* Writ. 1889 I. 315 The Jerseys and New Yorkers, I do not remember what it is they give. **1798** I. ALLEN *Hist. Vermont* 43 The New Yorkers..sent warrants into that county. **1859** G. H. LEWES *Let.* 6 Sept. in *Geo. Eliot's Lett.* (1954) III. 146 To-day a letter has come from the editor of a 'Parish Magazine'—and really G. E. was almost more likely to be tempted by that audience than by the New Yorkers. **1871** LONGF. in *Life* (1891) III. 181 It is a grand plan; I hope it will strike the New Yorkers. **1884** MATTHEWS & BUNNER *In Partnership* 127 'Are you a New Yorker, sir?' 'From the north of the State.' **1902** *Chambers's Jrnl.* July 450/1 The New Yorker defends this wretched state of affairs by a peculiar argument. **1916** H. L. WILSON *Somewhere in Red Gap* 398 The New Yorker was now sunk deep in a trance. **1934** *Fortune* Aug. 75/1 No advertising man is believed, by the editors, ever to have understood a *New Yorker* joke. **1948** *Hearst's International* May 175/1 Literary critics and editors of other magazines are always referring to 'The New Yorker style of writing'. **1948** *N.Y. Star* 30 June 14/3 The Board of Transportation is appealing to New Yorkers to put up patiently with the confusion. **1951** R. HOGGART *Auden* iii. 68 We consign much of this to the part of the mind which is tickled but put on its guard by the 'New Yorker' profiles. **1959** *Times Lit. Suppl.* 2 Jan. 4/2 He surveys the established Old Guard.., the new 'realists'.., the *New Yorker* School. **1974** *Times* 4 Mar. 14/8 Brenda Bedansky, a New Yorker, dressed to resemble a man trying to look like Marlene Dietrich.

Hence **New 'Yorkerish** *a.*, characteristic or reminiscent of the magazine *The New Yorker*; **New 'Yorkerism**, an idiom, expression, or word peculiar to *The New Yorker*.

1948 H. F. PRINGLE in *'48: Magazine of Yr.* Apr. 87/2 His [*sc.* H. W. Ross's] sense of comedy is properly *New Yorker*ish and fantastic. **1951** *Time* 22 Oct. 102/2 Many a New Yorkerism (e.g., Cartoonist Carl Rose's 'I say it's spinach, and I say the hell with it') has become a part of the language. **1961** *Punch* 4 Jan. 81/3 The drawings..[are] well suited to the captions, many of which have a *New Yorker*ish elliptical quality. **1967** *Guardian* 20 Oct. 7/4 Just another New Yorkerish monologue. **1970** D. L. EMBLEN *Peter Mark Roget* xv. 276 Punch in its *New Yorkerish* way, picking up a slip in some Scottish paper.

New 'Yorkese. [-ESE.] The regional form of English used in New York City. Cf. MANHATTANESE *sb.*

1894 *Harper's Mag.* Oct. 695/1 'Cafe'..is New Yorkese for dram-shop. **1935** F. M. FORD *Let.* 11 Sept. (1965) 242 Perhaps it is the latest New Yorkese which, I know, is always welcome in Hampstead. **1951** TRAGER & SMITH *Outl. Eng. Structure* I. 23 The sequence /əy/ has always been known to him as 'New Yorkese' or 'Brooklynese'. **1973** E.-J. BAHR *Nice Neighbourhood* vii. 71 'So continue,' said Don... He sometimes lapses into New Yorkese.

New-'Yorkish, *a.* [-ISH[1].] = next.

1913 F. H. BURNETT *T. Tembarom* xxiv. 305 How thoroughly New Yorkish it was that he should march into a fashionable shop and see that he got..the worth of his money! **1962** *John o' London's* 19 Apr. 385/3 That most New Yorkish of all musical comedies, *Guys and Dolls*.

New-'Yorky, *a.* [-Y[1].] Suggestive or characteristic of New York.

1908 E. WHARTON *Hermit* 150 To be compared to her! to be accused of being 'New-Yorky'! **1963** *Guardian* 25 Jan. 6/6 The 'Partisan', New York-y too, but out of a cosmopolitan liberal intelligentsia. **1973** R. L. SIMON *Big Fix* (1974) ix. 66 The accent was nasal and New Yorky, the voice scratchy.

New Zealand. 1. The name of an Australasian country, used *attrib.* to designate plants native there, as **New Zealand flax,** an evergreen plant, *Phormium tenax*, of the family Agavaceæ, cultivated for the fibre it produces or the ornamental value of its tufts of long, stiff, pointed leaves; **New Zealand passion flower**, a climbing plant, *Tetrapathæa tetrandra*, of the family Passifloraceæ; **New Zealand spinach**, an annual herb, *Tetragonia tetragonioides* (*T. expansa*), of the family Aizoaceæ, cultivated for its thick leaves which are used as a substitute for spinach.

1811 W. AITON *Hortus Kewensis* (ed. 2) II. 284 New Zealand Flax. Nat[ive] of New Zealand. Introd[uced] about 1789, by the Right Hon. Sir Joseph Banks. **1832** *Curtis's Bot. Mag.* LIX. 3199 The seeds brought home by Sir Joseph Banks in 1771 did not succeed, but the New Zealand Flax was introduced through the medium of the same enlightened individual in 1789, and thence has been liberally distributed. **1883** W. ROBINSON *Eng. Flower Garden* 195/1 New Zealand Flax (*Phormium tenax*). **1910** [see INANGA 2]. **1973** *Islander* (Victoria, B.C.) 4 Feb. 2/4 The harakeke or New Zealand flax..doesn't resemble its European cousin. **1853** J. D. HOOKER *Bot. Antarctic Voy.: Flora Novæ-Zelandiæ* I. 72. The New Zealand Passion-flower is a perfectly smooth climbing plant, with alternate, simple, petiolate leaves, axillary tendrils, and small axillary panicles of green flowers. **1951** LAING & BLACKWELL *Plants N.Z.* (ed. 5) 281 *Tetrapathaea tetrandra* (The New Zealand Passion-flower). A slender climber, with glossy leaves. **1822** J. ANDERSON in *Trans. Hort. Soc.* IV. 488 (*heading*) Account of a new Esculent Vegetable called *Tetragonia*, or New Zealand Spinach. **1867** E. SAUTER tr. *F. von Hochstetter's New Zealand* vii. 157 New Zealand Spinach..was first brought into notice by Captain Cook, who found it useful as an anti-scorbutic. **1898**, **1944** [see ICE-PLANT]. **1951** *Dict. Gardening* (R. Hort. Soc.) III. 1369/2 New Zealand Spinach is an excellent substitute for the common Spinach for use during the hot dry months. **1973** *Parade* (Melbourne) Sept. 35/1, I have seen New Zealand spinach..growing on the sandhills along the beach..north of Perth.

2. New Zealand rabbit, also **New Zealand black, New Zealand red, New Zealand white,** various American breeds of domestic rabbit. Also *absol.*

1914 ROTH & COLEMAN *Rabbit Culture* 95 Standard of the New Zealand Rabbit... Larger than the Belgian Hare and of a beautiful reddish buff color... Everybody's friend wherever known. **1917** C. P. GILMORE *N.Z. Red Rabbit* 8/1 The New Zealand Reds are..business rabbits for general or utility purposes. *Ibid.*, The New Zealand is practically a new rabbit in the American fancy. **1920** F. L. WASHBURN *Rabbit Bk.* ii. 43 The New Zealand Red. This rabbit is a close second to the Belgian and Flemish in the race for popularity. **1921** C. A. RICHEY *Rabbit & Cavy Bk.* (ed. 4) 21 A new breed..called the White New Zealand..having the type of the New Zealand, but a pure white coat with pink eyes. **1953** C. GOODCHILD *Keeping Rabbits* ii. 80 The New Zealand Red was first imported into this country around 1920. It was originated in the U.S.A., and was a breed much favoured by the Californian breeders for the frying trade. *Ibid.* 82 Although the New Zealand White has only recently been adopted in this country, they have been one of the most popular breeds in the U.S.A. for over a quarter of a century. **1965** *Amer. Rabbit Breeders' Assoc. Official Guide Bk.* 32 The New Zealand Rabbit had its origin in the United States in the early 1900's. *Ibid.* 33 The standard of perfection for all New Zealands is identical with the exception of the color of the fur, eyes and nails... The Black New Zealand is the newest variety of the New Zealand breed. Blacks were started in California in 1949. **1971** *Guardian* 28 Dec. 1/6 Half the consignment [of rabbits] will be New Zealand Whites which have red eyes. **1973** M. I. FAIVRE *How to raise Rabbits* i. 11 The New Zealand breed may be divided into three distinct categories: New Zealand Red, New Zealand Black, and New Zealand White... Although all three types are excellent meat rabbits, the New Zealand White fur is in greatest demand by garment makers because it takes a variety of dyes successfully.

New 'Zealander. [-ER[1].] **a.** One of the aborigines of New Zealand; a Maori. Also (occas.) *attrib.* **b.** One of the European settlers in New Zealand.

1773 CAPT. J. COOK *Jrnl.* (1961) II. 268 The New Zealanders cut and scar themselves on the same account. *a* **1791** WESLEY *Serm.* lxxiv. Wks. 1811 IX. 320 A Hottentot, a New-Zealander. **1837** *Sydney Gaz.* 11 Dec., in R. McNab *Old Whaling Days* (1913) ix. 167 They saw the chief officer, James George Bailey, a New Zealander. **1841** M. EDGEWORTH *Let.* 14 Mar. (1971) 586 A New Zealander boy with large head and frizzled black hair and face as yellow as dirty gold. **1842** PRICHARD *Nat. Hist. Man* 337 The skulls of the New Zealanders differ somewhat from those of the nations already mentioned. **1864** *Chambers's Encycl.* VI. 742/1 The New Zealanders, or Maories,..are located, with the exception of a few hundreds, in North Island. **1886** J. A. FROUDE *Oceana* xx. 323 The Australian, the New Zealander, the Californian will have as much in them..of the ancient 'Merry England' as the severely earnest Northern American. **1901** ROSE-INNES *With Paget's Horse* 174 All the other New Zealanders whom I met were..well educated. **1966** MRS. L. B. JOHNSON *White House Diary* 20 Oct. (1970) 430 We departed in a New Zealand airplane with the Prime Minister and Mrs. Holyoake to the tune of a thousand New Zealanders singing.

New 'Zealandism. [-ISM.] An idiom or word peculiar to the English spoken in New Zealand.

1957 *N.Z. Listener* 22 Nov. 4/3 'Creek' and 'paddock' are New Zealandisms, because they mean something quite different in the English of England. **1964** A. S. C. Ross in Ross & Moverley *Pitcairnese Lang.* 13 The two letters which I published in New Zealand about possible new zealandisms in Pitcairnese.

'nexal, *a.* [f. L. *nex-us* or *nex-um*, bond, obligation + -AL[1].] **1.** *Rom. Law.* Characterized by the imposition of servitude as a penalty on a defaulting debtor.

1886 *Encycl. Brit.* XX. 675/2 The nexal creditor's imprisonment of his defaulting debtor. *Ibid.* 681/1 The Pœtilian law of 428, abolishing the nexal contract. **1901** GREENIDGE *Rom. Public Life* 91 It is probable that in early times plebeian law recognised no debt except that created by the nexal contract.

2. *Linguistics.* Of or pertaining to a nexus (sense 1 c).

1933 *English Studies* XV. 148, I don't wish to speak to you ever again..is a more polite formula for: I wish never to speak to you again. We have here a very curious case of 'cleaving of *never*' and 'nexal attraction'. **1937** V. MATHESIUS in *Mélanges de Linguistique et de Philologie offerts à J. van Ginneken* 82 Professor Jespersen has repeatedly called attention to the difference between what he calls *special negation* and what he calls *nexal negation*.

†**nexe.** *Obs.* [app. ad. L. *nexus* NEXUS.] ? The cohesion existing between particles of matter.

1626 BACON *Sylva* §889 It appeareth plainly to be but a Motion of Nexe, which they call *Ne detur vacuum*... The Motion of Nexe did so claspe the Bottome of the Basen.

'nexible, *a.* *rare*$^{-0}$. [ad. late L. *nexibilis.*] 'Which may be knit' (Cockeram 1623; hence in Blount and later Dicts.).

ne'xility. *rare*$^{-0}$. [ad. late L. *nexilitas.*] 'Fastness, pithiness, compactness of speech' (Blount 1656; hence in Bailey 1721).

next (nɛkst), *a.*, *sb.*, and *adv.* Forms: α. 1 **néahst(a, néhst(a, next(a, nexsta, 2–6 nexte,** (3 **næxte,** 4 **nekste,** 5 **nextte), 3–5 nexste, 3– next,** (4 **nekist, neghst), 3–5 nexst,** (4 **nexist), 6–7 nex;** 1 **níehsta, nýhst(a, níhsta, nyxt(a,** 4 **nixte,** 5–6 *Sc.* **nixt,** (6 **nyxt).** β. 1 **nésta,** (*north.* **neesta, neista),** 3–5 **nest(e,** 3 **nesst,** 4 **neiste, neyste,** 4–5 **neest;** *north.* and *Sc.* 4–9 **neist,** (4 **neiest,** 4–5 **neyst),** 8–9 **niest, neisht.** [OE. *néahst*, *níęhst*, etc., superlative of *néah* NIGH, = OFris. *nest*, *neest* (mod.Fris. *nejst*, *neyst*), MDu. *naest* (Du. *naast*), OS. *nâhist*, *náist*, MLG. *nâgest*, *nâst*, *nêgest*, *nêist* (hence MDa. *nægest*, *negst*, MSw. *nägest*, *-ist*); OHG. *náhist-er* (adv. *nâhost*; MHG. *nâhest*, *nâst*, *næhest*, *næst*; G. *nächst*), ON. *næ̋st-r* (Sw. *näst*, Da. *næst*). The usual forms in OE. are those of the weak decl. *néhsta*, *nýhsta*, etc., corresponding to OFris. *neste*, *-ta*, OS. *nâ(h)isto*, OHG. *nâhisto*, *-esto*, *-osto* (MHG. *nâhste*, *næhste*), ON. *næ̋ste*, *-ti*.]

A. *adj.* and *sb.*

I. In attributive use, or absolutely as *sb.*

†**1. a.** Lying nearest in place or position. *Obs.*

In mod. use, as in ***the next house, town***, etc., the adj. no longer denotes simple proximity (which is expressed by ***nearest***), but involves the idea of sense 6.

c **950** *O.E. Chron.* (Parker MS.) an. 921 þa æfter ȝegadorode micel folc..of þam niehstum burȝum. *c* **950** *Lindisf. Gosp.* Mark i. 38 Gæ we..in ða neesto lond. *a* **1067** in Kemble *Cod. Dipl.* IV. 202 þæt ðridde swun of æuesan ðæs nextan wudes ðe liþ to kyngesbyriȝ. **1382** WYCLIF *Mark* i. 38 Go we in to the nexte townes and citees. *c* **1400** MAUNDEV. (1839) iv. 30 Whoso wil..come nerrer to Jerusalem, he schal go..to the port Jaff. For that is the nexte havene to Jerusalem. *a* **1450** *Fysshynge w. Angle* (1883) 16 þe next plume to the hoke schall be ther from a large fote & more. **1533** BELLENDEN *Livy* v. xii. (S.T.S.) II. 190 þe equis ..chasit him with grete effray & dredoure to þe nixt montanis. **1585** T. WASHINGTON tr. *Nicholay's Voy.* I. xii. 14 Two smal riuers, whereof the next and greatest hath a bridge of stone. **1652** NEEDHAM tr. *Selden's Mare Cl.* 497 They in debt seeking onely to serv the next Market. **1710** ADDISON *Tatler* No. 229 ¶3 They say, when a Fox is very much troubled with Fleas, he goes into the next Pool.

b. †***the next way***, the shortest, most convenient or direct way. *Obs.* Hence ***next ways*** adv.

a **1330** *Otuel* 437 He þoute þe nekste weie to ride. *c* **1386** CHAUCER *Man of Law's T.* 709 This messager..Unto the castel halt the nexte way. *a* **1450** *Knt. de la Tour* (1868) 63 They yode over a mareys for the next waye, but thei felle in the myre. **1525** LD. BERNERS *Froiss.* II. xv. 29, I wyll retourne into Englande the nexte waye. **1598** GRENEWEY *Tacitus, Ann.* XIII. ix. (1622) 191 The legions were not brought the next way,..but went ouer a farre off. **1678** BUNYAN *Pilgr.* I. (1862) 138 That comes down from our Country the next way into the way. **1767** *Cries of Blood* 10 The next way from that place to Mr. Harrison's house.

1789 COWPER *Let.* 5 Nov. in *Pearson's 81st Catal.* (1900) 24, I have transmitted it, as we say, next ways, to Johnson. **1809** BATCHELOR *Anal. Eng. Lang.* 139, I will go next ways home.

fig. *a* **1568** ASCHAM *Scholem.* I. (Arb.) 86 Thus bred vp.. to learne the next and readie way to sinne. **1601** SHAKS. *All's Well* I. iii. 63, I speake the truth the next waie. **1632** MASSINGER & FIELD *Fatal Dowry* v. i, To let you go, Were the next way.

2. a. Of persons: Living or dwelling nearest to one; happening to be nearest at a particular time. Now *rare* or *Obs.*

a **1000** *Daniel* 411 (Gr.), Ða þæt ehtode ealdor þeode..wið þam nehstum folcȝesiðum. **1377** LANGL. *P. Pl.* B. XIII. 373, I wolde Of my nexte neighbore nymen of his erthe. *c* **1440** *Generydes* 1894 To kynges and to princes all abought, The nexst that were marching on euery side. **1560** DAUS tr. *Sleidane's Comm.* 344 b, They publishe an other wryting, chiefly to the next inhabiters about them. **1598** MANWOOD *Lawes Forest* xix. §6. 144 An outcry unto the inhabitants and next dwellers within the same forest. **1630** *R. Johnson's Kingd. & Commw.* 414 To provide..against their next Enemies the Tartars, who make often incursions upon them. **1684** *Coll. Connect. Hist. Soc.* (1897) VI. 212 The Chimney veiwers..shall make presentment of what defects they find..to the next authority. **1771** GOLDSM. *Hist. Eng.* II. 257 He was obliged to make a short confession to the next priest that was at hand.

†**b.** *absol.* (One's) neighbour. *Obs.*

c **825** *Vesp. Psalter* xxvii. 3 Ða ðe spreocað sibbe mid ðone nestan. *c* **950** *Lindisf. Gosp.* Mark xii. 31 Lufa ðone neesta ðinne suæ ðec seolfne. *c* **1000** *Ags. Ps.* (Th.) cxxi. 8 Mine þa neahstan [ic] nemne swylce. *c* **1175** *Lamb. Hom.* 13 Ne spec þu aȝein þine nexta nane false witnesse. *c* **1250** *Gen. & Ex.* 3515 Ne gisce ðu nog ðin nestes ðing. **1297** R. GLOUC. (Rolls) 6729 Min frend & mi nexte ney stondeþ aȝe me. **1340** *Ayenb.* 145 Hi deþ man parfitliche louie his nixte ase himzelue.

c. ***the next man*** (***one, person***, etc.): the average man; a typical man; the next comer. orig. *U.S.*

1857 *Lawrence* (Kan.) *Republican* 18 June 2 The Judge.. will probably talk as long to a crowd without tiring them as the next man. **1897** KIPLING *Captains Courageous* i. 5 Guess I've as good right here as the next man. **1900** ADE *More Fables in Slang* 175 Lutie was just about as Nifty as the Next One. **1902** S. G. FISHER *True Hist. Amer. Revol.* 146 We do not surrender our property to the next man who is an abler business manager. **1925** S. O'CASEY *Juno & Paycock* II, in *Two Plays* 105 We have to live as well as th' nex' man. **1933** E. CALDWELL *God's Little Acre* iii. 37 Will can dig as good as the next one, if he wants to. **1938** G. GREENE *Brighton Rock* III. iv. 135 He'd been a loyal old geezer, he hadn't done as much harm as the next man. **1941** L. BROMFIELD in *Hearst's International* May 131/2 She thought: I'll show them that I'm as good as the next woman. I'll take care of myself. **1961** *Sunday Times* 5 Mar. 15/2 Cecil Beaton..can appreciate the 'excruciatingly bad taste' of a Lancashire living-room as well as the next designer. **1962** L. PETERS *Snatch of Music* ix. 155, I can read a paperback translation with the next man. **1966** A. E. LINDOP *I start Counting* xviii. 222, I can take a hint as well as the next person—and I know when I'm not wanted. **1973** *Sunday Bulletin* (Philadelphia) (Discover Suppl.) 14 Oct. 8/2, I feel you owe me a smidgin more than the next person.

3. a. Nearest in relationship or kinship. Also *absol.* in ***the next of*** (one's) ***blood, kin***, etc. (See KIN *sb.*[1] 8 c, and AKIN *adv.* 1.)

a **889** K. ÆLFRED *Charter* in *O.E. Texts* 451 Ȝif heo bearn nebbe, feo ðonne an hire reht federen sio neste hond to þem londe. *a* **1000** *Penit. Egbert* in Thorpe *Laws* II. 188 Gif hwylc man wifiȝe on his nehstan maȝan. *c* **1205** LAY. 22837 Nimeð al his nexte cun þa ȝe maȝen iuinden. *Ibid.* 32122 [The king] inemned was Alain, Cadwalader nexte mæi. *a* **1300** *Cursor M.* 13598 þe neist men of his oxspring Did þai þan be-for þam bring. *c* **1380** WYCLIF *Wks.* (1880) 440 Criste shulde be oure nexste fadir, & his chirche oure nexste modir. *c* **1400** MAUNDEV. (Roxb.) xxvi. 124 His sonne or þe next of his blude. *c* **1477** CAXTON *Jason* 48 Ye shalle assemble youre most next parentes and frendes. 1535 COVERDALE *Ruth* iii. 9 Thou art the nexte kynsman. 1603 OWEN *Pembrokeshire* ii. (1892) 30 All his inheritaunce came to his Nephewe Kinge Henry the seventh as next haire to the said Iasper. 1697 DRYDEN *Virg. Georg.* IV. 374 Their Friends attend the Herse, the next Relations mourn. 1766 BLACKSTONE *Comm.* II. 501 Till process hath first issued to call in the widow, or next of kin, to contest it. 1769 GOLDSM. *Hist. Rome* (1786) I. 13 Having previously communicated his intentions to his five next of kindred. 1818 CRUISE *Digest* (ed. 2) II. 352 Lands were devised to Robert Archer for life, afterwards to his next heir male. 1875 JOWETT *Plato* (ed. 2) V. 91 The betrothal of the parties shall be made by the next of kin.

b. ***next friend***, nearest friend or relative. In later use spec. in *Law*.

c 897 K. ÆLFRED *Gregory's Past. C.* xlix. 377 Hwæt, hie witon, ȝif hiera niehstan friend weorðað wædlan. *c* 1000 *Ags. Ps.* (Th.) lxxxvii. 18 þu me afyrdest frynd þa nyhstan. *c* 1175 *Lamb. Hom.* 17 ȝif þin nexta freond agult wið þe..bide hine luueliche þet he þe do riht. 13.. *Cursor M.* 11409 (Gött.), His sun for him was sett again, Or his neist frend þat was fere. 1387–8 T. USK *Test. Love* I. iv. (Skeat) l. 17 But enquyre of thy next frendes. *a* 1400–50 *Alexander* 619 So him neuyned was þe name of his next frendis. 1534 MORE *Comf. agst. Trib.* II. Wks. 1178/1 He maketh manye tymes oure next friendes our most foes. 1579 *Termes of the Law* 161 b, The next friende, or next of kynne to whom the lands cannot come or discende, shall haue the keepyng of the heire. 1720 T. WOOD *Instit. Laws Eng.* (1722) 13 An Infant, or Minor, shall sue by Prochein Amy (his next friend) or guardian,..but always defend by Guardian. 1883 *Rules Supreme Court* Order xvi. III. xvi, Infants may sue as plaintiffs by their next friends.

4. †**a.** Most pressing or important. *Obs. rare*$^{-1}$.

c 1205 LAY. 17153 Ich þe wulle ræden Of nexte þire neoden [*c* 1275 to þine nexste neode].

†**b.** Closest to hand, readiest, most convenient.

c 1449 PECOCK *Repr.* I. xiv. 75 The power of resoun..is not ordeyned..to be oure next and best and surest reuler. *c* 1538 in Ellis *Orig. Lett.* Ser. II. II. 99 The next remedys to refourme all thies enormyties after my pore conceyte is as followith. 1642 FULLER *Holy & Prof. St.* IV. vii. 273 Extremity makes the next the best remedy. 1679 PENN *Addr. Prot.* Pref., Whose duty therefore he shows..with the next and proper means to suppress it.

†**c.** Of ends, causes, etc.: Least remote, most proximate. *Obs.*

1628 T. SPENCER *Logick* 6 The remote end of Logick, is the very act it selfe of discoursing... The next end of Logick, is to prescribe a way, and rules of discoursing. 1654 Z. COKE *Logick* 56 Forms are always next causes of many faculties in subjects. 1705 STANHOPE *Paraphr.* I. 117 The Instruments and next Causes of their sufferings. 1754 EDWARDS *Freed. Will* I. i. 2 It should be considered what is the next and immediate Object of the Will, with respect to a Man's Walking, or any other external Action.

5. a. Of periods of time: Immediately following or succeeding. Also const. *after*, †*of* (quots. 1711).

In Sc. use, *next* is employed to designate the days of the following week; thus *next Friday*, the Friday of next week, is contrasted with *this Friday*, that of the present week. (Cf. the note to 10.)

a 1122 *O.E. Chron.* (Laud MS.) an. 1086 He swealt..on þone nextan dæȝ æfter natiuitas sancte Marie. *c* 1290 *Beket* 890 in *S. Eng. Leg.*, For-to þe nexte daie we biddez furst. 1377 LANGL. *P. Pl.* B. XIII. 154 þe Wednesday of þe nexte wyke after. *c* 1489 CAXTON *Sonnes of Aymon* iv. 129 The nexste morning after they departed. 1535 COVERDALE *1 Sam.* v. 3 Whan they rose vp early on the nexte morowe, they founde Dagon lyenge on his face. 1560 DAUS tr. *Sleidane's Comm.* 267 The Emperour..the nex daye came to Gieng. 1591 SHAKS. *Two Gent.* II. ii. 11 The next ensuing howre, some foule mischance Torment me for my Loues forgetfulnesse. 1653 HOLCROFT *Procopius, Goth. Wars* II. 40 The nex day..he ordered his Army for a fight. 1692 DRYDEN *Ep. Southerne* 31 Learn, after both, to draw some just design, And the next age will learn to copy thine. 1711 *Fingall MSS.* in *10th Rep. Hist. MSS. Comm.* App. V. 136 The next morning of the skirmish at the Boyn. *Ibid.* 154 The next day of the battle. 1771 *Antiq. Sarisb.* 5 They are arbitrary, often imposed..for reasons that did not exist the next hour. 1859 HELPS *Friends in C.* Ser. II. I. Addr. to Rdr. 10 What is written on public affairs in one week may be..obsolete..the next. 1894 HALL CAINE *Manxman* v. xxi. 344 Grannie came to Elm Cottage next morning.

β. 13.. *Cursor M.* 11377 (Gött.), Sum men sais þe neist ȝere Foluand, and sum..Sais tua ȝere efter þat þai come. 1596 DALRYMPLE tr. *Leslie's Hist. Scot.* x. 436 Not ane cannoune was schott or Lattne aff afor the neist day. 1722 RAMSAY *Elegy Ld. Carnegie* iv, Ae day gives joy, The neist our hearts maun bleed. 1794 *Piper of Peebles* 18 (E.D.D.) Niest afternoon he was inter'd. 1802 R. ANDERSON *Cumbld. Ball.* 42 A week at Gilsland tou salt try, Neist summer, if we're spar'd. 1876 C. GIBBON *Robin Gray* iv, I'll see how ye're getting on the morn or neist day.

b. Of persons, things, occasions, etc.: Coming directly after another in point of time; without anything of the same kind intervening.

? *a* 1400 *Arthur* 508 þe kyng Maxymyan,—þe next after Octauyan. *c* 1475 *Rauf Coilȝear* 758 The nixt vacant, be ressonabill richt, That hapnis in France. 1582 N. LICHEFIELD tr. *Castanheda's Conq. E. Ind.* I. viii. 21 He well knew, that at the next floud the ship would be afloate againe. 1672 LADY M. BERTIE in *12th Rep. Hist. MSS. Comm.* App. V. 26, I believe next news I heare will be that you are going to bee married. 1727 GAY *Begg. Opera* I. x, Have him peach'd the next Sessions. 1732 BERKELEY *Alciphr.* I. §7 Whoever escapes punishment in this life will be sure to find it in the next. 1818 CRUISE *Digest* (ed. 2) V. 614 At the next court the surrender was presented. 1840 *P. Parley's Ann.* I. 116, I promise never to do so any more, not till the next time. 1892 H. M. STEPHENS *Albuquerque* vii. 174 More extensive powers than were exercised by Albuquerque and his next successors.

c. *ellipt.* with omission of *letter*, *number* (†or *post*).

c 1645 HOWELL *Lett.* I. xvi. 26 In my next, I shall impart unto you what State-news France affords. 1655 *Nicholas Papers* (Camden) II. 282 My seruice to my beloued Lord Gerrard, to whome I will write by the next. 1733 BERKELEY *Let.* Wks. 1871 IV. 207 In your next let me know your thoughts on this and the whole affair. 1793 COWPER *Let. to Newton* 25 Apr., I..shall be obliged to you if, in your next, you will mention [etc.]. 1867 RUSKIN *Time & Tide* xxii. §145 To reserve suggestions of answer for my next. 1893 MCCARTHY *Red Diamonds* III. 172 Some serial story which stopped at an exciting point with the words—To be continued in our next.

6. a. Immediately succeeding or preceding in respect of position, order, arrangement, value, etc.

Precedence is denoted by the addition of *before*, etc., except in the second quot. from Wyclif.

c 1055 *Byrhtferth's Handboc* in *Anglia* VIII. 327 On þam circule fiftyne niht hiȝ onfoð on þære nextan linan. *a* 1300 *Cursor M.* 26877 Thinges thre þe quhilk i tald þe..In þe neist formast questiun. *c* 1380 WYCLIF *Sel. Wks.* II. 4 þis gospel tellip, as þe nexte bifore, how Joon made redy þe weye to Crist. *Ibid.* 318 As it is seid in þe nexte [= last] Sermon, of þis lore ben many gabbingis. *a* 1450 *Knt. de la Tour* (1868) 13 The good man that shroue the woman in the nexst tale afore. 1577 FULKE *Confut. Purg.* 363 When he him selfe in the next leafe before, affirmeth [etc.]. 1693 *Humours Town* 52 By that time one has done with his Intrigues, the next has fresh Adventures to impart. 1697 DRYDEN *Virg. Georg.* II. 688 My next Desire is, void of Care and Strife, To lead a soft, secure, inglorious Life. 1712 BUDGELL *Spect.* No. 425 ¶1 Such a Tranquility of Mind, as is I believe the next Happiness to that of hereafter. *a* 1756 ELIZA HEYWOOD *New Present* (1771) 254 In the next place, the chairs should be dusted. 1816 SCOTT *Antiq.* xl, I dinna mind the neist verse weel—my memory's failed. 1852 MRS. STOWE *Uncle Tom's C.* xvii. 167 The first one of you that comes..is a dead man, and the next, and the next. 1875 JEVONS *Money* (1878) 257 The organization of the Clearing House will be described in the next chapter.

b. Of persons in respect of position, birth, etc.

c 1380 WYCLIF *Wks.* (1880) 461 þe pope is holdun moost & nexst viker of iesu crist. 1390 GOWER *Conf.* I. 265 In good espeir To ben himself the develes heir, As he which is his nexte liche. 1560 DAUS tr. *Sleidane's Comm.* 15 The inheritaunce..came unto Jane the next syster. 1667 MILTON *P.L.* IV. 781 When Gabriel to his next in power thus spake. 1891 T. HARDY *Tess* iii, There was an interval of four years and more between Tess and the next of the family.

absol. 1607 TOURNEUR *Rev. Trag.* II. i, The Next of Italy commends him to you.

c. ***next best***, second-best.

a 1674 CLARENDON (J.), If the king himself had stayed at London, or, which had been the next best, kept his court at York. 1700 WALLIS in *Collect.* (O.H.S.) I. 318 Who did..out-leap..the next-best leaper..by seven inches. 1824 SCOTT *St. Ronan* ii, The Blue room is the best—and they that get neist best are no ill aff. 1870 LOWELL *Among my Bks.* Ser. I. (1873) 79 In poetry, to be next-best is, in one sense, to be nothing.

†**7. a.** ***on next, at (the) next***, in the next place, directly after or succeeding. *Obs. rare.*

a 1400–50 *Alexander* 2795 þen to Nostanda on next þus notis he a lettir. ? *a* 1400 *Morte Arth.* 2422 A-bowte the cete tha seuene they soughte at the nextte, To seke theme a sekyre place. *c* 1449 PECOCK *Repr.* II. vii. 177 Immediatli at next to the now bifore alleggid text of Peter this proces folewith.

†**b.** ***at the next***, directly at hand. *Obs. rare.*

c 1425 *Orolog. Sapient.* v. in *Anglia* X. 363/4, I see & know þat I maye no lenger lyue and þat deth is atte þe nexte. *c* 1449 PECOCK *Repr.* II. xx. 271 What a man mai not haue..at the next and immediatli, he wole be..weel plesid for to haue it mediatli.

†**8. a.** (OE. only.) Last. *Obs.*

c 825 *Vesp. Psalter* lxxii. 17 Oððæt ic ingae in godes haliȝ portic & ongete ða nestan heara [L. *novissima eorum*]. *c* 900 *Judith* 73 Wiȝgend stopon ut of ðam inne..þe ðone wærloȝan..læddon to bedde nehstan siðe. 971 *Blickl. Hom.* 21 Ne biþ he godes leof on þæm nehstan dæȝe.

†**b.** ***at next***, at (the) last. *Obs.*

c 825 *Vesp. Hymns* vii. in *O.E. Texts* 411 [Ic] oteawu hwet bið him ot nestan. *c* 950 *Lindisf. Gosp.* Matt. xxvi. 60 Æt nesta ða cuomon twoeȝe leaso..ȝewitneso. *c* 1000 ÆLFRIC *Hom.* II. 572 Ða æt nextan comon ða stuntan mædenu. *a* 1122 *O.E. Chron.* (Laud MS.) an. 1086 Æt nextan he ne sparode his aȝenne broðor.

II. In predicative use or following the sb.

Also const. *to*, *about*, etc., and sometimes in quasi-adverbial use with *adjoining*, *ensuing*, etc.

9. a. Nearest in place or position.

c 900 tr. *Bæda's Hist.* II. xvi. (Schipper) 177 (MS. B) Seo mæȝð nyhst on suðhealfe Humbre streames. *c* 900 *O.E. Chron.* (Parker MS.) an. 878 Ælfred..was winnende wiþ þone here, & Sumur sætna dæl se þær niehst wæs. *a* 1300 *Cursor M.* 1692 In þe ouermast stage [of the ark] þi self sal be, þe fouxules alþernest be þe. 1387 TREVISA *Higden* (Rolls) I. 293 ȝif þe water of þat welle is..i-helte vppon a stoon þat is next to þe welle. 1515 in *Vicary's Anat.* (1888) App. iii. 148 A Forge next to the Hertyshorn in Westsmyth-feld. *a* 1548 HALL *Chron., Hen. VII* 13 Then were his continuall enemyes next to the gate of his realme. 1596 DALRYMPLE tr. *Leslie's Hist. Scot.* Prol. 49 Than agane Marr lyes on the costsyde neist. 1631 GOUGE *God's Arrows* IV. §15. 396 This with-drawing chamber was next to his bed-chamber. 1662 STANLEY *Hist. Philos., Chaldaick* (1701) 14/1 From the places next about the Moon. 1765 BLACKSTONE *Comm.* I. 113 Wastes..when improved..are..to be assessed to all parochial rates in the parish next adjoining.

†**b.** *transf.* of help, accidents, attainment, etc.

a 1250 *Owl & Night.* 688 Hwenne þe bale is alre hekst, þenne is þe bote alre nest. *c* 1290 *Beket* 1534 in *S. Eng. Leg.*, ȝwane a man is In mest soruwe and teone, þanne is ore louerdes grace nest. 13.. *Cursor M.* 62 (Gött.), He þat wenis stiffest to stand, War him hijs fal is neist at hand. 1390 GOWER *Conf.* I. 108 For whanne I wende next have be,.. Thanne was I furthest ate laste. 1551 T. WILSON *Logike* (1580) 35 b, This rule holdeth in causes that are next adjoynyng. 1568 GRAFTON *Chron.* II. 839 When he is..next to his mischaunce for his offences and crimes.

c. As complement with verbs of rest or motion.

c 1420 LYDG. *Assembly of Gods* 1502 But nat in comparyson to Glose that sat next. 1567 *Gude & Godlie B.* (S.T.S.) 164 Deide to vs approachis neist. 1579 G. HARVEY *Letter-bk.* (Camden) 153 He put his hand into his pockit and pullid owt..sutch moony..as cam next to hande. 1676 HOBBES *Iliad* I. 387 Up you fetch'd Briareus..And set him next to Jove. 1711 STEELE *Spect.* No. 2 ¶4 Next to Sir Andrew in the Club-Room sits Captain Sentry. 1782 MISS BURNEY *Cecilia* VIII. vi, [She] drew a chair next to her.

10. a. Of days, etc.: Immediately following; coming directly after (the time in question).

In Sc. use, as applied to the days of the week, *next* (as in *Friday next*) is contrasted with *first*: see FIRST *a.* 1 h, and cf. the note to 5 above.

c 1250 *Gen. & Ex.* 3791 For al ðis, oðer day ðor was nest, Agenes moyses and is prest Gan al ðis folc wið wreðe gon. *a* 1300 *Cursor M.* 19135 þe toþer dai þat folud neist [*Fairf.* atte was neiste]. *c* 1386 CHAUCER *Shipman's T.* 307 The sonday next the marchaund was agoon. 1525 LD. BERNERS *Froiss.* II. viii. 18 To morowe next we shall haue a great assaute. 1596 SPENSER *F.Q.* VI. iii. 11 The morrow next, when day gan to uplooke. 1711 BUDGELL *Spect.* No. 67 ¶18 The Collection of Pictures which is to be Exposed to Sale on Friday next. 1818 CRUISE *Digest* (ed. 2) V. 466 Henry would, before the end of Michaelmas term then next, levy a fine. 1835 DICKENS *Let.* ? June (1965) I. 64 It will give me pleasure;..and I am sure will be excellent practice for you against Christmas next. 1850 CARLYLE *Latter-d. Pamph.* iv. 5 We know what France suddenly became in the end of February next.

b. With *after*, *before*, *ensuing*, *to come*.

1386 *Rolls of Parlt.* III. 225/1 Nichol Brembre..proposed hym the yere next after Johan Northampton Mair of the same Citee. 1424 *Paston Lett.* I. 12 The nyghte next biforne the feste. 1472–3 *Rolls of Parlt.* VI. 60/1 From the vi[th] day of Aprill next to come. 1474 *Ibid.* 108/2 In the Oeptas of Seint John Baptist next ensuyng the forseid xxi day of Januar'. 1542 UDALL *Erasm. Apoph.* 270 b, Beeyng the daye nexte before his death. *a* 1578 LINDESAY (Pitscottie) *Chron. Scot.* (S.T.S.) II. 296 So trewis and abstinacie was tane and proclemit..to the first day of January nixtocum. 1588 A. KING tr. *Canisius' Catech.* G viij b, Ye sonday nixt efter ye 14 change of ye moone.

11. a. Immediately following (or going *before*) in order or succession.

a 1300 *Cursor M.* 6948 Quen aaron was ded, þe priste, His sun eliazar was neist. 1390 GOWER *Conf.* I. 83 And next upon that other side..yit ther is The point seconde. *a* 1400–50 *Alexander* 1456 Sone sall I neuen ȝow þe note þat is next eftir. 1549 *Latimer's 2nd Serm. bef. Edw. VI* To Rdr. (Arb.) 46 Numa Pompilus, who was..created king [of] the Romaynes next after Romulus. 1583 STOCKER *Civ. Warres Lowe C.* III. 746 As more at large is set downe in the booke next before. 1600 J. PORY tr. *Leo's Africa* III. 165 Next of all are the stables, wherein their horses are marvellous well tended. 1645 GATAKER *God's Eye on Israel* 23 As he had spoken of in the verse next beforegoing.

b. As complement with *come* or *follow*.

c 1440 *Generydes* 1940 Nexst after come the kyng of Nicomede. 1533 GAU *Richt Vay* 9 This command followis nixt effter the iii commandis pertenand to god. 1667 MILTON *P.L.* I. 446 Thammuz came next behind, Whose annual wound [etc.]. 1884 tr. *Lotze's Logic* 452 The very criterion which follows next in order.

c. ***what next?*** as an exclamation of surprise.

1838 SHAFTESB. *Diary* 19 Oct. in *Life* (1886) I. vi. 237 As old ladies say, What next? 1858 *Punch* XXXIV. 2 Well, I'm sure! What next, I wonder!

12. a. Nearest in respect of kinship, intimacy, or other such relationship.

c 1307 *Elegy Edw. I*, iii, Helpeth mi sone, and crowneth him newe, For he is nest to buen ycore. *c* 1330 R. BRUNNE *Chron.* (1810) 92 William vnderstode, þat he said reson, & was next of blode. 1382 WYCLIF *Numb.* xxvii. 11 The herytage shal be ȝeue to hem that ben next to him. *c* 1400 tr. *Secreta Secret., Gov. Lordsh.* 96 Begynne at þe knawynge of þyn owen sawle, þat is nest to þe. *c* 1450 *St. Cuthbert* (Surtees) 6950 To serue þe saynt he was neste. 1620 J. WILKINSON *Coroners & Sherifes* 44 Make your pannels your selfe of such persons as bee most next, most sufficient, and not suspect.

b. Approaching most closely (*to* a person or thing) in rank or excellence; coming immediately *after* (another) in this respect.

1535 COVERDALE *Esther* x. 3 Mardocheus the Iewe was the seconde nexte [1611 was next] vnto kynge Ahasuerus. 1578 COOPER *Thesaurus* s.v. *Secundus, A rege secundus*, next in dignitie after the king. 1606 G. W[OODCOCKE] *Hist. Ivstine* XI. 48 Promising to performe all Darius request, if he would acknowledge himselfe as next vnto him. 1628 T. SPENCER *Logick* 197 That attribute bordreth next of all to mans particular essence. 1697 DRYDEN *Virg. Past.* v. 77 At least your lays Are next to his, and claim the second praise. 1849 MACAULAY *Hist. Eng.* iii. I. 335 Next to the capital, but next at an immense distance, stood Bristol. 1860 *Merc. Mar. Mag.* VII. 6 Next to an anemometric scale in value, is the Beaufort.

c. In phr. ***next after*** (or †***under***), ***next to***, used in loose apposition to the person or thing spoken of.

1561 WINȜET *First Tract.* Wks. (S.T.S.) I. 13 The weilfair of thy Maiestie, nixt efter God to vs..maist deirbelouit in erth. 1595 *Drake's Voy.* (Hakl. Soc.) 3 That quiet peace which wee, from the hands of Her Majestie (next under God) abundently enjoy. 1633 SIR J. BURROUGHS *Sov. Brit. Seas* (1651) 133 Next to the English they are now become the most redoubted Nation at Sea. 1700 S. PARKER *Six Philos. Ess.* 53 Physicians, of all people, gather most Money next to the Collectors of the Taxes. 1809 W. IRVING *Knickerb.* III. i. 154 They were never either heard or talked of—which, next to being universally applauded, should be the ambition of all sage magistrates and rulers. 1824 MISS MITFORD *Village* Ser. I. (1863) 187 He was, next after Lucy,

..by far the best news-gatherer of the country side. **1880** C. R. MARKHAM *Peruv. Bark* 438 The East Indian source of supply is now the most important next to Colombia.

13. a. next to, the nearest approach to; very nearly, almost.

1667 MILTON *P.L.* VI. 316 Together both with next to Almighty Arme, Uplifted imminent one stroke they aim'd. **1699** BENTLEY *Phal.* 140 The very facility and naturalness of every correction will be next to a Demonstration.., that the Observation must needs be true. **1719** DE FOE *Crusoe* II. (Globe) 329 It must have been next to miraculous if they had escaped. **1753** RICHARDSON *Grandison* (1811) II. xiii. 152 He loved his father, but next to adored his mother. **1815** W. H. IRELAND *Scribbleomania* 198 It was thought next to impossible. **1828** *Life Planter Jamaica* 86 It would therefore, be next to a miracle, if he should detect a single stranger among such a host. **1887** *Times* (weekly ed.) 12 Sept. 7/4 In such circumstances..it would be next to impossible to open the eyes.

b. With following negative.

1656 TUCKER in *Misc. Scott. Burgh Rec. Soc.* (1891) 5 They profered at first that which was next to nothing. **1706** E. WARD *Wooden World Diss.* (1708) 18 They may cost him next to nothing in the keeping. **1828** MOIR *Mansie Wauch* xi. 185 The old flute was for next to no use at all. **1849** GROTE *Greece* II. xlviii. (1862) IV. 219 Ships, they had few; trained seamen, yet fewer; wealth, next to none. **1885** *Manch. Exam.* 11 Nov. 5/1 In his letter he has contrived, without being defiant, to concede next to nothing.

c. *to get* (or *be*) *next* (*to* or *on*): to become acquainted or intimate with, to come to know; to find out about, to understand, to become worldly-wise, to acquire self-knowledge. Also *to put next* (*to*): to acquaint (one) (with). *U.S. slang.*

1896 [see BRASH *a.*[2] b]. **1896** ADE *Artie* xvi. 146 I've been next, I'll tell you those. **1900** —— *More Fables in Slang* 109 She knew that the Treasurer of the Shoe Factory was Next to all these Boarding School Tactics. **1902** 'D. DIX' *Fables of Elite* 85 'Do you get Next to my Meaning?' 'I am on..and I apprehend that a wink to the Wise is sufficient.' **1906** B. L. TAYLOR *Extra Dry* 24 Then along comes Paul Potter, and puts me next on how to write a play. **1908** K. MCGAFFEY *Show-girl* 72 You had better drop in your penny and get next to yourselves. **1910** W. M. RAINE *B. O'Connor* 225 Mrs. Mackenzie will put you next to the etiquette wrinkles where you are shy. **1910** WODEHOUSE *Gentleman of Leisure* vii. 66 Sure, he will... He'll be good. He's next to de game, sure. *Ibid.* x. 98 Boss, what's doin' here? Put me next to de game. **1913** E. C. BENTLEY *Trent's Last Case* vi. 59 'Has he any friends?' interjected Trent. Mr. Bunner [an American] glanced at him sharply. 'Somebody has been putting you next, I see that.' **1936** J. TULLY *Bruiser* iv. 41 She took me for a hundred before I got next. **1950** A. LOMAX *Mr. Jelly Roll* 19 If you could shoot a good agate.., I'm telling you you were liable to get next to that broad. **1957** R. STOUT *If Death ever Slept* (1958) vi. 73 Maybe you can get a lead to it through Brigham. Get next to him. **1969** 'H. PENTECOST' *Girl Watcher's Funeral* (1970) II. iii. 114 He found out I was an actor... He told me he could put me next to some guy who was making underground films. **1973** *Black World* Sept. 4/2 If he can't get next to what we're about, we'll just have to school him.

III. Governing a substantive (orig. in dative).

14. a. Nearest to (a thing, place, or person) in respect of situation.

c **888** K. ÆLFRED *Boeth.* xxxix. §7 Swa swa sio nafu færð neahst þære eaxe. *a* **900** CYNEWULF *Crist* 398 [Hy] þringað ȝeorne hwylc hyra nehst mæȝe ussum Nerȝende flihte lacan. *c* **1205** LAY. 24168 Her ich þe ȝeue Neustrie nexste mine riche. *a* **1240** *Sawles Warde* in *O.E. Hom.* I. 247 Strengðe stont nest hire. *c* **1330** R. BRUNNE *Chron. Wace* (Rolls) 7871 Handes on ȝour felawes lay, On ilka Breton þat sittes ȝou nest. **1377** LANGL. *P. Pl.* B. XVII. 286 Innocence is nexte god and nyȝte and day it crieth. *c* **1480** HENRYSON *Test. Cres.* 109 His chalmer was thaim neist. **1560** DAUS tr. *Sleidane's Comm.* 275 To invade the Emperours countrie next them. **1591** SPENSER *Virg. Gnat* 385 There next the vtmost brinck doth he abide. **1615** W. LAWSON *Country Housew. Gard.* (1626) 5 Euery soile hath his crust next day wherein trees and hearbs put their roots. **1687** A. LOVELL tr. *Thevenot's Trav.* I. 56 All of them..wear Drawers next their Skin. **1722** DE FOE *Plague* (1754) 177 A mad Dog..will fly upon and bite any one that comes next him. **1764** GOLDSM. *Hist. Eng. in Lett.* (1772) I. 23 All the trading and maritime towns next the continent. **1822** LAMB *Elia* Ser. I. *Roast Pig*, Tearing up whole handfuls of the scorched skin with the flesh next it. **1891** *Law Times* XC. 395/1 Placing wooden rails on the side next the glebe land and field stakes..on the side next the plaintiff's field.

b. In phr. *next* one's *hand*, nearest at hand. *next* one's *heart* (see HEART *sb.* 4).

a **1300** *Cursor M.* 62 He þat stitthest wenis at stand, Warre hym, his fall is nexst his hand. *a* **1774** GOLDSM. *Surv. Exp. Philos.* (1776) I. 212 Suppose I take any thing that is next my hand, a walking cane for instance.

15. a. Nearest to (a person or thing) in point of rank, condition, character, etc.

c **1200** *Trin. Coll. Hom.* 9 þe man mai be god next, þe him beð iqueme. **1297** R. GLOUC. (Rolls) 3321 þe erl aþ tueie men him next, briȝthoel & Iordan. **1377** LANGL. *P. Pl.* B. II. 202 Loue is leche of lyf and nexte oure lorde selue. *c* **1400** *Apol. Loll.* 5 Places ne orderis makun not vs nekist God, but oþer good meritis ioynun to gidir. **1572** *Satir. Poems Reform.* xxxviii. 20 Thy style was Treschristien, maist Cristen King, Baith heist and friest, and neist the impyre. **1620** T. GRANGER *Div. Logike* 230 A vehement asseveration, which is next an oath. **1667** MILTON *P.L.* I. 79 One next himself in power, and next in crime. **1750** JOHNSON *Rambler* No. 1 ¶9 A degree of solicitude next that of an author.

b. In loose apposition. = 12c.

a **1340** HAMPOLE *Psalter* cxxxii. 3 In thaim lightis the oynment of the halygaste, neste apostils. *c* **1375** *Sc. Leg. Saints* xxvii. (*Machor*) 461 For þu nixt god is my fadir. **14..** in *Tundale's Vis.* (1843) 123 Where neest thi son thou hast souerente. **1526** *Pilgr. Perf.* (W. de W. 1531) 82 To yᵉ whiche next mekenes and obedyence..we must apply our exercyse. **1568** GRAFTON *Chron.* II. 287 The thing that in this worlde I loue best, next my wyfe and children. *a* **1631** DONNE *Paradoxes* (1652) 86 Avarice is the greatest deadly sin next Pride.

B. *adv.*

†**1.** Last, on the last occasion. *Obs.*

a **900** CYNEWULF *Crist* 535 To Hierusalem..þonan hy God nyhst upstiȝende eaȝum seȝun. **971** *Blickl. Hom.* 125 Seo stow þe Drihten lichomlice nehst on stod her on middanȝearde. *a* **1000** *Cædmon's Gen.* 536 (Gr.), Ic wat, hwæt he me self bebead..þa ic hine nehst ȝeseah. *c* **1205** LAY. 5037 Nou hit is seoue ȝer at þou nexst wer her.

2. a. In the next place; immediately thereupon or thereafter.

α. *a* **1300** *Cursor M.* 26138 To quam I sal þe tell here nexist [*Fairf.* nest] þou sal þe scriue. **1390** GOWER *Conf.* I. 50 Bot next above alle othre schewe Of love I wol the propretes. *c* **1450** HOLLAND *Howlat* 378 Next the souerane signe was sekirly sene..The armes of the Dowglass. **1500–20** DUNBAR *Poems* lxxii. 41 Nixt all in purpour thai him cled. **1598** SHAKS. *Merry W.* II. ii. 263, I will first make bold with your money: next, giue mee your hand; and last [etc.]. **1649** MILTON *Eikon.* 90 First by his..mistrust.., Next by his hatred. **1664** BUTLER *Hud.* II. ii. 153 Did they not next compell the Nation To take and breake the Protestation? **1766** GOLDSM. *Vic. W.* xxv, I next attended the sheriff's officers to the prison. **1828** KIRBY & SP. *Entomol.* xii. I. 378 She next furnishes it with a store of pollen. **1860** TYNDALL *Glac.* I. xi. 76 Our way next lay up a steep incline. **1871** JOWETT *Plato* I. 146 Hippias the sage spoke next.

β. *a* **1300** *Cursor M.* 27148 Sumquat es to sai her nest þat falles to office o preist. *c* **1375** *Sc. Leg. Saints* l. (*Catherine*) 939 Syne þar neste I sall gere turment þe fulfaste. **1390** GOWER *Conf.* III. 121 Thanne nest He hath ek foure upon his brest. **1535** STEWART *Cron. Scot.* I. 58 Quhat hound.. bait neist and baid quhill he wes slane. **1721** RAMSAY *Prospect of Plenty* 103 A meaner phantom neist..Attacks with senseless fears the weaker head. **1728** —— *Archers diverting themselves* 95 Neist, Sir, you name. **1816** SCOTT *Antiq.* xxv, I wish we may get the light keepit in neist, wi' this fearsome wind.

†**b.** With *after* or *before*. *Obs.*

1511 *Guylforde's Pilgr.* (Camden) 39 Next after we come to yᵉ hous of Symyonis. **1545** RAYNOLD *Byrth Mankynde* 69 Of ye same..strength with the other pylles spoken of here nexte before. **1562** WINȜET *Third Tract.* Wks. (S.T.S.) I. 29 Can ȝe think him in ony vther gre, bot nyxt efter to speir gif Christ be borne?

3. On the first future or subsequent occasion.

1536 CROMWELL in Merriman *Life & Lett.* (1902) II. 43 When it shal fortune me next to speke with your lordship. **1542** UDALL *Erasm. Apoph.* 238 When he should nexte bee in dooyng sacrifice. **1667** MILTON *P.L.* VI. 439 Weapons more violent, when next we meet, May serve to better us. **1742** RICHARDSON *Pamela* III. 60 A few other Alterations.. are to be finished against we go down next. **1782** COWPER *Gilpin* 251 When he next doth ride abroad May I be there to see. **1875** TENNYSON *Q. Mary* III. v, When next there comes a missive from the Queen.

4. *Comb.*, as *next-born*, *-drawn*.

1612 DRAYTON *Poly-olb.* i. 339 The Oracles gaue out, that next borne Brute should bee His parents onelie death. **1898** MEREDITH *Odes Fr. Hist.* 10 Such enemies of her next-drawn breath she had.

next door. [NEXT *a.* 1.]

1. a. The (door of the) nearest or adjoining house. Also in *fig.* uses, and sometimes with omission of *the* (cf. 2).

c **1485** *Digby Myst.* (1882) II. 95 Yf on loke yow in the face that neuer se yow ere, Wold thynk ye were at the next dore by. **1548** UDALL, etc. *Erasm. Par. Mark* i. 9 A sinner whiche ..is at the next door to saluacion. **1628** EARLE *Microcosm., Good old man* (Arb.) 89 The next doore of death sads him not, but hee expects it calmely as his turne in Nature. **1634** SIR T. HERBERT *Trav.* 151 When they goe but to the next doore they doe it riding. **1643** TRAPP *Comm. Gen.* xix. 11 As if they were ambitious of destruction, which now was at next door by. **1760–72** H. BROOKE *Fool of Qual.* (1809) II. 137 The sweet babies at the next door! **1843** DICKENS *Chr. Carol* ii. 59 Trying to hide himself behind the girl from next door but one.

b. By extension, the occupant of the adjoining house; so *Mrs. next-door*. Also, *next-door-but-one*, the occupant of the house two doors away.

1855 DICKENS *Prince Bull* in *Household Words* 17 Feb. 51/1 One answered, 'I will if next door will;' and another, 'I won't, if over the way does.' **1933** D. C. PEEL *Life's Enchanted Cup* xi. 127 It..occurred to him that our extra pair of guests might belong to one of the 'next doors'. **1935** *Punch* 27 Nov. 590/1 Next-door-but-one was rather a strain. Have you ever imagined canvassing through a speaking-tube? **1951** W. MORUM *Gabriel* I. i. 20, I showed it to Mrs. Next-door. *Ibid.* vii. 95 Aunt Amy came in carrying a roast chicken... 'One of next-door's,' she said. **1960** WILLMOTT & YOUNG *Family & Class in London Suburb* ix. 107 Next door but one has pussy when we go on holiday. Last year she broke her arm and I used to go in and help her. **1962** *Guardian* 30 July 4/3 Most of us have had to pick up Mrs. Next-Door's torn-up letters.

2. In adverbial use (†rarely with *the*). **a.** Very close or near *to* (a state, condition, etc.); almost amounting *to* (something). †Also const. *by*.

1529 MORE *Dyaloge* 22 b/1 Those vyagys bene but..the nexte dore to Idoletry. **1542** UDALL *Erasm. Apoph.* (1877) 41 He meaneth..to make a good beginnyng not to bee a little, but to be nexte doore by a little, or nexte cousin to a little. **1628** T. SPENCER *Logick* 115 Such a one is next dore to salvation. **1656** [? J. SERGEANT] tr. *T. White's Peripat. Inst.* 62 Water..makes the body flaccid and loose, and next door to dissolution. **1699** R. L'ESTRANGE *Erasm. Colloq.* (1725) 202 This same Fawn I perceive is next door to a Fool. **1719** DE FOE *Crusoe* II. (Globe) 329 To be next Door to Starving. **1793** GOUV. MORRIS in Sparks *Life & Writ.* (1832) II. 380 The opera girl, Saunier, who is, though very beautiful, next door to an ideot as to her intellectual gifts. **1822–56** DE QUINCEY *Confess.* (1862) 161 Parliament had not then made it a crime next door to a felony. **1850** GLADSTONE *Glean.* (1879) II. 69 To speak of a thorough knowledge of Greek as being still next door to a miracle. **1878** SPURGEON *Serm.* XXIV. 713 The idea is next door to blasphemous.

b. In or at the next house (*to* a person or place). *boy next door*: see BOY *sb.*[1] 8; (*the*) *girl next door*: see GIRL *sb.* 2h.

1579 LYLY *Euphues* 131 It is an olde Prouerbe that if one dwell the next doore to a creple he will learne to hault. **1633** G. HERBERT *Temple, Praise* iv, A herb destill'd, and drunk, may dwell next doore..To a brave soul. **1669** STURMY *Mariner's Mag.* c 4 The Cross-daggers in Moor-fields, next door to the Popes Head Tavern. **1738** SWIFT *Pol. Conversat.* Introd. 8 At his Lodgings next Door to the Gloucester-Head. **1863** LADY HORNBY *Constantinople* 107 The Armenian lady next door, to whom the house belongs.

3. *attrib.*, as *next-door neighbour(dom)*, *town*.

1749 FIELDING *Tom Jones* IV. xii, Persons who live two or three miles distance in the country are considered as next door neighbours. **1806–7** J. BERESFORD *Miseries Hum. Life* (1826) VII. iv, A perpetual blister;—alias, a sociable next-door-neighbour. **1859** MRS. CARLYLE *Lett.* II. 394 When he had done with our next-door neighbour. **1882** H. C. MERIVALE *Faucit of B.* III. II. xix. 154 The arrangements of next-door-neighbourdom were of so casual a kind. **1897** MARY KINGSLEY *W. Africa* 330 He never eats it himself, but the next-door town does.

†**'nexter**, used for NEXT *a.*, perh. after *yester*.

1576 GASCOIGNE *Philomene* (Arb.) 111 Al that day, they fede in feare,..And in the nexter night Ful many times do crie, Remembring yet the ruthful plight.

†**nextfold**, *a. Obs. rare*[−1]. [Cf. OE. *néahfeald* (rare).] Nearest.

a **1225** *Juliana* 32 Al mi nest falde cun me heaneð þet schulden beon mine freond.

next hand, *adv.* and *a.* ? *Obs.* [f. NEXT *a.* + HAND *sb.* Cf. NEAR- and NIGH-HAND.]

A. *adv.* **1.** Nearest or first at hand.

a **1300** *Cursor M.* 26087 Grace it es be-for cumand And siþen him folus luue neist hand [*Fairf.* next hand]. **1603** HOLLAND *Plutarch's Mor.* 226 To set our mindes and knit our affections to those that come next hand. *a* **1641** BP. MOUNTAGU *Acts & Mon.* (1642) 12 Some part of them onely, which came next hand, not the choyce.

2. Nearest or next to (something).

a **1300** *Cursor M.* 9982 þe fundament þat first es laid Neist-hand þe roche. **13..** *St. Cristofer* 193 in Horstm. *Altengl. Leg.* (1881) 457 Vnto thi bedde when þou sall gaa Luk þat þou ly nexte-hand þe straa.

B. *adj.* Nearest, closest.

1642 ROGERS *Naaman* 147 Wedding our selves to our next hand props of children, wealth, meanes.

'nextly, *adv.* Now *rare.* [f. NEXT *a.* + -LY[2].]

1. In the next place; next.

1584 B. R. tr. *Herodotus* 53 To hym the chiefe gouernment of the army was nextly committed. **1616** J. LANE *Contn. Sq. T.* (1888) VI. 121 Nextlie, the kinge and Queene, with sadder eye then whilome wonted, viewd each mutualie. **1620** T. GRANGER *Div. Logike* 200 Chiefly in Arts where they are most accurately handled; and nextly in artificiall treatises. **1663** OWEN *Vind. Animadv.* Wks. 1851 XIV. 444 You add nextly, as my words, 'The eye' [etc.]. **1866** *Punch's Almanack*, The cry of dogs is nextly heard.

†**2.** Most immediately or directly. *Obs.*

1674 N. FAIRFAX *Bulk & Selv.* Ep. Ded., The Lord of the Soyl holds nextly of the King. **1754** EDWARDS *Freed. Will* I. i. (1762) 2 The Thing nextly chosen or prefer'd when a man wills to walk.

†**'nextmost**, *a. Obs. rare*[−1]. = NEXT *a.*

1576 GASCOIGNE *Philomene* (Arb.) 114 Hir next most note (to note) I neede no helpe at al.

'nextness. [f. NEXT *a.*] The fact or condition of immediate succession or proximity.

1875 MCCLELLAN *New Test.* 424 [St. Luke] promises to write 'according to nextness' in order, or consecutively. **1875** W. K. CLIFFORD *Lect.* (1879) I. 244 These elements of feeling have relations of nextness or contiguity in space.

†**nexure.** *Obs. rare.* [ad. med.L. *nexūra* (Du Cange), f. L. *nex-*, *nectĕre*: see next.] Connexion, combination.

1652 GAULE *Magastrom.* 151 The Series, order, nexure,.. disposition of second causes, &c. **1674** PETTY *Disc. Dupl. Proportion* A 5 An intelligible Account of the Nexures, Mixtures, and Mobilities of all the parts of the Universe.

‖**nexus** ('nɛksəs). [L. *nexus*, pl. *nexūs*, f. *nex-*, *nectĕre* to bind, connect.]

1. a. A bond or link; a means of connexion between things or parts.

1663 BOYLE *Usef. Exp. Nat. Philos.* II. 241 Changing the Motion and *nexus* or Juncture of their parts. **1709** *Brit. Apollo* No. 34. 2/1 What is the Nexus of Matter? **1776** J. ADAMS in Sparks *Corr. Amer. Rev.* (1853) I. 113 It is the *nexus* of the northern and southern colonies. **1839** CARLYLE *Chartism* vi. 149 Cash Payment had not then grown to be the universal sole nexus of man to man. **1877** E. CAIRD *Philos. Kant* I. 158 The nexus of cause and effect is not given in sensitive experience.

b. *causal nexus*, the necessary connexion between cause and effect.

1836–7 SIR W. HAMILTON *Metaph.* xxxix. (1859) II. 394 The phænomenon of necessity in our notion of the causal nexus. **1874** W. WALLACE *Hegel's Logic* §42. 75 The causal nexus between the two is..only evident to thought.

c. In Jespersen's terminology, a group of words containing a verb, or a predicative (with ellipsis of verb); a predicative relation or a construction treated as such. Freq. *attrib.*

1924 O. JESPERSEN *Philos. Gram.* vii. 97 If now we compare the combination *a furiously barking dog*..with *the dog barks furiously*, it is evident that the same subordination obtains in the latter as in the former combination... We shall call the former kind *junction*, and the latter *nexus*. *Ibid.* ix. 122 A nexus-object is often found: 'I found *the cage empty*', which is easily distinguished from 'I found *the empty cage*' where *empty* is an adjunct. *Ibid.* 126 The subject-part (primary) of a Latin nexus-subjunct may be an accusative-with-infinitive or a clause. *Ibid.* x. 138 Nexus-substantives are also often convenient in cases where idiomatic usage does not allow a dependent clause, as after *upon* in 'Close upon his resignation followed his last illness and death'. *Ibid.* xxii. 303 We may therefore call questions of this kind [i.e. yes-or-no] *nexus-questions*. **1928** —— *Internat. Lang.* II. 130 To form so-called 'abstracts' (i.e. in my terminology predicative nexus-words) from adjectives we use the suffix *-eso*. **1933** [see ADNEX]. **1936** J. R. AIKEN *Commonsense Gram.* xvii. 212 The clause is basically a nexus performing a single function within a communication. **1937** O. JESPERSEN *Analytic Syntax* 16 Nexus-substantive, e.g. work, kindness. **1946** —— *Mod. Eng. Gram.* VI. v. 47 Something looking like a nexus-tertiary is continued with its S[ubject] as the real subject of the sentence. **1951** A. GARDINER *Speech & Lang.* 261 Jespersen has given to this subject-predicate relation..the name of 'nexus'. **1957** S. POTTER *Mod. Linguistics* iii. 71 General or nexus-questions which may be answered by 'yes' or 'no'. **1966** *English Studies* XLVII. 55 Those with nexus-objects (e.g. I believe Williams the murderer = Williams to be the murderer).

2. A connected group or series.

1858 BIRCH *Anc. Pottery* II. 359 The letters are often united in nexus or ligatures. **1882** *N. Eng. Hist. & Gen. Reg.* XXXVI. 178 The constabulary office belongs to a nexus of court institutions..of immemorial antiquity.

ney, variant of NOY *v.*

†**neyard.** *Obs. rare*$^{-1}$. (See quot.)

1577 B. GOOGE *Heresbach's Husb.* III. (1586) 125 b, Those that are gotten betwixt a Horse and an Asse in olde time, were called Neyards.

†**ney-beer.** *Obs. rare*$^{-1}$. (See quot.)

1574 R. SCOT *Hop Gard.* (1578) 54 Experience hath taught them..to seeth them againe in the Woorte, which they call the Ney beere.

neyce, obs. f. NIECE.

neych(e, obs. varr. NIGH *v.*

neyder, -dyr, obs. ff. NEITHER.

neydlingis, var. NEEDLINGS *Obs.*

†**neye**, obs. form of EYE. (Also *pl.* nies.)

1641 BROME *Joviall Crew* II. Wks. 1873 III. 390 The pretty pretty pink Of her Neyes, that half wink. **1679** DRYDEN *Troil. & Cress.* III. ii, Do you lear indeed at one an other! do the Neyes twinkle at him! **1704** STEELE *Lying Lover* v, Till its pretty Nies be all blubber'd.

neye, obs. f. NEIGH *v.*, NIGH, NYE.

neyen, -þe, obs. ff. NINE, NINTH.

neyf, obs. f. NEIF, NIEVE.

neyger: see NEGRE.

neyghe, neyȝe, obs. ff. NEIGH *v.*, NINE.

neyghebur, etc., obs. f. NEIGHBOUR.

neyh(e, obs. ff. NEIGH *v.*, NIGH.

ney(h)lechen: see NEHLECHE.

†**neyle**, *v. Obs. rare.* In 4 **neȝle, neyhle, neyȝhele.** [f. *neȝ-* NIGH *a.* Cf. MLG. *nâlen, nêlen* (MDa. *nāle, naale*, MSw. *nāla*).] *intr.* To come near, approach.

1340 *Ayenb.* 105 Þe zaule..more propirliche neȝleþ to his riȝte uayrhede of his kende. **1393** LANGL. *P. Pl.* C xx. 58 He fleih a-syde, And wolde nat neyhle hym by nyne londes lengthe.

neyn(e, neynþe, obs. ff. NINE, NINTH.

†**neypur**, obs. variant of NEIGHBOUR.

a **1500** *Ten Commandm.* in Herrig *Archiv* LXXXV. 46 Covett þow not thy neypurs good. *Ibid.*, Thow shalt not desyre thy neypurys fere.

neys(e, obs. ff. NESE, NESH.

neysch(e, neyshe, etc., obs. ff. NESH.

neyst, dial. var. NEXT.

neyt, obs. f. AIT.

neyte, obs. f. NEAT *sb.*

neyþer, obs. f. NEITHER.

neyuen, obs. f. NEVEN.

neyuer, obs. f. NEVER.

neywat, var. of NIGHWHAT.

Nez Percé, Nez Perce (nɛz pɜːse, pɜːs). [Fr., lit. 'pierced nose'.] A member of a group of North American Indians; also, the language of this people. Also *attrib.*

1812 in *S. Dakota Hist. Coll.* (1908) IV. 157 The..Nez Perce nation have a tradition that the human race spring from this dog [*sc.* the prairie dog] and the beaver. **1832** in *Overland to Pacific* (1934) IV. 120 Here we found about 120 Lodges of the Nez Perces and about 80 of the Flatheads. **1841** G. CATLIN *Lett. on N. Amer. Indians* II. 108 The *Nez Percés* who inhabit the upper waters..of the Columbia,.. are seldom known to flatten the head. **1910** F. W. HODGE *Handbk. Amer. Indians* II. 67/1 Practically the only rupture in these relations was the Nez Percé war of 1877. **1926** L. A. CLARE tr. *Lévy-Bruhl's How Natives Think* iv. 157 With the Nez-percés, verbs assume different forms according to whether the subject or object is advancing or retreating. **1937** R. H. LOWIE *Hist. Ethnol. Theory* ix. 133 The Nez Percé myths dictated by an old native woman to her college-bred son form another notable instance. **1949** *Pacific Discovery* May–June 16/1 According to some it is derived from the Nez Percé word meaning 'muddy water'. **1959** E. TUNIS *Indians* 112/1 The northern Shoshone, the Nez Percé, and some other tribes obtained horses and were transformed into reasonable facsimiles of Plains Indians. **1965** *Canad. Jrnl. Linguistics* X. 78 Languages of sure affiliation...Nez Perce (Penutian). **1968** [see IBO *a.* and *sb.* B. 1 b]. **1969** *Language* XLV. 45 Sahaptian..has two members: Nez Perce and Sahaptin. Nez Perce was spoken in parts of present-day Oregon, Washington, and Idaho. **1973** *Times Lit. Suppl.* 23 Nov. 1425/1 Joseph, last of the Nez Percé, non-treaty chiefs, was restricted to a Washington reservation.

ngaio ('naɪəʊ, ‖'ŋaiɔ). Also 9 **ngaiho.** [Maori.] An evergreen shrub or small tree, *Myoporum laetum*, of the family Myoporaceæ, native to New Zealand and bearing clusters of white flowers. Also *attrib.*

1853 J. D. HOOKER *Bot. Antarctic Voy.: Flora Novæ-Zelandiæ* I. 205 *Myoporum lætum*... Nat[ive] name 'Ngaio', Col[enso]. (Cultivated in England.) **1861** A. S. ATKINSON *Jrnl.* 6 Mar. in *Richmond-Atkinson Papers* (1960) I. xii. 693 Sat down in the shade of the ngaiho's which bordered the beach. **1873** *Descr. Catal. Exhibits from N.Z. Vienna Exhib.* 24/1 *Myoporum lætum.* (Ngaio). A small ornamental tree. Wood light, white, and tough. Used for gun stocks. **1876** *Trans. N.Z. Inst.* IX. 206 A common New Zealand shrub, or tree, which may be made useful for shelter, viz. the Ngaio. **1921** H. GUTHRIE-SMITH *Tutira* xii. 102 In this light bush, tawa..mahoe or hinahina (*Melicytus ramiflorus*), ngaio (*Myoporum laetum*)..were the most common trees and shrubs. **1946** *Jrnl. Polynesian Soc.* LV. 161 Fancy ngaio not being in the Dictionary; ngaio, so reminiscent of the story of Ngaio and her translation to the moon with her calabash and the ngaio tree she clung to for support and stay. **1959** *Listener* 30 Apr. 769/2 The New Zealand 'properties'—ngaio, bluegum, etc.—enter naturally into what he [*sc.* J. K. Baxter] has to say. **1966** *Encycl. N.Z.* II. 681/2 Ngaio grows to a height of about 30 ft and is a much-branched, rounded tree. The leaves are bright green and somewhat fleshy... They are thickly studded with oil glands in which bacteria live. Flowers are small and appear as little clusters in the axils of leaves.

Ngala, var. LINGALA.

nganga, var. MGANGA.

‖**ngarara** (ŋɑː'rara, n-). [Maori.] A name used for various extinct, unidentified, New Zealand lizards; also, in Maori mythology, a lizard-like monster. Also *attrib.*

1874 J. W. STACK in *Trans. N.Z. Inst.* VII. 296 Ngarara burrows were frequently met with on the plains. *Ibid.*, A ngarara known as Te iha was kept a long time at Kaiapoi. **1882** W. D. HAY *Brighter Britain!* II. 115 There is a little emerald-green lizard in the bush, called by the Maori ngarara. It is dreadfully tapu. **1901** A. A. GRACE *Tales of Dying Race* 190 'The Ngarara—you never heard of him?' said the old woman. 'He is *the* Ngarara—the real one. Big body, eight feet long; big webbed feet; big wings like a bat's, with which he flies and catches fish; long tail like a *tuatara* lizard's, but bigger; skin like the bark of the red pine.' **1905** W. B. *Where White Man Treads* 38 His [*sc.* the Maori's] existence was burdened with the knowledge of huge reptilian monsters, ngarara on land, and taniwha in the water. **1949** P. BUCK *Coming of Maori* (1950) I. iv. 61 The crew and passengers of the [canoe] Mangarara consisted of reptiles and insects. The reptiles (*ngarara*) were lizards. **1966** *Encycl. N.Z.* I. 48/2 Less improbable were Maori tales of the *ngarara*, lizards which were larger than the tuatara... Certain prominent Maoris..claimed not only to have seen but also to have handled and eaten them. It seems that the *ngarara*, which frequented manuka scrub, varied in size from 2 to 3 ft in length and from 10 to 20 in. in girth. There was also a smaller *ngarara*, about 18 in. long, found in streams. The Maoris attributed the disappearance of the large *ngarara* to scrub-fires and the attacks of cats and.. perhaps the Norwegian rat.

Ngbaka (ŋ'bɑːkə). [Native name.] A Bantu language of the northern parts of Zaire.

1949 E. A. NIDA *Morphol.* (ed. 2) 63 Ngbaka, a language of the Belgian Congo. **1965** *Language* XLI. 347 A few short Ngbaka texts.

Ngbandi (ŋ'bændɪ). [Native name.] A Bantu language of the Central African Republic and northern Zaire.

1955 J. H. GREENBERG *Studies in African Linguistic Classification* 12 An enumeration of the membership of the Niger-Congo family by tentative genetic subfamilies follows:..14. Eastern Branch: Gbaya-Manjia,..Sango-Yakoma-Ngbandi. **1964** E. A. NIDA *Toward Sci. Transl.* ix. 199 In Ngbandi, a language of northern Congo, tense distinctions are generally indicated by tonal differences on the subject pronouns, while aspectual differences are signaled by differences of tone on the verbs. **1967** W. J. SAMARIN *Grammar of Sango* 17 Vernacular Sango, one of the dialects of the Ngbandi complex (which itself is a language of the Adamawa-Eastern group of Greenberg's Niger-Kordofanian), at one time came to be used as a lingua-franca. **1969** *Language* XLV. 659 Sango is a pidginized variant of a Ngbandi language of the Central African Republic.

‖**ngege** (ŋ'geɪgeɪ). [Native name.] A cichlid food fish, *Tilapia esculenta*, found in Lake Victoria in E. Africa. Cf. TILAPIA.

1928 *Times* (Weekly ed.) 12 Jan. 54/2 His nets were full of the prime fish of the lake, the carplike ngege. **1932** *Discovery* Jan. 16/1 The fish of economic importance is called the ngege, a carp-like species which is found in Lake Victoria.

Ngoko (ŋ'əʊkəʊ). [Native name.] The popular written or spoken form of modern Javanese.

1893, 1925 [see KROMO]. **1948** D. DIRINGER *Alphabet* vii. 424 Ngoko, the language of the commoner. **1963** R. T. MCVEY *Indonesia* x. 443 Semar..speaks to the god in Ngoko (low Javanese) and is answered in high Javanese.

‖**ngoma** (ŋ'gəʊmə). [Swahili *ngoma, goma*, drum, dance, music.] In East Africa, a dance, a social gathering where dancing is general, a night of dancing.

1926 *Glasgow Herald* 27 Jan. 10 They..console them for the temporary absence of their dancing partners at ngomas. **1935** E. HEMINGWAY *Green Hills of Africa* I. i. 16 That is what you should see. The big *ngomas*. The big native dance festivals. **1947** *E. African Ann.* 1946–7 57/1 Most include in their headdresses a 'halo' of giraffe or zebra hair, and one I saw at a Victory ngoma (dance) had his horned headdress crowned by a..teapot. **1960** *Spectator* 29 July 179 They would keep it up far into the night, drinking and drumming; a jolly social party not like the ngomas I used to see which always had a hint of magic and, it seemed, of menace. **1966** C. SWEENEY *Scurrying Bush* v. 65 It was not until I went to a *ngoma*, or beer-dance,..that I appreciated the tremendous volume of noise that human beings could produce. **1971** *Standard* (Dar es Salaam) 7 Apr. 1/8 There will be dances in all dancing halls,..competitions in ngomas and singing, [etc.].

Ngoni (ŋ'gəʊnɪ), *sb.* and *a.* [Native name.] **A.** *sb.* An African people belonging to the Nguni branch of the Bantu. (Groups of Ngoni migrated from their original home in Zululand in about 1830 and are now found in Malawi, Tanzania, Zambia, etc.) **B.** *adj.* Of or pertaining to this people.

1883 R. N. CUST *Mod. Lang. Africa* II. xii. 300 Bands of marauders, or Nomads, are met with as far North as the neighbourhood of the Victoria Nyanza under the names of ..Ba-Ngoni, Wa-Ngoni, and Ma-Ngoni. The uniform testimony of travellers is that they speak Zulu. **1891** W. A. ELMSLIE (*title*) Introductory grammar of the Ngoni (Zulu) language, as spoken in Mombera's kingdom. **1911** *Encycl. Brit.* XXVIII. 1050/2 In the 19th century various Zulu hordes successively invaded and overran a great part of east-central Africa... Throughout these regions they are variously known as Ma-Zitu, Ma-Ravi, Wa-Ngoni (Angoni), [etc.]. **1948** J. A. BARNES *Material Culture of Ft. Jameson Ngoni* i. 4 The principal difference between the Ngoni and their surrounding neighbours is in their form of centralised chieftainship, inherited from father to son. **1950** —— *Marriage in Changing Society* iv. 71 The Ngoni regard uxorilocal residence as part of the obligation a man has towards his wife's parents. **1966** C. G. SELIGMAN *Races of Africa* (ed. 4) ix. 141 Reflex movements northwards had produced disorder long before Arab raids and Ngoni incursions spread ruin and desolation.

†**ngou**, obs. variant of GNU.

1802 *Sporting Mag.* XX. 141 The n'gou and koudou are also inhabitants of Caffraria.

Nguni (ŋ'guːnɪ), *sb.* and *a.* [Zulu.] **A.** *sb.* A subdivision of the Bantu people which includes the Zulu-Xhosa tribes; also the languages spoken by this group, i.e. the Zulu-Xhosa-Swazi languages. **B.** *adj.* Of or pertaining to this group of peoples or languages.

1929 A. T. BRYANT *Olden Times in Zululand & Natal* i. 3 The natives of South-Eastern Africa we distinguish as of three separate families, which we call respectively Ngúni, in Zululand, the Transvaal, Natal and the Cape; Sutú..; and Tónga. *Ibid.* 5 Captured Bushwomen became common in their homes... And the children..adopted..in a Bantuized form, much of the slave-girl's speech... Hence the clicks in Ngúni speech. **1940** M. GLUCKMAN in Fortes & Evans-Pritchard *African Political Systems* i. 29 In the earlier period of Nguni history, political allegiance tended to coincide with kinship affiliation. **1950** RADCLIFFE-BROWN & FORDE *African Systems of Kinship & Marriage* 58 In the Nguni tribes the personal name that a woman has in her own family, as a daughter, may not be used by her husband's family. **1957** C. G. SELIGMAN *Races of Africa* (ed. 3) viii. 168 This group [*sc.* Eastern Southern Bantu] consists of two main subdivisions Nguni and Tsonga. The former include the Cape Nguni of the Ciskei and Transkei..together with the 'Fingo', fugitive remnants of tribes broken up in Natal ..; the Natal Nguni, or 'Zulu' of Natal and Zululand, with their offshoot the Ndebele (Tebele) of Southern Rhodesia; the Swazi of Swaziland and the Eastern Transvaal; and the 'Transvaal Ndebele' of Central and Northern Transvaal. **1970** W. SMITH *Gold Mine* xxxiv. 88 Basuto is also one of the fighting tribes of the N'guni group.

ngwee (ŋ'gweɪ). Pl. **ngwee.** [Chibemba, lit. 'bright'.] A small coin of Zambia.

1966 *Guardian* 10 Mar. 12/4 Zambia..is to go over, by January 1968, to a decimal currency based on the kwacha (worth 10s of the present pound), divided into 100 ngwee. **1969** *Reporter* (Nairobi) 16 May 12/4 Zambia's white farmers..appear fairly satisfied with the 38 ngwee per pound average. **1975** *Stand. Encycl. S. Afr.* XI. 573/1 The kwacha was equivalent to half of the pound and itself was made up of 100 ngwee.

nhabbe, see HAB *adv.* I (quot. 1542).

nhandu, var. of NANDU.

ni, obs. var. NE *adv.*

niacin ('naɪəsɪn). *Biochem.* [f. NI(COTINIC *a.* + AC(ID *a.* and *sb.* + -IN[1].] **a.** = *nicotinic acid*. **b.** The pellagra-preventing vitamin, which can be either nicotinic acid or nicotinamide.

1942 *Cooperative Consumer* 28 Feb. 5/3 'Niacin' is the new name for 'nicotinic acid', the ingredient of enriched bread which was first discovered as a potent preventive and cure for pellagra. The new name was found to be necessary because some anti-tobacco groups warned against using enriched bread because it would foster the cigaret habit... Federal Security Administrator Paul McNutt..approved the name. **1956** A. HUXLEY *Let.* 25 Dec. (1969) 814 Are there any published papers on the use of niacin in the treatment of high cholesterol conditions? **1968** PFEIFFER & MURPHREE in D. H. Efron *Psychopharmacology* 696/2 The majority of schizophrenic patients given niacin or niacinamide had fewer hospital readmissions..when compared to non-vitamin treated control groups. **1970** *Nature* 16 May 665/2 Niacin is now acceptably defined as a blanket word for the acid and amide. **1972** *Materials & Technology* V. xix. 676 The best dietary sources of niacin are yeast, liver, lean meat, poultry, and legumes.

niacinamide (naɪəˈsɪnəmaɪd). *Biochem.* [f. prec. + AMIDE.] = NICOTINAMIDE.

1951 *Addendum to Brit. Pharmacop.* 23 Injection of Nicotinamide. *Synonym.* Niacinamide Injection. **1955** W. W. DENLINGER *Compl. Boston* II. 34 The need for niacinamide, calcium pantothenate and pyr[i]doxine..has not yet been established as pertains to the nutrition of dogs. **1968** [see prec.]. **1972** *Arch. Dermatol.* CV. 574/2 In our patient, oral and parenteral administration of niacinamide.. led to rapid clearing of the pellagrous dermatitis.

Niagara (naɪˈægərə). [The name of a N. American river, flowing from Lake Erie into Lake Ontario, on which there is a famous waterfall.]

1. A cataract, torrent, deluge.

1841 F. A. KEMBLE *Let.* 28 Dec. in *Rec. Later Life* (1882) II. 153 Such a Niagara of information did surely never pour from the lips of mortal man! **1861** T. L. PEACOCK *Gryll Gr.* xiv, That Niagara of sound under which it is now the fashion to bury it. **1872** RUSKIN *Fors Clav.* (1896) I. xxiv. 492 Phlegethon falls into the abyss in a Niagara of blood. **1894** *Westm. Gaz.* 13 June 3/2 There is a deluge,..a very Niagara of concerts. **1909** *Chambers's Jrnl.* June 383/1 In the savage blizzards of a frozen Sahara this [ice-]drift becomes a roaring, hissing, blinding Niagara of snow, rising hundreds of feet into the air. **1912** I. S. COBB *Back Home* 321 Rivers of red pop had already flowed, Niagaras of lager beer and stick gin had been swallowed up. **1931** A. HUXLEY *Let.* 24 Aug. (1969) 352 We are reading *Monte Cristo* aloud. What a book! I had never read it before: it is a kind of Niagara! **1970** P. LAURIE *Scotland Yard* iii. 86 A Niagara of tinted hair. **1974** *Times* 9 Jan. 6/5 Mr Nixon was swept towards what the White House once called a 'Niagara' of accusations last spring.

2. *U.S.* (See quot.)

1864 SALA in *Daily Tel.* 10 June, One of her 'Niagaras' or 'cataract curls'—the name given to the shower of true or false ringlets the ladies are in the habit of wearing at the backs of their heads.

Hence **Niagara** *v.*, *intr.* to pour in a deluge. (In quot. stressed *nia'gara.*) Also **Niagaˈrean, Niagaˈrian** *adjs.*, resembling Niagara.

1799 SOUTHEY *St. Gualberto* xxii, The fountain streams.. Had niagara'd o'er the quadrangle. **1835** *Court Mag.* VI. 242/2 Retribution rushed upon me fiercely like a Niagarean torrent. **1839** REYNOLDS *Pickw. Abroad* lvi, A Niagarian fall of tears, and a Vesuvian eruption of sighs. **1882** J. G. HOLYOAKE in *19th Cent.* July 95 The Niagarian flood of denunciation which was poured out.

niaise, obs. form of NYAS.

‖**niaiserie** (nɪˈeɪzərɪ). Also 7 -ery. [F. *niaiserie*, f. *niais(e* simple, foolish.] Simplicity; foolishness; an instance of this.

1657 J. SERGEANT *Schism Dispach't* To Rdr. A iv b, The one makes his advantage from *niaisery* and shyness, the other from boldness. **1697** —— *Solid Philos.* a 6 Out of Niaiserie and Shamefastness. **1832** *Philol. Mus.* I. 651 As if a universal deluge of niaiserie..had whelmed the island. **1851** *Fraser's Mag.* XLIV. 632 The recollection of the little niaiseries of style in which he indulged..has vanished.

nialamide (naɪˈæləmaɪd). *Pharm.* [f. the proprietary name *Niamid* by insertion of *-al.*] A crystalline hydrazide, $C_{16}H_{18}N_4O_2$, which is a monoamine oxidase inhibitor used as an antidepressant.

1959 *Proc. Soc. Exper. Biol. & Med.* CI. 832 (*heading*) Pharmacological studies with nialamide, a new antidepressant agent. **1960** A. CARLSSON et al. in J. R. Vane et al. *Adrenergic Mechanisms* 434 Fig. 1 shows the action of nialamide, which is a very potent and long-acting monoamine oxidase inhibitor though its action sets in fairly slowly. **1971** *Brit. Med. Bull.* XXVII. 28/2 First nialamide ..and then tranylcypromine..began to be used for the treatment of depression.

Niam-Niam (ˈniːəmˈniːəm). [Dinka, lit. 'great eaters'.] = ZANDE.

1861 J. PETHERICK *Egypt, Soudan, & Central Africa* xxvi. 469 Attached to the girdle, a strong leather sheath containing a knife, hilt downwards, is worn by every Neam Nam. *Ibid.* 473 The Neam Nam recognise no superior chief; but, like the Dôr, the tribe is divided into numerous chieftainships. **1873** E. E. FREWER tr. *Schweinfurth's Heart of Africa* II. xiii. 3 The name Niam-niam is..so universally incorporated into the Arabic of the Soudan, that it seems unadvisable to substitute for it the word 'Zandey', the name by which the people are known among themselves. **1891** A. W. BUCKLAND *Anthrop. Studies* v. 59 In Africa, the typical home of the stalwart Negro..we find the Bushman and Hottentot in the South, and the Akkas and Niam-Niams in the centre, very small in stature and yellow in colour. **1902** *Encycl. Brit.* XXXI. 230/1 The Niam-Niam, or Zandeh people, as they call themselves..are now found to stretch, with interruptions, from the White Nile above the Sobat confluence to the Shari affluent of Lake Chad. **1931** J. G. LEYBURN *Handbk. Ethnography* 176/2 Niam-Niam. Between the Welle, a tributary of the Ubangi, and the Nile. **1966** R. & D. MORRIS *Men & Apes* viii. 238 The Niams-Niams, apparently, still adorn themselves with colobus monkey skins wound round the waist.

‖**niaouli** (niaˈuli). [Native name.] An evergreen tree, *Melaleuca quinquenervia*, of the family Myrtaceæ, native to New Caledonia. Also *attrib.* and *transf.*, a personification of New Caledonia.

1921 *Public Opinion* 29 July 109/2 A mat of pandanus leaves served for his sail and a paddle of niaouli wood for its helm. **1943** *Amer. Speech* XVIII. 14 It would be.. impossible to root them [*sc.* English words] out of the Niaouli's everyday language. *Ibid.* 15 Our expression 'to go bush' has its counterpart in Niaouli pidgin... Niaouli is the name of a tree which..has come to be regarded as a national symbol [of New Caledonia]. **1965** *Univ. Iowa Stud. Nat. Hist.* XX. VII. 52 (*caption*) This frequent burning maintains the enormous area of fire-resistant niaouli.

nias(se, obs. forms of NYAS.

niata (nɪˈɑːtə). [From some S. American language.] An abnormally small variety of cattle, found in South America. Also *attrib.*

1868 DARWIN *Anim. & Pl.* I. iii. 90 A niata bull and cow invariably produce niata calves. **1872** —— *Orig. Spec.* vii. (ed. 6) 177 At these times the Niatas perish, if not fed by their owners. **1879** tr. *De Quatrefages' Hum. Spec.* 71 The niata will unite indifferently in both senses with the ordinary ox.

Hence **ˈniatism**, a change or tendency towards a dwarfed condition in cattle or other animals.

1895 *Funk's Stand. Dict.*

niatt, obs. form of NEAT *sb.*

nib (nɪb), *sb.*[1] Also 7–8 nibb. [Corresponds in form and meaning to Fris. *nib*, MDu. *nib* (*nyb*), MLG. and MDa. *nibbe*, Norw. *nibba*, *nibb(e*, but is perh. only a later spelling of NEB *sb.*; in Sc. dial. the vowel is indistinct and there is no real difference in pronunciation between *neb* and *nib.*]

1. The beak or bill of a bird; the proboscis of an insect; the nose of a person. = NEB *sb.* 1, 2.

For Sc. examples (18–19th cent.) see *Eng. Dial. Dict.*

1585 HIGINS tr. *Junius' Nomencl.* 53 *Rostrum*, the bill, beake or nib. **1658** ROWLAND tr. *Moufet's Theat. Ins.* 1090 Their nib is sharper, they bite more, and tickle lesse. **1676** *Lond. Gaz.* No. 1076/2 Their Claws were like those of Indian Hens, Nibs crooked like Parrots.

2. a. The point of a pen. = NEB 3.

1611 MIDDLETON & DEKKER *Roaring Girl* III. ii, Let not you and I be tost On Lawiers pens; they haue sharpe nibs. **1676** MOXON *Print Letters* 9 Its Nib strikes a Lean stroke. **1786** [see PEN *sb.*[1] 4]. **1795** WOLCOT (P. Pindar) *Convention Bill* Wks. 1812 III. 376 The pen That with its lever nib of brass Tries from his power to heave Dundas. **1829** MRS. TROLLOPE in *Friendships Miss Mitford* (1882) I. vii. 193 Had I but the tenth of an inch of the nib of your pen, what pictures I might draw. **1865** *Chambers's Encycl.* VII. 368/1 Fitting small metal or even ruby points to the nib of the quill-pen. **1875** KNIGHT *Dict. Mech.* 1656/2 A pen with a broad flat nib made for marking packages.

b. A separate pen-point, now usually made of steel, intended for fitting into a pen-holder.

1837 WHITTOCK, etc. *Compl. Bk. Trades* (1842) 373 Steel nibs. **1840** *Penny Cycl.* XVII. 397/2 A few words upon the manufacture of 'quill nibs'. **1853** URE *Dict. Arts* (ed. 4) II. 367 Another class of workers who..make it concave, if a nib, and form the barrel, if a barrel pen. **1899** *N. & Q.* 9th Ser. III. 365 Nowadays nearly all ask for 'nibs' when they require pens.

c. Each of the divisions of a pen-point.

1840 *Penny Cycl.* XVII. 398/2 Pens made of gold with a small ruby at each nib seem to be perfect. **1875** KNIGHT *Dict. Mech.* 1525/1 Pens have usually two nibs, but Perry's have three.

3. a. The point of anything; a peak, tip, projecting part, or pointed extremity. = NEB *sb.* 3 b.

1713 DERHAM *Phys.-Theol.* x. *note*, Travellers cut the Nib off it, and presently a Spout of Water runs out from it, as clear as Crystal. **1788** SMEATON in *Phil. Trans.* LXXIX. 4 Its inside surface is made to agree with that of the horizon by means of a small thin nib of brass. **1826** in Hone *Every-day Bk.* (1827) II. 691 The nib of a jockey's cap. **1875** KNIGHT *Dict. Mech.* 1525/1 *Nib*,..2. A separate adjustable limb of a permutation key. *Ibid.*, *Nib*,..4 The point of a crow-bar. **1879** *Cassell's Techn. Educ.* IV. 413/1 There will also be a little swelling on the other end of the [spoon] handle, called the 'nib'. **1901** J. BLACK *Carp. & Builder Series: Slating & Tiling* 13 The ordinary pantile..is provided on the underside with a small projection known as a nib. **1940** *Chambers's Techn. Dict.* 578/1 *Nib*, a small projection, sometimes continuous, formed on the under-side at the top of each tile, enabling the tile to be hung on battens. **1955** *Railway Mag.* May 307/2 The main feature of the detachable nibs in the relay baseboards is that disconnection points are available without the necessity of providing independent terminal boards for each relay. **1962** *Gloss. Terms Glass Industry* (*B.S.I.*) 43 *Nib*, a small protrusion at the corner of a piece of flat glass due to faulty cutting. **1968** *Gloss. Formwork Terms* (*B.S.I.*) 17 *Kicker* (nib), a small concrete upstand cast above floor level to position wall or column forms for the next lift and to assist the prevention of grout loss.

†**b.** = NEB *sb.* 3 c. *Obs. rare*⁻¹.

a **1722** LISLE *Husb.* (1752) 115 The outward part of the nib ..sends forth the root.

4. *dial.* **a.** *pl.* The two short handles projecting from the shaft or sned of a scythe.

1673 *Col. Rec. Plymouth* (1856) V. 132 One gun, and one pair of old wheels, and one sythe & nibbs 01–00–00. [**1703** *Providence Rec.* (1894) VI. 226 Two sithes, sneds, nebbs, & Rings.] **1843** *Richardson's Historian's Table-bk., Leg. Div.* I. 213 A rest on the nibs, after sharping, was occasionally allowed [to the mower]. **1854–** in many dial. gloss. (Yks., Nhp., Worc., Glouc., Wilts., etc.). **1894** *Northumbld. Gloss.* s.v. *Scythe*, The handles projecting from the sned are called nibs.

b. The pole or draught-tree of an ox-cart or timber-carriage.

1808 *Beverley Lighting Act* 18 If any person..shall draw any timber..through any of the aforesaid streets..without any nib or carriage. **1886** ELWORTHY *W. Som. Word-bk.* 509 Two very high wheels, having an arched axle between them, with the nib proper projecting at right angles to it.

5. *pl.* The small pieces into which cocoa-beans are reduced by crushing.

1842 *Penny Cycl.* XXIV. 313/2 The simplest and best form is that of the seeds roughly crushed, termed cocoa-nibs. **1862** *Chamb. Encycl.* III. 108/2 When C[ocoa] nibs are infused with water like coffee, they yield a highly palatable beverage. **1878** *Encycl. Brit.* VI. 102/1 The seeds are reduced to the form of nibs, which are separated from the shells or husks by the action of a powerful fan blast.

6. A lump or knot in wool or raw silk.

1879 *Cassell's Techn. Educ.* IV. 378/2 Large quantities of this noil are exported to the Continent, where the.. machinery is better adapted to card and open out the small nibs which it contains. **1887** *Encycl. Brit.* XXII. 62/1 The silk..passes through a slit which is sufficiently wide to pass the filament but stops the motion when a thick lump or nib is presented.

7. A speck of solid matter in a coat of paint or varnish.

1940 in *Chambers's Techn. Dict.* **1958** *Listener* 11 Sept. 399/1 You can now tidy it [*sc.* the undercoat of paint] up with fine sandpaper—just enough to remove any dust nibs or brush marks. **1965** W. N. LAPPER in *Applic. Surface Coatings* (Oil & Colour Chemists' Assoc.) iii. 37 A coagulation of pigment can cause 'nibs' or bittiness in the film. **1968** *Pract. Motorist* Feb. 611/3 Once the first coat is fully dry rub it down very gently with wet-or-dry (grade 320) to remove any 'nibs' and runs.

†**nib**, *sb.*[2] *Obs. rare.* [See quots.]

a **1653** GOUGE *Comm. Heb.* iv. 13 They who..grow not.. in knowledge, may well be accounted babes, or young novices, or fresh-men (as they say in Schools), or nibs, or pages. [**1886** WILLIS & CLARK *Cambridge* III. 304 In King's College, Cambridge,..every new scholar being, on his arrival, looked after by an older one (his 'chum'), who was responsible for his 'nib's' strict observance of all college discipline.]

nib, *sb.*[3] *slang.* A gentleman.

1812 J. H. VAUX *Flash Dict.*, *Nib*, a gentleman or person of the higher order. **1834** H. AINSWORTH *Rookwood* III. v. (1878) 189 He's a rank nib. **1936** WODEHOUSE *Laughing Gas* viii. 81 You don't run to an English butler in Hollywood unless you are a pretty prominent nib.

Hence **ˈniblike** *a.*, **ˈnibsome** *a.*

1834 H. AINSWORTH *Rookwood* III. v, All my togs were so niblike and splash. **1839** REYNOLDS *Pickw. Abroad* xxvi. 224 Betray his pals in a nibsome game.

nib, *v.*[1] *Obs.* exc. *dial.* Also 6 knib. [App. related to NIBBLE *v.*; connexion with NIB *sb.*[1] is doubtful. Sense 4 may be a different word.]

†**1.** *trans.* To peck, pick, prick. Also *fig.* *Obs.*

1558 W. FORREST *Grysilde Seconde* 81 Theye nybbed Christes faithe after their pleasure. **1575** TURBERV. *Faulconrie* 360 Yee shall discerne the crampgout by your hawkes holding of hir one foote upon the other, and by hir often knibbing and iobbing of hir foote with hir beake. **1645** T. HILL *Olive Branch* (1648) 20 Conscience nibs thee, follows and dogs thee from place to place.

2. *intr.* and *trans.* To nibble. Now *dial.*

1613 DENNIS *Secrets Angling* I. xiv, When the Fish begins to nib and byte. **1720** *Humourist* 183, I had kept the Neat's Tongue..and every now and then I nibb'd a Bit on't. **1876** *Mid-Yorksh. Gloss.*, *Nib*, to nibble. **1888** *Cornh. Mag.* Nov. 530 You has to let 'em [geese] nib by the road.

†**3.** *intr.* To pick or pluck, in order to loosen.

1659 C. NOBLE *Inexpediency of Exped.* 15 That makes their fingers so busie, and to nib so about the Knot that ties up and is the very Bond of our Peace.

4. *slang.* To nab, to catch.

1775 in Farmer *Musa Pedestris* (1896) 54 For nibbing-culls I always hate. **1812** J. H. VAUX *Flash Dict.*, *Nibb'd*, taken in custody. **1870** ROBSON *Evangeline* 357 (E.D.D.), Up stackered Larty for a blaw, Fair on Ham's jug'lar nibb'd him.

nib, *v.*[2] Also 9 knib. [f. NIB *sb.*[1]] *trans.* To adapt the point of (a pen) for writing; to mend the nib of.

1757 MRS. GRIFFITH *Lett. Henry & Frances* (1767) IV. 28 Come, spread your Paper, sharpen your Wit, nib your Pen, and away with it. **1822** PRAED *Lillian* Poems 1866 I. 73, I drink my coffee and nib my quill. **1865** G. M. CRAIK *Winifred's Wooing* (1879) 85 [He] was..mending a pen for himself, and nibbing it with critical exactness.

transf. **1850** J. HAMILTON *Mem. Lady Colquhoun* iv. 134 It would be easy for an ordinary critic to..nib into a sharper paradox the pungent aphorism. **1885** MEREDITH *Diana* i, The sentence wants more working to line the thought; or, if you will, the thought to nib expression.

nibbed (nɪbd), *ppl. a.* [f. NIB *sb.*[1] + -ED[2]: cf. MDu. *genybt*, LG. *-nibbd*, MDa. *nibbet.*] Having a nib or point. Also ***hard-*, *long-nibbed***, etc.

1677 MIÈGE *Gt. Fr. Dict.* II. s.v., A hard nibbed pen. **1794** *Rigging & Seamanship* I. 55 *Nibbed-Hooks* are of iron, used to hang the yarn on. **1829** HOGG *Sheph. Cal.* I. 20 He had a large lang-nibbit staff in his hand. **1858** MRS. OLIPHANT *Laird of Norlaw* I. 215 It was a new pen, sharply nibbed, such as the minister loved.

nibber ('nɪbə(r)). *rare*⁻¹. [f. NIB *v.*² + -ER¹.] An instrument for nibbing or pointing a pen.

1886 *Athenæum* 31 July 138/2 A description [is added] of the pen or reed itself, the penknife and the nibber, the ruler, the ink, and the inkstand.

nibble, obs. or dial. variant of NIPPLE.

nibble ('nɪb(ə)l), *sb.* [f. the vb.]

1. The act or fact of nibbling; an instance of this, esp. on the part of a fish at a bait.

1658 ROWLAND tr. *Moufet's Theat. Ins.* 1102 They seek for the most tender places, and will not attempt the harder places with their nibble. **1820** W. IRVING *Sketch Bk.* I. 61 [To] fish all day.. though he should not be encouraged by a single nibble. **1867** F. FRANCIS *Angling* iii. (1880) 51 When you see a nibble do not be in a hurry.

fig. **1837** HT. MARTINEAU *Soc. Amer.* II. 114 To prevent any escape by a nibble in this circle. **1853** R. S. SURTEES *Sponge's Sp. Tour* (1893) 21 The ladies, to do them justice, are never at all suspicious about men—especially men on the 'nibble'.

2. A quantity (of grass) sufficient for a nibble.

1838 FR. A. KEMBLE *Resid. in Georgia* (1863) 46 The sheep perambulate also, in earnest search of a nibble of fresh herbage. **1860** MRS. GASKELL *Sylvia's Lovers* xii, There'll niver be a nibble o' grass to be seen this two month.

b. Pasturage, grass. Cf. BITE *sb.* 2 b.

1875 BLACKMORE *Alice Lorraine* III. v. 67 The moss had come over the herbage, and the sweet nibble of the sheep was souring.

nibble ('nɪb(ə)l), *v.* Also 5 nebyll, 6 *Sc.* nybbill, 6–7 (g)nible. [Corresponds in form and meaning to LG. *nibbelen*, also *gnibbelen*, *knibbelen*, = Du. *knibbelen* 'rodere, mussitare, altercari' (Kilian), app. an ablaut-variant of *knabbelen*, KNABBLE *v.* The immediate source in Eng. is not clear.]

1. a. *trans.* To take little bites of (a thing), to bite away little by little.

1500–20 DUNBAR *Poems* xxxiii. 93 Thay nybbillit him with noyis and cry. **1548** ELYOT, *Derodo*, to gnawe or gnibble. **1591** SPENSER *Virg. Gnat* 80 Some, clambring.. Nibble the bushie shrubs. **1649** G. DANIEL *Trinarch., Hen. IV*, ccxlviii, Like a Spring-taught Snayle, Was crauling to haue Nibbled the fresh leafe. **1712** STEELE *Spect.* No. 431 ¶3, I then nibbled all the red Wax of our last Ball-Tickets. **1756–7** tr. *Keysler's Trav.* (1760) I. 68 One sees the trouts and other fish.. nibbling the calves and ox livers with which they are fed. **1817** KEATS *Sleep & Poetry* 254 All tenderest birds there.. Nibble the little cupped flowers. **1865** KNIGHT *Passages Work. Life* III. iii. 56, I look upon the downs where flocks are peacefully nibbling the thymy grass. **1871** DARWIN *Desc. Man* I. iii. 75 Horses nibble, and cows lick, each other on any spot which itches.

transf. c **1460** *Towneley Myst.* xxx. 537 The meyn shalle ye nebyll, And I shalle syng the trebill. **1847** L. HUNT *Men, Women, & Bks.* I. ix. 162 [He] would nibble you the beginnings of half the odes of his favourite poet.

b. With complement: To strip *from*, take *off* or *away*, make *bare*, by means of little bites.

1602 MARSTON *Antonio's Rev.* Prol., Snarling gusts nibble the juyceles leaves From the nak't shuddring branch. **1617** MIDDLETON & ROWLEY *Fair Quarrel* v. i, All my baits nibbled off, And not the fish caught. **1796** H. HUNTER tr. *St. Pierre's Stud. Nat.* (1799) I. 591 They frequently nibble away the bait without touching the hook. **1867** TROLLOPE *Chron. Barset* I. xxxvii. 321 [He] nibbled off the end of a cigar, preparatory to lighting it. **1887** T. HARDY *Woodlanders* vii, The bases of the smaller trees were nibbled bare by rabbits.

c. To bring *into* (some state or form) by this means. Also *fig.*

1837 SYD. SMITH *Wks.* (1859) II. 280/2 If the Foreign Secretary were to retire, we should no longer be nibbling ourselves into disgrace on the coast of Spain. **1849** R. CURZON *Monast. Levant* viii. 100 The paint brush is made by chewing the end of a reed till it is reduced to filaments and then nibbling it into a proper form.

d. In lens-making: (see NIBBLING *vbl. sb.* 2).

e. To produce by nibbling.

1867 A. J. EVANS *St. Elmo* xxi. 296 Just see what a hole the pretty little wretch has nibbled in my new Swiss muslin dress!

2. a. *intr.* To take little bites; to eat or feed in this fashion. †Also const. *on*, *with*.

1582 STANYHURST *Æneis* Ded. (Arb.) 3 Not onlye by gnibling vpon thee outward ryne of a.. historie, but also by groaping thee pyth. **1643** MILTON *Divorce* Introd., Wks. 1851 IV. 7 To let them play and nibble with the bait a while. **1678** DRYDEN *All for Love* Pref., Ess. (ed. Ker) I. 193 Sucking critics, who would fain be nibbling ere their teeth are come. **1746** SMOLLETT *Reproof* 216 Th' unnumber'd shoals of smaller fry, That nibble round, I pity and defy. **1794** COWPER *Needless Alarm* 38 Some [sheep] with soft bosom pressed The herb as soft, while nibbling strayed the rest. **1867** F. FRANCIS *Angling* iii. 64 He cannot make up his mind to leave it, so he nibbles, and nibbles. **1878** A. H. MARKHAM *Gt. Frozen Sea* ii. 28 The 'wily cod'.. could not even be induced to 'nibble'.

b. Const. *at* (a thing). Also in fig. contexts, and *absol.*

1630 DEKKER *2nd Pt. Honest Wh.* I. i, His teeth water to be nibbling at my gold. **1660** PEPYS *Diary* 4 Nov., Mr. Mills did begin to nibble at the Common Prayer, by saying 'Glory be to the Father'. **1700** C. NESSE *Antid. Armin.* (1827) 134 The seed of the serpent may nibble at the heels of the seed of the woman. **1873** EARLE *Philol. Eng. Tongue* §359 Latin scholarship was, however, continually nibbling away at these monuments of the French reign. **1877** M. M. GRANT *Sun-Maid* viii, Nibbling at the sprouting edges of the path. **1921** W. J. LOCKE *Mountebank* xvi. 208 Moignon was in touch, on his behalf, with powerful American agencies... Moignon had said: 'They are nibbling for the winter.' **1973** *Times* 20 Mar. 21/3 Since the Broadspeed Turbo Bullit.. was announced in January, motor manufacturers have been nibbling at the idea.

c. To carp (*at* something), to make trifling objections or criticisms.

a **1591** H. SMITH *Serm.* (1592) 34 She will be nibling at his praier, and at his studie, and at his meditations, till she haue tyred his deuotions. **1641** MILTON *Reform.* II. Wks. 1851 III. 52, I need not say to nibble, but openly to argue against the King's Supremacie. **1699** BENTLEY *Phal.* 29 He will nibble at some Passages of this Section, to shew his own great Wit. **1719** J. WELWOOD *Pref. to Rowe's Lucan* 41 To humour the deprav'd taste of the Age, by nibbling at Scripture, or depreciating things in themselves Sacred. **1788** COWPER *Priv. Corr.* (1824) II. 143, I think I can give you an honest answer to your question, and without the least wish to nibble. **1824** BYRON *Juan* XVI. v, Who nibble, scribble, quibble, he Quiets at once with 'quia impossibile'. **1867** SWINBURNE *Ess. & Stud.* (1875) 162 The small troubles of spirits that nibble and quibble about beliefs living or dead. **1878** E. WHITE *Life in Christ* (ed. 3) Pref. 4 Reviewers have nibbled at phrases and special criticisms, but have avoided the principal questions.

d. *Cricket.* To play (indecisively) at a ball bowled outside the off stump.

1926 P. F. WARNER *Fight for Ashes* 16 Bardsley.. showed a distinct weakness in nibbling at good-length balls outside the off-stump. **1932** E. BLUNDEN *Face of England* 71 'Tom's out.' 'He shouldn't have nibbled at that.'

†**3. a.** *intr.* To fidget or play *with* the fingers. (Also said of the fingers.) *Obs. rare.*

1570 LEVINS *Manip.* 113/25 To Nibble with the fingers, *gesticulari*. **1573** BARET *Alv.* s.v., To nibble with the fingers, as vnmanerly boyes do with their pointes when they are spoken to. **1577** STANYHURST *Descr. Irel.* in *Holinshed* VI. 32 His fingers began to nibble, his teeth to grin.

b. *trans.* To fidget or play with (a thing).

1829 HOGG *Sheph. Cal.* vii, The hem of her jerkin, which she was nibbling with her hands.

4. *slang.* To catch, nab; to pilfer.

1608 MIDDLETON *Trick to catch Old One* I. iv, The Roague has spied me now, hee nibled me finely once, too. **1812** J. H. VAUX *Flash Dict.*, *Nibble*, to pilfer trifling articles, not having spirit to touch any thing of consequence. **1843** MONCRIEFF *Scamps of London* III. i, You are spliced—nibbled at last—well, I wish you joy. **1851** D. JERROLD *St. Giles* viii, A nice job I've had to nibble him.

nibbled ('nɪb(ə)ld), *ppl. a.* [f. NIBBLE *v.* + -ED¹.] That has been nibbled or cropped.

1865 R. D. BLACKMORE *Cradock Nowell* (1866) I. viii. 68 Over the nibbled sward.. came wandering the lightest foot that ever passed. **1905** J. B. FIRTH *Highways Derbyshire* viii. 119 The Dove flows between closely nibbled hill slopes. **1949** *U.S. Employment Service, Dict. Occup. Titles* 891 May file and grind excess metal and rough edges of nibbled parts to specified dimensions.

nibble-nip, *v.* [f. NIBBLE *sb.* or *v.* + NIP *v.*¹] *intr.* To give a nibble, a trifling nip (only *fig.*). So **nibble-nipped** *ppl. a.*

1883 G. MEREDITH *Poems & Lyrics of Joy of Earth* 26 Haggard Wisdom, stately once, Leers fantastical and trips: Allegory drums the sconce, Impiousness nibblenips. **1937** *Sunday Times* 10 Jan. 8/3 The conversation distinguished, sedate, and rather wintry (even Newman had at first felt nibble-nipped) of the Oriel Common Room.

nibbler ('nɪblə(r)). [f. NIBBLE *v.* + -ER¹.]

1. a. One who or that which nibbles, in various senses of the vb.

1598 FLORIO, *Rosicara*, a mouse, a rat, a nibbler. **1599** SHAKS., etc. *Pass. Pilgr.* iv, The tender nibler would not touch the bait. **1674** HICKMAN *Quinquart. Hist.* (ed. 2) 21 There is a late nibler at this Learned Doctor. a **1717** PARNELL *Battle of Frogs & Mice* III. 169 Then earth's inhabitants, the niblers, shake. **1759** WARBURTON *Lett. to Hurd* cxxx. (1809) 286 These are nibblers at the outside. **1800** HURDIS *Fav. Village* 195 Rich furze, erewhile By the last fleecy nibbler neatly trimmed. **1812** J. H. VAUX *Flash Dict.*, *Nibbler*, a pilferer or petty thief. **1867** F. FRANCIS *Angling* iii. 60 Although somewhat of a nibbler,.. the bream will almost always take the bait in the end.

b. *Engin.* A type of metal-cutting tool in which a rapidly reciprocating punch knocks out a line of overlapping small holes from sheet or plate.

1939 *Jrnl. R. Aeronaut. Soc.* XLIII. 144 Practically all of the standard means of cutting are used in all factories. These are the oxy-acetylene torch,.. the nibbler; the saw; and the uni-shears. **1958** *Engineering* 28 Mar. 409/2 A nibbler for sheet up to 16 s.w.g. **1961** *Aeroplane & Astronautics* CI. 272/3 On display is a complete range of tools, including drills, screwdrivers, nutrunners, grinders, rivet and bolt millers, nibblers and shears.

2. *U.S.* The Blue Perch (*Ctenolabrus adspersus*).

1859 BARTLETT *Dict. Amer.* s.v. *Burgall*, Other names.. are Nibbler, from its nibbling off the bait when thrown for other fishes, Blue Perch and Conner.

nibbling ('nɪblɪŋ), *vbl. sb.* [f. as prec. + -ING¹.]

1. The action of the verb, in various senses; an instance of this: a portion nibbled.

1590 NASHE *Pasquil's Apol.* I. A iv b, I tooke another nybling like a Minew about Bezaes Icones. **1672** H. MORE *Brief Reply* 46 There are some little nibblings and quibblings at my Transition which concludes this first Chapter. **1707** J. STEVENS tr. *Quevedo's Com. Wks.* (1709) 327 All this is but nibling of Fleas. **1738** *The Briton Described* 49 All the Nibblings in the World shall never be able to devour the Immortality of a Name. **1813** SIR. R. WILSON *Priv. Diary* (1862) I. 271 The promise of the Turkish nibblings being restored to Moldavia. **1893** SELOUS *Trav. S.E. Africa* 17 Mere surface nibblings.

2. *techn.* The gradual removal of small portions from the edge of a piece of glass, to reduce it to a circular form before it is ground for a lens.

1850 HOLTZAPFFEL *Turning* III. 1265 The process which is called shanking or nibbling is continued until the glasses are made circular.

nibbling ('nɪblɪŋ), *ppl. a.* [f. as prec. + -ING².]

1. That nibbles or takes little bites.

1602 MIDDLETON *Blurt, Master-Constable* IV. ii, The nibbling mouse is not asleep. **1624** QUARLES *Sion's Elegies* iii. 18 The treach'rous Angler strikes his nibbling pray. **1713** C'TESS WINCHILSEA *Misc. Poems* 292 When nibbling Sheep at large pursue their Food. **1762** BEATTIE *Pigm. & Cranes* 156 Careless of nibbling bills. **1799** SOUTHEY *Filbert*, The mouse Gnawing with nibbling tooth the shell's defence. **1819** WORDSW. *Waggoner* II. 138 You might have heard a nibbling mouse. **1868** MORRIS *Earthly Par.* (1870) I. I. 164 Nor took [he] heed Of how the nibbling dace might feed Upon the loose ends of his bait.

transf. **1823** LAMB *Elia* Ser. II. *Old Margate Hoy*, The nibbling pickpockets of your patience.

b. (See quot.)

1889 G. FINDLAY *Eng. Railway* 112 An interesting feature of this shop is the 'nibbling machine', designed for cutting out the 'throws' in the cranks.

2. Carping, captious.

1696 tr. *Du Mont's Voy. Levant* Pref. 5, I cou'd easily dispatch such nibbling Criticks. **1711** HEARNE *Collect.* (O.H.S.) III. 253, I say nothing about the nibling Criticks. **1887** H. MORLEY *Introd. T. L. Peacock's Crotchet C.* 8 The nibbling censure of the men whose wit is tainted with ill-humour.

3. Produced by nibbling.

1824 BYRON *Juan* XVI. xx, A mouse Whose little nibbling rustle will embarrass Most people.

Hence **'nibblingly** *adv.*

1847 in WEBSTER; hence in later Dicts.

'nibby, *sb. Sc.* [f. NIB *sb.*¹ 3.] A staff with a hook at the end. Also ***nibby staff***.

1812 GLASS *Cal. Parnassus* 53 (E.D.D.), By help o' their nibbies they fittet it weel. **1866** CARLYLE *Remin.* (1881) II. 260 Leaning on her nibby staff (a fine hazel, cut and polished from the Drumlanrig woods). **1886** J. RUSSELL *Remin. Yarrow* vi. 170 Two or three shepherds.. had to use their nibbies unmercifully.

'nibby, *a. rare*⁻¹. [f. NIB *sb.*¹ 6.] Of wool, etc.: Full of nibs or knots.

1879 *Cassell's Techn. Educ.* IV. 378/2 The 'noil'.. is valuable to the woollen cloth-maker.., but it is often very nibby and difficult to card.

nibcocked ('nɪbˌkɒkt), *a. rare*⁻¹. [f. NIB *sb.*¹ + COCK *sb.*¹ 20 + -ED².] ? Having a penis like the point of a pen.

1939 DYLAN THOMAS *Let.* Mar. (1966) 226 The English poets now are such a pinlegged, nibcocked, paperhearted crowd you could blow them down with one bellow out of a done lung.

nibful ('nɪbfʊl). *rare.* [f. NIB *sb.*¹ + -FUL.] As much as a nib can hold.

1930 V. WOOLF *Writer's Diary* 29 Apr. (1953) 158, I have just finished, with this very nib-ful of ink, the last sentence of *The Waves*.

'niblick, *sb.* [Of obscure formation.] A golf club having a small, round, heavy head, used when some force is necessary to take the ball out of a bad lie. Also *attrib.*

1857 H. B. FARNIE *Golfer's Manual* (1947) iii. 18 It is called a *Niblick*. **1862** *Rambling Rem. Golf* 18 The Niblick, or Track-Iron, is of very important service when the ball lies in a narrow cart-rut. *Ibid.*, The faces.. of the spoons, sand-iron, and niblick are hollowed or 'spooned'. **1886** H. G. HUTCHINSON *Hints on Golf* xiii. 33 In the typical niblick shot the ball lies in a heel-mark or other cup in the sand, with the face of the bunker in front. **1894** BLACK *Highl. Cousins* I. 35, I smashed my iron niblick clean in two. **1909** *Bystander* 13 Oct. 90/2 Herd.. saved an apparently lost hole by a most masterly niblick pitch. **1955** R. BROWNING *Hist. Golf* 145 Even the niblicks were originally wooden clubs: the first iron-headed niblicks were excessively short in the blade. **1961** M. SPARK *Prime of Miss Jean Brodie* v. 141 Sandy gave a hack with her niblick.

'niblick, *v. Golf.* [f. the sb.] *trans.* To hit (a ball) with a niblick.

1909 *Westm. Gaz.* 15 Jan. 4/2 If bunkered.. he would have to niblick the ball out sideways.

Nibmar, NIBMAR ('nɪbmɑː(r)). [f. the initials of '*no independence before majority African rule*'.] The policy of opposing recognition of the minority government which proclaimed the independence of Rhodesia in 1965.

1966 *Time* 23 Sept. 31 They demanded that he agree to something called NIBMAR. **1966** *Economist* 17 Dec. 1222/1 They suspect Britain is on the point of making a settlement with Mr Smith which would snatch from them the apple of Nibmar. **1970** *Times* 12 Nov. 6 Britain, he said, had never accepted a commitment to Nibmar from the United Nations.

nib-nib, variant of NEB-NEB.

‖**nibong** ('niːbʌŋ). Also nibung. [Malay *nībung*.] A Malaysian palm, *Oncosperma filamentosa*.

1779 T. FORREST *Voyage to New Guinea* ix. 121 We made very good curry; stewing it with the heart of the aneebong, or cabbage tree. **1783** W. MARSDEN *Hist. Sumatra* 77 The *neebong* or cabbage tree, a species of palm, grows wild in too great abundance to require being cultivated. **1820** J. CRAWFURD *Hist. Indian Archipelago* I. IV. 417 The *nibung* is the true mountain cabbage. **1839** T. J. NEWBOLD *Straits of Malacca* I. iv. 139 Thatch of Atap, and floors of split nibong, called lantei. **1866** *Treas. Bot.* 813/1 O[*ncosperma*] *filamentosa*, the Nibung or Nibong of the Malays, is a very elegant palm [etc.]. **1883** MRS. BISHOP in *Leisure Hour* 23/1 The *nibong*, a species of stemless palm, of which the poorer natives make their houses, and whose..fronds are often from twenty to twenty-two feet in length. **1898** CONRAD *Tales of Unrest* 275 Two tall nibong palms..leaned slightly over the ragged roof. **1907** F. SWETTENHAM *Brit. Malaya* vii. 151 The floor..is of planks, *nibong*, or split bamboos. **1954** R. H. HOLTTUM *Plant Life in Malaya* ii. 22 Other kinds of palm have many trunks; for example, the Sago palm and the Nibong. **1966** *Listener* 6 Oct. 502/3 Nearly 14,000 people live in wooden houses built on stilts of tough nibong palms.

nibs. *slang.* [Origin obscure.] = NABS. Esp. ***his nibs, His Nibs***, an employer, a superior; a self-important person.

1821 D. HAGGART *Life* Gloss. 172. **1846** *Swell's Night Guide* 57 She flokessed his nibs, and hooked it off to his crib. **1877** *Brooklyn Monthly* Oct. 21/2 Salute the hostess by saying: 'Cully, how's his nibs?' **1882** G. W. PECK *Sunshine* 131 A respectable merchant was going to the opera with a friend from the country, when a couple of sirens met them and one said to the other, 'Look at his nibs.' **1903** A. ADAMS *Log Cowboy* xxi. 333 Just to show his royal nibs that he's been thoughtless. **1906** E. DYSON *Fact'ry 'Ands* ii. 18 They're settin' her nibs t'-day. **1906** [see DILLY *a.*[1]]. **1919** G. S. GORDON *Let.* 30 June (1943) 115 We get on to the *Caesar*, and find their nibs strolling the quarterdeck after dinner. **1928** 'BRENT OF BIN BIN' *Up Country* ii. 33 Gifts..including a splendid meerschaum pipe for his Nibs. **1933** M. ALLINGHAM *Sweet Danger* xxi. 218 What if 'Is Nib's boy friends spot us before? **1944** [see HAMPSHIRE b]. **1957** H. CROOME *Forgotten Place* 175, I wish I could just lie on a bed and smoke, like His Nibs. **1967** A. WILSON *No Laughing Matter* I. 21 His father smiled. 'Trust His Nibs to have noticed that deficiency.' **1973** A. HUNTER *Gently French* i. 9 Since when were you on first-name terms with His Nibs? **1974** O. MANNING *Rain Forest* II. i. 141 Her nibs don't like me calling him 'old bugger'. There's a snobby bitch, if you like!

N.I.C., NIC, Nic (nɪk). [Acronym f. the initial letters of '*N*ational *I*ncomes *C*ommission'.] The name of a body giving advice to the government on economic policy. Cf. NICKY *sb.*[2]

1962 *Daily Tel.* 27 July 24/5 He saw the N.I.C. primarily as a means of 'educating public opinion'. **1962** *Times* 27 July 13/2 (*heading*) To Neddy add Nic.

Nicæan (naɪˈsiːən), *a.* and *sb.* [f. *Nicæ-a* (see NICENE) + -AN.] = NICENE *a.* and *sb.*

1706 PHILLIPS (ed. Kersey), *Nicean* or *Nicene*, belonging to that City. **1834** *Penny Cycl.* II. 341/1 Eusebianism was..as victorious in the east as the Nicæan Creed was..in the west. **1860** *Chamb. Encycl.* I. 403/2 Morally the victory was leaning to the side of the Nicæans.

nicampoop, obs. form of NINCOMPOOP.

Nicaragua (nɪkəˈrægjuːə). Also 8 nicar-, nicorago, 9 -guar. [The name of a republic in Central America.] ***Nicaragua wood***, a red dye-wood similar to Brazil wood, obtained from some species of *Cæsalpinia*; peach-wood.

1703 *Lond. Gaz.* No. 3891/3 Nicaragua and Mohogony Wood. **1708** *Ibid.* No. 4408/4 A Parcel of Nicorago Wood. **1725** SLOANE *Jamaica* II. 184 Nicaragua-Wood. This wood is almost as red, and as heavy as the true Brasile. **1756** P. BROWNE *Jamaica* (1789) 17 There are large quantities of logwood, nicarago, and..dry goods and bullion exported from thence. **1809** R. LANGFORD *Introd. Trade* 138 Our returns are..nicaragua wood,..hides, &c. **1845** *Encycl. Metrop.* XIX. 789/1 Its chief products are..turpentine, liquid amber, and Nicaragua wood. **1858** HOMANS *Cycl. Comm.* 1443/1 Nicaragua, or peach-woods, differ greatly in their quality as well as price.

Nicaraguan (nɪkəˈrægjuːən), *a.* and *sb.* [f. NICARAGUA: see -AN.] **A.** *adj.* Of, pertaining to, or characteristic of Nicaragua. **B.** *sb.* A native or inhabitant of Nicaragua.

1847 R. G. DUNLOP *Trav. Central America* iii. 105 The Caroline, a schooner chartered by the Nicaraguan government. **1852** E. G. SQUIER *Nicaragua* I. II. ii. 77 The average rate of duty exacted under the Nicaraguan tariff, is about 21 per cent. ad valorem. *Ibid.* 78 All its inhabitants were, and with the exception of a few.., still are Nicaraguans. **1868** F. BOYLE *Ride across Continent* I. p. xxi, The universal legend of the surrounding peoples—Indians, Caribs, Nicaraguans, and Costa Ricans,—declares the Guatuso race to be distinguished by fair hair and blue eyes. *Ibid.* iii. 120 He stayed with us through all our Nicaraguan experiences. **1884** *Encycl. Brit.* XVII. 478/2 The Nicaraguan fauna differs in few respects from that of the other Central-American states. **1923** LD. CHARNWOOD *Theodore Roosevelt* vii. 151 The Nicaraguan route would be cheaper for a canal. **1934** [see HONDURAN, HONDUREAN *a.* and *sb.*]. **1946** E. A. PEERS *Fool of Love* vii. 121 The Nicaraguan, Rubén Dario, took up the picturesque phrase. **1973** *Time* 25 June 17/1 Nicaraguan Ambassador Guillermo Sevilla-Sacasa said sympathetically [to Julie Nixon Eisenhower]: 'Your father still has one friend.'

†**niccanee.** *Obs.* Also nica-. [Origin obscure.] Some kind of piece-goods formerly imported from India.

1712 *Lond. Gaz.* No. 5051/3 Nillaes, Niccanees, Photaes. **1725** *Ibid.* No. 6388/2 The following Goods, viz... Bejutapants, Chelloes, Lemanees, Nicanees large, Nicanees small. **1727** W. MATHER *Yng. Man's Comp.* 411 Coral, Callicoes, Niccanees, Clouts [etc.]. **1788** CLARKSON *Impol. Slave Tr.* 104 In the second class may be reckoned..Callicoes, Cushtaes, Chintz, Chelloes, Nicamees [*sic*], Negampants.

ˈ**niccolic**, *a. rare.* [f. mod.L. *niccol-um* NICKEL.] Of nickel (see -IC 1 b).

1839 URE *Dict. Arts* 886 The niccolic suroxide has a dirty pale green colour. **1857** MAYNE *Expos. Lex.* 765/2 Double salts produced by the combination of a niccolic with an ammonic salt.

niccoliferous, variant of NICKELIFEROUS.

niccolite (ˈnɪkəlaɪt). *Min.* [f. mod.L. *niccolum* NICKEL + -ITE[1] 4.] Native arsenide of nickel; copper-nickel, nickeline.

1868 DANA *Syst. Min.* (ed. 5) 61 The name..should be written Niccoline, or better Niccolite, in place of Beudant's Nickeline. **1892** *Geol. Survey Canada* V. II. 45 R, Niccolite.., when pure, contains in one hundred parts 44·1 of nickel and 55·9 of arsenic.

niccolo, variant of NICOLO.

ˈ**niccolous**, *a. rare*[−1]. [f. mod.L. *niccol-um* NICKEL.] Of nickel (see -OUS c).

1839 URE *Dict. Arts* 886 The niccolous suroxide of Berzelius is black.

nice, obs. form of NICHE, NIECE.

†**nice**, *sb. Obs. rare.* [f. next.] A foolish or simple person; a fool.

c **1330** R. BRUNNE *Chron. Wace* (Rolls) 14420 After Malgo, Carice þei ches, A nyce þat louede no pes. **1390** GOWER *Conf.* II. 285 That wol with ydel hand reclame His hauk, as many a nyce doth. *c* **1430** *Hymns Virgin* 42 Out of þe wey y wole him lede, And make of him boþe fool and nyce.

nice (naɪs), *a.* Forms: 3–7 **nyce**, (4 **nycy**), 4–5 **nys**, 4–6 (8 *Sc.*) **nyse**, 4–6 **nise**, 5 **neys**, 6 **niece**, *Sc.* **nyss**, 7 **nies**, 9 *dial.* **nist(e, nyst(e**, 3– **nice**. [a. OF. *nice*, *niche* (now only dial.) = Prov. *nesci*, Catal. *neci*, Sp., Pg. *necio*, Pg., It. *nescio*:—L. *nescius*: see NESCIOUS *a.*]

The precise development of the very divergent senses which this word has acquired in English is not altogether clear. In many examples from the 16th and 17th centuries it is difficult to say in what particular sense the writer intended it to be taken.

†**1.** Foolish, stupid, senseless. *Obs.* (Common in 14th and 15th c.) **a.** Of persons.

c **1290** *S. Eng. Leg.* I. 476/493 And bot ich þe [seide] hou heo heold mi lif, for-soþe ich were nice. *c* **1350** *Will. Palerne* 491 Now witterly ich am vn-wis & wonderliche nyce. **1387** TREVISA *Higden* (Rolls) VI. 23 He made þe lady so mad and so nyce þat sche worschipped hym as þe grettest prophete of God Almyȝty. *c* **1450** LOVELICH *Grail* xlii. 73 They seiden he was a fool..and that they sien neuere so nise a man. **1500–20** DUNBAR *Poems* xxxix. 35 Quha that dois deidis of petie..Is haldin a fule, and that full nyce. *c* **1557** ABP. PARKER *Ps.* xlix. 141 As well the wyse as mad and nyse to others leave theyr port.

b. Of actions, etc.

13.. *Gaw. & Gr. Knt.* 323 Þyn askyng is nys, & as þou foly has frayst, fynde þe be-houes. **1390** GOWER *Conf.* III. 180 So is it bot a nyce Sinne Of gold to ben to covoitous. *c* **1460** J. RUSSELL *Bk. Nurture* 508 Cookes..þat provokethe þe peple..þrouȝ nice excesse of such receytes of þe life to make an endynge. **1494** FABYAN *Chron.* VI. ccxvi. 234 A nyce folysshe couenaunte ought nat to be holdin. **1560** ROLLAND *Crt. Venus* I. 739 [Quha did] reheirs ane certane nyse Sermonis, [With argu]mentis, and diuers questionis.

†**2.** Wanton, loose-mannered; lascivious. *Obs.*

a. Of persons.

c **1325** *Poem temp. Edw. II* (Percy) 10 These nyse prestes That playeth her nyse game By nyȝt. ? *a* **1366** CHAUCER *Rom. Rose* 1285 Nyce she was, but she mente Noone harme ne slight in hir entente, But oonely lust & jolyte. *c* **1412** HOCCLEVE *De Reg. Princ.* 1473 Þou woldest han as wantonly þe gyed As doþ þe nycest of hem. *c* **1430** *Hymns Virgin* (1867) 53 Dampned soulis..þat wolen not do wel, but euere be nyce. **1529** RASTELL *Pastyme, Hist. Brit.* (1811) 153 He..put out of his court all nyce and wanton people. **1588** SHAKS. *L.L.L.* III. 24 These are complements, these are humours, these betraie nice wenches that would be betraied without these.

absol. **13..** *E.E. Allit. P.* B. 1359 Hit is not innoghe to þe nice al noȝty þink vse Bot if all þe worlde wyt his wykked dedes. **1414** 26 *Pol. Poems* 60 God ȝeue ȝow grace..To cherische þe goode, and chastyse þe nys.

b. Of conduct, etc.

c **1330** R. BRUNNE *Chron.* (1810) 236 We..telle ȝow oþer tales..of þer nyce ribaudie. **1387** TREVISA *Higden* (Rolls) IV. 67 Þo it was i-doo wiþ foule songes and gestes and iapes and nyse menstralcie. **1423** JAS. I *Kingis Q.* cxxix, Gif thy lufe [be] sett alluterly Of nyce lust, thy trauail is in veyne. *a* **1450** MYRC 61 From nyse iapes and rybawdye Thow moste turne away þyn ye. **1529** MORE *Suppl. Soulys* Wks. 306/2 These nice and wanton wordes doo not verye wel wyth vs. **1587** GOLDING *De Mornay* Ep. Ded., Ouercome with nyce pleasures and fond vanities. **1606** SHAKS. *Ant. & Cl.* III. xiii. 180 When mine houres Were nice and lucky, men did ransome lives Of me for iests.

†**c.** Of dress: Extravagant, flaunting. *Obs.*

c **1430** *Pol. Rel. & L. Poems* (1903) 205 Þou studiest aftir nyce aray, And makist greet cost in cloþing. **1500–20** DUNBAR *Poems* xiv. 9 So nyce array, so strange to thair abbay, Within this land was nevir hard nor sene. **1563** *Homilies* II. *Idolatry* III. (1640) 72 An Image with a nice and wanton apparell and countenance.

†**d.** Very trim, elegant, or smart. *Obs. rare.*

1483 CAXTON *Gold. Leg.* 128 b/1 She chastysed them that were nyce and queynte, sayeng that suche nycete was fylthe of the sowle. *a* **1500** *Mylner of Abynton* in Hazl. *E.P.P.* III. 117 The wenche she was full proper and nyce; Amonge all other she bare great price. **1540** HYRDE tr. *Vives' Instr. Chr. Wom.* (1592) K ij, She shal not..use hir voyce to be feat and nice.

†**3.** Strange, rare, uncommon. *Obs.*

1413 *Pilgr. Sowle* (Caxton 1483) IV. xxiv. 70, I merueyled nought soo moche of no thyng..as I doo now of this nyce syght. **1500–20** DUNBAR *Poems* xxxv. 41 Quhen I awoik, my dreme it was so nyce, Fra every wicht I hid it as a vyce. **1535** COVERDALE *Ecclus.* xliii. 27 For there by straunge wonderous workes, dyuerse maner of nyce beestes and whall fishes. **1555** EDEN *Decades* (Arb.) 143 Frome hens-forth we shal neuer enuye nor reuerence the nyse frutefulnes of Stoidum, Taprobana, or the redde sea.

†**4. a.** Slothful, lazy, indolent. *Obs. rare*[−0].

c **1440** *Promp. Parv.* 355/2 Nyce, *iners.* **1604** R. CAWDREY *Table Alph.*, *Nice*, slow, lazie.

†**b.** Effeminate, unmanly. *Obs. rare.*

1573 BARET *Alv.* s.v., Men thinke they wax nice and effeminate. **1598** FLORIO, *Paranimpha*.., an effeminate, nice, milkesop, puling fellow. **1681** R. L'ESTRANGE *Tully's Offices* 64 Any thing that is Loose, Nice, and Effeminate.

†**c.** Not able to endure much; tender, delicate.

1562 BULLEYN *Bulwark, Sicke Men* 56 Soche be the weake, feble, nise stomackes of many. **1648** *Markham's Housew. Gard.* III. x. (1668) 80 The Bee is tender and nice, and only lives in warm weather. *a* **1674** CLARENDON in *Life* I. (1842) 927/2 He..was of so nice and tender a composition, that a little rain or wind would disorder him. *c* **1710** CELIA FIENNES *Diary* (1888) 26 But these are nice plants and are kept mostly under Glass's, ye aire being too rough for them.

†**d.** Over-refined, luxurious. *Obs.*

1621 BURTON *Anat. Mel.* I. ii. IV. ii. (1651) 145 We..spoile our childrens maners, by our overmuch cockering and nice education. **1720** OZELL *Vertot's Rom. Rep.* II. XII. 221 All the Roman Youth that had..grown effeminate with nice Living, joined and favoured Catiline.

†**5. a.** Coy, shy, (affectedly) modest, reserved. *Obs.*

14.. *Sir Beues* (S) 3199 Maydens at her first Weddyng Wel nyse al þe first nyȝt. **15..** *Christ's Kirk* 15 Thay wer sa nyss quhen men them nicht, Thay squelit lyke ony gaitis. **1592** KYD *Sol. & Pers.* I. ii, Then be not nice, Perseda, as women woont To hasty louers. **1634** MILTON *Comus* 139 Ere..The nice Morn on th' Indian steep From her cabin'd loop hole peep.

†**b.** Shy, reluctant, unwilling. Const. *to*, *in*, *of*, or with inf. *Obs.*

c **1560** A. SCOTT *Poems* (S.T.S.) iv. 91 The nycest to ressave Vpoun the nynis will nip it. **16..** BRYAN in Farr *S.P. Eliz.* (1845) II. 335 Straight bent to glorious deeds by kind, And to no braue acheiuements nice. **1617** MORYSON *Itin.* III. 40, I found the Italians nothing nice to shew their strong forts to me and to other strangers. *c* **1665** MRS. HUTCHINSON *Mem. Col. Hutchinson* (1846) 58 She is the nicest creature in the world of suffering her perfections to be known. **1668** MRS. BEHN *Oroonoko* Wks. (1718) 55 They are extreme modest and bashful, very shy, and nice of being touch'd. **1676** DRYDEN *Aurengz.* II. i, Virtue is nice to take what's not her own.

†**6.** Phr. ***to make* (*it*) *nice***, to display reserve or reluctance; to make a scruple. *Obs.*

1530 PALSGR. 624, I make it coye, or nyce as a daungerouse person doth, *je fais lestrange.* **1560** ROLLAND *Crt. Venus* III. 827 Raab and Ruth..War licht Ladeis, thocht ȝe it mak sa nice. **1595** SHAKS. *John* III. iv. 138 And he that stands vpon a slipp'ry place, Makes nice of no vilde hold to stay him vp. **1606** BIRNIE *Kirk-Buriall* (1833) 16 Although they seeme to make nyce in praying for dead. **1637** RUTHERFORD *Lett.* lxxxi. (1862) I. 205 Christ..cometh in..without ceremonies, or making it nice, to make a poor ransomed one His own. **1677** GILPIN *Demonol.* (1867) 168 They make not nice to tell him that there is no possibility of salvation but in their way.

7. a. Fastidious, dainty, difficult to please, esp. in respect of food or cleanliness; also in good sense, refined, having refined tastes.

1551 ROBINSON tr. *More's Utop.* II. (1895) 149 Anothere ys of so nyce and soo delycate a mynde that he settethe nothynge by yt. **1573** TUSSER *Husb.* (1878) 191 The slouen and the careless man, the roinish nothing nice. **1600** DEKKER *Fortunatus* Prol., Your nice soules, cloyd with dilicious sounds, Will loath her lowly notes. *a* **1656** BP. HALL *Rem. Wks.* (1660) 3 Nice ears are all for variety of Doctrines, as palates of meats. **1706** E. WARD *Wooden World Diss.* (1708) 99 He is not so nice as his Superiors, whom nothing will go down with, under right Nantz or Rum. **1751** JOHNSON *Rambler* No. 104 ¶9 The mind..becomes..nice and fastidious, and like a vitiated palate. **1805** R. W. DICKSON *Pract. Agric.* II. 1047 It is better, as fattening animals are very nice, to let them have rather too little than too much. **1836** C. SHAW in *Mem.* (1837) II. 593, I can eat anything, and am not very nice about the cleanliness. **1856** HAWTHORNE *Eng. Note-bks.* (1879) II. 318 Neither is it at all nice as to what it clutches, in its necessity for support.

Phrases. **1553** T. WILSON *Rhet.* (1580) 223, I knewe a Priest as nice as a Nonnes Henne. **1581** RICH *Farew.* (1846) 139 More nice than wise. **1653** H. MORE *Antid. Ath.* I. ii. (1712) 11 Suppose..the other more nice than wise should reply, Nay, it may possibly be otherwise. **1782** COWPER *Mut. Forbearance* 20 Some people are more nice than wise.

b. Particular, precise, strict, careful, in regard to some special thing.

1584 R. SCOT *Discov. Witchcr.* IX. i. (1886) 135 Some are so nise, that they condemne generallie all sorts of diuinations. **1625** BACON *Ess., Greatn. Kingd.* (Arb.) 479 The Spartans were a nice People in Point of Naturalization. **1661** MARVELL *Corr.* Wks. (Grosart) II. 59 The Parliament is alwayes very nice and curious on this point. **1724** WODROW *Corr.* (1843) III. 141, I find them very nice that no other..be admitted to this correspondence. **1839** URE *Dict. Arts* 107 He is extremely nice in selecting his malt and hops. **1861** LD. BROUGHAM *Brit. Const.* viii. 99 Like the old Romans, never very nice in weighing how large a proportion of the people influenced the government.

†**c.** Fastidious in matters of literary taste. *Obs.*

1628 WITHER *Brit. Rememb.* Premonit. 5, I had rather twenty nice Criticks should censure mee. *c* **1665** MRS. HUTCHINSON *Mem. Col. Hutchinson* (1846) 23 His judgement was so nice, that he could never frame any speech beforehand to please himself. **1709** POPE *Ess. Crit.* 286 Thus Critics, of less judgement than caprice, Curious not knowing, not exact but nice, Form short Ideas. **1770** LANGHORNE *Plutarch* (1879) II. 735/2 Such digressions as these the nicest readers may endure, provided they are not too long.

d. Precise or strict in matters of reputation or conduct; punctilious, scrupulous, sensitive.

1647 CLARENDON *Hist. Reb.* VII. §43 So difficult a thing it is to play an after-Game of Reputation, in that nice and jealous profession. 1709 SWIFT *Advancem. Relig.* Wks. 1755 II. I. 99 Women of tainted reputations find the same countenance..with those of the nicest virtue. 1784 COWPER *Task* III. 85 Men too were nice in honor in those days, And judg'd offenders well. 1826 DISRAELI *Viv. Grey* II. v, I am not very nice myself about these matters. 1843 MIALL in *Nonconf.* III. 227 The Duke of Wellington said..'Men who have nice notions about religion have no business to be soldiers'. 1887 BARING-GOULD *Red Spider* xvii, I should get it back again.., and not be too nice about the means.

e. Refined, cultured.

1603 DANIEL *Def. Rhime* H 2 b, Eloquence and gay wordes are..but the garnish of a nice time, the Ornaments that doe but decke the house of a State. *a* 1792 BURNS *Yon Wild Mossy Mountains* iv, Of nice education but sma' is her share. 1794 MRS. RADCLIFFE *Myst. Udolpho* i, As conversation awakened the nicer emotions of her mind, that threw such a captivating grace around her. 1818 SHELLEY *Julian* 536 As we could guess From his nice habits and his gentleness. 1874 GEO. ELIOT *Coll. Breakf.-P.* 56 'Truce, I beg!' Said Osric, with nice accent.

8. Requiring or involving great precision, accuracy, or minuteness.

1513 DOUGLAS *Æneis* III. iv. 138 Our fallowschip exerce palestrale play.., Nakit worsling and strougling at nyse poynt. 1590 NASHE *Pasquil's Apol.* I. D ij b, The pearle of the word, must not be weighed in those scales that men commonly vse to weigh their yron, it is a nicer work. 1665 BOYLE *Occas. Refl.* II. viii. (1675) 123 The Watch I use to measure the time with in nice Experiments. 1745 A. BUTLER *Lives Saints* (1836) I. p. xlvi, The indagation is often a task both nice and laborious. 1776 ADAM SMITH *W.N.* I. x. (1869) I. 108 A house carpenter seems to exercise rather a nicer and more ingenious trade than a mason. 1822 IMISON *Sci. & Art* I. 35 Those who are engaged in making nice philosophical experiments. 1840 *Penny Cycl.* XVI. 209/2 For nice purposes the metal may be obtained in a state of purity by the following process.

9. a. Not obvious or readily apprehended; difficult to decide or settle; demanding close consideration or thought; †intricate.

1513 DOUGLAS *Æneis* III. Prol. 14 Nyce laborynth, quhar Mynotaur the bull Was kepit. 1581 G. PETTIE tr. *Guazzo's Civ. Conv.* I. (1586) 19 The finer wit a man is of, the more he beateth it..about nice and intricate pointes. 1649 JER. TAYLOR *Gt. Exemp.* III. Sect. xiv. 51 The way to destruction is broad and plausible, the way to heaven nice and austere. 1689 POPPLE tr. *Locke's 1st Let. Toleration* L.'s Wks. 1727 II. 233 Opinions..about nice and intricate Matters that exceed the Capacity of ordinary Understandings. 1759 ROBERTSON *Hist. Scot.* I. 175 It was the work but of one day to examine and to resolve this nice problem. 1789 BELSHAM *Ess.* I. vii. 134 It becomes a very nice and curious question indeed. 1847–9 HELPS *Friends in C.* (1851) I. 21 One of the nicest problems for a man to solve. 1885 *Manch. Exam.* 3 June 5/1 Whether the agreement was actually violated is a question involving several nice points.

b. Minute, subtle; also of differences, slight, small.

1561 T. NORTON *Calvin's Inst.* I. xii. 29 Nowe leauyng nice suttleties, lette us wey the matter it selfe. 1612 T. JAMES *Corrupt. Scripture* IV. 6 They seeme to mince and slice the matter into certaine nice and subtile distinctions. 1662 STILLINGFL. *Orig. Sacræ* III. iii. §4 Without perplexing our minds about those more nice and subtile speculations. 1732 POPE *Ess. Man.* I. 223 Twixt that, and reason, what a nice barrier, For ever sep'rate, yet for ever near. 1784 JOHNSON *Let. to Mr. Sastres* 2 Sept., Your critick seems to me to be an exquisite Frenchman; his remarks are nice; they would at least have escaped me. 1855 BAIN *Senses & Int.* II. i. §22 The generality of people can appreciate far nicer differences than these. 1870 HOWSON *Metaph. St. Paul* ii. 41 When we desire to appreciate the nicer shades of meaning.

c. Precise, exact, fine.

1710 ADDISON *Whig Exam.* No. 4 ¶8 A very nice resemblance. 1746 HERVEY *Medit.* (1818) 127 You may observe..in its gently-bending tufts, the nicest symmetry. 1802 PALEY *Nat. Theol.* xii. (1819) 197 A nicer accomodation to their respective conveniency. 1841 MIALL in *Nonconf.* I. 1 No words could describe with nicer accuracy the political movements of English dissenters. 1867 DK. ARGYLL *Reign of Law* ii. (ed. 4) 92 The nice and perfect balance which is maintained between these two forces.

†10. a. Slender, thin. *Obs. rare.*

1590 SPENSER *F.Q.* III. ii. 6 As Ladies wont, in pleasures wanton lap To finger the fine needle and nyce thread. 1604 SHAKS. *Oth.* III. iii. 15 That policie may either last so long, Or feede vpon such nice and waterish diet.

†b. Unimportant, trivial. *Obs. rare.*

1592 SHAKS. *Rom. & Jul.* v. ii. 18 The Letter was not nice, but full of charge, Of deare import, and the neglecting it May do much danger. 1601 —— *Jul. C.* IV. iii. 8 In such a time as this, it is not meet That euery nice offence should beare his Comment.

11. †a. Critical, doubtful, full of danger or uncertainty. *Obs.*

1596 SHAKS. *1 Hen. IV*, IV. i. 48 To set so rich a mayne On the nice hazard of one doubtfull houre, It were not good. 1608 D. T[UVIL] *Ess. Pol. & Mor.* 64 b, Vnderstanding on what nice tearms the life of the Blacke-Prince..did stande. 1682 *Lond. Gaz.* No. 1711/4 We bless Propitious Heaven, which..has directed Your Majesty in these Nice and Critical times. 1710 WODROW *Corr.* (1843) I. 195 You know my itch after accounts of..the true state of things at this nice juncture.

b. Delicate, needing tactful handling.

1617 MORYSON *Itin.* IV. II. iii. (1903) 184 A Treatise to be written of purpose, and with deliberation, vppon that nice Subiect. 1664 J. WILSON *Projectors* v, Things of this nature are so nice, and kickish, the least Error renders them irretriveable. 1742 RICHARDSON *Pamela* III. 40, I hope you had Presence of Mind to do this,—For it was a nice Part to act. 1777 WATSON *Philip II*, III. (1793) I. 129 For several years in the nicest political negociations.

12. a. Entering minutely into details; attentive, close.

1589 PUTTENHAM *Eng. Poesie* II. xii[i]. (Arb.) 126 We imputed it to a nice and scholasticall curiositie in such makers. 1617 MORYSON *Itin.* III. 35 His company is like to be shunned, as of a nice observer of mens actions and manners. 1697 DRYDEN *Virg. Georg.* II. 358 Some Peasants, not t' omit the nicest Care, Of the same Soil their Nursery prepare. 1738 *Pref. J. Keill's Anim. Œcon.* 20 Nicer inquiries into the Structure of the Parts. 1789 G. WHITE *Selbourne* vi, Upon a nice examination..I could find nothing resinous in them. 1839 *Civil. Eng. & Arch. Jrnl.* II. 328/2 It fluctuates..perceptibly to a nice observer. 1864 BOWEN *Logic* xii. 397 The cases may be strictly parallel in every visible respect, as tested by the nicest observations.

b. Of the eye, ear, etc.: Able to distinguish or discriminate in a high degree.

a 1586 SIDNEY (J.), Such a man was Argalus, as hardly the nicest eye can find a spot in. 1755 J. SHEBBEARE *Lydia* (1769) II. 142 A nice pallate in good liquor had made my landlord a favourite companion. 1795 WOLCOT (P. Pindar) *Hair Powder* Wks. 1812 III. 304 Dull though thy tympanum, her nicer ear Catches a thunder-growl from yonder sphere. 1847 H. MILLER *Test. Rocks* v. (1857) 209 Gifted..with a peculiarly nice eye for detecting those analogies. 1873 BROWNING *Red. Cott. Nt.-cap* 273 The nice eye can distinguish grade and grade.

c. Of judgement, etc.: Finely discriminative.

1697 DRYDEN *Virg. Past.* Pref., Wks. 1721 I. 82 Virgil.. was of too nice a Judgement to introduce a God denying the Power and Providence of the Deity. 1742 SHENSTONE *Schoolmistr.* 237 With nice discernment see Ye quench not, too, the sparks of nobler fires. 1785 CRABBE *Newspaper* Wks. 1834 II. 126 We cannot call their morals pure, Their judgment nice, or their decisions sure. 1833 HT. MARTINEAU *Fr. Wines & Pol.* i. 16 No people on earth had so nice a sense of the morally graceful. 1845 S. AUSTIN *Ranke's Hist. Ref.* I. 297 His style is not above mediocrity, nor does he evince any nice sense of elegance and form.

d. Delicate or skilful in manipulation.

1711 ADDISON *Spect.* No. 83 ¶4 One Person at Work, who was exceeding slow in his Motions, and wonderfully nice in his Touches. 1764 REID *Inquiry* I. iii. 78 The nicest artist cannot make a feather or the leaf of a tree. 1806–7 J. BERESFORD *Miseries Hum. Life* (1826) II. xxxiv, Jobs that require both a nice hand and a contriving head.

13. a. Minutely or carefully accurate.

1599 SHAKS. *Much Ado* v. i. 75 Ile proue it on his body if he dare, Despight his nice fence, and his actiue practise. 1667 MILTON *P.L.* VI. 584 All at once thir Reeds Put forth, and to a narrow vent appli'd With nicest touch. 1699 BENTLEY *Phal.* Pref. 93 The largest and nicest knowledge of the English Language, of any man living. 1769 SIR J. REYNOLDS *Disc.* i. (1876) 309 That critical period of study, on the nice management of which their future turn of taste depends. 1805 COLLINGWOOD in Nicolas *Disp. Nelson* (1845) VII. 242 To pass them from the leeward..required nice steerage. 1849 LONGF. *Building of Ship* 17 With nicest skill and art..a little model the Master wrought.

b. Of instruments or apparatus: Showing minute differences; finely poised or adjusted.

a 1628 LD. BROOKE *Wks.* (1633) I. 54 To pease his deeds, by her nice weights and measure. 1666 BOYLE *Orig. Formes & Qual.* 397 Imploying a nice pair of Gold Scales..I found that this Powder weigh'd somewhat..more than twice so much common Water. 1704 J. HARRIS *Lex. Techn.* I. s.v. *Hygroscope*, You will find this plain and simple Instrument, the nicest Hygrometer of any, for it will show you very small Alterations. 1771 T. PERCIVAL *Ess.* (1776) III. 127 A watery dew..which being committed to a nice scale, may probably be found to be equal in gravity to a drop of rain. 1875 SEARS *Serm. Chr. Life* 29 Weigh arguments in the nicest intellectual scales.

14. Of food; Dainty, appetizing. *spec.* of a cup of tea.

1712 ARBUTHNOT *J. Bull* III. App. i, This was but a pretence to provide some nice bit for himself. *a* 1766 MRS. F. SHERIDAN *Sidney Bidulph* V. 193 We sent her up three or four plates of the nicest things that were at table. 1799 JANE AUSTEN *Lett.* (1884) I. 224 You must give us something very nice, for we are used to live well. 1852 ROCK *Ch. of Fathers* III. 103 A banquet which usually consisted of the nicest dishes then known. 1853 SOYER *Pantroph.* 284 Some of these pastries would appear very nice to us in the present day. 1899 R. WHITEING *No. 5 John St.* iv. 38 Her sex's universal restorative... 'You shall have a nice cup of tea.' 1928 R. KNOX *Footsteps at Lock* v. 41 You'd have got a nice cup of tea down at the Gudgeon. 1937 A. P. HERBERT *Nice Cup of Tea* (song), I like a nice cup of tea in the morning, For to start the day you see. 1937 'G. ORWELL' *Road to Wigan Pier* v. 88 There is generally a cup of tea going—a 'nice cup of tea'. 1961 I. FLEMING *Thunderball* iv. 38 The dimity world of the Nice-Cup-of-Tea. 1974 L. DEIGHTON *Spy Story* xxi. 221 'I'll pour him some tea,' said Dawlish. 'There's nothing so reviving as a nice cup of tea.'

absol. 1793 W. ROBERTS *Looker-on* No. 53 (1794) II. 287 To imitate our fashionable physicians in mixing up together ..the nauseous and the nice.

15. a. Agreeable; that one derives pleasure or satisfaction from; delightful. ***nice girl*** (of an adult); freq. somewhat derisive.

In common use from the latter part of the 18th cent. as a general epithet of approval or commendation, the precise signification varying to some extent with the nature of the substantive qualified by it.

1769 MISS CARTER *Lett.* (1817) II. 34, I intend to dine with Mrs. Borgrave, and in the evening to take a nice walk. 1780 BECKFORD *Biog. Mem. Extr. Painters* 110 A nice pocket edition. 1796 JANE AUSTEN *Lett.* (1884) I. 126 You scold me so much in the nice long letter which I have..received from you. 1837 MAJ. RICHARDSON *Brit. Legion* ix. (ed. 2) 220 The Commandant, whom I subsequently found to be a very nice fellow. 1860 B'NESS BUNSEN in Hare *Life* (1879) II. v. 270 Lilies of the valley, and I know not what nice things. 1876 C. M. YONGE *Womankind* xvi. 126 Though a well managed, innocent and select rink is quite possible, 'nice' girls would do well to abstain from those where a chance public shares the sport. 1897 MARY KINGSLEY *W. Africa* 654 How nice it must be to be able to get about in cars, omnibuses and railway trains again! 1901 W. D. HOWELLS *Heroines of Fiction* I. 12 They imagined the heroine who was after all a Nice Girl; who still remains the ideal of our fiction. 1905 E. WHARTON *House of Mirth* I. xiv. 239 He had never wanted to marry a 'nice' girl: the adjective connoting..certain utilitarian qualities..apt to preclude the luxury of charm. 1910 *National Police Gaz.* 16 July 3/1 That's what tells and it pulls the nice girls down with a sudden rush that takes their breath away. 1933 E. O'NEILL *Ah, Wilderness!* (1934) III. i. 89 You're a darned nice girl. 1938 N. MARSH *Artists in Crime* viii. 108 She tries to talk 'Slade'..but the original nice-girl gush oozes out. 1968–70 *Current Slang* (Univ. S. Dakota) III–IV. 86 *Nice Girl*, a sexually permissive girl. 1975 I. S. BLACK *Man on Bridge* ii. 26 'She's pretty.'.. 'More than that, she looked what used to be called a nice girl.'

Phr. 1796 MRS. M. ROBINSON *Angelina* I. 44 The parson's daughters are as nice as my nail and as clean as a penny! 1839 DICKENS *Let.* 5 Mar. (1965) I. 521 A capital bed, and all as nice as nice could be. 1937 G. & I. GERSHWIN *Nice Work if you can get It* (song), Holding hands at mid-night 'Neath a starry sky, Nice work if you can get it, And you can get it if you try. 1938 *Sun* (Baltimore) 20 June 8/2 Ruth said, 'Nice going, kid,' and that simple compliment pleased the young Cincinnati pitcher more than all of the other praises he received. 1954 R. BISSELL *High Water* xxiii. 279 'Nice going, George,' I said. 1958 *Listener* 2 Oct. 492/1 The Frenchman ..may well reply with impatience: 'Nice work if you can get it.'

b. *to look nice*, to have an agreeable, attractive, or pretty appearance.

1793 *Minstrel* II. 182 She was desirous of looking as nice as possible. 1836 *Going to Service* xii. 139 O, you look so nice,..any body would take you for an experienced servant. 1870 MISS BRIDGMAN *R. Lynne* II. xii. 255 Cuthbert liked her to look nice.

c. Kind, considerate, or pleasant (to others).

1830 MOORE *Mem.* (1854) VI. 152 She has, in the nicest and most delicate way, procured them. 1872 T. HARDY *Under Greenw. Tree* v. i, 'Not nice of Master Enoch', said Dick. 1887 I. R. *Lady's Ranche Life Montana* 165 When I say Van was good, I mean he was nice to me.

d. In ironical use. Also ***nice and.***

1836 DICKENS *Let.* 29 Dec. (1965) I. 217, I have been clearing off all the rejected articles to-day, and nice work I have had. 1846 D. JERROLD *Mrs. Caudle* ii, You'll be nice and ill in the morning. 1851 —— *St. Giles* viii, A nice job I've had to nibble him. 1892 I. ZANGWILL *Childr. Ghetto* I. I. xi. 248 Well, you're a nice friend of his, I must say. 1896 E. TURNER *Little Larrikin* xviii. 209 Aren't you going to stop and see Clem off?..you *are* a nice one. 1939 L. M. MONTGOMERY *Anne of Ingleside* v, S'posin' he et a lot of the little green apples..and got nice and sick?

16. As *adv.* Nicely. *rare.*

1540 J. HEYWOOD *Four P.P.* in Hazl. *Dodsley* I. 351 But prick them and pin them as nice as ye will. *c* 1557 ABP. PARKER *Ps.* cxix. 345 Curst be they all, from thy good love who wander wyll to nyse. *a* 1756 ELIZA HEYWOOD *New Present* (1771) 53 Take a fine piece of sturgeon, wash and clean it very nice.

17. *Comb.* as ***nice-conscienced, -eared, -fingered,*** etc.; ***nice-becoming, -looking, -spoken; nice-discerning, -judging; nice-driven, -preserved, -spun.***

a 1727 PATTISON *Crt. Venus* in *Prior's Poems* (1733) III. 106 Full in the midst, with *nice-becoming Grace, Stood Youth. 1642–4 VICARS *God in Mount* 18 These squemish and *nice-conscienced fellows. 1776 'JOEL COLLIER' (J. L. Bicknell) *Mus. Trav.* (ed. 4) App. 26 Should his lordship's *nice-discerning eye perceive any Jacobitical expressions in his works. 1630 *R. Johnson's Kingd. & Commw.* 39 That politike and *nice-driven negotiation of the peace betwixt England and Spaine. *a* 1843 SOUTHEY *Comm.-pl. Bk.* Ser. II. (1849) 33 The chilling fastidiousness of some *nice-eared critics. 1784 COWPER *Task* I. 202 One..whose notes *Nice-fingr'd Art must emulate in vain. 1818 JAMIESON *Burt's Lett. N. Scotl.* I. 322 It sets ye weel to be sae *nice-gabbit. 1571 GOLDING *Calvin on Ps.* xxii. 2 He was not so *nyce-harted as to make a cruell yelping out for some comon harme. 1583 —— *Calvin on Deut.* cxxxi. 806 Because yᵉ people were ouertender and nyceharted, they had need of helpe. 1728–46 THOMSON *Spring* 407 There throw, *nice-judging, the delusive fly. 1807 JANE AUSTEN *Lett.* (1884) I. 328 She is a *nice-looking woman. 1838 DICKENS *O. Twist* xiv, He is a *nice-looking boy, is he not? 1882 J. HAWTHORNE *Fort. Fool* I. xv, A portrait of a very nice-looking young lady. 1869 MISS BROUGHTON *Not Wisely* 11 Miss Chester was gifted with that sort of *nice-lookingness. 1618 N. FIELD *Amends for Ladies* III. iii. in Hazl. *Dodsley* XI. 132 A pox of these *nice-mouthed creatures! 1683 TRYON *Way to Health* 225 Foolish *Nice-pallated People and Gluttons. 1588 SHAKS. *Tit. A.* II. iii. 135 We will enjoy That *nice-preserued honesty of yours. 1777 POTTER *Æschylus* (1779) II. 88 This stranger seems, like the *nice-scented hound, Quick in the trace of blood. 1799 JANE AUSTEN *Lett.* (1884) I. 209 We have two very *nice-sized rooms. 1863 SALA in *Temple Bar* VIII. 73, I suppose there is nothing immodest (even in this wonderfully *nice spoken age) in confessing [etc.]. 1822–34 *Good's Study Med.* (ed. 4) I. 533 A few *nice-spun and chimerical speculations. 1815 MILMAN *Fazio* (1821) 17 Death's not *nice-stomach'd, to be cramm'd With such unsavoury offal.

†nicebecetur. *Obs.* Also 6 nyse-, nycebecetur (-byceter), nycibecetour. [Origin obscure; perh. a fanciful formation from NICE *a.* The earliest and latest quots. appear to show different stressings of the word.] A dainty, fine, or fashionable girl or woman.

c 1520 *Bk. Mavd Emlyn* 225 in Hazl. *E.P.P.* IV. 90 To gete gownes and furs, These nysebecetures, Of men sheweth theyr pyte. *a* 1530 HEYWOOD *Weather* (Brandl) 898 Another maner losse yf we sholde mys Then of such nyce-byceters as she is. 1542 UDALL *Erasm. Apoph.* 120 b, In suche did..the other nycibecetours or denty dames customably use..to bee carryed about. **1546** Heywood *Prov.* I. xi. (1874) 57 Betweene you and your Ginifinee Nycebecetur. [*a* **1553** Udall *Roister Doister* I. iv. 12.] **1584** in Cl. Robinson *Handful Pleasant Delights* (Arb.) 14 Farewel good Nicibicetur, God send you a sweeter.

So †**nicebice.** *Obs. rare*$^{-1}$.

1595 *Locrine* III. iv, No, by my troth, mistresse nicebice, how fine you can nickname me.

†**niced,** *ppl. a. Obs. rare.* [f. NICE *a.*] Made foolish or delicate.

a **1440** Burgh *Cato* 601 Dreede no dremys.. Thouh thei be caused of compleccioun, Or ellis of any nyced fantasie. **1577** Stanyhurst *Descr. Irel.* Ep. Ded. in *Holinshed*, If anie man his stomach shall be found so tenderlie niced, or so deintilie spiced, as that he maie not digest the grosse draffe of so base a countrie.

niced: see NYCETTE.

†'**nicefy,** *v. Obs.*$^{-0}$. [f. NICE *a.*] (See quot.)

1611 Cotgr., *Faire la sadinette*, to mince it, nicefie it, make it dainty, to be verie squeamish.

†**nicehead.** *Obs.*$^{-0}$. [f. NICE *a.*] (See quot.)

c **1440** *Promp. Parv.* 355/2 Nycehede, or nycete, *inercia*.

niceish ('naɪsɪʃ), *a.* Also **nicish.** [f. NICE *a.* + -ISH[1].] Somewhat or rather nice.

1835 Mrs. Carlyle *Lett.* I. 46 Talkative, niceish people. **1860** Trollope *Framley P.* xiv, He's a nicish cut of a horse. **1888** *Athenæum* 19 May 628/2 There is a niceish girl—not the mystic heroine born of fire and water.

'**niceling.** Now *rare.* [f. NICE *a.* + -LING[1].]

†**1.** An effeminate, tender, or delicate person.

1549 Coverdale, etc. *Erasm. Par. Jas.* i. 26 b, That.. we maye nether become tendre nycelynges through vayne pleasures, ne moued with terrible turmoylinges. **1583** Golding *Calvin on Deut.* xl. 238 There are a sorte of these nyce-lings which take greefe at it.

2. *arch.* A nice thing.

1884 Black *Jud. Shakes.* ii, I was showing you what nicelings and delicates my father was bringing.

nicely ('naɪslɪ), *adv.* Also 4 **nise-,** 5 **niceliche;** 4–6 **nycely,** (6 **-lie),** 5–6 **nysely.** [f. NICE *a.* + -LY[2], after OF. *nicement.*]

†**1.** Foolishly, unwisely. *Obs.*

c **1330** R. Brunne *Chron.* (1810) 297 Sir Hugh of Crissengham he did nycely & mys. **1387** Trevisa *Higden* (Rolls) I. 373 For no man schulde niseliche wende yn wiþ oute leue of þe bisshop. **1423** Jas. I. *Kingis Q.* xii, Impressioun Off my thoght causith this Illusioun, That dooth me think so nycely in this wise. **1494** Fabyan *Chron.* VII. 607 Eugeny the fourth,.. beyng admytted, demeaned hym so nycely in the begynnynge, yᵗ he was put out of Rome. **1523** Ld. Berners *Froiss.* I. cclxiii. 389 They thought nat to departe nysely out of their aduantage.

†**2.** Slothfully, sluggishly. *Obs. rare*$^{-0}$.

c **1440** *Promp. Parv.* 355/2 Nycely, *inerte*.

†**3. a.** Finely, elegantly, refinedly, daintily. *Obs.*

c **1400** *Chron. Eng.* (Caxton) ccxxxiii. 6 The women more nysely yet passed the men in aray & coriousloker. *c* **1440** *Gesta Rom.* lxxi. 388 (Add. MS.), His neghbores.. seydyn 'se this man! that late was a pore man, how nysely [he] arayes his childryn!' **1530** Palsgr. 839/2 Nycely, fetly, *coyntement*. **1576** Fleming *Panopl. Epist.* 311 Let not your gowne sitt vppon your backe too nicely, nor yet weare it too slouenly. **1601** Shaks. *Twel. N.* III. i. 17 They that dally nicely with words, may quickely make them wanton. **1690** Locke *Educ.* §7 How.. mortal a thing, taking Wet in the Feet is, to those who have been bred nicely. **1728** Young *Love of Fame* VI. 146 Aspasia's highly born, and nicely bred, Of taste refin'd, in life and manners read.

b. In an attractive, agreeable, pleasing, or pretty fashion.

1714 Mrs. Manley *Adv. Rivella* 119 A Bed nicely sheeted and strow'd with Roses, Jessamins or Orange-Flowers. **1766** Goldsm. *Vic. W.* iv, The walls on the inside were nicely white-washed. **1822** Byron *Vis. Judgem.* xcix, In two octavo volumes, nicely bound. **1830** Moore in *Mem.* (1854) VI. 138 A dinner-party at my mother's;.. All very nicely done. **1860** *Rutledge* 30 The tea tasted very nicely out of the thin china cup. **1881** 'Rita' *My Lady Coquette* iii, How nicely you have done your hair to-night.

c. Very well, satisfactorily.

In quots. 1935 and 1938 = 'merry from the effects of drinking'.

1829 Landor *Imag. Conv., Lucian & Timotheus* Wks. 1853 II. 31/2 Your flesh, properly cured, might hang up nicely against the forthcoming bean-season. **1852** Mrs. Stowe *Uncle Tom's C.* xiii, 'How is thee, Ruth?' she said... 'Nicely', said Ruth. **1880** Mrs. Forrester *Roy & Viola* I. 19 It is a great thing to have provided so nicely for yourself. **1935** G. Heyer *Death in Stocks* xvi. 178 It was quite obvious he'd been at a pub all the time, because he was quite nicely. **1938** N. Marsh *Death in White Tie* v. 55 I'm not inebriated ..but I am.. a little exalted. What I believe is nowadays called nicely thank you. **1943** *Times* 31 May 10/8 Aurelia Weatherbournes generally do quite nicely, thank you, on council estates. **1949** N. Marsh *Swing, Brother, Swing* ix. 207 'How are you, Mr. Fox?' 'Nicely, thank you, sir. And you?' **1954** A. S. C. Ross in *Neuphilologische Mitteilungen* LV. 43 Possible negative non-U answers are *I'm doing nicely, thank you* and (*Quite*) *sufficient, thank you.*

4. †**a.** With coyness or reserve; also, sparingly, grudgingly. *Obs.*

1530 Palsgr. 839/2 Nycely, straungly, *coyement, nicement*. **1579** Tomson *Calvin's Serm. Tim.* 418/2 He.. giueth it, but so nicely yᵗ men may but licke their fingers with it (as the Prouerbe is). *a* **1600** Hooker *Answ. Travers* §13 It is not their wont to speak so nicely of things definitively set down in that council. **1695** Ld. Preston *Boeth.* II. 44 She, who nicely conceals herself to others, is wholly displayed and open to thee.

†**b.** Fastidiously, squeamishly. *Obs.*

1547 *Homilies* I. *Good Wks.* II. D iv, Thei wold, as it wer nicely take a fly out of their cup, and drynke doune a whole camel. **1591** Harington *Orl. Fur.* Pref. ¶8 Some more nicely found fault with so many two sillabled and three sillabled rimes. **1618** Latham *2nd Bk. Falconry* (1633) 36 If you doe finde her to bee tutchie or nicely addicted. **1671** Milton *P.R.* IV. 377 Thou shalt have cause To wish thou never hadst rejected thus Nicely or cautiously my offer'd aid. **1791** Boswell *Johnson* an. 1781 Such small particulars are intended for those who are nicely critical in composition.

c. Scrupulously, punctiliously, in respect of conduct. Now *rare.*

1605 Shaks. *Lear* V. iii. 144 What safe, and nicely I might well delay, By rule of Knight-hood, I disdaine and spurne. *a* **1677** Manton *Serm. Ps. cxix*, civ. Wks. 1872 VIII. 5 To stand nicely upon terms of duty is to run in harm's way. **1709** Steele *Tatler* No. 11 ¶4 There are Women who are not nicely Chast, and Men not severely Honest, in all Families. **1741** Middleton *Cicero* I. v. 357 Nicely tender of his reputation. **1854** H. Miller *Sch. & Schm.* i. (1857) 9 For a man who had often looked death in the face, he had remained nicely tender of human life.

†**d.** Cautiously, gingerly, lightly, gently. *Obs.*

1590 Nashe *Pasquil's Apol.* I. D j, He treads nicelie, as one that daunceth vpon a lyne. **1606** Bp. Hall *Medit. & Vows* II. §12 As nettles, which if they bee nicely handled, sting and pricke. **1613** Donne *Epithal. Eliz.* 75 What mean those ladies which, as tho' They were to take a clock to pieces, go So nicely about the bride?

5. †**a.** With insistence on detail; strictly. *Obs.*

1599 Shaks. *Hen. V*, V. ii. 94 Happily a Woman's Voyce may doe some good, When Articles too nicely vrg'd, be stood on. **1659** Hammond *On Ps.* cxxxix. 13 It.. is not so strictly or nicely to be taken as to denote a creation.

b. With close attention, closely, minutely.

1690 Locke *Hum. Und.* IV. vii. §9 When we nicely reflect upon them, we shall find [etc.]. **1728** Pope *Dunc.* I. 163 Here studious I.. lost blunders nicely seek. **1739** Johnson *Wks.* (1787) IV. 324 It being his custom to draw a line under any passage which he intended more nicely to consider. **1858** Froude *Hist. Eng.* III. xiv. 198 The Privy Council had been obliged to levy men without looking nicely to their antecedents. **1871** Smiles *Charac.* iv. (1876) 115 His action becomes suspended in nicely weighing the pros and cons.

c. With particular care.

1697 Vanbrugh *Æsop* v. 477 Be clean in your clothes, but nicely so in your persons. *a* **1715** Burnet *Own Time* III. (1724) I. 553 He used to pare his nails very nicely. **1839** Ure *Dict. Arts* 592 Another workman is occupied in drying very nicely the surface of the glass that is to be silvered.

6. Accurately, precisely, exactly: **a.** With reference to adjustment, correspondence, etc.

1611 Shaks. *Cymb.* II. iv. 90 Two winking Cupids Of Siluer, each on one foote standing, nicely Depending on their Brands. **1697** Potter *Antiq. Greece* I. viii. (1715) 42 Amphitheaters.. were not nicely Orbicular, but Oval. **1715** Arbuthnot *Let. to Pope* 9 July, A Translation nicely true to the Original. **1745** P. Thomas *Jrnl. Anson's Voy.* 236 A small portable Balance.. so nicely made that.. the thousandth Part of a Crown will sensibly turn the Scale. **1866** Seeley *Ecce Homo* I. ii. 17 In its strangeness it is so nicely adapted to the character of Christ. **1866** R. M. Ferguson *Electr.* (1870) 23 It consists of a needle nicely poised on a point.

b. With ref. to judgement, discernment, etc.

1638 Junius *Paint. Ancients* 123 Such as are provoked, judge more nicely. **1683** Moxon *Mech. Exerc., Printing* xiii. ¶4 He.. Files off the Bur.. that he may the better and nicelier discern how well he has begun. **1705** Stanhope *Paraphr.* I. 68 A due Recompence nicely awarded, according to the Behaviour of each Man in Particular. **1755** B. Martin *Mag. Arts & Sci.* I. xvi. 110 If I do not nicely understand your Proportion of Squares, and such Things, you must excuse me, at present. **1839** *Civil Eng. & Arch. Jrnl.* II. 329/2 A wire.. being found suitable for enabling the eye to estimate very nicely the shade of the intercepted light. **1855** Bain *Senses & Int.* II. ii. §3 A very feeble impression cannot be nicely discriminated.

†**c.** Closely. *Obs. rare*$^{-1}$.

1690 Norris *Beatitudes* (1694) 73 It is not safe.. to nourish a Passion which.. borders so nicely upon Hatred.

†**d.** Slightly, very little. *Obs. rare.*

1698 Petiver in *Phil. Trans.* XX. 315 This nicely differs from the *Amaranthus Siculus spicatus*.. in having rounder Leaves. **1702** *Ibid.* XXIII. 1262 This and No. 271 are nicely different, if not the same.

7. *Comb.* as ***nicely-balanced, -bound, -established,*** †***-gauded, -laden.***

1607 Shaks. *Cor.* II. i. 233 Our veyl'd Dames Commit the Warre of White and Damaske In their nicely gawded Cheekes to th' wanton spoyle Of Phœbus burning Kisses. **1837** Howitt *Rur. Life* II. i. (1862) 93 The iron tray of nicely laden patty-pans goes into the oven. **1855** J. R. Leifchild *Cornwall Mines* 57 The man.. sent the nicely-balanced wonder of nature.. banging down the crags. **1858** W. Ellis *3 Visits Madagascar* viii. 220, I saw, amongst other nicely-bound books, 'The Women of England'. **1875** Whitney *Life Lang.* viii. 136 Under government of nicely-established rules.

Nicene ('naɪsiːn, naɪ'siːn), *a.* (and *sb.*) Also 6 **Nycene, Nicæne, Nicen.** Cf. Isnik. [ad late L. *Nīcēn-us, Nīcæn-us*, f. *Nīcēa, Nīcæa*, Gr. Νίκαια, the name of a town in Bithynia.]

1. a. ***Nicene Council***, one or other of two ecclesiastical Councils held at Nicæa, the first in the year 325 for the purpose of dealing with the Arian controversy, and the second in 787 to consider the question of images.

1432–50 tr. *Higden* (Rolls) V. 105 The legende of whom is had amonge scriptures apocriphate by the decrete of the cownesayle Nicene. **1526** *Pilgr. Perf.* (W. de W. 1531) 192 b, In the Crede of Nycene counsyle. **1564** *Brief Exam.* ****j, Certayne sectaries layde to the Fathers charge of Nicæne counsell, that they tooke an order.. for keping Easter day. **1660** Jer. Taylor *Duct. Dubit.* II. ii. rule 6 §35 As we learn from the acts of the second Nicene Council. **1727–38** Chambers *Cycl.* s.v. *Arianism*, Many.. returned to the faith of the first Nicene council, and anathematized the second. **1860** *Chambers's Encycl.* I. 403/1 The doctrines of A[rius] did not essentially differ from those of the Nicene Council. **1884** *Catholic Dict.* (1897) 53/1 In opposition to this error, the first Nicene Council defined [etc.].

†**b.** In the erroneous form ***Council of Nicene.***

1387 Trevisa *Higden* (Rolls) V. 105 He was i-martired under Dacianus þe iuge by doom of the counsaile of Nicene. **1432–50** tr. *Higden* (Rolls) V. 119 Whiche kepede the firste grete cownsayle of Nicene. **1563** *Homilies* II. *Sacrament* I. (1859) 445 Whereas, by the advice of the Council of Nicene, we ought to 'lift up our minds by faith'.

2. ***Nicene Creed***, a formal statement of Christian belief, based upon that adopted at the first Council of Nicæa, which was designed especially to combat the Arian heresy.

1567–9 Jewel *Def. Apol.* Wks. 1848 IV. 315. **1577** tr. *Bullinger's Decades* (Parker Soc.) I. 12 Excellent learned men who wrote the Creed commonly called the Nicene Creed. **1674** N. Fairfax *Bulk & Selv.* 201 When we read in the Nicene Creed [etc.]. **1781** Gibbon *Decl. & F.* xxvii. III. 17 He.. offered that Arian prelate the hard alternative of subscribing the Nicene creed, or of instantly resigning.. the cathedral. **1834** *Penny Cycl.* II. 340/2 A confession of faith, which seemed to be in unison with the Nicene Creed. **1884** *Catholic Dict.* (1897) 254/2 A creed.. identical with what we are accustomed to call the Nicene Creed.

3. Connected with, originating from, related to, the Nicene Council(s).

1597 Hooker *Eccl. Pol.* V. xlii. §2 They always professed love and zeal to the Nicene faith. **1719** Waterland *Vind. Christ's Div.* 210 The Nicene Fathers explain their meaning, both in the Creed it self, and in the Anathemas annex'd to it. **1781** Cowper *Hope* 394 By Athanasian nonsense, or Nicene. **1801** Ranken *Hist. France* I. II. ii. 195 The Nicene Christians were therefore most likely to prevail. **1884** *Catholic Dict.* (1897) 53/1 From which the whole of the Nicene definition follows by logical consequence.

4. *sb.* An adherent of the doctrine sanctioned by the first Nicene Council.

1882 *Athenæum* 9 Sept. 335/2 He has to treat of Arians, Semi-arians, Nicenes, Anomœans, Homœans,.. and others.

Hence **Ni'cenian, Ni'cenist.**

1663 Owen *Vind. Animadv.* Wks. 1851 XIV. 434, I presume you are well pleased with these Nicenians. **1891** F. W. Newman *Cdl. Newman* 53 Unless European Metaphysics or Philosophy could go back to 'Emanations', we cannot recover the position of the Nicenists.

nice-nellyism (naɪs'nɛlɪɪz(ə)m). *N. Amer. slang.* Also **nice-nellieism.** [f. *nice Nelly*, a conventional name for a respectable woman, a prude + -ISM.] Prudery; genteelism; excessive prudishness of speech or behaviour: usually applied adversely. Cf. NELLY[2] 3.

1936 *New Republic* 28 Oct. 337/1 Perhaps, it is true, as charged that the British press is displaying a brand of Nice Nellyism in refusing to mention the subject [*sc.* the divorce of Mrs Simpson, later Duchess of Windsor]. **1942** *Sun* (Baltimore) 17 June 10/7 Mr. Adams accused the editor [of a new book of soldier songs] of Nice Nellieism in dealing with the songs. **1947** *Sat. Rev.* (U.S.) 15 Feb. 9/2 It takes more than.. nice-Nellyism in the name of patriotism to obliterate that spirit. **1952** *New Yorker* 18 Oct. 159/1 Mr. Pyles attributes much of the nice-nellyism that blighted polite speech and writing during the nineteenth century to Webster's Puritan prudishness. **1956** *N. Y. Times Book Rev.* 30 Sept. 2/2 None of the words which Ned Sheldon.. found so obnoxious seems to me acutely distasteful, with the exception of 'funeral parlor', which carries nice-nellieism to the nth degree. **1960** I. Wallach *Absence of Cello* (1961) 174 'Experience', as absurd a nice-Nellyism for copulation as she could conceive. **1973** *Saturday Night* (Toronto) Oct. 15/1 The public had been made comatose by the greyness of Mackenzie King and the nice nellyism of Middle Powermanship.

niceness ('naɪsnɪs). [f. NICE *a.* + -NESS.] The quality or condition of being nice.

†**1.** Folly, foolish or wanton conduct, light behaviour, wantonness. *Obs.*

c **1530** Ld. Berners *Arth. Lyt. Bryt.* (1814) 70 Though I shewe thus vnto you my nysenes, I pray you think no folye in it. **1568** Grafton *Chron.* II. 32 He banished out of his Court nicenesse and wantonnesse. **1583** Stubbes *Anat. Abus.* I. (1879) 158 Was it.. to stirre vp filthie lust in them selues, or for nicenes onely, as our daunces bee.

†**2.** Luxury, effeminacy, delicacy; delicate or luxurious living. *Obs.*

1540 Morysine *Vives' Introd. Wysd.* C vj b, Cleane kepinge of the bodye (delicate nisenes of meates and drinkes leyed aparte). **1596** Spenser *F.Q.* IV. viii. 27 That age despysed nicenesse vaine, Enur'd to hardnesse and to homely fare. **1615** W. Lawson *Country Housew. Gard.* (1626) 49 A man.. degenerate cleane from his naturall feeding, to effeminate nicenesse. **1650** W. Brough *Sacr. Princ.* (1659) 423 So niceness of life ends often in retchlesnesse of conversation. **1697** Collier *Ess. Mor. Subj.* I. (1709) 58 This Niceness, though it renders them Insignificant to the great Purposes of Life, yet it polishes their Complexion.

†**b.** Elegance (in dress). *Obs. rare*$^{-1}$.

1693 Southerne *Maid's last Prayer* II. i, What you call handsomely, is a niceness wou'd.. ill become me.

†**3.** Inclination to idleness. *Obs. rare*$^{-1}$.

a **1557** Mrs. M. Basset tr. *More's Treat. Passion* M.'s Wks. 1366/1 If we growe so feble, that we wax lothe to goe foorth any further, and of slouthe and nycenesse begynne to stagger and stande styl.

†**4.** Reserve, shyness, coyness. *Obs.*

1567–9 Jewel *Def. Apol.* (1611) 167 Therefore leaue this nicenesse, M. Harding, and tell vs plainely [etc.]. **1579** Lyly *Euphues* (Arb.) 51 The Gentlewoman, whether.. for nicenesse, or for niggardnesse of courtesie, gaue him.. a colde welcome. **1631** *Celestina* vii. 91 What it is I will not tell you, because you make your selfe such a piece of nicenesse. *a* **1700** DRYDEN (J.), Unlike the niceness of our modern dames, Affected nymphs, with new affected names.

5. †**a.** Subtlety; over-refinement. *Obs.*

1592 PUCKERING in Ld. Campbell *Chancellors* xlvi. (1857) II. 304 Seek not advantages to trip one of you the other by covin or niceness. **1611** BIBLE *Transl. Pref.* ¶16 Nicenesse in wordes was alwayes counted the next step to trifling. **1664** EVELYN *Pomona* v. (1729) 67 The Royal Society approves more of Plainness and Usefulness than of Niceness and Curiosity.

b. Precision, accuracy, exactness.

1677 MOXON *Mech. Exerc.* 34 If the Nut be not to be cast in Brass, .. this niceness is not so absolutely necessary. **1696** WHISTON *The. Earth* (1722) 3, I shall wave that niceness, and set them down indifferently. **1726** LEONI *Alberti's Archit.* II. 17/1 All the lines and angles .. fit one another to the greatest niceness. **1764** HARMER *Observ.* i. §15. 38 The niceness of Russell's observations will not allow us to doubt the truth of what he says.

c. Delicacy, difficulty.

1642 in Rushw. *Hist. Coll.* III. (1692) I. 715 This is commonly the last Point in Treaties betwixt Princes, and of the greatest Niceness. **1689** POPPLE tr. *Locke's 3rd Let. Toleration* L.'s Wks. 1727 II. 408 Niceness and Difficulty there is, to hit that just Degree of Force. **1716** WODROW *Corr.* (1843) II. 193 He excused it a little from the importance of what was before us, and the niceness and tenderness of some things we had been on.

6. Fastidiousness; tendency to be over particular, susceptible, or squeamish.

1612 T. TAYLOR *Comm. Titus* iii. 1 The wisedome of godly teachers wil be not too much to yeeld vnto the nicenes of their hearers. **1650** J. COTTON *Sing. Ps.* 56 It were a sacrilegious nicenesse, to thinke it unlawfull lively to expresse all the artificiall elegancies of the Hebrew Text. **1705** BERKELEY *Cave of Dunmore* Wks. 1871 IV. 508 Neither need any one's niceness be offended on account of the bones. *a* **1791** WESLEY *Wks.* (1872) VIII. 321 Warn them all against niceness in hearing. **1851** HELPS *Comp. Solit.* vi. 113 Clerical niceness and over-sanctity.

†**b.** Fastidious taste or care. *Obs. rare*$^{-1}$.

1698 *Phil. Trans.* XX. 59 He remarks the Niceness of the Ancients, in having their Resemblances taken by none but exquisite Masters. **1714** J. MACKY *Journ. thro' Eng.* (1724) I. iii. 57 The late King William .. hath adorn'd it [Hampton Court], with all the Niceness imaginable.

7. Agreeableness, pleasantness.

1809 MALKIN *Gil Blas* x. iii. ¶8 The reason of its extreme niceness was that Don Cæsar .. took pleasure in improving and ornamenting it. **1840** MRQ. LONDONDERRY in *New Monthly Mag.* LX. 106 Sugared cakes of peculiar niceness, sweetmeats and grapes. **1871** WHITNEY *Real Folks* xx, They are in a fair way of learning the niceness of being nice.

†**'nicery.** *Obs. rare.* [f. NICE *a.*] A nicety.

1626 BERNARD *Isle of Man* (1627) 53 The fourth is the Doore of Smelling: at this enter foolish niceries, perfumings, and other allurements to dalliance. **1640** GLAPTHORNE *Ladies Priveledge* II. ii, But at the minute, reason may dispense Twixt us with such a nicery.

†**nicetery.** *Obs. rare*$^{-1}$. [ad. Gr. νικητήριον a prize of victory, f. νίκη victory.] A charm or talisman to secure victory.

1652 GAULE *Magastrom.* 192 Amulets, præfiscinals, phylacteries, niceteries, ligatures, suspensions, charmes.

nicety ('naɪsɪtɪ). Forms: 4–6 nyce-, 5– nice-; 4–5 nyse-, (5 *Sc.* nysse-), 5–6 nys-, 4 nise-; 5–7 nyci-, (6 nycy-), 6–8 nici-, 5 nisi-; also 4–6 -te(e, 5–7 -tie, (5 -tye). [a. OF. *niceté*: see NICE *a.* and -TY.]

I. †**1.** Folly, stupidity; a foolish action. *Obs.*

?*a* **1366** CHAUCER *Rom. Rose* 12 Who so sayth, or weneth it be A jape, or elles nycete To wene that dremes after falle. **1390** GOWER *Conf.* III. 7 Bot thanne it were a nycete To telle you hou that I fare. **1412–20** LYDG. *Chron. Troy* I. vi, I might .. be .. noted eke of wilfull nycetye So folylye to voyde away my grace.

†**2.** Foolish or wanton conduct; wantonness.

1303 R. BRUNNE *Handl. Synne* 4719 þe bysshope .. seyd .. þat he ne shulde make hys nycete Before the graces of þe charyte. *c* **1330** —— *Chron.* (1810) 123 Oþer afterward left of þer nycete. *c* **1380** WYCLIF *Wks.* (1880) 167 Litel sauour of holynesse .., but nycete & pleye & goynge to þe tauerne & oþere vanytes. *a* **1450** MYRC 1321 Hast thou, by malys or by nyste, I-made any mon dronke to be? *a* **1483** *Liber Niger* in *Househ. Ord.* (1790) 16 Ordinances for the house-holde, to kepe the ministres thereof from any breche, out-rage, reproche, or nicetie.

†**b.** Licentiousness, lust. *Obs.*

c **1386** CHAUCER *Wife's Prol.* 412 Than wold I suffre him doon his nycete. *c* **1412** HOCCLEVE *De Reg. Princ.* 3762 Plato .. dwelte in wildernesse, For to restreyne fleschely nycete.

†**3.** Reserve, shyness, coyness. Also *pl. Obs.*

c **1374** CHAUCER *Troylus* II. 1286 Lete be your nycete, and your foly, And spekith with hym in esyng of his hert; Let nycete not do yow bothe smert. **1590** SPENSER *F.Q.* II. ii. 3 So love does loath disdainefull nicitee. **1603** SHAKS. *Meas. for M.* II. iv. 162 Lay by all nicetie, and prolixious blushes That banish what they sue for. **1678** DRYDEN *All for Love* Pref., Ess. (ed. Ker) I. 193 Nicety and affectation; which is no more but modesty depraved into a vice. **1696** in Aubrey *Misc.* (1721) 198 Nay (says the Fellow) give over these Niceties, for he will be your first Husband. **1757** MRS. GRIFFITH *Lett. Henry & Frances* (1767) I. 200 Lady O—— was the only confidante made upon that occasion, .. on account of salving appearances to her nicety.

†**4.** Sloth, idleness, indolence. *Obs. rare.*

1387 TREVISA *Higden* (Rolls) I. 281 He was i-putte doun for grete nysete [L. *inertia*] and i-made a clerk. *Ibid.* V. 227 [The Romans] chargede þe Britouns to leve of un-manhede, and nysete [L. *ignavia*]. *c* **1440** [see NICEHEAD].

†**5.** Excessive refinement or elegance in dress or manner of living. *Obs.*

a **1450** *Knt. de la Tour* (1868) 165, I shalle telle you .. of a knightes doughter that lost her mariage bi her nisite. *c* **1520** *Treat. Galaunt* (1860) 16 The noble course of nature, nycete hath deuoured. **1542** UDALL *Erasm. Apoph.* 87 b, The robe or cope, and the tubbe of Diogenes, did .. vpbraide to the riche and welthie folkes their nycytee and their delices. **1603** B. JONSON *Wks.* (1616) 875 In his garbe he fauours Little of the nicety In the sprucer courtiery. **1652** CULPEPPER *Eng. Physic.* 76 Pride and Ignorance .. preferring nicity before health.

†**b.** Luxuriousness. *Obs. rare.*

1542 UDALL *Erasm. Apoph.* 104 b, To an ethnike philosopher it seemed nycitee .. that an ethnike or gentile should haue his shooes dooen on by his seruaunte. **1650** EARL MONM. tr. *Senault's Man bec. Guilty* 22 If we sleep, tis rather out of too much nicety than of necessity.

6. a. Delicacy of feeling, scrupulosity, punctiliousness.

1693 G. STEPNY in *Dryden's Juvenal* viii. 203 Nay when his Year of Honour's ended, soon He'll leave that nicety, and mount at Noon. **1711** STEELE *Spect.* No. 97 ¶2 It prevail'd only among such as had a Nicety in their Sense of Honour. **1768** STERNE *Sent. Journ.*, *Case of Delicacy*, As there was no other bed-chamber in the house, the hostess, without much nicety, led them into mine. **1816** SCOTT *Old Mort.* Introd., A fanciful nicety it was on the part of my .. friend. **1850** L. HUNT *Autobiog.* iv. I. 179 He had declined taking orders, from nicety of religious scruple.

b. Fastidiousness.

1723 STEELE *Consc. Lovers* I. i, What is it all of a sudden offends your Nicety at our House? **1797** JANE AUSTEN *Sense & Sens.* (1813) I. 232 My own nicety, and the nicety of my friends, have made me .. an idle, helpless being. We never could agree in our choice of a profession.

†**c.** Critical taste. *Obs. rare*$^{-1}$.

1780 JOHNSON in Boswell *Life* (1831) IV. 342 Sir, I beg to have your judgment, for I know your nicety.

d. Scrupulous care, particularity.

1718 LADY M. W. MONTAGU *Let. to C'tess of Mar* 10 Mar., The houses of the great Turkish ladies are kept clean with as much nicety as those in Holland.

7. Precision, exactitude, accuracy, minuteness.

1660 BARROW *Euclid* Pref., Some may have demonstrated most of these Propositions with more nicety. **1695** WOODWARD *Nat. Hist. Earth* IV. (1723) 204 With that exquisite Nicety as to express even the smallest and finest Lineaments of them. **1751** JOHNSON *Rambler* No. 155 ¶2 Those who can distinguish with the utmost nicety the boundaries of vice and virtue. **1787** BEST *Angling* (ed. 2) 123 If it is a proper fly for the season, and you cast it with a nicety, the fish is your own. **1832** BABBAGE *Econ. Manuf.* xi. (ed. 3) 83 Some nicety will be required in these operations. **1878** BOSW. SMITH *Carthage* 92 If the sea was running high the utmost nicety in steering .. would be essential.

b. A (specified) degree of precision.

1748 *Phil. Trans.* XLV. 114 They would be able to a very great Nicety to ascertain the absolute Velocity of Electricity. **1830** HERSCHEL *Stud. Nat. Phil.* 127 The pendulum affords a means of subdividing time to an almost unlimited nicety. **1866** —— *Fam. Lect. Sci.* 101 We know to a great nicety, by actual measurement of the earth's circumference, that its diameter is 7912½ miles.

c. Phr. ***to a nicety***, precisely, exactly, as closely or completely as possible.

1795 BURKE *Lett.* Wks. IX. 418 These things play the Jacobin game to a nicety. **1838** DICKENS *Nich. Nick.* iii, Fitting on his gloves to a nicety. **1862** CARLYLE *Fredk. Gt.* XI. iii. III. 64 All was arranged and concerted to a nicety.

8. The quality of requiring careful consideration or management; delicacy, difficulty, subtlety.

1707 *Lond. Gaz.* No. 4330/2 A Thing of too great Nicety and Difficulty to be accomplish'd in any other .. Reign. **1782** PRIESTLEY *Corrupt. Chr.* I. I. 103 The orthodox began to divide upon questions of great nicety. **1812** *Chron.* in *Ann. Reg.* 45 The learned judge told the jury that this was a case of great nicety. **1845** MᶜCULLOCH *Taxation* II. iv. (1852) 178 The question .. is one of considerable nicety and difficulty. **1869** J. MARTINEAU *Ess.* II. 99 Matters of the utmost depth and nicety.

b. The point in which accuracy or precision is required or which is difficult to hit.

1727 DE FOE *Eng. Tradesman* iii. (1841) I. 19 The nicety of writing in business consists chiefly in giving every species of goods their trading names. **1827** D. JOHNSON *Ind. Field Sports* 72 The great nicety is, to fix the bow, so that the arrow may fly quite horizontally. **1833** J. HOLLAND *Manuf. Metal* II. 290 Few of the scale makers, it seems, of his day, knew in what the nicety of a balance consists.

II. 9. Something choice, elegant, or dainty; an elegance or refinement.

1436 *Pol. Poems* (Rolls) II. 172 The commodites and nycetees of Venicyans and Florentynes. **1611** RICH *Honest. Age* (Percy Soc.) 15 Some foolish nicities that were vsed amongst women in his time. **1675** A. HUYBERTS *Corner-Stone* 16 The new Nicities serve for nought but ostentation and discourse. **1719** *Free-thinker* No. 118 ¶8 Mr. Gibbons could not have carved his Niceties with a Hatchet. *a* **1864** HAWTHORNE *Amer. Note-bks.* (1879) I. 10 Clean linen and other niceties of apparel.

b. Something nice or dainty for eating.

1755 JOHNSON s.v., Niceties, in the plural, is generally applied to dainties or delicacies in eating. **1793** *Friendly Addr. Poor* 13 Niceties do little towards filling the bellies of a hungry family. **1825** MRS. CAMERON *Honest Penny* (*Houlston Tracts* I. No. 10. 7) There were stuck up for sale apples, oranges, mintcakes, tarts, and many niceties of the same sort.

10. A nice or minute distinction; a subtle point or refinement in theory or practice.

1589 PUTTENHAM *Eng. Poesie* III. xxii. (Arb.) 258 The terme, though not greatly pertinent to the matter, yet not vn-pleasant to knowe for them that delight in such niceties. **1631** *Star Chamb. Cases* (Camden) 55 The Court would not rayse nycities out of the pardon and frame a third offence. **1652** R. SAUNDERS *Balm to heal Rel. Wounds* Ep. Ded. 2 When Satan is so busie .. there is no time to stick at nicities. **1706** E. WARD *Wooden World Diss.* (1708) 63 There's no standing upon Niceties .. with Fellows that have the Constitution of a Horse. **1788** BURKE *Impeachm. W. Hastings* Wks. XIII. 6 Not upon the niceties of a narrow jurisprudence, but upon the enlarged .. principles of state morality. **1834** MACAULAY *Ess.*, *Pitt* (1851) 295 These were niceties for which the audience cared little. **1880** T. A. SPALDING *Eliz. Demonol.* 16 Until the masses are more educated in theological niceties than they are at present.

b. A minute point or detail; a point or feature in which great precision or accuracy is involved.

1649 MILTON *Eikon.* 141 Above these twenty yeares he hath bin ruining the people about the niceties of his ruling. **1699** POMFRET *Dies Novissima* 36 'Tis not for you to ask, nor mine to say, The niceties of that tremendous day. **1754** SHERLOCK *Disc.* (1759) I. viii. 229 It will not be worth my Pains .. to enter into the Niceties of this Controversy. **1775** JOHNSON *Let. to Mrs. Thrale* 17 June, Her present qualifications for the niceties of needle-work being dim eyes and lame fingers. **1839** HALLAM *Hist. Lit.* II. i. §8 In the present state of philology there is incomparably more knowledge of grammatical niceties. **1875** *Chamb. Jrnl.* 23 Jan. 54 Young women .. do not know the niceties of legal proof.

nicey, nicy ('naɪsɪ), *a. colloq.* [f. NICE *a.* + -Y[1].] Nice. Also as *sb.*, a nice person or thing.

1859 TROLLOPE *Bertrams* I. vi. 120 The musty fusty people, and the nicy spicy people, and the witty pretty people do severally assemble and get together as they ought to do. Bertram's next-door neighbour was certainly of the nicy spicy order. **1879** C. M. YONGE *Burnt Out* viii. 132 Oh, you're a tell-tale-tit! Catch me giving you nicies again! **1914** *Conc. Oxf. Dict.* Add., *Nicy* .. (nursery), sweet, lollipop. **1922** JOYCE *Ulysses* 363 Go home to nicey bread and milky and say night prayers with the kiddies. **1959** *Listener* 3 Dec. 1008/1 Young nasties after lots of lolly, and young nicies to foil them at last.

†**nich**, contr. for *ne ich*, not I. *Obs.*

c **1160** *Hatton Gosp.* John xviii. 17 Ða cwæð he nich [*c* **1000** nicc] ne eom ich. *a* **1250** *Owl & Night.* 266 Thar to ne segge ich nich ne nai [*v.r.* nyk no nay].

niche (nɪtʃ, niːʃ), *sb.* Forms: 7 nice, niece, neech, 7–8 nitch, 7– nich(e. [a. F. *niche*, ad. It. *nicchia*, of doubtful origin (by Diez connected with *nicchio* mussel-shell). The Fr. form is also the source of Sp. and Pg. *nicho*, G. and Da. *nische*, Sw. *nisch*, Du. *nis*, Russ. *nish*.]

1. a. A shallow ornamental recess or hollow formed in a wall of a building, usually for the purpose of containing a statue or other decorative object.

1611 COTGR., *Niche*, a Niche; a hollow seat, or standing for a statue, or image, made into a wall. *a* **1612** B. JONSON *Pr. Henries Barriers* Wks. (1616) 966 There Porticos were built, .. The nieces filld with statues. **1624** WOTTON *Archit.* in *Reliq.* (1651) 292 That the Nices if they contain Figures of white Stone or Marble, be not coloured in their Concavity too black. **1670–98** LASSELS *Voy. Italy* I. Pref., Who can speak of Statues, but he must speak of Niches? **1713** STEELE *Englishm.* No. 40. 259 You have the blessed Virgin and a Child sitting in a Nitch. **1756–7** tr. *Keysler's Trav.* (1760) II. 310 The niches still remaining shew, that this temple formerly contained the statues of the gods. **1820** W. IRVING *Sketch Bk.* II. 184 Just over the grave, in a niche of the wall, is a bust of Shakespeare. **1838** LYTTON *Leila* I. v, Taking up a brazen lamp that burnt in a niche. **1874** MICKLETHWAITE *Mod. Par. Churches* 3 A tall niche in the wall, holding a processional cross.

b. A recess in the face of a dial. *rare*$^{-1}$.

1822 IMISON *Sci. & Art* I. 96 The small hand B, in the nich at top goes round once in a minute.

2. a. A small vaulted recess or chamber made in the thickness of a wall, or in the ground.

1662 J. DAVIES tr. *Olearius' Voy. Ambass.* 184 A certain number of Neeches Vaulted, in which there were rich beds. **1695** MOTTEUX tr. *St. Olon's Morocco* 20 Some Wicker Conveniencies cover'd with Linnen-Cloth, and contriv'd like Niches or Arches. **1753** HANWAY *Trav.* (1762) I. III. xxxiii. 152 Beds were taken out of nitches made in the wall for that purpose. **1822** BYRON *Werner* III. i, It leads through winding walls .. And hollow cells, and obscure niches, to I know not whither. **1848** BARTLETT *Egypt to Pal.* xx. (1879) 440 A third chamber had three connecting vaults, each with three raised niches for the dead.

b. A natural recess in a rock or hill.

1856 KANE *Arct. Expl.* I. vi. 54 We were fortunate enough to get out a whale-line to the rocks and warp into a protecting niche. **1865** W. G. PALGRAVE *Arabia* I. 153 We scramble up to a sort of niche near its summit.

c. = MIHRAB 2. In full, ***prayer niche***.

1911, etc. [see MIHRAB 2]. **1962** C. W. JACOBSEN *Oriental Rugs* 251 The prayer niche is typical and each is in this shape unless, by chance, it is one that has three prayer niches.

3. *fig.* **a.** A place or position adapted to the character or capabilities, or suited to the merits, of a person or thing.

1726 SWIFT *To a Lady* Wks. 1751 XIV. 227 If I can but fill my Nitch, I attempt no higher Pitch. **1779–81** JOHNSON *L.P.*, *Mallet* Wks. 1787 IV. 282 In the series of great men .. he should find a nich for the hero of the theatre. **1815** CHALMERS in Hanna *Mem.* (1849) I. 21 They have a niche assigned them in almost every public doing. **1869** W. M. ROSSETTI in *Q. Eliz. Acad.*, etc. II. 49 The work fills a niche of its own and is without competitor.

b. A place of retreat or retirement.

1725 BRADLEY *Fam. Dict.* s.v. *Spiders*, The way to destroy the Niches of Spiders in our Gardens. **1750** *Phil. Trans.* XLVII. 108 When the animal returns into its nich, the proboscis sinks into itself. **1860** RUSKIN *Mod. Paint.* V. VI. iii. §3. 12 Where the leaf-stalk forms a safe niche between it and the main stem. **1863** WOOLNER *My beautiful Lady* 20, I told of gourmand thrushes, which To feast on morsels oozy rich, Cracked poor snails' curling niche.

c. *Ecol.* The position of a plant or animal within its community.

1927 C. Elton *Anim. Ecology* v. 63 It is therefore convenient to have some term to describe the status of an animal in its community, to indicate what it is doing and not merely what it looks like, and the term used is 'niche'. *Ibid.* 64 The 'niche' of an animal means its place in the biotic environment, its relations to food and enemies. **1937** [see biotope]. **1960** N. Polunin *Introd. Plant Geogr.* xiv. 431 The large lianes comprise..by far the more numerous synusiae (groups of plants of similar life-form, each filling much the same ecological niche and playing a similar role). **1962** *Listener* 13 Sept. 388/2 Divergence is related to the existence of ecological niches. *Ibid.*, On the existence of niches, he [*sc.* Darwin] was already clear in 1837... Even more apposite is his question on how a niche is entered. **1965** B. E. Freeman tr. *Vandel's Biospeleology* i. 6 A number of terrestrial planarians are endogeans, occupying a similar niche to the earthworms. **1974** Bennett & Humphries *Introd. Field Biol.* (ed. 2) ii. 8 Each animal species has its own typical food relationships with other species, so in a given community at a given time each is said to have its characteristic food niche. *Ibid.* 12 Its habitat niche can be thought of as the sum total of its many effective environments throughout life. *Ibid.* 13 The term 'niche' on its own is much misused in ecological writing to mean food-niche, habitat-niche, habitat or microhabitat.

4. *attrib.* and *Comb.*, as ***niche-band***, ***-ornament***, ***work***; ***niche-like*** adj.

1841 *Civil Eng. & Arch. Jrnl.* IV. 412/2 The centre [opening]..forms a lofty arch to the niche-like loggia. **1848** Rickman *Styles Archit. Eng.* 228 The buttresses..are ornamented with various tiers of niche-work. **1851** Ruskin *Stones Ven.* I. xxiv. §10 This niche ornament of the north. **1867** A. Barry *Sir C. Barry* vii. 254 The top of the niche-band ranged with the cornice of the building. **1878** Bell *Gegenbaur's Comp. Anat.* 110 A fissure, or a niche-like depression of the edge of the disc.

niche (nɪtʃ, niːʃ), *v.* [f. the sb., or in some senses perh. partly ad. F. *nicher* to nest, nestle, place as in a nest:—pop. Lat. **nīdicāre*, f. *nīd-us* nest.]

1. *trans.* (in *passive*). To place (an image, etc.) in a niche or similar recess. Also *fig.*

1757 J. H. Grose *Voy. E. Indies* 326 Domestic idols.. which are niched in a conveyance that is to serve them for a triumphal car. **1798** Charlotte Smith *Yng. Philos.* IV. 66 You will never be niched with——faith, I have forgotten their names. **1838** Lytton *Lady of L.* iii. ii, No image of some marble saint, Nich'd in cathedral aisles, is hallow'd more. **1855** Dickens *Dorrit* ii. v, A family so conspicuously niched in the social temple as the family of Dorrit. **1880** 'Mark Twain' *Tramp Abroad* I. xxi. 198 A waxen Virgin niched in a little box against the wall.

b. To form as a niche. Const. *into*, *in*.

1818 J. C. Hobhouse *Hist. Illustr.* (ed. 2) 213 Half way up an open oratory has been niched into a wall. **1820** Byron *Juan* v. lxvi, A..cupboard niched in yonder.

2. To place in some recess or nook; to ensconce. In *passive*: **a.** of things or places.

1752 Watson in *Phil. Trans.* XLVII. 456 In the litho-phyton, the urtica, being niched in their crusts or barks, deposits a juice or liquor. **1819** Mrs. Jackson in *Sir G. Jackson's Diaries & Lett.* (1873) I. 131 Your fair divinity was a little earthly paradise niched somewhere in the mountains. **1862** T. A. Trollope *Lent. Journey* iv. 57 The little solitary convent..is niched into a little, low, damp-looking meadow.

b. of persons.

1824 Scott *Redgauntlet* let. x, They sat cosily niched into what you might call a bunker. **1847** Lytton *Lucretia* i. ii, Niched between two bouncing lasses, he had commenced acquaintance with them. **1876** M. Collins *From Midnight to Midn.* II. ii. 231 They got niched into a corner of the room.

3. *refl.* To settle or ensconce (oneself) quietly or comfortably. Also (rarely) of things.

1824 J. C. Hobhouse in *Athenæum* (1883) 4 Aug. 145/1 A corner or two for unobtrusive folks like ourselves to nitche themselves. **1853** Ruskin *Stones Venice* III. ii. §39. 60 It would not niche itself, wherever there was room for it, in the street corners. **1878** Mrs. Stowe *Poganuc P.* xvi. 140 Here Dolly loved to retreat and niche herself down in a quiet corner.

4. *intr.* To nestle, settle. *rare.*

1853 Miss Yonge *Heir of Redclyffe* xliii, Charlotte generally niched into Amy's old corner by Charles. **1883** K. S. Macquoid *Her Sailor Love* I. ii. vi. 115 Tufts of grass niching among the broken chalk.

Hence **niched** (nɪtʃt, niːʃt), *ppl. a.*

1771 T. Nugent tr. *Life Benv. Cellini* I. 450 My string of long slips, which I wanted to get about one of the nitched battlements. *a* **1837** Campbell *Departure of Emigrants* 92 Poet. Wks. (1837) 246 Niched statues breathing golden air. **1849** Ruskin *Sev. Lamps* i. §7. 15 Have we no..niched statuary in our corridors? **1855** Tennyson *Daisy* 38 Those niched shapes of noble mould.

nichel(l, *sb.* and *v.*: see nichil.

'nicher, *sb.* [Cf. next.] A neigh; a laugh.

a **1791** *Blind Harper of Lochmaben* xv. in Child *Ballads* IV. 18/1 There she [a mare] gave mony a nicher and sneer. **1844** *Richardson's Local Historian's Table-bk., Leg. Div.* II. 137 There was sic a queer eiry nicher, as o' some hundreds o' creatures laughin'. **1894** P. H. Hunter *J. Inwick* 249 A queer kind o' nicher o' a lauch.

nicher ('nɪxə(r)), *v. Sc.* and *north. dial.* [Imitative: cf. neigher *v.* and nicker *v.*] *intr.* (and *trans.*) To neigh; also *transf.* to laugh loudly.

a **1700** *Johnie Armstrang* in *Ever-Green* (1761) I. 192 These milk whyt Steids, That prance and nicher at a Speir. **1806** R. Jamieson *Ld. Randal* xxvii. in *Pop. Ballads & Songs* I. 169 Lord Randal's steed he nicher'd loud. **1822** Scott *Nigel* xxxi, Ye needna nicher that gait.., e'en though it was a pleasing jest. **1848** C. Bronte *Jane Eyre* (1857) 199 The old crone nichered a laugh under her bonnet and bandage. **1895** Crockett *Men of Moss-Hags* xiv, Above us the fitful, flying winds nichered and laughed like mocking fiends.

†'nichil, *sb. Obs.* Also 6 **nichel(l**. [a. med.L. *nichil*, class. L. *nihil* nothing: see nihil.]

1. Nothing, naught. *rare.*

1500–20 Dunbar *Poems* xxii. 74 He playis with totum and I with nichell. **1584** R. Scot *Discov. Witchcr.* xvi. vi. (1886) 406 The witches..that..give their soules to the divell..and their bodies to the hangman to be trussed on the gallows, for nichels in a bag. **1670** Ray *Prov.* 188 Nichils in nine pokes. Chesh[ire] *i.e.* Nothing at all. [Cf. nifle *sb.* 1.]

2. *Law.* The return made by the sheriff to the exchequer in cases where the party named in the writ had no goods upon which a levy could be made. Cf. nihil 2.

1585 *Act 27 Eliz.* c. 3 §3 After ten Months next after such two Nichils, or Garnishment returned, the same Lands.. shall be sold. **1684–1708** [see nihil 2]. *a* **1726** Gilbert *Treat. Exch.* viii. (1758) 133 A Roll of Nichils, or of the Debts which the Sheriff has nichilled. **1763** *Stat. at Large* (Ruffhead) I. 354 Accompts of Nichil shall be put out of the Exchequer.

b. ***Clerk of the Nichils***: a clerk of the exchequer who made a note of the Nichils returned by the sheriffs.

1642 C. Vernon *Consid. Exch.* 4 The nichelled issues are by the Clerke of the Nichells sent to the Treasurers Remembrancer. *a* **1661** Fuller *Worthies* xxiv. i. (1662) 75 The Clerk of the Nichils, who maketh a Roll of all such sums as are nichill'd by the Sheriff upon their Estreats of the Green wax. *a* **1726** Gilbert *Treat. Exch.* viii. (1758) 132 The Clerk of the Estreats and the Clerk of the Nichils meet and make up two Rolls.

†'nichil, *v. Law. Obs.* Also **nichel**. [f. prec.] *trans.* Of a sheriff: To mark or designate (a debt or sum) as illeviable through the absence of any goods to be taken. Hence **'nichilled** *ppl. a.*

1620 J. Wilkinson *Coroners & Sherifes* 75 Betweene the old Sherife which returned them, and the new Sherife which nichiled them, they must be payed. **1642–61** [see prec. 2 b]. *a* **1726** Gilbert *Treat. Exch.* v. (1758) 76 The Sheriff often gave Acquittances and Tallies to the Tenants and yet Nichil'd them on the Account.

†'nichillate, *ppl. a. Obs. rare*$^{-1}$. [ad. med.L. *ni(c)hilāt-us*, pa. pple. of *nihilāre*, f. *nihil* nothing.] Annulled.

1563 *Durham Wills & Inv.* (Surtees) 5 All other former wylls by hym maide to be voyde, frustrate and nichillate.

Nicholaite, -an: see Nicolaite, -an.

Nicholas ('nɪkələs). [The name of an early Christian saint (died 326 a.d.), bishop of Myra in Lycia, regarded as the patron of scholars, esp. of schoolboys.]

†1. ***St. Nicholas' bishop***, a boy-bishop elected by choir-boys or scholars on St. Nicholas' Eve (Dec. 5).

Cf. Puttenham *Eng. Poesie* iii. xxiii. (Arb.) 279; J. Gregory *Posthuma* (1650) 113–4; Brady *Clavis Calend.* (1813) II. Dec. 6; Bourne *Popular Antiq.* (ed. Brand) 362. **1501** *Acc. Ld. High Treas. Scot.* II. 128 Be the Kingis command, to Sanct Nicholais beschop of Coupir in Fiff xlijs. **1505** *Ibid.* III. 175 To Sanct Nicholas beschop in Linlithqw. xlijs.

2. ***St. Nicholas'(s) clerks***: **†a.** Poor scholars.

1553 T. Wilson *Rhet.* (1580) 155 Thei are no Churchemen, thei are masterlesse men, or rather S. Nicolas clarkes that lacke liuyng. **1581** Marbeck *Bk. of Notes* 204 To receive the Pope for his supreame head.., to receive S. Nicholas Clarkes, to have his beads, and to give to the high Altar.

b. Highwaymen. Now only *arch.*

See also clergyman 2.

1570 Foxe *A. & M.* (ed. 2) 2287, I haue heard of men robbed by S. Nicolas clerkes. **1596** Shaks. *1 Hen. IV*, ii. i. 68 If they meete not with S. Nicholas Clarks, Ile giue thee this necke. **1612** R. Daborne *Christian turn'd Turke* 1393 S'foot we are preuented; S. Nicolas Clearkes are stept vp before vs. **1662** J. Wilson *The Cheats* i. i, Who should I meet with but our old Gang, some of St. Nicholas's Clerks. **1819** Scott *Ivanhoe* xii, That I might at least see any of St. Nicholas's clerks before they spring on my shoulders.

Nichrome ('naɪkrəʊm). Also **nichrome**. A proprietary name of various alloys of nickel with chromium (10–20 per cent) and sometimes iron (up to 25 per cent).

1911 *Jrnl. Amer. Chem. Soc.* XXXIII. 190 The nichrome triangles..when used with city gas..lost, at most, one milligram an hour. **1933** *Official Gaz.* (U.S. Patent Off.) 4 July 18/1 Driver-Harris Company, Harrison, N.J... Nichrome. For alloys of nickel, chromium, and iron in the form of wire, ribbon, strip, [etc.]. **1937** *Jrnl. Brit. Interplanetary Soc.* IV. 7 The nozzles were machined from nichrome steel rod, threaded at the lower end so that they could be screwed into the exhaust end of the combustion chamber. **1947** J. C. Rich *Materials & Methods of Sculpture* ii. 46 For low-temperature firing, electric kilns equipped with nichrome wire heating elements are very efficient. **1950** *Jrnl. R. Aeronaut. Soc.* LIV. 20/1 For general purposes, the wire used in strain gauges is a straightforward cupro-nickel, or nickel-chrome alloy, such as Eureka, Brightray, Nichrome. **1951** *Trade Marks Jrnl.* 7 Mar. 228/1 'Nichrome'... Unwrought and partly wrought alloys composed mainly of nickel-chromium; and rods, tubes, bars, wire, sheets and pellets, all being goods..made from alloys composed mainly of nickel-chromium. British Driver-Harris Company Limited,..Manchester,.. manufacturers. **1964** S. H. Avner *Introd. Physical Metallurgy* xii. 387 Some nominal compositions are 80Ni-20Cr (Chromel A, Nichrome V, and others) used as electric heating elements for household appliances and industrial furnaces; 60Ni-16Cr-24Fe (Chromel C, Nichrome, and others) used as electrical heating elements for toasters..and hot-water heaters. **1968** E. R. Petty *Physical Metall. Engin. Materials* xiii. 276 There are two main groups of heater wire, one based on 80% nickel-20% chromium (Nichrome) with or without amounts of iron, and the other based on ferritic chromium steels... The former alloy is well known as the basis of the Nimonic high temperature alloys.

nicht, Sc. variant of night.

‖**nicht wahr** (nɪçt vaːr). [G., lit. 'not true'.] Is it not true?

1924 M. Kennedy *Constant Nymph* xii. 167 We should do very well without one [*sc.* a maid] for a little, *nicht war?* **1941** M. Treadgold *We couldn't leave Dinah* vi. 106 They are nice liddle horses, *nicht wahr*, Karl? **1948** W. Stevens *Let.* 25 Oct. (1967) 621 One has a sense that the world was never less new than now... Nicht wahr? **1967** 'G. Carr' *Lewker in Tirol* v. 69 Today it is so hot that tempers are not good—*nicht wahr?* **1971** J. Henderson *Copperhead* (1972) xiii. 162 He was going over to the other side. Such is truly a form of suicide, *nicht wahr?*

nicibicetur: see nicebecetur.

†'nicing, *ppl. a. Obs. rare*$^{-1}$. [f. nice *a.*] Disdainful, fastidious.

1581 T. Howell *Deuises* (1879) 233 With nising Nimphes I list not deale, Whose lookes aloft aspire.

nicish, variant of niceish *a.*

nick (nɪk), *sb.*[1] Also 5 **nyke**, 6 **nycke**, 6–7 **nicke**, 7 **nic**, **nike**, 8 **knick**. [Of obscure origin: appears earlier than the corresponding verb, but may be derived from it.]

I. 1. a. A notch, groove, or slit, cut into, or present in, something; an incision or indentation.

1483 *Cath. Angl.* 255/1 A Nyke, *tenus.* **1523** Fitzherb. *Husb.* §4 Somme plowes haue a bende of yron..that hath thre nyckes on the farther syde. **1578** Banister *Hist. Man* i. 32 Departyng from this corner, or deepe nicke,..there riseth a certaine sharpe Processe. **1609** C. Butler *Fem. Mon.* (1634) 118 It is best..in the edges on both sides, to cut little nicks. **1688** Holme *Armoury* ii. 68/2 The leaf 5 pointed, each cut with deep nicks, almost jagged. **1753** Bartlet *Farriery* 332 Holes must be made at certain distances in the groove,..and a nick cut to receive the billet from the strap. **1769** Mrs. Raffald *Eng. Housekpr.* (1778) 303 Fill one nick with chopped parsley, the second with fat pork,..and so on till you have filled all your nicks. **1815** J. Smith *Panorama Sci. & Art* I. 15 A nick is made in the wood or bone, to keep the work from being carried aside by the file. **1847** Le Fanu *T. O'Brien* 170 Deepening a nick with his penknife in the counter. **1888** Bottone *Electr. Instr. Making* §41 With a file, a nick is cut in this steel rod.

b. In various special applications (see quots.).

1562 Turner *Herbal* ii. (1568) 166 The sede layd to.. swageth the payne of the nickes or ryuinge of the fundamente. **1637** Suckling *Aglaura* ii. i, Like the string of a watch wound up too high, and forc'd above the nicke. *a* **1680** Butler *Rem.* (1759) II. 260 [He] has a different Humour for every Nick his drink rises to. **1688** Holme *Armoury* iii. 351/1 The Notch or Nick in the Arrow for the Bowstring to go in. **1791** *Young's Annals Agric.* XVI. 567 (E.D.D.), Instead of this ridge the new Leicester sheep are now breeding to have a furrow there, which is called the knick. **1841** *Penny Cycl.* XXI. 109/1 After which the nick, or groove [in a screw-head] to receive the end of the screw-driver, is cut with a circular saw. **1842** Lower *Eng. Surnames* (1875) II. App. 156 A nick is the mark cut in the mandible of a swan to distinguish its ownership.

c. *Printing.* A notch made on one side of the shank of a type, serving as a guide to the compositor in setting; †the part of the mould by which this is made.

1683 Moxon *Mech. Exerc., Printing* xv. ⁋8 In the upper half of the Mold..is fitted into the under side of the Body the Nick: It is made of a piece of Wyer. **1797** *Encycl. Brit.* (ed. 3) VII. 381/1 This wire, or rather half-wire, in the upper part makes the nick in the shank of the letter. **1824** J. Johnson *Typogr.* II. 6 The advantage to be derived from letter having a deep nick, and also that the nick should differ from other founts of that body. **1882** Southward *Pract. Printing* 11 The nick..distinguishes between letters of an equal size but of a different description.

d. *Squash* and *Real Tennis.* (See quot. 1961.)

1890 J. M. Heathcote et al. *Tennis, Lawn Tennis, Rackets, Fives* i. iv. 69 When the odds of touch-no-walls.. are given, a ball returned by the giver of odds, which makes a nick, is counted for the striker. **1926** C. Arnold *Handbk. on Squash Rackets* iii. 34 Winners can also be made by what is known as a dead service nick, the ball being made to meet the back or side wall and the floor at the same time. **1961** J. S. Salak *Dict. Amer. Sports* 296 *Nick* (court tennis)—the junction of the wall and the floor, or a return when the ball, as it drops or falls, touches the wall and the floor simultaneously. **1963** *Times* 8 Jan. 3/5 This Binns did with his usual touch strokes, boasting with precision and, on his forehand drops, turning his racket over like a butterfly net to impart top spin and make the ball die in the nick. **1973** R. Hawkey *Beginner's Guide Squash* iv. 41 One must avoid.. allowing a service to drop into the 'nick' between the back wall and the floor.

2. a. A notch used as a means of keeping a score; hence, †reckoning, account.

1483 *Cath. Angl.* 255/1 A Nyke of a tayle, *epimeridia.* **1530** Palsgr. 644/1, I make nyckes on a tayle, or on a stycke. **1587** Churchyard *Worth. Wales* (1876) 86 O fathers wise, and wits beyond the nicke. **1591** Shaks. *Two Gent.* iv. ii. 76 He lou'd her out of all nicke. **1611** Cotgr., *Hoche*, a nicke, or notch, on a Tallie, etc. **1887** Rider Haggard *Allan Quatermain* iv, A number of little nicks, each nick representing a man killed in battle. **1891** Kipling *Light that Failed* (1900) 34 That's another nick in the score. I'll jostle you later on.

b. One of the depressions between the rings which form on the horns of cattle, and afford some indication of their age. Also *fig.*

1788 PICKEN *Poems* (1813) I. 156 (E.D.D.), May..ilka new nick on her horn Some added pleasure yield her. *c* **1810** CROMEK in *Burns' Wks.* (1838–9) 62 It was his common practice to cut the nicks or markings from the horns of cattle, to disguise their age. **1862** HISLOP *Prov. Scot.* 192 There's ower mony nicks in your horn. That is, you are too knowing or cunning for me.

3. A gap in a range of hills.

1793 *Carlop Green* (1817) 112 Ending in a swelling know, Formed by King Charlie's Nick. **1860** KAY-SHUTTLEWORTH *Scarsdale* I. 117 The drivers of strings of gals [Galloway ponies] with lime sacks o'er the nick of Pendle. **1883** STEVENSON *Silverado Sq.* 66 There in the nick just where the foothills joined the mountain..was Silverado.

4. A cut; the act of cutting.

a **1816** WOLCOT (P. Pindar) *Middlesex Election* v. v. Wks. 1816 IV. 206 Our cock hath had a nick;..His droat is cut, and there he lieth. **1885** RIDER HAGGARD *K. Solomon's Mines* xiii, The fatal 'nick' of the artery was done..swiftly and painlessly.

II. †**5.** A verbal correspondence or resemblance; a pun. *Obs.* (Cf. NICK *v.*[2] 4.)

1561 T. HOBY tr. *Castiglione's Courtyer* II. (1577) K iij, The other sort of iestes..consisteth only in quicke and subtil sayings,..and in nickes. **1589** PUTTENHAM *Eng. Poesie* II. xvii[i]. (Arb.) 146 In these verses by reason one [word] of them doth as it were nicke another,..it behoueth..to place them where the nicke may be more expresly discouered.

6. In the game of hazard: A throw which is either the same as the main, or has a fixed correspondence to it (see quot. 1797).

a **1635** CORBET *Poems* (1807) 128 Amongst the gamesters, where they name thee thicke At the last maine, or the last pocky nicke. *c* **1696** PRIOR *Cupid & Ganymede* 32 The usual trick: Seven, slur a six; eleven, a nick. **1778** C. JONES *Hoyle's Games Impr.* 211 The Nick of Seven is seven to two, often laid ten to three. The Nick of Six and Eight is five to one. **1797** *Encycl. Brit.* (ed. 3) VIII. 347/1 Nicks are either when the chance is the same with the main,..or six and twelve, seven and eleven, eight and twelve. **1809** BYRON *Bards & Rev.* xxxii, The jovial caster's set, and seven's the nick. **1853** WHYTE MELVILLE *Digby Grand* I. vi. 164 'Seven's the main —seven!' The dice rattled, the box fell, and a dotted eleven turned its welcome surface upward. I need not say this was what is termed a nick. **1863** *Chambers's Encycl.* V. 274/2 If his throw be not a nick, or a crab, then, if he can repeat the same throw before the main turns up, he wins.

III. 7. ***the (very) nick*: a.** The precise or exact moment or point of time when something takes place or requires to be done; the critical moment. Chiefly used in phr. ***in* (†*at*, *upon*) *the nick*** (common from *c* 1580).

1577 HANMER *Anc. Eccl. Hist.* VI. vi, The Romane navie.. arrived at the very pinch, or as commonly we say, in the nicke. **1600** HOLLAND *Livy* XXX. xxv. 757 Thus the truce being doubtlesse broken..Lælius and Fulvius came in the verie nicke from Rome. **1622** MABBE tr. *Aleman's Guzman d'Alf.* II. (1623) 336 We at last came to the Gallies, just upon the very Nicke, [etc.]. **1638** COWLEY *Love's Riddle* v. Wks. 1711 III. 136 Philistus..just at the nick came in And parted us. **1648** EVELYN *Let.* in Wks. 1852 III. 11 Your Essex men, who (contrary to all expectations until the very nick) came in a body. **1724** SWIFT *Quiet Life* Wks. 1755 IV. I. 48 Ent'ring in the very nick, He saw virago Nell belabour..his peaceful neighbour. **1774** FOOTE *Cozeners* III. Wks. 1799 II. 196 Married..they would have been, if I had not come just in the nick. **1809** MALKIN *Gil Blas* IV. ii. ¶4 There passed by in the very nick one of his friends. **1868** NETTLESHIP *Ess. Browning* vi. 191 But the Pope and King returning in the nick, crucified him.

†**b.** The exact point aimed at; the mark. *Obs.*

1602 MARSTON *Ant. & Mel.* Induction, Wks. 1856 I. 3, I will so tickle the sense..with the titillation of hyperbolicall praise, that I'le strike it in the nick, in the very nick. **1621** FLETCHER *Pilgrim* III. vi, *Schol.* Does the sea stagger ye? *Mast.* Now ye have hit the nick. **1656** E. REYNER *Rules Govt. Tongue* 29 Right words are effectual; for they hit the mark, light in the nick, and strike on the right string.

†**c.** *slang* or *colloq.* The 'proper thing'. *Obs.*

1788 LD. R. SEYMOUR in *Murray's Mag.* I. 472 The word Ton is quite abolished. Everything that is fashionable is now called the Nick.

8. a. The precise moment or time *of* some occurrence or event.

1645 RUTHERFORD *Tryal & Tri. Faith* i. (1845) 3 It is unhappy, if, in the nick of the first breaking of the morning sky, the night-watch fall fast asleep. **1670** G. H. *Hist. Cardinals* II. III. 199 Dying just in the nick of the vacancy of the See. **1713** STEELE *Guard.* No. 82 ¶10 In the nick of being surprised, the lovers..escape at a trap-door. **1845** HOOD *True Story* xi, A tramper That came in danger's very nick. **1855** BROWNING *Childe Roland* xxix, In the very nick Of giving up, one time more, came a click.

†**b.** The essential part *of* something. *Obs.*

1577 STANYHURST *Descr. Ireland* Ep. Ded. in *Holinshed* (1808) VI, He was so crost in the nicke of this determination that his historie..wandred through sundrie hands. **1684** *Observator* No. 129 *Trim.* What's that to the Book here before us? *Obs.* Only the very Nick of the Case.

†**c.** The exact amount *of* something. *Obs.*$^{-1}$

1610 B. JONSON *Alch.* IV. iv, I knew, the Doctor would not leaue Till he had found the very nick of her fortune.

9. ***the* (*very*) *nick of time*** (or †***opportunity***) = 7 a. **a.** In phr. with *in* or *at*.

1612 R. CARPENTER *Soules Sent.* 40 [He] came in the nicke of opportunity to beg grace. **1643** [ANGIER] *Lanc. Vall. Achor* 19 [We] came in the nick of time to relieve the well-affected in Preston. **1687** A. LOVELL tr. *Thevenot's Trav.* II. 179 If he had not gone down at the very nick of time, the Ship could not have failed of being very quickly blown up. **1710** ADDISON *Tatler* No. 158 ¶1 In the very Nick of Time, in the Critical Moment. **1737** L. CLARKE *Hist. Bible* (1740) VIII. 539 Antiochus returning at the very nick of time, was unanimously declared King. **1818** HAZLITT *Eng. Poets* viii. (1870) 200 He unexpectedly appears just in the nick of time, after years of absence. **1840** DICKENS *Barn. Rudge* lxx, He.. had changed sides at the very nick of time. **1888** BURGON *Lives 12 Gd. Men* II. vii. 118 The following note..reached the young man's hands in the very nick of time.

b. In other constructions.

1644 *Lancash. Tracts Civil War* (Chetham Soc.) 177 Something must be done, and now was the nicke and joynt of time. **1681** FLAVEL *Meth. Grace* xi. 236 The wisdom of God..hits the very nick of time for his application. **1845** MIALL in *Nonconf.* V. 253 To turn to profitable account 'the nick of time'. **1867** TROLLOPE *Chron. Barset* I. xxxv. 299 It was simply the nick of time which gave it to him.

10. a. (With *a* and *pl.*) A critical point or moment. Now *rare*.

1628 FELTHAM *Resolves* II. viii. 19 There are some nicks in Time, which whosoeuer findes, may promise to himselfe successe. **1664** BUTLER *Hud.* II. iii. 622 With Symbols, Signs, and Tricks, Engrav'd in Planetary Nicks. **1730** T. BOSTON *Mem.* 293 They had come forth at such a nick for sale. *a* **1845** HOOD *Forge* II. xx, With whom, at that very particular nick, There is such an unlucky crow to pick. **1879** STEVENSON *Trav. Cevennes* 106 Certainly here was a man in an interesting nick of life.

†**b.** So ***nick of time***. Chiefly with *in* or *at*. *Obs.*

1642 *Declar. Lords & Comm. to Gen. Assembly Ch. Scot.* 12 In this nick of time. **1674** T. FLATMAN *Belly God* 8 'Tis a crime To interrupt at such a nick of time. *a* **1707** S. PATRICK *Autobiogr.* (1839) 179, I look upon it as a singular providence of God, that Dr. Harris..should come in at that nick of time. **1724** A. COLLINS *Gr. Chr. Relig.* Pref. 57 There is one season and nick of time, wherein they will allow [etc.].

†**c.** A point, stage, degree. ***to a nick***, to a nicety. *Obs.*

1636 RUTHERFORD *Lett.* (1862) I. lxx. 183 There is a nick in Christianity, to the which whosoever cometh they see and feel more than others can do. **1649** BULWER *Pathomyot.* II. i. 90 To fit its purpose in such an intricate nick of irresolution. *a* **1680** BUTLER *Rem.* (1759) I. 108 For who could choose but err, without some Trick To take your Elevation to a Nick.

†**d.** A chance, opportunity. *Obs. rare*$^{-1}$.

1664 J. WILSON *A. Commenius* v. i, He is so sensible of's danger, He catches at any thing—this is our nick.

IV. †**11.** (Precise sense not clear.) *Obs. rare*$^{-1}$.

1609 B. JONSON *Sil. Wom.* IV. iv, A very Sharke, he set me i' the nicke t'other night at primero.

†**12.** App., a fraudulent bottom in a beer-can, diminishing the quantity of liquor contained in it. (Cf. KICK *sb.*[2] 1.) Only in phr. ***nick and froth***. *Obs.*

In quot. *a* 1700 associated with sense 2 a, but compare quot. 1616 under NICK *v.*[2] 12.

1600–12 ROWLANDS *Four Knaves* (Percy Soc.) 48 With cannes of beere..And those they say are fil'd with nick and froth. **1630** J. TAYLOR (Water P.) *Trav. Twelvepence* Wks. I. 70/2 They vsed so much deceit with nick and froth. *a* **1658** CLEVELAND *Lenten Litany* ix, From the Nick and Froth of a Penny Pot-house, *Libera nos.* *c* **1665** *Nick & Froth* in *Roxb. Ball.* VI. 487 Now we'll..lay you all open to view, It's all for your Froth and your Nick (you slaves). *a* **1700** B. E. *Dict. Cant. Crew*, *Nick and Froth built the Pye at Aldgate*, sharping in the Reckonings and cheating in the Measure built that (once) Noted House.

attrib. **1741** *Poor Robin, Chron.*, She still continues the Nick and Froth Trade as usual.

V. 13. An instance of cross-breeding.

1824 D. BLAINE *Canine Pathol.* (ed. 2) 109 Some rearers of game fowls..are favourable to breeding from the third remove, which they call a nick. **1897** *Outing* (U.S.) XXIX. 484/1 Star, a good one in the field, was bred to Druid, and Mr. Wells made a record with this nick. Most of the puppies of this cross were handsome and excellent workers. **1927** J. E. PLATT *Thoroughbred Race-Horse* iv. 31 All the well-known nicks and blending of bloods must be observed, and the leading lines of sires and dams carefully considered. **1973** *Country Life* 15 Nov. 1545/1 The nick owed little to studies of genetics and line breeding [of harriers].

14. Phrases. ***in good nick*** (slang, orig. dial.), in good condition; **(*in the*) *nick*** (slang), (in) prison, (at a) police station.

1882 *Sydney Slang Dict.* 6/2 *Nick* (*The*), gaol. **1905** WRIGHT *Eng. Dial. Dict.* Suppl. 151/1 *In good nick*, in good condition. **1949** F. SARGESON *I saw in my Dream* 61 They [*sc.* tennis courts] seemed to be in good nick. **1952** 'N. SHUTE' *Far Country* 5 She's in good nick. **1957** *Railway Mag.* June 431/1 It does not mean..that an 'A4' in good 'nick'..is not capable of performances well up to the pre-war standard. **1957** P. WILDEBLOOD *Main Chance* 122 'Arrest me,' said Ron. 'Go on, take me to the nick.' **1959** *Listener* 9 Apr. 645/3 Sundry knaves have been routed and put in 'the nick'. **1962** R. COOK *Crust on its Uppers* i. 20 The boys down at Chelsea nick. **1968** *Listener* 8 Aug. 178/2 A second-'and British slave in good nick. **1968** J. LOCK *Lady Policeman* i. 7 An address much nearer than the 'nick'. *Ibid.* 8 Back at the nick the station officer was very cross. **1969** [see BUST *sb.*[3] f]. **1970** P. LAURIE *Scotland Yard* iii. 66 The Inspector calls the nick. **1971** 'F. CLIFFORD' *Blind Side* II. ii. 81 Reports are that he's in fair enough nick.

Nick (nɪk), *sb.*[2] [Prob. the familiar abbreviation of the name *Nicholas*, but the reason for the appellation is obscure. There is no evidence of connexion with any of the forms cited under NICKER *sb.*[1]] The devil. Usually ***Old Nick***.

a **1643** in Ebsworth *Merry Drollery* App. (1875) 394 For Roundheads Old Nick stand up now. **1668** [see OLD *a.* 9 b]. **1694** ECHARD *Plautus* 14 Wou'd Old Nick had these bloody-minded Fellows. *a* **1743** OZELL tr. *Brantome's Sp. Rhodomont.* (1744) 25 Old Nick himself was never painted half so ugly. **1774** GOLDSM. *Retal.* 58 We wished him full ten times a day at Old Nick. **1842** BARHAM *Ingol. Leg.* Ser. II. *St. Medard* Moral, Unless you're too Saintly to care about Nick. **1886** BESANT *Childr. Gibeon* I. viii, When you..made us laugh with your conceit, being always conceited as Old Nick.

†**nick**, *v.*[1] *Obs.* (exc. *arch.*) Forms: 4–6 (9) **nick**, (4 **nic**, ? **nickin**), 4 **nik(ke**, **nycke**, 4–5 **nyk(ke**, 5 **nek-**, 7 *Sc.* **neck**. [Of obscure origin: perh. f. *nic* = *ne ic* not I: see NICH. Connexion with Sw. *neka*, to deny, seems unlikely.]

1. a. *intr.* To make denial, to deny. *rare*$^{-1}$.

a **1225** *Ancr. R.* 308 Hit nis nout ine Godes kurt ase hit is iðe schire, þer ase þe þet nickeð [L. *negat*] wel mei beon iboruwen, and þe fule þet is icnowen is idemed.

b. *trans.* To deny (a person or thing). *rare*.

a **1300** *Cursor M.* 21078 Þat erth, þai say, vmstund Men seis vprisand fra þe grund..: þe landes folk it will noght nick. **13..** *Ibid.* 15566 (Gött.), Þu sal me nickin are.

2. *trans.* To answer (one) 'nay' or (usually) *with* 'nay'. Also const. *of*.

a **1300** *Cursor M.* 3917 Laban o leue þam nicked nai. [Also 6604, 19773.] *Ibid.* 4382 Has þou nicked me wit nay? *c* **1330** *Amis & Amil.* 2176 No wold thai nick him with no nay. *a* **1400** *Pistill of Susan* 148 Ȝif I nikke hem with nai, hit helpeþ me nouȝt. *c* **1470** *Gol. & Gaw.* 115 Lord, wendis on your way, Yone berne nykis yow with nay. **1515** *Scottish Field* in *Chetham Misc.* (1856) Introd. 13 But he nicked them with nay, and none of yt woulde. **15..** *King Estmere* xii. in Child *Ballads* II. 52/1 She nicked him of naye, And I doubt sheele do you the same. **1603** *Philotus* xxxii, Sweit sucker, neck me not with nay, Bot be content to tak him. [**1820** SCOTT *Abbot* xxxviii, I have but one boon to ask, I trust you will not nick me with nay.]

b. Without personal object. *rare*.

a **1310** in Wright *Lyric P.* viii. 32 Ant ever at neode y nycke nay, that y ner nemnede that heo nolde. *c* **1350** *Will. Palerne* 4145 Ȝif sche nickes wiþ nay & nel nouȝt com sone, ..I wol þat reaume ouer-ride.

nick (nɪk), *v.*[2] Also 6–7 **nicke**, 6 **nycke**, 7 **knick**. [Of obscure origin: there is no obvious connexion with similar forms in the cognate languages, as Du. *nikken*, G. *nicken*, to nod, beckon, G. *knicken* to break, snap. It is also uncertain whether all the senses really belong to the same word.]

I. 1. *trans.* To make a nick or notch in; to cut in nicks or notches; to indent.

1530 PALSGR. 644/1 It is no trewe poynte to nycke your tayle [more than mine]. **1573** TUSSER *Husb.* (1878) 189 Some cutteth the napkin, some trencher will nick. **1590** SHAKS. *Com. Err.* v. i. 175 His man with Cizers nickes him like a foole. *a* **1650** *Robin Hood & Guy of Gisborne* xlii. in Child *Ballads* III. 93/2 Robin pulled forth an Irish kniffe, And nicked Sir Guy in the fface. **1681** W. ROBERTSON *Phraseol. Gen.* (1693) 918 To nick or notch. **1764** E. MOXON *Eng. Housew.* 44 Nick your beef about an inch distance. **1815** J. SMITH *Panorama Sci. & Art* I. 122 Before a saw is employed .., nick the place with a paring chisel. **1856** MRS. BROWNING *Aurora Leigh* IX. 547 The falling beam Which nicked me on the forehead as I passed The gallery-door. **1879** *Cassell's Techn. Educ.* IV. 117/2 Each head came under a saw, and was nicked across the centre.

fig. **1881** *Harper's Mag.* July 249 A stiff palm-tree.. nicked the blue-blackness of the sky.

b. To record or score by means of a notch or notches made on a tally or stick. Also with *up*, *down*, and in fig. use.

1523 FITZHERB. *Husb.* §141 And yf he can not wryte lette hym nycke the defautes vpon a stycke. **1582** STANYHURST *Æneis* I. (Arb.) 22 Bee sure, this practise wil I nick in a freendlye memento. **1598** YONG *Diana* 484 Vpon our score You should nicke vp so many merie tides. **1613** DAY *Dyall* xii. (1614) 318 So is their reasoning again as silly, who upon the word Merit in the Fathers, nick up still our owne Deserts. **1641** BEST *Farm. Bks.* (Surtees) 98 With a knife wee nicke on a spell howe many cleane weathers. **1738** SWIFT *Pol. Conversat.* 5 I'll get a knife and nick it down, that Mr. Neverout came to our House. *a* **1845** HOOD *Tale of Trumpet* xiv, As for the clock the moments nicking, The Dame only gave it credit for ticking.

c. *absol.* or *intr.* To chip china.

1885 *Harper's Mag.* Feb. 477/1 As regards china..our servants are not in the least careful not to nick.

2. To cut into or through; to cut short.

1606 SHAKS. *Ant. & Cl.* III. xiii. 8 The itch of his Affection should not then Haue nickt his Captain-ship at such a point. **1787** BURNS *Death & Dr. Hornbook* xii, It's e'en a lang, lang time indeed Sin' I began to nick the thread. **1789** —— *Peregrin. Capt. Grose* viii, The knife that nicket Abel's craig. **1865** MRS. WHITNEY *Gayworthys* xxvi, Skylark grew to be her ordinary appellative; shortened, indeed to Skylie; the nickname nicked.

b. To fashion or mark out by cutting. Also with *out*, and in fig. use.

1605 CAMDEN *Rem.*, *Epitaphs* 42 A Monke of Duresme busied his braine in nicking out these nice verses vpon the death of W. de La-march. **1719** HAMILTON *Epist.* II. vi. in *Ramsay's Poems*, Thy verses nice as ever nicket, Made me as canty as a cricket. **1827** CLARE *Sheph. Cal.* 180 Nicking the 'Nine-peg morris' in the grass. **1838** *Civil Eng. & Arch. Jrnl.* I. 326/1 The breadth of land has been nicked out upon the ground.

c. *Mining.* (See quots.)

1847 HALLIWELL, *Nick*, to cut vertical sections in a mine from the roof. *North.* **1883** GRESLEY *Gloss. Coal-mining* 174 *Nick*, to cut or shear coal after holing.

d. To fasten with a click. *rare*$^{-1}$.

1856 MRS. BROWNING *Aurora Leigh* VI. 1067 The lady closed That door, and nicked the lock.

3. To make an incision at the root of (a horse's tail) in order to make him carry it higher.

1737 BRACKEN *Farriery Impr.* (1757) II. 4 Why should any Horse carry me better when his Tail is nick'd (as the Term is) than he did before? **1828** [H. BEST] *Italy as it is* 87 Most of the horses had their tails docked, nicked and cropped. **1887** HALL CAINE *Son of Hagar* I. vii, Anything from ploughing to threshing and nicking a nag's tail.

absol. **1859** MISS CARY *Country Life* (1876) 189 I'm a going to..learn to nick and dock.

b. To cut (a horse) at the root of the tail.

1753 J. BARTLET *Gentl. Farriery* 311 The art of nicking horses then chiefly consists in a transverse division of these depressing tendons of the tail. **1791** W. GILPIN *Forest Scenery* II. 268 The custom..of docking, nicking, and cropping their horses. **1815** *Sporting Mag.* XLVI. 115 Every man who nicks his horse, ought himself to be nicked elsewhere. **1896** *Daily News* 11 Feb. 9/1 Prosecuted..for 'nicking' two hackneys and a chestnut mare.

II. 4. †**a.** To tally with, correspond to, resemble, fit, suit exactly. *Obs.*

1589 PUTTENHAM *Eng. Poesie* II. xvii[i]. (Arb.) 146 By reason one [word] of them doth as it were nicke another. *Ibid.* III. xix. 212 Because the one [word] seemes to answere th'other by manner of illusion, and doth, as it were, nick him, I call him the Nicknamer. **1605** CAMDEN *Rem.* 140 Words nicking and resembling one the other, are appliable to diffrent significations. **1687** T. BROWN *Lib. Consc.* in *Dk. Buckhm.'s Wks.* (1705) II. 126 To this odd-conditioned Soul was tack'd a Body that nickt it like two Exchequer Tallies. **1702** MOTTEUX *Prol. Farquhar's Inconstant* 21 An opera, like an oglio, nicks the age.

b. *intr.*

1876 *Rep. Vermont Board Agric.* III. 132 There is another strain or peculiarity among these Canadians, that seems to nick well with the Morgans. **1974** *Country Life* 3–10 Jan. 43/3 The colour-marking Hereford 'nicks' well with virtually all beef and dairy breeds.

†**5.** To hit off or fit (a person or thing) *with* (or *in*) an appropriate name. *Obs.*

Perh. partly from *nickname*: cf. quot. 1889 in b.

1589 [? LYLY] *Pappe w. Hatchet* Biv, If anie be vnchristened, Ile nicke him with a name. **1602** CAREW *Cornwall* (1769) 88 Some of the idle disposed Cornish men nicke their townes with by words, as, the..pride of Truro, Gallants of Foy. **1605** CAMDEN *Rem.* 141 The Greekes..nicked Antiochus Epiphanes, that is, the famous, with Epimanes, that is, the furious. **1687** MONTAGU & PRIOR *Hind & P. Transv.* 24, I have so nickt his Character in a Name as will make you split. **1693** SOUTH *Serm.* 455 Take any Passion of the Soul of Man..and nick it with some lucky or unlucky Word.

b. To call by some (depreciative) name; to nickname. *Obs.* exc. as *nonce-wd.*

1605 CAMDEN *Rem.* 80 Goodith.., by which name King Henry the first was nicked in contempt. **1634** FORD *Perk. Warbeck* IV. iii, Warbeck, as you nick him, came to me. **1689** N. LEE *Princ. Cleve* II. iii, Believe me Sir, in a little time you'll be nick'd the Town-Bull.

1889 LANKESTER in *Nature* 21 Mar. 485 There is no ground for regarding the word 'Lamarckism' as a nickname. There can be no desire to 'nick' him or anyone else.

c. To criticize, censure.

1667 DRYDEN *Maiden Queen* 2nd Prol. 57 Those who write not, and yet all writers nick, Are bankrupt gamesters.

6. a. *to nick it*, to hit the mark, to make a hit; to guess rightly.

1624 MASSINGER *Parl. Love* v. i, Have I not nick'd it, tutor? **1681** HICKERINGILL *Black Non-Conf.* Concl., Wks. 1716 II. 151 Jezabel nick't it in Politicks, when..she made the Law [etc.]. **1705** VANBRUGH *Confederacy* Prol., All his decent plays, Where he so nicked it, when he writ for praise. **1740** RICHARDSON *Pamela* (1824) I. 182 So, Jackey, but we just nicked it, I find. *a* **1804** R. GRAVES tr. *Martial* II. vii, At every ball how prettily you nick it! **1823** MONCRIEFF *Tom & Jerry* I. iv, You've nicked it: the fact is this, Dicky—you must turn missionary. **1831** LAMB *Satan in search*, etc. I. xii, 'I wish my Nicky is not in love'.–'O mother, you have nicked it!'

b. To hit, arrive at with precision.

1673 [R. LEIGH] *Transp. Reh.* 6, I gad sir, and there you have nickt the present juncture of affairs. **1712** OLDISWORTH *Horace's Odes* VII. 29/1 Without doubt we have nick'd Horace's meaning. **1761** CHESTERF. *Lett.* ccclx. (1792) IV. 177 All things have their bound..; and I will endeavour to nick that point. **1800** LAMB *Let. to Manning* in *Final Mem.* (1848) I. 113 You just nicked my palate. **1853** LYTTON *My Novel* II. v, He..perceived the chances for and against.., and nicked the question between wind and water. **1889** DOYLE *Micah Clarke* xxvii, Mayhap you have nicked the truth.

†**c.** *to nick the pin*: (see quots.). *Obs.*

a **1700** B. E. *Dict. Cant. Crew* s.v. *Pin, Nick the Pin*, to Drink fairly. **1708** KERSEY, *To Nick the Pin*, to drink just to the Pin plac'd about the middle of a Wooden Bowl or Cup.

†**d.** To break (windows) by hitting with copper coins (cf. NICKER *sb.*[2] 3). *Obs. rare*⁻¹.

1717 PRIOR *Alma* III. 235 He starts up mohack; Breaks watchmen's heads, and chairmen's glasses, And thence proceeds to nicking sashes.

e. To hit *off* neatly or precisely.

a **1694** M. ROBINSON *Autobiog.* (1856) 6 His father..did admire to see how the boy would nick off the very sense of difficult passages. **1839** THACKERAY *2nd Lect. Fine Arts*, The chairs, tables, curtains, and pictures, are nicked off with extraordinary neatness and sharpness. **1856** —— *Christmas Bks.* (1872) 25 He dockets his tailor's bills, and nicks off his dinner notes in diplomatic paragraphs.

7. To hit or catch exactly (the proper time, season, etc. for something).

a **1664** FRANK in Spurgeon *Treas. Dav.* Ps. lxix. 13 Come we but to him in either of these, and we have nicked the time; we are sure to be accepted. **1677** W. HUGHES *Man of Sin* II. viii. 123 You must be sure to nick the Season; 'Tis at the Masse, just between the Elevation of our Lord, and the three Agnus Dei. **1725** T. THOMAS in *Portland Papers* (Hist. MSS. Comm.) VI. 139 We nicked the time very happily. **1759** GOLDSM. *Bee* No. 3 ¶12 He had, as he fancied, just nicked the time, for he came in as the cloth was laying. **1843** LE FEVRE *Life Trav. Phys.* I. I. iv. 75, I had nicked my time, and..I embarked. **1846** LANDOR *Exam. Shaks.* Wks. II. 269 Unless he nicked the time he might miss the monster.

†**b.** To catch, seize, take advantage of (an opportunity, etc.). *Obs.*

1634 SHIRLEY *Opportunity* v. i, Something will come on't, if he have The grace to nick this opportunity. **1672** MARVELL *Reh. Transp.* I. 4 None more ready to nick a juncture of Affairs than a malapert Chaplain. **1704** J. PITTS *Acc. Moham.* viii. 124 Had the Spaniards nick'd that opportunity ..they might have done great Execution.

c. To catch (a boat, train, etc.) just at the time of departure.

1841 LYTTON *Nt. & Morn.* II. iv, I must arrive just in time to nick the vessels. **1888** *Poor Nellie* 16 'Awfully glad we've nicked it' [*sc.* a train], said George.

d. Of a ball in squash, real tennis, etc.: to strike the floor and wall simultaneously.

1898 W. MORGAN *'House' on Sport* 251 By volleying the service you prevent the ball 'nicking', i.e., so pitching in the angle formed by floor and wall as to be unplayable. **1926** C. ARNOLD *Handbk. on Squash Rackets* iii. 34 It [*sc.* the ball] should be made just to nick on to the side wall and floor and there lie dead. **1960** *Times* 29 Nov. 17/3 Oddy was nicking the side wall more often. **1973** *Times* 31 Jan. 8/7 The pace was ferocious, the 22-year-old Jehan hitting a stream of nicked winners.

8. *slang.* To catch, take unawares; to nab or nail. In mod. use *spec.* of the police: to arrest, to put in gaol. Hence **'nicking** *vbl. sb.*

1622 FLETCHER & MASS. *Prophetess* III. i, We must be sometimes witty, To knick a knave. **1673** *S' too him Bayes* 83 Now will I nick thee here—worse than any where in all my book. **1706** E. WARD *Wooden World Diss.* (1708) 94 If he gets him dead drunk, then is the critical Minute to nick him. *a* **1734** NORTH *Lives* (1826) I. 204 There the Common Pleas thought they had nicked them. **1759** TOWNLEY *High Life below Stairs* II. i, You have just nick'd them in the very Minute. **1806** in *Spirit Pub. Jrnls.* IX. 379 He..stands a chance of getting nicked, because he was found in bad company. **1836** MARRYAT *Japhet* lvii, He has come to get off his accomplice, and now we've just nicked them both. **1893** P. H. EMERSON *Signor Lippo* xvii, All my pals got nicked, and I chucked it. **1958** *Encounter* May 11/2 He'd got nicked for ponceing off his old woman. **1959** 'M. CRONIN' *Dead & Done With* x. 152 They nicked your chum for killing his wife. **1962** *John o' London's* 25 Jan. 82/2 'Arrest' has many Cant synonyms including..*nick.* **1968** J. LOCK *Lady Policeman* iii. 30, I don't sleep rough any more. I've learnt a thing or two since you nicked me. **1970** G. F. NEWMAN *Sir, You Bastard* i. 28 Even on leave he looked for possible nickings. **1973** J. WAINWRIGHT *Devil you Don't* 32, I am talking to you, copper..either nick me..or close that bloody door.

†**b.** *nick me*, as an imprecation. *Obs. rare*⁻¹.

1760 FOOTE *Minor* I. Wks. 1799 I. 241 Nick me, but I have a great mind to tie up, and ruin the rascals.

c. To steal. Also, to rob.

1869 *Temple Bar* July 75, I bolted in and 'nicked' a nice silver tea-pot. **1896** *Daily News* 23 Apr. 2/2 Here is a pair of boots which Eliza has 'nicked'. **1901** 'J. FLYNT' *World of Graft* 220/1 *Nick*, to make a 'touch'. **1903** J. LONDON *People of Abyss* xxiii. 280 'At ten we 'ops the wag; at thirteen we nicks things; an' at sixteen we bashes the copper.' Which is to say, at ten they play truant, at thirteen steal, and at sixteen are sufficiently developed hooligans to smash the policemen. **1914** JACKSON & HELLYER *Vocab. Criminal Slang* 62 *Nick*... To surreptitiously extract something from the person. **1916** H. L. WILSON *Somewhere in Red Gap* vi. 236 'I did hear that you'd had your pocket picked.'.. 'That's right... Some lad nicked me for my roll and return ticket.' **1954** WODEHOUSE *Jeeves & Feudal Spirit* ix. 81 Despite this, you succeeded in nicking him for what must have been a small fortune. **1966** J. PORTER *Sour Cream* xiii. 169, I had Azatov's own pass which I had nicked from him at the airport. **1973** *Courier Mail* (Brisbane) 21 June 7/4 Nicking toys from chain stores. **1974** S. GULLIVER *Vulcan Bulletins* 29 The Libyans will try to nick Javits' shipment.

III. †**9.** In the game of hazard: To win against (the other players) by casting a nick. *Obs.*

a **1553** *Nice Wanton* 212 *Iniq.* Here, sirs, come on; seuen! (*They set him.*) Aleauen at all! *Ism.* Do ye nycke vs? **1668** DRYDEN *Even. Love* IV. i, My Don he sets me ten pistoles; I nick him: ten more, I sweep them too. **1673** —— *Marr. à la Mode* IV. iv, This is now the second time he has barr'd the dice when we were just ready to have nicked him. **1684** OTWAY *Atheist* III. i, I ha' not been robb'd, Sir, but I have been nick'd,..and that's as bad.

†**b.** In fig. use. *Obs.*

c **1620** FLETCHER & MASS. *Trag. Barnavelt* v. ii, We know you have..ministerd much Justice, Nickt many a worthie gamester. **1649** G. DANIEL *Trinarch., Hen. V*, cccx, France vnderhand pursues The Advantage of the Warre to nicke him out Ere he could prize his Chance; False Dice may doo't.

10. To make (a winning cast) at hazard; to get as a nick; to throw the nick of (a certain number).

1598 FLORIO *Legare*,..to binde, tie, or nick a cast at dice. **1611** COTGR. s.v. *Ambezatz*, hauing had that chance that no wise man would nicke. **1709** MRS. CENTLIVRE *Gamester* I. Wks. 1761 I. 140 Come, throw a Main, Sir, then I'll instruct you how to nick it. **1773** GOLDSM. *Stoops to Conq.* III, My old luck: I never nicked seven that I did not throw amesace three times following. **1815** *Chron.* in *Ann. Reg.* 289/2 A wager whether there are more ways than 6 of nicking 7 on the dice.

†**b.** *intr.* To make nicks; to gamble; also, to throw a nick. *Obs. rare.*

1676 WYCHERLY *Pl. Dealer* II. i, Thou art some..gaming Companion, and want'st some Widow's old Gold to nick upon. **1732** FIELDING *Lottery* Wks. 1775 I. 249 If I can but nick this time, ame's-ace I defy thee.

11. To trick, cheat: to defraud *of*, do *out of*. ? *Obs.*

1595 *Maroccus Ext.* 8 To nycoll you, or nicke you rather of an old peece of velvet hose. **1630** J. TAYLOR (Water P.) *Gt. Eater Kent* 8 Ale-houses nor tapsters cannot nick this Nick [Wood] with froth: curtoll cannes..could neuer cheate him. **1727** GAY *Begg. Op.* II. She rivetted a linen draper's eyes so fast upon her, that he was nick'd of three pieces of cambrick before he could look off. **1777** *Mme. D'Arblay's Early Diary* (1889) II. 279 He nickd us entirely and never came at all. **1818** SCOTT *Rob Roy* iii, The polite and accomplished adventurer, who nicked you out of your money at White's. **1818** —— *Hrt. Midl.* xx, Three words of your mouth would give the girl the chance to nick Moll Blood [the gallows].

absol. **1733** FIELDING *Quix. in Eng.* II. xiv, The mister and the man will trick, The mistress and the maid will nick.

†**12.** To provide (a beer-pot) with a nick. Also *intr.*, to employ this method of cheating. *Obs.*

1592 *Def. Conny Catching* in *Greene's Wks.* (Grosart) XI. 68 The Ale-wife unles she nicke her Pots and connycatch her guestes with stone Pottes..can hardly paye her Brewer. **1616** *Shirburn Ballads* (1906) 92 Though I be loth To nicke and to froth, That built the Pie at Algate. *c* **1665** in *Roxburghe Ballads* VI. 487 Bee't tankerd or flaggon,..we'l trust you to Nick and to Froth.

13. *intr.* In hunting, racing, or coursing: To cut *in*. Also with *past*, *up*, etc.

1852 R. S. SURTEES *Sponge's Sp. Tour* xxii, [He is] always nicking and skirting. **1883** E. PENNELL-ELMHIRST *Cream Leicestersh.* 133 Those [horsemen] who nicked in by means of a lucky road. **1883** *Standard* 22 Feb. 3/7 Glenlivet had a good winning balance when Strawberry Girl nicked past and killed. **1898** *Daily News* 16 June 2/3 That beautiful filly ..was lucky enough to nick in on the inside when the leaders ran out at the bend.

b. *Austral.* To slip away, depart hurriedly.

1896 E. TURNER *Little Larrikin* xxiii. 274 Trying to induce the driver of the motor, for whom he had a friendship, to promise at the end of the journey to 'nick away and come too'. **1928** 'BRENT OF BIN BIN' *Up Country* viii. 120 Bert and I could just nick down to Mungee. **1959** BAKER *Drum* II. 129 *Nick, do a*, to decamp, slip away unnoticed. Also, *nick off*.

IV. 14. Of animals, to mate with excellent results.

1865 *Jrnl. R. Agric. Soc.* I. II. 323 Colonel Cradock liked the sort for their size and milk, and they 'nicked' well both with the Booth and the Bates blood. **1868** *Ibid.* IV. II. 349 The native Shetland ewes..have 'nicked' so effectually with rams of the breed that the produce is bought up readily by a certain class of dealers. **1942** R. B. KELLEY *Sheep Dogs* 51 When the progeny of a bitch by a particular dog are outstanding the parents are said to have 'nicked'. **1959** *New Scientist* 22 Oct. 737/2 Where the offspring's performance is conspicuously superior to that of its parents the mating [of poultry] is said to 'nick'. **1971** *Daily Tel.* 4 Jan. 7/6 Breeders ..know from bitter experience that matings do not always 'nick' and that..they are sure to suffer many a disappointment.

15. To compare or compete.

1887 BURY & HILLIER *Cycling* 227 Only one sport 'nicks' with cycling, and that is fair toe and heel walking.

'nickar. Also nicker. [Of obscure origin: by early writers identified with NICKER, a marble, but perh. really a native name.] **a.** One of the hard round seeds of the Bonduc or *nickar-tree*. **b.** One or other of the species of Bonduc. (See quots.)

1696 SLOANE in *Phil. Trans.* XIX. 299 The Third kind of Bean..was that kind which in Jamaica is called Ash-coloured-Nickar from its being perfectly round and very like a Nickar, such as Boys use to play withal. **1750** G. HUGHES *Barbados* 195 The Horse-Nicker is a small groveling tree, growing chiefly in a loose, marly, or sandy soil. **1756** P. BROWNE *Jamaica* (1789) 228 The Grey Nickar. .. The seeds are of a gray colour, and commonly used instead of marbles by all the boys. *Ibid.*, The Yellow Nickar. The plant resembles the foregoing [the Grey Nickar] but it is not prickly. **1792** MARIA R[IDDELL] *Voy. Madeira*, The *guilandina moringa* or yellow nickar bears a berry like polished marble. **1866** *Treas. Bot.* 556/1 The seeds..are called Nicker nuts or Bonduc nuts.

c. In comb. *nickar-tree* = BONDUC.

1707 SLOANE *Jamaica* (1725) II. 40 Nicker Tree. It grows among shrubs in the Savannas everywhere. **1750** G. HUGHES *Barbados* 118 The Black Nicker-Tree. This grows to be a large tree covered with a bark of a greyish white. **1760** J. LEE *Introd. Bot.* App. 320 Nickar-tree, *Guilandina.* **1787** tr. *Linnæus' Fam. Plants* I. 282 *Guilandina.* Nickar-tree. **1838** *Econ. Veget.* 79 Some nuts and seeds are exquisitely polished, and of the most beautiful enamel, as those of..the bonduc, or nicker-tree. **1847** HAMILTON in *Pharmac. Jrnl.* VII. 225 On the medicinal and economic properties of the *Sapindus Saponaria*. Soap Berry, or Black Nickar Tree. **1849** BALFOUR *Man. Bot.* §851 The bark of *Guilandina Bonduc*, the Nicker-tree, is bitter, tonic, and its seeds are said to be emetic.

'nick-eared, *a.* Having the ears nicked.

1834 SIR H. TAYLOR *Artevelde* II. III. i, Hold thy peace, Thou nick-ear'd lubber; what have we to do With whys and wherefores?

nicked (nɪkt), *ppl. a.* [f. NICK *v.*[2] + -ED[1].] Having a nick or nicks; notched, indented, serrated. **a.** In predicative use.

1523 FITZHERB. *Husb.* §21 A pair of tonges made of wode, and in the farther ende it is nycked. **1562** TURNER *Herbal* II. 58 The roote beyng cut, nicked, or scotched. **1631** WIDDOWES *Nat. Philos.* 37 It hath leaves like Lawrell, nicked on the edge. **1656** W. COLES *Art of Simpling* x. 31 Saw wort is so called, for that the Leaves are nicked like a Saw. **1796** WITHERING *Brit. Plants* (ed. 3) I. 261 Cup 2-leafed, egg-shaped, nicked at the end. **1844** H. STEPHENS *Bk. Farm* II. 94 The back..literally becomes nicked, as it is termed; that is, the fat is felt through the skin to be divided into two portions. **1869** BLACKMORE *Lorna D.* xvii, Like a sleeve turned up, and nicked with brown at the corners.

b. In attributive use.

1615 MARKHAM *Eng. Housew.* II. v. (1668) 133 An open and wide toothed, or nickt brake, and a close and straight toothed brake. **1745** *Daily Advertiser* No. 4606. 4/1 A few white Hairs at the Tip of her Nose, and a nick'd Tail. **1791** W. GILPIN *Forest Scenery* II. 256 The most deformed one is nicked-tail; so named from a cruel operation used in forming it. **1867** F. FRANCIS *Angling* vi. (1880) 226 Taking two or three turns over the nicked end at the tail. **1890** *Lloyd's*

Weekly 14 Dec. 6/2 That suspicious sound which tells of a nicked edge.

Comb. *a* **1849** H. COLERIDGE *Ess.* (1851) I. 223 The nicked-bearded, huffing, hectoring, basket-hilted adventurer. **1890** W. J. GORDON *Foundry* 193 That ingenious nicked-type machine the Thorne.

nickel (ˈnɪk(ə)l), *sb.* [Named by the Swedish mineralogist Axel F. von Cronstedt in 1754, by abbreviation of G. *kupfernickel*, the mining name of the copper-coloured ore (niccolite) from which the metal was first obtained by Cronstedt in 1751.

The second element in *kupfernickel* is app. G. *nickel*, dwarf, rascal, mischievous demon, the name being given to the ore because it actually yielded no copper in spite of its appearance (cf. the etym. note to COBALT). Both KUPFERNICKEL and *copper nickel* (see COPPER *sb.*[1] 12) have been commonly employed in English as names of this variety of nickel-ore. For an earlier abbreviation in a different sense see NICOL[1].]

1. A hard silvery-white lustrous mineral, usually occurring in combination with arsenic or sulphur and associated with cobalt; it is both malleable and ductile, and is now largely employed for various purposes, esp. in alloys.

1755 *Gentl. Mag.* XXV. 541 From the name of this mineral [*kupfernickel*] he [Cronstedt] gives the metal the name of *Nickel*. **1772** PRIESTLEY in *Phil. Trans.* LXII. 249 Bismuth and nickel are dissolved in the marine acid. **1786** *Ibid.* LXXVI. 63 There are..persons who have denied the magnetism of purified nickel. **1800** tr. *Lagrange's Chem.* I. 396 It appears that nickel was employed by the Chinese long before it was proved to be a distinct metal. **1822** IMISON *Sci. & Art* II. 118 Nickel alloys with most of the metals. **1858** HOMANS *Cycl. Comm.* 1443/1 Nickel forms twelve per cent. of the new cent authorized by Congress in 1857. **1869** ROSCOE *Elem. Chem.* (1871) 230 German silver is an alloy of zinc, nickel, and copper.

2. *U.S.* †**a.** A one-cent piece partly made of nickel (see quot. 1858 above). *Obs.*

1857 *N.Y. Herald* 27 May (Bartlett), 'Nary red' will soon be an obsolete phrase among the boys, and 'nary nickel' will take its place. **1858** O. W. HOLMES *Aut. Breakf.-t.* ix. (1891) 221 A picture as big as a copper, or a 'nickel', rather, at the bottom of his eye.

b. A five-cent piece (containing one part of nickel to three of copper).

1883 *Century Mag.* Nov. 83/2 Even nickels cannot be had without labor. **1890** GUNTER *Miss Nobody* i, I can't go through Yale on nothing but a fifty-dollar note and two nickels.

c. Five dollars' worth of marijuana. *U.S. slang.*

1967 *Boston Sunday Herald* 26 Mar. 1/2 Nickel bags of marijuana (in hippie lingo a 'nickel' is $5 worth). **1968–70** *Current Slang* (Univ. S. Dakota) III–IV. 86 *Nickel*.., one-eighth to one-fourth of an ounce of marijuana costing about five dollars. Five dollars. (Drug users' jargon).

3. *attrib.* and *Comb.* **a.** Simple attrib. in various senses, as ***nickel anode, -candy, -cigar, electrotype, metal, mineral, plate, solution,*** etc.; objective, as ***nickel-bearing, -worker;*** instrumental, as ***nickel-coated, -faced*** (also ***-face*** vb.), ***-facing, -plate*** vb., ***-plated*** adj. (also *fig.*), ***-plater, -plating;*** **nickel-and-dime,** (*a*) rhyming slang for 'time'; (*b*) *adj.*, designating a store in which articles are cheaply priced; also *transf.* and *fig.*; **nickel bag** *U.S. slang*, a bag containing, or a measure of, five dollars' worth of a drug, esp. heroin or marijuana; **nickel-in-the-slot** *a.*, of a machine, etc.: operated by the insertion of a nickel; **nickel note** *U.S. slang* (see quots.); **nickel nurser** *U.S. slang*, a miser.

1935 A. J. POLLOCK *Underworld Speaks* 80/1 **Nickel and dime*, time. **1960** J. FRANKLYN *Dict. Rhyming Slang* 100/2 *Nickel and dime*, time. **1970** *New York* 16 Nov. 42/2 Pinned to its banks are proud, homely nickel-and-dime towns.. with sides made of asphalt shingles. **1972** *Times* 16 May 1/3 The first Mrs Wallace had worked in a nickel-and-dime store. **1974** 'E. LATHEN' *Sweet & Low* viii. 84 You've got a lot of members who do nickel-and-dime business. **1875** *Ure's Dict. Arts* (ed. 7) II. 221 The *nickel anodes are connected to the..carbon plates of the battery. **1967** WENTWORTH & FLEXNER *Dict. Amer. Slang* 672/1 The usual quantities or sizes of 'bags' are: 'trey' = $3 worth (esp. cocaine and heroin); '*nickel bag' = $5 worth (esp. marijuana, cocaine, or heroin). **1971** *Black World* Apr. 38/2 Black men and women and their children exchange expensive gifts of death—in small nickel bags. **1973** *Ibid.* June 79/2 If..he gets high and blurts it out to a stranger in some bar that he got his nickel bag from Joe, the pusher, then Joe's livelihood is endangered. **1877** RAYMOND *Statist. Mines & Mining* 283 Good *nickel-bearing pyrites. **1972** *Village Voice* (N.Y.) 1 June 13/4 *Nickel candy is 12 cents. **1894** R. KIPLING *Let.* 28 July in C. Carrington *Rudyard Kipling* (1955) ix. 217 There's a smell of horse-piss, Italian fruit-vendor, *nickel cigars. **1884** KNIGHT *Dict. Mech.* Suppl. 634/2 The articles to be *nickel-coated..are to be suspended in the solution. **1873** SPON *Workshop Rec.* Ser. I. 220/1 *Nickel electrotypes stand the wear and tear..better than the ordinary copper ones. **1894** *Amer. Dict. Printing & Bookmaking* 402/1 Electro-types are often *nickel-faced when they are to be used with colored inks, as copper injures the color. **1964** E. A. D. HUTCHINGS *Printing by Letterpress* I. xii. 207 The usual copper shell can be nickel-faced after the plate has been finished. This type of plate is termed a nickel-faced electrotype. **1892** A. POWELL *Southward's Pract. Printing* (ed. 4) lxxii. 696 (*heading*) Electrotyping.. finishing the plate..*nickel facing. **1946** W. H. CHURCH in H. Whetton *Pract. Printing & Binding* xiii. 169/1 No further finishing of the surface of the plate can be undertaken after the nickel facing is applied, without risk of the nickel peeling off when the plate is in use. **1889** *Tacoma* (Washington) *News* 13 Dec. 3/5 The latest *nickel-in-the-slot scheme is really a stroke of genius and is destined to revolutionize cheap literature in this country. **1893** *Harper's Mag.* Mar. 494 [In Jacksonville] there were the same..nickel-in-the-slot machines [as in Asbury Park]. **1901** *Daily Colonist* (Victoria, B.C.) 20 Oct. 10/3 So long as..there is no means of obtaining..official reports,..so long will mining stock investment remain on the level of 'nickel-in-the-slot' gambling. **1851** SMEE in *Ure's Dict. Arts* (1875) II. 220 The deposit..forms a great contrast to the common *nickel metal. **1874** RAYMOND *Statist. Mines & Mining* 309 This vein..contains in its ore an arsenical *nickel-mineral. **1926** *Amer. Speech* I. 652/1 **Nickel note*, five dollar paper bill. **1970** C. MAJOR *Dict. Afro-Amer. Slang* 85 *Nickel note*, five-dollar bill. **1926** MAINES & GRANT *Wise-Crack Dict.* 11/2 **Nickle nurser*, one who has a passion for seeing that his nickles don't stray. **1945** L. SHELLY *Jive Talk Dict.* 29 *Nickel nurser*, tightwad. **1875** *Ure's Dict. Arts* II. 223 A *nickel plate of the utmost purity. **1884** KNIGHT *Dict. Mech.* Suppl. 634/2 To *nickel-plate all pontys and molds for glass-making. **1884** *Encycl. Brit.* XVII. 488/2 The manufacture of cooking utensils and other useful articles out of..*nickel-plated iron. **1885** 'MARK TWAIN' in *Century Mag.* Dec. 194 He had some pathetic little nickel-plated aristocratic instincts. **1910** *Daily Chron.* 10 Dec. 9/5 This five-shilling watch..is made in cases of nickel or of gunmetal nickel-plated, with a crown bow. **1970** T. HUGHES *Crow* 39 The tears are nickel-plated. **1974** R. C. DENNIS *Conversations with Corpse* iii. 19 A revolver..or a pistol? Nickel-plated or blue steel? Regulation or snub-nosed? **1875** *Ure's Dict. Arts* II. 221 The veteran *nickel-plater of the states. *Ibid.* 220 It is only within the last few years that *nickel-plating has been brought prominently into notice. **1858** HOMANS *Cycl. Comm.* 1443/2 Mineralogists, chemists, and *nickel-workers.

b. Attrib. in names of natural or artificial compounds containing nickel, as ***nickel chloride, nitrate, ore, pyrites, regulus, salt, sulphate;*** **nickel-antigorite** [ad. G. *nickel-antigorit* (H. Strunz *Mineral. Tabellen* (ed. 3, 1957) 323)], a nickelian variety, $(Mg,Ni)_3Si_2O_5(OH)_4$, of antigorite; **nickel-bloom** = ANNABERGITE; **nickel bronze** (see quot.); **nickel-chlorite** [ad. G. *nickelchlorit* (H. Strunz *Mineral. Tabellen* (ed. 3, 1957) 317)], a basic silicate and aluminate of magnesium, iron, nickel, and aluminium, $(Mg,Fe,Ni,Al)_6(Si,Al)_4O_{10}(OH)_8$, which has been synthesized but whose natural occurrence is uncertain; **nickel glance** = GERSDORFFITE; **nickel green** = ANNABERGITE; **nickel gymnite**, a gymnite in which part of the magnesium is replaced by nickel; **nickel-iron**, any alloy of nickel and iron; freq. *attrib.*; **nickel ochre** = ANNABERGITE; **nickel silver**, an alloy similar to German silver; **nickel-skutterudite**, an arsenide of nickel and cobalt, $(Ni,Co)As_3$, with nickel predominating, found as white or grey isometric crystals; also, the cobalt-free compound $NiAs_3$; **nickel spinel** [ad. G. *nickelspinell* (H. Strunz *Mineral. Tabellen* (ed. 3, 1957) 137): see SPINEL], an artificially produced oxide of nickel and aluminium, $NiAl_2O_4$; **nickel steel**, an alloy of iron with nickel.

1961 *Mineral. Mag.* XXXII. 972 *Nickel-antigorite... An unnecessary name for nickelian antigorite. **1968** *Proc. Indian Acad. Sci.* B. LXVII. 178 The '*d*' spacings of this mineral can also stand a fair comparison with nickel-antigorite. Therefore, this sample could be either nepouite or nickel antigorite. **1861** BRISTOW *Gloss. Min.* 258 *Nickel-bloom. **1884** KNIGHT *Dict. Mech.* Suppl. 634/1 The pure metal is mixed with various proportions of copper, zinc, and tin, forming *nickel bronze. **1868** *Fownes' Chem.* (ed. 10) 464 *Nickel Chloride..is easily prepared by dissolving oxide or carbonate of nickel in hydrochloric acid. **1961** *Mineral. Mag.* XXXII. 972 *Nickelchlorite... Some of the natural nickel silicates may be members of the chlorite group. **1969** *Clays & Clay Minerals* XVII. 233 Nickel-chlorite has been obtained by the co-precipitation of nickelous hydrous oxide and montmorillonite at an OH/Ni ratio of 2·0. **1836** T. THOMSON *Min., Geol.*, etc. I. 529 Sulpho-Arsenide of Nickel. *Nickel glance. **1837** DANA *Syst. Min.* 245 *Nickel Green. *Niccolus prasinus.* Color a fine apple-green. **1853** *Amer. Jrnl. Sci.* Ser. II. XVI. 170, I described the mineral in 1851, under the name *Nickelgymnite. **1875** *Geol. Mag.* Decade II. II. 21 *Nickel-iron, containing 15·3 per cent. of nickel, constitutes 3·5 per cent. of the stone a less quantity than is found in the Pultusk meteorites. **1946** *Thorpe's Dict. Appl. Chem.* (ed. 4) VII. 458/1 Silicon-irons and nickel-irons with alloy additions are noteworthy. *Ibid.*, The nickel-iron alloys ('Permalloys') are used in compressed powder form at telephonic and radio frequencies. **1971** I. G. GASS et al. *Understanding Earth* viii. 116/1 Nickel-iron is practically absent from terrestrial rocks. **1971** *Gloss. Electrotechnical, Power Terms* (*B.S.I.*) I. iii. 14 *Nickel-iron sleeve*, longitudinally split sleeve of nickel-iron alloy, the use of which enables a winding to have a higher impedance at speech frequencies. **1796** KIRWAN *Elem. Min.* (ed. 2) II. 283 *Nickel Ochre and Vitriol of Nickel. **1861** BRISTOW *Gloss. Min.* 258 Nickel Ochre..occurs massive, earthy and friable. **1836** T. THOMSON *Min., Geol.*, etc., I. 523 The species of *nickel ores hitherto observed, amount only to eight. **1837** DANA *Syst. Min.* 399 Copper nickel. Prismatic *Nickel Pyrites. **1855** *Orr's Circ. Sci., Geol.*, etc. 497 Millerite. Sulphuret of Nickel. Nickel Pyrites. **1797** *Encycl. Brit.* (ed. 3) XII. 133/1 There is no copper, but a *nickel regulus is produced. **1852** FOWNES *Chem.* (ed. 4) 342 The artificial.. product, called *speiss*,..may be employed as a source of the *nickel salts. **1860** *Knight's Eng. Cycl., Arts & Sci.* V. s.v., Nickel..is extensively used in the manufacture of the so-called *nickel-silver. **1862** *Chambers's Encycl.* IV. 713/2 Britannia metal and nickel silver, which are used as substitutes for the true German silver. **1892** WALLER & MOSES in *School of Mines Q.* XIV. 51 This would be a mineral of the type of skutterudite $CoAs_3$... If further analysis confirms these results, the name **Nickel-Skutterudite* is suggested. **1935** *Amer. Mineralogist* XX. 723 Microscopic study of material from the Bullard's Peak district, New Mexico, shows native silver associated with nickel-skutterudite. **1968** I. KOSTOV *Mineralogy* II. 134 The analogous $NiAs_3$ (nickel-skutterudite) contains Ni 20·71%, As 79·29%. **1961** *Mineral. Mag.* XXXIII. 973 *Nickelspinel. **1963** *Jrnl. Amer. Ceramic Soc.* XLVI. 581/2 The other ternary phase assemblage, liquid, NiO, and nickel spinel, exists over wide ranges of temperature (1450° to ~1775° C) and composition (~20 to 100 mole % $NiAl_2O_4$). **1884** KNIGHT *Dict. Mech.* Suppl. 634/2 **Nickel Steel.* **1895** *Daily News* 14 Nov. 6/5 The nickel-steel gun forgings made ..in Pennsylvania. **1868** *Fownes' Chem.* (ed. 10) 465 *Nickel Sulphate..is the most important of the nickel salts.

Hence **ˈnickelic** *a.*, pertaining to, or containing, nickel. **ˌnickeˈliferous** *a.*, containing or yielding nickel. **ˈnickeline** *sb.* = NICCOLITE; (see quot. 1971); *a.*, consisting of nickel. **ˈnickelite** = NICCOLITE. **ˌnickeliˈzation**, the process of nickelizing. **ˈnickelize** *v. trans.*, to coat with nickel. **ˈnickelous** *a.*, containing nickel.

1828–32 WEBSTER s.v., The *nickelic acid is a saturated combination of nickel and oxygen. **1821** R. JAMESON *Man. Min.* 327 *Nickeliferous Grey Antimony. **1851** ASHBURNER tr. *Reichenbach's Dynamics* 594 Containing a great intermixture of this metallic nickeliferous iron. **1786** AIKIN tr. *Beaumé's Man. Chem.* 122 *note*, The ingredients which are usually separated from the *nickelline ores. **1796** KIRWAN *Elem. Min.* (ed. 2) II. 444 A solution of Sal Ammoniac would take up the nickeline part and leave the Cobaltic. **1835** SHEPARD *Min.* II. 83 Nickeline (Copper-Nickel). **1888** *Min. Mag.* VIII. 200 A few pieces of copper-nickel (nickeline) were obtained. **1971** *Mineral. Mag.* XXXVIII. 104 Recommendations of the Commission [on New Minerals and Mineral Names, of the International Mineralogical Association] on minerals for which more than one name is in common use:..Nickeline, not niccolite or nickelite. **1883** *Encycl. Brit.* (ed. 9) XVI. 392 *Nickelite (Copper Nickel). **1857** *Chamb. Jrnl.* VIII. 224 We have recently experimented upon the subject of *nickelisation. **1872** F. G. THOMAS *Dis. Women* (ed. 3) 349 The clamp.. may be made..of *nickelized steel. **1880** *Libr. Univ. Knowl.* VI. 511 Using a solution of *nickelous sulphate. **1899** *Nature* 20 Apr. 595/1 Complete analyses of nickelous bromide and cobaltous bromide were undertaken.

nickel, *v.* [f. the sb.] **a.** To coat with nickel.

a **1875** in Knight *Dict. Mech.* 1526/1 It being far easier to gild, plate, or copper an article than to nickel it.

b. To foul (the bore of a gun) with nickel off the bullet-casing; *intr.*, to become fouled.

1918, etc. [implied in NICKELING *vbl. sb.* below]. **1920** G. BURRARD *Notes on Sporting Rifles* 31 When a barrel has once been nickelled it is always liable to nickel again very quickly.

Hence **ˈnickeling** *vbl. sb.*, (*a*) the process of coating with nickel; (*b*) the fouling of the bore of a gun with nickel; metallic fouling; **ˈnickelled** *ppl. a.*, coated with nickel.

1875 KNIGHT *Dict. Mech.* 1526/1 Nickeling. **1884** HIGGS *Magn. & Dyn. Electr. Machines* 203 Gilding, silvering, nickeling and tinning have become so universal. **1885** *Bazaar* 30 Mar. 1272/2, 52 in. [bicycle],..nickelled, ball pedals. **1894** *Outing* (U.S.) XXIV. 132/2 Two of the nickeled hinges on my valise had been twisted off. **1918** E. S. FARROW *Dict. Mil. Terms* 407 *Nickeling*, in gunnery, metallic fouling caused by a portion of the cupro-nickel of the envelope of the bullet being left on the surface of the bore. **1920** G. BURRARD *Notes on Sporting Rifles* 30 Nickelling at first is impossible to detect with the eye. **1958** J. A. BARLOW *Elements of Rifle Shooting* (ed. 5) i. 6 It may be as well here to touch on the problem presented by metallic fouling, generally known as nickelling... Nickelling is mainly due to small particles of the bullet envelope being cut off by roughness or excrescence in the bore.

nickelian (nɪˈkiːlɪən), *a. Min.* [f. NICKEL *sb.* + -IAN 2.] Of a mineral: having a (small) proportion of a constituent element replaced by nickel.

1930 W. T. SCHALLER in *Amer. Mineralogist* XV. 571 Nickel—nickelian. **1951** C. PALACHE et al. *Dana's Syst. Min.* (ed. 7) II. 503 A nickelian variety [of kirovite] (2·5 per cent NiO) occurs in the Mt. Diablo district. **1974** *Encycl. Brit. Macropædia* XII. 41/1 There is simply a gradually thickening crust of iron oxides—a mixture of goethite, hematite, and nickelian magnetite.

nickelodeon (nɪkəˈləʊdɪən). *U.S.* [f. NICKEL *sb.* 2; app. after MELODEON.] **1.** A theatre or motion-picture show for which the admission fee is a nickel; a place containing automatic machines to provide amusement, which can be used for a nickel. Also *attrib.*

1921 *Ladies' Home Jrnl.* June 79/1 It is this class which first patronized the old nickelodeon, and undoubtedly it imposed its tastes and its traditions on the picture makers. **1927** F. HURST *Song of Life* 292 The nickelodeons and the gewgaw shops of the most terrific city in the world. **1930** *Time & Tide* 27 Sept. 1206 The film was..handed over by the scientists to the 'nickelodeons' of America. **1938** *Encycl. Brit. Bk. of Year* 422/2 The old nickelodeon programmes. **1939** C. MORLEY *Kitty Foyle* 68 A dance floor and a nickelodeon piano. **1955** G. GREENE *Quiet American* 188 It must have belonged to the same era as the nickelodeon. **1973** *Publishers Weekly* 10 Sept. 45/2 The development of American movies from nickelodeon days to the 1970s.

2. A 'jukebox'; a machine that automatically plays selected gramophone records on the insertion of a coin. Also *attrib.*

1938 *Florida Review* Spring 25/1 The requisites of a place entitling it to the name *jook* are..presence of the nickelodeon, and..of the dance-floor. **1949** *Sat. Even. Post*

15 Jan. 88/3 A nickelodeon at the end of the street emits a tinny piano tinkle. **1957** J. FRAME *Owls do Cry* 76 Putting money in the nickelodeon. **1971** *Daily Colonist* (Victoria, B.C.) 18 Aug. 8/2 The former shepherd boy who used a $4,000 nickelodeon as a springboard to the top.

ˈnicker, *sb.*[1] *Obs.* exc. *arch.* Forms: 1 (9) nicor, 3–4 niker, 4 nyker, 5 nycker, nykyr, 6 nicre, 9 nicer, nicker. [OE. *nicor*, *nicer-*, *nic(c)r-*, = MDu. and MLG. *nicker*, *necker* (Du. *nikker*), ON. *nykr* (Icel. *nykur*, Norw. *nykk*, Da. *nök*, Sw. *neck*) masc.:—OTeut. **nikwiz-*, **nikuz-*, also represented by OHG. *nichus*, *nih(h)us* masc. (glossing 'crocodillus'; MHG. *niches*, *nickes*, G. *nix*), and *nicchessa* fem. (MHG. *-nixe*, G. *nixe*): see NIX *sb.*[2] and NIXIE[1]. The root **niq-* may be identical with **nigw-* in Gr. *νίζειν*, *νίπτειν*, Skr. *nij-* to wash.]

1. An imaginary being supposed to live in the water; a water-demon, kelpie, river-horse (†hippopotamus); also in ME., a siren or mermaid.

Beowulf 422 þær ic..on yðum sloȝ niceras nihtes. **971** *Blickl. Hom.* 209 Under þæm stane wæs niccra eardung. *Ibid.* 211 þonne ȝewitan þa saula niðer..& him onfengon ða nicras. *c* **1000** in Cockayne *Narrat.* (1861) 11 Sona þæs ðe hie inna wæron swa wæron þa nicoras ȝearwe. *c* **1205** LAY. 21747 þat water is unimete brade; nikeres þer badieð inne. *c* **1330** R. BRUNNE *Chron. Wace* (Rolls) 1447 þer fond þey Nykeres [F. *seraines*] þat myry song, Out of þe weye to turne hem wrong. **1340** *Ayenb.* 61 þise byeþ þe tuo nykeren þet we uyndeþ in bokes of kende of bestes. Vor hy byeþ a ssewynge of þe ze, þet me klepeþ nykeren, þet habbeþ bodyes of wyfman and tayl of uissse. *c* **1440** *Promp. Parv.* 356/2 Nykyr, *Sirene.* **1568** WITHALS *Dict.* 9 a/1 A nicre, *remora, echeneis.*

1834 *Fraser's Mag.* X. 54 The Anglo-Saxons did not cease to believe in the existence..of the elves and the nicers. **1853** KINGSLEY *Hypatia* xii, 'What is a nicor, Agilmund?' 'A sea-devil who eats sailors'. **1892** BROOKE *Early Eng. Lit.* I. iii. 59 The nickers lie there on the sloping rocks of the ness, monsters that at mid-day go out into the open sea.

†**2.** [From Du. *nikker.*] A demon or devil. *Obs.*

1481 CAXTON *Reynard* (Arb.) 100 Alas me growleth of thyse fowle nyckers, come they out of helle?

ˈnicker, *sb.*[2] [f. NICK *v.*[2], in various senses.]

†**1.** One who cheats at play. *Obs. rare.*

1669 (*title*) The Nicker nicked; or, the Cheats of Gaming discovered. **1714** T. LUCAS *Lives Gamesters* 203 Call'd by the Nickers and Sharpers little Dick-Fisher.

†**2.** One who fits a thing neatly. *Obs. rare*⁻¹.

1676 MARVELL *Mr. Smirke* K b, Yet I am not neither one of the most credulous nickers or applyers of natural events to humain transactions.

3. One who hits in throwing; applied *spec.* in the early part of the 18th cent. to disorderly youths who made a practice of breaking windows by throwing coppers at them.

1716 GAY *Trivia* III. 323 His scatter'd Pence the flying Nicker flings, And with the Copper Show'r the Casement rings. **1849** MACAULAY *Hist. Eng.* iii. I. 361 At a later period arose the Nicker, the Hawcubite, and the yet more dreaded name of Mohawk. **1886** MISS BRADDON *Mohawks* ix, The *Flying Post* described how the Nickers had broken all Mr. Topsparkle's windows with halfpence.

4. One who, or that which, nicks or cuts.

a. One who nicks horses' tails.

1810 *Sporting Mag.* XXXV. 263 The defendant's witnesses, whom Mr. Serjeant Pell..described as croppers, dockers, nickers and trimmers.

b. That part of a centre-bit which cuts the circle of the hole made by the tool.

1846 HOLTZAPFFEL *Turning* II. 541 A thin shearing point or nicker, that cuts through the fibres like the point of a knife. **1865** *Routledge's Mag. for Boys* June 353 The nicker leads or prepares the way for the cutter throughout the entire depth of the hole.

c. *Telegr.* A recording apparatus which makes nicks in a strip of paper.

1871 *Echo* 2 Feb., Professor Morse's printing nickers and embossers.

ˈnicker, *sb.*[3] Also 7 **nickar**. [Perh. f. as prec., but cf. KNICKER.]

1. = KNICKER 1. Also *pl.* as a game.

1675 DUFFETT *Mock Tempest* IV. i, Now I can't teach my Wife to play Nickers. **1696** [see NICKAR]. **1727** BOYER *Dict. Royal* II, Marbles (round fine clay Nickers for Children to play withal). **1847** HALLIWELL, *Nicker*..(2) a little ball of clay or earth baked hard and oiled over for boys to play at nickers. **1893** J. INGLIS *Oor ain Folk* xii. (1894) 94 Every boy prided himself on having a favourite nicker.

2. = KNICKER 2.

1888 *Advance* (Chicago) 27 Dec., What's a nicker? 'A flat thick piece of lead..which you throw down at the buttons'. **1889** A. T. PASK *Eyes Thames* 119 The leaden 'nicker' is produced from the trousers pocket.

ˈnicker, *sb.*[4], variant of NICKAR.

ˈnicker, *sb.*[5] *Sc.* and *north. dial.* [f. the vb.] A neigh; also, a laugh, a snigger.

a **1791** *Lochmaben Harper* xiii. in Child *Ballads* IV. 19/2 His mare's away to Lochmaben, Wi' mony a nicker and mony a sneer. **1834** in Sharp *Bishoprick Garl.* 42 Settin up a greater nicker and a whinney. **1883** CLELAND *Inchbracken* xxvi. 210 She just leugh..an' syne she gae the ither nicker.

nicker (ˈnɪkə(r)), *sb.*[6] *slang.* [Origin unknown.] One pound sterling.

1910 *Sessions Papers* 1 June 128, I suppose this has cost you a couple of 'nickers'. **1939** [see CASER[2]]. **1960** D. LESSING *In Pursuit of English* ii. 66 It's a little matter. A hundred nicker. And it'd double itself in a year. **1966** F. SHAW et al. *Lern Yerself Scouse* 34 *Five nicker*, five pounds; five pound note. **1975** J. SYMONS *Three Pipe Problem* xv. 138 Who said there'd be trouble? Anyway, it's a hundred nicker.

ˈnicker, *v.* Chiefly *Sc.* and *north. dial.* [Imitative: cf. NEIGHER *v.* and NICHER *v.*]

1. *intr.* To neigh.

a **1774** FERGUSSON *Hallowfair* Poems (1821) 118 The cuissers prance and nicker, An' owre the ley-rig scud. **1820** SCOTT *Monast.* xxxiii, Mounted on nags that nicker at the clash of a sword. **1879** STEVENSON *Trav. Cevennes* (1886) 21 This other donkey..and Modestine met, nickering for joy. **1880** L. WALLACE *Ben-Hur* v. ii, One [horse]..nickered low and gladly at sight of him.

2. To laugh loudly or shrilly. Also *trans.*

1819 W. TENNANT *Papistry Storm'd* (1827) 22 He nicker't sic a lang gaffaw. **1829** HOGG *Sheph. Cal.* I. 329 She was sae glad that she fell a-nickering. **1863** in Robson *Bards of Tyne* 254 The keel-bullies nick'rd, but on Mally toddled.

Hence **ˈnickering** *vbl. sb.*

1881 K. BLIND in *Contemp. Rev.* XL. 199 With shrill nickering..the stallion ran..towards the lake.

nickerbocker, var. of KNICKERBOCKER.

ˈnicker-tree, var. of *nickar-tree* s.v. NICKAR.

†**ˈnickery.** *Obs. rare.* A nickname.

1823 'J. BEE' *Dict. Turf* s.v. *Nick*, Nickeries are the same [as nicknames] applied to actions and things. **1824** *Hist. Gambling* II. 37 This man, or this sharper, lived to a great age, little respected, under the nickery of 'Old Q.'

ˈnickety-ˈnock, *adv.* [Imitative.] With a clicking and knocking sound.

1812 H. & J. SMITH *Rej. Addr.*, *Rebuilding* (1873) 63 His head, as he tumbled, went nickety-nock, Like a pebble in Carisbrook well.

nickey (ˈnɪkɪ). [Of obscure origin.] A kind of boat with a lug-sail, used in the Isle of Man.

1883 *Fisheries Exhib. Catal.* (ed. 4) 132 This rig is rapidly superseding the class of boat for many years used in the Isle of Man, known as 'Nickeys', or lug sail boats. **1894** HALL CAINE *Manxman* 358 A Dandie..being smaller than a Nickey, and of yawl rig.

†**nick-fidge.** *Obs. rare*⁻¹. [Of obscure origin.] App., the person taken to task.

1608 H. CLAPHAM *Errour Left Hand* A iv, As for the Male-content, I make him the Nicke-fidge here, as I did the Flyer in the former [dialogue].

†**nick-hole**, obs. var. of HICKWALL.

Swainson gives *nickle* as a Notts form of the word.

1547 SALESBURY *Welsh Dict.*, *Kasec yddrickhin, ederyn*, a nycke hole.

nickie tam, nickie tom, varr. NICKY TAM.

nicking (ˈnɪkɪŋ), *vbl. sb.*[1] [f. NICK *v.*[2] + -ING[1].]

1. a. The action of notching or cutting.

1551 TURNER *Herbal* I. B vij b, The milky humour, that commeth out of yᵉ herbe, by scotching or nyckyng. **1611** COTGR., *Creneure*, a iagging, nicking, notching. **1828** MOIR *Mansie Wauch* xxiii, Baking and brewing—nicking of geese's craigs—hacking the necks of dead chickens. **1837** *Civil Eng. & Arch. Jrnl.* I. 72/1 The method of cutting this stone into sizes is by what the quarrymen call 'nicking'. A line is drawn across the stone with a chisel [etc.]. **1903** *Brit. Med. Jrnl.* No. 2205. 848 The 'nicking' of the stricture was followed by a large enema.

b. spec. in *Farriery* (see NICK *v.*[2] 3).

1753 J. BARTLET *Gentl. Farriery* 309 Before we describe the operation of Nicking, it may be necessary to enquire how the effect of it..is brought about. **1815** *Sporting Mag.* XLVI. 115 His condemnation of cropping and nicking. **1896** *Daily News* 14 Feb. 5/3 Nicking is a process supplemental to what is known as 'docking'.

c. A notch or indentation; a cutting or set of cuts. (See also quot. 1881.)

1844 H. STEPHENS *Bk. Farm* III. 1277 The nicking should extend all the way from the shoulder-top to the tail. **1881** RAYMOND *Mining Gloss.*, *Nicking*, the cutting made by the hewer at the side of the face. *Nickings* is the small coal produced in making the nicking. **1898** H. G. HUTCHINSON *Golf* (ed. 6) 69 The first gutta-percha balls were made smooth, without any of the 'nicking' which we now see upon them.

d. A method of pruning in which an incision is made below the base of a bud in order to curb its growth.

1949 C. R. THOMPSON *Pruning of Apples & Pears* ii. 53 The top bud should be prevented from growing vigorously by making a knife incision at its base, a treatment referred to as 'nicking'. **1972** G. E. BROWN *Pruning of Trees* ii. 24 Nicking is carried out below selected buds in order to reduce their vigour.

†**2.** The practice of fraudulently diminishing the capacity of a beer-can. *Obs. rare.*

1628 *Robin Goodfellow* (Percy Soc.) 29 There was a tapster, that with his pots smalnesse..had got a good summe of money together. This nicking of the pots he would never leave. *c* **1636** *London Chanticleers* v, The slight of nicking and frothing he scornes as too common.

3. The action of hitting (upon) or striking.

1668 DRYDEN *Dram. Poesy* Ess. (ed. Ker) I. 92 This nicking of him who spoke before both in sound and measure is so great an happiness. **1687** A. LOVELL tr. *Bergerac's Com. Hist.* 4 Because of the nicking of the time so patly. **1899** *N. & Q.* 9th Ser. III. 185/1 There was 'nicking', when one player's button touched another after rebounding from the wall when 'banged.'

4. See NICK *v.*[2] 8 a.

5. *attrib.*, as ***nicking board, buddle, trunk*** (for washing ores); ***nicking engine, file, saw, tool*** (for cutting the nick in screw-heads); ***nicking knife, machine*** (for horses' tails); ***nicking-process.***

1839 URE *Dict. Arts* 751 Alongside of this channel there is a slightly inclined plank, called *nicking board. *Ibid.*, The *nicking buddle is analogous to the tables called *dormantes* or *jumelles* by the French miners. **1831** HOLLAND *Manuf. Metal* I. 205 The pacha of Egypt obtained from this country ..six *nicking, and six cutting engines. **1875** KNIGHT *Dict. Mech.* 1526/2 **Nicking-file.* **1816** in Blaine *Veter. Art* (ed. 2) 665 *Nicking knives, with Lines and brass Pullies. **1753** J. BARTLET *Gentl. Farriery* 331 Directions for the Application of the *Nicking Machine. **1875** LOWER *Eng. Surnames* (ed. 4) II. App. 176 A Christian name unsusceptible of the *nicking or abbreviating process. **1884** KNIGHT *Dict. Mech.* Suppl. 634/2 **Nicking Saw.* **1875** —— *Dict. Mech.* 2067/2 The blank..is presented to the shaving tool, and then..fed to the *nicking tool. *Ibid.* 1526/2 **Nicking-trunk.*

†**ˈnicking**, *sb.*[2] *Obs.* (A doubtful form: see INKLING.)

a **1400–50** *Alexander* 2968 (D.), þis gouernour of grece.. Harde a nyckyng [*A.* a nyngkiling] of hys name & natys hym to ryse.

ˈnicking, *ppl. a.* [f. NICK *v.*[2] + -ING[2].] That nicks, in various senses of the vb.

1598 MARSTON *Sco. Villanie* III. ix. 218 O what a tricksie lerned nicking strain Is this applauded, senselesse, modern vain! **1631** WEEVER *Anc. Funeral Mon.* 208 The same Authour in another place..hath these nicking Hexameters. *Ibid.* 622 These nicking, nice, allusive verses. **1674** N. FAIRFAX *Bulk. & Selv.* To Rdr., Perhaps if we slip this tide, we shall never come again at such a nicking one. *a* **1734** NORTH *Exam.* II. iv. §40 (1740) 250 It might have proved a nicking Evidence against him.

nick-nack, variant of KNICK-KNACK.

nick-nackatory: see KNICK-KNACKATORY.

nick-nacket: see KNICK-KNACKET.

1820 SCOTT *Abbot* xix, This comes of carrying Popish nick-nackets about you.

nick-nackitarian, -nacky: see KNICK-.

nickname (ˈnɪkneɪm), *sb.* Also 5 **neke-**, 6–7 **nicke-**, 6 **nyck(e-**, 7 **nic-**. [Later form of EKE-NAME: see N 3.] A name or appellation added to, or substituted for, the proper name of a person, place, etc., usually given in ridicule or pleasantry.

c **1440** *Promp. Parv.* 352/2 Neke name, or eke name, *agnomen.* **1530** PALSGR. 248/1 Nyckename, *brocquart.* **1532** MORE *Confut. Tindale* Wks. 378, I shoulde here call Tindall by another name:..it were no nyek name at all. **1567** HARMAN *Caveat* (1869) 77 Men haue geuen all these nycke names to the places aboue sayde. **1617** MORYSON *Itin.* II. 63 James Fitz-thomas..was by a nicke-name called the Suggon Earle. **1674** R. GODFREY *Inj. & Ab. Physic* 138 Yee Independents, or yee Anabaptists, or yee Quakers, (which are all but Nick names). **1710** ADDISON *Tatler* No. 226 ¶4 He unfortunately got the Nickname of the Squeaking Doctor. **1789** BRAND *Newcastle* II. 313 *note*, Very improperly called cappers, a nick-name by which they are styled in some printed poll-books. **1806–7** J. BERESFORD *Miseries Hum. Life* (1826) VI. 118 A name for a stage coach which beats..every other English nick-name out of the field. **1849** MACAULAY *Hist. Eng.* i. I. 15 His own countrymen called him by a Saxon nickname. **1874** BURNAND *My Time* xxii. 201 He had an absurd nickname for every boy in the house.

Comb. **1888** *Spectator* 18 Feb. 239/2 Disraeli, senior, is an inexhaustible nickname-maker.

b. A familiar form of a Christian name.

1605 CAMDEN *Rem.* 114 From Nicknames or Nursenames, came these..Bill for William, Clem for Clement. **1837** DICKENS *Pickw.* xvi, A very good name it [*sc.* Job] is; only one, I know, that ain't got a nickname to it.

Hence **ˈnicknameless** *a.*, having no nickname.

1894 J. MENZIES *Our Town* xi. 115 John O'Meara, a nick-nameless native of the Emerald Isle.

ˈnickname, *v.* [f. the sb.]

1. *trans.* To call by an incorrect or improper name; to misname.

1536 *Rem. Sedition* 2 A certayne commune welth.. whiche if we baptyse righte and not nycke name it, we must nedes call a comon wo. **1580** LUPTON *Sivqila* 53 Are they called good men with you, that are stoute fighters?..Then surely they nickname them, unlesse evil be good. **1602** SHAKS. *Ham.* III. i. 151 You lispe, and nickname Gods creatures. **1655** GURNALL *Chr. in Arm.* I. 26 When we leave out this syllable All, we nick-name God, and call him by his creatures' name. **1680** HICKERINGILL *Curse ye Meroz* 5 It is (so) styled in this Text by the Spirit of God that Nick-names nothing. **1817** COLERIDGE *Biog. Lit.* (Bohn) 117 That compendious philosophy, which..contrives a theory of spirit by nicknaming matter. **1871** EARLE *Philol. Eng. Tongue* (1880) §107 The French and Germans have named the vowels, but the English have nick-named them.

b. With complement. Also with *as*, *so*.

1548 TURNER *Names Herbes* D iij b, Isatis, in english wad, & not Ode as some corrupters of the englishe tonge do nikename it. **1599** *Broughton's Let.* vii. 23 Which..the Apostle [calls]..ψευδωνυμονγνωσιν knowledge so nicknamed. **1621** QUARLES *Div. Poems*, *Esther* (1638) 117 Divine directions, Which oft (unseen through dulnesse of the mind) We nick-name Chance. **1656** G. COLLIER *Answ. 15 Quest.* 25 Publick sacramental examination is nick-named private popish confession. **1775** ROMANS *Florida* App. 72 You will see..a watch-house (nick-named a fort). **1813** SHELLEY *Q. Mab* III. 32 The fool Whom courtiers nickname monarch. **1824** BYRON *Juan* XV. xix, With no great care for what is nicknamed glory.

†**c.** To mention by mistake; to assert wrongly *to be* something. *Obs. rare.*

1588 SHAKS. *L.L.L.* v. ii. 349 *King.* The vertue of your eie must breake my oth. *Q.* You nick-name vertue: vice you should haue spoke. **1665** MANLEY *Grotius' Low C. Wars* 548 For preventing Princes of that sort of Dominion, which is nicknamed to be Power given them by Heaven.

2. To give a nickname to (one); to call by a nickname.

1567-9 JEWEL *Def. Apol.* (1611) 20 S. Hierome..nick-nameth S. Ambrose, sometimes calling him Coruus, sometimes Cornicula. **1589** R. HARVEY *Plain Perc.* (1590) 8, I will nicke-name no bodie: I am none of these tuft mockadoo mak-a-dooes. **1638** SIR T. HERBERT *Trav.* (ed. 2) 162 The Gowers that people it; nick-nam'd from their Idolatry. **1700** ASTRY tr. *Saavedra-Faxardo* I. 116 Alphonso, who was Nick-named from his broken Hands. **1856** KANE *Arct. Expl.* I. xxix. 383 They nicknamed and adopted all of us as members of their fraternity.

b. With complement. Also with *as, so.*

1577 STANYHURST *Descr. Irel.* i. in *Holinshed* (1587) 9/2 Whoso surpasseth others either in cauilling sophistrie, or subtile philosophie, is forthwith nicke named a Duns. **1610** HOLLAND *Camden's Brit.* I. 255 *marg.*, Nick-named John Lack-land. **1656** HEYLIN *Extraneus Vapulans* 227 The bitternesse of his Style against those poor men whom he so nick-nameth. **1728** MORGAN *Algiers* II. iv. 264 A notable Turkish Corsair, by the Spaniards nick-named Cacha-Diablo, i.e. Drub-Devil. **1760** WESLEY *Wks.* (1872) XIII. 388 They were soon nicknamed Methodists. **1825** BENTHAM *Ration. Reward* 41 You shall not be nicknamed projectors by the idle and the incapable. **1849** MACAULAY *Hist. Eng.* viii. II. 281 The satirists of the age nicknamed him Lord Allpride. **1894** J. T. FOWLER *Adamnan* Introd. 42 The Roman party nicknamed it Simon Magus's tonsure.

Hence **'nicknamed** *ppl. a.*, **'nicknaming** *vbl. sb.* Also **'nicknameable** *a.*, that can be nicknamed. **nickna'mee**, one to whom a nickname is given.

1618 SIR S. D'EWES *Autobiog.* (1845) I. 120 The common nick-naming and scoffing at religion. **1664** H. MORE *Myst. Iniq.* xiv. 161 The nick-naming of the true Christians by the odious Title of Hereticks. **1677** W. HUGHES *Man of Sin* II. v. 98 Come, ye..Heathens, and learn Idolatry from those Nick-nam'd Christians. **1794** C. PIGOT *Female Jockey Club* p. xxxv, Half a dozen Irish Chairmen..drove this nicknamed heaven-born Minister before them. **1888** *Spectator* 18 Feb. 239/2 No matter how obscure the nick-namer and nicknamee may be. **1898** L. STEPHEN *Stud. Biogr.* II. iv. 144 A man who is 'nicknameable' must be a good fellow.

nicknamer ('nɪkneɪmə(r)). [f. prec. + -ER^1.]

† **1.** The rhetorical figure Prosonomasia. *Obs. rare.*

1589 PUTTENHAM *Eng. Poesie* III. xix. (Arb.) 212 Ye have a figure by which ye play with a couple of words or names much resembling, and because the one seemes to answere th'other by manner of illusion, and doth, as it were, nick him, I call him the Nicknamer.

2. One who nicknames another person or thing.

1868 A. SMITH *Last Leaves* 172 The nicknamed and the nicknamer sleep in the same forgetfulness. **1894** HUXLEY in *Life* (1900) II. xxii. 385 The nicknamer of genius called this brand of genius 'pig philosophy'.

† **nick-ninny.** *slang. Obs.* (See quot.)

a **1700** B. E. *Dict. Cant. Crew, Nick-ninny*, an empty Fellow, a meer Cod's Head.

nickpoint, var. KNICKPOINT.

† **nick-pot.** *Obs. rare.* [f. NICK *v.*^{2}] **a.** An innkeeper or tapster. **b.** A fraudulent beer-pot.

1602 ROWLANDS *Greenes Ghost* (1860) 31 A necessarie caueat for victuallers and nickpots, how to beware of such insinuating companions. **1624** *Skelton's Ghost* 19 in S.'s Wks. 1843 II. 155 Our pots were full quarted, We were not thus thwarted With froth-canne and nick-pot.

nick-stick. Now *rare* or *Obs.* [f. NICK *v.*] A tally, a reckoning-stick.

1695 in *Trans. Antiq. Soc. Scot.* (1792) I. 558 You are to advert to keep an exact nickstick between you and the coalyier, of the number of deals of coals received in. **1816** SCOTT *Antiq.* xv. *note*, Each family had its own nick-stick, and for each loaf as delivered a notch was made on the stick. **1843** J. BALLANTINE *Gaberlunzie* (1875) 170 With her the baker required to keep no nickstick, the butcher no chalk-board.

transf. **1872** EGGLESTONE (*title*) The Weardale Nick-Stick, containing Floods, Thunderstorms, High Winds.

nick-tailed ('nɪkteɪld), *a.* Having the tail nicked.

1841 *Southern Lit. Messenger* VII. 219/1 Brenda, mounted on Paul Clifford, nick-tailed sorrel pacer. **1853** J. G. BALDWIN *Flush Times Alabama* 97 The horse, a nick-tailed trotter, Tom had raffled off. **1867** G. W. HARRIS *Sut Lovingood* 19 A nick tailed, bow necked, long, poor, pale sorrel horse.

† **nick-time,** *Obs. rare*$^{-1}$. The nick of time.

1650 A. B. *Mutat. Polemo* 16 In troth not too early, for it was in the nick-time.

† **'nickum.** *slang. Obs.* (See quot.)

In mod. Sc. dial. *nickum* is used in the sense of 'wag, mischievous or tricky person': see *Eng. Dial. Dict.*

a **1700** B. E. *Dict. Cant. Crew, Nickum*, a Sharper; also a Rooking Ale-house or Innkeeper,..or any Retailer.

nickum-poop, obs. var of NINCOMPOOP.

'nicky, *sb.*^{1} *dial.* Also nickee. (See quots.)

1854 *Jrnl. R. Agric. Soc.* XV. II. 414 The inferior [wood] going in sale faggots, bush faggots, and nickees, or small faggots used in lighting fires. **1882** W. BARNES in *Macm. Mag.* Mar. 418 When he wanted to chop up some small wood for nickies, as we call them in the West—some little bundles of wood for lighting fires.

Nicky ('nɪkɪ), *sb.*^{2} [f. N.I.C. (main entry), infl. by *Nicky*, dim. of *Nicholas*, a male name.] Colloq. name for the National Incomes Commission. Also *attrib.*

1962 *Daily Tel.* 27 July 1/1 The Commission, likely to be known as 'Nicky', will consider pay questions in both private and public sectors. **1962** *Ibid.* 10 Aug. 20/5 (*heading*) 'Nicky' report for TUC. **1963** *Ann. Reg. 1962* iii. 30 Nicky was expected to run the rule over wages claims.

nicky tam ('nɪkɪ tæm). *Sc.* Also **knicky tom, nickie tam, nickie tom,** and with hyphen. [f. K)NICK(ERS + -Y^6 + *tam* (see TAUM).] (See quot. 1965.)

1911 *Aberdeen Jrnl. N. & Q.* IV. 17/2 *Knicky-toms*, garters worn over trousers. **1917** E. S. RAE *Private John Macpherson* 54 An' Geordie, ma foreman, a dacenter lad Ne'er wore nickietoms, nor plooed up a fleed. *a* **1931** in E. MACCOLL *Scotland Sings* (1953) 96, I..buskit roond my nappin' knees a pair o' Nicky Tams. **1965** *Sc. Nat. Dict.* VI. 422/3 *Nickie-tam*... One of a pair of straps, or a piece of string in lieu, tied by farmworkers over the trousers-legs immediately below the knee to keep the legs clear of the soil and dust, etc. **1967** *Listener* 12 Oct. 472/3 The Scots word for 'a tying worn below the knee to keep the bottom of the trouser-leg lifted clear in dirty work or to exclude dust'. It is a nicky-tam. **1972** *Daily Mail* 29 July 6/3 We are about to lose the English word 'yorkers' or what the Scots called 'Nicky Tams'.

nicnac, nicname, obs. ff. KNICK-KNACK, NICKNAME.

Nicobarese (nɪkəbə'ri:z), *sb.* and *a.* [f. *Nicobar* (see below) + -ESE.] **A.** *sb.* **a.** The people of the Nicobar Islands in the Bay of Bengal. **b.** The Mon-Khmer language of this people. **B.** *adj.* Of or pertaining to this people. Also **Nico'barian** *sb.* and *a.*

1790 G. HAMILTON in *Asiatick Res.* II. 344 The people of Carnicobar have a tradition among them, that several canoes came from Andaman..and that the crews..killed several of the Nicobarians. **1846** *Jrnl. Asiatic Soc. Bengal* XV. 368 The Nicobarian Pigs appear to have been derived from the Chinese domestic species. **1859** *Sel. Rec. Govt. India Home Dept.* No. 25. 61 Their language bears no affinity to that of the Nicobarians. **1875** F. A. DE ROEPSTORFF *Vocab. Dial. Nicobar & Andaman Is.* (ed. 2) 14 The Nicobarese have all they want, yet they like very much to barter with foreigners. **1884** —— *Dict. Nancowry Dial. of Nicobarese Lang.* p. xiii, Nicobarese is a wholly uninflective tongue. **1889** E. H. MAN (*title*) Dictionary of the central Nicobarese language. **1924** G. WHITEHEAD *In Nicobar Is.* ii. 47 The Nicobarese keep a great number of domestic pigs, which they feed on coco-nut. **1972** W. B. LOCKWOOD *Panorama of Indo-European Lang.* 229 Nicobarese..is spoken by 15,000 islanders. *Ibid.*, The population of the Nicobars has been swollen in the last two decades by settlers from all parts of India, forming a polyglot element..about as numerous as the native Nicobarese.

† **Nico'demical,** *a. Obs. rare*$^{-1}$. [f. the name of *Nicodemus*, the Jewish ruler who came to Jesus by night (John iii. 1, etc.).] Characteristic of Nicodemus; of a literal type (cf. John iii. 4). So † **Nico'demically** *adv.*, in a literal sense. **Nico'demite**, one who resembles Nicodemus; a secret or timid adherent. † **Nico'demize** *v.*, to act or reason like Nicodemus. *Obs.*

1642 J. EATON *Honey-c. Free Justif.* 46 They fall a wrangling with *Nicodemicall conclusions. **1647** TRAPP *Comm. Matt.* xviii. 3 How absurd was that Anabaptist Aurifaber, who understanding this text *Nicodemically.. stirreth up the people..to carry themselves childishly. **1585** FETHERSTON tr. *Calvin on Acts* xxi. 26 False *Nicodemites.. goe about to colour their treacherous dissimulation. **1637** GILLESPIE *Eng. Pop. Cerem.* Ep. A2b, The lapped Nicodemite, holdes it enough to yeeld some secret assent to the trueth. **1691** BAXTER *Nat. Ch.* xv. 70 They will but be Nicodemites, and not venture on danger or difficulty. **1921** *Outward Bound* Apr. 29/2 This is no time to play the Nicodemite. **1624** DARCIE *Birth of Heresies* xxi. 98 Did he determin we should hereby Capernize & *Nicodemize, to enquire, or make doubt of Gods power?

† **'nicol**^{1}. *Obs. rare.* [var. of NICKEL; cf. the spelling *kupfer-nicol* in J. Hill *Fossils* (1748) 625, and *copper-nicol* (1728) s.v. COPPER *sb.*^{1} 12.] Nickel-green, annabergite.

1753 CHAMBERS *Cycl. Supp.*, *Nicol*,..a word used by the miners in Germany to express a greenish crust, covering several of the species of marcasites and cobalt.

Nicol^2 ('nɪkəl). *Opt.* Also nicol. [The name of the inventor, William *Nicol* of Edinburgh (died 1851).] A prism of Iceland spar, so constructed as to transmit only the extraordinary ray of doubly refracted light. (Also freq. called ***Nicol prism.***)

1843 *Phil. Mag.* XXII. 243, I find it a most material improvement to substitute a Nicol prism for the plate of glass. **1863** E. ATKINSON tr. *Ganot's Elem. Treat. Physics* VII. viii. 485 The Nicol's prism is one of the most valuable means of polarising light. **1875** TYNDALL *Heat* xv. (ed. 5) 517 The construction of the Nicol is such that it permits to pass through it vibrations which are executed in a certain determinate direction, and these only. **1878** LOCKYER *Stargazing* 448 If two Nicols are used instead of two simple crystals. **1906** *Jrnl. Chem. Soc.* LXXXIX. II. 1150 The nicols were rotated. **1937** *Discovery* Aug. 242/2 A Nicol prism (which is two portions of a rhomb of Iceland spar cemented together with Canada balsam). **1955** W. GADDIS *Recognitions* III. v. 874 If we can fix a microscope up with polarized light and put a particle of the pigment under it, we can see whether it's isotropic or anisotropic, for that we use nicol prisms.

Nicolaitan (nɪkə'leɪɪtən), *sb.* and *a.* Also 7 Nich-, 6, 9 -ane. [f. as next + -AN.]

A. *sb.* A member of an early Christian party or sect mentioned in Rev. ii. 6, 15, the precise nature of which is uncertain.

1526 TINDALE *Rev.* ii. 6 Butt this thou haste because thou hated the dedes off the Nicolaitans. **1546** BALE *Eng. Votaries* I. (1560) 64 b, Called there of them the heresy of Nicolaitanes. **1604** R. CAWDREY *Table Alph.*, *Nicholaitan*, an heretike, like Nicholas, who held that wiues should bee common to all alike. **1655** BAXTER *Quaker's Catech.* Pref. B j b, The Nicolaitans and the rest of the Gnosticks. **1702** ECHARD *Eccl. Hist.* (1710) 406 There appeared another sort of hereticks called the Nicolaitans,..a horrid brutish sect. **1831-3** E. BURTON *Eccl. Hist.* xii. (1845) 274 There were some Gnostics who did not scruple to eat things sacrificed unto idols: and these men were then known by the name of Nicolaitans. **1861** TRENCH *Comm. Ep. Churches Asia* 83 The Nicolaitans as we have seen are the Balaamites.

B. *adj.* Held by the Nicolaitans.

1874 J. H. BLUNT *Dict. Sects* 373 It may be concluded that the Nicolaitane doctrine was a doctrine of libertinism in religious rites.

Hence **Nico'laitanism.**

1882-3 SCHAFF *Encycl. Relig. Knowl.* II. 1655 The similarity of Nicolaitanism and the Antinomianism of Corinth.

† **Nicolaite.** *Obs. rare.* Forms: 4-5 **Nychol-**, 6 **Nichol-**. [ad. Gr. Νικολαΐτης (Rev. ii. 6), f. the personal name Νικόλαος.] = prec.

1382 WYCLIF *Rev.* ii. 6 But thou hast this good thing, for thou hatedist the dedes of Nycholaytis. *c* **1449** PECOCK *Repr.* v. iii. 497 Also the sect of Nycholaitis, which helden that weddid men myȝten chaunge to gidere her wyues. **1586** T. B. *La Primaud. Fr. Acad.* I. 463 The Nicholaites revived the same error in the primitive church.

Hence † **Nicolaitism.** *Obs. rare*$^{-1}$.

1669 H. MORE *Exp.* 7 *Epist.* iii. 42 This is allowed the Ephesine Church,..that they are free from Nicolaitism.

‖ **'nicolo.** Also niccolo. [ad. It. *niccolo*, aphetic for *oniccolo, a diminutive from L. *onyx.*] (See quot. 1874.)

1874 H. M. WESTROPP *Man. Prec. Stones* 104 The variety of onyx known as nicolo, consisting of a layer of a bluish tint over black. **1894** CHURCH in Smiles *Life Wedgwood* xiv. 152 Antique gems cut in onyx and niccolo. **1899** *Daily News* 29 June 6/7 An antique gem representing a bust..of Omphale, cut in a double nicolo.

attrib. **1877** W. JONES *Finger-ring* 23 One very massive [ring] of silver and gold, set with intaglio on nicolo onyx. **1899** *Daily News* 29 June 6/7 A nicolo-sardonyx with a fine head of Commodius in a cameo.

Niconian, var. NIKONIAN *sb.* and *a.*

nicor, variant of NICKER *sb.*^{1}

Nicorette (nɪkə'rɛt). [f. NICO(TINE + CIGA)RETTE.] The name (proprietary in the U.S.) of a type of nicotine-flavoured chewing-gum used to reduce dependency upon tobacco.

1980 *Jrnl. Amer. Med. Assoc.* 11 July 114/1 Nicorette (the gum's trade name) works on a pressure-release principle and must be chewed for at least 30 minutes to increase blood nicotine levels substantially. **1981** *Official Gaz.* (U.S. Patent & Trademark Office) TM507 AB Leo, Helsingborg, Sweden. .. *Nicorette*..for..medications for suppressing, reducing, or eliminating smoking and the urge to smoke... First use Jun. 22, 1973; in commerce Oct. 29, 1973. **1984** *Daily Tel.* 25 Oct. 19/6 Nicorette became available in 1980 and I have been challenging the authorities ever since to try to get it available on the National Health.

‖ **nicotia** (nɪ'kəʊʃ(ɪ)a). [mod.L., f. *nicot-* (see NICOTIANA) + -IA^1.]

1. a. Nicotianin. **b.** Nicotine.

1830 CONWALL in *Silliman's Jrnl.* XVII. 369 The most diagnostic property of Nicotia, is perhaps its entering into solution with vegetable acids, without forming with them any crystalline compound. **1857** MILLER *Elem. Chem.*, *Org.* 267 Nicotia [ed. 1862 Nicotylia] appears to belong to the class of nitrile bases. **1875** H. C. WOOD *Therap.* (1879) 363 When applied directly to the eye, nicotia produces a very marked contraction of the pupil.

2. *poet.* Tobacco.

1869 LOWELL *Winter Evening Hymn* vii, Nicotia, dearer to the Muse Than all the grape's bewildering juice.

† **ni'cotian,** *sb.*^{1} *Obs.* Also 6-7 -ane. [ad. F. *nicotiane* or mod.L. *nicotiana* (see below).] The tobacco-plant.

1577 FRAMPTON *Joyful News* II. 42 Thys hearbe is called Nicotiane of the name of him that gave the first intelligence thereof unto this Realme. **1597** LYLY *Wom. in Moon* III. i, Gather me balme and cooling Violets, And of our holly hearbe Nicotian. **1607** WALKINGTON *Opt. Glass* 105 To these I may..ioyn our adulterate Nicotian or Tobacco. **1672-3** GREW *Anat. Roots* II. §51 The Aer-Vessels having a predominion to keep it from growing deep; as in Stramonium, Nicotian, Beet, &c.

nicotian (nɪ'kəʊʃ(ɪ)an), *a.* and *sb.*^{2} [f. *nicot-* (see NICOTIANA) + -IAN.]

A. *adj.* Of, or pertaining to, tobacco; arising from the use of tobacco.

1825 SCOTT *Diary* in *Lockhart* (1839) VIII. 118, I..laid aside the use of the Nicotian weed for many years. **1851** HAWTHORNE *Snow Image*, etc. (1879) 287 Heedless of the nicotian atmosphere. **1890** *Spectator* 7 June, Here is a fair specimen of..light nicotian humour.

B. *sb.*^{2} **1.** (See quot.)

1840 *Penny Cycl.* XVI. 213/2 A tobacco-camphor, called nicotian, or nicotianin, which crystallizes, and is solid at the ordinary temperature of the air.

2. A tobacco-smoker.

1872 O. W. HOLMES *Poet Breakf.-t.* v. (1885) 120, [I] have been a Nicotian..more than half my days.

‖**nicotiana** (nɪkəʊʃɪ'eɪnə). *Bot.* [mod.L. (sc. *herba*), f. the name of Jacques *Nicot*, French ambassador at Lisbon, by whom tobacco was introduced into France in 1560.]

1. The tobacco-plant. Also personified.

1600 SURFLET *Countrie Farme* II. xliv. 281 This herbe is called Nicotiana, of the name of an ambassadour which brought the first knowledge of it into this realme. **1646** G. DANIEL *Poems* Wks. (Grosart) I. 51 Come my Nicotiana; weele renew Our free delights. **1688** HOLME *Armoury* II. 70/1 A Tobacco flower..is called the Nicotiana or Male petum, and Holy Hearbe. **1826** HENRY *Elem. Chem.* II. 329 The active properties of tobacco (nicotiana).

2. A genus of plants (chiefly American) of the nightshade family, to which the tobacco-plant (*N. Tabacum*) belongs.

1846 LINDLEY *Veget. Kingd.* 620 Tobacco..is the foliage of various species of Nicotiana.

nicotianin (nɪ'kəʊʃ(ɪ)ənɪn). *Chem.* Also -ine. [f. NICOTIAN-A + -IN[1].] (See quots.)

a. **1838** T. THOMSON *Chem. Org. Bodies* 498 Of Nicotianin. This concrete oily substance exists in tobacco, and gives it its characteristic odour. **1860** *Knight's Eng. Cycl., Arts & Sci.* V. 938/1 Nicotianin, or essential oil of tobacco. **1892** *Syd. Soc. Lex., Nicotianin,* a..camphorous bitter substance, obtained from the leaf of the tobacco by distillation with alkaline solutions.

β. **1839** URE *Dict. Arts* 886 *Nicotianine* is the name of an oil recently extracted from the leaves of tobacco, which possesses the smell of tobacco smoke. **1871** NICHOLS *Fireside Chem.* 44 A good cigar..should contain a large proportion of nicotianine.

ni'cotiant, *ppl. a. nonce-wd.* Smoking.

1877 HUXLEY in *Life* (1900) I. xxxii. 479 Froude and yourself nicotiant.

nicotic (nɪ'kɒtɪk), *a. Chem.* [f. *nicot-* (see NICOTIANA) + -IC.] Of or pertaining to nicotine. *nicotic acid*: (see quot. 1860).

1857 MAYNE *Expos. Lex.* 766/2. **1860** *Knight's Eng. Cycl., Arts & Sci.* V. 938/1 *Nicotic acid*, a peculiar acid allied with oxalic acid, and said to be contained in tobacco juice. **1871** NICHOLS *Fireside Chem.* 42 In tobacco it is called nicotic acid.

ni'cotidin(e. *Chem.* [Cf. NICOTINE and -ID[4].] A substance isomeric with nicotine.

1890 THORPE *Dict. Appl. Chem.* I. 334 The isomeric m-dipyridyl..boils at 293°, and yields on reduction with tin and hydrochloric acid nicotidine.

nicotina (nɪkə'taɪnə). *Chem.* [f. *nicot-* (see NICOTIANA) + -INA.] = NICOTINE.

1838 T. THOMSON *Chem. Org. Bodies* 284 Nicotina obtained in this way has the consistence of honey, an acrid taste, and a brown colour. **1840** *Penny Cycl.* XVI. 213/2 Nicotina, an alkaloid, which..does not exist at ordinary temperatures in a solid form, but in a fluid and volatile state, having an oily appearance. **1856** URE *Dict. Arts* (ed. 4) II. 269 From this distillation a quantity of nicotina and ammonia will be obtained in the receiver.

nicotinamide (nɪkəʊ'tɪnəmaɪd). *Biochem.* [f. NICOTIN(IC *a.* + AMIDE.] **a.** The amide, $(C_5H_4N)CONH_2$, of nicotinic acid, which can be converted into the acid *in vivo* and so can replace it in the diet.

1895 *Jrnl. Chem. Soc.* LXVIII. I. 391 On heating ethylic nicotinate with alcoholic ammonia..it is converted into nicotinamide, which melts at 121°. **1951** in M. McLuhan *Mech. Bride* (1967) 91/1 (Advt.), It is nicotinamide, an important component in the familiar Vitamin B Complex pill. **1957** A. HUXLEY *Let.* 12 Dec. (1969) 837 The Italians have been using massive doses of Nicotinamide (a variant on nicotinic acid) in psychological cases for some time. **1968** PASSMORE & ROBSON *Compan. Med. Stud.* I. v. 14/2 In Great Britain, the U.S.A. and many other countries, nicotinamide must by law be added to white flour used for bread making.

b. *Comb.* **nicotinamide-adenine dinucleotide**, a compound of adenosine monophosphate and nicotinamide mononucleotide which is a co-enzyme for the oxidation of a wide variety of substrates *in vivo*; NAD; co-enzyme I; diphosphopyridine nucleotide.

1961 *Biochem. Jrnl.* LXXX. 323/1 The rate of formation of nicotinamide-adenine dinucleotide from adenosine triphosphate..and nicotinamide mononucleotide..was measured. **1969** J. R. HOLUM *Introd. Org. & Biol. Chem.* xi. 381 Nicotinamide (niacinamide) is a vitamin used by the body in making the coenzyme nicotinamide adenine dinucleotide.

nicotinate ('nɪkəʊtɪneɪt). [f. NICOTIN(IC *a.* + -ATE[4].] The anion, or a salt or ester, of nicotinic acid.

1879 *Jrnl. Chem. Soc.* XXXVI. 809 If..potassium nicotinate is treated with phosphorus pentachloride, energetic action ensues. **1934** *Jrnl. Amer. Chem. Soc.* LVI. 2426/1 Folkers prepared ethyl nipecotate..by the hydrogenation of ethyl nicotinate. **1970** R. W. MCGILVERY *Biochemistry* x. 185 Nicotinate and its enzyme occur in all organisms.

nicotine ('nɪkətiːn). Also nicotin. [a. F. *nicotine*: see NICOTIANA and -INE[5].] **a.** A poisonous alkaloid forming the essential principle of tobacco, from which it is obtained as an oily liquid; in small doses it has a stimulating action, but in larger amounts it blocks the actions of autonomic ganglion cells and skeletal muscle fibres.

a. **1819** J. G. CHILDREN *Chem. Anal.* 290 Nicotin exists in the leaves of tobacco. **1826** HENRY *Elem. Chem.* II. 329 Nicotin. This is the principle in which reside the active properties of tobacco (nicotiana). **1880** J. W. LEGG *Bile* 176 Three drops of nicotin in 50 grammes of water..cause an immediate but short increase of the bile.

β. **1839** URE *Dict. Arts* 886 Nicotine is a peculiar principle, obtainable from the leaves and seeds of tobacco. **1855** BAIN *Senses & Int.* II. ii. §1 The volatile alkali, nicotine, the element of the snuffs. **1898** *Allbutt's Syst. Med.* V. 888 The view that nicotine has a more direct action. **1915** W. S. MAUGHAM *Of Human Bondage* xlvii. 231 She had long, beautiful hands, with fingers deeply stained by nicotine. **1940** H. A. MCGUIGAN *Appl. Pharmacol.* 589 When nicotine is injected intravenously, an enormous rise in blood pressure occurs. **1951** A. GROLLMAN *Pharmacol. & Therapeutics* xv. 285 Nicotine produces extreme nausea and vomiting when taken even in comparatively small quantities. **1966** *McGraw-Hill Encycl. Sci. & Technol.* IX. 100/2 Poisoning has occurred from accidental ingestion of insecticide sprays containing nicotine.

b. *attrib.* and *Comb.*, as ***nicotine-brown, -free, -like, -stained*** adjs.; ***nicotine poisoning***.

1945 DYLAN THOMAS *Let.* 30 July (1966) 278, I can hear ..my uncle Bob drinking tea and methylated spirits through eighty years of *nicotine-brown fern. **1967** *Daily Tel.* 20 Jan. 17/7 The pleasure of *nicotine-free smoking. **1898** *Allbutt's Syst. Med.* V. 888 The pallor..observed in *nicotine intoxication. **1914** *Nicotine-like [see MUSCARINE]. **1948** J. H. BURN *Lect. Notes Pharmacol.* 15 Nicotine is a substance which possesses the nicotine-like actions of acetylcholine. **1865** *Times* 15 Aug., One safe haven where no *nicotine perfume intrudes. **1898** *Allbutt's Syst. Med.* V. 905 *Nicotine poisoning being also excluded. **1951** A. GROLLMAN *Pharmacol. & Therapeutics* xv. 282 In the treatment of nicotine poisoning, artificial respiration should be instituted. **1936** C. DAY LEWIS *Friendly Tree* 12 A plump man with a *nicotine-stained moustache. **1967** A. MARSHALL in *Coast to Coast 1965–66* 121 He rubbed his chin with a nicotine-stained finger.

Hence **nico'tinean** *a.*, produced by the smoking of tobacco; **'nicotined** *a.*, full of tobacco-smoke; **nico'tinian** *a.* = NICOTIAN *a.*; **'nicotinism**, a diseased condition produced by the excessive use of tobacco; **ˌnicotini'zation**, subjection to the action of nicotine; **'nicotinize** *v. trans.*, to drug or saturate with nicotine; **'nicotinized** *ppl. a.*, containing or drugged with nicotine.

1873 W. S. MAYO *Never Again* xxiv, Lapped in *nicotinean elysium, the incautious worshippers of the weed recline in fancied security. **1889** C. C. R. *Up for Season* 193 A fragrance that purely Contrasts with this *nicotined air. **1879** *Cope's Tobacco Plant* July 356/1 The man that..is not sooth'd with *Nicotinian herb. **1898** *Daily News* 20 Sept. 6/3 Thackeray..wrote and sang in nicotinian mood. **1892** *Syd. Soc. Lex.*, **Nicotinism*, chronic tobacco poisoning. **1898** *Allbutt's Syst. Med.* V. 888 The less defined changes induced by alcoholism, nicotinism, and the like. **1945** *Amer. Jrnl. Physiol.* CXLIV. 192 The *nicotinization was maintained by adding nicotine (2 mgm./liter) to the perfusion fluid of the heart. **1966** *Punch* 9 Feb. 215/1 Today nicotinisation is complete with our own men taking the first breath of the day through a tube, lighting up automatically at the appearance of food, and thickening the bedroom air well into the early hours of the morning. **1865** *Reader* 1 Apr. 374/3 They narcotize, but do not *nicotinize, themselves. **1873** W. S. MAYO *Never Again* vi, Lanky, cadaverous, ..*nicotinized young men. **1911** *Jrnl. Physiol.* XLIII. 181 The partial contraction suggests an anodic inhibition in the nerve cell like that which occurs in certain nicotinized striated muscles. **1940** *Ibid.* XCIX. 73 Acetylcholine injections have been observed to produce vasoconstriction in the nicotinized as well as in the normal perfused guinea-pig lungs.

nicotinic (nɪkəʊ'tɪnɪk), *a. Chem.* and *Biochem.* [f. NICOTIN(E + -IC.] **1.** ***nicotinic acid*** [tr. G. *nicotinsäure* (H. Weidel 1873, in *Ann. d. Chem. und Pharm.* CLXV. 330)]: a white crystalline heterocyclic acid, $(C_5H_4N)COOH$, which is widely distributed (usu. in the form of a complex of its amide) in foods such as yeasts, wheat germ, and meat, is formed when nicotine is oxidized, and can be synthesized in the body from tryptophan; it is a B vitamin, deficiency of which causes pellagra in man; 3-pyridinecarboxylic acid. (Cf. NIACIN.)

1873 *Jrnl. Chem. Soc.* XXVI. 509 Acetyl chloride has no action on nicotinic acid. **1913** J. WALKER *Org. Chem.* 279 The *β* acid, or nicotinic acid, may also be produced by the oxidation of the alkaloid nicotine. **1942** *Industr. & Engin. Chem.* (*Analytical Ed.*) XIV. 663/1 The dietary position of cereals and cereal products in relation to their pellegra [*sic*]-preventive attributes has recently been given considerable prominence by the inclusion of nicotinic acid or niacin in the list of required components of enriched flour. **1968** PASSMORE & ROBSON *Compan. Med. Stud.* I. v. 14/2 Like thiamine, nicotinic acid is present in the whole-wheat grain in good quantities, but most is removed by the millers in preparing fine flours or polished rice.

2. Resembling (that of) nicotine; capable of responding to nicotine.

1941 [see MUSCARINIC *a.*]. **1961** A. GOTH *Med. Pharmacol.* iii. 44 The nicotinic receptors may be divided into the ganglionic receptors, which are hexamethonium sensitive, and the skeletal muscle receptors, which are sensitive to *d*-tubocurarine. **1970** *Nature* 5 Dec. 917/1 The pharmacological actions of acetylcholine..outside the central nervous system could be divided into two categories, nicotinic and muscarinic. **1973** *Jrnl. Pharmacol. & Exper. Therap.* CLXXXV. 649 The data..suggest that both stimulant drugs and competitive antagonists interact on a one-to-one basis with the nicotinic receptor of the guinea-pig lumbrical muscle.

'nicotism. *rare.* = NICOTINISM.

1899 *Allbutt's Syst. Med.* VII. 747 Alcoholism and nicotism..and Bright's disease are some of the conditions which fall under this head.

nicotize ('nɪkətaɪz), *v.* [f. NICOT-INE + -IZE.] *trans.* **a.** To bring *into* a certain state by smoking tobacco. **b.** To impregnate with nicotine.

1867 O. W. HOLMES *Guardian Angel* xxi, He can take to the philosophic meerschaum, and nicotise himself..into a kind of buzzing and blurry insensibility. **1890** *Spectator* 15 Nov., To see if his body was really as salt and as nicotised as the Feejeans used to say.

'nicotyl. *Chem.* [f. NICOT-INE + -YL.] A hydrocarbon found in nicotine.

1860 *Knight's Eng. Cycl., Arts & Sci.* V. 938 Ammonia in which the three equivalents of hydrogen are replaced by the teratomic radical nicotyl. **1862** MILLER *Elem. Chem., Org.* (ed. 2) 480 The hydrocarbon nicotyl which it [nicotylia] contains being equivalent in function to the 3 atoms of hydrogen in ammonia.

Hence **nico'tylia**, nicotine. *rare.*

1862 MILLER *Elem. Chem., Org.* (ed. 2) 479 Nicotylia is a limpid colourless oily liquid, with an extremely irritating and powerful odour of tobacco.

nicre, obs. f. NICKER *sb.*[1]

nicromancer, -mancy, obs. ff. NECROMANCER, -MANCY.

nictate ('nɪkteɪt), *v.* [f. L. *nictāt-*, ppl. stem of *nictāre* to wink.] *intr.* To wink. Cf. NICTITATE *v.*

1691 RAY *Creation* II. 35 The Eyes of Man..want the seventh Muscle, or the nictating Membrane. **1794** *Gentl. Mag.* LXIV. II. 648 A particular account of the Nictating Membrane in animals. **1870** GILLMORE tr. *Figuier's Rept. & Birds* Introd. 193 This pupil, or nictating membrane, placed at the internal angle of the eye. **1960** V. NABOKOV *Invitation to Beheading* iv. 40 Emmie was still squatting,..her long, pale, almost white lashes nictating as she looked across the table-top at the door.

nictation (nɪk'teɪʃən). [ad. L. *nictātiōn-em*, n. of action f. *nictāre* to wink.] The action or an act of winking or moving the eyelids.

1623 COCKERAM I, *Nictation*, the twinckling of the eye. **1650** BULWER *Anthropomet.* 71 Much more is their use in nictation when we are awake. **1678** CUDWORTH *Intell. Syst.* I. iii. §37 Our Nictations for the most part when we are awake..are performed with very little or no Consciousness. **1883** *Gd. Words* 265 As if a man should set himself to regulate or time the nictation of the eyelid.

nictitant ('nɪktɪtənt), *a. rare.* [ad. med.L. *nictitant-em*, pres. pple. of *nictitāre*: see next.] Nictitating.

1826 KIRBY & SP. *Entomol.* xlvi. IV. 287 Nictitant Ocellus... When the ocellus includes a lunular spot of a different colour. **1835** KIRBY *Hab. & Inst. Anim.* I. i. 34 Many reptiles..are furnished with a nictitant membrane like birds. **1857** MAYNE *Expos. Lex.* 766/2.

nictitate ('nɪktɪteɪt), *v.* [f. med.L. *nictitāt-*, ppl. stem of *nictitāre*, frequentative of L. *nictāre* to wink: see NICTATE *v.*] *intr.* Of the eyelids: To wink. *rare.*

1822–34 *Good's Study Med.* (ed. 4) III. 330 In dying people, whose eyelids are become torpid and do not nictitate. *Ibid.* 395 The eyelids nictitate with a quiver that is often difficult to follow-up.

Hence **'nictitating** *ppl. a.*, chiefly in ***nictitating membrane***, a third or inner eyelid present in many animals, serving to protect the eye from dust, etc., and to keep it moist.

1713 DERHAM *Phys.-Theol.* IV. ii. 110 To the Eye-lids, we may add another guard afforded the Eyes, of most Quadrupeds, Birds, and Fishes, by the nictitating Membrane. **1774** GOLDSM. *Nat. Hist.* (1776) VII. 209 The eye also [of the rattlesnake] is furnished with a nictitating membrane, that preserves it from dust. **1822–34** *Good's Study Med.* (ed. 4) III. 16 In the elephant, oppossum, seal, cat-kind, and various other mammals, all birds and all fishes, we find a third eyelid or nictitating membrane as it is usually called. **1899** *Allbutt's Syst. Med.* VIII. 39 Clonic spasm of the eye-lids.., sometimes spoken of as nictitating spasm.

nictitation (nɪktɪ'teɪʃən). [ad. L. type **nictitātiōn-em*: see NICTITATE *v.* and -ATION.] Winking; the action or habit of moving the eyelids. Also *transf.*

1784–6 E. DARWIN *Zoon.* (1801) I. 268 Other catenations of animal motion are gradually acquired..by disagreeable sensations, as in coughing or nictitation. **1831** *Fraser's Mag.* III. 653, I know by that satisfactory nictitation of your eye that you agree with me. **1899** *Allbutt's Syst. Med.* VIII. 107 There is often a nictitation of the lids. **1962** V. NABOKOV *Pale Fire* 160 A couple..whose blundering Cadillac half entered my driveway before retreating in a flurry of luminous nictitation.

nicy: see NICEY *a.*

nid. *rare.* [Later form of NIDE, perh. after F. *nid.*] A nest (of pheasants).

1808 COBBETT in *Friendsh. Miss Mitford* (1882) I. 41 The pheasants are all well, both nids. **1884** CARNEGIE *Game Preserving* 4 When quitting the 'nide' or 'nid', as the nest is technically termed, she instinctively scratches a covering of leaves or grass over it.

nidal ('naɪdəl), *a. rare*$^{-1}$. [See NIDUS.] Of or pertaining to a nest.

1850 *Tait's Mag.* XVII. 165/1 Like brooding halcyons calming the angry waters around their sacred nidal circle.

nidamental (naɪdə'mɛntəl), *a.* [f. L. *nīdāment-um* (see NIDUS) + -AL[1].]

1. *Zool.* Serving as a receptacle for the ova of molluscs or other marine animals; forming a collection of ova.

1835–6 *Todd's Cycl. Anat.* I. 557/1 The..oviducts have laminated glandular terminations, near to which are placed two detached nidamental glands. **1851** WOODWARD *Mollusca* I. iii. 20 The nidamental ribbon of the doris and eolis is attached to a rock. *Ibid.* iv. 50 The nidamental capsules of the cuttle-fish are clustered like grapes. **1877** HUXLEY *Anat. Inv. Anim.* viii. 534 The nidamental glands, composed of numerous vertical lamellæ,..are situated on the posterior wall of that cavity.

2. Of the nature of, serving as, a nest or nests.

1879 *Cassell's Techn. Educ.* IV. 123/1 Eggs, nests, nidamental structures..should be amalgamated into one series.

†**'nidary.** *Obs. rare*$^{-1}$. [See NIDUS and -ARY[1] B. 2.] A place for building nests.

a **1700** EVELYN *Diary* 27 Feb. 1644, In this rupellary nidary do the fowl lay eggs, and breed.

nidation (naɪ'deɪʃən). *Physiol.* [f. NID(US + -ATION.] †**a.** (See quots.) *Obs.*

1874 J. H. AVELING in *Obstetr. Jrnl.* II. 210 The act of nidation consists of the periodical development of the mucous membrane lining the interior of the body of the uterus. **1892** *Syd. Soc. Lex.*, *Nidation*,..Aveling's term for the monthly renewal of the epithelium of the mucous lining of the womb during the intermenstrual period.

b. = IMPLANTATION 6.

1892 *Syd. Soc. Lex.*, *Nidation*,..also, a term for the reception of the fertilised ovum in the uterine mucous membrane. **1921** B. M. ANSPACH *Gynecol.* iv. 72 These [changes] have for their purpose suitable nidation and nourishment of the ovum. **1966** *New Statesman* 17 June 880/1 Surely an abortifacient is something which interferes with an established pregnancy and not something which prevents the nidation of a fertilised ovum. **1970** *Sci. Jrnl.* June 63/2 It is apparently by this thickened trophoblastic plate that the penetration of the maternal tissues—called nidation or implantation—is accomplished.

niddecock, variant of NIDDICOCK *Obs.*

nidder, variant of NITHER *v.*

'niddering, *sb.* and *a.* Also **nider-**. [Erroneous form of NITHING, originating in the early printed text (1596) of William of Malmesbury, by misreading *niðing* as *nid'ing* (= nidering). The modern currency of the word is due to Scott.]

A. *sb.* A base coward or wretch. Also in predicative use, passing into *adj.*

1596 in Savile *Script. post Bedam* 68 Iubet, vt compatriotas aduocent ad obsidionem venire, nisi si qui velint sub nomine *Nidering*, quod nequam sonat, remanere. **1664** SPELMAN, *Niderling* seu *Nidering*. **1706** PHILLIPS (ed. Kersey), *Niderling*, *Nidering*,..an old English Word signifying a Coward, a sorry hen-hearted Fellow.

1819 SCOTT *Ivanhoe* xv. *note*, Threatening to stigmatize those who staid at home as *nidering*. *Ibid.* xliii, On pain of being held faithless, man-sworn, and *nidering*. **1848** LYTTON *Harold* x. iv, He who can be called niddering shall never be crowned king! **1864** KINGSLEY *Rom. & Teut.* 60 Niddering though he may have been called for coming back alive. **1864** DASENT *Jest & Earnest* (1873) I. 229 Though this was the deed of a niddering, it seems not to have raised the popular feeling against Sweyn so much as it ought. **1893** *Athenæum* 12 Aug. 226/1 It is difficult to be too severe with such a 'nidering'.

B. *adj.* Base, cowardly, vile.

1848 LYTTON *Harold* III. ii, Siward can give no niddering council to the king. **1866** BLACKMORE *Cradock Nowell* liii. (1883) 363 She learned her niddering wrong.

Hence, by further corruption, **'nidderling**. *rare.*

1664 [see prec.]. **1674** BLOUNT *Glossogr.* (ed. 4), *Niderling* or *Nithing* signifies an abject base-minded, false-hearted coward. **1678** PHILLIPS *Suppl.*, *Niderling*, a poor spirited, base, raskally sort of a fellow. **1887** BESANT *Kath. Regina* 218 Men who..call that man churl and nidderling and pitiful sneak and cur. **1895** CROCKETT *Men of Moss-Hags* 165 The men of the broad bonnet were neither cowards nor nidderlings.

'niddick. *dial.* Also 6 **nuddock**, 7 **niddock**, 9 **neddick**, etc. [Of obscure origin.] The nape of the neck.

Current in south-western dialects; see *Eng. Dial. Dict.*

1558 PHAER *Æneid* VII. Xj, Their nuddocks bolstred ben, and skulles of heads with barkes of corks. **1667** *Phil. Trans.* II. 480 It [a lamb] had two Eyes and as many Ears, in the usual places, and one extraordinary Eye in the Niddock. **1746** *Exmoor Courtship* (E.D.S.) 555 A Crick in ma Back and in ma Niddick. **1894** BLACKMORE *Perlycross* 376 The wick of a lamp that had dropped..on this man's collar, and burned a little hole in his niddick.

†**'niddicock.** *Obs. rare.* Also **nidde-**. [Of obscure formation: perh. a fanciful alteration of NIDIOT.] A fool, a ninny.

1586 HOOKER *Hist. Irel.* in *Holinshed* II. 94/1 They were neuer such fond niddicockes, as to offer anie man a rod to beat their owne tailes. **1654** GAYTON *Pleas. Notes* II. vi. 61 Thou..deservedst to be stak'd..for being such a Goose, Widgeon, and Niddecock to dye for love.

So †**'niddipol** = NODDYPOLL. *Obs. rare*$^{-1}$.

1582 STANYHURST *Æneis* IV. (Arb.) 98 What niddipol hare brayne Would scorne this couenaunt?

nidding, variant of NIDING.

'niddle, *v. Sc.* [Imitative.] *intr.* To move quickly.

1819 W. TENNANT *Papistry Storm'd* (1827) 15 The wyres were gowden..Wharewi' her fingers prettilie Did niddle i' their play. **1874** R. FORD in *Harp of Perthshire* (1893) 319 They whiddled aboot, they niddled aboot.

'niddle-'noddle, *a.* [A reduplicative formation on NOD *v.*: cf. NID-NOD *v.*] Having nodding heads. Also *fig.*

1761 *Brit. Mag.* II. 101 Who doats on pagods, and gives up vile man For niddle-noddle figures from Japan. **1820** COMBE *Syntax* III. i, What is said by state physicians, And niddle-noddle politicians.

'niddle-'noddle, *v.* [Cf. prec.] *intr.* To nod unsteadily to and fro; to nod the head rapidly. Also *trans.* with the head as object.

1840 HOOD *Kilmansegg, Christening* ix, Her head niddle-noddled at every word. **1845** *Punch* VIII. 138 He continually niddle-noddles his head like a toy mandarin. **1855** A. MANNING *O. Chelsea Bun-ho.* xv. 244 The Mandarin niddle-noddles, till it makes one's head spin to look at him.

niddy-noddy ('nɪdɪ'nɒdɪ), *v.*, *adv.*, and *sb.* [alt. f. prec.]

a. *v.* = prec. **b.** *adv.* to and fro, unsteadily.

1866 CARLYLE *Remin.* (1881) I. 324 The little phantasm of a creature—Sloane his name—who went niddy-noddying with his head. **1877** W. WATSON *Poems* 38 Ere we're half gate wi' our life, Our head plays niddy noddy.

c. A frame on which to skein and measure wool yarn.

1890 G. S. HALL in *Proc. Amer. Antiquarian Soc.* VII. 111 It was taken from the spindle sometimes on a niddy-noddy held in the hand, at two rounds per yard, but more commonly on a reel, in rounds of two yards each. **1927** M. N. RAWSON *Candle Days* ii. 28 The graceful 'swifts', the 'niddy noddy', or hand reels, was also of home construction in wood. **1968** *Beaver* Winter 43/1 A cross between the hand looms..has been found practical, as has been..the English niddy-noddy and butterfly yarn winders. **1969** E. H. PINTO *Treen* 318 The earlier device, which was in general use..was the cross reel, in English speaking countries almost universally known as a niddy-noddy. *Ibid.*, The niddy-noddy, which was held in one hand by the central stem, was wound with a waving motion, to the rhythm of a song, the opening line of which ran, 'Niddy-noddy, niddy-noddy, two heads and one body.'

nide (naɪd), *sb.* [ad. F. *nid* or L. *nīd-us*: the older F. *ni* is represented by NYE. Cf. NID.] A brood or nest of pheasants. Also *transf.* of geese.

1679 COLES *Eng.-Lat. Dict.*, A nide of pheasants, *phasianorum pullities*. **1706** PHILLIPS (ed. Kersey), *Nide*, a Term us'd in Falconry, for a Flock of Pheasants. **1790** *Loiterer* No. 57 ⁋5 My Father offered to conduct him to the best Nide of Pheasants on the Manor. ?**1810** A. MACKINTOSH *Driffield Angler* 294 Nide of pheasants, commonly called a Ni. **1834** *New Monthly Mag.* XLII. 119 The nides of pheasants are equally plentiful and well grown. **1896** *Blackw. Mag.* July 18 Mother Goose had brought a fine nide of eggs near to hatching on this island.

So **nide** *v. intr.*, to nest. *rare.*

1881 R. F. BURTON tr. *Camoens' Lusiad* II. 34 Those eyne wherein Dan Cupid aye doth nide.

nide, obs. f. NEED.

nideote, var. of NIDIOT[1].

nidering, variant of NIDDERING.

Niderviller (nidɛrvilɛr). The name of a town in Lorraine, east France, used, freq. *attrib.*, to designate the porcelain and faience made there from 1754.

1857 H. G. BOHN *Guide Knowl. Pottery, Porcelain* 480 *Niderviller*. Hard paste. Manufacture of François Lanfray, ..about 1790. Stencilled in blue. **1863** W. CHAFFERS *Marks Pott. & Porc.* 208 *Niderviller*, the letter N., for Niderviller, occurs on a set of plates, on one of which is the double C, and on another the letter N. **1903** M. L. SOLON *Hist. Old French Faïence* 112 The Niderviller faïence is amply represented in the Nancy Museum. **1948** A. LANE *French Faïence* ix. 39 The Niderviller figures belong to a class peculiar to the Lorraine region. **1960** R. G. HAGGAR *Concise Encycl. Cont. Pott. & Porc.* 329 The flower painting on Niderviller faience was of high quality and exploited the range of tints which 'purple of Cassius' crimson could be made to yield. **1963** *Times* 16 Feb. 4/4 A Niderviller part dinner-service of 37 pieces, painted with landscapes, the borders with butterflies, ladybirds and other insects, made £170. **1971** H. WYNTER *Introd. European Porc.* iii. 105 Niderviller characteristics..Hard-paste... Shapes and decoration.. similar to rococo Strasbourg.

nidge (nɪdʒ), *v.*[1] *rare.* [Of obscure origin.] *trans.* and *intr.* To shake, quiver.

1803 JANE PORTER *Thaddeus* xxvi. (1831) 225 The coxcomb, who stood nidging his head with anger. **1831** in *Mag. Amer. Hist.* Jan. (1888) 81 The majestic object is perpetually in motion, shaking and nidging and nodding this way and that.

nidge (nɪdʒ), *v.*[2] *Sc.* [Of obscure origin.] *trans.* To trim (stone) roughly by means of a sharp-pointed hammer. Hence **nidged** *ppl. a.*, **'nidging** *vbl. sb.*

1842 GWILT *Archit.* 519 In Aberdeen, where the stone is very hard,..they pick the stone until the surface has nearly acquired the requisite form. This sort of work is called nidged-work, and the operation nidging. *Ibid.* 1008 *Nidged Ashlar*, a species of ashlar used in Aberdeen. It is brought to the square by means of a cavil or hammer with a sharp point. **1850** in OGILVIE.

†**'nidgery.** *Obs. rare*$^{-0}$. [a. obs. F. *nigerie*, f. *niger* 'to trifle; to play the fop, or nidget'.]

1611 COTGR., *Nigeries*, nidgeries, fopperies, fooleries, trifles, nifles. [Hence in Blount *Glossogr.* (1656), etc.]

nidget ('nɪdʒɪt), *sb.*[1] Now only *arch.* Also 6 **nigeot**, 7 **nigit**, **nigid**, **niget**, **nigget**. [var. of NIDIOT: see note to IDIOT.] An idiot, a fool.

'As a modern word, if used, it signifies a trifler' (Smart).

α. **1579–80** NORTH *Plutarch* (1895) II. 50 This made men judge..that he would prove a very foole and nigeot [1595 idiote]. **1603** SIR C. HEYDON *Jud. Astrol.* xi. 244 Cleared from the imputation of [being] such a Nigit. **1621–3** MIDDLETON & ROWLEY *Changeling* III. iii, 'Tis a gentle nigget; you may play with him. **1638** HEYWOOD *Wise Wom.* II. i, I think he saith we are a company of fooles and Nigits. **1675** *Ballad* in *Luttrell Coll.* III. 107 Ridiculous Niget, to scoff at St. Bridget. *a* **1700** B. E. *Dict. Cant. Crew*, *Nigit*, a Fool.

β. **1605** CAMDEN *Rem.* 27 Abject, base minded, false harted, coward, or nidget. **1706** PHILLIPS (ed. Kersey), *Nidget*, an Idiot, a Ninny, or meer Fool. **1843** JAMES *Forest Days* ii, One of those men is a nidget.

nidget ('nɪdʒɪt), *sb.*[2] Also **-ett**, **niggett**. [Of obscure origin.] A triangular horse-hoe, used in Kent and Sussex.

1789 *Trans. Soc. Arts* I. 113, I have had what we call a brake and a nidget made..to move the earth in alleys. **1805** R. W. DICKSON *Pract. Agric.* II. 747 To admit of the ground between the plants being kept clean by the harrow and nidget. **1846** *Jrnl. R. Agric. Soc.* VII. II. 590 Guano..sown broadcast in the track made by the tines of the niggett. **1883** J. Y. STRATTON *Hops & Hop-pickers* 23 The garden is kept clear of weeds by means of a horse-hoe, or nidget.

nidget, *sb.*[3]: see NINE-HOLE.

nidget, *sb.*[4]: var. NIGGET.

'nidget, *v.*[1] [f. NIDGET *sb.*[2]]

1. *trans.* To work (land) with a nidget.

1805 R. W. DICKSON *Pract. Agric.* II. 758 Deduct summer digging... Add nidgetting. **1846** *Jrnl. R. Agric. Soc.* VII. II. 590 The portion..is niggetted or stirred as much before the 1st of April..as possible. **1848** *Ibid.* IX. II. 553 It should be nidgeted and got into a fine deep tilth.

2. To work *in* (lime, etc.) with the soil by means of a nidget.

1848 *Jrnl. R. Agric. Soc.* IX. II. 548 Lime,..nidgeted in after the hops are planted,..will be of greater benefit. **1881** WHITEHEAD *Hops* 33 Rape dust is a fine manure, and is nidgetted in with nidgetts.

nidget, *v.*[2] *dial.* (See quots.)

1745–60 ARDERON *Norwich Words* in Rye *E. Angl. Gloss.*, *Nigeting*, to call women to one in labour. **1764** *Low Life* 29 Poor labouring Men..are obliged to get up, put on Part of their Cloaths and go a Nigiting, i.e. fetching Mid-wives, Nurses and Gossips. **1895** RYE *E. Angl. Gloss.*, *Nidget*, to assist a woman in her travail.

'nidgetty, *a. rare*$^{-1}$. Trifling.

1798 JANE AUSTEN *Lett.* (1884) I. 177, I have been enabled to give a considerable improvement of dignity to [the] cap, which was before too nidgetty to please me.

'nidging, *a. rare*$^{-1}$. [Cf. NIDGE *v.*[1]] Restless, troublesome.

1796 MME. D'ARBLAY *Camilla* v. iii, I'd sooner have her than any of 'em, for all she's such a nidging little thing.

nidging, *vbl. sb.*: see NIDGE *v.*[2]

nidi, pl. of NIDUS.

nidicolous (nɪ'dɪkələs), *a. Ornith.* [f. mod.L. group name *Nidicolæ* (H. F. Gadow in A. Newton *Dict. Birds* (1894) 629) (f. L. *nīdus* nest + *col-ere* to inhabit) + -OUS.] Of a bird: bearing young which are helpless at birth and remain in the nest until they are sufficiently developed to live without parental care. So **'nidicole** *sb.*, a bird of this type.

1902 H. F. GADOW in *Encycl. Brit.* XXVI. 257/1 Order Sphenisciformes.—Nidicolous, marine. Flightless, wings transformed into rowing paddles. **1927** A. L. THOMSON *Birds* ix. 155 Birds may..be divided into two main types, those having nidifugous or 'nest-quitting' young, and those having nidicolous or 'nest-dwelling' young. **1945** S. SMITH *How to study Birds* iv. 74 Birds whose young are born naked, helpless and blind (the so-called nidicolous birds). **1962** J. C. WELTY *Life of Birds* xvii. 319/1 The altricial bird, is born naked, or nearly so, is usually blind, and is too weak to support itself on its legs... Such birds remain confined to the nest for some days or weeks. They are therefore called nidicoles or nest-dwellers. **1974** I. C. J. GALBRAITH tr. *Dorst's Life of Birds* I. xiii. 247 The parents are entirely responsible for feeding nidicolous young.

nidificate ('nɪdɪfɪkeɪt), *v.* [f. L. *nīdificāt-*, ppl. stem of *nīdificāre*, f. *nīdus* nest.] *intr.* To make a nest; to nidify.

1816 KIRBY & SP. *Entomol.* iv. (1818) I. 104 Getting.. between the skin and the flesh..where it nidificates and lays its eggs. **1835–6** *Todd's Cycl. Anat.* I. 267/1 All the Birds of Prey..nidificate in lofty situations. **1874** E. COUES *Birds N.W.* 313 This species may be shy and reserved, and consequently nidificates in out-of-the-way situations.

nidification (nɪdɪfɪ'keɪʃən). [See prec. and -ATION.] The operation of nest-building; the construction of a nest or nests; the manner in which this is done.

1658 PHILLIPS, *Nidification*, a building of a birds nest. **1659** H. MORE *Immort. Soul* (1762) 222 The Nidification of

Birds, as well as their Incubation. *a* **1676** HALE *Prim. Orig. Man.* (1677) 368 In the nidification of Birds, Bees, Silkworms, and divers others. **1713** DERHAM *Phys.-Theol.* IV. xiii. 228 That Method of Nidification doth abundantly Answer the Creatures Use and Occasions. **1773** G. WHITE in *Phil. Trans.* LXIV. 196 For some time after they appear, the *hirundines* in general pay no attention to the business of nidification. **1834** MUDIE *Brit. Birds* (1841) I. 192 If the tree affords no natural hole fit for the purpose of nidification. **1874** COUES *Birds N.W.* 389 Its nidification varies greatly with circumstances, the nest being placed indifferently on the ground, bushes, or trees.

Hence **nidifi'cational** *a.*, relating to nidification.

1888 J. T. GULICK in *Linn. Soc. Jrnl.* XX. 2262 Nidificational Segregation. Let us now consider the effects of divergent habits in regard to nest-building.

†**nidifice.** *Obs. rare*⁻⁰. [ad. late L. *nidificium.*] 'A nest, such as Birds make' (Blount *Glossogr.* 1656).

nidifugous (nɪ'dɪfjʊgəs), *a. Ornith.* [f. mod.L. group name *Nidifugæ* (H. F. Gadow in A. Newton *Dict. Birds* (1894) 629) (f. L. *nīdus* nest + *fug-ĕre* to flee) + -OUS.] Of a bird: bearing young which are well developed at birth and leave the nest almost immediately. So **'nidifuge** *sb.*, a bird of this type.

1902 H. F. GADOW in *Encycl. Brit.* XXVI. 257/1 Order Colymbiformes.—Plantigrade, nidifugous, aquatic. **1927** [see NIDICOLOUS *a.*]. **1945** S. SMITH *How to study Birds* iv. 74 Birds whose young are born strong, with plenty of down, and able to run within a few hours of the hatch (the nidifugous birds). **1962** J. C. WELTY *Life of Birds* xvii. 318/2 Nidifuges are often ground-nesting species that, as adults, are good runners or good swimmers and feed either on the ground or in the water. These precocial birds include such forms as the ostrich and its relatives, loons, grebes, ducks, [etc.]. *Ibid.* 319/2 (*caption*) The one-day-old, precocial, or nidifugous chick of the Ruffed Grouse. **1974** I. C. J. GALBRAITH tr. *Dorst's Life of Birds* I. xiii. 245 Nidifugous birds also have visual means of communication.

nidify ('nɪdɪfaɪ), *v.* [ad. L. *nīdificāre*, f. *nīdus* nest.] *intr.* To build a nest or nests.

1656 in BLOUNT *Glossogr.* **1720–1** *Lett. Mist's Jrnl.* (1722) II. 127 Birds, by Instinct,.. nidify, or make Nests after the same Manner. **1859** R. F. BURTON *Centr. Afr.* in *Jrnl. Geog. Soc.* XXIX. 396 Trees begin to bud, beasts to pair, and birds to nidify. **1880** J. COLQUHOUN *Moor & Loch* I. 249 The peregrine,.. nidifying on a giddy point.

Hence **'nidifying** *ppl. a.*

1871 DARWIN *Desc. Man* II. xv. 172 It is not necessary to suppose that each separate species had its nidifying instinct specially modified.

'niding. Now *rare.* Also 9 nidding. [Inexact form of *niðing*, used by Camden in citing from William of Malmesbury: cf. NIDDERING.] = NITHING.

1605 CAMDEN *Rem.* 28 Whosoever refused to come should be reputed a Niding. **1610** HOLLAND *Camden's Brit.* I. 333 Whosoever would not be reputed a Niding should repaire to recover Rochester Castle. **1642** HOWELL *For. Trav.* (Arb.) 79 He is worthy to be called a Niding, one, the pulse of whose soule beates but faintly towards Heaven. **1715** M. DAVIES *Athen. Brit.* I. 299 [from Camden]. **1866** T. BRUCE *Summer Queen* 148 To bondslave and low born knave And to the nidding too.

†**'nidiot**[1], obs. f. IDIOT. (Cf. NIDGET *sb.*[1])

1534 MORE *Comf. agst. Trib.* III. Wks. 1250/2 These folke as are verye nydeote fooles. **1586** A. DAY *Eng. Secretary* II. (1595) 47 After all these sporting deuises, he is but a Nideote. **1613** *Dodecahedron of Fortune* 5 This doting nidiot by his foolish desart Shall of his faire love at all have no part.

†**'nidiot**[2]. *Obs. rare*⁻¹. (See quot. and cf. NIGGET.)

1713 DERHAM *Phys.-Theol.* 190 *note*, One of the smallest, if not the very smallest of all the Gnat kind... Among us in Essex, they are called Nidiots, by Mouffet, Midges.

nid-nod, *v.* [A reduplicative formation on NOD *v.*: cf. NIDDLE-NODDLE *v.*]

1. *intr.* To nod repeatedly.

c **1787** BURNS *We're a' noddin*, We're a' noddin, nid nid noddin,.. at our house at hame. *c* **1817** HOGG *Tales & Sk.* I. 289 She sat nid-nodding. **1892** *Daily News* 18 June 3/3 A green straw hat with large roses nid-nodding from the crown. **1903** R. N. CAREY *Passage Perilous* xxiii, The two heads nid-nodded more closely.

2. *trans.* (with head as object).

1840 HOOD *Kilmansegg, Fancy Ball* xxiv, Lady K. nid-nodded her head.

Hence **nid-nodding** *vbl. sb.* and *ppl. a.*

1824 MISS FERRIER *Inher.* lxxix, That odd, little, nid-nodding face. **1833** HOOD *China Mender* 11 Great nid-noddin' mandarins, with palsies in the head. **1896** *Blackw. Mag.* Oct. 490/2 The nid-nodding of the red rose.

nid-nod, *a. poet.* [f. NID-NOD *v.*] That nid-nods.

1921 W. DE LA MARE *Veil* 88 Of whispering boughs, and feathery, nid-nod grass. **1937** —— *This Year, Next Year*, Poppy, cornflower, nid-nod wheat, The sheaves are ripe for rick. **1941** —— *Bells & Grass* 50 The nid-nod daffodil.

nidor ('naɪdə(r)). Now *rare.* Also 7 nidour. [a. L. *nīdor.*] The smell arising from animal substances (esp. of a fat or greasy nature) when burned, roasted, or boiled; †a strong smell, odour, or exhalation of any kind.

a **1619** FOTHERBY *Atheom.* I. xi. §4 (1622) 116 Who maketh .. his Caldron, his Sensor; his Nidor, his Incense; his Table, his Altar. **1662** H. STUBBE *Indian Nectar* iii. 29, I had my smell affected with such a nidor, as issues from fat, when broiled. **1678** CUDWORTH *Intell. Syst.* 810 That Evil Demons or Devils, were.. delighted with the Blood and Nidours of Sacrifices. **1707** FLOYER *Physic. Pulse-Watch* 264 In the Nidor of the Stomach there are hot Winds. **1746** JAMES *Moufet's Health Improv.* Introd. 43 A Nidor, or Stink, peculiar to Animal Substances in a State of Putrefaction. **1811** SYD. SMITH *Wks.* (1859) I. 203/2 The nidor of a human creature roasted for faith. **1923** *Blackw. Mag.* Feb. 159/2 A nidor was to him an agony impossible to endure.

†**nido'rose**, *a. Obs. rare.* [ad. late L. *nīdōrōs-us*: see prec. and -OSE.] Of the nature of a nidor; nidorous.

1707 FLOYER *Physic. Pulse-Watch* 104 If the Lungs be inflam'd they are subject to Suffocations;.. if the Stomach it self, to a nidorose Crudity. **1732** ARBUTHNOT *Rules of Diet* in *Aliments*, etc. I. 290 Hot nidorose Belchings, foulness of the tongue and Palate.

Hence †**nido'rosity**. *Obs. rare*⁻¹.

1696 FLOYER *On the Humours* (J.), The cure of this nidorosity is, by vomiting and purging.

nidorous ('naɪdərəs), *a.* Now *rare.* [ad. L. *nīdōrōs-us* (see prec.), or f. NIDOR + -OUS.] Of smells: Resembling that of cooked or burnt animal substances; strong and unpleasant.

1626 BACON *Sylva* §923 Incense, and Nidorous Smells, (such as were of Sacrifices,) were thought to Intoxicate the Braine. **1661** EVELYN *Fumifugium* Misc. Writ. (1805) II. 236 Horrid stinks, nidorous and unwholesome smells, which proceed from the tallow. **1698** FRYER *Acc. E. India & P.* 303 Stones of live Brimstone exhaling a nidorous Scent, stinking like that Water the Mariners call Bilge Water. **1757** A. COOPER *Distiller* I. xxiii. (1760) 95 It acquires an alcaline Disposition, and also a nidorous flavour.

b. Applied to stomachic crudities and eructations suggestive of such smells.

1651 BIGGS *New Disp.* ¶ 287 That an acid ructation, of a reparable ferment, superinduced upon a nidorous one, is good. **1710** T. FULLER *Pharm. Extemp.* 124 Steel Medicines thus taken.. stir up.. nidorous Belching. **1746** JAMES *Moufet's Health Improv.* Introd. 48 Nidorous Eructations, or Belches, which affect the Mouth with the Taste of putrefied Eggs. **1851** NOBLE tr. *Swedenborg's Heaven & Hell* (ed. 2) §488 Such nidorous exhalations as proceed from indigested substances in the stomach.

†**nidorulent**, *a. Obs. rare.* [f. NIDOR + -ULENT.] Of a nidorous nature.

1634 T. JOHNSON *Parey's Chirurg.* I. xiv. (1678) 20 The ventricle.. is troubled by its acid and nidorulent belchings. **1687** P. MADAN *Tunbridge Waters* 5 The Nidorolent Belches and Eructations after taking 'em.

nidulant ('nɪdjʊlənt), *a. Bot.* [f. L. *nīdulant-*, *nīdulans*, pres. pple. of *nīdulārī*, f. *nīdus* nest.] (See quots.)

1797 *Encycl. Brit.* (ed. 3) III. 447/1 Nidulant, nestling; seeds dispersed through a pulpy or soft substance. **1828–32** WEBSTER *Nidulant*,.. lying loose in pulp or cotton, within a berry or pericarp. **1857** MAYNE *Expos. Lex.* 767/1 *Nidulans*, embedded: nestling, as the seeds on the surface of the strawberry: nidulant. **1866** *Treas. Bot.*, *Nidulant*,.. lying free in a cup-shaped or nest-like body; as in the genus *Nidularia.*

†**'nidulate**, *v. Obs. rare*⁻⁰. [See prec.]

1623 COCKERAM I, *Nidulate*, to build a nest.

nidulation (nɪdjʊ'leɪʃən). *rare.* [f. prec.: see -ATION.] Nesting, nest-making, nidification.

1646 SIR T. BROWNE *Pseud. Ep.* 129 More especially remarkable in the time of their nidulation, and bringing forth their young. *a* **1682** —— *Tracts* (1683) 49 They were invited by such conveniences and prepared nests to relinquish their natural places of nidulation. **1845** SIR W. HAMILTON *Metaph.* I. App. 426 A convenient harbour for the nidulation, hatching, and nourishment of many parasitic animals.

‖**nidus** ('naɪdəs). Pl. nidi ('naɪdaɪ) and niduses. [L. *nīdus*:—**nizdus*: see NEST *sb.*]

1. *a. Zool.* A nest or place in which small animals, such as insects, snails, etc., lodge or deposit their eggs.

1742 H. BAKER *Microsc.* II. i. 70 The Eggs.. hatch and thrive when they happen to be lodged in a proper Nidus for them. **1760–72** tr. *Juan & Ulloa's Voy.* (ed. 3) I. 66 The cavity left, by the removal of the nidus, must be immediately filled.. with tobacco ashes. **1812** SIR J. SINCLAIR *Syst. Husb. Scot.* I. Add. 12 The insects and their nidi are.. exposed to the attacks of small birds. **1854** HOOKER *Himal. Jrnls.* I. ii. 46 The many-celled nidus of the leaf-cutter bee. **1871** T. R. JONES *Anim. Kingd.* (ed. 4) 152 Cystic parasites still enclosed in the nidus in which they are found in the omentum of rabbits.

b. *Bot.* A place or substance in which spores or seeds develop.

1796 WITHERING *Brit. Plants* (ed. 3) IV. 350 Though the fruit of such trees may be its more common nidus, I found it growing in large clusters on a rotten stick. **1859** T. MOORE *Brit. Ferns* 15 The spores.. would find a proper nidus for their development. **1868** HERSCHEL in *People's Mag.* Jan. 62 Forming a sort of vegetable honeycomb, and serving.. for a nidus to the spores.

c. *Phys.* and *Path.* A place of origin or development *for* some state or substance.

1804 ABERNETHY *Surg. Obs.* 68 The mammary gland seems to be the nidus for this diseased action. **1845** TODD & BOWMAN *Phys. Anat.* I. 88 In man, and the higher animals, cartilage is employed temporarily as a nidus for bone. **1879** *St. George's Hosp. Rep.* IX. 776 By purifying the cavity a fresh nidus for the disease is removed.

d. *fig.* A source or origin; a place where some quality or principle is fostered.

1807 *Edin. Rev.* IX. 415 The true *nidus* of the erroneous sentiments. **1817** KEATINGE *Trav.* II. 147 The Sorbonne, formerly the nidus of pedantry. **1845** R. W. HAMILTON *Pop. Educ.* i. (ed. 2) 9 It is the nidus of a new commonwealth. **1863** GEO. ELIOT *Romola* xi, The order of nature, which treats all maturity as a mere nidus for youth.

2. A place in which something is formed, deposited, settled, or located.

1778 KING in *Phil. Trans.* LXIX. 46 A proper nidus for the assemblage of the most valuable metals. **1846** CALLAWAY *Dislocations* (1849) 70 The bone again nearly always slips out from its nidus. **1876** *Trans. Clinical Soc.* IX. 165 The severe vomiting and purging probably dislodged the calculus from its nidus.

3. A collection *of* eggs, tubercles, etc.

1822–34 *Good's Study Med.* (ed. 4) II. 492 In many cases the cysts or niduses of tubercles possess so little energy of action as never to exceed the size of a small shot. **1826** KIRBY & SP. *Entomol.* xxix. III. 75 Reaumur had once brought to him a nidus of eggs clothed still more curiously.

nie, obs. f. NIGH, NINE; var. of NEYE.

niece, obs. form of NICE.

niece (niːs). Forms: 3–6 nece, 4–6 nese, (4 neese), 5–6 nees, 6–8 neece; 6 neise, neyce, neipce, 7 neice; 6 niese, niepce, nyepce, 6– niece; 4–7 nice, (4 nyce). [a. F. *nièce* (12th c.), † *nece*, *neice*, *nice*, *niepce*, etc. = Prov. *netsa*, obs. It. *nezza*:—pop. L. *neptia*, for L. *neptis* (related to NIFT): cf. Prov. *nepta*, Catal. and Pg. *neta*, Sp. *nieta*:—pop. L. **nepta.*]

1. †**a.** A grand-daughter, or more remote female descendant. *Obs.* **b.** A daughter of one's brother (brother-in-law) or sister (sister-in-law).

In older use, down to *c* 1600, the sense of 'grand-daughter' appears to have been common, but it is often difficult or impossible to make out which relationship is expressed by the word.

1297 R. GLOUC. (Rolls) 4160 Out of þe lond of spayne [he] come & adde ynome eleyne þat was so vair þe kinges nece. **13..** *E.E. Allit. P.* A. 233 Ho was me nerre þen aunte or nece. *c* **1374** CHAUCER *Troylus* II. 288 Good aventure, O bele nece, have ye Ful lightly founden. **1387** TREVISA *Higden* (Rolls) VI. 141 þat ȝere deide Hilda, abbesse of Whitby... Sche was kyng Edwyn his nese [1432–50 doȝhter of the doȝhter of kynge Edwinus]. **1422** *E.E. Wills* (1882) 50 Ion Skydmore, my newewe... Also.. Iane myn nece. **1470–85** MALORY *Arthur* XVII. xix. 717 Kynge Pelles and Elyazar his sone the whiche were holy men and a mayde which was his nece. **1513** DOUGLAS *Æneis* II. xii. 47, I, the nece of mychty Dardanus, And guide dochtir vnto the blissit Venus. **1542** UDALL *Erasm. Apoph.* 261 b, What Augustus would saie when any mencion was made either of Julia his doughter, or Julia his nice. **1576** GASCOIGNE *Steele Glas* (Arb.) 71 To tire his wearie wife, His daughters and his niepces euerychone. **1614** RALEIGH *Hist. World* III. (1634) 39 Taking two of Cyrus' daughters, and as many of his neeces for Wives. *c* **1657** SIR W. MURE *Hist. Ho. Rowallane* Wks. (S.T.S.) II. 254 Lord Hammiltoune who had to wife his Nice or sister daughter. **1673** CAVE *Prim. Chr.* I. iii. 45 His neece by the sister's side. **1723** GAY *Let. to Swift* 3 Feb., Mr. Maxwell, who married a niece of Mr. Meredith's. **1797** MRS. RADCLIFFE *Italian* i, Very cautious in her replies to his inquiries after her niece. **1847** TENNYSON *Princ.* II. 257 O by the bright head of my little niece, You were that Psyche.

c. Euphemistically applied to the illegitimate daughter of an ecclesiastic. Cf. NEPHEW 1 b.

1858 HOLMES *Aut. Breakf.-t.* vii. (1891) 161 Many a Holy Father's 'niece' Has softly smoothed the papal chair.

d. *niece-in-law*, the wife of one's nephew. *rare.*

a **1556** CRANMER *Wks.* (Parker Soc.) II. 329 Sister and sister-in-law, aunt and aunt-in-law, niece and niece-in-law.

†**2.** A female relative. *Obs.*

1297 R. GLOUC. (Rolls) 7252 Seint edwardes nece þat of is fader kunde com. *c* **1375** *Cursor M.* 10891 (Fairf.), Thyne old nyce Elizabeth hath gon with child vj moneth. *c* **1386** CHAUCER *Shipman's T.* 125 This monk bigan vp-on this wyf to stare, And seide, allas, my Nece; god forbede [etc.]. *c* **1400** *Lay le Freine* 288 Leman, he seyd, thou most lat be The abbesse thi nece, and go with me. *c* **1460** *Towneley Myst.* xi. 23 Ioachym thy fader at hame, And anna, my nese, and thi dame. **1508** DUNBAR *Flyting* 540 Thy trew kynnismen, Antenor & Eneas, Throp thy nere nece, and austern Olibrius.

†**b.** Used as a form of address to a woman. *Obs.*

c **1470** HENRY *Wallace* VII. 275 'Der nece', he said,.. 'Is my eyme dede, or hou the cace befell?'

†**3.** A nephew. *Obs. rare.*

c **1500** *Lancelot* 2200 The king.. said, 'Sir gawan, nece, why dois þow so? *Ibid.* 2720 The king.. of his necis lyf was in disspare. *a* **1592** GREENE *Alphonsus* II. Wks. (Rtldg.) 229/1 Seeking about the troops of Aragon, For to encounter with his traitorous niece. *Ibid.* III. 236/1 Belinus, my most friendly niece.

Hence **'nieceless** *a.*, **'nieceship.**

1834 SOUTHEY *Doctor* lxxii, She was a descendant of.. Japhet; she was allied to Ham, however, in another way besides this remote niece-ship. **1892** SIR E. B. HAMLEY *Let.* in Shand *Life* (1895) II. xxxi. 303, I then had a niece and a cat to comfort me—now I am nieceless and catless.

niede, nief(e, obs. ff. NEED, NEIF, NIEVE.

nieht, obs. form of NIGHT.

niel, var. of NIELLO. [Cf. Sp. *niel*, F. *nielle.*]

1873 SPON *Workshop Rec.* Ser. I. 219/1 The copy is hollow, and ready to receive the niel.

niellated (nɪˈɛleɪtɪd), *ppl. a.* [ad. It. *niellato*, pa. pple. of *niellare*, f. NIELLO.] Inlaid in niello.

1886 *Athenæum* 27 Feb. 301/3 They delineated numerous niellated works. **1901** *Chamb. Encycl.* VII. 498 The name niello is given not only to the engraved and niellated metal-work, but also to the paper proofs taken from them.

So **niˈelled** *ppl. a.*, nielloed.

1873 SPON *Workshop Rec.* Ser. I. 218/2 Nielled Silver.—This is a kind of inlaid enamel work, and is obtained by the sulphuration of certain parts of a silver object.

niellist (nɪˈɛlɪst). [f. next: see -IST.] A worker or artist in niello.

1841 *Gentl. Mag.* CXI. II. 21 The works of the Niellists did not cease on this discovery nor for some time after. **1883** C. C. PERKINS *Ital. Sculp.* 310 *note*, Highly reputed as a niellist, enamellist, and goldsmith.

‖**niello** (nɪˈɛləʊ), *sb.* Pl. nielli and niellos. [It. *niello*:—pop. L. **nigellum*, neut. of L. *nigellus*, dim. of *niger* black: cf. Prov. and Sp. *niel*, OF. *neel* (mod.F. *nielle* from It.).]

1. A black composition, consisting of alloys of silver, lead, copper, and sulphur, with which engraved designs on silver or other metals are filled in, so as to produce an ornamental effect.

1816 SINGER *Hist. Cards* 93 *note*, An impression from a Pax, engraved for the purpose of being filled with Niello. **1823** J. BADCOCK *Dom. Amusem.* 182 Enamel, called Niello. **1866** G. STEPHENS *Runic Mon.* I. 183 Much of the Niello has fallen away, and whole lines or parts of lines are now empty. **1877** W. JONES *Finger-ring* 55 The outer surface is engraved, and partly filled up with niello.

b. Ornamental work executed by the application of niello to engraved designs.

1842 BRANDE *Dict. Sci.*, etc. 399/1 It was the practice to decorate church and other plate with works in *niello*. **1845** MRS. JAMESON *Early Ital. Painters* I. 176 Maso Finiguerra.. became celebrated for the artistic beauty of his designs and workmanship in *niello*.

c. *attrib.* and *Comb.* as ***niello-cutting***, **-*plate***, etc.

1845 MRS. JAMESON *Early Ital. Painters* I. 175 The binding exhibits some beautiful specimens of niello-work. *Ibid.* 176 The earliest known impression of a niello plate. *Ibid.* 177 Maso Finiguerra, or any other niello-worker. **1864** *Chamb. Encycl.* VI. 765 Much interest attaches to the art of niello-cutting. **1884** KNIGHT *Dict. Mech.* Suppl. 635/1 The composition of the Russian tula or Niello silver.

2. A specimen of niello-work; an article ornamented with niello.

1840 *Civil Eng. & Arch. Jrnl.* III. 94/2 We see niellos upon bronze doors of Greek origin, even in Italy. **1841** *Gentl. Mag.* CXI. II. 21 They are not so fortunate as to possess a Niello in silver. **1895** *Pop. Sci. Monthly* Mar. 597 Our modern door plates are really nielli also.

3. An impression on paper of the design which is to be filled with niello.

1854 *Househ. Words* IX. 181 These impressions have in some few cases been preserved, as art-curiosities, and they, as well the plates themselves, are termed nielli. **1866** BRANDE & COX *Dict. Sci.*, etc. s.v., These impressions of the early fathers of copper-plate printing still exist, and are known also as *niellos*.

niˈello, *v.* [f. prec.] *trans.* To inlay with niello. Hence **niˈelloed** *ppl. a.*

1866 G. STEPHENS *Runic Mon.* I. 183 The whole runic inscription, and the two long lines.. are nielloed. **1877** W. JONES *Finger-ring* 58 There are various nielloed rings of the Saxon period. **1892** G. LAMBERT *Gold & Silversmith's Art* 45 All the gold, all the silver.. stamped, carved and chased, and nielloed.

nielsbohrium (ni:lzˈbɔərɪəm). *Chem.* [f. *Niels Bohr* (see BOHR) + -IUM, as ad. Russ. *nil'sboriĭ*, a name used by G. N. Flerov and co-workers (e.g. in Flerov & Zvara *Report D7-6013* (Joint Inst. Nuclear Res., Dubna, U.S.S.R., 1971) 56), though no explicit coinage of the word has been traced in the literature available.] (A name proposed for) an artificially produced transuranic element, of atomic number 105. (The name HAHNIUM has also been proposed for it.)

1973 *Nuclear Sci. Abstr.* XXVIII. 1209/2 Proposed names for Nos. 103–105 are Lawrencium (Lr), Kurchatovium (Ku), and Nielsbohrium (Bo). **1975** *Nature* 27 Mar. 288/2 As a sign of the rival claims elements 104 and 105 have been christened Rutherfordium and Hahnium in the USA and Kurchatovium and Nielsbohrium in the USSR.

Nielsen (ˈnɪəlsən). *U.S.* The name of Arthur Clarke *Nielsen*, used *attrib.* as ***Nielsen rating***, a popularity rating for radio and television programmes provided by A. C. Nielsen Co. and calulated from figures obtained from a sample survey of receiving sets fitted with a device (an Audimeter) to record automatically audience listening or viewing patterns (see quot. 1951). Similarly ***Nielsen index***, etc., and *absol.*

1951 E. E. WILLIS *Foundations in Broadcasting* 84 As does Hooper, Nielsen uses his sample to arrive at figures indicating the number of sets in use, the proportion of those sets tuned to a particular radio or TV show, and the percentage of the entire sample tuned to a specific program. It is this latter figure, the Nielsen rating, that has now superseded the Hooper rating as the most important national index of a network show's success. **1961** *Time* 6 Jan. 56/1 Last week's Nielsen ratings.. reported a total listenership of nearly 26 million homes per minute. **1975** *Sat. Rev.* (U.S.) 8 Mar. 12/1 The program is called 'Karen'. .. Even if 'Karen' fails its Nielsen test, ABC should be credited with spotting a significant trend. **1977** *Time* 10 Oct. 41/3 According to the Nielsen Index figures for TV viewing, Americans will have watched 18,000 TV murders by age 18. **1978** G. VIDAL *Kalki* vi. 139 CBS had racked up a Nielsen rating of 36.3, the highest ever in that particular time slot. *Ibid.* vii. 179 Dr. Lowell wants you to do a special show, guaranteed to hit a top Nielsen, maybe even in the high forties. **1982** *Amer. Speech* IV. 267 Television moguls apparently believe that copying shows that have already demonstrated their popularity is a sure-fire technique for increasing Nielsen ratings.

Niemann-Pick disease (ni:mənˈpɪk). *Path.* Also **Niemann-Pick's disease**. [f. the names of Albert *Niemann* (1880–1921) and Ludwig *Pick* (1868–?1944), German physicians, who described the disease in 1914 and 1926 respectively.] A rare, inherited metabolic disorder, usu. fatal in childhood, which is characterized by the accumulation within the body cells of a lipid (sphingomyelin).

1928 *Jrnl. Amer. Med. Assoc.* 7 Apr. 1166/1 (*heading*) Niemann-Pick disease. *Ibid.* 30 June 2077/2 The stored material in Niemann-Pick's disease is phosphatide. **1942** M. M. WINTROBE *Clin. Hematol.* xii. 521 The cells of Niemann-Pick's disease are round, oval, or polyhedral and are filled with small round hyaline droplets in clusters which give the appearance of foam or a honeycomb. **1966** WRIGHT & SYMMERS *Systemic Path.* I. v. 246/1 Niemann-Pick disease is considerably rarer than Gaucher's disease. **1973** *Sci. Amer.* Aug. 90/3 Another disorder involving enlargement of the liver and the spleen and mental retardation, Niemann-Pick disease, was shown.. to involve the accumulation of the phospholipid sphingomyelin.

nien(e, niend, nientene, -teþe, -ti, obs. ff. NINE, NINTH, NINETEEN(TH, NINETY.

niepce, obs. f. NIECE.

niepe, obs. f. NEAP.

Niersteiner (ˈnɪəʃtaɪnə(r)). [f. *Nierstein* a town in west central Germany near Mainz + *-er*, G. adj. suffix.] A much esteemed white Rhine wine produced at Nierstein.

[**1825** SCOTT *Talisman* in *Tales of Crusaders* IV. xi. 200 He invited them to a goblet of nierenstein.] **1833** C. REDDING *Hist. Mod. Wines* vii. 207 The wines of Bischeim.. are very pleasant wines; those of the most strength are.. Rüdesheimer, and Niersteiner. **1852** T. MCMULLEN *Handbk. Wines* xi. 112 Some are of opinion that the Marcobrunner, Rüdesheimer, and Niersteiner, possess more fulness and body. **1907** *Yesterday's Shopping* (1969) 99/3 Still Hock.. Niersteiner Pettenthal—Per doz. bots. 30/0. **1939** [see HEURIGE 2]. **1961** *Guardian* 3 Mar. 12/3 She was eating alone, with a bottle of Niersteiner. **1967** A. LICHINE *Encycl. Wines & Spirits* 447/2 Of some 550 parcels, about two dozen produce the soft, elegant, full-bodied, peak wines known around the world as Niersteiners. Look for Riesling on the label: the best Niersteiners are from the Riesling grape.

niese, obs. f. NEEZE, NIECE.

niess(e, obs. ff. NYAS.

niest, dial. var. of NEXT.

nieðe, obs. f. NINTH.

Nietzschean (ˈni:tʃɪən), *sb.* and *a.* Also **Nietzschian**. [f. the name of the German philosopher, Friedrich *Nietzsche* (1844–1900) + -AN.] **A.** *sb.* A follower, admirer, or imitator of Nietzsche; one who holds or supports Nietzsche's principles or views, esp. his theories of the superman, and the division of humanity into masters and slaves. **B.** *adj.* Of, pertaining to, or characteristic of Nietzsche or his views.

1904 *To-Day* XLIV. 49/2 This moustache.. was Nietzschean at the root, to end in the twirl of the sub-officer. **1908** G. B. SHAW *Sanity of Art* 6 The Nietzscheans were only too glad to see Tolstoy catching it. **1908** M. A. MÜGGE *Friedrich Nietzsche* III. ii. 331 There is no doubt that Goethe was a Nietzschean aristocrat. **1910** *Daily Chron.* 9 Feb. 6/3 The volumes of this edition are beginning to make me believe that Nietzsche's greatest enemies are the Nietzscheans. **1915** *London Q. Rev.* Jan. 92 One need only take up any of Nietzsche's books at random to see how alien this is to the 'Nietzschian' spirit. **1921** *Glasgow Herald* 24 Nov. 6 It is only fitting that the standpoint of that eminent Nietzschean, Mr A. M. Ludovici, should have an individuality of its own. **1932** D. B. W. LEWIS *Emperor of West* i. 22 The ironic pen of Machiavelli drew.. the portrait of the ideal Prince:.. the original Nietzschean Non-Moral Overman. **1959** [see BOUNDERISH *a.*]. **1968** *Times Lit. Suppl.* 25 Apr. 436/3 In his earlier years he [*sc.* Orage] was a Theosophist, a Nietzschean, and a Fabian Socialist. **1973** *Listener* 9 Aug. 170/1 The Nietzschean idea that since God is dead, everything is permitted.

Hence **ˈNietzscheanism**; **ˈNietzscheanite**; **ˈNietzscheism**; **ˈNietzscheite**.

1908 H. L. MENCKEN *Philos. Nietzsche* III. ii. 278 We have a hero who calls himself a dionysian and offers Nietzscheism as a substitute for Christianity. **1908** M. A. MÜGGE *Friedrich Nietzsche* I. ii. 82 It was the Dawn of Nietzscheanism. *Ibid.* III. ii. 352 Nietzscheanites hope their master's influence will create in England a sense for the true higher culture. **1909** CHESTERTON *Orthodoxy* iii. 73 If Nietzsche had not ended in imbecility, Nietzscheism would end in imbecility. **1910** —— *G. B. Shaw* 180 You must make sure of the presence of some Nietzscheite professor, who will explain to him that such a course might possibly serve to eliminate the unfit. **1914** *Times* 31 Oct. 7/1 Mistaken Nietzscheanism always tempts to the development of the devil in man. **1916** GALSWORTHY in *Scribner's Mag.* Jan. 21/2 The Neo-German conception of the State.. may be inverted Nietzscheism. **1968** *Times Lit. Suppl.* 25 Apr. 437/1 This untidy mixture of socialism, Nietzscheanism, and mysticism is a fair expression of Orage's untidy thought.

nieve (ni:v), **nief** (ni:f). Now *dial.* or *arch.* Forms: α. 4–6 neue, (9) neve, 5–6 newe, 5 (9) neeve, 6– neive, (7 neiue), nieve, 7–9 neave, (9 nee-), 8–9 nive, 9 niv, nev. (Also 9 **kneave**, etc.) β. 4–5 (9) nefe, 5 nef, 5–6 neff(e, 6 (9) neef; 6 (9) neif(e, 6 neiff, neyf, 7 (9) neiffe; 6 neafe, -ffe, 7, 9 neaf, (9 kn-), 9 neeaf; 6 nife, 7, 9 nief. γ. 5, 9 nave, 6 naif, 9 naive, neyv(e, knayve, etc. [ME. *neve*, *nefe*, ad. ON. *hnefi*, *nefi* (Norw. dial. *neve*, *növe*, *næva*, Sw. *näfve*, Da. *næve*). The γ-forms may correspond to the Norw. dial. var. *nava*, the relationship of which to *neve* is not clear. The word is not found in the other Teutonic languages.] A clenched hand; a fist.

Current in all northern and Sc. dialects; also used by Shakspere and B. Jonson (see NEUF) and hence sometimes by modern writers as an archaism. For the distribution of the mod. dial. forms see the *Eng. Dial. Dict.*

α. *c* **1300** *Havelok* 1917 So longe haueden he but and bet With neues under hernes set. **13..** *E.E. Allit. P.* B. 1537 When þat bolde Baltazar blusched to þat neue, al falewed his face. **1375** BARBOUR *Bruce* III. 581 Newys that stalwart war & squar, That wont to spayn gret speris war. *c* **1400** *Destr. Troy* 13889 He nolpit on with his Neue in the necke hole. **1456** SIR G. HAYE *Law Arms* (S.T.S.) 155 Gif he wald strike me.. I strike him agayne with my neve. **1573** *Satir. Poems Reform.* xlii. 427 The teindis will not cum in thair neuis, Sa lang as ony of vs leuis. *a* **1585** MONTGOMERIE *Cherrie & Slae* 1552 Quhois throt.. Ye may stap with your neive. **1609** SKENE *Reg. Maj.* II. 2 Gif he giues ane blow with his neiue .. he sall pay to the king sex kye. **1684** [MERITON] *Yorksh. Dial.* 599 She'l deal her Neaves about her, I hear tell. *a* **1758** RAMSAY *Fables* XVII. 4 A greedy Callan.. Shot his wee nive into the pot. **1785** BURNS *Death & Dr. Hornbook* xxvi, An honest Wabster.., Whase wife's twa nieves were scarce weel-bred. **1830** GALT *Lawrie T.* I. ii, Her nieve was said to be worse than a battering-ram. **1895** *Chamb. Jrnl.* XII. 779/2 He stepped forward a pace, his eyes flashing, his nieves clenched.

β. *c* **1375** *Cursor M.* 6682 (Fairf.), If.. þe tane þe toþer smyte wiþ nefe or stane. *a* **1400** *Sir Perc.* 2087 To Percevelle a dynt he ȝefe In the nekk with his nefe. *c* **1440** *York Myst.* xxix. 369 Dose noddil on hym with neffes That he noght nappe. **1513** DOUGLAS *Æneis* XII. viii. 106 Mesapus.. in hys left neif haldis all reddy Twa sowpill casting speris. **1570** *Satir. Poems Reform.* xxii. 60 Blind Hary with hir to sport and play, With fauldit neif. **1590** SHAKS. *Mids. N.* IV. i. 15 Giue me your neafe, Mounsieur Mustardseed. **1597** —— *2 Hen. IV*, II. iv. 195 Sweet Knight, I kisse thy Neaffe. **1674** RAY *N.C. Words* 35 A *Neive* or *Neiffe*: a Fist. **1825** BROCKETT *N.C. Gloss.*, *Neif*, the fist... *Double-neif*, the clenched fist. **1855** KINGSLEY *Westw. Ho!* (1889) 70/1 Come, give us thy neif, and let us part in peace. **1866** J. B. ROSE tr. *Ovid's Met.* 324 With clever neife And undegenerate cunning.

attrib. **1456** SIR G. HAYE *Law Arms* (S.T.S.) 155 Gif a man wald geve me a nef strake.

γ. **1375** BARBOUR *Bruce* XVI. 129 With ane trunsioune in [till] his nave, To schir Colyne sic dusche he gave. **1535** STEWART *Cron. Scot.* III. 518 This ilk Walter.. desirit for to haif That ilk falcone he buir vpoun his naif. **1841** HAMILTON *Nugæ Lit.* 337 A violent man threatens to have [heave] his nave. **1872** HARTLEY *Yorksh. Ditties* Ser. I. 130 He struck his naive o' th' table.

nieveful (ˈni:vfʊl). *Sc.* and *north. dial.* Forms: 5 neful, 7 niewfulle, neiffeful; 7, 9 nief-, 8 neaf-, 9 neef-ful (9 -fu'); 8–9 nieve-, 9 neive-, niveful, -fu'; also 8 niev'ow, 8–9 neffow, 9 neffu, etc. [f. prec. + -FUL.] A handful.

c **1375** *Sc. Leg. Saints* xxv. (*Julian*) 758 Iulyane.. his neful tuk of his blud red. **1665** SIR J. LAUDER *Jrnl.* (1900) 89 The beggar wives.. piking furth in neiwfulles on all sydes. **1686** G. STUART *Joco-ser. Disc.* 4 We'll have a pock pudding; Put a nief full of prunes in and make it a gude one. **1785** BURNS *2nd Ep. to J. Lapraik* xvii, Their worthless nievefu' of a soul, May in some future carcase howl. **1839** MOIR *Mansie Wauch* (ed. 2) xxv, I swept up two nievefuls o' dominoes off the table. **1863** J. L. W. *By-gone Days* 191 The alms.. generally consisted in a 'nievefou' or two of oatmeal.

nieveling (ˈni:vlɪŋ), *vbl. sb. Sc.* [Cf. NIEVE.] A method of milking cows (see quot. 1844).

1844 H. STEPHENS *Bk. Farm* II. 454 Nievling [is performed] by the whole hand doubled, or *fist*, pressing the teat steadily at one place. *Ibid.* III. 839 The easiest mode of milking them while under this complaint, is that described by nievling in. **1895** *Agric. Gaz.* 17 June 539/2 Of the four methods in use.. he thought the squeezing or 'nievling' was most suitable.

nievie (ni:vɪ). *Sc.* and *north. dial.* Also 6 nevie, 9 neevie, nievy, niv(v)y, etc. [f. NIEVE.] In ***nievie-(nievie-)nick-nack***, a guessing game played by children in which these words are used. (See *Engl. Dial. Dict.*)

c **1585** MONTGOMERIE *Misc. Poems* xxxii. 65 Can ȝe not play at 'nevie nevie nak'? **1821** *Blackw. Mag.* Aug. 37/2 Playing at nivy-nick-nack. **1824** SCOTT *St. Ronan's* xxx, I played it awa' at neevie-neevie-nick-nack. **1895** W. C. FRASER *Whaups* iii, The more advanced children.. played at 'Nievie, nievie, nick-nack'.

niewe, obs. form of NEW *a.*

†**nif**, for *ne if*, if not, unless. *Obs.*

13.. *E.E. Allit. P.* B. 21 Nif he nere scoymus & skyg & non scaþe louied. **13..** *Gaw. & Gr. Knt.* 1769 Gret perile bi-twene hem stod, Nif mare of hir knyȝt mynne.

nif, in south-western dial., for *an if.*

Nife (naɪf). Also **nife**. [f. *Ni* + *Fe*, chem. symbols for *ni*ckel and iron (L. *fe*rrum) respectively.] Nickel-iron; *spec.* [a. G. *Nife* (E. Suess *Das Antlitz der Erde* (1909) III. II. xxiv. 626)], the earth's core or the material composing it.

1909 H. B. C. & W. J. SOLLAS tr. *Suess's Face of Earth* IV. xv. 544 We assume the existence of three zones..as determining the structure of the earth, namely, the barysphere or the Nife (Ni-fe), Sima (Si-Mg), and Sal (Si-Al). *Ibid.* 547 A nucleus of Nife and heavy metals extends from the centre outwards for three quarters of the radius. *Ibid.* xvii. 606 We may suppose that..these gases and with them our volcanic eruptions do not proceed from the depth of the Nife but from Sima. **1924** J. G. A. SKERL tr. *Wegener's Orig. Continents & Oceans* x. 146 The core of the earth, probably composed chiefly of nickel and iron, has been termed the 'nife' by E. Suess. **1932** J. A. STEERS *Unstable Earth* iv. 159 Following Suess, Wegener assumed that the outer 'skin' of the earth was sial..; under this is the sima, and the interior core of the globe is the nife. **1927** *Wireless World* 19 Jan. 87/1 Batteries, Limited,..have recently drawn attention to the need of floating a layer of paraffin on the electrolyte of their Nife cells. [**1966** *McGraw-Hill Encycl. Sci. & Technol.* XIII. 158/1 In the original types of Ni-Cd (Jungner) cells the materials and structural features are quite similar to those described for the Ni-Fe cell.]

nife, obs. f. NIEVE.

nifel, var. of NIFLE.

niff (nɪf), *sb.*[1] *colloq.* and *dial.* Also **nif**. [Origin unknown.] Resentment, offence. Freq. in phr. ***to take a niff***, to take offence.

1777 *Horae Subsecivae* 303 Let her alone, her've o'ny a-got a bit of a niff her'll zoon come o' that again. **1865** R. HUNT *Pop. Romances W. of Eng.* 2nd Ser. 78 The woman took a nif, and for a long time never spoke to our John. **1903** in *Eng. Dial. Dict.* IV. 267/2 You're taking the niff. **1914** *Dialect Notes* IV. 77 *Niff*, a quarrel, grudge, or spite. **1946** *Amer. Speech* XXI. 308 To 'take a niff' at a person was to conceive a violent dislike for him.

niff (nɪf), *sb.*[2] *slang.* [Perh. f. S)NIFF *sb.*] A disagreeable smell; a whiff.

1903 in *Eng. Dial. Dict.* **1921** *Chambers's Jrnl.* Mar. 202/1 They found themselves within an outer circle of bee hive huts, fires that had died to red glimmers, and—a 'niff', if I may thus gently put it. **1960** D. FEARON *Murder-on-Thames* ii. 27 It wouldn't be nice for Rachel if some niff of ancient scandal caught up with her poor papa. **1975** *Draconian* Christmas 16922/1 The customary Oxford autumn niff, usually readily recognisable, redolent as it is of bonfires and long grass.

niff (nɪf), *v.*[1] *colloq.* and *dial.* [Origin unknown.] To quarrel, to be offended. So **niffed** (nɪft) *ppl. a.*

1875 W. D. PARISH *Dict. Sussex Dial.* 79 *Niff*, to quarrel; to be offended. **1880** COURTNEY & COUCH *Gloss. Words in Use in Cornwall* 40/1 She's gone away niffed. **1893** D. JORDAN *Forest Tithes* 99 Ye wunt feel niffed like when we meets ye, if we gives ye plenty o' elber-room, mister. **1906** E. PHILLPOTTS *Portreeve* III. xii. 310 Then—just because you'm niffed about something—you lift your hand to her to let out your bile. **1924** LAWRENCE & SKINNER *Boy in Bush* viii. 119 At last Monica..was niffed. She thought him a muff. **1927** W. E. COLLINSON *Contemp. Eng.* 116 Anger is expressed by such phrases as these in ascending order of intensity: he was niffed or peeved, he got shirty or hairy, he got his rag out, [etc.].

niff (nɪf), *v.*[2] *slang.* Also **nif**. [See NIFF *sb.*[2]] *intr.* To have a disagreeable smell.

1927 [see HUM *v.*[3]]. **1934** WODEHOUSE *Thank you, Jeeves* iii. 34 I've started breeding mice and puppies. And, of course, they nif a bit. **1938** —— *Code of Woosters* viii. 177 Scotties are smellie... You will recall how my Aunt Agatha's McIntosh niffed to heaven while enjoying my hospitality. **1950** A. BARON *There's no Home* v. 57 This ol' street may niff a bit, but it don't smell as bad as the water out of polluted wells. **1967** K. GILES *Death in Diamonds* iv. 66 It smelled... 'Niffs, don't it?' said one of the youths. **1974** WODEHOUSE *Aunts aren't Gentlemen* xvii. 145 'Nasty slinking-looking bleeder.'.. 'He don't half niff.'

ˈniffer, *sb. Sc.* [f. the vb.] An exchange. ***to put in a niffer***, to hazard.

1786 BURNS *Addr. to Unco Guid* iii, Ye see your state wi' their's compar'd, And shudder at the niffer. **1818** SCOTT *Hrt. Midl.* xviii, I wad make the niffer,..I wad gie a' these grey hairs..for her life. *Ibid.* xx, He put his life in a niffer, to break the prison to let me out. **1888** H. WARDROP *Poems & Sk.* 158 What could they gie as a niffer—This world has naething sae fine.

niffer (ˈnɪfər, ˈniːfər), *v. Sc.* and *north. dial.* Also **neifer**, **neiffer**, **-ar**, **neiver**. [Of obscure origin, perh. f. *nief*, NIEVE.]

1. *trans.* To exchange (a thing) *for* (†*with*) another. **b.** *intr.* in passive sense: To go in exchange.

1612 in Ritchie *Churches of St. Baldred* (1880) 108 Efter that ye said cow wald not niffer. **1637** RUTHERFORD *Lett.* I. lxxviii, A market where we might barter or niffer our lazy ease with a profitable cross. **1816** SCOTT *Antiq.* xxiii, I carried it for mony a year, till I niffered it for this tin ane. **1861** RAMSAY *Remin.* II. 168 'Oh', he said with great simplicity, 'my master niffered me for a pony'.

2. To make a mutual exchange of.

1721 RAMSAY *Answ. Burchet* 24 Proud czar, I wadna niffer fame With thee. *a* **1800** *Young Hyn Horn* x. in Child *Ballads* I. 203/2 You must niffer clothes with me. **1863** J. NICHOLSON *Kilwuddie* 74 Cuffs an' kicks they freely niffer't.

3. *intr.* **a.** To make an exchange.

1785 *Ferguson's Prov.* 17 He neiffers for the better. **1828** MOIR *Mansie Wauch* xxi, There being but small difference in the value of the cloths..I caused them to niffer. **1862** HISLOP *Prov. Scot.* 85 He's fond o' barter that niffers wi' auld Nick.

b. To bargain, haggle.

1818 SCOTT *Hrt. Midl.* xvi, I'll no stand niffering wi' ye. **1855** ROBINSON *Whitby Gloss.*, *Niffering* or *Niggling*, making a bargain in a hard or haggling manner.

Hence **ˈniffering** *vbl. sb.*

1541 *Aberd. Reg.* (Jam.), Be way of nyffering, coffing, & excambium. **1637** RUTHERFORD *Lett.* (1862) I. xcvii. 248 God forbid it come to bartering or niffering of crosses. **1897** CROCKETT *Lad's Love* iii, Profanin' the hoose o' God..wi' your cheep-dealin' and nifferin'!

niff-naff, *v. Sc.* and *north. dial.* [Of obscure formation: *niff-naff* as sb. in the sense of a trifling or unimportant thing is also common in north. dial. and Sc.] *intr.* To trifle.

1728 RAMSAY *There's my Thumb* iii, Dear lassie, it is but daffin To had thy wooer up ay niff naffin. *a* **1878** AINSLIE *Land of Burns* (1892) 318 Nif-naffin' at her apron strings. **1894** *Northumbld. Gloss.* s.v., He niffnaffed at the job.

So **niff(y)-naffy** *a.*, trifling, finical.

1796 W. MARSHALL *Yorksh.* (ed. 2) Gloss., *Niffy-naffy*. **1815** SCOTT *Guy M.* xliv, Thae niff-naffy gentles that gae sae muckle fash wi' their fancies. **1855** ROBINSON *Whitby Gloss.* s.v., 'A niffy naffy sort of a body', a person possessed of the opposite to business habits.

niffy (ˈnɪfɪ), *a. slang.* [f. NIFF *sb.*[2] + -Y[1].] Having a disagreeable or strong smell. Also as *sb.* Hence **ˈniffiness**.

1903 *Eng. Dial. Dict.* IV. 267/2 *Niffy*, adj. odorous. **1925** FRASER & GIBBONS *Soldier & Sailor Words* 209 *Niffy*, *a*, a strong nasty smell. **1934** 'BARON CORVO' *Desire & Pursuit of Whole* ix. 81 The niffy silted-up little Rio della Croxe. **1934** WODEHOUSE *Right Ho, Jeeves* x. 113 The garden was full of the aroma of those niffy white flowers. **1946** —— *Money in Bank* iv. 31 Well anyway, Stinker, putting aside for the moment the question of your niffiness, wasn't it notorious that you couldn't tell the truth without straining a ligament?

nifle (ˈnaɪf(ə)l). Now *dial.* Forms: 4, 7 **nyfle**, 5–6 **nyfel**, **-yl**, 6 **-ul**, **nifel**, 5–7 (8–9 *dial.*) **nifle**; 6 **niffel**, **niffle**. [Of obscure origin: perh. ad. med.L. *nichil* nothing (see NICHIL), influenced by *trifle*, with which it is often combined. There appears to be no other trace of the F. *nifle* given by Palsgrave. In mod. dialect the verb *nifle*, to trifle, is in common use (given by Ash, 1775).]

1. A trifle; a thing of little or no value; †a trifling or fictitious tale. (Common *c* 1550–1650).

c **1386** CHAUCER *Sompn. T.* 52 He served hem with nyfles and with fablis. **1436** *Libel Eng. Policy* in *Pol. Poems* (Rolls) II. 172 Apes, and japes, and marmusettes taylede, Nifles, trifles, that litelle have availede. **1526** SKELTON *Magnyf.* 1157, I am yet..as full of tryfyls, Nil, nihilum, nihil, anglice nyfyls. **1533** J. HEYWOOD *A Mery Play* 434, I wolde ye had harde the tryfyls, The toys, the mokkes, the fables, and the nyfyls, That I made thy husbande to beleue and thynke. **1562** *Apol. Priv. Masse* (1850) 22 You drive men to these trifles that the world may know you hang in nifels. **1610** HOLLAND *Camden's Brit.* I. 663 Might I not be thought..to catch at clouds, and fish for Nifles? **1657** J. WATTS *Baptism* 159, I..will give over spending my precious time about your nifles and trifles. **1868** WAUGH *Sneck-Bant* 89 She then took Betty's basket and crammed it with fruit, and with all sorts of sweet 'nifles'.

Phr. **1530** PALSGR. 850/2 Nyfels in a bagge, *de tout nifles.* **1622** MABBE tr. *Aleman's Guzman d'Alf.* II. 160 No wise man will adventure his person for nifles in a bagge.

b. Applied to a person. *rare*$^{-1}$.

1635 [GLAPTHORNE] *Lady Mother* III. ii. in Bullen *O. Pl.* II. 164 Will you goe?.. What stayes this nifle for?

†**2.** Some light or flimsy article of attire. *Obs.*

c **1460** *Towneley Myst.* xxx. 323 And nell with hir nyfyls of crisp and of sylke, Tent well youre twyfyls youre nek abowte as mylke. **1463–4** *Rolls of Parlt.* V. 505/2 That noo persone ..selle in any parte within this Reame eny Lawne, Nyfels, Uimple, or eny other manere of Kerchiefs.

ˈnifling, *a. rare.* [See prec. Some mod. dialects use *niffling*.] Trifling, worthless.

1649 J. E[LLISTONE] tr. *Behmen's Epist.* Pref., Whosoever beares not the Stamp, and Superscription of their.. Institutions, is but as Darkenesse and nifling Shaddows unto them. **1659** *Lady Alimony* II. vi. in Hazl. *Dodsley* XIV. 317 A poor nifling toy that's worse than nothing.

nifontovite (nɪˈfɒntəvaɪt). *Min.* [ad. Russ. *nifontovit* (Malinko & Lisitsyn 1961, in *Doklady Akad. Nauk SSSR* CXXXIX. 188), f. the name of P. V. *Nifontov*, 20th-cent. Russian geologist: see -ITE[1].] A hydrated borate of calcium, $CaB_2O_4 \cdot 2 \cdot 3H_2O$, found as colourless monoclinic crystals.

1961 *Mineral. Mag.* XXXII. 990 Nifontovite... Small anhedral grains in skarn deposits in the Urals. **1971** *Soviet Physics—Crystallogr.* XVI. 186/1 The description and investigation of a group of endogenic calcium metaborates: calciborite, korzhinskite, uralborite, nifontovite, frolovite, and pentahydroborite.

†**nift.** *Obs.* Forms: 1 **nift**, 3, 5 **nifte**, 4–5 **nyfte**, 5 **nypt(e**, **nyghte**. [OE. *nift* = OFris. *nift*, MDu. *nifte*, *nichte* (Du. *nicht*), MLG. *nifte*, *nichte* (hence G. *nichte*), OHG. *nift*, ON. *nift*, *nipt*:—OTeut. **niptiz* = L. *neptis*, Skr. *naptis*, from the stem *nept-*: cf. the etym. note to NEVE[1].] A niece. Also *forth-nift*, grand-niece.

c **825** *Epinal Gloss.* 734 in *O.E. Texts* 84 *Privigna*, *filia sororis*, nift. *c* **900** tr. *Bæda's Hist.* III. ix. (1890) 180 [Heo] wæs nift [L. *neptem*] þæs hiȝna aldres þe he sohte. **1030** *Will* in Thorpe *Diplomat.* 556 Ic an mine lauedy half marc goldes, an mine nifte ann ore wichte goldes. *c* **1250** *Gen. & Ex.* 1386 Of batuel ðis maiden cam; ȝhe was forð nifte of abraham. *c* **1330** R. BRUNNE *Chron. Wace* (Rolls) 11011 Neueus nyftes, sistres broþer, Ilka frend welcomede oþer. *c* **1440** *Promp. Parv.* 355/2 Nypte [*v.rr.* nifte, nyfte], *neptis. Ibid.*, Nypt [*v.r.* nyfte], broderys douter, *lectis.* **1447** BOKENHAM *Seyntys* (Roxb.) 97 Marculus a bysshop of grece..Wyth constance hys nyfte. *c* **1500** *Melusine* 179 Prayeng you right hertyly to haue me to my ryght dere & beloued nyghte your wyf to be recommanded.

niftily (ˈnɪftɪlɪ), *adv.* [f. NIFTY *a.* + -LY[2].] In a nifty manner.

1919 *Amer. Mag.* LXXXVII. 93/1 That was a clever girl you had against you tonight. I don't believe in pacifism much, myself, but she used it very niftily for her argument. **1960** P. MORTIMER *Saturday Lunch with Brownings* 202 She lay down on her stomach, lifting up the chest with one hand while niftily tucking the carpet down under its foot with the other. **1971** *New Yorker* 13 Nov. 126/3 (Advt.), Our famous Whale Tie..in a niftily contemporary 4½ inch width. **1974** D. SMITH *Look Back with Love* xi. 106, I..particularly liked one story..in which the hero fought his way through an army by niftily manipulating a chair.

niftiness (ˈnɪftɪnɪs). *colloq.* [f. NIFTY *a.* + -NESS.] The quality of being nifty; smartness, cleverness.

1923 M. WATTS *Luther Nichols* 27 His fixed purpose was to keep it so or to increase its niftiness. **1974** *Punch* 13 Feb. 268 Some have even been moved to congratulate him on the niftiness of his own footwork—particularly when it comes to the waltz.

nifty (ˈnɪftɪ), *a. U.S. slang.* [Of uncertain origin: see first quot.] Smart, fine, splendid. Also, clever, nimble, adroit.

1868 B. HARTE *Poems* 93 Smart, you bet your life 'twas that! Nifty! Short for magnificat. **1882** 'MARK TWAIN' *Innoc. at Home* ii, He was always nifty himself, and so you bet his funeral ain't going to be no slouch. **1907** C. E. MULFORD *Bar-20* ix. 107 I've heard of Smith of Topeka, an' he's mighty nifty with his hands. **1916** H. L. WILSON *Somewhere in Red Gap* v. 213 Hetty..looking so fresh and nifty and feminine. **1921** WODEHOUSE *Indiscretions of Archie* xiii. 141 Don't you think it's a nifty scheme? **1923** —— *Inimitable Jeeves* iii. 32 Roville..is a fairly nifty spot where a chappie without encumbrances in the shape of aunts might spend a somewhat genial week or so. **1930** CHESTERTON *Four Faultless Felons* iii. 196 He's awfully nifty with his fingers. **1933** G. ADE *Let.* 6 Apr. (1973) 166 You..tell a nifty little story at the finish. **1938** D. SMITH *Dear Octopus* II. i. 52 I'm very nifty on a step-ladder. **1949** N. MARSH *Swing, Brother, Swing* iv. 57 Now that's quite a nifty little idea. **1958** J. CANNAN *And be a Villain* i. 19, I..got the niftiest white overalls. **1968** *Globe & Mail* (Toronto) 3 Feb. 35/4 Bruce Kelly scored a tying goal..on a nifty pass from John DeDiana. **1973** R. HAYES *Hungarian Game* xxxi. 184 'Try that coffee now. Tell me if you like it.'.. It was good. 'It's nifty,' I said. **1975** *Observer* 19 Jan. 22/4 Duncan was nifty on occasions, indeed scored an immaculate goal, but was at other times rather daintily ineffective.

nifty (ˈnɪftɪ), *sb. slang.* [f. the adj.] A joke, a witty remark or story.

1925 WODEHOUSE *Carry on, Jeeves* vi. 145 Every time I started to pull a nifty, Sir Roderick swung round on me with such a piercing stare that it stopped me in my tracks. **1929** D. MACKAIL *How Amusing!* 237 He..released no less than six of the wisecracks or nifties which he had been carefully hoarding for his next story. **1957** O. NASH *You can't get there from Here* 65 Had he sought his answers just below where Broadway bisects the lower Fifties, He would have come up with some nifties.

†**nig**, *sb.*[1] *Obs. rare.* [Of obscure origin.

Agrees in meaning with Sw. *njugg* (dial. *nugg*, *nygg*) and with Icel. *hnögg-* (Norw. *nögg*), but there is no obvious connexion in form or history with these. Cf. also Norw. and Sw. dial. *nigla*, to live sparingly, to NIGGLE.]

A niggardly or mean person.

a **1300** *Vision of Paul* (MS. Laud 108) in Herrig *Archiv* LII. 36 He was an hokerere,..Foul nig and hard in al is liue. *c* **1400** *Plowman's Tale* 757 Some of them been hard nigges; And some of hem been proude and gaie. **1570** LEVINS *Manip.* 118/39 A Nigge, *parca mulier.* **1678** PHILLIPS (ed. 4) Suppl., *Nig*, a miserly, sordid, pinch-gut fellow.

nig, *sb.*[2] *dial.* and *slang.* [Of obscure origin.] (See quots.)

a **1700** B. E. *Dict. Cant. Crew*, *Nig*, the Clippings of Money. **1853** *N. & Q.* 1st Ser. VII. 366/2 In Essex, *nig* signifies a piece.

nig, *sb.*[3], an abbreviation of NIGGER. Now only in derogatory use.

c **1832** T. D. RICE *Jim Crow* x, De Nigs in ole Virginny Be so black dey shine. **1840** *Picayune* (New Orleans) 20 Sept. 2/2 Two little nigs..had a most scientific set-to at the corner. **1864** SALA in *Daily Tel.* 12 Aug., As through the crowded Wall-street pass'd A nig who bore..A green-back banner. **1879** MRS. A. E. JAMES *Indian Househ. Managem.* 43 Treat your servants as fellow-creatures, not as 'nigs'—a term too often applied..to the Indian natives. **1905** E. W. PRINGLE *Woman Rice Planter* 160 Her manner is what the 'nigs' call 'stiff'. **1916** J. B. COOPER *Coo-oo-ee* xvi. 245 He never wipes the glass slobbered over by dozens of dirty nigs! Gosh, it's a good place to get out of! **1939** J. CARY *Mister Johnson* 162 You don't know wot it costs us, you nigs, to tidy up things for you. **1961** C. WILLOCK *Death in Covert* i. 11 Like many of these nigs, he could shoot. Dammit, back home in steaming wogland he probably did nothing else. **1974** R. GADNEY *Something worth fighting For* xii. 85 Judd read National Front puts Britain First. Someone had scribbled Nigs Out.

†**nig**, *v.*[1] *Obs. rare*$^{-1}$. [Cf. NIG *a.*] *intr.* To be mean or niggardly.

1559 AYLMER *Harborowe* M iv b, By withholding thy hande, and nigging, to make her not hable to kepe out thine ennemy.

†**nig**, *v.*[2] *Obs. slang.* To clip money.

a **1700** B. E. *Dict. Cant. Crew, Nigging*, Clipping.

nigard, etc., obs. ff. NIGGARD, etc.

†**nigel.** *Obs. rare*$^{-1}$. Also 6 **nygelle, niggel.** [Anglicized form of NIGELLA.] = NIGELLA.

1578 LYTE *Dodoens* 275 The other wilde kinde..shall be hereafter described..amongst the Nygelles, or Larke spurres.

Hence †'**nigelweed.** *Obs. rare.* (See quots.)

1578 LYTE *Dodoens* 160 Cockle or Field Nigelweede hath straight slender hearie stemmes. **1598** FLORIO, *Micancolo*, cockle, or field niggel weed.

‖**nigella** (naɪ'dʒɛlə). *Bot.* [L., fem. of *nigellus*, dim. of *niger* black: hence also F. *nielle* and *nigelle*.] A genus of ranunculaceous plants, having numerous black seeds, of which the Fennel-flower (*Nigella sativa*) is a common species; also, the seeds of this used for medicinal purposes.

1398 TREVISA *Barth. De P.R.* XVII. lxxxi. (Bodl. MS.), Some meneþ þat þis herbe [*sc.* gith] is nigella. *Ibid.*, Nigella sleeþ if he be take in grete quantite. **1548** TURNER *Names Herbs* (E.D.S.) 40 Git is named in greeke Melanthion, in englishe herbe Git or Nigella romana. **1577** B. GOOGE *Heresbach's Husb.* (1586) 53 b, Smalledge, Leekes, Nigella, that being once sowed, come up every yere. **1611** COTGR., *Alesnes*, Cockle, Corne-rose, field Nigella, wild Nigella. **1662** *Stat. Irel.* (1765) II. 402 Nigella the pound 4^d. **1707** MORTIMER *Husb.* (1721) II. 384 You may continue to sow.. Nigella, Candy Tufts, Poppy, and such Annuals as are not prejudiced by Frosts. **1802** PALEY *Nat. Theol.* (1817) 169 In some cases (as in the nigella), where the shafts of the pistils or styles are disproportionably long. **1881** MRS. LYNN LINTON in Layard *Life* (1901) 206 Here there is nothing, excepting..that cottage flower (love in a mist)—the nigella.

Hence **ni'gellin**, 'a viscous substance obtained from *Nigella sativa*' (Watts *Dict. Chem.* 1866).

nigenti, obs. form of NINETY.

†'**niger**[1]. *Obs.* [a. L. *niger.*] = NEGER, NEGRO.

1574 HELLOWES *Gueuara's Fam. Ep.* (1584) 389 The Massgets bordering upon the Indians, and the Nigers of Aethiop, bearing witnes. **1584** R. SCOT *Discov. Witchcr.* VII. xv. (1886) 122 A skin like a Niger. **1676** S. SEWALL *Diary* 1 July, Jethro, his Niger, was then taken. **1698–9** *Par. Reg. Norton* (near Evesham) 6 Jan., John Langley a Niger of Jameca..was baptized. **1721** S. SEWALL *Diary* 20 Oct., Met a Niger Funeral. **1760** G. WALLACE *Princ. Law Scot.* in *Ann. Reg.* (1760) II. 265/1 Set the Nigers free, and, in a few generations, this vast and fertile continent would be crouded with inhabitants.

Niger[2] ('naɪdʒə(r)). Also written **niger**. **1.** The name of a West African river, used *absol.* or *attrib.* to designate a type of morocco produced in regions near the river and used for bookbinding.

1898 C. EYRE in *Bookbinding by Women* 4 From Chiswick there are a number of examples of the very beautiful Niger-morocco bindings. **1901** D. COCKERELL *Bookbinding* xix. 278 The leather that I have found most useful is the Niger goatskin, brought from Africa by the Royal Niger Company. *Ibid.* 279 It is to be hoped that before long some of the manufacturers interested will produce skins as good in quality and colour as the best Niger morocco. **1930** *Times Lit. Suppl.* 18 Dec. 1081/3 (Advt.), Bound in whole natural niger goat-skin. **1952** J. CARTER *ABC for Book Collectors* 124 True niger, which comes from West Africa, is a soft skin with an unemphatic, variable grain. It is locally tanned and dyed... The slight variations of grain and colour which give niger its character are seldom achieved in the imitations of it. **1963** B. C. MIDDLETON *Hist. Eng. Craft Bookbinding Technique* xi. 122 Niger goatskin..was popularized by Douglas Cockerell more than sixty years ago.

2. niger seed, the seeds of *Guizotia abyssinica*, of the family Compositæ, native to West Africa and cultivated elsewhere for the oil obtained from its seeds; also, the plant itself (cf. RAMTIL); **niger (seed) oil**, the oil produced from niger seeds.

1884 *Encycl. Brit.* XVII. 746/1 Niger oil is the produce of the seeds (properly achenes) of *Guizotia oleifera*, a plant native of the east coast of Africa, but cultivated throughout India and to some extent in Germany. The fruits, which are small, tooth-like in form, and shining black in colour, contain from 40 to 45 per cent. of oil... In Western countries niger oil is principally employed in soap-making and as a lubricant. **1889** G. S. BOULGER *Uses of Plants* 138 *Guizotia abyssinica*, Cass., Niger or Ramtil seeds, came into the English market about 1851. It is a native of Tropical Africa, but is cultivated in India and Germany. It is used in Europe for soap and lubricating oil. **1917** *Chambers's Jrnl.* May 293/2 Niger-seed oil is used as a substitute for linseed-oil when the latter is scarce. **1944** *Living off Land* ii. 40 Niger-seed..looks like a sunflower. **1974** F. N. HOWES *Dict. Useful & Everyday Plants* 175 Niger seed. *Guizotia abyssinica*, an oil seed and much favoured for cage birds. **1974** G. USHER *Dict. Plants used by Man* 288/2 The plant [sc. *Guizotia abyssinica*] is cultivated for the seeds which yield an oil (Niger Seed Oil, Ramtilla Oil, Werinnua Oil). The plant is cultivated mainly in India, but also in E. Africa, W. Indies and Germany... It is used for soap-making and cooking fats.

Niger-Congo ('naɪdʒə'kɒŋgəʊ). [f. the names of the rivers *Niger* and *Congo*.] A group of languages which includes those spoken by most of the indigenous peoples of western, central, and southern Africa.

1955 J. H. GREENBERG *Studies in African Linguistic Classification* 8 To the entire family consisting of the West Sudanic nucleus inclusive of Bantu, plus this eastward extension, I have preferred to adopt a new name of a non-committal geographic nature, Niger-Congo, from the two great rivers in whose basins these languages predominate. **1961** F. G. CASSIDY *Jamaica Talk* iii. 31 The Niger-Congo languages are characterised by differences of meaning which depend upon pitch—or 'tone'—and stress. **1970** R. FINNEGAN *Oral Lit. in Africa* iii. 55 In the opinion of some recent scholars, even this large Bantu group is only one subdivision within a much larger family, the 'Niger-Congo' group, which also includes most of the languages of West Africa. **1972** *Language* XLVIII. 273 Accounting for the various kinds of syntactic evidence in the Bantu languages, such as the consistent use of prefixes which often correspond to suffixes of the Niger-Congo languages, will require considerable historical study.

Nigerian (naɪ'dʒɪərɪən), *sb.* and *a.* [f. *Nigeria* (see below): see -AN.] **A.** *sb.* A native or inhabitant of Nigeria, a republic in West Africa occupying the basin of the lower Niger. **B.** *adj.* Of or pertaining to Nigeria or its inhabitants.

1860 W. COLE *Jrnl.* 6 May in *Life in Niger* (1862) 170 This is the general mode in which the Nigerians make known their losses. **1905** F. L. SHAW *Tropical Dependency* xlv. 425 The names, alas, of more than one of the first small Nigerian group are engraved now upon tombstones on that border of the Empire which they helped to make. *Ibid.* li. 481 There are now in all..about 400 white men in the Northern Nigerian service. **1908** *Daily Chron.* 31 Jan. 3/3 When she came back from her first journey still hale and happy, she was accepted as a full-fledged Nigerian. **1923** *Blackw. Mag.* Apr. 514/2 His early days have gone down in Nigerian history. **1954** R. ST. B. BAKER *Sahara Challenge* vii. 73 This is the secret of the successful growing of groundnuts, which has been known to the Nigerians for many generations. *Ibid.*, We slept just outside a Nigerian resthouse. **1973** *Listener* 14 June 782/1 There is a confidence and exuberance about Nigerians which lifts the spirits. **1973** *Guardian* 19 June 18/4 The Niger herdsmen are paid in Nigerian pounds. They buy Nigerian goods, recross the border and sell the goods.

Nigerianization (naɪ,dʒɪərɪənaɪ'zeɪʃən). [f. NIGERIAN *sb.* and *a.* + -IZATION.] The process of making Nigerian; *spec.* the transfer of posts in government and industry from foreigners to native Nigerians.

1954 *Rep. Lagos Conf.* 80 in *Parl. Papers 1953–4* (Cmd. 9059) XI. 122 We are determined to press forward with the Nigerianization of the Civil Service. **1955** *Times* 23 Aug. 7/4 The 'Nigerianization' of the public service had not kept pace with the speed of the advance of self-government. **1959** *Times* 4 Dec. 9/3 He..pursued a vigorous policy of Nigerianization, particularly in the Post and Telegraphs Department. **1960** *Economist* 8 Oct. 132/1 Nigerianisation will go on, as it ought to do. **1961** *Aeroplane* CI. 450/2 A programme of development has recently been agreed by the board of Nigeria Airways... Steps will be taken leading eventually to the complete 'Nigerianization' of all activities. **1973** *Times* 1 Oct. (Nigeria Suppl.) p. viii/3 Within Nigeria British business continues to play a highly significant role, despite the effects of Nigerianization.

Nigerianize (naɪ'dʒɪərɪənaɪz), *v.* [f. NIGERIAN *sb.* and *a.* + -IZE.] To make Nigerian in character. Hence **Ni'gerianized** *ppl. a.*

1960 *Guardian* 4 Nov. 10/3 The politicians..are themselves fully 'Nigerianised'. **1966** J. P. MACKINTOSH *Nigerian Govt. & Politics* iv. 175 The Eastern and Western Government were composed of men determined to Nigerianize their Public Services with the utmost speed. **1969** I. F. NICOLSON *Administration of Nigeria* ix. 251 There are several justifications for the somewhat arbitrary choice of the year 1948 as the starting point of the process of transforming alien 'administocracy' into the apparatus of modern, federal, parliamentary government, complete with Nigerian Ministers and 'Nigerianized' career public services. **1971** J. S. COLEMAN *Nigeria: Background to Nationalism* iv. 103 The first major effort to Nigerianize the clergy..was made by the Church Missionary Society.

nigerite ('naɪdʒəraɪt). *Min.* [f. *Niger-ia*, the name of the country in which it was discovered + -ITE[1].] A basic oxide of zinc, iron, magnesium, tin, and aluminium, $(Zn,Fe^{II},Mg)(Sn,Zn)_2(Al,Fe^{III})_{12}O_{22}(OH)_2$, found as brown or red hexagonal platelets.

1946 JACOBSON & WEBB in *Bull. Geol. Surv. Nigeria* No. 17. 11 The dykes to the south-east of Oke Oloke are of special interest on account of the discovery of a new tin-zinc mineral, nigerite, which occurs in quartz-andalusite-sillimanite veins associated with the albitized pegmatites. **1947** *Times* 2 Dec. 6/3 Specimens of nigerite, a new tin mineral, recently analysed and described by the Museum's Department of Mineralogy, have been given. **1974** *Mineral. Mag.* XXXIX. 837 (*heading*) Nigerite in the tin-tantalum pegmatites of Amapá, Brazil.

nigeshe, var. of NIGGISH *a. Obs.*

niget, var. of NIDGET.

nigga ('nɪgə). Also **niggah, nigguh niggur.** Repr. a Southern U.S. pronunciation of NIGGER *sb.* Cf. NIGRA.

Now virtually restricted to publication in which Black English vernacular is set down.

1925 L. R. HARRIS in A. Dundes *Mother Wit* (1973) 563/2 Howdy niggahs,..how's you all dis mawnin'. **1937** C. HIMES in *Black on Black* (1973) 139 Niggah, ef'n yo is talkin' tuh me, Ah ain' liss'nin'. **1968** *Amer. Speech* XLIII. 217 The mountain trapper..was *this Injun*,..*this niggur*, or *this hoss*. **1969** G. BROOKS in A. Chapman *New Black Voices* (1972) 202 Lord! Forgive these nigguhs that know not what they do. **1969** in A. Dundes *Mother Wit* (1973) 655/1 They end up losing all of their money to that big nigga who is supposed to be the epitome of 'nigga-ness'. **1970** J. CORTEZ in O. Coombs *We speak as Liberators* 17 Love Lives And I wanta taste myself inside Mmmmmmmm that pure nigguh pain. **1973** *Black World* Sept. 70 His sound now turns to nigguh notes. **1973** *Black World* Apr. 58 My wandering niggah done slipped up on me. **1974** *Ibid.* Dec. 23 In the grammaticality of the mid nighttime sky when them sweet blue nigga dialects of the flesh rise.

niggar, obs. form of NIGGER.

niggard ('nɪgəd), *sb.* and *a.* Forms: α. 4–5 **negarde**, 5–6 **negard**, 9 *dial.* **neeger, neager, niegre**, etc. β. 4–5 **nygard**, (4 **-art**), 4–6 **-arde**, (8) **nigard**, (6 **-arde**), 7 **nigatt**. γ. 4 **nyggard**, 5–6 **-arde**, 6– **niggard**, (6 **-arde**), 9 *dial.* **niggar(t, -er**, etc. [Of obscure etym.; an earlier synonym is NIGON, and the termination in both cases would normally indicate a French origin. The rareness of the sb. NIG makes it doubtful whether it is the base of both formations.]

A. *sb.* **1.** A mean, stingy, or parsimonious person; a miser; one who grudgingly parts with or expends anything.

α. *c* **1374** CHAUCER *Troylus* III. 1379 So parfite joye may no negarde have. *c* **1407** LYDG. *Reson & Sens.* 1498 Dame Venus Kan make folkys covetous to spend her good.., And the Negarde to be large. *c* **1510** MORE *Picus* Wks. 18/1 The negard then saith to his money.., my god arte thou.

β. **1377** LANGL. *P. Pl.* B. xv. 136 He was a nygarde that no good myȝte aspare. **1390** GOWER *Conf.* II. 289 This Viola largesce hath take And the nygard sche hath forsake. **1483** CAXTON *Cato* E vij b, Men saye comynlye that the nygarde expendeth more than the lyberalle. *a* **1548** HALL *Chron., Edw. IV*, 217 b, An extreme nigard, and a covetous extorcioner. **1579** NORTHBROOKE *Dicing* To Rdr., If a man will not dice & plaie, then he is a nigarde & a miser, and no good fellowe.

γ. *c* **1380** WYCLIF *Wks.* (1880) 243 He schal be holde a nyggard. *c* **1440** *Promp. Parv.* 355/2 Nyggarde (or muglard or nygun, or pynchar), *tenax.* **1529** MORE *Dyaloge* III. Wks. 225/2 If they kepe fewe seruauntes we call them nyggardes. **1576** FLEMING *Panopl. Epist.* 291 Some are pinchpenies & notable niggards. **1606** J. CARPENTER *Solomon's Solace* xliii. 168 That niggard, who for feare of loosing his wealth would hide it. **1675** TRAHERNE *Chr. Ethics* 481 He that does brave acts abroad, but is a niggard within doors. **1720** WELTON *Suffer. Son of God* I. XI. 280 As for the stingy Niggard, He benefits none, no, not even himself. **1748** RICHARDSON *Clarissa* (1811) I. xiii. 88 Riches left by one niggard to another. **1830** D'ISRAELI *Chas. I*, III. viii. 163 This monarch was no niggard when he once showered the largess of his royal friendship. **1886** JESSOPP in *19th Cent.* Apr. 519 It would not be permitted to a niggard to let the parsonage fall into disrepair.

transf. **1752** YOUNG *Brothers* V. i, 'Tis impious to be niggards in delight. **1776** PAINE *Com. Sense* (1791) 61 That narrowness of soul..which the niggards of all professions are so unwilling to part with. **1838** LYTTON *Leila* I. v, They shall not, at least, call the Jews niggards in revenge. **1878** BROWNING *La Saisiaz* 290 Praise or blame of its contriver, shown a niggard or profuse In each good or evil issue!

b. Const. *of.*

c **1386** CHAUCER *Wife's T.* 407 Old and angry nygardes of despense, God send hem sone verray pestilence. **1540–1** ELYOT *Image Gov.* (1544) 50 He was suche a nygard of tyme, that he was meruaylously greued, if he spente any day in solace. **1593** DRAYTON *Ecl.* ii. 48 Thy wasted lungs be Niggards of thy breath. **1633** P. FLETCHER *Poet. Misc.* 64 A crown of wood-nymphs..Sit round about, no niggards of their faces. **1660** F. BROOKE tr. *Le Blanc's Trav.* 56 They.. are not niggards of their lives in their Princes service. **1709** POPE *Ess. Crit.* 580 Be niggards of advice on no pretence, For the worst avarice is that of sense. **1772** MACKENZIE *Man World* I. v, He who never trusts, is a niggard of his soul. **1862** GOULBURN *Pers. Relig.* IV. xi. (1873) 349 So long as he thinks Him a niggard either of pardon or grace.

2. *dial.* A movable piece of iron or fire-brick placed in the side or bottom of a grate to economize fuel; a false bottom. Also ***niggard iron.***

1688 HOLME *Armoury* III. xiv. (Roxb.) 9/1 The seuerall parts of a great are these... The niggatt Irons, Irons to set further or closer to gather. **1820** C. R. MATURIN *Melmoth* I. i. 17 Go down and draw the niggers of the kitchen fire closer. **1851** MAYHEW *Lond. Labour* II. 6 Niggards, generally called niggers (*i.e.* false bottoms for grates). **1869–** in north. dial. glossaries (Northumbld., Cumbld., Lancs., Chesh.).

B. *adj.* **1.** Miserly, parsimonious, mean, sparing; unwilling to give or spend anything.

? *a* **1366** CHAUCER *Rom. Rose* 1172 A fulle gret fool is he, ywys, That bothe riche and nygart is. **1515** BARCLAY *Egloges* IV. C vj b, Though thou be nigard, & nought will geue of thine. *c* **1530** H. RHODES *Bk. Nurture* 761 in *Babees Bk.* (1868) 103 A man that is a niggard churle no tyme is lyberall. **1598** BARNFIELD *Compl. Poetrie* vi, What infernall furie late hath haunted Their niggard purses? **1623** PENKETHMAN *Handf. Hon.* I. xxix, Niggard or Couetous thou shalt not seeme. **1681** DRYDEN *Abs. & Achit.* 369 Why am I scanted by a Niggard Birth? **1725** POPE *Odyss.* XIV. 242 What by niggard Fortune was deny'd. **1794** COLERIDGE *Monody on Chatterton*, A prodigal nature and a niggard doom. **1825** BENTHAM *Ration. Reward* 35 Will they be supposed so mean as to be niggard with pence and lavish with millions? **1884** JENNINGS *Croker Papers* I. viii. 237 [He] paid off his personal grudges with no niggard hand.

b. Const. *of.*

1602 SHAKS. *Ham.* III. i. 13 Niggard of question, but of our demands Most free in his reply. **1812** BYRON *Ch. Har.* II. xlix, Here dwells the caloyer, nor rude is he, Nor niggard of his cheer. **1842** J. WILSON *Chr. North* (1857) II. 328 The heavens are niggard of their dues.

†**c.** Hard, unyielding. *Obs. rare*$^{-1}$.

1600 *Dr. Dodypoll* III. iii. in Bullen *O. Pl.* III. 131 Then thy soft feete Would be repining at these niggard stones.

2. Of actions and qualities: Niggardly, ungenerous, displaying reluctance to give anything.

1672 DRYDEN *Assignation* v. iv, To restore her to you, Is not an act of generosity, But a scant, niggard justice. 1794 SULLIVAN *View Nat.* V. 373 To pass over with niggard and reluctant mention, the illustrious virtues of those, who [etc.]. 1847 R. W. HAMILTON *Rewards & Punishm.* viii. (1853) 361 Ours are no niggard views. *a*1860 J. A. ALEXANDER *Gospel Jesus Christ* xv. (1861) 206 [They] held fast with a niggard grasp the keys of heaven.

3. Scanty; given in a grudging way.

1751 ELIZA HEYWOOD *Betsy Thoughtless* IV. 45, I confess myself utterly unable to maintain a family, like ours, on the nigard stipend you have allotted to that purpose. 1821–2 SHELLEY *Chas. I*, I. 159 To them who earn The niggard wages of the earth. 1877 GLADSTONE *Glean.* IV. 356 She obtained..but niggard measures either of aid or justice from the Powers of Europe.

b. Of a way, space, etc.: Narrow, small.

1595 DANIEL *Civ. Wars* I. xlviii, There was A niggard narrow way for men to passe. 1813 SCOTT *Rokeby* II. vii, A flinty footpath's niggard space. 1868 SILL *Poems, Hermitage* xix, Here is no niggard gap of sky above.

C. *Comb.*, as *niggard-like*, *-measured* adjs.

1741 RICHARDSON *Pamela* (1824) I. 169 What is my single happiness, if I suffer it, niggard-like, to extend no farther than to myself? 1881 H. PHILLIPS tr. *Chamisso's Faust* 5 In visions passed the niggard-measured hours.

† '**niggard**, *v.* *Obs. rare.* [f. prec.]

1. *intr.* To act in a niggardly fashion. Also with *it*.

*c*1600 SHAKS. *Sonn.* i, Thou..Within thine owne bud buriest thy content, And tender chorle makst wast in niggarding. 1609 ARMIN *Ital. Taylor* (1880) 146 Now not to niggard it at all, But ioyne as partner yit.

2. *trans.* To put off *with* a small amount of something; to treat in a niggardly fashion.

1601 SHAKS. *Jul. C.* IV. iii. 229 Nature must obey Necessitie, Which we will niggard with a little rest.

†**niggardess.** *Obs. rare*$^{-1}$. [f. NIGGARD *sb.* or *a.* + -ESS^2.] Niggardliness.

1632 SANDERSON *Serm.* 402 All base penurious nigardesse in saving their own purses.

niggardie, variant of NIGGARDY *Obs.*

†'**niggardise.** *Obs.* Forms: 6 nygardyse; 6 nigardise, 7 -ize, 8 -ice; 6–7 niggardise, -ize, 7 -ice. [f. NIGGARD *sb.* or *a.* + -ISE^2.] Niggardliness. (Common *c* 1580–1670.)

1502 *Ord. Crysten Men* (W. de W. 1506) IV. xxx. II j, For nygardyse, or also for the falsyte & decepcyon of the ware. 1579 FENTON *Guicciard.* (1618) 122 Not content with his niggardize in the expence and prouision of things necessary. 1621 BP. MOUNTAGU *Diatribæ* 238 A Patron and propugner of niggardise and wretchednesse in the seruice of God. *a*1683 OLDHAM *Wks.* (1686) 95 There where illib'ral Nature's niggardise Has set a Tax on Vice. 1750 W. ELLIS *Mod. Husbandm.* VI. I. 28 (E.D.D.), They had a peak against him on account of his nigardice.

†'**niggardish**, *a.* *Obs.* [f. NIGGARD *sb.* or *a.* + -ISH^1.] Niggardly.

1547–64 BAULDWIN *Mor. Philos.* (Palfr.) 161 Spend not too outragiously, nor be too niggardish. 1581 MULCASTER *Positions* v. (1887) 26 Which the most munificent God, by his no niggardishe nature, prouided for them both.

niggardize ('nɪgədaɪz), *v. rare.* [f. NIGGARD *sb.* or *a.* + -IZE.] **a.** *intr.* To play the niggard. **b.** *trans.* To give in a niggardly fashion. Hence '**niggardized** *ppl. a.*

*a*1634 CHAPMAN *Alphonsus* Plays 1872 III. 217 Fame I accuse thee, thou did'st niggardize, And faintly sound my loves perfections. 1877 BLACKIE *Wise Men* 160 Some [say] that stinted prayer And offering niggardised have turned the smile Of gods to frowning.

niggardliness ('nɪgədlɪnɪs). [f. NIGGARDLY *a.* + -NESS.] The state or quality of being niggardly; stinginess; parsimony.

1578 in *Priv. Prayers* (1851) 486 Let thy goodness supply that, which our niggardliness hath plucked away. 1621 BURTON *Anat. Mel.* I. ii. III. viii. (1651) 103 'Tis a sluggish humour..to..refrain from such places..through sloth, niggardliness, fear. 1688 PENTON *Guardian's Instruction* (1897) 49 Prodigality is a little more catching than Niggardliness with young Gentlemen. 1742 RICHARDSON *Pamela* III. 97 My Charge against you..is that of Niggardliness, and no other. 1802 MME. D'ARBLAY *Diary* 5 May, The niggardliness of my admiration was occasioned by my doubt of her assertions. 1848 MILL *Pol. Econ.* I. xiii. §2 (1876) 118 The niggardliness of nature..is the cause of the penalty attached to over population. 1868 FREEMAN *Norm. Conq.* (1877) II. vii. 62 Neither this bounty nor this niggardliness was a legal crime.

†'**niggardling**, *sb.* and *a.* *Obs. rare.* Also -lin. [f. NIGGARD *sb.* and *a.* + -LING.] **a.** *sb.* A niggard. **b.** *adj.* Niggardly.

1654 WHITLOCK *Zootomia* 81 What ever foolish and sordid Niggardlins think in these daies. 1704 N. N. tr. *Boccalini's Advts. fr. Parnass.* III. 311 Your being as niggardling in denying People those Titles which they expect, as you are covetous of receiving 'em.

niggardly ('nɪgədlɪ), *a.* Also 6 nigardly, 6 (9 *dial.*) niggerly. [f. NIGGARD *sb.* + -LY^1.]

1. Having a niggard's nature; meanly parsimonious, close-fisted, stingy; sparing.

1571 GOLDING *Calvin on Ps.* xxxv. 12 When the hande is bountifull, the heart may now and then be nigardly. 1621 T. WILLIAMSON tr. *Goulart's Wise Vieillard* 72 What a shame is it to young men..to shew themselues so pinching and niggardly in necessary beneuolences. 1666–7 PEPYS *Diary* 27 Feb., They going there..to eat his victuals, knowing him to be a niggardly fellow. 1766 GOLDSM. *Vic. W.* xxviii, Let us not be niggardly in our exhortation, but let all our fellow-prisoners have a share. 1831 MACKINTOSH *Hist. Eng.* II. 104 This hoard..was too great to be formed by frugality, even under the penurious and niggardly Henry. 1873 M. ARNOLD *Lit. & Dogma* (1876) 86 The Israelites..were perpetually slack or niggardly in the service of Jehovah.

b. Const. *of*.

1624 BP. HALL *Art Medit.* Ep. Ded., Wks. (1625) 102, I would his humilitie had not made him niggardly of his name. 1663 H. COGAN tr. *Pinto's Trav.* ix. 28 Fortune hath been exceeding niggardly to me of her goods. 1817 MALTHUS *Popul.* (ed. 4) II. 397 If the earth had been so niggardly of her produce as to oblige all her inhabitants to labour for it. 1844 RUSKIN *Mod. Paint.* I. Pref. (ed. 2), They are niggardly of the reputation which contributes to happiness.

2. Of actions, qualities, etc.: Characteristic of, or befitting, a niggard; mean, miserly.

1561 T. NORTON *Calvin's Inst.* II. i. 4 He accused God of lying, enuye, and niggardly grudgyng. 1583 BABINGTON *Commandm.* (1590) 381 The heart..by too neere and nigardlie keeping, transgresseth against this lawe of God. 1691 HARTCLIFFE *Virtues* 87 That they do not sink into a niggardly or covetous temper. 1759 FRANKLIN *Ess.* Wks. 1840 II. 156 By the niggardly treatment of good masters they have been driven out of the school. 1861 M. ARNOLD *Pop. Educ. France* 149 Where everything..is left to be done by the parish, there is niggardly pinching. 1875 MANNING *Mission H. Ghost* iv. 114 If we treat friends in this niggardly and ungenerous manner.

Comb. 1681 W. ROBERTSON *Phraseol. Gen.* (1693) 663 To give niggardly-wise.

3. Such as a niggard would give; meanly small; scanty, closely limited.

1599 NASHE *Lenten Stuffe* Wks. (Grosart) V. 239 The niggardliest mouse of biefe will cost him sixpence. 1624 CAPT. SMITH *Virginia* VI. 214 As I gathered from their niggardly relations in a broken language. *a*1628 PRESTON *Mt. Ebal* (1638) 42 It is not any scanty or niggardly kinde of love that hee will like of. 1696 S. PATRICK *Comm. Exod.* viii. 28 Which hath made some think this was but a niggardly Concession of Pharoah's. 1798 JANE AUSTEN *Northang. Abb.* xvi, A living..of about four hundred pounds yearly value, was to be resigned to his son;..no niggardly assignment to one of ten children. 1859 MEREDITH *R. Feverel* xxi, A niggardly confidence. 1878 HUXLEY *Physiogr.* 295 The most niggardly computation which lies within the bounds of possibility.

'**niggardly**, *adv.* Also 6 nyger-. [f. NIGGARD *a.* + -LY^2.] In the manner of a niggard; parsimoniously, grudgingly, sparingly.

1530 PALSGR. 839/2 Niggardly, *seichement*. 1534 MORE *Comf. agst. Trib.* III. Wks. 1226/1 Then shal he either nygerdly heape them vp together..or wastefully mysse spend theym. 1579 NORTHBROOKE *Dicing* 13 He is a couetous man that greedily & niggardly kepeth his own goods. 1630 *R. Johnson's Kingd. & Commw.* 9 The Spaniards, who in their owne Countries live most niggardly. 1703 MAUNDRELL *Journ. Jerus.* (1721) 42 Young Heirs that have been niggardly bred generally turn Prodigals. 1790 WOLCOT (P. Pindar) *Ep. Sylv. Urban* Wks. 1812 II. 261 If midst a vulgar mass his stars unkind Have placed most niggardly a pigmy mind. 1868 NETTLESHIP *Ess. Browning* vii. 253 Whose life is niggardly doled to us in twelve short pages.

niggardness ('nɪgədnɪs). Now *rare*. Also 6 *Sc.* nigar(t)-, nigirt-. [f. NIGGARD *a.* + -NESS.] Niggardliness.

1500–20 DUNBAR *Poems* xl. 12 ȝe tak that nigirtness [*v.r.* nigarnes] of ȝour muder. 1535 COVERDALE *Ecclus.* Contents xl, The vnfaithfullnes and nigardnesse of the vngodly. 1562 TURNER *Baths* 6 Some for nygardnes or for povertye..eat evell and unholsome meates. 1612 *Pasquil's Night-cap* (1877) 6 A liberall man, and void of niggardnesse. 1764 *Mem. G. Psalmanazar* 182, I have seen so many instances of his nigardness. 1799 ROBERTSON *Agric. Perth* 269 What might..appear..to be a niggardness in nature, or a defect in the bounty of heaven. 1849 ROCK *Ch. of Fathers* II. 315 To hinder the niggardness of surviving relatives from cheating the dead out of the Church's services.

†'**niggardous**, *a.* *Obs.* Also 5–6 nygardous(e. [f. NIGGARD *sb.* + -OUS.] Niggardly.

1491 CAXTON *Vitas Patr.* (W. de W. 1495) I. xxxvii. 46 b/1 Amonge the brethern there was one, whiche was merueyllously scarse and nygardouse. 1522 MORE *De quat. Noviss.* Wks. 94 This couetous gathering & nigardous keping. 1534 —— *Treat. Passion* Wks. 1305/1 To disdayne theyr symple nygardous rewarde.

niggardry: see NIGGARDY (quot. *c* 1412).

†'**niggardship.** *Obs.* Forms: see NIGGARD. Also 5 negardchepe, 6 nygerdeshyppe, negar-, niggarship. [f. NIGGARD *sb.* + -SHIP.] Niggardliness. (Freq. in 16th cent.)

1430–40 LYDG. *Bochas* III. i. (1554) 70/1 Whan..couetise put away largesse,..And nigardship exileth gentlenesse. *c*1440 *Jacob's Well* 121 þe thredde fote brede of wose of coueytise is nygardschippe. 1526 SKELTON *Magnyf.* 2518 Let neuer negarshyp your noblenesse affray. 1572 BOSSEWELL *Armorie* II. 85 b, Gentlemen, who..abhorre all suche auarice, churlishnesse, and niggardshippe. 1621 T. WILLIAMSON tr. *Goulart's Wise Vieillard* 73 Your rauenous niggardship, and base pinching. 1673 R. HEAD *Canting Academy* K 2 Niggardship, and covetousness.

†'**niggardy.** *Obs.* Forms: 4 negardye, nigardye, nygardie, 6 nygardy, nig(g)ardie, *Sc.* negartie. [f. NIGGARD *sb.* + -Y^3.] Niggardliness.

*c*1386 CHAUCER *Shipman's T.* 172 But yit me greveth most his nigardye. 1390 GOWER *Conf.* II. 288 His fortune.. Desdeigneth alle coveitise And hateth alle nygardie. *c*1412 HOCCLEVE *De Reg. Princ.* 1306 His nygardie [*Roxb.* nygardrye] Suffrith hys neghtburgh [*Roxb.* neighbore] by hym sterue and dye. 1517 *N. Love's Bonavent. Mirr.* xxxvi. (W. de W.) K iij b, Thyne owne fals couetyse in excusacion of thy nygardy. 1535 STEWART *Cron. Scot.* I. 392 The Romanis..haittit Cneo for his negartie. 1559 AYLMER *Harborowe* P j b, Sparing of your goodes, which is niggardie.

nigged, variant of *nidged*: see NIDGE *v.*^{2}

1836 PARKER *Gloss. Archit.* (1850) I. 326 *Nigged Ashlar*, stone hewn with a pick, or pointed hammer, instead of a chisel: this kind of work is also called 'hammer-dressed'. 1875 KNIGHT *Dict. Mech.* 1526/2.

niggel-weed: see NIGELWEED *Obs.*

nigger, dial. variant of NIGGARD *sb.*

nigger ('nɪgə(r)), *sb.* Also niggar. [Alteration of NEGER. Cf. also NIGER and NIGRE.]

1. a. A Negro. (Colloq. and usu. contemptuous.) Except in Black English vernacular, where it remains common, now virtually restricted to contexts of deliberate and contemptuous ethnic abuse.

1786 BURNS *Ordination* iv, How graceless Ham leugh at his Dad, Which made Canaan a nigger. 1811 BYRON in *Mem. F. Hodgson* (1878) I. 195 The rest of the world—niggers and what not. 1818 H. B. FEARON *Sk. Amer.* 46 The bad conduct and inferior nature of niggars (negroes). 1819 W. FAUX *Mem. Days Amer.* (1823) 9 Contempt of the poor blacks, or niggers, as they are there called, seems the national sin of America. *a*1849 H. COLERIDGE *Ess.* (1851) I. 164 A similar error has turned Othello..into a rank woolly-pated, thick-lipped nigger. 1867 LATHAM *Black & White* 127 Niggers (they are not 'coloured persons' yet in the South) are most artful flatterers. 1897 *Outing* (U.S.) XXIX. 333/1 What is wanted is a genuine nigger; not a colored person. 1931 D. L. SAYERS *Five Red Herrings* i. 11 Waters.., like all Englishmen, was ready enough to admire and praise all foreigners except dagoes and niggers. 1934 G. B. SHAW *On Rocks* II. 70 Pandranath: you are only a silly nigger pretending to be an English gentleman. *Ibid.* 71, I am called nigger by this dirty faced barbarian whose forefathers were naked savages worshipping acorns and mistletoe..whilst my people were spreading the highest enlightenment yet reached by the human race from the temples of Brahma... You call me nigger, sneering at my colour because you have none. The jackdaw has lost his tail and would persuade the world that his defect is a quality. 1936 M. MITCHELL *Gone with Wind* 401 'You're a fool nigger, and the worst day's work Pa ever did was to buy you,' said Scarlett slowly... There, she thought, I've said 'nigger' and Mother wouldn't like that at all. 1937 C. HIMES in *Black on Black* 132 Uncle Tomism, acceptance, toadying—all there in its most rugged form. One way to be a nigger. Other Negroes did it other ways—he did it the hard way. The same result—*a nigger*. 1948 [see COON *sb.* 2 c]. 1948 G. GREENE *Heart of Matter* I. i. 3, I hate the place. I hate the people. I hate the bloody niggers. Mustn't call 'em that you know. *Ibid.* II. i. 179 A clerk knocked and said, 'There's a nigger for you, Wilson, with a note.' 1949 B. A. BOTKIN *Treas. S. Folklore* p. xxiii, In turning his laughter on himself as well as the whites, the Negro has taken over the objectionable word 'nigger' (though not 'darky') and made it a term of praise or blame. 1964 L. HUGHES in J. H. Clarke *Harlem* iv. 251 A klansman said, 'Nigger, Look me in the face—And tell me you believe in The great white race.' 1966 *Stage & Television Today* 6 Oct., When 'Ten Little Niggers' opened for a week's run at Birmingham Theatre on Monday members of the co-ordinating committee against racial discrimination (CARD) staged a protest demonstration outside. 1968 C. BROWN in A. Dundes *Mother Wit* (1973) 232/1 Perhaps the most soulful word in the world is 'nigger'. 1969 D. L. LEE in A. Chapman *New Black Voices* (1972) II. 286 Change, stop being an instant yes machine. Change. Niggers don't change they just grow. That's a change; Bigger and better niggers. 1971 *Black World* Apr. 56 Who the hell you think, nigger? 1972 D. ONYEAMA *Nigger at Eton* iii. 83, I remember that in conversation, some boys occasionally used 'nigger' in reference to black people. I never dreamt that it was a racial name and generally used with contempt; I just reckoned it was a harmless slang word for a black man. 1973 *Black World* Aug. 61/1 Even credit-card niggers didn' really trust banks. 1973 *Times Lit. Suppl.* 14 Dec. 1536/1 You do not reduce to only a ticket-collector, only an asthmatic, only a voter, only a politician, only a pools-winner, only a nigger.

transf. 1889 RIDER HAGGARD *Allan's Wife* 262 As for that there claim, well, she's been a good nigger to me.

b. Loosely or incorrectly applied to members of other dark-skinned races.

1857 DUFFERIN *Lett. High Lat.* 251 This relationship with Polynesian Niggers, the native genealogists would probably scout with indignation. 1865 TREVELYAN *Cawnpore* 47 In the eyes of an English planter..bazaar-porters and Rajahs..are niggers alike one and all. 1891 *Melbourne Argus* 7 Nov. 13/5 The natives of Queensland are nearly always spoken of as 'niggers' by those who are brought most directly in contact with them. 1941 I. L. IDRIESS *Great Boomerang* xxii. 169 The cranky nigger who was on the job broke the only shovel. 1946 K. TENNANT *Lost Haven* (1968) 6 No grandson of mine,..is going to be brought up by them thieving, godless, nigger Detwinters. *Ibid.* xviii. 312 When that old nigger went past she turned up her nose.

c. *to work like a nigger*, to work exceptionally hard. orig. *U.S.*

1836 C. GILMAN *Recoll. Southern Matron* in *Southern Rose* 23 July 186/1, I have toiled night and day, I've worked like a nigger, and more than any nigger. 1861 GEO. ELIOT *Let.* 13 Apr. (1954) III. 404 Charles..will..work like a nigger at his music. 1880 'MARK TWAIN' *Tramp Abroad* 40 He laid into his work like a nigger. 1889 E. DOWSON *Let.* 19 May (1967) 80, I have simply worked like a nigger this week. 1920 R. FRY *Let.* 20 June (1972) II. 481, I have worked like a nigger to arrange it [*sc.* an exhibition] well. 1931 D. L. SAYERS *Five Red Herrings* ix. 99 Dalziel has been working like a nigger all day, getting him identified by his family and by the station-master at Pinwherry and by the people at Larne.

d. ***a nigger in the woodpile*** (or ***fence***): a concealed motive or unknown factor affecting a situation in an adverse way. orig. *U.S.*

1852 in *Kans. Hist. Quarterly* (1942) XI. 235 No 'nigger in the wood pile' here..; white men are at the bottom of this speculation. **1862** *Congress. Globe* 3 June 2527/1 [These gentlemen] spoke two whole hours.. in showing—to borrow an elegant phrase, the paternity of which belongs, I think, to their side of the House,—that there was 'a nigger in the wood-pile'. **1897** *Congress. Rec.* 18 Feb. App. 61/1 Like a great many others ignorant of facts, he finds 'a nigger in the wood pile' when there is neither wood pile nor nigger. **1911** Woodrow Wilson in *Outlook* 11 Aug. 944 If you go through the schedules you will find some nigger in every wood pile. **1930** *Cambridge Daily News* 24 Sept. 7/6 Unless .. there is a nigger in the wood pile, .. the shares ought to be worth a mild flutter at round 8s. 6d. **1952** A. Christie *They do it with Mirrors* xii. 109 Well now, let's have your point of view. Who's the nigger in the woodpile? The G.I. husband? **1958** *Listener* 13 Feb. 285/1 'The starry heaven that we know .. is inside us.'.. The nigger in the woodpile is to be found in the word 'know'. **1958** 'A. Gilbert' *Death against Clock* 72 The nigger in the woodpile on this occasion being an elderly spinster of decided views. **1960** *Daily Tel.* 16 Jan. 8 This seems to be the nigger in the woodpile—the woodpile being an industrial recovery and activity remarkable by any standard. **1974** M. Gilbert *Flash Point* ii. 19 It wouldn't have been easy to spot... It's taken Jonas himself all this time to spot the nigger in the woodpile.

1850 *California Courier* (San Francisco) 4 Sept. 2/6 The majority of the papers, however, think that there 'is a nigger in the fence' somewhere. **1888** B. Harte *Phyllis of Sierras* I. iii. 90 Ef he aint scooped up by Jenny Bradley he'll guess there's a nigger in the fence somewhere. **1911** H. Quick *Yellowstone Nights* xi. 286 He's always looking for a nigger in the fence.

2. a. The black caterpillar of the turnip saw-fly.

1840 *Cuvier's Anim. Kingd.* 584 *Athalia centifoliæ* is extremely destructive to turnips, its larva being known under the name of the Nigger, or Black Jack. **1844** H. Stephens *Bk. Farm* III. 774 The larvæ are known in different parts of the country by the names of black caterpillar, blacks, nigger, canker, etc. **1874** Lubbock *Orig. & Met. Ins.* i. 7 To this group belongs the nigger, or black caterpillar of the turnip.

b. (See quot.)

1855 Morton *Cycl. Agric.* II. 120 *Nigger*, the name of lady-bird larvæ in hop grounds.

c. (See quot.)

1855 Ogilvie *Suppl.*, *Nigger*, a species of holothuria, so called by the Cornish fishermen. It is very common in deep water off the Deadmen.

d. Used in Comb. to denote a dark shade of colour, as ***nigger-brown*** (also *ellipt.*), ***-grey***, ***-pink***.

1914 *Lady's Pictorial* 4 July p. v (Advt.), Soft Taffeta Hat .. In Black, .. Nigger, Mole, and White. **1915** *Home Chat* 2 Jan. 11/1 Nigger-brown cloth. **1917** *Ibid.* 3 Nov. 139/2 Nigger or, as it is now called, 'Zulu', is also to be seen. **1922** D. H. Lawrence *England, my England* 116 She was wearing a wide hat of grey straw, and a loose, swinging dress of nigger-grey velvet. **1923** [see *desert-brown* adj.]. **1930** J. Dos Passos *42nd Parallel* I. 124 On each table there were niggerpink and vermilion paper flowers. **1960** V. Williams *Walk Egypt* 89 A dry-goods store showed a dress of 'nigger-pink'. **1973** *Times* 12 Nov. 4/4 Decorations in autumnal colours, that is, coral pink and what used to be nigger brown.

3. *U.S.* **a.** A form of steam-engine used on ships; a steam-capstan employed in hauling river-boats over bars or snags. **b.** A strong spiked timber by which logs are canted in a saw-mill.

1867 J. A. Hosmer *Trip to States by Yellowstone & Missouri* 58 The boat.. struck the bar; they then began to work with the spars and nigger, and at two o'clock we got off. **1875** Knight *Dict. Mech.* **1878** J. H. Beadle *Western Wilds* 378 Then oaths, spars, 'nigger-engine' and all the other available machinery were set in operation. **1882** *Harper's Mag.* Jan. 175/2 One of the 'nigger' engines is suddenly called into service to tighten a two-inch rope, or wind up a discarded cable. **1890** *Cent. Dict.* **1900** *Atlantic Monthly* LXXXV. 103/2 'Carriages', bright with red and green lanterns.. rush to and fro, seizing the logs as they come from the 'kickers' and 'niggers'. **1910** S. E. White *Rules of Game* I. v. 32 When the car had flown back to its starting-point, the 'nigger' rose from obscurity to turn the log half-way round. **1929** *Encycl. Brit.* XIV. 482/1 A steam or air 'nigger' (mechanically operated steel arms) helps to place the log in the proper position.

4. a. In *Soap-making*: (see quot.).

1887 Dittmar & Paton in *Encycl. Brit.* XXII. 203 On settling a dark-coloured 'nigger', or under-lye separates out.

b. *U.S.* An impurity in the insulating covering of an electrical conductor.

a **1890** *Sci. Amer.* LIV. 308 (Cent.), The consequence.. might be that what the workmen call a nigger would get into the armature, and burn it so as to destroy its service.

c. *slang.* (See quot. 1960.)

1934 *Tit-Bits* 31 Mar. 12/1 The film world has a colourful compilation of expressions unlike those in other walks of life. 'Niggers' are not men of colour, but blackboards used to 'kill' unwanted reflections from the powerful lights. **1937** A. Buchanan *Film Making* iii. 52 'Niggers' are wooden oblong screens used to 'nigger-off' or shield light from faces, or shadows on walls, and so 'Her face needs a nigger' is not such an alarming statement as it sounds to the uninitiated. **1957** Manvell & Huntley *Technique Film Music* ii. 32 In silent film days we had all the apparatus we needed in the studios, with miles of cables, banks of arcs, and great screens (known in the industry as 'niggers') to reflect light and help shadow effects. **1960** O. Skilbeck *ABC of Film & TV* 89 *Nigger*, an adjustable Mask on a stand, used on the Floor to shield the camera from, or to achieve effects with, lights.

5. *Comb.*, chiefly objective, as ***nigger-breaker***, ***-chaser***, ***-dealer***, ***-driver***, ***-killer***, ***-lover***, ***-stealer***, ***trader***, ***worship(per***; ***nigger-driving***, ***-looking***, ***-loving*** adjs.

1845 F. Douglass *Narr. Life F. Douglass* 57 All of this added weight to his reputation as a '*nigger-breaker'. **1921** C. E. Mulford *Bar-20 Three* xvi. 217 Most likely they'll be *nigger-chasers th' way some folks'll be steppin' lively to get out of th' way. **1853** F. W. Thomas *John Randolph* 285 You know Robinson the *nigger-dealer, who has the pen down town. **1833** J. Neal *Down Easters* I. 70 When the *nigger-drivers falls out among themselves. **1861** Freeman in Stephens *Life* (1895) I. 270 Let the nigger-drivers go to the devil their own way. **1891** C. Roberts *Adrift Amer.* 198, I never came across such a beast of a nigger driver as this fellow Cole. **1856** Olmsted *Slave States* 108 If a man does not provide well for his slaves.. he gets the name of a '*nigger killer'. **1890** *Cent. Dict.* s.v. *Grampus*, The whip-tailed scorpion, .. also called mule-killer, nigger-killer. **1837** *Lett. fr. Madras* (1843) 99 He has a half-caste, dropsical wife, and a sickly *nigger-looking child. **1909** R. E. Knowles *Attic Guest* xiii. 178 'Then you can take what you deserve, curse you for a *nigger-lover,' I heard the Colonel retort madly. **1924** *American Mercury* Feb. 135/2 Shorty —Nigger-lover! *He throws the money in her face.* **1930** J. Dos Passos *42nd Parallel* II. 140 'Niggerlover,' yelled Joe in her ear... Janey began to cry. **1958** *Church Times* 21 Nov. 6/4 You can call a man a *Kaffir-Boetie* in Johannesburg and a nigger-lover in the Southern States; but both mean precisely the same thing and have the same accent. **1959** *Encounter* Dec. 45/2 They nick our boys and let the Spades go!.. Nigger-lovers! **1972** *Guardian* 3 July 8/2 Black Mountain College.. was a seat of free love, communism, and nigger-lovers. **1914** S. Lewis *Our Mr. Wrenn* 3 Mrs Zapp was too conscientiously dolorous to be much cheered by the sympathy of a *nigger-lovin' Yankee. **1962** *Guardian* 3 Oct. 1/6 It is still wise not to.. admit you represent such a Nigger-loving Red publication as the 'Guardian'. **1975** J. Rathbone *Kill Cure* III. iv. 106 You nigger-loving bitch. **1839** R. M. Bird *Adventures R. Day* I. xxv. 181, I was 'a kidnapper, a Georgeye *nigger-stealer'. **1884** 'Mark Twain' *Huck. Finn* xxxiii. 314 Only I couldn't believe it. Tom Sawyer a nigger-stealer. **1853** F. W. Thomas *John Randolph* 285 He's not in favor of these regular *nigger-traders is he? **1884** 'Mark Twain' *Huck. Finn* viii. 60 But I noticed dey wuz a nigger trader roun' de place considerable lately en I begin to get oneasy. **1862** Russell in *Times* 29 Jan., The Conservative masses, which lie between negrolatry or *nigger-worship and Secession. **1866** *Cornh. Mag.* Jan. 37 The contempt which they.. have expressed for *nigger-worshippers during the Jamaica troubles.

6. *attrib.* (passing into *adj.*).

a. Belonging to the Negro race; black-skinned. ***nigger-baby***, ***-blood***, ***boy***, ***girl***, ***-lips***, ***mouth***; also ***nigger-blooded***, ***-skinned*** adjs.; ***nigger-dead*** adj.; ***nigger minstrel***, one of a group of entertainers performing songs and dances typical of or based on plantation life in the Southern U.S., freq. by white men with blackened faces; also ellipt., *nigger*.

1872 De Vere *Americanisms* 117 The real *nigger baby is known under the name of pickaninny. **1833** J. Neal *Down-Easters* I. 66 If there's a drop of *nigger-blood in 'em, they'll always show it in their temper. **1932** W. Faulkner *Light in August* v. 96 'Take your black hand off of me, you damn *niggerblooded—' The hand shut down again. **1825** J. Neal *Bro. Jonathan* III. 207 Nobody there, I guess, but a *nigger boy. **1970** R. D. Abrahams *Positively Black* ii. 26 'Nigger boy,' he said to me, 'how'd you like to meet your maker right now?' **1970** W. Ford in O. Coombs *We speak as Liberators* 43, I would tell of being Black and Proud and Black and Loud and Black and Bowed and Black and *niggerdead. **1836** Marryat *Pirate* iv, You've been sweet upon that *nigger girl. **1842** Barham *Ingol. Leg.* Ser. II. *Broth. Birch.* xlv, Their *nigger inhabitants [devils] shook in their hoofs. **1922** Joyce *Ulysses* 219 From the hoardings Mr. Eugene Stratton grinned with thick *niggerlips at Father Conmee. **1860** A. J. Munby *Diary* 17 Mar. in D. Hudson *Munby* (1972) 56 My 'comic' friend suggested that I should apply to certain '*niggers', who had just bowed themselves off the stage... In this den were two or three men with blackened faces, taking off their shabby nigger costume. **1860** E. Cowell *Diary* 13 Sept. in *Cowells in America* (1934) 155 A Company of 'nigger minstrels' are to be here tomorrow night. **1883** Black *Shandon Bells* xvii, He.. made sure he was about to be serenaded by a nigger-minstrel. **1917** A. Waugh *Loom of Youth* II. i. 93 And do you think he really imagines he is doing any good to his form by giving that nigger minstrel entertainment up there? **1959** I. & P. Opie *Lore & Lang. Schoolch.* i. 13 Nellie Bligh.. was the heroine of a mid-nineteenth-century nigger minstrel song by Stephen Foster. **1922** Joyce *Ulysses* 365 The dark one [*sc.* girl] with the mop head and the *nigger mouth. **1938** *Nigger-skinned [see *fawn-eyed* adj.].

b. Of or belonging to, occupied by, Negroes, as ***nigger culture***, ***dialect***, ***emancipation***, ***land***, ***melody***, ***music***, ***quarters***, ***show***, ***song***. Also *transf.*

1970 J. B. Cole in A. Chapman *New Black Voices* (1972) III. 493 When blacks refer to '*Nigger culture', they often very explicitly speak of soul and style. **1834** *Knickerbocker* III. 445 And I would say too, that although *mighty smart*, and a *mighty smart chance*, *mighty big*, and *mighty little* was excellent '*nigger' dialect, yet it was not so refined, as an orator might use. **1844** Dickens *Mart. Chuz.* xxi, He has been, and is, the advocate.. of *Nigger emancipation. **1834** R. H. Froude in *Rem.* (1838) I. 380 *Niggerland is a poor substitute for the *limen Apostolorum*. **1846** *Knickerbocker* XXVIII. 244 Captain Marin would give a touch from a sea-song, or a specimen of a '*nigger-melody'. **1857** J. D. Borthwick *Three Yrs. in Calif.* xii. 212 My entertainers, producing two violins, favoured me with a selection of Nigger melodies. **1873** Miss Braddon *Lucius Davoren* I. Prol. ii. 21 Perhaps you could oblige us with a nigger melody. **1894** G. du Maurier *Trilby* I. III. 219 He.. can even scream with laughter at.. a nigger melody. **1948** A. Lomax in A. Dundes *Mother Wit* (1973) 472/1 If you like this *nigger music. **1856** Olmsted *Slave States* 61 You'll see some *nigger-quarters. **1856** C. E. De Long in *Calif. Hist. Soc. Q.* (1930) IX. 60 Went to a *nigger show. **1884** 'Mark Twain' *Huck. Finn* xxvi. 261 They never go to the circus, nor theatre, nor nigger shows, nor nowheres. **1909** R. E. Knowles *Attic Guest* xiii. 156 They'll be flaunting that Uncle Tom's Cabin nigger show under your noses. **1844** *United Service Jrnl.* XLIV. 21 He was never at rest,—now singing a *nigger song on the deck. **1851** H. Mayhew *London Labour* I. 273/1, I sell ballads and manuscript music .., which is 'transposed'.. from the nigger songs.

c. In special uses, as ***nigger caterpillar***, ***-hair***, ***-jockey***, ***Latin*** (see quots.); **nigger cloth** = *Negro cloth* (Negro 7); **nigger corner** *U.S.*, a part of a public building to which Negroes were confined; **nigger fish**, a small grouper, *Cephalopholis fulvus*, found in the West Indies and off the coast of Florida; = cony, coney *sb.* 7 b; **nigger goose** *N. Amer. local* (see quots.); **nigger heaven** *U.S. slang*, the top gallery in a theatre; **nigger heel** *Naut.* (see quot.); also **nigger-heeled** *a.* (see quot. 1961); **nigger hunt**, the organized pursuit of Negroes for the purpose of attacking them; so **nigger-hunter**, **-hunting**; **nigger lice** *U.S.*, informal name of the prickly awns of various species of plants, esp. of the genus *Desmodium*; **nigger luck**, exceptionally good luck; **nigger shooter** *U.S. slang*, a catapult; **nigger-stick** *U.S. slang* (see quot. 1974); **nigger toe** *U.S.*, a Brazil nut.

1850 Loudon *Encycl. Gard.* (ed. 2) 498 The black jack, or *nigger caterpillar, being the larva of Athalia centifoliæ. **1857** *Chambers's Jrnl.* 3 Jan. 3/2 The garments of.. copper-coloured *nigger cloth. **1860** J. G. Holland *Miss Gilbert's Career* iv. 61 You see he sells some of his nigger cloth for goods. **1955** W. Foster-Harris *Look of Old West* i. 38 Typically the cloth was linsey-woolsey... 'Nigger cloth' it was called. It had been much used for slaves' garments, [etc.]. **1894** 'Mark Twain' in *Century Mag.* June 233/1 In the '*nigger corner' sat Chambers. **1876** G. B. Goode *Catal. Fishes Bermudas* 60 The red form corresponds to *Terranus ouatalibe*, and is known as the *Nigger-fish. **1888** —— *Amer. Fishes* 321 Next in importance to the Plaice, comes the Flat Fish, *Pseudopleuronectes Americanus*... New York anglers call it the 'Nigger Fish'. **1917** T. G. Pearson *Birds of Amer.* I. 97/2 The Cormorants have many local names, such as 'Shag', 'Lawyer', and '*Nigger Goose'. **1941** R. Faherty *Big Old Sun* 313 You can eat curlew, or kill duck or coot or niggergoose if they come flying out yonder. **1947** *National Geographic Mag.* Sept. 339/1 A large flight of cormorants, called there [*sc.* in North Carolina] 'nigger geese', passed close aboard. **1957** W. L. McAtee *Folk-Names Canad. Birds* 5 Double-crested Cormorant.. nigger goose (in allusion to its colour and its goose-like appearance, especially when in flight in the V-formation so closely associated with the common Canada goose). **1852** *Smithson. Contrib. Knowl.* V. II. 41 This plant [*Polysiphonia arietina*] is common in various places in Long Island Sound... 'Pooh! that's what we call "*nigger-hair"'. **1878** A. Daly in J. F. Daly *Life A. Daly* (1917) 249 There is a '*Nigger Heaven' (as the third tier is called in Troy) here, & as 'tis very capacious I have been liberal with my pencilled passes. **1931** 'D. Stiff' *Milk & Honey Route* xiv. 151 These.. entertainments.. have raised their prices beyond the reach of the hobo, unless he wants to go to 'nigger heaven'. **1973** A. Dundes *Mother Wit* 222 This extension or transformation of the 'Nigger Heaven' stereotype has no doubt contributed to the continued currency of Harlem folk speech. **1901** *Rudder* XII. 302/2 The after leech would take an incurve or '*nigger heel', as sailmakers call it. **1922** C. G. Davis *How Sails are Made* (ed. 2) 63 A double-bighted sail would, if not carefully handled and hauled out too hard on peak and clew, become '*nigger-heeled', as a hollow leech was called. **1934** *Yachting Monthly* LVII. 11/1 We were watching a hawse-fallen sloop beating in under a badly nigger-heeled mainsail. **1961** F. H. Burgess *Dict. Sailing* 150 *Niggerheeled*, said of the leech of a sail that curves inward of a line from peak to clew, and is therefore not roached. **1834** *Chambers's Edin. Jrnl.* III. 135/3 When a slave runs away.. a party is made up for a *nigger hunt. **1940** E. Caldwell *Trouble in July* x. 165 This ain't no nigger-hunt—this here's a jawing match! **1959** *Encounter* Mar. 87 The young '*nigger-hunters' of Notting Hill. **1834** *Chambers's Edin. Jrnl.* III. 135/3 In Kentucky.. *nigger-hunting is a favourite sport. **1958** *Encounter* Dec. 4/2 They had then armed themselves, .. and had gone on what they described.. as a 'nigger-hunting expedition'. **1971** in C. Mullard *Black Britain* (1973) IV. xi. 142 The racists, who were no doubt nigger hunting, as they call it, felt that this was easy meat. **1838** Haliburton *Clockm.* Ser. II. iii, A *nigger-jockey.. is a gentleman that trades in niggers,—buys them in one state, and sells them in another, where they arn't known. **1859** M. Pattison *Ess.* (1889) I. 65 It is in perpetual conflict with the rules of good Latinity, .. partly from the addle-headed understanding of the characters supposed to write this *nigger Latin. **1933** *Sun* (Baltimore) 11 Sept. 6/7 The iron weed with its deep color, and.. great clumps of '*nigger lice'. **1940** H. L. Mencken *Happy Days* 43 Sometimes a black-hearted boy would sneak into the adjacent brickyard, which was covered in large part with Jimpson weeds, plantains and other such vegetable outlaws, and return with a large ball of nigger-lice. **1946** *Sun* (Baltimore) 2 Oct. 12/3 When I spoke the other day of 'nigger lice', I was referring to the tick trefoil, its scientific name. **1851** R. Glisan *Jrnl. Army Life* (1874) 90, I occasionally made him a little envious by my *nigger-luck, as he is pleased to term it. **1900** R. H. Savage *Midnight Passenger* (1901) 135 It has been a great stroke of nigger luck. **1909** *Dialect Notes* III. 352 You can't beat me playing dominoes. It's jest your nigger-luck that gets away with me. **1876** E. W. Heap *Diary* 26 Feb. in *Publ. Amer. Dial. Soc.* (1969) LII. 53, I had a job on hand making *Nigger shooters for Dr's children. **1883** Sweet & Knox *On Mexican Mustang through Texas* 339 Just about the time people have got used to tops buzzing about their ears, the 'nigger-shooter' mania breaks out. **1901** Ade *Forty Mod. Fables* 172 All you wanted to do was to tear out with those Toughs and kill Birds with Nigger-Shooters. **1963** R. I. McDavid *Mencken's Amer. Lang.* vi. 284 In the South it [*sc.* a slingshot] is still sometimes called a *nigger-shooter*. **1971**

Guardian 18 Sept. 11/7 Conditions inside American prisons. .. Prisoners live their lives at the end of gun barrels and what are often known as '*nigger-sticks'. **1973** *Black Panther* 15 Sept. 17/3 They were attacked and brutally beaten by 50 to 60 guards armed with tear gas, plexiglass shields and four-foot long 'nigger sticks'. **1974** *Guidelines to Volunteer Services* (N.Y. State, Dept. Correctional Services) 42 *Niggerstick*, officer's baton. **1896** *Dialect Notes* I. 421 *Nigger toes*: for *Brazil nuts*. **1958** J. M. LACY in A. Dundes *Mother Wit* (1973) 597/2 He buys .. nuts called 'nigger toes'. **1973** *Times* 27 Aug. 5/8 In Virginia brazil nuts are called *nigger-toes* and chewed with great relish.

Hence **'niggerdom**, Negroes collectively. **'niggerish** *a.*, pertaining to, characteristic of, the Negro. **'niggerism**, (*a*) Negro blood; (*b*) a term or expression peculiar to Negroes. **'niggerling**, a little Negro.

1862 *Congress. Globe* 28 Mar. 1414/2 New England, where they hate *niggerdom worse than the devil. **1868** *Good Words* 1 Oct. 603/2 The conquering nigger .. caught many of the Aborigines, blacked them over, and sent them off to proclaim the glories of Niggerdom. **1876** BESANT & RICE *Gold. Butterfly* xxx, The modern Arabs, the gipsies, niggerdom in general. **1825** J. NEAL *Bro. Jonathan* II. 67 Ye great *niggerish lookin', wap-sided haw. **1866** *Atlantic Monthly* XVIII. 79 When I say 'colored', I mean one thing, respectfully; and when I say 'niggerish', I mean another, disgustedly. *Ibid.*, My Auntie's piety was not of the niggerish kind. **1844** *Fraser's Mag.* XXIX. 656 An individual tainted even in the eighth degree with *niggerism. **1844** *St. Louis* (Missouri) *Reveille* 24 Nov. 2/4 Scrub and whitewash your spiritual niggerism, or you will forever rest in the valley of *Sheol*! **1856** *Illinois State Register* (Springfield) 19 June 2/1 For every democrat who deserts to niggerism, one hundred old line whigs join the democracy against it. **1873** *Porcupine* 19 Apr. 38/3 For the occasional dash or suspicion of niggerism in the mangling of the words, common custom and coincidence will quite account. **1883** WINTHROP *Edwin Brothertoft* II. v, [To] ventriloquize derisive niggerisms through the larynx. **1970** G. JACKSON *Let.* 10 June in *Soledad Brother* (1971) 33 He and my mother went to great pains to impress on me that it was the worst form of niggerism to hook and jab .. at other blacks. **1842** HOOD *Black Job* viii, All the little *Niggerlings emerge As lily white as mussels.

nigger ('nɪgə(r)), *v. U.S.* [f. prec.]

1. *trans.* **a.** (See quot. 1859.) **b.** To burn or char *off*.

1833 S. SMITH *Life & Writings J. Downing* 22 He laid sticks across the large logs .., and *niggered* them off with fire, and then roolled them up in piles. **1843** 'R. CARLTON' *New Purchase* I. xx. 188 In addition to the 'niggering off', it became necessary, as the cold increased, to chop off logs. **1859** BARTLETT *Dict. Amer.*, To *nigger out* land, signifies .. to exhaust land by the mode of tilling without fertilization pursued in the slave States. *a* **1890** in *Cent. Dict.*, They niggered the huge logs off with fire, which was kept burning for days. **1905** M. G. SHERK *Pen Pictures of Early Pioneer Life in Upper Canada* 49 To save the time and labor of cutting the fallen trees into lengths for being drawn together by the oxen, they were often 'niggered'.

2. To work 'like a nigger'; to work very hard; quasi-*trans.* with *it*.

1857 J. HYDE *Mormonism* v. 120 Many of the people express satisfaction in seeing these 'better-dressed fellers' obliged to 'nigger it' as well as themselves. **1878** J. H. BEADLE *Western Wilds* 349 Was it not more of an honor to be the 'bishop's fourth' .. than the 'slavey' of a poor mechanic, to 'nigger it on love and starvation'?

3. *refl.* To make (oneself) resemble a Negro, by blackening the face.

1881 M. CROMMELIN *Miss Daisy Dimity* I. ii. 21 Jemmy the third, was 'niggering' himself, by adorning his rosy cheeks with black.

nigge'rality. *rare*⁻¹. [f. *nigger* NIGGARD *sb.* + -ALITY.] Niggardliness.

1823 GALT *Entail* xci, Every farthing I can extortionate frae thee .. shall be pay't o'er to her .., just to wring thy heart o' niggerality.

'niggerhead. Also **nigger-head, nigger head.** [f. NIGGER *sb.* + HEAD *sb.*[1]]

1. a. *N. Amer.* (See quot. 1859.) Also, *N.Z.*, the tussocks formed in swampy ground by species of *Carex*, esp. *C. secta*.

1859 BARTLETT *Dict. Amer.*, *Nigger-Heads*, the tussocks or knotted masses of the roots of sedges and ferns projecting above the wet surface of a swamp. **1873** *Routledge's Young Gentlm. Mag.* Mar. 236/2 Stepping from one flax-bush or nigger-head to the other. **1882** T. H. POTTS *Out in Open* 76 Penetrating the dead massy root of an old plant of nigger-head (*carex virgata*). **1904** J. LYNCH *Three Yrs. Klondike* 41 We plunged into a mire of muddy water and 'nigger-heads'. 'Nigger-heads' are detachments of dark moss about a foot in diameter, lifting their heads just above the water or marshy subsoil. **1910** R. W. SERVICE *Ballads of Cheechako* 19 And there was the little lone moose trail... By muskeg hollow and niggerhead it wandered endlessly. **1921** H. GUTHRIE-SMITH *Tutira* xii. 103 The outer edges of these marshes were rough with nigger's-head (*Carex secta*). **1947** J. H. BROWN *Outdoors Unlimited* 314 The ptarmigan cackled in the manner of a Bronx cheer as it flew to a nearby nigger-head. **1950** *N.Z. Jrnl. Agric.* Apr. 356/3 Excellent crops and pastures .. where before only nigger-heads, rushes, and swamp plants were flourishing. **1958** P. BERTON *Klondike* 44 The great clumps of grass 'nigger-heads' that marked the mouth of Rabbit. **1961** C. VYVYAN *Arctic Adventure* xxi. 126 We had to negotiate about a mile of open country across nigger-heads.

b. *U.S.* A spherical prickly cactus belonging to the genera *Ferocactus* or *Echinocactus*.

1877 H. C. HODGE *Arizona* 244 The kind [of cactus] commonly called the nigger head is round, of the size of a cabbage, and covered with large, crooked, catlike thorns. **1881** [see *barrel cactus*]. **1940** E. C. JAEGER *Calif. Deserts* (rev. ed.) 181 Closely allied to this is the Mohavean niggerhead. **1966** E. Y. DAWSON *Cacti of Calif.* 51 (*heading*) Nigger Heads (*Echinocactus polycephalus*).

c. *U.S.* The black-eyed Susan, *Rudbeckia hirta*, a yellow composite flower with a dark centre.

1893 S. F. PRICE *Flora of Warren County, Kentucky* 15 *Rudbeckia .. fulgida*... Cone flower. 'Nigger-head'. **1931** W. N. CLUTE *Common Names of Plants* 45 A number of composites with yellow rays and dark centers are commonly known as niggerheads, though the more polite term is black-eyed Susan. **1966** *Publ. Amer. Dial. Soc.* 1964 XLII. 21 Niggerhead... The black-eyed Susan (*Rudbeckia hirta*).

2. A rock, stone, lump of coral, etc.

1847 H. HOWE *Hist. Coll. of Ohio* 569 It was a saw mill, with a small pair of stones attached, made of boulders, or 'nigger heads', as they are commonly called. **1876** J. MORESBY *Discov. New Guinea* 3 A crowd of 'nigger heads', black points of coral rock, peep up in places. **1877** RAYMOND *Statist. Mines & Mining* 56 The bowlders, composed of quartz, 'nigger heads', and micaceous schists, are not large. **1885** in *Amer. Speech* (1961) XXXVI. 295 The term 'Nigger head' is used by the Kanawha miners to designate a hard, heavy, impure coal often resembling cannel. **1886** *Ann. Rep. Smithson. Inst.* (1889) II. 523 *Nigger head.* (1) The black concretionary nodules found in granite; (2) Any hard, dark-colored rock weathering out into rounded nodules or bowlders; (3) Slaty rock associated with sandstone. **1898** MORRIS *Austral Eng.*, *Nigger-head.* Name given in New Zealand to hard blackstones found at the Blue Spur and other mining districts. **1901** *Chambers's Jrnl.* Sept. 634/1 He tightened his grip on the reins as he caught the dim outline of a treacherous nigger-head stone. **1908** E. J. BANFIELD *Confessions of Beachcomber* I. ii. 57 Nothing was left of the big ship save some distorted fragments of iron jammed in among the nigger-heads of coral. **1916** C. SANDBURG *Chicago Poems* 41 A boy passes and throws a niggerhead that chips off the end of the nose [of a statue]. **1948** E. N. DICK *Dixie Frontier* 4 Bears rolled 'nigger head' stones over and ate the grubs and field mice. **1956** M. L. WEST *Gallows on Sand* viii. 89 We moored the skiff to a niggerhead, one of those jutting stumps of dead coral which are found all over the reefs, and which have the look of a frizzled skull on top of a stumpy neck.

3. = NEGRO-HEAD 2. Also *attrib.*

1843 J. LUMSDEN *Amer. Memoranda* (1844) 14 My next communication will probably contain full details of the methods adopted by the Virginian planters in the manufacturing of the nigger-head, ladies'-twist, [etc.]. **1860** *Nor' Wester* (Red River Settlement) 28 June 4/5 After that I would smoke half a plug of 'nigger-head tobacco'. **1884** 'MARK TWAIN' *Huck. Finn* xxi. 194 You borry'd store tobacco and paid back nigger-head. **1893** J. A. BARRY *S. Brown's Bunyip*, etc. 24 He .. had accepted as much strong 'niggerhead' .. as would have stocked a tobacconist's shop. **1894** *Outing* (U.S.) XXIV. 355/1 Cigarettes .. made of native grown tobacco or the rank cheap stuff called niggerhead twist. **1936** *Beaver* Mar. 7/2 It is probably the lineal descendant of the nigger-head tobacco used in the Indian trade years ago, and as it came in ropes it was sold by the inch. **1956** CRATE & WILLIAMS *We speak for Silent* 3 Groceries—particularly tea and 'nigger-head' (a trade-tobacco for smoking and chewing)—are his more necessary 'luxuries'.

4. A variety of cowrie.

1895 MRS. F. A. STEEL *Rowans* x, Do you ever find niggerheads about here now?

5. *U.S. slang.* (See quot.)

1872 DE VERE *Americanisms* 281 They were Democrats, and retorted upon violent Union men by calling them Niggerheads. **1946** W. S. KNICKERBOCKER *20th Cent. English* 149 Niggerhead... After the Civil War it was used for a person in favor of full political equality for Negroes.

6. A type of fabric (see quot. 1950).

1892-3 *T. Eaton & Co. Catal.* Fall & Winter 10/2 In the plain cloth jackets the materials are beavers, niggerheads, serges and worsted. **1950** '*Mercury*' *Dict. Textile Terms* 366/1 *Niggerhead Curl*, a fancy dress cloth made from spiral yarn warp and mixture weft (cotton and wool).

7. (See quot.)

1927 G. BRADFORD *Gloss. Sea Terms* 119/1 *Niggerheads*, a name for bollards, and sometimes applied to winch heads.

'niggering, *vbl. sb.* [f. NIGGER *v.* + -ING[1].] The action of the verb in various senses.

1843 'R. CARLTON' *New Purchase* I. xx. 188 Niggering belongs mainly to very large timber, and pertains rather to the science of log-rolling than of preparing fuel. **1894** 'R. ANDOM' *We Three & Troddles* xix. 174 'Busking' be it known is the technical term for amateur niggering. **1948** E. N. DICK *Dixie Frontier* 126 Morning and evening dry limbs were laid in the widening gap until the log was burnt into length. After about a week the fires had done their work. This was called 'niggering off'.

niggerize ('nɪgəraɪz), *v.* [f. NIGGER *sb.* + -IZE.] *trans.* To make Negro in character; to treat (a Negro) with contempt. Also *intr.*, to act or dress up as a Negro.

1969 V. FERDINAND in A. Chapman *New Black Voices* (1972) 379 Blk people have done it to the english language, they have niggerized it. **1973** *Times* 13 Feb. 16/4 As people, we are tired of being niggerized, ostracized .. and ossified. **1974** 'J. MARKS' *Mick Jagger* 92 Mick niggerising with a fake, greasy dialect and a very heavy debt to Bo on 'I'm a King Bee'.

niggerly, obs. form of NIGGARDLY *a.*

†**'niggers,** used as an oath (cf. GOD *sb.* 14b). Also **niggers-noggers.** *Obs. rare.*

1633 ROWLEY *Match at Midn.* I. i, Niggers, and I had but dreamed of this. *Ibid.*, When we swear nothing but niggers-noggers. *Ibid.*, Niggers-noggers, I wonnot.

nigger's head. *Naut.* An ornamental knot; = TURK'S HEAD 2.

1925 *Glasgow Herald* 3 Oct. 4 The glittering ship's bell with its pendant of brightly painted niggershead knotting.

†**'niggery,** *sb. Obs. rare.* [ad. Du. *negerij*; cf. NEGERY.] An administrative division of the Dutch East Indies.

1800 *Asiatic Ann. Reg.* 201/2 The subordinate residents have from six to ten niggeries, or districts, under their charge. *Ibid.* 203/1 These .. niggeries are likewise called Regencies.

'niggery, *a.* [f. NIGGER *sb.* + -Y[1].] Of or belonging to, characteristic of, Negroes.

1855 'Q. K. P. DOESTICKS' *Doesticks, What he Says* xxiii 204 Coffee, which I sweeten with niggery brown sugar. **1862** *New York Tribune* May (Cent.), The dialect of the entire population is essentially and unmistakably niggery. **1881** M. A. LEWIS *Two Pretty Girls* II. 132, I wish you had small screwed-up eyes, and a niggery mouth. **1935** E. HEMINGWAY *Green Hills Afr.* (1936) IV. ii. 241 The long, clean niggery legs. **1936** M. MITCHELL *Gone with Wind* 427 The faint niggery smell which crept from the cabin increased her nausea. **1940** C. MCCULLERS *Heart is Lonely Hunter* (1943) I. iii. 43 Portia had a certain kind of niggery craziness, but she was O.K.

nigget ('nɪdʒɪt). *dial.* Also **nidget.** [Origin unknown.] A small insect; *spec.* one used by a witch or sorcerer as a familiar.

1875 W. D. PARISH *Dict. Sussex Dial.* 79 *Nidget*, a little bug. **1915** *Times* 3 Sept. 5/2 'Oh, what are niggets?' 'Why those creepy-crawly things that witches keep all over them. She was sitting down with her niggets all round her, feeding them with little bits of grass all chopped up.' **1925** R. O. WINSTEDT *Shaman, Saiva, & Sufi* ii. 21 But the best known of these familiars .. is of the nigget type and takes the shape of a house-cricket.

†**'niggish,** *a. Obs.* Also **nig(g)eshe, niggyshe, nygyshe, nyggish, -yshe.** [f. NIG *a.* or *sb.* + -ISH.] Niggardly. (Common *c* 1550–1600.)

1542 UDALL *Erasm. Apoph.* 74 Persones yᵗ dooe glorie & braggue of their niggyshe slooveny. **1577** tr. *Bullinger's Decades* (1592) 288 Let our wealthie pinchpence therefore .. leaue their niggish liues and insatiable couetousnesse. **1605** CAMDEN *Rem.* 196 Other maximes .. proceeding from a niggish olde wife.

Hence †**'niggishly** *adv.*; †**'niggishness.**

1562 TURNER *Baths* Ded., The extreme niggishness and illiberalite of sum that had most. **1580** HOLLYBAND *Treas. Fr. Tong.*, *Escharcement vivre*, to liue barely, to liue hardly, niggishly. **1598** GRENEWEY *Tacitus, Ann.* III. x. (1622) 78 The memory of Quirinius was nothing pleasing, by reason .. of .. miserable niggishness.

niggle ('nɪg(ə)l), *sb.* [f. NIGGLE *v.*[2]] **1.** Small cramped handwriting.

1834 HOOD *Tylney Hall* Introd., Sometimes it is a little close niggle, as if you studied economy in stationery. **1856** MISS YONGE *Daisy Chain* I. xviii, Ethel's best writing was an upright, disjointed, niggle. *Ibid.*, A still wilder combination of scramble, niggle, scratch, and crookedness.

2. A complaint or criticism, esp. one that is petty or trifling; a worry, annoyance; nagging or irritation.

1886 F. T. ELWORTHY *West Somerset Word-Bk.* 512 Her's always 'pon the niggle way un. **1956** I. BROMIGE *Enchanted Garden* III. iii. 144, I even feel a few little niggles of uneasiness myself. **1960** *Guardian* 11 June 1/5 The poor quality of contemporary furniture .. can be the only niggle. **1966** *New Statesman* 8 July 51/3 How much of us will be recognisable in the pages of the history books of 2066? This egoist's niggle spiralled up into my mind. **1972** M. GILBERT *Body of Girl* xii. 106 If the boys in blue can get in a niggle at you, they will. **1974** *Times Lit. Suppl.* 15 Feb. 158/3 In view .. of the fact that his book should .. go into a second edition .., one or two minor niggles may conveniently be ventilated.

†**niggle,** *v.*[1] *Obs. Cant.* Also 6 **nygle,** 7 **nigle.** [Of obscure origin: cf. next.] *intr.* and *trans.* (See quot. 1567.)

1567 HARMAN *Caveat* (1869) 84 To nygle, to haue to do with a woman carnally. **1608** DEKKER *Lanth. & Candle Lt.* Bij b, If we niggle, or mill a bowsing Ken .. If an ale-house we rob, or be tane with a whore. **1622** FLETCHER *Beggars' Bush* II. i, *Hub.* How long has she been here? *Snap.* Long enough to be .. nigled, an' she ha' .. good luck.

niggle ('nɪg(ə)l), *v.*[2] Also 8 **nigle.** [App. of Scandinavian origin, being current chiefly in northern dial., and corresponding both in form and meaning to Norw. *nigla* (Aasen and Ross), with the variants *nagla* and *nugla*. The precise meaning in some of the early examples is not quite clear; for the numerous variations of sense in dial. use, see *Eng. Dial. Dict.*]

1. a. *intr.* To work, or do anything, in a trifling, fiddling, or ineffective way; to trifle (†*with* a thing); to spend work or time unnecessarily on petty details; to be over-elaborate in minor points.

a **1616** BEAUM. & FL. *Little French Lawyer* IV. v, That Little Lawyer would so .. bite your honour by the nose, .. So niggle about your grave shins, lord Vertaigne. **1631** MASSINGER *Emperor East* V. iii, Take heed, daughter, You niggle not with your conscience. **1839** C. CLARK *J. Noakes* lxii, Long she'd niggle at her glass. **1854** MISS BAKER *Northampt. Gloss.* s.v., How you are niggling over your work; it is not worth the time. **1883** BLACK *Yolande* xlix, It was only to have been a sketch. And he has kept on niggling and niggling away at it. **1893** J. A. BARRY *S. Brown's Bunyip*, etc. 56 For a while they niggles away at the big butt, turn an' turn about.

b. To trot about, keep moving *along*, in a fiddling or ineffective manner.

1781 MME. D'ARBLAY *Diary* Aug., When I have nobody at all at my place but workmen; .. I niggle after them up and down. **1833** SIR F. B. HEAD *Bubbles fr. Brunnen* 246 The river, as one niggles along, is seen bit by bit from the steamboat. **1849** EASTWICK *Dry Leaves* 193 A fidgetty high-mettled steed, which dislikes a dozen of ragged galloways niggling along within a yard of its tail.

c. To get *on* in a kind of way *with* one.

1837 LADY DACRE in *Friendships Miss Mitford* (1882) II. 21, I shall try to niggle on with her; but I am too deaf and old, I fear, to scrape acquaintance with a young person.

d. To be unnecessarily critical or over-precise.

1844 W. BARNES *Poems Rural Life* 1st Coll. 330 *Niggle*, to complain of trifles from ill temper or bad humor. **1891** BLACK *Stand Fast, Craig-R.* vi, 'Come, come, aunt', said he, 'it isn't like you to niggle about nothing'. **1929** W. DEEPING *Roper's Row* xxviii. 312 He would niggle at his food. **1966** 'L. LANE' *ABZ of Scouse* 75 *Niggle*, to question; to raise objections. **1974** *Sunday Post* (Glasgow) 21 Apr. 16 (Advt.), Your accounts director won't niggle at the bill at the Ormonde Restaurant (just a high-speed lift away from your room).

2. Of girls: To be restless or fidgetty from wantonness or amorous inclination. ? *Obs.*

1706 ESTCOURT *Fair Example* IV. i, Had you been one of the fluttering Fops o' the Town, she had so wrigl'd and nigl'd, and have been so glad of your Company. **1793** PEARCE *Hartford Bridge* II. i, They giggle, simper, Niggle and whimper, And try to lure wherever they go. **1809** MALKIN *Gil Blas* IV. vii. ¶13 My little pet..niggled, nudged, toyed, and romped, like a school-girl in vacation.

3. *trans.* **a.** To cheat, trick.

1621 FLETCHER *Pilgrim* IV. iii, I shall so niggle you, And juggle you; and fiddle you, and firk you. **1719** D'URFEY *Pills* (1872) II. 111 To purge my sins, And buy me Pins, I've nigled an old Parson.

b. To draw *out* unwillingly.

1630 DEKKER *2nd Pt. Honest Wh.* Wks. 1873 II. 133, I had but one poore penny, and that I was glad to niggle out, and buy a holly-wand.

c. To execute in a petty trifling manner.

1860 E. FITZGERALD *Lett.* (1889) I. 276 Think of the Acres of Canvas Titian or Reynolds would have covered.. in the Time it has taken to niggle this Miniature!

d. To annoy, irritate; to criticize, nag.

1886 F. T. ELWORTHY *West Somerset Word-Bk.* 512 *Niggle*, same as to nag. To aggravate. Her'd niggle anybody's live out o' them, nif they'd let her to. **1959** I. & P. OPIE *Lore & Lang. Schoolch.* x. 178 A short-tempered person is spoken of as being..niggled or niggly. **1968** A. DIMENT *Great Spy Race* iv. 47 He is liable to start demanding mass executions when niggled. **1971** A. PRICE *Alamut Ambush* 6 He was mildly niggled that Maitland had found himself some other pressing engagement.

Hence **niggled** ('nɪg(ə)ld) *ppl. a.*, done with too much minuteness or petty detail; over-elaborated.

1884 *Century Mag.* Dec. 207 They..are niggled little drawings, carefully worked up with the point. **1888** *Art Jrnl.* II. 61/2 Its careful but not niggled workmanship. **1893** *Nation* (N.Y.) 19 Jan. 47/1 His more finished designs..are hopelessly niggled.

† **niggledigée**, obs. variant of NEGLIGEE.

1755 J. SHEBBEARE *Lydia* (1769) II. 29 Lady Betty Wriggle being dressed in what the tuneful part of the streets of London have distinguished in their songs by the polite term of the Niggledigée.

† **'niggler**[1]. *Obs. Cant.* [f. NIGGLE *v.*[1] + -ER[1].] A lascivious person.

1613 MARSTON *Insatiate C'tess* II. ii, With cleanly conveyance by the nigglers our maids, they shall be translated into our bed-chambers. **1641** BROME *Joviall Crew* II. Wks. 1873 III. 392 Heart and a cup of Sack, do we look like old Beggar-niglers? **1659** *Lady Alimony* II. v. in Hazl. *Dodsley* XIV. 313 Ha, ha, ha! this was a bold-fac'd niggler.

niggler[2] ('nɪglə(r)). [f. NIGGLE *v.*[2] + -ER[1].] One who niggles, *esp.* in artistic work.

1862 THORNBURY *Turner* II. 344 To the last he was rather a 'niggler' in oil. **1900** *Q. Rev.* Jan. 115 Bold effects must take the place of the niggler's puny scroll-work.

niggliite ('nɪglɪaɪt). *Min.* [f. the name of Paul *Niggli* (1888–1953), Swiss mineralogist + -ITE[1].] A mineral containing platinum and tin (or perhaps tellurium), found at Insizwa in Cape Province, Republic of South Africa.

1936 D. L. SCHOLTZ in *Publ. Univ. Pretoria* 2nd Ser. I. 184 (*heading*) Mineral F (niggliite). **1955** *Amer. Mineralogist* XL. 693 Niggliite..was found in a concentrate which was obtained by panning large amounts of oxidized sulphide ore from Waterfall Gorge, Insizwa, South Africa. **1968** I. KOSTOV *Mineralogy* 115 Various other formulae have been given to niggliite, PtTe, PtSn, and Pt_2Sn_3; its structure appears to be that of niccolite. **1972** *Mineral. Mag.* XXXVIII. 796 The close similarity of niggliite to synthetic PtTe..led Groeneveld Meijer (1955) to suggest that they were identical. Ramdohr (1960) suggests that the formula is Pt_2Sn_3 but in Ramdohr (1969) the composition is given as 'PtTe, perhaps a mixed crystal with isostructural PtSn'. Scholtz..reports that re-examination showed niggliite is essentially PtSn. *Ibid.* 798 Niggliite from the type locality has been shown to be an antimonian-bismuthian variety of PtSn.

† **'niggling**, *vbl. sb.*[1] *Obs. Cant.* [f. NIGGLE *v.*[1] + -ING[1].] (See quots.)

1608 DEKKER *Lanth. & Candle Lt., Cant. Dict., Niggling*, company keeping with a woman [**1610** ROWLANDS *Martin Mark-all* E 3, This word is not used now]. **1641** BROME *Joviall Crew* II. Wks. 1873 III. 391 The Autum-Mort finds better sport In bowsing then in nigling. *a* **1700** B. E. *Dict. Cant. Crew, Nigling*, accompanying with a Woman.

niggling ('nɪglɪŋ), *vbl. sb.*[2] [f. NIGGLE *v.*[2]]

1. Trifling or fiddling work; over-attention to details; mean or petty dealing.

1829 MARRYAT *F. Mildmay* viii, Cleanliness and good order are what seamen like; but niggling, polishing, scraping iron bars, and the like of that a sailor dislikes. **1840** THACKERAY *Catherine* x, The man was well fitted for the creeping and niggling of his dastardly trade. **1881** *Times* 5 Feb. 9/2 He will grant them some powers, but not all they are asking for... This of course is mere niggling.

2. Over-elaboration of detail in art.

1860 RUSKIN *Mod. Paint.* V. VI. v. §6. 37 So long as the work is thoughtfully directed, there is no niggling. **1886** R. C. LESLIE *Sea Painter's Log* 132 No amount of niggling will atone for the want of such touches.

'niggling, *ppl. a.* [f. as prec. + -ING[2].]

1. Trifling, mean, petty; deficient in force or vigour; lacking in breadth of view or feeling.

1599 NASHE *Lenten Stuffe* Wks. (Grosart) V. 203 All the King of Spaines Indies will not create me such a nigling Hexameter-sounder as he [Homer] was.

1827 SOUTHEY *Lett.* (1856) IV. 73 Neither did I like the niggling way in which they dealt with me. **1852** C. W. H[OSKINS] *Talpa* 126 Your unprofitable expense is ever peeping out in the niggling nature of your plans. **1876** STUBBS *Study Med. & Mod. Hist.* iii. (1886) 53 We do not want..niggling articles, which enumerate the mistakes and misstatements of a book. **1891** BARING-GOULD *Hist. Oddities* Ser. II. iii. 76 This little court..played a niggling game at petty intrigue.

b. Fiddling, troublesome, finicking.

1863 DARWIN in *Life* (1887) III. 312 It is just the sort of niggling work which suits me. **1877** ERICHSEN *Surg.* (ed. 7) II. 470 It is a niggling instrument, difficult to manage in this situation.

2. Showing too great elaboration of detail; deficient in boldness of execution.

1813 *Examiner* 10 May 229/2 The little, niggling pencilling of Mr. Glover's [landscapes]. **1860** RUSKIN *Mod. Paint.* V. VI. v. §6. 38 The whole hand [drawn] within the space of one of those 'niggling' touches of Hobbima. **1891** BARING-GOULD *In Troubadour-Land* xvii. 248 He has carried the face of his niggling little buttresses flush with the massive walls of the great towers.

b. Of handwriting: Consisting of short feeble strokes; cramped.

1854 MISS BAKER *Northampt. Gloss.* s.v., A niggling hand. **1890** *Spectator* 12 July 48/1 The most resolute person we know writes a niggling scrawl, hardly legible.

niggly ('nɪglɪ), *a.* [f. NIGGLE *v.*[2] + -Y[1].] = NIGGLING *ppl. a.*; also, irritable, short-tempered.

1840 W. HARCOURT *Let.* in A. G. Gardiner *Life W. Harcourt* (1923) I. ii. 24, I think his trees *niggly* as you would say, and he teaches an odd doctrine about trees. **1862** C. C. ROBINSON *Dial. Leeds* 40 Ah doant want to live soa as fowks could cawal us niggly. **1898** B. KIRKBY *Lakeland Words* 107 He was as niggly ower a penny as many a yan is ower a pund. **1952** M. TRIPP *Faith is Windsock* iii. 43 Well, aren't you a niggly old bastard? **1959** [see NIGGLE *v.*[2] 3 d]. **1967** E. SHORT *Embroidery & Fabric Collage* iv. 106 Care must be taken to avoid niggly detail and a temptation to imitate a pencil line or brush stroke exactly. **1973** A. ROSS *Dunfermline Affair* 65 'What about..going to get the bloody stuff?' Thomson said. He was niggly, and showed it.

niggon(ship, variants of NIGON(SHIP *Obs.*

niggot, app. a misprint for INGOT.

1579–80 NORTH *Plutarch* (1595) 415 For Itanus the historiographer writeth, that there was brought a maruellous great masse of treasure in niggots of gold, of three thousand seuen hundred and thirteen pound weight.

niggra: see NIGRA.

nigguh, niggur: see NIGGA.

nigh (naɪ), *adv.*, *a.*, and *sb.* Forms: *α.* 1 **néah**, (**néaȝ-**), **néh**, 2 **neoh**, 3 **næh**; 2–4 **neh**, 3 **nehȝ**, 3–4 **nehi**; 3–5 **neȝ**, (3 **neȝt**, 4 **neȝh**, **neeȝh**), 4–5 **neȝe**, **negh(e**; 3 (5–6 *Sc.*) **ne**, 6 **nee**. *β.* 3–4 **neih**, (3 **neiþ**, 4 **neich**), **nei**, (4 **neie**), 3–5 **neiȝ**, (4 **neiȝe**), 4 **neigh(e**, 6 **neight**; 3 **neyh**, 4–6 **ney(e**, 4 **neythe**, 5 **neyhe**, **neygh**, **neyȝt**. *γ.* 4 **niȝ**, **nieȝ**, **nyeȝ**, **nyh(e**, 4–5 **nyȝ(e**, 4–6 **nyghe**, (4 **nyȝghe**, 6 **nygghe**), 4–7 **nygh**, (6 **nyght**); 4–6 **nighe**, 4– **nigh**; 4–6 **ny(e**, 6–7 **nie**. [Common Teutonic: OE. *néah*, *néh* = OFris. *nei*, *nî*, MDu. *na*, *nae* (Du. *na*), OS. *nâh* (MLG. *nâge*, *nâ*), OHG. *nâh* adv., *nâher* adj. (MHG. *nâ*, *nâh-*, *nâch*, G. *nah*), ON. *ná-* (in combs. like *ná-búi* neighbour; Sw. and Da. *na-*), Goth. *nêhwa* (*nêhw*): the stem appears to be unrepresented outside Teutonic.

OHG. is the only one of the older languages in which a fully developed adjectival use of the word exists along with the adverbial. In OE. there are very scanty traces of adjectival inflexion, *néah* being commonly employed either as a simple adv. or with a dependent dative: in predicative use it may sometimes be taken as an adjective, but it is more probable that in such cases also it is an adverb. It is not till the 14th or 15th cent. that the attributive use becomes common.

The original comparative of *néah* as an adv. is *néar*, *néor*, NEAR *adv.*[1], while the adj. form *néarra* finally became *ner*, NAR *a.* The OE. superlative *níehst*(*a* is latterly represented by NEXT *a.* and *adv.* After phonetic changes had obscured the relationship of these forms to the positive, a new compar. and superl., *nigher* and *nighest*, were formed, and have been in common use since the 16th cent.]

= NEAR *adv.*[2] and *a.* (which in all senses has taken the place of *nigh* except in archaic or dialect use).

**Denoting proximity in place, time, etc.*

I. *adv.* With dependent dative (passing into *prep.*), or followed by *to* (see 4).

1. With verbs of motion, denoting approach to a place, thing, or person.

Beowulf 2290 He to forð ȝestop dyrnan cræfte dracan heafde neah. *c* **950** *Lindisf. Gosp.* Matt. xv. 29 And mið ðy oferfoerde ðona ðe hælend, cuom [he] æt *vel* neh sæ. *a* **1000** *Juliana* 635 (Gr.), Ða wæs [heo] ȝelæded londmearce neah. *c* **1205** LAY. 1609 Alle heo slowen þat heo neih comen. *a* **1300** *Cursor M.* 8041 Whenne þe kyng coom neȝe þo trees he kist hem. **1390** GOWER *Conf.* I. 120 The more he cam the welle nyh The nerr cam sche to him ayein. **1517** TORKINGTON *Pilgr.* 30 No Cristen man ys not suffered for to come ny it. **1590** SHAKS. *Mids. N.* II. ii. 18 Neuer harme, nor spell, nor charme, Come our louely Lady nye. **1681** DRYDEN *Abs. & Achit.* 162 He..for a calm unfit, Would steer too nigh the Sands. **1777** SHERIDAN *Trip Scarb.* v. ii, I am almost ashamed to come nigh 'em.

fig. *c* **1320** *Cast. Love* 320 Hit eode hire herte swiþe neih.

2. In prepositional use.

Beowulf 2831 Se widfloga wundum stille hreas on hrusan, hordærne neah. *a* **900** *O.E. Martyrol.* 22 Aug. 150 His lichoma is bebyrȝed neah sancte Paules ciricean þæs apostoles. *c* **1075** *O.E. Chron.* (Parker MS.) an. 1031 An scip flotiȝende swa neh þan lande swa hit nyxt mæȝe. *c* **1275** LAY. 27553 He..smot than eorl Beduer a-forn neȝen þan breoste. **13..** *Guy Warw.* (A.) 1508 To him he smot swiþe smert þurch þe bodi ful ney þe hert. **1393** LANGL. *P. Pl.* C. IX. 298 'By seynt paul', quath peers þo, 'thou poyntest neih þe treuthe'. **1413** *Pilgr. Sowle* (Caxton) I. xix. (1859) 19 Long tyme he had hyd hym self neyhe me. **1470–85** MALORY *Arthur* IV. xxvii. 156 She broughte hym there as was a turnement nyghe the marche of walys. **1610** SHAKS. *Temp.* I. ii. 216 *Pro.* But was not this nye shore? *Ar.* Close by, my Master. **1667** MILTON *P.L.* IX. 514 A Ship..Nigh Rivers mouth or Foreland, where the Wind Veres oft. **1770** in Picton *L'pool Munic. Rec.* (1886) II. 257 No gate shall be erected nigher Liverpoole than the four mile stone. **1826** J. F. COOPER *Mohicans* (1829) II. iii. 50 They had reached a bay, nigh the northern termination of the lake.

b. In complementary use with verbs.

c **825** *Vesp. Psalter* v. 6 Ne eardað neh ðe awerȝed. *c* **950** *Lindisf. Gosp.* Luke ii. 9 Engel drihtnes s[t]od neh ðæm. *a* **1122** *O.E. Chron.* (Laud MS.) an. 1105 Þa þe þam eorle Willelme of Mortoin ahwær neah wunedon. *a* **1225** *Ancr. R.* 312 Holde we him neih us mid smelle of swete werkes. *c* **1320** *Cast. Love* 370 Ich hit seih And tolde hit to Riht þat stood me neih. **1387** TREVISA *Higden* (Rolls) V. 357 In his ȝowþe he was..bismer to kynges þat wonede nyh hym. *c* **1440** *Gesta Rom.* ii. 6 (Harl. MS.), Ofte tyme he vsid to ligge ny þe fire.

3. In predicative use with the verb *to be*, or with ellipse of this: **a.** of locality.

c **950** *Lindisf. Gosp.* Luke xix. 11 Forðon [he] wære neh hierusalem. *c* **1000** *Ags. Ps.* (Th.) lxxviii. 4 Eallum.. ymbsittendum, þe us ahwær neah nu ða syndon. *c* **1175** *Lamb. Hom.* 95 Hit forðnimeð swa hwet him neh bið. *c* **1200** ORMIN 17918 He wass neh an casstelltun. *c* **1290** *S. Eng. Leg.* I. 1/4 Alle þe heþene men þat neiȝ him were. **1390** GOWER *Conf.* I. 197 He ferst loke out ate porte, That noman were nyh the stede. **1551** CROWLEY *Pleas. & Pain* 242 Such men as were nygh yon dwellynge. **1579** SPENSER *Sheph. Cal.* July 89 The hilles bene nigher heven. **1734** tr. *Rollin's Anc. Hist.* XV. ix. (1827) VI. 147 The drops which were nighest the torches taking fire.

b. In various *transf.* or *fig.* senses.

c **825** *Vesp. Psalter* xxxiii. 19 Neh is dryhten ðissum ða ȝeswencedre sind on heortan. *c* **1000** *Ags. Ps.* (Th.) liv. 20 Hit wæs his heortan ȝehyȝde neah. *a* **1250** *Owl & Night.* 1252 Hwanne ic iseo þat sum wrechede Is manne neyh, inouh ic grede. *c* **1320** *Sir Tristr.* 3016 Sir canados was þan Constable, þe quen ful neiȝe. **1380** WYCLIF *Sel. Wks.* III. 423 Nevereþoles summe godes ben more nyghe God. *c* **1440** *Gesta Rom.* lxxi. 388 (Addit. MS.), W[h]ere this woman was seke, and ney childe byrth. **1605** SHAKS. *Macb.* IV. ii. 72 To do worse to you were fell Cruelty, Which is too nie your person. **1875** MYERS *Poems* 63 When man's heart is nighest heaven.

c. Of time or events.

a **900** CYNEWULF *Crist* 782 Is þam dome neah. **971** *Blickl. Hom.* 95 Þonne..biþ neh þæm seofoþan dæȝe. *c* **1275** *O.E. Misc.* 142/45 Þis world is neyh þan ende. *a* **1300** *K. Horn* 494 Horn tok his leue, For hit was neȝ eue. **13..** *Sir Gaw. & Gr. Knt.* 1922 Þenne þay helden to home, for hit was nieȝ nyȝt. **1470–85** MALORY *Arthur* III. xiii. 116 He..leyd hym vnder the tree and slepte tyl it was nyghe nyght.

4. With *to* or *unto*, in uses similar to above.

c **950** *Lindisf. Gosp.* John vi. 19 [Hia] ȝeseað ðone hælend geongende..neh to scipp. *a* **1300** *Christ on Cross* 19 in *E.E.P.* (1862) 21 Man þou hast þe for-lor and ful neiþ to helle ibor. *c* **1330** R. BRUNNE *Chron. Wace* (Rolls) 1654 Þe Frankysch þenne cast a cry, þerfore men drowe to þeym ney. **1391** CHAUCER *Boeth.* IV. met. v. (1868) 132 Þe sterres of arctour ytourned neye to þe souereyne contre or point. *c* **1420** *Chron. Vilod.* 885 Edgar rode ouȝt..In to a Forest neyȝt to his place. **1484** CAXTON *Fables of Alfonce* i, [He] wente and lodged hym withynne a Temple nyghe to a Frendes hows. **1535** COVERDALE *John* vi. 23 There came other shippes from Tiberias, nye vnto yᵉ place where they had eaten the bred. **1581** MULCASTER *Positions* xl. (1887) 224 The scholers..be bourded at their charges somewhere verie nigh to the schoole. **1600** J. PORY tr. *Leo's Africa* v. 262 The citie of Tunis standing vpon a plaine hath no mountaines nigh vnto it. **1680** MORDEN *Geog. Rect., France* (1685) 163 Nigh to this place. **1704** *Col. Rec. Pennsylv.* II. 182 Being the neighest to their place of Abode. **1823** J. F. COOPER *Pioneers* v, The arm that was extended bent, and brought the hand nigh to his face.

transf. or *fig.* **1568** GRAFTON *Chron.* II. 785 They were good men, and true to the King and to nie to the Queene. **1611** BIBLE *Lev.* xxi. 3 His sister a virgin, that is nigh vnto him. **1826** J. F. COOPER *Mohicans* (1829) II. iii. 46 This change had brought them nigher to each other. **1896** MRS. CAFFYN *Quaker Grandmother* 183 We've crossed each other's paths these many years, for all..we haven't come very nigh to one another.

II. *adv.* Used absolutely as complement or predicate (passing into *adj.*).

5. Of place or position: **a.** With the verb *to be* expressed or understood.

c 897 K. ÆLFRED *Gregory's Past. C.* li. 399 Her is an lytele burȝ swiðe neah. c 950 *Lindisf. Gosp.* Mark xiv. 42 Seðe mec selleð neh is. a 1310 in Wright *Lyric P.* ix. 34 Heo hath browes bend an heh, Whyt bytuene, ant nout to neh. 1386 CHAUCER *Knt.'s T.* 668 Ful litel woot Arcite of his felawe, That was so ny. c 1450 tr. *De Imitatione* II. viii. 48 Whan ihesu is nye, all godenes is nye. 1501 DOUGLAS *Pal. Hon.* I. xxi, Thairby I vnderstude that scho was nie. 1590 SHAKS. *Com. Err.* II. i. 43 Heere comes your man, now is your husband nie. 1671 MILTON *P.R.* I. 332 We sometimes.. come forth To Town or Village nigh (nighest is far). 1821 SHELLEY *Aziola* i, Methinks she must be nigh. 1850 TENNYSON *In Mem.* cxxx, Far off thou art, but ever nigh.

b. With verbs of dwelling, standing, etc.

c 1200 *Trin. Coll. Hom.* 189 þe fleschliche lustes.. beoð þe smeðere him to biswikende for þan þe þei nehȝie wunion. 1382 WYCLIF *Jas.* v. 9 Lo! the iustise stondith nvȝ bifore the ȝat. 1513 DOUGLAS *Æneis* x. xiv. 5 Hys helm of steill besyde hym hang weil ne. 1567 MAPLET *Gr. Forest* 26 b, Doth not the Uine loue and embrace the Elme & prospereth the better, the nigher one is set by another? 1750 GRAY *Elegy* 78 Some frail memorial still erected nigh. 1791 COWPER *Iliad* IX. 248 Then bespake Patroclus standing nigh. 1833 TENNYSON *To J. S.* 33, I have not look'd upon you nigh, Since that dear soul hath fall'n asleep.

c. With verbs of motion.

c 1330 R. BRUNNE *Chron. Wace* (Rolls) 203 He ne wist it ȝolden was, tille he com so nehi. 1470–85 MALORY *Arthur* XII. i. 593 Come not to nyȝ for and thow doo.. I will slee the. 1667 MILTON *P.L.* v. 82 So saying, he drew nigh. 1772–84 *Cook's Voy.* (1790) V. 1618 They came so nigh, that we could discern, with our glasses, the deserters fastened together. 1825 J. NEAL *Bro. Jonathan* I. 332 The.. dog would not leave him; but crawled nigher. 1879 BROWNING *Ivan Ivanovitch* 92 What help, as nigher and nigher, The flames came furious?

†**d.** With verbs of striking, wounding, etc.

1535 COVERDALE *Bible* Prol., Euery one doth his best to be nyest the marke.., yet shuteth one nyer then another. 1590 GREENE *Palmer's Ode* Wks. (Rtldg.) 295/1 [He] with a dart that wounded nigh Pierc'd my heart as I did lie. 1671 MILTON *P.R.* IV. 489 Other harm Those terrors.. did me none,.. though noising loud And threatning nigh.

e. *Naut.* Close to the wind. *rare*$^{-1}$.

a 1687 VILLIERS (Dk. Buckhm.) *Cabin-Boy* Wks. 1705 II. 101 Nay he could Sail a Yatcht both nigh and large.

6. Of approaching or impending times or events.

Beowulf 1743 Bið se slæp to fæst.., bona swiðe neah. c 825 *Vesp. Hymns* vii. 68 Forðon neh is deȝ forlorenisse heara. 971 *Blickl. Hom.* 107 Maȝon we.. nu ȝeseon.. þæt þisses middanȝeardes ende swiþe neah is. a 1300 *Cursor M.* 14908 He þe time seis command nei. 1382 WYCLIF *Joel* ii. 1 For niȝ is the day of derknessis and myst. c 1400 *Destr. Troy* 7808 The night was so nighe, þat noyet hym sore. 1535 COVERDALE *Jas.* v. 8 The commynge of the Lorde draweth nye. 1559 *Mirr. Mag.* (1563) 35 Than wo and wrack, disease, and nede be nyest. 1666 DRYDEN *Ann. Mirab.* cii, Till the fresh air proclaimed the morning nigh. 1687 A. LOVELL tr. *Thevenot's Trav.* I. 45 Finding the Hour draw nigh, when it is lawful for them to drink and eat. 1866 NEALE *Sequences & Hymns* 130 The hour is nigh—far nigher may it be Than yet I deem.

7. Of relationship, friendship, or union. (Cf. 11.)

1382 WYCLIF *Ruth* iii. 12 Ne I denye me to be nyȝ, but there is another nerre than Y. c 1449 PECOCK *Repr.* II. xx. 272 More or lasse aftir that thilk ioynyng.. is more or lasse nyȝer or romber. a 1500 *Geste R. Hood* in Child *Ballads* III. 78/2 The pryoresse of Kyrkesly, That nye was of his kynne. 1549 COVERDALE, etc. *Erasm. Par. 2 Cor.* 51 b, [He] coumpteth hym nyghest of his kynne, whiche hath in his promisses moste affiaunce. 1628 SIR W. MURE *Domesday* 534 How more sublime the Object bee, The Union inward and more nie.

8. In phrases: †**a.** ***of*, *in*, or *from nigh***, close, near at hand. *Obs.*

a 1225 *Ancr. R.* 250 Derne nondunges, þet he scheoteð of feor, &.. tentaciuns keoruinde of neih. 1382 WYCLIF *Esther* ix. 20 The Jewis that in alle the prouyncis of the king dwelten, bothe in neeȝh set and afer. 14.. *Voc.* in Wr.-Wülcker 578/12 *Deprope*, fro ny. c 1489 CAXTON *Sonnes of Aymon* iii. 101 Charlemagne followed theym well of nyghe.

b. ***nigh at hand***. (See HAND *sb.* 25.)

a 1300 *Cursor M.* 15709 He es cumand negh at hand. c 1400 *Destr. Troy* 1948 Þere Nestor the noble Duke was negh at his hond. 1535 COVERDALE *2 Esdras* ii. 34 He is nye at hande, that shal come in the ende of the worlde. 1590 SPENSER *F.Q.* I. i. 7 To seeke some covert nigh at hand. 1671 MILTON *P.R.* I. 20 The great Proclaimer.. cri'd.. Heavens Kingdom nigh at hand. 1790 PALEY *Horæ Paul.* 271 He now regards the decision of his fate as nigh at hand.

†**c.** ***nigh and far***. (Cf. FAR *adv.* 1 b, and OE. *ȝe neah ȝe feor*.) *Obs. rare.*

1422 tr. *Secreta Secret., Priv. Priv.* 208 By the eyghen know we.. thynges neygh and ferre, meuynge and restynge. 1599 DAVIES *Immort. Soul* ii. (1742) 14 Mine Eyes, which view all Objects nigh and far.

9. *Comb.* as ***nigh-adjoinant*, *-coming*, *-dwelling*; *-dweller***. Also †***nigh-aimed***, hit by close aiming.

c 1400 tr. *Secreta Secret., Gov. Lordsh.* 97 Setyng, remuynge & neghcomyng, sterynge & rest. 1429 *Rolls of Parlt.* IV. 345/1 Nygh adjoynaunt to the Rever. 1553 GRIMALDE *Cicero's Offices* II. (1558) 100 Letting nye dwellynges and partie boundes, to be just and gentle. 1591 SPENSER *M. Hubberd* 742 Now his bright armes assaying,.. Now the nigh aymed ring away to beare. 1867 MUSGRAVE *Nooks & Corners Old France* II. 145 These quarrymen.. would prove more troublesome nigh-dwellers than they in fact are.

III. *adj.* In attributive use.

10. Of places, persons, or things. (In later use chiefly in comparative and superlative.)

c 900 tr. *Bæda's Hist.* IV. i. (Ca.), On þam neahȝum mynstre [*al.* neahnunnmynstre]. c 1330 R. BRUNNE *Chron. Wace* (Rolls) 5941 To ney neygheburs, & ferþer fro. c 1380 WYCLIF *Sel. Wks.* III. 175 Neyȝghe neiȝbores þat hadde riȝt to þese godes. 1432–50 tr. *Higden* (Rolls) I. 299 The nyer Speyne to theis costes begynnethe from the hilles Pirene. 1540–1 ELYOT *Image Gov.* (1556) 36 By the examinacion of theyr nighest neighbours. 1590 SPENSER *F.Q.* III. xii. 1 She heard a shrilling Trompet sound alowd, Signe of nigh battaill, or got victory. 1711 *Fingall MSS.* in *10th Rep. Hist. MSS. Comm.* App. V. 131 They had orders to remain at the nigher end of the four mile pass. 1798 COLERIDGE *Frost at Midn.* 69 The nigh thatch Smokes in the sun-thaw. 1827 J. F. COOPER *Prairie* I. i. 23 The distance from this place to the nighest point on the main river. 1868 MORRIS *Earthly Par.* I. 96 [He] seized the nighest ship.

fig. 1598 BACON *Medit., Hypocrites* Ess. (Arb.) 117 Vnto this ordinance that other Hipocrisie is a nigh neyghbour.

b. Of ways or roads. (See NEAR *a.* 5.)

1516 *Life St. Bridget* in *Myrr. our Ladye*, etc. p. li, Thy doughter by the nyghest waye shall goo vnto the kyngdome of heuyn. 1547 *Homilies* I. *Whoredom* I. (1640) 80 Is there any nigher way to lead unto damnation? 1765 R. ROGERS *Jrnl.* (1883) 136 The General.. ordered me.. to proceed across the Chestnut Plain the nighest and best way I could, to Lake Champlain. 1823 SCOTT *Quentin D.* xxxii, The nigher and the safer road to Liege.

†**c.** Of causes: Immediate, proximate. *Obs.*

1551 T. WILSON *Logike* (1580) 44 Good heede ought to bee had,.. that the nye causes and the farthest causes, be not taken al for one. 1620 T. GRANGER *Div. Logike* 49 The father is the nighest cause of the sonne.

d. = NEAR *a.* 3. Also *Comb.* as ***nigh-side***.

1722 *Lond. Gaz.* No. 6063/4 A white Heel on the Nigh Leg behind. 1823 J. F. COOPER *Pioneers* v, It was only pulling hard on the nigh rein, and touching the off flank of the leader. 1844 H. STEPHENS *Bk. Farm* I. 626 The nigh trace-chain of the nigh horse is hooked to the end.. of the swing-tree. *Ibid.* II. 540 The nigh-side shaft being laid upon the side-rail.

11. Of relatives or friends. (Cf. 7.)

c 1205 LAY. 10260 Ne bi-læfde he her neouðer suster ne broðer, ne quene ne næh cun. 1377 LANGL. *P. Pl.* B. XII. 95 Kynde Witte is of his kyn and neighe cosynes bothe To owre lorde. 1432–50 tr. *Higden* (Rolls) IV. 155 The grownde scholde be taken to the nyeste of his bloode. 1470–85 MALORY *Arthur* III. xii. 114 This lady is my kynneswoman nygh. c 1538 in Archbold *Somers. Rel. Houses* (1892) 93 Doctor Tregonwell.. hath obteigned the same for a nygh frende of his. 1650 TRAPP *Comm. Num.* xviii. 22 Gods Kinsmen,.. according to some translations, or his nigh-Ones.

absol. 1382 WYCLIF *Lev.* xxi. 2 Oonly in cosyns, and nyȝ [L. *propinquis*], that is, vpon fader and moder. —— *Prov.* xxiii. 11 The neeȝh [L. *propinquus*].. of them is strong.

** *Denoting approximation in degree, amount, etc.*

IV. *adv.* **12.** Nearly, almost, all but.

c 893 K. ÆLFRED *Oros.* I. i. 17 Þa Finnas.. & þa Beormas spræcon neah an ȝeþeode. c 1000 *Sax. Leechd.* I. 254 Heo hafað leaf neah swylce mistel. c 1200 ORMIN 3206 Till þatt he waxenn wass, & neh Of þrittiȝ winnterr elde. c 1250 *Gen. & Ex.* 1234 His moder wurð neȝ dead for friȝt. c 1290 *St. Brendan* 714 in *S. Eng. Leg.* I. 239 Þou schalt sone out of þis world, þi lijf is neiȝ at þende. 1340 *Ayenb.* 76 Huerof al þe wordle ys nyeȝ begyled. 1390 GOWER *Conf.* I. 33 This ymage is nyh overthrowe. c 1440 *Gesta Rom.* xii. 40 (Harl. MS.), By chaunce I was ny dreynt in a water. 1470–85 MALORY *Arthur* XI. viii. 582 Thenne the quene was nyghe oute of her wytte. 1523 LD. BERNERS *Froiss.* I. xviii. 25 They were nigh so feble that it shulde haue ben great peyne for them to haue goon any forther. 1590 SPENSER *F.Q.* I. iii. 13 Nigh dead with feare.. Shee found them both. 1667 MILTON *P.L.* x. 159 To whom sad Eve with shame nigh overwhelm'd,.. thus abasht repli'd. 1817 SHELLEY *Rev. Islam* x. xxxv, Kingly thrones, which rest on faith, nigh overturned. 1872 TENNYSON *Gareth & Lynette* 769 The wood is nigh as full of thieves as leaves.

b. With terms of quantity or number.

c 1055 *O.E. Chron.* (MS. C.) an. 1055 Ða gaderade man fyrde ȝeond eall Englaland swyðe neah. c 1200 ORMIN 1892 Acc Marrch was þa Neh all gan ut til ende. c 1250 *Gen. & Ex.* 833 Neȝ ilc burȝe hadde ise louereding. 1297 R. GLOUC. (Rolls) 4025 Hit is ney vif ȝer þat we abbeþ yliued in such vice. 1387 TREVISA *Higden* (Rolls) III. 147 He.. made fre ny fifty þowsand men. 1450–1530 *Myrr. our Ladye* 249 Nye all that knew him fleyng away from hym. 1559 *Mirr. Mag., Dk. Suffolk* vii, I gave nie five times five assaultes. 1672 SIR P. LEYCESTER *Hist. Antiq.* II. I. iii, Ethelred.. restored Caerleon,.. and made it nigh such two as it was before. 1890 BICKLEY *Surrey Hills* i, Nigh ten mile a day. 1896 CHANTER *Witch* i, Father he were huntsman.. for nigh forty year.

c. With *about* (*-but*), *on*, †*than*, *upon*.

c 1200 *Trin. Coll. Hom.* 33 Adam.. ledde after him neih þan al his ofspreng. c 1205 LAY. 22340 Þa Irisce men weoren nakede neh þan. 1632 LITHGOW *Trav.* IV. 149 Nigh about the same time it is obserued that Boniface the third begun his Empire. 1829 LANDOR *Imag. Conv., Chaucer*, etc. Wks. 1853 I. 405/1 Early on the second morning he was nigh upon twenty miles from home. 1854 DICKENS *Hard T.* I. xi, I were one-and-twenty myseln; she were twenty nigh-but. 1870 VERNEY *Lettice Lisle* x, I'm nighabouts twice eighteen. 1887 BARING-GOULD *Gaverocks* III. xlii. 10 It nigh on broke your dear mother's heart.

d. With negatives or *as*. (Cf. NEAR *adv.*^{2} 6, 8.)

c 888 K. ÆLFRED *Boeth.* xviii. §1 Eall moncynn & ealle netenu ne notiȝað nawer neah feorðan dæles þisse eorðan. a 1000 *Boeth. Metr.* xxx. 10 Ne mæȝ hio þeah ȝescinan... ahwærȝen neah ealla ȝesceafta. 1559 MORWYNG *Evonym.* 141 They attain un-to a certain incorruption as nye as may be. 1567 in *Vicary's Anat.* (1888) App. iii. 154 [To] make an estymate as neight as they can, what the Charges of the doyng thereof will amount vnto. 1691 NORRIS *Pract. Disc.* I The thorough Fool is not nigh so great a Prodigy as the Half-wise Man.

†**13.** Nearly, closely. (Denoting that little or nothing is left.) *Obs.*

c 1386 CHAUCER *Prol.* 590 His berd was schave as neigh as ever he can. c 1399 —— *Purse* 19 For I am shave as nye as is a frere. 1496 *Fysshynge w. Angle* (1883) 15 Kytte of the lynys ende & the threde as nyghe as ye maye. 1563 *Homilies* II. *Rogation Week* IV. (1640) 237 Charging the owners not to gather up their corne too nigh at harvest season.. but to leave behind some eares. 1587 MASCALL *Govt. Cattle, Oxen* (1627) 98 To heale the kibes, ye shall cut them forth as nie as ye can.

14. Near or close (to), in respect of attainment, resemblance, †likelihood, etc. †***nothing nigh***, nothing like.

c 1380 WYCLIF *Wks.* (1880) 339 Men þat.. ben full nyȝ to synne aȝeyne han no penaunce of her synne. 1500–20 DUNBAR *Poems* lxxxviii. 52 No Lord of Parys, Venyce, or Floraunce In dignytie or honoure goeth to hym nye. 1565 COOPER *Thesaurus* s.v. *A*, To be in case verie nie to be a banished man. 1666 BUNYAN *Grace Abound.* §154 This [sin] came nighest to mine of any that I could find. 1743 BULKELEY & CUMMINS *Voy. S. Seas* 119 We answered them that the Water was smoother without, and nothing nigh the Sea that runs within. 1847 L. HUNT *Men, Women, & B.* II. x. 225 Her sarcasms and self-will.. go nigh to confirm it. 1889 THEO. GIFT *Not for the Night-time* 45 [He] struck down and went nigh to murder the man.

15. As *adj.* Close, near; parsimonious.

1555 W. WATREMAN *Fardle of Facions* App. 325 There cometh not so greate profite to the owners by the nighe gatheryng. 1856 P. THOMPSON *Hist. Boston* 716 *Nye*, near, stingy, mean. 1866 BROGDEN *Prov. Words Linc.* s.v. *Nye*, Although holding a good position in the county he is a nye man.

†**b.** Coming near in amount. *Obs. rare*$^{-1}$.

1557 RECORDE *Whetst.* D ij b, Thei will helpe you to gesse at the nigheste rootes of nombers that be not square.

16. *Comb.*, as ***nigh-destroyed*, *-drowned*, *-ebbed*, *-naked*, *-spent***.

1598 F. ROUS *Thule* O 2 b, O cease (quoth they) to make an ouerflow Ouer the bounds of our ny-drowned mindes. 1649 OGILBY tr. *Virg. Georg.* II. (1684) 91 Nigh-destroyed Realms. 1768–74 TUCKER *Lt. Nat.* (1834) II. 638 The nigh-spent hour-glass of time. 1864 TENNYSON *En. Ard.* 677 On the nigh-naked tree the Robin piped. 1868 MORRIS *Earthly Par.* (1870) I. i. 125 The nigh-ebbed windless sea In the still evening murmured ceaselessly.

nigh (naɪ), *v.* Now *rare.* Forms: α. 3 **neh(h)ȝhenn, nehyen, neȝȝen, 3–5 nehe(n, neghe(n, 4 neghȝe, neȝhe, newhe, 4–5 neȝe**; *Sc.* 5 **nech(t, 6 nee.** β. 3–4 **neihen, 3–5 neiȝe(n, 4 neiȝhe, neiye, 4–5 (7, 9) neigh(e; 3–5 neye, (4 nay-), 4–5 neyhe, (5 -hhe), neyȝe, (4 -ȝþe), neyghe, 5** *Sc.* **neych.** γ. 4 **niȝe, 4–5 nyhe, 5 nyȝhe, nyegh, 4–6 nyghe, 5** *Sc.* **nycht, nicht, 5–6** *Sc.* **nich, 4–7 nye, 4– nigh.** [f. NIGH *adv.* Cf. MDu. *nahen* (rare), OS. *nâhian*, OHG. *nâhên* (MHG. *nâhen*, *nân*, G. *nahen*, *nahn*), ON. *ná* (Sw. *nå*, Da. *naa*), Goth. *nêhwjan*.]

1. *trans.* To go, come, or draw near to (a person, place, etc.); to approach closely. (Common c 1300–1500.)

c 1200 ORMIN 8077 Swa he stannc þat iwhillc mann Wass himm full laþ to nehhȝhenn. c 1220 *Bestiary* 147 Ðe neddre .. If he naked man se, ne wile he him noȝt neȝȝen. c 1330 R. BRUNNE *Chron. Wace* (Rolls) 3294 Als þey ryfled landes ay whore, Rome þey neighed ay þe more. 1377 LANGL. *P. Pl.* B. XVII. 58 Feith.. nolde nouȝt neighen hym by nyne londes lengthe. 1451 *Rolls of Parlt.* V. 216/2 If eny of the said persones be compelled.. to nygh youre persone. 1530 PALSGR. 644/1 Or it be nyght we shall nyghe the towne. 15.. *Christ's Kirk* 15 Thay wer sa nyss quhen men thame nicht, Thay squelit lyke ony gaitis. 1654 GAYTON *Pleas. Notes* IV. xxii. 274 Not Perseus horse.. Flies like to this (if any dangers nigh him). 1766 *Chron.* in *Ann. Reg.* 190/1 Jumping upon deck, and crying out 'She nighs us! she nighs us! she is standing this way!' 1806 J. GRAHAME *Birds of Scot.* 80 Now she nighs the carnage-freighted keel. 1817 SCOTT *Harold* IV. ix, Sooner than Walwayn my sick couch should nigh, My choice were, by leach-craft unaided to die.

†**b.** To approach so as to touch or handle. *Obs.*

c 1200 ORMIN 4491 Þatt tu nan oþerr manness wif Ne ȝeorne nohht to nehȝhenn Wiþþ unnclænnessess fule lusst. a 1225 *Ancr. R.* 134 He is þe achate þet atter of sunne ne neihede neuere. a 1300 *Cursor M.* 2422 Þat moght naman o licherie Hir body neght wit wilanie. *Ibid.* 10877 Womman þat neuer neghed man. c 1420 *Avow. Arth.* liv, Lye downe preuely hur by, Butte neghe noȝte thou that lady. c 1440 *Anc. Cookery* in *Househ. Ord.* (1790) 433 Take a faire urthen pot, and lay hit well with splentes in the bothum, that the flessh neigh hit not. 15.. *Adam Bell* iii. 258 But Cloudesle clefte the apple in twaine, His sonne he did not nee. 1674 RAY *N.C. Words* 34 *To nigh a thing*, to touch it. I did not nigh it: *i.e.* I came not nigh it.

†**c.** To take or accept. *Obs. rare*$^{-1}$.

13.. *Gaw. & Gr. Knt.* 1836 He nay[ed] þat he nolde neghe in no wyse Nauþer golde ne garysoun.

†**d.** To touch or concern (one) closely. *Obs. rare.*

c 1450 HOLLAND *Howlat* 276 Sen it nechit Natur.. Thai couth nocht trete but entent of the Temperale. c 1489 CAXTON *Blanchardyn* 135 The proude pucell.. reioysched her self.., by cause that this nyghed her at herte.

2. ***it nighs***: †**a.** It draws near or close to (a certain time). *Obs.*

The *it* appears orig. to be in apposition to the noun.

c 1200 *Vices & Virtues* 121 Nimeð scrifte of ȝewer sennes, hit neihedð heuene riche. a 1310 in Wright *Lyric P.* xxviii. 84 Me thynketh hit neȝyth domesday. c 1350 *Will. Palerne* 2599 Whan it neiȝet niȝt, þei nold no lenger a-bide. c 1430 *Syr Gener.* (Roxb.) 6989 Whan he saw it nighed night, Oute of the forest he went a right.

b. It draws *to* or *towards* a time. †Also with *at*.

a 1300 *Cursor M.* 14913 Fast it neghes to þe nede For his to suffur passion. 13.. *Gaw. & Gr. Knt.* 929 Hit was neȝ at þe niyȝt neȝed þe tyme. c 1400 *Destr. Troy* 672 Hit neght to þe night & the none past. c 1425 *Seven Sag.* (P.) 331 Hit neght fast toward nyght. 1821 *Blackw. Mag.* X. 124 When it nigh'd to Christmas-tide, I cut the holly's glorious bough.

3. *intr.* To draw or come near *toward* or *to* a person, place, etc.

c **1200** ORMIN 12794 Loc, here nehȝheþþ towarrd me.. An soþ Issraelisshe mann. *a* **1300** *Cursor M.* 11846 Moght nan for stinck negh til his bedd. *a* **1340** HAMPOLE *Psalter* xxxi. 8 Til him þai sall noght neghe. *c* **1400** MAUNDEV. (1839) v. 40 But it is fulle longe sithe that ony Man durste neyhe to the Tour. *c* **1450** tr. *De Imitatione* II. xii. 56 þan all þe seruauntes of þe crosse.. shul nye vnto crist þe Juge wiþ gret trust. **1496** *Dives & Pauper* (W. de W.) x. ii. 373/1 Ryght as theyr bodye by age nygheth to the erth. *a* **1821** KEATS *Hyperion* II. 103 The laden heart Is persecuted more.. When it is nighing to a mournful house.

transf. *a* **1300** *Cursor M.* 9977 [She] neghed neuer to wik dede, Bot euer sco liued in maiden-hede.

†**b.** To pierce *to*, to light *on*, the skin. *Obs. rare.*

a **1400–50** *Alexander* 4182 And quare it neȝes on þe nakid it noyis for euire. *c* **1400** *Destr. Troy* 6403 He shot þrough the shild & the shene maile..; Hit neghit to þe nakid.

4. To go, come, or draw near; to approach.

a **1300** *Cursor M.* 1009 Paradis is a.. land.. þar neuer neghes nede ne night. **13..** *Gaw. & Gr. Knt.* 132 An oþer noyse ful newe neȝed biliue. **1387** TREVISA *Higden* (Rolls) I. 101 No man durste neyhe, but he were purified and i-made all clene. *c* **1430** *Pilgr. Lyf Manhode* I. xxv. (1869) 16 þan is a welle closed þer neuere oon dar neighe ne aproche. **1551** CROWLEY *Pleas. & Payne* 425 Your wycked soule shall neuer nye, But lyue in payne for euermore. **1630** J. LANE *Contn. Sqr.'s T.* (Chaucer Soc.) 140 Looke how fast, at first, the Rebells nyed, so fast and faster now they rann to hide. **1898** T. HARDY *Wessex Poems* 71 The first battle nighed on the low Southern side.

b. Of time or events, etc.

c **1275** *O.E. Misc.* 142/42 þis world is neyh þan ende; þe deþ neyeþ blyue. **13..** *E.E. Allit. P.* B. 1754 Nyȝt neȝed ryȝt now with nyes fol mony. **1382** WYCLIF *Matt.* iii. 2 Do ȝe penaunce, for the kyngdom of heuens shal neiȝ. **1422** tr. *Secreta Secret., Priv. Priv.* 175 Many dayes Passyd, the terme neyghed, and he came not. *c* **1460** *Launfal* 829 The certayn day was nyghyng. **1515** *Scottish Field* 198 in *Chetham Misc.* (1856) Then nighed the night that byde must they nedes. **1595** SPENSER *Epithal.* 298 Now day is doen, and night is nighing fast.

†**5.** Followed by *nigh* adv. or prep. *Obs.* (Common *c* 1300–1450.)

a **1300** *Cursor M.* 21062 Iohn.. sei his ending dai him neghand nei [*Edinb.* neiȝand neich]. *c* **1350** *Will. Palerne* 1606 Whan þemperour of grece neiyed neiȝh rome. *c* **1400** *Destr. Troy* 4863 þai wete not.. þat we be neghit so negh. **1447** BOKENHAM *Seyntys* (Roxb.) 302 Whan hyr tym neyhyd ny, That ys to seyn whan she shuld deye.

†**b.** Similarly with *near* adv. and prep. *Obs.* (Very common *c* 1375–1450.)

a **1300** *Cursor M.* 5239 Quen iacob neghed egypte nere. *c* **1375** *Sc. Leg. Saints* xlix. (*Thecla*) 218 Syne come a lyone fel & fere & to sla tecle nichit nere. *c* **1425** WYNTOUN *Cron.* I. xiii. 1160 Thare is nane dar necht it nere. *c* **1450** *St. Cuthbert* (Surtees) 4395 It neghid nere þe tyme of none. **1530** *Hickscorner* 209 A knave catchpoll nyghed us nere.

Hence '**nighing** *vbl. sb.* and *ppl. a.*

1388 WYCLIF *Judith* xvi. 10 *marg.*, Bi this thing Judith schulde haue homeli neiȝing to him. **1434** *Rolls of Parlt.* V. 435/2 The neghing and dayly prees of the Werre therby to your gode Toune. *c* **1449** PECOCK *Repr.* II. viii. 182 A comoun place to which peple may haue her deuout neiȝing and accesse. **1596** LODGE *Marg. Amer.* 15 Midst thy pompe thy nying grave remember. **1818** KEATS in *Life & Lett.* (1848) I. 236, I look with hope to the nighing time when I shall have none.

nigh by, *adv.* (and *a.*) [f. NIGH *adv.* + BY: cf. MDu. *nabi* (Du. *nabij*) and see NEAR BY.]

†**1.** *adv.* Nearly, almost. *Obs. rare.*

c **1400** LOVE *Bonavent. Mirr.* xxxiv. (B.N.C. MS.) lf. 83 Not only lered and lewed seculeres, but also religiouse nyh by in alle astates. **1448** SHILLINGFORD *Lett.* (Camden) 141 Whiche brigge is of the lengthe, or negh by, and of the same mason werk as London brigge.

2. Near to; near by, near at hand. Also as *adj.*

c **1500** *Melusine* 244 They came & lodged them in the medow nygh by Lucembourgh. **1526** *Pilgr. Perf.* (W. de W. 1531) 3 There is a place here nye by, there y^u^ shalt stande. **1823** J. F. COOPER *Pioneers* xi, Benjamin.. posted himself nigh by. **1826** —— *Mohicans* (1829) II. iii. 37 They found the scout awaiting their appearance nigh by. **1889** A. T. PASK *Eyes Thames* 141 The waters of the nigh-by fountain would sound like gruesome whispers.

†**nighen**, *v. Obs. rare.* In 4 neiȝne, neyȝne. [f. NIGH *adv.* + -EN[5]: cf. MHG. *næhenen* (early mod.G. *nähenen*, *nähnen*, etc.).] To come near.

a **1400** *Prymer* (1891) 26 Ympne to alle his halwen.., to folk that neiȝneth to hym. *Ibid.* 53 Streyne thow here chekes that neyȝneth nouȝt to the.

nigh hand, *adv.* [f. NIGH *adv.* + HAND *sb.* Cf. NEAR HAND.]

1. Near or close at hand; close by.

a **1122** *O.E. Chron.* (Laud MS.) an. 1100 þa witan þe þa neh handa wæron, his broðer Heanriȝ to cynge ȝecuran. *a* **1225** *Ancr. R.* 424 Ancre þet naueð nout neih hond hire uode, beoð bisie two wummen. *c* **1275** *O.E. Misc.* 85/46 þat schal cume þe ilke day, and nv he is neyh honde. *c* **1320** *Cast. Love* 444 Pes ne bydyth in no londe Ther as Werre is nyȝhhonde. *a* **1400** *Pistill of Susan* 348 An angel is neih honde.. Wiþ a brennynge bronde. **1470–85** MALORY *Arthur* VII. xx. 244 His castel is here nyhe hand but two myle. **1551** ROBINSON tr. *More's Utop.* II. (1895) 161 They mayе be welcome to good and fyne fare so nyghe hande at the hall. **1588** PARKE tr. *Mendoza's Hist. China* 332 They of this towne.. fled vnto the mountaines that were nighest hande. **1600** FAIRFAX *Tasso* VI. xli, The shocke made.. woods and mountaines all nie-hand resound. **1667** MILTON *P.L.* III. 566 Amongst innumerable Starrs, that shon Stars distant, but nigh hand seemd other Worlds. **1890** W. A. WALLACE *Only a Sister?* 80, I shan't forget it till I die, but that's nigh hand now, I'm assured.

b. Governing a *sb.* Near, close to (a person or place).

a **1300** *Cursor M.* 12863 Ihesus to þat water yode, And sant Ihon neghand him stode. *c* **1330** R. BRUNNE *Chron.* (1810) 161 R. rode stilly neihand þe Emperour. *c* **1440** *Generydes* 951 He had them sett Nyhand the town. **1860** READE *Cloister & H.* lv, So forward, Bon Bec, for my life is not sure nigh hand this town.

2. Almost, nearly.

c **1350** *Will. Palerne* 1494 He þan swoned for sorwe & swelt neiȝhonde. **1398** TREVISA *Barth. De P.R.* xv. xx, Here londe is closid all aboute with nyȝe honde with woodes and mounteynes. *a* **1450** *Le Morte Arth.* 1591 In poynte had he nevir bene So nyghe hande for to haue be slayne. *a* **1548** HALL *Chron., Hen. VIII*, 123 b, All the peisants.. nye hand to the nomber of vii. or viii. score. **1592** G. HARVEY *Four Lett.* iii. 38, I had nigh-hand ouer-skipped the learned allegation in the margine. **1784** *Unfortunate Sensibility* II. 70 He said he could tell me of something that he dared say would go nigh hand to make me well. **1842** LOVER *Handy Andy* ix, Wasn't it enough for you to nigh-hand kill one of my horses? **1883** STEVENSON *Treas. Isl.* xvi, He came nigh-hand fainting, doctor, when he heard the cry.

So †**nigh hands** *adv.*, nearly. *Obs. rare*[−1].

c **1350** *Will. Palerne* 438, I mase al marred for mournyng neiȝh hondes.

nighly ('naɪlɪ), *adv.* Also 1 néalíce, 4 neli, 6 nyghly. [OE. *néalíce* = MDu. *nalike*, *-lijc*, *-lic*, OHG. *nâhlîcho* (MHG. *næhlîchen*), ON. *náliga*: see NIGH *adv.* and -LY[2].]

1. Nearly, almost.

971 *Blickl. Hom.* 207 On sumre stowe he wæs þæt man mid his handa nealice ȝeræcean mihte. *a* **1300** *Cursor M.* 7700 Oft þe chances sua þai fell, þat neli was þam noght e-mell. **13..** *Ibid.* 19124 (Edinb.), þe saduceis, namlic þat lede, for puprising walde neli wede. **1690** LOCKE *Hum. Und.* II. ix. §8 A Cube and a Sphere of the same metal, and nighly of the same bigness. **1744** MITCHELL in *Phil. Trans.* XLIII. 110 The Cuticle, which is separated, appears nighly of the same Colour on the Outside. **1832** L. HUNT *Sir R. Esher* (1850) 349 This old servant, old and nighly worn out. **1861** CDL. WISEMAN in *Ess. Relig. & Lit.* Ser. I. (1865) 15 Literature had apparently most nighly reached enervation.

†**2.** Nearly, closely. *Obs.*

1534 CROMWELL in Merriman *Life & Lett.* (1902) I. 377 That thing whiche semed to concerne his grace and his reigne so nyghly. **1589** COOPER *Admon.* 144 Now I must come to that which toucheth bishops most nighlie. **1651** N. BACON *Disc. Govt. Eng.* II. xxxi. (1739) 142 Especially such of them as most nighly related to Prerogative. **1691** W. NICHOLLS *Answ. Naked Gospel* 73 To suffer this.. for being so nighly related to a wicked Soul.

†**3.** Niggardly, sparingly. *Obs. rare.*

1548 ELYOT *Auare*,.. couetously, nyghly, nygardly. **1579** SPENSER *Sheph. Cal.* July 171 Theyr weedes bene not so nighly wore; Such simplesse mought them shend.

nighness ('naɪnɪs). ? *Obs.* [f. NIGH *a.* + -NESS.]

1. Nearness in place (or time), proximity.

1398 TREVISA *Barth. De P.R.* XI. i. (Bodl. MS.), Chaunginge of aiere comeþ of nyȝenes of þe see. **1432–50** tr. *Higden* (Rolls) I. 159 The nyȝhenesse of the sonne dothe brenne. **1450–1530** *Myrr. our Ladye* 243 The nynesse of thornes lessyth not the smelle of the florysshynge rose. **1548** UDALL, etc. *Erasm. Par. John* i. 19 By reason of the nyenesse of the night. **1581** MULCASTER *Positions* xl. (1887) 224 That the nighnes of his maisters house can be no great vantage. **1615** DAY *Festivals* xii. 328 The Neighbourhood, and Nighnes of such as dwell in the selfsame Streete. **1691** WOOD *Antiq.* II. *Fasti* 264 The nighness of her Father's house to which.. hindered any communication between them.

2. Nearness *of* kinship, blood, etc.

1398 TREVISA *Barth. De P.R.* XIII. xxvi. (Bodl. MS.), Bitwene fissche & water is nyȝenes to cosynage, for wiþoute water þei mowe not longe lyue. **1432** *Paston Lett.* I. 34 Suche persones as for nieghnesse of blood.. owe of reson to be suffred to speke with the King. **1471** *Rolls of Parlt.* VI. 233/2 The nighnes of blood which they be of unto hym. **1554** KNOX *Faythf. Admon.* G ij, Regardynge nothynge the affinitie nor nyghnese of bloud. **1577** tr. *Bullinger's Decades* II. x. 227/2 Let them be matched together, that are not seuered by.. nighnesse of affinitie. **1662** J. CHANDLER *Van Helmont's Oriat.* 161 It was not required for one to know another, or judge of the nighness of their kin, by a name.

3. Nearness *of* a possibility. *rare*[−1].

1425 *Rolls of Parlt.* IV. 270/2 Ye nyeghnesse of possibilite of the enheritaunce of ye Croune.

†'**nighsome**, *a. Obs. rare.* In 4 negh(t)som. [f. NIGH *adv.* + -SOME, used to render L. *propitius*, etc., f. *prope* nigh] Favourable, gracious. Hence †'**nighsomeness**.

a **1300** *E.E. Psalter* lxiv. 4 Til our quednesses neghtsom saltou [L. *tu propitiaberis*]. *Ibid.* xcviii. 8 Neghsom [L. *propitius*] was tou vnto þa. *Ibid.* cxxix. 4 For at þe neghtsomnes [L. *propitiatio*] es to be.

night (naɪt), *sb.* Forms: α. 1 næcht, næht, neaht, 1, 4 naht, (3 nahht), 3–5 naght, (4 naȝt), 3 naught, (5 nauȝt). β. 1–4 nyht, 3–5 nyth, 5–6 *Sc.* nycht; 4–5 nyȝt, (4 nyȝtt, -tht), 4–6 nyght, (4 nygth); 1, 4 niht, (3 nihht, nieht), 3–6 nicht, (4 nith); 3–5 niȝt, 5 neght, 5–6 nighte, 3– night. [Common Teut.: OE. *niht*, *nyht*, and *neaht*, *næht* fem. = OFris. and MDu. *nacht*, OS. *naht* (MLG. *nacht*), OHG. *naht* (G. *nacht*), ON. *nátt*, *nótt* (Norw. *natt*, *nott*, Sw. *natt*, Da. *nat*), Goth. *nahts*. The pre-Teut. stem **nokt-* is widely represented in the cognate languages, as in L. *noct-*, *nox*, OIr. *nocht*, Gr. *νυκτ-*, *νύξ*, Skr. *nákta*, *nákti*, Lith. *naktis*, O.Pruss. *naktin*, OSl. *noshtĭ* (Russ. *noch'*). The variation in OE. between *neaht* (Anglian *næht*) and *niht* (for **nieht*) is orig. due to umlaut in some of the cases; in the later language the mutated form finally displaces the other.]

I. 1. a. The period of darkness which intervenes between day and day; that part of the natural day (of 24 hours) during which no light is received from the sun; the time between evening and morning.

α. *c* **825** *Vesp. Psalter* ciii. 20 Ðu settes ðeostru & ȝeworden wes naeht. *c* **950** *Lindisf. Gosp.* Matt. xiv. 25 Ðiu feorða waccen næhtes cuom [he] to him ȝeongende ofer sæ. *a* **1000** *Boeth. Metr.* xx. 229 Ealle hi scinað ðurh þa sciran neaht. *c* **1200** ORMIN 16942 þe nahht maȝȝ ec bitacnenn uss All þatt stafflike lare Off moysæsess laȝheboc.

β. *Beowulf* 115 [Grendel] ȝewat ða neosian, syþan niht becom, hean huses. *c* **888** K. ÆLFRED *Boeth.* xxxix. §13 Sio sunne & se mona habbað todæled betwuht him þone dæȝ & þa niht. **971** *Blickl. Hom.* 207 Næs hweðre næniȝ man þe þær æfre nihtes tidum dorste on þære ciricean cuman. *c* **1000** *Sax. Leechd.* III. 242 Seo niht hæfð seofan dælas fram þære sunnan settlunge oð hire upgang. *c* **1055** *Byrhtferth's Handboc* in *Anglia* VIII. 298 On anum dæȝe & þære nihte beoð feower & twentiȝ tida. *a* **1225** *Leg. Kath.* 1682 For þer is a liht,.. Ne niht nis ter neauer. *c* **1300** *Havelok* 404 Ihesu crist, that makede mone On þe mirke nith to shine. **13..** *E.E. Allit. P.* B. 526 Sesounes schal you neuer sese; of sede, ne of heruest..; Ne þe nyȝt, ne þe day. **1422** tr. *Secreta Secret., Priv. Priv.* 245 Than wixen the dayes more schorte than they weryn, and the nyght more longyr. **1490** CAXTON *Eneydos* xxiv. 90 Y^e^ nyghte.. gyueth triews to alle labours, and by sleypyng maketh swete alle peynes and traueylles. **1548** FORREST *Pleas. Poesye* 183 in *Starkey's Eng.* p. xc, The daye in too the nyght shee can conuerte. **1566** *Reg. Privy Council Scot.* I. 447 Undir silence of nycht befoir day. **1602** SHAKS. *Ham.* I. v. 10, I am thy Fathers Spirit, Doom'd for a certaine terme to walke the night. **1638** JUNIUS *Paint. Ancients* 166 Images of young men.. with torches in their hands, for the use of the night. **1712** BUDGELL *Spect.* No. 425 ¶3, I reflected.. upon the sweet Vicissitudes of Night and Day. **1742** YOUNG *Nt. Th.* I. 102 Ev'n silent night proclaims my soul immortal. **1821** SHELLEY *Adonais* xxi, Evening must usher night, night urge the morrow. **1890** HALL CAINE *Bondman* II. vii, The night of the northern land had closed down.

b. In comparisons, ***as black***, ***dark***, etc., ***as night***.

c **1400** *Pol. Rel. & L. Poems* 151/244 Thow shalt go as derk as nyȝt, And þerfore þou most haue condell lyȝt. **1595** SHAKS. *John* IV. i. 15 Yong Gentlemen would be as sad as night Onely for wantonnesse. **1596** —— *Merch. V.* v. i. 86 The motions of his spirit are dull as night. **1667** MILTON *P.L.* II. 308 His look Drew audience and attention still as Night. **1795** J. BENSON in *Mem.* (1892) 284 They were all as silent and serious as night. **1821** BYRON *Juan* III. lxxv, Her eyelashes, though dark as night, were tinged. **1893** EARL DUNMORE *Pamirs* I. 4 Their hair.. was as black as night.

c. *poet.* Personified as a female being or deity.

1590 SHAKS. *Mids. N.* III. ii. 387 They.. must for aye consort with blacke browd night. **1632** MILTON *Penseroso* 121 Thus night oft see me in thy pale career. **1742** POPE *Dunc.* IV. 630 The sable Throne behold Of Night primæval and of Chaos old. **1788** COLERIDGE *To Autumnal Moon*, Mild Splendour of the various-vested Night. **1820** SHELLEY *Sensit. Pl.* II. 11 Like the lamps of the air when Night walks forth. **1845** LONGF. *The Day is done* i, The darkness Falls from the wings of Night.

d. The darkness which prevails during this time; the dark.

1855 TENNYSON *Maud* I. I. iv, I heard The shrill-edged shriek.. divide the shuddering night. **1879** E. ARNOLD *Lt. Asia* IV. (1883) 102 Then, lightly treading where those sleepers lay, Into the night Siddârtha passed.

2. In fig. contexts or uses.

c **950** *Lindisf. Gosp.* John ix. 4 Cymeð næht ðonne næniȝ monne mæȝe ȝewyrca. *c* **1200** ORMIN 1904 Crist ras upp.. Forr dæþess nahht to wannsenn. *c* **1250** *Gen. & Ex.* 89 For god ledde hem fro helle niȝt To paradises leue liȝt. *a* **1300** *Cursor M.* 3560 þe man þat sua wit eld es dight His day es turned him to night. **1382** WYCLIF *1 Thess.* v. 5 We ben not of nyȝt, nethir of derknessis. **1590** SHAKS. *Com. Err.* v. i. 314 Yet hath my night of life some memorie; My wasting lampes some fading glimmer left. **1593** —— *Rich. II*, III. ii. 218 Let them hence away, From Richards Night, to Bullingbrookes faire Day. *a* **1658** LOVELACE *Poems* (1659) 9 Some Ethiopian Queen,.. Whose ugly Night seem'd masked with days Skreen. **1697** DRYDEN *Æneid* IV. 992 Dido.. clos'd her Lids at last, in endless Night. **1720** J. HUGHES *Siege Damascus* v. (1777) 68 Look how he bleeds! Let's lay him gently down; Night gathers fast upon him. **1782** PRIESTLEY *Corrupt. Chr.* I. Pref. 5 Night.. has for many centuries obscured our holy religion. **1820** SHELLEY *Arethusa* 66 Where the shadowy waves Are as green as the forest's night. **1847** TENNYSON *Princ.* IV. 470 Robed in the long night of her deep hair.

3. The time at which darkness comes on; the close or end of daylight.

c **1205** LAY. 1680 þat com to þere nihte, þat lengre heo ne mighte. *c* **1300** *Havelok* 2669 So was bi-twenen hem a fiht Fro þe morwen ner to þe niht. **1340** HAMPOLE *Pr. Consc.* 2669 At morne, when þou sese lyght, Thynk als þou sal dygh ar nyght. **13..** *E.E. Allit. P.* B. 484 Hit was nyȝe at þe naȝt & Noe þen sechez. *c* **1470** HENRY *Wallace* I. 255 3hit this gud wiff held Wallace till the nycht. **1590** SHAKS. *Mids. N.* III. ii. 275 Since night you lou'd me; yet since night you left me. **1671** MILTON *P.R.* II. 260 It was the hour of night, when thus the Son Commun'd in silent walk. **1703** ROWE *Ulyss.* IV. i, Twice have I sought since Night To pass in private.

4. With *a* and *pl.* One of the intervals of darkness between two days.

a. Used with numerals to mark duration or lapse of time.

In OE. and early ME. the singular is used in place of the plural: cf. FORTNIGHT and SE(VE)NNIGHT.

a **900** CYNEWULF *Crist* 542 Bidon ealle þær.. in þære torhtan byriȝ tyn niht. *c* **900** *O.E. Chron.* (Parker MS.) an. 871 Ðæs ymb iii niht ridon ii eorlas up. *a* **1122** *O.E. Chron.*

(Laud MS.) an. 1004 Se here com þa to þeodforda..& þær binnon ane niht wæron. *c* **1205** LAY. 4506 Næuede heo bute þreo nihte feorst faren þat heo scolde. *c* **1275** *Serving Christ* 3 in *O.E. Misc.* 90 Ne beo we siker of þe lif on-lepy nauht. *a* **1300** *Cursor M.* 12926 Iesus..fasted..fourti night and fourti dais. *c* **1325** *Chron. Eng.* 157 in Ritson *Metr. Rom.* II. 276 Ther spac an ern [a] prophecie Thre dawes and thre nyht. *c* **1374** CHAUCER *Troylus* IV. 588 Ek wonder last but nine nyght nevere in towne. **1422** tr. *Secreta Secret., Priv. Priv.* 153 He makyd the cite of Rome afyre to sette, and Sewyn dayes and Sewyn nyghtes to brente. **1470–85** MALORY *Arthur* IV. xxvi. 155 Within seuen nyghtes his damoysel brought hym to an erles place. **1599** SHAKS. *Much Ado* II. iii. 18 Now will he lie ten nights awake caruing the fashion of a new dublet. **1634** W. TIRWHYT tr. *Balzac's Lett.* 352 One night in a bad Host-house were sufficient to finish the worke of my Death. **1667** MILTON *P.L.* IX. 63 The space of seven continu'd Nights he rode. **1725** POPE *Odyss.* VI. 205 Twice ten tempestuous nights I rolled. **1817** SHELLEY *Rev. Islam* XII. xxxviii, Three days and nights we sailed. **1891** *Daily News* 3 Mar. 3/1 A man was almost always five nights in bed before being called upon to spend a night out.

b. Used to mark an occasion or point of time. Also freq. with defining term, as *Christmas, Midsummer, ball, wedding night*, etc.; see these words.

c **900** tr. *Bæda's Hist.* I. xxxiii. (1890) 90 Æghwelce niht ofer his byrȝenne heofonlic leoht wæs æteawed. *a* **1122** *O.E. Chron.* (Laud MS.) an. 1110 On þære fiftan nihte on Maies monðe, ætwyde se mona on æfen beorhte scinende. *c* **1250** *Gen. & Ex.* 3142 Ðe tende dai it sulde ben laȝt, And ho[l]den in ðe tende naȝt. *a* **1300** *Cursor M.* 2712 þe trinite he sagh.. And gestend þam wit him þat night. *c* **1375** *Sc. Leg. Saints* xxxvi. (*Baptist*) 1168 þare þai wak þat nicht for sancte Ihonis sak. *a* **1400–50** *Alexander* 1084 þe same niȝt in his slepe Seraphis aperis. **1500–20** DUNBAR *Poems* xxvi. 1 Off Februar the fyiftene nycht..I lay in till a trance. **1568** GRAFTON *Chron.* II. 207 Wherefore he came on a night and declared all this to the Queene. **1653** tr. *Carmeni's Nissena* 39 Who by reason of his last nights waking..had a very sore fit of a Feaver. **1711** ADDISON *Spect.* No. 15 ¶7 The missing of an Opera the first Night. **1754** *Med. Obs. & Inq.* (1776) I. v. 37 The blisters which had been laid above her ancles the night before. *a* **1781** WATSON *Philip III* (1793) I. I. 79 Albert ..arrived on the same night at Bruges. **1890** *Law Times Rep.* LXIII. 765/1 The defendant only intended to represent the play on two nights.

c. As a division or period of time. Also with adjs. denoting the kind of weather prevailing or other natural feature.

c **1200** ORMIN 1901 Marrchess nahhtess wannsenn aȝȝ & Marrchess daȝhess waxenn. *a* **1250** *Owl & Night.* 523 Hwenne nyhtes cumeþ longe & bryngeþ forstes starke & stronge. *c* **1400** *Destr. Troy* 8684 With myche dole vppon dayes & on derke nightes Sum walt into wodenes. *a* **1568** *Satir. Poems Reform.* xlvi. 23 In moneless nichtis it is na mowis. **1591** SHAKS. *Two Gent.* IV. ii. 140 It hath bin the longest night That ere I watch'd. **1603** —— *Meas. for M.* II. i. 139 This will last out a night in Russia When nights are longest there. **1667** MILTON *P.L.* x. 680 Else had the Spring Perpetual smiled..Equal in Days and Nights. **1715** tr. *Gregory's Astron.* (1726) I. 64 To explain the Variety of the Days and Nights, and the Seasons of the Year thence arising. **1818** BYRON *Juan* I. cxxxv, 'Twas, as the watch-men say, a cloudy night. **1866** *Chambers's Encycl.* III. 86/2 Summer and autumn nights are freest of clouds. **1897** MARY KINGSLEY *W. Africa* 102 To my taste there is nothing so fascinating as spending a night out in an African forest.

transf. **1803** *Naval Chron.* XV. 154 The extra [working-time] was divided into nights and tides:—a night consisted of five hours, and a tide of an hour and an half. **1840** *Penny Cycl.* XVI. 326/1 The longest night [lasts] from the 19th of November to the 26th of January, which is two months and ten days.

d. With adjectives, denoting the quality of rest obtained, or the manner in which the time is spent. (Cf. GOOD-NIGHT.)

1594 SHAKS. *Rich. III*, I. iv. 2, O I haue past a miserable night, So full of fearefull Dreames. **1667** MILTON *P.L.* v. 31 Such night till this I never pass'd. **1671** —— *P.R.* II. 460 A Crown..Brings dangers, troubles, cares, and sleepless nights. **1775** *Med. Obs. & Inq.* (1784) VI. v. 38, I afterwards passed..a good night. **1887** *Brit. Med. Jrnl.* 12 Feb. 318/2 He had had a restless night, with intervals of sleep. **1894** *Lancet* 3 Nov. 1027 He had a very good night.

e. Phr. *to make* (or *have*) *a night of it* (or †*on't*): To spend the night in enjoyment or revelling. (Cf. MAKE *v.*[1] 18 c.)

[**1602** *Twelfth Nt. Merriment* (1893) 4 Youle make as good a night of it heere as if you had beene at all the houses in the towne.] **1693** CONGREVE *Old Bach.* IV. ix, I'm resolved to make a night on't. **1701** CIBBER *Love makes Man* I. i, Well! and didst thou make a Night on't, Boy? **1775** SHERIDAN *Duenna* III. i, I' faith, we'll have a night of it. **1809** MALKIN *Gil Blas* IV. vi. ¶8 He is going to make a night of it. **1885** *Scribner's Mag.* XXX. 393/2 Friends and neighbours also made a day of it, and then also a night of it, in honour of the departed.

f. An evening or night devoted to the performance of a play, or of music by a specified composer or artist, or celebrations in honour of a particular person, etc.; freq. with defining word prefixed, as in ***first night*** (see FIRST *a.* (*sb.*) and *adv.* C 2). Cf. quot. 1711 under sense 4 b.

1707 *Muses Mercury* Jan. 4 This Prologue was forbidden to be spoken the second Night of the Representation of the *Prophetess*. **1784** in C. B. Hogan *London Stage 1660–1800* (1968) v. 760 *Il Curioso Indiscreto*... This Night, the last of performing before the Holidays, will not be counted a Subscription Night, but the Tickets admitted as usual. **1793** in *Ibid.* v. 1584 *Othello*... Paid Music 4 Nights £35 19*s.* 4*d.* **1842** DICKENS *Let.* 12 Nov. (1974) III. 368 Mrs. Dickens begs me..to say that if you can oblige her with your box at Covent Garden on any of Miss Kemble's nights, she will be very thankful. **1847** *Punch* XIII. 60 (*caption*) Melancholy scene at the opera on a Jenny Lind night. **1859** G. A. SALA *Twice round Clock* 260, I have brought you to her Majesty's Theatre, and this is unfortunately a Verdi night. **1861** GEO. ELIOT *Let.* 6 Oct. (1954) III. 456 We are enjoying a great, great pleasure—a new grand piano; and last evening we had a Beethoven night. **1959** *Observer* 18 Jan. 14/4 The Burns Night circles the globe like a sputnik. **1969** M. R. BOOTH *Eng. Plays of 19th Cent.* II. 346 *Mrs. Dane's Defence* ran for 209 nights on its first appearance. **1970** *Listener* 10 Sept. 326/3 The years of the romantic biographers and the Beethoven pianists, of Beethoven nights at the old Queen's Hall.

g. ***the night***, the first occasion on which a play, entertainment, etc., is publicly performed; freq. in phr. (***it will be***) ***all right on the night***, an expression of optimism that a performance will go well when it is given publicly, even if rehearsals are unpromising; also *transf.*

1911 O. ONIONS *Widdershins* 26 I've not got on very well with it. But it will be all right on the night, as you used to say. **1938** R. G. COLLINGWOOD *Principles of Art* xiv. 322 In the rehearsal of any given passage..the actors may move and speak exactly as they will 'on the night'. **1939** S. BOX in J. W. Marriott *Best One-Act Plays of 1939* (1940) 296 *Juliet.* God-a-mercy! PROMPT!.. *Nurse.* Ah, well! 'Twill be all right on the night! **1949** *Economist* 23 July 172 The hope that the Atlantic Pact would 'turn out all right on the night'. **1967** J. GARDNER *Madrigal* ii. 22 Boysie..began to build up a mental block. It would be all right on the night, he thought with a nervous laugh. **1973** E. LEMARCHAND *Let or Hindrance* xiii. 165 Penny may fly off the handle, but she's always all right on the night.

h. (Also *'night.*) Ellipt. for GOOD NIGHT I. *colloq.*

1912 MULFORD & CLAY *Buck Peters, Ranchman* viii. 92 'Good-night. I'm goin' to roost.' 'Night, Dave.' **1922** JOYCE *Ulysses* 589 *Corny Kelleher.* Good night, men. *The Watch.* (*Saluting together.*) Night, gentlemen. **1933** A. THIRKELL *High Rising* vii. 151 'Good night. We're going to bed now.' 'Night,' said Stoker. **1967** K. GILES *Death & Mr. Prettyman* i. 21 'Seven ack emma tomorrow if you can manage.' 'Night, sir,' Honeybody lumbered off. **1972** 'H. HOWARD' *Nice Day for Funeral* v. 80 'I could sleep standing up.' 'Then let's call it a day...' ''Night...'

5. a. With possessive pronouns: The particular night on which a person performs some duty (†receives visitors), etc. (In quot. 1838 = benefit night.) Also ***night out***, the evening on which a domestic servant is free to go out; also, an evening or night spent in enjoyment or revelling away from one's home; a spree (cf. OUT *adv.* 15 b); so ***night off***, a night free from work or one's usual duties.

1525 *Aberd. Burgh Rec.* (1844) 112 Personis..to be gottin amangis the haill toun, euerie ilk man his nycht about. **1760** C. JOHNSTON *Chrysal* II. I. i. 7 The footman answered, that it was not his lady's night, and she was not at home. **1814** *New Brit. Theatre* I. 530 What glory might not any lady.. acquire for herself were she..to succeed in getting up a Masque..on one of her nights. **1838** DICKENS *Nich. Nick.* xxiii, Whenever the announce bills came out for her annual night. **1885** A. DALY in A. Nicoll *Hist. Eng. Drama 1660–1900* (1959) V. 333 (*play-title*) A night off; or, a page from Balzac. **1890** W. BOOTH *In Darkest Eng.* II. v. 190 The weekly Church service or 'night out' with nowhere to go. **1908** G. SANGER *Seventy Yrs. a Showman* ix. 30 For these people Lansdown Fair was, as they put it, their 'night out'. **1910** *Blackw. Mag.* Jan. 149/1 Mr. Lloyd-George declined to deliver a speech on the ground that it was 'the Prime Minister's night out'! **1916** E. V. LUCAS *Vermilion Box* 129 We have the pictures here, of course, and I go there regularly on my night out. **1943** J. B. PRIESTLEY *Daylight on Saturday* xix. 152 'I'm staying late tonight.' 'Then we can't have our night out,' she cried. **1947** N. CARDUS *Autobiogr.* 277 Whenever his 'night off' occurred he bought a ticket. **1961** H. PINTER (*title*) A night out.

b. The kind of night one has had, or usually has. *rare.*

1667 MILTON *P.L.* v. 93 Thus Eve her Night Related, and thus Adam answered sad. **1776** JOHNSON *Let.* 21 Oct. in *Boswell*, My nights are very restless and tiresome. **1847** C. BRONTE *J. Eyre* xxviii, My night was wretched, my rest broken.

II. In adverbial phrases.

6. a. ***night and day***, always, continually.

c **950** *Lindisf. Gosp.* Mark v. 5 Symle næht & dæȝe in byrȝennum & morum wæs. *c* **1200** ORMIN 4694 Beo þu ȝeornfull nihht & daȝȝ To follȝhenn Godess wille. *c* **1230** *Hali Meid.* 20 Alde feond..scheoteð niht & dei his earewen. *a* **1300** *Cursor M.* 10421 Sco..weped and mornd night and dai. **1390** GOWER *Conf.* I. 104 Bot nyht and day as I am now I schal alwey be such to yow. **1456** SIR G. HAYE *Law Arms* (S.T.S.) 175 He puttis..gude wache and warde apon him nycht and day. **1486** *Bk. St. Albans* E ij b, Thynke what I say, my sonne, nyght and day. **1530** *Hickscorner* 47, I ever with them went..Night and daye towarde the way of ryghtwysenes. *a* **1586** SIDNEY *Ps.* I. i, He blessed is who.. night and day..calls [God's law] to marking mind. **1828** MOIR *Mansie Wauch* xxii, Maybe—..rowing night and day [he] got home in a safe skin.

b. ***night* (*n*)*or day***, by night or by day.

13.. *Cursor M.* 19715 (Gött.), þair redis þarfor gun þai rune, ..Night or day to waite þe time. *a* **1450** LYDG. *Merita Missæ* in *Lay Folks Mass Bk.* 392 Which nyght nor day ne cesseth nought. **1707** FREIND *Peterborow's Cond. Sp.* 205 My Lord never rested night or day, till he came to Tortosa.

†**c.** ***the night***, during the night, by night. *Obs.*

1594 SHAKS. *Rich. III*, IV. iv. 118 Forbeare to sleepe the night, and fast the day. **1597** —— *2 Hen. IV*, IV. v. 126 Haue you a Ruffian that will sweare?.. Reuell the night?

7. a. ***all***, or ***the whole, night*** (***long***), throughout the night.

c **1205** LAY. 29309 þa burh born alle niht. **13..** *E.E. Allit. P.* B. 1002 þat alle naȝt [so] much niye hade no mon in his hert. **1382** WYCLIF *Isa.* lxii. 6 Al dai and al nyȝt euermar thei shul not be stille. *c* **1450** *Bk. Curtasye* 505 in *Babees Bk.*, A morter of wax..þat alle nyȝt brennes in bassyn clere. **1535** COVERDALE *Gen.* xix. 2 Turne in..into youre seruauntes house, and tarye all night. **1596** DALRYMPLE tr. *Leslie's Hist. Scot.* Prol. 5 The beimes of the Sone, al Scotland throuch, the hail nychte ar sein, the space of twa monethis. **1600** DYMMOK *Ireland* (1843) 41 The rebells..never ceased to disquiet our men, the whole night longe. **1667** MILTON *P.L.* IV. 603 She all night long her amorous descant sung. **1754** *Med. Obs. & Inq.* (1776) I. xiii. 111 He continued the whole night totally blind, and without a wink of sleep. **1802** MAR. EDGEWORTH *Moral T.* (1816) I. i. 5 He sat all night apart from the company. **1878** TENNYSON *The Revenge* viii, Ship after ship, the whole night long, their high-built galleons came.

b. So (***all***) ***the long night.***

13.. *E.E. Allit. P.* B. 807 Bot stylly þer in þe strete..þay wolde lenge þe long naȝt & logge þeroute. **1559** W. CUNNINGHAM *Cosmogr. Glasse* 36 But turne round about the pole, all the longe nyght.

III. In prepositional phrases.

8. †**a.** ***on night***, by night. *Obs.* (Cf. A-NIGHT.)

c **950** *Lindisf. Gosp.* Matt. xxviii. 13 Cueðende cuoðað gie þætte ðeȝnas his on næht cuomun. *c* **1000** *Sax. Leechd.* III. 242 Steorran æteowiað swilce on nihte. *c* **1200** ORMIN 2960 þatt godess enngell comm o nihht Till Josæp þær he sleppte. *c* **1250** *Gen. & Ex.* 1781 Laban hem bliscede, & on niȝt wente a-ȝen-ward. *a* **1300** *Cursor M.* 2973 Bot godd on night com to þe king in slepe. **13..** *E.E. Allit. P.* A. 243 Art þou my perle þat I haf playned, Regretted by myn one, on nyȝte? *c* **1375** *Sc. Leg. Saints* ix. (*Bartholomew*) 60 A hundre syis one day kneland, & als of[t] one nichte prayand. *c* **1450** *Bk. Curtasye* 506 in *Babees Bk.*, To saue þo chambur on nyȝt for fyre. **1508** KENNEDIE *Flyting w. Dunbar* 298 That cumis on nycht in visioun in my sleip. **1567** *Satir. Poems Reform.* vii. 66 Bludy boucheouris and throtcutters, on nycht.

b. ***by night***, during the night, in the night-time. Also ***by night and day***, always, at any time. (Cf. BY *prep.* 19 b.)

c **1220** *Bestiary* 63 A welle..ðat springeð ai boðe bi niȝt and bi dai. **13..** *Cursor M.* 6749 (Gött.), If..þe dede be don bi night, þe smyter þan sal haue na plight. **1340** *Ayenb.* 52 þet uolk þet late louieþ to soupi and to waki be niȝte. **1382** WYCLIF *Josh.* ii. 2 Men ben goon yn hythir bi nyȝt. **1466** *Anc. Cal. Rec. Dublin* (1889) 325 For perayles that ben imynent of horsemen by nyght. **1512** *Act 4 Hen. VIII*, c. 20 *Preamble*, Archbold with other xl. outlawes..come by night to..Penreth Cotes. **1590** SHAKS. *Com. Err.* IV. ii. 60 Time comes stealing on by night and day. **1667** MILTON *P.L.* III. 514 Jacob..Dreaming by night under the open Skie. **1770** GOLDSM. *Des. Vill.* 230 A bed by night, a chest of drawers by day. **1820** SHELLEY *Hymn Merc.* lxxxii, A joy by night or day —for those endowed With art and wisdom. **1885** *Law Times Rep.* LIII. 53/2 A tow which is being towed with a long scope of hawser by night.

c. ***at night***, at nightfall, in the evening. Also used to designate the hours from six p.m. to midnight. (Cf. 9 b.)

13.. *Sir Gaw. & Gr. Knt.* 1407 What nwez so þay nome, at naȝt quen þay metten. *c* **1375** *Cursor M.* 3931 (Fairf.), Iacob lay him stille atte naȝt. *c* **1450** *Bk. Curtasye* 487 in *Babees Bk.*, þo lorde schalle skyft hys gowne at nyȝt. **1523** LD. BERNERS *Froiss.* I. ccccxix. 733 The wednisday at night that ye bataylе was the next day. **1605** SHAKS. *Macb.* III. i. 42 Let euery man be master of his time Till seuen at Night. **1697** DRYDEN *Virg. Georg.* IV. 275 They give their Bodies due Repose at Night. **17..** in Herd *Coll. Songs* (1776) II. 159 By there came twa gentlemen At twelve o'clock at night. **1838** DICKENS *O. Twist* xxxii, At night, Oliver read a chapter or two from the Bible.

d. (See OVERNIGHT, TO-NIGHT.)

9. †**a.** ***on nights***, by night (habitually). Also ***o'*** and ***in nights***. *Obs.* (Cf. A-NIGHTS.)

1127–31 *O.E. Chron.* an. 1127 Soðfeste men heom kepten on nihtes. **1375** BARBOUR *Bruce* VII. 506 Fra Carleill all on nychtis ryde, And in covert on dayis byde. **1388** *Wyclif's Sel. Wks.* III. 488 Men mowe say þer Pater noster medefully under þo cope of heven, as Crist did in þo hille in nyȝttus. **1472** in *Surtees Misc.* (1890) 24 A ryotter on nyghtes. **1597** SHAKS. *2 Hen. IV*, II. i. 83, I will ride thee o'Nights, like the Mare. *Ibid.* iv. 252 When wilt thou leaue fighting on dayes, and foyning on nights..? **1708** *Bickerstaff Detected* in *Swift's Wks.* (1751) IV. 210 A pack of Rascals that walk the Streets on Nights. [**1823** LAMB *Elia* Ser. II. *Amicus Redivivus*, I have nothing but water in my head o' nights since this frightful accident.]

b. ***at nights***: (cf. prec. and 8 c).

1581 RICH *Farew.* (1846) 198 At nightes she was lodged in her father's chamber. **1720** *Humourist* 9 At Nights..they had the Shelter of a Barn. **1793** SMEATON *Edystone L.* §283 Having first established, that they should quit the work at nights. *Ibid.* §304 Which, indeed, except at nights, would generally be the case. **1883** J. W. SHERER *At Home & in India* 6 The stout, beaming man now appears quite distinctly—coming from somewhere at nights in a post-chaise.

c. ***of nights***: (see OF 52 b).

10. ***on*** (***upon***), ***in***, or ***of the night***, by night, during the night. Now only with *in*.

c **1205** LAY. 5601 Al makeden heore faren alse ha wolden a þare niht faren. *a* **1300** *Cursor M.* 6196 Drightin self þam ledd þair wai.. Wit firen piler on [*v.rr.* apon, vpon] þe niht. *c* **1375** *Sc. Leg. Saints* xxx. (*Theodera*) 288 To þat þing has he na sycht þat thocht or don is in þe nycht. *c* **1400** MAUNDEV. (Roxb.) xxv. 117 þis charbuncle lightnez all þe chaumbre on þe nyght. *c* **1440** *Alph. Tales* 115 He was tempid with grete ludificacions on þe nyght. *a* **1533** LD. BERNERS *Gold. Bk. M. Aurel.* (1546) E e vij b, She eateth her nothing on the dai nor slepeth in the nyght. **1559** W. CUNNINGHAM *Cosmogr. Glasse* 162 When you will verifie your nedle.., you shall use the healpe of the Sunne (and on the night) of some fixed sterre. **1590** SHAKS. *Mids. N.* II. i. 253 There sleepes Tytania, sometime of the night. **1596** DALRYMPLE tr. *Leslie's Hist. Scot.* I. 94 Thair heid..thay neuir couered in the nycht. **1753** CHAMBERS *Cycl. Suppl.*, *Night angling*, a method of catching..shy fish in the night. **1855** WHARTON *Crim. Law U.S.* 598 The breaking and entering must be in the night.

IV. *attrib.* and *Comb.*

11. a. Objective (and obj. genitive), as ***night-bringing, -cheering, -dispersing, -slayer, -swaying.***

1611 COTGR., *Nuicteux*, nightly, *night-bringing. 1824 FENBY *Lover's Good Night* vii, Softly, with *night-cheering beams, Yon moon rides thro' the cloudless sky. 1851 C. L. SMITH tr. *Tasso* v. lxxxv, When the *night-dispersing dawn arose. 1839–52 BAILEY *Festus* 137 Multitude of days Immortal as thy years, O *nightslayer! c1600 CHALKHILL *Thealma & Cl.* (1683) 19 *Night-swaying Morpheus clothes the East in black.

b. Instrumental, as ***night-clad, -cloaked, -cradled, enshrouded, hid***, etc.

1839–52 BAILEY *Festus* 10, I see the stars, *night-clad, all gathering In long and sad procession. 1851 H. MELVILLE *Whale* xxix, To visit the *night-cloaked deck. 1818 SHELLEY *Woodman* 18 The dull ear Of the *night-cradled earth. 1859 DICKENS *T. Two Cities* II. xxiii, Along the *night-enshrouded roads. 1601 *Death Earl Huntington* III. iv. in Hazl. *Dodsley* VIII. 279 This cage of *night-hid owls, light-flying birds. 1850 LYNCH *Theoph. Trinal* v. 79 Her beams come to a *night-mantled home. 1849 LONGF. *Lighthouse* v, It stands.. the *night-o'ertaken mariner to save. 1727–46 THOMSON *Summer* 1681 Whose mournful chambers hold (So *night-struck fancy dreams) the yelling ghost. 1776 MICKLE tr. *Camoens' Lusiad* 330 By *night-veiled art proud Sylves falls his prey. 1881 H. PHILLIPS tr. *Chamisso's Faust* 21 Yon night-veiled, hidden land of gloom. 1652 BENLOWES *Theoph.* Pref., Let them,.. being *night wildred in their Intellects, prosecute their sensuality. 1873 E. BRENNAN *Witch of Nemi* 118 Flames that made crimson all the *night-wrapt sky.

c. Similative, as ***night-black, -dark, -haired, -like, -swift.***

a1591 H. SMITH *Serm.* (1622) 467 As if we were *nightblacke rauens. 1817 SHELLEY *Rev. Islam* I. lii, On nightblack columns poised. 1872 TENNYSON *Gareth & Lynette* 1346 High on a nightblack horse, in nightblack arms. 1879 E. ARNOLD *Lt. Asia* 39 The *night-dark steed. 1839–52 BAILEY *Festus* 100 My *night-haired love! so sweet she was. 1821 SHELLEY *Adonais* (cancelled) 19 His dark and *night-like eyes. 1590 SHAKS. *Mids. N.* III. ii. 379 *Night-swift Dragons cut the clouds full fast.

12. Adverbial, in sense of 'by night', 'during the night': **a.** With pres. pples., as ***night-ambling, -blooming, -blowing, -contending***, etc.

1600 FAIRFAX *Tasso* IV. xxvii, Of their *night ambling dame the Syrians prated. 1835 LINDLEY *Introd. Bot.* (1839) 476 The flowers of the *night-blooming Cereus. 1866 SHUCKARD *Brit. Bees* 13 Our clients have nothing to do with these night-blooming flowers. 1804 CHARLOTTE SMITH *Conversations*, etc. II. 91 The..splendid Cactus Grandiflora, usually called the *night blowing Cereus. 1871 KINGSLEY *At Last* xvii, The Umbrella Rock, capped with.. night-blowing Cereus. 1817 SHELLEY *Pr. Athan.* I. 71 Tempest's war Is levied by the *night-contending winds. 17.. RAMSAY *Lure* 4 *Night-drinking sots [were] counting their lawin. 1714 GAY *Sheph. Week, Saturday* 57 Will a' wisp misleads *night-faring clowns O'er hills. a1887 JEFFERIES *Field & Hedgerow* (1889) 228 There is no *night-feeding bird to feed the fern-owl's young. 1824 SYMMONS *Agamemnon* 33 Dewy cover of *night freezing skies. 1632 LITHGOW *Trav.* I. 7 These *night-gaping foes, are trampled vnder foote. 1639 S. DU VERGER tr. *Camus' Admir. Events* 270 Who like unlucky *night-going fires lead him to precipitations. 1801 LAMB *Poems*, etc. (1884) 205 *Night-riding Incubi Troubling the fantasy. 1663 DRYDEN *Rival Ladies* I. iii, The lady..is seized by some *night-robbing villains. 1811 SHELLEY *St. Irvyne* II. i, The *night-rolling breath of the blast. a1631 DONNE *Holy Sonn.* iii. 9 Th' hydroptic drunkard, and *night-scouting thief. 1598 MARSTON *Satires* I. 61 *Night-shining Phœbe knowes what was begat—A monstrous Centaure, illegitimate. 1648 WILKINS *Math. Magic* II. xi, These *Noctilucæ* or Night-shining Bodies. 1802 BINGLEY *Anim. Biog.* (1813) III. 424 The night-shining Nereis. These minute creatures inhabit every sea. 1857 HOLLAND *Bay Path* xxxiii. 414 The *night-straying cow stumbled among them. 1642 H. MORE *Song of Soul* II. i. II. xi, His glowing sight..all *night-trifling sprights doth chase away with fear. 1596 SHAKS. *1 Hen. IV*, I. i. 87 Some *Night-tripping-Faiery had exchanged..our children. 1667 MILTON *P.L.* v. 40 Where silence yields To the *night-warbling Bird.

b. With verbal sbs., as ***night-angling, -breaking, -feeding, -firing, -fishing***, etc. (Cf. 13.)

1704 *Dict. Rust.*, *Night angling; for this Angling in the Night-time, take two great Garden-worms. a1625 SIR H. FINCH *Law* (1636) 217 Burglary is the *night-breaking of an house, with an intent to steale or kill. 1845 BLAINE in Youatt *Dog* ii. 37 More nutriment is derived from *night-feeding than by day. 1876 VOYLE & STEVENSON *Milit. Dict.* 82/2 *Collimator*, an instrument for laying guns and mortars..for *night-firing. 1653 WALTON *Angler* 126 You are to know, there is *night as well as day fishing for a Trout. 1802 DANIEL *Field Sports* II. 290 Night-fishing with a fly is best from May to the end of August. 1862 *N. Syd. Soc. Year-bk. Med. for 1861*, 173 Some Results of *Night-nursing. 1838 W. BELL *Dict. Law Scot.*, *Night Poaching. 1850 R. G. CUMMING *Hunter's Life S. Afr.* (1902) 139/1 This wound up my elephant *night-shooting. 1559 ASCHAM in *Babees Bk.* (1868) 361 Beware of secrett corners and *night sitting vp, the two nurses of mischiefe. 1644 MILTON *Areopag.* Wks. 1851 IV. 416 Excus'd in the genial cups of an Academick night-sitting. 1835 LONGF. *Outre-Mer* (1857) 375 This *night-travelling is..far from disagreeable.

c. With ppl. adjs., as ***night-born, -fallen, -folded, -foundered, -haunted, -scented, -swollen.***

1610 NICHOLS *England's Eliza* v, Error's *night-borne children. 1742 YOUNG *Nt. Th.* IX. 2090 My solemn night-born adjuration hear. 1839–52 BAILEY *Festus* 106 The cold pure radiance of the night-born light. 1798 BLOOMFIELD *Farmer's Boy, Winter* 333 And *night-fall'n Lambs require the Shepherd's care. 1820 MOORE *Ill Omens* iii, She..kiss'd off its night-fallen dew. 1820 SHELLEY *Prometh. Unb.* III. iii. 101 *Night-folded flowers Shall suck unwithering hues in their repose. 1634 MILTON *Comus* 483 Som one like us *night-founder'd here. 1667 —— *P.L.* I. 204 The Pilot of some small night-founder'd Skiff. a1593 MARLOWE *Edw. II* (Rtldg.) 191/2 The people..cannot brook a *night-grown mushroom. 1859 LD. LYTTON *Wanderer* (ed. 2) 224 A wild *night-haunted track. 1849 BALFOUR *Man. Bot.* §687 *Hesperis tristis*, or *night-scented stock. *Ibid.*, The white flowers of *Lychnis vespertina* are also night-scented. 1818 KEATS *Endym.* I. 215 Are not our lowing heifers sleeker than *Night-swollen mushrooms?

13. a. Attributive, in the senses 'of night', 'belonging or pertaining to the night', 'existing, prevailing, taking place, etc., during the night', as ***night-air, alarm, -ascent, -attack, -blast, -brawl, -calm, -city, -class, -damp, -duty, -fancy, -fear, -fight, -flight, -haunt, -hospital, -lunch, -music, -noise, -nursery, -perfume, -raid, -rate, -rehearsal, -road, -school, -self, -smell, -sound, -speech, -talk, -town, -train, -web, -wonder, -world***, etc.

1788 LD. AUCKLAND *Jrnl.* 25 June (1861) II. 55 He is afraid of the *night air. 1813 W. S. WALKER *Gustavus Vasa* 145 Breaking the night-air's still repose. 1861 FLOR. NIGHTINGALE *Nursing* ii. (ed. 2) 13 Another extraordinary fallacy is the dread of night air. 1606 SHAKS. *Tr. & Cr.* I. iii. 171 Now play him..Arming to answer in a *night-Alarme. 1693 CONGREVE in *Dryden's Juvenal* xi. (1697) 295 If you wou'd be free from Night-alarms, You must seem Fond. 1866 *Chambers's Jrnl.* Oct. 644/2 One *night-ascent has been made in this way. 1844 *Knickerbocker* XXIII. 117, I knew that Indians in a *night attack make signals by imitating the cry of some animal. 1893 F. ADAMS *New Egypt* 242 The most difficult and dangerous operation in warfare—a night attack. 1952 R. CAMPBELL tr. *Baudelaire's Poems* 127 Like enemies preparing night-attacks. 1813 SCOTT *Trierm.* III. viii, The *night-blast that wildy bore Its course along the hill. a1661 HOLYDAY *Juvenal* vi. (1673) 91 And so scape *Night-brawls. 1774 MASON *Poems* 169 (Jod.), Not a *night breeze wakes to blow. 1858 J. MARTINEAU *Stud. Chr.* 59 The night-breeze on his brow. 1817–19 WORDSWORTH *MS.* in E. de Selincourt *Prelude* (1959) 136 The *night-calm over sea and land. c1616 FLETCHER & MASS. *Thierry & Theod.* III. ii, They sit Upon my heart like *night charms, black and heavy. 1970 T. HUGHES *Crow* 55 Seeing the *night-city..He bellows laughter. 1891 A. BEARDSLEY *Let.* July (1971) 24 Two hours' daily work is quite sufficient for me, so, as you suggest, I mean to attend *night classes. 1936 N. COWARD *Fumed Oak* i, in *Tonight at 8.30* II. i. 47 Your father was a gentleman, which is more than your husband ever will be, with all his night-classes and his book reading—night-classes indeed! 18.. CAMPBELL *Soldier's Dream* Wks. (1837) 100 The *night-cloud had lowered. 1639 DRUMM. OF HAWTH. *Consid. to Parl.* Wks. (1711) 187 At all Assemblies, especially the *Night-conventions. 1851 H. MELVILLE *Moby Dick* III. xliv. 250 The unheeded *night-damp gathered in beads of dew upon that stone-carved coat and hat. a1661 HOLYDAY *Juvenal* (1673) 42 Now view *night-dangers, and the dreadful height Of our house-tops. 1645 RUTHERFORD *Tryal & Tri. Faith* (1845) 202 This is like the expelling of *night-darkness out of the whole body of the air, by the presence of the sun. 1665 DRYDEN *Ind. Emp.* III. ii, Sleeping Flowers beneath the *night-dew sweat. 1822–34 *Good's Study Med.* (ed. 4) I. 366 Sleeping in the open air.., while the serenados, or night-dews, were gathering around him. a1300 *E.E. Psalter* xc. 5 (Egerton), Noght saltou drede for *niht-drede. 1677 GALE *Crt. Gentiles* III. 58 The Pagan Diviners had their *night-dreams or day-visions whereby they divined things. 1894 *Daily News* 12 Sept., The first occasion on which he has done *night-duty alone. 1921 A. CHRISTIE *Mysterious Affair at Styles* viii. 170 She had kindly offered to remain on night duty. 1959 [see BEIGEL]. 1966 J. BINGHAM *Double Agent* vi. 93 The phone rang. It was the Night Duty Officer with a deciphered message from Vienna. 1973 'B. MATHER' *Snowline* vii. 83 Mukherjee wasn't at the [police] station, and the night duty havildar couldn't tell me where he was. 1863 LONGF. *Wayside Inn, Landlord's Tale* 43 Beneath, in the churchyard, lay the dead, In their *night-encampment on the hill. 1637 RUTHERFORD *Lett.* (1862) I. lxxxviii. 226 Dreams..and *night-fancies of a miserable life of sin. 1823 C. LAMB *Elia* 156 My night-fancies have long ceased to be afflictive. 1904 W. H. HUDSON *Green Mansions* xxii. 292 Half-delirious night-fancies. 1823 C. LAMB *Elia* 148 (*heading*) Witches, and other *night-fears. 1923 KIPLING *Irish Guards in Great War* I. 7 The 3rd Coldstream Guards..beat off that attack in a *night-fight. 1830 SCOTT *Ayrshire Trag.* II. i, You..saw, perhaps, the *night-flight which began it. 1918 *War Illustr.* 13 July 372/2 My first night-flight was during one of the earlier Zeppelin raids on London and the Eastern Counties. 1973 L. COOPER *Tea on Sunday* xxxi. 228, I must get a plane to Milan tonight..a night flight. 1582 STANYHURST *Æneis* IV. (Arb.) 115 Thus sayd, through *nightfog he vannisht. 1811 SCOTT *Don Roderick* II. ii, The river's night-fog rolling damp. 1576 BAKER *Jewell of Health* 64 The water also deliuereth the *night formes of Venus in sleepe. 1816 KIRBY & SP. *Entomol.* xxvi. (1818) II. 462 We not unfrequently have sharp *night-frosts in summer. 1798 SOTHEBY tr. *Wieland's Oberon* (1826) I. 93 Where chill the *night-gale blows. 1633 FORD *'Tis Pity* v. v, Hath your new sprightly lord Found out a trick in *night-games? 1820 KEATS *Isabella* xxxvi, Hoarse *night-gusts sepulchral briars among. 1817 *Edin. Rev.* XXIX. 9 In the..*night-halts of her luxurious progress. 1859 A. J. MUNBY *Diary* 20 Mar. in D. Hudson *Munby* (1972) 28 A large & still flourishing crop of secret dens & *night haunts. 1950 G. GREENE *Third Man* xi. 96 He might have been in any third-rate night haunt in any other shabby capital. 1821 BRYANT *Ages* xiv, Like the *night-heaven, when clouds are black with rain. 1963 '*Night' hospital [see *day-hospital* s.v. DAY *sb.* 23]. 1964 G. L. COHEN *What's Wrong with Hospitals?* viii. 174 He started a night hospital. .. Executives and professional men who would not otherwise contemplate treatment come by night to bare their unconscious. 1669 STURMY *Mariner's Mag.* II. x. 77 The upper half of the Circle..is the Day-hours, and the lower..half is the *Night-hours. 1830 MRS. HEMANS *Charmed Picture* Poems (1849) 459/1 The night-hour's haunted calm. 1849 C. BRONTE *Shirley* xviii, Another disturbance broke the *night-hush. a1649 DRUMM. OF HAWTH. *Hist. Jas. III*, Wks. (1711) 41 By *Night-journeys, shifting from Place to Place. 1933 M. PELL *S.S. Utah* 12 Anybody know where the *night lunch hangs out? 1945 *Seafarers' Log* 17 Aug. 6/5 Men coming back from shore leave are not able to get into night lunch. 1861 CLOUGH *Mari Magno* 918 Swift the *night-mail conveyed his missive on. 1884 PAE *Eustace* 110 The night mail from the north reached its destination in Edinburgh. a1806 FOX *Jas. II*, iii. 212 After the disastrous *night march from Killerne. 1849 GROTE *Greece* II. liii. (1862) IV. 509 He advanced by a night-march to the temple. 1614 PURCHAS *Pilgrimage* VIII. v. (ed. 2) 760 The many faults (as they report) of Mariners in priuate truckings and *night-marts. 1870 BRYANT *Iliad* II. XXIV. 407 They found the guard engaged With their *night-meal. 1662 HIBBERT *Body Div.* I. 252 The Protestants in their *night-meetings committed most abominable uncleannesse. 1853 KINGSLEY *Hypatia* xi, The..sun rose swiftly through the dim *night-mist of the desert. 1910 W. DE LA MARE *Three Mulla-Mulgars* ix. 128 It pleased Battle mightily, this *night-music—music of all the kinds they knew, white man's, Jaqquamusic, Nugga-music, and Mulla-mulgars'. 1952 M. J. WARD (*title*) A little night Music. 1954 J. R. R. TOLKIEN *Fellowship of Ring* I. xii. 214 He lay tossing and turning and listening fearfully to the stealthy *night-noises. 1844 T. WEBSTER *Encycl. Domestic Econ.* XXVI. i. 1189 *Night nurseries require little furniture beyond bedding, and utensils for washing and bathing. 1937 Night nursery [see BUDDY *sb.*]. 1974 J. POPE-HENNESSY *R. L. Stevenson* i. 34 Louis's night-nursery..was a small room to the east of the day-nursery. 1608 SHAKS. *Per.* v. iii. 70 Pure Dian..! I Will offer *night-oblations to thee. 1632 HEYWOOD *Four Prentices* I. Wks. 1874 II. 220 Making the darke *night-pathes shine bright as day. 1693 DRYDEN *Juvenal* i. (1697) 8 When *Night-performance holds the place of Merit. 1918 E. SITWELL *Clown's Houses* 7 Tulip-trees Spilling *night-perfumes on the terraces. 1677 GALE *Crt. Gentiles* III. 81 Content not thy self with..dark spurious, false, *night-philosophie. 1852 GROTE *Greece* II. lxx. IX. 124 Taking up their *night-post at a distance..from the Grecian position. 1932 AUDEN *Orators* 110 The shamming dead, the *night-raid, the feinted retreat. 1654 GAYTON *Pleas. Notes.* IV. xx. 268 Witches are confin'd in their *night rambles to egge shels. 1939 R. A. KNOX *Let Dons Delight* ix. 247 My host returned, voluble..in his anathemas over the cheap *night-rate for telephoning. 1975 J. R. L. ANDERSON *Death in North Sea* iv. 73 'Can you get a helicopter out tonight?' 'I can, but..night-rates for the crews make it rather expensive.' 1729 LAW *Serious C.* xxiii. (1732) 470 It should be a constant part of his *night recollection. 1726 POPE *Odyss.* XX. 172 In vain the Queen the *night-refection prest. 1812 *Dramatic Censor for 1811* 312 The Public are respectfully informed, that it being found absolutely necessary to have a general *night rehearsal of the new Burlesque Tragic Drama, there will be no performance in the Theatre this evening. 1866 M. MACKINTOSH *Stage Reminiscences* 98 We rehearsed the piece, without music, after which a night rehearsal, including the orchestra, was called. 1607 SHAKS. *Tim.* IV. i. 17 Domesticke awe, *Night-rest and Neighbourhood. 1933 W. DE LA MARE *Fleeting* 42 The empty *night-road to the sea. 1590 SHAKS. *Mids. N.* III. ii. 5 How now mad spirit, What *night-rule now about this haunted groue? 1529 MORE *Dyaloge* III. Wks. 240/1 Other could we not come by, whome we mighte further examine of that *nyghte scole. 1780 *New Jersey Jrnl.* 22 Nov. 4/2 Wanted, to be bound, a Boy;..he shall be..sent to night school if required. 1858 Night-school [see *cottage lecture* s.v. COTTAGE 6]. 1894 S. FISKE *Holiday Stories* (1900) 136 Will you go to night-school and learn? 1973 E.-J. BAHR *Nice Neighbourhood* i. 14, I met Don at night school. He was learning to be an accountant. 1922 D. H. LAWRENCE *Fantasia of Unconscious* xv. 271 The *night-self is the very basis of the dynamic self. 1965 *Punch* 3 Nov. 665/1 The struggle in man between the day-self and the night-self. 1650 STAPYLTON *Strada's Low C. Wars* III. 61 At..these *night-sermons, tumults were raised. 1594 in Nichols *Progr. Q. Eliz.* (1823) III. 284 All requisite service, be it *night-service or otherwise,..to all ladis. 1618 *Barnevelt's Apol.* G 2 b, Out yee Popish knaues, sonnes of darkenesse, and *night shadows. 1847 MARY HOWITT *Ballads* 380 Till the night-shadows dimmed the glen. 1629 MAXWELL tr. *Herodian* (1635) 302 Chariot-races, Stage-plaies, Feasts and *Night-shewes. 1865 MRS. WHITNEY *Gayworthys* iii. (1879) 32 Waiting in the *night-shine at the open door. 1605 SHAKS. *Macb.* v. v. 11 My sences would have cool'd To heare a *Night-shrieke. 1647 STAPYLTON *Juvenal* 41 Let me live where no night-shrieks terrify. 1398 TREVISA *Barth. De P.R.* VIII. ix. (Bodl. MS.), þese signes..that beþ watery and erthy beþ colde and femule and *nyȝt signes. 1790 BEATSON *Nav. & Mil. Mem.* II. 409 A very gross defect or impropriety in the *night-signals at present in use. 1812 *Chron.* in *Ann. Reg.* 2 At about ten o'clock the night-signal was made to alter the course. 1869 DUNKIN *Midn. Sky* 155 The summer *night-sky. c1000 ÆLFRIC *Saints' Lives* xxiii. 442 þæt ilce geþanc..þe heom amang þam *niht-slæpe wæs on heora heortan. 1835 LYTTON *Rienzi* I. i, Let us keep it for our night-sleep. 1936 C. MORGAN *Sparkenbroke* IV. 344 From the darkness of the garden came the soft patter of invisible rain and the earthy *night-smell of plants. 1904 W. H. HUDSON *Green Mansions* xx. 272 Nor had I any choice then but to listen to the *night-sounds of the forest. 1953 S. BECKETT *Watt* 33 Listening to the little nightsounds in the hedge behind him. 1954 J. R. R. TOLKIEN *Fellowship of Ring* II. vi. 352, I hear nothing but the *night-speech of plant and stone. 1849 GROTE *Greece* II. xlix. VI. 265 The Athenian captain had really gone back to take *night-station on his own coast. 1596 SPENSER *State Irel.* Wks. (Globe) 681/1 *Night stealthes which (are commonly driven in by-ways and by blinde foordes). 1811 SHELLEY *St. Irvyne* II. iii, Whilst the tide of the *night-storm is rolling. 1761 *Biogr. Dict.* II. 9 His constitution..was weakened still more by the intemperance of his *night-studies. 1910 W. DE LA MARE *Three Mulla-Mulgars* iv. 51 Soon the long-billed river-birds began their *night-talk across the water. 1811 SHELLEY *St. Irvyne* II. ii, Oft have I brav'd the chill *night-tempests fury. 1742 YOUNG (*title*) The Complaint: or, *Night-thoughts on Life, Death, and Immortality. 1831 CARLYLE *Sart. Res.* I. iii, The utterance of such extraordinary Night-thoughts. 1922 JOYCE *Ulysses* 422 The Mabbot street entrance of *nighttown. *Ibid.* 598 A word of caution *re* the dangers of nighttown, women of ill fame and swell mobsmen. 1971 *Guardian Weekly* 5 June 18 Where all seeing readers join is in delight at the architecture of his [*sc.* Maurice Sendak's] Manhattan nighttown of towering pots and packets and jars. 1848 C. BRONTË *Let.* 4 Sept. in *Studies in Bibliogr.* (1971) XXIV. 103 Anne & I..walked through a thunderstorm to the station, got to Leeds and whirled up by the *Night train to London. **1885** R. BUCHANAN *Annan Water* xxiv, To pack up his things for the night-train to Scotland. **1954** T. S. ELIOT *Confid. Clerk* I. 30 We took the night train, and did the Channel crossing. **1637** RUTHERFORD *Lett.* (1862) I. lxxxviii. 226 Bewitched with dreams, shadows,..*night-vanities. **1671** WOODHEAD *St. Teresa* II. xxxiii. 220 There were frequent *Night-Vigils kept there. **1827** CLARE *Sheph. Cal.* 111 The pale *Night-waggon driving through the sky. **1603** KNOLLES *Hist. Turks* (1638) 158 His Companions.. began to lead him forth..to *night walks also. **1687** NORRIS *Misc.* 38 Our Wiser Ghosts thy silent Night-walks love. **13..** *Seuyn Sages* (W.) 2621 He com to the galewes, armed wel ..For to make the first *night-ward. **1906** HARDY *Dynasts* II. VI. v. 276 Is it where sky-fires flame and flit, Or solar craters spew and spit, Or ultra-stellar *night-webs knit? **1909** E. POUND *Personae* 22 The strange *night-wonder of your eyes Dies not. **1939** DYLAN THOMAS *Map of Love* 75 The clean winter sounds of the *nightworld.

b. With names of things (intended to be) worn or used during the night, as ***night-attire, -bait, -basket, -bell, -express, -ferry, -latch, -refuge, -shelter, -sock, -stand, -suit, -wrapper***, etc.

1597 DRAYTON *Bar. Wars* VI. lv, She sat under an estate of lawn, In *night-attire. **1640** BRAITHWAIT *Lanc. Lovers* xv. (E.D.D.), She found a mammet or feature so artificially made up in her night-attire. **1716** J. S. *Compl. Fisher* title-p., Baiting of the Ground, and *Night Baits. **1814** *Sporting Mag.* XLIV. 103 You escape behind a lazarone's *night-basket. **1832** MARRYAT *N. Forster* xliv, A *night bell..was attached to one side of the street door. **1884** *Harper's Mag.* Mar. 562/1 You ought to break the wire of his night bell. **1811** *Ora & Juliet* I. 124 Then by her *night candle she.. began a letter. **1828** *Blackw. Mag.* XXIII. 297 The Hebrew women, who..had been accustomed to wear no *night-chemises at all. **1654** DOROTHY OSBORNE *Lett.* (1888) 246 Going out to walk in my *night-cloak and night-gown. **1885** WARREN & CLEVERLY *Wanderings Beetle* 69 The distant hills shaking off their *night-clothing of mist. **1578** in Nichols *Progr. Q. Eliz.* (1823) II. 78 A *night-coyf with a forehead clothe of..Spanysh worke of roses. **1855** KINGSLEY *Westw. Ho!* v, Lady Grenvile, putting her beautiful face in its night-coif out of an adjoining door. *a* **1586** SIDNEY *Arcadia* III. Wks. 1724 II. 682 The best..*night-deckings. *a* **1776** JAMES *Diss. Fevers* (ed. 8) 113, I took..a few *night draughts, to give me rest. **1821** SCOTT *Kenilw.* vi, Beside it stood a gold posset dish to contain the night-draught. **1731** *Gentl. Mag.* I. 167, 1 odd *Night Ear-ring, with 3 Brilliant Diamonds. **1877** J. BLACKWOOD *Let.* 25 June in *Geo. Eliot's Lett.* (1956) VI. 390 We propose to come down by the *night express. **1975** N. LUARD *Travelling Horseman* iii. 63 He was on the road to Edinburgh..to catch the night express back to London. **1954** I. MURDOCH *Under Net* xiii. 188, I set off to Victoria to catch the *night ferry. **1967** E. WYMARK *As Good as Gold* xiv. 200, I gave them Camilla's address on the Avenue Foch. I omitted to mention that she was already on the Night Ferry. **1769** PENNANT *Brit. Zool.* III. 191 *note*, Neither was any body to fish from sun-setting to sun-rising, that the fish might enjoy their *night-food. **1835** MARRYAT *Olla Podr.* (Routl.) 271 Remove my *night-gloves. **1897** E. L. TAUNTON *Eng. Black Monks* I. 78 He changed his *night-habit for his day one and washed. **1647** R. STAPYLTON *Juvenal* 84 Th' imperiall strumpet..stole out In her *night-hoods. **1663** *Roxb. Ball.* (1890) VII. 83 He gives her rings, and..fan or muff, or night-hood. **1653** WALTON *Angler* 121 This kind of fishing with a dead rod, and laying *night-hooks. **1772** FORSTER in *Phil. Trans.* LXIII. 153 After sunset, it is caught by a night-hook. **1821** *Sporting Mag.* IX. 69 Night-hooks for pike. **1838** DICKENS *Nich. Nick.* viii, Mrs. Squeers came in, still habited in the primitive *night jacket. **1860** WORCESTER, **Night Key*. **1888** A. K. GREEN *Behind Closed Doors* vi, I do not give night-keys to any one but the doctor. **1857** J. RAINE *Mem. J. Hodgson* I. 287 Sheep-folds, or *night-lairs as they were called. **1854** O. S. FOWLER *Home for All* 113 The front door..secured..with a *night-latch and two keys. **1967** KARCH & BUBER *Offset Processes* viii. 321 Turn night latch lever to 'night latch' position. *a* **1672** STERRY *Wks.* (1710) II. 261 The World is his *Night-Mantle, his Pavilion of Darkness. **1630** DRAYTON *Muses' Elys.*, *Nymphal* vii, Fine *night-masks, plaster'd well within, To supple wrinkles, and to smooth the skin. **1764** *Museum Rust.* III. 286 The game is wretchedly destroyed by poachers, who take it with *night-nets. **1809** E. S. BARRETT *Setting Sun* III. 145 The 'Wise Men of the East', bearing *night-pans as censers. **1897** *Allbutt's Syst. Med.* II. 433 A warmed night-pan should be used to prevent the patient getting out of bed. **1632** MASSINGER *Maid of Hon.* II. ii, Which of your grooms..ministers *Night-physic to you? **1832** G. DOWNES *Lett. Cont. Countries* I. 271, I speculated..on what appeared to be a short cut to our *night-quarters. **1852** GROTE *Greece* II. lxx. IX. 124 They could only reach their night-quarters. **1872** B. JERROLD *London* xxi. 185 We are in the receiving home of a *night refuge—the home of the ragged scholars whom Lord Shaftesbury has befriended—of the wild young clients of the devoted city missionaries. **1911** *Rep. Labour & Social Conditions in Germany* (Tariff Reform League) III. 223 We also had a visit to the Berlin night refuge. **1910** W. DE LA MARE *Three Mulla-Mulgars* xiii. 177 They would sneak off and hide in their *night-shelter. **1941** *Times* (Weekly ed.) 5 Feb. 4 Hours spent in night-shelters and tours of devastated areas. **1899** in A. Adburgham *Shops & Shopping* (1964) xxii. 261 *Night socks and hose. **1906** GALSWORTHY *Man of Property* III. iii. 305 To ask June whether she had worn night-socks up in those high hotels where it must be so cold of a night. **1961** *John o' London's* 28 Sept. 345/1 This won't be a show-off collection [of books]. Rather, a cross-section of what's on my *night-stand. **1939** C. DAY LEWIS *Child of Misfortune* 195 Oliver watched her fastening two children's *night-suits. **1788** HOLCROFT *Baron Trenck* (1886) ii. 59, I took care to make a stir in my *night-table. **1871** CARLYLE in *Mrs. C.'s Lett.* I. 208 The policeman's 'rattle' was a thing she actually had on her night-table. **1590** SHAKS. *Mids. N.* III. i. 172 The honie-bags steale from the humble Bees, And for *night-tapers crop their waxen thighes. **1623** FEATLY *Fisher Catched* Ep. Ded., Those glorious night-tapours, which were set so thick together in the streets. **1844** ALB. SMITH *Adv. Mr. Ledbury* (1856) I. x. 72 There are no *night-taverns, as in London. **1803** MARY CHARLTON *Wife & Mistress* I. 137, I stood upon the stairs with only my *night-things on. **1852** MRS. CARLYLE *Lett.* II. 166, I rendered myself at Paddington station..with my night-things in a bag. **1621** BRATHWAIT *Nat. Embassie* (1877) 102 Put a *night-tyre on it's ivorie head. **1863** KINGSLEY *Water-Bab.* 31 When she had put her head out of the window, her *night-wig fell into the garden. **1582** N. LICHEFIELD tr. *Castanheda's Conq. E. Ind.* 12 The other had a *night [w]rap of greene satten. **1863** A. D. WHITNEY *Faith Gartney's Girlhood* ix. 78 Miss Sampson entered..to put on her *night-wrapper and make ready for her watch.

c. With names denoting persons or agents, esp. such as act, or are on duty or abroad, during the night, as ***night-attendant, -brawler, -clerk, -editor, guard, nurse, -patrol, people, police, porter, sister, tourist***, etc.

1862 *N. Syd. Soc. Year-bk. Med. for 1861*, 173 Robertson requires the *night-attendants to visit all the habitually dirty patients at fixed times. **1604** SHAKS. *Oth.* II. iii. 196 You.. spend your rich opinion, for the name Of a *night-brawler. **1897** HOWELLS *Landlord at Lion's Head* 85 The witness of a hotel *night-clerk. **1377** LANGL. *P. Pl.* B. XIX. 140 [They] beden that men sholde Kepen it fro *niȝt-comeres. **1868** M. H. SMITH *Sunshine & Shadow in New York* lxxviii. 639 Henry Winson is city editor, and Governier Carr is *night editor. **1873** Night editor [see *day editor* s.v. DAY *sb.* 24]. **1949** *Time* 30 May 69/1 Stewart..had been night editor, sports editor and state editor of the Scripps-Howard *Press*. **1973** R. L. SIMON *Big Fix* (1974) xx. 174 Ask for the night editor. **1857** HUGHES *Tom Brown* I. ix, Hall and Brown were *night-fags last week. **1863** *Times* 16 June., That most indefatigable and restless of *night farers, the whip-poor-will. **1833** J. RENNIE *Alph. Angling* 49 Most fish are peculiarly *night-feeders. **1813** SCOTT *Rokeby* VI. iv, All the nameless tools that aid *Night-felons in their lawless trade. *a* **1810** SHELLEY *M. Nicholson, Despair*, 7 Can the fierce *night-fiends rest on yonder hill? **1816** KIRBY & SP. *Entomol.* xxi. (1818) II. 265 The infinite hosts of moths.., with few exceptions, are all *night-fliers. **1593** SHAKS. *3 Hen. VI*, IV. iii. 22 To defend his Person from *Night-foes. **1552** HULOET, Hegges or *nyght furyes.., which do sucke the bloude of children in the nyght, *striges*. **1642** W. MOUNTAGU in *Buccleuch MSS.* (Hist. MSS. Comm.) I. 302 The *night goers cause some suspicion, and presage no good. **1717** POPE *Iliad* x. 147 Between the trench and gates, Near the *night-guards, our chosen council waits. **1914** 'BARTIMEUS' *Naval Occasions* xvi. 128 'Night Guard,' said the Lieutenant curtly. **1784** G. WHITE *Selborne* ix, The deer ..are much thinned and reduced by the *night-hunters. **1810** *Sporting Mag.* XXXVI. 257 Night-Hunters or poachers..have, of late years, grown to be a very numerous body. **1865** DICKENS *Mut. Fr.* I. iii, Where they found the *Night-Inspector. **1764** *Museum Rust.* III. 286 Not a single *night-netter has been on his grounds on horse back. **1844** *Night-nurse [see *day-nurse* s.v. DAY *sb.* 23 c]. **1944** A. THIRKELL *Headmistress* ii. 36 The day nurse went off duty and the night nurse came on. **1971** 'F. CLIFFORD' *Blind Side* v. i. 190 Doctor O'Sullivan reckons Mrs. Lawrence needs a regular night nurse. *a* **1719** ADDISON tr. *Petronius Arbiter* (1736) 13 Must thou make a Noise, thou *Night-Pad? **1864** J. T. TROWBRIDGE *Cudjo's Cave* xxiii. 201 They discovered some horsemen drawn up before them beside the road. It was the *night-patrol. **1971** B. PATTEN *Irrelevant Song* 64 Leave it out among the night-patrols and the lovers. **1957** *N.Y. Post* 20 Sept. M4 *Night people, the professor and his wife used to retire at about 2.30 or 3 A.M. **1963** *Times* 8 Jan. 10/4 The 'night people', cleaners, maintenance men, and so on, who occupy the London Underground after the last train has gone. **1823** *Edin. Rev.* XXXIX. 51 *Night-poachers are transported for seven years. **1877** E. S. PHELPS *Story of Avis* 153 To recommend to the Faculty a stricter régime of *night police for those boys. **1861** DICKENS *Gt. Expect.* xliv, The *night-porter examined me with much attention. **1887** in C. E. Pascoe *Joyous Neighbourhood Covent Garden* 126 (Advt.), Rougemont hotel, Exeter... Night porter on patrol. **1963** N. MARSH *Dead Water* (1964) ix. 231 The night porter was reading behind his desk. **1969** H. MACINNES *Salzburg Connection* viii. 118 A little late, perhaps, to telephone but he knew the night porter there. **1646** TRAPP *Comm. John* vii. 50 Nicodemus was only a *night professor, Judas in the sight of all. **1813** BYRON *Giaour* 44 Rush the *night-prowlers on the prey. **1709** DAMPIER *Voy.* (1729) II. I. 77 There is a pair of Stocks by every Watch-House, to secure *Night Ramblers in. **1853** JAMES *Agnes Sorel* (1860) I. 4 A group of night-ramblers walked along. **1596** SPENSER *State Irel.* Wks. (Globe) 681/1 Wherby theeves and *night robbers might be more easely pursued. **1649** ROBERTS *Clavis Bibl.* 556 Edom shall be wholly spoiled, more then an house by Night-robbers. **1768–74** TUCKER *Lt. Nat.* (1834) II. 362 The hardiness of the night-robber. **1814** G. HANGER *To All Sportsmen* 96 That desperate gang of *night-shooters is totally broken up. **1886** E. C. E. LÜCKES *Hospital Sisters & their Duties* vi. 138 The *Night Sister's object is to help the Day sister by giving the supervision to her patients and Nurses which the latter cannot exercise both night and day. **1920** F. NORTON *Duties of Sisters in Small Hospitals* v. 54 The routine duties of the Night Sister consist in taking the day report, making periodical visits to the wards, supervising the admission of accidents and of emergency operation cases. **1934** P. BOTTOME *Private Worlds* 3 The door of the night-sister's room was open. **1958** Night-sister [see GARBO[1]]. **1973** 'E. PETERS' *City of Gold & Shadows* xii. 191 The night sister on duty was an old friend. **1611** FLORIO, *Ciuettini*,..wanton or effeminate lads, *night-sneakers. **1707** J. STEVENS tr. *Quevedo's Com. Wks.* (1709) 55 A Spark, who boasted he did not fear any Spirits or *Night-Specters. *a* **1591** H. SMITH *Wks.* (1866) I. 269 These *night-spirits begat purgatory.., as one serpent hatcheth another. **1601** HOLLAND *Pliny* II. 357 To sleepe securely, without any dread of night-spirits. *c* **1820** S. ROGERS *Italy* (1839) 97 To be proclaimed a ruffian, a *night-stabber. **1640** BP. REYNOLDS *Passions* Wks. (1679) 636 *Night-talkers, who cannot be said to be thoroughly asleep, nor perfectly awaked. **1382** WYCLIF *John* x. 10 A *niȝt theef cometh not, no but that he stele, and sle, and leese. **1681** W. ROBERTSON *Phraseol. Gen.* (1693) 1082 Night-thieves, house-breakers. **1963** L. DEIGHTON *Horse under Water* v. 28 They send me on a *Night Tourist aeroplane. **1971** P. PURSER *Holy Father's Navy* xviii. 88 The last plane will have gone, anyway. Unless there are night tourist flights. **1802** BLOOMFIELD *Rural Tales* 64 The lone *night-trav'ller's fancy. **1483** *Cath. Angl.* 255/1 A *Nighte waker, *noctivagus*.

d. With the names of animals, birds, etc. (sometimes in specific use), as ***night-ape, -beast, -butterfly, -churr, -cod, -crake, -cur, -dog, -fowl, -gnat, -herring, -monkey, -monster, -moth, -swallow, -wale, -warbler***. Also *fig.*, as ***night-bat, -hound, -howlet, -steed, -toad***. **night snake**, a name used for several nocturnal African snakes.

1863 BATES *Nat. Amazon* xii. (1864) 396 A third interesting genus of monkeys found near Ega are the nyctipitheci, or *night-apes. **1658** tr. *Bergerac's Satyr. Charac.* xii. 47, I send..the Hob-goblins, the haggs, the *night bats. **1847** HALLIWELL, *Night-bat*, a ghost. *North.* **1600** SURFLET *Countrie Farme* VII. xliii. 872 The flesh of *night-beastes, that is to say such as flie about in the night. **1577** B. GOOGE *Heresbach's Husb.* IV. (1586) 188 The *night Butterflie, that flieth about the candell. **1743** M. CATESBY *Nat. Hist.* (1754) II. 84 The four-eyed Night Butterfly ..(*Phalæna Luna*). **1855** *Orr's Circle Sci.*, *Org. Nat.* III. 343 It is to this note that the bird is indebted for its name of Nightjar or *Nightchurr. **1888** GOODE *Amer. Fishes* 343 Sometimes a school of Codfish will bite at night; these the fishermen call '*Night Cod'. *c* **1425** *Voc.* in Wr.-Wülcker 639/40 *Hec nicticorax*, *nyght-crake. **1576** FLEMING tr. *Caius' Dogs* in Arb. *Garner* III. 241 Farmers..call this kind of dog a *Night Cur; because he hunteth in the dark. **1598** SHAKS. *Merry W.* V. v. 252 When *night-dogges run, all sorts of Deere are chac'd. *c* **1616** FLETCHER & MASS. *Thierry & Theod.* I. i, Let night-dogs tear me..Ere I forsake my sphere! **1824** SYMMONS *Æschylus' Agamemnon* 3 Like a night-dog still Fix'd to my post. **1883** R. GROOM *Great Dane* 13 He has been used as a night-dog with great success. *a* **1225** *Ancr. R.* 142 Þe *nihtfuel ulið bi nihte, & biȝit ine þeosternesse his fode. **1830** TENNYSON *Mariana* 26 Waking she heard the night-fowl crow. **1530** PALSGR. 248/1 *Night gnat, *singalle*. **1758** BINNELL *Descr. Thames* 227 Fishers distinguish their Herrings into six different Sorts: As the Fat Herring,..the *Night Herring which is of a middle Size. **1673** R. HEAD *Canting Acad.* 30 The Constable..let loose a couple of his *Night-hounds. **1817** SCOTT *Rob Roy* xxxiv, O, the most egregious *night-howlets! **1871** KINGSLEY *At Last* xvii, A beautiful little *Night-Monkey, belonging to the Purser. **1896** O. FORBES *Hand-bk. Primates* I. 152 The Night-Monkeys are small and elegant animals covered with long hair. **1611** BIBLE *Isa.* xxxiv. 14 The shrichowle [*marg.*, Or, *night-monster] also shall rest there. **1859** MEREDITH *R. Feverel* xliii. A large white *night-moth flitted through the dusk. **1895** C. HOLLAND *Japanese Wife* 69 Huge, soft-winged night-moths which circle round the light of our lanterns. **1931** R. L. DITMARS *Snakes of World* ix. 93 The so-called Bush Snakes or *Night Snakes are rear-fanged species. **1954** J. A. PRINGLE *Common Snakes* 12 Olive Night-Snake..non-venomous..is a quiet, docile snake..mainly confined to the coastal belt from Cape Town to north of Durban. **1962** V. F. M. FITZSIMONS *Snakes S. Afr.* 112/1 *Lamprophis aurora*... Aurora- or Night-snake. **1841** BRYANT *Hunter's Serenade* Wks. (1891) 122 The *night-sparrow trills her song All night, with none to hear. **1629** MILTON *Hymn Nativ.* xxvi, The yellow-skirted Fayes, Fly after the '*Night-steeds, leaving their Moonlov'd maze. **1799** CAMPBELL *Pleas. Hope* Wks. (1837) 32 Chased on his night-steed by the star of day. **1840** *Penny Cycl.* XVI. 223/2 Night-Jars, the English name of those *Night-Swallows vernacularly termed Goat-suckers. **1681** OTWAY *Soldier's Fort.* V. i, Get ye gone, ye Dogs, ye Rogues, ye *Night Toads. **15..** *Parl. Byrdes* 161 in Hazl. *E.P.P.* III. 175 Then said the *night whale with his hed gray, He shameth us with his parlament aray. **1885** SWAINSON *Prov. Names Birds* 27 The name of *night warbler is also given to this bird [the reed-sparrow], because its cry may be heard at almost all hours.

e. With names of plants, as ***night-jasmine, -tree, -weed, -willow-herb***. **night-primrose** = *evening-primrose* (EVENING *sb.*[1] 5 b); **night stock** = *night-scented stock* (sense 14).

1866 *Treas. Bot.* 796/2 *Nyctanthes, Arbor tristis*, the *Night-Jasmine of India, is a shrub or small tree of the *Jasminaceæ*. **1881** CABLE *Mme. Delphine* ix. 49 The bush of night-jasmine. **1759** P. MILLER *Gardeners Dict.* (ed. 7) s.v. *Œnothera*. Tree Primrose... From the Flower opening in the Evening, many Persons call it the *Night Primrose. **1849** CRAIG, *Nightprimrose*. The plant Œnothera biennis is so called, because its flowers usually open between six and seven o'clock in the evenings. **1931** A. HUXLEY *Cicadas* 12 Your pallid beauty Like a pale night-primrose. **1918** D. H. LAWRENCE *New Poems* 33 The *night-stock oozes scent. **1849** *Southey's Comm.-pl. Bk.* II. 494 The Singadi, or *Night-Tree. **1796** CAMPBELL *Scene in Argylesh.*, The *night-weed and thorn overshadowed the place. **1847** DARLINGTON *Amer. Weeds* (1860) 136 Biennial Œnothera. Evening Primrose. *Night Willow-herb.

14. Special combs., as **night-adapted** *a.* = *dark-adapted* ppl. adj. s.v. DARK *sb.* 6; **night adder**, a nocturnal, venomous, African viper of the genus *Causus*, esp. *C. rhombeatus*, a grey snake with darker patches, common in southern Africa; **night-bag**, a travelling-bag containing necessaries for the night; †**night-blain**, a chilblain; **night-blood**, blood drawn from a patient by night, for microscopical examination; **night-blooming cereus**, one of several tropical plants belonging to the genera *Hylocereus* and *Selenicereus* of the family Cactaceæ, esp. *H. undulatus*, having very large, fragrant, white flowers that open only at night; **night-blue**, a recent name for various blues, esp. those which retain the colour under artificial light; also *attrib.* or as *adj.*; **night-boat**, (*a*) a boat used by night; (*b*) a passenger-boat which crosses by night; **night-bolt**, an inside bolt serving to secure a door by night; **night bomber**, an aircraft that drops bombs at night; also, the pilot of such an aircraft; hence ***night-bombing***;

†**night-book** (?); **night-bound** *a.*, bound, confined, or impeded by night or darkness; **night-box** = *boîte de nuit*; †**night-cape**, *fig.* a wife; **night-cart**, a cart used in removing filth by night; †**night-cat** (see quot.); **night chain**, a chain for securing a door at night; **night-climber**, one who climbs on buildings at night, esp. at the Universities of Oxford and Cambridge; so ***night-climbing***; **night clock**, a clock which is illuminated so that it can be seen in the dark; **night-cloud**, the form of cloud known as *stratus*; **night-club**, †(*a*) *U.S.* = *night-stick*; (*b*) a club or similar establishment that opens at night, usu. providing food, drink, and entertainment; also *attrib.*; hence **night-club** *v. trans.* and *intr.*, to take or go to a night-club; **night-clubber**, one who frequents night-clubs; **night-clubbing**, the frequenting of night-clubs; **night-clubby** *a.*, characteristic or fond of night-clubs; **night-coach**, (*a*) a coach that travels at night; (*b*) *U.S.*, a commercial aircraft providing a night service; **night crawler** *N. Amer.*, a large earthworm, esp. one caught at night to be used as bait in fishing; **night cream**, cosmetic cream that is applied to the face at night; **night-dial**, †(*a*) a transparent clock-dial or face which is lighted from behind at night; (*b*) a dial which shows the time by means of the moon's shadow (*Cent. Dict.*); **night-driving**, the driving of a motor vehicle at night; also *attrib.*; so **night-drive** *v. intr.*, to drive a motor vehicle at night; **night-eater** (*nonce-wd.*), a flea; **night effect**, irregularity of the strength and apparent direction of received radio waves of certain frequencies that is especially marked at night, owing to the reception of polarized waves reflected by the ionosphere; so **night error**; **night eye**, (*a*) *U.S.* = CHESTNUT 6; (*b*) an eye adapted for seeing in the dark (usu. *pl.*); **night-eyed** *a.*, capable of seeing in the night-time; †**night-farmer** = *gong-farmer* (GONG *sb.*[1]); **night-fighter**, a fighter (FIGHTER 3) used, or designed for use, at night; also, the pilot of such an aircraft; also *attrib.*; so ***night-fighting***; **night-flowering cereus** = *night-blooming cereus*; †**night-foe**, a chilblain; **night-fossicker** *Austral. Hist.*, a nocturnal thief of gold dust or quartz; so ***night-fossicking***; **night-herd** *N. Amer.*, the herding or guarding of cattle at night; hence as *v. intr.* and *trans.*, to herd or guard (cattle) at night; **night-herder**, one who night-herds; **night-herding**, the work of a night-herder; †**night-hooker**, one who steals by night; **night-horse**, (*a*) a horse used for work at night; (*b*) a punning alteration of NIGHTMARE *sb.*; **night-lark**, a person who goes about at night; **night-life**, manifestations of life at night; *spec.* the activities of, or urban entertainments open to, pleasure-seekers at night; **night-lifer**, one who enjoys night-life; †**night-lying**, bed-time; †**night-magistrate**, a constable (B.E. *Dict. Cant. Crew*, *a* 1700); **night-office** *R.C. Ch.*, (until 1971) the part of the canonical office performed during the night hours; **night-old** *a.*, done, gathered, etc., on the previous day; **night op** or **operation**, a military operation at night; **night paddock** *Austral.* and *N.Z.*, a field where stock, esp. dairy cows, are kept overnight; **night parrot** *Austral.*, a nocturnal green and yellow ground parrot, *Geopsittacus occidentalis*; **night rider**, one who rides by night, esp. on horse-back; *spec.* in *U.S.*, one of various gangs of mounted men who commit acts of violence in order to intimidate or punish (see also quots.); so ***night-riding*** vbl. sb. and ppl. adj.; †**night-runner** = NIGHTWALKER 1; **night-safe** (see quot. 1930); **night-scented stock**, a small annual herb, *Matthiola tristis* or *M. bicornis*, of the family Cruciferæ, whose fragrant lilac flowers open at night; **night-side**, (*a*) the dark or bad aspect of a person or thing; (*b*) *Shetland dial.*, in phr. *in the night-side*, in the evening; (*c*) (see quot. 1927); (*d*) the side of a planet that is facing away from the sun and is therefore in darkness; **night-sight**, (*a*) = NYCTALOPIA; (*b*) a rifle-sight designed for shooting at night; (*c*) = NIGHT-VISION 2 a; **night-singer**, a bird that sings by night; *spec.* the sedge-warbler; †**night-snap**, a night-thief; **night spot**, a night-club or similar place open to pleasure-seekers at night; **night-star**, (*a*) a star when shining by night; (*b*) the evening-star; **night starvation**, hunger at night; also *transf.*, lack of sexual gratification; **night-stick** orig. *U.S.*, a stick or truncheon carried by a policeman or the like, esp. at night; also *attrib.*; **night-stool** (see NIGHT-CHAIR); **night-stop**, a place where one stops for the night; the action of stopping at such a place; hence as *v. intr.*, to stop for the night; **night storage heater** or **radiator**, an electric heater in which heat can be accumulated at night and released during the day; so ***night-stored*** ppl. adj.; **night-terror**, a state of terror in which children sometimes awake during the night; †**night-trader**, a prostitute; †**night-tub**, a tub containing filth or night-soil; **night-watchman**, (*a*) a person employed to keep watch at night; (*b*) in *Cricket*, a batsman who goes in to bat just before the end of a day's play; **night-water**, water which collects or is stored during the night; †**night-worm**, (*a*) a treacherous comrade; (*b*) a prostitute; (*c*) a glow-worm; **night-yard** (see quot.).

1961 I. JEFFERIES *It wasn't Me!* x. 132 When the moon was up I let an hour pass to make sure my eyes were *night-adapted. **1972** J. POYER *Chinese Agenda* (1973) xi. 144 Just enough light for Gillon's night-adapted vision. **1834** PRINGLE *Afr. Sk.* 280 There are several species of snakes which have come under my own observation, such as the *nacht-slang* (*night-adder). **1915** *Chambers's Jrnl.* July 437/2 The night-adder, as its name implies, is most in evidence after sundown. **1947** J. STEVENSON-HAMILTON *Wild Life S. Afr.* xxxvi. 329 The Night Adder (*Causus rhombeatus*). *Ibid.*, I have often seen my cats eating night adders which they have caught and killed. **1966** C. SWEENEY *Scurrying Bush* vii. 98 The night adder was writhing in some discomfort. **1667** PEPYS *Diary* 13 June, They did go by the coach.., with about 1300*l.* in gold in their *night-bag. **1691** *Lond. Gaz.* No. 2666/4 A White Dimity Night-Bag..in which was Linnen, and other things. **1601** HOLLAND *Pliny* II. 37 Bloudie-falls or *night blains. **1897** *Allbutt's Syst. Med.* II. 1084, 56 slides of *night-blood from 56 cases of elephantiasis. **1832** J. LINDLEY *Introd. Bot.* IV. 402 Of a night (*nocturnus*); which appears during the night, and perishes before morning; as the flowers of the *night-blooming cereus. **1890** *Harper's Mag.* Mar. 613/1 My wife has a sweet face of her own, but one bearing the same relation to Miss Jasmine's as that existing between a sprig of mignonette and a night-blooming cereus. **1936** *Times Lit. Suppl.* 20 June 521/2 The flowering of the night-blooming cereus..is very lovingly described. **1971** E. L. WARDMAN *Bermuda Jubilee Garden* 199/2 Night-blooming cereus. A vine-like plant with triangular stems... Useful for clambering over a wall or rock face and even growing up a tree... Its very beautiful flowers open only after sunset and shrivel and die before morning. **1891** THORPE *Dict. Applied Chem.* II. 698 *Night-blue. **1908** *Paris Fashions* 18 Jan. 23/2 Costume of night-blue cloth. **1938** L. MACNEICE *I crossed Minch* II. viii. 106 The sky part of the landscape was night-blue. **1956** D. GASCOYNE *Night Thoughts* 45 That profound night-blue abyss of starry vacancy. **1970** R. P. WARREN *Incarnations* 17 On night-blue the tetter of cloud-scud. **1843** S. C. HALL *Ireland* III. 276 There is also a more cumbrous vessel called a '*night-boat'. **1891** KIPLING *Light that Failed* (1900) 153 They were going by the Dover night-boat. **1784** COWPER *Task* IV. 568 Ere you sleep..drop the *nightbolt. **1862** *Catal. Internat. Exhib., Brit. Div.* II. No. 5978 Mortise balance night bolt, and an improved night-latch. **1918** *Flying* 4 Sept. 221 (*caption*) A British *night-bomber photographed by searchlight. **1919** R. H. REECE *Night Bombing with Bedouins* 57 These calculations are all important to the long-distance night bomber. **1936** *Economist* 11 Jan. 85/2 The Fairey Company is an air-frame concern which is chiefly interested in the 'Hendon' night bomber. **1975** *Listener* 13 Mar. 335/1 Scheduled air services began on 25 August 1919..using ten- and 12-seated converted night bombers. **1942** W. S. CHURCHILL *End of Beginning* (1943) 118 These two great *night-bombing raids mark the introduction of a new phase in the British air offensive against Germany. **1809** *Sporting Mag.* XXXIV. 56 Suffering his name to remain upon the debtor side of a *night book for years. **1925** A. S. M. HUTCHINSON *One Increasing Purpose* I. xxvi. 161 As if the phrase were a path on which, *nightbound and groping, he suddenly had stumbled. *Ibid.* II. ii. 203 A finger-post whose word the nightbound traveller hates to obey yet may not disbelieve. **1954** L. MACNEICE *Autumn Sequel* 123 From my seat I see my night-bound double, slumped apart On a conveyor belt. **1938** *New Statesman* 23 July 154/1, I have very rarely been overcharged in France (except in the grotesque *night-boxes of Montmartre). **1973** E. MCGIRR *Bardel's Murder* iv. 108 Night boxes..came and they went, and the more crowded the more successful. **1604** SHAKS. *Oth.* II. i. 316, I fear Cassio with my *Night-Cape too. **1851** MAYHEW *Lond. Labour* (1865) II. 511/2 Who drive the *night-carts to and from..the cesspools. **1860** MASSEY *Hist. Eng.* (1865) III. 381 The prisoners were charged with having provided arms, and instruments called *night-cats, for impeding the action of cavalry in the streets. **1904** E. GLASGOW *Deliverance* 45 He had fastened the *night-chain and shot the heavy bolt. **1973** 'E. MCBAIN' *Let's hear It* xiv. 205 Kling heard the night chain being slipped off, the lock turning. **1968** J. M. WHITE *Nightclimber* iv. 28, I had repeated the whole series of safaris among the tiles and chimneypots pioneered by the *Night-climbers. *Ibid.* 27, I didn't realise you were interested in *night-climbing. **1911** F. J. BRITTEN *Old Clocks & Watches* (ed. 3) v. 266 A *night clock..is of ebony on oak, and the top lifts off to allow the insertion of a lamp. Showing through a curved slit in the upper part of the dial is a disc with perforated hour numerals so that the time can be seen at night. The light would also shine through a keyhole-shaped aperture above which serves as a pointer. **1972** *Times* 7 Nov. 25/4 (Advt.), A rare 17th century night clock, by Edward East, London. **1862** *Chambers's Encycl.* III. 86 Stratus, fall or *night-cloud,..is a widely extended horizontal sheet. **1882** J. D. MCCABE *New York* 383 The entire force on duty at the station dashed into the street, armed with their long *night clubs. **1894** W. J. LOCKE *At Gate of Samaria* (1903) xxvii. 319 They went together to East End music-halls,..night clubs in the West End, where ladies are admitted free on a member's introduction. **1906** R. MACHRAY *Night Side of London* i. 21 Finishing up, perhaps, at some night-club, or in some other den. **1915** Night club [see CABARET[1] 2 b]. **1928** F. B. YOUNG *My Brother Jonathan* II. viii. 355 A life of night-clubs and jazz-bands. **1938** *Amer. Speech* XIII. 194 Pleasure seekers at first went to night clubs; now, at least in the columns of the Broadway gossips, they simply *night-club*. **1965** *New Statesman* 9 Apr. 557/2 The sharp limitation in the circumstances in which businessmen can wine and dine and nightclub other businessmen. **1972** P. DRISCOLL *Wilby Conspiracy* (1973) xi. 138 That bitch of a nightclub singer. **1974** *Listener* 31 Jan. 131/1 The foreboding, the mounting menace, that we can trace through, say, the night-club songs of the Weimar republic. **1952** B. ULANOV *Hist. Jazz in Amer.* (1958) xv. 177 From the general hubbub of night clubs and the particular cries and grunts of *night-clubbers ..Bubber made his music. **1953** 'S. RANSOME' *Hear No Evil* (1954) xv. 138 Bendley, a confirmed night-clubber. **1936** R. LEHMANN *Weather in Streets* I. v. 90 No, she never married. .. Does some little odd jobs and goes lunching and dining and *night-clubbing. **1941** HERMER & MAY *Havana Mañana* p. xii, There have been no books about Havana that show tourists how to get more than their money's worth out of stopping, eating, sightseeing and nightclubbing. **1947** *Sun* (Baltimore) 4 Aug. 1/2 Senator Pepper (D. Fla.) today tabbed as possibly 'base judgment' the 1943 night clubbing activities which Elliott Roosevelt will be asked to explain tomorrow to senators investigating Howard Hughes's wartime plane contracts. **1971** D. BAGLEY *Freedom Trap* viii. 181 Too much damned night-clubbing. **1933** G. B. SHAW *Political Madhouse in Amer.* 48 You have become a wonderful *night clubby sort of nation. **1958** *New Statesman* 6 Sept. 314/2 A nightclubby girl 'with a spurious American accent' is a minor character in the recent *Sober as a Judge* by Henry Cecil. **1844** DICKENS *Mart. Chuz.* xi, The *night-coach had a punctual character. **1959** *Wall St. Jrnl.* (Eastern ed.) 7 Oct. 8/4 Standard first class Miami-New York fare oneway is $80.80, regular daycoach is $54.55 and regular nightcoach is $46.80 **1960** *Daily Progress* (Charlottesville, Va.) 6 Jan., A National Airlines night coach flying non-stop from New York to Miami crashed with 34 persons aboard. **1924** *Collier's* 2 Feb. 3/1 He could stay up till 10 and hunt *night crawlers in the garden with a lantern. **1948** *Esquire* Mar. 88 Members of the Huck Finn school of fishing..have been looking for some way to enliven the almost impossibly sluggish night crawler. **1951** T. CAPOTE *Grass Harp* (1952) ii. 64 Night-crawlers slithered away from its lurching light. **1971** B. MALAMUD *Tenants* 12 Lesser tried to scare off the nightcrawlers on his floor..by playing loud his hi-fi at night. **1973** *Islander* (Victoria, B.C.) 5 Aug. 13/2 Sympathy and practical help poured in from every direction. Small donations of native worms—night crawlers —were the most practical help. **1926–7** *Army & Navy Stores Catal.* 496/2 Day Cream... Massage Cream... *Night Cream. **1963** D. GRAY *Murder in Mind* iii. 23 Except for a thick night cream, she took so little [care] of her face. **1670–98** LASSELS *Voy. Italy* I. 30 The *Night-dial shews by a lighted lamp set behind it, the hours of the night. **1956** *This Week* 29 July 11/2 If you must *night-drive, keep the dash-lights as dim as possible—this particular glare is hypnotic. **1929** *Times* 31 Oct. 21/3 Those who have used this latest device under actual *night-driving conditions are unanimous in their praise. **1936** *Discovery* Oct. 302/1 The application of a sheet of..Polaroid..should remove one of the greatest inconveniences of night driving. **1962** L. S. SASIENI *Optical Dispensing* xiii. 327 There have been introduced from time to time certain glasses said to increase vision in low illumination—and so-called night-driving glasses. There are many arguments as to the merits and demerits of tinted glasses for night driving. **1626** BRETON *Fantastickes* Sept., The Innes now begin to prouide for ghests, and the *night-eaters in the stable pinch the Trauailer in his bed. **1914** R. STANLEY *Text-bk. Wireless Telegr.* x. 114 The difference between day and *night effects on the transmitted ether energy might possibly be caused by a change in the position of the upper conducting layer of atmosphere. **1932** F. E. TERMAN *Radio Engineering* xvi. 591 Since the sky wave is always strongest at night the errors that result from downcoming horizontally polarized waves are frequently referred to as 'night effects' although they are always present to some extent in daytime. **1962** J. H. & P. J. REYNER *Radio Communication* viii. 333 A phenomenon which considerably affects D.F. work is what is known as 'night effect'. **1921** *Flight* XIII. 664/1 Aircraft when within an area northward of the parallel of latitude 51° 10′ 00″ N., and westward of the meridian of longitude 8° 30′ 00″ W., should not ask for bearings from Carnsore, as such bearings ..will probably be unreliable on account of the effect of the coastline, the *night error in particular being of considerable magnitude. **1936** *Jrnl. R. Aeronaut. Soc.* XL. 161 These wave-lengths are subject to night error which affects the accuracy of bearings taken on medium wave direction finders. **1948** *Sat. Even. Post* 29 May 116/1 Six photographs are taken—a front view, side view and close-ups of the horse's four 'chestnuts', or '*night eyes', which are the rough protrusions of scaly, hardened skin that are on the inner side of each leg. **1954** J. R. R. TOLKIEN *Fellowship of Ring* II. ix. 402 It was dark, but not too dark for the night-eyes of Orcs. **1956** I. FLEMING *Diamonds are Forever* viii. 80 'The Jockey Club are going to change to photos of the night eyes [to help identify race horses].' 'What are night eyes?' 'They're those callouses on the inside of a horse's knees. The English call them 'chestnuts'. Seems they're different on every horse. Like a man's fingerprints.' **1957** 'J. WYNDHAM' *Midwich Cuckoos* ii. 21 The last customers to be persuaded out of The Scythe and Stone had lingered for a few minutes to get their night-eyes and gone their ways. **1963** M. A. STONERIDGE *Horse of your Own* ii. 75 Inside each of the horse's legs you will notice a sort of horny excrescence called Chestnuts or Night Eyes, which are vestigial toes (remember, prehistoric horses had four or five of them). Night Eyes vary in form with no two alike; they are as individual as human fingerprints and recorded as part of the identification system for thoroughbred race horses and registered trotters. **1603** B. JONSON *Sejanus* IV. v, I dare tell you..That our *night-eyed Tiberius doth not see His minion's drifts. **1620** MIDDLETON *World Tost at Tennis* C 2 'Tis a poor living... *Sol.* 'Tis somewhat better then the *night-farmer yet. **1647** LILLY *Chr. Astrol.* cxlix. 633 He makes Night-farmers, Slaughter-men, sweepers of channels, &c. **1941** *Aeronautics* Jan. 41/3 The effective range of fire of *night fighter aircraft will have to be increased. **1941** *Times* (Weekly ed.) 5 Feb. 15 The defence by night-fighter aeroplanes was the most difficult task of anti-aircraft defences. 1942 Tee Emm (Air Ministry) II. 62 That..is the gist, or guts, of the night-fighter pilot's training. Ibid. 85 Particularly important this for night-fighters. 1947 J. Mulgan Report on Experience vi. 80 Meeting sometimes night-fighters or flak coming back over the coast defences. 1933 Meccano Mag. Feb. 109/1 *Night fighting consists chiefly of individual attacks at close range. 1947 Crowther & Whiddington Science at War 60 The radar air interception equipments, used in the early night-fighting battles. 1789 W. Aiton Hortus Kewensis II. 152 Great *Night-flowering Cereus. Nat[ive] of Jamaica and Vera Cruz. 1601 Holland Pliny xx. xx. II. 70 Coriander.. cureth the *night-foes or chilblanes. 1853 C. R. Read What I heard, saw, & did at Austral. Gold Fields 150 (Morris), The man was what they called a *night fossicker, who slept, or did nothing during the day, and then went round at night to where he knew the claims to be rich, and stole the stuff by candle-light. 1889 Cent. Dict., *Night-fossicking. 1513 Douglas Æneis xii. Prol. 1 Dyonea, *nycht hyrd, and wach of day. 1884 R. Aldridge Life on Ranch 62 When on night-herd the men usually keep singing all the time as they ride round. 1903 A. Adams Log of Cowboy ii. 11 Forrest night herded them using five guards. Ibid. vii. 97 We night herded as usual. 1955 R. P. Hobson Nothing too Good for Cowboy viii. 71 Simrose and Rob came in from their night-herd shift. 1962 W. Stegner Wolf Willow iii. ii. 163 Everything he said or played or sang during his hours on the night herd was meant seriously. 1963 R. D. Symons Many Trails 37 We certainly did not propose to night herd. 1873 J. H. Beadle Undevel. West v. 98 The '*night-herder' Billy Keyes, and two other drivers..were Gentiles. 1891 C. Roberts Adrift Amer. 188 The night herders renewed it [the fire] from time to time. 1888 Chambers's Jrnl. Apr. 221/1 This is called *night-herding. 1890 L. C. D'Oyle Notches 55 That night-herding was becoming unpleasant work. 1908 Sat. Even. Post 24 Oct. 10/1 A long-eared, reddish, sleepy-eyed..mule frequently used in night-herding. 1933 J. V. Allen Cowboy Lore iv. 71 David went from night-herding to using a sling. 1601 Holland Pliny xix. iv. 12 These slie theeves and *night-hookers..committed such fellonious outrages. 1908 Sat. Even. Post 4 July 22/3 They made Blackie a *night horse, for his sure-footedness was remarkable. 1925 J. Farnol Loring Mystery xlii. 283 'Talking o' bed,' quoth Mr. Shrig.., 'do you ever dream —— d'ye ever have the night-'orse?' 1929 Amer. Speech V. 67 Usually the 'kept horses' or 'herding horses' are also 'night horses', those used for 'night herding'. 1937 Dialect Notes VI. 618 The night horse is one staked near the cowpuncher's bed for immediate use in some such emergency as a stampede. 1959 C. MacInnes Absolute Beginners 81 The capital was a night-horse dream. 1967 Coast to Coast 1965–66 195 The smell of the night-horse nearby and the cattle a little beyond will tie you to reality. 1895 G. Meredith Amaz. Marriage I. xxiii. 258 *Night-larks of different classes, both sexes. 1852 H. Melville Pierre xvi. i. 322 All the garish *night-life of a vast thoroughfare, crowded and wedged by day, and even now, at this late hour, brilliant with occasional illuminations. 1913 H. L. Mencken Let. 17 Aug. (1961) 32 The title 'Night Life in Vienna'..has the air of a lure held out to the Puritanical and dirty-minded. 1927 G. Ade et al. Let. 4 Mar. (1973) 119 Our fellow-passengers..were ashore last night, dancing and hunting up a second-rate African imitation of night life in Paris. 1929 D. L. Moore Pandora's Letter Box iii. 53 'Night life'—to use the popular expression for habitual nocturnal dancing and drinking. 1972 Sat. Rev. (U.S.) 25 Mar. 68/3 The Kabarett, with its sharp political satire, was part of Berlin night life. 1967 W. Soyinka Kongi's Harvest 13 A few *night-lifers pick up their drinks and go in. 1456 Paston Lett. I. 369 They avaunted of it when he of Lynne came by him at *ny3t lyeng. 1767 A. B. Short Acct. Life Mary of Holy Cross 84 In the Time of St. Peter Damian, only the Clergy rose to the *Night Office. 1909 M. B. Saunders Litany Lane i. iii. 34 A small chapel in which the brothers held their short night-office. 1957 Oxf. Dict. Chr. Church 960/1 Night office, another name for Mattins, the liturgical office prescribed for the night. c 1000 Laws of Ine 73 in Thorpe Laws I. 148 3if hit biþ *niht-eald þiefþ. 1362 Langl. P. Pl. A. vii. 296 Laborers..Deyne not to dyne a day niht olde wortes. 1916 W. Owen Let. 6 Apr. (1967) 388 We had '*Night Ops.' yesterday till 9.30! Ibid. 10 Apr. 390 We had *Night Operations again. 1930 Bulletin (Sydney) 29 Jan. 62/4 He strode up to the big, heavily-capped yards in the corner of the *night-paddock. 1950 N.Z. Jrnl. Agric. Jan. 71/2 Night paddocks on dairy farms showed least response [to potash topdressing]. 1966 Te Reo IX. 54 The apparently Australian innovation lies..in the adoption of the refined terminology of the home paddock and the night paddock. 1917 Chambers's Jrnl. Feb. 89/1 Even on moonlight nights I could never catch a glimpse of the flying *night-parrots. 1934 Bulletin (Sydney) 9 May 21/1 The night parrot..continues to hide itself from human ken, and is always referred to either as the elusive parrot or mystery bird. 1965 Austral. Encycl. VII. 27/2 A second remarkable parrot of the ground is one known as the night parrot, sole member of the genus Geopsittacus, which is, or used to be, distributed widely throughout the drier parts of the inland region. It is closely associated with the spiny spinifex or porcupine-grass, hiding in the thick clusters by day, feeding on their seeds at night. 1877 J. M. Wells Chisolm Massacre x. 118 They said that *night-riders had shot into the houses of the colored people. 1879 Congress. Rec. 20 May 1480/1 There was much said..of kuklux, white leagues, and night-riders... There are..no night-riders in the State of Louisiana. 1882 F. W. P. Jago Anc. Lang. & Dial.. Cornwall 226 Night-riders, Piskey (Fairy) people who have been riding Tom (the name of a horse) again. 1906 Kipling Puck of Pook's Hill 10 Leprechauns, night-riders, pixies, nixies. 1907 Lit. Digest 28 Dec. 976 The first appearance of the night riders was in November, 1906, when they destroyed some tobacco-barns and small factories in Todd County. 1911 J. Masefield Jim Davis ii. 12 They were the night-riders or smugglers. 1936 J. G. Miller Black Patch War 18 The Night Rider burnt his warehouse and his purchase with it. 1948 E. N. Dick Dixie Frontier 94 Patrols, called patterols by the slaves, were organized by the whites, and these night riders endeavored to enforce the regulations. 1970 New Yorker 12 Dec. 166/3 Night riders who fire shotgun blasts at the home of an anti-war leader..are routine. 1973 J. Cleary Ransom viii. 184 As a plainclothesman he had travelled on late trains out of Sydney to the suburbs, riding shotgun as it were against hooligans... Night riders, he guessed, were the same everywhere. 1875 Chicago Tribune 6 Nov. 3/6 To-night.. there is to be a '*night riding' and shooting..to arouse a degree of uneasiness in the darky's mind and cause him.. not to go to the election. 1909 Chambers's Jrnl. Feb. 104/1 Night riding began as soon as the farmers' associations were organised. 1952 C. Day Lewis tr. Virgil's Aeneid x. 215 The gentle Moon's Night-riding horses were pacing halfway across the heavens. 14.. Vergilius in Thoms E. Eng. Prose Rom. (1858) II. 40 How the *nyght ronners, and yll doers myght be ryd out of the stretes. 1930 W. Thomson Dict. Banking (ed. 7) 501/2 *Night safes. In order that customers may deposit cash or cheques after a bank has closed for the day or for the week-end, night safes were introduced in 1928. The entrance to these safes is in the outside wall of the bank, the opening being fitted with a locked cover to which customers who wish to avail themselves of the safe are supplied with a key. 1959 Times 18 Feb. 11/5 Night safes don't cash cheques. 1975 'M. Yorke' Small Hours iii. 31 Ray had tracked down one of the night-safe depositors. [1824 H. Phillips Flora Historica I. 336 We have no plant that exhales so delightful a fragrance in the night as the.. Night-smelling Rocket, or Night Odorous Stock.] 1849 *Night-scented stock [see night-scented, sense 12 c]. 1870 W. Robinson Wild Garden ii. 54 Night-scented Stock... May be established on the sunny sides of old ruins and walls. 1914 E. A. Bowles My Garden in Summer xiv. 259 The old Night-scented Stock of one's great-grandmother, is another half-hardy indispensable. 1972 Country Life 23 Mar. 690/1 Seeds of small annuals such as night-scented stock..I broadcast by scattering them over the ground. 1848 Mrs. Crowe (title) The *Night Side of Nature. 1855 G. Brimley Ess., Tennyson 99 The night-side of the soul. 1898 Shetland News 10 Dec., If Willie id been some boys, diel wird he'd sung i' da nicht side. 1900 Ibid. 26 May, Dis kirn is no laek ta brak i' da night side. 1927 Amer. Speech II. 242/2 On papers having both morning and afternoon editions one also hears references to the two divisions of the staff as the 'day side' and the 'night side'. 1951 A. C. Clarke Sands of Mars viii. 94 It was a live programme, beamed to Mars from somewhere on the night-side of Earth. 1970 Nature 7 Mar. 925/1 On the nightside of Venus at altitudes between 750 km and 1,450 km the presence of a light ion was inferred. 1973 G. Greene Honorary Consul v. iii. 285 Suppose the night-side of God swallows up the day-side altogether? Suppose it is the good side which withers away? 1974 Nature 4 Jan. 24/1 The orbit is near-polar with the north-going passes on the nightside at about 2230 LT, and the south-going passes on the dayside at about 1030 LT. 1822–34 Good's Study Med. (ed. 4) III. 144 Nyctalopia has necessarily been made to import day-sight instead of *night-sight. 1915 Chambers's Jrnl. Apr. 269/2 The night-sight does not interfere with the ordinary front-sight for daylight shooting. 1971 Guardian Weekly 6 Nov. 12 Our marksman..saw him clearly through his night-sight. 1972 B. Everitt Cold Front xv. 143 My night-sight is good and I drove on side-lights only. 1973 'D. Halliday' Dolly & Starry Bird ii. 29 At night the full lights in the cupola never go on. They would spoil the plate and ruin your night sight. 1816 Kirby & Sp. Entomol. xxiv. (1818) II. 401 The Fulgoræ appear to be *night-singers. 1840 Penny Cycl. XVI. 230/1 The Nightingale, or night singer, is a migratory bird. 1885 Swainson Prov. Names Birds 28 Sedge Warbler,..night singer (Ireland). 1620 Fletcher Chances ii. i, These fellows Were *night-snaps. 1936 Swing Music Mar. 9/1 The management at the Friar's Inn, well-known Chicago *night spot, was very anxious to feature this new type of music. 1947 Sun (Baltimore) 4 Aug. 1/2 He was the guest of John Meyer, publicity man, in a costly round of New York night spots. 1959 F. Usher Death in Error i. 18 They went to a night spot..where they drank champagne. 1973 Express (Trinidad & Tobago) 26 June 4/6 A flash fire..swept through a New Orleans night spot. 1811 Shelley St. Irvyne iii. vi, Till the *night-stars shone through the cloudless air. 1823 Joanna Baillie Poems 48 Where sober evening's primrose pale, To greet the nightstar, blows. 1838 Eliza Cook Away from the revel iv, It is twilight; the night-star is up. 1936 'G. Orwell' Keep Aspidistra Flying xii. 311 What they asked for was a really telling slogan; something in the class of '*Night-starvation' ..that would rankle in the public consciousness. 1949 Partridge Dict. Slang (ed. 3) Add. 1119/1 Night starvation, sexual deprivation, lack of sexual intimacy. 1970 Southerly XXX. 286 David's head is in the right place—night starvation—Horlicks—Venus de Milo. 1971 D. Lees Rainbow Conspiracy viii. 117 It wasn't as if I was suffering from night starvation. Val was easily one of the best screws in the business. 1974 Harpers & Queen Sept. 135/1 My bread rolls she secretes..against night starvation. 1887 W. E. S. Fales Brooklyn's Guardians ii. 30 In the wealthier thoroughfares the brawls were of so frequent occurrence that the sight of two watchmen..pounding each other with their *night-sticks, occasioned no comment. 1893 S. Crane Maggie xi. 102 The officer made a terrific advance, club in hand. One comprehensive sweep of the long night stick threw the ally to the floor. 1904 'No. 1500' Life in Sing Sing i. 10 Big clubs, heavier and more formidable than a policeman's night stick. 1905 N.Y. Times 15 July, San Juan Hill and the Gut were under nightstick law until early this morning. 1932 New Yorker 4 June 23 There's a lot of law at the end of a nightstick. 1963 T. & P. Morris Pentonville x. 209 Hospital officers do not carry night sticks. 1973 J. Wambaugh Blue Knight i. 18 A beat cop has to be big..or ..somebody'd take the night-stick off him and shove it up his ass. 1975 Daily Tel. 30 June 1/5 Police chased the demonstrators down the streets [of Delhi], stopping occasionally to swing at anyone in their way with heavy wooden nightsticks. 1854 Ronalds & Richardson Chem. Technol. (ed. 2) I. 246 Each cell..contains a gas-burner and a *night-stool. 1791 J. Byng Diary 3 July in Torrington Diaries (1935) II. 360 Dunnington, a small market-town, where I dined..in a quiet house, but not a *night-stop. 1951 'N. Shute' Round the Bend 232 Next day took us to Karachi, where we night-stopped before going on to Bahrein. 1959 New Statesman 8 Aug. 151/1 When coming back from India took five days, with agreeable night-stops along the way, it was quite pleasant. 1972 C. Kearey Last Plane from Uli ii. 34 'Are you night-stopping, sir?' the Immigration Chief asked curiously. 'No, I'm taking off for Lagos as soon as the refuelling's finished.' 1975 Daily Tel. (Colour Suppl.) 4 Apr. 16/1 Had the supervisors declared the plane unserviceable, another 747..due to night-stop in London would have been allocated to take her place. 1963 Good Housek. Setting up Home iii. 30 Electric *night storage heaters. These are electric heaters which..absorb and store heat during the night when off-peak rates for electricity are available, releasing it during the day. 1970 House & Garden Mar. 94/3 The eight-hour-charge night-storage radiators.. are able to store enough heat to give an even heat output for the rest of the day. 1973 Guardian 23 May 9/6 Night storage heaters are metal boxes filled with bricks wired for electric heating. 1962 Daily Tel. 20 Aug. 16/2 (heading) *Night-stored heat from electricity. 1897 Allbutt's Syst. Med. IV. 717 Suffocative '*night-terrors' often occur. 1899 Ibid. VIII. 218 Many excellent monographs on night terrors have appeared. 1629 Massinger Picture i. ii, All kinds of females, from the *night-trader I' the street..To the great lady in her cabinet. a 1616 B. Jonson Epigr., On Fam. Voy. 64 As at the muster Of all your *night-tubs, when the carts do cluster. 1863 A. D. Whitney Faith Gartney's Girlhood xxviii. 261 Michael Garvin, the *night-watchman,..had left. 1874 W. P. Mackay Grace & Truth iv, He is engaged to be a night-watchman. 1926 J. Masefield Odtaa xiii. 214 There must be at least a caretaker or night-watchman. 1949 Partridge Dict. Slang (ed. 3) Add. 1119/1 Night-watchman, a (usually a second-rate) batsman sent in to 'hold up an end' until the close of play. 1971 Sunday Times 2 May 24 The fifth [ball] was caught by Turner off the nightwatchman Wasim Bari's glove and shoulder. 1799 J. Robertson Agric. Perth 504 A drain half a mile long, and a reservoir for the *night-water. 1874 Raymond Statist. Mines & Mining 319 On the supposition that..the night-water was saved. 1430–40 Lydg. Bochas i. xix. (1554) 36 Suffre no *night worm within your counsell crepe. 1605 Daniel Queen's Arcadia i. iii, Bed-Brokers, Night-Worms and Impressitors. 1774 Mason Poems 222 (Jod.), Like a nest of night-worms they did glitter, Sprinkling the plain with brightness. 1851 Mayhew Lond. Labour II. 216 The *night-yards, or the places where the contents of the cess-pools are deposited.

night (naɪt), *v.* Forms: 4–6 **nyghte**, (4 **nyhte**, 5 **ny3te**, 6 **nyghtt-**), 5–6 *Sc.* **nycht, nicht**, (7 **nich**); 7– **night**. [f. the sb. Cf. OHG. *nahtên* (G. *nachten*, and dial. *nàchten*), ON. *nátta* (Norw. and MSw. *natta*, Da. *natte*).]

1. *intr.* To spend or pass the night; to remain or lodge for the night. Now *rare*.

1303 R. Brunne Handl. Synne 7730 He nyghtede yn a wasteyne, þere he sagh no stede certeyne. 1435 Misyn Fire of Love 46 For criste, to vs to pray, ensaumpyl gaf qwhen in prayer allon in þe hyll [he] nyghtyd. 1502 in Antiq. Rep. (1808) II. 256 Upon the morowe he nyghted at his castell of Wyndsore. 1632 Lithgow Trav. vii. 335 Leauing these Mountaynes..and passing the Townes of Antibo and Cana, to night at Furges. a 1670 Spalding Troub. Chas. I (1850) II. 6 Thay nicht for thair awin pay in the oldtoun. 1786 A. Gib Sacr. Contempl. i. v. i. 138 The words translated abideth not, strictly mean nighteth not, passeth not a night. 1818 Hogg Tales, Brownie of Bodsbeck (1866) 56 You and I shall never night thegither again in the same house. 1886 R. F. Burton Arab. Nts. (abr. ed.) I. 88 Would Heaven we had never entered this house, but had rather nighted on the mounds and heaps outside the city!

fig. c 1440 Gesta Rom. xlvii. (Add. MS.) 205 He entrede.. the wombe of the blissede Virgyne, and there he nyghted from the tyme of his conception vnto his birthe.

†**b.** To cease work for the night. *Obs. rare*⁻¹.

1529 Burgh Rec. Stirling (1887) I. 35 Till entyr to his werk at day lycht in the morwyng, laif at half hour to twelf at none, and nycht at ewyn.

†**2.** *impers.* To turn to night; to grow dark. Also with dat. of person. *Obs.*

c 1374 Chaucer Troylus v. 515 Into tyme that it gan to nyghte, They speken of Cryseyde. 1390 Gower Conf. II. 293 A while er it began to nyhte, A povere man..Cam forth walkende. c 1425 Wyntoun Cron. viii. xxvi. 3437 It nychtyd fast: and thai Thowcht till abyd thare to the day. c 1475 Rauf Coilȝear 40 Euill lykand was the Kyng, it nichtit him sa lait. 1500–20 Dunbar Poems v. 15 Att ane ailhous neir [hevin], it nyghttit thaim thare.

†**b.** Of the night: To come down, to fall. *Obs.*⁻¹

1422 tr. Secreta Secret., Priv. Priv. 153 Nero in ill tyme hym myght not Suffice the lordshupp of Solerne ther as the day dawyth, nethyr of galerne the baillie, ther as the nyght nyghtyth.

†**3.** In *passive*. To be overtaken by night, to be benighted. *Obs.*

c 1440 Bone Flor. 1437 They were nyghtyd in a wode thyck. 1470–85 Malory Arthur iv. xxv. 153 They cam in to a depe forest, and by fortune they were ny3ted. 1526 Pilgr. Perf. (W. de W. 1531) 133 b, Yf it fortune them to be nyghted, and the gates of the cite where they wold rest shutte. 1641 Best Farm. Bks. (Surtees) 101 Theire desire is to buy soone, that they may be goinge betimes, for feare of beinge nighted.

ˈ**night-bird.** [f. Night *sb.* + Bird *sb.*]

1. A bird of nocturnal habits; one that is chiefly (or only) heard or seen by night; *esp.* the owl or nightingale.

Also given as a local name for the Moorhen and the Manx Shearwater (Swainson).

1608 Shaks. Per. iv. Introd. 26 When to the lute She sung, and made the night-bird mute. 1657 Baxter Ministry §11. 6 The Owl will call the Lark a night-bird. 1752 W. Mason Elfrida Poems 5 The night-bird's 'custom'd spray What time she pours her wild, and artless song. 1797 Coleridge France i, Ye Woods! that listen to the night-birds singing. 1819 Shelley Similes ii, As two gibbering night-birds flit From their bowers of deadly yew. 1840 Cuvier's Anim. Kingd. 195 The Moth-hunters have the same light, soft plumage..that characterizes other night-birds. 1890 'R. Boldrewood' Col. Reformer (1891) 215 The..sound of the night-bird broke the profound..silence.

2. *transf.* Of persons: One who goes about at night; a night-thief.

c 1546 Crowley Confut. Shaxton E iij b, For the daye birdes can holde theymselues contente wyth thys lyght. As for the lurkinge night byrds that fle the lyghte [etc.]. 1618 Dalton Countr. Just. 66 For as one saieth, such Night-walkers (or night birds) are ominous. 1646 Boyle in Birch Life B's. Wks. 1772 I. p. xxix, These night-birds used to exercise their charity in easing weary travellers of..money and portmanteaus. *a* **1721** SHEFFIELD (Dk. Buckhm.) *Wks.* (1729) 122 When o'er his Cups this Night-Bird chirping sits. **1870** D. J. KIRWAN *Palace & Hovel* xxxii. 481 When the dancing places..close, this door remains open to catch all stray night birds who can find no other resting place. **1871** G. EASTON *Trav. Amer.* 41 In Boston the cars run till midnight, and after that time one car runs every hour through the principal thoroughfare for the accommodation of 'Night Birds'. **1900** [see BRUNCH]. **1939** JOYCE *Finnegans Wake* 438, I have every reason to know that rogues' gallery of nightbirds and bitchfanciers. **1974** 'J. LE CARRÉ' *Tinker, Tailor* xxxv. 313 It was nearly midnight... He was a night bird.

'night-blindness. *Path.* [f. NIGHT *sb.* + BLINDNESS. Cf. Du. *nachtblindheid*, G. *-heit*, Sw. *nattblindhet.*] = NYCTALOPIA.

1754 *Med. Obs. & Inq.* (1776) I. 120 Galen explains the word by a night-blindness. **1814** [see HEMERALOPIA]. **1834** *Cycl. Pract. Med.* III. 184/1 Night-blindness has been described as endemic in different countries. **1887** MOLONEY *Forestry W. Afr.* 375 In Travancore the juice from them is applied in cases of night-blindness. **1898** *Allbutt's Syst. Med.* V. 597 A man..will not show night-blindness, unless he be also exposed to very bright light.

So **night-blind** *a.*

1898 *Allbutt's Syst. Med.* V. 597 Perfectly vigorous well-fed men, if exposed to sufficient glare, become night-blind.

'night-cap. [f. NIGHT *sb.* + CAP *sb.*[1]]

1. a. A covering for the head, worn especially in bed.

c **1386** CHAUCER *Merch. T.* 609 She him saugh up sittinge in his sherte, In his night-cappe, and with his nekke lene. **14..** *Rule Syon Monast.* liii. in *Collect. Topogr.* I. (1834) 31 Up on ther hedes they may have a nyghte kerchyf and a nyghte cappe. **1523** FITZHERB. *Husb.* §142 Purse, dagger, cloke, nyght cap, kerchef. **1582** N. LICHEFIELD tr. *Castanheda's Conq. E. Ind.* I. iii. 9 Making exchaunge of certaine red night caps with the Negroes for Bracelets of Iuory. **1602** *2nd Pt. Return fr. Parnass* I. v, Ther's a fellow with a night cap on his head. **1655** CULPEPPER, etc. *Riverius* I. i. 7 If by Fumes he find pain in his head, you may only perfume his night-caps every evening. **1711** STEELE *Spect.* No. 260 ¶1 That some Ladies..may be persuaded to wear warm Night-Caps this cold Season. **1791** BOSWELL *Johnson* (1831) I. 234 With his little black wig on the top of his head, instead of a night-cap. **1836** MARRYAT *Japhet* xl, His head was covered with a white nightcap. **1887** BESANT *The World Went* i, His head, covered with a padded silk night-cap, was sunk deep in the pillows.

†**b.** ***night-cap wig***, ? a close-fitting wig resembling a night-cap. *Obs.*

1709 STEELE *Tatler* No. 26 ¶4 Some new Alteration in our Night-cap-Wigs and Pockets. **1711** ADDISON *Spect.* No. 129 ¶10 A Gentleman that had accoutered himself in a Night-Cap Wig [etc.]. **1829** LYTTON *Devereux* II. i, A tall, gaunt fellow, in a coat covered with tarnished lace, a night-cap wig [etc.].

2. a. In *transf.* or *fig.* applications. † ***horse('s) nightcap***, a halter.

1593, etc. [see HORSE *sb.* 28]. *c* **1667** *Roxb. Ball.* (1891) VII. 360 His Wife too will scoff, when he comes lamely off, And gave him a Night-cap of Horn. **1770** *Gentl. Mag.* XL. 560 To express the Condition of an Honest Fellow and no Flincher under the Effects of good Fellowship he is said to ..[have] Got his Night Cap on. **1850** THACKERAY *Pendennis* xxxix, Foker..voted Erith a prig and a dullard, the nightcap of the House of Commons.

†**b.** A nocturnal bully. *Obs. rare.*

1623 WEBSTER *Duchess Malfi* II. i, Be sure you are taken for one of the prime night-caps. —— *Devil's Law Case* II. i, Among a shoal or swarm of reeking night-caps.

c. A cloud of mist covering a mountain-top.

1626 BACON *Sylva* §819 They say in Wales, When certain Hills have their Night-caps on, they mean mischief. **1817** PAULDING *Letters from South* I. 160 It is a rainy morning; the mountains have all got on their nightcaps of mist.

3. An alcoholic drink taken immediately before going to bed in order to induce sleep. Also, a non-alcoholic drink taken at bedtime.

1818 *The Cook's Oracle* (ed. 2) 503 A pint of table beer, (or Ale, if you make it for a 'Night-Cap') [etc.]. **1829** MARRYAT *F. Mildmay* xxiii, A pint of hot brandy and water..by way of a nightcap. **1862** SALA *Accepted Addr.* 118 Drinks.. cunningly compounded..by way of night-caps. **1887** T. A. TROLLOPE *What I remember* II. ii. 21, I neither took, or cared to take, any wine with my dinner, and never wanted any description of 'nightcap'. **1930** *Daily Tel.* 9 Apr. 11/7 (Advt.), 'Ovaltine'... The world's best 'night-cap' to ensure sound, natural sleep. **1959** *New Statesman* 1 Aug. 141/3 A greater number of housewives than ever before realised the goodness of Bovril..for use as a beverage during the day, a night-cap, and for adding to savoury dishes. **1975** 'C. AIRD' *Slight Mourning* ii. 18 Sloan's own nightcap was usually milky coffee.

attrib. **1844** HEWLETT *Parsons & W.* xlv, The only glass that a man ought to take 'solus' is..the night-cap tumbler.

4. The final event in one day's series of sporting contests; *spec.* the second of two baseball games played by the same two teams on a single day. *N. Amer. colloq.*

1939 WEBSTER Add., *Nightcap*, the final race or contest of a day's sports. **1941** *Sun* (Baltimore) 22 Sept. 1/1 The Cardinals pulled the opening game out of the fire with a daring bit of base running..to win 6–5, and took the nightcap, 7–0. **1942** BERREY & VAN DEN BARK *Amer. Thes. Slang* §675/6 Second game of a 'double-header',..*nightcap.* **1969** *Internat. Herald Tribune* (Paris) 6 Nov. 13/1 In the nightcap, Baltimore's Wes Unseld..sat out much of the game because of foul trouble. **1970** *Toronto Daily Star* 24 Sept. 17/1 In the nightcap, Jerry Reuss permitted seven hits. **1974** *Union* (S. Carolina) *Daily Times* 22 Apr. 6/2 The Orioles edged New York 6–5 in 13 innings in the opener of a doubleheader and then protested the nightcap, which they lost 3–0.

Hence **'night-capped** (-kæpt) *a.*, covered with, or wearing, a night-cap or night-caps.

a **1658** LOVELACE *Poems* (1864) 230 When the sick sea with turbants night-cap'd was. **1826** POUNDEN *France & It.* 3 A squalid night-capped set of gentlemen. **1873** MRS. H. WOOD *Master of Greylands* ix, The window..was flung open.., and Mrs. Bent's night-capped head came out.

'night-cellar. [f. NIGHT *sb.* + CELLAR *sb.*] A cellar serving as a tavern or place of resort during the night for persons of the lowest class.

a **1743** SAVAGE *Wks.* 1775 II. 271, I generally..spend the evening with him at a night cellar in the Strand. **1796** BURKE *Regic. Peace* Wks. VIII. 188 By digging a night-cellar for such thieves, murderers, and house-breakers as ever infested the world. **1840** DICKENS *Barn. Rudge* xvi, Night-cellars..for the reception and entertainment of the most abandoned of both sexes. **1851** THACKERAY *Eng. Hum.* v. (1858) 243 How the thief divides has booty and drinks his punch at the night-cellar.

'night-chair. [f. NIGHT *sb.* + CHAIR *sb.*] A close-stool or commode for use by night.

1404 *Durham Acc. Rolls* (Surtees) 398, v nyght chares. **1763** C. JOHNSTON *Reverie* II. 259 He unluckily cast his eye on the night-chair..and never considering what it was, brought it out. **1825** GOOD *Study Med.* (ed. 2) II. 549 Four ..patients, of whom one had used the same night-chair. **1888** FAGGE & PYE-SMITH *Princ. & Pract. Med.* (ed. 2) I. 189 The same night-chairs were used by both sets of patients.

'night-clothes. [f. NIGHT *sb.* + CLOTHES. Cf. G. *nachtkleid*, Da. *natklæder*, Sw. *nattkläder.*]

1. Such clothes as are usually put on at night immediately before going to bed.

1602 MARSTON *Antonio's Rev.* III. i, 'Tis not yet proud day:..the unpranked world Wears yet the night-clothes. **1674** tr. *Scheffer's Lapland* 90 Besides these garments..they have also other which they use a nights, such as are called night-cloathes, for they have no feather beds. **1818** SCOTT *Br. Lamm.* xxxiv, Here they found the unfortunate girl..; her night clothes torn and dabbled with blood. **1846** MRS. CARLYLE *Let. to Carlyle* 23 Aug., Left me in total darkness, —to scramble into my night-clothes as I could. **1896** *Daily News* 17 Aug. 6/6 The bodies, which lay side by side in bed in night clothes, were in a composed attitude.

†**2.** Négligé or informal dress worn in the evening. *Obs.*

1667 PEPYS *Diary* 24 Dec., My Lady Castlemaine, who looked prettily in her night-clothes. **1709** STEELE *Tatler* No. 2 ¶2 These Nightclothes, Moll, become thee mightily. **1737** MRS. DELANEY *Life & Corr.* (1861) II. 6 The suit of night-clothes I have pitched on for you are charming: it is grounded Brussels. **1751** SMOLLETT *Per. Pic.* lxxxi, I dressed myself in a new pink sattin gown and my best laced night-cloaths.

'night-crow. Now *arch.* [f. NIGHT *sb.* + CROW *sb.*[1]] A bird supposed to croak or cry in the night and to be of evil omen; prob. an owl or nightjar. Cf. NIGHT-RAVEN.

c **1340** *Nominale* (Skeat) 794 Nytcrowe [F. *fresoie*] and watirfynch. **1382** WYCLIF *Lev.* xi. 16 An ostriche, and a nyȝt crowe [L. *noctua*], and a coote. *c* **1440** *Promp. Parv.* 356/1 Nyghte crowe, *nict(ic)orax.* **1508** FISHER *7 Penit. Ps.* cii. Wks. (1876) 152 The nyght crowe or the oule. **1545** ASCHAM *Toxoph.* (Arb.) 52 On the nighte time..nyghte crowes and poulcattes,..with all other vermine, and noysome beastes vse mooste styrringe. **1593** SHAKS. *3 Hen. VI*, v. vi. 45 The Owle shriek'd.., The Night-Crow cry'de, aboding lucklesse time. **1614** *Scourge Venns* (1876) 30 These goblins, lich-fouls, Owls, and night-crows to At murthers raile. **1631** P. FLETCHER *Piscatory Eclog.* i, No shrieking owl, no night-crow lodgeth here. **1825** SCOTT *Talism.* v, A voice.. resembling that of the night-crow more than any sound which is heard by daylight.

b. *transf.* Applied abusively to persons.

1570 FOXE *A. & M.* (ed. 2) 174 I neede not admonish thee to smell out the blinde practises of these night crowes. *c* **1613** ROWLANDS *Fours Knaves* (Percy Soc.) 88 Such night-crowes and owles, That lurke in bushes,..And cowardly upon a man will set. **1658** J. JONES *Ovid's Ibis* 27 The just judgment of God upon an unmerciful father provoked by the false suggestions of a femal night-crow.

'night-dress. [f. NIGHT *sb.* + DRESS *sb.*] **1.** A night-gown or other dress intended for wear during the night.

1712–14 POPE *Rape Lock* iv. 38 The fair ones feel such maladies as these, When each new night-dress gives a new disease. **1760–72** H. BROOKE *Fool of Qual.* (1809) IV. 38 [She] put on a sumptuous bedgown, with a suitable night-dress for her head. **1836** E. HOWARD *R. Reefer* li, Bounding down the hill, in her night-dress. **1865** TREVELYAN *Cawnpore* 9 A silk shirt and linen drawers, the universal night dress of the East. **1897** HUGHES *Medit. Fever* v. 188 The comfort of this form of garment, be it night-dress or suit, will be most evident.

2. *attrib.*, as **night-dress bag, case**, a bag or other container in which a night-dress can be placed when it is not being worn.

1975 *Times* 25 Nov. 2/6 He tried to punch her and hit a toy dog nightdress bag instead. **1907** *Yesterday's Shopping* (1969) p. xlvi/4 Night Dress Cases. **1932** D. C. MINTER *Mod. Needlecraft* 218/2 A triangular embroidered night-dress case. **1969** 'G. NORTH' *Procrastination of Sergeant Cluff* xv. 151 The night-dress case in the shape of a toy Koala-bear that growled when she lifted it.

So †**'night-dressing** = NIGHT-CLOTHES 2. *Obs.*

1622 MABBE tr. *Aleman's Guzman d'Alf.* II. 42 The Countesse put mee into a night-dressing; and a Smocke. **1662** PEPYS *Diary* 6 Jan., My wife's neglect in leaving of her scarf, waistcoat, and night-dressings in the coach.

'nighted, *ppl. a.* [f. NIGHT *v.* + -ED[1].]

1. Made dark or black as night. *rare.*

1604 SHAKS. *Ham.* I. ii. (Q. 2) 68 Good Hamlet, cast thy nighted [1623 nightly] colour off. **1605** —— *Lear* IV. v. 13 Edmund, I thinke, is gone In pitty of his misery, to dispatch His nighted life. [**1882** *Macm. Mag.* XLVI. 334/2 To show that Romeo ever had many moments in which he could naturally throw his nighted colour off.]

†**b.** Pertaining to the night. *Obs. rare*$^{-1}$.

1605 DRAYTON *Man in the Moone* 37 Now the goodly Moone Was in the Full, and at her Nighted Noone.

2. Overtaken by night, benighted. Also *fig.*

1640 GLAPTHORNE *Wallenstein* III. iii. Wks. 1874 II. 49 Like those fire drakes, Mis-guiding nighted travellers. **1765** [E. THOMPSON] *Meretriciad* 39 So have I seen a brilliant Star retire, And leave the nighted lover in the mire. **1819** SCOTT *Lady of L.* II. xxxii, Upon the nighted pilgrim's way. **1855** SINGLETON *Virgil* II. 67 His reeling ship,..him-self e'en steered her in the nighted waves.

†**'nighten,** *v. Obs. rare.* [f. NIGHT *sb.* + -EN[5].] *intr.* To grow dark, to become night.

1561 EDEN *Arte Nauig.* I. vii, To them it nyghteneth three houres soner then vnto vs in Spaine. **1570** LEVINS *Manip.* 61/31 To Nighten, *aduesperascere.*

'nighter. [f. NIGHT *sb.* + -ER[1].] A second element in certain combs., as ***all-nighter***, one who spends all the night in some occupation, etc.; ***first-nighter***, one who attends the first ordinary public performance of a play.

1882 DION BOUCICAULT in *Daily News* 23 Nov. 6/7 Persons who call themselves 'first nighters'..who attend the production of all important plays. **1895** *Outing* (U.S.) XXVI. 436/2 An 'all-nighter' and a 'rounder', a robber of hen-roosts and nests.

†**'nighterly,** *a. Obs. rare*$^{-1}$. [irreg. f. NIGHT *sb.*; cf. *easterly*, etc.] Nightly.

1559 MORWYNG *Evonym.* 94 If thou make a cake of meale knod with nighterly dew of saint John.

†**'nightern,** *a. Obs. rare.* [irreg. f. NIGHT *sb.*; cf. *eastern*, etc.] Nocturnal.

1615 BRATHWAIT *Strappado* (1878) 279 In this silent course of nighterne race, with quick recourse he runs vnto the place. *Ibid.* 305 The Nighterne owle, that night wil cease from prey, howling by night as she did howle by day.

†**'nightertale.** *Obs.* Chiefly *north.* and *Sc.* Forms: 4 **naghter-, naȝtter-; niht(t)er-, nither-, nyther-, niȝt(t)er-,** 4–5 **nyȝter-,** (4 **-tur**), 5 **nyght(t)er-,** *Sc.* **nichtir-, nychter-, (-tyr-),** 4–6 **nighter-,** (5 **-tir-**); also 4–5 **-tall(e,** 5 (7) **-taile, -tayl(l)e.** [Prob. of Scand. origin, and perh. an alteration of the synonymous ON. **nahtar-*, later *náttarþel* (f. *náttar* gen. of *nátt* night + *þel* groundwork, stuff, substance, heart, bottom), by substitution of the more familiar *tale* reckoning, count, for the original second element of the compound.] Night-time, the night. Only in phrases ***by, on, upon, a, with, of, (the) nightertale***, by night, during the night.

a **1300** *Cursor M.* 2991 Vp ras þe king, on nighter tale. *Ibid.* 11596 Wit naghtertale he went o tun. *c* **1300** *Havelok* 2025 Hwo mithe so mani stonde ageyn, Bi nither tale, knith or swein? *c* **1386** CHAUCER *Cant. T.* Prol. 97 By nightertale He sleep namore than dooth a nightingale. *c* **1412** HOCCLEVE *De Reg. Princ.* 3849 By nyghtertale he was slayn by kyng darie. **1455** *Anc. Cal. Rec. Dublin* (1889) 287 Hyt was ordeynyt that no maner beger..walke by nyghtertall abegyn. **1497** *North Riding Rec.* (1894) 189 [He] with Force and armz of the nyghtertall sent hys..seruantis to the Castell. **1530** PALSGR. 803 A nyghtertale, *de nuyct.* **16..** in Calthrop *Reports* (1670) 131 That yee do provide..that the Lanthornes with Light by Nightertaile in old manner accustomed be hanged forth.

'nightfall. [f. NIGHT *sb.* + FALL *sb.*[1]]

1. The coming on of night; the time of dusk.

1700 FARQUHAR *Constant Couple* II. iv, No man is seen to come into this house after nightfall. **1766** GOLDSM. *Vic. W.* xx, Whenever I approached a peasant's house towards nightfall, I played one of my most merry tunes. **1812** L. HUNT in *Examiner* 24 Aug. 538/1 By night-fall the enemy had betaken themselves to flight. **1855** MACAULAY *Hist. Eng.* xii. III. 342 The traveller at nightfall would have found the inn where he had expected to sup and lodge deserted. **1867** TROLLOPE *Chron. Barset* II. lvi. 133 Had he talked on the subject till nightfall no such word would have been spoken.

2. (See quot.) So **night-falling.** *rare*$^{-0}$.

1611 COTGRAVE, *La groüée des fruicts*, that fruit which falls in the night; wind-falls, night-falls, night-wind-falls. **1632** SHERWOOD, The night-fallings of fruites.

'night-fire. [f. NIGHT *sb.* + FIRE *sb.*]

†**1.** An ignis fatuus, will o' the wisp. *Obs. rare*$^{-1}$.

1633 G. HERBERT *Temple, Dotage* i, Foolish night-fires,.. Chases in Arras, guilded emptinesse.

2. A fire kindled at, or for the, night; a fire which burns by night.

1812 BYRON *Ch. Har.* II. lxxi, On the smooth shore the night-fires brightly blazed. **1839–52** BAILEY *Festus* 18 Unsaid thoughts, Which prey upon the breast like night-fires on A heath. **1851** *Zoologist* IX. 3125 Rough notes of a day's gleanings, scrawled by the light of the hissing night-fire.

'night-flower. [f. NIGHT *sb.* + FLOWER *sb.*] A flower that opens or blooms during the night.

1731 MEDLEY *Kolben's Cape G. Hope* II. 238 The Cape Europeans call all the Sorts [of *Geranium Africanum*] Night-Flowers. **1810** M. CUTLER in *Life*, etc. (1888) II. 343 Examined the night-flower, dissected it, and brought it home to preserve. **1866** Shuckard *Brit. Bees* 12 Although many flowers are night-flowers, yet the very large majority expand during the day. **1874** Lubbock *Wild Flowers* ii, Night-flowers, moreover, are generally pale.

ˈnight-flowering, *a.* [f. Night *sb.* 12a + Flowering *ppl. a.*] Blooming by night.

1810 M. Cutler in *Life*, etc. (1888) II. 342 Saw the cactus grandiflora, or night-flowering cereus. **1849** Balfour *Man. Bot.* §883 Some of the plants are noted as night-flowering. **1855** Miss Pratt *Flower. Pl.* I. 138 The Night-flowering Stock (*Matthiola tristis*).

ˈnight-fly. [f. Night *sb.* + Fly *sb.*[1]]

1. A fly which is active or frequent by night.

1597 Shaks. *2 Hen. IV*, iii. i. 11 Why rather (Sleepe) lyest thou in smoakie Cribs,..And huisht with bussing Night-flyes to thy slumber? **1767** G. S. Carey *Hills Hybla* 2 Chasing the night-fly and the buzzing gnat. **1824** Symmons *Agamemnon* 81 Scared by the night-fly's solitary buzz. **1895** Rider Haggard *Heart of World* xiv, Great fish rising in pursuit of some night-fly.

2. An artificial fly used in fishing.

1799 G. Smith *Laboratory* II. 306 White night-fly. This fly is, in my opinion, preferable to the former. **1856** 'Stonehenge' *Brit. Rural Sports* 246/1 The mealy-white night-fly. *Ibid.*, The mealy-brown night-fly.

ˈnight-flying, *a.* [f. Night *sb.* 12a + Flying *ppl. a.*] That flies by night.

1831 Rennie *Montagu's Ornith. Dict.* 337 Nocturnal moths and other night-flying insects. **1835–6** *Todd's Cycl. Anat.* I. 324/2 Digestion may be supposed to go on less actively in the..night-flying Owls. **1866** Shuckard *Brit. Bees* 13, I am not aware of a single instance of a night-flying bee.

ˈnight-flying, *vbl. sb.* [f. Night *sb.* + Flying *vbl. sb.*] Flying in an aircraft by night. Also *attrib.* Hence **ˈnight-fly** *v. intr.*

1907 A. C. Johnson *How to find Time at Sea* (ed. 6) 9 Steering by the stars, for night flying, night marching and night boat-work. **1918** *War Illustr.* 13 July 372/2 The petrol or electric flares, which are placed on all night-flying aerodromes for landing purposes. **1927** *Daily Tel.* 31 May 13/2 We night-fly regularly in America. It's the ideal time for flying in the States. **1935** [see directional *a.* 5]. **1945** *Tee Emm* (Air Ministry) V. 42 He thought the obstructions were left over from the previous night's night-flying taxi path. **1973** 'A. Hall' *Tango Briefing* xviii. 222 'Is there any chance of a flarepath on that strip?' 'No. They don't night-fly.'

†**ˈnightgale.** *Obs.* Forms: 1 necti-, **nectægalæ, næctægela, nacthegelæ, næcte-, nehtæ-, næhtegale, nihtegala,** 1–3 **nihte-,** 3–4 **nyhte-,** 5–6 **nyght(e)-,** 5 **nightgale,** (*Sc.* **nicht-**). [OE. *nęhte-, nihtegale*, etc. = OS. *nahta-, nahtigala* (MDu. *nachtegal, -gael*, Du. *-gaal*), OHG. *nahta-, nahte-, nahtigala*, etc. (MHG. *nahtegal*, G. *nachtigall*), ON. *nætrgali* (Da. *nattergal*, Sw. *näktergal*), f. Teut. *naht-* Night *sb.* + *galan* to sing, Gale *v.*[1]] The nightingale.

c **725** *Corpus Gloss.* (Hessels) L 330 *Luscinia*, naectegale. *Ibid.* A 121 *Achalantis*.., nehtęgale. *a* **1250** *Owl & Nightingale* (Jesus MS.) 4 Iherde ich holde grete tale An vle and one nyhtegale. *Ibid.* 13 Þe nihtegale bigon þo speke. *a* **1310** in Wright *Lyric P.* 92 When the nyhtegale singes, the wodes waxen grene. *c* **1400** Maundev. (Roxb.) xxv. 117 Laneres, sagres, sperhawkes, nyghtgales syngand, and papeiays spekand. **1435** Misyn *Fire of Love* 102 It is sayd þe nyghtgale to songe & melody all nyght is gyfyn. *c* **1450** Holland *Howlat* 715 The blyth Lark that begynnis, And the Nychtgalis. **1483** *Cath. Angl.* 254/2 A Nyghte gale; *filomena*.

ˈnight-gear. [f. Night *sb.* + Gear *sb.*]

1. = Night-clothes. †Also *pl.*

1560 Daus tr. *Sleidane's Comm.* 235 Havynge nothyng upon hym, but his cloke caste aboute hym, and hys nyghte gere. **1625** K. Long tr. *Barclay's Argenis* iii. viii. 179 Taking out my night-geare, he..placed mee in the Ship. *c* **1645** Howell *Lett.* I. v. vii, The Dutches..came in her night-geers from her Bed-Chamber. **1847** Lytton *Lucretia* (1853) 346 She stood in her long night-gear on the floor. **1861** *All Year Round* V. 13 The young Duke haled the old Duke..Thus, in his night gear, down the turret stair.

†**2.** Liquor for night-drinking. *Obs. rare*$^{-1}$.

1592 Nashe *Pierce Penniless* Wks. (Grosart) II. 79 Thou that vsest to drinke nothing but scalding lead and sulphur in hell, thou are not so greedie of thy night-geare.

ˈnight-glass. *Naut.* [f. Night *sb.* + Glass *sb.*[1]] A short refracting telescope especially constructed for use during the night.

1779 Nelson 13 May in *Nicholas' Disp.* (1845) I. 28, I have lost a very fine Brig,..I am sure for want of a Night-glass. **1812** Byron *Ch. Har.* i. xvii, The night-glass through the narrow bay Discovers where the Pacha's galleys lay. **1884** Pae *Eustace* xix. 242 Randolph stood upon the deck of his cutter with a night-glass at his eye.

nightglow (ˈnaɪtgləʊ). *Meteorol.* [f. Night *sb.* + Glow *sb.*] The faint light emitted by the upper atmosphere at night.

1951 Roach & Pettit in *Jrnl. Geophysical Res.* LVI. 325 Many investigators..have reported that the intensity of the green nightglow line at 5577 Å has a maximum near the observer's local midnight. *Ibid.*, The general term 'airglow' is used for radiations originating in the upper atmosphere. We use the term 'nightglow' to connote airglow at night to distinguish it from similar radiations which may be present (though not observable) in the daytime. **1955** *Sci. Amer.* Sept. 150/2 These studies show that the nightglow is faintest at the zenith overhead and grows in intensity down the sky until it reaches a maximum about 10 degrees above the horizon. **1967** R. W. Fairbridge *Encycl. Atmospheric Sci. & Astrogeol.* 9/1 It has become usual to distinguish these differing kinds of airglow by the names 'twilight glow' and 'dayglow', in distinction to the 'nightglow'. **1972** *Sci. Amer.* Jan. 78/2 The nightglow can be observed with a photometer or a spectrometer.

ˈnight-gown. [f. Night *sb.* + Gown *sb.*]

1. A loose gown specially used for putting on at (or during the) night in place of the ordinary clothes; a dressing-gown. Now only *Hist.*

a **1400** *Bk. Curtasye* 483 in *Babees Bk.*, Þen bryngis he forthe ny3tgoun also, And spredys a tapet and qwysshens two. **1541** *Rutland MSS.* (Hist. MSS. Comm.) IV. 321 Rydyng to Hwlle, to bere my Lorde a nyght gowne, iiijs. **1546** *Test. Ebor.* (Surtees) VI. 240 A gowne furrid withe lambe whiche is my nyghte gowne. **1582** N. Lichefield tr. *Castanheda's Conq. E. Ind.* 155 His night gowne was made of blacke Veluet, after the French use laced about, with lase of golde. **1607** Dekker & Webster *Sir T. Wyatt* Wks. 1873 III. 128 Pleaseth the Lady Iane, ile helpe her off with her night-Gowne. **1667** Pepys *Diary* 27 Aug., She..ran out in her smock into her aviary..; and thither her woman brought her her nightgown. **1683** *Lond. Gaz.* No. 1871/4 A Night-gown of striped Sattin cloth-colour and Buff, another for a man about the same colours. **1709** Mrs. Manley *Secret Mem.* (1736) I. 177 He starts up in the Bed, feels for his Night-Gown to rise..and see what was the matter. **1749** Smollett *Gil Blas* iv. x, She put on a thin night-gown which lay at the bed's feet. **1777** Sheridan *Trip Scarb.* i. Scene ii, a Dressing Room. Lord Foppington, in his Night Gown. **1808** Scott in *Lockhart* (1839) I. 27, I found him.. wrapped in a tartan night gown. **1881** Besant & Rice *Chapl. of Fleet* II. 43 The country parson went dressed in a grey-striped calamanco nightgown.

fig. **1728** Pope *Dunc.* ii. 38 No meagre, muse-rid mope,.. In a dun night-gown of his own loose skin.

†**2.** A kind of gown worn by ladies in the 18th cent., originally as an evening dress. *Obs.*

1700 Mrs. Centlivre *Perj. Husb.* iii. ii, But, Madam, what's to be done with your brocade night-gown you tore last night? **1745** in Dunbar *Social Life* (1865) 123 All plain silk night-gowns [are] worn with different coloured sattens sewed on the brest. **1756** Mrs. Delany *Life & Corr.* (1861) III 403 Long hoods are worn close under the chin, tied behind... Nightgowns worn without hoops. **1778** *Ibid.* Ser. ii. II. 380 The Queen was in a hat and an Italian night-gown of purple lutestring.

3. A light garment worn in bed, now *spec.* one worn by women and children.

a **1822** Byron *Juan* xvi. cxi, He was undrest, Saving his night-gown. **1851** Meredith *Love in the Valley* xi, When from bed she rises clothed from neck to ankle In her long night gown sweet as boughs of May. **1891** Hardy *Tess* (1900) 157/2 The skirts of her dressing-gown and the embroidery of her night-gown flowed upon the floor.

Hence **ˈnight-gowned** *a.*, dressed in a night-gown.

c **1860** Mrs. Spofford in *Casquet of Lit.* (1896) IV. 28 The four pattering night-gowned imps. **1899** Kipling *Stalky* 176 A nightgowned twelve-year-old leaped from his bed.

ˈnight-hag. Now *rare.* [f. Night *sb.* + Hag *sb.*[1]] A hag or female demon supposed to ride the air by night; the nightmare.

1666 Dryden *Ann. Mirab.* ccxlviii, Dire night-hags come from far to dance their round. **1667** Milton *P.L.* ii. 662 The Night-Hag, when call'd In secret, riding through the Air she comes Lur'd with the smell of infant blood. **1750** tr. *Leonardus' Mirror Stones* 86 A crisolete bound round with gold, and carried in the left hand, drives away night-hags. **1814** Scott *Wav.* xiii, When the Night-Hag wings the troubled air. **1834** L. Ritchie *Wand. by Seine* 59 The indefinite dread, which sits like the night-hag on their Souls.

ˈnight-hawk. [f. Night *sb.* + Hawk *sb.*[1]]

1. A name given to various birds; esp. **a.** The Nightjar or Goatsucker.

1611 Bible *Lev.* xi. 16 The owle, and the nighte-hauke, & the Cuckow. **1783** Latham *Gen. Synopsis Birds* II. 593 Dorr Hawk, Night Jarr, or Night Hawk. **1844** *Zoologist* II. 445, I had brought to me a pair of 'night-hawks', as goatsuckers are provincially termed in Kent. **1878** T. Hardy *Ret. Native* iv. vii, A night-hawk revealed his presence by whirring like the clack of a mill.

b. A predominantly nocturnal bird of the genus *Chordeiles*, esp. *C. minor*, belonging to the nightjar family, Caprimulgidæ.

1793 W. Bentley *Diary* 22 Aug. (1909) II. 48 We observed a great number of the birds, called here [*sc.* at Charlestown, N.H.] night hawks, playing in the air. **1812** A. Wilson *Amer. Ornith.* V. 65 On the last week in April, the night hawk commonly makes its first appearance in this part of Pennsylvania. **1851** Mayne Reid *Scalp Hunt.* xxxviii. 289 The night-hawk has filled his ravenous maw. **1868** Whittier *Among Hills* 209 We heard the night-hawk's sullen plunge. **1913** W. P. Pritchard *Barn Doors & Byways* 119 The naturalists tell us that the night-hawks nest on top of the Manhattan skyscrapers. **1962** O. L. Austin *Birds of World* 163/2 The plaintive buzzing calls of Nighthawks are now commonly heard above the traffic noises of many American cities as the birds course high over the rooftops in their buoyant, dancing search for flying insects. **1968** R. M. Patterson *Finlay's River* 123 The dew was starting to fall.. and the thrum of the night-hawk was sounding from the upper air. **1974** D. Sears *Lark in Clear Air* vi. 73 A night-hawk beeped high and out of sight.

c. A New Zealand owl (*Spiloglaux novæ-zealandiæ*), also called *morepork*.

1872 Domett *Ranolf* xi. iv, Two loud harsh notes assail her ear, The night-hawk's.

2. *fig.* One who seeks prey by night. Also, one who stays up late at night; a person who goes out or works at night; *spec.* = *night-herder* (see also quots.).

1818 Scott *Rob Roy* xxix, There are night-hawks abroad, so that I cannot give you..the meeting..whilk was my purpose. **1868** 'Mark Twain' *Let.* 8 Jan. (1920) 80 Jack Van Nostrand, Dan and I, (all Quaker City night-hawks,) had a blow-out at Dan's house. **1893** *Pall Mall G.* 3 Jan. 2/2 When Jack steps ashore with money in his pocket he is..the victim of the crimp and the night-hawk. **1903** W. D. Coburn *Rhymes from Round-up Camp* (rev. ed.) 18 Cotton-Eye, the night-hawk, Was then a top cow-hand. **1915** *Dialect Notes* IV. 209 *Night-hawk*, a thief or harlot. 'Those night-hawks ought to be taken up and sent home if they don't know enough to go.' **1929** F. Bowen *Sea Slang* 95 *Night hawks*, night watchmen stewards. **1934** A. Woollcott *While Rome Burns* 180 Your correspondent, a nighthawk of parts in those days, was within ear-shot. **1948** *Sierra Club Bull.* (San Francisco) Mar. 22 Ed Thistlethwaite..was our night hawk. It was to be his job..to get up and watch the dawn in the high and relatively high pasture lands to which the stock had been pushed, then to round them up and bring them down to work. **1972** J. Metcalf *Going Down Slow* vi. 108 As the hour wore on to eleven p.m. she excused herself and retired, always calling them 'night-hawks'.

ˈnight-heron. *Ornith.* [f. Night *sb.* + Heron.] A heron of the genus *Nycticorax*, represented in Europe by *N. griseus* or *europæus*; the common American species is *N. nævius* or *gardeni*, the Qua-bird.

1784 Pennant *Arct. Zool.* II. 450 Night Heron. **1813** Wilson *Amer. Ornith.* VII. 105 The food of the Night Heron, or Qua-bird, is chiefly composed of small fish. **1831** Rennie *Montagu's Ornith. Dict.* 338. **1883** *Harper's Mag.* Jan. 189/1, I have frequently found upon the breast of the night-heron a yellow oily powder.

ˈnight-house. [f. Night *sb.* + House *sb.*[1]] A tavern, public-house, etc. which remains open all night.

1734 Fielding *Univ. Gallant* iii. Wks. 1882 X. 70 They have put down all night-houses, and other places of rendezvous. **1764** *Ann. Reg.* i. 151/1 They went both to a night-house, where they sat drinking together till it was light. **1823** *Blackw. Mag.* XIV. 508 The wickets of the night-houses..open only to known customers. **1851** Mayhew *Lond. Labour* (1865) II. 511/2 The men..send to some night-house..to purchase a small quantity [of liquor].

nightie, nightie-night(ie): see Nighty *sb.*, Nighty-night *int.*

nightingale[1] (ˈnaɪtɪŋgeɪl). Forms: 3 **ni3tin-,** 4 **nihtyn-, nyhtin-,** 4–6 **nyghtyn-,** (5 **-yng, nygttyn-,** 6 **nyghtin-),** 4–5 **nytyn(g)-,** 5–6 *Sc.* **nycht(t)in-,** (6 **-yn-, nichtin-),** 4, 6 **nightyn-,** 6– **nightin-,** (7 **nitin-);** also 5–7 **-gal(l,** 6 *Sc.* **-gaill,** 7 **-ghale.** [Later form of *nightegale* Nightgale. For the insertion of the *n*, which has no etymological reason, cf. *farthingale.*]

1. a. A small reddish-brown or tawny migratory bird (*Motacilla* or *Daulias luscinia*), celebrated for the melodious notes which the male utters by night as well as by day during the breeding and nesting season.

By poets frequently called Philomel(a.

a **1250** *Owl & Night.* 4 (Cotton MS.) An hule and one ni3tingale. *Ibid.* 13 Þe ni3tingale bigon þe speche. *c* **1340** *Nominale* (Skeat) 788 Cote, houle, nytyngale. ?*a* **1366** Chaucer *Rom. Rose* 657 In many places were nyghtyngales, Alpes, fynches, and wodewales. **1390** Gower *Conf.* I. 54 He herde among the leves singe The Throstle with the nyhtingale. *c* **1440** *Promp. Parv.* 356/1 Nyghtyngale, *filomena*. **1484** Caxton *Fables of Alfonce* vi, He herd the songe of a nyghtyngale. **1523** Skelton *Garl. Laurel* 997 To here this nightingale..Warbelynge in the vale. **1555** Eden *Decades* (Arb.) 66 They harde nyghtingales synge in the thycke woodes. **1579** Spenser *Sheph. Cal.* Nov. 25 The Nightingale is sovereigne of song. **1661** Walton *Compl. Angler* (ed. 3) i. i, The Nightingale..breaths such sweet lowd musick out of her little instrumentall throat, that it might make mankind to think Miracles are not ceased. **1698** Fryer *Acc. E. India & P.* 248 The Nightingal, the sweet Harbinger of the Light, is a constant Chearer of these Groves. **1770** Gray in *Corr. w. Nicholls* (1843) 109 Trees blooming and nightingales singing all round us. **1821** Shelley *Adonais* xvii. 1 The lorn nightingale Mourns not her mate with such melodious pain. **1840** *Penny Cycl.* XVI. 230/2 In Ireland the Nightingale seems never to have been heard. **1894** Newton *Dict. Birds* 636 In great contrast to the Nightingale's pre-eminent voice is the inconspicuous coloration of its plumage.

b. Applied to other birds, as ***Cornish, Indian, Jamaica, Swedish nightingale***, etc. (see quots.).

mock, thrush, Virginian nightingale: see these words.

c **1710** Celia Fiennes *Diary* (1888) 227 The Cornish nightingales as they call them, the Cornish Chough. *a* **1818** M. G. Lewis *Jrnl. W. Ind.* (1834) 176 Two Jamaica nightingales have established themselves on the orange tree. .. This bird is also called the mocking-bird. **1855** *Orr's Circle Sci., Org. Nat.* III. 306 The *Kittacincla macroura*..is denominated the Indian Nightingale by some naturalists. **1884** Newton in *Encycl. Brit.* XVII. 499/1 The Redwing, strangely enough, has been often spoken of as the 'Swedish Nightingale'. **1885** Swainson *Prov. Names Birds* 28 Sedge Warbler, *Acrocephalus Phragmitis*,..Irish nightingale, Scotch nightingale.

c. ***Dutch nightingale***, a frog. Also ***Cambridgeshire nightingale***, the edible frog, *Rana esculenta*, which was introduced into East Anglia early in the nineteenth century.

1769 Pennant *Brit. Zool.* III. 5 The croaking of Frogs is well known, and from that in fenny countries they are stiled Dutch Nightingales or Boston Waites. **1812** Southey *Omniana* II. 33 Walton accuses the frogs of destroying them, but I cannot persuade myself to find a true bill against these poor persecuted Dutch nightingales. **1840** Spurden *Suppl. Forby, Dutch-Nightingale*, a frog, from its melodious note in the spring. **1881** *Brewer's Dict. Phr. & Fable* (ed. 12) 615/2 Cambridgeshire nightingales, edible frogs. **1975** *Country Life* 20 Feb. 455/2 The lakes, canals and meres of

East Anglia became well stocked with [edible] frogs... Locals called these invaders Cambridgeshire nightingales.

2. *transf.* Applied to persons, esp. to melodious singers or speakers. (See also quot. 1867.)

1500–20 DUNBAR *Poems* lxxxv. 34 Aue Maria!.. Haile, gentill nychttingale! *a* **1550** *Hye Way to Spittel Ho.* in Hazl. *E.P.P.* IV. 41 By my fayth, nyghtyngales of Newgate, These be they that dayly walkes and jettes. **1606** SHAKS. *Ant. & Cl.* IV. viii. 18 Mine Nightingale, We haue beate them to their Beds. *a* **1618** RALEIGH in Gutch *Coll. Cur.* I. 81 Basil, whom Nyssen calls the golden Nitingale of the church. *c* **1730** FIELDING *Pleasures of Town* Wks. 1771 I. 246 Soft Italians are nightingales, Sir, And a cock-sparrow mimics a beau. **1751** EARL ORRERY *Remarks Swift* (1752) 145 His voice in common conversation was so naturally musical, that I remember honest Tom Southerne used always to call him [Pope] The little nightingale. **1821** SHELLEY *Epipsych.* 10 This song shall be thy rose: its petals pale Are dead, indeed, my adored Nightingale! **1867** SMYTH *Sailor's Word-bk.* 643 *Spithead-Nightingales*, Boatswains and boatswains' mates, when winding their calls, especially when piping to dinner.

3. A popular or local name for certain flowers.

1862 *Monthly Pkt.* Oct. 435 Cuckoo flowers are called 'nightingales'. **1886** BRITTEN & HOLLAND 353 Nightingales, 1. *Geranium Robertianum.* 2. *Arum maculatum.* **1893** *Wilts. Gloss.* 110 Nightingale.., Greater Stitchwort.

4. *attrib.* and *Comb.*, as *nightingale-catcher*, *-like*; **nightingale floor**, in Japan, a floor that emits a high-pitched sound when it is trodden on; **nightingale-maggot, -pipe** (see quots.).

1611 COTGR., *Rossignolesque*, Nightingale-like, harmonious. **1626** BACON *Sylva* §172 In Regals (where they have a Pipe, they call the Nightingale-Pipe, which containeth Water) the Sound hath a continuall Trembling. **1750** W. ELLIS *Country Housew. Comp.* 193 Great Heats produce the Nightingale Maggot, that turns to a black wing'd Insect, that feeds upon and corrupts the Flower. **1752** MRS. DELANY *Life & Corr.* (1861) III. 86 Donnellan is tuning her nightingale pipes. **1773** BARRINGTON in *Phil. Trans.* LXIII. 283 One should suppose..that the nightingale-catchers had heard much of the French music. **1959** S. SITWELL *Bridge of Brocade Sash* v. 113 As for the squeaking,..the Japanese..will not allow it to be a 'nightingale floor', and leave it at that, but have to remark it is so constructed that 'at every step the boards emit a sound resembling that of *uguishu*, Japanese bush warbler'. **1964** I. FLEMING *You only live Twice* v. 62 This..is what the Japanese call a 'nightingale floor'... Imagine trying to get across here without being heard.

Hence **ˈnightingalize** *v.*, to sing like a nightingale. **ˈnightingaly** *a.*, suggestive of, adapted for, nightingales. (*nonce-wds.*)

1799 SOUTHEY *Eng. Ecl.* Poet. Wks. III. 78 He sings like a lark when at morn he arises, And when evening comes he nightingalizes. **1869** MRS. WHITNEY *We Girls* iii, Its expression was 'blossomy, nightingale-y', atilt with glee and grace. **1884** *Cent. Mag.* Mar. 775/2 The surrounding country..looked to me very nightingaly.

nightingale² (ˈnaɪtɪŋgeɪl). [f. the name of Miss Florence *Nightingale* (1820–1910).] **1.** A kind of flannel wrap used to cover the shoulders and arms of a patient while confined to bed.

1882 in OGILVIE. **1889** *Atalanta Mag.* Mar. Suppl. 1 A nightingale is such an easy thing to make: just two yards of flannel bound round and a short slit in the long side.

2. *attrib.*, as **Nightingale ward**, a type of hospital ward designed to accommodate several patients in one room.

1964 G. L. COHEN *What's Wrong with Hospitals?* ii. 37 Long after the austere open dormitory had been abandoned abroad, Britain doggedly went on building 'Nightingale wards'. **1970** *Guardian* 10 Sept. 13/1 Cubicles instead of Nightingale wards mean that nurses escape being constantly overseen.

† **ˈnightish**, *a. Obs. rare.* [f. NIGHT *sb.* + -ISH¹.] Pertaining to the night, nocturnal.

1495 *Trevisa's Barth. De P.R.* VIII. ix. (Caxton) 307 The sygnes of the Zodiacus..that ben watry and erthy ben colde and female and nyghtyssh sygnes. **1530** PALSGR. 319/2 Nyghtysshe or nyghty belongynge to the nyght, *nocturne.* **1567** TURBERV. *Epit* etc. 15 b, Thou shalt be worse detested then, than is the nightish Owle.

ˈnightjar. [f. NIGHT *sb.* + JAR *sb.*¹]

1. A common nocturnal bird, *Caprimulgus europæus* (see GOATSUCKER), so called from the peculiar whirring noise, something like that of a large spinning wheel, which the male makes during the period of incubation.

Similar names are *night-churr* (cf. Norw. dial. *nattekörre, -kurre*); *eve-churr* or *-jar*; *churn-, churr-*, and *jar-owl.*

1630 MAY *Contin. Lucan* VII. 470 Ill boding Owles, Night-iarrs, and Rauens with wide-stretched throats. **1783** LATHAM *Gen. Synopsis Birds* II. 593 Dorr Hawk, Night Jarr, or Night Hawk. **1802** MONTAGU *Ornith. Dict.* (1831) 337 The Nightjar is most plentiful in the wild tracts of uncultivated land. **1859** MEREDITH *R. Feverel* xx, The night-jar spinning on the pine-branch. **1888** MRS. H. WARD *R. Elsmere* 557 Suddenly they heard the purring sound of the night-jar.

2. Applied to other birds, esp. those belonging to species of *Caprimulgus* or to related genera.

1712 MORTON *Northampt.* 424 The Butcher-Bird.. breeds sometimes in Northamptonshire, and particularly in Whittlewood Forest, where 'tis called the Night-Jarr. **1840** *Penny Cycl.* XVI. 228/2 *Scotornis climaturus*, African Long-tailed Night-Jar. *Ibid.* 229/1 *Macrodipteryx Africanus*, Pennant-winged Night-Jar, or Long-shafted Goatsucker. **1894** NEWTON *Dict. Birds* 640 A second species of Nightjar, *C. ruficollis*,..is a summer visitant to the south-western parts of Europe. **1899** E. J. CHAPMAN *Drama Two Lives* 67 The nightjars wake their vesper note.

† **ˈnight-kerchief.** *Obs.* [f. NIGHT *sb.* + KERCHIEF *sb.*] A kerchief used to cover the head during the night.

Also †*night-kercher*: see NIGHT-RAIL, quot. 1554.

14.. [see NIGHT-CAP 1]. **1561** HOLLYBUSH *Hom. Apoth.* 14 b, Take a soft night kerchef and warme it. **1578** T. N. tr. *Conq. W. India* 9 He stripped himselfe naked, and tied a nightkercheffe about his head. **1599** A. M. tr. *Gabelhouer's Bk. Physicke* 105/1 Take nightkerchifs or Taffataye, and cover therwith the Cassiam and apply this plaster on the Brest.

ˈnight-lamp. [f. NIGHT *sb.* + LAMP *sb.*] A lamp which is kept burning during the night, esp. in a bedroom.

1821 SCOTT *Kenilw.* xxxii, Varney..placed a massive silver night-lamp..on a marble table which stood close by the head of the couch. **1842** TENNYSON *Locksley Hall* 80 Thou art staring at the wall, Where the dying night-lamp flickers. **1856** *Orr's Circ. Sci., Pract. Chem.* 494 The Common Floating Night-lamp..is nothing more than a small cup of metal pierced in the middle with a small glass tube.

b. Allusively, with reference to night-studies.

1895 in Anna Stoddart *J. S. Blackie* II. 234 He often warned us all against over-work and the night-lamp.

ˈnightless, *a.* [f. NIGHT *sb.* + -LESS.] Devoid of night, having no night.

1613 PURCHAS *Pilgrimage* (1614) 434 The Sun (whose presence they are long deprived of in the winter, which is recompensed in their night-lesse Summer). **1643** TRAPP *Comm. Gen.* xlvi. 29 Think of that glorious night-less day. **1825** HONE *Every-day Bk.* I. 772 Midsummer, or nightless days, now begin.

Hence **ˈnightlessness.**

1897 *Expositor* Sept. 208 All liberty is the result of nightlessness. *Ibid.* 209 The main feature of the city is the nightlessness.

night letter. [f. NIGHT *sb.* + LETTER *sb.*¹] **a.** In full **night telegraph letter**, a cheap-rate inland telegram delivered overnight. (Said in the 1945 P.O. Guide 'to be suspended'. The similar *overnight telegram* service was introduced in 1955.) Cf. LETTERGRAM.

1912 *Post Office Guide* Apr. 94 A service of night telegraph letters is in operation between London and Aberdeen and between London and Belfast. The rate is 6*d.* for 36 words or less and ½*d.* for every 3 words beyond 36. Night Telegraph letters are delivered (except on Sunday) by the first post next morning. **1912** *Times* 29 May 3/4 Night telegraph letters may be posted prepaid at the rates given above. **1938** E. T. CRUTCHLEY *G.P.O.* vii. 146 There are various by-products of the telegraph system about which the ordinary man-in-the-street remains strangely ignorant. For instance there is the Night Telegraph Letter which provides a means of communication after the usual posting hour, and at a cheaper rate than by the ordinary telegraph service. **1940** *Post Office Guide* Aug. 413 Night telegraph letters, which are accepted at any time and delivered by first postal delivery the next weekday or by special messenger shortly afterwards. Minimum charge 1*s.* 3*d.* for 36 words. **1953** H. ROBINSON *Britain's Post Office* xix. 258 A successful effort was made [*sc.* in the 1930s] to give the public a knowledge of the advantages of night-telegraph letters.

b. In full **night letter telegram**, a cheap-rate overseas telegram (see quots.). (Discontinued after 1949.)

[**1913** *Post Office Guide* Jan. 883 The Night and Weekend Cable Letter Services are not available viâ the Commercial or French Telegraph Cable Companies' routes... Night Cable Letters are accepted on the condition that they will not be delivered before the day after they are received at the Cable Companies' Stations.] **1914** *Ibid.* Apr. 896 (*heading*) Night and week-end letter telegrams for Canada, Newfoundland and the United States. *Ibid.*, Night Letter Telegrams are accepted on the condition that they will not be delivered before the day following that on which they are received at the Telegraph Companies' Stations. **1934** 'E. M. DELAFIELD' *Provincial Lady in America* 234 She gets such quantities of night letters and cables from abroad. **1949** *Post Office Guide* July 229 Night Letter Telegrams (NLT) may be sent to North and South America, British territories in Africa, Egypt, West Indies, certain British territories in the Far East, India, Pakistan and many other places outside Europe at one-third the rates for ordinary telegrams. They are normally delivered on the morning following the day of handing in. The minimum charge is as for 25 words. **1966** N. FREELING *King of Rainy Country* 33 The War Office in London..promised to get him off a night letter. **1973** T. TOBIN in Ade *Lett.* 1 George Ade sent the above night letter to Ashton Stevens in reply to the drama critic's request for an autobiographical sketch to insert in his *Chicago Herald and Examiner* column, April 30, 1930. The night letter to Stevens illustrates the image Ade manifested throughout his career.

ˈnight-light. [f. NIGHT *sb.* + LIGHT *sb.* Cf. MDu. (and Du.) *nachtlicht*, MLG. *-lecht*, OHG. *nahtlioht* (G. *nachtlicht*).]

1. The faint light which is perceptible during the night.

1648 HEXHAM, *Nachtlicht*, Night light, Night-shine. **1655** GURNALL *Chr. in Arm.* (ed. 2) I. 56 This night-light of Reason may save a person from some Ditch, or Pond. **1850** MRS. BROWNING *Poems* I. 13 Ever wave the Eden trees In the nightlight and the noonlight. **1865** DICKENS *Mut. Fr.* IV. xiv, By daylight, nightlight, torchlight. **1892** BRUCE *Apologetics* III. x. 496 The power to appreciate the difference between daylight and nightlight.

2. A light which burns or shines during the night. Also *fig.*

1839 *Civil Eng. & Arch. Jrnl.* II. 300/1 The absence of an universal system of night-lights or signals. **1895** ZANGWILL *Master* II. vii. 212 To watch..the river, mirroring a thousand night-lights, glide on.

b. A small thick candle, or other contrivance, constructed to burn dimly for a long period, and used by night, especially in sick-rooms.

1851 *Catal. Gt. Exhib.* 197 Wax and spermaceti lights, with plaited wicks, and other candles and night lights. **1857** W. COLLINS *Dead Secret* I. i, The night-light burning by the bed-side, displayed rather than dispelled the darkness. **1887** R. N. CAREY *Uncle Max* viii. 69, I had drawn the round table to the bed, and left the night-light..beside the sick woman.

ˈnight-line. [f. NIGHT *sb.* + LINE *sb.*²] A line with baited hooks set to catch fish by night.

1848 KINGSLEY *Yeast* viii, You were setting night-lines. I saw a minnow lie on the bank as I came up. **1857** HUGHES *Tom Brown* II. i, His pet plans of..making night-lines and slings. **1879** JEFFERIES *Wild Life in S. Co.* 359 Night-lines.. are the detestation of the true angler.

Hence **ˈnight-line** *v.*; **ˈnight-lining** *vbl. sb.*

1894 C. H. COOK *Thames Rights* 119 Owners have allowed their men to night-line to a large extent. *Ibid.* 121 Reserving netting and night-lining rights.

ˈnight-long, *a.* and *adv.* [f. NIGHT *sb.* + LONG *a.* Cf. OE. *nihtlǫng, -lang*; MHG. *nahtlanc* (G. *nachtlang*), ON. *náttlangt* adv.]

A. *adj.* That lasts or has lasted the whole night. Also *fig.*

1850 TENNYSON *In Mem.* lxxi, Thou hast forged at last A nightlong Present of the Past. **1872** HOWELLS *Wedd. Journ.* (1892) 42 Swelled the deep tide of life back from its night-long ebb. **1876** OUIDA *Winter City* vii, They returned to their night-long baccarat.

B. *adv.* All night; during the whole night.

1870 MORRIS *Earthly Par.* III. IV. 13 But night-long their ship lay..by the blossoms sweet. **1885** C. J. LYALL *Anc. Arab. Poet.* 82 Nightlong as we sat there.

† **ˈnight-long(s**, *adv. Obs. rare.* [See -LONG(S.] For the space of a night.

c **1000** ÆLFRIC *Gen.* xix. 2 Ic bidde eow, leof, þæt ȝe ȝecirron to minum huse and þær wunion nihtlanges. *c* **1205** LAY. 15504 Þe wal þe wes swa strong ne moste nihtlonges [*c* **1275** nih longe] nauere..istonden.

nightly (ˈnaɪtlɪ), *a.* Also 1, 4 nihtlic, 3 -lich, 4 nyȝtly. [OE. *nihtlíc* = MDu. *nachtelijc, -lic* (Du. *-lijk*), OHG. *nahtlîh* (G. *nächtlich*), ON. *náttligr* (Norw. *nattleg*, Sw. *nattlig*, Da. *natlig*): see NIGHT *sb.* and -LY¹.]

1. Coming, happening, or occurring during the night; accomplished or done by night.

c **897** K. ÆLFRED *Gregory's Past. C.* 433 Hæbbe eower ælc his sweord be his ðeo for nihtlecum eȝe. **971** *Blickl. Hom.* 11 Anra ȝehwylc hæfde sweord ofer his hype for nihtlicum eȝe. *a* **1300** *E.E. Psalter* xc. 5 (Harl.), Noght saltou drede fra nihtlic radnesse. *c* **1380** WYCLIF *Last Age Ch.* (1840) 24 Þat ben a nyȝtly drede, an arwe fleynge in day. *a* **1542** WYATT in *Tottel's Misc.* (Arb.) 49 Neuer was there nightly fantome So farre in errour. **1633** MILTON *Arc.* 48 All my Plants I save from nightly ill Of noisom winds and..vapours chill. **1721** YOUNG *Revenge* I. i, By nightly march he purpos'd to surprize The Moorish camp. **1760–72** H. BROOKE *Fool of Qual.* (1809) IV. 100 Killed in a nightly broil. **1826** KIRBY & SP. *Entomol.* xliii. IV. 193 The processionary caterpillars make only nightly sorties from their nests. **1856** KANE *Arctic Expl.* I. vii. 66 Its greatest nightly freezing has been three-quarters of an inch. **1894** GLADSTONE *Horace* II. xiii. 7 Such a man..shed the blood Of his own guest by nightly stroke.

b. Happening or occurring every night.

c **1705** POPE *Jan. & May* 15 This was his nightly dream, his daily care. **1794** LD. HOOD in Nicolas *Nelson Disp.* (1845) I. 400 Every boat assembled at sunset for orders, and the cheerfulness with which the Officers and Men performed this nightly duty is very much to be admired. **1812** BYRON *Ch. Har.* II. lix, Hark! from the mosque the nightly solemn sound The Muezzin's call. **1854** J. S. C. ABBOTT *Napoleon* (1855) I. ii. 52 There were daily and nightly skirmishes.

2. Belonging, pertaining, appropriate, or peculiar to the night; used by night; acting by night.

c **1200** *Trin. Coll. Hom.* 9 Hit is riht þat we forleten and forsaken nihtliche deden, þo ben þe werkes of þiesternesse. **1576** FLEMING *Panopl. Epist.* 221 So I say of nightly sleepings taken abusiuely. **1588** SHAKS. *Tit. A.* II. iii. 97 Heere nothing breeds, Vnlesse the nightly Owle, or fatall Rauen. **1604** —— *Oth.* IV. iii. 16 Good Æmilia, Giue me my nightly wearing, and adieu. **1617** tr. *A. de Dominis' Rom.* xiii. 12 If we be possessed with a nightly, drowsie silence in Gods businesse. **1682** DRYDEN *Rel. Laici* 8 As those nightly tapers disappear, When day's bright lord ascends our hemisphere. **1764** GOLDSM. *Trav.* 198 Some pilgrim, thither led, With many a tale repays the nightly bed. **1794** MRS. RADCLIFFE *Myst. Udolpho* iii, The voice of the shepherd calling his wandering flocks to the nightly fold. **1821** SCOTT *Kenilw.* xxxii, Am I but doomed to draw a brief and glittering train along the nightly darkness? **1875** JOWETT *Plato* (ed. 2) V. 109 Let the nightly hunters who lay snares and nets be everywhere prohibited.

b. Dark as, or with, night; resembling night.

1602 SHAKS. *Ham.* I. ii. 68 Good Hamlet cast thy nightly colour off. **1748** THOMSON *Cast. Indol.* xxxi. 277, I who have spent my nights and nightly days In this soul-deadening place. **1837** CARLYLE *Fr. Rev.* VII. iii, War-thunder mingling with the roar of the nightly main.

nightly (ˈnaɪtlɪ), *adv.* Also 5 neghtly, 5–6 nyghtly. [f. NIGHT *sb.* + -LY². Cf. MDu. *nachtelike*, G. *nächtlich*, Sw. *nattligen.*]

1. Every night. (Cf. DAILY *adv.*)

Some early examples might also be taken in sense 2.

1457 *Anc. Cal. Rec. Dublin* (1889) I. 296 Ther schold be viii. men ychos to wache neghtly betwen thys and Candylmas. **1496** *Naval Acc. Hen. VII* (1896) 170 Maryners dayly and nyghtly attendyng & awayting in keping the seid Ship in the dokke. **1540** *Act 32 Hen. VIII*, c 48 Euery of the same persons shal dayly and nightlye..do his office and duety. **1590** SHAKS. *Mids. N.* II. ii. 6 Some keepe backe The clamorous Owle that nightly hoots. **1615** G. SANDYS *Trav.* I Those of the Religion daily threatned, and nightly fearing a massacre. **1702** POPE *Sappho* 100 For those might Cynthia..bid Endymion nightly tend his sheep. **1796** BURKE *Regic. Peace* Wks. VIII. 394 The crowds that nightly flock to them. **1820** SCOTT *Abbot* xxxv, I dread the sentinel who is now planted nightly in the garden. **1862** SPENCER *First Princ.* II. iv. §52 (1875) 173 The comet.. nightly waxes larger. **1895** *19th Cent.* Aug. 337 A curious little ceremony that takes place nightly at a theatre.

2. At or by night; during the night.

1592 SHAKS. *Rom. & Jul.* IV. i. 81 Chaine me with roaring Beares Or hide me nightly in a Charnell house. **1634** SIR T. HERBERT *Trav.* 61 The other..speakes it selfe rather a Royal Carrauansraw, then a Temple, though nightly a thousand Lamps adorne it. **1667** MILTON *P.L.* II. 642 They on the trading Flood..Ply stemming nightly toward the pole. **1704** SWIFT *Batt. Bks.* Misc. (1711) 260 Two Mungril Curs..join in Partnership..nightly to invade the Folds of some rich Grazier. **1760–72** H. BROOKE *Fool of Qual.* (1809) I. 43 When morning appeared, they wondered to behold new ramparts raised, nightly erected, out of the ruins which the day had made. **1815** BYRON *Hebr. Mel., Sennacherib*, When the blue wave rolls nightly on deep Galilee.

'nightman. [f. NIGHT *sb.* + MAN *sb.* Cf. Da. *natmand*, †*nattemand* (1647).]

1. A man employed during the night to empty cesspools, etc., and to convey away the night-soil. Also *transf.*

1606 DEKKER *News fr. Hell* Wks. (Grosart) II. 121 More stinkingly musty..then the fists of night-men. **1665** *Orders of Ld. Mayor* in De Foe *Journ. Plague* (Rtldg.) 64 That no Nightman..be suffered to empty a Vault into any Garden. **1700** T. BROWN tr. *Fresny's Amusem.* (1709) 34 A Milch-Ass, to be sold at the Night-Man's in White-chapel. **1763** C. JOHNSTON *Reverie* II. 246 'We shall all want..our vaults emptied',—said the night-man. **1813** MOORE *Post Bag* iv. 291 Who now will be The Nightman of No-Popery? **1828** P. CUNNINGHAM *N.S. Wales* (ed. 3) II. 104 An odour to which that of a nightman's museum of foul abominations is myrrh and frankincense. **1869** PARKES *Pract. Hygiene* (ed. 3) 109 Nightmen, and the collectors and sorters of dust.

2. A man who does work during the night, or on a night-shift. (Usu. as two words.) Also, one who works illegally at night; a burglar.

1851 H. MELVILLE *Moby Dick* III. xlix. 293 The solitary night-man at the fore-mast-head. **1885** *Harper's Mag.* May 870/2 There is a day and a night man to each lock. **1887** *Pall Mall G.* 19 Feb. 8/2 The night men usually descend between half-past six and seven. **1928** *Amer. Mercury* May 78/1 *Rowdy-dowdy*..was borrowed from the more aristocratic *night-men*, who use it in this manner: 'Charge on a town, make as many clouts on the *kiester* (safe) as necessary, and then battle the irate citizens in a *rowdy-dowdy* get-a-way.' **1957** M. BANTON *W. Afr. City* v. 87 The people hated any type of investigator because so many of them were 'night men' (i.e. made an illegal living after dark). **1960** *Times* 29 Sept. 7/1 A company taxi is usually driven by both a day-man and a night-man.

nightmare ('naɪtmɛə(r)), *sb.* Also 6 **nightesmare.** [f. NIGHT *sb.* + MARE *sb.*[2] Cf. MDu. *nachtmare*, *-maere*, *-mer(i)e*, etc. (Du. *-merrie*), MLG. *nachtmar*, *-maer* (LG. *-moor*), MHG. *nahtmare* (G. *nachtmahr*, *-mähr*): some of these forms show assimilation to MARE *sb.*[1]]

1. a. A female spirit or monster supposed to beset people and animals by night, settling upon them when they are asleep and producing a feeling of suffocation by its weight.

c **1290** *S. Eng. Leg.* I. 306/228 Ofte huy ouer-liggez [men]: and men cleopiet þe niȝt-mare. *c* **1340** *Nominale* (Skeat) 701 Wolf, fox, and nytmare [F. *pesarde*]. *c* **1440** *Promp. Parv.* 356/1 Nyghte Mare (or mare, or wytche), *epialtes*. **1530** PALSGR. 248/1 Nightmare, *goublin*. **1561** *Chaucer's Miller's T.* C.'s Wks. (Speght) 13 Jesu Crist, and seint Benedight, Blisse this house..Fro the nightes-mare. **1608** TOPSELL *Serpents* (1658) 715 The spirits of the night, called Incubi and Succubi, or else Night-mares. **1696** AUBREY *Misc.* (1721) 147 It is to prevent the Night-Mare (viz.) the Hag, from riding their Horses. **1769** CHATTERTON *Ælla* cvi, The death-owl loud doth sing To the night-mares as they go. **1817** SHELLEY *Pr. Athan.* I. 120 Like an eyeless nightmare grief did sit Upon his being. **1842** TENNYSON *Morte d' Arth.* 177 King Arthur panted hard Like one that feels a nightmare on his bed.

fig. **1860** THACKERAY *Round. Papers, On half a loaf*, For weeks past this nightmare of war has been riding us.

b. As a term of abuse. *rare.*

1633 FORD *Broken H.* II. iii, Hold your chops, nightmare! **1824** BYRON *Def. Transf.* I. i, Out Thou incubus! Thou nightmare!

2. a. A feeling of suffocation or great distress felt during sleep, from which the sleeper vainly endeavours to free himself; a bad dream producing these or similar sensations.

1562 TURNER *Herbal* II. (1568) 84 A good remedy agaynst the stranglyng of the nyght mare. **1584** COGAN *Haven Health* ccxli. (1636) 274 The spirits being stopped, the night mare (as they call it) and palsie..be engendred. **1631** WIDDOWES *Nat. Philos.* 53 The Night-mare is a seeming of being choked or strangled by one leaping upon him. **1675** *Machiavelli's Belphegor* Wks. 527 This was no fantastick imagination, nor fit of the Night-mare. **1711** ADDISON *Spectator* No. 117 ¶8 Moll had been often brought before him for..giving Maids the Night-Mare. **1748** HARTLEY *Observ. Man* I. i. §i. 52 Which seems to be the Case in the Night-mare. **1826** SCOTT *Jrnl.* 29 Nov., I had the night-mare in short, and no wonder. **1852** MRS. STOWE *Uncle Tom's C.* xxxix, He stared at her like a man in the night-mare. **1874** L. STEPHEN *Hours in Library* (1892) I. vi. 234 He is above all things a dreamer, and his dreams resemble nightmares.

b. In *fig.* and *transf.* senses.

1831 CARLYLE *Sart. Res.* (1858) 71 Not till after long years ..did the believing heart..sink into spell-bound sleep, under the nightmare, Unbelief. **1840** DICKENS *Old C. Shop* xxix, Quilp indeed was a perpetual night-mare to the child. **1872** BAKER *Nile Trib.* ix, The night-mare of her life was the possibility that her daughter should be sold. **1909** *Chambers's Jrnl.* Feb. 75/2 From tip to tip of its outstretched arms this nightmare of the deep measured 56 feet. **1956** A. L. ROWSE *Early Churchills* 32 A great deal of genuine learning is displayed, a nightmare of authorities cited in the Elizabethan fashion. **1975** M. BABSON *There must be some Mistake* xiii. 100 'It's a nightmare,' Karen agreed. '..I wake up and it's still there.'

3. *attrib.* and *Comb.*, as ***nightmare-dream***, ***-dreamer***, ***-land***, ***-sleep***, ***-sleeper***, ***-weight***. Also ***nightmare-laden***, ***-ridden*** adjs.; ***nightmare-like*** adj. and adv.

1856 DELAMER *Fl. Gard.* (1861) 169 You may plant in safety, without *nightmare dreams of nipping frosts. **1954** KOESTLER *Invisible Writing* vii. 76, I am a chronic *nightmare-dreamer. **1865** *Macm. Mag.* XIII. 156 Like weird ghosts from the *nightmare-laden world I had left behind me. **1957** E. HYAMS *Into Dream* 246 For twenty-four hours he had been living in wonderland, *nightmareland. **1847** J. R. LOWELL *Let. from Boston* in *Pennsylvania Freeman* 1 Jan. 3/3 His words burn as with iron-searers, And *nightmare-like he mounts his hearers. **1919** WODEHOUSE *Damsel in Distress* xv. 176 This blister had become the one great Fact in an unreal nightmare-like universe. **1926** C. PLUMB in *Oxford Poetry* 36 Plagued, *nightmare-ridden by a million lusts. **1961** *Times* 10 Nov. 18/7 Schoenberg's nightmare-ridden territory. **1829** CARLYLE *Misc.* II. (1857) 116 Over our noblest faculties is spreading a *nightmare sleep. **1843** —— *Past & Pr.* (1858) 282 Awake, O *nightmare sleepers. **1847** TENNYSON *Princ.* VI. 281 This *nightmare weight of gratitude.

'nightmare, *v.* [f. the sb.]

1. *trans.* To beset as by a nightmare. Also *fig.* Hence **'nightmared** *ppl. a.*

1660 R. WILDE *Iter Boreale* 3 Hag of my Fancy,.. Nightmare my soul no more. *a* **1678** MARVELL *Poems* (1870) 136 Thus the State's nightmared by this hellish rout. **1856** R. A. VAUGHAN *Mystics* (1860) II. x. i. 154 Now she sat nightmared in company, nervous, stiff, and silent, the picture of stupidity. **1893** LELAND *Mem.* I. 110 The nightmared slumber of frozen orthodoxy.

2. To imagine as in a nightmare.

1839 LADY LYTTON *Cheveley* (ed. 2) I. xii. 269 The obscene trash and inconceivable horrors that are hourly night-mared in French garrets.

nightmarey, *a.* [f. NIGHTMARE *sb.* + -Y[1].] Resembling a nightmare; nightmarish.

1851 G. H. KINGSLEY *Sp. & Trav.* (1900) 531 A very nightmarey dream it promises to be. **1890** *Pall Mall G.* 21 Mar. 6/1 How the master ever wrote anything but nightmary stories..I cannot for the life of me imagine. **1934** H. NICOLSON *Diary* 24 Mar. (1966) 172, I am..very apprehensive and nightmarey.

'nightmarish, *a.* [f. as NIGHTMARE *v.* + -ISH[1].] Somewhat like a nightmare; apt to give one the nightmare.

1834 *Fraser's Mag.* X. 439 That wild, disjointed, nightmareish inspiration, which seems the essence of German romanticism. **1872** KING *Sierra Nevada* ix, After sleeping on the nightmarish brink of the falls. **1890** *Athenæum* 9 Aug. 189/2 The story is restrained..in tone, yet there are lurid and nightmarish touches.

Hence **'nightmarishly** *adv.*

1891 *Sat. Rev.* 4 Apr. 425/2 It is..unspeakably and nightmarishly dull. **1915** A. BENNETT *These Twain* (1916) II. xv. 297 The longer Hilda regarded, the more nightmarishly numerous seemed the doors. **1934** A. HUXLEY *Beyond Mexique Bay* 249 Then, nightmarishly proliferating, appear the Pittsburgs and Birminghams, the Osakas and Calcuttas of this unhappy world. **1973** *Nation Rev.* (Melbourne) 31 Aug. 1453/5 Backdrops as nightmarishly accurate as the best of Goya.

'nightness. *nonce-wd.* Darkness.

1839–52 BAILEY *Festus* 37/1 He strained His eyes to work the nightness which remained.

night-night ('naɪt,naɪt), *int.* Also **night, night.** [Cf. NIGHT *sb.* 4 h.] = GOOD NIGHT I.

1896 G. F. NORTHALL *Warwickshire Word-Bk.* 158 *Night-night*, good-night: spoken to children. **1905** R. FRY *Let.* 9 Jan. (1972) I. 229 Night, night, dear heart. Thanks for your cheering letter. **1945** W. DE LA MARE *Burning-Glass* 24 Night-night, my Precious!

night-old, *a.*: see NIGHT *sb.* 14.

'night-owl. [f. NIGHT *sb.* + OWL *sb.*] **1.** An owl which flies especially by night.

1593 SHAKS. *Rich. II*, III. iii. 183 For night-Owls shrike, where monting Larks should sing. **1601** —— *Twel. N.* II. iii. 60 Shall wee rowze the night-Owle in a Catch? **1691** *Vind. Top Knots* i. in *Bagford Ball.* (1876) I. 123 Like silly Night Owls They prate, and they talk of their Top-Knots. **1743** *Pol. Ballads* (1860) II. 301 The night-owl shrieks, the raven croaks. **1796** STEDMAN *Surinam* II. xxv. 239 The *strix* or night-owl of Guiana regularly paid us his nocturnal visits. **1845** *Encycl. Metrop.* XXV. 133/1 Night Owls..are of small size, but their habits are generally nocturnal, and their motions slow and noiseless.

2. A person who is up or out-of-doors late at night. orig. *U.S.*

1847 W. T. PORTER *Quarter Race Kentucky* 163 You no-souled, shad-bellied, squash-headed, old night-owl you! **1880** 'MARK TWAIN' *Tramp Abroad* 270 He calculated to be off before night-owls like me turned out of bed. **1963** M. MCCARTHY *Group* xii. 286 Her father, who was a night owl, was still awake. **1975** *Listener* 11 Sept. 343/3 Jazz lovers have to be night owls..for only two programmes feature early evening jazz.

'night-piece. [f. NIGHT *sb.* + PIECE *sb.* Cf. Du. *nachtstuk*, G. *nachtstück*.]

1. A painting or picture representing a night-scene. Also *transf.*

1605 B. JONSON *Masque Blackness* Wks. (Rtldg.) 545/1 The scene behind seemed a vast sea..to which was added an obscure and cloudy night-piece. **1655** VAUGHAN *Silex Scint.* 160 Some meek night-piece which day quails To candlelight unveils. **1692–3** NORRIS *Pract. Disc.* IV. 45 But I have drawn a sad, and black Night-piece of this already. **1711** ADDISON *Spect.* No. 83 ¶9 He had likewise hung a great Part of the Wall with Night-pieces. **1762–71** H. WALPOLE *Vertue's Anecd. Paint.* (1786) II. 195 Excelling particularly in night-pieces and candle-lights. **1797** HOLCROFT tr. *Stolberg's Trav.* II. li, Christ before Caiaphas. A night piece. *c* **1850** tr. *Hugo's Hunchback* I. iii, Faces..which Rembrandt has brought out so grave and so expressive from the dark ground of his night-piece.

b. Applied to an actual night-scene, or to a landscape as viewed by night.

1643 *Sober Sadness* 46 This plot was laid; and this designe in agitation (though it be a night-piece, which few have hitherto discover'd fully). **1646** J. GREGORY *Notes & Obs.* (1650) 109 So the Tradition, and so the Masters decribe the Night-peice of this Nativity. **1832** DOWNES *Lett. Cont. Countries* I. 54 The solitude..illumined by the bright and steady moon—I thought it the finest night-piece I had ever witnessed.

c. As a title of literary compositions.

1648 HERRICK *Hesp.*, The Night-piece to Julia. *a* **1718** PARNELL (*title*) A Night-piece on Death.

†**2.** *fig.* A mistress. *Obs. rare*[−1].

1620 MIDDLETON *Chaste Maid* I. ii, Some merchants would in soul kiss hell..To deck their night-piece.

'night-rail. Now only *Hist.* or *dial.* [f. NIGHT *sb.* + RAIL *sb.*[1]] A loose wrap, dressing-jacket, or dressing-gown, as worn by women when in undress.

1554 *Bury Wills* (Camden) 146 Oon of my night kerchers, and oon of my night railes. **1626** MIDDLETON *Mayor of Queenb.* III. ii, To see men wear stomachers or night-rails. *c* **1640** SHIRLEY *Capt. Underwit* I. in Bullen *Old Pl.* II. 327 What paid you for this dead mans hair? Where's your night rail? **1688** HOLME *Armoury* III. i. 12/2 He beareth Sable, a Set-Hood, laced, conjoyned to a Night raile... Some term this a Hooded Night-raile. **1710** STEELE *Tatler* No. 245 ¶2 Four striped Muslin Night-Rails very little frayed. **1753** RICHARDSON *Grandison* v. xliii, Does it not look as if she would have been an useful creature in the days of nightrail and notableness? **1793** *Regal Rambler* 24 The ragged remains of a nightrail. **1822** SCOTT *Nigel* xvii, I could wager a rose-noble..that she has clean head-gear and a soiled night-rail. **1852** THACKERAY *Esmond* I. vi, My lady sitting up in the bed, showing herself full dressed under her night-rail. **1891** T. HARDY *Tess* xxxiv, When we was packing your few traps and your Mis'ess's night-rail and dressing things.

'night-raven. Now only *poet.* [OE. *næht-*, *nihthræfn*, *-hrefn*, *-hremn*, etc. = MDu. *nachtraven*, *-rave* (Du. *-raaf*), MLG. *nachtraven*, OHG. *nachtraban*, *-(h)ram* (MHG. *nahtraben*, *-rabe*, G. *nachtrabe*), ON. *náttrafn* (Norw. *nattramn*, Da. *natte-*, *natravn*): see NIGHT *sb.* and RAVEN *sb.*] A nocturnal bird, variously identified as a night-owl, night-heron, or nightjar, or imagined as a distinct species. (Cf. NIGHT-CROW.)

In early use found only as a rendering of L. *noctua* or *nycticorax.*

c **725** *Corpus Gloss.* (Hessels) N 145 *Noctua*, naeht hraefn. *c* **825** *Vesp. Psalter* ci. 7 ȝeworden ic eam swe swe næht-hrefn [L. *nocticorax*] in husincle. *c* **1000** *Ags. Ps.* (Thorpe) ci. 5 Ic ȝenemned eam niht-hrefne ȝelic. *a* **1300** *E.E. Psalter* ci. 7 Made am i als nighte-rauen in housefes [that] esse. *a* **1400–50** *Alexander* 4531 A ratland niȝt ravyn is him to rent ȝolden. **1567** MAPLET *Gr. Forest* 94 (Cath. Angl.), The Nightrauen or Crowe is of the same maner of life that the Owle is. **1579** SPENSER *Sheph. Cal.* June 23 Here no night-ravenes lodge, more black then pitche. **1632** MILTON *L'Allegro* 7 Where brooding darknes spreads his jealous wings, And the night-Raven sings. **1678** RAY *Willughby's Ornith.* 279 The lesser Ash-coloured Heron, or Night Raven. **1755** tr. *Pontoppidan's Nat. Hist. Norway* II. 91 We have the Night Raven also here. **1808** SHELLEY *St. Irvyne* I. 4 Along the wild mountains night-ravens were yelling.

transf. **1673** KIRKMAN *Unlucky Citizen* 168 What good could I expect from my Father, who had such a Night-Raven as my Stepdame was?

'night-robe. [f. NIGHT *sb.* + ROBE *sb.*[1]] A garment worn during the night; a dressing-gown or night-gown.

1553 *Rutland Papers* (Camden) 119 Therle of Oxford claymeth..to haue the nighte robe with the which the Queene was clothed the night before. **1805** SCOTT *Last Minstr.* VI. xix, All in her night-robe loose she lay reclined. **1865** J. H. INGRAHAM *Pillar of Fire* (1872) 418 The queen came to the door hurriedly, in her night-robes, and opened it.

Comb. **1894** *Outing* XXIV. 110/1 Worthies, in white night-robe-like blouses protecting other clothing.

Hence **'night-robed** *a.*

1799 SHERIDAN *Pizarro* Prol., Where night-robed misses amble two by two.

nights (naɪts), *adv.* Now *colloq.* and *U.S.* [OE. *nihtes* = OFris. *nachtes*, *-is*, OS. *nahtes* (MDu. *nachtes*, *nachts*, Du. *'s nachts*), OHG. *nahtes* (G. *nachts*), an irreg. genitive form on the analogy of *dæges*, *dages*, etc. (see DAY *sb.* 1 b), but in later use prob. apprehended as a plural.] During the night, by night, at night.

Beowulf 422 Ic..on yðum slog niceras nihtes. *a* **900** CYNEWULF *Crist* 938 Mona þæt sylfe, þe ær moncynne nihtes lyhte, niþer ȝehreoseð. *c* **1000** *Boeth. Metr.* xiii. 59 Merecondel scyfð on ofdæle, uncuðne weȝ nihtes ȝeneðeð. *a* **1122** *O.E. Chron.* (Laud MS.) an. 1101 Se biscop Rannulf ..ut of þam ture on Lunden nihtes oðbærst. *a* **1250** *Owl & Night.* 591 Wan ich flo niȝtes after muse. *a* **1272** *Luue Ron* 60 in *O.E. Misc.* 95 If he dret þat me him stele, þenne doþ him pyne nyhtes wake. *c* **1375** *Sc. Leg. Saints* Prol. 102 Chosine knychttis seruand hyme bath day & nychtis. *c* **1400** *Laud Troy Bk.* 6443 Ȝe scholde sitte and wake nygthes, As hauke on perche that sittes in mewe. **1601** Weever *Mirr. Mart.* E ij, Aboue all nights, nights, dayes, each hower remember, To solemnize the twenteth of Nouember.

1786 *Exchange Advertiser* (Boston) 19 Oct. (Th.), Not a flute that has a hole in it, but that is employed very successfully nights. **1861** O. W. Norton *Army Lett.* (1903) 29 To-morrow we do guard duty. It is tiresome work. No sleep nights. **1866** Lowell *Biglow P.* Ser. II. Introd., So thievish they hev to take in their stone walls nights. **1899** F. J. Mather *Chaucer's Prol.* p. vii, Chaucer..returning nights to his home in chambers over Aldgate. **1938** T. Wilder *Our Town* 34 From my window up there I can just see your head nights when you're doing your homework over in your room. **1964** *Panorama* (Brisbane) Sept. 7/1, I don't know who writes the lyrics for their songs, but professionals can still sleep nights. **1970** *Globe & Mail* (Toronto) 25 Sept. 12/1 (Advt.), She wanted a place that would stay up nights to serve her.

night-scape, nightscape (ˈnaɪtskeɪp). [f. night *sb.* + scape *sb.*[3]] = night-piece.

1915 T. Burke *Nights in Town* 14 There is a short street in Walworth Road..which is as perfect as any nightscape ever conceived by any artist. *Ibid.* 272 Even as a child I was conscious of the call of these wicked nightscapes. **1949** *Archit. Rev.* CV. 248 (*caption*) Nightscape, suspended animation. **1958** L. Durrell *Mountolive* xiii. 250 The youthful figures of himself and Leila moved..to the punctuation of a single soft finger-drum across a violet night-scape.

ˈnight-scene. [f. night *sb.* + scene *sb.*] A scene viewed, or taking place, by night; a picture, or dramatic representation, of this.

1684 T. Burnet *The. Earth* II. 103 These things will make the day dead and melancholy, but the night-scenes will have more of horrour in them: when the blazing-stars appear. **1700** Rowe *Amb. Step-Moth.* IV. iii, A night Scene of the Temple of the Sun. **1711** Shaftesb. *Charac.* (1737) I. 317 A conversation of the same free nature as that recited by him in his night-scene. **1831** Scott in *Lockhart* (1839) X. 115 Garrick's acting, particularly in the night-scene, drew down universal applause.

night-school: see night *sb.* 13.

ˈnight-season. [f. night *sb.* + season *sb.*] The night-time.

1535 Coverdale *Luke* xxi. 37 In the night season he wente out, and abode all night vpon mount Oliuete. **1560** Daus tr. *Sleidane's Comm.* 51 The Captaine of Turege had taken in the night season John Oxeline. **1596** Dalrymple tr. *Leslie's Hist. Scot.* I. 93 In thir only mantilis in the nyᵗ seasone thay rowit thame selfes, and in thame sleipet sound. **1817** Coleridge *Biog. Lit.* (Bohn) 299 He calls up the breeze to chase away the usurping vapours of the night-season. **1860** Gosse *Rom. Nat. Hist.* 37 The aborigines holding their revels under the coolness of the night-season.

nightshade[1] (ˈnaɪtʃeɪd). Forms: 1 **nihtscada,** 5 **nyȝtschode, nichtheshod(e, niȝteschede,** 6 **nyghte-, nighteshad(e,** 6– **nightshade.** [OE. *nihtscada* = MDu. *nachtscade*, etc. (Du. *nachtschade*) and *nachtscadu(w)e* (Du. *-schaduwe*), MLG. *nachtschade, -schede, -scheide* (hence MSw. *natskada, -skàda, -skeda*, Da. *natskade*), OHG. *nahtscato, -schato* (MHG. *-schate*, G. *-schatte, -schatten*; ? hence Sw. *nattskatta, -skattegräs*), app. f. night *sb.* + shade *sb.*, perh. with allusion to the poisonous or narcotic properties of the berries. The variation of the second element in ME. and MLG. is prob. due to independent popular corruption.]

1. a. A plant of the genus *Solanum*, esp. *S. nigrum* (Black Nightshade), a herbaceous plant with ovate bluntly-toothed leaves, white flowers, and black poisonous berries, or *S. Dulcamara* (Woody Nightshade) with cordate or hastate leaves, purple flowers, and bright red berries. **b.** A plant of the genus *Atropa*, Deadly Nightshade or belladonna.

c **1000** Ælfric *Gloss.* in Wr.-Wülcker 135/3 *Strumus*, uel *uua lupina*, nihtscada. *c* **1400** *Lanfranc's Cirurg.* 55 Put to þis medycine þe jus of sum colde erbe: as morel, nyȝtschode, penywort. *c* **1450** *Alphita* (Anecd. Oxon.) 119 *Morella*.., *anglice* nichtheschode [*v.r.* niȝteschede] *vel* houndesberie. [Also 176 *Solatrum mortale*]. **1548** Turner *Names Herbs* (E.D.S.) 75 Solanum hortense which..is called in Englishe Nyghtshade. **1562** —— *Herbal* II. (1568) 141 Nighte shad or Petemorell..is a bushy herbe, whyche is vsed to be eaten. **1578** Lyte *Dodoens* 443 Nightshade hath rounde stalkes of a foote long, full of branches. **1657** S. Purchas *Pol. Flying-Ins.* 93 Those that are soporiferous, and Narcotick as..Night-shade. **1688** Holme *Armoury* II. 96/2 Night-shade..in most places..is called Gold-Knape, or yellow Crace, for the golden colour fruit. **1712** tr. *Pomet's Hist. Drugs* I. 138 Some will have them to grow on a kind of Night-shade. **1784** Cowper *Task* IV. 757 Some sprigs of mournful mint, Of nightshade, or valerian. **1810** Crabbe *Borough* xviii, Here the dull nightshade hangs her deadly fruit. **1846** Lindley *Veget. Kingd.* 619 The most immediate affinity of Nightshades seem to be with Oliveworts and Bindweeds. **1872** Macmillan *True Vine* vii. 295 The purple and yellow blossom of the nightshade is constructed exactly like the flower of the cyclamen.

attrib. **1821** Shelley *Epipsych.* 257 One, whose voice was venomed melody, Sate by a well, under blue nightshade bowers.

fig. *a* **1652** J. Smith *Sel. Disc.* i. 7 That venemous solanum, that deadly nightshade, that drives its cold poison into the understandings of men. **1850** O. Winslow *Inner Life* i. 15 Satan has ever sought to engraft the deadly nightshade of error upon the life-giving Rose of Sharon.

2. Used with specific names to denote species of *Solanum*, *Atropa*, or plants of other genera.

African, American, bastard nightshade (see quots.). † **bindweed n.** = *enchanter's n.* **black n.** (see 1 a). **climbing n.** (see quot.). **common n.** = *black n.* **deadly n.** (see deadly *a.* 4 c). **enchanter's n.** (see enchanter 2). **garden n.** = *black n.* † **mad n.** (see quot. 1578). **Malabar n.** = *climbing n.* † **red n.**, *Alkekengi*. **sleeping** or **sleepy n.** = *deadly n.* **stinking n.**, henbane. **three-leaved n.**, a N. American plant (*Trillium*) having simple stems with three leaves at the top. † **tree-n.** (see quot.). **woody n.** (see 1 a).

1839 Ure *Dict. Arts* 150 The berries of the *African nightshade (*solanum guineense*) have been of late years considerably applied to silk. **1760** J. Lee *Introd. Bot.* App. 320 Nightshade, *American, *Phytolacca*. *Ibid.*, Nightshade, American, *Rivinia*. *Ibid.*, Nightshade, *Bastard, *Rivinia*. **1597** Gerarde *Herbal* II. lix. 280 It is called in Latine ..*Circea lutetiana*; in English Inchaunters Nightshade, or *Bindweede Nightshade. **1846–50** A. Wood *Class-bk. Bot.* 448 *Solanum Nigrum*, *Black Nightshade. **1753** Chambers *Cycl. Suppl.* App. s.v., *Climbing Nightshade, a name sometimes used for the Basella or Cuscuta of botanists. **1578** Lyte *Dodoens* 447 This *solanum* cooleth..more strongly than the *Common Nightshade. **1707** Mortimer *Husb.* (1721) II. 231 Flowers like that of the common Nightshade. **1597** Gerarde *Herbal* II. li. 268 In English it [*Solanum hortense*] is called *Garden Nightshade; Morell, and petie Morell. **1578** Lyte *Dodoens* 447 The other is called *Solanum Manicum*, that is to say *Mad or Raging Nightshade. **1600** Surflet *Countrie Farme* II. xliv. 290 Diuers plants which haue the same vertue, as mad nightshade. **1760** J. Lee *Introd. Bot.* App. 320 Nightshade, *Malabar, *Basella*. **1578** Lyte *Dodoens* 444 Of *Red Nightshade, winter Cherie and Alkakengy. **1597** Gerarde *Herbal* II. li. 271 The red winter Cherrie is called..in Latine..*Solanum Vesicarium*: ..in English red Nightshade. **1664** Evelyn *Kal. Hort.* June (1729) 208 *Shrub Night-shade. **1707** Mortimer *Husb.* (1721) II. 231 Shrub Nightshade has a woody Stock and Branches, dark sad green Leaves. **1578** Lyte *Dodoens* 447 One is called..*Sleeping Nightshade. **1597** Gerarde *Herbal* II. li. 269 Dwale or sleeping Nightshade hath round blackish stalks sixe foote high. **1611** Cotgr., *Morelle somnifique*, *Sleepie Nightshade. **1688** Holme *Armoury* II. 75/2 The sleepy Night-shade hath a Sage-like leaf, with a purple Bell-flower. **1796** Withering *Brit. Plants* (ed. 3) II. 252 Deadly, or sleepy Nightshade. **1760** J. Lee *Introd. Bot.* App. 320 Nightshade, *Three-leaved, *Trillium*. **1597** Gerarde *Herbal* II. lxiv. 289 This rare and pleasaunt plant [*Solanum arborescens*] called *tree Night-shade is taken of some to be a kinde of Ginnie pepper, but not rightly. **1796** Withering *Brit. Plants* (ed. 3) II. 253 Bitter-sweet. *Woody Nightshade. **1849** Balfour *Man. Bot.* §961 *Solanum Dulcamara*, Bitter-sweet or woody Nightshade, has slightly narcotic properties.

ˈnight-shade[2]. [f. night *sb.* + shade *sb.*]

1. The shade or darkness of night.

1558 Phaer *Æneid* II. E iv, Through the dark night shade her self she drew from sight. **1621** Brathwait *Nat. Embassie* (1877) 164 Short was our sun-shine, but our nightshade long. **1839–52** Bailey *Festus* 237 The day hath nightshade long. **1878** Hardy *Ret. Native* VI. iv, The party drove off and vanished in the night-shades.

†**2.** *fig.* A night-walker, a prostitute. *Obs. rare*[−1].

1612 Beaum. & Fl. *Coxcomb* II. ii, Here comes a nightshade. A gentlewoman-whore.

ˈnight-shift. [f. night *sb.* + shift *sb.*]

1. A shift or garment worn by women at night.

1710 Steele *Tatler* No. 245 ¶2 [She] carried off the following Goods.., Eight Night-Shifts. **1727** G. Jacob *Rape Smock* 7 Cœlia..slips on her Night-Shift. **1863** Queen Victoria *Let.* 8 Apr. in R. Fulford *Dearest Mama* (1968) 192 Poor, dear Alice had the same night shift on which I had when you were all born! **1923** Conrad *Rover* v. 76 If she had a petticoat over her night-shift, that was all. **1958** *New Yorker* 13 Dec. 69/2 (Advt.), The beautiful night shift..by Barbizon in..nylon satin.

2. a. A shift, or gang of workers, employed during the night.

1839 Ure *Dict. Arts* 992 At 11 o'clock in the forenoon the night shift of miners was relieved by the day shift. **1887** *Pall Mall G.* 19 Feb. 8/2 There was consolation..in the fact that the whole of the night shift had not yet descended.

b. The time during which the shift lasts.

1860 Smiles *Self-Help* iv. 82 While working as an engine-man during the night-shifts. **1882** *Report Precious Metals U.S.* 18 To store the *débris* loosened during the night shifts.

ˈnight-shirt. [f. night *sb.* + shirt *sb.*] A shirt or loose garment worn by boys or men when in bed.

1857 Hughes *Tom Brown* I. iii, One of the ushers..caught the performer in his night-shirt. **1860** *All Year Round* No. 73. 543 The fetch or double of a man lying in his night-shirt in bed. **1891** *Spectator* 3 Jan. 3/2 One man was denuded of his night-shirt.

Hence **ˈnight-shirted** *a.*

1893 'B. Abbotsford' *But* 5 To run bang against two night-shirted little items.

ˈnight-soil. [f. night *sb.* + soil *sb.*] **1.** The excrementitious matter removed by night from cesspools, etc.

1770–4 A. Hunter *Georg. Ess.* (1804) II. 294 Night soil is found to be an excellent manure. **1844** Stephens *Bk. Farm* II. 30 A crop of the large orange carrot, manured with nightsoil. **1860** Reade *8th Commandm.* 343 They have toiled at scurrility day by day, year by year, like vendors of night soil, not like writers.

2. *attrib.* and *Comb.*, as ***night-soil cart, collector, man.***

1967 O. Wynd *Walk Softly, Men Praying* ix. 145, I had to steer past a chain of night-soil carts. **1960** *Spectator* 19 Feb. 244 The nightsoil collectors of Lagos's slums were so thoughtless as to go on strike. **1957** M. Banton *W. Afr. City* viii. 158 Loko men are ridiculed by other tribes for working as night-soil men. **1960** C. Achebe *No Longer at Ease* ii. 16 As soon as the night-soil-man passed swinging his broom.. and trailing clouds of putrefaction the boy quickly sprang to his feet and began calling him names. **1965** J. R. Hetherington *Selina's Aunt* 42/2, I then learned that he *worked* for the council—in the capacity of night-soilman.

ˈnight-song. [f. night *sb.* + song *sb.*]

1. A song sung by night.

1811 Moore *Irish Melodies* Poet. Wks. (1897) 102 The hour That awakens the night-song of mirth in your bower.

2. *Eccl.* [after OE. *niht-sang*.] The last of the seven canonical hours; compline.

1844 Lingard *Anglo-Saxon Ch.* (1858) I. vii. 272 The time for the night-song was, strictly speaking, midnight. **1853** Rock *Ch. Fathers* III. II. 10 Complin or night-song, which is rather a complement to, than a distinct hour by itself of, the divine office.

ˈnight-spell. [f. night *sb.* + spell *sb.*]

1. A spell used as a protection against harm by night.

c **1386** Chaucer *Miller's T.* 3480 The night-spel seyde he anon rightes, On the foure halves of the hous aboute, And on the threisshfold of the dore withoute. **1579** E. K. *Gloss. Spenser's Sheph. Cal.* Mar. 54 Spell, is a kinde of verse or charme,..as the Nightspel for theeues. **1608** Topsell *Serpents* (1658) 663 This is an excellent night-spell, and therefore I was loath to pretermit it. **1619** Fletcher *Mons. Thomas* IV. vi, Have at you with a night spell then!.. 'St. George, St. George,..He walks by day, so does he by night' [etc.]. **1674** Blount *Glossogr.* (ed. 4), *Night-spel*, was a Prayer against the Night-mar.

2. A spell used, or operating, to cause harm or trouble by night.

1589 R. Harvey *Pl. Perc.* (1590) 19 Such a one as speakes of gospels in the day: but vseth I know not what night-spels in the darke. **1612** J. Mason *Anat. Sorc.* 86 Binding some, that they cannot use their naturall powers and faculties, as we see in night-spels. **1827** *Gentl. Mag.* XCVII. 486 When the next morning's Sun had glistened upon the little stream, and the night-spell had thus been broken, one horse drew away with ease the waggon.

attrib. ? *c* **1600** *Distr. Emperor* I. i. in Bullen *Old Pl.* III. 169, I have seene Your conference with witches, night-spell knaves, Connivynge mountebanks.

ˈnight-sun. [f. night *sb.* + sun *sb.*[1]]

†**1.** A mock-moon, paraselene. *Obs. rare.*

1594 Constable *Diana* I. ii, Earthly vapours drawne up by the Sunne, Comets begun, and night-sunnes in the skie. **1601** Holland *Pliny* I. 18 Three Moones also appeared at once,..which most men called Night Sunnes.

2. *poet.* The moon.

1842 Longf. *Hiawatha* ix, The moon, the Night-Sun, eastward, Suddenly, starting from his ambush.

ˈnight-sweat. [f. night *sb.* + sweat *sb.*] Profuse perspiration occurring during the night, symptomatic of certain diseases. Also *fig.*

a **1754** Mead *Wks.* (1762) 487 In two months a hectick came on, attended with thirst, heat and night-sweats. **1789** *Med. Jrnl.* II. 19 The night-sweats, and other hectic symptoms, were now extreme. **1825** J. Neal *Bro. Jonathan* II. 176 Flowers that looked as if they had never had the night-sweat in all their lives. **1876** Bristowe *Th. & Pract. Med.* (1878) 600 With this are necessarily associated night-sweats and other characteristic features of hectic.

night telegraph letter: see night letter a.

ˈnight-tide. [f. night *sb.* + tide *sb.* Cf. MLG. *nachttît*, MHG. *nahtzît* (G. *nachtzeit*), MSw. *nattatidh* (Sw. and Da. *nattetid*).]

1. The time of night; night-time.

14.. *Sir Beues* (M) 3819 As Sabere slepud a nyght tide, Hym thought he sye Beues ride. **1849** Poe *Annabel Lee* vi, All the night-tide, I lie down by the side Of my darling..my bride. **1887** Morris *Odyss.* XII. 286 Ill too are the winds of the night-tide.

2. A tide of the sea occurring during the night.

1759 Saunders in Beatson *Nav. & Milit. Mem.* (1790) II. 374 To proceed with the first fair wind and night-tide above the town of Quebec. **1776** Cook in *Phil. Trans.* LXVI. 448 A notion..that the night-tide rises higher than the day-tide. **1853** J. Stevenson tr. *Beda's Eccl. Hist.* 575 The night-tide of the ocean had drifted in a beam of wood.

ˈnight-time. [f. night *sb.* + time *sb.*] The time between evening and morning; the time of night or darkness. Also *attrib.*

c **1400** Love *Bonavent. Mirr.* xxvi. (B.N.C. MS.) lf. 67 [He] cometh downe allone in the nyȝt time fro that trauaillous hille. **1538** Elyot *Dict.*, *Larna*, a spyrite whiche apperethe in the nyght tyme. **1588** in *Martin Marprel. Controv.* (Arb.) 39 [Taken] out of his bed in the nyght tyme. **1632** J. Hayward tr. *Biondi's Eromena* 72 She assailed the enemy in the night-time unawares. **1709** *Lond. Gaz.* No. 4527/1 He came up with them and attacked them in the Night-time. **1772** *Phil. Trans.* LXII. 94 The reason of the water's appearing so white in the night-time. **1829** Marryat *F. Mildmay* vii, Wandering about..in the night-time. **1856** R. A. Vaughan *Mystics* (1860) I. 82 The night-time of the body is the day-time of the soul. **1935** T. S. Eliot *Murder in Cathedral* ii. 76 The night-time heaping of the ashes. **1955** *Sci. News Let.* 26 Feb. 138/1 Sirius, the dog-star, brightest of all the stars in the nighttime sky.

fig. **1811** Moore *Irish Melodies* Poet. Wks. (1897) 102 Bright dreams of the past..Which come in the night-time of sorrow and care.

night-times ('naɪt,taɪmz), *adv.* Chiefly *dial.* [f. NIGHT-TIME + -S.] At night; during the night.
1884 'MARK TWAIN' *Huck. Finn* 41 Just tramp right across the country, mostly night-times. **1886** F. T. ELWORTHY *West Somerset Word-Bk.* 513, I goes to work, but I goes to school night-times. **1902** 'L. HOPE' *Garden of Kama* 18 We rested, night-times, on the sand By the rare waters of this weary land. **1940** *Sat. Even. Post* 20 Jan. 36/3 Cut the rest of his fence, nighttimes.

'night-vision. Also as two words. [f. NIGHT *sb.* + VISION *sb.*]
1. A vision or dream that comes during the night.
1382 WYCLIF *Isa.* xxix. 7 And shal be as a drem of a nyȝt viseoun [L. *visionis nocturnæ*]..the multitude..that foȝten aȝen Ariel. **1742** YOUNG *Nt. Th.* I. 162 Night-visions may befriend.., Our waking dreams are fatal.
2. a. The faculty of seeing during the night or in the dark. **b.** Ability to see only by night.
1822-34 *Good's Study Med.* (ed. 4) III. 146 Acuteness of night vision is natural to various animals that prowl in the dark. **1838** *Penny Cycl.* XII. 114/2 *Nyctalopia*, night-vision, or day-blindness, probably never occurs as a separate disease. **1946** V. TEMPEST *Near the Sun* vii. 53 The medical people were..confined to assisting the overcoming of..the effects of height and lack of oxygen,..the difficulties of night vision and the psychological approach to flying. **1961** *Housewife* (Ceylon) Dec. 19 Vitamin A..assists our eyesight, especially 'night vision'. **1969** P. KAVANAGH *Such Men are Dangerous* (1971) iii. 49 He might even wait until dark. Fine. My night vision was always good. **1973** J. ROSSITER *Manipulators* xxvi. 249 Ferris would have been watching his progress through his night-vision glasses.

†**'night-wake.** *Obs.* [f. NIGHT *sb.* + WAKE *sb.* Cf. MDu. *nachtwake* (Du. *-waak*), G. *nachtwache*, ON. *náttvaka.*] The action or fact of keeping awake, or watching, during the night; an instance of this; a wake or feast held at night.
a **1000** *Seafarer* 7 (Grein) þær mec oft biȝeat nearo nihtwaco æt nacan stefnan. **1483** *Cath. Angl.* 255/1 Nighte wakes, *vigelie, excubie.* **1521** *Knaresb. Wills* (Surtees) I. 13 For nyght wakes and hedemasse pennys viij d. **1587** GOLDING *De Mornay* xxi. (1592) 328 Their shamefull night-wakes and mysteries celebrated in the darke. *a* **1641** BP. MOUNTAGU *Acts & Mon.* (1642) 137 A tyrannical Prince, killed by his Satrapaes and Noblemen at that feast or drunken night-wake.
Hence **'night-waker; 'night-waking** *ppl. a.*
1483 *Cath. Angl.* 255/1 A Nighte waker, *noctivagus.* **1593** SHAKS. *Lucr.* 554 Yet, fowle night-waking Cat, he doth but dallie, While in his hold-fast foot the weak mouse panteth.

'night-walk, *v.* [f. NIGHT *sb.* + WALK *v.*[1]] *trans.* To walk or travel across (a place) by night. Also *transf.*
1845 THOREAU *Jrnl.* 6 Aug. in *Writings* (1906) VII. 377 Fallen spirits who once in human shape night-walked the earth. **1899** KIPLING *Five Nations* (1903) 8 Consider what toils we [*sc.* cruisers] endure, Night-walking wet sea-lanes, a guard and a lure.

'night-walker. [f. NIGHT *sb.* + WALKER *sb.*]
1. One who walks about by night, esp. with criminal intentions; a bully or thief. Now *rare.* (Common in 17th c.)
1467 *Nottingham Rec.* II. 264 Ricardus Colman..est communis noctivagus vocatus Anglice 'a nyghtwalker' contra formam Statuti. *c* **1500** *Virgilius* in Thoms *Prose Rom.* (1858) II. 41 The nyght walkers carede not a poynt for that crye. **1581** LAMBARDE *Eiren.* ii. vi. (1588) 196 Watches to be kept for arresting of suspected persons, and of nightwalkers. **1601** HOLLAND *Pliny* I. 400 Nero Cæ sar,.. vsing (as he did) to be a night-walker,..met otherwhiles with those that would so beat him. **1671** F. PHILIPPS *Reg. Necess.* 580 To lodge the remainder of the night among the debauched or unruly sort of people, calld Rats or Night-walkers. **1732** *Lond. Mag.* I. 334 Give some share of credit to the out-lying Night-walkers, and Suburbian ghosts. **1771** E. LONG in Hone *Every-day Bk.* II. 206 He never..hurt any body but rogues and night-walkers. **1808** *Sporting Mag.* XXX. 263 One of the night-walkers came in with his legs foremost. **1820** SCOTT *Abbot* xxxv, If he turns resetter of idle companions and night-walkers, the place must be rid of him.
b. A street-walker, a prostitute. Now *rare.*
1670-1 *N. Riding Rec.* VI. 152 A Huby woman presented for being a common night-walker. **1711** STEELE *Spect.* No. 8 ⁋3, I am very well acquainted with all the Haunts and Resorts of Female Night-walkers. *c* **1730** FIELDING *Pleasures of Town* Wks. 1771 I. 246 Young virgins are scarce as rails, sir; Plenty as batts the night-walkers go. **1825** *Act 6 Geo. IV*, c. 97 §3 Every common Prostitute and Night-Walker.
†**c.** 'A bell-man'. *Obs. rare*$^{-0}$.
a **1700** B. E. *Dict. Cant. Crew.*
2. An animal that moves about by night. Also in specific uses (see quots.).
1686 PLOT *Staffordsh.* 243 Most certain it is that Eeles are such night-walkers. **1691** RAY *Creation* (1692) 131 The Tamandua, or Ant-Bear, described by Marcgrave and Piso, who saith of them, that they are Night-walkers, and seek their Food by Night. **1754** STRYPE *Stow's Surv.* (ed. 6) I. I. xx. 124/1 What the Keepers call their School of Apes, which contains two Egyptian Night-walkers, and two Apes from Turkey. *a* **1779** COOK *Voy.* III. viii. (1784) I. 152 We caught ..another [fish].., of a reddish colour with a little beard, which we called night walkers, from the greatest number being caught in the night. **1894** *Outing* XXIV. 137/2 The huge nightwalkers or bob-worms.
3. A somnambulist. *rare*$^{-1}$.
1753 CHAMBERS *Cycl. Suppl.* s.v. *Noctambulatio*, Those.. afflicted with it..are by some called lunatic night-walkers.

'night-walking, *vbl. sb.* [f. NIGHT *sb.* + WALKING *vbl. sb.*] The action or fact of walking or going about by night; an instance of this. Also, sleep-walking.
1494 FABYAN *Chron.* VII. 400 Certayne persones yᵗ thyder were commytted by Sir Iohn Bryton, then custos or gardeyn of the cytie, for nyght walkynges. **1584** R. SCOT *Discov. Witchcr.* x. ix. (1886) 149 Witches night walkings are but phantasies and dreames. **1618** DALTON *Countr. Just.* (1630) 66 Such night-walkings are unfit for honest men, and more suiting to the theefe. **1621** BURTON *Anat. Mel.* I. ii. II. vii. 118 After hard meates, it [sleep] increaseth fearefull dreames, Incubus, night-walking. **1943** A. M. MAYNARD in D. Ibberson *Our Towns* 135 Look for signs of bitten finger-nails, night walking or excitability.

'night-walking, *ppl. a.* [Cf. prec.] That walks by night.
1594 SHAKS. *Rich. III*, I. i. 72 There is no man secure But the Queenes kindred, and night-walking Heralds. **1641** MILTON *Animadv.* Wks. 1851 III. 191 To stand to the courtesy of a night-walking cudgeller. **1658** ROWLAND tr. *Moufet's Theat. Ins.* 959 Those night-walking Butterflies batter with their wings and destroy those that fly by day. **1709** *Rambl. Fuddle-Caps* 8 To pleasure each Sot, like a Night-walking Lady. **1822** W. IRVING *Bracebr. Hall* (1890) 384 This night-walking old fellow of the Haunted House.

'night-wanderer. [f. NIGHT *sb.* + WANDERER *sb.*] One who or that which wanders by night; one who is travelling by night.
1576 FLEMING tr. *Caius' Dogs* (1880) 25 Theefes, robbers, spoylers, and night wanderers. **1590** SHAKS. *Mids. N.* II. i. 39 You..Misleade night-wanderers, laughing at their harme. **1667** MILTON *P.L.* IX. 640 A Flame, Which oft.. Misleads th'amaz'd Night-wanderer from his way. **1844** CARPENTER *Zool.* I. 193 There are few situations in the lower part of Java where this night wanderer is not constantly observed.

'night-wandering, *ppl. a.* [Cf. prec.] That wanders by night.
1593 SHAKS. *Lucr.* 307 Night-wandring weezels shreek to see him there. **1651** CLEVELAND *Poems* 55 When night-wandring Witches put on their pattins. **1720** POPE *Iliad* XIX. 414 So to night-wandering sailors, pale with fears, Wide o'er the watery waste, a light appears.
So **'night-wandering** *vbl. sb.*
a **1649** DRUMM. OF HAWTH. *Hist. Jas. V*, Wks. (1711) 98 Till after much Misery and Night-wandring at Home, they were constrained..to fly into England.

'nightward, *a.* [f. NIGHT *sb.* + -WARD.] Coming, taking place, etc., towards nightfall; leading towards night.
1631 MILTON in Birch *Life* M.'s Wks. 1738 I. 4, I am the bolder to send you some of my nightward Thoughts. **1644** —— *Educ.* 5 Their nightward studies wherewith they close the dayes work. **1863** MRS. WHITNEY *Faith Gartney's Girlh.* xxiii, To tread the nightward path under the old leaden sky.
So **'nightwards** *adv.*, towards the region of night, westwards.
1855 BAILEY *Mystic*, etc. 93 They scattered wide, From Hungria, to Golcond and isles Molucques, And nightwards, to Brasil.

'night-watch. [f. NIGHT *sb.* + WATCH *sb.*]
1. A watch or guard kept during the night; the time during which such a watch is kept.
c **1000** *Ags. Gosp.* Luke ii. 8 Hyrdas..waciende & niht wæccan healdende ofer heora heorda. **1611** COTGR., *Patrouille*, a still night-watch in warre. **1667** MILTON *P.L.* IV. 780 The Cherubim..stood armed To thir night watches in warlike Parade. **1671** F. PHILIPPS *Reg. Necess.* 580 The Constables of every Parish in London..can in their Night-watches command better men than themselves to the compters or London Prisons. **1812** S. ROGERS *Voy. Columbus* v. 25 Oft in the silent night-watch. **1829** MARRYAT *F. Mildmay* vii, I..determined to have one of those great coats..to keep me warm in night-watches. **1884** J. GILMOUR *Mongols* 5 Taking my turn in the night-watch against thieves.
attrib. **1588** SHAKS. *L.L.L.* III. i. 178 A Criticke, Nay, a night-watch Constable.
2. The person or persons engaged in watching by night.
c **1400** *Destr. Troy* 7352 Nightwacche for to wake, waites to blow. *c* **1400** *Siege Jerus.* 41/728 þe nyȝt wacche to þe walle & waytes to blowe. **1530** PALSGR. 248/1 Night watche, *eschaulnetes.* **1645** RUTHERFORD *Tryal & Tri. Faith* i. (1845) 3 If..the night-watch fall fast asleep. **1850** GROTE *Greece* II. lxv. VIII. 362 A little before day break, when the night-watch had just broken up. **1883** GRESLEY *Gloss. Coal-mining* 174 *Night Watch*, a trusty old collier who keeps guard on the surface during the night.
3. One of the (three or four) watches into which the night was divided by the Jews and Romans; hence, any similar period or division of the night. Usually in *pl.*
c **1200** *Trin. Coll. Hom.* 39 On þis niht beð fowuer niht wecches. **1535** COVERDALE *Ps.* cxix. 148 Myne eyes preuente yᵉ night watches. **1611** BIBLE *Ps.* lxiii. 6, I..meditate on thee in the night-watches. **1634** MILTON *Comus* 347 Might we but hear The..village cock Count the night watches to his feathery Dames. **1852** MRS. STOWE *Uncle Tom's C.* xxxvi, Flashing through the chambers of his brain, came all the fearful images of the night-watches.
So **'night-watcher; 'night-watching** *vbl. sb.* and *ppl. a.*
1568 GRAFTON *Chron.* II. 499 To auoyde all *night watchers adioyning to Paris. **1859** MEREDITH *R. Feverel* xli, He dismissed the night-watchers from the room. **1697** DRYDEN *Virgil* Life *2 His too great abstinence and *night-watchings at his Study. *a* **1839** PRAED *Poems* (1865) I. 384 Labour must be your doom, Night-watchings, days of gloom. **1856** *Orr's Circ. Sci., Pract. Chem.* 460 The best description of candle manufactured from wax is the mortar-light, which is used..for night-watching. **1579** NORTHBROOKE *Dicing* (1843) 46 You abused, and not vsed, your sleepe in due time and order, by reason of your ydle *night-watching playes. **1643** A. ROSS *Mel Helic.* 169 That he may not be found asleep By his night-watching enemy. **1820** SHELLEY *Hymn Merc.* ii, A night-watching and door-waylaying thief.

'night-wind. [f. NIGHT *sb.* + WIND *sb.*] A wind that blows during the night.
1812 BYRON *Ch. Har.* I. xiii. i, The night-winds sigh, the breakers roar. **1818** SCOTT *Hrt. Midl.* xvii, The moon, and the dew, and the night-wind. **1839-52** BAILEY *Festus* 29 A changeless tone Of sadness like the nightwind's.

'night-work, *sb.* [f. NIGHT *sb.* + WORK *sb.* Cf. OE. *nihtweorc* (Beowulf 827).] Work done, or which one has to do, during the night.
1594 PLAT *Jewell-Ho.* 67 To put some in minde of their grosse night-woorkes. **1599** B. JONSON *Ev. Man out of Hum.* v. v, I marle what piece of night-work you have in hand now. **1679** C. NESSE *Antichrist* 201 A work of darkness, moon or night-work. **1835** URE *Phil. Manuf.* 374 One ingenious physician, when asked about the effects of night-work on factory children, condemned it. **1869** E. A. PARKES *Pract. Hygiene* (ed. 3) 529 Among the duties of the soldier is some amount of night-work.
So †**'night-work** *v.*; **'night-worker.**
1654 GAYTON *Pleas. Notes* III. viii. 118 And for their Land-ladies, to Night-worke them into silence. **1714** MANDEVILLE *Fab. Bees* (1725) I 91 That the smell of gain was fragrant even to night-workers.

nighty ('naɪtɪ), *sb.* Also **nightie.** [f. *night-* (see def.) + -Y.] A familiar (orig. nursery) name for a night-gown or night-dress; also *transf.* of a surplice. Also *attrib.* and *Comb.*
1871 'S. MAY' *Prudy keeping House* 98 After a nice bath.. the little one was dressed in her nightie. **1894** S. HALE *Lett.* (1919) 286 A blind I opened (thereby drenching me and my nighty) banged and smashed a big pane. **1895** in *Funk's Stand. Dict.* **1897** FLANDRAU *Harvard Episodes* 205 A nice little boy at S. Timothy's,—piping liquidly in an angelic 'nighty' at Chapel. **1903** *Morn. Leader* 3 Dec. 7 The 'nighty' is smartened up..by being tied with narrow ribbons down the front. **1908** *Daily Chron.* 14 Sept. 5/5 So I folded up my nightie and went into the street. **1913** R. BROOKE *Let.* in *Coll. Poems* (1918) p. lxxx, We may only find each other in a whiter world, nighty-clad, harped, winged, celibate. **1934** R. NICHOLS *Fisbo* 36 Frivolous and frolicsome and flighty As the naughtiest flapper in her newest nightie. **1968** 'O. MILLS' *Sundry Fell Designs* iii. 29 Vicky's got a mangy old nightie-case she won't go to bed without. **1972** 'G. BLACK' *Bitter Tea* (1973) x. 157 The hospital nighty..felt slightly scratchy.

†**'nighty,** *a. Obs. rare.* [f. NIGHT *sb.* + -Y[1].] Pertaining to night; nightly, nightlike.
?*c* **1400** LYDG. *Æsop's Fab.* i. 19 To chase away [þe] nyghty [*v.r.* myghty] clowdes blake. **1530** [see NIGHTISH *a.*]. **1582** STANYHURST *Æneis* II. (Arb.) 55 Wee keepe thee midpath with darcknesse nightye beueyled.

'nighty-night, *int.* Also **nightie-night(ie), nighty-nighty.** [See -Y[6].] = GOOD-NIGHT I.
1876 A. F. PARKER *Gloss. Words Oxfordshire* 118 *Nighty-nighty*, good-night, a phrase used by *very old* people. **1888** *Texas Siftings* 7 Jan. 4/1 His nibs wants yer ter fire in yer stuff ter-morrow by eleven sharp. Nighty-night, dovey. **1929** E. BOWEN *Joining Charles* 193 Mrs. Moysey would say, 'Well nightie-night I suppose,' and get finally up. **1957** L. STERN *Midas Touch* II. xviii. 136 Nighty-night, Barbara. Sleep tight. **1959** I. & P. OPIE *Lore & Lang. Schoolch.* iii. 52 To one colloquially saying good-night 'Nightie, nightie', their good-humoured riposte is 'Pyjama, pyjama'. **1971** *Southerly* XXXI. 103 They kissed each other 'nightie night'.

†**nighwhat,** *adv. Obs. rare.* [f. NIGH *a.* + -WHAT; cf. *somewhat*, etc.] Almost, nearly.
c **1290** *Beket* 1924 in *S. Eng. Leg.* I. 161 Heo weren neiȝwat at þe se are þe king it wuste. **1297** R. GLOUC. (Rolls) 437 þe frensse were neiȝwat ibroȝt to gronde. *Ibid.* 1791 A louerding..& is men nei wat alle.

†**'nigion,** variant of NIDGET. *Obs. rare*$^{-0}$.
1570 LEVINS *Manip.* 164/9 A Nigion, *morio, ideota.*

nigirtness, obs. Sc. form of NIGGARDNESS.

nigiting, *vbl. sb.*: see NIDGET *v.*[2]

nigle, obs. variant of NIGGLE *v.*

†**nigmenog.** *Obs. rare*$^{-0}$. (See quot.)
a **1700** B. E. *Dict. Cant. Crew*, *Nigmenog*, a very silly Fellow.

nignay, -nye. *Sc.* Also 9 -noy, -naw. [Of obscure formation: cf. NICK-NACK.] A trifle; a trifling, useless thing or proceeding.
a **1689** CLELAND *Poems* (1697) 92 (Jam.), He was not for the French nignayes, But briskly to his brethern says [etc.]. **1730** RAMSAY *Fables, Cats & Cheese* 44 Poor Pousies now the daffin saw, Of gawn for nignyes to the law. **1788** PICKEN *Poems* (1813) I. 124 (E.D.D.), Naething now fills the bole or pantry, But some nignye that crams the gentry. **1835** WALKER *Rhymes* 195 (E.D.D.), Numerous Nig-naws from New Zealand. **1880** *Antrim & Down Gloss.* 73 *Nignays, Nignoys*, useless profitless doings.

nigneti, obs. form of NINETY.

nig-nog[1] ('nɪgnɒg). *slang.* [Perh. f. NIGMENOG fool.] A foolish person; hence, a raw and unskilled recruit. Cf. NING-NONG.
1953 *Punch* 9 Dec. 692/3 All must be represented on a strict basis of proportion of the number of citizens for whom they cater: Football-pool promoters (six representatives), barrow-boys (two representatives), share-pushers, erks, nig-nogs, [etc.]. **1962** A. WESKER *Chips with Everything* I. iii. 17 A straight line, you heaving nig-nogs, a straight line. **1967** *Times* 30 Nov. 10/8 'Nig-nog' was used on the railways

and elsewhere long before coloured immigrants appeared... It is usually taken as a mildly contemptuous but good-humoured name for an unskilled man or novice.

nig-nog² (ˈnɪgnɒg). [Redupl. shortened form of NIGGER *sb.*] A coarsely abusive term for a Negro.
1959 M. PUGH *Chancer* 85 First lot, and look lively. Lot of nig-nogs off the trees. **1971** J. GARDNER *Every Night's a Bullfight* xiii. 405 I'm talking about you and your precious Juliet, your beloved Carol bloody Evans that nig-nog tart. **1972** D. ONYEAMA *Nigger at Eton* x. 199 The word 'wog'.. was one racial name which I always seemed to fear at Eton. Together with 'nig-nog', it was the term of abuse which.. I did not, to start with, understand the meaning of. **1974** *Times* 14 Feb. 16/8 I'm not going to vote until they get me a house and get rid of the nignogs. **1975** J. SYMONS *Three Pipe Problem* v. 36 He wanted to send the nig nogs and the Pakis back where they belong, in the jungle.

† **nigon.** *Obs.* Forms: α. 4–6 **negon**, (5 **negyn**). β. 4–5 **nygun**, 5 **nyg(g)oun**, 5–6 **nygon**, 6 **niggon**. [Of obscure origin: see NIG *a.* and NIGGARD.] A niggard, miser.
α. **1303** R. BRUNNE *Handl. Synne* 6055 What seye ȝe by þese streyte negons þat se al day Goddes persones Before hem deye for mysese. **14..** *Sir Beues* (C) 1917 Þus men schal teche odur.. Of mete & drynke no negyn to be. *c* **1460** *Towneley Myst.* xxx. 571 The negons thai mowchid and had no will For hart fare. **1526** *Pilgr. Perf.* (W. de W. 1531) 19 b, He begynneth to spare his goodes, and waxeth a negon.
β. **1303** R. BRUNNE *Handl. Synne* 5575 Pers was.. swyþe coueytous, And a nygun and auarous. *c* **1330** —— *Chron. Wace* (Rolls) 5721 He was neuere nygon ne nyce. *c* **1386** CHAUCER *Cook's T.* 319 My brother is a nyggoun, I swer by Cristes ore. *c* **1412** HOCCLEVE *De Reg. Princ.* 2033 To you therof kan I be no nygon. **1520** *Caxton's Chron. Eng.* v. 64/1 He was a very nygon, and was exalted to his empire by the Grekes. **1570** LEVINS *Manip.* 164/8 A Niggon, *parcus.*
Hence † **ˈnigonry**, † **ˈnigonship**, niggardliness. *Obs.*
c **1400** LOVE *Bonavent. Mirr.* xxxvi. (B.N.C. MS.) lf. 87 Thyne owne false couetise in excusacioun of thyne nygunrye. *c* **1460** G. ASHBY *Dicta Philos.* 548 Be nat in youre expenses ouer large, Ne to sca[r]ce by maner of nygonship. **1526** *Pilgr. Perf.* (W. de W. 1531) 110 These be yᵉ vices contrary to these vertues,.. Auaryce or negonry.

nigra (ˈnɪgrə). *U.S.* Also **nigrah** (ˈnɪgrɑː). [f. NEGRO.] Variant form of 'Negro', used principally in the Southern States. Cf. NIGGA.
1944 *Amer. Speech* XIX. 166 In the South it is commonly heard as *nigrah*, and not only from white lips. Indeed *nigrah* is also used by Northern Negroes, including some of the most eminent. **1959** *New Statesman* 6 June 800/1 In the autumn of 1956 I asked a young plantation owner in Mississippi if he had noticed any change in his relations with Negro employees since the Supreme Court rulings against segregation. 'Well,' he said slowly, 'I guess you can say the nigra ain't loyal any more.' **1960** WENTWORTH & FLEXNER *Dict. Amer. Slang* 354/2 *Niggra* = nigger. A pronunciation used by Southerners of Southern breeding and ancestry. Conjuring up the period of Negro slavery, the pronunciation is even more derog. than 'nigger'. **1965** L. WHITTEN *Progeny of Adder* (1966) 69 The guy has some kind of funny accent, it ain't Jewish or Italian and it ain't Nigra or Southern. **1968** *Guardian* 25 Oct. 2/3 We know our niggras and we love them. **1969** P. CROSS in A. Dundes *Mother Wit* (1973) 654/2 They had the niggras on their plantation. **1969** F. RICHARDS *Risky Way to Kill* (1970) xi. 140 'Pretty little thing, as nigras go, Mrs. Prender said.' '"Nigras"? Like that, Henderson?' 'Way it sounded to me.' 'It's a Southern variant,' Heimrich said. 'Between "nigger", which they're beginning—some of them are beginning—not to use so much and "Negro", which a lot of them can't get used to.' **1973** L. HEREN *Growing up Poor in London* v. 109, I was with Martin Luther King Jr. on his 1961 freedom ride, and the church in which he preached in Montgomery, Alabama, was attacked. This led to a stopover of three or four days, during which several well-meaning whites, in spite of all the evidence, sought to persuade me that their niggers—or rather, nigras—were happy, well loved, and free to do whatever they wanted.

nigramancer, -mancy, obs. ff. NECRO-.

† **nigre**, variant of NIGER or NIGGER. *Obs.*
c **1700** T. BROWN *Lett. fr. Dead* (1707) II. 121 A manner that discover'd he had an ascendency over the rest of the immortal Nigres.

† **nigred**, a misprint for INGREDE *v.*
1657 TOMLINSON *Renou's Disp.* 325 The round [Aristolochia], which nigreds [L. *accedit ad*] the confection of Hiera Pacchii, califies and dries potently. [The *Phys. Dict.* compiled for the work gives '*Nigredes*, makes black'.]

† **niˈgredity.** *Obs. rare.* [f. late L. *nigrēdo* blackness.] Blackness.
1547 BOORDE *Brev. Health* lxxiii. 24 In whose urynes any nygreditie or blackenes hath dominion. **1597** A. M. tr. *Guillemeau's Fr. Chirurg.* 29/2 Ther remayneth somtimes a nigredítye or blacknes about the apertione.

† **nigrefaction.** *Obs.* *rare*⁻⁰. [Cf. NIGRIFICATION.] 'A making black' (Phillips 1658).

nigrefie, obs. form of NIGRIFY.

nigremansi, obs. form of NECROMANCY.

nigrescence (naɪˈgrɛsəns). [f. L. *nigresc-ĕre*: see next and -ENCE.] The process of becoming black, or the blackness produced.
1856 RUSKIN *Mod. Paint.* III. IV. x. §10 An imaginative observer may find, perhaps, more to amuse him in the erratic nigrescence than in many a laboured picture.
b. *spec.* Darkness of hair, eyes, or complexion.
1885 BEDDOE *Races Britain* 5 A ready means of comparing the colours of two peoples or localities is found in the Index of Nigrescence.

nigrescent (naɪˈgrɛsənt), *a.* [ad. L. *nigrescent-em*, pres. pple. of *nigrescĕre* to grow black, f. *niger* black.] Blackish, somewhat black.
1755 in JOHNSON. **1772** NUGENT *Hist. Fr. Gerund* I. 531 The nigrescent maculation of their pristine niveous candour. **1819** H. BUSK *Vestriad* I. 272 The glossy ermine, .. Or scarcer sable with nigrescent locks. **1822–34** *Good's Study Med.* (ed. 4) IV. 450 The Nigrescent Leprosy.. is improperly called black, though it was so named by the Greeks. **1882** *Entom. Mag.* Mar. 223 *A. gibbera*.. has black halteres, as well as nigrescent alulets and wings.

niˈgresceous, *a. rare.* [f. as NIGRESC-ENT + -EOUS.] Blackish.
1887 W. PHILLIPS *Brit. Discomycetes* 15 Variable in colour —brown spadiceous, violaceous, nigresceous.

nigrescite (ˈnɪgrəsaɪt). *Min.* [f. L. *nigrescĕre* (see above) + -ITE¹ 2. Named 1867.] A hydrous silicate of iron and magnesium, changing by exposure from green to black.

nigri-, combining form of L. *niger*, *nigr-*, as in ***nigricaulate***, or ***-cauline***, having a black stem, ***nigricollate***, having a black neck, ***nigricornate***, ***-crural***, ***-pennate***, etc.
1857 MAYNE *Expos. Lex.* **1892** *Syd. Soc. Lex.*

nigricant (ˈnɪgrɪkənt), *a.* [ad. L. *nigricant-em* blackish, swarthy, pres. pple. of *nigricāre* to be blackish, f. *niger* black.] Black. *Bot.* = NIGRESCENT.
1772 NUGENT *Hist. Fr. Gerund* II. 97 To dissipate the nigricant squadrons of darkness. **1887** W. PHILLIPS *Brit. Discomycetes* 182 Globose or hemispherical, nigricant.
So † **ˈnigricanting** *ppl. a.*, blackening. *Obs.*⁻¹.
1716 M. DAVIES *Athen. Brit.* III. Arianism 31 The better to carry on the nigricanting Art of sucking of Spiritual Venom out of Honey-suckles.

niˈgrific, *a. nonce-wd.* [Cf. *magnific.*] Black.
1804 *Something Odd* II. 89 He don't believe there is a devil. *Apropos* of his nigrific Majesty [etc.].

nigrifiˈcation. *rare*⁻⁰. [f. L. *nigrificāre*: see next and -ATION.] 'The act of making black' (Johnson 1755).

nigrify (ˈnɪgrɪfaɪ), *v.* Also 7 **nigrefie**. [ad. L. *nigrificāre* to blacken, f. *niger* black + *facĕre* to make.] *trans.* To blacken.
1656 in BLOUNT *Glossogr.* **1721** in BAILEY. **1800** LAMB *Lett.* v. 44 'Twould have been but giving a polish to lamp-black, not nigrifying a negro primarily. **1870** *Observer* 9 Oct., Using a tar brush to nigrify the white and shining celebrities. **1893** *Scott. Leader* 27 Sept., The old part.. has now become completely nigrified.

nigrine (ˈnɪgraɪn), *sb. Min.* Also **nigrin**. [f. L. *nigr-* black + -INE⁵. Named 1800.] A black ferriferous variety of rutile.
1805 JAMESON *Min.* II. 502 The red colour.. distinguishes it at once from nigrine. **1836** T. THOMSON *Min., Geol.*, etc. I. 468 Nigrin.. occurs at Ohlapian, in Transylvania, and was first described and analyzed by Klaproth. **1880** *Min. Mag.* IV. 70 They are of the variety of Rutile known as Nigrine.

nigrine (ˈnɪgraɪn), *a. rare.* [f. L. *nigr-* black + -INE¹.] Black.
1885 *Glasgow Herald* 4 May 9/5 Quite as satisfactory as any of Mr. Whistler's nigrine arrangements.

† **nigrite**¹. *Obs. rare.* [f. L. *nigr-* black + -ITE¹ 1.] A Negro.
1594 BLUNDEVIL *Exerc.* v. xii. (1636) 558 The Spaniards have not found either in Mexicana, or in Peruana any Nigrites or blacke Moores. **1597** J. KING *On Jonas* (1618) 179 The poore Nigrite their slaue.

nigrite² (ˈnɪgraɪt). *Chem.* [f. L. *nigr-* black + -ITE¹ 4.] ***nigrite core*** (see quot.).
1882 DREDGE *Electr. Illumination* I. 338 The 'Nigrite' core invented by Mr. Price.. is another combination of ozokerit and india-rubber (or gutta-percha)... Nigrite core has a high insulation resistance.

Nigritian (nɪˈgrɪʃ(ɪ)ən), *a.* and *sb.* [f. *Nigriti-a* (see def.) + -AN.]
A. *adj.* Of or belonging to Nigritia, a region in Central Africa nearly co-extensive with the Sudan, the home of the most pronounced types of Negro peoples; hence, of or belonging to the Negro race.
1757 J. DYER *Fleece* IV. 128 Sailing the western coast of Afric's realms, Of Mauritania and Nigritian tracts. **1856** J. L. WILSON *Western Africa* I. ii. 30 The inhabitants of Northern Guinea are known as the Nigritian family, from their supposed descent from the great Negro families living in the valley of the Niger. **1865** J. H. INGRAHAM *Pillar of Fire* (1872) 75 Two Nigritian lion-leopards of Rhodian marble. **1869** LUBBOCK *Preh. Times* (ed. 2) xii. 377 Negroes of the true Nigritian stamp. **1881** FEATHERMAN *Soc. Hist. Mankind* V. Introd. p. x, The Nigritian stock has branched out into four distinct races.
B. *sb.* An inhabitant of Nigritia.
1881 FEATHERMAN *Soc. Hist. Mankind* V. Introd. p. x, The Takroor Nigritians represent the original type without intermixture.

Nigritic (nɪˈgrɪtɪk), *a.* [f. L. *nigr-* black + -ITIC.] Of or pertaining to the Negro race, *spec.* the Oceanic Negroes (*Cent. Dict.* 1890).
1883 R. N. CUST *Sk. Mod. Lang. Afr.* I. iv. 54 Krapf.. became aware of the existence of two distinct Groups of Languages on the East Coast, about the line of the Equator, and called them Nilo-Hamitic, or Nilotic, and Nigro-Hamitic or Nigritic respectively. **1938** M. HAILEY *African Survey* iii. 76 Dr. Westermann.. proposes a four-fold division: (*a*) Nigritic, or Old Sudanic. **1963** C. J. MCCALL in A. Dundes *Mother Wit* (1973) 420 'Hoodoo represents the syncretistic blend of Christian and Nigritic religious traditions.

nigritude (ˈnɪgrɪtjuːd). [ad. L. *nigritūd-o*, f. *nigr-*, *niger* black: see -TUDE.] Blackness.
1651 CULPEPPER *Astrol. Judgem. Dis.* (1658) 194 Their colour is pale, shaddowed with a little nigritude or darknesse. **1657** TOMLINSON *Renou's Disp.* 211 Nigritude deturpates [the teeth]. **1822** LAMB *Elia* Ser. I. *Praise Chimney-Sweepers*, I like to meet a sweep..—one of those tender novices blooming through their first nigritude. *a* **1849** H. COLERIDGE *Ess.* (1851) II. 33 Reflections on the rear-ward nigritude of the kettle. **1889** *Q. Rev.* CLXVIII. 372 Our aged friends can well remember when the smoke of London was not equal to one-tenth of last year's nigritude.
b. A black thing or reputation.
1869 *Echo* 2 Sept., The subtle nigritudes born of the household fires. Upon our dwellings these nigritudes fall [etc.]. **1878** *Pall Mall G.* 6 Aug. 9 [Whitewashing], to be done effectively, must be attempted on such unmistakable nigritudes as Judas Iscariot or Judge Jeffries.
Hence **nigriˈtudinous** *a.*, black.
1849 J. G. SAXE *Poems, Devil of Names* 106 To whiten his nigritudinous legs.

† **ˈNigro.** *Obs.* Also 6 **nygro**. [ad. Sp. *negro* NEGRO, after L. *nigr-*, *niger.*] A Negro.
a **1548** HALL *Chron., Hen. VIII*, p. vii/1 Their faces, neckes, armes & handes, couered in fyne pleasaunce blacke .. so that the same ladies semed to be nygrost [*sic*] or blacke Mores. **1582** N. LICHEFIELD tr. *Castanheda's Conq. E. Ind.* iii. 9 Our men saw certaine little Nigroes. **1618** LITHGOW *Pilgr. Farewell* C j, I know these Nigroes, of the Austriale Sunne, Haue not endur'd such heat.

nigro-, combining form of L. *niger* black, used in *Ent.* and *Bot.* to indicate a mixture of black with some other colour, or some feature of a blackish tint.
1826 KIRBY & SP. *Entomol.* xlvi. IV. 303 When it is said of a body that it is nigro-æneous, it means that the æneous tint prevails. **1847** HARDY in *Proc. Berw. Nat. Club* II. No. 5. 235 Breast nigro-pubescent. *Ibid.* 244 Legs nigrofuscous. *Ibid.* 253 Elytra.. with a thickish nigro-pubescence. **1882** *Garden* 23 Dec. 553/3 Nigro-hirsute Dendrobes with rich orange blossoms are rare.

nigromancer, -mancy, varr. NECRO-.

nigromancian, -cien: see NECROMANCIEN.

nigrosine (ˈnɪgrəsɪn). *Chem.* Also **-in**. [f. L. *nigr-* black + -OSE + -INE⁵.] A blue-grey or blue-black colouring matter derived from aniline hydro-chlorate.
1892 in *Syd. Soc. Lex.* **1897** *Westm. Gaz.* 12 Aug. 2/3 One sample, made of nigrosine,.. contained quantities of fungi. **1899** *Allbutt's Syst. Med.* VIII. 882 They stain well.. with hæmatoxylin, congo-red, or acid nigrosin.

nigrous (ˈnɪgrəs), *a. Ent.* [f. L. *nigr-* black + -OUS.] Deep black.
[**1826** KIRBY & SP. *Entomol.* xlvi. IV. 303 Æneo-nigrous.] **1841** E. NEWMAN *Hist. Insects* III. ii. 173 Blacks:.. nigrous or niger, the colour of lamp black.

† **nigs.** *Obs.* (See GOD *sb.* 14 b, and OD¹ 2.)
1640 GLAPTHORNE *Wit in Constable* v. Wks. 1874 I. 231 Precise Taylors, that.. sweare cuds nigs over their wine. *a* **1643** W. CARTWRIGHT *Ordinary* IV. i, 'S nigs and well remember'd.

nigt, obs. form of NIGHT.

‖ **nigua** (ˈnɪgwə). Also 9 **negua**. [Sp. *nigua.*] The chigoe or jigger.
1622 CAPT. SMITH *Wks.* (Arb.) 580 Then had they a little flea called Nigua, which got betweene the skinne and the flesh before they were aware, and there bred and multiplied. **1760–72** tr. *Juan & Ulloa's Voy.* (ed. 3) I. 64 The insect of Carthagena called nigua, and in Peru pique, is shaped like a flea, but almost too small for sight. **1816** KIRBY & SP. *Entomol.* iv. (1818) I. 103, I am speaking of the celebrated Chigoe or Jiggers, called also Nigua. **1851** MAYHEW *Lond. Labour* (1861) III. 35 The most annoying species.. being a native of the tropical latitudes, and variously named in the West Indies, chigoe, jigger, nigua, tungua, and pique. **1868** F. BOYLE *Ride across Cont.* 68 'Neguas'.. better known in England by their West Indian name 'jiggers' or 'chigos'.

nihend, **nihȝeðe**, obs. forms of NINTH.

‖ **nihil** (ˈnaɪhɪl, ˈnɪhɪl). [L. *nihil* nothing.]
1. A thing of no worth or value. *rare.*
1579 G. HARVEY *Wks.* (Grosart) I. 124 Counters, which nowe and then stande for hundreds and thousands, by and bye for odd halfpens or farthinges, are other whiles for very nihils. *c* **1610** MIDDLETON, etc. *Widow* I. i, Look you, all these are nihils; They want the punction. **1623** I. BARGRAVE *Serm.* (1624) 22 While they would be both papists and protestants, they are, indeede, newters and nihils.
2. = NICHIL *sb.* 2.
1629–30 J. MEAD in *Crt. & Times Chas. I* (1848) II. 62 A commission was directed.. to inquire into his lands and goods, and to seize upon them for the king, but they returned a *nihil*. **1684** MANLEY *Cowell's Interpr.*, *Nihil* or *Nichil*, is a word which the Sheriff answers, that is opposed concerning Debts illeviable, and that are nothing worth, by reason of the insufficency of the Parties from whom they are

due. [Hence in Phillips (1706), *Termes de la Ley* (1708).] **1818** CRUISE *Digest* (ed. 2) V. 389 If the sheriff returned *nihil* upon the summons, an *alias* and a *pluries* issued.

Hence †**nihi'lagent**, one who does nothing.

1579–80 G. HARVEY *Lett.* Wks. (Grosart) I. 99 As if..we were borne to be the only Nonproficients and Nihilagents of the world.

†**nihi'larian.** *Obs. rare*$^{-1}$. [f. L. *nihil* nothing + *-arian*, as in *unitarian*, etc.] One who deals with things of no importance.

1705 BERKELEY *Commonpl. Bk.* Wks. 1871 IV. 426 If the wit and industry of the Nihilarians were employ'd about the useful and practical mathematiques.

†**'nihilate,** *v. Obs. rare*$^{-1}$. [ad. ppl. stem of med.L. *nihilāre*, f. L. *nihil* NIHIL.] To annul.

1545 *Act 37 Hen. VIII*, c. 13 §1 The said Act..[shall be] from henceforth frustrate and nihilated, and to be repealed for ever.

†**nihi'lation.** *Obs. rare.*$^{-1}$. [f. as prec.: see -ATION.] Nonentity.

1695 TRYON *Dreams* App. 260 He must..cease from all Motion and Action, and become an eternal Stillness, or Nihilation.

†**nihi'leity.** *Obs. rare.* [ad. late L. *nihileitas* (Du Cange). Cf. NIHILITY.] Nullity.

1603 HARSNET *Popish Impost.* 110 Choosing out such shadowes and Nihileities, to controll the Principalities and powers of Darkness. **1675** WOODHEAD, etc. *Par. S. Paul* 66 There being an inanity and nihileity in the called.

†**'nihilhood.** *Obs. rare*$^{-1}$. [f. L. *nihil* nothing + -HOOD.] Nullity, negation.

1602 J. DAVIES (Heref.) *Mirum in Modum* (Grosart) 23 Ill beeing but a meere defect of Good,.. Which is no more, but a meere Nihilhood.

nihili-, combining form of L. *nihil* nothing, as ***nihili-parturient***, producing nothing.

1812 SOUTHEY *Omniana* I. 314 A certain omni-pregnant, nihili-parturient genius of the editor's acquaintance.

ni'hilianism. *Theol.* [f. L. *nihil* nothing + -IAN + -ISM.] The doctrine that in the nature of Christ there was no human, but only a divine element. Cf. NIHILISM 4.

1895 GORE *Dissertations* III. iii. 279 What has been already described as nihilianism was the current mode of conceiving the Incarnation. **1896** *The Month* Apr. 466 What Canon Gore means by Nihilianism is the false theory of the Monophysite heretics.

nihilifi'cation. *rare.* [See next and -ATION.] The action of setting aside or slighting.

1678 PHILLIPS *Suppl.*, *Nihilifaction*, a setting at nought or slighting. **1820** *Examiner* No. 656. 705/1 The *Courier's* nihilification of the Learned Gentleman reminds us of the poet's panegyric.

†**nihilify,** *v. Obs. rare*$^{-0}$. [f. L. *nihilī facĕre.*] 'To set nothing by, to disesteem, to make no account of' (Blount 1656).

nihilism ('naɪhɪlɪz(ə)m, 'nɪ-). [f. L. *nihil* nothing + -ISM. Cf. F. *nihilisme*, Sp. *nihilismo*, It. *nichilismo*, G. *nihilismus*, Russ. *nigilizm.*]

1. Negative doctrines in religion or morals; total rejection of current religious beliefs or moral principles.

a **1817** T. DWIGHT *Trav. New Eng.*, etc. (1821) III. 238 Hence the transition is easy to mere Nihilism, and a total disregard of all moral obligation. **1854** BUCKNILL *Crim. Lunacy* 8 In Germany, rationalism ending in absolute nihilism has led to results of the same nature. **1881** BLACKIE *Lay Serm.* iii. (1886) 118 The hollow vacuities and negative absurdities of Atheism or Nihilism.

2. *Philos.* **a.** An extreme form of scepticism, involving the denial of all existence.

1836–7 SIR W. HAMILTON *Metaph.* xvi. (1859) I. 294 Of positive or dogmatic Nihilism there is no example in modern philosophy. **1842** —— *Diss.* in *Reid's Wks.* I. 129/2 Is the acknowledged result of the Fichtean dogmatism less a nihilism than the scepticism of Hume? **1857** MAX MÜLLER *Chips* (1880) I. xi. 284 Buddhism..cannot be freed from the charge of Nihilism. **1887** PATER *Imag. Portraits* 128 Actually proud at times of his curious, well-reasoned nihilism. **1909** A. M. LUDOVICI tr. *Nietzsche's Will to Power* I. 5 Nihilism, i.e., the absolute repudiation of worth, purpose desirability. *Ibid.* 16 The extremest form of Nihilism would mean that *all* belief—all assumption of truth—is false: because no real world is at hand. **1964** P. ROUBICZEK *Existentialism* vii. 125 Thus it is no cause for surprise that Sartre lands himself in complete nihilism. **1972** M. NATANSON in L. Embree *Life-World & Consciousness* 302 Value-free science as it has been interpreted by many contemporary social scientists does endorse a kind of *cultural nihilism.*

b. Nothingness, non-existence.

1856 R. A. VAUGHAN *Mystics* (1860) II. VII. ii. 15 [To] lose, in utter Nihilism, all sense of any existence separate from the Divine Substance. **1866** *Athenæum* No. 2006. 454/3 To aim at nihilism as the supreme good.

c. *Psychol.* In some forms of severe mental illness, the belief that the outside world, the patient's self, or parts of either, have ceased to function or to exist.

1889 *Jrnl. Mental Sci.* XXXIV. 137 Though not a mental affection in the strict sense of the word, nihilism is a psychical factor very liable to devolve into insanity. **1927** HENDERSON & GILLESPIE *Text-bk. Psychiatry* viii. 160 The most characteristic involutional qualities lie in the content of the psychosis, especially in the apprehension, hypochondriasis and nihilism. **1957** E. MAYER in P. A. Schilpp *Philos. K. Jaspers* xi. 451 Jaspers vividly describes nihilism as a symptom of mental illness or..as a manifestation of ultimate situations in which a human being can find himself in depressions and schizophrenias. **1965** J. POLLITT *Depression & its Treatment* iii. 33 The most extreme form of hypochondriacal delusion, referred to as 'nihilism'.

3. The doctrines or principles of the Russian Nihilists.

1868 G. DUFF *Glance over Eur.* 42 The Russian Tories.. have been assisted..by the spread among the half-educated of absurd and anti-social notions, to which the name of Nihilism has been given. **1882** *Macm. Mag.* XLV. 407 Nihilism in Russia is an explosive compound, generated by the contact of the Sclav character with Western ideas.

transf. **1880** *Fraser's Mag.* May 65 Atheism is, in many respects, the Nihilism of the intellect and conscience.

4. *Theol.* Nihilianism.

1882–3 SCHAFF *Encycl. Rel. Knowl.* II. 1656 Nihilism.. denotes in theology the view that the human nature of Christ had..no true subsistence.

nihilist ('naɪhɪlɪst, 'nɪ-). [f. as prec. + -IST. Cf. F. *nihiliste* (1797), Sp. *nihilista*, It. *nichilista*, G. *nihilist*, Russ. *nigilist.*]

1. One who holds the doctrine of nihilism in philosophy or religion.

1836–7 SIR W. HAMILTON *Metaph.* xvi. (1859) I. 294 Philosophers are divided..into Nihilists or Non-Substantialists [etc.]. **1854** tr. *Feuerbach's Ess. Chr.* 28 We must say with the oriental nihilist or pantheist. **1876** J. PARKER *Paracl.* II. xviii. 290 David Hume..has been correctly described as a nihilist; he denied everything and affirmed nothing.

2. (With capital initial.) A member of a Russian revolutionary party professing extreme principles.

1871 *Gen. Hist.* in *Ann. Reg.* 226 The 'Nihilists', as they called themselves, were an offshoot of Russian extravagance on the Socialist stock. **1880** *19th Cent.* VII. 1 It is because 'nothing' as it exists at present finds favour in their eyes that they have been called 'Nihilists'. **1887** T. A. TROLLOPE *What I remember* II. xiii. 235 He was a Nihilist of the most uncompromising type.

b. *attrib.* or as *adj.*

1880 *Standard* 22 Dec., Another Nihilist leader has been arrested. **1883** *Harper's Mag.* Jan. 315/2 Nihilist proclamations have continued to be placarded.

nihilistic (naɪhɪ'lɪstɪk, nɪ-), *a.* [f. prec. + -IC.] Of, relating to, characterized by, or professing, nihilism: **a.** in philosophy or religion.

1857 MAX MÜLLER *Chips* (1880) I. xi. 290 The more advanced views of the Nihilistic philosophers. **1871** ALABASTER *Wheel of Law* p. lii, I cannot decline to allow the term Nihilistic to be applied to it. **1873** WAGNER tr. *Teuffel's Hist. Rom. Lit.* II. 35 A kind of nihilistic resignation.

b. in Russian politics.

1868 G. DUFF *Pol. Surv.* 35 Nihilistic doctrines..contain a large proportion of sound tendencies. **1881** *Times* 11 Apr. 9/4 In Russia the outbreak of nihilistic fury has made humanitarian treatment impossible for the present. **1890** J. HATTON *By Order of Czar* 149, I thought she might have been a nihilistic spy.

c. *Psychol.* Of or characterized by delusions of nihilism (first described by J. Cotard *Du délire des négations* in *Archives Neurologiques* (1882) IV. XI. 152). See NIHILISM 2 c.

1925 STRECKER & EBAUGH *Pract. Clin. Psychiatry* iii. 45 Nihilistic ideas deny the existence of things. As an aspect of a depressive trend there may be self-depreciation. **1927** HENDERSON & GILLESPIE *Text-bk. Psychiatry* xi. 294 The feature of the depression is the frequency with which absurd nihilistic ideas are expressed. Patients claim that they are dead, that their blood has ceased to circulate,..that their bodies are utterly destroyed. **1944** LICHTENSTEIN & SMALL *Handbk. Psychiatry* ii. 34 Nihilistic delusions, in which there is a more or less complete denial of reality and existence. **1967** A. T. BECK *Depression* I. ii. 38 A typical nihilistic delusion is reflected in the following statement: 'It's no use... The world is empty. Everybody died last night.' **1974** M. ROHDE tr. *Cotard's Nihilistic Delusions* in Hirsch & Shepherd *Themes & Variations European Psychiatry* xiv. 354, I would tentatively suggest the name 'nihilistic delusions' (*délire de négations*) to describe the condition of the patients to whom Griesinger was referring.

nihility (naɪ'hɪlɪtɪ, nɪ-). [ad. med.L. *nihilitas*, f. *nihil* nothing: see -ITY. Cf. F. *nihilité* (Cotgr.).] The quality or state of being nothing; non-existence, nullity.

1678 GALE *Crt. Gentiles* IV. 514 This Nihilitie or Nothingnesse of the Creature is the same with its Passive power. **1725** WATTS *Logic* I. ii. §6 (ed. 2) 26 Not-Being is consider'd as excluding all Substance,..and this we call pure Nihility, or meer Nothing. **1794–6** E. DARWIN *Zoon.* (1801) IV. 90 Nor is there anyone..who has not at some moments felt the nihility of all things. **1831** I. TAYLOR in *Edward's Freedom of Will* Introd. v. 103 We will apply this method of resolving an illusory notion into its proper nihility. **1874** WHITNEY *Oriental & Ling. Stud.* 74 The basis ..relied upon to establish the date of Buddha's entrance upon nihility.

b. With *a* and *pl.* A mere nothing, a trifle; a non-existent thing; a nullity.

1765 *Lond. Chron.* 3 Jan. 11 After he had discharged all his nihilities, he returned with equal precipitation. **1794** MRS. PIOZZI *Synon.* II. 66 Della Crusca..had been asserting that all past actions were nihilities. **1824** DE QUINCEY *Analects* Wks. 1860 XIV. 134 This universe—in comparison of which the positive universe would be itself a nihility. **1878** F. FERGUSON *Life Christ* II. xv. 316 Not the Son of a mere abstraction, of an infinite nihility.

‖**nihil obstat** ('n(a)ɪhɪl 'ɒbstæt). [Lat., 'nothing stands in the way'.] Words appearing on the title-page or elsewhere in the preliminary pages of a Roman Catholic work indicating that it has been approved as free of doctrinal or moral error. Also *fig.*

1886 in P. Soulier *Life St. Philip Benizi* p. iv, Nihil obstat: Guglielmus T. Gordon, *Congr. Orat. Presbyter.* **1932** J. L. STOCKS in *Hibbert Jrnl.* XXX. 622 He loves beauty, he admires character, he feels the thrill of poetry and art. He believes in God. For all this the utmost that he can get out of science is a *nihil obstat.* **1933** *Times Lit. Suppl.* 21 Dec. 904/2 The selection [of anthems] carries with it the *nihil obstat* of two such eminent Church musicians as Sir Walford Davies and Dr. Henry Ley. **1938** *Mind* XLVII. 93 The parallel to the *Nihil Obstat* of Roman Catholic censorship is obvious. **1955** *Times* 6 July 11/4 Authoritarians wish that one dictionary enjoyed dictatorial rights. Reference to it then would finally close any argument; its *nihil obstat* would give the green light to *imprimatur.* **1958** *Spectator* 22 Aug. 260/1 This is a lucid, judicious book, with a '*Nihil obstat*' discreetly tucked away in the title pages. **1973** *Times* 11 Aug. 2/8 Mgr. Guazzelli said: 'The *nihil obstat* and the imprimatur were duly signed, and the censor and myself, as the responsible bishop, acknowledge this fact.'

niht, obs. f. NIGHT; var. of NITH *Obs.*

niinde, obs. f. NINTH.

-nik (nɪk), *suff.* from Russian (cf. KOLKHOZNIK, NARODNIK, SPUTNIK) and Yiddish, appended to sbs. and adjs. to denote a person or thing involved in or associated with the thing or quality specified, as *beatnik*, *folknik*, *no-goodnik*, NUDNIK, *peacenik*. Often with humorous or pejorative connotations.

1945 A. KOBER *Parm Me* 17 That stuck-upnick fomm the lodge, Sister Leshinsky..she's a regella Yenkee. **1958** *Amer. Speech* XXXIII. 154 On learning that a dog was in the Soviet Moon, the Detroit *News* (and almost every other paper)..referred to the satellite as *Muttnik*... From then on there was no end of -niks. **1959** *Observer* 14 June 22/7 It happened that Mr. Werth arrived in Columbus, Ohio, just as the Russian Sputnik soared into the cosmos; before he left the American flopnik had burnt out on its launching pad. **1965** *Newsweek* 1 Nov. 31/3 The crowded headquarters of the young draftniks and Vietniks pulse with an almost religious fervor. **1965** *Time* 12 Nov. 4 Those guitar-plunking protestniks whose St. Joan is Baez. **1966** *Economist* 5 Mar. 883/1 These protestants represent only a small faction, no more important politically than the nuclear disarmers were in Britain or the Vietniks are in America. **1966** *Sat. Rev.* (U.S.) 22 Oct. 59 Despite the alarums of the computerniks..the book would appear to be here to stay. **1968** B. FOSTER *Changing Eng. Lang.* ii. 110 This borrowing [*sc.* sputnik]..has given a new lease of life to the suffix *-nik* which had already made its appearance, at any rate in the U.S.A., as a loan from Yiddish... New creations..have usually been..humorous..; thus a device which failed to go into orbit was derided in..1957 as a Kaputnik (*Daily Express*), a Flopnik (*Daily Herald*), a Puffnik (*Daily Mail*), and a Stayputnik (*News Chronicle*). **1968** L. ROSTEN *Joys of Yiddish* 265 *-Nik* lends itself to delightful *ad hoc* inventions. A *sicknik* would be one who fancies 'sick' or 'black' humor. A *Freudnik* would be an uncritical acolyte of the father of psychoanalysis. And recently homosexuals began to refer to heterosexuals, with some amusement, as 'straightniks'. **1973** *Indexer* VIII. 227/2 Publishers and computerniks can create decadent search systems.

nikau ('ni:kaʊ). [Maori.] A New Zealand palm tree, *Rhopalostylis sapida*, or its leaves, once used as a sort of thatch. Also *attrib.*

1831 H. WILLIAMS *Jrnl.* 15 Nov. in H. Carleton *Life of Henry Williams* (1874) I. 100 We..erected a tent, with a shed of nikau for the boys. **1844** C. CHAPMAN *Let.* 30 Nov. in A. Drummond *Married & gone to N.Z.* (1960) 70 Another tree called the Nikau is said to be very good; I have tasted a little bit and found it very nice. **1847** *N.Z. Jrnl.* No. 191. 105/1 From Teapu southward the country is..wooded with rata and nikau, or cabbage palm, down to the high water mark. **1853** J. M. RICHMOND *Let.* 11 Nov. in *Richmond-Atkinson Papers* (1960) I. iii. 133 It [*sc.* their dwelling] is in fact a roof on the ground, thatched with nikau, a palm, the only one in N.Z. **1891** R. WALLACE *Rural Econ. Austral. & N.Z.* xvi. 242 The tree fern and the common Nikau Palm of the country dotted the hill-sides and gave..a semi-tropical appearance to the landscape. **1905** W. B. *Where White Man Treads* 16 He could supplement his dry fare with..the tender leaves of the nikau. **1920** J. MANDER *Story N.Z. River* 315 He built a nikau whare. **1935** J. GUTHRIE *Little Country* iv. 98 Nikaus, rata vine, and lycopodium..brought to the hall the charms of the New Zealand bush. **1949** P. BUCK *Coming of Maori* (1950) II. i. 87 The middle part of the top of the trunk of the *nikau* palm, just under the leaf spread, was eaten raw. **1959** M. SHADBOLT *New Zealanders* 66 He explained how easy it was to live off the bush if you wanted, eating..the juicy white insides of nikau palms. **1966** *Encycl. N.Z.* II. 690/1 The Maoris used the nikau leaves in their whares.

Nike ('naɪki:). [Gr. νίκη victory.] **1.** In Greek art: a winged statue representing Nike, the goddess of victory.

1867 H. M. WESTROPP *Handbk. Archæol.* 195 *Nike.—Victory.* Victory is represented in a short tunic, with wings, and usually carries a palm. She is also represented writing on a shield, and frequently sacrificing a bull. **1924** A. D. SEDGWICK *Little French Girl* IV. iii. 327 She's a Nike..on the prow of a Greek ship. **1960** R. CARPENTER *Greek Sculpture* v. 147 The running Nike is an interesting study in formal drapery. **1968** V. EHRENBERG *From Solon to Socrates* vii. 315 There are the figures of a number of winged *Nikai.*

2. Any of a range of surface-to-air guided missiles developed by the U.S., initially as defensive weapons.

1952 *Britannica Bk. of Year* 431/2 Limited production for operational trials of the U.S. army's Nike missile for the anti-aircraft artillery was begun in 1951. **1955** *Times* 4 July 9/7 Short-range guided weapons such as the American Nike are useless for the air defence of Britain. **1961** E. BURGESS *Long-Range Ballistic Missiles* vii. 194 On a recent tour of a

Nike-Zeus installation the writer saw..the tremendous complexity of the anti-missile missile system. **1970** J. W. R. TAYLOR *Rockets & Missiles* ii. 56 Typical of first-generation anti-aircraft missiles was America's two-stage Nike-Ajax, made up of a liquid-propellent second stage and a solid-propellent first-stage booster. **1974** *Encycl. Brit. Micropædia* VII. 344/1 Nike Zeus, first antimissile missile, was about 50 feet long... A further development was Nike X, which had a fixed radar antenna that could be electronically scanned. Nike Cajun, a sounding rocket, was capable of lifting a 50-pound payload of scientific instruments to a height of 90 miles.

niker, obs. f. NICKER *sb.*[1]

nikethamide (nɪ'kɛθəmaɪd). *Pharm.* [f. *ni*cotinic acid di*ethylamide*, its chemical name, by alteration.] A colourless or yellowish oily liquid or crystalline solid, $(C_5H_4N)CON(CH_2CH_3)_2$, which is used as a respiratory stimulant and analeptic.

1940 *Jrnl. Amer. Med. Assoc.* 20 Jan. 249/2 The Council consulted Ciba Pharmaceutical Products, Inc., and agreement was reached on the name 'Nikethamide'..as the nonproprietary name for the substance introduced in medicine under the proprietary name of Coramine. **1951** A. GROLLMAN *Pharmacol. & Therapeutics* viii. 168 Because of its analeptic action, nikethamide is used in acute respiratory depression of anesthesia, alcoholic intoxication, and overdosage with hypnotics. **1969** [see CORAMINE].

†**nikin.** *Obs. rare*⁻⁰. (See quot.)

a **1700** B. E. *Dict. Cant. Crew*, *Nikin*, a Natural or very soft creature.

Nikonian (nɪ'kəʊnɪən), *sb.* and *a.* Also **Niconian**. [f. *Nikon*, the name adopted by Nikita Minin (1605–81), 6th Patriarch of Moscow + -IAN.]

A. *sb.* An orthodox member of the Russian Church who accepted the reforms introduced by Nikon. **B.** *adj.* Of or pertaining to Nikon or his reforms. Hence **Ni'konianism**.

1874 J. H. BLUNT *Dict. Sects, Heresies* 373/1 *Niconians*, a name applied by Russian dissenters to the orthodox members of the Established Church who accepted the reforms introduced by the Patriarch Nicon in the year 1654. **1877** D. M. WALLACE *Russia* xx. 308 Believing these 'Nikonian novelties' to be heretical. **1888** S. M. KRAVCHINSKII *Russ. Peasantry* II. 454 They [*sc.* the Stranniky] look upon their co-religionists..with the same disgust and abhorrence as they lavish on the Niconians. **1957** *Encycl. Brit.* XIX. 695/2 A long struggle began between the faith of the Old Believers and the Nikonianism, as the official church was now generally called.

nil[1]. Now *rare* or *Obs.* Also 7 nill. [a. Arab. and Pers. *nīl*: see ANIL.]

1. The indigo plant; indigo dye.

1598 W. PHILLIP tr. *Linschoten* I. lxix. 117/2 Annil or Nil ..hath sky coloured leaves. **1625** FINCH in Purchas *Pilgrims* I. IV. iv. 428 The first of Nouember I was sent to buy Nill or Indico at Byana. **1640** PARKINSON *Theat. Bot.* 602 Else it was a worser kind of that Nil or Anil that grew in Turkey. **1753** CHAMBERS *Cycl. Suppl.* s.v., This is to be always understood as meaning that nil which is used in dying. **1846–50** A. WOOD *Class-Bk. Bot.* 442 Flowers..of a clear blue color (whence its specific name, Anil or Nil, Indigo).

2. A species of convolvulus with blue flowers.

1597 GERARDE *Herbal* II. ccciv. 715 There be also other sorts of Bindweeds,..which no doubt may be kinds of Nil. **1640** PARKINSON *Theat. Bot.* 170 The great blew Bindweede ..is taken by most to be the Nil of Avicen and Serapis. **1753** CHAMBERS *Cycl. Suppl.* s.v., It is probable that the convolvulus, or bindweed, called nil, obtained this name only from its flowers being of the same colour with the fine blue pigment obtained from the other nil, or woad.

‖**nil**[2] (nɪl). [L., contracted f. NIHIL.] **1. a.** Nothing.

1833 *Edin. Rev.* Oct. 14 Such a return from all the population..would be *nil*. **1849** KINGSLEY *Misc.* (1859) I. 404 Such attempts at it as we yet have seen, may be considered nil. **1899** *Allbutt's Syst. Med.* VII. 889 The locomotor effects of the spasms is either nil or but very slight. **1936** A. W. CLAPHAM *Romanesque Archit.* i. 5 Of all the various structures referred to or described by Isidore of Seville..the surviving remains are almost nil. **1952** C. DAY LEWIS tr. *Virgil's Aeneid* VIII. 172 Visibility was reduced to nil. **1955** *Times* 6 July 4/4 The British Isles Rugby Union tourists beat South West Africa by nine points to nil in their match here to-day.

b. ? = NICHIL 2.

1811 in *2nd Rep. Rec. Irel.* 132 The *Originalia* of Process, called the Schedules of Nils from the Pipe. *Ibid.* 141 The Process lodged by the Sheriffs..is of no further use after the Tots and Nils are discharged.

2. *Comb.*, as **nil-grade** *Philol.*, the most reduced form of weak ablaut grade, in which the vowel disappears; **nil norm** *Econ.*, during a wage-freeze a standard under which no wage increases are normally allowed.

1922–3 *Modern Philology* XX. 197 The *nil-grade of the root vowel is represented by OE *-tyllan* (in *fortyllan* 'to seduce'). **1928** *Language* IV. 163 It follows that *šd* is the nil-grade of ***sed-* 'sit'. **1935** *Mod. Lang. Notes* L. 523 Pre-English uncontracted *Lāamkô* (with nil-grade of the *k*-suffix). **1972** *Language* XLVIII. 9 The difficulty disappears if we start from a root *kʷerp*, whose nil-grade developed into Aryan *kṛp-* and Goidelic *kri*. **1966** *Sunday Times* 14 Aug. 8 For all the traditional wage demands some principle does need to be hammered out to establish who will be permitted to breach the *nil norm. **1967** *Economist* 23 Dec. 1204/1 Britain is still supposed to be operating in conditions of a 'nil norm' for wage increases. **1968** *Manch. Guardian Weekly* 1 Feb. 8 The £1 a week rise would not qualify as an exception to the nil norm laid down in the summer.

b. Passing into *adj.*, containing, reporting, or consisting of nothing.

1959 *Punch* 27 May 704/3 The thoughtless might suppose that hail-watching was dull work, with long blank intervals offering nothing better than a nil return. **1972** *Guardian* 14 Mar. 2/8 They..returned because of nil visibility. **1974** L. LAMB *Man in Mist* ix. 55 In view of my constable's nil report, *could* it be that nothing ever happened?

nil, var. NILL *sb.*; obs. f. NILL *v.*

‖**nil admirari** (nɪl ædmɪ'rɑːrɪ). [L.] An attitude of indifference to the distractions of the outside world, advocated by Horace (*Epistles* I. vi. 1): *nil admirari prope res est una..quae possit facere et servare beatum*, 'to wonder at nothing is just about the only way a man can become contented and remain so.' Hence, a person adopting this attitude. Also *attrib.* or as *adj.*

Also used erron. with the meaning 'to admire nothing'.

1748 CHESTERFIELD *Let.* 27 Sept. (1774) I. 345 This book ..will both divert and astonish you; and at the same time, teach you *nil admirari*. **1749** FIELDING *Tom Jones* III. VII. i. 8 The famous *Nil admirari* of Horace, or in the English Phrase, *To stare at nothing*. **1785** BOSWELL *Jrnl. Tour Hebr.* 118 But Dr. Johnson has much of the *nil admirari* in smaller concerns. **1821** BYRON *Don Juan* V. c. 185, I ne'er could see the very Great happiness of the 'Nil Admirari'. **1822** SHELLEY *Let.* 18 June (1964) II. 715 The *nil admirari*.. seems to me a bad sign in a young person. **1857** TROLLOPE *Barchester T.* III. xvi. 277 Very many men now-a-days.. adopt or affect to adopt the *nil admirari* doctrine. **1866** MRS. GASKELL *Wives & Daughters* I. xxii. 287 Every inflexion of the voice breathed out..admiration! And this from the *nil admirari* brother. **1935** J. BUCHAN *House of Four Winds* vi. 139 Mr. Glynde's *nil admirari* countenance..registered surprise. **1951** N. ANNAN *Leslie Stephen* x. 278 *Nil admirari* was his precept, the salute to genius his practice. **1961** M. KELLY *Spoilt Kill* iii. 193 Why was I always preaching *nil admirari*?

nild, obs. or dial. var. NEEDLE.

nild(e, would not: see NILL *v.*

‖**nil desperandum** (nɪl dɛspə'rændəm), *int.* Also ˌ**nihil despe'randum**. [L.] An exhortation to have hope in difficult circumstances and not to despair, deriving from Horace *Odes* I. vii. 27 *nil desperandum Teucro duce et auspice Teucro*, 'no need to despair with Teucer as your leader and Teucer to protect you'.

[**1617** T. ADAMS *Souldiers Honour* sig. A3v, Nil desperandū Christo Duce, & Auspice Christo.] **1628** R. BURTON *Anat. Melancholy* (ed. 3) III. ii. 527 *Nihil desperandum*, there's hope enough yet. **1749** FIELDING *Tom Jones* III. VIII. vi. 189 All I have is at your Service, and at your Disposal... Nil desperandum est Teucro duce et auspice Teucro. **1774** J. ADAMS *Wks.* (1851) IV. 12 *Nil desperandum* is a good motto. **1872** E. BRADDON *Life in India* iii. 75 But *nil desperandum* was the cry of the Vauxhall partisans. **1921** W. DE LA MARE *Memoirs of Midget* xx. 142 *Nil desperandum*, Mr. Crimble. And you know what they say about fish in the sea. **1955** *Times* 5 May 15/4 There is.. a key-note running through the essays and magazine articles here reprinted—'a note of *nil desperandum*'. **1974** J. MANN *Sticking Place* iii. 46 Edward had thought the job his for the asking... Well, *nil desperandum*..he might yet be moving in.

Nile (naɪl). The name of a river in North Africa, used *attrib.* to designate animals native to the region, as **Nile crocodile**, the African crocodile, *Crocodylus niloticus*; cf. CROCODILE 1; **Nile monitor** = IGUANA 2; **Nile perch**, a large food fish, *Lates niloticus*, found in the rivers and lakes of north and central Africa.

1860 T. H. HUXLEY in *Jrnl. Linn. Soc.* (*Zool.*) IV. 8, I could find neither in the British Museum, nor in the Museum of the Royal College of Surgeons, any authentic skeleton of this, the so-called Nilotic Crocodile.] **1898** J. ANDERSON *Zool. Egypt* I. 1 The *Nile crocodile was described, so long ago as 1699, by Oligeus Jacobæus. **1915** A. M. REESE *Alligator & its Allies* i. 39 The African or Nile Crocodile..is found throughout the continent of Africa. **1974** *BP Shield Internat.* Oct. 28/4 Nile crocodiles are a prominent feature of the lake fauna. **1900** H. A. BRYDEN *Animals of Africa* xv. 173 The *Nile Monitor, a big lizard, attaining a length of six feet,..is often miscalled an 'iguana'. **1964** C. WILLOCK *Enormous Zoo* vii. 125 The Nile monitor, an immense and really powerful lizard which sometimes reaches four feet in length, has a banquet when crocodile hatching time comes around. [**1905** A. SEDGWICK *Student's Text-bk. Zool.* II. 235 *Lates* C. and V., *L. niloticus*, the perch of the Nile.] **1931** J. R. NORMAN *Hist. Fishes* ix. 162 (*caption*) Skeleton of the *Nile Perch. **1949** L. J. MCCORMICK in Vesey-Fitzgerald & Lamonte *Gamefish of World* 367 In colour and form the Nile perch looks like an overgrown cod. **1965** A. J. MCCLANE *Standard Fishing Encycl.* 616/2 Various species of the Nile perch are distributed in the big rivers and lakes of tropical Africa. **1974** *Encycl. Brit. Macropædia* XIV. 46/2 The nile perches (Latidae) have been found as mummies in ancient tombs in Egypt.

nile, obs. f. NILL *v.*

nile-bird. *dial.* A local (Berks. and Bucks.) name for the Wryneck, from its cry.

1885 SWAINSON *Names Birds* 103.

Nile-blue, *sb.* and *a.* [f. the river *Nile*, after F. *bleu de Nil*.] **1.** A pale greenish blue. Also *ellipt.* **Nile.**

The ellipt. examples may represent *Nile-green*.

1873 *Young Englishwoman* Feb. 77/2 Dark maroon velvet and Nile blue silk rep. **1884** *Christian World* 4 Nov. 260/4 Amongst the favourite colours are imperial yellow, Nile blue, tea rose and cardinal. **1892** *Daily News* 29 July 3/3 Greenish Nile-blue is discordant with sky-blue. **1895** *Montgomery Ward Catal.* 7/3 Plain Crepe Picardie... Colors: Lilac,..nile, black [etc.]. **1926** *Daily Colonist* (Victoria, B.C.) 21 July 16/6 (Advt.), A 4-ply worsted wool in shades of pink..nile, [etc.]. **1950** MAERZ & PAUL *Dict. Color* (ed. 2) 199/1 Nile Blue.

2. Also **Nile blue**. A tetracyclic quaternary ammonium ion which is an azine dye and is used as a biological stain to colour fatty acids blue; also, a salt (usu. the sulphate) of this ion.

1888 *Jrnl. Soc. Dyers & Colourists* IV. 96/1 On wool and silk, Nile blue is applied in a neutral bath, and yields red shades of blue. **1920** *Physiol. Abstr.* VI. 617 The affinity of Nile blue sulphate for fat is small. Oleic acid and its esters are the most stainable. **1942** V. HAMBURGER *Man. Exper. Biol.* 46 A small particle of agar stained with Nile blue sulphate or neutral red is pressed against the surface of the blastula for a short period. **1971** AYYANGAR & TILAK in K. Venkataraman *Chem. Synthetic Dyes* IV. iii. 107 It has been shown that Rhodanile Blue is nothing but a mixture of Rhodamine B and Nile Blue.

So **Nile-green**.

1871 *Scribner's Monthly* June 209/1 'Nile green' will turn some people into oranges, though twenty empresses ordain its adoption. **1888** *Daily News* 7 June 5/8 A knot of Nile-green ribbons. **1944** R. CHANDLER *Lady in Lake* xvi. 93 The nile green tiles of the bathroom floor. **1969** 'I. DRUMMOND' *Man with Tiny Head* xv. 176 He used his palms against the nile-green hull. **1973** 'D. JORDAN' (*title*) Nile green.

Nileotic, variant of NILOTIC.

†**nilescope**, obs. variant of NILOSCOPE.

1642 HOWELL *For. Trav.* (Arb.) 223 There is a Castle in the grand Caire in Ægypt, called the Nilescope, where there stands a Pillar with certaine markes to observe the height of the River of Nile. **1738** T. SHAW *Trav.* 433 In the Middle of it is placed the Mikeas or measuring Pillar, which is divided, as the ancient Nilescopes may be supposed to have been, into Cubits.

nilgai ('niːlgaɪ). Also **-ghye**. [a. Hindī *nīlgāī*, f. *nīl* blue + *gāī* cow.] = NYLGHAU.

1882 *Mem. Gen. W. E. Baker* 11 (Yule), Occasionally.. one intruded on the solitude of a huge nilgai. **1890** S. W. BAKER *Wild Beasts* II. 157 In India we find one variety of large size, the nilghye (*Portax picta*). **1893** LYDEKKER *Horns & Hoofs* 145 The well-known nilgai, or more correctly nilgau,..of Peninsular India.

nilg(h)au, variant of NYLGHAU.

Nili ('niːliː). [Acronym f. Heb. *Netzach Israel lo Ishakare*, the strength of Israel will not lie (1 Sam. xv. 29).] A Jewish espionage group in Turkish-ruled Palestine during the 1914–18 war.

1930 H. B. SAMUEL *Unholy Memories of Holy Land* viii. 119 Aronson..leapt to prominence in the war by organizing the celebrated Nili Society..whose 'intelligence' was largely instrumental in the success of Lord Allenby's campaign. **1938** W. B. ZIFF *Rape of Palestine* vi. 66 Of..great importance was the voluntary intelligence service rendered by the celebrated Nili Society all over the Holy Land. **1959** A. ENGLE *Nili Spies* ix. 99 Nili became the name of the espionage group, adding a new word to the Hebrew language. *Ibid.* xi. 113 The actual details of Nili's work were never known... But the existence of a group of people carrying on espionage and plotting rebellion could not be concealed. **1973** *Jewish Chron.* 2 Feb. 12/4 The Nili Group ..sprang up during the First World War, when Turkish treatment of the Palestine Jewish community raised questions of its survival.

†**nill**, *sb.*[1] *Obs.* Also 6 nyll(e, 6–8 nil. [ad. med.L. *nil* (*nihil*), a rendering of G. *nichts*, taken in the usual sense of 'nothing', but in this connexion really a reduced form of *o'nychitis*, L. *onychītis* (Pliny), Gr. ὀνυχῖτις (Dioscorides).] White oxide or flowers of zinc (by early chemists called *nil* or *nihil album*).

There is no evidence that the term has ever been really current in English, but from being used to render *pompholyx* and *spodium* it has found its way into the dictionaries, in which it latterly appears with a number of erroneous definitions (see quots.).

1545 ELYOT, *Pompholix* is an herbe which (as Manardus writeth) is that which the Apothecaries dooe call Nill [*ed.* 1552 *omits* is an herbe whiche]. **1558** WARDE tr. *Alexis' Secr.* I. (1559) 8 Take..of Nill a dragme. **1565** COOPER *Thesaurus*, *Pompholix*.., the sperkles or ashes that commeth of brasse tried in the furneis, and is of Apothecaries called Nyll, much vsed in medicines of the Eyes. **1585** HIGINS tr. *Junius' Nomencl.* 408/1 *Pompholyx*.., the foile that commeth of brasse, and the ore of brasse, which is so light that it flieth like a feather in the aire, and is called Nil. **1611** COTGR., *Pompholige*, Nil; the light oare, or foyle of Brasse. **1632** SHERWOOD, Nill, *les escailles d'airain*. **1656** in BLOUNT *Glossogr.* [copying Cooper. Similarly Bailey, 1721.] **1696** PHILLIPS, *Nil*, the sparkles that flie from Metals tried in a Furnace. It is called in Greek *Pompholyx*, or *Spodium*. **1736** AINSWORTH, *Nil* [the shadings of brass in trying], *æris & cadmiæ favilla*. **1755** JOHNSON, *Nill*, the shining sparks of brass in trying and melting the ore. [Hence in Webster 1828–47, and Ogilvie 1850.] **1867** SMYTH *Sailor's Word-bk.* 497 *Nill*, scales of hot iron at the armourer's forge. Also, the stars of rockets.

†**nill**, *sb.*[2] *Obs.* Forms: 6 nyll, 7 nil(l. [f. the vb.] An instance of 'nilling'; a disinclination or aversion to something.

1526 *Pilgr. Perf.* (W. de W. 1531) 293 b, Where is one wyll and one nyll in all thynges. **1579** TWYNE *Phis. agst. Fortune* I. xxvii. 36 b, Some..haue fealt..yf a man may so tearme it, a wyll and a nyll at one instant. **1656** HOBBES *Liberty, Necess. & Chance* (1841) 362 Though a man have in every long deliberation a great many wills and nills. **1677** GALE *Crt.*

Gentiles IV. 262 God begins to wil or nil nothing; al his wils and nils are eternal.

nill, dial. var. of *neeld*, NEEDLE.

nill (nɪl), *v.* Now *arch.* Forms: (see below). [OE. (pres. t.) *nylle, nyle, nelle, nele*, etc., = OFris. *nil, nel(e, nelle*, f. *ne* NE 3 a + *wille, wile* WILL *v.* In the Lindisf. Gosp. the more original forms *nwill, nuill* also occur.

In early use another negative freq. occurs in the sentence.]

I. *intr.* To be unwilling, not to will.

1. Const. with infinitive (without *to*). Sometimes also denoting simple futurity.

a. *Present tense* (*and infinitive*).

α. *1st and 3rd sing.* 1 **nylle**, 1, 4 **nyle**, 1, 3-4 **nile**, 4-6 **nil, nyl(l**, 5 **nylle, nille**, 5- **nill**. *2nd sing.* 1, 4-5 **nylt**, 3-6 **nilt** (*Orm.* **nillt**), 6 **nillest(e**. *Pl.* 1 **nyllað**, **-eð**, 3 **nilenn**, 4 **nylen, nill**. *Inf.* 6-7 **nill**.

835 *Charter* in *O.E. Texts* 447 ȝif min wiif ðonne hia nylle mid clennisse swæ ȝehaldan. *a* **900** CYNEWULF *Christ* 683 Nyle he ænȝum anum ealle ȝesyllan gæstes snyttru. *c* **1000** *Ags. Ps.* (Thorpe) lxxiv. 8 Nyle he þa dærstan him don unbryce. *c* **1200** ORMIN 2091 Whase nile trowwenn þiss He slaþ hiss aȝhenn sawle. *Ibid.* 6278 ȝiff þu nillt nohht hatenn himm þatt hateþþ þe. *c* **1250** *Gen. & Ex.* 1806 Self his kinde nile ðat wune forȝeten. **13..** *E.E. Allit. P.* B. 1261 Nabuzardan nyl neuer stynt. **1388** WYCLIF *Isa.* i. 20 That if ȝe nylen,.. swerd schal deuoure ȝou. *c* **1420** *Chron. Vilod.* 3952 Y my-self nyl not be y-buryed þere. **1447** BOKENHAM *Seyntys* (Roxb.) 71 Yf thou nylt I shal.. [thee] never more doughtir calle. **1551** *Dr. Haddon's Exhort.* in Furnivall *Ball.* I. 325 Thow arte too bownde, that wake thow nillest, for no distres. **1579** SPENSER *Sheph. Cal.* May 151 If I may rest, I nill live in sorrowe. **1616** R. C. *Times' Whistle* 120 Marriage they nill admitt by any meanes.

β. *1st and 3rd sing.* 1-4 **nelle, nele**, 1, 3-5 **nel**, (3 **neolle, neole, neol**). *2nd sing.* 1-4 **nelt**. *Pl.* 1 **nellað**, 2 **nelleð**, 3 **-eþ**, 4 **nelen**.

Beowulf 679 Ic hine sweorde swebban nelle. **971** *Blickl. Hom.* 45 ðif hi nellaþ healdan Godes æwe. *c* **1000** ÆLFRIC *Exod.* v. 21 He nele þin word ȝehiran. *a* **1122** *O.E. Chron.* (Laud MS.) an. 1086 Hi nellað lufian God & rihtwisnesse. *c* **1200** *Trin. Coll. Hom.* 41 Synfulle men þe heued-synnes don habbeð and nelleð þerof no shrift nimen. *c* **1275** *Passion our Lord* 146 in *O.E. Misc.* 41 Ic nele neuer þe vorsake. *c* **1330** R. BRUNNE *Chron. Wace* (Rolls) 11518 ȝif hit be so ..þat þou nelt come at þy day. **1377** LANGL. *P. Pl.* B. XI. 22 Til þow be a lorde.. leten þe I nelle. *c* **1400** *26 Pol. Poems* 18/106 Many.. nelen non othere counscil crave. **1422** tr. *Secreta Secret., Priv. Priv.* 157 He wille not begyle, ne bigilid he nel not be.

γ. *1st and 3rd sing.* 2-3 **nulle, nule**, 3-4 **nul, nolle**, 4-5 **nol**. *2nd sing.* 3-4 **nult**, (6 *Sc.*) **nolt**. *Pl.* 3-4 **nulleð, -eþ, -eth, nolle(þ**, 7 *Sc.* **noll**.

c **1175** *Lamb. Hom.* 29 He nule nefre mare eft ȝedon þeo sunnen. *c* **1205** LAY. 1447 Nawit for his forbode nulle ich hit bileuen. *a* **1250** *Owl & Night.* 909 Hwi nultu fare to Noreweie? *Ibid.* 1764 Hwi nulleth hi nimen heom to rede? **1297** R. GLOUC. *Chron.* (Rolls) 7222 Hii nolleþ no god þing ihure ne yse. *a* **1310** in Wright *Lyric P.* viii. 32 Such tiding mei tide y nul nout teme. **1340-70** *Alex. & Dind.* 344 We nolle sclepe in no sclowþe. **1399** *Pol. Poems* (Rolls) I. 363 Ther nul no stych with odur abyde. *c* **1400** *Beryn* 189, I wol hym no thing spare That I nol touch his taberd. **1633** *Orkney Witch Trial* in *Abbotsford Club Miscell.* 161 He said to yow, Away wich, carling, devill a farthing ye noll fa.

b. *Past tense.*

α. *1st and 3rd sing.* 1-6 **nolde** (*Orm.* **nollde**, 3 **nulde**), 1-3 **nalde**, (2 **naldde**, 3 **nælde**), 4-6 **nold**, 6 **nould**, *Sc.* **nald**. *2nd sing.* 1 **noldes**, 1-3 **noldest**, 1, 3 **naldes**. *Pl.* 1 **noldon, naldon**, etc., 3-4 **nolden**, 4-5 **nolde**. β. 6 **nild(e, nilled**.

Beowulf 967 Ic hine ne mihte, þa metod nolde, ganges ȝetwæman. *a* **900** CYNEWULF *Christ* 1392 Ða þu lifes word læstan noldes. *c* **950** *Lindisf. Gosp.* Mark i. 34 Dioblas meniȝo he fordraf ut.. & nalde leta spreca hia. *c* **1000** ÆLFRIC in Assmann *Ags. Hom.* (1889) i. 229 For ðæs wintres cyle nolde se asolcena eriȝan. *a* **1122** *O.E. Chron.* (Laud MS.) an. 1106 Se cyng him nolde aȝifan þæt þe he.. uppon him ȝenumen hæfde. *c* **1175** *Lamb. Hom.* 5 He mihte ridan ȝif he walde on riche stede.. [yet] nalde he no. *a* **1225** *Ancr. R.* 234 [He] bed ure Louerd ȝeorne þet he dude hit from him, and he nolde. *c* **1250** *Gen. & Ex.* 3029 Ðe wicches hidden hem for-ðan, Bi-foren pharaun nolden he ben. *c* **1330** *Arth. & Merl.* 897 (Kölbing), Whi noldestow vnderstonde, Hou þi kin is brouȝt to schond? **1388** WYCLIF *Isa.* xlii. 24 Thei nolden go in hise weies. *c* **1420** *Chron. Vilod.* 1593 þe bysshopus nolde turne non other-weys. **1480** *Robt. Devyll* in Thoms *E. Eng. Prose Rom.* (1858) I. 33 Robert nolde ete nor drynke. **1501** DOUGLAS *Pal. Hon.* Prol. 52 Neptunus nold within that palice hant. *c* **1570** *Pride & Lowl.* (1841) 10 Whereas.. I them beheld.., But nold so much as touche them with my hand. **1590** GREENE *Wks.* (Rtldg.) 301/1 Unto the founts Diana nild repair. **1600** FAIRFAX *Tasso* v. xlvii, Thinke how I.. Was wronged, yet I nould reuengement take.

c. *Imperative* (*and subjunctive*).

Sing. 1 **nyl, nelle**, 4 **nil**, 4-5 (also *pl.*) **nile, nyle**. *Pl.* 1 **nyllað, nellað, nyllan, nelle**, 4 **nilles**.

Used only in renderings of L. *noli, nolite*.

c **825** *Vesp. Ps.* iv. 5 Eorsiað & nyllað synȝian. *Ibid.* xxxvi. 1 Nyl ðu elnian betwih awerȝde. *c* **1000** *Ags. Ps.* (Thorpe) lxi. 10 Nellað ȝe ȝewenan welan unrihte. *Ibid.* cii. 9 Nelle þu oð ende yrre habban. *a* **1300** *E.E. Ps.* lxi. 11 Nil þou hope in wickednes. *Ibid.* lxxiv. 5, I saide to wicked, Nilles do wicli. *c* **1380** WYCLIF *Serm.* Sel. Wks. II. 362 þerfore seiþ Poul aftir, Nyle ȝe ȝyve stede to þe devel. **1388** —— *Prov.* iii. 27 Nil thou forbede to do wel him that mai. *c* **1449** PECOCK *Repr.* i. xviii. 109 Nile ȝe deeme and ȝe schulen not be deemed.

†**2.** With ellipse of *go. Obs. rare.*

13.. *E.E. Allit. P.* C. 346 Nylt þou neuer to nunive bi no-kynnez wayez? **1377** LANGL. *P. Pl.* B. xv. 456 With foules þat fram hym nolde, but folwed his whistellynge.

†**3.** Const. *to* with infinitive. *Obs.*

c **1400** *Destr. Troy* 7585 Your self nold For mykill of þis medill erthe þat myschefe to se. **1471** RIPLEY *Comp. Alch.* Prol. ii. in Ashm. (1652) 117 Nylling to dwell where Syn is wrought. **1500-20** DUNBAR *Poems* lxvi. 85 Greit abbais grayth I nill to gather. **1621** QUARLES *Div. Poems, Esther* (1638) 99 The peoples patience nilling to sustaine The hard oppression. **1652** H. L'ESTRANGE *Amer. no Jewes* 74 'Tis a learned ignorance to nill to know What our great master does not will to show.

4. In the phrases *nill he, will he*; *nilling, willing*, etc. (Cf. WILL *v.*)

In these and other cases where *will* and *nill* are contrasted, the former usually precedes: for examples see WILL *v.*

a **1300** *Cursor M.* 23728 Ded has vs wit-sett vr strete, Nil we, wil we, we sal mete. *a* **1400-50** *Alexander* 301 Fleme he sall þe toþire [wife].., nyll he so will he. *c* **1440** *Gesta Rom.* II. xxvi. 354 Nylle he wille he, he shalle put forthe his honde. **1629** *Reg. Privy Counc. Scot.* III. 5 They sould caus fourtie knaves lyke himselffe bring him out nill he wald he. **1657** J. WATTS *Dipper Sprinkled* 73 To take a living from them, to the value of 100*l.* per annum,.. they nilling willing. **1787** BURNS *Let. to J. Skinner* 25 Oct., Your name will be inserted among the other authors—' Nill ye, will ye'. **1806** *Gazetteer Scot.* (ed. 2) 253/2 This puts the witch into such an agony, that she comes nilling willing to the house. **1850** STRUTHERS *Life* Poet. Wks. I. p. xli, Thoughts of this kind frequently.. forced themselves into his mind, nil he would he.

II. *trans.* **5.** Not to will (a thing); to refuse, reject; to negative, prevent from happening, etc.

c **1000** *Ags. Ps.* (Thorpe) v. 3 þu eart se ylca God þe nan unriht nelt. *c* **1205** LAY. 28103 ȝif hit weore ilimpe, swa nulle hit ure drihte [etc.]. *c* **1250** *Hymn to Virgin* ii. in *Trin. Coll. Hom.* App. 257 þu nult noþing bote richt. *a* **1300** *Vox & Wolf* 189 in Hazl. *E.P.P.* I. 64 Noltou, quod the wolf, thin ore? *a* **1330** *Roland & V.* 94 He brouȝt.. Gold & siluer, & riche stones, Ac þerof nold he nouȝt. *c* **1386** CHAUCER *Can. Yeom. Prol. & T.* 910 'Nay, nay', quod Plato, 'certein, that I nille'. *a* **1450** *Knt. de la Tour* (1868) 17 Y chese the yongest of the .iij. doughters, for y nille none other. **1577** tr. *Bullinger's Decades* IV. ii. 590/2 It.. nilleth, hateth, and repelleth the euil that the Lorde hath forbidden it. **1615** JACKSON *Creed* IV. vi. Wks. III. 64 Many divine truths.. we evidently refuse, or nill, when we come to question about their price. **1650** BAXTER *Saints' R.* IV. ix. §1 If it appeare evil to us, then we Nill it. **1683** J. CORBET *Free Actions* I. vi. 5 Though God doth not simply Nill the Existence of sin, yet he Nills it so far, as that he hates it. *a* **1708** BEVERIDGE *Priv. Th.* II. (1730) 94 So as to will what he wills.. and to nill what he nills. **1778** *Arminian Mag.* I. 196 He commanded Abraham to offer up Isaac, yet he nilled the execution of it. **1860** PUSEY *Min. Proph.* 20 When to will the same and nill the same, maketh of twain, one spirit.

†**b.** With dependent clause. *Obs.*

c **1175** *Lamb. Hom.* 105 God nele þet we beon gredie ȝitseras. *a* **1225** *Ancren R.* 8 þauh nullich nout þet ȝe bihoten ham ase heste to holden. **1297** R. GLOUC. (Rolls) 5055 Wanne god nel noȝt þat it be lengore in vre hond. ? *a* **1366** CHAUCER *Rom. Rose* 270 She nolde.. Hir owne fadir farede welle. **1513** DOUGLAS *Æneis* I. Prol. 271, I nald ȝe traist I saide this for dispyte. **1575** GASCOIGNE *Weedes* Wks. 112 Heaven it nolde that there they should them teint.

†**'nilla.** *Obs.* Also 7 **nilley.** [Of obscure origin.] A kind of Indian piece-goods (see quot. 1696 and BENGAL 1).

1696 J. F. *Merch. Wareho. laid open* 30 Nilleys, of which there is two sorts, strip'd and plain, by the Buyers are called Bengalls, because they come from the Bay of Bengal;.. it is of much use for Gowns and Petty-Coats, but does shrink in wearing unreasonably. **1712** *Lond. Gaz.* No. 5051/3 Nillaes, Niccanees, Photaes. **1725** —— No. 6388/2 The following Goods, viz... Herba Taffaties, Nillaes. **1757** tr. *Guyon's New Hist. E. Indies* II. 510 Prohibited goods. 50 allejars; 2650 nillaes.

'nilling, *vbl. sb.* Now *arch.* [f. NILL *v.* + -ING[1].] The fact of not willing (something); rejection, aversion.

c **1374** CHAUCER *Boeth.* III. pr. xi. (1868) 97 þe beestes þat han any manere nature of willynge or of nillynge. **1586** BRIGHT *Melanch.* xv. 79 Embraceth the same, impelled by the mindes willing, or reiecteth it.. according to her nilling. **1654** OWEN *Doctr. Saints' Persev.* Wks. 1853 XI. 528 The nilling of Sin was antecedent to the Sin. **1710** NORRIS *Chr. Prud.* v. 218 Our nilling of good has always a mixture of willing, tho' the nilling side be that which carries it. *Ibid.* vii. 323 More vehement or impetuous sorts of Willings or Nillings. **1865** NEALE *Hymns Paradise* 10 One in willing, one in nilling, Unity their spirits show.

So **'nilling** *ppl. a.*, that nills or can nill.

1620 T. GRANGER *Div. Logike* 37 Nilling with willing minde or willing with nilling mynd. **1710** [see prec.].

nilly-willy, *adv.* = WILLY-NILLY.

1880 'OUIDA' *Moths* III. 41 You belong to me, and you must continue to belong to me, nilly-willy. **1884** 'VERNON LEE' *Euphorion* II. 182 In these Italian Commonwealths,.. poets are forced, nilly-willy, to be platonic.

Nilo- (ˌnaɪləʊ). Used as combining form of *Nile* in names of language groups common to inhabitants of the Nile area and of some other specified area. Cf. next.

1932 W. L. GRAFF *Lang.* 434 *Kanuri*, of the Nilo-Chadian group. **1938** [see NILO-HAMITIC *a.*]. **1939** L. H. GRAY *Foundations of Language* 401 The Nobades (the supposed ancestors of the modern Nilo-Chadian Nuba). *Ibid.* 402 The divisions of *Sudano-Guinean*, according to Delafosse, may now be enumerated:.. (2) *Nilo-Abyssinian* (fifteen languages) with evident traces of classes and class-pronouns and tones, and including Shiluk, Dinka, etc. *Ibid.*, (5) *Nilo-Congolese* (nineteen languages) with traces of classes, and including Mangbetu, Mbuda, etc. **1966** J. H. GREENBERG *Languages of Africa* (ed. 2) 130 To the new grouping which consists of Songhai, Saharan, Maban, Fur and Coman in addition to Chari-Nile, the name Nilo-Saharan is given. **1969** *Language* XLV. 665 Of the 33 languages and language groups surveyed in *Hdbk 66*, 21 fall into Greenberg's Nilo-Saharan family.

Nilo-Hamite (ˌnaɪləʊˈhæmaɪt). [f. NILO-HAMITIC *a.*: see -ITE[1].] A member of the Nilo-Hamitic group of peoples.

1932 C. G. & B. Z. SELIGMAN *Pagan Tribes Nilotic Sudan* i. 5 There can be no doubt as to the persistent influence, physical and cultural, of the Hamites on the Nilotes and Nilo-Hamites. **1953** G. W. B. HUNTINGFORD *Southern Nilo-Hamites* 9 The majority of the Southern Nilo-Hamites are pastoralists practising.. a little agriculture. **1955** P. H. GULLIVER *Family Herds* iii. 55 Another tribe of the northern Nilo-Hamites, the Lotuko, makes the same distinction [of kinship terms]. **1966** C. G. SELIGMAN *Races of Africa* (ed. 4) vii. 102 The Nilo-Hamites.. speak Nilotic languages with Hamitic elements, and are predominantly pastoral Negroids. **1974** J. R. BAKER *Race* xiii. 226 The Aethiopids have hybridized secondarily with Nilotid Negrids to give rise to tribes referred to under the general title of Niloto or Nilo-Hamites (or sometimes Half-Hamites).

Nilo-Hamitic (ˌnaɪləʊhæˈmɪtɪk), *a.* Also **Niloto-Hamitic, Nilohamitic.** [f. NILO- + HAMITIC *a.*]

a. Used (originally by German philologists) to designate the groups of languages spoken by East African peoples of mixed Negro and Hamitic descent. **b.** Of, pertaining to, or designating any one or all of the peoples who speak a language belonging to this group.

1883 R. N. CUST *Sk. Mod. Lang. Afr.* I. iv. 54 Krapf.. became aware of the existence of two distinct Groups of Languages on the East Coast, about the line of the Equator, and called them Nilo-Hamitic, or Nilotic and Nigro-Hamitic or Nigritic respectively. **1920** G. W. MURRAY in *Jrnl. R. Anthrop. Inst.* L. 328 The Hamito-Semitic influence on these first three languages is so strong that we may certainly call them Niloto-Hamitic with Westermann. **1938** W. M. HAILEY *Afr. Survey* iii. 77 The Nilotic.. comprises tongues spoken in the Upper Nile region as far south as Lake Victoria. Two main branches are distinguished, Nilo-Sudanic.. and Nilo-Hamitic. **1955** J. H. GREENBERG *Studies in African Linguistic Classification* 66 The term Nilo-Hamitic has been used by different writers with widely varying meanings. **1955** P. H. GULLIVER *Family Herds* i. 1 In East Africa.. it so happens that many of the pastoral peoples are of the Nilo-Hamitic strain, which tends to give them a more striking physique than their Bantu neighbours. **1957** C. G. SELIGMAN *Races of Africa* (ed. 3) vii. 161 Their kinship is rather with the Nilo-Hamitic tribes of East Africa. **1967** M. J. COE *Ecol. Alpine Zone Mt. Kenya* 1 For centuries the peak of Mount Kenya has held a magical and religious significance for the Bantu and Nilohamitic peoples.

Nilometer (naɪˈlɒmɪtə(r)). [ad. Gr. Νειλομέτριον, on the analogy of words in -METER.] A graduated pillar or other vertical surface, serving as a scale or gauge to indicate the height to which the Nile rises during its annual floods.

The form *Nilometrion* is used in R. Cumberland's essay on *Jewish Measures and Weights* (1686) 13, etc.

1707 *Curios. Husbandry* 192 The Egyptians compute the Height to which the Nile rises by a Vessel which they call a Niloscope, or Nilometer. **1741-3** POCOCKE *Descr. East* I. 117 There was a temple to Cnuphis in this island [Elephantine], and a Nilometer to measure the rise of the Nile. **1790** BRUCE *Trav. Nile* III. 689 Omar.. destroyed the Grecian Nilometer from motives of religion. **1849** CURZON *Monast. Levant* 28 This Nilometer is an ancient octagon pillar of red stone in the island of Rhoda. **1887** RAWLINSON & GILMAN *Anc. Egypt* (ed. 2) vi. 114 Anxious eyes gaze daily on the sluggish stream, or consult the 'Nilometers'.

fig. **1848** *Blackw. Mag.* LXIV. 118 The Pyramids are the Nilometer of antiquity. **1876** J. MARTINEAU *Ess. & Addr.* (1891) IV. 270 A kind of Nilometer which shows the shifting levels and gathering floods of thought.

b. A small model of the above (see quots.).

1794 *Phil. Trans.* LXXXIV. 188 A mummy.. in which.. idols, beetles, frogs.. nilometers, &c. were found. **1848** COTTRELL tr. *Bunsen's Egypt's Place* I. vi. 382 [Phthah's] ordinary mode of representation is as a god holding before him with both hands the so-called Nilometer, or emblem of stability. *Ibid.* 416 Osiris.. appears with a barbaric countenance, the Nilometer, and large feathers of Ammon on his head.

So **'niloscope.** [ad. Gr. Νειλοσκοπεῖον.] *rare.*

An earlier form is NILESCOPE.

1707 [see above]. **1727-38** CHAMBERS *Cycl.*, *Nilometer*, or *Niloscope.* **1855** in OGILVIE *Suppl.*

Nilo'metric, *a.* [f. NILOMETER + -IC.] Of or pertaining to a Nilometer, or the measurement of the height of the Nile.

1921 G. A. F. KNIGHT *Nile & Jordan* ix. 96 The Second Cataract where Nilometric markings with his cartouche are recorded.

Nilot (ˈnaɪlɒt). Also **Nilote.** [f. NILE + -OT[2], or ad. Gr. Νειλώτης.] A native inhabitant of the banks of the Upper Nile.

1893 F. ADAMS *New Egypt* viii. 105 The Nilot is very different from the Cairene and the Alexandrian..; there is even a perceptible difference between the Delta man and the true Nilot of the upper river. **1896** HOGARTH in *Eng. Hist. Rev.* Jan. 8 The kings.. oppressed the Nilots with these haughty janissaries. **1932** C. G. & B. Z. SELIGMAN *Pagan Tribes Nilotic Sudan* i. 13 The Nilotes.. are essentially proud, aloof, tenacious of their old beliefs and ideas, intensely religious, and by far the most introvert of the peoples of the Sudan. **1934** D. WESTERMANN *African Today* ii. 24 The Masai and tribes related to them.. show strong Hamitic influence but are on the other hand relatives of the Nilotes. **1966** C. G. SELIGMAN *Races of Africa* (ed. 4) vii. 110 The second great group of hamiticized Negroes are the Nilotes.. geographically limited to the Nile Valley or its immediate neighbourhood.

Nilotic (naɪˈlɒtɪk), *a.* Also 7 -ik, -ick, 9 Nileotic. [ad. L. *Nīlōticus*, a. Gr. Νειλωτικός, f. Νεῖλος the Nile: see -OTIC.] **1. a.** Of or belonging to, peculiar to or characteristic of, the Nile, the Nile region, or its inhabitants.

1653 GATAKER *Vind. Annot. Jer.* 108 This Egyptian frog, crawling out of the mire and mud of some Nilotik mear. **1662** STILLINGFL. *Orig. Sacræ* Ded. i, The early felicitie of Moses, when exposed in an Ark of Nilotick papyre. **1680** BOYLE *Exp. Chem. Princ.* I. 30 This Nilotick Salt was very apt to imbibe the moist aire. **1822** DE QUINCEY *Confess.* 171 Laid..amongst reeds and Nilotic mud. **1865** J. H. INGRAHAM *Pillar of Fire* (1872) 147 The Egyptian or Nilotic race have a sharp and prominent face.

b. ***Nilotic crocodile, monitor*** (see quots.).

1840 *Cuvier's Anim. Kingd.* 274 Two species, in Egypt, have been considered the types of separate subdivisions; the Nilotic M[onitor]..and the Ground M[onitor]. **1855** *Orr's Circle Sci., Org. Nat.* III. 132 The best known species is the Nilotic Crocodile (*Crocodilus vulgaris*), which attains a length of twenty-five or thirty feet.

2. Of, pertaining to, or designating the group of East African Negro peoples including the Dinka, Luo, Nuer, and Shilluk, or the sub-group of Sudanic languages spoken by them.

1915 A. WERNER *Lang. Families of Africa* iii. 41 These.. may perhaps be grouped together as a 'Nilotic' subdivision of the Sudan family. **1930** C. G. SELIGMAN *Races of Africa* vii. 173 The Acholi and Belanda no doubt are of Nilotic origin. **1932** C. G. & B. Z. SELIGMAN *Pagan Tribes Nilotic Sudan* p. xxiii, In the Nilotic languages the *p* and *f* approach each other and seem to be interchangeable. **1949** tr. *L. Homburger's Negro-Afr. Lang.* ii. 42 Central Nilotic languages have no *s, z*; in them Arab *suk* becomes *šuk*. **1966** J. H. GREENBERG *Lang. of Africa* (ed. 2) 85 The closest relatives of these languages [*sc.* the Nilo-Hamitic languages] are the group of languages traditionally called Nilotic... The term Nilotic may be extended to include both the Nilotic and Nilo-Hamitic languages. **1973** *Sci. Amer.* July 74/2 The Sebei, a Southern Nilotic people who live on the northern slopes of Mount Elgon in Uganda. **1973** A. MANN *Tiara* xvii. 158 The indefinite tyranny of the Northern Arabs over the Nilotic and Nilo-Hamitic Southerners.

Nilotic (naɪˈlɒtɪk), *sb.* **a.** = NILOT. **b.** A subdivision of the Sudanic group of languages.

1924 *Chambers's Jrnl.* Jan. 11/2 The Nilotics are in nearly every case the aggressors. **1938** W. M. HAILEY *Afr. Survey* iii. 77 The third family included in the Negro division—namely Nilotic—comprises tongues spoken in the Upper Nile region as far south as Lake Victoria. **1963** *Times* 4 June 14/6 Hieroglyphics, and Demotics, and Nilotics, and Cryptics, and Cufics.

Nilous (ˈnaɪləs), *a.* [f. NILE + -OUS.] Resembling the alluvial deposit of the Nile.

1813 SIR R. WILSON *Priv. Diary* (1862) II. 448 They might live a little longer to enjoy this Nilous earth; for certainly it is more like Egypt's alluvium during the inundation than hard-set soil.

nilpotent (nɪlˈpəʊtənt), *a. Math.* [f. NIL[2] + L. *potent-, potens* powerful, POTENT *a.*[1]] Becoming zero when raised to some positive integral power (see also quot. 1949).

1870 B. PEIRCE in *Amer. Jrnl. Math.* (1881) IV. 104 When an expression raised to the square or any higher power vanishes, it may be called nilpotent. **1937** A. A. ALBERT *Mod. Higher Algebra* (1938) iv. 87 Two nilpotent matrices of index two are similar in F if and only if they have the same rank. **1949** S. KRAVETZ tr. *Zassenhaus's Theory of Groups* iv. 111 A group G is said to be nilpotent if the ascending central series contains the whole group as a member. **1971** I. T. ADAMSON *Rings, Modules & Algebras* xxiii. 194 We say that *I* is a nilpotent ideal if there exists a positive integer *n* such that I^n is the zero ideal. **1974** T. W. HUNGERFORD *Algebra* vii. 100 We obtain a sequence of normal subgroups of *G*, called the ascending central series of *G*: $\langle e\rangle < C_1(G) < C_2(G) < \ldots$ A group *G* is nilpotent if $C_n(G) = G$ for some *n*. *Ibid.* 102 A group *G* is said to be solvable if $G^{(n)} = \langle e\rangle$ for some *n*.. Every nilpotent group is solvable.

†**nim**, *sb.*[1] *Obs.* $rare^{-1}$. [f. the vb.] A thief.

1630 J. TAYLOR (Water P.) *Wks.* I. 71 To arrant Thieves ..To Sharkes, Stales, Nims, Lifts, Foysts, Cheats.

nim (nɪm), *sb.*[2] Also Nim. [Orig. uncertain: perh. suggested by NIM *v.* or G. *nimm* (imp. of *nehmen* to take).] A game in which two players alternately take one or more objects from any one of several heaps, the aim being to compel one's opponent to take the last remaining object (or, sometimes, to take it oneself).

1901 C. L. BOUTON in *Ann. Math.* III. 35 Nim. A game with a complete mathematical theory... The writer has not been able to discover much concerning its history, although certain forms of it seem to be played at a number of American colleges, and at some of the American fairs. It has been called Fan-Tan, but as it is not the Chinese game of that name, the name in the title is proposed for it. **1939** USPENSKY & HEASLET *Elem. Number Theory* i. 16 It should be interesting to present an application of the binary system ..to the theory of the game of Nim. **1955** *Sci. News Let.* 26 Feb. 134/2 A 17-year-old senior at Newton High School.. can boast of having an electronic player that almost never loses in the ancient game of wits, known as 'nim'. **1968** CORLETT & TINSLEY *Pract. Programming* iv. 66 In a game of Nim..two players move alternately and take any number of matches from one pile, the winner taking the last match. If a player can set up a winning position, he cannot lose unless he makes a mistake in a subsequent move.

nim, *v.* Now only *arch.* Forms: (see below). [A Common Teut. verb: OE. *niman, nioman*, etc. = OFris. *nima, nema* (*nam, nomen, nimen*; mod.Fris. *nimmen, nemmen*), MDu. *nemen* (*nam, namen, genomen*), OS. *niman, neman* (*nam, nâmun, ginoman* and *ginuman*), MLG. *nemen* (*nam, nêmen, genomen*), also *nomen, numen*, OHG. *neman, nemen* (*nam, nâmun, ginoman*; G. *nehmen*), ON. *nema* (*nam, námu, numinn*; MDa. *nemme, nimme*; MSw. *nima, nimma*), Goth. *niman* (*nam, nêmun, numans*); the root *nem-* is prob. identical with that of Gr. νέμειν to deal out, distribute, hold, possess, occupy.

In most of its applications *nim* corresponds to various senses of the later (Scandinavian) *take*, and remained in common use down to the 15th cent. During the 16th there are few traces of it, but immediately after 1600 it reappears (with weak pa. t. and pa. pple.) as a slang or colloquial word in the sense of 'to steal', and is very common in this use throughout the 17th cent.]

†**1.** *trans.* To take, in various senses of that verb.

For examples of the frequent ME. phrases *to nim gome, heed*, or *yeme*, see under the sbs.

a. *Infinitive, present tense, and imperative.*

Inf. 1 nioman, niom(m)a; 1–2 neoman; 1 nyman, 4 nymen, (5 -yn), 3–5 nyme, 4 nymme, 4–5 nym; 1–2 niman, (1 nimon), 2–4 nimen, (2 -in), 3–4 nime, 4, 7 nim, 7 nimme; 2 nemen, 3–4 neme. *Pres. Ind. 1st sing.* 1 nime, nyme, nimo, niomu: *2nd sing.* 2 nimes, 2–3 nimest, 3 nymest, nimst; *3rd sing.* 1 nimð, 1–3 nimeð, -eþ, 1–4 nymeð, -eþ; 1, 7 nimmes, 4 nymmes, -ez, nymez, 7 nims; *pl.* 1 niomað, -as, neomaþ, nymað, nimað, 2, 4 nemeð, -eþ, 4 nymes. *Subj.* 1 nyme, 2 nime, 4 nyme, 7 nimme. *Imper. sing.* 1–4 nim, 4–6 nym, 5 nyme, neme; *pl.* 1–2 nimað, 3 nimeþ, nemeþ, 4 nym(m)eþ, nymes.

c **825** *Vesp. Ps.* cxxxvi. 9 Eadiȝ se nimeð & ȝecnyseð ða litlan his to stane. **835** *Charter* in *O.E. Texts* 447 ȝif..hire liofre sie oðer hemed to niomanne. *c* **888** K. ÆLFRED *Boeth.* xx, þonne nimað hi hiora men mid him. **971** *Blickl. Hom.* 127 Maniȝe men þær þa moldan neomaþ on þæm lastum. *a* **1122** *O.E. Chron.* (Laud MS.) an. 1015 Se cyng..het nimon Siȝeferðes lafe. *c* **1126** *Ibid.* an. 1126 Let se kyning nimen his broðer Rotbert. *c* **1175** *Lamb. Hom.* 29 þas reueres ..nemeð oðres monnes eahte. *c* **1205** LAY. 26837 þu me woldest a-quellen, nimen mine castles alle. *c* **1250** *Gen. & Ex.* 2362 He bad cartes and waines nimen. *a* **1300** *Cursor M.* 17293 þai send sergantz for to nym both sir nichodem & him. *c* **1330** R. BRUNNE *Chron. Wace* (Rolls) 7869 Nymeþ out ȝour sexes when y so say. *Ibid.* 8697 At þe lewes ensample nymes. **1377** LANGL. *P. Pl.* B. XIII. 373 A fote-londe or a forwe..I wolde..nymen of his erthe. *c* **1430** *Two Cookery-Bks.* 6 þan neme þin grwel an do þer-to. *Ibid.* 14 Nym gode Almaunde Mylke. *c* **1450** *St. Cuthbert* (Surtees) 4100 Felgyld next come eftir him, þe lyfe of ankyr þare to nym. **1486** *Bk. St. Albans* b iiij, Go and retriue moo and she will nym plente. **1547** BOORDE *Introd. Knowl.* i. (1870) 122 Iche cham a Cornyshe man,..Nym me a quart of ale, that iche may it of sup.

b. *Past tense.*

α. *1st and 3rd sing.* 1 -noom, 1–5 nom, 3–5 nome; *2nd sing.* 1–4 nome; *pl.* 1 nomun, -an, -on, (noumun), 2–4 nomen, 3–5 nome, 4 nom.

c **725** *Corpus Gloss.* (Hessels) A 909 *Auserunt*, nomun [*Erf.* noumun], hlodun. *c* **825** *Vesp. Ps.* lxxii. 24 þu nome hond ða swiðran mine. *c* **825** *Vesp. Hymns* i, He sende engel his & nom mec of scepum feadur mines. *c* **900** *O.E. Chron.* (Parker MS.) an. 787 Her nom Beorhtric cyning Offan dohtor Eadburȝe. *c* **950** *Lindisf. Gosp.* Mark viii. 20 Huu moniȝ ceolas ðæra screadunga ȝie nomon? *c* **1175** *Lamb. Hom.* 3 Heo nomen þe asse and here colt. *c* **1205** LAY. 25447 Arður nom an honde fifti þusend cnihtes kene. *c* **1275** *Passion our Lord* 379 in *O.E. Misc.* 48 þe knyhtes hyne nomen. *Ibid.* 438 Hi nome twey þeoues. *a* **1300** *Cursor M.* 20690 Of hir bodi mi flexs i nom. *c* **1330** R. BRUNNE *Chron. Wace* (Rolls) 706 þe quene þorow treson þey nomen. **13..** *E.E. Allit. P.* B. 1613 Nabuzardan hym nome & now is he here. **1377** LANGL. *P. Pl.* B. xx. 9 Thow nome namore than nede þe tauȝ te. *c* **1420** *Chron. Vilod.* 23 He was þe twolthe kynge þ[t] in Westsex cristyndam nome. *c* **1450** *St. Cuthbert* (Surtees) 2056 Cuthbert to haly eland come And þe priory on him he nome. *c* **1470** HENRY *Wallace* IX. 1812 Maxwell..On to the Sotheroun the gaynest wayis nom.

β. *1st and 3rd sing.* 1–5 nam, 3 namm, næm, naam, 3–5 name; *pl.* 1 naamun, namon, -an, -en, 4 namen, 3 name, 4 nam.

c **825** *Epinal Gloss.* 113 *Hauserunt*, naamun. *c* **888** K. ÆLFRED *Boeth.* xxix. §2 Ða hlafordas naman swa hwæt swa hi hæfden. *c* **900** *O.E. Chron.* (Parker MS.) an. 866 [Hi] winter setl namon on East Englum. **971** *Blickl. Hom.* 31 þas cyþnesse Drihten nam of þisse wisan. *Ibid.* 69 Hie naman blowende palmtwiȝu. *a* **1122** *O.E. Chron.* (Laud MS.) an. 1010 þær namon [hi]..swa mycel swa hi woldon sylfe. *c* **1127** *Ibid.* an. 1127 þa nam he þes kynges wifes swuster.. to wife. *c* **1200** *Trin. Coll. Hom.* 23 He herewde helle and nam ut mid him alle [etc.]. *c* **1250** *Gen. & Ex.* 2840 Moyses ..hise childre wið him nam. *a* **1300** *Cursor M.* 20105 þan name þe apostil..In-til his keping þat maidan. *c* **1330** R. BRUNNE *Chron. Wace* (Rolls) 36 After þe Bretons þe Inglis camen, þe lordschip of þis lande þai namen. *c* **1386** CHAUCER *Can. Yeom. T.* 744 With the coper he came, And this chanon it in his hondes name. *c* **1400** *Destr. Troy* 792 Eneas it name & in note hade. **1447** BOKENHAM *Seyntys* (Roxb.) 32 To peter and poule his hors he nam, And unnethe that nyht to Souters cam.

γ. *Pl.* 3 neme(n, neomen. *Sing.* 4 nem; 5 nym(e; 7 nempt.

c **1275** LAY. 660 Hii neme [*c* 1205 nomen] anne herindrak þat god was to neode. *a* **1300** *K. Horn* 64 The pains come to londe And neme hit in here honde. **13..** *E.E. Allit. P.* B. 505 Bot Noe of vche honest kynde nem out an odde. *c* **1450** *St. Cuthbert* (Surtees) 3540 þis preste..what giftes he gaf or nym. *Ibid.* 7469 Grete tresure fra þe kyrke he nyme. [**1630** LANE *Contn. Sqr.'s T.* (Chaucer Soc.) 116 Ducello.. killd each one that in his mowth hee nempt.]

c. *Past participle.*

α. 1 ȝi-, ȝ enumen (-nummen), 2–3 inumen, 3 inomen, (4 y-); 1–4 numen, (4 -yn), 4–5 nummen, (4 -un, 6 -yn, 5 -yne), nomen, (-in, -yn, -yne), nommen, (-in, -yn, 5 -an).

c **825** *Epinal Gloss.* 100 *Adempto*, ȝinumni. *c* **888** K. ÆLFRED *Boeth.* xviii. §7 Eall þæt his fennas & moras ȝenumen habbað. *c* **950** *Lindisf. Gosp.* Matt. xiii. 12 þæt [he] hæfis, ȝenummen bið from him. *c* **1127** *O.E. Chron.* (Laud MS.) an. 1127 Willelm hæfde æror numen ðes eorles dohter of Anȝeow to wife. *c* **1175** *Lamb. Hom.* 29 þu eart numen in þon ilke þonke. *a* **1225** *Ancr. R.* 42 þeos psalmes beoð inumene efter þe uif lettres of vre lefdi nome. *c* **1250** *Gen. & Ex.* 2268 Wel faȝen he was of here come, for he was numen ðor to nome. *a* **1300** *Cursor M.* 5272 Wit il consail þan was i nummen. *Ibid.* 7059 In his time was troi nomyn. **1375** *Sc. Leg. Saints* xxvi. (*Nicholas*) 918 Quhen þe Iou ham wes cumyne, & fand his gudis a-way nummyne. *a* **1400–50** *Alexander* 1094 (Dubl.), So sall þi name owt of nowmbre be nomyn in-to mynde. ?*a* **1500** *Chester Pl.* (E.E.T.S.) 401 Which prophesy done shall be, when I my realm have nomman. **1513** DOUGLAS *Æneis* II. xi. 101 Nor neuir abak.. Blent I agane, nor perfite mynd has nummyn.

β. 3 inume, ynume, 3–4 inome, ynome.

c **1175** *Lamb. Hom.* 71 We habben him swa wel inume, þat þe saule mote to him cume. *c* **1275** *Passion our Lord* 206 in *O.E. Misc.* 43 So me doþ to þeoue þat schal beon ynume. *a* **1300** *Floriz & Bl.* 20 (Cambr. MS.), To þe hauene hi beoþ icume, And þer habbeþ here in inome. **1340** *Ayenb.* 165 Huo þet heþ þane guode way ynome, hit be-houeþ [etc.]. *c* **1386** CHAUCER *Cook's T.* 119 Whan that everich of hem a staf had i-nome. *a* **1450** MYRC 495 When body and soule to-geder schal come, And the gode to ioye be I-nome.

γ. 4, 6 num; 4 nom, 4–5 nome, nomme.

a **1300** *Cursor M.* 12730 We sal to heuen com Quen we o þis werld es nom [*Gött.* num]. *c* **1330** R. BRUNNE *Chron. Wace* (Rolls) 10824 Whilk of þem were ouer-come, Or slayn, or wyþ force nome. *c* **1385** CHAUCER *L.G.W.* 1777 *Lucretia*, Al allon hys way than hath he nome. *c* **1386** —— *Cook's T.* 580 They ben swore to-gidere that we schul be nome. *c* **1450** *Bk. Hawking* in *Rel. Ant.* I. 296 In kyndely spech ye schull say that your hawke hath nome a foule, and not i-take. *c* **1450** *St. Cuthbert* (Surtees) 1542 My heele, my tonge, bes fra me nome. *c* **1470** HENRY *Wallace* I. 124 At Canemor syne king Fergus has it nome. **1566** J. PARTRIDGE *Hist. Pand.* b iij b, Pandauola in her armes Her Alfyne hath up num.

†**2.** *intr.* To betake oneself, to go. *Obs.*

c **1100** K. *Ælfred's Boeth.* xvi. §1 (Bodl.), Se is eower aȝen, & þonan ȝe noman [*Cott.* comon]. *c* **1220** *Bestiary* 93 in *O.E. Misc.* 4 þus he neweð him ðis man, ðanne he nimeð to kirke. *c* **1250** *Gen. & Ex.* 744 In-to sichem..he nam And ðeðen he nam to mirie dale. *c* **1303** R. BRUNNE *Handl. Synne* 8164 Euery day to scole she nam [*glossed* ȝede]. *a* **1325** in Horstm. *Altengl. Leg.* (1878) 144 Out of her siȝt oway he nam; þai nist neuer whar he bicam. *c* **1430** *Syr Gener.* (Roxb.) 2400 The forster that with Sereyn came Rose erlie, and to hir chambre name.

3. *trans.* To steal, filch, pilfer.

1606 DAY *Ile Gulls* III. i, As I led him to his Chamber I nimde his Chayne and drew his Purse. **1630** J. TAYLOR (Water P.) *Wks.* III. 8/2 The thieuing knaue the purse he nimbly nims. **1663** BUTLER *Hud.* I. i. 598 They'll question Mars, and by his look Detect who 'twas that nimm'd a Cloke. **1692** R. L'ESTRANGE *Fables* (1694) 218 They..would still be nimming something or other for the very love of thieving. **1727** GAY *Begg. Op.* II. i, I expect the Gentleman about this snuff-box, that Filch nimm'd two nights ago in the Park. **1797** BRYDGES *Hom. Trav.* II. 403 A fellow that would nim a smock From off a hedge if it we loose. **1835** JAMES *Gipsy* ii, Tiny Dick..had very near been caught in nimming it off the edge of the common. **1898** HENLEY *Lond. Types, Beef-eater*, He shows that Crown the desperate Colonel nimmed.

transf. **1651** H. MORE *Enthus. Tri.* (1656) 81 Your quotation..is no new notion, but nimmed out of Philo.

†**b.** Const. with *away* or *off*. *Obs.*

1607 MIDDLETON *Five Gallants* I. i, You shall live at ease enough for nimming away jewels and favours from gentlemen. *a* **1635** CORBETT *Poems* (1807) 28 Looking in their plate He nimmes away their coyne. **1669** *Nicker Nicked* in *Harl. Misc.* (1744) II. 96 Some will nim off the Gold Buttons of your Cloke, or steal the Cloke itself.

4. *intr.* To steal, pilfer, thieve.

1622 MASSINGER & DEKKER *Virg. Mart.* II. iii, *Hir.* Spungius, y'are a picke-pocket. *Spun.* Hircius, thou hast nimb'd—..not so much money is left as will buy a louse. **1638** MAYNE *Lucian* (1664) 35 His mother sayes he stayes not in heaven by night, but that he may be nimming, goes down to hell, and pilfers there to. *a* **1763** BYROM *The Nimmers* 27 Nim? yes, yes, yes, let's nim with all my heart.

nim(b, variants of NEEM.

nimb (nɪmb). [ad. L. *nimbus* NIMBUS. Cf. F. *nimbe.*] A nimbus or halo.

1849 ROCK *Ch. of Fathers* II. 98 The nimb or circle, betokening endless, heavenly happiness, about the head of St. Dunstan. **1870** —— *Text. Fabr.* I. 44 The places, now bare, in the nimb and neck were..once filled in with fine seed-pearls. **1880** *Smith's Dict. Chr. Antiq.* s.v. *Nimbus*, The aureole..may be defined as the nimb of the body.

nimbated (ˈnɪmbeɪtɪd), *a.* [f. NIMB-US + -ATE[1] + -ED[1].] Furnished with a nimbus.

1901 *Archaeol. Jrnl.* Sept. 284 The sun, nimbated, with flying drapery, drives a quadriga.

‖**nimbe.** $rare^{-1}$. [Cf. NIMB.] A nimbus.

1830 *Anglo-French Coinage* 1 Surrounded by a double nimbe or glory.

nimbed (nɪmd), *a.* [f. NIMB + -ED[2].] Provided with a nimb.

1849 ROCK *Ch. of Fathers* I. iii. 258 In the middle of the furthermost border [of the super-altar] stands a nimbed lamb. *Ibid.* 259 A dove, nimbed, stands upon an altar. **1865** *Reader* No. 121. 462/2 A nimbed equestrian figure. **1877** W. JONES *Finger-ring* 394 A Saint, nimbed, clad in a monastic habit.

nim'biferous, *a. rare*⁻⁰. [f. L. *nimbifer* + -OUS.] 'That brings storms or showers' (Blount *Glossogr.* 1656).

nimbifi'cation. *rare*⁻¹. [f. L. *nimb-us* cloud.] The process of cloud-formation.

1814 MILLAR *Times Telescope* 341 The best time for viewing the progress of nimbification is by stormy weather.

nimble ('nɪmb(ə)l), *a.* (and *adv.*) Forms: *α.* 1 **næmel**, 4 **nemel, -il**, 5 **nemyl(l(e, nemble**, 6 **neem-, neamble**, 9 *dial.* **neamle.** *β.* 1 **numol, -ul, numel**, 5 **nymyl, -el**, 6 *Sc.* **nymill**, 9 *dial.* **nimmel, nummle**; 5 **nymbyll**, 5–6 **nymble**, *Sc.* **nymbil, nimbill**, 6– **nimble.** [The *α*-forms appear to represent OE. *næmel* (found only once), f. **næm-*, ablaut-variant of the stem (**nem-*) of *niman* to take, NIM *v.* + -EL, -LE 1. The *β*-forms represent the more usual OE. *numol, -ul, -el* (cf. also *scearpnumol* efficacious), f. the ppl. stem *num-* of the same verb. The OE. evidence is, however, very scanty, and the word only becomes common after the original sense had been obscured.]

†**1.** Quick at grasping, comprehending, or learning; hence, clever, wise. *Obs.*

α. c **1000** in Napier *Contrib. O.E. Lex.* (1906) 47 He wearð þa swiðe næmel þurh þæs Halȝan Gastes ȝife, þæt on litle firste he oferþeah his mæȝester on wisdome. **1483** *Cath. Angl.* 251/2 Nemylle; *cautus*; *vbi* wyse.

β. a **1000** *Gloss.* in Wr.-Wülcker 198 *Capax, qui multum capit*, andȝetul, gripul, numul. c **1000** ÆLFRIC *Gram.* ix. (Z.) 69 *Capax*, numol oððe ȝefyndiȝ. c **1440** *Promp. Parv.* 356/2 Nymyl, *capax*.

†**2.** Quick to seize or take hold of one. *Obs.*⁻¹

c **1000** in Napier *Contrib. O.E. Lex.* (1906) 49 Swa swa deaðes geferan, swa forfleoh þu þæt numele win [L. *mordax vinum*].

3. Quick and light in movement or action; agile, active, swift, rapid.

a. Of persons, animals, or things.

nimble lizard, the common or viviparous lizard.

α. a **1300** *Cursor M.* 21528 Of he kest al to his serk, To mak him nemel [*v.r.* nemil] til his werk. a **1400–50** *Alexander* 1065 þar was na man so nemyll þat him hit couthe. c **1430** LYDG. *Order Fools* 108 in *Bk. Precedence* 83 A biche Nemyl of mouthe for to mordyr A hare. a **1450** *Fysshynge w. Angle* (1883) 8 þus schall ye make yow a rode.. and hyt wyl be lyȝt & nemyll [1496 nymbyll] to fysche with. a **1500** *Sir Beues* (M) 2252 Syr Beuys was bothe nemble and wyght And start away from his dynt. **1535** COVERDALE *Wisd.* vii. 24 For wiszdome is neembler then all neemble thinges. **1570** LEVINS *Manip.* 208/23 Neamble, *agilis*. **1828** *Craven Gloss.* s.v., As neamle as a cat on a haat backstone.

β. **1470–85** MALORY *Arthur* VIII. xxvi. 312 Sire Tristram was lyght and nymel and voyded his hors lightely. **1509** FISHER *Funeral Serm. C'tess Richmond* Wks. (1876) 304 It [the risen body] shall be more nymble.. then is any swalowe. **1529** MORE *Dyaloge* I. Wks. 153/2 As the hande is the more nymble by the vse of some feates. a **1547** SURREY *Æneid* II. 1057 Like nimble windes, and like the flieing dreame. **1587** FLEMING *Cont. Holinshed* III. 1544/2 These were chosen of the strongest and nimblest men. **1609** ROWLANDS *Crew Kind Gossips* 3 Swift report hath very nimble wings. **1648** BURRELL *Cordial* 3 Being nimbler then the nimblest of them, he escaped. **1670** COTTON *Espernon* II. VIII. 409 Those of his followers who were nimblest of Foot. **1725** DE FOE *Voy. round World* (1840) 72 The rogues were too nimble for him and had got to his boat before him. **1782** COWPER *Gilpin* 78 Now see him mounted once again Upon his nimble steed. **1833** HT. MARTINEAU *Charmed Sea* iv. 53 She.. climbed a neighbouring pine like the nimblest of squirrels. **1857** WILLMOT *Pleas. Lit.* xv. 82 His nimble hand ranges over the keys. **1875** BUCKLAND *Log-bk.* 89, I am as nimble as most of them, and a deal nimbler.

transf. **1623** LISLE *Ælfric on O. & N. Test.* Pref. 19 Our language is.. become the fairest, the nimblest, the fullest. **1742** YOUNG *Nt. Th.* IV. 807 That hour, so late, is nimble in approach. **1781** COWPER *Conversat.* 152 Their nimble nonsense takes a shorter course.

b. Of actions, motion, qualities, etc.

1589 PUTTENHAM *Eng. Poesie* III. xxiv. (Arb.) 303, I haue seene him runne vp a paire of staires so swift and nimble a pace. **1627** *Lisander & Cal.* III. 53 With his nimble strength ..[he] lifted them both up from the ground. **1667** MILTON *P.L.* VI. 73 The passive Air upbore Thir nimble tread. **1728** POPE *Dunc.* I. 183 (Globe), As clocks to weight their nimble motion owe. **1794** COWPER *Moralizer Corrected* 20 Proceeding with his nimblest pace.

transf. **1681** *Relig. Clerici* 30, I believe the nimble Confession of Nathaniel.. was better approved of by Christ, than the.. deliberate advances of Judicious Nichodemus.

c. Of ships: Fast and easily handled.

1588 *Exhort. Faithful Subjects* in *Harl. Misc.* (1800) II. 100 Look to the amending and new building of ships. Make them strong, light, and nimble for the battle. **1627** CAPT. SMITH *Seaman's Gram.* ix. 43 Shee is a nimble ship that in .. tacking about will not fall to the Lee-ward of her wake. **1652** NEEDHAM tr. *Selden's Mare Cl.* 77 Antiochus should surrender his long ships..; and not have more than ten nimble Gallies. **1704** *Lond. Gaz.* No. 4001/3 The Enemy being a more nimble Sailer, got away from her. **1734** tr. *Rollin's Anc. Hist.* (1827) I. II. 376 As the Roman galleys.. were neither very nimble nor easy to work.

d. Applied to coins or sums of money, indicative of brisk circulation or return in business; chiefly in ***nimble ninepence***.

1851 MAYHEW *Lond. Labour* (1864) II. 263/1 The 'nimble ninepence' being considered 'better than the slow shilling'. **1860** EMERSON *Cond. Life, Wealth* Wks. (Bohn) II. 351 The farmer's dollar is heavy, and the clerk's is light and nimble. **1883** C. READE in *Harper's Mag.* June 94/2 He often sold his purchase on the road, for the nimble shilling tempted him. **1894** ASTLEY 50 *Years Life* II. 68 Not a bad instance of the nimble ninepence.

4. a. Of the mental faculties: Quick or ready in devising, designing, etc.; acute, alert.

1589 [? LYLY] *Pappe w. Hatchet* E ij b, If thy vaine bee so pleasant, and thy witt so nimble, that all consists in glicks and girds. **1600** HOLLAND *Livy* VII. xiv. 258 Having a subtle wit and nimble head. **1638** JUNIUS *Paint. Ancients* 62 Invited and drawne on by.. their nimble Imaginations. **1665** BOYLE *Occas. Refl.* 31 The faculties of the mind.. grow thereby the more vigorous and nimble. **1701** W. WOTTON *Hist. Rome* 270 He was a man of very nimble and dextrous parts. **1839** LD. BROUGHAM *Statesmen Geo. III*, Ser. II. 58 A subtlety so nimble, that it materially impaired the strength of his other qualities. **1885** *Manch. Times* 7 Feb. 5/5 The less nimble wits and the less educated intellects.

b. Of persons: Quick or ready-witted.

1604 T. WRIGHT *Passions* Pref., The Italians.. become very nimble in the managing all affaires. c **1645** HOWELL *Lett.* (1650) I. 253 There was there for the Queen, Gilpin, as nimble a man as Suderman. **1851** CARLYLE *Sterling* II. v, Every way a very human, lovable, good and nimble man. **1893** LIDDON *Life Pusey* I. 361 Whateley, indeed, was a nimble dialectician.

c. Cleverly or smartly contrived.

1602 FULBECKE *Pandects* 1 A briefe definition and verie nimble, if it be nimbly vnderstood. **1625** B. JONSON *Staple of N.* III. i, I do admire this nimble ingine, Picklock. **1751** JOHNSON *Rambler* No. 95 ¶2, I was.. initiated in a thousand low stratagems, nimble shifts, and sly concealments. **1868** KINLOCH *Ballad Bk.* 29 (E.D.D.), For the nimble trick to the Friar she play'd.

5. a. Quick or ready *at* or *in* (or *to* do) something.

a **1591** H. SMITH *Wks.* (1867) II. 144 Judas was nimble to betray Christ. **1628** FELTHAM *Resolves* II. xxxviii. 117, I know, wise men are not too nimble at an injurie. **1633** FORD *Broken H.* IV. iv, Nimble in vengeance, I forgive thee. **1686** HORNECK *Crucif. Jesus* xiv. 342 Make me.. nimble in religion without lightness. a **1703** BURKITT *On N.T.* Luke xxii. 32 Our Intercessor is full as nimble and speedy in our suit for us, as Satan is.. against us.

†**b.** Of physical agents: Acting rapidly. *Obs.*

1671 SALMON *Syn. Med.* III. x. 345 You may give nimble purging Physick. **1683** ROBINSON in *Ray's Corresp.* (1848) 138 [Volatile alkalies] destroy those nimble acids. **1744** J. PATERSON *Comm. Milton's P.L.* 288 Nimble mercury or quicksilver dissolved.

†**c.** Of actions: Taking place quickly. *Obs.*⁻¹

1707 MORTIMER *Husb.* (1721) II. 332 This is said.. to contribute much towards the nimble Precipitation of the Fæces.

†**6.** *sb. pl. Cant.* The fingers. *Obs. rare*⁻¹.

1621 B. JONSON *Gipsies Metam.* Wks. (Rtldg.) 619/2 Lay by.. using your nimbles In diving the pockets.

7. In special collocations, as **nimble-chaps** (or **-chops**), a talkative person (now *dial.*); so †**nimble-chop**, talkative; **nimble-come-quick** *a.*, of rapid growth; **nimble Dick**, *dial.* (see quot.); **nimble-fingers**, a juggler (*nonce-wd.*); †**nimble Jack**, an elusive person; **nimble-pimble** *v. intr.* (*nonce?*), to behave in a sentimental or trifling manner (toward); †**nimble-tail** (see quot.); **nimble-tailor**, *dial.* (see quots.); **nimble Will**, *U.S.* a slender grass, *Muhlenbergia schreberi*, found in the central United States and sometimes used for pasture.

1614 J. COOKE *Greene's Tu Quoque* c, Yes, *nimble-chappes; what say you to that? **1673** WYCHERLEY *Gent. Dancing-Master* III. i, How now, Mrs. Nimblechaps. **1662** HIBBERT *Body Divinity* II. 146 All the *nimble-chop Jesuites .. labour in vain to prove Peter prince of the apostles. **1863** KINGSLEY *Water-Bab.* viii, The hugest and softest *nimblecomequick turnip you ever saw. **1887** *Kentish Gloss.*, **Nimble Dick*, a species of horse fly or gadfly, differing somewhat from the Brims. **1781** C. JOHNSTON *Hist. J. Juniper* II. 158 Here you, master *nimble-fingers!.. let us have some of your tricks to divert us. **1682** BUNYAN *Holy War* 387 Mr. Unbelief was a *numble Jack, him they could never lay hold of. **1927** D. H. LAWRENCE *Let.* 6 Feb. in E. & A. Brewster *D. H. Lawrence: Reminisc. & Corr.* (1934) 115, I feel an infinite disgust at the idea of having to be there while the fools *nimble-pimble at the dialogue. a **1661** HOLYDAY *Juvenal* (1673) 69 The silurus being a vile fish,.. I render it, for defect of a proper name for it with us, a *nimble-tail. *Ibid.* 255 With half a stinking nimble-tail. **1854** MISS BAKER *Northampt. Gloss.*, **Nimble-tailor*, a field-pea. **1879** MISS JACKSON *Shropsh. Word-bk.*, *Nimble Tailor*, the Long-tailed Tit-mouse. **1816** D. THOMAS *Jrnl.* 10 July in *Travels through Western Country* (1819) 168 He pointed out to me a grass, of which I had heard much, known through all the western country by the name of *nimble Will. **1817** S. R. BROWN *Western Gazetteer* 109 This is the short, nutritious grass called 'nimble will', which has completely overspred with astonishing celerity, almost every spot of waste or uncultivated ground. **1847** DARLINGTON *Amer. Weeds*, etc. (1860) 375 Spreading Muhlenbergia. Drop-seed Grass... It is said to be known in Kentucky by the name of 'Nimble Will'. **1865** *Trans. Illinois Agric. Soc.* V. 863 The *Muhlenbergia diffusa*, or Nimble Will, is a common grass, which is rather known as a troublesome weed. **1894** J. M. COULTER *Bot. W. Texas* III. 523 Nimble Will... Dry hills and woods, northern Texas and northward.

8. *Comb.*, as ***nimble-brained, -eyed, -feathered, -headed, -heeled, -jointed, -mouthed, -pinioned, -spirited, -throated, -tongued, -toothed, -winged*** adjs. See also NIMBLE-FINGERED, -FOOTED, -WITTED.

1836–48 WALSH *Aristoph., Clouds* I. iv, Subtile disputes with *nimble-brained men. **1628** FELTHAM *Resolves* II. xxi. 69 His malice makes him *nimble-eyed. **1624** GATAKER *Transub.* 80 This *nimble-headed Doctor wanteth not an evasion for it. **1719** D'URFEY *Pills* V. 7 Such *nimble Heel'd Witnesses never were known. **1591** SPENSER *Muiopotmos* 121 Being *nimbler joynted than the rest. **1836–48** WALSH *Aristoph.* 176 *note*, Before thy *nimble-mouthed tongue-grievousness. **1592** SHAKS. *Rom. & Jul.* II. v. 7 Therefore do *nimble-Pinion'd Doues draw Loue. **1599** B. JONSON *Ev. Man. out of Hum.* II. i, These be our *nimble-spirited catsos, that.. will run over a bog like your wild Irish. **1930** BLUNDEN *Poems* 310 The girls are quicker, more *nimble-throated. **1608** DEKKER *Belman of London* Wks. (Grosart) III. 79 An old *nymble-tongd beldam. **1700** T. BROWN tr. *Fresny's Amusem.* 47 A nimble-tongu'd painted Sempstress. **1836–48** B. D. WALSH *Aristoph., Clouds* I. v, Bold, nimble-tongued, impudent. **1951** *Essays in Criticism* I. II. 165 She [*sc.* Mrs. Behn].. is nimble-tongued indeed at the expense of a military fop who was ready to damn her play. **1860** WYNTER *Curios. Civiliz.* 138 The grating.. is eaten through by this *nimble-toothed burglar. **1591** SYLVESTER *Du Bartas* I. ii. 346 [She] doth also feed th' air's *nimble-winged guests. **1960** S. PLATH *Colossus* (1967) 37 Each thumb-size bird Flits nimble-winged in thickets.

9. a. Quasi-*adv.* Nimbly.

1568 *Satir. Poems Reform.* xlviii. 44 Bayth thik and nymill gais the spwle. c **1600** SHAKS. *Sonn.* cxxviii, Those jacks that nimble leap To kiss the tender inward of thy hand. **1631** *Celestina* 196 That I may runne away the nimbler. **1683** MOXON *Mech. Exerc., Printing* xxiv. ¶6 That they may all perform their several offices the easier, lightlier, and nimbler. **1760–72** H. BROOKE *Fool of Qual.* (1809) II. 151, I turned much nimbler back again. *Ibid.* III. 94, I turned nimble upon him. **1771** SMOLLETT *Humph. Cl.* (1815) 210 Mr. Micklewhimmen.. came running as nimble as a buck along the passage.

b. *Comb.*, as ***nimble-moving, -shifting, -stepping***.

1591 SPENSER *Teares of Muses* 34 The joyous Nymphes.. Did learne to move their nimble-shifting feete. **1777** POTTER *Æschylus, Prom. Bd.* 21 With light foot now this nimble-moving seat.. I leave. **1845** MRS. NORTON *Child of Islands* (1846) 158 Thou supple-limbed and nimble-stepping slave.

'nimble, *v.* Now *rare*. [f. prec.]

†**1.** *trans.* To make nimble or supple. *Obs.*

1581 MULCASTER *Positions* x. (1887) 58 Certaine preparatives for nimbling, and spreding the vocall powers. *Ibid.* xvi. 75 We thinke it [dancing] beseemeth children best, to enable, and nimble their iointes therby. **1643** TRAPP *Comm. Gen.* xlvi. 5 His joynts oyled and nimbled.

†**2.** To do hastily. With *up*. *Obs. rare*⁻¹.

1612 [see *nimbling* vbl. sb. below].

3. *intr.* To move nimbly.

1598, 1640 [see *nimbling* ppl. a.]. **1827** CLARE *Sheph. Cal.* 64 The squirrel.. Who nimbles round from grain to grain. **1938** E. BOWEN *Death of Heart* II. ii. 191 She nimbled in with the tray.

Hence **'nimbling** *vbl. sb.* and *ppl. a.*

1598 MARSTON *Sco. Villanie* III. ii. 227 Torquatus, that nere op't his lip But in prate.. Of the nimbling tumbling Angelica. **1612** T. TAYLOR *Comm. Titus* iii. 5 The priuate nimbling vp of the matter in corners by some Priest or Minister. **1640** in Fuller *Abel Rediv., Luther* (1651) 46 Conserve with care, what ever is thine owne, Mischance sure footed comes like th' nimbling Hart.

nimble-fingered, *a.* Quick and dexterous with the fingers; light-fingered.

1621 QUARLES *Argalus & P.* (1678) 35 The nimble-fingered Lass Took the forg'd Letter. **1690** DRYDEN *Amphitryon* I. i, O, my nimble-fingered God of Theft, what make you here on Earth..? **1727** GAY *Begg. Op.* I. i, He.. is as nimble-fingered as a juggler. **1773** *Gentl. Mag.* XLIII. 593 It should seem.. that there are nimble-fingered ladies in all parts of the world. **1810** BENTHAM *Offic. Apt. Maximized, Extr. Const. Code* (1830) 65 *note*, Too simple to present any demand for instruction in the nimble-fingered art.

nimble-footed, *a.* Quick and light of foot.

1598 SHAKS. *Two Gent.* V. iii. 7 Being nimble footed, he hath out-run vs. **1618** *Barnevelt's Apology* F 4 Wee seldome vice so nimble-footed finde. **1735** BRACKEN in Burdon *Pocket Far.* 5 *note*, Choose a Horse that has never drawn, if you desire a Nimble-footed one. **1809** MALKIN *Gil Blas* VII. xii, The nimble-footed messenger of Don Rodrigo. **1848** BUCKLEY *Iliad* 252 They, mounting their nimble-footed steeds, pursued.

nimbleness ('nɪmb(ə)lnɪs). [f. NIMBLE *a.* + -NESS.] The quality of being nimble; quickness, agility; dexterity.

1535 COVERDALE *Isa.* xxx. 12 Ye haue.. conforted youre selues with power and nymblenesse. **1568** GRAFTON *Chron.* II. 868 For valiaunt courage.. and strength, and nymblenesse of bodie. **1581** MULCASTER *Positions* xvi. (1887) 75 Daunsing.. may be so full of nimblenesse and actiuitie. **1624** CAPT. SMITH *Virginia* III. i. 42 The Salvages by the nimblenesse of their heeles well escaped. **1676** MARVELL *Mr. Smirke* 18 As men set their Arms on their Plate, to prevent the nimbleness of such as would alter the property. **1732** LEDIARD *Sethos* II. IX. 325 He presum'd to depend on .. the nimbleness of his horse. **1776** HUNTER in *Phil. Trans.* LXVI. 422 This operation should be performed with all possible nimbleness. **1837** CARLYLE *Fr. Rev.* I. VII. vii, To retreat with accelerated nimbleness, through rank after rank. **1861** *Sat. Rev.* 20 July 63 Nimbleness in playing polkas or dancing them.

b. Of mind.

1561 T. NORTON *Calvin's Inst.* I. 51 The nimblenesse of the minde of man which veweth the heauen and earth. **1597** HOOKER *Eccl. Pol.* V. lvi, The personall wisedome of God is.. sayd to excell in nimblenesse or agilitie. **1602** FULBECKE *Pandects* 47 Men must not onely fight by warlike instruments, but by nimblenes of witte. a **1652** J. SMITH *Sel. Disc.* v. 147 The nimbleness and agility of our own reason. **1711** C. M. *Lett. to Curat* 50 With an Inimitable nimbleness he makes an Argument of him. **1839** LD. BROUGHAM *Statesmen Geo. III*, Ser. I. (ed. 2) 248 Nimbleness of mind and industry of application. **1889** *Spectator* 9 Nov., It increases nimbleness of mind, develops curiosity.

†**nimblesbie.** *Obs. rare*⁻¹. [f. NIMBLE *a.*: see -BY 2.] (See quot.)

1611 COTGR., *Passevolant*, a hireling whom a Captaine, on Muster dayes, foisteth into his companie; and generally, any such skipiacke or base nimblesbie.

†**nimbless(e.** *Obs. rare.* [f. NIMBLE *a.* + -ESS[2].] Nimbleness.

1596 SPENSER *F.Q.* v. ix. 29 Those litle Angels..on their purpled wings Did beare the pendants through their nimblesse bold. **1610** G. FLETCHER *Christ's Vict.* I. lxii, Those little sprights, through nimbless bold, The stately canopy bore on their wings. **1638** DRUMM. OF HAWTH. *Irene* Wks. (1711) 167 Neither will your Delusions and Tricks, by the Nimbless of your Hands, pluck it up.

nimble-witted, *a.* Quick-witted.

1613–16 W. BROWNE *Brit. Past.* II. v, The nimble-witted Mercury. **1687** SETTLE *Refl. Dryden* 84 What cannot a nimble witted Commentatour find out. **1879** CHRISTINA ROSSETTI *Seek & Find* 198 Many nimble-witted individuals of our lesser sex. **1899** *Q. Rev.* Apr. 459 The nimble-witted Voltaire. **1922** V. WOOLF *Jacob's Room* iv. 86 The talkative, nimble-witted people have taken themselves to towns.

nimbly ('nɪmblɪ), *adv.* Forms: α. 4 **nemely,** 5 **-lie, neemly, nemly,** 6 **neembly.** β. 6 *Sc.* **nimlie,** 6– **nimbly.** [f. NIMBLE *a.* + -LY[2].] In a nimble or agile manner; quickly, actively.

α. *a* **1350** *St. Mary Magd.* 567 in Horstm. *Altengl. Leg.* (1881) 87 He saw a childe..nemely for þe nones Playand it with precius stones. *c* **1400** *Destr. Troy* 1226 Duke Nestor anon nemly persayuit þat he was prinse of þe pepull. *c* **1440** *Alph. Tales* 448 He..put nemelie þe knyfe in hur hand. **1470–85** MALORY *Arthur* XII. iii. 596 Ther with the bore torned hym nemly. **1535** COVERDALE *Isa.* lxiii. 1 What is he this, that..cometh in so neembly with all his strength?

β. *a* **1585** MONTGOMERIE *Cherrie & Slae* 13 So trimlie and nimlie Thir birdis they flew me by. **1603** DEKKER *Wonderfull Yeare* Wks. (Grosart) I. 144 The Tinker..stript him starke naked, but first diude nimbly into his pockets. **1665** HOOKE *Microgr.* 12 On a very stiff Drum-head, which is vehemently or very nimbly beaten with the Drum-sticks. **1709** STEELE *Tatler* No. 93 ¶7, I recovered so quick, and jumped so nimbly into my Guard. **1766** GOLDSM. *Vic. W.* v, We saw a stag bound nimbly by. **1840** DICKENS *Old C. Shop* xix, The landlord bestirred himself nimbly. **1879** M. ARNOLD *Mixed Ess., Geo. Sand* 329 One alert figure..skips nimbly along at the horses' side.

Comb. **1605** SYLVESTER *Du Bartas* II. iii. III. *Lawe* 1146 Halfe a score of Reapers nimbly-neat.

†**b.** Lightly (armed). *Obs. rare*[−1].

1600 HOLLAND *Livy* XLIV. iv. 1172 The Romanes advanced forth to fight, nimbly appointed; and the enemies likewise were lightly armed.

nimbose, *a. rare*[−0]. [ad. L. *nimbōs-us*, f. *nimbus* cloud.] 'Stormy, tempestuous, cloudy' (Bailey, vol. II, 1727). So **nimbosity,** 'storminess' (Bailey 1721).

nimbostratus (nɪmbəʊ'strɑːtəs, -'streɪtəs). *Meteorol.* [mod.L., f. NIMB(US + -O + STRATUS.] A form of cloud, which usually occurs as a thick, low, extensive layer, which is grey and often dark, and from which rain, sleet, or snow falls (not necessarily reaching the ground) unaccompanied by lightning, hail, or thunder.

Quot. 1887 represents a different sense. The present use appears to have originated independently in 1932, and quot. 1909 is difficult to account for.

1887 R. ABERCROMBY *Weather* iii. 112 Weilbach..gives three varieties [of nimbus]—..and nimbo-stratus, the rain-cloud, in rear of cyclones, which we have designated cumulo-nimbus [i.e. a 'rocky cumulus cloud from which rain falls in squalls or showers']. **1909** *Cent. Dict.* Suppl., *Nimbo-stratus*, same as *nimbo-pallium* [*sc.* 'a broad sheet of cloud from which rain is falling']. **1932** *Internat. Atlas Clouds* (Internat. Meteorol. Comm.) (abridged ed.) I. 14 In the present Atlas it was intended to give the cloud (*a*) the new name of Nimbostratus, which is a better name than nimbus for a continuous layer which is formed by evolution from altostratus. **1940** W. J. HUMPHREYS *Physics of Air* (ed. 3) 295 The nimbostratus, formerly called nimbus, is any thick, extensive layer of formless cloud from which rain or snow is falling or seemingly on the point of falling. **1957** J. I. M. STEWART *Use of Riches* I. ii. 23 Charles pointed to the horizon. 'Nimbostratus. There's going to be rain.' **1967** R. W. FAIRBRIDGE *Encycl. Atmospheric Sci. & Astrogeol.* 687/1 Nimbostratus generally grows out of altostratus, thickening downward.

†**nimbrocado,** variant of IMBROCADO[1]. *Obs.*

1597 *Return fr. Parnass.* III. i. 887 Give mee a new knight of them all, in fenc-schoole, att a Nimbrocado or at a Stocado.

‖**nimbu-pani** ('nɪmbuː'pɑːnɪ). Also **nimboo-pani, nimbo-pani.** [Hindi; cf. Punjabi *nimbū* lemon, lime, Pali *pāna-* drink.] An Indian non-alcoholic drink comprising lemon-juice or lime-juice with sugar and ice or water.

1961 MRS. B. SINGH *Indian Cookery* 184 Nimboo pani or fresh lime juice and a little sugar dissolved in water is a very popular drink in India during the hot weather. **1968** P. LAL *Indian Recipes* 259 Rose-flavoured nimbu pani... Squeeze the juice out of the lemons and add the sugar... Add..iced water and the rosewater. Pour into serving glasses and serve with crushed ice. **1971** *Illustr. Weekly India* 4 Apr. 6/1 Portugal does not believe in *nimbu-pani*. *Ibid.* 25 Apr. 8/3 Nuzzling into a glass of nimboo-pani placed by his side. **1973** 'B. MATHER' *Snowline* xvi. 197 Nimbo-pani..is the juice of fresh limes squeezed on to cracked ice and sugar.

nimbus ('nɪmbəs). Pl. **nimbi** (rare), or **-uses.** [a. L. *nimbus* cloud, etc., perh. related to *nebula, nubes.*]

1. A bright cloud, or cloudlike splendour, imagined as investing deities when they appeared on earth. Also *fig.*

1616 B. JONSON *Masques* Wks. 927 In nature of those Nimbi, wherein..the Gods are fain'd to descend. **1874** H. R. REYNOLDS *John Bapt.* viii. 490 The manhood was lost in the nimbus of celestial glory.

b. *transf.* A cloud, halo, or atmosphere, investing a person or thing.

1860 MOTLEY *Netherl.* ii. (1868) I. 39 A nimbus of musk and violet-powder enveloping them as they passed before vulgar mortals. **1864** SALA *Quite Alone* i, There is the young lady herself, encompassed with a nimbus of petticoat. **1881** HUEFFER *Wagner* 20 The romantic old castle surrounded by the nimbus of both history and romance.

2. *Art.* A bright or golden disk surrounding the head, esp. of a saint. Cf. AUREOLE *sb.* 2, HALO *sb.* 2.

1727–38 CHAMBERS *Cycl.* s.v., The nimbus is seen on the medals of Maurice, Phocas, and others, even of the upper empire. **1843–5** WESTWOOD *Pal. Sacra* s.v. *Gk. Gospels* 2 A medallion of the bust of Christ, invested with the cruciferous nimbus and cross. **1854** FAIRHOLT *Dict. Terms Art* 58/1 As an attached attribute of power, the nimbus is often seen attached to the heads of evil spirits. **1887** RUSKIN *Præterita* II. 225 At Venice, one only knows a fisherman by his net, and a saint by his nimbus.

transf. **1863** MISS BRADDON *J. Marchmont's Legacy* i, A Nimbus of golden hair shone about his..forehead.

fig. **1834** KEIGHTLEY *Tales* ii. 32 The East.., imagination has always invested its front with a nimbus of splendour.

3. *Meteorol.* A rain-cloud.

1803 L. HOWARD *Modif. Clouds* (1830) 11 Of the Nimbus, or Cumulo-cirro-stratus. *Ibid.* 13 The nimbus, although in itself one of the least beautiful clouds [etc.] **1856** KANE *Arct. Expl.* II. xxv. 247 A rainy southwester too..was now spreading with its black nimbus over the bay. **1887** R. ABERCROMBY *Weather* iii. 111 Every kind of cloud from which rain falls is a nimbus, and there are practically two sorts—cumulo-nimbus..; and pure nimbus.

attrib. **1897** *Daily News* 9 Nov. 6/6 The nimbus clouds of the snowstorms covered it.

fig. **1858** O. W. HOLMES *Aut. Breakf.-t.* x. 241 Ah! but what if the stormy nimbus of youthful passion has blown by? **1865** BUSHNELL *Vicar. Sacr.* III. i. (1866) 193 Their whole internal state will be under a nimbus of confusion.

nimbused ('nɪmbəst), *a.* [f. prec. + -ED[2].]

1. Invested with, surrounded by, a nimbus.

1852 *Art Jrnl.* 112 The Virgin..nimbused by a coronet of stars. **1874** 'OUIDA' *Wooden Shoes* 44 Winged griffins and nimbused saints. **1892** A. AUSTIN *Fortunatus* I. iv, Persistent in Appearance; when approached, A nimbused nothingness. **1898** —— *Lamia's Winter-Q.* 55 Nimbused by sunlight or enwreathed in snow.

2. Formed into a nimbus.

1882 'OUIDA' *Maremma* I. 74 That perfect face which bends beneath its cloud of nimbus'd hair.

nimby: see NEMBIE.

nimeny-pimeny: see NIMINY-PIMINY.

†**nimfadoro.** *Obs.*[−1]. [It.] 'An effeminate fellow, a spruce ladies courting fellow' (Florio).

1599 B. JONSON *Ev. Man out of Hum.* II. i, What briske Nimfadoro is that in the white virgin boote there?

†**nim-gimmer.** *Obs. rare*[−0]. (See quot.)

a **1700** B. E. *Dict. Cant. Crew, Nim-gimmer*, a Doctor, Surgeon, or Apothecary, or any one that cures a Clap or the Pox.

nimiety (nɪ'maɪɪtɪ). [ad. late L. *nimietas*, f. *nimis* too much.] Excess, redundancy; an instance of this.

a **1564** BECON *Christmas Banquet* Wks. 1564 I. 20 Although ther ought not to be any sufficiency, much lesse any nimietie in spiritual things. **1625** GILL *Sacr. Philos., Trin.* 229 That nimietie, or excesse of goodness wherein it was created. **1657** REEVE *God's Plea* 204 Man may have his nimieties of expression, his diffluences, redundances..of speech. **1679** C. NESSE *Antid. agst. Popery* 8 Superstition, which is a nimiety and excess in religion. **1772** NUGENT *Hist. Fr. Gerund* II. 252 He was not only matchless, but even reached the line of nimiety. **1834** COLERIDGE *Table-t.* 2 June, There is a nimiety—a too-muchness—in all Germans. **1892** *Illustr. Lond. News* 17 Dec. 776/1 A more serious blemish..with most modern poetry, is nimiety, the tendency to dilute the general effect by..repetition.

'**niminy,** *a.* Abbrev. of next. *rare*[−1].

1878 STEVENSON *Inland Voy.* 182, I have never forgotten that girl... To call her a young lady, with all its niminy associations, would be to offer her an insult.

'**niminy-'piminy,** *a.* Also **nimeny pimeny, nimini pimini.** [Imitative of a mincing utterance. Cf. MIMINY-PIMINY.] Mincing, affected, trifling, lacking in force or spirit.

1786 J. BURGOYNE *Heiress* III. ii. 55 *Lady Emily*... You have only, when before your glass, to keep pronouncing to yourself nimini-primini. *Miss Alscrip*. Nimini-pimini-imini, mimini—oh, it's delightfully enfantine. **1786** G. WHITE *Let.* 25 Mar. in R. Holt-White *Life & Lett. G. White* (1901) II. 154, I hope you practice every day at your Glass; and that you are by this time perfect mistress of '*Nimini pimini*'. **1801** *Monthly Rev.* XXXV. 324 With..a smirking countenance, and 'nimeny pimeny' lisp. **1822** L. HUNT *Indicator* No. 23 I. 178 To see her proud, affected, niminy-piminy face in. **1830** J. JEKYLL *Corr.* (1894) 221 She..is an exquisite, her husband a nimini pimini gentleman. **1840** THACKERAY *Pict. Rhapsody* Wks. 1900 XIII. 345 But was there ever such a niminy-piminy subject treated in such a niminy-piminy way? *a* **1894** STEVENSON *St. Ives* xxv. 190 A niminy-piminy creature, afraid of a petticoat and a bottle.

Hence '**niminy-'pimininess;** '**niminy-'piminyism.**

1840 *Blackw. Mag.* XLVIII. 833 Such a pitiful piece of niminy-piminyism. **1884** W. C. HAZLITT *Offspring Th.* 56 There was no Niminy-pimininess about Johnson... He always said what he thought.

nimious ('nɪmɪəs), *a.* Also 5 **nemyows, nymyos.** [f. L. *nimius*, f. *nimis* too much: see -OUS.] Overmuch, excessive; †exceeding. Now chiefly as a Sc. legal term.

c **1485** *Digby Myst.* (1882) III. 857 My fathyr, of nemyows charyte sent me, his son. *Ibid.* 1112 Of yower nymyos charyte. **1622** S. WARD *Christ All in All* (1627) 23 With this Prouiso, that diuine and nimious adoration be not giuen. **1673** O. WALKER *Educ.* 37 In unseasonable, nimious, opprobrious chiding. **1826** SYD. SMITH *Wks.* (1850) 439 He is never nimious; there is nothing in excess. **1881** *Scotsman* 6 Jan., Nimious State interference is always and necessarily an evil thing. **1883** *Edin. Evening News* 20 Dec. 2/4 The action was *ex facie* so nimious and unreasonable as to excite prejudice against it.

nimite ('nɪmaɪt). *Min.* [f. *N*ational *I*nstitute for *M*etallurgy + -ITE[1].] A basic silicate, aluminate, and oxide of nickel, magnesium, iron, and aluminium (with nickel as the dominant cation), $(Ni,Mg,Fe,Al)_3(Si,Al)_2O_5(OH)_4$, which belongs to the chlorite group and is found as yellowish-green monoclinic crystals near the Scotia talc mine in Transvaal.

1968 HIEMSTRA & DE WAAL in *S. Afr. Nat. Inst. Metall. Res. Rep.* No. 344 (*title*) Nickel minerals from Barberton. II. Nimite, a nickelian chlorite. **1970** *Amer. Mineralogist* LV. 21 The exothermic reaction..at 921°C most probably is due to recrystallization of the nimite to a substance that by X-ray diffraction analysis proved to be mainly spinel.

nimmer ('nɪmə(r)). [f. NIM *v.* + -ER[1].] A pilferer, a petty stealer, a thief.

1608 *Penniles Parl.* in *Harl. Misc.* (1745) I. 179 To the great Impoverishing of all Nimmers, Lifters, and Cutpurses. **1655** tr. *Sorel's Com. Hist. Francion* x. 23 These are the Nimmers who would rob me of all my moveables. **1686** G. STUART *Joco-ser. Disc.* 59 This swindger at Saint Barthol's fair Where all the nimmers do repair. *a* **1763** BYROM *The Nimmers* 70 'Twixt right and wrong how many gentle trimmers Will neither steal nor filch, but will be plaguy Nimmers! **1882** COMPTON *Winscombe Sk.* (ed. 2) 103 The carrion crow..as a nimmer of chicken and ducklings.

nimming ('nɪmɪŋ), *vbl. sb.* [f. NIM *v.* + -ING[1].]

†**1.** The action of taking; the fact of being taken. *Obs.*

c **950** *Lindisf. Gosp.* Luke, Int. 5 Soecende of niming hera [*L. de vulsione spicarum*] in sabatum. *a* **1225** *Ancr. R.* 38 Iðen ilke flesche þet he nom of þe nes neuer sunne, ne i ðine.. efter þe ilke nimunge. *a* **1240** *Lofsong* in *O.E. Hom.* I. 207 Ich bide þe..bi his nimunge and bindunge. **13..** *K. Alis.* 1614 With launceynge and with rydyng, With throwyng, and with nymyng.

2. The action or practice of pilfering.

1607 S. COLLINS *Serm.* (1608) 66 What they haue done in Schooles for payring and nimming of the Arts. **1618** *Barnevelt's Apol.* F 3 You haue..ten times as much by nimming and iuggling. **1687** T. BROWN *Saints in Uproar* Wks. 1730 I. 77 A pack of vermin, bred up to plundering of hedges, nimming of cloaks. *a* **1734** NORTH *Exam.* II. iv. §49 (1740) 256 His Employments..were forging,..nimming, stealing and all Sorts of Villainy.

nimming ('nɪmɪŋ), *ppl. a.* [f. NIM *v.* + -ING[2].]

†**1. a.** Consuming. **b.** Taking bribes. *Obs.*

c **1175** *Lamb. Hom.* 97 God is, swa paul cweð, þet niminde fur. *c* **1250** in *O.E. Misc.* 184 King þat is wilful And domesmon niminde [*v.r.* nymynde].

2. Thieving, pilfering, stealing.

1603 T. MILLINGTON *Narr. Entertainm. Jas. I*, E 2, His Majestie, hearing of this nimming gallant, directed a Warrant..to haue him hanged. *a* **1693** *Urquhart's Rabelais* III. xxxviii. 316 Nimming and Filching fool. **1727** GAY *Begg. Op.* I. i, 'Twas only Nimming Ned. **1804** COLLINS *Scripscrap* viii, Those Nimming Neds and Crook-finger'd Jacks of the typographical Tribe.

nim-nosed ('nɪmnəʊzd), *a. rare*[−1]. [f. *nim* (dial. shortening of NIMBLE *a.*) + NOSED *a.*] Quick-nosed, swift to pick up the scent.

1936 J. MASEFIELD *Let. from Pontus* 68 The keeper with his nim-nosed dog.

Nimonic (nɪ'mɒnɪk). Also **nimonic.** A proprietary name of various nickel-based alloys similar to those known by the name INCONEL.

1941 *Trade Marks Jrnl.* 9 Apr. 136/2 *Nimonic*... Cast and wrought alloys of nickel sold in the form of bars, sheets, rods,..and other shaped pieces. Henry Wiggin & Company Limited,..London,..manufacturers. **1947** *Official Gazette* (U.S. Patent Office) 22 July 529/2 Henry Wiggin & Company Limited, London, England..*Nimonic*. **1947** A. W. JUDGE *Mod. Gas Turbines* iv. 79, 1270°C (abs.)..is about the limiting value for the turbine blades when made in Nimonic 80 alloy. **1957** *Technology* Aug. 213/1 Ordinary high-temperature alloys, like the nimonics, have reached the limits of development. **1966** [see INCONEL]. **1968** [see NICHROME]. **1968** D. R. CLIFFE *Technical Metall.* xvii. 357 Nimonic 75 contains approximately 80:20 Ni:Cr, with 0·2 to 0·6% Ti and up to 0·15% C. Nimonic 80 and 80A have, in addition, 0·5–1·8% Al, and Nimonic 90 and 95 have 15–21% Co replacing nickel. **1971** *New Scientist* 25 Mar. 667/1 Scientists within the UKAEA had been studying a selection of nickel-based alloys, and in particular a nimonic alloy called PE16.

†**nimp,** *v. Obs.* [Of obscure origin: cf. Sc. and north. *nimp*, a small piece.] To nibble, bite.

13.. *Metr. Hom.* (Vernon MS.) in Herrig's *Archiv* LVII. 283 Summe nymped wiþ feet and hondes As dogges don þat gnawen heore bondes. *Ibid.*, Þo þat nymped her fingres and hendes Are Bacbyteres bitwene frendes.

nimph, obs. form of NYMPH *sb.*

‖**n'importe** (nɛ̃pɔrt), *phr.* [Fr.] It does not matter, it is immaterial.

1775 H. WALPOLE *Let.* 16 Sept. (1904) IX. 257 *N'importe*; we know many sages that take great pains to pass their time with less satisfaction. **1779** [see SOMETHING *sb.* 1 b]. **1837** DICKENS *Let.* c 14 June (1965) I. 271 This is a bad look-out, but n'importe—we will mend it. **1856** S. O. BEETON *Let.* in N. Spain *Mrs Beeton* (1948) I. vi. 97 N'importe, a little more than a month, and I hope and think you will be a happy little wife. **1909** *Manch. Guardian* 24 Nov. 10/1 Dresses by the 'Maison N'Importe' and all the rest of it. **1929** R. HUGHES *High Wind in Jamaica* vii. 149 He imagined..rescuing Rachel—or Laura, *n'importe*—from new and complicated dangers. **1952** 'M. COST' *Hour Awaits* 113 'I'm so sorry, Fanchon.' '*N'importe*! You and Albert Augustus were cut out for tight-rope walking from birth.'

'nimpy-'pimpy, *a.* ? = NIMINY-PIMINY.

1825 C. WESTMACOTT *Eng. Spy* I. 256 Confound your nimpy-pimpy lass.

Nimrod ('nɪmrɒd). Also 6 **Nemroth, -rod.** [From the name of *Nimrod* (Heb. *Nimrōd*), described in Gen. x. 8–9 as 'a mighty one in the earth' and 'a mighty hunter before the Lord'.]

†**1.** A tyrannical ruler; a tyrant. *Obs.*

1545 BALE *Image Both Ch.* I. Pref. A vj, The boistuous tirauntes of Sodoma with their great Nemroth Winchester, ..wyll sturre about them. **1599** HAKLUYT *Voy.* II. I. 309 These mighty Nimrods fled some into holes and some into mountaines. **1607** HIERON *Wks.* I. 430 The griping Nimrods of the world reioyce in their taking men vpon aduantages. **1652** OWEN *Christ's Kingdom* Wks. 1851 VIII. 373 Pouring forth sundry vials of his wrath upon great Nimrods and oppressors. **1697** COLLIER *Ess. Mor. Subj.* I. (1703) 55 These Nimrods, say they, grew great by the strength of their limbs and their vices.

2. A great hunter; one who is fond of, or given to, hunting.

1712 ADDISON *Spect.* No. 371 ¶9 As I look upon you to be the greatest Sportsman, or, if you please, the *Nimrod* among this Species of Writers. **1769** BLACKSTONE *Comm.* IV. xxxiii. 409 The game laws have raised a little Nimrod in every manor. **1780** COWPER *Progr. Err.* 86 The sportsman and his train.., the Nimrod of the neighbouring lairs. **1835** W. IRVING *Tour Prairies* 139 The deer started up.., and our young Nimrods dash off in pursuit. **1863** KEARLEY *Links in Chain* xii. 261 That modern nimrod Captain Gordon Cumming.

Hence **'Nimrodded** *ppl. a.* (see quot.). **Nim'rodian** *a.*, resembling Nimrod, esp. as a hunter; characteristic of, or connected with, Nimrod; so **Nim'rodic(al** *a.* †**'Nimrodize** *v. intr.*, to act like Nimrod; to play the tyrant.

1836 *Fraser's Mag.* XIII. 233 The worthy old bishop might be said to be regularly *Nimrodded, as the term for a well summered hunter now is. **1631** R. H. *Arraignm. Whole Creature* viii. 57 Like the *Nimrodian builders of Babell. *Ibid.* xix. 330 The great Nimroddian Hunter the Divell. **1825** *Engl. Life* I. 214 Any of my father's Nimrodian friends. **1857** BREEN *Mod. Eng. Lit.* 138 The tally-ho, or Nimrodian style..of composition consists in starting some fresh idea at the beginning of every paragraph; in losing sight of it as soon as it is started; and in pursuing in its stead the first stray conceit that turns up. **1850** *Chamb. Jrnl.* XIV. 72 The *Nimrodic passion which haunts the mind of..Gordon Cumming. **1877** DAWSON *Orig. World* xii. 260 The more eastern remnants of the Nimrodic empire. **1796** *Mod. Gulliver* 79 Horsemen and all, in grand *nimrodical display, entered the court. **1598** SYLVESTER *Du Bartas* II. ii. II. 46 If ..now contagion of corrupted dayes Leave any tract of *Nimrodizing there. **1614** C. BROOKE *Ghost Rich. III*, Poems (Grosart) 81 For a crowne who would not Nimrodize?

Nimzo-Indian (ˌnɪmzəʊ'ɪndɪən), *a. Chess.* [f. *Nimzowitsch* (see next) + INDIAN *a.*]

Designating a form of Indian defence popularized by A. Nimzowitsch, in which Black plays his king's bishop to b4 (Kt5) instead of fianchettoing it.

1935 *Chess* I. 103/1 Nimzo-Indian Defence... White simply sought to *combat* and not to *refute* the Nimzo-Indian Variation. **1957** *Griffith & White's Mod. Chess Openings* (ed. 9) 261 The Nimzowitsch-Indian Defence, 'Nimzo-Indian' for short, was first worked out in detail by Aron Nimzowitsch, the Latvian-Danish Grandmaster. **1958** *Listener* 13 Nov. 803/3 If you prefer positional play..you will probably do best to specialize in some form of the Ruy Lopez or English with White, and with the French and Nimzo-Indian Defences with Black.

Nimzowitsch ('nɪmzəʊvɪtʃ). *Chess.* Also **Nimzovitch**, etc. The name of A. *Nimzowitsch* (1886–1935), Latvian-born chess-player, used *attrib.* and in the possessive to designate various methods of opening play introduced or popularized by him.

1925 *Griffith & White's Mod. Chess Openings* (ed. 4) 57 Nimzovitch's Defence. **1932** *Ibid.* (ed. 5) 105 Nimzovitch's Attack. **1957** Nimzowitsch-Indian [see NIMZO-INDIAN *a.*]. **1961** *Times* 25 Mar. 7/2 The game started with exactly the same variation of the Nimzovitch defence that was played in the first and third games. **1972** *Times* 2 Sept. 4/3 This had started with 1.P–Q4 and had been defended by Fischer, satisfactorily enough with a Nimzowitsch defence.

†**nin**[1]. *Obs., rare*$^{-0}$. Also **ninne**. (See quots.)

1611 FLORIO, *Bombo*... Also the word that children call their drinke by, as our children say Ninne or Bibbe. *Ibid.*, *Ninna*... Also children before they can speak will call drinke so, as oures say Nin.

nin[2] (nɪn). [ad. W. *nain* grandmother.] In Liverpool working-class use: grandmother.

1958 M. KERR *People of Ship Street* 48 The granny, or 'nin', or 'nanny', or 'nanna' or 'gran' as she is often called. **1966** P. MOLONEY *Plea for Mersey* 22 Every true wacker has three relations, viz. 'Me Mar, Me Nin, an me Anti-Mury'.

nin, north. dial. f. NONE; obs. f. NINE.

†**nin-a-kin.** *Obs. rare*$^{-1}$. ? A simpleton.

1787 *Minor* IV. v. 215 The one was Father Tady M'Carthy, a nin-a-kin.

†**'nincety-'fincety.** *Obs.*$^{-1}$ A trifling matter.

1566 DRANT *Horace, Sat.* I. x. E v, Fundanus may at his good luste, of nyncetie fynceties wryte.

nincom, -cum, abbrev. forms of NINCOMPOOP.

1807–8 W. IRVING *Salmag.* (1824) 61 Got fuddled and d——d the Professors for nincoms. **18..** *Odd People in Odd Places* xii. 101 His behaviour is that of the most consummate 'nincom' that ever was led with an apron-string. *a* **1845** HOOD *To J. Hume* iv, No one but a nincum.. Would furnish such wide trousers to the Sailors. **1873** HIGGINSON *Oldport Days* vii. 167 Tell 'em about Gerty, you nincum.

nincompoop ('nɪnkəmpuːp). Forms: α. 7 (8) **nicompoop, nickumpoop.** β. 8 (9) **nincum-**, 8– **nincompoop.** [Of obscure origin; prob. only a fanciful formation. Johnson's suggestion of *non compos* does not agree with the earliest forms.] A fool, blockhead, simpleton, ninny.

α. **1676** WYCHERLEY *Pl. Dealer* II. i, Thou senseless, impertinent..Nicompoop. **1685** CROWNE *Sir C. Nice* IV. Wks. 1874 IV. 322 Ay, for me, Nickumpoop. **1694** ECHARD *Plautus* 109 Thou..hast led me by the Nose, as if I had been the meerest Nicompoop in the World.

β. **1706** PHILLIPS (ed. Kersey), *Nincumpoop* or *Nickumpoop*, a meer Blockhead, Sot or Dolt. **1713** *Guardian* No. 109 (1756) II. 106 An old Ninny hammer, a Dotard, a Nincompoop. **1764** FOOTE *Mayor of G.* I. Wks. 1799 I. 174 Trot, nincompoop. **1782** MISS BURNEY *Cecilia* v. i, No, Mr. Nincompoop,..I put them on a stall. **1807** E. S. BARRETT *Rising Sun* I. 93 Fashion, though a goddess, is a fool, and all her worshippers..are nincompoops. **1851** D. JERROLD *St. Giles* xii. 117 To make him feel a coward, a nobody, a nincompoop. **1890** JESSIE FOTHERGILL *March in Ranks* xxviii, I know how to behave without making too great a nincompoop of myself.

Hence **'nincomˌpoopery**; **'nincomˌpoophood**; **'nincomˌpoopish** *a.*

1791 H. WALPOLE *Let. to Miss Berry* 26 May, The nincompoophood of her Prince. **1879** MEREDITH *Egoist* II. i. 235 His nincompoopish idealizations..would now be annoying. **1900** *Speaker* 3 Feb. 477/1 That glorious exemplar of nincompoopery.

nincompoopiana (ˌnɪnkəmpuːpiː'ɑːna). [f. NINCOMPOOP + -IANA.] (See quots.)

1895 BEERBOHM in *Yellow Bk.* Jan. 279 Long before this time there had been in the heart of Chelsea a kind of cult of Beauty... 'Nincompoopiana' the craze was called at first, and later 'Æstheticism'. **1970** *Sunday Times* 18 Oct. 49/3 'Nincompoopiana' began in the 1880s and was triggered off by the aesthetic movement which rebelled against the pretty and the respectable, and by the 'new woman'.

nincum, variant of NINCOM.

nind, obs. form of NINTH.

nine (naɪn), *a.* and *sb.* Forms: α. 1 **niȝon, -an, -en,** (*pl.* **-one, -ona, nyȝene**), 2–3 **niȝon,** 2–4 **niȝen,** (*Orm.* **niȝhenn**), 4 **neghen, neyen, neien.** β. 3 **niȝe,** 4 **nyȝe, ne(y)ghe;** 3 **nie,** 4 **nye.** γ. 1, 3 **nione,** 3–4 **niene, nyen,** 4 **nien.** δ. 4 **neyne, neine,** 4–5 **nene,** (4 **nen**), 5 (9 *dial.*) **neen.** ε. 4 **nin,** 4–7 **nyne,** 6–7 **nyn,** 4– **nine.** [OE. *niȝon*, etc. = OFris. *nigun, niugun, -en, -in, niogen*, OS. *nigun, -on, -en*, MDu. and MLG. *negen, neghen*:—**niȝun*, a variant of the OTeut. **niwun* which is represented by OHG. *niun* (*niwan*, MHG. *niun, neun*, also *niwen, newen*, G. *neun*), Goth. *niun*, ON. *níu* (Sw. *nio*, Da. *ni*). The Indo-Eur. stem **newn* is represented in all the cognate languages, as Skr. *náva(n)*, Gr. ἐννέα, L. *novem*, OIr. *nói(n)*, OPruss. *newin-*, Lith. *devynì*, OSl. *devętĭ*, etc.] The cardinal number next after eight, represented by the symbols 9 or ix.

A. *adj.* **1. a.** In concord with sb. expressed. (Also coupled with a higher cardinal numeral, as *nine and twenty*, etc.)

α. *c* **840** *Charter* 48 in *O.E. Texts* 454 [Ic]..sile Forðrede minum ðeȝne niȝen hiȝida lond in Wudotune. *c* **900** *O.E. Chron.* (Parker MS.) an. 898 Niȝon nihtum ær middum sumere. **971** *Blickl. Hom.* 9 He þa æfter niȝan monða fæce forðeode. *c* **1055** *Byrhtferth's Handboc* in *Anglia* VIII. 300 Ȝif se monð ne þearf habban buton niȝon & twentiȝ nihta. *c* **1200** ORMIN 1051 All ennglеþeod todæledd iss O niȝhenn kinne þeode. *c* **1205** LAY. 5149 Mid nihen hundred scipene heo commen in to hauene. *c* **1320** *Sir Tristr.* 364 Niȝen woukes and mare þe mariners flet on flod. **1340** HAMPOLE *Pr. Consc.* 729 Neghen hundreth wynter man lyfed þan. *c* **1375** *Cursor M.* 9179 (Fairf.), Ezechias..regned xxx. ȝere and neyen. *a* **1400–50** *Alexander* 4810 þus drafe þai furth.. a neȝen daies euen.

β. *c* **1205** LAY. 26603 To þan wuden þrungen niȝe þusende. *a* **1225** *Ancr. R.* 328 þis beoð nu nie reisuns. **1297** R. GLOUC. (Rolls) 3862 Wiþinne a nye ȝer al þis was ydo. *a* **1400** *Octouian* 536 The wynd gan blowe swyde schylle Neyghe dayes. *c* **1400** *Chron. R. Glouc.* (Rolls) 5413 (MS. α), In þe ȝer of grace nyȝe hundred ȝer & on.

γ. **13..** *Cursor M.* 1237 (Gött.), Adam had passid nien hundred ȝer. *c* **1400** *Ibid.* 28892 (Cott. Galba), Er þare nyen pointes to se.

δ. *a* **1300** *Cursor M.* 23265 And qui þar es þaa paines nene, here nu þe skil. **13..** *Ibid.* 18632 (Gött.), His lijf was in þis werld here Neine hundreth and thritti ȝere. *c* **1400** *Destr. Troy* 2638 My fader was..of fele yeres,—To the nowmber of nene skowre. **1483** *Cath. Angl.* 251/2 Neen tymes; *novies*.

ε. *a* **1300** *Cursor M.* 1455 Nine hundret yeir and seuen. *c* **1330** R. BRUNNE *Chron. Wace* (Rolls) 1377 Nyne syþe he ȝede aboute, & kiste þe auter. **1377** LANGL. *P. Pl.* B. XVII. 58 Feith..nolde nouȝt neighen hym ny nyne londes lengthe. *c* **1440** *Promp. Parv.* 357/1 Nyne Hundryd, *nonaginti*. *c* **1475** *Rauf Coilȝear* 961 Sic tythingis come to the King within thay nyne nicht. **1535** COVERDALE *Deut.* iii. 11 His yron bed is here.., nyne cubites longe. **1593** SHAKS. *3 Hen. VI*, I. i. 112 When I was crown'd, I was but nine moneths old. **1606** G. W[OODCOCKE] *Hist. Ivstine* xi. 46 Of Alexanders host, were slaine nine footemen. **1667** DUCHESS NEWCASTLE *Life Dk. of N.* (1886) II. 86 He was now able..to buy a coach and nine horses. **1727–28** CHAMBERS *Cycl.* s.v. *Ombre*, In ombre by three, nine cards are dealt to each party. *Ibid.*, If the ombre win all the nine tricks. **1819** SHELLEY *Peter Bell 3rd* VI. xv, I looked on them nine several days, And then I saw that they were bad. **1885** *New Bk. Sports* 106 In the skittles of our fathers, nine pins were used, but of different value.

†**b.** Forming a compound ordinal number. *Obs.*

c **1100** *O.E. Chron.* (MS. D.) an. 1052 þæt wæs on þam niȝon & brittiȝæðan ȝeare. *c* **1380** WYCLIF *Wks.* (1880) 160 þe neyne & twentiþe [default]. *c* **1380** —— *Last Age Ch.* (1840) 24 þe seuynty and nyne chapitre. **1579** FULKE *Heskins's Parl.* 491 The nine and fourtieth Chapter continueth the same exposition.

2. a. With ellipse of sb., which may usually be supplied from the context.

c **950** *Lindisf. Gosp.* Luke xvii. 17 Ahne teno ȝeclænsad woeron & ða niȝona [*Rushw.* nione] huer sint. *c* **1205** LAY. 26502 Sone heom after wenden iwepnede kempen, þer sixe þer seouene, þer æhte þer niȝene. **13..** *K. Alis* 2422 So Alisaundre among heore men Sleth doun ryght by nyne and ten. *c* **1380** WYCLIF *Serm.* Sel. Wks. I. 34 Where ben oþer nyne? *c* **1400** *Laud Troy Bk.* 4500 Thei turned aȝeyn on ther fomen And sclow hem doun by nyne and ten. *c* **1470** *Gol. & Gaw.* 227 Of the nobillest be-name, noumerit of nyne. **1526** *Pilgr. Perf.* (W. de W. 1531) 146 b, All the counseyles of our lorde Jesu Chryst may be reduced to these nyne. **1590** SPENSER *F.Q.* I. Introd. ii, Helpe then, O holy virgin! chiefe of nyne. **1611** SHAKS. *Wint. T.* III. ii. 183 Fancies too weake for Boyes, too greene and idle For Girles of Nine. **1726** SWIFT *Gulliver* I. viii, I..fastened them..to nine of the Vessels which attended me. **1790** MRS. WHEELER *Westmld. Dial* (1821) 65 Thear wor neen on us set off frae this side. **1828** SCOTT *F.M. Perth* xxxiv, Thus Eachin stood in the centre of nine of the strongest men of his band. **1868** *Chambers's Encycl.* X. 172/1 The same [holds] at long whist with players who are at nine.

b. *esp.* of the hour of the day, as ***nine o'clock***, etc. Also used with ref. to the horizontal position of the hour-hand of a clock at that time. *attrib.* ***nine o'clock news***: see NEWS *sb.* (*pl.*) 5 c; also *ellipt.*

1548 ELYOT, *Nonariæ meretrices*, commune harlottes, whyche vsed at ix. [*Cooper* nyne] of the clocke..to open theyr houses. **1592** SHAKS. *Rom. & Jul.* I. i. 167 But new strooke nine. **1598** —— *Merry W.* III. v. 47 Come to her betweene eight and nine. **1693** *Phil. Trans.* XVII. 673 Sometimes the Courses, Seams or Rakes..lie at Nine a Clock, and sometimes are perpendicular, which they call.. Twelve a Clock. **1765** *Ann. Reg.* I. 135 About nine at night an extraordinary phænomenon was seen. **1842** BORROW *Bible in Spain* vii, I started at nine next morning. **1861** PATTISON *Ess.* (1889) I. 47 The gates were closed at nine o'clock. **1942** T. RATTIGAN *Flare Path* II. i. 117 Anyone hear the nine o'clock? I clean forgot the time. **1952** M. LASKI *Village* i. 11 Since the King had spoken on the nine o'clock.

attrib. **1894** *Times* 17 July 8/1 To use a rifleman's expression, it was a '9 o'clock' wind... It blew from the left side of the rifleman.

c. ***the Nine.*** (i) The nine Muses.

c **1600** SHAKS. *Sonn.* xxxviii, Be thou the tenth Muse, ten times more in worth Than those old nine which rhymers invocate. **1635** F. QUARLES *Emblemes* v. iii. 254 'Tis not the sacred wealth of all the Nine Can buy my heart from Him. **1638** LISLE *Ælfric on O. & N. Test.* (ed. 2) To Prince, Yee Nine that leaue twi-pointed Pernas hill..Into my soule your honie-dew distill. **1693** DRYDEN *Persius* (1697) 401, I.. claim no part in all the Mighty Nine. **1708** POPE *Ode St. Cecilia* 1 Descend, ye Nine! descend and sing. **1757** J. DYER *Fleece* IV. 145 My Muse..Be thou the first of the harmonious Nine From high Parnassus. **1781** COWPER *Table-T.* 184 Nor would the Nine consent the sacred tide Should purl amidst the traffic of Cheapside. **1803** [see MUSE *sb.*[1] 1]. **1852** M. ARNOLD *Empedocles on Etna* 69 'Tis Apollo comes leading His choir, The Nine. **1887** BOWEN *Virgil Ecl.* IX. 32 For I, through grace of the Nine, Poet am also. **1933** KIPLING in *Times* 23 Feb. 16/1 He called the obedient Nine to aid The varied chase. And Clio kissed.

(ii) The group of countries forming the enlarged European Economic Community between 1973 and 1981.

In 1973, Denmark, the United Kingdom, and the Republic of Ireland were admitted to join the SIX *a.* 2 j. Cf. also *the Ten* (c) s.v. TEN *a.* 2 c.

1972 *Guardian* 18 Oct. 15/3 It will be necessary for the governments of the Nine to decide what kind of Europe they want to be. **1975** *Times* 18 Apr. 6/7 Nine safeguard New Zealand dairy products... The European Commission promises a new price review for New Zealand butter and cheese. **1979** *Dædalus* Winter 83 The nations of the Nine naturally partake of the problems..of the whole Western developed world.

d. ***nine-to-five, nine-till-five***, used *attrib.* (*a*) of a person working between 9 a.m. and 5 p.m.; so ***nine-to-fiver, nine-till-fiver***; (*b*) of an occupation pursued between these hours, or of the mentality concerned with such an occupation, or with work only between such hours. So *nine-to-five (it)* v., to work between such hours.

1959 *Manch. Guardian* 16 June 5/1 These people are just workers like everybody else.. they're all nine-to-fivers. 1960 *News Chron.* 13 Sept. 4/5 An electronic computer, working the nine-to-five shift. 1960 F. Raphael *Limits of Love* i. vi. 80 What do you want him to be? A nine till fiver? 1961 *Oxf. Mag.* 4 May 318/2 The so called '9 to 5' atmosphere and routine. 1962 R. Cook *Crust on its Uppers* i. 25 The game we play, it's got its risks, but it's.. better than nine-to-fiving it. 1965 *Listener* 10 June 856/2 Some 60 per cent. of the students are home-based—a statistic to which the president of the students' union attributes nine-till-five attitudes. 1966 O. Norton *School of Liars* i. 19 'I hate having my corn measured by someone else's bushel. Especially when it's a tinpot suburban bushel. The nine-to-five world.' That amused him. 'But you're a nine-to-fiver's wife.' 1969 *Times* 13 Mar. 20/3 (Advt.), 9 to 5 men come cheaper by the dozen. 1972 *Nature* 25 Feb. 412/3 The contract people tend to be exclusively '9 to 5' scientists whereas the scientists on grants have the traditional university attitude of ignoring the clock. 1972 F. Warner *Lying Figures* ii. 9, I couldn't stand a nine-to-fiver. 1975 P. G. Winslow *Death of Angel* i. 41 Wants a nine to five... That's her type, not a policeman coming in at all hours.

3. In special applications.

See also cat *sb.*[1] 13 b, order *sb.* 5, worthy *sb.*, etc.

a. In references to the time (*nine days* or *nights*) during which a novelty is proverbially said to attract attention. (Cf. 4 b.)

c 1374 Chaucer *Troylus* iv. 588 Ek wonder last but nine nyght nevere in towne. 1546 J. Heywood *Prov.* (1867) 90 This wonder lasted nine daies. 1579 Lyly *Euphues* (Arb.) 205 The greatest wonder lasteth but nine daies. 1600 Shaks. *A.Y.L.* iii. ii. 180, I was seuen of the nine daies out of the wonder, before you came. 1606 Bp. Hall *Medit. & Vows* iii. §18. 41 So those things.. shall be wonders to me; and that not for nine dayes, but for euer.

†**b.** *nine ways (at thrice)*, asquint, askew.

1542 Udall tr. *Erasm. Apoph.* (1877) 203 Squyntyied he was, and looked nyne wayes. 1649 G. Daniel *Trinarch., Rich. II*, 326 Passion flyes Squinting, and, as wee say, Nine wayes at Thrice.

c. *nine times* (etc.) *out of ten*, in the great majority of cases, as a rule.

1809 Malkin *Gil Blas* i. v. ⁋7 They.. nine times out of ten flogged me for nothing. *a* 1845 Hood *The Run-over*, It would have been a quietus for nine men out of ten. 1879 Mrs. A. E. James *Ind. Househ. Managem.* 43 In nine cases out of ten you will not find your confidence misplaced.

d. *nine points*: (see possession).

1880 Mrs. Lynn Linton *Rebel of Family* ix, 'You have it in your possession still'. 'My nine points? Rather shaky ones, I fear.'

4. a. Combined with sbs., forming attributive compounds, as *nine-feet*, *-foot*, *-hole*, *-hour*, *-inch*, *-knot*, *-mile*, *-pound*, *-share*, *-shillings*; also *nine-year-old* sb. and adj.

1828 P. Cunningham *N.S. Wales* (ed. 3) II. 299 A *nine-feet promenade is amply sufficient. 1897 P. Warung *Tales Old Regime* 81 The *nine-foot chain before mentioned. 1894 *Westm. Gaz.* 17 Nov. 7/1 A *nine-hole course has been laid out at Gavarnie. 1897 *Daily News* 13 July 8/5 A *nine-hour day is not so long as to be exhausting to a man. 1765 *Ann. Reg.* i. 103 All narrow wheels are to pay one-half toll more than the *nine-inch wheels. 1819 Shelley *Peter Bell 3rd* vi. xx, High trotting over nine-inch bridges. 1853 R. S. Hawker *Wks.* (1893) 28 There's a *nine-knot breeze above. 1780 *New Newgate Cal.* V. 139 Near the *nine-mile stone on the Hounslow-road. 1822–53 De Quincey *Confess.* Wks. 1853 I. 131 An easy nine-mile walk. 1711 *Lond. Gaz.* No. 4906/2, I had two *Nine pound Shots through my Fore-mast. 1893 J. Watson *Conf. Poacher* 63 She failed to jump a stone fence, with a nine-pound hare in her mouth. 1837 *Penny Cycl.* IX. 96/1 The *nine-share plough, or scarifier, has been found very useful in the light soils. 1683 Tryon *Way to Health* 340 Let your Drink at Meals be no stronger than *nine shillings Beer. 1828 Moir *Mansie Wauch* xi. 98 We.. read away like *nine-year-aulds. 1853 Miss Yonge *Heir of Redclyffe* xxxix, A long, thin, nine-year old child.

b. *nine days' wonder*, etc., applied to an event or thing of temporary interest. (Cf. 3 a.)

1594 *Spanish Trag.* iv. in Hazl. *Dodsley* V. 97 Which as a nine-days' wonder, being o'erblown. 1602 *How a Man*, etc. iv. ii. in *Old Eng. Dram.* (1824) 75 Her timeless death Is but a nine days' talk. 1625 Massinger *New Way* iv. ii, That were but nine days' wonder. 1764 Churchill *Ghost* iii. 547 He would be found.. A nine days' wonder at the most. 1818 Byron *Juan* i. clxxxviii, The nine days' wonder which was brought to light. 1861 Hughes *Tom Brown at Oxf.* xlii, His escape on the night of the riot had been a nine-days' wonder.

c. *nine-hours' day*: a working day of nine hours. So *nine-hours' movement*. Cf. *nine-hour*, sense 4 a.

1859 *Times* 5 Aug. 3/3 It appears that the 'Conference of the United Building Trades'.. is established for the special purpose of carrying the nine hours' movement. 1862 *Leisure Hour* 28 June 413/2 They agreed upon an effort to shorten working time, and fixed upon a nine-hours' day. The phrase includes nine hours' *actual* work.

5. a. In parasynthetic adjs., as *nine-banded*, *-circled*, *-cornered*, *-jointed*, *-lived*, *-spotted*, *-stringed*, *-tailed*, *-voiced*.

1909 *Biol. Bull.* XVII. 181 (*title*) A case of normal identical quadruplets in the *nine-banded armadillo [sc. *Dasypus novemcinctus*]. 1964 G. Durrell *Menagerie Manor* i. 34 The nine-banded armadillo.. trots about his cage. 1851 C. L. Smith tr. *Tasso* xviii. xlviii, Its grand *nine-circled stream opaque. 1809 W. Irving *Knickerb.* iv. iii, Some dozen huge, misshapen, *nine-cornered Dutch oaths. 1839 *Penny Cycl.* XV. 84/2 The antennæ.. are *nine-jointed. 1600 S. Nicolson *Acolastus* (1876) 46 Loue is *nine-liu'd; kill him ne'er so much, The Wanton Boy reuiueth with a tutch. 1861 *Trans. Illinois Agric. Soc.* IV. 347, I found numerous specimens of a *nine-spotted lady-bird (*Coccinella novemnotata*, Herbst,) under dry cow-dung. 1972 Swan & Papp *Common Insects N. Amer.* xx. 410 Nine-spotted lady beetle... In California.. they are heavy feeders on aphids in alfalfa. *a* 1649 Drumm. of Hawth. *Poems* Wks. (1711) 2/2 By the soft Touches of the *Nine-string'd Heaven. 1786 Burns *Ordination* xi, Hark, how the *nine-tail'd cat she plays! 1585 Jas. I *Ess. Poesie* (Arb.) 25 Her *nynevoced mouth resembled into sound The daunce harmonious making heauen resound.

b. In parasynthetic sbs., as *nine-pounder*.

1747 B. Robins *Prop. incr. Strength Navy* 8 Very lately the Six Pounders in some of the smaller Ships have been changed for Nine Pounders. 1834–47 J. S. Macaulay *Field Fortif.* (1851) 18 Supposing them to be armed with nine-pounders. 1876 Bancroft *Hist. U.S.* VI. xli. 242 Jones could only use three nine-pounders.

6. In special combs. (attrib. or absolute), as **nine-bark (spice or syringa)**, an American shrub, *Spiræa opulifolia*, having many layers of loose bark; **nine-days disease** (see quot.); †**nine-double**, ninefold; **nine-men's morris**: see morris; **nine-pegs**, **ninepins**; **nine-point(s) circle** (see quot. 1865); †**nine-worthiness**, valour like that of the nine worthies.

1796 Morse *Amer. Geog.* I. 576 Plum trees, *nine bark spice, and leather wood bushes. 1847 Darlington *Amer. Weeds* (1860) 120 A very showy ornamental species... Sometimes called 'Nine-Bark Syringa'. 1859 Bartlett *Dict. Amer.* (ed. 2), *Nine-bark*, a low shrub found in Maine, Canada [etc.]. Its old bark is loose, and separates in thin layers. 1799 Underwood *Diseases Children* (ed. 4) I. 159 A disorder, whose attack being within the first nine days after birth, has been denominated the *nine-days disease. 1598 Florio, *Nonoplo*, nine-fold, *nine double. 1675 Cotton *Burlesque upon B.* 56 Playing at *Nine peggs with such heat That mighty Jupiter did sweat. 1883 *Nature* XXVII. 607 In place of the well known '*nine-point' circle.. would not 'mid-point' circle be equally expressive? 1865 Brande & Cox *Dict. Sci.*, etc. I. 461 The circle which passes through the middle points of the sides of a triangle is referred to by Continental writers as 'the *nine-points circle'. 1663 Butler *Hud.* i. ii. 113 The Foe, for dread Of your *Nine-Worthiness, is fled.

B. *sb.* **1.** The abstract number nine; the figure or symbol representing this.

1398 Trevisa *Barth. De P.R.* xix. cxxii. (1495) 922 One addyd or putte to eyghte makyth the nombre of nyne. *a* 1400 in Halliwell *Rara Mathem.* 31 The figure of nyne that hath this schape 9. 1588 Shaks. *L.L.L.* v. ii. 488 Three times thrice is nine. 1611 Florio, *Nonarie*, of nine. 1798 Hutton *Course Math.* I. 10 Add the figures.. and find how many nines are contained in their sum.—Reject those nines, and set down the remainder. 1870 Sonnenschein & Nesbitt *Sci. & Art Arith.* i. xi. 132 Any number is an exact number of nines + the sum of its digits.

2. a. *Cards.* A card marked with nine pips. *nine of diamonds*: see curse *sb.* 4 c.

1599 Minsheu *Percival's Sp. Dict.* s.v. *Malilla*, a carde picked out and agreed vpon,.. that he that hath him may make him king, queene, knaue, ace, ten, nine. &c. 1680 Cotton *Compl. Gamester* (ed. 2) 77 Suppose you have in your hand a Nine and two Sixes. 1727–38 Chambers *Cycl.* s.v. *Ombre*, The whole ombre pack being only 40, by reason the eights, nines, and tens, are thrown aside. 1868 *Chambers's Encycl.* X. 173 Dropping the nine, and holding queen and knave.

b. A set of nine persons, players, etc.

a 1860 Alb. Smith *Med. Stud.* (1861) 69 A student.. assures him that.. the examiners never pluck two nines running. 1860 Campbell *Tales W. Highlands* (1892) III. 375 He could kill nine nines backwards with his sword. 1871 Cutting *Stud. Life at Amherst* 113 In 1866, the College Ball Club.. played against the 'Nine' of Brown University.

3. a. A shoe, or foot, of the ninth size.

1599 Minsheu *Percival's Sp. Gram.* 81 The.. size of shooes, as nines, tens, &c. 1607 Tourneur *Rev. Trag.* v. i, Courtiers haue feete a' th' nines & tongues a' th' twellues.

b. A thing or person marked or distinguished by the number nine.

1888 H. Morten *Hospital Life* 30 Voices repeat the fact.. that 'Nine' is going to be sent away for a change.

4. *long nine*: **a.** A nine-pounder gun.

1799 *Hull Advertiser* 19 Oct. 2/4 Corvette.. of thirty-two guns, twenty-four long nines. 1836 Marryat *Midsh. Easy* xxxviii, A couple of long brass nines. 1883 Stevenson *Treas. Isl.* xvii, We had entirely forgotten the long nine.

b. *U.S.* A kind of cigar. (See also long nine.)

1837 Hawthorne *Twice-told T.* (1849) vi. 59 The pedler .. having sold him many a bunch of long nines, and a great deal of pig-tail, lady's twist, and fig tobacco. 1858 O. W. Holmes *Aut. Breakf.-t.* ii. (1895) 51 Stable-boys smoking long-nines.

5. *nine point two*, a gun having a calibre of 9·2 inches.

1898 Kipling in *Morning Post* 10 Nov. 5/2 You'd need a nine point two to do that properly.

6. †**a.** *upon the nines*, ? at once. *Obs. rare*$^{-1}$.

c 1560 A. Scott *Poems* (S.T.S.) iv. 92 The moir degest and grave, The grydiar to grip it; The nycest to ressave, Vpon the nynis will nip it.

b. *(up) to the nines* (rarely *nine*), to perfection, to the highest degree or point.

1787 Burns *Answ. to Verses* v, 'Twad please me to the nine. *a* 1793 —— *Past. Poetry* vii, Thou paints auld Nature to the nines. 1821 Galt *Ayrsh. Legatees* xxv, He's such a funny man, and touches off the Londoners to the nines! 1836 Haliburton *Clockm.* (1862) 61 Praisin a man's farm to the nines. 1859 Hotten *Dict. Slang* 68 *Nines*, 'dressed up to the *nines*', in a showy or recherché manner. 1863 Reade *Hard Cash* I. 203 Being clad in snowy cotton and japanned to the nine. 1876 T. Hardy *Ethelberta* (1890) 3 When she's dressed up to the nines for some grand party. 1928 Galsworthy *Swan Song* i. viii. 63 Women then were defended up to the nines. 1963 N. C. E. Kenrick *Story Wiltshire Regiment* ix. 86 The 99th's sartorial perfection at this time [*c* 1850] is said to have given rise to the expression 'Dressed up to the nines' as the other Regiments in Aldershot were constantly trying to achieve the same standard. 1965 *Listener* 20 May 742/2 So there they are, whenever a concert is given by their own orchestra, dressed up to the nines and bursting with pride.

c. *nine-nine-nine*, a telephone number dialled in an emergency in order to obtain a connection to the ambulance service, fire brigade, police, etc.; also written *999*.

1937 *Rep. Proc. 14th Conf. ASLIB* 76 The first burglar caught by dialling 999—the new telephone alarm signal. 1939 G. Greene *19 Stories* (1947) 159 He chose.. a telephone box and dialled.. 999. 1954 I. Murdoch *Under Net* x. 136 'Better call the police if you ask me.'.. 'You go and dial nine nine nine.' 1954 M. Procter *Hell is City* i. i. 16, I stopped.. and dialled nine-nine-nine. *a* 1956 W. de la Mare *Compl. Poems* (1969) 713 Dial 999, and gain at once, Safety from fire, police and ambulance. 1966 'W. Haggard' *Power House* viii. 89 She staggered to the telephone.. dialled Nine Nine Nine. 1966 'A. York' *Eliminator* v. 85 Should something happen to him I don't see Lucinda dialling Nine-Nine-Nine. 1973 *Express* (Trinidad & Tobago) 17 Mar. 10/4 We have introduced the 999 system with four cars to cover Morvant, San Juan and Santa Cruz areas. 1974 'M. Innes' *Appleby's Other Story* vii. 55 He put through a 999 call to the police.

nine-eyed (ˈnaɪnaɪd), *a.* Having nine eyes.

†**1.** As an opprobrious epithet. *Obs. rare.*

1694 Echard *Plautus* Pref. A 3, I'll fetch ye out.. for a damnable, prying, nine-ey'd Witch. 1703 Farquhar *Inconstant* ii. ii, You son of a nine-eyed whore, d'ye come to abuse me?

2. *nine-eyed eel*, the lamprey. *Sc.*

1810 Neill *List Fishes* 30 (Jam.), Lesser Lamprey... The popular name Nine-eyed-eel arises from the spiracles being taken for eyes. 1838 Johnston in *Proc. Berw. Nat. Club* I. vi. 176 Sea-Lamprey. The Nine-eyed Eel.

So **nine-eyes.** *dial.* (*a*) The lamprey. (*b*) The butterfish (*Gunnellus vulgaris*).

Cf. MDu. *neghenoghe* (Du. *negenoog*), MLG. *negenoge* (hence Da. *negenöie*, Sw. *nejonöga*), OHG. *niunouga* (MHG. *-ouge*, G. *neunauge*).

(*a*) 1841 Hartshorne *Salop. Ant.* 517 Nine-eyes, the *Ammocætes branchialis* of Naturalists, so called from having a number of spiracles on each side, or branchial orifices in a lateral groove. 1880–4 [see nine-holes 3]. 1896 tr. *Boas' Text Bk. Zool.* 382 The Nine-eyes of Lampreys.. have a circular sucking mouth with horny teeth.

(*b*) 1863 Couch *Brit. Fishes* II. 236 Butterfish. Swordick, Gunnel, Nine eyes. 1879 Satchell *Gloss. Fish Names* 5 *Blennius gunnellus*, Butter-fish.., Nine-eyes.

ninefold (ˈnaɪnfəʊld), *a.*, *sb.*, and *adv.* [f. nine + -fold. Cf. MDu. *neghenvout* (Du. *negenvoud*), MLG. *negenvalt*, MHG. *niunvalt*.]

A. *adj.* **1.** Nine times as great or numerous.

c 1000 Ælfric *Gram.* xlix. (Z.) 285 *Nouenarius* niȝonfeald. 1557 Recorde *Whetst.* B ij, *Noncupla.* 9 to 1: 18 to 2.. Ninefolde. 1598 Florio, *Nonoplo*, nine-fold, nine double. 1817 Shelley *Rev. Islam* viii. xxi. 7 On all beside It turns with ninefold rage. *a* 1845 Hood *The United Family* xxii, A ninefold woe remains behind. 1892 *Pall Mall G.* 10 June 2/1 A ninefold fine should be exacted.

2. Consisting of nine folds or parts. Also (with sb. in *pl.*): Nine in number.

1594 Greene & Lodge *Looking Gl.* G.'s Wks. (Rtldg.) 129/2 Thy wickedness hath.. pierced through nine-fold orbs of heaven. 1598 Sylvester *Du Bartas* ii. i. iii. *Furies* 269 Th' ever-shaking nine-fold steely bars Of Stygian Bridge. 1629 Milton *Hymn Nativ.* xiii, With your ninefold harmony Make up full consort to th' Angelike symphony. 1667 —— *P.L.* ii. 436 This huge convex of Fire.. immures us round Ninefold. 1807 Crabbe *Par. Reg.* i. 93 Who simple truth with nine-fold reasons back. 1843 Carlyle *Past & Pr.* (1858) 102 The ninefold Stygian Marshes. 1854 Whittier *To Chas. Sumner* 9 He, for whom the ninefold Muses sang. 1896 Kipling *Seven Seas, Song of the English*, Draw now the threefold knot firm on the ninefold bands.

Comb. *c* 1590 Greene *Fr. Bacon* xv, When every charmer with his magic spell Calls us from nine-fold trenched Phlegethon.

B. *sb.* †**1.** An amount nine times as great.

1602 Fulbecke *Pandects* 80 If a thing of good value be taken awaie, they must render the nine-folde.

2. An attendant set of nine.

1605 Shaks. *Lear* iii. iv. 126 He met the Night-Mare, and her nine-fold. 1814 Scott *Wav.* xiii, On Hallow-Mass Eve the Night-Hag will ride, And all her nine-fold sweeping on by her side.

C. *adv.* To nine times the number.

1849 Macaulay *Hist. Eng.* iii. I. 286 In Lancashire the number of inhabitants appears to have increased nine-fold.

nine-holes.

1. a. A game in which the players endeavour to roll small balls into nine holes made in the ground, each hole having a separate scoring value. **b.** A similar game played with a board having nine holes or arches.

For a detailed account of the games see Strutt *Sports & Past.* (1801) 204–5 and the *Eng. Dial. Dict.*

1573 *New Custom* i. i. in Hazl. *Dodsley* III. 9 Playing at quoits or nine-holes, or shooting at butts. 1589 Greene *Menaphon* (Arb.) 56, Boies, that fell vpon one of their fellowes, and beate him most cruelly for playing false playe at nine holes. 1612 Drayton *Poly-olb.* xiv. 22 The vnhappy wags, which let their Cattell stray, At Nine-holes on the heath whilst they together play. 1648 Herrick *Hesper.*, *Upon Raspe*, Raspe plays at nine-holes; and t'is known he gets Many a teaster by his game, and bets. 1751 R. Paltock *P. Wilkins* xlv, One [game] like our bowls on a bowling-green, and at one somewhat like nine-holes. 1801 Strutt *Sports & Past.* iii. vii. 205, I have formerly seen a pastime practised by School-boys, called nine-holes. 1854 Miss Baker *Northampt. Gloss.*, Nine-holes, or Trunks.

attrib. 1593 G. Harvey *Pierce's Super.* 73 In time he may haply learne to play at nine hole nidgets. 1688 Holme

Armoury III. xvi. (Roxb.) 67/2 He beareth sable, a 9 Hole Board or, edged and linned of the first.

c. *in the nine-hole(s*: in a difficulty. *U.S.*

1863 'E. KIRKE' *My Southern Friends* 76 He owned har [*sc.* a slave] till he got in the nineholes one day, and sold har to the Gin'ral. **1877** *Congress. Rec.* 3 Nov. 230/1 We have put the gentleman in the 'nine-holes'; and there we intend to keep him. **1890** *Ibid.* 12 June 6002/1 The bill..has passed the Senate, and, to use a Western expression, it will put me 'in the nine-hole' if I do not get it through. **1906** B. L. RIDLEY *Battles & Sk. Army Tennessee* 295 The only time he ever got Johnston apparently in 'a nine hole' was at Resaca, on May 15, 1864.

2. *Sc.* 'That piece of beef that is cut out immediately below the brisket or breast, denominated from the vacancies left by the ribs' (Jam. 1825).

1842 J. AITON *Domest. Econ* (1857) 98 For boiling pieces of beef, the runner, the nineholes, and the breast are the best. **1844** STEPHENS *Bk. Farm* II. 169 The nineholes.. consists of layers of fat and lean without any bone.

3. The lamprey.

a **1825** FORBY *Voc. E. Anglia, Nine-holes*, a fish of the lamprey kind, not uncommon in our Fen ditches. **1880–4** DAY *Fishes Gt. Brit.* II. 360 Lampern,..nine-eyes, nine-holes, the eye and nasal orifice appear to be here counted.

'nine-killer. [A transl. of Du. *negendooder* or G. *neuntödter*.] The butcher bird or shrike (*Lanius excubitor* or *L. borealis*).

[**1678** RAY *Willughby's Ornith.* 87 In other parts of Germany it is called Neghen-doer, that is, Nine-killer.] **1801** *Nat. Hist.* in *Ann. Reg.* 442/2 Why is this bird of prey called the Nine-killer? **1808** A. WILSON *Amer. Ornith.* I. 77 Mr. Heckewelder..appears..to have been unacquainted that grasshoppers were, in fact, the favorite food of this Nine-killer. **1859** BARTLETT *Dict. Amer.* (ed. 2), *Nine-killer*, the popular name of the Northern Butcher-bird. **1866** *Fam. Her.* 511 The bird called a nine-killer is an arithmetician.

So †**nine-murder(er.** *Obs.* [LG. *negen-*, G. *neunmörder*.]

1544 TURNER *Avium Præcip.* I 5 b, *Tyrannus*, a nyn murder. **1565** COOPER *Thesaurus* s.v. *Molliceps*, a birde of bodie no bigger then a thrush... Some thinke a shrike or nyn murder. **1598** FLORIO, *Regéstola*, a kind of lanaret hawke called a shreeke or nine murtherer. **1611** COTGR., *Poul*,..the Ninmurder, a yellowish bird, and the smallest of birds.

ninepence ('naɪnpəns).

1. a. The sum of nine pence. Also in phrases, esp. *as neat*, etc., *as ninepence*.

to bring a noble to ninepence: see NOBLE *sb.*

1546 [see SHILLING 5]. **1606** *Proclam.* in Ruding *Coinage* (1840) I. 364 The said Harp Shillings should have..the name and value only of twelve Pence Irish,..being in true value no more than nine Pence English. **1607** DEKKER & WEBSTER *Sir Thos. Wyatt* W.'s Wks. (Rtldg.) 197/2 Henceforth the Harpers for his sake, shall stand But for plain ninepence throughout all the land. **1607** R. C. tr. *Estienne's World of Wonders* xv. 81 Hauing brought their twelue-pence to nine-pence, and their nine-pence to nothing. **1659** J. HOWELL *Eng. Proverbs* 11/1 As fine as fippence, as neat as nine pence. **1670** J. RAY *Coll. Eng. Proverbs* 206 As like as nine pence to nothing. *a* **1704** T. BROWN tr. *Æneas Sylvius Lett.* lxxxii. Wks. (1709) III. II. 80 The Devil and nine Pence go with her, that's Money and Company. **1850** F. E. SMEDLEY *Frank Fairlegh* l. 444 Well, let her say 'no' as if she meant it,..and then it will all be as right as ninepence. **1857** *Blackw. Mag.* LXXXI. 397 If I didn't see him whip a picture out of its frame, as neat as ninepence. **1865** DICKENS *Mut. Fr.* I. ix, As grand as ninepence. **1881** in *Lanc. Gloss.* s.v. *Hondrunnin*, He'd feight the whole lot on 'em,..as easy as ninepence. **1884** *Temple Bar* Aug. 525 The trick of alliteration if often useful to give point to old proverbs. In such familiar sayings as 'fine as fivepence', 'nice as ninepence', 'to lie by the legend', its importance is most curious. **1890** 'R. BOLDREWOOD' *Col. Reformer* (1891) 106, I thought I was as right as ninepence. **1968** 'C. AIRD' *Henrietta Who?* iv. 37 A rare old state it was in..but your mother..had it right as ninepence in next to no time.

b. (*nobbut, no more than*) *ninepence in the shilling*: of imperfect intelligence, mentally retarded. *dial.* and *colloq.*

1889 E. PEACOCK *Gloss. Words Manley & Corringham, Lincolnshire* (ed. 2) 370 *Nine-pence-to-the-shilling*, below the average in common sense. 'How's Mr..? Thaay do saay as he's nobut nine-pence-to-th'-shilling.'—M. F., *Scotton*, 1876. **1951** J. B. PRIESTLEY *Festival at Farbridge* III. ii. 521 She's got a husband who's..ninepence in the shilling, a bit barmy. **1957** M. KENNEDY *Heroes of Clone* II. iii. 97 She's ninepence in the shilling. **1964** 'A. GILBERT' *Fingerprint* v. 77 While they might be sympathetic, it was more likely they thought her child no more than ninepence in the shilling.

2. A coin of the value of nine pence. *nimble ninepence*: see NIMBLE *a.* 3 d.

In former English use applied to the Irish shilling, which passed current for ninepence (see quots. 1606–7 above). In the United States a name for the Spanish real.

1663 BUTLER *Hud.* I. I. 487 Like Commendation Nine-pence crookt With—To and from my Love—it lookt. **1679** *Exec. Bury* 6 They had an Art to make a Nine-pence or Groat just new made, look as if it had been Coined these hundred years. **1706** *Lond. Gaz.* No. 4234/5 Several old Nine-Pences and old Shillings, and many Milled Pence. **1722** DE FOE *Col. Jack* (1840) 46 With ninepences, and fourpence-halfpennies,..Scotch and Irish coin. **1812** BYRON *Waltz* xiii. *note*, A new ninepence—a creditable coin now forthcoming, worth a pound, in paper, at the fairest calculation. **1860** O. W. HOLMES *Poet Breakf.-t.* iii, Give me two fo'pencehappenies for a ninepence.

ninepenny ('naɪnpənɪ), *sb.* and *a.*

A. *sb.* **1.** A coin equal in value to nine pennies.

1830 SCOTT *Demonol.* iv. 138, I have several pieces to show, consisting of ninepennies, thirteen-pence-halfpennies.

2. Ale that costs ninepence a gallon.

1886 HARDY *Mayor of Casterbridge* I. xiii. 160 I'm in such a low key with drinking nothing but small table ninepenny this last week or two.

B. *adj.* **1.** Valued at or costing ninepence.

1894 *Outing* XXIV. 371/1 At Wrexham I passed the night in a nine-penny room. **1898** *Westm. Gaz.* 16 Feb. 3/1 A customer enters his shop and asks for ninepenny butter.

2. *ninepenny marl* = nine men's morris.

1826 HONE *Every-day Bk.* II. 983 There is an ancient game, played by the 'shepherds of Salisbury Plain,'..called 'Ninepenny Marl'.

ninepins ('naɪnpɪnz), *sb. pl.* [PIN *sb.*[1] 8.]

1. A game in which nine 'pins' are set up to be knocked down by a ball or bowl thrown at them.

1580 HOLLYBAND *Treas. Fr. Tong, Quilles*, as *iouër aux quilles*, to play at nine pins. **1610** BEAUM. & FL. *Scornf. Lady* IV. i, Thy dry bones can reach at nothing now, but gords or nine-pinnes. **1647** PEACHAM *Worth of a Penny* 31 The most ordinary recreations of the Countrey are football, skales or nine pins, shooting at butts [etc.]. **1663** PEPYS *Diary* 27 May, Afterwards to nine-pins, Creed and I playing against my Lord and Cooke. **1712** ARBUTHNOT *John Bull* I. iv, You Sot,..you spend your Time at Billiards, Ninepins, or Puppet-shows. **1774** *Westm. Mag.* II. 315 Swains appeared in fancy dresses, amusing themselves at the game of Ninepins. **1829** CARLYLE *Misc.* (1857) II. 4 A little boy was playing nine-pins on the streets of Mentz. **1856** 'STONEHENGE' *Brit. Rural Sports* 511 Skittles, nine pins, and Dutch pins, are modifications of the same game.

2. The pins with which this game is played; also in *sing.* of one of these.

1664 BUTLER *Hud.* II. i. 488 As when Merchants break, o'erthrown Like Nine-pins, they strike others down. **1691** J. WILSON *Belphegor* IV. iv, 'Tis a wonder, no more follow him: for it is often with Merchants, as Nine-Pins. **1697** DAMPIER *Voy.* (1699) 165 Some of these Trees..being big-bellied like Nine-pins. **1794** [see 3]. **1807** CRABBE *Par. Reg.* I. 661 The bowl that beats the greater number down Of tottering nine-pins. **1819** SCOTT *Ivanhoe* xli, When his holiness rolled on the green like a king of the nine-pins. **1864** G. MUSGRAVE *Ten Days in Fr. Parsonage* II. iii. 108 Little urchins.. tumbled about like ninepins.

b. Humorously applied to a child.

1862 MRS. H. WOOD *Channings* II. xix. 289 Little ninepins, would you like to get three-pence?

3. *attrib.* and *Comb.*, as *ninepin alley*, *yard*; *ninepin high*, *-like* adjs.; **ninepin block**, *Naut.* a block so called from its shape.

?**1756** WALPOLE *Lett. to Bentley* Aug., The bowling-green ..contains no less than four obelisks, as look like a Brobdignag *nine-pin-ally. **1758** JOHNSON *Idler* No. 28. ¶4 An alehouse.., with a ninepin alley. **1794** *Rigging & Seamanship* 156 **Nine-pin-blocks*. The shells..resemble the shape of a nine-pin... They are used to lead the running ropes in a horizontal direction. **1841** DANA *Seaman's Man.* 116 *Ninepin Block*, a block in the form of a ninepin, used for a fair leader in the rail. **1710** *Brit. Apollo* No. 100. 2/2 Little dirty Brats scarce *Nine-pin high. **1704** *Phil. Trans.* XXV. 1547 The *Nine-pin like Particles. **1709** *Lond. Gaz.* No. 4525/3 Bowling-Greens, and *Nine-pin Yards.

niner ('naɪnə(r)). *rare.* [-ER[1].] **1.** A criminal who is sentenced to imprisonment for nine years.

1897 WARUNG *Tales Old Regime* 219 Pedder was a 'sevener', Blake was a 'niner'.

2. Formerly, a senior naval cadet in the training-ship *Britannia*.

1914 'BARTIMEUS' *Naval Occasions* ix. 63 Jerry had to submit to strange indignities and stranger torments at the hands of Olympian 'Niners' (Fourth-term Cadets).

'ninesome, *sb.* and *a.* [f. NINE *a.* + -SOME.]

a. *sb.* A set of nine. **b.** *adj.* Consisting of nine.

?*a* **1400** *Morte Arth.* 523 Thy nedes..I notifiede myselfene, Be-fore þat noble of name and neynesome of kynges. **1887** SERVICE *Life Dr. Duguid* 224 She had an auchtsome or a ninesome family.

nineted ('naɪntɪd), *a. dial.* [var. of NOINTED.] Wicked, incorrigible.

a **1809** J. PALMER *Like Master* (1811) I. ii. 19 So prone to mischief, that his supposed aunt declared, 'it was beyond her to manage him—he was a nineted one'. **1841** HARTSHORNE *Salop. Ant.* 517 'A nineted youth', a youngster who is wicked and wilful.

nineteen (naɪn'tiːn, 'naɪntiːn), *a.* (and *sb.*) Forms: *α.* **1 nihȝon-, niȝontyne, 3 niȝen-, nien-, 3–4 neȝen-, 5 nyentene.** *β.* **3 nintene, 4 nynten, ninetene, nenteyn, 4, 6 nyn(e)tene, 6 nyne-, 7 nineteene, 7– nineteen.** [OE. *niȝontýne* = OFris. *niogentena*, *niugenten*, OS. *nigen-*, *nichentein*, MDu. and Du. *negentien*, OHG. *niunzehan*, *-zên* (MHG. *niunzehen*, G. *neunzehn*), ON. *nítján* (Sw. *nitton*, Da. *nitten*): see NINE and TEN.] The cardinal number composed of ten and nine, represented by 19 or xix.

1. In concord with sb. expressed.

α. *a* **1000** *Menologium* 71 Embe nihȝontyne niht þæs þe Easter monað to us cymeð. *c* **1055** *Byrhtferth's Handboc* in *Anglia* VIII. 300 He yrnð niȝontyne gear eall swa se oðer. *c* **1380** *Sir Ferumb.* 2699 Kyng heruer of Goran þe vitailes hadde y-sent..Be neȝentene vitaillers.

β. *c* **1330** R. BRUNNE *Chron. Wace* (Rolls) 14824 Mayster Edmond seis,..þat þe Engle hadde nynetene sones. *c* **1375** *Sc. Leg. Saints* xxii. (*Laurence*) 220 He baptist is þene, & of his nynten best men. **1603** SHAKS. *Meas. for M.* I. ii. 172 So long, that nineteene Zodiacks haue gone round. **1632** LITHGOW (*title*) The Totall Discourse of the rare Adventures..of long nineteen yeares Travayles from Scotland. **1770** BURKE *Pres. Discont.* Wks. II. 310 It was not untill he had reigned nineteen years. **1861** MILL *Utilit.* ii. 22 Happiness is done without involuntarily by nineteen-twentieths of mankind. **1892** E. REEVES *Homeward Bound* 277 The nineteen doors facing the court of oranges.

Comb. **1897** *Westm. Gaz.* 13 Dec. 9/2 Nineteen-day accounts on the Stock Exchange are proverbially wearisome affairs.

2. a. With ellipsis of sb., which may usually be supplied from context.

c **1205** LAY. 1850 þa niȝentene [*c* **1275** neȝentene] heo slowen. **1297** R. GLOUC. (Rolls) 10646 Tuelf hundered as in ȝer of grace & nintene, ich vnderstonde. *c* **1385** CHAUCER *L.G.W.* Prol. 186, I saw cominge of ladyes nyntene. **1426** LYDG. *De Guil. Pilgr.* 17730, I selle the wyke, I selle the day, ..Somtyme by twelue and by thryttene, By twenty ek, and by nyntene. *a* **1550** WRIOTHESLEY *Chron.* (Camden) I. 45 Which were nyneteene in number. **1611** SHAKS. *Wint. T.* III. iii. 65 Would any but these boylde-braines of nineteene and two and twenty hunt this weather? **1799** UNDERWOOD *Diseases Children* (ed. 4) III. 121 It will prove sufficiently nourishing for nineteen out of twenty. **1827** PUSEY in Liddon *Life* I. (1894) 42 An expression which I had used when nineteen. **1846** MRS. GORE *Eng. Char.* (1852) 39 The nineteen-and-sixpence she has netted incline her to return to the card-table.

b. Phr. *to talk (run) nineteen to the dozen*: to talk, or run on, at a great rate.

1785 E. SHERIDAN *Jrnl.* 7 Aug. (1960) ii. 63 The Mother good humour'd and Civil but talks nineteen to the dozen. **1852** READE *Peg Woff.* (1889) 50 He was talking nineteen to the dozen. **1860** SALA *Baddington Peerage* xliii, The ladies' maid's tongue was sure to run nineteen to the dozen. **1883** STEVENSON in *Longman's Mag.* II. 293 A very cheerful.. gentleman..who was talking away to me, nineteen to the dozen, as they say. **1916** 'BOYD CABLE' *Action Front* 187 They must be charging, I think, or our front line's fallen back, because the rifles is going nineteen to the dozen. **1936** A. CHRISTIE *Murder in Mesopotamia* v. 39 Presently Mr. Coleman bustled in and took the place beyond Miss Johnson... He talked away nineteen to the dozen. **1956** V. H. COLLINS *Bk. Eng. Idioms* 228 *Talk nineteen to the dozen*. .. Why 'nineteen'? The obvious numeral would be the round number 'twenty'. Possibly 'nineteen' was chosen just because, not being what might have been expected, it seemed to give a more striking effect.

†**3.** = Nineteenth. *Obs.*

c **1420** *Chron. Vilod.* 3090 Of Etheldrede þe nyentetene ȝere & nomore. **1523** LD. BERNERS *Froiss.* I. clii. 181 The nynetene day of February next after.

nineteen eighty-four. The year-date (freq. written in form *1984*): the title of an apocalyptic novel (1949) by 'George Orwell' portraying a society in which government propaganda and terrorizing destroy consciousness of reality; freq. used allusively. Also *1984-ish*. Cf. DOUBLETHINK, DOUBLE-THINK, NEWSPEAK.

1959 BENN & PETERS *Social Principles* x. 225 Our antipathy to nineteen eighty-four methods may be due in part to the evil ends with which we associate them, or with the physical and mental cruelty involved in particular techniques. **1959** *Times* 6 May 15/7 We had a constant 1984-ish feeling as we worked in these vast abandoned castles. **1961** L. MUMFORD *City in History* xvii. 527 Whether they extrapolate 1960 or anticipate 2060 their goal is actually '1984'. **1968** *Listener* 29 Feb. 261/1 David Brinkley.. pointed to the spokesman who claimed, 'We had to destroy that village to save it,' and commented that 1984 Newspeak had come to 1968. **1970** *Time* 16 Nov. 14 The political uses of television advertising and packaging of candidates were heralded by..doom-sayers as the ominous forerunner of 1984.

nineteenth (naɪn'tiːnθ, 'naɪntiːnθ), *a.* and *sb.* Forms: *α.* **1 niȝonteoða, -þe**, etc., **3 nien-, nyenteþe, 5 -tethe.** *β.* **4 nientend, 5 nyntende, -tenth, nintenth, 6 nynetenth, 6– nineteenth.** [OE. *niȝontéoða* = OFris. *niuguntinda*, MDu. (and Du.) *negentiende*, MHG. *niunzehende* (G. *neunzehnte*), ON. *nítjándi* (Sw. *nittonde*, Da. *nittende*): see NINETEEN *a.* (and *sb.*) and -TH[1].] The ordinal numeral corresponding to the cardinal NINETEEN.

A. *adj.* **1.** In concord with sb. expressed, or *ellipt.*

In quot. 1951 used in a quasi-*adj.* phr.

α. *a* **900** *O.E. Martyrol.* 24 On þone niȝonteoðan dæȝ þæs monðes. *Ibid.* 98 On þone nyȝenteȝðan dæȝ. *c* **900** *O.E. Chron.* (Parker MS.) an. 855 He ricsode niȝon teoþe healf ȝear. **1297** R. GLOUC. (Rolls) 5116 þe nyenteþe day of aueryl. *Ibid.* 8699 In þe nienteþe ȝere of is elde. *c* **1420** *Chron. Vilod.* 3820 Of kyng Knowde þe nyenthethe ȝere.

β. *c* **1330** R. BRUNNE *Chron.* (1810) 133 In his nientend ȝere of his regalte. **1382** WYCLIF *2 Kings* xxv. 8 It is the nyntenthe ȝeer of the kyng of Babiloyne. **1447** BOKENHAM *Seyntys* (Roxb.) 95 Petyr the nyntende pope. **1579** FULKE *Heskins' Parl.* 195 The nineteenth Chapter proceedeth vpon the same text. **1790** BURKE *Fr. Rev.* Wks. 1792 III. 192 In the nineteenth century. **1824** L. MURRAY *Eng. Gram.* (ed. 5) I. 135 See..the notes on the nineteenth rule of Syntax. **1836** HOOD (*title*) Song for the Nineteenth. **1886** MORLEY *Eng. Lit.* (ed. 12) Pref., Former Editions..touched very lightly on the Literature of the Nineteenth Century.

Comb. **1872** W. F. BUTLER *Gt. Lone Land* (ed. 2) xvi. 241 Terrible deeds..never perhaps more sickening than now in the full blaze of nineteenth-century civilization. **1879** *Temple Bar* Sept. 44 Glowering at each other in civil nineteenth-century fashion. **1923** J. W. HARVEY tr. *Otto's Idea of Holy* p. vii, A fair expression of the limitations and bias of the nineteenth-century mind. **1951** C. P. SNOW *Masters* xxxiv. 272 His views were eccentric for an old man, but his manners had stayed gentle and nineteenth century. **1956** R. C. ZAEHNER in A. Pryce-Jones *New Outl. Mod. Knowledge* 65 Nineteenth-century optimism, then, is comparable to Buddhism in the emphasis it lays on individual effort in the battle for salvation.

2. ***the nineteenth hole***: the bar-room in a golf club-house. Also *ellipt.* and in extended use. *slang* (orig. *U.S.*).

1901 W. G. VAN T. SUTPHEN (*title*) The nineteenth hole, being tales of the fair green. **1926** *Daily Colonist* (Victoria, B.C.) 11 July 4/3 The immeasurable distance of the nineteenth hole on standard courses is altogether beyond our physical capacity on these hot and golden Summer days. **1928** *Daily Express* 3 Jan. 9/2 Most courses have been completely unplayable, except at the nineteenth hole. **1948** 'J. TEY' *Franchise Affair* i. 7 A good chap who played a very steady game and occasionally, when it came to the nineteenth, expanded into mild indiscretions. **1956** [see EARBASH *v.*]. **1971** *Good Food Guide* 317 The Golf Tavern Nineteenth Hole.

B. *sb.* **a.** A nineteenth part. **b.** *Mus.* The interval of two octaves and a fifth.

1597 MORLEY *Introd. Mus.* 71 A vnison, a fift,..a fifteenth, a nineteenth, and so forth. **1609** DOULAND *Ornith. Microl.* 79 A nineteenth, which is equal to a fift, and a twelfth.

Hence **nine'teenthly** *adv.*, in the nineteenth place; *sb.* the nineteenth head of a sermon.

1681 H. MORE *Exp. Dan.* App. III. 304 Nineteenthly, The Curious may be prone to enquire why, etc. **1815** SCOTT *Paul's Lett.* (1839) 287 In the Nineteenthly of an afternoon's sermon. **1851** WHITTIER *To Schoolmaster* 124 As the long nineteenthlies poured Downward from the sounding-board.

nineteenth-'centuryism. The distinctive spirit, outlook, or character of the nineteenth century; a feature or trait suggestive of the nineteenth century.

1846 TENNYSON in H. Tennyson *Alfred Ld. Tennyson* (1897) I. 238 They seem to be very clever and full of a noble 19th century-ism (if you will admit such a word). **1891** 'L. MALET' *Wages of Sin* II. v. iii. 214 There is another of your perverted nineteenth-centuryisms!

nine-tenths. Nine parts out of ten; also loosely used to denote nearly the whole of any number or amount.

1812 SOUTHEY *Let. to J. White* 16 Feb., I apprehend that at least nine tenths of the business of B. Society relates to foreign countries. **1842** BORROW *Bible in Spain* xliv, Nine-tenths of the inhabitants had left this place. **1889** SKRINE *Mem. Thring* 102 A wretched nine-tenths of the place was the property of private owners.

nineth, obs. form of NINTH.

ninetieth ('naɪntɪɪθ), *a.* (*sb.*) Forms: 2 **niȝenteoþa**, 4 **nyntithe**, 6 **nin(e)teth**, 7- **ninetieth.** [f. next + *-eth* -TH[1].] The ordinal numeral corresponding to the cardinal NINETY.

a **1100** in Napier *O.E. Glosses* i. 2521 *Usque nonagenariam*, oþ þa niȝenteoþan. **1395** PURVEY *Remonstr.* (1851) 90 In Decrees, in one and nyntithe distinccioun. **1548** ELYOT, *Nonagesimus*,..the nineteth. **1570** LEVINS *Manip.* 88/43 Yᵉ Ninteth, *nonagesimus.* **1611** FLORIO, *Nonagesimo*, the ninetieth in order. **1751** JOHNSON *Rambler* No. 112 ¶9 He.. laughed obstreperously at the ninetieth repetition of a joke. **1826** SCOTT in *Lockhart* (1839) VIII. 383 My Aunt is now in her ninetieth year. **1877** TENNYSON *Harold* IV. i, This is my ninetieth birthday!

ellipt. **1901** *Munsey's Mag.* XXV. 342/1 He leaped upon the parapet of his pit and cheered the Ninetieth on.

ninety ('naɪntɪ), *a.* and *sb.* Forms: 1 **niȝon-**, 2 **niȝentiȝ**; 3 **niȝen-**, **niȝne-**, 4 **nene-**, **nineti**, **nynte**, 3 **nin-**, 4 **nen-**, **nyne-**, 6 **nynty**, **nyn(e)tie**, 7 **ninetie**, 7- **ninety.** [OE. *niȝontiȝ* = OFris. *nion-*, *niogen-*, *nogentich*, MDu. and MLG. *negentich* (Du. *negentig*), OHG. *niunzug*, *-zog* (MHG. *niunzec*, *-zic*, G. *neunzig*), ON. *níutigir* (Icel. *níutíu*, Norw. *nitti*, Sw. *nittio*): see NINE and -TY.]

1. a. The cardinal number equal to nine tens, represented by 90 or xc. Also with omission of sb., and in comb. with numbers below ten (ordinal and cardinal), as *ninety-one*, *ninety-first*, etc.

c **1000** *Ags. Gosp.* Luke xv. 7 Ma þonne ofer niȝon & niȝontiȝum [*Hatton* niȝentiȝ] rihtwisra. *c* **1250** *Gen. & Ex.* 1027 Ȝhe was niȝenti winter hold. **1297** R. GLOUC. *Chron.* (Rolls) 9931 In þe ȝer of grace..Endleue hundred & ninty. *a* **1300** *Cursor M.* 2699 His fader nineti and nine þat day. **1382** WYCLIF *Gen.* v. 9 Enos forsothe lyuede nynti ȝeer. *c* **1440** *Promp. Parv.* 357/1 Nynety, *nonaginta.* *c* **1470** HENRY *Wallace* VI. 107 Tuelff hundreth ȝer, tharto nynte and sewyn. **1596** DALRYMPLE tr. *Leslie's Hist. Scot.* I. 78 Sax-hundereth nyntie and fyue. **1611** FLORIO, *Nonagenario*, of ninety yeeres of age. **1769** BURKE *Late St. Nat.* Wks. II. 118 His subscription would be at ninety-nine per cent. discount the very first day of its opening. **1810** SOUTHEY *Kehama* VIII. i, Nine and ninety days are fled, Nine and ninety steeds have bled. **1894** SIR E. SULLIVAN *Woman* 13 In ninety-nine cases out of a hundred she is better.

Comb. **1852** R. S. SURTEES *Sponge's Sp. Tour* (1893) 365 This was ninety-shilling sherry. **1855** J. R. LEIFCHILD *Cornwall* 188 The great ninety-inch steam-engine on the Consolidated Mines. **1863** PRIOR *Pop. Names Brit. Plants* 162 *Ninety-knot*, see Knotgrass and Centinode.

b. ninety-day wonder *U.S. Services' slang*, a graduate of a ninety-day officers' training course; an inexperienced, newly-commissioned officer; also *attrib.* or as *adj.*

1917 R. LORD in *Captain Boyd's Battery, A.E.F.* (1919) ii. 23 Two tents of Shavetails (i.e...Ninety-Day Wonders..) have been attached to us for instruction purposes. **1919** K. M. CORTELYOU et al. *From Arizona to Huns* 106 'A ninty [*sic*] day wonder' fresh from O.T.S. **1921** F. L. FIELD *Battery Book* 15 The inexperience of officers was a circumstance of tremendous significance. The fact that we used to call them 'ninety-day wonders' indicates our attitude..at the time. **1926** L. H. NASON *Chevrons* 136 You ninety-day wonder!.. Haven't you got brains enough to know this brook runs east and west? **1928** A. C. HAVLIN *Hist. Company A, 102nd Machine Gun Battalion* 1 As usual, they were dubbed 'ninety-day wonders'. **1956** E. N. ROGERS *Queenie's Brood* 307 The draft law and the ninety-day-wonder officers came in for much discussion also. **1970** W. C. WOODS *Killing Zone* 5 A pale punk kid to run my company, another ninety day wonder.

2. ***the nineties.*** **a.** The degrees of a thermometer between ninety and a hundred. **b.** The years between ninety and a hundred in a particular century or in a person's life; *spec.* the years between 1890 and 1899. Also *attrib.*

1883 STEVENSON *Silverado Sq.* 21 The thermometer..had already climbed among the nineties. **1894** *Athenæum* 10 Feb. 176/1 Reinout is what Arthur Pendennis might have been in the nineties. **1897** WARUNG *Tales Old Regime* 207 He was an early arrival at the island away back in the 'Nineties. **1911** W. G. BLAIKIE MURDOCH *Renaissance of Nineties* 34 Subtlety and delicacy are not more prominent in the painting of the nineties than in the period's literature. *Ibid.* 45 If Life was the watchword of the men of the nineties, Freedom was the motto on their banner. **1913** H. JACKSON *Eighteen Nineties* i. 27 Max Beerbohm, in a delightful essay which could only have been written in the Nineties. *Ibid.* ii. 40 *The Yellow Book* and *The Savoy*..were the favourite lamps around which the most bizarre moths of the Nineties clustered. There were few essential writers of the Nineties who did not contribute to one or the other. **1920** B. MUDDIMAN (*title*) The men of the nineties. **1938** L. MACNEICE *Modern Poetry* i. 7 The nineties poets did to some extent criticize life. **1954** A. S. C. ROSS in *Neuphilologische Mitteilungen* LV. 32 It was apparently U and was certainly thriving in the nineties. **1971** P. MUIR *Victorian Illustrated Books* viii. 194 (*heading*) Other Nineties people. **1972** *Country Life* 23 Nov. 1414/3 The Nineties in Paris were not all decadence, can-can and absinthe. **1975** *Times* 5 Dec. 13/4 A mock-innocent return to the 'nineties.

ninetyish ('naɪntɪɪʃ), *a.* [f. NINETY *a.* and *sb.* + -ISH[1].] Of, belonging to, or characteristic of 'the nineties' of the nineteenth century; resembling, or suggestive of, what was then current. So **'ninetyism**, the spirit of 'the nineties'; **'ninetyishness**, ninetyish characteristics.

1909 *Westm. Gaz.* 2 Mar. 2/2 What the *Standard* had hoped was that 'there might be a return to the rule of the 'nineties, when the seat was won or lost by a margin between two and five hundred votes'. Certainly there is nothing ninety-ish about Saturday's figures. **1918** E. MARSH *Rupert Brooke* 13 He entertained a *culte*..for the literature that is now called 'ninetyish'—Pater, Wilde and Dowson. **1931** *Times Lit. Suppl.* 23 Apr. 327/4 Thus 'Proteus' in the *New Statesman* describes me as 'engagingly ninety-ish'. **1941** L. MACNEICE *Poetry of Yeats* iv. 66 He ceased to be 'ninetyish' with the Nineties. How saturated with 'Ninetyism' he had been can be seen [etc.]. **1959** *Times* 13 Feb. 13/4 Consider the subjects, or titles, of *Verklärte Nacht, Pierrot Lunaire, Wozzeck, Lulu*, all in varying measure products of a decadent romanticism, ranging from 'ninetyishness' to post-Freudian psycho-pathology. **1973** *Guardian* 28 Mar. 10/1 Firbank seemed negligible..his fictions artificial, *naughty* and Ninetyish.

Ninevite ('nɪnɪvaɪt). Also 6–7 **Ninivite.** [ad. L. *Ninivita*, f. *Ninive* Nineveh: see -ITE.] An inhabitant of Nineveh.

1550 LEVER *Serm.* (Arb.) 24 The same destruccion was tolde to the Sodomites, was tolde to the Niniuites. **1662** STILLINGFL. *Orig. Sacræ* II. vi. §11 Because the Ninivites might now suspect him to be no true Prophet. **1797** *Encycl. Brit.* (ed. 3) IX. 306/1 Jonah..was ordered to go and prophecy the destruction of the Ninevites. **1845** KITTO *Cycl. Bibl. Lit.* s.v. *Nineveh*, The Ninevites repented at the preaching of Jonah. **1888** *Academy* 7 Apr. 245/2 The Ninevites and the Babylonians, who spoke the same language, exhibit two distinct ethnical types.

Hence **'Ninevitish** *a.*

1846 THORPE *Ælfric's Hom.* II. 125 The old transgressions of the Ninevitish people.

ningid: see NINGUID *Obs.*

†**ningle**, *sb. Obs.* [See N 3.] = INGLE *sb.*[2] (Freq. in early 17th cent. plays.)

1598–9 B. JONSON *Case Altered* v. ii, Sirrah ningle, thou art a traveller, and I honour thee... Begin, find your tongue, ningle. **1602** DEKKER *Satirom.* B 4, Horace, my sweet ningle, is alwayes in labour when I come. **1622** MASSINGER & DEKKER *Virg. Mart.* II. i, Priapus..was the only ningle that I cared for under the moon. **1640** BROME *Sparagus Gard.* III. v, It may take your Nephew off his Ningle, who hath affected him with Poetry already.

So †**ningle** *v. Obs. rare*[−0] = INGLE *v.* I.

1659 TORRIANO *Zanzeráre*, to ningle [*Florio*, nigle] boyes, or wantonly to dally with them against nature.

ning-nong ('nɪŋnɒŋ). *dial.* and *Austral. slang.* Also **ning-nang.** [Origin unknown.] A fool, a stupid person. Cf. NIG-NOG[1].

1832 *Whitehaven Poll Bk.* 34 He looks parlish like a ning-nang. **1864** HOTTEN *Slang Dict.* 188 *Ning-nang*, horse-coupers' term for a worthless thorough-bred. **1881** J. SARGISSON *Joe Scoap's Jurneh through three Wardles* II. 189 Wad teh believe't noo, t'Ning-nang can nowder read ner write. **1957** 'N. CULOTTA' *They're a Weird Mob* (1958) i. 15, I 'ave ter get landed with a bloody ning nong who doesn't know where he's bloody goin'. **1973** *Telegraph* (Brisbane) 14 Mar. 71/1 Even ning-nongs can win prizes on Channel 0's daily quiz show.

Ningre Tongo ('nɪŋgreɪ 'tɒŋgəʊ). [prob. Taki-Taki, ad. Eng. NIGGER *sb.* + TONGUE *sb.*] An English-based creole language of Surinam, less divergent from English than *Jew Tongo.*

1933 L. BLOOMFIELD *Lang.* xxvi. 474 Ningre Tongo or taki-taki is spoken by descendants of slaves along the coast. **1939** L. H. GRAY *Foundations of Language* 37 The languages are termed *creolised*, examples being the *Taki-Taki* (or *Ningre Tongo*). **1968** [see *Jew Tongo* (JEW *sb.* 3 c)].

†**'ninguid**, *a. Obs. rare*[−0]. [ad. L. *ninguid-us*, f. *ninguis* snow.] (See quot.)

1656 BLOUNT *Glossogr.*, *Ningid* or *Ninguid*, where much Snow is.

ningyoite ('nɪŋgjəʊaɪt). *Min.* [f. *Ningyo*, the name of a pass in Tottori Prefecture, Japan + -ITE[1].] A hydrated phosphate of calcium and uranium, $CaU^{IV}(PO_4)_2.1\frac{1}{2}H_2O$, in which there is some replacement of uranium by lanthanons and which is found as brown or brownish-green orthorhombic crystals.

1959 T. MUTO et al. in *Amer. Mineralogist* XLIV. 634 The new mineral, ningyoite, is named for the locality, Ningyo Pass. *Ibid.* 649 The synthetic ningyoite ignited at 600°C. in air for 5–10 minutes still retained the original orthorhombic structure. **1962** *Mineral. Jrnl.* III. 306 Ningyoite contains almost all the rare earths and their abundance ratio resembles that of apatite. **1970** *Econ. Geol.* LXV. 470 For the formation of ningyoite, fixation of much sulfur in comparison with carbonaceous matter should occur before the penetration of uranium-carrying solutions.

ninhydrin (nɪn'haɪdrɪn). *Chem.* [prob. partially f. the chemical name, *triketohydrindene*, and app. first formed (as a trade name) in Ger.] A brown crystalline compound, $C_9H_6O_4$, which forms coloured products with amines and is particularly used for detecting and estimating amino-acids; triketohydrindene hydrate; 1,2,3-indantrione hydrate. Freq. *attrib.*

[**1912** *Warenzeichenblatt* Nov. 2500/2 Ninhydrin... Farbwerke vorm. Meister Lucius & Brüning, Aktiengesellschaft, Höchst a/M... Geschäftsbetrieb: Chemische Fabrik. Waren: Pharmazeutische und therapeutische Präparate.] **1913** *Chem. Abstr.* VII. 3765 Ninhydrin is a valuable reagent for the detection of non-biuret dialyzable amino acids. **1915** *Jrnl. Biol. Chem.* XX. 218 This discovery [of Ruhemann's] was confirmed and extended by Abderhalden, who applied it to the detection of pregnancy and cancer, triketohydrindene hydrate now being a commercial product under the name of 'ninhydrin'. *Ibid.* XXIII. 382 Free from soluble nitrogen capable of giving the ninhydrin test for amino-acids. **1949** ABRAHAM & HEATLEY in H. W. Florey et al. *Antibiotics* I. ii. 107 The positions of the separated amino acids on the paper were made visible by the coloration they gave with ninhydrin. **1962** DARDENNE & KIRSTEN in A. Pirie *Lens Metabolism Rel. Cataract* 416 In these hydrolysed lens extracts we detected some 30 non-protein-bound substances which could be determined by the ninhydrin reaction. **1974** W. J. BURLEY *Death in Stanley St.* x. 161 [We] decided to try a new test for latents. It's supposed to be better than the old ninhydrin test for some surfaces.

ninihammer, obs. form of NINNY-HAMMER.

†**niniversity.** *Obs. rare.* Also 7 **ninne-.** A humorous perversion of UNIVERSITY, after NINNY.

c **1590** GREENE *Fr. Bacon* vii, [I] will make a ship that shall hold all your colleges and so carry away the niniversity..to the Bankside in Southwark. **1654** E. JOHNSON *Wonderwrkg. Provid.* 96 A Woman that Preaches better Gospell then any of your black-coates that have been at the Ninneversity.

ninkling, obs. form of INKLING.

†**'ninnery.** *Obs. rare*[−1]. [f. NINN-Y + -ERY.] The behaviour of a ninny.

1600 *Hospit. Incurable Fooles* A 4 Folly was their mother, Buffonerie their sister, Ninnerie their companion.

ninny[1] ('nɪnɪ). Forms: 6–7, 9 **ninnie**, 7 **ninnee**, 7–8 **ninney**, 7- **ninny.** [Of obscure origin: perh. an abbreviation of *innocent* with prefixed *n* (see N 3).] A simpleton; a fool.

1593 *Passionate Morrice* (New Shaks. Soc.) 83, I should be quickly rid of a neere mishap, in being prevented of matching with a nice ninnie. **1609** ARMIN *Ital. Taylor* (1880) 143 Not long since I discouerd a nest of Ninnies in this great wombe the Worlde. **1621** BURTON *Anat. Mel.* I. ii. IV. iv. (1651) 149 He thought himself to be a man of most excellent skill (who was indeed a ninnie). **1669** PENN *No Cross* ix. §10 Being slighted of them as a Ninnee, a Fool, a Frantick. **1731** FIELDING *Mod. Husband* Epil., When ev'ry ninny Might put them on and off—for half a guinea. **1778** MISS BURNEY *Evelina* xxxiii, You needn't trouble yourself to make a ninny of me neither. **1812** H. & J. SMITH *Rej. Addr.*, *G. Barnwell*, The weak and incurable ninny. **1842** MRS. GORE *Fascination* 23 If my husband has been ninny enough to give your fascinating marquis credit. **1876** GEO. ELIOT *Dan. Der.* xlviii, He would not have liked a wife who..was ..a ninny, unable to make spirited answers.

b. *attrib.* and *Comb.*, as ***ninny-minded*** adj; †**ninny-broth**, coffee.

1696 *Poor Robin, Prognostication*, How to make coffee, alias Ninny-broth. **1705** *Hudibras Redivivus* I. i, Their wounded Consciences they heal With Ninny-Broth. **1849** E. P. GURNEY in Hare *Gurneys* (1895) II. 268 In this little ninny-minded world.

Hence **'ninnyish** *a.*, characteristic of a ninny; foolish. **'ninnyism**, behaviour characteristic of a ninny. **'ninnyship**, the fact of being a ninny.

1804 *Spirit Publ. Jrnls.* VII. 94 We shall never do well till a commission of ninnyism is grantable. **1822** *Blackw. Mag.* XII. 342 Had he been previously heard muttering sulky execrations, or ninnyish innuendoes, against the King. **1826** *Ibid.* XX. 419 Our gorge rises at the namby-pamby ninnyism. **1852** W. JERDAN *Autobiog.* I. 41, I felt the ninnyship of my ignorance and presumption.

†**'ninny²**. *Obs. rare*⁻¹. [ad. Sp. *niño, niña*.] A child.

c 1626 *Dick of Devonsh.* I. ii. in Bullen *O. Pl.* II. 15 Nurses still'd Their little Spanish Nynnies when they cryde 'Hush! The Drake comes'.

'ninny-,hammer. Also 6–7 nini-, 7 ninni-. [app. f. NINNY¹, but the force of the second element is not clear.] A simpleton.

1592 NASHE *Four Lett. Confut.* 60 Whoreson Ninihammer, that wilt assault a man and haue no stronger weapons. **1600** *Hospit. Incurable Fooles* A 3 b, Shallow-pates and ninnie-hammers. **1622** ROWLANDS *Good Newes & B.* 38, I might haue beene a scholler, learn'd my Grammar, But I haue lost all like a Ninnie-hammer. **1673** *S'too him Bayes* 3 A man ought not to talk like a ninny-hammer. **1712** ARBUTHNOT *John Bull* I. xii, That Clod-pated, Numskull'd Ninny-hammer of yours. **1767** STERNE *Tr. Shandy* IX. xxv, Numskulls, doddypoles, dunderheads, ninny-hammers, .. and other unsavoury appellations. **1812** MISS MITFORD in L'Estrange *Life* (1870) I. 198, I will be .. anythng now, to oppose these stupid, tasteless, ninny-hammers. **1853** *Blackw. Mag.* LXXIII. 748 The predominant feature of a ninny-hammer is the enormous development of his self-conceit.

So †**'ninny-whoop**. *Obs. rare*⁻¹.

1653 URQUHART *Rabelais* I. xxxii, They think to have to do with a ninnie-whoop to feed you thus with cakes.

ninon (ninɔ̃). [Fr.] A light-weight fabric, used esp. in dresses, made in a plain weave from silk, rayon, or nylon.

1911 *Daily Colonist* (Victoria, B.C.) 15 Apr. 24/1 (Advt.), Three large shipments just to hand making our stock replete with every desired line of silks .. Bengaline, .. Tamaline .. Ninon. **1913** W. J. LOCKE *Stella Maris* xiii. 160 Dressed in a soft grey ninon gown. **1923** *Daily Mail* 24 Feb. 11 Novel ninons are patterned with designs resembling finely worked embroideries. **1929** D. L. MOORE *Pandora's Letter Box* xiv. 254 Everything must be of silk, georgette, triple ninon and so forth. **1948** G. L. FRASER *Textiles by Britain* 165 *Ninon*, fine and closely woven plain-weave semi-transparent dress cloth made either in silk or rayon. **1968** HOLLEN & SADDLER *Textiles* (ed. 3) xvi. 140/1 *Ninon* is a filament sheer widely used for curtains.

nintene, -tenth, -teth, obs. ff. NINETEEN, -TEENTH, -TIETH.

ninth ('naɪnθ), *a.* and *sb.* Forms: *α.* 1. **niꝣ(e)oða, nyꝣoða,** 1–2 **niꝣeþe, nyꝣeþe,** 2–3 **niꝫeðe, (2 nihꝫ-),** 3 **neoꝫethe;** 1 **nioða,** 2–3 **nieðe,** 4 **nyeþe, nyþe, niþe.** *β.* 1 **niꝣend(e,** 3 **niꝫhennde,** 4 **ni(g)h-, neghend,** 4 **niend, nyend, neynd, neiuind, nend, nind, niinde, nynde.** *γ.* 4 **neghent, neuent, neynt, neent, nente;** *Sc.* 5 **ninte,** 5–6 **nynte,** 5–7 **nynt,** 6 **nint.** *δ.* 2 **niꝣonðe,** 3 **ninþe,** 4 **ney(e)nþe, nynethe,** 4–5 **nynþe,** 4–6 **-the,** 4–7 **nynth,** 6 **nienth, nineth,** 6– **ninth.** [Various formations from the numeral NINE are represented here. The *α*-forms, OE. *niꝣoða*, etc., correspond to OS. *nigudo*, MLG. *negede*, and are parallel with OE. *seofoða* seventh, *eahtoða* eight. The *β*-forms correspond to OFris. *niugunda, -enda*, OS. *nigundo*, MDu. and MLG. *negende*, OHG. *niundo, niunto* (MHG. *niunde, niunte*, G. *neunte*, †*neunde*), ON. *níonde, níundi* (Sw. *nionde*, Da. *niende*), Goth. *niunda*: it is possible that they may be due to Scand. influence. The anomalous *neiuind, neuent*, may be on the analogy of *seuend, -ent*, seventh. In the *δ*-forms the ordinal suffix *-th* is added to the full stem, as in *sixth, seventh, eighth, tenth*. With the *γ*-forms compare the obs. or dial. variants, *fift, sixt*, etc.]

The ordinal numeral corresponding to the cardinal number NINE.

A. *adj.* **1. a.** In concord with sb. expressed or understood.

α. a **900** *O.E. Martyrol.* 9 May 80 On þone nyꝣeðan dæꝣ þæs monðes bið sumeres fruma. c **950** *Lindisf. Gosp.* Matt. i. 3 In tal ða nioða. **971** *Blickl. Hom.* 141 On þa niꝣoþan tid þæs dæꝣes. a **1067** in Kemble *Cod. Dipl.* IV. 222 þa healf nyꝣoðe hundreda socne. c **1175** *Lamb. Hom.* 115 þe nihꝫeðe unþeau is þet þe king beo unrihtwis. a **1225** *Ancr. R.* 328 þe nieðe reisun is þis. **1297** R. GLOUC. (Rolls) 5406 þe niþe ꝫer of is kinedom. c **1300** *Beket* 617 The Neoꝫethe [law] was that Peteres Pans .. To the Pope nere not on isend. a **1400** *Minor Poems Vernon MS.* 245 þe Niþe [article] is wiþ-outen bost: þat in god is þe holy-gost.

β. a **1066** in Kemble *Cod. Dipl.* IV. 194/11 Ða niꝣend half hundred socne. c **1200** ORMIN 4488 þe niꝫhennde [commandment] wass sett þurrh Godd. a **1300** *Cursor M.* 26686 þe nend point þou vnderstand. **1340** HAMPOLE *Pr. Consc.* 4790 þe neghend day, gret erthedyn sal be. c **1357** *Lay Folks Catech.* 232 The neynd [commandment] is, that we noght yerne our neghtebur house. c **1400** *Rule St. Benet* (Prose) 14/21 Sain benet spekis .. of þe nihend degrece o mekenes. c **1400** MAUNDEV. (Roxb.) v. 14 At þe nynde moneth end a voice come to him.

γ. a **1300** *Cursor M.* 16767 + 59 About þe neghent oure of þe day. *Ibid.* 29470 þe neuent [case] es for þin aun pruu. **1375** BARBOUR *Bruce* XIX. 527 On the nynt day, The lord Dowglass hass spyit a vay. c **1400** *Destr. Troy* Title, Neynt Boke. c **1470** *Gol. & Gaw.* 1044 Na nane of the nynt degre haue noy of my name. **1513** DOUGLAS *Æneis* XII. Prol. 268 The nynt morow of fresche temperat May. **1563** WINȜET *Four Scoir Thre Quest.* Wks. (S.T.S.) I. 129 At the nynte hour of prayar. **1588** A. KING tr. *Canisius' Catech.* 12 Quhat expressis ye nynt artical?

δ. a **1122** *O.E. Chron.* (Laud MS.) an. 634 He rixade .ix. winter; man ꝣetealde him þæt niꝣonðe for þan heðenscipe þe hi druꝣon [etc.]. c **1290** *Beket* 617 in *S. Eng. Leg.* I. 124 þe Ninþe [law] was þat peteres panes .. þe pope nere nouꝫt on i-send. c **1380** WYCLIF *Wks.* (1880) 12 þei breken þe neynþe maundement of god. **1390** GOWER *Conf.* III. 123 The nynthe Signe .. Is cleped Sagittarius. **1541** COVERDALE *Old Faith* F vij b, In the nynth Chapter of Esaye. **1578** LYTE *Dodoens* 89 Theophrastus in his nienth Booke. a **1650** CRASHAW *Poems* (1858) 174 The ninth with awful horror hark'ned to those groans. **1688** R. HOLME *Armoury* III. 190/1 The Knights of St. Stephen .. instituted .. in honor of Pope Stephen the nineth. **1774** BURKE *Sp. Amer. Tax.* Wks. II. 383 The words of Governour Bernard's ninth letter. **1820** RANKEN *Hist. France* VIII. I. vi. 246 He should be established in the rank of ninth elector. **1873** MIVART *Elem. Anat.* 399 The ninth nerve is called the hypoglossal.

b. The ninth day (*of* a month).

1596 DALRYMPLE tr. *Leslie's Hist. Scot.* VIII. 147 Quhilk feild was strukne the nynt of September. **1596** SHAKS. *1 Hen. IV*, II. iii. 29 To meete me in Armes by the ninth of the next Moneth? **1653** WALTON *Angler* xiii. (repr.) 246, I shall long for the ninth of May. a **1845** HOOD (*title*), Ode for the Ninth of November.

2. *ninth part*, or † *deal*, one of the nine equal parts into which a thing may be divided.

971 *Blickl. Hom.* 53 Dæle [he] þeah his ælmessan forþ of þon niꝣeoþan dælon. c **1200** *Moral Ode* 342 (Trin. Coll. MS.), þe brode strate .. þe lat þe nieðe [*v.r.* niꝫeðe] dal to helle of manne. **1596** SHAKS. *1 Hen. IV*, III. i. 140 Ile cauill on the ninth part of a hayre. **1831** CARLYLE *Sart. Res.* III. xi, This is he, whom .. the world treats with contumely, as the ninth part of a man! **1846** MCCULLOCH *Acc. Brit. Empire* (1854) II. 309 There the adherents of the Established Church do not exceed one ninth part of the population.

3. Quasi-*adv.* In the ninth place. *rare.*

1526 *Pilgr. Perf.* (W. de W. 1531) 292 b, Nynth, they be mortifyed from all inwarde affeccyon & delectacyons.

B. *sb.* **1.** = Ninth part.

c **1275** *Moral Ode* 336 in *O.E. Misc.* 70 þeo brode stret .. þat lat þe nyeþe to helle of folke. **1557** RECORDE *Whetst.* B ii b, *Sesquinona* .. a nineth more. **1611** COTGR. *Neufaine*, a ninth. **1802** JAMES *Milit. Dict.* s.v. *Cannon*, If the fissure be 1-ninth of an inch deep. **1870** SONNENSCHEIN & NESBITT *Sci. & Art Arith.* II. 1 Find one ninth .. of £57.15*s.* **1897** GÜNTHER in Miss Kingsley *W. Africa* 702 The diameter of the eye .. is two ninths of the length of the head.

2. *Mus.* **a.** The interval of an octave and a second. Also, a note eight diatonic degrees above or below another note.

1597 MORLEY *Introd. Mus.* 71 *Phi.* Which distances make discord .. ? *Ma.* All such as doe not make concords: as a second, a fourth, .. a ninth. **1609** DOULAND *Ornith. Microl.* 21 Now a Tone with a Diapason is a perfect Ninth. **1753** CHAMBERS *Cycl. Supp.* App. s.v., When an upper part syncopates, the second is accented and treated as a Ninth. **1837** *Penny Cycl.* VII. 114/2 The most elegant form which the chord of the Ninth and Seventh assumes. **1864** BROWNING *Abt Vogler* 93, I blunt it into a ninth. **1880** PARRY in *Grove's Dict. Mus.* I. 459 The compound intervals called ninths exceed the octave either by a tone or a semitone; if the former the ninth is called 'major', if the latter it is called 'minor'.

b. In full, ***ninth chord***. The chord of such notes; a ninth added to a triad.

1845 *Encycl. Metrop.* IV. 799 As to pentachords, such as what have been called the major and minor ninth, and compound sharp sixth, .. they are .. only chords of the seventh .. with a fifth note violently forced in. **1876** STAINER & BARRETT *Dict. Mus. Terms* 303/1 *Chord of the major ninth*, a chord formed by a combination of thirds starting with the dominant or fifth of the scale, called by some writers the 'added ninth', because it consists of a chord of the dominant seventh, with the addition of the ninth; by others the 'dominant ninth', because it occurs on a dominant bass. *Ibid.* 303/2 *Chord of the minor ninth* .. consists of a dominant, its major third, major (perfect) fifth, minor seventh, and minor ninth. **1926** A. NILES in W. C. Handy *Blues* iii. 16 The device .. of ending up the tune on the diminished seventh chord .. lately sometimes on the chord of the ninth. **1934** [see ELEVENTH *sb.* 2]. **1949** L. FEATHER *Inside Be-Bop* ii. 50 By the 1920's it had become fashionable to end on a seventh or ninth chord. **1952** R. ELDRIDGE in B. Ulanov *Hist. Jazz in Amer.* (1958) xix. 238, I was full of ideas. Augmented chords. Ninths. **1969** *Rolling Stone* 28 June 17/3 In those days country music was very loose in both meter and lyrics. .. No one had ever heard of a ninth chord.

3. The ninth chapter. *rare*⁻¹.

1671 [R. MACWARD] *True Nonconf.* 244 In the Nynths of Ezrah, Nehemiah, and Daniel.

Hence **'ninthly** *adv.*, in the ninth place; also as *sb.* with ref. to the heads of a sermon.

c **1532** DU WES *Introd. Fr.* in *Palsgr.* 929 Nynthly, *neuuiésmement*. **1579** FULKE *Refut. Rastel* 770 Ninthly, that the lay people were not forbidden. **1648** D. JENKINS *Wks.* 38 Ninthly, wee maintaine that the politick capacity is not to be sevred from the naturall. **1681** H. MORE *Expos. Dan.* App. III. 298 Ninthly, If any one will again object. **1874** ALDRICH *Prud. Palfrey* x. (1885) 164 The poor old parson's interminable ninthlies and finallies.

ninty, obs. form of NINETY.

niobate ('naɪəbeɪt). *Chem.* [f. NIOB-IUM + -ATE¹.] A salt of niobic acid.

1845 H. ROSE in *Chem. Gaz.* III. 36 The niobate of soda indeed is almost insoluble in an excess of a solution of soda. **1849** D. CAMPBELL *Inorg. Chem.* 277 Niobates are obtained much in the same manner as tantalates. **1883** *Encycl. Brit.* XVI. 426/2 Pyrrhite from .. the Azores .. is in orange-red octahedra, and is a niobate of zirconia.

Niobe ('naɪəbiː). [f. Gr. Νιόβη.] In Greek legend, the name of the daughter of Tantalus, supposed to have been changed into stone while weeping for her children; hence applied to a woman or female comparable to her. Also *fig.*

In scientific use the name has been given to certain genera of trilobites, molluscs, and weaver-birds, and to one of the asteroids, discovered by R. Luther in 1861.

1589 GREENE *Menaphon* (Arb.) 62 A more than second Niobe, bewailing her seauen fold sorrow. **1606** SHAKS. *Tr. & Cr.* V. x. 19 There is a word will Priam turne to stone; Make wels, and Niobes of the maides and wiues. **1625** DRUMM. OF HAWTH. *Poems* Wks. (1711) 46/1 Justice weeps out her Eyes, now truly Blind; To Niobe's the remnant Vertues turn. **1778** FOOTE *Trip Calais* II. Wks. 1799 II. 352 Indeed, the poor gentlewoman was a perfect Niobe. **1781** COWPER *Truth* 174 The streaming tears Channel her cheeks —a Niobe appears. **1818** BYRON *Ch. Har.* IV. lxxiv, The Niobe of nations! there she stands, Childless and crownless, in her voiceless woe. **1842** TENNYSON *Walk. to Mail* 92 She was left alone Upon her tower, the Niobe of swine.

Hence **Niobean** (naɪə'biːən), *a.*, pertaining to, resembling that of, Niobe.

1847 TENNYSON *Princ.* IV. 352 A Niobëan daughter, one arm out, Appealing to the bolts of Heaven. **1857** DUFFERIN *Lett. High Lat.* (ed. 3) 321 The last survivor of this Niobean family.

niobian (naɪ'əʊbɪən), *a. Min.* [f. NIOB(IUM + -IAN 2.] Of a mineral: having a (small) proportion of a constituent element replaced by niobium.

1962 [see ILMENORUTILE]. **1972** *Nature* 31 Mar. 215/1 Terrestrial dysanalyte is a niobian perovskite which contains about 26% CaO and no detectable ZrO_2.

niobic (naɪ'əʊbɪk), *a. Chem.* [f. NIOB-IUM + -IC 1 b.] Of or pertaining to, derived from, niobium; esp. in ***niobic acid*** or ***oxide***.

1845 H. ROSE in *Chem. Gaz.* III. 36, I have called it Niobium, and its acid niobic acid. *Ibid.*, The niobic acid remains colourless. **1848** FOWNES *Chem.* (ed. 2) 310 The American tantalite contains niobic, pelopic, and tungstic acids. **1866** WATTS *Dict. Chem.* IV. 49 It is remarkable .. that niobic oxide cannot be formed from niobous oxide by direct oxidation. **1892** MORLEY & MUIR *Watt's Dict. Chem.* III. 506/1 Niobic oxide, Nb_2O_5, reacts with alkali oxides to form salts.

niobite ('naɪəbaɪt). [f. NIOB-IUM + -ITE¹.]

1. *Min.* = COLUMBITE.

1854 DANA *Syst. Min.* (ed. 4) II. 353 Columbite. Tantalite. Niobite. **1855** *Orr's Circle Sci., Geol.* 531. **1891** THORPE *Dict. Appl. Chem.* II. 698 Niobium occurs .. in niobite from the Isegebirge.

2. *Chem.* A niobic salt.

1866 WATTS *Dict. Chem.* IV. 49 Metallic niobium is obtained .. by heating niobite of sodium in hydrogen gas containing phosphorus vapour. **1885** RAMSAY *Min.* (ed. 3) x. 310 Columbite is usually regarded as a niobite of iron and manganese.

niobium (naɪ'əʊbɪəm). *Chem.* [f. NIOB-E, the daughter of Tantalus, + -IUM; named in 1845 by Heinrich Rose, who rediscovered it in the tantalites of Bavaria. The earlier name is COLUMBIUM.] A metallic element, occurring in tantalite and other minerals. Symbol Nb.

1845 H. ROSE in *Chem. Gaz.* III. 36 It is the oxide of a metal which differs from all known metals. I have called it Niobium, and its acid niobic acid, from Niobe, daughter of Tantalus. **1849** D. CAMPBELL *Inorg. Chem.* 277 The white chloride is the terchloride of niobium. **1866** WATTS *Dict. Chem.* IV. 49 Niobium occurs .. in columbite, which is a compound of niobous oxide with the protoxides of iron and manganese. **1880** CLEMINSHAW *Wurtz' Atom. The.* 147 The double fluoride of niobium and potassium.

attrib. and *Comb.* **1849** D. CAMPBELL *Inorg. Chem.* 278 The niobium and tantalum sulphides. **1863** *Fownes' Chem.* (ed. 9) 366 The examination of the niobium compounds. **1892** MORLEY & MUIR *Watts' Dict. Chem.* III. 505/2 The existence of three other metals in niobium-containing minerals has been asserted.

niobous (naɪ'əʊbəs), *a. Chem.* [f. NIOB-IUM + -OUS.] Derived from niobium (denoting a lower degree of oxidation than *niobic*).

1863 *Fownes' Chem.* (ed. 9) 366 With oxygen niobium forms two oxides of acid character, niobous acid, NbO, and niobic acid, NbO_2. **1866** WATTS *Dict. Chem.* IV. 49 The fused mass digested in water leaves niobous oxide.

niocalite (naɪəʊ'kælaɪt). *Min.* [f. NIO(BIUM + CAL(CIUM + -ITE¹.] A basic silicate and fluoride of niobium and calcium, $Ca_4NbSi_2O_{10}(OH,F)$, found as yellow orthorhombic crystals.

1956 E. H. NICKEL in *Amer. Mineralogist* XLI. 785 A new mineral species, for which the name 'niocalite' is here proposed, has been identified in rock from the Oka district, 20 miles west of Montreal, Quebec. **1958** *Canad. Mineralogist* VI. 264 The niocalite occurs as randomly oriented, coarse, prismatic crystals up to one centimetre in length, and occasionally even longer, embedded in the calcite. **1966** *Soviet Physics—Doklady* XI. 197/2 The Patterson projections show that niocalite does not have a screw axis.

nione, obs. form of NINE.

niopo (niː'əʊpəʊ). [Native name.] A narcotic snuff used by certain South American Indian tribes, prepared from the seeds of the tropical American trees, *Piptadenia peregrina* and related species. Also *attrib.*

1860 MAYNE REID *Odd People* 134 Snuffing the niopo is not exclusively confined to the Mundrucu. *Ibid.*, The niopo-taker who has one [*sc.* a device for taking snuff, made from the forked bone of a bird], esteems it as the most valuable item of his apparatus. **1900** DORLAND *Med. Dict.* 444/1 Niopo-snuff. .. An intoxicating snuff made from the seeds of *Piptadenia peregrina*, a tree of tropical America. **1966** *New Scientist* 21 Apr. 156/1 Some natives of tropical America use a snuff made from seeds of the tree *Piptadenia peregrina*. .. This is called cohoba, niopo or parica. **1969** R. R. LINGEMAN *Drugs from A to Z* 204 A hallucinogenic snuff is made by South American Indians by pulverizing the seeds of the legumes *Piptadenia peregrina, P. colubrina*, and *P.*

macrocarpa... Among different tribes it is known variously as yopo, niopo, cohoba, and huilca. These tribes are centered in the Orinoco basin of Columbia and Venezuela and in the Peruvian Andes.

nip, *sb.*[1] Also 6 **nyp(pe, nipp, 6–7 nippe.** [f. NIP *v.*[1]]

I. 1. a. The act of compressing sharply between two surfaces, edges, or points; a pinch; a sharp bite.

1551 CRANMER *Answ. Gardiner* (1580) 85 In the last booke you geue Christ such a nippe, that of that whole satisfaction, you pinch halfe away from him. **1573** TUSSER *Husb.* (1878) 206 What bobbed lips, what ierks, what nips! **1615** W. LAWSON *Country Housew. Gard.* (1626) 35 Snub his top with a nip betwixt your finger and your thumb. **1674** N. FAIRFAX *Bulk & Selv.* 181 The dreadfulness of a grim nip, and a dead-doing gripe. **1790** MORISON *Poems* 190 (E.D.D.), Ye'll find it smarter than an adder's nip. **1817** KEATS *'I stood tiptoe'* 144 What amorous and fondling nips They gave each other's cheeks. **1857** W. BROOKES in *Pat. Abridgm., Spinning* (1866) 1249 When by no nip thereof taking place the fibre will remain stationary. **1889** BADEN-POWELL *Pig-sticking* 133 A judiciously applied nip of his sharp little jaws.

fig. **1846** GREENER *Sci. Gunnery* 134 This fraudulent gain ..is called in Birmingham, 'a nip—biting the yokels'.

(*b*) In fig. phr. ***to put in the nips***, *Austral.* and *N.Z. colloq.* to cadge, to ask for a loan. Cf. NIP *v.*[1] 2 c.

1919 [see NIP *v.*[1] 2 c]. **1937** PARTRIDGE *Dict. Slang* 564/1 *Put the nips in*(*to*, to ask a loan (from a person): Australian and New Zealand: from ca. 1908. **1949** L. GLASSOP *Lucky Palmer* 230 You can't put the nips into old Alf. He's got death adders in his pockets. **1955** D. NILAND *Shiralee* 41 He was here yesterday, too. Put the nips into me for tea and sugar and tobacco in his usual style. **1963** B. PEARSON *Coal Flat* x. 190 'The woman's getting too serious,' he thought; 'she's putting the nips in.' **1973** F. HUELIN *Keep Moving* 48 Parsons, priests, doctors, lawyers and professional people generally were legitimate prey, and we had no scruples about 'putting the nips' into them.

b. *Naut.* Severe pressure exerted by ice on the sides of a vessel; the crushing effect of this.

1850 SCORESBY *Cheever's Whalem. Adv.* xiv. (1859) 203 These ships.., which are perpetually subject to heavy blows, and hard nips. **1878** A. H. MARKHAM *Gt. Frozen Sea* xxvi. 389 On the following morning we sustained a slight 'nip', caused by the ice setting rapidly in toward us. **1897** KIPLING *Capt. Cour.* v, That terrible 'nip' of '71, when twelve hundred men were made homeless on the ice.

c. *Naut.* The grip of a rope at a point where it is twisted round something; the part of a rope held fast in this way. ***to freshen the nip***: see FRESHEN *v.* 3.

1841 R. H. DANA *Seaman's Man.* 116 *Nip*, a short turn in a rope. **1859** GEN. P. THOMPSON *Audi Alt.* lxviii. II. 9 There wanted what sailors call 'freshening the nip'. Let us try how the new nip will hold, before we insist too rashly on returning to the old. **1862** *Catal. Internat. Exhib.* II. No. 2659 The nip of the blocks exists only when they sustain the weight of the boat, and ceases when it reaches the water.

d. *Coal mining.* (See quots.)

1839 URE *Dict. Arts* 965 Nips, occasioned by the gradual approximation of the roof and pavement, till not a vestige of coal is left between them. **1851** GREENWELL *Coal-trade Terms, Northumb. & Durh.* 37 *Nip.*—The effect produced upon coal pillars by creep; a crush or squeeze. Also, an approach of the roof and thill of a seam of coal towards each other. **1867** W. W. SMYTH *Coal & Coal-mining* 26 The thinning by a gradual depression of the roof till sometimes the entire coal is gone, but for a certain width only, is a kind of fault (*nip* or *want*).

2. A sharp saying, remark, or comment; a slight rebuke, reproof, or sarcasm. Now somewhat *rare* (very common *c* 1550–1620).

1549 CHALONER *Erasm. on Folly* R iv b, Herto serve the manyfolde nippes and taunts wherwith Christ in divers places..bayteth Pharisees, Scribes and Doctours of Law. **1589** PUTTENHAM *Eng. Poesie* I. xxvii. (Arb.) 68 A prety fashioned poeme..in which euery mery conceited man might..giue a prettie nip, or shew a sharp conceit in few verses. **1604** HIERON *Wks.* I. 476 It was truly said of him,.. that, amongst men, nothing can scape without a nippe. **1676** MARVELL *Mr. Smirke* Wks. (Grosart) IV. 25 Many a dry bob, close gird, and privy nip has he given him. **1738** tr. *Guazzo's Art Conversation* 56 The next kind of ill Tongues ..chop upon you with short nips. **1865** M. ARNOLD *Ess. Crit.* Pref. 13 Many a shrewd nip has he in old days given to the Philistines, this editor.

3. a. A severe check to vegetation caused by cold; the effect of a sharp cold upon plants or animals; the quality in wind or weather which produces this.

1614 D. DYKE *Mystery Selfe-Deceiuing* 87 The flattering of the Sunne raies often drawes forth the blossomes very earely; but afterward come colde nippes. **1631** MILTON *Ep. Marchioness Winchester* 36 So have I seen som tender slip Sav'd with care from Winters nip. **1684** STEPNEY *To Earl of Carlisle*, So hasty fruits and too ambitious flow'rs,..find a nip untimely as their birth. **1873** MRS. WHITNEY *Other Girls* iii, Dismal mornings of waterproofs..and blue nips and shivers. **1894** MRS. H. WARD *Marcella* II. 283 The nip of the east wind was not yet out of the air.

b. *Sc.* The quality of being pungent or stinging; a hot or pungent flavour.

1825 JAMIESON s.v., Bread, and especially cheese, is said to have a *nip*, when it tastes sharp or pungent. **1889** BARRIE *Window in Thrums* v, Lads, humour's what gies the nip to speakin'. **1894** A. S. ROBERTSON *Provost o' Glendookie* 62, I dinna like whiskey wi' a nip.

4. *Cricket* †**a.** A slight touch or stroke given to the ball by the batsman; a tip. *Obs.*

17.. *Laws of Cricket* in Grace *Cricket* (1891) 15 Each Umpire is ye Sole Judge of all Nips and Catches. **1755** *Game at Cricket* 9 A Stroke, or Nip over or under his Bat.

b. The quality in bowling which causes the ball to rise sharply from the pitch.

1963 A. ROSS *Australia 63* iii. 75 Coldwell had been varying pace and direction skilfully and only that lack of final nip which Bedser possessed prevented him from being even more troublesome.

5. *Naut.* (See quot.) *rare*$^{-1}$.

1803 *Man in Moon* (1804) 54 If they get to the windward of our cruizers, it must be with a Hammond's nip. *Note*, A Hammond's nip is a fine perfection in steering, by which it is possible to weather a point, or a vessel, not practicable to do by any other means.

6. ***nip and tuck*** (chiefly U.S.), neck and neck, a close thing. Also *attrib.* ***nip and tuck folder***: see quot. 1964.

1832 J. K. PAULDING *Westward Ho!* I. 172 There we were at rip *and* tuck [*sic*], up one tree and down another. **1847** W. T. PORTER *Quarter Race in Kentucky* 16 (Th.), It will be like the old bitch and the rabbit, nick and tack every jump. *Ibid.* 123 (Th.), Then we'd have it again, nip and chuck. **1857** *Knickerbocker* L. 498 (Th.), [I got the trout off the fire] by the head, and the dog got him by the tail, and it was nip and tuck, pull Dick, pull devil. *a* **1859** in Bartlett *Dict. Amer.* s.v., It was nip and tuck between us. **1884** *Harper's Mag.* Aug. 369/1 It was nip and tuck, neither animals gaining nor losing. **1890** in *Big Game N. Amer.* 92 It was a nip-and-tuck race. **1890** BARRÈRE & LELAND *Dict. Slang* II. 87/1 *Nip and tuck* (Cornwall), a close contest. An old term in wrestling. **1906** J. LONDON *Let.* 1 Dec. (1966) 226 This means..loss of money in the first months of the voyage, during which time things will be just nip and tuck with me. **1948** *Economist* 8 May 764/2 It is nip and tuck whether such a last great achievement of the bipartisan foreign policy can be ratified before..the Presidential race. **1964** *Gloss. Letterpress Rotary Print. Terms* (*B.S.I.*) 25 *Nip and tuck folder*, a type of folder in which the fold at right angles to the run of the web is formed by a blade thrusting the web between folding jaws. **1968** *Economist* 9 Nov. 28/3 The Vice President said that there were still several important states nip-and-tuck. **1974** *State* (Columbia, S. Carolina) 5 Mar. 6-A/1 It was nip and tuck the rest of the way with two straight Cunningham baskets to open the fourth quarter knotting the count, 40–40, with 7:28 left to play.

II. 7. Applied to persons. †**a.** A cutpurse or pickpocket. *Obs.*

1591 GREENE *Disc. Coosnage* To Rdr., The Nip, which the common people call a Cut-purse. **1592** —— *Groat's W. Wit* D iv b, He learned the legerdemaines of nips, foysts, conicatchers, crosbyters. **1630** J. TAYLOR (Water P.) *Wks.* III. 8/2 He..by sleight of hand Can play the Foist, the Nip, the Stale. *a* **1700** B. E. *Dict. Cant. Crew*, *Nip*, a Cheat.

b. *dial.* and *slang.* (See quots.)

1787 W. MARSHALL *E. Norf.* (1795) II. Gloss., *Nip*, a near, split-farthing house-wife. **1823** DE QUINCEY *King of Hayti* Wks. 1859 XII. 60 *note*, Passengers who are taken up on stage coaches by the collusion of the guard and coachman, without the knowledge of the proprietors, are called nips. **1853** COOPER *Sussex Gloss.* (ed. 2), *Nip*, one who is a close and sharp bargain maker, just honest and no more.

8. †**a.** (See quot.) *Obs. rare*$^{-0}$.

a **1700** B. E. *Dict. Cant. Crew*, *Nipps*, the shears with which Money was won't to be Clipt.

b. In wool- or silk-combing apparatus, a piece of mechanism which catches and carries forward the material. Also *attrib.* and *Comb.*

1884 W. S. B. MCLAREN *Spinning* (ed. 2) 109 The Noble combs are supplanting the nips. *Ibid.* 91 The Nip comb.. is in two parts: the screw gill box with the nip motion [etc.]. **1887** *Encycl. Brit.* XXII. 63/2 The silk is caught and cleaned off the endless comb by pairs of endless revolving nips. *Ibid.*, These laps..are taken to the circular nip combing machine.

c. The narrow gap or area of contact between two rollers; the rollers themselves.

1884 W. S. B. MCLAREN *Spinning* 250 Nip of rollers, the point where a pair of rollers touch each other, and where, consequently, they hold or nip the wool. *Ibid.* iii. 35 The lowest rollers..have their nip below the level of the suds. **1946** A. J. HALL *Stand. Handbk. Textiles* iv. 171 The fabric receives a light squeeze as it passes between the nip of the mangle rollers. **1969** W. R. R. PARK *Plastics Film Technol.* ii. 12 Aluminium foil is made by passing hot sheet through a series of hot, highly polished, precision finished metal roll nips. **1972** *Materials & Technol.* V. 515 The opening between the two rolls—the nip—is adjusted in such a way that when pieces of rubber are fed into the nip they are gripped and squeezed through the opening.

III. 9. A small portion, such as may be pinched off something; a fragment, little bit.

1606 CHARTERIS tr. *Rollock's Comm. 2 Thess.* 140 (Jam.), If thou hast not laboured,..looke that thou put not a nip in thy mouth. **1730** RAMSAY *Fables, Fox & Rat* 42 [He] chews the warrant a' in little nips. **1795** *Robin Hood & Beggar* xix. in Child *Ballads* III. 160/2 Think not..that I fear thee any whit For thy curn nips of sticks. **1828** MOIR *Mansie Wauch* xxiii, Water wi' twa or three nips o' braxy floating about in't. **1865** MASSON *Rec. Brit. Philos.* iv. 292 The minutest.. animalcule has its little nip of a cosmos. **1880** MEREDITH *Tragic Comm.* vii. (1892) 104, I will not fight him.., as I do not want to take his nip of life.

10. *Geol.* A low cliff cut along a gently sloping coastline by wave action; also, a notch cut along the base of a pre-existing coastal cliff by wave action.

1897 *Geogr. Jrnl.* IX. 542 Where the aggradation begins at the shoreline at the foot of the earlier formed 'nip'. **1919** D. W. JOHNSON *Shore Processes & Shoreline Development* v. 259 If the lagoon waves are too feeble, the nip may be entirely lacking. **1939** A. K. LOBECK *Geomorphology* x. 347 The smaller waves advance landward and cut low cliffs in the weak material of which the land is usually composed. Thus a nip is produced. **1942** C. A. COTTON *Geomorphology* (ed. 3) xxix. 409 Erosion may be so rapid that in cliffs of tough, unjointed rock a nip is cut—that is, a notch along the base, above which the cliff overhangs. **1958** SPARKS & KNEESE tr. *Guilcher's Coastal & Submarine Morphology* iii. 64 That notches or nips at the base of cliffs are due to mechanical erosion is often much more improbable.

nip, *sb.*[2] Also 8 **nyp.** [app. an abbreviation of NIPPERKIN: cf. NIPPER *sb.*[2]] **1.** †**a.** A half-pint of ale. *Obs.* **b.** A small quantity of spirits, usually less than a glass.

1796 *Grose's Dict. Vulg. Tongue* (ed. 3), *Nyp* or *Nip*, a half pint, a nip of ale; whence the nipperkin, a small vessel. *Ibid.* s.v., *Nyp Shop*..where Burton ale is sold in nyps. **1824** *Blackw. Mag.* XV. 441 Sit down to drink his Burton at 3*d.* the nip. **1869** TROLLOPE *He knew*, etc. xvi, A so-called nip of brandy will create hilarity, or, at least, alacrity. **1890** 'R. BOLDREWOOD' *Col. Reformer* (1891) 127 I'd have been all the better for a nip.

2. *Comb.* **nip bottle,** a miniature bottle of spirits (literally, one containing enough for one drink); **nip joint** *U.S.*, an establishment illegally selling (small quantities of) spirits.

1915 A. D. GILLESPIE *Lett. from Flanders* (1916) 150 The etcetera now includes goggles, respirators, and '*nip bottles' of chemicals. **1939** *Sun* (Baltimore) 18 Aug. 24/7 A hearing by the Liquor Board on the advisability of banning the sale of miniature, or 'nip' bottles of alcoholic drink. **1936** *Ibid.* 28 Jan. 9/1 The bills were opposed by..Raye O. Lawson,.. who said the legislation would increase bootlegging and '*nip joints'. **1938** *Ibid.* 10 Sept. 4/1 The court ordered restored to the owners a house which had been padlocked on conviction of a tenant for operating a 'nip joint'.

†**nip**, *sb.*[3] *Obs. rare.* In 4 **nippe, nype.** [Of uncertain origin and meaning; perhaps repr. OE. *ȝenip* gloom, darkness. Other senses suggested are 'place of piercing cold' and 'peak', 'hill-top' (Skeat *Gloss.*).]

1377 LANGL. *P. Pl.* B. XVIII. 162 Out of the nippe [C. XXI. 168 nype] of the north nouȝt ful fer hennes.

nip, *sb.*[4] Also 7 **nipp(e.** [variant of NEP *sb.*[1]: cf. MDu. *nippe.*]

1. Catmint, catnip. Now *dial.*

1651 FRENCH *Distill.* ii. 61 Take of the Leaves of..Nippe, Peny-royall, of each 2 handfull. **1683** TRYON *Way to Health* 562 They purge their nauseous Stomachs by eating of Grass, as Cats do theirs by eating the Herb Nipp. **1882** *Hardwicke's Science Gossip* 214/2 Suffolk Names— ..'brakes' (bracken); 'nip' (cat-mint); 'gottridge' (gelder-rose). **1895** *E. Anglian Gloss.*, *Nip*, the herb cat-mint, which being covered with a fine white down, has given rise to a common simile 'as white as nip'.

†**2.** Bryony. *Obs. rare*$^{-1}$.

1648 HEXHAM II, *Een Alf Pape*, a white Vine, or Nippe.

†**nip**, *sb.*[5], obs. variant of NIB *sb.* 2.

1721 BAILEY, *Nip*,..the sharp Part of a Pen. **1727** W. MATHER *Yng. Man's Comp.* 74 When you have done writing, set the Nips of your Pens in Water, for the Copperas in the Ink will fret the Nips.

Nip, *sb.*[6] and *a. slang.* [Abbrev. of NIPPONESE.] (A) Japanese. (Usually abusive.)

1942 *Time* 9 Feb. 23/3, I visited a command post in one sector where they had just rounded up a bunch of Nips. **1942** *R.A.F. Jrnl.* 31 Oct. 13 The Nip pilots. **1947** J. BERTRAM *Shadow of War* I. ii. 12 The Nips keep bombing the airfields. **1965** R. T. BICKERS *Scent of Mayhem* iii. 30 La belle Pauline was a secretary at the Nip Embassy in Paris. **1971** J. OSBORNE *West of Suez* I. 27 Few little Nips popping away with cameras. **1973** *Islander* (Victoria, B.C.) 19 Aug. 12/2 Who hadn't quite made up their minds about what should be done with Hitler and Mussolini and the Nips.

nip, *v.*[1] Also 4–6 **nyp(pe, 6–7 nippe, 8 knip.** [app. an ablaut-variant of the stem *nīp-*, which appears in Du. *nijpen*, to NIPE *v.*[2] The precise source of the word, and its relation to some foreign forms (as Da. *nippe* to twitch, to sip, Du. and G. *nippen* to sip, Du. *nippen* to wrangle), are uncertain. Cf. also GNIP and KNIP.]

I. *trans.* **1.** To compress or catch between two surfaces or points; to pinch, squeeze sharply, bite.

1393 LANGL. *P. Pl.* C. VII. 104 Thenne a-waked Wratthe with to white eyen, With a nyuylynge nose nyppyng hus lyppes. ? *a* **1400** in Horstm. *Altengl. Leg.* (1878) 202 Nyppyng his body withe pynsons. **1481** CAXTON *Reynard* (Arb.) 7 Ye haue byten and nypte myn vncle wyth your felle and sharp teeth. **1530** PALSGR. 644/1 He hath nypped me by the arme tyll it is blacke. **1535** COVERDALE *Eccl.* xxii. 24 He that nyppeth a mans eye, bryngeth forth teares. **1585** T. WASHINGTON tr. *Nicholay's Voy.* III. x. 86 They doe bite and with their teeth nip one another. **1633** SANDERSON *Serm.* II. 41 Biting, and nipping, and devouring one another. **1658** (*title*) Naps upon Parnassus: A Sleepy Muse Nipt and Pincht,..by Captain Jones and others. **1821** CLARE *Vill. Minstr.* II. 83 She..nips the portion of her snuff with tears. **1834** M. SCOTT *Cruise Midge* (1863) 178 A creature who would have thought it capital sport to have nipped you in two. **1871** TYNDALL *Fragm. Sci.* I. xxii. (1879) 501 Throwing one leg across the other I accidentally nipped a muscle.

fig. *a* **1548** HALL *Chron., Edw. IV*, 224 This thyng nipped kyng Edwarde hardly at the verie stomacke. **1590** SPENSER *F.Q.* I. x. 27 And sharp Remorse his hart did prick and nip. *a* **1649** CRASHAW *Carmen Deo Nostro* Wks. (1904) 289 Those ignoble stings That nip the bosome of the world's best things.

†**b.** To close up (a glass vessel) by pressing together the heated end of the neck or tube. *Obs.*

1594 PLAT *Jewell-ho.* 91 Howe to nip or close a Glasse with a paire of hot tongues, which is commonlie called *Sigillum Hermetis.* **1610** B. JONSON *Alch.* II. iii, Put 'hem in a Bolts-head, nipp'd to digestion. **1651** FRENCH *Distill.* i. 7 The way to nip up a glasse, or seal it up Hermitically is after this manner. **1665** HOOKE *Microgr.* 36 Nip up the slender Pipe and let it cool.

c. *Naut.* (See latest quots.) Also *absol.*

1667 Davenant & Dryden *Tempest* I. i, Nip well there; quartermaster, get's more nippers. 1850 Ogilvie s.v., *To nip the cable*, in marine language, is to tie or secure it with a seizing. 1876 Voyle & Stevenson *Milit. Dict.* (ed. 3) 488/2 *To Nip*, to stop ropes with a gasket, or with several turns of spun yarn round each, and the ends made fast.

d. *Naut.* Of ice: To squeeze or crush (the sides of a vessel).

1850 S. Osborn *Stray Leaves Arctic Jrnl.* (1852) 72 Penny had passed a long way inside of the spot the steamers had been beset and nipped in. 1853 Kane *Grinnell Exp.* xvi. (1856) 123 We momentarily expected it to 'nip' her sides, or bear her down with the pressure. 1886 Greely *Arct. Service* I. p. xiv, *Nipped*, the situation of a ship when forcibly pressed or jammed by ice. 1937 *Beaver* June 13/2 The 'Fort James', a Company schooner, was 'nipped' in the ice at Tuktuk. 1966 T. Armstrong et al. *Gloss. Snow & Ice* 29 *Nip*, ice is said to nip when it forcibly presses against a ship which is *beset*. A vessel so caught, though undamaged, is said to have been nipped.

2. To sever, remove, or take *off*, by pinching.

a 1400–50 *Alexander* 3940 Of sum þai nyppid fra þe nebb þe nose be þe eʒen. *a* 1450 *Fysshynge w. Angle* (1883) 23 Take þe red worme & nyp of þe hed. 1566 T. Stapleton *Ret. Untr. Jewel* Ep., As if he had nipped a saying of S. Gregory quite in the middest. 1617 Moryson *Itin.* II. 110 The Gardners.. did themselves nip of some buds. 1665 Hooke *Microgr.* 34, I nipped off the small top. 1707 Mortimer *Husb.* (J.), The small shoots.. must be nipt off. *a* 1810 Tannahill *Poems* (1846) 91 When our webs are at the close, He nips aff twa three shillings. 1839 Ure *Dict. Arts* 582 An assistant nips it off from the *punto* with a pair of long iron shears. 1872 H. Macmillan *True Vine* v. 220 Many of the tendrils of the vine require to be nipped off.

b. To strip or make bare by pinching or biting; to remove small portions of (a thing), to reduce the amount of. *rare*.

a 1585 Montgomerie *Flyting* 448 They kow'd all the kytrall, the face of it before; And nipped it sa doones neir, to see it was shame. 1736 Ramsay *Sc. Prov.* (1750) 126 Ye was set aff frae the oon for nipping the pyes. 1785 Grose *Dict. Vulgar T.* s.v. *Nip-cheese*, Those gentlemen being supposed sometimes to nip, or diminish the allowance of the seamen. 1839 Moir *Mansie Wauch* (ed. 2) xxii, The milk-cows were nipping the clovery parks.

c. To borrow, to obtain by wheedling. Cf. nip *sb.*[1] 1. *slang* (chiefly *Austral.*).

1919 W. H. Downing *Digger Dial.* 35 *Nip*, to cadge (or 'Put in the Nips'). 1925 Fraser & Gibbons *Soldier & Sailor Words* 209 *To nip*, to cadge.

† 3. *to nip by, in,* or *on the neck, head,* or *pate*: a. To overpower or overcome (a person) with, or as with, a sudden grip or pinch on these parts; to reduce to a state of helplessness. *Obs.*

c 1470 Henryson *Mor. Fab.* ix. (*Wolf & Fox*) xxxix, Deith cummis behynd, and nippis thame be the nek. 1580 Lyly *Euphues* (Arb.) 359 This question so earnestlye asked .. nipped him in the head. 1589 Greene *Menaphon* (Arb.) 38 Menaphon halfe nipte in the pate with this replie.. made this aunswere. 1620 Sanderson *Serm.* I. 142 This nipped him in the head, and strook cold to his heart. 1667 Dryden & Dk. Newcastle *Sir M. Mar-all* iv. i, Lord, sir, how you stand, as you were nipped i' the head!

†b. To give a decisive or final check to (something). *Obs.*

1594 T. B. *La Primaud. Fr. Acad.* II. To Rdr., This monstrous brood shalbe nipped in the head so soone as euer it shall dare to shew it selfe. 1603 Shaks. *Meas. for M.* III. i. 91 This outward sainted Deputie, Whose setled visage.. Nips youth i'th head, and follies doth emmew. 1642 Rogers *Naaman* 103 Ere ever Christ be truely closed with, sinne must be nipt in the necke.

4. † To check, stop, put an end to, cut short. *Obs.*

1600 Holland *Livy* v. xxx, More Tribes nipped that one law for going forward, than gave their voices to approove it. 1608 D. T. *Ess. Pol. & Mor.* 92 b, Wherewith he nipt the bloody instigations of those Parasits. 1625–8 tr. *Camden's Hist. Eliz.* III. (1688) 327 The Queen.. nipped the man at unawares in his swelling Pride by this one short letter.

†b. Of the wind: To catch and delay (a ship). *Obs.*

1669 Sturmy *Mariner's Mag.* I. ii. 18 Look well to the Westward, if you can see any Ships that have been nipt with the last Easterly Winds.

c. To defeat narrowly (in a sporting contest). *U.S.*

1942 Berrey & Van den Bark *Amer. Thes. Slang* §649/3 Defeat.. nick, nip, outbeat, outwin. 1942 *Sun* (Baltimore) 29 Apr. 19/1 Miss Goshen, under Eddie DeCamillis, came along in the stretch to take the second by two lengths. Sobriquet got up to nip Spare the Rod for second honors. 1951 *Amer. Speech* XXVI. 230/2 Oregon nips St. Mary's. 1966 *N.Y. Times* (Internat. ed.) 22 Apr. 12/1 The Pirates nipped the Reds, 3–2. 1969 *Eugene* (Oregon) *Register-Guard* 3 Dec. 1D/5 The Ducks.. will continue their three-game.. against highly rated Florida State, which nipped touring Oregon State 69–68 Tuesday night. 1974 *Anderson* (S. Carolina) *Independent* 19 Apr. 4B/2 Danny Ford banged out four hits and knocked in two runs as Augusta College nipped Erskine, 6–5, here Thursday.

5. To check the growth or development of (something), after the manner of pinching off the buds or shoots of a plant. Also with *off*.

1581 Mulcaster *Positions* xxxvii. (1887) 145 It is much better to nip misorder in the verie ground. 1682 Bunyan *Holy War* 40 It should be all our wisdoms and care, to nip the head of all such rumors as shall tend to trouble our people. *a* 1716 South *Serm.* (1727) VI. 157 God's Prescription is.. that we nip Sin when it begins to bud in the Thoughts. 1784 Cowper *Task* v. 439 That man should thus encroach on fellow-man,.. nip his fruitfulness and use.. Moves indignation. 1817 Coleridge *Sybil. Leaves*, Some sweet girl of too rapid growth Nipped by Consumption. 1871 R. Ellis tr. *Catullus* lxii. 52 Yet if a slender nail hath nipt his bloom to deflour it. 1880 Browning *Dram. Idyls* II. 78 Nip these foolish fronds Of hope a-sprout. 1902 *Chambers's Jrnl.* Nov. 742/2 Small establishments for the treatment of manufacturing refuse.. are nipped off by a rise in the price of fuel.

b. *to nip in the bud*: To arrest or check at the very beginning, or in a thorough fashion.

1606–7 Fletcher *Woman Hater* III. i, Yet I can frown, and Nip a passion, Even in the bud. 1639 Cokaine *Masque* Dram. Wks. (1874) 8 Dost thou approach to censure our delights, And nip them in the bud? 1677 *Govt. Venice* 307 Had not the Senat.. nipt their Animosity in the Bud. 1712 Steele *Spect.* No. 526 ¶2 Holding it extremely requisite that you should nip him in the Bud. 1746 Hervey *Medit.* (1818) 23 He has nipped infancy in its bud. 1844 W. Irving *Life & Lett.* (1866) III. 321 Insurrections have broken out .., and Government are taking strong measures to nip them in the bud. 1861 Buckle *Civiliz.* II. viii. (1873) 565 This and many other noble projects were nipped in the bud by the death of Charles III.

6. Of cold: To affect (persons, etc.) painfully or injuriously.

a 1548 Hall *Chron., Hen. V*, 48 If.. colde wether had not nipped them,.. they would have made their progress farther. [1579 Spenser *Sheph. Cal.* Dec. 133 The carefull cold hath nypt my rugged rynde.] 1665 *Phil. Trans.* I. 48 Men dangerously nipp'd by excessive cold. 1704 Steele *Lying Lover* I. (1747) 15 To see the dear things trip, trip along, and breathe so short, nipt with the Season. 1829 Col. Hawker *Diary* (1893) II. 4 One of the coldest nights that ever nipped a nose. 1844 Dickens *Mart. Chuz.* xii, The wind blew keenly, nipping the features.

fig. 1596 Drayton *Legends* II. 601 Nipt with cold Death. 1604 Middleton *Father Hubburd's T.* Wks. (Bullen) VIII. 54 A physical frost, that nips the wicked blood a little.

b. To check or destroy the growth of (plants, blossoms, etc.). Also in fig. context.

1588 Shaks. *L.L.L.* v. ii. 812 If frosts.. Nip not the gaudie blossomes of your Loue. 1615 W. Lawson *Country Housew. Gard.* (1626) 14 Roots being so weakly put, are soone nipt with drought or frost. 1671 Milton *Samson* 1577 The first-born bloom of spring Nipt with the lagging rear of winters frost. 1718 Rowe *Lucan* 128 To parch the fading Herb and nip the springing Green. 1778 Edwards 17 Apr. in Boswell *Johnson*, I am curious to see if this frost has not nipped my fruit-trees. 1814 Scott *Ld. of Isles* iv. xxx, Nipp'd by misfortune's cruel frost, The buds of fair affection lost! 1866–7 J. Thomson *Naked Goddess* 239 Storms in Spring nipped bud and sprout.

†7. To censure, reprehend, or rebuke sharply; to direct sharp remarks against (one). *Obs.* (very common *c* 1565–1600).

1548 Udall *Erasm. Par. Luke* viii. 93 He touched and nipped yᵉ pharisees and scribes. 1576 Fleming *Panopl. Epist.* 163 Nipping your people with sharpe reprehensions. 1602 Fulbecke *2nd Pt. Parall.* 26 He was.. more then nipped of Aristophanes. [1720 Strype *Stow's Surv.* (1754) I. I. xxii. 127 The boys of divers schools.., with Epigrams and Rhimes, nipping and quipping their fellows.]

8. To touch or concern (one) closely; to affect painfully, to vex. Now *rare*.

1553 Bradford *Treat. Prayer* Pref., These perilous days of necessity so nip us and provoke us to pray. 1574 tr. *Marlorat's Apocalips* 14 His hart is nipped with heauinesse. 1622 Rowlands *Good Newes & B.* 36 My wooing ouerthrowne, my horse play marr'd, As I am Gentleman, this nips me hard. 1633 Earle *Microcosm., Suspitious Man* (Arb.) 103 Not a word can bee spoke, but nips him somewhere. 1897 Beat. Harraden *H. Strafford*, etc. 199 It was just that which nipped me. I had done a wrong to her, and she had done a wrong to me.

9. To snatch, catch, seize or take smartly. Also with *away, out, up*. Chiefly *dial.* or *slang*.

c 1560 A. Scott *Poems* (S.T.S.) iv. 92 The moir degest and grave, The grydiar to grip it; The nycest to ressave Vpoun the nynis will nip it. 1601 F. Godwin *Bps. of Eng.* 123 That house.. belonged vnto the Archdeaconry, but.. was long since nipped away from the same. 1677 Nicolson *Gloss.* in *Trans. R. Soc. Lit.* (1870) IX. 316 *Nip*, to.. pilfer. 1768 Ross *Helenore* III. 122 Frae your ain uncles gate was nipt awa' That bonny bairn. 1870 E. Peacock *Ralf Skirl.* I. 113 'Why, if there isn't some o' them Bozzel chaps a nippin' up our rabbits.' 1880 C. B. Berry *Other Side* 105 He'd just nip out the pop-gun, and let him have it in the rear. 1894 *Columbus Disp.* 10 Sept., A business man.. from whom he nipped a $250 shirt stud.

b. *slang.* To arrest.

a 1566 R. Edwards *Damon & Pith.* in Hazl. *Dodsley* IV. 19, I go into the city some knaves to nip.., with their goods to increase the kings treasure. 1630 J. Taylor (Water P.) *Wks.* III. 10/2, I haue heard some Serieants haue beene mild, And vs'd their Prisoner like a Christians child; Nip'd him in priuate. 1851 Mayhew *Lond. Labour* III. 147 (Farmer), They'd follow you about, and keep on nipping a fellow.

c. *to nip a bung*, etc. (See quots. and bung *sb.*[2])

1573 Harman *Caveat* (1869) 84 *To nyp a boung*, to cut a pursse. 1592 Greene *Conny Catch.* III. Wks. (Grosart) X. 157 This crew of mates.. said there was no hope of nipping the boung because he held open his gowne so wide. 1621 B. Jonson *Gipsies Metam.* Wks. (Rtldg.) 619/1 Till.. he be able .. to nip a jaw, and cly the jark, 'tis thought fit he march in the infant's equipage. 1712 Shirley *Triumph Wit* (1724) 171 If the Cully he does meet, He nips all his Lour. 1740 *Poor Robin* (Farmer), The cut-purse in the throng, Hath a fair means to nyp a bung.

d. *Cricket.* To strike (a ball) with the edge of the bat, to tip. *rare*⁻¹.

17.. *Laws Cricket* in Grace *Cricket* (1891) 14 If a Ball is nipped up and he [the batter] Strikes her again Wilfully before She comes to ye Wicket, its out.

II. *intr.* 10. To give a nip or pinch; to cause or produce pinching.

c 1460 *Towneley Myst.* xiii. 161 Thay can nyp at oure hyre. *Ibid.* 290 If the flok be skard, yit shall I nyp nere. 1567 Drant *Horace, Ep.* x. Ej. The lesser shoe doth hurt thy foote for pardie it will nip. 1581 Mulcaster *Positions* xx. (1887) 87 The Eastwinde is hurtefull and nippes. 1865 Tester *Poems* 9 (E.D.D.), Words that nip like plasters. 1891 Kipling *City Dreadf. Nt.* iii, Machinery that planes and shaves,.. and punches and hoists and nips.

b. To ache, to smart.

1737 Ramsay *Sc. Prov.* (1750) 124 Ye're new risen and your young heart's nipping. 1806 A. Douglas *Poems* 26 (E.D.D.), O! but my heart nips for the pain, While thro' the green she wanders.

†11. *Cant.* To pick pockets, to steal. *Obs.*

1592 *Def. Conny Catch.* (1859) 4, I had consorts that could verse, nippe, and foyst. *a* 1634 Randolph *Hey for Honesty* III. i, I'll nip from Ruffmans of the Harmanbeck.

12. *slang.* To move rapidly or nimbly. (In quot. 1919 *trans.*) Const. with *in, out, up*, etc. Freq. *fig.*, as to cut *in*, and in extended use, to move informally or unobtrusively, often quickly, *away, out*, etc. Occas. without adv.

1825 Brockett *N.C. Gloss.*, *Nip up*,.. to move quickly. 1863 *Lanc. Fents* 27 So he nipt up th' tree like a cat. 1883 E. Pennell-Elmhirst *Cream Leicestersh.* 159 Pray nip out of the road as quickly as you can. 1889 D. C. Murray *Dangerous Catspaw* 147 'Nip in, sir', said the driver. 'Where do you want to go to?' 1908 H. G. Wells *War in Air* v. 155 She [*sc.* a ship] had.. nipped in between the *Susquehanna* and the *Kansas City*. 1909 A. Quiller-Couch *True Tilda* xiii. 169 'If they catch up with us we must nip into a gateway,' panted Tilda. 1919 *Times Lit. Suppl.* 27 Feb. 107/3 'The light-hearted snottie' who nipped in his piquet boat across the knife-edged ram of a fast travelling cruiser. 1920 *Blackw. Mag.* Jan. 111/2 Your friend.. nips in and takes up the running, and you are out of the hunt. 1920 D. H. Lawrence *Let.* 9 Apr. in C. Mackenzie *My Life & Times* (1966) V. 177 Nip over here for a short while! 1926 T. E. Lawrence *Seven Pillars* lviii. 355 So, watching the time, one or two of the quicker youths nipped across to drag back the saddle-bags. 1930 M. Allingham *Mystery Mile* xxi. 199 'Shall we nip off?' said Knapp nervously. 1930 W. S. Maugham *Bread-Winner* 115 If Uncle Alfred wants us to get out we'd better nip before Daddy comes back. 1930 J. B. Priestley *Angel Pavement* vi. 299 Now then,.. just nip back for the plates. 1947 *People* 22 June 7/5 Meantime, Club No. 2.. nipped in, handed the 'very famous footballer' the thousand smackers.., and clinched the transfer. 1955 M. Gilbert *Sky High* viii. 115 If you nip along now.. you could catch her before the practice starts. 1962 C. Oman *Mary of Modena* v. 187 All the visiting English who could manage it quietly nipped off to see the Prince of Wales. 1969 *Listener* 14 Aug. 205/2 Nipping out for a smoke during the odd bit of Schoenberg. 1973 A. Mann *Tiara* xiii. 118 Piccoli's will still be open. Shall I nip down and get pictures of all these types?

b. Of a cricket ball: to come sharply *off* the pitch; also *absol.*

1899 *Captain* I. 516/1 Another.. makes the ball nip off the pitch like a marble off a granite wall. 1903 P. F. Warner in H. G. Hutchinson *Cricket* xiv. 399 Matting on the bare grassless ground favours the batsman, though I am inclined to think that a really good bowler ought always to be able to make the ball 'nip' a bit.

13. *Comb.* as †**nip-bud** (see quot.); †**nip-cake, -crust, -farthing**, a mean or miserly person (cf. mod. dial. *nip-currant, -screed, -skin*, etc.); **nip-nosed** *a.*, having a small pinched nose; †**nip-shred**, a tailor; †**nip-skin** *v.*, to pinch severely; **nip-waisted** *a.*, having a pinched-in waist. Also nipcheese.

1658 Evelyn *Fr. Gard.* (1675) 101 There is also another kind of small worm, which they call the *Nip-bud. 1508 Dunbar *Flyting* 177 Nyse nagus, *nipcaik, with thy schulderis narrow. 1650 H. More *Observ.* in *Enthus. Tri.*, etc. (1656) 81 A *Nip-crust or Niggard of your precious speculations. 1566 Drant *Med. Morall* A vii, I woulde the not a *nipfarthinge Nor yet a niggarde haue. 1831 *Westm. Rev.* XIV. 424 The crow-footed, *nip-nosed spareness of thirty. 1661 K. W. *Charact. Coxcombs, Hyde-Pk. Lady* (1860) 58 Though her nimble *nipshred never medles with the garments. 1620 T. Granger *Div. Logike* 125 Finally render like for like, that may *nipskin her. 1899 *Crampton's Mag.* Jan. 113 A peevish, *nip-waisted, frizzle-fringed, flirty, flighty, governess.

nip, *v.*[2] [f. nip *sb.*[2] The resemblance to Du. and G. *nippen* (Da. *nippe*), to sip, is evidently quite accidental.]

1. *intr.* To take nips of liquor.

1887 Lady Bellairs *Gossips w. Girls* II. 64 A man who drinks to excess or habitually nips. 1896 Georgiana M. Stisted *True Life R. F. Burton* xi. 267 He could take his bottle after dinner with any man, but nip he could not.

2. *trans.* To take (liquor) in nips.

1897 W. H. Thornton *Reminisc. Clergym.* xi. 323 Some of our young men nip wine or spirits all day long.

†**nip**, obs. or dial. form of neap *v.*

1709 S. Sewall *Diary* 18 Nov., The Ship was on the Ground, and [Capt. Teat] fear'd he should be nip'd.

nipa (ˈniːpə, ˈnaɪpə). Also 6 **nypa, nyp-, niper, nipar, nipe,** 9 **nipah.** [a. Malay *nipah*. Early Portuguese writers call the wine *nipa* and the tree *nipeira*, whence app. the forms *niper, -ar*, etc.]

†1. A kind of toddy obtained from the spadix of the nipa-palm (see 2). Also *attrib. Obs.*

1588 Hickock tr. *C. Frederick's Voy.* 23 b, The greatest merchandise there is verzing, and nypa, which is an excellent Wine, which is had in the flowre of a tree called Nyper. *Ibid.*, Niper Wine is a most excellent drink. 1591 Barker in Hakl. *Voy.* (1599) II. II. 107 We found in her.. three hundred buts of Canarie wine, and Nipar wine, which is made of the palme trees. 1598 W. Phillip tr. *Linschoten's Voy.* 101/2 This *Sura*, being distilled, is called *Fula* or *Nipe*, and is as excellent *aqua vitæ* as any is made in Dort. 1616 R. Cocks *Diary* (Hakl. Soc.) I. 150 A jarr of *nipa* sent me for a present.

2. A kind of palm (*Nipa fruticans*), native to coastal regions in tropical Asia and Australia, having a creeping trunk with large feathery leaves, and bearing large round bunches of fruit; also, the foliage of this plant. Also *attrib.*

1779 T. Forrest *Voy. New Guinea* i. 16 She was covered almost entirely with the leaves of a certain Palm tree, called Nipa, such as the natives cover houses with on the south-west coast of Sumatra, and in almost all Malay countries. **1783** W. Marsden *Hist. Sumatra* 46 Those [people] of the lowest class have their fillet of the leaf of the *neepah* tree. **1817** [see attap]. **1839** Royle *Bot. Himalayan Mount.* 408 The Peruvian *Phytelephas*, with the Asiatic Palm-like *Nipa*. **1846** Lindley *Veget. Kingd.* 132 The juice of Nipa, as it flows from the pounded spadices, furnishes one of the inferior kinds of Palm wine. **1866** *Treas. Bot.* 790/2 The foliage, called Nipah, is used as thatch, and when burnt yields a supply of salt. **1882** De Windt *Equator* 20 Its river banks lined with mangroves and nipa palms. **1926** E. Blatter *Palms Brit. India* 553 Nipa is the vernacular name of the palm in the Philippines. **1954** R. H. Holttum *Plant Life in Malaya* ii. 23 One of the most peculiar of all palms is Nipah, which grows on muddy river banks near the sea. **1962** B. Harrisson *Orang-Utan* iv. 139, I had boarded ship at the mouth of the Rejang River where it had anchored alongside mud, mangrove and nipah-palms. **1966** D. Forbes *Heart of Malaya* xiii. 161 The wooden beach bungalows.. thatched with the nipa palm,.. were all empty. **1969** J. M. Gullick *Malaysia* iv. 160 *Nipah* is a type of palm whose fronds are plaited for use as thatch. **1973** *Telegraph* (Brisbane) 2 Apr. 12/1 They tied the two women up in a nipa (thatched grass) hut.

nipcheese (ˈnɪptʃiːz). [See nip *v.* 13.]

†**1.** *slang.* A ship's purser. *Obs.*

1785 Grose *Dict. Vulgar T.*, *Nip cheese*, a nick name for the purser of a ship. **1791–3** *Spirit Public Jrnls.* (1799) I. 21 The wonderful rise of this quondam nip-cheese has made him very proud of his own abilities. **1837** Marryat *Perc. Keene* xiii, 'That's our nipcheese.' 'Nipcheese!' 'Yes; nipcheese means purser of the ship.'

2. A mean or miserly person.

1825 Brockett *N.C. Gloss.*, *Nip-cheese*, a contemptuous designation for a parsimonious, covetous person. **1864** Sala in *Temple Bar* Jan. 183 Small good.. has the tasteless agitation of these churlish nipcheeses done them.

3. *attrib.* Mean, miserly, niggardly.

1819 *Hermit in London* I. 66 Like a nip-cheese purser of a man of war. **1860** Sala *Lady Chesterfield* v, This nip-cheese, candle-end saving, pebble-peeling.. principle.

†**nipe**, *sb. Obs. rare*$^{-1}$. [f. nipe *v.*^{2}] A nip.

1597 A. M. tr. *Guillemeau's Fr. Chirurg.* 39/2 With our cutting pinsers, we may with one nipe clippe it of.

†**nipe**, *v.*^{1} *Obs.* [OE. *hnipian*, related to ON. *hnípna*, *hnípa*.] *intr.* To bow down, bend, droop; to descend, get low.

c **897** K. Ælfred *Gregory's Past. C.* xxxiv. 234 Ða wearð Cain swiðe ierre, & hnipode ofdune. *a* **1000** *Boeth. Metr.* xxxi. 13 Bið ðeah wuhta ȝehwylc onhniȝen to hrusan, hnipað ofdune. *a* **1100** in Napier *O.E. Glosses* i. 1279 *Curva*, hnipendre, ȝebiȝedre. *c* **1160** *Hatton Gosp.* Matt. xxv. 5 Þa nipeden hyo ealle & slepen. *c* **1205** Lay. 31734 Þa hit wes uppen non, Þa sunne gon to nipen.

†**nipe**, *v.*^{2} *Obs. rare.* In 5–6 nype. [Corresponds to MDu. and MLG. *nipen* (Du. *nijpen*, from which quots. 1481 and 1597 are directly taken). Cf. nip *v.*^{1}] *trans.* To nip.

c **1430** Lydg. *Chorle & Birde* (Roxb.) 9 That smale birdes can nype by the hede. *c* **1440** *Promp. Parv.* 357/1 Nypyn, *premo, stringo.* **1481** Caxton *Reynard* (Arb.) 15 Bruyn the bere.. helde fast his heed and nyped both his fore feet. **1597** A. M. tr. *Guillemeau's Fr. Chirurg.* 20 b/1 The Chirurgiane must nype in the length of all the skinne and the fleshy pannickle.

Hence †**ˈniper**, one who nips; †**ˈniping** *vbl. sb.*

c **1440** *Promp. Parv.* 357/1 Nypare, *compressor, trusor. Ibid.*, Nypynge, *compressio.* **1546** Bale *Eng. Votaries* i. (1550) 75 b, Callynge them.. perjures, nypers, serpentes, deuourers, rauenours. **1597** A. M. tr. *Guillemeau's Fr. Chirurg.* 22 b/2 Avoydinge the nipinge of the little tonges. **1647** Hexham i, A Niper, *een nyper.*

Nipkow disc (ˈnɪpkɒf). *Television.* [f. the name of Paul *Nipkow* (1860–1940), Polish electrical engineer, who invented it in 1884.] A scanning disc used in some early television transmitters and receivers having a line of small apertures near the circumference arranged in a spiral of one complete turn, so that on each revolution of the disc an area is scanned equal in height to the radial distance between the first and last apertures.

1934 J. H. Reyner *Television* xiv. 161 Until recent times most of the Continental systems.. have been of the Nipkow disc type, and in that main respect similar to the Baird system. **1962** G. A. T. Burdett *Automatic Control Handbk.* xxi. 6 There are three types of scanning device in existence, .. the Nipkow disc, .. the flying-spot scanner and the pick-up tube. *Ibid.*, A development of the Nipkow disc has recently been produced in the U.S.A. for use as a slow-scan device for the transmission of documents. **1974** *Encycl. Brit. Macropædia* XVIII. 105/2 Until the advent of electronic scanning, all workable television systems depended on some form or variation (*e.g.*, mirror drums, lensed disks, etc.) of the mechanical sequential scanning method exemplified by the Nipkow disk.

†**ˈniplet.** *Obs. rare.* [f. nipple + -et^1.] A small nipple.

1648 Herrick *Hesp.*, *How Lillies came white*, The rubie niplet of her breast. —— *Upon the Nipples of Julia's Breast*, So like to this.. Is each neate Niplet of her breast.

nipped (nɪpt), *ppl. a.* [f. nip *v.*^{1} + -ed^1.] That has been, or is, pinched, compressed, severely checked, etc.

1535 [see nippet, nippit]. **1615** Jackson *Creed* v. iv, Human affections like to liquors kept in close vessels or nipt glasses secretly multiply their natural strength. **1759** *Compl. Lett.-Writer* (ed. 6) 223 Jenny Rowland's nipped short waist. **1816** Byron *Ch. Har.* iii. liv, In solitude Small power the nipp'd affections have to grow. **1820** Shelley *Autumn* ii, The chill rain is falling, the nipped worm is crawling. **1897** *Allbutt's Syst. Med.* III. 477 A nipped expression of face.

b. With *in* or *up*, denoting a compressed or contracted state.

1850 Ansted *Geol.* §1158 The levels at those places where the lode is narrow, or nipped in, are very narrow and confined. **1867** Waugh *Winter Fire* iii, Th' hinder-quarter's nipt in like a greyhound whelp. **1892** Mrs. Clifford *Aunt Anne* I. 184 She said I looked nipped-up, and asked me to sit down and get warm.

†**nipped** *a.*, obs. var. nibbed *a.* (Cf. nip *sb.*^{4})

1725 Bailey *Erasm. Colloq.* (1878) I. 103 Do you love to write with a hard-nip'd Pen or a soft?

nipper (ˈnɪpə(r)), *sb.*^{1} Also 6–8 nypper, 8 knipper. [f. nip *v.*^{1} + -er^1.]

I. 1. a. One who nips, in senses of the verb. Freq., down to *c* 1640, in citations or echoes of Isa. l. 5.

1535 Coverdale *Isa.* l. 5, I offre my backe vnto ẏ smyters, and my chekes to the nyppers. *a* **1568** Ascham *Scholem.* i. (Arb.) 85 Ready bakbiters, sore nippers, and spitefull reporters priuilie of good men. **1611** A. Stafford *Niobe* 93 Thou nipper of mirth, thou vnpleasant toyle. **1630** *R. Johnson's Kingd. & Commw.* 6 Cold [is] the great enemie and nipper of vegetation. **1661** Jer. Taylor *Serm. Opening Parl. Ireland* 8 May, [Jesus] gave his back to the smiters and his cheeks to the nippers.

b. A close-fisted, miserly person.

1573 L. Lloyd *Marrow of Hist.* (1653) 16 Amongst so many nippers of money, he onely shewed himself bountifull and liberall. **1879** F. W. Robinson *Coward Consc.* ii. xiii, That old, disagreeable nipper of a cousin of yours.

c. *U.S.* The Cunner, which nips the bait from the hooks, and the Bluefish, which nips pieces out of other fishes. (Cf. nibbler 2.)

1888 Goode *Amer. Fishes* 297 At Salem they [the Blue Perch] are called 'Nippers', and occasionally here and elsewhere 'Bait-stealers'.

†**2.** *Cant.* A thief or pickpocket. *Obs.*

1585 Fleetwood in Ellis *Orig. Lett.* Ser. i. II. 278 He that could take a peece of sylver out of the purse without the noyse of any of the bells, he was adjudged a judiciall Nypper. *Ibid.*, Nypper is termed a Pickepurse or a Cut-purse. *c* **1600** Day *Begg. Bednall Gr.* i. iii. (1881) 21 Your nipper, your foyst, your rogue, your cheat, your pander. **1785** Grose *Dict. Vulgar T.*, *Nypper*, a cut purse, so called by one Wotton, who in the year 1585, kept an academy for the education.. of pick-pockets.

3. a. A boy who assists a costermonger, carter, or workman.

1851 Mayhew *Lond. Labour* I. 33 Such lads.. are the smallest class of costermongering youths; and are sometimes called 'cas'alty boys', or 'nippers'. **1882** *Lanc. Gloss.*, *Nipper*, a carter's assistant; a lad who accompanies a lurry or cart. **1887** *Q. Rev.* Jan. 129 Thirty two spikers with a nipper to each pair drove 63,000 spikes. **1968** *Courier-Mail* (Brisbane) 21 Nov. 3/5 The men, employed by the Public Works Department, claimed the job foreman would not let their 'nipper' patronise the sandwich shop of his choice. A nipper is a boy or man who boils the billies, runs messages, buys lunches, and does similar jobs. **1971** R. Roberts *Classic Slum* viii. 125 The nippers, carters' helps. The nipper looked after the horse and sat guard over goods at the tail end of the vehicle.

b. *slang.* A boy, a lad. Also, a girl; a child of either sex; the smallest or youngest of a family.

[**1847** Dickens *Dombey* (1848) xxiii. 240 Florence endeavoured to believe that the Captain was right; but the Nipper.. shook her head in resolute denial.] **1859** Hotten *Dict. Slang* 68 *Nipper*, a small boy. **1872** *Daily News* 8 Apr. 5/4 When he was a 'nipper' the wages were 11*s.* a week, with victuals found. **1875** W. D. Parish *Dict. Sussex Dial.*, *Nipper*, a common nickname for the youngest member of the family, or for one who is unusually small for his age. **1886** R. C. Leslie *Sea Painter's Log* 26 Such a boy looks down upon mudlarks very much, calling them nippers and other scornful names. **1892** Williams *Round London* (1893) 85 The mind of the East End 'nipper' is equal to most emergencies. **1901** M. Franklin *My Brilliant Career* x. 81 By George, you're a wonderful-looking girl!.. You are such a little nipper. **1928** J. Mason *Before Mast in Sailing Ships* 128 Next to Clarke was a Scottish lad by the name of Nisbet, from Inverness-shire. He was the smallest, and was called the 'Nipper'. **1941** *Lilliput* Mar. 371/1 A family party.. arrived on the scene: Mother, aunty, two nippers—a girl and a boy. **1959** I. & P. Opie *Lore & Lang. Schoolch.* ix. 170 Little 'uns.. midge, nipper, penguin, pint-size. **1967** *Courier-Mail* (Brisbane) 3 Feb. 6/8 The establishment of 'nipper clubs' for boys aged from eight to 13 would guarantee the future of the surf club movement. **1969** Visct. Buckmaster *Roundabout* ii. 35 He [*sc.* a butler] was.. always in domestic trouble from the arrival of what he would call 'another little nipper'. **1972** *Times* 3 June 19/1 When I was a nipper at school in Glasgow [etc.].

II. 4. a. *pl.* An instrument, usually made of iron or steel, having two jaws by which a thing may be firmly seized and held, or cut through, by pressure exerted upon the handles; forceps, pincers, pliers. Frequently called ***a pair of nippers.***

Various forms and sizes are used for different purposes.

1541 R. Copland *Guydon's Quest. Chirurg.* A iii, A Cyrurgyen.. oughte to haue .v. [irons] as Cysers, Nyppers Launcettes, Rasoures, and Nedelles. **1580** Blundevil *Horsemanship* iv. 68 b, You may pull it out with a paire of nippers. **1658** Sir T. Browne *Hydriot.* 18 Brazen nippers to pull away hair. **1688** Holme *Armoury* iii. xxii. (Roxb.) 269/1 He beareth Or, a pair of Nippers, Sable. By the help of these any small peece of Tyn, corner or end, is nipt or cut off. **1752** Mrs. Delany *Life & Corr.* (1861) III. 179 They must be drawn out of their case with a pair of knippers, no fingers are small enough. **1765** *Chron.* in *Ann. Reg.* 158, 85 pair of shoemakers nippers and pincers. **1803** *Med. Jrnl.* X. 68 Two pair of nippers or small pincers for extracting filaments. **1832** Babbage *Econ. Manuf.* xi. (ed. 3) 87 The operator then pinches it between the ends of a pair of nippers. **1865** Livingstone *Zambesi* xv. 305 Its teeth are.. so arranged that the edges cut a hook like nippers.

sing. **1688** Holme *Armoury* iii. 309/1 A Glasiers Nipper or Grater. **1875** Knight *Dict. Mech.* 1528/1 *Nipper*, a grasping tool with cutting jaws.

b. An implement used for seizing large stones in order to move them freely.

1840 *Civil Eng. & Arch. Jrnl.* III. 29/1 The stones.. were first held fast by an implement, technically called nippers or devil's claws. **1898** *Daily News* 10 Oct. 9/3 A chain weighing several tons was being lowered down the pit shaft by means of nippers.

c. *slang.* Handcuffs.

1821 D. Haggart *Life* 94 That's one of the bulkies from Dumfries, wanting to clap the nippers on me. **1823** Egan *Grose's Dict. Vulgar T.* **1876** J. S. Ingram *Centenn. Exposition* viii. 235 The curious part of this [hardware] exhibit consisted in the police nippers. **1910** *Encycl. Brit.* X. 296/1 Several recently invented appliances are used as handcuffs, *e.g.* snaps, nippers, twisters. They differ from handcuffs in being intended for one wrist only... The nippers can be instantly fastened on the wrist. **1918** *Outlook* (N.Y.) 25 Sept. 126/1 A newly appointed policeman.. has to buy.. a pair of nippers. **1939** *Fortune* July 104/1 At 2145 one of the detectives put nippers on the prisoner's wrist. **1950** H. E. Goldin *Dict. Amer. Underworld Lingo* 145/2 We hit a scorf joint (went into an eating place), and the dick (detective) took the nippers off.

d. *slang.* Eyeglasses, pince-nez.

1876 Lowell *Lett.* (1894) II. 183, I am writing at this moment with spectacles (not nippers, mind you..) across my prosaic nose. **1899** *Westm. Gaz.* 28 Jan. 2/1 Miss Flint (slowly donning a pair of pince-nez): What's the good of nippers?

5. (Usually in *pl.*) **a.** One of the incisors, or cutting teeth of a horse.

1696 Sir W. Hope tr. *Solleysel's Parf. Mareschal* 19 There groweth then in the place of these four Foal-teeth.. four others which are called Nippers or Gatherers. **1727–38** Chambers *Cycl.* s.v. *Tooth*, *Nippers*, which are the two foremost teeth above, and as many below, which an horse first changes. *a* **1842** Sir C. Bell *Anat. Expression* (1844) ii. 53 The incisor teeth or nippers project. **1854** Owen in *Orr's Circ. Sci.*, *Org. Nat.* I. 285 The first deciduous incisor—'centre nipper' of veterinarians—.. usually cuts the gum between the third and sixth days.

b. One of the great claws or chelæ of the Crustacea.

1769 Bancroft *Guiana* 240 Five pair of legs,.. each.. armed at the end with a pair of red nippers. *a* **1774** Goldsm. *Nat. Hist.* (1776) VI. 369 The two nippers or claws resemble the thumbs. **1848** Johns *Week at Lizard* 259 The insertion of the point of a knife into the joint of the great claws.. renders the nippers powerless.

fig. **1877** Tennyson *Harold* ii. ii, Our great Count-crab will make his nippers meet in thine heart.

attrib. **1863** Wood *Illustr. Nat. Hist.* III. 585 The Nipper-crab (*Polybius Henslowii*) is a better swimmer than the fiddler-crab. **1863** Kearley *Links in Chain* vii. 153 Its great hairy nipper claws give it a very distinctive character.

6. a. A device to regulate the amount of tar used in tarring a rope.

1794 *Rigging & Seamanship* 55 A nipper is formed of two steel plates, eight inches square and half an inch thick, with a semi-oval hole in each four inches wide, which, by the upper plate moving, enlarges or contracts as the tarring of the yarn requires.

b. In wool-combing machinery, a device for seizing and holding the material.

1852 Lister & Ambler in *Pat. Abridgm.* (1866) 653 A thin plate of iron is inserted between the rows of the teeth so as to act as a nipper. **1889** J. Burnley *Wool & Wool Combing* 228 The nipper consists of a leather-covered jaw and a top jaw with three flutes.

7. *Naut.* **a.** A piece of braided cordage used to prevent a cable from slipping.

1627 Capt. Smith *Seaman's Gram.* ix. 44 [The cable] surges or slips backe vnlesse they keep it close to the whelps, and then they.. hold it fast with nippers. **1667** Davenant & Dryden *Tempest* i. i, Nip well there; quartermaster, get's more nippers. **1769** Falconer *Dict. Marine* (1780) s.v., These nippers are usually six or eight feet in length. **1825** H. B. Gascoigne *Naval Fame* 47 The gaining side and Cable bound in one, By pliant Nippers which the Boys hold on. **1867** Smyth *Sailor's Word-bk.* 498 The nipper is passed at the manger-board, the fore-end pressing itself against the cable.

attrib. **1769** Falconer *Dict. Marine* (1780) s.v. *Nipper*, The persons employed to bind the nippers about the cable and voyal, are called nipper-men. **1802** *Naval Chron.* 51 We have plenty of powder forward in the nipper-lockers.

b. (See quot.) *rare*$^{-0}$.

1867 Smyth *Sailor's Word-bk.*, *Nipper*, a hammock with so little bedding as to be unfit for stowing in the nettings.

c. A thick woollen mitten or glove used by codfishers to protect their wrists and hands.

1897 Kipling *Capt. Cour.* 56 A heavy blue jersey well darned at the elbows, a pair of nippers, and a sou'wester.

ˈnipper, *sb.*^{2} [abbrev. of nipperkin.] = nip *sb.*^{2}

1848 Lowell *Biglow Papers* Ser. i. ii, Step up and take a nipper, sir; I'm dreffle glad to see you. **1866** *Brit. Workman* xii. 78 He could not pass it without having what he termed his 'nipper', or what some of the good people of Scotland call their 'morning'.

'nipper, *sb.*³ [f. NIP *v.*²] One who takes nips.
1886 *Home Words* XVI. 21 The 'Nipper', says with confidence, 'the little drop which I take would hurt nobody'.

nipper ('nɪpə(r)), *v.*¹ [f. NIPPER *sb.*¹]
1. *Naut.* To secure (a rope) by means of cross-turns; to fasten with nippers.
1794 *Rigging & Seamanship* 190 The strap is nippered, with a heaver, round the block. **1841** R. H. DANA *Seaman's Man.* 43 Nippering, is fastening them [two parts of a rope] by taking turns crosswise between the parts, to jam them; and sometimes with a round turn before each cross. *c* **1860** H. STUART *Seaman's Catech.* 34 Heaving the two parts of the lanyard close together so as to nipper them.
2. *slang.* To take into custody.
1832 *Lincoln Herald* 18 Sept. 2/4 You had better nash (go away) unless you want to be nippered (taken into custody).

'nipper, *v.*² *rare*⁻¹. [Imitative.] *intr.* To whisper, gossip.
1840 LADY C. BURY *Hist. of Flirt* xxviii, What are you and the major 'nippering' about?

nipperkin ('nɪpəkɪn). Now *rare.* Also 7–8 kn-, 7 niper-. [Of obscure etym. The form points to a Du. or LG. origin: cf. MDu. *nypelkin*, the name of some game.]
1. A measure or vessel of small capacity used for liquors, containing half-a-pint or less.
1694 MOTTEUX *Rabelais* V. xxxiv. (1737) 152 Barrels, Nipperkins, Pint-Pots, Quart-Pots. **1739** R. BULL tr. *Dedekindus' Grobianus* 158 Some..puff in ev'ry Nipperkin of Ale. **1755** SHEBBEARE *Lydia* (1769) I. 350 The old song, which goes on with the gallon,..the pint, the half-pint, the nipperkin, and the brown bowl. **1796** [see NIP *sb.*²]. **1832** *Blackw. Mag.* XXXI. 320 The nipperkins, cups, and cans, The skillets, and kettles, and all.
2. The quantity of liquor that can be contained in such a measure; a small quantity of wine, ale or spirits. In later use chiefly *Sc.*
1671 MRS. BEHN *Amorous Prince* IV. iv, 'Tis something cold, I'le go take a Niperkin of wine. *a* **1700** B. E. *Dict. Cant. Crew*, *Nipperkin*, half a Pint of Wine, and but half a Quartern of Brandy, Strong waters, &c. **1792** BURNS *Let. to Cunningham* 10 Sept., I have set a nipperkin of toddy by me. **1813** WOLCOT (P. Pindar) *On Style of Johnson*, Such a clatter, To force up one poor nipperkin of water. **1856** STRANG *Glasgow & its Clubs* 530 Kindred spirits met to quaff their nipperkin of ale. **1890** SERVICE *Notandums* xi. 77 We juist hae time for a nipperkin o' yuill.

nippet, nippit. Sc. varr. NIPPED *ppl. a.* (chiefly in senses: miserly; scanty; starved; of restricted mental attitude; bitter, sarcastic).
1535 LYNDSAY *Satyre* 150 Howbeit my coat be schort and nippit, Thanks be to God, I am weill hippit. **1808** JAMIESON, *Nippit*, adj. 1. Niggardly, parsimonious... 2. Too small, scanty. **1814** C. I. JOHNSTONE *Saxon & Gaël* I. ix. 121 Na, na, I ne'er liket to be nippit or pinging, gie me routhrie o' a'thing. **1857** H. S. RIDDELL *St. Matthew* xxv. 24, I kennet thee that thou art ane nippet man, sheerin' whare thou hestna sawn, an' getherin' whare thou hestna strinklet. *c* **1860** in *Scotsman* (1912) 13 Sept., 'She is a puir nippet creater'—A poorly-fed child. **1875** N. ELLIOTT *Nellie Macpherson* 165 As regards the langidge, ye maunna be ower nippet on that point. **1924** A. DODD *Poppies in Corn* 33 Ye're naewise mean or nippit. **1925** *Glasgow Herald* 23 May 4/4 Nannie..rejected nothing—but oatcakes. The misguided and 'nippet' woman at the Sluices once offered these, conspicuously ill-baked. **1935** D. KIRKWOOD *My Life of Revolt* 222 Philip Snowden's views were precise, narrow, and moulded by the immediate circumstances. The Scotsmen used to call him 'nippet'. **1962** *Buchan Observer* 24 July 2 Nippet words an' soor ill-naiter Gart her man an' bairns behave!

'nippily, *adv.* [f. NIPPY *a.* + -LY².] In a nippy manner; sharply.
1650 A. B. *Mutat. Polemo* 21 Let such be nippily markt and taken notice of. **1972** *Guardian* 10 Nov. 11/1 The new 3-Door Renault 5..[will] take you nippily through the town traffic snarl-ups. **1974** *Times* 3 Jan. 23/3 The 128 [Fiat] handles nippily, with good roadholding.

nippiness ('nɪpɪnɪs). [f. NIPPY *a.* + -NESS.] Nimbleness, agility.
1923 U. L. SILBERRAD *Lett. J. Armiter* ii. 50 Jethro is smitten with admiration of her agility; 'nippiness' he calls it. **1932** *Daily Express* 2 July 11/2 Perry's volleys, Hughes' return of service and overhead smashing, and the perpetual nippiness of our two men, gave us the victory.

nipping ('nɪpɪŋ), *vbl. sb.*¹ [-ING¹.] The action of NIP *v.*¹ in various senses.
1572 HULOET, Nippes or nippinges, *compressiones.* **1606** *Proc. agst. Late Traitors* 25 For the blasting and nipping, both of the leaves, blossomes and buddes. **1626** BACON *Sylva* §388 In Orenges or Limons, the Nipping of their Rinde, giveth out their Smell the more. **1693** EVELYN *De la Quint. Compl. Gard.* II. 54 Pruning..with the Pruning-Knife, when the bare Trimming or Nipping is not sufficient. **1707** MORTIMER *Husb.* (1721) II. 42 It..preserves it self the best from the nipping of Deer. **1853** KANE *Grinnell Exped.* xxviii. (1856) 231 Wherever the nipping has caught two of the floes, they have been driven with a force inconceivable one above the other.
b. *concr.* A portion nipped off.
1766 *Compl. Farmer* s.v. *Rag* 6 I 1/2 Woollen Rags, and the nippings of the pitch-marks upon sheep, are a singularly good manure.

'nipping, *vbl. sb.*² [f. NIP *v.*² + -ING¹.] The action or practice of taking nips of liquor.
1883 *Longm. Mag.* June 180 A horrible Australian habit, ..is the practice of 'nipping' on bargains. **1896** GEORGIANA M. STISTED *True Life R. F. Burton* xi. 267 This nipping.. disagreed frightfully with Burton.

'nipping, *ppl. a.* (and *adv.*) [f. NIP *v.*¹ + -ING².] That nips, in various senses of the verb.
1. Of language: Sharp, stinging, sarcastic.
1547 LATIMER *Serm. & Rem.* (Parker Soc.) 426 After you had perused that my nipping and unpleasant letter. **1556** ROBINSON tr. *More's Utopia* (Arb.) 105 *marg.*, In this place seemethe to be a nipping taunte. **1581** J. BELL *Haddon's Answ. Osor.* 497 So much rayling in such scorpionlike nipping bitternesse. **1594** CAREW *Huarte's Exam. Wits* xv. (1596) 311 Hence tooke a certaine nipping prouerbe his originall. *a* **1693** *Urquhart's Rabelais* III. x. 80 Nipping Bobs, derisive Quips.
2. Of the weather, wind, etc.: Sharp, cold, biting; checking growth, blighting.
1563 B. GOOGE *Eglogs*, etc. (Arb.) 103 To keepe her feete from force of nyppynge colde. **1581** MULCASTER *Positions* xxxvi. (1887) 141 As there be faire blossomes, so there be nipping frostes. **1602** SHAKS. *Ham.* I. iv. 2 It is a nipping and an eager ayre. **1669** WORLIDGE *Syst. Agric.* (1679) 134 The sharp nipping winds. **1707** MORTIMER *Husb.* (1721) I. 308 Bleak Hills much exposed to high Winds and nipping Frost. **1764** HARMER *Observ.* i. §xvi. 40 Most nipping, pinching, unpleasant wind. **1828** SCOTT *F.M. Perth* xiii, It irks me the more to put on cold harness in this nipping weather. **1865** DICKENS *Mut. Fr.* I. xii, It was..a nipping spring with an easterly wind.
3. Causing pain or distress.
c **1550** *Pryde & Abuse Wom.* 181 in Hazl. *E.P.P.* IV. 242 We wonder moche at these nyppynge plages. **1583** STUBBES *Anat. Abus.* II. (1882) 52 They applie bitter potions, nipping medicines, gnawing corrosiues. **1608** WILLET *Hexapla in Exod.* 512 A biting, nipping, or deuouring vsurie. **1659** D. PELL in Spurgeon *Treas. Dav.* Ps. cvii. 28 Brought low by pinching and nipping afflictions.
†**4.** Affected, mincing. *Obs. rare*⁻¹.
1568 *Jacob & Esau* II. ii, So nipping, so tripping, so cocking, so crowing.
5. That nips, grips, or holds. ***nipping-fork*** (see quot. 1881), ***-roller.***
1831 YOUATT *Horse* 138 The colt's nipping teeth are rounded in front. **1858** HOLDEN & HUBNER in *Pat. Abridgm.* (1866) 1290 Two pairs of continuously operating and moving nipping surfaces. **1870** H. A. NICHOLSON *Man. Zool.* xxxvii. (1875) 269 The maxillary palpi..are converted into nipping-claws or chelæ. **1881** RAYMOND *Mining Gloss.*, *Nipping-fork*, a tool for supporting a column of bore-rods while raising or lowering them. **1920** *Discovery* Mar. 88/1 The padded goods are well squeezed through nipping-rollers, and then dried and 'backed'. **1964** *Gloss. Letterpress Rotary Printing Terms (B.S.I.)* 25 *Nipping rollers*, a pair of rollers adjustable to exert pressure to set a fold. **1967** V. STRAUSS *Printing Industry* vi. 382/2 The cutting cylinder cuts the web after it passes the nipping rollers.
6. *adv.* Nippingly.
1840 R. H. DANA *Bef. Mast* xxix. 99 The water was nipping cold.

nippingly ('nɪpɪŋlɪ), *adv.* [f. NIPPING *ppl. a.* + -LY².] In a nipping manner, in various senses of the adj.
1542 UDALL *Erasm. Apoph.* 184b, Nippyngly did he taunte..the foolishe ambicion of theim. **1586** T. B. *La Primaud. Fr. Acad.* I. (1589) 365 Stop the mouthes of such as are..impudent,..with a certaine meekenes and grave smiling, and somewhat nippingly. **1853** LYTTON *My Novel* I. xii, Pinching her husband's arm very nippingly. **1879** 'ANNIE THOMAS' *London Season* I. 19, 'I don't see it at all', Mrs. Varney nippingly replies. **1890** *Cornh. Mag.* Sept. 257 Though the wind blow nippingly from the snow.

†**'nippitate**, *sb. Obs.* Also -ato, -atum, -aty, (-ati). [Of obscure origin. The Latin and Italian endings are prob. only fanciful. The most usual form is that in *-aty.*] Good ale or other liquor of prime quality and strength.
α. **1575** LANEHAM *Lett.* (1871) 31 Az yet too the tast of a cup of Nippitate, his iudgement will be taken aboue the best in the parish.
β. **1576** FULWELL *Art Flattery* I. v. (1579) E iv b, The best Nippitatum in this towne, which is commonly called Hufcap. **1583** STUBBES *Anat. Abuses* E vij b, Though it will be a corrosive to their hautie stomacks and a nippitatum to their tender brests. *Ibid.* M iv b, When this Nippitatum, this Huf cap (as they call it), and this nectar of lyfe, is set abroach, well is he that can get the soonest to it.
γ. **1593** G. HARVEY *Pierce's Super.* 16 The nippitaty of the nappiest grape. *Ibid.* 63. **1600** NASHE *Summer's Last Will* in Hazl. *Dodsley* VIII. 60 Never cap of Nipitaty in London came near thy niggardly habitation! **1630** *Tincker of Turvey* Ep. Ded. 4 He loves that ale-house best, which washes his cheekes with the strongest nippitaty. *a* **1693** *Urquhart's Rabelais, Pantagr. Prognost.* ix, 'Tis all one to me, so we have but good Bub and *Nippitati* enough.
δ. **1611** BEAUM. & FL. *Kt. Burning Pestle* IV. ii, My father oft will tell me of a drinke In England found, and Nipitato cal'd. **1620** MELTON *Astrolog.* 32 They cannot put a Cup of Nippitato to their Snowts.
Hence †**nippitate** *a.*, strong, good, prime. *Obs.*
1600 *Look About You* xxi. in Hazl. *Dodsley* VII. 445 He was here to-day, sir, And emptied two bottles of nippitate sack. **1600** *Weakest goeth to Wall* (1618) B 2 Fresh ale, prime ale, nappie ale, nippitate ale! *a* **1634** CHAPMAN *Alphonsus* Plays 1873 III. 238 'Twill make a cup of Wine taste nippitate.

nipple ('nɪp(ə)l), *sb.* Forms: *α.* 6 **neble, nible,** 7 **nibble.** *β.* 6 **neapil, neaple, nypil,** 7 **nipl,** 6– **nipple.** [Of uncertain origin: there is no clear connexion with OE. *nypel*, used by Ælfric of an elephant's trunk.]
1. a. The small prominence, composed of vascular erectile tissue, in which the ducts of the mammary glands terminate externally in nearly all mammals of both sexes; esp. that of a woman's breast; a teat.
α. **1530** PALSGR. 247/2 Neble of a womans pappe, *bout de la mamelle.* **1598** HAYDOCKE tr. *Lomazzo* I. 30 The heades or extuberances whence the milke is sucked out, are called Nibles. **1611** COTGR., *Tetin*, the nibble or nipple of a dug. **1650** MASSEY *Glasse for Worldlings* 21 So much wormwood withall makes me nauseat the nibble. **1682** N. O. *Boileau's Lutrin* II. 114 Or Caucasus did form thee, of a Pebble, Or some fell Tigress nurs'd thee with her nibble.
β. **1538** ELYOT, *Papilla*, the nyppell or teate of a womannes breaste. **1570** LEVINS *Manip.* 125/26 A Nypil, *papilla. Ibid.* 209/8 A Neaple, teate, *papilla.* **1592** SHAKS. *Rom. & Jul.* I. iii. 30 It did tast the Worme-wood on the nipple of my Dugge. **1598** CHAPMAN *Iliad* IV. 568 Thoas..threw a dart, that did his pile convay Above his nipple, through his lungs. **1656** RIDGLEY *Pract. Physick* 156 The child will suck, and not touch the Nipple with his Lips. **1707** *Phil. Trans.* XXV. 2216 A small portion of it, in the form of a Nipple, did intrude itself as it were under the Tongue. **1803** *Med. Jrnl.* IX. 428 A tumour appeared under his left nipple. **1835** KIRBY *Hab. & Inst. Anim.* II. xxiv. 477 The elephant..has only two pectoral nipples. **1869** LADY LYTTON *Orval* 139 A finer babe was never Put to the nipple.
fig. **1642** FULLER *Holy & Prof. St.* V. xiv. 411 He infected the Universitie, from which he suck'd no milk but poysoned her nipples.
b. *transf.* A device used to cover the nipple while a child is sucking; also, the teat of a nursing-bottle.
1661 LOVELL *Hist. Anim. & Min.* 412 The paine in sucking may be prevented by an artificial nipple, covered with that of a young heifer. **1875** KNIGHT *Dict. Mech.* 1528/2 The nipple..has a stop-flange to keep it from passing too far into the infant's mouth.
2. a. Something resembling a nipple in function as well as form.
1573 BARET *Alv.* s.v., A little cocke, end, or nipple perced, ..which is put at the end of the cannelles of a fountayne, where through yᵉ water commeth forth. **1841** *Civil Eng. & Arch. Jrnl.* IV. 93/2 A stop cock..so adjusted as to allow any number of drops per minute to fall from the nipple. **1873** SPON *Workshop Rec.* Ser. I. 132/2 For filling the cases nipples of various sizes are employed, made preferably of metal.
b. A prominence on the surface of the skin which resembles a nipple; esp. such as marks the outlet of any secretory gland.
1713 DERHAM *Phys.-Theol.* VII. i. *note*, Two or three larger Cells, lying under the Nipple of the Oil-bag. **1730** CHAMBERLAYNE *Relig. Philos.* I. xiv. §3 Those little Protuberances, which they call the Papillae, or Nipples [of the tongue]. **1797** *Encycl. Brit.* (ed. 3) II. 192/2 Spiders have five tubercles or nipples at the extremity of the belly. **1826** KIRBY & SP. *Entomol.* xxx. III. 128 Between them also there is a lozenge-shaped opening, through which..protruded a circular sort of nipple.
c. A small protuberance on glass or metal; a projection of any kind having the appearance of a nipple.
1839 URE *Dict. Arts* 582 Another workman now applies the end of a solid iron rod tipped with melted glass..to the nipple or prominence in the middle. **1863** TYNDALL *Heat* iv. §115 (1870) 101 Whenever the hot metal comes into contact with its lead carrier, a nipple suddenly juts from the latter. **1880** *Spon's Encycl. Manuf.* II. 558 A nipple for attachment [of the button] to the garment.
d. A small rounded elevation on the summit of a hill or mountain.
1859 *Merc. Marine Mag.* (1860) VII. 106 Vessels..cannot fail..to recognize the mountain..by its..top, having several nipples. **1860** *Ibid.* 328 The western of these nipples is the higher. **1873** W. CORY *Lett. & Jrnls.* (1897) 343 The crests or nipples of the hill-line are crowned with the domes of the mosques.
3. A short perforated piece made upon, or screwed into, the breech of a muzzle-loading gun, on which the percussion cap is fixed and exploded.
1822 *Specific. S. Davis's Patent* No. 4648 My improvement consists in forming and constructing the pan and nipple of the lock. **1853** STOCQUELER *Mil. Encycl.* 126/2 A small copper capsule..which fits on the nipple of the touch-hole. **1897** F. M. CRAWFORD *Corleone* x, There was a percussion cap on the nipple of the lock.
4. *attrib.* and *Comb.* **a.** In sense 1, as ***nipple-chancre, -level, -line, -shield; nipple-like, -shaped.***
1897 *Allbutt's Syst. Med.* II. 271 A *nipple chancre..is not an infrequent result. **1893** GEE *Auscultation & Percussion* (ed. 4) I. i. 9 The maximum of difference, on the *nipple level, being an inch and a quarter. **1898** *Allbutt's Syst. Med.* V. 360 Two inches above the nipple level. **1826** KIRBY & SP. *Entomol.* xxx. III. 138 They are a mere retractile *nipple-like protuberance. **1879** *St. George's Hosp. Rep.* IX. 183 Apex beat in 5th sp. × *nipple line. **1844** H. STEPHENS *Bk. Farm* III. 875 A small *nipple-shaped knob. **1799** UNDERWOOD *Dis. Children* III. 111 This public recommendation of the *Nipple-Shield. **1860** SIMMONDS *Dict. Trade*, *Nipple shield*, a protection for the breast worn by females.
b. In sense 3, as ***nipple-lump, -seat, -wrench.***
1868 *Rep. to Govt. U.S. Munitions War* 35 Holding the breech-block firmly..by means of the thumb-piece and *nipple-lump. **1875** KNIGHT *Dict. Mech.* 1528/2 **Nipple-seat*, the hump on the side of a barrel on which the nipple is screwed. **1844** *Regul. & Ord. Army* 96 *note*, One *nipple Wrench. **1875** KNIGHT *Dict. Mech.* 1529/1 *Nipple-wrench*, the spanner..used for screwing it to and unscrewing it from the barrel.
c. In names of plants, etc., as †***nipple cowry,*** †***nipple peach;*** **nipple cactus**, a cactus of the genus *Mammillaria*, having nipple-like protuberances (*Cent. Dict.* 1890).

1876 *Encycl. Brit.* IV. 625/2 Mammillaria.—This group ..is called *Nipple Cactus. **1971** D. WENIGER *Cacti of Southwest* 122/1 *Mammillaria similis*... 'Nipple Cactus'. **1713** PETIVER *Aquat. Anim. Amb.* 4/1 *Gibba*...white *Nipple Coury. **1719** LONDON & WISE *Compl. Gard.* 83 These are condemn'd by the Author as the worst of Peaches. *Nipple Peach [etc.].

Hence **nipple** *v.*, to furnish with a nipple or nipples; to cover with nipple-like protuberances.

1882 in OGILVIE. **1892** *Daily News* 14 Nov. 6/2, I returned to the place, lest some portions of convexed nippled iron should..excite curiosity.

'nippleless, *a.* [f. NIPPLE *sb.*] Having no nipples. (Used *spec.* of the monotremes.)

1890 in *Cent. Dict.*

nipplewort ('nɪp(ə)lwɜːt). [f. NIPPLE *sb.*]

1. A common wayside annual (*Lapsana communis*) of the order *Cichoraceæ*.

1640 PARKINSON *Theat. Bot.* 811 It is good to heale the Vlcers of the nipples of womens breasts, and thereupon I have entituled it Nipplewort in English. **1666** MERRETT *Pinax* 69 *Lampsana*, Dock-cresses.., ordinary Niple-wort. **1711** PETIVER in *Phil. Trans.* XXVII. 381 Having..small yellow Flowers like Nipplewort. **1796** WITHERING *Brit. Pl.* (ed. 3) III. 693 Common Nipplewort,..Hedges, shady places, and on rubbish. **1863** MARG. PLUES *Rambles Wild Fl.* 164 The common Nipplewort..bears its small yellow flowers in panicles.

2. *dwarf nipplewort*, the plant *Arnoseris pusilla*, sometimes placed in the genus *Lapsana*.

1866 *Treas. Bot.*

Nippon ('nɪpɒn). [Jap., f. *ni*(*chi* the sun + *pon*, *hon* source.] **1.** The Japanese name for Japan.

1727 J. G. SCHEUCHZER tr. *Kæmpfer's Hist. Japan* I. I. iv. 58 This Empire is by the Europeans call'd *Japan*. The Natives give it several names and characters. The most common, and most frequently us'd in their writings and conversation, is *Nipon*, which is sometimes in a more elegant manner, and particular to this Nation, pronounc'd Nifon... It signifies, *the foundation of the Sun*. **1859** K. CORNWALLIS *Two Journeys to Japan* I. vii. 187 It was against the laws of Nipon—in speaking of their own country this was the invariable term and pronunciation. **1890** B. H. CHAMBERLAIN *Things Japanese* 174 Our word 'Japan', and the Japanese *Nihon* or *Nippon* are alike corruptions of *Jih-pên*,..literally 'sun-origin' a name given to Japan by the Chinese. **1914** M. KLEIN *By Nippon's Lotus Ponds* v. 62 Nippon's old custom wills that the..wife or..servant girl closely seal up the house with..big rain-doors. **1940** E. POUND *Cantos* lviii. 74 Sinbu put order in Sun land, Nippon, in the beginning of all things. **1942** *R.A.F. Jrnl.* 13 June 5 The sons of Nippon had become aware that their destiny was to establish a New Order in the East. **1975** O. SELA *Bengali Inheritance* xviii. 160 The Indians in Nippon dominated territory.

2. Nippon vellum = *Japanese vellum* (JAPANESE *a.* b).

1926 *Brit. Weekly* 3 June 185/3 They will simultaneously issue special editions on nippon vellum. **1958** J. R. BIGGS *Woodcuts* 91 *Nippon Vellum* and *Jappon Vellum*..are imitation vellum papers whose smooth, creamy kindly surface is just right for some prints.

Nipponese (nɪpə'niːz). [f. NIPPON + -ESE.]

a. The Japanese people; an individual Japanese. **b.** The Japanese language. Also *attrib.* or as *adj.*

1859 K. CORNWALLIS *Two Journeys to Japan* I. 205 Beyond..was to be seen the houses of the town of Napa.. wherein were moored several large junks, native and Niponese. **1860** R. H. DANA *Jrnl.* 24 Apr. (1968) III. 1027 This island, Yeso, is a conquest of the Japanese (Niponese). **1927** E. POUND *Let.* 9 Nov. (1971) 214 At present it is the scattered fragments left by a dead man, edited by a man ignorant of Japanese. Naturally any sonvbitch who knows a little Nipponese can jump on it or say his flatfooted renderings are a safer guide to the style of that country. **1931** *Lit. Digest* 16 May 45/1 Your Nipponese..looks as tho nothing short of an earthquake would startle him. **1935** J. JOYCE *Let.* c 18 Feb. (1966) III. 343 He wore a kimono and scarlet vest. I suppose the Nipponese evening dress. **1942** [see *crash-dive* vb.]. **1944** *Sun* (Baltimore) 25 Nov. 2/4 Nipponese planes were shot down. **1948** A. KEITH *Three came Home* i. 33 The war was coming to the East, and..the Nipponese were coming to Borneo. **1973** 'S. HARVESTER' *Corner of Playground* I. viii. 66 The apparent end of traditional Nipponese spiritual values under the steam-roller of post-war materialism.

Nipponian (nɪ'pəʊnɪən), *a.* [f. NIPPON + -IAN.] Of or pertaining to Japan, Japanese. So **'Nipponism**, the furtherance of Japanese nationalistic interests.

1909 *Daily Chron.* 19 Aug. 4/6 The best English account of the conflict from the Nipponian point of view. **1914** *Encycl. Relig. & Ethics* VII. 489/1 The cry of 'Nipponism' ..was raised in a somewhat extravagant fashion.

Nippy ('nɪpɪ), *sb.* [f. the adj.] Formerly, a waitress in one of the restaurants of J. Lyons & Co. Ltd., London; hence, any waitress.

1925 *Punch* 11 Feb. 167/2, I can't mike up me mind weyver to be a lidy's 'elp or a 'nippy'. **1941** J. SMILEY *Hash House Lingo* 39 *Nippy*, waitress. **1948** G. V. GALWEY *Lift & Drop* vi. 161 His hands stuck out in front of him like a Nippy carrying a tray. **1973** *Country Life* 22 Nov. 1736/1 Biba's shiny black tea boxes have three Nippies in gold decorating the label. **1974** W. FOLEY *Child in Forest* II. 251 The big brightly lit clean teashop in Oxford Street where I worked as a Nippy.

nippy ('nɪpɪ), *a.* [f. NIP *v.*[1] + -Y[1].]

1. Of a nipping nature or disposition; inclined to nip, in senses of the verb.

1575 TURBERV. *Faulconrie* 327 The more shee feedeth, the more greedie and nippie shee is. **1642** *View Printed Bk.* 40 Nippie reprehensions and sometimes imprisonment. **1816** SCOTT *Old Mort.* vii, His uncle, auld Nippie Milnwood has as close a grip as the deil himsell. **1898** BURLEIGH *Sirdar & Khalifa* xii. 189 Anything liquid and nippy would have been a rare treat. **1898** *Westm. Gaz.* 29 Dec. 3/3 The air is 'nippy', sure enough.

2. *slang.* Sharp, quick, active, nimble.

1853 R. S. SURTEES *Soapey Sponge* (1893) 131 Soapey.. overtook a fine nippy, satin-stocked, dandified looking gentleman. **1894** ASTLEY *50 Yrs. of Life* II. 70, I told him he would have to be pretty nippy. **1898** BURLEIGH *Sirdar & Khalifa* xi. 175 He..liked to see them keen and 'nippy' at every soldierly task.

† **'nipshot,** *adv. Obs. Sc.* [app. f. NIP *v.*[1] + SHOT *sb.*, but the force of the comb. is obscure.] Only in phr. *to shoot*, or *play, nipshot*, to miss the mark, or miss fire, in *lit.* and *fig.* use.

a **1568** *King Berdok* 12 in Laing *Anc. Poetry Scotl.* 269 Weill cowd he..bend ane aiprim bow, and nipschot schute. **1637–50** Row *Hist. Kirk* (Wodrow Soc.) 395 Now of thir Canons, one said merrilie, that all the Bishops' cannons were poysoned, they would misgive, and shoot nipshot. **1646** R. BAILLIE *Lett. & Jrnls.* (1841) II. 362 Our great hope on earth, the City of London, has played nipshott; they are speaking of dissolving the Assemblie.

† **nipsitate,** variant of NIPPITATE *sb. Obs.*

1639 DAVENPORT *New Trick to cheat the Devil* E, A cup of Nipsitate, briske and neate.

nirles. *Sc.* Also nirls. [Of obscure origin.] A kind of rash or efflorescence of the skin.

a **1585** MONTGOMERIE *Flyting* 325 With parles and plurisies opprest, And nipd with nirles. **1673** WEDDERBURN *Voc.* 19 (Jam.), *Morbilli*, the nirles. **1707** J. NIMMO *Narr.* (S.H.S.) 79 My child was sick..having a flix, the nirles and kink-host extreamly. **1822–34** *Good's Study Med.* (ed. 4) IV. 473 Like the measles of this modification, they are denominated nirles in some parts of Scotland. **1886** STEWART *Rem. Dunfermline* 48 Children suffering from the nirles.

† **nirt.** *Obs. rare*[−1]. [Of obscure origin: perh. related to Norw. dial. *nerta* to touch lightly.] A mark, scar, cut.

13.. *Gaw. & Gr. Knt.* 2498 Þe nirt in Þe nek he naked hem schewed.

‖ **nirvana** (nɜː'vɑːnə). Also **Nirwana.** [a. Skr. *nirvāṇa*, blowing out, extinction, disappearance, etc., f. *nirvā* to blow.] **1.** In Buddhist theology, the extinction of individual existence and absorption into the supreme spirit, or the extinction of all desires and passions and attainment of perfect beatitude.

α **1836** *Penny Cycl.* V. 531/1 The expression, which Bauddhas seem to be particularly fond of employing, is Nirvâna. **1864** MAX MÜLLER *Sci. Lang.* Ser. II. 346 The Nothing..under the name of Nirvána has become the highest goal of millions among the followers of Buddha. **1880** GOLDW. SMITH in *Atlantic Monthly* 204 In justice to Buddhism it must be remembered that there is more than one interpretation of Nirvana.

β. **1857** W. SMITH *Thorndale* IV. vii. 370 A Buddhist Saint sits motionless under his Bo tree to earn Nirwana. **1871** ALABASTER *Wheel of Law* p. xxxvii, Nirwana, the extinction of all this kind of existence, must therefore be the object of the truly wise man. **1876** M. DAVIES *Unorth. Lond.* (ed. 2) 309 Breathing such a tone of mystic devotion as suggested the Brahminical Nirwana.

b. *transf.* or *fig.*

1895 BALFOUR *Foundations Belief* 64 The very Nirvana of artistic imagination, without desire and without pain. **1902** 'LINESMAN' *Words Eyewitness* 341 Universal peace!..is a Nirvana unattainable until after the death of the weary, yearning bodies who desire it.

2. Nirvana principle *Psychol.*, in psycho-analytic theory, the attraction felt by the psyche for a state of non-existence, which Freud connected with the death-instinct, countering the tensions set up by the pleasure principle.

1920 B. LOW *Psycho-Analysis* (ed. 2) iii. 73 It is possible that deeper than the Pleasure-principle lies the Nirvana-principle, as one may call it—the desire of the newborn creature to return to that stage of omnipotence, where there are no non-fulfilled desires, in which it existed within the mother's womb. **1924** J. RIVIERE tr. *Freud's Econ. Problem in Masochism* in *Coll. Papers* II. xxii. 256 For this tendency that has been presumed by us Barbara Low has suggested the name Nirvana-principle, which we accept. But we have unquestioningly identified the pleasure-pain-principle with this Nirvana-principle. *Ibid.* 257 The *Nirvana*-principle expresses the tendency of the death-instincts. **1936** *Brit. Jrnl. Psychol.* Jan. 286 In the biological-physical conception of a tendency to death (for which they would reserve the name 'Nirvana principle') there is no room for Eros. **1973** L. BELLAK et al. *Ego Functions* II. xiv. 212 Do these data invalidate the Nirvana principle, or can that tenet be modified to include the seemingly contradictory clinical observations?

Hence **Nir'vanic** *a.*, of the nature of Nirvana; **Nir'vana-ing** *vbl. sb.*, experiencing the state of nirvana; **Nir'vanist**, one who experiences this state.

1893 E. F. BENSON *Six Common Things* 73 In spite of the nirvanic remoteness of its nature, it is not troubled by human emotions. **1898** G. B. SHAW *Perfect Wagnerite* 106 He rested himself as a Pessimist and Nirvanist. **1921** D. H. LAWRENCE in *Reminisc. & Corr.* (1934) 23 Nirvana-ing is surely a state of continuing as you are. **1922** —— *Aaron's Rod* xxi. 309 And you've never got to think you'll dodge the responsibility of your own soul's self, by loving or sacrificing or Nirvanaing. *a* **1930** —— *Sex, Lit. & Censorship* (1955) 101 Even the Nirvanists consider man as a fixed entity.

nis, *sb.* Also nisse, nys. [a. Da. and Sw. *nisse.*] In Scandinavian folk-lore, a species of brownie or friendly goblin which frequents barns, stables, and other buildings.

1833 KEIGHTLEY *Fairy Myth.* I. 222 The Nis is the same being that is called Kobold in Germany, Brownie in Scotland. **1855** BAILEY *Mystic.* etc. 147 Nisses, Noks, Kobolds, Kelpies, Norns, and Trolls. **1865** WHITTIER *Kallundborg Church* 28 The Neck and the Nis gave no reply.

† **nis,** is not: see NE and BE *v.* A. I. 3. *Obs.*

c **825** *Vesp. Psalter* iii. 3 Nis haelu hire in deo hire. *c* **888** K. ÆLFRED *Boeth.* v. §3 Hit nis ȝiet se tima. *c* **975** *Rushw. Gosp.* Matt. xxviii. 6 Nis he her forþon þe he aras. *c* **1000** ÆLFRIC *Gram.* (Z) 227 Nis hit swa? Hit nis. *c* **1175** *Lamb. Hom.* 23 Hit nis nan wunder. *c* **1200** ORMIN 6181 Inn all þatt niss nan sinne. *a* **1225** *Leg. Kath.* 282 Þer nis bot a Godd. *a* **1300** *K. Horn* 13 Fairer nis non þane he was. *c* **1320** *Sir Tristr.* 997 Nis þer non so bald. **1362** LANGL. *P. Pl.* A. I. 34 Al nis not good to the gost that the bodi lyketh. **1413** *Pilgr. Sowle* (Caxton 1483) IV. xx. 68 He and I oure herte nis but one. **1477** NORTON *Ord. Alch.* i. in Ashm. (1652) 13 This Science n'is holy in effect. **1579** SPENSER *Sheph. Cal.* June 19 Those hilles where harbrough nis to see. *a* **1586** SIDNEY *Arcadia* III. (1724) II. 714 Nothing can endure where order n'is. [**1634** W. CARTWRIGHT *Ordinary* IV. ii, I nis not Edmond Ironside, God wot.]

‖ **Nisan** ('nɪsən, 'niːsɑːn). Also †**Nysan.** [Heb. *Nīsān.*] The first month of the Jewish ecclesiastical year and the seventh of the civil year, formerly called ABIB.

1382 WYCLIF *Neh.* (2nd text) ii. 1 Forsothe it was doon in the monethe Nysan, in the twentithe ȝeer of Artaxerses, kyng. **1535** COVERDALE *Neh.* ii. 1 In the moneth Nisan of the twentieth yeare of kynge Artaxerses. **1611** BIBLE *Neh.* ii. 1 And it came to passe, in the moneth Nisan,..that wine was before him. **1737** W. WHISTON tr. *Josephus' Works* 9 Moses appointed that Nisan, which is the same with Xanthicus, should be the first month, for their festivals; because he brought them out of Egypt in that month. **1846** GEO. ELIOT *Let.* c Apr. (1954) I. 213 The evening of the 13th Nisan.. would be what Strauss calls the *Vorabend* des Pascha. **1934** T. S. ELIOT *Rock* i. 35 In Shushan the palace, in the month Nisan, He served the wine to the King Artaxerxes. **1972** C. RAPHAEL *Feast of History* i. 32/1 A hand-written Hebrew-Russian calendar..open at Nisan, the month of Passover.

† **nisberry,** obs. variant of NASEBERRY.

1756 P. BROWNE *Jamaica* (1789) 200 The Nisberry Tree.

nise, obs. form of NICE *a.*

nisei ('niːseɪ). Also **nissei**, and with capital initial. Pl. nisei. [Jap., f. *ni-* second + *sei* generation.] An American born of Japanese parents. Also *attrib.*

1943 S. MENEFEE *Assignment: U.S.A.* 191 The War Relocation Authority, after a delay of many months, finally began to release those Nisei, or American-born Japanese. **1945** MENCKEN *Amer. Lang.* Suppl. I. 608 The designation *nisei*..for Japanese of American birth was seldom heard, before Pearl Harbor, save on the Pacific Coast... *Nisei* is sometimes spelled *nissei*. **1948** *Newsweek* 30 Aug. 20/1 The 29-year-old Nisei claimed that she had taken a job with the Tokyo radio merely 'for the experience'. **1957** *New Yorker* 16 Nov. 125/1 It would be difficult for a Japanese born student to..date a nisei girl. **1972** J. BALL *Five Pieces of Jade* v. 51 The bespectacled, crew-cut, Babbitt-looking Nisei detective. **1973** *Publishers Weekly* 3 Sept. 48/3 This diary, kept for eight months in 1942 by a 26-year-old Nisei.

niset: see NYLET and NYSOT.

nisewurt, variant of NEEZEWORT *Obs.*

nisey, nisi, varr. of NIZY a fool. *Obs.*

nish, *U.S. dial.* var. NESH *a.*

‖ **nisi** ('naɪsaɪ). *Law.* [L. *nisi* unless.] A limiting term added to such words as *decree*, *order*, or *rule*, to indicate that these are not absolute or final, but are to be valid or take effect unless some cause is shown, or reason arises, to prevent this. (Cf. quots. 1860 and 1872.)

1836 SMART s.v. *Nisi prius*, A rule *nisi* is a rule *unless*, i.e. *unless* cause be shown to the contrary, as distinguished from a rule *absolute*. **1860** *Act 23 & 24 Vict.* c. 144 §7 Every Decree for a Divorce shall in the first instance be a Decree Nisi, not to be made absolute till after the Expiration of such Time not less than Three Months.., as the Court shall by General or Special Order from Time to Time direct. **1872** WILL *Wharton's Law Lex.*, *Decree Nisi*..remains imperfect for at least six months. **1877–9** SETON *Decrees* (ed. 4) I. p. xxvi, Order nisi for Claimant to appear. **1883** *Law Rep. 11 Q.B. Div.* 591 An order nisi was afterwards obtained for a new trial, on the ground of misdirection.

nisin ('naɪsɪn). *Pharm.* [See quot. 1947 and -IN[1].] A mixture of closely related polypeptides produced by the bacterium *Streptococcus lactis* which is active against Gram-positive bacteria and is used in some countries as a food preservative.

1947 MATTICK & HIRSCH in *Lancet* 5 July 5/1 We have already given some account..of the action in vivo of an inhibitory substance*, isolated from lactic streptococci, against streptococcal infections of the mouse. [*Note*] *Group N Inhibitory Substance: (G) Nisin. **1959** *Times* 9 Mar. (Britain's Food Suppl.) p. viii/2 Nisin is an easily digested protein. **1963** *B.S.I. News* Feb. 13/2 The bacteriological examination of butter, milk, cheese and ice-cream, and for the detection and assay of nisin. **1972** *Sci. Amer.* Mar. 18/3 A number of countries have permitted such antibiotics as tetracyclines, nystatin, nisin..as direct or indirect additives to chilled or raw fish.

nisinge, variant of NEEZING *vbl. sb.*

‖**nisi prius** ('naɪsaɪ 'praɪəs). *Law.* Also 8 nisi prise. [L. *nisi prius*, unless previously. The significance of the phrase is thus explained by Blackstone, *Comm.* (1768) III. 59:

'All causes commenced in the courts of Westminster-hall are by the course of the courts appointed to be there tried, on a day fixed in some Easter or Michaelmas term, by a jury returned from the county, wherein the cause of action arises; but with this proviso, *nisi prius justitiarii ad assisas capiendas venerint; unless before* the day prefixed the judges of assise come into the county in question.'

In the second statute of Westminster (1285) §30, by which the system was instituted, only the word *nisi* is used. The following is an early example of the full phrase:—

1297 *Coram Rege Roll* m. 5 *dorso* (1898) 30 Ideo Vicecomes habeat corpora omnium coram Rege ad prefatum terminum &c. Nisi prius R. le Brabanzon vel G. de Roubyr' vel eorum alter si prius ad partes illas &c.]

1. A writ directed to a sheriff commanding him to provide a jury at the Court of Westminster on a certain day, unless the judges of assize previously come to the county.

[**1347–48** *Rolls of Parlt.* II. 214/1 William de Thorp & ses Compaignons ne voillent granter le Nisi prius saunz garaunt de Graunt Seal. *Ibid.*, De grantier Brief de Nisi prius. **1443–44** *Durh. Acct. Rolls* 185 Quoddam breve vocatum Nisi prius.] **1495** *Act 11 Hen. VII* c. 24 §4 Nisi prius shalbe graunted by discrecion of the Justices upon the distres. **1535** *Fitzherbert's Natura Brev.* (1544) 183 b, A wryt of Nisi prius... This wryt is Judycyall and lyeth in case when thenquest is panel and retourned afore the Justices of yᵉ banke. **1596** BACON *Max. & Use Com. Law* I. (1630) 24 Of which words the writ is called a Nisi prius.

b. The clause, in such a writ, which is introduced by these words.

1543–4 *Act 35 Hen. VIII* c. 6 §2 Everie firste Writte of habeas corpora or distringas with a Nysi Prius delivered of Recorde to the Sherief. **1768** BLACKSTONE *Comm.* III. 353 Therefore it was enacted by statute Westm. 2.. that a clause of *nisi prius* should be inserted in all the aforesaid writs of *venire facias*.

c. The authority or commission to try causes conferred by this clause on justices of assize.

1596 BACON *Max. & Use Com. Law* I. (1630) 24 The Judges.. by their Commission of Nisi prius have authority [etc.]. **1768** BLACKSTONE *Comm.* III. 59 The.. authority.. of *nisi prius*, which is a consequence of the commission of assise.

2. An action tried under a writ of this kind.

[**1347** *Rolls of Parlt.* II. 195/1 Sur quoy le dit Priour.. ad suy plusours Nisi prius devant mons' William de Shareshull & autres Justices.] **1468** *Plumpton Corr.* (Camden) 18 As touching your *nisi prius* against Fulbaron. **1498–9** *Ibid.* 134, I understand William Babthorp will have a *nisi prius* at this next assizes. **1533** CROMWELL in Merriman *Life & Lett.* (1902) I. 359 The tryall of the saide Nisiprius. **1596** BACON *Max. & Use Com. Law* I. (1630) 23 These Nisi Prius happen in this sort. **1607** MIDDLETON *Phœnix* II. iii. F 2 b, Take heede I bring you not to a *Nisi prius*, sir. **1714** GAY *What d'ye call it* I. i, You ruined my poor Uncle at the Sizes, And made him pay nine Pounds for Nisiprises. **1748** SMOLLETT *Rod. Rand.* liv, He had suffered a *nisi prius* through the obstinacy of the defendant.

3. The trial or hearing of civil causes by the judges of assize; court-business of this kind. Hence *cause, court, justice*, etc., of *nisi prius*.

[**1347** *Rolls of Parlt.* II. 186/2 En quel suite Sire Alayn de Asch', Baron de la dit Escheqer, si ad este deux feitz per le Nisi Prius a Seint Martin graunt.] **1543–4** *Act 35 Hen. VIII* c. 6, An Acte concerninge thapparaunce of Jurors in the Nisi Prius. **1585** in Ellis *Orig. Lett.* Ser. III. IV. 57 The Lordes Chief Justices of either Benche do twise a weeke attend upon Nisi Prius for London and Middlesex. **1596** BACON *Max. & Use Com. Law* I. (1630) 23 A Commission to take Nisi Prius directed to none but to the Judges themselues and their Clerkes of Assizes. **1679** *Trials Green*, etc. *for Murder of Sir E. Godfrey* 87 No Brother, I am to sit at Nisi prius this Afternoon, and 'tis time we broke up the Court. **1709** *London Gaz.* No. 4508/3 A Postea, or Record of Nisi Prius, between Morris, Plaintiff, and Jordan, Defendant. **1793** *Chron.* in *Ann. Reg.* 13/1 The commission for opening the assizes.. for the trying of criminals, hearing causes of Nisi prius and for a general gaol delivery. **1840** *Penny Cycl.* XVI. 241/1 The judges of assize.. when sitting alone to try causes .. are said to be sitting at Nisi Prius. **1865** *Daily Tel.* 24 Aug., The learned serjeant drew an affecting picture, in the true style of nisi prius, of the happy results which would flow from the training ship. **1889** GRATTAN *Memory's Harkback* 135 Thus his legal life had been passed in Nisi Prius—he was quite a stranger to Chancery practice.

4. *attrib.* as *nisi prius clause, court, glory, laugh, -office* (1708), *record, sitting*.

1845 *Encycl. Metrop* XXI. 190/1 In Trials at Bar, which are actually conducted in the Court at Westminster, the *Nisi Prius clause is omitted. *a* **1734** NORTH *Exam.* I. ii. §118 (1740) 94 The *Nisiprius Courts, for Civil Trials. **1867** *Hampshire Chron.* 9 Mar., This case concluded the business of the *Nisi Prius* Court. **1852** DISRAELI *Ld. G. Bentinck* 277 Scarlett himself in the days of his *nisi prius glory had never shown more adroitness. **1841** LEVER *C. O'Malley* lxviii, A cunning leer of his eye, and a certain *nisi-prius laugh. **1848** WHARTON *Law Lex.*, **Nisi prius record*, an instrument in the nature of a commission to the Judges at *nisi prius* for the trial of a cause. **1864** *Chamb. Encycl.* VI. 777/1 The *nisi prius sittings are the jury sittings.

Niska: see NASS.

1895 F. BOAS in *Rep. Brit. Assoc. Adv. Sci.* 569 The customs of the Nîsk·a and those of the Tsimshian.. are practically identical. *Ibid.* 583 The Nîsk·a does not differ very much from the Tsimshian. **1973** *Times* 27 Dec. 6/4 There is also a portrait mask of an old woman (c 1825–1850) from the Niska of British Columbia, of wood inlaid with abalone shell.

†**'nisket.** *Obs. rare*$^{-1}$. (See quot.)

1725 DUDLEY in *Phil. Trans.* XXXIII. 264 The Whale.. got the Fluke into her Nisket, or the Orifice of the Uterus.

niskh(i), varr. NASKHI *sb. pl.*

Nissen ('nɪsən). [Name of the inventor, Lt.-Col. Peter Norman *Nissen* (1871–1930).] Used *attrib.* and *absol.* of a tunnel-shaped hut made of corrugated iron with a cement floor.

1917 E. F. WOOD *Note-Book of Intelligence Officer* 224 Recently I met the inventor of the now famous Nissen hut. **1932** AUDEN *Orators* III. 114 These nissen huts if hiding could Your eye inseeing from Firm fenders were. **1942** *R.A.F. Jrnl.* 16 May 3 In Nissen huts, with orders coming through from Flight Commander all day and night. **1948** G. GREENE *Heart of Matter* III. i. 191, I would never go back there, to the Nissen hut, if it meant that she were happy. *Ibid.* 192 The rain hammered on the Nissen roofs. *Ibid.* 222 He's living in one of the Nissens now. **1954** W. FAULKNER *Fable* (1955) 86 It was not the Nissen walls which trembled. **1973** J. WAINWRIGHT *Pride of Pigs* 72 There's a glorified Nissen hut—a bit of youth club—on the site.

Nissl ('nɪs(ə)l). *Med.* The name of Franz *Nissl* (1860–1919), German neurologist, used *attrib.* and in the possessive to designate esp. a methylene blue stain (***Nissl('s) stain***) used for the cell bodies of neurones; the application of this stain (***Nissl('s) method***); and hence the small cytoplasmic structures (***Nissl('s) bodies, granules***) revealed in the cell bodies of neurones by this method. Also **Nissl degeneration**, degeneration of the cell bodies of neurones, accompanied by disappearance of their Nissl bodies; **Nissl('s) substance**, the Nissl bodies collectively.

1898 *Jrnl. Mental Sci.* XLIV. 730 The Nissl bodies.., which stain deeply with basic dyes. **1899** *Jrnl. R. Microsc. Soc.* 448 (*heading*) New Nissl method. **1899** L. F. BARKER *Nervous System* 110 He thinks it very wrong that these should be thrown all together and designated either 'Nissl's substance' or 'tigroid substance'. **1901** *Jrnl. Exper. Med.* V. 551 The principles of Nissl's method are extremely simple. *Ibid.* 553 A definite reaction to the Nissl stain. *Ibid.* 554 He finds the Nissl granules embedded in a homogeneous coagulum-like mass. **1905** GOULD *Dict. New Med. Terms* 129/1 Staining with Nissl's stain (methylene-blue). **1911** STEDMAN *Med. Dict.* 586/2 Nissl degeneration. **1933** *Amer. Jrnl. Anat.* LIII. 153 The cells are indeed very light; the Nissl substance is scanty. **1943** STRONG & ELWYN *Human Neuroanat.* iii. 28/1 The significance of the Nissl stain.. lies in the fact that.. each type of nerve cell always presents the same appearance or 'equivalent picture' in normal conditions. **1966** WRIGHT & SYMMERS *Systemic Path.* II. xxxiv. 1147/1 In the cytoplasm of the neuron, certain polygonal, basiphile structures, known collectively as Nissl substance, are present. **1968** PASSMORE & ROBSON *Compan. Med. Studies* I. xiv. 2/2 Nissl granules are present in the perikaryons of all neurones. **1971** *Sci. Amer.* July 48/2 The Nissl method made it possible to outline and identify well-defined regions in the brain. **1971** J. Z. YOUNG *Introd. Study Man* xi. 147 Nerve cells are characterized by a large amount of ribonucleic acid in the cytoplasm—the basophilic Nissl bodies. **1974** PASSMORE & ROBSON *Compan. Med. Studies* III. II. xxxiv. 33/2 The parent cell bodies undergo central chromatolysis (Nissl degeneration).

†**nist**, for *ne wist*, knew not: see NE and WIT *v.* Forms: 1, 4–5 **nyste**, 1–2, 4 **neste**, 2–5 **nuste**, 3–4 **niste**, 4–5 **nist**, **nyst**. *Pl.* 1 **nyston (-ðon)**, 2 **nesten, nusten**, 2, 4 **nysten**, 4 **nisten**.

c **825** *Vesp. Psalter* lxxii. 22 Ic to nowihte ȝebeȝed eam & ic hit nyste. *c* **888** K. ÆLFRED *Boeth.* xxxviii. §1 Hi nyston nænne oðerne god on þæne timan. **971** *Blickl. Hom.* 79 Næs þæt na þæt he nyste hwæt se blinda wolde. *c* **1175** *Lamb. Hom.* 93 His wif.. nuste hwet hire were ilumpen wes. *a* **1200** *Moral Ode* 229 (Trin. Coll. MS.), Ic wille seggen hit þo þe hit hem self nesten. *c* **1230** *Hali Meid.* 59 Ha nuste hwuch wei ha come þeneward. *a* **1300** *K. Horn* 276 Þe stuard.. nuste what to do. *c* **1320** *Sir Tristr.* 246 He nist it whom to wite. **1377** LANGL. *P. Pl.* B. XIII. 25 There I say a maistre; what man he was I neste. **1390** GOWER *Conf.* I. 313 Thei nysten what fortune abide. **1447** BOKENHAM *Seyntys* (Roxb.) 52 She astoyned.. Was that she nyst what she myght seye.

nist(e, dial. forms of NICE *a.*

‖**nisus** ('naɪsəs). [L., noun of action f. *nītī* to strive, endeavour.] Effort, endeavour, impulse.

1699 *Phil. Trans.* XXI. 177 This condition of motion being chang'd, there is a lesser Nisus. **1741** MONRO *Anat. Nerves* (ed. 3) 34 This *Nisus* of the Mind to free the Body. **1752** HUME *Ess. & Treat.* (1809) II. 476 No animal can put external bodies in motion without the sentiment of a nisus or endeavour. **1851** SIR F. PALGRAVE *Norm. & Eng.* I. 39 Species and their varieties seem to have been produced by an inward nisus. **1899** *Allbutt's Syst. Med.* VIII. 248 When the nisus of web-spinning dominates the spider, when the nisus of nest-building dominates the bird.

nit, *sb.*[1] Forms: α. 1 **hnitu**, 4 **nite**, 5 **nyte**; 4–5 **nete**, 7 **neet**. β. 4–6 **nytte**, 5–6 **nitte**, 6 **nyt**, 7–8 **nitt**, 8 **knit**, 6– **nit**. [OE. *hnitu* fem. = MDu. *nete, nette* (Du. *neet*), MLG. *nete, neyt, nette, nit*, OHG. *niz* (MHG. *niz, nizze*, G. *niss, nisse*): cf. ON. *gnit* (Norw. *gnit, knit*, Sw. *gnet*, Da. *gnid*, Icel. *nit*). Outside of Teutonic related forms appear in Russ. and Pol. *gnida*, Czech *knida*, and Gr. κονιδ-, κονίς.]

1. a. The egg of a louse or other insect parasitic on man or animals; the insect itself in a young state.

α. *c* **825** *Epinal Gloss.* 590 *Lendina*, hnitu. *c* **1000** *Sax. Leechd.* I. 364 Hnite & wyrmas on weȝ to donne ðe on cildum beoð. **1340** HAMPOLE *Pr. Consc.* 651 And þou forth bringes of þi-self here Nites, lyse, and other vermyn sere. *c* **1340** *Nominale* (Skeat) 226 Woman in the seyme syketh the nete. **1398** TREVISA *Barth. De P.R.* XVII. xxii. (Tollem. MS.), It.. amendeþ and doþ awey nites and oþer unclennesse of þe heed. *c* **1425** *Voc.* in Wr.-Wülcker 642 *Hec lens*, nyte. [So *c* **1475** *ibid.* 767.] **1481** CAXTON *Reynard* (Arb.) 79 She can wel pyke out lyce and netis [Du. *neten*] out of mens hedis. **1638** SHIRLEY *Mart. Soldier* IV. in Bullen *O. Pl.* I. 236 There sits my wife kombing her hair, all the Neets in't are Spiders.

β. **1483** *Cath. Angl.* 255/1 A Nitte; *tinea capitis est.* **1493** *Festial* (W. de W. 1515) 174 Of trees cometh leves, floures, and fruyte, and of the lyce, nyttes, and fleen. **1547** BOORDE *Brev. Health* cclxxiii. 91 There be .iiii. kyndes, whiche be to say, head lyce, body lyce, crabbe lyce, and nits. **1573** TUSSER *Husb.* (1878) 58 Let season be drie when ye take them to house, for danger of nittes, or for feare of a louse. **1607** TOPSELL *Four-f. Beasts* (1658) 191 Goats are not troubled with Lice or Nits, but only with Tickes. **1664** PEPYS *Diary* 18 July, Thence to Westminster to my barber's, to have my Periwigg he lately made me cleansed of its nits. **1753** HANWAY *Trav.* (1762) I. v. lxiii. 290 Inferior silk has many nits and coarse stuff sticking to the threads. **1816** KIRBY & SP. *Entomol.* I. (1818) 84 Their nits or eggs are not hatched till the eighth day after they are laid. **1844** STEPHENS *Bk. Farm* II. 152 The egg or nit is pear-shaped, and may be seen attached to the hairs. **1884** *Med. Ann.* 44/2 Dilute Acetic acid destroys the pediculi and dissolves the nits.

Comb. **1672** MARVELL *Reh. Transp.* I. 160 The scold.. stretched up her hands with her two thumb-nails in the Nit-cracking posture.

fig. **1827** HOOD *Craniology* 34 The science thus—to speak in fit Terms—having struggled from its nit.

†**b.** A gnat, or small fly. *Obs. rare.*

1547 BOORDE *Brev. Health* §356 A nytte or a flye comming vnto a mannes mouth, when he doth take in his breth. **1684** OTWAY *Atheist* I. i, The Nits dance about on't like Atoms in the Sun-shine.

2. Applied to persons in contempt or jest. Now esp., a stupid or incompetent person. *colloq.*

Influenced by NITWIT.

1588 SHAKS. *L.L.L.* IV. i. 150 And his Page,.. Ah heauens, it is [a] most patheticall nit. **1596** —— *Tam. Shr.* IV. iii. 110 Thou Flea, thou Nit, thou winter cricket thou. *c* **1600** DAY *Begg. Bednall Gr.* IV. iii, Strowd, y'are a Nit, a Slave and a Pessant. **1622** MASSINGER & DEKKER *Virg. Mart.* II. iii, And so, sweet nit, we crawl from thee. **1632** BURTON *Anat. Mel.* I. ii. III. xiv. (ed. 4) 121 They are.. nitts and flies compared to his inexorable and supercilious, eminent and arrogant worship. **1941** BAKER *Dict. Austral. Slang* 49 *Nit*, a simpleton or fool. **1961** *Sunday Times* 17 Sept. 41/4 Livings's latest work, 'Sacred Nit'. **1962** *Melody Maker* 11 Aug 6/1 I could see he wasn't very impressed with this nit sitting across the table. **1963** [see COOT *sb.*[1] 4]. **1967** S. KNIGHT *Window on Shanghai* xxiii. 97 You ask a crazy question—Xmas???!!! The Chinese certainly enjoy celebrating, but for goodness sake! You nit, Mum—can you imagine them trooping to church on December 25? **1972** P. CLEIFE *Slick & Dead* II. ix. 70 If you think.. I would be willing to allow you.. to board my aircraft.. then you must be a nit.

3. In phr. ***as dead as a nit.***

1789 WOLCOT (P. Pindar) *Subj. for Painters* Wks. 1812 II. 191 Dead in a minute as a Nit. **1838** THACKERAY *Fash. F.* Wks. 1900 XIII. 254 Down he fell as dead as a nit. **1874** T. HARDY *Far fr. Mad. Crowd* xxi, [The sheep] will all die as dead as nits.

4. *Comb.*, as ***nit-comb.***

1943 D. IBBERSON *Our Towns* iii. 72 A square-toothed steel nit-comb.. is too expensive for the poorest. **1959** F. DONALDSON *Child of Twenties* iii. 39 My mother washed her head again and again, and combed her hair with a nit-comb.

nit (nɪt), *sb.*[2] *Austral.* [Origin unknown; but cf. NIX[1] 3, a parallel use.]

1. A word used as a signal that someone is approaching.

1899 H. LAWSON *If I could Paint* in *Stories* (1964) 3rd Ser. 416 I'd call it 'Nit! There's Mother.' **1911** L. STONE *Jonah* 8 Suddenly there was a cry of 'Nit! 'Ere's a cop!' and the push bolted like rabbits.

2. Usu. in phr. ***to keep nit***, to keep watch, to act as guard. Hence **'nitkeeper**, one who acts as sentinel, usu. while some illegal activity is being carried on.

1935 *Bulletin* (Sydney) 22 May 21/1 That outlaw the sulphur-crested cockatoo is not the only bird to post a 'nit-keeper' when transgressing against society. **1940** I. L. IDRIESS *Lightning Ridge* 20 Bill kept nit for his elder brother who was courting a girl, and earned a shilling. **1943** D. STEWART *Ned Kelly* II. i. 97 We keep nit and keep quiet. Ned's good watch-dogs! **1947** N. LINDSAY in B. James *Austral. Short Stories* (1963) 6 On condition of you kids scooting up the flat to keep nit, case the old man comes down this way. **1952** T. A. G. HUNGERFORD *Ridge & River* 10 Send two men a couple of hundred yards up and down the track to keep nit. **1963** F. HARDY *Legends from Benson's Valley* 108 An elaborate network of nitkeepers on all sides frustrated the new policeman for three weeks. **1971** D. IRELAND *Unknown Industrial Prisoner* 77 They had transgressed the unwritten law that you didn't let yourself go to sleep while you were keeping nit for your mates.

nit (nɪt), *sb.*[3] *U.S. colloq.* [Of obscure origin; perh. a corruption of NAUGHT *sb.*, NOUGHT *sb.*: cf. NIT *adv.*] None; nothing.

1910 'O. HENRY' *Strictly Business* v. 66 'You fool... Why did you do it? 'The Stuff,' explained Thomas briefly. 'You know. But subsequently nit. Not a drop.'

nit (nɪt), *sb.*[4] *Physics.* [a. F. *nit* (formally adopted in 1948 at the 11th meeting of the Commission internationale de l'Éclairage, and published in its *Recueil des travaux* (1950) 145),

f. L. *nit-ēre* to shine.] A unit of luminance equal to one candela per square metre.

1953 J. W. T. Walsh *Photometry* (ed. 2) v. 136 On the c.g.s. system the unit [of luminance] is the stilb, equal to one candela per sq. cm. or the nit, equal to one candela per sq. metre. There is no name for the corresponding unit on the British system; the candela per sq. inch or per sq. ft. is generally employed. **1965** G. A. Fry in R. Kingslake *Appl. Optics* II. i. 18 One nit of luminance is equal to one lux of illuminance per steradian of solid angle. **1965** R. Kingslake in *Ibid.* v. 198, 1 ft-L is equal to 3·43 nits. **1969** *Amateur Photographer* 19 Mar. 80/3 A brightness (or luminous intensity) of 1 Candela per square metre is termed a Nit. Therefore, for example, 60 Candelas per square centimetre equals 600,000 Nits.

†**nit**, *a.* *Obs. rare*$^{-0}$. (See quot.)

a **1700** B. E. *Dict. Cant. Crew, Nit*, wine that is brisk, and pour'd quick into a Glass.

†**nit**, *v.*[1] *Obs. rare.* [f. nit *sb.*[1]]

1. *intr.* To pore carefully *over* a book.

1596 Nashe *Saffron Walden* 15, I haue here tooke the paines to nit and louze ouer the Doctours booke. **1602** *2nd Pt. Return fr. Parnass.* I. ii. 149 Would it not grieue any good spiritt to sit a whole moneth nitting over a lousie beggarly Pamphlet?

2. To deposit nits. *rare*$^{-1}$.

1683 Tryon *Way to Health* 596 Bugs..harbour in Bedsteads, Holes and Hangings, Nitting and breeding as Lice do in Clothes.

nit (nɪt), *v.*[2] *Austral.* [Cf. nit *sb.*[2]] To escape, decamp; to hurry away.

1882 *Sydney Slang Dict.* 10/2 *Nit*, get away (usually from a foe), make tracks. **1897** W. T. Goodge *Hits! Skits! & Jingles!* (1899) 150 And to 'nark it' means to stop it, And to 'nit it' means to fly! **1941** Baker *Dict. Austral. Slang* 49 *To nit*, to decamp, get away (from a foe).

nit (nɪt), *adv.* [? f. Yiddish.] = not *adv.* Cf. nit *sb.*[3]

1895 W. C. Gore in *Inlander* Nov. 63 *Nit*.., not; sometimes an emphatic not. **1896** *Dialect Notes* I. 421 *Nit*, a decided negative, much stronger than *no*.

nit, obs. pa. pple. of knit, *v.*, pa. t. of nite *v.* *Obs.*

nital (ˈnaɪtæl). *Metallurgy.* Also **Nital**. [f. nit(ric *a.* + al(cohol.] An etchant consisting of a few per cent of concentrated nitric acid in ethyl or methyl alcohol.

1925 M. A. Grossmann tr. *Heyn's Physical Metallogr.* iv. 144 Alcoholic Nitric Acid (Martens)... Abbreviation HNO_3/Alc., or nital. **1936** *Metals Handbk.* (Amer. Soc. for Metals) 557 Nital brings out ferrite junction lines clearly while both Nital and Picral etch pearlite clearly. **1950** *Engineering* 24 Mar. 339/1 The barrel is etched with 7 per cent. nital solution. **1963** B. Harocopos *Princ. Structural Metall.* v. 55 Occasionally nital will produce pits in the vicinity of non-metallic inclusions, and in such cases amyl alcohol may be used as a solvent instead. **1975** *Nature* 21 Aug. 635/1 The Nital etch did not reveal recrystallisation in the taenite.

nitch (nɪtʃ), *sb. rare.* Also 8 **nich(e**. [Of obscure origin: cf. nick *sb.* and notch *sb.*] A slight break, notch, or incision.

1726 in Lowson *J. Guidfollow* (1890) App. 282 The Deponent afterward having seen the sword..perceived a nitch in it. **1726** Monro *Anat.* 80 Frequently a Hole is found on one Side, and a Niche [**1741** Nich] on the other. **1741** *Ibid.* (ed. 3) 28 *Niches* [**1782** *Nitches*] or *Notches*, small Breaches in the Bone. [**1839** Holloway *Dict. Prov.* s.v. *Nichilled*, One piece..has an incision made in it, but none cut out; this is called Nitch.]

nitch, var. of knitch, bundle; niche *sb.*

†**nitch**, obs. variant of niche *v.* 4.

1834 Mar. Edgeworth *Helen* III. iii. 35 Nicely adapted to her place in society to nitch and notch in, and to be of no sort of value out of it.

nitch (nɪtʃ), *v. rare.* [Prob. for *knitch* (recorded in this sense in Scottish dial. use): see knitch *sb.*] *trans.* To unite or connect together; to fix together, truss.

1824 Landor *Imag. Conv., Abbé Delille & Landor* I. 274 One of the beauties at which Boileau aimed, was the nitching of several names together in a verse, without any other word. **1880** Carnegie *Pract. Trap.* 10 Bend one hind leg, and make a slit behind the bone, place through this the other leg, nitch this one at the back of the knee, and the rabbit is ham strung.

nitched, obs. variant of niched *ppl. a.*

nitchie (ˈnɪtʃɪ). *Canad.* Also **neche, neechee, neejee, nichi, nichiwa, nidge, nitchee, nitchy.** [Algonquian.] Originally (among North American Indians), a friend; hence as a (usu. derogatory) term for a North American Indian.

1791 J. Long *Voy. & Trav. Indian Trader* 268 Neejee, or neecarnis, friend, or companion. **1838** A. Jameson *Winter Stud. & Summer Rambles Canada* III. 83 Thus, one man addressing another says 'nichi' or 'neejee', my friend. **1850** J. J. Bigsby *Shoe & Canoe* II. 161, I sallied forth, and found the Nidges loading the canoes, drest in their best. **1852** C. P. Traill *Canad. Crusoes* vi. 180 While she called Louis, 'Neechee', or friend. **1857** J. Palliser *Jrnls.* (1863) 52 Our Indian friend..to whom we had given the name Nichiwa, or friend. **1878** C. Hallock *Amer. Club List & Sportsman's Gloss.* p. viii, *Nitchee*, a common word among Indian tribes signifying brother. **1903** R. Cullum *Devil's Keg* xxii. 242 A neche was leisurely cleaning up round Lablache's store. **1910** R. W. Service *Ballads of Cheechako* 118 Then came I to a land I knew no man had ever seen, a haggard land, forlornly spanned by mountains lank and lean; The nitchies said 'twas full of dread, of smoke and fiery breath. **1930** J. Beames *Army without Banners* 131 Have to see if I can dig up a Nitchie an' trade whitefish for tobacco or something. **1947** *Beaver* Mar. 4 'These confounded nitchies,' he was wont to exclaim, 'are lazy, good-for-nothings.' **1956** *Saturday Night* 8 Dec. 16/2 And since when have Americans or British freely discussed Clear Grits, Digby chickens, Socreds, the Land of Little Sticks, separate schools, nitchies, longlinermen? **1960** in E. Fowke et al. *Canada's Story in Song* 127 They leave their homes on starving pay to take the nitchies' lives. **1973** R. D. Symons *Where Wagon Led* I. viii. 132 'Quick, you fellows,' he said, 'them Nitchies are crawling up all around.'

†**nite**, *sb.*[1] *Obs. rare*$^{-1}$. [f. the vb.] Denial.

c **1375** *Cursor M.* 23532 (Fairf.), If þou wille þou salle be tite, ne sal þer be þer-to na nite [*altered from* lite].

nite (naɪt), *sb.*[2] An arbitrary respelling of night *sb.* Also *attrib.* and *Comb.* Hence **ˈnitely** *a.* and *adv.*

A widespread vulgarism.

1931 *Amer. Speech* VI. 379 Write *rite* (for right) and *nite* (for night). **1934** B. J. Thompson in *Catholic World* Aug. 523 *Nite* connotes speakeasies, gin, cheapness and vulgarity. **1960** *Punch* 27 Apr. 584/1 Didn't you know? It's Rock Nite at the Darby and Joan. **1961** A. Berkman *Singers' Gloss. Show Business* 62 Nite Club, Nite Spot. **1968** *Blues Unlimited* Nov. 6 Both he and Myers were discovered by Johnny in Jackson 'nite-spots'. **1970** *Toronto Daily Star* 24 Sept. 32/2 (Advt.), Nitely dancing to an excellent European trio. **1970** *Globe & Mail* (Toronto) 25 Sept. 9/1 (Advt.), Train for Court Reporting..Special nite classes. **1971** *Times* 25 Aug. 11/7 (Advt.), Where it's at in Yorkshire... Mood with good food, nitely til 2... And for a romping, Bavarian-style nite out, visit the Intercon Bier Keller in Wakefield. **1971** *Leader* (Durban) 7 May 4/3 (*caption*) Elaine Meyers needs no introduction to nitelifers. *Ibid.*, Around the nitespots. **1973** *Black World* June 61 Sister Habiba knew how to give parties alright: three flights up—Saturday nite. **1974** *Marlboro Herald-Advocate* (Bennettsville, S. Carolina) 18 Apr. 7/8 (Advt.), Free parking in paved lot in rear of store. Open all day Wednesday. Open Fri. nite 'til 6:30.

†**nite**, *v. Obs. north.* and *Sc.* Forms: 4 **nite**, 5 **nyt**, 4–6 **nyte**, 6 **nyit**. *Pa. t.* 4 **nit, nitt(e**, 5 **nyt**. *Pa. pple.* 4–5 **nite**, 5 **nytit**. [a. ON. *níta*, related to *neita*: see nait *v.*[2]]

1. *trans.* To deny (a statement, etc.).

a **1300** *Cursor M.* 883 Al þat i sai mai sco noght nite. *c* **1325** *Metr. Hom.* 50 Sain Jon him prophet nitte, And said, prophet nan am I. *c* **1375** *Sc. Leg. Saints* viii. (*Philip*) 66 [Ebionites] þat throw wikit heresy nyttis, þat Criste had suthfaste flesche as man. *a* **1400** *Burgh Laws* §xxxviii. (Sc. Rec. Soc.) I. 19 Gif he nytis it and the playntyfe have na wytnes, than the tothir sall clenge hym. *c* **1470** *Gol. & Gaw.* 899 His name and his nobillay wes noght for to nyte.

absol. *c* **1450** Holland *Howlat* 70 Is nane bot dame Natur, I bid nocht to nyte, Till accuss of this caise. **1535** Stewart *Cron. Scot.* I. 208 Now at this tyme, I bid nocht for to nyit, On the he lais the haill caus and the wyit.

2. To deny, abjure (a person). Also *absol.*

a **1300** *Cursor M.* 15997 Quen he had nite his lauerd thris, he did him-seluen knau. *Ibid.* 19093 His sun..Yee suak and nitt be-for pilate. *Ibid.* 20871 Nitand he [Peter] fell, wepand he ras. *c* **1375** *Sc. Leg. Saints* xii. (*Mathias*) 401 þane, for he Criste nyt wald nocht, In-to þare consale þai hyme brocht.

b. To repudiate (an obligation, etc.).

c **1375** *Sc. Leg. Saints* xxvi. (*Nicholas*) 807 þane þe cristine mane vnwise..Nyt his det al wtrely.

3. To refuse (a request) to one.

c **1325** *Metr. Hom.* 137 Yef he the silc askinges nite. *c* **1375** *Sc. Leg. Saints* xxvii. (*Machor*) 1027 Fra quham he askit forgewine, & he had nytit hym his askine. *a* **1400–50** *Alexander* 1460 He had nite him a nerand noȝt bot o new time. **1513** Douglas *Æneis* ix. v. 164 Thy commancement ..Is sa douchty I may the nyte na thing.

b. To refuse *to* do a thing.

c **1375** *Sc. Leg. Saints* xxii. (*Lawrence*) 319 þane laurens cane nyt opinly Til fals godis to sacryfy.

†**niten**, for *ne witen* know not: cf. not *v.*

c **888** K. Ælfred *Boeth.* xiv. §3 þæt is þara monna unþeaw þæt hi niton hwæt hie sen. *c* **975** *Rushw. Gosp.* Matt. xxi. 27 þa onswarade to þæm hælende & cwædun, niton we. *a* **1200** *Moral Ode* 240 (Trin. Coll. MS.), Nabbeð hie none lisse; Niten hweðer hem doð wers.

†**ˈnitency**[1]. *Obs. rare.* [ad. L. type *nītentia, f. ppl. stem of *nītī*: cf. nisus.] Impulse.

1661 Boyle *Spring of Air* (1682) 93 Those Zones will have a strong Nitency to flie wider open. **1693** J. Beaumont *On Burnet's The. Earth* II. 105 The native Nitency of the Waters ..would much more strongly repel any Waters there rais'd above their level. **1768–74** Tucker *Lt. Nat.* (1834) I. 545 They talk of the tendencies and nitencies..of bodies.

ˈnitency[2]. *rare*$^{-0}$. [ad. L. type *nitentia, f. *nitent-*: see next.] 'Lustre; clear brightness.'

1755 Johnson [hence in later Dicts.].

†**ˈnitent**, *a. Obs. rare.* [f. L. *nitent-em*, pres. pple. of *nitēre* to shine.] Shining, lustrous.

1616 J. Lane *Contn. Sqr.'s T.* xii. 309 A blacke horse, nitent as the iett. **1657** Tomlinson *Renou's Disp.* 234 Whose branches are of a nitent black colour.

Hence †**ˈnitently** *adv.*, brightly. *Obs.*$^{-1}$

1657 Tomlinson *Renou's Disp.* 409 In form of a powder very nitently red.

†**ˈniter.** *Obs.*$^{-1}$ [f. nite *v.* + -er[1].] A denier.

a **1300** *Cursor M.* 20870 Petre was..luuer o lauerd, alsua niter. Nitand he fell, wepand he ras.

niter, obs. form of nitre.

†**ˈniterated, ˈniterous**, obs. varr. of nitrated, nitrous.

1605 Timme *Quersit.* I. v. 19 Such salts chymists call saltniter or niterous salts. **1678** Salmon *Pharm. Lond.* vi. viii. 834 The burning a matter to Ashes..by the help of Niter, as in the making of the Niterated Salt of Tartar.

nitery (ˈnaɪtərɪ). *U.S. slang.* Also **niterie**. [f. nite *sb.*[2] + -ery.] A night club.

1934 M. H. Weseen *Dict. Amer. Slang* x. 147 *Nitery*, a night club. **1935** *Vanity Fair* (N.Y.) Nov. 38/1 We'll never catch a wire in a decent nitery. **1938** *Amer. Speech* XIII. 239/1 The most recent market nose dive played hob with what Abel Green calls 'the niteries'. **1946** *Sat. Rev.* (U.S.) 19 Oct. 20/3 His reportage is accurate in capturing the contemporary nitery scene. **1955** Priestley & Hawkes *Journey down Rainbow* 129 All darkened niteries and dimmed hot spots. **1958** [see dream *sb.*[2] 4h]. **1962** *New Statesman* 19 Jan. 95/3 This negro comedian, who refuses to be winkled out of the grimy little niterie in which he made his reputation. **1967** *Boston Sunday Herald* 30 Apr. (Show Guide) 14/3 Our story begins in a narrow strip of niteries on 52nd Street. **1972** *Daily Tel.* (Colour Suppl.) 1 Dec. 62/3 The Body Shop..is a nitery of the topless/bottomless variety, and reminds one that this is..LA's own porno-strip. **1972** *Guardian* 13 Dec. 9/1 El Cubano (the New Niterie with the Olde Worlde Flavor).

ˈnit-grass. *Bot.* [f. nit *sb.*[1]] A species of grass, so called from its small nit-like flowers.

1847 W. E. Steele *Field Bot.* 184 *Gastridium.* Nitgrass. **1858** Bentham *Hdbk. Flora* 585 Awned Nitgrass...Britain, only in southern England.

nith, obs. form of night.

†**nith(e**, *sb. Obs.* Forms: 1–3 **nið, niþ**, 3 **nyð, nih**, 4 **nith(3), nyth, niht, nigh**; 3–4 **niþe, nithe**, 3–5 **nyþe**, 4–5 **nythe**. [OE. *nīð, nīþ* masc. = OFris. *nīth, nyd*, OS. *nīð*, MDu. *nijd-, nijt* (Du. *nijd*), MLG. *nîd, nît* (hence MSw. *niidh, niith*, Da. *nid*), OHG. *nīth, nîd, nît* (MHG. *nîd-, nît*, G. *neid*), ON. *níð* neut. ('satire, libel'), Goth. *neiþ* neut. The stem may be the same as that of L. *nītī* to strive.] Envy, malice, hatred.

c **825** *Vesp. Psalter* vii. 10 Sie fornumen nið ðeara synfulra. *a* **900** Cynewulf *Christ* 1669 Ðær is..sib butan niðe halȝum on ȝemonge. **971** *Blickl. Hom.* 171 þa woldan hie on ecnesse hæle & trume wið deofla niþum. *a* **1122** *O.E. Chron.* (Laud MS.) an. 1086 Ac he [wæs] swa stið, þæt he ne rohte heora eallra nið. *c* **1200** *Trin. Coll. Hom.* 191 Swo haueð þe deuel nið and onde to men. *a* **1250** *Owl & Night.* 417 Hit is for þine fule niþe, þat þu ne miȝt mid us bo bliþe. *c* **1275** Lay. 3934 Beine in niþe and honde wonede in þisse londe. *a* **1300** *Cursor M.* 1069 Vntil his broþer nith he bare. **1338** R. Brunne *Chron.* (1810) 237 Leulyn..werred also tite on him with nyth & onde. *a* **1425** *Cursor M.* 23279 (Trin.), þo þat euer had wraþþe & nyþe, And wiþ bacbytyng wolde kiþe.

Comb. *Beowulf* 194 Nydwracu niþgrim. *Ibid.* 683 þeah ðe he rof sie niþȝeweorca. *c* **1200** Ormin 13677 þurrh whatt he fell off heffne dun Inntill niþ hellepine. *c* **1205** Lay. 7116 Seoððen come Normans mid heore nið crafte.

†**nithe**, *v. Obs. rare.* [f. prec. Cf. MDu. *nīden, nyden*, MLG. *nîden, nîten* (hence MSw. *nidha*), OHG. *nîdôn, nîden* (G. *neiden*), ON. *níða* (to satirize).] **a.** *trans.* To envy, hate (a person). **b.** *intr.* To feel envy.

c **1250** *Gen. & Ex.* 1521 Niðede ðat folk him fel wel, And deden him flitten hise ostel. *a* **1300** *E.E. Psalter* xxxvi. 8 Blinne fra wreth, and lete breth swiþe; þat þou be liþered, nil þou niþe.

niþe, obs. form of ninth.

nither (ˈnɪðə(r)), *v. Obs.* exc. *north. dial.* and *Sc.* Forms: α. 1 **niðerian, nyðerian, (h)niðrian**, 2 **nytheren** (2–3 **niþeren**, 3 **niþþrenn**), 7– *Sc.* and *north.* **nither**; 6 *Sc.* **nydder**, 8 **nidder**. β. 3 **neoðerien**, 5, 7 *Sc.* and *north.* **nether**, 7 *Sc.* **nedder**. [OE. *niðerian*, etc. (also *ȝeniðerian*) = OFris. *(for)nedria*, MDu. *ned(e)ren, nideren*, MLG. *ned(d)eren*, OHG. *nideren, (gi)nidiran*, etc. (MHG. *nideren, -ern*, G. *niederen, -ern*), ON. *niðra* (Norw. *nedra*, Sw. *-nedra*, Da. *-nedre*), f. *niðer, niþer*, nether *adv.*[2]] *trans.* To bring or thrust down, to bring low, abase, humble, oppress, straiten, etc. (Also, in OE., to condemn.)

α. *c* **825** *Vesp. Psalter* xciii. 21 [Hie] ȝeheftað in sawle ðes rehtwisan, & blod unsceðende niðeriað. *c* **900** *Judith* 113 Gæst ellor hwearf under neowelne næs & ðær ȝenyðerad wæs. *c* **950** *Lindisf. Gosp.* Luke xiv. 11 Eghuelc seðe hine ahebbað ȝehniðrad bið [*c* **1000** bið ȝenyþerud, *c* **1160** byð ȝenyþered]. *a* **1122** *O.E. Chron.* (Laud MS.) an. 1100 Godes cyrcean he nyðerade. *c* **1175** *Lamb. Hom.* 117 Swa he bið eft iniþered on þan neoþemest pinan. *c* **1200** Ormin 8032 þe laþe gast Azz niþþrepþ Godess genge. *c* **1205** Lay. 25235 Iniðered wurðe þe ilke mon þe þer to nule helpen. **1513** Douglas *Æneis* viii. viii. 41 On ȝonder syde ar the Rutulianis rude, Nyddris our boundis. **1605** *Aberd. Reg.* (1848) II. 276 Thay find not onlie the Kingis gett to be nithered but also the aforesaid choip to be ane gryt.. preiudice to the gett. **17..** Ramsay *Genty Tibby* iii, We're obliged to nither Our spacious sauls' immense desires. **1768** Ross *Helenore* I. 46 Sair are we nidder'd, that is what ye ken. **1813** Picken in *Harp of Renfrewsh.* (1819) Pref. 71 Winter nithers a' below. **1876** *W. Yorks. Gloss.* s.v., I am nithered with cold.

β. *c* **1205** Lay. 5152 Heo commen in to þen lond and neoðerien þa leoden. *c* **1450** Holland *Howlat* 57 My neb is netherit as a nok, I am bot ane Owle. *Ibid.* 105, I am netherit ane Owll thus be Natur. **1603** *Prophecies* (Bann. Cl.) 28 Noroway hath neddered them and to neede brought. **1691** Ray *N.C. Words* 52 *Netherd*, starved with Cold.

Hence **'nithering** *vbl. sb.*

*c*900 tr. *Bæda's Hist.* IV. xiii. [xvii] (1890) 302 He hi fram yrmþum ecre nyþerunge..ʒenerede. *c*950 *Lindisf. Gosp.* Luke x. 19 Ic salde iuh mæht henisæs *vel* hniðrunges [*Rushw.* niðrunge] on-ufa nedrum. *a*1100 in Napier *O.E. Glosses* i. 1864 *Detrimenta*, niþerunga. 1375 BARBOUR *Bruce* XIX. 155 That on na wyss suld I Giff consaill till hys nethring. 1599 *Aberd. Reg.* (1848) II. 187 They had committit purpresture in niddering of the kingis commoun gett, and sawing of cornis theirvpon.

nither, obs. form of NEITHER.

niþer(e, niðer(e: see NETHER *a.* and *adv.*

nithertale, variant of NIGHTERTALE *Obs.*

† **'nithful**, *a. Obs.* Forms: 1–3 nið-, niþ-, 3 nyþ-, niht-, 4 nithful. [f. NITH(E *sb.* + -FUL. Cf. G. *neidvoll.*] Envious, malicious.

*c*1000 ÆLFRIC *Hom.* I. 606 Æfre bið se niðfulla wuniʒende on ʒedrefednysse. *c*1175 *Lamb. Hom.* 57 Prud ne wreiere ne beo þu noht, Ne niðful in þi þoht. *a*1225 *Ancr. R.* 404 þo þeo niðfule Giws offreden ure Louerde þis sure present o rode. *c*1250 *Gen. & Ex.* 1917 Ðo wex her hertes niðful & bold. *a*1300 *Cursor M.* 23750 þe flexs es ai to filthes fus, þe werld nithful and couatus. *Ibid.* 27658 Nithful man he luues lest þe quilk he wat es dughtiest.

nithing ('naɪðɪŋ). Now only *arch.* or *Hist.* [a. ON. *níðing-r* (MSw. *nidhinger*, Norw., Sw., and Da. *niding*), f. *níð* NITH(E *sb.* Cf. MHG. *nîdinc*, G. *neiding*.]

1. A vile coward; an abject or despicable wretch; a villain of the lowest type.

See also NIDDERING, NIDDERLING, and NIDING. The OE. negative form *unniðing*, of which two examples are given below, corresponds to an ODa. *úniþingr*, which occurs on a runic stone (of the early part of the 11th cent.) found in 1905 at Aarhus in Denmark. An *Edgarus dictus Unniþing* is also named in Dugdale's *Monast. Angl.* V. 400.

?*a*1000 in Liebermann *Gesetze Ang.* 392 Walreaf is niðinges dæde. *c*1050 *O.E. Chron.* (MS. C.) an. 1049 Se cing þa & eall here cwædon Sweʒen for niðing. *c*1125 WILL. MALMESB. *Gesta Regum* (Rolls) II. 362 Jubet, ut compatriotas advocent ad obsidionem venire, nisi si qui velint sub nomine Niðing, quod nequam sonat, remanere. Angli, qui nihil miserius putarent quam hujusce vocabuli dedecore aduri, catervatim ad regem confluunt. [Cf. *O.E. Chron.* an. 1087 þæt ælc man þe wære unniðing sceolde cuman to him.] *c*1205 LAY. 30389 Wurðe for niðing þe mon þe nule hine sturien. *a*1300 *K. Horn* 196 þanne spak þe gode kyng. I-wis he nas no Niþing. [1674 BLOUNT *Glossogr.*, *Nithing*, a Coward, Sluggard, or Out-law.] 1861 PEARSON *Early Mid. Ages Eng.* 164 The rebel was now proclaimed a 'nithing'. *Ibid.* 294 All who failed to appear were branded as 'nithings' or craven, and disgraced for life. 1868 FREEMAN *Norm. Conq.* II. vii. (1877) 104 The king and the army publicly declared the murderer to be Nithing. 1876 *Ibid.* V. xxiii. 77 The shameful name of nithing was to be the doom of every man..who failed to obey this summons of his lord.

† **2.** A mean or miserly person; a niggard. Also in comb. ***meat-nithing*** (= ON. *matníðingr*), one who gives food grudgingly. *Obs.*

*a*1150 in *Archiv Stud. neu. Spr.* CXVII. 22 and 25 *Munificus* (*i. largus*)..*non parcus*, unniding.

*a*1200 *Moral Ode* 234 (Trin. Coll. MS.), An helle hunger and þurst..þos pine þolieð þo þe ware meteniðinges here. *c*1250 *Kent. Serm.* in *O.E. Misc.* 30 Ure lord..habbeþ.. maked of þo euele manne good man,..of þe lechur chaste, of þe niþinge large. 13.. *K. Alis.* 2054 The large geveth; the nythyng lourith. 1303 R. BRUNNE *Handl. Synne* 6723 þat þey ne be no nythyng Of here mete, ne of here þyng. 1340 *Ayenb.* 109 þe milde..lovieþ an hondred ziþe more poverte þanne þe niþing deþ his richesse. 1426 AUDELAY *Poems* 16 He ys a nythying, a noȝt, a negard.

*attrib. c*1250 *Gen. & Ex.* 3432 He had him chesen steresmen..ðe soð-fastnesse lef ben, And ðe niðing giscing flen.

† **b.** Used predicatively: Niggardly, sparing.

*a*1300 *Cursor M.* 28741 For quat es þat spense mai be nithing þar þe lauerd es fre [*Cott. Galba* what nede es þat þe spenser be nithing of þat þe lord es fre.] 1450 MYRC 1285 Hast thou be hard and nythynge, To wythholden any thynge? 1674 RAY *N.C. Words* 34 *Nithing*, much valuing, sparing of, as Nithing of his pains: *i.e.* Sparing of his pains.

3. ***nithing-post***, or ***stake***, a post or stake set up as a form of insult to a person.

An inexact rendering of ON. *níðstöng*.

1847 BLACKWELL in Percy *Mallet's North. Antiq.* 155 Setting up what was called a Nithing-post or Nithing-stake. 1863 JANE SEWELL *Christian Names* II. 277 In the North such a pole was called a nithing post. 1890 W. MORRIS in *Eng. Illustr. Mag.* Sept. 894 His head on our hall-gable should be to us a nithing-stake, and a tree of reproach.

† **'nithinghead.** *Obs. rare*[−1]. [f. NITHING *sb.*] Niggardliness, miserliness.

*a*1300 *Cursor M.* 27842 O couaitise..cums..gredines and nithinghede, to be o goddes gyft to gnede.

Nithsdale ('nɪθsdeɪl). Now only *Hist.* Also 8 **Nithis-**. [f. the name of the Countess of *Nithsdale*, who enabled her husband to escape from the Tower in 1716 by disguising him in a riding-hood.] A large riding-hood worn in the 18th c.

1719 D'URFEY *Pills* II. 321 'Tis call'd a *Nithisdale*, since Fame Adorn'd a Countess with that Name. Whose Wit surmounting firmly stood All creatures with a Riding-hood. 1846 FAIRHOLT *Costume* I. 369 *note*, Such riding-hoods were thence called *Nithsdales*, and continued to be worn afterwards, but principally by elderly women.

nitid ('nɪtɪd), *a.* [ad. L. *nitid-us*, f. *nitēre* to shine.] Bright, shining, polished, glossy, in *lit.* or *fig.* senses.

1656 in BLOUNT *Glossogr.* 1661 H. D. *Disc. Liturg.* 5 Such an affectation of nitid words and curious phrases. 1671 FLAMSTEED in Rigaud *Corr. Sci. Men* (1841) II. 114 A perfect appearance of the sun..with a most nitid periphery. 1728 THOMSON *Spring* 30 The nitid Hues Which speck them o'er. 1760 LEE *Introd. Bot.* III. v. (1765) 183 *Nitid*, bright; when the smoothness of the Leaves causes them to shine. 1794 MRS. PIOZZI *Synon.* II. 320 Una resembles a pearl, loveliest in a strong and open daylight, where all her nitid beauties show most clearly. 1823 SYD. SMITH *Wks.* (1850) 376 Forth from his bill-case this votary of Plutus took his nitid Newlands. 1851 *Beck's Florist* 36 The flowers.. spring from a singularly nitid imbricated spike of large bracts.

Hence **ni'tidity**, 'cleanness, brightness, trimness' (Blount 1656); **'nitidous** *a.*, *Bot.* 'having a smooth and polished surface' (Ogilvie 1882).

† **'nitigram**, used for EPIGRAM, after NIT *sb.*[1]

1614 ROWLANDS *Fooles Bolt* 20 Yet theyle be busie with their make shift ryme,..And lay about with lowsie Nitigrams.

Nitinol ('nɪtɪnɒl). [f. *Ni*, chem. symbol for nickel + *Ti*, chem. symbol for titanium + the initial letters of *N*aval *O*rdnance *L*aboratory, Silver Spring, Maryland, U.S.A., the place of work of the metallurgists who discovered the alloy and invented its name.] An alloy of nickel and titanium; *esp.* one composed of equimolecular proportions of these elements, which has the property that after deformation it will return to its former shape when heated to a certain transition temperature.

1968 BUEHLER & WANG in *Ocean Engin.* I. 105 (*heading*) A summary of recent research on the Nitinol* alloys and their potential application in ocean engineering. [*Note*] *Name derived from Ni-Ti-NOL. Prefix numeral value (e.g., 55-Nitinol) indicates the nominal nickel content in weight per cent, balance titanium. *Ibid.*, The 55-Nitinol was found to be a single phase alloy containing only TiNi phase.., while nickel-rich TiNi alloys showed a $TiNi_3$ phase that co-existed in varying quantity with the TiNi phase. Nominal 55-Nitinol..exhibits a very unusual 'mechanical memory'. *Ibid.* 106, 55-Nitinol and 60-Nitinol must be considered as separate and distinct alloy types. 1969 *Nature* 29 Nov. 844/2 An object made of 'Nitinol' can be deformed to an arbitrary shape, briefly heated to 'fix' that shape, and then possesses a 'memory'. 1971 *Sci. Amer.* Mar. 48/1 At present the only commercial use of Nitinol is in a heat-shrinkable tube coupling.

nitkeeper: see NIT *sb.*[2] 2.

† **niton** ('naɪtɒn). *Chem. Obs.* [f. L. *nit-ēre* to shine + -ON[2].] = RADON.

1911 GRAY & RAMSAY in *Proc. R. Soc.* A. LXXXIV. 550 To show its relation to gases of the argon series, it should receive a similar name... The name 'niton', Nt, which has been used in this paper is suggested as sufficiently distinctive. 1912 *Bath & Wilts. Chron.* 12 Mar. 4/2 Solid niton causes the glass or silica tube in which it is necessary to confine it to glow with a brilliant light. 1926 G. BIRTWISTLE *Quantum Theory of Atom* xv. 154 The conclusions..agree with Bohr's general scheme, which gives niton orbits up to quantum number 6. 1947 *Science News* V. 157 In the six years 1894–1900 there were added to the periodic table five new elements, constituting a group soon to be completed by niton (the radioactive emanation).

† **'nitor.** *Obs.* Also nitour. [ad. L. *nitor.*] Brightness, brilliance. Also *transf.*

1607 TOPSELL *Four-f. Beasts* 527 The Amber..getteth that nitour and shining beauty, which we finde to be in it. 1637 POCKLINGTON *Altare Christ.* 42 Some excellent new Fucus to restore my complexion to a cleerer nitour. 1677 GALE *Crt. Gentiles* IV. 129 Virtue gives a Nitor, Lustre, Splendor, Beautie and Glorie to the Soul.

nitpicker ('nɪtpɪkə(r)). Also **nit-picker**. [f. NIT *sb.* + PICKER[1].] A pedantic critic; one who searches for and over-emphasizes trivial errors. Hence **'nitpicking, nit-picking** *vbl. sb.* and *ppl. a.* Hence (as back formations) **'nitpick** *v.* and *sb.*

1951 *Collier's* 24 Nov. 67/1 Two long-time Pentagon stand-bys are *fly-speckers* and *nit-pickers*. The first of these nouns refers to people whose sole occupation seems to be studying papers in the hope of finding flaws in the writing, rather than making any effort to improve the thought or meaning; nit-pickers are those who quarrel with trivialities of expression *and* meaning, but who usually end up without making concrete or justified suggestions for improvement. 1956 *Time* 16 Jan. 17 The members of the Cabinet commented on the draft of the message, then commented upon one another's comments. 'No nit-picking,' Vice President Nixon adjured his colleagues, but the Cabinet eventually sent out to the President a file of verbatim reaction that piled 1½ inches high. 1959 *Washington Post* 3 July A 12/2 When the nit-pickers and the parliamentary horse-traders had finished with it, the program had shrunk to much smaller proportions. 1961 *Flight* LXXX. 525 Contributions have not sought to attract the jackdaws nor the 'nitpickers'. 1962 W. SCHIRRA in *Into Orbit* 34 We all tried to avoid nit-picking with each other on these things. 1964 *New Statesman* 14 Feb. 261/3 Some of the..modern buildings..which provide a real feast for art-historical nit-pickers. 1968 *Listener* 4 July 22/1 Knox's essay was a stylistic send-up of German *apparatus criticus* nit-picking in the Bible and the classics. 1970 P. ST. PIERRE *Chilcotin Holiday* 93 Let us bring it down to the point where no nitpicking critic can disagree. 1970 *New Scientist* 10 Sept. 542/1 If I am giving an impression of nit-picking, I can only apologise. 1971 'D. SHANNON' *Ringer* (1972) vi. 108 Don't nitpick. 1972 *Times Lit. Suppl.* 18 Feb. 179/1 A savage, malicious, and nitpicking attack on Malone's great Variorum edition of 1790. 1972 *Guardian* 10 June 10/2 A nit-picking approach would be dangerous and impractical. 1972 *N.Y. Times* 19 Dec. 65/7 Every niggling detail is carefully nitpicked. 1973 *Times* 28 Nov. 4 Nit-picking is an occupational activity of MPs. 1974 *Sat. Even. Post* Jan.–Feb. 32/3 Protect yourself and your leaders from preoccupation with the trivial and the picayune: let people control their own time; don't nitpick procedures. 1975 *Time Out* 1 Aug. 3/3, I don't argue about the inaccuracies (though they're so nit-picking as to infer that everything about the film must be defended at all costs). 1975 *Times Lit. Suppl.* 15 Aug. 922/4 Professor Laqueur's nitpicks force me to comment.

nitracrol. *Chem.* [f. NITRE *sb.* + ACROL-EIN.] (See quot.)

1848 TILLEY in *Philos. Mag.* XXXIII. 82 Nitracrol. This substance was discovered by Redtenbacher among the products of the action of nitric acid on choloidinic acid... When œnanthol is distilled with nitric acid, nitracrol is found..mixed with fatty acids and dissolved in nitric acid.

nitragin ('naɪtrədʒɪn). [irreg. f. NITRATE or NITROGEN.] A fertilizer consisting of a culture of bacteria which abstract nitrogen from the air and transfer it to the tissues of leguminous plants.

1896 AIKMAN in *Contemp. Rev.* Aug. 210 Nitragin: an important advance in the science of agriculture. 1896 *Nature* 6 Aug. 326/1 To deliver, as an article of commerce, cultivations of..bacteria under the name of Nitragin wherewith to inoculate..various leguminous crops.

† **'nitral**, *a. Obs. rare*[−1]. [f. NITRE *sb.* + -AL[1].] Nitrous.

1742 *Lond. & Country Brew.* III. (1743) 166 Then the Pores of the Earth are unlocked, and the Aromatic Nitral Vapours set free.

Nitralloy ('naɪtrəlɔɪ). Also **nitralloy**. [f. *nitr*(*iding* vbl. sb. (s.v. NITRIDE *v.*) + ALLOY *sb.*] A proprietary name for any of a range of alloy steels specially manufactured for nitriding and usu. containing (among other elements) about one per cent of aluminium and 0·2 to 0·5 per cent of carbon.

1928 *Machinery* XXXI. 478/2 Nitralloys are suitable for crankshafts, camshafts, timing gears, wrist pins, worms,.. etc. 1930 *Flight* XXII. 170g/1 The Hispano-Suiza patents do not cover the actual hardening process, but its application to cylinder liners of an alloy steel known as Nitralloy, which is especially suitable for this form of heat treatment. 1952 J. WULFF et al. *Metall. for Engineers* x. 182 Steels (especially Nitralloy, which contains aluminium) may be case-hardened by heating in ammonia at 450–540°C. 1966 *McGraw-Hill Encycl. Sci. & Technol.* XIII. 314/1 The special alloy steels used for nitriding are known as nitralloy. 1972 *Trade Marks Jrnl.* 1 June 1059/1 Nitralloy... Unwrought and partly wrought nitriding steel. Firth Brown Limited,..Sheffield,..manufacturers and merchants.

ni'tramidin. *Chem.* [AMIDIN.] (See quot.)

1866 WATTS *Dict. Chem.* IV. 58 *Nitramidin*, an explosive substance produced by the action of strong nitric acid upon starch, also called Xyloïdin.

'nitran. *Chem.* [-AN 2.] (See quot.)

1866 WATTS *Dict. Chem.* IV. 58 *Nitran*, Graham's name for the radicle NO_3 which must be supposed to exist in the nitrates.

nitraniline (naɪ'trænɪlaɪn). *Chem.* [f. NITRE *sb.* + ANILINE.] Nitro-aniline (see quots.).

1846 MUSPRATT & HOFMAN in *Chem. Soc. Mem.* III. 111 On Nitraniline, a new Product of Decomposition of Dinitrobenzol. 1866 WATTS *Dict. Chem.* IV. 445 Mononitrophenylamine or Nitraniline,..of this base there are two isomeric modifications, the one called alpha-nitraniline,..obtained by reducing dinitrobenzene with sulphydic acid; the other called beta-nitraniline.

nitranisic (naɪtrə'nɪzɪk), *a. Chem.* [f. NITRE *sb.* + ANISIC *a.*] ***nitranisic acid***, a product of anisic acid (see quots.). So **ni'tranisíde, nitra'nisidine, ni'tranisol(e.** (Now *nitro-*.)

1852 *Fownes' Chem.* (ed. 4) 597 **Nitranisic acid*, a yellowish-white, crystalline, sparingly-soluble powder. *Ibid.*, **Nitraniside*, a resinous body produced by fuming nitric acid. 1854 *Ibid.* (ed. 5) 609 Treated with sulphuretted hydrogen these substances are converted into three organic bases, anisidine.., *nitranisidine.., and binitranisidine. 1857 MILLER *Elem. Chem.*, *Org.* 492 *Nitranisole..yields a base termed anisidine.

nitrate ('naɪtrət), *sb. Chem.* Also **nitrat**. [f. NITRE *sb.* + -ATE[1] 1 c, or ad. F. *nitrate* (1787).]

1. A salt produced by the combination of nitric acid with a base, or a compound formed by the interaction of nitric acid and an alcohol. **a.** With term specifying the base, as ***nitrate of mercury***, ***potash***, ***silver***, etc.

1794 *Phil. Trans.* LXXXIV. 396 Nitrate of mercury (solution of mercury in nitrous acid) produced a whitish turbid liquid. 1799 *Med. Jrnl.* I. 223 In this [case] the nitrat of silver has proved of..singular utility. 1822 IMISON *Sci. & Art* II. 89 Nitrate of lime is a very soluble salt. 1849 BALFOUR *Man. Bot.* §246 Nitrates of potash and soda have been recommended..on account of the nitrogen which they contain, in the form of nitric acid. 1876 HARLEY *Mat. Med.* (ed. 6) 253 Nitrate of Bismuth appears to be insoluble in the animal juices.

b. In generalized use.

1800 tr. *Lagrange's Chem.* I. 227 Nitrates. The generic characters of nitrates are [etc.]. 1807 T. THOMSON *Chem.* (ed. 3) II. 215 Nitric acid combines with alkalies, earths, and the oxides of metals, and forms compounds which are called nitrates. **1857** MILLER *Elem. Chem., Org.* 771 In..the carbonates, and the nitrates, but a single class has been recognized for each acid. **1872** FOX *Ozone* 29 Schonbein states that Nitrites can be changed into Nitrates by Ozone only.

2. *ellipt.* **a.** Potassium nitrate or sodium nitrate, used as a fertilizer.

1846 BAXTER *Libr. Pract. Agric.* (ed. 4) I. 35 The produce of the land treated with nitrate..did not fetch so high a price. **1849** BALFOUR *Man. Bot.* §246 The quantity of gluten is said to be increased by the use of nitrates. **1856** *Farmer's Mag.* Jan. 7 Guano, nitrates, and other manuring deposits.

b. Cellulose nitrate (i.e. nitrocellulose), used as a base for cinematographic films. Usu. *attrib.* (see 3).

1949 W. H. OFFENHAUSER *16-mm Sound Motion Pictures* iii. 20 The weight of nitrate, however, is but a fraction of one per cent of the total weight of the film. **1971** L. B. HAPPÉ *Basic Motion Picture Technol.* 348 *Nitrate*, cellulose nitrate, a highly inflammable material once used as film base.

3. *attrib.* and *Comb.* as ***nitrate base, deposit, film, reduction, solution***, etc.; ***nitrate-reducing*** adj.; **nitrate bath**, *Photogr.* (see quot. 1864); **nitrate reductase**, an enzyme or group of enzymes which brings about (the second step in) the reduction of nitrate to nitrite.

1936 A. B. KLEIN *Colour Cinematography* I. iii. 172 Standard *nitrate base for motion picture film is coated with three layers of emulsion containing dyes. **1858** T. SUTTON *Dict. Phot.* 304 Many of the failures in photographic operations..may be traced to the *nitrate bath being out of order. **1864** *Q. Rev.* Oct. 490 The solution of nitrate of silver into which he plunges his plate of iodised collodion, and which is known by the concise name of 'the Nitrate bath'. **1881** *Daily News* 22 Jan. 2/6 The *nitrate deposits, which are practically inexhaustible. **1925** *Chem. Abstr.* XIX. 728 Addn. of 16·6% camphor to one to [*sic*] the strongest *nitrate films increased the tensile strength from 3·43 to 8·56 kg. per sq. mm. **1975** *Oxford Jrnl.* 6 June 8 The old one [*sc.* projector room] was fireproof..because of the highly inflammable nitrate film that was used. **1927** S. A. WAKSMAN *Princ. Soil Microbiol.* vii. 180 The bacteria, which reduce nitrates only to nitrites or to ammonia, but not to nitrogen gas (elementary form and oxides), may be best spoken of as *nitrate reducing bacteria, reserving the term denitrifying bacteria for the other organisms. **1967** *Oceanogr. & Marine Biol.* V. 194 Inactivation of the nitrate-reducing system occurred on prolonged incubation at elevated pressures. **1939** *Chem. Abstr.* XXXIII. 2176 Reduction of $-NO_3$ to $-NO_2$ by this bacterium [sc. *E. coli*] involves 2 enzymes, an ordinary reductase and a special *nitrate reductase... The special reductase transfers the H [from an intermediate acceptor] to the $-NO_3$. **1964** *Oceanogr. & Marine Biol.* II. 216 Nitrate reductase is found in various green seaweeds. **1974** *Arch. Biochem. & Biophysics* CLX. 269 The enzymatic complex nitrate reductase from *Chlorella fusca* is inactivated by simple thiols. **1919** *Jrnl. Bacteriol.* IV. 267 (*heading*) The use of the *nitrate-reduction test in characterizing bacteria. **1973** *Jrnl. Gen. Microbiol.* LXXV. 419 The function of cytochromes in the metabolism of bifidobacteria seems to be associated with nitrate reduction. **1796** *Phil. Trans.* LXXXVI. 426 Concentrating by evaporation the *nitrate solution. **1883** *Pall Mall G.* 9 July 5/2 Before long..the *nitrate trade will have expanded.

nitrate ('naɪtreɪt), *v. Chem.* [See NITRE *sb.* and -ATE[3].] *trans.* To treat, combine, or impregnate with nitric acid.

1872 WATTS *Dict. Chem.* Suppl. 661 The woody fibre thus purified is nitrated by maceration for some hours in a mixture of nitric and sulphuric acid. **1881** *Athenæum* 12 Feb. 238/1 On the Position taken by the Nitro Group on nitrating the Dibromotoluenes. **1892** MORLEY & MUIR *Watts' Dict. Chem.* III. 523/1 Formed by nitrating acridine.

nitrated ('naɪtreɪtɪd), *ppl. a.* [Cf. prec.]

1. Chemically treated with nitric acid (†or nitre).

1694 SALMON *Bates' Dispens.* (1713) 473/2 Nitre with Tin, or, Jupiter nitrated. **1783** PRIESTLEY in *Phil. Trans.* LXXIII. 410 What I have called a nitrated calx of lead. **1805** SAUNDERS *Min. Waters* 443 Nitrated silver immediately renders it turbid. **1855** *Merc. Mar. Mag.* (1858) V. 334 A piece of burning nitrated paper is dropped. **1894** *Daily News* 30 Jan. 2/5 A combination of nitro-glycerine and nitrated cellulose.

2. Impregnated with nitre.

1799 KIRWAN *Geol. Ess.* 151 Common salt was also said to accompany the native nitre.., yet Klaproth in analysing this nitrated earth could find none.

3. Manured with nitrate of soda or potash.

1841 *Jrnl. R. Agric. Soc.* II. I. 139 The nitrated wheat was now observed to be mildewed. *Ibid.* 140 The nitrated part of the field continued to advance in its deep luxuriant colour.

nitratine ('naɪtrətɪn). *Min.* [f. NITRATE *sb.* + -INE[5].] Native sodium nitrate.

1849 NICOL *Min.* 335, 150,000 quintals of the refined nitratine were shipped. **1855** *Orr's Circ. Sci., Geol.*, etc. 539, Nitratine,..found in crystals in beds several feet thick, with clay and sand, in the district of Tarapaca in Peru. **1883** *Encycl. Brit.* XVI. 396 Nitratine,..used in the arts as a substitute for nitre; but diliquesces in moist air.

nitration (naɪ'treɪʃən). [f. NITRATE *v.*] The process of forming a nitrate or nitro-compound.

1887 *Sci. Amer.* 29 Jan. 69/2 Treating..pure cellulose to a bath of mixed nitric and sulphuric acids in which it undergoes the chemical change known as 'nitration'. **1890** *Nature* 4 Sept. 442/2 The lower products of nitration of cellulose.

nitrazepam (naɪ'treɪzɪpæm). *Pharm.* [f. NITR(O- + AZ(O- + *-ep(ine* (suffix designating an unsaturated seven-membered ring containing nitrogen) + AM(IDE.] A tricyclic, yellow, crystalline compound, $C_{15}H_{11}N_3O_3$, which is a rapidly acting non-barbiturate hypnotic. Cf. MOGADON.

1965 [see MOGADON]. **1970** PASSMORE & ROBSON *Compan. Med. Stud.* II. v. 35/1 Nitrazepam is also used as a night sedative and induces sleep without the hangover effects attributed to the barbiturates.

nitre ('naɪtə(r)), *sb.* Forms: 5 nytre(e; 6–7, 9 niter, (7 nither, nitour); 5– nitre. [a. F. *nitre* (13th c.), ad. L. *nitrum*, ad. Gr. νίτρον (also λίτρον), possibly of Oriental origin: cf. Heb. *nether*, which in Jer. ii. 22 is rendered by νίτρον in the Sept. and *nitrum* in the Vulgate. See also NATRON.]

1. †**a.** Native sodium carbonate; natron. *Obs.* (cf. 2 a). **b.** Potassium nitrate; saltpetre.

c **1400** *Lanfranc's Cirurg.* 60 þese medicyns ben compound: vreyne of a ȝong man wiþ nitre [*v.r.* nytre]. **1491** CAXTON *Vitas Patr.* (W. de W. 1495) I. i. 3b/2 The body is puryfyed and washyd by the Nytree, whyche is a specę of Salte puryfycatyff. **1560** BIBLE (Genev.) *Jer.* ii. 22 Though thou wash thee with nitre [*Cov., etc.* nitrus] and take thee muche sope, yet thine iniquitie is marked before me. **1563** HYLL *Art Gard.* (1593) 165 The decoction of the meat of the Gourde, with a litle honnie and Niter, and that drunke, doth loose gently the belly. **1617** MORYSON *Itin.* III. 91 Bohemia abounds with..Niter, which it is death to carry out. **1626** BACON *Sylva* §83 Snow and Ice especially being holpen and their cold activated by nitre. **1684** *Phil. Trans.* XIV. 615 When Nitre..is prescribed, that Nitre which is an ingredient of Gun-powder is not to be understood. **1704** F. FULLER *Med. Gymn.* (1711) 24 We know nothing in Nature that can afford Particles of..Elasticity as Nitre does. **1753** *Scots Mag.* Mar. 147/1 Small doses of nitre, and the mildest balsamics..relieved them. **1774** GOLDSM. *Nat. Hist.* (1776) II. 269 After these precautions, they salt the body with nitre. **1831** BREWSTER *Optics* xxiii. 202 Nitre, or saltpetre, is an artificial substance which crystallises in six-sided prisms. **1870** YEATS *Nat. Hist. Comm.* 112 Brazil produces iron and nitre abundantly.

fig. **1633** B. JONSON *Tale Tub* I. iii, She's..all dried earth, ..not a drop of salt, Or petre in her! All her nitre is gone.

†**c.** A supposed nitrous element in the air or in plants. *Obs.*

1661 SOUTH *Serm.* Wks. 1823 II. 328 In the rain, it is not the bare water that fructifies, but a secret spirit or nitre descending with it. **1676** GREW *Anat. Pl., Salts Pl.* (1684) 262 An Essential Salt or Nitre of Plants. **1704** J. HARRIS *Lex. Techn.* I. s.v., Some are mighty fond of the Notion of a Volatile Nitre, which abounds in the Air. **1725** N. ROBINSON *Th. Physick* 60 Frost or Ice arises from the Nitre of the Air crystallizing the spheres of Water. **1796** H. HUNTER tr. *St. Pierre's Stud. Nat.* (1799) I. 482 The nitre, ..which is diffused through the Atmosphere, is the cause of it.

d. A sediment produced during the refining of maple syrup.

1872 *Rep. Vermont Board Agric.* I. 219 The gritty sediment from maple syrup, commonly termed 'nitre'. **1882** *Ibid.* VII. 65 The higher the tree is tapped the more of nitre or malate of lime is found. **1949** *Highway Traveler* Feb. 39/1 Strainers..through which the hot syrup is passed to remove the 'nitre', or 'sugar sand', a fine gritty substance, before it is canned.

2. Used allusively: **a.** In sense 1 a. in echoes of Jer. ii. 22, where it is used to render Heb. *nether*.

1587 in *Marprelate Controv.* (Arb.) 61 The nitre that washeth purely, the word of the Lord, must doe it. **1612** T. TAYLOR *Titus* i. 15 Let them take much snow and nitre, yet of themselues can they neuer be cleane. **1647** WARD *Simp. Cobler* 34 When God shall purge this Land with Soap and Nitre, Woe be to the Crowne, woe be to the Mitre.

b. In sense 1 b, with ref. to the use of saltpetre as an ingredient in gunpowder.

1649 JER. TAYLOR *Gt. Exemp.* Disc. iv. §21. 130 Great flames kindled from a little spark, fallen into a heap of prepared nitre. **1667** MILTON *P.L.* II. 937 The strong rebuff of som tumultuous cloud Instinct with Fire and Nitre. *a* **1700** DRYDEN *Pythag. Philos.* 96 If..clouds, with nitre pregnant, burst above. **1762** FALCONER *Shipwr.* II. 49 The guns were primed;..The nitre fired. **1796** BURKE *Let. to Noble Lord* Wks. VIII. 60 To crystallize into true democratick explosive insurrectionary nitre.

†**3.** = NITRATE 1. *Obs. rare.*

1788 *Phil. Trans.* LXXVIII. 381 Nitrous acid, or cupreous nitre, mixed with iron filings. **1791** *Ibid.* LXXXI. 328 On adding to it 1/400 of a grain of nitre of mercury, the copper was rendered paler coloured.

4. ***cubic nitre***, sodium nitrate.

1782 *Phil. Trans.* LXXII. 336 Cubic nitre. **1801** *Encycl. Brit.* (ed. 3) Suppl. I. 367/1 Nitrat of soda. This salt was called formerly cubic nitre. **1875** *Ure's Dict. Arts* III. 417 Our imports of cubic nitre have been as follow.

5. *attrib.* as ***nitre-ball, -bed, -crystal, -flame, -heap, works***, etc.; **nitre-bush**, a species of *Nitraria*, a genus of plants so named because first noticed near Siberian nitre-works.

1753 BARTLET *Gentl. Farriery* (1754) 35 The *nitre-balls or drink may be continued. **1807** AIKIN *Dict. Chem. & Min.* II. 159/2 In France the *nitre-beds are composed of nitrous earth from farm-yards, stables, etc. **1839** *Nitrebed* [see NITRIARY]. **1887** MOLONEY *Forestry W. Afr.* 291 *Nitre Bush..Upper Guinea. **1873** LELAND *Egypt. Sketch Bk.* 180 If you will take a *nitre crystal, you will see that it consists of two pyramids joined at the base. **1637** N. WHITING *Albino & Bellama* 111 Had I..past through *Nitre-flames, that belch forth led. **1867** BLOXAM *Chem.* 416 The *nitre-heaps, which consist of accumulations of animal and vegetable refuse with limestone, old mortar, ashes, etc. **1611** FLORIO, **Nitraria*, a Salt-peter or *Niter-house. **1873** THOROWGOOD *Notes Asthma* (ed. 2) 51 *Nitre paper burnt in the patient's bedroom will prevent the asthmatic attack without awakening him. **1601** HOLLAND *Pliny* XXXI. x. II. 420 For feare it should resolve againe and melt in the *nitre pits. **1684** *Phil. Trans.* XIV. 612 The Nitre Pits grow full of Nitre. **1727–38** CHAMBERS *Cycl.* s.v. *Nitre*, There were nitre-pits in Egypt, as there are salt-pits among us. **1896** *Daily News* 9 Dec. 7/5 The *nitre ships commenced discharging to-day. **1877** A. B. EDWARDS *Up Nile* vii. 178 A series of stagnant *nitre-tanks. **1775** *South Carolina Hist. Soc. Coll.* (1858) II. 66 If he was assisted with a sufficient sum..he says he could bring the *nitre works to a great degree of perfection.

nitre ('naɪtə(r)), *v. rare.* [f. the sb.] *trans.* To treat with nitric acid in the manufacture of alkali. Hence **'nitring** *vbl. sb.*

1880 LOMAS *Alkali Trade* 52 But all these points may be guarded in solid nitreing, by careful work. *Ibid.* 54 Occasionally the chambers are steamed and nitred before the admission of burner gas.

nitred ('naɪtəd), *ppl. a.* [f. as prec. + -ED[1].] Manured with nitre; nitrated.

1841 *Jrnl. R. Agric. Soc.* II. I. 121 The nitred wheat yielded less than its proportion of flour.

†**'nitreous**, *a. Obs. rare*[−1]. [ad. L. *nitreus*, f. *nitrum* NITRE.] Nitrous.

1767 *Phil. Trans.* LVII. 464 Salt springs, that are impregnated with nitreous particles.

Nitrian ('nɪtrɪən), *a.* [f. the name *Nitria*: see -AN.] Of, pertaining to, or designating the desert region of Nitria in Egypt, *spec.* the Christian hermit monks, renowned for asceticism, who lived there in the fourth century.

1867 C. M. YONGE *Pupils of St. John* ix. 149 Christians.. are said to have preferred the Nitrian valley because of the words of Jeremiah—'though thou wash thee with nitre'. **1892** I. G. SMITH *Christian Monasticism* vii. 186 In the famous monastery of St. Gall, in Switzerland, as in the Nitrian monasteries of the fifth century, the whip..was suspended from a pillar in the chapter-house. **1904** J. O. HANNAY *Wisdom of Desert* 6 Journeying still southwards over about forty miles of utterly desolate land, he would come to a long valley extending east and west between two ranges of mountains.. covered with..dangerous rocks. This is the famous Nitrian desert... At the end of the fourth century the Nitrian mountains were dotted over with hermits' cells. **1923** T. E. LAWRENCE *Let.* 14 May (1938) 416 This sort of thing must be madness... It's terrible to hold myself voluntarily here, and yet I want to stay here till it no longer hurts me... It's a lurid flash into the Nitrian desert: seems almost to strip the sainthood from Anthony. **1958** L. DURRELL *Balthazar* iv. 80 His mind winged away like a swallow across the dunes into the Nitrian desert itself.

'nitriary. *rare.* [ad. F. *nitrière* (cf. Sp. *nitreria*, L. *nitrāria*): see NITRE *sb.* and -ARY[1].] An artificial nitre-bed.

1839 URE *Dict. Arts* 887 In France, Germany, Sweden, Hungary, etc., vast quantities of nitrous salts are obtained by artificial arrangements called *nitriaries*, or nitre-beds. **1892** DANA *Syst. Min.* (ed. 6) 871 Beds called *nitriaries* are arranged for this purpose..in France, Germany [etc.].

nitric ('naɪtrɪk), *a.* Chiefly *Chem.* [ad. F. *nitrique* (app. first in *acide nitrique*, 1787): see NITRE *sb.* and -IC.] Of or pertaining to, derived from, nitre. (In *Chem.* distinguished from NITROUS: see -IC 1 b.)

1. a. ***nitric acid***, a highly corrosive and caustic acid (HNO_3), which is usually obtained by treating potassium nitrate or sodium nitrate with sulphuric acid, and in its pure state is a clear colourless liquid with a very pungent smell and acrid taste; as used in the arts for dissolving metals, etc., it is commonly known as ***aquafortis***.

1794 *Phil. Trans.* LXXXIV. 421 Nitric acid added to the solution of that substance in muriatic acid, occasioned a decomposition. **1800** tr. *Lagrange's Chem.* I. 119 This property of the nitric acid to produce so intense a cold with ice. **1851** RICHARDSON *Geol.* vi. 135 It is easy to ascertain whether a rock be calcareous or not, by applying dilute nitric or sulphuric acid. **1881** ROUTLEDGE *Science* iii. 63 Nitric acid, which is one of the most important of Geber's discoveries.

attrib. and *Comb.* **1843** GRAVES *Syst. Clin. Med.* xxvii. 338 After a few days we proceeded to the use of nitric acid baths. **1875** KNIGHT *Dict. Mech.* 1529/1 The nitric-acid furnace consists of a number of parallel..retorts.

b. ***nitric oxide***, a colourless gas (formerly also called ***nitrous gas*** or ***air***) obtained by the action of nitric acid on metals, esp. copper.

1807 T. THOMSON *Chem.* (ed. 3) II. 134 When nitric oxide is converted into nitrous oxide by abstracting a portion of its oxygen. **1815** J. SMITH *Panorama Sci. & Art* II. 446 Nitric oxide (sometimes called nitrous gas)..is composed of 44 parts of nitrogen, and 56 of oxygen by weight. **1876** *Encycl. Brit.* V. 513/1 Nitric oxide immediately combines with oxygen when mixed with it.

attrib. **1821** URE *Dict. Chem.* s.v. *Laboratory*, The diminution produced by the addition of nitric oxide gas.

c. ***nitric ether***, a compound obtained by the interaction of ethyl alcohol and nitric acid, also called ***ethyl nitrate***.

1811 A. T. THOMSON *Lond. Disp.* (1818) 672 Nitrous, or rather nitric ether has a strong ethereal odour... Its taste is strong and peculiar; and its colour slightly yellow. **1831** DAVIES *Mat. Med.* 278 Nitric, or rather Nitrous Ether.. results from the combination of nitrous acid with alcohol. **1862** MILLER *Elem. Chem., Org.* (ed. 2) 196 Nitric ether is a colourless liquid of an agreeable odour.

2. In miscellaneous uses.

1794 *Phil. Trans.* LXXXIV. 420 A piece of paper dipped into this nitric solution. **1808** PIKE *Sources Missis.* (1810)

App. 5 A species of salt,..strongly impregnated with nitric qualities. **1823** J. BADCOCK *Dom. Amusem.* 84 Part of the nitric solution of mercury. **1871** TYNDALL *Frag. Sci.* (1879) I. xiv. 386 The rays..are intercepted by the nitric gas. **1884** *Encycl. Brit.* XVII. 519 Nitric esters, *i.e.* real nitrates formed from alcohols.

nitridation (naɪtraɪˈdeɪʃən). *Chem.* [f. NITRID(E + -ATION, after *oxidation*.] A reaction analogous to oxidation but involving nitrogen or its compounds rather than oxygen, water, etc.; *spec.* = NITRIDING *vbl. sb.*

1911 BROWNE & WALSH in *Jrnl. Amer. Chem. Soc.* XXXIII. 1728 One..purpose of this research has..been to study the phenomena of ammono-oxidation, or nitridation. **1929** *Chem. Abstr.* XXIII. 3888 (*heading*) Study of surface-hardening of steel by nitridation. **1931** *Jrnl. Amer. Chem. Soc.* LIII. 1478 Browne..applied the term 'nitridation' to all those reactions which for the ammonia system of compounds are essentially similar to oxidation reactions for the familiar water compounds... Nitridation reactions are today classed under the broader conception of oxidation reactions. **1974** *Jrnl. Materials Sci.* IX. 1362/2 Nitridations under identical conditions in tubes of two types of commercial sintered alumina resulted in the formation of greatly increased proportions of the beta phase.

nitride (ˈnaɪtraɪd), *sb. Chem.* [f. NITRE *sb.* + -IDE.] A compound of nitrogen with another element or radical.

1850 T. GRAHAM *Chem.* (ed. 2) 114 Thus, with the other elementary bodies,..Nitrogen forms nitrides. **1858** THUDICHUM *Urine* 46 A solution in nitric acid of the nitride of the sub-oxyde of mercury. **1881** *Nature* 6 Oct. 542/1 The nitride of silicon..is obtained by the direct union of nitrogen and silicon.

nitride (ˈnaɪtraɪd), *v.* [f. the sb.] *trans.* To convert into a nitride or nitrides; *spec.* to heat in the presence of ammonia or other nitrogen-containing gas so as to form nitrides near the surface and improve the hardness and corrosion resistance.

1928 *Machinery* XXXI. 479/1 The parts to be nitrided are placed in a gas-tight box. **1958** AITCHISON & PUMPHREY *Using Steel Wisely* I. ix. 155 A number of high-alloy steels —such as those employed for aero-engine exhaust valves —are nitrided with very beneficial results. **1966** *McGraw-Hill Encycl. Sci. & Technol.* XIII. 314/1 It is possible to nitride some of the common alloy steels which do not contain appreciable amounts of aluminium, although the hardness in this case is much lower than with nitralloy. **1972** *Nature* 28 Jan. 219/2 The alloys were nitrided in pure, dry nitrogen at 7 atmosphere pressure at 1,050°C.

Hence **ˈnitrided** *ppl. a.*, **ˈnitriding** *vbl. sb.*; ***nitriding steel***, steel made with a composition to fit it for nitriding.

1928 *Machinery* XXXI. 478/2 Standard electric furnaces can easily be adapted to the nitriding process. **1928** *Jrnl. Iron & Steel Inst.* CXVII. 855 Photo-micrographs show the nitrided case after nitriding for 90 hrs. at 900°F. **1931** *Ibid.* CXXIV. 615 With the exception of aluminium, all metals present in nitriding steels are transition elements, the nitrides of which have a metallic character. **1952** KIRK & OTHMER *Encycl. Chem. Technol.* IX. 26 Nitriding improves the fatigue endurance limit of the heat-treated nitriding steels. **1967** *Trans. Inst. Engin. & Shipbuilders Scotl.* CX. 32 A photograph of a frigate's fine-tooth coupling with barrelled, crowned and nitrided teeth. **1967** M. CHANDLER *Ceramics in Mod. World* vi. 171 Silicon nitride..is formed in the nitriding process, which consists of taking the element silicon, pressing it into the required form, and then heating to a temperature of about 1400°C in an atmosphere of nitrogen.

nitridizing (ˈnaɪtrɪdaɪzɪŋ), *ppl. a. Chem.* [f. NITRID(E + -IZ(E + -ING².] Bringing about nitridation.

1911 BROWNE & WALSH in *Jrnl. Amer. Chem. Soc.* XXXIII. 1728 In case the hydrogen pernitrides in liquid ammonia possess properties similar to those of hydrogen peroxide in aqueous solution it is to be expected that under proper conditions they should act in a sense as oxidizing agents, or more strictly as nitridizing agents. **1930** *Ibid.* LII. 2430 Mercuric nitride and bismuth nitride have been shown to have the properties of nitridizing agents.

nitriˈfaction. [f. *nitri-* as comb. form of L. *nitrum* NITRE *sb.* + *-faction* = -FICATION.] The formation of nitre.

1860 *Knight's Cycl., & Arts Sci.* V. 949/1 *Nitrifaction*, when organic matters containing nitrogen undergo decay.. a considerable quantity of the nitrogen becomes converted into a nitrate of the base.

niˈtriferous, *a. rare.* [f. as prec. + -FEROUS.] Bearing or yielding nitre.

1839 URE *Dict. Arts* 886 Such caverns exist..in Ceylon, where 22 nitriferous caverns are mentioned.

ˈnitriˌfiable, *a.* [f. NITRIFY *v.* + -ABLE.] Capable of being nitrified. Hence **ˌnitrifiaˈbility**, the property of being nitrifiable.

1827 *Phil. Mag.* I. 177 Tufa, chalk and nitrifiable materials act in nitrification both as absorbents of water and air, and as presenting a base which solicits the formation of nitric acid. **1842** T. GRAHAM *Chem.* 456 Nitrifiable rocks are never entirely destitute of organic matter. **1884** *Nature* 30 Oct. 645/1 A solution containing a nitrifiable substance. **1884** *Jrnl. Chem. Soc.* XLV. 651 Evidence of the nitrifiability of rape-cake. **1892** MORLEY & MUIR *Watts' Dict. Chem.* III. 522/1 All nitrogenous substances which yield ammonia by the action of organisms existing in fertile soils are nitrifiable.

nitrification (ˌnaɪtrɪfɪˈkeɪʃən). [a. F. *nitrification* (1797): see NITRIFY *v.* and -FICATION.]

1. a. The process of nitrifying; the production of nitre or nitrates.

1827 [see NITRIFIABLE *a.*]. **1828–32** in WEBSTER. **1842** T. GRAHAM *Chem.* 456 The latest writer upon nitrification is Professor Kuhlmann. **1869** ROSCOE *Elem. Chem.* 201 The process of nitrification, in which animal matter..is exposed in heaps, mixed together with wood-ashes and lime, to the action of the air. **1884** F. J. LLOYD *Sci. Agric.* 72 Nitrification causes the hydrogen to be taken away and its place supplied by oxygen. **1897** *Bull. Minnesota Agric. Exper. Station* No. 53. 7 Although a corn crop takes more nitrogen from the soil than a wheat crop, the cultivation of the corn crop favors nitrification (production of nitrates from humus) and results in leaving more available nitrogen in the soil. **1926** TANSLEY & CHIPP *Study of Vegetation* vii. 122 This process of nitrification..carried out by special bacteria, is of the first importance in humous soils. **1966** *McGraw-Hill Encycl. Sci. & Technol.* IX. 111/1 A well-aerated, fertile, neutral to slightly alkaline soil will provide optimum conditions for nitrification.

b. *fig.* with reference to the use of nitre as an ingredient of gunpowder.

1832 *Blackw. Mag.* XXXI. 92 In this blaze of cordons, and perpetual glow of homage, what female heart, not absolutely stone, could resist a little nitrification?

2. The process of impregnating with nitric acid.

1880 *Daily News* 27 Mar. 5/4 Practically gun-cotton and nitro-glycerine are the same thing, except that in the one case it is a liquid and in the other a solid that has been subjected to the so-called process of nitrification. **1892** GREENER *Breech Loader* 162 Nitro-explosives are..made from pulped wood which after nitrification [etc.].

nitrifier (ˈnaɪtrɪfaɪə(r)). *Biol.* [f. NITRIFY *v.* + -ER¹.] An organism or soil which nitrifies.

1903 *Lancet* 6 June 1590/1 The bacterial organisms themselves are..the real nitrogen bringers or nitrifiers. **1931** E. ASHBY tr. *Lundegårdh's Environment & Plant Devel.* viii. 241 Mycorhiza occur more commonly in soils which are poor nitrifiers, than in soils in which the nitrification is good. **1973** *Communications Soil Sci. & Plant Analysis* IV. 280 Greater populations of nitrifiers were found by the NPN method than by silica gel plating for most soils.

nitrify (ˈnaɪtrɪfaɪ), *v.* [ad. F. *nitrifier* (1777): see NITRE *sb.* and -FY.]

1. *trans.* To convert into, impregnate with, nitre; to make nitrous. *spec.* to convert (ammonia) into nitrite or nitrate. Also *absol.*

1827 *Phil. Mag.* I. 174 The putrescent blood was at the distance of two feet from the carbonate of lime, which it is pretended that it nitrified. **1828–32** WEBSTER, *Nitrify*, to convert into nitre. **1872** FOX *Ozone* 21 It may be said generally, that the direct spark passing through air nitrifies it. **1885** *Trans. Norfolk Nat. Soc.* IV. 18 The special organism which nitrifies ammonia exists in the surface soil of all fertile land. **1932** FULLER & CONARD tr. *Braun-Blanquet's Plant Sociol.* viii. 239 Probably all communities of the Molinion nitrify abundantly. **1957** G. E. HUTCHINSON *Treat. Limnol.* I. xvi. 837 A considerable part of the ammonia so formed is nitrified. **1962** H. S. MCKEE *Nitrogen Metabolism in Plants* iv. 112 These heterotrophs nitrify more completely than the autotrophic species.

2. *intr.* To turn to nitre; to become nitrous.

1827 *Phil. Mag.* I. 176 Chevraud met with compact chalks which did not nitrify. **1878** *Jrnl. Chem. Soc.* XXXIII. 46, 10 grams of a vegetable soil, known to nitrify with ease, were washed with water. **1884** *Nature* 30 Oct. 645/1 A thin layer of solution will nitrify sooner than a deep layer. **1892** MORLEY & MUIR *Watts' Dict. Chem.* III. 521/2 A little vegetable earth which was known to nitrify easily.

Hence **ˈnitrified** *ppl. a.*, **ˈnitrifying** *vbl. sb.* and *ppl. a.*

1827 *Phil. Mag.* I. 175 Why..does it exhibit no nitrifying power without the cooperation of carbonate of lime? **1839** URE *Dict. Arts* 888 Upon each of the four sides the nitrifying sheds are to be erected. **1867** BLOXAM *Chem.* 416 A few inches of the nitrified earth. **1882** *Nature* XXVI. 102 The.. use of this nitrifying organism is thus apparent. **1900** *Jrnl. Chem. Soc.* LXXVIII. II. 97 Experiments with amides, proteids, wine, &c., showed that the nitrifying organisms are not able to attack organic nitrogen; the nitrogen must first be converted into ammonia. **1932** FULLER & CONARD tr. *Braun-Blanquet's Plant Sociol.* viii. 236 The nitrogen compounds in the soil must generally be converted into nitric acid... But this transformation can only take place with the cooperation of nitrifying bacteria. **1969** F. E. ROUND *Introd. Lower Plants* i. 4 The nitrifying bacteria operate in the nitrogen cycle by utilizing ammonia ions which they convert into nitrite (nitrile bacteria), which is then excreted to be absorbed by nitrate bacteria which convert the nitrite into nitrate.

nitrile (ˈnaɪtrɪl). *Chem.* Also -yle, -il. [f. NITRE *sb.* + -ILE.] **1.** A cyanogen compound of an alcohol radical, in which the alkyl grouping is directly attached to carbon and in which the nitrogen atom may be regarded as trivalent.

1848 *Chem. Gaz.* VI. 449 On the Action of Sulphuretted Hydrogen upon the Nitryles. **1866** ODLING *Anim. Chem.* 112 In addition to aldehydes and acids, certain nitriles.. have been obtained by muscle oxidation. **1869** ROSCOE *Elem. Chem.* 349 Hydrocyanic is the nitril of formic acid.

attrib. **1857** MILLER *Elem. Chem., Org.* 267 Nicotia appears to belong to the class of nitrile bases.

2. Special Comb.: **nitrile rubber**, any of the copolymers of acrylonitrile with butadiene in various proportions, which have properties resembling those of natural rubber and are used esp. when oil resistance is necessary, as for fuel hoses, containers, and adhesives.

1947 *Mod. Plastics* Oct. 91/2 The particular difference between nitrile rubber and the more commonly used Buna-S or GR-S synthetic rubber is the use of acrylonitrile instead of styrene. **1954** W. L. SEMON in G. S. Whitby *Synthetic Rubber* xxiii. 818 One of the largest uses for nitrile rubber is in the form of latex, in which form it finds application as an adhesive, as a modifier for other water-dispersed resins, and as an impregnant for paper, textiles, and leather. **1972** *Materials & Technol.* V. xiv. 481 The first nitrile rubbers were hot polymerized; later on cold rubbers also became available, which are easier to process.

†**ˈnitrine,** *a.* [f. NITRE *sb.* + -INE¹.] Nitrous.

1778 [W. MARSHALL] *Minutes Agric., Digest* 110 Perhaps the food of Vegetables is neither principally nitrine, nor dangerously volatile.

ˈnitrion. *Chem.* [f. NITRE *sb.* + -ION¹.] The supposed radical of nitric acid.

1868 MILLER *Elem. Chem., Inorg.* (ed. 4) 95 The chlorine displaces the nitrion..from the argentic nitrate. *Ibid.* 96 Each atom of nitrion..requires one atom of a monad metal like potassium to neutralize it.

†**ˈnitrish,** *a. Obs. rare*⁻¹. [f. NITRE *sb.* + -ISH¹.] Impregnated with nitre.

1562 TURNER *Herbal* II 74b, The Date tre groweth..for the moste parte in a saltish or nitrishe ground.

nitrite (ˈnaɪtraɪt). *Chem.* [f. NITRE *sb.* + -ITE¹ 4.] A compound produced by the combination of a base or an alcohol with nitrous acid.

1800 tr. *Lagrange's Chem.* I. 129 This is the reason why chemists do not make nitrites, but only nitrates, with fixed alkalies and nitrous vapour. **1807** T. THOMSON *Chem.* (ed. 3) II. 224 Nitrous acid can exist only combined with a base. The genus of salts which it forms are called nitrites. **1847** *Chem. Gaz.* V. 76 An aqueous solution of nitrite of ammonia is decomposed by heat into nitrogen and water. **1871** TYNDALL *Frag. Sci.* (1879) I. iv. 113 Dry air was permitted to bubble through the liquid nitrite of butyl.

attrib. **1896** *Allbutt's Syst. Med.* I. 892 Emmerich.. explained cholera as a nitrite intoxication.

nitritoid (ˈnaɪtraɪtɔɪd), *a. Med.* [f. NITRIT(E + -OID.] Resembling the effect of nitrite; said of the crisis which may follow the administration of arsphenamine, which mimics the effect of nitrite poisoning.

1921 in STEDMAN *Med. Dict.* (ed. 6) 677/2. **1943** *Ann. Allergy* I. 144 Urbach was able to prevent nitritoid crisis from arsphenamine, for example, by a similar technique.

nitro- (ˈnaɪtrəʊ), combining form of G. *νίτρον* (as in *νιτροποιός* making nitre), used esp. in a large number of chemical terms.

a. In many names of acids, denoting the combination of nitric with an organic acid, as ***nitro-benzinic, -butyric, -caprylic, -cinnamic***, etc.

Only a few of these combs. are illustrated here.

1845 *Chem. Gaz.* III. 461 Researches on Azobenzide and *Nitrobenzinic Acid. **1857** MILLER *Elem. Chem., Org.* 401 Nitric acid converts the butyric into *nitrobutyric acid. **1873** *Fownes' Chem.* (ed. 11) 688 When boiled with nitric acid, it is converted into *nitro-caprylic acid. **1857** MILLER *Elem. Chem., Org.* 477 Nitric acid converts it into *nitro-cinnamic acid. **1868** *Fownes' Chem.* (ed. 10) 668 Fuming nitric acid dissolves it, forming..an acid called *nitro-frangulic acid. **1840** *Penny Cycl.* XVI. 243/1 A new acid is formed, which is the *nitrohematic acid. **1858** THUDICHUM *Urine* 145 It reappears as *nitrohippuric acid in the urine. **1845** *Chem. Gaz.* III. 2 *Nitrohumic acid is tetrabasic. **1828–32** WEBSTER, **Nitroleucic*, designating an acid obtained from leucine acted on by nitre. **1847** *Todd's Cycl. Anat.* IV. 165/1 A crystalline nitroleucic acid is formed. **1850** OGILVIE, **Nitromeconic acid*, an acid formed by the action of strong nitric acid, aided by a gentle heat, on meconine. *Ibid.*, **Nitronaphthalic acid*, an acid obtained by the action of alkalies on nitro-naphthalise. **1846** *Chem. Gaz.* IV. 237 The *nitrophenesic acid was prepared by treating pure hydrate of phenyle with nitric acid. **1845** *Chem. Gaz.* III. 229 In this manner *nitrophenissic acid is obtained in six-sided prisms. **1857** MILLER *Elem. Chem., Org.* 571 Carbazotic,..nitro-phenisic, or picric acid. **1840** *Penny Cycl.* XVI. 243/1 The protoxide of iron, separated, becomes peroxide at the expense of the *nitropicric acid. **1836–9** *Todd's Cycl. Anat.* II. 405/2 A peculiar crystallisable compound,..which he calls the *nitro-saccharic acid. **1847** *Chem. Gaz.* V. 214 Salicylic acid, when treated with sulphuronitric mixture, yields at first indigotic (*nitro-salicylic) acid. **1857** MILLER *Elem. Chem., Org.* 399 When valeric acid is boiled..a great part is converted into *nitro-valeric acid. **1796** KIRWAN *Elem. Min.* (ed. 2) II. 245 His *nitro-vitriolic acid also dissolves it.

b. In many names of chemical compounds or groupings, denoting the presence of the nitrogrouping NO_2 in place of hydrogen, as ***nitro-aniline, -anisol, -benzamide, -benzoate***, etc. **nitroˈfuran**, any of the furans having a nitro group attached to one of the carbon atoms of the furan ring, some of which (with the nitro group attached to a carbon atom next to the oxygen atom) are used as bacteriostatics; **nitroˈmethane**, an oily liquid, CH_3NO_2, which is used as a solvent, as a rocket fuel, and in the production of nitro-compounds; **nitroˈphenol**, any compound containing a nitro and a phenolic hydroxyl group; esp. any of the three possible compounds, $C_6H_4(NO_2)OH$, obtained by substituting a nitro group for one of the nuclear hydrogen atoms of phenol, *spec.* ***2-*** (or ***ortho-*)*nitrophenol***, a yellow crystalline compound used as a dyestuff intermediate, and

4- (or *para-*)-*nitrophenol*, a colourless or yellow crystalline compound used in the manufacture of phosphorus-containing pesticides and azodyes; **nitro'toluene**, any of the four possible compounds, $C_7H_7NO_2$, obtained by substituting a nitro- group for one of the hydrogen atoms of toluene, two of which (the *ortho* and *para* isomers) are used as intermediates for dyestuffs.

1892 *Syd. Soc. Lex.*, *Nitro-anilin. **1897** *Allbutt's Syst. Med.* II. 952 The presence of aniline, nitro-aniline or some coloured product due to the reduction of the nitro-benzole. **1854** FOWNES *Chem.* (ed. 5) 609 Three substitution-products, *nitro-, binitro-, and trinitro-anisol. **1848** *Chem. Gaz.* VI. 420 It is probably the *nitrobenzamide recently described by Field, which he obtained by heating the *nitrobenzoate of ammonia. **1844** *Ibid.* II. 185 Benzonitril is therefore isomeric with Laurent's *nitrobenzoile. **1857** MILLER *Elem. Chem.*, *Org.* 306 *Nitrobenzol and dinitro-benzol. **1847** *Chem. Gaz.* V. 215 Cumene, treated with fuming nitric acid, yields *nitrocumene and binitrocumene. **1868** *Fownes' Chem.* (ed. 10) 579 Cold fuming nitric acid converts it into liquid nitrocymene. **1930** *Jrnl. Amer. Chem. Soc.* LII. 2550 In connection with the preparation of aminofurans and their diazo-compounds, it was necessary to have a series of readily accessible *nitrofurans and their derivatives. **1950** *Jrnl. Pharmacol. & Exper. Therap.* XCVIII. 163 Of the nitrofurans fed in this study, the ones which result in appreciable antibacterial activity in the urine are characterized by a side-chain of the semicarbazone, semioxamazone, or closely related type in the 2-position of the furan ring. **1959** *Times* 7 Dec. (Agriculture Suppl.) p. vii/4 To prevent coccidiosis in chickens, nitrophenid, a sulfonamide, or a nitrofuran is added to the feed. **1970** W. H. PARKER *Health & Dis. in Farm Animals* xiii. 180 When the vaccine is used antibiotics and nitrofurans must only be used..for calves showing actual symptoms. **1840** *Penny Cycl.* XVI. 243/1 The *nitrohematate of ammonia. *Ibid.*, The *nitroleucate of lime and of magnesia. **1849** MAULE in *Q. Jrnl. Chem. Soc.* II. 116 For which I propose the name *Nitromesidine, instead of Nitromesitilidine. **1872** *Jrnl. Chem. Soc.* XXV. 804 *Nitromethane is a heavy oil, of a peculiar odour; it boils at 99°. **1896** *Allbutt's Syst. Med.* I. 225 Methyl-nitrite and nitro-methane have the same formula. **1950** *Sci. News* XV. 78 A third group..is the monergols, which contain the oxygen needed for their own combustion. Members of this group, such as nitromethane (CH_3NO_2), tend to be unstable, and research is now being intensively carried out with the object of making them safe to handle. **1972** *Materials & Technol.* IV. xv. 548 Nitromethane is used as a solvent for cellulose esters and vinyl resins. **1836** R. D. & T. THOMSON *Rec. Gen. Sci.* III. 295 *Nitro-naphthalase is formed by the action of boiling nitric acid upon naphthaline. **1866** WATTS *Dict. Chem.* IV. 48 *Nitronaphthalene. **1836** R. D. & T. THOMSON *Rec. Gen. Sci.* III. 296 *Nitro-naphthalese may be formed by boiling the preceding [nitro-naphthalase] with nitric acid for a long time. **1857** MILLER *Elem. Chem.*, *Org.* 574 A sulphur-yellow compound, termed *nitro-naphthalin. **1892** MORLEY & MUIR *Watts' Dict. Chem.* II. 578/1 Primary *nitro-paraffins. **1852** *Fownes' Chem.* (ed. 4) 646 Nitrophenasic acid = *Nitrophenol. **1905** CAIN & THORPE *Synthetic Dyestuffs* xviii. 149 The formation of these compounds [*sc.* the Nigrosines] is brought about by heating crude nitrophenol ..with aniline and aniline hydrochloride. **1949** P. W. VITTUM tr. *Fierz-David & Blangey's Fund. Proc. Dye Chem.* I. 148, *o-* and *p-*nitrophenols are the starting materials for *o-* and *p-*phenetidine and anisidine. **1972** *Materials & Technol.* IV. xv. 554 The nitrophenols are extremely hazardous materials; not only as a fire risk but also because the polynitrophenols are explosive. **1840** *Penny Cycl.* XVI. 243/2 *Nitrosaccharate of potash..crystallizes in needles. **1868** *Fownes' Chem.* (ed. 10) 686 Very strong nitric acid.. converts sugar into *nitrosaccharose. **1857** MILLER *Elem. Chem.*, *Org.* 288 Strychnia..yields a nitrate or a new substitution-base, *nitrostrychnia. *Ibid.* 292 Of these [products] the most remarkable are amalic acid.., and *nitro-theine or cholestrophan. **1871** *Jrnl. Chem. Soc.* XXIV. 871 (*table*) *Nitrotoluene. **1915** *Dyestuffs & Coal-Tar Products* i. 24 2-Nitrotoluene may be..reduced to *o*-azoxytoluene, which is then acidified..and reduced to tolidine sulphate. **1964** N. G. CLARK *Mod. Org. Chem.* xix. 377 A substituent in the side-chain of toluene may be designated 'α-'; for example, α-nitrotoluene, $C_6H_5.CH_2.NO_2$. **1972** *Materials & Technol.* IV. xv. 551 *para*-Nitrotoluene, a brownish-yellow solid.., is employed in the manufacture of *para*-toluidine. **1854** *Fownes' Chem.* (ed. 5) 615 Toluol..with nitric acid yields two products, *nitrotoluol..and binitrotoluol. **1857** MILLER *Elem. Chem.*, *Org.* 628 If cold dilute nitric acid be employed, nitrate of *nitrotyrosine..is formed.

c. In certain names of minerals, as **nitrobarite** (see quot.); **nitrocalcite**, native calcium nitrate; **nitroglauberite**, a compound of sodium nitrate and sodium sulphate; **nitromagnesite**, native magnesium nitrate.

1882 *Amer. Nat.* XVI. 78 Groth describes a natural nitrate of Baryta from Chili.. An appropriate..name for this mineral would be *Nitrobarite. **1835** SHEPARD *Min.* II. 84 *Nitrocalcite..is found in silky efflorescenses. **1861** BRITON *Gloss.* 260 Nitrocalcite..dissolves in one-fourth its weight of water. **1885** *Cassell's Encycl. Dict.*, **Nitroglauberite*, a mineral found in fibrous translucent masses, consisting of imperfect crystals. **1892** DANA *Min.* (ed. 6) 873 Nitroglauberite.. From the desert of Atacama. **1835** SHEPARD *Min.* II. 85 *Nitromagnesite. Magnesian earthysalt. **1893** CHAPMAN *Blowpipe Pract.* 194 Nitromagnesite..closely resembles nitrocalcite.

d. In miscellaneous combs., and without hyphen as quasi-adj., as **nitro-'acid**, a compound of nitric with an organic acid; †**nitro-a'luminous** *a.*, partaking of the natures of nitre and alum; †**nitro-atmo'spherical** *a.* = NITRO-AERIAL *a.*; **nitrobac'terium** [ad. F. *nitrobactérie* (S. Winogradsky 1891, in *Ann. de l'Inst. Pasteur* V. 92)], any nitrifying bacterium; *esp.* one of the genus *Nitrobacter*, which oxidizes nitrites to nitrates; **nitro'cellulose**, a compound of nitric acid and cellulose; **'Nitrochalk, 'nitrochalk**, the proprietary name of a fertilizer consisting of a mixture of ammonium nitrate and calcium carbonate; **'nitro-compound**, a compound substance resulting from the action of nitric acid; any compound containing a nitro group; **nitro-'cotton**, cotton treated with nitric acid; **nitro-ex'plosive**, an explosive prepared by means of nitric acid; **nitro-'gelatine** (see quot.); **nitro group**, the radical $-NO_2$, present in nitric acid; **'nitrolim(e** [LIME *sb.*[1]], calcium cyanamide, or a mixture of it with carbon, obtained by treating calcium carbide with nitrogen and used as a fertilizer; **nitro-'metal** (see quot.); †**nitro-neutral** *a.*, forming a nitrate without free nitric acid; **nitro-'powder**, a gunpowder prepared by means of nitric acid; **nitro-'substitute**, a compound in which nitrogen peroxide is substituted for hydrogen; so **nitro-substi'tution**; †**nitro-tar'tareous** *a.*, of the nature of nitre and tartar.

1857 MILLER *Elem. Chem.*, *Org.* 307 Many of the *nitro-acids obtained in this manner are yellow, and yield salts which have a yellow colour. **1670** W. SIMPSON *Hydrol. Ess.* 132 It consists of three ingredients, viz. the *nitro-aluminous salt. **1793** BEDDOES *Calculus*, etc. 258 Was not Mayow..infinitely nearer the truth..when he imputed muscular motion to the effervescence of his *nitro-atmospherical particles? **1891** *Jrnl. R. Microsc. Soc.* 680 M. Winogradsky, who at one time ascribed the nitrifying faculty to a single species of bacteria.., has..satisfied himself that morphological differences exist in these organisms, and they are now classed together in a group of '*Nitrobacteria', the common characteristic of which is the oxidation of the ammoniacal nitrogen. **1906** E. W. HILGARD *Soils* ix. 146 The oxidation of the nitrites into nitrates by.. rod-shaped bacilli, named nitrobacteria. **1965** B. E. FREEMAN tr. *Vandel's Biospeleology* xix. 335 The nitrobacteria have the effect of mineralising proteins. **1882** ALLEN *Comm. Org. Anal.* II. 366 The various *nitrocelluloses are soluble in strong caustic soda, undergoing partial saponification with formation of cellulose and sodium nitrate. **1911** E. C. WORDEN *Nitrocellulose Industry* I. xiii. 459 The nitrocellulose silks dissolve in concentrated sulphuric acid. **1931** *Economist* 28 Feb. 431/2 There is reason to believe that nitro-cellulose, lacquers, oils..are all being manufactured or obtained in France. **1955** F. D. MILES *Cellulose Nitrate* vi. 221 On account of its capacity to swell in nitroglycerine and to absorb it, nitrocellulose is an almost indispensable component of both the two principal classes of explosive—blasting explosives..and propellant explosives. **1962** F. T. DAY *Introd. to Paper* v. 53 Nitrocellulose finishing is now an established process for printing work, the smooth and polished surface being obtained by coating on the machine. **1972** *Materials & Technol.* V. xi. 336 Nitrocellulose paints and varnishes dry very fast to give hard, flexible, and reasonably durable films. **1927** *Daily Express* 7 Dec. 12/4 To replace Chilean nitrate we shall make..*nitrochalk, a rich mixture of nitrogen and calcium. **1936** *Trade Marks Jrnl.* 4 Nov. 1355/1 Nitro-Chalk... Artificial fertilisers for soils... I.C.I. (Fertilizer & Synthetic Products) Limited,..London,..manufactures. **1954** *Jrnl. Brit. Grassland Soc.* IX. 323 (*heading*) The influence of 'Nitro-Chalk' on established lucerne leys. **1966** WEBSTER & WILSON *Agric. in Tropics* viii. 197 It would seem wise to consider other types of nitrogenous fertilizer, such as nitro-chalk (15·5 per cent N) or ammonium nitrate.., as alternatives to the long-continued use of sulphate of ammonia. **1857** MILLER *Elem. Chem.*, *Org.* 306 The production of *nitro-compounds corresponding to nitrobenzol and dinitro-benzol. **1892** GREENER *Breech Loader* 160 The explosive used in shot guns is either black gunpowder..or a nitro-compound (carbon base, treated with nitric and sulphuric acids). **1928** ADKINS & MCELVAIN *Elem. Org. Chem.* x. 101 Many of these nitro compounds are of considerable importance. **1962** P. J. & B. DURRANT *Introd. Adv. Inorg. Chem.* xix. 679 The nitro compounds are made by the action of silver nitrite on the alkyl iodide. **1897** *Allbutt's Syst. Med.* II. 957 For the 'Kieselguhr'..he substituted *nitro-cotton. **1884** KNIGHT *Dict. Mech.* Suppl. 635/2 **Nitrogelatine*, an explosive agent invented by Nobel, formed by dissolving gun-cotton in nitroglycerine, with camphor added. **1886** E. F. SMITH tr. *V. von Richter's Chem. Carbon Compounds* 79 The *nitro-group always exerts such an acidic influence upon hydrogen linked to carbon. **1938** C. D. HURD in H. Gilman *Org. Chem.* I. vii. 628 The peculiar activity of the fourth nitro group in $C(NO_2)_4$ should be mentioned. **1964** J. W. LINNETT *Electronic Struct. Molecules* iv. 65 There is much evidence which suggests that the nitro-group (NO_2) is a very stable group in many different molecules. **1908** *Trans. Faraday Soc.* IV. 104 A great outcry was, and still is, made warning farmers against the use of calcium cyanamide, popularly known as *nitrolim, or at least advising that it should be employed with the utmost caution. **1909** *Jrnl. Chem. Soc.* XCVI. 893 (*heading*) Formation of 'Nitrolime'. **1923** J. HENDRICK *Farmer's Raw Materials* x. 156 When nitrolim is applied to the soil its nitrogen quickly turns to ammonia, and the ammonia in turn changes to nitrate. **1962** J. H. WHITE *Inorg. Chem.* xxi. 331 Nitrolime is a soluble fertilizer, rich in nitrogen. **1895** THOMSON & BLOXAM *Chem.* 155 No. 2 is absorbed by many finely divided metals, forming compounds called '*nitrometals*'. **1782** KIRWAN in *Phil. Trans.* LXXIII. 48 The decomposition of *nitro-neutral salts by the marine acid depends on the same principles. **1892** GREENER *Breech Loader* 163 *Nitro powders possess various advantages over black, the chief being the absence of smoke after the discharge. **1894** *Field* 9 June 814/3 Recent trials of nitro powders in an 8-bore gun. **1862** MILLER *Elem. Chem.*, *Org.* (ed. 2) 942 *Nitrosubstitutes of sugar, starch, &c. **1867** BLOXAM *Chem.* 128 The spaces thus left vacant have been filled up by the nitric peroxide.., producing what is termed a *nitro-substitution compound. **1663** BOYLE *Usef. Exp. Nat. Philos.* II. v. ii. 126 By this *Nitro-Tartareous Salt.. those Vegetables, whose Juice affords it..may be discriminated from those many others, from whence it is not to..be obtained.

nitro ('naɪtrəʊ). **1.** Abbrev. of *nitro-powder*: see NITRO- d.

1903 *Blackw. Mag.* Oct. 512/1 In most of the better brands of nitros, what used to be a positive danger has been reduced to a very occasional discomfort.

2. Abbrev. of NITROGLYCERINE. *slang.*

1935 N. ERSINE *Underworld & Prison Slang* 54 *Nitro*, nitroglycerine. **1950** R. CHANDLER *Let.* 18 May in *R. Chandler Speaking* (1966) 80 Opening a good safe (without a time lock) requires expensive and heavy tools, the finest drills either to drill out the lock or to get in the nitro if he is a peterman. **1972** J. GODEY *Three Worlds* (1973) iii. 30 They had an old-time safe... I hit it with a fat charge of nitro.

†**nitro-'aereous**, *a.* *Obs.* [ad. mod.L. *nitro-aereus* (Mayow 1674): see NITRO- d and AEREOUS *a.*] = next.

1682 GIBSON *Anat.* 117 The Nitro-aereous Particles may be carried..to the viscera. **1699** *Phil. Trans.* XXI. 236 Some will have the Menstruum to be a nitro-aëreous Spirit, that is, quick, and very penetrating.

nitro-'aerial, *a.* *Obs.* exc. *Hist.* [See prec. and AERIAL *a.*] Pertaining to, existing in, both nitre and the air. (See quots.)

1674 *Phil. Trans.* IX. 102 These Igneous particles, conceived by him [Mayow] to be common to Niter and Air, he calls Nitro-aerial, from whence the Spirit of Niter derives its caustique and corrosive nature. **1675** GREW *Anat. Pl.*, *Tastes Pl.* iv. (1684) 287 Those Roots which are Biting, have but few..Aer-Vessels; whereby fewer parts of the nitroaereal Sap are carryed off into the Trunk. **1744** *Phil. Trans.* XLIII. 20 Those from the Brain, he says, are nitro-aerial Particles, and the true Animal Spirits. **1799** *Med. Jrnl.* I. 252 He further adds, that the nitro-aerial spirit gives the red colour to bodies in which it exists, not unlike the fuming spirit of nitre. **1812** SIR H. DAVY *Chem. Philos.* 26 Mayow of Oxford, in 1674, published his treatises on the nitro-ærial spirit, in which he advanced opinions similar to those of Boyle and Hooke. **1892** *Syd. Soc. Lex.*, *Nitro-aerial particles*, Mayow's term for a substance indispensable to combustion, and which enters into the composition of nitre.

So **nitro-'aerian**, † **-'aerious** *adjs.*

1733 TULL *Horse-Hoeing Husb.* ii. (Dubl.) 15 The Nitro-aerious Particles may there enter, to keep up the vital Ferment or Flame. **1768–74** TUCKER *Lt. Nat.* (1834) I. 23 The nitro-aerious fluid pervading them. **1881** ROUTLEDGE *Science* x. 234 The water will arise within the jar as the candle removes the 'nitro-ærian' particles.

nitrobenzene (naɪtrəʊ'bɛnziːn). *Chem.* [NITRO- b.] A poisonous yellowish liquid, smelling like oil of bitter almonds, which is used in the preparation of aniline. Also *attrib.*

1868 *Fownes' Chem.* (ed. 10) 572 Benzene dissolves readily in strong nitric acid, and on adding water to the solution, nitrobenzene..separates out. **1891** THORPE *Dict. Appl. Chem.* II. 701 Nitrobenzene was first prepared by Mitscherlich in 1834 by the action of strong nitric acid upon benzene, and was termed by him 'nitrobenzide'. **1897** *Allbutt's Syst. Med.* II. 956 It was maintained that in complete combustion of the explosive no trace of nitrobenzene derivatives are [*sic*] left.

nitro'benzide. *Chem.* [NITRO- b.] = prec.

1835 R. D. & T. THOMSON *Rec. Gen. Sci.* I. 206 Nitrobenzide is the name given by Mitscherlich to the product of the action of fuming nitric acid upon benzine. **1857** MILLER *Elem. Chem.*, *Org.* 566 Nitrobenzol or nitrobenzide. **1891** [see prec.].

nitroben'zoic, *a.* *Chem.* [NITRO- a.] ***nitrobenzoic acid***, an acid produced by the action of nitric on benzoic acid.

1857 MILLER *Elem. Chem.*, *Org.* 462 Fuming nitric acid converts the benzoic into nitrobenzoic acid. **1867** BLOXAM *Chem.* 622 If [nitro-hippuric] acid be boiled with hydrochloric acid, it yields nitrobenzoic acid.

nitro'benzol. *Chem.* = NITROBENZENE.

1856 *Orr's Circ. Sci.*, *Pract. Chem.* 506 A rich perfume (nitro-benzole), which has the delicious odour of the essential oil of bitter-almonds. **1868** *Q. Rev.* Apr. 345 Benzol produces with nitric acid, nitro-benzol.., which is largely employed in perfuming soap. **1899** tr. *Rudolf & Jaksch's Clin. Diag.* i. (ed. 4) 79 A typical case of nitrobenzol poisoning.

'nitroform. *Chem.* [f. NITRO- d + -FORM.] A colourless crystallizable substance, with a bitter taste and unpleasant smell, which readily inflames and detonates.

1866 WATTS *Dict. Chem.* IV. 110 *Nitroform.* This compound discovered by Schischkoff..exhibits the relations of an acid. **1868** *Fownes' Chem.* (ed. 10) 662 Nitroform, a body analogous in composition to the methenyl ethers.

nitrofurantoin (ˌnaɪtrəʊfjʊə'ræntəʊɪn). *Pharm.* [f. NITRO- + *fur-furyl* (f. FURFUR-OL + -YL) + HYD)ANTOÏN in the chemical name of the compound, 1-(5-*nitrofur*furylideneamino)-hyd*antoïn*.] A yellow crystalline bicyclic compound, $C_8H_6N_4O_5$, which is an anti-bacterial agent used in treating infections of the urinary tract.

1953 *Antibiotics & Chemotherapy* III. 151 A new anti-bacterial nitrofuran, Furadantin, Eaton, brand of nitrofurantoin. **1963** *Amer. Rev. Respiratory Dis.* LXXXVIII. 712/2 Most tubercle bacilli with increased resistance to isoniazid also manifest increased susceptibility to nitrofurantoin. **1972** M. ROWLAND in Melmon & Morrelli *Clin. Pharmacol.* ii. 30/2 The most common side effect associated with nitrofurantoin is gastrointestinal irritation and occasional emesis due to a central action of the drug, probably dependent on high concentrations of nitrofurantoin in blood.

nitrofurazone (naɪtrəʊˈfɜːrəzəʊn). *Pharm.* [f. NITRO- + FUR(FURALDEHYDE + SEMICARB)AZONE in the chemical name of the compound, 5-*nitrofur*furaldehyde semicarb*azone*.] A yellow crystalline cyclic compound, $C_6H_6N_4O_4$, which is an antibacterial agent used locally on burns, wounds, and skin infections, and in veterinary medicine.

1947 F. K. OLDHAM et al. *Essent. Pharmacol.* xxiv. 323 5-nitro 2-furaldehyde semicarbazone (nitrofurazone) has been recently introduced under the name of furacin as a dressing for wounds and chronic ulcers. **1957** *Veterinary Rec.* LXIX. 1415/2 In Great Britain the drug nitrofurazone has been widely used and flocks of domestic poultry very commonly are given this drug continuously as a preventative measure against Eimeria infections. **1972** *Cancer Research* XXXII. 2623/1 Nitrofurazone chemotherapy was usually initiated after both surgery and radiotherapy had failed to arrest the metastatic invasion of testicular cancer to the lungs and its subsequent growth.

nitrogen (ˈnaɪtrədʒən). *Chem.* Also 8–9 **-gene**. [ad. F. *nitrogène* (Chaptal 1790): see NITRO- and -GEN 1.] **a.** A 'permanent' gas (symbol N), without colour, taste, or smell, which forms about four-fifths of the atmosphere.

1794 PEARSON in *Phil. Trans.* LXXXIV. 391 The remainder of the gaz extinguished flame, and was concluded to be nitrogen or azotic gaz. **1806** DAVY in *Phil. Trans.* XCVII. 11 Hydrogene, during its solution in water, seems to expel nitrogene. **1825** FARADAY *Exp. Res.* xxvii. 151, I have refrained from all reasoning on the probability of the compound nature of nitrogen. **1856** *Orr's Circ. Sci., Pract. Chem.* 306 Nitrogen, carbon, and hydrogen are to be found in all living bodies. **1870** EMERSON *Soc. & Sol., Clubs*, The flame of life burns too fast in pure oxygen, and nature has tempered the air with nitrogen.

b. *attrib.* and *Comb.* *nitrogen-containing* adj.; **nitrogen cycle** *Biol.*, the cycle of changes whereby nitrogen is interconverted between its free state in the air and combined states in organisms and the soil; **nitrogen fixation**, the conversion of free, gaseous nitrogen into a combined form; cf. FIXATION 2d; so **nitrogen fixer**, a nitrogen-fixing organism; **nitrogen-fixing** *ppl. a.*, bringing about nitrogen fixation; **nitrogen mustard**, any of the group of substances containing the group $-N(CH_2CH_2Cl)_2$, which are cytotoxic as a result of their alkylating property and some of which are used in treating neoplastic diseases, such as Hodgkin's disease and lymphosarcoma; **nitrogen narcosis**, a narcotic state, common among divers, induced by breathing air under pressure.

1894 *Field* 9 June 844/2 The *nitrogen-collecting power of leguminous crops. **1862** SPENCER *First Princ.* II. xiii. §101 (1875) 295 These *nitrogen-compounds are unusually prone to decomposition. **1956** *Nature* 4 Feb. 234/1 A *nitrogen-containing acid. **1967** *Oceanogr. & Marine Biol.* V. 168 If some of the nitrogen-containing gases (evolved during the digestion procedure) escape.. the values obtained may be too low. **1908** HALL & DEFREN tr. *Abderhalden's Text-bk. Physiol. Chem.* x. 198 The discovery that ordinary nitrogen can be directly assimilated closes the chain of the *nitrogen cycle, which had apparently been broken open by the discovery of the denitrifying organisms. **1931** E. ASHBY tr. *Lundegårdh's Environment & Plant Devel.* viii. 242 The nitrogen cycle.. lies to a great degree, though not exclusively, in the soil. **1966** *McGraw-Hill Encycl. Sci. & Technol.* IX. 111/2 The nitrogen cycle comprises the processes of ammonification, nitrification, denitrification, and nitrogen fixation. **1895** LAWES & GILBERT *Rothamsted Exper.* 164 Recently acquired knowledge in regard to *nitrogen fixation. **1938** *Nature* 12 Nov. 878/1 Diverse workers.. have previously affirmed nitrogen fixation by Blue-green Algæ. **1970** *Sunday Times* (Colour Suppl.) 16 Aug. 13/1 It is likely that Germany would have collapsed before 1918 but for the nitrogen fixation plants built in 1914–16. **1912** E. J. RUSSELL *Soil Conditions & Plant Growth* iv. 83 In all these cases leguminous plants are present in greatest extent where the gains in nitrogen are greatest, but they are not necessarily the only *nitrogen fixers. **1932** FULLER & CONARD tr. *Braun-Blanquet's Plant Sociol.* viii. 235 Anaerobic and aerobic nitrogen fixers often occur associated together in the same soil. **1968** *Jrnl. Gen. Microbiol.* L. 487 As these small colonies grew abundantly on nitrogen-poor agar, it was thought possible that some of them might be nitrogen-fixers. **1899** F. H. KING *Irrigation & Drainage* 233 The *nitrogen-fixing tubercles were already developed. **1929** WEAVER & CLEMENTS *Plant Ecol.* x. 249 Both nitrifying and nitrogen-fixing bacteria thrive in the humus. **1966** *New Statesman* 2 Dec. 826/1 The first new component isolated from the Du Pont nitrogen-fixing system. **1970** *Nature* 25 July 378/1 The nitrogen-fixing enzyme complex, nitrogenase, catalyses various reductions as well as the formation of ammonia from dinitrogen. **1815** J. SMITH *Panorama Sci. & Art* II. 348 *Nitrogen gas is most easily described by including many of its negative qualities. **1946** *Jrnl. Amer. Med. Assoc.* 21 Sept. 132/1 Although indications and contraindications for the use of the *nitrogen mustards remain to be established definitively, it is felt that these agents are deserving of further clinical trial. **1951** *New Biol.* XI. 97 In the treatment of leukaemia.. several different classes of chemicals show some value. There are some compounds, such as the nitrogen mustards, which imitate the action of radiation on the cell, and dislocate nuclear division. **1970** PASSMORE & ROBSON *Compan. Med. Stud.* II. xxix. 5/1 Chlorambucil.. can be given by mouth and is the slowest acting and least toxic of all the nitrogen mustards in clinical use. **1937** *U.S. Naval Med. Bull.* XXXV. 379 It is well known that if pressure is applied too quickly the diver becomes dizzy and often is so dazed as to require several minutes to orient himself. Consequently, if the cause were *nitrogen narcosis, the difficulty would increase with exposure rather than decrease. **1962** *Listener* 29 Mar. 562/1 Free deep-sea divers—that is to say, divers wearing cylinders filled with compressed air—may suffer at varying depths from a mild intoxicating effect, or 'rapture of the deep', known as nitrogen narcosis. **1972** *Aerospace Med.* XLIII. 1079 (*heading*) Diver performance: nitrogen narcosis and anxiety. **1869** ROSCOE *Elem. Chem.* 63 Nitric acid may be considered as a compound of *nitrogen pentoxide with water.

Hence **nitroˈgeneous** *a.*, **nitroˈgenic** *a.*, = NITROGENOUS. **nitrogeˈniferous** *a.*, producing nitrogen. **niˈtrogenize** *v. trans.*, to combine with nitrogen; *spec.* = NITRIDE *v.*; also **nitrogeniˈzation**, the action or result of nitrogenizing.

1836 SMART, **Nitrogeneous*. **1894** *Field* 9 June 844/2 The natural stores of nitrogeneous substances in the soil. **1889** *Nature* 25 July 312/1 The action of nitric acid on carbonic and *nitrogenic compounds. **1836–41** BRANDE *Man. Chem.* (ed. 5) 1256 An azotized or *nitrogeniferous substance. **1896** *Jrnl. Iron & Steel Inst.* L. 161 Iron specially *nitrogenised by the action of ammonia is materially altered in character. **1897** CHEYNE & BURGHARD *Man. Surg. Treat.* I. v. 97 The plan of inducing anæsthesia with nitrous oxide, and maintaining the narcosis with ether (nitrogenizing the ether). **1916** *Engineering* 3 Mar. 218/2 A sample of iron was taken, nitrogenised at 600 deg.,.. and then thrown out from the Heraeus furnace into very cold water. **1903** *Lancet* 6 June 1590/1 The increased *nitrogenisation of the soil by the widened use of phosphatic manures. **1922** *Engineering* 29 Sept. 413/1 To obtain positive evidence of nitrogenisation both unannealed and annealed specimens of armco iron were analysed for nitrogen. **1926** *Chem. Abstr.* XX. 2138 In Ni and Mn steels nitrogenization produced hardly any increase in hardness.

nitrogenase (naɪˈtrɒdʒəneɪz, -s). *Biochem.* [f. NITROGEN + -ASE.] The enzyme which combines with molecular nitrogen as the first step in biological nitrogen fixation.

1934 D. BURK in *Ergebnisse der Enzymforschung* III. 24 Nitrogenase is the specific enzyme within the azotase system that combines directly with N_2 with characteristic affinity. **1950** *Federation Proc.* IX. 548/1 The remarkable effect of molecular nitrogen appears to require activation of nitrogenase which in some way results in simultaneous activation of the dehydrogenases which are thereby enabled to compete successfully with the hydrogenase systems. **1975** *Nature* 3 Jan. 7/3 It is now a tacit assumption of all model studies that a metal ion, most probably molybdenum, is responsible for binding dinitrogen in nitrogenase.

nitrogenate (naɪˈtrɒdʒəneɪt), *v.* [f. NITROGEN + -ATE[3].] *trans.* To combine with nitrogen; *spec.* = NITRIDE *v.* So **niˈtrogenated** *ppl. a.* Also **nitrogeˈnation**, the action or process of nitrogenating.

1926 *Jrnl. Iron & Steel Inst.* CXIII. 600 Parts to be case-hardened by nitrogenation must be completely machined and finished off before case-hardening. **1927** *Ibid.* CXV. 893 Brinell tests were made on a chrome-aluminium steel nitrogenated by heating in ammonia. **1938** *Chem. Abstr. Third Decennial Index* 6205/3 *Nitrogenation*, see *nitridation*. **1967** *Biol. Abstr.* XLVIII. 1394/2 Ways of controlling nitrogenation [of soil] are.. treated. **1969** KUNII & LEVENSPIEL *Fluidization Engineering* xv. 517 (*heading*) Conversion of a particle in the nitrogenation of calcium carbide. **1971** *Biol. Abstr.* LII. 8948/2 (*heading*) Tests of the 'Pro-Milk Automatic Apparatus' for use in the serial determination of nitrogenated matter in milk.

nitrogenized (naɪˈtrɒdʒənaɪzd), *ppl. a.* [f. NITROGEN.] Combined or furnished with nitrogen.

1846 BAXTER *Libr. Pract. Agric.* I. 20 These azotized or nitrogenized principles. **1850** DAUBENY *Atom. The.* viii. (ed. 2) 245 The absorption of a nitrogenized substance would seem to be.. the starting point in the development of all living matter. **1866** ODLING *Anim. Chem.* 54 Ammoniated or nitrogenised principles are abundantly produced.

nitrogenous (naɪˈtrɒdʒənəs), *a.* [-OUS.] Containing, having the nature of, nitrogen.

1828–32 in WEBSTER. **1846** G. E. DAY tr. *Simon's Anim. Chem.* II. 195 The ammonia-salts, the urea, and nitrogenous extractive matters. **1880** BASTIAN *Brain* 8 Certain plants.. seem capable of discriminating nitrogenous from other substances.

nitroˈglucose. [NITRO- b.] A compound produced by the action of nitrosulphuric acid on cane or grape sugar, used esp. in photography.

1858 T. SUTTON *Dict. Photogr.* 307 Nitro-Glucose.. is made by acting on finely powdered cane sugar with nitro-sulphuric acid. **1883** HARDWICH *Photogr. Chem.* 162 Nitro-Glucose diminishes the sensitiveness of the film to weak rays of light, but increases the rapidity and intensity of the development in Negative pictures.

nitroglycerine, -in (naɪtrəʊˈglɪsərɪn). [NITRO- d.] A violently explosive substance, having the form of a yellowish oily liquid, which is obtained by adding glycerine to a mixture of nitric and sulphuric acids.

1857 MILLER *Elem. Chem., Org.* 92 Nitroglycerin.. and various other compounds may be obtained in this manner with facility. **1858** *Fownes' Chem.* (ed. 7) 504. **1879** H. GEORGE *Progr. & Pov.* VII. iv. (1881) 332 The other crowned heads of Europe sit, metaphorically speaking, upon barrels of nitro-glycerine. **1884** *Encycl. Brit.* XVII. 520 Nitro-glycerin is applied medicinally.. in cases of heart disease. **1898** tr. *Meyer's Hist. Chem.* 568 Nitro-glycerine had been known as a chemical preparation, discovered by Sobrero, for fifteen years before it began to find extended application in 1862, as the results of Nobel's researches.

attrib. **1881** *Times* 2 Mar., In 1869 the Nitroglycerine Act was passed. **1897** *Allbutt's Syst. Med.* II. 958 In nitro-glycerine factories the men.. do not work on Saturday.

nitrohydroˈchloric, *a.* *Chem.* [NITRO- a.] *nitrohydrochloric acid*, a mixture of nitric and hydrochloric acids, forming a powerful solvent, also called *nitromuriatic acid* and *aqua regia*.

1836–41 BRANDE *Man. Chem.* (ed. 5) 605 Rhodium is insoluble in acids, but, when alloyed with copper or lead, the nitrohydrochloric acid dissolves it. **1869** ROSCOE *Elem. Chem.* 252 Dissolving tin in cold nitro-hydrochloric acid. **1889** RAMSDEN *Inorg. Chem.* 281 The product of the action of nitro-hydrochloric acid upon a metal is the corresponding chloride.

niˈtroleum. [f. NITRO- d + L. *oleum* oil.] = NITROGLYCERINE.

1866 *Athenæum* 18 Aug. 212/2 The relative strength of nitroleum compared with gunpowder. **1875** KNIGHT *Dict. Mech.* 1529/2 Nitroleum.. is insoluble in and heavier than water.

nitrolic (naɪˈtrɒlɪk), *a.* *Chem.* [f. NITRE *sb.* + -OL + -IC.] *nitrolic acids* (see quots.).

1892 MORLEY & MUIR *Watts' Dict. Chem.* III. 578/1 Nitrolic acids.. are formed by the action of nitrons acid.. on the sodium derivatives of primary nitro-paraffins. **1895** THOMSON & BLOXAM *Chem.* 551 Nitrolic acids are colourless ..; they are very unstable, being decomposed into nitrous oxide and a fatty acid.

nitroˈmannite. [f. NITRO- d.] An explosive crystalline substance, obtained by treating mannite with nitric and sulphuric acids.

1857 MILLER *Elem. Chem., Org.* 91 It is insoluble in water, but is readily dissolved by boiling alcohol; the nitromannite .. crystallizes in fine needles as the solution cools. **1864** SPENCER *Biol.* I. 8 Explosiveness is a property of nitro-mannite, and also of nitro-glycerine. **1868** *Fownes' Chem.* (ed. 10) 670 By fuming nitric acid, or more easily by a mixture of nitric and sulphuric acids, mannite is converted into nitromannite.

nitrometer (naɪˈtrɒmɪtə(r)). [f. NITRO- d + -METER.] (See quots.)

1828–32 WEBSTER (citing URE), *Nitrometer*, an instrument for ascertaining the quality or value of nitre. **1878** LUNGE in *Chem. News* 12 July 19/2, I beg to hand you a sketch of the apparatus, which I have proposed to call 'Nitrometer'. **1890** THORPE *Dict. Appl. Chem.* I. 160 The nitrometer, originally devised by Lunge for the estimation of nitrogen oxides in oil of vitriol, is capable of being applied to gas analysis and a large number of other determinations. **1898** *Rev. Brit. Pharm.* 30 Allen's nitrometer test is retained.

nitroˈmuriate. *Chem.* [f. NITRO- b.] A compound (*of* a base) produced by treatment with nitromuriatic acid.

1796 PEARSON in *Phil. Trans.* LXXXVI. 421 With nitromuriate of gold.. this solution only produced a slight grey precipitation. **1806** DAVY *ibid.* XCVII. 26 Analogous results were obtained with.. nitrate of lead, and nitromuriate of tin. **1836–41** BRANDE *Man. Chem.* (ed. 5) 783 These solutions are generally known under the names of nitromuriate or oxymuriate of tin. **1849** NOAD *Electr.* 167 Dilute sulphuric acid, to which a few drops of nitromuriate of platinum should be previously added.

nitromuriˈatic, *a.* *Chem.* [NITRO- a.] *nitromuriatic acid*, nitrohydrochloric acid.

1795 NICHOLSON *Dict. Chem.* II. 519 *Nitro-muriatic acid*, the compound acid formed by uniting the nitrous and marine acids. **1796** *Phil. Trans.* LXXXVI. 333 The solution of cobalt in muriatic or nitro-muriatic acid, called sympathetic ink. **1847** SEYMOUR *Severe Dis.* I. 23 The nitro-muriatic acid was given internally, apparently with relief. **1873** *Fownes' Chem.* (ed. 11) 429.

attrib. **1843** GRAVES *Syst. Clin. Med.* xx. 231, I ordered the nitro-muriatic acid liniment to be rubbed over his chest. **1878** T. BRYANT *Pract. Surg.* I. 78 It should be sponged with some nitro-muriatic acid lotion.

nitron (ˈnaɪtrɒn). *Chem.* [ad. G. *nitron* (Busch & Mehrtens 1905, in *Ber. d. Deut. Chem. Ges.* XXXVIII. 4049), f. *nitro-* NITRO- + *-on*.] A heterocyclic compound, $(C_6H_5)_3C_2HN_4$, which is used in gravimetric analysis as a precipitant for nitrate, perrhenate, and some other ions.

1906 *Jrnl. Chem. Soc.* XC. I. 118 As a test for nitrates nitron is even more delicate than was stated previously. **1939** A. I. VOGEL *Text-bk. Quantitative Inorg. Analysis* i. 165 The following acids form slightly soluble salts with nitron.. perchloric, thiocyanic,.. and nitrous acids. **1971** *Mikrochim. Acta* 478 Small amounts of gold can be extracted into dichloroethane as nitron tetrachloroaurate.

nitronium (naɪˈtrəʊnɪəm). *Chem.* [mod.L. (coined in Ger. by A. Hantzsch 1925, in *Ber. d. Deut. Chem. Ges.* LVIII. 943): see NITRO- and -ONIUM.] †**a.** The cation which was supposed to be formed by ionization in pure nitric acid and formulated as $[NO(OH)_2]^+$ or $[N(OH)_3]^{2+}$. *Obs.*

1925 *Chem. Abstr.* XIX. 2312 The fairly high cond[uctivity] of pure HNO_3 is probably due not to ionization of H^+ and NO_3^-, but to formation of 'nitronium nitrate' $[NO(OH)_2][NO_3]$ or $[N(OH)_3][NO_3]_2$.

b. The cation NO_2^+, which is the nitrating agent in mixtures of concentrated nitric acid with another strong acid and is formed by the dissociation of nitric acid itself.

1946 R. J. GILLESPIE et al. in *Nature* 5 Oct. 480/1 The freezing point evidence..provides an unambiguous proof that the cation into which nitric acid is actually converted in sulphuric acid is..the nitronium ion, NO_2^+. **1961** *Aeroplane* CI. 549/2 New oxidizers such as nitronium perchlorate are being applied experimentally in propellents containing well established binder systems. **1972** S. J. WEININGER *Contemp. Org. Chem.* xv. 371 Salts of the nitronium cation containing nonnucleophilic anions may be prepared and..used as nitrating agents.

nitrophilous (naɪ'trɒfɪləs), *a. Bot.* [f. NITRO(GEN + -PHILOUS.] Of a plant: growing best in a habitat rich in nitrogen. So **'nitrophile** *sb.*, a plant of this type.

1909 GROOM & BALFOUR tr. *Warming's Oecol. Plants* xvii. 68 Nitrophilous plants..thrive best in soil where compounds of ammonium and nitric acid are abundant. **1932** FULLER & CONARD tr. *Braun-Blanquet's Plant Sociol.* iv. 63 Here [*sc.* among ecologically specialized forms] belong many mycotrophic species, saprophytes, nitrophiles. *Ibid.* viii. 240 Nitrophilous communities are very widely distributed in dry, subtropical regions. **1964** V. J. CHAPMAN *Coastal Vegetation* iv. 97 These [*sc.* marsh plants] are probably nitrophiles. **1967** M. E. HALE *Biol. Lichens* iv. 58 This phenomenon [*sc.* lichens growing on guano] has given rise to a large literature on nitrophilous or ornithocoprophilous lichens. **1972** A. MITCHELL in Leigh & Noble *Plants for Sheep in Australia* v. 42 In eastern Victoria ..the native perennial grasses could be maintained in the sward with the introduced clovers without the same tendency to invasion by nitrophilous weeds.

nitro'prusside. *Chem.* [NITRO- b.] One of a series of salts obtained by the action of nitric acid upon ferrocyanides.

1849 PLAYFAIR in *Phil. Trans.* CXXXIX. 485 The nitroprussides are salts with characters so decided, that they cannot be confounded with any known series of compounds. **1857** MILLER *Elem. Chem., Org.* 597 The nitro-prussides give a pale green precipitate with salts of copper. **1897** *Allbutt's Syst. Med.* IV. 313 A concentrated..solution of sodium nitro-prusside.

nitrosamine (naɪ'trəʊsəmiːn). [ad. G. *nitrosamin* (O. N. Witt 1875, in *Ber. d. deut. Chem. Ges.* VIII. 857): see NITROSO- and AMINE.] Any of the class of compounds containing the group >N–NO, which can be prepared by the action of sodium nitrite and a strong acid on secondary amines.

1878 O. N. WITT in *Jrnl. Chem. Soc.* XXXIII. 202 The term 'nitrosamine' I apply to any substituted ammonia which contains, instead of at least one atom of hydrogen, the univalent nitrosyl group, –NO, in immediate connection with the ammoniacal nitrogen. **1912** *Chem. Abstr.* VI. 2319 (*heading*) The nitrosamine of *p*-nitro-*o*-anisidine as a red resist under aniline black. **1942** FUSON & SNYDER *Org. Chem.* x. 118 The nitrosamines are really amides of nitrous acid and as such would be expected to be neutral compounds. **1954** *Chem. Abstr.* XLVIII. 7305 (*heading*) Printing of cotton with nitrosamine dyes using a neutral developer. **1975** *Daily Colonist* (Victoria, B.C.) 15 May 3/2 Animal research studies have shown that nitrate and nitrite preservatives may produce cancer-causing chemicals, called nitrosamines, in the stomach.

nitrosate ('naɪtrəʊseɪt), *v. Chem.* [f. NITROS(O- + -ATE[3].] *trans.* To introduce a nitroso group into (a compound).

1920 F. A. MASON tr. *G. von Georgievics's Text-bk. Dye Chem.* 66 The monoazo dyes derived from resorcinol can be nitrosated, but the mordant dyes obtained possess too slight tinctorial powers to be of much technical value. **1952** K. VENKATARAMAN *Chem. Synthetic Dyes* II. xxv. 783 Rhoduline Pure Blue 3G is prepared by nitrosating diethyl-*m*-phenetidine, and condensing with *m*-diethylaminophenol. **1973** *Nature* 12 Oct. 326/1 The mutagenicity of MG nitrosated in human gastric juice was studied by the spot test.

Hence **'nitrosated, 'nitrosating** *ppl. adjs.* Also **nitro'satable** *a.*, capable of being converted into a nitroso compound; **nitro'sation**, the process of converting into a nitroso compound.

1920 F. A. MASON tr. *G. von Georgievics's Text-bk. Dye Chem.* 66 On nitrosation, *p*-nitroso derivatives are obtained where the *para* position is free. **1968** R. O. C. NORMAN *Princ. Org. Synthesis* xi. 385 Nitrosation is limited to the very reactive nuclei of phenols and tertiary aromatic amines. **1970** R. PRICE in K. Venkataraman *Chem. Synthetic Dyes* III. vii. 371 Certain of the complexes which are disclosed are derived from nitrosated *o*-hydroxyarylazoresorcinol dyestuffs. **1972** *Science* 7 July 66/3 These are also the nitrosating species for secondary amines and alkylureas. *Ibid.* 67/3 Addition of ascorbate to certain foods containing nitrate or nitrosatable compounds might be worth considering. **1973** *Nature* 12 Oct. 326/1 Nitrosated MG was found to be mutagenic at up to sixteen-fold dilution of the original reaction mixture. **1974** *Ibid.* 8 Nov. 179/1 Ascorbate might be used to block *in vivo* formation of N-nitroso compounds from nitrosatable chemicals.

†**nitrose**, *a. Obs. rare.* [ad. L. *nitrōs-us*: see NITRE *sb.* and -OSE.] Nitrous.

1695 WOODWARD *Nat. Hist. Earth* IV. (1723) 226 Nitrose Stalactitæ. *a* **1754** MEAD *Wks.* (1762) 597 (Jod.), The calcareous and nitrose salts sweat out upon their surface of a colour almost as white as snow.

†**ni'trosity.** *Obs.* Also 6 -yte, 6–7 -itie. [Cf. prec. and -ITY. So F. *nitrosité* (16th c.).] Nitrous property or quality.

1551 TURNER *Herbal* I. F iij b, They have both..an euell iuice, by the reason of their nitrosyte or bytter saltishnes which thei haue like vnto saltpeter. **1634** T. JOHNSON tr. *Parey's Chirurg.* XXII. xxxv. (1678) 518 The sanies..doth by delay acquire greater acrimony and nitrosity. **1670** *Phil. Trans.* V. 2009 Without this Nitrosity the Sulphur of Seeds would lye dormant in the Earth. *a* **1693** *Urquhart's Rabelais* III. xxxii. 270 Their stinging Acrimony, rending Nitrosity.

nitroso- (naɪ'trəʊsəʊ), *Chem.*, used as a combining form to indicate the presence of nitrosyl (NO), as in ***nitroso-compound, -derivative, -substitution***, and in specific names such as ***nitrosonaphthaline*** **(-ene)**, ***-phenol***, etc. Also used without hyphen as quasi-*adj.*: **nitroso group**, the nitrosyl radical, –N:O.

1872 WATTS *Dict. Chem.* Suppl. 874 **Nitroso-compounds.* **1885** REMSEN *Org. Chem.* (1888) 101 The product..which is derived from the original substance by the substitution of the group NO for a hydrogen atom, is called a nitroso-compound. **1885** *Jrnl. Soc. Dyers & Colourists* I. 177/2 Tetramethyltolylenediamine seems to give a similar nitroso compound. **1938** C. D. HURD in H. Gilman *Org. Chem.* I. vii. 635 This tendency for nitroso compounds to change to oximes..is apparent even in the nitroso alcohols or acids. **1971** N. L. ALLINGER et al. *Org. Chem.* xxii. 604 Aliphatic nitroso compounds which bear at least one hydrogen on the carbon α to the nitroso group are isomerized rapidly and irreversibly by acid or base to oximes. **1890** *Anthony's Photogr. Bull.* III. 335 If..instead of using the azo derivative of Schaeffer's acid, we employ the *nitroso-derivative of the same, the process will be materially cheapened. **1911** I. W. FAY *Chem. Coal-Tar Dyes* v. 71 Naphthol green B. is a *nitroso dye which, unlike the other members of this class, does not require a mordant upon the fabric to be dyed. **1906** J. M. MATTHEWS tr. *Alexeyeff's Gen. Princ. Org. Syntheses* ii. 58 (*heading*) Substitution of the *nitroso group. **1864** *Reader* 8 Oct. 450 Ceruleine acid *nitrosonaphthaline. **1881** *Nature* XXIV. 293 *Nitroso-substitution compounds of what is apparent azoethane. **1866** WATTS *Dict. Chem.* IV. 116 *Nitrososulphates, commonly called Nitrosulphates. **1881** *Jrnl. Chem. Soc.* XXXIX. 40 With a view to producing by this means the *nitroso-sulphonic acids. **1890** *Anthony's Photogr. Bull.* III. 333 A nitroso-sulphonic acid of beta naphthol which..was the first known representative of the class of aromatic nitroso-sulphonic acids.

nitro'sulphate. *Chem.* [NITRO- b.] A compound (*of* a base) produced by the action of nitrosulphuric acid.

1827 BANCROFT in Hone *Every-day Bk.* II. 270 The result of these operations is the production of a fluid..which..I will call a nitro-sulphate of iron. **1838** T. THOMSON *Chem. Org. Bodies* 784 Nitrosulphate of potash is white, very soluble in water, insoluble in alcohol. **1891** THORPE *Dict. Appl. Chem.* II. 369/1 The iron mordant prepared by treating ferrous sulphate with nitric acid is sold as nitrosulphate or nitrate of iron, and is used in dyeing.

So **nitro'sulphide.**

1862 MILLER *Elem. Chem., Org.* (ed. 2) 689 By boiling the liquid, nitrosulphide of iron and of the alkaline metal is obtained.

†**nitrosul'phureous,** *a. Obs.* [NITRO- d.] Of the nature of nitre and sulphur.

1671 R. BOHUN *Wind* 31 Especially the nitrosulphureous and other Minerall or Metallic Concretes. **1695** S. PATRICK *Comm. Gen.* (1697) 318 Some of that dreadful Shower.. falling upon her, wrapt her Body in a sheet of Nitro-Sulphureous Matter. **1708** *Brit. Apollo* No. 21. 2/1 Lightning [is] nothing else but a very subtle Nitro-sulphureous Matter enflamed.

nitrosul'phuric, *a. Chem.* [NITRO- a.] Formed by the mixture of nitric and sulphuric acids.

1836 R. D. & T. THOMSON *Rec. Gen. Sci.* III. 304 Nitro-sulphuric acid. M. Pelouze formed this acid by causing the deutoxide of azote to act upon a solution of sulphite of potash and potash dissolved in water. **1840** *Penny Cycl.* XVI. 243/2 *Nitro-sulphuric acid.* This name has been applied to a mixture of nitric and sulphuric acid first proposed by Mr. Keir as a solvent for silver. **1856** *Orr's Circ. Sci., Pract. Chem.* 229 A preliminary experiment..will speedily indicate the actual strength of the nitrosulphuric acid.

†**nitrosul'phurious,** *a. Obs. rare*[−1]. = next.

1688 CLAYTON in *Phil. Trans.* XVII. 943, I conceive Tobacco to be a Plant abounding with Nitro-Sulphurious Particles.

†**nitro'sulphurous,** *a. Obs. rare.* Also 7 -erous. [NITRO- d.] = NITROSULPHUREOUS.

1656 S. HOLLAND *Zara* (1719) 44 Henceforth I will abjure the thought of that nefarious Nitrosulpherous Sex. *a* **1719** F. LEE *Diss.* (1752) II. 132 A sudden Induration of all the Parts of her Body..from the Abundance of the nitrosulphurous Particles penetrating the same throughout.

nitrosyl, -yle ('naɪtrəsɪl). *Chem.* [See NITROSO- and -YL.] The grouping NO.

1866 WATTS *Dict. Chem.* IV. 116 *Nitrosyl* or *Azotyl.* The name of nitric oxide in combination. **1880** CLEMINSHAW tr. *Wurtz' Atom. The.* 264 This is the case..with nitrogen dioxide or nitrosyl.

attrib. **1875** BLOXAM *Chem.* (ed. 3) 171 Nitrosyle chloride is also produced by mixing 2 volumes of nitric oxide with 1 volume of chlorine.

nitrous ('naɪtrəs), *a.* [ad. L. *nitrōsus*: see NITRE *sb.* and -OUS, and cf. F. *nitreux*.]

1. a. Having the nature or qualities of nitre; impregnated with nitre.

1601 HOLLAND *Pliny* I. 386 Forasmuch as Date trees delight in a salt and nitrous soile. **1657** S. PURCHAS *Pol. Flying-Ins.* 142 This falls out for want of a nitrous, and thereby a nutritive quality in the grain. **1692** RAY *Disc.* 142 The Air being..as much rarified, would contain but few nitrous Particles. **1748** *Anson's Voy.* I. vi. (ed. 4) 95 The land being generally of a nitrous and saline nature. **1774** J. BRYANT *Mythol.* I. 30 Hot streams either of water or bitumen: or else salt, and nitrous pools. **1884** LADY BRASSEY in *Good Wds.* June 403/1 The temple..submerged in the nitrous waters of the river.

b. Mixed or impregnated with nitre so as to form an explosive compound. Also *fig.*

1667 MILTON *P.L.* IV. 815 As when a spark Lights on a heap of nitrous Powder. **1714** GAY *Trivia* III. 383 The nitrous Store is laid, the smutty Train With running blaze awakes the barrell'd Grain. **1742** YOUNG *Nt. Th.* IX. 202 Sudden, as the spark From smitten steel; from nitrous grain, the blaze. **1806** J. GRAHAME *Birds Scot.* III. 84 The leaden bolt Slung from the mimic lightning's nitrous wing.

†**c.** As an epithet applied to the air, on the supposition that it was charged with particles of nitre. (Cf. NITRE *sb.* 1 c.) *Obs.*

1670 CLARKE *Nat. Hist. Nitre* 36 The nitrous Air receiv'd into the Lungs. **1720** WELTON *Suffer. Son of God* I. xiii. 342 My Blood requires the Nitrous Air, to preserve Life by the Respiration of my Breath. **1735** SOMERVILLE *Chase* I. 165 The nitrous Air, and purifying Breeze. **1784** COWPER *Task* III. 32 The nitrous air Feeds a blue flame, and makes a cheerful hearth.

d. Performed by means of nitre.

1800 *Med. Jrnl.* III. 429 My letter to Dr. Duncan, respecting nitrous fumigation.

2. In special applications: **a.** ***nitrous salt***, a salt containing nitre.

1662 R. MATHEW *Unl. Alch.* 20 Thy Salt doth also consist of three sorts, a fixed Salt, and a Nitrous, and a Volatil. **1718** QUINCY *Compl. Disp.* 113 For that reason it abounds with a nitrous Salt. **1732** ARBUTHNOT *Rules Diet* in *Aliments*, etc. 277 Nitres, and those Vegetables which have nitrous Salts in them. **1814** SIR H. DAVY *Agric. Chem.* 339 The nitrous Salts are too valuable for other purposes to be used as Manures. *a* **1828** PEARSON in *Brit. Husb.* (1834) I. 245 There is considerable waste in gases and ammoniacal and nitrous salt by their putrefaction.

b. ***nitrous acid***, an acid having nitrous properties; in later use *spec.* an acid (HNO_2) which contains less oxygen than *nitric acid*.

1676 GREW *Anat. Pl., Exper. Luctation* ii. (1682) 243 Upon its solution by a Nitrous Acid. **1779** *Phil. Trans.* LXIX. 396 Nitre is composed of two different ingredients, *viz.* an acid, called..the nitrous acid, and the vegetable alkali. **1804** ABERNETHY *Surg. Obs.* 139 The administration of nitrous acid, opium, and other remedies. **1849** D. CAMPBELL *Inorg. Chem.* 24 Nitrous acid pure is a colourless liquid at a low temperature, but becomes green on a slight elevation of heat. **1867** BLOXAM *Chem.* 134 The so-called nitrous acid of commerce is really nitric acid holding in solution a large proportion of nitric peroxide. **1871** TYNDALL *Frag. Sci.* (1879) I. iv. 101 The brown fumes of nitrous acid were seen.

attrib. **1812** SIR H. DAVY *Chem. Philos.* I. I. 113 Nitrous acid gas [is composed] of 1 of azote and 4 of oxygene. **1839** LINDLEY *Introd. Bot.* 386 Nitrous acid gas is probably as deleterious as the sulphurous and hydrochloric acid gases.

†**c.** ***nitrous air***, = next. *Obs.*

1775 PRIESTLEY *On Air* I. 109, I happened to distinguish it by the name of Nitrous air because I had procured it by means of spirit of nitre only. **1789** *Phil. Trans.* LXXX. 70 This salt, heated in close vessels, yields dephlogisticated nitrous air in great abundance.

d. ***nitrous gas***, a mixture of oxides of nitrogen, such as is obtained when most metals are acted on by nitric acid in the presence of air.

1794 PEARSON in *Phil. Trans.* LXXXIV. 389 A fresh discharge of nitrous gaz took place on adding more nitrous acid. **1800** tr. *Lagrange's Chem.* I. 121 The name of nitrous gas is given to that aeriform fluid which is disengaged by the action of iron, copper, silver, and mercury on the nitric acid. **1837** M. DONOVAN *Dom. Econ.* II. 227 Nitrous gas strongly resists putrefaction;..and after nitrous gas, carbonic acid gas is next in preservative power. **1880** *Jrnl. Soc. Arts* 445 Nitrous gas is passed through a solution of diphenylamine in acetic acid.

e. ***nitrous oxide***, a colourless gas (nitrogen protoxide, N_2O), with a faint odour and sweetish taste, which when inhaled produces exhilaration (hence called *laughing gas*) or anæsthesia.

1800 SIR H. DAVY *Res. Nitrous Oxide* 95 The nitrous oxide may be analised, either by charcoal or hydrogene. **1836–41** BRANDE *Man. Chem.* (ed. 5) 410 Nitrous oxide supports combustion, and a taper introduced into it has its flame much augmented. **1878** MEREDITH *Teeth* 205 The.. use of nitrous oxide for certain bodily complaints.

attrib. **1840** *Penny Cycl.* XVI. 244/1 Nitrous oxide gas is composed of one volume of oxygen and two volumes of azote. **1875** KNIGHT *Dict. Mech.* 1530/1 *Nitrous-oxide Apparatus.* **1892** *Syd. Soc. Lex.*, *Nitrous oxide water*, a solution..of five volumes of nitrous oxide in one of water.

f. ***nitrous ether***, nitric ether (NITRIC 1 c).

1811 [see NITRIC 1 c]. **1860** *Knight's Eng. Cycl.*, *Arts & Sci.* III. 980 Nitrous ether, dissolved in alcohol, is the sweet spirit of nitre of pharmacy. **1879** ALLEN *Comm. Org. Anal.* I. 153 Spirit of nitrous ether has often a great tendency to become acid. This may be due to the decomposition of nitrous ether.

g. ***nitrous vitriol***, a solution of oxides of nitrogen in sulphuric acid produced in the Gay-Lussac tower in the lead-chamber process.

1879 *Chem. News* 30 May 237/2 In a paper about to be published, I [*sc.* G. Lunge] have proved that denitration by hot water or steam is insufficient when the nitrous vitriol, by faulty work, contains nitric acid. **1933** W. T. READ *Industr. Chem.* xi. 165 A portion of the acid from the coolers is sent to the top of the cold tower. As it passes down the cold tower it picks up the oxides of nitrogen in the form of nitrosyl sulfuric acid and becomes..'nitrous vitriol'. **1954** KIRK & OTHMER *Encycl. Chem. Technol.* XIII. 472 The Glover tower receives the hot burner gas, and is fed at the top with the nitrous vitriol from the Gay-Lussac tower, and with 52° Bé. (65%) acid from the chambers.

† 'nitrousness. *Obs. rare*$^{-1}$. [f. prec. + -NESS.] Nitrous property.
1651 FRENCH *Distill.* v. 163 Which did attract, and condense the nitrousnesse of the aire.

† ni'troxide. *Obs. rare.* (See quot.)
1826 HENRY *Elem. Chem.* II. 130 This substance, commonly called red precipitate, is termed more properly the nitroxide of mercury.

nitroxyl (naɪ'trɒksɪl). *Chem.* [f. NITRO- + OX-IDE + -YL.] The radical NO_2.
1869 ROSCOE *Elem. Chem.* 68 The decomposition takes place in two stages, in the first a yellow liquid, called nitroxyl chloride, is formed. **1876** HARLEY *Mat. Med.* (ed. 6) 355 A great number of substitution products, formed as the above nitroxyl series, on the type of phenic acid.

nitruret ('naɪtrʊrɛt). *Chem.* [f. NITRE *sb.*; cf. *sulphuret.*] A combination of nitrogen with a simple body.
1836–41 BRANDE *Man. Chem.* (ed. 5) 737 Nitruret of Iron. .. When ammonia is passed over ignited ironwire..a portion of the nitrogen is retained in permanent combination with the iron. **1854** *Orr's Circ. Sci., Chem.* 491 Nitruret of Copper.

† 'nitry, *a. Obs.*$^{-1}$ [f. NITRE *sb.*] Nitrous.
1714 GAY *Trivia* II. 197 Winter my Theme confines; whose nitry Wind Shall crust the slabby Mire.

'nitryl. *Chem.* [f. NITRE *sb.* + -YL.] 'Nitric peroxide in combination' (Watts 1866).
1876 *Encycl. Brit.* V. 556/1 Nitro-substitution compounds in which hydrogen is replaced by nitryl (NO_2).

'nitta. *Bot.* Also **nutta.** [Native name.] A West African tree (*Parkia africana* or *biglandula*), also found in tropical Asia and introduced into the West Indies, bearing pods which contain edible pulp and seeds. Also ***nitta-tree.***
1797 MUNGO PARK *Trav.* (1799) 336 The yellow powder which is found in the pods of the nitta, so called by the natives, a species of mimosa. **1805** —— *Jrnl. Mission Africa* 14 May, One of the soldiers having collected some of the fruit of the Nitta trees. **1847** *Nat. Encycl.* I. 264 In the tropical regions of Africa we meet with..the nitta or doura tree. **1866** *Treas. Bot* s.v. *Parkia,* The African Locust tree (Nitta or Nutta of the negroes),..attaining thirty or forty feet in height. **1887** MOLONEY *Forestry W. Africa* 339.

nitte, obs. form of NIT *sb.*[1]

† nitte, nytte, varr. of NUTTE *v.* to use. *Obs.*
c **1200** ORMIN 5543 All hu mann birrþ weorelldþing Nittenn & tohh forrwerrpenn. *Ibid.* 12279 He cunneþþ þa to lærenn þe To nittenn swiþe litell. *c* **1300** *Havelok* 941 Þe wode fro the brigge he bar; Al that euere shulden he nytte, Al he drow, and al he citte.

'nitter. *rare*$^{-0}$. [f. NIT *v.*[1] + -ER[1].] 'The horse bee that deposits nits on horses' (Webster, 1828–32, citing *Med. Repos.*).

† 'nittical, *a. Obs. rare*$^{-1}$. [f. NIT *sb.*[1]] Infested by nits.
1607 MIDDLETON *Five Gallants* IV. viii, A filthy, slimy, lousy, nittical broker.

† 'nittify, *v. Obs. rare.* [f. NIT *sb.*[1] + -(I)FY.] **a.** *refl.* To make (oneself) nitty. **b.** *trans.* To bespatter as with nits.
In quot. 1596 the allusion is to hair-cutting.
1596 NASHE *Saffron Walden* Ep. Ded., Wks. (Grosart) III. 14 He, alas,..hath nittifide himselfe with a dish..any time this fourteene yeere to saue charges of sheep-shearing. **1647** *Maid's Petition* 5 Wyat the Prick-louse will nittifie our Corps with the small shot of reproofe.

† 'nittily, *adv. Obs.*$^{-1}$ [f. NITTY *a.*] Lousily.
1630 J. HAYWARD *Edw. VI* 103 Hee was a man nittily needy and therefore adventurous.

† 'nittiness. *Obs.*$^{-1}$ [f. NITTY *a.* 2.] The condition of being full of small air-bubbles.
1664 TAYLOR in Evelyn *Pomona* 50 It..comes into the glass..with a speedy vanishing nittiness (as the Vintners call it), which evaporates with a sparkling..noise.

† 'nittings. *Obs. rare*$^{-0}$. (See quot.)
1747 HOOSON *Miner's Dict.* N 3 b, *Nittings* [is] that Ore that stays in the Seive in washing of Smitham, which is something rounder than the Smitham it self.

nittle, variant of KNETTLE.

nitto ('nɪtəʊ), *v. Criminals' slang.* [Cf. NIT *sb.*[2]] (See quot. 1959.)
1959 J. GOSLING *Ghost Squad* ii. 25 'Nitto' means 'stop' or 'Be quiet'. **1962** D. WARNER *Death of Bogey* IV. vi. 169 You guys better nitto. The Sparrow's got a line to your run-in.

'nitty, *sb. Naut. slang.* [Etym. obscure.] A racket, disturbance.
1830 MARRYAT *King's Own* xxvi, I never seed a ship's company in such a farmant, or such a nitty kicked up 'tween decks, in my life. **1867** SMYTH *Sailor's Word-bk.* 498 *Nitty,* a troublesome noise; a squabble.

nitty ('nɪtɪ) *a.* Now *rare.* [f. NIT *sb.*[1] + -Y[1].]
1. Full of, abounding or infested with, nits.
1570 LEVINS *Manip.* 112/5 Nitty, *culicosus.* **1592** GREENE *Upst. Courtier* (1871) 36 As if he meant to give a warning to all the lice in his nitty locks. **1600** ROWLANDS *Lett. Humours Blood* v. 72 Goodly curld lockes; but surely tis great pitty, For want of kembing, they are beastly nitty. **1654** GATAKER *Disc. Apol.* 30 If..the poor Presbyter is left so needie, nittie, bare, and wors then beggerlie. **1671** MARTEN *Voy. Spitzbergen* III. xi. in *Acc. Sev. Voy.* II. (1694) 69 Here and there it hath some small knobs like nitty Hair. **1712** MRS. CENTLIVRE *Perplex. Lovers* III. iii, A nitty Son of a Whore, who does he call lousy? **1797** BRYDGES *Homer Travestie* II. 63 As easily I can ye souse As nitty tailors crack a louse.
transf. **1622** MASSINGER & DEKKER *Virg. Mart.* III. iii, Thy hungry tongue bit off these shreds of complaints, to patch up the elbows of thy nitty eloquence. **1666** J. SERGEANT *Lett. Thanks* 31, I may not trouble my Reader often with such nitty Exceptions with which your Book abounds.

† b. Used jocularly. (Cf. NIT *sb.*[1] 1.) *Obs.*$^{-1}$
1598 MARSTON *Pygmal., Sat.* III. 148 O dapper, rare, compleat, sweet nittie youth!

† 2. (Cf. NITTINESS.) *Obs. rare*$^{-1}$.
1654 GAYTON *Pleas. Notes* III. vi. 102 Before dinner again, refresh your Lamp..with the generous oyle of Sack, nitty, roapy, and razy.

nitty-gritty (ˌnɪtɪ'grɪtɪ). *slang* (orig. *U.S.*). [Etym. unknown.] The realities or basic facts of a problem, situation, subject, etc.; the heart of the matter. Also *attrib.* or as *adj.*
1963 *Time* 2 Aug. 14/2 The Negroes present would know perfectly well that the nitty-gritty of a situation is the essentials of it. **1963** *Wall St. Jrnl.* 12 Sept. 14/1 Says W. C. Patton, field secretary for..the National Association for the Advancement of Colored People. 'Now we're down to the nitty-gritty, the hard core who've never been interested in politics.' **1967** *Freedomways* VII. 186 All those 'nitty gritty' actions and styles which set Negroes off from the rest of American society. **1967** *N.Y. Times* 27 June 20 He's not afraid to get down to the nitty-gritty of unpleasant problems. **1968** *Times* 15 Nov. 17/2 To get down to what the American will call the 'nitty-gritty' of the matter—the heart, sir, the heart. **1969** *Listener* 25 Sept. 420/2 The Animals were already into the nitty-gritty of blues history. **1973** *Computers & Humanities* VII. 163 Most of the Harris work covers the nitty-gritty problems of subject analysis. **1974** *Financial Times* 6 Mar. 36/2 Mr Wilson is expected to appoint a trade union MP or two as junior Ministers at the Department of Employment to make up for Mr Foot's lack of experience in the 'nitty-gritty' of trade union negotiations. **1975** *Publishers Weekly* 13 Jan. 56/3 He still can startle the reader with his abrupt shifts from nitty-gritty reality to far-out fantasy.

nit-weed ('nɪtwiːd). [f. NIT *sb.* + WEED *sb.*[1]] A North American herb, *Hypericum gentianoides,* of the family Guttiferæ, having wiry stems, scale-like leaves, and yellow flowers; also called orange grass and pine-weed.
1818 A. EATON *Man. Bot.* (ed. 2) 422 Nit-weed, false john's wort... On the sandy plain west of Ball's spring, New Haven. **1843** J. TORREY *Flora N.Y.* I. 89 Ground Pine. Nitweed. Pine-weed. **1907** A. B. LYONS *Plant Names* (ed. 2) 414 Sarothra... Orange-grass, Pine-weed, Bastard Gentian, Ground Pine, Nit-weed, False Johnswort.

nitwit ('nɪtwɪt). *colloq.* [Perh. f. NIT *sb.* 2 + WIT *sb.*] A stupid person, a person of little intelligence. Also *attrib.* and *transf.*
1922 *Dialect Notes* V. 142 Nit-wit. **1926** L. NASON *Chevrons* v. 170 Listen, nit-wit. The rocket you want is a yellow smoke. **1928** *Daily Express* 1 June 9 The Vice-President announced loudly that he wanted a large cup of coffee with his dinner, and none of these 'nit-wit, pee-wee, demi-tasses'. **1930** *Musical Times* Nov. 987 Music..of the type that the nitwits who write..to the *Radio Times* call dry and highbrow. **1933** *Punch* 8 Feb. 157/2 *Barbara.* It's awful explaining to a nitwit. When you're out you put down. *Me.* Put what down? *Barbara.* Your cards, idiot! **1958** *Times Lit. Suppl.* 11 Apr. 193/3 Like some nitwit from a slapstick comedy, Turvey may be outwitted, but he is never really worsted. **1975** J. DRUMMOND *Slowly the Poison* II. 168 For God's sake, Beryl, don't be such a nitwit.

'nitwitted, *a.* [f. prec. + -ED[2].] Lacking in intelligence. Hence **nit'wittedness,** stupidity.
1931 *Observer* 6 Dec. 11 Many of the American films are just as shoddy, just as nitwitted. **1942** A. CHRISTIE *Body in Library* ix. 85 That half-baked nitwitted little slypuss. **1952** *Canad. Forum* XXXII. 13 These gems of phony surprise, of noxious nitwittedness.

nitwittery (nɪt'wɪtərɪ). [f. NITWIT + -ERY.] Imbecility, stupidity, lack of intelligence; foolish behaviour.
1936 *Punch* 29 Apr. 504/1 Eight of the stories are adventures which befell members of that singular focus of nitwittery, the Drones Club. **1949** C. FRY *Lady's not for Burning* 96 Last, vulgarity, cruelty, trickery, sham And all possible nitwittery. **1965** *New Statesman* 6 Aug. 194/1 It does not advance dramatic art to..tolerate nitwittery for the sake of a Cause.

Niuean (nɪ'uːən, 'njuːɪən), *sb.* and *a.* [f. *Niue,* native name (= 'world') of an island in the S. Pacific + -AN.] **A.** *sb.* **a.** A native or inhabitant of Niue. **b.** The language of the Niuean people. **B.** *adj.* Of or pertaining to Niue, the Niueans, or their language.
[**1893** *Jrnl. Polynesian Soc.* II. 11 The words were obtained from the New Testament translated into Niue by the Rev. Frank Lawes. *Ibid.* 13 The missionaries..'induced' two of the Niue youths to accompany them.] **1901** *Jrnl. R. Anthrop. Inst.* XXXI. 138 The Tongan mode of warfare was frontal attack by desperate charges; the Niuéan, a series of feints intended to frighten the enemy, and entice him into ambush. **1902** B. THOMSON *Savage Island* p. v, I went to the Niuéans in the name of the Queen and Empress whom the world is still lamenting. **1924** R. W. WILLIAMSON *Social & Pol. Syst. Cent. Polynesia* II. xiv. 53, I have..referred to Tregear's dictionary and to a Niuean vocabulary provided by Williams. **1954** K. B. CUMBERLAND *Southwest Pacific* vi. 270 It was native missionaries, Samoans mainly, who converted the Niueans. **1962** H. LUKE *Islands S. Pacific* xii. 222 In the latter half of the [19th] century..Niuean men would voluntarily leave the island..to work phosphate for good wages on Malden Island. **1968** *Encycl. Brit.* XVIII. 205/2 The best known of the dialects [of the Polynesian language] include Hawaiian,..Tongan, Tahitian, Niuean, ..and Tuamotuan. **1973** *Guardian* 21 May 13/4 The Cook Islanders and Niueans are New Zealand citizens, have free right of entry... The Fijians and Tongans need individual permits.

† 'niuell, *sb. Obs. rare*$^{-0}$. Also **niw-, neu-, new-.** [var. of NEWEL: cf. F. *noyau* in the same sense.] (See quots.) Hence **† 'niuell** *v.*
1611 FLORIO, *Anima di créta,* a long bar of iron luted with clay set vpright in the mold wherein ordinance is cast, called by our gunners the Niuell or Niwell. *Tiniuella,*..a neuell, a niuell among Gunners. *Tiniuellare,*..to boare or niuell thorow. *Tiniuellato,* a pi[e]ce niuelled or newelled. [Hence in Torriano, 1659, as *nivel,* etc.]

nival ('naɪvəl), *a. rare.* [ad. L. *nivālis,* f. *niv-, nix* snow: see -AL[1].] **a.** (See quot. 1656.) **b.** Growing among snow.
1656 BLOUNT *Glossogr., Nival,* pertaining to Snow, white or cold like Snow, snowy. **1894** *Science* IV. 475 Monte Rosa contains the richest nival flora.

nivation (naɪ'veɪʃən). *Geol.* [f. L. *niv-, nix* snow + -ATION.] Erosion of the ground beneath and at the sides of a snowbank, mainly as a result of alternate freezing and thawing.
1900 F. E. MATTHES in *21st Ann. Rep. U.S. Geol. Survey* II. 183 These névé effects..I shall, for the sake of brevity, speak of as effects of nivation. **1918** *Proc. Nat. Acad. Sci.* IV. 288 (*heading*) The importance of nivation as an erosive factor, and of soil flow as a transporting agency, in northern Greenland. **1957** G. E. HUTCHINSON *Treat. Limnol.* I. i. 59 A few cases may be found where nivation, or the freezing and thawing of water round patches of snow, has produced small closed depressions in jointed or fractured rocks. **1968** R. W. FAIRBRIDGE *Encycl. Geomorphol.* 123/2 When a deep snowdrift fails to melt away during summer, periodic freezing and thawing of the constantly moistened ground around and beneath it leads to the breakup of the rock particles which are then removed by meltwaters. This process is known as nivation.

nive, obs. form of NEW *adv.,* NIEVE.

† 'nivel, *v. Obs. rare.* In 3 **niuel,** 4 **nyuel, neuel.** [Of obscure origin: cf. SNIVEL *v.*] *intr.* To look downcast; to snivel.
a **1225** *Ancr. R.* 212 Hu heo schulen ham sulf grennen & niuelen, & makien sur semblaunt uor þe muchele angoise, iðe pine of helle. *Ibid.* 240 Þeonne spet heo & schekeð þet heaued, & foð on uorto niuelen, & makien sure & grimme chere. **1377** LANGL. *P. Pl.* B. v. 137 Now awaketh Wratthe with two whyte eyen, And nyuelynge [*v.r.* neuelynge] with the nose and his nekke hangynge.

nivel: see NIUELL *sb.*

ˌnivelli'zation. *rare.* [f. F. *nivel-er* to level + -IZATION.] A making level or equal.
1879 VIGFUSSON & POWELL *Icelandic Reader* 469 There is a nivellization of all vowels as to their quantities. **1947** R. WELLEK in H. Smith *Columbia Dict. Mod. Europ. Lit.* 186/1 There was after the war a most impressive expansion—with the concomitant dangers in a break with tradition, in commercialization and nivellization.

nivenite ('nɪvənaɪt). *Min.* [f. the name of W. *Niven* (see quot.) + -ITE.] A variety of uraninite, found in Texas.
1889 HIDDEN & MACKINTOSH in *Amer. Jrnl. Sci.* XXXVIII. 481 Nivenite, a hydrate thorium-yttrium-lead uranate. *Ibid.* 482 We have named this mineral nivenite, in recognition of the energy which Mr. Niven has displayed in this locality.

niveous ('nɪvɪəs), *a.* Also 7 **niuious, nivious.** [ad. L. *niveus,* f. *niv-, nix* snow.] Snowy, resembling snow.
1623 COCKERAM II, White as snow, *niuious.* **1646** SIR T. BROWNE *Pseud. Ep.* 338 Cinaber becomes red..which other-wise presents a pure and niveous white. **1800** HURDIS *Fav. Village* 113 Cottage and steeple in the niveous stole of Winter trimly dressed. **1826** KIRBY & SP. *Entomol.* xlvi. IV. 278 Niveous, the pure unblended white of snow.

Nivernois (nivɛrnwa). [f. the title of Louis Jules Mancini Mazarini, Duc de Nivernais or *Nivernois* (1716–98), f. Nivernais, *Nivernois,* a former province of central France.] A tricorn hat with a wide brim, fashionable in the late eighteenth century. Also *attrib.*
1765 in Cunnington & Beard *Dict. Eng. Costume* (1960) 147/1 He wears this large umbrella-like hat. This is the Nivernois. **1766** C. ANSTEY *New Bath Guide* x. 68 What with my *Nivernois'* Hat can compare? **1770** E. P. *Art of Dressing Hair* 8 For they to shining Balls the Camp prefer'd, Nor e'er of Powder and Pomatum heard, Of silken Suits, or Nivernois genteel. **1960** CUNNINGTON & BEARD *Dict. Eng. Costume* 147/1 *Nivernois hat,* a tricorne hat with broad spreading brim rolled over a flat crown; known as the 'Nivernois cock'. **1969** R. T. WILCOX *Dict. Costume* (1970) 248/1 *Nivernois,* a diminutive tricorne worn by the English Macaronies with the cadogan wig in in the 1770's.

‖ Nivose (nɪ'vəʊz). [F. *Nivôse,* ad. L. *nivōsus* snowy: see NIVOSITY.] The fourth month of the French revolutionary calendar, extending (in 1793–94) from 21 Dec. to 19 Jan.
1802 C. WILMOT *Let.* 3 Jan. in *Irish Peer* (1920) 21 Sunday —3rd Jany. 1802. 13 Nivose, An 10. **1838** H. NICOLAS *Chronol. Hist.* (ed. 2) 184 The French Republicans..used the number of the day of each month of their Calendar. For example: 1,2,..30 Nivose. **1884** *Encycl. Brit.* XVII. 266/2 He arrested and transported one hundred and thirty persons, whom he knew to be innocent of the plot... This is Nivose, an act as enormous as Fructidor, and with a perfidy of its own. **1957** *Ibid.* IX. 804/1 The winter months

were *Nivôse*, the snowy, *Pluviôse*, the rainy, and *Ventôse*, the windy month. **1972** R. Cobb *Reactions to French Revol.* iv. 134 On 7 Nivôse year VI (27 Dec. 1798), the *Ministre*.. reported to his colleague.

ni'vosity. [ad. L. type **nivōsitas* (f. *nivōsus* snowy), suggested by F. *nivôse*, the fourth month in the Republican calendar.] Snowiness.
1877 Morley *Crit. Misc.* Ser. II. 110 That faculty.. which had brought the forces of nature,—its pluviosity, nivosity, germinality, and vendemiarity,—under the yoke for the service of men.

niwe, obs. form of NEW *a.*

nix, *sb.*[1] *slang.* Also 8 nicks. [In sense 1 a. colloquial Du. and G. *nix*, for (*nichs*) *nichts*.]
1. a. Nothing; nobody. Also, = NO *adv.*[3]; not possibly.
1789 G. Parker *Life's Painter* (c 1800) 130 How they have brought a German word into cant I know not, but nicks means *nothing* in the cant language. **1812** J. H. Vaux *Flash Dict.*, *Nix*, or *Nix my doll*, nothing. **1824** Egan *Boxiana* IV. 444 (F.), Men who can be backed for large stakes do seldom fight for nix (comically called 'love'). **1858** Mayhew *Paved with Gold* III. i, Do you see all this land?.. the grandfather of this here Lord Southwark got it for 'nix'. **1890** Clark Russell *Ocean Trag.* ii, She has been exhorting me to choose a companion.., but it would have to be you or nix. **1909** *Dialect Notes* III. 352 *Nit*, *nix(y*, adv. Variants of *no*. Slang. **1926** J. Black *You can't Win* vi. 67 'I'll go to the farmhouse.. and buy something.' 'Nix, nix,' said one; 'buy nothin'.' **1929** A. Conan Doyle *Maracot Deep* 14 If I pull down fifty bucks a week it's not for nix. **1932** D. L. Sayers *Have his Carcase* xxiii. 309 As for getting an experienced actor and giving him a show in the part—nix! **1951** Green & Laurie *Show Biz* 570/1 *Nix*, no, veto, thumbs-down. **1959** 'J. R. Macdonald' *Galton Case* (1960) xvi. 132 'He.. wanted his old job back. Nix.' A gesture of his spread hand swept Lemberg into the dust-bin.
b. *U.S.* In pl. *nixes*, postal matter which cannot be forwarded from its not being properly addressed.
1885 in *Cent. Dict.*
c. Phr. *nix on*, enough of, have done with, no more of. *colloq.*
1902 'H. McHugh' *It's up to You* iii. 55 We decided before we stepped on the Pullman that it would be nix on the sweetheart talk. **1923** R. D. Paine *Comrades of Rolling Ocean* iv. 62 Camp Stuart at ten o'clock. Nix on that kid stuff. **1941** Baker *Dict. Austral. Slang* 49 *Nix on it!*: Stop it! Lay off!
d. = NO *a.*; none, negligible. (Also directly from G. *nix* (or *nichts*), in bilingual conversation.)
1906 E. Dyson *Fact'ry 'Ands* vii. 84 No man can reasonably expect t' live ther life iv er hindependent gent on er nix income. **1928** H. Crane *Let.* 31 Jan. (1965) 315 One can generally 'place' people to some extent; but out here it's mostly nix. **1945** G. Morgan *Only Ghosts can Live* xii. 144 'Nix Fish-Tins.' *Gefangener*—German for '*Nicht verstehen*': I don't get you. **1971** *Daily Tel.* (Colour Suppl.) 12 Nov. 21/2 Oh, I just said battery kaput, nix lights, nix motor... And we fix. But all European trucks stop for each other here.
2. ***nix my dolly***, a phrase (explained as meaning 'never mind') used by Ainsworth and echoed by other writers.
1834 Ainsworth *Rookwood* III. v, Nix my dolly, pals, fake away. **1840** Hood *Kilmansegg, Childhood* vi, The very puppet she had to pet, A bait for the 'Nix my Dolly' set, Was a Dolly of gold—and solid! **1844** Thackeray *Little Trav.* vi. [copying Ainsworth].
3. A word used as a signal that some one in authority is approaching. Also, as a children's 'truce-word'. Also ***keeping nix***, keeping watch.
1860 in Hotten *Dict. Slang* (ed. 2). **1869** *Routledge's Ev. Boy's Ann.* 229 'Keeping nix' was, in other words, keeping a look out that no person might catch us. **1885** *Indoor Paupers* 45 So the thing goes on until some one on the watch cries, 'Nix lads, buttons!'—the warning that the taskmaster is at hand. **1887** H. S. Brown *Autobiog.* x. 51 The word 'nix' saw every man and boy at his place. **1959** I. & P. Opie *Lore & Lang. Schoolch.* viii. 152 *Nicks* or *nix*. Prevailing term [as a truce-word] in Warwick.

nix, *sb.*[2] [a. G. *nix* masc., earlier *nicks*, *nichs*, MHG. *nickes*, *niches*, OHG. *nichus*: see NICKER *sb.*[1]] A water-elf. (Cf. NIXIE[1].)
1833 Keightley *Fairy Mythol.* II. 71 The female Nixes frequently go to the Market to buy meat. **1854** *Old Story-Teller* Pref. 3 The ideal regions inhabited by dwarfs, and nixes, and enchanted steeds. **1865** Kingsley *Herew.* Prel., He begins to people the weird places of the earth with weird beings and sees nixes in the dark linns as he fishes by night. **1883** 'Ouida' *Wanda* II. 149 There are nixes in the forests.

nix, *v.* [f. NIX *sb.*[1]] **1.** *trans.* To cancel, forbid, refuse. Freq. as imp., beware, cease (doing something).
1903 H. Hutchins *Autobiogr. Thief* viii. 180, I started in to talk about old times in the stir and.. he answered me by saying 'Nix', which meant 'Drop it'. **1914** [see EYEFUL *sb.* c]. **1934** M. H. Weseen *Dict. Amer. Slang* xxi. 371 *Nix*, to refuse an offer; a refusal; to deny a request; a denial. *Nixy* is a variant. **1945** in Wentworth & Flexner *Dict. Amer. Slang* (1960) 356/1 The blue-penciler nixed the story. **1961** *New Left Rev.* July/Aug. 53/1 Every time somebody nixes.. paid work to fulfil an unpaid commitment.. my faith.. is.. restored. **1969** R. V. Beste *Next Time I'll Pay* ii. 22 He could have been more explicit... If he had been his holiday would have been nixed, that was for sure. **1973** *Tucson* (Arizona) *Daily Citizen* 22 Aug. 11/1 (*heading*) Nude bathing nixed. **1974** *Maclean's Mag.* Dec. 19/1 It was the inner voice that nixed the deal—the savings contract that the salesman was pushing ensured that I wouldn't break even until after the first eight years.

2. ***nix out*** (*on*): *U.S. slang* in various senses (see quots.).
1940 *Music Makers* May 37/3 *Nix out*, to eliminate, get rid of. Ex. 'I nixed that chick out last week'. 'I nixed my garments' (undressed). **1945** L. Shelly *Jive Talk Dict.* 29/2 *Nix out*, to erase. **1946** Mezzrow & Wolfe *Really Blues* (1957) 84 The owner nixed big crowds out. **1969** Nix out on [see FADE *sb.*[1]]. **1970** C. Major *Dict. Afro-Amer. Slang* 85 *Nix out*, to throw away.

nixie[1] ('nɪksɪ). [ad. G. *nixe* fem.: see NIX *sb.*[2]] A female water-elf; a water-nymph.
1816 Scott *Antiq.* xxv, All the German superstitions of nixies, oak-kings, wer-wolves. **1821** —— *Pirate* xxviii, She who sits by haunted well, Is subject to the Nixie's spell. **1836** *Blackw. Mag.* XL. 146 Those Elves and Erles,.. those alps and goblins, those nixies and wood-nymphs. **1892** *Daily News* 16 Nov. 5/4 To the left and right, in the form of handles, are two nixies blowing shells. **1918** D. H. Lawrence *New Poems* 62 It seems to me The woman you are should be nixie, there is a pool Where we ought to be. **1952** R. Campbell tr. *Baudelaire's Poems* 214 If your gaze the gaze transfixes Of satyresses or of nixies.

nixie[2] ('nɪksɪ). Also nixy. [f. NIX[1] + -Y[6], -IE.]
1. = NIX[1] 1 b. Also *attrib.* *U.S.*
1890 *Cent. Dict.*, Nixy[2]. **1901** *Congress. Rec.* 17 Jan. 1145/6 These poor 'nixie' clerks in the postoffices of this country. **1904** *Springfield* (Mass.) *Republ.* 29 Oct. 4 He was made what is known in the office as a 'nixy' clerk.. one who looks up misdirected letters. **1905** *N.Y. Even. Post* 8 Feb. 5 What the railway postal clerks most dread is the class of mail they know as 'nixes'. **1929** *Lit. Digest* 5 Oct. 67/1 The similarity in appearance of the letters N.Y. and N.J... is responsible for many letters reaching the 'Nixie' division. **1949** *Amer. Speech* XXVI. 136/1 *Nixie*, a piece of mail so damaged or illegible that it can go no farther in the mails. The *Nixie* section rewraps and tries to discern the scribbled addresses on mail. **1956** *Daily Progress* (Charlottesville, Va.) 19 Sept. 28/1 '*Nixie*' is mail that can't be delivered because the address is incorrect, illegible, or insufficient.
b. = NIX *sb.*[1] 1 a.
1906 E. Dyson *Fact'ry 'Ands* xviii. 249 Er storm centre.. redooced.. land values t' nex' t' nixie.
2. *adv.* No, certainly not. Freq. as expletive.
1886 H. Baumann *Londinismen* 120/1 *Nixey*.. nein, nicht. **1903** *Pedagogical Seminary* X. 373 Nixy... Don't you believe it. Not much. **1914** G. Atherton *Perch of Devil* I. 108 They're all right to marry,.. but to sacrifice your life for, nixie.

†**'nixious**, *a.* *Obs.*[-0] [f. L. *nix* snow.] Snowy.
1623 Cockeram I, *Nixious*, white as snow.

Nixonian (nɪk'səʊnɪən), *a.* [f. the name of Richard M. *Nixon* (b. 1913), Vice-President of the United States 1953–61 and President 1969–74 + -IAN.] Of, pertaining to, or resembling Richard M. Nixon.
1959 *Listener* 10 Sept. 376/1 Thomas Edmund Dewey was a Nixonian sort of man. **1970** *Harper's Mag.* July 30/3 It was not, after all, critics of the Administration who defined Nixonian language for us—Don't watch what we say, watch what we do—it was the Administration spokesmen themselves. **1971** *Between Lines* (Newtown, Pa.) 1 Nov. 1/1 Voluntarism, the theme of the new Nixonian-economics, puts capitalism to its most severe test. **1972** *N.Y. Times Book Rev.* 29 Oct. 46/3 Herblock analyzes Nixonian techniques such as the Happening or Non-Event in which the Vice President is photographed standing at a podium addressing the President and full Cabinet and telling them what a great job they are doing. **1973** *Nation Rev.* (Melbourne) 31 Aug. 1445/1 Change indeed in nixonian Washington!
Hence **Nixonite** ('nɪksənaɪt), a supporter of Nixon or his policies; **Nixonization** (ˌnɪksənaɪ'zeɪʃən), development of a Nixonian character; subjection to the influence of or domination by supporters of Nixon; **Nixonomics** (nɪksə'nɒmɪks) *sb. pl.* [f. *econ*)*omics* (ECONOMIC *sb.* 2 c)], the economic policies of Nixon.
1958 *Time* 17 Nov. 22 A staunch Nixonite. **1960** *Guardian* 10 Nov. 10/7 There were some Nixonites present. **1969** *Demo Memo* (Washington, D.C.) 29 Oct. 1 Walter Heller.. challenges the soundness of 'Nixonomics'. **1971** *New Statesman* 16 Apr. 516/3 Alternatives to the Hobson's choice of possibly counterproductive street protest or mute acquiescence in the Nixonisation of the war. **1971** *N.Y. Times* 19 Sept. 2E/2 The President dredged up a term he had always treated with derision as a symbol of economic blundering by his Democratic predecessors and converted it to the dynamics of the new Nixonomics. **1972** *Newsweek* 16 Oct 89/1 Phase two of the new Nixonomics has changed nearly all the rules—and as one result, quite a few companies these days.. are going out of their way.. to cut profits down. **1973** *Black World* Mar. 68 There is certain to be greater Nixonization of government at every level. **1975** *Maclean's Mag.* Jan. 6/1 Richard Nixon was able to take dramatic economic action over a single weekend in August, 1971 (remember the new Nixonomics?) without a word of sass or backtalk from Congress.

nixt(e, obs. ff. NEXT.

nixto-cum, obs. Sc. spelling of *next to come.*

†**ni'xuriate**, *v.* *Obs.*[-0] [f. L. *nixurīre*.]
1623 Cockeram I, *Nixuriate*, to indeuour, to attempt.

niye, obs. form of NOY.

‖**Nizam** (nɪ'zɑːm). [Urdū and Turkish *nizām*, ad. Arab. *nidām*, order, disposition, arrangement, etc.; in sense 1 used as an abbreviation of the title *nizām-al-mulk* 'governor of the empire'.]
1. The hereditary title of the rulers of Hyderabad belonging to the dynasty founded by Asaf Jāh, Subahdar of the Deccan from 1713–48.
[**1601** R. Johnson *Kingd. & Commw.* (1603) 45 Nizzamuluc and Idalcam (for so the Portugals call the two princes of Decon). **1753** Hanway *Trav.* (1762) II. XIV. iii. 349 Nizam al muluch, governor of deccan,.. appropriated the revenues.] **1768** *Hist.* in *Ann. Reg.* 66/1 This bold adventurer worked upon the weakness of the Nizam of the Decan. **1796** Morse *Amer. Geog.* II. 539 The possessions of the Nizam or Soubah of the Deccan. **1817** Jas. Mill *Brit. India* II. IV. viii. 268 It is under the title of the Nizam, that the Subahdar of Deccan is commonly known. **1840** Macaulay *Ess., Clive* (1897) 509 Some glittering puppet dignified by the title of Nabob or Nizam. **1893** *Whitaker's Almanack* 454 Hyderabad is as large as.. Italy, and the Nizam enjoys a gross revenue of Rx. 3,340,000.
2. The Turkish regular army; the men, or one of the men, composing this. Also *attrib.*
1840 J. B. Fraser *Koordistan* II. xvii. 404 You see the slim figures of the Nizam flitting past you in their semi-European garb. **1845** Lady Stanhope *Mem.* I. vii. 258 She saw a man, in a *nizàm* dress. **1856** R. F. Burton *El-Medinah* xxxiii. (1879) 481 The Nizam, or Regulars, had not been paid for seven months. **1867** *Chamb. Encycl.* IX. 588/1 The total of the nizam is thus 156,480 men.
Hence **Ni'zamate**, the Nizam's territory.
1887 *Pall Mall G.* 24 Nov. 13/2 The Nizam, or at least the taxpayers of the Nizamate, were to pay the piper.

‖**Ni'zamut.** [Urdū *nizāmat*, f. prec.] The office or authority of the Nizam.
1764 *Ann. Reg.* I. 190 The treaty which I formerly concluded.. upon my accession to the nizamut.. I now confirm. **1783** Burke *Rep. Aff. India* Wks. XI. 259 He had dismissed the old established servants of the Nizamut. **1817** Jas. Mill *Brit. India* II. v. iii. 399 The incontestable right of the Nabob to all the powers of the Nizamut.

†**'nizy**, *sb.* and *a.* *Obs.* Forms: α. 7–8 nisey, 7 nisi, 8 nisy. β. 7–8 nizey (nize-), nizy. [Of doubtful origin: perh. f. NICE *a.* 1.]
A. *sb.* A fool or simpleton.
α. *c* **1684–6** *Roxb. Ball.* (1888) II. 558 There's none but meer Niseys that frets. **1693** *Oxford-Act* II. 10 Thus let him like a Nisi, But we intend more to surprize ye. **1706** E. Ward *Hud. Rediv.* II. IV. 9 So Politicians form Devices And raise new Whims, to please the Niseys.
β. *c* **1688** *Roxb. Ball.* (1892) VII. 497 We are on the Coast of France, Taking prizes from those Nizeys. *a* **1700** B. E. *Dict. Cant. Crew*, *Nizy*, a Fool, or Coxcomb. **1708** *Brit. Apollo* No. 66. 4/1 Be not such a Nizey.. to wed an Old Crony. **1710** *Galloper* 1 That their Looks may deceive the more credulous Nizies. *a* **1814** *Gonzanga* II. i. in *New Brit. Theatre* III. 111 You talk just like what you are—a nizy, a noodle!
B. *adj.* Foolish.
1709 *Brit. Apollo* No. 8. 3/2 Sometimes Saga as Solon, Oft Nizey as Ben. **1710** *Ibid.* No. 100. 3/2 Here lies a wretched, Nizey Wight.

nkonze, var. KONZE.

Nkrumahism (n'kruːməɪz(ə)m). Also **Nkrumaism**. [f. the name of 'Kwame *Nkrumah*' (Francis Nwia Kofi) (1909–72), Ghanaian political leader; see -ISM.] The principles and policies associated with Kwame Nkrumah; adherence to or support of these principles. So **N'kruma(h)ist** *a.* and *sb.*, (supporting, one who supports) the policies and principles of Nkrumah; of or pertaining to these policies and principles. Also **Nˌkrumahi'zation**, the making of changes in accordance with his policies and principles.
1960 *Sunday Times* 28 Aug. 5/1 Orgy of phrases... These phrases.. have cropped up constantly.. 'Nkrumahism' (off-stage among Ghanaians). **1962** *Listener* 23 Aug. 272/2 Bishop Roseveare had 'tried to subvert the Nkrumahist revolution'. **1964** *Economist* 1 Feb. 396/2 The forming of regional groups is not inimical to panAfrican unity (as Nkrumahism says it is). **1968** *Listener* 11 July 53/1 In 1964, 'local conditions'—that is to say, Kwame Nkrumah—demanded that the University appoint certain known 'Nkrumahists' to key positions. The sole specific intellectual content of 'Nkrumahism' was the implied infallibility of Kwame Nkrumah. *Ibid.*, At the University we had the choice of accepting 'Nkrumahisation' or 'sheltering behind political freedom.' **1973** *Ann. Reg. 1972* 247 There were those who saw the new military regime in Accra as returning to a form of 'Nkrumaism without Nkrumah'. *Ibid.*, General Nathan Aferi.. was reported as saying.. 'There are Busiaites and Nkrumaists and uncommitted.'

nname, obs. variant of YAM.

No., N°., an abbreviation of L. *numero*, abl. sing. of *numerus*, used in place of, and pronounced as, the word NUMBER. Also pl. ***Nos.*** 'numbers'. (Cf. F. *numéro*, It. and Sp. *numero*.)
In early use meaning 'in number'.
1661 Lovell *Hist. Anim. & Min.* 129 They goe two months, & then bring forth a blind off-spring like bitches, n°. eight or nine. **1693** tr. *Blancard's Phys. Dict.* (ed. 2) s.v. N, Take of Jujubes N° vi. that is, six in number. **1719** Quincy *Phys. Dict.* (1722), *N°.* In Prescription is often used to signify the Number of any Things, as Cariophyllorum N° vi. is six Cloves.
1753 *Chambers' Cycl., Suppl.* s.v. *Otis*, See Tab. of Birds, N° 28. **1797** *Encycl. Brit.* (ed. 3) XI. 721/2 When the magnifiers, N° 4, 5, or 6, are used. **1836–7** Dickens *Sk. Boz, Scenes* ii, Mrs. Macklin, of No. 4.. opened her little street

door. **1840** DICKENS *Let.* 4 Feb. (1969) II. 18, I am curious to see how the idea of the first No. of my projected work strikes you. **1873** TRISTRAM *Moab* vii. 131 They knew the sportsmen had only No. 7 in their barrels. **1888** *Pall Mall G.* 21 Sept. 2/2 'No. 9' is, of course, world-famous. **1905** *Strand Mag.* Apr. 376/1 George II.. made a present of No. 10 [Downing Street] to his Prime Minister, Sir Robert Walpole, and his successors. **1924** J. BUCHAN *Three Hostages* xvii. 242 It was eventually arranged that the district-visitor should call at No. 4 the following afternoon. **1937** N. MARSH *Vintage Murder* v. 47 He was advancing a No. 4 company in St. Helens. I was selling tickets for the worst show in England. **1972** *Oxford Times* 15 Sept. 18/1 Conversion of house into 2 No. self contained flats. **1974** M. GILBERT *Flash Point* ii. 14 It's No. 276 Coalporter Street.

b. *No.* 9 (Mil.): see quot 1917.

1911 *Pharmaceutical Formulas* (ed. 8) 922/2 (*heading*) Army Pill No. 9. **1917** A. G. EMPEY *Over Top* 301 'No. 9.' A pill the doctor gives you if you are suffering with corns or barber's itch or any disease at all.

no (nəʊ), *a.* Forms: α. 2–6 (9) **na**, (4 **nai**), 8–9 **naa, nae**, etc.; 6, 9 **nea**, 7 **neay**, 9 **neah, nee(a, ney(e, ne**, etc. β. 4–6 **noo**, 5, 7, **noe**, 3– **no**. [Reduced form of *nān, nōn* NONE *a.*, originally used only before consonants.]

No occurs in a considerable number of common phrases as *no bones, no end, by no means*, etc., which are treated under the various sbs. In some cases, as *no doubt, no wonder*, etc., there is often an ellipse of the verb. For *no other* see OTHER *a.* 5 b and 6 a; also OTHERWISE A.

I. 1. Not any.

a. Accompanied by other negatives (or redundant). Now only *dial.* or illiterate.

a **1200** *Moral Ode* 80 in *O.E. Hom.* I. 165 Nis na [*c* 1250 no] lauerd swich se is crist. *c* **1205** LAY. 25311 Na [*c* 1275 no] gauel he nule bringe. **1297** R. GLOUC. (Rolls) 304 þat deol þat made Innogen no tonge telle ne may. **1303** R. BRUNNE *Handl. Synne* 6802 For God no synne wyl þey nat lete. **1340** *Ayenb.* 83 No solas ne no confort me ne onder-vangþ bote of him. *c* **1385** CHAUCER *L.G.W.* 1749 *Lucretia*, By no crafte hire beaute was not feyned. *c* **1400** tr. *Secreta Secret., Gov. Lordsh.* 63 Ne gyf þou no credence to no wymmen. *c* **1475** *Rauf Coilȝear* 19 Thair micht na folk hald na fute on the heich fell. *a* **1548** HALL *Chron., Edw. IV*, 216 b, The communaltie coulde not be compelled by no commaundement to tarye at home. **1567** *Gude & Godlie B.* (S.T.S.) 144 Lat neuer na euill thing vs befall. **1596** SPENSER *F.Q.* v. xii. 11 Sith no redemption nigh she did nor heare, nor see. **1674** *Answ. States General* in *Phenix* (1708) I. 288 England had never no thoughts of securing this Right of the Flag by a formal Treaty. **1719** DE FOE *Crusoe* I. (Globe) 57, I had lost no time, nor abated no Diligence. **1871** MRS. H. WOOD *Dene Hollow* xxxi, "Tain't no good your stopping', he.. said. **1896** [see CON *v.*]. **1897** [see CLASS *sb.* 5 b]. **1968** *Listener* 20 June 796/3 He's not going to be put in no poorhouse.

b. Without other negative.

α. *a* **1300** *Cursor M.* 16 Wit sarazins wald þai na saght. *c* **1340** HAMPOLE *Pr. Consc.* 2462 Na syn þan unrekend sal be, þogh it war never swa prive. **1375** BARBOUR *Bruce* I. 371 Quhar it failȝeys, na wertu May be off price. *c* **1400** MAUNDEV. (Roxb.) Pref. 2 A flokk of schepe þat has na schephird. **1456** SIR G. HAYE *Law Arms* (S.T.S.) 167 Nychtbouris gude that he had na clame to. **1508** KENNEDY *Flyting w. Dunbar* 444 Thare is na lorde that will in seruice tak the. **1583** *Leg. Bp. St. Androis* 78 in *Satir. Poems Reform.*, He had nea toung for to denye it. **1596** DALRYMPLE tr. *Leslie's Hist. Scot.* I. 58 Another Ile,.. quhair nae kynd of cattail is fund. *Ibid.* 78 Maid abrogat, and of na effecte. **1684** [MERITON] *Yorksh. Dial.* 26 It'l git neay Cawd, it's bedded up to th' Een. **1721** RAMSAY *Prospect Plenty* 15 Nae nation in the warld. **1785** J. HUTTON *Bran New Wark* (E.D.S.) 184 Naa prawling wolf, naa cunning fox iver escap'd my eye. **1786** BURNS *Dream* vii, Let nae saving-fit Abridge your bonie Barges. **1804** GALLOWAY *Poems* 69 (E.D.D.), In argument ne papist e'er could ding him. **1827** J. WILSON *Noct. Ambr.* Wks. 1855 I. 353 There's nae kindness like kindness frae the haun o' a woman. **1833** *York Minster Screen* 60 T'other had ne'a business there.

β. **1362** LANGL. *P. Pl.* A. I. 9 Of þer heuene þen heer holde þei no tale. **1390** GOWER *Conf.* I. 7 The citees knewen no debat. *c* **1412** HOCCLEVE *De Reg. Princ.* 32 Deth, fro which no wight lyvyng Defendyn hym may. *c* **1449** PECOCK *Repr.* I. xviii. 102 Noo bischop or archideken or doctour. **1526** *Pilgr. Perf.* (W. de W. 1531) 1 b, Specyally to suche that vnderstande no latyn. **1542** UDALL in *Lett. Lit. Men* (Camden) 3 Noo sikenes, noo losse of worldly goodes, none ympresonyng, noo tormentes. **1597** SHAKS. *2 Hen. IV*, IV. i. 97 There is no neede of any such redresse. **1615** W. LAWSON *Country Housew. Gard.* (1626) 19 There is no tree like this for soundnesse. **1667** PEPYS *Diary* 9 Aug., I perceive Sir W. Coventry does really make no difference between any man. *a* **1687** PETTY *Pol. Arith.* (1690) Pref., That there is no Trade nor Employment for the People. **1712** W. ROGERS *Voy. R. World* 419 They added, that they had no Embarkations, but one Ship. **1790** BURKE *Fr. Rev.* 42 Our constitution has made no sort of provision towards rendering him.. responsible. **1815** JANE AUSTEN *Emma* xix, There is no comparison between them. **1839–52** BAILEY *Festus* 417 Thou hadst no need, no business to have loved me. **1891** *Law Times Rep.* LXIII. 691/1 There was no evidence that Nunney had authority to arrest.

c. In elliptic phrases.

For other phrases and proverbs, see the sbs.

1531 TINDALE *Expos. 1 John* Wks. (1573) 395/1 O Popishe forgiuenesse with whom it goeth after the common prouerbe, no peny no pardon. **1640** BAGSHAW in Rushw. (1721) III. II. 1343 Episcopacy is inseparable to the Crown of England; and therefore it is commonly now said, No Bishop no King, no Mitre no Scepter. *c* **1645** HOWELL *Lett.* II. xviii, I am of the Italians mind that said, *Nulla nuova, buona nuova*, no news, good news. **1701** *Lond. Gaz.* No. 3740/4 Deputations, commonly call'd 'No Purchase no Pay', for seizing Uncustomed and Prohibited Goods to certain Persons. **1751** J. BRIDGES (*title*) No foot, no horse. **1855** BAIN *Senses & Int.* I. ii. §25 It seems as if we might say, no currents, no mind.

†**d.** Any. *Obs. rare*$^{-1}$.

c **1500** *Melusine* 242 The Duches is brought to bed of the most fayrest sone that euer was seen in no land.

e. *no one*, nobody, no person. (See ONE 24.)

1601 SHAKS. *Twel. N.* II. iv. 58 My part of death no one so true did share it. *a* **1719** SMALRIDGE *Serm* (J.), No one who doeth good to those only.. can ever be fully satisfied of his own sincerity. **1829** SOUTHEY *Sir T. More* (1831) II. 421 Such transactions as no one,.. half a century ago, would have been ashamed of. **1861** PYCROFT *Agony Point* (1862) 35 No one has room to do much more than jostle together.

2. Qualifying a noun and adj. in close connexion, usually implying that an adj. of an opposite meaning would be more correct or appropriate.

For examples of *no such* (*thing*, etc.), see SUCH *a.*

c **1350** in Horstm. *Altengl. Leg.* (1878) 17/1 All þouh þei made no gret nois, He onswerd, as he hed herd heore vois. **1390** GOWER *Conf.* I. 46 Sche cast on me no goodly chiere. *c* **1449** PECOCK *Repr.* IV. viii. 468 Thei be not necessarie neither thei ben in no notable degree better. *c* **1500** *Trevelyan Papers* (Camden) 98 Whiche will amounte, yf hyt be well handelyd, to no lyttle summe. **1560** DAUS tr. *Sleidane's Comm.* 41 It is upon no lyght consyderation omitted. **1597** GERARDE *Herbal* I. ii. 3 This grasse is vnpleasant, and no wholesome food for cattell. **1641** BURGES *Serm.* 62 This is no Empiricall Dosis, but a *Probatum est.* **1671** MILTON *Samson* 650 This one prayer yet remains,.. No long petition. **1715** M. DAVIES *Athen. Brit.* I. 235 This sort of Meditation is still.. in no small esteem and practice. **1772** *Ann. Reg.* I. 91 It makes no inconsiderable addition to the revenue of the crown. **1826** DISRAELI *Viv. Grey* v. vii, With no pleased air. **1849** MACAULAY *Hist. Eng.* v. I. 528 On this man his party had long relied for services of no honourable kind. **1877** TENNYSON *Sir J. Franklin* 4 Thou.. Art passing on thy happier voyage now Toward no earthly pole.

b. Preceded by *the* or personal pronoun. Now only with *no small* or *little*.

1559 in Strype *Ann. Ref.* (1709) I. II. App. ix. 439 Falsifinge.. the scriptures, to the no small admiration of all the learned readers. **1581** MULCASTER *Positions* v. (1887) 26 Which the most munificent God, by his no niggardishe nature, prouided for them both. **1647** COWLEY *Mistr.*, *Request* vi, Dost thou deny onely to me The no-great privilege of Captivitie?

3. Qualifying a sb. in the predicate: Not (a).

1388 WYCLIF *Jer.* ii. 11 Certeynli thei ben no goddis. **1390** GOWER *Conf.* I. 340 Who that is of man no king, The remenant is as no thing. *c* **1450** HOLLAND *Howlat* 239 Thir ar na fowlis of reif. *a* **1500** in C. Trice-Martin *Chanc. Proc. 15th c.* (1904) 5 Saiying that it was noo season for a man of his ordre to walke so late. **1532** MORE *Confut. Tindale* Wks. 450/1, I take Moyses for no leder of yᵉ children of Israel. **1596** HARINGTON *Metam. Ajax* Pref. (1814) 10 A stream that seems to be no stream, by corn fields that seem no fields, down a street no street. **1634** SIR T. HERBERT *Trav.* 157 Great Personages, who otherwise are no Nymrods vpon earth. **1650** *Bounds Publ. Obed.* (ed. 2) 47 The remaining Members make no House. **1721** WODROW *Hist. Suff. Ch. Scot.* (1838) I. I. ii. 112 Mr. Dickson replied, he well knew his grace was no coward. **1749** SMOLLETT *Gil Blas* I. i, He chose a wife.. who, though she was no chicken, brought me into the world ten months after her marriage. **1798** FERRIAR *Illustr. Sterne*, etc. iii. 55 Sterne was no friend to gravity. **1815** ELPHINSTONE *Acc. Caubul* (1842) I. 329 Wanton cruelty and insolence are no part of the Afghaun character. **1839–52** BAILEY *Festus* 48 Inspiration cometh from above, And is no labour. **1895** *Bookman* Oct. 22/2 He was no ruler of consummate ability.

b. Denoting approximation to nullity, as in *it is no distance.*

1832 J. P. KENNEDY *Swallow Barn* II. xvii. 220 Which.. would produce a cure 'in almost no time'. **1868** G. G. CHANNING *Early Recoll. Newport R.I.* 143 The money was ..arranged as to facilitate the payments in 'no time', understood in my day, to mean the shortest period. **1891** L. FALCONER *Mlle. Ixe* vi. 165 [The mare] will get over to Carchester in no time.

4. Qualifying a verbal sb. or gerund in the predicate, denoting the impossibility of the action specified.

1560 BIBLE (Genev.) *Nahum* iii. 19 There is no healing of thy wounde. **1591** SHAKS. *Two Gent.* II. i. 161 *Val.* No, beleeue me. *Speed.* No beleeuing you indeed sir. **1641** SHUTE *Sarah & Hagar* (1649) 108 So the people were so impetuously set upon their lusts, that there was no speaking to them. **1650** TRAPP *Comm. Deut.* iv. 25 Thou thinkest there is no removing thee. **1719** DE FOE *Crusoe* II. (Globe) 345 There was no keeping Friday in the boat. **1753** *Gray's Inn Jrnl.* No. 54 There is no going any where without meeting Pretenders in this Way. **1820** W. IRVING *Sketch Bk., Little Britain*, Do what they might, there was no keeping down the butcher. **1850** THACKERAY *Pendennis* xv, There's no accounting for tastes, sir. **1895** SHAND *Life Sir E. B. Hamley* I. ii. 21 There was no mistaking the meaning of the invitation, and there was no declining it.

II. In combination with sbs. or adjs.

5. a. Denoting that the thing (or person) in question cannot properly be called by that name, owing to the absence of the specific qualities implied by it, as ***no-faith, no-form, no-jest***, etc. (Very common after 1600.)

1565 T. STAPLETON *Fortr. Faith* 103* Ye see a clere difference.. betwene the doctrine.. of our firste auncient faith, and of this vpstert no faith. **1610** B. JONSON *Alch.* I. i, A.. thredden cloake That scarce would cover your no-buttocks. **1631** WEEVER *Anc. Funeral Mon.* 54 Inuenting.. a new certaine no-forme of Liturgie to themselues. *a* **1704** T. BROWN *Praise Poverty* Wks. 1730 I. 98 Laugh immoderately at his own no-jest. **1742** FIELDING *J. Andrews* IV. vii, They.. have been thoroughly frightened with certain no-persons called ghosts. **1786** MRS. A. M. BENNETT *Juvenile Indiscr.* V. 220 Effeminacy, and these other nothings, that constitute the no-character of a modern beau. **1814** JEFFERSON *Writ.* (1830) IV. 239, I frankly confide to yourself these opinions, or rather no opinions of mine. **1850** MERIVALE *Rom. Emp.* I. (1865) VI. 182 The common story of Messalina's impudent no-marriage. **1880** CARNEGIE *Pract. Trap.* 13 A dog such as I have described, whatever be his breed or his no-breed.

b. Denoting entire absence of the thing named.

In quot. 1948 the sense is 'without the use of the hands'.

1603 FLORIO *Montaigne* II. xii. (1632) 247 To make them feele the emptinesse, vacuitie, and no worth of man. **1649** BP. HALL *Cases Conscience* III. ix. (1654) 262 Under the pain of a no-remission. **1680** DODWELL *Two Lett.* To Rdr. 18 Subjects would discover.. the no-necessity of those reasons produced for their Separation. **1700** T. BROWN *Lett. fr. Dead* II. 204 Walking in the Middle Temple.. to get them a Stomach to their No-dinners. **1796** MORSE *Am. Univ. Geog.* I. 214 Dobchick or Notail. **1835** *Court Mag.* VI. 9/2 His cab is the perfection of 'quiet' no-pretence. *Ibid.* 49/2 We have named its absolute no-pretension as regards the self-supposed claims of its owner. **1896** BOSCAWEN *Bible & Monum.* 166 The land of No-Return, the region of darkness. **1898** *Westm. Gaz.* 5 Sept. 3/3 It is the low prices which produce the 'no-profit'. **1940** *Ann. Reg. 1939* 253 A vote of no-confidence was carried in the Lower Chamber. **1948** D. BALLANTYNE *Cunninghams* I. xviii. 92 Ralph showed off, riding no-hands and skidding in the loose metal. **1954** F. C. AVIS *Boxing Reference Dict.* 75 *No contest*, a declaration of the referee that the fight is null and void, usually because both contestants are making no serious efforts at boxing. *Ibid.*, *No-count*, a slipping to the floor of the ring but getting up again before the count begins. **1956** J. G. PORTER in A. Pryce-Jones *New Outl. Mod. Knowledge* 142 Adaptable as he [*sc.* man] is, can he exist for any length of time under conditions of no-gravity? **1957** L. F. R. WILLIAMS *State of Israel* 158 The four years of the legislature's statutory life (which is, of course, always liable to be shortened by a vote of no-confidence). **1960** *Times* 5 July 18/2 Edwards has had 10 contests and won nine of them, featuring rather unluckily in a no-contest (or double disqualification). **1973** *Houston* (Texas) *Chron. Mag. People, Places, Pleasures* 14 Oct. 8/4 Agnew.. pleaded no contest—in effect, guilty—to cheating on his income tax.

c. With derivative sbs. in various senses, as ***no-poperist***, one who is for 'no popery'; ***no-religionist***, one who is of no religion; etc.

1827 SYD. SMITH in Lady Holland *Mem.* (1855) II. 273 Jesuits abroad—Turks in Greece—No-Poperists in England! **1838** HAWTHORNE *Amer. Note-bks.* (1883) 169 A group of Universalists and no-religionists sat around him. **1882–3** SCHAFF *Encycl. Relig. Knowl.* III. 2167 The wave of no-sabbathism now sweeping from Europe to America. **1886** *Pall Mall G.* 28 July 3/1 The right of the Government to deal with No-Renters as with rebels.

d. Used in various colloq. phrases, as ***no strings***, no conditions or obligations; also *attrib.* (cf. STRING *sb.*); ***no stuff***, no joking; ***no sweat***, no bother, no trouble.

1909 'O. HENRY' *Options* (1916) 50 I've told you.. my oral sentiments, and there's no strings to 'em. **1946** MEZZROW & WOLFE *Really Blues* (1957) 376 *No stuff*, no kidding. **1952** A. HUXLEY *Let.* 12 Oct. (1969) 658 The thing should start in a small way, but with adequate equipment, no strings and no red tape. **1955** *Amer. Speech* XXX. 118 *No sweat, no strain* n. phr. used adjectivally, easy, no trouble, no difficulty. **1960** *Ibid.* XXXV. 122 *No sweat*, the GI's reaction to an unpleasant, but necessary task. **1963** *Daily Mail* 11 Nov. 8/8 Mumble-mouth especially knows how to blow flicks that cop bread, no-sweat style (knows how to succeed in movies without really trying). **1965** *Economist* 6 Mar. 980/3 In effect, the family doctors will get a no-strings pay rise averaging 9 per cent. **1970** *Times* 18 Aug. 15 Following the February £13m no-strings pay deal.. union officials have been conducting a wages and conditions survey of motor plants in Britain. **1970** C. MAJOR *Dict. Afro-Amer. Slang* 85 *No stuff*, expression that implies sincerity. **1972** 'H. HOWARD' *Nice Day for Funeral* iii. 45 He respects me as a person. No strings. **1972** *Publishers Weekly* 16 Oct. 17/1 Mrs Wallach complains that she cannot use plastic book jackets on books with maps on the inside covers. No sweat! We paste the book pocket.. on the next inside page, [etc.]. **1973** K. GILES *File on Death* vi. 153 No sweat, mate... We're not looking for trouble.

e. Denoting the complete emptying of the mind described in Buddhist, and esp. Zen, philosophy as ***no-mind, no-thought***, etc.

1934 D. T. SUZUKI *Essays in Zen Buddhism* III. ii. 84 'Mind is still subject to measurement. Who is the Buddha?' 'No-mind is he.' **1949** —— *Zen Doctrine of No-Mind* 29 When.. the seeing of self-nature has no reference to a specific state of consciousness, which can be logically or relatively defined as a something, the Zen Masters designate it in negative terms and call it 'no-thought' or 'no mind', *wu-nien* or *wu-hsin*. **1956** A. HUXLEY *Adonis & Alphabet* 34 No-thought not-thinks about the world in terms of no-things. *Ibid.*, In Zen the virgin consciousness was called *Wu-nien* or *Wu-hsin*—no-mind or no-thought. **1959** C. C. CHANG *Practice of Zen* ii. 59 The so-called No-mind (Chinese: *Wu hsin*) is not like day, wood, or stone, that is, utterly devoid of consciousness; nor does the term imply that the mind stands still without any reaction when it contacts objects or circumstances in the world. It.. is natural and spontaneous at all times... There is nothing impure within it; neither does it remain in a state of impurity. When one observes his body and mind, he sees them as magic shadows or as a dream... When he reaches this point, then he can be considered as having arrived at the true state of No-mind. **1959** D. T. SUZUKI *Zen & Jap. Culture* iv. 74 All things are accomplished when one attains a mind of 'no-mind-ness' according to the great Zen master. **1960** A. KOESTLER *Lotus & Robot* II. x. 240 It [*sc.* Zen] proclaims to be the philosophy of no-mind (Wu-hsin), of no-thought (Wu-mien).. and of 'going ahead without hesitation'. **1966** P. KAPLEAU *Three Pillars of Zen* II. v. 201 Mindlessness, on the other hand, or 'no-mindness' as it has been called, is a condition of such complete absorption that there is no vestige of self-awareness.

6. In attrib. phrases: **a.** Denoting objection or opposition to the thing in question, as ***no-popery man***, etc.

1827 *Edin. Rev.* XLV. 437 Ready to join his No-Popery corps. **1840** DICKENS *Barn. Rudge* xxxviii, I'm a No-Popery man, and ready to be sworn in. **1855** L. HUNT *Old Crt. Suburb* I. 127 Just in his..'no-nonsense' style; what his opponents call 'heavy'. **1884** *Pall Mall G.* 10 Dec. 6/1 Stopping the supplies by adopting a No Rent manifesto. **1892** *Daily News* 11 Mar. 5/7 The no-surrender attitude which the vast majority of the men have assumed.

b. Denoting absence of the thing named, as ***no-school poet***, one belonging to no school; etc. Also, denoting absence of necessity for. See also NO-FINES *a.* (*sb.*)

1832 SOUTHEY in *Q. Rev.* XLVII. 95 The other of these no-school poets favoured us with some samples of his poetry. **1858** HOLMES *Aut. Breakf. T.* xii, A real, genuine, no-mistake Osiris. **1881** *Times* 6 Jan. 4/6 Similar volumes.. on the Pycnogonids or no-body crabs. **1898** *Daily News* 13 Oct. 4/4 The Cape Ministry has resigned in consequence of the No-Confidence Vote on Tuesday night. **1902** R. MACHRAY *Night Side of London* ii. 23 The clubs, both high-class and no-class, are not all closed. **1930** E. POUND *XXX Cantos* vii. 27 Brown-yellow wood, and the no colour plaster. **1936** 'J. BEYNON' *Planet Plane* 58, I didn't think we were going to hit the no-gravity zone so soon. **1939** No class [see *billiard-hall* (BILLIARDS 2)]. **1955** *N.Y. Times* 13 Feb. III. 8/1 The favorite fabric is the no-iron type. **1958** *Economist* 1 Nov. 435/2 Nobody really doubts that 'no deposit' business will also be done. **1961** P. WHITE *Riders in Chariot* viii. 233 For Chrisake! Who am I to know what is up to every no-hope Jew that comes to the country? **1963** B. FOZARD *Instrumentation Nuclear Reactors* xi. 132 The reading of the voltmeter may be corrected to zero under no-signal conditions. **1969** *New Statesman* 18 July 80/1 'It's a gas, man, it's a rave,' says a no-bra girl. **1970** *Globe & Mail* (Toronto) 26 Sept. 1/5 (*caption*) Empty cans and no-deposit bottles lie around a tree. **1971** *Flying* (N.Y.) Apr. 18/2 The evidence seemed clear that the no-accident day had been moved from Thursday to Tuesday. **1972** *Guardian* 2 Nov. 10/3 A no-hope telephonist with an invalid mother, an illegitimate child and a bad communication problem. **1973** *Times* 19 Mar. 21/1 The United States Justice Department filed both civil and criminal suits. Ford entered a 'no contest' plea and last month was fined a total of $7m. **1973** GAGNON & SIMON *Sexual Conduct* (1974) x. 291 The no-bra look is serving both males' fantasies and a return to naturalness.

7. With adjectives: †**a.** With the force of *non-* or *un-*, as ***no-concluding***, inconclusive; ***no-certain***, uncertain. *Obs.*

1650 CROMWELL *Decl. Ld. Lieut. Irel.*, To try this no-concluding argument,..but yet well enough agreeing with your learning,—I give you this dilemma. **1658** EARL MONM. tr. *Paruta's Wars Cyprus* 15 Being allured by the no-certain promises of Princes. **1751** COVENTRY *Hist. Pompey* II. ix. (1785) 66/1 A no-thinking scribbler of magazines.

b. In parasynthetic combs., as ***no-coated, -coloured, -shaped, -tongued***.

1836–7 DICKENS *Sk. Boz, Scenes* xvii, He was a brown-whiskered, white-hatted, no-coated cabman. **1875** LANIER *Symphony* 121, I speak for each no-tongued tree. **1887** MORRIS in Mackail *Life* (1899) II. 179 A queer little no-shaped slip cut off from some workshop. **1895** *Outing* XXVI. 338/1 This discolored, no-colored gown. **1916** JOYCE *Portrait of Artist* (1969) i. 50 His nocoloured eyes looking through the glasses.

no (nəʊ), *adv.*[1] [Several forms of different origin are included here. Those placed under *α* (in sense 1) represent OE. *nó*, f. *ne* NE + *ó* always, var. of *á*: see A *adv.* and O *adv.* The second group (*β*) contains the southern or midland representatives of OE. *ná* (see NA *adv.*[1]); the later examples, however, are somewhat uncertain, and some of them may be misprints for *not*. In early northern and Scottish texts (*γ*) *no* is prob. a scribal alteration of original *na* or *ne*; but the later Scottish *no* (from *c* 1600) appears to be a reduced form of *nōth* for *nocht* NOUGHT (cf. *dōther* for *dochter*, and *mou'* for *mouth*).] = NOT.

1. In ordinary uses. Now only *Sc.*

α. *c* **825** *Vesp. Psalter* liii. 5 Ða strongan..no foresettun god biforan ȝesihðe heara. *a* **900** CYNEWULF *Christ* 84 No ȝebrosnad wearð mæȝðhad se micla. **971** *Blickl. Hom.* 13 Ne herede heo hine no mid wordum anum. *Ibid.* 17 Se þe.. bideþ þæs ecan leohtes, & no ne ȝeblinneþ. *c* **1205** LAY. 7524 He ne blakede no. *Ibid.* 31816 Oðer brohte enne; þe oðer no brohte nenne. *a* **1225** *Leg. Kath.* 1963 Oðer, ȝef ha nule no, ha schal beon tohwiðeret.

β. *c* **1200** *Moral Ode* 77 (Trin. Coll. MS.), Nis him no þing forholen..Ne bie hit no swo derne idon. *a* **1225** *Ancr. R.* 340 Þauh, no þe later, 'Betere is þo þene no'. *c* **1250** *Gen. & Ex.* 2236 Us sal ben hard If we no holden him non forward. **13..** *K. Alis.* 6925 No shaltow heorte and flesch hardye. *c* **1330** *Arth. & Merl.* 5829 (Kölbing), For þai no seiȝen no socour. *Ibid.* 7224 No telle y ȝou nouȝt worþ an hawe. *c* **1350** *Will. Palerne* 1554, Alle men vpon molde no schuld my lif saue. *a* **1450** *Fysshynge w. Angle* (1883) 4 He may not gretly lose but a lyne.., so then hys loste ys no grevous. **1588** PARKE tr. *Mendoza's Hist. China* 8 They doe no leaue one foote of grounde vnsowen. **1628** DOUGHTY *Church Schismes* 22 Papistrie thwarts and cuts the very life-strings of a sauing beleefe. Semi-pelagianisme no so. **1661** P. HENRY *Diaries & Lett.* (1882) 79 My Father will no cease unlesse my Vncle acknowledge..that hee hath done him wrong. **1682** DRYDEN & LEE *Dk. Guise* II. ii, No yet, my Lord of Guise, no yet.

γ. *a* **1300** *Cursor M.* 7628 Awai þan drou him son daui, Bot saul dred him no for-þi. *c* **1325** *Metr. Hom.* 141 No gif thou of the self na tale. **13..** *Cursor M.* 11781 (Gött.), Þis child, if he no war god of might, vr goddes alle had standen up right. **1487** *Barbour's Bruce* IX. 471 (Cambr. MS.), That him sair repent sall he..May fall, quehen he no mend it may. *a* **1510** DOUGLAS *K. Hart* II. 303 Be no wraith with me, my lady deir! **1535** STEWART *Cron. Scot.* I. 272 At this time I no will Onto the Romanis do injure or ill. *Ibid.* II. 334 For caus that thai no wald Resist the wrang. **1596** DALRYMPLE tr. *Leslie's Hist. Scot.* II. 133 *marg.*, Be the law ȝoung and tendir of ȝeiris ar no permitted to haue the administratione of the Rep[ublic]. **1611** SIR W. MURE *Misc. Poems* Wks. (S.T.S.) I. 49 Cease, serpent, seik no to subdue And kill ane hert. **1629** *Ibid.* 218 To doe who care no, much delight to prat. **1725** RAMSAY *Gentle Sheph.* I. ii. 70 He's get his will: why no? *Ibid.* 131 The laird seeks in his rent: 'Tis no to gie. **1786** BURNS *Mount. Daisy* ii, Alas! it's no thy neebor sweet, The bonie Lark. **1799** MITCHELL *Scotticisms* 60, I have walked forty miles, and yet am no wearied. **1816** SCOTT *Antiq.* xliv, I maunna say muckle about them that's no weel and no very able. **1861** RAMSAY *Remin.* Ser. II. 182 Is it the fashion for them no to go on? *a* **1894** R. L. STEVENSON *Weir of Hermiston* (1896) viii. 245 Oh, my dear, that'll no dae! **1931** A. J. CRONIN *Hatter's Castle* II. xiii. 435 What was't he said, 'a loyal wife and a devoted mother,' wasn't no? **1973** *People's Jrnl.* (Inverness & Northern Counties ed.) 28 July 4/5 Who says the Scots are a dour lot? No' us anyway! **1975** M. RUSSELL *Murder by Mile* iii. 22 What's holding ye up?.. Was the tyre no' checked?

2. Expressing the negative in an alternative choice, possibility, etc. (Usu. ***whether..or no.***)

In earlier ME. *non* is employed in the same way (see NONE *adv.*); this makes it probable that the use originated in sentences (such as quots. *c* 1440 and 1708) in which *no* was adjectival.

1413 *Pilgr. Sowle* (Caxton) v. i. (1859) 71 To this hows all other ben subget, and seruauntes, whether they wylle or noo. *c* **1440** *Generydes* 2588, I will, she sayde, do as ye councell me: Comforte or no. **1535** COVERDALE *Judith* ix. 20 Yf no, then go fyre out from Abimelech. **1560** DAUS tr. *Sleidane's Comm.* 234 b, He causeth hym to take xiii Duckates, whether he wolde or noe. **1592** GREENE *Upst. Courtier* Wks. (Grosart) XI. 247 He..asketh whether he please to be shauen or no. **1664** POWER *Exp. Philos* I. 2 By which he tryes and feels all objects, whether they be edible or no. **1708** SWIFT *Sacram. Test* Wks. 1751 IV. 164 Many of them care not Three-pence whether there be any Church, or no. **1784** *Unfortunate Sensibility* I. 182 Whether or no, this coat shall be my favourite coat. **1813** PARR *Let. to J. C. Moore* 15 Oct., I am uncertain whether or no to notice very shortly some of his previous..exploits. **1853** WHEWELL in Todhunter *Acc. Writ.* (1876) II. 393 Whether or no there be virtue or vice in other worlds. **1892** MRS. H. WARD *David Grieve* I. vii, It was a half-baked eloquence... But half-baked or no, David rose to it greedily.

†**3.** Used in a rejoinder or retort having the form of a negative question. *Obs.*

1525 LD. BERNERS *Froiss.* II. cxix. [cxv.] 342, I wyll nat entre there... No wyll? quod Geronette. *a* **1553** UDALL *Royster D.* I. iv, *R.* This is not she. *M.* No is? *Ibid.* II. iv, *C.* What was his name? *An.* We asked not. *C.* No did? **1581** RICH *Farew.* (1846) 144 The Doctour..aunswered, that he never writte letter unto her... No have? (q, Mistres Doritie) read you then heare your owne lines. **1595** SHAKS. *John* IV. ii, *Io.* I had a mighty cause To wish him dead, but thou hadst none to kill him. *H.* No had (my Lord?). **1621** BP. MOUNTAGU *Diatribæ* 35 You professe your ignorance thus: *Non omnino capimus quid sibi velit.* No doe? That is marvell that you do not *capere*.

no (nəʊ), *adv.*[2] Also *α.* 1–6 **na**, 8–9 *Sc.* **nae**, *north.* **nea**. [OE. *ná*, identical with NA *adv.*[1] Cf. prec. 1 *β*.] With comparatives: Not any, not at all (better, etc.); ***no better than*** (one) ***should*** (or ***ought to***) ***be***: see BETTER *a.* 5. See also NO LESS, NO MO(RE.

α. *a* **1000** *Boeth., Metr.* xxv. 29 ȝif he wyrsa ne bið, ne wene ic his na beteran. *c* **1175** *Lamb. Hom.* 129 Heo weren ipult ut of paradise and ne mehten þer naleng etstonden. *c* **1200** ORMIN 13163 þeȝȝ nolldenn nohht tatt boc Flæshliȝ na lenngre follȝhenn. *a* **1300** *Cursor M.* 12366 For leons durst þai cum na nerr. *c* **1375** *Sc. Leg. Saints* xviii (*Egipciane*) 226 Hayre scho had, quhyt & streke, rekand na forthire na hir neke. *c* **1470** *Gol. & Gaw.* 109 Na forthir he faris, bot foundis away. **1508** DUNBAR *Tua Mariit Wemen* 200 He is at Venus werkis na war na he semys. **1580** HAY in *Catholic Tract.* (S.T.S.) 46 In the receaving of it thair is na farder profite. **1786** BURNS *Answ. Tailor's Ep.* x, Gelding's nae better than 'tis ca't. **1790** MRS. WHEELER *Westmld. Dial.* (1821) 12, I'll bide nea langer, sea gang I will.

β. *a* **1250** *Owl & Night.* 42 Heo [the owl] ne myhte no leng bileue. **13..** *E.E. Allit. P.* C. 85 At alle peryles..I aproche hit no nerre. *c* **1400** *Land Troy Bk.* 4186 Thei sayde thei myght no betre do. *c* **1440** *Jacob's Weil* 212 þou owyst to sellyn it hym no derere þan þou mayst haue þerfore in markett. **1461** *Paston Lett.* II. 5 We send no er un to you be cause we had non certynges tyl now. **1585** T. WASHINGTON tr. *Nicholay's Voy.* I. vi. 4 b, A small fountaine beeing no higher set then the pavement. **1590** SPENSER *F.Q.* II. ix. 21 No lenger time So goodly workemanship should not endure. **1621** BURTON *Anat. Mel.* (1652) 151 'Tis horse-play this, and those jests..are no better then injuries. **1697** DAMPIER *Voy.* 467 Being out of hopes to find their Habitations, we searched no farther. **1711** STEELE *Spect.* No. 80 ¶1 They now no longer enjoyed the Ease of Mind..in which they were formerly happy. **1790** BURKE *Fr. Rev.* Sel. Wks. II. 35 If they had been able to contrive no better remedy against arbitrary power. **1836** THIRWALL *Greece* II. xi. 59 The two factions had no sooner accomplished the object..than they began to quarrel. **1891** L. FALCONER *Mlle. Ixe* vi. 165, I hope that unfortunate fellow is no worse.

†**b.** None (*the* fairer, etc.). *Obs. rare* (except in NOTHELESS and NOTHEMO).

a **1000** *Exod.* 399 Fyrst ferhðbana no þy fæȝra wæs. **1297** R. GLOUC. (Rolls) 236 Hit com no þe later is he hadde iseyd.

no (nəʊ), *adv.*[3] and *sb.* Also 3 **noa**. [Southern and midland form of NA *adv.*[2]]

A. *adv.* **1.** A word used to express a negative reply to a question, request, etc., or to introduce a correction of an erroneous opinion or assumption on the part of another person.

On the distinction between *no* and *nay*, see NAY *adv.*[1]

a **1225** *Ancr. R.* 222 Noa, he seiðe, [I] ne mei nout makien þeos to suneȝen þuruh ȝiuernesse. *a* **1250** *Owl & Night.* 997 Yet þu ayschest hwi ic ne vare Into oþer londe & singe þare. No; hwat scholde ich among heom do? *c* **1320** *Cast. Love* 1099 No, ac er he dilyuered be, þou most al so muche delyuere me. *c* **1350** *Will. Palerne* 2701 No, madame, seide hire douȝter, marie þat graunt. **1382** WYCLIF *Zech.* iv. 5 Where thou wost not what ben these thingus? And Y saide, No, my lord. **1418** 26 *Polit. Poems* 63 To kepe his comaundement þey say no. **1535** COVERDALE *John* i. 21 Art thou the Prophet? And he answered: No. **1591** SHAKS. *Two Gent.* I. iii. 91 My heart accords thereto; And yet a thousand times it answers no. **1646** CRASHAW *Steps to Temple* Poems (1858) 78 When heav'n bids come, who can say no? **1695** *Anc. Const. Eng.* 4 No sure, not at all. **1718** G. SEWELL *Procl. Cupid* 8 The Fools say, Yes; but wiser Chaucer, No. **1766** GOLDSM. *Vic. W.* xiii, No, cries the Dwarf,..no, I declare off. **1817** *Parl. Deb.* 413 On the question that the bill do pass, being finally put, the cry of 'No', from the Opposition side, was very loudly pronounced. **1853** *Harper's Mag.* Feb. 402/1 This is the gentleman who can't say no. **1853** T. C. HALIBURTON *Sam Slick's Wise Saws* I. v. 119 You first of all force yourself into my cabin, won't take no for an answer, and then complain of oncivility. **1861** G. H. LEWES *Let.* 20 Aug. in Geo. Eliot *Lett.* (1954) III. 446 She allows herself to be preyed upon dreadfully by the boys—she can't say No. **1879** MEREDITH *Egoist* vii, He half refuses. I do not take no from him. **1884** TENNYSON *Becket* IV. i, *Eleanor.* Wilt thou love me? *Geoffrey.* No; I only love mother. **1930** W. S. CHURCHILL *My Early Life* iv. 74 Come on now, all you young men... Don't take no for an answer, never submit to failure. **1961** *Family Jrnl.* Dec. 15/3 'But he would not take "No" for an answer,' she went on. **1961** *Listener* 21 Dec. 1065/2 He was made Minister of Labour in a season when the Government's economic policy meant saying 'no' to wage demands. **1974** M. BUTTERWORTH *Man in Sopwith Camel* viii. 89 I'm warning you that I'm not taking no for an answer. **1975** C. STORR *Chinese Egg* vii. 41 'I can manage. You keep sitting down.' 'I shan't say, No. It's a long drag up to St. Monica's.'

ellipt. **1857** TOULMIN SMITH *Parish* 62 The whole number present at the meeting must range themselves, aye and no, on the two opposite sides of the room. **1893** GLADSTONE in *Daily News* 14 Feb. 4/6 Then I propose the question in Parliamentary form, 'Aye or no'.

†**b.** After verbs of thinking or implying. *Obs.*

1601 BP. W. BARLOW *Defence* 7 We dullard Protestantes thinke no. **1621** BP. MONTAGU *Diatribæ* 388 For my part I thinke no, vnlesse he held possessions in the Land of Promise. **1634** CANNE *Necess. Separ.* (1849) 243 His words import positively no, but we are sure yes, and so will every wise man..affirm too.

c. Used interrogatively.

c **1374** CHAUCER *Troylus* II. 1162 'Trewely I nil no lettre wryte.' 'No? than wol I', quod he. *a* **1553** UDALL *Royster D.* II. iv, *T.* Yet can I not yonder craftie boy see nor meete. *C.* No? **1884** TENNYSON *Becket* V. iii, Does he breathe? No? No, Reginald, he is dead.

2. Repeated for the sake of emphasis or earnestness.

a **1500** *Assembly of Ladies* 63 The povre pensees were not diloged there; No, no! god wot, her place was every-where! *a* **1548** HALL *Chron., Hen. V* 61 b, No, no, I wyll not so accomplishe your cloked request. **1630** DEKKER *2nd Pt. Honest Wh.* I. i, No, no, no, sir, no; I cannot abide to haue money ingender. **1667** MILTON *P.L.* IX. 913 Loss of thee Would never from my heart; no no, I feel The Link of Nature draw me. **1721** DE FOE *Mem. Cavalier* (1840) 70 No, no, I took care of that. **1791** BOSWELL *Johnson* an. 1775, I answered, also smiling, 'No, no, Sir; that will not do'. **1846** DICKENS *Battle Life* i, 'There is not a truer heart than Alfred's in the world!' 'No—no,..perhaps not'.

3. Introducing a more emphatic or comprehensive statement, followed by *not*, or *nor*. ***no, you don't***: see DO *v.* 29 b.

1369 CHAUCER *Dethe Blaunche* 280, I trowe no man hadde the wit To conne wel my sweven rede; No, not Ioseph. **1509** BARCLAY *Shyp of Folys* (1874) II. 304 No wylde beste: no: nat the mighty bere. **1581** FULKE in *Confer.* II. (1584) L iiij b, We are not iustified by them, no nor by faith, other-wise then instrumentally. **1601** HOLLAND *Pliny* I. 383 There growes nothing in it good to make ointments, no nor nothing throughout all Europe. **1636** HEYLIN *Hist. Sabbath* 57, I say there was none kept, no nor none commanded. **1721** DE FOE *Mem. Cavalier* (1840) 137 The Scots never appeared, no, not so much as their scouts. **1774** BURKE *Sp. Amer. Tax.* Sel. Wks. I. 135 He never stirred from his ground; no, not an inch. **1862** TENNYSON *Idylls of King, Ded.* 9 Who spake no slander, no, nor listened to it. **1884** —— *Becket* Prol., Thou art but deacon, not yet bishop, No, nor archbishop.

b. Introducing a correction or contradiction.

1616 DRUMM. OF HAWTH. *Poems, Sonn.* xiii, You her words, words, no, but golden chains. **1702** DE FOE *Shortest Way w. Dissenters* (1703) 2 Now they cry out Peace, Union, Forbearance, and Charity... No, Gentlemen, the Time of Mercy is past. **1825** *Spirit Publ. Jrnls.* 342 That class of persons was composed of men—no, he could not call them men..—of individuals.

B. *sb.* †**1.** ***without no***, beyond denial, certainly. (Cf. NAY *adv.*[1] 3.) *Obs.*

c **1330** *Arth. & Merl.* 118 (Kölbing), Ac Inglond was yhoten þo Michel Breteyne, wiþ outen no. *Ibid.* 307 So þai deden, wiþ outen no.

2. An utterance of the word *no*; an instance of its use; a denial.

1588 SHAKS. *L.L.L.* V. ii. 413 Henceforth my woing minde shall be exprest In russet yeas, and honest kersie noes. **1622** MABBE tr. *Aleman's Guzman d' Alf.* II. 202 It is hee that can giue you an I, or a No, whether I shall goe or stay. **1685** *Gracian's Courtier's Orac.* 15 The gracefull manner so guilds and sets off a No, as to make it more esteemed than an ill seasoned Yea. **1736** FIELDING *Pasquin* I. Wks. 1882 X. 139 Let the audience know they can speak, if it were buy an ay or a no. **1792** A. YOUNG *Trav. France* 129 She determined ..to go to church,..and give a solemn no instead of a yea. **1825** *Spirit Publ. Jrnls.* 183 As two noes will make a yes. **1831** CARLYLE *Sart. Res.* II. vii. (*heading*), The Everlasting No. **1865** RUSKIN *Ethics Dust* (1883) 97 Resolutely whispered 'No's'.

b. A negative vote or decision.

1589 *Marprel. Epit.* P iij, Here then is the puritans I, for the permanencie of this government, and M. doctors no. **1654** H. L'ESTRANGE *Chas. I* (1655) 119 When the same parity of reasoning was urged, Bellarmines No was produced. **1886** GLADSTONE *Election Address*, With you..it rests to deliver the great Aye or No, on your choice.

3. †**a.** The negative side or party. *Obs. rare.*

1620 *Jrnl. Ho. Comm.* 13 Feb. I. 520 Question whether the I or Noe to go out. The Noe yielded, before the Division of the House.

b. *pl.* Those who vote on the negative side in a division.

1657 *Burton's Diary* (1828) I. 324 A member stood up and said, that the Noes in the former question had it. **1669** MARVELL *Wks.* (Grosart) II. 289 The ayes proved 138 and the noes 129. **1710** *Acc. Distemper Tom Whigg* II. 50 The No's fronting to the East, the Yea's to the West. **1796** HATSELL *Prec. Proc. Ho. Comm.* (ed. 3) II. 82 *note*, If this question for adjournment takes place before four o'clock in the afternoon, and there is a division upon it, the Yeas go forth; if after four o'clock, the Noes. **1849** MACAULAY *Hist. Eng.* vi. II. 26 The Ayes were one hundred and eighty-two and the Noes one hundred and eighty-three.

Hence **no** *v.*, *intr.* to say no (*to* one); *trans.* to answer (one) with no. *nonce-uses.*

1820 *Blackw. Mag.* VIII. 271 Yes-ing and No-ing to the great man's will. **1835** *Court Mag.* VI. 168/1 It is of the utmost importance..that you should No the world.

†**no,** *conj.*[1] *Obs.* [var. of NA *conj.*[1]] Nor.

c **1205** LAY. 17053 Ne recche ich noht..his seoluer no his goldes no his claðes no his hors. *a* **1300** *Sarmun* xi. in *E.E.P.* (1862) 2 Silk no sendale nis þer none no bise no no meniuer. **1303** R. BRUNNE *Handl. Synne* 6734 He..to þe pore dyd euyl yn dede No halp hym noȝt yn hys nede. **1338** —— *Chron.* (1810) 56 Spare it neuer a dele, Noiþer man no beste, no manere no no toun. *c* **1400** *Gamelyn* 22 Had þei no rest nother nyght no day. *c* **1470** HENRY *Wallace* v. 779 That wood..was nothir thik no lang. **1535** STEWART *Cron. Scot.* I. 61 Stakkis no stoir into na stait ma stand.

†**no,** *conj.*[2] *Obs. Sc.* [var. of NA *conj.*[2]] Than.

1535 STEWART *Cron. Scot.* II. 346 Mekle mair..He said to him no I will tell ȝow heir. *Ibid.* III. 197 Moir sicker wes in gudlie haist to fle, No to remane.

No, Nō: see NOH.

noa ('nəʊə). [a. Hawaiian (Maori, Tahitian) *noa* (something) free from taboo, ordinary.] An expression substituted for a taboo word or phrase. Freq. in *Comb.*

1925 O. JESPERSEN *Mankind, Nation & Individual* ix. 169 This harmless word that has been substituted, the Polynesians call *noa*. *Ibid.* 179 Both the above Danish names for devil are originally noa-names. *Ibid.* 184 Certain words and expressions are taboo for certain persons and must therefore be replaced by other words, by noa-words. **1951** S. ULLMANN *Words & their Use* III. iii. 75 If a word is struck by a taboo ban, it must be replaced by a harmless alternative, a so-called *noa* term. **1956** *Trans. Philol. Soc. 1955* 1 The special terms used by the [Faroese] fishermen to replace ordinary words when these became tabooed are designated as noa words or noa names, etc. Noa denotes the opposite of taboo, in the present context it stands for what is allowed in contrast to that which is forbidden. **1975** W. B. LOCKWOOD *Lang. Brit. Isles* 55 [Cornish] *pajerpaw* 'newt', lit. 'four foot' ..clearly a noa name.

no-account, *a.* orig. *U.S.* Of no account, importance, value, or use; insignificant, worthless. (See also NO-'COUNT *a.*)

1845 *Spirit of Times* 1 Feb. 583/2 I'll just tell you that the land I'm after is a d-d, little, no-account quarter section, that nobody would have but me. **1886** *Pall Mall Gaz.* 29 Sept. 4/1 We submit to be..treated as no-account people in all affairs of State. **1898** H. S. CANFIELD *Maid of Frontier* 109 It seems to me..that Charlie is gettin mighty no account. **1900** CONRAD *Lord Jim* v. 47 The other two no-account chaps spotted their captain, and began to move towards us. **1902** G. H. LORIMER *Lett. Merchant* vi. 69 A mailing-clerk so no-account as to be writing personal letters in office hours. **1936** 'J. TEY' *Shilling for Candles* v. 51 'You mean she thinks he's a wrong 'un?' 'No. Just no account.' *Ibid.* vii. 71 We both felt no-account and were afraid people'd find it out. **1952** C. DAY LEWIS tr. *Virgil's Aeneid* XI. 246 Are we, we no-account souls, to litter the plains? **1973** M. MACKINTOSH *King & Two Queens* xii. 180 I'm only a no-account Irisher, but I like to pay my debts.

B. *sb.* A 'no-account' person.

1896 'MARK TWAIN' in *Harper's Mag.* Sept 523 Who ever had anything agin that poor trifling no-account? **1936** J. DOS PASSOS *Big Money* 169 The child of a no-account like Fred. **1970** W. GARNER *Puppet-Masters* xxx. 222 Why is a no-account like Lindsay collected from a police court by a Special Branch cop? **1973** *Philadelphia Inquirer* (Today Suppl.) 14 Oct. 43/2 Others—those Gypsies most respected and strongest in the community—will not challenge him because they believe he is a 'no-account'.

†'**Noachal,** *a. Obs. rare*[−1]. [f. as next + -AL[1].] Very ancient.

1661 K. W. *Conf. Charac., Pragm. Pulpit-filler* (1860) 85 The booksellers old obsolete and Noahcal [*sic*] sermons.. are the parchments he especially takes care of.

Noachian (nəʊ'eɪkɪən), *a.* [f. *Noach* = *Noah* + -IAN.] Of or relating to the patriarch Noah or his time, esp. ***Noachian deluge***, the Flood.

1678 CUDWORTH *Intell. Syst.* 451 Within eight hundred years after the Noachian Flood. **1711** *Brit. Apollo* No. 153. 2/1 After this Noachian Deluge, the Air..was changed. **1830** LYELL *Princ. Geol.* I. iii. (1837) I. 45 The universality of the Noachian cataclysm. **1876** PAGE *Adv. Text-bk. Geol.* vi. 113 Ascribing every phenomenon in the earth's crust to the operation of the Noachian deluge. **1879** FARRAR *St. Paul* I. 427 Four restrictions, which belonged to what was called the Noachian dispensation.

b. *transf.* Very ancient or old-fashioned.

1874 HARDY *Far fr. Mad. Crowd* lii, A..grey overcoat of Noachian cut.

Noachic (nəʊ'eɪkɪk), *a.* [f. as prec. + -IC.] Of or pertaining to Noah; Noachian.

a **1773** A. BUTLER *Feasts & Fasts* (1852) II. 114 *note*, The Noachick precepts are reduced to abstinence from blood and unclean meats. **1835** *Brit. Mag.* VII. 413 The Noachic Creation. **1863** J. G. MURPHY *Comm. Gen.* xx. 3–7 The Gentile world, who were under the Noachic covenant. **1892** J. TAIT *Mind in Matter* (ed. 3) 236 There is little question now of the deluge, but the disposition that once denied doubts if it was the Noachic one.

So **No'achical** *a.*

1669 W. PENN in *Life* Sel. Wks. 1825 I. 11 The utmost they required from strangers..was an acknowledgment to the Noachical precepts.

Noachid ('nəʊəkɪd). Also **-ide**. [Cf. prec. and -ID[3].] A descendant of Noah. Also *attrib.*

1856 J. HADLEY *Ess.* i. (1873) 10 In the tenth chapter of the book of Genesis, in the list of Noachids. **1877** RAWLINSON *Orig. Nat.* II. i. 173 The author of the Noachide genealogy.

Noa(h)ic (nəʊ'eɪɪk), *a.* = NOACHIC *a.*

1845 A. DUNCAN *Disc.* Pref. 7 An exposition of the Noahic, Abrahamic,..and Davidic covenants. **1861** J. G. SHEPPARD *Fall Rome* iii, 114 Even before the Noaic deluge.

Noah's Ark. [See *Genesis* vi. 14, etc.]

1. a. The ark in which Noah and his family, with many animals, were saved from the Flood.

1611 FLORIO, *Noale*, any place, roome, or thing that containeth varietie of things, as Noes Arke did. **1688** HOLME *Armoury* III. xv. (Roxb.) 27/1 Some blazon it Noahs Arke sable. **1725** WATTS *Logic* (1736) 321 All Animals were in Noah's Ark. **1777** SHERIDAN *Trip Scarb.* III. iii, The seat of our family looks like Noah's ark.

b. A small imitation of this, intended as a plaything for children.

1846 DICKENS *Cricket on Hearth* ii, Noah's Arks, in which Birds and Beasts were an uncommonly tight fit. **1883** RUSKIN *Art Eng.* 9 A Noah's Ark from the nearest toy-shop.

2. Something suggestive of the Ark in respect of size, shape, etc., *esp.* a large, cumbrous, or old-fashioned trunk or vehicle.

1829 MARRYAT *F. Mildmay* iv, I and my Noah's ark [= sea-chest] lay slap in the way. **1835** —— *Olla Podr.* iii, There was the pouring out of the Noah's Ark. **1880** MISS BRADDON *Just as I am* xxxiv, The barouche will hold us all. It is a regular Noah's Ark. **1884** *Harper's Mag.* Feb. 339/2 You hire a sort of floating Noah's ark, and live in it.

3. A small bivalve mollusc (*Arca Noæ*).

1713 PETIVER *Aquat. Anim. Amb.* 2/1 *Chama Noachina*, Noahs Ark. **1753** CHAMBERS *Cycl.* Suppl. s.v., Another shell of this genus which..resembles the *Noah's ark*,..is the oblong bucardium or ox heart shell, commonly called the *bastard Noah's ark.* **1823** in CRABB *Technol. Dict.* **1854** A. CATLOW *Conchol.* (ed. 2) 279 The *Arca Noæ* or Noah's Ark and several other species like it in form and character. **1871** KINGSLEY *At Last* i, Delicate prickly Pinnæ; 'Noah's arks' in abundance.

attrib. **1753** CHAMBERS *Cycl. Suppl., Noah's ark shell*,.. the name of a kind of sea shell [etc.]. **1882** *Standard* 26 Sept. 2/2 A near ally of the mussel, the Mediterranean Noah's Ark shell.

4. A cloud-formation having some resemblance to the outline of a ship's hull.

1787 BEST *Angling* (ed. 2) 145 Small black fragments of clouds like smoke, flying underneath, which some call messengers, and other Noah's Ark. **1821** CLARE *Vill. Minstr.* II. 27 As oft from 'Noah's Ark' great floods descend. **1866** BLACKMORE *Cradock Nowell* xxxi, Daubed with lumps of vapour which mariners call 'Noah's arks'. **1889** *Anthony's Photogr. Bull.* II. 279 Halos, 'Noah's Arks' and unusual clearness of sky are all good signs of rain.

5. *U.S.* An orchid of the genus *Cypripedium*, esp. the pink *C. acaule* and the yellow *C. calceolus* var. *pubescens*.

1826 W. DARLINGTON *Florula Cestrica* 95 *C[ypripedium] pubescens*... Noah's Ark. Yellow Mocasin [*sic*] flower. **1898** C. A. CREEVEY *Flowers of Field* 296 Stemless Lady's Slipper. Noah's Ark. Moccasin-flower. *Cypripedium acaule.* **1949** E. L. PALMER *Fieldbk. Nat. Hist.* 148/2 It bears a number of common names such as Noah's ark, squirrel's shoes, camel's foot, nerveroot, old goose, Indian moccasin, and two lips.

6. *Rhyming slang.* **a.** A police informer. **b.** *Austral.* A shark. (See also quots. 1941, 1960.)

1898 *Bulletin* (Sydney) 17 Dec. (Red Page), An informer or mar-plot is a nark or a Jonah or a Noah's Ark. **1941** BAKER *Dict. Austral. Slang* 49 *A Noah's ark*, a dull, witless fellow. A rhyme on 'nark'. **1941** 'V. DAVIS' *Phenomena in Crime* xix. 254 A stoolie, Noah's Ark, a grasshopper, a nark or informer. **1952** *Chambers's Shorter Eng. Dict.* 800/1 *Noah's ark (slang)*, a shark. **1960** J. FRANKLYN *Dict. Rhyming Slang* 101/1 *Noah's ark*, (1) nark (an informer), (2) park. (1) has been in use in England since the first decade of the 20 C. It is also used in the form of a Spoonerism '*oah's Nark*, the first word having the inference, '*whore's*' and when thus inverted it is the supreme expression of contempt.

7. (See quot. 1968.)

1945 *Archit. Rev.* XCVII. 59/3 In the 1920's an import from Germany, simpler in erection, faster and thus more thrilling, threatened the supremacy of the switch-back... This new machine—the Noah's Ark..had decorative features which continued the tradition of coarse splendour. **1965** *Observer* (Colour Suppl.) 29 Aug. 10/2 The showmen are setting up their stalls and heavy riding machines: Dodgems, Noah's Arks, Waltzers, Shows, and Hurricane Jets. **1968** D. BRAITHWAITE *Fairground Archit.* 153/2 The term 'Noah's Ark' referred to a circular ride having an undulating track..and a variety of fixed animals carried on segmental platforms, all contained within a static enclosure.

Also **Noah's Dove**, a constellation in the Southern hemisphere.

1594 BLUNDEVIL *Exerc.* IV. xix. (1636) 473 Other Images towards the South Pole, as the Crosse or Crosier, the South Triangle, Noahs Dove or Pigeon. **1665** SIR T. HERBERT *Trav.* (1677) 33 The Antartique constellations, some of which we took special notice of towards the Pole;..Noah's Dove, Polophylax.

noap, variant of NOPE, bullfinch.

†**noast,** obs. variant of OAST.

1656 W. DU GARD tr. *Commenius' Gate Lat. Unl.* 107 Having laid it on a kiln, or noast, scorcheth it, and converteth it into malt.

noat(e, obs. forms of NOTE.

†**nob,** *sb.*[1] *Obs.* [Of obscure origin: cf. Flem. *nobbeling*, the coarsest flax, of which sacking is made. See also NOBBLY *a.*] A knot (on thread).

1398 TREVISA *Barth. De P.R.* XVII. clxi. (Bodl. MS.) 230 b/2 Hurden..is clensing of offal of hempe oþer of flaxe ..þerof is þrede sponne þat is..vneuen and ful of nobbes.

nob (nɒb), *sb.*[2] *slang.* Also 8 **nobb.** [perh. a variant of KNOB *sb.*, in various senses of which the spelling *nob* is also used (see *Eng. Dial. Dict.*). Sense 3 may be unconnected.]

1. a. The head. (Cf. KNOB *sb.* 4.) ***bob a nob***: see BOB *sb.*[8] 2.

a **1700** B. E. *Dict. Cant. Crew, Nob*, a Head. **1733** K. O'HARA *Tom Thumb* I. iv, Do pop up your nob again, And egad I'll crack your crown. **1759** *Compl. Lett.-Writer* (ed. 6) 220 Miss Bennet had apparel'd her nob in a frightful Fanny Murry Cap. **1819** *Sporting Mag.* IV. 237 A tremendous lunging blow on his nob. *a* **1845** HOOD *Public Dinner* 17 A little dark spare man, With bald shining nob. **1894** MEREDITH *Ld. Ormont* i, Matey's sure aim..relieving J. Masner of a foremost assailant with a spanker on the nob. *fig.* **1782** G. PARKER *Hum. Sk.* 155 Here no despotic power shews Oppression's haughty nob.

b. *attrib.* and *Comb.* as ***nob-thatch***, hair; ***nob-thatcher***, a wig-maker (Grose 1796) or hatter.

1823 MONCRIEFF *Tom & Jerry* I. v, Some of our dashing straw-chippers and nob-thatchers in Burlington Arcade. **1866** YATES *Land at Last* vii, You've got a paucity of nob-thatch, and what 'air you 'ave is..gray.

c. A blow on the head.

1812 *Sporting Mag.* XXXIX. 153 By flush-hits, and nobs and fibs Who crack'd the jaw and broke the ribs Of fearless Thomas Molineux.

2. In *Cribbage*, the knave of the same suit as the turn-up card, counting one to the holder; esp. in phr. ***one for his nob***.

1821 LAMB *Elia* Ser. I. *Mrs. Battle's Opinions on Whist*, There was nothing silly in it, like the nob in cribbage. **1844** J. T. HEWLETT *Parsons & W.* liv, Fifteen two, and a pair's four, and his nob's five. **1870** HARDY & WARE *Mod. Hoyle, Cribbage* 18 If you hold in your hand or crib a knave of the same suit as the card turned up you peg one. In the familiar phrase, you take 'one for his nob'.

†**3.** The game of prick-the-garter. *Obs.*

1753 POULTER *Discov.* (ed. 2) 9 We defrauded a young Man of..four Guineas..at the old Nobb, or Pricking in the Belt. *Ibid.* 11.

nob (nɒb), *sb.*[3] *slang.* Also *Sc.* 8 **knabb**, 8–9 **nab.** [Of obscure origin: the Sc. forms are against the suggestion that it is an abbreviation of *nobleman.*] A person of some wealth or social distinction.

α. **1755** R. FORBES *Ajax Sp., Shop Bill* ii, Doughty geer That either knabbs or lairds may weer. **1796** LAUDERDALE *Poems* 75 (E.D.D.), A' the fat nabs through the countra. **1819** THOMSON *Poems* 29 (E.D.D.), The nabs will say, that duddy soul Shall no sit near, nor taste our bowl.

β. **1809** *MS. Lett. of W. Fowler*, My Drawings and Engravings..have recommended me to the notice of the first Nobbs of this Kingdom. **1825** C. WESTMACOTT *Eng. Spy* I. 255 Nob or big wig. **1837** DISRAELI *Henrietta Temple* v. xviii, The little waiter who began to think Ferdinand was not such a nob as he had imagined. **1850** HUXLEY in *Life* (1900) I. v. 63 [He] asked me to dine with him and meet a lot of nobs. **1872** *Punch* 3 Feb. 47/1 Why don't your nobs and swells get up poor's schools of their own?

nob, *sb.*[4], variant of KNOB *sb.*

nob, *sb.*[5], abbrev. of KNOBSTICK 2.

1870 J. K. HUNTER *Life Studies* xix. 136 They ha'e a strong society,..and hate nobs such as me. **1886** MACLEOD *Clyde Distr. Dumbart.* I. 22 The 'nobs' and their protectors proceeded to the works.

nob, *v.*[1] *Boxing slang.* [f. NOB *sb.*[1] 1.]

1. *trans.* To strike (one) on the head.

1812 *Sporting Mag.* XXXIX. 18 After Crib had again nobbed him. **1816** *Ibid.* XLVIII. 181 Ford..nobbed him severely. **1823** MONCRIEFF *Tom & Jerry* II. iv, I've nobb'd him on the canister.

2. *intr.* To deliver blows on the head.

1812 *Sporting Mag.* XXXIX. 153 Tom who cou'd both fib and nob. **1814** *Ibid.* XLIII. 55 Alexander kept nobbing with his left hand at the other.

Hence '**nobbing** *vbl. sb.*[1] and *ppl. a.*

1816 *Sporting Mag.* XLVIII. 87 Stephenson during these rounds..put in several nobbing hits. **1825** JONES *True Boxer* in Farmer *Musa Ped.* (1896) 92 With flipping and milling, and fobbing and nobbing.

nob, *v.*[2] *slang.* [Of obscure origin.]

1. To collect (money).

1851 MAYHEW *Lond. Labour* (1861) III. 135 We also 'nob', or gather the money. **1893** P. H. EMERSON *Signor Lippo* vi, I nobbed half a sovereign from a young visitor, besides a lot of small money.

2. To make a collection from (persons).

1851 MAYHEW *Lond. Labour* (1861) III. 206, I saw some men coming out of a chemical works, and we went to 'nob' them (that is get some halfpence out of them).

Hence '**nobbing** *vbl. sb.*[2] Also in concrete use.

1851 MAYHEW *Lond. Labour* (1861) III. 109 We'd take.. perhaps fifteen shillings of nobbings. **1895** MORTON *Adv. Arthur Roberts* 138 'Nobbing' is the professional euphuism for going round with the hat.

nob, in *hob and nob*, etc.: see HOB-NOB.

no ball, no-ball, *sb.* [f. NO *a.* + BALL *sb.*]

1. The words used by an umpire at cricket to denote that the ball has not been bowled in accordance with the rules of the game.

17.. *Laws of Cricket* in Grace *Cricket* (1891) 14 If he [the bowler] delivers ye ball with his hinder foot over ye Bowling crease, ye Umpire shall call no Ball. **1787** *Laws* §13 in Waghorn *Cricket-Scores* (1899), If the bowler's foot is not behind the bowling-crease when he delivers the ball, the umpire unasked must call 'no-ball'. **1890** *Laws of Cricket* §10 in Murdoch *Cricket* (1893) 87 The ball must be bowled: if thrown or jerked, the umpire shall call 'No Ball'.

2. A ball not bowled according to the rules.

1876 *Haygarth's Cricket Scores* V. 176 Mr. Hankey was bowled by a no ball..; he afterwards carried out his bat. **1884** *Lillywhite's Cricket Ann.* 48 Robertson delivered a no-ball. **1888** *Athenæum* 21 July 89/1 Why should the bowler in each instance deliver a palpable no-ball? **1955** *Times* 6 Aug. 4/3 The loping run, all arms and legs, and the no-ball were not forgotten. **1974** *Sunday Tel.* 3 Mar. 33/7 Hayes, his middle stump removed by a Holder no-ball.., remained to fight another day. **1975** *Cricketer* May 19/2 There were at least three occasions when he bowled batsmen with no-balls.

3. *fig.* (also *attrib.*).

1922 [see BEAVER[3]]. **1939** *John o' London's* 9 June 361/2 Mr. Chance's solution is much too complicated, and he does not play the game quite fairly, because he has two men who are related and can pass for each other, which..has been considered a 'no-ball' in detective fiction for a long time. **1966** *Sunday Times* (Colour Suppl.) 4 Dec. 73/2 GI Jargon. *No-ball Target*, Air Corps nickname for a German rocket launching site.

Hence **no-ball**, *v. trans.* (*a*) To condemn as a no-ball. (In quot. *fig.*) (*b*) To declare (a bowler) to have delivered a no-ball.

1862 *Baily's Mag.* Oct. 201 John Lillywhite..also 'No balled' the third, fourth, fifth, sixth, and seventh delivered by Willsher, who thereupon walked off the ground. **1867** G. H. SELKIRK *Guide to Cricket-Ground* iv. 60 Dean, as umpire, no balled Mr. C. D. Marsham three times in one over. **1878** *Sat. Rev.* 16 Nov. 617 The new destructive invention would be internationally 'no-balled'. **1883** *Standard* 8 May 3/7 It is their duty to 'no ball' any bowler as to the fairness of whose delivery they entertain any doubt. **1885** *Manch. Exam.* 18 July 5/2 Mr. Jowett, bowling for Lancashire, was no-balled on the ground of throwing.

nobbe, obs. variant of KNOB *sb.*

nobber[1] ('nɒbə(r)). *slang.* [f. NOB *v.*[1]]

1. A blow on the head.

1818 *Sporting Mag.* II. 23 Spring laughed and gave Painter a nobber. **1828** *Ibid.* XXII. 447 Crawley was about to give the party a second edition of 'nobbers' when Harry Holt interposed.

2. A pugilist skilled in nobbing.

1821 *Sporting Mag.* VIII. 263 Nature seems to have taken particular pains in qualifying Randall for a nobber of first-rate excellence.

'nobber[2]. *slang.* [f. NOB *v.*[2]] One who 'nobs' or collects money.

1890 *Echo* 30 Oct. (Farmer), Only a nobber can know the extraordinary meanness of the British public. **1893** P. H. EMERSON *Signor Lippo* vi, I have often met honourable nobbers since.

'nobbily, *adv.* [f. NOBBY *a.* + -LY[2].] In a nobby manner; showily; smartly (Ogilvie 1882).

1859 HOTTEN *Dict. Slang* 69 *Nobby*, fine or showy; *nobbily*, showily. **1877** 'MARK TWAIN' in *Atlantic Monthly* Nov. 591 Two hundred Bermudians..all of them nobbily dressed, as the poet says. **1880** *Punch* 25 Dec. 299/1 There wasn't a chap in the room so good-looking or nobbily drest.

'nobbiness. [f. NOBBY *a.* + -NESS.] Smartness; affected elegance.

1909 *N.Y. Even. Post* 7 Aug. 2 He unwittingly errs..on the side either of a certain scrubbiness or of an even more unfortunate 'nobbiness'. **1935** *Amer. Speech* X. 10/1 Around 1900 when the present-day elderly good-people were criminal Dapper Dans, their lingo was the last word in linguistic nobbiness.

nobbing, *vbl. sb.*: see NOB *v.*[1] and *v.*[2]

nobble ('nɒb(ə)l), *v. slang.* [Of obscure origin.]

1. a. *trans.* To tamper with (a horse), as by drugging or laming it, in order to prevent it from winning a race.

1847 [see NOBBLING *vbl. sb.*]. **1859** LEVER *D. Dunn* iv, A shadowy vision of creditors 'done', horses 'nobbled'. **1868** *Pall Mall G.* 4 May (Farmer), Buccaneer.. was nobbled, *i.e.* maimed purposely, before the Two Thousand in which he was engaged. **1881** *Standard* 22 June 3/4 The libel accused the Plaintiff of being a party to 'nobbling' a horse..with the object of raising the odds against it. **1933** WODEHOUSE *Heavy Weather* iii. 34 At any moment..the bounder was liable to come sneaking in, mask on face and poison-needle in hand, intent on nobbling the favourite. **1951** *News Chron.* 18 Dec. 1 Lord Rosebery confirms today that his horse which was nobbled was Snap.

b. To secure (a person, etc.) to one's own side or interest by bribery or other underhand methods. Also in somewhat weakened sense: to reduce the efficiency of (a person, etc.) by some means.

1856 LD. CLARENDON *Let.* in H. R. C. Wellesley *Paris Embassy* (1928) 103 Morny..seems to have talked with enthusiasm about the Empress-mother, and to have been quite nobbled by her. **1865** [see NOBBLING *vbl. sb.*]. **1884** *Manch. Exam.* 15 Oct. 5/5 He must be a very clumsy operator who, when he wishes to nobble a newspaper, does it by cash down. **1889** *Times* 2 May 9/5 A cool attempt to nobble the Council on the question of the licensing of music-halls. **1912** F. M. HUEFFER *Panel* I. ii. 31 'I want to point out to Miss Delamere that you can't reform the theatre without reforming the conventional idea about marriage.'.. 'Oh, I see,' the major said amiably, 'you want to nobble her before she makes any business arrangements with my uncle.' **1939** H. NICOLSON *Diary* 20 Sept. (1967) 36 Margesson insisted that..he [*sc.* Churchill] must be 'nobbled' by having a department which would occupy all his time. **1960** J. FINGLETON *Four Chukkas to Australia* xvii. 142 He was left bereft when this particular style of 'nobbling' the opposition was outwitted in the first Test. **1963** *Times* 13 May 6/6 Unions felt that if they were to take part in the work of the National Incomes Commission they would be 'nobbled at the start.' **1973** 'M. UNDERWOOD' *Reward for Defector* v. 39 What about the rest of the delegation?.. No chance of nobbling one of them?

2. a. To obtain by dishonest methods; to steal.

1854 THACKERAY *Newcomes* lvii, After nobbling her money for the beauty of the family. **1862** —— *Philip* xvi, The old chap has nobbled the young fellow's money. **1889** D. C. MURRAY *Catspaw* 207 A gentleman in your position might as well nobble the Griffin outside as steal them stones.

b. To swindle (one) *out of* something.

1854 THACKERAY *Newcomes* xxv, I don't know out of how much the reverend party has nobbled his poor old sister.

3. To get hold of, seize, catch. Also, to strike; to kidnap; to 'steal'.

1841 C. H. HARTSHORNE *Salopia Antiqua* 517 *Nobler*, a man whose duty it is to remind inattentive youths in church, of their misbehaviour, by '*nobling*' them, or hitting them on the head with a wand. **1865** MILTON & CHEADLE *N.-W. Passage by Land* xv. 306 His son had succeeded in 'nobbling' a brace of partridges, knocking the young birds out of the trees with short sticks, missiles they used with great dexterity. **1877** GREENWOOD *Dick Temple* I. ii. 73 There's a fiver in the puss, and nine good quid... Nobble him, lads, and share it betwixt you. **1888** 'R. BOLDREWOOD' *Robbery under Arms* (1890) 69 We're bound to be nobbled some day. **1922** JOYCE *Ulysses* 497 You once nobble that, congregation, and a buck joy ride to heaven becomes a back number. **1928** E. WAUGH *Decline & Fall* vii. 66 'What sort of job?' I says. 'Nobbling,' he says, meaning kidnapping. **1932** H. J. MASSINGHAM *World without End* 296 Off he goes to 'bibble' a mug of scrumpy and 'nobble' a hunk of cheese. **1968** M. WOODHOUSE *Rock Baby* viii. 64 We've got this Shackleton we've nobbled off Coastal Command.

Hence **'nobbled** *ppl. a.*

1891 *Review of Rev.* IV. 580/2 The nobbled managers were quite cowed. **1901** MCCARTHY 5 *Yrs. Irel.* xxxiv. 513 Secure, as they fondly thought, in a nobbled hierarchy.

nobble, variant of KNOBBLE *v.*

nobbler[1] ('nɒblə(r)). [f. NOBBLE *v.* + -ER[1].]

1. One who nobbles horses.

1854 WHYTE-MELVILLE *General Bounce* vii, Nobblers and noblemen—grooms and gentlemen—..apparently all layers and no takers. **1865** *Daily Tel.* 18 Apr. 3 It is to be hoped that the son of Orlando will speedily have the pen put through his name, and thereby mar the 'little game' of the 'nobblers'. **1881** *World* 6 July 15/1 It is dangerous to hastily append the word 'nobbler' to any man.

2. (See quot.)

1876 HINDLEY *Cheap Jack* 261 A lot of people called 'Nobblers', who used to work the 'thimble and pea rig' and go 'buzzing', that is, picking pockets.

nobbler[2] ('nɒblə(r)). Chiefly *Austral.* and *N.Z.* [Of obscure origin.] A small quantity of liquor. Also, a small glass or container for liquor.

1852 'G. F. P.' *Gold Pen & Pencil Sk.* XIV. (Morris), The summit gained, he pulls up at the Valley, To drain a fare-well nobbler to his Sally. **1853** J. SHERER *Gold-Finder of Australia* 177, I have only had two noblers (as they are called) since I came to the place, and paid 1s. 6d. per nobler. **1859** CORNWALLIS *New World* I. 300 People would drink nobbler after nobbler of spirits all day long. **1859** F. FOWLER *Southern Lights & Shadows* 52 (Morris), To pay for liquor for another is to 'stand' or to 'shout'... The measure is called a 'nobbler' or a 'break-down'. **1862** POLEHAMPTON *Kangaroo Land* 95 One fellow sold execrable rum at two shillings a nobbler, *i.e.* half a wine glass. **1873** TROLLOPE *Austral. & N.Z.* II. xi. 201 A nobbler is the proper colonial phrase for a drink at a public-house. **1885** R. C. PRAED *Austral. Life* 103 Having accepted at my hands the customary 'nobbler', he would sit down for half-an-hour, talking. **1888** 'R. BOLDREWOOD' *Robbery under Arms* (1890) 16 Every one wanted to be thought a man,..so we used to make a point of drinking our nobbler. **1908** D. FERGUSON *Bush Life in Austral. & N.Z.* (ed. 4) xxxv. 274 Nor did their thirst for ardent spirits appear to be in the least moderated by the price of the beverages..the good old colonial charge of one shilling per 'nobbler'. **1936** M. FRANKLIN *All that Swagger* xix. 181, I took a nobbler of your poisoned grog. **1949** D. M. DAVIN *Roads from Home* 216 He..was pouring it into two nobblers he had fished out of the pocket. **1957** D. NILAND *Call me when Cross turns Over* ii. 30 He poured himself nobbler after nobbler and drank them straight. **1971** *Walkabout* (Austral.) Nov. 73/1 Whisky costs around 300 rupiahs, or some 75 cents, for a generous nobbler.

'nobbler[3]. *rare.* [f. dial. *nobble* to strike on the head (f. NOB *sb.*[1] 1) + -ER[1].] **a.** A blow on the head (Ogilvie 1882). **b.** A short stick used for killing fish (cf. NOBBY *sb.* 1).

1888 SIR H. POTTINGER in *Fortn. Rev.* May 630 His final struggles are shortly ended with a single tap of the 'nobbler'.

nobbler, variant of KNOBBLER.

nobbling ('nɒblɪŋ), *vbl. sb.* [f. NOBBLE *v.* + -ING[1].] The action of the verb, in various senses.

1847 *Illustr. Lond. News* 6 Nov. 302/1 What is the play at a German watering-place compared with the..'nobbling' and 'hocussing' of a race course. **1865** *Pall Mall G.* 21 Aug. 11/2 Brickwood was umpire, in a London watermen's eight, and played his part well, despite various attempts at what is called nobbling. **1894** *Daily Tel.* 1 June 6/7 Cases of undoubted or suspected nobbling or attempts at nobbling. **1897** *Daily News* 25 Feb. 8/4 Filling empty sacks with small quantities of coke taken from each of the full sacks. The practice was known among coal men as 'nobbling'.

'nobbling, *a. rare*[−1]. [Cf. NOBBY *a.*] Well.

1825 *Spirit Public Jrnls.* 143, 'I hope you and your family are well', replied Sheridan. 'Ay, ay', answered the elector, 'they are pretty nobbling'.

†**'nobbly**, *a. Obs.* [f. NOB *sb.*[1]] Knotty.

1398 TREVISA *Barth. De P.R.* XVII. clxi. (Bodl. MS.) 230 b/2 Wiþ many brakingges..hurden beþ departed fro [the substance of] hempe oþer of flex and is grete when it is departed, nobly, schorte, and rowȝe.

nobbly, variant of KNOBBLY *a.*

nobbut ('nɒbət), *adv.* Now *dial.* Forms: 4 no bot, 4–5 (9) no but, 6 na but, 8–9 nobbut, 9 -at, -et, -it, etc. [f. NO *adv.*[1] + BUT *conj.* 4.]

1. Only, merely, just.

13.. *E.E. Allit. P.* B. 1127 No-bot wasch hir..in wyn as ho askes, Ho by kynde schal becom clerer þen are. **1388** WYCLIF 2 *Kings* xviii. 4 *marg.*, As if he seide, no thing of Godhed was in it,..no but copir was there. *c* **1425** *St. Mary of Oignies* II. x. in *Anglia* VIII. 177/45 No but elleuene tymes and in a litil quantite she toke bodily mete. **1567** DRANT *Horace, Ep.* II. ii. Hj, This boy ran once for feare of whip, And na but once from me. **1787** *Borrowdale Letter*, This is nobbut like t'clock when it gis warnin to strike twelve. **1804** R. ANDERSON *Cumbld. Ball.* (*c* 1850) 19 Nobbet sit your ways still, the truth I's tell. **1855** MRS. GASKELL *North & S.* xlv, I nobbut wanted to know if they'd getten him cleared? **1890** W. A. WALLACE *Only a Sister?* 87 He's but half a man that Missie, nobbut one of oursens dressed up like. **1929** J. B. PRIESTLEY *Good Companions* I. v. 196 It's nobbut Thursday, isn't it? Well, it seems like months. **1957** 'B. BUCKINGHAM' *Boiled Alive* xi. 61 There was nobbut a bunch of dirty foreigners here. **1963** *Times* 25 May 9/7 Mr. Vernon Horsfall still makes clogs. 'But it's a mak a finished is t'trade, you know. It's nobbut farmers and folk in weaving sheds.'

2. Except, unless; except that.

1382 WYCLIF *Mark* v. 37 He resceyuede not ony man to sue him, no but Petre, and James. **1388** —— *Gen.* xxviii. 17 Here is noon other thing no but the hows of God. **1395** PURVEY *Remonstr.* (1851) 37 [To] be deposid or degratid if he is a clerk no but he amende himself.

1870 E. PEACOCK *Ralf Skirl.* I. 36 This Billy hed a gran-father just such another man for all the warld as he is, no-but he wasn't lame.

nobby ('nɒbɪ), *sb.* [Of doubtful origin.]

1. = NOBBLER[3].

1887 *All Year Round* 22 Jan. 10 The fisherman's stick or nobby, used in the salmon fishing.

2. A Manx fishing boat of the smallest class. Also used more widely around the Irish Sea, and by the Royal Navy.

1899 S. GWYNN in *Blackw. Mag.* Oct. 489 The crews of forty-eight row-boats..and of eighteen nobbies and hookers. *Ibid.* 490 The nobby, a Manx type, has been largely introduced—a boat..provided with two short masts which can easily be a let down without being unstepped. **1936** E. VALE *Seas & Shores England* ii. 19 The Morecambe Bay fishermen with their specially evolved cutter-rigged smack called a *nobby* have been for generations famous throughout the three western seas of Britain. **1948** R. DE KERCHOVE *Internat. Maritime Dict.* 491/1 *Nobbie, nobby.* 1. A round-sterned, two-masted, lug-rigged fishing boat found on the south coast of Ireland... 2. A pointed-stern fishing boat of the Mersey estuary rigged with a jib, a dipping lug foresail, and a standing lug mizzen. **1953** J. MASEFIELD *Conway* (rev. ed.) IV. 209 We had three sailing dinghies—and the nobby—a heavier boat of about eighteen feet. **1970** E. J. MARCH *Inshore Craft Gt. Britain* II. viii. 280 The early smacks, 'nobbies' to use the local name, were about 36 ft long, and drew 4 ft of water. **1973** W. ELMER *Terminol. Fishing* i. 26 In the west, an impressive pattern is formed by the distribution of the *prawners* and *shrimpers* of the Cumberland and Lancashire coast, and the Lancashire *nobby*.

3. *Austral.* Black opal found as a silica drop (the characteristic form at Lightning Ridge, N.S.W.).

1924 T. C. WOLLASTON *Opal* I. ii. 10 Characteristic forms of the Black Opal are locally known as 'Nobbies'... pseudomorphs after sponges and corals. **1948** E. F. MURPHY *They struck Opal* 140 Nobbies are..scattered here and there like shells on the beach. **1963** A. LUBBOCK *Austral. Roundabout* 79 These petrified..bubbles are called 'nobbies'; and they are prised out..by the opal digger. **1967** S. LLOYD *Lightning Ridge Bk.* Introd., Dug out a cleanskin nobby. It was a bonza stone and a whopper too.

nobby ('nɒbɪ), *a. slang.* Also 8 *Sc.* **knabby.** [f. NOB *sb.*[3] + -Y[1].] Belonging to, or characteristic of, the 'nobs'; extremely smart or elegant.

a. Of persons.

1788 PICKEN *Poems* 178 The herds o' mony a knabbie laird War trainin' for the shambles. *c* **1810** *Broadside Ballad* (Farmer), A werry nobby dog's meat man. **1847** ALB. SMITH *Nat. Hist. Gent* x. 67 He would think that he was not 'nobby' if he did not have some wretched champagne. **1884** *Harper's Mag.* Jan. 230/2 How 'nobby' the Captain used to look..in the..silk suits.

b. Of places or things.

1844 C. SELBY *Lond. by Night* II. i, *Enter Ankle Jack, extravagantly dressed.* I fancy I shall do, my togs being in keeping with this nobby place. **1852** DICKENS *Bleak Ho.* liv, Respecting this unfortunate family matter, and the nobbiest way of keeping it quiet. **1862** *Punch* 29 Mar. 124/1 But..'the game's alive again', in the nobby new Westminster Pit. **1893** 'Q.' (QUILLER COUCH) *Delect. Duchy* 212 An outfit.. described as 'rather nobby'.

c. ***the nobby***, the smart thing.

1869 E. FARMER *Scrap Book* (ed. 6) 75 He went for the nobby, he heeded not price. **1905** *Daily Chron.* 18 Dec. 4/5 We pay sixpence..in the body of the hall, and ninepence if we do the nobby and ascend to the balcony.

nobby, variant of KNOBBY *a.*

nobchete, variant of NABCHEAT *Obs.*

no-being. [f. NO *a.* + BEING *sb.*] Negative existence; non-existence, non-entity.

1651 tr. *Kitchin's Jurisd.* (1657) Ep. Ded., I have fixt my hopes, that Ignorance..will lose its no-being in Judiciall Performances. **1653** MORE *Antid. Ath.* I. viii. Scholia (1712) 150 A most absolute necessity of Being, by which..it is different from a No-Being. **1733** W. CRAWFORD *Infidelity* (1836) 162 Have we not more need of no-being than being? **1864** BOWEN *Logic* iv. 90, I can certainly think a difference—that is, a relation—between being and no-being.

Nobel (nəʊˈbɛl, ˈnəʊbɛl). [The name of Alfred *Nobel* (1833–96), Swedish chemist and engineer, inventor of dynamite and other high explosives.] **Nobel prize**, one of five prizes, established by the will of Alfred Nobel, which are awarded annually to the person or persons adjudged by Swedish learned societies to have done the most significant recent work in physics, chemistry, medicine, and literature, and to the person or persons adjudged by the Norwegian parliament to have rendered the greatest service to the cause of peace. So ***Nobel award, bequest, laureate*** (see LAUREATE *sb.* 1 d), ***prize-man, prize-winner, prize-winning*** adj. Also *ellipt.*

A sixth prize, for economics, was first awarded in 1969.

1900 *Sci. Gossip* Nov. 164/2 Just before going to press we have been furnished..with copies of the official statutes and regulations of the Nobel Bequest. *Ibid.* Dec. 195/1 Each candidate for a Nobel prize must be proposed in writing by some one qualified to make such proposal. **1904** *To-day* 28 Dec. 252/2 (*heading*) The Nobel Prizemen. **1932** *Discovery* Oct. 327/2 Ross..was..awarded the Nobel Prize for Medicine. **1956** Nobel award [see GUGGENHEIM]. **1958** *Listener* 6 Nov. 749/1 His great discovery, a Nobel-prizewinning matter. **1962** *Ibid.* 8 Nov. 775/1 Deservedly a Nobel Prize winner, O'Neill..was perhaps the greatest twentieth-century dramatist writing in English. **1968** J. D. WATSON *Double Helix* xxii. 163 Though the odds still appeared against us, Linus had not yet won his Nobel. **1969** *Times* 29 Sept. 10/8 An award for economics is, I hear, to be added to the list of Nobel prizes for peace, literature, physics, chemistry, and medicine. It has been endowed after a bequest from the Royal Bank of Sweden, which has celebrated its 300th anniversary this year. **1973** D. ROBINSON *Rotten with Honour* 66 Our own people rate this man's work at Nobel standard. **1973** *Times* 19 Oct. 21/2 Professor Wassily Leontief, of Harvard University, yesterday won the Nobel Prize for Economics. He will receive an award of £41,000. **1975** J. AIKEN *Voices in Empty House* ii. 73 August's lab assistants gave him this set when he won his Nobel.

nobel, nobil, obs. forms of NOBLE *a.*

Nobelist (nəʊˈbɛlɪst). [f. NOBEL + -IST.] A winner of a Nobel prize.

1941 *Sci. News Let.* 30 Aug. 135/1 Prof. Enrico Fermi, Nobelist now working at Columbia University. **1965** *Amer. N. & Q.* Sept. 9/2 *Joseph Breuer as Nobelist*—Is there any evidence that Joseph Breuer (1842–1925), physiologist, was ever seriously considered as a candidate for a Nobel Prize? **1972** *Impact of Science on Society* (Unesco) XXII. IV. 282 Nobelists everywhere have emerged from the laboratory corner, the literary alcove or the private study to become involved with the plight of the race.

nobelium (nəʊˈbiː-, nəʊˈbɛlɪəm). *Chem.* [f. NOBEL + -IUM.] An artificially produced transuranic element, the longest-lived isotope of which has a half-life of about three minutes. Atomic number 102; symbol No.

1957 P. R. FIELDS et. al. in *Physical Rev.* CVII. 1461/2 We suggest the name nobelium, symbol No, for the new element in recognition of Alfred Nobel's support of scientific research and after the institute where the work was done. **1957** *Times* 10 Sept. 11/1 He compared the building up of new elements beyond uranium to the ascent of Everest... In the making of nobelium, the advanced camp had been curium 244, made in the materials testing reactor in Idaho, United States. **1963** *Sci. Amer.* Apr. 70/2 The investigators proposed the name 'nobelium' for element 102, and the name was accepted by the Commission on Atomic Weights of the International Union of Pure and Applied Chemistry. The acceptance turned out to be premature. All attempts.. to duplicate the Stockholm experiment have failed. **1974** *Encycl. Brit. Micropædia* VII. 368/2 Radiochemists have shown nobelium to exist in aqueous solution in both the + 2 and + 3 oxidation states.

nobiliary (nəʊˈbɪlɪərɪ), *sb.* and *a.* [ad. F. *nobiliaire*, L. type **nōbiliārius, -ium*: see NOBLE *a.* and -ARY.]

†**A.** *sb.* (See quot.) *Obs. rare*$^{-0}$.

1727–38 CHAMBERS *Cycl.*, *Nobiliary*, a collection, or historical account, of the noble families of a province, or nation. [Hence in Bailey, 1731, and some later Dicts., but prob. never in actual English use.]

B. *adj.* Of or pertaining to the nobility. ***nobiliary particle***, the preposition (as F. *de*, G. *von*) forming part of a noble title.

1762 tr. *Busching's Syst. Geog.* VI. 238 One is elected from among the whole body of the nobility, and one from among the nobiliary states of the canton. **1868** *Pall Mall G.* 21 Aug. 2 As for nobiliary pride, it is not known in Poland. **1871** *Member for Paris* II. 15 The law, which forbids persons to adopt nobiliary particles to which they have no right. **1889** H. D. TRAILL *Strafford* iv. 41 He was frankly proud of, frankly deferential to, nobiliary rank.

nobilich, obs. form of NOBLY.

noˈbilitate, *pa. pple.* and *ppl. a. Sc.* Now *rare* or *Obs.* Also 6–7 **-at**. [ad. L. *nōbilitāt-us*, pa. pple. of *nōbilitāre*: see next.] Ennobled; distinguished, renowned.

1596 DALRYMPLE tr. *Leslie's Hist. Scot.* Prol. 12 Farther it is nobilitate in fyne wole and quhyt. *Ibid.* 28 Westwarde lyes monteith, nobilitat and mekle commendet throuch the name of sik cheise. **1632** LITHGOW *Trav.* x. 499 A fruitfull, populous, and nobilitat planure. *a* **1670** SPALDING *Troub. Chas. I* (1850) I. 105 The Lord Ogiluy..being narrest the stock..and nobilitat before him. **1689** tr. *Buchanan's De Jure Reg.* 56 [He] thought him to be Nobilitate by the Slaughter of a Tyrant. **1722** NISBET *Her.* I. 76 The Branches of the principal Family of Douglass, which were nobilitate.

nobilitate (nəʊˈbɪlɪteɪt), *v.* Now *rare* or *Obs.* [f. ppl. stem of L. *nōbilitāre*, f. *nōbilis* NOBLE.] = ENNOBLE *v.* in various senses.

1542 UDALL *Erasm. Apoph.* 52 b, Sir kyng it is your pleasure..to nobilitate this place. **1577** HELLOWES tr. *Gueuara's Chron.* 58 The greatest of Traianes exercise was, to augment and nobilitate his armie and knighthood. **1598** HAYDOCKE tr. *Lomazzo* I. 6 There are two things, which doe specially dignifie and nobilitate a man. *c* **1610** SIR C. HEYDON *Astrol. Disc.* (1650) 69 Nature hath singularly nobilitated all the Aspects in the Motions of Saturn and Jupiter. **1665** J. WEBB *Stone-Heng* (1725) 3 A glorious Shew of Statues and Inscriptions..nobilitated the Memory of famous Citizens. **1699** T. BOSTON *Art Man-fishing* (1900) 44 My heart is nobilitated and tramples on the world.

b. To raise (one) to noble rank.

1538 [see below]. **1669** in Macfarlane *Genealog. Collect.* (1900) 65 He nobilitate Kenneth, making him by Patent Lord Kintail. **1724** J. MACKY *Journ. thro. Eng.* (ed. 4) I. i. 11 The Family..was Nobilitated into two Branches by King Charles II. **1763** *Chron.* in *Ann. Reg.* 62 William, lord Borthwick, was nobilitated in the year 1424.

Hence **noˈbilitated** *ppl. a.*; **noˈbilitating** *vbl. sb.* and *ppl. a.*

1538 LELAND *Itin.* (1769) VI. 38 The firste nobilitating of the Pophams, as it is saide, was by Matilde Emperes. **1729** E. ERSKINE *Serm.* Wks. 1871 I. 442 This law coming out of Zion is a dignifying or nobilitating law. **1753** *Scots Mag.* Nov. 530/1 The..nobilitating of rich commoners. **1791** *State P.* in *Ann. Reg.* 188* The law..which subjects all newly-nobilitated persons to certain civil restrictions.

nobiliˈtation. Now *rare* or *Obs.* [f. prec., or ad. med.L. *nōbilitātio* (Du Cange).] The action of ennobling.

1610 HOLLAND *Camden's Brit.* I. 175 A thing that evidently appeareth by the Patent or Instrument of Nobilitation. **1664** H. MORE *Antid. Idolatry* ii. 16 The Perfection and Nobilitation and Salvation of the Souls of men. **1775** C. JOHNSTON *Pilgrim* 86 The influence which this power of nobilitation might give him over them.

nobility (nəʊˈbɪlɪtɪ). Forms: 4–6 **nobylyte**, 6 **-ytye, -ite**; 5–6 **nobilite**, 6 **-yte, -itee**, 5–7 **-itie**. 6–7 **-itye**, 6 **-ity**. [ad. F. *nobilité* (12th c.), or L. *nōbilitās*, f. *nōbilis* NOBLE: see -ITY.]

1. a. The quality of being noble in respect of excellence, value, or importance. Now *rare*.

1398 TREVISA *Barth. De P.R.* v. i. (1495) 100 The nobylyte and precyousnesse of the eye. *c* **1400** *Rom. Rose* 5651 A book, that the Golden Verses Is clepid, for the nobilite Of the honourable ditee. *c* **1449** PECOCK *Repr.* I. xix. 114 What God is in hise dignitees, nobilitees and perfecciouns. **1514** BARCLAY *Cyt. & Uplondyshm.* (Percy Soc.) 24 Now juge.. whiche of these semeth the Of most avauntage, & most nobylyte? **1535** COVERDALE *Wisd.* viii. 3 Who so hath yᵉ company of God, commendeth hir nobilyte. **1567** MAPLET *Gr. Forest* 25 In Nobilitie aboue Stones and Mettals are Plants. **1578** BANISTER *Hist. Man* IV. 59 This tendon truly is of great nobilitie. **1604** E. G[RIMSTONE] *D' Acosta's Hist. Indies* v. i. 331 That other part of the worlde,..much inferiour in nobilitie. **1678** R. R[USSELL] tr. *Geber* II. i. III. ix. 77 It [silver] is a noble Body but wants of the nobility of Gold.

b. The quality of being noble in nature or character; nobleness or dignity of mind.

1595 W. JONES (*title*), Nenna's Nennio; or a Treatise of Nobility; wherein is discoursed what true Nobilitie is, with such qualities as are required in a perfect gentleman. **1604** SHAKS. *Oth.* II. i. 218, They say base men being in Loue, haue then a Nobilitie in their Natures, more then is natiue to them. **1641** J. SHUTE *Sarah & Hagar* (1649) 142 To labour for Vertue, which is true Nobility. **1687** DRYDEN *Hind & P.* III. 1220 They..named their pride nobility of soul. *a* **1711** KEN *Christophil* Poet. Wks. 1721 I. 462 He glories only in God reconcil'd, 'Tis his Nobility to be God's Child. **1851** LONGF. *Gold. Leg.* vi. *School Salerno* 266 All my divine nobility of nature By this one act is forfeited for ever. **1877** E. R. CONDER *Bas. Faith* v. 203 It is man's nobility, not his defect, that the most lofty and commanding part of him is his moral nature.

transf. **1860** TYNDALL *Glac.* I. xxv. 187 There was a nobility in this glacier scene.

c. *pl.* Instances of nobleness of nature.

1921 R. HICHENS *Spirit of Time* iv. 71 He pointed to the nobilities, the self-sacrifice,..the marvellous examples of courage.

d. The property (of an element) of being noble or relatively unreactive. Cf. NOBLE *a.* 7 b.

1907 [see NOBLE *a.* 7 b]. **1974** *Sci. Amer.* Aug. 48/2 The supposed 'nobility' of the elements that make up Group Zero in the periodic table was first compromised in 1962, when Neil Bartlett..synthesized xenon hexafluoroplatinate.

2. The quality, state, or condition of being noble in respect of rank or birth.

c **1440** *Gesta Rom.* xlvii. 202 (Harl. MS.), I was some tyme a worthi knight... Ande so when that I think of my grete nobilite that I haue bene inne [etc.]. **1560** DAUS tr. *Sleidane's Comm.* 3 b, Suche a one as was both in nobilitie of birth and in authoritie also right famous. **1596** DALRYMPLE tr. *Leslie's Hist. Scot.* I. 96 Of this cumis thair pryd..and bosting of thair nobilitie. **1621** BURTON *Anat. Mel.* II. iii. II. (1651) 316 This is it belike, which makes the Turkes at this day scorn nobility, and all those huffing bumbast titles. **1656** COWLEY *Pindar. Odes* Wks. 1710 I. 250 We draw a long Nobility From Hieroglyphick Proofs of Heraldry. **1705** ADDISON *Italy* (1733) 58 Their Merchants who are grown rich..buy their Nobility, and generally give over Trade. **1781** COWPER *Truth* 353 Royalty, nobility, and state Are such a dread preponderating weight. **1841** W. SPALDING *Italy & It. Isl.* III. 244 Nobles there are in abundance; but their nobility is valid only at court and in fashionable society. **1875** STUBBS *Const. Hist.* xv. II. 185 English nobility is merely the nobility of the hereditary counsellors of the crown.

transf. **1839** HALLAM *Hist. Lit.* IV. vii. §13 *note*, To observe the comparatively recent *nobility* of many things quite established by present usage.

3. a. (With *the*) The body of persons forming the noble class in any country or state.

1530 PALSGR. 889 Commodyouse and profytable vnto the nobylite of this realme. **1560** DAUS tr. *Sleidane's Comm.* 200 b, An especyall ornamente of the Frenche Nobilytye. **1606** WARNER *Alb. Eng.* XV. xcv. 379 The Prelacie, Nobilitie, States-men, and State betraide. **1671** MILTON *Samson* 1654 Lords, Ladies, Captains, Councellors, or Priests, Thir choice nobility and flower. **1726** SWIFT *Gulliver* II. vii, Farmers in the Country, whose Commanders are only the Nobility and Gentry. **1759** JOHNSON *Idler* No. 53 ⁋3 A street where many of the nobility reside. **1819** SHELLEY *Cenci* I. ii. 57 All our kin, the Cenci, will be there, And all the chief nobility of Rome. **1856** EMERSON *Eng. Traits, Wealth*, The introduction of these elements..draws the nobility into the competition.

†**b.** Without article. *Obs. rare.*

1581 MULCASTER *Positions* xxxvii. (1887) 147 If nobilitie and gentlemen would fall to diligence. **1596** SHAKS. *1 Hen. IV*, II. iv. 429 Stand aside, Nobilitie. **1603** JAS. I in Ellis *Orig. Lett.* Ser. I. III. 64 The Country [being] so full of Nobilitie and Gentlemen of the best sort. **1650** BULWER *Anthropomet.* 3 All the Children..born of Nobility.

c. *transf.* The pieces other than pawns in chess.

1656 W. HOWARD in Clarendon *Hist. Reb.* xv. §127. I have often observ'd that a desperate game at chess has been recovered, after the loss of the nobility, only by playing the pawns well.

4. a. (With *a*) A noble class; a body of nobles.

1612 BACON *Ess., Nobility* (Arb.) 192 A great..Nobilite addeth maiesty to a Monarch, but diminisheth power. **1662** STILLINGFL. *Orig. Sacræ* II. ii. §5 Strabo mentions no Nobility at all in Ægypt distinct from the Priests. **1735** BOLINGBROKE *On Parties* 192 The Saxons had a Nobility too, arising from personal Valour, or Wisdom. **1863** COWDEN CLARKE *Shaks. Char.* xvi. 405 The Venetians were a nobility of merchants.

b. One belonging to the noble class.

1840 CARLYLE *Heroes* vi. (1858) 342 One leaves all these Nobilities standing in their niches of honour. **1927** [see DIVINELY *adv.* 2].

noblay, variant of NOBLEY(E *Obs.*

noble (ˈnəʊb(ə)l), *a.* and *sb.*[1] Forms: 4–6 **nobul**, 4–5 **-ulle**, 6 **-ull**; 4–6 **nobyl**, 5 **-ylle**, 5–6 **-yll**; 4–6 **nobil**, (4 **-ile**), 4–7 **nobill**, (5 **-ille**); 5–6 **nobel**, **nowble**, 3– **noble**. [a. F. *noble* (= Sp. *noble*, It. *nobile*), ad. L. *nōbilis*, f. the stem *(g)nō-* to KNOW: see -BLE.]

A. *adj.* **I. 1. a.** Illustrious or distinguished by position, character, or exploits. (Usu. implying senses 2 and 4, and now merged in these.)

a **1225** *Ancr. R.* 54 Hire ueader & hire breðren, se noble princes alse heo weren. *c* **1290** *St. Kath.* 15 in *S. Eng. Leg.* I. 92 Riche Aumperour þou art, swiþe noble and hende. *a* **1352** MINOT *Poems* (ed. Hall) vii. 18 Þus haue I mater for to make For a nobill prince sake. **1390** GOWER *Conf.* III. 2 He is a noble man of armes. *a* **1400–50** *Alexander* 985 Lo! maisterlynges of massydon, so myghty & so noble. *c* **1475** *Rauf Coilȝear* 703 Sone besyde him he gat ane sicht of the Nobill King. *c* **1530** LD. BERNERS *Arth. Lyt. Brit.* I Gawyn, and Lancelotte, and many other noble knightes. **1560** DAUS tr. *Sleidane's Comm.* 14 b, Syns that so noble Princes had such an opinion of him. **1600** J. PORY tr. *Leo's Africa* 47 They esteeme themselues the most noble and worthy people vnder the heauens. **1750** GRAY *Long Story* 141 God save our noble King.

b. Of actions: Illustrious, great.

c **1470** HENRY *Wallace* I. 2 We suld..hald in mynde thar nobille worthi deid. **1535** COVERDALE *Ps.* cv. 1 Who can expresse yᵉ noble actes of the Lorde, or shewe forth all his prayse? **1568** GRAFTON *Chron.* II. 427 The noble feates of Chiualrie and Martiall actes. *c* **1586** *Mourn. Muse* 186 in *Spenser's Wks.* (Globe) 565/2 [He] doth tell Thy noble acts anew. **1606** SHAKS. *Ant. & Cl.* v. iii. 237 What poore an Instrument May do a Noble deede.

2. a. Illustrious by rank, title, or birth; belonging to that class in the community which has a titular pre-eminence over the others; *spec.*

belonging to, or forming, the nobility of a country or state.

In early use not clearly distinct from sense 1.

1297 R. Glouc. (Rolls) 701 Ich þe wole marie wel..To þe nobloste bacheler. a 1300 Cursor M. 17169 If þou neuer sa nobul war, Quat thing moght i giue þe mare? a 1352 Minot Poems (ed. Hall) viii. 65 Þe nobill burgase and þe best Come vnto him. c 1400 Maundev. (Roxb.) vi. 20 He gers bring before him all þe nobilest and þe fairest maydens. 1422 tr. Secreta Secret., Priv. Priv. 204 For the whyche proesses this nobill erle shold nat vaynglory haue. 1535 Coverdale 1 Macc. i. 6 He called for his noble estates..& parted his kyngdome amonge them. 1592 Shaks. Rom. & Jul. iii. iv. 21 A Thursday tell her, She shall be married to this Noble Earle. 1631 Heywood London's Jus Hon. Wks. 1874 IV. 265 More faire and famous it is to be made, then to be borne Noble. 1648 Nicholas Papers (Camden) I. 89 For many other reasons, which I presume those noble persons had in their consideracions. 1712 Steele Spect. No. 274 ¶2 The Copy of a Letter written..to a noble Lord. 1756–7 tr. Keysler's Trav. (1760) III. 68 The church..derives the last name from its noble founder. 1849 Macaulay Hist. Eng. vi. II. 47 All the noblest and most opulent members of their church.., except Lord Arundell. 1893 Wiggin Cathed. Courtship 58 Lady De Wolfe's husband has been noble only four months.

absol. a 1400–50 Alexander 481 Princes & dukis, With masterlingis of Messadone & many oþire noble.

b. Of birth, blood, family, etc.

c 1290 St. Kath. 1 in S. Eng. Leg. I. 92 Seinte Katerine of noble kunne cam. a 1374 Chaucer Boeth. iii. metr. vi. (1868) 79 Þanne comen alle mortal folk of noble seed. a 1533 Ld. Berners Huon xxi. 62, I slew a knyght of a noble blode. 1560 Daus tr. Sleidane's Comm. 2 b, This Thomas comming of a noble house, gave him self wholy to learning. 1611 Bible 2 Macc. xiv. 42 Chusing rather to die manfully, then ..to be abused otherwise then beseemed his noble birth. 1657 Earl Monm. tr. Paruta's Pol. Disc. 79 Any witty Citizen, or hopefull Young-man of noble extract. 1708 J. Chamberlayne St. Gt. Brit. ii. iii. iii. (1710) 437 The Noble Order of Knights of the Thistle..was revived by King James VII. 1808 Scott Marm. i. vii, Two gallant squires, Of noble name, and knightly sires.

c. Pertaining to, connected with, a person or persons of high rank. Also transf. in chess.

1390 Gower Conf. I. 155 Now amende He mai wel thurgh your noble grace. 1504 in Leadam Sel. Cas. Crt. Requests (Selden Soc.) 8 Your said Oratour..hadde begon to colour dyvers reed hides for your noble vse. 1534 More in Roper Life (1822) 118 The first lesson..that ever his Grace gave me at my first comming into his noble service. 1606 Shaks. Ant. & Cl. i. ii. 116 At your noble pleasure. 1680 Cotton Compl. Gamester (ed. 2) 46 When any Pawn..seats himself in any of his Noble houses, he is dignified with the..power of a Queen.

†3. Distinguished for genius or skill. Obs.

c 1400 Cursor M. 28846 (Cott.-Galba), Saynt Aniane, þat nobill clerk, Sais almus es goddes awin werk. a 1400–50 Alexander 3132 (Dubl.), He gart seke þair sarys, & þaim salue With surgers [v.r. surgens] noble. 1500–20 Dunbar Poems lxiii. 61 This noble cunning sort, Quhom of befoir I did report. 1596 Dalrymple tr. Leslie's Hist. Scot. Prol. 3 Thay being so noble Seymen, and sa expert in sayling.

4. a. Having high moral qualities or ideals; of a great or lofty character. (Also used ironically.) ***noble savage***, primitive man, conceived of in the manner of Rousseau as morally superior to civilized man.

1601 Shaks. Jul. C. v. v. 68 This was the Noblest Roman of them all. 1641 Baker Chron. (1653) 179 King Iohn..had the happinesse to fall into the hands of a Noble enemy. 1672 [see savage sb. 2]. 1778 Miss Burney Evelina lxxv, Tell me if he is not the noblest of men? 1829 Digby Broadst. Hon. I. Godefridus 223 The soldiers of Pavia were more noble than their Emperor Frederic II when they remonstrated against his barbarous execution of the Parmesan prisoners. 1871 R. Ellis tr. Catullus lxvii. 29 Truly a noble father, a glorious act of affection! 1892 19th Cent. July 118 The life of one of the noblest of a long list of noble names. 1914 C. Mackenzie Sinister Street II. iii. vi. 628 Every new writer who commands any attention drags out the old idol of the Noble Savage and invites us to worship him. Only now the Noble Savage has been put into corduroy trousers. 1933 J. Cary Amer. Visitor vii. 72 Her publisher..belonged to the most modern school of anthropologists and believed in the Golden Age, the noble savage, and all the other resuscitated fancies of Rousseau. 1947 English Studies XXVIII. 1 He is prevented from depicting the enemies..in..sinister colours by his interest in the romantic dream of the noble savage. 1954 W. S. Maugham Ten Novels i. viii. 201 Let us not forget that Typee is a glorification of the noble savage, uncorrupted by the vices of civilization, and that Melville looked upon the natural man as good. 1971 G. Steiner In Bluebeard's Castle iii. 52 The myth of the noble savage had interiorized a powerful hierarchic dogma. 1972 Daily Tel. 11 Dec. 11/1 They believe in the moral superiority of primitive over civilised man. As a potent idea, the Noble Savage died 100 years ago. But it lives for the Ardens in.. the Indian peasants, the exploited Irish.

b. Of the mind or nature.

1590 Spenser F.Q. i. i. 35 The noblest mind the best contentment has. 1613 Shaks. Hen. VIII, iii. ii. 419 Some little memory of me will stirre him (I know his Noble Nature). 1624 Wotton Elem. Archit. Pref. in Reliq. (1651) 195 Architecture can want no commendation where there are..Noble Mindes. 1700 Dryden Wife of Bath's T. 384 The nobleman is he whose noble mind Is filled with inborn worth.

5. a. Proceeding from, characteristic of, indicating or displaying, greatness of character.

1503 Dunbar Thistle & Rose 119 [The lion] Quhois noble yre is parcere prostratis. 1602 Shaks. Ham. iii. i. 57 Whether 'tis Nobler in the minde to suffer The Slings and Arrowes of outragious Fortune. 1630 R. Johnson's Kingd. & Commw. 218, I will not omit to speake of two Noble usages of the King of Swethland towards his Souldiers. 1729 Law Serious C. ii. (1732) 19 Then he will know that there is nothing noble in a Clergyman but a burning zeal for the Salvation of Souls. 1774 Goldsm. Nat. Hist. (1776) III. 218 Numberless accounts assure us that his anger is noble. 1809 Wordsw. Sonn. Liberty ii. xix. 12 To whose all-pondering mind a noble aim, Faithfully kept, is as a noble deed. 1851 Ruskin Stones Ven. (1874) I. i. 7 The noble pride which was provoked by the insolence of the emperor. 1872 Morley Voltaire (1886) 10 The too neglected list of good causes lost, and noble effort wasted.

b. Characterized by moral superiority or dignity; elevated, lofty.

1738 Gray Propertius ii. 53 You whose young bosoms feel a nobler flame. 1774 J. Bryant Mythol. II. 96 They..carry the sciences.., instruct the natives... These are to be sure noble occurrences. 1818 Byron Ch. Har. iv. cxlvii, Relic of nobler days, and noblest arts! 1831 Society I. 25 With a zeal worthy of a nobler cause. 1872 Morley Voltaire (1886) 4 The noblest collective tradition of free intellect which the achievements of the race could then hand down.

II. 6. a. Distinguished by splendour, magnificence, or stateliness of appearance; of imposing or impressive proportions or dimensions.

c 1290 S. Eng. Leg. I. 71 In þe priorie of wiricestre, þat noble hous and gret is. 1297 R. Glouc. (Rolls) 896 Romulus & remeus..Bigonne þo verst rome þat noble cite is. 13.. E.E. Allit. P. A. 1097 Þis noble cite of ryche enpresse. c 1384 Chaucer H. Fame i. 469 When I had seen al this syghte In this noble temple thus. c 1515 Cocke Lorell's B. 6 They wyll bylde at Colman hedge in space A nother noble mansyon. 1577 Harrison Descr. Brit. xi. in Holinshed I. 52 Being past Rochester, this noble riuer goeth to Chatham. 1662 J. Davies tr. Olearius' Voy. Amb. 228 We cross'd..over a very fair stone bridge, containing six noble Arches. 1703 Maundrell Journ. Jerus. (1732) 142 These noble Trees grow amongst the Snow. 1726 Swift Gulliver i. v, The rest of that noble Pile..[was] preserved from Destruction. 1779 J. Moore View Soc. II. lvii. 77 The gallery which contains them is a very noble room. 1826 Disraeli Viv. Grey vi. i, They ascended a noble stair-case. 1842 Borrow Bible in Spain xxxiv, It possesses a noble quay.

absol. 1741 C'tess Pomfret Corr. (1805) III. 202 Nor is this shore destitute of the noble as well as the agreeable.

b. Splendid, stately, magnificent. rare.

1297 R. Glouc. (Rolls) 1503 Þe oþer kinges echon Hit dude..& in so noble fourme non. c 1420 Lydg. Assembly of Gods 1159 The gret Alpha & Oo,..For that nobyll tryumphe, had hem thedyr sent. c 1500 Melusine 214 They were espoused & maryed togidre, & was the feste holden right grete & noble.

7. a. Having qualities or properties of a very high or admirable kind.

Freq. in the comparative and superlative, denoting superiority to other things of the same name.

c 1305 St. Kenelm in E.E.P. (1862) 55 Whan hit out of heuene com..What noblerere relik mizte þer beo. c 1375 Cursor M. 25116 (Fairf.), Þer is na praier þat is squa noble of þe mikilnes. 1387–8 T. Usk Test. Love ii. i. (Skeat) I. 106 A final cause is noblerer, or els even as noble, as thilke thing that is finally to thilke ende. 1390 Gower Conf. III. 146 The moste noble Creature Of alle tho that God hath wroght. 1508 Dunbar Tua Mariit Wemen 248 God..send me sentence to say, substantious & noble. 1577 B. Googe Heresbach's Husb. iii. (1586) 114 The Horse.., the noblest, the goodliest,..and the trustiest beast that we vse in our seruice. 1631 Widdowes Nat. Philos. 50 Sences of certaine parts are more or lesse noble. The nobler are Seeing, and Hearing. 1684 R. Waller Nat. Exp. 132 In Waters generally held the lightest, purest, and noblest, the little cloud is thinner. 1725 N. Robinson Th. Physick 211 Highly dangerous is it for those, that have been us'd to the most generous Wines, suddenly to abandon those Noble Liquors. 1774 Goldsm. Nat. Hist. (1776) II. 49 So we find that the noblest animals are ever the least fruitful. 1835 Penny Cycl. III. 421/2 The noble race of Barbary horses which we commonly call barbs. 1875 Jowett Plato (ed. 2) I. 16 In all bodily actions, not quietness, but the greatest agility and quickness, is noblest and best.

b. Of precious stones, metals, or minerals. Also (i) spec. of a metal: resisting oxidation; relatively unreactive. Hence of any element: low in the electrochemical series.

1390 Gower Conf. I. 57 He the Ston noblest of alle, The which that men Carbuncle calle Berth in his hed. 1398 Trevisa Barth. De P.R. xvi. xlvii. (Bodl. MS.), Precious stones..ben ifounde..in passinge grete vertue, whan þey bene noble and verrei. Ibid. xiv. iii, Noble metall is ymynyd oute of veynes and mountayns. 1666 Boyle Orig. Formes & Qual. 360 Our Menstruum may have a particular operation upon some Noble..parts of the Gold. 1708 J. C. Compl. Collier (1845) 17 Was it ever heard of, or known that this Noble, this Main-Coale, was sold..for 8s. per Chaldron? 1796 Kirwan Elem. Min. (ed. 2) II. 89 The three first [Gold, Platina, Silver] and Quicksilver commonly called Noble and Perfect metals. 1813 R. Bakewell Introd. Geol. 79 Many specimens have the characters of the precious or noble serpentine. 1842 Parnell Chem. Anal. (1845) 96 Silver and palladium are the only noble metals which dissolve in melted bisulphate of potash. Note. Noble metals are those which do not become converted into oxides, but remain bright when heated in the air. 1855 Orr's Circ. Sci., Geol. 510 Noble opal, or precious opal, includes all those specimens which exhibit the play of prismatic colours. 1907 E. S. Merriam tr. Danneel's Electrochem. v. 134 Metals whose solution pressure is less than that of hydrogen..have a negative potential. The same thing is meant when we speak of the 'nobility' of the metals; silver is more noble than zinc, and zinc is less noble than hydrogen, etc. 1938 R. W. Lawson tr Hevesy & Paneth's Man. Raidioactivity (ed. 2) xxii. 218 They can only be contemplated for those radio-elements which are to some extent electrochemically noble, and hence especially for the isotopes of lead, bismuth, and polonium. 1956 E. C. Potter Electrochem. x. 234 We may summarize this mode of corrosion..by saying 'it is unwise to permit a metal to contact an aqueous solution of a salt of a metal more noble than itself'. 1973 Nature 20 July 137/1 After a beta transformation the daughter element is electrochemically more noble than the mother element. 1974 Sci. Amer. Jan. 33/3 If..one puts the corroding metal in contact with a 'nobler' (less active) metal on which the cathodic reaction can proceed more easily, the corrosion current and hence the rate of dissolution of metal can be increased significantly.

(ii) ***noble gas***: = *inert gas* (b) s.v. inert a. 1 c. So ***noble liquid***, one of the noble gases in the liquid state.

noble gas is now the term officially preferred by the International Union of Pure & Applied Chemistry.

1902 J. I. D. Hinds Inorg. Chem. xviii. 151 The name Noble Gases has been given by Erdmann to the several rare and inactive elements which have recently been discovered. 1927 [see inert a. 1 c (b)]. 1950 Electronic Engin. XXII. 108 Electron tubes filled with a noble gas such as argon, neon or helium are now widely employed. 1971 Nomencl. Inorg. Chem. (I.U.P.A.C.) (ed. 2) 11 The use of the collective names..alkaline-earth metals (Ca to Ra), and noble gases [ed. 1 (1959): inert gases] may be continued. 1971 Nature 29 Oct. 617/1 We are working towards the development of a thin multiconductor chamber filled with a noble liquid. 1974 Sci. Amer. Aug. 48/3 Soon after Bartlett's announcement several other noble-gas compounds were made, chief among them the xenon flourides (XeF_2, XeF_4 and XeF_6) and xenon trioxide (XeO_3).

c. Of parts of the body, spec. of those without which life cannot be maintained, as the heart, lungs, etc.

1632 Sherwood s.v., The noble parts of the body. 1656 Ridgley Pract. Physick 12 Especially if it be near a noble part. 1668 Culpepper & Cole Barthol. Anat. Introd., The Bellies are certain remarkeable Cavities of the Body, wherein some noble bowel is placed. 1721 Bradley Acc. Wks. Nat. 67 The Flounder and many others will live a long time after their Bowels and more noble parts are taken out of them. 1733 Cheyne Eng. Malady ii. viii. §2 (1734) 193 Attended with no..Disease, or no noble Organ entirely spoil'd. 1843 Abdy Water Cure 44 A diseased function of one of the nobler organs. 1899 Allbutt's Syst. Med. VII. 100 The overgrowth of the neuroglia tissue at the expense of the noble elements.

d. Of hawks. (See ignoble a. 1 b.)

1614 Bp. Hall Recoll. Treat. 161 The Soule, like unto some noble Hauke, lets passe the crowes. 1833 Mudie Brit. Birds (1841) I. 79 The old division of noble and ignoble hawks. 1867 Dk. Argyll Reign of Law iii. (ed. 4) 166 The Hawks have been classified as 'noble' or 'ignoble', according to the length and sharpness of their wings.

e. In some specific names, as ***noble agrimony***, ***liverwort*** (q.v.), ***orange***.

1861 Bentley Man. Bot. (1887) 501 Other varieties are sometimes imported, as the Noble or Mandarin Orange and the Tangerine Orange.

f. ***noble rot*** = ***pourriture noble***.

[1924 H. W. Allen Wines of France ii. 114 The Botrytis produces a grey mould, which gives to other wines a most unpleasant taste, but in Sauternes that mould is the pourriture noble, the 'noble rottenness', which bestows on the grapes and the wines made from them their extraordinary richness of sweetness and perfume.] 1935 Schoonmaker & Marvel Compl. Wine Bk. i. 12 It is necessary to leave the grapes on the vine until they are.. over-ripe, sugary and shrunken, until that so-called 'noble rot' (la pourriture noble) has set in. 1959 W. James Word-Bk Wine 133 The noble rot also produces glycerine, which gives the wine a fine liqueur-like oiliness. 1965 A. Sichel Penguin Bk. Wines 194 To every hectolitre (22 gallons) off the fermenting must of the Furmint and Harslevelii grape they [sc. Hungarians producing Tokay] add 3, 4, 5 or 6 puttony of the grapes concentrated by the 'noble rot'. 1973 Country Life 15 Nov. 1535/3 The German vintage..lacking the 'noble rot' which produces the more luscious auslese and beerenauslese wines. 1975 P. Van-dyke Price Taste of Wine 53/1 The primarily sweet wines may have some grapes affected by noble rot, but there is a profundity and a distinctive after-taste to those that are chiefly made with nobly rotten grapes.

8. a. Splendid, admirable, surpassingly good.

a 1300 Cursor M. 11882 (Cott.), Medicine sal þou of vs take, A nobul bath we sal þe make. c 1375 Ibid. 3723 (Fairf.), Nobil venysoun þat I þe bringe. 1387 Trevisa Higden (Rolls) VIII. 21 Bernard wroot meny nobil bookes. c 1400 Maundev. (Roxb.) xiv. 61 Þer er þerin..grete medews and noble pasture for bestez. c 1440 York Myst. xxvi. 133 An oynement That nobill was and newe. 1470–85 Malory Arthur xxi. v. 849 Than hym thought synne and shame to throwe awaye that nobyl swerde. 1526 Pilgr. Perf. (W. de W. 1531) 5 We haue not taken theyr errours, but the noble verytees or treuthes of philosophy. 1577 B. Googe Heresbach's Husb. ii. (1586) 92 b, Of the Mulberie is made a verie noble medicine for the stomacke. 1626 Bacon Sylva §401 This is a noble Experiment; for, without this help, they would have been four times as long in coming up. 1662 J. Davies tr. Mandelslo's Trav. 99 When the president was to take leave of him, he presented him with a noble coverlet of Watte. 1759 Chron. in Ann. Reg. 61/2, I..gave him a noble dose of great guns and small arms. 1775 Sheridan Duenna iii. i, See that there be a noble supper provided. 1877 Dowden Shaks. Primer vi. 77 There is noble material for tragic poetry here. 1899 Besant Orange Girl i. i, He drank a great deal of port, of which he possessed a noble cellar.

†b. Notable, very great. Obs. rare.

1604 Supplic. Masse Priests i, As they affirme, and therein tell a most noble and remarkeable untruth. 1694 Salmon Bate's Dispens. (1713) 516/2 It cannot be done without a noble Diminution of some of their best parts.

9. ***the noble science*** (***of defence***) or ***art***, the art of (†fencing, or) boxing.

c 1588 in Tarlton's Jests (1844) p. xii, Richard Tarlton, master of the noble syence of deffence. c 1611 Beaum. & Fl. Knt. Burn. Pestle ii. i, A bold defiance Shall meet him, were he of the noble science. 1620 Melton Astrolog. 30 Like so many Masters of the Noble Science of Defence, they strive to breake the head of each other's reputation. 1726 in Hone Every-day Bk. II. 782 Professor of the Noble Science of Defence. 1749 Fielding Tom Jones iii. iv, Tom was much his superior at the noble art of boxing. 1839 Radcliffe (title) The Noble Science, with a few general ideas on Fox-Hunting.

10. *Comb.*, as ***noble-couraged, -gartered, -hearted (-ness), -natured, -spirited, -tempered; noble-ending, -looking*** adjs.; ***noble-wise*** adv.

1561 T. HOBY tr. *Castiglione's Courtyer* IV. (1577) Vj b, Wicked Tirans againste whome these *noble couraged Demi-gods kepte continuall..warre. **1599** SHAKS. *Hen. V*, IV. vi. 27 A Testament of *noble-ending loue. **1659** R. WILD *Poems* (1870) 16 The *noble-gartered 'Honi soit'. **1806** SURR *Winter in London* I. 227 A *noble-hearted, but unfortunate ..brother. **1856** LEVER *Martins of Cro' M.* 384 The people, the noble-hearted people, are the conquerors. **1879** L. SHEPHERD tr. *Guéranger's Liturg. Year* I. ii. 7 The *noble-heartedness of those defenders of the Law of God. **1800** MRS. HERVEY *Mourtray Fam.* I. 277 She was a tall *noble-looking woman. **1865** J. H. INGRAHAM *Pillar of Fire* (1872) 305, I regarded this noble-looking bond woman with surprise. **1872** TENNYSON *Gareth & Lynette* 456 The boy Is *noble-natured. **1617** HIERON *Wks.* II. 403 Well fare that *noble-spirited souldier. **1848** BUCKLEY *Iliad* 303 A lion coming among a herd, tawny, noble-spirited. **1654** WHITLOCK *Zootomia* 413 It hath been alwaies the Aimes of the *Noblest-temper'd Spirits. *a* **1618** SYLVESTER *St. Lewis* 576 Wks. (Grosart) II. 235 How happy is the Prince, who.. Thinks not himselfe to raign; save Noblewise.

B. *sb.*[1] **1. a.** A man of noble rank; a member of the nobility.

a **1340** HAMPOLE *Psalter* cxlix. 8 To bynde..þe nobils of þaim in manykils of yryn. **1390** GOWER *Conf.* II. 253 Ther stoden ek the nobles alle Forth with the comun of the toun. *c* **1400** *Destr. Troy* 13813 To þat noble, onone, ho neghit agayne. *c* **1450** HOLLAND *Howlat* 437 With his estatis in the steid, and nobillis ynewe. **1471** FORTESCUE *Wks.* (1869) 539 The councell and assent of the nobles temporals of the londe. **1538** STARKEY *England* I. iv. 129 Another yl custume among the nobyllys there ys, that euery one of them wyl kepe a court lyke a prynce. **1593** SHAKS. *Rich II*, II. i. 247 The nobles hath he finde For ancient quarrels, and quite lost their hearts. *c* **1645** HOWELL *Lett.* I. xviii, That regicide was hack'd to pieces..by the nobles. **1707** *Lond. Gaz.* No. 4364/1 The Princes of the Throne..are understood to act in the Solemnity as Nobles of Rome. **1752** HUME *Ess. & Treat.* (1777) I. 221 It consists chiefly of nobles and landed gentry. **1822** BYRON *Werner* IV. i, In league with the most riotous of our young nobles. **1844** H. H. WILSON *Brit. India* I. 65 The opposition..of the turbulent nobles and officers of the court. **1861** BUCKLE *Hist. Civ.* (1903) II. 89 In France..the great nobles held their lands, not so much by grant, as by prescription.

†**b.** A noble or famous person. ***nine nobles***, the nine worthies. *Obs. rare.*

c **1470** *Gol. & Gaw.* 1116 Than thei nobillis at neid yeid to thair note new. **1535** STEWART *Cron. Scot.* II. 698 This Godefryde..Quhilk numberit is amang the nobillis nyne. **1549** *Compl. Scot.* 4 To be ane of the principal of al the nyne noblis.

c. A leader or protector of men hired to replace striking workers. *U.S. slang.*

1930 *Amer. Mercury* Dec. 456/2 *Noble*, a guard for strike breakers. 'Me work? Don't be foolish. I'm a noble, I am.' **1937** *N.Y. Times* 22 Dec. 22 *Noble*, a lieutenant of strike operations usually in charge of a detachment of guards, sluggers and finks. **1950** H. E. GOLDIN *Dict. Amer. Underworld Lingo* 145/2 *Noble* (rare), a guard hired to protect strike-breakers. **1960** WENTWORTH & FLEXNER *Dict. Amer. Slang* 356/2 *Noble.* 1. A strike-breaker's guard. 2. The boss of a gang of strike-breakers; a chief fink.

2. a. A former English gold coin, first minted by Edward III: by 1550 its value had settled at 6*s.* 8*d.* Also *George-*, *thistle noble*; ANGEL, ROSE NOBLE: see these words.

[The following are some of the older statements relative to the value of the noble at different periods:—

1387 TREVISA *Higden* VI. 259 A duket þat is worþy half an Englisshe noble. *c* **1450** *Chron. Eng.* (MS. Bodl. 754) lf. 132 [The] floreyne that was cleped the noble, valewe vjs. and viijd. **1469** in *Archaeol.* XV. 167 One pece therof rennyng for x.s. of sterlings, which shalbe called the noble of gold. **1542** RECORDE *Gr. Artes* (1575) 197 An olde Noble, called an Henrye, is worthe 2 Crownes,..that is 10 *s.* *Ibid.*, A Noble, called a George, is worth 6 *s.* 8 *d.* **1596** SPENSER *State Irel.* Wks. (Globe) 666/1, I doe put onely seaven nobles rent and composition.., that is 40*s.* for composition, and 6*s.* 8*d.* for cheiferie to her Majestie. **1685** BAXTER *Paraphr. N.T.* Mark xiv. 45 Fifty two French crowns, and a half a crown is 6*s.* 8*d.*, our Noble. **1706** PHILLIPS (ed. Kersey), A Noble is also a Scotch Coin worth 6½*d.* English, and of which three make a Pound.]

1362 LANGL. *P. Pl.* A. III. 46 Heo tolde him a tale and tok him a noble, For to ben hire beode-mon. **1436** *Pol. Poems* (Rolls) II. 175 By iiij. pens lesse in the noble rounde, That is xij. pens in the golden pounde. **1496-7** *Act 12 Hen. VII*, c. 6 Preamble, Att whiche tyme the seid fyne was but of the value of halfe an olde noble sterling. **1523** LD. BERNERS *Froiss.* I. clxiii. 201 He payed for his raunsome sixe thousande nobuls. **1551** T. WILSON *Logike* (1580) 8 b, A Priest had a Noble for preachyng a funerall sermon. **1613** R. C. *Times' Whistle* IV. 1443 For a noble I'le stand thy friend, & healp thee out of trouble. **1677** YARRANTON *Eng. Impr.* 110, I would that I had met this Countrey-man Forty years ago, it had been Five hundred Nobles in my way. **1714** *Lond. Gaz.* No. 5207/3 John Meeres of Gosport..was.. Fined Twenty Nobles. **1821** SCOTT *Kenilw.* iii, She may aid me to melt my nobles into groats. **1873** DIXON *Two Queens* IV. XIX. i. 5 Henry heard him play, and tossed him twenty nobles.

b. In phr. ***to bring one's noble to ninepence***, etc., denoting wasteful extravagance. Now *rare* or *Obs.*

1568 FULWELL *Like Will to Like* D iv, Tom tospot since he went hence, Hath increased a noble iust vnto nine pence. **1660** HOWELL *Parly of Beasts* 59 You make the poor husband oftentimes to turn a noble to nine-pence. **1699** R. L'ESTRANGE *Erasm. Colloq.* (1711) 299, I have e'en brought a noble to nine-pence. **1782** V. KNOX *Ess.* clxx. (1819) III. 249, I do not bring my noble to ninepence and my ninepence to nothing.

'noble, *sb.*[2] *Sc.* [? f. prec.] (See quot.)

1808 JAMIESON, *Nobles*, the Pogge, or Armed Bullhead, a fish... This is the name at Newhaven. **1810** NEILL *List Fishes* 9 (Jam.).

†**'noble,** *v. Obs.* [f. NOBLE *a.* Cf. ENNOBLE *v.*, and OF. *noblir* (rare).] *trans.* To make noble, to ennoble. Also †**'nobled** *ppl. a.*

c **1386** CHAUCER *Second Nun's T.* 40 Thow nobledest so ferforth oure nature, That no desdeyn the makere hadde [etc.]. **1430-40** LYDG. *Bochas* I. xii. (1544) 23 This town was nobled by title of other thinges. **1493** *Festivall* (W. de W. 1515) 171 Almes..is a holy thynge, for it..multyplyeth thy eres & nobleth the mynde. **1550** BALE *Eng. Votaries* I. 77 b, Onlye is it Gods true knowledge, that nobleth yow before hym. **1554** in *Harington's Nugæ Ant.* (1804) I. 58 Suffer your nobled humanitie to overcome the contrarie perswasions. **1595** W. CLARKE *Polimanteia* T, Haue you not had..a Princesse truelie nobled with all vertues. **1621** BP. MONTAGU *Diatribæ* 353 Your nobling and divining him elsewhere would not serve your turne.

†**noblé.** *Obs. rare.* Also **noblee, nobullé.** [a. OF. *noblée*, f. *noble* NOBLE *a.*] Nobility.

c **1400** *Brut* ix. (E.E.T.S.) 16 If it were soþe þat men spoken of þe grete noblee and wisdome..of Kyng Salamon. **1422** tr. *Secreta Secret., Priv. Priv.* 199 Than he hym bethoght of the grete noble that he demenyd in Ierusalem. *a* **1440** *Sir Degrev.* 92 In ych place whaer he comme..They hade halowed hys name With gret nobullé.

†**'noblehead.** *Obs.* [f. NOBLE *a.* + -HEAD.] Nobleness.

1382-8 WYCLIF *Job*, 3rd Prol., Oon exsaumpler of noblehed. *c* **1425** *Cursor M.* 848 (Trin.), þat was not done al for nede But þourȝe his owne noble-hede. **1447** BOKENHAM *Seyntys* (Roxb.) 50 O soverayne evere lastyng majeste..Up on me rew for thy nobylhede. *c* **1475** *Partenay* 6339, I hire moche speke off hys roiall estate,..The which I hold of hug[e] noblehed.

nobleie, variant of NOBLEY(E *Obs.*

nobleite ('nəʊb(ə)laɪt). *Min.* [f. the name of Levi F. *Noble*, 20th-cent. U.S. geologist + -ITE[1].] A hydrated calcium borate, $CaB_6O_{10}.4H_2O$, found as colourless, monoclinic crystals at Furnace Creek, Death Valley, California.

1961 R. C. ERD et al. in *Amer. Mineralogist* XLVI. 560 The naturally occurring hydrous calcium borate, $CaO.3B_2O_3.4H_2O$..is named nobleite in honor of Dr. Levi F. Noble, geologist in the U.S. Geological Survey since 1909, in further recognition of his fundemantal contributions to geologic knowledge of the Death Valley region. **1964** *Ibid.* XLIX. 1549 Tunellite..is isostructural with the Ca analogue, nobleite. **1968** I. KOSTOV *Minerology* 435 Colemanite Group. The following minerals belong to this group:..nifontovite..tunellite..nobleite.

†**'noblely,** *adv. Obs.* Also 3-4 **-like, -lich(e.** [f. NOBLE *a.* + -LY[2].] Nobly.

c **1300** *Havelok* 2640 An erl, that he saw priken thore, Ful noblelike upon a stede. *c* **1320** *Sir Tristr.* 1536 So noblelich he hem hiȝt. *c* **1400** *R. Glouc.'s Chron.* (Rolls) 892 (MS. *a*), Cunedag..nobleliche þre & þritti ȝer huld þis kinedom. *c* **1400** *Destr. Troy* 10318 An nomly in þis note, so noblely, þou sayes [etc.]. *a* **1562** G. CAVENDISH *Wolsey* (1893) 101 To foresee all thyngs touchyng our rooms, to be noblely garnyshed accordyngly. **1565** COOPER *Thesaurus, Amplifice*, nobely.

nobleman ('nəʊb(ə)lmən). [f. NOBLE *a.* + MAN.]

1. One of the nobility; a peer.

1526 *Pilgr. Perf.* (W. de W. 1531) 210 Lyke as a noble man yᵗ hath a iourney to do of necessite. **1580** G. HARVEY in *Spenser's Wks.* (Grosart) I. 437 Any noblemans petitory or commendatorye letters. **1624** CAPT. SMITH *Virginia* I. 3 The Noblemen [had] fiue or sixe [pendants] in an eare. **1678** BUNYAN *Pilgr.* I. (1900) 88 There is not one of these Noblemen should have any longer a being in this Town. **1700** DRYDEN *Pref. Fables* Ess. (ed. Ker) II. 246 A certain nobleman.., beginning with a dog-kennel, never lived to finish the palace he had contrived. **1797** MRS. RADCLIFFE *Italian* i, A nobleman of one of the most ancient families of the kingdom of Naples. **1831** SIR J. SINCLAIR *Corr.* II. 350 Two Prussian noblemen who came to Scotland in 1806. **1855** KINGSLEY *Westw. Ho!* x, A condescension..on the part of a nobleman of Spain.

b. Formerly, a nobleman's son as a member of the University of Oxford or Cambridge. Also *attrib.*

1682 SHADWELL *Medal* 8 At Cambridge first your scurrilous Vein began, When sawcily you traduc'd a Nobleman. *Note.* A Lords Son, and all Noblemens Sons, are called Noblemen there. **1715** HEARNE *Collect.* (O.H.S.) V. 105 Three or four Scholars of note and Distinction, one of them being a Nobleman..of Worcester Coll. *Ibid.* 118 All the Noblemen Scholars in town. *a* **1814** BP. WATSON *Anecd.* (1817) 29 Some defects in the University education, especially with respect to Noblemen and Fellow-Commoners.

2. *pl.* The superior pieces in the game of chess.

1680 COTTON *Compl. Gamester* (ed. 2) 37 The Pawns are all alike, and each Nobleman hath one of them to wait upon him. **1761** HOYLE *Games, Chess* (1778) 145, I speak now, as supposing all the Noblemen are gone; if not, they are to attend your Pawns. **1797** *Encycl. Brit.* (ed. 3) IV. 639/2 The difference of the worth of pawns is not so great as that of noblemen.

Hence **'noblemanly** *a.*

1809-12 MAR. EDGEWORTH *Absentee* ix, I would give the contents of three such bills to be sure of such noblemanly conduct as yours. **1824** HEBER *Jrnl.* I. 196 Nothing was gaudy, but all extremely respectable and noblemanly. **1832** FR. A. KEMBLE *Rec. of Girlhood* (1878) III. 167 Being written in gentlemanly (noblemanly?) blank verse instead of turgid prose.

noble-minded, *a.* [f. NOBLE *a.* + MIND *sb.*] Possessed of or characterized by a noble mind, magnanimous.

1586 T. B. *La Primaud. Fr. Acad.* I. 372 Although this beseemeth not a noble-minded man. **1601** SHAKS. *Jul. C.* I. iii. 122 Some certaine of the Noblest minded Romans. **1713** ROWE *Jane Shore* I. ii, The noble-minded Hastings..Has kindly underta'en to be my Advocate. **1783** BOSWELL *Johnson* (1791) II. 448 He is, I really believe, noble-minded, generous, and princely. **1829** MARRYAT *F. Mildmay* ii, The courage..of a noble-minded boy is..broken down by ill-usage. **1855** MACAULAY *Hist. Eng.* XV. III. 514 The noble-minded Lady Russell.

Hence **noble'mindedness.**

1583 GOLDING *Calvin on Deut.* iii. 15 Good zeale, courage, and noblemindednesse. **1840** CARLYLE *Heroes* (1858) 220 The characteristic of noblemindedness. **1863** 'OUIDA' *Held in Bondage* (1870) 99 Praising me for my liberality and noble-mindedness.

nobleness ('nəʊb(ə)lnɪs). Forms: 5 **nobyl-, nobul-,** 5-6 **nobil-,** 4- **nobleness.** Also 5 **-nace,** 5-7 **-nes,** 4-7 **-nesse.** [f. NOBLE *a.* + -NESS.]

1. The state or quality of being noble, in various senses of the adj.; nobility.

14.. in *Tundale's Vis.* (1843) 105 To do honor to hys nobylnes With hem thei toke gold and grete ryches. **1470-85** MALORY *Arthur* XI. ix. 585 All kynges..may not fynde such a knyghte for to speke of his nobylnesse and curtosye. **1509** FISHER *Funeral Serm. C'tess Richmond* Wks. (1876) 290 This noblenes of blode they haue which descended of noble lynage. **1581** SIDNEY *Apol. Poetrie* (Arb.) 30 Wee can shewe the Poets noblenes. **1628** WITHER *Brit. Rememb.* VI. 1443 Whose vertues, and whose noblenesse, Brought honor to the seats they did possesse. **1660** SHARROCK *Vegetables* Ep. Ded., The whole piece..seems destitute of beauty, and without anything of worth, value, or nobleness. **1715** CHAPPELOW *Way to get Rich* (1717) 141 He tells you the lustre and nobleness of it, a jewel fit for the cabinet of a king. **1747** CARTE *Hist. Eng.* I. 21 Making his countrymen vye with the old Romans in the nobleness of their descent. **1775** JOHNSON in *Boswell* 1 Apr., A fighting cock has a nobleness of resolution. **1846** RUSKIN *Mod. Paint.* II. III. ii. §2 We must prove the nobleness of the delights, and thence the nobleness of the animal. **1874** GREEN *Short Hist.* iv. §3. 176 There was a nobleness in Edward's nature from which the baser influences of chivalry fell away.

†**b.** With personal pronouns as a title. *Obs.*

a **1400-50** *Alexander* 2777 Nostanday, to ȝour nobilnes þat ay my nek bowis,..my-selfe I comand. **1422** tr. *Secreta Secret., Priv. Priv.* 122 Y here translate to youre Souerayne nobilnes the boke of arystotle. **1528** ROY *Rede me* (Arb.) 84 As sone as my lady he dothe se..He saluteth her noblenes. **1568** GRAFTON *Chron.* II. 306 They desyred his noblenesse to haue some consideration of them. *a* **1592** GREENE *Jas. IV*, III. ii, We will attend your noblenes. **1760-72** H. BROOKE *Fool of Qual.* (1809) III. 143 So please your nobleness, I intend to leave London.

†**2.** Display, splendour; an occasion of this. *Obs.*

1523 LD. BERNERS *Froiss.* I. xxxiv. 48 Ther might haue been sene great noblenesse, and baners and penons.. wauyng in yᵉ wynde. **1657** HOWELL *Londinop.* 62 If any Triumph or Noblenesse were to be done,..the said Leaden-Hall is the most meet and convenient place. **1679** *Lond. Gaz.* No. 1453/4 The Entertainment was great and splendid, and all things performed with great Order and Nobleness.

†**3.** A noble person; *collect.* nobility. *Obs.*

c **1489** CAXTON *Sonnes of Aymon* i. 16 At the which battaylle..dyed greate noblenesses of kinges, princes, Dukes [etc.]. *Ibid.* 17 We have loste there ryghte greate chevalry and noblenesse. **1523** LD. BERNERS *Froiss.* I. ccxxxv. 332 The church that day was so full of noblenesse, that a man might nat a remoued his fete.

noblesse (nəʊ'blɛs). Forms: 3-4 **noblesce,** 5-8 **-less,** 5-6, 8 **-les,** 5 **-lisse;** 4 **-lesse.** [a. OF. *noblece, -esce, -esse*, = Prov. *noblessa, -eza*, Sp. *nobleza*, Pg. *nobreza*, obs. It. *nobilezza*:—Rom. type **nobilitia*: see NOBLE *a.* and -ESS[2].

Common in ME. and frequent down to the 17th cent. In later use mainly, if not entirely, a direct re-adoption from F.]

1. Noble birth or condition; nobility, nobleness.

a **1225** *Ancr. R.* 166 þe ueorðe reisun is preoue of noblesce & or largesse. ? *a* **1366** CHAUCER *Rom. Rose* 1108 Upon the tresses of Richesse Was sette a cercle for noblesse. *c* **1384** —— *H. Fame* I. 471 Yet sawgh I neuer suche noblesse Of ymages. *c* **1407** HENRY SCOGAN *Moral Ballad* 73 Here may ye see that vertuous noblesse Cometh not to you by way of auncestrye. **1470-85** MALORY *Arthur* IX. xxxi. 387 Whan sir Tristram beheld the noblesse of these xx Knyghtes he merueiled of their good dedes. **1538** CROMWELL in Merriman *Life & Lett.* (1902) II. 118 The good affection whiche I bere towardes her for her vertues wisedome and noblesse. **1594** KYD *Cornelia* II. 297 True noblesse neuer doth the thing it should not. **1611** SPEED *Hist. Gt. Brit.* IX. xii. (1623) 707 It being a thing perpetuall and solemne not to fight without those signes of Noblesse. **1653** JER. TAYLOR *Serm. for Year* I. iii. 38 His arms of honour are extinguished, the noblesse of his Ancestours is forgotten. **1709** MRS. MANLEY *Secret Mem.* (1720) III. 227 Had he had a Noblesss of Soul.., what might he not have done? **1887** RUSKIN *Preterita* II. 210 The noblesse of thought which makes the simplest word best.

†**b.** As a form of address. *Obs.*

1412-20 LYDG. *Chron. Troy* I. vii, We praye to your hygh noblesse To our purpose for to condiscende. **1425** *Rolls of Parlt.* IV. 271/2 Ye protestation made by Sir Wauter Beauchamp..by your noblesse amitted and graunted.

2. The nobility; persons of noble rank.

1598 DALLINGTON *Meth. Trav.* S iv, The French Noblesse, glorying in their Armes, call themselves The Arme of their country. **1615** G. SANDYS *Travels* (1637) 1 The Princes of the blood discontented, the noblesse factious. **1666** DRYDEN *Ann. Mirab.* Pref., That advantage

..which the noblesse of France would never suffer in their peasants. **1683** TEMPLE *Mem.* Wks. 1720 I. 405 A Scum of the mean People, that hated and spoil'd the Noblesse of the Province. **1753** *Scots Mag.* Oct. 481/1 In France one of their noblesse must not marry a *roturiere.* **1796** MICHELL *Princ. Legis.* 153 A very few years ago, the opinions..of Europe were decidedly in favour of a monarchy, a noblesse and a census. **1813** *Sporting Mag.* LXI. 243 Some of the first families of our Noblesse. **1846** GROTE *Hist. Greece* II. II. iii. (1849) 370 The abundance of corn and cattle from the neighbouring plains sustained..a proud and disorderly noblesse. **1898** BODLEY *France* I. I. iii. 170 Few of the local noblesse under the old Monarchy bore titles.

‖**noblesse oblige** (nəʊ'blɛs əʊ'bliːʒ), *phr.* [Fr.] Phrase suggesting that noble ancestry constrains (to honourable behaviour); privilege entails responsibility. Also in extended use. Also as *sb.* and *attrib.*

1837 F. A. KEMBLE *Let.* 1 Aug. in *Rec. Later Life* (1882) I. 86 To be sure, if 'noblesse oblige', royalty must do so still more. **1864** J. H. NEWMAN *Apol.* I. 10 Do you think I can let you go scot free instead of myself? No; *noblesse oblige.* Go to the shades, old man. **1873** C. M. YONGE *Pillars of House* IV. xxxix. 150, I always regarded you as a sacred personage, condemned to *noblesse oblige,* and all that! **1896** BEERBOHM *Happy Hypocrite* in *Yellow Bk.* Oct. 12 *Noblesse oblige*..an aristocrat should be very careful of his good name. **1903** CHESTERTON *Robert Browning* v. 114 When someone excused coarseness..on the ground of genius, he said, 'That is an error: Noblesse oblige.' **1923** D. H. LAWRENCE *Birds, Beasts & Flowers* 65 Blessed are the pure in heart and the fathomless in bright pride; The loveliness that knows *noblesse oblige.* **1932** J. M. S. TOMPKINS *Popular Novel in England 1770–1800* iv. 153 The Magdalens of gentle blood ..descend..to the family vault. It is a clear case of *noblesse oblige.* **1968** *Listener* 6 June 713/2 *Noblesse oblige* Toryism.. is giving way to..managerial Conservatism. **1973** J. SHUB *Moscow by Nightmare* xiii. 150 He was pleased to inform the servants of his whereabouts; it simplified their reporting for the KGB. *Noblesse oblige.*

†'**noblety.** *Obs.* Forms: 4 noblete, 4–5 nobilte; 5 nobylte, nobeltee, -di; 6 nobiltie. [a. OF. *nobleté* (*-ti*): see NOBLE *a.* and -TY.] Nobility, nobleness; splendour.

1340–70 *Alex. & Dind.* 192 Þe kidde king alixandre..Þat name haþ of noblete. **1387** TREVISA *Higden* (Rolls) I. 235 For to hiȝte þe noblete of þe citee þe Romaynes made a wommans ymage in bras. *Ibid.* VIII. 15 Nyh al þe nobilte of Cristen men deide þat tyme. **1422** tr. *Secreta Secret., Priv. Priv.* 179 Precious stones, riche clothis, and grete nobeldi. *Ibid.* 203 Of dyuers..necessary nobilteis of the vertu of orison. *a* **1450** *Knt. de la Tour* (1868) 110 The feste, where there was gret nobeltee and plente of richesses. **1500–20** DUNBAR *Poems* xxi. 26 All gentrice and nobiltie Ar passit out of he degre.

noblewoman ('nəʊb(ə)lwʊmən). [Cf. NOBLEMAN.] A woman of noble birth or rank.

1575 LANEHAM *Lett.* (1871) 59 A Noblewooman that I am ..mooch boound vntoo. **1607** ROWLANDS *Hist. Earl Warw.* L 2 Who unto Pilgrims did more bounty show, Than any Noble-woman in the Land. **1641** *Lords Spiritual* 13 Then would it also follow.., That Noble-women should have no Lords to be their tryers. **1762** *Biogr. Dict.* IX. 227 A noblewoman of the county of Avignon. **1861** THACKERAY *Four Georges* i. (1862) 52 The countess was a large-sized noblewoman. **1896** ECKENSTEIN *Wom. under Monasticism* 149 The young noblewoman stayed at home.

†**nobley(e,** *sb. Obs.* Forms: α. 3–4 nobleie (4 nobel-), 4–5 nobleye. β. 4. noblei, 4–5 nobley (5 nobeley). γ. 4–5 noblay (4 nobel-), nobillay. [a. F. *nobleie, -leye* fem., or *noblei, noblai* masc., f. *noble* NOBLE *a.*]

1. Nobility of nature or rank; noble quality, condition, or estate; splendour, pomp.

α. *c* **1290** *Beket* 245 in *S. Eng. Leg.* I. 113 Al-to nobleie of þe worlde his continaunce he brouȝte. *c* **1330** R. BRUNNE *Chron. Wace* (Rolls) 105 Þai sayd it for pride & nobleye. *c* **1380** WYCLIF *Wks.* (1880) 204 ȝif þei lyuen in pride of herte for nobeleie of blood or kyn. *c* **1400** tr. *Secreta Secret., Gov. Lordsh.* 58 Þe nobleie of þy free wyl.

β. *c* **1300** *St. Kenelm* 284 in *E.E.P.* (1862) 55 [To] do þat wiþ gret nobley þat hi ischryned were. **1338** R. BRUNNE *Chron.* (1810) 44 With mykelle nobley ageyn Eilred he nam. *c* **1380** WYCLIF *Serm.* Sel. Wks. I. 257 Noblei of oure prelatis shulde not lette hem to be pore. **1425** *Rolls of Parlt.* IV. 268/2 Ye princely nobley of you my said Lord. **1470–85** MALORY *Arthur* VIII. xxix. 316 Anone they were rychely wedded with grete nobley. *c* **1530** *Crt. of Love* i, Me list my writing to convey, In that I can to please her high nobley.

γ. *c* **1330** *Arth. & Merl.* 2468 (Kölbing), Par ma fay, Þis is a begger of noblay. **13..** *Gaw. & Gr. Knt.* 91 Anoþer maner meued him eke, þat he þurȝ nobelay had nomen. **1375** BARBOUR *Bruce* VIII. 211 As man of gret noblay He held toward the trist his vay. *a* **1400–50** *Alexander* 2716, I haue herd..Of þi noblay now o newe time a-nentes my modire. *c* **1470** *Gol. & Gaw.* 899 His name and his nobillay wes noght for to nyte.

2. Articles of value; valuable possessions.

a **1350** *St. Matthew* 196 in Horstm. *Altengl. Leg.* (1881) 134 Gold and siluer and precius stanes, And oþer nobillay for þe nanes. *c* **1400** MAUNDEV. (Roxb.) xxxii. 147 Mykill ricches and nobillay of tresour and precious stane. *c* **1400** *Ywaine & Gaw.* 3566 It es no man that haves So mekil tresor ne nobillay.

3. Persons of noble rank.

1390 GOWER *Conf.* I. 110 With lordes and with gret nobleie Of lusti folk that were yonge. **1459** *Rolls of Parlt.* V. 348/2 All the Lordes, Knightes and Nobley in your Host.

Hence †**nobley** *v.*, to ennoble. *Obs. rare.*

c **1450** tr. *De Imitatione* III. lx. 141 Grace or charite, wher-wiþ who þat be nobleied shal be worþy euerlastyng lif.

†**noblier,** obs. compar. of NOBLE *a.*

1398 TREVISA *Barth. De P.R.* IV. ix. (1495) 93 Soo flewme is noblyer than colera or malencolia. *c* **1400** *Apol. Loll.* 106 Þe patriarkis, þat were þa nobliar of þe Jewis, herdid bestis. **1602** WARNER *Albion's Eng.* Epit. 367 Likewise in euery Shire of the Noblier and of chiefe note was a yeerely choise of a Shire-Reeue.

†'**noblify,** *v. Obs. rare*$^{-1}$. [f. NOBLE *a.* + -FY.] *trans.* To ennoble.

1600 HOLLAND *Livy* XXII. xxxiv. 453 Those who of commoners are now noblified are all..of the same profession.

†'**noblish,** *v. Obs. rare*$^{-1}$. [Cf. ENNOBLISH *v.*] *trans.* To ennoble.

1483 CAXTON *Gold. Leg.* 99/2 The blessyd saynt Stephen was noblysshid by many myracles.

nobly ('nəʊblɪ), *adv.* Forms: α. 3 noblyche, 3–4 -liche, 4 -lich, 5 -leche; 4 nobeliche, -lyche. β. 4 nobely, 4–5 -illy, 5 -elly, -ully, -ylly, -yly, 6 -ily; 4– nobly. See also NOBLELY. [f. NOBLE *a.* + -LY^{2}.] In a noble manner.

1. With noble courage or spirit; gallantly, bravely; in a lofty or exalted manner.

1297 R. GLOUC. (Rolls) 5545 Þis noble king aþelston.. Nobliche & wel he faȝt. *c* **1330** *Arth. & Merl.* 4880 (Kölbing), No herd men neuer so fewe in lond, Noblicher so fele wiþstond. **1387** TREVISA *Higden* (Rolls) IV. 73 Þe consuls of Rome sette busshementes for hym, and he defendede hym nobeliche. *c* **1420** LYDG. *Assembly of Gods* 1073 Nobully theym bare and faught myghtyly. **1470–85** MALORY *Arthur* VIII. iv. 278 Syr Marhaus the good knyght that was nobly preued. **1607** HARINGTON in *Nugæ Ant.* (1804) II. 243 The arch-bishop did much noblier to hazard this obliquie of some idle tongues. **1654–66** EARL ORRERY *Parthen.* (1676) 717 His Navy could not have been Noblier lost. **1692** E. WALKER tr. *Epictetus' Mor.* Introd., His rich Soul aloft did soar, And nobly left the drossy ground. **1776** GIBBON *Decl. & F.* xi. I. 375 No general had more nobly deserved a triumph than Aurelian. **1784** COWPER *Task* v. 705 Patriots have toiled, and in their country's cause Bled nobly. **1856** FROUDE *Hist. Eng.* (1858) I. ii. 177 His impulses, in general nobly directed, had never known contradiction. **1886** —— in *Good Wds.* July 378 If we believe nobly about ourselves we have a chance of living nobly.

2. Splendidly, magnificently, finely.

1297 R. GLOUC. (Rolls) 3279 Þis feste was noble ynou, & nobliche ydo. *c* **1330** R. BRUNNE *Chron. Wace* (Rolls) 9761 Nobliche his court he ledde. *c* **1375** *Cursor M.* 7408 (Fairf.), Dauid cowde..nobely harpe and sing wiþ rote. *c* **1394** *P. Pl. Crede* 128 Þi name schall noblich ben wryten & wrouȝt for the nones. *c* **1430** *Pilgr. Lyf Manhode* I. cxxxix. (1869) 72 She hadde now arayed me queyntliche and nobleche. *c* **1450** *Mirour Saluacioun* (Roxb.) 2 The temple Salomon belded to god noblyie. *a* **1533** LD. BERNERS *Huon* lxxxi. 241 Thus.. kyng Charlemayn nobly accompanyed rode..by his iourneyes. **1568** GRAFTON *Chron.* II. 247 The two Cardynals went thorough Henault at the desire of yᵉ erle, who feasted them right nobly. **1613** SHAKS. *Hen. VIII,* IV. i. 90 The Rod, and Bird of Peace, and all such Emblemes Laid Nobly on her. **1668** PEPYS *Diary* 2 Nov., There I was stopped and dined mighty nobly at a good table. **1724** SWIFT *Drapier's Lett.* vii. Wks. 1751 IX. 93 The Painted Chamber, and Court of Requests,..are never so nobly filled, as when an Irish Appeal is under Debate. **1871** B. TAYLOR *Faust* (1875) II. iii. 185 Cheerful and brave and bold, and nobly formed is he. **1890** 'R. BOLDREWOOD' *Col.-Reformer* (1891) 161 A nobly proportioned..apartment.

3. In that manner which is involved in noble breeding, connexions, or descent; esp. ***nobly born.***

1591 SPENSER *Teares Muses* 446 What bootes it then to come from glorious Forefathers, or to have been nobly bredd? **1592** SHAKS. *Rom. & Jul.* III. v. 182 A Gentleman.. Of faire Demeanes, Youthfull, and Nobly Allied. **1684** DRYDEN *Ep. Earl Roscommon* 55 Now will invention and translation thrive, When authors nobly born will bear their part. **1719** J. T. PHILIPPS tr. *Thirty-four Confer.* 283 That our Souls are nobly and heavenly descended, I allow. **1822** BYRON *Werner* I. i, I, born nobly also,..was taught a different lesson. **1854** RUSKIN *Arch. & Paint.* ii. 94 Thinking it better to be nobly remembered than nobly born.

4. *Comb.*, as ***nobly-born, -dowered, -mannered, -minded, -peopled, -privileged, -sacred.***

1620 T. GRANGER *Div. Logike* 340 A man of noble mind begetteth noblie-minded children. **1648** J. BEAUMONT *Psyche* I. iii, By free Carrowsing in these nobly-sacred Streams. *Ibid.* VII. cxcii, O nobly-privileg'd Poverty. **1789** CHARLOTTE SMITH *Ethelinde* (1814) V. 103 The nobly-born, and nobly-minded Montgomery. **1822** BYRON *Werner* III. i, Asking after you With nobly-born impatience. **1859** TENNYSON *Guinevere* 332 These two Were the most nobly-manner'd men of all. **1870** BRYANT *Iliad* I. v. 158 Who quickly will destroy Your nobly-peopled city. *Ibid.* vi. 202 The nobly-dowered Andromache Came forth to meet him.

nobob, variant of NABOB.

Nobodaddy ('nəʊbəʊdædɪ). [Blend of NOBODY + DADDY.] Used by William Blake, and others after him: a disrespectful name for God, esp. when regarded anthropomorphically. Also *transf.*, someone no longer held in esteem, and *attrib.*

c **1793** W. BLAKE in *Compl. Writings* (1972) 171 (*title*) To Nobodaddy. *Ibid.* 187 Then again old Nobodaddy swore He ne'er had seen such a thing before, Since Noah was shut in the ark. **1921** G. B. SHAW *Back to Methuselah* p. lxiii, It did not occur to us that Old Nobodaddy, instead of being ridiculous fiction, might be only an imposter. *Ibid.* p. lxvi, The moment Nobodaddy was slain by Darwin, Public Opinion, as divine deputy, lost its sanctity. **1922** JOYCE *Ulysses* 203 Whether these be sins or virtues old Nobodaddy will tell us at doomsday leet. *Ibid.* 388 But the braggart boaster cried that an old Nobodaddy was in his cups it was muchwhat indifferent and he would not lag behind his lead. **1926** A. MACLEISH (*title*) Nobodaddy. **1962** *Listener* 29 Nov. 932/1 Goethe is in danger of turning into a Nobodaddy —a booming, boring member of that depressed class, the Illustrious Dead. **1976** *Guardian* 8 Jan. 12/7, I believe we see here [*sc.* in the poetry of Tristan Tzara] the great Nobodaddy Dadaist losing out to the truthful inclusiveness of our women's contemporaries.

nobody ('nəʊbədɪ). [f. NO *a.* + BODY *sb.* 13.] Written as two words from the 14th to the 18th c., and with hyphen in the 17th and 18th.

1. a. No person; no one.

1338 R. BRUNNE *Chron.* (1810) 183 No body bot he alone vnto þe Cristen cam. **1484** CAXTON *Fables of Alfonce* xi, I wyll wel, yf thow wilt swere that thou shalt neuer reherce it to no body. *c* **1489** —— *Sonnes of Aymon* iv. 120 And thenne the foure brethern wente vp to the hall, and met wyth noo bodi. **1535** COVERDALE *2 Kings* vii. 5 And whan they came to the vttemost ende of yᵉ tentes, beholde, there was no body. **1568** GRAFTON *Chron.* II. 268 There was no body in them, but two fayre Damoselles. **1621** S. WARD *Life Faith* 8 Hee ingrosseth the common God to himselfe, as if his and no bodies else. **1663** COWLEY *Ess., Obscurity,* In Places where they are by no body known. **1693** NORRIS *Pract. Disc.* (1698) IV. 10 That a thing that is so much every Body's Concern, should be almost no Body's Discourse. **1721** AMHERST *Terræ Fil.* No. 40. 210 The advantages..are so palpable, that, at the bare mention of it, no body can be at a loss to perceive them. **1754** SHERLOCK *Disc.* I. iii. (1759) 135 Mysteries... Things which no-body can under-stand. **1791** MRS. RADCLIFFE *Rom. Forest* x, Your father nor nobody else has ever sent after you. **1813** WELLINGTON in Gurw. *Desp.* (1838) XI. 136, I can send..nobody from hence to relieve you. **1860** TYNDALL *Glac.* I. xvi. 108 Nobody knew anything of the state of the snow this year. **1885** *Manch. Exam.* 6 Nov. 5/3 The effort to please every-body usually results in pleasing nobody.

Prov. **1611** COTGRAVE *Dict.* s.v. *Ouvrage,* Euerie bodies worke is no bodies worke. **1661** WALTON *Angler* (ed. 3) ii. 52 A wise friend of mine did usually say, That which is every bodies businesse is no bodies businesse. **1709** STEELE *Tatler* No. 18 ¶1 Because a Thing is every Body's Business, it is no Body's Business. **1725** DEFOE (*title*) Every-body's business is no-body's business. **1828** MACAULAY in *Edin. Rev.* Sept. 103 The business of every body is the business of nobody. **1829** COBBETT *Advice to Young Men* vi. 345 Public property is never so well taken care of as private property; and this, too, on the maxim, that 'that which is every body's business is no [*sic*] nobody's business'.

b. Followed by *they, their,* or *them.*

1548 UDALL, etc. *Erasm. Par. Luke* 94 b, No bodye will receiue you into their house. **1628** tr. *Mathieu's Powerfull Favorite* 108 No body should dare to stretch out their arme, or present their bosome to receiue him. **1704** N. N. tr. *Boccalini's Advts. fr. Parnass.* II. 13 Such Confusion, that no body knew what they were to do, or what to let alone. **1755** WARBURTON in W. & Hurd *Lett.* (1809) 201 Nobody has yet written against me, but at their own expence. **1831** WHEWELL in Todhunter *Life* II. 112 Nobody will know the origin of pliocene, &c., till you tell them. **1856** F. E. PAGET *Owlet of Owlst.* 9 Nobody likes to be turned out of quarters where they have lived snugly and comfortably for scores of years. **1874** L. STEPHEN *Hours in Library* III. 333 Nobody ever put so much of themselves into their work.

2. a. A person, or persons, of no importance, authority, or social position. Phr. ***nobody's business*** (see BUSINESS 16 f); ***nobody's fool,*** a person who cannot be taken advantage of.

1581 PETTIE tr. *Guazzo's Civ. Conv.* II. (1586) 58 Let them come to writing any thing, and they are no bodie. **1599** *Broughton's Let.* vii. 21 To accompt all besides themselues.. babish,..riffaffe, nobodie. **1607** HIERON *Wks.* I. 170 If another had risen by him, and come from no body to be a man of some fashion and ability. **1608** WILLET *Hexapla Exod.* Ded. 2 Others being of sound judgement in the new Testament, are no bodie in the olde. **1778** BURNEY *Evelina* lxiv, Since I, as Mr. Lovel says, am Nobody, I seated myself quietly. **1797** GODWIN *Enquirer* I. viii. 66 A child usually feels that he is nobody. **1839** *Spirit of Times* 8 June 163/1 As to eating, jist go to Snowden's, and the way you can git good things is nobody's business. **1847** FR. A. KEMBLE *Later Life* III. 335 Miss ——, being only a banker's daughter, was of course 'nobody'. **1871** BLACKIE *Phases Mor.* 6 According to our aristocratic way of talking, she was nobody. **1923** H. C. WITWER *Fighting Blood* xi. 323 He's a little too big..for us. .. And, another thing, Ryan is nobody's fool. **1940** N. MARSH *Surfeit of Lampreys* (1941) xv. 232 They've displayed a surprising virtuosity. They're nobody's fools. **1942** [see DEATH *sb.* 17 c]. **1956** *Times* 12 Sept. 1 What she could do with a pencil, notebook, and typewriter was simply nobody's business. **1959** 'A. FRASER' *High Tension* x. 103 He smiled slightly, and I made a note that he was nobody's fool. **1962** 'E. PETERS' *Funeral of Figaro* i. 32 'He can sing like nobody's business,' said Stoker positively. **1975** *Times* 20 Sept. 9/7 Poirot..adds..' Never do I pull the leg.' That, alas, is not true. He teased poor Hastings like nobody's business.

b. Similarly with *a* and *pl.*

1583 STOCKER *Civ. Wars Low C.* IV. 6 Persones..by whom the true enheritors..are disturbed, made no bodies, or vtterly disenherited. **1657** TRAPP *Comm. Neh.* iv. 4 We are..nullified, as a company of No-bodies. **1770** FOOTE *Lame Lover* I. Wks. 1799 II. 59 There are..in this town a great number of nobodies. **1807** *Sporting Mag.* XXIX. 239 The nobodies were never above a day behind in their imitations. **1856** MRS. BROWNING *Aur. Leigh* v. 280 Being wronged by some five hundred nobodies. **1886** G. MEREDITH *Let.* 15 Nov. (1970) II. 838 In origin I am what is called here a nobody. **1899** *Educ. Rev.* Oct. 222 Which exasperates somebodies who feel they are treated as nobodies. **1922** JOYCE *Ulysses* 316 And who was he, tell us? A nobody. **1950** G. B. SHAW *Farfetched Fables* 67, I replied that if he did not realize that without them he would be a nobody he was no gentleman. **1961** NEW ENG. BIBLE 2 Cor. xii. 11 In no respect did I fall short of these superlative apostles, even if I am a nobody. **1975** *Listener* 4 Dec. 752/2

Out there, he could become a 'somebody'; in London, he felt he was a 'nobody'.

3. nobody-crab, a marine arachnid of the order Pantopoda (or Pycnogonida), having a small body and four pairs of very long, thin legs; = *pycnogonid* (s.v. PYCNO-), SEA SPIDER 1 b.

1881 [see *pycnogonid* (s.v. PYCNO-)]. **1935** *Discovery* Sept. 282/1 Those queer creatures the Pycnogonida, the so-called No-body Crabs, real Tom Noddies, with only enough body to hold together the legs, in which are situated the vital organs. **1945** T. H. SAVORY *Spiders Brit. Isles* (ed. 2) 20 Sea-spiders or nobody-crabs are found only in the sea, where they range from the littoral regions to the depths of the ocean.

Hence **ˈnobodyness**, anonymity. *rare*$^{-1}$.

1886 REES *Pleasures Book-Worm* v. 176 By far too many 'stabs in the dark' are inflicted under cover of editorial nobodyness.

no bon (nəʊ bɔ̃), *adj. phr. slang.* [NO *adv.*[1] + BON *a.*] No good.

1918 W. OWEN *Let.* 29 May (1967) 554 Music—no bon! Painting—nah pooh! **1929** *Papers Mich. Acad. Sci., Arts, & Lett.* X. 310/2 *No bon*, no good.

†**nob-pitcher.** *Obs. slang.* (See quot. 1812.)

1812 J. H. VAUX *Flash Dict.*, *Nob-pitchers*, a general term for those sharpers who attend at fairs, races, &c., to take in the flats at prick in the garter, cups and balls, and other similar artifices. **1819** *Sporting Mag.* V. 123 The cup-and-ball Macers,.. the Nob-Pitchers,.. and the Rampers.

†**nobs.** *Obs. rare.* [Of obscure origin.] A term of endearment applied to a woman; (one's) dear or darling.

a **1529** SKELTON *E. Rummyng* 225 He calleth me..His nobbes and his conny, His swetyng and his honny. *a* **1530** J. HEYWOOD *Love* (Brandl) 395 Fynde the best and next way.. And except your nobs for malous do nede ye Make brefe returne. **1567** *Trial of Treas.* Ej, My mouse, my nobs, and cony swete, My hope, and ioye, my whole delight.

So †**ˈnobsey**, a mistress. *Obs. rare*$^{-1}$.

c **1555** HARPSFIELD *Divorce Hen. VIII* (Camden) 275 Sometime [he] carried her about with him in a great chest full of holes, that his pretty nobsey might take breath at.

nobull(e, nobyl(e, obs. forms of NOBLE *a.*

nocake (ˈnəʊkeɪk). *U.S.* Forms: α. 7–9 **nocake**, 7, 9 **nokake**. β. 7–8 **nokehick**, 8 **-hock**, **nuichicke**. [American Indian: Narragansett *nokehick*, Natick *noohkik*, maize.] Indian corn parched and pounded into meal.

α. **1634** W. WOOD *New Eng. Prosp.* 68 The best of their victuals for their journey is *Nocake* (as they call it), which is nothing but Indian Corne parched in the hot ashes. *a* **1676** *New Eng. Hist. & Gen. Reg.* (1883) XXXVII. 366, 300 small baggs for each man to carry nokake,.. 50 bush. Indian corne parched and beaten to nokake. **1760** [see β]. **1859** BARTLETT *Dict. Amer.*, *Nocake*, an Indian word still used in some parts of New England. **1875** TEMPLE & SHELDON *Hist. Northfield* 46 Corn was parched and beaten fine; and sometimes was made into balls with suet. Thus prepared it was called nokake.

β. **1643** R. WILLIAMS *Key* 11 Nókehick, parch'd meal, which is a readie very wholesome food, which they eate with a little water. **1691** C. MATHER *Life Eliot* 79 Their diet has not a greater dainty than their nokehick, that is a spoonful of their parched meal. **1760** T. HUTCHINSON *Hist. Mass.* (1765) 465 A small pouch of parched corn, ground or rather pounded into meal, and called Nuichicke, which is well enough translated Nocake. **1766** *Gazetteer* 2 Jan. 2/1 Samp, hominy, succatash, and nokehock, made of it, are so many pleasing varieties.

no-ˈcalorie, *a.* [f. NO *a.* + CALORIE.] Of a food substance or diet: free from, or very low in, calories. Abbrev. **no-cal.**

1961 S. PRICE *Just for Record* x. 101 Morosely munching their no-calory diet. **1969** *Guardian* 6 Oct. 11/4 Young mothers..whose entire diet consists of cottage cheese, yogurt, and gallons of 'no-cal' pop. **1971** *Petticoat* 17 July 5 They are no-cyclamate, no-calorie, no-aftertaste sweeteners.

no can do, *colloq. phr.* [f. NO *adv.*[1] + CAN *v.*[1] + DO *v.*] It is not possible; it is not within the power of (the speaker).

1914 'SAKI' *Beasts & Super-Beasts* 289 'Sorry, my dear, no can do,' said Suzanne. **1915** A. D. GILLESPIE *Lett. from Flanders* (1916) 69 'Nap poo'..was once 'il n'y a plus', but now it's used like the Chinese 'no can do' for everything. **1923**, **1958** [see CAN *v.*[1] 8 c]. **1962** 'E. FERRARS' *Busy Body* v. 53 Sorry, no can do—not tonight.

nocardiosis (nəʊkɑːdɪˈəʊsɪs). *Path.* [f. mod.L. *Nocardi-a*, the name of a genus of actinomycetes (f. the name of E. I. E. *Nocard* (1850–1903), French veterinary pathologist + -IA[1]) + -OSIS.] Infection with, or a disease caused by, an actinomycete of the genus *Nocardia*, esp. *N. asteroides*, which is occas. pathogenic in humans, producing local lesions or more often generalized disease beginning in the lungs but tending to spread to other organs, esp. the brain, and often proving fatal.

1907 J. H. WRIGHT in Osler & McGrae *Mod. Med.* I. xvi. 341 It has been pointed out that if the name Actinomyces be not used for these microörganisms then the only permissible generic term to apply to them..is Nocardia, and disease processes produced by them should be called nocardiosis. **1920** *Arch. Dermatol. & Syphilol.* II. 137 (*heading*) Nocardiosis cutis resembling sporotrichosis. **1949** *Amer. Jrnl. Path.* XXV. 1 (*heading*) Pure granulomatous nocardiosis: a new fungus disease distinguished by intracellular parasitism. **1963** C. W. EMMONS et al. *Med. Mycol.* ix. 75 Nocardiosis is recognized in the dog oftener than in other domesticated animals. **1974** PASSMORE & ROBSON *Compan. Med. Stud.* III. I. xii. 90/2 Nocardiosis and mucormycosis are infections usually acquired by inhaling dusts.

†**ˈnocence.** *Obs. rare*$^{-1}$. [See -ENCE.] = next.

c **1620** T. ADAMS *Fatal Banquet* ii. Wks. 1861 I. 212, I would iniquity was not bolder than honesty, or that innocence might speed no worse than nocence.

†**ˈnocency.** *Obs.* [ad. L. *nocentia*: see next and -ENCY.] Guilt.

1611 FLORIO, *Nocenza*, nocency, wittingnesse, knowledge. **1650** WELDON *Crt. Jas. I*, 112 His greatnesse fortified with innocency would carry their nocencies through all dangers. **1693** G. FIRMIN *Rev. Davis's Vind.* i. 1 Offering himself to him in a State of Nocency. **1736** CARTE *Ormonde* II. 263 To make the proof of nocency so easy and general that none..might be able to escape censure.

nocent (ˈnəʊsənt), *a.* and *sb.* Now *rare.* [ad. L. *nocent-*, *nocens*, pres. pple. of *nocēre* to hurt.]

A. *adj.* **1.** Harmful, injurious, hurtful.

c **1485** *Digby Myst.* (1882) II. 321 Infecte with venom nocent. **1568** SKEYNE *The Pest* A iij, The maist nocent Sterres to mankynd. **1597** A. M. tr. *Guillemeau's Fr. Chirurg.* 4 b, Nothinge nocente or daungerous to the lyfe of the patient. **1618** BARET *Horsem.* I. 98 Though many things are now become nocent and hurtfull to man, which at the first was..seruiceable to him. **1667** MILTON *P.L.* IX. 186 Not yet in horrid Shade or dismal Den, Not nocent yet. **1708** J. PHILIPS *Cyder* I. 26 Whilst the warm limbec draws Salubrious waters from the nocent brood. **1746** W. HORSLEY *Fool* (1748) II. 9 A kind of Sheep only rendered terrible by their outside Apparatus, but not very nocent or hurtful.

Comb. **1641** R. BROOKE *Eng. Episc.* 90 Some can dispence with one of the three Grand Nocent-innocent ceremonies, some with another, some with neither.

2. Guilty; criminal.

a **1566** R. EDWARDS *Damon & Pithias* in Hazl. *Dodsley* IV. 48 He is not innocent, whom the king judgeth nocent. **1618** STUKELEY *Petit.* in *Harl. Misc.* (Malh.) III. 390 He was.. uncapable of another trial, by which he might have been found as nocent as before. **1640** HABINGTON *Edw. IV*, 227 Publique mischiefes seldome happen, but that the Prince, though not actually nocent, is in some degree guiltie. *a* **1677** BARROW *Serm.* Wks. 1716 I. 340 This manner of suffering was..unworthy of a freeman, however nocent and guilty. **1866** J. B. ROSE tr. *Ovid's Met.* 168 Fed with her innocent his nocent fire.

b. *absol.* as sing. or plural.

1568 GRAFTON *Chron.* II. 412 But now drewe on the time, the Innocent must perishe with the Nocent, and the vngiltie with the giltie. **1592** WYRLEY *Armorie* 137 Many an innocent with the nocent died. **1647** N. BACON *Disc. Govt. Eng.* I. xxv. (1739) 43 These twelve were to be sworn, neither to condemn the Innocent, nor acquit the Nocent. **1678** CUDWORTH *Intell. Syst.* I. v. § 19. 877 The innocent and the nocent, the Pious and the Impious.

B. *sb.* A guilty person.

1447 BOKENHAM *Seyntys* (Roxb.) 234 He wold me Do forsakyn to ben an innocent That he me myht makyn a nocent. *a* **1548** HALL *Chron.*, *Hen. IV* (1809) 19 That an Innocent with a Nocent, a man ungilty with a gilty, was pondered in an egall balaunce. **1606** *Proc. agst. Late Traitors* 128 Taking away some Innocents with many Nocents. **1654** tr. *Martini's Conq. China* 201 Involving in the Slaughter as well the innocents as the nocents. *c* **1685** *Lett. to Jas. II*, in *N. & Q.* 6th Ser. (1882) V. 361/2 To Kil al that came in their way without discriminating nocents from Innocents.

Hence **ˈnocently** *adv. rare*$^{-1}$.

1646 J. COOKE *Vind. Law* 21 Hadst thou rather thy husband should dye nocently than innocently.

nocerite (ˈnəʊsəraɪt). *Min.* [f. its locality, *Nocera* in Italy: named *nocerina* by Scacchi in 1881.] 'Oxyfluoride of calcium and magnesium, found in white, acicular crystals, in volcanic bombs' (Chester).

1883 DANA *Syst. Min.* App. III. 85 Nocerina—nocerite. Announced by Scacchi. **1892** E. S. DANA *J. G. Dana's Syst. Min.* (ed. 6) 175 The bombs of Nocera which have yielded the Nocerite.

†**ˈnoces.** *Obs. rare.* Also 3–4 **neoces**, 4 **neces.** [a. F. *noces* (OF. also *noeces*, *nueces*, etc.; AF. *neoces*) for *nopces*:—pop. L. **noptias*, L. *nuptias*, *-iæ*: see NUPTIALS.] Wedding.

a **1225** *Ancr. R.* 78 þe þridde time þet heo spec, þet was et te noces [*v.r.* neoces], & þer, þurh hire bone, was water iwend to wine. *c* **1320** *Cast. Love* 1263 For atte neces [*v.r.* neoces]..At þe Caane of Galylee..he torned water to wyn.

‖**noceur** (nɔsœr). [Fr.] A reveller, rake, libertine; one who stays up late at night.

1908 NEVILL & JERNINGHAM *Piccadilly to Pall Mall* iv. 157 The French *noceur* is only too pleased to show himself in the company of some well-known 'horizontale'. **1918** J. AGATE *Buzz, Buzz!* i. 11 In Ibsen the characters who bother themselves about the arts are invariably humbugs or hypocrites or *noceurs*. **1931** W. ROTHENSTEIN *Men & Memories* I. ix. 94 Though I could, on occasion, sit up most of the night, I was not a *noceur*.

noch, obs. Sc. var. *nocht*, NOUGHT.

†**noche**, variant of *nouch*, OUCH *sb.*

[**1391** *Earl Derby's Exped.* (Camden) 105/12 Cuidam homini..eo quod inuenit vnum noche domini ibidem.] **1540** *Invent.* in V. Green *Worcester* (1796) II. App. II. 5 Item, a noche, called Lyttultons noche, of gold and precious stones.

nochell, variant of NOTCHEL *v. Obs.*

nocht, Sc. variant of NOUGHT.

noci- (nəʊsɪ), comb. form of L. *noc-ēre* to do harm, used in a few terms, esp. in neurology, as **nociˈceptive** *a. Physiol.* [RE)CEPTIVE *a.*], (of a stimulus) painful; responding to or caused by such a stimulus; hence **nociˈceptor** [(RE)CEPTOR], any sensory receptor for painful stimuli; **nociˈfensor** *a.* [L. *dē-fens-*, ppl. stem (in DEFENSIVE *a.*, etc.): cf. L. *dēfensor* defender] (of a nerve) concerned in the transmission of the sensation of pain.

1904 C. S. SHERRINGTON in *Nature* 8 Sept. 463/1 In this reaction the reflex arc is (i) the receptive neurone ..(nociceptive) from the foot to the spinal segment, (ii) perhaps a short intraspinal neurone, and (iii) the motor neurone..to the flexor muscle. *Ibid.*, Stimulation (nociceptive) of the foot causes flexion of its own leg and extension of the opposite. **1956** *Nature* 18 Feb. 340/1 In the lightly anæsthetised preparations, nociceptive stimuli, twisting the pinna and electrical stimulation of the reticular activating system produced transient changes in the cortical blood-flow. **1961** *Lancet* 2 Sept. 546/2 Dr. W. Koll.. described his work on the action of various pharmacological substances on nociceptive spinal reflexes. **1974** *Sci. Amer.* Jan. 43/1 The nociceptive (*N*) cells require still stronger mechanical stimuli. **1906** C. S. SHERRINGTON *Integrative Action Nervous Syst.* ix. 330 The reaction initiated by a nociceptor..is to be regarded as consummatory. **1967** *Jrnl. Physiol.* CXC. 541 Seventy-four fibres conducting between 6 and 37 m/sec were classified as nociceptors because they responded only to damaging mechanical stimulation of the skin. **1936** T. LEWIS in *Clin. Sci.* II. 402 It will be evident that any system of nerve fibres, which in the exercise of its function gives rise to no obvious and distinctive external manifestations, will tend to escape recognition... The need to postulate a new system of nerves has arisen to explain hitherto unrecognised phenomena. The nerves of this system are at present unnamed. Because they are associated with local defence against injury I propose to call them the 'nocifensor nerves'. **1964** J. Z. YOUNG *Model of Brain* xiii. 209 They are presumed to be nocifensor (pain) fibres, coming either direct from the periphery or after synapse in the sub-vertical lobe.

†**ˈnocible**, *a. Obs. rare*$^{-1}$. [ad. med.L. *nocibilis*, f. *nocēre* to hurt: cf. NUISIBLE.] Harmful.

1490 CAXTON *Eneydos* xiii. 49 To eschew alle thynges that in this caas myghte be nocible and contrarye to her.

†**noˈciferous**, *a. Obs. rare*$^{-1}$. [f. L. type **nocifer*, f. *nocēre* to hurt + -OUS.] Harmful.

1702 EVELYN *Sylva* (1776) 342 Not that there are no nociferous trees as well as saniferous.

nocin, variant of NOWCIN, need. *Obs.*

no-city, *a.* Also **no-cities.** [NO *a.*] Of a strategy in a nuclear war: (see quot. 1966).

1962 *Economist* 8 Dec. 1014/1 Many Americans are sceptical of this 'no cities' doctrine. **1965** H. KAHN *On Escalation* vi. 124 If the war were conducted as a no-city, war. **1966** SCHWARZ & HADIK *Strategic Terminol.* 102 *No-cities strategy*, strategy based on the principle that only the enemy's forces are to be targets of nuclear strikes, and that enemy population centers are to be avoided completely or as much as possible.

†**nocive**, *a. Obs.* [ad. L. *nocīvus*, f. *nocēre* to hurt: see -IVE.] Harmful, injurious.

1538 *Abbess of Godstow* iii. 71 It is very nocive for them.. to go two mile about. *a* **1560** ROLLAND *Crt. Venus* III. 313 The man is ȝit on liue: And neuer had, na hes ane wound nociue. **1610** HOLLAND *Camden's Brit.* II. 34 All nocive things to Muses, hence repell. **1644** DIGBY *Nat. Soul* xi. § 4. 436 Ouergrowne with hidropicall and nociue humours.

So †**noˈcivous** *a. Obs. rare.*

1616 R. C. *Times' Whistle* (1871) 147 Phisitions..That know what is nocivous, and what good. **1651** BIGGS *New Disp.* ⁋ 192 Such a refrigeration becomes nocivous.

nock (nɒk), *sb.*[1] Forms: 4–7 **nocke**, 5–6 **nokke**, 6 *Sc.* (**k**)**nok**, 6– **nock.** [Of obscure origin, but possibly the same word as next, although the specific meaning does not appear to be recorded in MDu. or MLG.

Florio gives It. *nocca*, *nocchia*, *nocco*, *nocchio*, as meaning 'the nocke of a bow', but the genuineness of this is extremely doubtful. Kilian's '*Nocke, kerfken in den pijl*, crena,.. incisura sagittæ quæ neruum admittit' is not otherwise certified, and is rendered suspicious by his citing 'Ang. *nock*'. The origin of Sw. *nock* or *nokk* in the sense of notch or incision is quite obscure.]

1. *Archery.* **a.** Originally, one of the small tips of horn fixed at each end of a bow and provided with a notch for holding the string (*obs.*); in later use, the notch cut in this or in the bow itself.

In the *Promp. Parv.* (quot. 1440) app. also applied to the tip of a spindle; but cf. NOCK *sb.*[3]

1398 TREVISA *Barth. De P.R.* XVIII. xiii. (Bodl. MS.), Of hornes beþ made tippinges and nockes for arblastes and bowes and arowes. *c* **1440** LYDG. *Hors, Shepe, & G.* 380 Of the sheepe is cast a-way no thyng: His horn for nokkis, to haftis goth the bone. *c* **1440** *Promp. Parv.* 357/2 Nokke of a bowe, or a spyndylle, or other lyke, *tenorculus*,.. *clavicula*. **1513** DOUGLAS *Æneis* XI. xvi 60 Hir hornit bow [she] has bent,.. Syne halis vp..Quhill that the bowand nokkis met almaist. **1530** PALSGR. 248/1 Nocke of a bowe, *oche de larc.* **1545** ASCHAM *Toxoph.* (Arb.) 119 Whan the strynge is..put croked on, or shorne in sundre wyth an euell nocke. **1548** ELYOT, *Tenus*, Seruius iudgeth it to be the nockes or endes of a bowe. **1625** LISLE *Du Bartas, Noe* 32 A bow that shines aloft..and bending ore the rocks Against a misly Sun i' th' Ocean dips her nocks. **1856** 'STONEHENGE' *Brit. Rural Sports* 505/1 In each of the tips of horn is a notch for the string, called 'the nock'.

b. A small piece of horn fixed in the butt-end of an arrow, provided with a notch for receiving the bowstring; also, the notch itself.

1530 PALSGR. 248/1 Nocke of a shafte, *oche de la flesche*. [See also NOCK *v.* 2.] **1545** ASCHAM *Toxoph.* (Arb.) 127 The nocke of the shafte is dyuersly made, for some be greate and full, some hansome and lytle, some wyde, some narowe. *a* **1585** MONTGOMERIE *Misc. Poems* xvii. 6 Quhais Turkie bou and quaver bleu, Quhairin appeirit noks aneu. **1612** BRINSLEY *Lud. Lit.* 33 His ruling pen..is to be made with a nocke in the neb or point of it, like the nocke of an arrow. **1840** HANSARD *Bk. Archery* 387 The nock of English arrows, for a century past, has been a piece of taper horn glued into the wood. **1856** 'STONEHENGE' *Brit. Rural Sports* 507/2 The feathers..may be smoothed down by passing them through the hand from the point towards the nock. **1884** F. R. STOCKTON *Lady or Tiger?* etc. 69 'When you draw your bow; bring the nock of your arrow'—he was always very particular about technical terms—'well up to your ear'.

†**c.** The notch in a cross-bow for receiving the string when the bow is bent for shooting. *Obs.*

1535 STEWART *Cron. Scot.* II. 569 Greit corce bowis,.. Fast to the knok war buklit vp in bend. *Ibid.*, The bent bowis..Out of the nok ane ganȝe wald lat go. **1620** SHELTON *Quix.* II. xxxv. 237 For my soul indeed is trauersed in my throte, like the nocke [Sp. *nuez*] of a crosse-bow.

†**d.** In phrases, ***out of nock***, out of order; ***above*** or ***beyond the nock***, above or beyond measure. *Obs.*

15.. *Parl. Byrdes* 80 in Hazl. *E.P.P.* III. 171 Then crowed agayne the More Cocke, The Hauke bringeth much thing out of Nocke. *a* **1530** J. HEYWOOD *Love* (Brandl) 484 Where or whan she lyst gyue a mock, She coulde and wolde do it beyonde the nock. **1530** PALSGR. 489/2 He commendeth hym by yonde the nocke, *il le prise oultre bort*, or *oultre mesure*. **1553** T. WILSON *Rhet.* (1580) 60 On now, praise we, a Gods name, the single life aboue the nocke.

†**2.** The cleft in the buttocks; the breech or fundament. *Obs.*

1533 J. HEYWOOD *Play of the Wether* (Brandl) 1065 Yf hys tale be not lyckly Ye shall lycke my tayle in the nocke. **1611** COTGR., *La raye du cul*, the nock, fould, or dint betweene the buttocks. **1668** *Cleveland's Old Gill* ii, Her Breath smells like Lox, Or unwiped Nocks. *a* **1704** T. BROWN *Imit. Satire Persius* Wks. 1730 I. 52 To have..Your precious lines serv'd up to nocks, or pye. **1708** *Brit. Apollo* No. 17. 3/2 Victoria's thin Smock, Tho' but down to your Nock.

Comb. **1610** HOLLAND *Camden's Brit.* I. 186 He had unreverently plaied upon Cornishmen as if they were seated in the nocke-hole of the world. **1632** QUARLES *Divine Fancies* Wks. (Grosart) II. 252 Thy nock-shorn Cloake, with a round narrow Cape. **1653** URQUHART *Rabelais* I. xiii, You will thereby feel in your nockhole a most wonderful pleasure.

†**b.** Used without article. *Obs. rare.*

1663 BUTLER *Hud.* I. i. 285 Noses, which Wou'd last as long as parent breech; But when the date of Nock was out, Off dropt the sympathetick snout. **1674** T. FLATMAN *Belly God* 50 The Muscle, or the Cockle will unlock Thy bodies trunck, and give a vent to nock.

nock (nɒk), *sb.*² *Naut.* Also 6 nok. [a. the synonymous Du., Flem., and Fris. *nok* or LG. *nokk*, whence also G. and Sw. *nock*, Da. *nok*. These words also occur in other special senses, denoting a projection, point, or tip of some kind: cf. prec.]

†**1.** *Sc.* The tip or extremity of a yard-arm. *Obs.*

1513 DOUGLAS *Æneis* III. viii. 83 Anon the nokkis of our rays we writh; Doun fallis the schetis of the salis swith. *Ibid.* v. xiv. 9 Thai..Set in a fang, and threw the ra abak, Baith to and fra all did thar nokkis wry. **1549** *Compl. Scot.* vi. 41 Pul doune the nok of the ra in daggar vyise.

2. In sails: (see quot. 1794).

1794 *Rigging & Seamanship* 84 The nock and peek are lashed by the earings. *Ibid.* 88 *Nock*, the foremost upper corner of boomsails, and of staysails cut with a square tack. **1841** DANA *Seaman's Man.* 116 *Nock*, the forward upper end of a sail that sets with a boom. **1851** KIPPING *Sailm.* (ed. 2) 24 To determine the height of the nock of the sail. **1867** SMYTH *Sailor's Word-bk.* 498.

attrib. **1794** *Rigging & Seamanship* 7 *Nock-earing*, the rope that fastens the nock of the sail. *Ibid.* 93 Mizens..have ..a nock-piece and a peek-piece. *Ibid.* 108 If the depth of the nock-seam be subtracted.

†**nock**, *sb.*³ *Obs. rare.* Also 6 **nok**. [Of Scand. origin, corresp. to Icel. *hnokki*, Fær. *nokki*, Norw. and Da. *nokke*, Sw. *nocke*, with the same meaning.] A small hook fixed upon a spindle.

c **1450** HOLLAND *Howlat* 57 My neb is netherit as a nok, I am bot ane Owle. **15..** *Wooing of Jock* 54 in Laing *Anc. Poet. Scot.* 360 Ane spindill wantand ane nok.

attrib. **1577** GASCOIGNE *Grief of Joy* Wks. (Grosart) II. 265 The strongest thryd yᵉ ever yet was sponne..Is nock-throwen yet even with yᵉ spindles twyst.

nock, variant of KNOCK *sb.*¹ 2, a clock.

1853 READE *Chr. Johnstone* 294 Flucker informed her that the nock said 'half eleven'.

nock (nɒk), *v.* [f. NOCK *sb.*¹]

1. *trans.* To provide (a bow or arrow) with a nock or notch. Usu. in pa. pple. *nocked*.

? *a* **1366** CHAUCER *Rom. Rose* 942 Ten brode arowis hilde he there,..they were shaven wel and dight, Nokked and fethered aright. *c* **1500** *Robyn Hode* cxxxii. in Child *Ballads* III. 62/6 Euery arowe..With pecok wel idyght, Inocked all with whyte siluer. **1545** ASCHAM *Toxoph.* (Arb.) 111 You must looke that youre bowe be well nocked for fere the sharpnesse of the horne shere a sunder the strynge. **1590** SIR J. SMYTH *Disc. Weapons* 46 b, Their bowes of Yeugh, long and well nocked and backed. **1611** COTGR., *Oché*,..nocked, notched. *Rencocher*, to nocke the second time.

2. To fit (the arrow) to the bowstring ready for shooting.

1513 DOUGLAS *Æneis* v. ix. 44 With arrow reddy nokkit than Evritioune Plukkis wp in hy his bow. **1530** PALSGR. 644/1, I nocke an arrowe, I put the nocke in to the strynge, *je encoyche*. **1561** BRENDE *Q. Curtius* VIII. 81 Their arrowes were so longe and heavy, that they could not nocke them within theyr bowes. **1590** SIR J. SMYTH *Disc. Weapons* 20 b, To drawe their arrowes out of their cases..to nocke them in their Bowes. ? **1613** SPELMAN in *Capt. Smith's Wks.* (Arb.) I. p. cxiv, Till they can nocke another arrow they make the trees ther defence. **1647** HERRICK *Noble Numb.* Poems (1902) 331 God..doth show No Arrow nockt, onely a stringlesse Bow. *a* **1835** MOTHERWELL *Poems* (1847) 178 Nock a shaft and strike down that proud doe. **1856** 'STONEHENGE' *Brit. Rural Sports* 507/2 In shooting at the target, the first thing to be done is to nock the arrow.

absol. **1545** ASCHAM *Toxoph.* (Arb.) 132 As it were to gyue a man warning to nocke ryght. *Ibid.* 148 To nocke well is the easiest poynte of all. **1611** SIR W. MURE *Misc. Poems* ii. 26 Wks. (S.T.S.) I. 10 The blindit god arywed, His bow bent in his hand ready to nocke. **1875** *Encycl. Brit.* II. 377/2 Always nock on the same place.

Hence **nocked** (nɒkt), *ppl. a.*; **'nocking** *vbl. sb.* ***nocking point***, the point of the bowstring to which the notch of the arrow is applied.

1545 ASCHAM *Toxoph.* (Arb.) 109 To haue a goose quyll splettyd and sewed againste the nockynge, betwixt the lining and the ledder. *Ibid.* 148 Vnconstante nockynge maketh a man lesse hys lengthe. **1611** FLORIO, *Accoccatura*, a nocking. [**1801** STRUTT *Sports & Past.* II. i. 56 A proper attention was to be paid to the nocking, that is, the application of the notch at the bottom of the arrow to the bow-string.] **1856** 'STONEHENGE' *Brit. Rural Sports* 507/2 Turn the arrow.., and fix it on the nocking point of the string. **1859** R. F. BURTON *Centr. Afr.* in *Jrnl. Geogr. Soc.* XXIX. 332 Flourishing his spear and agitating his bow, probably with nocked arrow.

†**nockandro.** *Obs. rare.* [f. NOCK *sb.*¹ 2, with obscure ending.] The breech.

1611 COTGR., *Cul*,..[a] tayle, nockandroe, fundament. **1653** URQUHART *Rabelais* II. xix. 139 Panurge put one finger of his left hand in his nockandrow. **1654** GAYTON *Pleas. Notes* 14 Blest be Dulcinea, whose Favour..Rescu'd poore Andrew, and his Nock-Andro from breeching.

‖**nockerl** ('nɒkərl). Pl. **nockerln**. [Austrian G., little dumpling.] A small, light dumpling, made with a batter including eggs, and usually fried; **Salzburger nockerl**, a sweet version of this dumpling, using extra eggs which make the mixture puff up when it is cooked.

1855 E. ACTON *Mod. Cookery* (rev. ed.) xxxii. 620 (*heading*) A Viennese soufflé-pudding, called Salzburger Nockerl. **1954** G. BEER *Austrian Cooking* 89 A *Nockerl* is tiny to medium-sized, oval in shape and not really a dumpling at all. The only reason why I continuously refer to them as such is for want of a better name. *Ibid.* 90 The *Nockerln* must not brown. *Ibid.* 106 Salzburger Nockerl... Remove *Nockerln* carefully with a palette knife... Dust liberally with icing sugar... The centre should be light and creamy, the outside golden brown and puffed. **1958** J. GROSSINGER *Art Jewish Cooking* (1960) 31 Soup Nockerl... Beat the eggs, water and salt together. Mix in the flour and baking powder. Drop by the teaspoon into boiling salted water. Cook until they rise to the surface.

nocket, *dial.*: see NACKET *sb.*²

nock-hole: see NOCK *sb.*¹ 2.

nocking, *vbl. sb.*: see NOCK *v.*

†**nock-saw.** *Obs. rare*⁻⁰. [f. NOCK *sb.*¹] A small saw for cutting nocks in bows or arrows.

1659 HOWELL *Vocab.* LI, A thwitting knife, nocksaws, a rasp, a riper.

†**'nocky.** *Obs. rare*⁻⁰. 'A silly, dull fellow'.

a **1700** in B. E. *Dict. Cant. Crew*.

no claim(s, *attrib. phr.* [NO *a.*] Designating a discount allowed on a motor-vehicle insurance premium if no claim has been submitted during the preceding year(s).

1933 G. W. GILBERT *Motor Insurance* iii. 66 (*heading*) No claim bonus. This is allowed..only at a flat rate of 10 per cent of the renewal premium. If more than one cycle is insured the bonus is payable 'per cycle'. *Ibid.* iv. 75 No Claim Bonus is paid..if the policy as a whole runs free of claim for one or two or three succeeding years. **1955** *Times* 24 Aug. 7/3 The 'tariff' companies are credited with the intention of still further increasing the 'no-claims' bonus. **1968** D. DEVINE *Sleeping Tiger* i. 15 'Take it up with the insurance company, would you?..' 'It's not worth losing your no-claim bonus. I'll pay for it to be resprayed myself.' **1970** *Motoring Which?* July 91/1 Before no-claims bonus and other discounts, fully comprehensive insurance will probably cost you around £45 to £90 for the 3-litre. **1975** *Times* 24 Sept. 3/2 The no-claim bonus is no longer, because of inflation, a sufficient incentive.

no comment: see COMMENT *sb.* 2 c. Also (with hyphen) as attrib. phr.

1966 S. B. JACKMAN *Davidson Affair* iii. 22, I thought he was strictly a no-comment man. **1971** 'L. BLACK' *Death has Green Fingers* iii. 32 The police simply didn't know any more yet. When they did, the 'no comment' answers would begin. **1971** E. FENWICK *Impeccable People* xix. 103 Ben wore his no-comment expression.

no-'count, *a.* Aphetic form of NO-ACCOUNT *a.* Cf. 'COUNT. Also as *sb.*

1853 'P. PAXTON' *Stray Yankee in Texas* 282 (Th.), Yes, Massa, dem no 'count calves done fool me again. **1885** H. JACKSON *Zeph* iii. 82 Ye miserable, mean-spirited, no-'count critter! **1902** A. D. MCFAUL *Ike Glidden* xviii. 145 It wasn't enough for your sickly, no-'count mother to waste my grub and money in idleness. **1920** C. E. MULFORD *Johnny Nelson* xiii. 135 Judgin' from th' way those no-'count hosses was pullin' when they come over th' hill..I reckoned you got th' hides. **1936** M. MITCHELL *Gone with Wind* iv. 65 Dey is de shiflesses, mos' ungrateful passel of no-counts livin'.

noct-, combining form of L. *nox*, *noctis*, used in words based on L. *ambulāre* to walk, also as used in place of NOCTI- in words in which the following element begins with a vowel; **noc'tambulant** *a.*, night-walking; **noc'tambulate** *v. intr.*, to walk at night; **noctambu'lation**, somnambulism; sleep-walking; **noc'tambulator**, one who walks at night; **noctambu'latory** *a.* = *noctambulous* adj.; **noc'tambule** [cf. F. *noctambule*], a sleep-walker; **noc'tambulism** [F. *-isme*], somnambulism; **noc'tambulist**, a somnambulist; a night-walker; **noctambu'listic** *a.*, connected with night-walking; †**noc'tambulo** (also *pl.* **-ones**), a somnambulist; **noc'tambulous** *a.*, given to night-walking; **noc'turia** [-URIA], the condition of being aroused from one's sleep abnormally often by the need to urinate;

1819 H. BUSK *Vestriad* I. 467 *Noctambulant, aloof, Pads the patrole with solitary hoof. **1891** *Harper's Mag.* Aug. 430/2 His face is ascetic, with a large forehead, two noctambulant eyes sheltered behind spectacle glasses. **1955** H. SPRING *These Lovers fled Away* 206 Now and then I would *noctambulate through the city. **1721** BAILEY, **Noctambulation*, a walking in ones Sleep. **1799** C. B. BROWN *Edgar Huntly* xxv, Men have employed anxious months in search of that which, in a freak of noctambulation, was hidden by their own hands. **1962** V. NABOKOV *Pale Fire* 221 If you..pull up the window, and..roll out.. there is always the chance of knocking clean through into your own hell a pacific *noctambulator walking his dog. **1913** C. MACKENZIE *Sinister Street* I. II. vii. 259 Conversations with Brother Aloysius were sufficiently thrilling journeys, and Michael was always ready to follow his footsteps as one might follow a *noctambulatory cat. **1825** R. P. WARD *Tremaine* III. xv. 345 He says, all are mad, foolish, dreaming, *Noctambules, fit patients for Monroe. **1860** WORCESTER (citing HOBLYN), **Noctambulism*. **1881** COLQUHOUN *Hist. of Magic* I. 55 The phenomena of the natural somnambulism or Noctambulism. **1731** BAILEY (vol. II.), **Noctambulist*, a Person who walks in the Night, properly in Sleep. **1803** BEDDOES *Hygëia* IX. 130 The proneness of noctambulists to loss of consciousness. **1852** MUNDY *Antipodes* i. (1855) 18 If a noctambulist yourself, you may indeed encounter, towards the small hours, an occasional night-errant. **1887** T. HARDY *Woodlanders* II. xvii. 319 She decided that her fellow-noctambulist, even if a poacher, would not injure her. **1890** *Temple Bar* Jan. 116 A *noctambulistic escapade. **1624** DONNE *Serm.* xlvi. 467 That our *Noctambulones, men that walke in their sleepe, will wake if they be called by their names. **1643** SIR T. BROWNE *Relig. Med.* 180 Those Noctambuloes and night-walkers, though in their sleep, do yet injoy the action of their senses. **1733** ARBUTHNOT *Air* (J.), Respiration being carried on in sleep, is no argument against its being voluntary. What shall we say of noctambulos? **1731** BAILEY (vol. II), **Noctambulous*, of or pertaining to walking in the Night. **1786** *Nat. Hist.* in *Ann. Reg.* 51/2 By nature melancholy,..carnivorous and noctambulous. **1899** *Speaker* 25 Nov. 188/1 Hardy, unscoured, fraternal, noctambulous..the Bohemian is part born, part made. **1911** DORLAND *Med. Dict.* (ed. 6) 558/2 **Nocturia*, excessive urination at night. **1928** EISENDRATH & ROLNICK *Text-bk. Urology* xlvi. 707 The patient has noticed that..there has been an increase in the number of times, he or she, experienced the desire to void urine. This may have occurred only at night i.e. nocturia, or during the day. **1961** *Lancet* 12 Aug. 335/2, 1 patient was troubled by nocturia. **1971** GOLDEN & MAHER *Kidney* ii. 36 Nocturia may thus be an early symptom of renal failure.

nocti-, comb. form of L. *nox*, *noctis*, used in certain words, as **noc'tidial** [L. *dies* day] *a.*, comprising a night and a day. †**'noctifer** [cf. L. *noctifer* evening star], a bringer of night or darkness. †**noc'tiferous** *a.* (see quot.). **nocti'florous** *a.*, *Bot.* night-flowering (Cassell 1886). **nocti'lucent** *a.*, shining by night; *spec.* in ***noctilucent cloud***, a cloud of a kind occas. seen at night in summer in high latitudes, which occurs at a height of about 80 kilometres (at the mesopause) and which some authorities believe is composed purely of cosmic dust and others of ice condensed round cosmic dust particles; cf. *mother-of-pearl cloud*; so **nocti'lucid** *a.* (*Cent. Dict.*). †**noc'tipotent** *a.* (see quot.). Also NOCTILUCA, NOCTIVAGANT, etc.

1694 HOLDER *On Time* 98 The *Noctidial Day, the Lunar Periodic Month, and the Solar Year are Natural and Universal. **1884** *Punch* 1 Mar. 102 Farewell to noctidial sittings. **1667** WATERHOUSE *Fire Lond.* 140 Lest..he hurl you Lucifers out of the Heaven of your sinful felicity, and make you *Noctifers and Mortifers of misery and contempt. **1656** BLOUNT *Glossogr.*, **Noctiferous*.., that betokens or brings night, the evening Star. **1890** *Cent. Dict.*, **Noctilucent*, shining by night or in the dark; noctilucid; as, the noctilucent eyes of a cat. **1910** W. L. MOORE *Descriptive Meteorol.* xi. 198 Certain clouds that are seen about midnight in summer have for twenty years received considerable attention from Abbe and others..; sometimes they are called nacreous..at other times noctilucent, because they shine at night. **1936** N. SHAW *Man. Meteorol.* (ed. 2) II. iii. 44 The lower type, known as Perlmutter or iridescent clouds, show brilliant prismatic colours and occur at heights between 20 and 30 kilometres. They differ from noctilucent clouds by appearing almost exclusively in winter. **1940** *Chambers's Techn. Dict.* 581/1 *Noctilucent*

(*Zool.*), phosphorescent, light-producing. **1956** *Nature* 18 Feb. 308/1 The technique of observing noctilucent clouds has been improved recently. **1963** *New Scientist* 25 July 169/2 There has been considerable dispute in the past about whether the noctilucent clouds are composed of ice particles or dust particles. **1678** PHILLIPS *2nd Suppl.*, **Noctipotent*, powerful in the night.

noc'tilionine, *a. Zool.* [See def. and -INE.] Of bats: Belonging to the genus *Noctilio*.

1844 A. GRAY *Zool. Voy. Sulphur* I. 29 A very good character for the determination of the genera among the Noctilionine and Pteropine Bats.

‖**noctiluca** (nɒktɪ'lu:kə). Pl. -lucæ (-lu:si:). [ad. L. *noctilūca* moon, lantern, f. *nocti-*, *nox* night + *lūcēre* to shine. Cf. F. *noctiluque*.]

†**1.** A species of phosphorus. *Obs.*

1680 BOYLE *Aerial Noctiluca* 5 This [phosphorus] by some Learned Men has been call'd, to discriminate it from the former, a Noctiluca. **1681–2** —— *New Exp. Icy Noctiluca* 19 Our Icy Noctiluca or Phosphorus is manifestly heavier in Specie than common Water. **1706** PHILLIPS, *Noctiluca*, a certain Substance, chymically perpared, such as will shine of it self in the dark. **1727–38** in CHAMBERS *Cycl.*

2. *Zool.* A marine animalcule, of a nearly spherical shape, which produces a phosphorescent appearance in the sea.

1855 *Orr's Circ. Sci., Org. Nat.* II. 227 In some localities the Noctiluca..also plays an important part in the production of this phenomenon. **1865** *Pop. Sci. Rev.* 179 The Noctiluca, which causes the sea waves to sparkle with phosphoric light. **1883** *Harper's Mag.* Jan. 182/2 A gobletful of the noctilucæ produces light sufficient to read by at a distance of two feet.

Hence †**nocti'lucal** *a.*, phosphorescent. **nocti'lucan**, an animalcule of the genus *Noctiluca* (Cassell 1886). **nocti'lucence**, marine phosphorescence due to noctilucæ (*Stand. Dict.* 1895). **nocti'lucin(e** [F. *noctilucine*], the light-giving substance in phosphorescent animalcules.

1681–2 BOYLE *New Exp. Icy Noctiluca* 46 A conjecture I had made about the great diffusedness of the Noctilucal Matter. **1880** *Libr. Univ. Knowl.* X. 659 Noctilucine has a syrupy consistence at ordinary temperatures.

nocti'lucous, *a. rare.* [f. NOCTILUCA + -OUS.] Shining at night, phosphorescent.

1681–2 BOYLE *App. Aerial Noctiluca* 1 Till more Noctilucous Matter could be prepared. **1774** PENNANT *Tour Scotl.* II. *Voy. Hebrides* 345 Myriads of noctilucous Nereids that inhabit the ocean..and..give a fine light. **1777** —— *Brit. Zool.* (ed. 2) IV. 38 Nereis Noctilucous. These are the animals that illuminate the sea, like glow-worms. **1832** MACGILLIVRAY *Trav. Humboldt* xi. (1836) 131 The thorny bushes covered with noctilucous insects.

noctivagant (nɒk'tɪvəgənt), *a.* (and *sb.*) [f. NOCTI- + VAGANT *a.*] Wandering by night.

c **1620** T. ADAMS *Sinner's Passing-bell* Wks. 1861 I. 347 The lustful sparrows, noctivagant adulterers, sit chirping about our houses. **1633** —— *Com. 2 Peter* i. 4 If our affections be noctivagant, night walkers, they will easily come home quick with child. **1656** in BLOUNT *Glossogr.* **1721** in BAILEY. **1819** H. BUSK *Vestriad* IV. 8 What if a noble P—— ..Noctivagant perambulate the street? **1860** *Macm. Mag.* II. 222 To put some check on any noctivagant propensities of their lodgers. **1881** W. WILKINS *Songs of Study* 21 The noctivagant student head-dress being rife to-night.

b. *sb.* One who wanders by night. *rare*$^{-1}$.

1633 T. ADAMS *Com. 2 Peter* i. 19 Noctivagants are negligent in their habits.

†**noctivagating.** *Obs. rare*$^{-1}$. = next.

1633 T. ADAMS *Exp. 2 Peter* iii. 3 For a hypocrite to decline open..noctivagating,..and revels, is no wonder.

†**noctiva'gation.** *Obs.* [f. NOCTI- + VAGATION.] Wandering or rambling by night, as an unlawful or prohibited practice subject to a fine.

1632 MARMION *Holland's Leaguer* IV. iii, No farther than to prison, where you shall pay But forty shillings for noctivagation. **1637** ABP. LAUD *Wks.* (1853) V. 164 You shall do well to have a care of noctivagation and other disorders. **1678** WOOD *Life* 25 Apr. II. 403 The townsmen acknowledge 6*s.* 8*d.* to be paid for noctivagation,..but not 40*s*.

b. In general use.

1645 HOWELL *Twelve Treat.* (1661) 337 Thus have you a rough account of a rambling Noctivagation up and down the world. **1654** GAYTON *Pleas. Notes* IV. xv. 253 When upon the entrance of his adventures this vertigo of noctivagation, and watching his Armes, seized him.

†**noctivagator.** *Obs.* [f. NOCTI- + *vagātor*, agent-noun f. L. *vagārī* to wander.] One who walks by night; a night-walker.

1640 FEATLY *Abbot* in *Fuller's Abel Rediv.* (1651) 544 After prayers he commanded the gates to be locked, to prevent or at least discover all noctivagators. **1654** GAYTON *Pleas. Notes* III. v. 99 Who..ask'd this noctivagator, where he had been so late. *a* **1703** in Gutch *Coll. Cur.* II. 47 To search and seize Noctivagators and other suspicious persons.

noctivagous (nɒk'tɪvəgəs), *a.* [f. NOCTI- + L. *vagus* wandering.] = NOCTIVAGANT.

1801 COL. HANGER *Life* I. 212 They became ambulatory and noctivagous. **1843** F. E. PAGET *Pageant* 144 Beasts of prey, burglars, and ladies of fashion are the only three kinds of noctivagous mammalia. **1854** *Fraser's Mag.* XLIX. 158 As she is noctivagous, that poor invalid..must have a disturbed time of it.

'**noctograph.** [irreg. f. L. *noct-*, *nox* night + -GRAPH.] A writing-frame for a blind person.

1864 TICKNOR *Life Prescott* 134 This framework of wires is folded down upon a sheet of paper thoroughly impregnated with a black substance... The whole apparatus is called a noctograph.

noctourne, obs. form of NOCTURN *sb.*

‖**noctua** ('nɒktjʊə). *Entom.* [a. L. *noctua* night-owl.] A moth of the genus *Noctua*.

1840 *Cuvier's Anim. Kingd.* 612 The palpi [are] generally nearly similar to those of the Noctuæ. **1892** *Athenæum* 15 Oct. 520/1 A curious noctua taken on the sandhills at St. Anne's-on-Sea. **1905** *Westm. Gaz.* 19 May 4/2 The Noctuas are sugar-lovers above all the others.

†'**noctual**, *a. Obs. rare*$^{-1}$. = NOCTURNAL.

1632 LITHGOW *Trav.* I. 10 A noctuall den of theeues.

†'**noctuary.** *Obs. rare.* [f. L. *noct-*, *nox* night, *noctū* by night, after *diary*.] An account of what passes during the night.

1714 BYROM *Spect.* No. 586 ⁋10, I have got a Parcel of Visions and other Miscellanies in my Noctuary. **1812** SOUTHEY *Omniana* II. 61 It stands thus in a diary or rather noctuary of dreams. **1829** J. MILLER *Sibyl's Leaves* II. 365 [He] might have been a profound philosopher in spite of his noctuary. **1910** *Chambers's Jrnl.* Sept. 594/2 My sceptical friends..say I kept myself awake on purpose to write this noctuary.

noctuid ('nɒktjʊɪd), *a.* and *sb. Entom.* [f. mod.L. *Noctuidæ*: see NOCTUA and -ID.]

a. *adj.* Belonging to the family of moths named *Noctuidæ*. **b.** *sb.* A noctuid moth.

1880 *Libr. Univ. Knowl.* I. 706 The larva of a noctuid moth. **1894** *Harper's Mag.* Mar. 555 The evening primrose ..hangs a golden necklace about the welcome murmuring noctuid. **1899** D. SHARP *Insects* II. 415 The majority of Noctuid larvæ have the usual number of legs.

noctule ('nɒktjʊl). *Zool.* [a. F. *noctule* (Buffon), ad. It. *nottola*, *-olo*, bat: hence mod.L. *noctula*.] The largest British species of bat (*Vesperugo noctula*); the great bat. Also ***noctule bat***.

1771 PENNANT *Synopsis Quadrup.* 369 Noctule Bat with the nose slightly bilobated. *Ibid.* 370, I never saw but one specimen of the Noctule. **1802** BINGLEY *Anim. Biog.* (1813) I. 110 The length of the Noctule Bat is about 5½ inches to the tip of the tail. **1840** *Cuvier's Anim. Kingd.* 70 The Noctules are allied to the true Bats (*Vespertilio*). **1863** KEARLEY *Links in Chain* xi. 244 The Noctule, or great high flying bat, is the earliest to retire, being seldom seen after July. **1896** LYDEKKER *Brit. Mammals* 32 The Noctule is spread over the greater part of temperate Europe and Asia. *Ibid.* 35 A solitary pair of Noctules.

†**noctuolent**, *a. Obs. rare.* [f. L. *noctū* by night + pres. pple. of *olēre* to smell.] Of plants: Smelling strongest in the night-time.

1753 CHAMBERS *Cycl. Supp.* s.v. *Dog-rose*, The noctuolent plants, of which there are several kinds, as some of the geraniums, and of the jasmines, etc.

nocturlabe: see NOCTURNLABE.

nocturn ('nɒktɜ:n), *sb. Eccl.* [a. F. *nocturne*, ad. late or med.L. *nocturna* fem. sing. of *nocturnus*: see next.]

1. In the Roman Catholic Church, one of the divisions of the office of matins (see quot. 1526).

The first quot. may belong to sense 2.

a **1225** *Ancr. R.* 270 Seie ȝet, he seið, one nocturne. *a* **1400** *Prymer* (1891) 83 Here bygynneþ þe þridde nocturne. *c* **1425** *St. Elizabeth of Spalbeck* in *Anglia* VIII. 108/31 And so..she solempnyzes þe watches of the firste nocturne. *Ibid.* 109/22 Þe firste nocturne of matyns. **1482** *Monk of Evesham* (Arb.) 34 The next night after when y was at matens aboute the begynnyng of the thirde nocturne. **1526** *Pilgr. Perf.* (W. de W. 1531) 248 In matyns communly be iii orbes, otherwyse called iii nocturnes, of yͤ whiche euery orbe conteyneth iij psalmes, iii lessons, and iii responsories. **1671** WOODHEAD *St. Teresa* I. xxxi. 222 Being at that time in Oratory, and having recited the Nocturn, and saying those very devout prayers which are at the end thereof. **1706** in Cotes tr. *Dupin's Eccl. Hist.* (1725) II. v. 43 He says..that the Name Mattins is very improperly given to the Night-Office..; that the Night-Office is divided into three Nocturns, which are said at three different times. **1840** BROWNING *Sordello* IV. 969 Some brother spoke, Ere nocturns, of Crescentius. **1884** *Catholic Dict.* (1897) 101/2 The lections of the second nocturn which contain the history of the Saints.

†**2.** (See quots. 1546 and 1548–9.) *Obs.*

1483 CAXTON *Gold. Leg.* 435/1 He begynneth and saith a psalme that is in the thyrd nocturne of the psaulter. **1525** LD. BERNERS *Froiss.* II. xxvi. 30/1 He sayd many orisons, euery daye a nocturne of the psalter, matyns of our lady. **1546** LANGLEY tr. *Pol. Verg. de Invent.* VI. ii. 114 The diuision of Dauids Psalter into vii partes called noctournes according to the seuen daies in the weke was the worke of Hierome. **1548–9** (Mar.) *Bk. Com. Prayer* Pref., The auncient fathers had deuided the psalmes into seuen porcions: whereof euery one was called a nocturne.

†**nocturn**, *a. Obs. rare.* [ad. F. *nocturne* or L. *nocturnus*: see next.] Nocturnal.

15.. in *Dunbar's Poems* (S.T.S.) App. xi. 26 We may nocht in this vale of bale abyd, Ourdirkit with the sable clud nocturn. **1636** BRATHWAIT *Rom. Emp.* 214 Vesuvius.. covered the face of Italy..with nocturne darknesse in the day. **1677** GALE *Crt. Gentiles* III. 78 A cloudy, dark, nocturne Philosophie. **1762** C. DENIS in *St. James's Mag.* I. 133 What would be this nocturn sprite.

nocturnal (nɒk'tɜ:nəl), *a.* and *sb.* [ad. late L. *nocturnāl-is*, f. *nocturnus* (see prec.), f. *noct-*, *nox* night. Cf. obs. F. *nocturnal*, *-nel*.]

A. *adj.* **1.** Of or pertaining to the night; done, held, or occurring by night; etc. ***nocturnal arc***: (see quot. 1704 and ARC *sb.* 2).

1485 CAXTON *St. Wenefryde* 20, I shold haue begonne my nocturnal offyce. **1537** LATIMER *Serm. Convocation* Ej, The solempne and nocturnal bacchanals. **1599** A. M. tr. *Gabelhouer's Bk. Physicke* 4/2 When you intende to take your nocturnalle rest. **1602** MARSTON *Ant. & Mel.* III. Wks. 1856 I. 34 To see if the nocturnall court delights Could force me envie their felicitie. **1634** MILTON *Comus* 128 Hail Goddesse of Nocturnal sport Dark vaild Cotytto. *a* **1691** BOYLE *Hist. Air* (1692) 32 He observed the nocturnal air to be very damp. **1704** J. HARRIS *Lex. Techn.* I, *Nocturnal Ark*, is that Space in the Heavens which the Sun, Moon, or Stars, run thro' from their Rising to their Setting. **1759** JOHNSON *Idler* No. 49 ⁋11 In this dismal gloom of nocturnal peregrination. **1792** COWPER *Let. to W. Hayley* 29 July, I have told you something of my nocturnal experiences. **1835** THIRLWALL *Hist. Greece* ix. I. 349 The victim of a nocturnal sacrifice to the powers below. **1875** JOWETT *Plato* (ed. 2) V. 12 A nocturnal council is instituted for the preservation of the state.

b. ***nocturnal emission***: involuntary ejaculation of sperm during sleep.

1821 J. WILSON *Lect. Struct. & Dis. Male Urinary & Genital Organs* xv. 424 He had experienced repeated erections, attended with nocturnal emissions. **1928** H. B. ENGLISH *Student's Dict. Psychol. Terms*, *Nocturnal emissions*, loss of semen during sleep. **1948** A. C. KINSEY et al. *Sexual Behavior Human Male* xv. 516 In the male, nocturnal emissions or wet dreams are generally accepted as a usual part of the sexual picture. **1951** M. MCLUHAN *Mech. Bride* (1967) 47/1 The [sexual] 'outlets' are..'nocturnal emission', [etc.]. **1958** M. ARGYLE *Relig. Behaviour* x. 123 *Nocturnal emissions* for Kinsey's devout males were insignificantly more frequent, for his devout females sex dreams to the point of orgasm were less frequent.

2. *Zool.* **a.** Active during the night.

1726 POPE *Odyss.* XXIV. 10 Some rifted den, Where flock nocturnal bats, and birds obscene. **1768** PENNANT *Brit. Zool.* I. 107 The hedge hog is a nocturnal animal. **1774** GOLDSM. *Nat. Hist.* (1776) VIII. 38 This tribe of insects has therefore been divided into Diurnal and Nocturnal Flies. **1826** KIRBY & SP. *Entomol.* XXXV. III. 639 In the Crepuscular and Nocturnal Lepidoptera this fold..is very slight. **1849** *Sk. Nat. Hist., Mammalia* IV. 15 In their habits they are nocturnal. **1870** NICHOLSON *Man. Zool.* (1875) 548 The Nocturnal Birds of Prey, which..have the eyes directed forward.

b. Capable of vision by night.

1840 *Cuvier's Anim. Kingd.* 62 The Dourocouli..only differ from the Sagouins by their great nocturnal eyes.

3. *Mus.* Of the nature of a nocturne.

1896 *Peterson's Mag.* Jan. 43/2 There is a nocturnal symphony between the first and second acts.

B. *sb.* †**1.** A night-piece. *Obs. rare*$^{-1}$.

a **1631** DONNE (*title*), A Nocturnal upon St. Lucy's Day, being the shortest day.

2. An astronomical instrument adapted for taking observations by which to ascertain the hour of the night, etc.

1627 CAPT. SMITH *Seaman's Gram.* xiv. 65 An Astrolabe, a Nocturnal. **1669** STURMY *Mariner's Mag.* II. 46 A Nocturnal so ordered, that it shall give you the Hour of the Night by the North-Star.., whereby you may take the true Declination. **1690** LEYBOURN *Curs. Math.* 617 There are several sorts of Nocturnals, of which some are Projections of the Sphere. *a* **1748** WATTS *Geogr. & Astron.* §20 (1760) 206 The Instrument called a Nocturnal, wherein the most remarkable Stars are fixed in their proper Degrees of Declination and Right Ascension. **1769** FALCONER *Dict. Marine* (1780), *Alidade*, the index of a nocturnal or sea-quadrant. **1884** *Chamb. Jrnl.* 1 Nov. 695/1 Astrolabes, nocturnals, and other astronomical instruments..are largely represented.

†**3.** A night-service; a nocturn. *Obs. rare*$^{-1}$.

1670 G. H. *Hist. Cardinals* I. III. 91 All the Fryeries..say the Offices for the dead, and cause a Nocturnal to be rehearsed.

4. A night-walker; a night-hag.

1693 TATE in *Dryden's Juvenal* (1697) 32 Such vile Practices..As makes our Matrons lewd, Nocturnals chast. **1823** *Spirit Public Jrnls.* 40 Amongst a group of nocturnals, from St. Martin's watch-house. **1861** T. L. PEACOCK *Gryll G.* xxxiv, We implored the nocturnals to keep themselves to themselves, while we were returning from supper.

5. *pl.* **a.** The nocturnal birds of prey; the night-owls. **b.** The nocturnal Lepidoptera; the moths.

1842 BRANDE *Dict. Sci.*, etc.

Hence **noc'turnally** *adv.* (Webster 1847).

nocturne ('nɒktɜ:n), *sb.* Also -urn. [a. F. *nocturne* (It. *notturno*): cf. NOCTURN *sb.* and *a.*]

1. *Mus.* A composition of a dreamy character.

'A name and form of composition the origin of which is due to John Field' (*Grove's Dict. Mus.* II. 460).

1862 T. A. TROLLOPE *Marietta* I. vii. 130 He had attempted to compose some words for his nocturn. **1882** MISS BRADDON *Mt. Royal* I. viii. 254 Christabel was playing slow sleepy nocturnes.

2. *Painting.* A night-piece, night-scene.

1874 R. TYRWHITT *Sketch Club* 300 Don't be bothered with symphonies and nocturns. *c* **1880** WHISTLER *Let. to Leyland* in *Art Jrnl.* Aug. 252, I can't thank you too much for the name 'Nocturne' as the title for my moonlights. *Ibid.*, The Nocturne in blue and silver is one you don't know at all. **1882** *Cornh. Mag.* Feb. 168 One is tempted to linger over these strange dream-pictures, these nocturnes [etc.].

3. *Zool.* (See quot.)

1900 *Nature* 5 Apr. 552/2 In constant darkness, a nocturne (that is, a prawn in the nocturnal colour-phase) recovers to its diurnal colour.

Hence **ˈnocturne** *v. intr.*, to assume the nocturnal colour.
1900 *Nature* 5 Apr. 553/1 Blinded prawns nocturne and recover as completeley as normal ones.

†**nocturnlabe.** *Obs. rare.* [irreg. f. NOCTURN *a.*, after *astrolabe.*] = NOCTURNAL *sb.* 2.
1594 BLUNDEVIL *Exerc.* VII. xxxix. (1636) 717 To know by the Northstar and his guards, with the helpe of an instrument called a Nocturnlabe, the houre of the night. [**1704** J. HARRIS *Lex. Techn.* I, *Nocturlabe*, is an Instrument used to find how much the North Star is higher or lower than the Pole at all Hours of the Night.]

†**nocˈturnous,** *a. Obs. rare*$^{-0}$. [f. L. *nocturnus* + -OUS.] 'Pertaining to the night.'
1727 BAILEY, vol. II.

†**ˈnocument.** *Obs.* [ad. med.L. *nocumentum*, f. *nocēre* to hurt.] Harm, damage; evil.
1550 BALE *Image both Ch.* II. K vii, All these noyfull nocumentes are the holy frutes of the whordome of that.. churche. **1604** T. WRIGHT *Passions* v. 189 The dammage or nocument, which casually was annexed. *c* **1650** *Contemp. Hist. Irel.* (1879) I. 192 Nocuments are documents, and greate afflictions are good lecturers to reformation of life and maners. **1657** TOMLINSON *Renou's Disp.* 595 By whose quality the head will..be armed against the nocuments of Opium.
Hence †**nocuˈmental,** †**nocuˈmentous** *adjs.*
1644 HUNTON *Vind. Treat. Monarchy* ix. 65 For it so fals out to the best physicke, where the nocumentous humours are prevailing. **1657** TOMLINSON tr. *Renou's Disp.* To Rdr., To correct their nocumental qualities.

nocuous (ˈnɒkjuːəs), *a.* [a. L. *nocuus*, f. *nocēre* to hurt: cf. *innocuous.*] Noxious, hurtful; venomous, poisonous.
1635 SWAN *Spec. M.* ix. §1 (1643) 480 Though this be a nocuous creature, it much magnifieth the power of God. **1656** in BLOUNT *Glossogr.* **1721** in BAILEY. **1883** *Brit. Q. Rev.* July 19 Anything of the kind which has such power is.. nocuous for constant use. **1890** LUMHOLTZ *Cannibals* 23 This change is due..to a nocuous kind of grass, namely the dreaded spear-grass.
Hence **ˈnocuously** *adv.*; **ˈnocuousness.**
1847 WEBSTER, *Nocuously.* **1894** *Westm. Gaz.* 15 Jan. 2/3 It proves neither nocuousness nor innocuousness.

nod (nɒd), *sb.*[1] [f. the vb.]
1. a. A short, quick inclination of the head used as a sign, esp. to convey salutation or recognition, to express assent or approbation, or to direct attention to something. In phrases which imply approval, as ***to get*** or ***give the nod*** (chiefly *U.S.*).
1540-1 ELYOT *Image Gov.* 40 Notwithstandynge..they received nothing in conclusion but noddes with the head. **1565** COOPER *Thesaurus, Nutus*, a signe that one maketh with his eyes or head; a becke; a nodde. **1594** SHAKS. *Rich. III*, I. iii. 49 Because I cannot..Ducke with French nods, and Apish curtesie. **1617** MORYSON *Itin.* I. 40 A Doctor.. commanded me to draw water for his horse, giving me no reward presently but only a nod. **1642** FULLER *Holy & Prof. St.* IV. viii. 276 The Jurie being wise men (whose apprehensions could make up an whole sentence of every nod of the Judge). **1692** LOCKE *Educ.* §77 A Look or Nod only ought to correct them, when they do amiss. **1711** BUDGELL *Spect.* No. 77 ¶5 Those Nods of Approbation which I never bestow unmerited. **1782** MISS BURNEY *Cecilia* v. i, [The] smirk..was converted into a familiar nod. **1818** SHELLEY *Tasso* 14 Those nods and smiles were favours worth the zechin. **1821-30** LD. COCKBURN *Mem.* v. (1874) 241 The speculations and conjectures, and nods and winks, ..were endless. **1887** RUSKIN *Præterita* II. 278 Delivering the last words of each paragraph with two or three energetic nods of his head. **1948** W. O'SULLIVAN in *Thrilling Sports* July 55/1 Rebel felt sure of his surmise on the hidden-crew game when his bunch got the nod to start against the highly regarded Tiger crew. **1953** *Wall St. Jrnl.* 23 Apr. 1/3 Paul L. Troast got the G.O.P. nod, beating his nearest rival, State Sen. Malcolm Forbes, by more than 53,000 votes. **1962** *New Yorker* 17 Nov. 43/2 Industry has at last given literature the nod. **1967** *Boston Globe* 20 May 2/2 (*heading*) Desalting funds get U.S. nod. **1970** *New Yorker* 28 Nov. 151/1 We will not be surprised if the museum gives this piece the nod. **1973** *Bulletin* (Sydney) 25 Aug. 30/2 Perhaps he sees himself —if he gets the nod—as a natural successor to Sir Kevin Ellis in the Speaker's chair of the Assembly. **1975** *Cleveland* (Ohio) *Plain Dealer* 31 Mar. 2-D/2 The five outfielders certainly will include regulars Charlie Spikes, George Hendrick, and Oscar Gamble, meaning the two other jobs will be fought for among Ken Berry, Leron Lee and Rick Manning, with Berry and Lee probably getting the nod.
fig. **1649** BULWER *Pathomyot.* I. §6. 37 All the ready variations of his cunning fingers being done by the Nods of the Soule. **1653** H. MORE *Antid. Ath.* I. xi. §8 To move itself and by its motions and nods to determinate the course of the Spirits.
Prov. (See also WINK *sb.*[1] 2.)
1794 GODWIN *Caleb Williams* I. viii. 171 A nod is as good as a wink to a blind horse. **1809** MALKIN *Gil Blas* II. ix. ¶5, I shall say no more at present, a nod is as good as a wink. **1834** MARRYAT *P. Simple* li, A nod's as good as a wink to a blind horse. **1893** MCCARTHY *Red Diamonds* II. 28 A nod is as good as a wink to such a dark horse as you are. **1935** T. S. ELIOT *Murder in Cathedral* i. 24 My Lord, a nod is as good as a wink. A man will often love what he spurns. **1974** N. FREELING *Dressing of Diamond* 200 All right; a nod's as good as a wink.. You've got these people in mind.
b. A sign of this kind conveying an imperative command, or expressive of absolute power.
1567 MAPLET *Gr. Forest* 29 The race of this life was..eche moment at death his nod and beck. **1596** DRAYTON *Legends* iii. 471 Whose very Nod acts with a thousand Hands. **1641** MILTON *Ch. Gov.* Concl., They stood upon their own bottom, without their main dependance on the royal nod. **1684-5** SOUTH *Serm.* (1692) 395 Masaniello..with a Word, or a Nod, absolutely Commanding the whole City of Naples. **1718** PRIOR *Solomon* II. 944 Nations obey my word, and wait my nod. **1781** GIBBON *Decl. & F.* xxxiv. (1787) III. 361 They watched his nod; they trembled at his frown. **1787** JEFFERSON *Writ.* (1859) II. 332 In Turkey, where the sole nod of the despot is death. **1826** E. IRVING *Babylon* II. 365 The whole western empire was at his nod. **1850** MAZZINI *Royalty & Repub.* 152 You have..multitudes of men dependent on your nod. **1870** BRYANT *Homer* I. I. 28 That thou Mayst be assured, behold, I give the nod.
†**c.** One who is nodded at. *Obs. rare*$^{-1}$.
c **1586** C'TESS PEMBROKE *Ps.* CIX. xii, Alas! I am their scorn, their nod, When in their presence I me show.
d. ***on the nod***, on credit.
1882- in FARMER *Slang.* **1897** *Westm. Gaz.* 11 June 5/3 We went into a..shop and wanted to be served on the nod. **1907** 'IAN HAY' *Pip* ix. 286 He looked all round the room, and I *knew* he knew everything in it had been got on the nod. **1934** *Bulletin* (Sydney) 25 July 46/4 Drunks with determined minds to get bacon, bread, cheese, on the nod. **1945** B. NAUGHTON in C. Madge *Pilot Papers* I. 106 Edith..got them a house,..and Edith filled it with furniture on the 'nod'.
e. ***on the nod***, with a merely formal assent; by abstention from voting.
1959 *Times* 14 Mar. 4/2 The Bill..was given a second reading 'on the nod' by the House. **1969** *Sunday Times* 12 Jan. 4 The agenda, usually the cause of great friction, was accepted 'on the nod'. **1973** C. MULLARD *Black Britain* III. vii. 85 The late Lord (Learie) Constantine, then a member of the Board, opposed the appointment of John Lyttle on the nod, and urged that the job should be advertised in the press.
2. a. An involuntary forward movement of the head in one who has fallen asleep or is drowsy; hence, a short sleep, a nap. Also *transf.*, a lapse.
c **1610** *Lives Wom. Saints* 111 She permitted her bodie to take a little nodd or sleepe. **1625** FLETCHER & SHIRLEY *Nt. Walker* IV. ii, Common-wealths men Are ever subject to the nods; sit down, Sir, A short nap is not much amiss. *a* **1704** T. BROWN *Walk round Lond.* Wks. 1709 III. II. 21 When the Spewing-fit is over, he'll sit down to take a Nod. **1793** *Regal Rambles* 69 Even Homer had his nods now and then. **1894** ANNIE RITCHIE *Chapters fr. Mem.* vi. 70 My own head.. came down with a sleepy nod.
b. ***the land of Nod***, sleep. [A pun on the biblical place-name, *Gen.* iv. 16.]
1731-8 SWIFT *Pol. Conversat.* 214 I'm going to the Land of Nod. **1818** SCOTT *Hrt. Midl.* xxx, There's queer things chanced since ye hae been in the land of Nod. **1863** READE *Hard Cash* xviii, [It] had my lady into the land of Nod in half a minute. **1900** *Chamb. Jrnl.* III. 642/2 In the night-time, when human beings..are absent in the Land of Nod.
c. A state of drowsiness brought on by narcotic drugs. *Esp.* in phr. ***on the nod.***
1942 BERREY & VAN DEN BARK *Amer. Thes. Slang* §509/22 *Play the nod*, to be drowsy as a result of over-indulgence in narotics. **1946** B. TREADWELL *Big Bk. of Swing* xvi. 125/1 *Nod*, tired feeling, sleepy, fatigued. **1951** *Life* 11 June 126/2 Instead of a warming, bright 'charge', he merely becomes comatose and lethargic (goes on the nod in junkie parlance). **1953** W. BURROUGHS *Junkie* (1972) iv. 43 Don't ever invite him to your home... He'll go on the nod in front of your family. He's got no class to him. *Ibid.* xiv. 147 When he arrived in Mexico, I gave him half a grain of M and he went on the nod. **1962** K. ORVIS *Damned & Destroyed* v. 37 While I was on the nod. **1965** *New Statesman* 20 Aug. 248/3 In addict's language—'going on the nod' (becoming senseless). **1969** H. WAUGH *Young Prey* (1970) xxiii. 180 Once you went into the nod, the surroundings no longer mattered.
3. A forward or downward movement. *rare.*
1594 SHAKS. *Rich. III*, III. iv. 102 Like a drunken Sayler on a Mast, Readie with euery Nod to tumble downe. **1692** BENTLEY *Boyle Lect.* 257 By those surprizing nods of the pole we might be tossed backward or forward in a moment from January to June.

†**nod,** *sb.*[2] *Obs. rare*$^{-1}$. = NODDY *sb.*[1] 1.
c **1563** *Jack Juggler* in Hazl. *Dodsley* II. 130 For it would grieve my heart, so help me God, To run about the streets like a masterless nod. **1606** WARNER *Alb. Eng.* XIV. To Rdr. 331 [The poets] most-what but for Nods doe cense Saints, senselesse of more Recompence.

nod, *sb.*[3] *dial.* = NODDLE *sb.*[1] 1 b.
1695 KENNETT *Par. Antiq.* s.v. *Coppire*, The knape or nape.., in Kent the Nod of the neck. **1838** HOLLOWAY *Prov. Dict.* s.v. *Niddick*, The node of the neck is the nape of the neck. *Hants.* **1875** PARISH *Sussex Gloss.* s.v., It catched me right across the nod of my neck. **1884** J. C. EGERTON *Sussex Folk & Ways* 112 A bit of hair from the 'nod'.

nod, obs. form of NEED *sb.*

nod (nɒd), *v.* Also 4-7 nodde. [Of obscure origin: no equivalent form with the same sense is found in any of the cognate languages. Connexion with MHG. *notten* (G. dial. *notteln*) to move about, shake, is doubtful.]
I. 1. *intr.* To make a quick inclination of the head, esp. in salutation, assent, or command.
c **1386** CHAUCER *Manciple's T.* Prol. 47 With this speche the Cook wax wrooth.., And on the Manciple he gan nodde faste For lakke of speche. *c* **1440** *Promp. Parv.* 357/2 Noddynge wythe the heed, *conquiniscio.* **1483** *Cath. Angl.* 255/2 To Nodde; *conqui[n]escere.* **1500-20** DUNBAR *Poems* xxxiv. 39 The Dyvill luche and on him qwoth nod, Renunce thy God and cum to me. **1530** PALSGR. 644/1, I nodde with the heed, *je fais signe de la teste.* When I nodde upon the, than go. **1590** SHAKS. *Mids. N.* III. i. 177 Nod to him, Elues, and doe him Curtesies. **1638** SIR T. HERBERT *Trav.* (ed. 2) 138 Young Ganimeds..went up and downe..to powre out wine to such as noded for it. **1635-56** COWLEY *Davideis* I. Note §29 The Poets are so civil to Jupiter, as to say no less when he either Spoke, or so much as Nodded. **1711** ADDISON *Spect.* No. 12 ¶2 Upon which my Land-lady nods, as much as to say she takes my Meaning, and immediately obeys my Signals. **1828** SCOTT *F.M. Perth* vii, Some of the citizens..began to nod and look exceedingly wise upon the advocate of acquiescence. **1842** TENNYSON *Godiva* 30 And nodding, as in scorn, He parted. **1877** MRS. FORRESTER *Mignon* I. 65 Sir Tristram nods and smiles at her and goes off to the garden.
transf. **1583** GOLDING *Calvin on Deut.* clxx. 1057 Like the Asse which can well ynough nodde with his Eares.
2. a. To let the head fall forward with a quick, short, involuntary motion when drowsy or asleep.
1562 J. HEYWOOD *Prov. & Epigr.* (1867) 91, I nother nod for sleepe.., nor blisse for spirites. **1601** SHAKS. *Jul. C.* IV. iii. 271 If thou do'st nod, thou break'st thy Instrument. **1617** MORYSON *Itin.* I. 247 We not used to this watching, were so sleepy..as we could not abstaine from nodding. **1651** HOBBES *Leviath.* I. ii. 7 As one that noddeth in a chayre. **1711** ADDISON *Spect.* No. 112 ¶3 If he sees any Body else nodding, [he] either wakes them himself, or sends his Servant to them. **1783** S. CHAPMAN in *Med. Comm.* I. 303 Oppressed with inclination to sleep, he frequently nodded. **1840** DICKENS *Barn. Rudge* I, She would be seen..to nod a little way forward, and stop with a jerk. **1870-74** J. THOMSON *City Dreadf. Nt.* IX. ii, A man sits nodding on the shaft.
fig. **1633** G. HERBERT *Temple, Divinitie* i, For fear the starres should sleep and nod, And trip at night. **1648** CRASHAW *Steps to Temple* Wks. (1904) 88 Our Harpes.. Nodding on the willowes slept.
transf. **1879** THOMSON & TAIT *Nat. Phil.* I. I. §106 It is the case of a common spinning-top..; not sleeping upright, nor nodding, but sweeping its axis round [etc.].
†**b.** To wink *at*, overlook, a thing. *Obs. rare*$^{-1}$.
1607 TOURNEUR *Rev. Trag.* II. ii, It well becomes that Judge to nod at crimes.
c. To be momentarily inattentive or inaccurate; to make a slip or mistake. In echoes of Horace *Ars Poet.* 359 (*dormitat Homerus*).
1677 W. HUGHES *Man of Sin* I. v. 20 We see a Jesuite may sometimes nod as well as Homer. **1709** POPE *Ess. Crit.* 180 Those oft are stratagems which errors seem, Nor is it Homer nods, but we that dream. **1796** BURKE *Let. to Noble Lord* 35 Homer nods; and the duke of Bedford may dream. *a* **1876** G. DAWSON *Shaks.*, etc. (1888) 50 If Homer sometimes nods, Johnson snores. **1887** HUXLEY in *19th Cent.* Feb. 196 Scientific reason, like Homer, some-times nods.
d. (See quot.)
1968-70 *Current Slang* (Univ. S. Dakota) III-IV. 86 *Nod*, to drift in and out of consciousness while under the influence of a drug.
3. a. To swing or sway from the perpendicular, as if about to fall.
1582 STANYHURST *Æneis* I. (Arb.) 21 Theire ships too larboord doo nod, seas monsterus haunt them. **1631** GOUGE *God's Arrows* II. §25. 169 Tottering to and fro, nodding and sliding much like carved pictures without life. **1681** DRYDEN *Abs. & Achit.* 801 If ancient Fabricks nod, and threat to fall. **1718** PRIOR *Solomon* II. 732 Porches and schools.. Uncover'd, and with scaffolds cumber'd stood, Or nodded, threatening ruin. **1732** POPE *Essay on Man* I. 255 Heav'n's whole foundations to their centre nod. **1816** H. G. KNIGHT *East. Sketches* (ed. 3) Pref. xii, A fragment of a palace which is nodding to its fall. **1849** RUSKIN *Sev. Lamps* v. §10. 145 The arches nodding westward and sinking into the ground.
b. In fig. context.
1752 YOUNG *Brothers* I. i, His empire shakes, And all her lofty glories nod to ruin. **1770** *Ann. Reg.* I. 7 This vast, ill-founded, and unwieldy empire seems indeed nodding to its fall. **1821** SHELLEY *Hellas* 870 A later Empire nods in its decay.
4. To bend or incline downward or forward with a swaying movement.
1606 SHAKS. *Ant. & Cl.* IV. xiv. 6 A forked Mountaine.. With Trees vpon't, that nodde vnto the world. **1744** AKENSIDE *Pleas. Imag.* II. 203 The shade More horrid nodded o'er me. **1784** COWPER *Task* v. 26 The bents And coarser grass,..fledged with icy feathers, nod superb. **1805** SCOTT *Last Minstr.* I. xxv, Green hazels o'er his basnet nod. **1841** LOWELL *Rosaline*, With long black garments trailing slow, And plumes anodding to and fro.
transf. **1899** CROCKETT *Kit Kennedy* 28 The little green bank..nodding with fern and queen-of-the-meadow.
†**5.** To incline or tend *to* something. *Obs. rare*$^{-1}$.
1599 B. JONSON *Ev. Man out of Hum.* II. i, My brother, sir, for want of education, sir, somewhat nodding to the boor, the clown.
II. 6. *trans.* To incline (the head). Also *transf.*
1553 T. WILSON *Rhet.* (1580) 223 Some noddes their hedde at euery sentence. **1581** G. PETTIE tr. *Guazzo's Civ. Conv.* (1586) I. 34 They nodde theyr heads, and abase their eyes. **1666** DRYDEN *Ann. Mirab.* ccxxii, He..nods at every house his threatening fire. **1695** CONGREVE *Taking of Namur* v, Craggy Cliffs..Nod impending Terrours o'er the Plain. **1840** DICKENS *Barn. Rudge* x, John contented himself with nodding his head in the affirmative. **1898** RIDER HAGGARD *Dr. Therne* 20, I nodded my head.
7. To signify by, to say with, a nod.
1713 STEELE *Englishm.* No. 8. 50 Ay, ay nodded the Porter; but, Sir, whom must I say I came from? **1775** SHERIDAN *Rivals* Epil., She..Curtsies a pension here—there nods a place. **1819** SCOTT *Leg. Montrose* xvi, The general laid his hand upon his nose, and nodded intelligence. **1847** MARRYAT *Childr. N. Forest* ix, The keeper nodded adieu to Edward. **1863** GEO. ELIOT *Romola* III. xxi, He nodded assent, and Romola set out. **1883** *Harper's Mag.* Apr. 741/2 The officer nodded an affirmative.
8. To invite, send, or bring, by a nod.
1606 SHAKS. *Ant. & Cl.* III. vi. 66 Cleopatra Hath nodded him to her. **1647** TRAPP *Comm. 1 Pet.* v. 6 If God can..nod us to destruction. **1684** BROOK *Prec. Remedies* 266 God can speak or nod you to hell in a moment. **1742** YARROW *Love at First Sight* 74 He cries play; the Harper uncases, the Drawer is nodded out. **1821** CLARE *Vill. Minstr.* II. 82 The

beckoning lover nods the maid away. **1889** F. BARRETT *Strange Mask* II. xv. 96, I nodded him out of the room.

9. To cause to bend or sway.

1818 KEATS *Endym.* I. 261 By every wind that nods the mountain pine.

Hence **'nodded** *ppl. a.*

1887 MEREDITH *Ballads & P.* 131 And thou perform The nodded part of pantaloon.

nodal ('nəʊdəl), *a.* [f. NODE *sb.* + -AL[1]; cf. F. *nodal.*] Pertaining to, of the nature of, a node or nodes, in various senses, esp.

1. ***nodal line*** or ***point***, a line or point of absolute or comparative rest in a vibrating body or surface. Similarly ***nodal surface***. Cf. NODE *sb.* 6 a.

1831 FARADAY *Exp. Res.* xlvi. 318 Neither sand nor filings could rest on the quiescent, or nodal, lines. **1838** in *Eng. Mech.* (1869) 24 Dec. 356/3 It was situated at a nodal or quiescent point during some tones. **1873** W. LEES *Acoustics* I. iii. 25 We have not only nodal points in a vibrating string, but we may have nodal lines in a vibrating plate. **1937** J. W. T. SPINKS tr. *Herzberg's Atomic Spectra & Atomic Struct.* i. 41 For $n > 1$, ψ goes once, or more than once, through the value zero before the exponential decrease sets in; that is, on certain spherical surfaces about the nucleus, the ψ function is always zero. These are the nodal surfaces of the ψ function corresponding to the nodes of a vibrating string.

2. *Bot.* and *Biol.* Pertaining to, of the nature of, a node in a vegetable or animal organism.

1842 WILLSHIRE in *Ann. Nat. Hist.* IX. 85, I have examined portions of the plant both young and old, and at all portions of the nodal places. **1875** HUXLEY & DYER in *Encycl. Brit.* III. 683/1 An inter-nodal cell, which elongates greatly,..is succeeded by a nodal cell, which elongates but little. **1882** VINES tr. *Sachs' Bot.* 191 Each nodal disk consists of the anterior half of an older segment [etc.]. **1888** ROLLESTON & JACKSON *Anim. Life* 572 The cirri are borne.. upon certain joints of the stem, hence termed nodal.

3. ***nodal point***, a stopping- or starting-point; a centre of convergence or divergence; a point constituting a node of any kind.

1845 GROVE *Contrib. to Sci.* 298 Forming the nodal point or zero of the table. **1862** M. HOPKINS *Hawaii* 238 These nodal points [in history] determine the length of his chapters. **1863** DANA *Man. Geol.* 598 These species occupy nodal points, as they may be called, or points of divarication. **1880** LE CONTE *Sight* 29 This point of ray-crossing is called the nodal point.

4. *Astron.* Pertaining to planetary nodes.

1868 LOCKYER *Guillemin's Heavens* (ed. 3) 220 It is enough to look out for the body at one or other of these nodal passages. **1872** PROCTOR *Ess. Astron.* ix. 125 The nodal shifting of the meteor-band.

nodality (nəʊ'dælɪtɪ). [f. NODAL *a.* + -ITY.]

a. The degree to which a place is a point of convergence for routes, roads, or the like.

1897 *Geogr. Jrnl.* IX. 78 A higher degree of 'nodality', to use Mr. Mackinder's term, is found where several such furrows [*sc.* shallow valleys in the chalk] meet to form a well-marked though by no means deep hollow. **1902** H. J. MACKINDER *Britain & British Seas* xix. 330 A spot upon which more numerous land and water roads converge, as in a defile past some natural obstacle, may be said to have a higher degree of nodality. **1953** J. M. HOUSTON *Social Geogr. Europe* ix. 205 In cities of long history, such as Paris, it is easy to point out the geographical advantages of the site and the elements of nodality, whether at a bridge-head, a crossing of routes or at a transfer point.

b. The number of nodes of an oscillation.

1905 *Trans. R. Soc. Edin.* XLI. 602 In any given lake, seiches of all degrees of nodality, i.e. uninodal, binodal, trinodal, etc., are possible. **1957** G. E. HUTCHINSON *Treat. Limnol.* I. v. 299 In the case of Loch Earn, periods have been identified which may belong to a nodality as high as the sixteenth.

nodalize ('nəʊdəlaɪz), *v. rare.* [f. NODAL *a.* + -IZE.] *trans.* To make nodal in form or arrangement; to concentrate in a node.

1915 D. H. LAWRENCE *Rainbow* xv. 412 For what purpose were the incalculable physical and chemical activities nodalised in this..speck under her microscope?

nodated, *ppl. a.* ? *Obs.* [f. L. *nōdāt-us*, pa. pple. of *nōdāre* to knot + -ED[1].] Knotted.

1710 J. HARRIS *Lex. Techn.* II, *Nodated Hyperbola*: so Sir Is. Newton calls a peculiar kind of Hyperbola, which by turning round decussates or crosses itself. **1783** HERSCHEL in *Phil. Trans.* LXXIII. 279 A similar curve is to be delineated in the southern hemisphere, in the nodated part of which the same appearances will take place. **1797** *Encycl. Brit.* (ed. 3) II. 483/1 All the stars in the northern hemisphere, situated within the nodated part of the conchoid, will seem to go to the north.

†**no'dation.** *Obs. rare.* [ad. L. *nōdātio*, f. *nōdāre*: see prec.] A knotted part; knottiness.

1597 A. M. tr. *Guillemean's Fr. Chirurg.* 2 b/2 The nodation of the gorge or throte, or Adam's bitte. **1623** COCKERAM I, *Nodation*, Knottinesse.

†**'nodcoke.** *Obs. rare.* [Cf. NOD *sb.*[2]] A fool.

1582 BRETON *Flourish upon Fancie* Wks. (Grosart) I. 17/2 The Cooke that drest the meate: then Nodcoke naturall, Then Jacke-an-apes. *Ibid.* 22/1 So nodcoke I, that longe haue serued thee like a slaue,..Repentaunce gained haue.

nod-crafty *a.* [f. NOD *sb.*[1]] Able to nod with an air of great wisdom.

1608 BACON in Spedding *Life & Lett.* (1868) IV. 92 Solemne goose, stately, leastwise nodd crafty.

†**'noddant.** *Obs. rare*$^{-1}$. [f. NOD *v.* + -ANT[1].] One who nods.

1589 WARNER *Alb. Eng.* v. xxvii, Soothly nodds to Poets now wear largisse, and but lost, Since for the Noddant they observe no pen note worth the cost.

†**'noddary.** *Obs. rare*$^{-1}$. [f. NOD *sb.*[2] or NODDY *sb.*[1] 1 + -ARY[1].] A foolish action.

1647 WARD *Simp. Cobler* 49 Peoples prostrations of these things..are prophane prostitutions, ingnorant ideotisms, under-naturall noddaries.

noddee (nɒ'diː). *rare.* [f. NOD *v.* + -EE[1].]

†**a.** One who causes nodding or drowsiness. *Obs.* **b.** One who is nodded to.

a **1680** H. MARTYN in Aubrey *Lives* (1898) II. 46 Mr. Speaker, a motion has beene to turne out the Nodders; I desire the Noddees may also be turn'd out. **1810** *Sporting Mag.* XXXV. 250 Nodding his head at him [he] significantly added, 'I am the nodder and you are the noddee'.

†**'nodden,** *ppl. a.*, perh. for *knodden* (pa. pple. of KNEAD *v.*) in the sense of 'compact'.

1748 THOMSON *Cast. Indol.* I. x, They neither plow, nor sow; ne, fit for flail, Ere to the barn the nodden sheaves they drove.

nodder ('nɒdə(r)). [f. NOD *v.*] One who nods, in various senses of the verb.

1625 in *Cosin's Corr.* (Surtees) I. 54 You delt bravely with that nodder with his grave head you wrote of. **1653** H. MORE *Conject. Cabbal.* (1713) p. iii, Which those drowsie Nodders over the Letter of the Scripture have very oscitantly collected. *a* **1680** [see NODDEE]. **1747** *Gentl. Mag.* 59 Even the furr'd nodders on the B—h have benefited by these young Scotch pleaders. **1848** LOWELL *Biglow P.* Poems (1890) II. 98 With a congregation of fifty thousand .., and never so much as a nodder, even, among them!

noddie, obs. for NODDY *sb.*[1]

noddiepeake, -poope: see NODDYPEAK, -POOP.

noddil, obs. variant of NODDLE *sb.*[1] and *v.*[1]

nodding ('nɒdɪŋ), *vbl. sb.* [f. NOD *v.* + -ING[1].]

a. The action of the verb. Also = NOD *sb.*[1] 2 c.

1495 *Trevisa's Barth. De P.R.* XVIII. lix. 815 The harte calfe hyghte Hinnulus..& hath that name Hinnulus of.. beckynge other noddynge. **1548** ELYOT, *Nutatio*, noddynge, as a mans head dooeth, whan he sytteth slepyng. **1562** J. HEYWOOD *Prov. & Epigr.* (1867) 91 What thing is it..That bringeth this busy blissing and noddyng? **1615** G. SANDYS *Trav.* 146 They pray silently with ridiculous and continual noddings of their heads. **1649** BULWER *Pathomyot.* II. i. 56 Nodding to us is a gesture of invitation. **1668** DRYDEN *Even. Love* II. i, For all your noddings. and your mathematical grimaces. **1812** L. HUNT in *Exam.* 19 Oct. 657/1 Mr. Sheridan..assures him, with a hearty nodding of the head.. , that they all drank his health. **1844** MARY HOWITT *Own Story* viii. 73 With sundry winks of his large eyes, and upward noddings of his chin. **1882** *Garden* 11 Mar. 167/1 The constant nodding of the florets, even in the calmest weather, is delightful. **1970** H. E. ROBERTS *Third Ear* 10/2 Nodding out, a drug stupor. **1972** C. WESTON *Poor, Poor Ophelia* (1973) xxiv. 149 He's high on something. Nodding, I think they call it.

b. *Comb.*, esp. ***nodding acquaintance***, a slight acquaintance (*with* a person), extending no further than recognition by a nod.

1711 ADDISON *Spect.* No. 124 ¶1 The most severe Reader makes Allowances for many Rests and Nodding-places in a Voluminous Writer. **1825** H. WILSON *Mem.* (ed. 2) II. 108 Having only a sort of bowing, nodding acquaintance with him. **1861** HUGHES *Tom Brown at Oxf.* iv, Many with whom he had scarcely a nodding acquaintance. **1868** DICKENS *Uncomm. Trav.* xxi, I am on nodding terms with a meditative turncock. **1894** D. C. MURRAY *Making of Novelist* 140 A group of men with whom I had a nodding acquaintance. **1959** I. & P. OPIE *Lore & Lang. Schoolch.* viii. 122 Childhood is on nodding terms with the supernatural. **1969** *Times* 22 July p. ii/6 Nobody volunteers that they are not at least on nodding terms with their hero. **1972** H. C. RAE *Shooting Gallery* ii. 74 Three thousand students in this establishment. I know, on nodding terms, about forty of them. **1972** *Times* 7 Aug. (Jamaica Suppl.) p. ii/5 A health care plan..should give many Jamaicans at least a nodding acquaintance with health services.

nodding ('nɒdɪŋ), *ppl. a.* [f. NOD *v.* + -ING[2].]

1. That nods; esp. of plants, trees, etc.

1590 SHAKS. *Mids. N.* II. i. 250, I know a banke..Where Oxslips and the nodding Violet growes. **1634** MILTON *Comus* 38 This drear Wood, The nodding horror of whose shady brows Threats the forlorn..Passinger. **1697** DRYDEN *Virg. Past.* x. 38 A Country Crown Of Fennel, and of nodding Lillies. **1700** —— *Pal. & Arc.* III. 370 At length the nodding statue clash'd his arms. **1725** POPE *Odyss.* IX. 224 Crown'd with rough thickets, and a nodding wood. **1754** GRAY *Progr. Poesy* 12 The rocks and nodding groves. **1792** R. KERR tr. *Linnæus's Anim. Kingd.* 69 Nodding Monkey. **1820** SHELLEY *Ode Liberty* iv, The nodding promontories, and blue isles, And cloud-like mountains. **1871** MEREDITH *H. Richmond* III. 197 He collapsed in speech, and became what he used to call 'one of the ordinary nodding men'.

b. Of the nature of nodding.

1899 *Allbutt's Syst. Med.* VII. 909 Nodding movements of the head accompany these 'Salaam convulsions'.

2. a. Swaying, inclining, tottering.

1693 SOUTHERNE *Maid's last Prayer* II. ii, Sure, Granger, thou lovest a nodding wall, that will bury thee in its ruins. **1715** POPE *Iliad* II. 18 Destruction hangs o'er yon devoted wall, And nodding Ilion waits the impending fall. **1840** DICKENS *Barn. Rudge* lxviii, The tumbling down of nodding walls and heavy blocks of wood. **1853** KANE *Grinnell Exped.* xlviii. (1856) 452 Nodding, pendulous, stalactitic hummocks were not unfrequent.

b. Drowsy, sleepy.

1875 JOWETT *Plato* (ed. 2) III. 38 So to order their lives as to have no need of a nodding justice.

3. *Bot.* (and *Entom.*) Bent or curved downward.

1776 J. LEE *Introd. Bot.* 378 *Nutans*, nodding, the Top or Head bent downwards. **1796** WITHERING *Brit. Pl.* (ed. 3) II. 160 Panicle nodding. **1826** KIRBY & SP. *Entomol.* xlvi. IV. 300 Nodding horn (*Cornu nutans*). When a horn bends forwards. **1870** HOOKER *Stud. Flora* 232 *Erica*... Flowers usually nodding. **1886** A. H. CHURCH *Food Grains Ind.* 40 With..hairy leaves and a much divided nodding panicle.

b. In plant-names.

1789 J. PILKINGTON *View Derbysh.* I. 451 *Bidens cernua*, Nodding Double-tooth. **1855** MISS PRATT *Flower. Pl.* III. 256 Nodding Bur Marigold. **1857** A. GRAY *First Lessons Bot.* (1866) 193 Nodding Trillium or Wake-Robin.

Hence **'noddingly** *adv.*

1882 in OGILVIE. **1885** CLARK RUSSELL *Strange Voy.* II. vii. 110, I was gazing at the distant speck,..and noddingly wondering how far distant [etc.].

noddle ('nɒd(ə)l), *sb.*[1] Forms: 5–6 **nodle**, 5 **-el**, **-ul(le**, **-yl(e**; 6–7 **nodell**, 6 **-il**; 6 **noddel** (7 **-ell**), *Sc.* **-ill**; 6– **noddle**, 9 *dial.* **nuddle**. [Of obscure origin. No similar form appears in any of the cognate languages.]

†**1. a.** The back *of* the head. *Obs.*

c **1425** *St. Elizabeth of Spalbeck* in *Anglia* VIII. 108/46 Sche smytes hir-selfe in þe nodel of the hede byhynde. *c* **1440** *Promp. Parv.* 357/2 Nodyl, or noddle of þe heed (or nolle), *occiput*. **1548** VICARY *Anat.* iii. (1888) 27 A bone of the hinder part of the head called the Noddel of the head. **1567** J. MAPLET *Gr. Forest* 6 They rippe in sunder the noddle of his head. **1676** HOBBES *Iliad* 62 His strong sharp-pointed spear..lighting Behind upon the noddle of his head.

b. The back *of* the neck. (Cf. 2 c.) Now *dial.*

1564 P. MOORE *Hope Health* I. v. 9 Memorie is placed in the hindermost parte of the braine aboue the noddle of the necke. **1567** GOLDING *Ovid's Met.* (1593) v. 108 To Petales he lendeth such a souse Full in the noddle of the necke. **1590** BARROUGH *Meth. Physick* I. xxiv. (1639) 42 After that fasten cupping glasses to the noddle of the neck. **1823** E. MOOR *Suffolk Words* s.v. *Nuddle*, Cut a lock of hair from the nuddle of the neck. **1889** *Macm. Mag.* Sept. 358 Last winter I suffered terrible with the misery in my head—just in the noddle o' the neck it fared to lay.

2. *absol.* †**a.** The back of the head. *Obs.* **b.** The head or pate. (Colloq. or jocular.)

c **1425** *Voc.* in Wr.-Wülcker 633 *Hoc occipud*, A[e] nodulle. *c* **1450** *M. E. Med. Bk.* (Heinrich) 65 As ofte þou anoynte þyne heued in þe nodul be hynde wyþ hoot watur. **1509** HAWES *Past. Pleas.* xliv. (Percy Soc.) 213 On his noddle darkely flamyng Was set Saturne..And Jupiter amiddes his foreheade. **1533** ELYOT *Cast. Helthe* (1541) 10 b, Imagination in the forheed: Reason in the braine: Remembrance in the nodell. **1582** STANYHURST *Æneis* III. (Arb.) 91 His nodil in crossewise wresting downe droups to the growndward. **1607** MARKHAM *Caval.* v. (1617) 21 From the noddle or crowne of his head downward vnto his mayne. *c* **1645** HOWELL *Lett.* (1650) I. 360 The late Queen of Spain took off one of her chapines and clowted Olivares about the noddle with it. **1664** BUTLER *Hud.* II. i. 532 Quoth he, My Head's not made of brass As Friar Bacon's noddle was. **1713** ARBUTHNOT *John Bull* II. v, If they offered to come into the warehouse, then strait went the yard slap over their noddle. **1755** J. SHEBBEARE *Lydia* (1769) II. 191 Master Doctor, having thatched his noddle with his enormous periwig,.. sallied forth. **1825** SCOTT 16 May in *Fam. Lett.* (1894) II. xxi. 267 The fine bust he cut of my poor noddle three years ago. **1864** THACKERAY *D. Duval* i, Many a smart rap with the rolling-pin have I had over my noddle.

†**c.** The back of the neck. (Cf. 1 b.) *Obs. rare.*

1599 BRETON *Will of Wit* 3, I suddenly stept to him, tooke him by the Noddle and turned him to my work. **1612** WOODALL *Surg. Mate* Wks. (1653) 22 Cupping-glasses..are used..to set in the nodell, and on the upper part of the shoulder-blades.

3. The head as the seat of the mind or thought. (Colloq., and usually with playful or contemptuous suggestion of dullness or emptiness.)

1579 TOMSON *Calvin's Serm. Tim.* 656/1 The diuell.. putteth into their braines and foolishe noddles to make great shewes. **1594** LYLY *Moth. Bomb.* II. i, Let me alone,.. there's matter in this noddle. **1611** W. BAKER *Paneg. Verses* in Coryat *Crudities*, Thy worke (which is the moddell Of most the wit enskonsed in thy noddell). **1654** VILVAIN *Theor. Theol.* vii. 193 He frams a new Moon-calf-model of Heaven..after his own Pythagorean Noddle. **1709** STEELE *Tatler* No. 178 ¶2 These Reflections..seize the Noddles of such as were not born to have Thoughts of their own. **1755** B. MARTIN *Mag. Arts & Sci.* 123 All the senseless Whimsies that have possessed the Noddles of the credulous Vulgar. **1793** COWPER *Let. to W. Hayley* 27 July, Laying his own noddle, and the carpenter's noddle together. **1840** BARHAM *Ingol. Leg.* Ser. I. *Acc. New Play*, Lady Arundel..Perplexes her noddle with no such nice queries. **1869** TROLLOPE *He knew*, etc. xxxvi, Slatternly girls, with-out an idea inside their noddles!

†**b.** By extension: A person. *Obs. rare.*

1705 HICKERINGILL *Priest-cr.* 43 John Calvin, a cunning Man, a great Scholar; and, above all, a reaching Noddle. **1711** SHAFTESB. *Charac.* (1737) I. 148 If they can produce a set of Lancashire noddles, remote provincial head-pieces,.. to attest a story of a witch upon a broomstick.

4. *attrib.* and *Comb.*, as †***noddle-pate***; †**noddle-bone**, the occipital bone; †**noddle-case**, a wig; †**noddle-thatcher**, a wig-maker.

1611 COTGR., *Os occipital*, the *noddle bone. **1615** CROOKE *Body of Man* 442 The fourth is called *Os Occipitis* the Noddle or Nowle-bone. **1681** W. ROBERTSON *Phraseol. Gen.* (1693) 271 The hind-head bone, or, the noddle-bone. **1702** T. BROWN *Wks.* (1760) II. 197 Next time you have occasion for a new *noddle-case,..I'll recommend you to the honestest perriwig-maker in Christendom. **1712** STEELE

Spect. No. 518 ¶9 A Pinch of right and fine Barcelona.., and a Noddle-case loaden with Pulvil. **1622** BRETON *Strange News* Wks. (Grosart) II. 11/1 Naturall capacities,..such as they were, and fitted the humour of his *noddle pate. **1716–20** *Lett. fr. Mist's Jrnl.* (1722) I. 84 To deprive 20000 *Noddle-Thatchers of their Livelihood.

ˈnoddle, *sb.*² *rare.* [f. NODDLE *v.*] A nodding movement of the head.

[**1756** FULKE GREVILLE *Max., Charac. & Reflections* 70 His head goes noddle noddle, like a Chinese figure.] **1765** LADY S. LENNOX *Life & Lett.* (1901) I. 172 She has a noddle with her head that makes some people reckon her like me.

†**ˈnoddle**, *v.*¹ *Obs. rare.* [? f. NODDLE *sb.*] *intr.* and *trans.* To beat, pummel (? on the head).

c **1440** *York Myst.* xxix. 369 Dose noddil on hym with neffes That he noght nappe. **1623** WEBSTER *Devil's Law-Case* III. iii, Some women..have long'd to beat their husbands; what if I..exercise my longing Upon my tailor that way, and noddle him soundly?

noddle (ˈnɒd(ə)l), *v.*² [A frequentative of NOD *v.*: see -LE, and cf. NIDDLE-NODDLE.]

1. *trans.* To nod (the head) quickly or slightly.

1733–4 in Mrs. Delany *Life & Corr.* (1861) I. 428 Who should I see at Court last night, noddling her head, but Molly Winnington? **1772** GRAVES *Spir. Quix.* I. 222 She noddled her head, was saucy, and said rude things to one's face. **1822** T. L. PEACOCK *Maid Marian* xiii, Robin struck up and played away merrily, the bishop..noddling his head, and beating time with his foot. **1865** *Routledge's Mag. for Boys* Feb. 109 What a pretty horse yours is, Sir..; he noddles his head so cheerfully.

b. To bring *into* (a state) by noddling; to beat (time) by nodding the head.

1788 ANNA SEWARD *Lett.* (1811) II. 90 The profession of this personage is music,..his height and proportion..well enough by nature, but fidgeted and noddled into an appearance not over prepossessing. **1887** J. ASHBY-STERRY *Lazy Minstrel* (1892) 201, I sit..And noddle time with languid beat.

2. *intr.* To nod or shake the head. (Now *dial.*)

a **1734** NORTH *Lives* (1826) I. 144 He walked splay, stooping and noddling. **1737** BRACKEN *Farriery Impr.* (1757) II. 20 Like the Goose in the Fable, he will still waddle and noddle. **1753** JANE COLLIER *Art Tormenting* 160 You must noddle, and laugh, and pretend to be very merry.

Hence **ˈnoddling** *ppl. a.*

1790 JOANNA BAILLIE *Fugitive Verses* (1840) 89 Up-hoisted arms and noddling head.

†**no(d)dock**, obs. var. of *nuddock* NIDDICK.

Cf. also NOD *sb.*³ and NODDLE *sb.*¹ 1 b.

1594 CAREW *Huartes Exam. Wits* iii. (1596) 25 The man who hath his forehead very plaine, and his nodocke flat. *Ibid.*, A certaine masse of things, which rise from the noddocke vpward. **1650** BULWER *Anthropomet.* Pref., Whilst the blind Nodock wants it ornament. *Ibid.* 6 When ..the Nodock is made flat..the brain [has] not wit.

noddy (ˈnɒdɪ), *sb.*¹ Forms: 6–7 **nody, -dye,** 6–7 **-die;** 6–7 **noddie,** 7 **-dye;** 6– **noddy.** [Of obscure origin; perh. a sb. use of NODDY *a.*¹]

1. A fool, simpleton, noodle.

a **1530** J. HEYWOOD *Love* (Brandl) 798 Why, where the deuyll is this horeson nody? **1550** BALE *Apol.* 30 b, O beastly nody wythoute brayne. **1580** LUPTON *Sivquila* 14 Mighte not he been counted a verye noddy, that woulde pay suche a fine for a Farme? **1621** BURTON *Anat. Mel.* I. ii. IV. iv, Soft fellows, stark noddies, and such as were foolish. **1648** GAGE *West Ind.* 101 In his carriage and experience in the World a simple noddy. **1682** N. O. tr. *Boileau's Lutrin* III. 94 And there they sneaking stand like baffled Noddies. **1705** HICKERINGILL *Priest-cr.* II. iii. 36 The cringing old Noddies and Cathedral-Men, that adore unlighted Candles at the Altar. **1794** WOLCOT (P. Pindar) *Sun & Peacock* Wks. 1812 III. 265 To credit such a tale I'm not the noddy. **1838** DICKENS *Nich. Nick.* vii, To think that I should be such a noddy! **1871** B. TAYLOR *Faust* (1875) I. xxii. 197 A gray and wrinkled noddy.

2. A soot-coloured sea-bird (*Anous stolidus*) of tropical regions, having the figure of a tern, but with shorter wings and tail less forked.

1578 BEST *Frobisher's Voy.* III. (Hakl. Soc.) 232 Certayne fowles, as wylmots, nodies, gulles, etc., which there seeme only to live by sea. **1670** NARBOROUGH *Jrnl.* in *Acc. Sev. Late Voy.* I. 16 Small Sea-Fowls, call'd Black Nodies, flying to and fro. **1697** DAMPIER *Voy.* (1699) 53 The Noddy is a small black Bird, about the bigness of the English Black-bird. **1707** SLOANE *Jamaica* I. 31 We had also Boobies.., as well as Noddies..; they are so called by Seamen,..because they suffer themselves to be catch'd by the Hand. **1777** G. FORSTER *Voy. round World* I. 550 Shearwaters, terns, noddies, gannets,..appeared numerous about us. **1819** BYRON *Juan* II. lxxxii, At length they caught two boobies, and a noddy. **1842** *Penny Cycl.* XXIV. 233/1 The Noddies may be distinguished from the other Sea-Swallows. Their tail is not forked. **1880** *Q. Rev.* Jan. 202 The noddies were torn in pieces and swallowed raw as they were caught.

attrib. **1703** DAMPIER *Voy.* III. 142 We also saw some Boobies, and Noddy-birds. **1707** SLOANE *Jamaica* I. 31 The Noddy Bird was Eleven Inches long from the end of the Bill to that of the Tail.

noddy (ˈnɒdɪ), *sb.*² Also 7 **noddie.** [Of obscure origin: connexion with prec. is not clear.]

1. A card game resembling cribbage (see quot. 1688). Also *noddy-fifteen.* Now *rare.*

1589 [? NASHE] *Almond for Parrat* 52 Let not me take you at noddy anie more, least I present you to the parish for a gamster. **1602** MIDDLETON *Blurt, Master-Constable* III. ii, She'll sit up till you come, because she'll have you play a game at noddy. *c* **1610** J. DAY *Peregr. Schol.* (1881) 77 By plaieing to much at primeroe and noddy he lost Time and his monie to. **1688** HOLME *Armoury* III. xvi. (Roxb.) 72/2 The principall games at cards..8. Noddy, and Cribbidge-Noddy. 2 or 4 persons may play at it, 61 being vp, Each person hath 3 cards and one turned vp to which he makes as many casts as he can. *c* **1780** in Gilpin *Pop. Poet. Cumbld.* (1875) 68 She..lost nineteen-pence at noddy. **1823** E. MOOR *Suffolk Words* s.v., We have also..a game called noddy, the same, I believe, which we call niddy-noddy; another name of which is the Lord Mayor of Coventry. **1828** *Craven Gloss., Noddy-fifteen*, a game at cards. **1875** *Encycl. Brit.* VI. 575/2 Cribbage seems to be an improved form of noddy.

†**2.** The knave in various card games. Also *knave noddy. Obs.*

1611 *Vadianus' Paneg. Verses* in Coryat *Crudities*, Noddie turn'd up, all made, yet lose the tricke. **1680** COTTON *Compl. Gamester* (ed. 2) 76 If you have a knave of that suit which is turned up, it is knave Noddy. **1757** FOOTE *Author* II. Wks. 1799 I. 147 You want four, and I two, and my deal: Now, knave noddy—no, hearts be trumps. **1799** *Spirit Public Jrnls.* II. 14 A noddy, the reader will observe, has two significations—the one, a Knave at all-fours, the other a fool, or Booby.

noddy (ˈnɒdɪ), *sb.*³ [Possibly f. NOD *v.*]

1. A light two-wheeled hackney-carriage, formerly used in Ireland and Scotland (see quots.).

1767 BUSH *Hiber.* (1769) 23 They have an odd kind of hacknies here, that is called the Noddy. **1776** R. TWISS *Tour Irel.* 28 There are many single-horse two wheeled chaises, which constantly ply in the streets in Dublin; they are called noddies. **1825** J. WEDDELL *Voy.* 220 A conveyance was provided such as by us is called a noddy, having but two wheels and being drawn by two horses abreast, on one of which rode the driver. **1844** W. H. MAXWELL *Sports & Adv. Scotl.* ii. (1855) 31 A vehicle, which in Scotland..is called a noddy. **1889** TAIT *Two Cent. of Border Ch. Life* 288 The noddy was a rather cumbrous looking box set on two wheels, entered by a door in the rear, and with a seat for the driver in front.

Comb. **1843** W. WHITE *Jrnls.* (1898) 44 The noddy-drivers were equally noisy..in making their wants known.

2. An inverted pendulum fitted with a spring which tends to restore it to a vertical position.

1846 MALLET in *Trans. R. Irish Acad.* (1848) XXI. 107 They [instruments] have been upon the principle of the inverted pendulum or watchmaker's noddy.

†**ˈnoddy**, *sb.*⁴ *Obs. rare*⁻¹. [f. NOD *v.*; prob. suggested by NODDY *sb.*²] *at noddy*, nodding, napping, asleep.

1665 R. HEAD *Engl. Rogue* (Pearson) I. 110 In Paternoster-row we found a fellow at noddie upon a stall, with his Lanthorne and Candle by him.

†**ˈnoddy**, *a.*¹ *Obs. rare.* [Of obscure origin; perh. f. NOD *v.* Cf. NODDY *sb.*¹] Foolish, silly.

a **1529** SKELTON *Col. Cloute* 1245 That no man shulde se Nor rede in any scrolles Of theyr dronken nolles, Nor of theyr noddy polles. **1645** PAGITT *Heresiogr.* (1661) 60 Ignorant Idiots, noddy Nabalites. **1648** *British Bellman* 6 You present us with an inane nihil, a new Directory of a noddy Synod.

ˈnoddy, *a.*² [f. NOD *v.*] Drowsy, sleepy.

a **1864** HAWTHORNE *S. Felton* (1883) 351 I'll..try to go to sleep. I feel very noddy all at once.

†**ˈnoddy**, *v. Obs. rare*⁻¹. [f. NODDY *sb.*¹] *trans.* To make a fool of.

1600 BRETON *Pasquils Fooles-cappe* lxxvii, If such an Asse be noddied for the nonce,..Let him but thanke himselfe for lacke of Wit.

noddy-board. *rare.* [f. NODDY *sb.*² 1.] A board for playing the game of noddy on.

1654 GAYTON *Pleas. Notes* 196 Billiards, Kettle-pins, Noddy-boards, Tables, Truncks, Shovell-boards, Fox and Geese, or the like. *Ibid.* 239 Here is a Chesse-board to my Hosts Noddy-board. [**1875** *Encycl. Brit.* VI. 575/2 The game was..marked with counters, occasionally by means of a noddy-board.]

†**ˈnoddypeak.** *Obs. rare.* Also 7 **noddi(e)-.** [var. of HODDYPEAK (see N 3), perh. under the influence of *noddypoll.*] A fool. Also *attrib.*

1611 COTGR., *Bauc*, a sot, asse, doult, dull-pated noddipeake. **1653** URQUHART *Rabelais* I. xxv. 116 Ninnie-hammer flycatchers, noddiepeak simpletons. **1694** MOTTEUX *Rabelais* IV. lxvi. (1737) 271 Thou mangy Noddy-peak!

Hence †**noddy-peaked** *a. Obs.*

1694 MOTTEUX *Rabelais* IV. xxix. (1737) 119 A great Noddy-peak'd Youngster.

†**ˈnoddypoll.** *Obs. rare.* In 6 **nody-, nodi-.** [f. NODDY *a.*¹ + POLL *sb.*¹] A blockhead, noodle.

a **1529** SKELTON *Sp. Parrot* 319 There is none that your name woll abbrogate Then nodypollys and gramatolys of smalle intellygens. *a* **1529** —— *Agst. Garnesche* iii. 88 Yt fallyth [not] for..seche a nody polle A pryste for to controlle. **1532** MORE *Confut. Tindale* Wks. 709/1 So foolyshe, that a verye nodypoll nydyote myght be ashamed to say it. **1598** R. BERNARD tr. *Terence, Andria* III. i, I now at length hardly understand.., whorson nodipol that I am.

So †**noddypoop** *sb.* Also †**noddypoop** *v. trans.*, to befool. *Obs.*

1598 FLORIO, *Fatappi*, doltes, fooles, noddies, guls, noddie-poopes. **1640** BROME *Sparagus Gard.* II. iii, Sdaggers, if ever man that had but a mind to be a Gentleman was so noddy poopt!

node (nəʊd), *sb.* [ad. L. *nōd-us* knot, NODUS.]

1. A knot or complication; an entanglement.

1572 BOSSEWELL *Armorie* III. 4, I will not here dissolue the node, ne yet maye not, but..I will partly declare my simple iudgement therein. **1828–32** WEBSTER, *Node*, in poetry, the knot, intrigue or plot of a piece, or the principal difficulty. **1851** C. L. SMITH tr. *Tasso* IV. xxiii, To her are known all frauds with tangled node. **1872** GEO. ELIOT *Middlem.* xix, There are characters which are continually creating collisions and nodes for themselves in dramas which nobody is prepared to act with them.

2. a. A knot, knob, or protuberance, on a root, branch, etc.

1582 HESTER *Secr. Phiorav.* III. lxv. 89 If ye take those nodes or knottes that are on the rootes, and stampe them and boile them. **1611** FLORIO, *Nocchio*, any..nodositie, node,.. or ruggednesse in any tree or wood. **1677** GREW *Anat. Seeds* I. §13 This Seed,..near the Radicle, hath a very small and round Node, like a Navel. **1829** J. L. KNAPP *Jrnl. Nat.* 348 The alburnum or sap wood, being thus wounded, rises up in excrescences and nodes all over the branch. **1842** SELBY *Brit. Forest Trees* 319 The smooth nodes upon the trunk and larger branches.

b. *Bot.* The point of a stem from which the leaves spring.

1835 LINDLEY *Introd. Bot.* I. ii. (ed. 2) 53 At the nodes [1832 *nodi*].., vessels are sent off horizontally into the leaf. **1849** BALFOUR *Man. Bot.* §169 There are regular nodes or points on the stem..at which leaves appear. **1861** BENTLEY *Man. Bot.* 99 Generally the arrangement of the tissue of the stem at the nodes is somewhat different from that of the internodes. **1878** A. H. GREEN, etc. *Coal* iii. 75 Towards the pointed end the nodes are often closely crowded together.

3. a. *Path.* A hard tumour; a knotty swelling or concretion upon some part of the body, esp. on a joint affected by gout or rheumatism.

1610 HEALEY *Theophrastus* (1636) 68 This fellow having ulcers in his legges, nodes or hard tumors in his fingers. **1661** LOVELL *Hist. Anim. & Min.* 2 It wonderfully helpeth the swellings and nodes of the joynts,..making them plain and smooth. **1691** WOOD *Ath. Oxon.* II. 417 The node, which was almost as big as a Pullets egg, was suppurated. **1745** P. THOMAS *Jrnl. Anson's Voy.* 137 Scorbutick Symptoms, such as Blackness of the Skin, hard Nodes in the Flesh. **1779** FORREST *Voy. N. Guinea* 348 His hands and feet were..so contracted, that they grew quite crooked and full of nodes. **1804** ABERNETHY *Surg. Obs.* 145 Ulcerated sore throats, eruptions, and nodes on the bones. **1856** KANE *Arct. Expl.* II. ii. 33 Severe purpuric blotches, and nodes in limbs. **1899** *Allbutt's Syst. Med.* VIII. 467 Nodes select the shins especially.

Comb. **1898** *Allbutt's Syst. Med.* V. 313 The periarteritic and peribronchial granulations may occur as separate nodules of node-like foci.

fig. **1672** MARVELL *Reh. Transp.* I. 135 The Mind too hath its Nodes sometimes, and the Stile its Buboes.

b. Any knot, lump, or knotty formation.

1753 TORRIANO *Midwifery* 20 [It] has Nodes or Glands in it, which perhaps may secrete or prove Receptacles for some Humours. **1791** E. DARWIN *Bot. Gard.* I. 184 Hence dusky Iron sleeps in dark abodes, And ferny foliage nestles in the nodes. **1827** *Gentl. Mag.* XCVII. II. 499 The breaks or decorative nodes which appear in the middle of these characters. **1841** EMERSON *Lect. Conservative* Wks. (Bohn) II. 266 Each of the convolutions of the sea-shell, each node and spine marks one year of the fish's life. **1863** BARING-GOULD *Iceland* 136 A huge node of crag, which is now nearly severed from the cliff.

c. *Anat.* Any small mass of differentiated tissue; also applied to the interruptions (called *nodes of Ranvier*: see RANVIER) of the myelin sheath of myelinated nerve fibres.

1885 *Encycl. Brit.* XIX. 23/2 The medullary sheath shows at certain intervals interruptions called the 'nodes of Ranvier'. **1892**, etc. [see *lymph node* (LYMPH 5)]. **1902** *Trans. Chicago Path. Soc.* V. 151 (*heading*) Are the hemolymph nodes organs *sui generis*? **1917** *Amer. Jrnl. Anat.* XXI. 375 The frequent close association of lymph and hemal nodes makes differentiation of the early stages in development naturally very difficult. **1962** *Gray's Anat.* (ed. 33) 89 At its [*sc.* the primitive streak's] headward end a further area of exceptionally active growth forms a knob-like thickening which is termed the primitive node. **1968** PASSMORE & ROBSON *Compan. Med. Stud.* I. xxviii. 9/1 The part of the heart with the highest spontaneous rate..provides the source of excitation of the whole heart, and this pacemaker is normally the sinuatrial (SA) node. *Ibid.* 10/1 Situated low in the right atrium, near the opening of coronary sinus and tricuspid valve, is another group of cells with a specialized conducting function, the atrioventricular (AV) node.

4. *Astr.* **a.** One of the two points at which the orbit of a planet intersects the ecliptic, or in which two great circles of the celestial sphere intersect each other. ***ascending*** and ***descending node***: (see the adjs.).

1665 *Phil. Trans.* I. 38 The said Circle inclined to..the Nodes towards the beginning of Gemini and Sagittary. **1676** *Ibid.* XI. 682 These Observations will serve to verifie the Nodes of the Orbes of the Satellites with the Orb of Jupiter. **1728** PEMBERTON *Newton's Philos.* 177 The motion of the aphelion and nodes, which continually increase, become sensible in a long series of years. **1748** *Phil. Trans.* XLV. 11, I consider'd..the Situation of the Ascending Node of the Moon's Orbit. **1812–16** PLAYFAIR *Nat. Phil.* (1816) II. 125 The line in which the plane of the moon's orbit cuts the ecliptic, is called the Line of the Nodes. **1834** MRS. SOMERVILLE *Connex. Phys. Sci.* (1849) 12 When the planet is in the plane of the ecliptic, its latitude is zero: it is then said to be in its nodes. **1864** HERSCHEL in *Gd. Words* 58/2 Nineteen years, the period of the circulation of the nodes of the moon's orbit.

†**b.** A small ball representing a planet on the Ptolemaic sphere. *Obs. rare.*

1674 MOXON *Tutor to Astron. & Geog.* (ed. 3) App. 204 Bring each respective Node which represents each respective Planet, to those several places you find them in the Ephemeris. *Ibid.*, The little golden Node on the Suns Orb.

5. *Dialling.* (See quot. and NODUS *sb.* 2.) ? *Obs.*

1704 J. HARRIS *Lex. Techn.* I, *Nodus* or *Node*, in Dyalling, is a certain Point in the Axis or Cock of the Dial, by the shadow of which, either the Hour of the Day,..or the Parallels of the Sun's Declination, his Place in the Ecliptick,

. . &c. are shown. [Also in Chambers *Cycl.* (1727-38), and some later Dicts.]

6. a. A point or line of absolute or comparative rest in a vibrating body. Hence also, a point at which a spherical harmonic or similar function has the value zero. Cf. NODAL *a.* 1.

1831 BREWSTER *Nat. Magic* viii. (1833) 182 This stationary point is called a node. **1869** SIR E. REED *Shipbuild.* i. 13 Knowing that with flexible ships the edge of the bulkhead was a sort of node to the flexure. **1873** W. LEES *Acoustics* I. iii. 24 Ventral segments . . are separated from each other by points of apparent rest, called nodes. **1879** G. PRESCOTT *Sp. Telephone* 95 There will be two equal vibrating segments and a point of rest or node at the centre. **1884** HAWEIS *Musical Life* I. 83 To hit upon the lesser nodes for single harmonics was one of the recognised violin difficulties. **1905** *Trans. R. Soc. Edin.* XLI. 601 At these points, which are called nodes, the level of the surface [of the lake] is unaltered by the seiche. **1927** T. M. MACROBERT *Spherical Harmonics* iii. 59 The middle point . . is always at rest, and this point is called a node, the end-points also being nodes. For the *n*th mode there are $n - 1$ nodes, as well as the two end nodes. **1957** G. E. HUTCHINSON *Treat. Limnol.* I. v. 299 While the periods and positions of the nodes depend on the form of the lake basin, the amplitude of the seiche depends only on the source of energy that generates it. **1964** J. W. LINNETT *Electronic Struct. Molecules* i. 6 For $n = 3$, the $l = 0$ function would be multiplied by a radial function varying with *r*, the distance from the nucleus, which had two nodes (i.e. it may be considered, rather approximately, as made up of 3 half-waves).

b. *Electr.* A point on an aerial or in a circuit where the current or voltage is zero.

1915 A. E. SEELIG tr. *Zenneck's Wireless Telegr.* ii. 25 In a lineal oscillator . . the current amplitude is greatest at the middle and zero at the ends of the oscillator. In other words, there are 'current nodes' at each end and a 'current anti-node' at the middle. . . The 'potential' or 'voltage anti-nodes' occur at each end of the oscillator, the 'potential node' being at the middle. **1947** E. K. SANDEMAN *Radio Engin.* I. xvi. 645 At the voltage anti-nodes (current nodes) the incident and reflected voltages are in phase and therefore add, while the incident and reflected currents are 180° out of phase and therefore subtract. **1968** *Radio Communication Handbk.* (ed. 4) xiii. 3/1 The positions of maxima are usually known as current (or voltage) anti-nodes or loops and the intermediate positions as nodes or zeros.

7. a. *Geom.* A point at which a curve crosses itself; a double or multiple point; also, a similar point on a surface. Also *attrib.*

1850 in OGILVIE. **1866** BRANDE & COX *Dict. Sci.*, etc. II. 675/2 In the theory of surfaces, nodes are also called conical points. **1877** *Encycl. Brit.* VI. 720/2 If the given curve has a node, the first polar passes through this node. *Ibid.* 721/1 A cusp of the second kind, or node-cusp.

b. A point or vertex of a network or graph (sense 1). Also ***node point.***

1864 H. J. S. SMITH in *Rep. Brit. Assoc. Adv. Sci. 1863* I. 768 Let an infinite plane area be divided by two systems of parallel lines into similar and equal parallelograms. The vertices of these parallelograms we shall call nodes. **1892** G. B. MATHEWS *Theory of Numbers* I. iv. 124 Let the plane of reference be divided up into a system of equal and similar parallelograms . .; such a system will be called a net, . . and each joint, where two lines cross, a node. **1941** *Proc. Cambr. Philos. Soc.* XXXVII. 194 Let *N* be a network (or linear graph) such that at each node not more than *n* lines meet (where $n > 2$), and no line has both ends at the same node. **1957** N. CHOMSKY *Syntactic Structures* vii. 68 The phrase structure of a terminal string is determined from its derivation, by tracing segments back to node points. **1964** J. J. KATZ in Fodor & Katz *Struct. of Lang.* 526 The amalgam is assigned to the set of paths associated with the node (i.e., the point at which an *n*-ary branching occurs) that immediately dominates the sets of paths from which the paths amalgamated were drawn. The amalgam provides one of the meanings for the sequence of lexical items that the node dominates. **1964** A. BATTERSBY *Network Analysis* ii. 14 The beginning and end of a job are events; they are represented as numbered circles called nodes. *Ibid.* 19 The nodes which represent the events are numbered successively from the beginning to the end of the network. **1966** S. BEER *Decision & Control* ix. 194 In the first place, the nodes in the network which now represent individuals are not very tidily placed in ranks of equivalent importance. **1967** *Electronics* 6 Mar. 132/1 The feedback loop is formed by connecting the amplifier's inverting input . . to potentiometer R_3. When power is first applied . . the voltage at the common node rises quickly to 6·6 volts. **1971** [see GRAPH *sb.*[1] 1]. **1972** *Sci. Amer.* June 52/3 By last month the network . . included 24 computer centers ('nodes' in the terminology of the system), ranging from Massachusetts to California. **1975** *Language* LI. 388 The use of the empty node in the derivation of truncated passives is not motivated empirically, but rather is a way of retaining a transformational analysis of passives.

†**node**, *v.* *Obs. rare*$^{-0}$. [ad. It. or L. *nōdāre.*] *intr.* To form a knot.

1611 FLORIO, *Nodare*, to knot, to knit, to node, to knur.

node, obs. form of NEED *sb.*

'noded, *ppl. a.* [f. NODE *sb.* 6 a.] Divided into nodes.

1897 *Pop. Sci. Monthly* Nov. 138 On reflecting light from such a noded plate the proper light alone was reflected.

noder, obs. variant of OTHER *a.*

†**'nodgecock, -comb.** *Obs. rare.* [Of obscure formation.] A ninny, simpleton.

1566 PAINTER *Pal. Pleas.* I. 211 b, This poore Nodgecock contriving the time in sweete and pleasaunt wordes with his dareling Simphorosia. **1593** NASHE *Four Lett. Confut.* Wks. (Grosart) II. 212 Confesse thy selfe a flat nodgcombe before all this congregation. **1596** —— *Saffron Walden* M 4 So was he counted and bad stand by for a Nodgscombe.

†**'nodhead.** *Obs. rare*$^{-1}$. [f. NOD *sb.*[2]] A foolish head or wit.

1652 H. BELL tr. *Luther's Colloq.* 292 They will all triumph, and show their nodheads in writing books.

nodi-, comb. form of L. *nōd-us* knot, NODE, used in some scientific (*Bot.* and *Entom.*) terms, as **'nodicorn** [F. *nodicorne*] *a.*, having nodose antennæ (*Cent. Dict.* 1890). **no'diferous** *a.*, bearing nodes. **nodi'florous** [F. *nodiflore*] *a.*, having flowers springing from the nodes of the stem. **'nodiform** *a.*, having the form of a node or knot (esp. of joints).

1713 PETIVER in *Phil. Trans.* XXVIII. 188 Capitated and Nodiflorus Plants. **1856-8** W. CLARK *Van der Hoeven's Zool.* I. 75 Polyps with scattered tentacles, nodiferous or globose at the tip.

nodical ('nəʊdɪkəl), *a.* *Astr.* [f. NODE *sb.* 4 a + -ICAL.] Of or pertaining to the nodes.

1839 *Penny Cycl.* XV. 373/2 The average nodical month, or from a node to a node of the same kind. **1842** BRANDE *Dict. Sci.*, etc. s.v. *Moon*, The interval from node to node is called the nodical period, and is shorter than any of the other periods. **1868** LOCKYER *Elem. Astron.* 102 One period being 27 d. 5 h. 6 m., called the nodical revolution of the Moon.

nodie, obs. f. NODDY *sb.*[1]

nodipol, var. of NODDYPOLL *Obs.*

nodock: see NOD(D)OCK.

nodosarian (nəʊdəʊ'sɛərɪən), *a.* and *sb.* [f. mod.L. *Nodosaria* (see def.) + -AN.]

a. *adj.* Belonging to a family (*Nodosaria*) of vitreous-shelled foraminifera, the individuals of which are composed of a rectilinear succession of similar chambers. **b.** *sb.* An individual of this family.

1858 W. C. WILLIAMSON *Foraminifera Gt. Britain* 16 Where a group of large and strong Nodosarian shells abound. **1865** PARKER & JONES in *Phil. Trans.* CLV. vi. 347 A higher specialization of the simple repetitive Nodosarian form. **1884** BRADY in *Challenger Rep., Zool.* IX. 492 These two drawings . . illustrate . . its relation to the other straight Nodosarians.

So **no'dosarine** *a.* and *sb.*

1862 W. B. CARPENTER *Introd. Foraminifera* 165 The Nodosarines are not so common in littoral deposits. **1865** PARKER & JONES in *Phil. Trans.* CLV. vi. 340 Several of the Nodosarine forms are well represented in the northern seas. **1884** BRADY in *Challenger Rep., Zool.* IX. 489 A mixed group, the Nodosarine members of which are now included in . . Rhabdogonium.

nodose (nəʊ'dəʊs), *a.* [ad. L. *nōdōs-us*: see NODE *sb.* and -OSE.] Knotty; knotted or knobbed; furnished with, or characterized by, knot-like swellings.

1721 BAILEY, *Nodose*, knotty, full of knots. **1752** J. HILL *Hist. Anim.* 580 The Capra, with nodose horns, bending towards the back, the Ibex. **1767** GOOCH *Treat. Wounds* I. 165 A plaster compress, . . with the well adapted nodose bandage. **1822-34** *Good's Study Med.* (ed. 4) I. 274 The head of the thread-worm is subulate, nodose and divided into three vesicles. **1846** DANA *Zooph.* (1848) 504 Branches . . often irregularly inflated or nodose. **1880** V. L. CAMERON *Future Highway* II. xii. 263, I found the horn of a male [mountain sheep] . . which was recurved, flattened, and nodose. **1897** *Allbutt's Syst. Med.* II. 48 The nodules may coalesce into large irregular, nodose, or flattened masses.

transf. **1880** BLACKMORE *Mary Anerley* III. iii. 38 His enemy arose slowly with grunts, and action nodose and angular, rather than flexibly graceful.

nodosity (nəʊ'dɒsɪtɪ). [ad. L. *nōdōsitas* (whence also F. *nodosité*, It. *nodosita*), f. *nōdōs-us*: see prec. and -ITY.]

1. The state or quality of being nodose or knotty.

1611 FLORIO, *Nodosita*, . . knottinesse, nodosity. **1656** BLOUNT *Glossogr.*, *Nodosity*, . . knottiness, knobbiness. **1805** *Med. Jrnl.* XIV. 275 The Clinical History of the Nodosity of the Joints. **1837** CARLYLE *Mirabeau* Misc. 1869 V. 133 It is very beautiful, this mild strength, . . in contrast with his brother's nodosity. **1839-47** *Todd's Cycl. Anat. & Phys.* III. 255/1 A tumour . . like a shelled walnut in point of size and nodosity.

2. A knotty swelling or protuberance.

1601 HOLLAND *Pliny* II. 311 The same ointment . . abateth the tumors & nodosities vpon the ioints. **1646** SIR T. BROWNE *Pseud. Ep.* v. v. 239 That tortuosity, or complicated nodosity, we usually call the Navell. **1677** PLOT *Oxfordsh.* 171 Such are the Nodosities . . to be found in Ash as well as Maple. *a* **1791** BURKE in Boswell *Johnson* an. 1781, It has all the nodosities of the oak without its strength. **1828** STARK *Elem. Nat. Hist.* I. 165 A dorsal fin in some species; nodosities on the back in others. **1872** COHEN *Dis. Throat* 182 These nodosities . . are softer than the rest of the substance. **1899** *Allbutt's Syst. Med.* VIII. 468 Tender nodosities or nodes on the shins.

fig. **1808** KNOX & JEBB *Corresp.* (1834) I. 461 There does not seem to remain in him a single doctrine nodosity. **1892** *Academy* 6 Feb. 125/1 These nodosities upon the golden thread of an otherwise fine diction.

†**no'dosous**, *a.* *Obs.*$^{-0}$ Nodose.

1623 COCKERAM I, *Nodosous*, full of knots.

nodous ('nəʊdəs), *a.* [ad. L. *nōdōs-us*: see NODE *sb.* and -OUS.] Full of knots, knotty.

1646 SIR T. BROWNE *Pseud. Ep.* 183 This [finger] is seldome or last of all affected with the Gout, and when that becometh nodous, men continue not long after. **1679** EVELYN *Sylva* xxxi. (ed. 3) 201 The nodous, and knotty part of these sort of Trees. **1709** STEELE *Tatler* No. 36 ¶4 He has not a Bone sound, but a Thousand nodous Parts for which the Anatomist have not Words. **1835-6** *Todd's Cycl. Anat. & Phys.* I. 611/2 At the nodous parts of the tube were slight vortices in the current.

nodre, variant of NOTHER, neither.

nodular ('nɒdjʊlə(r)), *a.* [f. NODULE + -AR.]

1. *Min.* and *Geol.* Having the form of, occurring in, nodules.

1794 SULLIVAN *View Nat.* II. 6 Nor will I say, that they were originally created in nodular forms. **1796** KIRWAN *Elem. Min.* (ed. 2) II. 270 Found massive, . . very rarely specular, or Botryoidal, or nodular. **1802-3** tr. *Pallas's Trav.* (1812) II. 222 We observed . . veins of red, nodular iron-ore. **1863** DANA *Man. Geol.* 239 The structure of the limestone is often nodular or concretionary. **1878** RAMSAY *Phys. Geogr.* xi. 160 Layers and nodular masses of gypsum.

2. Of zoophytes: Having nodes on the stem.

1846 DANA *Zooph.* (1848) iv. 83 The germ-polyp . . gives rise to the various branching and nodular zoophytes.

3. *Path.* Of the nature of, characterized by, knotty tumours.

1872 COHEN *Dis. Throat* 205 The surface of implantation at the basilary apophysis remained unequal and nodular. **1878** T. BRYANT *Pract. Surg.* I. 700 A spongy nodular feel of the mucous membrane. **1898** P. MANSON *Trop. Diseases* 394 The essential element in nodular leprosy is the leproma.

4. *Metallurgy.* Of cast iron: containing all the graphite in the form of small spheroids rather than flakes, which results in increased strength and ductility and can be brought about by adding a suitable inoculant. Cf. SPHEROIDAL *a.*

1947 *Machinery* LXX. 420/1 (*heading*) Nodular cast iron. **1950** [see INOCULATION 3]. **1967** A. H. COTTRELL *Introd. Metallurgy* xxv. 520 In nodular cast irons the structure is developed directly, in an as-cast grey iron, by adding a small amount of magnesium or cerium alloy to the metal in the ladle.

nodularity (nɒdjʊ'lærɪtɪ). [f. NODULAR *a.* + -ITY.] The state or condition of being nodular.

1948 L. MARTIN *Clin. Endocrinol.* x. 200 Nodularity so extreme as to be obviously pathological. **1953** *Brit. Jrnl. Urology* XXV. 27 Radial striation on the fractured surface of a calculus is often associated with nodularity of the external surface. **1971** *Amer. Jrnl. Public Health* LXI. 241 (*heading*) Thyroid nodularity in southwestern Utah school children exposed to fallout radiation.

nodulate ('nɒdjʊleɪt), *v.* *Bot.* [f. NODUL(E + -ATE[3], or back-formation from NODULATED *a.*]

a. *trans.* To produce root nodules on.

1939 *Soil Sci.* XLVII. 67 A velvet bean culture . . produced nodules on six plant species included within the cowpea group yet did not nodulate three other plant members. **1973** *Nature* 17 Aug. 460/1 The *Trema* root nodule bacterium is the first of the rhizobia known to effectively nodulate a non-legume.

b. *intr.* Of a plant: to undergo nodulation.

1956 *Biol. Rev.* XXXI. 111 The degree to which an individual plant can be induced to nodulate earlier by root exudates depends wholly upon its normal nodulating habit in their absence. **1968** GIBBS & SHAPTON *Identification Methods for Microbiologists* 61 Only about 1200 species have been examined for the presence of nodules and not all of these nodulate.

Hence **'nodulating** *vbl. sb.* and *ppl. a.*

1944 *Proc. Soil Sci. Soc. Amer.* IX. 95 (*heading*) The nodulating performance of three species of legumes. **1960** *Dissertation Abstr.* XX. 3003/1 Experiments using . . nodulating and non-nodulating soybeans were established. **1971** M. ALEXANDER *Microbial Ecol.* xi. 259 The nodulating habit is particularly prominent among genera of Podocarpaceae, a family that includes trees important as timber.

nodulated ('nɒdjʊleɪtɪd), *a.* [ad. L. type **nōdulāt-us* (cf. NODULATION) + -ED[1].] Furnished with, characterized by, nodular growths. (Cf. NODULATE *v.*)

1835-6 *Todd's Cycl. Anat. & Phys.* I. 409/1 Among the invertebrata its surface is uneven and nodulated like that of a raspberry. **1849** BALFOUR *Man. Bot.* §70 These tubers occasionally become nodulated, or elongated, or curved in various ways. **1876** BRISTOWE *Th. & Pract. Med.* (1878) 276 The nodulated thickening of the eyebrows and adjacent parts of the forehead. **1932** E. B. FRED et al. *Root Nodule Bacteria & Leguminous Plants* ii. 17 In 1905 Norton & Walls . . . suggested that the wild Leguminosae, nearly all of which are nodulated in Maryland, are important agents for adding nitrogen and humus to the soils. **1957** *Canadian Jrnl. Microbiol.* III. 120 In the nodulated plants the nitrogen content was fully twice the seed nitrogen. **1971** M. ALEXANDER *Microbial Ecol.* xi. 259 In addition to the plants cited, several gymnosperms are nodulated, and they may be capable of assimilating N_2.

nodulation (nɒdjʊ'leɪʃən). [f. L. type **nōdulāre* (f. *nōdulus* NODULE) + -ATION.] The process of becoming nodulated, or the result of this. (Cf. NODULATE *v.*)

1872 COHEN *Dis. Throat* 138 To the touch the tumor appeared but little hard, without nodulations. **1897** *Allbutt's Syst. Med.* II. 50 After the stage of nodulation has lasted for a variable period, the final stage of ulceration sets in. **1924** *Soil Sci.* XVII. 439 Fellers found that under many conditions nodulation was increased by an application of phosphorus, calcium, or potassium. **1973** *Nature* 17 Aug. 459/1 Roots of *Trema aspera* Decaisne plants growing between rows of tea in . . New Guinea showed abundant nodulation, similar to the nodules found on many tropical legumes.

nodule ('nɒdju:l). [ad. L. *nōdulus*, dim. of *nōdus* knot: see -ULE. Hence also F. *nodule*.]

†**1.** A small quantity of some medicinal substance tied up in a bag. *Obs.*

1600 SURFLET *Countrie Farme* II. lxx. 420 Hang in the vessell a nodule or knot full of cinnamome [etc.]. **1634** T. JOHNSON tr. *Parey's Chirurg.* (1678) XXVI. xxiii. 644 Nodules have the same use with Suppositories and are oftentimes substituted in stead of Glysters. **1694** SALMON *Bate's Dispens.* 716/2 Tie it up in a Bit of Silk, in Form of a Nodule. **1713** *Phil. Trans.* XXVIII. 229 They smell to black Cummin-seed bruised and tyed up in a Nodule. **1756** C. LUCAS *Ess. Waters* II. 65 Applied warm, in nodules or sacks, it assuages pain.

2. *Min.* and *Geol.* A small rounded lump of some mineral or earthy substance.

1695 WOODWARD *Nat. Hist. Earth* IV. (1723) 207 Strata compiled of metallick and mineral Nodules. **1766** BORLASE in *Phil. Trans.* LVI. 36 A large cake, or nodule, of tin ore, weighing about six pounds. **1794** SULLIVAN *View Nat.* I. 439 It is never found crystallized, but rather, in separate irregular nodules, scattered through other strata. **1815** BAKEWELL *Geol.* 191 In some of the beds of clay over coal detached nodules of iron-stone occur. **1880** GÜNTHER *Fishes* 196 Devonian fishes are frequently found under peculiar circumstances, enclosed in the so-called nodules.

fig. **1885** *Academy* 24 Oct. 265/1 A single point of literature, one shining nodule broken off the rock.

3. *Bot.* A small node or knot in the stem or other part of a plant. Esp., one formed on the root of a leguminous plant by symbiotic bacteria. Also *attrib.*

1796 WITHERING *Brit. Plants* (ed. 3) IV. 141 Branches very fine,..nodules of fructifications small. **1839** LINDLEY *Introd. Bot.* I. ii. (ed. 3) 79 Those nodules which are so well known in the bark of the Beech, and some other trees. **1867** J. HOGG *Microsc.* II. i. 308 These plants are produced by.. minute cellular nodules called gemmæ or buds. **1890** *Proc. R. Soc.* XLVII. 104 The limited growth in pot 1..is coincident with the entire absence of nodule-formation. **1922** *Encycl. Brit.* XXX. 72/1 The so-called 'nodule' organisms (*Pseudomonas radicicola*)..live in symbiosis with the leguminous plants. **1965** BELL & COOMBE tr. *Strasburger's Textbk. Bot.* 303 In the development of the nitrogen-fixing nodules on the roots of the Leguminosae the first process is a normal infection of the rootlets by various races of the aerobic *Rhizobium leguminosarum*..living saprophytically in the soil.

4. *Anat.* **a.** (See quots.)

1839-47 *Todd's Cycl. Anat. & Phys.* III. 690 The anterior extremity of the inferior vermiform process projects into the cavity of the fourth ventricle, and serves to close it at its inferior extremity... Reil has named it *the Nodule.* **1840** G. V. ELLIS *Anat.* 49 The apex of the uvula, which projects into the fourth ventricle, is the nodule.

b. A small knot or knotty tumour in some part of the body.

1845 BUDD *Dis. Liver* 108 By its contraction the lobular substance of the liver is drawn into round nodules. **1865** LIVINGSTONE *Zambesi* xiii. 275 The true skin next thickens and rises in nodules. **1880** BASTIAN *Brain* 27 The groups of nerve cells..are usually aggregated so as to form distinct and separate nodules known as 'ganglia'.

Hence **'noduled** *a.*, formed into nodules. Also **nodu'liferous** *a.*, bearing or yielding nodules; **'noduliform** *a.*, having the form of a nodule.

1791 E. DARWIN *Bot. Gard.* I. 398 As you now dissect with hammers fine The granite-rock, the nodul'd flint calcine.

nodulize ('nɒdjʊlaɪz), *v.* *Metallurgy.* [f. NODUL(E + -IZE.] *trans.* To convert (esp. finely-divided iron ore) into nodules. So **'nodulized** *ppl. a.*, **'nodulizing** *vbl. sb.*

1905 *U.S. Patent* 794,673 1/1 A new and useful Improvement in Methods or Processes of Purifying and Nodulizing Metalliferous Materials. **1905** *Iron Age* LXXVI. 590/1 The National Metallurgic Company has erected what it terms an ore purifying and nodulizing plant. **1906** *Jrnl. Iron & Steel Inst.* LXXI. 359 One rotary kiln.. has produced an average of 75 to 90 tons of nodulised desulphurised pyrites cinder per day of twenty-four hours. **1921** W. GOWLAND *Metallurgy of Non-Ferrous Metals* (ed. 3) 139, 62 per cent. of the concentrate is nodulized, 14 per cent. sintered, and 24 per cent. reduced direct. **1968** E. N. SIMONS *Outl. Metallurgy* i. 3 Nodulizing..passes the ore too fine for use through a rotary kiln, in which it is heated with a relative movement between an internal rotary drum and an outer shell. Nodulizing has some advantages over sintering. *Ibid.* iii. 34 The graphite is present as tiny round balls, i.e. it is nodulized.

Hence **noduli'zation**, the process of nodulizing.

1915 *Chem. Abstr.* IX. 590 Nodulizing iron ores..by subjection first to a reducing flame at a temp. only slightly below that required for nodulization and then to an oxidizing flame which suddenly raises the temp. of the material above the nodulizing point. **1921** W. GOWLAND *Metallurgy of Non-Ferrous Metals* (ed. 3) 138 In the process of nodulization the proportion of sulphur has been reduced from 28 to 18 per cent. **1968** E. N. SIMONS *Outl. Metallurgy* iii. 34 Nodulization or spheroidization renders the iron stronger and more ductile.

nodulle, obs. form of NODDLE.

nodulose (nɒdjʊ'ləʊs), *a.* *Bot.* and *Zool.* [f. NODULE + -OSE.] Having little knots or knobs.

1828 STARK *Elem. Nat. Hist.* II. 45 Shell ovate,..wrinkles nodulose. **1835** LINDLEY *Introd. Bot.* I. ii. (1839) 109 If the fibres have occasionally dilatations at short intervals, they are called nodulose. **1852** DANA *Crust.* I. 131 All joints of legs..nodulose. **1870** BENTLEY *Man. Bot.* (ed. 2) 124 In the Common Dropwort the root is nodulose.

nodulous ('nɒdjʊləs), *a.* [f. NODULE + -OUS: cf. F. *noduleux*.] = NODULOSE.

1841 JOHNSTON in *Proc. Berw. Nat. Club* I. ix. 271 The ribs..[are] sometimes only to be traced in a nodulous line along the suture. **1850** DANA *Geol.* App. I. 728 Whorls of the spire angulated and nodulous in the middle. **1864** *Reader* 240/1 Subplicate character..inclining to nodulous.

†**'nodulus.** *Obs. rare.* = NODULE 1.

1651 CULPEPPER *Astrol. Judgem. Dis.* (1658) 222 Also you may make a Nodulus with any of these oyles. **1688** HOLME *Armoury* III. 424/2 The Nodus, or Nodulus, is a Bag of Ingradients..put into Beer, Ale, or Wine, the tincture whereof the Patient is to drink.

nodum ('nəʊdəm). *Ecology.* Pl. **noda.** [mod.L., perh. f. L. *nōdus* knot.] (See quot. 1955.)

1955 M. E. D. POORE in *Jrnl. Ecol.* XLIII. 243 The additional term Nodum has been introduced to apply to an abstract unit [of vegetation]..of uncertain status. *Ibid.* 259 The term nodum is being adopted to apply to abstract vegetation units of any category. It corresponds to the term taxon in systematics. *Ibid.*, Both the *Rhacomitrium-Carex bigelowii* and the *Nardus* noda..are clearly defined communities. **1961** *Watsonia* V. 76 The nodum is only developed on south- to west-facing slopes of 10 to 15°, fully exposed to wind and salt spray. **1971** *New Phytologist* LXX. 1155 The noda are related to environmental factors. *Ibid.*, A strongly marked relationship between the percentage of maritime species in a nodum and the sodium-organic ratio is noted. **1973** H. J. B. BIRKS *Past & Present Vegetation of Skye* iv. 24/2 A community is any aggregation of plants constituting a certain spatial whole... It is regarded as synonymous with Poore's general term 'nodum'. *Ibid.* 25/2 Where the vegetational unit is rather heterogeneous, it is termed a *nodum*. The word is italicised when it is used to refer to a specific vegetational unit that does not merit the rank of association.

‖**nodus** ('nəʊdəs). Pl. **nodi.** [L. *nōdus*. Cf. F. *nodus* (16th c., Paré).]

†**1.** *Path.* A knotty swelling. = NODE *sb.* 3 a. *Obs.*

c **1400** *Lanfranc's Cirurg.* 252 Nodus is a knotte, & þus comeþ in þe iȝe liddis. **1650** J. F[RENCH] *Chym. Dict.* s.v., Nodi are hard tumours of the joints. **1672** *Phil. Trans.* VII. 4062 Not long after his landing, he found a certain Nodus or hard lump in the very place whence this stone was cut. **1706** in PHILLIPS (ed. Kersey), *Nodus* or *Node*,..a kind of gummy Swelling, made by the settling of a gross Humour between the Bone and the Periosteum.

†**2.** *Dialling.* (See quot. and NODE *sb.* 5.)

1668 MOXON *Mech. Dyalling* 39 The point in the middle of this Glass we will mark A, and for distinction sake call it Nodus. Through this Nodus you must draw a Meridian Line. *Ibid.* Fasten a string just on the Nodus.

3. The base of a numerical system. *rare*$^{-1}$.

1677 LOCKE 28 Aug. in Ld. King *Life & Lett.* (Bohn) 73 Monsieur Bernier told me that the heathens of Hindoostan pretend to great antiquity,..that their nodus in their numbers is ten, as ours, and their circuit of days seven.

†**4.** (See NODULUS, quot. 1688.) *Obs.*

5. A knotty point, a difficulty or complication.

1727-38 CHAMBERS *Cycl.* s.v., Nodus in Poetry, &c. **1763** BLAIR *Diss.* in *Ossian's Poems* (1796) II. 300 We find..a Nodus, or intrigue in the poem. **1808** *Edin. Rev.* XI. 369 Beleaguer'd and beset by what they call the nodus, or difficulty of his situation. **1828** CARLYLE *Misc.* (1857) I. 126 The whole nodus may be more of a logical cobweb, than any actual material perplexity. **1872** GEO. ELIOT *Middlem.* li, Neither the Parliamentary Candidate Society nor any other power..seeing a worthy nodus for interference.

†**'nody**, *a.* *Obs.*$^{-0}$ [f. NODE *sb.*] Nodose.

1611 FLORIO, *Gropposo*, knottie, nodie, full of knots.

nody(e, obs. ff. NODDY.

nodylle, obs. f. NODDLE.

nodypoll(e, obs. ff. NODDYPOLL.

noegenesis (nəʊi:'dʒɛnɪsɪs). [f. Gr. νόη-σις NOE(SIS + -GENESIS.] The generating of new knowledge from experience through the apprehension of experience, the eduction of relations and the eduction of correlates; the obtaining of knowledge thus. So **noege'netic** *a.*, of, pertaining to, or concerned with, noegenesis.

1923 C. SPEARMAN *Nature of 'Intelligence'* iv. 61 'Noegenesis'. Another basal property of the manifestations of all the principles is that they, and they alone, are generative of new items in the field of cognition. If then, it be desired to depict these three principles summarily, taking into account both their noetic and their generative properties, we must compound some such name as 'noegenetic'. **1931** F. AVELING in W. Rose *Outl. Mod. Knowl.* viii. 336 The noegenetic principles, though accounting for the origin of knowledge, do not cover the entire cognitive field. **1936** F. BANKS *Conduct & Ability* xii. 232 Clearly some word like *eduction* was needed to distinguish this noegenetic process from the 'merely associative'. *Ibid.* xv. 308 The third principle of noegenesis will also be found adequate to explain the inventions of science. **1938** *Mind* XLVII. 378 Very proper complaint is registered to the effect that Psychologists have always neglected the problem of the perception of relations. Here again Prof. Spearman may reflect with pride on his own contribution in the shape of the 'noegenetic laws'. **1972** L. S. HEARNSHAW in Cox & Dyson *20th-Cent. Mind* I. vii. 235 Spearman contributed a powerful and erudite analysis, and though once again his theory of noegenesis, or creative intelligence, has not altogether stood up to subsequent scrutiny, it proved practically useful. **1973** H. J. EYSENCK *Inequality of Man* ii. 45 Spearman (1927) tried to lay down in his 'noegenetic laws' the essence of this cognitive ability.

‖**noel** (nəʊ'ɛl). Also **noël.** [F. *noël*: see NOWEL.] A Christmas carol.

1811 BUSBY *Dict. Mus.*, *Noels*, certain canticles, or songs of joy, formerly sung at Christmas in the country churches in France. **1880** *Grove's Dict. Mus.* II. 462 The French Noëls will, of course, bear no comparison with those written in Italy in point of excellence. **1903** *Speaker* 3 Jan. 324/2 The singing of noels must be heard to be really appreciated.

noell, obs. variant of NEWEL[1].

noem ('nəʊɛm), **noeme** ('nəʊi:m). *Philos.* and *Linguistics.* [f. Gr. νόημα thought.] A term used to denote that aspect of a unit of speech which is concerned with meaning as distinguished from sound.

a **1866** J. GROTE in *Jrnl. Philol.* (1872) IV. 55 It will be necessary for me to make use of one or two new-coined words, which I will begin by defining as accurately as I can. .. When I mean words as thought I shall use the term *noem.* *Ibid.* 56 Logically, a noem may be called a concept, a notion, or what we will; but I would have the term bear simply a relation to language, and mean the thought-word, that, whatever it is, which the sound stands for. **1926** L. BLOOMFIELD in *Language* II. 161 The meaning of a glosseme is a noeme. **1940** *Mod. Lang. Q.* June 178, I have recently encountered the *enthymeme*,..the *noeme*, the *philosopheme*, [etc.]. **1966** M. PEI *Gloss. Ling. Terminol.* 180 *Noeme*, the meaning of a glosseme.

noema (nəʊ'eɪmə, nəʊ'i:mə). *Philos.* Pl. **noemata** (nəʊ'i:mətə). [ad. Gr. νόημα thought.] A term first used by Husserl for that which is perceived or thought as the self experiences it. (See quot. 1966.)

1931 W. R. B. GIBSON tr. *Husserl's Ideas* III. iii. §88. 258 Corresponding at all points to the manifold data of the real (*reellen*) noetic content, there is a variety of data displayable in really pure (*wirklich reiner*) intuition, and in a correlative '*noematic content*', or briefly '*noema*'—terms which we shall henceforth be continually using. **1957** B. LONERGAN *Insight* p. xxv, The *noêma* or *intentio intenta* or *pensée pensée*, illustrated by the lower contexts, *P*, *Q*, *R*,...and by the upper context that is Gödel's theorem. **1966** A. GURWITSCH *Stud. Phenomenology & Psychol.* vii. 132 What has just been described by these allusions is the *noema* of perception—namely the object just (exactly so and only so) as the perceiving subject is aware of it. *Ibid.* 133 Noemata are not to be found in perceptual life alone. There is a noema corresponding to every act of memory, expectation, representation, [etc.]. **1972** H. DREYFUS in L. Embree *Life-World & Consciousness* 138 If the noema were an abstract entity, we could indeed reflect on the higher order noemata involved in reflecting on the first-order noema.

noematic (nəʊi:'mætɪk), *a.* [f. Gr. type νοηματικός, f. νόημα thought.] **a.** Of or pertaining to a noem. **b.** Of, pertaining to, or connected with a noema.

1860 in WORCESTER. *a* **1866** J. GROTE in *Jrnl. Philol.* (1872) IV. 55, I shall use the adjectives *phonal* and *noematic*; and I shall give the name of phonal or noematic *schematisms* to modifications of the primary noems and phones. **1931** [see NOEMA]. **1934** *Mind* XLIII. 310 Kant obviously contemplated the possibility of a noematic 'given'. **1943** M. FARBER *Found. Phenomenology* xvi. 526 The *noematic* side (referring to what is correlatively involved, as 'that which is experienced, thought, etc.'). **1957** B. LONERGAN *Insight* II. xiv. 415 The pure forms of noetic experience terminating in noematic contents. **1973** J. N. MOHANTY in Carr & Casey *Explor. Phenomenology* 212 An awareness of the truth of its own noematic content.

†**noe'matical**, *a.* *Obs. rare.* [f. Gr. type *νοηματικός, f. νόημα thought: see -ICAL.] Originating, or existing, in thought, or in the mind alone; noetic.

1682 H. MORE *Annot. Glanvill's Lux O.* 253 If we distinguish those two Attributes in God, namely, of Wisdom and Knowledge; as if the one were Noematical, the other Dianoetical. *a* **1688** CUDWORTH *Immut. Mor.* (1731) 143 So are the Cogitations that we have of Corporeal things usually both Noematical and Phantasmatical together, the one being as it were the Soul, and the other the Body of them.

Hence †**noe'matically** *adv.*, intellectually. *Obs.*

1659 H. MORE *Immort. Soul* I. ii. Ax. 3 By Common Notions I understand whatever is Noematically true, that is to say, true at first sight to all men in their wits, upon a clear perception of the Terms. **1661** [G. RUST] *Origen & his Opinions* in *Phœnix* (1721) I. 19 There are Moral Axioms Noematically true, as well as Geometrical. **1672** H. MORE *Brief Reply* 138 Which is an Axiome noematically true.

'noemics, *sb. pl.* [irreg. f. Gr. νόημα thought.] 'The science of the understanding; intellectual science' (Ogilvie *Suppl.* 1855).

noem-noem, var. NUM-NUM.

no entry. [ENTRY 1.] Used *attrib.* to designate an area to which entrance is forbidden; also, to designate a sign marking this instruction.

1967 *Guardian* 15 Dec. 3/5 Bollards and no-entry signs to deflect vehicles. **1968** *Ibid.* 13 Aug. 5/3 Potential suicides swerve into 'No entry' streets. **1969** S. COULTER *Embassy* xviii. 195 They had reversed the traffic along the Avenue Gabriel. No Entry signs—white-barred red discs—were now planted in concrete bases on either sidewalk. **1971** *Guardian* 30 Oct. 20/1 Mrs. Joy Johnson..demolished a 'No Entry' sign while driving a double-deck bus.

noesis (nəʊ'i:sɪs). Pl. **noeses.** [a. Gr. νόησις, f. νοεῖν to have mental perception or intelligence, f.

νόος mind, thought.] **a.** (See quot. 1881.) **b.** An intellectual view of the moral and physical world.

1881 MIVART *Cat* 386 The sum-total of the mental action of a rational animal may be called its noesis. **1905** RAMSAY in *Expositor* Nov. 361 Jewish ritual stands to Christian spirituality in the same relation as Phrygian ritual to educated Noesis.

c. *Philos.* In phenomenology, that which is involved in the act of thinking or perceiving. Cf. NOEMA.

1931 W. R. B. GIBSON tr *Husserl's Ideas* III. iii. §92. 268 Our glance, instead of passing through the noeses of perception.. goes through a noesis of remembrance into a world of memory. **1957** B. LONERGAN *Insight* p. xxv, There is also the *noêsis* or *intentio intendens*, or *pensée pensante* that is constituted by the very activity of inquiring and reflecting, understanding and affirming, asking further questions and reaching further answers. **1967** B. JAGER tr. *Kockelmans's Edmund Husserl's Phenomenological Psychol.* v. 244 A consideration and analysis of the related *noeses*, of the different acts in and through which the ego is conscious of something. **1970** PIVČEVIĆ *Husserl & Phenomenology* vi. 67 'Noesis'.. must of course be strictly distinguished from the sensory content of an experience.

Noetian (nəʊˈiːʃ(ɪ)ən), *sb.* and *a.* [ad. L. type **Noētiānus*, f. *Noētus*, a native of Smyrna and presbyter of the church in Asia Minor (*c* 230 A.D.).]

A. *sb.* A follower of Noetus in acknowledging only one person (the Father) in the Godhead. (Cf. PATRIPASSIAN and MONARCHISM.)

1585 T. ROGERS *39 Art.* 4 Men.. which do graunte the name of three sondrie persons, and denie their persons, as did the Noëtians. **1719** WATERLAND *Vind. Christ's Div.* 334 The Noetians had so high an Opinion of the Divinity of Christ.. that They had no way of solving the difficulty, but by making Father and Son one Person, and, in Consequence, were Patripassians. **1765** MACLAINE tr. *Mosheim's Eccl. Hist.* III. II. v. §13 The Sabellians.. [were] called Patripassians.. in a different sense from that in which this name was given to the Noetians. **1853** W. E. TAYLER *Hippolytus* vi. 51 The Noetians.. accused the orthodox with believing in two Gods. **1876** PLUMMER tr. *Döllinger's Hippolytus & Callistus* 10 It is not true that.. the Noëtians are cited as the last heresy.

B. *adj.* Of, pertaining or relating to, Noetus or Noetianism.

1719 WATERLAND *Vind. Christ's Div.* 334 He has been thought to have refined upon the Noetian Scheme. **1765** MACLAINE tr. *Mosheim's Eccl. Hist.* III. II. v. §12 The Noetian controversy. **1876** PLUMMER tr. *Döllinger's Hippolytus & Callistus* 10 Our author.. treats the Elchasaite heresy.. as a short appendage to the Noëtian school. **1884** 'EDNA LYALL' *We Two* xxiv, I consider that he has Noetian tendencies.

Hence **No'etianism**, the heresy of Noetus.

1874 J. H. BLUNT *Dict. Sects* 374/2 The derivation of Noëtianism from the doctrine of Heracleitus.

Noetic (nəʊˈɛtɪk), *a.*¹ *rare.* [f. *Noe* (Vulgate), Noah.] Noachian, Noachic.

1695 WOODWARD *Nat. Hist. Earth* I. (1723) 126 Ever since the time of the Noetick Deluge. **1803** G. S. FABER *Cabiri* I. 131 The mutual resemblance of the Cabiri, the Titans, the Rishis, and the Noëtic family, is too striking to be the effect of mere accident.

noetic (nəʊˈɛtɪk), *a.*² and *sb.* [ad. Gr. νοητικ-ός, f. νόησις NOESIS.]

A. *adj.* **1. a.** Of or pertaining to the mind or intellect; characterized by, or consisting in, mental or intellectual activity.

1653 WATERHOUSE *Apol. Learning* 12 All Learning, whether Noetick or Manual, of book or hand, proceeds from God. **1677** GALE *Crt. Gentiles* III. 92 Another attribute.. of Pagan Philosophie is, that it be νοητικη, noetic or intelligent, i.e. comprehensive of the first and highest principles. **1852** SIR W. HAMILTON *Discuss.* 4 The noetic faculty, intellect proper, or place of principles. **1872** *Contemp. Rev.* XX. 75 Noetic intuition involves some discursive thought. **1890** MASSON *Edinb. Sketches* 220 There was little in his mind of what may be called the purely *noetic* organ—that faculty which speculates, investigates [etc.]. **1907** W. JAMES *Pragmatism* v. 166 This is the hypothesis of *noetic pluralism*, which monists consider so absurd. **1925** *Brit. Jrnl. Psychol.* Oct. 106 In the following pages the word 'noetic' is used for brevity's sake instead of the more elaborate though more correct 'noegenetic'. *Ibid.* 115 The tests.. measure the 'Noetic' and the 'Generative' powers of the subject. **1957** J. S. HUXLEY *Relig. without Revelation* (rev. ed.) ix. 204 Some new term.. in which communicable mental activities play a predominant rôle. If so, I suggest the term *noetic*. *Ibid.*, Religions are thus noetic organs of evolving man. **1972** *Encycl. Psychol.* II. 327/2 *Noetic superstructure*, a term applied by strata theorists.. to individual thought processes (power of abstraction, judgment, logical reasoning, etc.) that take place, together with voluntary activities, above the endothymic basis.

b. In phenomenology, that which is concerned with or pertains to the act of thinking or perceiving (see NOESIS c). Cf. NOEMATIC *a.* b.

1931 [see NOEMA]. **1943** M. FARBER *Found. Phenomenology* xvi. 526 This applies to the *noetic* side ('I think', 'I experience', etc.) as well as to the *noematic* side. **1969** R. MCKEON in R. Klibansky *Contemp. Philos.* III. 105 The difference of knower and known disappear in the description of the experiencing (or the 'noetic') and experienced (or the 'noematic').

2. Originating or existing in the mind or intellect; purely intellectual or abstract.

c **1810** COLERIDGE in *Lit. Rem.* (1838) III. 263 Reduce it to the noetic pentad, or universal form of contemplation. **1836-7** SIR W. HAMILTON *Metaph.* xxi. (1859) II. 33 That the sensible or ectypal world.. stands to the noetic or archetypal world.. in the same relation [etc.]. **1881** W. R. SMITH *O. Test. in Jewish Ch.* 32 Those doctrines higher than reason, those noëtic truths, as they were called, of a divine philosophy.

3. Given to intellectual speculation. (See quots.)

1882 MOZLEY *Reminis.* I. iii. 19 The new Oriel sect was declared to be Noetic, whatever that may mean. **1882** *Church Times* 6 Oct. 674 The so called 'Noetic' school at Oriel was far advanced in Rationalism before Newman became a Fellow. **1893** *Month* Dec. 563 It is the noetic school of Whately which is really responsible for this evil.

B. *sb.* **1.** A science of the intellect. Also *pl.*

1825 COLERIDGE *Aids Refl.* (1848) I. 137 The universal Noetic, in which we require terms of most comprehension and least specific import. *a* **1834** —— in *Lit. Rem.* (1838) III. 416 In short, a transcendental aesthetic, logic, and noetic. **1875** T. HILL *Order Stud.* 1 Gymnastics, or care of the body; noetics, or training of the mind. **1931** W. R. B. GIBSON tr. *Husserl's Ideas* II. iv. §59. 176 So too.. we cannot suspend general Noetics, which expresses our essential insight into the rationality or irrationality of the judging activity generally.

2. That which has a purely intellectual existence or basis.

1854 MAURICE *Mor. & Met. Philos.* (ed. 2) 59 To separate that in man which is capable of converse with the noetic, the essentially pure, from that which is.. earthly. **1876** WILDER *R. P. Knight's Symbolic Lang.* 4 The end of which is the Knowledge of the First, the Lord, and the Noëtic.

3. A member of the noetic school (see A. 3).

1882 M. PATTISON in *Academy* 1 July 1 The old Oriel school—the Noetics—had no dogmas, and left no books. **1885** —— *Mem.* 78 The Noetics knew nothing of the philosophical movement which was taking place on the continent.

Hence **no'etical** *a.*

1644 BP. MAXWELL *Prerog. Chr. Kings* xiv. 137 In him who in sharpnesse of wit approacheth nearest to Angelicall and Noeticall spirits. **1661** K. W. *Conf. Charac., Pragm. Pulpit-filler* (1860) 83 Their noetical faculties devoid of philosophick irradiations. *a* **1688** CUDWORTH *Immut. Mor.* (1731) 296 Those that arise from the pure noetical Energies of the Soul it self. **1931** W. R. B. GIBSON tr. *Husserl's Ideas* III. iii. §87. 256 It is a long.. way that leads from meaning, from ontological and noetical insights.

no-fault. *U.S.* Used *attrib.* to designate a form of motor vehicle insurance (see quot. 1973¹).

1967 *Wall St. Jrnl.* 7 Nov. 1 Support for no-fault auto insurance in the U.S. **1968** *Economist* 13 July p. xviii/2 American motor insurance is now to be put under the microscope. And a no-fault compensation system is being discussed. **1973** C. L. BARNHART et al. *Dict. New Eng.* 318/7 *No-fault*, of or relating to a form of automobile insurance by which an accident victim is compensated for damages or expenses by his own insurance company, whether the accident was his fault or not. **1973** *Washington Post* 13 Jan. A.22/2 Governor Holton's call for a strong no-fault insurance bill. **1974** *Aiken* (S. Carolina) *Standard* 22 Apr. 1-A/2 The bill, to come up today, would assure that victims are paid for their losses regardless of who is at fault. It would require every car owner to buy insurance to protect himself and his family against losses arising from traffic accidents. The no-fault bill heads the Senate agenda for the week as Congress returns from a 10-day recess.

no-fines (nəʊˈfaɪnz), *a.* (*sb.*) [f. NO *a.* + pl. of *fine* sb. (FINE *a.* B).] Applied to concrete made from an aggregate composed of lumps larger than about 9 mm. (and smaller than about 18 mm.), which results in increased porosity and better thermal insulation. Also as *sb.*

1946 A. F. BOYD *Rep. Tests No-Fines Concrete* (Commonwealth Exper. Building Station, Sydney) 1 Little technical information was available on the strength of no-fines concrete as applied to building construction. **1954** *Archit. Rev.* CXVI. 410/3 Hills themselves also made no-fines walling blocks about 7 in. thick.. for facing their steel-framed houses. **1955** *Times* 5 July 17/3 (Advt.), We handed over during the year some 19,500 permanent dwellings, most of them built by the Wimpey 'No-Fines' technique, which continues to make a wide appeal to those wanting speed combined with a high standard of construction. **1960** M. BOWLEY *Innovations in Building Materials* ix. 209 Dense concrete properly made is impervious to moisture.. but provides poor heat insulation... 'No fines', on the other hand, is more pervious.. but provides better heat insulation. **1969** E. C. ADAMS *Sci. in Building* III. viii. 139 No-fines is made by mixing a coarse aggregate with cement and water. *Ibid.*, No-fines concrete is not subject to capillarity, and can .. provide a weatherproof wall in one thickness.. if rendered externally.

†noforsooth, *v. nonce-word.* (See quot.)

a **1644** QUARLES *Virg. Widow* (1649) 53 She charg'd me, that when any sued for my love, I should be coy, and say Noforsooth,.. which I ha' done so long that I have almost Noforsooth'd away all my fortunes.

no-frills. [FRILL *sb.*¹ 1 e.] Also **no-frill.** Used *attrib.* to designate a lack of ornamentation or embellishment.

1960 *Farmer & Stockbreeder* 16 Feb. 3/2 A no-frill piggery. **1967** 'E. LATHEN' *Murder against Grain* iv. 48 The no-frills exterior of Halloran's garage. **1969** *Listener* 27 Mar. 436/2 *World in Action* has an aggressive investigatory policy combined with tight editing and a no-frills presentation. **1969** *Daily Tel.* (Colour Suppl.) 3 Oct. 20/4 The 61st is a no-frills working regiment that spends most of its time in khaki field uniforms.

nog (nɒg), *sb.*¹ Also **nogg.** [Of obscure origin.] A peg, pin, or small block of wood serving for various purposes; chiefly *techn.* in special applications (see quots.). Also, a knag, snag, or stump on a tree or branch.

1611 COTGR., *Frayoire*, the racke-staffe, or nog of a mill; the little peece of wood which rubbing against the hopper makes the corne fall from it. **1688** HOLME *Armoury* III, 287/2 The Bobbin or Nogg, a piece of round Wood with an handle to begin to wind or make the Clew on. *Ibid.* 332/2 The Noggs, are the handles of the Sythe. **1711** W. SUTHERLAND *Shipbuild. Assist.* 162 *Nog*; a Trenel drove in at the Foot of each Shore, or the Props that support the Ship in the Nature of trigging the Shores. **1747** HOOSON *Miner's Dict.* G iij b, We.. therein put two Nogs of Wood and these keep the Forks from being pressed inward by the side Weight. *a* **1802** *Jock o' the Syde* xi. in Scott *Minstrelsy Border* I. 158 A tree they cut, wi' fifteen nogs on each side. **1841** *Civil Eng. & Arch. Jrnl.* IV. 234/2 The three holding nogs or dies are attached by screws to dove-tail slide-pieces. **1842** GWILT *Archit.* 1008 *Nogs*, the same as Wood Bricks... The term is chiefly used in the north of England. **1844** H. STEPHENS *Bk. Farm* III. 986 The lifting-bar *f*, which rests at each end on wooden noggs tenoned into the bars. **1856** BAINBRIDGE *Law Mines & Min.* (ed. 2) Gloss., *Nog*, square bits of wood piled to support the roof of coal mines.

attrib. **1747** HOOSON *Miner's Dict.* G iij b, We put a Sill under them,.. and drive them fast up against the Head-tree, so far till the Nog-holes appear on the inside of the Forks.

nog (nɒg), *sb.*² Also **nogg.** [Of obscure origin.]

1. A kind of strong beer, brewed in East Anglia.

1693 PRIDEAUX *Lett.* (Camden) 161 A bottle of old strong beer, wᶜʰ in this countrey [Norfolk] they call 'nog'. **1723** SWIFT *French Dog* Wks. 1755 IV. I. 35 Walpole laid a quart of nog on't He'd either make a hog or dog on't. **1743** *Lond. & Country Brew.* III. (ed. 2) 227 In Suffolk and Norfolk they run very much upon a light brown, or deep Amber colour'd Butt-Beer, which in the latter Place is called Nogg. **1774** *Westm. Mag.* II. 319 The Sailor toasts thy charms in flip and grog; The Norwich Weaver drinks Thee deep in nog. **1847** STEPHENS in Johnston & Browne *Life* (1878) 222 Our landlady sent round some nogg a while ago. **1893** ZINCKE *Wherstead* 261 Here 'nog' is a kind of strong ale.

2. = EGG-NOG.

1851 A. O. HALL *Manhattaner* 10, I tremble to think of the juleps, and punches, and nogs, and soups. **1881** A. W. TOURGÉE *Zouri's Christmas* in *Royal Gentleman* viii. 527 Then he tried to drain the glass, but a part of the foamy nogg remained in it despite his efforts. **1896** *Harper's Mag.* XCII. 783/2 Mrs. Raker was holding a foaming glass to the sick man's lips. 'There; take another sup of the good nog', she said.

nog, *v.* [f. NOG *sb.*¹]

1. *trans.* To secure by nogs or pegs.

1711 W. SUTHERLAND *Shipbuild. Assist.* 26 Then nog all the Shores very secure.

2. To build with timber-framing and brick.

1805 DUNCUMB *Agric. Heref.* 30 They [cottages] are raised with stone two feet above the ground, and then carried to the roof with timber and brick in squares, or as it is here termed *nogged together*.

Hence **nogged** (nɒgd) *ppl. a.*, consisting of a timber framework filled in with brick. (Usu. in comb. *brick-nogged.*)

1688 R. HOLME *Armoury* III. 457/1 A Nogged Wall, being only of a Brick breadth. **1842** GWILT *Archit.* §2024 When the spaces between the timbers or quarters are bricked up, it is called a bricknogged partition.

Nogai, var. NOGAY.

‖**nogaku** (ˈnoːgaku). [Jap. *nōgaku*, f. *nō* talent, accomplishment, NOH, NO + *gaku* music.] The Japanese dramatic form called Noh; the genre of the Noh drama.

1916 JOLY & TOMITA *Jap. Art & Handicraft* 7 The *Nô Gaku* originated in the Oyei era close upon the beginning of the XVth century. **1932** B. L. SUZUKI (*title*) Nōgaku: Japanese Nō Plays. **1938** D. T. SUZUKI *Zen Buddhism & its Influence on Jap. Culture* I. v. 101 The beginning of *haiku*, nōgaku theatre,.. is to be sought in them. **1948** *Introd. Classic Jap. Lit.* (Kokusai Bunka Shinkokai) p. xvi, The earliest theatrical performances were those of the *nôgaku* (Noh drama), and the *nô-kyôgen* (Noh farces). **1959** W. P. MALM *Jap. Music* iv. 105 (*heading*) Nohgaku, the music of the noh drama.

nogat, variant of NOUGAT.

no-gate, *adv. north.* and *Sc.* Forms: α. 4 **nan-gat, nane-, none-gate.** β. 4-5 **na-, no-gat, -gate,** 9 **nae-gate, -gait.** [f. NO *a.* or NONE *a.* + GATE *sb.*²]

a. Nowhere. **b.** In no way, no-wise.

α. *a* **1300** *Cursor M.* 1078 Þe bodi moght he nan-gat hide. *c* **1325** *Metr. Hom.* 57 This sawel.. Mai nangat cum til hevin blis. *a* **1400** *Harrow. Hell* 1087 (Harl. MS.), He may noght lif ogayne nanegate [*v.r.* nonegate].

β. **13..** *Cursor M.* 9794 (Gött.), Hou miht þai man of sin ma clene? Certis na gate, als i wene. *Ibid.* 12900 Bot might it nogat þe witslipp þat he self said. *c* **1375** *Sc. Leg. Saints* xliii. (*Cecilia*) 548 Bot we, þe haly name þat wat of god, ma nyt it na-gat. *a* **1400** *Harrow. Hell* 1071 (Harl. MS.), He bad: 'no gate luke þ ou go hethen, Till fourty days be past'. **1489** *Barbour's Bruce* (Edin. MS.) x. 230 Swa that men mycht it spar na gat.

1815 SCOTT *Guy M.* xxxii, We turned nae gate at a', but just keepit straight forward. **1879** G. MACDONALD *Sir Gibbie* xxvii, I div not ken hoo it'll be poassible, an' you naegait 'ithin my sicht or my cry.

So †**no-gates** *adv. Obs.*

a **13..** *Cursor M.* 5054 (Gött.), No-gates miht þair bodijs ly. *a* **1400** *Sir Perc.* 2226 Be that so nere getis he, That scho myghte nangatis fle. *c* **1400** *Destr. Troy* 612 And ye.. No gatis me begyle, ne to grem brynge, I hete you.., þat I you helpe shall.

Nogay (nəˈgaɪ). Also †Na-, Nogai. **a.** A Turkic-speaking people inhabiting the north-western Caucasus region of the U.S.S.R. **b.** The language of this people, a member of the Kipchak branch of Turkic languages. Also *attrib.* or as *adj.* So **Noˈgaian** *a.*

1652 Nagaian [see Kirghiz *sb.* and *a.*]. **1840** *Penny Cycl.* XVI. 248/1 The Nogays are a Tartar or Turkish nation, dispersed over the steppes which extend between the lower course of the river Dnieper and Mount Caucasus. **1886** [see Kazakh]. **1888** [see Kirghiz *sb.* and *a.*]. **1948** D. Diringer *Alphabet* 568 The Arabic character has also been adopted for..Nogai Turkish, spoken by nearly 200,000 people to the north-west of the Caucasus and in the Crimea. **1958** *Everyman's Encycl.* IX. 268/1 *Nogay*, Turkic-speaking people of N. Caucasus, who live in the Groznyy oblast and Circassian Autonomous Oblast. **1974** *Encycl. Brit. Micropædia* VII. 376/1 Nogay belongs to the northwestern, or Kipchak, division of the Turkic languages, along with such languages as Kazakh and Tatar.

noger, variant of *nauger*, auger *sb.*[1]

1747 Hooson *Min. Dict.* s.v. *Boring*, First make a Place or Stope in the Stone with a Pick, to set the Noger Point in. **1802** Mawe *Min. Derbysh.* Gloss., *Noger*, or Jumper.

ˈnoggen, *a.* and *sb.* Now *rare* or *Obs.* [f. western dial. *nog(s)* refuse of flax or hemp + -en[4].]

a. *adj.* Made of coarse flax. **b.** *sb.* Coarse linen.

1492 *Will of P. Hall* (Somerset Ho.), A noggen shete. **1564** in Noake *Worc. Relics* (1877) 12, j table clothe of noggen. **1625** in Miss Jackson *Shropsh. Word-bk.* (1879) 302 Eyghtenne payre of hempten sheets and six paire of noggen sheets. **1660** Sir T. Blount *Boscobel* 18 His Majesty ..put on a noggen course shirt which was borrowed of Edw. Martin. *Ibid.* 41 A noggen shirt, of the coursest linnen. **1879** in Miss Jackson *Shropsh. Word-bk.*

noggin (ˈnɒgɪn). also 7 -ing, 8 knoggin, noggan, 8–9 naggin. [Of obscure origin: Gael. *noigean*, Ir. *noigin* are no doubt from Eng.]

1. a. A small drinking vessel; a mug or cup.

1630 *Tincker of Turvey* Ep. Ded., Of her ale, her custome was to set before me two little noggins full. *a* **1648** Digby *Closet Opened* (1677) 45 You have the yeast in a large noggin with a handle. **1716** T. Ward *Eng. Ref.* 50 Plate, Candlesticks, and Silver Flaggons were turn'd to Brass and Peuter Noggins. **1753** *Stewart's Trial* 208 The noggin in which he had carried the drink to Allan Breck. **1773** *Poetry* in *Ann. Reg.* 234 The milky store..Crowns the clean noggin. **1824** Doddridge *Notes* 109 The settler's furniture consisted of a few pewter dishes,..wooden bowls, trenchers, and noggins. **1859** Sala *Tw. round Clock* (1861) 53 The pewter counters and the brass-work of the beer-engines, the funnels and the whisky noggins.

b. The head. orig. and chiefly *U.S.*

1866 J. Finley *Hoosier's Nest* 90 But Matty's top-knot.. Wasn't there, for his noggin was bald. **1885** 'Phudge Phumble' *Adventures Greenhorn in Gotham* 25 The full force of it against his noggin. **1931** D. Runyon *Guys & Dolls* (1932) 286 She smacks Rusty Charley on the side of the noggin with the bat. **1951** *Landfall* V. 202 'Thanks, chum,' said Vic, 'You used your noggin.' **1957** *New Yorker* 2 Nov. 34/3 The Right Honourable Our Man Stanley, his Lock hat set firmly on his noggin, dropped by the office the other day and deposited the following dispatch. **1972** J. E. Franklin in W. King *Black Short Story Anthol.* 354 Her hair was short,..and a dozen of those little twig-plaits tucked under and pinned looked like knots rising on her noggin. **1975** P. G. Winslow *Death of Angel* iv. 86 A rap on the back of the noggin that knocked her out.

c. A pail or bucket. *local U.S.*

1885 'C. E. Craddock' *Prophet Gt. Smoky Mts.* x. 175 Mirandy Jane, seated on an inverted noggin, listened tamely to the conversation. **1889** —— *Despot of Broomsedge Cove* xviii. 324 Isabel sat idle on an inverted noggin.

2. A small quantity of liquor, usually a quarter of a pint.

1693 *Humours Town* 101 The poor Curate..is the Humble Servant of ev'ry one that Treats him with a Noggin of cool Nants. *a* **1700** B. E. *Dict. Cant. Crew*, *Noggin*, (of Brandy) a Quarter of a Pint. **1745** *Gentl. Mag.* 425 He drank about a quart a day, a naggin at each time. **1798** *Sporting Mag.* XI. 284 A man..drank no less than four noggins of gin. **1810** Vandeleur *Lett.* (1894) 14 Our army has very good rations: 1 pound of beef, 1 pound of bread, and about a naggin of rum each day. **1853** Kane *Grinnell Exp.* xii. (1856) 94 While we were joking about his adventure over a quiet little noggin of whisky-punch. **1863** Hawthorne *Our Old Home* (1879) 233 No doubt many a noggin of whiskey is here quaffed.

3. *attrib.*, as ***noggin-bottle, -glass, -pot, -stave.***

1663 Wood *Life* 1 Feb., At Short's the coffee-man..in chocolate, 6*d.*, for a noggin pot, 5*d.* **1804** R. Anderson *Cumbld. Ball.* (*c* 1850) 68 To monie a bonnie Carel lass.. The noggin glass went roun. **1855** Kingsley *Westw. Ho!* xix, If the Lord had not fought for us, she'd have been beat to noggin-staves there on the beach. **1894** Hall Caine *Manxman* vi. x. 394 With a noggin bottle of brandy in his fist.

nogging (ˈnɒgɪŋ), *sb.* and *vbl. sb.* Also noggin. [f. nog *sb.*[1] or *v.* + -ing[1].]

1. *sb.* (Usually ***brick-nogging.***) Brickwork built up between wooden quarters or framing.

1825 J. Nicholson *Operat. Mechanic* 354 A brick wall built in panels between timber quarters is called brick nogging. **1833** Loudon *Encycl. Archit.* §79 To fill in the cross partitions with four-inch brick nogging flat. **1842** Barham *Ingol. Leg.* Ser. ii. *Jerry Jarvis' Wig*, A fanciful arrangement of brick and timber..in the 'Weald' is a 'noggin'. **1857** [see brick *sb.*[1] 10]. **1904** A. Griffiths *50 Yrs. Public Life* xvii. 232 A wooden framework, its external sides filled in with brick 'nogging'.

b. ***nogging-pieces***, horizontal pieces of wood nailed to the quarters to strengthen the work in brick-nogging.

1825 J. Nicholson *Operat. Mechanic* 354 The..nogging pieces being included in the measure. **1833** Loudon *Encycl. Archit.* §83 Nogging pieces, four by two inches.

2. *vbl. sb.* (See quots.)

c **1850** *Rudim. Navig.* (Weale) 135 *Nogging*, the act of securing the heels of the shores. **1867** Smyth *Sailor's Word-bk.* 499 *Nogging*,..securing the shores by tree-nails.

nogh(t, obs. forms of nought *sb.* and *adv.*

nog-head. *dial.* [f. nog *sb.*[1]] A blockhead.

c **1800** Wolcot (P. Pindar) *Horrors Bribery* Wks. 1816 IV. 287 Zounds! what a noghead and a fool. **1893** Kennard *Diogenes' Sandals* xiii, Wosbird and noghead were the epithets bestowed.

So **nog-headed** *a.*, thick-headed, stupid.

1891 Miss Tuttiet *Heart Storm* i. ii, 'Matt Meade's that nog-headed',..Cousin Jane used to say. **1893** Raymond *Gentl. Upcott's Daughter* 117 Muttering complaints in which..'pig-headed', 'nog-headed', constantly recurred.

noghtihod: see noughtihood.

nogli, obs. variant of ugly *a.*

no-go. Also no go. [A sb. use of the phrase *no go*: see go *sb.*[1] 8.] **a.** An impracticable situation; an impasse; an indecisive contest, etc. Freq. *attrib.*

1870 Lowell *Among my Bks.* Ser. i. (1873) 150 They have ..arrived at a happy positivism as to its structure, though at the risk of bringing it to a no-go. **1884** *Western Daily Press* 16 Apr. 7/2 The first 'fly' resulted in a 'no go'. **1946** *Ann. Computation Lab. Harvard Univ.* I. 26 If..the calculator finds that all multiples of the divisor are greater than the dividend or the remainder under consideration, a zero or 'no-go' is entered in the quotient counter and a new comparison made one column to the right. **1961** *Flight* LXXX. 542/1 A self-checking capability was therefore built into the machine so that, whenever a 'No Go' condition occurred, this part..carried out a self-checking routine to ensure that the fault was in the aircraft and not in the tester. **1962** A. Shepard in *Into Orbit* 170 When a particular station is on a 'No Go' status, the appropriate symbol lights up to indicate which of the several systems there is non-operative. **1966** *Electronics* 17 Oct. 93 Usually one test was sufficient to provide a go or no-go indication. **1969** *Guardian* 14 June 7/3 The astronauts would have had to end the mission there for, in space jargon, this was potentially a 'no-go' situation.

b. Used *attrib.* of an area: impossible to enter (because of barricades, etc.); to which entry is forbidden for specified persons, groups, etc.

1971 *Guardian* 13 Nov. 1/6 For journalists and others, the Bogside and Creggan estates are 'no-go' areas, with the IRA in total effective control. **1972** *Times* 24 May 16/1 The UDA organized the Protestant 'no go' areas in Belfast last weekend. **1972** *Guardian* 29 May 8/1 The Duke of Norfolk has decreed the Royal Enclosure at Ascot a 'no-go' area for the miniskirted or hotpanted lass. **1972** *Times* 3 June 2/7 Gypsy Council Names Four 'No-Go' Districts. The first four English boroughs likely to be designated as 'no-go' areas for gypsies were named yesterday. **1972** *Daily Tel.* 11 Nov. 2/5 As a result, soldiers have been injured in rioting in the former 'no go' areas. **1974** *Times* 12 Feb. 2/8 Since the dispersal of the IRA leadership from inside the city to Donegal, after the British Army moved into the 'no-go areas' in 1972.

So **no-goism.** *nonce-wd.*

1850 Dickens *Lett.* (1880) I. 220 As to two comic articles ..out of me, that's the intensest extreme of no-goism.

no-God. Used *attrib.* of a set of beliefs, etc., based on atheism. Also (*nonce-wd.*), a personified non-deity. So **no-Goddism, no-Goddite.**

1931 Belloc *Essays of Catholic* viii. 174, I have seen one very monstrous Myth reach maturity..and..explode. That was the Myth of Natural Selection. The enthusiasm which supported it and gave it the atmosphere in which to grow was no-Goddism. **1933** Chesterton *St. Thomas Aquinas* iv. 126 The Bolshevist No-God movement in the twentieth century. **1940** L. MacNeice *Last Ditch* 15 The horses ride ..To a place where God and No-God Play at pitch and toss. **1952** R. A. Knox *Hidden Stream* vii. 60 If your atheist friend was a really reasoned no-Goddite, he would hoot with laughter.

no-good. *orig. U.S.* [A sb. use of the phr. *no good*: see good C. 5 g.] **1.** A useless or valueless person or thing. Also *attrib.* Hence **no-ˈgooder,** (*U.S. slang*) **no-goodnik** [-nik], a no-good person.

1908 E. J. Banfield *Confessions of Beachcomber* ii. i. 250 A no-good-boy wantonly brought about a big wind. **1924** A. J. Small *Frozen Gold* i. 14 I'll learn you half-suckled no-goods what it means. **1931** M. Allingham *Look to Lady* v. 59 A pack of crazy no-goods—strutting about in funny clothes. **1936** S. P. Spivey in P. Oliver *Screening Blues* (1968) vi. 246 Oh you dirty no-gooder, you don't mean me no good. **1944** *This Week Mag.* 22 Oct. 21/2 Any newspaper reader of the late '20's would remember this no-gooder. **1944** S. J. Perelman *Crazy like Fox* (1945) 9 A parasite, a leech, a bloodsucker—altogether a five-star nogoodnick! **1947** D. M. Davin *Gorse blooms Pale* 28 Taking that no-good Calaghan girl to every dance. **1948** J. Steinbeck *Russ. Jrnl.* (1949) 100 The slovenly, no-good girl. **1958** 'A. Gilbert' *Death against Clock* 67 He recognized her almost at once for what she was, a gold-digger, a no-good. **1958** R. Graves in *Times Lit. Suppl.* 15 Aug. p. x/2 And the committee would, I am sure, be a snuggery of all the no-goods and do-goods whom I have spent half my life successfully avoiding. **1958** *Listener* 9 Oct. 569/2 A splendid comic performance by Alberto Sordi as a no-gooder from the city. **1959** *News Chron.* 19 June 8/2 Holly..gets herself involved with a no-good hoofer in a low night club. **1960** *Sunday Express* 10 July 15/6 He is a lazy no-good. **1960** *Guardian* 23 Sept. 11/7, I know their type... Bums and nogoodniks, the lot of them. **1968** *N.Y. Times* 3 Mar. 37 Lew Archer's job is to find a 17-year-old girl who has run off with a 19-year-old no-goodnik. **1971** *Black Scholar* Sept. 38/2 It was snowin' when your no good daddy left me for that hussy. **1973** W. M. Duncan *Big Timer* x. 67 This no-good whom I do not even see for weeks on end.

2. Phr. ***no good to Gundy***: (see quots.). *Austral.*

The explanation in quot. 1945 seems improbable.

1919 W. H. Downing *Digger Dial.* 35 *No good to gundy*, of no advantage. **1945** Baker *Austral. Lang.* iv. 90 *No good to Gundy*, an elaboration of the simple 'no good', has been current since 1907 or before, and probably had its origin in America... The origin is more likely to be found..in the old U.S. phrase, *according to Gunter*. Gunter was a noted mathematician who gave his name to works of precision and accuracy. **1966** G. W. Turner *Eng. Lang. Austral. & N.Z.* vi. 118 The unexplained phrase *no good to Gundy*, meaning simply 'no good' perhaps appeals because of its alliteration.

nogt, obs. form of nought.

Noh, No (nəʊ). Also Nō. [Jap.] The traditional Japanese masked drama evolved from the rites of Shinto worship and substantially unchanged since the 15th c.; the oldest form of drama in Japan. Freq. *attrib.*

1871 A. B. Mitford *Tales of Old Japan* I. 156 A kind of classical opera, called Nô, which is performed on stages specially built for the purpose. **1899** [see kyogen]. **1911** *Encycl. Brit.* XV. 169 Briefly speaking, the Nō was a dance of the most stately character, adapted to the incidents of dramas. **1917** W. B. Yeats *Lett.* (1954) IV. 631 The music to my Noh play *The Dreaming of the Bones.* **1927** E. Pound *Let.* 9 Nov. (1971) 214, I wonder if Iwasaki is trained in No or if you and he want to undertake revision of my redaction of Fenollosa's paper on the Noh (or No; better I think spelled with the 'h'). **1938** D. T. Suzuki *Zen Buddhism & its Influence on Jap. Culture* i. iv. 70 The Noh-play 'Kokaji' gives us some idea about the moral and religious significance of the sword among the Japanese. **1958** [see kyogen]. **1960** B. Leach *Potter in Japan* vii. 155 A grey, wooden, thatched, open-air Nō stage where the monks still perform under an August moon. **1964** I. Fleming *You only live Twice* i. 15 'Grey Pearl'..was so thickly made up that she looked like a character out of a No play. **1973** *Times* 20 Mar. 9/5 The bare events of the tragedy are retained and acted out in trance-like, Noh-play fashion. **1974** S. Marcus *Minding the Store* (1975) xiv. 281 Billie gave me..a Noh mask from Japan.

no hit. 1. *Cricket.* (See quot. 1835.)

This rule no longer applies.

1827 *Sussex Weekly Advertiser* 9 July, The umpire called no hit. **1835** *Hoyle's Games* 426 When the striker shall hit the ball, one of his feet must be on the ground, and behind the popping crease, otherwise the umpire shall call *no hit.*

2. *Baseball.* (See quots. 1961.) So **no-hitter.**

1948 *Richmond* (Va.) *Times-Dispatch* 15 Mar. 17/4 Even without this new delivery Blackwell..came within two outs of pitching two successive no-hitters. **1949** [see *left field* (left *a.* 3 c)]. **1955** A. Budrys in D. Knight *100 Yrs. Sci. Fiction* (1969) 255 Walker's a good pitcher, all right—but he didn't pitch any no-hitters. And he only won eighteen games. **1961** J. S. Salak *Dict. Amer. Sports* 298 *No-hit no-run game*, a game in which the pitcher permits the opposing team no base hits and no runs for the entire game or for at least the first nine innings of the game. **1961** Webster, *No-hitter*, a no-hit game in baseball. **1973** *Tucson* (Arizona) *Daily Citizen* 22 Aug. 60/2 Bahnsen said he was aware he had a no-hitter going and started bearing down in the seventh inning. **1974** *News & Reporter* (Chester, S. Carolina) 22 Apr. 10-A/8 Blackwell struck out 13 batters in the contest and pitched five innings of no-hit ball before Burton ended his hopes for a no-hitter.

no-ˈhoper. *Austral. slang.* [f. no *a.* + hoper.]

a. A horse with no prospect of winning, an outsider. **b.** A useless or incompetent person, one from whom no good can be expected.

1943 Baker *Dict. Austral. Slang* (ed. 3) 54 *No-hoper*, an outsider. (Racing slang.) **1945** T. Ronan *Strangers on Ophir* (1966) 79 There were actually eight runners in it: the three favourites, three no-hopers hardly up to hack-race standard, [etc.]. **1953** [see drongo 3]. **1957** D. Niland *Call me when Cross turns Over* i. 27 This son was not a no-hoper. **1959** Baker *Drum* (1960) iii. 33 The suggestion that a heart of gold beats in the breast of every no-hoper. **1959** *Times Lit. Suppl.* 25 Dec. 753/2 Shanty towns where the 'no-hopers' drink their big cheques away. **1967** J. Morrison in *Coast to Coast 1965–66* 137 He's a bit of a no-hoper. **1971** *Sunday Australian* 8 Aug. 5/1 He prefers that they go north to the mining towns to..staying in the cities where they are dragged down to the level of no-hopers they pick up with.

ˈnohow, *adv.* (and *a.*) [f. no *a.* + how *adv.*; cf. *somehow, anyhow.*]

1. a. In no manner, by no means; not at all.

1775 in *Priv. Lett. Ld. Malmesbury* (1870) I. 300 A course of habitual improvement which nohow else is to be acquired. **1795** *Montford Castle* II. 42 Edmund..could nohow insert the point of his sword. **1829** Landor *Imag. Conv., Emp. China & Tsing-Ti*, Not being his father, the misfortune could nohow be attributed to me. **1841** Herschel *Ess.* (1857) 212 This is a modification of the idea of cause, which we can no-how bring ourselves to conceive. **1877** Mrs. Oliphant *Makers Flor.* xiv. 348 Genius has strange gifts in it,..knowledge nohow conveyable by teaching of man.

b. In uneducated speech frequently used with another negative. Esp. in phr. ***no how you (they) can fix it.*** Cf. fix *v.* 14 c. Chiefly *U.S.*

1833 J. Hall *Harpe's Head* 91 (Th.), They don't raise such humans in the Old Dominion, no how. **1835** W. G. Simms *Partisan* 506 It won't be an easy journey, ma'am, no how, I tell you. **1836** [see fix *v.* 14 c]. **1840** *Knickerbocker* XVI. 19, I mean my name ain't G. Washington Mortimer, no how. **1843** 'R. Carlton' *New Purchase* I. xviii. 141, I.. couldn't read a chapter in the Bible no how you could fix it. **1851** D. Jerrold *St. Giles* x. 98 You don't call that justice, no-how, do you? **1863** Reade *Hard Cash* II. 246 That don't dovetail nohow. **1884** *Harper's Mag.* Feb. 410/1 He wouldn't let it stand nohow. **1929** H. W. Odum in A. Dundes *Mother Wit* (1973) 187 Boys jes' natchelly tired an' don't want to work no-how. **1970** R. P. Warren *Incarnations* 48 Did he merely blow, and never Was rightly your husband, no how. **1973** C. Williams *Man on Leash* (1974) x. 146 You won't be thinkin' about yore hairdo nohow.

2. a. In no particular manner or condition; with no distinctive appearance or character.

In quots. 1779 and 1853 with suggestion of b.

1779 Mme. D'Arblay *Diary* (1842) I. 161, I could not speak a word; and I dare say I looked no-how. **1853** Whewell in Mrs. Douglas *Life* (1881) 430 The air has been filled.. with a dense fog, which has made everything look ill, or more properly speaking, look *no-how*. **1888** Freeman in Stephens *Life & Lett.* (1895) II. 283 New York.. is just now nohow, an uninteresting mass of houses.

b. With *all*: Out of order, out of sorts.

1852 Mrs. Carlyle *Lett.* II. 174 You were 'decidedly better', and now again 'all nohow'. **1865** Dickens *Dr. Marigold* vii, Ain't Mr. B. so well this morning? You look all nohow.

3. *adj.* Having no distinctive character. *rare.*

1828 Lady Granville *Lett.* (1894) II. 29 She is a comfortable, no how, little, good-natured thing.

Hence 'nohowish *a.*

1826 Disraeli *Vivian Grey* II. xii. 171, I was altogether *no-howish* by the time I got home. **1867** Smyth *Sailor's Word-bk.* 499, *No-Howish*, qualmy; feeling an approaching ailment without being able to describe the symptoms. *a* **1897** [see all A. 10 a]. **1935** J. M. Murry *Between Two Worlds* viii. 110 Within a fortnight I was feeling nohowish.

noht, nohut, obs. forms of nought.

‖**noia** ('nɔiə). [It.] Boredom, weariness, ennui.

1944 'Palinurus' *Unquiet Grave* I. 22 The secret of happiness lies in the avoidance of Angst (anxiety, spleen, noia, guilt, fear, remorse, cafard). **1962** *Encounter* XIX. 69 Let us hear what Moravia has to say about *noia*, the fundamental.. situation of all his books. **1967** *Listener* 2 Nov. 583/2 The revenge play is the pretext for all that Renaissance introspection and *noia* and *Angst*.

noiance, variant of noyance.

noice, noie, obs. forms of noise, noy.

noik, obs. Sc. form of nook *sb.*

noil (nɔil). Also noyl. [Of obscure origin.] *pl.* and *sing.* The short pieces and knots of wool combed out of the long staple.

pl. **1623–4** *Act 21 Jas. I*, c. 18 §3 Many ill disposed persons.. have used to mixe and putte Flockes and Thrumes and alsoe Noiles and Haires and other deceivable thinges into.. broad Woollen Cloths. **1793** *Spec. Wright & Hawksley's Patent* No. 1956. 2 A circular brush.. revolving quick to take the noils off the teeth. **1835** Ure *Philos. Manuf.* 150 The noyls, or short refuse wool, which remains entangled among the teeth, being removed. **1872** *Daily News* 26 Mar., Noils and brokes are in steady demand, and prices are firm. **1884** W. S. B. McLaren *Spinning* (ed. 2) 94 The very short fibres of wool.. fall over naturally into a box or can placed to receive them. This short wool is called 'noils'.

sing. **1805** Luccock *Nat. Wool* 159 The fragments collect in the instrument and form only a noil, an article of no use in the fabrication of worsteds. **1844** G. Dodd *Textile Manuf.* iv. 127 This, under the name of noyl or noil, is afterwards carded and spun into coarse woollen yarn. **1894** *Times* 12 Mar. 13/5 The machine which separates the long fibres for fine spinning from the waste or 'noil', which is used for spinning heavy numbers.

attrib. **1884** W. S. B. McLaren *Spinning* (ed. 2) 104 The noil knives in the small circles. *Ibid.* 109 Noil knots are dragged over the pin points.

Noilly Prat (nwaji pra). [Name of the manufacturers.] The proprietary name of a French vermouth; a drink of this.

1906 *Hatch, Mansfield Price List* May 32 Liqueurs... Vermouth (Noilly, Prat).. 2/7-litre. **1907** *Yesterday's Shopping* (1969) 100/3 Vermouth... French, Noilly Prat —Per bot. 2/7. **1950** D. Ames *Corpse Diplomatique* i. 10, I found Dagobert.. sipping a *Noilly Prat*. **1964** E. Bowen *Little Girls* I. iv. 53 We are also right at the end of the Noilly Prat. **1965** *Harper's Bazaar* Jan. 80/3 Haut Savoie, historically the cradle of French vermouth, though Noilly-Prat has always been made well to the west of it. **1966** J. Pearl *Crucifixion of Pete McCabe* (1967) v. 65 He uncorked the Noilly Prat vermouth. **1974** D. Winsor *Death Convention* v. 40, I want a very dry martini. With Noilly Prat.

noint, 'noint, aphetic forms of anoint *v.*

13.. *Cursor M.* 7286 (Gött.), He was.. þe first þat noyntid man to king. **1432–50** tr. *Higden* (Rolls) V. 23 That man scholde be sleyne and the body of Faustina.. be noyntede with the bloode of hym. **1495** *Trevisa's Barth. De P.R.* xii. xxxix. (W. de W.) 436 The blode of a reremouse noynted [*Bodl. MS.* i-smered] vpon the lyddes suffreth not the heere to growe agayn. **1508** Fisher 7 *Penit. Ps.* li. Wks. (1876) 109 The forheed of the chylde is noynted with holy creme. **1577** B. Googe *Heresbach's Husb.* iv. (1586) 144 The vlcerous places must be nointed with Vineger. **1611** Chapman *May Day* Plays 1873 II. 339 One that noints his nose with clowted creame. **1647** R. Stapylton *Juvenal* 77 The oyle.. which those country-men nointed with, when they bathed. **1689** N. Lee *Princess Cleve* iii. i, They are.. suspected for Witches, mine noints her self ev'ry Night.

1821 Scott *Kenilw.* vii, He would.. fling him a handful of silver groats,.. to 'noint the sore withal. **1822** Shelley *Faust* ii. 182 We are washed, we are 'nointed, stark naked are we.

Hence **'nointed** *ppl. a.* (see quot. 1855 and cf. nineted *a.*); **'nointer,** one who anoints; **'nointing** *vbl. sb.*; **'nointment,** ointment.

13.. *Cursor M.* 9338 (Gött.), Quen he þat haliest es comen, ȝour noynting sal fra ȝou be nomen. **1432–50** tr. *Higden* (Rolls) VI. 159 He was confermede by hym by the noyntynge of holy creame. *c* **1485** *Digby Myst.* (1882) iii. 640 Her xal mary.. a-noynt hym with a precyus noy[n]ttment. **1565** Cooper *Thesaurus, Circunlitio*,.. noyntyng. **1647** R. Stapylton *Juvenal* 89 Their Tyrian cassocks, nointings for the field, Who knowes not, sees not? *Ibid.* 36 A rhetorician, a grammarian, A painter, nointer, augur, geometrician. **1855** Robinson *Whitby Gloss.* s.v., 'A nointed youth', a young man apparently destined to, or determined upon, evil courses.

noious(e, obs. forms of noyous *a.*

‖**noir** (nwar), *a.* [F. *noir.*] **1.** *Heraldry.* Black. *rare.*

1871 Tennyson *Last Tourn.* 433 A shield Showing a shower of blood in a field noir.

2. a. The black numbers in the game of roulette.

1850 *Bohn's Hand-bk. Games* 348 The other chances are also designated on the green cloth.., 'le pair, le passe, et le noir'. **1928** M. Carol *How to play Roulette* ii. 21 Among other divisions, or spaces for the stakes, you will find *Passe, Pair, Manque, Impair, Noir, Rouge*. **1939** T. King *Twenty-one Games to play for Money* 31 Even chances are given when a stake is placed on:.. *Noir*, meaning any black number that turns up. **1964** A. Wykes *Gambling* ix. 215 The European betting table is divided into six areas labelled *pair, impair, passe, manque, rouge,* and *noir* (even, odd, high, low, red, black). **1971** P. O'Neil-Dunne *Roulette for Millions* iv. 36 You may be regarded as socially inferior in French casinos, if you do not understand the following French expressions: *Rouge*: Red *Noir*: Black *Impair*: Odds [etc.].

b. The black colour in the game of *rouge et noir* (cf. *rouge et noir* s.v. rouge *sb.*[1] 4).

1850 *Bohn's Hand-bk. Games* 343 The first parcel of cards played, is usually for noir, the second for rouge. **1850** [see inverse *sb.* 3]. **1928** M. Carol *How to play Roulette* iv. 56 The even money chances are Rouge or Red, Noir or Black, Colour [*sic*] and Inverse. **1964** A. Wykes *Gambling* vii. 171 (*caption*) The dealer lays out two rows of cards (*le noir* and *le rouge*) until each totals 31 or more. Players bet that one or the other row will be nearer to 31 by placing chips on *rouge* or on *noir*.

nois, obs. Sc. form of nose *sb.*

†**'noisance.** *Obs.* Forms: 5–6 noysaunce, 5, 7 -ance, 5 -ans, 6 -auns, 6- noisance; also 5 nosaunce, -awnce. [a. OF. *noisance*, var. of *nuisance* nuisance.]

1. Trouble, molestation, annoyance.

c **1400** tr. *Secreta Secret., Gov. Lordsh.* 112 Þe konyng þat þe sawle folowys.. whenne it ys deliured of noysance. *c* **1450** Lovelich *Merlin* 2256 To hym maden they here Surawnce him there to bryngen with-owten Nosawnce. *c* **1450** *Merlin* 456 Yef ye take eny [men] of owres, thei shull helpe yow to oure noysaunce. *a* **1500** *Chaucer's Dreame* C.'s Wks. (1598) 357 Without sicknes or displeasaunce, Or thing that to you was noysaunce. *a* **1548** Hall *Chron., Hen. VIII*, 71 b, Those that shall bryng vitailes necessarie to the saied assembly, maie without daunger, trouble, impechement or noysaunce go and come. **1610** Holland *Camden's Brit.* ii. 63 Howbeit much noisance they have everywhere by Wolves. **1656** Prynne *Resol. Import. Queries* 21 A Writ is granted.. for a thing done to the noysance of another.

b. In phr. *to do noisance.*

c **1412** Hoccleve *De Reg. Princ.* 810 To me this longe walke it dothe noisance. **1449** in *Wars Eng. in France* (Rolls) I. 489 Robbeurs and pirates.. whiche dayly do alle the noysance thay canne. *a* **1548** Hall *Chron., Hen. VIII*, 46 b, The mayre.. declared to them the noysaunce done to the Citezens.

2. Nuisance.

1473–4 *Sarum Church-w. Accts.* (1896) 15 For the clansyng of a noysance abowte the church. **1657** Howell *Londinop.* 392 Any thing of noisance in the River of Thames.

†**'noisant,** *a. Obs. rare.* [a. OF. *noisant*, var. of *nuisant* nuisant.] Troublesome, grievous.

a **1440** Burgh *Cato* 723 If she be noysaunt, ful of greuaunce, Constreyne hir nat to biden in thi yerde. *c* **1475** *Partenay* 1045 Iff it be, ye shall haue gretly to doo huge noisaunt pannes with aduersite.

noise, obs. form of nose.

noise (nɔiz), *sb.* Forms: 3–7 noyse, 4–6 noys, 5–6 noyes, *Sc.* noyis, 6 noyse; 4 nois, 6 noiz, 3- noise. Also 4 nouse, nowse, 5 nose. [a. F. *noise* (11th cent.; OF. also *noyse, nose*) = Prov. *noysa, nosa, nausa*, of uncertain origin: L. *nausea* and *noxia* have been proposed, but the sense of the word is against both suggestions.]

1. a. Loud outcry, clamour, or shouting; din or disturbance made by one or more persons.

In this and other senses freq. in the phrase ***to make*** (more rarely †***keep***) ***a noise***: cf. sense 6.

a **1225** *Ancren R.* 66 Þe wreche peoddare more noise he makeð to ȝeien his sope, þen a riche mercer al his deorewurðe ware. **1297** R. Glouc. (Rolls) 8167 Of trompes & of tabors þe sarazins made þere So gret noyse þat cristinemen al destourbed were. *a* **1300** *Cursor M.* 6535 He hard þe gret nois was þare Abute þis calf. *c* **1330** R. Brunne *Chron. Wace* (Rolls) 11531 At þat word was noise & cry Of þe Bretons þat stoden ney. ? **1370** *Robt. Cicyle* 174 (Horstm.), He gan crie and make nois, He swor þei schulde alle abye [etc.]. **1390** Gower *Conf.* III. 321 With this noise and with this cry, Out of a barge faste by.. Men sterten out. **1455** *Paston Lett.* I. 351 They sette an hous on fyer.., and cryed and mad an noyse as though they had be sory for the fyer. **1481** Caxton *Godfrey* v. 23 Of the noyse that sourded emonge the hethen men discordyng in theyr lawe. *a* **1533** Ld. Berners *Huon* lix. 207 They all made great ioy with suche a ioyfull noyse that the paynyms without dyd here it. **1590** Shaks. *Com. Err.* iii. i. 61 Who is that at the doore yt keeps all this noise? **1622** Mabbe tr. *Aleman's Guzman d'Alf.* ii. 42 It did mightily vexe me,.. that I could not call vnto them to keepe lesse noise. **1633** G. Herbert *Temple, Redemption* 12 At length I heard a ragged noise and mirth Of theeves and murderers. **1702** Rowe *Tamerl.* iv. i, Thou hast thy sexes Virtues, Their Affectation, Pride, Ill Nature, Noise. **1775** tr. *Scarron's Com. Rom.* I. 286 Zounds, sir, don't keep such a noise about your boots, but rather take mine, so you will but let us sleep. **1844** Dickens *Mart. Chuz.* xxv, I wish you'd hold your noise! **1850** Browning *Bp. Blougram's Apol.* 19 When dinner's done, And body gets its sop and holds its noise And leaves soul free a little.

†**b.** ***without noise***, in a quiet manner; without any display, privately. *Obs.*

1390 Gower *Conf.* I. 100 Prively withoute noise He bringth this foule grete Coise To his Castell. **1560** Daus tr. *Sleidane's Comm.* 114 b, She would be buried without any pompe or noyse. **1614** Raleigh *Hist. World* ii. 508 After this time Ezechia had rest, and spending without noyse that addition which God had made unto his life. **1662** J. Davies tr. *Olearius' Voy.* 110 They were married on Shrove-Sunday.. but without any noyse.

†**c.** Strife, contention, quarrelling. *Obs.*

1484 Caxton *Fables of Æsop* ii. xii. 48 Oftyme it happeth that of a fewe wordes euyll fette, cometh a grete noyse and daunger. **1491** —— *Vitas Patr.* (W. de W. 1495) i. cxix. 141/1 Neuer to haue noyse with a nother it is angels lyfe. **1530** Palsgr. 248/1 Noyse, frayeng, *castille*.

2. †**a.** Common talk, rumour, report; also, evil report, slander, scandal. *Obs.*

1297 R. Glouc. (Rolls) 6383 He let caste þis traitour in þe eueninge late At an fenestre in temese, noise vorto abate. *c* **1400** *Rom. Rose* 3971 To me it is gret hevinesse, That the noyse so fer is go, And the sclaundre of us two. **1426** *Paston Lett.* I. 26 To declare aught of this matier in stoppyng of the noyse that renneth in this case. **1461** *Ibid.* II. 50 Ther is gret noyse of this revell that was don in Suffolk be Yelverton and Jeney. *c* **1478** *Plumpton Corr.* (Camden) 38 The great rumor, slaunder, & full noyse of your tenants.. att they shold be untrew peopell. **1523** Ld. Berners *Froiss.* I. ccliv. 571 The castell.. the whiche the Gauntoyse hadde brente, as the noyse ranne. *a* **1572** Knox *Hist. Ref.* Wks. 1846 I. 92 The noyse of the death of King James divulgat,.. the hartes of men begane to be disclossed. **1655** *Nicholas Papers* (Camden) II. 179 All agree in the noise of more plotts. **1683** Sir W. Temple *Mem.* Wks. 1720 I. 423 The Noise that ran of the magnificent Preparations.. design'd by the Marquess. **1711** Addison *Spect.* No. 164 ¶1 The Noise of this intended Marriage soon reached Theodosius. **1734** tr. *Rollin's Anc. Hist.* (1827) VII. xvii. 223 The noise of this accident was immediately spread in all parts.

†**b.** Repute, reputation. *Obs.*

c **1460** *Towneley Myst.* xiii. 224 Thou has an yll noys of stelyng of shepe. **1470–85** Malory *Arthur* viii. vii. 282 By cause of that noyse and fame that thou hast. **1549–62** Sternhold & H. *Ps.* lxxxix. 16 Through thy righteousness have they a pleasant fame and noyce. **1556** *Aurelio & Isab.* (1608) N vj, Myn ill noise makes me worthey that all the wordes ill saide againste them be unto me attributede.

†**c.** Distinction, note. *Obs. rare*[−1].

1670 G. H. *Hist. Cardinals* ii. iii. 201 They were persons of no great noise, but resolute, modest, courteous.

d. An utterance, usu. in phr. ***to make noises***: to express (something) vocally; freq. with defining adj. prefixed.

1951 N. Marsh *Opening Night* vii. 152 Dr. Curtis said: 'I'd better go and make professional noises at him.' **1955** *Times* 21 July 8/6 If this is so, 'why then the noise about the 12 German divisions in W.E.U. and N.A.T.O.?' **1956** N. Marsh *Off with his Head* (1957) v. 91, I suppose I ought to make a polite noise. **1965** *N.Y. Times* 15 Sept. 42 Leftwing Liberals have made neutralist noises in the past. **1967** *New Scientist* 22 June 718 General Electric and Alcoa, for example, are making noises about getting into city building. **1969** S. Hyland *Top Bloody Secret* iii. 232, I made the right kind of encouraging noises. **1971** *Guardian* 14 May 24/2 There is a temptation to see the hand of Tate and Lyle and Mr Cube in any political noises from the sugar trade. **1971** P. Worsthorne *Socialist Myth* iii. 32 The Labour Party cannot make the classical patriotic noises as convincingly as the Tories. **1973** *Times* 8 Jan. 3/3 Although the city council is, as they see it, making more friendly noises, its policies on development and road building.. set it on a collision course.

3. a. A loud or harsh sound of any kind; a din.

c **1290** *St. Barnabas* 51 in *S. Eng. Leg.* I. 28 Al þat on half daschte a-doun.. of þis temple with gret noyse and soun. **13..** *E.E. Allit. P.* B. 849 Þe god man glyfte with þat glam & gloped for noyse. **1390** Gower *Conf.* III. 216 Many an other tente mo With gret noise, as me thoghte tho, It threw to grounde. *c* **1400** Maundev. (Roxb.) xxxi. 138 Þer es herd noyse as it ware of trumppes. *a* **1450** *Fysshynge w. Angle* (1883) 5 Þe noyse of houndes & blastes of hornes. *a* **1533** Ld. Berners *Huon* xxiii. 68 The water.. made suche a noyse that it myght be herde .x. leges of. *a* **1548** Hall *Chron., Hen. VI* 95 By the noyes of a spanyell was on a night a man espied and taken. **1582** Lichefield tr. *Castanheda's Conq. E. Ind.* 73 b, The tackling.., with the great force of the winde, made such a terrible noyse, and was so fearefull to heare. **1624** Quarles *Job* xvii 54 Who ever heard the voyce Of th' angry heavens, unfrighted at the noyse? **1653** tr. *Carmeni's Nissena* 124 By the noise of Trumpets and beating up of Drums. **1710** J. Clarke tr. *Rohault's Nat. Philos.* (1729) I. 185 Gunpowder when it takes Fire in a Cannon.. makes such a prodigious Noise. *a* **1774** Goldsm. *Nat. Hist.* (1776) I. 160 This motion continued the remaining part of the day..; nor did the noise cease during the whole time. **1848** L. Hunt *Jar of Honey* ii. 23 A noise is heard like the coming of a thousand chariots. **1888** Miss Braddon *Fatal Three* I. iv, I never heard any one make such a noise on a piano.

b. The aggregate of loud sounds arising in a busy community.

c **1450** tr. *De Imitatione* i. xx. 25 Þat he wiþdrawiþ him fer fro seculer noyce. *c* **1610** *Women Saints* (1880) 44 Ill brooking secular noise, and worldlie companie of the towne.

1651 Hobbes *Leviath.* I. ii. 5 Obscured and made weak; as the voyce of a man is in the noyse of the day. **1676** Hale *Contempl.* I. 286 In shady Privacy, free from the Noise And busles of the World. **1730** Berkeley *Lett.* Wks. 1871 IV. 173 Preferring quiet and solitude to the noise of a great town. **1784** Cowper *Task* III. 379 A life all turbulence and noise may seem To him that leads it, wise. **1816** Shelley *Dæmon* I. 28 Seek far from noise and day some western cave.

c. ***noises off***: sound effects, usu. loud or confused, produced off the stage but to be heard by the audience at the performance of a play. Also *transf.*

1924 H. A. Vachell *Quinney's Adventures* 46 As he did so, he heard what is called in stageland a 'noise off'. 'Put them in your pocket,' commanded madame, in a hurried whisper. **1932** Wodehouse *Hot Water* ii. 66 He's got a job with the British Broadcasting Company... He does the noises off. **1934** *B.B.C. Year-bk.* 44 Plays, for example, need their effects, which in their turn call for the studio and staff allocated specially for producing 'noises off'. **1937** N. Marsh *Vintage Murder* xi. 122 'And what..is Scotland Yard's part in the proceedings?' 'Noises off, Mr Ackroyd,' replied Alleyn good-humouredly. **1940** 'G. Orwell' *Inside Whale* 38 The aristocracy and the big bourgeoisie exist in his books chiefly as a kind of 'noises off', a haw-hawing chorus somewhere in the wings. **1949** F. Maclean *Eastern Approaches* III. v. 359 After some time had elapsed, there were 'noises off' from which those of us who remained concluded that the attention of the enemy was fully engaged elsewhere. **1958** *Times* 7 July 9/4 There are 'noises-off', however, that add to the harmony. **1972** *Daily Tel.* 31 May 10/4 In fact the rustlings of the wind-blown trees were perfect noises-off for Shakespeare's uninhabited island.

d. ***noise and number index***: a quantity used in evaluating aircraft noise in terms of its intensity and duration.

1963 *Final Rep. Comm. Probl. Noise* 218 in *Parl. Papers 1962–3* (Cmnd. 2056) XXII. 657 During the Social Survey made in 1961 in the vicinity of London (Heathrow) Airport, measurement of noise levels and studies of the numbers of aircraft likely to be heard were made... The results have been combined..to form a Noise and Number Index (NNI). **1971** *Physics Bull.* Nov. 660/3 An exposure index for aircraft noise has been developed from this survey, called the noise and number index. This index is a combination of the average noise level measured at a point on the ground and the number of times a person is exposed to aircraft noise during a given period of time.

4. A sound which is not remarkably loud.

c **1375** *Sc. Leg. Saints* xxvi. (*Nicholas*) 121 þane of þe noys of his fet he waknyt þane. **1387** Trevisa *Higden* (Rolls) III. 275 Democritus was woned to seie þat þe hestes of schrewes and þe noyse of þe wombe beeþ in oon place. **1560** Daus tr. *Sleidane's Comm.* 232 b, That noise..whan a man doeth rattle or shake together a nomber of dead mens bones. **1617** Moryson *Itin.* I. 196 We tooke some rest,..but with such feare, as wee were ready to flie upon the least noise. **1642** Fuller *Holy & Prof. St.* I. xii. 36 Some report of sheep, that when they runne they are afraid of the noise of their own feet. **1697** Dryden *Virg. Georg.* IV. 801 A buzzing noise of Bees his Ears alarms. **1732** Arbuthnot *Rules Diet* in *Aliments*, etc. 315 A soft Noise of Water distilling by Drops into a Bason. *a* **1774** Goldsm. *Nat. Hist.* (1776) VII. 28 The noise which the snail makes in moving the water. **1833** Tennyson *Lady of Shalott* IV. iii, Thro' the noises of the night She floated down to Camelot. **1876** Bristowe *Th. & Pract. Med.* (1878) 364 The noises which attend the acts of coughing.

fig. **1660** South *Serm.* (1727) IV. 31 One would think, that every Letter was wrote with a Tear, every Word was the Noise of a Breaking Heart.

5. a. An agreeable or melodious sound. Now *rare.*

?*a* **1366** Chaucer *Rom. Rose* 79 Than doth the nyghtyngale hir myght To make noyse and syngen blythe. *Ibid.* 1416 The water, in renning, Gan make a noyse ful lyking. *c* **1403** Lydg. *Temple Glas* 1362 þe noise and heuenli melodie Which þat þei made in her armonye. **1500–20** Dunbar *Poems* xlvi. 25 Nevir suetar noys wes hard with levand man, Na maid this merry gentill nychtingaill. **1535** Coverd. *Ps.* xlvi. 5 God is gone vp with a mery noyse. *a* **1553** Udall *Royster D.* I. iv. 20 Up wyth some mery noyse, Sirs, to bring home the bride! **1585** T. Washington tr. *Nicholay's Voy.* III. ix. 84 Diuers cymbals..made a very plesant and delectable noyce. **1798** Coleridge *Anc. Mar.* 368–9 It ceased; yet still the sails made on A pleasant noise till noon, A noise like of a hidden brook.

†**b.** A company or band of musicians. *Obs.*

1558 in Nichols *Progr. Q. Eliz.* I. 39 Nere unto Fanchurch was erected a scaffolde richely furnished, whereon stode a noyes of instrumentes. **1594** Lyly *Moth. Bomb.* III. iv, Then I wish'd for a noyse Of crack-halter Boyes, On those hempen strings to be twanging. **1598** Chapman *Blinde Beg. Alexandria* Plays 1873 I. 17 Oh that we had a noyse of musitions to play to this anticke as we goe. **1609** B. Jonson *Sil. Wom.* III. iii, The smell of the venison, going through the street, will inuite one noyse of fidlers, or other. **1636** R. Griffin in *Ann. Dubrensia* (1877) 52 A Virgin-crew of matchlesse choyce,..attended with a noyse Of musique sweet. **1668** Dryden *Maiden Queen* III. i, I hear him coming, and a whole noise of fiddles at his heels.

transf. **1676** Wycherley *Pl. Dealer* I. i, I cou'd as soon suffer a whole Noise of Flatterers at a Great Man's Levee.

6. ***to make*** (or †***keep***) ***a noise*** (in other than literal senses): **a.** To make an outcry, to talk much or loudly, *about* a thing.

1668 Sir W. Temple *Let. to Ld. Arlington* Wks. 1720 II. 163 Many Persons in England..had made a Noise about the Marine Treaty. *c* **1680** Beveridge *Serm.* (1729) I. 300 For all the great noise that is made about it, there is but little true faith in the world. **1753** *Scots Mag.* XV. 67/1 The French made a great deal of noise about advantages they had gained. **1782** A. Monro *Compar. Anat.* (ed. 3) Introd. 9 Anatomists have made a noise about the different structures of the same part.

b. To be much talked of; to be the object of general notice and comment. Also (without preceding *make* or *keep*) used of a person, esp. in phr. ***the*** (or ***a***) ***big noise***: a person of great importance (orig. *U.S.*).

?**1618** Howell *Lett.* (1650) I. 5 The news that keeps greatest noise here now, is the return of Sir Walter Rawleigh. **1677** *Hist. MSS. Comm., 12th Rep.* App. V. 36 Lord Burghley's chalange sent by Sir Scroope Howe makes a great deal of noyse. **1707** Addison *Pres. St. War* Wks. 1766 III. 258 Blenheim was followed by a summer that makes no noise in the war. **1788** Nelson in Nicolas *Disp. & Lett.* (1845) I. 275 The capture of a Privateer makes more noise taken in the Channel, than a Frigate..afar off. *a* **1862** Buckle *Civiliz.* (1869) III. ii. 107 In 1596, David Black.. delivered a sermon, which made much noise. **1908** G. H. Lorimer *Jack Spurlock* vii. 153 A lot of people are beginning to think that Teddy's a mere noise. **1911** R. W. Chambers *Common Law* vi. 169 Well, sister, take it from muh, she thinks she's the big noise in the Great White Alley. **1927** T. E. Lawrence *Let.* 8 Feb. (1938) 506 Drill Parades bi-weekly when a big noise draws near—Sir Sam. **1931** Galsworthy *Maid in Waiting* vi. 42 Saxenden is a big noise behind the scenes in military matters. **1939** C. Day Lewis *Child of Misfortune* III. iii. 296 Elderton was the big noise in the Home Office. **1942** J. B. Priestley *Black-out in Gretley* iii. 32 He's rather a big noise here. Landed man really, but has a seat on our Board, and a local J.P. **1957** M. Kennedy *Heroes of Clone* I. v. 50 Say you don't want him. You're the big noise here.

c. ***to make a noise in the world***, to attain to general notoriety or renown.

1662 Stillingfl. *Orig. Sacræ* II. ii. §6 Their Hieroglyphical and mystical Learning hath made the greatest noise in the world, and hath the least of substance in it. **1685** Burnet *Let.* in *Trav.* (1687) II. 42 Those publick scandals that make a noise in the World. **1702** Addison *Dial. Medals* Misc. Wks. 1736 III. 14 Such persons as have made a noise in the world. **1751** Earl Orrery *Remarks Swift* (1752) 191 The first of these, *The Tale of a Tub*, has made much noise in the world.

d. Joc. phr. ***to make a noise like***, to pretend to be.

1920 'Sapper' *Bull-Dog Drummond* v. 126 Make a noise like a sturgeon, and he'll think it's caviare. **1928** D. L. Sayers *Lord Peter views Body* 87, I s'pose I'd better make a noise like a hoop and roll away. Night, night, everybody. **1961** Partridge *Dict. Slang.* Suppl. 1199/1 *Noise like a—, make a*..dates from ca. 1908. Baden Powell, in his *Scouting for Boys*, instructed scouts in danger of detection to take cover and make a noise like a (say) thrush.

7. In scientific use, a collective term (used without the indef. article) for: fluctuations or disturbances (usu. irregular) which are not part of a wanted signal or which interfere with its intelligibility or usefulness.

1923 *Telegraph & Telephone Jrnl.* IX. 119/2 The variations in noise were plotted, and their effect at times was to reduce the intelligibility to 20 or 30 per cent. **1930** *Proc. IRE* XVIII. 253 Circuit for measuring noise on the plate side of a vacuum tube. *Ibid.* 259 The ratio of signal to noise in the input circuit. **1932** F. E. Terman *Radio Engin.* vi. 207 The output currents obtained..in the absence of a signal voltage produce what is commonly referred to as 'noise' when flowing through a..loudspeaker, and it is also common practice to apply the term 'noise' to the corresponding radio-frequency currents obtained in the output of a radio-frequency amplifier, although these lie above the range of audible frequencies. **1940** Zworykin & Morton *Television* vi. 194 If the noise is appreciable compared with the picture signal, it appears in the reproduction as a myriad of constantly changing bright specks. **1953** J. B. Carroll *Study of Language* vii. 201 It is ..necessary to study the effect of the signal-to-noise ratio on the efficiency of communication, noise being defined as that part of a received transmission which is extraneous to the original message. **1962** A. Nisbett *Technique Sound Studio* 262 In all electronic components and recording or transmission media the signal must compete with some degree of background noise. **1966** *New Scientist* 16 June 714/3 In this way a radar echo which may otherwise be hidden by 'noise' is rendered visible. **1968** J. Lyons *Introd. Theoretical Linguistics* ii. 88 The distortions produced in one's handwriting in a moving train can be attributed to 'noise'. **1970** O. Dopping *Computers & Data Processing* i. 21 Information theory deals largely with what happens when a random interference ('noise') is superimposed on the desired signal. **1973** *Computers & Humanities* VII. 160 Knisbacher uses a generalized (context-free) grammar in his algorithm [for machine translation] but avoids the 'noise' of too many resultant analyses for each sentence by simulating context sensitivity within that context-free framework. **1974** *Nature* 10 May 192/1 As normally viewed, displays of video noise ('snow') have the appearance of fields of small speckles which seem to dart about at random.

8. *Comb.*, as ***noise abatement, control, level, -maker, -making, measurement, meter, pollution, reduction, suppression; noise-free, -measuring*** adjs.; **noise check** *Motor Rallying*, the use of a decibel metre to ensure that cars do not make too much noise; **noise contour**, an imaginary line or surface joining points where the noise level is the same; **noise factor** or **figure** *Electronics*, a quantity representing the additional noise introduced by a signal-processing device such as an amplifier (see quots.); **noise filter** *Electronics*, a filter for selectively reducing noise; **noise limiter** *Electronics*, a circuit or device for selectively reducing certain types of noise, esp. by momentarily reducing the output or the gain during peaks of greater amplitude than the desired signal; **noise-money** (see quot. 1883); **noise storm** *Astr.*, a radio emission from the sun consisting of a succession of short bursts or pips in the megahertz range that lasts for a period of hours or days and is associated with sunspots.

1923 *Health* II. 438 A real want, a very great want, and a very immediate want is a Noise-Abatement Society. **1973** *Scotsman* 13 Feb. 8/3 It would be very hard to sustain a reasonable argument against them on noise abatement grounds. **1960** S. Turner *Rallying* vi. 68 One other sort of check which you must treat with respect is a noise check. **1963** [see *dust-raising* adj. (Dust *sb.*[1] 8 b)]. **1963** P. Drackett *Motor Rallying* iii. 37, I was remarkably unimpressed by the secrecy displayed by noise-check marshals on one big rally. **1971** *Physics Bull.* Nov. 656/1 During design studies of rotorcraft the noise of various designs is assessed by predicting an appropriate noise contour (usually 90 PN dB) and comparing it with the design noise target. **1973** *Times* 25 Apr. 19/6 If there were a prospect of drastically curtailing operations from Heathrow and Gatwick..before the time when the noise contours will start contracting through the increasing use of quieter aircraft, then there would be some point..in building Maplin. **1960** *McGraw-Hill Encycl. Sci. & Technol.* IX. 120/1 The first step in noise control is an analysis of the nature and extent of the problem. **1937** A. G. Tynan in *Radio Engin.* July 21/2 Such a factor is very easily arrived at by multiplying the noise-signal ratio..by the sensitivity of the receiver in microvolts. This may be conveniently christened the noise factor. **1952** *Wireless World* June 224/1 There are various slightly different definitions of noise factor (in America, 'noise figure'). *Ibid.*, The noise factor is 3. It means that the result of amplifier noise is to make the noise 3 times as bad as in the ideal case where the signal source is the sole noise generator. *Ibid.*, In an ideal amplifier or receiver the noise factor..would be 1. **1962** *Rep. Comm. Broadcasting 1960* 333 in *Parl. Papers 1961–2* (Cmnd. 1753) IX. 259 The Band V tests have also shown that the noise factor of receivers in this Band is at present relatively high. **1944** *Proc. IRE* XXXII. 420/2 The noise figure *F* of the network is defined as the ratio of the available signal-to-noise ratio at the signal-to-generator terminals to the available signal-to-noise ratio at its output terminals. **1952** Noise figure [see *noise factor* above]. **1968** *Wireless World* Dec. 455/2 Noise figure = Total noise output power/Noise output power due to sources only. *Ibid.* 457/2 Negative feedback..has no effect whatever on the noise figure of an amplifier at any given frequency. *Ibid.* 458/2 A noise figure at 1,000 Hz of 0·02 dB. **1960** *McGraw-Hill Encycl. Sci. & Technol.* IX. 130/1 The tone control of a radio or record player can act as a noise filter, as when high-frequencies are cut down to reduce record noise. **1967** E. L. Gruenberg *Handbk. Telemetry & Remote Control* ix. 15 The characteristics of the noise filter are determined by the sampling rate, the overall system accuracy, and the allowable crosstalk between successive samples. **1934** *Discovery* Dec. 348/1 Standard practice in noise-free construction is now available for architects. **1966** D. G. Brandon *Mod. Techniques Metallogr.* 162 Careful design of the collection system for backscattered electrons yields practically noise-free images. **1925** *Sci. Amer.* June 422/3 The limit of radio..is the static—what the radio engineers call the 'noise level' of the disturbances in the ether. **1932** V. O. Knudsen *Archit. Acoustics* ix. 257 The average street noise level in New York varies from about 47 to 80 db. **1959** *Daily Tel.* 24 Apr. 20/7 It must be shown that helicopter operations can be carried out at a noise level tolerable to the public. **1972** R. Adams *Watership Down* xix. 111 Nowadays, among fields and woods, the noise level by day is..too high for some kinds of animal to tolerate. **1939** *Wireless World* 5 Jan. 15 (*heading*) Noise limiters suppressing interference in the receiver. **1954** E. Molloy *Radio & Television Engineers' Ref. Bk.* xxxiii. 8 Noise limiters tend to be less efficient when used in receivers possessing extremely high selectivity. **1574** Howse in *Hist. Fam. Fortescue* (1869) II. 231 They found nobody there, for the noise-makers were gone back. **1610** Shaks. *Temp.* I. i. 47 You whoreson insolent Noyse-maker. **1654** Whitlock *Zootomia* 533 Of so much more Concernment is one suffering Saint, than all the Noise-makers in the World. **1815** Moore *Mem.* (1853) II. 78 Among chatterers, drinkers, and all sorts of noise-makers. **1422** tr. *Secreta Secret., Priv. Priv.* 187 Thou shalte lagh wythout grynnynge, speke wyth-out cry or noyse-makynge. **1934** *Discovery* Dec. 345 Efforts..are being made to provide standards of noise-measurement. *Ibid.* 347/1 The expert with his noise-measuring gear. **1964** R. F. Ficchi *Electr. Interference* vii. 120 About twenty years ago, a new approach to the problem of measurement was taken when it was stated that the most practical type of noise-measuring instrument is, essentially, a radio receiver with an indicating means. **1931** *Proc. IRE* XIX. 1953 This instrument, which has been called a 'circuit noise meter', consists of an amplifier, a frequency weighting network, a rectifier, and an indicating meter. **1950** *Jrnl. R. Aeronaut. Soc.* LIV. 699/1 The microphone..has been calibrated by the makers in conjunction with the noise meter. **1883** *Chamb. Jrnl.* 8 Dec. 770/2 So disagreeable is this fog-signalling duty..that..the whole crew receive what they call 'Noise-money',..for the time the signal is actually in operation. **1970** *Britannica Bk. of Year 1969* 798/3 *Noise pollution*, pollution consisting of annoying noise (*noise pollution* caused by automobile traffic, a jet airplane, or a vacuum cleaner); called also *sound pollution.* **1970** *Sci. Jrnl.* Mar. 5 The greatly improved noise pollution characteristics of VTOL compared not only with conventional aircraft (CTOL) but with short take off and landing craft (STOL). **1972** J. Maddox *Doomsday Syndrome* iv. 98 'Noise pollution' is a phrase in everyday use. **1931** *Proc. IRE* XIX. 1763 The noise reduction advantage of the arrays..is some 15 decibels over that of a nondirectional antenna. **1959** W. S. Sharps *Dict. Cinematogr.* 114/2 In photographic recording and reproducing, noise reduction is a process whereby the average transmission of the sound track of the print..is decreased for signals of low level and increased for signals of high level. **1947** C. W. Allen in *Monthly Notices R. Astron. Soc.* CVII. 391 All solar noise storms..in Figs. 2 and 3 coincide with near meridian passage of spots. **1974** G. L. Verschuur *Invisible Universe* iii. 36 Sunspots also produce characteristic radio bursts, called storm bursts or bursts of type I. These are very short-lived intense pips of radio emission, each lasting only a fraction of a second, although thousands of these might be emitted every hour and the noise storm (a string of bursts) may last for days. **1933** *Practical Wireless* II. 37/2 (*heading*) Noise suppression on the short waves. **1968** *IEEE Jrnl. Quantum Electronics* IV. 644 (*heading*) Noise suppression in the Argon FM Laser.

noise (nɔɪz), *v.* Also 5–7 noyse, 5 noyce, 6 noyz. [f. NOISE *sb.*, or ad. OF. *noisier*, *noiser*, to make a noise, to quarrel, wrangle.]

1. *trans.* To report, rumour, spread (*abroad*). Now somewhat *rare*.

a. In phr. ***it is noised that***, etc.

c **1400** *Destr. Troy* 1173 Hit was noiset anon þat a noumbur hoge Of Grekes were gedret. **1465** *Paston Lett.* II. 206 It is noyced here that my Lord of Norffolk hathe taken partye in thes mater. **1470–85** MALORY *Arthur* VI. x. 197 Hit is noysed that ye loue quene Gueneuer. *a* **1548** HALL *Chron., Hen. VIII*, 126 The Frenche kyng..caused it to be noysed that he would besege the toune of Valencyen. **1599** *Warn. Faire Wom.* ii. 786 Tis noysd at London, that a marchant's slain. **1684** BUNYAN *Pilgr.* II. 201 It was noised abroad that Mr. Valiant-for-truth was taken with a Summons. **1849** MACAULAY *Hist. Eng.* iv. I. 506 It was noised abroad that he had more real power to help and hurt than many nobles.

b. In ordinary passive use.

c **1400** *Destr. Troy* 12271 The noy of þat noble was noyset thurgh the ost. **1489** CAXTON *Faytes of A.* II. v. 99 He made wordes to be noysed about. **1535** COVERDALE *1 Chron.* xiv. 17 And Dauids name was noysed out in all londes. **1560** DAUS tr. *Sleidane's Comm.* 228 Rumour was noysed abrode, that Themperour shoulde secretly mynde warre. **1614** RALEIGH *Hist. World* III. 62 That of the battell against the Tarquinians..was presently noised at Rome. **1665** MANLEY *Grotius Low-C. Wars* 431 These things, as soon as they were noysed through Brabant [etc.]. **1744** OZELL *Brantome's Sp. Rhodom.* 78 Our other Man retir'd, for the Thing began to be nois'd abroad. **1779** in *Hist. Pelham, Mass.* (1898) 138, I think its Noised by some as if it was not Desired. **1879** BUTCHER & LANG *Odyssey* 74 My true lord whose fame is noised abroad from Hellas to mid Argos.

c. In active use.

1463 *Paston Lett.* II. 134 He noyseth and seyth,..ye have caused a mad woman to take apell a yens hym. **1470–85** MALORY *Arthur* XXI. i. 840 Where ye noyse [that] my lord Arthur is slayne & that is not so. **1555** in Strype *Eccl. Mem.* (1721) III. App. xlvi. 142 And they have noyzed and bruted abrode most shamefull sklaunders. **1588** SHAKS. *L.L.L.* II. i. 22 All-telling fame Doth noyse abroad Nauar hath made a vow. **1641** MILTON *Ch. Govt.* I. vi. Wks. 1851 III. 126 Noise it till ye be hoarse, that a rabble of Sects will come in. **1689** G. HARVEY *Curing Dis. by Expect.* vi. 37 They so highly advance the Credit of a milk Diet, by noising it to be the sole grand sweetner of the Blood. **1896** *New York Weekly Witness* 30 Dec. 13/2 The welcome cooled when we noised-about the object of our visit.

†**2.** To spread rumours or a report concerning (a person, etc.); *esp.* to defame, speak ill of. *Obs.*

1424 *Paston Lett.* I. 17 The seyd Walter..in divers other maneres hath noysed and sklaundered the seyd William. **1447–8** SHILLINGFORD *Lett.* (Camden) 87 To noyse and disslaundre the said citee. **1470–85** MALORY *Arthur* X. xlvi. 488 Euer this Corsabryn noysed her and named her that she was oute of her mynde. **1530** PALSGR. 644/2, I noyse one, I gyve hym a name or brute, good or badde, *je donne le bruit*. He is noysed to be an yvell lyver.

†**3. a.** With *it*: To clamour, cry out. *Obs. rare.*

1662 HICKERINGILL *Distr. Innoc.* Wks. 1716 I. 291 Thus did they furiously noise it against our Saviour.., Crucifie him.

†**b.** To force *out of* by clamour. *Obs. rare.*

a **1734** NORTH *Lives, Ld. Kpr. North* (1826) I. 322 He was not a little concerned to see men noised out of their lives, as the twelve priests were, and that nothing could resist the fury of the people, that, like a hurricane, pursued them.

4. *intr.* **a.** To talk loudly or much *of* a thing.

c **1374** CHAUCER *Boeth.* III. met. vi. (1868) 7 Thanne comen alle mortal folk of noble sede; why noisen ye or bosten of youre eldres? *c* **1475** *Partenay* 1556 The peple merily ioyng As off the good rule noysed of thaim to. **1837** CARLYLE *Fr. Rev.* I. II. II. iii. 290 A plan, much noised of in those days,..has been devised. **1858** —— *Fredk. Gt.* v. v. (1872) II. 101 Much noised of in the..Prussian Books.

b. To make a noise or outcry.

a **1400–50** *Alexander* 4744 Vmquile he noys[is] as a nowte, as a nox quen he lawes. **1441** *Plumpton Corr.* (Camden) p. lx, Upon whom the said misdoers followed,..noising & crying, Sley the Archbishop' Carles! *a* **1578** LINDESAY (Pitscottie) *Chron. Scot.* (S.T.S.) I. 166 Quhen thir tydingis..came abrode and noyssed throw the countrie. **1671** MILTON *P.R.* IV. 488, I never fear'd they could, though noising loud And threatning nigh. *a* **1814** *Forgery* I. i. in *New Brit. Theatre* I. 435 Thou hast noised as much as if thou wert Sir Robert. **1827** CLARE *Sheph. Cal.* 4 Rook, crow, and jackdaw—noising loud, Fly to and fro to dreary fen. **1857** BORROW *Rom. Rye* (1858) I. 110 What's the bird noising yonder, brother?

Hence **noised** *ppl. a.*; **'noising** *vbl. sb.* and *ppl. a.*; †**'noisingly** *adv.*

1425 *Rolls of Parlt.* IV. 298/2 Thourgh which langage and noysyng, I fele my name..emblemysshed. **1426** *Paston Lett.* I. 26, I am foule and noysyngly vexed with hem, to my gret unease. **1453** in *Epist. Acad. Oxon.* (1898) I. 320 The first publisheris of the seide sclandirful noysyng. **1568** GRAFTON *Chron.* II. 521 He declareth you a true man to hym,..the sayde dislaunder and noysing notwithstanding. **1641** QUARLES *Enchyrid.* I. c, A victory whose noys'd renowne may fill the world with your eternall glory. **1656** *Burton's Diary* (1828) I. 103 But the great noising argument is, That we are under Gospel dispensation. **1681** H. MORE in *Glanvill's Sadducismus* I. Postscr. (1726) 1 Therefore he expected the Issue of that noised Story of the Spectre at Exeter. **1828** *Sporting Mag.* XXI. 227 Hot-headed, hot-horsed, noising, coffee-housing friends. **1864** *Good Wds.* 790/2 The latest books only, the noised books of the season. **1871** MEREDITH *H. Richmond* xxxvi, Making the low noising of the leaves an intolerable whisper of lovers.

noiseful ('nɔɪzfʊl), *a.* [f. NOISE *sb.* + -FUL.]

1. Full of noise; noisy.

1382 WYCLIF *Prov.* xx. 1 A leccherous thing [is] win, and noiseful drunkenesse. *c* **1425** *Found. St. Bartholomew's* (E.E.T.S.) 3 Amonge the noysefull prese of that tumultuous courte. **1608** SYLVESTER *Du Bartas* II. iv. IV. *Decay* 264 Either side in their seem-Rights' defence Was hot and earnest at the noise-full Bar. **1644** SIR E. DERING *Prop. Sacr.* C iij, These proud fastuous wayes of humility, this noisefull piety. **1674** DRYDEN *Epil. Univ. Oxford* 5 Content of mind; Which noiseful towns and courts can never know. **1725** POPE *Odyss.* XV. 557 From noiseful revel far remote she flies. **1858** BEECHER *Life Thoughts* (1859) 51 The forest is quiet or only so much noiseful as the insects make it.

†**2.** Full of slander or evil report. *Obs.*

1459 *Paston Lett.* I. 499 Bothen have answerid Wyndham, not aldermoste to hise plesir, becaus of his noiseful langage. **1463** *Ibid.* II. 134 With ougth evydent proffe the mater schall be but noysefull to you.

Hence **'noisefully** *adv. rare*$^{-1}$.

c **1611** CHAPMAN *Iliad* II. *Comm.*, Λιγεως..signifieth shrillie, or noisefullie, squeaking.

noiseless ('nɔɪzlɪs), *a.* [f. as prec. + -LESS.]

a. Silent, quiet; making no stir or commotion.

1601 SHAKS. *All's Well* V. iii. 41 Th' inaudible, and noiseless foot of time. **1605** —— *Lear* IV. ii. 56 France spreads his banners in our noiseless land. *a* **1667** COWLEY *On the late Civil War* Wks. (Grosart) I. p. cxxxvii, His Treasons restless, and yet noiseless Heart. **1699** GARTH *Dispens.* 11 Midnight Silence guards the noiseless Doors. **1750** GRAY *Elegy* 76 They kept the noiseless tenour of their way. **1784** COWPER *Task* IV. 346 The wain..in its sluggish pace, Noiseless, appears a moving hill of snow. **1816** BYRON *Ch. Har.* III. lxxxv, This quiet sail is as a noiseless wing To waft me from distraction. **1853** KANE *Grinnell Exp.* (1856) xxvii. 221 It is no fun..to sit motionless and noiseless as a statue, with a cold musket in your hands. **1875** HOWELLS *Foregone Conclusion* 1 The canal, where he could see the noiseless black boats meeting and passing.

b. Characterized by a virtual absence of noise (sense 7).

1931 A. NADELL *Projecting Sound Pictures* xiv. 244 The recently developed 'noiseless recording' is achieved by passing a 'bias' current through the value ribbons, in addition to the usual speech current. The effect of the bias is to eliminate the former spacing of 2, or 1½ mils, and to keep the ribbons always closed when no speech current is passing. **1944** *Phil. Mag.* XXXV. 394, *r* must be regarded as a noiseless shunting resistance. **1957** *Sci. Amer.* Feb. 82/2 The maser would..be useful in astronomy and cosmology. As a noiseless amplifier it would eliminate the noise generated in the circuits of radio telescopes. **1972** J. M. TAYLOR tr. *Meyer & Neumann's Physical & Applied Acoustics* ix. 351 In variable-area recording..the bright side of the sound track is darkened for small amplitudes in the region that does not contribute to sound generation (noiseless recording).

noiselessly ('nɔɪzlɪslɪ), *adv.* [f. prec. + -LY².] Silently, quietly, without noise.

1835 MARRYAT *Olla Podr.* iv, We glided noiselessly.. along. **1860** MOTLEY *Netherl.* i. (1868) I. 2 A clerk or two, noiselessly opening and shutting the door.

noiselessness ('nɔɪzlɪsnɪs). [f. as prec. + -NESS.] The state or quality of being noiseless.

1847 in WEBSTER. **1855** J. R. LEIFCHILD *Cornwall* 50 Let us listen in perfect noiselessness for a few moments. **1893** F. F. MOORE *Gray Eye or So* II. 130 The butler..disappeared with the noiselessness of a shadow.

†**'noiser.** *Obs. rare.* [f. NOISE *v.* + -ER¹.] A slanderer; a spreader of a report.

1434 MISYN *Mending Life* 118 Þi noysurs wrechidar þou sal se, & with all þi mynde to criste þou salt draw. **1460** CAPGRAVE *Chron.* (Rolls) 278 This langage sesid mech aftir tyme that a prest, on of the first noyseres, was take.

noisette¹ (nwɑː'zɛt). [f. the name *Noisette* (see quot. 1837).] A variety of rose, being a cross between a common China rose and a muskrose. Also in *attrib.* use.

1837 RIVERS *Rose Amateur's Guide* 80 The 'Blush Noisette' rose, was raised from seed in America, by M. Ph. Noisette, and sent by him to his brother M. Louis Noisette ..in 1817. *Ibid.* 81 Belle Antonine is a pillar Noisette. **1850** MRS. GASKELL *Moorland Cottage* i, Clustering noisettes, and fraxinellas, and sweet briar. **1857** KINGSLEY *Two Y. Ago* i. 3 The great yellow noisette swung its long canes across the window. **1892** *Daily News* 12 Sept. 3/1 Rose bushes and rose trees, tea-roses and noisette roses.

noisette² (nwɑː'zɛt). [Fr.] *pl.* Small pieces of beef or mutton, with various additions, prepared as a dish.

1891 MRS. MARSHALL *Cookery Book, Extra Rec.* 150 Noisettes of Mutton à la Parisienne.

noisily ('nɔɪzɪlɪ), *adv.* [f. NOISY *a.* + -LY².] In a noisy manner, with noise.

1779 JOHNSON *L. Poets, Milton* I. 158 They, who could so noisily censure it,..could contrive what they wanted to accuse. **1856** KANE *Arctic Explor.* I. xvii. 213 When I turned in, he was still noisily disconsolate. **1870** MISS BRIDGMAN *R. Lynne* I. iii. 28 You do everything so noisily. **1897** MARY KINGSLEY *W. Africa* 504 The African is usually great at dreams, and has them very noisily.

noisiness ('nɔɪzɪnɪs). [f. as prec. + -NESS.] The quality of being noisy; loudness of sound.

1727 in BAILEY (vol. II). **1877** M. M. GRANT *Sun-Maid* i, Baptiste rang a huge bell with much noisiness. **1899** SIR R. TEMPLE *Ho. Comm.* iii. 55 The noisiness, restlessness, and casual conversation of the Members.

noising, *vbl. sb.* and *ppl. a.*, **noisingly** *adv.*: see NOISE *v.*

noisome ('nɔɪsəm), *a.* Forms: 4 noȝesum, 5–8 noysome (6–7 -som, 6 -sum), 6–8 noisom, 6– noisome. [f. NOY *sb.*¹ or *v.* + -SOME.]

1. Harmful, injurious, noxious.

1382 WYCLIF *Prov.* i. 22 Hou longe..foolis tho thingus that ben noȝesum to them shul coueiten? **1514** BARCLAY *Cyt. & Uplondyshm.* (Percy Soc.) 9 Nought is more noysom to flocke, cotage, ne folde, Than sodayne tempeste, and unprovyed colde. **1542–3** *Act 34 & 35 Hen. VIII*, c. 1 Suche bokes, writynges,..teachinges, and instructions, as be pestiferous, and noysome. **1578** LYTE *Dodoens* 516 That with the red flowers groweth in moyst medowes, and is very noysome to the same. **1609** HOLLAND *Amm. Marcell.* XXII. v. 193 No savage beasts are so noisom and hurtful to men, as Christians are to themselves. **1650** VENNER *Via Recta* 98 All fat is of itself ill and noysome to the stomack. **1693** EVELYN *De la Quint. Compl. Gard.* II. 4 Those Branches which, as noisom and useless, must be taken from it. **1718** PRIOR *Solomon* III. 125 The noisome pestilence..marches through the midday air. **1784** COWPER *Task* III. 671 The rank society of weeds, Noisome, and ever greedy to exhaust Th' impoverish'd earth. **1845** HIRST *Poems* 50 Begirt with noisome ivy vines That shroud me like a pall. **1868** MORRIS *Earthly Par.* I. I. 50 Fair streams we saw,..But nothing noisome for a man to fear.

2. Offensive to the sense of smell; ill-smelling.

1577 *Nottingham Rec.* IV. 169 We do present the yssue.. to be vere noysum and nedefull to be scoured. **1579** W. WILKINSON *Confut. Fam. Love* 60 b, The more myer is stirred, the sauour is the noysomer. **1600** DEKKER *Gentle Craft* 19 Sweepe me these kennels that the noysome Stench offende not the nose of my neighbours. **1642** ROGERS *Naaman* 28 Held under with his filthy noysome malady. **1678** R. L'ESTRANGE *Seneca's Mor.* (1702) 324 When we are abroad,..we can bear well enough with..nasty streets, noisom Ditches. **1712** ARBUTHNOT *John Bull* I. xvi, Such a noisome infectious Breath, as threw all the servants, that dressed her, into consumptions. **1748** *Anson's Voy.* I. v. 58 These operations were extremely necessary for correcting the noisom stench. **1785** BURKE *Sp. Nabob of Arcot's Debts* Wks. 1842 I. 345 A bloated, putrid, noisome carcass, full of stench and poison. **1818** MRS. SHELLEY *Frankenst.* xiii. (1865) 169 His blind and aged father..lay in a noisome dungeon, while he enjoyed the free air. **1879** H. GEORGE *Progr. & Pov.* VII. ii. (1881) 318 In squalid garrets and noisome cellars women work away their lives.

3. Disagreeable, unpleasant, offensive.

c **1440** *York Myst.* xxxii. 99 Sir, a noysomemare note newly is noysed. **1542** *Lam. & Piteous Treat.* in *Harl. Misc.* (1745) IV. 511 The Waye is altogether in a Maner noysome, croked ouertwhart, and in many Places narowe. **1573** TUSSER *Husb.* (1878) 89 Where plots full of nettles be noisome to eie, Sowe thereupon hemp seed, and nettle will die. **1589** R. HARVEY *Pl. Perc.* (1860) 10 Me thinks the clacke of thy mill, is somewhat noisome to the whole countrey. **1607** TOPSELL *Hist. of Four-f. Beasts* (1658) 511 She roareth, ..and uttereth such a fearfull, noysome, and terrible clamor. **1632** J. HAYWARD tr. *Biondi's Eromena* 131 Seeing melancholy makes a man noysome, both to him-selfe and others. **1861** J. TULLOCH *Eng. Puritanism* 231 He poured forth the vials of his most noisome wrath in reply. **1899** W. JAMES *Talks to Teachers* (1904) 58 Even such a noisome thing as a collection of postage stamps.

†**4.** Annoying, troublesome. *Obs. rare.*

1548 PATTEN *Exped. Scotl.* P j, The church of Annan, a strong place, and uery noysum alway vnto oure men. **1570** *Satir. Poems Reform.* xiii. 116 Ane noysum nychtbour proude in oppressioun. **1653** MORE *Antid Ath.* III. ix. (1712) 114 One that..was often infested with the noisom occursions of that troublesome Ghost.

Hence **'noisomely** *adv. rare.*

1589 RIDER *Bibl. Schol.*, Noisomely, *infeste, perniciose*. **1633** BP. HALL *Occas. Medit.* §86 Now that it is stuffed thus noysomely, all helpes are too little to countervaile that sent of corruption.

noisomeness ('nɔɪsəmnɪs). [f. prec. + -NESS.] The quality or condition of being noisome; unwholesomeness, offensiveness.

1530 PALSGR. 248/1 Noysomnesse or ykesomnesse, *ennuy*. **1561** DAUS tr. *Bullinger on Apoc.* (1573) 299 b, In heauen is founde no noysomenes, no obscure darckenes. **1591** SAVILE *Tacitus, Hist.* III. xxxv. 135 The ground being infected with the noysomenesse of the dead carcases. **1617** MORYSON *Itin* III. 35 All the objects of humane life, are more often accompanied with noysomenesse then pleasure. **1698** FRYER *Acc. E. India & P.* 63 Poysoned partly by the noisomeness of the Air. **1836** THIRLWALL *Greece* III. 457 Their unburied corpses still adding to the ever growing noisomeness of the crowded dungeon. **1864** C. MAYO *Vac. Tour.* 391 The drainage of Washington can only be known to exist by its extreme noisomeness.

noisy ('nɔɪzɪ), *a.* [f. NOISE *sb.* + -Y¹.]

1. a. Making, or given to making, a loud noise; clamorous, turbulent.

1693 DRYDEN *Epist. to Sir G. Kneller* 83 A noisy crowd, Like women's anger, impotent and loud. **1700** ROWE *Amb. Step-Moth.* I. i, Stir the simple hinds to noisie Faction. *a* **1774** GOLDSM. *Nat. Hist.* (1776) III. 335 It is more noisy in its pursuits even than the dog. **1838** THIRLWALL *Greece* IV. 139 The noisiest advocates of the most violent measures were probably its retainers. **1869** *Daily News* 22 Dec., That noisier section of the agitators.

b. noisy scrub bird *Austral.*, a ground-dwelling bird, *Altrichornis clamosus*, found in parts of Western Australia.

[**1848** J. GOULD *Birds Austral.* III. tab. 34 (*heading*) *Altrichia clamosa*, Gould. Noisy Brush-bird.] **1901** A. J. CAMPBELL *Nests & Eggs Austral. Birds* I. 504 The Noisy Scrub Bird..lives in the thickets of undergrowth. **1933** *Bulletin* (Sydney) 1 Feb. 21 One of the rarest and most curious of Australian birds is the 'noisy scrub-bird'..whose home, if perchance the secretive creature survives, is in the dense forest of the Leeuwin Peninsula. **1966** *Evening Standard* 14 July 18/2 One of Australia's rarest birds, the noisy scrub bird, has forced the Western Australian State Government to abandon plans to establish a new town. The town..was to have been in the heart of the noisy scrub bird country near Albany, 300 miles south of Perth. *Ibid.* 18/3 Between 1889 and 1961 the bird was neither seen nor heard. But then it reappeared... The noisy scrub bird is extremely elusive. The male has a call like the crack of a whip. **1972** G.

DURRELL *Catch me a Colobus* x. 218 In Australia they rediscovered the Noisy Scrub Bird which had been thought to be extinct.

2. a. Full of, characterized by, noise.

1693 DRYDEN *Juvenal* iii. (1697) 43 In quiet Cumæ fixing his Repose: Where, far from noisie Rome secure he lives. **1718** ROWE tr. *Lucan* I. 61 Where thousands crowded in the noisie street. **1751** JOHNSON *Rambler* No. 153 ¶4 With little envy of the noisy happiness which my elder brother had the fortune to enjoy. **1796** H. HUNTER tr. *St.-Pierre's Stud. Nat.* (1799) II. 338 Aquatic birds have shrill and piercing cries.. in perfect correspondence with their noisy situations. **1849** MACAULAY *Hist. Eng.* iii. I. 358 In Covent Garden a filthy and noisy market was held close to the dwellings of the great. **1877** M. ARNOLD *Sonn., Quiet Work*, Labour, that in lasting fruit outgrows Far noisier schemes.

Comb. **1798** B. JOHNSON *Orig. Poems* 187 Gay Mirth, and Laughter noisy-loud.

b. (In the sense of NOISE *sb.* 7.)

1944 *Phil. Mag.* XXXV. 394 If [the resistance] *r* were thermally 'noisy'. **1949** *Proc. R. Soc.* A. CXCVII. 480 (*facing caption*) Noisy background chiefly due to imperfections of illuminating objective. **1951** *Sci. Amer.* Aug. 14/3 Transistors.. were 'noisy'. **1973** *Nature* 5 Oct. 258/1 In the galactic plane, the 1,420 MHz line is noisy, which decreases its attractiveness.

3. *transf.* Very loud in colour.

1900 *Westm. Gaz.* 9 Aug. 3/2 The effect from the reverse of the simple serge costume was not the least noisy.

noit, obs. Sc. form of NOTE *sb.* and *v.*

noither, variant of NOTHER *conj.*

‖**noix** (nwa). [F., lit. 'nut'.] (See quot. 1961.)

1845 E. ACTON *Mod. Cookery* ix. 210 That part of the fillet [of veal] to which the fat or udder is attached;.. Called by them [*sc.* French cooks] the *noix*. **1893** *Encycl. Pract. Cookery* II. 699/2 Beat the noix well, trim it to a nice shape, and lard with thin fillets of fat bacon. **1906** A. FILIPPINI *Internat. Cook Bk.* 162 (*heading*) Noix of veal, braisée, fermière. **1923** C. H. SENN *Cent. Cookery Bk.* (new ed.) 565 Noix de veau à la Viart.. 1 small cushion or kernel part of veal [etc.]. **1960** E. DAVID *French Provincial Cooking* 371 A *noix* of veal, the cut approximating to the topside of the leg in beef. **1961** N. FROUD et al. tr. *Montagné's Larousse Gastronomique* 993/1 The *noix* of veal is the topside (rump), the fleshy upper part of the leg, cut lengthwise. **1967** A. WILSON *No Laughing Matter* III. 193 They hungrily devoured the noix de veau and carrots at lunch. **1974** *Times* 2 Nov. 11/5 Everything from stewing steak to dainty noix de veau.

nok(e, obs. forms of NOCK, NOOK, and OAK.

†**noker-tree.** *Obs. rare*$^{-1}$. [ad. MDu. *nokerboom.*] A walnut-tree.

c **1481** CAXTON *Dialogues* 34 Asshe, nokertree, olyvetree.

†'**nokes.** *Obs. rare*$^{-0}$. (See quot.)

a **1700** B. E. *Dict. Cant. Crew*, *Nokes*, a Ninny or Fool.

nokhoda: see NAKHODA.

†**no kin**, *a. Obs.* Forms: α. *north.* and *Sc.* 4 **nan(e) kin, 4–6 na kin, kyn (4 kyne, 5 kine).** β. 4 **none kunne, 5 noone kynne; 4 noe kinne, noo kyn, 4–5 no kyn(e.** [f. NO *a.* and KIN *sb.* 6 b. Cf. next.]

1. No kind of, not any.

α. *c* **1300** *Cursor M.* 3753 And es þar nakin [*Fairf.* nankin] blessing left? *Ibid.* 14664 We thoru nakin [*Gött.* nane-kin] art Mai be made in sundre part. **1375** BARBOUR *Bruce* v. 362 He him sparit na kyn thing. *a* **1400–50** *Alexander* 4583 Is þer non Instrumentis of Iren in all þat Ile founden, Ne nakin metall. *c* **1470** HENRY *Wallace* II. 149 His kyn mycht nocht him get for na kyn thing.

β. *c* **1386** CHAUCER *Shipman's T.* 338 (Harl.), Nought for to borwe of him no kyn monay. **1393** LANGL. *P. Pl.* C. XI. 250 For no kyne catel, ne no kyne byheste Suffren hus seed seeden with Caymes seed. *c* **1440** *Gesta Rom.* xxxiv. 132 He also had a sone passyngly wyse.. and no man myght be likenid to him in no kynne sciens. *c* **1470** HENRY *Wallace* VIII. 901 To wait yow with na ill, Be no kyn meyn.

2. In the adverbial phrases (*on* or *in*) *no kin gate, way(s), wise.*

α. *a* **1300** *Cursor M.* 10761 Bot stint he ne moght nankinwai [*Gött.* na kin way]. **13..** *Ibid.* 17951 (Gött.), He mai get it nakin wais. **1375** BARBOUR *Bruce* v. 268 He.. saw he mycht, on nakyn wiss, Warray his fais. *c* **1375** *Sc. Leg. Saints* xvi. (*Magdalene*) 852 He mycht nakine gat cum nere þe place. *c* **1470** HENRY *Wallace* VII. 730 Fra thine to pass he suld on nakyn wys, Quhill he had tane Stirlyng, the castell strang. **1567** *Gude & Godlie B.* (S.T.S.) 8 Thou sall not slay, in na kin wyse.

β. *c* **1400** *Destr. Troy* 13881 þai denyet hym onone, o no kyn wise. *c* **1425** *Seven Sag.* (P.) 203 For in noone kynne wyse, The flore ne may nouȝt aryse. *c* **1475** *Babees Bk.* 5 Vnto him that brouhte yt yee hit take.., for yt in no kyn wyse Auhte comvne be.

†**no kins**, *a. Obs.* Forms: α. 2–3 **nanes, 3–4 nones, 4 non s-, no s-.** β. 3 **nane, 4 nan, na.** γ. 3–4 **none, 4 non, 4–5 no, 5 noo.** Also 2–3 **cunnes** (4 **cunes**), 3–4 **kunnes, 4 kunus; 2 cinnes, kinnes, 4 kines, 4–5 kins; 3 kynnys, 3–5 kynnes, 4–5 kyns.** [f. as prec. For the history of the forms see the note to KIN *sb.*[1] 6 b.]

1. No kind of, not any.

α. *a* **1122** *O.E. Chron.* (Laud MS.) an. 675 Ne ȝeold ne feording ne nanes cinnes ðeudom. *Ibid.* Ne biscop wite ne sinað ne nanes kinnes þing. *c* **1200** ORMIN 274 Nan man, Ne naness kinness shaffte. *a* **1225** *Leg. Kath.* 1912 Ȝet ne seh Katerine nanes cunnes pine þet ha oht dredde. *c* **1275** *Passion our Lord* 446 in *O.E. Misc.* 50 Hi nolden þer-of makie nones cunnes dol. *c* **1320** *Cast. Love* 855 þat nones kunnes assaylyng Ne may derue þe tour for no þing. *c* **1384** CHAUCER *H. Fame* III. 1794 These ben that wolden honour Haue, and do no skynnes labour. *a* **1400** *St. Alexius* (Vernon) 412 With non scunes [*Laud MS.* nones kynnes] ginne.. miȝte he hit not out winne.

β. *c* **1205** LAY. 25456 þurh nane cunnes spelle ne cuðe heom na mon telle. *a* **1300** *Cursor M.* 5575 Na man mai, for nankins chance, For-do þat lauerds purueance. **13..** *Ibid.* 10408 (Gött.), May nakines nede be funden þare. **13..** *Seuyn Sag.* (W.) 2882 For nankins gode thou wald him gif.

γ. *c* **1275** LAY. 25456 þorh none cunnes spelle. *a* **1300** *Havelok* 860 Neyþer hosen ne shon, Ne none kines oþer wede. **13..** *Cursor M.* 1226 (Gött.), [Caym] alsua.. Lued vr lauerd non kines thing. *Ibid.* 4369 Of þe haue i no kines miht. *a* **1400** *Rowland & O.* 376 Late hym noghte skape for nonkyns thynge. *a* **1400** *Launfal* (Ritson) 363 That thou make no bost of me For no kennes mede. *c* **1475** *Babees Bk.* 7 The salte also touche nat in his salere Withe nokyns mete.

2. In phrases (*by, on, in*) *no kins ways* or *wise.*

13.. *E.E. Allit. P.* C. 346 Nylt þou neuer to Nunive bi no-kynnez wayez? ? **1370** *Robt. Cicyle* 54 For he wende, on no kyns wyse, That myghtfulle God cowde devyse [etc.]. *c* **1450** HARDYNG *Chron.* Pref. p. vi, Ȝour patent cowthe I haue in nokyns wyse. **1458** *Test. Ebor.* (Surtees) II. 226 That thei putte not away non of the said juelles.. in noo kynswise.

no-knock. *U.S.* Used *attrib.* (occas. *absol.*) of a search or raid by the police made without permission or warning.

1970 *Atlantic Monthly* Oct. 57 John Mitchell puts on a happy face and suggests that the name of the 'no-knock' law be changed to something more felicitous, like 'quick-entry'. **1971** *New Yorker* 10 Apr. 30 The 'no-knock' and 'preventive-detention' provisions of the District of Columbia Crime Control Act have violated, respectively, the public's right to be secure against unreasonable searches and seizures and the traditional presumption of innocence. **1973** *Black Panther* 8 Sept. 8/3 The California State Supreme Court last week refused to decide in favor of a no-knock rule. In a four to three decision the court held that a search warrant specifically providing that a police officer can enter a home without announcing himself cannot be issued. **1973** *Houston* (Texas) *Chron. Mag. People, Places, Pleasures* 14 Oct. 4/6 Can't the people see the implications of a thing like 'no knock'? It's a Gestapo tactic.

nol, obs. f. NOLL *sb.*, NILL *v.*

nold(e, would not, see NILL *v.*

nolder, var. of NOTHER *adv.*

†'**nolence, 'nolency.** *Obs. rare.* [ad. late L. *nōlentia*, f. *nōlo, nolle*: see -ENCE, -ENCY.] Unwillingness.

1652 N. CULVERWEL *Lt. Nature* I. xi. (1661) 98 It makes a willingness.. where there was an absolute nolency.. before. *Ibid.* II. iii. 49 Grace.. takes away that Nolence and Reluctancy that is in the hearts of men.

‖**nolens volens** ('nəʊlənz 'vəʊlənz). [L. *nōlens* unwilling, pres. pple. of *nōlo, nolle*; and *volens* willing, pres. pple. of *volo, velle*.] Willing or unwilling, whether willing or not, willy-nilly.

1593 PEELE *Edw. I*, Wks. (Rtldg.) 394/2 A little serves the friar's lust, When *nolens volens* fast I must. **1612** *Proc. Virginia* in *Capt. Smith's Wks.* (Arb.) 155 Had they not beene forced nolens volens perforce to gather and prepare their victuall. **1665** SIR T. HERBERT *Trav.* (1677) 124 He would profer them a little money for what he liked, which if they refused, then *nolens volens* he would have it. **1727** A. HAMILTON *New Acc. E. Ind.* II. xxxiii. 17 But, nolens volens, Perrin must take them, and sign Bills of Loading. **1815** SCOTT *Guy M.* I, Well, *nolens volens*, you must hold your tongue. **1837** HOOD *Ode to Rae Wilson* 455 Tugg'd him neck and crop Just *nolens volens* thro' the open shop. **1881** NICHOLSON *Sword to Share* xii. 80 (Stf.), Who placed me, nolens volens,.. under the wing of an ample-skirted American matron.

no less, *adv.* and *a.* [NO *adv.*[2] + LESS *a.*] Not less, as much, in various uses.

1. Used absolutely.

a **1300** *Cursor M.* 6915 Fourti winter, an nales. **1500–20** DUNBAR *Poems* xxvi. 102 The feyndis gaif thame hait leid to laip, Thair lovery wes na less. **1559** W. CUNNINGHAM *Cosmogr. Glasse* 139, I confesse no lesse. **1655** FULLER *Ch. Hist.* IX. 192 That fatall year generally foretold that it would be wonderfull, as it proved no less. **1798** COLERIDGE *Anc. Mar.* VI. xvii, The rock shone bright, the kirk no less. **1818** SHELLEY *Eugan. Hills* 302 The dun and bladed grass no less, Pointing from this hoary tower. **1847** MRS. CARLYLE *Lett.* II. 10 John had bid me take two glasses (no less) of Madeira. **1871** R. ELLIS tr. *Catullus* viii. 9 Now she resigns thee; child, do thou resign no less.

2. Constr. with *than*: **a.** In reference to number.

a **1121** *O.E. Chron.* (Laud MS.) an. 897 þy ilcan sumera forwearð no læs þonne xx. scipa mid monnum.

1596 SHAKS. *Tam. Shr.* II. i. 379 No lesse Then three great Argosies, besides two Galliasses. **1613** PURCHAS *Pilgrimage* (1614) 321 The sacred servants, which were no lesse then sixe thousand. **1709** STEELE *Tatler* No. 46 ¶12 No less than Ten People produced the following Poem. **1801** MAR. EDGEWORTH *Cast. Rackrent* (*c* 1880) 20 No less than three ladies in our county talked of for his second wife. **1841** MACAULAY *Warren Hastings* Ess. (*c* 1853) III. 174 Matter for no less than twenty Articles of impeachment.

b. In reference to comparison or degree.

1561 WINȜET *Cert. Tractates* Wks. (S.T.S.) I. 8 Thay ar na les than the vtheris degenerat ignorantis. **1578** TIMME *Calvin on Gen.* 87 She accounted him no lesse than a domesticall beast. **1613** PURCHAS *Pilgrimage* (1614) 230 The Pilot directed their journey by the Compasse.. no lesse then if it had beene at Sea. **1667** MILTON *P.L.* VIII. 248 Pleas'd with thy words no less then thou with mine. **1711** ADDISON *Spect.* No. 55 ¶4 The Aim of each of them was no less than Universal Monarchy. **1767** FORDYCE *Serm. Yng. Wom.* I. Pref. 7 Dictated by friendship no less than by conviction. **1822** SHELLEY tr. *Calderon's Mag. Prodig.* I. 250, I am Held no less than yourselves to know the limits Of honour and of infamy. **1882** FARRAR *Early Chr.* II. 236 In the Books of Esdras, Enoch and Baruch, no less than in St. John—there are for us some necessary difficulties.

3. Directly preceding the word qualified (usually with *than* following): **a.** With verbs.

1559 W. CUNNINGHAM *Cosmogr. Glasse* 11 Plato (which otherwyse is a grave Philosopher) did no lesse erre then the other, imagining [etc.]. **1611** SHAKS. *Wint. T.* I. ii. 392 Clerke-like experienc'd, which no lesse adornes Our Gentry, then our Parents Noble Names. **1667** MILTON *P.L.* II. 848 Death Grinnd horrible a gastly smile... No less rejoyc'd His mother bad.

b. With adjectives.

1542 UDALL *Erasm. Apoph.* 200 b, Auouchyng hymself to bee no lesse beholdyng to the said Aristotle then to his father. **1585** T. WASHINGTON tr. *Nicholay's Voy.* I. xv, A history no lesse lamentable then full of dispayre. **1605** SHAKS. *Macb.* III. i. 136 Whose absence is no lesse materiall to me, Then is his fathers. **1652** MILTON *Sonn.* xvi. *To Cromwell*, Peace hath her victories No less renownd then warr. **1711** ADDISON *Spect.* No. 128 ¶7 The same female Levity is no less fatal to them after Mariage than before. **1766** GOLDSM. *Vic. W.* v, My little ones were no less busy. **1861** PATTISON *Ess.* (1889) I. 47 The export trade of the Steelyard was no less extensive than its import. **1892** N. SMYTH *Chr. Eth.* I. iii. 158 A moral order no less infrustrable, and as universal in its dominion.

c. With substantives.

1711 STEELE *Spect.* No. 33 ¶1 The Father received his Intelligence with no less Joy than Surprize. **1874** GLADSTONE *Glean.* (1879) II. 235 He spoke no less a number of them than twenty-three. **1882** *Nature* XXVI. 147/2 The no less fertility of ingeniously-devised experiment.

no-licence. A stipulation that no licence is granted, e.g. for the sale of liquor. Freq. *attrib.*

1908 *Daily Chron.* 24 Apr. 4/3, I have been a police officer for thirty-seven years, and am consequently quite familiar with the conditions prevailing before the no-license law.. came into effect. **1909** *Ibid.* 27 Feb. 5/7 A no-license resolution, which means that no certificate for the sale of excisable liquors shall be granted. **1921** E. O'FERRALL in Murdoch & Drake-Brockman *Austral. Short Stories* (1951) 163 I've decided to reform and join the No-licence crowd. *Ibid.*, I'm goin' t' vote No-licence! **1969** *Austral. Encycl.* V. 312/1 There was to be no compensation for licensees in the event of a vote for no-licence.

‖**noli me tangere** ('nəʊlaɪ miː 'tændʒərɪ). Also 6 noly. [L., 'touch me not', occurring in the Vulgate, *John* XX. 17: cf. sense 5.]

1. *Path.* An eroding ulceration attacking the face: in later use = LUPUS.

1398 TREVISA *Barth. De P.R.* VII. lix. (Bodl. MS.), Noli me tangere is a cankery posteme in þe face and freteþ.. lasse þanne oþer. **1527** ANDREW *Brunswyke's Distyll. Waters* B iij, The same water heleth that evyll soore named noly me tangere. **1577** FRAMPTON *Joyful News* 42 b, An vlcer.. comming of a *Noli me tangere*, which began to take roote alredy at the gristles of the Nose. **1601** HOLLAND *Pliny* II. 200 The very ill-fauoured Polype and Noli-me-tangere in the nosthrils, the juice of this root doth cvre and heale wonderfully. **1661** LOVELL *Hist. Anim. & Min.* 257 The dried skinne.. helps the paine of a hot cause; and any impostume or *noli me tangere*. **1674** JOSSELYN *Voy. New Eng.* 184 Head-aches are frequent, Palsies, Dropsies, Worms, Noli-me-tangeres. **1707** *Curios. in Husb. & Gard.* 144 A Spoonful of it.. cures the *Noli me tangere*, all Shankers. **1762** R. GUY *Pract. Obs. Cancers* 114 Lydia Goldsbury came with an obstinate *Noli me tangere* on the Nose. **1834** *Cycl. Pract. Med.* III. 169/1 The terms lupus and noli me tangere are synonymous in British medicine, and have always signified the same thing since they have been used in any definite sense.

fig. **1650** B. *Discolliminium* 6 Some of his arguments are mortally sick of the *Polypus* or *Noli me tangere*; I shall not meddle with them. **1771** SMOLLETT *Humph. Cl.* 6 May ii, She's a *noli me tangere* in my flesh, which I cannot bear to be touched or tampered with.

2. *Bot.* A species of balsam, growing in the North of England, so called from the peculiarly forcible expulsion of its ripe seeds, which occurs when it is touched. Now only as part of the full botanical name, *Impatiens Noli (me) tangere.*

1563 T. GALE *Antidot.* 35 b, And also, Noli me tangere all diseases brede of fleame and colde humours it healeth them. **1578** LYTE *Dodoens* I. 76 There is yet an other herbe founde called *Noli me tangere*, the whiche also is reduced and brought vnder the kindes of Mercury. **1704** *Collect. Voy. & Trav.* III. 824/2 There grows another Tree in Ceylon like our *Noli me tangere*. **1741** *Compl. Fam.-Piece* II. iii. 362 You may now sow, in Natural Ground, the wild spirting Cucumber, and the Noli me tangere.

3. A person or thing that must not be touched or interfered with.

a **1635** NAUNTON *Fragm. Reg.* (Arb.) 18 He was wont to say of them, that they were of the Tribe of Dan, and were *noli me tangere's*; implying, that they were not to be contested with. **1654** WHITLOCK *Zootomia* 166, Sure Learning was no such *Noli me tangere*, in the Apostles account. **1692** T. WATSON *Body of Div.* (1858) 460 Herod could not brook to have his incest meddled with—that was a *noli me tangere*. **1782** BURNEY *Hist. Mus.* II. 15 [They] rather chuse to impoverish the melody, by making a fourth of the Key a *noli me tangere*, than admit this innovation. **1828** LYTTON *Pelham* iii, Mr. Wormwood, the *noli-me-tangere* of literary lions—an author who sowed his conversation.. with.. thorns.

4. A warning or prohibition against meddling or interference, etc.

1634 W. WOOD *New Eng. Prosp.* (1865) 24 The Porcupine .. stands upon his guard and proclaimes a *Noli me tangere*, to man and beast. **1641** MAISTERTON *Serm.* 18 The forbidden fruit, upon which God hath set a *Noli me tangere*. **1792** CHARLOTTE SMITH *Desmond* II. 129 Every attempt at redress is silenced by the *noli-me-tangere*, which our constitution has been made to say. **1806** J. BERESFORD *Miseries Hum. Life* X. xxi. (ed. 5) I. 219 Every dish, as it is brought in, carrying a 'noli me tangere' on the face of it. **1817** BYRON *Let.* 15 Nov. in Moore *Lett. & Jrnls.* (1875) 605, I used to think that *I* was a good deal of an author in *amour propre* and *noli me tangere*.

5. A painting representing the appearance of Christ to the Magdalen at the sepulchre.

1680 EVELYN *Diary* 2 Sept., The *Noli me tangere of our blessed Saviour to Mary Magdalen after his Resurrection*, of Hans Holbein. **1722** RICHARDSON *Statues Italy* 173 *Noli me tangere*..is a Magnificent Picture. **1800** DALLAWAY *Anecd. Arts Eng.* 481 The 'noli me tangere' at All Souls College was painted by Raffaelle. **1859** HAWTHORNE *Marb. Faun* xxxvii, Half of the other pictures are Magdalens,..Noli-me-tangeres.

6. *attrib.*, as ***noli me tangere face, manner***, etc.

1822 DE QUINCEY *Confess.* 28 A sort of *noli me tangere* manner, nervously apprehensive of too familiar approach. **1842** C. WHITEHEAD *R. Savage* (1845) II. iv. 221 A sort of noli me tangere sensitiveness. **1877** READE *Wom. Hater* x, A trick of putting on *noli me tangere* faces among strangers.

Hence **noli-me-tangere'tarian**. *nonce-wd.*

1846 LANDOR *Exam. Shaks.* Wks. 1853 II. 294/1 If a dean is not on his stilts,..he stands on his own ground: he is a noli-me-tangeretarian.

no-limit. Used *attrib.* of a game, betting, etc., in which no limits are laid down.

1915 *Munsey's Mag.* LIV. Apr. 485/1 Poker game tonight... We'll have a real game this time—a no-limit game. **1954** F. C. AVIS *Boxing Ref. Dict.* 75 *No-Limit Boxer*, a heavyweight, from the fact that there is no restriction of weight among the 'heavies'. **1962** K. ORVIS *Damned & Destroyed* xv. 110 Play on the no-limit table was completed. **1973** *Times* 12 Apr. 12/6 Ladbroke..aside from the £50m spending spree planned on hotels, is quite happy to welcome no-limit betting.

†**no'lition.** *Obs.* [f. L. *nōlo*, *nolle*, to be unwilling: cf. VOLITION.] Unwillingness; absence of willing.

1653 J. TAYLOR *Serm. for Year* I. v. 65 So long as the prayer is fervent, so long the man hath a nolition, and a direct enmity against the lust. **1678** GALE *Crt. Gent.* IV. III. 18 Molina..tells us that these signs of the Divine wil signifie properly and formally some nolition or volition in God. **1683** J. CORBET *Free Actions* I. vi. 5 Between Volition and Nolition there is a middle thing, viz. Non-volition. **1857** in *Appleton's Illustr. Handbk. Amer. Trav.* 237 Do not allow.. the nolition of your womankind..to prevent you.

noll (nəʊl). Now *dial.* Forms: α. 1 hnoll, 4–6 nolle, 4–9 noll, 4, 6–7 nol, 6 nole. β. 6 noule, 6–7, 9 nowle, 9 *dial.* nowl, noul. [OE. *hnoll* = MDu. *nolle*, OHG. *hnol* (MHG. *nol*) top, summit, crown of the head.]

1. The top or crown of the head; the head generally; the noddle.

In later use freq. with the epithet *drunken*.

α. *c* **825** *Vesp. Ps.* vii. 17 In hnolle his unrehtwisnis his astiȝeð. *c* **1000** ÆLFRIC *Hom.* II. 452 Se deofol..sloh Iob mid þære wyrstan wunde, fram his hnolle..oð his ilas. *c* **1380** WYCLIF *Sel. Wks.* III. 92 Mowe þou not be helid fro þe sole of þe foot unto þe nolle. *c* **1400** *Turnament of Tottenham* 60 Thay set on ther nollys For to kepe ther pollys, Gode blake bollys. *a* **1529** SKELTON *Col. Cloute* 1244 That no man shulde se Nor rede in any scrolles Of theyr dronken nolles. **1559** *Mirr. Mag.* (1563) M iv, The bastard law broode, which can mollyfie All kynd of causes in theyr crafty nolles. **1577** HARRISON *England* II. vi. (1877) I. 161 He carrieth off a drie dronken noll to bed with him. **1600** HOLLAND *Livy* XXXIII. xlviii. 851 When..they awoke and roused themselues, with their drunken and drousie nols. **1626** BRETON *Fantasticks* Wks. (Grosart) II. 14/2 The nappy Ale makes many a drunken Noll.

β. **1567** DRANT *Horace, Ep.* B ij, All the pothigaries stuffe can scarcely purge his nowle. **1596** SPENSER *F.Q.* VII. vii. 39 Then came October full of merry glee; For yet his noule was totty of the must. **1653** MIDDLETON & ROWLEY *Sp. Gipsy* III. i, Peter-see-me shall wash thy noul And malaga glasses fox thee. **1657** TRAPP *Comm. Ps.* VII. vi, Priests with their drunken Nowls said Mattens. **1823–** in dial. glossaries (Suff., Worc., Som., Cornw.).

†**b.** *transf.* A (dull, drunken, etc.) person. *Obs.*

1399 LANGL. *Rich. Redeles* I. 20 Though þis be derklich endited ffor a dull nolle, Miche nede is it not to mwse þer-on. **1566** DRANT *Horace, Sat.* I. III, B iv b, We call him goose, and disarde doulte, and fowlye fatted nowle. **1598** BARRET *Theor. Warres* I. ii. 9 Drunken nowls are apt..in their drunken pangs to haue their throates cut. **1600** HOLLAND *Livy* IX. xxx. 335 Neither perceived they ought, senselesse druncken nols they.

†**2.** The nape of the neck; the back of the head.

1382 WYCLIF *Acts* xv. 10 What tempten ȝe God, for to putte a ȝok on the nol, or necke, of disciplis? **1398** TREVISA *Barth.* V. xxv. (Bodl. MS.), If þe heed be temperatlich greete, and þe nolle of þe nekke somedele greet. *a* **1400–50** *Alexander* 807 þe noll of Nicollas þe kyng he fra þe nebb partis. *c* **1550** LLOYD *Treas. Health* H 4 Aplye it to the nape of yᵉ necke beneth the nol. **1598** HAYDOCKE tr. *Lomazzo* I. 30 The hinder parte vnder the crowne, some do call..the nape or nolle. **1615** CROOKE *Body of Man* 21 The veynes of the forehead, the nowle or backe part of the head. *c* **1720** W. GIBSON *Farrier's Guide* I. iv. (1738) 35 It is..about two inches within the Head before it passes out at the Noll.

†**3.** *transf.* The extreme point. *Obs. rare*⁻¹.

1387 TREVISA *Higden* (Rolls) II. 9 For þis lond lieþ vnder þe norþ nolle [L. *vertex*] of þe world.

4. *Comb.*, as †**noll-bone**, the occiput. *Obs.*

1615 CROOKE *Body of Man* 581 The knub of the nowle-bone inarticulated or ioyned to the first rack-bone of the necke. **1683** SNAPE *Anat. Horse* IV. xiii. (1686) 167 The Muscles ascend upward as far as to the Occiput or Noll-bone. *c* **1720** GIBSON *Farrier's Guide* (1722) 62 All which [nerves] uniting together are inserted into the Noll-bone.

Hence †**nolled** *a.*, having a noll (or peak) of a certain kind. *Obs. rare.*

1388 WYCLIF *Ecclus.* xvi. 11 If oon hadde be hard nollid, wondur if he hadde be giltles. **1398** TREVISA *Barth. De P.R.* XVIII. lxxviii. (Bodl. MS.), Onocentaurus..is a beste.. stronge nekked and nolled as a boole. **1602** MARSTON *2nd Pt. Ant. & Mel.* IV. i, A mount of mischief..As weighty as the high-noll'd Apennine.

†**noll,** obs. variant of KNOLL *v.*

1620 T. GRANGER *Div. Logike* 170 Noll, or to noll a bell.

nollah-nollah, variant of NULLAH NULLAH.

‖**nolle** ('nɒliː), *sb. U.S.* Abbrev. of NOLLE PROSEQUI.

1871 E. EGGLESTON in *Hearth & Home* 23 Dec. 1010/3, I now enter a *nolle* in his case..and I ask that this court adjourn. **1878** J. H. BEADLE *Western Wilds* xxxi. 507 He had been indicted along with the others, and a *nolle* entered.

nolle, *v. U.S.* Abbrev. of NOLLE PROSS *v.*

1896 *Watertown Republican* 18 Nov., The criminal libel suit pending against W. T. Rambusch was nolled. **1910** *Springfield* (Mass.) *Weekly Republ.* 24 Nov. 10 (*headline*) Case against Haskell Nolled.

‖**nolle pros.** = NOLLE *sb.*

1895 *Denver Times* 5 Mar. 1/3 John Doyle was dismissed on a nolle pros in both cases against him.

‖**nolle prosequi** ('nɒlɪ 'prɒsəkwaɪ). *Law.* Also 7–8 noli, 9 nolo. [L., 'to be unwilling to pursue'.] An entry made upon the record of a court, when the plaintiff or prosecutor abandons part, or all, of his suit or prosecution against a defendant or defendants. Also (quot. 1971) *joc.*

1681 LUTTRELL *Brief Rel.* (1857) I. 70 A privy seal, commanding Mr. atturney generall to enter a nolle prosequi to the said indictment. **1700** CONGREVE *Way of World* IV. viii, My lady came in like a *noli prosequi*, and stopped the proceedings. **1712** ARBUTHNOT *John Bull* I. xi, [Fees for] Entries, Declarations, Replications, Recordats, *Nolle Prosequis.* **1809** JEFFERSON *Writ.* (1830) I. 130 Mr. Huntington..had determined to enter *nolle-prosequis.* **1811** *Hist.* in *Ann. Reg.* 28/2 The case of a *nolo prosequi* having been granted on a prosecution for libel. **1842** BRANDE *Dict. Sci.*, etc. s.v., On the defendant's demurring to one count in a declaration, the plaintiff may enter a nolle prosequi as to that count. **1884** *Encycl. Brit.* XVII. 532/2 In proceedings either by indictment or by information, a *nolle prosequi* or stay of proceedings may be entered by the attorney-general. **1946** [see NUT *sb.*[1] 7 e] **1964** *Mod. Law Rev.* XXVII. 268 The jury failed to agree whether there was a trade dispute. The Attorney-General entered a *nolle prosequi*, but wished it to be 'clearly understood' that strikes not in pursuit of trade disputes had no statutory protection. **1971** WODEHOUSE *Much Obliged, Jeeves* x. 104 When an aunt has set her mind on a thing, it's no use trying to put in a nolle prosequi.

Hence **nolle-pross(e)**, etc. *v. trans.*, to abandon (a suit or indictment) by a 'nolle prosequi'. *U.S.*

1880 G. A. PIERCE *Zachariah* 436 Judge Spalding informed Zach..that the case could be 'nolle prossed' when it came up. **1883** *N. York Even. Post* 13 May, All of the indictments were nolle-prossed late last evening. **1905** *Springfield* (Mass.) *Weekly Republ.* 15 Dec. 2 The court heard petitions for a new trial, and upon these being granted the cases were nol prossed and the brothers set free. **1926** D. L. COLVIN *Prohibition in U.S.* 505 In the two years 14,567 cases were nolle-prossed or dismissed. **1974** D. TIDYMAN *Dummy* ix. 127 The State would move to *nolle prosse* the case against Donald Lang.

noll-kholl. *rare.* Also nol-kole, knolkhol. [ad. Du. *knolkool* or G. *knollenkohl*: see KNOLL *sb.*[1] 4 and note.] The turnip-cabbage; kohl-rabi.

1812 SIR J. SINCLAIR *Syst. Husb. Scot.* 261 A new plant of the turnip sort has been lately introduced into Scotland, called noll-kholl. **1886** YULE & BURNELL *Hobson-Jobson* 830/2 *Nol-kole*..is the usual Anglo-Indian name of a vegetable a good deal grown in India.

no-load (ˌnəʊ'ləʊd), *attrib. phr.* [NO *a.* 6 b.]

1. *Electr.* Corresponding to or involving an absence of any load.

1907 G. W. O. HOWE tr. *Thomälen's Text-bk. Electr. Engin.* viii. 180 The no-load loss for a given excitation can generally be looked upon as a constant loss. **1951** W. SLUCKIN *Princ. Alternating Currents* vii. 175 Calculation of the..iron losses is based on the results of the so-called open-circuit or no-load test. **1966** N. JONES *Basic Electrotechnology* xi. 150 The motor exhibits a practically constant speed characteristic, the full-load speed being about 5% less than the no-load speed.

2. Of shares: sold at net asset value. Also as *sb.*

1964 P. WYCKOFF *Dict. Stock Market Terms* 174 *No load fund*, a mutual fund which charges little or no commission (*load charge*) to the buyer of its shares. No sales organization is involved. **1968** *Maclean's Mag.* Oct. 22 A handful or so Canadian funds are 'no-loads'—are offered without any sales charge and are generally available through investment dealers. **1969** *Times* 5 May (Suppl.) p. vi/3 No-loads are more likely to be performance funds because they have no salesmen to sell them. **1972** *National Observer* (U.S.) 27 May 8/6 (Advt.), The Scudder Special Fund is a no-load mutual fund seeking above-average growth of capital and may invest in securities with above-average risk. You pay no sales commission when you invest in this Fund.

‖**nolo contendere** ('nəʊləʊ kɒn'tɛndəreɪ). [L., 'I do not wish to contend'.] 'A plea by the defendant in a criminal prosecution that without admitting guilt subjects him to a judgment of conviction as in case of a plea of guilty but does not preclude him from denying the truth of the charges in a collateral proceeding' (Webster, 1961).

1872 G. P. BURNHAM *Memo. U.S. Secret Service* p. vii, *Nolo contendere*, don't wish further to contend. **1960** *Times* 9 Dec. 11/2 Counsel for these companies told the court that their pleas of Guilty and *nolo contendere* were not an admission of all allegations on the indictment, but were made with a desire to terminate what would otherwise be protracted and expensive litigation. **1972** *N.Y. Law Jrnl.* 24 Nov. 3/1 [He] entered a plea of nolo-contendere to ten counts of securities fraud of an indictment charging him with sixteen counts of securities law violations.

†**nolp,** *sb. Obs. rare.* [Of obscure origin: see next.] A blow or stroke.

c **1400** *Destr. Troy* 6753 Was non so bold..Forto..negh hym with noy, for nolpis of his hond. *Ibid.* 14037 Eneas also auntrid to sle..Neron the noble with a nolpe alse.

†**nolp,** *v. Obs. rare.* [Of obscure origin.

Both sb. and vb. correspond in meaning to mod. north. dial. *nawp*, *noup*, *nope*, but the variation of vowel in these forms normally indicates a Scand. **naup* sb., **naupa* v., which in the *Destr. Troy* would appear as **nawpe*.]

a. *trans.* To strike down. **b.** *intr.* To give a blow *to*, to keep *on* giving blows.

c **1400** *Destr. Troy* 1257 Castor the king conceyuit..That Nestor with noy was nolpit to ground. *Ibid.* 7475 Neptolemus, the noble, nolpit to Archilagon. *Ibid.* 13889 He nolpit on with his Neue in the necke hole.

nolt (noult, nɒlt). *Sc.* Also 6 noult. [Originally only a graphic variant of NOWT, by false analogy with *bowt* BOLT, *cowt* COLT, etc., but latterly accepted as a distinct word.]

1. Neat, cattle; oxen or cows.

c **1470** HENRY *Wallace* x. 551 Off nolt and scheip thai tuk at sufficiens. **1500–20** DUNBAR *Poems* xxii. 73 Twa curis or thre hes vpolandis Michell,..Thocht he fra nolt had new tane leif. **1535** STEWART *Cron. Scot.* III. 218 Baith scheip and nolt, gait and all vther gair. *a* **1585** POLWART *Flyting w. Montgomerie* 182 On ruites and runches in the fielde, With nolt thou nurishde was a ȝeir. **1609** SKENE *Reg. Maj.* 155 Na maner of gudes, horse, meiris, nolt, sheip, or vther cattell. *a* **1670** SPALDING *Troub. Chas. I* (Bann. Club) 25 Ther came doun certain hielanders..and took away three-score nolt. **1716** *Wodrow Corr.* (1843) II. 135 Nor did they spare the very nolt that were for plowing the ground. **1822** W. J. NAPIER *Pract. Store-farming* 254 Turning out a parcel of half-starved nolt upon the hill. **1865** CARLYLE *Fredk. Gt.* V. XIII. v. 67 Who dares me..insult, Him will I serve like this fat head of nolt. **1895** CROCKETT *Men of Moss-Hags* 356 A good stock both of nolt and sheep.

2. *attrib.*, as ***nolt-beast, -byre, -fold, -foot***, etc.

1513 DOUGLAS *Æneis* XI. xv. 100 Quhen that he hes.. weryit the nolt herd on the plane. ? *a* **1550** *Freiris Berwik* 260 in *Dunbar's Poems* (1893) 294 Ane sowsit nolt fute, and scheipheid. **1581** BURNE *Disput.* in *Cath. Tract.* (S.T.S.) 138 Ye vill that thair be na difference betuix your kirkis, and als monie noult faldis. **1595** DUNCAN *App. Etym.* (E.D.S.) 67 *Bubile*, a nolte byer: *boum stabulum.* **1681** *Min. Baron Crt. Stitchill* (1905) 89 Taking out of some nolt beasts out of..his stabls. **1739** A. NICOL *Nature without Art* 85 That Station now had been much better Than Nolt-herd or a Shepherd either. *c* **1817** HOGG *Tales & Sk.* VI. 194 [That loading] was of nolt-hides; that is, of cow-hides, oxen-hides, bull-hides and all sorts of hides.

nolt, wilt not: see NILL *v.*

nolt(e, know not: see NOT *v.*

‖**nom** (nɔ̃). [F. *nom* a name.] Used in expressions denoting a pseudonym, a false or assumed name; esp.

a. ***nom de guerre*** (nɔ̃ də gɛr), lit. 'war-name', a name assumed by, or assigned to, a person engaged in some action or enterprise.

1679 DRYDEN *Limberham* I. i, Mr. Woodall, you Rogue! that's my *nom de guerre*. You know I have laid by Aldo. **1709** MRS. MANLEY *Secret Mem.* (1720) IV. 318 When they went upon private Adventures, to prevent Discovery, each had her *Nome de Guerre.* **1750** GRAY *Long Story* 35 Melissa is her *Nom-de-Guerre.* **1829** W. IRVING in *Life & Lett.* (1864) II. 369, I have adopted a *nom de guerre*, as allowing me a freer scope. **1883** *Harper's Mag.* July 236/2 Fox..being designated Reynardo, and other..characters introduced by ..*noms de guerre.*

b. ***nom de plume*** (nɔ̃ də plym), lit. 'pen-name', a name assumed by a writer.

1823 DE QUINCEY *The Incognito* Wks. 1859 XI. 1 A living author.., not known at all under that name, but under the *nom-de-plume* of Friederich Laun. **1876** TREVELYAN *Macaulay* (1883) II. 293 *note*, Sylvanus Urban was the *nom de plume* adopted by the editor of the Gentleman's Magazine. **1886** RUSKIN *Præterita* I. 413 The nom-de-plume I chose, 'According to Nature'.

c. ***nom de Dieu*** (nɔ̃ də djø), a mild oath.

1867 'OUIDA' *Under Two Flags* III. ix. 228 'Nom de Dieu, Miladi!' she swore in her teeth. **1922** E. E. CUMMINGS *Enormous Room* viii. 176 *Nom de dieu*, I thought vaguely. Am I or am I not completely asleep? **1961** *Amer. Speech* XXXVI. 35 Another basic oath is *nom de Dieu.*

d. ***nom de théâtre*** (nɔ̃ də teatr), a stage name.

1874 W. P. LENNOX *My Recollections* I. viii. 189 After leaving the army, he appeared on the regular boards under the *nom de théâtre* of Calcraft. **1935** WODEHOUSE *Blandings Castle* xi. 278 A short list of names, one of which she proposed as a *nom de théâtre* as soon as her screen career should begin. **1952** GRANVILLE *Dict. Theatrical Terms* 122 *Nom de théâtre*, a stage name. These were adopted at the time when connection with the stage was not considered respectable. **1974** *Times* 6 Apr. 14/2 Erik Weisz..in 1890.. set himself up as a stage musician under the *nom de théâtre* of Harry Houdini.

e. ***nom de vente*** (nɔ̃ də vɑ̃t), a name assumed by a buyer at an auction who wishes to remain anonymous.

1955 *Times* 21 May 5/4 This, it is understood, is the *nom-de-vente* for a member of the nobleman's family. **1959** *Times* 26 Feb. 12/5 All three bought by Felham, a *nom de vente*.

‖**noma** (ˈnəʊmə). *Path.* [L. *noma* (*nomē*), a. Gr. νομή, f. νομ-, νέμειν to feed.] A gangrenous ulceration of the throat, occurring mainly in young children.

1834 Carswell in *Cycl. Pract. Med.* III. 138/2 There is one other form of sphacelus from general debility..which has received the names of *noma*; *cheilocace* [etc.]. **1861** *N. Syd. Soc. Year-bk. for* 1860, 224 Dissertation on Noma. **1876** Bristowe *Th. & Pract. Med.* (1878) 632 More pain and discomfort than are usually associated with noma.

nomad (ˈnɒmæd, ˈnəʊmæd), *sb.* and *a.* [ad. L. *Nomad-*, *Nomas*, a. Gr. νομαδ-, νομάς, f. νομ-, νέμειν to pasture. Cf. nomades.]

1. A person belonging to a race or tribe which moves from place to place to find pasture; hence, one who lives a roaming or wandering life.

1587 Golding *De Mornay* viii. (1592) 99 The life of the people called the Nomads or Grazyers. *c* **1618** Moryson *Itin.* iv. ii. v. 198 The people build no houses but like Nomads living in Cabins remoue from one place to an other. **1843** Carlyle *Past & Pr.* ii. (1858) 286 Wise men pestered with nomads. **1856** Kane *Arct. Expl.* I. xxviii. 372 We are absolutely nomads, so far as there can be any..pastoral life in this region. **1873** Hamerton *Intell. Life* xii. i. 430 The civilized English nomad is usually..a person of independent means.

2. *attrib.* or *adj.* **a.** Living as a nomad; leading a roaming or wandering life; nomadic.

1798 *Brit. Critic* Feb. 223 These last and most authentic observations on this Nomad tribe. **1853** Newman *Hist. Sk.* (1873) II. i. ii. 54 This horde of Turks, the Chozars, was nomad and pagan. **1862** Johns *Brit. Birds* (1874) 235 The breeding season over, they become nomad in their habits.

b. Belonging to, characteristic of, nomads.

1835 Lytton *Rienzi* ix. vi, As of old, from the Nomad tents was built up the stately Babylon. **1850** W. Irving *Mahomet* II. 476 They readily amalgamated with the Arabs, having the same nomad habits. **1873** Farrar *Fam. Speech* iv. 117 In every stage of nomad unprogressiveness.

c. *Comb.*, as ***nomad-pastoral***.

1880 *Fortn. Rev.* Feb. 303 The nomad-pastoral age.

nomade (ˈnɒmeɪd, ˈnəʊmeɪd), *sb.* and *a.* [var. of prec.; in later use prob. after F. *nomade*.]

†**1.** A nomadic band. *Obs. rare*⁻¹.

c **1630** G. Sandys *Ps.* lxxxiii. (1636) 136 Idumæans, who in Nomades stray, And shaggy Ismaelites, that live by prey.

2. = nomad 1.

1775 Johnson *West. Isl.* Wks. X. 357 He differed from some of the ancient nomades. **1798** W. Taylor in *Monthly Mag.* VI. 554 The future ruler of men now the hireling of a nomade. **1835** W. Irving *Tour Prairies* i, The Pawnees, the Comanches, and other fierce..tribes, the nomades of the prairies. **1837** Sir F. Palgrave *Merch. & Friar* i. (1844) 21 The Arab yielded to a fiercer nomade. **1880** L. Oliphant *Land of Gilead* ii. 26 A long caravan of mules laden with tents and baggage, to tempt the needy nomade.

3. *attrib.* or *adj.* **a.** = nomad 2 a.

1817 G. S. Faber *Eight Diss.* (1845) II. 237 A warlike nomade horde of herdsmen and shepherds. **1851** D. Wilson *Preh. Ann.* I. ii. i. (1863) 300 The wanderings of his nomade fathers. **1872** Hardwick *Trad. Lanc.* 209 This outcast nomade race which wandered from forest to forest.

b. = nomad 2 b.

1819 G. S. Faber *Dispens.* (1823) I. 108 Cain..being doomed to a nomade state of life. **1862** Merivale *Rom. Emp.* lxv. (1865) VIII. 160 To close the sources of the perennial stream of nomade savagery. **1865** W. G. Palgrave *Arabia* I. 31 The advantages of nomade license and the insolent lawlessness of the clans.

nomades (ˈnɒmədiːz), *sb. pl.* Now *rare.* [a. L. *Nomadēs*, ad. Gr. Νομάδες, pl. of νομάς: see nomad.] **a.** The nomad tribes or peoples mentioned by ancient writers. **b.** Such tribes as move about from place to place.

In later use it is somewhat uncertain whether this form, or the pl. of prec., is intended.

1555 W. Watreman *Fardle Facions* G viij, The Arabiens named Nomades occupie much Chamelles, bothe in warre, and burden. **1578** Banister *Hist. Man* Pref. 11 The Scythians, named Nomades, are very corpulent, and fleshy. **1592** Moryson *Let.* in *Itin.* (1617) I. 25 Methinks I am one of the Nomades, every day changing my dwelling. **1609** Holland *Amm. Marcell.* 402 They keepe a great way asunder, and wander like unto the Nomades. **1649** G. Daniel *Trinarch., Rich. II*, ccxcix, Like the Race Of Nomades, wee shift from place to place. **1662** J. Davies tr. *Olearius' Voy.* 67 Though the Samojedes have indeed no Cities, yet are they not Nomades. **1728** Morgan *Algiers* I. i. 10 The Sabæan Arabs, like all other Nomades or Scenites, ..ranging about with Tents, Families and Droves. **1764** Harmer *Observ.* xvi. §16. 422 The ancient Nomades, or the present Arabs.

no'madian. *rare*⁻⁰. [f. nomad + -ian.] A nomad. (Worcester, 1860, citing *N. Brit. Rev.*)

nomadic (nəʊˈmædɪk), *a.* [ad. Gr. νομαδικός, f. νομαδ- nomad: see -ic.]

1. Characterized by, or leading, a wandering life.

1818 Todd, *Nomadick*,..having no fixed abode [etc.]. **1850** W. Irving *Mahomet* II. 476 Persians and Copts, and nomadic Africans. **1859** Marcy *Prairie Trav.* vi. 218 The mode of life of the nomadic tribes. **1882** Pitman *Mission Life Gr. & Palest.* 298 A large..nomadic population.

transf. **1864** Lowell *Fireside Trav.* 97 The American is nomadic in religion, in ideas, in morals. **1869** Landreth *Adam Thomson* I. 64 Seceders were far from being 'nomadic' hearers.

b. Of birds or beasts.

1876 E. White *Life in Christ.* i. v. 45 Vast battalions of nomadic birds. **1877** J. A. Allen *Amer. Bison* 465 The buffalo is quite nomadic in its habits.

2. Peculiar to, distinctive of, a wandering people or manner of life.

1825 Coleridge in *Lit. Rem.* (1836) II. 326 Their brethren..who still sojourned in the nomadic state. **1835** Sir J. Ross *Narr. 2nd Voy.* xl. 530 Our march had a very nomadic..appearance. **1856** Stanley *Sinai & Pal.* 125 The patriarchs could here gradually exchange the nomadic life for the pastoral. **1872** Baker *Nile Trib.* vi, In their nomadic habits they retain the..formalities of the distant past.

3. *Path.* (See quot.)

1842 Dunglison *Med. Lex.* s.v. *Nomad*, The word Nomadic has been applied to spreading ulcer.

So **no'madical** *a.*; **no'madically** *adv.*

1799 *Chron.* in *Ann. Reg.* 421 A numerous nomadical nation, who derived their subsistance from their flocks of sheep. **1862** R. H. Patterson *Ess. Hist. & Art* 124 When Europe was thinly and nomadically peopled, and tribes migrated in mass.

nomadism (ˈnɒmədɪz(ə)m, ˈnəʊ-). [f. nomad.] The practice, fact, or state of living a wandering life.

1841 Emerson *Ess., History*, In the early history of Asia and Africa, Nomadism and Agriculture are the two antagonist facts. **1854** Latham *Native Races Russ. Emp.* 74 As the former displaces the latter, agriculture encroaches on nomadism. **1872** C. King *Sierra Nevada* xi. 242, I have felt all the pathos of nomadism, from the Aryan migration down. **1963** *Punch* 13 Nov. 721/1 Centuries of fierce nomadism. **1964** Gould & Kolb *Dict. Social Sci.* 724/2 Usages of transhumance..agree in contrasting the term with *pastoral nomadism*. **1974** *Environmental Conservation* I. 12/1 If traditional nomadism finally disappears..it will be impossible to recreate it.

transf. **1841** Emerson *Ess., History*, This intellectual nomadism, in its excess, bankrupts the mind.

nomadization (nɒmədaɪˈzeɪʃən, ˈnəʊ-). *rare.* [f. as next + -ation.] **a.** The establishment of nomadic conditions; the abolition of a settled mode of life.

1897 W. M. Ramsay in *Contemp. Rev.* Aug. 235 The Turks triumphed by bringing about the nomadisation of Asia Minor.

b. A making or becoming nomadic in character or nature.

1920 H. G. Wells *Outl. Hist.* 606/2 What we now call democracy, the boldness of modern scientific inquiry and a universal restlessness, are due to this 'nomadization' of civilization.

nomadize (ˈnɒmədaɪz, ˈnəʊ-), *v.* [f. nomad + -ize.]

a. *intr.* To live, or roam about, as nomads.

1799 W. Tooke *View Russian Emp.* II. 100 The Tunguses ..nomadize about the coasts of the Eastern-ocean. **1842** Prichard *Nat. Hist. Man* 203 They have occupied..or rather nomadised over contiguous regions from immemorial times. **1873** Burnaby *Ride Khiva* xvi. 150 The tribes which nomadised on the Sam.

b. *trans.* To make nomadic in character.

1902 D. G. Hogarth *Nearer East* 156 The incomers 'nomadised' the south-east. *Ibid.* 272 The southern oases are the most 'nomadised'.

nomady (ˈnəʊmədɪ). [f. nomad *sb.* and *a.* + -y³.] The state, condition, or life of a nomad.

1909 Beerbohm *Yet Again* 126 Had nomady been my business, had I been a commercial traveller or a King's Messenger. **1920** —— *And Even Now* 263 The Bohemian, as tending always to nomady, feels that [etc.].

no man. Forms: α. 1 **nán man** (2 **nan-**, **namman**), 2 **non man** (1–3 **mon**), 4–5 **none man.** β. 2 **namon**, 2–4 **na mon**; 4–5 **naman** (5 *Sc.* **-mane**), 4, 6 *Sc.* **na man**, 8–9 *Sc.* **nae man.** γ. 3–5 **nomon, no mon**; 3–6 **noman** (5 **-manne**), 3– **no man.** [f. *none*, no *a.* + man *sb.* In early use both words have their ordinary inflections.]

1. a. No one, nobody.

α. *c* **888** K. Ælfred *Boeth.* xi. § 1 Hie næfre to nanum men ne becumaþ. *Ibid.* xiii, Hi nan mon fullice habban ne mæᵹ, ne hie nanne mon ᵹeweᵹian ne maᵹon. **971** *Blickl. Hom.* 43 Ne for feo, ne for nanes mannes lufon. *a* **1000** *Ags. Gosp.* Luke x. 22 Nan man [*Hatton* namman] nat hwylc is se sunu buton se fæder. *a* **1067** in Kemble *Cod. Dipl.* IV. 228 Ic nelle nanum men ᵹeðafian ðæt him æniᵹ ðara þinga ofnime ðe ic him ᵹeunnen hæbbe. *a* **1175** *Cott. Hom.* 217 3if non man ne þoht of Gode, non ne spece of him. *c* **1200** Ormin 16164 Swa þatt nan mann ne þurrfte off himm, Ne nimenn gom, ne rekkenn. *a* **1225** *Ancr. R.* 68 Ut of chirche þurle ne holde 3e none tale mid none monne. *c* **1315** Shoreham iii. 103 Coueyte none mannes wyf. **1482** *Monk of Evesham* (Arb.) 15 That none man shuld dowte or mystruste of anothir life and world.

β. *a* **1200** *Moral Ode* 22 in *O.E. Hom.* I. 161 Ne lipnie na mon to muchel to childe ne to wiue. *c* **1205** Lay. 7000 Ne cuðe na mon swa muchel of song. *a* **1300** *Cursor M.* 12381 Forth in þes he bad þam ga, To noi naman ne naman þaim. *c* **1375** *Sc. Leg. Saints* xxxviii. (*Adrian*) 204 Tel me..quhy þu fled, seand na payne, na namane fichtand þe agane. **1483** *Cath. Angl.* 248/2 Naman; *nemo, nullus.* **1508** Dunbar *Flyting* 129 Commirwald crawdoun, na man comptis the ane kerse. **1567** *Satir. Poems Reform.* iii. 20 Vnto na man was he odious. **1728** Ramsay *Monk & Miller's Wife* 66 I'll unbar my door to nae man. **1791** Burns *Tam o' Shanter* 67 Nae man can tether time or tide. **1818** Scott *Hrt. Midl.* v, There was nae man pinned down to sic a slavish wark as a saddler's.

γ. *c* **1200** *Moral Ode* 119 (Trin. Coll. MS.), Drihte ne demeð noman after his biginninge. *a* **1250** *Owl & Night.* 1539 Nis nomon þat ne may ibrynge his wif amys myd suche þinge. *c* **1275** Lay. 13259 Nas þar neuere no man þat don þar mihte cristendom. *c* **1380** Wyclif *Serm.* Sel. Wks. I. 4 þere nys no man but 3if he longe sum weie after blise. **1426** Lydg. in *Pol. Poems* (Rolls) II. 135 Ageins which noman may maligne. *c* **1475** *Childr. Lytil Bk.* in *Babees Bk.* (1868) 20 At the tabylle..Loke þou rownde not in nomannys ere. **1535** Coverdale *Acts* i. 20 The habitacion be voyde & noman be dwellinge therein. **1560** Daus tr. *Sleidane's Comm.* 60 b, No man ought to be judge in his owne cause. **1606** G. W[oodcock] *Hist. Ivstine* xxiii. 85 The country became so dangerous, that no man durst hardly stir abroad. **1642** Eaton *Honey-c. Free Justif.* 249 No man almost receiveth his testimonie. **1781** Cowper *Convers.* 62 Well known, or such as no man ever knew. **1864** Tennyson *Enoch Arden* 851 His head is low, and no man cares for him.

b. [see no *adv.*³ and *sb.*] A man who says 'no'; one who is accustomed to disagree or to refuse requests in a resolute manner. *colloq.*

1953 Berrey & Van den Bark *Amer. Thes. Slang* (1954) §400/3 Obstinate person..'no' man. *Ibid.* §421/1 Critic; opposer..'no' man (*vs.* 'yes man'). **1959** *Listener* 30 July 168/1 He [*sc.* Metternich] was the great 'No-man'. One can make a long list of the changes he did not like. **1961** *Sunday Express* 19 Feb. 8/4 Prince Philip..attacked what he called the 'no-men' who stood in the way of those with energy and imagination. **1967** *Listener* 26 Jan. 143/1 The only role of the abominable no-men of Whitehall was to frustrate him at every turn.

2. ***no man's land***: **a.** A piece of waste, or unowned, land; in early use as the name of a plot of ground, lying outside the north wall of London, and used as a place of execution. See also quots. 1966 and 1972.

1320 *Ann. Paul.* in *Chron. Edw. I & II* (Rolls) I. 291 Quædam domina nomine Juliana..fuit combusta apud Nonesmanneslond extra Londonius. **1326** *Ibid.* 321 Quidam Arnoldus..a communitate ductus fuit..extra civitatem apud Nonesmanneslonde, et ibi decapitatus fuit. **1598** Stow *Survey of London* 356 Ralph Stratforde Bishop of London, in the yeare 1348. bought a peece of ground called no mans land, which he inclosed with a wall of Bricke. **1719** De Foe *Crusoe* ii. (Globe) 563 This was a kind of Border, that might be called no Man's Land. **1881** T. Hughes *Rugby, Tennessee* 50 A small lot of noman's land in the woods. **1876** H. Brooks *Natal* 234 In 1866..the Government of the colony took possession of 'No-man's-land'. **1890** Dilke *Prob. Gt. Brit.* I. 517 The country is not a no-man's land. **1902** *Chambers's Jrnl.* Jan. 34/1 The independent warlike tribes formerly sandwiched in a No Man's Land between Afghanistan and India. **1909** *Westm. Gaz.* 21 Aug. 14/1 This place has a higher attraction..for it is no-man's-land, eligible for building on, threatened, but as yet unoccupied. **1910** *Chambers's Jrnl.* Aug. 495/1 These cottages had been built..on ground between two roads, which was a kind of 'no man's land' and rent free. **1921** C. A. W. Monckton *Some Experiences New Guinea Resident Magistrate* xxvi. 306 The country we were camped in was a sort of 'no man's land' or border land lying between the Baruga tribe and their mountain enemies. **1966** G. E. Evans *Pattern under Plough* xiii. 136 The belief that a piece of land in the parish should be left untilled. In English villages this is sometimes called *Jack's Land* or *No-Man's Land*. **1972** P. Newton *Sheep Thief* 187 *No Man's Land*, those areas of wild rough country, bounding the Southern Alps, which are not stocked. **1975** *Country Life* 19 June 1637/1 Until the Dutchman Vermuyden came on the scene..to control..the river Great Ouse..much of the region was a marshy no-man's-land through which..the only means of transport was by boat.

b. *Naut.* (See quot.)

1769 Falconer *Dict. Marine* (1780). *No Man's Land*, a space between the after-part of the belfrey and the fore-part of a ship's boat, when the said boat is stowed upon the booms... The space called No man's land is used to contain any blocks, ropes, tackles, &c. which may be necessary on the forecastle.

c. *fig.*

1870 H. A. Nicholson *Man. Zool.* I. 6 Some observers have established an intermediate kingdom, a sort of no-man's-land, for the reception of those debatable organisms. **1888** H. A. Strong tr. *Paul's Princ. Hist. Lang.* ii. 28 This 'no man's land' forms a boundary wall through which the influences cannot pass from one side to the other. **1892** *Month* July 445 The objectionable no-man's-land of Haeckel is likely..to remain for some time. **1954** M. Beresford *Lost Villages* v. 166 The crucial years lie half in a no-man's-land of English historical research. **1959** *Wall St. Jrnl.* 9 Nov. 16/4 One aim of the new law was to abolish the so-called 'no-man's-land' between Federal and state authority in labor cases. **1973** *Archivum Linguisticum* IV. 51 This is indeed a No Man's Land, virgin territory one might say. **1974** 'H. Carmichael' *Motive* iv. 53 One question chased another..questions that got lost in a no-man's-land of conjecture. **1974** *Kingston* (Ontario) *Whig-Standard* 11 Jan. 7/1 Dossers are..men and women squeezed into a no-man's-land by an increasingly affluent society.

d. *Mil.* The terrain between the front lines of armies entrenched opposite one another.

1908 *Blackw. Mag.* Dec. 761 Here and there in that wilderness of dead bodies—the dreadful 'No-Man's-Land' between the opposing lines—deserted guns showed up singly or in groups. **1915** G. Adam *Behind Scenes at Front* 101 Perilous work it is repairing wire in the No Man's Land between trenches. **1936** M. Plowman *Faith called Pacifism* 97 The order I received..to go out across No-man's-land, and cut the throat of the nearest German lad on sentry. **1973** R. Hill *Ruling Passion* iii. ii. 173 They were keeping steadily on neutral ground and she was finding it a pleasant experience. Like football in no-man's-land during a Great War Christmas.

e. *Lawn Tennis.* (See quot. 1931.)

1931 Doeg & Danzig *Elem. Lawn Tennis* 65 If you hesitate you are caught in what is known as 'No Man's Land', the territory between the service line and the baseline. **1969** *New Yorker* 14 June 68/3 Graebner, in no man's land, drives the ball far into Ashe's backhand corner.

nomancy. *rare.* [ad. F. *nomancie*, aphetic f. *onomancie*.] = ONOMANCY.

1727–38 CHAMBERS *Cycl.* [app. from the *Dict. de Trévoux*]. **1866** REDDING *Past Celebr.* II. 160 Have you studied astrology, Nomency,..and the long list of et ceteras once considered as attaching to the study of medicine?

no-mar ('nəʊ,mɑː(r)), *attrib. phr.* [f. NO *a.* + MAR *v.*] That is designed not to mar, spoil, etc.

1970 *Globe & Mail* (Toronto) 26 Sept. 52/4 (Advt.), Trays..of stain-resistant woodgrain, with raised frame and no-mar, plastic tipped feet. **1973** *Washington Post* 13 Jan. A. 19/1 (Advt.), Round extension table with..walnut bronze no-mar top table.

nomarch ('nɒmɑːk). Also 7 -ar(c)k. [ad. Gr. νομάρχης or νόμαρχος, f. νομός NOME *sb.*[2] + ἄρχειν to rule: cf. *monarch*, etc.]

†**1.** A local ruler or governor. *Obs. rare*$^{-0}$.

1656 BLOUNT *Glossogr.*, *Nomark*, he that hath the preheminence in the ministration of Laws, as a Major or other like Officer. **1678** PHILLIPS, *Nomarch*, the chief Administrator of the Laws in any particular City or Province.

2. The governor of an ancient Egyptian nome.

1846 GROTE *Greece* I. xx. (1862) II. 490 The Nomarch or chief of each Nome. **1875** BIRCH *Rede Lect.* (1876) 34 The nomarchs divided the country amongst themselves, like feudal barons. **1895** SAYCE *Egypt of Hebrews* 137 Before leaving Egypt Alexander appointed the nomarchs who were to govern it.

3. The governor of a modern Greek nomarchy.

1880 *Encycl. Brit.* XI. 85/2 The nomarchs are assisted in the administration of the province by a council. **1884** *Macm. Mag.* Oct. 431/2 The nomarch of the Cyclades, who superintends the course of justice in the eight Eparchies into which the islands are divided.

nomarchy[1] ('nɒmɑːkɪ). [ad. Gr. νομαρχία: see prec. and cf. *monarchy*.]

†**1.** (See quot.) *Obs. rare*$^{-0}$.

1656 BLOUNT *Glossogr.*, *Nomarchie*, a jurisdiction or Majoralty, a Law, a County or Shire, a Territory about some city.

2. One of the provinces into which modern Greece is divided.

1863 *Chambers's Cycl.* V. 81 By the arrangements of 1852, modern Greece is divided into ten provinces or nomarchies. **1880** *Encycl. Brit.* XI. 85/2 For purposes of local government Greece is divided into 13 nomarchies, under officers called nomarchs.

'nomarchy[2]. *nonce-wd.* [f. Gr. νόμος law.] The legal class in a state.

a **1843** SOUTHEY *Doctor* ccxli. (1848) 661 The chiefs of the Hierarchy, the Iatrarchy, the Nomarchy and the Hoplarchy, ..were, like our Bishops, Peers of the realm by virtue of their station.

nomber, -bre, obs. ff. NUMBER.

nomble, obs. f. NUMBLE.

nombrary, var. of NUMBRARY.

‖**'nombril.** *Her.* [F. *nombril* the navel.] That point on an escutcheon which lies midway between the true centre (or Fesse Point) and the Base Point. Sometimes vaguely alluded to as the centre of the escutcheon. Also *attrib.*

1562 LEGH *Armory* (1597) 25 The letter H. is termed the Fesse point. The letter I. is called the Nombril. For it is euen opposite to the nauel. **1610** GUILLIM *Heraldry* I. vii. 30 The Nombrill is next vnderneath the Fesse Point, answering in a like distance from the Fesse Point. **1661** MORGAN *Sph. Gentry* III. vi. 57 All meeting or centring about a round plate of the same in the Nombril of the Shield. **1727** BAILEY (vol. II.) s.v., The first of those [parts] is the *Nombril*, and the lowest the *Base*. **1797** *Encycl. Brit.* (ed. 3) VIII. 441/2, E the fess point. F the nombril point. **1868** CUSSANS *Her.* ii. 44 In English Heraldry, mention is seldom made of the Honour and Nombril points.

nombry, obs. f. NUMBER *v.*

nombur, -byr, obs. ff. NUMBER *sb.*

nome, obs. f. NAME *sb.* and *v.*, NUMB *a.*; obs. pa. t. and pa. pple. of NIM *v.*

†**nome,** *sb.*[1] *Obs. rare.* [Related to NIM *v.*]

a. The act of seizing. **b.** A captive, a prisoner.

c **1220** *Bestiary* 800 In water ȝe is wis of heuekes come, & we in boke wið deules nome. *c* **1250** *Gen. & Ex.* 2268 Wel faȝen he was of here come, for he was numen ðor to nome.

nome (nəʊm), *sb.*[2] [ad. Gr. νομός, f. νέμειν to divide.] One of the thirty-six territorial divisions of Ancient Egypt.

a **1727** NEWTON *Chronol. Amended* (1728) 22 Sesac. distributes Egypt into xxxvi Nomes, and in every Nome erects a Temple. **1773** MONBODDO *Lang.* III. xiii. (1774) I. 638 They were so particular as to name the nome or district in Egypt. **1840** MILMAN *Hist. Christianity* II. 435 Seven hundred virgins of Alexandria, and of the Mareotic nome. **1869** RAWLINSON *Anc. Hist.* 234 The division of the whole country into nomes was maintained; and most of the old nomes were kept. **1895** SAYCE *Egypt of Hebrews* 188 The Egypt which lay north of the Theban nome and Lake Mœris.

nome (nəʊm), *sb.*[3] [ad. Gr. νόμος, f. νέμειν to divide.] An ancient Greek form of musical composition. (Cf. quots.)

1753 CHAMBERS *Cycl. Supp.* s.v., Nome is also used for a kind of song, or hymn, in honour of the gods, said to have been invented by Terpander. **1776** BURNEY *Hist. Mus.* I. 359 Hyagnis..was the inventor of the Nomes, or airs, that were sung to the mother of the Gods, to Bacchus [etc.]. **1789** *Ibid.* (ed. 2) I. ix. 152 Aristotle says that dithyrambics, nomes, tragedies, and comedies use alike number, verse, and harmony. **1847** GROTE *Greece* II. xxix. IV. 102 Olympus as well as Klonas taught many new nomes or tunes on the flute. **1850** MURE *Lit. Greece* III. 37 The term Nome appears..to have borne a more immediate reference to the music or air, than the poetry or words, of a song.

nome, *sb.*[4] *Math.* [a. F. *nôme*, the second element in *binôme*, etc.: see BINOMY.] (See quots.)

1665 COLLINS in Rigaud *Corr. Sci. Men* II. 458 The limits of such equations as have but two nomes. **1704** J. HARRIS *Lex. Techn.* I, *Nome*, in Algebra, is any Quantity with a Sign prefixed to it, and by which 'tis usually connected with some other Quantity, and then the whole is called a *Binomial*, a *Trinomial*, &c. **1727–38** CHAMBERS *Cycl.* s.v., *a* + *b* is a binomial, whose names or nomes are *a* and *b*.

†**nome,** *v. Obs.* Also 5–6 nomme. [var. of NIM *v.*, by assimilation to the preterite forms: cf. MLG. *nomen*.] **a.** *trans.* To take. **b.** *intr.* To go or pass (quot. *c* 1390).

a **1225** *Ancr. R.* 68 Bereð wurðschipe þerto, uor þe holi sacrament þet ȝe iseoð [*v.r.* nomeð] þer þurh. *c* **1315** SHOREHAM I. 1647 Two manere speches beþ iwoned þer two men for to nomene. *Ibid.* IV. 72 And þat a-combreþ swyþe fele þat none kepe nomeþ. *c* **1390** *Constit. Masonry* 546 (Halliw.), Thaȝgh suche a flod aȝayne schulde come, Over the werke hyt schulde not nome. **1486** *Bk. St. Albans* a viij b, If yowre hawke Nomme a fowle and the fowle breke away fro hir. [**1530** PALSGR. 644/2, I nomme, I take (Lydgate), *je prens.*]

no-meaning. [f. NO *a.* + MEANING *sb.*] The absence of, or want of, meaning or purpose; unmeaningness; nonsense.

1735 POPE *Ep. Lady* 114 True No-meaning puzzles more than Wit. **1784** COWPER *Task* IV. 74 Cat'racts of declamation thunder here; There forests of no meaning spread the page. **1818** SCOTT *Rob Roy* i, Owen..endeavoured..to explain my no-meaning, and to cover my retreat. **1834** L. RITCHIE *Wand. by Seine* 167 A little ugly, incongruous brick erection ..the nature and no-meaning of which we cannot tell. **1882** MRS. OLIPHANT *Lit. Hist. Engl.* III. 107 The quaint and delightful no-meaning of some of Shakspeare's snatches of spirit-song.

nomecuðe, nomekowthe, varr. NAMECOUTH.

nomeliche, -ly, obs. forms of NAMELY *adv.*

nomen ('nəʊmən). [L.] **1.** *Taxonomy.* **nomen nudum** ('njuːdəm) [L., naked name], a Latin name which has no standing because it was introduced without publication of the full description demanded by the rules governing botanical and zoological nomenclature. Also occasionally used for a popular name that cannot be attached to a definite species (see quot. 1957).

1906 *Verhandl. Int. Bot. Kongr. Wien 1905* VIII. 205 A genus or any other group of higher rank than a species, named or announced without being characterised conformably to article 37 cannot be regarded as effectively published (*nomen nudum*). **1925** A. S. HITCHCOCK *Methods of Descriptive Systematic Bot.* xii. 114 A new name appearing without description is called a *nomen nudum*. **1957** *N. & Q.* Feb. 83/2 Since, however, no such variety has been described or bred, Chub-eel (× *Aminguilla*) remains a *nomen nudum*. **1963** DAVIES & HEYWOOD *Princ. Angiosperm Taxonomy* viii. 290 It is permissible..to use a name for a new species that already exists as a *nomen nudum*—i.e. has never been validated by a description and there-fore has no standing under the Rules [of botanical nomenclature]. **1969** E. MAYR *Princ. Systematic Zool.* xiii. 347 A name published without satisfying the conditions of availability is generally called a *nomen nudum*... A *nomen nudum* has no standing in zoological nomenclature and is best never recorded, not even in synonymy.

2. *Philol.* In phrases: **nomen actionis** (ækʃɪ'əʊnɪs), a noun of action; **nomen agentis** (æ'dʒɛntɪs), an agent noun.

1928 C. BERGENER *Contrib. to Study of Conversion of Adjs. into Nouns* ii. 18 When a nomen agentis is contrasted with an absolute past participle of the corresponding verb (as in Galsw., Flower I, ch. vi: *the tortured does not salute her torturers*). **1930** T. SASAKI *On Lang. Bridges' Poetry* III. ii. 80 The use of the gerund and the noun of action (nomen actionis)..have in common certain grammatical functions. **1932** A. GARDINER *Theory of Speech & Lang.* iii. 107 In all these languages..the equivalent of 'speech' is a *nomen actionis* for the activity of which the most evident symptoms are articulation and audibility. **1963** F. T. VISSER *Hist. Syntax Eng. Lang.* I. iv. 357 With a plural subject the ending *-end* of the nomina agentis appeared as *-ende*. **1966** *English Studies* XLVII. 53 This is an old trait in Germanic where the pres. participles had the character and regimen of nomina agentis. **1970** *Archivum Linguisticum* I. 9 One other class of words seems to have had fluctuating secondary stress: these are the nomina agentium in *-ari, eri, -iri*.

nomenclate ('nəʊmənkleɪt), *v. rare.* [Back-formation from NOMENCLATURE.] *trans.* To assign a name or names to; to call by a certain name.

1801 CATH. M. FANSHAWE *Ep. to Ld. Harcourt*, 'Twould try Don Quixote's patience To nomenclate this mob of nations. **1868** TUCKERMAN *Collector* 127 The natural history of the doctor has not yet been written, but the classes are easily nomenclated. **1881** *Daily Tel.* 6 June 2 The institution nomenclated the Chelsea Hospital for Women.

†**nomen'clation.** *Obs. rare.* [ad. L. *nōmenclātiōn-em* (rare): cf. prec. and -ATION.] Name or nomenclature.

1638 SIR T. HERBERT *Trav.* (ed. 2) 184 Buried..in oblivion, or wrapt up in other nomenclations. *Ibid.* 343, I may conferre the nomenclation upon some adventurous Cambryan. **1651** BIGGS *New Disp.* ¶291 The nomenclation of a disease.

nomenclative ('nəʊmənkleɪtɪv), *a.* [f. as NOMENCLATE + -IVE.] Concerned with, or relating to, the action of naming.

1875 WHITNEY *Life Lang.* xiv. 299 The conception first, then the nomenclative act. **1884** *Field* 25 Oct. 556/1 The same poverty of nomenclative invention is a marked characteristic of the times.

nomenclator ('nəʊmənkleɪtə(r)). Also 6 *Sc.* -our. [a. L. *nōmenclātor* (also *-culātor*), f. *nōmen* name + *calāre* to call.]

†**1.** A student appointed as a kind of monitor or prefect over a certain part of his class. *Obs. rare.*

1563–7 BUCHANAN *Reform. St. Andros* Wks. (S.T.S.) 8 The nomenclatouris to haif charge to gather the lessons writtin, euery ane in hys awyne decurio, and bring thayme to the regent, and schaw hym quha has faltis. And geif the regent find falt quhairof the nomenclator has nocht advertysit hym, than he sal punyss baith the writar and the nomenclator.

†**2.** Used as the title of works containing collections or lists of words; hence, a book of this kind; a vocabulary. *Obs.*

1585 HIGINS (*title*), The Nomenclator, or Remembrancer of Adrianus Junius, Physician. ? **1608** BODLEY in *Reliq. B.* (1703) 79, I have sent you, by this Carrier, three several *Nomenclators*, which I have only borrowed. **1635** JACKSON *Creed* VIII. xxxi. 363 The full importance of this word..will not be easily found in ordinary Lexicons or Nomenclators. **1698** *Phil. Trans.* XX. 355 'Tis then most natural..to furnish him..with a Nomenclator; containing a competent number of Names. **1707** R. BROWNE (*title*), The English Expositor improv'd, a Complete Dictionary,..also an Index and Nomenclator.

†**b.** A compiler of such a work. *Obs. rare.*

1609 [BP. W. BARLOW] *Answ. Nameless Cath.* 330 Let all the Onomastiks, and Nomenclators, or Mathematicians, or Schoolemen be searched, and 'twill not be found. **1622** FOTHERBY *Atheom.* Pref. 21 Any Nomenclator, or Dictionarie maker.

3. *Rom. Antiq.* **a.** A servant or dependent whose business it was to inform his master or patron of the names of persons, esp. when engaged in canvassing for office. **b.** A steward or usher who assigned or indicated the places of guests at a banquet.

1601 HOLLAND *Pliny* II. 437 A certain Nomenclator or Controller belonging to one of our prodigall and wastful spendthrifts here at Rome. **1605** CAMDEN *Rem.* 96 Do not looke that I should as the Nomenclators in olde time marshall every name according to his place. **1656** *North's Plutarch* 639 *note*, This Prompter is usually call'd Nomenclator, Monitor and Factor. **1713** ADDISON *Guardian* No. 107 ¶2 When a great man stood for any publick office, ..he had always one of these Nomenclators at his elbow. **1741** MIDDLETON *Cicero* I. II. 77 The use of these Nomenclators was contrary to the laws. **1781** GIBBON *Decl. & F.* xxx. (1787) III. 208 The nomenclators, who are commonly swayed by interested motives, have the address to insert in the list of invitations, the obscure names of the most worthless of mankind. **1834** LYTTON *Pompeii* IV. iii, Diomed..had appointed a nomenclator, or appointer of places, to each guest. **1839** DE QUINCEY *Lake Poets, Wordsw.* Wks. 1889 II. 235 There needed no Roman nomenclator to tell me that this *he* was Wordsworth.

4. One who announces, or imparts to another, the names of persons or guests.

1599 B. JONSON *Cynthia's Rev.* V. iii, *Cup.* Hedon thy master is next. *Mer.* What, will Cupid turn nomenclator, and cry them? **1609** —— *Sil. Wom.* III. ii, *Daw.* My ladie Havghty, this my lady Centavre, mistresse Dol Mavis.. *Mor.* What nomenclator is this! **1625** K. LONG tr. *Barclay's Argenis* IV. ii. 275 Are you so forgetful of Astioristes that you need a Nomenclator? **1641** MILTON *Animadv.* Wks. 1851 III. 187 Their names are knowne to the all-knowing power above, and..doutlesse they wreck not whether you or your Nomenclator know them or not. **1713** ADDISON *Guardian* No. 107 ¶2, I have with much pains..qualified myself for a Nomenclator to this great city. **1811** L. M. HAWKINS *C'tess & Gertrude* II. 49 She began to speculate, with the great advantage of a most intelligent nomenclator. **1816** SCOTT *Old Mort.* iii, 'You forget..,' said her nomenclator, 'that the young gentleman comes here to discharge suit and service in name of his uncle'. **1827** LYTTON *Pelham* xl, Let me despatch Lady Babbleton, and I'll then devote myself to being your nomenclator.

†**b.** One who reckons up or recounts. *Obs. rare.*

1628 EARLE *Microcosm.* (Arb.) 53 Hee is a great Nomenclator of Authors. **1692** WASHINGTON tr. *Milton's Def. People* viii. M.'s Wks. 1851 VIII. 191 You are become of a sudden a wonderful Nomenclator of our Statutes.

5. One who gives a name to, or invents a designation for, something: *spec.* one who

classifies natural objects under appropriate designations.
1644 BULWER *Chiron.* 124 The Nomenclators seeme to have excluded the left hand from all actions of decencie and importance. **1647** COWLEY *Mistr., Her Name* v, Adam (God's Nomenclator) could not frame One that enough should signify. **1680** H. MORE *Apocal. Apoc.* 337, I will ask R. H. whether he takes himself to be a more wise and just Nomenclator than the Holy Ghost. **1785** MARTYN *Rousseau's Bot.* viii. (1794) 77 The science which distinguishes the true botanist from the mere herbarist or nomenclator. **1811** PINKERTON *Petral.* I. Introd. 18 Those who collect, and the nomenclators properly so called, do not like these doubtful sorts, which it is too difficult to arrange under the known genera. **1852** S. BAILEY *Disc. Var.* 70 Our scientific nomenclators glue long words together with little or no abridgment. **1875** WHITNEY *Life Lang.* v. 77 Reasons which were satisfactory to the nomenclators.
fig. **1708** SWIFT *Agst. Abol. Christ.* Wks. 1751 IV. 110 Are Envy, Pride, Avarice, and Ambition such ill Nomenclators, that they cannot furnish Appellations for their Owners?
Hence **'nomen,clatorship.** *rare*$^{-1}$.
1695 J. EDWARDS *Perf. Script.* 184 This nomenclatorship of Adam.

no,mencla'torial, *a.* [See -ORIAL.] In connexion with, in relation to, nomenclature.
1885 NEWTON in *Encycl. Brit.* XIX. 149/2 Nomenclatorial purists, objecting to the names..as 'barbarous'. **1897** *Nature* 19 Aug. 364/1 To distinguish those [references] that relate to habits and biology from those that are systematic and nomenclatorial. **1935** *Jrnl. Heredity* XXVI. 461/1 It has been..a continuing nomenclatorial tragedy that parents.. label helpless infants..with the cognomen of the political (or other) hero popular at the moment of birth. **1946** F. E. ZEUNER *Dating the Past* viii. 271 This [*sc.* a difference in dating Chinese geological formations] appears to be due to nomenclatorial rather than factual differences. **1953** *Parasitology* XLII. 260/2, I wish also to make reference to another nomenclatorial problem. **1970** *Nature* 5 Sept. 1065/2 Fortunately, the informational content of volume eight of *Primates* is in no way affected by these nomenclatorial niceties.

no'menclatory, *a. rare*$^{-1}$. [Cf. prec. and -ORY.] Pertaining to nomenclature.
1875 WHITNEY *Life Lang.* viii. 139 Every conceptual act is so immediately followed as to seem accompanied by a nomenclatory one.

'nomen,clatress. *rare*$^{-1}$. [f. NOMENCLATOR + -ESS.] A female nomenclator.
1713 ADDISON *Guardian* No. 107 ¶3, I have a wife who is a Nomenclatress, and will be ready, on any occasion, to attend the Ladies.

nomen'clatural, *a.* [f. next + -AL^1.] Relating to, or concerned with, nomenclature.
1803 *Edin. Rev.* III. 53 Having devised the most superlative specimen of nomenclatural absurdity. **1825** P. W. WATSON *Dendrol. Brit.* Introd. 19 Nomenclatural Conspectus. **1866** BRANDE & COX *Dict. Sci.*, etc. II. 633/2 The nomenclatural difficulties in which they are involved. **1937** N. N. PUCKETT in A. Dundes *Mother Wit* (1973) 167/1 The enticement may have been the ceremony [of baptism] rather than a delusion of nomenclatural grandeur. **1939** [see HOMOTYPE 1]. **1951** G. H. M. LAWRENCE *Taxon. Vascular Plants* ix. 196 In many countries the nomenclatural patterns and practices were set by botanists of considerable prestige. **1961** G. G. SIMPSON *Princ. Animal Taxon.* i. 29 Personal preferences and emphases also frequently affect rearrangements of supraspecific taxa..although this is not an important cause of nomenclatural change. **1972** *Nature* 24 Nov. 239/1 The difference between them is more apparent than real and stems from nomenclatural rather than biological considerations. **1974** *Ibid.* 1 Nov. 85/3 He has kindly and lucidly drawn attention to the intricacies of the correct nomenclatural procedures to be used.
Hence **nomencla'turally** *adv.*
1944 S. A. CAIN *Found. Plant Geogr.* xxx. 473 The first described form in a group is the species and the later forms are varieties, nomenclaturally. **1967** R. E. BLACKWELDER *Taxonomy* xx. 423 Nomenclaturally it [*sc.* the type specimen] serves as an anchor for the name.

nomenclature ('nəʊmənkleɪtjə(r), nəʊ'mɛnklətjə(r)), *sb.* [ad. L. *nōmenclātūra* (Pliny): see NOMENCLATOR and -URE. Hence also It., Sp., and Pg. *nomenclatura*, F. *nomenclature*.]
1. A name, appellation, designation. Now *rare.*
1610 *Histrio-mastix* I. 142 *Scri.* Your appellations? *Post.* Your names he meanes. The man's learn'd... *Scri.* Your nomenclature? *Post.* O stately Scrivener! That's: where dwell ye? **1626** BACON *Sylva* §839 To say..that there wanteth a term or Nomenclature for it. **1666** G. HARVEY *Morb. Angl.* xi. 121 A moist Consumption receives its nomenclature from a moist..expectoration that attends it. **1862** E. BURTON *Bk. Hunter* (1863) 243 Societies there are.. which identify themselves through their very nomenclature with misfortune and misery. **1891** *Daily News* 11 Nov. 3/3 A certain species of cactus... Its nomenclature is Stapelia gigantea.
†**2.** The act of assigning names to things. *Obs.*$^{-1}$
1622 FOTHERBY *Atheom.* II. xiii. 347 The Heathen haue reckoned this nomenclature, and imposition of names, for one of Gods owne works.
3. A list or collection of names or particulars; a catalogue, a register.
1635 HEYWOOD *Hierarchy* I. 26 He rank't in the Nomenclature of Fooles. **1641** J. JACKSON *True Evang. T.* I. 30, I cannot now give you a nomenclature or list of the particulars. **1683** DRYDEN *Life Plutarch* in *P.'s Lives* 75 The catalogue or nomenclature of Plutarch's Lifes, drawn up by his son. **1812** W. TAYLOR in *Monthly Rev.* LXVIII. 297 The nomenclature is certainly very copious, and for his materials the author must have consulted a multitude of books. **1846** ROBERTSON tr. *Schlegel's Philos. Hist.* 69 At first, indeed, it is merely a nomenclature of celebrated personages and events.
†**b.** A list or collection of words or terms, *esp.* those connected with a particular language or subject; a glossary, a vocabulary. *Obs.*
1659 HOWELL *Lex., To the tru Philologer*, The second Volume is a large Nomenclature of the peculiar and proper termes in all the fower languages belonging to severall Arts. **1672** tr. *Comenius' (title)*, Visible World: or, A Picture and Nomenclature of all the chief Things that are in the World. **1710** ADDISON *Tatler* No. 257 ¶7 There was at the end of the Grammar a little nomenclature, called 'The Christian Man's Vocabulary'. **1745** *Observ. Conc. Navy* 70 A Nomenclature, Italian and English.
4. The system or set of names for things, etc., commonly employed by a person or community.
1664 H. MORE *Myst. Iniq.* 211 If therefore we will stand to the Nomenclature of the Ancients [etc.]. **1691** NORRIS *Pract. Disc.* 243 There's an unimaginable difference even in the very Nomenclature..of Earth and Heaven. **1811** *Poet.* in *Ann. Reg.* 609 No name so sad as your's is seen In sorrow's nomenclature. **1857** KINGSLEY *Two Y. Ago* x, He had played, to use his nomenclature, two trump cards running. **1875** LUBBOCK *Orig. Civiliz.* iv. (ed. 3) 167 No other part of the world where the nomenclature of relationships is so primitive.
b. The terminology of a science.
1789 JEFFERSON *Writ.* (1859) III. 16 The new nomenclature has..been already proved to need numerous and important reformations. **1815** BAKEWELL *Geol.* Pref. 9 The pedantic nomenclature and frivolous distinctions recently introduced into mineralogy. **1863** LYELL *Antiq. Man* i. (ed. 3) 3 Some preliminary explanation of the nomenclature adopted in the following pages will be indispensable. **1899** *Allbutt's Syst. Med.* VIII. 833 To whom we owe the nomenclature and most of our knowledge of the disease.
c. The collective names given (or to be given) to places in a district or region.
1828 *Edin. Rev.* XLVIII. 438 The nomenclature of the frozen regions is a task which has exercised the ingenuity of all their explorers. **1856** KANE *Arct. Expl.* I. v. 44, I had no difficulty now in justifying the somewhat poetical nomenclature which Sir John Franklin applied to this locality. **1876** FREEMAN *Norm. Conq.* V. xxiii. 111 The local nomenclature of modern Glamorgan, with its strongly marked British, English, and French elements.
5. (Without article.) Names or designations forming a set or system.
1785 MARTYN *Rousseau's Bot.* Introd. (1794) 4 Such a chaos of nomenclature, that the Physicians and Herbarists no longer understood each other. **1810** W. TAYLOR in *Monthly Mag.* XXX. 345 That fund of nomenclature for visual ideas, which is afterwards extended to the abstract ideas. **1856** R. A. VAUGHAN *Mystics* (1860) I. 205 Are not your differences mere disputes about nomenclature? **1883** *19th Cent.* May 857 Fraudulent nomenclature is one of those fine arts in which false science is an adept.
6. (With *a* and *pl.*) A particular set or system of names or designations.
1809–10 COLERIDGE *Friend* (ed. 3) III. 134 Artificial classification for the preparatory purpose of a nomenclature. **1840** CARLYLE *Heroes* (1858) 191 Atheistic science babbles poorly of it, with scientific nomenclatures, experiments and what-not. **1872** MINTO *Eng. Prose Lit.* Introd. 28 We have as yet no nomenclature or notation for describing it technically. **1882** A. MACFARLANE *Consang.* 4 In a systematic nomenclature, it is convenient to extend the meaning of the term.
Hence **nomenclature** *v.*, to name or designate. Also **nomenclaturing** *vbl. sb.*
1803 *Edin. Rev.* III. 109 Nomenclaturing is likewise a new word. **1816** SCOTT *Vis. Paris* (ed. 5) 284 That the ticketing of a heap of oyster shells is carrying the system of nomenclaturing a little too far. **1824** *Examiner* 547/2 That part of the frame nomenclatured by little wits the understanding. **1826** *Sporting Mag.* XVIII. 134 The complaint was, by the old jockeys, nomenclatured 'dropping in the joints'.

nomen'claturist. [f. prec. + -IST.] One who devises a nomenclature.
1809 *Edin. Rev.* XV. 140 His acquaintance with species.. can never entitle him to rank higher than as a nomenclaturist. **1898** *Rev. Brit. Pharm.* 40 Chemical nomenclaturists will be satisfied by the change of hydrobromates and hydrochlorates to the respective 'ides'.

nomer, obs. form of NUMBER.

'nomial. *rare*$^{-1}$. [f. BI-NOMIAL, etc.] **a.** An algebraic expression consisting of a given number of terms. **b.** 'A single name or term in mathematics' (Webster 1828–32).
1717 *Phil. Trans.* XXX. 611 All Radical Expressions of Binomials, Trinomials, or of any other Nomial.

'nomian, *a. rare*$^{-1}$. [f. Gr. νόμ-ος law + -IAN.] Accepting the Mosaic Law.
1800 W. TAYLOR in *Monthly Mag.* VIII. 797 Those who receive that law as of divine authority, the nomian christians, as they might be called.

nomic ('nɒmɪk), *a.*^{1} [f. Gr. νόμος NOME *sb.*^{3}: cf. next.] Pertaining to, having the character of, Greek musical nomes.
1727–38 CHAMBERS *Cycl.* s.v. *Mode*, The antients had like-wise their *modi melipœiæ*, of which Aristides names these: dithyrambic, nomic and tragic. **1789** TWINING *Aristotle's Treat. Poetry* (1812) I. 210 He, particularly, mentions the Persians and the Cyclops as imitated in the Dithyrambic and Nomic Poetry of Timotheus and Philoxenus. **1850** MURE *Lit. Greece* III. 33 A wider compass and nobler character had been imparted to the nomic order of composition, through the medium of the flute or clarionet.

nomic ('nɒmɪk), *a.*^{2} and *sb.* [ad. Gr. νομικός, f. νόμος law: cf. prec.] **A.** *adj.* Of spelling: Customary, usual.
B. *sb.* **1.** The customary spelling.
1870 A. J. ELLIS in *Trans. Philol. Soc.* 89. **1880–1** *Ibid.* 303 Forming an introduction to nomic, and not at all.. superseding the use of nomic. *Ibid.*, Nomic spelling must always be a matter of memory.
2. *Philos.* and *Math.* That pertains to or is concerned with a discoverable scientific or logical law.
1892 K. PEARSON *Gram. of Sci.* iii. 114, I shall, for convenience, however, speak of natural law in the old sense, or, as a mere routine of perceptions, as law in the *nomic* sense. Law in the nomic sense is thus no product of the reason, but a pure *order* of perceptions. **1905** *Nature* 30 Mar. 517/2 The correlation..is..of nomic heteroscedasticity. **1921** W. E. JOHNSON *Logic* I. iv. 61, I should propose that *nomic* (from νόμος, a law) should be substituted for necessary as contrasted with contingent. Thus a nomic proposition is one that expresses a pure law of nature. **1959** K. R. POPPER *Logic of Sci. Discovery* 434 A 'necessary conditional' or a 'nomic conditional'. **1961** E. NAGEL *Structure of Sci.* iv. 51 The distinction between accidental and nomic universality can be brought out in another way. **1973** N. RESCHER *Conceptual Idealism* iv. 59 This nomological necessity of laws is generally called 'nomic necessity'.
Hence **'nomically** *adv.*
1921 W. E. JOHNSON *Logic* I. iv. 61, The nomically possible.

nominable ('nɒmɪnəb(ə)l), *a.* [f. L. *nōmināre* NOMINATE + -ABLE: cf. med.L. *nōminābilis* (Du Cange).] Capable or worthy of being named.
1743 FIELDING *Juv.* vi. Misc. I. 101 Some smaller crimes, which seem scarce nominable. **1834** SOUTHEY *Lett.* (1856) IV. 371 Another nominable person who has not been named yet is William Bankes.

nominal ('nɒmɪnəl), *a.* and *sb.* Also 5 **-alle,** 6–7 **-all.** [ad. L. *nōmināl-is*, f. *nōmin-*, *nōmen* name. So F. *nominal* (1521).]
A. *adj.* **1.** *Gram.* Of the nature of, pertaining to, a noun or nouns. (See also quots.)
c **1430** *Art Nombryng* 8 The nombre to be multipliede resceyvethe a nominalle appellacioun, as twies .5.;—5. is the nombre multipliede, and twies is the nombre to be multipliede. **1843** *Proc. Philol. Soc.* I. 27 Their scheme of terminations..is more or less applicable to every case of nominal inflexion. **1874** SAYCE *Compar. Philol.* ii. 80 Accadian seems to have nominal as well as verbal roots. **1924** O. JESPERSEN *Philos. of Gram.* ix. 120 Here we first encounter the so-called nominal sentences, containing a subject and a predicative, which may be either a substantive or an adjective. **1928** H. POUTSMA *Gram. Late Mod. English* (ed. 2) I. i. 2 Predicates are of two kinds, viz.: (*a*) verbal predicates..; (*b*) nominal predicates, i.e. such as are made up of a copula or link-verb and a nominal. **1929** *Ibid.* x. 557 *And* is used to..bring about a junction of a sentence with an undeveloped nominal- or infinitive-clause. **1939** L. H. GRAY *Foundations of Lang.* 230 There is only one case in which the sentence does not require a verb, i.e., the nominal sentence of the type of the Latin *omnia praeclara rara* 'all splendid things (are) rare'... Contrary to popular opinion, the nominal sentence does not omit the copula, and none is to be supplied. **1949** *Archivum Linguisticum* I. 183 The hybrid nature—nominal-verbal—of the participle. **1954** PEI & GAYNOR *Dict. Ling.* 147 *Nominal sentence*, a sentence in which the principal part..is a noun or nominal form. **1973** *Archivum Linguisticum* IV. 3 Some verbal forms occur as nominal modifiers, others not.
2. Belonging or pertaining to the nominalists; holding views akin to these. *rare.*
1528 TYNDALL *Obed. Christian Man* Wks. 104/1 One is reall, an other nominall. What wonderfull dreams haue they of their predicamentes, uniuersales, &c. **1663** BUTLER *Hud.* I. i. 155 Profound in all the Nominal And Real ways beyond them all. **1711** SHAFTESB. *Charac.* (1737) II. II. ii. 257 Others, one may say, are only nominal Moralists, by making Virtue nothing in itself, a Creature of Will only.
3. a. Of the nature of, consisting in, pertaining or relating to, a name or names (in distinction to things).
1620 T. GRANGER *Div. Logike* 158 Primortiues are either nominall and simple, or reall and compound. **1690** LOCKE *Hum. Und.* III. vi. §2, I call it by a peculiar name, the nominal essence, to distinguish it from that real constitution of substances, upon which depends this nominal essence. **1727–38** CHAMBERS *Cycl.* s.v. *Character*, Nominal characters are those we properly call letters, which serve to express the names of things. **1796** MORSE *Amer. Geog.* I. 232 The time, however, is anticipated..that all nominal distinctions shall be lost in the general and honourable name of Americans. **1887** MAX MÜLLER *Sci. Thought* x. 595 By nominal attributes I mean those by which a name stands or falls. **1898** J. HUTCHINSON *Arch. Surg.* IX. 305, I will not venture on any diagnosis of the disease, whether nominal or essential.
b. ***nominal definition***: (see quot. 1864).
1697 tr. *Burgersdicius' Logic* II. i. 2 Nominal definition appears to be threefold. **1725** WATTS *Logic* 160 Those propositions whose predicate is a nominal or real definition of the subject. **1864** BOWEN *Logic* iv. 86 A Nominal Definition is a distinct explication of all the Marks which are connoted in the name of the Concept by general consent, as evinced in the use of language.
4. a. Existing in name only, in distinction to *real* or *actual*; merely named, stated, or expressed, without reference to reality or fact.
1624 LD.-KPR. WILLIAMS in *Fortescue Papers* (Camden) 203 Whereby he may be a nominall Judge of the Common Pleas, with his place in Wales, he disclayminge from all fees and profitts of the place in the Common Pleas. **1701** *Lond.*

Gaz. No. 3758/3 We shall at all times be most ready..to assert Your undoubted Right to these..Realms.., against the Nominal Prince of Wales. **1747** CHESTERF. *Lett.* cxix. I. (1792) 323 Thus seduced by fashion, and blindly adopting nominal pleasures, I lost real one's. **1776** ADAM SMITH *W.N.* I. v. (1869) I. 34 Labour, like commodities, may be said to have a real and nominal price. **1799** *Monthly Rev.* XXX. 128 Their Pacha..is an officer tolerated and nominal, but neither obeyed nor respected. **1833** HT. MARTINEAU *Manch. Strike* v. 57, I said the nominal amount of your wages mattered little. I said nothing about the real amount. **1883** *19th Cent.* May 890 The nominal effect of this treaty was to place Annam at the complete dependence of France.

b. With limiting words, as *mere(ly, only, but,* or with implication of these, denoting entire contrast to something real or substantial.

1799 *Sporting Mag.* XIV. 175 An action for mere nominal damages. **1817** JAS. MILL *Brit. India* II. v. vii. 592 To this, with only a nominal modification, the Council agreed. **1849–50** ALISON *Hist. Europe* I. Introd. §23. 18 The Franks acknowledged but a nominal allegiance to their chief. **1863** D. G. MITCHELL *Sev. Stor., My Farm of Edgewood* 300, I bought a cord or two at a nominal rate. **1885** *Law Times Rep.* LIII. 484/2 Where an insolvent sues as a mere nominal plaintiff, as a mere shadow of another person, security is required.

5. a. Containing explicit mention of a name.

1788 in E. D. Dunbar *Soc. Life* (1865) I. 392 Nominal prayers for the King are to be authoritatively introduced.

b. Consisting of, containing, a set of names.

1802 JAMES *Milit. Dict., Nominal Call,* which corresponds with the French *appel nominatif*; and, in a military sense, with our roll call. **1844** *Regul. & Ordin. Army* 178 A Nominal Return of such Men as from time to time join the Depôt. **1884** *Manch. Exam.* 30 Sept. 4/6 The Secretary..has forwarded to us a nominal list..of the officers and crew of the gunboat Wasp.

c. Giving the names of persons dealt with.

1849 FRUSE *Comm. Class-bk.* 105 The nominal accounts will show, without constant reference to the Store or Warehouse books, the value of goods sold.

d. Assigned to a person by name.

1869 *Bradshaw's Railway Manual* XXI. 369 The nominal capital now consists of 92,000 original shares of 5*l* each; 38,000 preference shares of 4*l* each: and 32,000 obligations of 4*l* each. **1882** *Times* 8 Feb. 11/1 These shares are still nominal, and the original subscribers, as well as subsequent holders are liable on them. **1964** *Lebende Sprachen* IX. 98/2 The amount of capital stated in the memorandum of association which a joint-stock company may issue is called *nominal* or *authorized capital*.

e. ***nominal note*** = NOMINAL *sb.* 3.

1884 *Encycl. Brit.* XVII. 103/2 Sounds of a higher pitch than the nominal note, in fact the harmonics, of which the nominal note is the fundamental.

6. (See quot. 1970[2].)

1966 *Aviation Week & Space Technology* 5 Dec. 30/1 The mission is to launch the 800-lb. Prime vehicle to effect a nominal re-entry at 400,000 ft. following injection at 26,000 fps. **1970** N. ARMSTRONG et al. *First on Moon* vi. 124 An example of misuse is our use of the word 'nominal', which most of the English-speaking world interprets as meaning small, minimal—and we usually use it in the sense of being average or normal. **1970** R. TURNILL *Lang. Space* 94 *Nominal*, a favourite word, meaning within prescribed limits; anything from 'perfect' to acceptable. **1972** *Daily Colonist* (Victoria, B.C.) 26 July 3/1 As one engineer said, 'She is phenomenally nominal'—nominal being space jargon for operating-as-planned.

B. *sb.* **1.** A nominalist. Now *rare* or *Obs.*

1519 HORMAN *Vulgaria* 93 The wey of the nomynallys and reals is dyuers. **1565** JEWEL *Repl. Harding* (1611) 294 He should haue remembred..That Scotus is against Thomas: ..and the Nominals against the Reals. **1604** [see REAL C. 1]. **1640** GLAPTHORNE *Wit in Constable* II. Wks. 1874 I. 187 The Nominalls, the Thomists, all the sects Of old and moderne Schoole-men. **1680** BAXTER *Answ. Stillingfl.* Pref. A 3 b, A Nominal, who contracteth all his Syllogisms into simple terms of art. **1725** WATTS *Logic* II. iii. §4 (1892) 235 In the colleges of learning, some are for the nominals, and some for the realists. **1772** O'HALLORAN *Introd. Hist. & Antiq. Irel.* I. iv. 38 William Halloran, head of the Nominals at Oxford.

†**2.** A thing existing in name only. *Obs. rare.*

a **1625** BOYS *Wks.* (1629) 261 Deuills are not Nominals onely but Reals. *a* **1626** [see REAL C. 2]. **1661** GLANVILL *Van. Dogm.* 134 Euery Religion hath its bare Nominals.

3. *Mus.* A note giving its name to a scale.

1811 BUSBY *Dict. Mus.* (ed. 3), *C*, the nominal of one of the two natural modes. **1895** *Pall Mall Mag.* VII. 191 The tones of nominals, fundamentals, and hum-notes, seem to move, as it were in three separate spheres.

†**4.** (See quot.) *Obs. rare*$^{-1}$.

a **1813** A. MURRAY *Hist. Europ. Lang.* (1823) II. 281 Nominals are verbs formed from nouns which undergo the addition of the consignatives peculiar to the future participles.

5. *Gram.* (See quot. 1972.)

1928 H. POUTSMA *Gram. Late Mod. Eng.* (ed. 2) I. i. 2 A nominal (a noun or adjective) or a nominal equivalent (i.e. a word or word-group doing duty as a nominal). **1935** H. STRAUMANN *Newspaper Headlines* 49 Words of these formal characteristics will be called nominals. **1961** *Amer. Speech* XXXVI. 159 It is customary to describe the English nominal as consisting of a sequence of constituents: predeterminers, determiners, adjectives, the noun head, and finally certain postnominal modifiers, such as relative clauses. **1968** J. LYONS *Introd. Theoretical Linguistics* 347 Let us..draw a distinction between what we will call *first-order* and *second-order* nominals in English, and say that only second-order nominals may occur in sentences whose underlying structure is Nominal + Time. **1972** HARTMANN & STORK *Dict. Lang. & Ling.* 151/2 *Nominal*, a name given ..to a word which functions as a..noun, but does not have all the formal characteristics of a noun (i.e. in English the distinction between singular and plural and between common and possessive cases). **1974** *Nature* 25 Oct. 705/1 One could defend the thesis that sentences are remembered by forming an associative structure linking representations of their nouns and verbs by arguing that the associative machinery deals with nominals derived from verbs in a very similar way to verbs themselves.

nominalism (ˈnɒmɪnəlɪz(ə)m). [ad. F. *nominalisme* (1752); see NOMINAL B. 1. and -ISM.] **a.** (See quot. 1836.) **b.** The view which regards universals or abstract concepts as mere names without any corresponding reality.

1836 KEBLE *Serm.* viii. (1848) 215 The Nominalism of our days; I mean, the habit of resolving the high mysteries of the faith into mere circumstances of language. **1846** [see REALISM 1]. **1864** BURTON *Scot Abr.* II. i. 16 In some shape or other, Nominalism and Realism still divide between them the empire of thought. **1885** PATTISON *Mem.* 166 In these years Whately's Logic, or some form of nominalism, predominated in the schools.

nominalist (ˈnɒmɪnəlɪst), *sb.* (and *a.*) [f. NOMINAL *a.* 2 + -IST. Cf. F. *nominaliste* (1752).] One who maintains or accepts the doctrine of nominalism. Also *attrib.* or as *adj.*

1654 JER. TAYLOR *Real Pres.* 89 This was the sense of Ocham the Father of the Nominalists. *a* **1695** [see REALIST 2]. *a* **1751** BOLINGBROKE *Ess.* IV. xli. Wks. 1754 IV. 624 The dispute..between the nominalists and realists about the nature of universals. **1816** COLERIDGE *Lay Serm.* (Bohn) 356 Laodiceans in spirit, Minims in faith, and Nominalists in philosophy. **1839** HALLAM *Hist. Lit.* III. iii. §153 Hartley also resembles Hobbes in the extreme to which he has pushed the nominalist theory. **1843** MILL *Logic* I. vi. §1 The doctrine of the extreme nominalists that it is an expression of an agreement or disagreement between the meanings of two names. **1880** HUTH *Life Buckle* I. ii. 123 Horne Tooke was a nominalist and sensationalist. **1885** PATTISON *Mem.* 170, I had not yet abandoned my nominalist foundations. **1965** *Listener* 9 Dec. 942/1 How much more nominalist, in a way, the whole society is.

nominaˈlistic, *a.* [f. prec. + -IC.] Of the nature of, pertaining to, nominalism. Hence **nominaˈlistically** *adv.*

1863 KINGSLEY *Water-Bab.* iii. 88 The one true.. nominalistic, realistic..doctrine of this wonderful fairy tale. **1870** MAX MÜLLER *Sci. Relig.* (1873) 399, I call this the nominalistic as opposed to the realistic method of comparative mythology. **1878** SYMONDS *Shelley* 35 He adopted the negative conclusions of a shallow nominalistic philosophy. **1932** C. C. J. WEBB *John of Salisbury* 154 In philosophy he favoured the views of the Nominalistic school. **1939** *Mind* XLVIII. 246 To save himself he would have to read 'satisfaction' nominalistically.

nomiˈnality. *rare*$^{-1}$. [f. NOMINAL *a.* 4 b.] A merely nominal thing.

1880 MRS. WHITNEY *Odd or Even?* i, Slidden from his old-fashioned, steady inherited business into the nominalities.

ˈnominalize, *v.* [f. NOMINAL *a.* 1 + -IZE.] *trans.* To convert into a noun. Hence **nominaˈlizable** *a.*; **nominaliˈzation**; **ˈnominalized** *ppl. a.*; **ˈnominalizer**; **ˈnominalizing** *ppl. a.*

1659 *Instructions Oratory* 32 Verbs..nominalized, do admit one termination familiarly, that suffer not another. **1951** Z. S. HARRIS *Methods in Structural Linguistics* xvi. 277 There is no noun class in Hidatsa, only a stem class (neither noun nor verb), a class of nominalizing suffixes, and a class of verbalizing suffixes. **1955** T. BURROW *Sanskrit Lang.* iv. 125 Such transference is common in nominalised adjectives throughout the system. **1960** R. B. LEES in *Internat. Jrnl. Amer. Linguistics* XXVI. (*title*) The grammar of English nominalizations. **1965** N. CHOMSKY *Aspects of Theory of Syntax* ii. 87 Nominalizable adjectives. **1965** *Canad. Jrnl. Linguistics* X. 117 The nominalizer *-ma* is attached directly to the future durative suffixes. *Ibid.* 160 These articles are obligatory with every noun or nominalization appearing as subject or object of a verb. **1967** Z. VENDLER *Linguistics in Philos.* v. 124 In technical terms, we will end up with a list of nominalized sentences. **1968** J. LYONS *Introd. Theoretical Linguistics* 265 The constituent-string is transformed ('nominalized') into an N[oun] P[hrase] of the form A[djective] + N[oun]. **1972** A. MAKKAI *Idiom Structure* 140 *The king stepped down*, nominalizable as **the downstepping of the king*. **1972** *Science* 23 June 1306/2 When a surgeon uses a phrase such as the [*sic*] 'the bleeding of the vessels', the only admissible origin for the nominalization 'bleeding' would be 'the vessels bled' and not 'someone (that is, the surgeon) bled the vessels'. **1972** J. W. BRESNAN in *Language* XLVIII. 334 It must be noted that *-ation* is not an isolated case... Many other nominalizing affixes affect internal stress: continue, continúity; oppóse, opposítion; [etc.]. **1974** H. ESAU (*title*) Nominalization and complementation in modern German.

nominally (ˈnɒmɪnəlɪ), *adv.* [f. NOMINAL *a.*]

1. By name; as regards a name or names.

1665 MANLEY *Grotius Low C. Wars* 973 It consisted with the Honour of the Commonwealth nominally to include the House of Nassau, which had so well deserved of Liberty. **1736** LEDIARD *Life Marlborough* I. 28, I shall only recount one memorable Story..without applying it nominally to the Persons. **1783** W. F. MARTYN *Geog. Mag.* II. 325 The kings of England and of France are both nominally prayed for in the Churches of Geneva. **1822** DE QUINCEY *Confess.* Pref., He was nominally known to the public as Dean of Carlisle.

†**2.** As a noun, substantively. *Obs. rare*$^{-1}$.

1674 N. FAIRFAX *Bulk & Selv.* 200 World, whether it be in the singular number or plural, may betoken plurally or indefinitely, and as much adverbially as nominally.

3. In name, as opposed to *really*.

1748 HARTLEY *Observ. Man* II. iv. Concl. 440 The nominally Christian States of these Western Parts. **1776** ADAM SMITH *W. N.* II. iv. (1869) I. 358 The profits of stock would be the same, both nominally and really. **1822** BYRON *Werner* IV. i. 50 The country (nominally now at peace) Is over-run with—God knows who. **1884** J. GILMOUR *Mongols* xxxi. 361 Many a lama who has nominally a sufficient income never receives more than half of his due.

†**ˈnominance.** *Obs. rare*$^{-1}$. [See next and -ANCE.] Name, designation.

1642 H. MORE *Song of Soul* II. iii. III. lxv, The Medicean foure reel about Jove; Two round old Saturn without Nominance.

nominate (ˈnɒmɪneɪt), *pa. pple.*, *ppl. a.*, and *sb.* Also 6 **nomynate, nominat.** [ad. L. *nōmināt-us*, pa. pple. of *nōmināre*: see next.]

A. *pa. pple.* †**1.** Named, called, entitled. *Obs.*

c **1485** *Digby Myst.* (1882) II. 414 By name I am nominate the god belyall. **1513** BRADSHAW *St. Werburge* 2338 The yssue..Was a noble prynce, nomynate Colrede. **1567** *Trial Treas.* (1850) 30 As I, being properly nominate Juste, Am here associate with Contentation.

†**2.** *Sc.* Mentioned by name; noted. *Obs.*

1570 *Satir. Poems Reform.* xx. 92, I pans and muse how thay excuse This murther..Quhair it is nominate. **1583** *Reg. Privy Council Scot.* III. 621 The uthers persones quhilkes wer present specialie nominat in the uther tickit gevin to us. **1596** DALRYMPLE tr. *Leslie's Hist. Scot.* Prol. 56 The maist nominat amang thame is this.

†**3.** Nominated, appointed. *Obs.*

1546 *Yorks. Chantry Surv.* (Surtees) 276 Incumbent.. nominate by the mayor and bretherne. **1590** H. BARROW in *Confer.* III. 57 Your Parsons are nominat by the Patron. *a* **1648** LD. HERBERT *Hen. VIII* (1683) 370 Sir Thomas More, or the Bishop of London, to be nominate by the King.

B. *ppl. a.* **1.** †**a.** Having the character of a descriptive name. *Obs. rare*$^{-1}$. **b.** Having a special name. **c.** Mentioning a particular name.

1610 W. FOLKINGHAM *Art of Surv.* III. i. 65 Vocall Propriety denotes the Properties of particulars by due Appellation, which is either Nominate or Cognominate. The first is..either Generall; as Up-land and Maritime..; or Speciall; as Wealdes, Woulds, Plaines. **1818** COLEBROOKE *Obligations* 18 Those, which have an appropriate denomination and distinctive proper name, denoting their particular effect and esential properties, are nominate or named contracts. **1838** W. BELL *Dict. Law Scot.* 674 A nominate right is a right possessing a *nomen juris*, the use of which defines its boundaries. *Ibid.*, The nominate and innominate contracts illustrate the doctrine. **1880** MUIRHEAD *Gaius* II. §128 A nominate disherison..might either precede or follow the institution.

d. *Taxonomy.* (See quot. 1967.)

1948 A. L. RAND *Mammals Eastern Rockies* 100 The Alberta form is the nominate subspecies [of badger]: *Taxidea taxus taxus* Schreber. **1967** R. E. BLACKWELDER *Taxonomy* xix. 398 A nominate taxon is the subordinate taxon which contains the type of the subdivided 'higher' taxon. **1968** PERRING & SELL *Critical Suppl. Atlas Brit. Flora* 146 The question of the use of the nominate subspecies in this case [sc. *Eleocharis palustris*] is complex and disputed. **1971** *Nature* 10 Dec. 360/1 The European stock [of the Atlantic salmon], binomially named by Linnaeus, must become the nominate subspecies and, therefore, should bear the name *Salmo salar salar* Linnaeus. **1974** *New Phytologist* LXXIII. 802 The presence of the nominate subspecies in some cases..and not in others..is not explained.

2. Nominated to an office. Chiefly *Sc. Law.*

1681 STAIR *Instit.* I. vi. §5. 56 There be three kinds of Tutors... The first is, Tutor Testamentar, or nominate. *a* **1768** ERSKINE *Instit. Law Scot.* I. vii. §1 (1773) 114. **1838** W. BELL *Dict. Law Scot.* 395 The executor, in the former case, being called an executor-nominate. *Ibid.* 1016 A tutor-nominate or testamentary is he whom the father..has nominated, either in a testament, or in some other writing. **1864** *Standard* 16 Apr., The bishop nominate..was once a slave boy.

†**C.** *sb.* A nominee. *Obs. rare*$^{-1}$.

1599 SANDYS *Europæ Spec.* (1632) 148 After two Monethes imprisonment in the Conclaue [they] were forced to relent and to choose one of his nominates.

nominate (ˈnɒmɪneɪt), *v.* Also 6 **nomynate**, 6–7 **nominat.** [f. L. *nōmināt-*, ppl. stem of *nōmināre* to name, f. *nōmin-*, *nōmen* name.]

1. *trans.* To call by the name of; to call, name, entitle, designate. Now somewhat *rare.*

1545 RAYNOLD *Byrth Mankynde* 7 The fourth be nominatyd the ouerthwart muskles. **1582** STANYHURST *Æneis* I. (Arb.) 21 Theese rancks the Italian dwellers doo nominat altars. **1626** MIDDLETON *Anything for Quiet Life* I. i, She has a book, which I may truly nominate Her Black Book. **1657** J. SERGEANT *Schism Dispach't* 92 The same men who nominate us Papists for onely acknowledging the Pope's authority. **1748** *Anson's Voy.* I. x. 141 This Ocean being nominated Pacific. **1799** C. COOKE in Beddoes *Contrib. Phys. & Med. Knowl.* 393 These are all the diseases that can with propriety be nominated constitutional. **1824** SCOTT *St. Ronan's* iv, It must stand Munt-grunzie in the stamped paper, being so nominated in the ancient writs and evidents thereof. **1868** HELPS *Realmah* (1876) 90 Those animals whom we are pleased to nominate 'the lower creation'.

†**b.** To give a name or names to; to provide with a name. *Obs.*

1597 HOOKER *Eccl. Pol.* v. lxxviii. §2 If they that first doe impose names, did alwayes vnderstand exactly the nature of that which they nominate. **1658** SIR T. BROWNE *Hydriot.* 16 The City of Norwich..was enlarged, builded, and nominated by the Saxons. **1697** J. SERGEANT *Solid Philos.* 294 We do not nominate them precisely according to what we do then actually know.

2. To mention or specify by name. (Very common *c* 1600–80; now somewhat *rare.*).

1593 G. HARVEY *Pierce's Super.* 205, I could nominate the man, that could teach the Delphical Oracle, and the Ægyptian Crocodile to play their parts. **1601** DENT *Pathw. Heaven* 141, I pray you, nominate the oathes which are so rife and common amongst vs. **1620** E. BLOUNT *Horæ Subs.* 378 There be in this towne multiplicity of Palaces.., of which I will but nominate two. **1680** COTTON *Compl.*

Gamester (ed. 2) 13 Consider how many persons have been ruined by play. I could nominate a great many. **1801** ELIZ. HELME *St. Marg. Cave* III. 185 He ordered him to hasten to an obscure part of the city which he exactly nominated. **1846** MCCULLOCH *Acc. Brit. Empire* (1854) I. 423 Leases held on the longest of two lives..expire at an average..every 64 years, if boys and girls of 4 years of age are nominated.

3. To name, fix, appoint, specify. Now *rare*. **1564** *Child-Marriages* 197 Richard..said, 'by my trouth, I will marry the bie such a Day',—& did nominate the day. **1596** SHAKS. *Merch. V.* I. iii. 150 Let the forfeite Be nominated for an equall pound Of your faire flesh. **1637** PRYNNE *Will* in *Documents* (Camden) 98 The somme of tenne pounds, to be imployed..as my nephew..shall nominate and directe. **1680** AUBREY *Lives* (1898) II. 143 Being the challengee it belonged to him to nominate place and weapon. **1716** WODROW *Corr.* (1843) II. 187 Their scruples of keeping the day the King nominates without a church appointment. **1751** ELIZA HEYWOOD *Betsy Thoughtless* IV. 32 Sir Ralph Trusty..had the honour of nominating the day for the celebration of their nuptials.

4. To appoint (a person) by name to hold some office or discharge some duty. **1560** DAUS tr. *Sleidane's Comm.* 366 That the king shoulde within vi monethes nominate some man to the Bishop of Rome. **1582** N. LICHEFIELD tr. *Castanheda's Conq. E. Ind.* I. lxiii. 128b, First he would nominate him that should remaine in the Indias for Captaine generall. **1603** KNOLLES *Hist. Turkes* (1621) 976 To honour him the more, [he] nominated him the Generall of his armie against the Persians. **1653** *Clarke Papers* (Camden) III. 5 They proceede in nominating persons in the severall counties to sitt as a Counsell. **1681–2** WOOD *Life* 3 Feb. (O.H.S.) III. 4 Henry Aldrich..nominated or elected Canon of Ch. Ch. by the commissioners. **1765** BLACKSTONE *Comm.* I. ix. 330 The judges could not meet there..to nominate the sheriffs. **1841** W. SPALDING *Italy & It. Isl.* I. 114 The decurions, who had nominated a magistrate, were..held bound as sureties for him. **1874** GREEN *Short Hist.* vii. §1. 341 The House of Commons was crowded with members nominated by the Royal Council.

absol. **1688** *Pr. of Orange's Declar., w. Animadv.* 23 Whether before he nominate, he do not satisfy himself that his Nominê be a Man on whom he may rely. **1761** HUME *Hist. Eng.* (1806) IV. lxii. 622 They chose seven persons, who should nominate to such commands as became vacant.

b. To propose, or formally enter, (one) as a proper person or candidate for election. **1601** R. JOHNSON *Kingd. & Commw.* (1603) 101 The nomination being ended, the chiefe of the Companies demaunde of the people which of these three thus nominated, they are willing to elect. **1774** JOHNSON 21 Feb. in *Boswell*, We are thinking to augment our Club, and I am desirous of nominating you. **1828–32** WEBSTER, s.v., Any member of the assembly or meeting *nominates*, that is, proposes to the chairman the name of a person whom he desires to have elected. **1857** TOULMIN SMITH *Parish* 171 It is declared that any person nominated may send in, before the day of election, his refusal to act. **1875** JOWETT *Plato* (ed. 2) V. 83 Any one may challenge the person nominated and start another candidate.

5. In horse breeding, to choose (a mare) as suitable for mating *to* a particular stallion. **1950** H. WYNMALEN *Horse Breeding* vi. 109 The considerations set out in the preceding chapter will be found helpful in selecting a suitable stallion to which to nominate our mare. **1972** *Harper's Bazaar* Apr. 63/1 [The mare] gave the stallion she was nominated to such a hell of a time he wouldn't touch her with a barge-pole.

'nominated, *ppl. a.* [f. NOMINATE *v.* + -ED[1].]

1. Named (for a position or office), appointed. *a***1548** HALL *Chron., Hen. VI*, 148 Many honorable personages..sailed into Fraunce, for the conveyaunce of the nominated Quene, into the realme of England. **1693** WOOD *Life* 25 Nov., The new nominated warden of Merton Coll. **1892** SIR H. PARKES *50 Yrs. Austral. Hist.* II. 264 To appoint fifteen new members to the nominated Council.

†**2.** Noted, famous. *Obs. rare*. **1642** MILTON *Apol. Smect.* 75 Such of them as were thought the chief and most nominated opposers on the other side. **1645** —— *Tetrach.* 97 The most nominated Fathers of the Church.

'nominately, *adv. rare*. [f. NOMINATE *pa. pple.* + -LY[2].] †**a.** Especially, particularly. *Obs.* **b.** By name. **1630** SPELMAN *De Sepult.* 13 *Locus religiosus* is that which is assigned to some office of Religion, and especially that where the body of a dead person hath been buried. **1880** MUIRHEAD *Gaius* III. §63 The Senate decreed that the estates..should belong..in the next place to the latter's descendants not nominately disinherited.

'nominating, *ppl. a.* [f. NOMINATE *v.* + -ING[2].] That nominates or names. **1597** MIDDLETON *Wisd. Solomon* x. 15 Shall we call her wisdom, by her name, Or new-invent a nominating style? **1677** MARVELL *Corr.* Wks. (Grosart) II. 554 Some rather desiring that they might only be generall words, and not nominating. **1888** BRYCE *Amer. Commw.* III. lx. II. 422 A Nominating Convention..is a representative body composed of delegates from all the primaries within its limits, who have been chosen at those primaries for the sole purpose of..selecting the candidates.

nomination (nɒmɪ'neɪʃən). Also 5 **nomynacioun,** 6 **-ion,** 5–6 **nominacion,** 6 **-atioun.** [a. OF. *nominacion, -ation* (1305), or ad. L. *nōminātiōn-em*, n. of action f. *nōmināre* to nominate.]

†**1. a.** The action of mentioning by name. *Obs.* **1425** *Rolls of Parlt.* IV. 269/2 To yat blode and armes was drawen ye nomination of him above all othyr Erles. *c***1425** *Found. St. Bartholomew's* (E.E.T.S.) 21 At the nomynacioun of the glorious Apostle, the same fyre semyd to suffre violence. **1563** FOXE *A. & M.* 1357/2 To put your hand to your head, and at the nomination..of the Popes holynesse vncouer the same. **1623** AILESBURY *Serm.* 49 Christian eares would be offended at the nomination of those things that are done in secret. **1665** *Intelligencer* No. 80 in Willis & Clark *Cambr.* (1886) I. 621 That great and wise Prelate..is so well known, that the sole nomination of the Founder is a sufficient accompt of the elegance..of the Foundation.

†**b.** The action of naming, specifying, or appointing; the fact of being appointed. *Obs. rare*. **1594** SHAKS. *Rich. III*, III. iv. 5 *Buck.* Is all things ready for the Royall time? *Darb.* It is, and wants but nomination. *Ely.* Tomorrow then I judge the happie day. *c***1710** CELIA FIENNES *Diary* (1888) 141 When plaite was in nomination to pay a tax, ye Earle..sold it all. **1753** RICHARDSON *Grandison* VI. xxx, The nomination of a day.

2. a. The action (or right) of appointing a person by name to some office or duty; in early use *spec.* of ecclesiastical appointments. **1454** *Rolls of Parlt.* V. 253/2 Nominations of Abbays, Prioryes, Hospitals, Churches. **1491** *Act 7 Hen. VII*, c. 19 The same Griseld at the nominacion and desire of the same late Cardynall therof enfeoffed Laurence late Bisshoppe of Duram. **1539** *Act 31 Hen. VIII*, c. 13 §2 All the..advousons, nominacions, patronages, annuityes..and other hereditamentes whatsoeuer. **1573** G. HARVEY *Letter-bk.* (Camden) 3 After nine was the congregation for the nomination. **1601** LD. MOUNTJOY *Let.* in Moryson *Itin.* (1617) II. 122 To informe you that Sir Hen. Dockwra hath had greater favour in the nomination of Captaines then he. **1699** BENTLEY *Phal.* 377 If I might have the Nomination, it should be He. **1726** AYLIFFE *Parergon* 91 In England the King has the Nomination of an Archbishop; and after such Nomination, he sends..to the Dean and Chapter, to elect the Person thus named by him. **1758** J. S. *Le Dran's Observ. Surg.* Introd. (1771) p. v, The Honour conferred upon me by his Majesty's Nomination. **1856** FROUDE *Hist. Eng.* (1858) II. vi. 3 He had absolute power over every nomination to an English benefice.

attrib. **1863** H. COX *Instit.* I. viii. 108 Mr. Pitt took the opportunity of abolishing many of the smaller nomination boroughs.

b. The action of proposing as a candidate, or as a suitable person to be elected. **1601** [see NOMINATE *v.* 4b]. **1857** TOULMIN SMITH *Parish* 171 Otherwise, the election is at an end with the act of secret nomination. **1861** *Illustr. Lond. News* 17 Aug. 153/3 On Tuesday the nomination of a member for South Lancashire took place at Newton. The show of hands..was declared to be in favour of..the Conservative candidate.

3. a. The fact or position of being nominated. Freq. in phrase ***in nomination***. **1494** FABYAN *Chron.* VII. 361 The best of the cytie gaue the nominacion vnto Aleyn Sowch, and dyuerse of ye other cryed vpon Thomas Fiz Thomas. **1612** *North's Plutarch, Cæsar Augustus* 1170 Giuing order that none should be put in nomination but such as were vertuous. **1699** LUTTRELL *Brief Rel.* (1857) IV. 485 The commons yesterday, after they expelled Mr. Woollaston, had in nomination some others. **1768** SIR J. GRAY in *Priv. Lett. Ld. Malmesbury* (1870) I. 171 My acquaintance with Mr. Harris your father..made me readily acquiesce in your nomination. **1837** MCCULLOCH *Acc. Brit. Empire* II. 232 A candidate is not precluded from offering himself, because he is not put in nomination the first day. **1890** 'R. BOLDREWOOD' *Col.-Reformer* (1891) 147 The London Club, to which he had been elected about five years after nomination.

b. A set of nominees. *rare*[−1]. *a***1817** T. DWIGHT *Trav. New Eng.* etc. (1821) I. 257 At the same time, and place, they vote, also, for twenty persons as a Nomination for the Council of the ensuing year.

†**4.** Name, designation, denomination. *Obs.* **1502** ARNOLDE *Chron.* (1811) 283 Ye shulde leue your right, your tytle,.. and nominacion of you [as] Kyng of Fraunce,..and be content only in wryting wyth Rex Anglie. **1553** *Respublica* I. iv, *Avar.* Oh, I shoulde have sayde, helpe, sir Reformacyon. *Oppr.* Yea, Marye, sir, that is my Nomynacion. **1579** FENTON *Guicciard* VI. (1599) 243 Abhorring such nomination, they had reuerenced the name of the Duke Valentinois. **1658** SIR T. BROWNE *Hydriot.* 44 Who cares to subsist..under naked nominations without deserts and noble acts. **1683** SNAPE *Anat. Horse* I. vi. (1686) 77 By these several nominations or names it goes. **1771** SMOLLETT *Humph. Cl.* (1815) 230 The North Briton..observed, that he himself had the honour of a scriptural nomination. **1794** T. TAYLOR *Pausanias's Descr. Greece* III. 251 They found themselves unable to discover the cause of their nomination; but were informed that the one was called Eros.., and the other Anteros.

5. a. Assignation of a name or names. **1552** ABP. HAMILTON *Catech.* (1884) 13 How thair is goddis be false nominatioun. **1601** R. CHESTER *Love's Mart.*, etc. (1878) 179 What shall I call this creature..? All nomination is too straight of sence. **1756** CLUBBE *Hist. Wheatfield* Misc. Tracts (1770) I. 30 From that moment, according to the capricious and licentious nomination of men and things of those times, called it Whatfield. **1863** J. G. MURPHY *Comm., Gen.* xii. 8, 9 The name, then, was not first given at the second nomination by him.

b. Designation *by* a certain name. **1865** *Cornh. Mag.* Aug. 194 The general mediæval usage of Italy, in the popular nomination of artists by their Christian names alone.

6. In horse breeding, the planned mating of a particular mare and a particular stallion. **1912** *Bloodstock Breeders' Rev.* I. 169/2 (*heading*) Free nominations for mares. *Ibid.*, The Board, in 1911, allotted for award by County Committees 777 nominations for the free service of mares by the King's Premium stallions. **1927** J. E. PLATT *Thoroughbred Race-Horse* iv. 29 It is necessary to book nominations for two, three, or even four years ahead. **1950** H. WYNMALEN *Horse Breeding* vi. 110 If the horse is of a type and character that pleases you..you are not likely to go wrong in fixing upon your nomination. **1969** G. E. EVANS *Farm & Village* x. 118 They gave them assisted nominations to encourage horse-breeding. **1974** *Country Life* 14 Mar. 584/1 The highest price was given for a nomination to the American horse, Never Bend.

nominatival (nɒmɪnə'taɪvəl), *a.* [f. next + -AL[1].] Pertaining to, connected with, the nominative case; having the character of a nominative. **1843** *Proc. Philol. Soc.* I. 73 We need not therefore feel surprise if sometimes the Old-English definite adjective takes *en* as a nominatival ending. **1876** EADIE *Thessalonians* 234 The apposition is nominatival.

nominative ('nɒmɪnətɪv), *a.* and *sb.* Also 4 **nomen-, nominatyf,** 5 **nominatif(e, -iffe,** 5–6 **-iue,** 6 **-yve.** [a. F. *nominatif, -ive* (13th c.), or ad. L. *nōminātīv-us* (*casus*): see NOMINATE *v.* and -IVE.]

A. *adj.* **1.** *Gram.* **a.** ***nominative case***, that case of nouns, adjectives, and pronouns, which stands as, or is connected with, the subject of a verb. **1387** TREVISA *Higden* (Rolls) I. 327 Þat ylond of Ynde hatte Tilis in þe nomenatyf caas; and þe ilond of occean hatte Tyle in þe nominatyf caas. *c***1440** *Gesta Rom.* xci. 416 (Add. MS.), And so we han the nominatif case. ?**1481** in Flügel *Neuengl. Lesebuch* (1895) 297 Sum tymys they be verbys parsonallys and haue nominatiffe casys before them. **1520** WHITINTON *Vulg.* (1527) 1 The verbe shall accorde with his nominative..case. **1588** FRAUNCE *Lawiers Log.* II. i. 86 The nominative case and the verbe be placed grammatically, according to the prescription of Syntaxis. **1668** WILKINS *Real Char.* III. ix. 355 The Nominative Case before the Verb, and the Accusative after. **1751** HARRIS *Hermes* (1841) 168 Hence the reason why every verb..has in language a necessary reference to some noun for its nominative case. **1817** SELWYN *Law Nisi Prius* (ed. 4) II. 835 Doubts had been entertained whether the words *other person* in this statute should be taken to be in the nominative or in the genitive case. **1886** T. M. DOUSE *Introd. Gothic* 209 Its inflectional characteristic is the Nominative case.

b. Of the nature of, characteristic of, pertaining to, the (*or* a) nominative case. **1824** L. MURRAY *Eng. Gram.* (ed. 5) I. 219 These sentences, or clauses, thus constituting the subject of an affirmation, may be termed nominative sentences. **1872** MORRIS *Hist. Eng. Accid.* 101 The nominative ending *s*..is connected with the demonstrative pronouns.

2. Nominated; appointed by nomination. **1660** *Trial Regic.* 124 The case is instant in Philip who was a nominative King. **1735** *Col. Rec. Pennsylv.* IV. 45 Even so this Nominative Court may pass with the learned as Justifiable. **1883** W. E. BAXTER *Winter in India* ii. 21 The municipality of Bombay is partly elective and partly nominative. **1892** *Daily News* 6 Aug. 4/8 The Second Chamber was still nominative in parts where it should have been elective.

3. Appellative, denominative. *rare*[−1]. **1844** TUPPER *Heart* xi. 115 Their latest *noms de guerre* will serve all nominative purposes as well as any other.

4. Bearing the name of a person. **1872** *Daily News* 30 Sept., A nominative personal invitation from M. Vogeli to meet M. Gambetta. **1879** *Standard* 10 June, The Shares are nominative, but they can be converted into Share Warrants 'to Bearer'.

B. *sb.* **1.** The nominative case. *c***1620** A. HUME *Brit. Tongue* (1865) 29 The nominative hath no other noat but the particle of determination. **1751** HARRIS *Hermes* (1786) II. iv. 281 The Nominative is that Case, without which there can be no regular and perfect Sentence. **1768** HOLDSWORTH *Virg.* 161 This is certainly used in the nominative plural. **1841** LATHAM *Eng. Lang.* 216 The Nominative Plural and the Genitive Singular are, in the present language of England, identical. **1872** MORRIS *Hist. Eng. Accid.* 101 The nominative and accusative have no formative particles to distinguish them.

2. a. A word in the nominative case; a form which is the nominative case of a word. **1668** WILKINS *Real Char.* 448 Some words requiring a Nominative, others a Dative, others an Accusative. **1699** BENTLEY *Phal.* 320 To put Nominatives instead of Oblique Cases. **1751** HARRIS *Hermes* (1841) 193 Hence..arises the grammatical regimen of the verb by its nominative, and of the accusative by its verb. **1797** *Encycl. Brit.* (ed. 3) VIII. 51 *note*, The preposition in this case..governs a nominative and a verb. **1889** *Proc. Philol. Soc.* 322 Brugmann explains the Nominatives *ager, ācer* as standing for **agros*, **ācris*.

b. A subject (*to* a verb). **1824** L. MURRAY *Eng. Gram.* (ed. 5) I. 225 That a sentence, or part of a sentence, may be the nominative to a verb, is undoubtedly true.

3. ***nominative absolute***. **1843** *Proc. Philol. Soc.* 153 Other idioms..have the indeterminate pronoun preceded by a nominative absolute. **1858** C. P. MASON *Eng. Gram.* 97 This adverbial relation may be sustained... By a substantive (accompanied by some attributive adjunct) in the nominative absolute; as '*The sun having risen*, we commenced our journey'. **1916** E. A. SONNENSCHEIN *New Eng. Gram.* III. 44 The nominative absolute construction is an equivalent of an adverb-clause: *We sitting*, as I said, the cock crew loud. **1949** BAILEY & HORN *Eng. Handbk.* vii. 266 Begin some sentences with a nominative absolute... Dr. Carver having proved his point, sweet potatoes and peanuts were planted in abundance. **1963** PENCE & EMERY *Gram. Present-Day Eng.* ii. 62 The nominative absolute is a perfectly proper construction as far as grammar is concerned... Although a nominative absolute has no *grammatical* function in the statement in which it appears, it should have a logical function. **1972** HARTMANN & STORK *Dict. Lang. & Linguistics* 152/2 *Nominative absolute*, absolute construction.

Hence **'nominatively** *adv.*, 'in the manner of the nominative' (Webster 1847).

‖**nominativus pendens** (ˌnɒmɪnə'taɪvəs 'pendɛnz). [L.] (See quot. 1926.) **1867** WHARTON *Law-Lexicon* (ed. 4) 647/2 *Nominativus pendens*, a nominative case grammatically unconnected with the rest of the sentence in which it stands. **1926** FOWLER *Mod. Eng. Usage* 611/2 *Nominativus pendens*.., 'hanging nominative'. A form of anacoluthon in which a sentence is begun with what appears to be the subject, but before the verb is reached something else is substituted in word or in thought, & the supposed subject is left in the air. **1929** C. MACKENZIE *Gallipoli Memories* viii. 124 And I would have turned a gerund into a participle here and there..and probably there would be a vile *nominativus pendens*. **1929** BLUNDEN *Near & Far* 12 While the pallid herd Of Grecians limit their pedantic gaze To some prodigious *nominativus pendens*. **1963** F. T. VISSER *Hist. Syntax Eng. Lang.* I. I. i. 61 This subject is sometimes called 'nominativus pendens' or 'dangling subject'.

nominator (ˈnɒmɪneɪtə(r)). [ad. late L. *nōminātor*, agent-noun f. *nōmināre*: see -ATOR.]

1. One who nominates to office or for election.

1659 *Clarke Papers* (Camden) IV. 299 The Counceil.. agreed on 7 to be Nominators of Officers. **1714** BENTLEY *Rem. Free-thinking* II. §52 (1717) 66 While Tiberius Gracchus was creating new Consuls; one of the Nominators suddenly fell down dead. **1772** *Ann. Reg.* 203 To oppose Lord Dysart, the first and improper nominator. **1831** *Lincoln Herald* 6 May, The radical organ of the council of nominators. **1885** *L'pool Daily Post* 30 June 4/8 Sir Richard's nominator and seconder and his election agent.

†**2.** *Math.* A numerator. *Obs. rare*⁻¹.

1674 JEAKE *Arith.* (1696) 41 This is called the Numerator, and sometime Nominator.

Hence **nomiˈnatrix**, a female nominator.

1899 *Westm. Gaz.* 1 April 6/3 It requires a holding of £3,000 even to be a nominator or nominatrix [of directors].

‖**nominatum** (nɒmɪˈneɪtəm). [L., neut. of *nōminātus*, pa. pple. of *nōmināre* NOMINATE *v.*] 'The thing that is named by a sign, word, or linguistic expression' (Webster, 1961).

1947 R. CARNAP *Meaning & Necessity* iii. 96 The customary method of meaning analysis regards an expression as a *name* for a (concrete or abstract) entity, which we call its *nominatum*. **1949** H. FEIGL tr. G. Frege in Feigl & Sellars *Readings in Philos. Analysis* 89 A proper name (word, sign, sign-compound, expression) expresses its sense, and designates or signifies its nominatum. We let a *sign express* its sense and *designate* its nominatum. **1962** W. & M. KNEALE *Devel. of Logic* viii. 496 'Nominatum' is too obviously artificial. **1966** S. CECCATO in *Automatic Transl. of Lang.* (NATO Summer School, Venice 1962) 77 However, since thought is always constituted by correlations made up of correlata in a given order, it is clear that the second example requires a repetition of the nominatum of 'water' which is not required in the first example.

ˈnominature. *rare*⁻¹. = NOMINATION.

1864 *Daily Tel.* 12 July, Three or four active supporters of the straight nominature.

no-mind: see NO *a.* 5 e.

nominee (nɒmɪˈniː). Also 7 **nominê**. [f. NOMINATE *v.* + -EE¹.]

†**1.** (See quot. 1675.) *Obs.*

1664 EARL ORRERY in *State Lett.* (1743) I. 174, I..beg you that he may be in the first rank of the nominees. **1675** EARL ESSEX *Lett.* (1770) 144 By the Act of Explanation, all the rest of those thirty-eight persons who had not upon the first act been restored to their estates, together with as many more as make up in all fify-four persons (who are commonly called Nominees) are provided for [etc.].

2. The person who is named in connexion with, or as the recipient of, an annuity, grant, etc.

1697 *Lond. Gaz.* No. 3338/4 If he receives any quarterly Payment beyond the Death of the Nominee, he shall forfeit treble the value of the Money received. **1723** *Ibid.* No. 6169/3 After the Decease of the respective Nominees. **1766** BLACKSTONE *Comm.* II. xxii. 368 Upon the original surrender the nominee hath..such a possibility, as he may when-ever he pleases be reduced to a certainty. **1802–12** BENTHAM *Ration. Judic. Evid.* (1827) III. 294 Nominee in a life-annuity. **1844** WILLIAMS *Real Prop.* (1877) 18 The heir was thus a nominee in the original grant.

attrib. **1883** *Manch. Guard.* 17 Oct. 5/4 That nominee life policies are often effected which are altogether invalid is only too evident.

3. One who is nominated for some office.

1688 [see NOMINATE *v.* 4. *absol.*]. *a* **1768** ERSKINE *Inst. Law Scot.* I. vii. §2 (1773) 114 Though such nominee gets the name of a tutor.., the appellation is improper. **1790** [see NOMINOR]. **1810** BENTHAM *Offic. Apt. Maximized, Def. Econ.* (1830) 22 This power of parcelling out the property of the public among the nominees of Kings and Ministers. **1878** LECKY *Eng. in 18th C.* I. iii. 433 A Parliament consisting in a very large measure of the nominees of great families.

attrib. **1865** *Sat. Rev.* 5 Aug. 160/1 A nominee member for a little market town.

4. One in whose name, though he is not the owner, a stock or registered bond certificate is registered. Also *attrib.*

1869 *Bradshaw's Railway Manual* XXI. 157 The directors ..be authorised to offer such new shares to the holders of ordinary stock..or to the nominees of such holders. **1930** *Economist* 22 Mar. 634/2 Again, many securities registered in the names of British banks or even individuals, as nominees, are really the property of foreigners. *Ibid.* 15 Nov. 896/1 Our own figures for 1929 are on the low side owing to the growth of nominee holdings in recent years. **1960** *Times* 24 Oct. (Financial Review) p. xvii/4 The nominee companies endeavour to facilitate the handling and supervision of portfolio investment. **1964** *Financial Times* 12 Mar. 19/5 Nominee..is a holder who, as respects the exercise of any rights in respect of a security, is not entitled to exercise those rights except in accordance with instructions given by the owner. **1975** *Guardian* 24 Feb. 20/7 Mr Marcus Lipton, the Labour MP for Lambeth Central will, however, ask the Government this week to outlaw nominee shareholding.

Hence **nomiˈneeism**, the system of nominating persons to offices or posts.

1831 *Lincoln Herald* 13 May, Opposed to nomineeism in every shape. **1892** SIR H. PARKES *30 Yrs. Austral. Hist.* I. 302 The vicious principle of nomineeism.

†**noˈminion.** *Obs. rare*⁻¹. = NOMINATION.

1513 BRADSHAW *St. Werburge* I. 179 The realme of Mercyens..Thre hundreth yeres endured in auctoryte, Vnder eyghtene kynges worthy nomynyon.

‖**nominis umbra** (ˈnɒmɪnɪs ˈʌmbrə), *phr.* [L. (Lucan I. 135).] The shadow or appearance of a name; a name without substance.

1856 BAGEHOT in *National Rev.* Apr. 363 Taylor's theorem will go down to posterity,..but what does posterity know of the deceased Taylor? *Nominis umbra* is rather a compliment; for it is not substantial enough to have a shadow. *c* **1874** W. JAMES in R. B. Perry *Tht. & Char. W. James* (1935) I. xxxi. 525 The British school say that the laws are nil—*nominis umbra*. **1896** [see BOOKFUL *a.* 2]. **1959** JOWITT *Dict. English Law* II. 1230/2 *Nominis umbra*, the shadow of a name, *e.g.*, a one-man company.

†**ˈnominor.** *Obs. rare.* = NOMINATOR.

1765 BLACKSTONE *Comm.* I. 341 Among the Goths the twelve nominors were first elected by the people themselves. **1790** BENTHAM *Mem. & Corr.* Wks. 1843 X. 229 The terms of connexion..between a nominor and a nominee.

nominy (ˈnɒmɪnɪ). *north. dial.* [perh. ad. L. *nomine* in the formula *in nomine patris*, etc.] A rhyming formula; a set or form of words in popular use; a rigmarole, long story. Also *Comb.*

1814 *Costume of Yorks.* 63 in Brand *Pop. Antiq.* (1849) II. 188 He..repeats a speech, or what they term a *nominy*, which..is here subjoined. **1846** *M. A. Richardson's Historian's Table-bk., Leg. Div.* III. 160 It was formerly the custom, in the more remote parts of the county of Durham, to address complimentary verses to a newly married couple. .. This was called 'saying the Nominy'. *Ibid.*, Pray remember the Nominy sayer! **1889** NICHOLSON *Folk-Sp. Yorksh.* 8 Should the boy be unable to recite this rhyme, he would be told 'he didn't knaw his nominy'. **1892** NORTHALL *Folk-Rhymes* 319 Nominies or Formulas.

nomir, obs. Sc. form of NUMBER.

nomism (ˈnəʊmɪz(ə)m). [f. Gr. νόμ-ος law + -ISM.] (See quots.)

1905 *Jewish Encycl.* IX. 326/1 *Nomism*, that religious tendency which aims at the control of both social and individual life by legalism, making the law the supreme norm. **1917** *Encycl. Relig. & Ethics* IX. 380/1 'Nomism' or 'legalism' is the name given to the view that moral conduct consists in the observance of a law or body of laws.

nomisma (nəʊˈmɪzmə). Pl. **nomismata**. [ad. Gr. νόμισμα money, f. νομίζ-ειν to use customarily, f. νόμος usage, custom.] = BEZANT I.

1908 W. WROTH *Catal. Imperial Byzantine Coins Brit. Mus.* p. lxxiv, Under Alexius I, the nomisma..was issued in several different metals simultaneously. **1957** *Encycl. Brit.* XV. 699/1 The principal coin, the *nomisma*, popularly called bezant, was derived from the Roman gold solidus. **1959** E. POUND *Thrones* xcvii. 24 Vasa Klipped for the people, Lycurgus, nomisma, And 'limitation is the essence of good nomisma'. **1960** H. HAYWARD *Antique Coll.* 200/1 *Nomisma*, the gold coin of the later Byzantine Empire. Usually scyphate in form with types of the Emperor, Christ, the Virgin and saints.

nomistic (nəˈmɪstɪk), *a.* [f. Gr. νόμ-ος law + -ISTIC.] Based upon law.

1877 tr. *Tiele's Hist. Relig.* 3 Not until a later period did polytheism give place here and there to nomistic religions. **1883** *Encycl. Brit.* XX. 368 Nomistic or nomothetic communities, founded on a law or Holy Scripture. **1894** *Thinker* V. 438 Instead of the principle of faith, the nomistic principle was substituted.

nomly, obs. var. NAMELY *adv.*

nomme, *v.*: see NOME *v. Obs.*

nommen, obs. pa. pple. of NIM *v.*

nommer, obs. Sc. f. NUMBER.

nommet, var. NUMMET *dial.*

nomo-, ad. Gr. νομο-, combining form of νόμος law, occurring in a few words, as **ˈnomocanon** [med.Gr. νομοκανών, -κάνονον], a collection of the canons of Church councils, together with civil laws relating to ecclesiastical matters. **noˈmocracy**, a system of government based on a legal code; the rule of law in a community. **noˈmogenist**, a believer in, or advocate of, nomogeny. **noˈmogenous** *a.*, produced by, or resulting from, the operation of natural laws. **noˈmogeny**, the origination of life as a natural (opp. to miraculous) process. **noˈmographer** [Gr. νομογράφος], (*a*) a writer of laws, a legislator; (*b*) one who is skilled in nomography. **noˈmography**, (*a*) (see quot. 1731); (*b*) (see quot. 1830); (*c*) the expression of law in a written form. **nomoˈlogical** *a.*, of or pertaining to nomology; also as *sb.*; hence **nomoˈlogically** *adv.* **noˈmologist**, one who is interested or versed in nomology. **noˈmology** (see quots.). †**nomoˈtechnic**, **nomoˈtheism**, †**noˈmothesy** (see quots.).

1727–38 CHAMBERS *Cycl.* s.v., The first *nomocanon was made by Johannes Scholasticus in 554. **1797** *Encycl. Brit.* (ed. 3) XIV. 630/2 He [Photius] wrote..the *Nomocanon* under 14 titles. **1884** *Catholic Dict.* (1897) 660/2 The Nomocanon which goes under the name of St. Wladimir, and is accepted as the basis of canon law in Russia. **1837** *Fraser's Mag.* XVI. 95 If the Hebrew common-wealth was not a theocracy, it was a *nomocracy. **1894** *Thinker* V. 439 Nomocracy, pure and simple, reigned supreme. **1868** OWEN *Comp. Anat. Vertebr.* III. 817 The *Nomogenist is reduced to enumerate the existing elements into which the simplest living jelly..is resolvable. **1869** *Student* II. 428 The terms '*nomogenous' and miraculous are only contrasted by a limited school of theologians. **1868** OWEN *Comp. Anat. Vertebr.* III. 814 *Nomogeny or Thaumatogeny? **1656** BLOUNT *Glossgr.*, *Nomographer, a writer of the Law: a Legislator. **1716** M. DAVIES *Athen. Brit.* II. Addenda, The Law-writers..belong to the Scotch Nomographers. **1731** BAILEY (vol. II.), *Nomography, a Description of, or Treatise of the Laws. **1830** BENTHAM *Offic. Apt. Maximized* Pref. 26 *Nomography*..is an appellation, which presented itself as capable of being made to serve, with most convenience, for the designation of the *logic of the will*. *a* **1832** —— (*title*), Nomography; or the Art of Inditing Laws. **1895** *19th Cent.* July 152 English law still remains.. conspicuous for its defects of form,..and no one would pretend that the art of 'nomography' is not capable of further material development. **1845** *Nomological [see *Nomology* below]. **1886** *Westm. Rev.* July 126 It would take too long in this place to analyze in nomological terms this remarkably opaque utterance. **1947** H. REICHENBACH *Elements of Symbolic Logic* viii. §61. 360 We shall call these formulas *nomological formulas*. The term 'nomological'..is chosen to express the idea that the formulas are either laws of nature or logical laws... The term 'nomological' is therefore a generalization of the term 'tautological'. **1961** E. NAGEL *Structure of Sci.* iv. 51 Such use is characteristic of all nomological universals. *Ibid.* 53 They contend only that genuine nomologicals are logically necessary. **1967** *Philosophy* XLII. 134 My theory permits me nomologically to derive the statement. **1970** J. N. FINDLAY tr. *Husserl's Logical Investigations* I. xi. 230 One could say..that these sciences are *nomological*, in so far as their unifying principle, as well as their essential aim of research, is a law. **1973** *Jrnl. Genetic Psychol.* CXXIII. 11 The beginnings of a nomological network may have been laid in this experiment. **1973** [see NOMIC *a.*²]. **1886** *Westm. Rev.* July 135 Parental love is a fact which *nomologists must accept as a datum. **1845** SIR W. HAMILTON *Metaph.* vii. (1859) I. 122 If, again, we analyse the mental phænomena with the view of discovering and considering..the Laws by which our faculties are governed,..we have a science which we may call the *nomology of mind,—nomological psychology. **1866** *Treas. Bot.* 792/1 *Nomology*, that part of Botany which relates to the laws which govern the variations of organs. **1886** *Westm. Rev.* July 143 Rather what may be termed nomology, or the inductive science of law. **1901** *Month* May 497 Nomology would be that which deals with the conformity of actions to rules. **1594** R. ASHLEY tr. *Loys Le Roy* 32 *Nomotechnicke for knowledge, exposition or interpretation of Lawes. **1872** BIRKS *Doctr. Creation* 185 The view may also be held along with *Nomotheism, or that modified Theism, which reckons all direct, periodic interference of God with the universe an impeachment of His perfect foresight. **1656** BLOUNT *Glossogr.* [from Cotgrave], *Nomotheste, the making, publishing, or proclaiming a Law.

†**no mo**, *sb.* and *a. Obs.* Forms: α. 1 **ná má**, 3–4 (6 *Sc.*) **na ma**, 3–4 **nama**, 3–5 (6 *Sc.*) **no ma**, 6 *Sc.* **na mea**, 9 **nae mae**. β. 3–4, 6 **na mo**, 3–4 **nāmo**; 4–5 **no moo** (5 **noo**), **nomo**, 4–6 **no mo**, 6–7, 9 **no moe**. [f. *ná* NO *adv.*² + *má* MO, quasi-*sb.*¹ and *a.* For adverbial uses see MO *adv.*] No more (in number).

α. **971** *Blickl. Hom.* 35 Ne bið þara fæstendaʒa na ma þonne syx & þritiʒ. *c* **1000** ÆLFRIC *Gram.* xiv. (Z.) 89 Sume naman..habbað tweʒen mislice casus and na ma on ʒewunan. *c* **1205** LAY. 91 Nefede he boten ane sune... nefede he bern no ma. *a* **1300** *Cursor M.* 2269 þe first bot an was and nama [*Gott.* na ma]. *c* **1330** R. BRUNNE *Chron. Wace* (Rolls) 6523 A doughter had Dianot, & no ma. *c* **1440** *Bone Flor.* 1104 Now my lorde ys fro me tane, Y wyll love no ma But hym that boght me. *a* **1560** ROLLAND *Crt. Venus* II. 823 In till hir Court (quod he) is thair na ma Bot sex Ladeis! **1570** BUCHANAN *Admonit.* Wks. (S.T.S.) 31 Scho sould beir na ma childrene to debar þame fra þe croun. **1583** *Leg. Bp. St. Androis* 614 Of honest men he had na mea. **1809** T. DONALDSON *Poems* 40 Like her alake? I hae nae mae, Now Muffie's dead.

β. *c* **1200** *Trin. Coll. Hom.* 109 On [þing] is þat þe sunne is on and nāmo. **1297** R. GLOUC. (Rolls) 527 Ȝwanne þe geans were alle aslawe þat þer ne bileuede na mo [*v.rr.* nāmo, no mo]. *c* **1350** *Will. Palerne* 1271 Strokes was þer delt na mo fram þe duk was take. **1377** LANGL. *P. Pl.* B. II. 234 Saue Mede þe Mayde na mo [*v.rr.* nama, no moo] durst abide. *c* **1450** *Merlin* 56 At this counseile were no mo but Pendragon and Vter. **1485** CAXTON *Paris & V.* (1868) 35 He had but hyr onely and no moo sones ne doughters. **1535** COVERDALE *Eccl.* iv. 8 There is one man, no mo but himself alone. **1570–6** LAMBARDE *Peramb. Kent* (1826) 217 In that day, there issued no moe, but these three, out of the place of paines. **1611** SHAKS. *Cymb.* III. i. 36 There is no mo such Cæsars. **1619** T. TAYLOR *Comm. Titus* i. 6 God's action in creating one man, and one woman, and no moe. **1813** HOGG *Queen's Wake* 255 My twenty men, I have no moe.

nomogram (ˈnɒməgræm). [ad. F. *nomogramme*, f. Gr. νομο- NOMO- + F. *-gramme* -GRAM.] A diagram representing a relationship between three or more variables in the form of a number of (straight or curved) scales, so arranged that the value of one variable corresponding to given values of the others can be read off by means of one or more straight lines drawn to intersect the scales at the appropriate values.

1909 in *Cent. Dict.* Suppl. [with Fr. reference]. **1910** R. K. Hezlet in *Jrnl. R. Artillery* XXXVI. 460 Fig. 5 shows..the 'nomogram' constructed for the formula on this plan. [*Note*] Coining an equivalent to the French 'nomogramme'. **1918** *Inst. Automobile Engin. Proc.* XII. 191 When..this 'intersection' diagram is changed to a 'nomogram' or 'alinement' diagram, all these difficulties disappear and the reading is rendered much more accurate. **1920** *Chem. Abstr.* XIV. 2440 (*heading*) Nomograms for the functions log $p = -(Q_0/4{\cdot}57T) + 1{\cdot}75 \log T + C$ and log $P = -(Q_0/4{\cdot}57T) + 1{\cdot}75 \log T - aT + 3{\cdot}3$. **1938** *Jrnl. R. Aeronaut. Soc.* XLII. 8 Nomograms for picking the best airscrew diameter. **1947** *Electronic Engin.* XIX. 100 Line drawings, tables, charts and nomograms are liberally used. **1957** G. E. Hutchinson *Treat. Limnol.* I. ix. 582 (*caption*) Nomogram for determining O_2 saturation at different temperatures and altitudes. **1965** A. S. Levens *Graphical Methods Res.* II. 39 There are two general types of nomograms: one recognized as a Cartesian coordinate chart (or concurrency chart) and the other as an alignment chart.

nomograph ('nɒməgrɑːf, -æ-). [f. nomo- + -graph.] = prec.

1909 in *Cent. Dict.* Suppl. **1921** *Chem. Abstr.* XV. 3233 The methods of calcg. and plotting nomographs are explained. **1939** *Nature* 4 Mar. 371/2 In the third chart a third series of horizontal and vertical lines leading to a final nomograph either confirms the horizontal shear strength as adequate or shows the correction required. **1965** A. S. Levens *Graphical Methods Res.* II. 81 The nomographs provide a means for the rapid evaluation of the relative merit of various materials for the design of ablating shields on re-entering vehicles. **1975** G. J. King *Audio Handbk.* ii. 30 The intrinsic noise of the power amplifier is always fed to the loudspeaker, and the attenuated preamplifier noise adds in vector sum (see the nomograph in Fig. 1.5).

nomography (nə'mɒgrəfɪ). [ad. F. *nomographie* (M. d'Ocagne *Nomographie. Les calculs usuels effectués au moyen des abaques*, etc. (1891)), f. Gr. νομο- nomo- + F. *-graphie* -graphy: cf. *nomography* s.v. nomo-] The technique of using or devising nomograms.

1909 in *Cent. Dict.* Suppl. [with Fr. reference]. **1913** R. K. Hezlet (*title*) Nomography. **1918** *Inst. Automobile Engin. Proc.* XII. 187 Nomography can be an aid to efficiency in the drawing office and factory. **1951** *Engineering* 3 Aug. 160/1 Although nomography is by no means a new branch of mathematics, the use of nomograms seems never to have become widespread. **1965** [see nomographic *a.* below].

Hence **no'mographer**, one who employs nomography; **nomo'graphic** *a.*, involving or being a nomogram; **nomo'graphically** *adv.*, by means of a nomogram.

1915, 1918 Nomographic [see alignment 6]. **1947** Douglass & Adams *Elem. Nomography* p. v, This book uses the term 'nomographic chart' in the popular sense to refer to alignment diagrams. *Ibid.* p. vii, However, the successful rule-of-thumb or short-cut nomographer is not to be criticized for his approach. **1965** W. H. Burrows *Graphical Techniques for Engin. Computations* p. ix, A modification of existing theory..pointed the way towards the development of a new theory of nomographic representation, the hyperbolic coordinate method from which have grown generalizations and extensions covering the entire field of nomography. **1965** A. S. Levens *Graphical Methods Res.* II. 81 The amount of material given up during ablation..can be determined nomographically for heat input rates from 100 to 5,000 Btu/ft.^{2}-sec.

‖**nomoli** ('nɒmɒlɪ). Also **nomori**, **numori**. [Mende.] (See quots.)

1910 T. J. Alldridge *Transformed Colony* xxix. facing p. 286 (*caption*) Numori... Steatite figures found in caves and supposed to be of very great antiquity. **1925** T. N. Goddard *Handbk. Sierra Leone* III. iii. 56 Another superstition of much interest is that associated with the steatite stone figures known locally as 'Nomori'... A Nomori is venerated for its supernatural powers and the good luck it is supposed to bring. **1926** F. W. H. Migeod *View Sierra Leone* xiv. 180 Owing to the demand of Europeans for steatite images which, of unknown origin, have frequently been dug up in various parts of Mende country, the manufacture of them has begun again... Their name in Mende is Nomoli. **1951** K. L. Little *Mende of Sierra Leone* xi. 223 The steatite *nomoli* which the farmer turns up when he is hoeing in old bush are looked upon as the genii's handiwork and can be used to make the rice prosper. **1954** R. Lewis *Sierra Leone* xvii. 161 Small soapstone figures of men and animals called Nomoli, which are found only in Sierra Leone, are not the artistic productions of any existing tribe, though they are greatly valued as bringers of good luck and fertility; at the time of planting rice they are whipped to make them 'work'. They are, apparently, the handi-work of an earlier bush culture and are found in the gravel of rivers or in the bush. They have, however, been convincingly counterfeited by Mende craftsmen for European collectors. **1961** *Times* 12 Aug. 10/5 Called 'Nomoli' by the Mende, these [figures] are credited with a supernatural origin.

no more, *sb.*, *a.*, and *adv.* Forms: α. 1 **ná** (**nó**) **máre**, 2 **nam mare**, 2–4 **namare** (4 **namar**), 3–5 **na mare**; *Sc.* 5 **nomar(e**, 6 **na mair**, 8–9 **nae mair**. β. 2–3 (**nā**) **nam mor**, **nam more**, 3–4 (**nā**) **nammore**, **na more**, 3–5 **namore** (4 **-moore**), 4–6 **nomore** (4–5 **-mor**), 4– **no more** (5 **mor**, 6 *Sc.* **moir**). [f. *ná* no *adv.*[2] + more *sb.* etc. Cf. no less.

It is possible that the forms *nam* and *nā* (the latter frequently read and printed as *nan*) properly belong to none *adv.* 1 a. A curious change of vowel appears in the form *nūmor* (printed *nunmor*), which occurs several times in *Gen. & Ex.*]

A. *sb.* **1.** Nothing more or further.

α. *c***888** K. Ælfred *Boeth.* xxvi. §1 Swa weligne þæt he ʒenoȝ hæbbe & no maran ne ðyrfe. *c***1000** *Ags. Gosp.* Mark xv. 5 Ða ne andswarode se hælend him na mare [*Hatton* nam mare]. *c***1175** *Lamb. Hom.* 37 Soðliche ne þerft þu bidden namare. *c***1205** Lay. 15737 Nat ich na mare to suggen þe of mine sune. *c***1375** *Sc. Leg. Saints* iii. (*Andrew*) 67 þai tynt þe sycht, & mycht nomare do, as for þane. **1486** *Bk. St. Albans* e iij b, Of this ilke hare Speke we no mare. **1508** Dunbar *Poems* vi. 34 Of varldis gud I bad na mair. **1786** Burns *Ep. to J. Smith* xxix, I shall say nae mair, But quat my sang. **1816** Scott *Antiq.* xii, I beg nae mair at ony single house than a meal o' meat.

β. *c***1154** *O.E. Chron.* (Laud. MS.) an. 1132, þa he nā mor ne mihte, þa uuolde he ðæt his nefe sculde ben abbot in Burch. *Ibid.* an. 1137, þa þe uurecce men ne hadden nā more to ȝyuen, þa ræueden hi. *a***1225** *Ancr. R.* 246 Nullich of bonen siggen her nam more. **1297** R. Glouc. (Rolls) 638 Me ..deþ a lettre þer to & namore [*v.rr.* nāmore, no more] iwis. **1340** *Ayenb.* 270 Nammore ne is be-tuene ane manne and ane beste bote ine onderstondynge. **1390** Gower *Conf.* I. 158 So that ther is nomor to seie Touchende of that. **1401** *Pol. Poems* (Rolls) II. 113 Therfor, Daw, I sey nomore to the at this tyme. *c***1470** *Gol. & Gaw.* 1049 Of me gettis thou na more, Doutles this day. **1500–20** Dunbar *Poems* xxiii. 34 No moir thy pairt dois fall, Bot meit, drynk, clais. **1558** Cavendish *Poems* (1825) II. 18 This is my last complaynt, I can say you no more. **1600** Heywood *1st Pt. Edw. IV*, D ij, I can no more but giue you mine aduise. **1680** H. More *Apocal. Apoc.* 332 Nor has R. H. produced anything material against any part of Mr. Mede's Interpretations, no more no[r] so much as against his Synchronisms. **1719** De Foe *Crusoe* II. (Globe) 328 They had no more to do then, but to get into their Boats. **1742** Young *Nt. Th.* I. 27 Fate! drop the curtain; I can lose no more. **1818** Cobbett *Pol. Reg.* XXXIII. 406 There was no more of blasphemy in the publication than there was of witchcraft. **1872** Morley *Voltaire* (1886) 2 Who asked no more from them meanwhile than that they should prove their love.

b. *ellipt.* as a command or request.

*c***1460** *Towneley Myst.* xvi. 385 Peasse now, no more! **1610** Shaks. *Tempest* I. ii. 246 Before the time be out? no more. **1822** Byron *Vis. Judgm.* xcii, The monarch.. exclaimed 'What! what!..No more—no more of that!'

2. *ellipt.* (See next.)

1895 tr. *Jusserand's Eng. Ess.* 151 No more Don Japhet, no more verses..; of all these no mores, the last is the worst.

B. *adj.* Not any more; no further.

1377 Langl. *P. Pl.* B. XII. 279 Ergo saluabitur, quod he, and seyde namore Latyne. *c***1400** *Rom. Rose* 3237 Be wel ware to take nomore Counsel, that greveth aftir sore. *c***1470** Henry *Wallace* I. 196 Eftir to Scottis that did no mor grewance. **1535** Coverdale *Acts* xxiv. 11 There are yet nomore but twolue dayes sence I came vp to Ierusalem. **1576** Fleming *Panopl. Epist.* 70 Surely there is no more but one course of wel gouerning the common wealth. *a***1662** Heylin *Laud* (1668) 157 Laud was resolved that there should be no more but one Bishop in that City. **1692** R. L'Estrange *Fables* ccccxxviii. (1708) 463, I know no more Reason I have to Obey my Husband, than my Husband has to Obey me. **1709** Steele *Tatler* No. 176 ⁋8 Having no more Children than one Daughter. **1829** T. L. Peacock *Misfort. Elphin* ii, The least honourable of the two is next in honour.., because there are no more but two. **1855** Browning *Bp. Blougram's Apol.* 1 No more wine? Then we'll push back chairs and talk. **1895** [see A. 2].

b. With implication of *adv.* 1.

1719 De Foe *Crusoe* I. (Globe) 57 In the Morning when I look'd out, behold no more Ship was to be seen.

C. *adv.* **1.** No longer. (Passing into 2.)

*c***1205** Lay. 1949 þa nolde Brutus na mare [*c* 1275 na more] þat hit swa ihaten weore. *c***1250** *Owl & Night.* 213 Nv him ne lust namore pleye; he wile gon a rihte weye. *a***1300** *Cursor M.* 1401 Quen he herd he suld liue namare, þan he logh. *c***1400** Maundev. (Roxb.) xxxii. 148 He wald na mare be called Kyng. **1500–20** Dunbar *Poems* xxv. 96 Cum hame and dwell no moir in Striuilling. **1585** T. Washington tr. *Nicholay's Voy.* IV. i. 114 b, They resorted with the elders and were no more subiect to goe vnto the warres. **1601** Shaks. *All's Well* III. vi. 2 Hold me no more in your respect. **1697** Dryden *Virg. Georg.* IV. 671 Th' unhappy Husband, Husband now no more, Did on his tuneful Harp his Loss deplore. **1757** Gray *Bard* III. i, No more our long-lost Arthur we bewail. **1796** Macneill *Waes o' War*, Up wi' frantic haste she started; Cauld nor fear she felt nae mair. **1803–6** Wordsw. *Ode Intim. Immort.* 9 The things which I have seen I now can see no more. **1877** Ruskin *Arrows of Chace* (1880) II. 216 Military distinction is no more possible by prowess.

Comb. **1820** Shelley *Prometheus Unb.* III. iv. 169 The ghosts of a no-more-remembered fame.

b. As predicate: No longer existent; departed, dead, gone.

1601 Shaks. *Jul. C.* v. iii. 60 But Cassius is no more. **1667** Milton *P.L.* IX. 827 But what if God have seen And Death ensue? then I shall be no more. **1712** Addison *Spect.* No. 471 ⁋4 When the Heavens and Earth shall be no more. **1795** Burke *Corr.* (1844) IV. 296 While I was discussing the merits of a single measure of a government, the government itself was no more. **1821** Clare *Vill. Minstr.* I. 152 Last spring he was living but now he's no more. **1871** Browning *Balaust.* 833 No, for I have to die:..but now, even now, I shall be reckoned among those no more.

2. Never again; nevermore.

1297 R. Glouc. (Rolls) 7823 He wep..& bihet ȝif he moste libbe þat he nolde misdo nammore. **13..** *Guy Warw.* (A.) 414 Go heþen, ..& cum nam-more in mi purpris. *c***1350** *Will. Palerne* 2556 William ne is swete wiȝt seie hem na more. *a***1400–50** *Alexander* 725 (D.), Fro he had hym þis worde sayd he wakens no more. *c***1440** *Alph. Tales* 91 þis old man..bad hur be a gude womman, & temp no mor no men. **1587** *Mirr. Mag., Albanact* vi, Commaunded neuer to retourne no more. **1742** Young *Nt. Th.* I. 7 How happy they who wake no more! **1820** Shelley *Chas. I*, II. 415 The waters..are gone, and can return no more. **1846** Keble *Lyra Innoc.* 235 No more to rest in sabbath shade.

3. To no greater extent; in no greater degree. (Followed by *than.*)

*a***1225** *Ancr. R.* 380 ȝe owen uorte unnen þet no word ne kome of ou, nanmore þen of deade. *a***1300** *Cursor M.* 502 þai mai neuermar held til il, Namar þan þe wick mai to god will. **1340** *Ayenb.* 27 þe enuious ne may ysy þet guod of opren nāmore þanne þe oule..þe zonne. *c***1385** Chaucer *L.G.W.* Prol. 190 No more than of the corne agayn the sheef. **1523** Ld. Berners *Froiss.* I. xxviii. 42 Eche of them..spared no thynge, no more than yf the Kynge of Englande had bene there in proper persone. **1633** Bp. Hall *Occas. Medit.* (1851) 186 Thou..canst no more be absent than not be thyself. **1721** Bradley *Philos. Acc. Wks. Nat.* 130 These Creatures cannot bear Heat no more than the Snails. **1808** Ashe *Trav.* I. 298 We majors, colonels, and generals..are so cheap and common here, that people don't mind us no more than nothing. **1850** Thackeray *Pendennis* xxi, [Laura's eyes] could no more help..looking and shining than one star can help being brighter than another.

4. Just a little; neither.

*c***1400** Maundev. (1839) xx. 221 He schalle not trowe it lightly; and treuly, no more did I my self, til I saughe it. *c***1440** *Alph. Tales* 106 þan þe abbott said; 'No more may þou lett þoghtis to com in þi harte & þi mynde'. *a***1533** Ld. Berners *Huon* lxxxiii. 260 He..durst speake no worde.., and no more durst none of his men. **1598** Shaks. *Merry W.* II. i. 7 You are not yong, no more am I. **1865** Kingsley *Herew.* i, 'I do not understand thee,' quoth the Abbot. And no more he did. **1870** M. Arnold *St. Paul & Protestantism* (1900) 63 You have not righteousness... No more have you, though you think you have.

nomori, var. nomoli.

nomos ('nɒmɒs). *Theol.* [ad. Gr. νόμος usage, custom, law.] The law; a law of life.

1938 P. S. Watson tr. *Nygren's Agape & Eros: Part 2* I. 35 The *Commandment* of love was easier to grasp, and it led back to the Old Testament level, so that Agape was again brought under the scheme of Nomos. **1948** J. L. Adams tr. *Tillich's Protestant Era* iv. 56 The words 'autonomy', 'heteronomy', and 'theonomy' answer the question of the *nomos* or the law of life in three different ways. **1954** *Scottish Jrnl. Theol.* VII. 260 The Church follows Christ as justified, reconciled, and risen with Him, and is therefore differently related to the *nomos*- form of this age.

nomotechnic, -theism, -thesy: see nomo-.

†**nomothete.** *Obs. rare.* [ad. Gr. νομοθέτης.] A lawgiver or legislator.

1586 Sir. E. Hoby *Polit. Disc. Truth* xi. 34 Such officers as were wont to bee in Greece, called Nomothetes. **1641** H. L'Estrange *God's Sabbath* 92 The matter it self was first debated and resolved upon by the Nomothetes or Legislatours in their counsel-house.

nomo'thetic, *a.* [ad. Gr. νομοθετικός.] = next; that pertains to or is concerned with the study or discovery of general (scientific) laws, esp. as contrasted with idiographic study.

1658 Manton *Exp. Jude* 4 Lusts cannot endure to hear of a restraint, and therefore we oppose most Christ's nomothetic power. **1816** Bentham *Chrestomathia* Wks. 1843 VIII. 94 Division of Internal Government and Politics, into Nomothetic..and Aneunomothetic. **1883** [see nomistic]. [**1894**: see *idiographic* adj. s.v. idio-.] **1904** *Jrnl. Philos., Psychol. & Sci. Methods* 21 Jan. 42 This is the same distinction as that made by Windelband under the names nomothetic and idiographic sciences. *a***1943** R. G. Collingwood *Idea of Hist.* (1946) 166 Windelband..laid it down that history and science were two different things... There were two kinds of science..: nomothetic science, which is science in the common sense of the word, and idiographic science, which is history. **1948** *Brit. Jrnl. Psychol.* XXXVIII. 160 (*heading*) Nomothetic and idiographic [perspectives in psychology]... Two aims: the discovery of general laws of mind, or the description..of the unique undivided personality... Well-balanced psychologists ought to keep in mind both the nomothetic and idiographic aims. **1955** F. H. Allport *Theories of Perception* xi. 263 Conditions that are truer to life than those in which the exact or 'nomothetic' laws of nature are sought. **1964** *Listener* 16 Apr. 617/2, I [*sc.* G. Freeland] have coined ..the term 'nomothetic corrections'. This group of corrections is intimately tied up with scientific laws. **1970** *Daily Tel.* 19 Sept. 9/7 Is musicology—or rather *musikwissenschaft*, which means science of music—a nomothetic or an idiographic discipline?. Ought it to emulate physics and concern itself with establishing generally applicable laws or must it, like history, describe what is unrepeatable?

nomo'thetical, *a.* [See prec. and -al[1].] Law-giving; legislative.

1619 T. Morton *Def. Innoc. 3 Cerem.* 60 Nomotheticall authority. **1637** Gillespie *Eng. Pop. Cerem.* III. viii. 123 It includeth no such thing as a nomotheticall power, to prescribe..such sacred..Ceremonies as he shall thinke good. **1683** Renwick *Reply to Langton* in *Serm.* (1776) 576 Not in an authoritative and nomothetical yet in a material and principal sense. **1854** P. Fairbairn *Typol. Script.* (1857) II. III. vii. 189 The nomothetical authority of the Mosiac law is abolished, but its didactical authority remains. **1880** L. Oliphant *Land of Gilead* xiv. 392 The latter..were obliged to adopt their nomothetical laws outwardly.

nomparell, obs. form of nonpareil.

nompere, -peyr, variants of noumpere.

-nomy, a second element in compounds, representing Gr. -νομία (related to νόμος law, νέμειν to distribute), occurring in words either adopted from Greek, as *autonomy* αὐτονομία, *economy* οἰκονομία, *astronomy* ἀστρονομία, *gastronomy* γαστρονομία, or formed on the analogy of these, as *agronomy*, *geonomy*, *phytonomy*, *zoonomy*.

nomyn, obs. pa. pple. of nim *v.*

‖**non** (nɒn). [L. = not.]

1. The first word in a large number of Latin phrases, chiefly legal, some of which have been in more or less frequent use in English contexts. The most important are entered as Main words.

Many others will be found in the Law Dicts. of Cowell, Blount, Bell, Bouvier, and Wharton, and in the Stanford Dictionary of Anglicized Words and Phrases.

†**2.** as *sb.* A negation or prohibition.

1551 Latimer *Serm.* (1562) 116 Neither in chamberyng and wantonnes. Beware of S. Paules *nottes* and *Nons.* For when he saieth *Non*, we cannot make it yea.

†**3.** Short for non placet. Also *attrib.* in ***non-party.***

1679 Wood *Life* 24 Jan., The non partie being most, the bishop was sent for, who though he pleaded hard for his owne man.., yet the non's prevailed. **1712** Hearne *Collect.* (O.H.S.) III. 345 There were a great many Nons, but 'twould not do.

non, obs. form of none, noon, nun.

non- (nɒn), *prefix* (also 4–6 **noun-**, **noon-**, 5 **nom-**, 5–6 **nowne-**, 5–7 **none-**, often written separate), used to express negation. One of the great formative elements in English. The earlier formations were either directly adopted from, or modelled upon, Anglo-French compounds in *noun-* = OF. *non-*, *nom-*, *nun-*, *num-* (mod.F. *non-*):—L. *nōn* 'not' used as a prefix; from about 1500 the predominant form of the prefix is that of the L. *nōn*. It appears first in English towards the end of the 14th c. in *non-power* (Chaucer, Langland, Wyclif), and *non-residence*, *nonsuit* (Wyclif). In the 15th and 16th c. a considerable number of compounds (chiefly nouns of action and gerunds) were in use, most of them being of a legal character. Until about the middle of the 17th c. the compounds formed with *non-* are mostly of a special or technical kind, but from that time the prefix became less restricted in its use and began to be prefixed freely to substantives, adjectives and adverbs, participles, and verbal sbs. (rarely to infinitival forms). To the political and religious movements of the 17th and 18th c. are due many new formations, some of which, as *nonconformist*, *non-juror*, *non-resistance*, have a permanent place in the language.

In the majority of the compounds of *non-* the hyphen is usually retained; but it is commonly omitted in the case of a few, such as *nonconformist*, *nonentity*, *nonsense*, in which the etymology has been to some extent lost sight of. Normally the prefix is unstressed, but in the disyllables *nonage*, *nonclaim*, *nonsense*, *nonsuit*, and in *nonchalance*, *-ant*, *nondescript*, the *non-* receives the stress. It is also liable to be stressed when the compound and the simple word are coupled together, as *to act or 'non-act*, *distribution or 'non-distribution*, *being and 'non-being.*

Formations having an independent status or a continuous history during any period are entered as Main words; a small proportion of the remainder are illustrated in this article, no attempt having been made to represent with any degree of fullness the very extensive development in the use of the prefix during the last hundred years.

1. Prefixed to nouns of action, condition, or quality, as ***non-accomplishment*** = failure to accomplish, ***non-acquaintance*** = want of acquaintance, ***non-adherence*** = the condition or quality of not being adherent. Also ***non-achievement***, ***-activity***, ***-ambiguity***, ***-aspiration***, ***-availability***, ***-candidacy***, ***-class***, ***-commitment***, ***-communication***, ***-commutativeness***, ***-commutativity***, ***-comparability***, ***-comprehension***, ***-conservation***, ***-contemporaneity***, ***-creativity***, ***-deposition***, ***-derivability***, ***-disclosure***, ***-discrimination***, ***-employment***, ***-equilibrium***, ***-equivalence***, ***-finality***, ***-happening***, ***-implication***, ***-inclusion***, ***-independence***, ***-influence***, ***-invitation***, ***-involvement***, ***-occurrence***, ***-pathogenicity***, ***-planarity***, ***-possession***, ***-reality***, ***-reception***, ***-recognition***, ***-recurrence***, ***-simultaneity***, ***-stationarity***, ***-stoich(e)iometry***, ***-support***, ***-transitivity***, ***-uniformity***, ***-uniqueness***, ***-universality***, ***-validity***, etc.

c **1465** *Plumpton Corr.* (Camden) 15 Excuseing the *non accomplishment of her desire in such wis as yee can well enough. **1934** Webster, *Nonachievement. **1946** *Nature* 17 Aug. 236/2 The residual carbon dioxide in the inhibited oxidation gases..is shown in the graph by the non-achievement of 100 per cent inhibition. **1884** *Manch. Exam.* 27 Aug. 6/3 Owing to their *non-acquaintance with the English tongue. **1752** Carte *Hist. Eng.* III. 282 Alarming her with the evil consequences of her *non-acquiescence. **1836–41** Brande *Chem.* (ed. 5) 367 The *nonaction of this gas on copper-leaf. **1897** Gladstone *E. Crisis* 2 The concerted action, or non-action of the Powers of Europe. **1847** W. Smith tr. *Fichte's Characteristics Present Age* 6 Every one would accept the proof of *non-existence* at a particular time, as equivalent to the proof of **non-activity* at the same time. **1715** *Life Earl Halifax* in *Wks.* 208 The same Members could not be as much as suspected for *Non-adherence to the same Principles. **1848** Lindley *Introd. Bot.* (ed. 4) II. 45 This character of the aril, viz., its non-adherence to the testa. **1414** *Rolls of Parlt.* IV. 58/1 The forseide Priour and Chanons hav cleymed of hem.. custumes, for her singuler profyt and *non avauntage to the Kyng. **1862** Ansted *Channel Isl.* I. i. 8 The practical difference between them amounts to little more than a *non-agreement as to their rates of decomposition. **1766** Blackstone *Comm.* II. xx. 301 The feodal doctrine of *non-alienation without the consent of the heir. **1949** A. Pap *Elem. Analytical Philos.* iii. 74 How could we..insure *non-ambiguity of a proper name? *a* **1797** Walpole *Geo. II* (1847) I. v. 138 What he had said regarded the clause of *non-amotion. **1579** *Reg. Privy Council Scot.* III. 187 Finding himself be his *non-apprehensioun disappointit of his weikit purpois. **1808** T. Chalmers in *Mem.* (1849) V. 133, I..am much mortified by the *non-arrival of my copies. **1821** Mar. & R. L. Edgeworth *Mem.* I. 59 My articulation, or *nonarticulation of the letter R. **1958** E. Fischer-Jørgensen in Saporta & Bastian *Psycholinguistics* (1961) 140/1 The *non-aspiration of final /t/ and the non-closure of final /d/ should be considered as part of the syllable boundary. **1784** R. Bage *Barham Downs* II. 16, I got him to repeat this maxim, and then ventured upon a little *non-assentation. **1731–8** Swift *Pol. Conversat.* Introd. 57 The Mind being wholly taken up, and the Consequence of *Non-attention so fatal. **1975** *Aviation Week & Space Technol.* 17 Feb. 24/3 *Non-availability of spare parts in many areas. **1985** *Data Communications* Jan. 126/2 The uninterrupted period of time that network or computer resources are..available to a user; time between failures or periods of nonavailability. **1968** *Gainesville* (Florida) *Sun* 16 Jan., All this randomly built superstructure of his *non-candidacy could..come tumbling down. **1971** *New Yorker* 4 Dec. 47 In addition to repeatedly asserting his non-candidacy, [Senator Edward] Kennedy had made some forceful speeches in recent months. **1940** W. V. Quine *Math. Logic* 123 The distinguishing feature of *non-class *y* is this: '*x* ∈ *y*' amounts, for every object *x*, to '*x* = *y*'. **1973** 'Trevanian' *Loo Sanction* (1974) 11 A dour young man.. flaunting his non-class by drinking beer. **1853** J. Martineau *Ess.*, etc. (1891) III. 472 Infinite non-commencement and infinite *non-close are impossible to thought. **1827** Sir J. Barrington *Pers. Sk.* II. 20 A snap or a *non-cock is to be considered a miss-fire. **1788** T. Taylor *Proclus* II. 157 Such as affirm the *non-coincidence of lines extended from angles less than two right. **1650** *Exercit. conc. Usurped Powers* 72 The people's *non-commitance of any power to their Representees. **1959** *Brno Studies in English* I. 133 This is not so much *non-commitment..as withdrawal. **1962** W. Nowottny *Lang. Poets Use* iv. 94 A tone of non-commitment is established. **1781** Lutwyche *Reports* Table of Entries, Plea of *non-commorancy. **1960** *News Chron.* 28 July 6/6 Critics talk a lot about the problem of *non-communication amongst my characters. **1973** *N.Y. Times* 11 Aug., One is struck by the talent of the lawyers for non-communication. **1940** *Mind* XLIX. 459 It is not always the case that *ab* = *ba*. This *non-commutativeness is quite essential to its use in physics. **1964** E. A. Power *Introd. Quantum Electrodynamics* vi. 83 The order of the factors **p** and **A**(**q**) in the first term of (56) is immaterial despite the *non-commutativity of p_a and q_a in the quantum theory. **1909** W. James *Pluralistic Universe* 335 The only real relations in comparison are absolute identity and absolute *non-comparability. **1973** *Computers & Humanities* VII. 158 A. A. Lyne..spoke on 'The Problem of Non-Comparability of Word-Frequency Counts'. **1741** Richardson *Pamela* II. 311 He was..out of Humour at her supposed *non-complaisance. **1910** *Daily Chron.* 3 Mar. 4/4 To *non-comprehension of the true meaning of that golden rule..can be traced practically every defect of our system. **1962** *Times* 15 Feb. 15/2 Across a vast abyss of non-comprehension. *a* **1641** Bp. Mountagu *Acts & Mon.* (1642) 532 Her [*sc.* the Virgin's] *non-conception of humane seed. *a* **1716** South *Serm.* (1744) X. 85 It sees the *non-concludency of those arguments, that it rested upon before. **1830** Lindley *Nat. Syst. Bot.* 207 The *non-connivence of their anthers. **1941** *Physical Rev.* LIX. 441 A natural consequence of this *nonconservation of spin angular momentum is a dependence of the scattering cross section upon the spin magnetic quantum number of the incident beam. **1968** M. S. Livingston *Particle Physics* vii. 146 As another example of nonconservation of parity in a weak interaction, it shows a correlation between spin and direction for the product photon. **1691** Norris *Pract. Disc.* 307 A *Non-consideration of his [*sc.* God's] Presence and Inspection. **1657** *North's Plutarch, Add. Lives* 52 Her very Palace was distastefull unto her, by reason of the *non con-society of her dead Lord and King. **1950** F. E. Zeuner *Dating Past* (ed. 2) iv. 78 This evidence bears out what has been said on p. 54, that the land rose faster than the sea-level in the northern Baltic region, and that the *non-contemporaneity of the maximum in different parts of the Baltic may be due to this fact. **1969** Bennison & Wright *Geol. Hist. Brit. Isles* i. 5 The noncontemporaneity of geological events..makes some scale of reference imperative. **1677** Gilpin *Demonol.* (1867) 247 The suspicions of *non-conversion are more common, and not so dangerous. **1673** S. Parker *Reproof Reh. Transp.* 416 Some ..protest their *non-conviction of any guilt. **1831** Scott *Let.* in *Lockhart* (1839) X. 126 Our habits of *non-correspondence are so firmly established. **1957** P. Suppes *Introd. Logic* 154 Criterion of *Non-creativity. **1965** B. Mates *Elem. Logic* xi. 190, *ϕ* will satisfy the criterion of non-creativity. **1864** Pusey *Lect. Daniel* (1876) 494 They.. assume..the *non-credibility of the Gospels. *a* **1859** De Quincey *Posth. Wks.* (1893) II. 154 If the *non-culture of the human race allowed them to break out into war with little or no preparation. **1698–9** in Willis & Clark *Cambridge* (1886) II. 105 The great difficulties which soon arose from the *non-currency of Money. **1845** Whately *Logic* (1850) III. §17 146 This *non-decision is practically the very same thing as a decision in favour of the existing state of things. **1742** Gilbert *Cases Equity* 254 The Plaintiff, by assigning a particular Breach in the *Non-delivery at any one Time, may bring the whole Matter in Question. **1843** Mill *Logic* I. III. ix. 499 The presence or absence of an uninterrupted communication with the sky causes the deposition or *non-deposition of dew. **1969** Bennison & Wright *Geol. Hist. Brit. Isles* i. 8 The older strata may be tilted..during the period of non-deposition. **1957** A. N. Prior *Time & Modality* ii. 14 If we wish to express the *non-derivability of *CMpp*. **1964** G. Kreisel in Benacerraf & Putnam *Philos. of Math.* 157 Hilbert emphasized the consistency problem which is so to speak the weakest non-derivability result. **1835–6** *Todd's Cycl. Anat.* I. 507/1 In consequence of *non-development of the pelvis. **1651** C. Cartwright *Cert. Relig.* I. 41 In vaine is their excuse, if *non-disagreement in fundamentalls. **1768–74** Tucker *Lt. Nat.* (1834) II. 486 The *non-discernment, if owing to inability, being not a wickedness committed. **1908** *Westm. Gaz.* 24 July 8/4 Defendants resisted the plaintiff's claim under the policy upon the grounds of the misstatement and *non-disclosure. **1950** *Mind* LIX. 248 There is always a possibility..of non-disclosure or lies. **1923** *19th Cent.* Jan. 135 Shinto favours racial *nondiscrimination. **1958** *Listener* 16 Jan. 88/1 To say that the Communists, who claim world brotherhood,.. practise non-discrimination in the fullest sense on the racial side, [etc.]. **1540** in *Eng. Gilds* (1870) 256 A reasonable accompt of the distribucioun and *non-distribucioun thereof. **1845** Whately *Logic* (1850) I. §5. 28 The fallacy.. consisting in the 'non-distribution of the middle term'. **1864** Pusey *Lect. Daniel* iii. 103 The objection tacitly assumes the thing to be proved, the *non-Divinity of prophecy. **1663** Boyle *Usef. Exp. Nat. Philos.* I. v. 108 The Divisibleness or *non-Divisibility of each Corporeal Substance into infinite Material Parts. **1683** J. Corbet *Free Actions* III. xxviii. 48 Though the meer *Non-donation of more special..Grace be arbitrary with God. **1843** Mill *Logic* II. v. iv. 398 It is not the nature of the faculties..but the *non-employment of them. **1966** A. Battersby *Math. in Management* iii. 74 The quick answer 'use machinery wherever possible because it is cheaper' is not necessarily the best when the non-employment of labour is unjustified on social or moral grounds. **1864** Bowen *Logic* v. 139 We have an equation, or *non-equation, established between these Terms. **1790** *Phil. Trans.* LXXX. 526 The *non-equilibrium of the particles in motion. **1938** J. Newton *Introd. Metallurgy* vi. 162 The iron-carbon equilibrium diagram..is the best diagram to illustrate the meaning of equilibrium and non-equilibrium. **1971** *Contrib. Mineral. & Petrol.* XXXII. 165 Some magnetites..that show a wide variation of Cr content also give very erratic oxygen isotopic results, suggesting non-equilibrium. **1894** J. N. Keynes *Stud. & Exerc. Formal Logic* (ed. 3) II. iii. 111 To establish their *non-equivalence we may proceed as follows. **1955** A. N. Prior *Formal Logic* 212 The connected non-equivalence of $\Pi x M\phi x$ and $M\Pi x\phi x$. *a* **1676** Hale *Prim. Orig. Mankind* I. iv. (1677) 99 The *Non-eternity of Mankind. **1760** *Chron.* in *Ann. Reg.* 94 The *non-exercise of the mind contributes not a little to the increase of the scurvy. **1647** H. More *Song of Soul* II. iii. III. xviii, Rash man that doth inferre negation From thy dead ear, or *non-experience. **1896** W. Caldwell *Schopenhauer's System* viii. 370 Religion alone pretends to answer the question, why it is that *non-finality and non-attainment and illusoriness seem to characterise all human experience and all human life. **1971** D. Crystal *Linguistics* 133 The.. sentence ends with a rising movement.. , giving the impression of non-finality. **1740** Cheyne *Regimen* 181 This ..supposition of God's..*Non-foreknowledge of his finite free Intelligences future actions. **1658–9** in *Burton's Diary* (1828) IV. 176 All that sit on that foot of *non-freedom or non-residency. **1802–12** Bentham *Ration. Judic. Evid.* (1827) II. 494 The amount of damage..that might result from the *non-fulfilment of it [*sc.* a contract]. **1656** Jeanes *Mixt. Schol. Div.* 15 A certaine perswasion of the *non futurition of the evill. **1657** Baxter *Pres. Thoughts* 11 It is not the Impossibility but the *non-futurity that God decreeth. **1664** Power *Exp. Philos.* II. 136 His third Argument is from the *Non-gravitation of the Mercurial Cylinder. **1892** W. James *Coll. Ess. & Rev.* (1920) 319 Our conscious states are temporal *events*,..the conditions of whose happening or *non-happening from one moment to another, lie certainly in large part in the physical world. **1968** *Gainesville* (Florida) *Sun* 13 Feb., The [TV] medium's extraordinary ability to suggest that a true happening resides in a non-happening. **1808** *Phil. Trans.* XCIX. 36 The *non-identity of the common electricity, and that given out by the Voltaic apparatus. **1878** H. MacColl in *Proc. London Math. Soc.* IX. 180 Thus in a *non-implication, as in an implication, the rule is *Transpose and change signs.* **1887** J. N. Keynes *Stud. & Exerc. Formal Logic* (ed. 2) II. ii. 77 The implication or non-implication of existence in propositions. **1932** Lewis & Langford *Symbolic Logic* ix. 281 Facts like these about non-implication and independence. **1972** M. A. Boden *Purposive Explanation in Psychol.* viii. 318 The logical characteristics of indeterminacy,..and non-implication of embedded clauses. *a* **1703** Burkitt *On. N.T.*, Mark iv. 25 He that hides his talent..is in danger of being punished severely for the *nonimprovement of it. **1885** J. Veitch *Institutes of Logic* §383 *All* are thus excluded, through the *non-inclusion of *any.* **1952** *Mind* LXI. 526 We interpret the non-inclusion of a conjunction as the exclusion of one *or* the other of the conjuncts. **1677** Grew *Exper. Sol. Salts* in *Anat. Plants* (1682) 296 Whether the Solution of a smaller quantity of several Salts, doth consist with the *non-increase of the bulk of the Water? **1874** W. Wallace tr. *Hegel's Logic* 293 A mean which combines in itself the centrality with the *non-independence of the objects. **1965** Hughes & Londey *Elem. Formal Logic* xviii. 131 (*heading*) PM (IV)—independence and non-independence. **1838** W. Howitt *Rural Life of Eng.* I. I v. 79 Those who..believe in the nonsense of the economists on the *non-influence of absenteeism. **1907** W. James *Pragmatism* iv. 138 All these systems of influence or non-influence may be listed under the general problem of the world's *causal unity.* **1824** Miss Mitford *Village* Ser. I. (1863) 151 To..leave our daughters..to Mrs. C.'s system of *non-instruction. **1646** Browne *Pseud. Ep.* III. xxi. 157 Where we finde such Instruments, wee may with strictnesse expect their actions, and where we discover them not, wee may with safety conclude the *non-intention of their operations. **1688** Norris *Love* I. iv. 35 If in this Absolute *non-invincibility he will have our..Freewill to consist. **1908** *Daily Chron.* 24 July 4/3 Invitations would be robbed of their grace, and *non-invitations be invested quite unnecessarily with the air of a slight. **1940** *Economist* 11 May 853/1 Japan's policy, for all her declarations of '*non-involvement' (a new type of non-belligerency?) is bound to be that of fishing in troubled waters. **1970** *Guardian* 31 Dec. 7/8 A devastating..argument for non-involvement as a starting-point for social research. c1661 *Papers on Alter. Prayer-Bk.* 95 That its uncharitableness to punish any Infants for the Parents faults, and that a *non-liberation is such a punishment. **1866** Odling *Anim. Chem.* 142 The loss, or rather non-liberation, of force resulting from the merely half-burning..of the excess of carbon. **1846** Landor *Imag. Conv.* Wks. 1853 II. 73/2 Johnson's remarks..on the *non-materiality or non-immateriality of Satan. **1863** De Morgan *Pref.* in *From Matter to Spirit* 12 The civilised man of *non-nescience—a word I take the liberty of using for science, since two negatives make an affirmative. **1741** Richardson *Pamela* II. 212 Her *Non-observance of my Lessons. **1646** Browne *Pseud. Ep.* I. ii. 6 The Pelagians.., who peremptorily maintaining they can fulfill the whole Law, will insatisfactorily condemne the *non-observation of one. **1807** R. Kirwan *Logick* I. 178 Their occurrence or *non-occurence being consonant to common observation. **1963** J. Lyons *Structural Semantics* i. 8 The non-occurrence of the large set of grammatical, but nonsensical, sentences. **1646** Browne *Pseud. Ep.* VII. xviii. 383 So must..the *non opposition of our reasons procure our..acquiescence in the other. **1971** *Nature* 12 Mar. 97/8 It should..be possible to improve greatly the efficacy of live cholera vaccines by preparing them from bacteria in which *non-pathogenicity has been induced by a very specific genetic mutation. a**1635** Naunton *Fragm. Reg.* (Arb.) 51 A violent indulgencie of the Queen..towards this Lord; all which argued a *non-perpetuity. **1967** A. Battersby *Network Analysis* (ed. 2) xi. 177 There are, however, some minor ones [*sc.* obstacles], including integer restrictions and *non-planarity. **1687** Dryden *Hind. & P.* II. 462 No union, they pretend, but in *Non-Popery. **1843** Mill *Logic* I. I. ii. 52 The *non-possession of any given attribute is also an attribute, and may receive a name as such. **1959** D. Cooke *Lang. Mus.* ii. 69 The feeling is..of non-possession, non-acceptance, need. **1674** Hickman *Hist. Quinquart.* (ed. 2) 38 Any who was under a *non-predestination unto effectual and infallible means of eternal life. **1808** Toller *Tithes* (1816) iii. 53 By *non-presentation of a vicar for a long series of years. **1879** M. Pattison *Milton* 88 All artists have intervals on *non-productiveness. **1650** Bp. Hall *Cases Consc.* Addit. i. 397 To give Testimony to the *non-prohibition of this marriage. **1842** Lover *Handy Andy* x. 95 His..*non-pronunciation of the letter R. **1680** *Lond. Gaz.* No. 1522/4 [He] was, in regard of his long Imprisonment, and *non-Prosecution, Bailed out. **1650** *Non-protection [see non-obedience]. **1572-3** *Reg. Privy Council Scot.* II. 195 In respect of *non-publiccatioun of the said abstinence. **1495** *Act 11 Hen. VII*, c. 2 §3 The penaltie lymytted..to be forfeited by any officer..for *noun punysshement of Vagaboundes. **1571** Golding *Calvin on Ps.* xlv. 7 How great myscheefs bred of non-punishment and libertie. **1583** *Reg. Privy Council Scot.* III. 601 Tueching the *non-persute of Alexander Lawder. **1885** *Law Times* LXXVIII. 385/1 The *non-rateability of empty houses. a**1866** J. Grote *Treat. Moral Ideals* (1876) 360 We may assume four degrees of reality or *non-reality in the moral ideals. **1909** W. James *Pluralistic Universe* iv. 234 Zeno..has no alternative but to say that our intellect repudiates motion as a non-reality. **1924** W. E. Johnson *Logic* III. i. 7 A verbal formula that.. gives the true test of non-reality. **1802-12** Bentham *Ration. Judic. Evid.* (1827) V. 656 To the account of loss, or of *non-receipt of gain. **1878** Trollope *Is he Popenjoy?* II. ii. 20 Mr. Holdenough had made no attempt after the reception—or rather *non-reception—awarded to his wife. **1963** *Times Lit. Suppl.* 1 Mar. 152/4 His [*sc.* Chopin's] reception—or non-reception—by the English. **1659** Rushw. *Hist. Coll.* I. 537 This Message for *non-recess, was not well pleasing to the House. **1539** *Act 31 Hen. VIII*, c. 13 §16 For mysrecitall or *non-recitall of leases. **1885** *Law Times Rep.* LI. 803/1 The non-recital of the Act of 1845. **1838** J. S. Mill in *London & Westm. Rev.* Aug. 484 His *non-recognition of them does not put them out of existence. **1848** Mill *Pol. Econ.* III. ii. §3 (1876) 271 The complete non-recognition and implied denial of it. **1862** Bagehot *Coll. Works* (1965) II. 257 Its non-recognition by what is called the public. **1946** *Nature* 9 Nov. 679/1 A further factor which stems progressive action is the non-recognition of the educational potentialities of museums. **1965** A. J. P. Taylor *Eng. Hist. 1914-45* x. 373 In February 1932 Stimson, the American secretary of state, announced that the United States would not recognize territorial changes brought about by force... 'Non-recognition' became a League [of Nations] principle. **1847** A. De Morgan *Formal Logic* xiii. 278 The demand for *non-recurrence of words arises from the public (I beg its pardon) not knowing how to read. **1911** J. Ward *Realm of Ends* xv. 335 In place of the existing certainty of evil, there will be an even chance of its non-recurrence. **1824** Miss Mitford *Village* Ser. I. (1863) 119 Any little *non-resemblance may be noted after-wards. **1855** Kingsley *Westward Ho!* xxi, The doctor talked mere science, or *nonscience, about humours, complexions, and animal spirits. **1412-20** Lydg. *Chron. Troy* IV. xxix, Their hope is fully put abake And dispeired in *nonsecurytye. **1855** H. Spencer *Princ. Psychol.* II. v. 121 The simultaneity or *non-simultaneity of certain events. **1904** *Mind* XIII. 214 The non-simultaneity of perception and object, where internal perception is concerned, need cause no difficulty. **1953** C. E. Bazell *Linguistic Form* 44 Non-simultaneity has different degrees of validity. **1643** Milton *Divorce* II. iv. Wks. 1851 IV. 74 If we cannot be contented with his *non-solution. **1965** *Math. in Biol. & Med.* (Med. Res. Council) IV. 158 *Non-stationarity of the EEG signals during each of the 10-second epochs does not pose the same limitations. **1974** *Jrnl. of Business* (Chicago) XLVII. 518 (*heading*) Investigations of nonstationarity in prices. **1962** Simpson & Richards *Physical Princ. Junction Transistors* iii. 35 In the latter materials any unbalance (*non-stoichiometry) between constituents degrades physical properties such as mobility and lifetime to a marked extent. **1763** Burn *Eccles. Law* (1767) I. 409 He was suspended, and after-wards upon his *non-submission deprived. **1909** *Daily Chron.* 20 Jan. 6/2 The English woman makes a charge of *non-support against her husband. **1481** Botoner *Oracion of Flammeus Cayus* (Caxton) e8 They euery day put it in peryll and *nonsurete. **1833** Coleridge *Table-t.* 16 Feb., Wordsworth and Goethe..have this peculiarity of utter *non-sympathy with the subjects of their poetry. a**1641** Bp. Mountagu *Acts & Mon.* (1642) 82 Iudah transgressed, and the Promise failed, as not to be verified but upon Supposition of *non-transgression. **1939** *Mind* XLVIII. 532 Obviously true of *non-transitivity since that is 'ambiguous' with respect to transitivity or intransitivity. **1974** *Sci. Amer.* Oct. 120/2 If the nontransitivity is so counter-intuitive as to boggle the mind, we have what is called a nontransitive paradox. **1902** *Encycl. Brit.* XXVIII. 456/2 *Non-uniformity of convergence of the series does not necessarily imply discontinuity in the sum. **1962** Simpson & Richards *Physical Princ. Junction Transistors* vi. 116 For high-power transistors, other factors such as the non-uniformity of current distribution across the base region may become important. **1957** J. D. O'Connor in Saporta & Bastian *Psycholinguistics* (1961) 102/1 The acceptance of the *nonuniqueness of phonemic solutions. **1974** *Physics Bull.* Dec. 587/3 Questions of nonuniqueness and stability in nonlinear continuum mechanics. **1846** J. D. Morell *Hist. View Philos.* I. ii. 102 He attempts to prove their *non-universality. **1893** W. Minto *Logic* 70 The expression of Quantity, that is, of Universality or non-universality, is all-important. **1600** W. Watson *Decacordon* (1602) 343 The *non validity of bulles. **1952** W. V. Quine *Methods of Logic* §9. 50 Interchange of equivalents..preserves consistency, nonvalidity, nonimplication, and nonequivalence. **1964** P. F. Anson *Bishops at Large* viii. 271 The validity or non-validity of Anglican orders. **1683** J. Corbet *Free Actions* I. 5 Between Volition and Nolition there is a middle thing, viz. *Non-volition.

2. a. Prefixed to agent-nouns and designations of persons and objects, as ***non-abstainer*** = one who is not an abstainer or does not abstain, ***non-accent*** = absence or lack of accent. Also ***non-actor, -addict, -body, -breeder, -candidate, -Christian, -clitic, -cognitivist, -dancer, -drinker, -driver, -electrolyte, -fact, -friend, -Jew, -joiner, -linguist, -motorist, -musician, -owner, -participant, -people, -philosopher, -reader, -scientist, -self, -sentence, -slave-holder, -socialist, -speaker, -structuralist, -swimmer, -theist, -theorem, -visualizer, -writer***, etc.; **non-se'cretor**, a person whose saliva and other secretions do not contain his blood-group antigens.

1882 *Med. Temp. Jrnl.* L. 53 Any thoughtful person, whether abstainer or *non-abstainer. **1872** *Routledge's Ev. Boy's Ann.* 73 'Incompetence'..takes an accent on the 'com', and a sort of sub-accent—different from a *non-accent—on the 'tence'. **1937** *Times* 17 Aug. 8/3 The air of reality, the judicious use of non-actors, the social consciousness of the Russian film. **1955** *Publ. Amer. Dial. Soc.* xxiv. 34 The natural revulsion which *nonaddicts feel toward addicts. **1787** Hawkins *Johnson* 166 The instruction of *non-adults in the elements of literature. **1802-12** Bentham *Ration. Judic. Evid.* (1827) I. 506 What the *non-advocate is hanged for, the advocate is paid for. **1632** H. Seile *Augustus* 34 His being a *Non agent in the busines, would bring his honor off without staine. **1933** Dylan Thomas *Lett.* (1966) 72 The life of the *non-body..is capable..of creating an artistic progeny. **1949** G. Ryle *Concept of Mind* vi. 189 Perhaps it is because of the absurdity of such collocations that so many people have felt driven to describe a person as an association between a body and a non-body. **1944** J. S. Huxley *On Living in Revolution* ix. 99 About 17,000 breeding pairs: with the *non-breeders, about 40,000. **1950** *Chem. Engin. Progress* XLVI. 112/1 The nonbreeders are pointed essentially toward power production. **1967** *Time* 22 Sept. 22 (*heading*) The *non-candidates. **1972** *Daily Colonist* (Victoria, B.C.) 12 Jan. 16/5 Miami—Sen. Edward Kennedy, a steadfast noncandidate, was one of a dozen Democrats whose names have been entered in the..primary. **1671** A. Woodhead *Consid. Council of Trent* xv. 240 Nor may such separation be understood from Infidels, Heathens, or *non-Christians only. **1941** W. Temple *Citizen & Churchman* iv. 68 Children grow up in it who are schoolfellows of non-Christians. a**1871** Grote *Eth. Fragm.* vi. (1876) 230 Aristotle's ideas are miserably defective as regards obligation towards *non-citizens. **1949** *Nonclitic [see additive *sb.*]. **1952** *Mind* LXI. 546 The *non-cognitivists are usually regarded as a relatively homogeneous group. **1963** R. Carnap in P. A. Schilpp *Philos. R. Carnap* 1008 Both cognitivists and non-cognitivists agree that beliefs play a very important role in the origin of attitudes and decisions. **1965** Noncognitivist [see imperativism]. **1638** Featley *Strict. Lyndom.* I. 135 Priests..in the institution of this Sacrament..were *nonconficients. a**1631** Donne *Serm.* lvii. 579 All *Non-confitents, That thinke not of confessing their sinnes at all. **1643** *Plain English* 23 The Ordinance for assessing the *Non-contributors. a**1680** Charnock *Attrib. God* (1834) I. 527 If there were any thing ..in the whole creation, or *non-creation,..unknown to him. **1636** Brathwait *Rom. Emp.* 93 Being an Infidel and *non-credent. **1863** Trollope *Rachel Ray* I. vii. 136 Now the room was partially cleared, the *non-dancers being pressed back. **1868** Pardon *Card Player* 16 The *non-dealer then cuts the pack into two parts. **1929** L. Bettany in W. J. Temple *Diaries* p. lxxiv, Bored as a Whig, as a *non-drinker, as a scholar, and as an opponent of blood sports, by the only society he could generally enter. **1975** E. Mosbacher tr. *Herlin's Commemorations* 4 A tall, thin, fair man.., a non-smoker and non-drinker. **1953** *Essays in Criticism* III. 422 The customary impression of the *non-driver, that handling a car by night involves merely the switching on of headlights, and the turning of a wheel. **1891** *Jrnl. Chem. Soc.* LX. II. 971 (*heading*) Freezing points of dilute aqueous solutions of *non-electrolytes. **1964** N. G. Clark *Mod. Org. Chem.* i. 4 With salts very much in mind, he probably associates inorganic chemistry with electrolytes... However,..this branch of chemistry embraces..many compounds which neither dissolve in water nor produce ions, i.e. typical non-electrolytes. **1884** *Bookseller* 7 Oct. 1002/1 A reproduction..so closely similar in form and appearance as to appear to *non-experts one of the originals. **1926** Fowler *Mod. Eng. Usage* 576/1 Utopia, the realm of *non-fact or the imaginary. **1964** *Listener* 9 Jan. 48/2 Our opinions..should not be based on non-facts, or dubious facts. **1886** *Mind* Jan. 29 A non-god, a non-spirit, a non-person, a *non-form. **1622** Malynes *Anc. Law-Merch.* 430 It is vniust to punish all promiscuously as well frauders as *non frauders. **1760** T. Hutchinson *Hist. Mass.* i. (1765) 147 A petition..from about five and twenty *non-freemen. **1971** *Harper's Mag.* Sept. 57 'There are people here who are not our friends.' The *nonfriends were expelled. **1973** *Jrnl. Genetic Psychol.* CXXIII. 70 Cliques of friends and nonfriends. **1687** *Lond. Gaz.* No. 2282/1 Though of somewhat differing Persuasions in *Non-fundamentals. **1818** Cobbett *Pol. Reg.* XXXIII. 89 All Journeymen and Labourers,..whether *non-house-holders or house-holders. **1870** *Sat. Rev.* 2 Apr. 443 All *non-infallibilists are but half-Catholics. **1828** Miss Mitford *Village* Ser. III. (1863) 4 The grief of the children on losing this most indulgent *non-instructress. **1967** W. Q. de Funiak *American-British Dict.* 115 **Non-Jew*, Gentile. **1973** R. Perry *Nowhere Man* 6 For a non-Jew to have risen so high [in Israel] was testimony enough to his ability. **1964** R. Miliband in I. L. Horowitz *New Sociology* 78 Mills was a determined *non-joiner, with an intense dislike of togetherness. **1974** *Listener* 14 Feb. 210/2 It was an efficient way of getting people into a group, turning non-joiners into joiners. **1936** *Language* XII. 93 *Non-linguists..constantly forget that a speaker is making noise, and credit him, instead, with the possession of impalpable 'ideas'. **1965** *English Studies* Feb. 58 A terminology as simple and as familiar to the non-linguist as possible. **1908** *Westm. Gaz.* 31 Dec. 4/1 *Non-motorists can join on equal terms. **1936** *Discovery* Apr. 108/2 Even the non-motorist may enjoy the adventure, as a comfortable bus service has been established. **1949** *Penguin Music Mag.* Feb. 40 This is utterly meaningless to a *non-musician, and obvious and therefore unnecessary to a musician. **1754** *Ess. Manning Fleet* 27 The Luxuries, or *Non-necessaries of Life. **1912** Belloc *Servile State* 3 This principle of compulsion applied against the *non-owners. **1948** *Mind* LVII. 228 The political opinions of automobile-owners are not very symptomatic of the political opinions of non-owners. **1883** 'Mark Twain' *Life on Mississippi* 379 Could you come nearer to reproducing it [*sc.* the siege of Vicksburg] to the imagination of a *non-participant? **1971** *Jrnl. Gen. Psychol.* LXXXV. 266 All three categories (doublers, singlers, nonparticipants) are compared. **1967** B. Kaufman in S. Henderson *Understanding New Black Poetry* (1973) III. 206, I am writing these lines to the responsible *non-people. **1969** *Guardian* 26 Sept. 11/2 His shiny, plastic world of nonpeople attending nonevents. **1897** W. James *Will to Believe* 210 In all this the philosopher is just like the rest of us *non-philosophers. **1956** F. C. Copleston in H. D. Lewis *Contemp. Brit. Philos.* 122 By the term 'ordinary man' ..I mean simply the non-philosopher. **1711** G. Hickes *Two Treat. Chr. Priesth.* (1847) I. 272 The mission..which the ministers of some Presbyterian Churches..derive from *non-presbyters or mere lay-men. **1857** R. Tomes *Amer. in Japan* ix. 210 Most of the higher classes..form a large body of indolent *non-producers. **1884** tr. *Lotze's Logic* 77 Any subject, whatever it may mean, must be either *Q* or *non-*Q*, either straight or not-straight. **1857** Trollope *Barchester T.* xxxv, The quality..were to eat a breakfast, and the *non-quality were to eat a dinner. **1938** S. Beckett *Murphy* 162 Murphy, a strict *non-reader. **1964** M. Critchley *Developmental Dyslexia* iv. 16 Monroe, too, preferred the old-fashioned phonic approach, saying darkly that it was better to be a slow reader than a non-reader. **1848** Mill *Pol. Econ.* II. li. §3 Collaterals have no real claims, but in cases which may be just as strong in the case of *non-relatives. **1600** W. Watson *Decacordon* (1602) 109 A..dissembling wilinesse, with a relation to Atheisme or a *non-religion. a**1653** Gouge *Comm. Heb.* vi. 8 The opposition is..between Saints and *non-Saints. **1897** W. James *Will to Believe* 320 We all, scientists and *non-scientists, live on some inclined plane of credulity. **1959** C. P. Snow *Two Cultures* i. 5 The non-scientists have a rooted impression that the scientists are shallowly optimistic. **1950** *Sci. News* XV. 111 Most people secrete the appropriate blood group substances (antigens) in bodily secretions such as saliva and tears. About one-seventh of the population, however, do not do this, and are called '*non-secretors'. **1971** J. Z. Young *Introd. Study Man* xl. 586 Those who get duodenal ulcers include more group O than would be expected. Non-secretors are more liable to the disease than secretors. **1874** J. Cunningham *New Theory of Knowing* 98 The bodily organism is *the 'debateable land' between self and *non-self. **1897** *Daily News* 28 May 8/4 The boat lost at Kingstown had been replaced by a *non-self-righter of the Southport type. **1949** Koestler *Insight & Outlook* viii. 120 Our understanding of other personalities, of the nonself by the self. **1970** *New Scientist* 19 Feb. 345/1 When a foreign protein enters the body the immune system recognizes the invader as non-self and produces antibodies which destroy it. **1940** Bryant & Aiken *Psychology of Eng.* 21 The phrase is any other group of words with a unitary idea, within a sentence or a *nonsentence. **1966** M. Gross in *Automatic Transl. of Lang.* (NATO Summer School, Venice 1962) 124 Certain strings on *V* are clearly understood by speakers of *L* as sentences of *L*, others are clearly recognized as nonsentences. **1832** T. J. Randolph *Speech on Abolition of Slavery* 16 The burden of this defence..is to fall upon the less wealthy class of our citizens; chiefly upon the *non-slaveholder. **1895** G. B. Shaw *Let.* 15 Dec. (1965) 578 The third division falling to Horobin, a *non socialist. **1964** M. A. K. Halliday et al. *Linguistic Sciences* 63 A *non-speaker of the language. **1971** J. Z. Young *Introd. Study Man* xxxvi. 518 The selection of those individuals who were competent in such skills became unusually severe at the expense of the non-speakers. **1874** Heath *Croquet-Player* 59 The *non-striker's ball, off which the croquet is taken. **1952** *Archivum Linguisticum* IV. 89 To the *non-structuralist at least, the book appears to throw less light on the essential nature of the French language than on the present state of structural linguistics. **1849** D. Campbell *Inorg. Chem.* 21 Nitrogen.. being a *non-supporter of respiration. **1932** Blunden *Face of England* 159 Our young men are *non-swimmers. **1962** J. F. Powers *Morte d'Urban* xiii. 285 Paul, the non-swimmer, had probably been thinking of the return voyage when he pinched the life preserver. **1865** Dickens *Mut. Fr.* IV. v, As an out-sider and *non-sympathizer. **1908** *Lit. Guide* 1 Sept. 141/2 This false charge—viz., that *non-theists are morally inferior persons. **1944** W. Temple *Let.* 6 Mar. (1963) 148 But there is a Christian way of living and it is possible for non-theists to appreciate it and try to follow it. **1954** I. M. Copi *Symbolic Logic* vi. 185 A purely formal criterion for distinguishing between theorems and *non-theorems of the system. **1972** A. Church in Rudner & Scheffler *Logic & Art* x. 198 The expected consequences of any assertion, even of a non-theorem. **1648** Gage *West. Ind.* (1655) xv. 102 They will be sure to vent out some *non-truth. **1881** *Times* 17 Jan. 6/2 Many conventional non-truths (to speak kindly) must..

be excused. **1924** B. G. Shaw *St. Joan* p. xxi, Some other people see imaginary diagrams and landscapes..and are thereby able to perform feats of memory and arithmetic impossible to *non-visualisers. **1953** A. Huxley *Let.* 21 June (1969) 676, I am a non-visualizer, and got very little in the way of imagery. **1940** V. Woolf *Writer's Diary* 29 Mar. (1953) 330 All the detail that seems to the *non-writer so easy..to me is torture. **1958** *New Statesman* 15 Nov. 664/2 It might even lure some of the great non-writers in the historical profession into putting pen to paper.

b. *spec.* Prefixed to a sb. with an implication of pretence, to denote a person who, or thing which, is not wholly, adequately, or genuinely what is specified by the sb.; used esp. of forms of art or literature, freq. with the implication that they are new or unconventional forms of the things specified (cf. ANTI-[1] 2 c); as ***non-answer***, ***-architecture***, ***-book***, ***-budget***, ***-conversation***, ***-country***, ***-debate***, ***-drama***, ***-film***, ***-information***, ***-issue***, ***-lecture***, ***-music***, ***-news***, ***-newspaper***, ***-novel***, ***-play***, ***-policy***, ***-problem***, ***-sherry***, ***-story***. See also NON-ART, NON-EVENT, NON-HERO.

1966 *Listener* 21 July 84/1 Public men have learned to apply the technique of the non-answer, a technique in many cases mastered and perfected at the Commons dispatch-box. **1968** *Gainesville* (Florida) *Sun* 11 Mar. 8 They were non-answers—words calculated solely as a physical response to solve the immediate need for some kind of a response generated in a news conference. **1960** *20th-Cent.* Oct. 357 Manchester..is a city with no architecture, only an inert mass of *building*. I believe that the adherents of the Betjemanesque cult of Victorian bad taste find things to admire in examples of Manchester non-architecture. *Ibid.* May 441 Technical language and presentation are necessary; they do not excuse so many non-books. **1972** *Scholarly Publishing* III. 101 Non-books are of several kinds; but their differences notwithstanding, they all share two common features: they tend to be written for market rather than for intellectual reasons, and they are all means rather than ends. **1967** *Observer* 16 Apr. 10/2 The crescendo of the roll call of defeat..came just two days after the Chancellor of the Exchequer's non-Budget. **1960** *News Chron.* 28 July 6/8 Pinter is..a writer over-occupied with the externals of behaviour. The non-conversations..can stale into nothingness. **1970** *Gainesville* (Florida) *Sun* 24 Sept. A6 Jordan was and remains a non-country, created out of sandscape by Britain to pay off a dynastic debt. **1971** *Britannica Bk. of Year* (U.S.) 779/3 *Noncountry*, a country whose size, location, and economic resources are inadequate for economic self-sufficiency and development. **1970** *Times* 21 May 8 The debate on the amendments to end the Indo-China war was the usual non-debate. **1968** *Sat. Rev.* (U.S.) 20 Jan. 33 Most of the noise is made by Mailer, who, as principal player in a turgid nondrama..barks sometimes like a dog and sometimes like a seal. **1963** *Listener* 31 Jan. 201/1 Their [*sc.* the Situationists'] violent and derisory manifestations—such as the non-film *Hurlements en faveur de Sade*—are all intended to create situations..such as will produce certain kinds of human behaviour, usually disgust or disorientation. **1970** *Times* 16 Apr. 5 The ritual exchange of non-information. **1965** *New Society* 9 Sept. 5/3 The brain drain is a non-issue. **1972** *Time* 20 Nov. 28 Unfortunately for the country, there were a lot of non-issues in this campaign. **1953** E. E. Cummings (*title*) I: six nonlectures. **1958** *Publ. Amer. Dial. Soc.* xxx. 41 There has always been a tendency in some circles to regard jazz as non-music. **1969** *Listener* 3 July 26/1 Easily the most interesting and successful work in the programme was the one which kept consistently and coherently to the realms of non-music, and could thus be listened to without difficulty on its own terms. **1963** Non-news [see NON-EVENT]. **1972** *Wall St. Jrnl. Index* 681/1 President Nixon clears desk with sweep of proclamations and orders, other (yawn) nonnews items. **1973** *Nation Rev.* (Melbourne) 31 Aug. 1443/4 There's a new type of newspaper occurring in the world: the *non newspaper*. **1961** *Guardian* 27 Oct. 6/5 Henry Miller's two remarkable non-novels. **1963** *New Yorker* 8 June 120 A non-novel, 'Why Not Try God?' **1968** *Ibid.* 28 Dec. 2 Dustin Hoffman does his brave best to make us believe that this non-play by Murray Schisgal is a touching comedy about the ignominy of young manhood. **1962** E. Cleaver in A. Dundes *Mother Wit* (1973) 20/1 The fallacious stupidity of the non-policy of segregation. **1969** *Guardian* 7 Nov. 12/2 The apostles of relevance..bring massive expertise to bear on non-problems. **1967** *Economist* 5 Aug. 477 The non-sherries have carved themselves out healthy chunks of the fortified wine market on the basis of what they really are, more than by pretending to be the real Spanish thing. **1967** *Gainesville* (Florida) *Sun* 19 Mar., The latest non-story out of New Orleans on the Kennedy assassination 'plot'. **1968** *Listener* 11 July 49/2 The House of Lords vote on Rhodesia ..was the great 'non-story' of recent weeks. **1971** M. Russell *Deadline* xiii. 157 This promises to be the non-story of the month. **1973** L. Heren *Growing up Poor in London* vii. 179 The coming and going of ships were regularly reported by local stringers, but tarantula spiders among the bananas and other non-stories were always available.

3. Prefixed to adjectives, as ***non-absorbable***, ***-academic***, ***-actinic***, ***-adaptive***, ***-addictive***, ***-æsthetic***, ***-alcoholic***, ***-alphabetic***, ***-alphabetical***, ***-ambiguous***, ***-analytic***, ***-antigenic***, ***-aquatic***, ***-aqueous***, ***-articular***, ***-assertive***, ***-assimilable***, ***-atomic***, ***-auditory***, ***-automatic***, ***-axiomatic***, ***-basic***, ***-behavioural***, ***-binary***, ***-biodegradable***, ***-British***, ***-calcareous***, ***-causal***, ***-causative***, ***-cellulosic*** (also as *sb.* (*sc.* fibre)), ***-chemical***, ***-Christian***, ***-chromosomal***, ***-circular***, ***-classical***, ***-cognitive***, ***-coherent***, ***-coital***, ***-collinear***, ***-combustible***, ***-commercial***, ***-communicative***, ***-Communist***, ***-communistic***, ***-commutative***, ***-compact***, ***-competitive***, ***-complementary***, ***-complex***, ***-compound***, ***-conceptual***, ***-concrete***, ***-conscious***, ***-conservative***, ***-consonantal***, ***-constructive***, ***-contiguous***, ***-continuous***, ***-contrastive***, ***-controversial***, ***-corrosive***, ***-critical***, ***-crystalline***, ***-cumulative***, ***-cyclic***, ***-deductive***, ***-degenerate***, ***-delinquent***, ***-demonstrative***, ***-denominational***, ***-denumerable***, ***-derivative***, ***-descriptive***, ***-designative***, ***-deterministic***, ***-diffusible*** (also ***-able***), ***-directive***, ***-discriminatory***, ***-dispersive***, ***-dispositional***, ***-disruptive***, ***-dissipative***, ***-dominant***, ***-dramatic***, ***-economic***, ***-electrolytic***, ***-electronic***, ***-elementary***, ***-emotional***, ***-emphatic***, ***-English***, ***-enumerative***, ***-enzymatic***, ***-enzymic***, ***-equivalent***, ***-ethical***, ***-exclusive***, ***-existential***, ***-explanatory***, ***-explosive***, ***-extensional***, ***-factual***, ***-fatty*** (cf. *non-fat* in 4), ***-final***, ***-finite***, ***-finitist***, ***-fissile***, ***-fissionable***, ***-formal***, ***-functional***, ***-generic***, ***-genetic***, ***-geometrical***, ***-German***, ***-Germanic***, ***-grammatical***, ***-gravid***, ***-habitual***, ***-hæmolytic***, ***-Hermitian***, ***-historical***, ***-homogeneous***, ***-identical***, ***-ideological***, ***-illusory***, ***-imitative***, ***-independent***, ***-indigenous***, ***-individual***, ***-Indo-European***, ***-inductive***, ***-industrial***, ***-infectious***, ***-infective***, ***-inferential***, ***-inflammable***, ***-inflected***, ***-inflexional***, ***-initial***, ***-insightful***, ***-integral***, ***-intellectual***, ***-intuitive***, ***-involved***, ***-irritant***, ***-Jewish***, ***-judg***(e)***mental***, ***-kosher***, ***-lethal***, ***-lexical***, ***-linguistic***, ***-literary***, ***-local***, ***-magnetic***, ***-manual***, ***-marine***, ***-material***, ***-mathematical***, ***-measurable***, ***-mechanical***, ***-medical***, ***-Mendelian***, ***-mental*** (also as *sb.*), ***-mentalistic***, ***-metabolizable***, ***-metaphorical***, ***-metaphysical***, ***-metrical***, ***-migratory***, ***-military***, ***-mimetic***, ***-minimal***, ***-modal***, ***-molecular***, ***-monetary***, ***-motile***, ***-musical***, ***-mystical***, ***-national***, ***-native***, ***-Nazi***, ***-negative***, ***-negligible***, ***-negotiable***, ***-null***, ***-numerical***, ***-nutritious***, ***-observational***, ***-official***, ***-operational***, ***-organic***, ***-pathogenic***, ***-perceptual***, ***-perfective***, ***-perishable*** (also as *sb.*), ***-permissive***, ***-phallic***, ***-phenomenal***, ***-philosophical***, ***-phonemic***, ***-phonetic***, ***-physical***, ***-planar***, ***-poetic***, ***-poisonous***, ***-polarizable***, ***-porous***, ***-predicative***, ***-predictable***, ***-pregnant***, ***-prepositional***, ***-prescriptive***, ***-productive***, ***-professorial***, ***-progressive***, ***-propositional***, ***-psychological***, ***-public***, ***-purposeful***, ***-purposive***, ***-quantitative***, ***-racial***, ***-radioactive***, ***-reactive***, ***-realistic***, ***-reciprocal***, ***-recurrent***, ***-redundant***, ***-relational***, ***-relative***, ***-relativistic***, ***-religious***, ***-renewable***, ***-representational***, ***-representative***, ***-reproducible***, ***-revolutionary***, ***-Roman***, ***-roman***, ***-routine***, ***-saponifiable***, ***-sceptical***, ***-sectarian***, ***-selective***, ***-sensational***, ***-sensory***, ***-sensuous***, ***-sentential***, ***-sharp***, ***-shrinkable***, ***-simultaneous***, ***-social***, ***-socialist***, ***-spatial***, ***-spherical***, ***-stationary***, ***-statistical***, ***-statutory***, ***-steady***, ***-structural***, ***-subjective***, ***-suppurative***, ***-syllogistic***, ***-symbolic***, ***-symmetric***(***al***, ***-synchronous***, ***-synonymous***, ***-syntactic***, ***-systematic***, ***-tautologous***, ***-technical***, ***-teleological***, ***-temporal***, ***-terminal***, ***-theatric***(***al***, ***-theistic***, ***-theological***, ***-theoretical***, ***-tonal***, ***-totalitarian***, ***-toxic***, ***-traditional***, ***-transitive***, ***-turbulent***, ***-typical***, ***-ultimate***, ***-uniform***, ***-urban***, ***-utilitarian***, ***-vacuous***, ***-valid***, ***-veridical***, ***-visual***, ***-vital***, ***-vocal***, ***-vocalic***, ***-vocational***, etc.; **non-'clinical**, not clinical; *esp.* not accompanied by directly observable symptoms; **non-di'mensional**, (of a quantity) = DIMENSIONLESS *a.* 1 d; (of an equation) composed of dimensionless terms; **non-ho'mologous**, not homologous; *spec.* in *Genetics* (cf. HOMOLOGOUS *a.* 4 b); **non-'Ohmic** *Electr.*, not obeying or in accordance with Ohm's law; ˌ**non-stoich(e)io'metric** *a. Chem.*, containing or representing atoms of the different elements in numbers that do not bear a simple ratio to one another.

Such compounds are very common in scientific use.

1808 *Phil. Trans.* XCVIII. 361 A..quantity of *non-absorbable gas. **1797** *Ibid.* LXXXVIII. 16 The only distinction of earths, till about the last half century, was into absorbent and *non-absorbent. **1918** *Nation* (N.Y.) 28 Mar. 335 The real trouble with American universities has been their inability to 'get it across' to the 'man in the street', the 'roughnecks', and all those other fearsome beasts that inhabit the *non-academic jungles. **1937** *Mind* XLVI. 124 That ease, forcefulness, and felicity of expression which made him so welcome a speaker, alike to academic and to non-academic audiences. **1957** C. S. Lewis *Let.* 16 Mar. (1966) 275 In *writing* I do regard all non-academic works.. as being leisure occupations. **1975** *Times* 6 Dec. 3/2 To chop £500,000 off the budget of a college means fewer jobs for staff, academic and non-academic. **1909** *Westm. Gaz.* 16 Oct. 14 The real essential in comfort..is the use of one of the scientifically prepared light screens which gives us all the possible *non-actinic light. **1935** *Discovery* Apr. 97/1 The non-actinic paper in which photographic plates were wrapped. **1883** *Law Rep.* 27 Chanc. Div. 528 Where parties have been merely *non-active. **1646** Sir T. Browne *Pseud. Ep.* IV. xi. 207 The Pygmies of Paracelsus; that is, his *non-Adamicall men, or middle natures betwixt men and spirits. **1926** J. S. Huxley *Ess. Pop. Sci.* xviii. 276 An artificial and *non-adaptive tendon. **1955** *Sci. Amer.* Apr. 93/1 The modification of T2 is 'nonadaptive'; that is, the modified virus cannot grow in the host that changed it. **1967** *Economist* 7 Oct. 20/1 The 'non-medical', *non-addictive drugs such as marijuana and LSD. **1870** H. A. Nicholson *Man. Zool.* xxix. (1875) 218 Sometimes the tube is free and *non-adherent..; more commonly it is attached to some submarine object. **1934** C. Lambert *Music Ho!* iv. 251 Music for organized and *non-aesthetic action such as military marches and fox-trots. **1957** T. Veblen *Theory of Leisure Class* 164 The limits..are fixed by requirements of a non-aesthetic kind. **1848** Mill *Pol. Econ.* III. vi. §2 The *non-agricultural, or rather the non-peasant population. **1907** *Yesterday's Shopping* (1969) 59/2 Hop Bitter Beer, *non-alcoholic. **1909** [see BEERLESS *a.*]. **1966** B. Kimenye *Kalasanda Revisited* 58 There he was..nursing a glass of non-alcoholic, fizzy liquid. **1960** E. Delavenay *Introd. Machine Translation* vi. 90 A meaningful group of signs, alphabetic and *non-alphabetic (spaces, hyphens, etc.). **1973** *Computers & Humanities* VII. 151 A provision must be made for the concurrent appearance of any number of non-alphabetic characters in any position. **1948** D. Diringer *Alphabet* 21 The crudest forms of writing..are *non-alphabetical. **1964** E. Palmer tr. *Martinet's Elem. General Linguistics* iv. 114 A *non-ambiguous form. **1971** J. Anderson in A. J. Aitken et al. *Edin. Stud. Eng. & Scots* 76, I want now to turn to the (non-ambiguous) distinction hinted at above. **1890** W. James *Princ. Psychol.* II. xxii. 351 In certain stages of the hypnotic trance the subject seems to lapse into the *non-analytic state. **1939** *Mind* XLVIII. 202 The class *k* of non-analytic declarative sentences formulable in a given language. **1949** A. Pap *Elem. Analytical Philos.* viii. 152 A synthetic statement would simply be defined as a non-analytic statement. **1934** Webster, *Nonantigenic. **1948** J. H. Burn *Lect. Notes Pharmacol.* 75 The protein must, of course, be non-antigenic. **1951** Whitby & Hynes *Med. Bacteriol.* (ed. 5) vi. 69 Enzymic digestion of antitoxic sera is also used, and by this means even the antibodies themselves may be split into non-antigenic fractions without loss of activity. **1963** D. W. & E. E. Humphries tr. *Termier's Erosion & Sedimentation* xvii. 338 Sediments of *nonaquatic origin, such as those of deserts, can receive rain water. **1904** R. A. Lehfeldt *Electro-Chem.* I. i. 84 These laws..are only very partially applicable to *non-aqueous solutions. **1957** G. E. Hutchinson *Treat. Limnol.* I. iii. 202 The only other non-aqueous natural liquids are the complex mixtures of hydrocarbons and other organic compounds known as petroleums. **1967** G. M. Wyburn et al. *Conc. Anat.* iv. 111/1 The [parotid] gland occupies the *nonarticular part of the mandibular fossa of the temporal bone. **1901** A. Sidgwick *Use of Words* viii. 224 Some statement of theirs is ambiguous, and therefore..*non-assertive. **1940** *Kenyon Review* II. 282 The poetic statement ..falls between the two poles of full assertion..and pure non-assertive tension between plurisigns. **1920** H. G. Wells *Outl. Hist.* 563/1 There has hitherto existed in the States no organization for and no tradition of what one may call *non-assimilable possessions. **1972** P. Green *Shadow of Parthenon* 70 Everything that conventional historiography finds non-assimilable, from science to tragedy. **1829** Lamb *Let. to Gillman* 30 Nov., *Non-assistive to partition of natures. **1943** *Mind* LII. 26 It is supposed that..all complex or *non-atomic assertions are just aggregates of atomic propositions linked by 'and', 'on', or 'if—then'. **1955** Koestler *Trail of Dinosaur* 239 The value of an atomic stockpile against non-atomic, local aggression. **1890** W. James *Princ. Psychol.* I. ii. 50 The momentary loss..of our **non*-auditory images..makes us mentally deaf. **1938** *Times Lit. Suppl.* 8 Oct. 649/3 Calvin was not hostile to art as such, but merely to the use of any non-auditory art in connexion with worship. **1953** C. E. Bazell *Linguistic Form* i. 1 *Non-automatic alternations between phonemes differing in respect of one minimal feature alone are seldom more frequent than similar alternations between phonemes differing in respect of several features. **1964** E. Bach *Introd. Transformational Gram.* iii. 44 The number suffixes show different forms for these two classes (nonautomatic). **1896** L. T. Hobhouse *Theory of Knowl.* 480 We shall have to discard any other principle..as *non-axiomatic in character. **1966** *Jrnl. Philos.* LXIII. 435 We are not inclined to admit intuition or nonaxiomatic knowledge about sets. **1939** *Mind* XLVIII. 489 The discrimination of basic from *non-basic predicates. **1964** R. H. Robins *Gen. Linguistics* 235 Non-basic endocentric constructions. **1946** C. Morris *Signs, Language & Behavior* 201 The explanation has the merit of not invoking *non-behavioral factors. **1953** *Mind* LXII. 231 We have not yet enquired whether a machine is essentially distinct from a man in non-behavioural respects. **1887** Farrar , etc. (*title*), *Non-Biblical Systems of Religion. **1947** *Math. Tables & Other Aids to Computation* Oct. 361 It is convenient to use as many selections as there are basic binary places in the computer, or in *nonbinary machines as many as on-off signal channels. **1962** F. I. Ordway et al. *Basic Astronautics* vi. 287 By taking an inventory of nonbinary, solar-type stars with low angular momenta, we may at the same time be taking an inventory of stars with planetary systems. **1967** *New Scientist* 31 Aug. 440/1 Organic substances which are largely or totally *nonbiodegradable are currently being used in both domestic and industrial applications. **1971** *Ibid.* 27 Apr. 260/1 Pollution created by non-biodegradable products has created immense environmental problems. **1859** Geo. Eliot in Cross *Life* (1885) II. 130 A genuine *non-bookish man like Captain Speke. **1955** *Times* 2 May 18/4 The pressing need of giving *non-British immigrants to the Dominions some idea of British standards and culture. **1934** Webster, *Noncalcareous. **1946** *Nature* 21 Sept. 421/2 The non-calcareous type of surface waters, chiefly found in mountainous areas of the north and west, requires little or no treatment in the best cases. **1964** V. J. Chapman *Coastal Vegetation* vi. 139 Two main types of dune, i.e. calcareous and non-calcareous. **1765** *Phil. Trans* LVI. 232 When the rocks below are mixed, calcary and *noncalcary. **1911** W. James *Some Probl. Philos.* xii. 201 *Non-causal sequences can be reversed; causal ones follow in conformity to rule. **1939** *Mind* XLVIII. 422 But very often in determining the dates of events we use non-causal Law-propositions. **1959** *Archivum Linguisticum* XI. 15 *Feed* can also have the *non-causative sense: 'we feed at eight'. 1931 Jrnl. Physical Chem. XXXV. 469 The walls [of Corallines] are *non-cellulosic. 1959 Times Rev. Industry Sept. 4/1 Man made fibres.. have seen the development of non-cellulosic fibres. 1964 Financial Times 25 Feb. 2/2 Output of all man-made fibres, including non-cellulosics, in the U.K. was 15 per cent. higher in 1963. 1964 N. G. Clark Mod. Org. Chem. vii. 119 This and other *non-chemical uses of acetylene today account for only about 20 per cent of the amount consumed. 1974 Verbatim Dec. 1/1 The elements for which there is likely to be a nonchemical.. name. 1936 T. S. Eliot Ess. Anc. & Mod. 132 There may always be schemes, initiated by *non-Christian and non-Catholic minds with purely temporal motives and aims, to which we can give unqualified support. 1965 English Studies Feb. 3 Such scenes in earlier non-dramatic narrative, where the roots are probably non-Christian. 1975 Times 18 Dec. 10/8 The beauty of ancient non-Christian mystical texts. 1960 New Biol. XXXI. 109 The special value of Paramecium for genetics depends not on its use in the analysis of heredity by Mendelian methods but on its revelation of other hereditary or quasi-hereditary systems, based on *non-chromosomal or cytoplasmic elements. 1922 A. D. Udden tr. Bohr's Theory of Spectra III. iii. 100 The *non-circular orbits will correspond to a firmer binding than the circular orbits having the same value for the principal quantum number. 1935 Mind XLIV. 373 This interpretation.. shows the appeal to the divine veracity to be both non-circular and epistemologically necessary. 1926 S. R. James Seventy Years ix. 72 In those days the *non-classical masters [at Eton College] who held houses were known as 'Dames'. 1955 A. N. Prior Formal Logic 258 A non-classical calculus developed by the Russian logician A. Kolmogorov in 1925. 1934 Webster, *Nonclinical. 1960 Farmer & Stockbreeder 9 Feb. 77/1 The prohibition has been made since the discovery that a form of non-clinical rhinitis exists in pigs in Ireland. 1971 Brit. Med. Bull. XXVII. 33/1 The range of conditions is gradually progressive, from normal veins to veins that are elongated, tortuous and dilated but which give rise to no symptoms or to one symptom referable to the legs; these have been termed 'non-clinical' varicose veins. 1890 W. James Princ. Psychol. II. xvii. 9 Plato's earlier pupils used to admit Sensation's existence, grudgingly, but they trampled it in the dust as something corporeal, *non-cognitive, and vile. 1963 R. Carnap in P. A. Schilpp Philos. R. Carnap 45 The view that these sentences and questions are non-cognitive was based on Wittgenstein's principle of verifiability. 1962 F. I. Ordway et al. Basic Astronautics v. 207 (caption) Coherent and *non-coherent converters. 1967 M. Chandler Ceramics in Mod. World iii. 98 The glaze at this stage is a feeble layer of noncoherent particles. 1789 T. Taylor Proclus II. 155 A right line cutting *non-coincident right lines. 1971 G. H. Bourne Ape People x. 255 Among humans the amount of sexual play.. and.. *noncoital sex in general seem to be related to the social level.. and intelligence in the individual concerned. 1973 I. Singer Goals Human Sexuality i. 35 Claiming that all coital orgasms are physiologically indistinguishable from noncoital ones. 1914 S. E. Rasor tr. Burkhardt's Theory of Functions i. 24 Three points A, B, C in the plane such that oA, oB, oC are *non-collinear. 1918 Veblen & Young Projective Geom. II. iii. 96 The triads of points.. are all triads of noncollinear points. Ibid. 97 A, B, C are any three noncollinear points. 1966 Ogilvy & Anderson Excursions in Number Theory vi. 69 How many non-collinear points in a plane can be spaced at integral distances each from each? 1888 Rolleston & Jackson Anim. Life 755 The Hydroidea.. the second order of Craspedota, contains both *non-colonial and colonial hydroids. 1969 Gloss. Terms Fire (B.S.I.) I. 7 *Non-combustible, not capable of undergoing combustion. 1975 B.S.I. News May 10 The term 'incombustible' as a synonym for 'non-combustible' is deprecated in BS 4422: Part 1: 1969 and should not be used in standards. 1901 Edin. Rev. Apr. 492 The 'dumping' abroad at *non-commercial prices of goods manufactured in excess of the requirements of the protected home market. 1933 Dylan Thomas Let. Jan. (1966) 14 It is prose.. but an utterly non-commercial prose. 1973 Listener 30 Aug. 295/3 This concern to tailor the news to the listener has even spread.. to National Public Radio, the non-commercial radio network. 1953 C. F. Hockett in Saporta & Bastian Psycholinguistics (1961) 63/2 Information theory does not deal with the way in which a source maps a *noncommunicative stimulus into communicative output. 1920 B. Russell Pract. & Theory Bolshevism v. 76 If they elected a *non-Communist representative he could not obtain a pass on the railway. 1972 'G. Black' Bitter Tea (1973) vi. 82 Singapore is now the real focal point for the whole of non-Communist Chinese life. 1852 Mill Pol. Econ. (ed. 3) I. II. i. 258 The two elaborate forms of *non-communistic Socialism known as St. Simonism and Fourierism. 1863 Rep. Brit. Assoc. Adv. Sci. 1862 II. 7 An algebra of *non-commutative symbols. 1964 E. Bach Introd. Transformational Gram. vii. 159 Ordinary arithmetical multiplication and addition form groups of a special character called commutative (or Abelian) groups, since they obey the commutative law: $x + y = y + x$; semi-groups are in general noncommutative. 1954 Proc. Nat. Acad. Sci. XL. 1150 The quotient G/K of a simple *noncompact group with center reduced to $\{e\}$ by a maximal compact sub-group carries a Hermitian symmetric structure invariant under G if and only if K has a nondiscrete center. 1959 E. M. Patterson Topology iii. 63 The transformation operates on a non-compact space. 1964 E. Bach Introd. Transformational Gram. v. 114 It is only at the lowest levels that the noncompact nature of the morphemes appears. 1632 Star Chamb. Cases (Camden) 125 [He] was excepted against by Mr. Hudson for a *non-competent witnesse. 1906 Daily Chron. 10 Aug. 8/7 This club is extending the idea of holding a long-distance *non-competitive run to Bath and back. 1935 Discovery Mar. 64/1 We have never ceased advocating this non-competitive use of available idle labour. 1953 C. E. Bazell Linguistic Form 40 Non redundancy (*non-complementary distribution). 1961 R. B. Long Sentence & its Parts i. 22 But the distinction between complementary and noncomplementary contained modifiers can generally be disregarded. 1936 Mind XLV. 316 The third class.. actually includes *non-complex ideas revived by imagination. 1972 Jrnl. Social Psychol. LXXXVI. 36 Complex groups perform better than noncomplex groups. 1887 J. N. Keynes Formal Logic (ed. 2) vi. 381 The proposition.. is supposed to be *non-compound. 1954 I. M. Copi Symbolic Logic iv. 66 We must develop methods for analyzing non-compound statements.

1897 W. M. Urban Hist. Princ. Sufficient Reason iv. 41 The postulate of ground.. is not.. unlogical, and *non-conceptual, as Schopenhauer later maintained. 1929 A. N. Whitehead Process & Reality 344 Physical feelings form the non-conceptual element in our awareness of nature. 1964 F. Bowers Bibliogr. & Textual Criticism I. v. 27 Not as words that have meaningful values—but, instead, as impersonal and non-conceptual inked prints. 1641 Sir E. Dering Sp. conc. Laud iii. 11 Wee may prosecute *non concludent Arguments. 1928 E. & C. Paul tr. Marx's Capital II. iii. 117 The money serves as an ideal, as a *non-concrete, means of purchase. 1667 Primatt City & C. Builder Pref., If the *Non-confident Author hath been any ways defective. 1846 Mill Logic I. ii. §5 A *non-connotative term is one which signifies a subject only, or an attribute only. 1912 J. S. Huxley Individual in Animal Kingdom iii. 84 To discriminate between conscious and *non-conscious brains. 1972 Computers & Humanities VII. 111 We propose to do a feasibility study to see if the role of language in the formation of nonconscious belief systems can be ascertained. 1867 Thomson & Tait Treat. Nat. Philos. ii. 280 It is easy to arrange a system artificially, in connexion with a source of energy, so that its forces of position shall be *non-conservative. 1962 Corson & Lorrain Introd. Electromagn. Fields vi. 219 We shall now extend the discussion to include time-dependent magnetic fields and the nonconservative electric fields which accompany them. 1965 H. Kahn On Escalation xii. 241 Almost everybody looks for ways to improve a situation, and 'non-conservative' behavior.. becomes very possible. 1964 R. H. Robins Gen. Linguistics 157 Opposed acoustic features:.. consonantal, *non-consonantal. 1775 in Chase Hist. Dartmouth Coll. (1891) I. 350 Furious *non-constitutional men. 1908 Westm. Gaz. 8 Aug. 14/1 Non-resistance is for the *non-constructive man. 1964 G. Kreisel in Benacerraf & Putnam Philos. of Math. 158 Brouwer ignores non-constructive mathematics altogether. 1863 H. Cox Instit. II. xi. 567 Those courts which have a voluntary or *non-contentious jurisdiction. 1964 Language XL. 24 *Noncontiguous dialect areas. 1865 G. M. Hopkins Jrnls. & Papers (1959) 103 All figures must be composed of continuous or of *non-continuous lines or of both. 1973 Archivum Linguisticum IV. 4 A past time auxiliary which refers to recent non-continuous actions. 1964 R. H. Robins Gen. Linguistics 130 The equally *non-contrastive [t] and [p[h]]. 1928 J. Reith Diary 13 Apr. (1975) i. 100 Winston Churchill.. said he would like to.. speak for 15 minutes the next night, factual and *non-controversial. 1943 Mind LII. 274 This covers only the elementary, non-controversial portions of the system. 1960 E. L. Delmar-Morgan Cruising Yacht Equipment v. 66 A modern sextant is.. made of *non-corrosive light metal alloy. 1969 Jane's Freight Containers 1968–69 472/2 Floor screws, flat head, self-tapping with non-corrosive finish. 1893 G. B. Shaw Let. 3 Mar. (1965) 386 Assuring you, in our personal, non-artistic and *non-critical relations, of my unmitigated defiance. 1967 A. Battersby Network Analysis (ed. 2) iii. 26 The systematic analysis of a network sorts out the individual jobs into two main classes, critical and non-critical. 1861 Beresf. Hope Eng. Cathedr. 19th C. 241 The *non-cruciform Llandaff Cathedral. 1851 Phil. Mag. I. 178 It is.. desirable that a complete theory of magnetic induction in crystalline or *non-crystalline matter should be established independently of any hypothesis of magnetic fluids. 1966 D. G. Brandon Mod. Techniques Metallogr. ii. 64 In electron microscopy the contrast is most commonly caused by elastic scattering only, that from non-crystalline replica materials being due to non-coherent scattering, that from thin crystalline films being diffraction contrast. 1908 Westm. Gaz. 15 Aug. 15/1 Home Railway Preference stocks are *non-cumulative. 1954 G. I. M. Swyer Reproduction & Sex xiv. 173 An efficient spermicide.. should be non-toxic, non-irritating, and non-cumulative;.. it should preferably be non-absorbable. 1946 F. E. Zeuner Dating the Past xi. 341 There are superimposed cycles, or *non-cyclic changes of a considerably longer duration. 1962 Corson & Lorrain Introd. Electromagn. Fields v. 203 If the vectors are permuted in noncyclic order, the sign is changed. 1914 B. Russell Our Knowl. External World ii. 34 The ultimate result of the introduction of the inductive method seems not the creation of a new kind of *non-deductive reasoning. 1968 R. A. Lyttleton Mysteries Solar Syst. vii. 250 An intricate subjective psychological process must be concerned, of a non-deductive character. 1900 Trans. Amer. Math. Soc. I. 462 This represents the most general *non-degenerate quadric. 1929 Non-degenerate [see degenerate a. B. 3 a]. 1968 C. G. Kuper Introd. Theory Superconductivity xi. 183 The n-fold degenerate pair state has been split into an $(n - 1)$-fold level and a non-degenerate lower state. 1839 Ure Dict. Arts 948 The *non-deliquescent sulphates.. such as sulphate of soda, &c. 1941 Manch. Guardian Weekly 14 Mar. 214/4 Now is my chance .. to synthesize the ideology and emotional attitudes of juveniles and adolescents (cross-sectional and non-delinquent) during their vacational activities. 1970 Jrnl. General Psychol. LXXXII. 265 Delinquent and nondelinquent subjects. 1944 Mind LIII. 344 We must admit *non-demonstrative principles of inference which are not derivable from experience. 1965 P. Caws Philos. of Sci. xxvi. 193 The most common name for such non-demonstrative inference is induction. 1908 Daily Chron. 19 Nov. 4/4 The Churches.. together with all the ethical and *non-denominational societies should be summoned to co-operate. 1953 E. Smith Guide to Eng. Traditions & Public Life 17 A non-denominational chapel was commonly provided for religious services. 1905 Ann. Math. VI. 175 An example of a *non-denumerable class is the class of all non-terminating decimal fractions. 1937 Mind XLVI. 59 The properties of integers are non-denumerable. 1968 J. J. C. Smart Between Sci. & Philos. vii. 245 A non-denumerable infinity of points. 1902 W. James Let. 29 July in R. B. Perry Tht. & Char. W. James (1935) II. 650, I may maximize unduly the *non-derivative character of these forces, which you minimize. 1956 J. Whatmough Language 39 The derivative manly as compared with the simple 'non-derivative' word man. 1892 A. Sidgwick Distinction 182 Normally all proper (or *non-descriptive) names have once been general (or descriptive). 1925 L. P. Smith Words & Idioms iii. 83 The non-descriptive, non-explanatory, and purely identifying term of the French Précieuses, je ne sais quoi. 1944 Mind LIII. 241 A formal distinction can be made ..between descriptive symbols on the one hand and nondescriptive or logical symbols on the other. 1946 C. Morris Signs, Language & Behavior 116 Knowledge about the adequacy of *non-designative signs is a powerful factor in their control. 1952 Mind LXI. 459 These theories proposed that ethical terms function like 'hurrah' and 'blast', as non-designative expressions. 1960 Encounter XV. v. 42 A markedly *non-deterministic interpretation of psycho-analysis. 1965 A. Shimony in M. Black Philos. in America 260 As a result of the measurement there is a non-deterministic transition from the initial state to a final state. 1885 *Non-diffusible [see particulate a.]. 1951 Whitby & Hynes Med. Bacteriol. (ed. 5) iv. 57 The toxins of bacteria which do not produce exotoxins are termed endotoxins and are thought to be firmly bound to the bacterial proteins in a non-diffusible form. 1962 H. Heath in A. Pirie Lens Metabolism Rel. Cataract 362 Nondiffusable high polymers. 1967 Oceanogr. & Marine Biol. V. 380 Part of the calcium content of the blood is in the form of non-diffusible compounds of calcium with protein. 1956 A. A. Townsend Struct. Turbulent Shear Flow v. 91 By substituting in the equation of mean motion.., the *non-dimensional equation is obtained. 1956 Nature 24 Mar. 548/2 The rather bewildering array of non-dimensional numbers that confronts the student in this subject [sc. combustion]. 1971 Ibid. 13 Aug. 447/3 The system is then arranged so that the equations of motion have the same form whether they are dimensional or non-dimensional. 1951 Mind LX. 398 The Rogerian *non-directive technique is of no avail. 1954 J. A. C. Brown Social Psychol. of Industry 78 'Non-directive' interviewing in which the interviewer listens rather than talks. 1961 Ann. Reg. 1960 467 The expansion of world trade on a multilateral *non-discriminatory basis. 1962 W. B. Thompson Introd. Plasma Physics ii. 11 These oscillations have the unusual character of being *non-dispersive. 1966 D. G. Brandon Mod. Techniques Metallogr. 155 Such needle counters hold great promise in the field of 'non-dispersive' analysis. 1941 Mind L. 339 So it does not seem as if ϕ can be a *non-dispositional, non-relational characteristic. 1949 A. Pap Elem. Analytical Philos. xii. 289 The dispositional predicate is said to be reducible, by means of the reduction-sentence, to non-dispositional predicates. 1970 Manch. Guardian Weekly 24 Oct. 9 The colleges on their side would agree to permit *non-disruptive occupations and boycotts of classes. 1940 Chambers's Techn. Dict. 582/1 *Non-dissipative network, a network designed as if the inductances and condensers are free from dissipation, and with components of minimum loss. 1964 R. F. Ficchi Electr. Interference iv. 38 A cavity resonator is described as a cylindrical box with perfect conductivity and containing within itself a nondissipative medium. An oscillation, once started within the box, should continue indefinitely. 1961 Amer. Speech XXXVI. 204 The reasons for the persistence of *non-dominant languages. 1972 Jrnl. Social Psychol. LXXXVII. 92 Ring electrodes were slipped onto two fingers of the subject's nondominant hand. 1947 C. Gray Contingencies v. 120 Avoiding.. the pitfall of *non-dramatic music-making into which so many of his contemporaries and predecessors had fallen. 1965 English Studies Feb. 3 It is possible to find such scenes in earlier non-dramatic narrative. 1871 Kingsley Lett., etc. (1877) II. 359 Flax and hemp would be the only *non-eatable crops here. 1920 B. Russell Pract. & Theory Bolshevism II. 123, I do not think that *non-economic factors can be neglected. 1965 J. D. Chambers in Glass & Eversley Population in Hist. xiii. 344 There is more reason to relate the change to non-economic causes. 1853 Phil. Mag. V. 398 Nothing is known with certainty regarding the *non-electrolytic resistance of liquid conductors. 1964 R. F. Ficchi Electr. Interference v. 55 Capacitors, both electrolytic and nonelectrolytic. 1964 Times Rev. Industry & Techn. Jan. 22/2 The operation was put straight on to a computer without an intervening *non-electronic stage. 1964 Language XL. 191 The simple words which by our definitions are *nonelementary. 1965 Hughes & Londey Elem. of Formal Logic xxiii. 177 Even the full Lower Predicate Calculus.. raises problems of a non-elementary nature. 1941 Mind L. 168 Expressed in non-metaphoric and *non-emotional words. 1961 R. B. Long Sentence & its Parts vi. 147 This occurs in subordinate-declarative clauses following ideas of appraisal, emotional or non-emotional. 1901 W. James Let. (1920) II. 153 The optimism and healthy-mindedness are yours... But the moderate and *non-emphatic way of putting things is not. 1966 English Studies XLVII. 257 The normal non-emphatic character of the subject. 1877 E. Caird Philos. Kant II. xiv. 514 The power of *non-empirical ideas over the human mind. 1955 Publ. Amer. Dial. Soc. XXIV. 20, I have on tape some argots which might at first appear to be *non-English. 1941 Mind L. 129 We know the truth of a universal *non-enumerative proposition, All A is B, only by apprehending, in a particular instance, that the universal A-ness necessitates the universal B-ness. 1956 J. O. Urmson Philosophical Analysis v. 63 The case becomes still more favourable to general facts if we take the non-enumerative universal proposition of traditional logic—'All As are B'. 1960 New Biol. XXXI. 26 A mutation (change) of a single chromosomal gene can lead to a corresponding chemical change in a *non-enzymatic protein. 1964 Oceanogr. & Marine Biol. II. 347 Luciferin.. is a non-enzymatic protein which luminesces in the presence of calcium ions. 1934 Webster, *Nonenzymic. 1946 Nature 28 Sept. 433/2 Mackworth finds the other –SH enzymes.. much less sensitive, requiring concentrations of the order of $M/1{,}000$, and this was also found by Morgan and Dixon for –SH groups in non-enzymic proteins. 1965 Peacocke & Drysdale Molecular Basis Heredity x. 115 Work on non-enzymic proteins. 1816 J. W. Mason Plea Cath. Comm. (ed. 2) 206 The inconsistency of the government of England in supporting.. the *non-episcopal churches abroad. 1885 J. Veitch Institutes of Logic §560 What are equivalent, or *non-equivalent, to a common third term, are equivalent or non-equivalent to each other. 1973 J. J. Zeman Modal Logic v. 80 The systems which have an infinite number of non-equivalent irreducible modalities will generally be called 'absolutely strict' systems, while systems containing only a finite number of non-equivalent modalities will, in general, be called 'systems of complete modalization'. a 1676 Hale Prim. Orig. Man. I. vi. (1677) 124 A limited or *non-eternal time. 1925 C. D. Broad Mind & its Place xi. 487 Purely ethical characteristics.. cannot be identified with or defined in terms of *non-ethical or 'natural' characteristics. 1964 E. A. Nida Toward Sci. Transl. v. 93 It might seem strange at first glance that in the above treatment of jwok in Anuak we have not indicated such traditional componential contrasts as ethical vs. non-ethical and secular vs. sacred. **1847** A. De Morgan *Formal Logic* iv. 75 We may say that each is *participant*, or *non-exclusive*, of the other. **1963** Auden *Dyer's Hand* 402 Friendship is a nonexclusive, nonpossessive relationship. **a1674** Clarendon *Hist. Reb.* x. §131 The not having a ship ready, if it were intended, was *non-excusable. **1903** B. Russell *Princ. Math.* I. li. 450 The consideration of existence itself leads to *non-existential propositions, and so contradicts the theory. **1949** A. Pap *Elem. Analytical Philos.* iv. 85 Such discourse about connections of properties without any regard to particulars exemplifying them, is often called 'non-existential'. **1901** A. Sidgwick *Use of Words* iv. 119 Some kind of *non-explanatory verbiage. **1966** *Jrnl. Philos.* LXIII. 446 The author's typical non-explanatory explanations. **1946** F. E. Zeuner *Dating the Past* xii. 381 The *quality* of the species-steps during the period of explosive evolution differs from those of the period of ordinary, *non-explosive evolution. **1971** I. G. Gass et al. *Understanding Earth* xxi. 301/2 Non-explosive fissure eruptions. **1641** Prynne *Antipathy* Ep. Ded. 3 A now-*non-extant Booke, written..in King Edward the 6. his dayes. **1831** Carlyle *Sart. Res.* ii. viii, Two little visual Spectra of men..simultaneously..explode one another into Dissolution; and off hand become Air, and Non-extant! **1949** *Mind* LVIII. 63 We need a modal or *non-extensional language which contains such words as 'necessarily' or 'accidentally'. **1955** A. N. Prior *Formal Logic* 269 Modal operators (and non-extensional operators generally). **1934** Webster, *Nonfactual. **1936** *Mind* XLV. 359 According to Mr. Ayer every significant, non-factual proposition is analytic; every factual proposition is synthetic. **1879** *St. George's Hosp. Rep.* IX. 720 Medical officers of health hear of all the fatal cases of any infectious disease.., but by no means of all the *non-fatal cases. **1934** Webster, *Nonfatty. **1935** *Discovery* June 170/1 For analytical purposes, milk is divided into three parts: fat or cream; non-fatty solids..; and water. **1870** Rolleston *Anim. Life* 59 A point corresponding to the junction of the fimbrate with the *non-fimbriate portion of the mantle. **1953** C. E. Bazell *Linguistic Form* iv. 47 The opposition in French between 'close e' and 'open e' in *non-final syllables is similarly marginal. **1973** *Word* 1970 XXVI. 103 In such compounds, nonfinal primary stress is supposed to become secondary. **1923** J. S. Huxley *Ess. Biologist* vii. 264 Man's ideals are in themselves unlimited, *non-finite. **1971** *Computers & Humanities* V. 307 Stylistic uses of the non-finite verb clause in Shakespeare's plays. **1940** *Mind* XLIX. 248 The theory that the *non-finitist symbols used in pure mathematics are to be interpreted as 'ideal elements'.. would provide a fruitful starting-point for a consideration of certain aspects of scientific method. **1956** J. H. Woodger tr. *Tarski's Logic, Semantics, Metamath.* 260 On account of its non-finitist nature the rule of infinite induction differs fundamentally. **1909** Webster, *Non-fissile. **1953** Non-fissile [see fissile *a.* 2]. **1961** J. E. Radford *Nuclear Energy Simplified* ii. 29 The non-fissile isotope U^{238}..has now become exceedingly valuable because plutonium can be transmuted from it. **1950** *Chem. Engin. Progress* XLVI. 110/1 An immediate concern should be to make use of the relatively large amount of *nonfissionable U-238. **1974** *Sci. Amer.* June 36/1 The fusion neutrons can also be used to convert nonfissionable isotopes of uranium or thorium to fissionable isotopes. **1731** Bailey vol. II, **Non-floriferous*.. bearing no Flowers. **1903** B. Russell *Princ. Math.* I. iii. 41 This is simply an instance of the *non-formal principle of dropping a true premiss. **1964** R. H. Robins *Gen. Linguistics* v. 194 Those [definitions of the word unit] relying on non-formal, extra-grammatical criteria..are of little value. **1833** Darwin in *Life & Lett.* (1887) I. 243 The country is *non-fossiliferous. **1926** J. S. Huxley *Ess. Pop. Sci.* xviii. 301 The embryonic or *non-functional period. **1965** *English Studies* XLVI. 420 The attempt to save the *Gesetz* by saying that in all these cases the alliteration of the verb is non-functional can hardly be taken seriously. **1959** *Brno Studies in English* I. 42 The *non-generic indefinite article. **1932** J. S. Huxley *Probl. Relative Growth* vii. 207 The bulk of the observable differences in size and proportions between the existing Scottish strain of Red deer and (a) the existing Carpathian strain and (b) the sub-fossil Scottish type are *non-genetic and of no taxonomic significance. **1964** *Oceanogr. & Marine Biol.* II. 314 Others imply a nongenetic character of the changes involved or a combination of both genetic and non-genetic components. **1926** A. Huxley *Essays New & Old* 131 The grandest sight I saw in *non-geometrical Holland was Zaandam. **1936** *Mind* XLV. 466 Some non-geometrical kind of analysis. **1861** Mill *Repr. Govt.* xvi. 292 East Prussia..must..be either under a *non-German government, or the intervening Polish territory must be under a German one. **1964** *English Studies* XLV. 395 The use of *Textbuch* in the non-German sense may be due to carelessness of translation. **1937** *Jrnl. Eng. & Gmc. Philol.* 4 Oct. 463 Rules are given..and a comparison made between the vocabulary of German and English and the *non-Germanic languages. **1965** *English Studies* XLVI. 419 This [*sc.* Gregorian chant] is of non-Germanic origin. **1955** J. L. Austin *How to do Things with Words* (1962) i. 3 The mistake of taking as straightforward statements of fact utterances which are *either* (in interesting *non-grammatical ways) nonsensical *or else* intended as something quite different. **1965** *Canad. Jrnl. Linguistics* XI. 47 The moment a 'non-grammatical' sentence is uttered or written, it ceases to be 'non-grammatical'. **1961** L. C. Martin *Clinical Endocrinol.* (ed. 3) i. 15 Oxytocin has little or no effect either upon the *non-gravid human uterus or upon the gravid uterus until the time of parturition. **1967** *Oceanogr. & Marine Biol.* V. 161 The perivisceral fluid..constitutes only 25% of the mass of a small (non-gravid) sea urchin. **1964** C. Barber *Present-Day Eng.* vi. 142 This habitual/*non-habitual criterion is not typical. **1946** *Nature* 31 Aug. 294/1 It is *non-hæmolytic and does not produce any pyrogenic effect on intramuscular injection in man. **1964** W. G. Smith *Allergy & Tissue Metabolism* v. 61 They also caused the formation of hæmolytic lysolecithin-like substances and non-hæmolytic SRS. **1657** *Rec. Presb. Dingwall* (S.H.S.) 291 The *nonharmonious concurrence of the parochiners to that transplantatione. **1955** W. Pauli *Niels Bohr* 37 This group distinguishes two kinds of complex (*non-Hermitian) fields..which are multiplied by gauge-transformations with opposite phase factors. **1970** G. K. Woodgate *Elem. Atomic Struct.* 207 We find it convenient to use two non-Hermitian operators. **1896** W. Caldwell *Schopenhauer's System* ix. 508 A metaphysical analysis of the world must naturally always be taken in a timeless or ideal (*non-historical) sense. **1935** *Mind* XLIV. 235 The historical essays..are mostly concerned with Greek philosophy..; and two of the essays are ostensibly non-historical. **1957** L. Fox *Two-Point Boundary Probl.* vii. 190 A change..in the *non-homogeneous part of the equation. **1927** *Jrnl. Heredity* XVIII. 269/1 One might suppose that a portion of one chromosome has become attached to a member of a *non-homologous pair. **1956** *Nature* 25 Feb. 386/1 'Centric fusion' of non-homologous autosomes. **1971** *Perceptual & Motor Skills* XXXII. 639 Synchrony of bimanual wrist movements by 12 normal Ss was compared when homologous muscles (e.g., left and right wrist flexors) and when non-homologous muscles (e.g., left flexors and right extensors) were simultaneously active. **1971** *Chromosoma* XXXV. 247 Rieger (1957) reported a high level of pairing between non-homologous chromosomes in haploid forms of *Antirrhinum majus*. **1890** R. Adamson in W. S. Jevons *Pure Logic* p. xi, *Non-identical contents presented to it. **1965** *Language* XLI. 280 The nonidentical subject constituents. **1964** Rousseas & Farganis in I. L. Horowitz *New Sociology* 270 The *non-ideological liberal is uncommitted. **1975** *Times* 25 Nov. 8/8 The [Chinese] authors..have been writing cultural books, largely non-ideological, since the 1930s. **1932** H. H. Price *Perception* v. 110 Some few and as it were privileged expanses (normal or *non-illusory ones). **1928** L. P. Smith *Words & Idioms* 114 The *non-imitative arts, architecture and music. **1973** *Jrnl. Genetic Psychol.* CXXIII. 145 The reinforced group emitted significant more physical, verbal, and nonimitative aggression than the nonreinforced group. **1874** W. Wallace tr. *Hegel's Logic* 208 The *non-independent and changeable. **1965** Hughes & Londey *Elem. of Formal Logic* xviii. 131 A4..can be proved from the other axioms... We express this fact by saying that A4 is a non-independent axiom. **1894** C. Dixon (*title*) The nests and eggs of *non-indigenous British birds. **1964** *Language* XL. 93 Regional and nonindigenous influence. **1926** D. H. Lawrence *Plumed Serpent* vii. 128 Men, dark, collective men, *non-individual. **1949** A. Pap *Elem. Analytical Philos.* iv. 88 The use of non-individual variables commits the logician to the use of names of abstract entities, like properties, classes or propositions. **1934** Priebsch & Collinson *German Lang.* ii. v. 251 A residue of untraced words which have led some scholars..to postulate a *non-Indo-European strain in the early vocabulary. **1965** W. S. Allen *Vox Latina* i. 13 Many of the words..are probably non-Indo-European. **1899** *Jrnl. Inst. Electr. Engin.* XXVIII. 17 A practically *non-inductive wire resistance. **1957** G. Ryle in C. A. Mace *Brit. Philos. in Mid-Cent.* 259 Pure mathematics is a non-inductive..science. **1938** *Mind* XLVII. 247 It is this aspect of Dr. Myers' essay that is of interest to the *non-industrial reader, though there is much of value in it about the prevention of accidents in industrial occupations. **1909** Webster, *Noninfectious. **1956** *Nature* 21 Jan 131/1 The purified protein alone was found to be non-infectious. **1965** McKeown & Brown in Glass & Eversley *Population in Hist.* xii. 291 Infectious and non-infectious cases. **1956** *Nature* 18 Feb. 304/1 Extracts from infected plants contain a range of specific proteins that resemble the virus..but are not infective... Beans appear to contain an unusually large proportion of *non-infective protein. **1971** *Brit. Med. Bull.* XXVII. 9/1 It may have a predominantly non-infective allergic origin. **1897** B. Russell *Essay on Foundations of Geometry* ii. 61 This element must be *non-inferential. **1935** *Mind* XLIV. 48 The last phrase suggests a less positive stand in regard to the non-inferential apprehension of the objective. **1849** D. Campbell *Inorg. Chem.* 71 *Non-inflammable gas is prepared by distilling in a retort fragments of phosphorus with a solution of potash in alcohol. **1936** *Discovery* Apr. 106/2 Helium gas is used as a non-inflammable substitute for hydrogen in balloons and airships. **1969** *Jane's Freight Containers 1968–69* 476/2 Both achieved by in-situ foamed non-inflammable urethane. **1837** J. S. Mill *Let.* Sept. in *Wks.* (1963) XII. 350 Our *non-inflected language. **1928** *Mod. Lang. Rev.* Apr. 136 Then we shall have two genitives in English, one inflected and one non-inflected. **1924** H. E. Palmer *Gram. Spoken Eng.* 81 All other classes of qualificatives..form the comparative..and superlative by the *non-inflexional method. **1940** *Mind* XLIX. 436 The syntax of the Aryan languages differs fundamentally from that of non-inflectional languages, in particular Chinese. **1953** K. Jackson *Lang. & Hist. in Early Britain* ii. 286 He gives substitution by AS. *i*, *y*, or *e* in all cases, apparently not considering Pr.W. stressed *ï* in *non-initial syllables. **1965** *Language* XLI. 453 Medial (i.e. noninitial and nonfinal) dissyllabic sequences. **1962** *Listener* 20 Sept. 436/2 The differences between insightful and *non-insightful problem-solving behaviour. **1968** M. S. Livingston *Particle Physics* ii. 18 The *non-integral atomic weights were explained as isotopes. **1897** W. James *Will to Believe* 11 Evidently..our *non-intellectual nature does influence our convictions. **1946** *Mind* LV. 51 This, so far as it depends on denying the possibility of other sorts of non-intellectual intuition than the sensible, is certainly dogmatic. **1957** N. Chomsky in Saporta & Bastian *Psycholinguistics* (1961) 41/2 Our ultimate aim is to provide an objective, *non-intuitive way to evaluate a grammar. **1960** *Suppl Oxf. Med. Treatment of Disease* VIII. 804 *Non-involved. **1973** S. Fisher *Female Orgasm* xv. 434 A signal for potential future sexual difficulties is..a distant, non-involved relationship with the father. **1946** *Nature* 14 Dec. 876/2 Physiological effect on man: *non-irritant. **1963** J. Osborne *Dental Mechanics* (ed. 5) i. 9 It [*sc.* the impression material] should be non-irritant to the mouth tissues. **1860** Wharton *Law Lex.* (ed. 2), **Non issuable pleas*, those upon which a decision would not determine the action upon the merits, as a plea in abatement. **1935** Huxley & Haddon *We Europeans* iii. 96 In each country the Jewish population overlaps with the *non-Jewish. **1973** *Guardian* 17 Apr. 15/8 The Passover meal, to which non-Jewish passengers like me were invited. **1965** M. Morse *Unattached* i. 44 His impartial and *non-judgemental attitute. **1972** *Jrnl. Social Psychol.* LXXXVI. 224 Low authoritarian subjects are..flexible and nonjudgmental. **1949** Koestler *Promise & Fulfilment* iii. iii. 317 The Cabinet has capitulated to the rabbis and no *non-kosher meat will be imported into Israel. **1968** D. Hopkinson *Incense-Tree* iv. 38, I was considered by Jews to be a Jewess. Accordingly I ought not to..eat non-kosher food. **1849** Balfour *Man. Bot.* §921 *Non-lactescent herbs or undershrubs. **1930** R. A. Fisher *Genetical Theory of Natural Selection* iii. 64 With *non-lethal mutants..a process of modification of the homozygote may be expected to commence. **1965** H. Kahn *On Escalation* xii. 234 The 'nonlethal central confrontations'..were not repeated. **1955** P. Strevens *Papers in Lang. & Lang. Teaching* (1965) ix. 118 The *non-lexical effects arise chiefly from the absence of a system of interdependent stress and intonation. **1971** *Archivum Linguisticum* II. 131 The terms Pre-article and Post-article can be used when talking about arrangements of non-lexical formatives in surface structure. **1927** *Mod. Philology* Nov. 217 An ear trained to other languages will hear differences between the [t]'s of [tik, stik, botr, bit] which are not distinctive, that is, in English *non-linguistic. **1956** J. Whatmough *Language* 7, May 'thought' be not merely sub-linguistic, but also non-linguistic, or both? **1960** W. V. Quine *Word & Object* 270 Discourse about non-linguistic objects would have been an excellent medium. **1971** D. Crystal *Linguistics* 72 Modern linguists..do not want to gear their descriptions to non-linguistic standards of correctness. **1889** *Granta* 17 May 9/1 To a *non-literary man, like myself, the post of Editor offered temptations well-nigh irresistible. **a1943** R. G. Collingwood *Idea of Hist.* (1946) 258 Non-literary sources, such as coins and inscriptions. **1965** *English Studies* XLVI. 256 These three themes are all copiously illustrated with quotations, the vast majority being drawn from non-literary sources. **1908** *Westm. Gaz.* 3 Feb. 2/2 He has in three weeks done all that any *non-local candidate could do. **1965** *English Studies* Apr. 140 Non-local forms of their names can hardly..affect the outcome of an investigation. **1831** Brewster *Optics* Introd. 1 *Non-luminous bodies are those which have not the power of discharging light of them-selves. **1829** *Phil. Mag.* VI. 146 This ore is remarkable on account of its being entirely *non-magnetic. **1903** Non-magnetic [see oersted b]. **1968** C. G. Kuper *Introd. Theory Superconductivity* ii. 22 Since the normal phase has been assumed to be nonmagnetic g_n is independent of the field. **1884** Britten *Watch & Clockm. Handbk.*, *Non-Magnetizable Watch. **1869** E. A. Parkes *Pract. Hygiene* (ed. 3) 475 Its frequent occurrence in *non-malarious places. **1956** J. E. Floud *Social Class & Educational Opportunity* i. i. 7 In South West Hertfordshire the *non-manual occupations are much better represented. **1946** *Nature* 31 Aug. 299/1 The *non-marine Lamellibranchs have become of extreme economic importance in the correlation of seams in British and Continental coalfields. **1965** G. J. Williams *Econ. Geol. N.Z.* xviii. 324/2 The non-marine Orauea mudstone consists in the lower part of grey to brown sandy mudstone. **1937** R. H. Lowie *Hist. Ethnol. Theory* vii. 83 Tylor's mistake sprang from the difficulty of applying the evolutionary scale to elements of *non-material culture. **1967** Cox & Grose *Organiz. Bibliogr. Rec. by Computer* ii. 41 E.D.P. offers both the low data input rate and the non-material manipulation required. **1847** A. De Morgan *Formal Logic* xii. 232 The terms by which the *non-mathematical logician indicates his degrees of belief. **1937** *Mind* XLVI. 38 The rejection from the interpretation of nature of everything *non*-mathematical. **1973** *Sci. Amer.* Apr. 103/3 Nonmathematical scholars tend to view with profound indifference the tortures that mathematicians suffer over such basic issues as the nature of number. **1920** A. S. Eddington *Space, Time & Gravitation* 4 What you are comparing it with is not some *non-measurable ideal of length, but some attainable, or at least approachable, ideal of material constitution. **1949** A. Pap *Elem. Analytical Philos.* vii. 128 The only legitimate distinction between 'primary' and 'secondary' qualities is that between measurable qualities..and non-measurable qualities. **1855** H. Spencer *Princ. Psychol.* iii. ix. 416 The *non-mechanical sequences occurring in them [*sc.* organisms]. **1939** L. H. Gray *Found. Language* 144 Language..has two aspects: physiological or mechanical, and psychological or non-mechanical. **1834** Mill in *Monthly Repos.* VIII. 818 The most important facts of the human organization, explained in a manner peculiarly well suited..even to *non-medical readers. **1967** Non-medical [see *non-addictive* above]. **1902** W. Bateson *Mendel's Princ. Heredity* p. xiii, *Non-Mendelian phenomena. **1968** H. Harris *Nucleus & Cytoplasm* i. 7 Where there is good evidence that the specifications for a particular characteristic are encoded in cytoplasmic DNA, as, for example, in the case of the chloroplast, genetic analysis reveals a non-mendelian or cytoplasmic form of inheritance. **1878** W. James *Coll. Ess. & Rev.* (1920) 62 It is perfectly possible to express the existence of interests in *non-mental terms. **1936** *Mind* XLV. 182 From these three assertions, it would immediately follow that a mental act, in being experienced, is an *-ed* as well as an *-ing*, that is to say, is non-mental as well as mental. **1959** *Encounter* Jan. 3 It prepares the philosophical student for the belief that mind has some kind of supremacy over the non-mental universe. **1973** *N.Y. Times* 22 Aug. 1/6 The Secret Service continued today to press its investigation of what was described as a 'very serious, very large' conspiracy by 'nonmentals' to assassinate President Nixon during his visit to New Orleans yesterday. **1936** L. Bloomfield in *Language* XII. 95 Now let us re-word the statement in *non-mentalistic terms. **1968** P. M. Postal *Aspects Phonol. Theory* p. xv, The recent attempt of C. F. Hockett to formulate an antimentalistic theory of sound change within the general framework of a nonmentalistic interpretation of autonomous phonemics. **1962** R. van Heyningen in A. Pirie *Lens Metabolism Rel. Cataract* 400 The interconversion of sugars..can, in certain micro-organisms, enable the incorporation into a major metabolic pathway of an otherwise *non-metabolizable sugar. **1973** *Nature* 9 Mar. 122/2, 3-MG is a non-metabolizable sugar which is transported into brain but does not react with hexokinase. **1962** W. Nowottny *Lang. Poets Use* iv. 85 *Non-metaphorical poetry. **1865** Mill *Exam. Hamilton's Philos.* xiii. 249, I ask..whether to the natural, or *non-metaphysical man, it is not as great a paradox [etc.]. **1892** W. Wallace tr. *Hegel's Logic* (ed. 2) 66 In these material, non-metaphysical surroundings, thought is free. **1937** *Mind* XLVI. 120 He lays stress on the resolution made by the Congress to produce an International Encyclopaedia which is to represent in a unified, physicalistic, non-metaphysical terminology the Unity of Science. **1933** A. N. Whitehead *Adventures of Ideas* viii. 142 Geometry, developed in this fashion, has been termed '*Non-metrical Projective Geometry'. **1963** *Times* 22 Feb. 16/5 The original non-metrical notation. **1909** Webster, *Non-migratory. **1926** J. S. Huxley *Ess. Pop. Sci.* 171 This occupation of territory [by birds] takes place in..the same way in migratory and *non-migratory forms. **1964** *Oceanogr. & Marine Biol.* II. 186 That it is independent of species is apparent from comparison of examples such as the brown trout and sea trout, non-migratory and migratory forms respectively of the species, *Salmo trutta*. **1869** Mill *Subj. Women* iv. 158 Gentleness, generosity, and self-abnegation, towards the *non-military and defenceless classes generally. **1956** A. H. Compton *Atomic Quest* 239 A nonmilitary demonstration. **1965** G. McInnes *Road to Gundagai* i. 20 His decision to pursue what the A.I.F. called Non-Military Employment. **1957** N. Frye *Anatomy of Criticism* 290 Farce, being a *non-mimetic form of comedy, has a natural place in the masque. **1959** J. L. Austin *Sense & Sensibilia* (1962) xi. 137 Consider, he says, the statement, 'I hear a car'. This is *non-minimal, he says. **1966** G. N. Leech *Eng. in Advertising* viii. 84 A complete measure of grammatical complexity would require a similar calculation for all non-minimal units. **1875** Max Müller *Chips* IV. 317, I had divided the six great religions of the world into Missionary and *non-Missionary. **1928** H. Poutsma *Gram. Late Mod. Eng.* (ed. 2) I. I. i. 37 Also *non-modal *may* is frequently attended by emotional *perhaps*. **1953** *Mind* LXII. 398 The philosophical character of a modal system turns in the first place on which non-modal expressions are flagged as necessary. **1957** A. N. Prior *Time & Modality* 60 The non-modal part of the theory of reference..could be..formalized. **1961** *Lancet* 19 Aug. 435/1 No constant abnormality was observed in the non-modal cells. **1971** J. Anderson in A. J. Aitken et al. *Edin. Stud. Eng. & Scots* 102 Note, however, that the complex modals can have only the future interpretation, as is also the case with their non-modal equivalents. **1890** W. James *Princ. Psychol.* I. viii. 215 Fichte calls it [*sc.* the soul] the inner body, Ulrici likens it to a fluid of *non-molecular composition. **1965** Phillips & Williams *Inorg. Chem.* I. vi. 193 Most non-molecular solids give this type of spectrum, but salts do not. **1951** R. Firth *Elements of Social Organization* iv. 133 A *non-monetary economy does provide for a great deal of direct matching of goods and services. **1909** *Cent. Dict.* Suppl., *Non-motile. **1956** *Nature* 11 Feb. 257/2 One of the strains—*Proteus X* I—..was under some conditions motile and under others non-motile. **1902** W. James *Var. Relig. Exper.* xvi. 421 Music gives us ontological messages which *non-musical criticism is unable to contradict. **1965** *B.B.C. Handbk.* 200 Suggestions for non-musical light entertainment programmes. **1902** W. James *Var. Relig. Exper.* iv. 90 More ordinary *non-mystical conditions of rapture suffice for my immediate contention. **1941** *Mind* L. 128 One would like there to be a uniformity of knowing-power in such straight-forward non-mystical matters. **1879** Whitney *Skr. Gram.* 50 Before another *non-nasal mute or before a sibilant. **1937** S. Spender *Forward from Liberalism* 272 The U.S.S.R. offers the world the example of the *non-national state. **1942** L. B. Namier *Conflicts* 11 A line of independent States arose between Austria and Turkey which, with the backing of Russia, were to become a menace to both these non-national Empires. **1909** *Westm. Gaz.* 2 Sept. 2/1 The country which is..dependent upon intelligent work for *non-native wealth. **1968** P. M. Postal *Aspects Phonol. Theory* vi. 126 When languages borrow large bodies of vocabulary they very often borrow nonnative phonological matrices. **1975** *Verbatim* May 5/2 Nonnative speakers seem to lack the security of being able to admit they are ignorant of a word. **1934** *Political Q.* V. 135 For expressions of *non-Nazi opinion we have to go outside Germany. **1939** *War Illustr.* 9 Dec. 394 Written by a non-Nazi German who was interned in England. **1621** Burton *Anat. Mel.* I. ii. iv. i, Of those remote..necessary causes, I have sufficiently discoursed in the precedent member, the *non-necessary follow. **1885** J. Veitch *Institutes of Logic* xxxiv. 464 Our expectation of recurrence in the future is determined by the condition that we do not know that any negative or destructive cause has been at work. The theory of the Inductive Principle is at once' positive and negative, or rather is positive and *non-negative. **1937** *Mind* XLVI. 58 Gödel's procedure of arithmetization consists essentially of the establishment of a one-one correlation between all possible series of symbols belonging to the 'object language' (*i.e.*, a certain system of mathematics) and certain non-negative integers. **1966** *Mathematical Rev.* XXXI. 22/1 Representations of natural numbers as sums of nonnegative *k*th powers. **1957** L. Fox *Numerical Solution Two-Point Boundary Probl.* vii. 180 This involves..a *non-negligible difference correction in the finite-difference equations. **1972** *Science* 27 Oct. 407/1 Account had to be taken of the very small, but nonnegligible, declination motion of the satellite. **1927** Haldane & Huxley *Animal Biol.* ix. 177 In the higher animals, the living capital is locked up in *non-negotiable forms to a much greater extent. **1969** *Listener* 8 May 632/1 These demands are almost always called 'non-negotiable', so that the university's offer to negotiate is..meaningless. **1973** M. & G. Gordon *Informant* xxv. 101 About the securities, even the theft of the non-negotiable ones could hurt us badly. **1873** Ralfe *Phys. Chem.* p. xv, *Non-nitrogenous fatty acids. **1959** E. M. Patterson *Topology* (ed. 2) iii. 49 The only *non-null open set is the whole space, and so no separation condition is possible. **1974** *Canad. Jrnl. Linguistics* XIX. 198 Substitution rules are defined as including both deletion rules and rules substituting a non-null element for a term in the Structural Index. **1903** B. Russell *Princ. Math.* xxxii. 264 Other instances of *non-numerical functions are afforded by dictionaries. **1940** W. V. Quine *Math. Logic* 68 The analogous use of letters in non-numerical fields. **1973** *Computers & Humanities* VII. 173 It conveys an erroneous impression to science students concerning the present state of so-called non-numerical data processing. **1964** *Oceanogr. & Marine Biol.* II. 260 Reeve (1963) working with *Artemia salina*..showed that it does not discriminate between nutritious and *non-nutritious particles when filter-feeding. **1973** *Sci. Amer.* Dec. 66/1 It is then given over to savannas of coarse, non-nutritious grasses, bamboo thickets and stands of bracken and other ferns. **1767** *Phil. Trans.* LVII. 435 To swallow it, digest it, and return the *non-nutritive parts back again by the same way. **1945** *Mind* LIV. 4 The theory [of matter] itself contains a large number of highly abstract, *non-observational terms such as 'atom', 'electron', 'nucleus', 'dissociation', 'valence'. **1960** W. V. Quine *Word & Object* 47 He can translate the non-observational occasion sentences. **1850** *Punch* Aug. 57/2 We subjoin a specimen of the two styles of reports, the one official, and the other *non-official. **1970** *Jrnl. General Psychol.* LXXXII. 215 Analyses of a variety of official and non-official documents. **1874** Garrod & Baxter *Mat. Med.* 283 Inferior *non-officinal cinchona barks. **1946** *Nature* 23 Nov. 742/1 (*heading*) Silicon carbide *non-ohmic resistors. **1973** *Physics Bull.* Dec. 741/1 The final chapter..describes the nonohmic behaviour observed in several semiconductors. **1942** *Tee Emm* (*Air Ministry*) II. 63 The C.M.E. has passed me 'fit for *non-operational flying at home'. And the Blitz has started! **1949** A. Pap *Elem. Analytical Philos.* v. 97 A non-operational definition. **1946** C. Morris *Signs, Language & Behavior* 18 The *non-organic world. **1968** C. A. Doxiadis *Between Dystopia & Utopia* 34 Cities continued to spread in what seems to be a non-organic pattern. **1835–6** *Todd's Cycl. Anat.* I. 202/2 In the *non-parasitic species [of arachnids]. **1884** E. Klein *Micro-Organisms & Disease* xviii. 169 (*heading*) Vital phenomena of *non-pathogenic organisms. **1964** M. Hynes *Med. Bacteriol.* (ed. 8) ii. 10 Fæcal streptococci resist 60° C. for 30 minutes and non-pathogenic thermophilic bacteria may actually grow at 75° C. **1904** W. James *Ess. Radical Empiricism* (1912) i. 16 These *non-perceptual experiences have objectivity as well as subjectivity. **1963** P. Gardiner *Schopenhauer* ii. 52 Attempts to describe or explain the physical world in non-perceptual terms. **1962** B. M. Strang *Mod. Eng. Structure* viii. 142 Thus, *he is eating* is non-interrogative, non-negative, non-passive, *non-perfective, but is durative. **1973** *Archivum Linguisticum* IV. 34 The behaviour of transitive verbs in non-perfective sentences is exactly parallel to that of intransitive verbs in both perfective and non-perfective sentences. **1922** Joyce *Ulysses* 287 *Nonperishable goods. **1962** R. B. Fuller *Epic Poem on Industrialization* 212 The 'non-perishables', chiefly the industrial metals. **1974** *Times* 21 Dec. 9/4 Shop for all non-perishable foods this weekend. **1975** *Times* 9 Dec. 16/6 Non-perishables, such as grain and butter. **1967** *Punch* 27 Dec. 976/1 We can't simply go back one square, trying to apply to Them what our *non-permissive parents practised on Us. **1973** S. Fisher *Female Orgasm* iv. 102 Femininity seemed to be maximized by a parental orientation that was nonpermissive and punitive. **1928** D. H. Lawrence *Let.* 13 Mar. (1932) 711, I feel one still has to fight for the phallic reality, as against the *non-phallic cerebration unrealities. **1973** S. Fisher *Female Orgasm* iii. 69 The female experiences her body as nonphallic, in contrast to the male whose body feelings are saturated with phallic qualities. **1879** W. James *Coll. Ess. & Rev.* (1920) 94 Such relations, represented as *non-phenomenal entities, become thus the *bête noire* and pet aversion of many thinkers. **1954** R. Wells in Saporta & Bastian *Psycholinguistics* (1961) 276/1 In that case we invent or postulate some non-phenomenal circumstance. *a***1866** J. Grote *Exam. Utilitarian Philos.* (1870) xvi. 243 Only the older utilitarianism..has any sympathy with this *non-philosophic spirit. **1965** *Language* XLI. 511 A nonphilosophical writer like Euripides? **1933** L. Bloomfield *Language* ix. 147 *Non-phonemic, gesture-like features may become fairly fixed. **1953** C. E. Bazell *Linguistic Form* 22 This is most strikingly illustrated in Zoque, where the impermissibility of many sequences of consonants leads to a non-phonemic transposition of phoneme-order in the event of suffixation. **1965** *Canad. Jrnl. Linguistics* X. 147 The illusion of objective non-phonemic recording. **1964** *Archivum Linguisticum* XVI. 43 The main *non-phonetic or non-French features of the *graphie occitane*. **1973** *Sci. Amer.* Feb. 60/2 Given the nonphonetic nature of the Chinese writing system, it may seem an impossible task to reconstruct how the language was spoken many centuries ago. **1920** A. S. Eddington *Space, Time & Gravitation* xii. 194 The matter ..can only differ in a mysterious *non-physical quality—that of identity. **1957** G. Ryle in M. Black *Importance of Lang.* (1962) 166 All three maintained the doctrine of a third realm of non-physical, nonpsychological entities. **1880** Haughton *Phys. Geog.* vi. 266 The *non-placental Mammals contain two great subdivisions, viz., the Marsupials and the Monotremes. **1934** Webster, *Nonplanar. **1945** *Jrnl. Inst. Electr. Engin.* XCII. I. 163/2 This procedure breaks down if the old circuit cannot be drawn without crossings between some of its branches ('non-planar' networks). **1964** N. G. Clark *Mod. Org. Chem.* xviii. 366 This work suggests that the basic units of vitrinite consist of small benzenoid groups joined together. .. These elongated, non-planar, rather rigid units have a molecular weight of 1000 to 3000. **1925** I. A. Richards *Princ. Literary Criticism* 250 In ordinary, *non-poetic, non-imaginative experience. **1964** W. S. Allen in D. Abercrombie et al. *Daniel Jones* 7 Sequences of words in the course of non-poetic utterance. **1935** *Discovery* Nov. 316/1 White *non-poisonous pigments. **1968** *Times* 2 Oct. 12/6 Butterflies reared on non-poisonous plants. **1878** *Non-polarizable [see polarizable *a.*] **1966** Phillips & Williams *Inorg. Chem.* II. xxv. 243 (*caption*) Upper plot (type A) corresponds to a non-polarizable ligand, lower plot (type B) to a polarizable ligand. **1946** *Nature* 5 Oct. 475/1 Compact, *non-porous sorbing media such as wool. **1966** A. W. Lewis *Gloss. Woodworking Terms* 62 *Non-porous woods*, woods from conifers, i.e. softwoods, which do not contain vessels or pores. **1950** *Mind* LIX. 262 This book..claims to show how the predicative activities of judgment arise out of earlier, *non-predicative forms of awareness. **1964** E. Palmer tr. *Martinet's Elem. General Linguistics* iv. 133 Units which are all capable of assuming predicative and non-predicative functions. *Ibid.* iii. 88 An accent with a *non-predictable position. **1946** *Nature* 26 Oct. 590/1 The sera studied were taken from umbilical blood, infants up to the age of eighteen months, and adults in the pregnant and *non-pregnant state, as controls. **1954** G. I. M. Swyer *Reproduction & Sex* vi. 83 The normal non-pregnant uterus is approximately 7·5 cm. (3 in.) long. **1904** H. Poutsma *Gram. Late Mod. Eng.* I. I. iii. 130 Both the objects are *non-prepositional. **1933** M. Callaway *Consecutive Subjunctive in O.E.* i. 11 In the *Lindisfarne Gospels* we find few Consecutive Subjunctives Introduced by Non-prepositional Correlative Particles. **1964** E. Palmer tr. *Martinet's Elem. General Linguistics* i. 15 In the case of linguistics it is particularly important to insist on the scientific and non-prescriptive character of our approach. **1658** Phillips, **Non-principiate*,..not having a beginning. **1864** Bowen *Logic* ix. 295 The petitio principii ..consists in assuming..a *non-probable principle as probable. **1922** *Non-productive [see direct *a.* 6 f]. **1961** *Brno Studies in English* III. 18 The type to which they belong is a traditional, non-productive one. **1974** P. H. Matthews *Morphology* xii. 221 The formation of *breadth* is wholly non-productive. **1802–12** Bentham *Ration. Judic. Evid.* (1827) II. 308 An inferior and *non-professional sort of judge called a justice of the peace. **1862** Lytton *Strange Story* I. xxii. 156 Among readers as non-professional as myself. **1946** *Nature* 26 Oct. 578/1 Several departments in the College have *non-professional heads. **1969** H. Perkin *Key Profession* i. 15 Non-professorial tutors and lecturers. **1909** Webster, *Non-progressive. **1950** B. Russell *Unpopular Essays* ix. 166 Learning in Babylonia seems..to have become stereotyped and non-progressive. **1973** *Archivum Linguisticum* IV. 7 The action involved is of a continuous nature as is clear..from a comparison with a non-progressive future. **1937** *Mind* XLVI. 103 Of course, she could not discuss in detail the question of *non-propositional truth in so short a volume. **1903** B. Russell *Princ. Math.* iii. 35 If I may be allowed to use the word *assertion* in a *non-psychological sense. **1965** B. Mates *Elem. Logic.* i. 7 Leibniz..wishes to use the..word [*sc.* 'inconceivable'] in what may be termed a 'non-physchological' sense. **1946** *Nature* 14 Sept. 381/2 Within the scope of *non-public management lie such special fields as industrial administration, commercial or business administration, [etc.]. **1938** *Mind* XLVII. 251 In any case I cannot see any other way of *defining* a 'higher' centre than by saying that it is a class of happenings which facilitate 'purposeful' series and inhibit '*non-purposeful' ones. **1926** J. S. Huxley *Essays of Biologist* (ed. 3) i. 41 Apparently purposive structures could arise by means of a *non-purposive mechanism. **1965** P. Caws *Philos. of Sci.* xl. 312 The goal itself may emerge from an originally nonpurposive activity. **1940** W. V. Quine *Math. Logic* 7 To the scientist longing for *non-quantitative techniques,..mathematical logic brings hope. **1971** *Computers & Humanities* V. 317 Quantitative data covering this aspect of the story are supplemented by a narrative based on traditional (non-quantitative) sources. **1909** *Westm. Gaz.* 7 Apr. 3/1 It is to be conducted on 'absolutely *non-racial and non-party lines'. **1971** *Rand Daily Mail* 3 Apr. 1/3 We stand for nonracial not multiracial cricket and..believe in selection on merit, irrespective of colour. **1972** *Jrnl. Social Psychol.* LXXXVII. 150 It may be that these nonsignificant results were due to the nonracial nature of the communications. **1904** E. Rutherford *Radio-Activity* 397/2 Preparation of *non-radio-active thorium. **1937** *Discovery* Apr. 127/1 An isotope of a non-radioactive element. **1909** Webster, **Nonreactive*, without inductance or capacity. **1962** Simpson & Richards *Physical Princ. Junction Transistors* vi. 107 Another non-reactive extrinsic effect is sometimes added to the low-frequency equivalent circuit. **1969** *Jane's Freight Containers 1968–69* 550/1 The braking safety and non-reactive road holding characteristics required by today's operators. **1941** *Mind* L. 163 A difficulty which Price doubts whether any *non-Realistic theory can completely remove is that quite specific statements may be made purporting to be about unperceived objects for the existence of which there is no evidence. **1965** J. Lawlor in J. Gibb *Light on C. S. Lewis* 75 The non-realistic nature of a large part of Shakespearian characterization. **1949** *Mind* LVIII. 3 A 'determining' element which qualifies it in some *non-reciprocal way. **1788** T. Taylor *Proclus* II. 181 That which is rectangular, is shewn to be greater than that which is *non-rectangular. **1935** B. Russell *Relig. & Sci.* ii. 45 What was unusual or *non-recurrent was assigned directly to the will of God. **1973** *Univ. Oxf. Ann. Rep. 1970–71* 6 The Institute received £150 as a non-recurrent supplement to the departmental grant. **1939** *Mind* XLVIII. 399 Russell long ago emphasised that Peano's axioms, for instance, could be satisfied in infinitely many ways by objects other than the integers. The same is true of all *nonredundant sets of axioms. **1972** J. L. Dillard *Black English* iii. 93 Non-redundant tense marking... This system of tense marking persists into Black English today. **1903** B. Russell *Princ. Math.* iv. 49 Subject—predicate propositions are distinguished by just this *non-relational character. **1954** I. M. Copi *Symbolic Logic* v. 145 The non-relational premiss that all greyhounds are dogs. **1843** Mill *Logic* I. ii. §7. 1. 53 The fifth leading division of names is into *relative* and *absolute*, or let us rather say, *relative* and **non-relative*; for the word absolute is put upon much too hard duty in metaphysics, not to be willingly spared when its services can be dispensed with. **1934** *Mind* XLIII. 202 Such an independence of non-relative properties is what the operationalist theories, with the exception of Mead's, come to. **1930** *Nature* 20 Dec. 954/1 *Non-relativistic wave mechanics. **1970** G. K. Woodgate *Elem. Atomic Struct.* ii. 12 Schrödinger's equation is equivalent to the non-relativistic form of the classical equation of conservation of energy. **1902** W. James *Var. Relig. Exper.* viii. 176 In these *non-religious cases the new man may also be born either gradually or suddenly. **1929** D. H. Lawrence *Pansies* 66 The mind is non-religious. **1964** E. A. Nida *Toward Sci. Transl.* v. 109 It would have been possible to use the label 'religious vs. nonreligious'. **1956** Ld. Boyd-Orr in A. Pryce-Jones *New Outl. Mod. Knowledge* 539 This great accelerating rate of increasing consumption of *non-renewable sources of energy. **1974** *Guardian* 27 Aug. 14/6 Human time..is the ultimate non-renewable resource. **1923** *Gramophone* June 25/2 Music to assert itself has become representational; painting to assert itself has become *non-representational. **1958** *Times* 20 Aug. 11/1 The non-representational third symphony. **1855** S. Bailey *Lett. on Philos. Human Mind* 212 Ideas of a *non-representative character. **1925** I. A. Richards *Princ. Literary Criticism* 159 From Raphael..to Rembrandt..all degrees of participation between non-representative form and represented subject..can be found. **1942** W. Churchill *End of Beginning* (1943) 180 The outstanding fact which has so far emerged from the violent action of the Congress Party has been their non-representative character. *a***1910** W. James *Some Probl. Philos.* (1911) v. 82 What I am contending for is that the *non-reproducible part of reality is an essential part of the content of philosophy. **1832** *Planting* (Libr. Usef. Knowl.) iii. 33 *Non-reproductive or resinous trees. **1868** Swinburne *Blake* 132 François Villon and Aphra Behn, the two most inexpressibly *non-respectable of male or female Bohemians. **1805** Saunders *Min. Waters* 27 Water..that is impregnated with a *non-respirable gas. **1908** *Daily Chron.* 4 May 3/3 If Socialism was to come in England,..it must needs have come in a slow, quiet, *non-revolutionary, almost invisible way. **1959** *Brno Studies in English* I. 121 The non-revolutionary Fabian standpoint. **1905** *Tablet* 14 Oct. 608/2 Some mission or other that called itself Catholic but confessed itself *non-Roman. **1964** R. H. Robins *Gen. Linguistics* v. 193 The use of orthographic spaces, or other marks as in some non-roman scripts. **1956** *Nature* 31 Mar. 610/2 Professional advisory service of a *non-routine nature. **1964** F. Bowers *Bibliogr. & Textual Criticism* III. i. 69 The occurrence of error through non-routine operation. **1934** Webster, *Non-saponifiable. **1946** *Nature* 28 Dec.

950/1 Prelog, Ruzicka and Stein isolated a compound.. from the non-saponifiable portion of extracts of pig spleen. **1967** *Oceanogr. & Marine Biol.* V. 173 Using alcoholic KOH, lipids may be separated into a saponifiable fraction.. and a non-saponifiable fraction including the sterols, carotenoids, wax-alcohols, and hydrocarbons. **1875** W. JAMES *Coll. Ess. & Rev.* (1920) 4 (As is almost always the case with *non-skeptical systems) it simply ends by 'indorsing' common-sense. **1941** N. K. SMITH *Philos. of D. Hume* p. v, This doctrine is the key to the non-sceptical, realist teaching which Hume has expounded. **1865** *What is Wine* vii. 9 A crude and *non-scientific treatment of the must. **1831** J. S. MILL *Lett.* (1910) I. 4 The clergy of a *non-sectarian church. **1937** J. M. MURRY *Necessity of Pacifism* v. 81 The Adelphi Centre is a centre of non-sectarian Socialism. **1948** E. WAUGH *Loved One* 138 All non-sectarian services expeditiously conducted at competitive prices. **1975** G. SEYMOUR *Harry's Game* xiii. 180 Most of the farmers round were Prods but.. the market was 'non-sectarian', as they'd say these days. **1927** R. H. WILENSKI *Mod. Movement in Art* 95 It was the artist's duty to rival the camera in purely mechanical *non-selective vision. **1958** *Observer* 20 July 21/5 The danger lies in the enforcement of the non-selective principle in the vast majority of schools which will continue as separate units in existing buildings. **1909** W. M. URBAN *Valuation* iv. 98 The *non-sensational aspects of any experience are.. describable in functional terms. **1921** B. RUSSELL *Analysis of Mind* iv. 81 (*heading*) Non-sensational elements in perception. **1937** *Mind* XLVI. 307 Kant holds that we are never acquainted with existence in a wholly non-sensory way. **1855** J. M. D. MEIKLEJOHN tr. *Kant's Critique Pure Reason* II. i. 56 The understanding was defined above only negatively, as a *non-sensuous faculty of cognition. **1934** *Mind* XLIII. 364 Locke taught that we can have a non-sensuous intuition of agreement and disagreement of ideas. **1939** *Mind* XLVIII. 483 It is full sentences that serve for communication, not isolated or *non-sentential signs. **1966** *Jrnl. Philos.* LXIII. 665 Propositions in a nonsentential sense were unavailable,.. so facts seemed all the more needed. **1812** SOUTHEY *Omniana* II. 251 The.. opinion that animals are *non-sentient. **1822** LAMB *Elia* Ser. I. *Distant correspondents*, In the latter [*sc.* puns], I include all *non-serious subjects. **1836–9** *Todd's Cycl. Anat.* II. 432/1 Reproduction may be divided into *non-sexual and sexual. **1960** *Amer. Speech* XXXV. 232 Correlates of Central Romance palatals.. are best interpreted as members of a three-way set: plain (*nonsharp).., sharp.., and palatal. **1967** E. CHAMBERS *Photolitho-Offset* vii. 80 An anastigmatic lens gives a flat field and corrects any spherical shape of the image area which otherwise is non-sharp towards the edges of the image. **1897** *Sears, Roebuck Catal.* 239/2 Men's heavy winter weight.. wool shirts... *Non-shrinkable. **1963** A. J. HALL *Textile Sci.* v. 242 This shrunk non-shrinkable finish is then set by passing it (with drying) around the hot cylinder of a Palmer machine P. **1890** W. JAMES *Princ. Psychol.* I. xi. 411 The 'difficulty', in the cases of which Wundt speaks, is that of forcing two *non-simultaneous events into apparent combination with the same instant of time. **1953** C. E. BAZELL *Linguistic Form* 44 The fact that the units concerned may occur as units in a functionally discrete sequence is one criterion for treating the units as non-simultaneous. **1877** CAYLEY in *Encycl. Brit.* VI. 724/1 The classification mixes together *non singular and singular curves. **1944** J. S. HUXLEY *On Living in Rev.* ii. 18 Powerful monopolies develop, which, from being merely *non-social, may become definitely anti-social. **1964** M. ARGYLE *Psychol. & Social Probl.* xiv. 176 Social structures often change as the result of non-social factors in the situation—technical, economic and so on. **1949** KOESTLER *Promise & Fulfilment* III. i. 305 The political record of the only strong *non-Socialist opposition Party in Israel is one of frustration and sterility. **1959** *New Statesman* 13 June 833/2 The idea of a planned hospital service had been developed by non-socialist doctors by 1920 (Dawson Report). **1888** W. JAMES *Let.* 22 Aug. in R. B. Perry *Tht. & Char. of W. J.* (1935) II. 86 By the Kantian view.. *I* mean the doctrine of a *supersensational* construction. For Kant there is a *non-spatial sensational chaos before there is space in the mind. **1897** B. RUSSELL *Essay on Foundations of Geometry* iv. 181 The argument rests on a *petitio principii*, for only if sensations are necesarily non-spatial does their projection demand a subjective space-form. **1851** *Phil. Mag.* I. 177 Poisson.. does not overlook the possibility of these magnetic elements being *non-spherical and symmetrically arranged in crystalline matter. **1971** I. G. GASS et al. *Understanding Earth* vii. 98/1 The uneven attraction of the non-spherical Earth. **1668** WILKINS *Real Char.* 375 The *non-spiritous, or breathless Consonants, P, T, C. **1940** S. GLASSTONE *Text-bk. Physical Chem.* xiii. 1063 One of the results of *non-stationary chains is the phenomenon of explosion limits. **1968** P. A. P. MORAN *Introd. Probability Theory* iii. 173 This is a non-stationary pure birth process. **1922** A. D. UDDEN tr. *Bohr's Theory of Spectra* II. i. 22 This is of great importance, since it represents the first instance in which the quantum theory was applied to a phenomenon of *non-statistical character. **1949** A. PAP *Elem. Analytical Philos.* ix. 179 We use the word 'probable' in a non-statistical sense. **1963** *Higher Educ.* (Cmnd. 2154) 315 The form of government, including financial and other relations with central and local government, with *non-statutory bodies and with industry. **1946** *Nature* 5 Oct. 475/2 He laid the foundation for a fundamental study of the kinetics of dyeing by deriving four differential equations to describe the *non-steady state of flow. **1960** *Times* 1 Sept. 2 Application of non-steady flow theory. **1975** *Sci. Amer.* Nov. 81 The muscle-powered flight of birds, bats and insects depends on the flapping of the wings, which introduces a degree of nonsteady airflow. Nonsteady aerodynamics is thus inherent in natural flapping flight. **1946** *Nature* 24 Aug. 275/2 Some years ago, LeBlanc and Eberius reported that in the decomposition of lead dioxide, PbO_2, a range of homogeneous oxides of *non-stoichiometric formulae was formed. **1965** PHILLIPS & WILLIAMS *Inorg. Chem.* I. viii. 267 There are compounds of the type $Fe_{0.95}O$, $GeTe_{1.025}$, $Ti_{1.103}S_2$. Such non-stoicheiometric compounds are found largely amongst minerals, alloys, and those compounds which contain one or more elements giving rise to at least two valence states. **1954** U. WEINREICH in Saporta & Bastian *Psycholinguistics* (1961) 379/2 The interplay of structural and *non-structural factors. **1965** HUGHES & LONDEY *Elem. of Formal Logic* iii. 16 In doing this we have by-passed the non-structural features, i.e. the particular content of the propositions. **1902** W. JAMES *Var. Relig. Exper.* xviii. 433 Logical reason drawing rigorous inference from *non-subjective facts. **1965** F. SARGESON *Memoirs of Peon* vii. 192 Unless there had been some non-subjective displacement in the timing of events. **1848** JOHNSTON in *Proc. Berw. Nat. Club* II. vi. 301 The structure of the mouth.. proves it to be a *non-suctorial insect. **1907** J. H. PARSONS *Diseases of Eye* xi. 258 (*heading*) *Non-suppurative keratitis. **1951** WHITBY & HYNES *Med. Bacteriol.* (ed. 5) xv. 273 Prostration is extreme, with.. a characteristic non-suppurative arthritis floating from joint to joint. **1849** H. L. MANSEL *Aldrich's Artis Logicæ* App. 38 Aquinas.. admits the ἔκθεσις as a *non-syllogistic process, being an appeal to the senses, not to the reason. **1971** *Jrnl. Gen. Psychol.* Apr. 239 This was an effort to present deductive reasoning demands in a nonsyllogistic form. **1903** B. RUSSELL *Princ. Math.* I. ii. 18 There are much greater difficulties in the way of *non-symbolic exposition of the ideas embedded in our symbolism. **1933** CHAPMAN & HENLE *Fundamentals of Logic* 226 There has been a complete separation between the 'informal' non-symbolic postulates and the 'formal' symbolic ones. **1961** L. F. BROSNAHAN *Sounds of Language* viii. 182 Features of sound complements (which are, of course, non-symbolic). **1964** E. BACH *Introd. Transformational Gram.* vii. 155 It [*sc.* a relation] is *nonsymmetric if there is at least one pair such that $R(x, y)$ and not $R(y, x)$... *Loving* is nonsymmetric, as numerous poems testify. **1948** H. REICHENBACH *Elem. Symb. Logic* iii. 119 We include both mesosymmetrical and asymmetrical functions in the group of *nonsymmetrical functions. **1955** H. LEBLANC *Introd. to Deductive Logic* 188 A relation R is said to be non-symmetrical in a class A if it is neither symmetrical nor asymmetrical in A. **1912, 1940** *Non-synchronous [see ASYNCHRONOUS *a.*]. **1971** *Engineering* Apr. 6/1 With synchronous or non-synchronous controls. **1953** in M. Macdonald *Philos. & Analysis* (1954) 63 Some clearly *non-synonymous names or predicates apply to exactly the same objects. **1965** B. MATES *Elem. Logic* v. 79 The indicated procedure can lead to different, and plainly non-synonymous, translations for the same formal sentence. **1957** R. W. ZANDVOORT *Handb. Eng. Gram.* IX. i. 283 Such a *non-syntactic group as *happy-go-lucky*. **1965** N. CHOMSKY *Aspects of Theory of Syntax* iv. 158 One can cite cases of perfectly grammatical strings that are incongruous on nonsyntactic grounds. **1960** *Non-systematic [see IMPRESSIONISTIC *a.* 2]. **1964** E. A. NIDA *Towards Sci. Transl.* v. 87 It must be recognized, however, that semantic space may be orthogonal, i.e. regular and systematic, or it may be nonorthogonal, i.e. irregular and nonsystematic. **1949** *Mind* LVIII. 69 This simply begs the central question at issue, *viz.* whether there can be any necessary *non-tautologous propositions. **1955** A. N. PRIOR *Formal Logic* 139 'Analytic' and 'synthetic' are now often used as synonyms for 'tautologous' and 'non-tautologous' respectively. **1833** ARNOTT (*title*), Elements of Physics.. written.. in Plain or *Non-technical Language. **1920** A. S. EDDINGTON *Space, Time & Gravit.* xii. 180 But this mode of development of the theory cannot be described in a non-technical book. **1944** W. TEMPLE *Let.* 5 Jan. (1963) 132 The non-technical mind of the ordinary Churchman. **1971** *Engineering* Apr. 26/1 He spends his time on non-technical activities. **1949** KOESTLER *Insight & Outlook* x. 153 Like all means towards an end (or subfunctions in *nonteleological language). **1972** M. A. BODEN *Purposive Explan. in Psychol.* v. 180 The nonteleological factors involved may include learnt motor habits. **1924** R. M. OGDEN tr. *Koffka's Growth of Mind* v. § 1. 244 The images that occur can scarcely be called *non-temporal. **1933** A. N. WHITEHEAD *Adventures of Ideas* xiii. 209 The everlasting nature of God, which in a sense is non-temporal and in another sense temporal. **1954** I. M. COPI *Symbolic Logic* v. 132 The words 'always', 'never', and 'sometimes' frequently have a strictly non-temporal significance. **1962** H. C. CONKLIN in Householder & Saporta *Problems in Lexicography* 129 The same segregates may be classed.. as terminal or *nonterminal categories in another taxonomy. **1965** *Language* XLI. 292 Certain nonterminal constituents. **1959** *New Statesman* 14 Nov. 661/1 The film was made by the BBC Television Service, and is scheduled for *non-theatric distribution; which means that it will only be seen by film societies and non-paying audiences. **1966** *BBC Handbk.* 39 The distribution of programmes for non-theatric use in schools. **1927** T. S. ELIOT in *Newton's Seneca* (Tudor Translations) I. p. xi, This curious freak of *non-theatrical drama. **1964** F. BOWERS *Bibliogr. & Textual Criticism* VI. i. 160 A non-theatrical manuscript such as an author's 'foul papers'. **1879** *Dublin Rev.* Apr. 263 It seems to be the wish of the prominent *non-theistic writers of our own day to be called Agnostics. **1964** E. FROMM in I. L. Horowitz *New Sociology* 191 Marx's theory.. is close to Pelagius' heresy; it is a doctrine of salvation in non-theistic terms. **1962** H. R. LOYN *Anglo-Saxon England* (1963) vi. 285 Interest was also shown in *non-theological matters. **1943** *Mind* LII. 130 Clearly the outcome of a maze learning experiment is completely devoid of any significance in the latter, *non-theoretical sense. **1963** P. GARDINER *Schopenhauer* v. 216 At a non-theoretical level, Schopenhauer suggests, such features of aesthetic awareness are.. recognized by sensitive and perceptive persons. **1959** D. COOKE *Lang. of Music* p. xiii, The new *non-tonal language.. must be restricted to expressing what chromaticism always was restricted to expressing. **1963** *Listener* 21 Feb. 345/3 Schoenberg went on from there to write first non-tonal and later twelve-note music. **1964** R. H. ROBINS *Gen. Linguistics* iii. 111 English, a non-tonal language. **1941** J. S. HUXLEY *Uniqueness of Man* xi. 235 The T.V.A. in America is perhaps the largest social experiment ever undertaken, at any rate in a *non-totalitarian country. **1967** H. ARENDT *Orig. Totalitarianism* (new ed.) ix. 279 Non-totalitarian countries.. generally have shied away from mass repatriations. **1946** *Nature* 31 Aug. 294/1 Animal experiments with guinea pigs and rabbits have shown polyporin to be completely *non-toxic. **1971** *Engineering* Apr. 30/1 Since the introduction of plastics enabled the use of non-tainting, non-toxic, and non-staining materials. **1938** WYNDHAM LEWIS *Let.* 1 May (1963) 253 A *Non-traditional (and so a 'fashionable') policy. **1957** MANVELL & HUNTLEY *Technique Film Music* iii. 169 The term 'synthetic sound' is generally used to cover a wide variety of new, non-traditional methods of making noise, sound effects, music, and speech, by electronic, magnetic, mechanical, optical, and other means. **1914** B. RUSSELL *Our Knowl. External World* ii. 48 A relation is said to be *non-transitive whenever it is not transitive. Thus 'brother' is non-transitive, because a brother of one's brother may be oneself. All kinds of dissimilarity are non-transitive. **1964** E. BACH *Introd. Transformational Gram.* vii. 155 *Friend* is nontransitive if you are my friend and have friends who are not my friends. **1974** *Sci. Amer.* Oct. 120/1 Familiar games abound in transitive rules (if poker hand A beats B and B beats C, then A beats C), but some games have nontransitive (or intransitive) rules. **1946** *Nature* 14 Sept. 361/2 Another means of attaining greater efficiency in flight.. is to design the wing section so that the flow in the very thin 'boundary-layer' of air near the wing surface remains *non-turbulent over as much of the surface as possible. **1964** J. C. CATFORD in D. Abercrombie et al. *Daniel Jones* 30 Airflow through the glottis is non-turbulent and consequently silent. **1890** W. JAMES *Princ. Psychol.* I. iii. 93 When we begin to react in the 'extreme sensorial' way, Lange says that we get times so very long that they must be rejected from the count as *non-typical. **1959** *Brno Studies* I. 106 The non-typical nature of his [*sc.* Bulwer's] figures. **1874** W. WALLACE tr. *Hegel's Logic* 299 Finite things as finite ought in justice to be viewed as *non-ultimate. **1935** *Mind* XLIV. 351 He ought to say that such facts as 'orange is between red and yellow' are incomplete or non-ultimate. **1886** G. S. CARR *Synopsis Elem. Results Pure & Appl. Math.* I. II. 905/1 (Index), *Non-uniform functions. **1920** A. S. EDDINGTON *Space, Time & Gravit.* ii. 40 An absolute non-uniform motion through space is just as impossible to imagine as an absolute uniform motion. **1968** *Economist* 23 Mar. 48/2 The 40-month contract.. reportedly gives workers giant but nonuniform wage increases. **1909** *Daily Chron.* 12 Apr. 4/4, I revisit America and wander off into the *non-urban—there are no really rural—parts. **1953** K. JACKSON *Lang. & Hist. in Early Britain* 230 A state of affairs that was essentially non-urban. *a* **1866** J. GROTE *Exam. Utilit. Philos.* (1870) p. xvii, Mr. Mill gives up points objected to in the old utilitarianism, and approximates to *non-utilitarian schools. **1965** F. SARGESON *Memoirs of Peon* i. 10 My grandmother was entirely non-utilitarian, a dreamer. **1939** *Mind* XLVIII. 202 And if *s* does express a proposition, thereby being subject to *non-vacuous application of this [verification] principle, it could be the case [etc.]. **1965** N. CHOMSKY *Aspects of Theory of Syntax* i. 39 At least one rule $A \to x$ being obligatory for each category A, so as to guarantee that each cycle is nonvacuous. **1881** MAX MÜLLER tr. *Kant's Critique Pure Reason* (1896) 323 All those predicates are with regard to intuition *non-valid, entailing no consequences with regard to objects of experience. **1935** *Mind* XLIV. 504 The content of a sentence is said to be the class of its non-valid consequences. **1870** H. A. NICHOLSON *Man. Zool.* lxiii. (1875) 473 The *non-venomous and most typical Snakes. **1919** A. C. DOYLE *Vital Message* iii. 102 Thus though '*non-veridical', to use the modern jargon, they do conform to all our canons of evidence. **1942** *Mind* LI. 43 But if there need be no 'intrinsic difference'.. between veridical and non-veridical experiences, then how can you tell, at any given time, whether your perceptual experience is veridical or non-veridical? **1890** W. JAMES *Princ. Psychol.* II. xx. 212 Berkeley.. concluded that distance could not possibly be a visual sensation, but must be an intellectual 'suggestion' from 'custom' of some *non-visual experience. **1971** J. Z. YOUNG *Introd. Study Man* xxx. 421 Some lemurs have scent-glands on the fore-limbs; these are common among non-visual mammals. **1933** *Discovery* Sept. 278/1 It is, in fact, not an *aposeme* to frighten an enemy away.. but an *episeme*, to distract attack from a vulnerable to a fortified or *non-vital region. **1936** J. R. KANTOR *Objective Psychol. Gram.* xiii. 184 There is still left the question of interjectional acts or even *non-vocal behavior. **1946** C. MORRIS *Signs, Language & Behavior* 192 That there are non-vocal languages is not generally disputed. **1964** R. H. ROBINS *Gen. Linguistics* iv. 157 Opposed acoustic features: vocalic, *non-vocalic. **1930** *Times Educ. Suppl.* 15 Feb. 70/2 What was known as *non-vocational education. **1963** *Higher Educ.* (Cmnd. 2154) 317 Courses of a mainly non-vocational character.

4. Prefixed to a sb. (or vbl. sb.) forming a phrase used attributively, as ***non-citizen, -class, -combat, -copyright, -corridor, -county, -craft, -dollar, -equilibrium*** (see also sense 1), ***-fat*** (cf. *non-fatty* in 3), ***-food, -image, -jazz, -kernel, -language, -league, -narrative, -pedigree, -print, -profit, protein, -speech, -structuralist, -teaching, -title, -vintage***, etc.; **non-association** (see quot. 1940).

Occas. such phrases are used predicatively (as in quot. 1956 for *non-protein*).

1909 *Installation News* II. 180 The standard qualities listed are:— (1) A class equivalent to what is generally designated throughout the trade as *Non-Association Cable. (2) A grade equivalent to that manufactured by members of the Cable Makers' Association, and sold by the latter under the Association's label as Association-made Cable. **1940** *Chamber's Techn. Dict.* 582/1 *Non-association cable*, cable which is not manufactured or designed in accordance with the standards of the Cable Makers' Association. **1906** *Westm. Gaz.* 11 Apr. 10/3 Charming Semi-detached *Non-basement Houses. **1892** in Greener *Breech Loader* 285 [Greener's No. 12 choke-bore] kills on an average at least 20 yards further than a *non-choke bore. **1882** *Contemp. Rev.* Aug. 301 The wish on the part of the *non-church people to relieve themselves of all Church questions. **1970** *East African Standard* 2 Jan. 15/2 In the Market Square in Kampala, which is one of the areas proscribed for *non-citizen businessmen, there are several empty shops. **1957** R. N. CAREW HUNT *Guide to Communist Jargon* xxxii. 111 The ideologists of the imperialist bourgeoisie, hypocritically screening themselves behind a *non-class approach. **1971** *Jrnl. Gen. Psychol.* Apr. 313 Centred on each of these cards was a column of 12 words, one of which was the correct response, the other 11 words being nonclass, low associate, masking words. **1944** D. WECTER *When Johnny comes marching Home* 547 He must also be persuaded that an important job waits for him, either in *non-combat duty or in civil life. **1971** *Fremdsprachen* XV. 209 In the last three months of 1970, aircraft accidents were the chief cause of noncombat deaths. **1879** WHITNEY *Skr. Gram.* 60 The tip of the tongue,.. reverted into the loose lingual position by the utterance of a *non-contact lingual element. **1947** *Penguin Music Mag.* Dec. 37 British *non-copyright masterpieces such as *David Copperfield*. **1908** *Daily Chron.* 31 July 1/7 The door on the *non-corridor side of the train was found open. **1966** M. Catto *Bird on Wing* vi. 93 It was one of those old-fashioned non-corridor trains. **1909** *Westm. Gaz.* 1 May 9/2 Property owned and leased by county and *non-county boroughs. **1963** *Times* 7 June 3/7 It contains a detailed breakdown of the rates levied by the 83 county boroughs and 28 metropolitan boroughs, and there is also a representative selection of 226 non-county boroughs, 219 urban districts and 144 rural districts. **1961** *Spectator* 7 Apr. 474/2 These craft divisions, particularly those between what is considered 'craft' and '*non-craft' work, are apparently carried much further in Britain than elsewhere. **1958** *Ann. Reg. 1957* 88 Japan was placed on the same footing as other ..*non-dollar countries. **1951** S. R. de Groot *Thermodynamics of Irreversible Processes* xi. 220 (*heading*) *Non-equilibrium thermodynamical functions. **1962** Simpson & Richards *Physical Princ. Junction Transistors* i. 2 The higher energy states will be empty except in a non-equilibrium condition when an electron is excited to a higher state by some external influence. **1971** *Nature* 17 Dec. 393/1 Nonequilibrium thermodynamics, as developed by Onsager and others, has been successful in correlating many physical, chemical and biological phenomena. **1835** Ure *Philos. Manuf.* 335 The embroidery of bobbin-net, called lace-running,.. a *non-factory household work. **1969** *Listener* 30 Jan. 159/3 The bonus payments scheme takes into account not merely the important nutrients in milk (protein, vitamins and minerals, commonly known as the '*non-fat solids') but also fat content, which doesn't matter a hoot to anyone who doesn't want to make butter or cheese. **1946** *Nature* 7 Sept. 324/1 Possible *non-food industrial utilizations of the wheat protein. **1974** *Index-Jrnl.* (Greenwood, S. Carolina) 19 Apr. 1/5 Sharply higher food prices and a record jump in nonfood commodities pushed the cost of living up 1.1 per cent in March. **1654** Gataker *Disc. Apol.* 96 And a thousand more *non-Gospel phrases. **1853** R. S. Surtees *Soapey Sponge* (1893) 291 D—n you, sir, I'll fight you, sir, any *non-hunting day you like, sir, except Sunday. **1953** Kirk & Othmer *Encycl. Chem. Technol.* XI. 139 The moisture film produced on the plate is continuous on the *nonimage areas of the plate. **1964** *Gloss. Letterpress Rotary Printing Terms* (*B.S.I.*) 9 *Blacking up*, printing of the non-image areas. **1926** Whiteman & McBride *Jazz* viii. 168 The orchestrations for bands, jazz and *non-jazz are almost as important as the song plugger himself. **1958** P. Gammond *Decca Bk. Jazz* xv. 189 His fault at the moment ..is his quick switching from jazz to non-jazz phrasing. **1963** *Amer. Speech* XXXVIII. 295 *Nonkernel, derived sentences such as 'The man is on the corner'. **1936** J. R. Kantor *Objective Psychol. Gram.* vi. 74 B's action may be connected with a *non-language response—namely, handing over the book. **1946** C. Morris *Signs, Language & Behavior* 6 The differences between non-language and language signs. **1938** C. E. Sutcliffe et al. *Story of Football League* 12 The boycott of *non-League clubs..was withdrawn. **1963** *Times* 28 Jan. 3/3 Nairn county, another non-league club still in the competition, came down from the Highlands on Saturday to cause a surprise by holding Hamilton Academicals, leaders of the second division, to a draw. **1975** *Liverpool Echo* (Football ed.) 11 Jan. 8/3, I cannot recall..so many non League clubs doing so well [in the F.A. Cup]. **1884** *Law Rep.* 14 Q.B. Div. 262 Persons who were doing on *non-market days that which they could only do legally on market days. **1964** M. A. K. Halliday et al. *Linguistic Sci.* 237 It shows the written language in use in *non-narrative registers. *a* **1687** Petty *Pol. Arith.* i. (1691) 26 Jews, and *Non-Papist Merchant-Strangers. **1880** *Standard* 15 Dec., Mr. Fawcett's..speech..was..almost entirely of a *non-party character. **1931** *Times Lit. Suppl.* 13 Aug. 620/4 Others in favour are the Border, the Lakeland, the Fox, the Sealyham (but with these two it is generally specified that they must be '*non-pedigree' or 'old type'). **1960** *Farmer & Stockbreeder* 9 Feb. 85/3 The few non-pedigree cattle on offer were of moderate class and sold to 130gs. **1971** *Computers & Humanities* VI. 96 Such classes of material as technical reports, government documents, and microforms and other *non-print media. **1972** *Guardian* 5 Dec. 9/7 The shift to non-print means of communication —television, the telephone. **1942** *Agenda* Oct. 305 The T.V.A...is required by statute to give preference to States, counties, municipalities, and *non-profit co-operative associations. **1972** *Accountant* 28 Sept. 389/2 The interest rates are high, being 11 per cent for a with-profit policy and 10 per cent for a non-profit policy. **1974** *Spartanburg* (S. Carolina) *Herald* 25 Apr. C. 2/5 Kawamura's laboratories are in the Mitsubishi Chemical Co.'s nonprofit Institute of Life Sciences which it set up in 1971 at a cost of $6·6 million. [**1934** Webster, *Nonprotein, *n.*] **1946** *Nature* 2 Nov. 610/1 The now demonstrated ability of ruminants to utilize non-protein nitrogen in the form of urea. **1956** *Ibid.* 28 Jan. 190/2 Binkley..obtained a soluble fraction..which was apparently non-protein in nature. **1967** *Oceanogr. & Marine Biol.* V. 159 The biochemical analysis of marine invertebrates, especially their content of macromolecules.. and reserves (lipids, carbohydrates, non-protein nitrogenous compounds (NPN)). **1890** W. J. Gordon *Foundry* 26 The breech-block is linked to the body and mounted on a *non-recoil carriage. **1846** *Penny Cycl.* Suppl. II. 234/1 The *non-restraint system [in asylums]. **1954** F. G. Cassidy *Robertson's Devel. Mod. Eng.* iv. 54 The phonetician..must include the entire range of speech sounds... Pike would have him investigate *non-speech sounds too. **1953** C. E. Bazell *Linguistic Form* 5 The earlier distinction of morpheme and semanteme is obsolete except in *non-structuralist circles. **1893** *Times* 25 Apr. 9/3 The total produce of *non-tax revenue would be 85,000 more than last year. **1959** *New Statesman* 21 Feb. 259/3 Hours are wasted each week in administrative, *non-teaching duties such as special staff meetings, frequent house meetings, tutorial group meetings. **1851** Mayhew *Lond. Lab.* II. 39/2 Other small *non-thoroughfare courts, some-times called blind alleys. **1973** *N.Y. Times* 28 Jan. 21/2 This is a *nontitle fight and there is no weight restriction on heavyweights. **1836** Pusey in Liddon *Life Pusey* (1893) I. xviii. 421 He argues..against the *non-transmission doctrine. **1953** D. Parry *Going Up—Going Down* vi. 318 At dinner Clive ordered up four bottles of *non-vintage champagne. **1959** *Listener* 5 Mar. 422/1 Bratby is here, of course, a non-vintage work half way between the 'larder' period and what is happening at his current exhibition. **1975** *Country Life* 2 Oct. 838/3 No non-vintage champagne may be sold until it has been a year in bottle.

5. a. Prefixed to an infinitive, as ***non-act*** = not to act, to refuse, neglect, or omit to act.

1645 *Non-act [see non-consent]. **1818** Bentham *Ch. Eng. Catech. Exam.* 294 Keeping eyes shut or open at pleasure, to *non-answer or false answer to questions. **1846** De Quincey *Wellesley* Wks. 1858 VIII. 28 A war administration, that ever feebly misapplied or lazily *non-applied the resources of a mighty empire. **1676** W. Hubbard *Happiness of a People* 40 The civill power..ought to *non-licentiate him that shall take upon him..to prescribe to the people poysonous Drugs.

b. Prefixed to an infinitive forming a phrase used attributively in the sense 'that does not——', 'that is designed not to——', as ***non-crease***, ***-crush***, ***-dazzle***, ***-shrink***. Cf. non-skid *a.*, non-slip *a.*, non-stick *a.*

1944 A. Thirkell *Headmistress* ix. 200 Utility non-crease (though they were neither) ready-made dresses. **1969** *Punch* 5 Feb. 195/1 You *should* wear non-crease clothes. **1924** *Times Trade & Eng. Suppl.* 29 Nov. 247/2 It must be remembered that the heavy weight non-crush costume linens absorb an enormous quantity of flax in spinning. **1961** *Times* 4 Dec. (Agric. Suppl.) p. iii/5 An optional extra to be combined with a non-crush cab. **1962** *Times* 5 May 9/4 A non-dazzle protective covering for our remaining pictures. **1965** *Economist* 27 Feb. 929/2 An alternative pair of non-dazzle lamps..[for] meeting other traffic. **1962** J. T. Marsh *Self-Smoothing Fabrics* xv. 256 The anti-shrink effect so often ignored by later publications on non-shrink processes. *a* **1963** L. MacNeice *Astrology* (1964) vii. 237 The Zodiac..signs are featured..in advertisements for.. non-shrink cottons.

6. a. Prefixed to ppl. adjs., as ***non-articulated***, ***-aspirated***, ***-associated***, ***-budding***, ***-centralized***, ***-ciliated***, ***-classified***, ***-clogging***, ***-coloured***, ***-committed***, ***-corroding***, ***-defining***, ***-dividing***, ***-fabricated***, ***-fattening***, ***-flying***, ***-glottalized***, ***-graphitizing***, ***-growing***, ***-increasing***, ***-interacting***, ***-introduced***, ***-ionized***, ***-ionizing***, ***-living***, ***-medullated***, ***-nasalized***, ***-overlapping***, ***-palatalized***, ***-playing***, ***-polarized***, ***-polluting***, ***-proliferating***, ***-recurring***, ***-referring***, ***-reflecting***, ***-scripted***, ***-slaveholding***, ***-specialized***, ***-teaching***, ***-terminating***.

Such compounds are very common in scientific use.

1861 Bentley *Man. Bot.* I. iii. §3 When a leaf separates from the stem, it either does so by decaying upon it, when it is said to be *non-articulated; or [etc.]. **1934** Priebsch & Collinson *German Lang.* I. iii. 42 The *non-aspirated mediae are treated differently from the aspirated mediae. **1964** E. A. Nida *Toward Sci. Transl.* vi. 132 In one language in Central Africa there is a contrast between aspirated and nonaspirated consonants. **1934** C. Lambert *Music Ho!* ii. 78 Surrealism may conveniently be defined as the free grouping together of incongruous and *non-associated images. **1974** *Information Handbk. 1974–5* (Shell Internat. Petroleum Co.) 85 Non-associated gas — either from structures capable of producing only gas economically or from condensate reservoirs which yield relatively large amounts of gas per barrel of light liquid hydrocarbons. **1836** J. M. Gully *Magendie's Formul.* (ed. 2) 186 A *non-azotized animal or vegetable substance. **1846** Dana *Zooph.* (1848) 69 The lateral *non-budding polyps of the branch. **1893** G. B. Shaw *Let.* 11 Jan. (1965) 377 My present intention is to go uncompromisingly for..*non-centralized local organization of the Labor Party. **1956** *Nature* 3 Mar. 432/1 A well-defined zone of *non-ciliated epithelium which lies along the medial sides of the lips of the endostylar groove [in *Ciona intestinalis*]. **1958** *New Statesman* 19 Apr. 494/1 The Columbia Inspection Project, a private, *non-classified study of disarmament techniques. **1973** A. Price *October Men* x. 136 He is in charge of the non-classified printed material—newspapers, periodicals and journals. **1910** *Daily Chron.* 12 Mar. 8/5 A truly efficient *non-clogging lubricant has been used. **1960** *Farmer & Stockbreeder* 16 Feb. 106/2 Automatic recoil-starter eliminating the use of loose starting rope; special non-clogging, fast-cutting blades, 18 in. cutting width. **1962** E. Cleaver in A. Dundes *Mother Wit* (1973) 15/1 Blue eyes, long straight blonde hair, and *non-colored skin. **1964** S. M. Miller in I. L. Horowitz *New Sociology* 306 That can be done most effectively by outsiders—non-colored, non-poor —coming into the impoverished areas. **1901** R. Fry *Let.* 14 Mar. (1972) I. 180 Shannon, coming to such design from the Impressionist side,..goes off into vague *non-committed tastefulness. **1970** Non-committed [see non-alignment]. **1908** *Daily Chron.* 21 Nov. 9/3 As evidence of their *non-corroding quality specimens are shown in glass bottles immersed in water uninjured. **1967** E. Chambers *Photolitho-Offset* xii. 189 The turntable consists of a non-corroding alloy. **1756** C. Lucas *Ess. Waters* III. 314, I poured off the *non-crystallised liquor. **1926** Fowler *Mod. Eng. Usage* 635/2 The closer connexion between a defining, (or *that-*) clause & the antecedent than between a *non-defining (or *which-*) clause & the antecedent. **1970** *Dict. Sci. Biogr.* I. 250/2 His [*sc.* Aristotle's] distinction..between defining and non-defining characteristics. **1876** *Clinical Soc. Trans.* IX. 167 The tissue having become firm, even, and *non-discharging. **1945** Koestler *Yogi & Commissar* III. iv. 242 *Non-dividing organic constituents (proteins, enzymes, hormones, etc.). **1864** Pusey *Lect. Daniel* ix. 561 A *non-enquiring acquiescence in doubt, which is the peril of this day. **1701** Norris *Ideal World* I. v. 279 The supposed exception..according to the rule makes the affirmation hold the more strongly in the *non-excepted instances. **1939** *Mind* XLVIII. 170 The first objection asserts that all universals are fabricated, and no *non-fabricated universals exist. **1971** *Woman's Own* 27 Mar. 30/2 It's expensive to eat *non-fattening foods. **1941** N. Macmillan *Air Strategy* 53 Safeguarding the health and efficiency of the *non-flying personnel. **1849** Noad *Electricity* (ed. 3) 240 The *non-galvanized rabbit wheezed audibly, and made frequent attempts to vomit. **1949** E. A. Nida *Morphology* (ed. 2) 287 The contrasts in such changes are..glottalized, *non-glottalized. **1973** *Word 1970* XXVI. 6 A regular interchange ..between nonglottalized and glottalized stops. **1693** *Oxford Act* II. 11 For Graduates, and *Non-graduated... the Gall'ries are reserved. **1951** *Non-graphitizing [see graphitizable *a.*]. **1971** *Nature* 30 July 306/2 The graphitizable carbon fibres probably have superior tensile properties..than the equivalently heated non-graphitizing carbon fibres. **1937** *Discovery* June 173/1 The *non-growing tip must have some control over the growing region below it. **1968** H. Harris *Nucleus & Cytoplasm* iii. 54 In cells growing exponentially, ribosomal RNA appears to be essentially stable, and in non-growing cells, it turns over at a very much slower rate than the rapidly labelled RNA. **1671** Flavel *Fount. Life* II. 3 The glorious condition of the *Non-incarnated Son of God. **1962** D. R. Cox *Renewal Theory* i. 3 Clearly $\mathscr{F}(0) = 1$, $\mathscr{F}(\infty) = 0$ and $\mathscr{F}(x)$ is a *non-increasing function of *x*. **1951** A. C. Ewing *Fundamental Questions Philos.* vi. 125 The same substance appearing under parallel *non-interacting aspects. **1962** W. B. Thompson *Introd. Plasma Physics* viii. 170 For the case of non-interacting particles..eq. (8.1.1) may be integrated to yield the collisionless Boltzmann equation. *a* **1661** Fuller *Worthies Shropshire* III. (1662) 3 They have flourished the owners thereof, by an *noninterrupted succession, from the time of King Edward the Confessor. **1957** R. W. Zandvoort *Handbk. Eng. Gram.* v. ii. 217 Note the following example of a *non-introduced clause (with *so*): *I paid him double, I was so pleased.* **1966** *English Studies* XLVII. 262 The non-introduced type is normal in adjunct clauses and verbs, and in adjunct clauses to adjectives. **1902** *Encycl. Brit.* XXVIII. 15/1 In the case of non-electrolytes and of all *non-ionized molecules this analogy completely represents the facts, and the phenomena of diffusion can be deduced from it alone. **1963** B. Fozard *Instrumentation Nuclear Reactors* viii. 78 Thus glow transfer can be caused by applying a negative pulse to the cathode of the non-ionized gap. **1974** M. C. Gerald *Pharmacol.* iii. 39 At the physiological pH of body fluids, drug molecules exist as a mixture of the nonionized or uncharged molecular form and the ionized or charged form. **1903** *Nature* 3 Dec. 103/2 If *non-ionising solvents like the hydrocarbons be substituted for water, the absence of effects attributable to ionisation might be discernible. **1968** M. S. Livingston *Particle Physics* iv. 83 Nonionizing neutral particles..were assumed also to be produced. **1926** J. S. Huxley *Ess. Pop. Sci.* 261 For Haldane, regulation places organisms in a different category from any *non-living systems. **1971** J. Z. Young *Introd. Study Man* ii. 14 It is not enough to base our biology only on familiar concepts with which we describe the non-living world. **1861** H. Kingsley *Ravenshoe* xxxvii, A *non-marrying man, as the slang goes. **1881** J. Ross *Treat. Dis. Nervous Syst.* I. I. i. 22 (*heading*) *Non-medullated nerve-fibres. *Ibid.* 23 A fatty material of a very special character accumulates in the interior of the protoplasm..in order to account for the development of the medullated from the non-medullated fibres (Ranvier). **1949** J. B. Speakman in J. M. Preston *Fibre Science* xvi. 277 Turning..to non-medullated fibres, Chamberlain found that the sulphur content of human hair, which had been descaled..was identical with that of the original untreated hair. **1962** *Gray's Anat.* (ed. 33) 50 Fibres with a myelin sheath are described as myelinated, medullated or white. Those devoid of it are termed unmyelinated, amyelinated, non-medullated or grey fibres. **1953** K. Jackson *Lang. & Hist. in Early Britain* 642 (Apparently) *non-nasalised spellings are found in MW. beside nasalised (non-nasalised even occurring in later MSS. when the earlier MS. copied has nasalised). **1843** Pereira *Treat. Food & Diet.* 36 That *non nitrogenised foods alone are incapable of supporting animal life. **1873** Spencer *Stud. Sociol.* iii. 61 Minute *non-nucleated portions of protoplasm. **1950** *Mind* LIX. 202 The division is exhaustive and *non-overlapping. **1968** P. A. P. Moran *Introd. Probability Theory* iv. 185 A set function, ϕ (A). is said to be σ-additive on a σ-field, if $\phi(\Sigma A_i) = \Sigma\,\phi(A_i)$ for every finite or enumerable set of non-overlapping sets A_i such that $\phi(\Sigma A_i)$ is bounded. **1801** Davy in *Phil. Trans.* XCI. 399 The wire from the *non-oxidating surface. **1956** Jakobson & Halle in Saporta & Bastian *Psycho-linguistics* (1961) 348/2 Consonants: palatalized vs. *non-palatalized. **1776** Da Costa *Elem. Conchol.* x. 187 Their shape so much resembles the Sea Ears, that most authors..call them *non-perforated Sea Ears. **1888** Rolleston & Jackson *Anim. Life* 122 The pigmented cells are widest at their inner, the *non-pigmented at their outer ends. **1898** H. E. Byers in W. A. Morgan '*House' on Sport* 206 The *non-playing men alternately shout their approbation and make heavy bets. **1958** *Atlantic Monthly* Nov. 184/2 One solution is to.. subsidize a trip to the movies for the nonplaying members of the family. **1959** *Times* 11 Sept. 9/3 The British team's non-playing captain. **1826** Hood *Irish Schoolm.* ix, Below he wears the nether garb of males, Of crimson plush, but *non-plushed at the knee. **1876** Preece & Sivewright *Telegraphy* iii. 60 A *non-polarized relay..is not much used in England. The forms of relay more largely used are called polarized, because their armatures are either permanent magnets or are maintained in a magnetized condition. **1946** *Nature* 30 Nov. 794/2 The erythrocytes become dipoles..and form chain-like aggregates... Sedimentation-rates of such red-cell aggregates will be greater than those of single non-polarized blood cells. **1967** *Economist* 8 July 107/3 Tenants in some rural areas had to prostrate themselves at a safe, *non-polluting distance on the one day they saw their Brahmin landlord, rent day. **1974** *Listener* 14 Feb. 212/2 What is needed is..cycleways and encouragement for people to use this non-polluting form of transport. **1622** in Rushw. *Hist. Coll.* (1659) I. 64 Not onely for a help for the *Non preaching, but withall for a pattern..for the Preaching Ministers. **1885** *Spectator* 10 Jan. 51/2 The cynical and unprincipled, or at least *non-principled, time of which he writes. **1761** *Chron.* in *Ann. Reg* 101 At Malta the bailiff Marulli has just made a call of all the knights professed and *non-professed. **1946** *Nature* 21 Dec. 900/1 The processes listed are mainly brought about by *non-proliferating suspensions of bacteria or yeasts. **1797** *Monthly Mag.* III. 266 The qualifications, which entitle a person to be a candidate for the medals, wholly preclude the *non-reading men from a competition. **1824** *Gradus ad Cantabr.* **1780** *Chron.* in *Ann. Reg.* 262/2 Many..killed themselves with drinking *non-rectified spirits. **1910** *Daily Chron.* 7 Mar. 1/7 They did not mix up recurring and *non-recurring expenditure. **1973** *Ann. Rep. Curators Bodl. Libr. 1971–2* 49 A total balance of £1,614 from special non-recurring grants for stock-piling. **1957** A. N. Prior *Time & Modality* 61 Genuinely *non-referring names..are excluded. **1963** F. T. Visser *Hist. Syntax* I. iii. 236 Another [construction] of very recent introduction, in which *it* is non-referring. **1946** *Nature* 21 Sept. 422/1 The anti-reflexion or *non-reflecting thin transparent film deposited on the surface of the lens. 1962 L. S. SASIENI *Optical Dispensing* x. 271 Coating the lens surfaces with a non-reflecting coating. 1974 *Country Life* 21 Mar. 659/2 The black non-reflecting surface. 1684 E. CHAMBERLAYNE *Pres. St. Eng.* II. (ed. 15) 138 The rest of his Majesties established Forces..being *non-regimented. 1836 J. M. GULLY *Magendie's Formul.* (ed. 2) 130 *Non-saturated hydrochloric acid. 1972 P. BLACK *Biggest Aspidistra* III. iv. 179 The *non-scripted shows made an important contribution to the art of radio. 1973 *Nation Rev.* (Melbourne) 31 Aug. 1453/1 *Lonesome cowboys* is a collection of heads playing themselves in non scripted situations. 1819 *Deb. Congress U.S.* 17 Feb. (1855) 1235 A line..shall divide the slaveholding from the *non-slaveholding States. 1909 S. & B. WEBB *Break-up of Poor Law* I. i. 11 Here and there we meet exceptionally gifted natures, whose faith and love..enable them..to withstand the deadening influence of the *non-specialised institution. 1964 M. A. K. HALLIDAY et al. *Linguistic Sci.* 37 'Context'..thus corresponds roughly to 'meaning' in the general, non-specialized sense of the term. 1853 R. S. SURTEES *Soapey Sponge* lxiii. (1893) 337 The *non-sporting inmates of Non-such House. 1868 CARPENTER *Microscope* §570 (ed. 4) 729 The 'smooth' or *Non-striated form of Muscular fibre. 1963 *Times* 5 Feb. 6/3 Other factors are £880,000 for aid to pupils and £621,000 for *non-teaching staff. 1975 *Listener* 4 Dec. 757/2 Non-teaching Fellows and professors. 1936 *Mind* XLV. 105 Popper, indeed, recognises that falsification, too, is a *non-terminating process. 1966 OGILVY & ANDERSON *Excurs. Number Theory* x. 121 Therefore if the irrationals have continued fraction expansions (and indeed they do), these must be nonterminating. 1776 DA COSTA *Elem. Conchol.* IV. 80 Univalves, in which they comprehend both the *non-turbinated and turbinated. 1864 E. YATES *Broken to Harness* xxxii, The first drops..causing an immediate consternation..among the *non-umbrellaed spectators. 1892 J. TAIT *Mind in Matter* (ed. 3) 336 Bipeds and quadrupeds, winged and *non-winged beasts.

b. Prefixed to combs. formed with ppl. adjs., as ***non-English-speaking, -habit-forming, -information-carrying, -interest-bearing, -profit-making***, etc.

1866 AITKEN *Pract. Med.* II. 43 In the *non-beer-drinking countries. 1949 M. MEAD *Male & Female* xvi. 330 The division of labour among *non-English-speaking immigrants. 1975 *Nature* 20 Feb. p. xiv/1 (Advt.), The work..involves..language correction of contributions written by non-English-speaking authors. 1877 RAYMOND *Statist. Mines & Mining* 66 The..*non-gold-producing strata of serpentine. 1933 *Radio Times* 14 Apr. 112/2 This pleasant, gentle laxative..is *non-habit-forming. 1949 M. LOWRY *Let.* 16 Feb. (1967) 169 One or other of the non-habit-forming barbiturates should be often used in preference to strychnine or chloral. 1974 M. C. GERALD *Pharmacol.* xi. 198 Virtually all of these nonbarbiturate compounds have been initially promoted as being nonhabit-forming. 1967 COX & GROSE *Organiz. Bibliogr. Rec. by Computer* iv. 85 These are a set of words which the user defines as *non-information carrying words. 1937 E. SNOW *Red Star over China* vi. 233 Some $70,000 in *non-interest-bearing loans had been invested by the Government in the co-operatives. 1959 E. POUND *Thrones* ciii. 85 Trying (T.C.P.) 50 years later to keep some of the non-interest-bearing etc. in circulation as currency. 1888 BRYCE *Amer. Commw.* II. App. 640 The *non-office-holding delegates from the same States. 1933 *Planning* I. VIII. 11 A *non-profit-making organisation for this purpose could probably obtain a large interest in British farming. 1971 *Guardian* 16 Dec. 1/8 A railway porter..has been told to stop his non-profit making early-morning hot drink service to passengers. 1848 MILL *Pol. Econ.* III. vi. §3 Slave-grown will exchange for *non-slave-grown commodities [etc.]. 1837 CALHOUN *Sp.* Wks. 1864 III. 118 The people now receive the notes of *non-specie-paying banks.

7. Prefixed to gerunds and vbl. sbs., as ***non-accompanying*** = failure or neglect to accompany.

1573 *Reg. Privy Council Scot.* II. 227 For *nonaccumpaneing him to ane raid. 1657 *Burton's Diary* (1828) II. 37 The clause about the *non-alienating the revenue was read. 1657 BAXTER *Pres. Thoughts* 8 The *non-apostatizing of the Elect. 1683 J. CORBET *Free Actions* III. xxxiii. 52 The *non-ascertaining of an Event doth not render it impossible. 1444 *Paston Lett.* I. 50 [He] is right sory of the matier that is cause of your *noun comyng hedir. a1641 BP. MOUNTAGU *Acts & Mon.* (1642) 532 Her [the Virgin's] *non-conceiving of humane seed. 1564 *Reg. Privy Council Scot.* I. 304 For *non desisting of the landis of Castellwod. 1547 *Act 1 Edw. VI*, c. 14 §34 It shall not be lefull..to enter into..anny Landes..for the *non doing not naming or none fyndinge of anny such preist. 1665 BOYLE *Occas. Refl.* (1848) 35, I could never suspect that the *Non-employing of their thoughts could be their Choice rather than their Punishment. 1525 *Sc. Acts Jas. V* (1814) II. 298 In caiss of *Non-finding souirtie. 1901 *Essex Herald* 9 Apr 2/4 Many of the cases are for *non-labelling margarine. 1472-3 *Rolls of Parlt.* VI 49/2 Charged in defaute of *non-makyng of the said pavement. 1472-5 *Ibid.* 155/2 If any Custumer..be necligent..in *noon pakkyng of the same Clothes. 1650 WEEKES *Truth's Conflict* i. 25 If everlasting life imply *non perishing. 1422 tr. *Secreta Secret., Priv. Priv.* 160 Whos neclygence in *non-Punyshynge of hare nacionys and Subiectes. 1571-2 *Reg. Privy Council Scot.* II. 125 For *non-putting the said Maister Allane Stewart to libertie. 1439 *Rolls of Parlt.* V. 27/1 For ye *nounreceivyng of ye saide ordre. 1538 *Aberd. Reg.* XV. 651 (MS), The *nonredding of his buycht [= booth]. a1548 HALL *Chron., Hen. VIII* 30 The greate wronges..quhilk we haue suffred..in vpberyng, maynsweryng, *nounredressyng of Attemptates. a1680 CHARNOCK *Attrib. God* (1834) I. 94 By the *non-regarding of God men rush into evil. 1791 PAINE *Rights of Man* (ed. 4) 15 A law not repealed continues in force..because it is not repealed; and the *non-repealing passes for consent. 1533 *Acc. Ld. High Treas. Scot.* VI. 131 Lettrez..to be send to my lord Maxwell for *non-ryding on the bordouris. 1651 BAXTER *Inf. Bapt.* Apol. 14 He had so sharply dealt with Mr. Marshall for *non-syllogizing. 1833 CHALMERS in *Mem.* (1851) III. 409 We had as much talk as his *non-understanding of my dialect could admit. 1681 WOOD *Life* 3 July, His dispensation for *non visiting and not circuiting.

8. Prefixed to adverbs, as ***non-adaptively, contentiously, -denumerably, -enzymatically, -enzymically, -inferentially, -relativistically, -spatially, -uniformly***, etc.

1931 *Brit. Jrnl. Psychol.* XXII. 126 The reaction is not adaptive. It is one in which the past..does not function; or if it does function at all, it does so inefficiently, *non-adaptively. 1885 *Manch. Exam.* 28 Mar. 5/4 Everything is plain when it is looked at *non-contentiously. 1945 E. T. BELL *Devel. of Math.* (ed. 2) viii. 171 *Non-denumerably infinite classes of rational numbers. 1965 B. MATES *Elem. Logic* viii. 141 The question thus arises whether one could find a consistent set of sentences that is satisfiable only by interpretations having non-denumerably infinite domains. In view of the Löwenheim-Skolem theorem, the answer is negative. 1953 *Adv. in Protein Chem.* VIII. 169 Labelled amino acids may combine *nonenzymatically with certain proteins in other ways than through sulfur linkage. 1974 *Nature* 4 Jan. 4/1 The inhibitory alcohol also reacts, non-enzymatically, with the antennal protein. 1962 H. HEATH in A. Pirie *Lens Metabolism Rel. Catatact* 366 Glutathione readily and *non-enzymically reduces dehydroascorbic acid to ascorbic acid. 1875 J. H. COLLINS *Metal Mining* 105 The steam is used *non-expansively. 1860 A. DE MORGAN *On Syllogism* 214 *Non-inferentially and immediately seen. 1956 J. O. URMSON *Philosophical Analysis* iii. 42 Now some of these philosophers..inferred the existence of such things as God, substance, universals, the ego, which they did not claim to be non-inferentially discoverable. 1879 THOMPSON & TAIT *Nat. Phil.* I. I. §107 A symmetrical cup..when..set spinning *non-nutationally. 1814 SIR R. WILSON *Priv. Diary* (1862) II. 308 It is..believed to have been printed *non-officially by the connivance of government. 1957 BETHE & SALPETER *Quantum Mechanics of One- & Two-Electron Atoms* I. xix. 97 We treat the electron *nonrelativistically throughout. 1822 LAMB *Elia* Ser. I. *Distant correspondents*, Subjects serious in themselves, but treated..*non-seriously. 1882 VINES tr. *Sachs' Bt.* 235 The new plants..have the power..of propagating *non-sexually by the formation of gonidia. 1934 *Mind* XLIII. 299 What confronts the mind, in this sense..is (perhaps *non-spatially) *there* to be found, or haply to be found out, by searching. 1873 LELAND *Egypt. Sk. Bk.* 37 He shook his head *non-understandingly. 1893 HARKNESS & MORLEY *Treat. Theory of Functions* iii. 72 A *non-uniformly convergent series may be continuous. 1969 *Listener* 2 Jan. 11/1 Stars generally spin non-uniformly, rotating faster near the equator than at the pole. 1882 MINCHIN *Unipl. Kinematics* 181 Energy of *non-vortically moving Liquid.

non-, form of NONA- used before a vowel.

nona- (before a vowel **non-**), comb. form of L. *nōnus* ninth. **a.** In scientific words, as NONAGON, NONAPEPTIDE, NONIC *sb.* and *a.* **b.** *spec.* in *Chem.*, used in naming the alkane with nine carbon atoms in its molecule, NONANE, and compounds and radicals which contain a similar carbon chain, as NONOIC *acid*, NONYL.

non-a'bility. [NON- 1.] Inability, incapacity; *spec.* inability to commence a suit at law.

c1477 CAXTON *Jason* 27 b, Jason..thanked..the nobles..for their goode purchase in excusing gretly him self of non-habilite. 1531 *Dial. on Laws Eng.* II. 75 So that the title of examinacion of habilite be nat therby taken fro the ordinaries. 1612 DAVIES *Why Ireland*, etc. (1787) 72 The infancy of King Edward the Sixth, and the coverture of Queen Mary (which are both non abilities in the law) did in fact disable them to accomplish the conquest of Ireland. 1646 SIR T. BROWNE *Pseud. Ep.* VII. xiii. 364 Nor will it be easie to obtrude such desperate attempts unto Aristotle, upon a non ability or unsatisfaction of reason, who so often acknowledged the imbecility thereof. c1697 AUBREY *Lives* (1898) I. 124 For want of management, and his non-ability, it came to nothing.

non-ab'juror. *Hist.* [NON- 2. After *non-juror*.] One who refused to take the oath of ABJURATION imposed in 1703.

1893 *Dict. Nat. Biogr.* XXXIV. 426 In the winter of 1705 an information was sworn against him [*sc.* John McBride] as a non-abjuror.

† **non-'able**, *a. Obs.* [NON- 3.] Impotent.

1552 HULOET, Nonable, *impotens*.

non-'absolute, *a.* (*sb.*) [NON- 3.] Not absolute; (with *the*) that which is not absolute.

1830 COLERIDGE *Table-t.* 1 May, A fall of some sort or other—the creation, as it were, of the non-absolute—is a fundamental postulate of the moral history of man. 1879 NOAD & PREECE *Electr.* 209 The common non-absolute unit of work involving the product of a weight into a length is styled kilogramme or foot pound.

non-ac'ceptance. [NON- 1.] Neglect or refusal to accept.

1682 SCARLETT *Exchanges* 35 He that hath a Bill of Exchange in Possession, which was not accepted,..and so is protested for Non-Acceptance. 1766 BLACKSTONE *Comm.* II. xxx, The payee, or indorsee may protest it for non-acceptance. 1809 R. LANGFORD *Introd. Trade* 22 Re-exchange means the damages incurred by non-acceptance and non-payment. 1892 J. TAIT *Mind in Matter* (ed. 3) 33 Non-acceptance of the findings of perception unsettles the judgment.

So **non-ac'ceptant** *a.*, refusing to accept.

1718 *Freethinker* No. 56 ⁋3 It forces the Non-acceptant Party of that Kingdom, zealously to espouse the Interests of the Duke Regent.

non-accep'tation. *rare.* [NON- 1.] = NON-ACCEPTANCE.

1622 MALYNES *Anc. Law-Merch.* 403 The Notarie doth make the Protest, both for the non-acceptation, and for the non-payment, reciting the Bill of Exchange *verbatim*.

non-'access. *Law.* [NON- 1.] Impossibility of access for sexual intercourse, as in the case of a husband being abroad or at sea.

1799 *Sporting Mag.* XIII. 333 A declaration of non-access within a certain time. 1857 GREENLEAF *Treat. Law Evidence* I. §28. 38 *note*, Non-access is not presumed from the fact that the wife lived in adultery with another. 1891 *Daily News* 19 Dec. 7/2 The paternity was denied by the petitioner on the ground of non-access.

non-act, *sb.* [NON- 1.] Something which is not an act; failure to act.

1645 RUTHERFORD *Tryal & Tri. Faith* (1845) 288 Faith..turneth all these acts..half to non-acts. 1726 AYLIFFE *Parergon* 195 'Tis not a Non-act, which introduces a custom. 1848 WHARTON *Law Lex.*, *Non-act*, a forbearance from action, the contrary to act.

† **non-a'ddress.** *Obs.* [NON- 5.] Refusal to join in the address of Parliament to the King. So † **non-a'ddresser**, † **non-a'ddressing** *vbl. sb.*

1657-8 in *Burton's Diary* (1828) II. 432 The Parliament, after the vote of non-addresses, did declare for a House of Lords. 1681 LUTTRELL *Brief Rel.* (1857) I. 100 Who agreed with the nonaddressers that the proceedings of the addressers was unwarrantable. 1681 T. FLATMAN *Heraclitus Ridens* No. 23 (1713) I. 155 That..the Non-Addressers [be accounted] as true Protestants as those who voted the Non-Addresses to the late King. 1687 *Reply Oxf. Clergy* in Somers *Tracts* I. (1745) 246 Is Non-addressing a Matter of Faith; or Addressing, contrary to the Rule of good Manners?

non-ad'mission. [NON- 1.] Neglect or refusal to admit.

1681 WOOD *Life* (O.H.S.) II. 541 Mr. vice-Chancellor..not returning.., occasion'd the D^or's non-admission till the day after. 1726 AYLIFFE *Parergon* 65 In the Imperial Chamber this vulgar answer is not admitted... And the reason of this Non-admission is, because of its great uncertainty. 1802-12 BENTHAM *Ration. Judic. Evid.* (1827) III. 262 *note*, For the purpose of forming a pretence for non-admission.

non-ad'vertence. [NON- 1.] Want of advertence or attention (*to*). So **non-ad'vertency.**

1536 BELLENDEN *Cron. Scot.* (1821) I. 209 In aventure thay nuris sic displesour to thaimself, be thair non-advertence. a1677 MANTON *Serm. Ps. cxix*, liv. Wks. 1872 VII. 18 Non-advertency to heavenly doctrine is the bane of many. 1826 R. HALL *Wks.* (1832) VI. 385 In a state of disunion from God, and non-advertence to the prospect of eternity.

nonage[1] ('nəʊnɪdʒ). Forms: 4-5 **nownage**, 5 **noun age, nounage**, 5-6 **nowne age, noneage, non(e) age**, 6 **nonai(d)ge, noon aege, nonadge, noonage**, 7 **nonnage**, 6-8 **non-age**, 5- **nonage.** [a. AF. *nounage* = OF. *nonage*, f. *non-* (see NON-) + *age* AGE *sb.*]

1. The condition of being under age; the period of legal infancy; minority.

In the first quot., app. a payment due to the King when an estate fell to a minor.

1399 LANGL. *Rich. Redeles* IV. 6 Ne þe nownagis þat newed him euere, As marche and moubray and many mo oþer. 1424 *Plumpton Corr.* (Camden) p. l, The farme of our tenants..quilk to us perteyns because of nonage of the heire of Sir Robert Plompton. c1450 *Chron. Eng.* ccliii. (Caxton) 326 b, The duk of gloucestre vmfrey the kynges vncle had ben protectour of Englond alle the none age of the kyng. 1523 *Act 14 & 15 Hen. VIII*, c. 14 §2 That the feoffees or executours..have..the Londes and Tenementes..during the nonage of every such heir. 1633 EARL MANCH. *Al Mondo* (1636) 121 Christ..went up to the Temple in his Nonage. 1690 LOCKE *Govt.* II. vi. §57 To inform the Mind, and govern the Actions of their yet ignorant Nonage, till Reason shall take its Place. 1768 BLACKSTONE *Comm.* III. 332 In case of a suit to reverse a fine for non-age of the cognizor, or to set aside a statute or recognizance entered into by an infant. 1821 SCOTT *Kenilw.* i, I have..permitted..all of you to use your pleasure with the frolics of my nonage. 1877 MISS YONGE *Cameos* IV. xvii. 178 She viewed as invalid all that was done in her brother's nonage. 1892 STEVENSON *Across the Plains* 179 He had passed a riotous nonage.

† **b.** Phr. *of nonage*: minor. *at, in nonage*: in one's minority. *Obs.*

1484 *10th Rep. Hist. MSS. Comm.* App. v. 318 If he be a childe of none eage. 1565 COOPER *Thesaurus* s.v. *Deponere*, To committe the money of..children in none age, to the..keping of the citee. 1638 SIR T. HERBERT *Trav.* (ed. 2) 109 At that time Zeifadin was King (in nonage) ruled by Atar a spitefull Eunuch. 1715 CHAPPELOW *Way to get Rich* (1717) 171 You are like heirs at non-age. 1788 REID *Active Powers* IV. v. 614 Children in nonage act voluntarily.

c. *transf.* of plants.

1660 SHARROCK *Vegetables* 18 [Plants] able to abide the sharp winter in their nonage. 1697 DRYDEN *Virg. Georg.* II. 497 In their tender Nonage, while they spread Their Springing Leafs. a1720 J. HUGHES *Claudianus*, That folded in its tender nonage lies, A beauteous bud.

2. *fig.* The period of immaturity; the early stage in the growth or development of anything.

1584 LYLY *Sappho* IV. ii. 39 She is in her Nonage for affections. 1586 A. DAY *Eng. Secretary* I. (1625) A 2 This booke rudely digested, and then roughly delivered I did in the very nonage thereof recommend unto your patronage. 1639 FULLER *Holy War* v. xxviii. (1647) 277 The loadstone to draw their affection, (now out of non-age) must present itself necessary. c1645 HOWELL *Lett.* II. lv. (1655) 47 In the nonage of the world, men and beasts had but one buttery which was the fountain and river. **1700** DRYDEN *Fables* Pref. *B 2 b, Even after Chaucer there was a Spencer, a Harrington, a Fairfax, before Waller and Denham were in being; And our Numbers were in their Nonage till these last appear'd. **1814** CARY *Dante, Inf.* XXIV. 1 In the year's early nonage. **1820** SCOTT *Monast.* xx, A song, 'which..the inimitable Astrophel, whom mortals call Philip Sidney, composed in the nonage of his muse'. **1871** FARRAR *Witn. Hist.* iii. 116 Nations outgrew their spiritual nonage.

3. *attrib.*, as ***nonage time, youth.***

1619 T. TAYLOR *Comm. Titus* ii. 11 This present world is our nonage time, wherein we must be schooled to these lessons. **1628** WITHER *Brit. Rememb.* VII. 231 Those non-age Youths, to whom our Lawes deny A pow'r in things that smaller trust imply.

nonage[2] ('nəʊnɪdʒ). [ad. eccl. L. *nōnāgium*, f. *nōn-us* ninth: see -AGE.] (See quot.)

1848 WHARTON *Law Lex.*, *Nonagium* or *Nonage*, a ninth part of moveables which was paid to the clergy on the death of persons in their parish.

† **'nonaged,** *a. Obs.* [f. NONAGE[1] + -ED[2]. Cf. OF. *nonaagé.*] Belonging to the period of nonage; in one's nonage, minor. Also *fig.*

1601 *Acts Privy Council* XXXI. 241 In the behalfe of Peter de la Rocque and his nonaged bretheren. **1613** W. BROWNE *Brit. Past.* I. v, Here could I..tell the world, the Muses loue appeares In nonag'd youth, as in the length of yeeres. **1643** QUARLES *Embl.* III. xiii, My nonag'd day already points to noon. **1645** —— *New Distemper* Wks. (Grosart) I. 155/1 We might have taken an advantageous leisure and mature deliberation to ripen every Bill, and, by degrees, to rectifie every nonag'd Grievance.

nonagenarian (nɒnədʒɪ'nɛərɪən), *a.* and *sb.* [f. L. *nōnāgēnāri-us* (f. *nōnāgēnī* ninety each): see -IAN.]

A. *adj.* Ninety years old, or between ninety and a hundred. **B.** *sb.* A person of such age.

1804 [R. GRAVES] (*title*), The Invalid: with the obvious means of enjoying..long life. By a Nonagenarian. **1817** BYRON *Let.* 9 Apr., This nonagenarian..must be one of the 'deux fils'. **1865** *Morning Star* 4 Jan., Eight nonagenarians died in the week. The oldest were two widows aged 95 and 96. **1893** *Nation* 20 July 49/3 Her nonagenarian Béarnese grandmother.

† **nona'genary.** *Obs. rare*$^{-1}$. [ad. L. *nonāgēnāri-us*: see prec.] (See quot.)

1601 HOLLAND *Pliny* I. 10 As for Mars, as he is neerer vnto the Sun, so feeleth he the Sun beames by a quadrant aspect, to wit ninetie degrees, whereupon that motion tooke the name, called the first and second Nonagenarie from both risings.

nonagesimal (nɒnə'dʒɛsɪməl), *a.* and *sb. Astr.* [f. L. *nōnāgēsim-us*, ordinal of *nōnāginta* ninety: see -AL[1]. Cf. F. *nonagésimal.*]

A. *adj.* ***nonagesimal degree, point***: that point of the ecliptic which is highest above the horizon at any given time, being 90° above the point at which the ecliptic intersects the horizon.

1704 J. HARRIS *Lex. Techn.* I, *Nonagessimal Degree*, is the highest Point, or 90th Degree of the Ecliptick. **1797** *Encycl. Brit.* (ed. 3) II. 522/2 Sometimes she stands, as it were, upright on her lower horn, and then such a line [*sc.* touching the points of the moon's horns] is perpendicular to the horizon: when this happens she is in what the astronomers call the nonagesimal degree. **1833** HERSCHEL *Astron.* iv. 182 The altitude of its highest point or as it is sometimes called, the nonagesimal point of the ecliptic. **1862** G. C. LEWIS *Astron. Ancients* IV. §1 The angle of the east, which is now called the nonagesimal degree.

B. *sb.* The nonagesimal degree.

1789 *Phil. Trans.* LXXIX. 59, I have calculated them two different ways, viz. by the method of parallactic angles, and by the method of the nonagesimal. **1815** BURNEY *Falconer's Marine Dict.* s.v., The altitude of the nonagesimal is equal to the angle of the east, and, if continued, passes through the poles of the ecliptic. **1834** *Nat. Philos.* III. *Astron.* (Libr. Usef. Knowl.) xii. 252/1 What we have here called the longitude of the zenith, is often called the longitude of the nonagesimal.

† **nona'gesime,** *a.* [ad. L. *nōnāgēsim-us*: see prec. Cf. F. *nonagésime.*] = prec. A.

1653 SHAKERLEY *Tabulæ Britan.* 73 Finde the Node ascendent, and subtract it from the Nonagesime degree. **1771** *Phil. Trans.* LXI. 438 To find the nonagesime or 90th degree of the ecliptic from the horizon.

non-a'ggression. [NON- 1.] Absence of the will, desire, or intention to show aggression on the part of nations, governments, or politicians; freq. *attrib.*, esp. in phr. ***non-aggression pact.***

1903 J. MORLEY *Life of Gladstone* III. x. viii. 508 Then he would go on—'..—My name stands in Europe as a symbol of the policy of peace, moderation, and non-aggression.' **1925** A. TOYNBEE *Survey Internat. Affairs* 26 The proposed pledge of non-aggression would not have power to deprive the Allies of the right conferred on them by the Treaty of Versailles. *Ibid.* 31 Mr. Lloyd George broached to the French delegation his project for a Pact of Non-aggression. **1935** *Ann. Reg. 1934* [217] The Polish Ambassador in Moscow signed a Protocol extending the Non-Aggression Pact between the two countries till December 31, 1945. **1941** KOESTLER *Scum of Earth* 19 The classical form for non-aggression treaties had been so far to promise neutrality. **1955** *Ann. Reg. 1954* 106 The two countries [*sc.* India and China] based their relationship on..mutual non-aggression.

nonagon ('nɒnəgən). *Geom.* [irreg. f. L. *nōn-us* ninth, after *hexagon*. Cf. OF. *nongone.*] A figure having nine angles; an enneagon.

1688 R. HOLME *Armoury* III. xvi. (Roxb.) 98/1 An Henneagon, or Enneagon or Nonagon, a fort of nyne corners. *a* **1696** SCARBURGH *Euclid* (1705) 174 Of the.. Nonagon, Euclide makes no mention. **1817** COLEBROOKE *Algebra* 93 Next the proof of the side of the nonagon is shown. **1842** GWILT *Archit.* 1008.

b. Used *adj.* Nine-angled.

1754 POCOCKE *Trav.* (Camden) I. 72 They are making a nonagon building..where poultry..are to be kept.

non-a'ligned, *a.* [NON- 6.] Of a country, government, etc.: pursuing a policy of non-alignment. Also *absol.* as *sb.* Hence **non-a'lignedness, non-a'ligner.**

1960 *New Left Rev.* Nov.–Dec. 10/2 The non-aligned powers have grown in strength. **1962** *Guardian* 7 Nov. 18/7 The concept of political non-alignedness. **1963** *Economist* 28 Dec. 1325/1 India's professional non-aligners. **1965** *Times Lit. Suppl.* 25 Nov. 1056/4 The attitudes of allies and of the non-aligned. **1966** *Guardian* 14 Oct. 12/2 The Canadians.. believe that there is a real strategic danger of a nonaligned block composed of Austria, Switzerland, and France cutting Europe into two. **1970** *Guardian Weekly* 30 May 6 The two groups in Indonesia opposing each other are the 'nonaligneds' and the 'interventionists'. **1973** *Caribbean Contact* Feb. 9/3 The need..for the Non-Aligned world to probe beyond the detente between the big powers.

non-a'lignment. [NON- 1.] Lack or absence of alignment; *spec.* in *Politics*, absence of political or ideological affiliations with other nations, esp. with the most powerful nations. Also *transf.*

1934 in WEBSTER. **1955** *Times* 6 May 11/4 He extolled 'non-alignment' and co-existence. **1963** M. BRECHER *New States of Asia* iv. 111 *Non-alignment*..is a political status. It refers to a state that declares itself aloof from bloc conflicts; nothing more. It proclaims itself free from *a priori* alliances, notably military entanglements with any bloc or Great Power anywhere in the world. **1970** E. BULLINS *Theme is Blackness* (1973) 153 My non-alignment with reality is quite evident and explainable..my being Black and non-committed to any political truths. **1973** 'D. JORDAN' *Nile Green* xx. 81 The Egyptians..prefer to hang on to what's left of their non-alignment status and not rely on the Russians.

non-a'llergic, *a.* [NON- 3.] Not allergic; *spec.* not causing allergy.

1936 H. GOODMAN *Cosmetic Dermatol.* xxv. 368 In the field of cosmetics and beauty-application preparations, the words *allergy* and *nonallergic* are mentioned more and more often. **1938** *Words* Jan. 11/2 'Cosmetics are non-allergic.' Donna Ray broadcast Oct. 24 [19]37. **1954** L. MARTIN *Clin. Endocrinol.* (ed. 2) vii. 150 The eosinophil count will..be lowered by..50 per cent or more in non-allergic subjects. **1964** W. G. SMITH *Allergy & Tissue Metabolism* iii. 42 Inflammation of non-allergic origin. **1972** *Islander* (Victoria, B.C.) 18 June 7/3 Dacron fibrefill II is non-allergic and moth, vermin and mildew resistant.

no-name ('nəʊneɪm), *a.* and *sb.* orig. and chiefly *U.S.* Also **noname.** [f. NO *a.* + NAME *sb.*]

A. *adj.* **1.** Of commercial products, etc.: having no brand-name; generic or 'own-brand'.

1977 *Washington Post* 20 Oct. E1/5 Two new concepts in supermarketing..: discounting and 'no-name brands'. **1977** *Time* 21 Nov. 45/2 No-name groceries have become hot items, and they could herald a change in the way that Americans shop. **1979** *Washington Post* 12 Apr. E1/2 A & P was the first to offer generics—or noname products—here. **1982** *Times* 26 Jan 15/3 Within the grocery industry, such products are usually known as 'generics', but they are also sometimes referred to as 'brand-free' or 'no-name' items.

2. Of a person: unknown; not having made a name in a particular profession, etc.

1979 *Washington Post* 21 Nov. D4/1 Hard work, with a group of noname receivers, has produced a 60 percent completion rate, five touchdowns and no interceptions in the last two games. **1982** *N.Y. Times* 25 Apr. II. 17/4 There are those who would even say that the situation..is better nowadays than it was..when no-name singers came and went so fast. **1983** *Washington Post* 22 Apr. C2/1 Bud Light gets competent, no-name athletes, puts them in real-life game situations, and lets them enact the American Dream.

B. *sb.* **1.** A generic product; an 'own brand'.

1984 *Money* Sept. 114/2 Choose a model that is durable and a brand name that will hold its value. House brands and nonames are risky. **1985** *Financial Times* 22 July I. 10/7 The devastating challenge posed by suppliers of generics ('no-names').

2. One who has not yet made a name in a particular profession or activity; an unknown.

1984 *Gainesville* (Florida) *Sun* 26 Mar. 113/2 The Longhorns had one superstar in backstroker Rick Carey, but mainly relied on relative 'no-names'. In the end, Florida's no-names were better.

non-American, *a.* (*sb.*) [NON- 3.] Not American. Occas. as *sb.*, one who is not an American.

1904 G. SAINTSBURY *Hist. Criticism* III. 640 The poet who seems to some possibly rash non-American persons to divide with Poe the prize due to the worthiest in American poetry, was also a critic—less of the professional kind, much more *borné*, but more concentrated. **1924** S. P. SHERMAN *Genius of America* 213 He laughed at all the non-American world. **1936** *Mind* XLV. 15 Insufficiently known and appreciated, not only among non-American philosophers, but even among his own colleagues in the United States. **1962** H. A. GLEASON in Householder & Saporta *Problems in Lexicography* 88 Dictionaries with good..citations..have been mostly produced by people outside the fraternity—non-American linguists, or people laying no claim at all to the title of linguist. **1965** J. POTTER in Glass & Eversley *Population in Hist.* xxvii. 631 For non-Americans,..it can have an important bearing on their own attempts to interpret the European..data.

† **'nonan,** *a. Obs. rare.* [ad. L. *nōnān-us*, f. *nōn-us* ninth: see -AN. Cf. OF. *nonain.*] Applied to a fever recurring every ninth (*i.e.* eighth) day.

1657 *Expert Physician* 123 The Quintan, Sextan, Septan, and Nonan Feavers, differ not from intermitting Feavers. **1892** *Syd. Soc. Lex.*, *Nonane*..Formerly applied to an erratic fever returning on the ninth day.

nonane ('nəʊneɪn). *Chem.* [f. L. *nōn-us* ninth + -ANE 2 b.] A hydrocarbon (C_9H_{20}), being the ninth of the methane series. Hence **nona'noic** *a.* = NONOIC *a.*; **nona'noate,** the anion, or an ester or salt, of nonanoic acid.

1868 FOWNES *Chem.* 551. **1947** K. S. MARKLEY *Fatty Acids* xv. 407 Armstrong and Hilditch described a method for the disruptive oxidation of methyl oleate in acetone solution which they claim yields 80% to 90% of the theoretical amount of nonanoic acid. **1967** I. L. FINAR *Org. Chem.* (ed. 5) ix. 211 Nonanoic acid is obtained by the oxidation of oleic acid. **1974** *Ber. der Bunsen-Gesell. für physikal. Chem.* LXXVIII. 874 (*heading*) X-ray-studies of cholesteric-smectic-pretransitions in mixtures of cholesteryl chloride and cholesteryl nonanoate.

nonapeptide (nɒnə'pɛptaɪd). *Biochem.* [f. NONA- + PEPTIDE.] Any peptide composed of nine amino-acid residues.

1960 *Helv. Chim. Acta* XLIII. 1358 The synthesis of a nonapeptide exhibiting bradykinin-like properties is described. **1972** *Science* 22 Sept. 1108/3 Animals were given the nonapeptide Pyr-Trp-Pro-Arg-Pro-Gln-Ile-Pro-Pro, a potent inhibitor of the angiotensin-converting enzyme.

non-a'pparent, *a.* [NON- 3.] Not apparent. Also *absol.* with *the.*

1748 RICHARDSON *Clarissa* (1811) IV. 188 Dorcas no sooner found them, than she assembled these ready writers of the non-apparent. *a* **1835** McCULLOCH *Attributes* (1843) II. xxxiv. 306 We do not know whether it is dormant or acting when it is non-apparent. **1880** *Contemp. Rev.* Feb. 199 Nature being at most a secondary manifestation of that which is now non-apparent and supernatural.

non-a'ppearance. [NON- 1.] Failure or neglect to appear, *esp.* in a court of law, as a party to a suit or as a witness.

1475 *Rolls of Parlt.* VI. 134/1 Londes..which they forfetted by their noun apperaunce. **1562** *Act 5 Eliz.* c. 9 §12 The Loss..that the Party..shall sustain by reason of the Non-appearance of the said Witness. *a* **1676** HALE *Prim. Orig. Man.* (1677) 161 Arts and Sciences..have their non-appearances for some Ages, and then seem first to discover themselves where before they were not known. **1768** BLACKSTONE *Comm.* III. x. 193 Through their default or non-appearance in a possessory action, they were..without any remedy. **1846** BROWNING *Luria* i, The non-appearance of our foe's ally. **1874** STUBBS *Const. Hist.* (1897) I. iii. 60 Although it does not follow that it was unknown to them, its non-appearance is a presumptive evidence of superior simplicity of organisation.

So **non-a'ppearer,** one who fails to appear.

1755 MAGENS *Insurances* II. 145 The Proceedings.. against the Non-Appearers..shall be from three Days to three Days, for the first, second, and third Default.

non-'arcing, *ppl. a. Electr.* Also **-arcking.** [f. NON- 6 + ARC *sb.* 5.] Of a metal: That does not form a voltaic arc or allow it to be formed.

1895 *Standard Dict.*, *Non-arcing.* **1899** *Min. Proc. Inst. Civil Engin.* CXXXVI 44 Arresters of the short-gap type having a resistance in series are of more value than the non-arcking metal type.

non-art. [NON- 2 and 2 b.] Something that is not art; *spec.* a form of art which avoids artifice or which rejects conventional modes and methods.

1936 L. DURRELL *Spirit of Place* (1969) 49 It [*sc. Tropic of Cancer*] bore out a few theories about writing that I had been trying to formulate. The art of non-art... Real art being absolutely devoid of 'artifice', in the literary sense. **1949** *Horizon* XIX. 379 The great artists of the past..are not replaced by others because we are moving into a world of non-art. **1958** *New Statesman* 20 Sept. 377/1 The great illusion of current non-art lies in the belief that numerous meanings can be expressed without searching. **1965** ZIGROSSER & GAEHDE *Guide Coll. Orig. Prints* iii. 35 The distinction..between art (as we know it now) and non-art might lose its force. **1971** R. A. CARTER *Manhattan Primitive* (1972) xxii. 215 You haven't transformed it into art—you've just set it down. It's non-art, Bess. Anti-art.

nonary ('nəʊnərɪ), *a.* and *sb.* [ad. L. *nōnāri-us*, f. *nōn-us* ninth.] **A.** *adj. Arith.* ***nonary scale***: a scale of notation having nine as its basis.

1870 SONNENSCHEIN & NESBITT *Sci. & Art Arith.* I. 114 Add..in the nonary scale 1235, 7834 [etc.]. **1883** *Encycl. Brit.* XV. 215 The numbers..being kept in the nonary scale.

B. *sb.* **1.** A group of nine.

1666 BP. S. PARKER *Free & Impart. Censure* (1667) 83 This Ternary of Hierarchies, and Nonary of Orders do Circulate about the three fold Essence of God. **1839** *Fraser's Mag.* XX. 205 The terrestrial gods and demigods will.. form two ogdoads, and not a septenary and nonary, as Manetho has them.

2. A fever recurring every ninth (*i.e.* eighth) day.

1747 tr. *Astruc's Fevers* 63 A tertian may also seem to be a nonary, its paroxysms being suppressed, except those which fall on every 9th day.

non-'Aryan, *a.* and *sb.* [NON- 3, 2.] **A.** *adj.* Of a language or a person: not Aryan or of Aryan descent; used *spec.* of Jews in Nazi Germany.

1878 [see ARYAN *a.*]. **1878** *Encycl. Brit.* VIII. 698/2 The Basques, the Esthonians, and the Finns, who have retained their non-Aryan speech. **1898** R. BROWN *Semitic Influence in Hellenic Mythol.* III. iii. 86 The mixed peoples of Asia Minor, Aryan, and non-Aryan. **1931** *Times Lit. Suppl.* 11 June 461/2 It is interesting..to encounter variants of familiar ballads in a non-Aryan language. **1933** *New Statesman* 15 Apr. 465/2 A slight relief has been given by a Reich decree which allows an increase in the number of 'non-Aryan' lawyers who may practise. **1942** L. B. NAMIER *Conflicts* 133 More logical were those who attempted amalgamation: but even this, as a mass movement, merely produces Marranos or 'non-Aryan Christians'. **1964** *Archivum Linguisticum* XVI. 76 *Nicula-*, probably non-Aryan.

B. *sb.* One who is not an Aryan; used *spec.* of Jews in Nazi Germany.

1933 [see ARYAN *sb.* 2]. **1935** AUDEN & ISHERWOOD *Dog beneath Skin* II. i. 75 Rumour-monger!.. Non-Aryan! **1944** J. S. HUXLEY *On Living in Rev.* 174 It is thus absurd to distinguish between 'non-Aryans' and 'Europeans'.

non-a'script, *a.* [ad. mod.L. (*scholaris*) *non-ascriptus*, unattached student.] = NON-COLLEGIATE.

1897 ESCOTT *Social Transform. Vict. Age* xiv. 181 The formal consent to his life in lodgings of his parents..was.. required from the non-ascript undergraduate.

‖**non assumpsit** (nɒn əˈsʌmpsɪt). *Law.* [L. = 'he did not undertake'.] A plea in an action of assumpsit by which the defendant denies that he made any promise or undertaking.

1631 *Star Chamb. Cases* (Camden) 78 That the plaintiff had brought an action of the case against Rickby, the defendant, and upon *non assumpsit*. **1678** W. BROWN *Entring Clerk's Vade Mecum* 108 *marg.*, As to the first, second, and third promises the Defendant pleads Non assumpsit. **1768** BLACKSTONE *Comm.* II. xx. 305. **1824** STEPHEN *Pleading* 175 In Trespass on the case (in the species of *assumpsit*), the general issue is called the plea of *non assumpsit*.

no-'nation, *a. dial.* [f. NO *a.* 6 b + NATION *sb.*[1]] (See quots.)

1825 J. JENNINGS *Observ. Dial. W. Eng.* 57 *Nonation*, difficult to be understood; not intelligent; incoherent, wild. **1856** P. THOMPSON *Hist. Boston* XVI. 716 *No-nation place*, an out-of-the-way locality, or lawless neighbourhood. **1868** J. C. ATKINSON *Gloss. Cleveland Dial.* 357 *No-nation*, strange, remote, out-of-the-way; scarcely known, geographically; and, hence, uncivilised and rough. **1914** *Dialect Notes* IV. 77 *No-nation*,.. worthless. 'You *no-nation* cuss!' **1932** *Times Lit. Suppl.* 27 Oct. 792/1 He was a 'no-nation' boy and he had no name other than Duke.

non-a'ttached, *ppl. a.* [NON- 6.] Not attached; *spec.* unconcerned or uninvolved with material things. So **non-a'ttachment**.

1856 *Oxford & Camb. Mag.* Apr. 237/2 The non-attached students no longer receiving help from the religious houses, fell away. **1937** A. HUXLEY *Ends & Means* i. 3 The ideal man is the non-attached man. Non-attached to his bodily sensations and lusts. Non-attached to his craving for power and possessions... Non-attached to his anger and hatred. *Ibid.* 4 The practice of non-attachment entails the practice of all the virtues. **1940** AUDEN *Another Time* 23 Over the talkative city like any other Weep the non-attached angels. **1950** 'G. ORWELL' *Shooting an Elephant* 108 In this yogi-ridden age, it is too readily assumed that 'non-attachment' is ..better than a full acceptance of earthly life.

non-a'ttendance. [NON- 1.] Failure or neglect to attend.

1687 LD. HALIFAX *Cautions Choice M.P.* 5 Non-Attendance in former Parliaments ought to be a Bar against the Choice of Men who have been guilty of it. **1763** *Chron.* in *Ann. Reg.* 94 Penalties for non-attendance as militia men. **1824** SYD. SMITH *Wks.* (1867) II. 55 The weekly fines levied upon Catholics for non-attendance upon public worship. **1884** *Law Times Rep.* LI. 103/1 A judge should have power to commit for non-attendance as a witness.

†**non-a'ttendancy.** *Obs.* [NON- 1.] Inattention.

a **1677** MANTON *Serm. Ps.* cxix, c. (1687) 217 Non-attendency, or inadvertency, prejudicate opinions and rooted lusts.

So †**non-a'ttendingly** *adv.*, inattentively.

1678 CUDWORTH *Intell. Syst.* I. iii. §37. 160 We have all experience of our doing many animal actions non-attendingly, which we reflect upon afterwards.

‖**non avenu** (nɔnavny). Also *erron.* -ue. [Fr.] Not having happened.

1840 THACKERAY *Paris Sk. Bk.* I. 123 Otherwise the deed became null and non-avenue. **1887** BARON H. DE WORMS *Mem. Ct. von Beust* I. Introd. p. lvii, The incident was considered, in diplomatic language, as *non avenu*.

non-bank, *a.* [NON- 4.] Not connected with, or transacted by, a banking house; of an institution: not being a bank.

1946 C. C. ABBOTT *Managem. Federal Debt* v. 87 Should a boom or a price inflation develop and conditions call for a restriction of deposits, this policy of relying upon increases of bank credit to take up obligations not wanted by nonbank holders would aggravate the situation. **1961** *Ann. Reg. 1960* 485 The Bank of England commented..that..in the light of the need to attract purchases of stock by 'non-bank' investors, 'a somewhat higher level of gilt-edged yields would now be appropriate'. **1961** *Economist* 25 Nov. 822/3 The gilt-edged market (which provides the Exchequer with non-bank finance). **1964** GOULD & KOLB *Dict. Soc. Sci.* 438/2 Like every other nonbank institution, savings and loan associations..must keep accounts with commercial banks. **1973** *N.Y. Law Jrnl.* 4 Sept. 3/5 (Advt.), We are.. the largest non-bank firm—providing complete corporation securities services.

non-being. [NON- 7.]

1. a. The condition of not being; non-existence.

c **1449** PECOCK *Repr.* II. xvi. 242 These men..concludiden ..that al the bodili heuen..was euer withoute bigynnyng of tyme, and schal euer be withoute corrupcion and withoute noon being. **1645** BALL *Sphere Gov.* 8, I conceive..power.. to consist rather in reason positive then negative, in beeing rather then in non-beeing. **1765** HARRIS *Three Treat.* Notes 267 Contingents..were equally susceptible both of Being and Non-being. **1899** DZIEWICKI *Wyclif's De Logica* III. p. xxxv, Whether the non-being of the world preceded its being.

b. A non-existent thing.

1662 J. CHANDLER *Van Helmont's Oriat.* 25 Of a non-Being, no conception, no figure, and no understanding, doth answer. **1793** T. TAYLOR *Sallust*, etc. xvii. 83 It is impossible that any thing can be generated from non-beings.

†**2.** Not being present. *Obs.*

1455 *Rolls of Parlt.* V. 335/2 For his nounbeyng at this your present Parlement.

non-be'lligerent, *a.* and *sb.* [NON- 3, 2.] **A.** *adj.* Not actively engaged in hostilities; not aggressive. **B.** *sb.* A country which abstains from active involvement in a war but which more or less openly favours one side. Hence **non-be'lligerence, -be'lligerency**, the status or attitude of a non-belligerent country.

1909 *Westm. Gaz.* 14 June 5/3 When the defence has been on anything like a great scale, the non-belligerent defenders have very largely exceeded in number the armed defenders. **1940** *War Illustr.* 5 Jan. 556 'The position assumed by Italy on September 1,' he [*sc.* Count Ciano, the Italian Foreign Minister] said, 'was a position of non-belligerency strictly in conformity with the German intention of localizing the conflict.' **1940** *Manch. Guardian Weekly* 1 Mar. 162 Today all the Balkan states are neutral, Italy is a 'non-belligerent', Turkey is a firm friend, Russia is uncertain. **1946** *Ann. Reg. 1945* 76 The Spanish Government had publicly followed a policy not of neutrality but of non-belligerence. **1953** P. C. BERG *Dict. New Words* (ed. 2) 115/1 A non-belligerent attitude between contending parties or powers. **1975** *Times* 19 Aug. 13/2 A formal pledge of non-belligerency is something which President Sadat cannot or will not give.

non-bio'logical, *a.* [NON- 3.] Not belonging to biology or forming part of its subject matter; not occurring in, involving, or pertaining to living organisms.

1931 J. S. HUXLEY *What dare I Think?* i. 32 There have been Boards of Pest Control which were not too anxious to find their occupation gone with the going of their particular pest. Leaving such non-biological or hyper-biological considerations on one side, there have been many pests which have so far baffled research. **1956** *Nature* 21 Jan. 110/2 Photochemistry in higher plants and in non-biological systems. **1957** G. E. HUTCHINSON *Treat. Limnol.* I. xvi. 866 The existence of non-biological mechanisms of oxidation of ammonia. **1962** F. I. ORDWAY et al. *Basic Astronautics* vi. 247 An understanding of much corollary evidence and supposition from nonbiological fields. **1971** I. G. GASS et al. *Understanding Earth* ix. 125/1 All known extra-terrestrial environments and many geological environments are still non-biological.

Hence **non-bio'logically** *adv.*

1974 *Nature* 6 Sept. 43/1 A rapid, routine, new tool for the differentiation of biologically and nonbiologically produced dicarboxylic acids.

non-black, *a.* and *sb.* [NON- 3, 2.]

A. *adj.* Not black; *spec.* (also *non-Black*), of, pertaining to, or being a person or persons who are not Black. **B.** *sb.* A non-Black person.

1926 D. M. LIDDELL *Handbk. Non-Ferrous Metallurgy* I. ix. 283 No radiation pyrometer has been found to be very useful for measuring temperatures of non-black bodies. **1930** *Social Sci. Abstr.* June 1011 In the non-black land the rush toward individual appropriation was naturally less than in the black soil belt. **1970** *Guardian Weekly* 22 Aug. 7 At the University of Natal, non-white students..refer to whites as 'non-blacks'. **1971** *Black Scholar* Jan. 27/2 The argument goes that black artists..must move beyond race in their work to some mythical human (non-black) understanding. **1973** *Black World* Apr. 20/2 Expertly directed by a non-Black, the musical played to standing-room audiences. **1973** S. HENDERSON *Understanding New Black Poetry* 9 Is it possible that, given a Black Poetic Structure, a non-Black can create in this form—as whites play jazz, for example?

non-'capital, *a.* [NON- 3.] Of a murder or other offence: for which a convicted person is not punishable by the death penalty.

1898 C. ILBERT *Government of India* i. 15 The Company were in the habit of procuring for each voyage a commission to the 'general' in command, empowering him to inflict punishments for non-capital offences, such as murder or mutiny. **1956** *Hansard Commons* 15 Nov. 1237/1 The distinction between non-capital murders and capital murders which is made in this part of the Bill must lead to many inconsistencies and anomalies. **1964** MORRIS & BLOM-COOPER *Calendar of Murder* viii. 328 The legislature.. sought..to mitigate considerably the incidence of the death penalty..by declaring certain categories of murder non-capital. **1968** *Globe & Mail* (Toronto) 13 Feb. 3/8 Two men were jointly charged yesterday with the non-capital murder of..a taxi driver.

non-'Catholic, *sb.* and *a.* [NON- 2, 3.]

A. *sb.* One who is not a Roman Catholic.

1793 BURKE *On Policy of Allies* Wks. VII. 178 His toleration was granted to non-catholicks—a dangerous word, which might signify any thing. **1859** MILL *Liberty* iv. 154 What do Protestants think of these perfectly sincere feelings, and of the attempt to enforce them against non-Catholics? **1971** J. C. HEENAN *Not Whole Truth* i. 12 His church was half-filled every Monday evening with enquirers who came to hear his talks to non-Catholics.

B. *adj.* That is not Roman Catholic.

In a somewhat wider sense in quot. 1936.

1823 C. BUTLER *Continuation of A. Butler's Lives of Saints* p. lxii, Their anti-christian and non-catholic adversaries. **1867** F. OAKELEY in H. E. Manning *Ess. Relig. & Lit.* 2nd Ser. 130 The world persists in thinking that the Catholic and non-Catholic ideas are in diametrical opposition. **1936** T. S. ELIOT *Essays Ancient & Modern* 132 There may always be schemes, initiated by non-Christian and non-Catholic minds..to which we can give unqualified support. **1966** *Publ. Amer. Dial. Soc.* XLII. 35 To recall many abusive terms for non-Catholic Christians.

nonce[1] (nɒns). Forms: 3 [to þan anes], *Ormin* naness, 4–5 nonis, 4–6 nones, nonys, nons, nonest (5 nownes, noones, -ys, 6 nonst(e, 6–7 nonse, 8–9 *dial.* noance; *Sc.* and *north.* 4 nanyse, 4–5 nanes, 5–6 -is), 6– nonce. [orig. in the ME. phrases *to þan ane*, **for þan ane*, *to þan anes*, **for þan anes*, the last of which was altered by wrong division (as in *a newt* for *an ewt*) to *for þe nanes*, *nones*, literally = for or with a view to the one (thing, occasion, etc.). The genitival form *anes* was substituted for the original dative *ane* probably by analogy with the synonymous pairs *ane* and *anes*, *ene* and *enes* = ONCE. For the forms *nonest*, *nonst*, cf. *onest*, *onst* for *ones*, ONCE *amidst* for *amiddes*.]

1. for the nonce: **a.** For the particular purpose; on purpose; expressly. Often with inf. or clause expressing the object or purpose. *Obs.* exc. *dial.*

c **1200** *Ormin* 7160, & wel itt mihhte ben þatt he Wass gramm.. All forr þe naness, forr þatt he Swa wollde don hiss lede To ben all þess te mare offdredd Off himm & off hiss eʒʒe. **1297** R. GLOUC. (Rolls) 5795 He com & mette him in a wode & bed him abyde, & he adde uor þe nones tueye suerdes bi is syde. **1338** R. BRUNNE *Chron.* (1810) 108 Steuen com for þe nons, þis lond to haf he þouht. *c* **1386** CHAUCER *Prol.* 381 A Cook they hadde with hem for the nones, To boille the chiknes with the mary-bones. *c* **1440** *Promp. Parv.* 173/2 For the nonys, *idcirco, ex proposito*. *c* **1450** *Merlin* 420 For the dredde that theire beerdes sholde growe she lete a-noynte her chynnes with certeyn oynementes made for the nones. **1533** MORE *Answ. to poysoned Bk.* Wks. 1055/1 Thys bread is bread descending from heauen for the nones that whoso may eate and be fedde of that, shall not perish by euerlasting death. *a* **1548** HALL *Chron., Hen. VIII*, 216 She withdrewe her into a litle place made for the nones on the one side of the quere. **1548** UDALL, etc. *Erasm. Par. John* ii. 5–8 Jesus deferred y[e] myracle for the nonest, because the lacke of wyne should be the better perceiued of euery body. **1596** SHAKS. *1 Hen. IV*, I. ii. 201, I haue Cases of Buckram for the nonce, to immaske our noted outward garments. **1600** HOLLAND *Livy* XXIII. xxiii. 490 Trifling out the time for the nonce and of purpose [orig. *sedulo*]. **1670** LASSELS *Voy. Italy* II. 128 They buryed her alive in a low vault made for the nonce. **1760–72** H. BROOKE *Fool of Qual.* (1809) I. 80 The least locomotive faculty, in the meanest reptile, must..be provided with.. nerves, tubes, reservoirs, levers, and pulleys, for the nonce. **1853** W. D. COOPER *Sussex Gloss.* (ed. 2), *Nonce*, purpose, intent, design. 'He did it for the nonce.' Still in frequent use in S. and Hants. **1887** *Kentish Gloss.*

b. In ME. poetry (and later, more or less archaically) used as a metrical tag or stop-gap, with no special meaning; frequently riming with *bones* and *stones*.

c **1315** SHOREHAM *Poems* v. 233 Þare he fond flesch and blod myd þe bones, An nou he gan to crye loude for þe nones: 'My lord ich abbe y-founde.' **13..** *Gaw. & Gr. Knt.* 844 A hoge haþel for þe nonez, & of hyghe elde. **1375** BARBOUR *Bruce* x. 58 The folk off Lorne..tumlit on hym stanys, Richt gret and hevy for the nanys. **1390** GOWER *Conf.* II. 102 A stille water for the nones Rennende upon the smale stones. *c* **1400** *Destr. Troy* 1502 Of hir ffeturs & fairhed is ferly to telle, Alse noble for þe nonyst as nature cold deuyse. *c* **1400** *Ywaine & Gaw.* 2051 The lyon hungerd for the nanes, Ful fast he ete raw fless and banes. *c* **1440** *Generydes* 3289 His helme was wele ordeynyd for the nonys, Right wele garnysshed with perle & precious stonys. **1513** DOUGLAS *Æneis* VIII. i. 67 Eneas..hymself doun layd.. for the nanis, And gave schort rest vnto his wery banis. **1557** *Tottel's Misc.* (Arb.) 169 Behold my picture here well portrayed for the nones, With hart consumed and fallyng flesshe, lo here the very bones. **1591** SPENSER *Vision Bellay* vi, I saw her litle ones In wanton dalliance the teate to crave, While she her neck wreath'd from them for the nones. *a* **1635** CORBET *Poems* (1647) 50 Here for the nonce, Came Thomas Jonce, In St. Jileses Church to lye. **1832** L. HUNT *Poems* 289 A cup of good Corsican Does it at once; Or a glass of old Spanish Is neat for the nonce.

c. For the occasion; hence (in modern use), for the time being; temporarily.

1589 PUTTENHAM *Eng. Poesie* II. xvi. (Arb.) 143 If your word polysillable would not sound pleasantly whole, ye should for the nonce breake him. **1672** MARVELL *Reh. Transp.* I. 98 To make a Conscience fit for the nonse, he sayes [etc.]. **1775** WESLEY *Wks.* (1872) VII. 406 Do we not continually tell lies for the nonce, without gaining thereby either profit or pleasure? **1819** SCOTT *Ivanhoe* xxvi, I fear.. there is no one here that is qualified to take upon him, for the nonce, this same character of Father Confessor. **1848** DICKENS *Dombey* vi, Converting the parlour, for the nonce, into a private tyring room. **1859** JEPHSON *Brittany* iv. 42, I therefore made a virtue of necessity, and was a good Catholic for the nonce. **1888** BRYCE *Amer. Commw.* III. lvi. (1890) II. 376 They will take the often more profitable course of fusing for the nonce with one of the regular parties.

†**2. a.** *to þan ane(s, o' the nonce* = 1 a. ***with the nones***: on condition (that). *Obs.*

c1205 LAY. 17304 þa þet word him com to þet Brutes wolden þer don, & comen to þan anes to fæchen þa stanes. *Ibid.* 21506 Mid spæren and mid græte wa3en to þan ane icoren. **c1384** CHAUCER *H. Fame* III. 1009 And here I wol ensuren thee With the nones that thou wolt do so, That [etc.]. **c1385** —— *L.G.W.* 1540 *Hypsipyle*, As wolde almighty god that I had yive My blood and flesh, so that I mighte live, With the nones that he hadde o-wher a wyf For his estat. **c1400** *Gamelyn* 206, I wold geve ten pound,.. With the nones I fand a man to handil him sore. **1665** COTTON *Poet. Wks.* (1765) 116 She kept Sichæus' Bones In a great Coffer made o' th' nonce.

†**b.** ***in the nonce***: at that moment, at once.

c1475 *Hunt. Hare* 266 Y wold that.. In the nownes ye had me the coppe gene, For therof had Y nede.

3. †***for the very nonce***: for the express purpose. ***at the very nonce***: at the very moment.

1627 J. CARTER *Plain Expos.* 55 When they fasted,.. instead of disfiguring their lusts, they disfigured their faces, for the very nonce; affecting rather the seeming then the substance of sanctimony. **1681** HICKERINGILL *Black Non-Conf.* iii. Wks. 1716 II. 36 If they stray, thou art a good Shepherd, reduce them; thou are well kept and paid for the very nonce. **1705** —— *Priest-cr.* I. ibid. III. 4 So fitted and accoutred by Providence for the very nonce. **1855** BROWNING *Childe Roland* xxx, Fool, to be dozing at the very nonce, After a life spent training for the sight!

4. *attrib.*: **nonce-word**, the term used in this Dictionary to describe a word which is apparently used only for the nonce (see vol. I, p. xxvii); similarly ***nonce-use***, etc.; similarly ***nonce-borrowing, -combination, -form, -formation, -meaning***.

1954 U. WEINREICH in Saporta & Bastian *Psycholinguistics* (1961) 385/1 At the time of his utterance, it is a 'nonce-borrowing'. **1943** *Amer. Speech* XVIII. 301 A number of them.. also meet the condition of not being independent words used in some nonce-combination. **1962** H. A. GLEASON in Householder & Saporta *Problems in Lexicography* 88 A dictionary-maker need not include a non-idiomatic nonce-form. **1957** *Archivum Linguisticum* IX. 122 It clearly functions morphemically as everyday nonce-formations testify. **1943** C. L. WRENN *Word & Symbol* (1967) 97 The most surprisingly beautiful result of Spenser's experimenting in poetic language is in the use.. of the word *Cheuisaunce*, which may be described as having acquired for special purpose what I would call a nonce-meaning. **1884** Nonce-wd. [see ANOTHERNESS]. **1927** *Englische Studien* Nov. 99 If an alternative explanation presents itself, topographical nonce-words ought to be avoided. **1957** R. W. ZANDVOORT *Handbk. Eng. Gram.* I. ii. 43 Some of them are nonce-words, i.e. spontaneous creations by a speaker or writer, coined for the occasion.

nonce[2] (nɒns). *Criminals' slang.* [Origin uncertain: see quot. 1984 and *nonce* good-for-nothing fellow (*Eng. Dial. Dict.* Suppl.).] A sexual deviant; one convicted of a sexual offence, esp. child-molesting.

1975 *Time Out* 3 Jan. 7/1 What he told *Seven Days* about his experiences as a sex offender in prison raises a number of urgent questions on the subject of treatment and attitudes to 'nonces', the term used for them by other prisoners. **1977** *Community Care* 2 Nov. 19/3 After the officer had finished his rounds he came back, stormed into my cell and pushed me over the bed. He said: 'You're a f... nonce, you raped a nurse and you want heating!' **1984** *Police Rev.* 18 May 975/3 *Nonce*, prison term for a child molester. The very bottom of the prison pecking order, the 'nonce' is usually segregated from ordinary prisoners at all times for his own protection. Originally derived from 'nancy-boy'. **1986** *Sunday Tel.* 29 June 21/2 As what prisoners call a 'nonce', he now faces years of solitary confinement and regular assaults from fellow inmates.

nonce, variant of NUNCE, nuncio.

non-'central, *a.* [NON- 3.] **1.** *Statistics.* Having or corresponding to a non-zero mean.

1928 *Proc. R. Soc.* A. CXXI. 670 This interpretation of the distribution.. is seen to replace the χ^2 distribution of the analysis of variance for cases in which the sum of squares corresponding to n_1 degrees of freedom is derived theoretically for non-central deviations with fixed central displacements. **1949** *Biometrika* XXXVI. 202 In the case of the well-known tests using χ^2, *t* and *F*, the evaluation of their power functions involves the use of what have been called non-central distributions. **1968** P. A. P. MORAN *Introd. Probability Theory* vii. 323 The quantity χ^2 in (7.121) is then said to have a non-central χ^2-distribution.

2. *Physics.* Of a force: not central, i.e. not in general directed along the line joining the bodies it acts between.

1948 *Physical Rev.* LXXIII. 1403/1 (*heading*) The effect of non-central forces on the collisions of high energy neutrons with protons. **1962** *Encycl. Dict. Physics* V. 610/1 The magnetic forces due to electric currents also have this non-central character. **1966** D. L. LIVESEY *Atomic & Nuclear Physics* ix. 414 There are noncentral forces between neutron and proton. **1970** G. K. WOODGATE *Elem. Atomic Struct.* vii. 107 In the central-field approximation we neglected the residual electrostatic term in the Hamiltonian which represents a non-central force.

Hence **non-cen'trality**, the property of being non-central.

1959 H. SCHEFFÉ *Anal. of Variance* 412 The ordinary or central chi-square distribution is the special case of the noncentral distribution when the noncentrality parameter δ = 0. **1969** H. O. LANCASTER *Chi-Squared Distribution* xi. 231 It is required to determine the parameters of non-centrality of the test of independence in two dimensions.

†**non-cer'tain**, *sb. Obs.* [f. NON- 1 + CERTAIN B. 2.] Uncertainty. Chiefly in phr. ***in non-certain***.

1387-8 T. USK *Test. Love* III. i. (Skeat) l. 61 Opinion is whyl a thing is in non-certayn, and hid from mens very knowleging. **1390** GOWER *Conf.* III. 348 Al the whiles that I hove In noncertein betwen the tuo. **c1392** CHAUCER *Compl. Venus* 46 In noun certaine we langwisshe in penaunce. **1422** tr. *Secreta Secret., Priv. Priv.* 176 Hit is a grete noun certayne of good renoune, that a man Putte hym of anothyr manys mouthe to be Praysid. **1426** LYDG. *De Guil. Pilgr.* 24103 Wherfore I stonde in nonecerteyn. **c1430** —— *Min. Poems* (Percy Soc.) 245 This sesoun Ver stant evir in nouncerteyne.

†**non-'certain**, *a. Obs.* [NON- 3.] Uncertain.

1602 FULBECKE *1st Pt. Parall.* 9b, When a graunt is non-certaine. *Ibid.* 37 This estate is determined, and it was certaine, but a thing non-certaine was the cause of the determination of it.

†**non-'certainty.** *Obs.* [AF. *non-certeintee*: see NON- 1 and CERTAINTY.] Uncertainty.

1475 *Rolls of Parlt.* VI. 129/2 By cause of the noun certeynte of the lyfe of the said Galiard. **1523** FITZHERB. *Bk. Survey.* v b, The declaracyon of this statute is doubtfull, bycause of the none certentie therof.

†**non-cer'tificate.** *Obs.* [NON- 1.] The act or fact of not certifying. Also **non-'certifying** *vbl. sb.*, in the same sense.

1455 *Rolls of Parlt.* V. 334/1 To be forfette, for the non-certificate therof. **1474** *Ibid.* VI. 116/1 For their noncertifiying lymyted and sette as is aforesaid. **1503** *Act 19 Hen. VII*, c. 13 If the same Justices.. have no resonable excuse for non certefying of the same.

nonchalance ('nɒnʃələns; as Fr., nɔ̃ʃalɑ̃s). [a. F. *nonchalance*, f. *nonchalant*: see next.] The condition of being nonchalant; want of warmth of feeling or enthusiasm, lack of interest; indifference, unconcern.

1678 SAVILE *Corr.* (Camden) 73 She.. is at last tired with the King's nonchalance in the prosecution of it. **1758** *Case Authors Stated* 28 With the true *Non-Chalance* of the Indifferent. **1774** MME. D'ARBLAY *Early Diary* (1889) I. 306 All the sisters then poured the incense of praise upon this Ode, to which he listened with the utmost nonchalance. **1844** DISRAELI *Coningsby* III. i, All this, too, without any excitement of manner; on the contrary, with repose amounting almost to nonchalance. **1865** *Cornh. Mag.* July 29 Neglected dames were sublime in a wretched nonchalance. **1874** L. STEPHEN *Hours in Library* (1892) I. vi. 203 Allusions to his old characters are thrown in with a calculated nonchalance.

nonchalant ('nɒnʃələnt; as Fr., nɔ̃ʃalɑ̃), *a.* [a. F. *nonchalant*, pres. pple. of *nonchaloir*, f. *non-* + *chaloir* (:—L. *calēre*) to be warm.] Wanting in warmth of feeling; lacking in enthusiasm or interest; indifferent.

a1734 NORTH *Exam.* II. iv. §147 (1740) 310 To be *non chalant* and insipid in such Matters. **1813** BYRON *Let. to Moore* 8 July, The *nonchalant* deities of Lucretius. **1841** W. GRESLEY *Portr. Churchman* (ed. 6) 83 The irreverent nonchalant demeanour of many of those who form our English congregations. **1893** *Nation* 6 July 17/3 Along with this nonchalant dealing with broad generalities, goes naturally the most careless handling of specific facts.

Hence **'nonchalantly** *adv.*, with nonchalance or indifference; **'nonchalantness** *rare*, nonchalance.

1840 BROWNING *Sordello* IV. 427 You would say, 'Twas a youth nonchalantly looked away Through the embrasure. **1878** DOWDEN *Stud. Lit.* 473 There is a manner of powerful nonchalantness. **1893** VIZETELLY *Glances Back* I. xx. 398 Our artistic friend nonchalantly lighted up his cigar and smoked in the royal bed-chamber.

†**noncha'loir.** *Obs.* In 5 none shaloyre. [a. OF. *nonchaloir* (see NONCHALANT), inf. used as sb.] Neglect, disregard.

c1495 *Epit. Dk. Bedford* in *Skelton's Wks.* (1843) II. 392 Gewellys of late poysyd at grete valoyre,.. Stykynge on stakes as thynges of none shaloyre.

nonchion, obs. form of NUNCHEON.

†**non-church**, *v. Obs.* [NON- 5.] *trans.* To deprive of the status of a church.

a1679 J. BROWN *Life of Faith* (1824) II. xxi. 393 We cannot understand why He should continue the gospel long with one people and remove it quickly from another, and non-church them.

'non-claim. *Law.* [a. AF. *nounclaim*: see NON- 1 and CLAIM *sb.*] Failure or neglect to make a claim within the time limited by law.

1488-9 *Act 4 Hen. VII*, c. 25 The Kyng.. considereth that fynes ought to be of.. fynall ende and conclusion, and of suche effecte were taken afore a statute made of noun cleyme. **1532** *Dial. on Laws Eng.* II. l. 128 To these cases may be resembled yᵉ case of a fine with none clayme. **1594** WEST *2nd Pt. Symbol.* §51 Fine and nonclaime by the space of a yeere and a day was a peremptory barre to al men. **1766** BLACKSTONE *Comm.* II. 354. **1769** *Aclome Inclos. Act* 13 The non-claim or non-acceptance of any guardian. **1858** LD. ST. LEONARDS *Handy-Bk. Prop. Law* xiii. 84 The Courts would not permit any guardian entering as such, afterwards to set up a title by non-claim against his ward.

†**non-claimer.** [Cf. prec. and -ER[4].] = prec.

1701 *Expedient Propos'd* 19 Unless it be.. lost by disusage and nonclaimer beyond the memory of Man.

non-coll. *colloq.* Short for NON-COLLEGIATE.

[**1874** *Non-collegiate Memoranda* 16 The score was as follows: Non-coll. 1st Innings, 124... Trinity. 1st Innings, 132.] **1879** *Durham Univ. Jrnl.* 13 Dec. 13 The Cambridge 'non-colls' have had to take their boat off the river. **1902** *Non-Collegiate Stud. Mag.* II. 118, I can't see why a clergyman because he is a Non-Coll. man shouldn't get a curacy on the same terms as any one else.

non-co'llegiate, *a.* and *sb.* [NON- 2, 3.]

A. *adj.* Not belonging to a college; belonging to the body of students (in certain universities) not attached to any particular college or hall (*scholares nulli collegio vel aulæ ascripti*). Also, occas. of a university: Not having a collegiate system.

1874 *Non-collegiate Memoranda* 2 The Board for superintending Non-collegiate Students, appointed by the University [of Cambridge]. **1876** G. W. KITCHIN *Scholares non ascripti* 5 The advantages they would certainly enjoy in a non-Collegiate University. **1884** *Add. ad Corpus Stat. Univ. Oxon.* 907 Whereas it is expedient that students in the University who are not members of any College or Hall should be designated as Non-Collegiate Students.

B. *sb.* One not educated or trained in a college; one of a non-collegiate body.

1683 (*title*), A Plea for the Chymists or Non-Colegiats. **1897** ESCOTT *Soc. Transform. Vict. Age* xiv. 186 Mr. J. A. Froude's successor in the Chair of Modern History was, throughout the greater portion of his career, a non-collegiate.

non-com. Colloquial abbreviation of *non-commissioned officer*.

[**1747** *Gentl. Mag.* XVI. 336 For 15196 commission'd and non com. in Flanders.] **1883** in *Harper's Mag.* Aug. 398/2 One mess of 'non-coms' had the addition of a.. dish of roast hare. **1894** SALA *London up to Date* 178 He left the army with the rank of sergeant-major; his old commanding officer.. appreciated the worth of the valiant old non-com.

non-'combatant. [NON- 2.] One who is not a combatant, as a civilian in time of war; *spec.* in the army and navy, one whose duties do not include that of fighting, as a surgeon, purser, or chaplain.

1811 WELLINGTON in Gurw. *Desp.* (1838) VIII. 493 The.. pay of non-combatants and pensioners. **1813** *Ibid.* XI. 78 In former wars, a person in your situation would have been considered a non-combatant and would have been immediately released. **1897** GEN. PORTER in *Cent. Mag.* Feb. 494 Many of the non-combatants had gone away.

b. *attrib.* or as *adj.*

1868 *Rep. to Govt. U.S. Munitions War* 196 Hospital attendants.. employed in the transport of wounded.., while non-combatant and solely occupied in these duties [etc.]. **1881** E. ROBERTSON in *Encycl. Brit.* XIII. 194/1 That the non-combatant portions of the two communities should remain as though they were in a state of peace.

non-come. Taken by some to be a nonsensical abbreviation of NON-COMPOS, but perhaps intended as a substitute of NONPLUS.

1599 SHAKS. *Much Ado* III. v. 67 Wee will spare for no witte I warrant you: heere's that shall driue some of them to a non-come.

†**non-commission.** *Obs.* [NON- 4. See COMMISSION *sb.*[1] 13.] = next.

1693 *Royal Proclam.* 9 Feb. in *Lond. Gaz.* No. 2844/1 To the Non-Commission-Officers. **1698** LUTTRELL *Brief Rel.* (1857) IV. 333 Six dayes full pay to each private trooper and non commission officer of the horse and dragoons. **1764** *Chron.* in *Ann. Reg.* 100 The petty officers of the navy and non-commission officers of the army.

non-co'mmissioned, *a.* [NON- 6.]

1. Of officers of the army (†and formerly of the navy): Not holding a commission.

1703 *Lond. Gaz.* No. 3906/4 The Noncommissioned Officers and private Troopers of the Honourable Lieutenant-General Lumley's Regiment of Horse. **1764** *Low Life* 72 The Non-Commissioned Officiers, and Fore-Mast Men of all the Royal Yachts moored about Greenwich. **1813** WELLINGTON in Gurw. *Desp.* (1838) X. 469 As to the non-commissioned officers,.. they are as bad as the men. **1875** *Encycl. Brit.* II. 592/2 Recruiting is carried on by parties detached, or by non-commissioned officers and men on furlough.

2. Of a ship: Not put in commission.

1868 *Rep. Neutrality Law Comm.* in *Morn. Star* 2 June, Any foreign non-commissioned ship despatched from this country after having come within it.

non-co'mmittal, *sb.* (*a.*) [NON- 1.] **a.** Refusal to commit oneself to a particular view or course of action. (orig. *U.S.*)

1836-40 HALIBURTON *Clockm.* (1862) 449 Not lettin' on as if I know'd that he was there, for there is nothin' like a non-committal. **1876** SARAH INGHAM *White Cross* lii, The youth was reticent, and the maiden remarkable for non-committal. **1885** *Daily News* 23 Jan. 5/1 Caution,.. hesitancy, non-committal—these are.. the virtues of the hour.

b. *attrib.* or *adj.* Characterized by refusal to commit oneself to a particular view or course of action; (*esp.* of words and actions) implying neither consent nor dissent.

1829 H. ORNE *Lett. of Columbus* 18 The non-committal system prevailed. **1851** *Fraser's Mag.* Sept. 287/2 A successful politician here [New York] is.. either a blind partisan, who knows nothing outside of 'the regular ticket', or a 'non-committal' man, who says everything to everybody. **1879** J. HAWTHORNE *Laughing Mill*, etc. 112 It was written in an ordinary business hand, quite characterless and non-committal. **1890** 'R. BOLDREWOOD'

Col.-Reformer (1891) 174 The two sailors had the ordinary non-committal expression always observable in trained seamen. **1973** *Archivum Linguisticum* IV. 18 The same applies in..(5), which may be interpreted as a 'non-committal' statement.

Hence **non-co'mmittally** *adv.*, in a non-committal manner; without committing oneself.

1885 HOWELLS *Rise Silas Lapham* I. 187 'She's a pretty girl', said Corey non-committally. **1890** *Harper's Mag.* Mar. 515/2 'Oh, yes,' she said, non-committally.

non-co'mmittalism. [f. NON-COMMITTAL + -ISM.] Non-committal action, practice, state of mind, etc. (orig. *U.S.*)

1855 OGILVIE *Suppl.*, *Non-committalism*, in American politics, the practice or doctrine of not committing or pledging one's self. **1859** BARTLETT *Dict. Amer.* (ed. 2) s.v. (citing *N.Y. Commercial Advertiser*), On many points he.. expresses his opinion with so many qualifications as to subject himself to the charge of non-committalism. **1891** *Review of Rev.* May 456/1 An agnostic non-committalism.

non-co'mmunicant, *sb.* (*a.*) [NON- 2.] One who is not a communicant or does not communicate (e.g. at a particular service); in the 17th c. often *spec.*, one who did not communicate according to the rites of the Church of England.

1602 R. T. *Five Godlie Serm.* 146 As for the common sort of them, which are contemptuous recusants and Non communicants. **1642** *Act Gen. Assemb. Ch. Scot.* (1682) 120 The Assembly would enjoin every Presbyterie to proceed against Non-communicants, whether Papists or others, according to the Act of Parliament made thereanent. **1690** NORRIS *Beatitudes* (1694) I. 115 There is such a thing as an Unworthy Non-Communicant, as well as an Unworthy Communicant. **1708** *Brit. Apollo* No. 89. 2/1 Persons, who have been hitherto Non-Communicants. **1855** SCUDAMORE *Comm. Laity* 65 The other non-communicants being dismissed by the proclamation of the deacon. **1864** (*title*), The Pastor to the Non-communicant. **1876** *Prayer-bk. Interleaved* 169 Non-communicants then left the quire.

b. *adj.* Not communicating.

1901 *Westm. Gaz.* 6 June 8/1 The idea of a non-communicant people was a mediæval corruption.

So **non-co'mmunicating** *vbl. sb.* (also *attrib.*) and *ppl. a.*

1691 BAXTER *Nat. Ch.* xiv. 60 All the Parish Churches are to distinguish Communicating Members from Non-communicating Inhabitants. **1861** J. E. VAUX *Pres. Whole Congreg. Holy Euch.* 5 Such non-communicating attendance was agreeable to..those divines who had the chief share in the construction of the Book of Common Prayer. **1917** A. S. PRINGLE-PATTISON *Idea of God* iii. 57 It is impossible to treat the world of religious belief and the world of fact..as if they were two non-communicating spheres. **1960** K. AMIS *New Maps of Hell* (1961) i. 20 Some excellent stories have been written about non-communicating aliens, from *The War of the Worlds* onwards. **1972** *Where* May–June 158/2 The parent who protested that her LEA was sending her non-communicating child 200 miles away from home and so she would not be able to visit, when the child could not write or use a phone, had a real case.

†non-co'mmunion. *Obs.* [NON- 1.]

1. Lack of communion or fellowship.

1648 GAGE *West. Ind.* xii. 63 Non-communion of prayers.

2. Refusal to communicate, *esp.* according to the rites of the Church of England. Hence **†non-co'mmunionist**, one who practises such abstention.

1644 J. DURY *Epist. Disc.* 20 Except they can make clearly appear..that the Church way of Non-Communion (for I know not what else to call it) is the only true way of God. *Ibid.* 41 The scrupulosities of the Non-Communionists.

3. Exclusion from communion.

1723 in *Narr. Proc. Synods Presbyt. Irel.* (1727) 73 For prescribing a particular form of Confession to Intrants under the penalty of Non-communion.

non-com'pearance. *Sc. Law.* Also 6 -perence, -ance, -peirance, 7 -parence. [NON- 1.] Failure to appear in a court of law.

1532 *Acc. Ld. High Treas.* VI. 62 Certane unlawis in the quhilkis he was adjugit for non-compeerence in the Tolbwith of Perth. **1582–8** *Hist. & Life Jas. VI* (1825) 66 The Duc of Chattellarault, the Abbot of Kilwynning,..and Mr. Thomas Maitland, war denouncit rebellis to the King, for noncomperance before the Regent. **1619** DR. BALCANQUAL *Let.* in Hales *Gold. Rem.* (1673) II. 108 No mans charge in private can excuse him for noncomparence before a judge, when he is cited. **1693** J. WALLACE *Descr. Orkney* 82 He being..forefaulted for non-compearance to the Parliament. **1774** *Scots Mag.* XXXVI. 720/1 Elizabeth Bruce..was fugitated for non-compearance. [**1893** STEVENSON *Catriona* 98 The remeid is to summon the principal and put him to outlawry for the non-compearance.]

Also **†non-com'pearing** *vbl. sb.* = prec.

1566 *Reg. Privy Council Scot.* I. 463 Put to the horne for noncompering befoir thair majesteis.

non-com'pliance. [NON- 1.] Failure or refusal to comply.

1687 LD. HALIFAX *Let. to Dissenter* 9 You are let loose only upon Bayl; the first Act of Non-compliance, sendeth you to jayl again. **1740** RICHARDSON *Pamela* (1824) I. 203 He was so out of humour at her supposed non-compliance, that [etc.]. **1750** BEAWES *Lex Mercat.* (1752) Pref. p. viii, The Trials about Noncompliance with accepted Bills. **1884** *Law Times Rep.* LI. 79/2 As soon as there is any..non-compliance with the rules..there is an absolute forfeiture. **1885** *Law Times* LXXVIII. 166/1 The instrument was..void for non-compliance with the Act.

Also **non-com'pliant** *a.*, in quot. used subst., one who refuses to comply; **non-com'plying** *vbl. sb.*, non-compliance.

1687 H. HOLDEN in *Magd. Coll.* (O.H.S.) 175 None of them, though the danger of noncomplying was intimated to them,..would comply. **1896** *Daily News* 16 Jan. 5/5 To carry out the threat of dismissing non-compliants.

non 'compos. Short for NON COMPOS MENTIS.

1628 COKE *On Litt.* 247 So it is of a *Non compos*, and so it is of him *qui gaudet lucidis interuallis.* **1711** *Vind. Sacheverell* 41 Any Jury..will bring him in *Non Compos.* **1771** SMOLLETT *Humph. Cl.* (1815) 176 The Templar affirmed, that the poor fellow was 'non compos'; and exhorted the justice to discharge him as a lunatic. **1814** CHALMERS *Sp.* in *Life* (1849) I. 503 They.., like a non-compos, have resigned the management of their affairs into other hands. **1817** T. L. PEACOCK *Melincourt* I. 89 Your learned mythologist appears to be non compos. **1858** O. W. HOLMES *Aut. Breakf.-t.* ii. (Rtldg.) 45 If they were not the most stupid or the most selfish of human beings, they would become *non-compotes* at once.

‖**non compos mentis** (nɒn 'kɒmpɒs 'mɛntɪs). [L. = 'not master of one's mind'.] Not *compos mentis*; not in one's right mind. Also as *sb.*

1607 COWELL *Interpr.*, *Non compos mentis* is of foure sortes. **1628** COKE *On Litt.* 246 b, Here Littl. explaneth a man of no sound memory to be *Non compos mentis.* **1692** *Jacobite Conventicle* Postscr., These men are sure *Non compos mentis*, And Bedlam must be sure Enlarg'd. **1695** CONGREVE *Love for L.* IV. xii, His son is *non compos mentis*, and thereby incapable of making any conveyance in law. **1732** FIELDING *Miser* IV. ix, Heyday! sure you are non compos mentis! **1765** BLACKSTONE *Comm.* I. viii. 294 A lunatic, or *non compos mentis*, is one who hath had understanding, but by disease [etc.] hath lost the use of his reason. **1815** W. H. IRELAND *Scribbleomania* 129 Never was scribe yet so *non compos mentis*, And ranking of Bathos more sterling apprentice. **1864** NICHOLS *Forty Years Amer. Life* II. 123 A crazy man, or one decided to be *non compos mentis*, might be challenged and his vote denied.

non-com'pounder. [NON- 2.] One who does not compound; *spec. Hist.* a member of that section of the Jacobite party shortly after the Revolution which desired the restoration of James II without imposing any conditions on him.

1651 BIGGS *New Disp.* 41 ¶77 Those [herbs] who are.. listed in the bills of mortality, excepted against in the list of non-compounders with the State of our vital Œconomy [etc.]. **1827** [see COMPOUNDER 2 b]. **1855** MACAULAY *Hist. Eng.* xx. IV. 385 The Non-compounders thought it downright Whiggery, downright rebellion, to take advantage of His Majesty's unfortunate situation for the purpose of imposing on him any condition. **1886** A. FERGUSSON *Laird of Lag* v. 103 This incorrigible offender against Whig Rule and inveterate 'non-compounder'.

non-con[1] ('nɒnkɒn). *colloq.* Abbreviation of NONCONFORMIST.

1681 T. FLATMAN *Heraclitus Ridens* No. 34 (1713) I. 223 I'll say that for our Non-cons, they are in as fair a way to undo themselves, as they have been this forty Years. **1710** *Last Distemper Tom Whigg* II. 17 A Tall Two-handed Squint-ey'd Non-Con waving a Banner in the Air with all his Force. *a* **1825** PARR in Field *Mem.* (1828) I. 137 You non-cons have done well to exchange the word meeting-house for chapel. **1862** *Westm. Rev.* Jan. 89 A chapel [in Keighley] for some section of the Methodists..who were popularly known as 'Noncons'.

attrib. **1681** T. FLATMAN *Heraclitus Ridens* No. 72 (1713) II. 191 Methinks you have much of the obscurity of a Non-Con Parson in this talk. *a* **1734** NORTH *Exam.* (1740) 645 One Rosewell, a Non-Con Teacher, convict of High Treason. **1819** PARR *Lett. to Mr. Berry* 19 Dec. Wks. 1828 VIII. 481 The undisciplined curiosity of non-con sciolists.

non-con[2]. Abbreviation of NON-CONTENT.

1847 WEBSTER (citing JOHN FOSTER), *Non-content*... The word is sometimes abridged into Non-con, and applied to any one who dissents or expresses dissatisfaction.

non-con'cur, *v. U.S.* [NON- 5.] **a.** *trans.* To refuse to concur in or agree to. ? *Obs.*

1703 S. SEWALL *Diary* 24 July, Bristol business is Non-concurr'd by the Deputies. **1760** T. HUTCHINSON *Hist. Mass.* iii. (1765) 256 Then they non-concurred the vote. **1775** —— *Diary* 23 Mar., The only way for the Commons, they say, is to non-concur the Amendment. **1823** W. TUDOR *Life of James Otis* 239 The Council non-concurred this resolve.

b. *intr.* To fail or refuse to concur; to disagree. Usu. const. *in* or *with.*

1855 *Chicago Times* 3 Mar. 3/5 The House non-concurred with the Senate amendment. **1862** *Congress. Globe* 9 July 3214/1, I hope the house will non-concur in that amendment of the Senate. **1907** *Springfield* (Mass.) *Weekly Republican* 20 June 1 The Senate has non-concurred with the House amendments. **1911** PARTON & MANNING in C. E. Persons et al. *Labor Laws* 53 The House went on record as favorable to the resolution. The State nonconcurred. **1974** *Spartanburg* (S. Carolina) *Herald* 18 Apr. A. 2/4 Arthur was one of several House members to take the floor Tuesday to urge the legislators to non-concur in the Senate amendments.

non-con'currence. [NON- 1.] A refusal to concur (*with*).

a **1691** PIERCE (L.), Bishop Sanderson's last judgement concerning God's concurrence or non-concurrence with the actions of men. **1711** G. HICKES *Two Treat. Chr. Priesth.* (1847) I. 288 The non-concurrence of the upper house of convocation with the lower.

†non-con'currency. *Obs.* [NON- 1.] The quality of not running together in space. So **†non-con'curring** *ppl. a.*

a **1696** SCARBURGH *Euclid* (1705) 31 The Attribute of these Strait Lines is Nonconcurrency. *Ibid.*, The Geometrical Notion to be conceived under that name of Parellels is Nonconcurring Strait Lines.

non-con'densing, *ppl. a.* [NON- 6.] Applied to a kind of steam-engine in which the steam on leaving the cylinder is not condensed in a condenser but is discharged into the atmosphere.

1841 BREES *Gloss. Civil Engin.* 122 High-Pressure, or Non-Condensing Engine, an engine in which the cylinders are worked by the elastic force of the steam alone, without the aid of a vacuum. **1856** *Orr's Circ. Sci., Mech. Philos.* 421 Non-condensing engines are generally of the form called beam-engines. **1895** *Mod. Steam Engine* 43 Chaplin's Non-condensing Vertical-Action Steam Engine.

non-conducti'bility. [NON- 1.] The quality or condition of being a non-conductor.

1844 LARDNER & WALKER *Electr., Magn.*, etc. II. Index, Comparative non-conductibility of individuals. **1863** TYNDALL *Heat* vii. 231 The same quality of non-conductibility manifests itself when we wrap flannel round a block of ice.

non-con'ducting, *ppl. a. Physics.* [NON- 6.] That does not conduct heat or electricity; that is a non-conductor.

1771 *Phil. Trans.* LXI. 650 If any body is surrounded on all sides by the air, or other non-conducting substances, it is said to be insulated. **1821** URE *Dict. Chem.* s.v. *Electricity*, The crystalline arrangement always introduces non-conducting qualities. **1835–6** *Todd's Cycl. Anat.* I. 265/1 An adequate protection of the surface of the body by means of non-conducting down and imbricated feathers.

fig. **1871** MORLEY *Condorcet* in *Crit. Misc.* Ser. I. (1878) 34 If to be of this non-conducting temperament is impossible in the greatest characters.

non-con'duction. *Physics.* [NON- 1.] Failure to conduct.

1828–32 WEBSTER (citing URE). **1867** GROVE *Correl. Phys. Force* (ed. 5) 134 Sonorous vibrations, which might be called conduction and non-conduction of sound.

non-con'ductor. *Physics.* [NON- 2.] A substance or medium that does not permit the passage of any form of energy (as heat or electricity).

1751 [see CONDUCTOR 11]. **1759** *Phil. Trans.* LI. 317 Wax, when it is once in good order, will continue a non-conductor for a long time. *Ibid.* 896 Wood, properly dried, till it becomes very brown, is a non-conductor of electricity. **1857** LARDNER *Anim. Phys.* §587 Fat..is nearly a non-conductor of heat. **1890** *Nature* 16 Oct. 601 Volcanic ash..forms one of the most effective non-conductors known.

†non-con'form, *a. Obs.* [NON- 5. See CONFORM *a.* 3.] Nonconforming.

?**1679** *Scotl. Grievances Lauderdale's Ministry* 36 He plainly turns this new Indulgence, ino a universal confinement, of the whole non-conform Ministers. **1680** *Spirit of Popery* 16 The Nonconform Ministers scornfully rejected them. **1784** J. BROWN *Hist. Brit. Ch.* (1820) II. 112 The Nonconform ministers..presented a Supplication for liberty to administer the Lord's supper.

non-con'form, *v.* [NON- 5.] *intr.* To fail to conform (*to*).

1681 T. FLATMAN *Heraclitus Ridens* No. 45 (1713) II. 37, I can shew you one little Yelper that Nonconforms to the whole Party. **1847** HELPS *Friends in C.* Ser. I. ii, When we talk of non-conformity, it may only be that we non-conform to the immediate sect of thought or action about us. **1852** LYNCH *Orthodoxy* in *Lett. to Scattered* (1872) 273 What.. liberty of soul may belong to the men who non-conform to the world.

†non-con'formable, *a. Obs.* [NON- 3. See CONFORMABLE 3 c.] Nonconforming.

1647 CLARENDON *Hist. Reb.* III. 257 The non-conformable party of the kingdom. **1672** BAXTER *Bagshaw's Scand.* iii. 32 In 1640 there were not found near half so many Non conformable Ministers as are Counties in England. **1691** WOOD *Ath. Oxon.* I. 610 Afterwards shewing himself nonconformable he was deprived of his Archdeaconry.

transf. **1670** BROOKS *Wks.* (1867) VI. 417 How wonderfully did he preserve the three children, or rather the three non-conformable champions, from burning in the midst of the flames! **1673** [R. LEIGH] *Transp. Reh.* 43 Schismatick in Poetry, though nonconformable in point of Rhyme.

Comb. **1637** W. SALTONSTALL *Eusebius' Constantine* 17 Declaring that hee should bee glad to see the Church settled in peace and concord, hating those that were stubborne, refractory, and non-conformable minded.

noncon'formably, *adv.* [NON- 8.] Not in accordance *with.*

1860 I. TAYLOR *Ess.* 42 Whatever is done conformably with order and also nonconformably with order.

non-con'formance. [NON- 1.] Failure to conform *to.*

1843 *Civil Eng. & Arch. Jrnl.* VI. 118/1 The monks,..on account of their nonconformance to the Catholic observance of Easter, were expelled the monastery.

†non-con'former. *Obs.* [NON- 2.] = NONCONFORMIST.

1619 [see CONFORMER]. **1676** *Pkt. Advices to Men of Shaftesbury* 35 All other Nonconformers lay no claim to a Church-National.

noncon'forming, *vbl. sb.* [NON- 7.] Failure to conform; *esp.* to the rites and discipline of the Church of England.

1682 *2nd Plea Nonconformists* 14 The Original Crime is Nonconforming; the next is not taking the Oxf. Oath. **1716** M. DAVIES *Athen. Brit.* II. 212 [He] had been turn'd out.. for Non-Subscribing or Non-Conforming.

noncon'forming, *ppl. a.* [NON- 6.] Not conforming to the Church of England (or any established church); pertaining to or supporting nonconformity; = NONCONFORMIST *attrib.* Also in non-religious contexts; *spec.* (see quot. 1961).

1646 SALTMARSH *(title)*, Groanes for Liberty: presented from the Presbyterian (formerly Non-conforming) brethren. **1682** WOOD *Life* (O.H.S.) III. 23 Mr. John Fairclough *vulgo* Featly, a non-conforming minister. **1790** BURKE *Fr. Rev.* 12 Doctor Richard Price, a non-conforming minister of eminence, preached at the dissenting meeting-house of the Old Jewry. **1876** BANCROFT *Hist. U.S.* III. iv. 355 No non-conforming Catholic could buy land, or receive it by descent, devise, or settlement. **1886** *Encycl. Brit.* XXI. 82/1 The nonconforming sects, while helping to preserve several advantageous features of Russian life, have had a powerful influence in maintaining.. the old system of the Muscovite family. **1899** 'MARK TWAIN' *Man that corrupted Hadleyburg* (1900) 273 Worn officially, our nonconforming swallow-tail is a declaration of ungracious independence in the matter of manners. **1961** E. A. POWDRILL *Vocab. Land Planning* iv. 67 When industry of this nature [*sc.* general industry] is located in an area the primary use of which is residential, shopping, or other non-industrial uses, it is said to be 'non-conforming', in that it does not conform, in usage, to the primary use. **1972** *Jrnl. Social Psychol.* LXXXVI. 16 When a non-conforming response was made by an *S* in the low or high reward condition.. he automatically received a coin. **1973** *N.Y. Law Jrnl.* 26 July 2/2 The effect of such a zoning law change is to make the property a non-conforming use.

noncon'formism. [f. next: see -ISM.] The system of nonconformity.

1844 *Fraser's Mag.* XXX. 687/1 The banner of Nonconformism was unfurled. **1894** *Dubl. Rev.* July 210 Anglicanism.. was created, while Nonconformism was crushed.

nonconformist (nɒnkən'fɔːmɪst). [NON- 2.]

1. a. (Usually with capital *N.*) Orig. in the early part of the 17th century, one who, while adhering to the doctrine of the Church of England, refused to conform to its discipline and practice (chiefly in the matter of certain ceremonies). Now *Hist.* **b.** Later, *esp.* after the passing of the Act of Uniformity of 1662 and the consequent ejection from their livings of those ministers who refused to conform, a member of a religious body which is separated from the Church of England; in modern use, usually = Protestant Dissenter.

The term has been sometimes applied analogically to the Puritan section of the Church of England in the reigns of Edward VI and Elizabeth.

1619 T. MORTON *(title)*, A Defence of The Innocencie of the three Ceremonies of the Church of England, viz. The Surplice, Crosse after Baptisme, and Kneeling at the receiuing of the blessed Sacrament. Diuided into two Parts. In the former whereof the Generall Arguments vrged by the Non-conformists.. are answered. **1634** CANNE *Necess. Separ.* To Rdr., There is not ten of an hundred which separate from the Church of England, but are moved first thereto.. by the Doctrines of the Nonconformists. **1655** FULLER *Ch. Hist.* VII. xvi. §30. 406 Three Classes of Non-conformists:.. 1. Antient Non-conformists, here in King Edward's daies... 2. Middle Non-conformists, in the end of Queene Elizabeth and beginning of King James... 3. Modern Non-conformists. **1662** PETTY *Taxes* 7 Pecuniary mulcts such as every Conscientious Non-conformist would gladly pay. **1665** *Act 17 Chas. II*, c. 2 *(title)*, An Act for restraining Non-Conformists from inhabiting in Corporations. **1672** MARVELL *Reh. Transp.* I. 125, I suppose the Nonconformists value themselves tho upon their Conscience and not their numbers. **1732** NEAL *Hist. Purit.* I. 57 The Garments were continued which soon after divided the Reformers among themselves, and gave rise to the two parties of Conformists and Non-conformists. **1849** MACAULAY *Hist. Eng.* vi. II. 6 That salvation might be found in the Church of Rome.. was admitted by all divines of the Anglican communion and by the most illustrious Non-conformists. **1885** *Ch. Quart.* XXI. 126 Cartwright was a Nonconformist, not a Separatist; he hated schism as much as episcopacy.

c. *gen.* One who does not conform to the doctrine or discipline of an established church.

1672 MARVELL *Reh. Transp.* I. 74 Which of these two [*sc.* Guelphs and Ghibellines] were the Nonconformists in those dayes. **1769** BLACKSTONE *Comm.* IV. iv. 51 Non-conformists are of two sorts: first, such as absent themselves from the divine worship in the established church, through total irreligion. **1837** LOCKHART *Scott* I. 205 Andrew Macdonald .. then officiated as minister to a small congregation of Episcopalian nonconformists. **1886** *Encycl. Brit.* XXI. 82/1 The nonconformists [in Russia] enjoying, as a rule, a greater degree of prosperity than their Orthodox neighbours.

2. One who does not conform to a particular practice or course of action.

a **1677** BARROW *Serm.* (1700) III. ix. 94 Is it just.. that I should be a Non-conformist either in publick sorrow or joy? *a* **1680** BUTLER *Rem.* (1759) II. 57 They are State-Recusants, politic Nonconformists, that.. cannot comply with the present Government. **1685** CROWNE *Sir C. Nice* II. Wks. 1874 III. 277 He.. comes hither hourly to perform his devotions to me, but in such a slovenly manner; 'tis such a non-conformist to all decent ceremonies. **1952** [see FEATHER-BEDDING *vbl. sb.*].

3. *attrib.* or as *adj.* Nonconforming; pertaining to or characteristic of Nonconformists. Esp. in phr. ***nonconformist conscience.***

1641 R. BROOKE *Eng. Episc.* 90 The Church of England hath three maine Divisions: the Conformist, the Non-Conformist and the Separatist. **1669** WHITEHEAD *(title)*, The Glory of Christ's Light within expelling Darkness; being the sun of the controversie between the.. Quakers, and some Non-conformist Priests. **1752** CARTE *Hist. Eng.* III. 422 These non-conformist ministers were desirous to justify their conduct by the opinions of foreign divines. **1868** M. PATTISON *Academ. Org.* 2 How are the nonconformist Children to be provided for? **1890** *Let.* in *Times* 28 Nov. 8/6 The minimum demand of the great Nonconformist party is the.. abdication of Mr. Parnell... Nothing less will satisfy the Nonconformist conscience now. **1890** *Times* 28 Nov. 8/6 The *minimum* demand of the great Nonconformist party is the unconditional abdication of Mr. Parnell, and his immediate retirement from Parliamentary life... Nothing less will satisfy the Nonconformist conscience. **1893** O. WILDE *Lady Windermere's Fan* III. 90 There is nothing in the whole world so unbecoming to a woman as a Nonconformist conscience. **1894** BEERBOHM in *Yellow Bk.* III. Oct. 250 The Non-conformist Conscience makes cowards of us all. **1931** *Times Lit. Suppl.* 10 Sept. 670/1 The difficulties of governing Ireland and keeping the Nonconformist conscience quiet.

4. A moth, *Lithophane lamda*, found in northern Europe, Russia, and North America.

1869 E. NEWMAN *Illustr. Nat. Hist. Brit. Moths* 428/2 The Nonconformist... Their colour is bluish-gray in some specimens, prettily varied with darker and lighter gray in others. **1961** EDELSTEN & FLETCHER *South's Moths Brit. Is.* (ed. 4) 228 The Nonconformist (*Lithophane lamda*, Fab.).

Hence **nonconfor'mistical** *a.*, characteristic of Nonconformists; **nonconfor'mistically** *adv.*, in the manner of Nonconformists.

1808 SOUTHEY *Lett.* (1856) II. 66 The 'Monthly Review' .. notices the book with civil Non-conformistical dullness. **1891** *Sat. Rev.* 21 Mar. 343/1 It is.. the most Nonconformistically conscientious thing in the world.

†**noncon'formitan.** *Obs.* [NON- 2.] = NONCONFORMIST. Also †**noncon'formitant.** Hence †**noncon'formitancy**, nonconformity.

1618 DONNE *Serm.* (1661) III. 25 Here is the true Recusant, and the true Non-conformitan. **1627** JACKSON *Chr. Obed.* vi. Wks. 1844 XII. 299 Admit then any refractory nonconformitant could.. justly presume of immunity from any temporal punishment. **1647** [J. HART] *Trodden Down Strength* 117 Being a Non-conformitan in judgment.. [he] was contented.. to accept of that poore Living. *a* **1670** HACKET *Abp. Williams* II. (1692) 43 It was his judgment.. to allow some of the chief.. among the Non-Conformitants with some of the dignities of the Church. *Ibid.* 44 Officers Ecclesiastical did prosecute Presentments, rather against Non-conformitancy of Ministers and People, than for Debaucheries.

nonconformity (nɒnkən'fɔːmɪtɪ). [NON- 1.]

1. Refusal to conform to the doctrine, discipline, or polity of an established church, orig. and now *esp.* of the Church of England; the principles or practice of Nonconformists; in modern use, usually = Protestant dissent. Also, Nonconformists as a body. (Usually with capital *N.*)

1618 DONNE *Serm.* (1661) III. 25 He confesses that he hath received good instruction, but he refuses to conform himself unto it; there's Non-conformity. **1641** R. BROOKE *Eng. Episc.* 96 In Queen Elizabeths time many good men were cut off from the Church... And all this for one word of their owne compounding, Non-conformity. **1655** FULLER *Ch. Hist.* VII. 401 Non-conformity in the daies of King Edward. **1663** HEATH *Flagellum* (1672) 13 Orthodox Divines, no way given to that Schisme of Non-Conformity, into which Oliver soon after fell. *a* **1731** CALAMY *Life* (1829) I. i. 65 My father, in the year 1662,.. was for his nonconformity ejected from a good living. **1860** L. HARCOURT *Diaries G. Rose* II. 278 The ultimate designs of political nonconformity. **1886** *Encycl. Brit.* XXI. 82/1 Nonconformity, which formerly had no hold upon Little Russia,.. has suddenly begun to make progress there in the shape of the 'Stunda', a mixture of Protestant and rationalisitc teaching. **1898** *Times* 29 Oct. 13/6 The Bishop said that.. neither Rome on the one hand nor Nonconformity on the other trusted their ministers as the Church confided in the priesthood of England.

2. Want of conformity or refusal to conform to a rule, practice, or requirement. Const. *to*, *with*.

1682 *2nd Plea Nonconformists* 13 Their Nonconformity to the Act of Uniformity. *a* **1720** SEWEL *Hist. Quakers* (1795) I. II. 142 Their nonconformity with the Vulgar Salutation, and their saying Thou and Thee. **1841** CATLIN *N. Amer. Ind.* lviii. (1844) II. 233 In case of non-conformity to this indispensable form. **1879** SPENCER *Data Ethics* vi. §37. 95 The.. sufferings caused by nonconformity to the laws of life.

3. Want of correspondence, agreement, or adaptability between persons or things.

1672 MARVELL *Reh. Transp.* I. 269 Never was there such Incongruity and Nonconformity in their furniture. **1763** JON. MAYHEW *(title)*, Observations on the Charter and Conduct of the Society for the Propagation of the Gospel..; designed to shew their nonconformity to each other. **1846** DE QUINCEY *Shelley* Wks. 1890 XI. 372 Nonconformity of tastes might easily arise between two parties, without much blame to either. **1853** G. JOHNSTON *Nat. Hist. E. Bord.* I. 240 The girl.. was apt to meet his seriousness with something savouring of coquetry... But the nonconformity was more evanescent than the early dew. **1886** *Law Rep., Weekly Notes* 188/1 The nonconformity of the complete specification with the provisional specification.

non-con'junction. [NON- 1.] **1.** *Cytology.* The failure of homologous chromosomes to pair at meiosis. *rare.*

1925 J. BELLING in *Jrnl. Genetics* XV. 256 Non-conjunction. This term is used instead of non-conjugation, because in most cases it cannot be told whether conjugation, that is, parasynapsis, has taken place or not, with regard to the chromosome pair in question... Non-conjunction cannot be distinguished from true non-disjunction, in the later stages.

2. *Logic.* The relation of the terms in a proposition asserting the negative of a conjunctive proposition ('not both.. and..').

1926 H. M. SHEFFER in *Isis* VIII. 229 The authors consider one of the cardinal improvements in the new edition to consist in their substitution, for the two operations of propositional *negation* and *disjunction*, of the single operation of *non-conjunction*. **1956** A. CHURCH *Introd. Math. Logic* (rev. ed.) I. ii. 134 Sheffer uses the sign of disjunction, ∨, inverted as a sign of non-disjunction; he introduces non-conjunction only in a footnote and uses no special sign for it. *Ibid.* 135 Taking non-conjunction as the only primitive connective, give definitions of the singulary and remaining binary connectives. **1957** *Encycl. Brit.* XIV. 306/1 We shall use.. the sign | to denote non-conjunction ('$p|q$' to mean 'not both p and q'). *Ibid.*, If the sign of non-conjunction (Sheffer's stroke) is taken as primitive, all the other connectives can be defined from this one. **1965** HUGHES & LONDEY *Elem. Formal Logic* viii. 54 The following are valid: (i) $(p \uparrow q) \equiv \sim (p.q)$, (ii) $(p\downarrow q) \equiv \sim (p \vee q)$, which suggests the names 'non-conjunction' and 'non-disjunction' for '↑' and '↓' respectively.

†**non-con'sent**, *v. Obs. rare.* [NON- 5.] *intr.* To withhold consent.

1645 BALL *Sphere Gov.* 8, I conceive.. power.. to consist rather in.. the King's power to consent, and Act, rather than in his power to non-consent and non-act.

†**non-con'senter.** *Obs.* [NON- 2.] One who withholds consent; a dissenter.

1661 BAXTER *Moral Prognost.* (1680) II. 46 Consent is made by Christ, the Condition of Pardon and Covenant-Benifits, which no Non-consenter hath a Title to.

So †**non-con'senting** *ppl. a.*, dissenting.

1680 BAXTER *Answ. Stillingfl.* xxxiv. 56 How prove you.. that the Relation of the Ejected London Ministers, and their Flocks was Dissolved, and that the Succeeders were true Pastors to the Non-consenting Flocks? **1805** EUGENIA DE ACTON *Nuns Desert* I. 280 Love, which he saw was received with smiles and curtsies, though her lips spoke a non-consenting language.

†**non-con'sentient.** *Obs.* [f. NON- + CONSENTIENT used subst.] One who does not consent.

1625 BP. MOUNTAGU *App. Cæsar* 143 What Parliament, Law.., or Edict did ever command it to be professed, or have imposed penaltie upon.. non-consentients unto it?

non-'consequence. [NON- 1.] Want of consequence in reasoning; also, an instance of this, a *non sequitur*.

1649 CANNE *Golden Rule* 12, I find some to frame their objection thus... It is a great non-consequence. **1666** BP. S. PARKER *Free & Impart. Censure* (1667) 40 His Circular arguings,.. contradictions, non-consequences. **1856** DOVE *Logic Chr. Faith* I. §1. 35 We must.. endeavour.. to lay bare .. the non-consequence of his conclusion.

non-con'sumption. [NON- 1.] Refusal to consume certain articles of food (in *U.S. Hist.*: cf. *non-importation*). Also *attrib.*

1774 *Chron.* in *Ann. Reg.* 215 As a non-consumption agreement.. will be an effectual security for the observation of the non-importation, we.. solemnly agree.. that we will not purchase or use any tea imported on account of the East-India company [etc.]. **1774** J. ADAMS *Wks.* (1854) IX. 347, I believe we shall agree to non-importation, non-consumption, and non-exportation. **1961** L. E. DAVIS et al. *Amer. Econ. Hist.* iii. 54 The net.. addition to a nation's capital stock.. must be the result of nonconsumption of national product.

non-con'tagion. *Med.* [NON- 1.] The condition or property of being non-contagious.

1808 *Med. Jrnl.* XIX. 113 The non-contagion doctrines have been familiar in America some time. **1845** *Encycl. Metrop.* Index, Non-contagion of cholera. **1864** W. T. FOX *Skin Dis.* 39 Non-contagion, hereditary transmission [etc.].

Hence **non-con'tagionist**, one who holds the doctrine of non-contagion with regard to certain diseases.

1822–34 *Good's Study Med.* (ed. 4) I. 232 Facts of this kind.. are easily explained by the non-contagionists. **1845** *Encycl. Metrop.* VII. 817/1 Of 250 officers, comprising the medical staff in Bengal, all but one are non-contagionists.

non-con'tagious, *a.* [NON- 3.] Not contagious or propagated by contagion. So **non-con'tagiousness** = NON-CONTAGION.

1817 W. TAYLOR in *Monthly Mag.* XLIV. 313 Certificates of non-contagiousness. **1845** R. WILLIAMS *Princ. Med.* in *Encycl. Metrop.* VII. 817/1 The evidence of the non-contagious nature of cholera.

'non-content. [NON- 2. See CONTENT *a.* 3 c and B.] **a.** In the House of Lords, one who votes 'Not content'.

1778 *Chron.* in *Ann. Reg.* 181 On the chancellor's putting the question,.. the non-contents were 20, and the contents only 4. **1863** H. COX *Instit.* I. vii. 92 The equality of votes is held equivalent to a majority of non-contents.

b. One who is not content.

1860 J. BROWN *Rab, Let. to J. Cairns* (1906) 289 There was one man who held out against his 'call'. Mr. Brown meeting him.., the non-content said [etc.].

non-con'tingent, *a.* [f. NON- 3 + CONTINGENT *a.* 4.] That does not happen by chance or depend on a variable.

1890 J. RANKINE *Erskine's Princ. Law Scotl.* (ed. 18) III. vii. 405 The running of prescription is suspended during the minority of the person who is *verus dominus*, being lawfully vested with a non-contingent title to compete for possession, or of him who is the true creditor. **1939** KURTZ & EDGERTON *Statistical Dict. Terms & Symbols* 99 *Mathematically independent*, unaffected by the happening of another event or by the size of another variable. Also called independent, non-contingent, and uncontingent. **1971** *Jrnl. General Psychol.* Apr. 326 *S*s were given either 30%, 50%, or 70% noncontingent positive *E*-administered reinforcement. **1973** *Jrnl. Genetic Psychol.* Sept. 16 The final design contained two levels of noncontingent preference value within subjects.

non-contra'diction. [NON- 1.] The absence of contradiction; in Logic, ***principle*** or ***law of non-contradiction*** = 'principle of contradiction' (see CONTRADICTION 4 c).

1836-7 [see CONTRADICTION 4 c]. **1882** ADAMSON in *Encycl. Brit.* XIV. 782/2 The stricter followers of the Kantian logical idea.. recognize, as sole principles which can be said to be involved universally in the action of thought, the laws of identity, non-contradiction, and excluded middle. **1892** HUXLEY in *Pop. Sci. Monthly* XLI. 601 This non-natural sense may.. be manipulated into some sort of non-contradiction of scientific truth.

non-con'tributory, *a.* [NON- 3.] Of a pension, a pension-scheme, or the like: not involving contributions from the pensioner or beneficiary.

1911 *Q. Rev.* July 198 The provision for old age in our system is non-contributory and wholly paid by the State. **1935** *Planning* II. XLII. 5 The first of these is the non-contributory State pension of 10s a week available at 70 subject to a declaration of means. **1975** *Times* 1 Dec. 12/8 The question of moving from a non-contributory to a contributory [pensions] scheme has been reopened in Whitehall.

non-co-ope'ration. [NON- 1.] Failure or refusal to co-operate; *spec.* used as a means of resistance or protest, esp. against the British in India before 1947. Also *attrib.*

1795 NELSON 17 Sept. in Nicolas *Disp.* (1846) VII. Add. 22 The non-co-operation of the British Fleet and the Sardinian Army. **1860** RUSKIN *Unto this Last* (1862) IV. 141 The most accurately nugatory labour is.. that of which not enough is given to answer a purpose effectually... Also, labour which fails of effect through non-co-operation. **1920** A. BESANT (*title*) Gandhian non-co-operation; or, shall India commit suicide? **1922** *Telegraphic Corr. India* 3 in *Parl. Papers* (Cmd. 1586) XVI. 578 The origins of the non-co-operation movement. **1937** J. M. MURRY *Necessity of Pacifism* vi. 91 The only possible creative issue for the German Socialist movement was by way of non-violent non-co-operation. **1946** J. S. HUXLEY *Unesco* i. 7 The non-cooperation or even withdrawal of a number of nations. **1973** C. MULLARD *Black Britain* IV. xiii. 156 This resistance has been passive in the tradition of civil disobedience and of Martin Luther King's philosophy of nonco-operation.

Hence **non-co-'operate** *v. intr.*, to refuse to co-operate; **non-co-'operating** *ppl. a.*, **non-co-'operative** *a.*, that refuses or fails to cooperate; **non-co-'operator**, one who practises or advocates non-co-operation.

1921 *Daily Tel.* 28 Sept. 9/1 The leaflet.. asks the Moplahs actively to non-co-operate with the Government. **1922** J. T. GWYNN *Let.* 17 May in *Indian Politics* (1924) iii. 17 A Non-Co-operating politician. *Ibid.*, Non-Co-operative propaganda. *Ibid.* 18 The first-raters may be looked for either among the Co-operators or among the practising Non-Co-operators. **1928** *Observer* 19 Feb. 17/3 The non-co-operators expected to win in the division. **1958** *Punch* 29 Jan. 187/2 The water-fowl are non-co-operative, bobbing about indistinguishably on the far side of the water.

non-'crossover. *Biol.* [NON- 2, 4.] A gamete or individual which does not exhibit the results of crossing-over between any two genetic loci. Also *attrib.*

1916, **1919** [see CROSS-OVER 4]. **1962** *Lancet* 12 May 1026/1 In the three families there were six children who could be considered non-cross-overs. **1971** LEVITAN & MONTAGU *Textbk. Human Genetics* x. 379 To whom the *AB*/*ab* parent contributed non-crossover gametes. *Ibid.*, The former could identify a noncrossover gamete of the *AB*/*ab* parent.

noncupative, obs. form of NUNCUPATIVE.

†**noncuple**, *a.* and *sb. Obs.* [f. L. *nōnus* ninth + *-uple* as in *quadruple*, with *c* inserted on the analogy of *decuple*.] **A.** *adj.* Ninefold. ***noncuple to***: nine times as great as. **B.** *sb.* A quantity nine times as great as another.

1557 RECORDE *Whetst.* E iij b, 36 vnto 4 is a noncuple proportion. **1570** BILLINGSLEY *Euclid* XVI. prop. 30. 454 To proue that a trilater equilater Pyramis, is noncuple to a cube inscribed in it. **1674** PETTY *Disc. Dupl. Proportion* 22 A quadruple Sail is requisite to double Swiftness, and noncuple to treble. **1674** JEAKE *Arith.* (1696) 182 Both triples added together.. make the proportion or amounting Ratio Noncuple, or ninefold. **1690** LEYBOURN *Curs. Math.* 181 And so on to the ninth and last [row], in which you shall find the noncuple of the number given.

Hence †**noncupli'cation**, multiplication by nine.

1674 JEAKE *Arith.* (1696) 25 Noncuplication, or to multiply by 9.

noncu'rantist, *a.* [f. It. *noncurante* not caring, careless + -IST.] Marked by indifference. Also **noncurance**, indifference; **noncurant** *a.*, indifferent.

1882 W. S. BLUNT *Future of Islam* 42 The faith of Mecca .. was giving place to a noncurantist infidelity. **1904** F. ROLFE *Hadrian the Seventh* iii. 84 He began to undress.. with the noncurance of one accustomed to swim in Sandford Lasher. *a* **1913** —— *Desire & Pursuit of Whole* (1934) viii. 78 The most elegant young stranger.., exquisitely noncurant in carriage. *a* **1913** —— *Nicholas Crabbe* (1958) iii. 28 In the matter of money, he was extravagant, chimerical, quixotic, noncurant, to a degree. *Ibid.* xxiii. 158 Some unknown boy, noncurant, saucy, shrilly whistling. **1928** *Times Lit. Suppl.* 12 July 510/4 He contrasts the Italian measures against manifestations in favour of Enosis (union with Greece) with the completely noncurantist tolerance of them by the British authorities in Cyprus. **1931** *Ibid.* 5 Nov. 870/3 Some of the [Masonic] symbols and ceremonies discarded in the days of uninquiring ignorance and self-satisfied noncurance.

noncyen, obs. form of NUNCHEON.

nonda ('nɒndə). [Native name.] A rosaceous tree, *Parinarium Nonda*, of north-eastern Australia, yielding an edible fruit.

1847 LEICHHARDT *Jrnl.* x. 315 We called this tree the 'Nonda' from its resemblance to a tree so called by the natives in the Moreton Bay district. **1886** *Encycl. Brit.* XX. 174/1 (Queensland), The nonda.. grows up to 60 feet.

non-day. Nonce-translation of DIES NON.

1858 MERIVALE *Rom. Emp.* xlix. V. 502 His measure for curtailing the numerous non-days of the calendar.

nondescript ('nɒndɪskrɪpt), *a.* and *sb.* [NON- 3.]

A. *adj.*

†**1.** *Nat. Hist.* Of a species, etc.: Not hitherto described. *Obs.*

1683 RAY *Corr.* (1848) 134 The description.. is scarce sufficient to determine.. whether it be a nondescript species. **1772** *Phil. Trans.* LXII. 386 This fine non-descript owl lives upon hares. **1793** JEFFERSON *Writ.* (1859) IV. 64 They agree it is a nondescript disease, and no two agree in any one part of their process of cure. **1806** T. ASHE (*title*) Memoirs of Mammoth.. Bones, of Incognita or Nondescript Animals. **1812** BRACKENRIDGE *Views Louisiana* (1814) 54 Mr. Bradbury has discovered nearly one hundred and fifty non-descript plants.

transf. **1820** SOUTHEY *Wesley* II. 260 Sectarians of every kind, descript and non-descript, had been introduced in Cromwell's time.

2. Not easily described or classified; of no particular class, kind, or form; that is neither one thing nor another.

1806-7 J. BERESFORD *Miseries Hum. Life* (1826) IX. i, The dry rank remains of some non-descript cheese. *a* **1822** BYRON *Juan* VII. ii, A non-descript and ever-varying rhyme. **1851** MAYHEW *Lond. Labour* II. 51 A cottage of wood, nondescript in shape, but pleasant in locality. **1876** C. M. DAVIES *Unorth. Lond.* (ed. 2) 77 Those nondescript animals that are neither boys nor young men.

B. *sb.*

†**1.** *Nat. Hist.* A species, etc., that has not been hitherto described. *Obs.*

1693 *Phil. Trans.* XVII. 730 Some curious Plants.., amongst which are few Non-descripts, or such as have not been taken notice of by other Writers. **1783** HERSCHEL in *Phil. Trans.* LXXIII. 279 This curve, to borrow a term from natural history, is a non-descript as far as I can find at present. **1794** KIRWAN *Elem. Min.* I. 107 He gives a much fuller account of this stone, which he considers as a non-descript. **1817** J. BRADBURY *Trav. Amer.* 81 A few scattered shrubs of a species of *Artemisia*, apparently a nondescript.

transf. **1790** BURKE *Fr. Rev.* 15 A valuable addition of non-descripts to the.. known classes, genera and species, which .. beautify the *hortus siccus* of dissent. **1800** WEEMS *Life of Washington* i. (1877) 6 A perfect nondescript of baseness.

2. A person or thing that is not easily described, or is of no particular class or kind.

1811 SOUTHEY in *Edin. Ann. Reg.* II. I. 289 The House contains about 250 country gentlemen, 120 courtiers [etc.]. The rest are non-descripts. **1813** *Weekly Reg.* (Baltimore) IV. 149/2 The British, now, affect to consider our frigates a sort of 'terrible non-descripts'. **1836-7** DICKENS *Sk. Boz, Tales* viii, A few ostlers and stable nondescripts were standing round. **1883** STEVENSON *Treas. Isl.* III. xv, I was now, it seemed, cut off upon both sides; behind me the murderers, before me this lurking nondescript [*sc.* the maroon].

non-de'structive, *a.* [NON- 3.] That does not involve destruction, esp. of an object or material that is tested.

1929 *Trans. Amer. Soc. Steel Testing* XVI. 771 (*heading*) Nondestructive testing. *Ibid.*, A number of independent investigators have been working on various methods of nondestructive inspection. **1930** *Mining & Metallurgy* XI. 308 (*heading*) Destructive and non-destructive tests of welds. **1946** *Nature* 19 Oct. 539/2 It was pointed out that the X-ray method is the only non-destructive way of determining surface residual stresses. **1959** *Jrnl. Iron & Steel Inst.* CXCI. 299/2 The economic importance of non-destructive testing is emphasized. **1962** *Gloss. Terms Automatic Data Processing* (*B.S.I.*) 63 *Non-destructive reading*, a reading process which does not change the record of the data which has been read. **1962** *B.S.I. News* June 12/1 Points covered in the section on welding are the quality of welds, tests on welds.. and non-destructive examination. **1971** *Engineering* Apr. 37/1 Facilities at Harwell have become available to industry through the Nondestructive Testing Centre. **1975** G. BRAM *Manufacturing Technol.* ii. 66 Research and development of methods of non-destructive testing has increased considerably over the past thirty years.

Hence **non-de'structively** *adv.*

1930 STOUGHTON & BUTTS *Engin. Metallurgy* (ed. 2) iii. 54 (*heading*) Tests sometimes made non-destructively. **1945** A. N. SACHANEN *Chem. Constituents of Petroleum* iii. 130 Petroleum fractions are completely and non-destructively hydrogenated so that the ring structure of the naphthenes formed corresponds to the original ring structure. **1969** P. B. JORDAIN *Condensed Computer Encycl.* 336 Magnetic tapes, disks, drums, and cards are usually read nondestructively. **1971** *Engineering* Apr. 33/1 To be able to examine critically the insides of welds or castings non-destructively has improved fabrication technology.

non-di'rectional, *a.* (*sb.*) [NON- 3.] Lacking directional properties; *esp.* equally sensitive, intense, or the like, in all directions. †Also as *sb.*

1903 *Nature* 22 Oct. 610/1 In Prof. Henrici's algebra the products of two vectors α, β are:—($\alpha\beta$) a non-directional or 'scalar',.. and [$\alpha\beta$] a vector perpendicular to the plane drawn through α and β. **1931** *Proc. IRE* XIX. 1754 When the noise comes from more than one direction the effects produced by sunrise or sunset upon the noise intensity as received on a nondirectional antenna become somewhat involved. **1946** H. JACOB *On Choice of Common Language* iii. 107 In addition to the primarily spatial directives, *for*, *of*, and *till* are used on the same analogy, as non-directional prepositions. **1964** *Oceanogr. & Marine Biol.* II. 448 The usual response of untrained fish in aquaria to non-directional sounds is one of non-orientated quickened swimming, often momentary. **1967** E. SHORT *Embroidery & Fabric Collage* iii. 59 This non-directional type of design is important in an article which may be carelessly thrown down.

non dis. day. *Hist.* (See quot. and DIS.)

1904 C. WORDSWORTH *Anc. Kal. Oxf. Univ.* (O.H.S.) 18 A table of 'Non Dis. days', i.e. holidays on which the formal academic exercises called 'disputations' were not allowed to be held for qualifying a student for his degree.

non-dis'junction. [NON- 1.] **1.** *Cytology.* The failure of one or more pairs of homologous chromosomes (at meiosis) or sister chromatids (at mitosis) to separate and move away normally from the equatorial plate during nuclear division, usu. with the result that one of the daughter nuclei has too few chromosomes and the other too many.

1913 *Jrnl. Exper. Zoöl.* XV. 587 (*heading*) Non-disjunction of the sex chromosomes of Drosophila. **1925** *Jrnl. Genetics* XV. 251 Non-disjunction was long ago observed in the diploid *Oenothera*. **1961** *Lancet* 5 Aug. 319/2 The mosaicism reported here could have originated in several ways. Mitotic nondisjunction in a normal diploid embryo could result in 1 cell with forty-eight chromosomes (trisomy for chromosome 21 and chromosome 19 or 20) and 1 non-viable cell with forty-four chromosomes. **1962** *Ibid.* 15 Dec. 1270/1 Three types of meiotic non-disjunction have been recognised. **1971** LEVITAN & MONTAGU *Testbk. Human Genetics* iii. 63 Changes in the total number of chromosomes most frequently result from the occasional failure of chromosomes to move to opposite poles or disjoin during anaphase of cell division. Such a failure is called non-disjunction.

Hence **non-dis'junctional** *a.*

1913 *Jrnl. Exper. Zoöl.* XV. 589, 10 per cent of the eggs of such a female matured in a non-disjunctional manner. *Ibid.* 590, I counted the offspring of the non-disjunctional male only with respect to white and pink. **1930** *Genetics* XV. 11 These seven non-disjunctional males were red. **1971** LEVITAN & MONTAGU *Textbk. Human Genetics* iii. 66 Nondisjunctional error in meiosis could involve *all* 23 pairs of chromosomes.

2. *Logic.* The relation of the terms in a proposition asserting the negative of a disjunctive proposition ('neither.. nor..').

1956, **1965** [see NON-CONJUNCTION 2].

non-di'stinctive, *a. Linguistics.* [NON- 3.] Not distinctive (see DISTINCTIVE *a.* 1 b).

1916 JONES & PLAATJE *Sechuana Reader* p. xiv, The consonant sounds c, ʃ, ɥ, and the vowel sound ʉ are probably 'non-distinctive'... By this we mean that the substitution of the sounds t, l, w, u respectively.. would probably never change the meaning of any word. **1933**, **1942** [see DISTINCTIVE *a.* 1 b]. **1964** L. S. HULTZÉN in D. Abercrombie et al. *Daniel Jones* 92 There is of course a great deal of grammatically non-distinctive variation in utterance.

nondo ('nɒndəʊ). A tall umbelliferous plant, *Ligusticum actæifolium*, found in North America.

1860 GRAY *Man. Bot.* 155.

nondry, obs. form of NUNNERY.

none (nəʊn), *sb.* [a. F. *none* or ad. L. *nōna*: see NOON and NONES. ME. examples of the form belong to NOON *sb.*]

†**1.** (See quots.) *Obs.*

1656 BLOUNT *Glossogr.*, *None of the day*, is the third quarter of the day beginning at Noon and lasting till the Sun be gone half way towards setting. **1706** in Cotes tr. *Dupin's Eccl. Hist.* (1725) II. v. 43 The last [part of the day], which began at the middle of the Afternoon, i.e. at half the Time between Noon and Sun-setting, was called None, because it began at the Ninth Hour.

2. = NONES 2.

1845 LINGARD *Anglo-Sax. Ch.* I. vii. 297 *note*, The third of these hours was called.. terce; the sixth, midday; and the ninth, none. **1877** J. D. CHAMBERS *Div. Worship* 129 Including also Sext and None from Septuagesima to Easter.

attrib. **1845** LINGARD *Anglo-Sax. Ch.* I. vii. 296 The prime-song,.. none-song and even-song for [the service] of the day. **1853** ROCK *Ch. Our Fathers* III. 65 As soon as they hear the none-bell, they take to meat.

none (nʌn), *pron.*, *a.*, and *adv.* Forms: α. 1 **nán** (*pl.* **náne**), 2–4, *Sc.* 5–6 (*north.* 9) **nan** (2–4 *pl.* **nane**), 4–5, *Sc.* 6–9 **nane**, 8–9 *north.* **naan(e**; 4, *Sc.* 6 **nain**; *Sc.* 5 **nayne**, 6 **naine, neyn(e**, 9 **neen**; *north.* 7 **neane**, 9 **neean, nin**. β. 2–6 (9 *dial.*) **non** (*pl.* 2–**none**), 4–6 (9 *dial.*) **noon**, 4–5 **noone**, 5 **noyn**, 5–**none**; 9 *dial.* **noan(e, nooan**. [OE. *nán*, f. *ne* NE + *án* ONE *a.* = OFris. *nên* (*nin, nan*), ON. *neinn*: cf. OS. *nên*, MDu. (Du.) *neen*, OHG. (G.) *nein*, no!

In OE. *nán* was inflected in the same way as *án* (see ONE); the forms which chiefly survive in early ME. (down to *c* 1300) are the acc. sing. masc. *nænne, nenne, nanne, nonne*, and the dat. sing. fem. *nare* (OE. *nánre*), *nore*.]

In early use commonly accompanied by another negative.

A. *pron.* **1. a.** No one, not any (one), *of* a number of persons or things. Also, neither *of* two persons or things (now *dial.*).

In later use commonly with pl. verb: cf. 2 b.

α. **835** *Charter* 41 in *O.E. Texts* 448 Ȝif þæt ȝesele..ðæt ðer ðeara nan ne sie ðe londes weorðe sie. *c* **937** *O.E. Chron.* (Parker MS.) an. 937, Myrce ne wyrndon heardes hond-plegan hæleþa nanum. *c* **1000** ÆLFRIC in Assmann *Ags. Hom.* (1889) ii. 205 Heora nan ne sealde swylce leafe næfre. *c* **1200** ORMIN 13931 Ne chæs himm nohht te Laferrd Crist Till nan off hise posstless. *c* **1205** LAY. 26589 Ne mihten heo ..heore nenne [*c* 1275 none of ȝam] adun bringe. *c* **1375** *Sc. Leg. Saints* Prol. 104 He had þame inflammyt swa, þat nan of þaim vald part hym fra. *c* **1450** *St. Cuthbert* (Surtees) 4981 Nane of þair bodys on bra ne banke, Was neuir aftir sene. *c* **1560** A. SCOTT *Poems* (S.T.S.) II. 26 Thay wer sa haisty.., That nane of thame wald ȝeild. **1588** A. KING tr. *Canisius' Catech.* 86 b, þat nain of Christs sacraments ar vsit to saluatione. **1640** *King & a poore Northerne Man* 346 in Hazl. *E.P.P.* IV. 306, I wod all may win and neane of you leese. **1721** RAMSAY *Prospect of Plenty* 115 Dare she nane of her herrings sell..? **1785** HUTTON *Bran New Wark* (E.D.S.) 142 Hes naane of ye seen a young thing, giggling and laughing? **1818** SCOTT *Hrt. Midl.* xviii, I want naething from nane o'ye. **1865** MRS. LYNN LINTON *Lizzie Lorton* II. 215, I mind when nin on 'us daur say bo til a guse afore my mither.

β. *c* **1275** [see quot. *c* 1205 above]. **1388** WYCLIF *John* xvii. 12 Thilke that thou ȝauest to me, Y kepte, and noon of hem perischide. *c* **1400** *Three Kings Cologne* (1886) 56 þey noon of hem ȝit knewe oþir. **1470–85** MALORY *Arthur* IX. xi. 355 That neuer none of hem shold fyghte ageynst other. **1557** NORTH *Gueuara's Diall Pr.* 4 None of these two were as yet fiftene yeares olde. **1626** W. FENNER *Hid. Treasure* (1652) 28 None of the wicked in all the world know it. **1680** DODWELL *Two Lett.* (1691) To Rdr. §2 None of them..ever enduring to hear of any Laical encroachments on the Calling itself. *a* **1774** GOLDSM. *Surv. Exp. Philos.* (1776) II. 42 None of these however are known to us. **1820** SOUTHEY *Wesley* I. 400 Except Whitefield, none of them had devoted themselves body and soul to the work. **1849** MACAULAY *Hist. Eng.* iii. I. 389 None of these was published oftener than twice a week. **1885** SWINBURNE *Misc.* (1886) 339 None of their own countrymen were so competent to control, alike by wisdom and by valour.

b. In predicative use, denoting exclusion from a certain class: Not any; not one. (Cf. 3 b.)

c **1440** *York Myst.* xlviii. 176 Ȝe weryed wightis, ȝe flee hym froo, On his lefte hande as none of his. **1526** *Pilgr. Perf.* (W. de W. 1531) 30 b, As though he sayd,..ye were none of my seruauntes. **1551** T. WILSON *Logike* (1580) 83 He will eate his meate I warraunt you, he is none of these scrupulous consciences. **1634** W. TIRWHYT tr. *Balzac's Lett.* 143 You are none of those who will finde fault with the Ayre. **1690** LOCKE *Hum. Und.* III. ix. §16 Liquor..which, I think, too, none of the most perplex'd Names of Substances. **1722** DE FOE *Col. Jack* (1840) 79, I am none of their gang. **1823** LAMB *Ess. Elia* II. *Old Margate hoy*, He was none of your hesitating half story-tellers. **1850** TENNYSON *In Mem.* lxxxix, Tho' their sons were none of these.

c. Followed by a superlative used absolutely.

1599 PORTER *Angry Wom. Abingd.* (Percy Soc.) 42 *M. Bar.* Canst thou read? *Nich.* Forsooth, though none of the best, yet meanly. **1609** HOLLAND *Amm. Marcell.* 125 The circuit of the citie, which was none, ywis, of the greatest. **1656** HEYLIN *Surv. France* 219 The Jesuits have divers Colledges founded for them, and they are known to be none of the poorest. **1690** LOCKE *Hum. Und.* IV. vii. §9 The general Idea of a Triangle (which is..none of the most.. difficult). **1718** FELTON *Classicks* (T.), The most glaring and notorious passages are none of the finest. **1814** BYRON *Wks.* (1837) III. 105 You know, I suppose, that T..is none of the placidest. **1888** RIDER HAGGARD *Mr. Meeson's Will* ix, His understanding was none of the clearest.

2. a. No one, no person, nobody. Also ***none other***, no other person (now *arch.*).

Now more commonly as *pl.*: see b.

α. *c* **960** *Rule St. Benet* (Schröer) xlii. 67 Æfter þæm nihtsange ne sy nanum alyfed, þæt he æniȝ word cweþe. *c* **1000** *Ags. Gosp.* John xv. 24 Ȝif ic nane weorc ne worhte on him þe nan oðer ne worhte. *a* **1122** *O.E. Chron.* (Laud MS.) an. 1066, He dyde swa mycel to gode..swa nefre nan oðre ne dyde toforen him. *c* **1200** ORMIN 493 Þatt nan ne shollde wurrþenn þa sett to wurrþenn prest, butt iff He prestess sune wære. *a* **1225** *Leg. Kath.* 123 Nes þer nan þet mahte neauer eanes wrenchen hire..ut of þe weie. *a* **1300** *Cursor M.* 1968, I bad al-sua Nain be sa bald þat oþer sla. *c* **1320** *Sir Tristr.* 899 Aȝaines him stod þer nan In land. **1340** *Ayenb.* 237þe ilke þet is uoul ne may nenne oþrenne klensy. *a* **1400** *Pol., Rel. & L. Poems* 259 He is boþe god and man: swilc ne sawe neuere nan. *c* **1470** HENRY *Wallace* x. 140 Thow thinkis nan her at suld thi falow be. **1533** GAU *Richt Vay* 27 Faith is sa neidful that neyne kane be saiff without it. **1588** A. KING tr. *Canisius' Catech.* App., To defende the pure mans cause, quhen thair is nan to take it in hand by him. **1725** RAMSAY *Gentle Sheph.* IV. ii, I'll wed nane else. **1788** BURNS *I Hae a Wife* i, I'll tak cuckold frae nane, I'll gie cuckold to nae-body. **1818** SCOTT *Rob Roy* xix, Nane could ever say that o' the trades o' Glasgow.

β. *a* **1175** *Cott. Hom.* 217 Ȝif non of him ne spece, non hine ne lufede. Ȝif non hine ne lufode, non to him ne come. *c* **1250** *Gen. & Ex.* 223 Ne was ðor non lik adam. **1297** R. GLOUC. (Rolls) 9604 To him þe king truste mest, ne þer nas non so hey. **1338** R. BRUNNE *Chron.* (1810) 6 To write Inglis gestes fond he non his pere. *c* **1380** WYCLIF *Wks.* (1880) 23 Almost noon shal be so nyse and worldly proude as þes stynkynge heretikis. **1447** BOKENHAM *Seyntys* (Roxb.) 51, I noon but the Know, lorde, that may my comfort be. *c* **1489** CAXTON *Blanchardyn* xxxix. 148 Noon was there, my self nor noon other, that myghte recomforte her. **1509** BARCLAY *Shyp of Folys* (1570) 58 Wisedome will that we should refrayne From foolishe deming, and nones death discus. *a* **1586** SIDNEY *Arcadia* (1622) 323 A vow..that I would neuer marry none, but such one as was able to with-stand mee in armes. **1608** HEYWOOD *Lucrece* (1638) 179 His willfull Edicts..In which nones tongue is powerfull save the Kings. **1677** LADY CHAWORTH in *12th Rep. Hist. MSS. Comm.* App. V. 37 All from Court say the House will infailibly sit, but none dares warrant how long. **1766** FORDYCE *Serm. Yng. Wm.* (1767) I. ii. 74 The ladies..would be the apes of none in dress. **1805** HARRAL *Scenes of Life* I. p. vii, Let none attempt to excuse himself. **1855** TENNYSON *Maud* I. XVIII. i, There is none like her, none. **1880** SWINBURNE *Stud. Shaks.* 209 None other..than him-self alone could have mingled.. such human passion.

Comb. **1601** SHAKS. *All's Well* III. ii. 108 Is't I That.. expose Those tender limbes of thine, to the euent Of the none-sparing warre?

b. *pl.* No persons.

Now the commoner usage, the sing. being expressed by *no one*.

c **888** K. ÆLFRED *Boeth.* xxvii. §1 þæt þær nane oðre an ne sæton buton þa weorðestan. *c* **1200** *Trin. Coll. Hom.* 31 Ne doð hit none swo ofte se þe hodede. *c* **1205** LAY. 766 Alle to gadere he heom nom, nane he ne lafde. *a* **1300** *Cursor M.* 11396 A folk ferr.., Wonnand be þe est occean, þat bi-yond þam ar wonnand nan. **1357** *Lay Folks Catech.* 112 We, thas ilke, and nane othir than we er now,..sal rise up. *c* **1530** LD. BERNERS *Arth. Lyt. Bryt.* 409 He strake none but that they lost their lyves. **1582** N. LICHEFIELD tr. *Castanheda's Conq. E. Ind.* I. i. 2 b, Of which Religion wer then none other but Portingales. *a* **1641** BP. MOUNTAGU *Acts & Mon.* (1642) 65 None have all; all must have some. **1697** DRYDEN *Virg. Georg.* Ded., None have been so greedy of Employments.. as they who have least deserv'd their Stations. **1759** GOLDSM. *Bee* No. 8 ¶ 5 None but they alone could have either skill or strength to bring the prisoners back again. **1790** BURKE *Fr. Rev.* 69 None but traitors would barter it away for their own personal advantage. **1813** SOUTHEY *Nelson* I. 37 The contagion had become so general, that there were none who could work at it. **1887** STEDMAN *Victorian Poets* (ed. 13) 37 None but sentimentalists and dilettanti confuse their prose and verse.

†**c.** ***none other***, no other thing (or course); nothing else. *Obs.* (See OTHER B. 7.)

a **1300** *Cursor M.* 4147 Quen ruben sagh þair was nan oþer Bot algat for to sla þer broþer. **1388** WYCLIF *1 Sam.* xxi. 9 Here is noon other outtakun that. *a* **1400–50** *Alexander* 735* (Dubl.), Dame, now is þar none other to do bot deme it þi seluen. **1611** BIBLE *Gen.* xxviii. 17 This is none other, but the house of God. **1645** CROMWELL *Let.* 14 June, Sir, this is none other but the hand of God.

3. *ellipt.* **a.** Not any (such thing or person as that previously or subsquently mentioned).

α. **971** *Blickl. Hom.* 169 Se þe hæbbe twa tunecan, selle oðre ðam ðe nane næbbe. *a* **1122** *O.E. Chron.* (Laud MS.) an. 443, Brytwalas..heom fultumes bædon wið Peohtas, ac hi þær nefdon nænne. *Ibid.* an. 1116, Þis ȝear wæs swa gæsne on mæstene, swa þæt on eallon þison lande..ne ȝehyrde me of nanan seȝcean. *c* **1205** LAY. 15819 Ich habbe lim & stan, on leode nis betere nan. **1375** BARBOUR *Bruce* I. 173 For litill enchesone or nane, He was arestyt syne and tane. *c* **1470** HENRY *Wallace* IV. 201 He bad him gyftis ser: Wallace wald nayne. **1500–20** DUNBAR *Poems* lxvi. 54 Vnworthie I..Ane kirk dois craif, and nane can haif. **1596** DALRYMPLE tr. *Leslie's Hist. Scot.* Prol. 7 The grettest parte of the Ile hes sa plentiful feildes that nane mair plentiful. *c* **1620** A. HUME *Brit. Tongue* (1865) 13 This symbol can be no reason serve that sound, nor nane of that kynd. **1785** BURNS *Halloween* v, Then, straught or crooked, yird or nane, They roar.

β. *c* **1290** *Beket* 24 in *S. Eng. Leg.* I. 107 Þat Amiral ane faire douȝter hadde..none mo for-soþe he nadde. *c* **1330** R. BRUNNE *Chron. Wace* (Rolls) 2447 Y hadde richesse; now haue y non! *c* **1400** *Gamelyn* 165 The knight thoughte on tresoun and Gamelyn on noon. *c* **1485** *Digby Myst.* (1882) III. 501 In wynter a stomachyr, In somer non att al. **1562** J. HEYWOOD *Prov. & Epigr.* (1867) 131 Better an akyng eye then none. **1583** STUBBES *Anat. Abus.* II. (1882) 72, I thinke it is better to haue meane fare than none at all. **1658** BAXTER *Saving Faith* v. 34 A Belief and Love indeed he hath, but morally..it is as none. **1697** SIR T. P. BLOUNT *Ess.* 108 The Egyptians seem to have had only knowledge enough to know that their neighbours had none at all. **1718** *Freethinker* No. 22 ¶ 101 It seems to be a much greater Affront..to have an ill opinion of him, than to have none at all. **1796** H. HUNTER tr. *St.-Pierre's Stud. Nat.* (1799) II. 250 That the cocoa-trees which have houses around their roots become much more beautiful than those where there are none. **1813** SHELLEY *Q. Mab* II. 85 None but a spirit's eye Might ken that rolling orb. **1859** FITZGERALD *Omar Khayyám* liv, Better be jocund with the fruitful Grape Than sadden after none, or bitter, Fruit.

b. In predicative use, denoting lack of the essential qualities of the thing or person mentioned. (Cf. 1 b.) †Also, null, of no effect.

c **888** K. ÆLFRED *Boeth.* xxx. §1 Forhwy þe haten dysiȝe men mid leasre stemne wuldor, nu ðu nane neart. *c* **1386** CHAUCER *Miller's T.* Prol. 54 Yet nolde I..demen of my-self that I were oon; I wol beleve wel that I am noon. **1442** *Rolls of Parlt.* V. 43/2 That it be voide and non in lawe. **1551** T. WILSON *Logike* (1580) 3 Thei bee like those that goe for honest men, and are none. **1592** WEST *1st Pt. Symbol.* §11 e, If there be any error or deceipt.., that Contract is either made altogether none, or of none effect. **1604** SHAKS. *Oth.* III. iii. 126 Men should be what they seeme, Or those that be not, would they might seeme none. **1653** WALTON *Angler* To Rdr., How to make a man that was none, an Angler by a book.

c. ***none of***, not at all, not in the least.

1571 CAMPION *Hist. Irel.* (1633) 175, I am none of Henryes Deputy. **1638** FEATLY *Strict. Lyndom.* I. 81 The Church of Rome I grant is a mother,..but shee is none of our mother. **1712** STEELE *Spect.* No. 455 ¶4 This Match was none of her own choosing. **1719** DE FOE *Crusoe* I. (Globe) 236 It was none of my Business. **1764** FOOTE *Patron* III. Wks. 1799 I. 359, I am determined he shall be none of the man.

4. No part or amount *of* some thing, quality, etc.

a **1300** *Cursor M.* 9916 O gret suetnes [*Gött.* suete grennes] þar wantes nan. **13..** *Coer de L.* 3547 Off thy golde wolde he take non. **1553** T. WILSON *Rhet.* (1580) 29 Seleucus would none of that in any wise. **1560** DAUS tr. *Sleidane's Comm.* 114 b, This woman wold have none of this gere done for her. **1610** SHAKS. *Temp.* II. i. 51 Of that there's none, or little. **1638** BAKER tr. *Balzac's Lett.* (vol. II.) 182 Beelief it cannot be without contesting, I will none of it. **1656** A. WRIGHT *Five Serm.* To Rdr., This Pulpit aye hath so much of the New light, as it hath almost none of the Old day of the Gospel. **1742** RICHARDSON *Pamela* III. 169 My Lady said, None of your reproaching Eye, Pamela. **1779** J. MOORE *View Soc. Fr.* (1789) II. xcvi. 433 No!..says John, none of your coaxing. **1872** MORLEY *Voltaire* (1886) 6 Yet we recognise that none of it was ever the dreary still-birth of a mind of hearsays.

B. *adj.* **1. a.** Not any; = NO *a.* 1. Now *arch.*

In later use only before vowels and *h*, and after 1600 almost entirely supplanted by the reduced form *no*. For examples of OE. *nán man, þing*, see NO MAN, NOTHING.

α. *c* **888** K. ÆLFRED *Boeth.* iii. §4 þæt was þæt nan anweald nære riht butan rihtum þeawum. **971** *Blickl. Hom.* 21 þæt leoht on nanre tide ne ablinneþ. *Ibid.* 33 Ne þincþ us þæt nan wundor. *c* **1055** *Byrhtferth's Handboc* in *Anglia* VIII. 301 Þonne þæs ȝeares ne beoð nane epactas. *a* **1122** *O.E. Chron.* (Laud MS.) an. 1013, Mycel his folces adranc on Temese, forðam hi nanre brycȝe ne cepton. *c* **1200** ORMIN Ded. 274 Nan wihht, nan enngell, nan man, Ne naness kinness shaffte. **1297** R. GLOUC. (Rolls) 9121 Of engelond ne can ich nanne red. *c* **1375** *Sc. Leg. Saints* ix. (*Bartholomew*) 24 Of þare god gat þai nan answere. *c* **1400** MAUNDEV. (Roxb.) Pref. 1 He desserued neuer nane euill. *c* **1470** *Gol. & Gaw.* 286 Thair gat he nane homage, For all his hie parage. **1513** DOUGLAS *Æneis* VIII. i. 106 Thus I declayr the nane vncertane thing.

β. *c* **1200** *Trin. Coll. Hom.* II. 165 Nis nower non trewðe. *c* **1205** LAY. 5658 Ne nomen heo nonne cniht quic. *c* **1275** *Passion Our Lord* 676 in *O.E. Misc.* 56 Hi nolden þo bileue ..vor nore pyne heore prechynge. *c* **1330** R. BRUNNE *Chron. Wace* (Rolls) 10555 He was told of non honour Bot he had ben wyþ kyng Arthour. *c* **1380** WYCLIF *Serm.* Sel. Wks. I. 169 Þis lore þat Cristis scole axiþ loveþ none gabbingis. *c* **1430** *Two Cookery Bks.* 35 Ȝif þou wolt make it in spycery, þen putte non chykonys þer-to. **1484** CAXTON *Fables of Æsop* VI. xv, Men ought not to leue none euyll vnpunysshed. **1535** COVERDALE *Esther* (Apocr.) xvi. 17 Ye shal do well, yf ye holde them of none effecte. **1579** FULKE *Heskins' Parl.* 91 The vsage of the Church..will prooue it to bee none abuse. **1641** J. SHUTE *Sarah & Hagar* (1649) 174 You are inimicitious to those that offer you none injury. **1755** *Connoisseur* No. 98 ¶7 This extravagant and ill-judged Generosity renders all her numerous excellencies of none effect. **1801** STRUTT *Sports & Past.* I. i. 10 Henry the second ..endeavoured to render these grants of none effect.

b. Followed by *other*. Now *arch.* (See also NOTHER and OTHERWISE.)

c **888** K. ÆLFRED *Boeth.* v. §1 Ne ȝebrohte ðe eac nan oþer man on þam ȝedwolan. *c* **1200** ORMIN 5714 Ne þurrh nan oþerr flæshess lusst. *c* **1205** LAY. 12628 Nes þer nan oðer [*c* **1275** non oþer] andswere. **1338** R. BRUNNE *Chron.* (1810) 5 Sorow & site he made, ther was non other rede. **1390** GOWER *Conf.* I. 87 As be that weie..Bot trewliche in non othre thinges. **1470–85** MALORY *Arthur* IX. xxxvii. 399 Sire Tristram sawe none other boote but rode ageynst hym. **1535** COVERDALE *1 Macc.* ii. 36 Neuerthelesse they gaue them none other answere. **1568** GRAFTON *Chron.* II. 146 They perceyued well that there was none other meane. **1611** BIBLE *Transl. Pref.* ¶2 Brought to vntimely death for none other fault, but [etc.]. **1713** SWIFT *Frenzy of J. Denny* Wks. 1755 II. I. 140, I have none other disease, than a swelling in my legs. **1827** SOUTHEY *Hist. Penins. War* II. 287 Those journalists taught..that Europe should have none other Lord but him.

c. Placed after (or separated from) the noun.

α. *c* **950** *Lindisf. Gosp.* John x. 41 Meniȝo..cuoedon þætte Iohannes..becon worhte nan. *a* **1000** *Phœnix* 51 Nis þær on þam londe..weatacen nan. *c* **1205** LAY. 600 Nes castel nan swa strong i þon londe of Griclond. *a* **1300** *O.E. Misc.* 200 Idel adh ne swere þu Nan. *c* **1375** *Sc. Leg. Saints* xviii. (*Egipciane*) 999 Vthyr clathis had I nane. *c* **1400** MAUNDEV. (Roxb.) xxxi. 140 Housez hafe þai nane. *c* **1450** *St. Cuthbert* (Surtees) 7183 [That] his monkes nane ne some..Suld fra gude leuyng skypp. **1513** DOUGLAS *Æneis* IV. xii. 27 Geif that neuir nane At our cost had arrivit schip Troiane. **1573** *Satir. Poems Reform.* xlii. 154 Suld their pepill Preiching haue nane?

β. *c* **1330** R. BRUNNE *Chron. Wace* (Rolls) 15805 Of alle þise, heires com þer non. *c* **1374** CHAUCER *Anel. & Arc.* 148 Natheles gret wondre was it noone. *c* **1400** *Gamelyn* 396 Two dayes and two nightes mete had he noon. *c* **1475** *Litt. Red Bk. Bristol* (1900) I. 141 Also right shall I none lett. **1535** COVERDALE *Acts* iii. 6 Syluer and golde haue I none. **1630** *R. Johnson's Kingd. & Commw.* 79 Fortresses they build none. **1676** HOBBES *Iliad* I. (1686) 12 Remedy was none. **1721** DE FOE *Mem. Cavalier* (1840) 296 Hay for our horses we got none. **1817** JAS. MILL *Brit. India* II. v. ix. 708 Motives to application..can be discovered none. **1845** M. PATTISON *Ess.* (1889) I. 2 Poetry we have almost none. **1885–94** R. BRIDGES *Eros & Psyche* Aug. iv, Harbour knew she none, where her distress Might comfort find.

C. *adv.* **1.** With comparatives:

†**a.** = NO *adv.*[2] *Obs. rare.*

a **1122** *O.E. Chron.* (Laud MS.) an. 1114, Þæs ȝeares syððan he ne heold hired nan oftar. *c* **1290** *S. Eng. Leg.* I. 359/18 Ȝif we þe habbez ouȝt mis-don we ne schullen none more. *a* **1300** *Cursor M.* 328 For-þi es godd, als sais scripture, Nan [*Gött.* non] elder þan his creature. **1340** *Ayenb.* 262 Þeruore ich nelle non more zigge, ac hier ich wille endi mine matire. **1465** *Paston Lett.* II. 218 On Friday last and non er. *c* **1475** *Rauf Coilȝear* 546, I neid nane airar myne erand. *a* **1682** SIR T. BROWNE *Tract viii* (1683) 146 Words..of common use in Norfolk, or peculiar to the East Angle Countries; as..Noneare. [Hence in Hickes (1689) and Ray (1691).]

b. With *the*: In no way, to no extent.

Common in 19th c., esp. ***none the better, worse***. See also NONETHELESS *adv.*

1799 *Spirit Publ. Jrnls.* II. 134 When she found his studying politics made us none the richer. **1820** BYRON *Wks.* (1837) IV. 325 To my mind, they look none the worse for their nudity. **1841** MACAULAY *Speeches* (1853) 237 My circumstances are to be worse, and Johnsons's none the better.

†**2.** ***or none***, or no, or not. (Cf. NO *adv.*[1] 2.) *Obs.*

This usage, which is common in Chaucer, may have originated in sentences similar to quot. *c* 1330.

a **1300** *Cursor M.* 6618 O þis watur he gert ilkan Drinc, quer he wald or nan. *c* **1330** R. BRUNNE *Chron. Wace* (Rolls) 14909 'Wheþer ar þei Cristen', he seide, 'or non?' **1390** GOWER *Conf.* I. 46 So that I may finde in this place If thou be gracious or non. **1452** *Paston Lett.* I. 229 Whethir it be thus or non I can not say.

3. a. By no means, not at all. Now usually followed by *so* or *too* and an adjective forming combs. used *attrib.*

1651 C. CARTWRIGHT *Cert. Relig.* I. 202 His own righteousnesse can none be justified. ?*c* **1750** in Child *Ballads* II. 129/1 All was blythe, and all was glad, But Lady Maisery she was neen. **1824** GALT *Rothelan* II. III. ii. 20 After some questioning, by which he saw that I was none informed regarding the page. **1879** *Spectator* 31 May 680 The Horse Guards are none so fond of him. **1885** *Law Times* LXXIX. 169/2 Their merits are none too liberally recognised. **1928** H. CRANE *Let.* 31 Jan. (1965) 315 Crowds of ambitious but none-too-successful strumpets of moviedom. **1941** *Amer. Speech* XVI. 57/2 This none-too-accurate article on the DAE. **1963** D. BALLANTYNE in C. K. Stead *N.Z. Short Stories* (1966) 151 His none-too-searching questions had already disclosed that the psychologist.. was sophisticated enough to take an irreverent view of Freud. **1970** 'M. HEBDEN' *Mask of Violence* (1971) i. 3 He was dressed in shabby jeans and a none-too-clean shirt. **1974** *Country Life* 26 Dec. 2016/2 Its class of none-too-hardy evergreens.

b. As complement with verbs, esp. *sleep* and *worry*.

1719 DE FOE *Crusoe* I. (Globe) 23 We.. lay still all Night; I say still, for we slept none! **1752** *Scots Mag.* (1753) Sept. 450/1 He had slept none for two nights. **1800** ALEX. CARLYLE *Autobiogr.* (1861) 95 He seemed as torpid as George Murray..: he conversed none. **1821** SCOTT *Pirate* xviii, By my advice, you will quarrel nane with Captain Cleveland. **1852** J. B. JONES *Col. Vanderbomb* xv. 198 Our adventurers slept none that night. **1890** J. SERVICE *Thir Notandums* i. 3, I would weary nane. **1906** *Advocate of Peace* Mar. 52 Has civilization advanced none from the barbaric days of the 5th century? **1956** B. HOLIDAY *Lady sings Blues* (1973) xviii. 151, I had never cared what the hell people thought, and jail hadn't changed that none. **1973** E. BULLINS *Theme is Blackness* 65 Now, now, don't you worry none about that, Mother. We'll find a way.

†**none**, *a.*[2], obs. variant of OWN.

See N 3, NAIN *a.*, and OWN *a.* 1 *c*.

c **1420** *Sir Amadace* (Camden) lx, Lette vs leng to-gethir here,.. As alle thi none hit ware. **1549** Q. ELIZABETH in Ellis *Orig. Lett.* Ser. I. II. 156 You write that I seme to Stande in my none witte in beinge so wel assured of my none selfe. **1616** BRETON *Good & Bad, Effem. Fool* Wks. (Grosart) II. 13/1 His father's loue, and his mother's none-child. **1655** FULLER *Ch. Hist.* VI. 283 Adrian the fourth, our none Countrey-man. **1679** *Licentiousness Times* in Ebsworth *Bagford Ball.* (1878) 718 His Worship so wise,.. Is by [his] none dear Wife at home made a Fool.

none, obs. form of NOON, NUN.

†**non-edificant.** *Obs.* [f. NON- 2 + EDIFICANT used subst.] One who does not edify.

a **1625** BOYS *Wks.* (1629) 682 Hee.. that is a non-edificant, is vnworthy to bee called an Apostle [etc.].

non-e'ffective, *a.* and *sb.* [NON- 3.]

A. *adj.* **1.** Producing no effect.

1862 SPENCER *First Princ.* II. xvii. (1875) 399 Any incident force is primarily divisible into its effective and non-effective portions. **1875** KNIGHT *Dict. Mech.* 1532/1 *Non-condensing Steam-engine*,.. in which the steam on the non-effective side of the piston is allowed to escape into the atmosphere.

2. Of soldiers and sailors: Not fit or qualified for active service.

1802 JAMES *Milit. Dict.* s.v. *Naic*, Every battalion of native infantry has two drill havildars or serjeants, and two drill-naicks, called Non-Effective, attached to it. **1811** WELLINGTON in Gurw. *Desp.* (1838) VIII. 129 That measures should be taken to replace those become non-effective on account of ill health. **1853** KANE *Grinnell Exp.* ii. (1856) 22 Our little corps of officers numbered four for each ship, including that non-effective limb, the doctor.

3. [attrib. use of B.] Pertaining to, consisting of, connected with non-effectives or their maintenance.

1756 WASHINGTON *Lett. to Captain Hog* Writ. 1889 I. 293 *note*, I hope you will account for all the non-effective money you have received. **1833** HT. MARTINEAU *Three Ages* III. 113 The expenses of the non-effective service being considerably greater than the maintenance of the actual army. **1849** MACAULAY *Hist. Eng.* iii. I. 306 The non-effective charge, which is now a heavy part of our public burdens. **1901** *Daily Chron.* 20 Sept. 5/2 The men on the non-effective list.

B. *sb.* A soldier or sailor who is not fit or qualified for active service.

1800 DUNDAS in Owen *Wellesley's Desp.* (1879) 559 Whatever the establishment is, one fourth must be deducted for non-effectives. **1825** BENTHAM *Ration. of Reward* 159 In some countries the emoluments of the commanders of regiments increase in proportion to the number of non-effectives. **1859** *War Office Circular* in *Volunteer Almanac* (1861) 68 Enrolled members, consisting of Effectives, Non-Effectives, and Supernumeraries.

fig. *c* **1800** R. CUMBERLAND *John de Lancaster* (1809) III. 156 Those.. idlers, those non-effectives in creation's roll.

†**non-e'fficience.** *Obs.* [NON- 1.] Absence or want of efficient power.

1683 J. CORBET *Free Actions* III. v. 29 All sin of Omission and Commission is resolved at least into Gods Non-Volition and Non-efficience, as the prime Reason thereof.

non-e'fficient, *a.* (*sb.*) [NON- 3.] Of volunteers: Not efficient (see quot. 1876). Also *sb.*

1863 *Regul. Volunteer Force* 59 Enrolled Members are classed as Efficients or Non-Efficients. **1876** VOYLE & STEVENSON *Milit. Dict.* 456/1 Volunteers are.. classed as 'efficients' and 'non-efficients'. Efficients must have received certificates from the commanding officer and adjutant, certifying that they have acquired a knowledge of their duties and attended certain drills. **1884** *Manch. Exam.* 4 Nov. 5/4 A number of the London Volunteers have been.. returned as non-efficient on account of failure in their musketry practice.

non-ego (nɒn'iːgəʊ, -'ɛgəʊ). *Metaph.* [NON- 2.] All that is not the ego or conscious self; the object as opposed to the subject.

1829 SIR W. HAMILTON *Discuss.* (1852) 9 In every act of consciousness we distinguish a Self, or Ego, and something different from self, a Non-ego. **1869** SPENCER *Princ. Psychol.* (1872) I. II. viii. 263 External feelings are.. distinguished as sequences belonging to the Non-ego. **1876** *Encycl. Brit.* V. 224/2 The determination of the Ego presupposes.. the Non-Ego.

Hence **non-ego'istical** *a.*, pertaining to or concerned with the non-ego.

1842 SIR W. HAMILTON *Diss.* in *Reid's Wks.* (1846) II. 817 The scheme of Non-Egoistical Idealism, which, in all its forms, is necessarily hyperphysical. *Ibid.* 818 This cruder form of egoistical representationism substantially coincides with that finer form of the non-egoistical, which views the vicarious object as spiritual.

non-e'lastic, *a.* [NON- 3.] Not elastic.

1759 SMEATON in *Phil. Trans.* LI. 130 Non-elastic bodies, when acting by their impulse or collision, communicate only a part of their original power. **1798** HUTTON *Course Math.* (1828) II. 238 [A fluid] is non-elastic, when it is not compressible or expansible, as water. **1883** DAY *Indian Fish* 44 (Intern. Fish. Exhib.), Fixed engines constructed of non-elastic substances are still more destructive to fish than are such as are made of net.

So **non-ela'sticity**, inelasticity.

1848 LINDLEY *Introd. Bot.* (ed. 4) II. II. ii. 156 The non-elasticity of the flower-stalk.

non-e'lect, *a.* [NON- 3.] Not elect (chiefly in the theological sense). Usually *absol.*

1674 HICKMAN *Quinquart. Hist.* (ed. 2) 38 Never did any of non-elect become elect. **1678** GALE *Crt. Gentiles* IV. III. 208 The non-elect are always permitted to fail in the performance of the condition. **1700** C. NESSE *Antid. Armin.* (1827) 17 Some grant.. to the non-elect only a prescience or naked foresight. **1820** KEATS *Lamia* II. 6 A doubtful tale from faery land Hard for the non-elect to understand.

non-e'lection. [NON- 1.] The state of not being elect; failure to elect or to be elected.

1651 C. CARTWRIGHT *Cert. Relig.* I. 228 That foreseene unbeliefe is not the cause of non election. **1677** GILPIN *Demonol.* (1867) 250 These suspicions of non-election prevailing, all promises and comforts are urged in vain. **1772** FLETCHER *Logica Genev.* 100 The emptiness of the pleas which some urge in favour of unconditional reprobation, or if you please non-election. **1847** WEBSTER (citing JEFFERSON).

non-e'lective, *a.* [NON- 3.] Not appointed by election.

1909 W. S. CHURCHILL in *Westm. Gaz.* 9 Oct. 9/4 The claim of the House of Lords—that is, the claim of a non-elective and unrepresentative Chamber—to make and to unmake Governments. **1910** *Blackw. Mag.* Aug. 283/1 The independent opinion of men formed in the comparatively 'dry light' of the non-elective chamber has a value of its own.

†**non-e'lectric**, *a.* and *sb.* *Obs.* [NON- 3.]

A. *adj.* Not electric; incapable of developing electricity when excited by friction.

1751 FRANKLIN *Lett.* Wks. 1840 V. 260 The terms *electric per se* and *non-electric* should be laid aside as improper..; the terms *conductor* and *non-conductor* may supply their place. **1755** B. MARTIN *Mag. Arts & Sc.* 305 The electric Fluid,.. ready to be dispensed in small Quantities to every Non-electric Body that shall approach it, in the Form of a Spark. **1797** *Encycl. Brit.* (ed. 3) VI. 432/2 There is a very remarkable difference between substances with regard to their non-electric or conducting power.

B. *sb.* A non-electric substance.

1739 DESAGULIERS in *Phil. Trans.* XLI. 205 An Iron Bar suspended by a silken Thread,.. when an excited Electric *per se* is brought near it, will both attack and send out its Effluvia to a Non-electric held near it. **1745** [see CONDUCTOR II]. **1752** FRANKLIN *Lett.* Wks. 1887 II. 253 New flannel, if dry and warm, will draw the electric fluid from non-electrics. *c* **1790** IMISON *Sch. Arts* I. 94 Conductors.. are also called non-electrics, because no electric powers can be excited in them by friction. **1832** *Handbk. Nat. Philos., Electr.* i. §5. 2 (U.K.S.).

So †**non-e'lectrical** *a.* and *sb.*

1739 DESAGULIERS in *Phil. Trans.* XLI. 204 Electricals *per se* communicate their Virtue to any of the Non-electrical, when brought near them; in which Case the Non-electricals attract and repel like the Electricals *per se*. *Ibid.* 206 If a long Non-electrical String be fasten'd to an Electrical *per se*.

non-e'lectrified, *a.* [NON- 6.] Not electrified. So †**non-e'lectrized** *ppl. a.*

1761 *Phil. Trans.* LII. 340 He gives us his idea of non-electrised bodies electrised *plus*. **1765** CROKER *Compl. Dict.* II. F, Another non-electrified light body. **1779** *Phil. Trans.* LXX. 17 The two electricities are certainly contrary to one another; but either of them attracts a non-electrified body. **1824** J. WEBSTER *Nat. Philos.* 126 They are said to be in a non-electrified state.

†**nonelike**, *a.* and *sb.* *Obs. rare.* [f. NONE *a.* + LIKE *a.*] A scalene (triangle).

1551 RECORDE *Pathw. Knowl.* I. Def, These [triangles] the Greekes and latine men do cal scalena and in englishe theye may be called nonelekes, for thei haue no side equall.. to ani other in the sam figur. *Ibid.* No. 2 In a nonelike triangle you must take ij. lengthes besyde the fyrste lyne.

non-'empty, *a.* *Math.* and *Logic.* [NON- 3.] Not empty; having at least one member or element.

1937 *Mind* XLVI. 375 There is another non-empty sub-set.. of sentences of C_2 which are nonsensical but not α-nonsensical. **1956** E. M. PATTERSON *Topology* vi. 113 A complex *K* is said to be connected if it is not the union of two non-empty subcomplexes which have no simplexes in common. **1957** P. SUPPES *Introd. Logic* 198 At least one of the three small regions is non-empty. **1965** P. CAWS *Philos. of Sci.* xvii. 130 The restriction must be added that the domain be non-empty. **1971** G. GLAUBERMAN in Powell & Higman *Finite Simple Groups* i. 54 Let $\mathscr{A}$ be a non-empty set of subgroups of *S*.

Hence **non-'emptiness**, the property of being non-empty.

1937 A. SMEATON tr. *Carnap's Logical Syntax of Lang.* 261 We introduce conditions which require for symmetrical, reflexive, and transitive relations the property of non-emptiness. **1950** W. V. QUINE *Methods of Logic* (1952) 80 The bar.. can be made to lie across a boundary and thus indicate non-emptiness of a compound region. **1957** P. SUPPES *Introd. Logic* ix. 198 Another kind of symbol is needed for non-emptiness. **1965** HUGHES & LONDEY *Elem. Formal Logic* xlvi. 339 Each schema.. is valid under the hypothesis of the non-emptiness of some one term.

nonene ('nɒniːn). *Chem.* [f. L. *nōn-us* ninth + -ENE.] = NONYLENE.

1868 *Fownes' Chem.* (ed. 10) 555.

‖**non-ens** (nɒn'ɛnz). *Obs.* Pl. **no'nentia** (-'ɛnʃ(ɪ)ə). [mod.L., f. *nōn* not + *ēns* (see ENS).] Something which has no existence; a nonentity.

1603 J. DAVIES *Microcosm.* Wks. (Grosart) I. 69/2 Withoute Favoure, Loue is a non Ens; For, Favoure waites vpon Love's excellence. **1628** WITHER *Brit. Rememb.* VIII. 668 Who preach Non-sense, and oft *nonentia* too. **1650** HOWELL *Lett.* III. xxiii. 33 To waste their brains in making laws against Chymeras, against *non entia*. **1659** BAXTER *Key Cath.* II. iii. 430 A true General Council now no man can know, because it is a *non ens*. *a* **1734** NORTH *Examen* II. iv. §81 (1740) 270 A false Fact is a *Non-Ens*, and cannot be revealed. **1762** KAMES *Elem. Crit.* ii. I. iii, Cessation of bodily pain is not of itself a pleasure, for a *non-ens* or a negative can neither give pleasure nor pain. **1803** *Gradus ad Cantabr.*, *Non ens*, a Freshman in Embryo! one who has not been matriculated,.. consequently is not considered as having any being!

nonent ('nɒnɛnt). *Philos.* [ad. mod.L. *nonent-* NON-ENS.] That which is not.

1885 JACKSON in *Encycl. Brit.* XVIII. 315/2 In the truism 'the Ent is, the Nonent is not', ὄν ἔστι, μὴ ὄν ὀυκ ἔστι, Parmenides breaks with his predecessors.

†**no'nented**, *ppl. a.* [f. mod.L. *nonent-* NON-ENS + -ED.] Made non-existent.

1643 R. O. *Man's Mortality* i. 3 The Resurrection restoreth this non-ented Entitie to an everlasting Being.

no'nentitize, *v.* [f. NONENTITY + -IZE.] *trans.* To make into a nonentity.

1903 G. B. SHAW *Man & Superman* I. 21 We're beaten—smashed—nonentitized, like her mother. **1913** R. W. SERVICE *Rhymes of Rolling Stone* 176 Sober am I nonentitized; drunk am I more than half a god.

nonentity (nɒ'nɛntɪtɪ). [NON- 1.]

1. The quality or condition of not being or existing; non-being, non-existence.

1643 DIGBY *Observ. Relig. Med.* (1644) 34 Who understandeth the nature of contradiction, will find Non Entity in one of the termes. *a* **1652** J. SMITH *Sel. Disc.* v. 135 These black opinions of death and the non-entity of souls. **1760–72** H. BROOKE *Fool of Qual.* (1809) I. 79 He wished to deprive them of their very existence, and laboured to persuade himself.. of their non-entity. **1824** BYRON *Juan* XVI. cxx, How odd, a single hobgoblin's non-entity, Should cause more fear than a whole host's identity. **1837** LANG *New South W.* II. 30 It becomes a matter of importance to prove either the death or the nonentity of the English husband. **1899** DZIEWICKI *Wyclif's De Logica* III. p. xxv, The non-entity of the world did not precede its entity.

2. Something which does not exist; a non-existent thing; hence, a thing existing in the imagination only; a figment, a nothing.

c **1600** EDMONDS *Observ. Cæsar's Comm.* 38 Our commanders, to whom particular fortunes are esteemed non-entities, and men in seueral of no valew. **1642** SIR E. DERING *Sp. on Relig.* xvi. 81 It is a fancy, a dream, a meer non entity. **1653** WHITFIELD *Treat. Sinf. Men* iii. 7 Sin being a defect or privation, and so a kinde of none entity. **1726** DE FOE *Hist. Devil* II. ix. 347 Satan was not such a Fool as not to know that Baal was a Non Entity, a Nothing. **1838** SIR W. HAMILTON *Logic* v. (1866) I. 77 What.. has no qualities, has no existence in thought,—it is a logical nonentity. **1849** C. BRONTE *Shirley* xiii, We are aware that mermaids do not exist: why speak of them as if they did? How can you find interest in speaking of a nonentity?

b. What does not exist.

1655–87 H. MORE *App. Antid.* vii. §1 (1712) 199 Non-entity can have no affection or property. **1690** LOCKE *Hum. Und.* IV. x. (1695) 354 No more than I would argue with pure nothing, or endeavour to convince Non-entity, that it were something. **1892** J. TAIT *Mind in Matter* (ed. 3) 17 Total unfamiliarity with entity coming out of non-entity, by mental process.

3. A person or thing of no significance, consequence, or importance.

1710 STEELE *Tatler* No. 118 ¶6 The Esquire of a neighbouring village, who had been a long time in the number of non-entities, is entirely recovered by them. **1751** SMOLLETT *Per. Pic.* lxxxviii. III. 104 The insignificance of lord ——, who, tho' a nominal husband, was, in fact, a mere non entity. **1827** LYTTON *Pelham* iii, He was an atom, a nonentity, a very worm, and no man. **1883** CHALMERS & HOUGH *Bankruptcy Act* p. ix, An Act was passed which very much limited their duties, and practically reduced them to nonentities.

Hence **non-'entitative, non-'entitive, non-'entit(i)ous** *adjs.*, that is a nonentity; non-existent. Also **non-'entityism.**

1831 MANNING *Let.* in Purcell *Life* (1895) I. vi. 76 My present routine of non-entitous existence. **1846** MRS. GORE *Eng. Char.* (1852) 5 Byron..characterized our century as 'the Age of Bronze'. The truth..would be far greater, were it defined as 'the age of non-entityism!' **1872** J. WALKER *Theol. Scot.* iii. 86 Dr. Chalmers has accepted the nonentitive conception of sin. **1889** *Microcosm* Sept. 146 A shadow, the non-entitative effect of light, has no existence before the light-force is applied. **1951** W. SANSOM *Face of Innocence* (1954) 77 The girls nubile and the men nonentitous. **1954** C. E. M. JOAD *Folly Farm* vi. 143 Henry, the husband, a decent civil servant, utterly non-entitious—another character without a face..without a body of any kind. **1968** *Listener* 15 Aug. 212/3 Much of the rebuilding is elephantine and nonentitious.

†non-'entres(se. *Sc. Law. Obs.* [NON- 1.] Failure of the heir of a deceased vassal to renew investiture. (The lands in such a case were said to be ***in non-entres.***) Also, the feudal casualty due to the immediate superior upon such failure.

1494–5 *Acc. Ld. High Treas.* I. 211 Ane composicione maid wyth Thomas Kennede..for the none entress of the are of Crorswell. **1546** *Reg. Privy Council Scot.* I. 51 The said Schir Neill sall alwayis defend and keip..the saidis landis fra decrete of nonentres. **1552** *Ibid.* 130 All waird landis, terce & conjunct fie landis, and landis in nonentres. **1566** *Ibid.* 471 Giftis of eschetis, wardis, nonentressis, mariages, new infeftmentis. **1597** SKENE *De Verb. Sign.* (1681) 90.

non-'entry. [NON- 1.]

1. *Sc. Law.* = prec. Also *attrib.*, as ***non-entry duty, mail.*** Now *Hist.*

1497 *Acc. Ld. High Treas.* I. 315, I ressauit fra Schir James of Levingstoune..of ane termez male of his landis, being in the Kingis handis for his nonentree. *a* **1578** LINDESAY (Pitscottie) *Chron. Scot.* (S.T.S.) I. 351 He fand money of the saidis landis in non entrie. **1681** STAIR *Instit.* II. xiv. §20. 299 Non-entry taketh place whenever the Fee is void, whether it be holden Ward, Blanch or Feu. *Ibid.* §21. 300 To pay the Non-entry Mails. *a* **1768** ERSKINE *Inst. Law Scot.* II. v. §46 (1773) 232 A charter of Novo-damus..imports a release to the vassal..of all nonentry-duties prior to the grant. **1837** SKENE *Highlanders Scot.* II. iv. 103 A gift of the nonentries of Knoydart to Cameron. **1860** C. INNES *Scot. in Middle Ages* iv. 122 The feudal casualties of ward, relief, marriage, and non-entry.

2. The act or fact of not entering; no entrance.

1599 B. JONSON *Cynthia's Rev.* v. iii, You must pardon your non-entry: Husbands are not allow'd here. **1616** —— *Love Restored*, I am sure he concluded all in a nonentry. **1962** H. R. LOYN *Anglo-Saxon Eng.* ix. 359 A factor that determined entry or non-entry in Domesday Book.

nonery, obs. form of NUNNERY.

nones (nəʊnz). Also 5 **nonys.** [In sense 1, a. F. *nones* (12th c.), or ad. L. *nōnæ* (acc. *nōnās*), fem. pl. of *nōnus* ninth. In sense 2, pl. of NONE *sb.*: cf. *matins, vespers.*]

1. *Rom. Antiq.* The ninth day (by inclusive reckoning) before the Ides of each month, being thus the 7th of March, May, July, and October, and the 5th of all other months.

c **1420** *Pallad. on Husb.* III. 1031 Thai been ripe atte Jules nonys. [**1485** CAXTON *St. Wenefryde* 12 The day of the thyrdde Nonas of Nouembre.] **1555** EDEN *Decades* 5 The daye before the nones of Aprel, he came to the courte him selfe. **1560** DAUS tr. *Sleidane's Comm.* 461 b, About yᵉ nones of November..the Lantgraves daughter died. **1601** HOLLAND *Pliny* I. 224 From the rising of the Dolphin starre, vnto the day before the Nones of Ianuarie. **1631** WEEVER *Anc. Funeral Mon.* 811 The day before the Nones of May, 1196. **1679** MOXON *Math. Dict.* 26 The Roman Month its several days divides By reckoning backwards, Calends, Nones, and Ides. **1840** *Penny Cycl.* XIII. 173/1 The mode of fixing any particular day was by saying that it was so many days before the kalends, nones, or ides, next immediately following. **1870** *Eng. Gilds* (E.E.T.S.) 181 Given at Lincoln, on the Nones of September, A.D. 1337.

2. *Eccl.* A daily office, originally said at the ninth hour of the day (about 3 p.m.), but in later use sometimes earlier.

1709 J. JOHNSON *Clergym. Vade M.* II. 101 That the same Liturgy of prayers be used both at Nones and Vespers. [*Note.* Nones was what we call three o'clock in the afternoon.] **1805** SOUTHEY *Madoc in W.* xiii, From noon till nones The brethren sate. **1838** LONGF. *Drift-wood* Pr. Wks. 1886 I. 395 After this we sang the service of mid-day,..and slept, and got up again, and sang Nones. **1865** SWINBURNE *Poems & Ball., St. Dorothy* 282 It were good game betwixen night and nones For one to sit and hearken to such saws. **1873** DIXON *Two Queens* I. iii. I. 20 The Virgin was supposed to love and listen to their nones and vespers.

none-schenche, -shyne, obs. ff. NUNCHEON.

none shaloyre: see NONCHALOIR.

none-so-pretty, *sb.* (and *a.*)

1. Some article of haberdashery. Also as *adj.* Now only *Hist.*

c **1700** in *N. & Q.* 9th Ser. X. 88/1 Webb-Cane and Leather Hooping, Gartering of all Sorts, Nonesopretties, Pins and Needles, Inkle and Spinnel. **1759** *St. Papers* in *Ann. Reg.* 201, 1 [piece] cotton romals, 4 ditto, none-so-pretties, 8 lb. coloured thread. **1771** in A. M. Earle *Costume Col. Times* (1894) 173 None-so-Pretty Tapes. **1804** W. CLARK in *Orig. Jrnls. of Lewis & Clark Exped.* (1905) VI. 271 For Indians Presents..10 pieces Nonsoprettys. **1969** R. T. WILCOX *Dict. Costume* 248/1 *None-so-pretties*, fancy, decorative tapes used for trimming garments in the eighteenth century in the American Colonies.

2. The plant London Pride. (Cf. NANCY-PRETTY.)

1731 MILLER *Gard. Dict.* s.v. *Geum*, London Pride, or None so Pretty. **1753** CHAMBERS *Cycl.* Supp. *App.*, None-so-pretty, a popular name for the Geum of botanical authors. **1760** J. LEE *Introd. Bot.* App. 320 None so pretty, *Saxifraga.* **1796** WITHERING *Brit. Plants* (ed. 3) II. 404. **1884** BLACK *Jud. Shakespeare* xii, Pansies, snapdragon, none-so-pretty.

‖**non esse** (nɒn 'ɛsiː). [L. (used subst. by Wyclif, *De Logica* III. x): see NON and ESSE.] Non-being, non-existence.

1654 WHITLOCK *Zootomia* 404 Passing from a *Non esse* not being, over the Stage of a short *Est*, or Duration, to an everlasting Non-existence. *a* **1680** CHARNOCK *Immunt. God* Wks. 1864 I. 416 What an unhappiness is it to have our affections set upon that which retains something of its *non esse* with its *esse.*

†non-'essence. *Obs. rare*⁻¹. [NON- 1.] Non-existence.

a **1618** J. DAVIES *Wittes Pilgr.* Wks. (Grosart) I. 23/2 What ioy is so great but the conceipt Of falling to his Infinition (Of blacke Non-essence) will confound it streight?

non-e'ssential, *a.* and *sb.* [NON- 3.]

A. *adj.* Not essential (in various senses).

1751 EARL ORRERY *Remarks Swift* (1752) 71 He answered her in the non-essential modes. He talked of friendship [etc.]. **1846** MILL *Logic* I. vi. §4 Non-essential or accidental Propositions, on the contrary, may be called Real Propositions in opposition to Verbal. **1866** LITTLEDALE *Incense* 9 The..abandonment..of a non-essential, though primitive, custom. **1875** POSTE *Gaius* I. Introd. 18 The error is held to be non-essential and does not avoid the disposition. **1883** BLACK *Shandon Bells* xxxii, I say that he is careless about what is non-essential.

B. *sb.* A thing that is not essential, absolutely necessary, or of the utmost consequence.

1806 SURR *Winter in Lond.* III. 16, I..only dissented from my amiable Rebecca in what she termed non-essentials. **1833** *Tracts for Times* No. 3. 3 Shall not we pass from non-essentials to essentials? *a* **1857** R. A. VAUGHAN *Ess. & Rem.* (1858) I. 51 He [*sc.* Schleiermacher] made manifest..the distinctions between essentials and non-essentials in religion. **1900** *Daily News* 7 May 6/6 In essentials Unity, in non-essentials Liberty, in all things Charity.

‖**non est** (nɒn 'ɛst). *colloq.* Short for NON EST INVENTUS.

1870 BREWER *Dict. Phr. & Fable.* **1882** OGILVIE, *Non est*, a contraction of the legal phrase *Non est inventus*.., and popularly used to signify, he was not there, he was absent. **1945** MRS. BELLOC LOWNDES *Let.* 21 July (1971) 261 *Eggs* are practically *non est*, unless one has hens. **1959** R. FULLER *Ruined Boys* I. v. 34 The weights you put on it at the end of the arm thing were *non est.*

nonest(e, obs. forms of NONCE¹.

nonestedyng: see NOONSTEADING.

‖**non est factum** (nɒn ɛst 'fæktəm). *Law.* [L. = 'it was not done'.] (See quot. 1607.)

1607 COWELL *Interpr.*, *Non est factum* is an aunswer to a declaration, whereby a man denyeth that to be his deed, whereupon he is impleaded. **1712** ARBUTHNOT *John Bull* II. xvi, Expences of the Suits,..To Esquire South's Accompt for *post Terminums*; To ditto for *Non est Factums.*

‖**non est inventus** (nɒn ɛst ɪn'vɛntəs). *Law.* [L. = 'he was not found'.] The answer made by the sheriff in the return of the writ when the defendant is not to be found in his bailiwick. In 16–17th c. often allusively.

Sometimes abbreviated ***non est invent.*** (See also NON INVENTUS, and NON EST.)

c **1475** *Mankind* 774 in *Marco Plays* 29 ȝe must speke to þe schryne for a 'cepe coppus', Ellys ȝe must be fayn to retorn with 'non est inventus'. **1583** STUBBES *Anat. Abus.* Kj, Sheriffes & officers wil returne writs with a *tarde venit*, or with a *non est inuentus.* **1590** GREENE *Never too Late* (1600) H 3 So long put he his hand into his purse, that at the last the empty bottome returned him a writ of *Non est inuentus.* **1662** [H. P. DE CRESSY] (*title*), A non est inventus return'd to Mr. Edward Bagshaw's Enquiry and vainly boasted discovery of weakness in the grounds of the Churches infallibility. **1688** SHADWELL *Sqr. Alsatia* I. Wks. 1720 IV. 20, I plead to all this matter *Non est inventus* upon the Pannel. **1712** ARBUTHNOT *John Bull* II. xvi, Esquire South's Quota for a Return of a *Non est invent*, and *Nulla habet bona.* **1780** *Chron.* in *Ann. Reg.* 212/1 For having returned a warrant *Non est inventus* in an action..when in fact the defendent Henwood had been arrested. **1827** DE QUINCEY *Murder* Wks. 1854 IV. 50 He inquired after the unfortunate reporter..: the answer was..from the under-sheriff of our county—'Non est inventus'.

nonesuch ('nʌnsʌtʃ), *sb.* and *a.* [f. NONE *pron.* and *a.* + SUCH *a.* See also NONSUCH, which is now the usual form.]

I. 1. †a. Without article. As a designation of persons or things, implying sense 2. *Obs. rare.*

1598 TOFTE *Alba* (1880) 68 An Ornament [*sc.* a bracelet] th' art to be seene Of her white Hand, yclept of right Nonesvch. *a* **1618** SYLVESTER *Urania* xlii, Therefore did Plato from his None-Such banish Base Poetasters. **1649** CANNE *Golden Rule* 24 Princes (specially of late) haue deem'd themselves to be None-such, and..unlike other men.

†b. As a place-name, prob. with allusion to *Nonsuch* near Epsom in Surrey. *Obs.*

1599 *Broughton's Let.* ii. 8 As if you were borne at *None-such*, you are not contented to be accompted..a great Diuine. **1645** WITHER *Vox Pacifica* 74 A spotlesse Church, or perfect Disciplines Go seek at None-such.

c. ***Nonesuch*** (or ***Nonsuch***) ***chest***: a type of wooden chest made in the 16th and 17th centuries, inlaid with stylized designs supposedly representing views of Nonsuch Palace (see 1 b); also ***Nonesuch ornament.***

1905 F. S. ROBINSON *Eng. Furnit.* v. 71 A somewhat rare type of chest..called a 'Nonesuch' chest. **1920** *Connoisseur* Dec. 205 The 'Nonsuch chest'..possesses the flat surface unrelieved by mouldings, which is characteristic of many of the earlier inlaid pieces. **1960** H. HAYWARD *Antique Coll.* 200/1 *Nonesuch chest*, chest, dating from the second half of the 16th cent., decorated with an inlaid design representing an ideal building resembling the Palace of Nonesuch. **1970** D. ASH *Dict. Eng. Antique Furnit.* 107/2 Ornament of this kind probably originated in Italy, but quite possibly reached England from Germany without any connection with the palace from which its name is derived. Some pieces of furniture bearing Nonsuch ornament and long regarded as English may well have been imported. **1973** *Country Life* 7 June 1690 English oak chest, with..bands of stylised zig-zag ornament reminiscent of so-called None-such chests... Circa 1630.

2. a. An unmatched or unrivalled thing.

1590 GREENE *Menaphon* (Arb.) 74 This Paragon, this nonesuch, this Eaw, this Mistres of our flockes. **1616** R. CARPENTER *Christ's Larumbell* 12 His love..may rightly be termed and entituled, A None-such. **1650** FULLER *Pisgah* III. viii. 425 The Scripture itself..presenteth Solomon's [temple] as a Nonesuch, or peerless structure. **1674** N. FAIRFAX *Bulk & Selv.* Ep. Ded., I know whatever is a Nonesuch, will draw enough as 'tis. **1731** MEDLEY *Kolben's Cape G. Hope* II. 39 'Tis well provided with game, and may indeed be call'd a None-such at the Cape. **1745** T. SMITH *Jrnl.* (1849) 269 This month [March] has been like February; a nonesuch; wonderful pleasant, and like April.

b. A person who has no equal; one to whom no other can be compared; a paragon.

1647 TRAPP *Expos. Matt.* i. 10 This man was (till converted) as very a nonesuch in Iudah as Ahab was in Israel. **1702** C. MATHER *Magn. Chr.* VII. App. (1852) 647 The giddy people had cried him up for a nonesuch. **1741** RICHARDSON *Pamela* (1824) I. 96 Come to bed, purity! said she; you are a nonesuch, I suppose. **1771** T. HULL *Sir W. Harrington* (1797) II. 38 His equal..I never met with before:..he is a none-such. **1821** A. ROYALL *Lett. from Alabama* (1830) ii. 123, I went to hear this none such. **1927** 'S. ROHMER' *Moon of Madness* 18 He was a poisonously handsome none-such. *Ibid.* 26 Da Cunha danced perfectly, with all the sensuous grace of a none-such.

c. In depreciatory sense. *rare.*

1705 HICKERINGILL *Priest-cr.* II. Pref. A 2 Some quarrel with my Style, saying, It is a none-such, and like no bodies.

†3. The most eminent person or thing *of* some class, kind, place, etc. *Obs.*

c **1613** ROWLANDS *More Knaues Yet?* (Hunterian Cl.) 4 The very Nonesuch of true courtesie. **1649** ROBERTS *Clavis Bibl.* Introd. ii. 13 The None-such of all the Prophets in Israel. **1652** H. L'ESTRANGE *Amer. no Jewes* 40 His Glory and Wisdome cryed up for the None-such and wonder of the world. **1670** LASSELS *Voy. Italy* I. 27 Fountainbelleau, where I saw that Kingly house, the Nonesuch of France.

†4. *adj.* Unrivalled, unequalled, incomparable.

1641 J. TRAPPE *Theol. Theol.* viii. 326 Not like that None-such Ahab, or those perverse Pharisees. **1681** HICKERINGILL *Sin Man-catching* Wks. 1716 I. 192 These are the great Plagues, the none-such Pests of all Society. **1715** in *Roxb. Ball.* (1888) VI. 620 A conjunct company, both of Scots and Dutch men..; they're almost all non-such Men.

II. *spec.* **5.** The Scarlet Lychnis. ? *Obs.*

1597 GERARDE *Herbal* II. cxix. 380 It is called..of some Flower of Bristowe, and Nonesuch. **1629** PARKINSON *Parad.* 11 The flower of Bristow or None-such is likewise another kinde of Campion. *Ibid.* 253 Single None-such, or Flower of Bristow, or Constantinople. **1688** HOLME *Armoury* II. 95/1 None-such, or Flower of Bristow, is a small flower of many leaves. **1753** CHAMBERS *Cycl. Suppl.* App., *None-such*, a name sometimes given to the Lychnis of botanists.

6. = NONSUCH 6 a.

1762 B. STILLINGFL. *Misc. Tracts* 315 Several plants still in flower, as..black nonesuch. **1764** *Museum Rust.* II. 359 About ten pounds per acre of nonesuch, or white Dutch clover-seed. **1847** DARLINGTON *Amer. Weeds* (1860) 100 Hop-like Medicago. Black Medick. Nonesuch.

nonet (nəʊ'nɛt). Also in It. form. [ad. It. *nonetto*, f. *nono* ninth: see -ET¹.]

1. *Mus.* A composition for nine instruments or voices.

1865 tr. *Spohr's Autobiogr.* 180 A Nonet concerted for the ..Violin, Viol, Violincello and Double-Bass; and the..Flute, Oboe, Clarinet, Horn and Bassoon. **1880** ROCKSTRO in Grove *Dict. Mus.* II. 464. **1896** *Godey's Mag.* Apr. 422/2 A curious and elaborate *allegro molto*.. ends the 'Nonet'.. with an abrupt major chord.

2. *Nuclear Physics.* A multiplet (sense b) of nine sub-atomic particles.

1963 S. OKUBO in *Physics Lett.* V. 166/2 We have to take into account of [*sic*] the ninth boson ϕ together with the octet. This means that we are dealing with a nonet rather than an octet, and a singlet. **1970** *New Scientist* 29 Oct. 211/3 To reconcile the A2 meson with current theory, it is necessary to show that the other members of its SU(3) nonet display similar double structure.

nonetheless (nʌnðəˈlɛs, ˈnʌnðəlɛs), *adv.* Also none the less, none-the-less. [See NONE *adv.* 1 b, LESS *adv.* 1 a.] Nevertheless.

1847 DICKENS *Dombey* (1848) xlii. 419, I thank you none the less. **1875** RUSKIN *Fors Clav.* lv, The children none the less knew their love. **1924** G. B. SHAW *St. Joan* v. 66 But you will be none the less alone: they cannot save you. **1930** *Principal's Rep., Armstrong College* (*Newcastle*) *1929–30* 4 The elevation of Sir William Noble.. to the peerage.. has been a matter of pride and pleasure.. which nonetheless has been qualified subsequently. **1955** *Times* 13 July 7/5 Later than *Nabucco*.., it is, nonetheless, not such a good opera. **1972** *Nature* 8 Dec. 327/1 Although some research fields seem to grow from a single, germinal experiment, others take root in accidents set off by workers stumbling from one preserve to another—and are none-the-less interesting for that.

†**nonett.** *Obs.* [a. F. *nonnette*, dim. of *nonne* NUN.] A titmouse.

1601 HOLLAND *Pliny* I. XI. xxxvii. 331 The pretie Titmouse or Nonett is filletted or coifed vpon the head. *Ibid.* 601.

nonetyde, obs. form of NOONTIDE.

non-Eu'clidean, -ian, *a.* [NON- 3.] Not Euclidean or in accordance with the principles of Euclid.

non-Euclidean geometry: a system of geometry involving the study of the consequences which follow from denying (or, in a wider use, merely dispensing with) any of the assumptions on which the Euclidean system is founded. (See also METAGEOMETRY, PANGEOMETRY.) ***non-Euclidean space***: the kind of space with which this geometry deals.

1874 LEWES *Probl. Life & Mind* Ser. I. I. 59 A non-Euclidian geometry. **1878** NEWCOMB *Pop. Astron.* IV. iii. 505 Several geometrical systems have been constructed in recent times, which are included under the general appellation of the non-Euclidian Geometry. **1900** R. S. BALL *Theory Screws* 439 The.. basis of the mensuration of non-Euclidian space.

non-Euro'pean, *a.* and *sb.* [NON- 3, 2.]

A. *adj.* Not European.

1907 W. JAMES *Pragmatism* v. 182 At this stage of philosophy all non-European men without exception have remained. **1923** D. H. LAWRENCE *Birds, Beasts & Flowers* 31 A set, stoic endurance, non-European. **1967** *Guardian* 15 May 6/6 Another such Russian idea.. is that all 'non-European' nuclear weapons should be banned from European soil and seas.

B. *sb.* A person who is not European; esp. in South Africa: a non-white.

1926 M. NATHAN *South Africa from Within* viii. 166 According to this [*sc.* a 1921 census in British S. Africa], there were 1,519,488 Europeans.., and 5,409,092 non-Europeans. **1935** A. M. CARR-SAUNDERS in Huxley & Haddon *We Europeans* viii. 242 In the Union of South Africa there are under 2 million Europeans and about 6 million non-Europeans. **1939** J. S. MARAIS *Cape Coloured People* p. vii, This book is.. a study.. of the relations between the Europeans and that group of non-Europeans with whom the former have been longest.. in contact. **1958** *Ann. Reg. 1957* 95 The so-called 'open' universities, Cape Town and the Witwatersrand, had a long tradition of admitting non-Europeans. **1970** *Cape Times* 28 Oct. 18/2 (Advt.), Personal loans, for Europeans and non-Europeans.

non-e'valuative, *a.* [NON- 3.] Of or pertaining to that which does not evaluate but is concerned only with fact.

1937 *Jrnl. Philos.* XXXIV. 237 It is a basic rule of valuational logic that an evaluative conclusion can not be deduced from non-evaluative, that is to say factual, premises. **1958** W. STARK *Sociol. of Knowl.* I. iv. 152 'Knowledge' in the context of gnosio-sociology is a non-evaluative term. **1973** 'J. PATRICK' *Glasgow Gang Observed* xxi. 219 Adolescents.. did not know how to react to the non-evaluative, non-judgmental approach of the street worker.

non-e'vent. [NON- 2 b.] An unimportant or unexciting event, *spec.* one which was expected or intended to be important; occas., something that did not happen.

1962 *Spectator* 30 Nov. 853/1 The chief non-event of Gilmour's campaign was also, he says, the product of the 'serious' press. **1963** I. GILMOUR in *Hansard Commons* 7 May 272 Drugged by their normal diet of non-news stories and non-events, the newspapers tend to lose their heads when.. faced with.. a news story. **1965** *Listener* 30 Sept. 480/2 For all its admirable achievements in science and technology and the arts, the Soviet Union is still a great place for the non-event and the non-person, a category in which Mr. Khrushchev is at present languishing. **1966** K. AMIS *Anti-Death League* 186 To find this view supported by events, or as now by non-events, was depressing. **1967** *Listener* 23 Nov. 679/2 Here was a non-event to compare with those other annual and totally insignificant English non-events—Ascot, the Boat Race and the Queen's Speech. **1972** *Guardian* 22 Jan. 15/3 The exchange of signatures is a non-event.. it is neither truly historic nor of much practical significance.

non-exe'cution. [NON- 1.] Neglect of execution; omission or failure to execute.

a **1663** SOUTH *Serm.* 5 Nov., The Non-execution of the Laws upon such Hypocrites. **1690** CHILD *Disc. Trade* (1698) 94 Much of this mischief happens by the non, or ill execution of the laws. **1758** *M.P.'s Lett. on Navy, Let. to Mayor* 6 The Non-execution of it [*sc.* an Act of Parliament] appearing to have taken Place soon after the Death of the Lord Torrington. *c* **1850** *Arab. Nts.* (Rtldg.) 317 The captain had nothing to reply to this command, the non-execution of which was to involve him.. in so severe a punishment.

non-e'xistence. [NON- 1. Cf. Fr. *non-existence*.]

1. The condition of being non-existent; non-being, nonentity.

1646 SIR T. BROWNE *Pseud. Ep.* I. vii. 27 The omission hereof affords some probability it was not used by the Ancients, but will not conclude the nonexistence thereof. **1662** STILLINGFL. *Orig. Sacræ* III. iii. §3 A possibility of non-existence, or annihilation in a creature. **1728** MORGAN *Algiers* I. vi. 175 Some I never heard of; tho' that is no Argument of their Non-Existence. **1807** G. CHALMERS *Caledonia* I. I. i. 3 Empires successively arose.. and sunk into non-existence. **1854** K. H. DIGBY *Compitum* VII. iii. 255 Books of dogmatic scepticism, and expositions of the non-existence of virtue and honour. **1968** P. A. P. MORAN *Introd. Probability Theory* vi. 269 The fact that this is not analytic at t = 0 corresponds to the non-existence of the moments in this case.

2. A non-existent thing. Also (indefinitely), that which has no existence.

1646 SIR T. BROWNE *Pseud. Ep.* IV. x. 20 A method of many Writers, which much depreciates the esteeme and value of miracles, that is, therewith to salve not onely reall verities, but also non-existences. **1678** CUDWORTH *Intell. Syst.* 249 They were all made ἐξ οὐκ ὄντων, from an antecedent Non-existence or Nothing brought forth into being. **1866** J. MARTINEAU *Ess.* I. 230 An existence without predicates is a non-existence. **1892** J. TAIT *Mind in Matter* (ed. 3) 74 Men are asked to believe that the whole dog and the whole pigeon.. were produced from non-existence, by opportune additions to an invisible speck of living matter.

non-e'xistent, *a.* and *sb.* [NON- 3.]

A. *adj.* Not existent or having existence.

1682 SIR T. BROWNE *Chr. Mor.* (1716) 75 What is and will be latent is little better than non-existent. **1787** HAWKINS *Life Johnson* 160 He sometimes raised subscriptions for non-existent poems. **1818–60** WHATELY *Comm.-pl. Bk.* (1864) 82 The bread which I ate a year ago and the ambrosia of Homer's Gods are both equally non-existent at this moment. **1891** HARDY *Tess* l, This sound of a non-existent coach can only be heard by one of D'Urberville blood.

absol. **1836–7** SIR W. HAMILTON *Metaph.* xvi. (1859) I. 294 Concerning Nature or the Non-Existent. **1875** JOWETT *Plato* (ed. 2) I. 230, I and all the world are in a difficulty about the non-existent.

B. *sb.* A person or thing that does not exist.

1658 BAXTER *Saving Faith* §7. 53 This is no more their fault, then it is that they see not non-existents. **1734** WATTS *Reliq. Juv.* (1789) 133 Confus'd ideas Of non-existents and impossibles. **1824** COLERIDGE *Aids Refl.* (1848) I. 186 The champion's challenge to all the non-existents, that.. dispute his [*sc.* a prince's] rights and royalty. **1885** MARTINEAU *Types Eth. The.* I. I. i. (1886) 27 That of which there should be no idea would be *ipso facto* a non-existent.

non-e'xisting, *ppl. a.* [NON- 6.] = prec. A.

1797 HOLCROFT tr. *Stolberg's Trav.* (ed. 2) II. lx. 446 Non-existing phantoms.. are pointed to as realities. **1826** MISS MITFORD in L'Estrange *Life* (1870) II. x. 223 Was not this a most absurd difficulty? To have written a charade upon a non-existing word! **1897** *Westm. Gaz.* 25 May 7/3 He treated evidence which was not forthcoming as non-existing.

non-expor'tation. [NON- 1.] Refusal to export (in *U.S. Hist.*: cf. *non-importation*).

1774 JEFFERSON *Wks.* (1853) I. 144 The heavy injury that would arise to this country from an earlier adoption of the non-exportation plan. **1774** [see NON-CONSUMPTION]. **1876** BANCROFT *Hist. U.S.* IV. v. 351 They.. proposed non-importation and, if necessary, non-exportation as means of temporary resistance.

non-feasance (nɒnˈfiːzəns). *Law.* [NON- 1.] Omission of some act which ought to have been done. (Distinguished from MALFEASANCE, MISFEASANCE.)

1596 BACON *Max. Com. Law* (1630) 2 If the grantee commit treason, wherby he is imprisoned, so that the grantor cannot have access unto him for his counsel, yet nevertheles the annuity is not determined by this non-feasance. **1622** CALLIS *Stat. of Sewers* (1824) 211 No permission, sufferance, neglect, or non-feasance, can be found to be by force, because they consist not *in agendo*. **1765** [see MALFEASANCE]. **1781, 1875** [see MISFEASANCE]. **1845** POLSON *Eng. Law* in *Encycl. Metrop.* II. 813/2 Misconduct of officers of justice, being what the law terms malfeasance, that is, wrong-doing,—or culpable non-feasance. **1891** MORLEY in *Times* 30 Oct. 7/2 If your colleague.. of to-day.. is to be at liberty to-morrow to turn round and reproach you with supposed misfeasances and non-feasances.

transf. **1773** *Observ. State Poor* 27 There is one infallible way to put an end to begging,.. which consists merely in a nonfeasance: give them nothing.

†**non-'feelingness.** *Obs.* [f. NON- 1 + FEELING *ppl. a.* + -NESS.] Absence of sensation.

1650 GENTILIS *Considerations* 212 To overcome a feigned non-feelingnesse of griefe attempts a greater mischiefe.

non-'ferrous, *a.* [NON- 3.] Containing no iron; of or pertaining to metals other than iron.

1887 [see FERROUS *a.* 2]. **1909** *Westm. Gaz.* 4 Sept. 4/3 The non-ferrous metal trades. **1936** *Times Educ. Suppl.* 13 June p. iv/1 A non-ferrous survey ship.. is being fitted out and will probably start work in the Southern Indian Ocean. **1940** LAING & ROLFE (*title*) Non-ferrous foundry practice. **1963** H. R. CLAUSER *Encycl. Engin. Materials & Processes* 120/1 Nonferrous centrifugal castings are produced from copper alloys, nickel alloys, and tin and lead-base bearing metals. **1971** *Nature* 23 July 215/1 Britain's imports of non-ferrous metals cost £600 million annually.

†**non-'fiance.** *Obs. rare*$^{-1}$. [NON- 1.] Want of confidence.

1643 BAILLIE *Lett. & Jrnls.* (1841) II. 99 Essex much suspect, at least of non-fiance and misfortoune.

non-'fiction. [NON- 2.] Prose writings other than fiction (see FICTION 4). Also *attrib.* or as *adj.*, esp. in **non-fiction novel**, a novel written about real situations or characters.

1909 *Westm. Gaz.* 2 June 5/2 In Capetown the percentage of non-fiction to the total number of volumes is 58. **1922** HOLLIDAY & VAN RENSSELAER *Business of Writing* 174 Successful works of non-fiction not infrequently are later issued in cheaper forms by the original publisher. **1930** *Times Educ. Suppl.* 31 May 248/3 One of the most pleasing features was an increase of 344 issues of non-fiction literature. **1951** L. Z. HOBSON *Celebrity* (1953) xvi. 255 In this bad slump, nonfiction's the only thing selling—apart from one or two novels a year. **1965** *Vogue* 15 Oct. 94 [Truman] Capote is an experimenter, an adventurer. His newest experiment is *In Cold Blood*, a unique book, for it is the first non-fiction novel, a precise documentary, in many ways brilliantly composed. **1967** *New Mexico Q.* Autumn 243 (*heading*) The 'non-fiction' novel. **1969** *Times* 30 Oct. 10/7 Non-fiction paperbacks.

Hence **non-'fictional** *a.*, of, pertaining to, or characteristic of non-fiction.

1903 *Library World* Mar. 227 Mr. Doubleday's allusions to the expedients that have been adopted to advertise the non-fictional wares remind me of another point. **1911** A. BENNETT *Let.* 28 July (1966) I. 159 This clause would prevent me from publishing anything whatever non-fictional until they issued the book. **1938** D. BAKER *Young Man with Horn* II. i. 92 The author's right, as author, to furnish himself, as hero, with everything he lacked in his non-fictional life. **1966** G. N. LEECH *Eng. in Advertising* v. 54 Credibility is a dominant consideration in both fictional and non-fictional indirect address. **1967** *Britannica Bk. of Year 1966* 803/3 *Nonfictional novel*, a completely factual narrative characterized by the use of fictional techniques; *nonfictional novelist*.

non-'figurative, *a.* [NON- 3.] Not figurative; *spec.* in art = ABSTRACT A. 4 d. So **non-figu'ration**.

1927 O. JESPERSEN *Mod. Eng. Gram.* III. xiv. 294 *Play* in the non-figurative sense has often *to*: he played Beethoven to us. **1934** *Burlington Mag.* Aug. 94/1 Cubism or non-figurative art is dismissed as an ephemeral movement. **1955** P. HERON *Changing Forms of Art* iii. 40 Until painting became non-figurative, the spatial configuration which the painter registered upon his canvas consisted of forms that could be read as illusionistic references to real objects; objects, that is, that were external to the picture. *Ibid.* 41 In 1945 pure non-figuration began to predominate in Paris. **1961** *Guardian* 16 Nov. 7/4 Abstract pattern deriving from Islamic ornament.. to transcend.. Western non-figuration. **1962** *Listener* 19 July 94/1 The non-figurative painter avoids stereotypes by means of marks and shapes, the interpretation of which is arbitrary, since the truly non-figurative is infinitely ambiguous.

non-flam, *a.* [NON- 3.] That is not inflammable. Hence as *sb.*, something that is not inflammable. So **non-'flammable** *a.*

1906 *Chambers's Jrnl.* 24 Nov. 831/2 A British firm, the patentees of 'Non-Flam' goods, of Aytoun Street, Manchester, points out that however efficacious Professor Doremus's prescription may be, it will need to be applied to the curtains every time they are washed. **1908** *Daily Chron.* 20 Oct. 3/6 It would be a good thing if the Government would.. prohibit the use of any but 'non-flam' or other permanently incombustible flannelette for infants' garments. **1909** *Ibid.* 27 Feb. 4/7 'Non-Flam'.. will not flare when brought into contact with fire. **1927** *Daily Tel.* 25 Oct. 14 In France from Jan. 1 next no celluloid film may be used unless made from this so-called 'non-flam' film. **1961** *Daily Mail* 20 July 9/4 A resolution urging the association to do more to promote the use of non-flammable clothing was accepted. **1968** *Punch* 17 Jan. 77/2 (*caption*) You've sure got a point there, Senator—non-flam draft cards. **1970** N. ARMSTRONG et al. *First on Moon* iii. 65 It was made of foam and covered with nonflammable tape. **1975** L. DEIGHTON *Yesterday's Spy* xxx. 221 Non-flam helium would not have burned.

non-fraterni'zation. [NON- 1.] An absence of fraternization (see FRATERNIZATION b). Also abbrev. (*slang*) **non-frat**. Also *attrib.*

1945 F. GILLARD in Hawkins & Boyd *War Report* (1946) xx. 383 The Germans don't like our non-fraternization rule, and they don't like the way in which our troops are obeying these rules. *Ibid.* 384 The attitude of these people makes our non-fraternization policy more necessary than ever. **1945** Non-fraternisation [see FRATERNIZATION b]. **1945** Non-frat [see FRATTING *vbl. sb.*]. **1957** *Wiener Beiträge* LXV. 280 Soldiers abbreviated the long words *fraternisation* and *non-fraternisation* to *frat* and *non-frat*.

nong (nɒŋ). *Austral. slang.* Also **nong-nong**. [Origin unknown.] A fool; a stupid person. Cf. NING-NONG.

1953 BAKER *Australia Speaks* vii. 171 *Nong*, a simpleton or fool. **1959** —— *Drum* viii. 61 'Nong' (or the duplicated form 'nong-nong') was equivalent not only to dill, but also to drube, dope, and drongo. **1961** *Sunday Mail Mag.* (Brisbane) 5 Feb. 5/1 Nicholson and Fenton were not complete nongnongs. **1970** M. KELLY *Spinifex* vii. 113 Todd whirled, rifle at hip, 'You nong!' 'That's what they call me,' Reid commented affably. **1972** *Telegraph* (Brisbane) 5 Dec. 3/4 Mrs. Margaret Whitlam today emphatically denied that she had referred on Saturday night to journalists as 'nongs'.

†**nongain'standing,** *prep. Obs.* [See NON- and GAINSTAND *v.* b.] Notwithstanding.

1456 SIR G. HAYE *Law Arms* (S.T.S.) 137 Nongaynstanding thir argumentis.

nongenary (nɒn'dʒiːnərɪ). [f. L. *nongēnārius* containing nine hundred, after CENTENARY *sb.* 3.] A nine hundredth anniversary, or the celebrations connected with it.

1926 FOWLER *Mod. Eng. Usage* 72/2 A list of not intolerable forms is here offered... Centē'nary,.. octingē'nary, nongē'nary, millē'nary. **1965** E. GOWERS *Fowler's Mod. Eng. Usage* (ed. 2) 83/1 Nor is anyone, however passionate a supporter of etymological correctness, likely to try to introduce *sescenary, septingenary, octingenary*, or *nongenary*. **1966** *New Statesman* 8 Apr. 511/2 The painters are in no way concerned with the nongenary of the Battle of Hastings.

non-'greasy, *a.* [NON- 3.] Not greasy.

1907 *Yesterday's Shopping* (1969) 537/1 Violet Oatmeal Skin Cream... Non-greasy and without stickiness. **1937** *Discovery* Oct. 297 An offset—a print made in a non-greasy powdered chalk. **1967** E. CHAMBERS *Photolitho-Offset* xvi. 242 Gravure inks are difficult in make-up, being very fluid, finely ground, non-greasy and drying mainly by evaporation. **1974** *Harpers & Queen* Sept. 112 Some foundations are non-greasy, ideal for oily skins.

non-'gremial. [NON- 2.] One who is not a resident member (of the university of Cambridge). Also *attrib.* or *adj.* in ***non-gremial examinations***, an early name for the 'local' examinations.

1841 PEACOCK *Stat. Cambr.* App. A. 17 *note*, Non gremials ..were suspended *ab omni gradu*. **1858** *Guardian* 29 Dec. 1042/3 At Bristol last week there was a public meeting in support of the Cambridge non-gremial examinations. **1865** *Sat. Rev.* 25 Feb. 220/1 That girls as well as boys might be ..admitted to what are called the 'non-gremial' examinations.

non-habence (nɒn'heɪbəns). *rare*⁻¹. [f. NON- 1 + **habence*, ad. L. *habentia*, f. *habent-*, pres. ppl. stem of *habēre* to have.] The condition of not having a thing.

1865 J. GROTE *Moral Ideals* (1876) 27 The degrees of withoutness are (1) simple non-habence [etc.].

non-'hearer. *Hist.* [NON- 2.] (See quots.)

1853 J. H. BURTON *Hist. Scot.* II. 69 A portion of them [*sc.* the Cameronians]..isolated themselves as 'non-hearers'. **1855** MACAULAY *Hist. Eng.* xvi. III. 707 The number of these zealots [*sc.* Presbyterian nonjurors] went on diminishing till..they were nowhere numerous enough to have a meeting house, and were known by the name of the Non-hearers.

'non-hero. [NON- 2 b.] One who is the opposite or the reverse of a hero; one who is not genuinely a hero. Cf. ANTI-HERO.

1940 *Sun* (Baltimore) 7 Sept. 10/7 In my list of non-heroes, Carol of Rumania stands close to the top. **1948** E. E. CUMMINGS *Let.* 27 Jan. (1969) 181 Since our (as he's doubtless already boasted to you) non-hero was once a candidate for honours. **1959** *Times Lit. Suppl.* 13 Nov. 657/1 These two novels..take lovable, weak, defeated men as non-heroes. **1972** *Sat. Rev.* 17 June 52/3 Our existential nonhero wanders through the story.

non-'human, *a.* [NON- 3.]

1. Not of the human race, not a human being.

1839 J. ROGERS *Antipopopr.* vi. §2. 210 He is quite different from the whole human family, or is nonhuman. **1852** M. ARNOLD *Empedocles* I. ii, Though the non-human powers Of Nature harm us not. **1865** LUBBOCK *Preh. Times* 114 The non-human bones met with in their researches.

2. Not natural or proper to human being.

1853 KINGSLEY *Hypatia* xxi, Celibacy and asceticism, utterly non-human as they were. **1891** HARDY *Tess* xx, At those non-human hours they could get quite close to the waterfowl.

nonic ('nəʊnɪk), *sb.* and *a. Math.* [f. NON(A- + -IC.] **A.** *sb.* A nonic curve or equation. **B.** *adj.* Of the ninth order or degree.

1879 *Amer. Jrnl. Math.* II. 233 (*heading*) Nonic. **1894** *Phil. Trans. R. Soc.* A. CLXXXV. 103 The nonic was proved..to have only three real roots. **1958** *New Biol.* XXV. 16 By an elementary transformation I have thrown his rather formidable nonic equation into a form which allows numerical tabulation.

nonillion (nɒ'nɪljən). [a. F. *nonillion* (16th c.), f. L. *nōn-us* ninth, after *million*.] The ninth power of a million, denoted by 1 followed by 54 cyphers. In American use, an octillion multiplied by 1000, denoted by 1 followed by 30 cyphers. Hence **no'nillionth** (in recent Dicts.).

1690 [see BILLION 1]. **1828–32** WEBSTER, *Nonillion*, the number of nine million millions. *a* **1835** McCULLOCH *Attributes* (1843) II. xxxix. 476 Words effect less than figures; especially in the higher numbers. A Nonillion is scarcely more than a million to our conceptions.

non-impor'tation. [NON- 1.] Neglect or refusal to import. **b.** *attrib.* in ***non-importation agreement*** or ***act***, applied to various agreements or acts made by the American colonial governments (from 1768 to 1774) to prevent the importation of goods from Great Britain and her colonies.

1770 *Chron.* in *Ann. Reg.* 159 We [at Charles Town] have agreed to stop all commercial intercourse with New-York, on account of that Province breaking the Non-Importation Agreement, which we strictly adhere to. **1774** [see NON-CONSUMPTION]. **1774** (*title*) A Friendly Address to all Reasonable Americans,..in which the Necessary Consequences..of a General Non-Importation are Fairly Stated. **1833** C. REDDING *Mod. Wines* 213 The non-importation of the pure wine took place about 1815. **1849–50** ALISON *Hist. Europe* VII. xlii. §54. 135 Congress.. passed a non-importation act against the manufactures of Great Britain. **1876** BANCROFT *Hist. U.S.* IV. xxxii. 79 The certainty that the country could not as yet manufacture for itself, and consequently..that the schemes of non-importation would fail.

So **non-im'porting** *ppl. a.* (Webster, 1847.)

nonino: see NONNY-NO.

non-in'telligence. [NON- 1.]

†1. Failure to understand. *Obs.*

a **1674** TRAHERNE *Poet. Wks.* (1903) 33 My non-intelligence of human words Ten thousand Pleasures unto me affords.

2. Want of intelligence.

1905 J. M. ROBERTSON *Chamberlain* x. 52/2 It was the apotheosis of notional non-intelligence.

non-in'telligent, *a.* (*sb.*) [NON- 3.] **A.** *adj.* Not intelligent. **B.** *sb.* One who is not intelligent.

1628 FELTHAM *Resolves* II. xx. 67 Mercurie himselfe may moue his tongue in vaine, if hee has none to heare him, but a Non-intelligent. **1768–74** TUCKER *Lt. Nat.* (1834) I. 332 If we had declared Him non-intelligent, it would have conveyed the same idea we have of senseless matter. **1860** GEN. P. THOMPSON *Audi Alt.* cxxii. III. 70 The puerile display of non-intelligent imbecility.

non-'intercourse. [NON- 1.] Want of intercourse. **b.** *attrib.* in ***non-intercourse act***, in *U.S. Hist.*, an act of 1809 prohibiting ships from France and Great Britain from entering American ports. Also humorously allusive.

1809 JEFFERSON *Writ.* (1829) IV. 131 This view is derived from the former non-intercourse law only. **1809** MALKIN *Gil Blas* XI. vii. ¶5 You must submit to an embargo on your wit, and a non-intercourse act between you and the faculty of writing. **1826** MISS MITFORD *Village* Ser. II. (1863) 371, I intend to try the effect of non-intercourse, and to break with her outright. **1888** A. JOHNSTON in *Encycl. Brit.* XXIII. 759/1 The use of non-intercourse agreements as revolutionary weapons against Great Britain.

non-inter'ference. [NON- 1.] Failure or refusal to interfere, *esp.* in politics.

1830 GEN. P. THOMPSON *Exerc.* (1842) I. 284 The more cases you can produce of non-interference on the other side, the more easily you may say that non-interference cannot last for ever, and you must interfere in this. **1866** CRUMP *Banking* ii. 60 Banking, above all other professions, is that which under entire freedom and non-interference would soonest be placed in the most perfect position. **1907** *Standard* 19 Jan. 8/1 If the Downing Street people would only give us [in South Africa]..a little continuity of non-interference.

attrib. **1859** J. TAYLOR *Logic in Theol.* 227 The 'non-interference' statesmen, who rule India.

So **non-inter'ferer,** one who favours non-interference; **non-inter'fering** *ppl. a.*, that does not interfere.

1860 GEN. P. THOMPSON *Audi Alt.* cxxvi. III. 83 To note the way in which the non-interferers can turn round when it suits them. **1897** MARY KINGSLEY *W. Africa* 442 A non-interfering and therefore a negligeable quantity.

non-inter'vention. [NON- 1. So in Fr.] Absence of intervention; in international politics, systematic non-interference by a nation in the affairs of other nations except where its own interests are directly involved.

1831 [see INTERVENTION 1.]. **1835** MARRYAT *Olla Podr.* vii, The French marched an army of non-intervention down to the citadel. **1849** S. P. CHASE *Let.* 30 July in J. Schuckers *Life of Chase* (1874) xii. 102 For what will be the cost to the Democracy of the alliance with the slaveholders in a presidential campaign?.. It is non-intervention upon the subject of slavery. **1881** E. ROBERTSON in *Encycl. Brit.* XIII. 192/1 Premature recognition of a struggling rebellion would be regarded as a breach of the principle of non-intervention. **1888** MARQ. SALISBURY in *Times* 11 Apr. 12/2 That spirit of haughty and sullen isolation which has been dignified by the name of 'non-intervention'. **1937** H. NICOLSON *Diary* 27 July (1966) 309 Anthony Eden..says that the French really did take the initiative in non-intervention [in Spain] and were not put up to it by us. **1939** S. SPENDER *Poems for Spain* 10 Satire, like Edgell Rickword's on Non-Intervention, in which the fundamental ideas are turned against the politicians. **1959** *Ann. Reg. 1958* 51 A discreet non-intervention in the debate was observed by the Leader of the Party. **1975** *Times* 16 Oct. 15/2 The Soviet Union feels free to propagate its ideas in the west, so the west should not be shy about propagating its ideas in the east... The passages on non-intervention are aimed..at..physical intervention.

attrib. **1846** MRS. GORE *Eng. Char.* (1852) 85 An intervention and non-intervention war is waged between the parties. **1896** *Daily News* 17 Nov. 5/4 The renewal of Bismarck's Non-intervention Alliance.

Hence **non-inter'ventionist,** also **non-inter'ventionalist** (*rare*⁻¹), one who favours non-intervention; also *attrib.* **non-inter'vene** *v. intr.*, not to intervene; **non-inter'vener,** one who does not intervene or who advocates non-intervention; **non-inter'vening** *ppl. a.*

1859 RUSKIN *Arrows of Chace* (1880) II. 13 We English non-interventionalists. **1860** *Sat. Rev.* X. 483/1 The Greek ecclesiastics are non-interventionists. **1884** *L'pool Mercury* 14 Feb. 5/6 The non-interventionist peace party. **1901** K. D. BEST *Victories of Rome* (ed. 4) p. xii, The State..is exhibiting to a non-intervening circle of Catholic kingdoms the newest and latest development of Liberté, Egalité, Fraternité. **1937** A. P. HERBERT in *Punch* 8 Sept. 275/1 The Non-Intervention Committee are meeting, The Non-Interveners are meeting again. *Ibid.* 275/2 So let every soldier go non-intervening—Oh, fly with me Southward and non-intervene! **1942** 'A. BRIDGE' *Frontier Passage* iv. 53 Mr. Crumpaun..was playing bridge with the elderly clergyman and two Non-Interveners. **1969** *Guardian* 29 Aug. 8/4 Mr Chamberlain..threatened to..'non-intervene' on Hitler's side against Czechoslovakia, as they were doing in favour of General Franco in Spain.

non-in'trusion. [NON- 1.] Absence of intrusion; *spec.* in the Church of Scotland, applied to the principle of resisting the intrusion by patrons of unacceptable ministers upon objecting congregations. Also *attrib.*

1840 J. ROBERTSON *Observ. Veto Act* 5 The observations now offered to the public on the non-intrusion enactment of the Assembly, 1834. **1841** DE QUINCEY in *Blackw. Mag.* Aug. 128 All those laymen who profess principles of Non-intrusion. *Ibid.*, In Edinburgh, the peace of the city was sought to be disturbed, by setting up the Non-intrusion Lord Provost against Mr. Macaulay. **1841** MACAULAY in Trevelyan *Life* (1880) II. 93 A Non-intrusion opposition has been talked of... The leading Non-intrusionists..have had a conference with me. **1879** *Encycl. Brit.* IX. 744/1 That the church..should reaffirm the principle of non-intrusion as an integral part of the constitution of the Reformed Church of Scotland.

Hence **non-in'trusionism,** the tenets and practice of non-intrusionists; **non-in'trusionist,** one who favours non-intrusion; also *attrib.*

1841 DE QUINCEY in *Blackw. Mag.* Aug. 128 To vote for a Non-intrusionist was a matter of divine duty. *Ibid.* 129 To such partisans..Christianity itself is scarcely more important than Non-Intrusionism. *Ibid.* 132 The sentiments and language of the Non-Intrusionist Lord-Advocate.

‖**non inventus** (nɒn ɪn'vɛntəs). [L. = 'not found'.] = NON EST INVENTUS.

c **1670** HACKET *Abp. Williams* II. (1693) 88 They [*sc.* commissioners] broke up with a *Non-inventus*. **1760–72** H. BROOKE *Fool of Qual.* (1809) II. 124 The return of *non invent*, generally made upon writs. **1880** J. PAYN *Confident. Agent* xxiii, It is rumoured that the assistant of a well-known jeweller..is *non inventus*.

non-i'onic, *a.* and *sb.* [NON- 3.] **A.** *adj.* Not ionic; *spec.* (esp. of a detergent) not dissociating into ions in aqueous solution.

1943 *Chemical Industries* LII. 327/1 Non-ionic surface active agents, as their name implies, are not ionizable and owe their effectiveness to a proper balance between certain hydrophilic (polar) and lyophilic (non-polar) groups in their molecules. **1959** *Spectator* 4 Sept. 294/1 Together with the nonionic 'Nonidet' products, they have scores of applications throughout industry both for cleaning and maintenance. **1963** A. J. HALL *Textile Sci.* vi. 296 Surface active agents or surfactants can be usefully classified into three main groups—anion-active, non-ionic, and cation-active. **1964** M. HYNES *Med. Bacteriol.* (ed. 8) vii. 90 It depends on such forces as attraction between polar non-ionic groups..and van der Waal[s] attraction. **1965** PHILLIPS & WILLIAMS *Inorg. Chem.* I. v. 171 The difference between the equilibrium lattice energies U and U_i is seen to be approximately equal to the additional non-ionic binding energies.

B. *sb.* A non-ionic substance or detergent.

1952 *Mod. Sanit. & Build. Maint.* IV. 63/1 Considerable interest has been shown as to just what happens when iodine is dissolved in nonionics... It has been observed that nonionics render iodine soluble in aqueous solutions providing the amount of iodine does not exceed 25% based on the nonionic. **1972** *Materials & Technol.* V. x. 308 In several of the different classes of these non-ionics, it is possible to obtain products ranging from completely oil-soluble to completely water-soluble.

non-iron, *a.* [Cf. NON- 5 b.] Of clothes, fabrics, etc.: that does not require ironing after being washed.

1957 *Woman* 16 Nov. 25/4 Cottons and rayons with a special finish—that is ones that have been made crease-resistant, drip-dry or non-iron cannot be dyed at home. **1971** *Vogue* 15 Sept. 43/1 Thick soft American towels, non-iron sheets. **1975** *Times* 27 Sept. 16/1 Easily washable and non-iron fabrics.

nonius ('nəʊnɪəs). [mod.L., being the latinized form of the name of Pedro *Nuñez*, a Portuguese mathematician (1492–1577).] A contrivance for the graduation of mathematical instruments, invented by Nuñez and described by him in his work *De Crepusculis* (1542 A.D.). Often inaccurately used for the VERNIER, which is an improved form of Nuñez' instrument.

1750 *Phil. Trans.* XLVI. 515 In this Method another Observer will be generally necessary to note the Degree cut by the Nonius. **1781** M. CUTLER in *Life*, etc. (1888) I. 86, I went to Salem to get a nonius fitted to my barometer. **1804** CT. VON RUMFORD in *Phil. Trans.* XCIV. 78 Their scales were divided with the greatest care; and, by means of a nonius, they show eighth parts of a degree very distinctly. **1881** SERPA PINTO *How I crossed Africa* II. II. ii. 160, I read in the nonius 50° 10′.

b. *attrib.*, as ***nonius plate, scale, screw***.

1732 *Phil. Trans.* XXXVII. 274 The Nonius Plate moves with the Index, and subdivides each of the small Divisions of the Arch into ten equal Parts or Minutes. **1837** Brewster *Magn.* 350 The lever or clamp, connected with the nonius screw on one of the deflectors. **1867** Smyth *Sailor's Word-bk., Nonius Scale, or Vernier.*

non-'joinder. *Law.* [non- 1.] The omission to join, as a party to a suit.

1833 *Act 3 & 4 Will. IV*, c. 42 §10 The.. Defendants who shall have so pleaded in Abatement the Nonjoinder of such Person. **1845** Stephen *Comm. Laws Eng.* (1874) II. 100 Each is entitled if sued alone to object to the non-joinder of the other partners. **1887** *Law Times Rep.* LVIII. 112/1 Under the old practice.. their non-joinder could have been made the subject of a plea in abatement.

†**non-'jurable,** *a. Obs.* [f. non- 3 + **jurable*, ad. L. type **jurābilis* (f. *jurāre* to swear: see -able).] That cannot be sworn, e.g. as a witness.

a **1734** North *Examen* (1740) 264 If.. they were brought to the View of this Fellow's Saltinbanco Tricks, they would have.. pined at his being such a Nonjurable Rogue.

non-jurancy (nɒn'dʒʊərənsɪ). *Hist.* [f. non-jurant: see -ancy.] The condition of being a non-juror; the principles of the non-jurors.

1715 Wodrow in *Wodrow's Corr.* (1843) II. 21 To show it was neither disloyalty nor Non-jurancy hindered him, he went over.. and preached at Lanark with Mr. Orr. **1720** —— *Ibid.* 486 The other thing insisted on is a declaration of the reasons of our Non-jurancy. **1895** Raven *Hist. Suffolk* 229 Archbishop Sancroft's non-jurancy.

non-'jurant, *a.* and *sb. Hist.* Also 8 erron. -and. [f. non-juror: see -ant and cf. jurant.]

A. *adj.* That is a non-juror; belonging to or characteristic of non-jurors.

1696 Luttrell *Brief Rel.* (1857) IV. 138 One Glascome, a nonjurant parson. **1788** in *N. & Q.* 8th Ser. VIII. 16 Nov. (1895) 385/1 Upon the 24th of April 1788 at a Meeting of the Protestant Nonjurand Bishops at Aberdeen they unanimously resolved to pray for George the Third. **1791** Newte *Tour Eng. & Scot.* 372 A non-jurant place of worship. **1900** J. Dowden in C. E. G. Wright *Gideon Guthrie* Pref. xiv, Guthrie, an Episcopal and non-jurant clergyman.

transf. **1837** Carlyle *Fr. Rev.* III. I. iv. 36 Poor Abbé Sicard, with some thirty other Nonjurant Priests. **1866** *Pall Mall G.* 14 Sept. 5 The annexation of Hanover to Prussia seems likely to give rise to a class of non-jurant clergy in the former country.

B. *sb.* = non-juror.

1702 *Reasons for addr. his Majesty to invite Electress* 9 Those of 'em who pretend to be Protestants are particularly stil'd High-Flyers, High-Churchmen, a few of 'em Non-jurants, and all of 'em Torys. **1703** *Moderation a Virtue* 21 These are the Nonjurants, who reserve their Allegiance for the young Gentleman at St. Germans. **1848** Thomson *Hist. Sk. Secession Ch.* 8 The non-jurants.. were supported.. by the general voice of the people, who, looking upon the oath [of abjuration] as a badge of slavery [etc.]. **1881** Agnew *Theol. Consol.* 287 The most earnest ministers.. refused to swear [the oath of allegiance to William and Mary]. To distinguish them from the Episcopal Non-jurors,.. they were usually called non-jurants.

transf. **1837** Carlyle *Fr. Rev.* III. I. iv. 37 A poor Non-jurant, of quicker temper, smites the horny paw with his cane.

Hence †**non-'jurantism** = non-jurancy.

1706 Baynard *Cold Baths* II. 268 Now to reason a little why Men.. should even against Conviction oppose Cold Bathing, is a Paradox, surely the reason must be the same with that of Nonjurantism.

†**non-'juress.** *Obs. nonce-word.* [f. non-juror + -ess.] A female non-juror.

1723 Dk. Wharton *True Briton* No. 21. I. 182 So great a Reinforcement of Nonjuresses as they will now have.

non-'juring, *ppl. a. Hist.* [f. non-juror: see -ing².] Refusing the oath of allegiance; belonging to the party of non-jurors.

1691 Wood *Life* 21 Apr. (O.H.S.) III. 359 Non-juring bishops: Sancroft [etc.]. **1747** J. Owen (*title*) Jacobites and Nonjuring Principles freely examined. **1779** Boswell *Let.* 2 Feb. in *Johnson*, I.. had solemn conversation with the Reverend Mr. Falconer, a nonjuring bishop. **1814** Scott *Wav.* xi, The nonjuring clergyman was a pensive and interesting old man, with much the air of a sufferer for conscience sake. **1855** Macaulay *Hist. Eng.* xiv. III. 495 Some non-juring assembly, where the service which he loved was performed without mutilation. **1882–3** Schaff *Encycl. Relig. Knowl.* II. 1666 Nonjuring congregations continued to exist until the death of the last bishop Boothe, in 1805.

non-'jurist. *Hist.* [f. non-juror: see -ist.] Used *attrib.* = prec. Also **non-ju'ristical** *a.*

1723 *Poor Robin* (title-p.) The Roundheads, Fanaticks, Muggletonians, Nonjuristical and Papistical Account. **1871** Fraser *Life Berkeley* ii. 49 Non-resistance and passive obedience were.. supported in Queen Anne's reign in Non-jurist tracts and pamphlets.

non-ju'ristic, *a.* [non- 3.] Not juristic.

1875 Poste *Gaius* IV. 508 We.. find *manus injectio* spoken of by non-juristic writers as an act of self-redress.

non-juror, nonjuror (nɒn'dʒʊərə(r)). *Hist.* [non- 2.] Orig., one of the beneficed clergy who refused to take the oath of allegiance in 1689 to William and Mary. Also, in wider use (see quot. 1769).

1691 Wood *Life* 14 Oct. (O.H.S.) III. 373 To justifie his proceedings in not expelling the non-jurors or non-swearers. **1696** Evelyn *Diary* 26 Feb., A Conspiracy of about 30 Knights, [etc.].. many of them Irish and English Papists and Nonjurors or Jacobites (so call'd), to murder K. William. **1714** Swift *Pres. St. Aff.* Wks. 1751 IV. 276 Excepting those who are Nonjurors by profession, I have not met with above two persons who appeared to have any scruples concerning the present Limitation of the Crown. **1769** Blackstone *Comm.* IV. ix. 124 Every person refusing the same [oaths of allegiance, supremacy, and abjuration] who is properly called a non-juror, shall be adjudged a popish recusant convict. **1827** Hallam *Const. Hist.* xv. (1876) III. 109 Eight bishops,.. with about four hundred clergy,.. chose the more honourable course of refusing the new oaths; and thus began the schism of the nonjurors. **1852** Thackeray *Esmond* xi, So my Lord Castlewood remained a nonjuror all his life nearly. **1879** L. Stephen *Hours in Library* III. 289 When Macaulay attacks an old non-juror or modern Tory.

Hence **non-'jurorism**, the principles of the non-jurors.

1882 in Ogilvie.

non-jury. [non- 4.] *attrib.* in *non-jury action, case*, an action or case not requiring a jury. Also *absol.* = non-jury case.

1897 *Daily News* 9 Mar. 8/4 Two non-jury cases from Mr. Justice Matthew's court. **1898** *Westm. Gaz.* 19 May 2/1 To try Special, Common, and non-juries. **1901** *Scotsman* 11 Mar. 9/2 Mr. Justice Bucknill sat to try non-jury actions.

non-'knowledge. [non- 1.] Want of knowledge.

1503 *Rolls of Parlt.* VI. 532/2 For the serche and non knowlege of their severall Tenures. **1600** W. Watson *Decacordon* (1602) 277 A Non-knowledge, what catholiks were guiltie, and who were free. **1612** Heywood *Apol. Actors* Ep. Ded. A 2 b, They have either wandred through spleene, or erred by non-knowledge. **1898** *Westm. Gaz.* 1 April 4/1 His non-knowledge of the customs of the country led to a very funny situation.

non'leaded, *ppl. a.* [f. non- 6 + leaded *ppl. a.* e.] Of petrol: containing no added tetraethyl lead to counteract 'knocking'.

1955 *Sci. News Let.* 22 Jan. 54/1 The best way to remove carbon monoxide from auto fumes appears to be the use of nonleaded gasoline and a catalytic converter, Dr. W. L. Faith, chief engineer of the Southern California Air Pollution Foundation, said. **1971** *McGraw-Hill Yearbk. Sci. & Technol.* 212 The two most desired types of gasoline components for nonleaded gasolines are highly branched paraffins and the common aromatic components such as benzene, toluene, and xylene. **1971** J. D. Roberts et al. *Org. Chem.* iii. 58 The manufacture of engines capable of running on nonleaded gasoline is also being undertaken.

non le day. *Hist.* [See non- 2 and le.] A day on which ordinary exercises were not read in the schools; hence, a day of rest, a holiday.

1635 Heylin *Sabbath* (1636) II. 114 [That] the Lords day .. should be a non-lee day, a day of rest and ease unto them. **1904** Wordsworth *Anc. Kal. Univ. Oxf.* (O.H.S.) 181 There were in old times many holy days which intervened to stop lectures, and these were accordingly called *non Le*, or *non Dis* days (or both at once).

‖**non licet** (nɒn 'lɪsɛt). [L. = 'it is not lawful'.]

†**1.** A refusal of permission. *Obs.*

1622 Mabbe tr. *Aleman's Guzman d'Alf.* 50, I was dismist with a *non licet*.

2. *attrib.* (hyphened). Not allowed, unlawful.

1628 Prynne *Brief Surv.* 80 These non-licet times of Marriage. **1637** Heylin *Antid. Linc.* Pref. 2 This and such like lawlesse, and non-licet Pamphlets. **1672** Wood *Life* 9 Feb. (O.H.S.) II. 242 Dye.. keeps a non-licet coach,.. notwithstanding the vicechancellor had prohibited him. **1891** Wrench *Winchester Word-bk., Non-licet* adj., illegal: unbefitting a Wykehamist. *Ex.*—Don't sport non-licet notions.

'non-life. [non- 2.] Absence or negation of life.

1733 W. Crawford *Infidelity* (1836) 186 Here there is a progress from a non-life to a life. **1862** J. Brown *Rab, Mystery of Black & Tan* (1906) 59 That shudder, by which he leapt out of non-life into life. **1899** Dziewicki *Wyclif's De Logica* III. p. xxii, The instant of death.. viewed from different standpoints: as the end of life, and the beginning of non-life.

non-'linear, *a.* [non- 3.] Not linear, in sense 3 of the adj.; involving terms of an equation that are not of the first degree; involving or possessing the property that the magnitude of an effect or output is not linearly related to that of the cause or input.

1844 *Phil. Trans. R. Soc.* CXXXIV. 282 The integration of non-linear differential equations. **1905** *Drapers' Company Res. Mem. Biometric Ser.* II. 21 In the cases of non-linear regression.. I have.. had to deal with, I find that parabolæ of the 2nd or 3rd order will suffice as a rule to describe the deviation from linearity. **1925** F. C. Mills *Statistical Methods* xii. 432 (*heading*) Non-linear correlation. **1930** T. E. Shea *Transmission Networks & Wave Filters* ii. 43 Waves would tend to lose character in propagation, because of what is called non-linear distortion. **1949** O. G. Sutton *Sci. of Flight* ii. 43 The inertia terms in these equations contain both squares and products of the velocities and the equations are thus non-linear. **1968** Fox & Mayers *Computing Methods for Scientists & Engineers* i. 7 The Runge-Kutta method, or one of its variants, is a useful general-purpose routine for non-linear first-order equations. **1969** *Sci. Jrnl.* Apr. 53/3 Non-linear optics.. is the study of the behaviour of materials subjected to light of such intensity as to change some of the parameters of the material. **1973** [see linearize *v.*].

b. *Linguistics.* = *suprasegmental* adj.

1947 C. F. Hockett in *Internat. Jrnl. Amer. Ling.* XIII. 258/2 Features of stress or tone, for example, which normally stretch over more than a single vowel or consonant, have been called non-linear or suprasegmental, in contrast to the linear or segmental vowels and consonants. **1947** —— in *Jrnl. Amer. Oriental Soc.* LXVII. 258/1 Since it is inconvenient to transcribe other than linearly, we derive the symbols for inclosure between solidi from the symbols defined above in such a way as to eliminate the need for non-linear notation.

Hence **non-'linearly** *adv.*

1943 *Jrnl. Amer. Chem. Soc.* LXV. 381/2 The ratio π/c of osmotic pressure to concentration has been found.. to vary non-linearly with concentration. **1964** R. F. Ficchi *Electrical Interference* iii. 24 Components should not be permitted to operate nonlinearly since this causes harmonics to generate. **1973** *Jrnl. Genetic Psychol.* CXXII. 325 Body proportions.. vary nonlinearly with figure age.

non-line'arity. [non- 1.] The property of not being linear; *esp.* lack of proportionality between two related quantities (as input and output).

1929 *Physical Rev.* XXXIII. 633 (*heading*) Non-linearity of photoelectric response near long wave-length limit. **1937** J. Orr tr. *Iordan's Introd. Romance Linguistics* iv. 379 Non-linearity of structure is shown to be present when a sign 'cumulates' more than one function. **1948** *Proc. IRE* XXXVI. 37/1 Any transmission system containing vacuum tubes is more or less nonlinear, with the degree of nonlinearity increasing with increasing signal level. **1965** *Math. in Biol. & Med.* (Med. Res. Council) VI. 266 In some cases, such as an excessively branching syncytial network, the gross non-linearities may be completely smoothed out and virtually linear polarizing current-voltage relations could then be obtained. **1967** *Oceanogr. & Marine Biol.* V. 30 Part of the non-linearity in the latter equations arises from the assumption that the bottom friction is proportional to the square of the bottom current. **1973** *Sci. Amer.* July 29/3 The presence of such nonlinearity in the control characteristics gives rise to additional frequencies at double, triple and quadruple the frequency of the basic oscillation.

‖**non liquet** (nɒn 'lɪkwɛt). [L. = 'it is not clear'.] A condition of uncertainty as to whether a thing is so or not; *spec.* in *Law*, a verdict given by a jury in cases of doubt, deferring the matter to another day for trial. Also *attrib.* = uncertain as to the side to which one belongs.

1656 Blount *Glossogr.* **1679** *Trials of White, & other Jesuits* 63 It is still a Non liquet whether you were here in July or no. *c* **1700** J. Wodrow in *Life* (1828) 109 The Non-liquet men further those that are for the negative. [*a* **1734** North *Examen* (1740) Pref. vi, Here is a Yesterday's Tale out of the best Writers, and who they are non liquet.] **1802** Coleridge *Unpubl. Lett. to J. P. Estlin* 86 (Stanf.), A non liquet concerning the nature and being of Christ. **1952** *Archivum Linguisticum* IV. II. 99 Hofmann.. has also returned a verdict of *non liquet* on the question of etymology.

non-'literate, *a.* *Anthropol.* [non- 3.] Denoting a person or culture that has no written language. Hence as *sb.*, a non-literate person.

1948 M. J. Herskovits *Man & his Works* II. v. 75 The.. form, *nonliterate*, simply describes the fact that these people do not have written languages... Nonliterate, because it is colorless, conveys its meaning unambiguously, and is readily applicable to the data it seeks to delimit, is thus to be preferred to all the other terms we have considered. **1956** R. Redfield *Peasant Society & Culture* i. 6 Among these non-literates there was no history to learn. **1958** A. R. Radcliffe-Brown *Method in Soc. Anthropol.* II. iii. 155 The customs of ancient times might be better understood in the light of the resemblances they show to customs of non-literate peoples of later times. **1970** G. A. & A. G. Theodorson *Mod. Dict. Sociol.* 276 Sometimes the term *preliterate* is used as synonymous with nonliterate; however, preliterate is associated with certain theoretical assumptions .. that are no longer accepted.

non-'logical, *a.* [non- 3.] Not logical; *spec.* in *Logic* = material *a.* 2.

1845 Whately *Logic* in *Encycl. Metrop.* I. 225/1 The Non-logical (or material) Fallacies. **1899** *Westm. Gaz.* 31 Aug. 3/3 There are many non-logical arguments.. which may.. be made to do a lot of good.

non-'member. [non- 2.] One who is not a member. So **non-'membership**.

1650 J. Cotton *Sing. Psalms* 49 Neither doe the members of the Church.. lay aside this dutie, and leave it to Non-Members. **1653** Firmin *Sober Reply* 37 He is under cure, but his cure is non-membership, a member cut off from the body. **1847** in Webster. **1901** *Scotsman* 8 Mar. 6/7 There were forty non-members in the place. **1903** *Daily Chron.* 23 Mar. 5/4 On account of membership or non-membership of a labour union.

non-'metal. *Chem.* [non- 2.] A non-metallic element.

1866 Odling *Anim. Chem.* 14 The chlorides of the metals, like those of the non-metals, must also be divided into monochlorides. **1871** Roscoe *Elem. Chem.* 6 The number of the metals is much larger than that of the non-metals.

non-me'tallic, *a.* [non- 3.] Not metallic, not consisting of metal; *Chem.*, that is not a metallic element.

1815 Aikin *Man. Min.* (ed. 2) 55 Class I.—Non-Metallic Combustible Minerals. The substances of this class (with the exception of Diamond) are of low specific gravity. **1845** F. Lunn *Chem.* in *Encycl. Metrop.* IV. 646/2 Non-Metallic (Electronegative?) Elements. **1856** *Orr's Circ. Sci., Mech. Philos.* 3 Silicium is sometimes regarded as a non-metallic body. **1872** Schellen *Spectrum Anal.* §23 The spectrum of any non-metallic substance.

nonmete, variant of noonmeat.

non-'moral, *a.* [NON- 3.] Not moral; having no moral standard; wanting in moral instinct or sense. So **non-mo'rality**.

a **1866** J. GROTE *Exam. Utilit. Phil.* xxi. (1870) 355 Whether what we are to expect of human action is that it should be non-moral. **1886** SWINBURNE *Misc.* 66 Keats,.. the most absolutely non-moral of all serious writers. **1891** LOUNSBURY *Stud. Chaucer* III. viii. 352 Those who insist that art, while it is not immoral, is non-moral. **1902** *N. & Q.* Ser. IX. IX. 79/2 The *naïveté* of their non-morality.

nonn, obs. form of NUN.

non-nant (nɒn'nænt). [f. NON- 6 + L. *nant-*, pres. ppl. stem of *nāre* to swim.] At Eton College: A boy who is not a swimmer. Also *attrib.*

1869 *Eton Boating Bk.* Introd. 2 No check was put upon those who belonged to the Boats, nor were they prohibited to 'Non-nants'. **1900** BRODRICK *Mem. & Impr.* 31 At the beginning of each summer half [at Eton] a 'non-nant list' was printed.

nonnat ('nɒnæt). [a. dial. F. *nonnat, noun(n)at.*] A name given on the Mediterranean coast of France to the young of fish of the families *Gobidæ* and *Atherinidæ*.

1868 *Mus. Nat. Hist.* II. 131. **1880** GÜNTHER *Fishes* 501.

non-'natural, *a.* and *sb.* [NON- 3.] **A.** *adj.*

† **1.** ***non-natural things*** [medical L. *res non-naturales*] = 'non-naturals' (see B). *Obs.*

1621 BURTON *Anat. Mel.* I. ii. 86 Necessary.. are those six non-naturall things, so much spoken of amongst Physitians. **1704** J. HARRIS *Lex. Techn.* I, Non-Natural Things, or the Non-Natural Cause of Diseases, as the Physicians reckon them are six. **1727–38** CHAMBERS *Cycl.* s.v. *Medicine*, The fourth branch considers the remedies, and their use, whereby life may be preserved, whence it is called hygieine. Its objects are what we strictly call non-natural.

2. Not belonging to the natural order of things; not according to or dependent upon nature; deviating from the natural course or order.

1826 LAMB *Elia* Ser. II. *Sanity of true Genius*, For the super-natural, or something super-added to what we know of nature, they give you the plainly non-natural. **1839** J. ROGERS *Antipopopr.* vi. §2. 210 Whoever comes not from or through Eve or her female posterity, is to be deemed non natural. **1862** McCOSH *Supernatural* II. i. §4. 150 *note*, A miracle is non-natural. **1874** M. ARNOLD in *Contemp. Rev.* Oct. 797 The God of this religion of the future will be still a magnified and non-natural man. **1887** *Challenger Rep.* XIX. IV. 1 The majority of zoologists continued for a long time to divide the Pteropoda into non-natural groups. **1898** *Green's Encycl. Law Scot.* X. 292 The duty of a proprietor making a non-natural use of his lands is extremely strict, and negligence is presumed from the fact of damage.

3. Not in accordance with the natural interpretation or meaning.

1844 W. G. WARD *Ideal Chr. Ch.* 479 Our twelfth Article is as plain as words can make it on the 'evangelical' side.. I subscribe it myself in a non-natural sense. **1864** PUSEY *Lect. Daniel* 471 When they strive so hard, in non-natural ways, to force other meanings on the words. **1884** LD. SELBORNE in *Law Rep.* 25 Chanc. Div. 688 It is not that the word 'wife' is taken in a non-natural sense.

B. *sb. pl.*

1. *Old Med.* The six things necessary to health, but liable, by abuse or accident, to become the cause of disease, *viz.* air, meat and drink, sleep and waking, motion and rest, excretion and retention, the affections of the mind.

1708 WAINEWRIGHT (*title*), A Mechanical Account of the Non-Naturals: Being a Brief Explication Of the Changes made in Humane Bodies, by Air, Diet, &c. **1725** ROBINSON *The. Physick & Dis.* 71 None of the Evacuations will be irregular, if the Air, our Aliment, or some other of the Non-naturals do not disaffect 'em. **1788** COWPER *Let.* in *Priv. Corr.* (1824) II. 144, I rather suspect that you do not allow yourself sufficient air and exercise. The physicians call them non-naturals, I suppose to deter their patients from the use of them. **1826** SCOTT *Diary* 9 June in *Lockhart*, Slept well last night. By the way, how intolerably selfish this Journal makes me seem—so much attention to one's naturals and non-naturals! **1833** *Cycl. Pract. Med.* I. 597/2 On the relations of diet to the non-naturals.

2. The department of study concerned with non-natural objects. *rare.*

1874 M. ARNOLD in *Contemp. Rev.* Oct. 818 If any science is likely to be able to demonstrate to us the magnified and non-natural man, it must be the science of non-naturals.

Hence **non-natu'rality, non-'naturalness**, the condition of being non-natural.

1802–12 BENTHAM *Ration. Judic. Evid.* (1827) III. 55 He denied some of the facts by which the non-naturality of the death was indicated. **1878** *N. Amer. Rev.* CXXVII. 330 The non-naturalness of the thought.

non-'naturalism. [NON- 1.] **1.** Non-natural style; also, a non-natural feature or characteristic.

1895 SAINTSBURY in *Academy* 29 June 541/3 Non-naturalisms and over-embroideries in style. **1895** *Blackw. Mag.* Feb. 175 The.. non-naturalism of 'les deux Goncourt'.

2. *Philos.* A theory of ethics which opposes naturalism; intuitionalism in ethics.

1939 *Mind* XLVIII. 464 The practitioners of a certain kind of ethical theory, which is dominant in England and capably represented in America, and which is variously called objectivism, non-naturalism, or intuitionism, have frequently charged their opponents with committing the naturalistic fallacy.

non-'naturalist, *a.* and *sb.* [NON- 4.]

A. Used *attrib.* or *adj.* **a.** Not versed in, or disposed to the study of, Natural History.

1858 DARWIN in *Life & Lett.* (1887) II. 138 Being quizzed by my non-naturalist relations. **1873** TAYLOR *Half-hours in Green Lanes* 2 The most non-naturalist of pedestrians.

b. *Philos.* Of or pertaining to non-naturalism.

1966 *Amer. Philos. Q.* III. 299/2 Such a derivation, if valid, might be.. a counter-example to the non-naturalist thesis.

B. *sb.* [NON- 2.] *Philos.* An adherent of non-naturalism.

1939 *Mind* XLVIII. 5 It is not indeed the only sense of good which the non-naturalist will hold incapable of reduction to naturalistic terms. **1966** *Amer. Philos. Q.* III. 305/2 Both non-naturalists and their critics seem to be seriously mistaken.

Hence **non-natura'listic** *a.*; **non-natura'listically** *adv.*

1902 W. JAMES *Var. Relig. Exper.* vi. 143 Brahmans, Buddhists, Christians, Mohammedans, twice-born people whose religion is non-naturalistic. **1939** W. D. ROSS *Foundations of Ethics* i. 6 If you define 'good' as meaning 'such that it *ought* to be desired', you are putting forward a non-naturalistic definition. Consequence theories also may be either naturalistic or non-naturalistic. **1940** *Mind* XLIX. 228 In the Introduction Ross divides attempted definitions of ethical terms into 'attitudes-theories' and 'consequence-theories', and then sub-divides each of these into a naturalistic and a non-naturalistic sub-class. **1952** *Mind* LXI. 544 Any moral system is taken to be grounded non-naturalistically which is deduced from principles held to be certain and inviolable.

nonne, obs. form of NUN.

non-ne'cessity. [NON- 1.] The condition of being unnecessary; absence of necessity.

1594 HOOKER *Eccl. Pol.* Pref. ii. §9 Beza most truly maintaining the necessitie of excommunication, Erastus as truly the non-necessitie of lay elders to be ministers thereof. *c* **1661** *Papers on Alter. Prayer-Bk.* 103 The Common-Prayer-Book plainly speaks of the non-necessity of Unction. **1802–12** BENTHAM *Ration. Judic. Evid.* (1827) III. 388 An attempt to prove supposes the necessity of proof, and assumption supposes the non-necessity of proof. **1880** BARWELL *Aneurism* 59 *note*, The non-necessity of tying soluble ligatures tight enough to cut through the outer and middle coat.

nonnerie, -ye, obs. forms of NUNNERY.

non-net, *a.* [NON- 3.] Of a book: not subject to the normal conditions of sale of net books.

1939 in F. D. Sanders *Brit. Bk. Trade Organisation* 79 The sale of books published at non-net prices is not covered by the terms of the Net Book Agreement. **1951** B. N. LANGDON-DAVIES *Practice of Bookselling* ii. 21 In respect of non-net books the only condition is that the bookseller may not sell them at less than the price he gave for them. **1963** 'R. FINDLATER' *What are Writers Worth?* 11 'Non-net' books are mainly educational ones, sold in bulk for use in schools by contractors rather than through the bookshops. **1972** *Bookseller* 2 Dec. 2545/2 Many of them [*sc.* textbooks] will be non-net, and not have prices printed on them.

non-New'tonian, *a.* [NON- 3.] Not Newtonian, in sense 1 of the adj.; used esp. in connection with the flow of fluids (see quot. 1937).

1913 *Phil. Mag.* XXV. 157 The Einstein transformation equations, and the other principles of non-Newtonian mechanics. **1937** *Rep. Progress Physics* III. 22 It is rather with impure liquids, semi-liquids and semi-solids, that we have to deal in every-day life. Of these a large proportion may be described as 'non-Newtonian', i.e. the rate of shear is not proportional to the shearing stress, and they do not obey Poiseuille's or Stokes's law. **1943** *Amer. Speech* XVIII. 220 We are.. on the threshold, he says, of a third stage: the 'non-aristotelian', non-Euclidean, non-Newtonian stage. The complete revolution Einstein has produced in physics is only part of a general revolution that must eventually affect all human knowledge. **1946** *Nature* 17 Aug. 245/1 The measurement of viscosity of non-Newtonian liquids. **1971** *Biorheology* VIII. 79 The 'overall vicosity'.. exhibited non-Newtonian behavior.

‖**non nobis** (nɒn 'nəʊbɪs). The first words of the psalm (cxv in the English versions, part of cxiii in the Vulgate) beginning *Non nobis, Domine, non nobis* 'Not unto us, O Lord, not unto us', used as an expression of humble gratitude or thanksgiving for mercies vouchsafed.

c **1475** *Mankind* 480 in *Macro Plays* 18 'No[n] nobis, domine; non nobis', by sent Deny! **1599** SHAKS. *Hen. V*, IV. viii. 128 Let there be sung *Non nobis*, and *Te Deum*, The dead with charitie enclos'd in Clay. **1814** COLERIDGE *Unpubl. Lett. to J. P. Estlin* 86 (Stanf.), For ourselves we hold it sufficient to say: *Non nobis*! **1838** D. JERROLD *Men of Char., J. Applejohn* v, 'After dinner, we must have—humph! —what d'ye call it?' whispered Benjamin. '*Non nobis*', replied Oldjoe. *a* **1845** HOOD *Public Dinner* 22 Then silence is wanted, Non Nobis is chanted.

non-'normal, *a.* [NON- 3.] Not normal; *spec.* in *Statistics* (cf. NORMAL *a.* and *sb.* A. 2 e).

1929 *Biometrika* XXI. 124 (*heading*) On the distribution of the ratio of mean to standard deviation in small samples from non-normal universes. **1966** *English Studies* XLVII. 194 In this last phrase [*sc.* 'Mallice domestique'] the contrasting adjective 'domestique', given emphasis by its non-normal position, brings into full prominence the 'hatred' which the noun contains. **1968** P. A. P. MORAN *Introd. Probability Theory* vii. 300 The distributions.. converge to a proper distribution, $F(x)$, which can be chosen to be non-normal if the theorem is false. **1973** J. J. ZEMAN *Modal Logic* ix. 146 The PC connectives behave in non-normal worlds precisely as they do in normal ones.

So ˌ**non-nor'mality**, the property or state of being non-normal.

1935 *Proc. Cambr. Philos. Soc.* XXXI. 230 The test of significance of a correlation coefficient has been shown.. to be little vitiated by non-normality. **1962** E. S. KEEPING *Introd. Statistical Inference* viii. 208 If there is reason to suspect non-normality, from the nature of the data, it is advisable to try a transformation. The logarithm of the variate, or the square root,.. may be more nearly normal. **1968** *Brit. Med. Bull.* XXIV. 212/1 The emphasis placed so far on non-Normality is somewhat misleading, in that other kinds of departure from the usual statistical model are often more important.

non-'nuclear, *a.* [NON- 3.] That is not nuclear (in various senses); *spec.* not possessing nuclear weapons; esp. in ***non-nuclear club***, a group of nations that agrees not to possess nuclear weapons. Hence as *sb.*, something non-nuclear; *spec.* a nation that has no nuclear weapons.

1920 W. W. STRONG *New Philos. of Mod. Sci.* 103 Present day theories of the atom assume that the positive charge on the nucleus is equal in magnitude to the charge of the non-nuclear or planetary electrons. **1932** H. H. PRICE *Perception* viii. 258 If the sense-datum is a non-nuclear one, we cannot possibly move *towards* it. **1950** *New Biol.* VIII. 20 The unequal distribution of some non-nuclear hereditary substance. **1956** *Bull. Atomic Sci.* June 204/1 The nonnuclear nations may have the feeling that they alone constitute the stakes in the great struggle for world hegemony that the East is waging with the West. **1957** *Ibid.* Sept. 260/2 The U.S. on June 26 also proposed a reduction of nonnuclear weapons. **1959** *Daily Tel.* 6 July 6/2 His [*sc.* Mr. Gaitskell's] promise to try to form a non-nuclear club under British leadership. **1961** Y. OLSSON *Syntax Eng. Verb* vi. 95 The most restricted collocability gives the nucleus and the most general collocability gives the non-nuclear elements. *Ibid.* 127 The N^v-expansion contains no non-nuclears. **1966** *Economist* 13 Aug. 634/1 Keeping the devices out of non-nuclear hands (and sight), but providing the service at a much lower cost than the non-nuclears would face. **1967** *Observer* 26 Feb. 10/6 The current leader of the non-nuclear club is Germany. **1968** MRS. L. B. JOHNSON *White House Diary* 1 July (1970) 692 The United States, Great Britain, and the Soviet Union, as well as fifty-eight non-nuclear nations, signed the Treaty.

nonny bag, var. NUNNY-BAG.

† **nonny-no.** *Obs.* Also 6–7 **nonino**, 7 **nonne-, nonni-no.**

1. Used as a refrain, like NONNY-NONNY.

1593 DRAYTON *Ecl.* iii. C 3 These noninos of filthie ribauldry. **1600** SHAKS. *A. Y. L.* v. iii. *song*, With a hey, and a ho, and a hey nonino. *a* **1650** *Percy Folio MS.*, Loose & Hum. Songs (1867) 58 Cupid bidds itt shold bee soe, Because all men were made for her hynonino.

2. A trifle, bagatelle.

1681 HICKERINGILL *Black Non-Conf.* Introd. (1682) A 2, I was not so soon Thunderstrook with Excommunication for a Nonne-no, but I was sooner Absolv'd. **1682** *Ibid.* xvi. 48, I lost my time, detain'd for a Nonni-no above a Fortnight at London.

nonny-nonny ('nɒnɪ'nɒnɪ). *Obs.* exc. *arch.* Also 6 **noney nony.** A meaningless refrain, formerly often used to cover indelicate allusions.

1533 J. HEYWOOD *Play of the Wether* (Brandl) 1041 Gyue boys wether, quoth a nonny, nonny. *a* **1540**, **1599** [see HEY 2]. **1553** *Respublica* III. vi, *Cantent*, Hey noney nony houghe for money. **1602** SHAKS. *Ham.* IV. v. 165 Hey non nony, nony, hey nony. **1605** —— *Lear* III. iv. 103. *a* **1625** FLETCHER *Hum. Lieut.* IV. iv, That noble mind to melt and moulder For a hey-nonny-nonny. **1823** PRAED *Lillian* 12 Nonny Nonny!—who shall tell Where the Summer breezes dwell? **1832** L. HUNT *Poems* 182 Ah little ranting Johnny, For ever blithe and bonny, And singing nonny, nonny.

no-no ('nəʊnəʊ). *colloq.* (orig. *U.S.*). [Redupl. NO *sb.*] Something that must not be done, used, etc.; something that is forbidden, impossible, or not acceptable; a failure.

1942 BERREY & VAN DEN BARK *Amer. Thes. Slang* §310/1 *No-no*,.. something that should not be done. **1968** *Washington Post* 30 Sept. A. 20/2 What she was doing was a no-no, the protectors of our health announced... She must stop baking things for sale. **1970** *Islander* (Victoria, B.C.) 25 Oct. 16/3 Colonial Secretary Young at Victoria had to remind them that the Admiralty timber reserve was a 'no-no'. **1972** *New Yorker* 17 June 29/1 Our people in Accounting tell me that cash payments are a no-no. **1972** *Observer* 17 Sept. 34/8 *Nationwide*.. has my strict instructions never to touch the subject of rock music again: its piece on Bob Dylan was a total no-no. **1975** *Sunday Advocate-News* (Barbados) 15 June 3/1 Plants that require a great deal of moisture are no-noes unless you have your own well.

non-o'bedience. [NON- 1.] Neglect of obedience; failure to obey.

1582 *Reg. Privy Council Scot.* III. 469 For allegit non-obedience thairof. **1650** A. A[SCHAM] *Reply to Sanderson* 10 Non-obedience can expect nothing but non-protection. **1847** WEBSTER (citing MILNER). **1884** *Law Rep.* 9 Prob. Div. 52 The petitioner asked for an attachment against the respondent for such non-obedience.

So † **non-o'beisance**, in the same sense.

1447 *Shillingford Lett.* (Camden) 134 That for the nonn-obeisaunce therof thei be putte in no vexacon, hurt, trouble ne losse. **1567** *Reg. Privy Council Scot.* I. 577 For his non obeysance of the command.

non-object. **1.** [NON- 2.] **a.** Something which is not a material body.

1914 C. D. BROAD *Perception* i. 8 We must accept the possibility of real non-objects, though there cannot be apparent non-objects.

b. The condition of not being a grammatical object.

1964 E. A. NIDA *Toward Sci. Transl.* v. 109 Semantic markers are primarily of two types: (1) those which mark positive-negative dichotomies, e.g. nonobject vs. object and verbal vs. nonverbal.

2. *attrib.* [NON- 4.] **a.** Not corporeal. **b.** Not functioning as grammatical object.

1963 F. T. VISSER *Hist. Syntax of Eng. Lang.* I. iv. 429 For its [*sc.* 'the self's'] use in non-object relations see 1959 Carstensen p. 226. **1971** *Gloss. Electrotechnical, Power Terms (B.S.I.)* IV. ii. 9 *Non-object (perceived) colour*, colour perceived as non-located in depth, such as that perceived as filling a hole in a screen.

non-ob'jective, *a.* [NON- 3.] Not objective; *spec.* in art = ABSTRACT A. 4d. Hence **non-ob'jectivism, non-ob'jectivist, non-objec'tivity.**

1905 W. JAMES in *Jrnl Philos., Psychol. & Sci. Methods* II. 286 That..is enough to save them from being classed as absolutely non-objective. **1936** *Amer. Mag. of Art* Mar. 154 (*heading*) Non-objectivity at Charleston. **1936** *Design* June 13 (*heading*) Definition of non-objective painting. **1937** H. READ *Art & Society* vii. 260 A heightened sensibility to the purity of form..can best be induced and refined by the creation and appreciation of non-objective works of art. **1946** D. D. RUNES *Encycl. Arts* 680/1 The non-objectivist used his medium, line and color..to create freely following his intuition. **1952** *Time* 16 June 61 He enjoys swimming against the current of non-objectivism. **1958** *Times* 24 Nov. (Canada Suppl.) p. xvi/6 In our contracting world few countries can escape the impact of the international artistic trend towards non-objectivity. **1959** *Listener* 3 Dec. 980/2 The non-objectivist Alexander Rodchenko painted three canvases, one red, one blue, one yellow, and announced 'the death of art'. **1960** E. H. GOMBRICH *Art & Illusion* viii. 286 Even nonobjective art derives some of its meaning and effects from the habits and mental sets we acquired in learning to read representations. **1962** J. SÖDERLIND in F. Behre *Contrib. Eng. Syntax* 110 Non-objective *of*-groups offer some difficulties.

†**non-'obstant,** *prep.* (*conj.*) *Obs.* [a. OF. *nonobstant* (from 14th c.), repr. L. *non obstante*: see next.] Notwithstanding.

c **1400** *Beryn* 2467 Non-obstant his drede, yet part of sapience Stremyd in-to his hert. **15..** *Aberd. Reg.* (Jam.), Non obstant that [etc.]. **1591** J. ELIOT tr. *De Loque's Disc. Warre* 7 This is to be vnderstod of the true Church, *non-obstant* the abuse vsed vnder the popish empire.

‖**non-obstante** (nɒnɒb'stænti:). [mod.L. = *nōn* not + *obstante* (abl. sing. of pres. pple. of *obstāre* to be in the way), orig. agreeing with a sb. in the abl. absol. const., e.g. *non obstante veredicto* 'the verdict being no hindrance', 'notwithstanding the verdict'.]

†**1.** as *adv.* or *prep.* Notwithstanding. *Obs.*

non upstant in Ben Jonson's *Gipsies Metam.* Wks. (1641) 67 is prob. intended as an ignorant corruption of this word.

1646 HAMMOND *Wks.* (1674) I. 254 That men were then saved *non obstante* this want of greater light. **1653** COLLINGES *Caveat for Prof.* 138 If..the Church did enjoyn it (possibly) it might be observed, this exception *Non obstante*.

2. as *sb.* (*Law.*) The first two words of a clause formerly used in statutes and letters patent, which conveyed a licence from the sovereign to do a thing notwithstanding any statute to the contrary (*non obstante aliquo statuto in contrarium*); hence (in full, *clause of non-obstante*), a clause of this nature. Now *Hist.*

In England this form of dispensation was first used by Henry III in his charters (see 2b, quot. 1669); it was abolished by the Bill of Rights.

1444 *Rolls of Parlt.* V. 104/2 No patent of the seide offices ..to be made, all be it yat yei be with this clause non obstante. **1601** SIR G. MOORE *Sp.* in Townsend *Hist. Collect.* (1680) 234 Admit we should make the Statute with a non Obstante; yet the Queen may grant a Patent with a non Obstante to cross this non Obstante. **1628** COKE *On Litt.* 99a, When he [the King] licenceth expressly to alien an Abbot, &c. which is in Mortmaine, he needs not make any *non obstante* of the Statutes of Mortmaine. **1642** C. VERNON *Consid. Exch.* 62 The Non-obstantes in the Leases of Recusants lands. **1668** *Ormonde MSS.* in *10th Rep. Hist. MSS. Comm.* App. V. 65 To draw up..a pardon..and to insert therein all such clauses and *non-obstantes* as in like cases are usual. **1686** LUTTRELL *Brief Rel.* (1857) I. 380 The King's power of dispensing with all penall lawes by a clause of non obstante. **1688** *Act I Will. & Mary* c. 2 §52 That.. after this present Session of Parlyament noe dispensation by Non obstante of or to any Statute..shall be allowed. **1744** NORTH *Life Dudley North* 184 What should hinder the great Seal from sending forth Commissions,..with *non obstante's* in the Body of them, against the Test Laws?

attrib. **1810** A. LUDERS *Tracts* v. 334 In the next year (1251) the King..executed his design of imitating the Pope by a *nonobstante* grant. *Ibid.* 338 The *nonobstante* clause was not long confined to one statute or to one branch of the royal prerogative.

b. With reference to papal use.

1625 PURCHAS *Pilgrims* II. VIII. vi. §3. 1257 But what is this to the Popes *Non obstante*? a plenitude of power to dispense with Oathes, Vowes, and whatsoeuer Diuine or Humane, standing in the way of his Monarchie? **1669** PRYNNE *Animadv. Fourth Pt. Inst.* 132 King Henry the 3, though he at first detested..these..*Non-obstantes* in Popes Bulls..yet at last he began to imitate them. **1726-31** TINDAL tr. *Rapin's Hist. Eng.* (1743) I. 527/1 It was a mortal blow to the court of Rome, to whom the clause of *Non-obstante*, so frequently used by the Popes, became fruitless, at least with regard to the collation of benefices.

†**3.** *transf.* and *gen.* **a.** A dispensation from or relaxation of a law or rule. Const. *on*, *of*, *to*. **b.** An exception to a rule. *Obs.*

1604 JAS. I in *Egerton Papers* (Camden) 397 Some warrant ..wherein there may be some words inserted with a *non obstante* of this our absolute restraint. *a* **1631** DONNE *Poems* (1654) 28, I do not sue from thee to draw A Non obstante on natures law. **1678** T. JONES *Heart & its Soveraign* 498 A God devoid of all Divine Attributes..so shamefully mash'd with contradictions, and *non-obstante's*. **1720** S. PARKER *Biblioth. Bibl.* I. 264 The Rule deliver'd down to us from the Beginning with our *Non obstantes* and Notwithstandings. **1742** NORTH *Lives of Norths* 45 The Chief Justice..would not break a Law with a *Non obstante*.

†**c.** *with a non-obstante to*: notwithstanding.

1659 SOUTH *Serm.* (1727) I. 88 These Words import the Hindrance of the Duty enjoyned; which therefore is here purposely enforced with a *Non-obstante* to all Opposition. **1667** *Ibid.* II. 37 With a *non obstante* to all their Revels, their Profaneness, and scandalous Debaucheries of all sorts, they continue Virtuoso's still. **1710** *Chuse which you Please* 2 These Men allow of a Mental Reservation, with a *Non Obstante* to their express Oath to the contrary thereunto.

nonoic (nəʊ'nəʊɪk), *a.* *Chem.* [f. L. *nōn-us* ninth, after *octoic*.] The ninth in the series of fatty acids.

1891 THORPE *Dict. Appl. Chem.* II. 100.

no-'nonsense, *a.* [The phr. *no nonsense* (NONSENSE *sb.* 1c) used as an adj.] That does not tolerate foolish or extravagant conduct; sensible, business-like, realistic, practical.

1928 *Sat. Even. Post* 12 May 25/1 From a no-nonsense business man he has become a romantic. **1943** J. B. PRIESTLEY *Daylight on Saturday* xiii. 92 Her own breezy, no-nonsense line. **1957** *Observer* 27 Oct. 16/3 The tunes are vigorous no-nonsense affairs. **1959** W. MCGIVERN *Savage Streets* (1960) i. 7 A blunt, no-nonsense sort of person. **1963** [see *go-anywhere* adj. s.v. GO *v.* VIII]. **1973** J. WAINWRIGHT *Pride of Pigs* 113 Its bare-brick walls were painted white. Its floor was no-nonsense concrete.

†**non-or'ganical,** *a.* *Old Anat.* [NON- 3.] (See quots.)

1682 GIBSON *Anat.* 4 A non-organical part is that which has only an use, and no action. **1704** J. HARRIS *Lex. Techn.* I, *Non-Organical Part* of an Animal,..as a Gristle, Bone, Foot, &c.

non-'orientable, *a.* *Math.* [NON- 3.] Of a surface: such that a figure in the surface can be continuously transformed into its mirror image by taking it round a closed path in the surface; not orientable.

1949 S. LEFSCHETZ *Introd. Topology* ii. 76 The combination of the first type is called nonorientable. **1952** P. NEMENYI tr. *Hilbert & Cohn-Vossen's Geom. & Imagination* vi. 306 The classification of surfaces into two-sided and one-sided surfaces is identical with the classification into orientable and non-orientable. *Ibid.*, A surface is non-orientable if and only if there exists on the surface some closed curve *s* which is such that a small oriented circle whose center traverses the curve continuously will arrive at its starting point with its orientation reversed. **1965** S. BARR *Exper. Topology* ii. 22 The Moebius strip is what is called non-orientable—which is less open to misinterpretation than saying it is 1-sided.

Hence ˌ**non-orienta'bility,** the property of being non-orientable.

1949 S. LEFSCHETZ *Introd. Topology* ii. 83 A closed surface ..is completely characterized by the value of its Betti number..and by its orientability or nonorientability. **1964** H. LEVY *Projective & Related Geometries* v. 38 We shall derive two properties of L_2 that are strongly suggestive of its nonorientability.

nonose ('nəʊnəʊs, -z). *Chem.* [a. G. *nonose* (E. Fischer 1890, in *Ber. d. Deut. Chem. Ges.* XXIII. 934): see NONA- and -OSE[2].] Any monosaccharide having nine carbon atoms in the molecule, esp. when these are all in an unbranched chain.

1890 *Jrnl. Chem. Soc.* LVIII. 1234 (*table*) Nonose. **1915** *Jrnl. Biol. Chem.* XXIII. 327 When it was found later that the glucon준nose was not fermentable, the configurations of the two nonoses became of great interest. **1945** *Adv. Carbohydrate Chem.* I. 7 Distinctly different nonoses were obtained in the two researches by the reduction of the respective lactones. **1972** BRIMACOMBE & WEBBER in Pigman & Horton *Carbohydrates* (ed. 2) IA. xiv. 497 Extension of the cyanohydrin synthesis to this nonose have a decitol.

non-paid. [NON- 6.] A letter that has not been prepaid.

1829 LAMB *Lett.* (1837) II. 236 Three two penny post non-paids in a week.

†**non-parallel.** *nonce-wd.* Alteration of NONPAREIL.

1641 R. BRATHWAIT *Eng. Gentlewoman* 350 Art thou persuaded that this non-parallel thou thus affectest hath dedicated his service only to thee?

non-para'metric, *a.* *Statistics.* [NON- 3.] Not involving any assumptions as to the form or parameters of a frequency distribution.

1942 J. WOLFOWITZ in *Ann. Math. Statistics* XIII. 264 Most of these developments have this feature in common, that the distribution functions of the various stochastic variables which enter into their problems are assumed to be of known functional form, and the theories of estimation and of testing hypotheses are theories of estimation of and of testing hypotheses about, one or more parameters..the knowledge of which would completely determine the various distribution functions involved. We shall refer to this situation..as the parametric case, and denote the opposite case, where the functional forms of the distributions are unknown, as the non-parametric case. **1956** S. SIEGEL (*title*) Nonparametric statistics for the behavioral sciences. **1957** KENDALL & BUCKLAND *Dict. Statistical Terms* 87 Distribution-free inference or distribution-free tests are sometimes known as nonparametric but this usage is confusing and should be avoided. It is better to confine the word 'non-parametric' to the description of hypotheses which do not explicitly make an assertion about a parameter. **1962** E. S. KEEPING *Introd. Statistical Inference* x. 251 Non-parametric tests are generally simple to apply... In those cases where a parametric test would also be applicable a non-parametric test will naturally be less powerful than the parametric one. **1966** *Lancet* 31 Dec. 1434/1 To avoid making assumptions concerning normality and homogeneity, the non-parametric one-way analysis [of] variance by ranks..was carried out. **1972** *Jrnl. Social Psychol.* LXXXVIII. 204, I have typically used a nonparametric correlation to illustrate the association between awareness and experimental performance.

nonpareil (nɒnpə'rɛl), *a.* and *sb.* Forms: 5 nonparaille, 6 -parreille, 6–7 -parel(e, 6–8 -pareill(e, 7 -paril, -parell, -peril(l, -perel, 7, 9 -pariel, 6– non(-)pareil. *β.* 6 **nompareille**, 7 **-parell**, **numparell** (9 **numparel**). (See also B. 1b.) [a. F. *nonpareil*, †*nompareil*: see NON- and PAREIL *a.* and *sb.*]

A. *adj.* Having no equal; unequalled, peerless.

1477 CAXTON *Jason* 32b, O right noble and nonparaille Myrro, she is without peer. **1594** GREENE & LODGE *Looking Gl.* G.'s Wks. (Rtldg.) 117 Beauty nonpareil in excellence. **1645** TOMBES *Anthropol.* 8 Some magnified Peter, as non-paril. **1654** WHITLOCK *Zootomia* 204 The most *Non-pareille* Beauty of the World, Beauteous Knowledge. **1730** (*title*) A Treatise of Buggs..By John Southall, Maker of the Non-pareil Liquor for destroying Buggs and Nits. **1818** *Amer. Monthly Mag.* III. 181/2 Now for a picture of the *non-pareil* De Courcy—this Adonis, Apollo, and Hercules of eighteen. **1834** SOUTHEY *Doctor* I. 70 A truth which..will be.. elucidated in this nonpareil history. **1893** F. ADAMS *New Egypt* 211 The great and famous nonpareil champion.

B. *sb.* **1.** A person or thing having no equal; something unique.

1593 NASHE *Four Lett. Confuted* Wks. (Grosart) II. 265 Euermore maist thou be canonized as the Nonparreille of impious epistlers. **1596** LAMBARDE *Peramb. Kent* 349 [Name of a ship] Non Pareille. **1599** *Broughton's Let.* vii. 24 You accompt your selfe the *Non parel* for knowledge. **1601** SHAKS. *Twel. N.* I. v. 273 Though you were crown'd The non-pareil of beautie. **1612** CAPT. SMITH *Virginia* I. Wks. (Arb.) 169 Pocahontas, Powhatans daughter..was the very Nomparell of his kingdome, and at most not past 13 or 14 yeares of age. **1748** HARTLEY *Observ. Man* II. iii. §4. 267 That Tendency which Every Man has to think himself a Non-pareil. **1768–74** TUCKER *Lt. Nat.* (1834) II. 615 People are apt to think their children nonpareils, the sole object deserving admiration and regard. **1817** MAR. EDGEWORTH *Ormond* xxii, Miss Annaly, who was to have been a non-pareil of an heiress in case of the brother's death, will have but a moderate fortune. **1887** STEDMAN *Vict. Poets* (ed. 13) v. 162 'The Talking Oak',..the nonpareil of sustained lyrics in quatrain verse.

b. In quasi-It. forms **nonpareillo, -parella.**

1672 VILLIERS (Dk. Buckhm.) *Rehearsal* I. (Arb.) 41, I think you'l say this is a *non pareillo*: I'm sure no body has hit upon it yet. **1673** [R. LEIGH] *Transp. Reh.* 7 To all these Reasons, our Farce-monger might have added another, which is a *non pareillo*. **1687** PRIOR & HALIFAX *Hind & P. transv.* P.'s Wks. 1892 II. 319 I'le be bold to say, the exactest piece the world ever saw, a *non pareillo*, I' faith. **1899** *Atlantic Monthly* June 728/2 A nonparella of all grace and beauty!

2. *Printing.* A size of type intermediate between emerald and ruby (in America, between minion and agate). †Also as *adj.* (following the sb.) = Printed in nonpareil. (Cf. F. *nonpareille*.)

1647 *Pref. Verses* in Lilly *Chr. Astrol.*, Heaven is his book; The Stars both great & smal Are letters Nonperill and Capitall Disperst throughout. **1683** MOXON *Mech. Exerc.*, *Printing* ii. ¶2 Letter of all Bodies..viz. Pearl, Nonparel, Brevier. **1686** *Lond. Gaz.* No. 2109/4 The Bible Nonperil, in Twelves. **1825** HANSARD *Typogr.* 382 Ruby..was.. originally a Nonpareil with short ascenders and descenders, cast on a smaller body.

attrib. **1824** J. JOHNSON *Typogr.* II. 72 Unless Nonpareil figures can be conveniently had. *Ibid.* 84 The founders.. cast one sized type upon another body: *viz.* a Nonpareil face on a Minion body, and a Minion on a Nonpareil.

3. A kind of comfit. (Cf. F. *nonpareille*.)

1697 *C'tess D'Aunoy's Trav.* (1706) 250 Certain little Comfits, which in France we call Non-pareil. **1712** tr. *Pomet's Hist. Drugs* I. 56 Nonpareille, which is nothing but Orrice-Powder cover'd with Sugar. **1747–96** MRS. GLASSE *Cookery* xxi. 328 Strew different coloured nonpareils over it. **1821** LAMB *Elia* I. *My first play*, I remember the waiting at the door..with the cry of nonpareils, an indispensable play-house accompaniment in those days... The fashionable pronunciation of the theatrical fruiteresses then was, ..'Chase..some numparels'..—chase *pro* chuse. **1843** PEREIRA *Food & Diet* 120 Sugar constitutes the base of an almost innumerable variety of hard confectionary, sold under the names of Lozenges, Brilliants, Pipe, Rock, Comfits, Nonpareils. **1862** FRANCATELLI *Confectioner* 327.

4. A kind of apple. (Cf. F. *nonpareille*.)

1731 MILLER *Gard. Dict.* s.v. *Apple Tree*,..Nonpareil. **1761** *Phil. Trans.* LII. 73 Non-pareil apple-trees. **1783** JOHNSON in *Boswell* 18 Apr., Sir, you can no more have nonpareils than you can have grapes. **1821** MRS. SHELLEY in Dowden *Life Shelley* (1886) II. 366 He produces something as like Dante as a rotten crab-apple like a fine non-pareil. **1834** *Penny Cycl.* II. 190/1 Braddick's nonpareil. Old nonpareil. **1866** *Treas. Bot.* 945/2 Scarlet Nonpareil.

attrib. **1839** LINDLEY *Introd. Bot.* II. xiii. 389 A nonpareil branch 2 feet long.

5. a. A small beautifully coloured finch of the southern United States, *Cyanospiza* (*Emberiza*) *ciris*. **b.** The rose parrakeet, *Platycerus eximius*. (Cf. F. *nonpareil, nonpareille.*)

1758 G. EDWARDS *Gleanings* I. 132 The Painted Finch.., more generally known to the curious in London by the name of Nonpareil and Mariposa. **1853** GOULDING *Young Marooners* xxxvi, A nonpareil, hidden in the branches, sat whistling plaintively to its mate. **1895** *Outing* XXVI. 70/2 Cane-brakes gay with cardinals and nonpareils.

6. A kind of wheat.

1805 DICKSON *Pract. Agric.* I. 540 The nonpareil is a sort said to be brought into this country from America; it has a bright straw with a brown ear; and the grain is very white.

7. A name for several beautiful moths.

1819 SAMOUELLE *Entom. Compend.* 422 The Nonpareil, *Noctua sponsa.* **1832** RENNIE *Butterfl. & Moths* 206 The Nonpareil (*Œcophora eximia*, Stephens). A most beautiful species. **1875** HOUGHTON *Brit. Insects* 88 The splendid Clifden Nonpareil (*Catocala fraxini*).

non-parti'san, *a.* [NON- 3.] Not partisan. Also as *sb.*, one who is not a partisan. Hence **non-parti'sanship**.

1885 *Century Mag.* Apr. 823 A citizens' ticket, largely non-partisan in character, was run for certain local offices. **1888** *Voice* 9 Feb., The non-partisans have for some time been making Mr. Johnson's position very uncomfortable for him. **1888** G. H. CARROW (*title*) Non-partisanship; or, do not take temperance into politics. **1932** *Times Lit. Suppl.* 11 Feb. 95/4 Critical, non-partisan, and bright in style, this book is a veritable compendium of the theories, claims, and actual achievements of psychology. **1952** G. SARTON *Hist. Sci.* I. xii. 319 His nonpartisanship, objectivity, and honesty. **1957** *Economist* 7 Sept. 850/2 For most of the time, he has put on a determined show of nonpartisanship. **1964** *Ann. Reg. 1963* 215 The latter..dealt in a relatively non-partisan spirit with contemporary Western culture. **1974** *Nature* 25 Jan. 169/1 The inferior quality of the recent Commons debate on the fuel shortage does not bode well for informed non-partisan discussions.

†**non-pass.** *Backgammon.* [NON- 1.]

1688 HOLME *Armoury* III. xvi. (Roxb.) 64/1 A nonpasse, is when the adverse men are so set that you cannot passe with your man or men till he giue you liberty.

non-passive, *a.* and *sb. Gram.* [NON- 3, 2.]

A. *adj.* Not in the passive voice.

1962 C. L. BARBER in F. Behre *Contrib. Eng. Syntax* 26 Of these [finite verbs], 28% are passive, and 72% non-passive. **1963** F. T. VISSER *Hist. Syntax of Eng. Lang.* I. iv. 562 In the non-passive construction the predicative adjunct is usually preceded by *for*: 'Hig hæfdon hyne for ænne witegan'. **1965** *Language* XLI. 107 The non-passive aorist in Greek.

B. *sb.* A construction not in the passive voice.

1962 C. L. BARBER in F. Behre *Contrib. Eng. Syntax* 27 A much smaller number of passives—only 3%, against 97% non-passives.

non-past. *Gram.* [NON- 2.] A tense that is not the past tense; usually, the present tense, or the present and future tenses. Also *attrib.* or as *adj.*

1946 *Language* XXII. 213 The non-past indicative of the copula, *dá*, is replaced by a zero alternant (i.e. drops out). **1951** TRAGER & SMITH *Outl. Eng. Structure* II. 60 Verbs are inflected for 3D Person SG. Non-past, Past, Past Participle, Present Participle. **1962** S. E. MARTIN in Householder & Saporta *Problems in Lexicography* 157 In many parts of the world, verbs are usually entered under the plain present (or non-past) form. **1966** *Amer. Speech* XLI. 201 The present, which many structuralists have preferred to call the 'nonpast'. **1971** *Achivum Linguisticum* II. 25 It is important to notice that [in Classical Latin] both potential and unreal conditions could refer to past and to non-past time. *Ibid.* 27 It is possible to visualize, in Old Spanish, the maintenance of the category of 'non-past, unreal', a category which.. existed in Latin. **1972** *Language* XLVIII. 473 One feature of emphatic transformations from verbal bases is the replacement of the verb form of the base clause by an emphatic form; this is a special form in the non-past or past corresponding to the simple forms in the same tenses.

†**non-patience.** *Obs.* [NON- 1.] Alleged term for a 'company' of wives.

1486 *Bk. St. Albans* f vj, A Noonpaciens of wyues.

non-'patrial, *sb.* and *a.* [NON- 2, 4 + PATRIAL *a.* (*sb.*) 3.] **A.** *sb.* One who is not a patrial. **B.** *adj.* Applied to a person who is not a patrial.

The 1971 Immigration Act does not use the term 'non-patrial'.

1971 *Telegraph* (Brisbane) 25 Jan. 5/3 Under the Government's new Immigration Act, everyone who regards himself as a UK citizen is to be defined as a 'patrial' or 'non-patrial'. **1971** *Daily Tel.* 11 Oct. 1/5 The Police Federation asked the Government four months ago to drop the proposal in the Bill for 'non-patrial' Commonwealth citizens to register with and report to the police, as aliens do. **1972** *Guardian* 25 Nov. 10/2 A non-patrial Commonwealth citizen who wants to work here. **1973** C. MULLARD *Black Britain* II. v. 63 Others—'non-patrials'—do not have an automatic 'right of abode'.

non-'payment. [NON- 1.] Failure or neglect to pay; the condition of not being paid.

c **1447-8** SHILLINGFORD *Lett.* (Camden) 82 The seide wronge of nonpayement of the seide dymes. **1530** RASTELL *Bk. Purgat.* III. iii, The hurte & hynderaunce that I have had for the none payment of the .c. li. **1579-80** NORTH *Plutarch* (1657) 411 This Miltiades,..being condemned by the state to pay the sum of fifty Talents, was for non-payment cast into prison. **1593** SHAKS. *Ven. & Ad.* 521. **1686** PLOT *Staffordsh.* 435 Earle Robert obliging himself upon non paiment, to forfeit all his lands. **1764** *Chron.* in *Ann. Reg.* 100 The non-payment of Canada bills by the French government. **1837** LOCKHART *Life Scott* VI. 106 That if anything should..befall Constable, Sir Walter would suffer a heavier loss than the nonpayment of some one novel. **1901** *Scotsman* 3 Apr. 10/1 He had protested strongly against the non-payment of sums due to Americans.

So **non-'paying** *vbl. sb.*, in the same sense; **non-'paying** *ppl. a.*, that does not pay.

1407 *Waterf. Arch.* in *10th Rep. Hist. MSS. Comm.* App. V. 329 For the nonpaying of the Kings chief rent. **1659** *Burton's Diary* (1828) IV. 412 Their non-paying of the several debts charged upon them. **1877** RAYMOND *Mines & Mining* 347 Much time, labor, and money were thrown away upon non-paying lodes.

non-per'ception. [NON- 1.] Want of perception; failure to perceive.

1692 NORRIS *Curs. Reflect.* 10 Which utterly silences that argument taken from the Non-perception of them in children. **1704** —— *Ideal World* II. iii. 131 The proper defect of the understanding is ignorance or non-perception. **1802-12** BENTHAM *Ration. Judic. Evid.* (1827) V. 645 Misconception or non-perception. **1882** B. NICHOLSON in *Trans. New Shaks. Soc.* (1880-2) 355 Such non-perception of moral responsibility is one of the clearest proofs of madness.

non-per'formance. [NON- 1.] Failure or neglect to perform or fulfil a condition, promise, etc.; the condition of not being performed.

1509-10 *Act 1 Hen. VIII*, c. 19 *Preamble*, For nonperfourmance of the said condicions. **1611** SHAKS. *Wint. T.* I. ii. 261 Fearefull To doe a thing, where I the issue doubted, Whereof the execution did cry out Against the non-performance. **1635** JACKSON *Creed* VIII. vii. 68 His non-performances of what hee often seriously intended. **1727** ARBUTHNOT *John Bull* III. xvii, Exasperated at the Non-performance of John Bull's Promise. **1751** SMOLLETT *Per. Pic.* III. xcii. 284 It would be a meritorious action to put the rascal to the proof, and then toss him in a blanket for non-performance. **1790** *Amer. State Papers* (1833) I. 124 Delay is always a kind of breach, since, as long as it lasts, it is the non-performance of stipulations. **1802-12** BENTHAM *Ration. Judic. Evid.* (1827) II. 306 The performance or non-performance of the ceremony called swearing, or taking an oath. **1845** POLSON *Eng. Law* in *Encycl. Metrop.* II. 831/1 The breach or nonperformance of lawful conditions.

Hence **non-per'former**, one who is guilty of non-performance; **non-per'forming** *vbl. sb.*, failure to perform.

1675 WOODHEAD, etc. *Paraph. S. Paul* 22 With a curse to the non-performers. **1773** SALKELD *Cases King's Bench* III. 374 The Jury found, that the Plaintiff was damnified 10*l.* by the Defendant's Non-performing his Promise.

non-peri'odic, *a.* [NON- 3.] Characterized by or exhibiting a lack of periodicity; without regular recurrence; = APERIODIC *a.*

1843 *Scientific Mem.* III. 221 (*heading*) On the non-periodic variations in the distribution of temperature on the surface of the earth. **1902** *Encycl. Brit.* XXVII. 161/2 The non-periodic comets appearing since 1700 are nearly all in the hands of computers. **1932** W. L. GRAFF *Language & Languages* 17 Many so-called musical tones are nonperiodic. **1965** *Math. in Biol. & Med.* (Med. Res. Council) IV. 141 If the time occupied by one complex cycle is assumed to increase to infinity, then a Fourier Integral..may be developed which describes, again in terms of sines and cosines, the waveform of a transient or nonperiodic function.

'non-person. [NON- 2.] A person who is regarded as nonexistent or unimportant; someone who is ignored, humiliated, or forgotten.

1959 *Times Lit. Suppl.* 2 Oct. 555/3 The belief that all Africans, students and dockers alike, are the same; the notion that they are 'non-persons', with a kind of animal anonymity which relieves whites of their inhibitions. **1965** [see NON-EVENT]. **1968** *Daily Tel.* 7 Nov. 22/4 Pets are in highest demand in the wealthy Protestant West, with all its rejects and 'non-persons'. **1973** R. HAYES *Hungarian Game* xxiii. 145 Neither AVH nor KGB had a watch on Mityas' house. He'd become such a non-person that not even they worried about whom he saw.

non-'personal, *a.* and *sb.* [NON- 3, 2.]

A. *adj.* Not personal. **B.** *sb.* Something that is not personal, or not a person; *spec.* a pronoun representing a non-personal noun.

1902 W. JAMES *Var. Relig. Exper.* xx. 500 The contention of the survival-theory that we ought to stick to non-personal elements exclusively. **1925** GRATTAN & GURREY *Our Living Lang.* 189 With Non-Personals the idea of possession is commonly not present—for example—I have recovered this book and mended *the* (not *its*) back. **1928** O. JESPERSEN *Internat. Lang.* II. 128 If there is an apparatus called in this way, the word belongs to the non-personal class: *telegrafe* (the apparatus), *telegrafa* vb, *telegrafo* telegraphing. **1933** L. BLOOMFIELD *Lang.* ix. 146 *It* has the class-meanings of substantives, singulars, non-personals. *Ibid.* xv. 253 The English definite or third-person pronouns..differ.., in the singular, for *personal* and *non-personal* antecedents: personal *he, she*, versus non-personal *it*. **1957** R. W. ZANDVOORT *Handbk. Eng. Gram.* IX. ii. 315 The addition of *-ish* to other personal nouns: *boyish, girlish* (= proper to the nature of), and to a few non-personal nouns (*feverish*). **1965** *English Studies* XLVI. 228 It perfectly focusses the gap between a personal standard and the non-personal sonorities of Roman 'honor'.

‖**non placet, non-placet** (nɒn 'pleɪsɛt) [L.: see NON and PLACET.] The Latin for 'it does not please' (*scil.* me, us), being the formula used in the older universities and in ecclesiastical assemblies in giving a negative vote upon a proposition; hence, as *sb.*, a negative vote in a legislative assembly of a university, etc., and †*gen.*, an expression of dissent or disapproval.

1589 GREENE *Menaphon* (Arb.) 42 When I craued a finall resolution to my fatall passions, shee filde her..eyes full of furie, turned her backe, and shooke me off with a *Non placet*. **1596** NASHE *Saffron Walden* G 2 b, Because I would cut his cloake with the Wooll, though Lilly and Nashe neuer so, cry *Non placet* thereat. **1620** BRENT tr. *Sarpi Counc. Trent* (1676) VI. 500 There were 57 who said *Non placet.* *a* **1635** SIBBES *Christian's End* (1639) v. 110 When flesh and bloud shall put up a petition,..give it a *Non placet*, deny the petition. **1880** *Daily News* 12 Nov. 2/6 There voted on grace (a)—Placets, 145; non-placets, 185. **1888** ORELLI in *Encycl. Brit.* XXIV. 208/1 The 'placet of the temporal power for church affairs—when it occurs—also involves in this manner in itself the veto or non placet'.

attrib. **1896** *Daily News* 11 Mar. 4/4 One of the signatories of the non-placet notice.

Hence **non-'placet** *v. trans.*, to vote *non placet* upon (a proposition); to throw out (a measure).

1807 THOMASON in *Memoirs of Simeon* (1847) 239 On the whole, it seems to me that we should *non placet* the measure. **1843** WHEWELL in *Life* (1881) 287 To-day I brought in a Grace with that view: it is non-placeted. **1870** *Daily News* 25 Nov., The non-placeting of Graces without notice having been previously given.

non-'plevin. *Law.* [a. AF. *nounplevine.*] Failure to replevy land in due time.

[**1335** *Act 9 Edw. III*, c. 2 Que nul ne perde sa terre desore par cause de nounplevine.] **1706** PHILLIPS (ed. Kersey), *Non-Plevin.* **1848** WHARTON *Law Lex.*

non-'plural, *sb.* and *a.* [NON- 2, 3.] **A.** *sb.* The fact or condition of being only one in number.

1941 N. K. SMITH *Philos. of D. Hume* xxiii. 500 Tending to equate 'unity' with 'the simple', in the sense of the non-plural.

B. *adj. Linguistics.* Not in the plural form.

1958 L. KRASNER in Saporta & Bastian *Psycholinguistics* (1961) 81/1 When used to reinforce nonplural responses, both stimuli tended to increase the frequency of such responses. **1961** R. B. LONG *Sentence & its Parts* viii. 184 The 'singular' forms are really nonplural rather than singular in the strict sense. **1970** *Jrnl. Gen. Psychol.* July 7 Greenspoon noted that both of these reinforcing stimuli effected an increase in the emission of nonplural responses.

nonplus ('nɒnplʌs), *sb.* and *a.* Also 8 corruptly -plush. [f. L. phr. *nōn plūs* not more, no further. Cf. obs. F. (17th c.) *mettre à nonplus* to nonplus.]

A. *sb.* **1.** A state in which no more can be said or done; inability to proceed in speech or action; a state of perplexity or puzzle. Almost always in phr. *to be at* (rarely *in*) *a nonplus* = to be nonplussed; *to put, bring, drive, reduce to a nonplus*, † *to set at a nonplus*, also occas. † *to set a nonplus on*, † *to give nonplus to*: = NONPLUS *v.*

1582 R. PARSONS *Def. of Cens.* Ep. to Charke 8 Beynge now brought to a *non plus* in argueing. **1588** *Marprel. Epist.* (Arb.) 5 If you be not set at a flat *non plus*, and quite ouerthrowen. *c* **1590** GREENE *Fr. Bacon* (1630) E 3, I haue giuen *non-plus* to the Paduans. **1602** FULBECKE *2nd Pt. Parall.* 74 Though I bee in questioning at a nonplus. **1614** BEAUM. & FL. *Wit at Sev. Weapons* I. ii, Gentlemen, I have done! any man, that can, go further! I confess myself at a non-plus. **1621** QUARLES *Div. Poems, Esther* (1638) 94 Whose even poys'd valour..Had set a *Non-plus* on their doubtfull tongues. *a* **1626** BACON *Civil Convers.* Mor. & Hist. Wks. (Bohn) 198 Hasty speech..oftentimes..drives a man either to a nonplus or unseemly stammering. **1657** LIGON *Barbadoes* 85 Their often failings had put them to often stops and nonplusses in the work. **1692** SOUTH *12 Serm.* (1697) I. 50 The Nonplus of my Reason will yield a fairer opportunity to my Faith. **1702** C. MATHER *Magn. Chr.* I. App. (1852) 96 The people found themselves plunged into a sad non-plus what way to take for a subsistence. **1745** P. THOMAS *Jrnl. Anson's Voy.* 143 The Mortality..put our scheming Doctor to a sad Nonplus. **1775** S. J. PRATT *Liberal Opin.* liv. (1783) II. 151 You put me quite to a nonplush, I am quite out of cash. **1811** W. IRVING *Life & Lett.* (1864) I. 262 Here was a non-plus enough to startle any man of less enterprising spirit. **1863** COWDEN CLARKE *Shaks. Char.* xv. 378 The manner of York reveals the old man in a nonplus and perturbation. **1889** JESSOPP *Coming of Friars* vii. 325 Prophets are never at a nonplus, and never surprised by a question.

¶**b.** *at a nonplus*: unprepared, unawares.

1803 MAR. EDGEWORTH *To-morrow* ii, He can never find our larder at a nonplus. **1811** *Ora & Juliet* I. 9, I did think it was but a frugal sort of a dinner,..but as I took you at a non-plus, it did very well.

†**2.** Short for NON PLUS ULTRA. *Obs.*

1670 LASSELS *Italy* II. 178 A world of such rich work, which makes this bedstead the nonplus of art and magnificence.

†**B.** *adj.* [app. a shortening of *at a nonplus.*] At a nonplus; perplexed, embarrassed. *Obs.*

1589 WARNER *Alb. Eng.* VI. xxx. 132 Soone his wits were *Non plus*, for his wooing could but spell. *c* **1590** GREENE *Fr. Bacon* (1630) C, Set him but *non-plus* in his magicke spels, And make him yeeld in Mathematicke rules. **1600** HOLLAND *Livy* XLIV. xxvi. 1187 When he could make no answere thereto, but was set *nonplus*. **1631** R. H. *Arraignm. Whole Creature* xvi. 289 Apollonius Rhodius imposed voluntary Exile on himselfe,..because he was Nonplus in one of his Poems.

'nonplus, *v.* [f. NONPLUS *sb.*] *trans.* To bring to a nonplus or standstill; to perplex.

1591 SYLVESTER *Du Bartas* I. ii. 9 Mans Reason *nonplust* in some Accidents. **1598** *Ibid.* II. ii. I. 290 Now *nonplust*, if to re-inforce thy Camp, Thou fly for succour to thine Ayrie

Damp. **1639** FULLER *Holy War* v. x. (1840) 261, I know it will nonplus his power to work a true miracle. **1649** ROBERTS *Clavis Bibl.* 506 Expounding Nebuchadnezzars dreams, and Belshazzars vision, when all the wise men in Chaldea were non-plus'd with them. **1678** BUTLER *Hud.* III. II. 442 In which [*sc.* wrangling] his Parts were so accomplisht, That right, or wrong, he ne'r was non-plust. **1712** ADDISON *Spect.* No. 476 ¶5 He has been non-plus'd on a sudden by Mr. Dry's desiring him to tell the Company what it was that he endeavoured to prove. **1738** tr. *Guazzo's Art Conversation* 11 At first,.. I must own, I was a little nonplushed. **1840** E. FITZGERALD *Lett.* (1889) I. 58, I wrote a good bit of a letter to you three weeks ago: but, being non-plussed suddenly, tore it up. **1894** J. KNIGHT *Garrick* vii. 115 A continued struggle for supremacy in which the audience found itself nonplussed to decide.

b. With a thing as obj.: To render ineffective or inoperative.

1640 J. GOWER *Ovid's Festivalls* III. 64 Winds non-plus art [orig. *Vincitur ars vento*]. **1674** R. GODFREY *Inj. & Ab. Physic* 83 The Remedies being thus non-plust [etc.]. **1681** *News fr. Doctor's Commons* 5 It non-plust all reply. **1891** *Pall Mall G.* 7 Dec. 5/2 Such behaviour quite nonplusses measures of repression.

nonplussation (nɒnplʌˈseɪʃən). *rare.* [f. NONPLUS *v.* + -ATION.] The action of nonplussing; the condition of being nonplussed.

1833 M. SCOTT *Tom Cringle* i. (1842) 34 When the *voiture* stopped at the village, there seemed to be a nonplusation, to coin a word for the nonce, between my friend and his sisters. **1898** E. H. AITKEN *Tribes on my Frontier* (ed. 6) 61 They stared after it with a gape of utter nonplussation.

nonplussed (ˈnɒnplʌst), *ppl. a.* [f. NONPLUS *sb.* or *v.* + -ED.] Brought to a nonplus or standstill; at a nonplus; perplexed, embarrassed.

1606 WARNER *Alb. Eng.* XIV. lxxxix. 363 So many Incantations, lyes, feares, hopes instanced shee,.. As lastly did the *non-plust* Nunne vnto her Charmes agree. **1826** J. WILSON *Noct. Ambr.* Wks. 1855 I. 140 [He] stares round the company with his vacant and nonplussed eyes. **1828** CARLYLE *Misc.* (1857) I. 137 'Blown up' by nonplussed and justly exasperated Review-reviewers! **1886** BYNNER *A. Surriage* xvii, She swept from the room, leaving the nonplussed artist to puzzle over the cause of her.. behavior.

‖**non plus ultra** (nɒn plʌs ˈʌltrə). [L. = 'not more beyond'. So used in Fr. (from 17th c.).] = NE PLUS ULTRA 2, 2b.

[**1608** MIDDLETON *Trick to catch Old One* IV. F3b, Alwaies when we striue to be most politique we proue most cocskombs, *Non plus vltra*.] **1676** *Life Sarpi* in Brent tr. *Counc. Trent* p. xci, The two Pyramides which were carved and ingraven by the knife of all the judicious with a *non plus ultra*. **1727** POPE, etc. *Art of Sinking* i, The central Point, the *non plus ultra*, of true Modern Poesy. **1775** *Phil. Trans.* LXVI. 136 No trace.. of Roman servitude is to be met with in this district, except the ambiguous name of one mountain, .. generally thought to have been the *non plus ultra* of the Roman arms on the Italian side. **1858** CARLYLE *Fredk. Gt.* v. vi. I. 595 Seckendorf.. witnesses with unfeigned admiration the non-plus-ultra of manœuvring.

non-ˈpolar, *a.* [NON- 3.] Not polar; *spec.* in *Chem.* and *Physics*, (composed of molecules) having no electric dipole moment.

1892 *Electrician* 29 Jan. 329/1 He [*sc.* G. Forbes] had carried out some encouraging experiments with a dynamo.. built on his 'non-polar' principle. **1896** FISHER & SCHWATT tr. *H. Durège's Elem. Theory Functions* vii. 126 A non-polar discontinuity. **1913** *Jrnl. Amer. Chem. Soc.* XXXV. 1443 Polar and non-polar bonds may.. appear in the same formula. *Ibid.*, There are two distict types of union between atoms: polar, in which an electron has passed from one atom to the other, and non-polar, in which there is no motion of an electron. *Ibid.*, Characteristics of the non-polar type [of substance] are the ability to form chain compounds, and the existence of separable isomers. **1951** *New Biol.* X. 124 Water molecules, being polar, that is, with electric charges not distributed uniformly, are attracted by other polar molecules or parts of molecules but have no affinity for non-polar groups. **1965** PHILLIPS & WILLIAMS *Inorg. Chem.* I. iv. 135 Polar molecules will have higher.. boiling points than otherwise similar non-polar molecules. **1967** E. CHAMBERS *Photolitho-Offset* i. 8 Lithographic etches produce non-polar deposits not capable of absorbing an acid.

non-poˈlitical, *a.* and *sb.* [NON- 3, 2.]

A. *adj.* Not political. **B.** *sb.* One who is not involved in politics.

1860 DICKENS *Uncommercial Traveller* (1958) xvii. 172 If the prisoner.. had committed every non-political crime in the Newgate Calendar.. nothing would have been easier than.. to obtain his release. **1882** E. W. HAMILTON *Diary* 27 July (1972) I. 312 It appears that H. M., regarding the matter as 'non-political', has also taken the advice of Lord Cranbrook and Northcote about it. **1920** B. RUSSELL *Practice & Theory Bolshevism* I. ii. 25, I was able.. to find out how the whole system appears to the ordinary non-political man and woman. **1926** R. MACAULAY *Crewe Train* (1967) II. iii. 67 She enjoyed her mother's party, though she found at it too many non-politicals. **1958** *New Statesman* 1 Feb. 131/1 Even in South Africa (I would argue) it was all right for us to live our non-political lives. **1962** *Guardian* 22 Dec. 3/1 The other non-politicals contented themselves with brief speeches.

‖**non possumus** (nɒn ˈpɒsjuːməs). [L. = 'we can not'.] A statement or answer expressing inability to act or move in a matter.

1883 *Standard* 15 Sept. 5/1 Their answer to all applications consisting in a *non possumus*, and nothing more. **1885** LOWE *Bismarck* II. 347 To give up diplomatising, and return to a policy of *non possumus*. **1890** *Athenæum* 25 Jan. 124/3 Some time ago it was proposed to the Royal Academy to do this; the answer was a sort of 'non possumus'.

†**non-power.** *Obs.* Also 4 noun-, nom-power, 5 non-, nown-poiar. [a. AF. *nonpoair*, OF. *nonpooir*: see NON- 1 and POWER.] Lack of power; impotence.

*c*1374 CHAUCER *Boeth.* III. pr. v. (1868) 75 Ryȝt on þat same side nounpower entriþ vndirneþ þat makeþ hem wreches. **1377** LANGL. *P. Pl.* B. XVII. 310 Nouȝt of þe nounpowere of god þat he ne is myȝtful To amende al þat amys is. *c*1380 WYCLIF *Serm.* Sel. Wks. II. 374 God mai not faile on his side for noun-power or unwitt. *c*1400 *Laud Troy Bk.* 17341 And ȝe ar now of nom-power, Ne vs comes no help fer ne ner. *c*1460 FORTESCUE *Abs. & Lim. Mon.* vi. (1885) 121 All thes poiars comen of impotencie. And therfore thay mey properly by callid nown poiars. **1483** CAXTON *Gold. Leg.* 301b/2, I haue herd thy commaundement and haue sene the nonpower of hym but I shal amende it.

non-proˈficience. *rare*$^{-1}$. [NON- 1.] = next.

1709–11 KEN *Anodynes* xxviii. Poet. Wks. 1721 III. 450 The Graces which God's Image forme survey, In each my Non-proficience to display.

non-proˈficiency. [NON- 1.] Failure to make progress or improve.

1592 HARVEY *Pierce's Super.* Wks. (Grosart) II. 13 He shall finde a cold aduersary of him, that.. might easely be induced to be the Inuectiue of his owne Nonproficiency. **1607** R. C[AREW] tr. *Estienne's World of Wonders* 30 He twits his auditors not so much for their non-proficiencie.. as for their deficiency. **1666** ABP. SANCROFT *Lex Ignea* 10 Our foul and shameful Non-proficiency under so plentiful a Grace. **1671** J. WEBSTER *Metallogr.* i. 16 The reasons of the non-proficiency of the knowledge of Minerals and Metals in general. **1721** in BAILEY.

non-proˈficient. [NON- 2.] One who fails to make progress or improve.

1579–80 [see NIHILAGENT]. **1608** DOD & CLEAVER *Expos. Prov.* 24 Reproofe of Non-proficients which are taught much and learne little. **1647** TRAPP *Comm. Matt.* xiii. 47 Christ is an incessant teacher: learn then, for shame, lest he turn us off for non-proficients. **1665** BOYLE *Occas. Refl.* IV. ix. 61 If a Sermon leave us Devouter than it found us.. we may be Despondents, but are not altogether Non-proficients.

non-prolifeˈration. [NON- 1.] The prevention of an increase in the number of countries possessing nuclear weapons. Freq. *attrib.*

1965 *Times* 13 July 12/3 It would, however, only be prepared to subscribe to an east-west agreement on non-proliferation when the problem of nuclear security within the Atlantic Alliance had been satisfactorily settled. **1965** *Newsweek* 26 July 36/2 The price for a Russian agreement on a non-proliferation pact. **1974** *Friend* 1 Feb. 114/2 The premier.. is committed under the Non-Proliferation Treaty to negotiate an end to the nuclear arms race. **1974** *Times* 20 May 15/2 Some Afro-Asian countries.. maintained that the non-proliferation treaty was.. a plot to maintain the hegemony of those who already had the bomb.

†**non-promovent,** *a. Obs. rare*$^{-1}$. [f. NON- + L. *prōmovent-*, pres. ppl. stem of *prōmovēre* (see PRO- and MOVE *v.*).] Not moving forward.

1605 BACON *Adv. Learn.* II. 65 If he make them [*sc.* axioms] not withall Circular, and Non promouent, or Incurring into themselues.

non-pros (nɒnˈprɒs). *Law.* Abbreviation of NON PROSEQUITUR.

1675 MARVELL *Corr.* Wks. (Grosart) II. 439 A clause for regulating the Atturney Generall as to his entring *Non-Pros* against Papists. *a*1734 NORTH *Examen* II. v. §83 (1740) 366 Exempted from the Law.. by *non pros*, or Pardon *toties quoties*. **1769** BURROWS *Rep.* IV. 2418 The Plaintiff not declaring within the limited Time, the Seven Defendants signed Seven distinct Judgments of *Non-pros* against him. **1817** W. SELWYN *Law Nisi Prius* (ed. 4) II. 687 Defendant shall pay to plaintiff the costs of the non-pros.

Hence **non-prossed** (nɒnˈprɒst) *pa. pple.* (said of the suit or of the plaintiff).

1755 MAGENS *Insurances* I. 545 *note*, The Defendant brought a Writ of Error. But, despairing of success, suffered it to be non-prossed. **1768** [see NON-PROSEQUITUR]. **1774** HALLIFAX *Anal. Rom. Law* 99 In case of omission or neglect by the Plaintiff, he loses the benefit of his Writ, and is said to be nonsuited, or nonpros'd.

non-prosequitur (nɒnprəʊˈsɛkwɪtə(r)). *Law.* [L. = 'he does not prosecute'.] A judgement entered against a plaintiff in a suit in which he does not appear to prosecute.

1768 BLACKSTONE *Comm.* III. xx. 296 A *nonsuit*, or *non prosequitur*, is entered; and he is said to be *nonpross'd*.

non-ˈproven, *pa. pple.* [NON- 6.] Occasional substitute for *not proven* = Not proved.

1847 FR. A. KEMBLE *Later Life* III. 242 The main question of progress.. was non-proven. **1896** *Allbutt's Syst. Med.* I. 110 It is quite possible—but 'non-proven'—that the muscular coats of the small arteries are likewise capable of self-regulation.

non-proˈvided, *a.* [NON- 6.] Of schools or education: that is not provided (see PROVIDED *ppl. a.* 4b).

1918 A. QUILLER-COUCH *Foe-Farrell* 44 He.. zigzagged off into Education 'Provided' and 'Non-Provided', lunging and floundering with the Church Catechism and the Rate-book. **1921** *Act 11 & 12 Geo. V.* c. 51 §29 *marg.*, Conditions to be observed in conduct of non-provided schools. **1960** R. WILLIAMS *Border Country* 162 The entrance to the school, Glynmawr Non-Provided.

non-ˈrandom, *a.* [NON- 3.] Not random. Hence **non-ˈrandomly** *adv.*; **non-ˈrandomness.**

1942 *Genetics* XXVII. 531 (*heading*) The non-random distribution of mutants in the progeny of certain flies. **1943** J. S. HUXLEY *Evolutionary Ethics* 73 A non-random sample of the population. **1958** *Oxf. Univ. Gaz.* 27 Jan. 524/2 A model of non-randomness in threshold experiments. **1961** L. F. BROSNAHAN *Sounds of Language* v. 90 Sounds.. occur in apparently non-random distributions which unite languages of different language groups. **1966** D. G. BRANDON *Mod. Techniques Metallogr.* 251 Spatial non-randomness may be either orientation-dependent or orientation-independent. **1972** *Science* 5 May 545/1 Alleles of polymorphic loci, in the absence of direct selection, will tend to become nonrandomly associated with closely linked overdominant loci. **1972** *Jrnl. Soc. Psychol.* Aug. 223 A nonrandom sample of collective behaviour. **1973** *Nature* 16 Mar. 166/1 Human chromosomes are segregated non-randomly into hybrid clones.

non-ˈrational, *a.* [NON- 3.] Not rational. Also *absol.* as *sb.* Hence **non-ratioˈnality.**

*a*1871 G. GROTE *Eth. Fragm.* (1876) v. 183 Aristotle classifies the phenomena of.. the non-rational soul into three. **1896** W. CALDWELL *Schopenhauer's System* i. 16 His experience of life was such as to bring the *non-rational* side of things prominently before his mind. **1902** W. JAMES *Var. Relig. Exper.* iii. 74, I do not yet say that it is *better* that the subconscious and non-rational should thus hold primacy in the religious realm. *a*1910 —— *Some Probl. Philos.* (1911) viii. 136 The only alternative allowed by monistic writers is to confess the world's non-rationality—and no philosopher can permit himself to do that. **1951** R. FIRTH *Elements of Social Organization* vii. 245 The possibilities of intellectual and emotional satisfaction to be derived from religious belief are increased by the resort of that belief to non-rationality. **1957** J. S. HUXLEY *Relig. without Revelation* iii. 52 Mythical thought, which is basically non-rational. **1972** *Listener* 21 Dec. 854/2 Reliance on the non-rational means that courses of action are followed without regard for their long-term consequences.

†**non-reason.** *Sc. Obs.* [f. NON- 1 + REASON *sb.*] Unlawful action; = UNREASON.

1609 SKENE *Reg. Maj.* 3 They sal not hald Courts of life and limme; but onely of injuries, and non reason; that is, wrang and vnlaw.

non-refeˈrential, *a.* [NON- 3.] Of hypothesized mental events, such as the awareness of thought or of an image: having no reference to anything beyond themselves.

1925 C. D. BROAD *Mind & its Place* vi. 305 Purely inspective situations would belong to the latter class. So would pure sensation, the mere awareness of an image, etc. .. I am inclined to think that pure sensations, etc., are ideal limits rather than actual facts.. . Let us call situations of the .. second kind 'non-referential'. **1943** *Mind* LII. 176, I.. shall say something more about the non-referential interpretation of 'copy'. **1971** J. Z. YOUNG *Introd. Study Man* x. 125 All the words of the mental language are said to be 'non-referential'.

non-reˈflexive, *a.* [NON- 3.] **1.** *Gram.* Not reflexive (REFLEXIVE *a.* 5).

1949 O. JESPERSEN *Mod. Eng. Gram.* VII. 170 As a reflexive use of the *self*-forms we must also reckon the predicative in 'he is quite himself again' = 'in a normal condition', though NED takes it to be the emphatic, i.e. non-reflexive use. **1965** D. WARD *Russ. Lang. Today* v. 139 As a general rule, such nouns are formed from imperfect non-reflexive verbs. **1968** J. LYONS *Introd. Theoretical Linguistics* 361 Many languages.. have a set of reflexive pronouns distinguished for person and number..; others.. draw a distinction between reflexive and non-reflexive objects only in the third person.

2. *Philos.* Of a relation which may, but need not, hold between a thing and itself. Cf. IRREFLEXIVE *a.*, REFLEXIVE *a.* 3.

1947 H. REICHENBACH *Elem. Symbolic Logic* iii. 120 The nonreflexive functions comprise the irreflexive and the mesoreflexive functions. **1954** I. M. COPI *Symbolic Logic* v. 143 Relations which are neither reflexive nor irreflexive are said to be non-reflexive. The phrases: 'loves', 'hates', and 'criticizes' designate non-reflexive relations. **1955** A. N. PRIOR *Formal Logic* III. iii. 274 Not everybody is a shaver of himself, but some are. These [relations] are sometimes called 'non-reflexive'. **1964** E. BACH *Introd. Transformational Gram.* vii. 155 If there is at least one term in its domain that does not bear the relation to itself, then it is classed as *nonreflexive*... *Admiring* is presumably non-reflexive; i.e, there are people who admire someone and do not admire themselves. **1965** HUGHES & LONDEY *Elem. of Formal Logic* xxxix. 274 Every dyadic relation must be either reflexive or irreflexive or non-reflexive.

†**non-reˈgardance.** *Obs. rare*$^{-1}$. [NON- 1.] Failure to regard.

1601 SHAKS. *Twel. N.* v. i. 124 Since you to non-regardance cast my faith.

non-ˈregent. Now *Hist.* [NON- 2.] A master of arts whose regency has ceased.

In the Statutes of the University of Oxford the division of *magistri* into *regentes* and *non-regentes* is still retained.

1504 [see REGENT *sb.* 3a]. **1659** RUSHW. *Hist. Coll.* I. 371 His chief strength consisted in the Doctors.. and in the Non-Regents, who are Masters of Art of five years standing and upward. **1689** *Lond. Gaz.* 2496/2 *Cambridge, Octob. 8.* On Sunday last the Vice-Chancellor, the Heads of Colledges,.. with several Regents and Non-Regents,.. waited upon His Majesty at Newmarket. **1841** PEACOCK *Stat. Cambr.* 15, *note.* **1845** T. MYERS in *Encycl. Metrop.* XVI. 184/2 The Senate is divided into two Houses, respectively denominated Regents and Non-Regents.

b. *attrib.* or as *adj.*

1773 *Ann. Reg.* 153 The grace for the reconsideration of the question of annual examinations in the University of

Cambridge was voted in the non-regent house. **1831** Sir W. Hamilton *Discuss.* (1852) 392 In Paris, the non-regent graduates were only assembled on rare..occasions. **1845** *Encycl. Metrop.* XVI. 184/2 A..Non-Regent Master of Arts.

non-regu'lation. [NON- 4.] Applied to provinces of India in which the ordinary laws are not in force.

1845 Stocqueler *Handbk. Brit. India* (1854) 122 The whole of the provinces, regulation and non-regulation, cover 325,652 square miles. **1881** Sir W. Hunter in *Encycl. Brit.* XII. 769/1 Alike in regulation and in non-regulation territory the unit of administration is the district.

†**non-'replicate,** *a.* Not folded back.

1647 H. More *Song of Soul* II. ii. II. xviii, Forme bodily Non-replicate, extent, not setten free.

non-'residence. [NON- 1.]

1. Failure of a clergyman to reside where his official duties require him to reside; systematic absence of a clergyman from his benefice or charge.

c **1380** Wyclif *Wks.* (1880) 424 He seiþ þat propring of chirchis is leeueful, & noun residense is excusid bi siche a viker þat holdiþ his stede. **1425** *Rolls of Parlt.* IV. 290/2 Because of noun residens of Persons of holy Chirche, opon theire Personages, mykell pepull lakkes bothe gostely fode, and bodely. **1530** *Act 21 Hen. VIII*, c. 13 §17 Provyded alwais that this Acte of none resydence shall not in any wyse extende ne be prejudiciall to any such spirituall person [etc.]. **1587** in *Marprel. Controv.* (Arb.) 65 Non-residences haue cut the throte of our Church. **1653** Milton *Hirelings* Wks. 1851 V. 385 Thir Pluralities, thir Nonresidences, thir odious Fees [etc.]. **1723** Swift *Argts. agst. Power of Bps.* Wks. 1751 IX. 42 As to Non-Residence, I believe there is no Christian Country upon Earth, where the Clergy have less to answer for upon that Article. **1808** Syd. Smith *Wks.* (1867) I. 126 A law..fixing what shall be legal and sufficient causes for non-residence. **1892** J. C. Blomfield *Hist. Heyford* 68 The last [century]..so sadly notorious for the pluralism and non-residence of the parochial clergy.

†**b.** *fig.* Departure *from. Obs.*

1615 T. Adams *Englands Sickness* 8, I might here inferre to your obseruation (without any non-residence from the Text) that the Church is called *Filia Jerusalem*.

2. *transf.* and *gen.* The fact of not residing in a particular place.

1585 *Reg. Privy Council Scot.* IV. 39 The lang want of the administratioun of civile justice be non-residence of the Lords of Sessioun, quhilk hes happynnit throw occasioun of the lait plague. **1827** *Gentl. Mag.* XCVII. II. 594 The gradual decay of the castle, through neglect and the non-residence of the Earls. **1884** *Law Times Rep.* L. 177/2 The non-residence of the applicant [a foreigner] is a cogent argument against such interference.

†**non-'residency.** *Obs.* [NON- 1.] = prec.

The first example may belong to prec.

1545 Brinklow *Compl.* 30b, Lycence to eate flessh in lent, non-residencys, and such other. **1584** D. Fenner *Def. Ministers* (1587) 5 Your Nonresidencie, double benefices [etc.]. **1604** Tooker *Fabrique Ch.* 57 Wilfull and continuall Non-residency from their cures. **1658–9** *Burton's Diary* (1828) III. 499 In case of non-residency of a Burgess or Knight, *lex et consuetudo parliamenti* dispenseth it. **1668** *2nd Disc. Relig. Eng.* 47 To discourage Pluralities, Nonresidencies,..and Idleness in all Sorts. **1696** in Phillips.

non-'resident, *sb.* [NON- 2.]

1. A clergyman who does not reside where his official duties require him to reside; an absentee incumbent or church dignitary.

1583 *Acts Gen. Assemb. Ch. Scot.* (Maitland Cl.) II. 635 That the Commissioners present give up the names of the non residents upon Munday afternoone. **1588** Udall *Diotrephes* (Arb.) 27 See that he be such a one as hath bene a non-resident before, and let him haue diuers liuings. **1608** Willet *Hexapla Exod.* 774 Idle pastors and secure non-residents. **1692** [see pluralist 1]. **1723** Swift *Argts. agst. Power of Bps.* Wks. 1751 IX. 42, I am confident there are not ten Clergymen in the Kingdom, who, properly speaking, can be termed Non-Residents. **1835** Marryat *Olla Podr.* xi, So many of our clergymen are..non-residents.

2. One who does not reside in a particular place.

1819 (*title*) A Letter to a Member of Convocation..on the present state of the Catholic Claims, by a Non-Resident. **1863** Cox *Instit.* III. ix. 729 The usurpations of corporations, the extensive rights of their councils, and the interference of non-residents. **1869** Tozer *Highl. Turkey* II. 119 A few of the non-residents..took part [in the dance].

3. A person who uses some of the facilities of a hotel without residing there.

1910 *Bradshaw's Railway Guide* Apr. 1081 Sea and fresh water baths in the hotel..are open to non-residents. **1960** *Harper's Bazaar* Oct. 101/1 Even at the Dorchester..the bar is closed at 11 p.m. to non-residents. **1971** 'A. Gilbert' *Tenant for Tomb* vii. 132 A printed invitation to non-residents to use the bar and the dining-room.

non-'resident, *a.* [NON- 3.]

1. a. Of a clergyman: Not residing where his official duties require him to reside; culpably absent from his benefice or charge.

1530 *Act 21 Hen. VIII*, c. 13 §16 Yf any Person or Persons procure..any maner of lycence..to be none resydent at their said Dygnytees, Prebende [etc.]. **1588** J. Udall *Demonstr. Discip.* (Arb.) 27 If the priests might not dwell farre from the temple, then may not ministers be nonresident. **1642** Milton *Apol. Smect.* Wks. 1851 III. 307 The non-resident and plurality-gaping Prelats. **1766** Blackstone *Comm.* II. xx. 322 Licensed pluralists, who are allowed to demise the living, on which they are non-resident, to their curates only. **1868** J. H. Blunt *Ref. Ch. Eng.* I. 403 Preventing the Pope from conferring English benefices on non-resident foreigners.

†**b.** *fig.* Divergent or deviating *from. Obs.*

1616 Adams *Soul's Sickness* xxv. Wks. 1861 I. 473 When as yet himself is more non-resident from his theme than a discontinuer is from his charge. **1631** W. Foster *Hoplochrismaspongus* 3 That Divine which takes into consideration, whether this [cure]..be not done by.. witchcraft, cannot properly bee said to be Non-resident from his profession.

2. *transf.* and *gen.* Not residing at home or on one's estate; not resident in a particular place.

1540 *Act 32 Hen. VIII*, c. 27 Divers of the kinges subjectis ..have..obteynid..lycences for to be absent and none resident in and uppon their ordinary offices within the said townes. **1641** *Rec. Elgin* (New Spalding Cl.) I. 271 Ane non-resident burges. **1845** Disraeli *Sybil* (1863) 54 The monks were never non-resident. They expended their revenue among those whose labour had produced it. **1846** *Penny Cycl.* Suppl. II. 235/1 In the Irish district asylums,..the non-resident physician is the principal officer. **1869–70** *Ann. Rep. Deleg. Stud. not attached* 11 If any Student desires ..to be entirely non-resident for a Term.

3. *U.S.* Of land: owned by a person who does not reside on it.

1849 E. Chamberlain *Indiana Gaz.* (ed. 3) 313 The large amount of non-resident lands has hitherto retarded improvements. **1881** *Mich. Gen. Statutes* (1882) I. 385 Such notice to owners of such non-resident lands, shall be served by posting up the same in three public places.

non-'residenter. *rare.* Also 7 *Sc.* -are. [f. NON-RESIDENT + -ER[1].] A non-resident.

1637–50 Row *Hist. Kirk* (Wodrow Soc.) 28 No beneficed persone may be a non-residentare. **1828** *Life Planter Jamaica* 197 Landed proprietors, most of whom are non-residenters in the country. **1842** J. Aiton *Domest. Econ.* (1857) 71 The minister has become a non-residenter.

non-resi'dential, *a.* [NON- 3.] Not residential, as a college or university.

1898 *Daily News* 17 May 3/7 Non-residential Mansfield [College at Oxford]. **1906** *Westm. Gaz.* 11 May 2/1 The non-residential University of his friend.

non-resi'dentiary, *sb.* and *a.* [NON- 2.]

A. *sb.* A church dignitary who is not residentiary. **B.** *adj.* Not residentiary.

c **1630** Risdon *Surv. Devon* §107 (1810) 109 The dean,.. the chanter, the chancellor, and the treasurer of the church; ..every of these being non-residentiaries, have sufficient livelihoods of themselves. **1898** *Westm. Gaz.* 31 Mar. 6/3 One of the non-residentiary prebends.

non-re'sistance. [NON- 1.] **a.** The practice or principle of not resisting authority, even when it is unjustly exercised formerly esp. with reference to the ***doctrine of non-resistance*** as held in England in the 17th c. (Cf. *passive obedience*.)

1643 Diggs *Unlawf. Taking up Arms* 50 Their severall exceptions and corrupt glosses by which they endeavour to avoyd this plaine obligation of non resistance. **1685** *Acc. Execution Dk. of Monmouth* 1 My Lord, if you be of the Church of England, you must acknowledge the Doctrine of Non-resistance to be True. **1687** Dryden *Hind & P.* III. 663 Your sons are malcontents, but yet are true, As far as non-resistance makes them so. *c* **1720** *Vicar of Bray* iii, Passive obedience was a joke, A jest was non-resistance. **1791** Burke *App. Whigs* Wks. VI. 154 Sir John Hawles..positively affirming the doctrine of non-resistance to government to be the general, moral, religious, and political rule for the subject. **1838** W. L. Garrison in *Liberator* (Boston) 28 Sept. 154/5 We shall adhere to the doctrine of non-resistance and passive submission to enemies. **1855** Macaulay *Hist. Eng.* xiv. III. 453 Ken,..in the times when nonresistance and passive obedience were the favourite themes of his brethren,..had scarcely ever alluded to politics in the pulpit. **1861** W. Rowntree *War & Christianity* 6 The great principle of non-resistance. **1871** Fraser *Life Berkeley* ii. 49 Non-resistance and passive obedience were then associated with Jacobitism. **1878** Gardiner in *Encycl. Brit.* VIII. 348/2 The Five Mile Act (1665) forbade the expelled clergyman to come within five miles of a corporate borough,..unless he would swear his adhesion to the doctrine of non-resistance. **1898** [see internationalism]. **1934** G. B. Shaw *On Rocks* 155 It is easy to suggest that they [*sc.* evildoers] should be reformed by gentleness and shamed by non-resistance. **1973** R. V. Sampson *Tolstoy: The Discovery of Peace* vi. 109 It is very rare for a writer to allow Tolstoy's arguments in support of the doctrine of non-resistance to evil—the essence of Tolstoy—to be heard.

attrib. **1844** Emerson *New Eng. Reformers* Ser. II. 169 Temperance and non-resistance principles. **1856** Olmsted *Slave States* 225 Charles II. ordered a shipment of Quakers to Virginia... Their non-resistance principles must have added much to their value.

b. *gen.* (const. *to*.)

1821 Lamb *Elia* Ser. I. *Witches & Night Fears*, The non-resistance of witches to the constituted powers. **1824** Miss Mitford *Village* Ser. I. (1863) 76 An operation which that sagacious quadruped endured with the most perfect passiveness, the most admirable non-resistance.

non-re'sistant, *a.* and *sb.* [NON- 2, 3.]

A. *adj.* Not resistant; †pertaining to or involving the doctrine of non-resistance.

1702 De Foe *Test Ch. Eng. Loyalty* 20 This Doctrine of Absolute, Passive, and Non-resistant Obedience. *a* **1735** Arbuthnot *State Quacks* Misc. Wks. 1751 I. 159 [To] teach Passive-Obedience and Non-Resistant Principles. **1796** Coleridge *Lett.* (1895) 201 It commands them never to use the arm of flesh, to be perfectly non-resistant. **1853** Kane *Grinnell Exp.* xxxi. (1856) 272 We, so utterly helpless, hampered, and non-resistant, must await the inevitable action of the ice. **1871** Spencer *Princ. Psychol.* II. vi. xiv. (1872) 179 The two being distinguished as resistant extension—and non-resistant extension. **1873** T. H. Green *Introd. Pathol.* (ed. 2) 165 The tissue..being soft and non-resistant.

B. *sb.* One who does not resist authority or force (occas. = NON-COMBATANT); one who holds or practises the doctrine of non-resistance.

1755 in S. M. Hamilton *Lett. to Washington* (1898) I. 91 The fighting Faction..threaten to put to Death all the Non-resistents—Dunkers, Moravians, Dutch and Quakers. *c* **1850** Saxe *Poems* (1874) 20 When for their dogmas Non-Resistants fight. **1863** W. Phillips *Sp.* xvii. 385, I confess I am not a non-resistant. **1870** T. W. Higginson *Army Life* 231 Released on parole as a non-resistant.

non-re'sister. [NON- 2.] = NON-RESISTANT *sb.*

1851 J. A. Quitman in J. F. H. Claiborne *Life & Corr. J. A. Quitman* (1860) II. 147 By the election of Non-resisters to the Convention, a majority of the people have declared against the course of policy on the slavery questions.

non-re'sisting, *ppl. a.* [NON- 3.] = NON-RESISTANT *a.* A.

1712 Berkeley *Pass. Obed.* Wks. III. (1871) 137 Absolute non-resisting obedience to government. **1715** Addison *Freeholder* No. 15 ¶2 The Non-resisting women..think no post tenable against an army, that makes so fine an appearance. **1801** Nelson 22 Apr. in Nicolas *Disp.* (1845) IV. 346 God forbid I should destroy a non-resisting Dane. **1814** Southey *Lett.* (1856) II. 389 Scenes ensue, in the course of which Oliver drops his nonresisting principles, and cuts down the renegade with a tomahawk. **1884** Spencer *The Man v. the State* 3 The Non-Resisting Test Bill, which proposed for legislators and officials a compulsory oath that they would in no case resist the king by arms.

non-re'strictive, *a.* [NON- 3.] Not restrictive; *spec.* in *Gram.*, denoting a word, phrase, or clause that does not restrict or limit the meaning of the word or words to which it is added.

1924 O. Jespersen *Philos. of Gram.* viii. 111 Next we come to *non-restrictive adjuncts* as in *my dear little Ann!* **1927** —— *Mod. Eng. Gram.* III. iv. 82 Restrictive or defining clauses, ..give a necessary determination to the antecedent, and thereby make it more precise... Non-restrictive or loose clauses..might be discarded without serious injury to the precise understanding of the sentence as a whole. **1953** J. S. Huxley *Evolution in Action* vi. 142 What is difficult is to discover just how any one step is effected, still more to distinguish desirable from undesirable change, and restrictive from non-restrictive improvement. **1966** G. N. Leech *Eng. in Advertising* xiv. 132 Proper nouns do occasionally combine with modifiers of non-restrictive force: 'fair Helen'..; 'beautiful Britain'. **1971** *Archivum Linguisticum* II. 14 To separate non-restrictive progressive relative clauses from the preceding clause.

non-re'turn. [NON- 1.] Failure or neglect to return; the condition of not being returned.

1547 *Act 1 Edw. VI*, c. 10 §5 For everye suche faulte of non Retourne, everie suche Sherife..shall..forfaite Five Powndes. **1812** *Examiner* 7 Sept. 570/1 He is entitled to one moiety in case of a non-return of any taxable article. **1845** Lytton *Night & Morn* v. xiv, The alarm of Sarah at her non-return. **1898** *Westm. Gaz.* 19 Mar. 2/4 The borrowing of your cherished books and their non-return.

attrib. **1906** *Motor Boat* 12 July 18 Carburetted air drawn in through a non-return valve.

non-re'turnable, *a.* [NON- 3.] That may not be returned; *spec.* of containers, bottles, etc.: that may not be returned empty to the suppliers. Also *absol.* as *sb.*

1903 T. E. Young *Insurance* x. 265 The premiums in the event of death happening prior to the adult age agreed upon may be either non-returnable..or returnable in full. **1907** *Yesterday's Shopping* (1969) p. x/1 All empties, except 'non-returnable cases'..must be returned within a reasonable period. **1926–27** *Army & Navy Stores Catal.* p. ix/1 Goods sent by Rail or by Carter Paterson are packed in non-returnable cases for which no charge is made. **1961** *New Scientist* 16 Mar. 700/2 The milk bottle..is about five times cheaper than the non-returnable carton. **1968** *Economist* 27 Jan. 59/3 Now that the non-returnable bottle—and breathalysers—are here to stay, grocery stores are the growth point in drink sales. **1971** *Wall St. Jrnl.* 5 Mar. 26/4 About 70 such laws were debated last year by various local, state and federal bodies. Bowie, Md., actually banned nonreturnables. **1971** *Nature* 6 Aug. 359/2 Potential customers should..make appropriate non-returnable deposits as marks of their good faith. **1973** *Times* 11 Dec. 6/4 It is absurd for continuance of non-returnable bottle production still to be allowed.

nonrew'ard. *Psychol.* [NON- 1.] In learning experiments: deliberate withholding of an expected reward. Hence **non'rewarded** *ppl. a.*

1951 N. E. Miller in S. S. Stevens *Handbk. Exper. Psychol.* 458/1 The cues produced by nonreward. *Ibid.*, The interspersing of a number of nonrewarded trials during training with primary drive and reward (i.e. partial reinforcement) may increase the resistance of a learned reward to experimental extinction. **1970** *Jrnl. General Psychol.* Oct. 185 The role of frustrative nonreward in instrumental escape conditioning. **1973** *Jrnl. Genetic Psychol.* Mar. 89 Association with frustrative nonreward alters the affective value of the stimulus.

nonrie, -y, nons, obs. ff. NUNNERY, NONCE[1].

non-'rigid, *a.* [NON- 3.] Not rigid; *spec.* denoting an airship which has no framework to support the envelope, and whose shape is maintained solely by the pressure of the gas inside. Also occas. as *sb.*, an airship of this kind.

1909 A. BERGET *Conquest of Air* I. v. 108 These airships are non-rigid. **1909** *Daily Chron.* 3 Aug. 1/7 The two non-rigids that are to come from France. **1930** *Daily Express* 6 Oct. 2/4 He..was captain of non-rigid airships in home waters and the East Mediterranean. **1961** *B.S.I. News* Dec. 20/2 Rigid plastics; semi-rigid plastics; non-rigid plastics.

non-sane, nonsane (nɒn'seɪn), *a. Law.* [ad. law-French *non sane* (*memorie*), law-Latin *non sanæ* (*memoriæ*): see NON- 3, SANE *a.*, MEMORY *sb.* 2 b.] Not sane; of unsound mind.

1628 COKE *On Litt.* 247 If such a man of Non sane memorie make a Feoffement. **1766** BLACKSTONE *Comm.* II. 291 Idiots and persons of nonsane memory. **1818** CRUISE *Digest* (ed. 2) IV. 85 All persons incapable of binding themselves by any other contract, such as persons of nonsane memory. **1855** DUNGLISON *Dict. Med. Sci.*

Hence †**non-'sanity**, insanity.

1675 *Act 27 Chas. II*, c. 1 §2 Disability in respect of Coverture, Infancy, Non sanity of memory. *a* **1734** NORTH *Lett.* (1826) II. 128 Non-sanity of mind.

nonsant: see NONSUNT.

non-'scheduled, *a.* orig. *U.S.* [NON- 6.] Not scheduled; *spec.* of an airline: operating without fixed or published flying schedules; of or pertaining to such an airline. So **non-sched, -sked** (nɒn'skɛd), a non-scheduled airline; also *attrib.* or as *adj.*

1946 *Harper's Mag.* Oct. 324/1 The non-scheds naturally look with envy at the mail subsidies now granted to the big airlines. **1949** *Aviation Week* 30 May 7/1 The nonsked may barely break even as a result. **1949** *Industrial Arts Index* June 7/2 Air carriers: non-scheduled operations. **1960** *Wall St. Jrnl.* 12 Jan. 30/2 The ultimate outcome of the case apparently will affect several other suits brought by 'non-skeds' which seek an additional $154.6 million in damages. **1961** *Flight* LXXX. 645/1 The Flying Tiger Line has leased an L.1049H Super Constellation to Trans-International Airlines Inc, a Florida-based 'non-sked'. **1971** *Flying* Apr. 113/2 Cargo and non-scheduled carriers described. **1975** *Publishers Weekly* 3 Mar. 73/2 This is like being stuck on a nonsched junket to the most obvious European spots.

†**non-'scriber.** *Obs.* = NON-SUBSCRIBER.

1650 (*title*) Plea for Non-Scribers, or Grounds and Reasons for many Ministers in Cheshire, Lancashire, &c. refusing the late Engagement. **1651** ELCOCK (*title*) Animadversions on a book called a Plea for Non-Scribers.

†**non-script**, *a.* [f. NON- 6 + L. *script-us* SCRIPT.] Unwritten.

1657 J. WATTS *Dipper Sprinkled* 65 The Trine immersion is a nonscript Tradition of the Apostles.

nonse, obs. form of NONCE[1].

non-seat. *Coal-mining.* (See quot.)

1883 GRESLEY *Gloss. Coal-mining, Non-seat.* See *D Link.* [A flat iron bar attached to chains, and suspended from a hemp rope to a windlass at surface.]

nonsenche, obs. form of NUNCHEON.

nonsense ('nɒnsəns), *sb.* Also 7–8 **-sence**, 8 **-scense**. [f. NON- 2 + SENSE *sb.* Cf. F. *nonsens* (from 12–13th c.).]

1. a. That which is not sense; spoken or written words which make no sense or convey absurd ideas; also, absurd or senseless action. *to knock the nonsense out of*: see KNOCK *v.* 6 e.

Often used exclamatorily to express disbelief of, or surprise at, a statement.

1614 B. JONSON *Bart. Fair* IV. iv, Here they continue their game of vapours, which is Nonsense. *a* **1643** VISC. FALKLAND, etc. *Infallibility* (1646) 121 You leave out those words..and so make non-sence of that period. *a* **1680** BUTLER *Rem.* (1759) I. 222 For learned Nonsense has a deeper Sound, Than easy Sense, and goes for more profound. **1707** LADY M. W. MONTAGUE *Lett.* II. xlvi. 33, I understand architecture so little, that I am afraid of talking nonsense in endeavouring to speak of it particularly. **1711** ADDISON *Spect.* No 35 ¶1 If they speak Nonsense, they believe they are talking Humour. **1790** BURKE *Fr. Rev.* 17 This doctrine..either is nonsense, and therefore neither true nor false, or it affirms a most..dangerous..position. **1816** SCOTT *Antiq.* xiii, Come, let us have no more of this nonsense. **1859** HAWTHORNE *Fr. & It. Note-bks.* (1871) II. 345, I am writing nonsense, but it is because no sense within my mind will answer the purpose. **1894** FENN *In Alpine Valley* I. 28 'You are not [dying], John dear. It's all stuff and nonsense,' said the little lady.

b. In particularized use: A piece of nonsense; also *concr.* and = a muddle, fiasco, esp. in phr. *to make a nonsense* (*of*).

a **1643** VISCT. FALKLAND, etc. *Infallibility* (1646) 98 Every new nonsense will be more acceptable..then any old sense. **1655** tr. *Sorel's Com. Hist. Francion* II. 36 He understood not French very well, nor I his Fustian Language, so our discourse was a perpetuall Nonsense. **1803** SCOTT *Let.* 14 Sept. (1932) I. 204, I daresay I shall go on scribbling one nonsense or another to the end of the chapter. **1942** E. WAUGH *Put Out More Flags* iii. 212 Everyone said, 'Lyne made a nonsense of the embarkation.' *Ibid.* 242 'It was all rather a nonsense' said the subaltern, in the classic phraseology of his trade which comprehends all human tragedy. **1957** *Listener* 30 May 873 Size is essential for efficiency. A small steel works..is an economic nonsense. **1960** L. COOPER *Accomplices* II. i. 71 He's made a complete nonsense of the whole thing and got the sack. *Ibid.* vi. 135, I knew you'd make a nonsense of it so I told Wallis to be ready to take over. **1962** *Movie* June 6/2 Ambitious nonsenses like *The Entertainer* and *Flame in the Streets.* **1966** A. PRIOR *Operators* xv. 225 An occasion that could make a nonsense of any Op. Bad intelligence, weather, flak. **1970** *New Statesman* 16 Jan. 88/3 'Structure' is one of those useful nonsenses in the vocabulary of the fiction critic, the mystery ingredient with the secret formula.

c. *no nonsense*: no foolish or extravagant conduct; no foolery or humbug. Chiefly in phr. *stand no nonsense* (also used as adj.).

1821 *Sporting Mag.* VIII. 233 Smith would stand *no nonsense.* **1836** SIR G. STEPHEN *Search of a Horse* i. (1841) 4 There was 'no nonsense about him' [*sc.* a horse],..but he unluckily moved like a castle! **1849** MISS MULOCK *Ogilvies* ii, Mr. Ogilvie would allow 'no nonsense' of late rising. **1904** SLADEN *Lovers Japan* xiii, Rich was the only stand-no-nonsense Englishman of the lot.

d. Used, usu. in the spelling *non-sense*, without connotations of absurdity: something that is not sense or that differs from sense.

Not clearly separable from sense 1 a.

1942 T. S. ELIOT *Music of Poetry* 14 His [*sc.* Lear's] non-sense is not vacuity of sense: it is a parody of sense, and that is the sense of it. **1943** *Amer. Speech* XVIII. 221 Men struggle over non-sense questions. **1965** *English Studies* XLVI. 322 A 'steep ford' is quite obvious non-sense.

2. Absurdity, nonsensicalness.

1630 W. BEDELL in *Ussher's Lett.* (1686) 421, I shewed the false Latin, Non-sence, injustice of it. **1660** T. PIERCE *Inq. Nat. Sin* To Rdr. *marg.*, Compare the non-sense with the impiety of the expression. **1841** L. HUNT *Seer* II. 2/1 The nonsense of ill-will.

3. Unsubstantial or worthless stuff or things.

1638 COWLEY *Love's Riddle* IV. Wks. 1711 III. 113 Our Desires..are Love's Nonsence, wrapt up in thick Clouds. **1648** J. BEAUMONT *Psyche* V. i, What royal Nonsence is a Diadem Abroad, for One who's not at home supreme? **1687** NORRIS *Coll. Misc.* 24, I find This busie World is Non-sense all. **1900** *Westm. Gaz.* 2 Feb. 12/1 Six dollars a week for slippers, and three more for 'ribbons and bits of chiffon nonsense'.

4. A meaning that makes no sense.

1650 WEEKES *Truth's Conflict* i. 11 This is to put a nonsense upon the place, and to destroy the savor that is in it. **1711** POPE *Lett.* (1735) I. 166 How easy it is to a Caviller to give a new Sense, or a new Nonsence to any thing.

†**5.** Want of feeling or physical sensation. *Obs.*

1621 in T. Bedford *The Sinne*, etc. A i b, Disquietnesse of Conscience [growes] into a numbdnesse or non-sense.

6. *attrib.* and *Comb.* **a.** *gen.* *nonsense-proof* adj., *talker*, *-writer*; **nonsense-book**, a book of nonsense or nonsense verses; **nonsense-name** (see quot.); **nonsense syllable**, a syllable formed by putting a vowel between any two consonants, used in memory experiments and tests; **nonsense verses**, verses consisting of words and phrases arranged solely with reference to the metre and without regard to the sense; also *nonsense song*, etc.; also **nonsense verse**, comically nonsensical or whimsical verse; *spec.* a limerick; **nonsense word**, a word which has no accepted meaning; also = *nonsense syllable*.

1887 *Spectator* 17 Sept. 1251 Lear's *Nonsense Books. **1842** *Rep. Brit. Assoc.* 118 *Nonsense names.—Some authors..have adopted the plan of coining words at random without any derivation or meaning whatever. **1778** *Love Feast* 12 Led by the Spirit to John's pantil'd Roof, Which many a vagrant Paul makes *Nonsense-Proof. **1871** E. LEAR (*title*), *Nonsense Songs, Stories, Botany and Alphabets. **1968** *Radio Times* 28 Nov. 65/2 A nonsense song from Virginia, 'Poor Howard'. **1975** *Listener* 6 Mar. 305/2 When Charlie finally opened his mouth in *Modern Times*, out came a nonsense song no one needed to understand. **1890** W. JAMES *Princ. Psychol.* I. xvi. 667 Mr. Burnham..suggested ..one ought to test one's self *à la* Ebbinghaus on series of *nonsense-syllables. **1924** R. M. OGDEN tr. *Koffka's Growth of Mind* i. 29 Impressing certain material (preferably nonsense-syllables in an ordered series)..upon the observer. **1971** *Jrnl. General Psychol.* LXXXV. 139 Ss were allowed to work 10 nonsense-syllable examples. *a* **1832** BENTHAM *Deontol.* ii. (1834) I. 26 The moralist..would call his enemy..hypocrite, and *nonsense-talker. **1799** *Public Characters* II. 423 Although few *men* in England could equal him in writing *sense* prose, yet many *boys* might surpass him in writing *nonsense* verses. **1819** KEATS *Let.* 17 Sept. (1931) II. 438, I cannot get on without writing as boys do at school a few nonsense verses. **1830** COLERIDGE *Table-t.* 5 Oct., I did not seem much interested with a piece of Rossini's, which had just been performed. I said, it sounded to me like nonsense verses. **1851** [see AMPHIGOURI, -GORY]. **1870** *Spectator* 26 Dec. 30 Mere musical sounds are no other than nonsense verses are in poetry. **1898** [see LIMERICK]. **1938** A. DAVIDSON *Edward Lear* ii. 18 It is possible that these extemporized nonsense-verses were in the limerick form. **1940** *Essays & Studies* XXV. 7 The nonsense verse also was well worth having—who had believed, else, that Housman had it in him either to be happy or to write nonsense. **1919** J. B. WATSON *Psychology* ix. 336 *Non-sense words or syllables are made by separating two consonants with a vowel as *ver*, *gax* and *moc.* **1935** B. MALINOWSKI in M. Black *Importance of Lang.* (1962) 72 Have we to imagine that magical speech starts from sheer non-sense words..? **1954** J. R. R. TOLKIEN *Fellowship of Ring* I. vi. 130 Out of a long string of nonsense-words (or so they seemed) the voice rose up loud and clear and burst into this song. **1887** *Spectator* 17 Sept. 1251 The parent of modern *nonsense-writers.

b. That is nonsense; full of nonsense; †in the 17th c. often used as *adj.* = Nonsensical.

1621 BURTON *Anat. Mel.* II. iv. I. v. (1651) 375 A few simples well..understood are better than such an heap of nonsense confused compounds. **1638** CHILLINGW. *Relig. Prot.* I. iv. §47. 217 Some empty unintelligible non-sense distinction. **1642** ROGERS *Naaman* 191 Put case the way of washing in Jordan bee irrationall and non-sense to thy wit and reason. **1757** FOOTE *Author* I. (1782) 23 You are a Non-sense man, and I won't agree to any such Thing. **1858** MRS. OLIPHANT *Laird of Norlaw* II. 127 This is not a nonsense letter—will you read it, mother? **1862** PALGRAVE in *Times* 15 May, A learned mockery, a nonsense sculpture.

c. *Biol.* Denoting a codon that does not specify any amino-acid, or a mutation which gives rise to such a codon (and may thus prematurely bring about a blocking of polypeptide synthesis).

[**1957** F. H. C. CRICK et al. in *Proc. Nat. Acad. Sci.* XLIII. 418 We shall assume that there are certain sequences of three nucleotides with which an amino acid can be associated and certain others for which this is not possible. Using the metaphors of coding, we say that some of the 64 triplets make sense and some make non-sense.] **1961** [see MISSENSE *a.*]. **1964** G. H. HAGGIS et al. *Introd. Molecular Biol.* xii. 318 They then calculated that the sixty-four triplets could be divided..into two classes, with twenty meaningful triplets in one class and forty-four nonsense triplets in the other. **1969** A. M. CAMPBELL *Episomes* ix. 122 Nonsense mutations of *lacZ*..produce reduced levels of the permease coded by *lac Y.* **1974** *Encycl. Brit. Micropædia* IV. 464/2 It is now known that there may be several codes for one amino acid and that there are nonsense codes that do not code anything.

Hence †**nonsensely** *adv.*, nonsensically.

1656 DUCHESS NEWCASTLE *Nature's Picture* XI. *Epistle*, Others in one discourse speak mixtly, now rational, then nonsensely.

nonsense ('nɒnsəns), *v. rare.* [f. the sb.] *intr.* To talk nonsense.

1822 M. EDGEWORTH *Let.* 30 May (1971) 404 We have given most elegant repasts as I shall have the honor of describing to you soon when we are all together nonsenseing round Lucys sofa. **1909** R. A. WASON *Happy Hawkins* 67, I nonsensed a while, tryin' to get her to laugh an' cut up, but not her.

non-'sensible, *a.* [NON- 3.] Not sensible.

1851 MILLAIS in *Life* (1899) I. iv. 124 Forgive this nonsensible scribble. **1875** WHITNEY *Life Lang.* viii. 137 Every figurative transfer which ever made a successful designation for some non-sensible act or relation..rested upon a previous perception of analogy.

nonsensical (nɒn'sɛnsɪkəl), *a.* and *sb.* [f. NONSENSE + -ICAL.]

A. *adj.* That is nonsense; of the nature of, or full of, nonsense; having no sense; absurd.

1655 *Nicholas Papers* (Camden) II. 221 They haue such nonsensicall conceipts that there is some impossibility to please their humours. **1668** PEPYS *Diary* 12 Oct., A ridiculous nonsensical book set out by Will. Pen for the Quakers. **1684** WOOD *Life* 28 Dec. (O.H.S.) III. 120 Lord Hawley, the great bull-maker or maker of nonsensicall puns. **1742** RICHARDSON *Pamela* IV. 11 Canst thou not forbear letting thy discerning Lord see thy nonsensical Emotions? **1816** SCOTT *Antiq.* xiv, The knight's a punctilious old fool, but I promise you his daughter is above all nonsensical ceremony and prejudice. **1869** AINSWORTH *Hilary St. Ives* II. i, Put aside all nonsensical feeling, and accept Sir Charles. **1885** *Law Times* LXXVIII. 186/2 This sentence is certainly the worst.., and it would be hard to invent a more nonsensical one.

b. Of persons.

1682 *Enq. Elect. Sheriffs* 24 Stupid and nonsensical Fops. **1704** SWIFT *Batt. Bks.* Wks. 1751 I. 220 A Pack of..confounded Loggerheads and illiterate Whelps, and nonsensical Scoundrels. **1815** MISS AUSTEN *Emma* xxvi, 'Nonsensical girl,' was his reply. **1852** MRS. STOWE *Uncle Tom's C.* xv. 141 Come, now, Marie, what do you think of the likeness? Don't be nonsensical, now.

B. *sb.* A nonsensical, absurd, or trifling thing.

1842 *Peter Parley's Ann.* III. 246 Silks and satins..and the host of nonsensicals with which little minds pride themselves. **1856** FERRIER *Inst. Metaph.* App. I. 498 It does not..hold the mind thus circumstanced..to be a nonentity, but only a non-sensical, an absolutely inconceivable.

Hence **non'sensically** *adv.*; **non'sensicalness, nonsensi'cality**.

1654 WHITLOCK *Zootomia* 83 If they misapply words..never so non-sensically, they passe for fine Fellowes. **1674** R. GODFREY *Inj. & Ab. Physic* 186 Observing the nonsensicalness of the Compound, and the multitude of Simples, mixt without Reason. **1702** C. MATHER *Magn. Chr.* VII. App. (1852) 644 A certain silly scribbler, the very first-born of Nonsensicality. **1754** EDWARDS *Freed. Will* I. iii. (1762) 15 If any Man uses these Terms in such Cases, he either uses them nonsensically, or in some new Sense. *a* **1850** HAWTHORNE in *Hawthorne & his Wife* (1885) I. 498 She..keeps our little nonsensicalities from ourselves. **1850** SIR W. HAMILTON *Discuss. Philos.*, etc. (1852) 624*, I admit, that had we thus spoken, we had spoken, not only ungrammatically, but nonsensically. **1891** *Spectator* 9 May 665/1 Good nonsense is very difficult to write, for it ought to express gaiety of heart even in its very nonsensicalness.

non'sensify, *v.* [f. NONSENSE + -IFY.] *trans.* To make nonsense of. So **nonsensifi'cation**, the production of nonsense.

1649 H. LAWRENCE *Some Consid.* 13 They have..nonsensifyed a Scripture with their Figures and Allegories. **1816** SCOTT *Antiq.* xxii, Simple suffumigation? simple nonsensification—planetary hour? planetary fiddlestick!

non-'sensitive, *a.* and *sb.* [NON- 3.] **a.** *adj.* Not sensitive. †**b.** *sb.* A thing without feeling.

1628 FELTHAM *Resolves* II. xviii. 56 Whatsoeuer we preach of Contentednesse in want; no precepts can so gaine vpon Nature, as to make her a non-sensitiue. **1836** SMART, *Non-sensitive*, wanting sensation. **1898** *Westm. Gaz.* 14 June 2/1 A wife of the sturdy, enduring, non-sensitive type.

So **non-'sensitiveness**.

1890 SIR F. A. ABEL in *Nature* 4 Sept. 444/2 Comparative non-sensitiveness to explosion by friction or percussion.

non-'sequence. *Geol.* [NON- 1.] An interruption in the deposition of adjacent comformable strata that was too short (in geological terms) for significant erosion to take place and consequently has to be inferred from a gap in the fossil record.

[**1895** S. S. Buckman in *Q. Jrnl. Geol. Soc.* LI. 391 Non-sequential strata, when the sequence is incomplete, but the planes of the deposits are practically parallel.] **1904** *Ibid.* LX. 349 (*heading*) Evidence for a non-sequence between the Keuper and Rhætic series in North-West Gloucestershire and Worcestershire. **1933** *Ibid.* LXXXIX. 163 If..the oolitic and nodular beds are at this horizon..their position immediately overlying slates with *Didymograptus bifidus* would indicate that they mark a considerable non-sequence. **1969** Bennison & Wright *Geol. Hist. Brit. Isles* i. 7 Naturally non-sequences are unprovable in barren unfossiliferous rocks..or in rocks so altered that fossils have failed to be preserved.

‖**non sequitur** (nɒn 'sɛkwɪtər). [L. = 'it does not follow'.] An inference or a conclusion which does not follow from the premisses.

1564 *Brief Exam.* ***** ij b, After this you bring in a patch of Gratians decrees. *Caus. 21 Quest.* 4..This is a *Non sequitur.* **1643** Prynne *Sov. Power Parl.* iii. 90 The proper argument then that can be thence deduced by our Opposites, is but this *Nonsequitur.* *a* **1726** Gilbert *Cases in Law & Equity* (1760) 98 (Stanf.), The Justices need not set forth any Reason of their Judgment, therefore a *Non sequitur* will not vitiate. **1817** *Parl. Deb.* col. 1070 (Stanf.), This was so inconsequent, such a *non sequitur* in reasoning, that he left it to the noble lord, and the other logicians on the Treasury-bench, to solve the problem. **1863** Kirk *Chas. the Bold* II. 403 *note*, The delicious *non sequitur* of this conclusion need scarcely be pointed out.

transf. and *fig.* **1533** Elyot *Pasquill* A iij, Thou haste the strangest apparaile that euer I loked on... This longe estrige fether doeth wonderly wel... But this longe gowne with strayte sleues is a *non sequitur.* **1855** Geo. Eliot *Ess.* (1884) 150 His practice is in many respects an amiable *non sequitur* from his teaching.

nonsicut. *nonce-word*, f. L. *nōn* not + *sīcut* so, after nonesuch.

1621 Bp. Mountagu *Diatribe* 28 And so be δακτυλόδεικτοι, of all passengers by, for absolute Nonsicuts in intolerable arrogancy.

nonsien, obs. form of nuncheon.

non-sig'nificant, *sb.* [non- 3.] A sign, symbol, or statement that is not significant.

1605 Bacon *Adv. Learn.* ii. 61 The Simple Cyphars with Changes, and intermixtures of Nulles, and Nonsignificants. **1654** Whitlock *Zootomia* 387 With many such non-significants, or mean-nothings.

So **non-sig'nificance, non-sig'nificative** *a.*

1633 Ames *Fresh Suit agst. Human Cerem.* 84 He shall perceave some non significative to be the speciall to the Genus of a significative cere[mony]. **1846** *Proc. Philol. Soc.* III. 9 Respecting the significance or non-significance of those elements.

non-sig'nificant, *a.* [non- 3.] Not significant. Also *absol.*

1902 S. H. Butcher *Aristotle's Theory of Poetry & Fine Art* (ed. 3) x. 377 In Plautus the number of names etymologically significant and appropriate largely preponderates over the non-significant. **1903** C. G. D. Roberts *Barbara Ladd* 219 His wife was a non-significant, abundant, gently acquiescent pudding of a woman. **1923** J. S. Huxley *Ess. Biologist* iv. 139 These differences may be biologically speaking non-significant, mere accidents of the primary difference. **1973** *Jrnl. Genetic Psychol.* CXXIII. 10 A nonsignificant correlation of −.10 was obtained. **1974** *Nature* 22 Nov. 272/2 Unobserved objects (black holes, dead white dwarfs and so on) must only make up a non-significant percentage of the galactic mass.

†**non-sin'cere**, *a. Obs. rare.* [non- 3.] Not decided for or against a measure.

1656 Harrington *Oceana* (1700) 132 The Suffrage being gather'd and open'd before the Signory, if the red Box, or Nonsincere had above half the Suffrages [etc.]. *Ibid.* 156 Three Boxes, the Negative, the Affirmative and the Non-sincere. [Cf. p. 119 *bossolo di non sinceri.*]

non-sked: see non-scheduled *a.*

non-skid, *a.* and *sb.* [non- 4 or 5 b.] **A.** *adj.* That does not skid, or is designed to prevent skidding. **B.** *sb.* A tyre, substance, etc., designed to prevent skidding. So **non-'skidding** *ppl. a.*

1908 *Sears, Roebuck Catal.* 169/1 We have added to this tire a link chain non-skid tread, the most practical and scientific tread ever made. **1908** *Daily Report* 12 Sept. 8/4 It is absolutely incumbent upon all owners of such cars to only use this sort of non-skid in the winter. **1909** *Chambers's Jrnl.* June 404/1 A perfect non-skidding wheel. **1911** *Daily Colonist* (Victoria, B.C.) 2 Apr. 10/1 (Advt.), Michelin 'Semelle' Non-Skids, unlike so-called non-skids made wholly of rubber, do not wear down into ordinary smooth treads. **1920** *Motor Cycle* 29 July 129/2 Non-skid chains. **1925** *Public Opinion* 11 Dec. 588/3 We want light-coloured, waterproof, nonskid surfaces. **1937** [see autostrada]. **1944–45** *Jane's Fighting Ships* (1946) 459 Armoured flight deck is..covered with non-skid surface material. **1972** *Country Life* 15 June 1577/2 A useful top oddments shelf with non-skid surface. **1972** *Islander* (Victoria, B.C.) 25 June 2/2 Many busy weeks and months were spent painting and putting non-skid on the decks.

non-slip, *a.* [non- 4 or 5 b.] That does not slip, or is designed to prevent slipping. So **non-'slipping** *ppl. a.* and *vbl. sb.*

1904 G. B. Shaw *Common Sense of Municipal Trading* vii. 56 To ride bicycles through greasy mud..on tires advertized as 'non-slipping'. **1909** Webster, Nonslip. **1912** *Chambers's Jrnl.* Jan. 78/2 The gyroscope non-slipping device has been subjected to many exacting tests, but has established its capabilities to overcome skidding. **1933** *Archit. Rev.* LXXIII. 219 The staircase is in concrete, and the steps are rendered non-slip on the nosings. **1956** [see granolithic *a.*]. **1959** *Times* 27 Apr. (Suppl. Rubber Industry) p. vi/7 Special non-slipping mineral grain-filled flooring is used for safety walks and service corridors. **1973** *Times* 19 Oct. 14/3 (*caption*) Non-slip. They are unlikely to get pushed across the kitchen floor.

non-'smoker. [non- 2.] A person who does not smoke.

1846 in H. C. Webster *Railways for All* (1950) xv. 114 Smokers and non-smokers should be apart, but why should smokers exclusively be indulged with the use of the best carriages on the line? **1860** *Pharmaceutical Jrnl.* II. iii. 190 Dividing the pupils..into..the smokers and the non-smokers, it is shown that the smokers have proved themselves in the various competitive examinations far inferior to the others. **1891** W. Morris *News from Nowhere* vi. 37 Bob is always telling me that we non-smokers are a selfish lot. **1898** K. Baedeker *Spain & Portugal* p. xv, Every train is bound to have a first-class compartment..and another for non-smokers. **1921** G. B. Shaw *Back to Methuselah* ii. 84 They believe the tee-totallers and non-smokers live longer. **1973** K. Giles *File on Death* i. 10 No car, two suits a year, non-smoker, allows more than he should afford on drink.

b. A compartment in a railway carriage, or other conveyance, where smoking is not permitted. *colloq.*

1962 J. Braine *Life at Top* v. 74 All the first-class compartments seemed to be full; finally I got a seat in a non-smoker. **1971** 'L. Black' *Death has Green Fingers* iii. 29 When the woman angrily lit a cigarette, he pointed out to her..that she was in a non-smoker.

non-'smoking, *a.* [non- 4, 6.] Denoting a railway compartment, carriage, etc., in which smoking is not permitted.

1891 H. Spencer *Let.* 27 Mar. in G. S. Layard *Mrs. Lynn Linton* (1901) xx. 278 One may persist in putting down smoking in a non-smoking compartment of a railway carriage. **1909** *Daily Chron.* 17 Sept. 4/7 A well-known clergyman was travelling in a non-smoking compartment of a train. **1922** C. E. Montague *Disenchantment* (1924) vi. 86 Trains are divided into 'non-smoking' and 'smoking'. **1936** *Punch* 5 Feb. 141/3 Discovering as we finish lighting our pipes that we are in a Ladies Only Non-Smoking carriage. **1963** *Mod. Railways* May 359/1 The sliding door to the non-smoking compartment is often left open by passengers.

b. Denoting a person who does not smoke.

1946 *R.A.F. Jrnl.* May 178 Les, non-smoking but not teetotal,..will never fail to stand by for a duty. **1972** J. Mosedale *Football* v. 65 The non-smoking, non-drinking Graham, of whom it was said, 'His idea of a big night is eating chocolate ice cream.' **1975** V. Canning *Kingsford Mark* v. 74 Are you still non-smoking and non-drinking?

non-so'ciety. [non- 4.] *attrib.* Not belonging to a society; *spec.* applied to a workman who is not a member of a trade-union, or to an establishment in which such men are employed.

1851 Mayhew *Lond. Labour* (1861) III. 222/2 The slopworkers of the different trades—the cheap men or non-society hands. **1886** *Pall Mall G.* 22 Oct. 10/2 The Board had paid more for printing in 'non-society' houses than in society houses. **1890** W. J. Gordon *Foundry* 192 Its [*The Times*] being a non-society office.

non-'solvency. [non- 1.] Failure or inability to pay what is owing; insolvency.

1708 *Brit. Apollo* No. 83. 2/1 The Non-solvency of such a trifle. **1732** Swift *Proposal National Debt* Wks. 1751 IX. 188 Some of the Purchasers..may be content to live cheap in a worse Country, rather than be at the Charge of Exchange and Agencies; and, perhaps of Non-solvencies in Absence, if they let their Lands too high. **1734** —— *Reasons agst. settling Tythe of Hemp* Ibid. 261 The Tythes..have..sunk..at least one Fourth of their former Value, exclusive of all Non-solvencies.

non-'solvent, *a.* (*sb.*) [non- 3.] **A.** *adj.* Not solvent; unable to pay debts; insolvent.

1625 B. Jonson *Staple of N.* iv. Interm., *Cen.* For a decay'd wit— *Exp.* Broken— *Tat.* Non-soluent. **1644** Heylin *Stumbling-block* Tracts (1681) 679 Unless,..being one of the Farmers of the Tolls and Taxes,..he became non-solvent, and had not cleared his accompt with the Common-wealth. **1669** Owen *Doctr. Trin. Vind.* (1851) II. 437 The debt which He took upon Himself, and discharged for us, when we were nonsolvent, in His love.

B. *sb.* One who is unable to pay his debts.

1647 Trapp *Comm. Luke* vii. xlii, We are all non-solvents, stark beggars.

non-'specialist, *a.* and *sb.* [non- 3, 2.] **A.** *adj.* That is not a specialist. **B.** *sb.* One who is not a specialist.

1919 W. Lewis *Caliph's Design* iii. 53, I am..only giving so much general matter..as is necessary to remind a non-specialist public of the rough points of the position. **1933** *Discovery* Sept. 286/2 He has just written a remarkable book, where the non-specialist will find much of interest. **1958** *Times Lit. Suppl.* 24 Jan. 46/2 An editor whose speciality is to be non-specialist. **1971** J. Spencer *Eng. Lang. W. Afr.* p. viii, If our explorations prove to be of interest to the non-specialist, while at the same time stimulating the specialist to embark upon further research, we shall be very well satisfied. **1975** *Listener* 28 Aug. 280/3 The performance criteria were clear to non-specialists.

non-'specie. [non- 4.] Used *attrib.*, Not payable in specie.

1697 *Lond. Gaz.* No. 3345/7 The said Trustees shall pay to such Person or Persons Money for the said Bills, if they be Specie Bills; Or deliver other Bills of like value, if they be Non-Specie Bills. **1711** Luttrell *Brief Rel.* (1857) VI. 677 A supply..to enable her majestie to make all non specie exchequer bills specie.

non-spe'cific, *a.* [non- 3.] Not specific; esp. in *Med.*, not specific as regards cause or effects. Hence ˌ**non-speci'ficity.**

1938 R. W. Lawson tr. *Hevesy & Paneth's Man. Radioactivity* (ed. 2) xv. 147 Non-specific adsorption forces do not play a part in this process. **1939** H. Kogan et al. in Saporta & Bastian *Psycholinguistics* (1961) 534/2 Gestalt psychology..left unaltered the postulate of its non-specificity. **1942** Darlington & Mather *Genes, Plants & People* (1950) iv. 37 The difference between activity and inertness would then be the difference between specificity and non-specificity. **1964** W. G. Smith *Allergy & Tissue Metabolism* ii. 29 Promethazine produces considerable antagonism, but the effect is probably a non-specific one. **1971** *Brit. Med. Bull.* XXVII. 61/1 This group of diseases might be referred to as 'chronic non-specific lung disease'. **1971** J. Z. Young *Introd. Study Man* xxvi. 372 The first organism included only one enzyme, a non-specific phosphokinase. **1975** I. K. Martin *Regan & Manhattan File* 88 He made some non-specific enquiries to the FBI.

nonsse: see ounce *sb.*[1]

nonst, obs. f. nonce[1].

non-'standard, *a.* [non- 3.] Not standard; esp. of language that is not standard (see standard *a.* 3).

1924 *Simplified Practice Recommendation* (U.S. Nat. Bureau Standards) XVI. 61 These tables include certain illustrative combinations of standard, and nonstandard, widths and thicknesses. **1927** *Reliable Poultry Jrnl.* Feb. 33 Whatever may be said of the policy of showing the non-Standard colors, there can be no doubt..that a class of all Standard colored birds makes a much better impression on the lay visitor than a class of mixed shades of color. **1933** L. Bloomfield *Language* iii. 48 'Bad' or 'vulgar' or, as the linguist prefers to call it, *non-standard* English. **1962** A. Battersby *Guide to Stock Control* viii. 77 Another multiplier of stock items is the non-standard product. **1971** *Engineering* Apr. 117 Diameters can be altered slightly to produce non-standard sizes. **1973** *Archivum Linguisticum* IV. 107 It might well only give evidence of a socially determined Nonstandard English.

b. *Math.* Involving infinitesimals and infinities, as quantities which are not defined in the real number system but can be rigorously accommodated in a model which includes that system.

1961 A. Robinson in *Proc. K. Nederlandse Akad. v. Wetensch.* A. LXIV. 432 (*heading*) Non-standard analysis. *Ibid.* 437 Let $f(x, t)$ be a standard function defined in a standard set S_1, and let $g(x) = f(x, \omega)$, where ω is non-standard, e.g. infinite or infinitesimal. **1966** —— *Non-Standard Analysis* p. vii, In the fall of 1960 it occurred to me that the concepts and methods of contemporary Mathematical Logic are capable of providing a suitable framework for the development of the Differential and Integral Calculus by means of infinitely small and infinitely large numbers. I first reported my ideas in a seminar talk at Princeton University (November 1960) and, later, in an address at the annual meeting of the Association for Symbolic Logic (January 1961) and in a paper published in the Proceedings of the Royal Academy of Sciences of Amsterdam... The resulting subject was called by me Non-standard Analysis since it involves and was, in part, inspired by the so-called Non-standard models of Arithmetic whose existence was first pointed out by T. Skolem. **1972** *Sci. Amer.* June 86/2 We define the instantaneous velocity not as the ratio of infinitesimal increments, as L'Hôpital did, but rather as the standard part of that ratio; then *ds, dt* and their ratio *ds/dt* are nonstandard real numbers. We have as before $ds/dt = 32 + 16dt$, but now we immediately conclude, rigorously and without any limiting argument, that *v*, the standard part of *ds/dt*, equals 32.

non-'starter. [non- 2.] One who does not start something; esp. one who fails to start in a race or other contest; hence, a useless or ineffective person or thing; an impracticable idea.

1909 in Webster. **1932** *Brit. Jrnl. Psychol.* July 31 Besides the 33 non-starters, only two made no attempt at this test. **1934** Wodehouse *Right Ho, Jeeves* ii. 27, I reminded myself that this non-starter and I had been at school together. **1942** 'A. Bridge' *Frontier Passage* iii. 49 That's one reason why non-intervention is such a non-starter. **1952** A. J. Ayer *Philosophical Essays* (1954) iii. 42 A statement..might be a non-starter, in the sense that the question of its truth or falsehood did not arise. **1973** C. Mullard *Black Britain* iii. ix. 109 People begin to dub the council a nonstarter.

non-stick, *a.* [non- 5 b.] That does not stick or allow sticking; *spec.* of a cooking utensil: to which food does not adhere.

1958 *Listener* 4 Dec. 967/1 Silicones are used..for..coating cooking pans to make them 'non-stick'. **1960** *Farmer & Stockbreeder* 1 Mar. 153/2 (Advt.), Men's non-stick P.V.C. plastic oilskin coats. **1968** *Guardian* 9 July 7/3 The cost of the non-stick oven lining adds £6 10s to the price of a cooker. **1973** 'D. Jordan' *Nile Green* ii. 14 Sticky non-stick frying pans in the sink.

non-stop, *a.*, *sb.*, and *adv.* [non- 4 or 5 b.]

A. *adj.* That does not stop; *spec.* of a railway train or other conveyance: that travels between two (usually distant) places without stopping at intermediate ones; of a journey, etc.: made or done without a stop; of a variety show or the like: in which there is no interval between the various acts.

1903 *Work* 11 July 364/1 The L. & N.W. Railway long non-stop run..presents no difficulty. **1904** *Windsor Mag.* Dec. p. ix (Advt.), Awards gained for Glasgow to London non-stop trials. **1910** *Punch* 15 June 441/2 *Platelayer* (to passenger who has jumped from the London-Plymouth Non-stop Express). Jumped aht? did yer.—Wof for? **1914** *Whitaker's Almanack 1915* 822/1 Britannia trophy awarded to Capt. Longcroft, R.F.C., for non-stop flight Montrose to Farnborough. **1923** WODEHOUSE *Inimitable Jeeves* xv. 192, I was fairly tired, having swung a practically non-stop shoe from shortly after dinner till two a.m. **1932** *Sunday Express* 3 July 17/6 Of all the people in non-stop variety, the one I should most hate to annoy is Veronica, the dancer. She can do fifty high kicks in twenty-five seconds. **1938** *Times Lit. Suppl.* 15 Jan. 44/1 A job as chorus girl in a very undressed non-stop revue. **1957** *Economist* 28 Dec. 1120/2 The sum total of his economics is that a non-stop increase in money wages is.. a Good Thing. **1967** G. F. FIENNES *I tried to run a Railway* vii. 86 Averages of 75 m.p.h. for the non-stop business expresses. **1973** 'I. DRUMMOND' *Jaws of Watchdog* i. 9 The party will be out to sea. A seventy-two hour trip, way the hell out, a non-stop party. **1973** *Country Life* 23 Aug. 476/2 The Windmill Theatre.. became famous as the home of live, non-stop revue.

B. *sb.* A non-stop train; a non-stop journey or run; (see also quot. 1925; *obs. slang*).

1909 *Westm. Gaz.* 8 Sept. 2/1 The innovation and growth of 'non-stops' upon the Metropolitan and District electric lines. **1911** *Motor Cycle* 27 Apr. 428/1 He.. has now made six successive non-stops. **1922** V. WOOLF *Jacob's Room* ix. 183 The hordes crossing Waterloo Bridge to catch the non-stop to Surbiton. **1925** FRASER & GIBBONS *Soldier & Sailor Words* 210 *Nonstop, a,* a trench expression used of a long range shell passing high overhead. **1957** *Railway Mag.* Jan. 22/2 Thus the non-stops to and from Sheffield were suspended. **1958** J. BETJEMAN *Coll. Poems* 202 They.. caught the first non-stop to Willesden Green.

C. *adv.* Without stopping.

1920 'IXION' *Motor Cycle Remin.* 15 The beastie [*sc.* a motor cycle] did the outward journey non-stop. **1927** *Daily Tel.* 14 June 11/3 The second attempt to fly non-stop to India. **1942** *R.A.F. Jrnl.* 16 May 9 The test pilot.. flew the aircraft non-stop from Moscow to Baku and back. **1953** A. UPFIELD *Murder must Wait* xvii. 147 We were talking non-stop. **1963** *Ann. Reg. 1962* 447 One station in New York (WBAI) gave the whole *Der Ring des Nibelungen* in 17 hours non-stop. **1965** W. SOYINKA *Road* 21 Have you known any other driver take an oil-tanker from Port Harcourt to Kaduna non-stop since Muftan died? **1968** M. BRAGG *Without City Wall* x. 112 Both he and Richard went on non-stop about London, their friends, politics, anything that came up.

non-sub'scriber. Also *Sc.* 7 -scriver, -scryver. [NON- 2.]

1. One who refuses to subscribe to an undertaking, a religious creed, etc.

(*a*) In Scottish Church History, one who did not subscribe to the National Covenant of 1638; (*b*) one of the section of Irish presbyterians which arose in 1720 and opposed the imposition of subscription to the Westminster Confession. Now *Hist.*

1599 (*title*), A Triall of Subscription, by way of a Preface vnto certaine Subscribers; And, Reasons for lesse rigour against non-subscribers. **1621** *1st & 2nd Bks. Discipl.* (Calderwood) 11 That whosoever hath borne office in the ministerie of the Kirke within this Realme.. shall be charged.. to subscrive the heads of the discipline of the Kirk of this Realme.., under the paine of excommunication to be executed against the non-subscrivers. **1638** R. BAILLIE *Lett. & Jrnls.* (1841) I. 78 That day was a solemne Fast over all our Kingdome... Some of our non-subscryvers refused to joyne. **1650** (*title*), A brief Apology for all non subscribers, and looking glasse for all apostate, perjured prescribers, and subscribers of the new engagement. **1727** *Narr. Prov. Synods Presbyt. Irel.* 36 The Ministers, who in a few days after [in June, 1721] were distinguish'd by the name of Non-subscribers.

2. One who does not pay a subscription.

1713 *Lond. Gaz.* No. 5131/4 Subscribers pay one Guinea, and Non-Subscribers five Guineas Entrance. **1816** T. J. HOWELL *Stranger in Shrewsbury* 65 The public libraries in Shrewsbury are wretchedly furnished except one, and to *that* entrance is almost denied to strangers and non-subscribers. **1884** *List of Subscribers* (London & Globe Telephone Co.) [3] Subscribers.. must not allow non-subscribers to use their instruments for the transmission of messages.

So **non-sub'scribing** *vbl. sb.*, **non-sub'scription**, refusal or failure to subscribe (e.g. to a religious creed); also **non-sub'scribing** *ppl. a.*

1662 WOOD *Life* 24 Aug. (O.H.S.) I. 453 What heads of houses was turned out upon non-subscribing to the Act of Uniformity. **1716** [see NONCONFORMING *vbl. sb.*]. **1727** *Narr. Prov. Synods Presbyt. Irel.* 58 An anonymous Pamphlet, called, *The Mind of the Synod*, which contained many grievous Aspersions on the Non-subscribing Ministers. **1736** CHANDLER *Hist. Persec.* 395 The two great evils of the Church, Non-subscription and Arianism. **1747** H. WALPOLE *Lett.* (1846) II. 199 The non-subscribing at the time of the rebellion has been most successfully played off upon the Jacobites. **1827** *Christian Moderator* I. (*title of article*), Progress of Nonsubscription to Creeds. **1879** WITHEROW *Mem. Presbyt. Irel.* 166 Opening of the non-Subscription Controversy. **1895** *Daily News* 24 Oct. 3/3 Unitarians.. were.. Non-Subscribing—i.e. their trust deeds did not provide that ministerial officers.. should subscribe to a creed.

non-sub'stantial, *a. Philosophy.* [NON- 3.] Not substantial. Hence **non-sub'stantialism**, the theory that there is no substance underlying phenomena; = NIHILISM 2. Also **non-sub'stantialist**, one who holds the doctrine of non-substantialism; = NIHILIST 1.

1836-7 SIR W. HAMILTON *Metaph.* xvi. (1859) I. 294 Philosophers.. are divided into Realists or Substantialists, and into Nihilists or Non-Substantialists. **1865** MASSON *Rec. Brit. Philos.* 66 The system of Nihilism or, as it may be better called, Non-substantialism. **1875** MᶜLAREN *Serm.* Ser. II. i. 13 They are non-substantial and non-permanent.

non-suc'cess. [NON- 1. Cf. F. *non-succès.*] Want of success.

1665 NEEDHAM *Med. Medicinae* 282 The Non-Successes of the common Methods and Medicins. **1837** DE QUINCEY *Coleridge* Wks. 1854 II. 167 It was natural to impute his non-success exclusively to his own irregular application. **1897** *Westm. Gaz.* 1 Apr. 2/1 That impatience of non-success which was often noted as a defect in his character. **1902** *Outing* June 278/1 The success or non-success of the finished picture from an artistic standpoint.

So **non-suc'cessful** *a.*, not successful.

1867 *Routledge's Ev. Boy's Ann.* Dec. 769 If non-successful, there comes a smash. **1901** *Scotsman* 13 Mar. 12/2 The publication of the non-successful estimates.

nonsuch ('nɒnsʌtʃ), *sb.* and *a.* [var. of NONESUCH, and now the usual form.

The change of *none* (nʌn) to *non-* would be natural in a compound of this form, but may have been partly helped by association with the prefix NON-.]

I. †1. = NONESUCH 1. *Obs. rare*$^{-1}$.

1620 R. N. *Sonn.* in *Sylvester's Du Bartas*, Then by right Rare Muses Non-Such shall thy Worke be hight.

2. = NONESUCH 2.

1657 S. PURCHAS *Pol. Flying-Ins.* 13 For every Hive, or Commonwealth, endeavours to be a Non-such, and to engross all within its own circumference. **1677** W. HUGHES *Man of Sin* I. i. 2 We have therein a very Nonsuch, for the enriching that Ægypt, which it passeth through. **1710** T. FULLER *Pharm. Extemp.* 106 An Oliose Draught.. is a Nonsuch for a Pleurisy. **1820** AMELIA OPIE *Tales of Heart* IV. 274, I have got a little pot of honey and some rob.., as 'tis reckoned a nonsuch for a cough.

b. = NONESUCH 2 b.

1655 GURNALL *Chr. in Arms.* I. (1665) 132 Was not Job the Devil's hypocrite, whom God vouch't for a non-such in holinesse. **1670** BROOKS *Wks.* (1867) VI. 30 Job was a non-such in his day for holiness. **1753** RICHARDSON *Sir C. Grandison* I. xxii. (1781) 152 Then you are, as indeed I have always thought you, a nonsuch of a woman. **1819** KEATS *Let. to G. Keats* 14 Feb., A young gentleman.. leaves his unfortunate Bride and follows this nonsuch. **1850** DOBELL *Roman* v. Poet. Wks. (1875) 61 Nay, everybody! Write me up a nonsuch! I can beat everybody. **1895** 'SARAH TYTLER' *Macdonald Lass* 172 As for your Prince,.. he's not a nonsuch.

c. In depreciatory sense.

1836 *Gentl. Mag.* V. 423/2 The audience were insulted by the mis-representation of a nonsuch called the Fate of War, which caused a tremendous disturbance in the Theatre.

†3. = NONESUCH 3. *Obs.*

1635 BRATHWAIT *Arcadian Princess* II. 11 He was esteemed the Non-such of his time. **1660** W. SECKER *Nonsuch Prof.* 9 Beleivers in the world, they are the Non-such's of the world. **1673** JANEWAY *Heaven upon Earth* (1847) 212 Those brave worthies who were.. the nonsuches of their age, and a pattern to future generations.

†4. *adj.* = NONESUCH 4. *Obs.*

1667 WATERHOUSE *Fire Lond.* 3 This spoil and non-such disappointment. **1711** *10th Rep. Hist. MSS. Comm.* App. V. 186 A non-such contempt of the world in a monarch. **1728** P. WALKER *Life Peden* Pref. (1827) 7 Ere that tremendous non-such stroke came upon Jerusalem.

II. *spec.* **5.** = NONESUCH 5. ? *Obs.*

1760 J. LEE *Introd. Bot.* App. 320 Nonsuch, *Lychnis.*

6. a. A species of Lucern (see quot. 1844). Also called ***black nonsuch***.

1668 *Phil. Trans.* III. 725 Of 7 acre of Non-such or Hopp-Clover. **1669** WORLIDGE *Syst. Agric.* (1681) 31 It's better to sowe three [bushels] mixt with Nonsuch. **1705** *Lond. Gaz.* No. 4111/4 Broad Clover and Trefoil, alias Non-such. **1768-74** TUCKER *Lt. Nat.* (1834) I. 501 Every country fellow makes the distinction between natural grass, and clover, nonsuch, or others that are sown. **1778** *Eng. Gazetteer* (ed. 2) s.v. *Worplesdon*, A sort of grass was lately much cultivated in these parts, called Nonsuch, which is equal to St. Foin. **1844** STEPHENS *Bk. Farm* II. 556 *Medicago lupulina* is the hop-clover, or black nonsuch, which is.. sown by some farmers amongst their grass.

attrib. **1766** *Museum Rust.* VI. 338 We find it useful, also, when we sow any saintfoin, to throw in about a gallon of nonsuch seed.

b. ***white nonsuch***, rye-grass seed. ? *Obs.*

1787 MARSHALL *E. Norfolk* (1795) Gloss.

7. A variety of apple (†and pear). Also *attrib.*

1676 WORLIDGE *Cyder* (1691) 210 The Non-such [apple] is a long-lasting fruit, good at the table. *Ibid.* 216 The Non-such, Dionier,.. are all very good winter-pears. **1846** MRS. GORE *Eng. Char.* (1852) 112 With lustrous, rosy, and whiskerless face, round as a Nonsuch apple. **1859** F. G. WHITE *Addr. Cape Town Fine Arts Exhib.* 13 No man in his senses would eat sour crabs when he could get ribstone pippins or nonsuch apples.

†nonsue, *v. Obs.* [NON- 5.] = NONSUIT *v.*

1437 *Rolls of Parlt.* IV. 509/2 He woll be nonsued; and theruppon he wolle begynne a newe feyned suite. **1487** *Act 3 Hen. VII*, c. 10 Yf.. that persone.. that sueth Writte.. of errour be nonsued [AF. *nonsuez*] in the same.

†non-su'fficient. *Obs.* [NON- 1. Cf. INSUFFICIENT *sb.* 1.] Insufficiency.

1425 *Rolls of Parlt.* IV. 276/2 Knowlech of the suffisante or nonsuffisante of swiche [persones] as ye Kyng.. offrid. **1477** *Ibid.* VI. 186/1 For non sufficiente of the said Gardeyn and Wyrker to answere of the forseid forfeiture.

†nonsuing, *vbl. sb. Obs.* [NON- 7.] Failure to sue.

1620 J. WILKINSON *Coroners & Sherifes* 51 That he shall .. discharge.. the said J. H... from.. all maner of troubles.. either by nonsuing, or unlawfull returning.. of any precepts.

nonsuit ('nɒnsjuːt), *sb. Law.* [a. AF. *no(u)n-sute*: see NON- 1 and SUIT *sb.*] In early use, the cessation of a suit resulting from the voluntary withdrawal of the plaintiff; in modern use, the stoppage of a suit by the judge, when, in his opinion, the plaintiff fails to make out a legal cause of action or to bring sufficient evidence. (See also quot. 1884.) †Also *fig.*

c **1380** WYCLIF *Wks.* (1880) 410 But ech prest may liȝtly þus sue crist ȝif he lette not hym silf, & þus synne excusiþ hym not þat he synne not in þis noun suyt. **1488** *Rolls of Parlt.* VI. 417/2 The said discontinuance, or any Nonsuyt of or in the said Atteint. **1566** PAINTER *Pal. Pleas.* (1569) I. 42 Menalippus ouer came him in law. and the noble men which were the frends of Phalaris, would giue no sentence, but brought the matter to a nonsuite. **1606-7** *Act 4 Jas. I*, c. 3 (*title*), An Act to give Costes to the Defendant uppon a Nonsuite of the Plaintiffe. **1632** *Star Chamber Cases* (Camden) 128 The Kinges Bench afterwardes discharged the costes upon the nonsuit. **1741** *Act 14 Geo. II*, c. 17 §1 That all Judgments given by virtue of this Act shall be of the like Force and Effect as Judgments upon Nonsuit. **1768** [see NON-PROSEQUITUR]. **1803** SYD. SMITH *Wks.* (1859) I. 50/1 A proof of non-residence might be made to operate as a nonsuit in an action for tithes. **1883** *Law Rep.* 11 *Q.B. Div.* 591 Watkin Williams, J., was of opinion that the words above mentioned were privileged.. and directed a nonsuit. **1884** *Encycl. Brit.* XVII. 534/2 s.v., The matter now is of no great importance, for, although judgment of nonsuit still exists, it has, since the Judicature Acts, the same effect as a judgment on the merits, unless the court otherwise directs.

†'nonsuit, *a. Law. Obs.* [app. intended as a pa. ppl. form on the analogy of words like *execute*. AF. had *nounsuy*.] Subjected to a nonsuit; nonsuited.

c **1476** *Plumpton Corr.* (Camden) 35 Ailmer wife was like to have bene non suit in her appeale. **1531-2** *Act 23 Hen. VIII*, c. 2 §4 The same partie so nonsuite or so discontynueng the said Atteynt. **1594** WEST *2nd Pt. Symbol.* §43 When one hath bin nonsuit he may begin againe. **1660** BONDE *Scut. Reg.* 58 The King in a manner is every-where. .. And therefore it is that he cannot be non-suite. **1720** *Lond. Gaz.* No. 5868/5 The Officers become Non-suit. **1768** BLACKSTONE *Comm.* III. 376 If the plaintiff does not appear, no verdict can be given, but the plaintiff is said to be nonsuit, *non sequitur clamorem suum.* **1817** SELWYN *Law Nisi Prius* (ed. 4) II. 857 In case the plaintiff become nonsuit, or discontinue his action.

fig. **1581** MULCASTER *Positions* xxxviii. (1888) 174 They will rather retire for shame and proue to be nonsuite, then confesse themselues faulty. **1589** WARNER *Alb. England* VI. xxxi. (1612) 155 Better at first be Non-sute, than at length not to subdue.

†b. *transf.* Of a project: Interrupted, balked.

1679 'TOM TICKLEFOOT' *Obs. Trials of Wakeman*, etc. 8 The Plot is Non-suit, *Semel insanivimus omnes.*

'nonsuit, *v.* [f. NONSUIT *sb.* or *a.*] *Law. trans.* To subject to a nonsuit.

1531-2 *Act 23 Hen. VIII*, c. 15 (*title*), An Acte that the Defendaunt shall recover Costes ageinste the Pleyntif, if the Pleyntif be nonsuited, or if the verdicte passe ageinste him. **1593** NASHE *Christ's T.* 51 b, If hee haue but a quarter of an enemy in the Court, it [*sc.* his suit] is casheird and non suted. **1606-7** *Act 4 Jas. I*, c. 3 Cases where the Plaintiff.. should become Nonsuited. **1709** STEELE *Tatler* No. 39 ¶4 The University has been Nonsuited in their Action against the Booksellers for printing Clarendon in Quarto. **1768** BLACKSTONE *Comm.* III. xx. 295 Formerly they [*sc.* common pledges] were of use to answer to the king for the amercement of the plaintiff, in case he were non-suited. **1818** CRUISE *Digest* (ed. 2) IV. 304 Ld. Ch. Just. de Grey thought such parol evidence inadmissible, and nonsuited the plaintiff.

absol. **1818** BYRON *Juan* I. clxxxix, The pleadings Of counsel to nonsuit, or to annul.

†b. *transf.* and *fig.* (sometimes with a pun).

1604 SHAKS. *Oth.* I. i. 16 But he.. Euades them, with a bumbast Circumstance..; Non-suites my Mediators. **1608** TOPSELL *Serpents* 99 Lest.. he [*sc.* a lover] should turne Crauen.. or else be vtterly non-suited. *a* **1652** BROME *Covent Garden* II. i, [A tailor says:] I can do no lesse then take you by default and non-suit you. **1714** MANDEVILLE *Fable Bees* (1725) I. 317 Your sly sinners that.. hope that it will expiate their guilt, and Satan be nonsuited by it at a small expence.

Hence **'non-suiting** *vbl. sb.*

1662 HIBBERT *Body Divinity* I. 92 They are sure of.. the non-suting of all actions and accusations.

non-'summons. *Law.* [NON- 1.] Failure to serve a summons in due time.

1630 EARL MANCH. in *Buccleuch MSS.* (Hist. MSS. Comm.) I. 273 Putting in of dilatory pleas, as non-summons. **1845** E. V. WILLIAMS *Saunders' Rep. K.B.* II. 1. 45 c, The summons must be served fifteen days before the day of the return of the writ, otherwise the tenant may wage his law of non-summons.

†nonsunt. *Sc. Obs.* Also -sount, ? -sant. [Two words of the legend on the reverse of the coin, which runs IAM . NON . SVNT . DVO . SED . VNA . CARO . 'they are no more twain, but one flesh' (Matt. xix. 6).] The twelve-penny groat coined under Francis and Mary (1558-9).

1564 in Pitcairn *Crim. Trials* I. 440 Tressonabill cunȝeing off diuerse fals Testonis, half Testonis, Non suntis, and Lyones callit Hardheidis. **1567** *Sc. Acts Parl.* (1814) III. 43/2 It is thocht neidfull that all nonsunt be proclamit to vj d, babeis to iij d, plakis to ij d, hardheidis to half pennyis. **1584** *Reg. Privy Council Scot.* III. 706 Fals and adulterat cunyie of nonsantis.

†**non-su'rrective**, *a. Obs.* [L. *surrect-*, ppl. stem of *surgĕre* to rise + -IVE.] (See quot.)
1668 WILKINS *Real Char.* 341 A Person.. Unwalkative, is a Cripple; Non surrective, is Bedrid.

nonsute, obs. form of NONSUIT.

†**non-'swearer.** *Obs.* [NON- 2.] = NON-JUROR. Also *attrib.*
1690 *Let. to Dissenting Clergyman* 10 Some of the Gentlemen.. are such as have admired even the meanest of the Non-Swearers. **1691** [see NON-JUROR]. **1691** LUTTRELL *Brief Rel.* (1857) II. 326 One Wilcox, a nonswearer parson. **1692** *Let. to Friend* in *Harleian Misc.* (1746) VII. 296 All our Non-swearers could not hinder the late Revolution, nor can they make another. *c* **1693** *Mem. Cnt. Teckely* Pref. p. xi, The best Use of this is to be made by the Non-swearers.
So †**non-'swearing** *vbl. sb.* and *ppl. a.*, non-juring.
1691 LUTTRELL *Brief Rel.* (1857) II. 162 The other non-swearing bishops. **1692** *Let. to Friend* in *Harleian Misc.* (1746) VII. 296 Could their Non-swearing restore him to his Throne again, it would [etc.]. *a* **1704** T. BROWN *Satire upon French King* Wks. 1730 I. 59 A non-swearing parson.

non-sy'llabic, *a.* and *sb. Linguistics.* [NON- 3, 2.] **A.** *adj.* **a.** = ASYLLABIC *a.*; *spec.* denoting a speech-sound that does not constitute the predominant sonority of the syllable in which it occurs. **b.** Not syllable-timed. **B.** *sb.* A non-syllabic speech-sound.
1909 WEBSTER, Nonsyllabic, *a.* **1933** L. BLOOMFIELD *Language* vii. 120 Some of the phonemes are more sonorous than the phonemes (or the silence) which immediately precede or follow... Any such phoneme is a *crest of sonority* or a *syllabic*; the other phonemes are *non-syllabic*. Thus the [e] in *red* and the [r] in *bird* are syllabics, but the [r] in *red* and the [d] in *red* and *bird* are non-syllabics. **1947** K. L. PIKE *Phonemics* 30/1 The acoustic quality is quite similar to that which is found when they are acting as nonsyllabics. **1957** H. WHITEHALL in N. Frye *Sound & Poetry* 143 The first distinction would be drawn between syllabic and non-syllabic rhythms. **1961** R. B. LONG *Sentence & its Parts* xvii. 382 Such monosyllabic complexes employing nonsyllabic suffixes as *truth* and *fourth*. **1965** *Language* XLI. 32 Since the first element of these clusters always represents the syllable peak.., I have not separately indicated the nonsyllabic nature of the second element. *Ibid.* 476 According to their function in the syllable, the consonants are non-syllabics or syllabics.

nont, dial. variant of NAUNT.
1777 *Antiq.* in *Ann. Reg.* 147. **1888** *Sheffield Gloss.*

non-'tenure. *Old Law.* [a. AF. *nountenure*: see NON- 1 and TENURE.] 'A plea in bar to a real action, by saying that he (the defendant) held not the land in the plaintiff's count or declaration, or at least some part thereof' (Wharton).
1574 tr. *Littleton's Tenures* 128 b, If anye manne sue a Precipe quod reddat againste anye tenaunte of free hold, in whiche action.. the tenaunte pledeth not nontenure. **1602** FULBECKE *2nd Pt. Parall.* 57 Seuerall tenancie, or non-tenure is no plea in a *Nuper obijt*, because of the priuitie of bloud. **1628** COKE *On Litt.* 362 b, If the Tenant pleade non-tenure or disclaime. **1652** tr. *Fitzherbert's Nat. Brev.* 256 And Nontenure hath been pleaded, and admitted a good plea divers times in an Attaint. **1865** NICHOLS *Britton* II. 84 In this plea there lies neither view, nor voucher to warranty, nor abatement of writ for non-tenure.

†**non-term.** *Obs.* [NON- 1.] The time of vacation between two terms; the cessation of term; hence *gen.*, a period of inaction.
1607 COWELL *Interpr.*, *Non terme* (*non terminus*) is the time of vacation between Terme and Terme. **1648** SPARKE *Ep. Ded.* to *Shute's Sarah & Hagar* a j b, By thus improving an enforced Non-term, and over-long Vacation, in such a promulgating the best Laws. *a* **1658** CLEVELAND *For Sleep* Wks. (1687) 295 The Senses Non-Term, Life's serenest Shore. **1664** POWER *Exp. Philos.* I. 71 During this Interval and Non-tearm of Sensation (for so we may.. call Sleep). **1824** *Gradus ad Cantabr.* s.v., When any Member of the Senate dies within the University during Term, on application to the Vice-chancellor, the University bell rings an hour; from which period Non Term, as to public lectures and disputations, commences for three days.

‖**non-'terminus.** [NON- 1.] = prec.
1573 G. HARVEY *Common-pl. Bk.* (Camden) 52 It is the smalist matter of an hundrid with them, for the schollars to want a Greek lecture a fortniht or thre weeks togither besides non-termjnus. **1607** [see prec.].

non-the'matic, *a.* [NON- 3.] **1.** *Linguistics.* = ATHEMATIC *a.* 1.
1933 E. H. STURTEVANT *Compar. Gram. Hittite Lang.* vi. 217 There is also, as in I[ndo-] E[uropean], a distinction between thematic and non-thematic conjugation. **1955** T. BURROW *Sanskrit Lang.* vii. 318 The verbs are divided into two major types, (a) non-thematic.. and (b) thematic.
b. Not conveying new information; constituting part of the rheme; = RHEMATIC *a.*
1959 *Brno Studies in English* I. 43 The indefinite article and its zero plural variant.. play an important part in that co-operation of means which may render non-thematic even such a subject as occurs at the very beginning, or very near the beginning, of the sentence.
2. *Mus.* = ATHEMATIC *a.* 2.
1946 G. ABRAHAM in A. L. Bacharach *Brit. Mus.* 55 *Neptune, the Mystic*, which shares with *Saturn* the distinction of being one of the most remarkable purely impressionistic, practically non-thematic pieces of music ever written.

nontid(e, obs. forms of NOONTIDE.

non-'treaty. *N. Amer.* [NON- 4.] Used *attrib.* or *absol.* to designate an American Indian who is not subject to a treaty made with the Government.
1878 *Saskatchewan Herald* (Battleford) 18 Nov. 2/2 The non-treaty Indians invade them. **1885** J. L. ONDERDONK *Idaho* 15 Councils were held at Lapwai to apportion lands to the various chiefs of the Non-treaties. **1945** *Beaver* Mar. 12/1 Some four hundred Chipewyans and one hundred Crees, the latter being mixed treaties and non-treaties. **1956** C. RELANDER *Drummers & Dreamers* 121 The intruders occupied the scurfy land along the Columbia where the non-treaty people lived. **1964** W. DUFF *Indian Hist. Brit. Columbia* I. 70 The generalization, often heard, that the Indians of British Columbia are 'non-treaty' Indians is not wholly true.

non-'trivial, *a.* [NON- 3.] Not trivial; significant; *spec.* in *Math.*, such that not all variables or terms are zero.
1915 R. D. CARMICHAEL *Diophantine Analysis* ii. 52 Prove that a non-trivial solution does not exist when *b* is a square number. **1940** *Mind* XLIX. 366 This view has non-trivial consequences. **1948** F. D. MURNAGHAN *Introd. Applied Math.* i. 12, *n* plane vectors are linearly dependent when, and only when, there exists a nontrivial linear combination of the *n* vectors which is the zero vector. **1953** C. E. BAZELL *Linguistic Form* 19 It is only when there are relations of conversion between constructions that complementary distribution is non-trivial. **1971** *Amer. Jrnl. Physics* XXXIX. 486/1 Our aim.. is to derive a list of all values of $\Omega > 0$ for which there exist nontrivial *q* satisfying (11) and (12). **1973** *Sci. Amer.* Feb. 81/2 The ratio of those who received nontrivial injuries was 70 percent higher among the unbelted than among the belted.
So **non-'trivially** *adv.*
1940 W. V. QUINE *Math. Logic* 222 We can speak non-trivially of *the x* of *y*. **1971** POWELL & HIGMAN *Finite Simple Groups* i. 2 A conjugate class of *G* that interests *S* non-trivially.

nontronite ('nɒntrənaɪt). *Min.* [ad. F. *nontronite* (Berthier 1827), f. *Nontron* (in France), its locality.] A pale-yellow variety of chloropal. Now the usual name for the mineral.
1832 SHEPARD *Min.* 246 Nontronite... Soft; opake: unctuous and tender. **1837** DANA *Syst. Min.* 224. **1928** *Amer. Jrnl. Sci.* CCXV. 10 A large number of names have been proposed for the hydrous silicates of ferric iron; and of these nontronite, chloropal, pinguite, fettbol, and graminite are recognized by most mineralogists as belonging to the species nontronite. **1935**, etc. [see MONTMORILLONITE]. **1945** *Prof. Papers U.S. Geol. Survey Paper* No. 205-B. 28/1 The name chloropal has a slight priority over nontronite. However, the material has been shown to be definitely crystalline by both optical and X-ray methods, and the name chloropal, suggesting a deeply colored opaline mineral, is unsuitable. Dana (1892, p. xliii) has laid down the rule that a name having priority may properly be set aside when its signification is glaringly false. Mineralogists for some time have used the name nontronite as the most suitable for this mineral. **1963** M. H. HEY *Index Min. Species* (ed. 2) App. 117 *Nontronite*... The older name Chloropal has passed out of common use.

non-U (nɒn'juː, 'nɒnjuː), *a.* and *sb.* [f. NON- 3 + U 4.] **A.** *adj.* Not upper-class; not characteristic of upper-class people; esp. with reference to linguistic usage. **B.** *sb.* Non-U persons or characteristics collectively; non-U language. Hence **non-U-ness**.
1954 A. S. C. ROSS in *Neuphilologische Mitteilungen* LV. 21 (*title*) U and non-U. *Ibid.*, In this article I use the terms *upper class* (abbreviated: U), *correct, proper*,.. to designate usages of the upper class; their antonyms (*non-U, incorrect, not proper*,..) to designate usages which are not upper class. *Ibid.* 22 As a boy I heard *not quite a gent*.. used by non-U speakers. *Ibid.* 23 The non-U slang phrase *He's left his visiting card*. *Ibid.* 27 The U-rules for ending letters are very strict; failure to observe them usually implies non-U-ness. *Ibid.* 45 *Pardon*! is used by the non-U in three main ways. **1956** *Times* 13 Jan. 9/4 The cosh is, of course, definitely non-U, whereas the old-fashioned blunt instrument was perfectly *comme il faut*. **1957** O. NASH *You can't get there from Here* 16 The Wicked Queen said 'Mirror, mirror on the wall' instead of 'Looking glass, looking glass on the wall'... So the Wicked Queen exposed herself as not only wicked but definitely non-U. **1958** *Times Lit. Suppl.* 18 July 411/2 They phrase their advice just seriously enough to encourage the uninitiated, or non-U, yet just facetiously enough to reassure the *cognoscenti*. **1960** R. LISTER *Decorative Cast Ironwork* iv. 141 Letter racks, tobacco jars, spittoons ('salivaria' in non-U). **1964** H. KÖKERITZ in D. Abercrombie et al. *Daniel Jones* 140 These pronunciations .. might.. be classified as U rather than non-U. **1967** M. ARGYLE *Psychol. Interpersonal Behaviour* iii. 47 Others may be divided simply into the 'saved' and the 'not-saved', U and non-U, or into finer sub-groups. **1973** *Listener* 29 Nov. 755/2 Empty-headed chat, mixed with non-U euphemisms.

†**non 'ultra.** *Obs.* [L. = 'not beyond'.] = NE PLUS ULTRA 2, 2 b. Also *attrib.*
Formerly the name of a 'walk' in Oxford (see Wood *Antiq. Oxford* O.H.S. I. 344, 576; III. 221).
[**1589** GREENE *Tullies Loue* Ep. Ded. Wks. (Grosart) VII. 99 Suche as read *Non vltra*, on Hercules pillers. *c* **1600** *Timon* I. iv, At Gades I washt away *Non vltra* writt with Hercules owne hand.]
1611 CORYAT *Crudities* sig. b 3ᵛ, To give the *Non vltra* of him in a word, he is so Substantive an Author as will stand by himselfe. *a* **1666** EVELYN *Diary* 8 Feb. an. 1645 (1955) II. 354, I left this Ode.. as the Non ultra of my Travells. **1672** VILLIERS (Dk. Buckhm.) *Rehearsal* IV. i, Is not that good language now? is not that elevate? It's my *non ultra*, I gad. **1682** SIR T. BROWNE *Chr. Mor.* (1716) 62 Let not the law of thy country be the *non ultra* of thy honesty. *a* **1700** EVELYN *Diary* 8 Feb. 1645, This I made the *non ultra* of my travels. **1704** NORRIS *Ideal World* II. vii. 357 Now light is at our journey's end, arrived at its *non ultra*, there being no part.. disposed to transmit it any further.

non-'union.
1. [NON- 1.] Failure to unite.
1892 *Syd. Soc. Lex.*, *Non-union*, the condition of a fractured bone, or other divided tissue, the ends of which fail to unite. **1909** *Daily Chron.* 17 Feb. 1/6 Dr. Jameson.. warned his hearers of the dangers of non-union, which might possibly lead to internecine war. **1963** *Lancet* 12 Jan. 86/2 There are only two cases of delayed union or non-union of fractures.
2. *attrib.* [NON- 4.] Not belonging to a trade-union; also, manufactured by non-union men.
1863 FAWCETT *Pol. Econ.* II. ix. (1876) 244 A non-union man is subjected to so many petty annoyances that his life not unfrequently becomes a burden to him. **1890** *Daily News* 13 Sept. 5/5 It was affirmed that the unionists would refuse to handle non-union wool. *c* **1926** 'MIXER' *Transport Workers' Song Bk.* 28 Your ranks are broken through By the carping critic 'ringnecks'. And non-union alienage. **1964** S. M. MILLER in I. L. Horowitz *New Sociol.* 309 The importance of organizing the non-union and rapidly growing white-collar workers. **1973** L. SNELLING *Heresy* II. i. 61 Even if they stayed away I'm sure you could shoot the thing [*sc.* a film] with non-union people. **1974** *Times* 10 May 11/6 The *Daily News*.. has continued to be printed.. by non-union staff.
Hence **non-'unionist**, one who does not belong to a trade-union; also used *attrib.*; **non-'unionism**, the principles of non-unionists; **non-'unionize** *v. trans.*, to make non-union in character; to supply with non-union employees in place of union members; also **non-'unionized** *ppl. a.*
1861 *Illustr. Lond. News* 7 Dec. 576/3 A non-unionist workman has been employed on the premises. **1884** *Manch. Exam.* 2 Sept. 4/6 The miners are now encamped near the mines in order to prevent non-unionists from working. **1895** *Standard Dict.*, *Non-unionism*. **1901** *Daily Chron.* 17 July 7/5 Strongholds of non-unionism. **1926** *Glasgow Herald* 26 July 7 A motion was carried condemning the action of those Scottish newspaper proprietors who had non-unionised their offices since the strike. **1961** W. SHEED *Middle Class Education* xviii. 334, I resent every last butler of yours. And when I think of those non-unionized chambermaids—cheezt! **1968** *Economist* 20 July 19/2 If no union can attain 50 per cent of the votes, the plant remains non-unionised. **1974** *Black Panther* 16 Mar. 15/4 Many non-unionized enterprises were forced to close down as well.

non-u'nited, *ppl. a.* [NON- 6.] Applied to that part of the Greek Church which is not in union with Rome.
1777 *Char.* in *Ann. Reg.* 47 They [*sc.* Wallachians] confess the non-united Greek religion. **1886** W. J. TUCKER *Life in E. Europe* 199 The Church [in Hungary].. has the majority of the aristocracy.. on its side,.. not to mention the United and Non-united Greek Church to back it.

†**nonupar'tition.** *Obs.* [irreg. f. L. *nōnus* ninth + PARTITION.] The taking of a ninth part.
1674 JEAKE *Arith.* (1696) 34 Nonupartition, or to take the ninth part of a number.

†**'nonupla.** *Mus. Obs.* [mod.L., fem. of *nōnuplus*, f. *nōnus* ninth + *-plus* as in *duplus* DUPLE.] The 'time' which has nine crotchets or quavers in a bar.
1597 T. MORLEY *Introd. Mus.* I. 54 The tripla broken in the more prolation, maketh nine minimes for one stroke, which is our common Nonapla. **1656** BLOUNT *Glossogr.*, *Nonupla*, a quick time in Musick peculiar to Gigs and such like; having nine Crotchets between Bar and Bar. **1753** CHAMBERS *Cycl. Supp.* **1811** BUSBY *Dict. Mus.*

nonuplet ('nɒnjʊplɛt). *Mus.* [f. L. *nōnus* ninth + *-plet* as in *triplet*.] A group of nine notes to be performed in the time of eight or six.
1876 STAINER & BARRETT *Dict. Mus. Terms.*

non upstant: see NON-OBSTANTE 1 *note*.

non-'usage. [NON- 1.] Cessation of the use of something; failure to use.
1552 HULOET, Non vsage, *dissuetudo*. *c* **1600** EDMONDS *Observ. Cæsar's Comm.* (1604) 31 As usage continueth the property of a tenure, so non-usage implieth a forfeiture. *a* **1693** URQUHART *Rabelais* III. xxvii. 221 Non-usage oftentimes destroys ones Right. **1838–42** TUPPER *Proverb. Philos.* (1853) 427 For use will mould and mark it, or non-usage dull and blunt it. **1900** *Westm. Gaz.* 22 Feb. 3/2 The point of non-usage was brought forward, and.. it was distinctly laid down that 'omission is not prohibition'.

non-'usager. *Hist.* [NON- 2.] A member of that section of non-jurors which rejected 'the usages' in the celebration of the Holy Communion.
1874 J. H. BLUNT *Dict. Sects, Heresies*, etc. 381/2 A division thus sprung up in the now small body of Nonjurors, .. the former party being called 'Non-Usagers' and the latter 'Usagers'.

†**non-'usance.** *Obs.* [NON- 1.] Non-usage.
1646 SIR T. BROWNE *Pseud. Ep.* IV. xiii. 232 Yet were it not reasonable to inferre.. a non-usance or abolition.

non-'use. [NON- 1.] Failure or neglect to use.
1605 L. HUTTEN *Aunswere* 104 He doth conclude the abuse of one Ceremony by the Non vse of another. **1761** in Entick *London* (1766) IV. 369 They shall lose no privilege for non use, or even abuse. **1816** G. S. FABER *Orig. Pagan Idol.* I. 470 The.. distinction.. between.. clean and unclean animals;.. which relates.. to their use or non-use in

sacrifice. **1875** JOWETT *Plato* (ed. 2) I. 204 The wrong use of a thing is far worse than the non-use. **1884** *Manch. Exam.* 20 Aug. 5/3 The discussion of the Manchester Ship Canal Bill has suggested..some reflections on the use and non-use of canals.

non-ˈuser. *Law.* Also 8 erron. -usure. [NON- 1.] Neglect to use a right, by which it may become void. Also *transf.*

1650 *Abridgm. Coke's Rep.* IX. 340 Admitting that he cannot make a Deputy, this *Non user* is no cause of forfeiture. **1691** T. H[ALE] *Acc. New Invent.* 89 Whose so long Non-user of their power [etc.]. **1709** J. JOHNSON *Clergym. Vade M.* II. cv, Unless they [*sc.* Canons] be antiquated by a long non-usure. **1768** BLACKSTONE *Comm.* III. xvii. 263 A writ of *quo warranto*..lies..in case of non-user or long neglect of a franchise. **1844** WILLIAMS *Real Prop.* (1877) 459 The rights above mentioned may be lost by abandonment, of which non-user for twenty years or upwards is sufficient evidence. **1862** MARSH *Lect. Eng. Lang.* viii. 179 The mere non-user of a word is not likely to be noticed until it has been so long out of currency that [etc.]. **1885** *Law Rep.* 14 Q.B. Div. 203 Such power could not be lost by mere non-user.

†**non-using,** *vbl. sb.* [NON- 7.] Non-use.

1533 FRITH *Mirr. to know thyself* B, That the none vsynge of them maye be thy greater damnacyon. **1688** *Vox Cleri Pro Rege* 26 Does their non-using argue a non-Right in them of such a Power, that they may never..make use of it?

non-uˈtility, *a.* [NON- 3.] Not utility or not for utility; used chiefly of clothes that are of better quality than UTILITY garments.

1948 *News Chron.* 7 Apr. 1 Children's non-utility garments. *Ibid.*, Non-utility tables, desks, chairs. **1950** *Engineering* 6 Jan. 11/3 'Nonutility generation' is defined as 'generation by producers..for the purpose of supplying electric power required in the conduct of their industrial or commercial operations'. **1957** R. CAMPBELL *Portugal* 82 In Portugal there are still the regional dresses of the people (strictly non-utility). **1960** I. JEFFERIES *Dignity & Purity* iv. 55 My suits happened to be new and very non-utility.

non-ˈvalent, *a. Chem.* [f. NON- + -VALENT.] **a.** Not capable of entering into chemical combination; inert.

1908 *Athenæum* 28 Mar. 390/1 All the 'non-valent' elements—I should prefer to describe them as the elements which are inert at atmospheric pressure and temperature—should sublime.

b. Having a formal oxidation state of zero.

1950 N. V. SIDGWICK *Chem. Elements & their Compounds* II. 1429 Nickel is of course non-valent in the carbonyl $Ni(CO)_4$. **1962** P. J. & B. DURRANT *Introd. Adv. Inorg. Chem.* xxiv. 981 None of the elements [of sub-Group VI T] forms any compounds in which it is non-valent.

non-ˈvanishing, *ppl. a. Math.* and *Physics.* [NON- 6.] Not becoming zero, or not zero.

1907 M. BÔCHER *Introd. Higher Algebra* v. 54 The non-vanishing *r*-rowed determinant stands in the upper left-hand corner of the matrix. **1922** G. N. WATSON *Theory Bessel Functions* xix. 636 Schlömilch series with non-vanishing coefficients. **1956** *Physical Rev.* CIV. 257/1 The particle has a nonvanishing spin. **1962** CORSON & LORRAIN *Introd. Electromagn. Fields* ii. 76 In Eq. 2-197 it must include all regions of space in which the field intensity *E* is nonvanishing.

non-ˈvascular, *a. Anat.* [NON- 3.] Destitute of vessels for the circulation of fluids.

1857 HOLDEN *Hum. Osteol.* 17 Bone so thin as to need no Haversian canals is called 'nonvascular' bone. **1862** SPENCER *First Princ.* II. xiii. §104 (1875) 302 The low rate of change going on in dry non-vascular tissues, such as those which form hairs, nails, horns, &c. **1879** *St. George's Hosp. Rep.* IX. 526 Localised non-vascular ulceration of the cornea.

non-ˈverbal, *a.* [NON- 3.] **a.** Not employing or including words; unskilful in the use of words.

1927 B. RUSSELL *Outl. Philos.* xxiv. 271 This keeps us in the verbal realm, and does not get us outside it to some realm of non-verbal fact. **1934** H. C. WARREN *Dict. Psychol.* 181/2 *Non-verbal test*, a type of mental (generally intelligence) test, in which no words are used in the test content, but the directions for giving the tests may be either verbal or by pantomime. **1953** W. BURROUGHS *Junkie* (1972) xv. 152 What I look for in any relationship is contact on the non-verbal level of intuition and feeling, that is, telepathic contact. **1972** J. L. DILLARD *Black English* i. 33 There may be many reasons, most of them cultural, why a child may appear 'non-verbal' in certain contexts.

b. Not employing or including a verb; not a form of a verb.

1932 A. H. GARDINER *Theory of Speech & Lang.* iv. 219 Old Egyptian dispensed with the copula in more than one common sub-class of nominal or, as I prefer to call them, non-verbal sentences. **1965** D. WARD *Russ. Lang. Today* iv. 102 Non-verbal predicators include НЕ and НЕТ, as in ОН НЕ ТАМ *He is not there. Ibid.* v. 123 Пред is productive, however, in non-verbal derivatives. **1973** *Archivum Linguisticum* IV. 49 In respect of their association with a verbal or non-verbal form in the sentence, the suffixes often alternate more or less freely.

So **non-ˈverbalized** *ppl. a.*, not verbalized; **non-ˈverbally** *adv.*, not verbally.

1949 KOESTLER *Insight & Outlook* xxiv. 342 It is in the very nature of this type of nonverbalized experience that ordinary language..is insufficient to convey it. **1955** J. L. AUSTIN *How to do Things with Words* (1962) ix. 118 The means for achieving its ends non-verbally must be conventional. **1958** B. BERNSTEIN in J. A. Fishman *Readings Sociol. Lang.* (1968) 233 The child is born into a world in which personal qualifications are established non-verbally in the sense that the personal qualifications are left out of the structure of the sentences. **1961** *Countryman* LVIII. III. 462 Most of his waking life the berger is communicating with animals in grunts, cries and other non-verbalized sounds.

non-ˈviable, *a.* [NON- 3.] Not viable; *spec.* (*a*) of living beings or living matter: = INVIABLE *a.*; (*b*) not economically viable.

1879 *Premature Death* 61 The liability to give birth to immature and non-viable children. **1946** *Nature* 9 Nov. 678/1 The cells become non-viable. **1956** A. HUXLEY *Adonis & Alphabet* 204 The wall, which now divides the ancient city from the new, the non-viable state of Jordan from the non-viable state of Israel. **1959** *Times* 6 Mar. 11/5 Her Majesty's Government..is struggling..to build up a primitive people in a non-viable country to a point where they may one day hope to achieve a genuine form of democracy. **1959** *Economist* 18 Apr. 218/1 Agricultural policy is belatedly growing more rational, which means tougher towards the 'non-viable' farm. **1971** J. Z. YOUNG *Introd. Study Man* xxvii. 385 Producing a new version that is not a non-viable freak. **1974** *Nature* 1 Nov. 64/2 The consideration that cells defective for such processes should be non-viable.

non-ˈviolence. [NON- 1.] The principle or practice of abstaining from the use of violence.

1920 M. K. GANDHI in J. Nehru *Autobiogr.* (1936) xii. 83, I believe that non-violence is infinitely superior to violence, forgiveness is more manly than punishment. **1936** [see CONSCIENTIOUS *a.* 2]. **1942** KOESTLER in *Horizon* June 384 His [*sc.* Gandhi's] slope..gradually made him slide down to his present position of non-violence towards the Japanese aggression. **1968** M. LUTHER KING *Trumpet of Conscience* iv. 77 Nonviolence is no longer an option for intellectual analysis, it is an imperative for action. **1974** *Peace News* 1 Feb. 3/1, I knew myself pretty well and knew a little about nonviolence.

So **non-ˈviolent** *a.*, characterized by, believing in, or practising non-violence; **non-ˈviolently** *adv.*, in a non-violent manner.

1920 M. K. GANDHI *Non-Violence* 9 Mar. (1922) in *Young India 1919–22* 288 We must not intend harm to the English or to our co-operating countrymen, if and whilst we claim to be non-violent. **1923** C. M. CASE (*title*) Non-violent coercion. **1937** J. M. MURRY *Necessity of Pacifism* i. 22 A Socialism of voluntary community and absolute but non-violent resistance to war. **1948** A. HUXLEY *Ape & Essence* (1949) 2 Gandhi..just couldn't do anything but resist oppression non-violently. **1971** M. MCCARTHY *Birds of America* 82 Peter replied non-violently. 'It's for my mother.' **1973** J. FERGUSON (*title*) The politics of love: the New Testament and non-violent revolution.

non-ˈvocoid. *Linguistics.* [NON- 2.] A speech sound that is not a vocoid; = CONTOID *sb.*

1943 K. L. PIKE *Phonetics* vii. 143 All nonvocoids are contoids. **1952** A. COHEN *Phonemes of English* 37 Pike suggests using the terms vocoids and non-vocoids in phonetic, and vowels and consonants in phonemic analysis.

non-ˈvolatile, *a.* [NON- 3.] Not volatile. **a.** Of substances (cf. VOLATILE *sb.* and *a.* B. 3).

1866 WATTS *Dict. Chem.* IV. 230 They possess a bitter taste, are non-volatile, and do not suffer any change when exposed to air. **1903** *Phil. Mag.* V. 577 In other cases..the new matter is itself non-volatile. **1957** G. E. HUTCHINSON *Treat. Limnol.* I. viii. 553 Evaporating the water to dryness, so obtaining the total solids per unit mass or volume, and then igniting the residue to obtain the non-volatile solids per unit mass or volume. **1971** I. G. GASS et al. *Understanding Earth* 114 It is widely believed that the average composition of meteoric matter provides the best information on the relative abundances of the non-volatile elements.

b. *Computers.* Of a store or storage (cf. VOLATILE *a.*).

1950 W. W. STIFLER et al. *High-Speed Computing Devices* xiv. 313 The storage unit is said to be nonvolatile because it can sustain loss of power without losing all the information stored. **1962** *Gloss. Terms Automatic Data Processing* (*B.S.I.*) 65 A non-volatile store..retains its content when the power supplies are switched off normally, but the content may be lost if power failure occurs. **1969** P. B. JORDAIN *Condensed Computer Encycl.* 563 Non-volatile storage (almost all magnetic; some optical and some punched-hole media) will hold onto its data through any mishaps.

Hence **non-volaˈtility**, the property of not being volatile.

1964 N. G. CLARK *Mod. Organic Chem.* v. 67 The highest members [of the paraffin series], e.g. the waxes, because of their non-volatility, possess no smell.

non-white, *a.* and *sb.* Also non-White. [NON- 3, 2.] **A.** *adj.* Not having a white skin; of or pertaining to people who are not white. **B.** *sb.* A non-white person. Also *collect.*

1921 *Sci. Amer.* 20 Aug. 125 The States that have the greatest proportion of non-white residents. **1952** B. DAVIDSON *Rep. S. Afr.* I. i. 27 No serious South African will argue any longer (at least in private) that *apartheid*, the complete and geographical segregation of the white from the non-white at all levels, can work. **1953** P. ABRAHAMS *Return to Goli* II. iii. 57 They are the most prejudiced and colour conscious of all the non-White groups. **1956** *Time* 9 Jan. 61/2 The rarity of skin cancer among non-whites..is thought to be caused by a 'true racial difference in susceptibility'. **1959** V. PACKARD *Status Seekers* (1960) vi. 86 If white residents of an area are in no hurry to leave, but non-whites are eager to come in, the pressure of non-white demand may bid up the price of houses. **1973** E. BULLINS *Theme is Blackness* 3 America's educational institutions are predicated upon keeping Black men ignorant of themselves and the other nonwhite four-fifths of the world. **1973** *Black Panther* 5 May 5/2 Eleven non-whites and five civil rights organizations last week charged the San Francisco Police Department with discriminatory employment practices against non-whites and women.

†**non-will,** *v. Obs. rare*⁻¹. [f. NON- 5 + WILL *v.*] *trans.* To will the annihilation of.

1788 *New Lond. Mag.* 434 To nonwill the existence of anything he once willed into being.

†**nonwit.** *Sc. Obs. rare*⁻¹. Nonage.

1570 BUCHANAN *Admon.* (S.T.S.) 30 To be to him as curatour and gouernour during all ye tyme of his nonwit.

ˈnon-word. [NON- 2.] A word that is not recorded or not established.

1961 *Life* 27 Oct. 4 (*heading*) A non-word deluge. **1963** *Punch* 16 Jan. 95/1 The aesthetically displeasing non-word 'annoyment'. **1967** D. G. HAYS *Introd. Computational Linguistics* v. 87 But for that to be practical, the memory would have to be large enough so that every string of letters shorter than the longest word in the language could serve as a cell index, and almost all the cells in the memory would be empty—since almost every letter string is a nonword. **1970** *Sun* (Gainesville, Florida) 8 Jan., The School Board's petition to the Supreme Court contained an error, the non-word 'predominately'.

non-ˈworker. [NON- 2.] One who does not work. Also **non-ˈworking** *ppl. a.*

1851 MAYHEW *Lond. Labour* III. 2 The Workers and Non-Workers. *Ibid.* 3 The members of every community may be divided into the..hardworking and the non-working.

non-woven, *a.* and *sb.* [NON- 3, 2.] **A.** *adj.* Not woven (see quot. 1968). **B.** *sb.* A nonwoven fabric or material.

1945 *Forbes* (N.Y.) 15 Oct. 16/2 The new non-spun and non-woven cloth will be cheaper, not only because it eliminates so many operations but also because it requires much less of the basic fiber to cover a given area. **1959** A. J. HALL *Standard Handbk. Textiles* iii. 156 It is obvious that non-woven fabrics can never entirely take the place of woven or knitted fabrics. **1961** *New Scientist* 20 Apr. 115/2 The methods are seen as a means of up-grading such ordinary fabrics as..non-wovens. **1963** A. J. HALL *Textile Sci.* i. 11 The characteristics of non-woven fabrics are capable of wide variation. **1968** J. IRONSIDE *Fashion Alphabet* 242 *Non-woven fabrics.* A 'non-woven' ought..to refer to any fabric not made on a loom, but the generally accepted meaning..is that it is any fabric which is not woven, knitted or spun but built up by interlocking fibres by means of chemical bonding agents, and (for fusible fibres) by mechanical means, chemical action, moisture and heat... Paper is also included in this definition. **1970** *Cabinet Maker & Retail Furnisher* 23 Oct. 173/2 The chemically or adhesively bonded non-wovens use bonding elements that behave as glueing binders. **1973** *Times* 28 Aug. 17/7 That other branch of the disposable paper industry, nonwovens, is being addressed in the same optimistic tones.

nonyl (ˈnɒnɪl). *Chem.* [f. L. *nōn-us* ninth + -YL.] The ninth in the series of alcohol radicals of the general formula C_nH_{2n+1}. Also *attrib.*

1866 WATTS *Dict. Chem.* IV. 134 *Nonyl.* C^9H^{19}... It is also called Pelargonyl. **1868** *Fownes' Chem.* (ed. 10) 632 Nonyl Alcohol, $C_9H_{20}O$. **1872** WATTS *Dict. Chem.* Suppl., *Nonane* or *Nonyl Hydride*, C^9H^{20}.

Hence **ˈnonylamine** [see AMINE], a compound in which one atom of the hydrogen in ammonia is replaced by nonyl; **ˈnonylene**, a hydrocarbon produced in the decomposition of lime soap; whence **nonyˈlenic** *a.*; **nonylic** (nɒˈnɪlɪk) *a.*, pertaining to or derived from nonyl.

1866 WATTS *Dict. Chem.*, **Nonylamine.* $C^9H^{21}N$. Obtained by the action of ammonia on chloride of nonyl. **1857** MILLER *Elem. Chem., Org.* (1862) 247 *Nonylene, or Elaene ($H_{18}C_{18}$) was obtained mixed with hexylene, by Fremy, during the distillation of several fatty acids. **1889** *Watts' Dict. Chem.* II. 431 Ennenoic acid.., *Nonylenic acid. **1866** WATTS *Dict. Chem.* IV. 134 Chloride of Nonyl.. when boiled with potash yields hydrate of nonyl, *nonylic or pelargonic alcohol. **1873** *Fownes' Chem.* (ed. 11) 689 Nonylic acid is obtained by the action of boiling alcoholic potash on primary octyl cyanide.

nonys, obs. form of NONCE[1].

non-ˈzero, *a.* [NON- 4.] Not equal to zero.

1905 *Proc. London Math. Soc.* III. 273 This assumption is valid in the case of functions of finite (non-zero) order. **1925** C. E. CULLIS *Matrices & Determinoids* III. I. xxvii. 440 Two sets of non-zero positive integers whose sums are respectively *m* and *n*. **1951** *Physical Rev.* LXXXIII. 1235/1 Small but nonzero errors in the results. **1970** G. K. WOODGATE *Elem. Atomic Struct.* vii. 132 The admixture of the $^1P_1$ level accounts for the non-zero intensity of the line 2,537 Å.

noodle (ˈnuːd(ə)l), *sb.*[1] [Of obscure origin.]

a. A simpleton, a stupid or silly person.

1753 HAWKESWORTH *Adventurer* No. 25 ¶6 The words ninnyhammer, noodle, and numscull, are frequently bandied to and fro betwixt them. **1764** FOOTE *Mayor of G.* II. Wks. 1799 I. 184 To take up at last with such a noodle as he! **1802** *Sporting Mag.* XX. 118 The Buck, who scorns the City Puts, And thinks all rich men noodles. **1826** SCOTT *Woodst.* iii, Thou wouldst..trip, like the noodles of Hogs-Norton, when the pigs play on the organ. **1875** HELPS *Soc. Press.* viii. 113, I say he is a noodle if he has not previously determined how and when to leave off.

b. *slang.* The head. cf. NODDLE *sb.*[1] 2 b, 3.

1914 JACKSON & HELLYER *Vocab. Criminal Slang* 62 *Noodle*.., the human head; brains; savoir faire; mentality. **1923** T. FANE *What's wrong with Movies* vi. 101 To the masses the cinema is only an entertainment, and using their noodles has long been classed..as one of life's hard labors. **1945** M. TRIST in *Coast to Coast 1944* 207 Take no notice... She's off her noodle.

Hence **ˈnoodle** *v.*, to fool. *rare*⁻¹.

1803 *Censor* 1 Feb. 23 To descend from my grammatical stilts in order to inform her that her mistress has completely noodled her!

noodle, *sb.*[2] [a. G. *nudel*, of uncertain etymology.] A strip or ball of dough made with wheat, flour, and eggs, and served in soup. Also *attrib.* in ***noodle-soup***.

1779 LADY MARY COKE *Jrnl.* Oct. (1892) III. 243 A noodle soup—this I begged to be explained and was told it was made only of veal with lumps of bread boiled in it. **1850** B'NESS TAUTPHŒUS *Initials* (1853) 139 That's the soup, and the Noodles will be all squashed if you work them up after that fashion. **1859** BARTLETT *Dict. Amer.* (ed. 2), *Noodles*, dumplings or vermicelli. They are used in Pennsylvania, and are made by rolling into very thin sheets the dough, which differs from the Italian preparation by the addition of eggs. *Ibid.*, Noodle-Soup. **1876** M. B. EDWARDS *John & I*, vii. 56 He had almost got reconciled to the frequent recurrence of sausage and noodle soup.

noodle ('nu:d(ə)l), *sb.*[3] *Jazz.* [Origin unknown.] A trill or improvisation on an instrument. Cf. NOODLE *v.*[3] below.

1926 WHITEMAN & MCBRIDE *Jazz* x. 220 'Noodles', that is, fancy figures in saxophone such as triple trills, often crowd out the melody. **1958** *Jazz Review* Nov. 25 My one complaint is that Monk here allows too many of his favourite piano 'noodles' (all pianists seem to have them).

noodle ('nu:d(ə)l), *v.*[2] *Austral.* [Origin unknown.] **a.** *intr.* and *trans.* To search for opals (in opal dumps or 'mullock'). **b.** *trans.* To obtain (an opal) in this way. So **'noodling** *vbl. sb.*[1]

1902 *Geol. Survey* No. 177 (Queensland Dept. Mines) 20 Some splendid opal is found..by turning over and searching the old heaps and mullock—'noodling'. **1931** M. S. BUCHANAN *Prospecting for Opal in Austral.* 10 Produced ten thousand pounds, with what was 'noodled' or picked up from the dumps. **1940** I. L. IDRIESS *Lightning Ridge* (1948) xiii. 79 Send the dirt up in the bucket where his mate.. would carefully 'noodle' it, seeking tell-tale potch and colour. **1962** R. WEBSTER *Gems* I. x. 191 The practice of picking over old mine dumps for overlooked opal is another form of 'mining'. Such procedure is termed 'noodling'. **1963** A. LUBBOCK *Austral. Roundabout* 79 Anyone can poke about..and 'puddle' or 'noodle' in the gravelly tailings of the mines. **1967** *Sunday Mail Mag.* (Brisbane) 8 Jan. 6/7 If you do the work by hand, sitting on the mullock heap like a shag on a rock, and patiently sift through the dirt, you are 'noodling'.

noodle ('nu:d(ə)l), *v.*[3] orig. *U.S.* [f. the sb.; cf. NOODLE *sb.*[3]] *intr.* To improvise or play casually on a musical instrument, esp. in jazz; to play an elaborate or decorative series of notes; also occas. *trans.* Freq. as **'noodling** *vbl. sb.*[2] Also *fig.*

1937 *Printers' Ink Monthly* May 39/3 *Noodling*, the tuning up of musical instruments with practice runs, trills, scales, etc. **1941** *Sun* (Baltimore) 19 July 8/3 There is something rather exciting about the notion of 'Old Man River', already a folk song, being poured out by the whole choir of woodwinds, with the strings noodling away in the background like rolling waters. **1946** R. BLESH *Shining Trumpets* (1949) ix. 212 Shield's clarinet part..revolves in little runs around lead notes (this is called 'noodling'). **1957** *Nugget* Dec. 5 Every time a jazz musician noodles a passable break these days he is followed by a show of bravura on an open Underwood fingered by a jazz writer. **1960** H. O. BRUNN *Story of Orig. Dixieland Jazz Band* 164 Larry Shields will go down in history as the father of the 'noodling' style and possessor of one of the most powerful clarinet tones on record. **1966** AUDEN *About House* 44 In the half-dark, members of an avian orchestra Are already softly noodling, limbering up for An overture at sunrise. **1970** *Globe & Mail* (Toronto) 26 Sept. 27/2 Each piece [of writing] has the feel of jazz, the sense of building, of noodling around here, improvising there and finally resolving.

'noodledom. [f. NOODLE *sb.*[1] + -DOM.]

1. The world or aggregate of noodles; a collection of noodles.

1810 SYD. SMITH in *Edin. Rev.* XV. 305 These two phrases, the delight of Noodledom, are grown into common-places upon the subject. **1825** —— *Wks.* (1859) 417 How impossible it appeared to Noodledom to repeal them! **1867** G. GILFILLAN *Night* viii. 294 A noodledom of blood now governs France. **1878** BROWNING *Poets Croisic* cvi, 'Yes,' you sneer, 'Ninnies stock Noodledom.'

2. Foolishness, stupidity; an instance of this.

1827 *Blackw. Mag.* XXI. 820 It is the most entire piece of noodledom that can be perpetrated. **1837** *Fraser's Mag.* XVI. 640 They are sufficiently bored with the solemn noodledoms of pretension. **1865** *Star* 5 Jan., The noodledom of the magistrates is the one feature of the case. *attrib.* **1886** *Athenæum* 23 Jan. 138/2 Mr. Thomson's collection of noodledom stories for the Folk-lore Society.

So **'noodledum**, noodledom; a noodle. *rare.*

1826 *Examiner* 727/1 A piece of noodledum that was even attributed to Louis XIV. **1883** HALL CAINE *Cobwebs Crit.* v. 145 Ridiculous..squabbles among the tribes of Noodledums.

'noodleism. [f. NOODLE *sb.*[1] + -ISM.]

1. Silliness, stupidity.

1831 *Examiner* 562/2 Written in a congenial strain of noodleism. **1865** CARLYLE *Fredk. Gt.* XXI. v. (1872) X. 90 Some gleams of Kinghood for us under Marlborough: — after whom Noodleism and Somnambulism.

2. A silly action or idea.

1829 *Examiner* 145/2 Lord Eldon..rose to disavow participation in such extreme noodleisms. **1834** GEN. P. THOMPSON *Exerc.* III. 55 It is manifestly an old-wifery, a noodleism, and all the world for fifty years has held it so.

noodler ('nu:dlə(r)). *Austral.* [f. NOODLE *v.*[2]] One who 'noodles' (see NOODLE *v.*[2]).

1940 I. L. IDRIESS *Lightning Ridge* (1948) xvi. 96 All stones thus missed were regarded as the legitimate prey of the noodlers. **1945** *Walkabout* (Austral.) 1 Mar. 15 Other noodlers use a wire-screen and a shovel. **1967** S. LLOYD *Lightning Ridge Bk.* 38 A champion noodler. First to use shear blade to cut opal dirt on dumps.

noodly ('nu:dlɪ), *a.* *rare*⁻¹. [Presumably f. NOODLE *sb.*[1] + -Y[1].] Stupid, silly.

1922 JOYCE *Ulysses* 646 A big foolish nervous noodly kind of a horse.

noogenesis (nəʊəʊ'dʒɛnɪsɪs). [ad. F. *noögenèse*, f. Gr. νόο-ς mind + GENESIS.] The coming into being of the stage or sphere of the mind, according to Pierre Teilhard de Chardin's theory of evolution (see quot. 1959).

1959 B. WALL tr. *Teilhard de Chardin's Phenomenon of Man* III. i. 181 Psychogenesis has led to man. Now it effaces itself, relieved or absorbed by another and a higher function —the engendering and subsequent development of all the stages of the mind, in one word *noogenesis*. **1966** C. F. MOONEY *Teilhard de Chardin* ii. 43 'Noogenesis' will therefore be spiritual and social, that is to say, it will concern itself with the development of individuals as persons and with society on the level of interpersonal relationships.

noogenic (nəʊəʊ'dʒɛnɪk), *a.* [ad. F. *noögénique*, f. Gr. νόο-ς mind + -GENIC.] Pertaining to or connected with noogenesis, or to that which exists in the sphere of the mind.

1959 B. WALL tr. *Teilhard de Chardin's Phenomenon of Man* 307 Without doubt, the 'noogenic' forces of compression, organisation and interiorisation, under which the biological synthesis of reflection operates, do not at any moment relax their pressure on the stuff of mankind. **1964** I. LASCH tr. *V. E. Frankl's Man's Search for Meaning* (rev. ed.) II. 102 Existential frustration can also result in neuroses. For this type of neuroses, logotherapy has coined the term 'noögenic neuroses' in contrast to..psychogenic neuroses. Noögenic neuroses have their origin..in the noölogical (from the Greek 'noos' meaning mind) dimension of the human existence. **1968** *Time* 2 Feb. 38 Dr Frankl makes great play with words beginning with noö—, from the Greek *noös* (mind), as in noödynamics and noögenic neuroses.

Noogoora (nu:'gu:rə). The name of a Queensland sheep station, used attrib. in **Noogoora burr** to designate a composite plant, *Xanthium chinense*, treated as a noxious weed in Australia because of its hooked burrs which become entangled in wool.

1883 F. M. BAILEY *Synopsis Queensland Flora* 259 *X[anthium] strumarium*,..known as 'Noogoora Burr', and supposed injurious to stock. **1900** —— *Queensland Flora* III. 857 Noogoora Burr. A tall wide-spreading annual... A widespread weed of warm countries. **1934** *Bulletin* (Sydney) 12 Sept. 22/1 Through not obeying a Lands Department order to clear his holding of Noogoora burr, a N[orth] Q[ueensland] grazier has been served with a notice of forfeiture. **1961** *Times* 7 June 3/1 A cerambycid beetle..[is] to be liberated in Queensland in 1962 against the important weed Noogoora burr. **1961** *Coast to Coast 1959–60* 41 When we saw how he looked at our note-book, we knew he was a dairy farmer, because his eyes classified us—with drought, fire, the pear, flood and Noogoora burr. **1965** *Austral. Encycl.* IX. 227/2 One of the worst offenders [*sc.* plants whose burrs cling to wool] is noogoora burr (*Xanthium chinense*) which causes annual wool losses of at least £50,000. Since the 1860s it has occupied sheep country from the Gulf of Carpentaria to Sydney... Noogoora burr, indigenous to South America, is supposed to have been introduced with cotton seed.

nook (nʊk), *sb.* Forms: α. 3–4 **nok**, 4–6 **noke**, 5–7 **nooke**, 6– **nook**; 6 **noque**, 4, 6–7 **nouke**. β. *north.* and *Sc.* 5–6 **nuk**, **nwke**, 5–7, 9 **nuke**, 6 **nucke** (9 **nuck**); 5 **noik**, 6 **nwik**, **nuike**, 6–7, 9 **nuik** (9 **nuick**); 6, 8–9 **neuk** (9 **neuck**), **newk** (6 **newke**), 9 **niuk**; 8–9 *north.* **neak**. [Of obscure origin; the early examples are northern, and the word has most dialect currency in the north, but the earliest trace of it appears in Layamon in the adj. *four-nooked.*

The forms prove a ME. *nōk*, to which the only parallel seems to be a Norw. dial. *nōk*, recorded by Aasen & Ross with the sense of 'hook, bent figure, bent or contracted person', etc.; whether this is the same word is very doubtful, although a Scand. origin seems probable. Ir. and Sc. Gaelic *niuc* is clearly from northern of Sc. *neuk*, *newk*.]

1. A corner of a square or angular thing (such as a piece of cloth or paper), or of a figure bounded by straight lines. Now *rare.*

α. *a* **1300** *Cursor M.* 19845 A mikel linnen clath four squar ..At nokes four, four listes lang. **13..** *On learning Music* in *Rel. Antiq.* I. 292 Summe notes arn shorte and somme a long noke. **13..** *Gaw. & Gr. Knt.* 660 Vchone halched in oþer, ..& fyched vpon fyue poyntez,..With-outen ende at any noke. *a* **1440** *Sir Degrev.* 165 He held the lettre by the nooke. **1551** RECORDE *Pathw. Knowl.* I. Def., A cantle..cutte out with two lynes drawen from the centre to the circumference ..if it be not parted from the reste of the circle..is called a nooke. **1605** VERSTEGAN *Dec. Intell.* (1634) 150 A nooke or corner being in our ancient language called a kant or cantell. **1640** GLAPTHORNE *Wit in a Constable* II. Wks. 1874 I. 189 The custard with the foure and twenty Nooks At my Lord Majors feast. *a* **1795** in Child *Ballads* III. 163/1 In every hand he took a nook Of that great leathern meal [= bag]. **1824** BYRON *Juan* XVI. xxvii, Couch'd all snugly on his pillow's nook, With what he had seen his phantasy he fed. **1897** AUSTIN CLARE *Rise of River* 194 The lamb was slung in the nook of his plaid.

β. *c* **1520** M. NISBET *N.T.* Acts x. 11 A vessel cummand doun, as a gret schete with iiij newkis. **1583** *Leg. Bp. St. Androis* 819 in *Satir. Poems Reform.* 380 Ten pundis stirling furth he tuike, And knit it in a neapkyn nucke. *a* **1600** [see PLAID 5]. *c* **1800** *Auld Maitland* xxviii. in Scott *Minstr. Border* (1869) 155 He..caught the standard by the neuk. **1826** T. WILSON *Pitman's Pay* (1843) 10 For dishclout serves her apron nuik. **1871** W. ALEXANDER *Johnny Gibb* x. 76 A laddie wi' a tartan plaid.., an' a' 's [= all his] spare claise i' the neuk o't.

b. A corner of a thing regarded as a separate portion; a piece or fragment; a part. Now *rare.*

In early use only in ***farthing('s) nook***; in later examples chiefly of a pie or pasty.

c **1300** *Havelok* 820 Al þat he þer-fore tok, With-held he nouth a ferþinges nok. **1303** R. BRUNNE *Handl. Synne* 5810. **1338** —— *Chron.* (1810) 28 Siluer for Southwales not a ferþing noke; Oþer treuage he sette, a þousand kie he toke. **1513** DOUGLAS *Æneis* X. xii. 27 A stane..Quhilk of a montane semyt a gret nuike. **1728** VANBR. & CIB. *Prov. Husb.* II. i, The Nook that's left o' th' Goose Poy. **1819** SCOTT *Ivanhoe* xvii, Thou shalt be welcome to a nook of pasty. **1887** *S. Cheshire Gloss.* s.v., A good nook o' the money was gone.

c. A corner or angular piece of land; a small triangular field; †also, in early use, a certain measure of land (see quot. *a* 1634).

[? *a* **1300** in Madox *Form. Anglic.* (1702) 424 Legavit Christinæ filiæ suæ unam Nocham terræ. **1331** in Blount *Law Dict.* (1670) s.v. *Nok*, Tradidi..Henrico Adams unum mes & unam nokam terræ. *a* **1400** in Dugdale *Monast. Angl.* (1671) II. 331 Unam virgatam terræ..et tres nocas terræ.] **1603** *Laing Charters* (Anderson) 351 Lands..of which..the other portion lies in the 'Conyflett' and is called the 'nuik'. **1606** in *Trans. Cumb. & West. Archæol. Soc.* (N.S.) III. (1903) 153 His gapp or Yaite between the Meare Stone and the Intake Nooke. *a* **1634** NOY *Compl. Lawyer* 57 You must note, that two Fardells of Land make a Nooke of Land, and two Nookes make halfe a Yard of Land. **1665** *Hist. Springfield* (1899) II. 214 There is grannted to Lawrence Bliss Some Small nookes & Strappets of Meddow & Swamp lying in the corners of his meddow. **1753** *MS. Indenture* (Mappleton, Derby), Land..called Tibdale goats nook. **1899** *Cumberld. Gloss.* s.v., A designative term for a small field or farm—Low Wood Nook, High Nook.

†**d.** One of the 'corners' of the earth. *Obs.*⁻¹

a **1400–50** *Alexander* 4831 ȝit fand he clouen þurȝe þe clynt twa crasid gatis, Ane to þe noke of þe north, a-nothire to þe est.

e. A point of land running into the sea; a headland or promontory; also, a piece of ground projecting from one division into another and terminating in a point. Now *rare.*

1487 *Barbour's Bruce* IV. 556 (Cambr. MS.), Gif he seis we land ma ta, On Turnberyis nwk [*v.r.* snuke] he may Mak a fyre. **1536** BELLENDEN *Chron., Cosmogr.* vi. (1821) I. p. xxix, Galloway rinnis with ane gret snout of craggis..in the Ireland seis. This snout is callit be the peple the Mulis Nuk. **1577** HARRISON *Descr. Scotl.* iii. in *Holinshed*, As for Galloway it selfe, it yeeldeth out a great point promontory or cape (which the Scots call a Mule or Nuke) into the Irish Sea. **1596** DALRYMPLE tr. *Leslie's Hist. Scot.* I. 5 That syde quhilke lyes to ffrance hes twa nuikes, of quhilkes the ane lyes to Kent, the vther to the South. **1610** HOLLAND *Camden's Brit.* (1637) 323 Britaine heere [in Kent] runneth out with a mightie nooke, or corner into the East, and I haue observed, that such a kind of nooke in Scotland is called, Cantir. **1667** PRIMATT *City & C. Build.* 106 A Platform for two Houses, the ground lying with a Nuke. *Ibid.* 163 Any Map or Plat of ground, if it hath never so many Nukes and Corners, may be reduced into Triangles. **1713** ARBUTHNOT *John Bull* II. iv, He wants my poor little Farm, because it makes a Nook in his Park-wall. **1855** ROBINSON *Whitby Gloss.*, *Neuk*, an angle of a field.

fig. **1671** M. BRUCE *Gd. News* (1708) 48, I trow in stead of Waiting, many a one of us be come to the far nook of our Patience.

2. A corner of a house or other building, of any erection or upright object, of a street, etc. Chiefly *north.* and *Sc.*

a **1300** *Cursor M.* 17675 Bi nokes four þe hous up hang. *a* **1300** *E.E. Psalter* cxvii. 22 þe stane whilk biggand forsoke, It es made in heved of þe noke. *c* **1375** *Lay Folks Mass Bk.* (MS. B) 88 þo prest..stands turnande his boke at þo south auter noke. *c* **1520** NISBET *N.T.* Matt. vi. 5 Ypocritis that luvis to pray standand in synagogis and newkis of stretis. **1579** *Reg. Privy Council Scot.* III. 189 The inner barmkin of the said hous, and the tour upoun the south nuke of the samin. **1785** BURNS *Ep. W. Simpson* Postscr. v, 'Twas the auld moon turn'd a newk An' out o' sight. **1811** *Sporting Mag.* XXXVII. 131 He offered V.C. a shilling to..shoot at me as I turned a hedge nook. **1851** GREENWELL *Coal-trade Terms, Northumb. & Durh.* 37 *Nook* (*Neuk*).—One of the corners of a working place at the face; also, the corner of a pillar of coal. **1880** WATT *Poet. Sketches* 113 Roun' the first nook we gang he'll be standin'.

3. An interior angle formed by the meeting of two walls or similar boundaries; a corner in a room or other enclosed space.

See also *chimney-nook* (CHIMNEY *sb.* 11) and INGLE-NOOK.

α. **13..** *E.E. Allit. P.* C. 278 He lurkkes & laytes where was le best, In vche a nok of his nauel. *c* **1440** *Alph. Tales* 91 þis womman layde hur down in a noke of his cell & slepyd. *c* **1450** *St. Cuthbert* (Surtees) 3519 þen oute of his bedd noke Fyue vnyons þeyn he toke. **1601** HOLLAND *Pliny* II. 492 The Statues..were set vp in the cornered nouke of the Comitium at Rome. **1617** FLETCHER *Mad Lover* III. ii, Not a nook of hell, Not the most horrid pit, shall harbour thee. **1725** DE FOE *Voy. round World* (1840) 59, I caused him to be set down in a nook of the cabin. **1812** H. & J. SMITH *Rej. Addr.*, *Tale of Drury Lane*, Forth from thy nook John Horner come. **1822** GALT *Sir A. Wylie* xlix, I'll take a nook in the carriage wi' you as far as the road lies in my way. **1877** MRS. FORRESTER *Mignon* I. 4 There were so many nooks and corners in the..room.

β. *c* **1375** *Sc. Leg. Saints* xviii. (*Egipciane*) 609 Bot of þe ȝard in til a nuke I restyt me. *c* **1470** HENRY *Wallace* II. 372 A rousty suerd in a noik he saw stand. **1500–20** DUNBAR

Poems xxvi. 111 Syne ran a feynd to feche Makfadȝane, Far northwart in a nuke. **1575–6** *Durham Depos.* (Surtees) 267 The said Thomas laye in a newke nigh the fier. **1725** RAMSAY *Gentle Sheph.* II. i, A large ham hangs reesting in the neuk. **1787** BURNS *Holy Fair* xx, While some are cozie i' the neuk, And forming assignations. **1802** R. ANDERSON *Cumbld. Ball.* (c 1850) 49 My fadder started i' the nuik. **1894** R. REID *Kirkbride* vii. Poems 4 I'll wait for the comin' o' God..In a neuk o' the auld Kirkbride.

b. An out-of-the-way corner in or among buildings or similar surroundings.

a **1352** MINOT *Poems* (ed. Hall) vii. 5 Ȝit in many priue nokes May men find of Merlin bokes. **1375** BARBOUR *Bruce* XVII. 93 Thai..held thame in ane nwke preue, Quhill at the nycht suld passit be. *c* **1400** MAUNDEV. (Roxb.) xi. 44 In a nuke of þe citee es þe bathe of oure Lord. **1500–20** DUNBAR *Poems* xx. 33 Be thow not ane roundar in the nwke. *c* **1560** A. SCOTT *Poems* (S.T.S.) iv. 3 Hant nocht in hoile or nuke, To hurt ȝour womanheid. **1620** *Nottingham Rec.* IV. 369 Greatte disorder as ther is in divers places..in nookes and back sides. *a* **1677** BARROW *Serm.* Wks. 1716 II. 155 As if the King should cause his Edicts to be set up in the blindest and dirtiest nook of the Suburbs. **1785** COWPER *Let. to J. Hill* 25 June, I write in a nook that I call my *boudoir*. **1828** SCOTT *F.M. Perth* xxxii, Others dragged from some nook the stupified Bonthron. **1852** MRS. STOWE *Uncle Tom's C.* xiv. 121 He would climb to a nook among the cotton-bales of the upper deck.

c. Any small corner or recess. Also *fig.*

a **1400–50** *Alexander* 506 Fast scho flekirs about his fete.. And þar it nestild in a noke as it a nest were. **1576** NEWTON *Lemnie's Complex.* (1633) 92 They that have the nookes and cells of their braine slenderly moist. **1582** STANYHURST *Æneis* IV. (Arb.) 106, I doe craue (yf toe prayers as yeet soom nouke be reserued). **1667** MILTON *P.L.* I. 705 A third..had form'd..A various mould, and from the boyling cells..fill'd each hollow nook. **1721** RAMSAY *Lucky Spence* vi, Ryp ilka pouch frae nook to nook. **1818** SCOTT *Br. Lamm.* v, Shame be in my meal-poke,..and your hand aye in the nook of it! **1851** GOOLD in *Owen's Wks.* VI. 88 No nook of the heart is left unsearched.

d. A place or spot having the character of a recess shut in by rocks, trees, etc.; a secluded or sheltered place among natural scenery.

1555 W. WATREMAN *Fardle Facions* Z j, He vanisshed in a noque of the hille, beynge soubdenly ouercaste with a cloude. **1581** DERRICKE *Image Irel.* D iij, So do thei [eagles] kepe in wildest Nokes. **1628** WITHER *Brit. Rememb.* II. 1635 Through Nookes, & Corners, she pursu'd the Chase. **1667** MILTON *P.L.* IX. 277 As in a shadie nook I stood behind. **1794** COWPER *Needless Alarm* 40 The hasty brook, Struggling, detain'd in many a petty nook. **1810** SCOTT *Lady of L.* I. viii, In the deep Trosachs' wildest nook His solitary refuge took. **1856** STANLEY *Sinai & Pal.* ii. (1858) 141 These trees,..secluded as they are in their retired nooks on the heights of Lebanon. **1873** HAMERTON *Intell. Life* I. v. 29 He explored the whole neighbourhood, looking into every nook and cranny of it.

e. A small or sheltered creek or inlet.

1582 STANYHURST *Æneis* I. (Arb.) 22 Theare stands far stretching a nouke vplandish: an Island..hath framed an hauen. **1610** SHAKS. *Temp.* I. ii. 227 Safely in harbour Is the Kings shippe, in the deepe Nooke. **1661** *Proclamation Chas. II* 1 The great plenty of Fish, wherewith the..Nooks and Lakes of our Dominions doth abound. **1725** *Portland Papers* (Hist. MSS. Comm.) VI. 116 A large nook or recess in those banks..which they are informed by tradition was formerly a Haven. **1884** PAE *Eustace* 8 In a sheltered nook close under the high bank lay a boat.

4. An outlying, remote, or secluded part of a country, region, etc., or of the world.

c **1375** *Sc. Leg. Saints* xxvii. (*Machor*) 658 Hou ma we þane þis word fulfil þat in a nuk here lyis stil. **1536** BELLENDEN *Cron. Scot.* (1821) I. 161 Ye, quhilkis ar heir in the farrest nuik of the warld. **1581** BURNE *Disput.* in *Cath. Tract.* (S.T.S.) 140 He meruellis hou that Scotland being bot ane nuke of the varld [etc.]. **1609** HOLLAND *Amm. Marcell.* XXXI. iii. 404 A strange and unknowne kind of people before time,..risen from out of a secret nooke. **1631** BOLTON *Comf. Affl. Consc.* vi. (1635) 37 That thou shouldest bee borne and bred and brought up, in this little neglected nooke of the world. **1702** C. MATHER *Magn. Chr.* I. vi. (1852) 83 As genteel persons as most that ever visited these nooks of America. **1784** COWPER *Task* II. 207 While yet a nook is left Where English minds and manners may be found. **1842** TENNYSON *The Epic* 9 How all the old honour had from Christmas gone,..or dwindled down to some odd games In some odd nooks like this. **1878** BROWNING *La Saisiaz* 12 The news of that rare nook Yet untroubled by the tourist.

fig. **1632** MILTON *Penseroso* 90 What vast Regions hold The immortal mind that hath forsook Her mansion in this fleshly nook.

5. *attrib.*, as †**nook-cantle** (see quot.); **nook-rib**, *Arch.* a rib in the corner of a vault; **nook-window**, a window in the corner of a room next the fire-place.

1551 RECORDE *Pathw. Knowl.* I. Def., Sometimes..a cantle is cutte out with two lynes drawen from the centre to the circumference,..and then maie it be called a nooke cantle. **1835** WILLIS *Archit. Middle Ages* 367 Sometimes octagon nook-ribs are used with cylindrical shafts. **1885** HALL CAINE *Shadow of a Crime* 118 They put her in a great armchair and wheeled her into her place by the neuk window.

nook (nʊk), *v. rare.* [f. the sb.] **a.** *intr.* To hide in a corner. **b.** *trans.* To chip *off*, so as to form corners. **c.** To set in a corner; to conceal.

1611 MIDDLETON & DEKKER *Roaring Girl* H, *Hang.* Shall the ambuscado lie in one place? *Curt.* No, nooke thou yonder. **1789** BRAND *Newcastle* II. 681 The hewer first digs as far as he can into the bottom of the stratum; then he nooks or corners off the part measured off. **1840** *Tait's Mag.* VII. 345 The elder tree, growing by the little wicket, or nooked in a corner of the garden. **1899** *Birmingham Daily Post* 29 Apr. (E.D.D.), He heard them talk about 'nooking' the boots, by which he understood they meant to hide them.

nook, var. NUKE *sb.*[2]

nooked (nʊkt), *a.* [f. NOOK *sb.*]

1. Having (so many) corners, esp. in ***four-nooked***, square, ***three-nooked***, triangular. Now *dial.*

c **1205** LAY. 21999 Þer þis water wendeð, is an lutel wiht mære... Feower noked [*c* **1275** Four nokede] he is. **1513** DOUGLAS *Æneis* VII. iii. 20 Ne spair thai nocht..Thair fatale four nukit trunschowris for to eit. **1536** [see FOUR *a.* C. 2]. **1596** DALRYMPLE tr. *Leslie's Hist. Scotl.* Prol. 4 The Ile almaist is thrie nuiket. *Ibid.* I. 98 Thay far starker do make, four nuiked, of earth only. **1616** *Aberd. Burgh Reg.* (1848) II. 340 To..leave ane four nuikit hoill in the croun of the said voult. **1640** NABBES *Bride* I. iv, A Citty feast with a Ram-mutton pasty, and a twelve nookt custard. **1816** SCOTT *Antiq.* xxxvi, A three-nookit handkercher is the maist fashionable overlay. **1821** —— *Kenilw.* xxix, The loss of a four-nooked bit of paper. **1857** J. STEWART *Sketches Scot. Character* 118 Thae shapeless, mony-nookit blocks.

2. Having points, peaks, or corners; angular.

1549 *Compl. Scot.* vi. 54 Sum tyme it [the moon] aperit neukyt, heffand hornis, and sum tyme it vas al rond. **1567** *Gude & Godlie B.* (S.T.S.) 195 Preistis, cut ȝour gowne, Ȝour nukit bonet put away. **1610** HOLLAND *Camden's Brit.* I. 651 Such variety it hath of nouked bayes. **1632** GUILLIM *Heraldry* III. xx. (ed. 2) 238 By the Beake of an Hawke, is vnderstood the vpper part which is nooked. **17..** RAMSAY *Carle came o'er Croft* ii. (1877) II. 208 A siller broach..To fasten on my curtchea nooked. **17..** —— *To Starrat* 13 *ibid.* 276 Lang mayst thou teach, with round and nooked lines, Substantial skill.

'nookery. [f. NOOK *sb.* + -ERY.] A snug nook.

1824 in L. M. Hawkins *Mem.* I. 269 In this nookery were to be found..such men as the Rev. Mr. Cracherode, Mr. Southwell [etc.]. **1835** IRVING *Life & Lett.* III. 75 My idea is to make a little nookery somewhat in the Dutch style.

'nooking. [-ING[1].] A nook, ingle-nook.

Current in north. dial. in forms *neukin*, *newkin*, *nuikin*.

1865 KNIGHT *Passages Work. Life* II. ix. 183 Cheap literature was not then, as now, to be found in every out-o'-the-way nooking.

'nooklet. [-LET.] A little nook or corner.

1847 *Tait's Mag.* XIV. 854 Hope from out of some sweet nooklet Of the heart sends forth its lay. **1874** HOLLAND *Mistr. Manse* ii. 20 Every nooklet and retreat..Shall wear a charm.

'nook-shaft. *Arch.* [f. NOOK *sb.*] A shaft placed in the internal angle formed by the meeting of two contiguous faces in a compound archway.

1835 WILLIS *Archit. Middle Ages* 36 The archway..consists of three orders of square-edged banded arches, with two interposed nook-shafts. **1840** *Penny Cycl.* XVI. 275/2 The larger arches below..spring from nook-shafts or slender attached pillars. **1865** STREET *Gothic Archit. Sp.* 69 There are nook-shafts at the angles.

'nook-shotten, *a.* Now *arch.* or *dial.* [f. NOOK *sb.*] Running out into corners or angles.

1599 SHAKS. *Hen. V*, III. v. 14 A slobbry and a durtie Farme In that nook-shotten Ile of Albion. **1688** HOLME *Armoury* III. 385/2 Querke, is a nook shoten Pane, or any Pane whose sides and top run out of a square form. *a* **1800** PEGGE *Anecd.* (1814) 391 *Nook-shotten*, spoken of a wall in a bevil, and not at right angles with another wall. [**1834** DE QUINCEY *Autobiog. Sk.* Wks. 1853 I. 231 The provinces, to the very furthest nook of these 'nook-shotten' islands.] **1879** MISS JACKSON *Shropsh. Word-bk.* s.v., An old farmer cautioned a certain person against taking a short cut across some fields because the way was very 'neuk-shotten'.

nooky ('nʊkɪ), *sb. slang.* Also nookie. [Orig. uncertain; perh. f. NOOK *sb.* 3.] Sexual intercourse; hence also, a woman or girl considered as a sex object.

1928 HECHT & MACARTHUR *Front Page* I. 46 *Mollie Malloy enters. She is a North Clark Street tart...* Well, well! Nookie! **1930** J. DOS PASSOS *42nd Parallel* v. 400 Hendriks said he'd picked up with a skirt that was a warm baby and he was getting his nookie every night. **1932** J. T. FARRELL *Young Lonigan* vi. 242 Schreiber was a good guy, but you know he liked his nooky, and he was always mixed up with some woman or other. **1948** N. MAILER *Naked & Dead* (1949) II. v. 161 A woman that likes her nookie ain't gonna be satisfied with one man after she gits used to him. **1953** *Landfall* VII. 250 But I've had my bit of nookie on toast... A sheila of thirty, hot and spry. **1960** A. WEST *Trend is Up* (1961) iii. 95 Still nooky was nooky he told himself, and who cared what the woman was like if the lay was good. **1964** W. MARKFIELD *To Early Grave* (1965) vi. 108 He starts telling me how tough it is for him to break in another nookie, how he's tired of having to make up reading lists for them. **1972** M. WOODHOUSE *Mama Doll* vii. 83 All the money he'll make as well as the nooky.

nooky ('nʊkɪ), *a.* [f. NOOK *sb.* + -Y.] Abounding in nooks; nook-like.

1813 M. EDGEWORTH *Let.* 19 Apr. (1971) 19 Railed-in nice gardens, little *nooky* green spots. **1827** CLARE *Sheph. Cal.* 43 Or race around the nooky church. **1847** LYTTON *Lucretia* ii, Two windows..helped to give that irregular and nooky appearance to the apartment. **1871** MISS MULOCK *Fair France* i. 25 A nooky hollow of blue and white violets.

noological (nəʊəʊ'lɒdʒɪkəl), *a.* [See NOOLOGY and -ICAL.] Pertaining to noology.

1811–31 BENTHAM *Logic* Wks. 1843 VIII. 245 The leading words of many ethical, noological, or pathological works. **1816** —— *Chrestom.* ibid. 75 By imagination, the idea and practice of logical, noological, metaphysical analysis, was deduced from that of physical.

noologist (nəʊ'ɒlədʒɪst). [See next and -IST.] One who refers the origin of certain ideas to the mind itself and not to experience.

1857 T. E. WEBB *Intellect. Locke* i. 17 When with reference to 'the origin of the pure cognitions of Reason' Kant divided philosophers into Noologists and Empiricists, he regarded Aristotle as the head of the Empiricists.

noology (nəʊ'ɒlədʒɪ). [f. Gr. νόο-ς mind + -LOGY.] The science of the understanding.

1811–31 BENTHAM *Logic* App. Wks. 1843 VIII. 289 The field of the corresponding branch of science may be termed the field of noology. **1816** —— *Chrestom.* ibid. 88 Alegopathematic, or say Alego-aesthetic Pneumatology has for its single-worded synonym the not unexpressive appellation Noology. **1836–7** SIR W. HAMILTON *Metaph.* vii. (1859) I. 123 We have several deservedly forgotten treatises of an older date, under the inviting name of Noologies.

noomble, obs. form of NUMBLE.

no'ometry. *nonce-wd.* [f. Gr. νόο-ς mind + -METRY.] The measurement of mind.

1817 T. L. PEACOCK *Melincourt* I. 184 The same distinction is conferred on all capacities by the academical noometry not of merit but of time.

noon (nuːn), *sb.* Forms: α. 1 nón, 2–5 non, 4 noen, 3–6 none, 4–7 noone, 3– noon. β. *north.* and *Sc.* 4 noun(e, nown, 5 novne, nowne, noyn(e; nun, nvne, 7– nune. [OE. *nón* neut. = ON. *nón* (MSw. and Norw. *non*) neut., OS. **nôn* (*noon*, *nuon*), MDu. (and Du.) *noen*, obs. G. *non* fem., ad. L. *nōna* (sc. *hōra*), fem. sing. of *nōnus* ninth: cf. NONE *sb.* and NONES. A weak fem. form, more directly representing the L., appears in OS. and OHG. *nôna* (MLG. and MHG. *nône*), ON. *nóna*, MDu. *none*, *noene*: cf. also F. *none*, †*nonne*.]

†**1. a.** The ninth hour of the day, reckoned from sunrise according to the Roman method, or about three o'clock in the afternoon. *Obs.*

Chiefly as a direct rendering of L. *nona* (*hora*), and in later use most frequent in accounts of the Crucifixion.

Beowulf 1600 Ða com non dæges: næs ofgeafon hwate Scyldingas. *c* **900** tr. *Bæda's Hist.* III. v. (Schipper) 204 Þæt hi þy feorðan wicdæge & þy syxtan fæstan to nones. *c* **1000** *Sax. Leechd.* II. 140 Sele drincan on þreo tida, on undern, on middæg, on non. *c* **1175** *Lamb. Hom.* 45 Ic ham ȝeue reste.. from non on saterdei a þa cume monedeis lihting. *c* **1275** *Passion our Lord* 478 in *O.E. Misc.* 50 Hit wes welneyh mydday, þo þusternesse com, In alle Middenherde fort þet hit wes non. *a* **1300** *Cursor M.* 988 He was wroght at vndern tide, At middai eue draun of his side,..þai war bath don out at none. **13..** *Sir Beues* 3237 Þe sonne schon, hit drouȝ to vnder,..Middai com, hit drouȝ te noune. **1382** WYCLIF *Mark* xv. 33 Derknessis ben maad..til in to the nynthe our, that is, noon. *c* **1420** *Pol. Rel. & L. Poems* (1866) 277 Ȝet he was in suffryng..Tyl it was pacyd non.

†**b.** *Eccl.* The hour or office of NONES. *Obs.*

c **960** ÆTHELWOLD *Rule St. Benet* (Schröer 1885) 40 Eornostlice on þysum tidum we herien urne scyppend.., on middæg, on non, on æfen. *a* **1000** *Colloq. Ælfric* in Wr.-Wülcker 101 We..sungon non, *cantauimus nonam*. *a* **1225** *Ancr. R.* 20 Siggeð non efter mete þe hwule þet sumer lested. *c* **1300** *St. Brandan* 225 in *S. Eng. Leg.* I. 225 Þe foweles sunge ek here matyns..& vnderne siþþe & middai & afterwardes none. **1303** R. BRUNNE *Handl. Synne* 928 Þey shuld nat werche Lengyr þan þey rong none at þe chyrche. *c* **1380** WYCLIF *Wks.* (1880) 41 But late lewid freris seie..for prime, tierce, vndren & noon, for eche of hem seuene pater nostris. *c* **1420** *Anturs of Arth.* xvii, Were thritty trentalles done, By-twyxene vndrone and none, My saule were saluede fulle sone. **1481** CAXTON *Reynard* (Arb.) 10, I haue yete to saye my sexte, none, and myn euensonge. **1526** *Pilgr. Perf.* (W. de W. 1531) 164b, The chirche..entendeth to honour & worshyp at vij tymes in the daye, that is to saye, in matyns,..none, euensonge & complyn. **1561** BP. PARKHURST *Injunctions*, Whether they..vse muche iangling in festiuall daies in ringing none or curphew.

2. a. Twelve o'clock in the day; mid-day.

The same change in the time denoted by *noon*, probably due to anticipation of the ecclesiastical office or of a meal-hour, has taken place with Du. *noen*, and with F. *none* in older (and still in dialect) use. By the 14th cent. it appears to have been the ordinary sense of the word in English, although in many examples there is no clear indication of the time intended. The common phrases (*be*)*fore noon* and *after noon* have given rise to the sbs. FORENOON and AFTERNOON. *high noon*: see HIGH *a.* 11.

α. *c* **1205** LAY. 14039 Þa þe non wes icumen, þa weoren Peohtes ouer-cumen..& alle dai heo fluȝen. *c* **1290** *St. Michael* 403 in *S. Eng. Leg.* I. 311 Þe sonne..is euene a-boue þin heued riȝt atþe nones stounde. *c* **1320** *Sir Tristr.* 890 Bitvene þe none and þe niȝt Last þe batayle. *c* **1391** CHAUCER *Astrol.* II. §3 From .xi. of the clokke byforn the howre of noon til on of the clok next folwyng. *c* **1410** HOCCLEVE *Compl. Virg.* 135 O sonne, with thy cleere bemes brighte, þat seest my child nakid this nones tyde. **1470–85** MALORY *Arthur* XX. xxi. 835 Euery day..from vnderne tyl hyhe none hys myght encreaced tho thre houres. **1472–3** *Rolls of Parlt.* VI. 23 The houre of XII, comenly called the houre of none, of the seid fourty day. **1529** CROMWELL in Merriman *Life & Lett.* (1902) I. 324 Whiche I trust shalbe to morow at nyght or wenesday by none. **1565** *Reg. Privy Council Scot.* I. 332 Fra sex houris in the morning to XI houris at none, and fra ane eftir none to sex houris at evin. **1577** B. GOOGE *Heresbach's Husb.* II. (1586) 81 b, Before noone when it waxeth hotte..you must digge it. **1625** N. CARPENTER *Geogr. Del.* I. x. (1635) 232 When the one hath his Noone, the other inioyes his midnight. **1656** HEYLIN *Surv. France* 423 It was full noon before we were under sail. **1697** DRYDEN *Virg. Georg.* IV. 615 'Twas Noon; the sultry Dog-star from the Sky Scorch'd Indian Swains. **1710** STEELE *Tatler* No. 232 ¶1 The Noons have been of late pretty warm. **1784** COWPER *Task* VI. 58 Now at noon..The season smiles,..And has the warmth of May. **1812** WOODHOUSE *Astron.* i. 5 Noon is determined by the Sun being on the meridian. **1836–7** DICKENS *Sk. Boz, Scenes* i, We come to the heat, bustle, and activity of Noon. **1863** LONGF. *Wayside Inn, Prel.* 23 But noon and night, the panting teams Stop under the great oaks.

fig. **1819** SHELLEY *Cenci* IV. i. 82 She shall stand shelterless in the broad noon Of public scorn. **1839–52** BAILEY *Festus* 160 Whose hearts have a look southwards, and are open To the whole noon of nature.

β. **1375** BARBOUR *Bruce* XVII. 659 Apon sic maner can thai ficht Quhill it wes neir noyne of the day. *c* **1375** *Sc. Leg. Saints* xl. (*Ninian*) 769 Fasting..fryday fra þe novne til sonday at þe mes be done. *c* **1460** *Towneley Myst.* ix. 81 Or noyn of the day, I dar you hyght, to bryng hym by the hand. *c* **1470** HENRY *Wallace* VII. 611 Be ane our nowne at Bothwell ȝeit he was. **1609** SKENE *Reg. Maj.* 154 It is not lesum to pack, or peill fish, bot fra eleven houres, to twa after nune.

b. *transf.* The most important hour of the day.

1712 STEELE *Spect.* No. 454 ¶2 The fashionable World, who have made Two a Clock the Noon of the Day. **1848** THACKERAY *Bk. Snobs* xxxv, At the noon of London time you see a light-yellow carriage. **1855** —— *Newcomes* vi, It is 5 o'clock, the noon in Pall Mall.

c. The mid-day sun.

1858 SEARS *Athan.* vi. 53 The noon is blazing down upon the Syrian plain.

†**3.** The mid-day meal. (Cf. NOONMEAT.) *Obs.*

a **1175** *Cott. Hom.* 231 Me..sceolde..ȝiefe him his formemete, þat him to lang ne þuhte to abiden oð se laford to þe none inn come. *c* **1205** LAY. 16595 þa þe þridde dæi com & þat folc hafde imaked non. **1377** LANGL. *P. Pl.* B. v. 378, I..ouer-seye me at my sopere and some tyme at nones. **1393** —— *P. Pl.* C. IX. 290 Let hem abyde..Til alle þyn nedy neihebores haue none ymaked. *a* **1483** *Liber Niger* in *Househ. Ord.* (1790) 56 For hys chambre brekefast, none, soupers & lyvery for all nyght vii loves.

4. a. The time of night corresponding to mid-day; midnight. Chiefly in phr. *(the) noon of night.*

1603 BEN JONSON *Sejanus* V. vi, When arrived you? About the noon of night. **1648** HERRICK *Hesper., The Hag* iii, While mischiefs,..At noone of Night are a-working. **1697** DRYDEN *Æneid* IV. 744 Hoary simples,..With brazen sickles reap'd at noon of night. **1745** WARTON *Pleas. Melanch.* 50 Nor undelightful is the solemn noon Of night. **1796** MOSER *Hermit Caucasus* I. 21 At the noon of night their ears were assailed by the..sound of a trumpet. **1820** SHELLEY *Witch Atl.* xlvii, When the weary moon was in the wane, Or in the noon of interlunar night. **1830** TENNYSON *Poems* 123 Night hath climbed her peak of highest noon. **1867** JEAN INGELOW *Dreams that came true* xliv, For the moon Was shining in, and night was at the noon.

b. The place of the moon at midnight.

1605 DRAYTON *Man in the Moone* 37 Now the goodly Moone Was in the Full, and at her Nighted Noone. **1632** MILTON *Penseroso* 68 To behold the wandring Moon, Riding neer her highest noon. **1638** QUARLES *Elegies* xiv. Wks. (Grosart) III. 25 The Queen of light,..in her young Noone of night.

5. The culminating or highest point.

c **1600** SHAKS. *Sonn.* vii, Thou, thyself out-going in thy noon, Unlook'd on diest. **1624** DONNE *Serm.* xliii. 429 But the meridianall noone is in faith. **1671** MILTON *Samson* 683 Thou oft Amidst thir highth of noon, Changest thy countenance. **1817** SHELLEY *Rev. Islam* VIII. xxix, In the bright wisdom of youth's breathless noon. **1844** MRS. BROWNING *Drama of Exile* 1960 In the set noon of time, shall one from Heaven..Descend before a woman. **1869** MARTINEAU *Ess.* II. 229 Shadows..deaden the colors of the noon of life.

6. a. *attrib.* and *Comb.*, as *noon-beam, -bell, -dew, -height, -reek, rest, -scape, -top,* etc.; *noon-bright, -clear, -fierce, -hot, -maned, -slight, -wandering, -wide, -wild* adjs.; *noon-aglow* adv.

1919 W. DE LA MARE *Flora* 33 Her billowing summits heaving *noon-aglow. **1776** MICKLE tr. *Camoens' Lusiad* 407 The sultry *noon-beam shines the lovers' aid. **13..** *Sir Beues* (A.) 2250 So stod Beues in þat þring, Til *noun belle be-gan to ring. **1858** BONAR *Hymns Faith & Hope* 120 My sky was once *noon-bright. **1874** HARDY *Far from Madding Crowd* II. i. 5 In her *noon-clear sense that she had never loved him she forgot for a moment, [etc.]. **1953** E. SITWELL *Gardeners & Astronomers* 9 Holding small stars for seeds And planets of *noon-dew. **1656** W. DU GARD tr. *Comenius' Gate Lat. Unl.* 190 Leav a breakfast, & *noon-dinner to labourers. **1954** W. FAULKNER *Fable* (1955) 42 He would whisper the one word *noon-fierce stone under his face. **1869** D. G. ROSSETTI *Let.* 26 Aug. (1965) II. 720 Every sense..Now labours o'er the stark *noon-height To reach the sunset's desolate disarray. **1940** AUDEN *Another Time* 37 Every crevice of the *noon-hot landscape. **1946** DYLAN THOMAS *Deaths & Entrances* 17, I see the togron in tears In the androgynous dark, His striped and *noon maned tribe striding to holocaust. **1468** *Medulla Gram.* in *Promp. Parv.* 361 *note, Anticenia,* a *nonemele. **1578** *Chr. Prayers* in *Priv. Prayers* (1851) 444 That sun of thine..is always at *noon-point with them, ever bright, ever shining. **1922** JOYCE *Ulysses* 155 The heavy *noonreek tickled the top of Mr Bloom's gullet. **1538** ELYOT, *Meridiatio,* *noone reste. **1873** J. H. BEADLE *Undevel. West* xxviii. 615 We found water enough for our noon rest in the hollowed surface of a rock. **1926** V. SACKVILLE-WEST *Land* 71 Then, with the *noonscape, underneath the hedge..the random reaper drains his pint of ale. **1461** *Paston Lett.* I. 540 Yowr letter was delyveryd to me the xxiii. day of Januar abowthe *none seasson. *a* **1646** J. GREGORY *Posthuma* (1650) 300 Of Oxford the Sign-Regent is Capricorn, the *Noonshadows are Heteroscian. **1807** MONTGOMERY *West Indies* IV. (1810) 63 Where the noon shadow shrinks beneath the sun. **1936** L. B. LYON *Bright Feather Fading* 16 He loved to shoulder A far cloud or brush the *noon-Slight sickle moon. **1868** WHITTIER *Among Hills* 11 The locust by the wall Stabs the *noon-silence with his sharp alarm. **1671** MILTON *P.R.* II. 156 Many are in each Region passing fair As the *noon Skie. **1933** C. DAY LEWIS *Magnetic Mountain* 9 Spirit mating afresh shall discern him On the world's *noon-top purely poised. **1820** SHELLEY *Witch Atl.* xlvi, A *noon-wandering meteor flung to heaven. **1935** —— *Time to Dance* 25 Buoyed, embayed in heaven's *noon-wide reaches. **1936** L. B. LYON *Bright Feather Fading* 41 Battlement that once glowed *Noon-wild is warier lit.

b. Special combs., as **noon-basket** *U.S.*, a lunch-basket; †**noon-devil** (see MERIDIAN *a.* 1 b); **noon-flower**, a name given to plants of the genus *Mesembryanthemum*, and to the Goat's-beard (*Tragopogon pratensis*); †**noon-hall**, ? a dining-hall; **noon-halt**, a halt made in the middle of the day; **noon-hour**, *U.S.* the hour of dinner or rest in the middle of the day; **noon-house** *U.S.*, a house used for rest and meals at midday; now *Hist.*; **noon-line**, the line marking the hour of noon on a sun-dial; **noon-mark**, a mark which indicates when it is noon; midday; now *Hist.*; **noonshine**, joc. form of NUNCHEON; **noon-spell** *U.S.*, a rest taken in the middle of the day; **noon-sprite** (cf. *noon-devil* above); †**noon-tender** (see quot. 1684).

1865 A. D. WHITNEY *Gayworthys* vi. 71 Don't you remember what we used to say at school, when we opened our *noon-baskets? **1560** DAUS tr. *Sleidane's Comm.* 30 b, The Scripture warneth us, to beware of the *noone Devill, & the fliynge Arrowe. **1621** MOLLE *Camerar. Liv. Libr.* IV. ii. 265 At this day the Russians feare and reuerence the noone deuil. **1856** DELAMER *Fl. Gard.* (1861) 95 *Noon Flower.——An immense genus of succulents, mostly shrubby. **1864** PRIOR *Plant-n., Noon-flower,* or *Noon-tide,* from its closing at midday, and marking the hour of noon. **1665** PEPYS *Diary* 20 Apr., This night I am told the first play is played in White Hall *noon-hall, which is now turned to a house of playing. **1843** J. C. FRÉMONT *Rep. Exploring Expedition* 15 At our *noon halt, the men were exercised at a target. **1854** J. R. BARTLETT *Pers. Narr. Explor. Texas* II. xxxvii. 395 On our return we made a noon halt on the banks of the river. *a* **1918** G. STEWART *On Frontier* I. 115 John Dickery rode ahead from our noon halt to try to kill a sage hen. **1889** *Charity Organis. Rev.* Aug. 341 He asked a few men to call every day at his *noon hour at the place where he worked. **1845** S. JUDD *Margaret* I. 110 Several elderly men and women retired to what was called a '*Noon House', a small building..where they ate dinner and had a prayer. **1891** A. EARLE *Sabbath* 102 There might have been seen a hundred years ago, by the side of many an old meeting-house in New England, a long, low, mean, stable-like building... This was the 'noon-house', or 'Sabba-day house'... It was a place of refuge in the winter time, at the noon interval between two services. **1596** BLAGRAVE *Vran. Astrolabe* E 3 The *noone-line brought to the sunnes chief Apex. **1669** STURMY *Mariner's Mag.* VII. iii. 4 The Gnomon ..erected upon the Noon-line, or Line of 12 a Clock. **1854** B. F. TAYLOR *Jan. & June* I. 131 The sun..has reached the *noon-mark on the threshold. **1889** R. T. COOKE *Steadfast* xxv. 275 Goodness! tis most noon-mark and I haven't took a step towardst dinner. **1948** *Amer. N. & Q.* Nov. 121/2, I should like to know whether..the term 'noon mark' was once common. **1808** JANE AUSTEN *Let.* 20 June (1952) 195 The Moores came..between one & two o'clock, &..after the *noonshine which succeeded their arrival, a party set off for Buckwell. *Ibid.* 24 Oct. 228 The tide is just right for our going immediately after noon-shine. **1839** C. M. KIRKLAND *New Home* xlv. 300 Even the '*noon-spell' shines no holiday for the luckless subjects of her domination. **1887** J. KIRKLAND *Zury* 18 Wait till noon-spell, then we'll see! **1889** R. T. COOKE *Steadfast* ii. 30 Its nigh about noonspell now. **1892** CHILD *Ballads* IV. 440/2 The Wends have the proverbial phrase, to ask as many questions as a *noon-sprite. **1684** E. CHAMBERLAYNE *Pres. St. Eng.* II. (ed. 15) 245 Sixteen *noon-tenders, who attend the goods on the keys whilst the other officers go to dinner. **1710** J. CHAMBERLAYNE *St. Gt. Brit.* II. III. 494 Noon-tenders, at 16*l.* each *per Ann.*

noon (nuːn), *v. U.S.* [f. NOON *sb.* Cf. W. Flem. *noenen,* G. dial. *nonen,* Norw. dial. *nona, nöna.*] *intr.* (also with *it.*) To halt or rest at noon, or in the middle of the day; to stop for, or partake of, the mid-day meal.

1806 LEWIS & CLARK *Exped.* (1893) 1061 We arrived.. where we had nooned it on the 12th of Sept. last. **1850** B. TAYLOR *Eldorado* xix. 135 We nooned at Sanchez' Ranche. **1880** L. WALLACE *Ben-Hur* VII. v. 459 The third day of the journey the party nooned by the river Jabbok.

noon, obs. form of NONE.

†**noon**, obs. aphetic form of ANON.

1462 *Paston Lett.* II. 102 And noon upon thys same langwage, yong Debnam spake hys fader.

noonchine, obs. variant of NUNCHEON.

noonday (ˈnuːndeɪ). [f. NOON *sb.* + DAY *sb.* Cf. ONorw. *nóndagr.*]

1. The middle of the day; mid-day.

1535 COVERDALE *Job* xi. 17 Then shulde thy life be as cleare as the noone daye. *c* **1586** C'TESS PEMBROKE *Ps.* XXXVII. iv, The glory of noone day. **1660** *Trial Regic.* 53 It is as clear as the Noon-day, that this was not the House of Commons. **1706** E. WARD *Wooden World Diss.* (1708) 47 It's Noon-day with them, and they look no farther. **1821** BYRON *Heav. & Earth* iii. 917 The pleasant trees that o'er our noonday bent. **1893** FORBES-MITCHELL *Remin. Gt. Mutiny* 26 It was clear as noonday to the meanest capacity.

fig. **1869** CRAIK *Hist. Eng. Lit.* II. 1 Our national literature ..had its noonday in..the last quarter of the sixteenth and the first of the seventeenth century.

b. Freq. in phr. *at (†the) noonday.*

1535 COVERDALE *2 Sam.* iv. 5 He laye vpon his bed at the noone daie. **1596** DALRYMPLE tr. *Leslie's Hist. Scot.* VI. 317 As may be seine ouer all cleirer than the sone at Nune day. **1651** H. L'ESTRANGE *Answ. Mrq. Worc.* 12 [That] we must not walk abroad at high noon-day without a Torch. **1700** T. BROWN *Lett. fr. Dead* 234 My *Minor* is as plain as the Sun at Noon-day. **1780** COWPER *Progr. Err.* 451 Judgment drunk,..Winks hard, and talks of darkness at noon-day. **1850** MARSDEN *Early Puritans* (1853) 141 Prisons in..which he could not see his hand at noonday. **1867** TROLLOPE *Chron. Barset* I. iv. 31 That he was not a thief was as clear to her as the sun at noonday.

†**c.** So *at noondays. Obs.*

1537 LATIMER *Serm. Convocation* A vij b, They are to be lyghted with waxe candelles,..yea at noone dayes. **1574** G. HARVEY *Letter-bk.* (Camden) 66 Is it not cleerer than the sun at noondayes. **1611** COTGR. s.v. *Midi,* He that looks for night at noone-dayes may well be tearmed mad, or blind.

2. *attrib.*, as *noonday comfort, dream, light,* etc.; †**noonday devil** (see NOON *sb.* 6 b).

1651 JER. TAYLOR *Serm. for Year* II. 350 At this day some of the Russians fear the Noon-day Devil. **1656** EARL MONM. tr. *Boccalini's Advt. fr. Parnass.* 80 The noon-day comfort of a great Tree standing in his Court-yard. **1674** *Ch. & Crt. of Rome* 5 In this Noon-day Light of Christian Knowledge. **1712** ADDISON *Spect.* No. 441 ¶11 My Noon-day Walks he shall attend. **1781** COWPER *Charity* 398 Di'monds..Reflect the noon-day glory of the skies. **1791** BURKE *Let. to Member Nat. Assembly* Wks. VI. 20 The then noon-day splendour of the civilized world. **1815** SHELLEY *Alastor* 420 The noonday sun Now shone upon the forest. **1820** —— *Cloud* 4, I bear light shade for the leaves when laid In their noonday dreams. **1873** 'OUIDA' *Pascarèl* I. 69 They would run out.. to fetch me a noonday meal of coffee..and little patties.

noone, obs. f. NONE, NOON, NUN.

noonery, obs. f. NUNNERY.

noones, obs. f. NONCE[1].

nooning (ˈnuːnɪŋ). Also 5 noynyng. [f. NOON *sb.* + -ING[1] 1.]

1. Noontide. Now *U.S.*

c **1460** *Towneley Myst.* xxiv. 65 He has myster of nyghtys rest that nappys not in noynyng.

1880 L. WALLACE *Ben-Hur* VII. iv. 379 And so to them the nooning came, and the evening.

2. A noonday meal. Now *dial.* and *U.S.*

a **1652** BROME *Mad Couple* V. ii, Seaven constant ordinaries every night, Noonings, and intermealiary Lunchings. **1695** KENNETT *Par. Antiq.* Gloss. s.v. *Ad Nonam,* A great piece, enough to serve for a nooning or dinner of any common eater. **1711** ADDISON *Spect.* No. 72 ¶3 If he be disposed to take a Whet, a Nooning, an Evening's Draught, or a Bottle after Midnight. **1797** R. GURNEY in A. J. C. Hare *Gurneys* (1895) I. 71 Kitty would not let us go to nooning till we had finished a lesson we were about. *a* **1833** J. T. SMITH *Bk. for Rainy Day* (1845) 260 At this time the servant announced Nooning. **1849** MRS. RUNDELL *Dom. Cookery* Pref. p. xii, Where noonings or suppers are served, care should be taken [etc.]. **1880** 'MARK TWAIN' *Tramp Abroad* ii. 18 A German gentleman and his two young lady daughters had been taking their nooning at the inn.

3. A rest or repose at noon. Now *U.S.*

1552 HULOET, Noonynge, or noone rest, *meridiatio.*

1850 LOWELL *Lett.* I. 193, I mean to take a nooning and lie under the trees looking at the sky. **1883** ROLLINS *New Eng. Bygones* 94 The noonings were bright features of a haying landscape.

b. *U.S.* An interval in the middle of the day, esp. for rest or food.

1865 *Reader* 12 Aug. 172/3 In the 'nooning', as it is called in New England—that is, in the space between Sunday morning and afternoon services. **1884** *Harper's Mag.* Nov. 830/2 The workmen, during their noonings, show equal interest.

4. *attrib.*, as *nooning-meal, -place.*

1865 MRS. WHITNEY *Gayworthys* v. (1879) 52 The simple nooning meal, that needed intervention of neither knife nor fork, was eaten. **1884** J. G. BOURKE *Snake-Dance Moquis* viii. 77 [He] confirmed this story by telling another of a sorcerer killed near this very nooning-place.

'noon-light. [f. NOON *sb.* + LIGHT.] The light of noon; the brightest or clearest light of the day. Also *fig.*

1598 BARCKLEY *Felic. Man* v. (1603) 421 A spirit not onely of the day, but also of noone-light. **1645** RUTHERFORD *Tryal & Tri. Faith* (1845) 269 The noon-light that is in the great body of the sun. *a* **1672** P. STERRY *Freed. Will* (1675) 205 The Noon-Light of Knowledge is the sight of things in their eternal Ideas. **1810** MONTGOMERY *Bolehill Trees* Poems 125 Through the blue dazzling distance of noon-light. **1845** WHITTIER *Lines* 1 With a cold and wintry noon-light. **1861** DORA GREENWELL *Poems* 64 Within the noon-light Of one illimitable Present.

†**noonmeat.** *Obs.* Forms: 1 nónmete; 4–5 none mete (5 nun, nvne), 6 none, noone meat(e. [f. NOON *sb.* + MEAT *sb.* Now represented in dial. by NAMMET and NUMMET.] A meal taken at noon, a luncheon.

a **1000** *Sal. & Sat.* lix, On xii monðum ða scealt sillan ðinum þeowan men vii hund hlafa, and xx hlafa, buton morȝenmetum, and nonmetum. *c* **1000** *Ælfric's Voc.* in Wr.-Wülcker 147 *Merenda,* nonmete. *a* **1400** *Gloss.* in *Rel. Antiq.* I. 6 *Merenda,* nonemete. **1428–9** *Rec. St. Mary at Hill* (1904) 71 Also payd for þe none mete on þe morwe of iij carpenters & ij plomers, a sholdere & a brist of moton. *c* **1440** *Promp. Parv.* 360/2 Nunmete, *merenda.* **1495** *Act 11 Hen. VII,* c. 22 §4 Laborers..longe sitting at ther brekfast at ther dyner and nonemete. **1548** THOMAS *Ital. Gram., Merenda,* breakefast, or noone meate. **1591** PERCIVALL *Sp. Dict., Merendar,* to take the noonemeat.

noonshun, obs. form of NUNCHEON.

noonstead. *Obs.* exc. *dial.* Forms: 6–7 noonestead (6 -steede, 7 -sted), 6 none-, noonsteed, 6– **noonstead.** [f. NOON *sb.* + STEAD *sb.*] The station or position of the sun at noon.

1559 *Mirr. Mag.* (1563) P iij, Pale Cinthea..was past the Noonesteede syxe degrees in sight. **1598** DRAYTON *Heroic. Ep.* (1695) 127 The worlds great light.. Would at our Noonstead ever make aboad. **1612** J. DAVIES *Muse's Sacr.* Wks. (Grosart) II. 83/2 The Sunne..stands..fixt in the Noonestead of Eternities. **1670** FLAMSTEED in Rigaud *Corr. Sci. Men* (1841) II. 77 The moon was scarce an hour removed from the noonstead. **1876** *Mid Yorksh. Gloss.* s.v. *Folkstead.* *attrib.* **1551** RECORDE *Cast. Knowl.* (1556) 22 A circle.. whiche is called therefore the Meridiane circle, and may be named well the Noone steede cyrcle. **1601** HOLLAND *Pliny* I. 191 In the 12 tables of Romane lawes, there is no mention at all made but of East and West; after certain yeres the noon-stead point in the South quarter also was obserued.

Hence †'**noonsteading**, the time of coming on the meridian.

1570 DEE *Math. Pref.* 42 Foreseeing the Rising, Settyng, Nonestedyng..of certaine..fixed Sterres.

noon-sun. [f. NOON *sb.* + SUN *sb.*[1]] The sun at its meridian.

1601 HOLLAND *Pliny* I. 372 By the reflection of the beames of the Noon-sun. **1626** BACON *Sylva* §898. 19 In Making of Vinegar, they..set Vessels of Wine over against the Noonesunne. **1846** PROWETT *Prometh. Bound* 3 Roasted in the noon-sun's glare. **1872** TENNYSON *Gareth & Lynette* 619 Morning-Star, and Noon-Sun, and Evening-Star.

noontide ('nu:ntaɪd). Forms: 1–2 **nóntid;** 4 **nonetyde,** 6 **-tyd;** 6–7 **noonetide,** 6 **-tyd;** 6– **noontide.** [OE. *nóntíd* = MDu. *noentijt* (*-tide,* also *noene-, none-*; Du. *noentijd*), MHG. *nôn(e)zît* (G. *none-, nonzeit*), MSw. *nonstidh*: see NOON *sb.* and TIDE *sb.*]

1. The time of noon; in later use, mid-day.

971 *Blickl. Hom.* 47 þriddan siþe on midne dæȝ, feorþan siþe on nontid, fiftan siþe on æfen. *c* **1000** in Assmann *Ags. Hom.* (1889) XI. 65 Sona swa hy þæt belltacen ȝehyrað þære nigoðan tide, þæt is seo nontid. **1154** *O.E. Chron.* (Laud MS.) an. 1140, þer efter..þestrede þe sunne & te dæi abuton non tid dæies þa men eten. *c* **1325** *Orfeo* 457 A morewe at the none-tyde He made the quene there abyde. *a* **1440** *Sir Eglam.* 364 Ageynys the none-tyde, Yn a foreste there he can ryde. **1576** FLEMING *Panopl. Epist.* 409 All noontide to solace yourself in the refreshing shadowe. *c* **1586** C'TESS PEMBROKE *Ps.* CII. xiii, Turne not to night the noonetide of my day. **1625** N. CARPENTER *Geogr. Del.* I. x. (1635) 223 The Sunne at Noonetide is alwayes on the South of those which dwell vnder the Arcticke Circle. **1675** DRYDEN *Epil. Crowne's Calisto,* Whose morning rays like noontide strike and shine. **1768** BEATTIE *Minstr.* I. xlvii, Dark even at noontide is our mortal sphere. **1796–7** COLERIDGE *Lines Autumnal Even.* vi, To shield my love from noontide's sultry beam. **1844** MRS. BROWNING *Drama of Exile* 625 The noontide's hush and heat and shine. **1868** MISS BRADDON *Dead Sea Fr.* I. 20 In the blazing July noontide.

b. *attrib.*, as ***noontide sun***, etc.

1593 SHAKS. *3 Hen. VI*, I. iv. 34 Now Phaeton hath.. made an Euening at the Noone-tide Prick. **1610** —— *Temp.* v. i. 42 By whose ayde..I haue bedymn'd The Noone-tide Sun. **1667** MILTON *P.L.* II. 309 Still as Night, Or Summer's Noon-tide air. *Ibid.* IV. 246 Where the unpierc't shade Imbround the noontide Bowrs. **1697** DRYDEN *Virg. Georg.* III. 233 Mossy Caverns for their Noontide Lare. **1725** POPE *Odyss.* IV. 548 Th' enormous herd..taints the noon-tide gales. **1781** COWPER *Truth* 540 The splendour of a noon-tide ray. **1810** SCOTT *Lady of L.* III. vii, Of noon-tide hag, or goblin grim. **1865** BARING-GOULD *Werewolves* viii, Some reapers lay down in the field to take their noon-tide sleep.

2. a. *transf.* The middle *of* night; the position *of* the moon at midnight.

c **1560** A. SCOTT *Poems* (S.T.S.) iv. 66 Sum monebrunt madynis myld, At nonetyd of the nicht. **1823** BYRON *Juan* XII. lxiii, The noontide of the moon. **1847** DE QUINCEY *Secr. Soc.* Wks. 1863 VI. 244 Meeting in secret chambers, at the noontide of night.

b. *fig.*, esp. the culminating point *of* something.

1578 *Chr. Prayers* in *Priv. Prayers* (1851) 506 O noontide of fervent love. **1649** T. FORD *Lusus Fort.* 78 Whose eyes, in the noone-tide of the Gospell, are wandring about in every corner. **1680** *Life Edward II* in *Select. fr. Harl. Misc.* (1793) 30 Making the noon-tide of his sovereignty full of tyrannical oppressions. **1823** LAMB *Elia* Ser. II. *Poor Relations*, A Poor Relation—is..a preposterous shadow, lengthening in the noontide of your prosperity. **1876** MORRIS *Sigurd* I. 2 His dawning of fair promise, and his noontide of the strife.

3. The Noon-flower or Goat's-beard. ? *Obs.*

1597 GERARDE *Herbal* (1636) 736 Goats-beard is called.. in English..Noon-tide, and Go to bed at noone. **1640** PARKINSON *Theat. Bot.* 413 *Tragopogon*..in English Goates beard..or Noone tide. **1864** in PRIOR *Plant-names.*

noon-time. Now *rare.* [f. NOON *sb.* + TIME.] = NOONTIDE. Also *fig.* and as *adv.*, **noontimes** *U.S.*, at mid-day.

1377 LANGL. *P. Pl.* B. xv. 278 Antony a dayes about none tyme, Had a bridde that brouȝte hym bred. *a* **1400–50** *Alexander* 563 Fra þe none tyme Till it to myddày was meten. *a* **1450** *Fysshynge w. Angle* (1883) 19 Mony poyl fysche wyl bytte beste yn none tyme.

1883 *Harper's Mag.* Aug. 371/2 At noontime all Germans had assembled. **1938** T. WILDER *Our Town* 11 Quarter of nine mornings, noontimes, and three o'clock afternoon's, the hull town can hear the yelling and screaming from those schoolyards. **1951** E. PAUL *Springtime in Paris* i. 3, I concluded that he was posting the Dove bills noontimes, on a volunteer basis. **1965** *Times Lit. Suppl.* 25 Nov. 1036/3 The noon-time of the genre [*sc.* the musical] was over.

noop[1] (nu:p). *north. dial.* Also 8 **knupe,** 9 **knope.** [Of obscure origin: cf. *knout-* KNOTBERRY and NUB-BERRY.] The fruit of the Cloudberry, *Rubus Chamæmorus.* Also *attrib.*

a **1800** R. W. *Cheviot* (1817) 3 The little hills the humble knupes produce. **1843** *M. A. Richardson's Borderer's Table-bk., Leg. Div.* I. 403 (Cloudberry)—whose orange fruit is locally called 'noops'. **1859** W. WHITE *Northumbld.* 355 The shepherds call them knout, or knope-berries.

noop[2]. *Sc. rare*[−1]. [? Cf. Norw. dial. *knōp* knuckle, short bone.] The point of the elbow.

1818 SCOTT *Hrt. Midl.* xvii, A'body has a conscience... I think mine's as weel out o' the gate as maist folk's are; and yet it's just like the noop of my elbow, it whiles gets a bit dirl on a corner.

†'**noorie.** *Obs. rare.* Also **noorrie.** [var. of NOURRY.] A fosterling.

1567 TURBERV. *Epit.*, etc. 60 The nymph..in hir armes the naked noorie strainde: Whereat the boy began to strive a good. **1567** —— *Ovid's Epist.* X. iij b, Ne was I then so proude..: ne I my selfe king Priams noorrie knewe.

noorse, dial. variant of NURSE.

nooscopic (nəʊəʊ'skɒpɪk), *a.* and *sb.* [f. Gr. νόο-ς mind + -SCOPIC.] **a.** *adj.* Pertaining to the examination of the mind. **b.** *sb. pl.* = NOOLOGY.

1816 BENTHAM *Chrestom.* Wks. 1843 VIII. 88 Division of Pneumatology into Alegopathematic (Nooscopic) and Pathematoscopic (Pathoscopic). *Ibid.* 90 Division of Nooscopics or Noology into Plasioscopic and Cœnonesioscopic.

noose (nu:s), *sb.* Also 7–8 **nooze.** [Of obscure origin: in common use only since 1600. If quot. *a* 1450 belongs here, it may be a. OF. *nos, nous, nuz,* etc. (:—L. *nodus*), nom. sing. of *no, neu, nu,* etc. (:—L. *nodum*), later *noud,* mod. *nœud.* Prof. Skeat suggests that the equivalent Prov. *nous* may have been the source (*Notes Eng. Etym.* 198).]

1. A loop, formed with a running knot, which tightens as the string or rope is pulled, as in a snare, lasso, hangman's halter, etc.; a loop, a folding or doubling of a string or rope. ***running noose***: see RUNNING *ppl. a.*

a **1450** *Fysshynge w. Angle* (1883) 8 Double the lyne & frete hyt fast yn þe top with a nose [**1496** bowe] to fasten an your lyne.

1600 HOLLAND *Livy* XXXVIII. xxix. 1001 It went..away, as sent and driven out of the noose of a stone-bow. **1610** —— *Camden's Brit.* I. 293 To lay grins for birds, to set snares to allure them with nooze or pipe. **1680** MOXON *Mech. Exerc.* x. 188 On this Crook is slipt the Noose of a Leather Thong. **1735** SOMERVILLE *Chase* IV. 80 Behind he lags, doom'd to the fatal Noose. **1774** GOLDSM. *Nat. Hist.* (1776) III. 86 The hunter..fixes a noose round the horns of the tame gazelle. *Ibid.* VII. 151 The sportsman..fastens his nooze round its neck. **1808** PIKE *Sources Mississ.* (1810) App. III. 42 They will catch another horse with a noose and hair rope, when both are running full speed. **1842** TENNYSON *St. Sim. Styl.* 64, I wore The rope..Twisted as tight as I could knot the noose. **1881** JOWETT *Thucyd.* I. 145 The Plataeans dropped nooses over the ends of these engines and drew them up. *transf.* **1812** [see NOOSE *v.* 1]. **1826** S. COOPER *First Lines Surg.* (ed. 5) 456 When this viscus is a noose of intestine. **1859** FITZGERALD *Omar Khayyám* i, The Hunter of the East has caught The Sultán's Turret in a Noose of Light.

b. In references or allusions to hanging.

1663 BUTLER *Hud.* I. ii. 116 Where the Hangman does dispose To special friends the Knot of Noose. **1813** SCOTT *Rokeby* VI. xvii, He..looked as if the noose were tied, And I the priest who left his side.

2. *fig.* **a.** The marriage tie.

c **1600** *Timon* II. iv. (1842) 33 Wilt thou putte thy necke Into a marriage nooze? **1609** B. JONSON *Sil. Wom.* II. i, [They] desire that you would sooner commit your grave head to this knot, than to the wedlock nooze. **1693** DRYDEN *Juvenal* (1697) 118 To choose to thrust his Neck into the Marriage Noose! **1709** STEELE *Tatler* No. 77 ¶4 Your Marriage-Haters, who rail at the Noose. **1746** SMOLLETT *Advice* 6 Divorc'd, all hell shall not re-tie the noose! **1826** T. I. WHARTON in *Pa. Hist. Soc. Mem.* I. 112 They are usually married before they are 20 years of age; and when once in that noose, are for the most part a little uneasy.

b. A snare or bond.

1624 FLETCHER *Rule a Wife* III. iv, Am I trickt now? Caught in mine own nooze. **1652** TATHAM *Scotch Figgaries* IV. i, I fall Into the noose of taverns like a pigeon. *a* **1687** H. MORE in Norris *Lett.* 181 Methinks you run yourself into an unnecessary noose of Fatality. **1800** WEEMS *Life Washington* ix. (1877) 102 To choke the colonies by a military noose.

noose (nu:s), *v.* Also 7 **nooze.** [f. the sb.]

1. *trans.* To secure as by a noose; to ensnare.

? *c* **1600** *Distr. Emperor* v. i. in Bullen *O. Pl.* III. 240 Am I then noosd!..am I lymed! **1665** MANLEY *Grotius' Low C. Wars* 547 He endeavours by this League..to noose as many of us as he can. **1694** CROWNE *Regulus* IV. 37 Pox o' your tricks, you have noos'd me. **1710** PALMER *Proverbs* 127 He, that loves at first sight, nooses himself by vows. **1765** FOOTE *Commissary* III. i, When once he is noos'd, let him struggle as much as he will, the cord will be drawn only the tighter. **1812** W. TAYLOR in *Monthly Mag.* XXXIV. 235 Her from the noose of death I freed, And noos'd her soul for aye. **1865** CARLYLE *Fredk. Gt.* V. XIX. vi. 557 Amherst..is diligently noosing, and tying up, the French military settlements.

b. In allusions to marriage.

1700 T. BROWN tr. *Fresny's Amusem.* vii. Wks. 1709 III. 60 Those who are not Noos'd in the Snare, will thank me for giving a Comical Description of it [*sc.* marriage]. **1771** SMOLLETT *Humph. Cl.* 18 July, I. ¶5 Where there was a parson who dealt in this branch of commerce, and there they were noosed, before the Irishman ever dreamt of the matter. **1813** *Examiner* 17 May 319/1 When I was noosed, my father began to equivocate. **1821** COMBE *Syntax, Wife* v, On the third or fourth day after: They were both noos'd in Hymen's garter.

2. To hang; to put to death by hanging.

1673 R. HEAD *Canting Acad.* 192 If they catch him horse-coursing, he's noozed. **1676** SHADWELL *Libertine* IV, Oh! I am noos'd already; I feel the Knot, methinks, under my left ear. **1686** F. SPENCE tr. *Varillas' Ho. Medicis* 127 This unfortunate Prelate was noos'd up in the pontifical robes he happened to have on. **1809** SCOTT *Poacher* 16 Our buckskinn'd justices expound the law,..And for the netted partridge noose the swain.

3. To catch or capture by means of a noose; to cast or put a noose round.

1748 *Anson's Voy.* I. vi. 66 In the same manner they noose horses, and..even tygers. **1784** COWPER *Task* IV. 462 Oh for a law to noose the villain's neck Who starves his own. **1808** PIKE *Sources Mississ.* (1810) II. 159 We equipped six of our fleetest coursers with riders and ropes, to noose the wild horses. **1843** MARRYAT *M. Violet* xxi, G. had..noosed the animal with his lasso. **1885** HORNADAY *2 Yrs. in Jungle* xxxi. 369 Trying to noose a deer.

transf. **1823** LOCKHART *Sp. Ballads, Zara's Ear-rings* iv, Some other lover's hand, among my tresses noosed.

4. To make a noose on (a cord); to place *round* in a noose; to arrange like a noose or loop.

1814 SCOTT *Ld. of Isles* v. xxv, 'He plays the mute.' 'Then noose a cord.' *a* **1860** ALB. SMITH *Med. Student* (1861) 92 A piece of whipcord is then noosed round the victim's neck. **1886** *Athenæum* 27 Feb. 303/2 The sleeves are noosed and laced over the shoulder and arm.

Hence **noosed** (nu:st), *ppl. a.*; '**noosing** *vbl. sb.* and *ppl. a.*

1624 CAPT. SMITH *Virginia* VI. 231 Bradford was suddenly caught by the leg in a *noosed Rope. **1859** TENNENT *Ceylon* II. IX. iv. 473 No arms or apparatus of any kind, except a noosed rope. **1818** SCOTT *Br. Lamm.* xxi, I am going to let you into a secret—a plot—a *noosing plot. **1835** W. IRVING *Tour Prairies* 310 Finding it impossible to get within noosing distance. **1840** HOOD *Kilmansegg, Marriage* v, There's nothing so draws a London mob As the *noosing of very rich people. **1878** JEFFERIES *Gamekeeper at H.* 163 Here the art of noosing lingers; the loop being..slipped over the bird's head while at roost.

noos(e, obs. forms of NOSE.

noosel(l, variants of NUZZLE, to train.

nooser ('nu:sə(r)). [f. NOOSE *v.*] One who uses a noosed rope, *esp.* for catching elephants.

1859 TENNENT *Ceylon* II. VIII. v. 357 The headman of the 'cooroowe' or noosers crept in. **1885** HORNADAY *2 Yrs. in Jungle* xx. 222 The tame elephants and the noosers are introduced at the gate.

noosphere ('nəʊəʊsfɪə(r)). [a. F. *noösphere*, f. Gr. νόο-ς mind + SPHERE *sb.* 7.] The name given by Pierre Teilhard de Chardin in his theory of evolution to the stage or sphere characterized by the emergence of consciousness and mind which follows the stage of the establishment of human life (see quot. 1959). Also *fig.* Hence **noosp'heric** *a.*

1953 J. S. HUXLEY *Evolution in Action* iv. 110 It provides a new kind of environment for life to inhabit. It needs a name of its own: following Père Teilhard de Chardin, the French paleontologist and philosopher, I shall call it the *noösphere*, the world of mind. **1959** B. WALL tr. *Teilhard de Chardin's Phenomenon of Man* III. i. 182 Much more coherent and just as extensive as any preceding layer, it is really a new layer, the 'thinking layer', which..has spread over and above the world of plants and animals. In other words, outside and above the biosphere there is the noosphere. **1962** M. MCLUHAN *Gutenberg Galaxy* 32 This externalization of our senses creates what de Chardin calls the 'noosphere' or a technological brain for the world. **1965** *Times Lit. Suppl.* 6 May 350/5 Linguistic anthropologists are at least asking questions about language which pull that phenomenon down from its cold noosphere back into the warm current of social living. **1966** *New Statesman* 6 May 659/2 Stock fictional characters in some kind of noöspheric organisation run by Conchis for his own enlightenment. **1967** *New Scientist* 26 Jan. 227/2 In practice we all act as if the mental aspect of Chardin's noösphere really is a guiding and determining factor in human existence. **1970** *Sci. Amer.* Sept. 53/3 Just before his death on January 6, 1945, he wrote..'I think that we undergo not only a historical, but a planetary change as well. We live in a transition to the noosphere.' By noosphere Vernadsky meant the envelope of mind that was to supersede the biosphere.

noost, variant of NOST, knowest not. *Obs.*

noost, var. NOUST.

'**noosy,** *a. rare*[−1]. [f. NOOSE *sb.* + -Y[1].] Acting like a noose.

1658 FRANCK *Northern Mem.* (1821) 96 Yet are their rivers and rivulets replenished with trout because undisturbed with the noosy net.

noot, var. of NOT, knows not. *Obs.*

noote, obs. f. NOTE.

Nootka ('nu:tkə, 'nɒtkə), *sb.* and *a.* [f. *Nootka* Sound, an inlet on the coast of Vancouver Island, British Columbia.] **A.** *sb.* **a.** A North American Indian people of north-western Washington state and Vancouver Island; a member of this people. **b.** The Wakashan language of the Nootka people.

[**1841** *Jrnl. R. Geogr. Soc.* XI. 221 The second or Southern Family of the insular tribes may be also denominated *Nootka-Columbian*, from the two places in which they have had most intercourse with Europeans.]

1846 H. HALE *Rep. U.S. Exploring Exped.* VI. 198 (*heading*) The North-Oregon division. All the tribes north of the Columbia..belong to this division... The *Nootkas*..also belong to it. **1868** G. M. SPROAT *Scenes Stud. Savage Life* iv. 22 The men (the Nootkahs) are below the middle height, with thick-set limbs, broad faces..and rough, coppery, and tanned skins. **1875** H. H. BANCROFT *Native Races of Pacific States* I. iii. 176 The Nootkas are of less than medium height ..but rather strongly built. **1910** F. W. HODGE *Handbk. Amer. Indians* II. 82/1 The Nootka form one branch of the great Wakashan family. **1915** E. SAPIR *Abnormal Types of Speech in Nootka* 1 In Nootka there are special words used in speaking of obscene matters to or in the presence of women. **1934** *Language* X. 122 In Nootka a monosyllabic word may end in a consonant or a long vowel, but never in a short vowel. **1959** *Chambers's Encycl.* I. 339/2 The tribes of the coast and islands of north-west Canada comprise.. southward, coast Salish, Nootka, Chinook, [etc.]. **1972** *Language* XLVIII. 274 Languages like Nootka, in which it seems difficult to distinguish between nominal and verbal roots.

B. *adj.* **1.** Pertaining to or designating the Nootkas or their language.

1846 H. HALE *Rep. U.S. Exploring Exped.* VI. 220 We might..add to the synopsis and map the *Nootka Family*, comprising the tribes of Vancouver Island. **1875** H. H. BANCROFT *Native Races of Pacific States* I. iii. 177 The Nootka complexion..is decidedly light. **1890** J. G. FRAZER *Golden Bough* II. iii. 113 Amongst the Nootka Indians of British Columbia, when a bear had been killed, it was brought in and seated before the head chief. **1915** E. SAPIR *Abnormal Types of Speech in Nootka* 3 More specialized Nootka examples to be given presently. **1955** P. DRUCKER *Indians of Northwest Coast* 12 They [*sc.* the Chinook Indians] traded slaves from the Californian hinterland up the coast for Nootka canoes.

2. Designating trees native to the Pacific coast of North America, as **Nootka (false-) cypress, Nootka Sound cypress**, a coniferous tree, *Chamæcyparis nootkatensis*, of the family Cupressaceæ, also known as the yellow cedar; **Nootka fir** = *Douglas fir* (DOUGLAS[1]).

1892 A. C. APGAR *Trees Northern U.S.* 195 Nootka Sound Cypress... Tree 100 ft. high in Alaska. **1897** G. B. SUDWORTH *Nomencl. Arborescent Flora U.S.* 79 Yellow Cedar... [Also called] Nootka Cypress... Nootka Sound Cypress. **1957** M. HADFIELD *Brit. Trees* 116 The Nootka cypress grows on the Pacific coast of North America, from southern Alaska to southern Oregon. **1969** T. H. EVERETT *Living Trees of World* 33/2 The Nootka false-cypress..has quadrangular, drooping branchlets and leaves without white markings on their undersides. A native from Oregon to Alaska, this slender tree is often 120 feet tall. **1974** *Country Life* 12 Dec. 1855/1 Two big Nootka cypresses (*Chamaecyparis nootkatensis*). **1803** A. B. LAMBERT *Descr. Genus Pinus* I. 51 Nootka Fir... A specimen in the Banksian herbarium, brought home by Mr. Menzies, by whom it was discovered on the North-west coast of America. **1889** G. S. BOULGER *Uses of Plants* vii. 186 *Pseudotsuga Douglasii*, Carrière, the Oregon Pine, or Douglas or Nootka Fir, abundant in North-west America, furnishes fine, straight, and durable timber. **1957** *N.Z. Timber Jrnl.* Dec. 59/2 *Nootka fir*, Douglas fir.

So **'Nootkan** *a.* and *sb.*

1841 *Jrnl. R. Geogr. Soc.* XI. 224 Whoever will compare the list of Nootkan words..with the Tlaoquatch vocabulary ..will find that there is very little difference between them. *Ibid.* 225 The Kawitchen tribe..appears..to be a mixed race, compounded of Shahaptans and Nootkans. **1848** *Jrnl. Ethnol. Soc. London* I. 234 Nootkans. **1973** *Amer. Speech 1969* XLIV. 232 Chinook jargon [has]..Nootkan and Algonkian lexical elements.

nooze, obs. f. NOOSE *sb.* and *v.*

noozel, var. of NUZZLE, to train.

†**nop**, obs. north. and Sc. form of NAP *sb.*[3] Hence **nop-bed, nop-sack** [= MDu. and MLG. *noppensack*], a bed or sack stuffed with nap.

a. **1465** *Acc. Rolls Durham* (Surtees) 243 Item j fedyrbed. .. Item iiij nopsekez. **1472** *Ibid.* 246, j nopseke. **1478** *Act. Audit.* (1839) 67 The ruf of a bed, þe courtingis of þe samyn, a nop sek. **1541** *Aberd. Reg.* (1844) I. 175 Ane nop seke.., quhilk scho lay vpoune.

b. **1477** *Aberd. Reg.* (1844) I. 408 Ane pair of schetis, ane nop bed, a bowster. **1541** *Ibid.* 175 Ane standand bed, ane nop bed, ane pair of scheittis.

nopal ('nəʊpəl). [a. Sp. *nopal* (also Pg. and F.; It. *nopale*), ad. Mexican *nopalli* cactus.

The compound *nopalnocheztli*, given in some Dicts. as the source of *nopal* or *Nopalea*, is really the name for cochineal.]

1. An American species of cactus (*Opuntia* or *Nopalea cochinellifera*) cultivated for the support of the cochineal-insect.

1730 RUTTY in *Phil. Trans.* XXXVI. 265 These Pastles are then placed upon the Plants of the Nopal, or Prickly Indian Fig. **1783** JUSTAMOND tr. *Raynal's Hist. Indies* III. 351 This shrub, which is know'n by the name of nopal, or Indian fig, is about five feet high... There are several species of nopal. **1851** MAYNE REID *Scalp-Hunt.* i. 14 It is a forest of the Mexican nopal. **1876** *Encycl. Brit.* IV. 626/2 Plantations of the nopal and the tuna, which are called nopaleries.

attrib. **1808** *Naval Chron.* XXII. 376 The Nopal Plantations in his district. **1855** KELLY tr. *Cervantes' Exempl. Novels* 241 Seated together under a nopal-tree. **1866** *Treas. Bot.* 187/2 *O. cochinellifera*, the Nopal plant.

2. A plant of this kind.

1808 *Naval Chron.* XXII. 377 The Nopals being agreeably acid. **1832** MACGILLIVRAY *Trav. Humboldt* vi. 81 The negro..led them through a wood of nopals to the hut of an Indian. **1861** HULME *Moquin-Tandon* II. III. i. 73 A certain number of nopals are planted around the houses.

nopalry ('nəʊpəlrı). Also **-ery**. [f. NOPAL + -RY, after Sp. *nopalera*, F. *nopalerie, nopalière*.] A plantation of nopals where the cochineal-insect is bred.

α. **1783** JUSTAMOND tr. *Raynal's Hist. Indies* III. 352 A spot thus planted, and distinguished by the name of Nopalry, is usually no more than one or two acres in extent. **1789** J. ANDERSON *Corr. Introd. Cochineal Insects* (1791) 4 The establishment of a public Nopalry. **1861** HULME tr. *Moquin-Tandon* II. III. i. 75 In 1853, in the province of Algiers alone, there were fourteen nopalries.

β. **1815** KIRBY & SP. *Entomol.* I. x. 323 They plant their nopaleries in cleared ground on the slopes of mountains or ravines. **1866** *Treas. Bot.* 792/2 Plantations for rearing the cochineal insect..are called nopaleries. **1876** [see NOPAL 1].

no parking. [PARKING *vbl. sb.*] Used *attrib.* and *absol.* to designate an area, place, etc., where vehicles may not be parked; also, to designate a sign bearing this instruction.

1946 *Rep. Departmental Comm. Traffic Signs 1944* (Ministry of Transport) 51 We do not consider it desirable that the words 'Halt' or 'No Parking' should be marked on the carriageway. **1956** F. CASTLE *Violent Hours* (1966) x. 97 The car was in a no-parking zone. **1964** I. FLEMING *You only live Twice* iv. 51 A smart Toyopet saloon waiting in a no-parking area. **1964** J. MASTERS *Trial at Monomoy* ii. 49 That's a *No Parking* zone. **1968** S. B. HOUGH *Sweet Sister Seduced* iv. 15 He reached the grass, the No Parking signs. **1971** A. PRICE *Alamut Ambush* i. 12 A parked car is just a parked car if it's not in a 'no parking' zone. **1972** M. SINCLAIR *Norslag* x. 85 A 'No Parking' sign by the kerb.

nop-bed: see NOP.

nope (nəʊp), *sb.*[1] Also 7 **nowpe, noap.** [app. a var. of ALP, OLP: see N 3.] The bullfinch.

1611 COTGR., *Chochepierre*, a kind of Nowpe, or Bullfinch. **1612** DRAYTON *Poly-olb.* xiii. 74 The Red-sparrow, the Nope, the Red-breast, and the Wren. **1655** MOUFET & BENNET *Health's Improv.* (1746) 185 The Nope feedeth upon Mast, Nuts, and Cherries. **1678** RAY *Willughby's Ornith.* 247 The Bulfinch, Alp or Nope. [Hence in various later works.] **1848** *Zoologist* VI. 2191 In Warwickshire, as elsewhere,..the bullfinch [is] a 'nope'. **1879-** in dial. glossaries, esp. West Midland and E. Anglian.

attrib. **1668** in T. C. Smith & J. Short *Hist. Ribchester* (1890) 110 To Richard Ward for 13 Noap heades.

nope (nəʊp), *sb.*[2] *north. dial.* Also 9 **noap(e.** [See note to NOLP *sb.*] A knock on the head.

1725 *New Cant. Dict.*, *Nope*, a Blow, a Knock on the Pate. **1785** W. HUTTON *Bran New Wark* 157 In some churches the sidesmen gang about with staaves, and give ivvery sleeper a good nope. **1869-** in northern glossaries.

nope (nəʊp), *adv. slang* (orig. *U.S.*). Extended form of NO *adv.*[3] Cf. YEP.

1888 *N.Y. Life* 12 May, Cover 3/2 'I suppose you will be a literary man, like your father, when you grow up.' 'Nope,' said the little boy..'Literary nuthin'! I'm goin' to be a ten-thousand-dollar cook.' **1891** *Harper's Mag.* Nov. 970/1 The professor, wishing to express negation, made use of the objectionable form 'nope'. **1908** C. E. MULFORD *Orphan* ii. 24 Nope, I reckon not—seven husky Apaches are too much for one man to go out of his way to fight. **1918** E. WALLACE *Down Under Donovan* x. 129 'Have you been in Europe before?' 'Nope,' she replied shortly. **1941** R. STOUT *Red Threads* iii. 30 'You don't paint in oils, do you?' 'Nope.' **1956** E. POUND tr. *Sophocles' Women of Trachis* 27 Nope, no proof without data. **1964** MRS. L. B. JOHNSON *White House Diary* 8 Apr. (1970) 103 And General George Marshall said, 'I'll be damned if I will have people calling me "Marshal Marshall". Nope, we'll just have five-star Generals.' **1971** H. C. RAE *Marksman* I. viii. 72 'Anybody asking for me?' 'Nope.'

no-place, *sb.* and *adv.* [f. NO *a.* + PLACE *sb.*]

A. *sb.* A place which does not exist.

1929 E. BOWEN *Last September* xi. 131 To be enclosed in nonentity, in some ideal no-place. **1934** L. B. LYON *White Hare* 12 Now is the new page turned and the new light falling From the no-place of the spirit. **1958** *Listener* 28 Aug. 304/2 Neither to accept nor to rebel Is that no-place which I call hell. **1963** *Colorado Portfolio* No. 1 31/3 And in some noplace in some notime he would take out a tiny book..and write.

B. *adv.* (usu. *colloq.*) Nowhere; (in double negative) anywhere. Chiefly *U.S.*

1934 in WEBSTER. **1942** PARTRIDGE *Usage & Abusage* 211/1 *No place* is illiterate for *nowhere*, as in 'The jewel was no place to be found'. **1956** H. GOLD *Man who was not with It* (1965) ix. 74 'Where are you going?' I..cried out: 'Noplace!' **1969** M. PUGH *Last Place Left* xxv. 187 You're going no place until Herb gets here. **1971** D. E. WESTLAKE *I gave at the Office* (1972) 192 We was in two trucks, packed in tight so you couldn't hardly sit down noplace.

noppe, obs. f. KNOP; obs. var. of NAP *sb.*[3] and *v.*[2]

nopping, obs. f. NAPPING *vbl. sb.*[2]

noppy, obs. f. NAPPY *a.*

noppyd, obs. f. NAPPED *a.*

nop-sek(e: see NOP.

†**'nopster.** *Obs.*[−1] [a. MDu. *nopster*, f. *noppen* NAP *v.*[2]] A woman who puts a nap on cloth.

c **1481** CAXTON *Dialogues* 33 Clarisse the nopster Can well her craft..Cloth for to noppe.

noquar, -quer, -qwer(e, obs. forms of NOWHERE.

noque, obs. f. NOOK *sb.*

nor (nɔː(r)), *conj.*[1] [probably a contraction of NOTHER, like the equivalent OFris. *noer* for *noder*.] A negative conjunction employed as follows:—

I. 1. a. Continuing the force of a negative (as *not, never*, etc.) attached to some word in the preceding clause, and extending it to the corresponding word which follows.

13.. *Cursor M.* 7361 (Gött.), I here noght of þat iesse tel, Nor his sonis ne him i knaw. *a* **1400-50** *Alexander* 316 Þis myȝty god..is of a meddill age, Noȝt of ȝouth nor of eld nor ȝerris to many. *c* **1440** *Alph. Tales* 6, I may not eate your benys nor your cale. *c* **1460** FORTESCUE *Abs. & Lim. Mon.* xiv. (1885) 144 The kynge shalnot be greved be importunite of suytours, nor thai shall..optayne any vnresonable desires. **1538** STARKEY *England* I. iv. 126 Wherfor to pyl theyr cuntreys for thys purpos, ys not just nor resonabul. **1590** SPENSER *F.Q.* I. iii. 11 She could not heare, nor speake, nor understand. **1622** WITHER *Philarete* (1633) 617 No others high degree, Nor beauteous looke shall change me. **1688** HOLME *Armoury* III. 251/2 It is said of the French that they Speak not as they Write, nor Write as they Speak. **1740** RICHARDSON *Pamela* I. xxv. 30 Is there no Constable nor Headborough, tho', to take me out of his House? **1766** GOLDSM. *Vic. W.* i, We had no revolutions to fear, nor fatigues to undergo. **1821** SCOTT *Pirate* Adv., The inhabitants..not possessing arms nor means of resistance. **1870** GLADSTONE *Glean.* (1879) IV. 252 Not a vessel, nor a gun, nor a man, were on the ground to prevent their landing.

†**b.** Followed by another negative. *Obs.*

13.. *Cursor M.* 6788 (Gött.), [To] wydw, na child fadirless, Do ȝe na wrang nor na maless. *c* **1400** *Apol. Loll.* 1, I haue not ben, nor is, nor neuer schal,..to sei any þing aȝen þe general feiþ. *c* **1440** *Alph. Tales* 6, I may not eate your benys.., nor I may not drynk your thyn ale. **1509** FISHER *Funeral Serm. C'tess Richmond* Wks. (1876) 298 It is not loked for.., nor none abydynge stroke..falleth vpon them. **1568** GRAFTON *Chron.* II. 130 No man was called to aunswere, nor no question put vnto any person by the sayd enquest. **1598** GRENEWEY *Tacitus, Ann.* XIII. iv. (1622) 183 He could lay no iust cause against him, nor openly durst not commaund the murdering of his brother. **1668** MARVELL *Corr.* Wks. (Grosart) II. 263 Wise..he saith hath not yet bin with him, nor dares not. **1739** CHESTERF. *Lett.* xxv. (1792) I. 92 It requires no rhymes nor no certain number of feet or syllables. *a* **1774** GOLDSM. *Hist. Greece* I. 224 No skill could obviate, nor no remedy dispel the terrible infection.

†**c.** Following upon *as...so. Obs. rare.*

1548 UDALL, etc. *Erasm. Par. Acts* 29 b, Lyke as the Israelites perceyued not this in Iesus, euen so nor than dyd they vnderstande that in Moyses. **1657** MOSSOM *Preacher's Tripartite* I. 17 As I look not upon my merit, so nor do thou look upon my demerit.

2. a. As correlative to a preceding *neither, nother*, or *nouther*. (For examples see these words.)

b. Introducing both alternatives. Chiefly *poet.*

1576 GASCOIGNE *Steele Gl.* (Arb.) 59 How many pore (which nede nor brake nor bit) Might therwith al..be fedde. **1591** SHAKS. *Two Gent.* V. iv. 80 Who by Repentance is not satisfied, Is nor of heauen, nor earth. **1615** DAY *Festivals* xii. 338 Nor Papists with their Miracles, nor Puritans with their Presbytery, shall ever put life into it againe. **1654-66** EARL ORRERY *Parthen.* (1676) 9 Nor my weakness, nor my tongue ..shall ever confess you have any advantage over me. **1697** DRYDEN *Virg. Georg.* III. 393 Nor Bits nor Bridles can his Rage restrain. **1725** POPE *Odyss.* XV. 478 Now let our compact made Be nor by signal nor by word betray'd. **1798** COLERIDGE *Anc. Mar.* I. xiv, Nor shapes of men nor beasts we ken. **1807** J. BARLOW *Columb.* III. 349 But we nor fear his frown, nor trust his smile. **1839-52** BAILEY *Festus* 410 Perfection To imperfection leaves nor choice nor mean.

3. With omission of *neither*.

a. With preceding or following negative.

a **1400-50** *Alexander* 46 Þer preued neuer nane his prik for passing of witt, Plato nor Piktagaras. **1484** CAXTON *Fables of Æsop* V. xii, Certaynly I nor none other canne give the Jugement. *a* **1586** SIDNEY *Arcadia* (1613) 41 She concealed her sorrow, nor cause of her sorrow, from no body. **1791** MRS. RADCLIFFE *Rom. Forest* x, Your father nor nobody else has ever sent after you.

b. Without other negative expressed.

a **1548** HALL *Chron., Hen. VIII* 144 [He] would sende them no woorde of his affaires,..for he ought their master, nor yet them suche service. **1594** MARLOWE & NASHE *Dido* V. ii, Though thou nor he will pity me a whit. **1621** LADY M. WROTH *Urania* 532 The most ignorant proud woman liuing, caring for, nor respecting any but her selfe and hers. **1649** LOVELACE *Poems* 64 Yet Servants knowing Minikin nor Base, Are still allow'd to fiddle with the Case. *c* **1750** SHENSTONE *Elegy* iii. 6 Pageant nor plume distinguish Alcon's bier. **1813** BYRON *Br. Abydos* I. xii, A heart his words nor deeds can daunt. **1827** JARMAN *Powell's Devises* II. 229 It was his will that they, nor either of them, should take any thing under his will. **1872** TENNYSON *Last Tourn.* 203 Great brother, thou nor I have made the world.

†**4.** = OR. *Obs. rare.*

c **1489** CAXTON *Blanchardyn* viii. 32 Blanchardyn..was moche abasshed how nor by what manere he sholde mowe passe hit ouer. **1615** WADSWORTH in Bedell *Lett.* (1624) 7 It could neuer sinke into my braine how..members sound nor vnsound [could be] participant each of other.

5. Following upon an affirmative clause, or in continuative narration, with the force of *neither* or *and...not*.

1523 LD. BERNERS *Froiss.* I. cxxxv. 162, I greatly desyre to se the kynge my maister, nor I wyll lye but one nyght in a place, tyll I come there. *a* **1578** LINDESAY (Pitscottie) *Chron. Scot.* (S.T.S.) I. 26 To mak hir purgatione that scho was frie of all misrewlle..nor gave na counsall thairto. **1631** MAY tr. *Barclay's Mirr. Mindes* I. 39 The whole coast is most sweetly verdant,..nor hardly, is there ground any where more abundantly fruitfull. **1667** MILTON *P.L.* III. 626 A golden tiar Circl'd his head, nor less his Locks behind..Lay waving round. **1697** DRYDEN *Virg. Georg.* III. 161 His Age and Courage weigh: Nor those alone. **1738** JOHNSON *London*

260 Then shall thy friend, nor thou refuse his aid, . . forsake his Cambrian shade. **1788** *Trifler* No. 22. 291 The little creature cried and laid down, nor could all our beating raise it. **1821** BYRON *Heaven & Earth* iii. 673 Away! nor weep! **1871** R. ELLIS tr. *Catullus* lxi. 205 Come nor tarry to greet her. **1875** JOWETT *Plato* (ed. 2) I. 423 Nor among the friends of Socrates must the jailer be forgotten.

II. 6. As *sb.* or *adj. Computers.* (Written in capitals.) A Boolean function of two or more variables that has the value unity if all the variables are zero and is otherwise zero; 'neither . . nor . .'. Usu. *attrib.*

1957 *Trans. Amer. Inst. Electr. Engin.* LXXVI. I. 263/1 The transistor NOR circuit was introduced because of the desire to have a single logic element which would combine well in logic configurations with a minimum concern for matching and element loading. A NOR element has a signal output only if there are no input signals. *Ibid.*, P-n-p and n-p-n transistor NOR circuits . . cannot be readily intermixed. **1958** [see NAND]. **1969** J. J. SPARKES *Transistor Switching* iv. 96 For NOR gates the Boolean expression is first reduced to its simplest form containing the product of sums. **1971** J. H. SMITH *Digital Logic* iv. 42 The NOR function is used extensively, especially in resistor-transistor logic systems. **1972** *IEEE Trans. Computers* XXI. 153/1 Optimal networks consisting of NOR-OR gates (each gate produces the NOR and/or the OR of its inputs) are tabulated for all Boolean functions of three variables.

nor, *conj.*[2] *Sc.* and *dial.* [Of obscure origin: cf. NA *conj.*[2]] Than.

c **1400** *Sc. Troy-bk.* (Horstm.) II. 2402 Pirrus was of þat thing richt wo And mor of his grantschire in deid Nor of hime self. *c* **1475** *Rauf Coilȝear* 546, I neid nane airar myne erand nor none of the day. **1508** DUNBAR *Flyting* 133 Thow . . beggis mair beir and aitis Nor ony cripill in Karrik land. **1558** KENNEDY *Compend. Treat.* in *Wodrow Soc. Misc.* (1844) 151 Ar nocht thaye quha sulde gyde the peple mair ignorante nor the simple pepyll self? **1573** TYRIE *Refut.* in *Cath. Tract.* (S.T.S.) 15 He apperis mair wicked nor Sathan him self. **1637** RUTHERFORD *Lett.* (1862) I. cxliv. 342 So then I see that Christ can triumph in a weaker man nor I. *a* **1658** DURHAM *Comm. Revelation* (1660) i. 5 His Kingly Office extendeth no further nor his Priestly and Prophetical Office. **1792** BURNS *My Tocher's the Jewel* ii, Ye'll crack your credit wi' mae nor me. **1840** THACKERAY *Catherine* iv, You're no better nor a common tramper. **1859** GEO. ELIOT *A. Bede* xxx, I know better nor you. **1883** W. BLACK *Shandon Bells* xxxii, There'll be more grey nor red in my beard by that time.

†**nor,** *conj.*[3] *Sc. Obs.* [Cf. prec. and NA *adv.*[1]] **a.** In imprecations: = MAY. **b.** If . . not.

1500–20 DUNBAR *Poems* xxxiv. 32 Nor I be hangit be the nek. *Ibid.* 77 God . . Nor ane stark widdy gar me gaip. **1552** LYNDESAY *Monarche* 5039 It maruellis me, He, haueand sic prosperite, . . Nor he had infynite plesoure.

nor (nɔː(r)), *a. Organic Chem.* [f. prec.] Applied to compounds or groups of compounds conventionally named by adding the prefix NOR- to the name of a parent compound, esp. with a prefixed numeral indicating the methyl group lacking or a prefixed capital letter indicating the ring which is contracted as compared with the parent compound.

1940 *Chem. Abstr.* XXXIV. 5455 Diminution from a 6-ring to a 5-ring by loss of C atoms . . in rings A, B and C gives rise to the corresponding A-nor, B-nor and C-nor compds. **1946** *Jrnl. Biol. Chem.* CLXII. 589 The nor, bisnor, and etio homologues of 3,11-dihydroxy-12-ketocholanic acid have been prepared. **1954** *Jrnl. Amer. Chem. Soc.* LXXVI. 4092/2 The efficacy of this 19-nor analog . . in human females has been established. **1972** *Adv. Steroid Biochem. & Pharmacol.* III. 93 Two of the 19-nor steroids, norgestrel and allylestrenol, appear to show differences from norethisterone and lynestrenol.

nor', abbrev. f. NORTH.

nor- (nɔː(r)), *prefix. Organic Chem.* [f. NOR(MAL *a.* and *sb.*] **1. a.** Prefixed to the names of organic compounds to denote the replacement of one or (esp. in terpenes) all the (methyl) side-chains by hydrogen atoms.

The use arose from the designation of a compound $C_8H_6O_5$ as 'normal opianic acid', of which opianic acid was supposed to be a dimethyl derivative: **1868** MATTHIESON & FOSTER in *Jrnl. Chem. Soc.* XXI. 358 We therefore propose to call the compound $C_9H_8O_5$ monomethyl-normal opianic acid, or if the contraction is admissible, methylnoropianic acid.

nor'bornane [*bornane* f. BORN(EOL + -ANE], the crystalline bicyclic hydrocarbon, C_7H_{12}, which is obtained by replacing the three methyl groups of bornane (camphane) by hydrogen atoms and is the parent compound of a number of terpenes; bicyclo[2.2.1]heptane; **nordi͵hydroguaia'retic acid** [f. *guaiaretic acid*, f. GUAIA(C + Gr. ῥητ-ίνη resin of the pine], a crystalline phenol, $C_{18}H_{18}(OH)_4$, which is used as an antoxidant for oils and fats; **no'rephedrine**, the crystalline, optically active compound, $C_9H_{13}NO$, which is obtained by replacing the methylamino group of ephedrine by an amino group and has actions and uses resembling those of ephedrine; **nore'thisterone**, a crystalline compound, $C_{20}H_{26}O_2$, which has actions similar to those of progesterone and is used as a contraceptive and in the treatment of amenorrhœa and functional uterine bleeding; (*β*-)**nor'nicotine** [a. F. *nornicotine* (M. & M. Polonovski 1927, in *Compt. Rend.* CLXXXIV. 1333)], an optically active liquid alkaloid, $C_9H_{12}N_2$, found with and resembling nicotine; **norsy'nephrin(e** = OCTOPAMINE; **norte'stosterone**, the 19-norsteroid derived from testosterone.

1952 *Chem. & Engin. News* 3 Mar. 930/3 Corresponding to these six types [of bicyclic compounds] are the four-parent ring systems northujane . ., norcarane . ., norpinane . . and norbornane. **1962** E. L. ELIEL *Stereochem. Carbon Compounds* x. 302 Norbornane, despite its easy accessibility, is an appreciably strained system. **1974** *Jrnl. Chem. Soc.: Perkin Trans. II* 322 (*heading*) Inhibition of ring expansion reactions in the norbornane system by neighbouring methyl groups. [**1919** *Chem. Abstr.* XIII. 991 Schiff's norguaiaretic acid is shown to be norhydroguaiaretic acid.] **1944** *Oil & Soap* XXI. 33/1 An investigation was made of the antioxydant properties of nordihydroguaiaretic acid. **1945** *Jrnl. Amer. Pharm. Assoc.* (*Sci. Ed.*) XXXIV. 81/1 One, if not the most active, of the bactericidal agents present in [the shrub] *Larrea divaricata* Cav. has been characterized as nordihydroguaiaretic acid. **1956** M. K. SCHWITZER *Margarine & Other Food Fats* viii. 323 Nordihydroguaiaretic acid . . was permitted to be used in the United States in December, 1943 at the rate of 0·01 per cent. The antioxidant effect is very marked in animal fats. . . It is less effective in vegetable fats. **1971** P. TOOLEY *Fats, Oils & Waxes* iv. 125 Oxidation can cause serious deterioration in a lipstick producing unpleasant rancid odours and taste. . . This can be largely prevented by the use of antioxidants such as . . nordihydroguaiaretic acid. **1929** *Chem. Abstr.* XXIII. 2431 Reduction of $PhCH(OH)CH(NO_2)Me$ with Zn dust and dil. H_2SO_4 gave norephedrine . . and nor-*ψ*-ephedrine. **1943** *Jrnl. Lab. & Clin. Med.* XXVIII. 704 Norephedrine and pseudonorephedrine together constitute propadrine, of which the commercial preparation contains also a small amount of ammonium chloride. **1973** *Biochem. Jrnl.* CXXXVI. 769/1 Norephedrine is extensively metabolized in the rabbit but not in man. **1956** *Proc. Soc. Exper. Biol. & Med.* XCI. 419/2, 10 mg nor-ethisterone given twice daily represents a reproducibly effective dose in women for the production of marked progestational changes. **1964** Norethisterone [see ETHINYLŒSTRADIOL]. **1973** *Nature* 10 Aug. 351/1 If inferences can be drawn from this preliminary study using mouse foetal hearts, it would seem that the concentration of norethisterone acetate in the pill should be kept to a minimum. **1927** *Chem. Abstr.* XXI. 3905 (*heading*) *β*-Pyridyl-*α*-pyrrolidine (nornicotine). **1936** *Jrnl. Econ. Entomol.* XXIX. 854 Macht & Davis . . observed that *β*-nornicotine was more toxic for certain vertebrates . . than natural nicotine. **1951** A. GROLLMAN *Pharmacol. & Therapeutics* xv. 281 Nornicotine, which has similar actions to nicotine, lacks only the CH_3 group in the pyrrolidine nucleus. **1968** LARSON & SILVETTE *Tobacco* Suppl. I. 682/1 Nornicotine inhibited development of the chick-embryo, and was even more potent than nicotine in causing hydrops. **1952** Norsynephrine [see OCTOPAMINE]. **1952** *Ricerca Sci.* XXII. 1576 Sympatho-mimetic amines (tyramine, norsynephrine, adrenaline, noradrenaline). **1960** *Biochim. & Biophys. Acta* XLIII. 568 The enzyme responsible for norsynephrin formation is dopamine *β*-oxidase. **1950** *Jrnl. Chem. Soc.* 367 This *βγ*-unsaturated ketone has now been isomerised . . to the *αβ*-unsaturated ketone . ., which is a 10-nortestosterone. **1955** H. HIRSCHMANN *Hormones* III. xi. 544 19-Nortestosterone on the other hand, is inferior to testosterone as an androgen but equal to it in its myotrophic . . effect. **1973** *Jrnl. Appl. Physiol.* XXXV. 378/2 Nortestosterone esters are more potent than testosterone in their capacity to stimulate erythropoietic activity in mice.

b. Denoting the contraction of a chain or ring of carbon atoms by one methylene group, as **norcho'lanic acid** [*cholanic* f. CHOL- + -AN + -IC], a crystalline, optically active compound, $C_{23}H_{38}O_2$, obtained by shortening the side-chain of cholanic acid by one methylene group; **nor'pinic acid**, a crystalline dicarboxylic acid, $C_8H_{12}O_4$, existing in *cis* and *trans* isomers and differing from pinic acid in having a carboxyl group attached to the cyclobutane ring in place of a carboxymethyl group.

1927 *Chem. Abstr.* XXI. 590 Oxidation of I [*sc.* cholanic acid] by CrO_3 in AcOH yielded the next lower homolog, norcholanic acid. **1958** C. W. SHOPPEE *Chem. Steroids* iv. 192 Similar reactions have been carried out in the norcholanic acid . . series. **1909** *Jrnl. Chem. Soc.* XCV. 1170 Our experiments have, however, shown that this ring, in norpinic acid, exhibits quite unusual stability. **1932** J. L. SIMONSEN *Terpenes* II. iii. 129 By the action of dilute hydrochloric acid at 180° [on the *cis*-isomer], an equilibrium mixture of *cis*- and *trans*-norpinic acids is obtained. **1960** A. R. PINDER *Chem. of Terpenes* v. 91 The molecular formula and properties of norpinic acid suggested it was derived from *cyclo*butane.

2. Denoting the normal (unbranched chain) isomer of the compound to whose name it is prefixed, as **nor'leucine** [ad. G. *norleucin* (E. Abderhalden et al. 1913, in *Zeitschr. f. physiol. Chem.* LXXXVI. 455)], an optically active, crystalline, non-essential amino-acid, $CH_3(CH_2)_3CH(NH_2)COOH$; **nor'valine** [ad. G. *norvalin* (Abderhalden & Kürten 1921, in *Fermentforschung* IV. 328)], an optically active crystalline amino-acid, $CH_3(CH_2)_2CH(NH_2)COOH$.

1913 *Jrnl. Chem. Soc.* CIV. I. 1049 The acid, for which the name norleucine is proposed, has been combined with glycine and leucylglycine to form polypeptides. **1932** *Jrnl. Biol. Chem.* XCVII. 342 Norleucine has been isolated from spinal cord protein. **1961** D. M. GREENBERG *Metabolic Pathways* II. xiv. 111 Norleucine is readily oxidized to CO_2 in the intact animal. **1971** *Nomencl. Org. Chem.* (I.U.P.A.C.) (ed. 2) C. 42 193 (*table*) Norleucine . . Norvaline. [*Note*] Use of 'nor' in these names to denote a 'normal' (unbranched) chain conflicts with more recent usage. **1921** *Jrnl. Chem. Soc.* CXX. I. 547 *dl*-*α*-*Amino-n*-valeric acid, . . to which the name *norvaline* is given, is prepared by the usual methods from *n*-valeric acid. **1933** *Ann. Rev. Biochem.* II. 73 Further evidence of the occurrence of norvaline in proteins has been furnished by Abderhalden & Heyns . . who report its occurrence in steer horn. **1969** *Biochem. Jrnl.* CXV. 621 Kinetic studies of glutamate dehydrogenase were made with wide concentration ranges of the coenzymes NAD^+ and $NADP^+$ and the substrates glutamate and norvaline.

noradrenaline (nɔːræ'drɛnəlɪn, -æ'driːnəlɪn). *Med.* Also **-in.** [f. NOR- 1 a + ADRENALINE.] An amine, $(HO)_2C_6H_3{\cdot}CHOH{\cdot}CH_2NH_2$, related to adrenaline, having a hydrogen atom in place of the methyl group; 1-(3, 4-dihydroxyphenyl)-2-aminoethanol; *spec.* the lævorotatory isomer, which is the transmitter substance of sympathetic nerves and at some synapses in the central nervous system, is also synthesized in the adrenal medulla, and whose acid tartrate is used, usu. by intravenal infusion, as a vasoconstrictor for raising blood pressure.

1932 *Arch. Internat. de Pharmacodynamie et de Thérapie* XLI. 366 This compound . . is referred to occasionally as nor-adrenaline. **1948** *Science* 6 Aug. 135/2 The facts . . point to the existence of two highly active sympatho-mimetic substances: nor-adrenaline and adrenaline. **1962** A. HUXLEY *Island* xiii. 206 The power generated by fear or envy or too much noradrenalin. **1965** J. POLLITT *Depression & its Treatment* iv. 53 Monoamines are neuro-hormones . ., and two substances of this group playing particularly important roles in mood regulation are serotonin and noradrenalin. **1968** [see DRIP *sb.* 2 b]. **1971** J. Z. YOUNG *Introd. Study Man* xliii. 629 Carnivorous animals are said to secrete large amounts of noradrenalin, which makes them aggressive. **1973** *Daily Colonist* (Victoria, B.C.) 30 June 12/1 Both humans and rats secrete a large amount of noradrenaline when they shiver.

Hence **noradre'nergic** *a.* [after ADRENERGIC, CHOLINERGIC *adjs.*], (of a nerve-cell) stimulated by or liberating noradrenaline; **noradre'nergically** *adv.*

1963 *Arch. Internat. de Pharmacodynamie et de Thérapie* CXLII. 257 The hindleg vasoconstriction, spleen contraction and cardioacceleration, which occur in response to a threshold stimulation of the corresponding post-ganglionic noradrenergic nerve supply, are not sensitized by intravenous infusion of noradrenaline. **1973** *Naunyn-Schmiedebergs Arch. Pharmakol.* CCLXXIX. 53 An *α*-receptor-mediated feed-back control of noradrenaline release, previously demonstrated in postganglionic sympathetic nerves, also operates in central noradrenergic neurones. **1975** *Nature* 21 Aug. 659/2 Peripheral, noradrenergically innervated tissue.

noraghe: see NURAGH.

Noraid ('nɔːreɪd). orig. *U.S.* Also **NORAID.** [Shortened f. *Irish Northern Aid Committee.*] An organization whose principal purpose is to raise funds for Northern Irish Republican causes among sympathizers in the U.S. Also *attrib.*

[**1971** *N.Y. Times* 20 Oct. 8/1 The Times of London . . quoted Toomas Enright of the United States-based Irish Northern Aid Committee as denying that the arms shipped on the Queen Elizabeth 2 came from the committee.] **1974** G. FITZGERALD in *Irish Times* 28 Sept. 8/4 A tiny minority of Irish Americans . . has been misled into subscribing on a significant scale to I.R.A. front organisations like Noraid. **1976** *Economist* 10 Jan. 52 Mr. Wilson estimated that 85% of the IRA's arms come from the United States, and held the Irish Northern Aid Committee (Noraid) largely responsible. **1979** *N.Y. Times* 24 Sept. B4/3 These officials regard Noraid as the I.R.A.'s best-organized and most fervent ally in the United States. **1982** *Government & Opposition* XVII. 149 There is little doubt that many of the contributors to Noraid's funds were under the misapprehension that the money was solely being used for the welfare of Republican prisoners' families. **1983** *Guardian* 8 Aug. 11/2 Noraid . . is thought to have sent almost £2 million to the province over the past 10 years. **1984** *Newsweek* 27 Aug. 49/2 In New York NORAID director Michael Flannery said 'It was a plus for us.' **1986** *Washington Post* 26 Jan. (Book World) 9/1 This is a novel with a thesis, and one that will not endear Benedict Kiely to the supporters of NORAID—or of Ian Paisley.

norate (nə'reɪt), *v. U.S. dial.* Also **norrate.** [? Corruption of NARRATE *v.*] **a.** To announce; to spread (information) by word of mouth. **b.** To denigrate. So **no'ration, norration.**

1853 J. W. PAGE *Uncle Robin* 231 Der's some folks who tells de people, dar, dat massers in dis country [*sc.* in the South], when der niggers runs away, puts out a noration, dat dey will give four hundred dollar' to anybody who will bring one o' der runaway niggers to um, dead or live. **1895** *Dialect Notes* I. 373 'We will *norate* the preaching' (i.e. announce the services to be held). **1905** *Ibid.* III. 89 [Arkansas] A French specialist has given out the '*noration*' that kissing is not a hurtful process. **1914** *Ibid.* IV. 110 Norate. . . Also, norration, noration, *n.* **1921** J. C. CAMPBELL *Southern Highlander & his Homeland* 145 [In the Southern Appalachians] a man wishing to hold a public meeting has it *norated*, that is, the announcement of it spread by report. **1938** *Amer. Speech* XIII. 6/2 [S.E. Arkansas] It is norated about that he is a crook. **1941** H. SKIDMORE *Hawk's Nest* 22 Norratin' it round bout them wanten men to work. **1949** H. HORNSBY *Lonesome Valley* 10 'You're planning to norate the word,' he said. . . 'More than apt they'll expect me to do the preaching.' **1954** *Publ. Amer. Dial. Soc.* XXI. 33 [South Carolina] *Norate*: *v.t.*, to depreciate. Usually of persons.

norbergite ('nɔːbɜːgaɪt). *Min.* [f. *Norberg*, the name of the village in Sweden near which it was discovered + -ITE[1].] A basic silicate and fluoride of magnesium, $Mg_3SiO_4(F,OH)_2$, which is found as pink or whitish orthorhombic crystals.

1926 P. GEIJER in *Geol. Fören. Stockholm Förhand.* XLVIII. 84 Norbergite. Only in massive aggregates, crystal system unknown... The proposed name is derived from the name of the district, since that of the mine is unsuitable for an international nomenclature. **1928** *Amer. Mineralogist* XIII. 349 The norbergite occurs in a coarsely crystalline limestone from the Nicoll Quarry, and grains or crystals are commonly several millimeters across. **1968** *Mineral. Mag.* XXXVI. 966 The polyhedral distortions in norbergite are smaller than in forsterite in accord with the decreased number of shared edges.

Norbertine ('nɔːbətɪn, -aɪn), *sb.* and *a. Eccl.* [f. *Norbert*, the founder of the order + -INE.]

A. *sb.* A member of the Premonstratensian order.

1674 BLOUNT *Glossogr., Norbertins*, a Religious Order, otherwise called Præmonstratenses. **1727–38** CHAMBERS *Cycl., Premonstrantes*, ..a religious order of regular canons instituted in 1120 by S. Norbert; and thence also called Norbertines. **1884** *Catholic Dict.* (1897) 746/1 The habit of the Norbertines was white; hence they were commonly called in England the White Canons.

B. *adj.* Of or pertaining to this order.

1865 *Chambers's Encycl.* VII. 745/2 Premonstratensian (called also Norbertine) Order. *c* **1880** *Archit. Soc. Dict.* s.v., Norbertine monks were Premonstratensians. **1902** MISS SPEAKMAN in *Owens Coll. Hist. Ess.* 73 The Norbertine house of Whithorn in Wigtonshire.

norce, norcery, obs. ff. NURSE, NURSERY.

norche, variant of NORSH *v. Obs.*

nordcaper ('nɔːd,keɪpə(r)). Also **-kap(p)er**. [ad. Du. *noordkaper* or G. *nordkaper* (f. Du. *noordkaap*, G. *nordkap*, the North Cape), formerly used as a specific name (*Balæna Nordcaper*): hence also F. *nordcaper*.] A North Atlantic species of whale, variously identified with *Balæna mysticetus* and *B. biscayensis*. Cf. NORTH-CAPER.

1822 GOOD *Study Med.* I. 4 The Greenlander feeds voraciously on the skin and fins of the nord-caper [*printed* -capon]. **1868** *Chambers's Encycl.* X. 152/1 The *Nordkaper* ..has by some naturalists been described as a distinct species, although it is more generally regarded as a variety of *B. mysticetus*. **1886** *Sci. Amer.* LIV. 24 The great Arctic or Greenland whale..and the Atlantic right whale, nordcaper, sletbag and sarde of the old authors.

'Nordenfelt. The name of a Swedish engineer, used *attrib.* and *absol.* to designate a form of machine-gun invented by him.

1880 *Encycl. Brit.* XI. 287 Nordenfelt gun... The barrels are here placed horizontally, and have no movement. **1885** *Pall Mall G.* 23 Feb., Six of the Nordenfelts will be worked amidships, on the top of the high bulwark.

nordenskiöldine (nɔːdən'ʃɜːldiːn, -skiː'ɜːldiːn). *Min.* [ad. Sw. *nordenskiöldin* (W. C. Brögger 1887, in *Geol. Fören. Stockholm Förhand.* IX. 255), f. the name of Baron Nils Adolf Erik *Nordenskiöld* (1832–1901), Swedish geologist and explorer: see -INE[5].] A borate of calcium and tin, $CaSnB_2O_6$, found as colourless or yellow rhombohedral crystals.

1890 *Jrnl. Chem. Soc.* LVIII. 1078 Nordenskiöldine, named after the celebrated traveller, is of great rarity in the Norwegian veins. **1935** *Mineral. Abstr.* VI. 46 An ore pipe in marble near a granite contact at Arandis, South-West Africa.., contains near its margin cassiterite, tourmaline, and small colourless plates of the rare mineral nordenskiöldine. **1966** *Doklady Earth Sci.* CLXIV. 131/1 Macroscopically, the nordenskiöldine synthesized is a dense white mass in which hexagonal, heavily tabular crystals up to 0·005 mm in size are discernible under the microscope.

Nordhausen ('nɔːdhaʊz(ə)n). The name of a town in Thuringia (formerly in Prussian Saxony), used *attrib.* in designations of sulphuric acid, which is made there.

1849 D. CAMPBELL *Inorg. Chem.* 56 Nordhausen, or fuming sulphuric acid. **1875** *Ure's Dict. Arts* (ed. 7) III. 962 Anhydrous Sulphuric Acid..is most easily obtained by subjecting the Nordhausen sulphuric acid to a gentle heat in a glass retort. **1895** THOMSON & BLOXAM *Chem.* 220 The Nordhausen oil of vitriol is an important article of commerce. *Ibid.*, The Nordhausen acid.

Nordic ('nɔːdɪk), *a.* and *sb.* [ad. F. *nordique* (J. Deniker 1898, in *L'Anthropologie* IX. 127) f. *nord* NORTH: see -IC.] **A.** *adj.* Of or pertaining to the Scandinavian people or their languages; *spec.* of or pertaining to a physical type of northern Germanic peoples characterized by tall stature, bony frame, light colouring, and dolichocephalic head.

In Nazi doctrine the 'Nordic race' was regarded as essentially 'superior' to other races.

1898 W. Z. RIPLEY in *Pop. Sci. Monthly* Oct. 744 A direct physical relationship between the three [peoples], referring them all to a so-called nordic race, is confirmed by the very latest and most competent authority [*sc.* J. Deniker]. **1921** *Contemp. Rev.* Jan. 56 All the talk about Nordic supremacy is vanity when we look at the facts in Europe. **1929** CHESTERTON *Thing* xiv. 113 Englishmen who now call themselves Nordic used to call themselves Teutonic. **1937** [see sense B. 1 below]. **1938** G. HEYER *Blunt Instrument* ii. 37 You ought to have seen me giving my impression of a Nordic public-school man with a reverence for good form and the done-thing. **1939** H. G. WELLS *Holy Terror* IV. ii. 419 The new generation of Germans were ashamed of the Hitler period and the Nordic legend. **1940** —— *All Aboard for Ararat* i. 24 The third, Japhet, was what the Germans would consider a Nordic type, all milk and roses. **1957** M. BELOFF *Europe & Europeans* iv. 86 The Nordic languages, especially Old Norse, borrowed important words from Anglo-Saxon. **1959** *Chambers's Encycl.* XIV. 319/1 The term viking is Nordic in origin. **1966** W. P. LEHMANN in Birnbaum & Puhvel *Anc. Indo-Europ. Dialects* 16 The most striking innovation common to Gothic and the Nordic languages is the development of a stop in geminate *j* and *w* clusters. **1968** G. JONES *Hist. Vikings* 69 As Wessén says, at the beginning of his history of the Swedish language:..We have then come to the *Primitive Nordic language*, the parent tongue of the present Nordic vernaculars, common to the Scandinavian countries down to the beginnings of the Viking Age. **1970** FOOTE & WILSON *Viking Achievement* 3 Some of the Nordic provinces had sent out tribes in the Migration Age to join the more southerly Germanic peoples as they cut their way through the old domains of the Roman Empire. **1973** G. BEARE *Snake on Grave* vii. 36 A crowd of Nordic drunks at a table near him was singing. **1974** *Encycl. Brit. Micropædia* VII. 386/3 *Nordic Council*, organization of the Nordic states of Denmark, Finland, Iceland, Norway, and Sweden for the purpose of consultation and cooperation on matters of common interest.

b. Of a skiing competition involving cross-country or jumping events.

1954 *Brit. Ski Yr. Bk.* XVI. 70 The greatest of all of the Nordic competitions—Holmenkollen. **1960** *Ski-ing* ('Know the Game' series) 24/2 The Nordic events include cross-country races and jumping competitions. **1966** S. ERIKSEN *Come ski with Me* 44 Norwegian had won the Nordic Combination and the 18 km. cross-country in Holmenkollen. **1969** M. HELLER *Ski* xiii. 170 Nordic ski-ing is the original and basic form of ski-ing... The fundamental techniques are self-evident—the diagonal stride, double poling with and without a stride and uphill strides—in other words, walking on skis. **1972** *Evening Telegram* (St. John's, Newfoundland) 24 June 23/1 Rolf Kjaernsli of Norway has been named nordic skiing program director to develop nordic and cross-country skiing in Canada.

B. *sb.* **1.** A person of the Nordic type.

1901 *Cassell's Mag.* June 110/2 The tall blonde race of northern Europe, sometimes called 'Teutons', but more scientifically 'Nordics'. **1928** WODEHOUSE *Money for Nothing* ii. 32 Well, all I can say is,..it's no life for a refined Nordic. **1936** H. G. WELLS *Anat. Frustration* xv. 176 It is for the treatment of the Jews that we are most frequently urged to condemn Hitlerism... Their [*sc.* the Jews'] racial purity is as much a falsehood as the racial purity of the 'Nordics'. **1937** A. HUXLEY *Ends & Means* xiii. 242 Hitlerian theology affirms that there is a Nordic race, inherently superior to all other. Hence it is right that Nordics should organize themselves for conquest.

2. The northern branch of the Germanic languages.

1955 T. BURROW *Sanskrit Lang.* 8 Germanic..may be divided into East Germanic or Gothic (extinct), Nordic or Scandinavian, and West Germanic. **1967** *Scandinavian Studies* XXXIX. 16 (*title*) Proto-Scandinavian and Common Nordic. **1972** in Van Coetsem & Kufner *Toward Gram. of Proto-Germanic* 78 The close relationship of 'Nordic' and 'Gothic'.

Nordicism ('nɔːdɪsɪz(ə)m). [f. NORDIC *a.* and *sb.* + -ISM.] **a.** The state or condition of being Nordic; the characteristics of the Nordics. **b.** The belief in or doctrine of the cultural and racial supremacy of the Nordic people. Hence **'Nordicist**, one who believes in the supremacy of the Nordic people.

1923 J. H. ECKENRODE *Jefferson Davis* (1924) ii. 24 The modernism of the North and the Nordicism of the South came more and more into conflict. **1924** *Glasgow Herald* 7 Apr. 8 Doubtless he was not as strong on Nordicism as his biographer. **1925** *Nation* (N.Y.) CXX. 516/1 The transition from Aryanism to Nordicism in Germany. **1929** R. HUGHES *High Wind in Jamaica* vii. 151 The Nordicism of captain and mate kept the rest looking clean enough. **1934** A. TOYNBEE *Study of Hist.* I. II. 221 The Nordicists claim it [*sc.* the monopoly of the unique magical quality in Mankind] for all White Men with fair hair and blue eyes. **1957** G. CLARK *Archaeol. & Society* (ed. 3) viii. 259 Much..was corrupted by doctrines which stemmed directly from Gustaf Kossinna (1858–1931), an ardent exponent of Pan-Germanism and Nordicism.

nordite ('nɔːdaɪt). *Min.* [ad. Russ. *nordit* (V. I. Gerasimovsky 1941, in *Doklady̆ Akad. Nauk SSSR* XXXII. 496): see quot. 1941 and -ITE[1].] A silicate of sodium, strontium, manganese, calcium, and lanthanides, found as light brown orthorhombic crystals.

1941 V. I. GERASIMOVSKY in *Compt. Rend.* (*Doklady*) *de l'Acad. des Sci. de l'URSS* XXXII. 496 A more detailed study of the mineral has shown that it cannot be identified with any of the minerals already known, and therefore it was given a new name—nordite (because of its northern origin). **1958** *Chem. Abstr.* LII. 12701 The predominance of La over Ce in nordite is an exception to the Oddo-Harkins rule. **1970** *Amer. Mineralogist* LV. 1167 The structure of nordite is closely related to the structures of melilite and datolite-gadolinite, and can be considered as an unusual combination of both.

nord-kap(p)er, varr. of NORDCAPER.

nordmarkite ('nɔːdmɑːkaɪt). [f. *Nordmark*, name of an area in Sweden + -ITE[1].]

1. *Min.* A brown manganesian variety of staurolite.

1868 J. D. DANA *Syst. Min.* (ed. 5) v. 389 *Manganese-Staurolite, Nordmarkite* (anal. 28); from dolomite in Nordmark, Sweden, of chocolate-brown color, with H. = 6·5, G. = 3·54, and presenting the usual crystalline form. Its easy fusibility is reason for here giving this variety the distinctive name *Nordmarkite*. **1968** I. KOSTOV *Mineralogy* 289 Staurolites rich in manganese are termed nordmarkite.

2. *Petrogr.* [a. G. *nordmarkit* (W. C. Brøgger 1890, in *Zeitschr. f. Kryst. und Mineral.* XVI. I. 55).] A syenite composed mainly of microperthite, with lesser amounts of quartz and usu. oligoclase and biotite, which has a trachytoid or granitic texture.

1895 *Mineral. Mag.* XI. 115 The corresponding abyssal or plutonic rock is nordmarkite. **1928** *Mineral. Abstr.* III. 498 The differentiation of the Lung Wang Miao åkerite has given rise to a whole series of granitic derivatives: nordmarkite, alkali-granite-aplite, and quartz-porphyry. **1942** *Amer. Jrnl. Sci.* CCXL. 362 Nordmarkite porphyry from a dyke at Blindern, by Oslo, Norway. **1970** *Meddelelser om Grønland* CXC. II. 15 The nordmarkites are grey or fawn in colour and are fairly coarse-grained rocks. *Ibid.* 16 In most of the nordmarkites the ferromagnesian minerals occur in small clusters.

Hence **nordmar'kitic** *a.*, composed of, or having the nature of, (the rock) nordmarkite.

1947 *Mineral. Mag.* X. 90 At Dorowa [S. Rhodesia] nordmarkitic granite occurs with syenite in the outer ring. **1953** *Q. Jrnl. Geol. Soc.* CIX. 161 Keratophyres, kersantites and nordmarkitic rocks occur on both sides of the outcrop of the Moine thrust-plane.

nordstrandite ('nɔːdstrəndaɪt). *Min.* [a. F. *nordstrandite* (D. Papée et al. 1958, in *Bull. Soc. chim. de France* 1306/2), f. the name of Robert A. van *Nordstrand*, 20th-cent. U.S. chemist: see -ITE[1].] One of the phases of aluminium hydroxide, $Al(OH)_3$.

1962 *Nature* 20 Oct. 265/1 The nordstrandite varies from almost colourless to coral pink and reddish-brown, the coloration being largely due to inclusions of finely divided goethite. **1968** *Mineral. Abstr.* XIX. 176/2 Nordstrandite occurs in all (6) Hungarian brickclays examined and is the only phase in the Debrecen clay.

nore, variant of ORE[1], favour.

†**nore**, obs. variant of *nor'*, NORTH. (Cf. NOREAST, -WEST.)

1612 DEKKER *If it be not good* Wks. 1873 III. 293 *Nat.* How blowes the winde Syr? *Leaf.* Wynde! is Nore-Nore-West. **1688** *Phil. Trans.* XVII. 784 The Nore and Nore-West are very nitrous and piercing. **1709** *Brit. Apollo* No. 73. 3/1 A Town's erected on a Bank to th' Nore. **1718** ROWE tr. *Lucan* I. 728 *note*, Circius..is placed as a Nore-west or Nore-nore-west.

†**noreast**, obs. form of *nor' east*, NORTH-EAST.

1594 J. DAVIS *Seamans Secr.* (1645) D, Noreast by North raiseth a degree in sayling 24 leagues.

nor'-easter, variant of NORTH-EASTER.

1836–48 B. D. WALSH *Aristoph., Knights* I. iii, Slack your sheet. A strong nor'-easter's groaning.

Noregan, variant of NORGAN *Obs.*

norelin, variant of Sc. *norlin*, NORLAND.

†**Norenish**, *a. Obs.* Also **Norein(n)-, Norwen-, Norn-**. [f. OE. *Noren*, NORN *a.* + -ISH: cf. MLG. *norrensch*.] Norwegian. Also *absol.* in *pl.*

c **1205** LAY. 12854 Peohtes inowe & Scottes vnifohȝe, Densce & Norenisce [*c* **1275** Norwenisse]. *Ibid.* 23198 Heo ..sumneden uerde, ȝeond Nornisce ærde. *Ibid.* 23229 Noreinisce men þer feollen.

norepinephrine (,nɔːrɛpɪ'nɛfrɪn). *Biochem.* [f. NOR- + EPINEPHRINE.] = NORADRENALINE.

1948 *Jrnl. Pharmacol. & Exper. Therap.* XCII. 369 Norepinephrine ('Arterenol'), a racemic compound,..is 1·5 times more pressor than racemic epinephrine. **1951** A. GROLLMAN *Pharmacol. & Therapeutics* xi. 205 Norepinephrine is a vasoconstrictor and unlike epinephrine does not decrease the peripheral resistance or increase the cardiac output. **1962** J. GLENN et al. *Into Orbit* 115 The flow of norephinephrine [*sic*] from his adrenal glands during the flight had been more than 2¼ times what it had normally been. **1971** *Nature* 2 Apr. 330/1 Some, if not all, states of mental depression may be associated with a deficiency in norepinephrine..at functionally important receptor sites in the brain.

nores(se, obs. forms of NOURICE, NOURISH.

noreshoure, obs. form of NOURISHER.

norethynodrel (nɔːrɛ'θɪnədrɪl). *Pharm.* [f. NOR- + ETH(ANE + -YN(E + *-odrel*, of unknown origin.] A synthetic hormone, $C_{20}H_{26}O_2$, with actions and uses similar to those of norethisterone, with which it is isomeric.

1957 *Endocrinology* LX. 804 Norethynodrel has been examined for its ability to produce endometrial gland development in the estrogen-primed spayed or immature rabbit. **1962** *New Scientist* 7 June 506/3 Most contraceptive pills consist of a mixture of two steroids obtained from yams. One is norethynodrel..which is believed to inhibit ovulation. The other is an oestrogen. **1970** PASSMORE & ROBSON *Compan. Med. Stud.* II. xii. 6/1 Shift of the double bond in the A ring of norethisterone from the 4–5 to the 5–10 position produces the isomer, norethynodrel.

noreture, obs. form of NOURITURE.

Norfolk ('nɔːfək). Also 5–7 **Northfolk.** [OE. *Norðfolc.*] **a.** The name of an English county on the East Coast, used *attrib.* to designate things peculiar to or characteristic of the district.

1407 *Nottingham Rec.* II. 52 Pro ij. volets de Northfolkthred, *xd.* **1573** TUSSER *Husb.* (1878) 209 For Norfolke wiles, so full of giles, Haue caught my toe. *c* **1600** [see DUMPLING]. **1609** DEKKER *Ravens Alm.* Ep., Of the nature of Dogs, & more nimble then Norfolke tumblers. **1663** DRYDEN *Wild Gallant* II. i, A parcel of melted flints set in gold, or Norfolk pebbles. **1728** VANBR. & CIB. *Prov. Husb.* I. ii, Sir, here's Norfolk-nog to be had at next door. **1840** *Penny Cycl.* XVI. 262/1 Norfolk turkeys are well known as of peculiar size and delicacy. **1889** A. J. ELLIS *Early Eng. Pron.* v. 260 Every one has heard of the Norfolk 'drant', or droning and drawling in speech.

b. In special applications, as **Norfolk capon**, a red herring (cf. CAPON *sb.* 3); **Norfolk crag** (see CRAG *sb.*[1] 3); **Norfolk dumpling**, (*a*) a native or inhabitant of Norfolk; (*b*) a plain dumpling made from bread dough; **Norfolk jacket**, a loosely fitting jacket having a waistband, and used chiefly in shooting, fishing, cycling, etc.; **Norfolk plover**, the Stone Curlew; **Norfolk reed**, the common reed, *Phragmites australis*, grown in East Anglia for use as thatching material; **Norfolk spaniel**, a name formerly used for the English springer spaniel, a breed once associated with the estates of the Duke of Norfolk; **Norfolk suit**, a suit with a Norfolk jacket and knee breeches; **Norfolk terrier**, the drop-eared variety of the Norwich terrier (see NORWICH); **Norfolk turkey**, a native or inhabitant of Norfolk.

1836 SMITH *Individual* 4 (Farmer), A *Norfolk capon is jolly grub. **1880–84** DAY *Fishes Gt. Brit.* II. 210 A red herring..is also known as a Norfolk capon. **1846** BUCHANAN *Techn. Dict.*, **Norfolk Crag*, an English tertiary formation belonging to the older pliocene, and consisting of irregular beds of ferruginous sandy clay mixed with marine shells. *c* **1600**, etc. *Norfolk dumplin [see DUMPLING I a]. *a* **1661** FULLER *Worthies, Norfolk* (1662) 247 Norfolk Dumplings. .. This..relates to the fare they commonly feed on. **1747** H. GLASSE *Art of Cookery* ix. 112 *Norfolk Dumplings.* Make a good thick batter... Eat them hot. **1787** GROSE *Prov. Gloss.*, *Norfolk Dumpling*, a jeering nick-name for Norfolk-men. **1877** *Cassell's Dict. Cookery* 458/1 Norfolk Dumplings... When bread is made at home, take a little of the dough.., make it up into small balls.., drop them into fast-boiling water... Send melted butter, sweetened and flavoured with lemon juice, to table with them. **1933** C. H. SENN *Century Cookery Bk.* (ed. 10) 1013 *Norfolk Dumplings,*—Make an ordinary bread dough... Serve with a boat of rich gravy or other suitable sauce. **1972** *Mrs. Beeton's Family Cookery* 449 Norfolk Dumplings.. Boiling water, Salt, Bread, Dough... Make the dough... Cream the yeast with the sugar and add the warm water and the melted fat... Serve with..jam, treacle, golden syrup, *or* butter and sugar. **1866** J. MACGREGOR *Thousand Miles in Rob Roy Canoe* i. 9 The '*Norfolk jacket' is a loose frock-coat, like a blouse, with shoulder-straps, and belted at the waist, and garnished by six pockets. **1893** EARL DUNMORE *Pamirs* II. 276 An English-made Norfolk jacket. **1898** G. B. SHAW *Widowers' Houses* Plays I. 4 You have nothing but that Norfolk jacket. **1969** *Queen* 17–30 Sept. 76 Norfolk jacket in cream leather; long side vents; belt..45 gns. **1768** PENNANT *Brit. Zool.* II. 378 The *Norfolk Plover. **1840** *Cuvier's Anim. Kingd.* 235 This is the Stone Curlew, Whistling or Norfolk Plover, as it is variously designated. **1877** NEWTON in *Encycl. Brit.* VI. 712/1 The..Stone-Curlew—called also, by some writers, from its stronghold in this country, the Norfolk Plover. [**1925** E. G. BLAKE *Roof Coverings* ii. 18 The reeds are grown principally in the eastern counties, especially on the Norfolk Broads.] **1952** *Oxf. Jun. Encycl.* VI. 440 A well-bedded thatch of *Norfolk reed..has been known to last as long as 50 years. *Ibid.*, Although Norfolk reed is by far the most durable, it is also the most expensive. **1965** P. WAYRE *Wind in Reeds* ix. 111 Norfolk reed is in much demand for thatch, being most durable and of good length—often exceeding eight feet. **1971** *Country Life* 18 Nov. 1403/1 The great tithe barn at Tisbury, in Wiltshire, has just been re-thatched with Norfolk reed. **1859** *Field* 5 Mar. 180/3 Will any of the readers of *The Field* kindly inform me what *spaniels are considered the best for woodcock-shooting—the Sussex, Clumber, Norfolk, &c.? **1867** 'STONEHENGE' *Dogs Brit. Is.* I. iii. 40 The Norfolk is one of the four descriptions of spaniels known as 'springers'. *Ibid.*, The Norfolk spaniel is now seldom to be obtained mute. **1945** C. L. B. HUBBARD *Observer's Bk. Dogs* 65 The old name of Norfolk Spaniel.. is obsolete. **1896** *Junior Army & Navy Stores Catal.* p. xxxvi/2 *Norfolk Jackets..Suits. **1913** C. MACKENZIE *Sinister St.* I. I. vii. 112 An exciting Monday spent in buying a Norfolk suit and Eton collars. **1938** J. CARY *Castle Corner* iii. 116 He was seen every day walking about Knockeen with his solemn, fierce air and his smartest norfolk suits. **1964** *Kennel Gaz.* 419/2 On September 22, 1964, the General Committee of the Kennel Club agreed to register drop-eared Norwich Terriers as *Norfolk Terriers, a separate breed and not a variety. **1968** C. G. E. WIMHURST *Bk. Terriers* xxi. 154 The Norfolk Terrier is one of the smallest of the terriers. **1971** F. HAMILTON *World Encycl. Dogs* 463 The Norfolk Terrier was, until September 1964, the drop-eared Norwich Terrier. *Ibid.* 467 There is little or no difference in character between the Norwich and the Norfolk. **1811** *Ora & Juliet* I. 100, I shall..shew them the difference of a highly-educated person, and the boorish manners of those *Norfolk turkeys.

c. *ellipt.* The dialect of Norfolk.

1895 W. RYE *Gloss. E. Anglia* p. vii, The following specimens of modern Norfolk have been handed to me.

d. *ellipt.* A Norfolk jacket. In *pl.*, a Norfolk suit.

1902 E. NESBIT *Five Children & It* ii. 47 Nine pockets in my Norfolks. *Ibid.* viii. 215 A giant little boy—in Norfolks like my brother's. **1904** *T. Eaton & Co. Catal.* Spring & Summer 87/1 Brownie Norfolks, made of dark green Tweed. **1969** R. T. WILCOX *Dict. Costume* 248/1 The coat of the Duke of Norfolk's hunting suit, the first 'Norfolk', appeared in the 1880's with knickerbockers, a revival of knee breeches for day wear. **1970** S. J. PERELMAN *Baby, it's Cold Inside* 28 Where'd you get that Norfolk?.. Brooks hasn't carried that model in years.

Norfolk Howard ('nɔːfək 'haʊəd). [From an advertisement in the *Times* of 26 June, 1862, professing to be a declaration by one Joshua Bug that he had assumed the name of Norfolk Howard.]

A bed-bug.

1865 in HOTTEN *Slang Dict.* (ed. 2). **1870** *Figaro* 19 Oct. (Farmer), Those entomological pests that are euphemistically called Norfolk Howards. **1888** LEES & CLUTTERBUCK *B.C.* 1887, xxii, In one bag the Norfolk Howards, In one bag the fleas, the Jumpers.

Norfolk Island ('nɔːfək 'aɪlənd). The name of a South Pacific island about five hundred miles north-west of New Zealand, used *attrib.* in **Norfolk (Island) pine** to designate a large conifer, *Araucaria heterophylla* (formerly *excelsa*), of the family Araucariaceæ, native to this island.

[**1778** J. R. FORSTER *Observations made during Voyage round World* v. 174 In the opposite, or Westernmost part of the South-Sea, lies a small isle, which has obtained the name of Norfolk-Island... Peculiar to this isle, and to the Eastern end of Caledonia, we found a species of coniferous tree, from the cones probably seeming to be a cypress: it grows here to a great size, and is very heavy but useful timber.] **1803** A. B. LAMBERT *Descr. Genus Pinus* I. 87 Norfolk Island Pine... This tree..is the tallest at present known. **1836** *Agriculturist's Manual* (P. Lawson & Son) 354 The Norfolk Island Pine..was first discovered by the celebrated circumnavigator Captain Cook, in his second voyage, on Norfolk Island and New Caledonia. **1854** J. C. PATTESON *Let.* 24 Aug. in C. M. Yonge *Life J. C. Patteson* (1874) I. v. 175, I shall write to you very often, and send you ferns and seeds, and tell you about the Norfolk Island pines. **1920** C. COLTMAN-ROGERS *Conifers* vi. 227 The Norfolk Island Pine ..is fast becoming quite a common corner-window side-show in many English homes. **1933** *Bulletin* (Sydney) 27 Dec. 20/4 Almost as well known overseas as the eucalypts is the Norfolk Island pine. **1940** F. SARGESON *Man & his Wife* (1944) 91 A very old settled place with a row of Norfolk pines planted along the beach. **1966** *Times* 28 Mar. (Austral. Suppl.) p. xv/2 The home unit blocks are growing taller than the two Norfolk pines. **1968** *Southerly* XXVIII. 172 Halfway up the west face of the valley was a double row of Norfolk Island pines. **1974** A. MITCHELL *Field Guide Trees Britain* 57 One tender species, the Norfolk Island Pine, *A*[*raucaria*] *heterophylla* (*excelsa*), frequent as a pot plant and growing to 30 m at Tresco, Isles of Scilly.

† **'Norfolkize**, *v. Obs. rare*⁻¹. [f. NORFOLK + -IZE.] *intr.* To assume a Norfolk character.

1655 FULLER *Hist. Cambr.* 46, I confess some have complained of this Matthew Parker, that, in favour to his native county, he made all this College to Norfolkize, appropriating most Fellowships thereto.

† **'Norgan**, *sb.* and *a. Obs.* Forms: 4 **Nore-, Norigan(e**, 4, 6 **Norgane**. [ad. med.L. *Noreganus*, f. ON. *Noreg-r* Norway.] = NORWEGIAN.

1387 TREVISA *Higden* (Rolls) VII. 229 In þe mene tyme [þe] kyng of Noreganes..cam wiþ þre hondred schippes. *Ibid.* 239 þey moste haue no part of þe prayes at þe bataile of þe Norganes. **1586** WARNER *Alb. Eng.* III. xvi, When the Norgane Prince and Peeres were seated. *Ibid.*, The.. Norgane Ladies Shippe was tossed to the Coste.

norgestrel (nɔː'dʒɛstrəl). *Pharm.* [f. NOR- + PRO)GEST(OGEN + *-rel*, prob. after NORETHYNODREL.] An artificial steroid hormone, $C_{21}H_{28}O_2$, which has actions similar to those of progesterone and is used in some contraceptive pills.

1966 R. A. EDGREN et al. in *Internat. Jrnl. Fertility* XI. 389 Norgestrel..is a highly potent, totally synthetic progestogen chemically related to norethisterone and norethynodrel. **1974** *Nature* 8 Mar. 98/3 Ovranette contains a progestogen called norgestrel which is not converted to oestrogen in the body. In fact it is actively anti-oestrogenic, reversing some of the changes brought about by oestrogen.

‖ **nori** ('nɔərɪ). [Jap.] A Japanese food prepared from fronds of a seaweed of the genus *Porphyra*, eaten either fresh or dried, when they stick together to form small sheets. Cf. LAVER *sb.*[1] 2.

1892 E. ARNOLD *Japonica* II. 86 Large slices of broiled *tai*, and *tsubo* or *nori*, sea-weed,..of which the Japanese are fonder than the foreigner is likely to prove. **1966** P. S. BUCK *People of Japan* (1968) xiv. 167 Rice covered with shredded egg and *nori.* **1973** A. BROINOWSKI *Take One Ambassador* xi. 174 We all collected *nori*, the seaweed along the beach.

‖ **noria** ('nɔərɪə). [Sp. *noria*, ad. Arab. *nāʿūrah.*] A device for raising water, used in Spain and in the East, consisting of a revolving chain of pots or buckets which are filled below and discharged when they come to the top.

1792 J. TOWNSEND *Journ. thro. Spain* I. 103 Every farm has its Noria, a species of chain-pump, which from its extreme simplicity, seems to have been the invention of the most remote antiquity. **1845** FORD *Handbk. Spain* I. 430 The common and most picturesque *noria.* **1875** KNIGHT *Dict. Mech.* 1534/1 The true Spanish noria has earthen pitchers secured between two ropes which pass over a wheel above and are submerged below.

norice, obs. variant of NOURISH *v.*

norice, -iche, obs. variants of NOURICE, nurse.

noricerie: see NOURICERY.

norie[1] ('nɔərɪ). Also 9 **Norrie, nory.** [See def.] A copy of the *Epitome of Navigation* by J. W. Norie, originally published in 1803.

1828 P. CUNNINGHAM *N.S. Wales* (ed. 3) II. 200 Having acquired a thorough knowledge of navigation by the occasional perusal of a stray Norrie. **1831** TRELAWNY *Adv. Younger Son* II. 282, I cursed my improvidence..in not having provided myself with a knife, a compass, a quadrant and a nory.

norie[2], the puffin: see TAMMIE-NORIE.

1793 *Statist. Acc. Scotl., Kirkwall* VII. 546 Among these we may reckon..the tyste, the pickternie, the norie [etc.].

no-right ('nəʊraɪt). [f. NO *a.* + RIGHT *sb.*[1] 7.] In Jurisprudence, an obligation not to prevent the exercise of a privilege.

1913 W. N. HOHFELD in *Yale Law Jrnl.* XXIII. 32 As indicated in the above scheme of jural relations, a privilege is the opposite of a duty, and the correlative of a 'no-right'. **1923** —— *Fundamental Legal Conceptions* i. 39 The correlative of X's right that Y shall not enter on the land is Y's duty not to enter; but the correlative of X's privilege of entering himself is manifestly Y's 'no-right' that X shall not enter. **1938** M. RADIN in *Harvard Law Rev.* LI. 1150 The phrase 'no right' was subjected to a great deal of critical and destructive comment. 'A "no-right"', one critic once declared, 'might be an elephant.' **1972** W. A. WILSON in *Juridical Rev.* Aug. 162 The correlative of a liberty is a no-right. The jural opposite of a right is a no-right.

norimon ('nɒrɪmɒn). Also 7 **nere-, norri-.** [ad. Jap. *norimono*, f. *nori* to ride + *mono* thing: cf. KAKEMONO.] A kind of litter or palanquin used in Japan. Also *attrib.*

1616 R. COCKS *Diary* (Hakl. Soc.) I. 164 He kept hym selfe close in a *neremon.* **1662** J. DAVIES tr. *Mandelslo's Trav.* 202 After them came one and twenty other *Palanquins* of a kind, which they call *Norrimones*, varnish'd with black and gilt. **1727** tr. *Kæmpfer's Hist. Japan* v. i. 402 The *Norimon* itself is a small room, of an oblong square figure.., curiously twisted of fine thin split *Bambous*, sometimes Japan'd and finely painted, with a folding-door on each side. All these *Norimon*-men are clad in the same livery. **1780** *Phil. Trans.* LXX. App. p. vii, We were carried by men in a kind of palankins, called Norimons, covered, and provided with windows. **1863** FORTUNE *Yedo & Peking* 67 A norimon containing an official or person of rank.

noris(e, -ishe, -isse, obs. varr. NOURICE.

† **'Norish**, *a. Obs. rare*⁻¹. [var. of NORSE.] Norwegian.

a **1688** J. WALLACE *Descr. Orkney* (1693) 90 An explication of some Norish words used in Orkney and Zetland.

norishe, -ysh(e, etc., obs. forms of NOURISH.

'norite ('nɔəraɪt). *Geol.* and *Min.* [f. *Nor*(*way*) + -ITE.] A variety of gabbro or granite.

1878 tr. *Cotta's Rocks* 143 The norite of Scheerer is a compound of hypersthene or diallage, labradorite, orthoclase (containing soda), and even some quartz. **1885** GEIKIE *Text-bk. Geol.* (ed. 2) 154 Norite. Under this name Rosenbusch has proposed to group all the older gabbro-like rocks in which any rhombic pyroxene..is conjoined with a plagioclase felspar.

noriture, obs. form of NOURITURE.

nork (nɔːk). *Austral. slang.* [See quot. 1966.] A woman's breast. Usu. *pl.*

1962 C. ROHAN *Delinquents* 157 Hello, honey, that sweater —one deep breath and your norks will be in my soup. **1966** BAKER *Austral. Lang.* (ed. 2) x. 215 *Nork*, a female breast, usually in plural. (Ex Norco Co-operative Ltd., a butter manufacturer in N.S.W.). The form *norg* is reported from Melbourne. **1969** *Private Eye* 21 Nov. 14 She's a top model with norks out to here. **1972** I. HAMILTON *Thrill Machine* iii. 17 She's only a body, all she's got is big norks. **1973** P. WHITE *Eye of Storm* 593 Hits herself in the eye with an independent nork it isn't any laughing matter.

norland[1] ('nɔːlənd). Also *Sc.* 8–9 **norlan'**, 9 **norlin', norelin.** [Reduced form of NORTHLAND.]

1. The north-country; the land in the north.

a **1578** LINDESAY (Pitscottie) *Chron. Scot.* (S.T.S.) I. 202 He was to ryde to the norland amangis his lordis. **1844** MRS. BROWNING *Drama of Exile* 1707 As the storm-wind blows bleakly from the norland. **1880** SWINBURNE *Songs of Four Seasons* i, Our noisy norland.

b. *attrib.* Belonging to the north.

a **1578** LINDESAY (Pitscottie) *Chron. Scot.* (S.T.S.) I. 202 The norland lordis that fawored him. *Ibid.* 205 The norland men and wastland men. **1786** BURNS *Earnest Cry* xiv, Erskine, a spunkie norland billie. *c* **1792** —— *Here's a health to them that's awa*, Here's a health to Tammie, the Norland laddie. **1830** TENNYSON *Oriana* xi, When Norland winds pipe down the sea. **1864** *Daily Tel.* 25 Oct., In these norland woods and groves.

2. A northerner; a north-country person, esp. one from the north of Scotland.

1771 J. MACPHERSON *Introd. Hist. Grt. Brit. & Irel.* 129 The appellation of Southerons and Norlands are not hitherto totally extinguished among the Scots. **1798** CRAWFORD *Poems* 27 (E.D.D.), Kirsty was a Norlan' bred.

1817 J. GILCHRIST *Intell. Patrimony* 159 The journeyman carpenter..possessed all the quaint shrewdness which is among the Scotch implied in the word Norelin.

Hence **'norlander** = prec. 2; **'norlandism**, a characteristic of a northern dialect.

1716 in Maidment *Spottiswoode Misc.* (1845) II. 449 They met with a bold Norlander of Aberdeenshire. *c* 1795 SCOTT in Child *Ballads* (1892) IV. 387 *note*, I recollect several of them as recited in the south of Scotland divested of their Norlandisms.

Norland[2] ('nɔːlənd). The name of the *Norland* Institute (see below), now the Norland Nursery Training College, used *attrib.* to designate the methods of child care taught there, a nurse trained in these methods, or a nursery following them. Also *ellipt.*, a Norland nurse.

[1892 *St. James's Gaz.* 28 Sept. 12/2 It will be interesting to watch the experiment being made by Mrs. Walter Ward, who has just opened the Norland Institute for the training of kindergarten nurses. 1893 *Farm, Field & Fireside* 10 Feb. 460/1 The Norland Institute is situated at 9, Norland Place, Holland Park Gardens, London, W. It was started by Mrs. Walter Ward (Miss Emily Ford) for the training of ladies as children's nurses on Froebelian principles.] 1894 *Nursing Record & Hospital World* 7 Apr. 234/2 As a Norland Nurse, I have now had opportunity of seeing the value of the work to both employer and employée. 1899 *West-End* 23 Aug. 14/1 [The nurse] must receive a certificate, and do a further three months as probationer in a family.., or at some special Institution, before she dons her pretty neat brown uniform, and sallies forth as a fully-fledged Norland nurse. 1945 N. STREATFEILD *Saplings* ii. 19 Lena would have liked..a young Norland or the equivalent, looking smart in her uniform. 1959 *Times* 29 Sept. 2/7 Norland/Trained Nurse required. 1972 J. GATHORNE-HARDY *Rise & Fall of Brit. Nanny* vi. 178 From the first a Norland Nurse was forbidden to hit a child... This enlightened view..has remained a key feature of the Norland training. 1975 *Harpers & Queen* May 139/2 When they were eighteen months old they went to a Norland nursery. 1975 *Times* 4 Aug. 5/6 Each weekend they go to Barnwell with [the baby] Alexander and his Norland nanny.

norm (nɔːm), *sb.* [Anglicized form of NORMA: cf. also NORME.] **1. a.** A standard, model, pattern, type. (Common since *c* 1855.)

1821 COLERIDGE in *Blackw. Mag.* X. 257 Each after its own norm or model. 1828 PUSEY *Hist. Enq.* I. 21 Every expression of his upon controverted points became a norm for the party. 1857 P. FREEMAN *Princ. Div. Serv.* II. 143 The norm and measure of all our eucharistic thoughts, and words, and actions. 1877 E. CAIRD *Philos. Kant* iv. 66 The mind must find in itself the norm or principle of unity upon which it works. 1911 R. BROOKE *Coll. Poems* (1918) 154 All of the accents upon all the norms!—And ah! the stress on the penultimate! We never knew blank verse could have such feet. 1941 J. P. MARQUAND *H.M. Pulham, Esquire* iv. 44 Beatrice considered that I was utterly characteristic, completely true to type; once she called me a norm. 1961 S. R. HERMAN in J. A. Fishman *Readings Sociol. of Lang.* (1968) 505 Frequently the newcomer arrives with the belief that the prevailing norm about using Hebrew to the exclusion of other languages is more rigidly observed than is actually the case... Soon, however, the newcomer becomes aware of the wide range of deviations from the norm. 1964 M. ARGYLE *Psychol. & Social Probl.* iii. 38 One particular respect in which a group equilibrium develops is in the formation of norms—shared patterns of behaving, feeling and thinking. All social groups develop norms, particularly about matters connected with the group's main purposes and activities... When group members deviate from the norms, various kinds of persuasion, pressure and sanctions are exerted in order to make them conform. 1965 *Economist* 13 Feb. 645/2 The other vital point will be the 'norms' or 'guiding lights' [for incomes] recommended for each year.

b. *Algebra.* (See quots.) Also defined analogously for other quantities. [Introduced as L. *norma* by Gauss 1832, in *Commentationes Recentiores Soc. R. Scient. Gottingensis* VII. Class. math. 98.]

1856 W. R. HAMILTON *Notebook* in Halberstam & Ingram *Math. Papers Sir W. R. Hamilton* (1967) III. 657, $a + ib$ is said to be a complex number, when a and b are integers, and $i = \sqrt{-1}$; its norm is $a^2 + b^2$; and therefore the norm of a product is equal to the product of the norms of its factors. 1866 BRANDE & COX *Dict. Sci.*, etc. II. 228/2 The product $a^2 + b^2$ of a complex number $a + b\sqrt{-1}$, and its conjugate $a - b\sqrt{-1}$ is called its norm. 1932 TURNBULL & AITKEN *Introd. Theory Canonical Matrices* iv. 38 This fundamental Hermitian inner product of $\bar{x}$ and x is often called the norm of the complex vector x... The square root of the norm, taken with positive sign, $(\bar{x}x)^{\frac{1}{2}}$, is sometimes denoted by $|x|$. 1949 A. ALBERT *Solid Analytic Geom.* i. 3 The norm of a vector P is defined to be the inner product $P{\cdot}P = x_1{}^2 + \ldots + x_n{}^2$. 1952 C. MØLLER *Theory of Relativity* iv. 99 It then follows..that the 'square of the magnitude of the four-vector', or the norm of the vector, $\sum_i a_i{}^2 = \sum_i a'_i{}^2$, is an invariant. 1967 MACLANE & BIRKHOFF *Algebra* v. 187 Each quadratic field $Q(\sqrt{d})$, with the elements $\sigma = r + s\sqrt{d}$, has as automorphisms the identity and $\sigma \mapsto \bar{\sigma} = r - s\sqrt{d}$. The product $\sigma\bar{\sigma} = r^2 + s^2d$ is called the norm $N(\sigma)$ of σ.

(ii) The positive square root of the quantity defined above; more generally, a quantity defined on a vector space over the real or complex field which represents a generalization of the concept of length or magnitude and has the properties that $\|u\| > 0$ if $u \neq 0$ ($\|u\|$ being the norm of the vector u), $\|u\| = 0$ if $u = 0$, $\|au\| = |a|\,\|u\|$ (a being a real number), and $\|u + v\| \leqslant \|u\| + \|v\|$ (v being another vector).

1921 *Proc. Nat. Acad. Sci.* VII. 84 The notion of norm or numerical value of a complex quantity, $c = a + b\sqrt{-1}$, namely, $|c| = \sqrt{(a^2 + b^2)}$, as it arises in algebra, has a more or less immediate generalization to more extensive matric systems. 1951 P. R. HALMOS *Introd. Hilbert Space* i. 13 The norm of a vector α in the inner product space..coincides with the absolute value of the complex number α. 1955 L. F. BORON tr. *I. P. Natanson's Theory of Functions of Real Variable* I. vii. 199 Let $f(x) \in L_p$. The number $\|f\| = \sqrt[p]{(\int_a^b |f(x)|^p dx)}$ is called the norm of the function $f(x)$ (considered as an element of L_p). 1962 KACINSKAS & COUNTS tr. *L. S. Pontryagin's Ordinary Differential Equations* iv. 152 The maximum modulus of this function.. will be called its norm. 1965 PATTERSON & RUTHERFORD *Elem. Abstract Algebra* v. 184 A norm can be defined in a vector space having an inner product by writing $\|x\| = \sqrt{(x{\cdot}x)}$... There exist norms which cannot be expressed in this way in terms of an inner product. In the case where an inner product exists, it is clear that the length of a vector satisfies the requirements for a norm. *Ibid.* 185 Let $M_{2,2}(C)$ be the vector space of 2×2 matrices over the complex field. Then the mapping $\left[\begin{smallmatrix} a & b \\ c & d \end{smallmatrix}\right] \to \max(|a|, |b|, |c|, |d|)$ defines a norm in $M_{2,2}(C)$. The mapping $\left[\begin{smallmatrix} a & b \\ c & d \end{smallmatrix}\right] \to \sqrt{(|a|^2 + |b|^2 + |c|^2 + |d|^2)}$ defines another norm. 1970 F. A. MATSEN *Vector Spaces & Algebras* i. 11 The norm N_c of c is defined by $N_c = (cc^*)^{1/2} = \sqrt{(a^2 + b^2)}$.

c. In Communist countries, a standard unit of work prescribed.

1935 S. & B. WEBB *Soviet Communism* II. ix. 706 They [*sc.* piece-work rates] are, in some cases, even progressive, the rate rising by stages for output beyond the norm. 1952 *Manch. Guardian* 6 June, Stakhanovite women miners in the Donetz basin are performing four, nine, and eleven norms each. 1959 *Times* 12 Mar. 13/6 This moulding process may vary from the crudest regimentation and subordination..to factory-like specification and 'norms' to mere pilotage..towards the Marxist haven.

2. *Petrol.* A hypothetical mineral composition of a rock calculated by assigning the compounds present to certain relatively simple minerals in accordance with prescribed rules.

1902 [see MODE *sb.* 5 b]. 1932 A. JOHANNSEN *Descr. Petrogr. Ign. Rocks* II. 272 (*heading*) Table 135. Norms of rhyolites. 1973 *Jrnl. Petrol.* XIV. 35 The norms used are not based on stoichiometric formulae..but approach the compositions of the constituents as actually found in natural rocks. *Ibid.* 250 The C.I.P.W. norms which accompany the analyses were calculated using an Fe_2O_3/FeO ratio estimated to be appropriate for the quartz-fayalite-magnetite-buffered charges.

3. *attrib.* and *Comb.*

1934 *Archit. Rev.* LXXVI. 42/1 It represents a return to the machine, regarded realistically and as mechanism to produce mechanical norm-types. 1958 M. ARGYLE *Relig. Behaviour* v. 57 All these findings can be regarded as instances of social learning, mediated by the usual processes of persuasion, imitation and norm-formation. 1961 J. N. FINDLAY *Values & Intentions* ix. 399 The religious object.. must tend more and more towards the pattern of a detached, suprapersonal, norm-setting *mind*. 1964 I. L. HOROWITZ *New Sociology* 32 Why do people choose rapid industrialization with its attendant psychological turmoil over social stability and norm adherence? 1966 *Mathematical Rev.* XXXI. 8/2 Since norm-sentences are neither true nor false, logical connectives undergo re-interpretation. 1969 J. F. SZWED in Halpert & Story *Christmas Mumming in Newfoundland* 116 During socialization, each person acquires an awareness of social sanctions and at the same time becomes 'norm-oriented'.

norm (nɔːm), *v. Math.* [f. the sb.] **1.** *trans.* = NORMALIZE *v.* 3 a. ? *Obs.*

1931 P. DIENES *Taylor Series* viii. 274 We 'norm' the mapping with respect to $u = a$ by requiring that $a_1k = 1$. 1941 R. V. CHURCHILL *Fourier Series* iii. 38 The functions of the set are normed by dividing each function $g_n(x)$ by $[N(g_n)]^{1/2}$.

2. *trans.* [back-formation from NORMED *a.*] To define a norm on (a space).

1959 L. F. BORON tr. *Naimark's Normed Rings* i. 73 The space $X/\mathfrak{M}$, normed by formula (1), will be called a normed factor-space. 1964 D. E. BROWN tr. *Kantorovich & Akilov's Functional Analysis in Normed Spaces* ii. 51 The metric spaces..are also linear sets and can be normed. 1972 A. G. HOWSON *Handbk. Terms used in Algebra & Analysis* xxii. 111 The vector space $\mathscr{L}(E, F)$ can be normed in the following way.

Hence **'norming** *vbl. sb.*

1967 L. RÉDEI *Algebra* I. iv. 307 In different rings norming is carried out in different ways.

‖**norma** ('nɔːmə). Also pl. **normae** ('nɔːmiː). [L. *norma*, carpenter's or mason's square; hence, pattern, rule, etc. So in Sp., Pg., and It.]

1. = NORM *sb.*

a 1676 HALE *Prim. Orig. Man.* (1677) 344 Again, will they suppose it a *Norma*, Rule, or Law of a most excellent frame and order. 1830 M. DONOVAN *Dom. Econ.* I. 211 He is cautious, and never willingly varies from that *norma* which he has once found successful. 1842 GROVE *Corr. Phys. Forces* (1874) p. xiv, We can only understand the normæ of their action. 1881 BRIDGETT *Holy Eucharist* I. 47 A norma or standard to which discipline should be reformed.

2. One of the southern constellations.

1840 *Penny Cycl.* XVI. 274/2 *Norma*, the Rule, a constellation of Lacaille, situated between Scorpio and Lupus.

normal ('nɔːməl), *a.* and *sb.* [ad. L. *normālis*, f. *norma* (see prec.): cf. F. (15th c.), Sp., It. *normal*, It. *normale*.]

A. *adj.* **1. a.** Right (angle), rectangular. *rare.*

1650 BULWER *Anthropomet.* 55 Those determined bounds of the hair, which are called by our Barbars the Normal Angels. 1901 WATERHOUSE *Conduit Wiring* 53 The angle not being suited to either a right angled (normal) or half-normal bend.

b. Standing at right angles; perpendicular.

a 1696 SCARBURGH *Euclid* (1705) 15 To which therefore It is said to be a Normal Line. 1704 J. HARRIS *Lex. Techn.* I, *Normal*, the same with Perpendicular, or at Right Angles, and 'tis usually spoken of a Line or a Plane that Intersects another Perpendicularly. [Also in Phillips (1706), Chambers, etc.] 1879 NEWCOMB & HOLDEN *Astron.* 203 The line ZN', perpendicular to HR, and therefore normal to the earth at Q. 1882 *Engineering* 13 Jan. 24/1 These being in directions always normal to the surface of the pulsating sphere—that is to say, in lines radiating from its centre.

2. a. Constituting, conforming to, not deviating or differing from, the common type or standard; regular, usual. (Common since *c* 1840.)

Blount *Glossogr.* (1656) gives '*Normal*, right by rule, made by the square or Rule'.

1828 STARK *Elem. Nat. Hist.* II. 216 Two superior groups, which he denominates normal or typical. 1843 R. J. GRAVES *Syst. Med.* xii. 135 Temperature of the body normal. 1860 TYNDALL *Glac.* I. vii. 54 The veining, whose normal direction would be transverse to the glacier. 1877 BROCKETT *Cross & Crescent* 28 War seemed to be its normal condition.

b. *Chem.* (i) Of a salt: containing no acidic hydrogen.

1860 W. A. MILLER *Elements Chem.* (ed. 2) II. x. 338 The most usual form of salt, in which 1 atom of a protoxide is united with 1 atom of an acid to form the normal salt. 1869 ROSCOE *Elem. Chem.* 189 If all the replaceable hydrogen in an acid is exchanged for metal, a normal salt is said to be formed. 1915 P. W. OSCROFT *Adv. Inorg. Chem.* iv. 38 It must not be understood that normal salts are always neutral bodies with regard to their action with litmus; this is far from being the case. 1965 B. J. MOODY *Comp. Inorg. Chem.* xiii. 188/2 Both sodium sulphate and trisodium orthophosphate are normal salts.

(ii) Of (the concentration of) a solution: having one gramme-equivalent of solute per litre.

1863 F. SUTTON *Syst. Handbk. Volumetric Anal.* 19 The normal solutions prepared on the gramme system are equally applicable for that of the grain, and *vice versâ*. 1892 COOLEY *Cycl. Pract. Rec.* s.v., A so-called 'normal' (or 'N.') solution is one which, at a temperature of 16° C., contains per litre the hydrogen equivalent of the active reagent weighed in grammes. 1915 P. W. OSCROFT *Adv. Inorg. Chem.* v. 48, 25 c.c. of a caustic potash solution required 15 c.c. of a normal sulphuric acid solution for neutralization. 1955 C. R. N. STROUTS et al. *Analyt. Chem.* I. xii. 258 A solution of one-tenth normal strength is designated as N/10. 1967 R. FULTON *Course in Titrimetric Anal.* ii. 7 Normal solutions are more widely used [than molar solutions].

(iii) (Composed of molecules) containing an unbranched chain of carbon atoms in an alkane molecule or alkyl radical.

1869 C. SCHORLEMMER in *Proc. R. Soc.* XVII. 373, I had obtained the normal propyl alcohol by this method. 1871 —— *Ibid.* XIX. 487 The first group, which I called normal paraffins, contain the carbon atoms linked together in a single chain. 1876 *Encycl. Brit.* V. 557/2 *Normal paraffins*, in which no carbon atom is combined with more than two other carbon atoms. 1932 I. D. GARARD *Introd. Org. Chem.* ii. 20 At average room temperature, those normal paraffin hydrocarbons containing four carbon atoms or less are gaseous, and those from five to seventeen, liquids. 1968 J. A. MONICK *Alcohols* iii. 86 If the [parent] hydrocarbon consists of an unbranched carbon chain, the equivalent primary alcohol is called normal.

c. *Physics.* Of, pertaining to, or being a mode of vibration in which every particle executes simple harmonic motion at the same frequency and in phase (or 180° out of phase).

1867 THOMSON & TAIT *Treat. Nat. Philos.* ii. 274 There are in general..*i* distinct determinate displacements, which we shall call the normal displacements, fulfilling the condition, that if any one of them be produced alone, and the system then left to itself for an instant at rest, this displacement will diminish and increase periodically according to a simple harmonic function of the time, and consequently every particle of the system will execute a simple harmonic movement in the same period. 1877 [see MODE *sb.* 4 c]. 1927 TOFT & KERSEY *Theory of Machines* xiv. 362 Any type of oscillation other than a normal mode may be considered as being the sum of a number of motions each of which is a normal mode. 1942 SYNGE & GRIFFITH *Princ. Mech.* vii. 209 The periods and frequencies of normal modes are called normal periods and normal frequencies. 1962 P. J. & B. DURRANT *Introd. Adv. Inorg. Chem.* viii. 229 There may be several normal vibrations of different frequencies characteristic of a given molecule. 1971 *Amer. Jrnl. Physics* XXXIX. 484/2 The major purpose of this paper is to determine .. the normal-mode longitudinal-vibration frequencies of the chain.

d. *Geol.* Applied to a fault and to faulting in which the relative downward movement occurred in the strata situated on the upper side of the fault plane. So ***normal-faulted*** adj.

1876 A. H. GREEN *Geol.* xi. 382 The direction of the hade in a normal fault. 1878 J. LECONTE in *Amer. Jrnl. Sci. & Arts* XVI. 99 Thus arise two distinct slips: In the one, the more common or normal, the strata drop on the hanging-wall side of the fissure, in the other or reverse fault, the strata on the hanging-wall side is slidden up and over the other side by the sheer force of the horizontal pressure. 1902 *Jrnl. Geol.* X. 873 Orographic blocks may..display an arrangement in zigzags or *en échelon*, which it is difficult to explain upon any other basis than that of normal faulting. 1944 A. HOLMES *Princ. Physical Geol.* vi. 79 Normal faults involve an extension of the faulted beds. 1974 FLINT & SKINNER *Physical Geol.* iv. 293/2 Normal faults are caused by tensional forces that tend to pull the crust apart, and also by forces tending to expand the crust by pushing it upward from below. *Ibid.* 294/1 In the Earth's crust are many zones that have been deformed repeatedly by normal faulting. 1975 *Nature* 1 May 22/2 This part represents a tensional arm..bifurcating into normal-faulted shear zones south of Sinai.

e. *Statistics.* = GAUSSIAN *a.* b.

1893 K. Pearson in *Nature* 26 Oct. 615/2 As verification note that for the normal probability curve $3\mu_2^2 = \mu_4$ and $\mu_3 = 0$. **1894** —— in *Phil. Trans. R. Soc.* A. CLXXXV. 72 A frequency-curve, which, for practical purposes, can be represented by the error curve, will for the remainder of this paper be termed a normal curve. **1897** *Proc. R. Soc.* LXII. 176 A random selection from a normal distribution. **1920** [see Gaussian *a.* b]. **1928** T. C. Fry *Probability & its Engin. Uses* viii. 244 Both the Binomial and the Poisson Laws, under suitable conditions, approach the Normal Law as a limit. **1938** A. E. Waugh *Elem. Statistical Method* vi. 94 Many phenomena of biology, economics, psychology, education, etc., even though not exactly normal in distribution, can be described roughly by the normal curve. **1951** Dixon & Massey *Introd. Statistical Anal.* v. 63 Many practical problems have statistical answers based on the 'assumption' that the distribution of the population is normal... The truth of this assumption may be checked by plotting the sample cumulative-percentage points on normal-probability paper. **1968** *Brit. Med. Bull.* XXIV. 211/1 One of these [alternatives for small samples] consists simply in plotting the individual sample values..on 'Normal-probability' graph paper—this is a special graph paper whose vertical scale has been 'stretched' in such a way that the S-shaped cumulative Normal curve is transformed graphically into a straight line.

f. *Med.* Of a saline solution: containing the same concentration of sodium chloride as the blood.

1895 *Jrnl. Physiol.* XVIII. 50 Neither can the injection of normal saline be of much benefit. **1924** L. Clendening *Mod. Methods Treatment* ii. 153 Normal salt solution given in subcutaneous areolar tissue (beneath the breasts or in the thighs) or intravenously is very frequently used in surgical shock. *Ibid.*, In normal salt solution with glucose any concentration could be used, without hemolysis. **1970** F. N. Douglas *Essentials Pharmacology in Clinical Nursing* iii. 22 Physiologic normal saline (0·9 per cent) is used for treating dehydration in the absence of acidosis.

g. Physics. ***normal state*** = *ground state* (ground *sb.* 18).

See also sense 2 i.

1914 [see N I. 4 b]. **1922** A. D. Udden tr. *Bohr's Theory of Spectra* ii. ii. 32 All the atoms exist in that stationary state in which the value of the energy is a minimum. This state I shall call the normal state. **1952** R. W. Ditchburn *Light* xvii. 550 The atom very quickly makes a transition back to the normal state re-emitting the radiation. **1963** G. F. Lothian *Electrons in Atoms* iii, Mercury atoms have quantized energy levels..above the normal or 'ground' state.

h. *spec.* = heterosexual.

1914 E. M. Forster *Maurice* (1971) xxii. 106 Against my will I have become normal. I cannot help it.

i. *Physics.* Pertaining to or characteristic of a substance that is not in the superconducting state.

1927 *Nature* 3 Dec. 818/2 The resistance became normal at a certain critical value of the magnetic field. **1938** D. Shoenberg *Superconductivity* i. 4 Apart from the loss of resistance the metal appeared to have identical properties both in the superconducting and normal states. **1955** H. B. G. Casimir in W. Pauli *Niels Bohr* 119 The theory describing the normal state when the absolute temperature tends towards zero is extremely simple. **1968** C. G. Kuper *Introd. Theory Superconductivity* i. 6 An upper bound for the resistance in the superconducting state can be established. If R_n is the resistance of the specimen when normal, then $R/R_n < 10^{-15}$.

j. ***normal forest***, a collection of trees at various stages of development, organized to provide a regular yield of timber.

1928 R. S. Troup *Silvicultural Systems* i. 1 With the object of ensuring future sustained yields the ideal of the normal forest has been created. Such a forest contains a regular and complete succession of age-classes..in correct proportion, density, and distribution... The normal forest can hardly be said to exist in reality; rather it should be regarded as an ideal to be aimed at. **1962** C. E. Hart *Practical Forestry* vi. 109 The term normal forest is used for a forest or woodland or group of woodlands containing a regular and complete succession of age classes, from the youngest to the oldest.

k. *Physics.* Applied to a component of a superfluid that is regarded as not having the properties of a superfluid and as co-existing at the atomic level with a component that does have them, in a proportion that decreases with decreasing temperature.

1947 L. Tizas in *Physical Rev.* LXXII. 842/2 The density [of the Bose-Einstein liquid]..will be subdivided into two parts: $\rho = \rho_n + \rho_s$ where ρ_n is the density connected with the 'molecules' of the gas and ρ_s refers to the 'background' in which the molecules are moving. The subscripts refer to 'normal' and 'superfluid', a terminology which will be explained below. *Ibid.* 853/2 In this 'anomalous' region [*sc.* between about 1°K and 2·19°K] the liquid is a mixture of a normal component (like helium I) and a superfluid component. **1967** J. Wilks *Properties of Liquid & Solid Helium* iii. 39 Two baths of liquid helium II..at slightly different temperatures..are connected by a fine capillary. The capillary almost completely inhibits the flow of the normal fluid, on the other hand the superfluid having zero viscosity, may pass freely. **1975** *Nature* 10 Apr. 480/3 At a finite temperature the superfluid phase [of ^{4}He] behaves like a mixture of two fluids: a 'normal' component, behaving like an ordinary viscous liquid..; and a 'superfluid' component, ..closely associated with the atoms in the Bose condensate.

3. ***normal school*** [after F. *école normale* (1794)], a school for the training of teachers. Also *ellipt.*

1834 *Edin. Rev.* LIX. 491 The system of Primary Schools, which the French..have..denominated Normal. **1842** Brande *Dict. Sci.*, etc. 1089/1 Normal schools form a regular part of the establishments for education in many Continental states. **1885** *Harper's Mag.* Jan. 199/2 Polly..had been a pupil in the Normal School. **1888** *Nat. Educ. Assoc. U.S. Addresses & Proc. 1887* 478 We say that normal-school training is as essential to good teaching as the work of a medical school to the physician. *Ibid.* 502 A course of normal instruction. **1925** in P. W. Slosson *Great Crusade* (1931) xv. 431 Unlawful for any teacher in any of the universities, normals, and all other public schools..to teach ..that man has descended from a lower order of animals. **1939** H. G. Wells *Holy Terror* iv. i. 359 An increasing number of women are taking up professions now; at architecture, catering, various industries, normal teaching ..they are practically as good as men or better. **1960** P. E. Burrup *Teacher & Public School Syst.* iv. vii. 275 'Normal Schools' for the preparation of teachers..have been replaced by teachers' colleges, liberal-arts colleges, and universities, each with a college of education. **1960** Curtis & Boultwood *Introd. Hist. Eng. Educ.* xii. 277 In that year [*sc.* 1836] a normal school of design was established. *Ibid.* 278 The Normal School of Design became the Royal College of Art in 1896.

4. Philos. ***normal form*** (see quot. 1950).

1948 *Mind* LVII. 173 He [*sc.* Boole] introduced two notions which are of the greatest importance, namely, that of a *truth-function* and that of a *normal form.* **1950** L. M. Hammond et al. tr. *Hilbert & Ackermann's Math. Logic* i. §3. 11 (*heading*) Normal form for logical expressions. *Ibid.* 12 Any combination of sentences can be brought into a certain normal form by means of equivalence transformations;.. this normal form consists of a conjunction of disjunctions in which each component of the disjunction is either an elementary sentence or the negation of one. **1952** *Mind* LXI. 564 The procedure is to be applied to normal forms, reduction to which is a matter of propositional logic. **1965** E. J. Lemmon *Beginning Logic* 189 Normal forms have a certain interest in connection with the truth-table method, since they provide an independent test as to whether a wff is tautologous, contingent, or inconsistent; and they are also used in certain proofs of the completeness of the propositional calculus. **1973** J. J. Zeman *Modal Logic* viii. 117 The normal-form theorem holds for systems LS1° and LS1.

B. *sb.* †**1.** A regular verb. *Obs. rare*$^{-1}$.

1530 Palsgr. 394 If the verbe in this tonge be nat a normal.

2. *Geom.* A perpendicular; a straight line at right angles to the tangent or tangent plane at any point of a curve or curved surface.

1727–38 Chambers *Cycl.* s.v. *Subnormal*, The point in the axis of a curve, where a normal or perpendicular..cuts the axis. **1797** *Phil. Trans.* LXXXVIII. 381 The lines so drawn ..shall be normals to the parabolas at their intersections with the ellipse. **1816** tr. *Lacroix's Calculus* 81 It is often more convenient..to consider the tangent and the normal, by means of their equation. **1877** *Encycl. Brit.* VI. 676/1 How crystals might be represented..by their normals, that is, by lines drawn from the centre of the system vertical to the faces.

3. *Physics.* The average or mean of observed quantities.

1859 Bache *Discuss. Magn. & Meteorol. Obs.* i. 4 The last mean thus obtained for each observing hour and each month has been called 'the normal'. **1890** *Nature* 9 Oct. 603 The barometer normals fall more as we approach the Antarctic.

4. a. The usual state or condition.

1890 *Daily News* 11 Oct. 5/4 It does not require a very strong gale to..raise the level of the Neva three or four feet above its normal. **1896** *Current Hist.* (Buffalo) VI. 373 The importation of raw sugars last year did not reach normal, or what it was in 1892. **1957** M. Spark *Comforters* v. 114 She snapped back at him. And so, in his need for their relations to return to a nice normal, he said peaceably, [etc.].

b. *ellipt.* Normal temperature.

1896 *Allbutt's Syst. Med.* I. 149 The dictum..that in fever the organism is adjusted to a higher normal.

5. a. A normal variety of anything; that which, or a person who, is healthy and is not impaired in any way.

1894 W. Bateson *Study of Variation* 17 For the belief that such races are descended from the putative normal scarcely ever rests on proof. **1901** *Amer. Jrnl. Psychol.* XII. 235 The blind rats learned the original task as well as the normals. **1908** *Daily Chron.* 14 Oct. 4/4 We might divide them [*sc.* criminals] into three groups:—Normals, Juveniles and children; and The degenerate. **1916** J. S. Haldane *Organism & Environment* (1917) iv. 102 The normals of anatomy are not mere physical structures, nor are the normals of physiology mere averages: they are manifestations of the life of an organism regarded as a whole. **1940** *Psychol. Bull.* XXXVII. 425 Scales may be successively discovered and standardized on a reservoir sample of normals. **1964** M. Critchley *Developmental Dyslexia* vii. 40 Measuring the reaction time..in normals and in dyslexics. **1973** *Nature* 12 Jan. 99/1 The response of lymphocytes from normals or leukaemics to low (7μg ml.$^{-1}$) doses of PHA.

b. A heterosexual person.

1966 *New Statesman* 29 Apr. 623/3 He [*sc.* Coward]'s working for the same kind of audience—Knightsbridge normals—and still going as near the knuckle as he thinks they can abide. **1971** M. McCarthy *Birds of America* 304 A female *clocharde* had reason to shrink from 'normals'.

Hence **'normalcy** chiefly *U.S.* = normality; **'normalist.**

1857 Davies & Peck *Math. Dict.* 386 If we denote the co-ordinates of the point of contact, and normalcy, by *x''* and *y''*. **1878** Bellingham tr. *Haulleville's Aspects Cath. & Protestantism* 184 The fellow-countrymen of Ovid, of Horace and of Virgil, were not all normalists. **1893** *Nation* 30 July 47/1 Believers..in the mathematical normalcy of the female mind. **1920** W. G. Harding in F. L. Allen *Only Yesterday* (1931) ii. 41 America's present need is not heroics but healing; not nostrums but normalcy; not revolution but restoration. **1929** G. N. Clark in *S.P.E. Tract* xxxiii. 417 If..'normalcy' is ever to become an accepted word it will presumably be because the late President Harding did not know any better. **1932** G. K. Chesterton *Sidelights* ii. xiv. 182 Life in a modern town, whatever else it is, is not Normalcy. **1939** *John o' London's* 9 June 369/1 That insistent normalcy of men who cannot afford to permit themselves to be thrown off balance. **1951** M. McLuhan *Mech. Bride* 47/1 Professor Kinsey's surveys, with their economist-like normalcy charts. **1957** V. J. Kehoe *Technique Film & T.V. Make-up* i. 17 On stage, where strong lights and distance of the actors from the audience wash out and flatten the features, make-up restores to the face the look of normalcy in both color and contour. **1965** *New Statesman* 7 May 733/1 A kind of spectral normalcy.

normalism ('nɔːməlɪz(ə)m). *rare.* [f. normal *a.* and *sb.* + -ism.] The quality or state of being normal.

1891 F. W. Bain *Antichrist* ii. 113 The planing away of all gnarled and knotty characteristics, the reducing each individual to precisely the same external appearance. This is the essence and the consequence of the impulse to normalism.

normality (nɔː'mælɪtɪ). [f. normal *a.* + -ity: cf. F. *normalité*, It. *-ita*, Sp. *-idad.*]

1. a. The character or state of being normal.

a **1849** Poe *Eureka* Wks. 1865 II. 153 In a condition of positive normality or rightfulness. **1866** *Athenæum* 29 Dec. 873 Normality..gives us only the negative notion of the absence of defect. **1896** *Allbutt's Syst. Med.* I. 150 Those parts in which it is their business to maintain constancy, that is normality.

b. *spec.* in *Statistics* (cf. normal *a.* and *sb.* A. 2 e).

1928 *Amer. Jrnl. Psychol.* XL. 348 We can change 0·93 into a P.E. [*sc.* probable error] by multiplying by 0·845 (assuming normality of distribution). **1938** A. E. Waugh *Elem. Statistical Method* vi. 95 In most statistical problems there is no a priori reason for expecting normality of distribution—no reason for believing in advance that the data will be distributed as are the coefficients of the expansion $(\frac{1}{2} + \frac{1}{2})^n$. **1968** *Brit. Med. Bull.* XXIV. 211/1 The assumption of Normality is central to the most powerful statistical techniques. **1974** *Nature* 22 Mar. 288/1 A weighted least squares analysis of the two sets of correlations ..provides (given normality) a test of goodness of fit of the model.

2. *Chem.* The concentration of a solution as a proportion of the normal concentration.

1903 *Sci. Abstr.* VI. 315 Boric acid was agitated..with an excess of aqueous hydrochloric acids of different normalities. **1928** A. W. Wellings *Volumetric Analysis* ii. 41 The normality of the acid solution will be 0·1N. × 18·6/50. **1966** *McGraw-Hill Encycl. Sci. & Technol.* III. 361/2 In double-decomposition reactions normality may be an ambiguous concept unless referred to a specific reaction. **1972** *Nature* 8 Sept. 69/3 At higher concentrations of the salt ..the viscosity was considerably smaller (1·60 at a normality of 0·50).

normalizable ('nɔːməlaɪzəb(ə)l), *a.* [f. normaliz(e *v.* + -able.] Capable of being normalized.

1939 V. Rojansky *Introd. Quantum Mech.* i. 37 If *u* and all of its derivatives approach zero when $|x| \to \infty$, and if $\int_{-\infty}^{\infty} \bar{u}u\, dx$ is finite, we call *u* a normalizable function (this use of the term is not standard in the literature). **1955** O. Klein in W. Pauli *Niels Bohr* 116 There may be some reason to expect that the most obvious formulation of the interaction problem on these lines should already give rise to a normalizable theory, the effect of the 'wrong' states being limited to further infinite contributions to the mass and charge of the electron. **1968** *Physics Bull.* Nov. 373/2 A normalizable state ϕ_0.

normali'zation. [f. normalize *v.* + -ation.]

a. The action or process of making normal or of normalizing (in any sense).

1882 in Ogilvie. **1892** tr. *Schäffle's Impossib. Soc. Democracy* 107 This whole process of normalization. **1894** J. R. C. Hall *A.-S. Dict.* Pref., Normalisations have..been generally avoided. **1916** *Jrnl. Iron & Steel Inst.* XCIV. 10 It is not suggested to abandon the term 'normalise', but to define normalisation as a treatment which will give equalisation and not metal of abnormal variations. **1929** [see normalize *v.* 3 a]. **1944** Gregory & Simons *Heat-Treatment Steel* xx. 273 The steels not requiring normalization after forging should be cooled off in lime, then annealed. **1959** E. M. McCormick *Digital Computer Primer* xi. 155 To facilitate normalization, many computers have a special instruction..that counts the positions the number must be shifted left to be normalized. This count is then used to modify the exponent. **1967** C. L. Wrenn *Word & Symbol* p. xii, The problem of normalisation for Old English still requires scholarly attention. **1972** Bergman & Bruckner *Introd. Computers & Computer Programming* vi. 169 The only exception to the normalization rule is zero; there are many ways in which we can represent zero. **1972** P. W. Williams *Numerical Computation* ix. 162 One method of normalization is to divide all the elements of a vector by the largest element so that vectors have unity as the largest element. Alternatively, each element could be divided by the sum of the squares of the elements of the vector in which case vectors have unit length. **1973** *Amer. Speech 1969* XLIV. 220 Two sociolinguistic problems: immigrant bilingualism and language normalization.

b. *Psychol.* The subconscious process whereby the mental image of a shape, pattern, etc., is changed to resemble something more familiar; also *attrib.* See normalizing *vbl. sb.* b.

1935 K. Koffka *Princ. Gestalt Psychol.* xi. 499 Autonomous changes occur against the forces of normalization and pointing. **1971** J. Hochberg in Woodworth & Schlosberg *Experimental Psychol.* (1972) xii. 469 The normalization effects might thus simply be instances of the figural after effects produced by satiation.

c. *Politics.* The achieving of 'normal' or stable political relationships between two countries, freq. between a major power and a weaker or dependent country.

1938 *Times Review of 1937* p. vii/1 The 'normalization' of Polish-German relations. **1955** *Times* 22 Aug. 5/3 The Yugoslav Press has been complaining for some time that the process of 'normalization' with Albania was lagging behind other east European countries. **1956** *Ann. Reg. 1955* 260 'Normalization' of relations with the satellites. **1962** *Daily Tel.* 18 Sept. 12/2 President Tito can be well pleased. 'Normalisation' has been attained without compromise of Jugoslavia's freedom of action, in defence of which he broke with Stalin. **1968** *Economist* 7 Sept. 33/1 It will permit Mr. Dubcek, his party leadership and government to resume the road towards what is laughingly called 'normalisation' just so long as they stick to Moscow's interpretation of normality.

normalize ('nɔːməlaɪz), *v.* [f. NORMAL *a.* + -IZE.] **1. a.** *trans.* To make normal or regular.

1865 *Pall Mall G.* No. 175. 1/1 To normalize an abnormal condition. **1880** R. G. WHITE *Every-Day Engl.* 72 A scheme for simplifying and normalizing orthography.

absol. **1892** tr. *Schäffle's Impossib. Soc. Democracy* 100 We must normalize also according to work.

b. *intr.* To become normal.

1923 *Contemp. Rev.* Mar. 366 If a rise in the price of tin should follow on the already normalising price of materials.

2. *Metallurgy. trans.* To heat (steel) to above the transformation range (about 700°C or more) and allow to cool in still air at room temperature, so as to remove any effects of strain-hardening, produce a finer grain structure, and improve the mechanical properties and machinability.

1902 *Jrnl. Iron & Steel Inst.* LXI. plate XIV (*caption*) Mr. Stead's Austenite normalized. **1916** *Ibid.* XCIV. 26 (*heading*) Effect of heating to 850°C., quenching in oil and tempering at 550°C., compared with the same steels simply normalized by heating to 1000°C. and cooling in air. **1937** R. T. ROLFE *Steels for User* vi. 114 Since quenching in a liquid medium was for a long time prohibited, these castings were either annealed or normalised, followed by a tempering process. **1970** E. N. SIMONS *Dict. Ferrous Metals* 155 The rate of cooling differs according to the mass of the piece, a thin cross-section cooling more rapidly than a thick, so that in the large masses the core is annealed rather than normalized. **1971** B. SCHARF *Engin. & its Lang.* ii. 13 Steel is often normalised before hardening or machining.

3. a. Chiefly *Math.* and *Physics.* To multiply (a series, function, or variable) by a factor that makes the norm or some associated quantity (as an integral) equal to a particular value, usu. unity.

1921 *Proc. Lond. Math. Soc.* XX. 125 The sequence $\{\psi_n(x)\}$ being normalised and orthogonal. **1929** CONDON & MORSE *Quantum Mech.* i. 30 Of course, when $\Psi\bar{\Psi}$ is to be used as probability it has to be so normalized, by choice of a constant multiplier for Ψ, that $\int\Psi\bar{\Psi}\,dv = 1$... The same normalization is required from the distributed charge standpoint to express the fact that the total charge is *e*. **1934** W. V. HOUSTON *Princ. Math. Physics* ix. 134 A function can be normalized by multiplying it by a constant. When it is normalized, $\int_a^b R_i^2\,dx = 1$. **1956** *Math. Tables & Other Aids to Computation* X. 2 The fundamental sequence was normalized so that $-1 \leqslant u_j \leqslant 1$. **1961** POWELL & CRASEMANN *Quantum Mech.* ix. 286 A vector of unit norm is said to be normalized... Every nonzero vector can be normalized. **1975** *Nature* 13 Feb. 563/1 To normalise variations among tissues, responses are reported as percentage of the maximum increase, calculated for each preparation.

b. *Computers.* To express (a number in floating-point representation) in the standard form as regards the position of the radix point, which is usually immediately preceding the first non-zero digit.

1946 *Ann. Computation Lab. Harvard Univ.* I. 495 The quantity to be normalized lies in storage counter A. **1957** D. D. MCCRACKEN *Digital Computer Programming* xvii. 205 The first two steps convert the code number into an unnormalized floating point form. The third does nothing but normalize it, i.e., it brings the first nonzero digit into position three of the accumulator. **1962** HUSKEY & KORN *Computer Handbk.* xv. 23 It is desirable to obtain as many significant figures in the answers as possible. In floating-point systems this can be accomplished by normalizing the nonzero numbers at each step. **1973** H. DINTER *Introd. Computing* v. 167 The decimal exponent will be a value that is adjusted for normalizing the number. For example, if the number 26·5 is to be expressed in normalized form, it will be presented as $\cdot 265 \times 10^2$.

Hence '**normalized** *ppl. a.*

1880 *Academy* 9 Oct. 256 Prose texts in a consistently normalised spelling. **1894** J. R. C. HALL *A.-S. Dict.* Pref., Prof. Toller has chosen a..normalised form.

normalizer ('nɔːməlaɪzə(r)). [f. NORMALIZE *v.* + -ER[1].] Someone or something that normalizes.

1926 *Heating & Ventilating Mag.* (U.S.) Oct. 110/1 (*caption*) The Sjostrom Atmospheric Normalizer. *Ibid.* 110/2 When the Normalizer is operating it moves about 800 cu. ft. of air per minute. **1946** *House Beautiful* Nov. 290 If you live in a hard-water area, it helps to use a good water normalizer..in the water. **1960** P. DORF tr. M. M. Guxman in J. A. Fishman *Readings Sociol. of Lang.* (1968) 773 The puristic strivings of the German normalizers of the 17th and 18th centuries were ridiculed, the striving of many normalizers both in Western as well as Eastern countries to counteract the appearance of the new vital tendencies of the colloquial variety of the language was underscored. *Ibid.* 777 It is a known fact that the French normalizers of the 15th and 16th centuries oriented themselves towards the language of Paris, but towards the form in which it was spoken at court.

normalizing ('nɔːməlaɪzɪŋ), *vbl. sb.* [f. NORMALIZ(E *v.* + -ING[1].] The action of the vb. NORMALIZE.

1909 *Jrnl. Iron & Steel Inst.* LXXIX. 350 (*heading*) Normalising. **1935** A. B. KINZEL in *Symp. Welding Iron & Steel* (Iron & Steel Inst.) II. iii. 424 Complete normalising or stress-relieving of the entire structure should be considered essential if high internal stress exists. **1970** O. DOPPING *Computers & Data Processing* vii. 112 In computers with built-in operations for floating-point arithmetic..normalizing usually occurs as a special operation.

b. *Psychol.* = NORMALIZATION b.

1929 J. J. GIBSON in *Jrnl. Experimental Psychol.* XII. 3 The first kind [of change] he [*sc.* Wulf] calls *normalizing* (Normalizierung), *i.e.* a change (presumably in the reproductions) in the direction of a familiar object. **1935** K. KOFFKA *Princ. Gestalt Psychol.* xi. 499 Normalizing occurs when the reproductions approach successively a familiar form. **1970** L. ZUSNE *Visual Perception of Form* vii. 312 Making the reproduced figure resemble some well-known shape (normalizing).

normally ('nɔːməlɪ), *adv.* [f. NORMAL *a.* + -LY.]

†**1.** In a regular manner; regularly. *Obs. rare.*

1597 A. M. tr. *Guillemeau's Fr. Chirurg.* 50/2 Thervnto are many thinges reqvired, which I heere normallye and rightlye will prosecute. **1599** —— tr. *Gabelhouer's Bk. Physicke* 102/2 Applye the same on his Breste, 3 or 4 nightes normallye after other.

2. Under normal or ordinary conditions.

1853 CARPENTER *Princ. Hum. Physiol.* (ed. 3) §224 The mode in which the first production of tendons and ligaments is normally accomplished. **1861** GOSCHEN *For. Exch.* 94 Every kind of produce, which normally..would have risen in value. **1882** FARRAR *Early Chr.* I. 161 Normally, and as a whole, human law is on the side of divine order.

3. In a normal manner; in the usual way.

1871 BLACKIE *Four Phases Mor.* I. 70 Constant action and reaction in every normally developed human mind.

4. At right angles.

1869 TYNDALL in *Fortn. Rev.* Feb. 246 When we look normally, or perpendicularly, at an incipient cloud.

5. *Statistics.* In accordance with the normal distribution.

1928 T. C. FRY *Probability & its Engin. Uses* viii. 243 It is absurd to speak of a man of negative height:..it simply cannot occur. Yet if height were distributed normally, the second property of the Law would assign a finite probability to this absurdity. **1951** DIXON & MASSEY *Introd. Statistical Anal.* v. 63 Often a research worker has sufficient data and enough experience..to be able to specify the type of transformation of measurement which will give a normally distributed variable. **1971** *Nature* 3 Sept. 19/1, I take as my datum the fact that Englishmen are normally distributed in height with a mean of 5 feet 8 inches.

normalness ('nɔːməlnɪs). *rare.* [f. NORMAL *a.* and *sb.* + -NESS.] = NORMALITY.

1854 GEO. ELIOT tr. *Feuerbach's Essence Christianity* xvi. 159 The agreement of others is therefore my criterion of the normalness, the universality, the truth of my thoughts. **1972** *Language* XLVIII. 314 We suspect that for some speakers, some of the sentences that we have claimed to be 'odd' will sound quite normal. This is to be expected if the oddness or normalness of a given stress contour depends partly on the speaker's ability to provide a satisfactory context.

Norman ('nɔːmən), *sb.*[1] and *a.* Also 4 **noreman, normen**, 7 **Normane**. [Orig. in pl., a. OF. *Normans, -manz* (AF. *-maunz*), pl. of *Normant* (later *-mand*) NORMAND, a reduced form of the Teut. or Scand. NORTHMAN 1, which also appears as *Norman* in OE., OFris., OHG., MDu., and MSw. (mod.G. *Normann*, Du. *Noorman*, Norw. *Norrman*). Hence med.L. *Normannus*.]

A. *sb.* **1. a.** A native or inhabitant of Normandy; one belonging to, or descended from, the mixed Scandinavian and Frankish race inhabiting that part of France.

c **1205** LAY. 7116 Seoððen comen Normans mid heore nið crafte and nemneden heo Lundres. **1297** R. GLOUC. (Rolls) 7498 þus was in normannes hond þat lond ibroȝt. *Ibid.* 7500 Of þe normans beþ heyemen..of engelonde. **1338** R. BRUNNE *Chron.* (1810) 75 þe Normans in þe South wer in so grete affray. **1387** TREVISA *Higden* (Rolls) I. 29 þe sixte [book is] from þe Danes to þe Normans. þe seuenþe fro Normans to oure tyme. *c* **1425** *Engl. Conq. Irel.* 140 Thay anoon..of the Normannes weren shamefully receyued. **1538** STARKEY *England* I. iv. 123 Therby ys testyfyd our subiectyon to the Normannys. **1602** SHAKS. *Ham.* III. ii. 36 Neyther hauing the accent of Christians, nor the gate of Christian, Pagan, or Norman. **1736** THOMSON *Liberty* IV. 739 The haughty Norman seiz'd at once an isle, For which ..The Roman, Saxon, Dane had toil'd and bled. **1818** CRUISE *Digest* (ed. 2) III. 157 The next name of dignity is *comes*, earl, which was also introduced here by the Normans. **1874** STUBBS *Const. Hist.* (1897) I. 270 Of the constitutional history of the Normans of Normandy we have very little information.

Comb. **1876** TENNYSON *Harold* (Show-day at Battle Abbey), Here fought, here fell, our Norman-slander'd king.

†**b.** A Northman, a Norwegian. *Obs. rare.*

Cf. the OE. pl. *Normen* in this sense.

1605 [see NORWEGIAN B. 1]. **1797** *Encycl. Brit.* (ed. 3) I. 570/2 A people so versed in maritime affairs, and so adventurous, as the ancient Normans were.

2. = Norman-French (see B. 3 b).

†Also in Sc. form *Normans*, after *Scots* = Scottish.

1646 DRUMM. OF HAWTH. *Wks.* (1711) 213 The Laws of England, which William the Conqueror imposed.., mufled up in barbarous Normans. **1797** *Encycl. Brit.* (ed. 3) VI. 667/2 Our language..is now a mixture of Saxon,..Danish, Norman, and modern French. **1819** SCOTT *Ivanhoe* iv, I sufficiently understand Norman to follow your meaning. **1879** WALFORD *Londoniana* II. 98 The upper classes spoke Norman and lived as Normans.

B. *adj.* **1.** Belonging or pertaining to, characteristic of, the Normans.

1589 PUTTENHAM *Eng. Poesie* II. xii. (Arb.) 130 Scholers .., who not content with the vsuall Normane or Saxon word, would conuert the very Latine..word into vulgar French. **1640** BAKER *Chron.* (1653) 38 Footsteps remaining of the Norman language in the English tongue. **1698–9** DRYDEN *Sigism. & Guisc.* 1 While Norman Tancred in Salerno reigned. **1736** THOMSON *Liberty* IV. 773 The Barons .., Both those of English and of Norman race. **1797** *Encycl. Brit.* (ed. 3) II. 229/2 The rage of building fortified castles ..among the Norman princes. **1819** SCOTT *Ivanhoe* v, The fantastic fashions of Norman chivalry. **1879** HARLAN *Eyesight* viii. 112 What are called Norman Capitals, in which the characteristic strokes are excessively heavy, and the others but lightly traced.

Comb. **1877** TENNYSON *Harold* I. i, I say not this, as being Half Norman-blooded.

2. ***Norman Conquest***, the conquest of England by the Normans under William I, which took place in 1066. (Cf. CONQUEST *sb.* 3.)

1605 CAMDEN *Rem.* (1623) 144 Many approoued customes, lawes, manners,..haue the English alwayes borrowed of..the French..by the Norman Conquest. **1708** J. CHAMBERLAYNE *Pres. St. Gt. Brit.* I. II. xiii. (1710) 100 Our Ancestors, who after the Norman Conquest, were generally skill'd in the French tongue. **1755** JOHNSON *Dict.*, Hist. E i/2 This change seems not to have been the effect of the Norman conquest. **1827** *Gentl. Mag.* XCVII. I. 607 The Norman-Conquest is one of the most splendid events in history. **1874** STUBBS *Const. Hist.* (1897) I. 269 The effect of the Norman Conquest on the character and constitution of the English was threefold.

3. ***Norman-English*** or ***-Saxon***, English as spoken by the Normans, or as influenced by them. *rare.*

1589 PUTTENHAM *Eng. Poesie* II. xii. (Arb.) 130 Our Normane English which hath growen since William the Conquerour. **1819** SCOTT *Ivanhoe* vii, The following [ejaculations] were distinctly heard in the Norman-English, or mixed language of the country. **1845** STODDART *Gram.* in *Encycl. Metrop.* I. 74/2 *Strong*..seems to have been anciently adopted in the Noman-Saxon Adverbially.

b. ***Norman-French***, the form of French spoken by the Normans, or the later form of this in English legal use (Law French).

1605 CAMDEN *Rem.* (1623) 26 By setting downe their lawes in the Norman-French. **1797** *Encycl. Brit.* (ed. 3) VI. 667/2 After that the Saxon blended with the Norman French. **1865** NICHOLS *Britton* I. p. xlvi, The jargon..of our legal writers,..which has also been commonly termed Norman French. **1900** TOLLER *Hist. Eng. Lang.* 209 For some time the natural speech of the Norman was Norman-French.

4. The distinguishing epithet of a form of architecture, or its details, developed by the Normans and employed in England after the Conquest.

1797 *Encycl. Brit.* (ed. 3) II. 221/2 There seems to be little or no grounds for a distinction between the Saxon and Norman architecture. **1815** J. SMITH *Panorama Sci. & Art* I. 134 In many small churches..the Norman door has been suffered to remain. **1828** *Gentl. Mag.* XCVIII. II. 519 The noble structures of Norman architecture, as it is called in this country. **1842** GWILT *Archit.* §392 That called the Norman style, which continued from 1066 to nearly 1200. **1889** MERRIMAN *Slave of Lamp* xviii, The narrow Norman windows had been framed with unpainted wood.

5. ***Norman line, shell, thrush*** (see quots.).

1713 PETIVER *Anat. Anim. Amb.* 4/1 *Auris marina*.., Long Sea Ear or Norman Shell. **1883** JONCAS *Fish. Canada* 12 (Intern. Fish. Exhib.), The bank fishing is made with long lines which our fishermen call 'Norman lines'. **1891** *Cent. Dict.* s.v. *Thrush*, Norman thrush, the mistle-thrush.

norman ('nɔːmən), *sb.*[2] *Naut.* [= Du. *noorman*, G. *normann*, Sw. *norman*, Da. *normand*; perh. the same word as prec., but the connexion is not clear.] (See quots.)

1769 FALCONER *Dict. Marine* (1780), *Norman*, a name given to a short wooden bar, thrust into one of the holes of the windlass in a merchant-ship, whereon to fasten the cable. *c* **1850** *Rudim. Navig.* (Weale) 135 *Norman*, a square fid of oak, or short carling, fixed through the head of the rudder of East India ships, to prevent the loss of the rudder in case of its being unshipped. **1865** *Dubl. Even. Mail* 22 Sept., The bight of the chain flew over the norman (this is an iron bar that goes through the windlass to keep the chain clear when running out).

attrib. **1874** THEARLE *Naval Archit.* 66 An iron forging, termed a 'spider', with a square hole or a socket in the top to receive the norman head, is let down over the..rudder.

†**Normand**. *Obs.* Also 4 -mant, 6 -mund. [a. OF. *Normand, -mant*.] = NORMAN *sb.*[1] 1 a.

1338 R. BRUNNE *Chron.* (1810) 59 William þe Normant aryued vp at Douer. *Ibid.* 70 Toward þis lond þei drouh.. With Normandes inouh, of Flandres & of France. **13..** *Cursor M.* 24781 (Gött.), In-till ingland þan for to fare, Apon þe normandes [*Cott.* normanz] for to fight. *c* **1420** *Chron. R. Glouc.* (Rolls) 6701 þeruore of Normandes with him so muche folc he broȝte. *c* **1425** WYNTOUN *Chron.* I. xiv. 1371 þe Normandeis [*v.r.* Normundis] eftyr wan Inglande.

Normandy ('nɔːməndɪ). [Name of a region of northern France.] ***Normandy butter***: butter made in Normandy. Also *ellipt.*

1902 J. T. LAW *Grocer's Man.* (ed. 2) 632/2 Normandy butter. **1962** L. DEIGHTON *Ipcress File* ii. 19, I..bought.. some Normandy butter and garlic sausage. **1973** *Guardian* 26 Jan. 9/1 'Butter is half the price here, even French butter,' she said, packing pounds of best cream Normandy into her shopping trolley. **1975** R. BUTLER *Where all Girls are Sweeter* i. 5 There was still a slab of Sainsbury's Normandy butter.

b. ***Normandy vellum***, a strong, hand-made paper designed to imitate the qualities of parchment.

1935 S. BECKETT *Echo's Bones*, This edition is limited to 327 copies of which 25 on Normandy vellum signed by the author are numbered 1 to xxv. **1968** *Amer. N. & Q.* VI. 158/1 There were only 212 copies [of the magazine *Pages*] of which 12.. are on Normandy vellum.

Normanesque (nɔːməˈnɛsk), *a.* [f. NORMAN *sb.*¹ + -ESQUE.] Suggestive of, similar to, the Norman style of architecture.

1844 *Civil Eng. & Arch. Jrnl.* VII. 125/2 The towers themselves have a Normanesque air. **1880** A. L. RITCHIE *Churches of St. Baldred* 57 Two Norman or Normanesque arches.

ˈ**Normanish**, *a. rare*⁻¹. [-ISH.] = NORMAN *a.*

1586 FERNE *Blaz. Gentrie* 229 Many a name of a Normanish signification liued landles in their new habitations in Neustria.

Normanism (ˈnɔːmənɪz(ə)m). [f. NORMAN *sb.*¹ + -ISM: cf. F. *normanisme*, Sp. and Pg. *normandismo*.] Prevalence of Norman rule or characteristics; tendency to favour or imitate the Normans.

1647 J. HARE (*title*), Plaine English to our wilfull Bearers with Normanisme. **1837** SKENE *Highland. Scotl.* (1902) II. 261 Previous to his accession in 1124 there is not a trace of Normanism, if I may be allowed the expression, in Scotland. **1866** *Cornh. Mag.* May 547 In looking for traces of Normanism in our national genius.. we do but lose our labour. **1877** TENNYSON *Harold* III. i, Edward too is English now, He hath clean repented of his Normanism.

ˈ**Normanist**, *sb.* (and *a.*) [f. NORMAN *sb.*¹ + -IST.] **a.** A favourer of the Normans.

1611 SPEED *Hist. Gt. Brit.* IX. ii. §14 Goodwin and Edmund.. fought with Adnothus (sometime Master of their Fathers horse, but now a Normanist).

b. (See quot. 1970.) Also as *adj.*

1943 G. VERNADSKY *Anc. Russia* VII. iv. 276 Let us then turn to an appraisal of the results of the tournement of the *Norsephiles* ('Normanists') and *Mysosnorses* ('Anti-Normanists'), so famous in the annals of the Russian historiography. *Ibid.* 277 The whole argument of the first Normanists was based on the premise that the very name of Rus spread from north to south and not otherwise. **1968** G. JONES *Hist. Vikings* III. iv. 247 The most readable 'Normanist' statement is still V. Thomsen's *Relations*. G. Vernadsky presents a summary of evidence for the 'anti-Normanist' view. *Ibid.* 264 To the disengaged it may well seem that the Normanist case has been as over-presented by a majority of Scandinavian historians as it has been played down by a majority of the historians of Russia. **1970** FOOTE & WILSON *Viking Achievement* vi. 220 Scholars have tended to side with one of two factions; the first firmly believing in the importance of the Scandinavian element in the founding of Russian towns and of the Russian state itself, the second discounting this influence almost completely (these two schools of thought are labelled in technical literature by the unfortunate terms 'Normanist' and 'anti-Normanist'). *Ibid.*, Discussion of the validity of this evidence is at the basis of the Normanist controversy. *Ibid.* 222 Both Normanists and anti-Normanists are more or less agreed that Ladoga was at one time dominated by Scandinavian traders.

Normaniˈzation. [f. next + -ATION.] The process of Normanizing.

1901 J. E. MORRIS *Welsh Wars Edw. I*, i. 4 A group of lords marchers co-operated in the work of Normanisation on the Welsh borders.

Normanize (ˈnɔːmənaɪz), *v.* [f. NORMAN *sb.*¹]

1. *intr.* To adopt the Norman tongue or manners.

1623 LISLE *Ælfric on O. & N. Test.* To Rdr. p. xiii, Hee would neuer haue borrowed so many words from abroad,.. except it were to please the Prince and Nobles, then all Normanizing. **1877** TENNYSON *Harold* III. ii, This lightning before death Plays on the word,—and Normanizes too!

2. *trans.* To make Norman or like the Normans.

a **1861** SIR F. PALGRAVE *Norm. & Eng.* V. 3 He never strove to Normanize the English people. **1875** LOWER *Eng. Surnames* (ed. 4) I. p. xxvii, The author's fault.. lies in Normanizing whatever he can.

Hence ˈ**Normanized** *ppl. a.*; ˈ**Normanizer**; ˈ**Normanizing** *vbl. sb.* and *ppl. a.*

1848 LYTTON *Harold* I. v, The Norman knights and youths profusely scattered amongst the Normanised Saxons. **1861** PEARSON *Early & Mid. Ages Eng.* 271 Others ..were Normanized Englishmen. **1868** FREEMAN *Norm. Conq.* (1875) II. vii. 82 If they were not Normanizers, they were at least Romanizers. **1878** *Encycl. Brit.* VIII. 289/2 Had the Normanizing schemes of the Confessor been carried out. **1885** *Dict. Nat. Biogr.* I. 260/1 A step in the direction of normanising and feudalising the civil government.

Normanly (ˈnɔːmənlɪ), *adv.* [-LY².] In the Norman manner; like the Normans.

1870 LOWELL *Among my Bks.* Ser. I. (1873) 152 His impartial brain—one lobe of which seems to have been Normanly refined and the other Saxonly sagacious.

Normannic (nɔːˈmænɪk), *a.* [f. NORMAN *sb.*¹ + -IC. Cf. F. *normannique*.] Of or belonging to the Normans.

1710 HEARNE *Collect.* (O.H.S.) II. 386 A sword.. in the Normannic Form. **1711** MADOX *Exch.* Ded. A ij b, That Imperial Crown, which from the Renowned Saxon and Normannick race rightfully descendeth to Your Majesty. *a* **1843** SOUTHEY *Comm.-pl. Bk.* (1849) I. 446 Before the conquest the popular language had been invaded by the Normannic.

Norˈmanno-, comb. form of NORMAN *a.*, as in ***Normanno-Gallican, -Saxonic.***

1724 WATERLAND *Athanasian Creed* v. 67 The inter-linear version which Mr. Wanley calls Normanno-Gallican. **1813** *Gentl. Mag.* I. 604/2 An original poem on the Battle of Hastings, in the Normanno-Saxonic of Turgotus.

ˈ**normated**, *ppl. a.* [f. L. *normāt-us*, f. *norma* NORM *sb.*] Conformed to a standard.

1893 FAIRBAIRN *Christ in Mod. Theol.* I. viii. 160 The theology was primary and normative, the church secondary and normated.

norˈmatic, *a. rare*⁻¹. [f. L. *norma* NORM *sb.* + -ATIC.] Conducted according to rule.

1597 A. M. tr. *Guillemeau's Fr. Chirurg.* 1 b/2 An artificialle and normaticke applicatione.. wherwith the decayed health is restored.

normative (ˈnɔːmətɪv), *a.* [ad. L. type **normātīv-us* (see NORMA and -ATIVE), or a. F. *normatif, -ive*.] **1. a.** Establishing or setting up a norm or standard; deriving from, expressing, or implying a general standard, norm, or ideal. Also *absol.*

1880 W. WALLACE *Epicureanism* 136 The aim which they assigned to the legislator in his normative action on Society. **1884** D. HUNTER tr. *Reuss's Hist. Canon* x. 171 The normative character of scriptures divinely inspired. **1897** J. H. GULLIVER et al. tr. *Wundt's Ethics* I. 1 The normative point of view considers objects with reference to *definite rules*, which find expression in them, and to which they are at the same time required to conform. *Ibid.*, From the normative point of view, it is the purpose of the inquirer to estimate the relative values of facts. **1912** L. BLOOMFIELD in *Jrnl. Eng. & Germ. Philol.* XI. 622 The scientific study of language has nothing to do with the normative (i.e. purely pedagogic) purpose of teaching people of ('fixing') the use or the better use of a literary language. **1931** M. R. COHEN *Reason & Nature* III. iv. 403 Instead of refuting the normative standpoint of the old natural law, these writers substitute an unconscious natural law of their own. **1932** E. C. TOLMAN *Purposive Behav.* v. xxiii. 389 Relations to pre-individual or 'normative psychology'. *Ibid.* 397 Normative psychologies.. tend to take an average (normal) individual or.. sample of individuals.. and then to apply all sorts of different stimuli. **1941** [see GENETIC *a.* 1 f]. **1954** *Mind* LXIII. 264 As examples of 'normatives' he gives 'I ought to go' [etc.]. **1963** H.-N. CASTAÑEDA in Castañeda & Nakhnikian *Morality & Lang. of Conduct* vii. 279 A complete elucidation of the nature and structure of normatives requires an understanding of the logic of imperatives. **1968** A. ETZIONI in Lindzey & Aronson *Handbk. Social Psychol.* (ed. 2) V. xliii. 547 The world situation warrants an approach that would emphasize common interests—above all, peace—as the key normative principle. **1970** R. C. ZAEHNER *Concordant Discord* iii. 46 It is the custom of nature mystics to assume that their own experience, even though it last only for a few moments, must be normative of all such experiences. **1973** *Archivum Linguisticum* IV. 107 It is hazardous to state correlations between social status and speech behaviour, especially if it is done in this normative fashion.

b. In special collocations: ***normative grammar***: grammatical rules set up as a fixed standard to which language in use must conform; also, a treatise setting out such rules; so ***normative grammarian***; ***normative science***: a discipline such as ethics or æsthetics which aims at evaluation as well as description; ***normative system***: a system based on what is established as the norm.

1901 H. OERTEL *Lect. on Study of Lang.* ii. 87 Normative or didactic grammar sets up a certain standard as correct. **1933** L. BLOOMFIELD *Language* i. 7 This gave the authoritarians their chance: they wrote *normative grammars*, in which they often ignored actual usage in favor of speculative notions. **1966** L. J. COHEN *Diversity of Meaning* (ed. 2) i. 9 The late eighteenth century was the first period to treat words' meanings as raw material for historians as well as normative grammarians. *Ibid.*, Some bold spirit had to cry down the pretensions of normative grammar and lexicography. **1968** *Word* XXIV. 387 Normative grammarians come into being when a society begins to concern itself with its language. **1895** F. THILLY tr. *Paulsen's Introd. Philos.* 26 Three normative sciences are added: Logic, practical philosophy based on psychology, and technology based on physics. **1921** W. E. JOHNSON *Logic* I. xiv. 224 Any study of which imperatives constitute the subject-matter has been called a normative science. **1934** COHEN & NAGEL *Introd. Logic* vi. 110 Logic has.. been defined as the normative science which studies the norms distinguishing sound.. from unsound thinking. **1953** G. E. M. ANSCOMBE tr. *Wittgenstein's Philos. Investigations* I. 38ᵉ F. P. Ramsey once emphasized in conversation with me that logic was a 'normative science'. **1966** *Mathematical Rev.* XXXI. 8/2 (*title*) The principles of a logic of normative systems. **1967** C. MARGERISON in Wills & Yearsley *Handbk. Management Technol.* 31 The normative system is a central factor in securing group participation. *Ibid.* 32 Various studies have indicated how the group's activity can be structured and led to bring about a normative system consonant with the organizational goals. **1973** *Jrnl. Genetic Psychol.* Mar. 56 Internalization was defined as correspondence between the child's normative system (i.e., his generalized expectations) and the parent's behavior or own normative system.

2. *Petrol.* Of or pertaining to the norm of a rock.

1902 W. CROSS et al. in *Jrnl. Geol.* X. 604 The standard minerals which make up the norm are to be called the normative minerals, not the normal ones, since the latter adjective has the meaning of usual or common. **1909** J. P. IDDINGS *Ign. Rocks* I. II. iii. 420 Normative minerals are frequently not the normal ones in certain rocks, though they may be the normal minerals in many others. **1962** *Jrnl. Petrology* III. 353 The normative components in basalts closely approximate the mode in most cases. **1973** *Ibid.* XIV. 35 (*heading*) Normative composition.

Hence ˈ**normatively** *adv.*; ˈ**normativeness**; ˈ**normativist**; **normaˈtivity**.

1945 Normativity [see FACTICITY]. **1948** J. TOWSTER *Pol. Power in U.S.S.R.* 16 The normativists (Kelsen etc.), too, say that every law is state (public) law. **1953** J. G. PERISTIANY in *Durkheim's Sociol. & Philos.* p. xv, The generality of a fact.. is significant in this context only in relation to its generality, in the sense of its normativeness. **1957** *Archivum Linguisticum* IX. I. 75 Among the normativists both Gaertner/Passendorfer and Slonski admit of both genders. **1958** W. J. H. SPROTT *Human Groups* ix. 144 Normativeness as such is a prerequisite for continuous interaction. **1964** GOULD & KOLB *Dict. Soc. Sci.* 495/2 This rules out.. any items of conduct which are not founded on past experience (in their words 'normatively regulated'). **1970** J. N. FINDLAY tr. *Husserl's Logical Investigations* I. ii. 78 Has not the concept of normativity got an inherent relation to a guiding aim. **1973** *Nature* 23 Nov. 228/2 The intent of these very simple models is neither to forecast, even implicitly, the levels reached in either population or food, or to forecast 'normatively', to set a target and then to deduce what is needed to achieve it.

†**norme**. *Obs. rare.* [ad. L. or It. *norma*, or a. F. *norme*.] = NORM *sb.*

1635 J. HAYWARD tr. *Biondi's Banish'd Virg.* 169 These conditions which serve for a norme and a patterne.. to forme their lives and actions by. **1649** G. DANIEL *Trinarch., Hen. IV*, xxv, There is a Line Springs from All humane Actions to informe A nearer Way then by the written Norme.

normed (nɔːmd), *a. Math.* [f. NORM + -ED².] Having a norm.

1935 *Trans. Amer. Math. Soc.* XXXVIII. 360 We now add the permanent assumption that $\mathfrak{B}$ is 'normed', that is, that there is associated with $\mathfrak{B}$ a rule assigning to every $\xi \in \mathfrak{B}$ a number $\|\xi\|$ called the 'norm' of ξ, and satisfying [etc.]. **1947** *Ibid.* LXII. 193 A normed linear vector space is a Banach space.. if it is furthermore complete. **1959** L. F. BORON tr. Naimark (*title*) Normed rings. **1962** C. WEXLER *Analytic Geom.* ii. 29 The most important normed linear spaces are those that have one additional property, that of completeness. **1972** A. G. HOWSON *Handbk. Terms used in Algebra & Analysis* xxii. 111 A space with a norm is known as a normed space; it is.. a metric space with metric $d(x, y) = \|x - y\|$.

ˈ**normlessness**. [f. NORM + -LESS + -NESS.] Without any relevant standard or norm.

1944 H. P. FAIRCHILD *Dict. Sociol.* 206/1 *Normlessness*, the absence of any appreciable norm. **1951** R. K. MERTON *Soc. Theory & Soc. Structure* II. iv. 128 There develops what Durkheim called 'anomie' (or normlessness). **1961** B. R. WILSON *Sects & Society* IV. v. 350 The individual is sheltered from the wider social anomie.. the normlessness of the modern world. **1964** I. L. HOROWITZ *New Sociology* 20 All agree that anomie is defined by a 'condition of normlessness'. **1969** R. BLACKBURN in Cockburn & Blackburn *Student Power* 198 Seeman suggests reducing the concept [*sc.* alienation] to five psychological dimensions (feelings of normlessness, meaninglessness, powerlessness, isolation and self-estrangement).

normo- (ˈnɔːməʊ), comb. form of L. *norma* (see NORMA) used in several biological and medical words, esp. in physiology, to express the condition of being close to the average in respect of any particular character which varies (often contrasted with HYPER- and HYPO-). **normoˈchromic** [Gr. χρῶμ-α colour] *a.*, having the normal amount of hæmoglobin; (of anæmia) characterized by the presence of red blood cells with the normal content of hæmoglobin; ˈ**normocyte** [-CYTE], an erythrocyte which is normal (esp. in size); so **normoˈcytic** *a.*, of or pertaining to a normocyte; (of anæmia) characterized by the presence of erythrocytes which are normal in size, etc., but reduced in numbers; **normoglyˈcæmia** (*U.S.* -ˈemia), a normal concentration of sugar in the blood; so **normoglyˈcæmic** *a.*, characterized by normoglycæmia; **normoˈtensive** [HYPER-, HYPO)TENSIVE *adjs.*] *a.*, having, or being, a normal blood pressure; hence as *sb.*, one who has such a blood pressure; **normoˈthermic** *a.* [Gr. θέρμ-η heat], characterized by or occurring at a normal body temperature; **normovoˈlæmia** (*U.S.* -ˈemia) [VOL(UME *sb.* + Gr. αἷμα blood], the condition of having a normal volume of circulating blood in the body; so **normovoˈlæmic** *a.*, characterized by or pertaining to normovolæmia.

1935 WHITBY & BRITTON *Disorders of Blood* iii. 48 The technical terms used are, firstly, 'hypochromic', 'normochromic' and 'hyperchromic', which indicate whether the cells contain an amount of hemoglobin which is less than, equal to, or more than normal. **1958** Normochromic [see HYPOCHROMIC *a.* 1]. **1974** *Nature* 7 June 551/1 Clinically the disease is characterised by proteinuria, corneal opacities and normochromic anaemia with decreased erythrocyte life span. **1900** *Buck's Handbk. Med. Sci.* (rev. ed.) I. 273/1 The red cells.. are spoken of as microcytes, normocytes, and megalocytes, according to their size. **1935** WHITBY & BRITTON *Disorders Blood* iii. 49 Hypochromia may be found with microcytes and normocytes. **1969** W. R. PLATT *Color Atlas & Textbk. Hematol.* ii. 28/1 The erythrocyte (normocyte or red blood cell) measures 6–8 μ in diameter. **1911** DORLAND *Med. Dict.* (ed. 6) 559/2 Normocytic. **1935** WHITBY & BRITTON *Disorders of Blood* iii. 48 The technical terms used are

..'microcytic', 'normocytic' and 'macrocytic', which indicate whether the [red] cells are smaller than, equal to, or larger than normal. **1971** *Indian Jrnl. Med. Res.* LIX. 427 In 60% of the cases the anemia was of the normocytic normochromic type. **1932** DORLAND & MILLER *Med. Dict.* (ed. 16) 871/2 Normoglycemia. **1961** *Lancet* 16 Sept. 637/2 To maintain normoglycæmia a [diabetic] woman of 81 needed 45 units P.Z.I. before the course but only 15 units after it. **1973** *Nature* 17 Aug. 447/2 Direct injection of pancreatic islets into the portal vein resulted in normoglycaemia and normal urine volumes in the five rats studied. **1933** *Stedman's Med. Dict.* (ed. 12) 733/2 Normoglycemic. **1961** *Diabetes* X. 322/1 The ketonuria may ..represent the relatively benign normoglycemic ketosis of hunger or starvation which usually responds to increase in the amount of carbohydrate in the diet. **1969** *Hormone & Metabol. Res.* I. 266 (*heading*) Insulin levels during pregnancy or obesity in normoglycemic women with a positive history of diabetes mellitus. **1941** DORLAND & MILLER *Med. Dict.* (ed. 19) 982/1 *Normotensive*, marked by normal blood pressure. **1948** *Federation Proc.* VII. 41/2 (*heading*) The immediate pressor effect of desoxycorticosterone acetate in hypertensive and normotensive subjects. **1953** *Lancet* 12 Sept. 541/2 None of the other normotensives exceeded 0·9 ml. per minute. *Ibid.* 543/2 Ten normotensive women. **1962** *Ibid.* 26 May 1092/1 Possible sources of irregularity in the distribution of blood-pressure include..the observer's subconscious distinction between normotensive and hypertensive levels of pressure. **1972** *Aerospace Med.* XLIII. 1225 (*heading*) Effect of hydrochlorothiazide on + G_z tolerance in normotensives. **1959** *Surg., Gynecol. & Obstetr.* CIX. 721 (*heading*) Normothermic perfusion and replantation of the excised dog kidney. **1960** *Amer. Jrnl. Physiol.* CXCIX. 163/1 The heart was cooled while maintaining the rest of the body normothermic. **1974** *Nature* 22 Feb. 568/2 Obviously the destruction of cells by growth of virus may also be different in hypothermic and normothermic conditions. **1925** Normovolemia [see *hypervolæmia* s.v. HYPER- IV]. **1966** *Ann. Surg.* CLXIV. 51 (*heading*) Effects of adrenergic blocking agents on renal blood flow in normovolemia and experimental hypovolemia. **1947** *Acta Cardiologica* II. 134 This method..permitted comparisons of sequential cardiovascular changes which occurred in the same animal during oligemic shock and normovolemic shock (i.e., shock with essentially normal blood volume). **1966** *Amer. Jrnl. Physiol.* CCXI. 878/1 Normovolemic anemia was produced by removing from a femoral artery 40 ml/kg blood while infusing an equal volume of 6% dextran in saline into a femoral vein.

'normoblast. *Path.* [f. *normo-*, as comb. form of L. *norma* + -BLAST.] A nucleated red blood-corpuscle of a normal size.

1890 GOULD *Med. Dict.* 119 Corpuscles of the blood have been distinguished, according to their size—into normoblasts (normal in size), megaloblasts of excessive size [etc.].

Hence **normo'blastic** *a.*

1905 *Brit. Med. Jrnl.* 25 Feb. 401 All that I came across were of normoblastic character.

Norn (nɔːn), *sb.*[1] Also 8–9 erron. **Nornie**, 9 **Norne.** Also with non-naturalized pl. **Nornir.** [a. ON. *norn* (pl. *nornir*), of obscure etym.; hence also Sw. *norna*, G., Da., F. *norne.*] One of the female Fates recognized in Scandinavian mythology. Chiefly in *pl.*

1770 PERCY tr. *Mallet's Northern Antiq.* II. 51 These [virgins] are they who dispense the ages of men; they are called Nornies, that is, Fairies or Destinies. **1855** M. ARNOLD *Balder* I. 24 He has met that doom, which long ago The Nornies, when his mother bare him, spun. **1859** G. W. DASENT *Pop. Tales from Norse* p. xli, The worshippers of Odin and the Nornir were gradually converted into votaries of the Virgin Mary. **1861** F. METCALFE *Oxonian in Iceland* xix. (1867) 281 Yonder float the white swans—an Icelandic story-teller would say they are Norns, presiders over destiny. **1875** *Encycl. Brit.* I. 211/1 The three principal Norns or Nornir are Urd, past time; Verdandi, present time; and Skulld, future time. **1878** P. W. WYATT *Hardrada* 18 The thread of Fate By grey Nornes spun hung o'er the Raven's flight. **1959** R. W. V. ELLIOTT *Runes* vii. 105 Other possibilities occur to one: such as that the figures represent the Nornir, the 'three fatal sisters' of Northern mythology.

Comb. **1886** *Edin. Rev.* July 158 The norn-like daughters of Regner Lodbrok.

Norn, *a.* and *sb.*[2] Also 7 **Nourne.** [a. ON. *norrœnn* adj., or *norrœna* sb.: see NORREN *a.*]

a. *adj.* Norwegian. Also, of or pertaining to Norn. **b.** *sb.* The Norwegian dialect formerly spoken in Orkney and Shetland. Also formerly spoken on parts of the northern mainland of Scotland. Also ***the Orkney*** (or ***Shetland***) ***Norn.***

1633 *Orkney Witch Trial* in *Abbotsford Club Miscell.* 151 Scho aundit in bitt, quhilk is ane Nourne terme, and to expon it into right languag is alse mikill as, scho did blew hir breath thairin. *a* **1688** J. WALLACE *Descr. Orkney* 92 *Norn*, the Language spoken by the ancient Inhabitants of Orkney and Zetland. **1774** LOW *Tour Orkney & Schetland* (1879) 107 He spoke of three kinds of poetry used in Norn. *Ibid.* 163 One of the company all the while singing a Norn Visick. *Ibid.* 196 They speak the English language with a good deal of the Norn accent. **1888** SAXBY *Lads of Lunda* 210 Reciting some grand Norn veisic..after the manner of the ancients. **1932** *Times Lit. Suppl.* 6 Oct. 712/3 Jakobsen's great dictionary of the Norn language in Shetland. **1956** 'H. MACDIARMID' *Stony Limits & Scots Unbound* 48 The old Norn words. **1966** E. W. MARWICK in J. Shearer et al. *New Orkney Book* iv. 25 At the beginning of the eighteenth century some of them were still speaking the old Norn language. **1966–69** *Saga-Book* XVII. 11 In Appendix II he printed specimens of the Orkney Norn of the fourteenth and fifteenth centuries. **1972** W. B. LOCKWOOD *Panorama Indo-Europ. Lang.* vii. 122 Norse obliterated the Pictish of Orkney and Shetland and hastened its demise on the mainland. Known locally as Norn, the language lived on there and across the Pentland Firth in Caithness until modern times. *Ibid.* 127 On the Scottish mainland generally, Norn was ousted by Gaelic during the Middle Ages, except in the North-East of Caithness where it appears to have lingered on until the sixteenth century. **1970–73** *Saga-Book* XVIII. 382 The section on the Orkney and Shetland Norn..is most noteworthy in this respect.

'Norna, Latinized form of NORN *sb.*[1]

1840 CARLYLE *Heroes* (1858) 199 At the foot of it, in the Death-kingdom, sit Three *Nornas*, Fates,—the Past, Present, Future; watering its roots from the Sacred Well. **1848** LYTTON *Harold* VIII. vi, Day by day from the rill The Nornas besprinkle The ash Ygg-drasyll.

nor'narcotine. *Chem.* (See quots.)

1869 ROSCOE *Elem. Chem.* 430 Narcotine yields nornarcotine and methyl iodide. **1892** MORLEY & MUIR *Watt's Dict. Chem.* III. 495/1 *Nornarcotine*, obtained by heating narcotine with fuming HIAq.

norne, var. of NURN *v. Obs.*

Nornisce: see NORENISH *a. Obs.*

nor'-nor'-east, abbrev. form of NORTH-NORTH-EAST. (Cf. *nore-nore-west* s.v. NORE.)

1594 J. DAVIS *Seamans Secr.* (1645) D, Nor-nor-east raiseth a degree in sayling 21 leagues and two miles. **1891** *Pall Mall Gaz.* 16 Nov. 1/2 He changed his course and steered Nor'-Nor'-East. **1891** CLARK RUSSELL *Marr. at Sea* v, 'How is the wind?' 'About nor'-nor'-east, Sir'.

norree, var. of NORRY *v. Obs.*

†Norreis, *sb. pl. Obs. rare.* [a. ONF. *noreis*, usually *norois, norrois*, f. *nor-* north + *-eis, -ois*:—L. *-ensis*: cf. NORWAY[2].] Norwegians.

c **1275** LAY. 23226 Þe Norreis euere folle. **1338** R. BRUNNE *Chron.* (1810) 27 Þei nomen Inglis & Danes, & þe gode Norreis. *Ibid.* 32 Upon þe fals Norreis Edmunde wan inouh.

norreis, obs. variant of NOURICE, nurse.

†'norrel. *Obs. rare*⁻⁰. (See quot.)

1656 BLOUNT *Glossogr.*, *Norrel ware*, corruptly so called in some part of England for Lorimers.

†Norren, *a. Obs. rare.* Also (1 **Norn-,**) 3 **Nor(r)ein.** [a. ON. *norrœnn* (MSw. *noren, norän, norn-*), for **norðrœnn*, f. *norðr* NORTH. Cf. NORN *a.*] Norwegian. Also *absol.* in *pl.*

c **1100** *O.E. Chron.* (MS. D) an. 1066, Olafe þæs Norna cynges suna. *a* **1122** *Ibid.* (Laud MS.), Hine ȝemette Harold se Norrena cyng. *c* **1205** LAY. 23226 Þe Norrene þer feollen. Bruttes weoren balde; þa Noreine [*c* **1275** Norreine] heo aqualden. *c* **1275** *Ibid.* 23282 Mid him he nam forþrihtes his Noreine cnihtes.

norrie: see NORIE[1].

'norril. *rare*⁻¹. [Survival of NARELL.] *pl.* The nostrils (of a game-cock).

1832 JOHNSON *Sportsman's Cycl.* 146 They have their combs and gills taken off, and are marked in the eyes, norrils, and feet.

norrishe, obs. f. NOURISH.

norriture, obs. var. of NOURITURE.

Norroway, Sc. f. NORWAY.

Norroy ('nɒrɔɪ). Also 5 **Norrey.** [f. AF. *nor-* NORTH + *rey, roy* king.] The title of the third King of Arms, whose jurisdiction lies to the north of the Trent.

1485 *Rolls of Parlt.* VI. 349/2 John More, otherwise called Norrey, Chief Herauld and Kyng of Armes of the North parties of this oure Realme. **1503** *Lett. & P. Rich. III & Hen. VII* (Rolls) I. 418 The said Norroy shall well note the manner and words that the said king shall use. **1631** WEEVER *Anc. Funeral Mon.* 687 Norroy, king of Armes of the north parts. **1686** ASHMOLE *Diary* (1774) 374 The Duke of Norfolk proposed to me, to give my brother Dugdale the place of Norroy. **1722** *Lond. Gaz.* No. 6084/5 His Grace's Surcoat of Arms, carried by Norroy King of Arms. **1796** BURKE *Let. to Noble Lord* Wks. VIII. 37 Prouder by far than all the Garters, and Norroys and Clarencieux, and Rouge Dragons. **1806** A. DUNCAN *Nelson's Funeral* 33 Norroy, King of Arms, (in a Mourning Coach). **1895** *Whitaker's Almanack* 171/2 Kings of Arms. Garter,..Clarenceux,.. Norroy.

†'norry, *sb. Obs.* Also norre(y. [a. OF. *norri*, pa. pple. of *norrir*: see next and cf. NORY.]

1. A foster-child, pupil.

a **1374** CHAUCER *Boeth.* I. pr. iii. (1868) 10 O quod sche my norry scholde I forsake þe now. **1387** TREVISA *Higden* (Rolls) VI. 79 He took his noble norrey Beda, a childe of sevene ȝere olde, and tauȝte hym whiles he was onlyve.

2. A fosterer, nourisher.

1387 TREVISA *Higden* (Rolls) VII. 393 Herbert Lesang, þat..was þo bisshop of Teddeforde, was a greet norrey [*v. rr.* norry, nory: L. *fomes*] of symonye, for he hadde i-bouȝt his bisshopriche of þe kyng. *c* **1450** LOVELICH *Grail* xxvi. 55 An old vauasour..that Inne sche trosted.., For norre he was to hire sone so dere.

†'norry, *v. Obs. rare.* Also norree. [ad. OF. *norrir*: see NOURISH *v.*] *trans.* To nurse.

c **1450** LOVELICH *Merlin* i. 997 Thus the modyr gan hym norree, tyl ten mounthes old he was, Sekerle. *Ibid.* v. 6532 Thanne took sche the child and leide it hire by,..& hire owne to norrye putte owt thus son.

norryshe, obs. f. NOURISH.

norryture, obs. f. NOURITURE.

nors(e, obs. ff. NURSE.

Norse (nɔːs), *sb.* and *a.* [prob. ad. Du. *noorsch*, variant of *noordsch*, MDu. *no(o)rdsch, no(o)rtsch*, f. *noord* NORTH + *-sch* -ISH: cf. OFris. *norsch, nordsch, northesk*, MLG. *norrisch*, MSw. *norsker* (1436), Icel. *norskur* (16th c.), mod. Sw., Da., and Norw. *norsk.* Cf. NORISH.]

A. *sb.* **†1. a.** A Norwegian. **b.** The Norwegian people or king. *Obs. rare.*

1598 HAKLUYT *Voy.* I. 3 The Norses haue possessed many lands and Islands of this Empire. *a* **1719** LADY WARDLAW *Hardyknute* ix, The king of Norse..Landed in fair Scotland. *Ibid.* xx, Now that Norse dois proudly boast Fair Scotland to inthrall.

2. As *pl.* (The) Norwegians. Also, any native or inhabitant of ancient Scandinavia.

1848 LYTTON *Harold* I. i, A simple song, that..betrayed its origin in the ballad of the Norse. **1902** A. MACBAIN in Skene *Highland. Scotl.* 396 Erp, son of Meldun, was captured by the Norse. **1972** W. B. LOCKWOOD *Panorama Indo-Europe. Lang.* vii. 126 As many as 5,000 Norse are believed to have lived in Greenland.

3. The Norwegian tongue. ***Old Norse***, the language of Norway and its colonies down to the 14th cent.; also, the North Germanic language which was the immediate ancestor of the Scandinavian languages.

a **1688** J. WALLACE *Descr. Orkney* 33 All speak English with a good Accent, only some of the common People among themselves speak Norse or the old Gottish Language. **1703** BRAND *Descr. Orkney* 69 The Norse hath continued ever since the Norvegians had these Isles in Possession. **1763** BLAIR *Diss.* in *Ossian's Poems* (1796) II. 323 Their ancient language..is called the Norse, and is a dialect..of the Scandinavian tongue. **1809** EDMONDSTON *Zetland Isl.* I. 142 Pure Norse or Norwegian is now unknown in it [*sc.* Zetland]. **1844** LATHAM in *Proc. Philol. Soc.* I. 236 Even in the very earliest stages of the Old Norse. **1874** R. COWIE *Shetland* (ed. 2) 24 In 1774, some of the people in Foula could repeat the Lord's Prayer in Norse. **1927** E. V. GORDON *Introd. Old Norse* p. xvi, The structure of Gothic.. reveals its affinity with Norse, but the differences between the oldest surviving Gothic..and Norse of the same period are too great for Gothic to be included in the Norse group of tongues.

B. *adj.* Norwegian; belonging to, originating from, Norway. Also, of or pertaining to ancient Scandinavia or the Norse peoples as a whole.

1768 GRAY *Odes* vii. (*heading*), The Fatal Sisters, from the Norse Tongue. **1774** LOW *Tour Orkney & Schetland* (1879) 105 The Norse Language is much worn out here..; it was the language of the last age. **1821** SCOTT *Pirate* i, Land..in the possession of the Norse inhabitants. **1844** LATHAM in *Proc. Philol. Soc.* I. 236 The examples drawn from the oldest Norse composition. **1874** R. COWIE *Shetland* (ed. 2) 10 The first of the famous Norse jarls of Orkney and Zetland. **1885** *Encycl. Dict.* V. I. 216/1 *Norse*,..of or pertaining to ancient Scandinavia or its inhabitants; Norwegian. **1927** E. V. GORDON *Introd. Old Norse* p. xv, The home of the oldest Norse culture and the oldest Norse traditions was Sweden. *Ibid.* p. xxxv, The oldest Norse poetry preserved traditions which belonged not merely to the Norse peoples but to the Germanic race as a whole. **1970–73** *Saga-Book* XVIII. 208, I may insert a word of warning on Dr Marwick's old-fashioned and narrowly correct use of the term 'Norse'—to him it translates *norsk*, Norwegian and then especially *landsmål.*

Hence **'Norseness,** the state or quality of being Norwegian or Scandinavian.

1961 *Listener* 7 Sept. 363/3 Ibsen's characters are always about to take flight into fantasy but their manner, their stubborn Norseness, holds them fast in a two-dimensional theatre. **1968** G. JONES *Hist. Vikings* III. iv. 264 The adoption of Slavonic customs had quietly eroded the Norseness of the Rus.

'norsel, *sb.* Also 7 **nossel, nozzel, orsell, ossel, ossil, ozzel,** etc. [Later form of NOSTEL.] (See quots.) Hence **'norsel** *v.*, to fit with norsels.

1615 E. S. *Britain's Buss* in Arber *Garner* III. 630 Each net is to be fastened to her ropes with short pieces of cords or lines, of two feet long a piece, called Nozzels. These nozzels are tied very thick... So each net takes 150 nozzels. **1641** S. SMITH *Herring Buss Trade* 4 For Norsels at 8*d.* a Net, being 130 to a Net. *Ibid.* 11 To bring the Nets to their ropes, and Norsell and Corke them. *c* **1682** J. COLLINS *Making Salt in Eng.* 112 To each of these are fastned 20 Snoods, *alias* Nossels, which are small Lines, with Hooks and Baits at them. **1750** in *Sc. Nat. Dict.* (1965) VI. 495/3 The Ossels..each 18 inches long..are fixed to two Mashes at one end by an Eye. **1881** *Proc. Soc. Antiquaries Scotl.* III. 150 The nets..are attached to a strong..rope by means of thinner cords known as 'ozzels'. **1883** *Fish. Exhib. Catal.* 7 Simple Machine, for making Norsels or Snoods of any length. **1921** [see NORSELLER]. **1972** M. F. WAKELIN *Patterns Folk Speech Brit. Isles* 18 Figure 2 shows the *sole-rope* as made fast to the net by the *ossils*. *Ibid.* 24 There are four fairly well-defined usages. *Ossil* extends, with one or two breaks, from Burnmouth as far as Lossiemouth. **1973** W. ELMER *Terminol. Fishing* ii. 54 The bait..is put on a *skewer* ..or hung on an *orsle*..(a short piece of line), and the whole is weighted with stones.

'Norseland. [f. NORSE *a.*] Norway.

1840 CARLYLE *Heroes* (1858) 211 Hynde Etin, and..Red Etin of Ireland, in the Scottish Ballads, these are both derived from Norseland. **1877** TENNYSON *Harold* v. i, Have we not broken Wales and Norseland?

norseller (ˈnɔːs(ə)lə(r)). Also orseller. [f. NORSEL *sb.* and *v.* + -ER[1].] A person who fits nets with norsels.
1921 *Dict. Occup. Terms* (1927) §398 *Net orseller, norseller,* attaches orsells or norsels (short lines about ten inches long) to top and bottom of fishing net at regular intervals.

ˈNorseman. [f. NORSE *a.*] A Norwegian. Also, any native or inhabitant of viking-age Scandinavia.
1817 SCOTT *Harold* I. i, Count Witikind.. roved with his Norsemen the land and the main. **1840** CARLYLE *Heroes* (1858) 205 Writing by Runes has some air of being original among the Norsemen. **1864** *Chambers's Encycl.* VI. 792/2 The first Danish Norsemen made their appearance on the eastern and southern coasts of England in 787. *Ibid.* 793/2 The Swedish Norsemen directed their expeditions chiefly against the eastern coasts of the Baltic. **1874** R. COWIE *Shetland* (ed. 2) 10 When the nautical daring.. had become so much developed in the Norsemen. **1935** *Chambers's Encycl.* VII. 527/2 *Northmen,* or Norsemen, were the sea-rovers who came from the north—Denmark, Norway, Sweden. **1943** G. VERNADSKY *Anc. Russia* VII. iii. 273 It seems highly probable that.. a band of Norsemen—more exactly, of Swedes—established their control over the lower Don and Azov area. **1948** *Oxf. Jun. Encycl.* I. 137/1 *Danes.* These are a Scandinavian people, as are their neighbours the Swedes.. and Norwegians... The ancestors of all three were the Norsemen or Vikings. **1968** G. JONES *Hist. Vikings* IV. iii. 395 Ireland was different. The Norsemen (part Danes, part Norwegians) had established a number of important trading towns in the southern half of the island. **1970** FOOTE & WILSON *Viking Achievement* i. 14 Saxon political influence went hand in hand with Saxon efforts to convert the Danes to Christianity. The archbishopric of Hamburg-Bremen.. was intended as a missionary outpost with prime responsibility for bringing the heathen Norsemen to the true faith.

norserye, obs. form of NURSERY.

norsethite (ˈnɔːsəθaɪt). *Min.* [See quot. 1959[2] and -ITE[1].] A carbonate of barium and magnesium, $BaMg(CO_3)_2$, that is found as whitish crystals with a vitreous or pearly lustre, similar to calcite and dolomite.
1959 C. MILTON et al. in *Bull. Geol. Soc. Amer.* LXX. 1646 Norsethite, $BaMg(CO_3)_2$, was found in dolomitic, black oil shale below the main trona bed in the Westvaco trona mine. *Ibid.*, Norsethite is named in honor of Mr. Keith Norseth, engineering geologist of the trona mine at Westvaco, Sweetwater County, Wyoming. **1967** *Amer. Mineralogist* LII. 1770 The occurrence of norsethite, $BaMg(CO_3)_2$, in large quantities in a newly discovered zinc-lead-copper deposit in South West Africa, is reported. It is one of the major gangue minerals of the deposit, is closely associated with calcite and is apparently of hydrothermal origin. **1968** I. KOSTOV *Mineralogy* II. xi. 540 Norsethite is probably trigonal-trapezohedral with distinct rhombohedral {10$\bar{1}$1} cleavage.

†**norsh,** *sb.*, obs. variant of NOURISH *sb.*, nurse.
1382 WYCLIF *Ruth* iv. 16 Noemy putte the takun child in hir bosum; and vside the office of norshe. **1480** *Robt. Devyll* in Thoms *E. Eng. Prose Rom.* (1828) 8 He bote the norshes pappes.

†**norsh,** *v. Obs.* Forms: 3–4 norss(i, 4 norsshe, 5 norshe, 4–5 norsche, norche. [var. of NOURISH *v.*] *trans.* To nurse or nourish.
1297 R. GLOUC. (Rolls) 1450 He spac engliss vor he was at rome inorssed biuore. *Ibid.* 1567 [Nero] let hit rere a noble court.. to norssi þe ssrewe þer inne. *a* **1380** WYCLIF *Wks.* (1880) 42 Ȝif a modir norscheþ & loueþ here fleschly child. **1387** TREVISA *Higden* (Rolls) IV. 99 It is grete enemyte to werriours forto norsche sleuþe and leccherie. **1422** tr. *Secreta Secret., Priv. Priv.* 195 She was of a child I-norshit with venym. **1460** CAPGRAVE *Chron.* (Rolls) 30 So vas he.. thus norchid up onto mannes age.
Hence †**ˈnorshing** *vbl. sb.* Also †**ˈnorsher,** nourisher. †**ˈnorshery,** nursery.
c **1374** CHAUCER *Boeth.* II. pr. v. (1868) 47 Þe fruytes of þe erþe owen to ben on þe norssinge of bestes. **1387** TREVISA *Higden* (Rolls) VI. 219 He was i-take to norschynge and to lore to Benet Bisshop. **1442** tr. *Secreta Secret., Priv. Priv.* 139 This byth the norchynges of lechurie. *c* **1440** *Promp. Parv.* 358/2 Norschynge, in manerys and condycyons ..*educacio.* *c* **1450** *Cov. Myst.* (Shaks. Soc.) 239, I am norssher of synne to the confusyon of man. *a* **1500** *Promp. Parv.* 358/2 Norshery, where ȝong childyr ben.

Norsk, *a.* and *sb.* [a. Scand. *norsk.*] = NORSE.
1851 *Zoologist* IX. 2978 Our Norsk guide soon collected some heather. **1861** F. METCALFE *Oxonian in Iceland* (1867) 22 After the fashion of the old Norsk kings. **1875** JEVONS *Money* iv. 23 In the Norsk, Anglo-Saxon, and English, *scat* or *scot* has been specialized to denote tax or tribute.

norsse, obs. form of NURSE.

norsteroid (nɔːˈstɪərɔɪd, -ˈstɛrɔɪd). *Biochem.* [f. NOR- + STEROID.] A steroid lacking a methyl side chain (esp. the one containing the carbon atom numbered 19), or having one of its rings contracted by one methylene group.
1950 *Jrnl. Chem. Soc.* 367 The synthetic approach to nor-steroid hormones has now been greatly simplified by Birch and Mukherji's method of reduction. **1954** *Ibid.* 1984 Values for 2-substituted A-norsteroids.. may be considered. **1970** *Indian Jrnl. Biochem.* VII. 116/1 Since the introduction of 19-norsteroids as the synthetic progestational agents, it has become necessary to know their role as regulators of metabolic processes.

nort, variant of NURT *v.*, to thrust.

†**ˈnortelry.** *Obs. rare*[−1]. [irreg. f. stem of ME. *nortour* NURTURE.] Education.
c **1386** CHAUCER *Reeve's T.* 47 What for hir kynreed and hir nortelrye, That sche had lerned in the nonnerye.

norter, obs. form of NURTURE.

‖**nortes** (ˈnɔːtiːz), *sb. pl.* Also in *sing.* norte. [Sp. *nortes*, pl. of *norte* NORTH.] Violent gales from the north prevailing in the Gulf of Mexico from September to March. (Cf. NORTHER.)
1843 PRESCOTT *Mexico* (1850) I. 249 The island.. would shelter him from the *nortes* that sweep over these seas with fatal violence in the winter, sometimes even late in the spring. **1864** G. A. SALA in *Daily Tel.* 20 July, One of those tremendous gales called 'Nortes', or 'Northers', which spring up at ten minutes' notice. **1883** R. H. SCOTT *Elem. Meteor.* xix. 383 The 'Nortes' of the Gulf of Mexico are Northerly winds, which blow with great force, and are often dangerous to shipping. **1926** *British Weekly* 21 Jan. 398/5 We hear of the *norte*, the wind from the Equatorial belt... When the *norte* blows, many temperamental folk are apt to become unbalanced.

north (nɔːθ), *adv.*, *sb.*, and *a.* Forms: 1–3 **norð,** 1–4 **norþ** (*Orm.* **norrþ**), 3– **north,** 5–6 **northe,** *Sc.* **northt.** Also *abbrev.* **N.** [Common Teutonic: OE. *norð, norþ* = OS. *nord,* OFris. *north, noerd,* MDu. *nort, noort* (Du. *noord*), MLG. *nort,* OHG. *nort, nord* (G. *nord*), ON. *norðr* (Sw. *nord, norr,* Da. *nord*): not recorded in Gothic, and of uncertain relationship. From Teutonic come F. *nord* (OF. also *nort, north*), It. *norte, nort, nord,* Sp. *norte, nord,* Pg. *norte.*
In OE. and OS. *north* appears only as an adv., in OHG. only as a sb.; in OFris., MDu., and ON. it had both functions. For the development of the adjectival use in Eng. see below. OE. had also the adv. form *norðan* 'from the north', = OHG. *nordana,* ON. *norðan* (Sw. *nordan,* Da. *norden-*), whence *be norðan,* which survived in the later language as BENORTH.]
A. *adv.* **1.** Towards, or in the direction of, that part of the earth or the heavens which (in the northern hemisphere) is most remote from the midday sun. Also with qualifications, as ***north by east,*** etc.
a. With ref. to movement, extent, or direction.
a **900** *O.E. Chron.* (Parker MS.) an. 823, Hie Baldred þone cyning norþ ofer Temese adrifon. *a* **1000** *Boeth. Metr.* xiii. 59 Merecondel scyfð on ofdæle.. norð eft & east. *a* **1122** *O.E. Chron.* (Laud MS.) an. 1064, Fela hund manna hi namon & læddon norð mid heom. *c* **1205** LAY. 16442 Hengest is ifaren norð. *a* **1250** *Owl & Night.* 921 Ac ich fare boþe norþ & soþ. *c* **1300** *Havelok* 1255 She lokede norþ, and ek south. *c* **1391** CHAUCER *Astrol.* II. §17 Fro which lyne alle planetes som tyme declinen north or south. *c* **1470** HENRY *Wallace* IV. 324 Northt so our Ern throuch out the land thai went. **1559** W. CUNNINGHAM *Cosmogr. Glasse* 80 Can they not in like maner, draw paralleles from th' Æquinoctiall Southward as they do North? **1612** CAPT. SMITH *Descr. Virg.* Wks. (Arb.) 53 There is one [river] that commeth due north. **1725** DE FOE *Voy. round World* (1840) 175, I changed my course a little, and went away north-by-east. ? **1788** COWPER *Mischievous Bull* 21 Therefore go—I care not whether east or north. **1863** KINGSLEY *Water-Bab.* iv, I wandered north and north.. till I met with cold icebergs. **1894** MISS STEEL *Flower Forgiveness* 79 If you will take my advice, come up north.
Comb. **1891** *Scribner's Mag.* Sept. 282/1 The traveller boards the north-bound steamer.
b. With reference to place or location. Also ***north-away,*** in the north.
Beowulf 858 Monig oft ȝecwæð, þætte suð ne norð be sæm tweonum.. oþer nænig selra nære. *c* **893** K. ÆLFRED *Oros.* I. i. 17 Þa wæs he swa feor norþ swa þa hwæl-huntan firrest faraþ. **971** *Blickl. Hom.* 209 Wæron norð of ðæm stane awexene swiðe hrimiȝe bearwas. *c* **1205** LAY. 3443 Leir þe king wende forh to is dohter [þat] wunede norð. *c* **1250** *Gen. & Ex.* 278 Min fliȝt.. ic wile up-taken, Min fete norð on heuene maken. *c* **1391** CHAUCER *Astrol.* I. §17 Tak kep of thise latitudes north and sowth. *c* **1425** WYNTOUN *Cron.* I. xi. 985 Þe hil of Cawcasus,.. North on til Ewrop marchande nere. *a* **1539** *Cartul. Abb. Rievalle* (Surtees) 341 The iij romys north therof seelyd round with waynscot. **1607** WALKINGTON *Opt. Glass* ii. 15 The rudenes and simplicitie of the people, that are seated far north. **1667** MILTON *P.L.* IV. 569 In the Mount that lies from Eden North,.. he first lighted. **1719** DE FOE *Crusoe* II. (Globe) 379 They saw another Island on the Right-Hand North. **1738** —— *Tour* (ed. 2) III. 337 North of the Mouth of this River is.. Cromarty Bay. **1878** W. MORRIS in Mackail *Life* (1899) I. 370 The heap of grey stones with a grey roof that we call a house north-away. **1955** J. R. R. TOLKIEN *Return of King* 197 Going swiftly to lesser posts and strongholds north-away.
c. In phr. ***north and south.***
14.. *Sailing Directions* (Hakluyt) 11 Fro Vamborugh to the poynt of the Ilond the cours lieth north and South. **1612** CAPT. SMITH *Descr. Virg.* Wks. (Arb.) 48 This Bay lieth North and South. *c* **1630** RISDON *Surv. Devon* §249 (1810) 260 Whom though they accounted an heretick, yet buried they him in the church-yard, north and south. **1720** HEARNE *Collect.* (O.H.S.) VII. 169 A certain Chapell.. which he plac'd North and South, in opposition to all other Churches and Chapells.
attrib. **1839** *Penny Cycl.* XIV. 288/1 The deviation of which from the true north-and-south line is the declination of the needle.
d. In *slang* phrases: ***too far north,*** too clever, too knowing. ***a little more north*** (see quot. 1864).
1748 SMOLLETT *Rod. Rand.* (1780) I. 124 It shan't avail you, you shall find me too far north for you. **1797** MRS. A. M. BENNETT *Beggar Girl* (1813) III. 28 She was what I call too far north for that. **1864** *Glasgow Her.* 9 Nov., An old salt delights to order his steward to make his grog 'a little more North', 'another point, steward'.
2. a. quasi-*sb.* = B. 1. In early use chiefly in ***from north to south.*** Also † ***at north,*** from the north.
c **1200** ORMIN 11258 All þiss middellærd iss ec O fowwre daless dæledd Onn Æst, o Wesst, o Suþ, o Norrþ. **13..** *Cursor M.* 22330 (Gött.), Þan sal fra north a folk rijs. *c* **1391** CHAUCER *Astrol.* I. §15 From est to West, fro sowth to north. *c* **1425** WYNTOUN *Cron.* I. ix. 553 Fra north on south þe streme it strekis. **1570** DEE *Math. Pref.* aiij b, Of the Variacion of the Compas, from true North. **1625** PURCHAS *Pilgrims* I. II. 60 The first of March a storme took vs at North. **1743** BULKELEY & CUMMINS *Voy. S. Seas* 138 This Morning.., had a fresh Breeze at North. **1748** HUME *Ess., Nat. Characters,* Most Conquests have gone from North to South. **1821–2** SHELLEY *Chas. I,* II. 421 The rainbow hung over the city.. from north to south. **1859** TENNYSON *Elaine* 525 His party, knights of utmost North and West. **1870** LOWELL *Study Wind.* Ser. I. *Good Word for Winter,* You must have plenty of north in your gale.
†**b.** ***by north,*** in the north, on the north side.
Perhaps representing OE. *be norðan* BENORTH.
c **1205** LAY. 21043 Arður wes bi norðe, and noht her of nuste. *c* **1305** *Oxford Student* 1 in *E.E.P.* (1862) 40 A kniȝt þer was in Engelond, by norþe her biside. **1387** TREVISA *Higden* (Rolls) I. 57 Þe grete see Ponticus þat passeþ by north by Thracia. *a* **1425** *Cursor M.* 12131 Of any mon bi norþ or souþ who herde euer suche selcouþ? **1570** LEVINS *Manip.* 174/1 By Northe, *Boreas.*
c. ***by north:*** (see BY *prep.* 9 b).
14.. *Sailing Directions* (Hakluyt) 14 Seint Mary of Cille and Uschante lien northwest and by north. **1612** CAPT. SMITH *Descr. Virg.* Wks. (Arb.) 50 The first of those rivers ..hath his course from the West and by North. **1795** COWPER *Pairing Time* 51 The wind.. Now shifted east and east by north. **1848** LOWELL *Biglow P.* Ser. I. vii, This.. leaves me frontin' South by North.
B. *sb.* (Usually with *the.*)
1. a. That one of the four cardinal points which is directly opposite to the sun at mid-day.
The ***true north*** and ***magnetic north*** correspond respectively to the north, and north magnetic, pole (see POLE *sb.*[2] 2 and 5 b).
c **1290** *St. Kenelm* 12 in *S. Eng. Leg.* I. 345 Abouten eiȝte hondret mile Engelond long is Fram þe South into þe North. *a* **1300** *E.E. Psalter* lxxxviii. 12 Þou grounded þe north to be. **1390** GOWER *Conf.* III. 310 Out of the North they sihe a cloude. *a* **1450** *Fysshynge w. Angle* (1883) 21 Yf hyt be by the northe or north est. **1533** GAU *Richt Vay* 53 He sal.. gader to gider al his chosine barnis.. fra the sutht to ye northt. **1594** BLUNDEVIL *Exerc.* III. xix. (1636) 319 How much any Mariners Compasse doth vary from the true North and South. **1625** N. CARPENTER *Geogr. Del.* I. iii. (1635) 62 The magneticall needle will vary from the true point of the North. **1667** MILTON *P.L.* VI. 79 Farr in th' Horizon to the North appeer'd.. a fierie Region. **1725** DE FOE *Voy. round World* (1840) 145 We were obliged to.. go away after it to the north or north-by-west. **1786** H. TOOKE *Purley* II. iv. (1829) II. 302 Directing his view to the North rather than to the East. **1812** WOODHOUSE *Astron.* xli. 409 The Magnetic North, almost always, differs from the true. **1878** HUXLEY *Physiogr.* 6 It is a common practice to draw maps in such a position that the north is towards the top.
Comb. **1648** J. BEAUMONT *Psyche* LX. xxxix, The piercing stroke Of barbarous North-begotten Boreas. **1730–46** THOMSON *Autumn* 890 To where the north-inflated tempest foams O'er Orca's.. highest peak.
b. *Bridge.* A person occupying a position opposite 'South'.
1926 [see EAST *sb.* 4]. **1958** *Listener* 2 Oct. 541/2 North bid Three Clubs. **1965** *Ibid.* 20 May 758/2 The bidding should have made it clear to him that North was hoping to play in Two Hearts doubled. **1973** *Country Life* 21 June 1842/3 Study this deal... Dealer, North. North-South vulnerable.
2. The northern part of a country or region; *spec.* **a.** of England (beyond the Humber), Great Britain, Scotland, or Ireland; the North Country.
c **1205** LAY. 2134 Albanac hefde al þat norð. *c* **1275** *Ibid.* 2659 He.. eode forþ, and droþ [= drew] him in to þat norþ. **1338** R. BRUNNE *Chron.* (1810) 25 Ȝit a noþer Danes kyng in þe Norþ gan aryue. *c* **1386** CHAUCER *Reeve's T.* 95 Of a toun .. Fer in the North, I can nat telle where. *c* **1400** *Brut* xxii. (1906) 26 Anoþere [way] fram þe Northe into þe Southe, þat was callede Ikenyle strete. **1596** SHAKS. *1 Hen. IV,* II. iv. 369 The same mad fellow of the North, Percy. **1665** SIR J. LAUDER *Jrnl.* (1900) 58 A constrainct on that house of Huntly, the Cock of the North. **1674** RAY *Coll. Words* To Rdr., Local words.. in divers Counties,.. especially of the North. **1786** H. TOOKE *Purley* II. iv. (1829) II. 241 The word [scale] is still used in the North. **1855** TENNYSON *Daisy* 104, I forgot the clouded Forth,.. And grey metropolis of the North.
attrib. **1828** CUNNINGHAM *N.S. Wales* (ed. 3) II. 239 The 'Cork boys', the 'Dublin boys', and the 'North boys'.
b. Of Europe: The northern lands.
1579 FULKE *Heskins's Parl.* 119 Peter acknowledged no Pagans, but such as dwell farthest in the North. **1667** MILTON *P.L.* I. 351 A multitude, like which the populous North Pour'd never from her frozen loyns. **1748** HUME *Ess., Nat. Characters,* All strong Liquors are rarer in the North, and consequently are more coveted. **1784** COWPER *Task* I. 617 Thus fare the shiv'ring natives of the north. **1838** CRICHTON *Scandinavia* I. 9 The religion, laws, and literature of the ancient North. **1847** TENNYSON *Princ.* IV. 80 Dark and true and tender is the North.
c. *U.S.* The northern States, those in which there was no slave-holding, bounded on the south by Maryland, the Ohio River, and Missouri.
1796 WASHINGTON *Messages & Papers* (1898) I. 217 The North, in an unrestricted intercourse with the South. **1831** J. M. PECK *Guide for Emigrants* II. 81 The result would be more disastrous to the south and west, than the influx of foreign goods was to.. the north.. in 1816. **1835** in Ht. Martineau *Soc. Amer.* (1837) II. 132 Men of property and

intelligence in the north. **1861** LD. R. MONTAGU *Mirror Amer.* 91 Between the North and South there will be feelings of implacable hatred. **1884** J. QUINCY *Figures Past* 343 Characteristic of slaveholders when upon their good behavior at the North.

3. a. The northern part *of* any country, etc.

c **1425** WYNTOUN *Cron.* I. xiii. 1183 In to þe northe of Europe is A rywere þat hat Canays. **1622** in *Capt. Smith's Wks.* (Arb.) 303 A thousand yeares agoe they were in the North of America. **1738** [see C. 1 b]. **1863** MORRIS *Hampole's Pr. Consc.* Pref. 8 In the Local-names of the North of England.

fig. **1601** SHAKS. *Twel. N.* III. ii. 28 You are now sayld into the North of my Ladies opinion.

b. ***North-of-England***, used *attrib.*, of, pertaining to, or characteristic of, the north of England.

1816 SCOTT *Antiq.* III. ii. 34 His father was a north-of-England gentleman. **1847** C. BRONTË *Jane Eyre* I. xii. 212 A North-of-England spirit, called a 'Gytrash'; which,.. haunted solitary ways. **1907** F. E. E. BELL *At Works* vi. 127 Watching football matches, a comfortless thing enough to do in a North of England winter. **1973** J. WAINWRIGHT *High-Class Kill* 221 North-of-England conformity —— best-clothes-on-Sunday-speak-when-you're spoken-to.

4. a. The north wind. (Chiefly *poet.*)

1382 WYCLIF *Song Sol.* iv. 16 Ris, north, and cum, south; bloȝ thurȝ my gardyn.

1604 SHAKS. *Oth.* v. ii. 220, I will speake as liberall as the North. *c* **1648–50** BRATHWAIT *Barnabees Jrnl.* II. (1818) 45 Sure thou know'st the North's uncivill. **1766** GRAY *Kingsgate* 9 Here reign the blustering North and blighting East. **1786** BURNS *Mountain Daisy* iii, Cauld blew the bitter-biting North Upon thy early, humble birth. **1817** SHELLEY *Rev. Islam* VIII. i, The north breathes steadily Beneath the stars. **1871** R. ELLIS tr. *Catullus* xxvi. 3 'Tis not showery south,.. North's grim fury, nor east.

b. A north wind, esp. one of those northern gales which blow in the West Indies.

1699 DAMPIER *Voy.* II. III. 60 In the West Indies there are three sorts, *viz.* Norths, Souths and Hurricanes. **1707** SLOANE *Jamaica* I. p. xxxii, Hail.. comes with very great Norths, which.. throw down everything before them. **1775** ROMANS *Florida* App. 11 At the season when Norths are frequent. *a* **1818** M. G. LEWIS *Jrnl. W. Ind.* (1834) 113 The drying quality of these norths is still more detrimental than the want of rain. **1851** BLYTH *Rem. Mission. Wk.* v. 205 Even the norths which occasionally prevail are mild.

5. north and south *Rhyming slang*, mouth; **north canoe**, a birchbark canoe once used north and west of Lake Superior, North America; **northpaw** *U.S. slang* (see quot. 1960).

1858 A. MAYHEW *Paved with Gold* II. x. 169 'I'll smash your "glass case", and damage your "north and south",' roared Bill, referring to the *face* and *mouth* of his opponent. **1928** M. C. SHARPE *Chicago May* 287/2 North and South, mouth. **1958** F. NORMAN *Bang to Rights* 36 Dust floating about in the air, which gets in your north and south. **1972** *Lebende Sprachen* XVII. 8/2 *North and south*, mouth. **1819** W. F. WENTZEL *Let.* in L. F. R. Masson *Bourgeois de la Compagnie du Nord-Ouest* (1889) I. 134 Sir Alexander Mackenzie has suggested that one north canoe with Canadian voyageurs, and six small Indian canoes, would be a fitter outfit. **1879** H. M. ROBINSON *Great Fur Land* 31 The North canoe.. is a light graceful vessel about thirty-six long, by four or five broad, and capable of containing eight men and three passengers. **1956** V. FISHER *Pemmican* 250 A north canoe; twenty-five foot long and from four to five feet wide, it could carry a crew of eight or nine men and their supplies, as well as three passengers. **1969** *Islander* (Victoria, B.C.) 23 Nov. 12/3 Ahead roared the Rapids of the Drowned. They gained their name after one of the Hudson's Bay Company's large north canoes capsized there with the loss of several men. **1960** WENTWORTH & FLEXNER *Dict. Amer. Slang* 358/1 *Northpaw*.., a right-handed baseball pitcher; any right-handed person. **1968** *Listener* 19 Sept. 357/1 A skilful person is 'dextrous': in its way as insulting to left-handers (they call us southpaws, though I have never heard anyone described as a northpaw) as 'white man', for someone of worthy character, is offensive to Negroes. **1972** *Daily Mail* 1 Aug. 2/6, 20 per cent of Americans are tired of grappling with things designed for northpaws.

C. *adj.*

Developed from the OE. use of *norð-* as the first element of compounds: see examples in 1, and in the main words NORTHDEAL, -END, -HALF, etc. Similar compounds also occur in the cognate tongues, but have not given rise to a purely adjectival use of the word.

1. With proper names:

a. Denoting the northern division of a race or nation. (See also NORTHUMBER.)

Beowulf 783 Norð-denum stod atelic eȝesa. *c* **900** tr. *Bæda's Hist.* III. xxiv, þa syndon tosceadene mid Trentan streame wið Norðmyrcum. *c* **922** *O.E. Chron.* (Parker MS.) an. 922, þa cyningas on Norþ Wealum.. hine sohton him to hlaforde. **1577–87** HOLINSHED *Chron.* I. 118/2 The countrie of the Northmercies conteined in those daies 7000 housholds. **1670** MILTON *Hist. Eng.* v, Imploring his Aid against the North-Welch. **1841** LATHAM *Eng. Lang.* 40 The situation of the North Frisians has been indicated.

b. Denoting the northern part of a country, land, or region, or the more northern of two places having the same name. Also *attrib.*

c **1205** LAY. 29923 Inne Norð Wales wes a king. **1387** TREVISA *Higden* (Rolls) II. 69 Caerleel is a citee in þe contre of Norþ Engelond. *c* **1450** *Godstow Reg.* 290 Half an acre in northlonglond. **1547** BOORDE *Introd. Knowl.* ii. (1870) 127 North Wales and Sowth Wales do vary in there speche. **1615** BRATHWAIT *Strappado* (1878) 110 Where he encountred a North-britaine man. **1708** *Lond. Gaz.* No. 4422/7 Where-ever they should be called within North-Britain. **1738** DE FOE *Tour* (ed. 2) III. 335 That which we truly call the North of Scotland, and others the North Highlands. **1845** KEMBLE in *Proc. Philol. Soc.* II. 132 The Danish isles, and much of North Germany.

transf. **1801** *Sporting Mag.* XVIII. 101 *North Allertons* —Spurs; that place.. being famous for making them.

c. With sbs. and adjs. derived from the names of countries or districts.

1708– [see NORTH BRITON]. **1766** [see NORTH AMERICAN]. **1796** MORSE *Amer. Geogr.* I. 654 The North Carolinians are mostly planters. **1845** KEMBLE in *Proc. Philol. Soc.* II. 119 On the North Anglian Dialect.

d. ***North Oxford***, of, pertaining to, or characteristic of the suburban part of Oxford north of the university area, where many dons and their families live. Also as *sb.*

1935 N. MITCHISON *We have been Warned* IV. 462 She had.. a Sybil Dunlop moonstone on a long silver chain. A bit North Oxfordy? Well, she was North Oxford! **1950** A. WILSON *Such Darling Dodos* 79 The whimsical humour of North Oxford. *Ibid.* 97 Why you should have to drag Coleridge in, only your staunch North Oxford spirit can explain. **1973** *Country Life* 13 Sept. 720/1 The houses behind (Carolean or North Oxford Gothic?).. seem oddly familiar. **1974** F. EMERY *Oxfordsh. Landscape* vii. 214 Between the rustic variety of Summertown and the old suburbs of St Giles lies the Victorian perfection of North Oxford proper.

2. a. With ordinary nouns: Lying towards the north; situated on the side next the north.

a **1122** *O.E. Chron.* (Laud MS.) an. 565, Columba.. com to Pyhtum.. þæt sind þone wærteres be norðum morum. **1382** WYCLIF *Num.* xxxiv. 7 To the north plage [**1388** at the north coost] fro the greet see teermes shulen begynne. *c* **1391** CHAUCER *Astrol.* II. §21 Fro the pool artik vn-to the north Orisonte. **1432–50** tr. *Higden* (Rolls) I. 93 That cuntre of Media towchethe Parthia of the northe parte. **1486** *Rec. St. Mary at Hill* (1904) 14 On the North part of the Chirch. **1513** BRADSHAW *St. Werburge* I. 452 Kynge of the North regyon. *Ibid.* 473 Penda.. to the North partyes went. **1591** SHAKS. *Two Gentl.* III. i. 380 Thy Master staies for thee at the North gate. **1601** HOLLAND *Pliny* I. 121 Being once past the vtmost quarter of the North-point. **1612** CAPT. SMITH *Descr. Virg.* Wks. (Arb.) 47 The degrees of 34 and 44 of the north latitude. **1726** DART *Canterb. Cathedr.* 60 In the North-Cross or Martyrdom, where are the Tombs of the Archbishops. **1837** *Penny Cycl.* VII. 146/2 A north transept.. longer than the south transept.

Comb. **1862** ANSTED *Channel Isl.* I. i. 5 A north-central group, including Guernsey, Herm, Sark [etc.].

b. Facing the north. Also *Comb.*

1642 FULLER *Holy & Prof. St.* III. vii. 167 A North-window is best for Butteries and Cellars. **1706** LONDON & WISE *Retir'd Gard.* 69 Plant no more than two sorts against a North-aspected Wall. **1727–38** CHAMBERS *Cycl.* s.v. *Dial*, A north dial shews the hours before six in the morning, and those after six in the evening. **1796** C. MARSHALL *Gardening* iii. (1813) 29 The North wall is greatly advantaged, by having more sun.

c. Northern; of a northern type.

1820 KEATS *Isabella* xxxii, Before he dares to stray From his north cavern. **1836** F. S[YKES] *Scraps from Jrnl.* 106 The building is very neat..; it is peculiarly north.

Comb. **1837** CARLYLE *Fr. Rev.* II. I. xi, Considerate North-blooded Mountaineers of Jura.

d. North Circular (Road), a road passing through the northern outskirts of London.

1944 M. LASKI *Love on Supertax* xi. 102 After a prolonged.. journey by 'bus, Clarissa alighted way out on the North Circular Road. **1968** J. LLOYD *Death at Roman Farm* xviii. 171 You go straight through town and send the other car round the North Circular. **1974** 'A. GARVE' *File on Lester* xxxi. 118 He became silent, concentrating on his driving on the busy North Circular.

3. Of the wind: Blowing from the north.

Perhaps representing OE. *norðanwind*.

c **1340** *Nominale sive Verbale* (Skeat) 565 Northwynde, Estwynde. **1483** *Cath. Angl.* 256/1 Þe Northe wynde; *boreas, septemtrio*. **1535** COVERDALE *Song Sol.* iv. 16 Vp thou northwynde, come thou southwynde. **1608** SHAKS. *Per.* IV. i. 52 When I was born, the wind was north. **1667** MILTON *P.L.* II. 489 The dusky clouds Ascending, while the North wind sleeps. **1712** ARBUTHNOT *John Bull* I. xvi, You might argue as well with the North wind, as with her ladyship. **1797** *Encycl. Brit.* (ed. 3) XIII. 106/1 The north wind is generally accompanied with a considerable degree of cold. **1833** TENNYSON *Two Voices* 259 He will not hear the north-wind rave. **1857** EMERSON *Poems* 42 Without the baffled north-wind calls.

fig. **1656** EARL MONM. tr. *Boccalini's Advts. fr. Parnass.* II. vi. (1674) 145 They should sail with the safe North-wind of *Ne-quid nimis*.

4. *Comb.*, **north-facing** *a.*, facing the north; *spec.* of a window.

1952 A. G. L. HELLYER *Sanders' Encycl. Gardening* (ed. 22) 205 Position, semi-shaded or north-facing. **1973** 'I. DRUMMOND' *Jaws of Watchdog* xii. 156 A large window. North-facing so I guess a studio.

north (nɔːθ), *v. rare.* [f. prec.]

1. *intr.* Of the wind: To begin to blow from the north; to turn or veer towards the north.

1866 in GREGOR *Banffsh. Gloss.* **1880–1** in JAMIESON.

2. *trans.* To steer to the north of (a place).

1887 MORRIS *Odyss.* III. 170 Whether northing Chios the craggy, our ships we so should lay.

north a'bout. *Naut.* By a northerly route, *spec.* round the north of Scotland.

Cf. OE. *norþ ymbutan* in *O.E. Chron.* an. 894.

1710 *Lond. Gaz.* No. 4685/3 Four Galleys from the River of Thames, bound North about to New-England. **1785** J. PHILLIPS *Treat. Inland Navig.* 48 They are now obliged to be brought.. down the English Channel..; or else they must go North-about, which is a long and dangerous voyage. **1796** MORSE *Amer. Geogr.* I. 139 To coast north-about in small vessels, between the great flakes of ice and the shore. **1851** *Beck's Florist* 13 Jan., Off the coast of Scotland (for we were going north about). **1858** *Merc. Marine Mag.* V. 240 It was desirable to go.. north-about.

North African, *a.* and *sb.* [f. *North Africa* the countries of northern Africa, *spec.* the region including Morocco, Algeria, Tunisia, Libya, and Egypt.] **A.** *adj.* Of or pertaining to North Africa or its inhabitants. **B.** *sb.* A native or inhabitant of North Africa.

1867 'OUIDA' *Under Two Flags* II. iii. 56 The blaze and heat of the North African day. **1932** KIPLING *Limits & Renewals* 321 His speech—to suit his hearers—ran From pure Parisian to gross peasant, With interludes North African If any Legionnaire were present. **1961** E. WAUGH *Unconditional Surrender* II. v. 140 Stirred by the heavy North African wine de Souza's imagination rolled into action. **1962** P. BRICKHILL *Deadline* vi. 88 The noise made by four North Africans on a dais. *Ibid.* 89 Belly dancing seemed to be the forte of the North African smart spots in Paris. **1972** D. LEES *Zodiac* 107 The couscous was being ladled out by a grinning North African.

North American, *sb.* and *a.* [f. *North America* the name of the northern part of the continent of America including Central America, Mexico, U.S., and Canada.] **A.** *sb.* A native or inhabitant of North America, esp. of the United States or Canada.

1766 FRANKLIN *Observ.* Wks. 1887 III. 501 Did ever any North-American bring his hemp to England for this bounty? **1783** A. STOKES *Brit. Colonies* 144 The North Americans will refuse them their assistance. **1825** J. NEAL *Bro. Jonathan* II. 1 The man of America—the Original North American.. the 'Indian' as he is called. *Ibid.* III. 413 The brave North American was dead. **1974** 'E. ANTHONY' *Malaspiga Exit* ii. 25 You could disguise every feature except the magnificent dentistry of the North Americans.

B. *adj.* Of or pertaining to North America or its inhabitants; belonging to or characteristic of North America, living in North America, etc.

1770 J. OTIS in W. Tudor *Life J. Otis* (1823) 476 My humble North American word of honour for it, my lord, these volumes will hurt neither thee, nor thy master. **1771** FRANKLIN *Autobiogr.* (1909) 171 This was the mother of all the North American subscription libraries, now so numerous. **1775** BURKE *Speech on Conciliation with America* 22 Mar. in *Wks.* II (1792) 31 The export trade to the colonies consists of three great branches. The African.. the West Indian; and the North-American. **1776** (*title*) The North-American and the West-Indian Gazetteer. **1783** (*title*) The North-American Calendar. **1837** *Southern Lit. Messenger* III. 695 A declaration of the independence of the North American States. **1880** G. W. CABLE *Grandissimes* iv. 23 She had.. the nerve of the true North American Indian. **1916** G. B. SHAW *Androcles & Lion* p. li, Jesus himself had referred to that psalm (LXXXII) in which men who have judged unjustly and accepted the persons of the wicked (including by anticipation practically all the white inhabitants of the British Isles and the North American continent, to mention no other places) are condemned. **1923** A. L. KROEBER *Anthropol.* xiii. 356 It would be extravagant to maintain that throughout the North American continent every matrilineal tribe was culturally more advanced than every patrilineal one. **1949** *Chicago Tribune* 8 Nov. 1. 12/2 The very rich head of a business is vanishing as rapidly as the North American Indian. **1952** *Oxf. Jun. Encycl.* X. 105/1 The example of the North American colonists roused other oppressed colonists to bid for freedom. **1959** M. SCHLAUCH *Eng. Lang.* iii. 78 Words connected with the life of North American Indians also appeared after 1600. **1974** E. AMBLER *Dr. Frigo* II. 96 He was still speaking Spanish but adulterating it now with.. North American business jargon. **1975** *Country Life* 6 Nov. 1250/3 *Q[uercus] coccinea* is the North American scarlet oak.

north-bound, *a.* Also northbound. [NORTH *adv.*] Bound for the north; travelling northwards; also, intended for such travellers, serving as a point of departure for the north. Also as *sb.*, a north-bound train.

1903 KIPLING *Five Nations* 115 We gather and wait her coming—The wonderful north-bound train. **1904** W. N. HARBEN *Georgians* 217 The young man was at the seven-o'clock north-bound train when it stopped in the antiquated brick car-shed. **1939** G. HOUSEHOLD *Rogue Male* 78 At the bottom of the Piccadilly escalator you turn left for the north-bound trains... I ran on to the north-bound platform. **1973** *Sci. Amer.* June 26/2 A slowing of the northbound Coastal Current. **1975** D. BEATY *Electric Train* 232 'When's the next train?' 'No more northbounds tonight.'

North 'Briton. Also 8 Britain. [See NORTH *a.* 1 c.] A native of Scotland; a Scot.

1708 *Lond. Gaz.* No. 4409/4 Geo. Bremar, a North Britain,.. well set and fat. **1717** PRIOR *Alma* I. 216 North Britons thus have Second Sight. **1822** SCOTT *Nigel* ii, 'I see nae gude it wad do me to speak ought else but truth,' said the worthy North Briton. **1862** BORROW *Wales* xxii, A tall lathy North Briton with a keen eye and hard features.

Hence **North-'Britonize** *v.*

An allusion to the title of Wilkes' newspaper, *The North Briton*, published in 1762–3.

1764 H. WALPOLE *Let. to Earl Hertford* 12 April (1846) IV. 406 Mr. Wilkes would have been glad to have North-Britonised for our little Bishop of Osnaburgh.

† **north-caper**, obs. variant of NORDCAPER.

1743 *Phil. Trans.* XLII. 611 There is another sort of Whale in these Seas, called North-Capers, which feed on Herrings. **1796** STEDMAN *Surinam* II. 384 We also saw.. above the water a large north-caper. This fish, which very much resembles the Greenland whale, is more dangerous.

north 'country. [NORTH *a.* 2.]

1. The northern part of any country; *spec.* of England (beyond the Humber) or Great Britain; the country or region towards the north.

1297 R. GLOUC. (Rolls) 7978 Hii.. barnde & destrude þe norþ contreie vaste. **1338** R. BRUNNE *Chron.* (1810) 32 Men say he was fonden in þe North cuntre At Hexham now late. **1387** TREVISA *Higden* (Rolls) II. 163 ȝif þey gooþ to þe norþ contray þey gooþ wiþ greet..strengþe. **1458** in Gardner *Hist. Dunwich* (1754) 149 To Will. Roper when he went to the norre Contre for the Kyngs Viage. **1535** COVERDALE *Zech.* vi. 8 These that go towarde the north, shal still my wrath in the north countre. **1577** HARRISON *England* II. v. (1877) I. 108 Here in England, especiallie in the north countrie. **1611** BIBLE *Zech.* vi. 6 The blacke horses..goe forth into the North countrey. **1681** GLANVILL *Sadducismus* 5 It was, and sometimes yet is, as much discoursed of in the North-Countrey, as any thing. **1768** BEATTIE *Minstr.* I. xi, But he, I ween, was of the north countrie. **1840** CARLYLE *Heroes* (1858) 198 In a greater proportion along the east coast; and greatest of all, as I find, in the North Country.

2. The dialect of the north of England. Also a native of the north country of England.

1698 *Lond. Gaz.* No. 3357/4 He..speaks broad North Country. **1706** *Ibid.* No. 4214/4 Speaks North Country. **1823** J. G. LOCKHART *R. Dalton* II. v. v. 289 You're north-country, I believe. **1966** *Listener* 7 Apr. 501/1, I can play cockney, I can play north country. **1972** C. DRUMMOND *Death at Bar* ii. 60 'If you borrow you make bad friends'—a flash of honest north-country peeped through the trained accent. **1974** *Times* 30 Dec. 4/7 Gracie Fields..reverts to the characteristic mixture of North Country, standard English and American overtones. **1975** J. MITCHELL *Smear Job* x. 69 Her accent was harshly Sicilian, but lurking in it was a hint of the North Country she had picked up from the soldiers.

3. *attrib.* **a.** (Frequently hyphened.)

1674 RAY *Coll. Words* (heading), North-countrey Words. **1684** SYMSON in Ramsay *Remin.* (1874) 212 Contrary to some north country people, they oftentimes pronounce 'w' for 'v'. **1703** *Lond. Gaz.* No. 3898/4 Strong Voice, a North Country Pronunciation. **1753–4** RICHARDSON *Grandison* (1781) V. 48 Aunt Nell, who has naturally a good blowzing north country complexion. **1838** *Civil Eng. & Arch. Jrnl.* I. 341/2 Eleven hundred and sixty-five pounds of 'north country coals'. **1871** RUSKIN *Munera P.* Pref. (1880) 19 A quiet north country town. **1896** D. C. MURRAY (*title*) A capful o' nails: a North-Country story. **1933** M. ALLINGHAM *Sweet Danger* x. 129 A comfortable, homely voice with an unexpected North Country accent. **1959** R. LONGRIGG *Wrong Number* ii. 30 They..left in a gruff welter of north-country gratitude. **1964** V. S. NAIPAUL *Area of Darkness* ix. 243 The newcomer was a commercial Englishman, middle-aged, fat and red-faced. He spoke with a North Country accent.

b. ***North-countryman***, a native of the north of England.

1706 *Lond. Gaz.* No. 4252/4 Jonathan Shipton, a North-Countryman. **1711** J. GREENWOOD *Eng. Gram.* 276 A Word common with the Scotch, and our North countreymen. **1834** MARRYAT *P. Simple* (1863) 196 The master, an old north-countryman, who knows his duty. **1876** L. STEPHEN *Eng. Th. in 18th C.* vi. II. 121 Paley is a hard-headed North-countryman.

Hence **north-'countriness**.

1888 *Pall Mall G.* 8 Mar. 3/2 There is a chill north-countriness over everything.

†**northdeal, -dole.** *Obs.* [See NORTH *a.*, and cf. Du. *noorderdeel*, G. *nordtheil*.] The northern part *of* a place.

c **893** K. ÆLFRED *Oros.* I. x. 44 Mid firde farende on Sciþþie on ðа norðdælas. *c* **1000** ÆLFRIC *Hom.* I. 10 He wolde..sittan on þam norð-dæle heofenan rices. *c* **1100** *O.E. Chron.* (MS. D) an. 926, Her oðeowdon fyrena leoman on norð dæle þære lyfte. *c* **1200** ORMIN 16412 Norrþdale off all þiss werelld iss Arrctoss bi name nemmnedd.

†**northdown.** *Obs.*$^{-1}$ Some kind of liquor.

1670 SIR T. CULPEPER *Necess. Abating Usury* 12 Accustomed to swill in Spirits, Brandy, Sack, Metheglin, Northdown, and Mum.

north-east (nɔːθ'iːst), *adv.*, *sb.*, and *a.* [f. NORTH and EAST: cf. MDu. *noortoost* (Du. *noordoost*), G., Sw., Da. *nordost*; also F. (13th cent.), It., and Sp. *nordest*, Sp. and Pg. *nordeste*.

OE. had also *norðanéastan*, from the north-east, = MDu. *noortoosten-*, OHG. *nord-*, *northostan*.]

A. *adv.* **1.** In the direction lying midway between north and east.

931 in W. de Gray Birch *Cartul. Sax.* II. 358 Swa norð east to ðære lytlan riðe. *a* **1122** *O.E. Chron.* (Laud MS.) an. 1106, Swilce ormæte beam ʒeþuht norð east scinende. **14..** *Sailing Directions* (Hakluyt) 11 It flowith on the londe of Holdernes northest. **1555** EDEN *Decades* (Arb.) 348 Neyther shulde the needle make any chaunge..in saylynge northeeste. **1612** CAPT. SMITH *Descr. Virg.* Wks. (Arb.) 52 The river it selfe turneth North east. **1725** DE FOE *Voy. round World* (1840) 174 We stood away now north-east and north-east-by-north. **1762** FALCONER *Shipwr.* I. 726 North-east a league, the Isle of Standia bears. **1846** DICKENS *Cricket on Hearth* i, It's been blowing north-east, straight into the cart, the whole way home. **1872** RAYMOND *Statist. Mines & Mining* 11 The mines are situated 42 miles north east of the town of San Diego.

Comb. **1875** BEDFORD *Sailor's Pkt.-bk.* (ed. 2) §5. 172 The north-east going stream..makes to the eastward.

2. quasi-*sb.* With prepositions, as *on*, *from*, *at*.

c **1122** *O.E. Chron.* (Laud MS.) an. 1122, Feole scipmen ..sædon þæt hi sæʒon on norð east fir micel. **1481** CAXTON *Godfrey* clxxiii. 256 Fro the yate toward northeste..vnto the tour on the corner. *c* **1500** *Lancelot* 677 Richt as he spred his bemys frome northest, The king wprass. **1599** HAKLUYT *Voy.* II. II. 329 In the 41 degrees we met with the winde at Northeast. **1725** DE FOE *Voy. round World* (1840) 146 So I ran on, having an easy gale at north-east.

B. *sb.* **1.** The direction, or point of the horizon, lying midway between north and east.

1387 TREVISA *Higden* (Rolls) I. 61 Þe secounde [sea] is i-cleped Caspius, and entreþ toward þe norþ est. **1398** —— *Barth. De P.R.* XV. ix. (Bodl. MS.), He haþ..in þe norþe este þe grickissche see. *a* **1450** [see NORTH B. 1]. **1535** COVERDALE *Ezek.* xl. 23 Ouer agaynst the dore, that was towarde yᵉ north east. **1604** E. G[RIMSTONE] *D'Acosta's Hist. Indies* III. v. 134 Mestrall they call the northeast. **1725** DE FOE *Voy. round World* (1840) 302 The wind came about to the north-east and blew very hard. **1778** W. ROBERTSON *Hist. Amer.* Wks. 1851 V. 139 [He] directed his course towards the north-east. **1844** *Mem. Babylonian Princess* II. 134 On the north-east, the lake of Genesareth. **1856** BOND *Russia at Close 16th C.* (Hakluyt) Introd. 3 They despatched expeditions..in the direction of the north-east.

2. The north-east wind.

1382 WYCLIF *Acts* xxvii. 14 The wynd Tiffonyk, that is clepid north eest, or wynd of tempest.

1711 PRIOR *Henry & Emma* 368 Can they resist The parching dog-star, and the bleak north-east? **1728–46** THOMSON *Spring* 142 The North-east spends his rage. **1865** ALLINGHAM *50 Mod. Poems, Winter Cloud*, With snow Driv'n by a sharp north-east on bough and stem.

C. *adj.*

1. Of the wind: Blowing from the north-east. Perhaps representing OE. *norðanéastan wind.*

1398 TREVISA *Barth. De P.R.* XI. iii. (Bodl. MS.), Anoþer ..hatte chorus, þe norþe este winde. **1483** *Cath. Angl.* 256/1 Þe Northe est wynde, *uroaquilo*. **1581** PETTIE tr. *Guazzo's Civ. Conv.* I. (1586) 17 b, I thinke the Northeast winde doth not so driue in sunder the clouds. **1667** MILTON *P.L.* IV. 161 North-East windes blow Sabean Odours from the spicie shoare. **1707** MORTIMER *Husb.* (1721) II. 112 The Eastern [aspect] is subject to the North-East Winds. **1797** *Encycl. Brit.* (ed. 3) XVIII. 862/2 It appears..that the north-east wind blows much more frequently in April, May, and June ..than at any other period. **1861** F. METCALFE *Oxonian in Iceland* x. (1867) 152 A north-east wind is called a 'land-north' wind.

2. Lying or situated in or towards the north-east. Also *fig.*

1501 DOUGLAS *Pal. Hon.* I. xxvi, And sa appeirit to my fantasie, A schynand licht out of the north eist sky. **1560** *Astrol.* in *Chaucer's Wks.* 251/2 The Sterres..ben cleped Sterres of the North, for they arisen by the Northeast line. **1675** *Phil. Trans.* X. 457 A Noarth East and South West Moon. **1709** *Brit. Apollo* No. 56. 2/2 Turn the North-East Side of your Face to them and blast their Expectations. **1726** SWIFT *Gulliver* I. viii, Walking..to the North-East Coast of the Island. **1821** SCOTT *Kenilw.* xxvi, A small but strong tower, occupying the north-east angle of the building. **1900** J. V. BARTLET *Apost. Age* I. vi. 157 Rhodes, lying to the northeast corner of its fine island.

b. ***north-east passage***, a passage for vessels along the northern coasts of Europe and Asia, formerly thought of as a possible course by which to make voyages to the East.

1600 HAKLUYT *Voy.* III. A 6 b, Great probabilities of a North, Northwest, or Northeast passage. *a* **1625** FLETCHER *Woman's Prize* II. ii, As many servants..as the North-East passage Has consum'd sailors. **1697** DAMPIER *Voy.* (1699) 274, I would take the same method if I was to go to discover the North East Passage. **1725** [see PASSAGE *sb.* 11]. **1885** *Encycl. Brit.* XIX. 325 The achievement of the north-east passage.

Hence **north-'east** *v.* Of the compass: To vary in the direction of north-east. *rare*$^{-1}$.

a **1646** J. GREGORY *Posthuma, Maps & Charts* (1650) 311 At the Straits of Magellan the Roundlet there saith..That the Needle North-easteth six Degrees.

north-'easter. [f. as prec. + -ER¹.] A wind blowing from the north-east.

1774 FITHIAN *Jrnl.* in *Amer. Hist. Rev.* V. 315 This is a true August Northeaster, as we call it in Cohansie. **1839** LONGF. *Life* (1891) I. 347 It means a storm-wind—or a north-easter, coming over the sea. **1870** KINGSLEY in *Gd. Words* 203/2 Thanks to the brave north-easter, we have gained in five days thirty degrees of heat.

north-'easterly, *a.* and *adv.* [f. NORTH + EASTERLY.] **A.** *adj.*

1. Of the wind: Blowing from the north-east.

1743 WOODROOFE in Hanway *Trav.* (1762) I. II. xxiii. 101 Hard gales of north easterly winds. **1806** *Med. Jrnl.* XV. 581 The north and north-easterly wind has lately prevailed in an unusual degree. **1878** *Encycl. Brit.* XVI. 149/1 In the New England States..north-easterly winds are cold.

2. Lying towards the north-east.

1825 J. NEAL *Bro. Jonathan* III. 85 A ridge of hills, running quite across the island, in a north easterly direction. **1872** RAYMOND *Statist. Mines & Mining* 11 In a north-easterly direction from San Diego City.

B. *adv.* From or towards the north-east.

1739 *Encour. Seaf. People* 38 The Admiral followed them ..., with small Gales NEtly. **1796** MORSE *Amer. Geogr.* I. 117 [Raleigh] coasted northeasterly as far as Chesapeak Bay. **1877** RAYMOND *Statist. Mines & Mining* 112 A branch of Buck's Creek, flowing northeasterly.

north-'eastern, *a.* [f. NORTH + EASTERN.] Lying on the north-east side.

1841 EMERSON *Misc.* 226 Walking here on our North-eastern shores. **1861** F. METCALFE *Oxonian in Iceland* x. (1867) 148 The wild reindeer frequent mostly the north-eastern parts of the island. **1878** GLADSTONE *Homer* 59 The great northern and north-eastern mass of Europe.

†**north-'easting,** *vbl. sb. Obs.* [f. NORTH-EAST + -ING¹.] The variation of the compass from the true north in the direction of north-east.

1555 EDEN *Decades* (Arb.) 348 Neyther shulde the needle make anye chaunge or dyffer in northestinge. **1561** —— *Arte Navig.* A iij, The maner and causes of the Northeastinge & Norwesting (commonly called the variation of the compasse). **1594** BLUNDEVIL *Exerc.* III. vii. (1636) 384 In every other place the Compasse doth vary from the true North, either by Northeasting or Northwesting. *a* **1646** J. GREGORY *Posthuma, Maps & Charts* (1650) 311 The several Degrees of Variation of the Compass in North-easting or North-westing.

north-'eastward, *adv.*, *a.*, and *sb.* [f. NORTH-EAST + -WARD. Cf. MDu. *noortoostwert*, G. *nordostwärts*.] **A.** *adv.* Towards the north-east; in a north-eastern direction.

1553 EDEN *Treat. Newe Ind.* (Arb.) 26 Northeastwarde to the citie of Lop. **1839** THACKERAY *Major Gahagan* i, I travelled..north-eastward. **1849** DANA *Geol.* I. (1850) 19 This chain extends northeastward from Hawaii. **1884** *Harper's Mag.* Sept. 513/1 The sand and lava..extend northeastward from the Dalles.

B. *adj.* Situated towards the north-east.

1766 ENTICK *London* IV. 60 The king's-arms [are] on the north-eastward, and the arms of London on the south-eastward pillar.

C. *sb.* The north-east quarter.

1892 *Daily News* 27 Apr. 3/5 Wind was..from the northward or north-eastward.

north-'eastwardly, *a.* and *adv.* [-LY¹.]

A. *adj.* Blowing from, situated or leading towards, the north-east.

1796 *Phil. Trans.* LXXXVI. 351 The north-eastwardly end of the tunnel. **1805** *Ibid.* XCVI. 245 North-eastwardly winds..were the next that prevailed. **1860** MAURY *Phys. Geogr.* ii. §65 The isothermal lines..run off in a northeastwardly direction.

B. *adv.* Towards the north-east.

1796 MORSE *Amer. Geogr.* I. 609 Nearly parallel with the sea coast, though rather approaching it as they advance northeastwardly. **1807** VANCOUVER *Agric. Devon* (1813) 25 Returning north-eastwardly from Tiverton.

†**'northen,** *a. Obs.* Also 2 **norðen**, 5 **-þen**, 4 **norþin**, 5 *Sc.* **-thyne**, 6 **-thin**. [f. NORTH + -EN⁴. Cf. MDu. *norden*, *noorden*.] Northern.

c **1175** in Assmann *Ags. Hom.* (1889) VII. 109 Of iaphet.. com þæt norðene mennisc. **13..** *Cursor M.* 20063 (Edinb.), Turnid ic haue it til ur awin language of the norþin lede. **1398** TREVISA *Barth. De P.R.* XVII. lxi. (Bodl. MS.), The norþen winde greueth þe fige tree more þan þe soþen winde. *c* **1450** tr. *De Imitatione* III. xxvii. 97 Sey to þe see, 'be in reste,' & to þe norþen wynde, 'blowe not'. **1513** DOUGLAS *Æneid* VII. Prol. 15 Brym blastis of the northyne art. **1588** *Marprel. Epist.* (Arb.) 25 His grace hearing this northen logicke, was mooued on the sodaine. *c* **1625** FLETCHER *Nice Valour* I. i, He has almost beate The Northen fellow blind. **1660** tr. *Amyraldus' Treat. conc. Relig.* III. i. 304 As if a man should purpose to sail from the South with a Northen Wind. **1709** H. BLUNT in Garth *Dispens.*, The People of the Northen Zone. **1772** D. TAITT in N. D. Mereness *Trav. Amer. Col.* (1916) 541 The Inhabitants of the Tuskigees are a remnant of Northen Indians and speak a different Language from the Creek. **1773** C. CAROLL *Let.* 26 Mar. in *Maryland Hist. Mag.* (1920) XV. 58 Keep the Boy if the Northen Post be not Come in untill Monday.

north-end. [OE. *norðende*, f. *norð* NORTH *adv.*; cf. MDu. *nortende*, Du. *noordeinde*, G. *nordende*. In later use f. NORTH *a.*, and properly unhyphened, except when used attributively.]

1. The northern end or extremity of anything.

c **888** K. ÆLFRED *Boeth.* xxxix. §3 Hi sint swa neah þam norðende þære eaxe þe eall þes rodor on hwerfð. **971** *Blickl. Hom.* 93 Seo eorþe on þæm norþ-ende & on þam east-ende sprecaþ him betweonum. *c* **1205** LAY. 12729 Heo habbeoð of ure londe al þene norð ende. *a* **1352** MINOT *Poems* ix. 3 Þe north end of Ingland teched him to daunce. **1641** in Nalson *Impart. Collect.* (1683) II. 399 At the North-end of the Table so standing Altar-wise. **1707** [see NORTHERMOST]. **1840** *Origines Par. Scotiae* I. 327 Near the north end of the present parish. **1861** F. METCALFE *Oxonian in Iceland* v. (1867) 81 Occupying what I believe to have been once the north end of the lake.

attrib. **1902** *Protest. Observer* Sept. 131/1 The Archbishop of Canterbury very properly took the North-end position at the Table.

b. (See quot.)

1883 GRESLEY *Gloss. Coal-mining* 175 *North End*, the rise side of the coal in North Yorkshire.

†**2.** The north of England. *Obs.*

c **1100** *O.E. Chron.* (MS. D) an. 1052, Man bead þa folce þider ut ofer ealne þisne norðende. *c* **1205** LAY. 28982 Þa wunede bi-ȝeonde þere Hunbre..in þan norð ende drenches sume sixe. *c* **1300** *Havelok* 734 In humber grim bigan to lende, In lindesaye, Rith at þe north ende. **1338** R. BRUNNE *Chron.* (1810) 32 Alle þe north ende was in his kepyng, & alle þe South ende tille Edmund þei drouh.

northen-spell, corrupt var. of *knurr and spell*: see KNUR 3.

1801 STRUTT *Sports & Past.* II. iii. 86 Northen-spell is played with a trap, and the ball is stricken with a bat or bludgeon.

†**'northenwards,** *adv. Obs.* From the north.

1591 *Child-Marriages* 155 Richard Ince hath receyued into his howse diuers parcelles of Red and white harnes northenwardes within the said Citie.

†**'norther,** *a. Obs.* [OE. *norþerra*, *norðra*, a comparative formed on *norþ*, *norð* adv. = OFris. *northera*, MDu. *nordere*, *noordre*, ON. *nordari*. Cf. MLG. and MHG. *norder-*, Du. *noorder-* in combs. In sense 2 perh. for *northern*.]

1. The more northerly of two places or things; situated or lying to the north.

901 in Birch *Cartul. Sax.* II. 242 Þonne andlang steðes þæt be neoðan beamwær on þone norðere steð. *c* **922** *O.E. Chron.* (Parker MS.) an. 922, Ðæt folc eal ðe to ðære norþerran byriȝ hierde. **947** in Birch *Cartul. Sax.* II. 601 Ðone licgað ðær ða þreo hida on ðan norðran denceswurðe undælede. *c* **1290** *St. Edmund* 361 in *S. Eng. Leg.* I. 441 In alle halewene church-ȝerd, in þe norþure side. **1497** HEN. VII in Ellis *Orig. Lett.* Ser. I. I. 35 Whereupon Perkin and his company went to the East gate, and to the Norther gate.

2. Northern; belonging to the north.

1375 BARBOUR *Bruce* XVII. 846 Bot Northir men wald no-thing swa.

†ˈ**norther**, *adv. Obs. rare.* [Cf. prec. and ON. *norðarr.*] Further north.

*c*893 K. ÆLFRED *Oros.* I. i. 18 þæt byne land is easteweard bradost, & symle swa norðor swa smælre. *c*1275 LAY. 2674 þo ferde he norþer, and one neuwe borh makede.

norther (ˈnɔːθə(r)), *sb.* [f. NORTH + -ER[1].]

1. A northerly wind; esp. a strong north wind accompanied with intense cold, which blows, during the autumn and winter months, over Texas, Florida, and the Gulf of Mexico.

1827 *Western Monthly Rev.* I. 320 We were struck by a gale, that they call a norther. **1831** M. HOLLEY *Texas* (1833) i. 19 Our voyage..is..not without hazard, on account of the Northers; as they are called. **1844** MRS. HOUSTON *Yacht. Voy. Texas* II. 147 During the continuance of a norther, the cold is intense. **1857** OLMSTED *Journ. Texas* 169 These northers upon the open prairies are exceedingly trying. **1891** V. STUART *Adv. Equat. For.* 132 The Northers on rare occasions carry frost even as far south as Cape Sable. **1946** *Sun* (Baltimore) 30 Dec. 11/1 St. Mary's football squad arrived in Houston early this morning to be greeted by a Texas 'norther'. **1969** 'J. MORRIS' *Fever Grass* xiii. 121 A fresh 'norther' was blowing from the Gulf. **1973** *Houston* (Texas) *Chron.* 21 Oct. 1/3 (*caption*) A delightfully persistent Indian Summer lingered over Houston, luring people to parks for langorous hours of contentment before looking ahead to winter and the prospect of rain and blue northers.

2. A strong north wind blowing in other parts, esp. on the Pacific seaboard of North America.

1835 J. F. COOPER *Monikins* II. iii. 71 It may be even now questioned whether the ship would claw off..with a sending sea, and this heavy norther. **1850** in *Harper's Mag.* (1878) Jan. 279 We met a norther in coming out of the Gulf of California. **1891** *Scribner's Mag.* X. 283 The weather along the Pacific highway has been uniformly pleasant, for northers are infrequent. **1893** KIPLING *Seven Seas* (1896) 28 We've slipped from Valparaiso With the Norther at our heels. **1903** —— *Five Nations* 53 That night the Norther found me—Froze and killed the plains-bred ponies.

norther (ˈnɔːðə(r)), *v.* [f. NORTH *adv.* + -ER[5].] *intr.* Of the wind: To shift or veer northward. Hence ˈ**northering** *ppl. a.*

1628–9 DIGBY *Voy. Medit.* (Camden) 93 It was extreme cold, and the wind northered vpon vs. **1672** *Lond. Gaz.* No. 682/4 The wind was very high, and Northering. **1889** *Daily News* 9 July 3/6 In a northering breeze the Valkyrie had just the better of the Irex. **1893** F. ADAMS *New Egypt* 86 The hills..run inland with a slight northering tendency.

ˈ**northerliness.** *rare*[−0]. 'The state of being northerly' (Ogilvie *Suppl.* 1855).

ˈ**northerling.** *rare*[−1]. [f. NORTH; cf. EASTERLING.] A native or inhabitant of the north.

1616 *Manifest. Abp. Spalato's Motives* App. III. 1 Stooping so low, as in our owne Language to conuerse with vs..rude Northerlings.

northerly (ˈnɔːðəlɪ), *a.* [f. NORTH; cf. *easterly, westerly.*]

1. Situated towards the north; northern.

1551 RECORDE *Cast. Knowl.* (1556) 263 The one sorte are called Northerlye constellations. **1577** B. GOOGE *Heresbach's Husb.* I. (1586) 17 In colde and Northerlye Countreys. **1624** CAPT. SMITH *Virginia* v. 174 In the height of thirty degrees of Northerly latitude. **1671** J. GAILHARD *Pres. St. Italy* (ed. 2) 196 Northerly people do blame the wayes which they [Italians] use to be avenged. **1730** A. GORDON *Maffei's Amphith.* 323 The northerly Circus in Constantinople. **1776** SEMPLE *Building in Water* 39, I then stood on the northerly Part of the Bridge. **1862** J. M. LUDLOW *Hist. U.S.* 105 Faster..on the more Northerly than on the more Southerly parallels. **1880** GEIKIE *Phys. Geog.* iv. 182 The most northerly swell of the Rocky Mountains.

fig. **1599** B. JONSON *Cynthia's Rev.* II. i, A..smooth and overflowing face that Seems as it would run and pour itself into you: Somewhat a northerly face.

2. Of the wind: Blowing from the northward.

1555 EDEN *Decades* (Arb.) 382 We mette northerly wyndes and greate roostynge of tydes. **1602** SHAKS. *Ham.* v. ii. 99 Beleeue mee 'tis very cold, the winde is Northerly. **1664** EVELYN *Kal. Hort.* (1729) 197 The sharp Easterly and Northerly Winds transpierce, and dry them up. **1702** *Lond. Gaz.* No. 3835/3 The Wind proving Northerly.., they stood..to the Westward. **1748** *Anson's Voy.* II. i. 115 The northerly winds seldom blow in that climate. **1840** MARRYAT *Olla Podr.* III. 19 All the winds which have northerly in them are coarse. **1878** MARKHAM *Gt. Frozen Sea* v. 60 We encountered a fresh northerly wind dead in our teeth.

northerly (ˈnɔːðəlɪ), *adv.* [Cf. prec. and ON. *norðarliga.*] To the northward; towards the north; on the north side.

1596 DALRYMPLE tr. *Leslie's Hist. Scot.* Prol. 66 Vthiris mair northirlie, nocht ȝit haue bene inhabited. **1635** PAGITT *Christianogr.* 32 Scattered farre and wide.., both Northerly in Cataya, and Southerly to India. **1644** MILTON *Educ.* 3 We Englishmen being farre northerly. **1705** W. PENN in *Pa. Hist. Soc. Mem.* X. 15, I would have the same county to be marked northerly by stones. **1725** DE FOE *Voy. round World* (1840) 304 We weighed and stood northerly along the shore. **1812** WOODHOUSE *Astron.* xiii. 112 The star will be more northerly in the position E. **1845** STOCQUELER *Handbk. Brit. India* (1854) 18 As we proceed northerly, the climate becomes more temperate.

†ˈ**northermore**, *adv.* Also 3 **norður-ma.** [See NORTHER *a.* and -MORE.] Further north.

*c*1205 LAY. 2674 þa ferde þe king norður ma, & ane neowe burh makede. **1338** R. BRUNNE *Chron.* (1810) 77 Ʒit Northermore þei ȝed vntille Bethlyngton.

†ˈ**northermost**, *a. Obs.* [Cf. *northmost* and *eastermost.*] Most northerly.

1557 W. TOWRSON in Hakluyt *Voy.* (1589) 113 Betwixt the northermost two hilles. **1707** *Lond. Gaz.* No. 4350/3 The Northermost Black Buoy lieth on the North End of the outer middle. **1760** T. HUTCHINSON *Hist. Mass.* i. (1765) 108 The northermost part of the..river.

northern (ˈnɔːðən), *a.* and *sb.* Forms: 1–3 **norþern-**, 2–3 **norðern-**, 4–7 **northerne**, 6– **northern**; 4–5 **northeren**, 5 **-erin**, 6 **-iren**; 4 **northrin**, 6–7 **-ren.** [f. NORTH + -ERN: cf. OHG. *nordrôni* 'septentrio', ON. *norrœnn.*] **A.** *adj.*

1. a. Of persons or peoples: Living in, originating from, the north, esp. of England or of Europe.

*c*890 *O.E. Chron.* (Parker MS.) an. 890, Godrum se norþerna cyning forþferde. *c*1000 ÆLFRIC *Hom.* II. 356 Hine ʒelæhton ða sume þæs norðernan folces. *a*1122 *O.E. Chron.* (Laud MS.) an. 1064, þa norðerne men dydan mycelne hearme abutan Hamtune. *c*1205 LAY. 31333 He þat norðerne uolc hæuede ineouðered ful swiðe. *a*1300 *Cursor M.* 20063 Our aun Langage o northrin lede. **1338** R. BRUNNE *Chron.* (1810) 33 Bot þe Northeren men held him no leaute. **1568** GRAFTON *Chron.* II. 652 Meaning to have..a southrene Byll, to counteruayle a Northren bastard. **1577–87** HOLINSHED *Chron.* III. 873 Divers northern-men borne. **1610** HOLLAND *Camden's Brit.* (1637) 533 Contention betweene the Northren and Southren Students at Oxford. **1671** MILTON *P.R.* III. 338 When Agrican with all his Northern powers Besieg'd Albracca. **1712** ADDISON *Spect.* No. 415 ¶3 Frosts and Winters, which make the Northern Workmen lie half the Year Idle. **1773** JOHNSON 24 Feb. in *Boswell*, My northern friends have never been unkind to me. **1861** M. PATTISON *Ess.* (1889) I. 34 A powerful coalition of northern princes to resist the encroachments of Rome. **1884** PENNINGTON *Wiclif* ii. 52 Wiclif, as a northern-man, had made common cause with the northern party.

b. *U.S.* Belonging to the northern States.

1836 J. Q. ADAMS 10 June in Ford *Adams & Monroe Doctr.* (1902), The change of dynasty from the Tennessean Hero to the Northern Man with Southern principles. **1849** LYELL *2nd Visit U.S.* II. 35 These Northern settlers are compelled to preserve a discreet silence..when in the society of Southern slave-owners. **1890** HENTY *With Lee in Virg.* 96 In Virginia it was very seldom that the Northern generals could obtain any trustworthy information.

c. ***northern canoe*** = *north canoe.*

1820 R. HOOD *To Arctic* (1974) 110 Late on the 21st Mr. Robertson, of the Hudson's Bay Company arrived, and furnished us with a guide, but desired that he might be exchanged when we met the northern canoes. **1860** S. HANCOCK *Narr.* (1927) 163 What is termed a northern canoe is much larger and differently shaped from those made and used by the Indians south of the Straits of Fuca. **1867** J. T. ROTHROCK *Flora Alaska* 434 From it the celebrated 'northern canoes' are made. These canoes, 'dug' from a single trunk and afterwards steamed into shape, will often carry four tons. **1938** *Beaver* Dec. 13/1 The northern canoe carried a crew of five or six men, apart from passengers. **1954** M. W. CAMPBELL *Nor' Westers* 44 Each northern canoe held twenty-five ninety-pound packs instead of the sixty loaded into the Montreal canoes.

2. Of the wind: Blowing from the north.

*a*1000 *Boeth. Metr.* vi. 14 Eac þa ruman sæ norþerne yst nede ʒebædeð. *c*1290 *S. Eng. Leg.* I. 209 A norþerne wind faste blevȝ. *a*1310 in Wright *Lyric P.* xvi. 51 Blow, northerne wynd, Sent thou me my suetyng. **1398** TREVISA *Barth. De P.R.* XI. iii. (Bodl. MS.), Borias þe norþeren winde..ariseþ vnder þe sterre þat hat polus articus. **1480** *Chron. Eng.* (Caxton) ccxxxii. 252 That northren wynde is euer redy and destinat to all euell. **1598** GRENEWEY *Tacitus, Ann.* II. xiii. (1622) 51 The northren winds droue him backe againe. **1638** SIR T. HERBERT *Trav.* (ed. 2) 219 Another cold northern blast benummed her. **1748** *Anson's Voy.* II. i. 116 The northern winds are never to be apprehended. **1784** COWPER *Task* VI. 60 Where the woods fence off the northern blast. **1820** SHELLEY *Sensit. Pl.* III. 110 A northern whirl-wind..Shook the boughs.

3. a. Of things: Belonging or pertaining to, found in, produced by, characteristic of, the north.

northern dozens, morn(ing), whites: see the sbs.

1387 [see B. 1 a]. **1428–9** *Rec. St. Mary at Hill* (1904) 70 A tonne..of northerin ston for þe new chirche porche. **1611** BIBLE *Jer.* xv. 12 Shall yron breake the Northren yron, and the steele? **1682** DRYDEN *Mac-Fl.* 170 Sir Formal..attends thy quill And does thy northern dedications fill. **1748** HUME *Ess., Nat. Characters*, The more southern [languages] are smooth and melodious, the northern harsh and untuneable. **1786** H. TOOKE *Purley* II. iv. (1829) II. 272 The Northern origin [of language] is totally out of sight. **1813** SCOTT *Trierm.* III. xxiv, Pallid beams of northern day. **1882** 'OUIDA' *Maremma* I. i. 23 The old woman with the northern eyes.

b. In the specific designations of animals or plants, as ***Northern diver, holy-grass, sea-cow***: see the sbs. ***Northern Spy***, an American variety of red-skinned, late-ripening, dessert apple.

1847 J. M. IVES *New England Bk. Fruit* 46 Northern Spy.—This new native fruit, originated near Rochester, N. York. It is a fine winter apple, and is one of the most popular fruits in New York. **1850** *New England Farmer* II. 404 Northern Spy Apple. We had hoped to be able to test the qualities of this apple ourselves. **1860** HOGG *Fruit Man.* 19 Northern Spy... An American apple, which ripens well in this country. **1860** O. W. HOLMES *Elsie V.* i, A seedling apple, like the Northern Spy. **1917** D. CANFIELD *Understood Betsy* iii. 61 Those Northern Spies are just getting to be good about now. When they first come off the tree in October you could shoot them through an oak plank. *Ibid.* xi. 241 A basket..half full of striped red Northern Spies. **1944** *Poetry Chap Bk.* Fall 14 And fragrant windrows of crisp Northern Spies are scattered in the tumbled twisted sheaves. **1965** MRS. L. B. JOHNSON *White House Diary* 15 Jan. (1970) 221 'What are your best brands [of apple]?' asked Gromyko. Without hesitation and with honesty General McNaughton replied, 'Our best brands are Northern Spies and McIntosh Reds.'

4. a. Lying or situated to the northward; having a position relatively north.

northern car, crown, hemisphere: see the sbs.

1590 SPENSER *F.Q.* II. x. 14 Albanact had all the Northerne part. **1594** BLUNDEVIL *Exerc.* IV. xix. (1636) 466 The crowne of Ariadna..is commonly called..the Northerne Crowne. **1600** FAIRFAX *Tasso* III. lxiv, Against the northren gate his force he bent. **1697** DRYDEN *Virg. Georg.* I. 210 The Pleiads, Hyads, and the Northern Car. **1719** DE FOE *Crusoe* II. (Globe) 572 The Northern Ocean bounds the Land also on that side. **1748** *Anson's Voy.* II. ii. 136 We espied a sail in the northern quarter. **1818** SHELLEY *Apennines* 4 Like the sea on a northern shore. **1872** MORLEY *Voltaire* (1886) 4 The Reformation, the great revival of northern Europe.

b. ***Northern star*** = NORTH STAR.

1601 SHAKS. *Jul. C.* III. i. 60, I am constant as the Northerne Starre. **1700** S. L. tr. *Fryke's Voy. E. Ind.* 353 We saw again the Northern Star to our great Joy. **1748** GRAY *Alliance* 68 The influence of the northern star. **1847** TENNYSON *Princ.* I. 4 On my cradle shone the Northern star.

c. ***Northern Lights***, the Aurora Borealis.

1721 *Phil. Trans.* XXXI. 215 If any enquire farther, Why the Northern Lights have of late been so unusually frequent. **1775** *Ibid.* LXVIII. 410 Northern lights to Northward. **1805** SCOTT *Last Minst.* II. viii, He knew, by the streamers that shot so bright, That spirits were riding the northern light. **1860** *Chambers's Encycl.* I. 558 The term Polar Lights would be more appropriate than Northern Lights to designate the aurora.

5. Taking place, carried on, in the north.

1589 COOPER *Admon.* 248 In the Northren rebellion. **1669** LADY CHAWORTH in *Hist. MSS. Comm.* 12th Rep. App. V. 12 They talk heere as if the King would goe a northerne progresse this summer.

6. quasi-*adv.* In the northern manner.

*a*1613 OVERBURY *A Wife*, etc. (1638) 97 He speakes Northerne, what Country-man soever.

B. *sb.* †**1. a.** Northern men. *Obs. rare.*

1338 R. BRUNNE *Chron.* (1810) 26 þorȝh þe gode Northeren slayn wer ilkaman. **1387** TREVISA *Higden* (Rolls) II. 163 Men of myddel Engelond..vunderstondeþ bettre þe side langages, norþerne and souþerne, þan northerne and souþerne vnderstondeþ eiþer oþer. **1622** DRAYTON *Poly-olb.* xxii. 958 He durst not trust The Northern, which so oft to him had been unjust. *Ibid.* 968 To whom by this revolt, they many Northern drew.

†**b.** Northern cloth. *Obs. rare*[−1].

*a*1592 GREENE *Jas. IV*, IV. iii, Let my doublet be white northern, five groats the yard.

2. a. A native of the north.

1774 LOW *Tour Orkney & Schetl.* (1879) 107 This kind of poetry being..most fitted to the genius of the Northerns. **1813** EUSTACE *Class. Tour* (1821) III. iv. 123 In the opinion of a phlegmatic northern. **1855** KINGSLEY *Westw. Ho!* (1865) II. 73 Cold Northerns, you little dream how a Spaniard can love. **1871** *Daily News* 16 Aug., Sir Walter Scott..is our common countryman. He made us northerns and us southerns conscious of one flesh and blood.

b. A north wind.

1818 KEATS *Endym.* III. 750 He tore it into pieces small as snow That drifts unfeather'd when bleak northerns blow.

Hence ˈ**northern** *v.*, to become more northern.

1757 GROSE *Voy. E. Indies* 365 As the land northerns, the continent grows broader and broader. **1830** *Blackw. Mag.* XXVIII. 131 The finer wools,..as the latitude northerns, become thicker and more plentiful.

ˈ**northerner.** [f. NORTHERN *a.* + -ER[1].]

1. *U.S.* One belonging to the northern States.

1831 J. M. PECK *Guide for Emigrants* II. 60 Such for beauty and splendor and fragrance, the *Northerners* have never seen. **1840** J. BUEL *Farm. Compan.* 19 Let not the Northerners take credit to themselves from this outline of old Virginia husbandry. **1890** HENTY *With Lee in Virg.* 119 The Northerners protected by the strong fortifications they had thrown up round Washington. **1928** I. C. WARD *Phonetics of English* i. 3 A Northerner's pronunciation of *but*..is called 'broad'. **1945** *Chicago Daily News* 1 Feb. 8/7 It's about time we long-suffering Northerners got it off our chest.

2. A native or inhabitant of the north, or of the northern part of any country.

1841 EMERSON *Ess.* Ser. I. *Prudence*, The northerner is perforce a householder. **1867** HATTON *Tallants of Barton* i, These northerners are a rare practical race.

northernism (ˈnɔːðənɪz(ə)m). [f. NORTHERN *a.* and *sb.* + -ISM.] Northern quality; a Northern characteristic, esp. a Northern form of expression.

1930 *Times Lit. Suppl.* 9 Jan. 28/4 Anything tainted with northernism or 'Lutheranism' is poison for Italy. **1964** *English Studies* XLV. 249 Identified..as a northernism. **1965** H. KÖKERITZ in Bessinger & Creed *Medieval & Linguistic Stud.* 294 Notwithstanding a few seeming northernisms..there is no vestige of his father's dialect.

ˈ**northernize**, *v.* [f. NORTHERN *a.* + -IZE.] *trans.* To make northern in respect of feelings, character, or form. Hence ˈ**northernized** *ppl. a.*

1859 *Charleston Mercury* 21 June, Washington had, long previously to his death,..become perfectly Northernized. **1899** PLUMMER *Sax. Chron.* II. p. cxix, Before this northernised recension had extended beyond the original limits.

ˈ**northernly**, *a.* Now *rare.* [f. NORTHERN *a.* + -LY[1].] = NORTHERLY *a.*

1574 NEWTON *Health of Mag.* 25 In winter and beginninge of the Springe, and Northernly seasons. **1594** BLUNDEVIL *Exerc.* III. II. viii. (1636) 387 By taking his said declination, because it is Northernly, out of his Meridian altitude. **1632** LITHGOW *Trav.* III. 94 Storme-sted with

Northernely winds. **1658** W. BURTON *Itin. Anton.* 37 The frequent inrodes of the more Northernly Britains, called the Picts. **1703** J. SAVAGE *Lett. Antients* xxxix. 101 You have travell'd from the more Northernly Nations, even to our Region. **1893** *Academy* 25 Nov. 467/2 In Yezo, a northernly island of Japan.

† **'northernly**, *adv. Obs.* [f. as prec. + -LY².]

1. = NORTHERLY *adv.*

1576 NEWTON *Lemnie's Complex.* (1633) 208 Among honest substantiall Traffiquers, and namely, of those that dwell Northernly. **1594** BLUNDEVIL *Exerc.* VI. XXX. 639 Every degree of any of the Southerne signes riseth Southernly, and not Northernly. **1613** PURCHAS *Pilgrimage* 60 These [constellations] Northernely are seene. **1652** EARL MONM. tr. *Bentivoglio's Hist. Relat.* 87 Islands..which are seated so far Northernly. **1679** OATES *Narr. Popish Plot* 48 If the wind blew northernly.

2. In a north country dialect or accent.

1579 E. K. *Gloss. Spenser's Sheph. Cal.* May 177 *The Gate*, the Gote: Northernely spoken. **1632** BROME *North. Lass* II. i, And sings, and speaks so pretty Northernly they say.

'northernmost, *a.* [f. as prec. + -MOST.] Most northern or northerly; furthest north.

1719 DE FOE *Crusoe* II. (Globe) 571 The great River Tartarus, named so from the Northernmost Nations of the Mongul Tartars. **1725** —— *Voy. round World* (1840) 106 The northernmost land of Grand Tartary. **1830** LYELL *Princ. Geol.* II. vi. (1837) I. 392 The northernmost group of the British Islands. **1870** PROCTOR *Other Worlds* iv. 93 At its northernmost end it turns sharply westward.

'northernness. [f. as prec. + -NESS.] **1.** The state of being in a northern situation.

1853 KANE *Grinnell Exped.* xix. (1856) 149 Eight hundred miles from the Polar limit of all northernness. **1856** —— *Arct. Explor.* I. x. 108 This indication of our extreme northernness.

2. The quality of being from the north.

1939 C. S. LEWIS *Rehabilitations* ii. 37, I knew one who could come no nearer to an explanation of Morris's charm than to repeat 'It's the Northernness—the Northernness'. **1955** E. BLISHEN *Roaring Boys* ii. 74 To our grey northernness they brought a southern gleam. **1968** G. JONES *Hist. Vikings* 2 Though they had many ties..to remind them of a shared northernness, they had but little sense of a separate Danish, Swedish, or Norwegian nationality. **1975** C. N. MANLOVE *Mod. Fantasy* iv. 100 Despite lifelong fascination for 'Northernness', and interests in the medieval School of Chartres and in the Renaissance, he never felt the urge to visit their sources in Scandinavia, France or Italy.

'northest, *a.* [Superl. of NORTH *a.*; cf. ON. *norðastr.* First quot. doubtful.] Most northerly.

c **1470** HENRY *Wallace* VII. 558 Behynd thaim cum, and in the Northast [*v.r.* North eist] raw. **1749** H. WALPOLE *Lett.* (1846) II. 300 We thought ourselves in the northest part of England.

† **north-half.** *Obs.* [OE. *norðhealf* (see NORTH *a.* and HALF *sb.* 1) = MDu. *nordalf*, OLG. *northalva*, OHG. *nordhalba*, ON. *norðrhálfa.*] The north side or part; the north.

c **893** K. ÆLFRED *Oros.* I. i. 12 On norþhealfe is seo sæ Euxinus. **971** *Blickl. Hom.* 209 On þa norðhealfe þæs weofodes. *c* **1131** *O.E. Chron.* (Laud MS.) an. 1131, Ðis ʒear ..wæs se heouene o ðe norð half eall swilc hit wære bærnende fir. *c* **1205** LAY. 15937 þe an is a norð half, þe oðer a suð half. **1297** R. GLOUC. (Rolls) 11685 Sir Edward..sone come þo ride To þe norþhalf of þe toun. *c* **1315** SHOREHAM VII. 395 He wolde sette hys sete ryche Of north half, and be god ylyche. **1393** LANGL. *P. Pl.* C. XIX. 66 Tho that selde hauen the sonne and sitten in the north-half. *c* **1425** WYNTOUN *Cron.* I. xiii. 1214 On northe half is it rynnande syne A wattyr þat is callit Albeus.

northing ('nɔːθɪŋ), *vbl. sb.* [f. NORTH + -ING¹.]

1. (Chiefly *Naut.*) Progress or deviation towards the north made in sailing or travelling; difference in latitude due to moving northwards. Freq. in phr. ***to make*** (so much) ***northing.***

1669 STURMY *Mariner's Mag.* IV. iii. 154 Northing, Southing, Easting, and Westing,..is the Difference of Latitude and Departure from the Meridian. **1690** LEYBOURN *Curs. Math.* 641 You shall find 15.31 Leagues, for the Northing. **1709** *Lond. Gaz.* No. 4632/4 Discovering the Certainty of the Easting and Westing of the Globe, as exactly as the Northing and Southing already are. **1793** *Phil. Trans.* LXXXIII. 196 On the following day, the observation shewed two miles northing. **1807** PIKE *Sources Missis.* (1810) I. App. 12 The head of Lake Pepin is in 44° 58′ 8″ N. and we have made very little northing since. **1857** DUFFERIN *Lett. High Lat.* (ed. 3) 204 During the whole of that afternoon..we made but little Northing at all. **1891** J. WINSOR *Columbus* App. 651 Baffin, exceeding the northing of Davis, found lying before him the great expanse of Baffin's Bay.

2. Of heavenly bodies: Apparent movement towards the north.

1808 J. WEBSTER *Nat. Philos.* 225 When the moon has northing or southing the shade is elliptical. **1883** PROCTOR *Gt. Pyramid* iii. 139 The..northing of heavenly bodies.

So **'northing** *ppl. a.*, moving northwards.

1859 R. F. BURTON *Cent. Afr.* in *Jrnl. Geog. Soc.* XXIX. 207 Following the northing sun,..the rains reach Western India in June.

northland ('nɔːθlənd). [OE. *norðland* (see NORTH *a.*) = G., Da., Sw. *nordland*, ON. *norðrland.*] The northern part of a country, etc.; also *pl.* the lands lying in the north.

c **893** K. ÆLFRED *Oros.* I. ii. 30 He..for mid miclum ʒefeohtum on Scieðie þa norðland. *c* **1052** *O.E. Chron.* (MS. C) an. 1052, Hi hwendon þa mid þam scypon wið þæs norð landes. *c* **1470** HENRY *Wallace* IX. 574 On to the se thai send Schyr Jhon Sewart, that weyll the northland kend. **1533** *Acc. Ld. High Treas.* VI. 123 To ane boy that postit nycht and day in the northland with lettrez. **1738** DE FOE *Tour* (ed. 2) III. 336 The North-land, being all the Country beyond Inverness. *Ibid.*, The third Division of Scotland, called the North-land. **1873** MORRIS *Love is enough* 48 Sure the northlands shall know of the blessings she bringeth. **1896** *Harper's Mag.* Apr. 717/1 The roughest country in all the North-land.

attrib. **1552** *Reg. Privy Council Scot.* I. 129 The hevynnis or portis of this realme, at the eist and northland seyis. *a* **1578** LINDESAY (Pitscottie) *Chron. Scot.* (S.T.S.) II. 12 Vther hieland men and mony northland men in the meirnis and angus. **1738** DE FOE *Tour* (ed. 2) III. 349 Those whom I have been describing in the North-Land Division. **1840** CARLYLE *Heroes* (1858) 197 The primary characteristic of this old Northland Mythology.

Hence **'northlander**, one from the north.

1845 THORPE tr. *Lappenberg's A.S. Kings* II. 13 An incessant outpouring of Northlanders over the North and Baltic Seas, in quest of booty and a home.

'north-light. Also north light. [Cf. Du. *noorderlicht*, G. *nordlicht*, ON. *norðrljós* (Da. *nordlys*).]

1. (Usu. *pl.*) The Aurora Borealis. Also *fig.*

1706 PHILLIPS (ed. Kersey), *North-Light*, a wonderful Meteor, which usually appears in Greenland [etc.]. **1794** MRS. RADCLIFFE *Myst. Udolpho* vi, I stood looking up at the North-lights, which shot up the heaven to a great height. **1827** CLARE *Sheph. Cal.* 111 With shooting North-lights, 'tokening bloody wars. **1839** LOWELL *Lett.* (1894) I. 47 Two north-lights are there in the Soul that beam, Truth's steady ray and Fancy's waving gleam.

2. Light coming from the north.

1870 LOWELL *Among my Bks.* Ser. I. (1873) 346 Flashes.. of very different quality from the equable north-light of the artist.

3. A window, esp. in a roof, that faces north. So ***north-light roof.***

1904 F. E. KIDDER *Architects' & Builders' Pocket-Bk.* (ed. 14) 1304 With the 'Maze' glass, the artist may have, in all weather and in all directions, what is in effect a much-desired 'north-light'. **1919** R. FRY *Let.* 29 Nov. (1972) II. 473, I went to his tiny studio..he'd simply put a high north light in the roof of a small bedroom. **1931** *Engineering* 9 Jan. 33/2 The older bays had roofs of the saw-tooth pattern, with north lights. **1940** *Chambers's Techn. Dict.* 583/1 *North light roof*, a pitched roof of unequal slopes, of which the steeper is glazed and arranged to receive light from the north. **1958** *Times* 20 Aug. 13/6 Where only day shifts are worked the cost of installing fittings to produce the whole of the necessary illumination, instead of only those required to supplement daylight from windows or north-light roof must also be reckoned. **1961** E. E. CUMMINGS *Let.* 22 July (1969) 272, I asked a firstrate carpenter..to make me a real—with a North Light—studio in the barn. **1972** E. LEMARCHAND *Cyanide with Compliments* ix. 117 Could be a studio... I can't make out if it's got a north light, though.

† **'northly**, *a. Obs.* [f. NORTH + -LY¹. Cf. OE. *norðlic*, MDu. *noordelijc* (Du. *-lijk*), *noortlijc*, G. *nord-*, *nördlich*, Da. and Sw. *nordlig.*] Northerly, northern.

1557 RECORDE *Whetst.* a iij, The olde attempte for the Northlie Nauigations. **1573** TUSSER *Husb.* (1878) 62 In tempest (the wind being northly or east). **1576** TURBERV. *Trag. Tales* (1837) 143 Those warlike wights That earst from Almaine came, And other Northly parts beside. **1622** DRAYTON *Poly-olb.* xix. 316 To fortie three Degrees of North'ly Latitude.

† **'northly**, *adv. Obs. rare.* [f. NORTH + -LY². Cf. MDu. *noortlike*, Du. *noordelijk*, G. *nord-*, *nördlich*, Sw. *nordligt.*] Northwards.

a **1490** BOTONER *Itin.* (Nasmith) 178 So contynewyth the seyd laane to the seyd kay northly. **1654** VILVAIN *Epit. Ess.* iii. 74 Sevn Stars stand Northly in set clusters framed.

Northman ('nɔːθmən). [OE. *Norðman* (see NORTH *a.*) = OFris. *North-*, *Nord-*, OHG. *Nort(h)-*, *Nordman*, ON. *Norðmaðr* (pl. *-menn*), mod.G., Da., and Sw. *Nordman*: see also NORMAN *sb.*¹ The history of the word in Engl. is not continuous.] **1.** (Chiefly *pl.*) An inhabitant or native of Norway or of Scandinavia.

c **893** K. ÆLFRED *Oros.* I. i. 17 Ohthere sæde..þæt he ealra Norðmonna norþmest bude. *c* **937** *O.E. Chron.* (Parker MS.) an. 937, þær ʒeflemed wearð Norðmanna bregu. *c* **1000** ÆLFRIC *Saints' Lives* xxix. II. 180 Him onbuʒon þa francan and þa fyrlenan norðmenn to þam wynsuman iuce wuldres cynincʒes. **1605** VERSTEGAN *Dec. Intell.* vi. 165 Their habitation was in Norway, so called for the northern situation there-of, and themselues Northmen,..vpon lyke reason. **1817** SCOTT *Harold* III. vi, O'er Eric, Inguar's son, Dane and Northman piled the stone. **1845** [see NORTHUMBRIAN A]. **1887** HAWEIS *Lt. of Ages* vii. 199 Wherever the North-man landed, he settled.

2. *U.S.* = NORTHERNER 1.

1836 *Southern Lit. Messenger* II. 434 From my very heart, northman as I am, I admire and affect this good remnant of olden time. **1837** *Ibid.* III. 337 Between the Virginians and the North-men there was a wide variance.

'northmost, *a.* Now *rare.* Also 1, 6 -mest. [See -MOST.] Most northerly, northernmost.

c **893** K. ÆLFRED *Oros.* I. vii. 40 Sciþþie þa norðmestan hæfdon unʒewunelice hæton. *a* **1000** *Boeth. Metr.* ix. 43 Oð ða norðmestan næssan on eorðan. **1535** STEWART *Cron. Scot.* II. 303 To this Eufride the northmest part tha gaif. **1564** MAITLAND *Let.* in Sir J. Melvil *Mem.* (1735) 86 Upon my Progress towards the Northmost Parts of our Realm. **1632** LITHGOW *Trav.* III. 109 The Northmost Ile of the Syclades. **1720** DE FOE *Capt. Singleton* (1906) 72 The great river..at the northmost part of the coast of Mozambique. **1743** BULKELEY & CUMMINS *Voy. S. Seas* 118 Bearing from the Northmost Point S. by E. about eighteen Leagues. **1888** SWINBURNE *Armada* III. i, Darker far than the tempests are that sweep the skies of her northmost clime. **1921** R. L. JACK (*title*) Northmost Australia.

'northness. [f. NORTH + -NESS.] The quality or state of being relatively north.

1854 *Orr's Circ. Sci., Chem.* 263 Experimenters believed that either northness or southness in a magnet..might be capable each of an individual existence. **1867** HAYES *Open Polar Sea* xxxv. 345 Long lines of cackling geese..winging their way to some more remote point of northness.

north-north-east, *adv.*, etc. [= Du. *noordnoordoost*, G. and Sw. *nordnordost*; also F. *nord-nord-est*, It. *nortnortest*, Sp. and Pg. *nornordeste.*] In the direction lying midway between north and north-east. Also as *sb.* and *adj.* (cf. NORTH-EAST).

14.. *Sailing Directions* (Hakluyt) 13 Ye must rere at a North north est moone. **1555** EDEN *Decades* (Arb.) 66 The northnortheaste wynde roughely tossed the shyppes. **1588** SHAKS. *L.L.L.* I. i. 248 It standeth North North-east and by East. **1604** E. G[RIMSTONE] tr. *D'Acosta's Hist. Indies* III. v. 134 They divide amongst them the rest of the winds,..as North-northwest, North-northeast. **1691** *Lond. Gaz.* No. 2708/3 The Wind being at North-North-East. **1725** DE FOE *Voy. round World* (1840) 304 The coast running from port St. Julian north-north-east. **1849** J. D. DANA *Geol.* ix. (1850) 468 The main mountain range has in general a northeast to north-northeast course. **1870** LOWELL *Study Wind.* Ser. I. *Good Wd. for Winter*, The vast blur of a north-north-east snow storm.

north-north-west, *adv.*, etc. [= Du. *noordnoordwest*, G. *nordnordwest* (Sw. *-vest*); also F. *nord-nord-ouest*, Sp. *nornorueste.*] In the direction lying midway between north and north-west. Also as *sb.* and *adj.*

c **1381** CHAUCER *Parl. Foules* 117 As wisly as I saw the northe northe west When I beganne my sweuene for to write. **1398** TREVISA *Barth. De P.R.* XV. XV. (Bodl. MS.), þis londe haþ in þe norþe norþewest side þe see Occian. *Ibid.* xxvii, Toward norþe norþeweste. **14..** *Sailing Directions* (Hakluyt) 11 The cours is North northwest and South South est. **1602** SHAKS. *Ham.* II. ii. 396, I am but mad North, North-West: when the Winde is Southerly, I know a Hawke from a Handsaw. **1662** J. DAVIES tr. *Mandelslo's Trav.* 259 The contrary wind forc'd us to laveering to the North-north-west. **1719** DE FOE *Crusoe* I. (Globe) 59 It was on the N.N.W. Side of the Hill. **1824** SCOTT *St. Ronan's* xvii, Twenty-three miles north north-west. **1877** RAYMOND *Statist. Mines & Mining* 65 A line drawn through its center would run north-northwest and south-southeast.

Hence **north-north-westward** *adv.*

1784 *Phil. Trans.* LXXIV. 203 From about 45° of elevation north-north-westward.

north-polar, *a.* [f. *north pole*: cf. POLAR *a.*] Of or pertaining to the north pole (see POLE *sb.*²).

1784 HERSCHEL in *Phil. Trans.* LXXIV. 255 The bright north-polar spot in fig. 26. **1849** NOAD *Electricity* (ed. 3) 298 A south pole at E, which either destroys or neutralizes the north-polar magnetism previously induced by N.

North Sea. [Cf. (= 1 b) MDu. *Nort-*, *Noortzee* (Du. *Noordzee*), G. *Nordsee*, Da. *-sö*, Sw. *-sjö.*]

1. † **a.** The Bristol Channel. *Obs. rare.*

c **894** *O.E. Chron.* (Parker MS.) an. 894, [Hi] ymbsæton an ʒeweorc on Defnascire be þære norþ sæ. *a* **1490** BOTONER *Itin.* (Nasmith) 123 Le north-see. Villæ principales super mare boriale sitæ. Primo Seyt Hyes.

b. The German Ocean.

c **1290** *St. Kenelm* 17 in *S. Eng. Leg.* I. 345 To þe Northse hombur geth. **1720** RAMSAY *Prosp. Plenty* 2 In lays immortal chant the North-sea's praise. **1753** HANWAY *Trav.* (1762) II. I. iii. 17 The mouth of the Elbe, at the north-sea, is about thirteen..miles distance. **1841** *Penny Cycl.* XXI. 147/2 The Baltic..receives so great a supply of river-water, that its level is higher than that of the North Sea. **1859** TENNYSON *Elaine* 481 A wild wave in the wide North-sea.

attrib. **1705** *Lond. Gaz.* No. 4103/4 Newfoundland Bank-Fish,..equal to the North-Sea Cod. **1720** RAMSAY (*heading*), Prospect of Plenty: A Poem on the North-Sea Fishery. **1891** CLARK RUSSELL *Marr. at Sea* v, A staunch little craft..built for North Sea weather.

c. ***North Sea gas, oil***: raw materials discovered beneath the North Sea.

1965 *Times* 22 Sept. 10/6 The BP gas find radically alters the North Sea oil and gas search. **1967** *Guardian* 4 Jan. 3/1 Bringing North Sea gas ashore in Norfolk. **1972** *Ibid.* 8 June 9/1 The tests were carried out in households supplied by North Sea gas and those supplied by town gas. **1973** *Ibid.* 2 Mar. 15/7 North Sea oil will go a long way to reducing Britain's dependence on the volatile Middle East. **1974** *Sunday Times* (Colour Suppl.) 28 Apr. 20 It is a feature of the story of North Sea oil that men encountering its immensities can find themselves in conflict with their previous positions. **1975** *Sat. Rev.* 25 Jan. 16/3 Britain retiring into a new insularity fueled by North Sea oil.

† **2.** The sea to the north of (central) Europe; the Baltic. *Obs. rare.*

c **1000** ÆLFRIC *Vet. Test.* (Gr.) 4 Of Iaphet..com þæt norðerne mennisc be þære norðsæ. **1398** TREVISA *Barth. De P.R.* x. viii. (Bodl. MS.), þe norþe see is but litel salt. *Ibid.* XIV. ii, Londe þᵗ is nyʒe to þe [souþe] see is more [hot] and moiste þanne londe þat is nyʒe to þe norþe see.

3. *pl.* The seas of the northern hemisphere.

1601 R. JOHNSON *Kingd. & Commw.* (1603) 33 In these places they made the north and south seas their bounds. **1726** SWIFT *Gulliver* I. viii, An English Merchant-man, returning from Japan by the North and South Seas.

4. (See quot.)

1867 SMYTH *Sailor's Word-bk.* 500 *North Sea*, the Jamaica name for the north swell.

† **'north-shine.** *Obs. rare*⁻¹. [Cf. G. *nordschein*, Da. *nordskin*, Sw. *norrsken*.] The Aurora Borealis.

1738 [G. SMITH] *Cur. Relat.* II. 447 It shoots forth from the North, for which Reason it is call'd the North-Shine.

north-side. [ME. *norðside* (see NORTH *a.*) = MDu. *nort-*, *noor(t)side* (Du. *noordzijde*), OHG. *nordsîta* (G. *nordseite*), MSw. *norrsijda*, Sw. *nordsida*, Da. *-side*. In later use also simply a collocation of NORTH *a.* and SIDE *sb.*] The side lying towards the north.

c **1205** LAY. 24515, I þere chireche..bi þere norð side [sat] Wenhæiuer þa quene. *a* **1300** *Cursor M.* 17288 + 137 þer was our lord sepulcre, in þe northside I-wis. *c* **1305** *Edmund Conf.* 350 in *E.E.P.* (1862) 80 In alle halewe churchȝerd, in þe norþ side. **1387** TREVISA *Higden* (Rolls) I. 61 By twene þe norþside of India and Scythia. **1535** COVERDALE *Ezek.* xlviii. 1 The trybes that lye vpon the northsyde. **1552** *Bk. Comm. Prayer, Communion*, The Priest standing at the north-syde of the Table, shal saye the Lordes prayer. **1612** CAPT. SMITH *Descr. Virg.* Wks. (Arb.) 50 From the North side is the river of Chickahamania. **1641** in Nalson *Impart. Collect.* (1683) II. 399 The Minister, who is by the Law to officiate at the North-side of the Table. **1754** T. GARDNER *Hist. Dunwich* 125 John Baret..on the North-Side. **1836** PARKER *Gloss. Archit.* (1850) I. 132 On the north side of the chancel is placed a chantry chapel. **1866** F. G. LEE *Direct. Angl.* 356 *North-side*, the part of the altar to the left of the Midst as the Priest stands in the front facing the east. **1887** MORRIS *Odyss.* XIII. 110 The one to the north-side facing.

North star. [ME. *north sterre* = MDu. *noirdstern*, Du. *noordster*, G. *nordstern*, Da. *-stjerne*, Sw. *-stjerna*.] The Pole-star.

1398 TREVISA *Barth. De P.R.* VIII. ii. (Bodl. MS.), The moste norþe sterre, the whyche norþe sterre we clepeþ schyppeman-sterre. **1530** PALSGR. 248/2 Northe starre, *pol articque*. **1559** W. CUNNINGHAM *Cosmogr. Glasse* 96 By findinge the height of the Northe starre. **1599** SHAKS. *Much Ado* II. i. 258 If her breath were as terrible as [her] terminations,..she would infect to the north starre. **1625** PURCHAS *Pilgrims* I. II. ii. 34 When they had sayled past the Equinoctiall Line, they lost the sight of the North starre. **1661** BOYLE *Style of Script.* (1675) 61 The North star..doth better guide the pilot, than ev'n the moon herself. **1719** DE FOE *Crusoe* II. (Globe) 605 Our..Guide, who..steer'd himself by the Pole, or North Star. **1779** JOHNSON *L.P., Milton* (1868) 66 The pensive man..outwatches the North Star, to discover the habitation of separate souls. *c* **1808** SURTEES in G. Taylor *Mem. R.S.* (Surtees) 244 The witching spell..That lur'd the north star from the sky. **1848** LOWELL *Biglow P.* Ser. I. ix, He..axed ef I could pint The North Star out.

fig. **1639** S. DU VERGER tr. *Camus' Admir. Events* 232 In such tender years they are ships without North-starre, Rudder, or anchor. **1656** EARL MONM. tr. *Boccalini's Advts. fr. Parnass.* I. xxix. (1674) 32, [I] resolved to steer..by the assured North-Star of the afore-said Sentence. **1730** FIELDING *Rape upon Rape* III. vi, A widow with fourscore thousand pounds in her pocket—There's a North star to steer by!

North Star State. *U.S.* The state of Minnesota.

1862 *American Odd Fellow* I. 196/2 In the North Star State here, we rejoice in having a Grand Master, who knows no such word as fail. **1909** *World To-Day* Oct. 1108 The North Star State has been the scene of her greatest usefulness. Mrs. Potter commenced her educational work in Minneapolis. **1946** C. MCWILLIAMS *Southern Calif. Country* 173 Floats move through the streets of Long beach with captions as 'Corn is King',..'Minnesota: The North Star State'.

Nor'thumber. Now *rare.* [OE. *Norðhymbre* (also *Norðan-*), f. *norð-* NORTH + *Humbre* the Humber. The ME. *a*-forms appear to represent the OE. gen. or dat. pl., but may have been taken in the sense of 'Northumberland'.] *pl.* The ancient inhabitants of Northumbria, or that part of England lying north of the Humber.

α. *a* **900** *O.E. Chron.* (Parker MS.) an. 601, Edwine Norðhymbra cyning. *a* **1122** *Ibid.* (Laud MS.) an. 1095, Se eorl Rodbeard of Norðhymbran. *c* **1205** LAY. 30379 Cadwaðlan gon liðe..touward Norð-humbre. **1297** R. GLOUC. (Rolls) 4683 þe verste king of norþhumber. **1387** TREVISA *Higden* (Rolls) II. 81 þis is þe citee þat Ethelfride, kyng of Norþhumber, destroyed.

β. **1387** TREVISA *Higden* (Rolls) II. 163 Al þe longage of þe Norþhumbres, and specialliche at ȝork, is..scharp, slitting, and frotynge and vnschape. **1568** GRAFTON *Chron.* II. 15 While king William was thus occupied in Normandy, the Northumbers rebelled. **1601** WEEVER *Mirror Mart.* VI. i, He pierst the eie Of the Scots king, and set Northumbers free. **1631** —— *Anc. Funeral Mon.* To Rdr. 4 Ceonulph, King of the Northumbers. **1705** J. TAYLOR *Journ. Edenb.* (1903) 51 Edwin, king of the Northumbers, a Pagan. **1756–9** BUTLER *Lives Saints* (1836) II. 205 The English Saxon kingdom of the Northumbers. **1854** WATERWORTH *Eng. & Rome* 182 His pious and zealous son, the King of the Northumbers.

Northumbrian (nɔːˈθʌmbrɪən), *a.* and *sb.* [f. prec. + -IAN.]

A. *adj.* Of or pertaining to Northumbria or Northumberland.

1622 DRAYTON *Poly-olb.* xxiv. 937 The Roll of these Northumbrian Kings. *Ibid.* 1238 Of the Northumbrian Line so have we many more. **1776** SIR D. DALRYMPLE *Annals Scotl.* I. 7 Maerleswegen, Gospatrick, and other Northumbrian nobles. **1818** SCOTT *Rob Roy* v, The monsters of heraldry, embodied by the art of some Northumbrian chisel. *Ibid.* xviii, A snug comfortable Northumbrian cottage. **1845** R. GARNETT in *Proc. Philol. Soc.* II. 78 This admixture of the Northmen in the population of the Northumbrian provinces. **1884** *Encycl. Brit.* XVII. 567/2 The management of many Northumbrian farms is excellent.

B. *sb.* **1.** An inhabitant or native of ancient Northumbria or modern Northumberland.

1752 *Life Bernard Gilpin* 207 These wild Northumbrians indeed went beyond the ferocity of their ancestors. **1797** *Encycl. Brit.* (ed. 3) XIII. 111/2 The Northumbrians were anciently stigmatized as a savage, barbarous people. **1828–43** TYTLER *Hist. Scot.* (1864) I. 56 The Scots.. delayed their advance; and the Northumbrians..returned home. **1884** *Encycl. Brit.* XVII. 567/1 In physique the Northumbrian is stalwart and robust.

2. The northern dialect of English current in ancient Northumbria; also, the modern dialect of Northumberland.

1845 KEMBLE in *Proc. Philol. Soc.* II. 125 The most extensive monument of pure Northumbrian which we possess. **1889** SKEAT *Gospels* Introd., The other three Gospels are glossed in Old Northumbrian.

Hence **Nor'thumbrianism.**

1845 R. GARNETT in *Proc. Philol. Soc.* II. 84 The Northumbrianisms *swa, gude, sall, swilke, til.*

northupite ('nɔːθəpaɪt). *Min.* [Named after its discoverer, C. H. *Northup*.] (See quots.)

1895 *Amer. Jrnl. Sci.* L. 481 The name Northupite is proposed for this new species. **1896** CHESTER *Dict. Min.*, *Northupite*,..chloride and carbonate of sodium and magnesium, found in regular octahedrons.

northward ('nɔːθwəd), *adv.*, *sb.*, and *a.* Forms: 1 **norðw(e)ard**, 3–4 **norþ-**, 5 **norþe-**, 3– **northward** (6 *Sc.* **-wart**); 4 **northe-**, 5–6 **northwarde**. [f. NORTH + -WARD: cf. MDu. *nortwart*, *-wert*, *noort-*, *noordewaert*.]

A. *adv.* **1.** Towards the north; in a northern direction: **a.** of motion or aspect.

a **1100** *O.E. Chron.* (MS. D) an. 1016, Ða Uhtred ȝeahsode þis, þa forlet he his herȝunge & efste norðweard. *c* **1290** *Beket* 1119 in *S. Eng. Leg.* I. 138 Al North-ward he drouȝ him furst, a-wei al fram þe se. **1338** R. BRUNNE *Chron.* (1810) 207 Jon Northward him sped, his lond for to visite. **1387** TREVISA *Higden* (Rolls) I. 57 þanne þe see schedeþ norþward, and makeþ þe see Propontides. **1470–85** MALORY *Arthur* I. xi. 51 He had the hoost Northward..vnto the foreist of Bedegrayne. **1568** GRAFTON *Chron.* II. 653 Making prouision to go Northwarde agaynst his aduerse faction. **1596** SHAKS. *1 Hen. IV*, III. i. 79 To you The remnant Northward, lying off from Trent. **1682** DRYDEN *To Duchess of York* 10 Love..wander'd northward to the verge of day. **1709** STEELE *Tatler* No. 93 ¶5 He had a better Stomach when he moved Northward. **1784** JOHNSON 12 July in *Boswell*, I am going Northward for a while. **1858** DASENT in *Oxford Ess.* 193 Its doors look northward. **1878** GLADSTONE *Homer* 61 From hence round to the Black Sea, passing east and northward.

b. of relative position.

c **1384** CHAUCER *H. Fame* III. 62 This hille, that Northewarde lay. **1398** TREVISA *Barth. De P.R.* XV. xliii. (Bodl. MS.), Wiþin þese londes esteward is rodus and norþeward Cenode. *c* **1420** *Palladius on Husb.* I. 120 Northward in placis hoot; in placis colde, Southward. **1535** COVERDALE *Ezek.* xl. 44 There stode one also, besyde the east dore north warde. **1596** SHAKS. *Merch. V.* II. i. 4 Bring me the fairest creature North-ward borne. **1612** CAPT. SMITH *Descr. Virg.* Wks. (Arb.) 53 Thirty leagues Northward is a river not inhabited. **1669** STURMY *Mariner's Mag.* VII. xvi. 25 Those that live 90 deg. from us Northward or Southward. **1885** *Manch. Exam.* 9 Mar. 5/1 On the Downs northward of Brighton.

2. quasi-*sb.* = next.

1864 TENNYSON *En. Ard.* 102 Ten miles to northward of the narrow port. **1865** CARLYLE *Fredk. Gt.* V. 546 To northward of Bautzen forty miles.

B. *sb.* That direction or part which lies to the north (*of* a place or thing).

1624 in *Capt. Smith's Wks.* (Arb.) 337 A relation of a Discovery towards the Northward of Virginia. **1644** BULWER *Chiron.* 43 The hand..leapeing back to the Northward of the Body. **1702** *Lond. Gaz.* No. 3831/3 Two Men of War to the Northward of the Fleet gave him Chase. **1748** *Anson's Voy.* II. iii. 147 To fit up the boats..and to proceed with them to the northward. **1820** W. SCORESBY *Acc. Arctic Reg.* II. 208 Some ships have sailed to the northward of the seventy-eight degree of latitude. **1864** TENNYSON *Aylmer's F.* 415 The tall pines That darken'd all the northward of her Hall. **1880** HAUGHTON *Phys. Geogr.* iii. 126 The vapour..flows to the northward and southward.

C. *adj.* That moves or looks northward; extending or situated towards the north.

Not historically connected with OE. *norð(e)weard* or *norðanweard*.

1597 SHAKS. *2 Hen. IV*, II. iii. 13 When your owne Percy ..Threw many a Northward looke. **1622** DRAYTON *Poly-olb.* xxiv. 28 Whence Lestershire she leaves upon the Northward side. **1707** *Lond. Gaz.* No. 4395/3 The Northward Part of the Goodwin Sands. **1853** KANE *Grinnell Exp.* xxv. (1856) 200 The observations which I noted during our northward drift. **1892** LEE *Hist. Columb.* II. 222 In 1868, the northward growth of the city began to be notable.

'northwardly, *adv.* and *a.* [f. prec. + -LY².]

A. *adv.* In a northward direction.

1796 MORSE *Amer. Geogr.* I. 609 European geographers.. extended the name northwardly. **1807** VANCOUVER *Agric. Devon* (1813) 38 Proceeding northwardly through the remainder of East Allington. **1853** *Jrnl. R. Agric. Soc.* XIV. I. 18 Travelling northwardly from this..plain.

B. *adj.* That has a northern situation or direction; of the wind, blowing from the northward.

c **1682** J. COLLINS *Making Salt in Engl.* 75 The most Northwardly part is Rag-Point. **1805** *Phil. Trans.* XCVI. 251 These northwardly winds I take to have been the north-east wind in the offing. **1858** *Merc. Marine Mag.* V. 161 A slowly moving northwardly current.

northwards, *adv.* and *sb.* [Cf. Du. *noordwaarts*, G. *nordwärts*.] Northward.

c **894** *O.E. Chron.* (Parker MS.) an. 894, þa woldon [hie] ferian norþweardes ofer Temese in on East Seaxe. **1375** BARBOUR *Bruce* VIII. 406 His wiage northwardis he tais. **1461** *Paston Lett.* I. 540 My Lord Fitzwater is ryden northewards. **1511** *Guylforde's Pilgr.* (Camden) 22 It marcheth..northwardes to the kyngdome of Surrey. **1574** W. BOURNE *Regiment for Sea* 31, I doe take the heigth of the Sunne vnto the Northwardes. **1624** in *Capt. Smith's Wks.* (Arb.) 337 The winds so crossed vs [that] wee fell more Northwards. *a* **1700** EVELYN *Diary* (1645) Apr., Minding us of returning Northwards. **1806** A. DUNCAN *Nelson* 153 It stretched northwards. **1887** BOWEN *Virg. Æneid* I. 391 Sped to a sheltering haven by winds that have northwards turned.

† **'Northway,** obs. variant of NORWAY².

1387 TREVISA *Higden* (Rolls) I. 287 þan Norþways and Danes made hem cheef citees in Gallia.

north-west (nɔːθ'wɛst), *adv.*, *sb.*, and *a.* [f. NORTH and WEST: cf. MDu. *noortwest* (Du. *noord-*), OHG. *nord-*, *northuuest*, G. *nordwest*, Da. and Sw. *nordvest*; also F. *nordouest* (†*north-*, *nort-*, *nor-*), Sp. *nordovest*, *norueste*, Pg. *noroeste*.

OE. had also *norðanwestan*, from the north-west.]

A. *adv.* **1.** In the direction intermediate between north and west.

c **893** K. ÆLFRED *Oros.* I. i. 24 An ðæra garena lið suðwest ..& se ðridda norðwest onȝean Brigantia. **931** in Birch *Cartul. Sax.* II. 358 Of ðære flodan norð west to ðære miclan apoldre. **14..** *Sailing Directions* (Hakluyt, 1889) 11 The streme settith North West and Southest. **1509** HAWES *Past. Pleasure* xiv. (Percy Soc.) 53 In the stormy pery Mercury northwest thou mayst se appere. **1594** BLUNDEVIL *Exerc.* IV. xxiii. (1636) 479, I find..that the said starre setteth Northwest and by West. **1612** CAPT. SMITH *Descr. Virg.* Wks. (Arb.) 52 The greatest [river]..is called Quiyough and trendeth north west. **1703** MAUNDRELL *Journ. Jerus.* (1721) Add. 6 Our Course..was North West and by North. **1725** DE FOE *Voy. round World* (1840) 303 We stood northward again, and then north-west. **1809** [see the sb.]. **1880** C. R. MARKHAM *Peruv. Bark* 371 The valley runs north-west and south-east.

b. From this direction.

1870 MORRIS *Earthly Par.* II. III. 382 The south-east wind..changed, and northwest now it blew.

2. quasi-*sb.* = next.

14.. *Sailing Directions* (Hakluyt, 1889) 11 Yif..the wynde be at Northwest your cours is Southest. *Ibid.* 14 Bery land est and by north west. **1725** DE FOE *Voy. round World* (1840) 301 A fresh gale at north-west-by-west. **1806** A. DUNCAN *Nelson* 61 The French had sailed..with a fresh gale at north-west.

B. *sb.* The direction or region lying between north and west; *spec.* the North-west Territories of Canada.

1387 TREVISA *Higden* (Rolls) II. 69 A citee in þe contre of Norþ Engelond toward þe norþ west. **1432–50** tr. *Higden* (Rolls) II. 71 A place..at the northe weste of hit. **1610** HOLLAND *Camden's Brit.* (1637) 631 In the utmost angle.. toward the North-West. **1662** J. DAVIES tr. *Mandelslo's Trav.* 248 The wind changed, and came to the north-west. **1719** DE FOE *Crusoe* II. (Globe) 571 Till we came round the Pole, and consequently into the North-West. **1778** W. ROBERTSON *Hist. Amer.* (1783) I. 142 After this..he advanced towards the north-west. **1809** A. HENRY *Trav.* 239, I was now in what is technically called the north-west; that is, the country north-west of Lake Superior. **1874** *Encycl. Brit.* IV. 766/1 The vast prairie lands of the great north-west thus embraced within the Dominion.

C. *adj.* **1.** Of the wind: Blowing from the north-west.

Perhaps representing OE. *norðanwestanwind*.

1398 TREVISA *Barth. De P.R.* XI. iii. (Bodl. MS.), Borias.. haþ bi his sides..þe norþeweste winde. **1483** *Cath. Angl.* 256/1 þᵉ Northe west wynde; *circius*. **1572** HULOET s.v., Ptol. calleth the Northweast wynde *Chorus*. **1612** CAPT. SMITH *Descr. Virg.* Wks. (Arb.) 48 The Northwest winde is commonly coole. **1725** DE FOE *Voy. round World* (1840) 13 We met with..a north-west blast, which carried us..a great way off to sea. **1806** A. DUNCAN *Nelson* 60 The enemy had sailed with a north-west wind.

2. ***North-west Passage***, a passage for vessels along the north coast of America, formerly thought of as a possible channel for navigation between the Atlantic and the Pacific.

1600 HAKLUYT *Voy.* III. A4, The voyage of Sebastian Cabota.., for the discouery of a Northwest passage. **1631** J. DONE *Polydoron* 152 The Philosophers Stone is like the Northwest Passage lockt up in Strechio Davies, but not so cold in Seeking. **1697** DAMPIER *Voy.* (1699) 273, I know there have been divers attempts made about a North West Passage and all unsuccessful. **1725** [see PASSAGE *sb.* 11]. **1753** CHAMBERS *Cycl. Suppl.* s.v., A north-west passage by Hudson's bay, into the pacific ocean. **1820** W. SCORESBY *Acc. Arctic Reg.* I. 17 The existence of a 'north-west passage' is not yet either proved or refuted. **1857** ARMSTRONG (*title*), A Personal Narrative of the Discovery of the North West Passage. **1867** SMYTH *Sailor's Word-bk.* 500 The north-west passage..was..solved by H.M.S. Investigator..reaching the western end of Barrow's Straits. *fig.* **1670** CLARENDON *Ess.* Tracts (1727) 145 It [industry] is the North-west Passage that brings the merchant's ships ..to him. **1823** BYRON *Juan* XIII. xxxix, They are a North-West Passage Unto the glowing India of the soul. **1831** CARLYLE *Sartor Res.* II. v, That shorter North-west Passage to thy fair Spice-country of a Nowhere.

b. Hence ***North-west discovery***. Also *fig.*

1600 HAKLUYT *Voy.* III. 45 Certaine Gentlemen that went with M. Frobisher in his North west discouerie. **1638** CHILLINGW. *Relig. Prot.* I. v. §91. 292 Search your storehouse, M. Brerely, who hath travailed as farre in this Northwest discovery, as it was possible for humane industry.

3. Pertaining to the north-west; situated in the north-west part of a country, etc.

1827 *Gentl. Mag.* XCVII. II. 390 The nearly ascertained site of the North-west Magnetic pole. **1836** W. IRVING *Astoria* (1849) 120 Numbers of men of this class were scattered throughout the northwest territories. **1864** *Chambers's Encycl.* VI. 797 The area of the North-West Provinces is 116,493 square miles.

north-'wester, *sb.* [f. prec. + -ER¹.]

1. A wind or gale blowing from the north-west.

1737 T. SMITH *Jrnl.* (1849) 267 There has been no north-westers this fall nor winter. **1751** FRANKLIN *Lett.* Wks. 1840 V. 261, I question whether the strongest north-wester would dissipate it. **1807** W. IRVING *Salmag.* (1824) 271 The brisk north-westers, which prevailed not long since. **1860** *Merc. Marine Mag.* VII. 199 There is no protection from the heavy swell setting in with a north-wester.

2. = NOR'-WESTER 2.

1830 MARRYAT *King's Own* xx, Pouring him out a north-wester.

†**north-wester,** *a. Obs.* = NORTH-WEST *a.* 1.

c **1450** tr. *Giraldus Cambrensis' Hist. Irel.* (1896) 14 Storkes & swalewes & oþer somer foules..comen, & wyth þe cold north-westre wynd þay ben awey ywent.

north-'westerly, *a.* [f. NORTH-WEST, after WESTERLY.] **a.** Of the wind: Blowing from the north-west. **b.** Tending north-west.

1611 COTGR., *Galerneux*, north-westerlie. **1708** *Lond. Gaz.* No. 4446/3 We have Tided it with the Merchant Ships ..to this Place with small Gales North-Westerly. **1778** W. ROBERTSON *Hist. Amer.* (1783) II. 9 A north-westerly wind and excessive cold are synonymous terms. **1828** SCOTT *F.M. Perth* xxvii, Directing his course in a northwesterly direction. **1870** LOWELL *Study Windows* Ser. I. *Good Word for Winter*, The avant-courier of a northwesterly gale.

north-'western, *a.* and *sb.* [Cf. WESTERN and OHG. *northuuestrôni.*]

A. *adj.* Situated or extending towards the north-west.

1612 SELDEN in *Drayton's Poly-olb.* 125 Japhet..had the North-westerne Part of the World. **1632** LITHGOW *Trav.* III. 105 These North-westerne Ilands..are neither hot nor cold. **1846** MᶜCULLOCH *Brit. Empire* (1854) II. 58 Among the greater lines of railway now existing, may be specified the London and North Western. **1860** VENABLES *Isle of Wight* 338 The woodland of the north-western district.

B. *sb.* (See quot.)

1701 WOLLEY *Jrnl. New York* (1860) 23 A thick winter Coat there is commonly called a North-western.

†**north-'westing,** *vbl. sb. Obs.* [f. NORTH-WEST + -ING¹.] The variation of the compass from the true north in the direction of north-west.

1594–1646 [see NORTH-EASTING].

north-'westward, *adv.* and *sb.* [f. NORTH-WEST + -WARD.]

A. *adv.* In a north-westerly direction; towards the north-west.

1387 TREVISA *Higden* (Rolls) II. 71 A place foure score myle out of York norþwestward. **1599** HAKLUYT *Voy.* II. II. 17 We met with the winde at Northeast, and so we ran Northwestward. **1686** PLOT *Staffordsh.* 402 Which he makes Northwestward from Coventry. **1728** MORGAN *Algiers* I. iii. 70 North-Westward of Costantina..there is a Mountain. **1760** T. HUTCHINSON *Hist. Mass.* iv. (1765) 390 A line to run northwestward. **1858** H. D. ROGERS *Geol. Pennsylv.* I. 124 The Matinal shale manifestly declines in thickness as it spreads north-westward.

B. *sb.* = NORTH-WEST *sb.*

1796 MORSE *Amer. Geogr.* I. 128 To the northwestward of Hudson's Bay is an extensive chain of lakes. **1820** W. SCORESBY *Acc. Arctic Reg.* I. 76 After doubling Cape Farewell, they stood to the north-westward. **1892** *Daily News* 27 April 3/5 Wind was light..from the north-westward in the west of France.

Hence **north-'westwardly** *a.* and *adv.*

1796 MORSE *Amer. Geogr.* I. 223 A northwestwardly course. **1863** MRS. WHITNEY *Faith Gartney's Girlh.* xxvi, Looking off, northwestwardly, across the head of the Pond.

north wind: see NORTH *a.* 3.

nortour, -ure, obs. forms of NURTURE.

Norvegian, obs. form of NORWEGIAN.

norward ('nɔːwəd), *adv.* and *sb.* [f. *nor'* NORTH + -WARD.]

A. *adv.* In a northern direction; northward.

a **1618** SYLVESTER *Little Bartas* 274 Wks. (Grosart) II. 87 The more that they are Nor-ward driven. **1681** VISC'TESS CAMPDEN in *Hist. MSS. Comm.* 12th Rep. App. V. 56 They do not like to come norward so late in the yeare. **1839–48** BAILEY *Festus* 68 Norward now we'll hold our course. **1865** TENNYSON *Captain* 35 Stately, lightly, went she Norward, Till she near'd the foe.

B. *sb.* The northern part or region.

a **1618** SYLVESTER *Job Triumph.* 85 Wks. (Grosart) II. 162 To the Norward, where hee worketh rife. **1698** FRYER *Acc. E. India & P.* 22 A fair Wind soon set us once more to the Norward of the Equinoctial. **1700** GOV. NICHOLSON in W. S. Perry *Hist. Coll. Amer. Col. Ch.* I. 118 In Pennsylvania and to the Norward.

So **'norwards** *adv.*

1855 BAILEY *Mystic* 106 And those, Hrimthursar hight, who norwards held Frore Jotunheim.

Norway¹ ('nɔːweɪ). [Repr. ME. *Norwey, -wei*, OE. *Norweᵹ*, ad. ON. *Norvegr* (earlier *-*wegr*), f. *nor-, norðr* NORTH + *veg-r* WAY.] The name of one of the Scandinavian countries, used *attrib.* to designate special kinds or varieties of plants or trees, animals, or things, as ***Norway berry, birch, fir, maple, spruce; Norway crow, haddock, rat; Norway deal, neckcloth, ragstone, skiff, yawl.*** (See quots. and the various sbs.) Also **Norway lobster** = *Dublin (Bay) prawn* (DUBLIN); **Norway pine** (see PINE *sb.*² 2).

1674 tr. *Scheffer's Lapland* 141 Berries, the chief are those which the Swedes call *Hiortron*, some Dew-berries, or the *Norway Berry. **1887** BENTLEY *Man. Bot.* 668 The common Birch yields the timber known as *Norway Birch. **1848** *Zoologist* VI. 2258 The hooded crow is the *Norway crow. **1731** MILLER *Gard. Dict.* s.v. *Abies*, The Common Firr, or Pitch Tree, sometimes called, The *Norway or Spruce Fir. **1847** CARPENTER *Zool.* §556 The Sebastes, or *Norway Haddock, which inhabits the northern seas, and is an important article of food. **1777** T. PENNANT *Brit. Zool.* (ed. 4) IV. 17 Cancer Novegicus...*Norway. L[obster] with a long spiny snout. **1800** SHAW *Naturalist's Misc.* XII. pl. 464 Norway Lobster... This species is nearly equal in size to the common Lobster, and is principally found in the Northern ocean. **1911, 1963** [see *Dublin (Bay) prawn* (DUBLIN)]. **1797** *Encycl. Brit.* (ed. 3) I. 60/2 The platanoides, or *Norway-maple, grows naturally in Norway, Sweden, and other northern countries of Europe. **1882** *Garden* 25 Nov. 459/2 The Norway Maple is a beautiful tree. *a* **1790** POTTER *Cant. Dict.* (1795), **Norway neckcloth*, the pillory. **1720** R. PALMER *Let.* 4 Oct. in M. M. Verney *Verney Lett.* (1930) II. xxiv. 81, 36 *Norway Pines and Yews for a Hedge of 38 yards long. **1784** M. CUTLER *Jrnl.* 22 July in Parker & Cutler *Life & Corr. M. Cutler* (1888) I. iii. 99 We rode five miles over pitch and Norway-pine plains, with very low shrubs. **1829** J. C. LOUDON *Encycl. Plants* 804 The pitch pine, *P[inus] resinosa* is generally known in its native country by the name of Norway pine; sometimes, particularly among the Canadian French, red pine. **1838** J. F. COOPER *Homeward Bound* I. xvi. 252 [He] applied his knife to try the quality of the wood, and pronounced the Norway pine of the spars to be almost equal to anything that could be found in our own southern woods. **1896** M. E. WILKINS *Madelon* I There were evergreens—Norway pines, spruces and hemlocks—bordering the road. **1969** T. H. EVERETT *Living Trees of World* 51/1 Eastern American species with paired leaves include the red pine or Norway pine (*P. resinosa*). It may at first seem to be misnamed, but its popular designation refers to the Maine village of Norway and not to the land of the Vikings. **1973** *Saint Croix Courier* (St. Stephen, New Brunswick) 26 July 1 Dories are planked with Norway (Red) Pine and clench-fastened with galvanized boat nails. **1858** SIMMONDS *Dict. Trade*, **Norway Ragstone*, the coarsest variety of the hone-slates, or whetstones. **1753–9** *Norway rat [see RAT *sb.*¹ 1]. **1781** PENNANT *Hist. Quadrup.* II. 439 Norway Rat (the Brown Rat). **1867** SMYTH *Sailor's Word-bk.* 501 **Norway Skiff*, a particularly light and buoyant boat, which is both swift and safe in the worst weather. **1797** *Encycl. Brit.* (ed. 3) XIV. 762/1 The.. European spruce fir..includes the *Norway spruce and long-coned Cornish fir. **1832** *Planting* 124/1 (L.U.K.), The Norway spruce is considered to attain..one hundred and fifty feet in height. **1882** *Garden* 20 May 350/3 Dwarf varieties of the Norway Spruce. **1867** SMYTH *Sailor's Word-bk.* 501 **Norway Yawl*, this, of all small boats, is said to be the best calculated for a high sea.

†**Norway².** *Obs.* Forms: *pl.* 2 **Norweis,** 4 **-weies, -weyes,** 5 **-weys;** 4–5 **-wais,** 4, 6 **-wayes;** *Sc.* 5 **Norowais,** 6 **Norrowa(y)is.** [Prob. ad. AF. *Norays*, ONF. *Noreis*, with assimilation of form to prec.] *pl.* Norwegians.

a **1200** *O.E. Chron.* (MS. C) an. 1066, Harold..& hys furde..þere michel wel ᵹesloᵹon, ᵹe Norweis ᵹe Flæming. **1338** R. BRUNNE *Chron.* (1810) 38 þe Danes vp aryued..þat with Norwais Kerlion was destroied. **1387** TREVISA *Higden* (Rolls) I. 347 Turgesius, duke and ledere of Norweyes, brouȝt þider Norwayes. *c* **1440** *Partonope* 1252 The Norweys are at his ledyng. *c* **1470** HENRY *Wallace* x. 794 + 9 At Dunmoir, quhair first Norowais come in. **1535** STEWART *Cron. Scot.* III. 125 That tha supportit..The Norrowayis agane thair awin king. **1596** SPENSER *State Irel.* Wks. (Globe) 678/1 The Muscovites, the Norwayes, the Gothes,..and many others doe witness the same.

Norwegian (nɔː'wiːdʒən), *a.* and *sb.* Also 7–8 **Norvegian.** [f. med.L. *Norvegia*, with assimilation to NORWAY¹. Cf. F. *Norvégien.*]

A. *adj.* **a.** Of or pertaining to Norway; belonging to, found in, Norway.

1607 TOPSELL *Four-f. Beasts* (1658) 13 Of the Norvegian Monsters. **1622** DRAYTON *Poly-olb.* xix. 183 Of th' huge Norwegian hills. **1644** MILTON *Areop.* (Arb.) 33 A Hunnish and Norwegian statelines. **1667** —— *P.L.* I. 293 The tallest Pine Hewn on Norwegian hills. **1776** DALRYMPLE *Annals Scotl.* I. 44 *note*, He has no other authority than some Norvegian chronicles. **1781** COWPER *Expost.* 470 Rock'd by many a rough Norwegian blast. **1821** SCOTT *Pirate* xvi, Singing the achievements brave Of many an old Norwegian earl. **1874** R. COWIE *Shetland* (ed. 2) 21 Their dwellings were commodious erections of Norwegian timber.

b. In special applications (see quots. and sbs.). ***Norwegian steam*** (see quot. 1960).

1880–84 DAY *Fishes Gt. Britain* I. 43 Norway haddock and *Norwegian carp. **1792** KER tr. *Linnæus* 241 *Cuniculus norwegicus*, or *Norwegian Coney. **1883** *Leisure H.* 147/1 Tea..is ready all day long in teapots kept hot in covered baskets very thickly padded, such as are known with us as '*Norwegian Kitchens'. **1792** KER tr. *Linnæus* 241 *Mus norwegicus*, *Norwegian Mouse, or Lemming. *Ibid.* 228 *Mus norwegicus*, or *Norwegian Rat. **1944** *Amer. Speech* XIX. 106 *Norwegian steam is brute manpower,..from the tradition of the fine sailing ships. **1947** R. O. BOYER *Dark Ship* vii. 53, I heard another sailor say 'We got there by Norwegian steam' and asked him what he meant. 'By rowing,' he said. **1958** E. S. LAND *Winning War with Ships* iv. 66 The power on deck for such work as weighing anchor was 'Norwegian steam'. **1960** WENTWORTH & FLEXNER *Dict. Amer. Slang* 358/1 *Norwegian steam*, manpower; muscle power. A little jocular use, esp. maritime use. **1970** *Sea Breezes* Nov. 717/2 All the hoisting and hauling is done by hand—'Norwegian steam' as we used to say years ago. **1875** KNIGHT *Dict. Mech.* 1534/1 **Norwegian Stove*..consists of a square wooden box lined with a soft, non-conducting substance. **1899** *Outing* XXX. 229/1 The arrangement of the sliding-seat, the deck tiller, and the '*Norwegian' tiller. The latter is a device adapted from the Norwegian fishing boats. **1836** T. THOMSON *Min., Geol.*, etc. I. 200 *Norwegian Tremolite..in amorphous masses, having a white colour passing into bluish grey.

B. *sb.* **1.** A native of Norway.

1605 VERSTEGAN *Dec. Intell.* vi. 177 In the North parte of England the Norwegians or Normannes were ouerthrown. **1703** J. BRAND *Descr. Orkney* 71 The Norse hath continued ever since the Norvegians had these Isles in Possession. **1757** BURKE *Abridgm. Eng. Hist.* Wks. X. 286 Assisted by the Norwegians, and other people of Scandinavia. **1848** LYTTON *Harold* I. ii, Swede, Norwegian, and Dane, had one common character viewed at a distance. **1884** *Encycl. Brit.* XVII. 590/1 The director of the Danish national theatre in 1771 was a Norwegian.

2. The language of Norway.

1605 VERSTEGAN *Dec. Intell.* vii. 195 The Danish, Norwegian, and Swedish do again differ from these, and some litle each from other. **1797** *Encycl. Brit.* (ed. 3) XIV. 564/2 The Swedish is more nearly related to the Icelandic than either the Danish or Norwegian. **1841** LATHAM *Eng. Lang.* 13 In Danish, Swedish, and Norwegian the form is [etc.].

3. *U.S.* A kind of fishing-boat. (See quots.)

1872–3 J. W. MILNER in *Rep. U.S. Fish Commission* (1874) 9 At Milwaukee, for a time, the most of the boats were the sloop-rigged 'Norwegians', afterwards abandoned, and the square stern adopted. *Ibid.* 14 The 'Norwegian' is a huge, unwieldy thing, with flaring bows, great sheer, high sides, and is sloop-rigged... She is only used by the Scandinavian fishermen.

So †**Nor'wegic** *a. Obs. rare*⁻¹.

1681 GREW *Musæum* III. §i. v. 304 The Relation given at large by Wormius of the Norwegick Mouse.

Norwenisse: see NORENISH *a. Obs.*

nor'-west, reduced form of NORTH-WEST *a.* and *sb.* Also *ellipt.* (quot. 1895).

14.. *Piers of Fullham* 14 in Hazl. *E.E.P.* II. 2 Ther comythe a noyes norweste wynde. *c* **1485** *Digby Myst.* (1882) III. 1876 þe wynd is nor west! **1533–4** *Act 25 Hen. VIII*, c. 8 All cariages, caried from west and Nor-west parties of the realme. **1647** WARD *Simp. Cobler* 18 A new-sprung Sect of Phrantasticks, which would perswade themselves and others, that they have discovered the Nor-west passage to Heaven. **1786** BURNS *On a Sc. Bard* vi, He saw Misfortune's cauld Nor-west Lang mustering up a bitter blast. **1816** SCOTT *Antiq.* xxvi, I wad rather hail the coble half a mile aff, and the norwast wind whistling again in my teeth. **1854** P. B. ST. JOHN *Amy Moss* 141 The dark clouds from the nor'-west came bodily down. **1895** *Outing* XXVI. 30/2 There were..nineteen 'native' duck, ten 'nor'-wests', five spoonbills, and three sprig.

nor'-wester. [Reduced f. NORTH-WESTER.]

1. A wind or gale from the north-west. Esp. in the South Island of New Zealand (in full, ***Canterbury nor'-wester***).

1703 DAMPIER *Voy.* III. 9 These norwesters give notice of their coming. **1871** LADY BARKER *Christmas Cake in Four Quarters* IV. ii. 267 How many of us would be in that valley on a Christmas Day in the far future, when these trees would have struggled up against their enemy the Nor'-wester. **1879** FARRAR *St. Paul* (1883) 711 Fair Havens afforded a shelter from the norwester. **1933** L. G. D. ACLAND in *Press* (Christchurch) 2 Dec. 15/7 The ordinary man in the paddock in Canterbury recognises only three winds: east (from N.E.), sou'-wester (from S.E., S., etc., S.W., etc.), and nor'-wester. **1959** A. MCLINTOCK *Descr. Atlas N.Z.* 22 In summer the hot, dry 'Canterbury Nor'wester' is generally a most unpleasant wind. **1966** G. W. TURNER *Eng. Lang. Austral. & N.Z.* viii. 163 The Canterbury *nor' wester* resembling the European *Föhn* wind..and the *three-day sou'wester* in New Zealand.

2. A glass of strong liquor.

1840 MARRYAT *Olla Podr.* III. 34 Jack poured out the rum till the tumbler was half full. 'Why, Littlebrain,' said his messmate, 'that is a dose, that's what we call a regular Nor-wester'. **1884** 'H. COLLINGWOOD' *Under Meteor Flag* 191 Pouring them out a stiff 'nor'-wester' each to cheer them up a little.

3. An oilskin hat worn by sailors in rough weather; a sou'wester. Also, a strong oilskin or waterproof coat worn in rough weather (in full ***norwester coat***).

1689–90 J. GREENVILL in W. S. Pelletreau *Early Long Island Wills* (1897) 46 My will is that my norwester Coat.. may be given to Christopher Leaming. **1851** MAYHEW *Lond. Labour* (1861) III. 302 The doors nearly blocked up with hammocks and 'well-oiled nor'-westers'. **1853** MOODIE *Life Clearings* 21 A leather hat like a sailor's nor'-wester, with a long peak behind.

†**norwesting,** var. of NORTH-WESTING. *Obs.*

1561 [see NORTH-EASTING *vbl. sb.*].

Nor'weyan, *a. rare.* [f. NORWAY + -AN.] Norwegian.

1605 SHAKS. *Macb.* I. ii. 31 But the Norweyan Lord.. Began a fresh assault. *Ibid.* iii. 95 He findes thee in the stout Norweyan Rankes. **1817** SCOTT *Harold* I. xiii, The war-songs of Danesmen, Norweyan, and Finn.

Norwich ('nɒrɪtʃ, -ɪdʒ). [The name of the city and county town of Norfolk.] Used *attrib.* in various collocations, as ***Norwich crape*** (see CRAPE *sb.* 1); ***Norwich damask, poplin, shawl***; also ***Norwich school***, an English school of painting of the early nineteenth century associated with Norwich; ***Norwich stuff***, a textile fabric manufactured, or as manufactured, in Norwich; ***Norwich terrier***, a small, thickset, red or black-and-tan, rough-coated terrier with pricked ears, belonging to a breed developed in East Anglia; in North America and formerly in Britain also used for the drop-eared variety of the breed, now called the Norfolk terrier; also ellipt. *Norwich*.

1618 T. Roe *Advise for Goodes* in *Embassy* (1899) II. 487 Some light coullored Norwich stuffes wrought in flowers for triall, the lighter the better. **1685**, **1709** [see crape *sb.* 1]. **1741** Richardson *Pamela* IV. xiii. 75 So many Yards of Norwich Stuffs for Gowns and Coats for Girls. **1774** H. Walpole *Descr. Strawberry-Hill* 65 The room is hung with crimson Norwich damask. **1790** M. Dunsford *Hist. Mem. Tiverton* iv. 235 This year [*sc.* 1752] was introduced to Tiverton the manufacture of Norwich stuffs, camblets, tarborates, [etc.]. **1816** J. Crome *Let.* Jan. in W. F. Dickes *Norwich Sch. Painting* (1906) v. 111 You wish me to give you my opinion of your picture... How pleased I was to see so much improvement in the figures, so unlike our Norwich School; I may say they were good. **1821** *Times* 15 Aug., The ladies to wear..dark Norwich crape. *c* **1860** in A. Adburgham *Shops & Shopping* (1964) ix. 100 Paisley, Norwich and French shawls. *Ibid.*, Irish and Norwich poplins. **1877** *Encycl. Brit.* VII. 596/2 *John Crome* (1769–1821), English landscape painter, founder and chief representative of the 'Norwich School'. **1906** W. F. Dickes *Norwich Sch. Painting* 11 The Norwich School has had a powerful influence upon the Art of Great Britain. **1929** *Official Guide to City of Norwich* 25 The..Jacquard loom for the weaving of the beautiful Norwich shawls of coloured silks. **1931** J. Lucas *Hunt & Working Terriers* xxiii. 189 In 1880 a Mr. Nichols of Wymondham, Norfolk, was breeding a small red dog which he called the Norwich terrier. **1950** '*Mercury' Dict. Textile Terms* 368/1 *Norwich crepe*, a cloth very similar to georgettes, and made from fine silk warp and cotton weft, the crepe being produced by the weave. **1950** A. C. Smith *Dogs since 1900* xi. 179 Some of their admirers.. asked permission to have them registered at the Kennel Club as Norwich Terriers. In 1932 they were admitted to registration. **1951** *Short Guide Norwich School Pictures* 3 The old masters of Holland..influenced so profoundly the Norwich School. **1958** *Times* 12 Dec. 1/7 (Advt.), Norwich Terrier for sale. **1967** R. M. R. Young *Guide to Bridewell Museum* 11 The traditional Oriental design now often called 'the Paisley pattern' was also used by the Norwich shawl makers. **1971** F. Hamilton *World Encycl. Dogs* 466 From these red East Anglian terriers..sprang the breed which was recognized..as the Norwich terrier. *Ibid.* 467 The Norwich is very hardy and adaptable. **1972** *Times* 21 June 16/5 Two large, fine views by Henry Bright, the late Norwich school landscapist. **1974** *Country Life* 28 Nov. 1652/1 The Castle Museum at Norwich has long specialized in the..Norwich School.

†**'nory**, *sb. Obs.* Also nori(e. [a. OF. *nori*, pa. pple. of *norir*, var. of *nourrir* to nourish. Cf. norry *sb.*] A foster-child; a pupil.

13.. *K. Alis.* (Weber) 4730 His owen noryes to deth hym broughth. *c* **1350** *Will. Palerne* 1511 His del þan he made, how william hire worþi nory was neiȝe atte deþe. **1387** Trevisa *Higden* (Rolls) VII. 379 Wolstoun gropede þe heved of oon Nichol, þat was his owne norie.

†**'nory**, *v. Obs. rare*$^{-1}$. [a. OF. *norir*, var. of *nourrir* to nourish.] *trans.* To bring up.

c **1450** *Gesta Rom.* lxi. 260 (Harl. MS.), Fro that tyme I have bene norisshid, noried, norturid, and tauȝte in the same contre.

nory: see newry and norie.

noryce, -ys(e, etc., varr. of nourice *Obs.*

norysshe, obs. f. nourish *v.*

noryture, var. of nouriture.

†**nos.** *Obs.* [Of obscure origin.] ? An opening.

13.. *E.E. Allit. P.* C. 451 [Jonah's booth was] Happed vpon ayþer half a hous as hit were, A nos on þe north syde & nowhere non ellez.

nosawnce, variant of noisance *Obs.*

†**'noscible**, *a. Obs. rare*$^{-1}$. [ad. late Lat. *noscibilis* knowable, f. *noscĕre* to know: see -ible.] (See quot.)

1654 Z. Coke *Logick* 76 Noble is he which by vertue is noscible, famous or well known.

nose (nəʊz), *sb.* Forms: 1–2 nosu, 3–4 nos, 5–6 noos, 5 noose, noys(e, 6 noise, nois, noss, 3– nose. [OE. *nosu* fem. = OFris. *nosi*, *nose*, *nosa*, *nos*, MDu. *nose*, *nuese*, *neuse* (Du. *neus*), MLG. *nose*, nose; MSw., Sw., and Norw. *nos* (*nōs*) snout, muzzle. The relationship to OE. *nasu* nase and to nese is not clear.]

I. 1. a. That part (usually more or less prominent) of the head or face in humans and animals which lies above the mouth and contains the nostrils. Also, the corresponding part, or some similar formation, in lower forms of animal life.

In *Saxon Leechd.* I. 88 the plural appears to be used in the sense of 'nostrils'.

c **897** K. Ælfred *Gregory's Past. C.* xi. 64 Ȝif he..to micle nosu hæfde, oððe to lytle. *c* **1000** Ælfric *Hom.* I. 568 Ic ȝeslea ænne wriðan on his nosu, & ænne bridel on his weleras. *a* **1122** *O.E. Chron.* (Laud MS.) an. 1014, Cnut.. let þær up þa gislas..& cearf of heora handa & heora nosa. *c* **1220** *Bestiary* 393 Te gandre & te gos, bi ðe necke & bi ðe nos, [the fox] haleð is to hire hole. *c* **1290** *Beket* 2177 *S. Eng. Leg.* I. 169 A smal rewe þere was of blode þat ouer is nose drouȝ. *c* **1340** *Nominale* (Skeat) 152 Man snyfterith and nose snyt. **1398** Trevisa *Barth. De P.R.* v. xiii. (Bodl. MS.), þe nose is in þe myddel of þe foremest partye of þe hed. **1422** tr. *Secreta Secret., Priv. Priv.* 228 Tho that haue grete Noosys lyghtely bene talentid to couetise. *c* **1470** Henry *Wallace* ix. 1928 His lyppys round, his noys was squar and tret. **1561** Hollybush *Hom. Apoth.* 15 Fyll a fylberts shell full of it, and draw it so in through the nose. **1590** Lodge *Rosalind* (Hunt. Cl.) 38 His nose on the sodaine bled, which made him coniecture it was some friend of his. **1600** Shaks. *A.Y.L.* ii. i. 39 The big round teares Cours'd one another downe his [the stag's] innocent nose. **1650** Bulwer *Anthropomet.* 77 Great is the ornament that the Face receiveth by the Nose. **1687** A. Lovell tr. *Thevenot's Trav.* i. 52 All the Figures that were carved upon her for ornament, had the noses cut off. **1760** Sterne *Tr. Shandy* iii. xxxii, Pressing up the ridge of his nose with his finger and thumb. **1798** Ferriar *Illustr. Sterne* iv. 103 The nose furnishes the principal expression of derision in the countenance. **1826** Kirby & Sp. *Entomol.* xxxiv. III. 477 To enable you to distinguish the nose of insects..it is the terminal middle part that sometimes overhangs the upper lip. **1855** Tennyson *Maud* ii. 10 The least little delicate aquiline curve in a sensitive nose. **1872** Ruskin *Eagle's N.* §182 Some animals have to dig with their noses.

†**b.** Applied to an elephant's trunk. *Obs. rare.*

1601 Holland *Pliny* I. 196 It will with the nose or trunke ..turne aside whatsoeuer beast commeth in his way. **1727** A. Hamilton *New Acc. E. Ind.* II. xli. 110 He put in his Trunk at the Window, and blew his Nose on the Taylor with such a Force and Quantity of Water, that the poor Taylor and his Life-guard were blown off the Table.

c. ***parson's nose***, the rump of a fowl (see parson *sb.* 6); so ***recorder's nose***.

1825 C. Westmacott *Eng. Spy* II. 112 Shall I send you the recorder's nose?

d. That part of a pair of spectacles or eye-glasses which crosses the nose; the bridge.

1895 *Funk's Stand. Dict.*

e. In Horse-racing: the nose of a horse used as an indication of the distance between two finishing horses. Phr. ***to bet*** (etc.) ***on the nose***: to back a horse to win (as opposed to betting for a place, or betting each way).

1908 L. Mitchell *New York Idea* i. 11 Flying Cloud slipped by the pair and won on the post by a nose in one forty nine! **1951** *Publ. Amer. Dial. Soc.* xvi. 13 Bet on the nose. **1955** *Amer. Speech* XXX. 26 Laymen..will say that a horse won by a neck, head, or nose to describe any race which was extremely close. In this country a bet on a horse to win..is said to be on the nose. **1963** 'J. Prescot' *Case for Hearing* iv. 71 Every afternoon that lad of mine is in the betting shop slapping as much as fifty quid a time on the nose. **1973** *Times* 12 Apr. 12/6 Ladbroke..assured me that I could lay £30,000 on the nose if I wished.

2. a. The organ of smell.

a **1400–50** *Alexander* 4380 Quare-of þe breth as of bawme blawis in oure noose. **1526** *Pilgr. Perf.* (W. de W. 1531) 184 Was dulcet & swete to ye mouth..& sauoured wele to the nose. **1588** Shaks. *L.L.L.* v. ii. 569 Your nose smels no, in this most tender smelling Knight. **1601** —— *All's Well* v. ii. 11 *Par.* Nay you neede not to stop your nose sir... *Clo.* Indeed sir, if your Metaphor stinke, I will stop my nose. **1697** Dryden *Virg. Georg.* iv. 67 Nor rost red Crabs t' offend the niceness of their Nose. **1735** Somerville *Chase* i. 324 His snuffling Nose, his active Tail Attest his Joy. **1784** Cowper *Task* ii. 259 That no rude savour maritime invade The nose of nice nobility!

fig. **1589** *Marprel. Epit.* B ij, I am sure their noses can abide no iest. **1591** Lodge (*title-p.*), Catharos, A Nettle for Nice Noses. **1792** Boswell *Johnson* an. 1784, 27 June, He entered upon a..discussion of the difference between intuition and sagacity;..one he observed was the *eye* of the mind, the other the *nose* of the mind.

b. The sense of smell; a (good, bad, etc.) faculty of smell or power of tracking by scent.

c **1350** *Will. Palerne* 92 Wiȝtly þe werwolf þan went bi nose euene to þe herdes house. **1573** Baret *Alv.* s.v. *Smell*, He hath a very good nose: or he can smell very quickly. **1611** Cotgr. s.v. *Nez*, A dog of a deepe nose, or good sent. **1711** E. Ward *Vulgus Brit.* ii. 131 All tho' the Puppies have no Noses They'l with them Hunt thro' Woods and Closes. **1732** Berkeley *Alciphr.* v. §1 You shall often see among the dogs a loud babbler, with a bad nose, lead the unskilful part of the pack. **1856** 'Stonehenge' *Brit. Rural Sports* 28/1 The hunting power of the spaniel, its delicacy of nose [etc.]. **1897** *Outing* XXIX. 543/2 He had a wonderful nose and as much bird-sense as I have ever known one dog's head to contain.

fig. **1549** Latimer *5th Serm. bef. Edw. VI* (Arb.) 142 He was a gentilman of a longe nose... Thys Shyryffe was a couetuouse man. **1875** W. Hyde in C. F. Wingate *Views & Interviews on Journalism* 196 The 'nose for news', by which is meant unwearying alertness and insatiable hunger for something 'ahead of the other papers'. **1876** E. Jenkins *Blot on Queen's Hd.* 10 Keen noses for their own interest. **1934** C. Lambert *Music Ho!* ii. 86 He had an astounding 'nose' for the growth of any particular movement of taste or snobbism. **1942** E. Waugh *Put out More Flags* ii. 118 One does not work in the East without acquiring a nose for a deal. **1960** *Times* 20 June 4/1 The crowds who always have a nose for personality. **1972** 'J. Cassells' *Profit for Picaroon* v. 36 He was a damned good reporter..and he had a nose for a story.

c. Smell, odour, perfume; esp. of wines.

1894 Blackmore *Perlycross* 61 The room was like a barn after a bad cold harvest, with a musty nose to it. **1899** Haggard *Farm. Year* 8 July 265 Otherwise it [the hay] would lack 'nose' and flavour. **1936** F. C. Lloyd *Art & Technique Wine* xv. 146 The bouquet, or 'nose' to use a more technical word, is very important and serves to reveal the characteristics of wines to a connoisseur. **1952** A. Lichine *Wines of France* x. 107 Its tremendous nose—*bouquet* is too delicate a word—makes it [*sc.* Chambertin] a veritable Cyrano. **1971** *Guardian* 12 Nov. 9/2 The dry white of Beaucaire..has an aromatic 'nose' and plenty of body.

d. ***on the nose*** (Austral.): offensive, annoying; smelly.

1941 Baker *Dict. Austral. Slang* 49 *Nose, on the*: (said of things) disliked, offensive. **1945** T. Inglis Moore *We're going Through* 18 Withdraw! That's on the nose! **1946** K. Tennant *Lost Haven* (1947) vi. 86 'Christ! Alec,' he complained. 'This bait's a bit on the nose, ain't it?' He spat over the side as the reek of fish-heads a week old..caught his stomach. **1953** D. Cusack *Southern Steel* 138 The beer's on the nose and the plonk'd make a willy-wagtail fight an emu. **1974** *Australian* 12 Dec. 13 She renounced her Australian citizenship and swore everlasting loyalty to the Stars and Stripes. A bit on the nose, we think.

3. As an organ by which speech-sounds may be produced or affected. Chiefly in phrases ***in*** or ***through the nose***.

1530 Palsgr. 2 They sounde hym..a lyttell in the noose. **1588** Shaks. *L.L.L.* iii. i. 16 Sing a note,..sometime through [the] nose. **1604** —— *Oth.* iii. i. 4 Haue your Instruments bin in Naples, that they speake i' th' Nose thus? **1648** *Visitation Oxford* 4 Langley (the new made Yeoman Bedell of Divinity) with Paper, Spectacles, and Nose proclaimed a Convocation. **1741** A. Monro *Anat. Nerves* (ed. 3) 86 People labouring under a *Coryza*, or stopping of the Nose from any other Cause,..are by the Vulgar..said to speak through their Nose. **1850** Dickens *Dav. Copp.* xxii, He..pays as he speaks..—through the nose. **1888** [see nasally].

4. ***a nose of wax***, a thing easily turned or moulded in any way desired; a person easily influenced, one of a weak character.

Very common *c* 1580–1700, esp. in allusions to wresting the Scriptures.

1532 Tindale *Expos. Matt.* vi. 23 If the Scripture be contrary, then make it a nose of wax and wrest it this way and that way till it agree. **1589** Cooper *Admon.* (Arb.) 58 Affirming..that the Scriptures are darke.., because they may bee wrested euery way, like a nose of waxe, or like a leaden Rule. **1657** *Burton's Diary* (1828) II. 162 This Bill is not worth a second reading. It is a nose of wax. **1686** Horneck *Crucif. Jesus* ix. 167 Oral Tradition, that nose of wax, which you may turn and set, which way you list. **1748** *Lond. Mag.* 259 Are the laws for preventing the growth of popery only a nose of wax? **1801** Huntington *God Guard. of Poor* 139 He turned his text into a nose-of-wax, in order to make it fit my face. **1821** Galt *Annals Parish* xii, Her ladyship..said that I was a nose-of-wax. **1880** Disraeli *Endym.* III. xxx. 300 He was a nose of wax with this woman.

5. *slang.* A spy or informer; one who supplies information to the police. (See also quot. 1812.)

1789 G. Parker *Life's Painter* xv. 151 Nose.—Snitch. **1812** J. H. Vaux *Flash Dict.*, *Nose*, a thief who becomes an evidence against his accomplices;..also a spy or informer of any description. **1830** *Boston Gaz.* 26 Oct. 1 The first issue of forged notes, it is stated by a nose (an informer), amounted to 500. **1888** *Pall Mall G.* 11 Oct. 88 The co-operation of the..policeman with female 'pals' and 'noses'. **1928** E. Wallace *Gunner* xviii. 145 He was just a little thief and a nose. **1954** [see grass *sb.*[1] 12]. **1961** *John o' London's* 30 Nov. 610/3 Other words used for him [*sc.* an informer] include *grass*, *nose*, [etc.]. **1974** R. Edwards *Dixon of Dock Green* 7 He knew that CID men are allowed to drink on duty because much of their time is spent with 'noses' or informants.

II. In phrases more or less figurative.

6. a. In various colloquial or allusive expressions.

to make a long nose (see long *a.*[1] 1 c). ***to have***, or ***take***, ***pepper in the nose*** (see pepper *sb.* 4 b).

1297 R. Glouc. (Rolls) 2090 Maximian was suþþe aslawe maugre is nose. **13..** *K. Alis.* 7812 (MS. Laud 622), þe kyng hym dude quyk dispose, Wiþ harme to his owen nose. **1338** R. Brunne *Chron.* (1810) 95 A Breton (daþet his nose) for Roberd þider sent. **1377** Langl. *P. Pl.* B. iv. 164 But he be knowe for a koke-wolde kut of my nose. **1526** Skelton *Magnyf.* 835 Pryde hath plucked thé by the nose. **1577** *F. de Lisle's Legendarie* F vij b, If she [the Queen-mother] had not supported them, their noses had then kissed the ground. **1589** *Pasquil's Ret.* B ij b, They prooue so ridiculous.., that I am ready to stand on my nose. **1605** *Tryall Chev.* i. iii, Tary, sir, tary, we want the length of your nose. **1632** Strafford in Browning & Foster *Life* (1892) App. ii. 301 The Commission of the Peace, (the instrument of terroure by which he pulled them on along with him by the noses). **1687** T. Brown in Villiers (Dk. Buckhm.) *Wks.* 1705 II. 126 He durst hardly show his Nose over his hatch. **1734** Pope *Ess. Man* iv. 224 Onward still he goes, Yet ne'er looks forward farther than his nose. **1837** Carlyle *Fr. Rev.* III. ii. i, Seeing clearly to the length of its own nose, it is not paralysed. **1861** Hughes *Tom Brown at Oxf.* vi, You've always got your nose in the manger. **1917** R. Fry *Let.* 23 Nov. (1972) II. 420 Millions of people..catch me on the telephone the moment I just put my nose inside the Omega. **1922** Joyce *Ulysses* 322 In Shanagolden where he daren't show his nose. **1935** J. Buchan *House of Four Winds* i. 42, I should like to put my nose inside Evallonia just to say I'd been there. **1947** M. Lowry *Under Volcano* i. 25 Geoffrey's 'nose was always in a book'. **1963** Nose wide open [see fox *sb.* 2 c]. **1968** M. Jones *Survivor* ii. 33 It was considered anti-social to 'have your nose stuck in a book'. **1970** C. Major *Dict. Afro-Amer. Slang* 85 '*Nose wide open*' is to be in love.

Comb. **1882** Floyer *Unexpl. Baluchistan* 245 There was a general nose-in-the-air, defiant kind of aspect.

b. (***in***) ***spite of one's nose***, notwithstanding one's opposition or objection. Also in ME. ***maugre his nose*** (see prec., quot. 1297). ? *Obs.*

1570 *Satir. Poems Reform.* x. 183 Than come ȝour king.. And reft him from hir in spyte of his nois. **1579** Fulke *Heskins' Parl.* 286 In spite of his nose, he must confesse al this speach to be figuratiue. **1659** Hammond *On Ps.* cxxxviii. 7 Our English usual expression, in spite of the nose of mine enemies. **1664** Cotton *Scarron.* Wks. (1725) 110 He would go, spite of all their Noses. **1675** —— *Burlesque upon B.* ibid. 182 Spight of your Nose, and will ye, nill ye, I will go home again, that will I.

c. In comparisons denoting that something is perfectly plain or obvious. Also ironically.

1591 Shaks. *Two Gent.* ii. i. 142 Oh Iest vnseene: inscrutable: inuisible, As a nose on a mans face, or a Wethercocke on a steeple. **1655** H. More *Second Lash* 200

As plain as the nose on a mans face. **1695** CONGREVE *Love for L.* IV. viii, 'Tis as plain as the nose in one's face. **1773** GRAVES *Spir. Quix.* v. xix, The Gentleman..has made it as plain as the nose in one's face, if one did but understand him. **1821** CLARE *Vill. Minstr.* I. 157 It's as plain as the nose on your face for to see't. **1873** HARDY *Pair Blue Eyes* iii, It is as plain as the nose in your face that there's your origin.

d. ***to count,*** or ***tell, noses,*** denoting the counting of persons, esp. those on one side or party.

1657 *Leveller* in *Harl. Misc.* (1745) IV. 515 The Leveller's Designs, to make all Men's Estates to be equal, and to divide the Land by telling Noses. **1691** *New Disc. Old Intreague* xxxiv, Tells how in Common Hall he counted Noses. **1711** SHAFTESB. *Charac.* (1737) I. 148 Some modern zealots appear to have no better knowledg of truth, nor better manner of judging it, than by counting noses. *a* **1734** NORTH *Examen* III. vii. §29 (1740) 523 As if there had been none better than Number, or telling Noses.

7. In prepositional phrases, chiefly denoting closeness or proximity to a person or thing.

a. ***at one's (very) nose.*** (Still *colloq.* or *dial.*)

1526 *St. Papers Hen. VIII*, VI. 543 That citie stondith in a very strong place hard at his [the Pope's] nose. **1568** GRAFTON *Chron.* II. 695 Because the war was ouert at his nose, with the French kyng. **1659** B. HARRIS *Parival's Iron Age* 45 The taking of so important a place; just at the nose of so strong an Army. **1704** N. N. tr. *Boccalini's Advts. fr. Parnass.* II. To Rdr., They make 'em believe, Rewards and Honours are just at their very Noses.

b. ***under one's (very) nose.***

Freq. implying that an action is done in defiance of a person, or without his perceiving it.

a **1548** HALL *Chron., K. Hen. V* 38 Why doth your grace ..covet a countrey farre from your sight, before a realme under your nose? **1577** HARRISON *England* II. i. (1877) I. 30 In some places where the kings and princes dwelled not under his [the Pope's] nose. **1607** NORDEN *Surv. Dial.* I. 7 You are but a meane obseruer of the course..of things passing dayly under your nose. **1670** COTTON *Espernon* I. IV. 153 They..suffer'd the Duke..to continue his work under their noses. **1707** FREIND *Peterborow's Cond. Spain* 240 His Lordship procur'd and bought near 800 Horses, under the Enemies nose. **1775** SHERIDAN *Duenna* III. vi, They continue to sin under my very nose. **1856–7** GEO. ELIOT *Sc. Clerical Life* II. i, A parson, always under your nose on your own estate.

c. † ***by one's nose,*** very close to one. † ***to one's nose,*** before one's face. † ***on the nose of,*** immediately before, on the eve of. ***on the nose*** (U.S.): accurately, precisely, to the heart of the situation; accurate, precise (esp. of time). ***nose to nose,*** closely face to face, directly opposite.

1549 LATIMER *5th Serm. bef. Edw. VI* (Arb.) 142 She had hir landes by the Shiriffes nose. **1588** SHAKS. *Tit. A.* II. i. 94 What, hast not thou full often strucke a Doe, And borne her cleanly by the Keepers nose? **1607** —— *Cor.* IV. vi. 83 To see your Wiues dishonour'd to your Noses. **1681** SIR J. LAUDER *Scot. Affairs* (Bann. Cl.) 304 That they, on the nose of a Parliament, came so near the deciding on dubious elections. **1732** *Buccleuch MSS.* (Hist. MSS. Comm.) I. 382 You sit down quite close as ever you can, nose to nose. **1781** COWPER *Conv.* 270 In contact inconvenient, nose to nose. **1855** THACKERAY *Newcomes* II. 283 The two parties would often meet nose to nose in the same street. **1937** *Printers' Ink Monthly* May 40/1 *On the button*, a program ending exactly on time... *On the nose*, see 'On the button'. **1943** *New Yorker* 30 Oct. 21/1 I'll meet you there happest twelve, but on the nose. **1944** W. C. GREET *World Words* p. v, This book has been prepared in great haste. To be readily understood, and, in radio parlance, to be on the nose, were its prime requirements. **1958** B. HOLIDAY *Lady sings Blues* (1973) ii. 27 'You were supposed to be out weeks ago,' they told one girl. But I got out right on the nose at the end of four months. **1959** N. MAILER *Advts. for Myself* (1961) 240 Malcolm Cowley was right on the nose when he wrote that *The Deer Park* was a far more difficult book to write than *The Naked and the Dead.* **1962** P. GREGORY *Like Tigress at Bay* i. 14 'That's it.' he said. 'You've hit it right on the nose.' **1972** R. H. COPPERUD *Dict. Contemp. & Colloq. Usage* (Eng.-Lang. Inst. Amer.) 21/1 *On the nose*, right on target; exactly; accurately; on the button. **1974** HAWKEY & BINGHAM *Wild Card* xxii. 176 The cerebroid was properly docked in the flight couch. 'Right on the nose,' Stillman said.

d. ***before one's nose,*** right in front of one.

c **1600** *Distr. Emperor* v. iv, What a lardge passage.. Theise prynces make to come unto the way Which lyes before their nosses! **1883** STEVENSON *Treas. Isl.* xiii, I ran straight before my nose, till I could run no longer.

8. In phrases with verbs, implying something done to, or with, one's own nose:

a. ***to follow one's nose,*** to go straight forward; *fig.* to be guided by instinct.

1591 GREENE *Art Conny catch.* Wks. (Grosart) X. 35 Who so hath not some sinister way to help himselfe, but foloweth his nose alwaies straight forward. **1605** SHAKS. *Lear* II. iv. 70 All that follow their noses are led by their eyes, but blinde men. **1664** COTTON *Scarron.* 60 There lies your way, follow your Nose. **1692** BENTLEY *Boyle Lect.* ii. (1724) 79 The main Maxim of his [Epicurus's] Philosophy was to trust to his Senses, and follow his Nose. **1742** FIELDING *J. Andrews* II. ii, Adams asked him if he could direct him to an alehouse. The fellow..bade him follow his nose. **1822** BYRON *Juan* VIII. xxxii, Juan, following honour and his nose. [**1860** LD. LYTTON *Lucile* II. i. § I. 40 To pay through his nose just for following it.]

b. ***to poke, put,*** or ***thrust, one's nose,*** to poke or pry *into* something, esp. a matter which does not properly concern one. Conversely ***to keep one's nose clean,*** to behave properly, keep out of trouble (see also quot. 1909).

1611 COTGR. s.v. *Nez, Mettre le nez par tout*, to thrust his nose into euery corner. **1648** HEXHAM, *Besnoffelen*, to See Prie, or Have his nose in every thing. **1755** JOHNSON s.v., To thrust one's Nose into the affairs of others, to be meddling with other people's matters; to be a busy body. **1809** W. IRVING *Knickerb.* (1861) 86 In those days nobody..thrust his nose into other people's affairs. **1850** THACKERAY *Pendennis* II. xxxvi. 347 Beck! leave the room. What do *you* want poking your nose in here? **1856** READE *Never too Late* xv, If he hadn't been a fool and put his nose into my business. **1883** M. PATTISON *Mem.* (1885) 190 A flourishing Evangelical, who poked his nose into everything. **1887** *Lantern* (New Orleans) 13 Oct. 5/3 There's worse fellows than you looking for it, and if you only keep your nose clean, we'll let you have it. **1909** J. R. WARE *Passing Eng.* 162/1 *Keep your nose clean* (Army), avoid drink. **1934** J. O'HARA *Appointment in Samarra* ii. 54, I give you the sawbuck because you've just got out of the can. Keep your nose clean. **1945** P. CHEYNEY *I'll say she Does!* i. 12 You're a guy who has gotta reputation for keepin' his nose clean, but..you're in bad with the big boy. **1959** N. MAILER *Advts. for Myself* (1961) 350 You boys on Channel Five want to keep your nose clean, now don't you? **1960** C. MACINNES *Mr. Love & Justice* 15 What we're offering you is—well, influence... How you manage there, provided you keep your nose clean, is really up to you. **1970** N. ARMSTRONG et al. *First on Moon* i. 23 Do what people tell you, keep your nose clean and work out your academic progress. **1974** A. ROSS *Bradford Business* 64 Denis Fitzgerald..a known associate of villains, but managed to keep his own nose clean.

c. ***to turn up one's nose,*** to show disdain. Also, ***to look down one's nose.***

1818 BYRON *Juan* I. clix, Antonia.., turning up her nose, with looks abused Her master. **1845** FORD *Handbk. Spain* I. 28 The better classes turn up their noses at these odoriferous delicacies of the peasantry. **1879** B. TAYLOR *Germ. Lit.* 7 What learning there was in those days..turned up its nose at the strains of the native minstrels. **1921** GALSWORTHY *To Let* III. xi. 306 That chap Jolyon's water-colours were on view there. He went in to look down his nose at them—it might give him some faint satisfaction. **1932** *Sun* (Baltimore) 24 Oct. 8/1 It is getting more difficult for a lawyer to look down his nose at the courtroom, with consequent impairment of the prestige of the courts. **1956** A. WILSON *Anglo-Saxon Att.* I. iv. 102 When you were all little babies, I used to sing and dance all day. The English neighbours would say 'That young Mrs Middleton's quite mad', and look down their noses—so! **1973** *Times* 24 Apr. 5/4 The portrait of the famous widow, who invented the topsy-turvy logic of *remuage* and *dégorgement*..looks down her nose down the stairs at her successors in the craft.

d. † ***to hold up one's nose,*** to be proud or haughty. † ***to hang a nose,*** to have an inclination or hankering. † ***to fuddle one's nose*** (see FUDDLE *v.* 2 b). ***to cut off one's nose,*** etc., to do something to one's own hurt or loss.

1579 TOMSON *Calvin's Serm. Tim.* 228/1 Let women holde vppe their noses no more: for all their presumption is sufficiently beaten downe here. **1649** G. DANIEL *Trinarch. Hen. V* cxxv, Chuse his Bread, And hang a Nose to Leekes, Quaile-Surfetted. **1655** tr. *Sorel's Com. Hist. Francion* VIII. 19 If there be in my kitchin any thing better than another.. this Gallant wil hang a nose after it. **1796** *Grose's Dict. Vulgar Tongue* (ed. 3) s.v., He cut off his nose to be revenged of his face. Said of one who, to be revenged on his neighbour, has materially injured himself. **1867** TROLLOPE *Chron. Barset* xxiv, I make it a rule never to cut the nose off my own face.

e. ***to hold one's nose***: to compress the nostrils between the fingers in order to avoid perceiving a (bad) smell. Also *fig.*

a **1592** GREENE *Jas. IV* (1905) II. I. ii. 102 A stiffe docket, —hold your nose, master. **1830** COLERIDGE *Table-T.* 8 July (1884) 102 Son of Jacob! Thou stinkest foully. See the man in the moon! he is holding his nose at thee at that distance. **1900** *Fortn. Rev.* Jan. 74 Surely there are times when he is forced to hold his nose and shut his eyes to shut out the abominable visions he conjures up for us. **1973** *Times* 18 Sept. 18/2 Then abolish all alternatives to this public system of education, at which they hold their noses.

f. ***to thumb one's nose***: to put one's thumb to one's nose and extend the fingers as a gesture of derision: to 'cock a snook'. Also *fig.* orig. *U.S.*

1903 R. DUNN *Diary* 25 July (1907) ix. 109 He thumbed his nose at us. **1929** A. C. & C. EDINGTON *Studio Murder Myst.* iv. 37 Underlings in the studio thumbed their noses at his back. **1947** W. MOTLEY *Knock on any Door* 119 Behind Ma's back Ang thumbed her nose at him and stuck out her tongue. **1973** J. WAINWRIGHT *High-Class Kill* 163 They are already thumbing their snotty, aristocratic noses at us.

g. ***to get it up one's nose***: in P. G. Wodehouse (*a*) to become angry; (*b*) to become infatuated.

1925 WODEHOUSE *Carry on, Jeeves!* iii. 67 This lad seems to have chucked all the principles of a well-spent boyhood. He has got it up his nose! **1934** —— *Right ho, Jeeves* xvii. 220 So thoroughly had Gussie got it up his nose by now that it seemed to me that had he sighted me he might have become personal about even an old school friend. **1961** —— *Service with Smile* (1962) ix. 135, I have seldom seen a man who has got it so thoroughly up his nose. **1971** —— *Much Obliged, Jeeves* iii. 20 He had spoken of her..with devotion in every syllable. Plainly he had got it up his nose and didn't object to being bossed. **1973** —— *Bachelors Anonymous* viii. 92 'See what I mean?.. Got it right up his nose,' said Mr. Llewellyn. 'I have seldom seen a case where the symptoms were more clearly marked,' said Mr. Trout. 'He is taking her to dinner.'

h. ***to get up someone's nose***: (see quot. 1951).

1951 PARTRIDGE *Dict. Slang* 1120/2 *Nose, get up one's*, to upset, annoy, irritate, render 'touchy'. **1975** *Daily Mail* 6 Aug. 7/1 The implication that granny was a little winning knockout with a system that couldn't be bettered..does, I'm afraid, get rather up my nose. **1975** *Times Lit. Suppl.* 26 Sept. 1102/2 The police pulled them [*sc.* homeless alcoholics] in whenever they got up the public's nose too much.

i. ***to get one's nose down*** (*to*): to work arduously and concentratedly (at). Cf. GRINDSTONE 2 b.

1962 *Times* 31 May 4/1 Getting their noses really down to business. **1966** WODEHOUSE *Plum Pie* i. 11 One would certainly have expected him by this time to have raised the price of a marriage licence and had the Bishop and assistant clergy getting their noses down to it.

9. In phrases with verbs, implying something done to another person.

† **a.** ***to cast in,*** or ***lay to, one's nose,*** to reproach or upbraid one with. *Obs.* (Cf. CAST *v.* 65.)

1526 *Pilgr. Perf.* (W. de W. 1531) 10 He wyll obiecte it to the, and cast it in thy nose. **1579** TOMSON *Calvin's Serm. Tim.* 256/1 Let euery one of us..take such heede to him selfe, that this reproch bee not laide to our noses. *a* **1600** *Flodden F.* (1664) 75 Let it never be laid unto our nose, That Scotchmen made us turn our back.

b. ***to put*** (or †***thrust***) ***one's nose out of joint,*** etc., to displace or supplant one; to spoil one's plans; to throw out or disconcert in some way.

1581 RICH *Farew. Milit. Profess.* K iv, It could bee no other then his owne manne, that had thrust his nose so farre out of ioynte. **1598** R. BERNARD tr. *Terence, Eunuch* I. ii, Fearing now lest this wench..should put your nose out of joynt. **1662** PEPYS *Diary* 31 May, The King is pleased enough with her: which, I fear, will put Madam Castlemaine's nose out of joynt. **1754** GOODALL *Exam. Lett. Mary Q. of Scots* 9 This method of proceeding..thrust their noses quite out of joint. **1781** J. ADAMS in *Fam. Lett.* (1876) 403 Burgoyne don't seem to be affronted that his [= Cornwallis's] nose is out of joint. **1840** MRS. TROLLOPE *Widow Married* xi, She won't put my nose out, any how. **1860** THACKERAY *Lovel* vi, My dear, I guess your ladyship's nose is out of joint.

c. ***to bite*** or ***snap one's nose off,*** to answer snappishly.

Cf. Robinson tr. *More's Utopia* (Arb.) 25, and Shaks. *Much Ado* v. i. 115.

1599 NASHE *Lenten Stuffe* 47 Shee was a shrewish snappish bawd, that wold bite off a mans nose with an answere. **1709** MRS. CENTLIVRE *Busie Body* I. i, I..ask'd him if he was at leisure for his Chocolate,..but he snap'd my Nose off; no, I shall be busy here these two Hours.

d. ***to make a bridge of one's nose*** (see quots.).

a **1700** B. E. *Dict. Cant. Crew* s.v., *You make a Bridge of his Nose*, when you pass your next Neighbor in Drinking, or one is preferr'd over another's Head. **1731–8** SWIFT *Pol. Conversat.* II. Wks. 1751 XII. 242 Pray, my Lord, don't make a Bridge of my Nose. **1768** *Ray's Prov.* 180 To make a bridge of one's nose, i.e. To intercept one's trencher, cup, or the like; or to offer or pretend to do kindnesses to one, and then pass him by, and do it to another; to lay hold upon and serve himself of that which was intended for another. **1828** in *Craven Dial.* s.v.

e. † ***to bite by the nose,*** to treat with contempt. † ***to bore one's nose,*** to cheat, swindle. † ***to joint one's nose of,*** to trick one out of. † ***to play with one's nose,*** to make game of one. ***to make one's nose swell,*** to make one jealous or envious. ***to rub*** (occas. ***push***) ***one's nose in it***: to remind (someone) humiliatingly of his error; to make (someone) acutely aware of (a fault, etc.).

See also GRINDSTONE 2 b, and LEAD *v.*[1] 4 c.

1584 B. R. tr. *Herodotus, Euterpe* (1888) 163 Apyres was perswaded that neither god nor the diuell coulde haue ioynted his nose of the Empyre. **1590** GREENE *Arcadia* (1616) 29 Pesana hearing how pleasantly Melicertus plaide with her nose, thought to giue him a great bone to gnawe vpon. **1603** SHAKS. *Meas. for M.* III. i. 109 Has he affections in him, That thus can make him bite the Law by th' nose? **1611** COTGR., *Nasarder*, to fillip;..also, to frumpe, or breake a ieast on; play with the nose of. **1625** FLETCHER & SHIRLEY *Nt. Walker* II. iii, I'll take order she shall ne'er recover To bore my nose. **1642** HOWELL *For. Trav.* (Arb.) 44, I have known divers Dutch Gentlemen grosly guld by this cheat, and som English bor'd also through the nose this way. **1743** in Howell *St. Trials* (1813) XVII. 1187 He heard lord Altham say,..my wife has got a son, which will make my brother's nose swell. **1963** P. M. HUBBARD *Flush as May* xiii. 121 I'm sorry. I've said I'm sorry... Don't rub my nose in it. **1967** 'M. HUNTER' *Cambridgeshire Disaster* vii. 47 It makes a change, I suppose,..having your nose rubbed in it. **1971** D. LEES *Rainbow Conspiracy* i. 18 Using me on a hard news story would be pushing their noses in it—treating them like a branch office with printing facilities. **1972** *Times Lit. Suppl.* 3 Mar. 234/1 Discontinuity will not do on its own for a resolute dualist and Bataille wants to rub our noses in the idea of the continuous.

10. a. In allusions to the act of wiping the nose.

1437 *Pol. Poems* (Rolls) II. 176 Thus they wold, if we will beleve, Wypen our nose with our owne sleve. **1562** J. HEYWOOD *Prov. & Epigr.* (1867) 80, I may..make you wype your nose vpon your sleeue. **1575** *Gamm. Gurton* v. i, She will..byd you seeke your remedy, and so go wype your nose. **1611** COTGR. s.v. *Nez*, They wipe his nose with his owne sleeue, his taile with his owne shirt; they allow him meat, or meanes, out of his owne money. **1630** *R. Johnson's Kingd. & Commw.* 160 It was used in that good old world, when men wiped their nose on their sleeve (as the French man sayes).

† **b.** ***to wipe one's nose of,*** to deprive, defraud, or cheat one of (anything). *Obs.*

1598 R. BERNARD tr. *Terence, Eunuch* I. i, The very destruction of our substance: who wipes our noses of all that we should have. **1630** *R. Johnson's Kingd. & Commw.* 362 Many thinke his nose will be wiped of it. **1667** PEPYS *Diary* 17 July, That..the King [might] own a marriage before his contract..with the Queene, and so wipe their noses of the Crown. **1721** CIBBER *Rival Fools* Wks. II. 1754 I. 29, I durst lay my Life thou wipest this foolish Knight's Nose of his Mistress at last.

11. ***to pay through the nose,*** to pay excessively; to be charged exorbitantly.

1672 MARVELL *Reh. Transp.* I. 270 Made them pay for it most unconscionably and through the Nose. *a* **1700** B. E. *Dict. Cant. Crew.* **1782** MISS BURNEY *Cecilia* x. vi, She knows nothing of business, and is made to pay for every thing through the nose. **1809** MALKIN *Gil Blas* I. ii. ¶ 10 But paying through the nose was not the worst of it. **1860** [see 8 a]. **1893** BARING-GOULD *Cheap Jack Zita* I. 136 Something for which the public had that day paid, and paid through the nose.

III. In transferred uses.

12. † **a.** A socket on a candlestick, into which the lower end of the candle is inserted. *Obs.*

1431 *Rec. St. Mary at Hill* (1904) 27 A kandelstyk of laton with foure nosis. **1534** MORE *Comf. agst. Trib.* II. Wks. 1172/1 The snuffe of a candle that burneth wᵗ in the candlestickes nose. *Ibid.*, A flame halfe an ynch aboue the nose. **1577** tr. *Bullinger's Decades* III. v. (1592) 347 Christ is the shanke or shaft of the candlesticke, vpon which shanke many snuffers or noses do sticke, which holde the light vp to the Church.

b. The open end of a pipe or tube; the muzzle of a gun, the nozzle of a pair of bellows, etc.

1598 BARRET *Theor. Warres* III. i. 34 Holding the nose of his peece somwhat vpward. **1625** B. JONSON *Staple of N.* II. iv, A wretched rascall, that will binde about The nose of his bellowes, lest the wind get out When hee's abroad. **1664** EVELYN *Kal. Hort.* (1729) 231 The Thermometer hanging over the Nose of the Ground-pipe, by which to govern the Heat. **1690** *Lond. Gaz.* No. 2609/4 A streight Key with a Steel Nose. **1730** CHAMBERLAYNE *Relig. Philos.* II. xvii. §21 Take a Syringe;..put the End or Nose of it in Water. **1757** A. COOPER *Distiller* I. xxi. (1760) 85 A large glass..placed under the Nose of the Worm. **1844** *Regul. & Ordin. Army* 97 A plug of wood is then to be put into the nose of the Barrel. **1890** W. J. GORDON *Foundry* 143 The gatherer dips his pipe or tube inside this ring, and with a twirl collects on the end, or 'nose', a pear-shaped lump.

c. The beak or rostrum of an alembic, retort, or still.

1651 FRENCH *Distill.* v. 146 Take a Caldron with a great and high cover having a beake or nose. **1678** R. RUSSELL tr. *Geber* II. I. x. 107 An Alembeck with a wide nose or beak. **1758** REID tr. *Macquer's Chym.* I. 396 Let the nose of the retort enter about half an inch into the water.

d. The neck of a globe of glass when detached from the blow-pipe.

1844 *Civil Eng. & Arch. Jrnl.* VII. 35/2 The nose of the glass is heated in a furnace constructed at one side, which is called the nose-hole. **1880** *Spons' Encycl. Manuf.* I. 1064 The end of the piece which was next the now detached pipe, is called the nose.

e. = NOSE-HOLE 2.

1839 URE *Dict. Arts* 581 The outside is built of common brick,..and the mouth or nose of Stourbridge fire-clay.

f. = NOSE-PIPE 2.

1874 RAYMOND *Statist. Mines & Mining* 306 The throat had to be kept dark, the 'noses' also dark, and about 6 inches in length.

13. The prow, bow, or stem of a ship or boat. Hence, the corresponding part of an aeroplane, motor vehicle, torpedo, surfboard, etc.

1538 ELYOT, *Coronis*.., the nose of a shippe. **1569** STOCKER tr. *Diod. Sic.* III. viii. 114 He..embarqued..great store of Shot and Engines.., planting them in the Noses of his Gallies. **1583** —— *Civ. Warres Lowe C.* III. 112b, The nose of one of them so touched vpon the shore of the Ryuer, as that she was not able well to turne her selfe about. **1613** PURCHAS *Pilgrimage* (1864) 53 One of the Gallies lost her Nose with a shot. **1749** *Naval Chron.* III. 206 The Ship rode with a whole cable before her nose. **1853** KANE *Grinnell Exp.* xxxii. (1856) 277 The brig remains as she was—her nose burrowing in the snow. **1889** J. K. JEROME *Three Men in Boat* xviii, The nose of our boat had got fixed under the woodwork of the lock. **1899** *Royal Mag.* Jan. 251/1 In the 'nose' of the torpedo. **1899** H. G. WELLS *When Sleeper Wakes* xxiv. 320 The nose of the machine jerked upward steeply. **1903** *Science Siftings* 7 Nov. 68/1 When the operator wishes to descend he pulls on a line which lowers the nose of the kite. **1906** *Strand Mag.* May 516/2 In such cases they put the nose of the machine to the opposite side. **1914** *War Illustr.* I. 406 A British Army biplane that collapsed and fell with its nose in the earth. **1942** *R.A.F. Jrnl.* 13 June 33 Always face the nose of the bomb. When I say 'nose' I mean the end which is away from the explosive charge. **1962** S. CARPENTER in *Into Orbit* 57 The engineers designed the capsule so that the blunt-nose would come down first. **1962** T. MASTERS *Surfing made Easy* 64 *Nose*, the front of the surfboard. **1968** W. WARWICK *Surfriding in N.Z.* 3/2 The nose was rounded with a slight uplift or rocker. **1971** M. TAK *Truck Talk* 110 *Nose*, the foremost part of a trailer.

14. a. A prominent or projecting part; the point or extremity of anything.

In technical use in a number of special applications.

1592 LYLY *Gallathea* I. iv, The Lode-stone that alwaies holdeth his nose to the North. **1676** MOXON *Print Lett.* 48 The Nose of Small Letters project also 3 parts. **1688** HOLME *Armoury* III. 239/2 Their Shooes do turn up at the Nose, after the manner of a hook. *Ibid.* 289/1 The Nose is either ends of the Shuttle, which are ever tipt with Iron. **1747** HOOSON *Miner's Dict.* Qj, Bringing up the Earth upon the Nose or end of his Spade. **1829** *Sporting Mag.* XXIII. 388 What we call a wheel-iron, placed, as usual, on the nose of an axle-tree. **1871** L. STEPHEN *Playgr. Eur.* (1894) v. 118 Blue crevasses..were drawn across the protruding nose of ice.

b. A projecting part of a shell; also *spec.* of tortoise-shell (see quot. 1858).

1681 GREW *Musæum* I. vi. i. 128 It is not properly the Nose or Beak of the Snail, but of its shell. **1705** *Phil. Trans.* XXIV. 1953 The Nose lies in the midst of its hinge. **1858** SIMMONDS *Dict. Trade*, *Noses*, a name given to some of the smaller shell plates from the edges of the carapace of the sea-tortoise.

c. *Arch.* The projecting part or edge of a moulding, stair-tread, or mullion.

c **1815** MAR. EDGEWORTH *Parent's Assist.* (1854) 320 He broke off in the midst of a speech about the nose of the stairs. **1847** SMEATON *Builder's Man.* 184 All cornices and mouldings, and all works where the running mould is used, are measured from the nose of the moulding to the wall. **1876** *Encycl. Brit.* IV. 475/1 Draw lines, showing the face (or what the workmen call the *nose*) of the mullion.

d. *Bookbinding*: (see quot.).

1865 HANNETT *Bibliopegia* Gloss. 399 In glueing up a volume, if the workman has not been careful to make all the sheets occupy a right line at the head, it will present a point either at the beginning or end, which point is called a nose.

e. A projecting part of an electric traction motor by which it is suspended from the framework of the bogie or vehicle.

1907 PARSHALL & HOBART *Electric Railway Engin.* x. 451 In the case of a heavy motor there is usually a nose in the frame casting which rests on a bar carried by springs on the transom. **1927** R. E. DICKINSON *Electric Trains* vi. 110 On the other side of the motor case a projecting 'nose' is cast and this nose is fixed on the bogie transom with a stiff spring above and below it. **1955** E. A. BINNEY *Electric Traction Engin.* vii. 126 The nose end of the motor is resiliently supported on the bogie transom.

15. The 'eye' of an apple, gooseberry, etc.

1718 MRS. EALES *Receipts* 24 To preserve Green Jennitins. Cut out the Stalk and Nose, and put 'em in cold Water on a Coal-Fire 'till they peel. **1736**, **1879** [implied in NOSE *v.* 5 a]. **1887** *S. Cheshire Gloss.*, *Nose*, the blossom on the ends of ripe gooseberries or currants.

16. ***white nose***, a small white wave-crest.

1866 CRICHTON *Ramble Orcades* 110 Many a 'white nose' chequering the blueness of the more open water.

IV. *attrib.* and *Comb.*

17. General combs. **a.** Attributive, as ***nose-bleeding, -bone, -breadth, -carbuncle, -cloth, -jam, -net, -peg, -pin, -tip, weight***, etc.

1578 LYTE *Dodoens* Table Nature Herbs, [To] Stanche *Nose bleeding. **1897** *Allbutt's Syst. Med.* III. 461 Nose-bleeding and other strange effects. **1890** W. F. BUTLER *Sir Charles Napier* xiii. 188 Others..have not had the nerves torn by a jagged ball passing through, breaking *nose-bones and jaw-bones, and lacerating nerves. **1956** H. GOLD *Man who was not with It* (1965) i. 7 Even if the sharpest nosebones worked *their* way into my cheeks. *a* **1667** C. HOOLE *School-Colloq.* 98 You are deceived your *nose-breadth, for we are repeating together. **1572** HULOET, *Nose-bridge, or the particion whiche standeth between the twoo nosethryllles. **1652** BENLOWES *Theoph.* I. xx. 4 When our *nose-carbuncles, like link boys blaze before 'um. **1589** NASHE *Introd. Greene's Menaph.* (Arb.) 15 Hee made his moist *nosecloth, the pausing intermedium, twixt euerie nappe. *c* **1000** ÆLFRIC *Gloss.* in Wr.-Wülcker 157 *Internasus*, ..*nosegristle. **1641** BEST *Farm. Bks.* (Surtees) 1 The space betwixt eyebrow and the nose grissles. **1785** J. COLLIER *Mus. Trav.* (ed. 4) 30 The clerk of the parish..has the finest nasality, or *nose-intonation, that ever was given to a psalm-tune. **1922** JOYCE *Ulysses* 168 Sheepsnouts bloodypapered snivelling *nosejam on sawdust. **1862** M. E. ROGERS *Dom. Life Palestine* 381 These *nose-nails are worn by the younger girls, and are very fashionable. **1883** *Illustr. Sporting & Dramatic News* 6 Jan. 407/2 He calls it a '*nose net'. It consists of an ordinary bag net, just large enough to encircle the muzzle of a horse... The effect..is to make a horse keep his mouth shut and.. to prevent him pulling. **1963** E. H. EDWARDS *Saddlery* xii. 88 A very simple device is the nose-net... It is put over the nose and fastened fairly tightly to the noseband and will stop the majority of tearaways. **1695** J. EDWARDS *Perfect. Script.* 243 So much of this..*nose-ornament. **1909** *Cent. Dict.* Suppl. II. 875/1 **Nose-peg*, a pin or stud attached to the quadrant-arm in a spinning-mule to effect an acceleration of the spindle in forming the cop. **1935** H. H. FINLAYSON *Red Centre* xii. 118 The nose-peg..is a hardwood cylinder expanding to a disk at one end and a smaller pointed cone at the other... The young camel is thrown, the cartilage of the left nostril pierced.., and the peg pushed through the wound. **1966** G. W. TURNER *Eng. Lang. Austral. & N.Z.* iii. 39 Cook noticed the *nose-pins worn by native men. **1971** *World Archaeology* III. 140 There might be an occasional stone nose-pin. **1844** H. STEPHENS *Bk. Farm* II. 694 The colt..should be led out to walk..by the *nose-rein of the cavesson. **1656** *Twa Sisters* ix. in Child *Ballads* I. 126/2 What did he doe with her *nose-ridge? Unto his violl he made him a bridge. **1572** HULOET, *Nose-tippe, or the ball of the nose. **1927** W. DE LA MARE *Told Again* 246 The Fox then brushed himself nose-tip to stern with his brush. **1959** '*Motor' Man.* (ed. 36) xiii. 270 A caravan with a heavy *nose weight tows more steadily than one without. **1601** HOLLAND *Pliny* II. Index, *Nose ulcers. **1597** A. M. tr. *Guillemeau's Fr. Chirurg.* 29/4 The sixt is the *nose vayne, in the middest of the end of the nose, betweene the two gristles or cartilages.

b. Objective, or obj. genitive, as ***nose-borer, -maker, -mender***, etc.; ***nose-blowing, -making, -painting, -pulling***, etc.; also ***nose-pulled***, †***nose-wring***.

1864 J. S. LE FANU *Uncle Silas* I. xxiv. 292 The boisterous *nose-blowing that suddenly resounded from the passage. **1967** E. A. GOLLSCHEWSKY in *Coast to Coast 1965–6* 87 The vehement nose-blowing..that marked her progress from room to room. **1760–2** GOLDSM. *Cit. W.* iii, Your *nose-borers, feet-swathers, tooth-stainers, eyebrow-pluckers. *a* **1879** LAWRENCE in *Life* (1883) I. 320 The least I could do was to summon the *nose-maker, and let him try his skill. **1829** *Gentl. Mag.* XCVII. II. 535 Taliacotius has the credit of bringing the art of *nose-making into fashion. **1760** STERNE *Tr. Shandy* III. xxxviii, This Ambrose Paræus was chief surgeon and *nose-mender to Francis the Ninth. **1807–8** W. IRVING *Salmag.* (1824) 46 Agreeably painted and mottled by Mr. John Frost, *nose-painter-general. **1605** SHAKS. *Macb.* II. iii. 31 What three things does Drinke especially prouoke? Marry, Sir, *Nose-painting, Sleepe, and Vrine. **1862** THACKERAY *Philip* xxvii, His old comrade ..whom he had insulted and *nose-pulled. **1712** J. HEYWOOD *Spect.* No. 268 ¶2 A thing that..renders the *Nose-puller odious. **1807–8** W. IRVING *Salmag.* (1824) 229 They should be guaranteed from all dangers of..*nose-pulling, whipping-post, or prosecution for libels. **1682** OTWAY *Venice Preserved* III. (1735) 50 Common Stabbers, *Nose-slitters, Alley-lurking Villains! **1861** MRS. LANKESTER *Wild Flowers* 32 Nasturtium is a name given to all these biting plants; each being a *nasus tortus*, or *nose-twitcher. **1601** HOLLAND *Pliny* II. 29 Cresses tooke the name in Latine Nasturtium, *a narium tormento*, as a man would say, *Nose-wring, because it will make one writh and shrink vp his nosthrils. **1712** STEELE *Spect.* No. 268 ¶2 One of these *Nose-wringers overhearing him, pinched him by the nose.

c. Miscellaneous, as ***nose-belled, -leafed; nose-grown, -high, -wards***, etc.; ***nose-dropping***.

1646 G. DANIEL *Poems* Wks. (Grosart) I. 60 Let vs rather Chuse Long *nose-bell'd Horses, such as Children vse. **1905** J. JOYCE *Let.* 19 Jan. (1966) II. 78 O, blind, snivelling, *nose-dropping, calumniated Christ. **1611** COTGR. s.v. *Avantagé, Bien avantagé en nez*, nosed with aduantage, well *nose-growne. **1567** DRANT *Horace Ep.* II. Eij, In hote August a *nosehigh fyer wil do the as much good. **1657** THORNLEY *Daphnis & Chloe* 110 About the Cock's crowing, made their fires nose-high. *c* **1685** in Dk. Buckhm. *Wks.* (1705) II. 48 She..made him a fire nose high. **1884** *Standard Nat. Hist.* V. 173 The Phyllostomines are those *nose-leafed bats which have a long and narrow muzzle, a tongue of moderate length. *a* **1661** HOLYDAY *Juvenal* (1673) 79 He thinks thee *nose-led by his kitchin's smell. **1826** SCOTT *Woodst.* viii, I will not be thus nose-led by him. **1885** W. L. BLACKLEY *Thrift* II. xx. 108 The members of bad Friendly Societies are nose-led by their interested officials. **1869** *Eng. Mech.* 3 Dec. 271/2 If by any means they are not drawn '*nosewards'.. they take a short cut and 'well' over the eyelid. **1881** *Graphic* 5 Nov. 474/3 Her chin was drawn up nosewards.

18. Special combs.: **nose-ape**, the proboscis-monkey; **nose-bridge**, (*a*) = NOSE *sb.* 1 d; (*b*) *Archæol.* denoting a type of handle found on pottery of the Copper Age in southern Europe; **noseburn tree**, a pungent tropical American tree (*Daphnopsis tenuifolia*), belonging to the spurge-laurel family (*Treas. Bot.* 1866); **nose-candy** *U.S. slang*, a drug that is inhaled (illegally), *spec.* cocaine; **nose-clip**, a clip excluding water from the nose of a swimmer or diver; †**nose-compasses**, eye-glasses; **nose door** *Aeronaut.*, a forward-facing door in the nose of an aeroplane; **nose drive**, the positioning of the engines at the front of a space rocket; so **nose-driven** *a.*; **nose drops**, a medicament intended to be administered as drops into the nose; **nose-fish** (see quots.); **nose-fly**, (*a*) (see quot. *a* 1793); (*b*) the bot-fly which infests the nose-passages of sheep (*Cent. Dict.*); **nose-fuse**, a fuse inserted in the nose of a shell; **nose-glasses** *U.S.*, eye-glasses held on the nose by a spring; †**nose-gunpowder**, snuff; **nose hangar** *Aeronaut.* (see quot. 1960); **nose-heavy** *a.* *Aeronaut.*, having a tendency for the nose to drop relative to the tail; hence **nose-heaviness**; †**nose-herb**, a herb for smelling at; †**nose-hold**, a device to grasp the nose; †**nose-hook**, a hook for leading an ox by the nose-ring; †**nose-horn**, a beetle having a horn on the nose (cf. *nasicornous*); **nose job** *colloq.* (orig. *U.S.*), an operation involving rhinoplasty or cosmetic surgery on a person's nose; also *fig.*; **nose-leaf**, the foliaceous appendage of the nostrils in certain bats; †**nose-man** (see quot.); **nose-monkey**, the proboscis-monkey; **nose-nippers** *pl.* = PINCE-NEZ; **nose-paint** *slang*, intoxicating liquor; also, a reddening of the nose ascribed to habitual drinking (cf. *nose-painter, -painting* s.v. NOSE *sb.* 17 b); **nose paste** = *nose putty* below; **nose-pinch**, a pince-nez; **nose print**, a drawing of the facial characteristics of an animal, used as a means of identification; so **nose-printing** *vbl. sb.*; **nose putty**, a putty-like substance used in the theatre for altering the shape of the nose, etc.; **nose-rag**, a pocket-handkerchief (*slang*); **nose-ride** *v. intr.*, to stand on the nose (cf. NOSE *sb.* 13) of a surfboard (usu. as *vbl. sb.*); **nose-riders** *pl.*, spectacles; **nose suspension**, a method of supporting a traction motor from the framework of the bogie or vehicle at one end and on an axle at the other (cf. sense 14 e); so **nose-suspended** *a.*; †**nose-tent**, a medicinal plug for insertion in the nose; **nose-thumbing** *vbl. sb.*, the action of thumbing one's nose (NOSE *sb.* 8 f); an instance of such behaviour; so (as a back-formation) **nose-thumb** *sb.*; **nose-to-tail** *adv.* and *a.*, (of motor vehicles) travelling, or placed, behind one another and very close together; **nose-trick**, the inadvertent inhalation or expulsion of liquid through the nose when drinking; **nose-tube**, a tube used for feeding a patient through the nose; **nose wheel** *Aeronaut.*, a wheel under the nose of an aircraft; **nose-wipe** *v.*, to cheat, deceive (cf. 10 b); *sb.* = *nose-wiper*; **nose-wiper**, a pocket-handkerchief (*slang*); **nose-worm**, the larva of the sheep-bot.

1923 A. HUXLEY *Antic Hay* x. 156 Shell rims with gold ear-pieces and gold *nose-bridge. **1939** V. G. CHILDE *Dawn Europ. Civilization* (ed. 3) xiv. 245 In the pottery [of Sardinia before the nuragic age] we might distinguish:.. carinated cups and other vessels with nose-bridge handles, which persist into the nuragic age. **1935** A. J. POLLOCK *Underworld Speaks* 81/1 **Nose candy*, cocaine. **1935** C. F. COE *G-Man* ii. 25 I'll lay off the booze an' you lay off the organizin', the nose-candy and the stick-ups. **1960** *Time* 25 Jan. 88/2 Cocaine..is put into crystalline form. This enables users to sniff it ('nose candy'). **1974** *Globe & Mail*

(Toronto) 28 Sept. 33/4 The movie omitted the morphine and left the cocaine because nose candy is the trendy drug. 1959 *Elizabethan* Apr. 9/2 Following the orders of the sergeant I had..fitted the *nose clip in place [on an under-water breathing apparatus]. 1971 A. DIMENT *Think Inc.* vii. 123, I bit on the rubber mouth-piece, put on the nose-clip and flipped down my face mask. 1654 GAYTON *Pleas. Notes* I. v. 17 She read without Spectacles, and could..see lost pins without the help of a paire of *Nose-compasses. 1960 *Nose door [see *beaver-tail* s.v. BEAVER[1] 6]. 1969 *Jane's Freight Containers 1968–69* 454/1 Loading is via a vizor-type, straight-in, nose-door with full-width integral ramps. 1937 *Discovery* Sept. 270/2 First he [*sc.* Goddard] directed his attention to the so-called '*nose-drive' construction. 1947 W. LEY *Rockets & Space Travel* (1948) v. 134 The gases were to be ejected through a system of nozzles at the top of the rocket; the nozzles were to pull the rocket upward, instead of pushing it upward as planned in the original Oberth Rocket... This system, known as 'nose drive'.., offered a great number of advantages. The rocket did not have to be constructed as sturdily nor did it require an elaborate steering mechanism. 1952 E. BURGESS *Rocket Propulsion* v. 131 It has been stated that *nose-driven rockets..are inherently more stable than those in which the motor is situated at the extreme rear. This is another common fallacy, for providing the thrust line of the motor passes through the centre of gravity of the rocket, the actual position of the motor cannot affect stability. 1942 T. SOLLMANN *Man. Pharmacol.* (ed. 6) 165 '*Nose drops', *i.e.*, solutions in liquid petrolatum for instillation into the nares, should not contain more than 1 per cent of eucalyptol or camphor. 1970 *Women's Household* July 12/1 When he needed nose drops badly he would come over to one of us and stick up his nose. 1828–32 WEBSTER, **Nose-Fish*,..a fish of the leather-mouthed kind, with a broad flat snout; called also *broad-snout*. 1890 *Cent. Dict.*, *Nose-fish*, the bat-fish, *Malthe vespertilio*. *a*1793 G. WHITE *Selborne* (1837) 472 A species of fly..which proves very tormenting to horses, trying still to enter their nostrils and ears... Country people call this insect the *nose fly. 1839 HOLLOWAY *Prov. Dict.*, *Nose-fly*, a very fine, delicately made fly, which gets into horses' noses, and stinging them, frequently causes them to run away. 1888 *Times* 2 Oct. 3/2 The shape of the heads [of shells] which were suitable only for a *nose fuse. 1890 *Cent. Dict.* V. 4020/2 *Nose glasses. 1901 ADE *Forty Mod. Fables* 22 He said 'Whom,' and wore Nose Glasses. 1929 D. RUNYON in *Hearst's International* Oct. 64/1 To look at Judge Henry G. Blake, with his..nose glasses. 1971 *Lebende Sprachen* XVI. 11/2 US nose glasses—BE/US pince-nez. 1706 BAYNARD in Floyer *Cold Baths* II. 197 A charge of *Nose Gun-Powder, Snuff 'twixt Finger and Thumb. 1948 *Jrnl. R. Aeronaut. Soc.* LII. 573 In the civil field the '*nose hangar', such as that used successfully by KLM for the Constellation last winter, is a realistic effort to provide shelter where it is needed, instead of enclosing space at random. 1960 G. BLANCHET *Search in North* v. 66 Nose hangars were built—sheds in which the front of a plane could be sheltered and work done on its engines. 1970 R. & J. PATERSON *Cranberry Portage* xiv. 87 A great deal of time was spent warming aircraft engines with roaring fire-pots inside the canvas nose-hangars. 1919 A. KLEMIN *Text-bk. Aeronaut. Engin.* xv. 178 The down stream from the propellers..is said to increase the safety from the point of view of longitudinal balance, giving tail heaviness with power, and *nose heaviness without power. 1930 R. DUNCAN *Stunt Flying* iii. 26 Nose-heaviness, or tail-heaviness, can be corrected by adjusting the horizontal stabilizer. 1959 *Times* 8 Sept. 13/6 There is no feeling of nose-heaviness, and the steering does not have any tricks on corners. 1914 S. L. WALKDEN *How to understand Aeroplanes* ii. 5 This 'front-heavy,' or '*nose-heavy' machine..is devoid of a self-righting effect. 1917 *Flying* I. 217/1 A stable aeroplane has its centre of gravity well forward, and normally the centre of pressure is behind the centre of gravity. Without a fixed tail plane it would therefore be nose heavy. 1945 R. VON MISES *Theory of Flight* xvii. 501 If the state of motion changes or the loads are shifted, the airplane will become slightly nose- or tail-heavy so that the pilot has to operate the elevator. 1601 SHAKS. *All's Well* IV. v. 20 They are not [salad] hearbes you knaue, they are *nose-hearbes. 1797 *Monthly Mag.* XLVI. 215 Prejudice is the *nose-hold for certain purposes, of the otherwise intractable. 1778 [W. MARSHALL] *Minutes Agric.* 4 Aug. 1775 Hoed the late-planted cabbages with one ox and the *nose-hook. 1658 ROWLAND tr. *Moufet's Theat. Ins.* 1008 We have seen four kindes of *Nose-horns, the chiefest and greatest of all lives in India, it is very black, it hath a nose on its face crooked horn'd like to the stern of a ship. 1963 T. PYNCHON *V* iv. 95 Chapter four. In which Esther gets a *nose job. 1978 *Detroit Free Press* 16 Apr. (Detroit Suppl.) 11/1 Cosmetic plastic surgery..will cost you about $1,000 for a nose job;..$1,000 for an eye lift [etc.]. 1979 *Observer* 11 Feb. 33/2 A hammer-wielding Australian..had given the Madonna a nose-job. 1984 *Which?* Aug. 346/3 It was what the trade calls a 'nose job' with the fashionable aim of smoothing the passage of the car through the air. 1837 *Penny Cycl.* VII. 22/1 *Nose-leaf simple, solitary. 1864 H. ALLEN *Bats N. Amer.* Introd. 15 There is some doubt whether the nose leaves hold the same relation to the olfactory sense. 1599 H. BUTTES *Dyets Drie Dinner* P 3b, Plinies *Nosemen (mouthles men) surnam'd, Whose breathing nose supply'd Mouths absence. 1883 *Cassell's Nat. Hist.* I. 88 The newly born *Nose Monkey is a most extraordinary object. 1895 J. DAVIDSON *Old Aberdeenshire Ministers* 26 The *Aberdeen Journal*, which he read aloud..in a loud monotone, nasalised by the light grip of a large pair of *nose-nippers worn low. 1900 CONRAD *Lord Jim* v. 40 He saw the old man lift his head from some writing so sharp that his nose-nippers fell off. *a*1913 F. ROLFE *Desire & Pursuit of Whole* (1934) vii. 61 Smirking female with the thinnest of pinched lips and nose-nippers. 1880 A. A. HAYES *New Colorado* (1881) xi. 158 We saw..a sign, in which a name which I have never encountered elsewhere was given to stimulating beverages. This sign was '**Nose-paint* and *Lunch*'. 1901 F. E. TAYLOR *Folk-Speech S. Lancs.*, *Nose-paint*, a jocular term for alcoholic drink. 1922 JOYCE *Ulysses* 615 A strong suspicion of nosepaint about the nasal appendage. 1968 *Amer. Speech* XLIII. 303 He [*sc.* the cowman] drinks..*nose paint* instead of 'whiskey'. 1951 N. MARSH *Opening Night* vii. 156 One cardboard box containing false hair, rouge, substance labelled '*nose paste'. 1961 BOWMAN & BALL *Theatre Lang.* 233 *Nose paste*, a plastic substance used to alter the appearance of an actor's nose, chin, etc. 1896 *Punch* 4 Apr. 160/2 The tall, meagre females..in abbreviated hair and a *nose-pinch. 1939 *Sun* (Baltimore) 15 Sept. 15/2 The '*nose print' of a dog is as distinctive as the finger print of a human being. 1952 *Ibid.* 8 Dec. 10/4 Three dairy scientists of the South Dakota Agricultural Experiment Station at Brookings, S.D., have worked out a system of nose prints by means of which it is possible to identify one individual cow from a million others. 1970 B. KNOX *Children of Mist* iii. 56 Sometimes breeders..try to work a switch of animal. So we keep one nose-print on file in special cases..ready for comparison. 1973 *Times* 26 Nov. 17/5 Four investigators followed the trail of the animals, to establish 'contact' with them and where possible, to draw 'noseprints'—simple drawings of nostril shape and facial wrinkles—to identify the particular animals and their approximate stages of development. 1939 *Sun* (Baltimore) 15 Sept. 15/2 A plan for nation-wide identification of dogs by '*nose printing' to eliminate 'dognapping'. 1960 A. CHRISTIE *Adventure of Xmas Pudding* 223 Why did I feel..I was talking to..an actor playing a part!.. What did I see..the beaked nose (faked with that useful substance, *nose putty), [etc.]. 1969 K. VONNEGUT *Slaughterhouse-Five* v. 88 Rosewater was a big man, but not very powerful. He looked as though he might be made out of nose putty. 1838 HALIBURTON *Clockm.* (1862) 367 Tickle, tickle goes my boscis agin, and I had to stop to sarch my pocket for my *nose-rag. 1965 FARRELLY & MCGREGOR *This Surfing Life* 138 **Nose-ride*, to ride on the nose of the surfboard. 1875 E. H. DERING *Sherborne* II. xviii. 53 Sir Thomas..put on a pair of those glasses which are popularly known as *nose-riders. 1962 *Austral. Women's Weekly* Suppl. 24 Oct. 3/3 **Nose-riding*, standing right at front of the board while riding a wave. 1971 *Studies in English* (Univ. Cape Town) Feb. 25 Until the end of the nose-riding era, the run of Cape Town surfers identified with the Californian scene as portrayed in *Surfer*. 1927 R. E. DICKINSON *Electric Trains* vi. 111 Fig. 48 shows a bogie with two *nose-suspended motors in place. 1948 D. W. & M. HINDE *Electric & Diesel-Electric Locomotives* ii. 25 During the past few years, however, nose-suspended motors mounted on bogies have become standard practice on all American diesel-electric locomotives. 1894 K. HEDGES *Amer. Electr. Street Railways* vii. 75 In the case of the G.E. 800 type when the side suspension is used, the whole of the weight is taken off the axle, whereas by the older method half the weight only was on the cross bar, resting on springs, and the remainder on the axle. One method is known as the End or *Nose Suspension, the other as the Side Bar Suspension. 1927 R. E. DICKINSON *Electric Trains* vi. 111 For multiple unit trains the nose suspension is practically universal. 1948 D. W. & M. HINDE *Electric & Diesel-Electric Locomotives* ii. 24 Where hammer-blow on the track and axle-loading are not limiting factors and provided that there is one motor per driven axle, nose-suspension is the simplest form of drive obtainable. 1601 HOLLAND *Pliny* II. 61 Cumin reduced into the form of trochisks or *nose-tents, put vp into the nosthrils, stancheth bloud. 1963 *Guardian* 11 Feb. 2/6 Their medical officer of health..is leaving his post because of the council's continued *nose-thumb at the Clean Air Act. 1959 I. & P. OPIE *Lore & Lang. Schoolch.* xiv. 317 That peculiar form of recognition variously known as 'the five-finger salute', '*nose thumbing',..'cocking a snook', or 'taking a sight' used, thirty years ago, to be demonstrated by every child in the country. 1970 *Globe & Mail* (Toronto) 26 Sept. 23/5 A nose-thumbing gesture comes as a blessed relief in a movie so painfully earnest. 1959 *Manch. Guardian* 20 July 2/5 Four L-drivers *nose to tail on a busy road. 1960 *Guardian* 7 June 6/1 The accustomed queues of nose-to-tail traffic on main roads. 1963 *Times* 11 June 5/4 Yet above the garage cars sit nose-to-tail on free space within the park, and scour Mayfair for vacant meters. 1974 C. FREMLIN *By Horror Haunted* 48 The nose-to-tail crawl along the motorway. 1954 P. FRANKAU *Wreath for Enemy* II. i. 58 It was the 'Prendergast' that made me do what is vulgarly called the *nose-trick with my lemonade. 1972 P. DICKINSON *Lizard in Cup* ix. 132 Pibble almost did the nose-trick with the dung-smelling local brandy. 1899 *Allbutt's Syst. Med.* VIII. 300, I..feed the patient by the *nose-tube if she cannot be got to take enough nourishment otherwise. 1934 *Flight* 6 Dec. 1301 A castor *nose wheel allows the fullest use to be made of the wheel brakes of the Hammond Model Y. 1940 *Illustr. London News* CXCVII. 315 (*caption*) The 'Boston' has..an undercarriage of the tricycle type—two rear wheels retracting into the rear of the engine nacelles and the nosewheel retracting rearwards and upwards into the fuselage. 1974 *Daily Tel.* 5 Oct. 1 A Belgian airliner..pitched on to its nose on the main runway at Southend airport when the nosewheel collapsed shortly before takeoff. 1919 W. DEEPING *Second Youth* ii. 13 Yer dirty little wretch yer; ain't yer got a *nose-wipe? 1628 H. BURTON *Israel's Fast* Ded. 13 Cheated and *nosewiped euen to their face. *a*1895 LD. C. E. PAGET *Autobiog.* (1896) i. 4 Charged with my relay of *nose-wipers, I was close to his Majesty on the steps of the throne. 1861 HULME tr. *Moquin-Tandon* II. VII. i. 326 The œstrus of the sheep.., called by Reaumur 'Fly of the *Nose-worm'.

nose (nəʊz), *v.* [f. the sb.]

I. *trans.* **1. a.** To perceive the smell of (something); to discover or notice by the sense of smell.

1577–87 HARRISON *Descr. Scotl.* viii. in *Holinshed*, He neuer ceasseth to range till he haue nosed his footing. 1602 SHAKS. *Ham.* IV. iii. 38 You shall nose him as you go vp the staires into the Lobby. 1614 B. JONSON *Barth. Fair* I. iii, There cannot be an ancient Tripe or Trillibub i' the Towne, but thou art straight nosing it. 1795 *Sporting Mag.* V. 85 A partner in a banking-house, who lives near enough..to nose his lordship's kitchen. 1815 SOUTHEY *Jrnl. Tour in Netherlands* (1903) 153 You might nose them [cheeses] at a considerable distance. 1861 FLOR. NIGHTINGALE *Nursing* (ed. 2) 7 Although we 'nose' the murderers in the musty, unaired, unsunned room.

b. *fig.* To find out, detect, discover, as if by means of a keen scent.

1767 S. PATERSON *Anoth. Trav.* I. 368 If a pickpocket noses a peer upon the turf. 1824 *Blackw. Mag.* XV. 335 We nosed him as the prime contributor to the New Monthly. 1893 W. A. SHEE *My Contemp.* viii. 219 The parliamentary 'busybody'..nosing a job in every Ministerial move.

c. To scent or smell *out* (in *lit.* and *fig.* uses).

*c*1630 B. JONSON *Underwoods* lxi. 139 The Brethren they straight nosed it out for news. 1828 SCOTT *F.M. Perth* iii, My daughter and I could nose out either a fasting hypocrite or a full one. 1856 KANE *Arct. Expl.* I. xxix. 388 Began..to turn them over and nose out their fatness. 1877 *Scribner's Mag.* XV. 170/2, I have seen a pack..nose out the scent under an inch of light snow.

2. a. To confront, reproach, or upbraid (a person) *with* something. Now only *dial.*

1625 BURGES *Pers. Tithes* 60 None of the best Proctors for vs Tithing-men, but One with whom we poore Vicars are daily nosed. 1641 J. SHUTE *Sarah & Hagar* (1649) 71 This..frequent fault in the world; which is, when men haue done kindness to others, to nose them with it. 1733 *Revol. Politicks* II. 51 What is this,..but affronting and noseing the Bishops with Popery to their very Faces? 1753 JANE COLLIER *Art Torment.* 123 If he loves company,..nose him with your great love of needle-work and housewifery. 1889 *N.W. Linc. Gloss.*

b. To confront, face, or oppose (a person, etc.) in an impudent or insolent manner. (Cf. BEARD *v.* 3.)

1629 RANDOLPH *Jealous Lovers* I. iv, Y'are an arrant Coxcomb To tell me so. My daughter nos'd by a slut! 1649 QUARLES *Virgin Widow* II. i, When Pertenax..Could nose the King, and beard him to his face. 1673 BP. S. PARKER *Reproof Reh. Transp.* 157 You began to lift up your heads, and to nose your Governours. 1733 KILLIGREW in *Jrnl. R. Inst. Cornwall* IX. II. (1887), Mr. Rogers made him town sergeant and mace bearer, to nose Sir Peter and his interest. 1796 BURKE *Let. to Noble Ld.* Wks. VIII. 14 A sort of national convention..nosed parliament in the very seat of its authority. 1824 *Hist. Gaming* 16 Is not the thought appalling, that a monarch..should thus be..nosed in his own courtly dwelling?

c. To sit opposite and close to (one); to meet, encounter, come in one's way.

1812 COLMAN *Br. Grins, Luminous Hist.* xiii, Nosing Eudoxus, blue-eyed Agnes sat. 1831 *Blackw. Mag.* XXX. 324 The French noblesse had no grandeur. No man could be impressed reverentially by titles which nosed him in every corner of every street.

†3. To cheat or defraud (one) *of* something. *Obs.*

*a*1652 BROME *Eng. Moor* I. ii, 'Twould anger any man to be nos'd of such a match. 1679 BRIAN *Pisse-prophet* 60, I am like to be nosed of a patient.

4. a. To utter with a nasal twang; to sing through the nose.

*a*1643 W. CARTWRIGHT *Ordinary* III. v, It makes far better musick when you nose Sternold's, or Wisdom's meeter. 1748 RICHARDSON *Clarissa* (1811) VI. 220 After he has nosed and mumbled over his responses.

b. To puff out through the nose. *rare*$^{-1}$.

1658 OSBORN *Adv. Son* Wks. (1673) 23, I..cannot approve nosing, or swallowing it [tobacco] down. 1693 LITTLETON *Dict.*, To nose Tobacco, *peti fumum per nares efflare*.

5. a. To pick the noses off (gooseberries, etc.).

1736 BAILEY *Househ. Dict.* 309 Nose your gooseberries. 1879 MISS JACKSON *Shropsh. Word-bk.*, We nosed about eight quarts o' black curran's after milkin' time.

b. To put a nosing on (a step).

1884 HOR. SMITH *Negligence* (ed. 2) 185 *note*, Slipping on steps nosed with brass.

6. a. To rub with the nose; to press the nose close to, thrust the nose into (something).

1777 G. FORSTER *Voy. round World* I. 224 They immediately saluted the family of natives on board, with the usual application of noses, or as our sailors expressed it, they nosed each other. 1839–48 BAILEY *Festus* VIII. 81 Nosing each-other like a flock of sheep. 1868 TENNYSON *Lucretius* 100 Lambs are glad Nosing the mother's udder.

transf. 1876 C. D. WARNER *Mummies & Moslems* xix. 250 It does not need our eyes to tell us when the bow of the boat noses the swift water.

b. To examine with the nose; to put the nose close to (a thing) in examining.

*a*1851 MOIR *Highlander's Return* ix, Old Stumah fawning fain, First nosed him round, then licked his hand. 1873 *Routledge's Young Gentlm. Mag.* Apr. 280/2 A serious accident may repay you for nosing it too closely. 1882 STEVENSON *New Arab. Nts.* I. 91 The New-Englander nosed all the cracks..with the most passionate attention.

c. To push (one's way) with the nose.

1894 HALL CAINE *Manxman* V. iii. 288 Cranching among the boats as they nosed their way to the harbour mouth. 1926 E. F. SPANNER *Naviators* i. 9 The car nosed its way ahead on bottom gear, and at a snail's pace. 1937 *Discovery* Feb. 38/2 We nosed our way through the reeds. 1973 P. MOYES *Curious Affair* i. 14 The station wagon nosed its way along the narrow road.

d. To direct the nose of (a motor vehicle, etc.) in a certain direction.

1954 'N. SHUTE' *Slide Rule* iv. 89 The elevator coxswain nosed her [*sc.* an airship] upwards to about a thousand feet. 1972 D. DELMAN *Week to Kill* 139, I nosed the car out of town and on to 118, where I zapped it into high.

7. To lead *about* by the nose.

1885 HOWELLS *Silas Lapham* (1891) I. 258 As long as you live you'll have to be nosed about like..I don't know what!

II. *intr.* **8. a.** To apply or employ the nose in examining or smelling; to sniff, smell.

1783 WOLCOT (P. Pindar) *Ode to R.A.'s* vii, Closely nosing, o'er the Picture dwell, As if to try the goodness by the smell. 1823 *Blackw. Mag.* XIV. 530 Panting and open mouth'd and nosing. 1871 BLACKIE *Four Phases Mor.* i. 42 You expect your dog to nose well. 1891 MISS DOWIE *Girl in Karp.* 141 One of the horses woke me by nosing at my arm in a friendly way.

b. Const. with *about* or *round*. Chiefly *fig.*

1869 BLACKMORE *Lorna D.* iii, Our two pads..began to nose about and crop. 1879 'MARK TWAIN' *Let.* 21 Jan. (1920) I. 187 The detectives were nosing around after Stewart's loud remains. 1887 *Lantern* (New Orleans) 3 Dec.

2/3 We nosed around to try and find out why. **1895** CABLE *John March* 259 If that fellow's still nosing round here with his gun. **1898** *Daily Tel.* 22 Aug. 5/3 The whole duty of a dog is to keep other dogs from nosing round its master's garden. **1917** WODEHOUSE *Uneasy Money* iv. 43 There's no harm in my nosing round, is there? Be a good chap and give me the address. **1925** —— *Carry On, Jeeves!* i. 28 He began to nose about. He pulled out drawer after drawer. **1955** A. HUXLEY *Let.* 25 Sept. (1969) 766 While in Guildford I read, or rather nosed about in, Penfield's book on Epilepsy. **1958** P. KEMP *No Colours or Crest* iii. 36 We nosed around the Islands, sometimes less than a mile off shore, searching for indications of our quarry.

c. To pry or search (*after* or *for* something); also with *among*. ***to nose upon*** (see quot. 1812).

1648 *Regall Apol.* 11 They go nosing and smelling after faults. **1812** J. H. VAUX *Flash Dict.*, To *nose*, is to pry into any person's proceedings in an impertinent manner. To *nose upon* any one, is to tell of any thing he has said or done with a view to injure him, or to benefit yourself. **1871** MEREDITH *H. Richmond* III. 122 What the deuce they do here nosing after my grandson! **1899** HEWLETT in *Blackw. Mag.* Feb. 326/1 Franciscans..and Dominicans..who got wind of something amiss, and began to nose for a scandal. **1936** R. LEHMANN *Weather in Streets* II. 189, I thought of her nosing in my room for signs. **1941** A. CURNOW in Chapman & Bennett *N.Z. Verse* (1956) 148, I am the nor'west air nosing among the pines.

d. To inform; †to turn king's evidence. *Criminals' slang.*

1811 [see TWIST *v.* 9c]. **1822** *J. Mackcoull Mem. Life* 112 *Nosed*,..watched and informed against. **1846** tr. *E. Sue's Myst. of Paris* cli. 743/1 Gros Boiteux..has already wanted to *escarper* him, (make him a stiff 'un—kill him,) because he has *mangé* (nosed, informed upon some one). **1923** E. WALLACE *Missing Million* xix. 156 When a copper comes to one of the 'boys' for expert advice, it means he wants him to 'nose'. **1930** —— *White Face* x. 147 You come down 'ere an' expect us to 'nose' for you, and everybody in the court knows we're 'nosing'.

9. To push with the nose. Also *transf.* with *ahead*, to go into the lead by a small margin.

1891 MEREDITH *One of our Conq.* I. i. 12 A steamer slowly nosing round off the wharf-cranes. **1898** *Daily News* 7 May 7/5 The Morrill, which had been nosing up towards us, swung across the path of the liner. **1960** *Times* 1 July 18/1 So Miss Truman had nosed ahead at last. **1971** WODEHOUSE *Much Obliged, Jeeves* xiii. 134 If the McCorkadale nosed ahead of him in the voting, Florence would in all probability hand him the pink slip.

10. Of strata or veins: To dip *in*, to run *out*.

1879 GEIKIE in *Encycl. Brit.* X. 301/1 When a fold diminishes in this way it is said to 'nose out'... Hence the anticline noses out to the north and the syncline to the south. **1883** GRESLEY *Gloss. Coal-Mining* 175 A stratum is said to nose in when it dips beneath the ground or into a hill-side in a V or nose form.

11. nose down *Aeronaut.*: to direct the nose of an aircraft downwards, to produce or undergo a (downward) steepening of the flight path.

1916 H. BARBER *Aeroplane Speaks* 85 If a sharp turn necessitates banking beyond that angle, he must 'nose-down'. *Ibid.* 88 The C.G. being forward of the C.P...causes the aeroplane to nose-down. **1938** V. W. PAGÉ *Airplane Servicing Man.* xxiv. 818 It is considered advisable, if the engine should stop, that the plane will nose down automatically, instead of tending to stall. **1958** R. D. BLACKER *Basic Aeronaut. Sci.* xi. 195/1 The vertical portion of the lift was not as great as the weight of the airplane and it nosed down, losing altitude. **1974** J. MONTGOMERIE *Implosion* xii. 86 We crossed the coast, nosing down over pewter sea... Runway rose towards us.

12. Of an aircraft: to fall *over* on its 'nose'. Of a surfboard: to plunge downward nose first.

1928 V. W. PAGÉ *Mod. Aircraft* xii. 523 Always pick as smooth and level a piece of ground as possible when making a landing, as, if the ground is very soft or if there are hummocks or ditches, the machine is very likely to 'nose over'. **1953** BERG *Dict. New Words* 115/2 *Nose over*... *Flying.* To fall nose forward. **1963** *Surfing Yearbk.* 42/2 *Nosing*, when the nose of the surfboard goes under water while riding a wave. **1965** J. POLLARD *Surfrider* ii. 20 Don't let your board 'nose'. This is what happens when the front of the surf board digs in.

¶ Johnson's '*Nose*, v.n. To look big; to bluster', copied with variations by later Dicts., is based on the misreading *noses* for *noises* in the passage quoted by him from Shaks. *Ant. & Cl.*

Hence **'nosing** *vbl. sb.* and *ppl. a.*; also *Comb.*, as **nosing motion** (see quot. 1940).

1593 G. HARVEY *Pierce's Super.* Wks. (Grosart) II. 125, I cannot stand nosing of Candlestickes, or euphuing of Similes. **1775** ASH, *Nosing*, the act of taking by the nose. **1828** P. CUNNINGHAM *N.S. Wales* (ed. 3) II. 228 If they suspect any one of nosing [*note*, informing], they will conceal some of their own things in his bag. **1883** H. E. WALMSLEY *Cotton Spinning* 30 The terminal velocity of the spindles may be increased in the same ratio, as their diameter decreases. This object is attained by Platt's automatic nosing motion. **1884** R. MARSDEN *Cotton Spinning* ix. 264 The last invention.., which seems to answer all needs, is the automatic nosing motion brought out by Messrs. Platts, and which consists of a scroll placed upon the end of the winding-on drum. **1888** STEVENSON in *Scribner's Mag.* III. 768 Perpetual nosing after snobbery at least suggests the snob. **1897** KIPLING *Capt. Cour.* iii, The nosing bows slapped and scuffled with the seas. **1932** W. SCOTT-TAGGART *Cotton Machinery Sketches* (ed. 4) p. xviii, Diagram of Cop, etc., illustrating Principle of Nosing Motion. **1940** *Chambers's Techn. Dict.* 583/2 *Nosing motion* (Cotton Spinning), a motion on the mule spinning frame which, as the diameter lessens, increases the speed of the tapering spindle on which a cop is being wound.

nose, obs. form of NOISE *sb.* and *v.*

nosean ('nəʊzɪən). *Min.* Also noseane, nosian(e. [Named (*nosian*) by Klaproth, 1815, after K. W. *Nose*, a German geologist who had described it.] A silicate of aluminium and sodium, occurring in crystals in volcanic rocks. (Also called *noselite, nosin*, and *nosite.*)

1836 T. THOMSON *Min., Geol.*, etc. I. 257 Sodalite. Hauyne, noseane, spinellane. *Ibid.* 675 Nosiane. **1842** PARNELL *Chem. Anal.* (1845) 401 Silicates decomposable by Hydrochloric Acid. Nosian. **1879** RUTLEY *Stud. Rocks* x. 112 Sodalite, hauyne, and nosean are all silicates of alumina and soda.

'nose-bag. [f. NOSE *sb.*]

1. a. A bag, usually made of strong canvas and leather, which is suspended from a horse's head (the open end covering his nose) so that he may eat the provender contained in it.

1796 *Grose's Dict. Vulgar Tongue* (ed. 3), *Nose Bag*, a bag fastened to the horse's head, in which the soldiers of the cavalry put the oats given to their horses: whence the saying, I see the nose bag in his face; i.e. he has been a private man, or rode private. **1844** H. STEPHENS *Bk. Farm* II. 178 Every man takes his pair of nose-bags, and supplies his own horses. **1873** TRISTRAM *Moab* vi. 112 The muleteers are not scrupulous about stealing from each other's nosebags.

transf. **1889** *Pall Mall G.* 22 Jan. 6/2 It is often said that these public institutions are largely used as 'nose-bags'—that they afford a comfortable corner for persons to lunch in or otherwise shelter themselves.

b. *slang.* (See quot. 1860.) Also, the practice among holiday-makers of taking their own food or refreshments with them; *attrib.*, as ***nose-bag crowd.***

1860 *Slang Dict.*, *Nose-Bags*, visitors at watering places, and houses of refreshment, who carry their own victuals. **1908** *Daily Chron.* 4 Aug. 3/4 Neither was it, as one of Messrs. Lyons's managers observed with appreciation, a 'nose-bag' crowd. **1909** *Ibid.* 7 June 5/2 The 'nose-bag' grows and flourishes.

2. A net placed over a horse's nose to protect it from flies.

1839 HOLLOWAY *Prov. Dict.* s.v. *Nose-fly*, Nose-bags or nets are used to protect the horses' noses.

3. Food, a meal. Also allusively. Phr. ***to put*** (occas. ***get***) ***on the nose-bag***, to eat. *slang.*

1874 HOTTEN *Slang Dict.* 239 To 'put on the nose-bag' is to eat hurriedly, or to eat while continuing at work. **1886** F. T. ELWORTHY *West Somerset Word-Bk.* 521 Well! hon I zeed zo many o' they there whit-neckangkecher fullers comin', I thinks to mysul, there's a bit of a nose-bag a-gwain on in there. **1898** J. D. BRAYSHAW *Slum Silhouettes* 155 Come in, we'll jist 'ave five minutes wiv the nose-bag. **1921** R. LARDNER *Big Town* v. 201 We couldn't stop to put on the nose bag at the Graham. **1925** WODEHOUSE *Carry On, Jeeves!* vi. 145 Biffy's man came in with the nose-bags and we sat down to lunch. **1926** *Amer. Speech* I. 652/1 *Nose-bag*, lunch handed out in paper bag. **1930** D. L. SAYERS *Strong Poison* xi. 137 Thanks awfully, I've had my morning nosebag. **1962** *New Statesman* 21 Dec. 897/3 The precise time the family get the nose-bag on. **1973** WODEHOUSE *Bachelors Anonymous* xiv. 185, I must rush. I'm putting on the nosebag with a popsy.

4. A gas-mask. *colloq.*

1915 D. O. BARNETT *Let.* 11 May 135 Every one was ready and had their nose-bags on, and the gas had no effect whatever. **1940** *Everybody's Weekly* 2 Mar. 4/1 Londoners call their masks 'Dicky-birds', 'Canaries' and 'Nose-bags'.

nose-bagger. [f. NOSE-BAG + -ER[1].] = NOSE-BAG 1 b.

1931 *Morning Post* 17 Oct. 12/5 The friendly little South Coast town, where only the 'nose-baggers'..are frowned upon.

'nose-band. [f. NOSE *sb.*] The lower band of a bridle, passing over the nose, and attached to the cheek-straps; a musrole. = NOSE-PIECE *sb.* 1 b.

1611 COTGR., *Museliere*,..the nose-band of a bridle. **1753** CHAMBERS *Cycl. Supp.* s.v., Nose-band..is that part of the head-stall of a bridle that comes over a horse's nose. **1775** R. TWISS *Trav. Port. & Sp.* 205 The horses have no bits in their mouths, but are governed by *caveçons* or nose-bands. **1833** *Regul. & Instr. Cavalry* I. 71 The strap..should act both as a noseband and curb. **1889** BADEN-POWELL *Pigsticking* 128 The noseband..in place of the bit, as it saves the horse's mouth from the jobbing and dragging.

'nose-bit. [f. NOSE *sb.* + BIT *sb.*[1]]

†**1.** *Sc.* A metal nose-band for a horse. In quot. *fig.* (Cf. *nese-bit* s.v. NESE *sb.* c.) *Obs. rare*$^{-1}$.

1583 *Leg. Bp. St. Androis* 1105, I sall leave blankis for to imbrew thame, That he a nosebitt may beleive thame Whome to my buik salbe directit.

2. (See quots.)

1794 *Rigging & Seamanship* 152 *Nose-bit*, a bit similar to a gouge bit, having a cutting edge on one side of the end. **1846** HOLTZAPFFEL *Turning* II. 540 The nose-bit.., called also the slit-nose-bit, and auger-bit, is slit up a small distance near the center. **1875** *Carpentry & Join.* 31 A is a shell augur, which, if made smaller and used with a brace, goes by the name of a nose-bit.

†**nose-bledels, -bledles.** *Obs. rare.* [f. OE. *blédan* to bleed: see -ELS.] = NOSE-BLEED.

c **1450** *M.E. Med. Bk.* (Heinrich) 232 Tak millefoyle .i. nose-bledels or yarow, stampe hyt smal. *c* **1450** *Alphita* (Anecd. Oxon.) 190/1 *Millefolium*,..nosebledles.

'nose-bleed. [f. NOSE *sb.* + stem of BLEED *v.*]

1. The plant Miltoil or Yarrow. Also *attrib.*

There is no clear evidence of the name being actually current after 1600.

14.. *Voc.* in Wr.-Wülcker 596 *Millefolium*, Myllefoyle *vel* Noseblede. *c* **1450** *Alphita* (Anecd. Oxon.) 118/1 *Miriofillos siue..millifolium*,..noseblede. **1567** [see MILFOIL 1]. **1597** GERARDE *Herbal* 913 Of Yarrowe or Nose-bleede,..The leaues being put into the nose, do cause it to bleede. **1611** COTGR., *Millefueille* [sic], nose-bleed Yarrow, common Yarrow. **1657** C. BECK *Univ. Character* M 4 b, Yarrow or nose-bleed. **1731** MILLER *Gard. Dict.*, *Millefolium*, Yarrow, Milfoil, or Nose-bleed. **1753** CHAMBERS *Cycl. Suppl.* App., *Nose bleed*, in botany, a popular name for the Millefolium of botanical writers. **1855** MISS PRATT *Flower. Pl.* III. 325 Several of the old names of this plant are very significant of its former uses: Souldier's Wound-wort, Knyghten Milfoil, and Nose-bleed.

2. A bleeding at the nose. Also *fig.*

1848 *Asmodeus* (N.Y.) 73 (Th.), What's the best cure for nose-bleed, doctor? **1852-6** in WRIGHT *Univ. Pron. Dict.* IV. **1890** CHILD *Ballads* IV. 117/2 The omen of nose-bleed occurs in the ballad of 'The Mother's Malison'. **1914** G. S. GORDON *Let.* 11 Aug. (1943) 59 Germany will get the nose-bleed of her life. **1953** 'J. R. MACDONALD' *Imaginary Blonde* in *Manhunt* (1964) XII. 138/1 It was a little scuffle. One of the guests suffered a nosebleed. **1960** WODEHOUSE *Jeeves in Offing* xv. 161 Half way through the second act..Catsmeat Potter-Pirbright, who was playing Lord Fancourt Babberley, left the stage abruptly to attend to an unforeseen nose bleed. **1972** 'L. EGAN' *Paper Chase* (1973) x. 160 Just a nosebleed... Somebody banged me on the nose.

'nose-cap. [f. NOSE *sb.* + CAP *sb.*[1]] **1.** A metal cap on the nose of a gun-stock.

1844 *Regul. & Ordin. Army* 99 For nose-cap, when supplied by the Armourer..6*d.* **1860** *All Year Round* No. 71. 500 The stock is divided into the nose-cap, the upper, middle, and lower bands [etc.].

2. *Aeronaut.* **a.** (See quot. 1950.)

1909 KIPLING *Actions & Reactions* 112 From her North Atlantic Winter nose-cap (worn bright as diamond with boring through uncounted leagues of hail, snow, and ice) to the inset of her three built-out propeller-shafts is some two hundred and forty feet. **1950** *Gloss. Aeronaut. Terms* (*B.S.I.*) I. 49 *Bow cap* (*nose cap*), a structure forming the extreme forward end of the envelope or hull.

b. (See quots.)

1919 BLACKBURN & NEWBY *All about Aircraft* 106 *Nose cap*, a conical cap placed over the propeller boss to reduce head resistance. **1949** *Gloss. Aeronaut. Terms* (*B.S.I.*) II. 19 *Nose cap*, a boss or hub fairing filled co-axially and rotating with the propeller. It does not extend aft of the front of the blade roots.

3. The metal cap on the nose of a shell or bomb which contains the device for setting the time fuse.

1917 A. G. EMPEY *Over Top* 301 *Nosecap*, that part of a shell which unscrews and contains the device and scale for setting the time fuse. **1919** W. DEEPING *Second Youth* xxix. 244 St. Roman was not a nice place that night, with 'dud Archies' and nose-caps falling into it, as well as bombs. **1942** 'R. CROMPTON' *William carries On* iii. 65 Rich in nose-caps and time-fuses and casings.

4. A cover protecting the nose.

1973 *Times Lit. Suppl.* 18 May 544/2 The middle-aged on the beaches clearly felt no self-consciousness in wearing little paper nose-caps as protection from the sun.

nose cone. Also **nose-cone, nosecone.** [f. NOSE *sb.*] A conical nose-cap; *spec.* the cone-shaped front part of a rocket, which is designed to withstand the severe heating caused by atmospheric friction and generally contains any instruments that may be carried.

1949 *Jrnl. Brit. Interplanetary Soc.* VIII. 233 A diagram of the rocket is shown in Fig. 1. The equipment space is within a thin ogival-shaped aluminium nose-cone. **1956** *Spaceflight* I. 26/1 At this stage..the ballistic nose-cone (which protects the satellite package from aero-dynamic heating) can be thrown off. **1963** *Guardian* 30 Mar. 1/5 The plane was struck by lightning..A hole was made in the fibre nosecone. **1964** J. L. NAYLER *Dict. Astronautics* 177 The nose cone may become the satellite itself..or, after shielding the satellite.., be separated by an explosive cartridge. **1974** A. PRICE *Other Paths* II. ii. 128 They were trying to take the brass nose-cone off one of our howitzer shells.

'nose count. [f. the phr. *to count noses* (NOSE *sb.* 6 d).] An enumeration, esp. of votes; a decision by majority vote. Hence **'nose-counting** *vbl. sb.*, assessment by numbers.

1938 *Life* 6 June 22/3 Meantime in London peace-yearning Prime Minister Chamberlain again tried to quarantine the Spanish war by proposing a nose-count and withdrawal of foreign troops. **1951** *True Police Cases* (U.S.) Nov. 42 At nose-counting time in the..hoosegow. **1958** *Listener* 30 Oct. 708/1 Was that nose-counting success due only to some adventitious notion..that *Salome* is salacious? **1960** *Times* 14 Sept. 12/6 There was much talk just then of the coming 'Nose Count' over the U.S.A. which was one way of making their census sound more personal and pointed. **1966** *Economist* 29 Oct. 450/1 The prospects of an effective tightening of Rhodesian sanctions must depend far more on the major powers' real readiness to apply a tighter squeeze than on the nominal nose-count in the Security Council. **1967** M. McLUHAN *Medium is Massage* 22 Nose-counting, a cherished part of the eighteenth-century fragmentation process, has rapidly become a cumbersome and ineffectual form of social assessment.

nosed (nəʊzd), *a.* [f. NOSE *sb.*]

Such combs. as *bottle-, flat-, hawk-, hook-, long-nosed*, are given as main words or under the first element.

1. Having a nose *like* that of some other person or animal.

1505 in *Facsimiles Nat. MSS.* (1865) I. 92 She ys myche lyke nosid vnto the quyn hir moder. **1563** B. GOOGE *Eglogs* (Arb.) 123 A myghty face..Muche nosed lyke a Turky Cocke. **1622** FLETCHER *Sea-Voy.* v. ii, The slaves are nos'd like vultures: how wild they look!

b. (Also *well-nosed.*) Keen-scented.

1604 MIDDLETON *Witch* I. ii, There's no knavery but is nosed like a dog, and can smell out a dog's meaning. **1625** tr. *Gonsalvio's Sp. Inquis.* 147 The Inquisitors well nosed like the diuell. **1709** STEELE *Tatler* No. 73 ¶8 They have Dogs as well nos'd and as fleet as any.

2. Having a prominent nose.

1896 H. O. FORBES *Handbk. to Primates* I. 252 In the second Sub-family are included the Nosed-Monkeys (*Nasalis*) of Borneo.

'nose-dive, *sb.* Also **nose dive, nosedive.** [f. NOSE *sb.* + DIVE *sb.*] **1.** *Aeronaut.* A sudden or rapid descent by an aircraft nose first. Also *transf.*

1912 *Flight* 31 Aug. 787/1 The machine at once started a spiral nose-dive. **1914** HAMEL & TURNER *Flying* iii. 57 M. Adolphe Pégoud introduced side-slips, tail-dives, and nose-dives into his exhibition repertory of flying. **1917** 'I. HAY' *Carrying On* i. 17 Next moment she [*sc.* the aeroplane] lurched again, and then took a 'nose-dive' straight into the British trenches. **1922** *Encycl. Brit.* XXX. 21/2 The aeroplane may..drop one wing and pass into a steep spiral glide known as a 'spinning nose-dive'. *a* **1930** D. H. LAWRENCE *Last Poems* (1932) 15 The dolphins leap..and flip! they go! with the nose-dive of sheer delight. **1932** AUDEN *Orators* II. 52 *Nose-dive*—Nightmare to nerves And needed by no one And dash toward death. **1952** R. S. PORTEOUS in *Coast to Coast 1951–1952* 146 If this tub rolls over or takes a sudden nose-dive to the bottom. **1955** H. KLEIN *Winged Courier* viii. 52 It looked as if the 'Pioneer' was crashing to its doom in an uncontrolled nose-dive. **1975** *Aeroplane Monthly* Nov. 572 When a down-draught was encountered or the control column was pushed forward.. this resulted in a nose-dive to earth.

2. *fig.*

1920 R. MACAULAY *Potterism* VI. iv. 241 If you chuck the *Fact* you take away its last chance. It'll do a nose-dive now! **1946** *Sun* (Baltimore) 8 Nov. 21 An unexplained nose dive in surplus sales occurred in the July-August-September quarter. **1973** *Guardian* 28 May 6/6 After a really splendid first week, the Festival took a nosedive from which it never recovered.

'nose-dive, *v.* Also **nosedive.** [f. prec. sb., or DIVE *v.*] **1. a.** *intr.* To perform a nose-dive.

1915 *Sphere* 24 July 94/2 Its engines stopped, and it nose-dived to a level of 2,000 ft. **1920** *Chambers's Jrnl.* Mar. 208/1 Checking any tendency [of a motor-boat] to nosedive. **1923** *Daily Mail* 27 Mar. 9 His aeroplane nose-dived from a height of about 150 feet and crashed on to the aerodrome. **1930** E. BLUNDEN *Poems* 42 A hundred feet he nose-dives. **1930** *Daily Express* 6 Oct. 3/3 Then with all the lights on the airship nose dived. **1930** J. S. HUXLEY *Bird-Watching & Bird Behaviour* (1949) ii. 35 They [*sc.* birds] must be protected against side-slipping and nose-diving. **1968** W. WARWICK *Surfriding in N.Z.* 2 He then ran to the front of the board so that it nosedived.

b. *trans.* To put into a nose-dive.

1919 PIPPARD & PRITCHARD *Aeroplane Structures* vi. 55 There is a moment upon the wings tending to nose dive the aeroplane still further. **1928** *Daily Tel.* 16 Oct. 17/5, I have nose-dived this machine at 250 miles an hour.

2. *fig.* Esp. to drop or decrease abruptly.

1920 R. MACAULAY *Potterism* VI. iv. 241, I can't stop it [*sc.* a newspaper's collapsing]. But I'm jolly well not going to nose-dive with it. I'm clearing out. **1926** *Spectator* 13 Mar. 492/1 We will nose-dive straight into the middle of Mr Cobham's book. **1954** *Sun* (Baltimore) 16 Dec. 24/1 Business..has nosedived since the expressway was opened to intercity traffic. **1958** S. HYLAND *Who goes Hang?* xviii. 78 'Is that all you wanted to ask me?' He said it falsetto. 'Well, as a matter of fact, no.' 'Good.' His voice nose-dived. **1969** *Daily Tel.* 23 Jan. 4/1 Allied Investments nosedived again yesterday. The market pushed the shares down another 2s to 3s 6d.

Hence **'nose-diving** *vbl. sb.* and *ppl. a.*

1917 E. W. WALTERS *Heroic Airmen* xii. 102 He was compelled to resort to nose-diving. **1931** *Handbk. Aeronautics* (R. Aeronaut. Soc.) iv. 288 The fuselage must have a load factor the same as for the main planes in nose diving. **1958** *Engineering* 7 Mar. 295/1 Nose diving under hard braking is no more than on more conventional vehicles. **1970** T. HUGHES *Crow* 39 The nosediving aircraft concludes with a boom.

nose-'down, *a.* and *sb. Aeronaut.* [f. NOSE *sb.* + DOWN *adv.* or the phr. *to nose down* (NOSE *v.* 11).]

A. *adj.* With the nose directed downwards. Also as quasi-*adv.*

1916 H. BARBER *Aeroplane Speaks* 87 [An inclinometer] will indicate a nose-down position by increase in airspeed. *Ibid.* 113 The aeroplane may have a tendency to fly 'nose-down'. **1933** *Jrnl. R. Aeronaut. Soc.* XXXVII. 67 She.. goes into a second dive, being 1,160 ft. below her starting height at $t = 80$, and 1,440 ft. below at $t = 100$, when she is 13·5° nose down. **1965** C. N. VAN DEVENTER *Introd. Gen. Aeronaut.* v. 88 If the engine fails the airplane will automatically assume a slightly nose-down position ready for a glide.

B. *sb.* A descent.

1942 *Tee Emm* (Air Ministry) II. 94 That steep nose-down which is often so dangerous if the sea is met sooner than expected. **1944** J. R. HOYT *Safety after Solo* xii. 217 It is time to start the nose down toward point 3.

no-see-em (nəʊ'siːəm). *N. Amer.* Also **no-see-um.** [Corruption of *no see them.*] A name used for several small, blood-sucking insects, esp. biting midges of the family Ceratopogonidæ.

1848 THOREAU *Maine Woods* 2 In the summer myriads of black flies, mosquitoes, and midges, or, as the Indians call them, 'no-see-ems', make travelling in the woods almost impossible. **1902** W. D. HULBERT *Forest Neighbors* (1903) 129 The mosquitoes and black-flies and no-see-'ems had bitten him until his skin was covered with blotches. **1903** S. E. WHITE *Forest* 154 The midge, again, or punkie, or 'no-see-'um', just as you please, swarms down upon you suddenly. **1934** A. CHRISTIE *Parker Pyne Investigates* 198 The no-see-ums are biting good and hard. **1939** K. PINKERTON *Wilderness Wife* xvi. 166 No-see-ums are after dark prowlers. **1964** *Atlantic Advocate* July 67/1 Near the bottom we struck swamp ground, a paradise for no-see-'ems, those minute flies whose burning bites are inversely related to their size. **1970** *Observer* (Colour Suppl.) 19 Apr. 59/1 Down on the banks [of a Canadian river] there were awful blood-sucking insects called 'no-see-um', giant mosquitoes. **1975** *New Yorker* 24 Feb. 82/3 No-see-ums are so small they go right through the screening of the tent. They home on flesh.

nose-end. [NOSE *sb.* 17 a.] **a.** The tip of the human nose. **b.** The end of a nose in any of the transferred senses.

1611 COTGR. s.v. *Prendre*, You may take your selfe by the nose end; viz...you are as guiltie, faultie, or farre in, as the rest. **1681** GREW *Musæum* I. §ii. i. 20 Not above five Inches and ½ from his Nose end to his Buttocks. *c* **1728** EARL AILESBURY *Mem.* (1890) 573 Brave he was, but saw not his nose end. **1960** S. PLATH *Colossus* (1967) 65 The nose-end that twitches. **1961** *Times* 16 Dec. 11/5 Make sure..that mud does not enter the nose-ends [of a gun].

Hence **nose-ender,** (*a*) a straight blow on the nose; (*b*) (see quots. 1929, etc.).

1854 'C. BEDE' *Verdant Green* II. 25, I couldn't..give a straight nose-ender. **1929** F. C. BOWEN *Sea Slang* 96 *Nose ender*, a strong head wind. **1946** J. IRVING *Royal Navalese* 123 *Nose-ender*, a head wind and sea; regular Destroyer Weather. **1962** W. GRANVILLE *Dict. Sailors' Slang* 82/1 *Nose-ender*, wind blowing from dead ahead, literally into one's nose.

'nose-flute. [f. NOSE *sb.*] A musical instrument blown with the nose; used in Thailand, the Fiji and Society Islands, etc., and subsequently also in North America and Europe.

1775 *Phil. Trans.* LXV. 72, I have also examined the nose-flute of Otaheite. **1864** ENGEL *Mus. Anc. Nat.* 16 The nose-flutes of the Society and Feejee Islanders. **1882** *Macm. Mag.* XLVI. 81 The nose-flute is played in Siam. **1962** *New Yorker* 21 July 68/2 They are the manzello and the stritch, early forbears of the saxophone; a pocket-sized nose flute; the..melodica, a kind of accordion that is blown, not pumped. **1963** *Economist* 23 Nov. 775/2 Invented [jazz] instruments like the stritch and a nose-flute. **1969** *Listener* 3 Apr. 470/3 He has a large gong, a kind of..battery-run accordion, various whistles, and a nose flute.

nosegay ('nəʊzgeɪ). Also 6–7 **-gaye, -gaie.** [f. NOSE *sb.* + GAY *sb.*]

1. A bunch of flowers or herbs, esp. sweet-smelling flowers; a bouquet, a posy. Also, an imitation or representation of this.

c **1420** LYDG. *Assembly of Gods* 380 A nosegay she had made full pleasauntly. **1530** PALSGR. 698/2 Assay, this nose-gaye savoureth swetely. **1578** LYTE *Dodoens* 88 At the toppe ..growteth small tuftes, or as it were nosegeyes of ten or xii floures or more. **1600** SURFLET *Countrie Farme* II. xlvii. 301 These..flowers for nosegaies shall be set in order vpon beds and quarters. **1672** MARVELL *Reh. Transp.* I. 203 'Tis a Flower of the Sun, and might alone serve both for a Staff and a Nose-gay for any Noble mans Porter. **1704** *Collect. Voy.* (Churchill) III. 690/1 Also a Nosegay of Gold to be worn by the Emperor only. **1753** HOGARTH *Anal. Beauty* viii. 43 Observe the well composed nosegay, how it loses all its distinctness when it dies. **1837** HOWITT *Rur. Life* (1862) 231 Almost every person..had a nosegay in hand. **1877** A. B. EDWARDS *Up Nile* xv. 396 The damsels..in holiday apparel, with nosegays in their hands.

b. *fig.* or in fig. context.

1570 DEE *Math. Pref.* bj, To make this Preface, to be a little swete, pleasant Nosegaye for you, to comfort your Spirites. **1626** T. H[AWKINS] tr. *Caussin's Holy Crt.* 3 The Nose-gay of the Elect, called in holy Scripture *Fasciculus viventium.* **1651** C. CARTWRIGHT *Cert. Relig.* I. 103 Will you forsake the Rose of Sharon, and the Lillie of the Vallies for such a Nose-gay? **1731–8** SWIFT *Pol. Conversat.* Introd. Wks. 1751 XII. 160 It hath become a choice Flower in the Nosegay of Wit and Politeness. **1778** MME. D'ARBLAY *Early Diary, Let. to Susan Burney* 16 June, I design to make you a present of Miss Couss's letter when we meet for your nosegay, if you think her praise worth having.

c. *transf.*, with ref. to scent or show.

1768 GOLDSM. *Good-n. Man* v, I have a drop in the house of as pretty raspberry as ever was tipt over tongue..; the last couples we had here, they said it was a perfect nosegay. **1853** DICKENS *Bleak Ho.* xviii, The smell of sweet herbs and all kinds of wholesome growth..made the whole air a great nosegay. **1889** W. MORRIS in Mackail *Life* (1899) II. 222 The country is one big nosegay, the scents wonderful.

d. A perfume or scent (*spec.* one artificially prepared; see quot. 1881); an odour, smell.

1855 PIESSE *Art Perfum.* vi. 115 The formulæ for preparing the most favourite 'bouquets' and 'nosegays'. **1881** *Spons' Encycl. Manuf.* II. 1530 Nosegays or Bouquets. —By far the greatest part of the scent consumed is in this form being as the names indicate, mixtures of a number of odoriferous extracts. **1889** GRETTON *Memory's Harkback* 53 The lodgers had, to boot, the nosegay from the drains.

†**2.** A gay bunch or cluster. *Obs. rare*⁻¹.

1592 NASHE *P. Penilesse* (ed. 2) 13 b, These aged mothers of iniquitie will..weare nosegayes of yeolow haire on their furious foreheads.

3. *attrib.* and *Comb.*, as ***nosegay-dance, -flowers, -garden, -like*** (adj. and adv.), ***-maker***; **nosegay-plant** (see quot. 1837); **nosegay-tree,** the red jasmine of Tropical America, *Plumeria rubra*, or the related species *P. alba.*

1597 BRETON *Figure of Four* Wks. (Grosart) II. 7/1 Foure sweet Trades in a Citie: Sugar-men, Comfit-makers, Perfumers and Nose-gay-makers. **1600** SURFLET *Countrie Farme* II. xlvii. 301 Nosegaie flowers..shall be sowen,..no otherwise then the potherbes. *Ibid.*, [This] may be called the nosegaie garden. **1611** COTGR. s.v. *Bouquet, Bransle du bouquet*, the nosegay daunce. *Ibid.*, *Bouquetier*, of, or belonging to, nosegayes, nosgay-like. **1837** *Penny Cycl.* VII. 215/1 The French gardeners call it [the curled-leaved Bigarade] *Le Bouquetier*, or Nosegay plant. **1856** MRS. BROWNING *Aur. Leigh* I. 630 All the fields are tied up fast with hedges, nosegay-like.

†**nosegent.** *Obs. Cant.* (See quot.)

1567 HARMAN *Caveat* 83 *Nosegent*, a Nunne. *Ibid.* 87 There was a proude patrico and a nosegent.

nose-high, *a.*: see NOSE *sb.* 17 c.

'nose-hole. [f. NOSE *sb.*]

1. A nostril. Now *dial.*

1527 ANDREW *Brunswyke's Distyll. Waters* N ij b, Cotton wet in the same water and put in the nose holes is good against Polippus. **1716** *Phil. Trans.* XXIX. 519 The right Nose-hole, at the Root of the upper Beak. **1875–** in many dial. glossaries. **1922** JOYCE *Ulysses* 51 His leprous nosehole snoring to the sun. **1950** R. MOORE *Candlemas Bay* 242 You know how Candy looks when she's mad, like death, them black eyes and her noseholes thin.

2. In *Glass-blowing*, the open mouth of a side furnace at which the nose of a bulb of crown-glass in process of manufacture is softened by heating.

1832 G. R. PORTER *Porcelain & Gl.* 158 On either side of each bocca is a smaller circular opening, sometimes called a *boccarella*, but more generally..nose-hole. **1844** [see NOSE *sb.* 12 d]. **1881** *Spons' Encycl. Manuf.* III. 1064 The end of the piece [of iron]..is called the nose, and gives its name to the furnace or nose-hole.

'nose-jewel. [f. NOSE *sb.*] A valuable ornament worn in or attached to the nose.

1611 BIBLE *Isa.* iii. 21 In that day the Lord will take away ..The rings, and nose-iewels. **1695** J. EDWARDS *Perfect. Script.* 241 Their frontal jewel..fastned on their foreheads .., call'd..a nose-jewel. **1760–72** tr. *Juan & Ulloa's Voy.* (ed. 3) I. 465 Among the gold pieces are the nose-jewels. **1813** *Gentl. Mag.* LXXXIII. II. 351 Nor could even Fatima's beautiful face reconcile me to the nose jewel. **1862** M. E. ROGERS *Dom. Life Palestine* 381 An artificial clove made of gold, with a pearl..at the top, is a very favourite nose-jewel.

b. *transf.* A pig-ring.

1844 H. STEPHENS *Bk. Farm* II. 705 The best material for making the nose-jewels of swine is horse-shoe nails.

nosel(l, variants of NUZZLE *v.*¹ and *v.*²

noseless ('nəʊzlɪs), *a.* [f. NOSE *sb.*] Destitute or deprived of a nose; that has lost the nose.

1398 TREVISA *Barth. De P.R.* XVIII. xlvii. (Bodl. MS.), Somme beþ all heedles and noseles. **1509** BARCLAY *Shyp of Folys* (1570) 88 For he that is sure, and to a fray will renne, May fortune come home agayne noselesse or lame. **1606** SHAKS. *Tr. & Cr.* v. v. 34 His mangled Myrmidons, That noselesse, handlesse, hackt and chipt, come to him; Crying on Hector. **1646** *J. Hall's Poems* To Mr. Hall, Thou need'st no nose-lesse monuments display. **1727** GAY *Fables* I. xlvii, My shanks, sunk eyes, and noseless face Prove my pretension to the place. **1800** W. TAYLOR in *Monthly Mag.* VIII. 727 O'er the pale picture, and the noseless bust, Oblivion strews a soft sepulchral dust. **1862** *Temple Bar* V. 524 A noseless face would have no divinity.

Hence **'noselessly** *adv.*; **'noselessness.**

1752 RICHARDSON *Let. to Mrs. Donnellan* 22 Feb., Amelia, even to her noselessness, is again his first wife. **1855** THACKERAY *Newcomes* xxxv, Senators namelessly, noselessly, noiselessly seated. **1870** *Daily News* 6 June, The causes leading up to the..noselessness of 'the brigands' heads'.

†**'noseling(s,** *adv. Obs.* In 5 **noselyng(e, -lyng(g)ys.** [f. NOSE *sb.* + -LING².] On the nose, face downwards.

14.. *Sir Beues* (Naples MS.) 649 He leide him noselyng on þe grounde. *c* **1440** *Promp. Parv.* 358/2 Noselynggys (*S.* noslyngys), *suppinus* (S. *resupinus*). **1470–85** MALORY *Arthur* XVII. iv. 695 He was smyten with a swerd on the ryghte foote that he felle doune noselynge to the shyps bord.

'noselite. *Min.* [ad. G. *noselith* (Francke, 1890).] = NOSEAN.

1892 DANA *Min.* 432.

nosema (nəʊ'siːmə). [mod.L. (C. W. von Nägeli 1857, in *Amtlicher Bericht über die Versammlung Deutscher Naturforscher* XXXIII. 133), f. Gr. νόσημα disease.] A microsporidian protozoan parasite of the genus so called, esp. *Nosema apis*, identified in 1909 as the cause of an infectious dysentery affecting bees; also, the disease itself. Also *attrib.*

1911 FANTHAM & PORTER in *Proc. Zool. Soc.* 625 That *Nosema apis* was fatal to bees and allied Hymenoptera had been shown..by feeding healthy hive-bees, mason-bees, and wasps with honey infected with *Nosema* spores. **1912** *Ann. Trop. Med. & Parasitol.* VI. 149 Bees infected with *Nosema* seem unable to preserve their spotless cleanliness. *Ibid.* 159 Wasps have been observed carrying away bees dead of *Nosema* and then feeding their larvae on the corpses. **1914** *Bull. U.S. Dept. Agric.* no. 92, 6 The name 'Nosema disease', which the writer [*sc.* G. F. White] suggests as the common name for this disease, is, it will be observed, only a translation of the German name used by Zander. *Ibid.*, One is justified in at least drawing the conclusion that Nosema infection in a colony tends to weaken the colony. **1937** W. HERROD-HEMPSALL *Bee-Keeping* II. xxx. 1427 Nosema Disease is caused by a microscopical animal parasite (*Nosema apis*) infesting the food canal of the bee. *Ibid.* 1429 Nosema infected bees do not, as a rule, lose the power of flight. **1955** *Sci. News Let.* 1 Oct. 214/3 Antibiotics ..will give successful control over the destructive diseases, American and European foul-broods, that attack larval bees, and nosema, a killer of adults. **1973** *Times* 19 Apr. 27/5 It is against these very diseases [of bees], notably the two 'foul brood' types, but not forgetting acarine and nosema, that the Ministry is acting.

†**'noseness.** *nonce-wd.* (See quot.)

1598 FLORIO, *Nasaggine*, a nosenes or qualitie of ones nose.

nose'ology. Also **nosology.** [f. NOSE *sb.* + -(O)LOGY.] (See quot. 1819.)

1819 *Blackw. Mag.* V. 157 Noseology, a dissertation on the Intellectual Faculties, as manifested by the various configurations of the Nose. **1822** *Blackw. Mag.* XI. 427 If ever we should possess a classified nosology, my nose must be ranked in the order..which shall comprise the pitch-delighting olfactories. **1825** C. WESTMACOTT *Eng. Spy* I. 295 Fancy lectures on noseology.

Hence **noseo'logical** *a.*, pertaining to noseology.

1819 *Blackw. Mag.* V. 159 We denounce that man as an enemy to candid noseological disquisition.

'nose-pick. [PICK *sb.*[1] 5.] An instrument for clearing the nose of mucus, etc. **'nose-picker** [PICKER[1]], a person who picks his nose (with his fingers); **'nose-picking** *vbl. sb.* and *ppl. a.*

1825 *Kaleidoscope* 11 Oct. 114/3 Appended to it, by a silver chain, was..an ivory nose-pick. **1959** I. & P. OPIE *Lore & Lang. Schoolch.* iii. 47 To a nose-picker they chant: Friday, pie-day, Keep your nose tidy. **1960** KOESTLER *Lotus & Robot* I. i. 62 Only the nose-picking disciple kept up his activities. **1975** J. AIKEN *Voices in Empty House* iv. 116 The nose-picking in itself made me feel sick... *Nobody* in polite society *ever* picked their nose.

'nose-piece. Also **nose piece.** [f. NOSE *sb.*]

1. a. A part of a helmet or turban serving as a guard for the nose; a nasal.

1611 COTGR., *Nazal*, the nose-peece of a helmet; the part thereof which couereth the nose. **1800** *Asiat. Ann. Reg.* 344/2 The nose-piece of the turban has several Arabic inscriptions. **1865** KINGSLEY *Herew.* I. x. 226 The small space on either cheek which was left bare between the nose-piece and the chain-mail.

b. A nose-band for a horse; also, a similar part of a dog's muzzle.

1865 *Routledge's Mag. for Boys* Feb. 111 However you may fancy the appearance of a nose-piece.., never use a headstall or Gaveston martingale. **1893** K. SANBORN *S. California* 178 The headstall is covered with fluted silver, with large engraved silver rosettes at the sides,..with an elaborate nose-piece with silver engraving. **1899** *Daily News* 16 Dec. 6/3 He took the nose-piece between his teeth and pulled manfully.

c. A piece of wood inserted to form the nose of a stuffed animal.

1894 *Outing* XXIII. 408/2 Make a nose-piece of pine or soft wood. Drive it up into the skull and tack it there.

2. a. (See quot.)

1858 SIMMONDS *Dict. Trade, Nose-piece*, the nozzle of a hose or pipe.

b. *Optics.* The part of a microscope to which the objective (or object-glass) is attached.

1867 HOGG *Microsc.* I. ii. 71 Mr. Brooke's double nose-piece, or Baker's treble, is a useful piece of mechanism. **1899** tr. *Jaksch's Clin. Diagn.* (ed. 4) x. 436 The tube of the microscope is provided with a 'revolver' or 'nose-piece', to which lenses of different magnifying powers are fixed.

3. a. *Aeronaut.* (See quot.)

1918 W. E. DOMMETT *Dict. Aircraft* 32 *Nose piece*, conical metal piece attached to the propeller boss, its contour being continuous with the engine cowling.

†**b.** *Astronautics.* = NOSE CONE. *Obs.*

1946 H. HARPER *Dawn of Space Age* III. viii. 113 During the initial thrusting period, while the space-vessel is ascending from the earth, the heat resisting carapace—or nose-piece..will obscure any view forward.

'nose-pipe. [f. NOSE *sb.*]

1. A pipe, or piece of piping, forming a nose or terminal to another pipe, a vessel, etc.

1784–5 *Usef. Projects* in *Ann. Reg.* (1795) 55/2 By these means the branch or nose-pipe of the Engine is conveyed into the window of any room. **1853** URE *Dict. Arts* I. 594 The nose-pipe of the worm tub terminates in, and is firmly cemented to the side of the glass globe.

2. *spec.* The blast-pipe nozzle inside the tuyère of a blast furnace.

1839 URE *Dict. Arts* 825 Each of these tubes ends in a leather pocket, and an iron nose-pipe *K*, adjusted in the tuyère of the furnace. **1854** RONALDS & RICHARDSON *Chem. Techn.* (ed. 2) I. 314 The gas is not ignited immediately as it issues from the nose-pipes, but passes over a bridge..into the hearth of the furnace. **1875** KNIGHT *Dict. Mech.* 1534/2 The nose-pipes..vary in size with the nature of the coke and the ore.

noser ('nəʊzə(r)). [f. NOSE *sb.* + -ER.]

1. A blow or fall on the nose.

1851 MAYHEW *Lond. Labour* I. 12/2 The winner is the man who gives the first 'noser'; a bloody nose however is required to show that the blow was veritably a noser. **1862** *Country Gentl.* II. 42 That Irish Baronet had a noser at the same place.

2. A strong head wind; a wind in one's face; *esp.* in phr. ***a dead noser.***

1852 *Beck's Florist* 13 The fair wind..soon shifted into an adverse quarter, and off the coast of Scotland..it became a dead noser. **1873** W. CORY *Lett. & Jrnls.* (1897) 303 The hurricane born of Captain Rice's 'noser' came on us fourteen hours after.

'nose-ring. [f. NOSE *sb.*]

1. A ring fixed in an animal's nose.

1778 [W. MARSHALL] *Minutes Agric., Digest* 49 Nose rings will reclaim them, be they ever so riotous.

2. A ring-shaped ornament worn in the nose.

1819 KEATS *Cap & Bells* (1848) II. 227 His turban wreath'd of gold,..Mustachios, ear-ring, nose-ring, and his sabre keen. **1839** THACKERAY *Major Gahagan* i, I..carried away Scindiah's nose-ring with a pistol-ball. **1864** SPENCER *Illustr. Progress* 90 From nose-rings to ear-rings. **1877** A. B. EDWARDS *Up Nile* xix. 545 The bride..wears a gold brow-pendant and nose-ring. **1964** S. M. SHDEEK *Windswept & Other Stories* (1969) 14 Earrings and nose-rings twinkled.

Hence **'nose-ringed** *ppl. a.*

1925 E., O., & S. SITWELL *Poor Young People* 7 Like my black Nose-ringed lumbering bear.

'nose-smart. ? *Obs.* [f. NOSE *sb.* + SMART, after L. *nasturtium.*] The plant Cress.

1589 J. RIDER *Bibl. Schol.* 1749 The hearb nose smart, *Nasturtium.* **1598** FLORIO, *Nasturcio*,..the hearbe wilde mint, or nose-smart. **1611** COTGR., *Nasitort*, Nose-smart, garden Cresse. **1655** STANLEY *Hist. Philos.* I. (1701) 105/2 The magnetick vertue of the Earth Would draw away the humour of my Brain, Just as we see in Nose-smart. **1755** in JOHNSON [hence in later Dicts.].

nose-thirl, †**nose-thrill.** *Obs.* exc. *dial.* Forms: α. 4–6 (9) **nose-thurl,** (5 **-thurll**), 4–6 (9) **-thyrl,** 4–6 **thirl,** 4 **-therl.** (Also 5 **noos-,** 4–5 **noose-,** 6 *Sc.* **nois-.**) β. 4–6 **nose-thryl,** (5–6 **-thryll,** 6 **-thrylle**), 4–7 **-thrill,** (5 **-þrill**), 6–7 **-thril,** 6 **-threl(l.** γ. 5 **nosetril,** 6 **-trel(l;** 5 **-sterl,** 6 **-strell,** 7 **-strill.** [f. NOSE *sb.* + THIRL *sb.*, a new comb. in place of OE. *nosþyrel* NOSTRIL *sb.*, to which the γ-forms show some assimilation: compare the parallel ME. formation NESE-THIRL. The β-forms are very common from *c* 1400 to 1600.] A nostril.

α. *c* **1340** *Nominale* (Skeat) 20 Nose gristul and nose-thurles. *c* **1386** CHAUCER *Prol.* 559 His nose-thurles blake were and wyde. **1422** tr. *Secreta Secret., Priv. Priv.* 234 Who-so hath the noose-thurlis moche opyn, he is strongly angry. **1480** *Caxton's Trevisa* I. xxii. (1527) 20 Sponges watred and holden at theyr nosethyrles. **1567** *Gude & Godlie B.* (S.T.S.) 110 Thair nois thirlis can nouther sauer nor smell. **1856** P. THOMPSON *Hist. Boston* 716 *Nose-thurls*, the nostrils. **1866** BROGDEN *Linc. Words* s.v., He is very broad in the nose-thurles.

β. **1382** WYCLIF *Num.* xi. 20 To the tyme that it come out bi ȝoure noose thrillis. *c* **1400** *Destr. Troy* 7727 He neyt as a nagge, at his nose thrilles! **1485** CAXTON *Chas. Gt.* 151 His nosethrylles large & ample. **1534** FITZHERB. *Husb.* §84 Pursy is a dysease in an horses bodye,..and appereth at his nosethrilles. **1584** R. SCOT *Discov. Witchcr.* XII. xx. (1886) 227 Conveied through the nosethrels and mouth. **1609** HOLLAND *Amm. Marcell.* 13 Snuffing and drawing back their wind inwardly at their broken nose-thrils. **1656** HEYLIN *Surv. France* 132 Not yielding the least offence to the most curious nosethrill.

attrib. **1632** tr. *Bruel's Praxis Med.* 8 An oyntment.. wherewith anoynt the forehead & nose-thrill holes.

γ. *c* **1400** *Trevisa's Higden* (Rolls) I. 185 Sponges i-watred and i-holde at hir nostrilles [MS. α, nosetrils]. *c* **1400** tr. *Secreta Secret., Gov. Lordsh.* 115 A nose þat hauys nosesterles oft greuant, & harde openynge. **1545** RAYNOLD *Byrth Mankynde* 132 Powre..into the chyldes nosetrelles of oyle of castorium. *a* **1569** KINGESMYLL *Man's Est.* xii. (1580) 87 Wee have but borrowed breathe and that liyng in our nosetrels. *a* **1617** BAYNE *Lect.* (1634) 105 Icekles hanging at his Nosestrills.

'nose-up, *a. Aeronaut.* [f. NOSE *sb.* + UP *adv.*[2]] With the nose directed upwards.

1933 *Jrnl. R. Aeronaut. Soc.* XXXVII. 60 The lighter [air]ship..takes 20 seconds longer than the neutral ship to return to the horizontal, beyond which it only proceeds to 1° nose up. **1971** *Flying* Apr. 35/3 All you have to do is open the throttles, accelerate to that speed, rotate to a 10- or 12-degree nose-up attitude, and blast on out of the aerodrome. **1975** *Flight Internat.* 2 Oct. 506/2, I..adjusted the attitude..because it was more markedly nose-up than expected.

†**'nose-wise,** *a. Obs.* [f. NOSE *sb.* + WISE *a.*, perh. after Du. *neuswijs*, LG. *näsewîs*, G. *nase(n)weis* (MHG. *nasewîse*): cf. *nese-wise* s.v. NESE *sb.*]

1. Conceited; clever in one's own opinion.

1566 *Pasquine in Traunce* To Rdr., But nowe me thinketh I heare some nose wise papist, make a very vnnecessarie obiection. **1598** BP. HALL *Sat.* IV. i. 12 My rimes rellish of the Ferule still..Some nose-wise Pedant saith. **1630** J. TAYLOR (Water-P.) *Wks.* II. 13/2 Ther's not a Puritan, Or any nose-wise foole Precisian. **1787** W. TAYLOR *Scots Poems* 174 On the pride of a Nose-wise S***er.

2. Keen-scented.

1613 PURCHAS *Pilgrimage* IV. ix. 391 One more nose-wise then the rest, smelled the sent of flesh. **1630** G. GRAEME *Let.* in *Miscell.* (S.H.S.) II. 253, I think you to nosvyse that has smellid Your father's..falsety so far off.

†**'nosewort.** *Obs. rare.* Also 6 **noswort.** [f. NOSE *sb.*] **a.** Neeze-wort, Hellebore. **b.** Nasturtium (cf. NOSE-SMART).

1563 HYLL *Art Garden.* (1593) 21 The root Hellebor, or otherwise Noswort. **1608** TOPSELL *Serpents* 37 Of green hogs-fennell, take the lowest branches, Of nosewort sharpe [L. *acris nasturci*], so much. **1661** LOVELL *Hist. Anim. & Min.* 253 The root of centaury or hartwort, nosewort, gentian, or sesamine.

nosey ('nəʊzɪ), *sb.* [f. NOSE *sb.* + -Y.] One who has a large nose. (Used as a nickname.)

1788 GOV. POWNALL in *Archaeol.* IX. 148 There is an admirable caricatura of a musician, what the vulgar of this day would call *Nosey*, playing on a violin. **1804** *Naval Chron.* XI. 100 Pye..was always called *Nozey.* **1819** *Metropolis* III. 89 The calling a noseless man, nosey, is adding insult to the injury which he has sustained. **1851** MAYHEW *Lond. Labour* I. 474/1 Had heer'd of the Duke of Wellington; he was Old Nosey. **1887** SQUIRE in *Dict. Nat. Biog.* IX. 428/2 It is said that the gallery cry, 'Play up, nosey', owes its origin to his appearance.

nosey ('nəʊzɪ), *a.* and *sb.* Also **nosy.** [f. as prec. Cf. NOSY *a.*]

A. *adj.* **1. a.** Evil-smelling, emitting a bad odour.

1836 HALIBURTON *Clockm.* (1862) 53 It's so everlasting bad—it's near about as nosey as a slave ship of niggers. **1867** *Jrnl. R. Agric. Soc.* III. II. 620 [The corn] was left, heated a good deal, and came out clammy and 'nosey'.

b. Fragrant.

1892 WALSH *Tea* 161 Many teas that may be 'new and nosey' in the hand will be thin and flat in the cup.

2. Sensitive to bad smells.

1894 *Daily News* 17 Jan. 3/1 It is a great compliment to the management to state that the most nosey visitor has no legitimate ground for offence from organic causes.

3. *slang.* **a.** Inquisitive, esp. objectionably so; curious.

1882 F. W. P. JAGO *Anc. Lang. & Dial. Cornwall* 226 *Nosey*, impertinent, intrusive. **1910** H. G. WELLS *Hist. Mr. Polly* vi. 163 I'm not such a blooming Geezer..as not to be able to sell goods a bit. One has to be nosy over one's buying, of course. **1928** *Daily Express* 11 Sept. 7 Marylebone man: Being nosey, I goes to 'ave a look. Magistrate: Being what? Clerk: Nosey; meaning curious. **1957** M. SPARK *Comforters* iv. 91 She saw Laurence examining Eleanor's cigarette case in his nosey way. **1973** P. EVANS *Bodyguard Man* xv. 104 'A nosey man...' 'Very nosey, very smart, very perceptive.'

b. ***Nosey Parker, nosey parker***: an inquisitive person. Hence ***Nosey-Parkering, nosey-parkering*** ppl. adj. and vbl. sb. and (as a back-formation) ***nosey-park*** v. intr.; ***nosey-parkerdom, Nosey-Parkerism, nosey-parkery,*** the display of inquisitive behaviour, the exercise of oppressive questioning; ***nosey-parkerishness,*** inquisitive tendencies.

1907 *Picture post card* (London View Co. Ltd.) (*caption*) The adventures of Nosey Parker. **1912** C. MACKENZIE *Carnival* xxi. 217 'I saw you go off with a fellah.' 'What of it, Mr. Nosy Parker?' **1915** WODEHOUSE *Something Fresh* v. 163 'But Nosey Parker is what *I* call him,' she said. 'He minds everybody's business as well as his own.' **1925** W. DEEPING *Sorrell & Son* xxx. 302 A rodent, a nasty, acute little man of the Nosey Parker genus. **1929** H. A. VACHELL *Virgin* xviii. 280 I'm a pestering nosey-parkering, shilly-shallying sort of an idiot, eh? **1930** J. B. PRIESTLEY *Angel Pavement* iv. 156 That's what takes your time, my boy—doing your bit of nosy-parkering. **1932** H. WILLIAMS in *Hansard Commons* CCLXII. 1359/2 What I call the modern spirit of 'nosey-parkerism' in legislation and administration. **1937** N. MARSH *Vintage Murder* viii. 86 Shut up, Gordon... Don't nosy-park. **1939** —— *Overture to Death* xi. 118 Asking questions..out of..nosey-parkerishness. **1947** T. H. WHITE *Mistress Masham's Repose* xx. 150 'Good-bye.' 'And none of your Nosey-Parkering.' **1958** E. HYAMS *Taking it Easy* II. iii. 195 Is Bachelor still connected with military intelligence, or security, or whatever fancy name they have for official nosey-parkering? **1961** *Economist* 4 Nov. 426/3 This kind of officious nosey-parkery gives the British immigration authorities a bad name. **1966** C. MACKENZIE *My Life & Times* V. 157 The original 'nosy parker'..was one who played Peeping Tom to love-making couples in Hyde Park. **1969** *Daily Tel.* 25 Apr. 18 Goodness knows what all this massive exercise in nosey parkerdom is costing in terms of printing, manpower, administration, etc. **1971** L. LAMB *Worse than Death* iii. 29 Mrs Marshman nosey-parked..in Mrs Marble's cupboard. **1973** *Times* 17 Feb. 14/8 As ducks are 'parkers', it is easier to understand why exploratory and curious ducklings became 'nosy parkers'. **1974** 'D. CRAIG' *Whose Little Girl are You?* i. 19 All nosey parkers in this street. **1974** J. COOPER *Women & Super Women* 23 The social security ladies come nosy-parkering round.

B. *sb.* An inquisitive person, a 'Nosey Parker'.

1937 N. MARSH *Vintage Murder* xiv. 155 He may be a bit of a nosy, but he doesn't look like a murderer. **1942** BERREY & VAN DEN BARK *Amer. Thes. Slang* §399/1 *Meddler or inquisitive person*,..nosy. **1975** H. R. F. KEATING *Remarkable Case* ii. 25 Tomorrow she would be out there in time, before all the noseys come out.

noseyness ('nəʊzɪnɪs). Also **nosiness.** [f. NOSEY *a.* + -NESS.] Impertinent curiosity.

1919 F. HURST *Humoresque* 14 Haven't I learned it to you often enough a slummer must pay for her nosiness? **1941** *Penguin New Writing* X. 10, I do not think the men read these letters out of pure noseyness. **1952** J. STEINBECK *East of Eden* xviii. 179 This isn't nosiness. This is the law. **1973** *Daily Tel.* 5 Oct. 17/3 Noseyness was the main motive; we always spent a lot of time speculating about other people's marriages. **1975** L. DEIGHTON *Yesterday's Spy* viii. 60 Curiosity—even nosiness—is not yet against the law.

nosh (nɒʃ), *sb. colloq.* [Yiddish; cf. next word.]

a. A restaurant; a snack-bar. More usually ***nosh bar, -house.***

1917 R. FRY *Let.* 11 May (1972) II. 411 Come with me to Kettners' nosh at 8.0. **1959** C. MACINNES *Absolute Beginners* 154 After a quick bite at a Nosh, and two strong black coffees, I felt up to the ordeal. **1969** I. DRUMMOND *Man with Tiny Head* i. 21 We're going to your nosh-house. **1970** *New Scientist* 2 Apr. 5/2 What dishes will they have at the epicurean nosh-houses up west? **1973** *Jewish Chron.* 2 Feb. 22/4 The quasi-kosher-culture of the nosh bar. **1974** J. GARDNER *Corner Men* viii. 67 Wanted to set up a couple of class nosh houses in the Smoke, here.

b. Food, a meal. Also ***nosh-up,*** a (good) meal. The more usual sense in the U.K.

1963 *Daily Mail* 15 May 4/1 Why is it that whenever I read anything about freedom from hunger it's accompanied by pictures of people having a nosh-up? **1964** *Cherwell* 4

Nov. 12 At the unofficial opening..two old ladies were dragged in off the street and given free nosh and free coats. **1968** *Punch* 14 Feb. 220 I've always found Chinese nosh both cheap and filling. **1968** A. DIMENT *Great Spy Race* ii. 19, I like him enough to buy him some alcohol and the occasional cheap nosh. **1970** A. DRAPER *Swansong for Rare Bird* ix. 79 Like most birds she didn't want to lose out on a nosh-up. **1972** C. DRUMMOND *Death at Bar* vi. 159 Burglars go for plain, healthy English nosh.

c. A snack eaten between meals; a titbit. Chiefly *U.S.*

1965 *N.Y. Times* 9 Apr. 40 Advertising copy will stress that the company makes everything from 'soup to nosh'. (A nosh is a snack.) **1968** L. ROSTEN *Joys of Yiddish* 267 Many delicatessen counters display plates with small slices of salami, or pieces of halvah, with a legend affixed to a toothpick: 'Have a nosh.'

nosh (nɒʃ), *v. colloq.* [Yiddish; cf. G. *naschen* to nibble, eat on the sly.] **1. a.** To nibble, to eat a snack between meals. Chiefly *U.S.*

1957 *Observer* 3 Nov. 8/5 One eats breakfast or lunch, but one noshes in between. *Ibid.*, 'Women don't know how to nosh,' he continued, 'except chocolate and sweets.' **1958** I. BROWN *Words in Our Time* 76 Women, the salesman complained, only nosh chocolates and the true nosher is a connoisseur of cheeses at once sharp and ripe. **1968** L. ROSTEN *Joys of Yiddish* 267 To *nosh* is to 'have a little bite to eat before dinner is ready', or to 'have a little something between meals'. **1970** *Time* 12 Oct. 42 The politician, equipped with a trowel and the Fixed Smile, gobs mortar on a cornerstone, or noshes his way along the campaign trail. **1973** *Impetus* (Toronto) June 44/2 By nightfall, when mosquitoes as large as vampire bats were noshing on my exposed flesh, I had hoed a row and a half.

b. More generally, to eat; occas., to drink.

The more usual sense in the U.K.

1962 R. COOK *Crust on its Uppers* ii. 34, I finally bought a quart of grappa... Mrs. Marengo had noshed her half down. **1965** G. MELLY *Owning Up* xiv. 170 After our huge meal, we were forced to refuse although, as Mick said, 'I'd have noshed the lot if I could have done.' **1972** *Annabel* Jan. 8/3 There I sat in my steaming bath, noshing my favourite food. **1972** C. DRUMMOND *Death at Bar* v. 122 The Sergeant ..morosely noshed the veal-and-ham pie.

2. To practise fellatio (with). *coarse slang.*

1965 *Listener* 18 Nov. 803/1 Such typical modernisms as *snog, nosh, dildo,* [etc.]. **1968** [see GAMAHUCHE *v.*]. **1972** B. RODGERS *Queens' Vernac.* 142 *Nosh*.., to suck cock.

Hence **'noshable** *a.*; **'noshing** *vbl. sb.*

1957 *Observer* 3 Nov. 8/5 Noshing—derived from the German verb *naschen*—is to sample desirable food voluptuously, surreptitiously. **1965** J. P. CARSTAIRS *Concrete Kimono* i. 12 Too much noshin' and drinkin' the night before. **1965** W. YOUNG *Eros Denied* xiv. 137 *Gamming*, from the French *gamahucher*, or *blowing*, or *plating*, or *noshing*, from the Yiddish *nosh*, to nibble, or eat between meals. **1966** M. WADDELL *Otley* xi. 114 A particularly noshable repast—chop and peas and potatoes. **1966** *Crescendo* Nov. 10/1 This saga of happy noshing.

nosher ('nɒʃə(r)). *colloq.* [f. NOSH *v.* + -ER¹.] A person who samples food before buying it; one given to eating snacks; a customer at a restaurant.

1957 *Observer* 3 Nov. 8/5 He jerked his head towards a round-bellied, cheerful man..who was biting large segments of Gruyère held lovingly in his hand. 'A nosher,' said the shopkeeper sentimentally. **1958** I. BROWN *Words in Our Time* 76 The salesman's much-liked noshers paid up properly as they nosed and nuzzled and chewed their way from one of his cates to another. **1969** *Sunday Times* 23 Mar. 28 Hot meal vending machines in the lobby for late night noshers. **1974** *Ibid.* 20 Jan. 24/7 Gourmet foods to salivate the palates of jaded British noshers.

noshery ('nɒʃərɪ). *colloq.* [f. NOSH *v.* + -ERY 2 b.] A restaurant; a snack-bar.

1963 R. I. McDAVID *Mencken's Amer. Lang.* v. 261 Miami Beach and similar outposts of civilization are full of *nosheries*... A *Chinese Noshery* was opened in the posh Georgetown section of the District of Columbia, *c.* 1955. **1970** A. DRAPER *Swansong for Rare Bird* ix. 78 Let's skip your noshery and I'll take you out for some grub. **1972** K. O'HARA *Company of St George* xiii. 118 The place I'm thinking of for lunch..has the reputation of a very superior noshery. **1975** *Spectator* 11 Jan. 36/1 A chain of nosheries have just sent out a drinks guide that shows sherry in that abominable receptacle known as an 'Elgin' or 'schooner'.

noshi ('nɒʃɪ). Also **nosi**. [Jap.] A Japanese token of esteem, originally a piece of dried awabi or more recently a specially folded piece of paper, forming part of the wrapping of a Japanese gift.

1855 R. HILDRETH *Japan* xli. 434 *Nosi*, a species of edible sea-weed, of which small pieces are attached to every congratulatory present. **1891** A. M. BACON *Japanese Girls & Women* i. 2 Tied with a peculiar red and white string, in which is inserted the *noshi*, or bit of dried fish daintily folded in a piece of coloured paper, which is an indispensable accompaniment of every present. **1954** J. M. MORRIS *Wise Bamboo* iv. 61 It was wrapped as a Japanese wedding gift, tied with gold and white cords in the traditional knot and with a paper *noshi*, the Japanese sign of a gift, on the wrapping. **1971** R. HARBIN *More Origami* 39 A simple Noshi which is a good luck item given with anything.

no show, *sb.* orig. *U.S.* Also **noshow**, (with hyphen) **no-show**. [f. NO *a.* + SHOW *v.*] A person who reserves a place on a train, boat, or esp. an aircraft, and fails to claim or cancel it. Also *transf.* and *attrib.*

1941 *Collier's* 27 Sept. 67 He's what the Airlines call a 'no show'. **1946** *Sun* (Baltimore) 3 Sept. 6 (Advt.), The traveling public has long been aware of the so-called 'no show'. He is the person who reserves airline space, buys a ticket and then neglects to cancel his reservation when he decides not to go. **1948** *Time* 10 May 89/3 Last week ship lines were still accepting tentative bookings—but only to replace last-minute no-shows. **1949** *Birmingham* (Alabama) *News* 17 Feb. 40/3 Many passengers who were denied seats could have occupied those left empty by 'noshows'. The airlines are in the red largely because of 'noshow' passengers. **1959** *Economist* 17 Jan. 248/1 To be sure of a seat or a sleeping berth, the 'no show' traveller books on several different services and sits back to decide at leisure which booking to take up. **1961** *Flight* LXXX. 489/1 IATA announce that transatlantic operators, in order to alleviate the no-show problem, are to introduce a reconfirmation rule. **1963** *Times* 8 Feb. 19/6 Booking and cancellation charges and 'no-show' charges. **1972** R. K. SMITH *Ransom* i. 25 The phone rang... Another 'no show', the Cable boy. Wasn't that on Ben Carter's route? **1973** *Daily Colonist* (Victoria, B.C.) 7 July 9/2 No-shows, passengers who simply fail to turn up for flights they've booked, have long been a major headache for airlines. **1974** *Index-Jrnl.* (Greenwood, S. Carolina) 19 Apr. 6/5 The regulatory agency said there was an increase in the number of no-shows, fans who purchase tickets but don't attend the game.

no side. *Rugby.* [SIDE *sb.*¹ 20 b.] The (announcement of the) conclusion of a game.

1857 T. HUGHES *Tom Brown's School Days* I. v. 125 Five o'clock strikes. 'No side' is called, and the first day of the School-house match is over. **1874** *Rugby Union Football Ann. 1874–75* 39 Glasgow were again compelled to touch the ball down before the call of 'No-side', when the match was declared drawn in favour of Edinburgh. **1882** *Standard* 20 Nov. 2/8 When 'no side' was called, the University were left the winners. **1904** WODEHOUSE *Gold Bat* xi. 126 The whistle blew for no-side. **1931** *Times* 16 Feb. 5/1 They had looked a beaten team when, a quarter of an hour from 'no side', England at last managed to score a try. **1957** *Times* 14 Nov. 17/1 When no-side arrived the Australians had had all that they wanted. **1968** *Listener* 8 Aug. 189/1 The Lions took the lead ten minutes from no side, at which point the referee began awarding penalty kicks at goal to the Transvaal side.

'nosin. *Min.* ? *Obs.* = NOSEAN.

1825 HAIDINGER *Moh's Min.* III. 157 The name of Nosin has been given to it in honor of Mr. Nose. **1836** THOMSON *Min., Geol.*, etc. I. 675 Nosin.

nosiness, var. NOSEYNESS.

nosing ('nəʊzɪŋ). [f. NOSE *sb.* + -ING¹.] **1.** The rounded edge of a bench, or of a step projecting over the riser; also, a metal shield for the same; the prominent edge of a moulding or drip.

1775 ASH, *Nosing*,..that which is put on at the end of anything resembling a nose. **1778** *Encycl. Brit.* (ed. 2) 618/2 The rail cannot be fixed less than one fourth part from the nosing or front of the step. **1823** P. NICHOLSON *Pract. Build.* 185 The meeting of the sides which form the external angle of the steps is called the line of nosing. **1839** *Civil Eng. & Arch. Jrnl.* II. 363/1 A nosing, or rebated piece of iron, is made fast to the step of wood by iron studs. **1876** *Arch. Inst. Jrnl.* XXXIII. 21 The nosing of the wall-bench..has been cut away flush with the riser.

2. The keeper of a lock, which receives the bolt.

1884 KNIGHT *Dict. Mech.* Suppl. 636/1.

nosing, *vbl. sb.* and *ppl. a.*: see NOSE *v.*

no sir: see NOSSIR.

no siree (nəʊ sɜːˈriː). *U.S. colloq.* Also **no sirree**. [f. NO *adv.*³ + SIRREE.] No indeed; certainly not. Cf. YES SIREE.

1848 RUXTON *Far West* i, No sirre-e; I went out when Spiers lost his animals. **1851** *Knickerbocker* XXXVIII. 496 'Can you take two to Whitlockville by five o'clock?'..No, Siree!' **1861** G. F. BERKELEY *Eng. Sportsman* ix. 146 To say No sirree-e-e-e-e is to convey the sentence of No you infernal rogue [etc.]. **1883** *Wheelman* Apr. 2/2 No, sir-e-e, you can't have any of my boats. **1936** J. DOS PASSOS *Big Money* (1937) 83 No more of that stuff, nosiree. **1973** J. DI MONA *Last Man at Arlington* (1974) 49 The senator wouldn't protect him. No siree.

nosism ('nɒsɪz(ə)m). [f. L. *nos* we + -ISM.]

1. An attitude of mind in a group of persons, corresponding to egotism in the individual.

1819 *Blackw. Mag.* V. 97 The egotism or *nosism* of the other luminaries of the Lake School, is at times extravagant enough, and amusing enough withal.

2. The use of 'we' in stating one's own opinions.

1829 *Examiner* 162/1 We will be consistent according to the fashionable virtue of the day in *nos*-ism. **1864** *Edin. Rev.* July 52 It tempts a man to indulge in *Nos*-ism, where modesty..would have made him shrink from undisguised egotism.

'nosite. *Min. rare.* = NOSEAN. (Dana, 1868.)

no-sky (nəʊˈskaɪ), *adj. phr.* [f. NO *a.* 6 b + SKY *sb.*¹] ***no-sky line***: a line in a room behind which no sky is visible from table height.

1927 *Illumination Res. Techn. Paper* (Dept. Sci. & Industr. Res.) No. 7. 12 This experience of adequacy and inadequacy in front of and behind the 'no-sky' line appears to be more or less independent of weather, so long as no sun is shining into the room. **1961** J. W. T. WALSH *Sci. Daylight* xi. 255 The first step in preparing a daylight plan is, usually, to plot the no-sky line.

nosle, obs. variant of NOZZLE *sb.*

no smoking, *vbl. sb.* [NO *a.* 4.] Usu. *attrib.*, = NON-SMOKING *a.*; also a formula used on a notice, sign, etc., indicating that smoking is not permitted.

1944 J. GUNTHER *D Day* i. 13, I wanted to smoke, but fell asleep before the No SMOKING sign was switched off. **1952** T. J. MULVEY *These are your Sons* v. 108 The light over the cabin door flashed red. NO SMOKING. FASTEN YOUR SEAT BELTS—the glass panel warned. **1955** G. WILLANS *Fasten Your Lapstraps!* i. 17 Inside the airport there are more notices. 'No Entry', 'No Smoking', 'Staff Only'. **1961** *John o' London's* 1 June 608/3 One doesn't always notice the no-smoking sign. **1970** *New Yorker* 16 May 46/3 The no-smoking lights go out and the loud-speaker confirms that the passengers may now unfasten their seatbelts and smoke. **1971** P. AUDEMARS *Stolen like Magic Away* i. 15 The No Smoking notice was prominently displayed. **1973** J. ASHFORD *Double Run* vi. 44 He reached..for a pack of cigarettes. 'This is a no-smoking compartment,' said the woman.

noso- ('nɒsəʊ), combining form of Gr. νόσος disease, used in a number of compounds, chiefly pathological, as † **'nosocome** [a. F. *nosocome*, ad. L. *nosocomium*, Gr. νοσοκομεῖον], a hospital. *Obs.*⁻¹ **noso'comial** [cf. prec.] *a.*, belonging or pertaining to a hospital. † **nosogno'monic** *a.* (see quot.). *Obs.*⁻¹ **nosoma'thete** [Gr. μαθητής], a student of diseases. **no'someter** (see quot.). **no'sonomy**, 'the doctrine of the natural laws by which diseases occur' (Mayne, 1857). **'nosophile** *rare* [-PHIL, -PHILE], a person who is morbidly attracted by sickness or disease. **noso'phobia**, morbid apprehensiveness of disease. **'nosophyte** (see quot.). **nosopo'etic** *a.*, producing or causing disease. **noso'taxy**, the distribution and classification of diseases (Dunglison, 1855). **noso'theory**, the theory of disease (Mayne, 1857). **nosotoxi'cosis** (see quot.). **no'sotrophous** *a.*; **no'sotrophy** (see quots.).

Various other combs. of doubtful currency, such as *nosogenesis*, *-genetic*, *-geny*, *-mania*, are given in the *Syd. Soc. Lex.* and some recent Dicts.

1653 URQUHART *Rabelais* I. li. 227 Gargantua..gave order that the wounded should be drest and had care of in his great Hospital or **Nosocome*. **1855** DUNGLISON *Med. Lex.* s.v., *Nosocomial or hospital fever. **1891** C. CREIGHTON *Hist. Epidem. Brit.* 95 The purely nosocomial part of these charities was in not a few instances for the immediate relief of the monasteries themselves. **1655** STANLEY *Hist. Philos.* (1687) 165 Medicine is of five kinds.. *Nosognomonick discerns diseases. **1841** J. T. HEWLETT *Parish Clerk* I. 106 Whether the state of the stomach depends on the state of the mind, or vice versa, I am not *nosomathete enough to say. **1822–34** *Good's Study Med.* (ed. 4) I. 543 The pulse becomes a sort of *nosometer, or measurer of the violence and danger of the disease. **1665** DRAGE (*title*), A Physical *Nosonomy; or, A new and true Description of the Law of God (called Nature) in the Body of Man. **1855** DUNGLISON *Med. Lex.*, Nosonomy. **1895** tr. *M. Nordau's Degeneration* v. i. 539 Sadists, 'bestials', *nosophiles, and necrophiles, etc., find legal opportunities to gratify their inclinations. **1905** *Smart Set* Sept. 113/2 Names of Satanic painters from Hell-Fire Breughel to Arnold Böcklin..passed through the halls of this nosophile's memory. **1889** *Lancet* 9 Nov. 966/1 *Nosophobia is certainly much more frequent in man, probably because women act as nurses, and consequently have no fear of infection. **1890** GOULD *Med. Dict.*, **Nosophyte*,..a term applied to any pathogenic microbe, or minute parasitic organism which produces disease. **1733** ARBUTHNOT *On Air* vi. §23. 156, I shall make a few Observations upon the Qualities of the Air, so far as they are *Nosopoetick, that is, have a Power of producing Diseases. **1834** *Fraser's Mag.* X. 569 Least of all can we explain the nosopoetic effects of atmospherical changes. **1892** *Syd. Soc. Lex.*, **Nosotoxicosis*, a condition in which morbid symptoms are exhibited, which are dependent on the presence of toxic bases in the blood [etc.]. **1857** MAYNE *Expos. Lex.*, *Nosotrophus*.., nourishing or maintaining disease: *nosotrophous. *Nosotrophia*.., the nourishment or nutrition of disease; *nosotrophy.

nosography (nəˈsɒgrəfɪ). [f. NOSO- + -GRAPHY, or ad. mod.L. *nosographia*: cf. F. *nosographie* (1798), Sp. *nosografia*.] A (*or* the) systematic description of diseases.

1654 WHITLOCK *Zootomia* 110 The Diseases of the Mindes of Patients..; to sum up which, would be a Nosography..as large as any, treating of the Bodies distemper. **1847** tr. *Feuchtersleben's Med. Psychol.* 11 The nosography which aims at exhibiting the phenomena, the natural history, and the so called system of psychosis. **1851–9** *Man. Sci. Enq.* 243 These again should lead to a more useful nosography than is generally adopted. **1861** *Sat. Rev.* XI. 431/1 Dr. Fuller's work..on the subject of rheumatism, the nosography, pathology, statistics, and treatment of which are illustrated [etc.].

So **no'sographer**; **noso'graphic(al** *adjs.*; **noso'graphically** *adv.*

1859 SEMPLE *Diphtheria* 134 To trace,..after the manner of nosographers, the specific characters of the different kinds of Angina. **1888** *Amer. Jrnl. Psychol.* I. 497 Charcot's famous three states or nosographic groups were formulated in 1882.

nosological (nɒsəʊˈlɒdʒɪkəl), *a.* [f. NOSOLOGY. Cf. F. *nosologique*, It. and Sp. *nosologico*.]

1. Of or pertaining to nosology.

1777–84 CULLEN *First Lines Physic* (1808) I. §805 My reasons for differing from these authors, must be left to a nosological discussion. **1805** SAUNDERS *Min. Waters* 460 In acute diseases, the thirst after water..is sufficiently constant to be a basis of nosological description. **1843** R. J. GRAVES *Syst. Clin. Med.* 20 Will you from this very excellent nosological definition venture to prescribe for this case of dropsy? **1899** *Allbutt's Syst. Med.* VII. 384 He founded his nosological classification on certain cases observed by himself.

2. Dealing with nosology.

1807 *Med. & Phys. Jrnl.* XVIII. 535 A close application to the perusal of the late Nosological authors.

Hence **noso'logically** *adv.*

1836 E. HOWARD *R. Reefer* liii, I don't know whether I have described this fever case..nosologically. **1859** SEMPLE *Diphtheria* 316 Speaking nosologically, Diphtherite is a phlegmasia.

nosologist (nə'sɒlədʒɪst). [f. as prec. + -IST. Cf. F. *nosologiste.*] One who is occupied with, or learned in, nosology.

1777–84 CULLEN *First Lines Physic* (1808) I. §734 The Petechia has been, by all our Nosologists, enumerated amongst the exanthemata. **1800** tr. *Cullen's Nosology* Pref. 18 The characters of former Nosologists appear to me, in general, too short and defective. **1843** R. J. GRAVES *Syst. Clin. Med.* 20 'Tell me the name of the disease' was the motto of the nosologist, 'and I will tell you the remedy'. **1884** M. MACKENZIE *Dis. Throat & Nose* II. 339 Nasal hemorrhage was classed by the nosologists of the last century as a substantive disease.

nosology (nə'sɒlədʒɪ). [ad. mod.L. *nosologia* (so Sp. and It.; F. *nosologie*), a. Gr. type *νοσολογία: see NOSO- and -LOGY.]

1. A classification or arrangement of diseases.

1721 BAILEY, *Nosology*,..a Treatise concerning Diseases. **1777–84** CULLEN *First Lines Physic* (1808) Introd. §2 To establish a Methodical Nosology, or an arrangement of diseases according to their genera and species. **1804** ABERNETHY *Surg. Obs.* 5 In Dr. Cullen's Nosology we find diseases of arteries, veins, glands, &c., brought together under one order. **1857** T. WATSON *Lect. Phys.* (ed. 4) 12 That phantom—a perfect methodical nosology. **1860** TANNER *Pregnancy* i. 7 Such an expression should hardly have a place in any scientific nosology.

transf. **1785** REID *Intell. Powers* VI. viii. 652 It were to be wished that we had also a nosology of the human understanding.

b. A collection or combination *of* diseases.

1823 DE QUINCEY *Lett. on Self-Educ.* (1860) 139 A sentence..liable to a whole nosology of malconformations. **1851** CARLYLE *Sterling* I. i, All this fatal nosology of spiritual maladies, so rife in our day.

c. The list or catalogue of known diseases.

1839 CARLYLE *Chartism* ix, There is no disease in the Nosology but he can trace in himself some symptoms of it. **1899** *Times* 25 Aug. 8/2 [Plague] is one of the easiest of the great epidemic diseases to combat in our whole nosology.

2. Systematic or scientific classification or investigation of diseases; that branch of medical science which deals with this.

1727–38 CHAMBERS *Cycl.* s.v. *Medicine*, The second branch considers the diseases of the human body, their differences, causes, and effects; and is called..*nosology*, when it examines their differences. **1799** *Med. Jrnl.* I. 42 There is little hope of seeing a theory of medicine, or a System of Nosology established, which..will..stand the test of ages. **1827** *Lancet* 17 Nov. 252/2 Nosology is of course frequently taught without therapeutics. **1881** G. MACDONALD *M. Marston* III. xiv. 256 Nosology is a science doomed, thank God, to perish. Health alone will at last fill the earth.

transf. **1849** SIR J. STEPHEN *Eccl. Biog.* (1850) I. 345 Phenomena in the science of mental nosology. *Ibid.* II. 406 Ecclesiastical Nosology, or the Morbid Anatomy of the Church.

3. The special character *of* a particular disease, or the views current with regard to this.

1825 *Sporting Mag.* XVI. 355 A satisfactory conclusion is, to agree on the nosology of the disease. **1876** *Trans. Clinical Soc.* IX. 91 With a reference to the divided state of the nosology of leuchæmia.

nosology, var. NOSEOLOGY.

nossel: see NOSTEL, NOZZLE *sb.*, NUZZLE *v.*[2]

†**nossen**, obs. variant of NOISING *vbl. sb.*

1504 *Plumpton Corr.* (Camden) 186 And so they have.. arrest him; the which is a great nossen in the country.

nossir (nəʊ'sɜː(r)). Chiefly *U.S. colloq.* Also no sir. [Corruption of *no sir.*] A formula of emphatic denial or refusal: certainly not. Cf. NO SIREE.

1856 *Knickerbocker* XLVII. 544 *Examiner*: Has it effected that object? *Student*: No, Sir-r-r! I don't think it has. **1930** I. LOW *His Master's Voice* ii. 15 Most of his replies to questions were in the nature of 'Yessir!' 'Nossir!' or their present-day Russian equivalent. **1932** MRS. P. CAMPBELL *Let.* 29 Mar. in *B. Shaw & Mrs. Campbell* (1952) 298 Please don't think..that I am such a foolish creature as to look upon these letters as bouquets to *me* 'No, Sir'—as the Americans say, with the accent on the 'sir'. **1939** A. HUXLEY *After Many a Summer* I. iv. 43 She really cared for her old Uncle Jo, and cared for him, what was more, not merely as an old uncle—no, *sir.* **1955** POHL & KORNBLUTH *Space Merchants* xv. 156 'I want to look at your books.' He shook his head emphatically. 'Nossir. Only the old man himself gets to see the books.' **1968** E. MCGIRR *Lead-lined Coffin* ii. 51 Joe Silverman don't like his neck being breathed down. Nossir. **1970** R. CRAWFORD *Kiss Boss Goodbye* II. ii. 64 '*Nobody* gave you an answer?' 'Nossir,' Dell said. **1973** *Listener* 19 Apr. 501/3 In Texas, do you think they're going to inquire about the hanging of the venison..? No, sir. They wonder if there's any shepherd's pie.

†**nost**, for *ne wost*, knowest not; see NOT *v.*[2]

a **1310** in Wright *Lyric P.* 102 When thou shalt deȝe, ner thou nost. *c* **1384** CHAUCER *H. Fame* 2047 Nost nat thou That is betyd late or now? **1388** WYCLIF *Ecclus.* xxxiii. 33 Thou noost whom thou schalt seke. **1390** GOWER *Conf.* II. 61 Thou nost what chance schal betyde.

nost, obs. variant of OAST.

nostalgia (nɒ'stældʒɪə). [a. mod.L. *nostalgia* (so It., Sp., Pg.; F. *nostalgie* (1802)), f. Gr. νόστος return home + ἄλγος pain.] **1.** *Path.* A form of melancholia caused by prolonged absence from one's home or country; severe home-sickness.

1770 J. BANKS *Jrnl.* in J. Cook *Jrnls.* (1955) I. 409 The greatest part of them [*sc.* the ship's company] were now pretty far gone with the longing for home which the Physicians have gone so far as to esteem a disease under the name of Nostalgia. **1780** THACHER *Mil. Jrnl.* (1823) 242 Many perplexing instances of indisposition,..called by Dr. Cullen *nostalgia* or home sickness. **1786** R. HAMILTON in *Edin. Med. Comm.* XI. 343 History of a remarkable Case of Nostalgia. **1818** SYD. SMITH *Wks.* (1867) I. 250 What a dreadful disease Nostalgia must be on the banks of the Missouri! **1856** KANE *Arct. Expl.* I. xiii. 145 He looked as wretched as any lover of a milder clime. I hope I have treated his nostalgia successfully. **1877** OWEN in *Wellesley's Desp.* p. xlv, One who was to spend so much of his life in the East..should not be hampered by ties and habits calculated ..to foster nostalgia.

transf. **1842** J. WILSON *Chr. North* I. 57 That pond has.. about half-a-dozen trouts, if indeed they have not sickened and died of Nostalgia. **1861** *Times* 24 Sept., The principal object thought of appears to be the health of the trees,..that they might not suffer too much from nostalgia.

2. *transf.* Regret or sorrowful longing *for* the conditions of a past age; regretful or wistful memory or recall of an earlier time.

1920 D. H. LAWRENCE *Lost Girl* xv. 344 The terror, the agony, the nostalgia of the heathen past was a constant torture to her mediumistic soul. **1928** A. WAUGH *Nor Many Waters* vi. 231 He pictures with a sense of nostalgia, too acute almost to be endured, all that marriage to Marian would have meant. **1933** D. GARNETT *Pocahontas* xx. 234 Seeing all these things again filled her heart with that violent sentimental nostalgia..felt by the very young about the very recent past. **1943** KOESTLER in *Tribune* 26 Nov. 13/1 Even the names of Paris underground stations..become the nostalgia-imbued stimuli of conditioned reflexes. **1945** AUDEN *For Time Being* 37 We and They are united in the candid glare of the same commercial hope by day, and the soft refulgence of the same erotic nostalgia by night. **1951** L. P. HARTLEY *My Fellow Devils* xxxiii. 339 The faults for which she had been obliged to sack him no longer counted: ..she was free to dwell with some nostalgia on his virtues. **1957** *Listener* 3 Oct. 512/1 When grown-ups become passionately interested in them [*sc.* children's books] some kind of nostalgia is involved. **1957** B. & C. EVANS *Dict. Contemp. Amer. Usage* 322/2 Now a vogue word, *nostalgia* has come to mean any vague yearning, especially for the past and especially..when tinged with tenderness and sadness. **1959** *Observer* 8 Feb. 7/5 Nostalgia for one's childhood does not necessarily mean that the childhood was a happy one. **1971** *Sunday Times* 30 May 32/2 Nostalgia's all right, But it's not what it was.

nostalgic (nɒ'stældʒɪk), *a.* [f. prec. + -IC. Cf. F. *nostalgique*, It., Sp., and Pg. *nostalgico.*]

1. Of the nature of, characterized or caused by, nostalgia.

1806 T. ARNOLD *Insanity* (ed. 2) I. 208 A variety of pathetic insanity, to which, from nostalgia its most usual appellation, I have given the epithet nostalgic. **1894** DU MAURIER *Trilby* (1895) 331 The desire to hear it once more became nostalgic—almost an ache! **1898** *Daily News* 24 Feb. 3/1 The French songs..were invariably nostalgic.

2. Affected with nostalgia; home-sick.

1869 O. W. HOLMES *Cinders fr. Ashes* (1891) 244 We jogged soberly along,—kind parents and slightly nostalgic boys,—towards the seat of learning. **1877** BLACK *Green Past.* xl, We dragged these nostalgic persons out on to the pleasant little iron balcony.

3. a. That evokes a wistful and sentimental yearning for the past. **b.** Feeling or indulging in nostalgia.

1944 *Evening News* 11 Dec. 1/3 Britain, that nostalgic lover of vanished thrones. **1950** A. L. ROWSE *England of Elizabeth* v. 184 That nostalgic figure, the Town Crier, was becoming familiar. **1952** *N.Y. Herald Tribune* 28 Aug. 16/7 The Empire Theater, fifty nine years old and 'one of the fine old nostalgic houses' will be torn down next spring. **1958** B. NICHOLS *Sweet & Twenties* viii. 112 The charming thing snapped open, releasing a cloud of dust and a host of memories. The very sound of it was nostalgic. **1959** *Observer* 18 Jan. 19/1 It had a sudden sharp nostalgic appeal for me because I immediately recognised in one of the chief testifiers a former assistant master at my preparatory school. **1965** *Church Times* 18 June 6/4 The departure on Friday afternoon of the last train to be drawn out of Paddington Station..by a steam locomotive was..a nostalgic occasion.

nostalgically (nɒ'stældʒɪkəlɪ), *adv.* [f. NOSTALGIC *a.*: see -ICALLY.] In a nostalgic way; in evocation of the past.

1928 GALSWORTHY *Swan Song* III. xi. 298 A long time he sat there, nostalgically bemused, strangely unwilling to move. **1937** A. HUXLEY *Ends & Means* i. 2 The poor and downtrodden have always dreamed nostalgically of a man ideally well-fed, free, happy and unoppressed. **1945** *John o' London's Weekly* 24 Aug. 216 Its style of binding is nostalgically akin to that of those A.A. handbooks which one used to find (sometimes) in seaside hotels. **1957** A. E. COPPARD *It's Me, O Lord!* iii. 37 There is something nostalgically primitive about the woodwind instruments. **1958** *Listener* 20 Nov. 842/2 Mesens..uses these elements lyrically and nostalgically. **1975** J. MELDRUM *Semonov Impulse* iii. 57 You're going nostalgically north?.. See the boys?

‖**nostalgie de la boue** (nɔstalʒi də la bu). [Fr., lit. = yearning for mud (Émile Augier *Le Mariage d'Olympe* (1855) I. i).] A desire for degradation and depravity.

1897 G. B. SHAW *Our Theatres in Nineties* (1932) III. 168 To him those habits were 'morality'; and what was counter to them was 'nostalgie de la boue'. **1905** H. A. VACHELL *Hill* vi. 121 She..said that I suffered from what the French call *la nostalgie de la boue*; that means, you know, the homesickness for the gutter. **1920** G. DICKINS *Hellenistic Sculpture* ii. 27 The Hellenistic sculptors..suffered as much as any modern decadent from 'la nostalgie de la boue'. **1928** D. H. LAWRENCE *Lady Chatterley* xix. 358 You're one of those half-insane, perverted women who must run after depravity, the *nostalgie de la boue.* **1957** C. MACINNES *City of Spades* II. xii. 181 It's the crude animal type that attracts you... It's simply another form of *nostalgie de la boue.* **1965** *Listener* 9 Sept. 391/2 A cultural *nostalgie de la boue* for the nonsense of the 'thirties is surely perverse. **1969** R. LOWELL *Notebook 1967–68* 105 The Muse shouts vacation in my ear: *Nostalgie de la boue* that shelters ape And protozoa from the rights of man. **1971** *Southerly* XXXI. 11 There may be a suggestion of *nostalgie de la boue* in his choice of sexual partners.

Similarly ***nostalgie de la banlieue*** [Fr., = suburbs], ***des adieux*** [Fr., = farewells], ***du divin*** [Fr., = divine], ***du pavé, trottoir*** [Fr., = pavement], etc.

1933 D. L. SAYERS *Murder must Advertise* iii. 41 There is a *nostalgie de la banilieu* [*sic*] as well as *de la boue.* **1941** Nostalgie des adieux [see FAUTE DE MIEUX]. **1944** *Horizon* IX. 13 My reaction to everything not urban has been either one of acute melancholy or an urgent *nostalgie du pavé.* **1944** M. LASKI *Love on Supertax* ix. 88 'Every man has an urge to go Mayfairing once in his life.'..'*Nostalgie du trottoir*,' agreed Tatiana. **1948** W. STEVENS *Let.* 6 May (1967) 596 He speaks of the nostalgie du divin, (which is obviously epidemic in Dublin). **1972** *Times* 27 Sept. 5/3 The archetypal early twentieth-century laboratory scented evocatively with *Nostalgie de la Bunsen Burner.*

no'stalgy, anglicized form of NOSTALGIA.

1846 in BUCHANAN *Technol. Dict.* **1874** O'SHAUGHNESSY *Disease of Soul, Music & Moonlight* 105 The nostalgies of dim pasts seize me. **1882** A. W. WARD *Dickens* iii. 64 Longing with a nostalgy that was specially strong upon him at periods of mental excitement.

†**'nostel.** *Obs.* Forms: 1 **nostle, nosle,** 5 **nostylle, -tul.** [OE. *nostle, nosle*, related to OFris. *nestla, nesla*, MDu. *nastel, nestel*, OHG. *nastila* fem., *nastilo* masc. (G. *nestel*), of uncertain etymology. The Teut. type **nastil-* appears in med.L. as *nastulus, -ula, -ulum, nastola, nastale, -ile*, and in It. as *nastro.*]

1. A band or fillet. (OE. only.)

c **897** K. ÆLFRED *Gregory's Past. C.* xiii. 76 [Hit] sceolde beon awriten..on ðæm hræȝle þe mon hæt rationale, & mid nostlum [*Hatt.* noslum] ȝebunden. *c* **1000** ÆLFRIC *Gloss.* in Wr.-Wülcker 125 *Fascia*, nostle. *Ibid.* 153 *Fasciola*, nosle.

2. A short piece of cord fastened to a net; a NORSEL.

c **1440** *Promp. Parv.* 359/1 Nostylle of nettys (*H.* nostul), *nastula, instita, nasculus.*

Hence †**'nostelling** (see quot.). *Obs.*

Cf. MDu. *nastel-, nestelinc, -ing.*

1615 E. S. *Britain's Buss* in Arb. *Garner* III. 630 Round about the head and two sides of each net, but not at the bottom, must be set a small cord, about the bigness of a bow-string, which is called [the] Head-Roping or Nostelling.

Nostoc ('nɒstɒk). *Bot.* Also 7–8 nostoch, 8 -ock. [A name invented by Paracelsus.] A genus of unicellular *Algæ*, having the cells arranged in rows which intertwine with each other and form a gelatinous mass; *esp.* the ordinary species of this, *Nostoc commune*, formerly believed to be an emanation or deposit from the stars.

1650 CHARLTON tr. *Van Helmont's Paradoxes* Transl. Suppl. 98 Nostoch understandeth the nocturnall Pollution of some plethoricall and wanton Star, or rather excrement blown from the nostrills of some rheumatick planet,..in consistence like a gelly, and so trembling if touched. **1650** J. FRENCH *Chym. Dict.*, *Nostoch* is that which we call a falling star, a kind of gelly or slime found oftentimes in the Summer in fields, and meadowes. **1701–2** DE LA PRYME *Let.* in *Diary* (Surtees) 247 A bottle of Nostock..called Star Slough, or Star Shot Gelly,..a substance that falls from the starrs. **1753** CHAMBERS *Cycl. Suppl.*, *Nostoch*, the name of a vegetable substance which seems to differ from most of the other bodies of that kind, in several particulars. **1834** W. MACGILLIVRAY *Lives Zoologists* 208 This phlegm is a vegetable called nostoc. **1843** *Penny Cycl.* XXVII. 805/2 The species of *Nostoc* are found on damp earth, as well as in sea and fresh water. Most of them are gelatinous,..and shrink almost to nothing in drying. **1895** VINES *Text-bk. Bot.* III. 234 Nostoc is constantly found in the tissue of certain Hepaticæ.

attrib. **1872–3** W. ARCHER in *Grevillea* I. 23 Fibres, from which break forth, through the 'Nostoc-jelly', the first root hairs. **1874–5** H. WOOD *ibid.* III. 43 The development of the distinguishing threads of the Collema out of the ordinary Nostoc-cell. **1892** *Syd. Soc. Lex.* s.v. *Nostoc commune*, Nostoc colonies occur as pseudoparasites in the intercellular spaces and cavities of other plants.

b. An individual plant of this genus.

1851 HARVEY *Nereis Boreali-Amer.* 19 Nothing can well be less star-like than a Nostoc, as it lies on the ground. **1882–4** M. C. COOKE *Brit. Fresh-Water Algæ* I. 221 Nostocs should be dried as quickly as possible after they are collected.

Hence **nosto'c(h)aceous, 'nostochine** *adjs.*

1857 BERKELEY *Introd. Cryptogamic Bot.* 146 Sometimes ..a connecting cell is formed, as in the Nostochine genus *Sphærozyga.* **1872–3** W. ARCHER in *Grevillea* I. 25 Such nostochaceous plants as live in moist or wet habitats.

nosto'mania. *Path.* [mod.L.; see NOSTALGIA and -MANIA. So Sp. and Pg. *nostomania*, F. *nostomanie*.] A kind of madness, an aggravated form of nostalgia.

1855 in OGILVIE *Suppl.*

nosto'maniac. *rare.* [f. NOSTOMANIA: see -AC.] A person affected with nostomania.

1913 R. W. SERVICE *Rhymes of Rolling Stone* 50 The Nostomaniac.

nostos ('nɒstɒs). Also **Nostos.** Pl. nostoi. [Gr. νόστος a return home.] A homecoming, applied *spec.* to the homeward journeys of Odysseus and the other heroes of Troy. Also, the story of such a homecoming or return, esp. as the conclusion of a literary work.

In quots. 1883, 1901, and 1962[1] *Nost(o)i* is the title of a lost poem of the Epic Cycle dealing with the return of the Greek heroes from the Trojan War.

1883 D. B. MUNRO in *Jrnl. Hellenic Studies* IV. 319 A passage of Pausanias (x. 28, 7), mentions, as the poems which contain descriptions of the infernal regions, the *Odyssey*, the *Minyas*, and the *Nostoi*. **1901** —— *Homer's Odyssey Bks. XIII–XXIV* 380 We may regard the *Nosti* as a tragic *Odyssey*. **1920** J. JOYCE *Let.* 12 July (1957) I. 143 A great part of the Nostos or close was written several years ago and the style is quite plain. **1924** T. W. ALLEN *Homer: Origins & Transmission* 333, I have found a reference to their Nostos in Plutarch. **1957** N. FRYE *Anat. of Criticism* iii. 159 It is rare, in literature as in life, to find even a domesticated animal peacefully living through its full span of life... The exceptions, such as Odysseus' dog, are appropriate to the theme of *nostos* or full close of a cyclical movement. **1962** M. BOWRA in Wace & Stubbings *Compan. to Homer* iii. 40 The tradition that he composed the *Iliad* and the *Odyssey* becomes less impressive when he is credited by different authorities with the *Thebais*, *Epigonoi*, *Cypria*, and *Nostoi*. **1962** THOMAS & STUBBINGS in *Ibid.* ix. 292 Agamemnon, on his *nostos*, was carried away as he approached Malea. **1968** C. R. BEYE *Iliad, Odyssey & Epic Tradition* v. 161 The story of homecoming had a name: *nostos*. The several *nostoi* are a leitmotiv throughout the *Odyssey* which is over-all a *nostos*, being the return of Odysseus. There is a hint in the *Odyssey* that epics of *nostoi* were currently fashionable.

Nostra'damic, *a.* [f. next.] Similar to that of Nostradamus.

a **1834** SURTEES in G. Taylor *Mem. R. S.* (Surtees) 263 For much of Nostradamic lore The aged dame still kept in store.

Nostradamus (nɒstrə'deɪməs). [Latinized form of the name of Michel de *Nostredame*, a French physician (1503–1566) who published a collection of prophecies in 1555.] One who professes to foretell future events; a seer comparable to Nostradamus.

1668 DRYDEN *Even. Love* II. i, There's nothing more uncertain than the cold Prophecies of these Nostradamusses. **1810** *Q. Rev.* IV. 250 The Nostradamuses of opposition altered their tone, and began to foretel the final success of the French. **1859** WRAXALL tr. *R. Houdin* v. 59, I need not a Nostradamus to predict that you will devote yourself to it some day. **1870** BREWER *Dict. Phr. & Fable* s.v., The Nostradamus of Portugal. Gonçalo Annës Bandarra.

Nostraine, obs. var. NASRANI.

Nostratic (nɒ'strætɪk), *a.* Also **Nostratian.** [ad. G. *nostratisch*, f. L. *nostrās, -ātis* of our country: see -IC.] (See quots.)

1931 J. W. SPARGO tr. *Pedersen's Linguistic Science in Nineteenth Century* viii. 338 As a comprehensive designation for the families of languages which are related to Indo-European, we may employ the expression *Nostratian Languages* (from Latin *nostrās* 'our countryman'). **1966** B. COLLINDER in Birnbaum & Puhvel *Anc. Indo-Europ. Dial.* 199 Holger Pedersen used to speak about a 'nostratic' family of languages, comprising Indo-European, Semitic-Egyptian-Hamitic, Uralic, Altaic, Yukagir, and Eskimo. **1966** M. PEI *Gloss. Linguistic Terminol.* 136 *Japhetic*, a hypothetical language family claimed to include North Caucasian, South Caucasian, Sumerian, Elamite, Asianic, Basque, Etruscan, etc... *Synonyms*: Alarodian, Nostratic. **1973** *Jrnl. R. Asiatic Soc.* 46 The term Nostratic is defined by the words in brackets following the title of the book, 'Semito-Hamitic, Kartvelian, Indo-European, Uralian, Dravidian, Altaic'.

'nostrificate, *v. rare.* [ad. mod.L. *nostrificāre*, f. *nostri-*, *noster* our + *-ficāre* (see -FY).] *trans.* Of Austrian universities: To admit (foreign degrees) to the same status as the native ones. So **nostrifi'cation.**

1885 *U.S. Cons. Rep.* No. 54. 482 (Cent.), There are no definite rules for the nostrification of foreign diplomas [in Austria]. **1889** *Lancet* II. 810 Buda Pesth—A special examination..for the purpose of 'Nostrificating' the Edinburgh M.D. held by Dr. John Brodie.

no-strike, *adj. phr.* orig. *U.S.* Also **no strike.** [STRIKE *sb.* 9.] Applied in industrial relations to agreements, etc., in which there is a guarantee that the workforce will not strike as long as certain conditions are met.

1942 *Federal Reporter* 2nd Ser. CXXVII. 31/2 Neuhoff.. objected to a no-strike clause. **1963** *U.S. News & World Rep.* 6 May 92/2 Another proposal calls for working out a no-strike agreement, with disputes to be settled by a 'labor court' if unions and publishers are unable to agree. **1965** H. KAHN *On Escalation* i. 10 A 'no strike' policy..rarely works for any length of time. **1973** *N.Y. Law Jrnl.* 27 July 1/7 Participation by employees in a strike in violation of a 'no-strike' clause..did not constitute misconduct. **1976** *CQ Almanac 1975* 487/2 Amendments..allowed employers to seek an injunction against common site picketing that violated a no-strike clause. **1981** *Business Week* 7 Dec. 35/1 McBride has been meeting with U.S. Steel officials to negotiate a no-strike pledge to be used in 1983 bargaining in the steel industry. **1984** *Financial Times* 13 Nov. 9/3 The main English clearing banks will reject a no-strike undertaking to be offered by the 97,000-strong Clearing Bank Union.

nostril ('nɒstrɪl), *sb.* Forms: α. 1 **nosþyrl, -ðyrl,** 5 **-thirl,** 6–7 **-thril(l,** 7 **-threl.** β. 1 **nosterl,** 4–6 **-trell(e,** 5–7 **-trel;** 4, 6–7 **nostrill,** 6 **-teril,** 7– **nostril.** [OE. *nosþyrl*, f. stem of *nosu* NOSE: cf. NOSE-THIRL and OFris. *nosterle*.]

1. One of the two openings in the nose in man and most vertebrate animals; an opening serving a similar purpose in other forms of animal life.

α. *c* **1000** ÆLFRIC *Hom.* II. 98 Se bræþ on heora nosþyrlum. *c* **1050** *Sax. Leechd.* I. 72 (B), Do on þa nosþyrlu. *Ibid.* 352 Do on þæt nosþyrl. *c* **1500** *Yng. Childr. Bk.* in *Babees Bk.* 25 Wype not thi nose nor þi nos-thirlys. **1565** COOPER *Thesaurus, Naris*, the nosthrille. **1597** BEARD *Theatre God's Judgem.* (1612) 150 See what a hooke the Lord put in the nosthrils of this barking dogge. **1626** BACON *Sylva* §63 When the Spirits, that come to the nosthrils, expell a bad Sent [etc.]. **1669** W. SIMPSON *Hydrol. Chym.* 95 Vapours..distill..by the nosthrils.

β. *c* **1000** ÆLFRIC *Gloss.* in Wr.-Wülcker 117 *Vibrissæ*, nosterla hær. *Ibid.* 157 *Pinnulae*, uteweard nosterle. **1387** TREVISA *Higden* (Rolls) I. 185 Sponges i-watred and i-holde at hir nostrilles. *Ibid.* III. 11 Precious stones þat schulde.. be i-holde to þe nostrelle of men. **1486** *Bk. St. Albans* c vij, Castyng wat thorogh her Nostrellis or hir nares. **1535** COVERDALE *Job* xxvii. 3 As longe as the wynde..is in my nostrels. **1576** FLEMING *Panopl. Epist.* ¶iij, My nostrells [were fed] with most comfortable sauours. **1586** MARLOWE *2nd Pt. Tamburl.* IV. iv. 8 And blow the morning from their nosterils. **1607** DEKKER & MARSTON *Northw. Hoe* v. D.'s Wks. 1873 III. 67 Out of my nostrils, tapster, thou smelst like Guild-hall two daies after Simon and Jude. **1667** MILTON *P.L.* x. 280 So sented the grim Feature, and upturn'd His Nostril wide into the murkie Air. **1709** STEELE *Tatler* No. 35 ¶2 To supply his weak Brain with Powder at the nearest Place of Access, viz. the Nostrils. **1777** PRIESTLEY *Matt. & Spir.* (1782) I. v. 54 Could we have had any idea..of smell without the nostrils, and the olfactory nerves? **1834** MᶜMURTRIE *Cuvier's Anim. Kingd.* 36 His nostrils, more complicated than those of the monkey, are less so than those of all other genera. **1877** BRYANT *Odyss.* v. 548 The brine gushed forth From mouth and nostrils.

transf. **1854** BREWSTER *More Worlds* iii. 39 The lofty peak with its cap of ice or its nostrils of fire.

b. *fig.* with reference to persons.

1644 MILTON *Areop.* (Arb.) 54 An imposition which I cannot beleeve how he that..is but of a sensible nostrill should be able to endure. **1678** BUNYAN *Pilgr.* I. 110 That makes Religion to stink in the nostrils of many. **1771** BURKE *Middlesex Election* Wks. X. 65 Our judgments stink in the nostrils of the people. **1844** EMERSON *Nature* Wks. (Bohn) II. 231 There is no end..so sacred or so large, that, if pursued for itself, will not at last become carrion and an offence to the nostril. **1887** LOWELL *Democracy* 78 Its moral nostrils were of an equally masculine temper.

c. *techn.* in smelting (see quot.).

1839 URE *Dict. Arts* 825 Below this narrow part, eight holes..are perforated obliquely through the substance of the trompe, called the vent-holes or nostrils, for admitting the air, which the water carries with it in its descent.

2. *attrib.*, as †**nostril(s)-dropping** (see quot.); **nostril-piece**, a part between the nose and lip of an insect, supposed to correspond to the nostrils of quadrupeds.

1708 KERSEY, *Nostrils-Dropping* [**1726** BAILEY, *Nostril*], a Distemper in Cattel. **1826** KIRBY & SP. *Entomol.* xxxiv. III. 481 A part of the nose [*sc.* of an insect]..which I have.. named the *Rhinarium* or nostril-piece.

Hence **no'strility**, prominence of nostril. *rare.*

1885 J. JACOBS in *Jrnl. Anthropol. Inst.* XV. 54 It is not alone this 'nostrility' which makes a Jewish face so easily recognizable. **1899** —— in *Pop. Sci. Monthly* LV. 510 Jewish 'nostrility', as I have termed it,..can not be affected by change of environment.

nostril ('nɒstrɪl), *v.* [f. the sb.] To look like or function as a nostril; to inhale or exhale through one's nose. So **'nostrilled** *ppl. a.*, having nostrils, freq. of a particular kind.

The *transf.* use in quot. 1942 is unusual.

1909 *Athenæum* 31 July 125/1 The characteristically Irish 'nostrilled' portraits of the four Evangelists. **1939** E. HEMINGWAY *Fifth Column* 131 His outstretched, wide-nostrilled muzzle. **1942** A. L. ROWSE *Cornish Childhood* (1943) 36 The blue summer sea curling round the ships of those emigrant miners, the water nostrilling the stem. **1971** A. HUNTER *Gently at Gallop* v. 49 He was smoking a small, sooty briar... He nostrilled a couple of wisps of smoke.

nostrum ('nɒstrəm). [ad. L. *nostrum*, neut. sing. of *noster*, our.]

1. A medicine, or medical application, prepared by the person recommending it; *esp.* a quack remedy, a patent medicine.

1602 F. HERRING *Anat.* 15 Setting to sale their witlesse Nostrums. [**1654** WHITLOCK *Zootomia* 103 He will put *Nostrum*, to *Album Græcum*.., *Pilulæ de Tribus*, or the like he wraps up in this blind *Nostrum*.] **1704** SWIFT *T. Tub* v, A certain curious Receipt, a Nostrum, which..I found among his Papers. **1754** *Phil. Trans.* XLVIII. 854 The kermes mineral, once altogether as much celebrated..as any antimonial nostrum now-a-days. **1795** WOLCOT (P. Pindar) *Hair Powder* Wks. 1812 III. 301 No Nostrum gives the bloom of health again. **1852** THACKERAY *Esmond* I. ii, The doctors and quack-salvers..experimenting on his poor little body with every conceivable nostrum. **1883** *Law Rep.* 23 Chanc. Div. 735 The owner of a nostrum of some kind, called a patent food.

fig. **1713** *Guardian* No. 36, I look upon punning as a Nostrum, a *Medicina Gymnastica*, that throws off all the bad humours. **1787** BURNS *Holy Fair* xvi, In guid time comes an antidote Against sic poosion'd nostrum.

b. A recipe. *rare*⁻¹.

1742 *Lond. & Country Brew.* I. (ed. 4) 67 This then is the true Nostrum of Brewing.

2. A special means or device for accomplishing something; *esp.* a pet scheme, or favourite remedy, for bringing about some social or political reform or improvement.

1749 FIELDING *Tom Jones* x. Chapter iv, Containing infallible nostrums for procuring universal disesteem and hatred. **1780** COWPER *Progr. Error* 595 Swallow the two grand nostrums they dispense, That scripture lies, and blasphemy is sense. **1816** 'QUIZ' *Grand Master* IV. 83 The parson's holy nostrum, Must be proclaimed, from a rostrum. **1850** KINGSLEY *Alt. Locke* x, Another party's nostrum is, more churches, more schools, more clergymen. **1884** *Sat. Rev.* 7 June 731/2 The incurable faith of some English Liberals in the party nostrums.

3. *Comb.*, as **nostrum-monger**, one who deals in nostrums; hence **nostrum-mongership, -mongery.** Now *rare* or *Obs.*

1706 BAYNARD *Cold Baths* II. 203 Your *Nostrum-monger Dr. Stew-Toad. **1775** SHERIDAN *St. Patrick's Day* II. iv, Will you submit to be cured by a quack nostrum-monger? **1802** *Spirit Public Jrnls.* VI. 254 A bottle of his nostrum, in compliment to the greatest nostrum-monger of the age [= Pitt]. **1748** RICHARDSON *Clarissa* (1811) III. xxi. 134 Should I be outwitted with all my sententious boasting conceit of my own *nostrum-mongership.., I should certainly hang, drown, or shoot myself. **1812** *Examiner* 30 Nov. 764/1 That pernicious system of *nostrum-mongery which is so prevalent.

nostul, nostylle: see NOSTEL.

†**nosul, nosylle,** obs. variants of OUZEL.

14.. *Lat. & Eng. Voc.* in Wr.-Wülcker 597 *Nodosa*, a nosul, *avis est.* **1483** *Cath. Angl.* 256/2 A Nosylle; *quedam Auis, merulus, merula.*

'nosy, *a. rare*⁻¹. [f. NOSE *sb.* + -Y: cf. NOSEY *a.*] Having a prominent nose.

1620 SHELTON *Quix.* II. xiv. 90 The Story leaves them, to tell who was the Knight of the Glasses and his nosie Squire.

nosy, var. NOSEY *a.*

nosyll, obs. variant of NUZZLE *v.*[1]

not (nɒt), *a.* and *sb.*[1] Now *dial.* Forms: 1 **hnot,** 4, 6– **not,** 6, 9 **nott,** 9 **knot;** 6, 9 **nat,** 9 **natt.** [OE. *hnot*, of obscure origin.]

†**1.** Close-cropped, short-haired. *Obs.*

c **1000** ÆLFRIC *Gram.* ix. (Z.) 35 *Glabrio*, calu oððe hnot. *c* **1386** CHAUCER *Prol.* 109 A not-heed hadde he, with a broun visage. **1399** LANGL. *Rich. Redeles* III. 46 Thanne comeþ þer.. As not of his nolle, as he þe nest made, Anoþer proud partriche. **1620** B. JONSON *News fr. Moon* (Rtldg.) 616/2 Not heads and broad hats, short doublets and long points.

†**b.** *Comb.*, as *not-headed, -pated* adjs. *Obs.*

1596 SHAKS. *1 Hen. IV*, II. iv. 78 Wilt thou rob this Leatherne Ierkin, Christall button, Not-pated, Agat ring? **1611–2** CHAPMAN *Widowes T.* Wks. 1873 III. 18 Your not-headed Countrie Gentleman. **1633** B. JONSON *Tale Tub* I. iii, The incorrigible Nott-headed beast, the clowns, or constables, Still let them gaze.

†**2.** Of a willow: Pollard. *Obs. rare*⁻¹.

931 in Birch *Cartul. Sax.* II. 357 þam lange grafette suðeweardon to ðon hnottan seale on Searleage stent.

3. Of sheep or cattle: Hornless, polled.

1587 MASCALL *Gov. Cattle, Sheep* (1627) 237 Some say, that a horned ram is ill to get lambs:..therfore the nat ram is counted the better. **1596** HARINGTON *Metam. Ajax* Prol., He massacred a whole flocke of good nott-ewes. **1601** HOLLAND *Pliny* I. 50 They have not all of them hornes, but some are nott;..the nott she goats are more free of milk. **1787** GROSE *Prov. Gloss.*, *Not*, smooth, polled or shorn. *Not-sheep*, sheep without horns. *Essex.* **1807** VANCOUVER *Agric. Devon* (1813) 347 The Old Devonshire dim-faced nott sheep. **1868–** in southern dial. glossaries, of sheep and cows. **1891** HARDY *Tess* xvii, Why do nott cows give less milk in a year than horned?

b. *sb.* A hornless sheep.

1837 YOUATT *Sheep* vii. 253 The Devonshire notts, or polled sheep, used..to be at least middle-woolled, if not short-woolled sheep. **1875** PENGELLY *Verbal Prov.* 113 (E.D.D.), A cross of the new Leicester with the Bampton nott.

†**4.** Of wheat or barley: Awnless, beardless. *Obs.*

1602 CAREW *Cornwall* 20 Of Wheate there are two sorts, French, which is bearded,..and Notwheate, so termed because it is vnbearded. *c* **1680** *Enquiries* 2/2 Do you sow Aleppo wheat,..Not wheat, Pendule wheat?.. Have you.. Not Barleys sown here, or any other Barleys?

†**not,** *v.*[1] *Obs.* Also 6 **notte, nott.** [f. prec.] *trans.* To clip or cut short (the hair or beard).

1530 PALSGR. 645/1, I have notted my heed nowe that sommer is come. **1565** COOPER *Thesaurus* s.v. *Tondeo*, They notted their fathers head and bearde. **1570** FOXE *A. & M.* (ed. 2) III. 1702 Now was hys head notted euil fauordly, and clypped much lyke as a man would clippe a fooles head. **1592** STOW *Ann.* (1631) 570 Hee caused..from thence forth his beard to be notted and no more shauen. **1674** RAY *Coll. Words* 73 To *Not*: and *Notted*: i.e. polled, shorn. *Essex.* [Hence in Ainsworth (1736), etc.]

b. With personal object.

1541 *Rutland MSS.* (Hist. MSS. Comm.) IV. 313 To Mr. Markham, barber, for nottyng my Lordes children, ijs. **1567** GOLDING *Ovid's Met.* x. 204 His Barbare who Was wont to nott him spyed it. **1606** HOLLAND *Sueton.* 19 He would not onely be notted & shaven very precisely, but also have his haire plucked.

†**not**, *v.*², **note**, for *ne wot* know(s) not: see NE and WIT *v.* Forms: α. 2–3 **nat.** β. 3–7 **not,** 6 **nott.** γ. 4–6 **note,** 6 **nolte.** δ. 4, 6 **noot.**

For other parts of the verb *wit* with prefixed negative, see NETE, NIST, NITEN, NOST, NUTE(N.

α. *c* **888** K. ÆLFRED *Boeth.* v. §3 Ic nat ful ȝeare ymb hwæt þu ȝiet tweost. *c* **1000** *Ags. Gosp.* John xii. 35 He nat hwyder he gæð. *c* **1175** *Lamb. Hom.* 31 ȝif he nat to soðe þet heo beoð liues. *c* **1230** *Hali Meid.* 9 Nat tah na mon bute ham self hwat ham sticheð ofte.

β. *a* **1225** *Ancr. R.* 178 þis is þe ancre þet not nout hwat is fondunge. *a* **1250** *Owl & Night.* 1621 Ich not neauer to hwan þu miȝt. *c* **1320** *Sir Tristr.* 92 In to þis londes ende Y not non better kniȝt. **1390** GOWER *Conf.* I. 43 He not, til that the chance falle, Wher he schal lese. **1413** *Pilgr. Sowle* (Caxton) I. xv. (1859) 13, I not to whome I shal my seluen dresse! *c* **1480** *Paston Lett.* III. 302 For the peyne I not me wher to hold. **1552** LYNDESAY *Monarche* 19, I nott quhome to thy Simpylnes to sende. **1576** GASCOIGNE *Philomene* (Arb.) 90 As yet I not, what proper hew it bare. **1614** J. DAVIES (Heref.) *Commend. Poems*, etc. Wks. (Grosart) II. 21/2, I not how I shall thriue therein.

γ. *a* **1300** *E.E.P.* (1862) 153 Soch an oþir an erþe i note. *c* **1425** *Seven Sag.* (P.) 126 Thay hym nome I note how mykil out of Rome. **1494** FABYAN *Chron.* VI. clviii. 147 To bryng his malycious purpose aboute, I note by what sorcery. *a* **1542** WYATT *Ps.* li. Prol., I note whether he cries or sings. **1590** SPENSER *F.Q.* I. xii. 17, I note whether [to] praise or pitty more. **1600** FAIRFAX *Tasso* XVIII. l, But loe (from whence I nolte) a falcon came.

δ. **1377** LANGL. *P. Pl.* B. XI. 207 Noot no man how neighe it is. **1387** TREVISA *Higden* (Rolls) III. 55, I noot ȝif þat was i-doo by his broþer wil. *a* **1425** *Cursor M.* 5265 (Trin.), What cloop was hit . . þat blody was & I noot how.

not (nɒt), *adv.* and *sb.*² Also 4–6 nott, 5 nut, 7– n't. [Abbreviated form of NOUGHT *adv.*: cf. NAT *adv.*] The ordinary adverb of negation.

A. *adv.* **1.** Modifying a simple tense or form of an ordinary verb.

a. Following the verb. Now *arch.*

1362 LANGL. *P. Pl.* A. Prol. 29 As Ancres and Hermytes . . Coueyte not in Cuntre to carien a-boute. **1390** GOWER *Conf.* III. 159 So that here kinges yhe is blent And wot not hou the world is went. *c* **1489** CAXTON *Sonnes of Aymon* iv. 120 They wyst not what folke they were. *Ibid.*, See ye not what folke we ben? **1530** TINDALE *Answ. More* I. Wks. (1573) 276/1 As long as yt signification bode, it hurted not. **1590** SPENSER *F.Q.* I. i. 30 With holy father sits not with such thinges to mell. **1628** BP. HALL *Old Relig.* 194, I differ not from the iudgement of our best . . Classical Diuines. **1653** WALTON *Angler* IV. v, Let not your line exceed . . three or four hairs at the most. *a* **1700** DRYDEN (J.), Let each man do as to his fancy seems; I wait not, I, 'till you have better dreams. **1789** *Triumphs Fortitude* I. 101, I doubt not but they will greatly contribute [etc.]. **1798** COLERIDGE *Anc. Mar.* IV. ii, Fear not, fear not, thou Wedding Guest! This body dropt not down. **1821** BYRON *Sardanap.* IV. i, I seek . . no pleasure but in parting not. **1870** MORRIS *Earthly Par.* I. I. 424 Thou shalt see the day Unharmed, if that dread box thou openest not.

b. Preceding the verb. Chiefly *poet.*

c **1400** *Laud Troy Bk.* 3092 Whan Troyens dede this trespas, Menelaus at home not was. **1483** *Cath. Angl.* 256/2 To Nott moghe; *nequire, non posse.* **1608** SYLVESTER *Du Bartas* II. iv. *Schisme* 617 (Saving Henoch) onely hee not-dies. **1610** SHAKS. *Temp.* II. i. 121, I not doubt He came aliue to Land. **1650** GENTILIS *Considerations* 45, I (to not wonder at it) doe rather consider whence it proceeds. **1740** JOHNSON *Life Drake* Wks. IV. 419 They . . possessed the island, but not enjoyed it. **1816** BYRON *Ch. Har.* III. lxv, Making a marvel that it not decays.

c. With ellipsis of dependent clause after certain verbs, as *do, have, know, say not.* colloq.

1906 KIPLING *Puck of Pook's Hill* 147 'Did *you* have a governess, then?' 'Did we not? A Greek too.' **1918** C. MACKENZIE *Early Life Sylvia Scarlett* II. vii. 450 '. . Do you remember a man called Leopold Hansberg?' 'Do I not?' Sylvia exclaimed. **1936** M. ALLINGHAM *Flowers for Judge* iv. 74 'I suppose they've been questioning you . .?' 'Have they not!' Mike spoke explosively. **1973** C. AIRD *His Burial Too* ii. 28 Your father always puts it in the book . . I've never known him not.

2. a. Following an auxiliary verb. Also in the reduced form *n't*, usually written as one word with the verb.

α. *a* **1340** HAMPOLE *Psalter* xxxiv. 22 þai sall not ouercum þaim. **1382** WYCLIF *Luke* x. 42 The beste part, which schal not be take a wey fro hir. *c* **1450** *Merlin* 243 He nys no knyght that will not deffende his londe. **1508** KENNEDIE *Flyting w. Dunbar* 433 Thou may not pas Mount Barnard for wild bestis. **1577** FULKE *Answ. True Christian* 25 You can not proue that your church hath canonized the Apostles. **1632** B. JONSON *Epigr.* xxxiii, I'll not offend thee with a vain tear more. **1710** SHAFTESB. *Adv. to Author* II. i, The Arts and Sciences must not be left Patron-less. **1766** GOLDSM. *Vic. W.* xiv, His presence did not interrupt our conversation. **1820** KEATS *Eve St. Agnes* xxxviii, Though I have found, I will not rob thy nest. **1884** tr. *Lotze's Logic* 323 The act of severance has not produced any lasting . . excitement.

β. **1652** TATHAM *Scotch Figgaries* IV. i, But mayn't I Bar points, being the Challenged? **1672–1774** [see DO *v.* 29]. **1674** N. FAIRFAX *Bulk & Selvedge* 130 They can't strike sail . . in a trice. **1834** MAR. EDGEWORTH *Helen* III. v. 160 'No no, I can't sit, can't stay,' said Lady Cecilia. **1852** THACKERAY *Esmond* III. ii, That was . . one [duty] that she wouldn't have broke her heart in trying to do. **1895** GISSING *Eve's Ransom* 110 You mustn't tell me anything.

b. *ellipt.* in replies. Freq. with *that.*

1629 MASSINGER *Picture* I. ii, *Eubulus.* Have you ne'er read The story of Semiramis and Ninus? *Honoria.* Not as I remember. **1866** MEREDITH *Vittoria* xxxix, 'Carlo Ammiani will marry her, I presume,' said Lena. 'Not before he has met Captain Weisspriess [etc.].' **1939** 'N. BLAKE' *Smiler with Knife* i. 13 You never knew when . . Nigel [would] be dragged into some queer criminal tangle. Not that they really needed the substantial fees he charged. **1967** *Listener* 7 Dec. 762/3 We should recall our initial experience of a creative personality as strong as Mahler's . . Not that Koechlin is a Mahler, but at best he is an original.

3. a. Following the substantive verb. Also as *n't.*

α. **1362** LANGL. *P. Pl.* A. IX. 75 Ho . . is not dronkeleuh ne deynous Dowel him folewęþ. **1475** *Paston Lett.* III. 130 Iff the market be nott goode yit, I hope it shall be better. **1596** SHAKS. *Merch. V.* V. i. 35 *Mes.* I pray you is my Master yet return'd? *Loren.* He is not. **1597** —— *2 Hen. IV*, I. ii. 238 There is not a daungerous Action . . but I am thrust vpon it. **1645** MILTON *Colasterion* 20 These matters are not for pragmatics . . to babble in. **1685** LOVELL *Gen. Hist. Relig.* 8 Amongst them Laicks are not constrained to confess once a year. **1710** STEELE *Tatler* No. 181 ¶2 At which Time I was not quite Five Years of Age. **1791** BURKE *Corr.* (1844) III. 282 This is not the cause of a king, but of kings. **1821** SHELLEY *Epipsych.* 52, I am not thine: I am a part of thee. **1898** ILLINGWORTH *Div. Immanence* iii. (1904) 35/2 This is unquestionably not the case.

β. **1701** FARQUHAR *Sir H. Wildair* IV. ii, I an't to be believed. *a* **1703** POMFRET *Cruelty & Lust* (1724) 70 Since in Battle you can greater be, That over, be'nt less merciful than he. **1706–** [see AN'T, AIN'T, and IN'T]. **1895** MISS MONTRESOR *Highw. & Hedges* I. vi, It isn't true.

b. With ellipse of verb, esp. after *if*, or in replies.

1399 LANGL. *Rich. Redeles* III. 151 But [they] beggith and borwith . . And not þe better of a bene. **1671** MILTON *Samson* 971 Fame if not double-fac't is double-mouth'd. **1740** CHEYNE *Regimen* 311 Body and Spirit . . will eternally be *disparata*, if not contradictory. **1864–8** BROWNING *J. Lee's Wife* IV. iv, No Love! not so indeed! **1883** 'ANNIE THOMAS' *Mod. Housewife* 143 'Not to be done!' Mrs. Sampson said decidedly.

c. *not the* (. .): an introductory formula used humorously in the titles of publications, etc., to qualify the name of something that is being parodied or satirized. (Chiefly in allusion to the name of the 'alternative' British television comedy programme referred to in quot. 1979.)

1979 *Daily Tel.* 18 Oct. 15/8 The postponement of *Not The Nine O'Clock News* (BBC-2) earlier in the year because of the General Election would seem to suggest that the BBC is over sensitive about sensitivities of politicians. **1981** *Not the Church Times* 22 Sept. 1/2 We apologise for the statement in last week's edition of Not The Church Times that the Archbishop of Canterbury is a Methodist. This was wrong. **1984** T. HEPBURN (*title*) Not the 1984 Olympics.

4. Preceding an infinitive or gerundial clause. Esp. with imperative force; freq. in colloq. phr. ***not to worry***, do not worry.

c **1440** *Alph. Tales* 135 To ly in his bed & not com att matyns at mydnyght. **1469** *Anc. Cal. Rec. Dublin* (1889) 333 [That] hit be lawfull to any suche swyne to be killet, and the killers of them note to be empechit. **1582** N. LICHEFIELD tr. *Castanheda's Conq. E. Ind.* 128 He praied him not to say him nay. **1639** AINSWORTH *Pentateuch* 44 They failed in not casting out the inhabitants. **1673** RAY *Journ. Low C.* 159 It seldom happens the Council-chamber not to be full. **1719** DE FOE *Crusoe* II. (Globe) 321, I knew neither what to do, or what not to do. **1751** JOHNSON *Rambler* No. 175 ¶9 It is, indeed, impossible not to hear . . of wrongs and falsehoods. **1812** BYRON *Ch. Har.* I. vii, It was a vast and venerable pile; So old, it seemed only not to fall. **1853** MRS. GASKELL *Cranford* ix, Miss Pole clutched my arm, and begged me not to turn. **1872** TENNYSON *Gareth & Lynette* 1207 One who came to help thee, not to harm. **1872** GEO. ELIOT *Middlem.* II. xxxvii. 258 And he objects to a secretary: please not to mention that again. **1958** *Daily Mail* 24 July 6/5 Not to worry. By the time he . . had finished with me . . I'd be doing long division. **1965** L. MEYNELL *Double Fault* I. iii. 31 'We'll send it for you.' 'Not to bother. I'm going down to the country this evening.' **1967** *Spectator* 11 Aug. 160/1 In short, to borrow one of Mr. William's own favoured colloquialisms, not to worry. **1970** V. CANNING *Great Affair* xiv. 269 He gave me a big grin and said, 'Not to be overcome, son.'

5. †**a.** Used redundantly after verbs of forbidding, dissuading, or preventing. *Obs.*

c **1380** WYCLIF *Wks.* (1880) 106 þei forbeden not vtterly þat men schulden not preche þe gospel. **1430–40** LYDG. *Bochas* (1554) 22 b, Bochas forbade husbandes . . Without prefe not leve to sone their wyves. *c* **1540** *Pol. Verg. Eng. Hist.* (Camden) 118 The earle had diswadyd the king not to place his syster Margaret in maryage unto Charles. **1569** J. SANFORD tr. *Agrippa's Van. Artes* 81 A lawe whiche did forbidde that they shoulde not woorshippe images. **1677** GILPIN *Demonol.* (1867) 414 Contrary to other plain scriptures prohibiting not to tempt the Lord.

b. Coupled with other negatives, or repeated. Now *dial.* or *vulgar.*

1426 AUDELAY *Poems* 10 Thai wold not on us have no pete. **1471** *Paston Lett.* III. 15 Take heede . . that they be not in noon place wher that sykenesse is regnyng. **1503** HAWES *Examp. Virt.* I. xii, I wyll not medle with no duplycyte. **1568** GRAFTON *Chron.* II. 739 They should not neede no more to feare him then his shadowe. **1606** HOLLAND *Sueton.* 105 Hee absented not himselfe in no place. **1632** LITHGOW *Trav.* I. 24 Rauenna, which for antiquity will not bow her top to none in Italy. **1654** tr. *Scudery's Curia Pol.* 149 We resolve then to . . render her incapable not to offend us.

6. Preceding a sentence, clause, or word.

a. In introductory phrases, as ***not but*** (***that***), ***not that***, † ***not for-thy***, etc. (See also BUT C. 18.)

a **1340** HAMPOLE *Psalter* xxxiv. 22 Not forthi thai takyn with eȝhen, as thai lufid me. **1382** WYCLIF *John* vi. 46 Not for ony man syȝ the fadir, no but this that is of God. *Ibid.* 59 Not as ȝoure fadris eeten manna, and ben deed. *c* **1420** *Pallad. on Husb.* XII. 224 Yet not for thy thei may endure in colde. **1470–85** MALORY *Arthur* X. xxx. 463 Not for thenne they bothe lyghtely aroos. **1601** SHAKS. *Jul. C.* III. ii. 23 Not that I lou'd Cæsar lesse, but that I lou'd Rome more. **1678–9** DRYDEN & LEE *Œdipus* IV. i, Not but you were adorned with all the riches That empire could bestow. **1766** GOLDSM. *Vic. W.* i, Not but that we sometimes had those little rubs [etc.]. **1784** COWPER *Task* VI. 981 Not that he peevishly rejects a mode Because that World adopts it. **1856** F. E. PAGET *Owlet of Owlst.* 52 Not but what I consider discretion to be the better part of valour. **1864** MEREDITH *Belloni* xxv, Not that she conceived him designedly base.

b. Placed first for the sake of emphasis.

1554 PHILPOT *Exam. & Writ.* (Parker Soc.) 384 Not for this we bring in a church like to thilk city of Plato. **1578** TIMME *Calvin on Gen.* 180 Nevertheless . . not they are called righteous, which are perfect in each point. **1667** MILTON *P.L.* III. 26 Yet not the more Cease I to wander. **1697** DRYDEN *Virg. Georg.* III. 413 Nor cou'd his Kindred . . change his fatal Course. No, not the dying Maid. **1747** P. FRANCIS tr. *Hor. Ep.* I. xvii, Not every one shall reach the wisht-for port. **1804** DR. PARR in *Bentham's Wks.* (1843) X. 417 Not so doth Godwin and his French followers. **1885–94** R. BRIDGES *Eros & Psyche* I. xiii, Not long, I wot, shall that poor girl of Crete God it in my despite.

c. In contrast with a following *but.*

1579 SPENSER *Sheph. Cal.* July 115 The hylls . . I reverence and adore: Not for themselfe, but for the sayncts [etc.]. **1611** BIBLE *John* i. 13 Which were borne, not of blood, . . but of God. **1635** J. HAYWARD tr. *Biondi's Banish'd Virg.* 148 Discovering what it not hid but vailed. **1768** TUCKER *Lt. Nat.* II. 460, I may believe myself—not a perceptivity but a perceptive spirit. **1849** MACAULAY *Hist. Eng.* vi. II. 104 To use their arms in defence, not of the mass book, but of the Bible. **1874** L. STEPHEN *Hours in Library* (1892) I. vi. 201 He has peopled not a country town but a metropolis.

d. Emphasizing a pronoun after a negative statement, or in a reply.

c **1625** DEKKER, ROWLEY, & FORD *Witch Edmonton* IV. i, He is no Witch, not he. **1722** DE FOE *Col. Jack* (1840) 218, I challenge you, sir! not I, I made no challenge. **1783** BECKFORD *Dreams*, etc. viii. 51 They had no notion, not they, of admiring barren crags and precipices. **1846** DICKENS *Battle of Life* i, 'Did you never hear [etc.]?' 'No, father!' 'No, not you, of course; you're a woman.' **1889** J. K. JEROME *Three Men in Boat* xvii, They are not to be 'had' by a bit of worm on the end of a hook, . . not they!

7. a. With terms of number or quantity.

c **1325** *E.E. Allit. P.* A. 343 For anger gaynez þe not a cresse. *Ibid.* 351 þy mendez mountez not a myte. ? *a* **1366** CHAUCER *Rom. Rose* 451 Povert . ., That not a peny hadde in wolde. *a* **1400** *Pistill of Susan* 247, I charge hit not a pere. **1585** JAS. I *Ess. Poesie* (Arb.) 52 Sen though they stay, it harmes him not a hair. **1591** SHAKS. *Two Gent.* IV. ii. 67 *Ho.* I perceiue you delight not in Musique. *Iu.* Not a whit. **1634** MILTON *Comus* 585 Not a period Shall be unsaid for me. **1663** BUTLER *Hud.* I. i. 8 Not a man of them knew wherefore. **1719** DE FOE *Crusoe* II. (Globe) 346 He spoke not a Word. *Ibid.* 496 All this while they fir'd not a Gun. **1817** C. WOLFE *Burial Sir J. Moore* i, Not a drum was heard, not a funeral note. **1849** MACAULAY *Hist. Eng.* x. II. 599 He solemnly assured them that not a hair of their heads should be touched.

b. ***not a little***, a good deal, considerably.

1470–85 MALORY *Arthur* XVII. xvii. 714 Thenne was not he a lytel sory, for launcelot loued hym. *a* **1548** HALL *Chron., Hen. IV*, 24 He not a littell mused but muche more mervailed that the duke [etc.]. **1712** POPE *Spect.* No. 408 ¶7 Young Men whose Passions are not a little unruly. **1838** in Trevelyan *Macaulay* (1876) II. vii. 2 His visits served not a little to enliven. **1845** MCCULLOCH *Taxation* I. ii. (1852) 169 The policy of laying heavy taxes on necessaries is not a little questionable.

c. ***not half*** (see HALF *adv.* 3).

d. ***not all that***, not exceptionally (so).

1964 T. WHITE tr. *Simenon's Maigret & Saturday Caller* iv. 70 'Were they heavy?' . . 'Quite heavy, but not all that.' **1970** *Guardian* 24 Jan. 1/5 Asked how he assessed the capacity of the present relief system of the Federal authorities to cope with widespread starvation, Lord Hunt said: 'Now I don't feel all that confidence in the Nigerian Government's ability to do this.' *Ibid.* 28 Jan. 8/3 Without her voice, Callas is not all that impressive an actress. **1974** *Sat. Rev. World* (U.S.) 19 Oct. 56/2 Several years ago . . I asked him, 'How was the picture?' He . . said, 'Not all that good.' The expression 'not all that good', as far as I know, was fairly new at the time.

8. After *or, if,* or *as*, with ellipse of words expressed or implied in the preceding clause.

c **1400** *Apol. Loll.* 52 A prest weþer he be beneficid or not, he howiþ not to sett to hire his gostly warks. **1503** in *Trans. R. Hist. Soc.* (1902) 152 Ye knowe whether ye maye truste me or not. **1535** COVERDALE *Gen.* xxiv. 21 Tyll he knewe whether the Lorde had prospered his iourney or not. **1611** BIBLE *Gen.* xviii. 21, I will goe downe now, and see whether [etc.]: and if not, I will know. **1724** DE FOE *Mem. Cavalier* (1840) 125 Shall we give battle . . or not? **1738** POPE *Universal Prayer* 47 Thou know'st if best bestow'd or not. **1857** M. ARNOLD *Rugby Chapel* 45 Conscious or not of the past. **1875** JOWETT *Plato* (ed. 2) I. 290 If virtue is of such a nature, it will be taught; and if not, not. **1887** F. M. CRAWFORD *Saracinesca* III. xxxiv. 299, I would just as soon give you up to the Holy Office as not.

9. Denoting contrast or opposition to what precedes, with or without *and.*

1471 *Litt. Red Bk. Bristol* (1900) II. 130 Punyshing the principall sturrers of rebellion ayenst vs, and not a generalte. **1552** *Bk. Com. Prayer, Communion*, They are in heauen and not here. **1621** BURTON *Anat. Mel.* To Rdr. 76, I hate their vices, not their persons. **1649** MILTON *Eikon.* 36 Some of thir Friends, and in the Roman not the pettifogging sense thir Clients. **1678** SHADWELL *Timon* IV. ii, They govern for themselves and not the people. **1837** NEWMAN *Par. Serm.* (ed. 2) III. x. 148 It was a respite, not a resurrection. **1892** TENNYSON *Doubt & Prayer* 12 Till this . ., My prison, not my fortress, fall away!

10. a. With adverbs or adverbial phrases.

1475 *Paston Lett.* III. 123 The Emperor hathe besegyd also, not fferr from these, a castell. *c* **1500** *Melusine* 297 And whan Raymondyn perceyued it, wete it wel that he was ryght dolaunt and sorowful & not without cause. **1559** AYLMER *Harborowe* Bj, Happening therfore not long agone to rede a lytle booke. *a* **1648** LD. HERBERT *Hen. VIII* (1683)

369 Not long after which..the King sent George Bolen. **1774** Goldsm. *Nat. Hist.* (1776) II. 296 His method is still, and not without reason, adopted by many. **1818** Coleridge in *Lit. Rem.* (1836) I. 167 The titles of the poet..and the general not seldom formed a garland round the same head. **1852** Tennyson *Death Wellington* viii, Not once or twice.. The path of duty was the way to glory.

b. Modifying adjectives or participles in agreement with a preceding substantive or pronoun.

1529 Cromwell *Will* in Merriman *Life & Lett.* (1902) I. 63 The residue of all my goodes catalles and debttes not bequethed. **1596** B. Griffin *Fidessa* 37 Whil'st I..doe sit in heauie plight.., Not daring rush into so rare a place. **1614** R. Tailor *Hog hath lost Pearl* in Dodsley (1780) VI. 408 Where penitency, not disturb'd may grieve. **1820** Lamb *Elia* Ser. I. *Christ's Hospital*, The remnants left at his table (not many, nor very choice fragments). **1844** Kinglake *Eothen* (1845) 186, I rose from a state of half-oblivion, not much unlike to sleep. **1889** Jerome *Idle Thoughts* 112 You have got to be regarded as not quite right in your head.

c. With negative adjectives or adverbs, implying the affirmative term. (See also bad *a.* 1 c.) Also as *sb.*, **not-bad**.

1657 W. Rand tr. *Gassendi's Life Peiresc* I. 69 The study of antiquity was not unusefull towards the knowledge of the Lawes. **1671** H. M. tr. *Erasm. Colloq.* 85 We say well and elegantly, not ungrateful, for very grateful. **1765** Dickson *Treat. Agric.* (ed. 2) 200 The damage done by this is not inconsiderable. **1794** Earl Malmesbury *Diaries & Corr.* III. 117 Not unclever but importunate. **1824** Landor *Imag. Conv.*, *Johnson & Tooke*, Perhaps the learned author..was not undelighted with the pleasurable vices of poetry in such company. **1843** Thoreau *Let.* 24 Jan. in *Corr.* (1958) 77 He is, at any rate, one of the not-bad. **1871** Geo. Eliot *Middlem.* I. I. ix. 128 She had got nothing from him more graphic about the Lowick cottages than that they were 'not bad'. **1900** G. C. Brodrick *Mem.* 168 A certain air of dignity, not unmingled with insolence. **1973** A. Ross *Dunfermline Affair* 41 A not-bad job, Farrow. Not bad at all. **1975** *Times* 20 Sept. 8/5 Brian Armstrong's *Bags of Swank* consisted of three not-bad scripts about his National Service.

†**11.** ***not but***, only. = nobbut. *Obs.*

For other forms of sentence in which *not* is followed by *but*, see but *conj.* 4 c, 7 b, c, 9, 16.

c **1374** Chaucer *Compl. Mars* 121 Not but two pases within the yate hit stode. *c* **1400** Maundev. (1839) viii. 96 Betwene that Mount and the Cytee, is not but the Vale of Josaphathe. *c* **1477** Caxton *Jason* 14 All his desir is not but for to mowe come to your goode grace. **1560** Rolland *Crt. Venus* II. 975 Quhair I gat not bot ansueir detestine.

B. *sb.* †**1.** Nought, nothing. *Obs.*

c **1380** Wyclif *Wks.* (1880) 216 þe lord þat made alle þingis of not. *c* **1380** —— *Serm.* Sel. Wks. I. 94 He haþ drede of þing of not. *c* **1400** Love *Bonavent. Mirr.* (1907) 92 It was nouȝt for not that they tauȝten..hem [etc.]. *a* **1450** *Knt. de la Tour* vi. (1868) 9 In suche wise that euer after the housholde yede to not. **1508** Kennedie *Flyting w. Dunbar* 508 Tak the a fidill,..thou art ordanyt to not ellis!

2. The word 'not'; a negation or negative.

1601 Shaks. *All's Well* III. ii. 24, I haue wedded her, not bedded her, and sworne to make the not eternall. **1608** H. Clapham *Errour Left Hand* 82 They still doe returne us a not. **1621** Lady M. Wroth *Urania* 420 Come backe to me, who neuer knew the plot To crosse your minde, or to thy will an nott. **1866** Lowell *Biglow P.*, Introd., Poems 1890 II. 201, I guess ef I was to leave the *nots* out o' some o' the c'man'ments, 't 'ould soot you full ez wall!

3. *Computers.* (Usu. written in capitals.) A Boolean function of one variable that has the value unity if the variable is zero, and *vice versa*. Usu. *attrib.* or as *adj.*

1947 *Proc. IRE* XXXV. 758/2 The 'not' operation is.. performed by an inverter tube. **1950** W. W. Stifler *High-Speed Computing Devices* xiii. 270 This device, called a half adder, will consist of *and*, *or*, and *not* circuits..arranged so as to carry out the operations exemplified in Table 13-1. **1955** R. K. Richards *Arithmetic Operations in Digital Computers* ii. 29 A fundamental concept which is found in Boolean algebra and which has no counterpart in ordinary algebra is the 'not' function, as indicated by a line over a symbol. **1957** Goode & Machol *System. Engin.* xxv. 394 There is..evidence that certain synapses are inhibitory, i.e. not gates. **1969** P. B. Jordain *Condensed Computer Encycl.* 341 NOT is a unary operation since it has only one argument, and it is one of the most fundamental logic operators. **1970** O. Dopping *Computers & Data Processing* i. 26 All logical connections between two-valued variables can be expressed by means of the three functions NOT, AND, and OR. **1972** *IEEE Trans. Computers* XXI. 153/2 When digital computers are synthesized with gates other than AND, OR, and NOT gates, it is difficult to design optimal..networks directly from the Boolean expressions.

C. *Comb.* **1. a.** With verbal substantives.

1561 T. Norton *Calvin's Inst.* I. 3 b, If the notknowing of God be any where to be found. **1587** Golding *De Mornay* xvi. (1592) 262 Goodnes is not a defect or a notdooing of things. **1606** Shaks. *Tr. & Cr.* III. iii. 270 Heele answer no body: he professes not answering. **1652** Gataker *Antinom.* 25 The not drowning of the whole world again. **1695** J. Edwards *Perfect. Script.* 50 The difference of the idiom was sufficient to beget a not-understanding of one another. **1749** Fielding *Tom Jones* VIII. vi, Danger might attend the not dressing his wound. **1816** Byron *Let. to Murray* 20 Feb., You must not mistake my *not* bullying for dejection. **1858** H. W. Beecher *Life Thoughts* (1859) 130 His rests and not-doings seem even more significant than that which was overt.

†**b.** With nouns of action. *Obs.* (Common in 17th cent.; now expressed by *non-*.)

1582 *Reg. Privy Council Scot.* III. 531 His dissobedience in not comperance befoir the Kingis Majestie. **1590** *Ibid.* IV. 521 For not-payment of ministeris stipendis. **1613** Shaks. *Hen. VIII*, IV. i. 30 For not Appearance, and The Kings late Scruple,..she was diuorc'd. *a* **1643** Dudley Digges *Unlawf. Armes* (1647) 102 [They] redeemed their not obedience to him, by offering up their bodies. **1675** J. Smith *Chr. Relig. App.* II. 44 They could not impute their not-recovery to their want of will, but skill.

†**c.** With agent-nouns. *Obs.* (Now *non-*.)

1596 Spenser *Hymn Love* 159 How falles it then that.. Thou doest afflict..the not-deserver? **1619** Sanderson *Serm.* I. 11 The eater despised the not-eater, and the eater judged the not-eater. **1651** *Rec. Communion* §4 To communicate with not-discerners. **1680** H. More *Apocal. Apoc.* 213 If both the Beheaded and the Not-worshippers of the Beast were of the same kind.

d. With other types of nouns. Also not-self.

1575 Fenton *Gold. Epist.* (1582) 85 Our merite or not merite standes not in the seruices which we do to God. **1599** Sandys *Europæ Spec.* (1632) 180 The not possibilitie of erring being..peculiar unto God. **1627** W. Sclater *Exp. 2 Thess.* (1629) 14 It's something, at least a not-nothing. **1645** Howell *Twelve Treat.* (1661) 360 Issuing rather from his not-knowledge of me, than from malice. **1740** Cheyne *Regimen* 311 It must be actually brought to be not-matter. **1818** Bentham *Ch. Eng. Catech. Exam.* 171 In case of not-guiltiness. **1860** Pusey *Min. Proph.* 452 What He attributes to idols, i.e. not-gods. **1867** Mill *Exam. Hamilton's Philos.* (ed. 3) xiii. 289 A complete idea of a closed figure, and of the boundary which incloses it—the outline separating object from not-object.

2. a. With adjectives or past participles.

1587 Golding *De Mornay* i. 3 Wether was first,..of Sensible or Notsensible, of Reasonable, or Notreasonable? **1599** [see next]. *a* **1643** Dudley Digges *Unlawf. Armes* (1647) 124 By the unspeakable scandal of these not-Christian courses. **1663** Boyle *Usef. Exp. Nat. Philos.* I. 15 And I have..made in that admirable Stone a not-inconsiderable Experiment. **1774** Hallifax *Anal. Rom. Law* 117 Punishments..short of Natural or Civil Death, were called Not-Capital. **1819** *Hermit in London* III. 171 Her not-stinted foot was pinched into pink satin shoes. **1874** Darwin in *Life & Lett.* (1887) III. 191 The product of a cross between not-related ants. **1875** Jowett *Plato* (ed. 2) III. 376 Evil is a greater enemy to good than to the not-good.

b. With present participles.

1599 Sandys *Europæ Spec.* (1632) 115 Their not-erring and not controllable Lord of Rome. **1611** Shaks. *Cymb.* II. iv. 19 You shall heare The Legion..sooner landed In our not-fearing-Britaine. **1654** Gataker *Disc. Apol.* 48 Some not-preaching Ministers. **1675** Woodhead, etc. *Par. St. Paul* 17 It was a law then which made not-knowing infants also guilty. **1730–46** Thomson *Autumn* 1226 The village toast..Darts not-unmeaning looks. **1762** Bp. Forbes *Jrnl.* (1886) 215 He asked me how the not-swearing clergy lived now. **1853** Markham *Skoda's Auscult.* 204 The sound produced by striking together two hard, not-ringing (*nicht-klingend*) bodies. **1863** J. Brown *Marjorie Fleming*, *Rab & F.* (1906) 85 A man..to give a second and not-forgetting look at.

c. With adjectival phrases.

1570 Foxe *A. & M.* (ed. 2) III. 1365 Accept my thankes, though they proceed out of a not enough circumcised heart. **1678** Vaughan *Thalia Rediv.*, *The World* (1858) 234 The not-to-be-repented Shares Of time and business. **1863** A. C. Ramsay *Phys. Geogr.* 13 The not-long extinct volcano of the Island of Ascension. **1882** Wallace in *Nature* XXVI. 86 Close individual resemblance of not-nearly-related species of butterflies.

d. Freq. with *so* or *too* and an adj. forming combs. used as *sb.*, *adv.*, or *adj.*

1748 Richardson *Clarissa* II. xiii. 72, I [say]..she is too wise; that is to say..Not so young as she has been. **1851** Lytton (*title*) Not so bad as we seem. **1866** Mrs. Gaskell *Wives & Daughters* I. xxi. 235 It was also evident to her that Osborne was not too happy at home. **1870** Geo. Eliot *Let.* 15 Nov. (1956) V. 120 We..cannot yet decide whether we should..have a modest little refuge in the not-too-distant country. **1931** J. S. Huxley *What dare I Think?* vi. 190 Man believing himself the inhabitant of the Universe's central globe,..looking forward to a not-too-distant end of this terrestrial home, cannot well have the same religion as man knowing himself descended by slow evolution from the brutes. **1935** *Discovery* Sept. 262/1 The not-so-distant days of the pirates. **1941** M. Allingham *Traitor's Purse* xx. 229 'I say, it's pretty serious, isn't it?' He nodded. 'Not so hot. Time's short.' **1943** G. Ade *Let.* 5 Feb. (1973) 238 The not-so-good-news in regard to the soy bean crop does not come as a surprise. **1945** [see atomic *a.* 2 f]. **1945** *Sun* (Baltimore) 29 Oct. 4 A British rubber inspection committee sent out to the plantations of Malaya..reported today that conditions were 'not too bad'. **1951** S. Spender *World within World* iii. 143 One of their not-too-distant neighbours was Lytton Strachey. **1952** A. G. L. Hellyer *Sanders' Encycl. Gardening* (ed. 22) 270 Soil, cool, slightly moist, and a not-too-hot position in the rock garden. **1955** *Radio Times* 22 Apr. 5/1 Where the making of home entertainment is not just a pleasant memory of the not-so-young. **1957** *Times Lit. Suppl.* 13 Dec. 762/5 The not-so-rich lady in the subway solemnly knitting a double-necked jersey. **1960** *Guardian* 20 May 4/5 Access is limited for the not-so-young, the not-so-robust, and those who like to amble. **1962** R. H. Smythe *Anatomy of Dog Breeding* iv. 77 Bred from ancestors of not-so-long-ago. **1965** *Listener* 27 May 766/2 They accepted all the good things..and the not-so-good things, with fatalistic acquiescence. **1971** *Good Motoring* Sept. 3 This incredible phenomenon is the Giant's Causeway, known to most people by pictorial sight but, oddly, not too many know its location. **1972** E. Lemarchand *Cyanide with Compliments* i. 3 Olivia watched the launch filling up. The not-so-young predominated. **1974** *Sat. Rev. World* (U.S.) 19 Oct. 41/1 All of this is seen through the eyes of a not-too-bright country boy.

3. With adverbs. *rare.*

1648 Boyle *Seraph. Love* xvii. (1700) 106 The not-wilfully refusing it. **1726** S. Lowe *Lat. Gram.* 33 Interrogatives us'd not-interrogatively.

4. With infinitives after *does not*, etc. *rare.*

1626 W. Fenner *Hid. Manna* (1656) 62 A wicked man doth not, not repent, because hee cannot, but because he will not. **1656** [? J. Sergeant] tr. *T. White's Peripat. Inst.* 227 He that knows a thing exists knows that it does not not-exist. **1890** Stirling *Gifford Lect.* xvi. 318 The very thought of God is of that which is, and cannot not-be.

not, obs. variant of nut *sb.*

‖**nota**, *sb.* *Obs.* *rare.* [L. *nota*.] A mark; a stigma.

1715 *Wodrow's Corr.* (1843) II. 111 After such a nota put upon our brethren's halving of the oaths and declaration. **1800** tr. *Cullen's Nosology* Wks. 1827 I. 454 Symptoms, every particular of which, in the language of methodical writers, is a *nota* or mark.

‖**nota**, *v.* *Obs.* [L. *notā*, 2nd sing. imperative of *notāre* to mark.] Observe, take notice.

c **1391** Chaucer *Astrol.* II. §26 And nota, þat this forseid rihte orisonte, þat is clepid *orison rectum* [etc.]. **1527** Andrew *Brunswyke's Distyll. Waters* a iij, Nota a lutynge for a glasse that ryveth upon the fyre. **1569** *Reg. Privy Council Scot.* II. 50 *marg.*, Nota the Lard of Amysfeild wes chargit to present thame. **1625** Purchas *Pilgrims* I. 341 Nota, you must bring the high Church East Northeast Easterly, before you shall be cleered of the shoale.

‖**nota bene** (ˈnəʊtə ˈbiːniː, ˈbɛneɪ). [L. *notā* (see prec.) and *bene* well. So F. *nota benè*.] Mark well, observe particularly. (Abbrev. N.B.: see N. II. 2.)

a **1721** Prior *Daphne & Apollo* 65 Next, nota bene, you shall never rove. **1758** Lady M. W. Montagu *Lett.* (1893) II. 348 *Nota bene.* You have dispossessed me of the real devils who haunted me. **1818** Moore *Fudge Fam. Paris* v, *Nota Bene.*—Papa's almost certain 'tis he. **1863** C. Reade *Hard Cash* i. I. 35 Like an animal frequently mentioned in Scripture; but, nota bene, never once with approbation.

b. Used substantivally.

1731–8 Swift *Pol. Conversat.* Introd. 11 To set down.. certain Marks, Asterisks, or *Nota-bene's* (in English, Mark-well's) after most Questions, and every Reply or Answer.

notability (nəʊtəˈbɪlɪtɪ). Also 4–5 -ite(e, 5 -yte, 6 -ylitie. [a. OF. *notabilité* (= It. *-ità*, Sp. *-idad*, Pg. *-idade*) or ad. med.L. **notabilitas*: see next and -ity.]

1. †**a.** A notable fact or circumstance. *Obs.*

a **1380** *St. Augustine* 1739 in Horstm. *Altengl. Leg.* (1878) 91 Hit is an old notabilite þat þreo þingus þer be þat worldliche men disiren here. *c* **1386** Chaucer *Nun's Priest's T.* 389 He in a cronycle saufly myght it wryte, As for a souereyn notabilitee. *c* **1449** Pecock *Repr.* IV. ix. 474 These iij. notabilitees weel considerid..is worth.. a buyschel ful of gold. *c* **1470** Harding *Chron.* Proem v, Vnto your sapience I wyll remember a notabilyte Of your elders rule and regymence.

b. A noteworthy object or feature. *rare*$^{-1}$.

1858 Hawthorne *Fr. & It. Note-bks.* (1872) II. 41 The old sacristy, with the peculiarities or notabilities of which I am not acquainted.

c. A notable or prominent person.

1832 J. S. Mill *Lett.* (1910) I. 33 There is need that the march of mind should raise up new spiritual notabilities; for it seems as though all the old ones with one accord were departing out of the world together. In a few days or weeks the world has lost the three greatest men in it in their several departments—Goethe, Bentham, and Cuvier. **1851** *Fraser's Mag.* XLIII. 257 Along with other ancient 'notabilities', Cleopatra and Mark Antony were addicted to the pastime. **1857** Kingsley *Two Y. Ago* I. 206 Various other little notabilities of the neighbourhood. **1897** 'Sarah Tytler' *Lady Jean's Son* 193 Another notability was the gypsy beauty.

2. The quality of being notable.

a. Housewifely industry or management.

1788 Mrs. Hughes *Henry & Isabella* IV. 93 This grand quality was, in her estimation, divided into two heads, modesty and notability. **1800** Mrs. Hervey *Mourtray Fam.* III. 141 Mrs. Mourtray, who had resumed all her former notability, bustled about her house as usual. **1842** Orderson *Creoleana* iii. 25 She would..send over little presents of various articles, that served also to show her own notability and domestic skill. **1866** Mrs. Gaskell *Wives & Daughters* I. 530 Mary has infected me with her notability, and I'm going to work Mama a footstool.

b. Note, distinction, prominence.

1881 Froude *Short Stud.* (1883) IV. II. iv. 207, I need not mention names which have no historical notability.

notable (ˈnəʊtəb(ə)l), *a.*, *sb.*, and *adv.* Also 4 (6 *Sc.*) -abil(e, 5 -abille, 6 -abyll; 5 -abull(e, 6 -abul; 5 -abel. [a. F. *notable* (13th c.) = Sp. *notable*, Pg. *notavel*, It. *notabile*, ad. L. *notābilis*, f. *notāre* to note: see -able.

Sheridan (1789) gives the pron. as (ˈnɒtəb(ə)l), and this is retained by Walker, Smart, Webster, and Worcester, as the correct pron. in sense 4 b.]

A. *adj.* **1.** Worthy or deserving of note for any reason, esp. on account of excellence, value, or importance; remarkable, striking, eminent.

a. Of things, actions, etc.

a **1340** Hampole *Psalter* lxv. 7 He þat lufis god, luf his neghbure, shewand til him þat is notabile for him. *c* **1386** Chaucer *Doctor's T.* 156 It is no fable, But knowen for a storial thing notable. **1432–50** tr. *Higden* (Rolls) V. 405 Hit was made open by the manifestacion of a notable signe. **1483** Caxton *Gold. Leg.* 192/1 They..edefyed ouer thys holy corps a moche notable chyrche. **1538** Starkey *England* II. i. 151, I thynke in few yerys the pepul schold increse to a notabul noumbur. **1571** Golding *Calvin on Ps.* ii. 8 David obteyned notable victories. **1612** Woodall *Surg. Mate* Wks. (1653) 38 A notable cordial water for comforting the head and heart. **1665** Hooke *Microgr.* 155 Methinks Nature does seem to hint some very notable virtue or excellency in this Plant. **1712** Steele *Spect.* No. 508 ¶2 They support it by Acts of notable Oppression and Injustice. **1750** Berkeley *Wks.* (1871) IV. 323 Learning continues to make notable advances in your College. **1775** Sheridan *Duenna* I. i, So! a notable hour for one of my regular disposition. **1829** Lytton *Devereux* I. ii, He would shake his head with a notable archness. **1873** Symonds *Grk. Poets* i. 17 The first who achieved a notable success in the new and difficult art of Prose Writing.

Comb. **1630** DEKKER *2nd Pt. Honest Wh.* I. i. Wks. 1873 II. 97 This Lodouico is a notable tounged fellow.

b. Of persons. Also const. *at* (quot. 1677).

c **1420** LYDG. *Assembly of Gods* 897 Ther were notable and famous doctours. *c* **1450** *Merlin* 27 Ther myght noon knowe the cause why, but it were notable clerkes. **1535** COVERDALE *Matt.* xxvii. 16 At the same tyme he had a notable presoner called Barrabas. **1596** SPENSER *State Irel.* Wks. (Globe) 636/1 At the execution of a notable traytour at Limmericke. *a* **1661** FULLER *Worthies* xxiv. (1662) 73 You have mingled many Unworthies among them, rather Notorious than Notable. **1677** GILPIN *Demonol.* (1867) 180 They have also a cunning of ascribing effects to wrong causes... Austin tells us the heathens were notable at this. **1711** SHAFTESB. *Charac.* I. ii. (1737) I. 62 The ablest Negotiators have been known the notablest Buffoons. **1798** W. TAYLOR in *Monthly Mag.* V. 352 You summoned a meeting of your more notable creditors, relations, and friends. **1835** THIRLWALL *Greece* (1839) I. 429 The Megarian demagogues procured the banishment of many of the notable citizens. **1851** DIXON *W. Penn* vi. (1872) 54 Fox and Loe were notable for the purity of their lives.

2. †**a.** Easily noted; attracting notice; conspicuous. *Obs.*

1533 SIR T. MORE *Debell. Salem* Wks. 945/1 The variaunce betwene priests & priests is more marked & more notable then any of yͤ tother, because the priests go more abrod. **1580** FULKE *Stapleton Confut.* II. v. Wks. (Parker Soc.) II. 100 Their habit..Augustin in his virgins forbiddeth to be notable, or differing from other women. **1621** BURTON *Anat. Mel.* I. ii. III. xiv. (1651) 125 To avoid such things as are more notable in themselves: as a rugged attire, hirsute head, horrid beard.

b. Capable of being noted or observed; noticeable, perceptible. Now *Chem.*

1551 RECORDE *Pathw. Knowl.* I. Defin., There is a notable and sensible angle..which euermore is made by the meetyng of two seuerall lynes. *Ibid.* No. 5 If your line be of any notable length, deuide it into fiue partes. And if it be not so long that it maie yelde fiue notable partes [etc.]. **1638–9** *Laws Maryland* in *Arch. Maryland* I. (1883) 53 Drinking with excess to the notable perturbation of any organ of sence or motion. **1662** RAY *Three Itin.* III. 171 We did not observe any notable taste in it, neither would it tincture siluer. **1698** HEARNE *Duct. Hist.* (1714) I. 2 Chronology is the Regulation of Times, shewing by notable Signs or Tokens..the exact Time when every Action happen'd. **1818** ACCUM *Chem. Tests* 109 Suppose..we wish to know whether it contains a notable quantity of oxide of manganese. **1857** MILLER *Elem. Chem., Org.* (1862) 536 The kernels of the peach, the plum, the cherry,..also yield this essence in notable quantities.

†**3.** ***notable goods***, a legal term applied to testamentary goods when of a certain amount. *Obs.*

Various opinions on the precise import of the phrase are given by Swinburne.

1590 SWINBURNE *Testaments* 222 What is ment by Notable goods, in this place, or when they are so to be tearmed, diuers authors haue bene of diuers opinions.

4. †**a.** Of men: Industrious, energetic, businesslike. *Obs. rare.*

1666 SOUTH *Serm.* (1823) I. 138 That such an one is a wise and a thriving, or, in the common phrase, 'a notable man'. **1732** LAW *Serious C.* iii. (ed. 2) 37 Penitens was a busy, notable Tradesman, and very prosperous in his dealings.

b. Of women: Capable, managing, bustling; clever and industrious in household management or occupations.

In common use from *c* 1750, but now rare or obs. On the pronunciation see note above.

1718 *Free-thinker* No. 121. 84, I remember to have heard of a notable Woman, who was thoroughly sensible of the intrinsick Value of Time. **1745** ELIZA HEYWOOD *Female Spect.* No. 10 (1748) II. 192 Supposing her an excellent œconomist, in every respect what the world calls a notable woman. **1811** L. M. HAWKINS *C'tess & Gertr.* II. 370 Notable housewives have occasional 'family rummages'. **1865** *Cornh. Mag.* Oct. 409 Lady Cuxhaven, notable from girlhood, was using the blind-man's holiday to net fruit-nets. **1874** MRS. EWING *Lob* 34 Notable people complain, very properly, of thoughtless and untidy ones.

Comb. **1866** MRS. GASKELL *Wives & Daughters* II. 242 The little notable-looking brown hands, with the wedding-ring for sole ornament.

c. Of the nature of, connected with, household management or industry.

1787 *Generous Attachment* II. 24 Engaged in every notable exercise which love and conjugal affection inspire. **1800** MRS. HERVEY *Mourtray Fam.* I. 74 She had learned to detest all needlework of the notable kind. **1835** MOTLEY *Corr.* (1889) I. iii. 60, I thought the whole scene at first too tidy, too notable, too housewifish. **1852** THACKERAY *Esmond* III. ix, Both ladies were perfect housewives,..keeping a notable superintendence over the Kitchen.

B. *sb.* **1.** A noteworthy fact or thing. *rare.*

1483 CAXTON *G. de la Tour* e j, She gaf them these two notables to thende they shold know their faute. **1653** H. WHISTLER *Upshot Inf. Baptisme* 17 Helping against you by many Notables in the very Text. **1705** ADDISON *Italy* (R.), Varro's aviary is still so famous, that it is reckoned for one of those notables, which foreign nations record.

b. A person of eminence or distinction.

1815 SOUTHEY in *Q. Rev.* XIII. 19 The notables of Egypt. **1823** SCOTT *Quentin D.* xix, The notables of the town were fast assembling. **1878** GLADSTONE *Glean.* (1879) I. 201 The straitened philosophy of a local notable.

transf. **1892** HUDSON *La Plata* 221 Amongst the feathered notables..is the Crested Screamer from South America.

2. *pl.* During the Ancien Régime: a number of prominent men from the various estates of the realm of France, summoned by the king as a deliberative assembly in times of national emergency.

1568 GRAFTON *Chron.* II. 482 All worthy nobles and estates of the same realme of Fraunce, as well spirituals as temporals, and also Cities, notables and commonalties. **1634** W. TIRWHYT tr. *Balzac's Lett.* (vol. I) 4 This is a trueth.. which you so solidly confirmed at the last assembly of Notables. **1789** *Hist. Europe* in *Ann. Reg.* 201/1 Mr. Necker had at the beginning of winter summoned a new convention of Notables. **1792** A. YOUNG *Trav. France* 275 From the very commencement of the revolution, at the first meeting of the notables. **1845** *Encycl. Metrop.* XIII. 8/1 It was thought advisable to calm such feelings by summoning an assembly of Notables, who met at Rouen late in the year. **1864** KIRK *Chas. the Bold* I. vi. 317 An article..providing for the appointment of thirty-six 'notables'.

transf. **1818** J. C. HOBHOUSE *Italy* (1859) II. 360 When Bonaparte, in the year 1801, convoked at Lyons the Notables of the Cisalpine Republic. **1855** MACAULAY *Hist. Eng.* xiv. III. 471 An extraordinary meeting of the privy council, or rather an assembly of Notables, which had been convoked at Whitehall.

†**C.** *adv.* Notably. *Obs. rare.*

1586 A. DAY *Eng. Secretary* II. (1625) 82 Here 'never die' seemeth superfluous, and yet notable well adorneth the sentence. **1646** SIR T. BROWNE *Pseud. Ep.* 227 Some season of the year more notable hot then other.

'notableness. [f. prec. + -NESS.] The quality of being notable or remarkable.

1563 *Homilies* II. II. i. (1640) 16 The notablenesse of the place, being the very beginning of the very loving Lord's law. **1745** MRS. DELANY *Life & Corr.* (1861) II. 358, I don't at all doubt my sister's notableness. **1799** R. WARNER *Walk* (1800) 53 A perseverance and notableness..unknown amongst the fair ones of modern days. **1856** RUSKIN *Mod. Paint.* IV. v. xvi. §6 In notableness of lateral precipice, the Matterhorn..stands..unrivalled among the Alps.

†**notablety**, obs. variant of NOTABILITY.

c **1380** WYCLIF *Serm.* Sel. Wks. I. 99 þan shal þe liȝt of Crist..shyne in þe toþer worlde..for notablete of Crist.

notably ('nəʊtəblɪ), *adv.* Also 4 -li, 6 -lye; 5 -ely, -ully, 6 -uly. [f. NOTABLE *a.* + -LY[2].] In a notable manner; remarkably, strikingly.

c **1380** WYCLIF *Sel. Wks.* III. 343 Of þis Chirche þes wordis ben soþli seid, and notabli to mannis kynde. *c* **1400** *Apol. Loll.* 74 Notably is Sichem callid þe son of Emor, þat is interpretid an asse. **1433** LYDG. *St. Edmund* Prol. 66 By pronostyke notably souereyne. **1477** *Rolls of Parlt.* VI. 193/2 His lifelode and richesse notably exceded any other within his Lande. **1526** *Pilgr. Perf.* (W. de W. 1531) 4 All was but fygures yͭ god notably wrought & shewed to them. **1571** GOLDING *Calvin on Ps.* li. 8 Beinge so notablye furnished with trew understandinge. **1641** J. JACKSON *True Evang. T.* I. 43 A Prophecy..that..the Roman Empire should notably flourish. **1680** H. MORE *Apocal. Apoc.* Pref. 6 The Excellency whereof is notably set out. **1711** ADDISON *Spect.* No. 105 ¶6 If you mention either of the Kings of Spain or Poland, he talks very notably. *a* **1732** T. BOSTON *Crook in Lot.* (1805) 15 Bright souls.., notably bemisted and darkened from the crazy bodies they are lodged in. **1856** RUSKIN *Mod. Paint.* IV. v. xiv. §19 The true hard rock or precipice is notably a thing cut. **1897** MARY KINGSLEY *W. Africa* 439 They are notably deficient in all mechanical arts.

†**no'tado.** *Obs. rare*[−1]. [a. Sp. *notado*, pa. pple. of *notar* to NOTE.] A mark or sign.

1647 WARD *Simp. Cobbler* 30, I am also sure Souldiers use to weare other marklets or notadoes in time of battell.

†**notaire.** *Obs. rare.* Also **notayre.** [a. F. *notaire.* Cf. NOTAR.] = NOTARY *sb.*

1474 CAXTON *Chesse* (1883) 93 The Notayres, skynners, coryours, and cardewaners werke by skynnes and hydes. *Ibid.* 94 That aduocate or notaire that hath charge to wryte and kepe sentence.

†**no'tairely,** *adv.* *Obs.* *rare*[−1]. [ad. OF. *notairement*, f. *notaire* variant of *notoire*: see NOTORIOUS and NOTOUR.] = NOTARILY.

c **1480** CAXTON *Scipio's Oration* e ij, Their famous deedes be to theyr infynyte lawde notairely knowen of you alle.

notal ('nəʊtəl), *a.*[1] [f. Gr. νῶτ-ον the back + -AL[1].] Dorsal.

1855 DUNGLISON *Med. Lex.*

notal ('nəʊtəl), *a.*[2] [f. NOTE *sb.*[2] + -AL.] Of, pertaining to, or employing notes.

1884 *Encycl. Brit.* XVII. 85/1 The treachery of tradition is exemplified in the loss of the rules for this once generally understood practice of notal inflexion. **1924** LUCAS & BONAR tr. *Knapp's State Theory of Money* ii. 113 There are metalloplatic and papyroplatic notal money systems, with or without hylodromy.

‖**notalgia** (nəʊ'tældʒɪə). *Path.* [mod.L., f. Gr. νῶτ-ον back + ἄλγος pain. Cf. F. *notalgie.*] Pain in the back without inflammatory symptoms. Hence **no'talgic** *a.*

1855 DUNGLISON *Med. Lex.* **1892** *Syd. Soc. Lex.*

notam ('nəʊtəm). [f. initial letters of *no*tice *t*o *a*ir*m*en.] A (warning) notice to pilots of aircraft.

1946 F. HAMANN *Air Words* 38/1 *Notam*, notice to airmen. **1955** R. J. SCHWARTZ *Compl. Dict. Abbrev.* 128/2 *Notam*, International Notices to Airmen. **1963** *Times* 25 Jan. 4/4 He added that until two months ago 'notams'—notices warning aviators and mariners to keep out of the way of Nato exercises—were also issued and had nearly a worldwide circulation. **1967** *Times* 16 May 10/3 All went well until the second Spanish 'notam' (notice to airmen), a week ago.

'notamy, etc., aphetized form of *anotamy*, obs. var. of ANATOMY, skeleton. (Cf. It., Sp., and Pg. *notomia.*) Now *dial.*

1487 *Ann. Barber-Surgeons* (1890) 102, xviij men and ij women hanged; the Barber-surgeons had one of them to be a notheme at ther halle. **1577** HOLINSHED *Chron.* I. 1816/2 A man chylde.., the heade, armes and legges whereof were like a notamie. **1598** TOFTE *Alba* (1880) 111 Who then can rid me (Notamie of Woe) From these hell plagues? **1790** *Bystander* 391 My leg was at last as thin as Tom Muggins's, the notamy in surgeon's hall. **1825** BROCKETT *N.C. Gloss.*, *Nottamy, ottamy*, a skeleton. **1889** ELWORTHY in *N. & Q.* *Somerset & Dorset* 27 Aug., Throughout the Western Counties the usual term for a Skeleton is *Nottomy* or *Notamy*.

NOT AND (nɒt ænd). *Computers.* [f. NOT *adv.* + AND *conj.*] = NAND.

1960 [see NAND]. **1962** SIMPSON & RICHARDS *Physical Princ. Junction Transistors* xvi. 402 Parallel *p-n-p* inverters form a 'NOT AND' gate, for which all must be one to maintain a zero output.

‖**notandum** (nəʊ'tændəm). Also pl. **notanda.** [L., gerund of *notāre* to NOTE, used to introduce a memorandum, e.g.

1605 BEN JONSON *Volpone* IV. i, What is here? *Notandum*, A rat had gnawne my spurre-lethers.]

An entry or jotting of something to be specially noted; a memorandum, observation, note.

α. **1685** SIR J. LAUDER *Chron. Notes* (1822) 53 By way of notandum, he gave himself two wounds when taken by Graeme of Dougalstoun's men. **1715** M. DAVIES *Athen. Brit.* I. 242 The interludes are compos'd of divers notandums. **1800** *Asiatic Ann. Reg.* II. 17/1 A notandum to the account remarks, that this sum was taken from the Bengal statements. **1858** W. ARNOT *Laws fr. Heaven* II. xxiv. 197 His fellow-disciple John..adds to his name the significant notandum 'Not Iscariot'.

β. **1702** HOWE *Wks.* (1834) 63/1 (Stf.), And now for his *notanda*..by which he would conclude [etc.]. **1787** HAWKINS *Life Johnson* 266 He feigns to have dropped his paper of Notanda. *a* **1847** CHALMERS in Spurgeon *Treas. Dav.* (1874) IV. 367 Verses 11 and 12 are both most savoury and precious notanda.

notaphily (nəʊ'tæfɪlɪ). [f. NOTE *sb.*[2] 18 + -PHILY.] The collecting of bank-notes as a hobby. Hence **no'taphilic** *a.*; **no'taphilism**; **no'taphilist.**

1970 *Daily Tel.* 7 Nov. 15/2 Stanley Gibbons has created a new word, 'Notaphilly' [*sic*], which derives from Latin and Greek meaning 'lover of notes'... A banknote is a notaphilic item and the collector is a notaphilist. (Say it like 'philatelist'.) **1970** *Guardian* 2 Dec. 11/2 The charm of bank notes..is their history... Notaphily is the name of the hobby. **1972** *Daily Tel.* 28 Oct. 29/4 Colin Narbeth compares the position of today's notaphilist with that of Edward Stanley Gibbons..when he bought a kit bag containing thousands of Cape Triangulars for £5. **1973** *Times* 13 Dec. 17/8 Collectors have coined the ugly name notaphilists to describe themselves. About twenty of the highest-denomination notaphilists came to the auction. **1976** *Times* 27 Jan. 17/4 Biafran £1 notes..found their way on to the notaphilic market.

'notar. *Sc.* Now *rare.* Also 5–6 **notare,** 6 **notair(e,** 6–7, 9 **noter,** 7 **nottar.** [Sc. variant of NOTARY *sb.*: see -AR[2].] A notary.

1439 in *Charters etc. Edinb.* (1871) 65 In presens of Robert Mechelson of Hyrdmanston public notare vnderwrytin. **1469** *Sc. Acts Jas. III* (1814) II. 95 His hienes may mak notaris & tabellionis. *c* **1480** HENRYSON *Mor. Fab.* VI. (*Sheep & Dog*) v, The foxe wes clerk and notare in the cause. **1533** BELLENDEN *Livy* IV. iv. (S.T.S.) II. 63 Vnder þe quhilk suld be notaris and writaris to bere þe charge of tabillis and registeris. **1546** *Reg. Privy Council Scot.* I. 46 Neill Layng, and Alexander Gibsoun, noteris publict. **1588** A. KING tr. *Canisius' Catech.* 9 Sinnes that maye be done by notaires. **1678** SIR G. MACKENZIE *Crim. Laws Scot.* II. xiii. §2 (1699) 209 The Clerks of all other Courts must be Notars. **1708** J. CHAMBERLAYNE *St. Gt. Brit.* (1710) II. II. iv. 409 The Lord Register..has the Power of appointing Clerks for Registration of Seasines and Admissions of Nottars. *a* **1773** FERGUSSON *Will* Poems (1788) I. 101 These presents wrote are By William Blair, the public notar. **1822** HIBBERT *Desc. Shetl. Isl.* (1891) 61 Filled with all the clauses and quirks that the lawyer and noter could invent.

'notaress. *rare*[−1]. [f. NOTAR-Y *sb.* + -ESS.] A female notary or clerk.

1622 T. ROBINSON *Anat. Eng. Nunnery* 31 Iosepha Bingham, Portresse, Lucy Iohnson, Notaresse.

notarial (nəʊ'tɛərɪəl), *a.*[1] [ad. L. type **notāriāl-is*, f. *notārius* NOTARY *sb.* So F. *notarial.*]

1. Of or belonging to a notary.

1482 in Rymer *Fœdera* (1711) XII. 165/1 We have.. commaunded the said Notary to set his signe Notariall to the same. **1818** CRUISE *Digest* (ed. 2) V. 129 A certificate..was signed by two persons, who stated themselves to be public notaries; but no notarial seal was annexed. **1866** CRUMP *Banking* v. 115 It was not allowed by the law to recover the notarial charges against the acceptor unless special damage was made in the declaration. **1888** *Century Mag.* Nov. 94 Several pairs were kept waiting by the notarial table while the commandant was served.

b. Characteristic of, peculiar to, notaries.

1828 CARLYLE *Misc.* (1857) I. 68 He examines and records with a certain notarial strictness. **1844** S. R. MAITLAND *Dark Ages* 15 A subscription..which may, at the same time, be a specimen of notarial eloquence. **1894** *19th Cent.* July 80 The odd grammar and the notarial style of this memorial present some difficulties at first sight.

2. Drawn up, framed, or executed by a notary.

1622 MALYNES *Anc. Law-Merch.* 125 Hereupon likewise passeth a Notariall Contract. **1682** SCARLETT *Exchanges* 79 It is not usual to make a formal Notarial Protest. **1726** AYLIFFE *Parergon* 305 Thro' want of a Notarial Evidence. *a* **1768** ERSKINE *Inst. Law Scot.* (1838) 615 Solemnities requisite to Notarial Instruments. **1818** CRUISE *Digest* (ed. 2) V. 129 The notarial certificate required in the case of a fine acknowledged in a foreign country. **1837** CARLYLE *Fr. Rev.* II. II. v, M. de Malseigne 'takes act', due notarial protest, of such refusal. **1889** *Century Mag.* Aug. 597/1 Madame Lalaurie, we know by notarial records, was in Mandeville ten days after.

b. esp. ***notarial act*** (see ACT *sb.* 6).

1752 CARTE *Hist. Eng.* III. 3 He caused him to sign a notarial act protesting against it. **1839** BROOKE *Office of Notary* 7 The expression notarial act..has a technical meaning. **1897** *Times* 16 Jan. 6/2 Sir James Parker Deane, Q.C.,..signed and sealed the customary notarial acts.

Hence **no'tarially** *adv.*

1847 in WEBSTER. **1901** *Westm. Gaz.* 17 June 8/2 Documents..translated into English and notarially certified.

†**no'tarial,** *a.*[2] *Obs. rare*$^{-1}$. [Cf. prec.] Of the nature of notes.

1753 N. TORRIANO *Gangr. Sore Throat* p. ix, The little notarial Scholia I have here and there made upon it.

no'tariate. *rare.* [= F. *notariat*, Sp. *-ato*, Pg. *-ado*, med.L. *-atus*: see NOTARY *sb.* and -ATE[1].] The profession of notary.

1888 H. C. LEA *Hist. Inquisition* I. 379 *note*, Peculiar importance attached to the notariate, and the limitations imposed on its membership are seen in the papal privileges.

notarikon (nəʊ'tærɪkən). *Jewish Lit.* Also notaricon. [late Gr. *νοταρικόν*, f. L. *notārius* shorthand-writer, NOTARY *sb.*] In cabalistic phraseology, the art of making a new word from letters taken from the beginning, middle, or end of the words in a sentence.

1880 [see ONOMANCY]. **1911** 'SEPHARIAL' *Kabala of Numbers* I. iii. 31 *Notaricon.*—Selection was made of certain letters according to the rules of the art, these letters being taken from the beginning, middle, or end of the words in a sentence, so as to produce a single word from their combination. **1941** G. G. SCHOLEM *Major Trends Jewish Mysticism* iii. 90 Techniques..popularly supposed to represent the heart and core of Kabbalism, such as *Gematria* .., *Notarikon*, or interpretation of the letters of a word as abbreviations of whole sentences. **1951** *John o' London's Weekly* LX. 716/2 Hempe..is a Tudor notarikon... Hempe is formed of the initial letters of the Tudor sovereigns Henry, Edward, Mary, Philip and Elizabeth.

†**'notarily,** *adv. Obs.* [f. NOTARY *a.* + -LY[2].] Notoriously; commonly (known).

1459 *Rolls of Parlt.* V. 367 Such persones..ben notariely and universally thorough oute all this your Realme famed and noysed..for open Robbers. **1487** HEN. VII in *Epist. Acad. Oxon.* (1898) II. 514 Seynge, as itt ys notaryly knowen, that he cann nott be accepted as a scolare. **1697** *Phil. Trans.* XIX. 728 A poor Man of Rowdil, in the Isle Harries, notarily known by the Name of St. Clements Blind.

notarize ('nəʊtəraɪz), *v.* [f. NOTAR(Y *sb.* + -IZE.] *trans.* To have (a document) legalized by a notary. Usu. in **'notarized** *ppl. a.*

1935 *Sun* (Baltimore) 22 Nov. 10/1 In a series of notarized cases a prominent journal recently stated that in the installation of industrial machinery totaling $8,000,000 the savings effected by these installations were approximately $55,000 per plant per year. **1939** W. FAULKNER *Wild Palms* 19 There was no sworn notarised statement attached. **1960** *Times* 2 Aug. 7/4 Boys under 21 and girls under 18 must be accompanied by their parents to obtain a marriage licence, or else present a notarized letter of consent. **1972** *Scholarly Publishing* III. 182 Sometimes..he has practically to sign his life away to get his meagre five dollars or so. In extreme cases the publisher once even had to get the form notarized.

notary ('nəʊtərɪ), *sb.* Also 4–7 **notarie,** 4–5 **-arye,** 5 **-ory, -ery.** [ad. L. *notārius* shorthand-writer, clerk, secretary, f. *notāre* to note, *nota* a note. Hence also Sp. *notario*, Pg. *notario, -airo*, It. *notaro, -aio*, F. *notaire*.]

†**1.** A clerk or secretary to a person. *Obs.*

In quot. 1474 applied to the bishop's pawn in chess.

1303 R. BRUNNE *Handlyng Synne* 5748 Pers kalled to hym hys clerk þat was hys notarye. **1377** LANGL. *P. Pl.* B. xv. 32 þanne am I conscience ycalde, goddis clerke and his notarie. **1422** tr. *Secreta Secret., Priv. Priv.* 212 Of Notaries... To chese the be-houeth, to write thy Pryuyteis.., wyse men of Parfite eloquence. **1474** CAXTON *Chesse* (1883) 92 Hit is reson that the alphyn or juge haue his notarye, by whom y[e] processe may be wreton. **1600** J. PORY tr. *Leo's Africa* III. 160 Where the gouernor of the mint with his scribes and notaries haue their aboad. **1609** HOLLAND *Amm. Marcell.* XIV. v. 8 The principall and of greatest note was one Paulus a Notarie, borne in Spaine.

fig. **1593** SHAKS. *Lucr.* 765 O comfort-killing Night,.. Dim register and notary of shame! **1615** BRETON *Charac. Ess., Knowledge* Wks. (Grosart) II. 6/1 Knowledge..is the Notary of Time, and the tryer of Truth.

2. A person publicly authorized to draw up or attest contracts or similar documents, to protest bills of exchange, etc., and discharge other duties of a formal character.

1340 *Ayenb.* 40 Þe ualse notaryes, þet makeþ þe ualse lettres, and ualseþ þe celes. *c* **1386** CHAUCER *Pars. T.* ¶ 721 Ware yow, questemongers and notaries. **1423** *Coventry Lett.-bk.* (E.E.T.S.) 59 Whethur he be Notary impereall, or he be not; and if so be he be a Notary sworen & admyttyd [etc.]. **1480** *Caxton's Chron. Eng.* (1520) VII. 126 b, Whan they hadde thus sworne they toke theyr crosses that theyr othes were comprehended into the notaryes. **1513–4** *Act 5 Hen. VIII*, c. 1 Preamble, Divers officers..called Notaries ..to accepte take and recorde the Knowlege of all contracts. **1592** WEST *1st Pt. Symbol.* § 100 e, It sufficeth not our notarie to know only what Instruments and contracts be. **1621** BURTON *Anat. Mel.* To Rdr. (1651) 26 Notaries alter sentences, and for money lose their deeds. **1720** STRYPE *Stow's Surv.* (1754) II. v. xv. 328/2 There were sixteen Notaries in the Mayoralty of Sir James Haws..in 1574. **1797** MRS. RADCLIFFE *Italian* xvii, The Inquisitor merely bade the notary write down her name. **1841** ELPHINSTONE *Hist. India* I. 123 He acts as notary in drawing up deeds for them. **1871** MARKBY *Elem. Law* §480 The resort..to a notary to draw up the documents relating to any business in hand.

b. More fully ***notary public, public*** (or †***common***) ***notary.***

1494 FABYAN *Chron.* VII. 546 Thomas Feryby and Denys Lopham, notaryes publyque. **1555** EDEN *Decades* (Arb.) 204 The subscription of a common notarie therunto requyred. **1578** T. N. tr. *Conq. W. India* 5 The office of Publike notarie in Azua. **1655** FULLER *Ch. Hist.* III. 65 Made a Count Apostolick, whereby he had the Priviledges to appoint publick Notaries. **1682** SCARLETT *Exchanges* 72 Protest is ordinarily made by a Notary Publick in the presence of two credible Witnesses. **1712** *Lond. Gaz.* No. 4954/4 The Employment of Advocate, Writer to the Signet, Notary Publick. **1818** CRUISE *Digest* (ed. 2) V. 128 Authenticated by his certificate or attestation, as a notary public. **1866** CRUMP *Banking* v. 116 In the absence of a notary-public, a protest may be made by any inhabitant of the place.

†**3.** A noter or observer. *Obs.*

1589 NASHE *Anat. Absurd.* Wks. (Grosart) I. 32 You know them without my discourse,..though I be not the Notarie of their iniquitie. **1645** MILTON *Tetrach.* Wks. 1851 IV. 234 The words of Christ shall be asserted from such elementall notaries, and resolv'd by the now-only law-giving mouth of charity. **1685** DUNTON *Lett. fr. New-Eng.* (1867) 18 All that this Starry Notary can tell her, is that the Stars prognosticate a Boy.

†**4.** A note-book. *Obs. rare*$^{-1}$.

1651 BAXTER *Inf. Bapt.* 255 You have nothing but the weakness of your memory and notaries to excuse all these palpable untruths.

†**'notary,** *a.*[1] *Obs.* Also 5 **-arye,** 5–6 **-arie,** 6 **-eri, -erye.** [ad. med.L. *nōtārius* for *nōtōrius*, perh. after F. *notaire*.]

1. Notorious.

1388–9 in *Wyclif's Sel. Wks.* III. 468 If hit be knowen þat persouns..lyven in notary fornicacione. **1433** *Rolls of Parlt.* IV. 447/1 Many murdererys of men, and notarye theves. **1502** ARNOLDE *Chron.* (1811) 276 Any other Notary and open causes vpon the which ony subget, clerke, or leyman be diffamyd. **1527** in Fiddes *Wolsey* (1726) II. 171 It is also verey notarie that thei dyd lye together.

2. Well-known; notable.

1419 in Ellis *Orig. Lett.* Ser. II. I. 87 To remembre his notarie proclamation made thorgh his Roialme. **1423** *Rolls of Parlt.* IV. 257 Expert persones, havyng notary conyng in the craft of Goldsmyth. **1494** FABYAN *Chron.* VII. 518 Where both hoostis thus lyinge, w[t]out notary feate of warre, a treatye of accorde was yet agayne moued.

†**'notary,** *a.*[2] *Obs. rare*$^{-1}$. [ad. L. type **notārius*, f. *nota* a mark. Cf. NOTORIOUS and NOTORY.] Dealing with marks or signs.

1584 R. SCOT *Discov. Witchcr.* XV. xlii. 393 Hereunto [to Theurgie] belongeth..the art of Paule, the art of Revelations, and the art Notarie.

not at all. = *don't mention it* (see MENTION *v.* 1 c).

1936 WODEHOUSE *Laughing Gas* ii. 19, I was not-at-alling and shoving the handkerchief up my sleeve again. **1963** 'E. MCBAIN' *Ten plus One* vii. 88 'Well, thank you,' Carella said. 'Not all. My pleasure,' Richardson answered. **1973** J. BURROWS *Like an Evening Gone* i. 13 She..pretty well knocked him flying... 'So sorry.' 'Not at all.'

'notate, *a. Bot.* [ad. L. *notātus* pa. pple. of *notāre*: see NOTATION.] (See quot.)

1857 A. GRAY *First Less. Bot.* (1866) 223 *Notate*: marked with spots or lines of a different color.

notate (nəʊ'teɪt), *v.* [f. as NOTATE *a.*] **a.** To set down in musical notation. **b.** To record, note. So **no'tated** *ppl. a.*; **no'tating** *vbl. sb.*

1922 W. J. LOCKE *Tale of Triona* xii. 128 He could play, ..by ear—knowledge of notated music he disclaimed. **1965** *Listener* 16 Dec. 990/2, I would say it would help any composer to conduct if he had the gift, because, in the first place, you learn how to notate your music more precisely, so that a performing musician will know exactly what you mean. **1971** S. CAVELL *World Viewed* ii. 17 Such troubles in notating so obvious a fact. **1974** *Times Lit. Suppl.* 13 Dec. 1411/2 To sing through the variants of even a single song —for example, of the beautiful 'Seeds of Love', the first which [Cecil] Sharp notated—is an enlargement of the spirit... Once notated versions of the songs exist, are the rhythmic quirks ironed out?

not at home, *adv. phr.* Not prepared to receive visitors or accessible to callers. Also as *sb.* or *adj.*

1829 [see AT HOME 1 b]. **1831** *Society* I. 307 He was on that young lady's not-at-home list. **1874** HARDY *Far from Madding Crowd* I. ix. 123 'I can't see him in this state. Whatever shall I do?' Not-at-homes were hardly naturalized in Weatherbury farm-houses, so Liddy suggested—'Say you're a fright with dust, and can't come down.' **1923** *Mrs. Beeton's Bk. Househ. Managem.* i. 35 When visitors present themselves the servant charged with the duty of opening the door will..answer without hesitation if the family are 'not at home', or 'engaged'.

notatin (nəʊ'teɪtɪn). *Biochem.* [f. L. *notāt-us*, pa. pple. of *notāre* to mark, NOTE *v.*[2] + -IN[1].] A flavoprotein produced by the mould *Penicillium notatum* which is an enzyme that catalyses the direct oxidation of glucose to gluconic acid and hydrogen peroxide and is used in the detection and estimation of glucose; = PENATIN, PENICILLIN A, B.

1942 C. E. COULTHARD et al. in *Nature* 28 Nov. 634/2 When a selected strain of *Penicillium notatum* Westling is grown on a Czapek-Dox medium an anti-bacterial substance is produced which differs in the majority of its properties from penicillin. This anti-bacterial substance was originally named 'Penicillin A', but in order to avoid confusion with penicillin we now prefer the name 'notatin'. **1949** N. G. HEATLEY in H. W. Florey et al. *Antibiotics* I. iii. 136 For the assay of 'notatin' (known also as 'penicillin B' or 'penatin') the medium must contain glucose, for this so-called antibiotic is an enzyme..and exerts its effect purely through the hydrogen peroxide which is formed. **1954** A. WHITE et al. *Princ. Biochem.* xii. 264 A curious example of an antibiotic isolated from the mold *Penicillium notatum* is the substance notatin, which was later found to be the enzyme glucose oxidase containing flavin adenine dinucleotide. **1963** R. BENTLEY in P. D. Boyer et al. *Enzymes* (ed. 2) VII. xxiv. 568 The following materials, originally described as antibiotics, are actually enzymes similar to, or identical with, the glucose oxidase of Müller: notatin (originally penicillin A).., penatin.., and penicillin B. *Ibid.* 569 Much of the work described in this chapter has been carried out with purified preparations of notatin, and an unqualified reference to glucose oxidase in the rest of this chapter will indicate notatin.

notation (nəʊ'teɪʃən). [ad. L. *notātiōn-em*, n. of action, f. *notāre* to NOTE. Hence also F. *notation* (14th c.), Sp. *notacion*, It. *notazione*, Pg. *notação*.]

†**1.** The explanation or exposition of a term in accordance with its etymology; the etymological or primary sense of a word. *Obs.* (common in 17th cent.).

1570 J. DEE *Math. Pref.* b j, This Description, or Notation, is brief. **1588** FRAUNCE *Lawiers Log.* I. vi. 35 b, As for conjugates and notation,..I dare not admit them into the text. **1609** DOWNAM *Christ. Lib.* 30 This..error they seeke to iustifie by the like notation of the Latine words. *a* **1654** GATAKER *Antid. Errour* (1670) 7 If we respect the Notation or Original of the word *Justifie*, it should signifie *to make just*. **1690** *Andros Tracts* II. 32 If we may Admit that Gentleman's Notation of a Libell (a Lie because False, and a Bell because Loud).

2. A note or annotation. Now *rare.*

1584 FENNER *Def. Ministers* (1587) 96 We may lett passe the sifting of these notations altogither vnworthie to be noted. **1685** *Boston Rec.* (1881) VII. 175 Some articles.. which wee have thought fit to leave some notations or memorandum with the Selectmen about. **1706** J. SERGEANT *Chapter Bp. Chalcedon* (1853) 122 Neither was there any room for inferences, or many notations. **1762–71** H. WALPOLE *Vertue's Anecd. Paint.* (1786) V. 150 No other notation at all concerning any designer, engraver, or publisher whatever. **1822** GALT *Provost* xxxv, Intending these notations for the instruction of posterity. **1845** R. W. HAMILTON *Pop. Educ.* i. (ed. 2) 3 The Sacred Volume has gathered up certain notations of this great study of our nature. **1929** J. GALLISHAW *Twenty Probl. Fiction Writer* 228 The wise writer depends upon recorded observations, and makes notations. **1932** L. C. DOUGLAS *Forgive our Trespasses* (1937) vii. 128 The papers submitted on Tuesday were, in the main, satisfactory. They would be returned, with notations, to their makers, at the close of the hour.

3. The action of taking or making note of something. *rare.*

1646 SIR T. BROWNE *Pseud. Ep.* I. iv. 13 Although there be no lesse then six, yet are there but two onely thereof worthy our notation. **1667** WATERHOUSE *Fire London* 43 He..would not himself have set a foot this work..upon that day..But that the Notation of the day might lesson us displeasure extraordinary. **1866** CRUMP *Banking*, etc. v. 113 A different operation from the 'notation of protest', as regards foreign bills of exchange.

†**4.** A mark or indication. *Obs. rare*$^{-1}$.

a **1661** FULLER *Worthies* (1840) I. xxi. 81, I have endeavoured..to time eminent persons by one of these notations; first, that of their morning, or nativity [etc.].

5. The process or method of representing numbers, quantities, etc., by a set or system of signs; hence, any set of symbols or characters used to denote things or relations in order to facilitate the recording or considering of them.

a. *Arith.* and *Algebra.*

1706 PHILLIPS (ed. Kersey), *Notation*... In Arithmetick, it is that part which shows how to express, read, or declare ..any Number written. **1730** BAILEY (folio), Notation (with Algebraists), the representing quantities by Letters of the Alphabet. **1806** HUTTON *Course Math.* (ed. 2) I. 241 Avoiding the short ways of notation, which..are..less useful to the pupil. **1847** EMERSON *Repr. Men, Uses of Gt. Men* Wks. (Bohn) I. 276 The inventor of decimal notation. **1882** MINCHIN *Unipl. Kinemat.* 93 If (*A*) denotes the area traced out by *A*, and (*X*) the area of *D*, we have, with the previous notation [etc.].

b. *Music.*

1776 BURNEY *Hist. Mus.* I. 7 As the notation of the Greeks was imagined in the infancy of the art of music. **1811** BUSBY *Dict. Mus.* s.v., The literal notation for the lute is constantly called the Tablature. **1876** STAINER & BARRETT *Dict. Mus. Terms* (1888) 309 The ecclesiastical notation of the Greek Church..is supposed to have originated in the Greek accents.

c. In miscellaneous uses.

1831 BREWSTER *Nat. Magic* xi. (1833) 293 A system of mechanical notation invented by Mr. Babbage. **1837** WHEWELL *Induct. Sci.* (1857) III. 185 The various methods of notation by which it has been proposed to represent the faces of crystals. **1855** ABP. THOMSON *Laws Th.* §101 A mode of notation to be able to represent to the eye by figures the relation which subsists in thought between conceptions. **1871** WATTS *Dict. Chem.* IV. 136 The system of chemical notation now in use among chemists belongs exclusively to modern times.

6. *Logic.* (See CONNOTATION 2, quot. 1829.)

no'tational, *a.* [f. NOTATION + -AL[1].]

1. Of, pertaining to, or characterized by notation (esp. in *Logic*).

1880 *Libr. Univ. Knowl.* X. 736 All [early numerals] seem to have been once used without notational place, that is without the zero. **1955** A. N. PRIOR *Formal Logic* 293 Introducing 'classes' as merely a notational device. **1964** P. K. BOCK in J. A. Fishman *Readings Sociol. of Lang.* (1968) 217 The structural description of any one situation occurring in a human community must, necessarily, refer to other situations; therefore, a notational system was devised to facilitate cross-referencing. **1964** E. BACH *Introd. Transformational Gram.* vii. 145 A certain amount of facility in handling symbols and practice in manipulating the notational conventions is all that is needed. **1965** HUGHES & LONDEY *Elem. of Formal Logic* xxxvi. 249 We can..reduce the welter of bracketing..by the following notational convention. **1965** *Language* XLI. 485 Using the same notational devices as before. **1970** J. D. MCCAWLEY in P. L. Garvin *Cognition* x. 231 A system of semantic representation that is along the lines of the notational systems used in symbolic logic. **1973** J. HINTIKKA *Logic, Language-Games & Information* xi. 252 A formula which is like one of the constituents or a-constituents we have defined..will be called its *notational variant.* We shall call two constituents or a-constituents *different* only if they are not notational variants of each other.

b. *spec.* Of or pertaining to musical notation.

1925 P. A. SCHOLES *Second Bk. Gramophone Record* 162 Under the notational description of 6/8 we get sometimes *two groups* in a bar, sometimes *three groups.*

Hence **no'tationally** *adv.*

1896 *Musical Herald* 1 Feb. 43/1 With regard to *ba*, Mr. McNaught admitted that, notationally, there was something to be said in favour of abolishing the name, but, educationally, it was better to keep it. **1940** W. V. QUINE *Math. Logic* 33 A mode which consists notationally of compounding the statements by means of 'implies' and the two pairs of quotation marks.

no'tationist. [f. NOTATION + -IST.] One who uses or advocates a particular style of musical notation.

1896 *Musical Herald* 1 Feb. 41/2 Every singer should be a two-notationist. **1897** *Ibid.* 1 June 188/2 There is no reason why..Sol-faists and staff notationists should not come to a common understanding and agreement. **1928** *Musical Times* July 619 All those brought up on the Staff would benefit by a grounding in Tonic Sol-fa... The dual notationist is, in fact, the best-equipped musician.

notative ('nəʊtətɪv), *a.* [ad. L. type **notātīvus*: cf. CONNOTATIVE *a.*] (See quot. 1867.)

1842 *Penny Cycl.* XXIII. 444/1 The simplicity of notative distinctions must bear some proportion to that of the real differences they are meant to represent. **1867** ATWATER *Logic* 67 A Notative Conception..suggests its own marks (*notæ*) by its very name.

notator (nəʊ'teɪtə(r)). *rare.* [f. L. *notāt-, notāre,* to note; cf. *annotator*, and Sp. *notador*, It. *notatore.*]

†**a.** An annotator. *Obs.* **b.** A noter, recorder. **c.** One skilled in musical notation.

1691–2 WOOD *Ath. Oxon.* (1820) IV. 460 The notator Dr. Potter in his epistle before it to the reader saith thus. **1830** CHAMBERS *Life Jas. I,* II. x. 273 'She is generally well-wished' says a notator of passing events. **1896** ASHBY-STERRY *Tale Thames* (1903) 98/1 You..would appear to be beyond the grasp of the most subtle of musical notators.

not-being, *sb.* [NOT *adv.*]

1. Absence of being; non-existence.

a **1586** SIDNEY *Arcadia* (1622) 265 A base and vilest degree of being, and next to a not-being. **1587** GOLDING *De Mornay* (1592) 13 Afore the which there went a Not-beeing. **1623** WEBSTER *Duchess Malfi* IV. ii, Did any ceremonial form of law Doom her to not-being? **1683** J. CORBET *Free Actions* I. viii. 6 No more is needful to a Not-being, than Gods not Willing and not Effecting. **1725** WATTS *Logic* (1728) 28 As being is divided into substance and mode, so we may consider not-being with regard to both these. **1850** MAURICE *Mor. & Met. Philos.* (ed. 2) 185 Being had been confounded with truth, Not-being with falsehood. **1871** TYLOR *Prim. Cult.* II. 97 He may find in utter dissolution and not-being a refuge even from heaven. **1907** J. R. ILLINGWORTH *Doctrine of Trinity* i. 8 We cannot possibly conceive a passage from not-being to being, as the Greeks phrased it,..except through the operation of some energy which is already actual,..and adequate. **1917** D. H. LAWRENCE *Look! We have come Through!* 147 It wounds me to death with my own not-being. **1933** C. DAWSON *Enquiries Relig. & Culture* III. ii. 194 The element of nothingness or not-being which is inherent in the world of sensible experience.

2. A non-existent thing. *rare*[−1].

1725 WATTS *Logic* (1736) 27 Then they rank them also under the general Head of Not-Beings.

So **not-being** *a.*, non-existing. *rare*[−1].

1594 J. DICKENSON *Arisbas* (1878) 83 The extremitie of fortunes malice, which seemed to ease me with a shadow of not-being solace.

notch (nɒtʃ), *sb.* Also 7–8 **noch,** 8 **knotch.** [app. ad. older F. *oche* (mod.F. *hoche*) of the same meaning, with *n* of the article prefixed (see N 3). There is thus no original connexion with NOCK *sb.*[1]

Examples of the verb OCHE occur in the alliterative *Morte Arthur* (*c* 1400), but the sb. has app. not been recorded.]

1. a. A V-shaped indentation or incision made, or naturally occurring, in an edge or across a surface.

1577 HARRISON *England* II. xi. (1877) I. 227 Which being drawne vp to the top of the frame is there fastned by a woodden pin (with a notch made into the same after the manner of a Samsons post). **1597** BARLOWE *Navigators Supply* D 3 b, Prepare a little Notche or slit of equall depth in the two sights of the sight-Ruler. **1624** CAPT. SMITH *Virginia* II. 31 To make the noch of his arrow he hath the tooth of a Beaver, set in a sticke, wherewith he grateth it by degrees. **1648** WILKINS *Math. Magic* I. ix. 60 A little wheel, with some notches in it, equivalent to teeth. **1697** DAMPIER *Voy.* (1699) 41 The other end..is jagged with notches like a Harpoon. **1719** DE FOE *Crusoe* I. (Globe) 83 With much chopping..hard Wood, they were all full of Notches and dull. **1774** M. MACKENZIE *Maritime Surv.* 45 A crooked Bit of Brass, with a Notch in it. **1825** J. NICHOLSON *Operat. Mechanic* 306 Each circle..is divided into eleven parts, and at each a rectangular notch is cut. **1844** H. STEPHENS *Bk. Farm* III. 1276 Every year after the horn is protruded from the head, with a notch on it. **1870** BRYANT *Homer* I. IV. 110 Grasping the bowstring and the arrow's notch He drew them back.

b. In fig. uses.

Quot. 1970 perh. belongs to 1 a.

1644 QUARLES *Sheph. Orac.* viii, We cut out doctrines, and from notch to notch, We fit our holy Stuffe. **1670** LASSELS *Voy. Italy* Pref., Traveling takes my yong noble-man four notches lower in his self-conceit and pride. **1790** R. TYLER *Contrast* v. i. (1887) 92 Ho, ho, ho! There the old man was even with her; he was up to the notch—ha, ha, ha! *c* **1817** HOGG *Tales & Sk.* II. 242 To bring them forward to the same notch of time. **1853** KANE *Grinnell Exped.* xxxviii. (1856) 349 We..tumbled over, no matter how often; but we hit the ships to a notch. **1897** *Outing* XXX. 266/2 When you have girded yourself up to the last notch, go to speak. **1929** W. FAULKNER *Sound & Fury* 399 Luster took still another notch in himself and gave the impervious Queenie a cut with the switch. **1947** *Sun* (Baltimore) 15 May 2/8 The notch, instead of $67, is $38.50, and it stops at $265.52. **1958** *Sunday Times* (Johannesburg) 21 Sept. 4/9 Each of the Transvaal's 13,000 teachers will have their pay raised by at least one notch on October 1. **1958** *Cape Times* 29 Oct. 15/5 Applicants must have auctioneering experience... The notch for appointment will depend on previous experience. **1970** E. MCGIRR *Death pays Wages* vii. 146 He turned up the central heating a notch.

†**c.** = NOCK *sb.*[1] 1 a. *Obs. rare*[−1].

1621 BURTON *Anat. Mel.* II. ii. IV. (1651) 266 This present Sultan makes notches for bows.

d. A slit in the ground made to take the roots of a seedling tree.

1891 W. SCHLICH *Man. Forestry* II. ii. 126 An enlarged notch may be produced by swaying it [*sc.* the notching spade] to and fro. **1934** *Forestry* VIII. 21 A deep vertical notch..with adequate firming, is the best method of planting. **1970** H. L. EDLIN *Collins Guide to Tree Planting & Cultivation* vii. 107 In its simplest form, the notch is just a slit cut into the ground, into which the tree's roots are inserted.

e. An incision made in a twig to stimulate the growth of a bud lower down the twig.

1916 tr. K. Koopmann in L. H. Bailey *Pruning-Manual* v. 127 Notches are made on twigs of one year's growth or more, to influence a particular bud in various ways. **1974** R. GROUNDS *Practical Pruning* iii. 28 Cut a notch just above the buds that you wish to form branches during April.

2. a. A nick made on a stick, etc., as a means of keeping a score or record. (Cf. NICK *sb.*[1] 2 a.) Also *fig.*

† *out of all scotch and notch*: (see SCOTCH *sb.*).

1580 HOLLYBAND *Treas. Fr. Tong, Vne oche, vn cren,* or *crenne,* a notch in a skore. **1676** MARVELL *Mr. Smirke* Wks. (Grosart) IV. 60 The Exposer..hath payed him exactly, though not in as good billet, yet in as many notches. **1719** DE FOE *Crusoe* I. 64 Upon the Sides of this square Post, I cut every Day a Notch with my Knife. **1784** COWPER *Tiroc.* 560 Th' indented stick, that loses day by day Notch after notch. **1817** J. BRADBURY *Trav. Amer.* 41 *note,* It is customary amongst the Missouri Indians to register every exploit in war, by making a notch for each on the handle of their tomahawks. **1876** GEO. ELIOT *Dan. Der.* II. xxv. 155 He felt sure that there was a notch made against him—and that somehow or other he was intended to pay.

b. A run in cricket. Now *rare.*

1737 in Waghorn *Cricket Scores* (1899) 17 Kent side went in first and got 99 notches. **1755** *Game at Cricket* 10 If in running a Notch, the Wicket is struck down by a Throw; it's out. **1812** *Sporting Mag.* XL. 246 A match..which was won by Burley, ninety-seven notches against sixty-five. **1835** W. HOWITT in *Friendsh. Miss Mitford* (1882) I. xii. 293 The sudden shout..of the crowd when the last decisive notch was gained. **1881** *Sportsman's Year-bk.* 137, 1,163 notches have been placed to his credit by the scorers.

3. *U.S.* A narrow opening or defile through mountains; a deep narrow pass. (Common in local names in the New England States.)

1718 S. SEWALL *Diary* 15 Sept., About half way between the Notch of the Mountain and Hartford. **1760** *New Eng. Hist. & Gen. Reg.* (1882) XXXVI. 32 On arriving on the Lake, I took the bearing of a Notch or Break in the Mountains. **1812** MELLISH *Trav. U.S.* I. 98 There is a singular curiosity in the state [of New Hampshire] called the Notch, which is a pass through the mountains. **1838** HAWTHORNE *Amer. Note-bks.* (1883) 197 This Notch is otherwise called the Bellowspipe, being a long and narrow valley, with a steep wall on either side. **1890** J. H. WARD *White Mts.* 45 The Crawford Notch is so much in the heart of the mountains that it offers unusual facilities for seeing them.

4. a. An opening; a break or breach.

1794 S. WILLIAMS *Hist. Vermont* I. 25 The direction of this passage is oblique, and full of stops or notches. **1804** BROWN tr. *Volney's View* 66 The gaps, whose sides..exhibit those notches occasioned by the first overflowings of the lake.

b. *spec.* An opening extending above the water level in a surface placed across a stream like a weir; also, the surface itself.

1789 T. WRIGHT *Meth. Watering Meadows* (1790) 20 Keep it [the water] high enough to flow through the notches, (or what we improperly call sluices). **1845** *Encycl. Metrop.* III. 238/1 Theoretically the quantity discharged through a rectangular notch, which reaches to the surface, is two-thirds of what would issue through an equal orifice placed at the whole depth below the level of the fluid. **1907** W. C. UNWIN *Treat. Hydraulics* v. 96 Notches for measuring purposes are weirs fitted with a plate in which an open notch is formed through which the water passes. **1908** A. H. GIBSON *Hydraulics* v. 137 (*heading*) Flow over notches and weirs. **1914** W. M. WALLACE *Hydraulics* xii. 188 Where it is possible to provide an artificial section for the stream the gauge notch is used, of which there are three standard forms, viz., (1) rectangular, (2) circular, (3) triangular. **1959** [see FLUME *sb.* 3 a]. **1974** J. A. FOX *Introd. Engin. Fluid Mech.* iii. 99 In the case of orifices and rectangular notches the coefficient of discharge varies with both the Reynolds number and the value of *l/h*.

5. An act of notching or cutting.

1844 H. STEPHENS *Bk. Farm.* I. 506 Small holes made in the ground with three or four notches of the spade.

6. *attrib.* and *Comb.*, as ***notch-eared, -flowered, -leaved***; **notch-back,** (*a*) a back on a motor car that extends approximately horizontally from the bottom of the rear window so as to make a distinct angle with it; a car having such a back; also *transf.*; opp. *fast back*; (*b*) s.v. FAST *a.* 11; **notch-bar test** *Engin.* = *notched-bar test* (NOTCHED *ppl. a.* 1); **notch-block** *Naut.*, a snatch-block; **notch-board,** (*a*) a board grooved to receive the ends of the steps in a stair; (*b*) a board with notches placed as a stop in a water-channel; **notch-brittleness** *Engin.*, susceptibility to fracture at a notch when a sudden load is applied; hence (as a back-formation) **notch-brittle** *a.*; **notch effect** *Engin.*, the increase in the susceptibility of a specimen to fracture caused by the presence of a notch; **notch factor** *Engin.* (see quot. 1968); **notch filter** *Electronics*, a filter that attenuates signals within a very narrow band of frequencies; **notch-head,** an ornamental incision in stone; **notch-house** *slang*, a brothel (cf. NAUTCH *sb.* 2); **notch-ladder** (see quot.); **notch-planting** = NOTCHING *vbl. sb.* 3; **notch-ringing** (see quot.); **notch-sensitive** *a. Engin.*, characterized by a high notch sensitivity; **notch-sensitiveness** or **-sensitivity** *Engin.* (see quot. 1970); **notch-sight, -stick** (see quots.); **notch-toughness** *Engin.*, the opposite of *notch-brittleness*; *spec.* the result (in units of energy) of a notched-bar test on a specimen; **notch-weed** (see quots.); †**notch-wheel,** the locking- or count-wheel in a clock; **notch-wing,** a name of various moths.

[**1959** *Motor* 28 Oct. 447/2 The Special Continental saloon..was notable for the abandonment of the sloping tail in favour of a notched back treatment.] **1965** J. LAWLOR *How to talk Car* 76 **Notch-back,* body design with a separate distinct rear deck. The term is used to distinguish conventional styling from fast-back design. **1967** *Wall St. Jrnl.* 24 Apr. 6/3 The Charger will drop its fast-back roofline in 1968 in favor of a 'notchback' in which the roofline slopes more abruptly to the rear fender. **1971** *Flying* (N.Y.) Apr. 40/1 In 1962, the Cessna 182 got the Omni-Vision treatment, with a notchback after fuselage and auto-style rear window. **1972** *Practical Motorist* Oct. 69/2 In 1961..a Capri based on the notch-back Ford Classic was introduced. **1957** *Financial Times Ann. Rev. Brit. Industry* 61/4 To predict the service behaviour of the steel..the information derived from small *notch bar tests is being amplified. **1966** *McGraw-Hill Encycl. Sci. & Technol.* VIII. 272/2 Notch-bar tests are usually made in either of two convenient arrangements, in both of which the specimen is broken by a freely swinging pendulum. **1846** A. YOUNG *Naut. Dict.* 38 Snatch-Blocks (or *Notch-Blocks) which are single blocks with a notch cut in one cheek, to receive the bight of a rope. **1823** P. NICHOLSON *Pract. Build.* 189 A *notch-board is a board into which the ends of the steps are let. **1844** H. STEPHENS *Bk. Farm* III. 1024 Notch-boards injure the edges of feeders, besides causing deep holes to be scooped beyond them by the fall of water. **1958** A. D. MERRIMAN *Dict. Metallurgy* 212/1 In *notch brittle materials the notch or crack is propagated with great rapidity under sudden loading conditions. **1963** ALEXANDER & BREWER *Manuf. Prop. of Materials* i. 16 There is a fairly well-defined threshold value of temperature below which the steel is notch-brittle and above which it exhibits relatively ductile behaviour. **1929** *Jrnl. Iron & Steel Inst.* CXX. 514 The authors first discuss two diagrams representing the ratios of the *notch-brittleness obtained by means of Mesnager test-pieces and large Charpy test-pieces for a large number of steels. **1965** MATSUO & INOUE tr. *T. Yokobori's Strength, Fracture & Fatigue of Materials* vii. 162 The classical theory of Griffith explains notch brittleness as the increase of the plastic constraint factor *qe* arising from fibrous cracks induced in the early stages of the process. **1840** *Cuvier's Anim. Kingd.* 74 *note,* *Notch-eared Bat (*V. emarginatus*).—The fur reddish-grey above, ash-coloured beneath. **1925** M. A. GROSSMANN tr. *Heyn's Physical Metallogr.* v. 299 With decreasing *b*, hence with increasing *notch effect, the values for *q* and ϵ_e decrease. **1970** C. C. OSGOOD *Fatigue Design* iii. 104 The scale of notch sensitivity for a material then varies between no notch effect, $q = 0$, and full theoretical notch effect at $q = 1$. **1939** *Jrnl. R. Aeronaut. Soc.* XLIII. 728 The *notch-factor was plotted against the notch-depth, and the resulting curve indicated that, as the notch-depth increases, the notch-factor increases up to a critical value of the notch-depth, and thereafter decreases. **1968** F. A. D'ISA *Mechanics of Metals* vii. 326 The actual effectiveness of stress concentration on fatigue strength is measured by the fatigue notch factor, K_f, which is defined as the ratio of the fatigue strength of a specimen with no stress concentration to the fatigue strength at the same number of cycles with stress concentration for the same conditions. [**1950** *Electronics* July 75/3 (*heading*) Notching filters.] **1962** *Electronic Technol.* XXXIX. 332/1 At v.h.f. it is desirable to construct *notch filters from coaxial elements. **1974** *Physics Bull.* Mar. 107/3 A fully tunable notch filter for removing line frequency pick-up. **1886** CASSELL, **Notch-flowered*,.. having the flowers notched at the margin. **1843** *Civil Eng. & Arch. Jrnl.* VI. 320/1 An ornamental parapet, with a cornice of *notch-heads, or dog-tooth, or corbels. **1931** *Amer. Mercury* Nov. 353/2 **Notch house*, a house of prostitution. **1956** H. GOLD *Man who was not with It* (1965) xxx. 277 Nancy ran a notch-house for travelers who loved to see things. **1902** *Chambers's Jrnl.* Oct. 657/2 A notable feature of these smaller mines is the *notch-ladder system of conveying the ore from the interior to the pit-head. Two masts, notched like bear-poles, form the means of ascent and descent for a more or less continuous chain of *peons*. **1822** *Hortus Anglicus* II. 468 *Alnus Serrulata*, *Notch-leaved Alder. **1953** H. L. EDLIN *Forester's Handbk.* ix. 145 *Notch planting..is the simplest and cheapest method, by which the majority of forest trees are planted today. **1970** —— *Collins Guide to Tree Planting & Cultivation* vii. 107 (*heading*) Notch planting. **1884** *Australasian* 8 Nov. 875/1 In *notch-ringing, a belt of bark is not only removed, but a notch running round the tree is cut in the sap-wood about 2 in. deep. **1946** *Metallurgia* XXXIII. 250/1 A forthright statement of which material is the more *notch sensitive seems impossible. **1956** M. C. SMITH *Princ. Physical Metallurgy* x. 377 Because a notch creates locally a condition of triaxial tension, all metals are notch-sensitive. **1967** LEE & NEVILLE *Handbk. Epoxy Resins* iv. 9 Cyclization, together with randomly occurring areas of low bond density for other reasons.., will lead to internal flaws within the polymer network to create notch-sensitive defects. **1934** *Jrnl. Iron & Steel Inst.* CXXX. 653 The investigation of *notch sensitiveness, the use of the index of notch sensitiveness.. and the connection between the index and the chemical composition..are discussed. **1934** *Jrnl. Res. Nat. Bureau of Standards* (U.S.) XIII. 535 Even for annealed copper, notch sensitivity evidently is equal to that of steels with tensile strength five times as great. **1970** C. C. OSGOOD *Fatigue Design* iii. 104 The ratio between the apparent increase in local stress [due to the presence of a notch or other stress concentrator] in fatigue and the increase predicted by the elastic theory of stress concentration has been defined..as *notch sensitivity. **1867** SMYTH *Sailor's Word-bk.*, **Notch-sight of a gun*, a sight having a V-shaped notch, wherein the eye easily finds the lowest or central point. **1883** GRESLEY *Gloss. Coal-mining*, **Notch Sticks*, short pieces of stick notched or nicked, used by miners as records of the number of tubs of coal, &c., they send out of the pit during the day. **1926** *Jrnl. Iron & Steel Inst.* CXIII. 624 This method of testing enables it to be judged whether a material has been brought to its best condition in regard to *notch-toughness. **1972** E. N. SIMONS *Testing of Metals* v. 85 A component designed for a hot climate may not give the same degree of notch toughness in a cold one if the temperature of the latter lies below the transition temperature. **1736** AINSWORTH, *Notch weed, *Atriplex olida*. [Hence in Johnson, etc.] **1866** *Treas. Bot.* 793/2 Notchweed, *Chenopodium Vulvaria*. **1611** COTGR., *Roüe de compte*, a *Notch-wheele in a Clocke. **1819** SAMOUELLE *Entomol. Compend.* 435 The shallow *Notchwing.. The common Notchwing. **1832** J. RENNIE *Butterfl. & Moths* 180 The Chequered Notch-Wing.

† **notch**, obs. variant of NAUTCH *sb.*

1796 ELIZA HAMILTON *Lett. Hindoo Rajah* (1811) I. 222, I was invited by the Governor-General to a notch, or, as they express it, a ball.

notch (nɒtʃ), *v.* Also 6 **noch**, 9 **knotch**. [f. the sb.]

† **1.** *trans.* To cut (hair) unevenly. *Obs. rare.*

Cf. Percivall *Span. Dict.* (1591) '*Trasquilones*, notches in the hair'.

1597 BP. HALL *Sat.* III. vii, All Brittish bare upon the bristled skin Close noched is his beard, both lip and chin. **1611** COTGR., *Bertauder*,..to notch, or cut the haire vneuenly. **1687** MIÈGE *Gt. Fr. Dict.* II. s.v., To notch Hair, *couper les cheveux d'une maniere ridicule*. **1747** P. FRANCIS *Horace, Epist.* I. i. 136 If some unlucky Barber notch my Hair.

2. a. To cut or make notches in; to cut or mark with notches.

1600 HEYWOOD *1st Pt. Edw. IV* (1613) C 2 b, Whose recreant limbs are notcht with gaping scarres. **1607** SHAKS. *Cor.* IV. v. 199 He scotcht him, and notcht him like a Carbinado. **1672** SIR W. TALBOT *Discov. J. Lederer* 25 You must not forget to notch the trees as you go along with your small Hatchet. **1737** POPE *Hor. Epist.* I. i. 84 From him whose quills stand quiver'd at his ear, To him who notches sticks at Westminster. **1766** *Compl. Farmer* s.v. *Madder* 5 I. 3/1 They are seven inches broad, notched half the thickness of the stocks of the beetles. **1814** JANE AUSTEN *Mansf. Park* III. 280 Her eyes could only wander to..the table, cut and knotched by her brothers. **1862** MORRALL *Hist. Needle-m.* 2 You may see men grinding long steel bars to the necessary fineness,..then notching them at the required lengths.

fig. **1649** G. DANIEL *Trinarch., Hen. V* ccxxi, Greiv'd, that the Tallies of his Fame was Seene Notch't, with a Debt. **1871** MEREDITH *H. Richmond* xlvi, The place is notched where it occurred and for ever avoided.

transf. **1864** LOWELL *Fireside Trav.* 144 Pines, whose pointed summits notched the rosy west in an endless black *sierra*. **1878** HUXLEY *Physiogr.* xvii. 274 The eastern end is notched by the estuary of the Thames.

b. To convert *into* (some form) by the process of making notches.

1768–74 TUCKER *Lt. Nat.* (1834) II. 319 Persons..might notch a stick into something that could be fancied a human face. **1832** HT. MARTINEAU *Hill & Valley* ii. 28 Another would notch it into a saw. **1862** SCROPE *Volcanoes* 136 Notching it into..fantastically-shaped eminences.

c. *absol.* To make notches.

1848 DICKENS *Dombey* i, Remorseless twins they are for striding through their human forests, notching as they go.

3. a. To score, mark, record, by means of notches. Also with *up* or *down*, and in fig. contexts.

1623 MIDDLETON *More Dissemblers* v. i, I'll notch your faults up. **1645** FULLER *Good Th. in Bad T.* (1841) 43 He had no leisure to eat for notching up the men he met. **1649** G. DANIEL *Trinarch., Hen. V* cclxxxiv, Let Harrie's Fate (Notch'd sure with Time) Spin to a Softer Bed. **1837** DICKENS *Pickw.* vii, The umpires were stationed behind the wickets; the scorers were prepared to notch the runs. **1848** LOWELL *Biglow P.* Poet. Wks. 1890 II. 138 We notched the votes down on three sticks. **1860** EMERSON *Cond. Life, Fate* Wks. (Bohn) II. 320 As children stand up against the wall.. and notch their height. **1879** *Princeton Rev.* May 478 The cataract itself has notched the records of the ages of its retrocession upon the rocks by its side. **1911** *Chambers's Jrnl.* Oct. 702/1 A speed of one hundred miles an hour has been notched on more than one occasion. **1963** *Sunday Express* 6 Jan. 23/5 Her earnings now are well above the £10,000 she was notching up a few years ago. **1969** 'D. RUTHERFORD' *Gilt-Edged Cockpit* i. 17 In about three minutes Mascot would have notched up the victory they so desperately needed. **1973** *Daily Tel.* 23 Apr. 5/4 When ..'Andre Previn's Music Night' notched up audiences of six million last year, he was understandably delighted and encouraged. **1974** *Nature* 29 Mar. 373/3 Albright and Wilson managed to notch up an increase in profits.

absol. **1837** DICKENS *Pickw.* vii, They notch in here..it's the best place in the whole field.

b. To score, succeed in getting (a run, etc.).

1837 DICKENS *Pickw.* vii, All-Muggleton had notched some fifty-four. **1895** *Daily News* 18 Dec. 9/4 The nearest they could get to scoring was a corner, whilst their opponents notched two goals.

c. To mark *off* by effacing a notch.

1831 LANDOR *Andria of Hungary* Wks. 1846 II. 2 Notched off like schoolboy's days Anxious to see his parent.

4. a. To fix, secure, or insert, by means of notches.

1768 C. BEATTY *Jrnl.* 72 *note*, Logs of wood laid upon one another, notched at the corners into each other. **1837** *Civil Eng. & Arch. Jrnl.* I. 2/2 Longitudinal sleepers of timber.. on which are notched down transverse bearers. **1838** *Ibid.* 104/1 Cross-ties notched on to the waling. **1857** THOREAU *Maine W.* (1894) 23 One directly above another, and notched together at the ends. **1875** *Carpentry & Join.* 62 You can notch in the corners, like E, as it cannot get out of place when the top is nailed on.

fig. **1824** SCOTT *St. Ronan's* i, The houses were notched as it were into the side of the steep bank.

b. To chop *off*, cut *out*.

1820 SCOTT *Abbot* iii, Have they hands, and fight not for the land which bore them? They should be notched off at the elbow! **1896** *Allbutt's Syst. Med.* I. 192 Rhombic in shape with a corner notched out.

5. To fit the arrow to the bowstring; to nock.

1635 QUARLES *Embl.* I. vii. 30 His bow is bent, and he hath notch'd his dart. **1649** G. DANIEL *Trinarch., Hen. V* clxxix, Other well-notch their Arrowes; trye their Stringes And draw their Bowes. **1720** DE FOE *Capt. Singleton* xvii. (1840) 292 Their arrows being soon notched upon their bows. **1767** *Poetry* in *Ann. Reg.* 230, I bent my bow,..and strait Notch'd on the nerve the messenger of fate.

6. To stop or jam (a wheel). *rare*$^{-1}$.

1674 N. FAIRFAX *Bulk & Selv.* 130 They can't strike sail, or notch the wheels,..in a trice.

7. *intr.* To become jagged or indented. *rare*$^{-1}$.

1693 EVELYN *De La Quint. Compl. Gard.* II. 15 Their matter must be of good temper'd Steel, so that the edge may neither turn, or notch easily.

notched (ˈnɒtʃt), *ppl. a.* [f. prec. + -ED^{1}.]

1. a. That has a notch or notches cut in it; nicked, indented; marked with a notch.

1602 MARSTON *Ant. & Mel.* I, He lookes like a may-pole, or notched stick. **1683** CROWNE *City Politiques* v, Because a knight's notch'd in the crown, and the doctor's a little crack'd there. **1744** JOHNSON *Diary N. Wales* (1816) 74 At an iron-work I saw round bars formed by a knotched hammer and anvil. **1779** FORREST *Voy. N. Guinea* 110 They ascended with great agility, by a long notched stick. **1821** CLARE *Vill. Minstr.* I. 112 The oak-tree, gnarl'd and notch'd, Lifts its..furrow'd side. **1847** SMEATON *Builder's Man.* 163 To describe an Ellipse by Means of..a piece of notched Lath. **1887** HALL CAINE *Deemster* xxxiii, The notched door of the portcullis was open.

b. *Bot.* Coarsely dentate or serrate.

1676 GREW *Anat. Pl., Fruits* 176 The Belly'd [flowers] are also Even Edged, as in Convolvulus; or Notched, as in Trachelium. **1748** *Anson's Voy.* III. ii. 310 The leaves of this tree are..notched about the edges. **1796** WITHERING *Brit. Plants* (ed. 3) I. 200 Petals..heart-shaped, bent inwards, and notched at the end. **1824** SIR J. E. SMITH *Eng. Fl.* (1828) II. 345 Petals 5, flat, spreading, notched. **1870** HOOKER *Stud. Flora* 51 Petals notched, and with a notched scale.

c. *Zool.* Having notches or incisions.

1713 PETIVER *Aquat. Anim. Amboinæ* 1/2 *Echinus planus*, ..Double notch'd Sea Pan-cake. **1774** GOLDSM. *Nat. Hist.* (1776) VI. 359 The two great claws..are usually notched, like a saw. **1837** *Penny Cycl.* VII. 26/1 Ears..a little notched on their external border. **1880** GÜNTHER *Fishes* 330 Pectoral fins not notched at their origin.

Comb. **1871** *Cassell's Nat. Hist.* I. 307 The Notched-eared Bat (*Vespertilio emarginatus*), found in Central and Southern Europe, and extending eastward into Persia.

d. ***notched-bar test***: any of several impact tests (as the Izod or the Charpy test) in which the energy absorbed in breaking a notched specimen in a single blow is measured.

1918 *Proc. Inst. Automobile Engin.* XII. 250 Untreated bright drawn mild steel bar..usually gives a low result on the notched bar test. **1966** *McGraw-Hill Encycl. Sci. & Technol.* VIII. 272/2 Notched-bar tests are made to estimate the ductility that may be expected in the presence of defects in structures.

† **2.** Having unevenly or closely cropped hair.

1611 COTGR., *Bertaudé*, curtalled; also, notched, or cut vneuenly. *c* **1648** DAVENANT *Vac. in London* Wks. (1673) 289 For Prentice notch'd he strait does call. **1681** DRYDEN *Span. Friar* Prol., Even as notch'd prentices whole sermons write. [**1820** LAMB *Elia* Ser. I. *Oxford in the Vacation*, A votary of the desk—a notched and cropt scrivener.]

notchel (ˈnɒtʃəl), *sb. dial.* Also 7 **nochell**, 9 **nochil(d, knotchell**, etc. [Of obscure origin. Now current only in Chesh., Lanc., and W. Yks.] ***to cry (one) notchel***, to proclaim publicly that one will not be responsible for debts incurred by the person named. Also in ***notchel-crying***, ***-notice***.

1681 *Dial. betw. Sam. & Will.* in *Harl. Misc.* (1744) II. 101 The King's Majesty,..him they cryed Nochell. *Sam.* What, as Gaffer Block of our Town cryed his Wife? **1839** LEWIS *Gloss. Heref.*, In Lancashire, 'cry'd nochild' means a woman cried down by her husband. **1859** in *N. & Q.* 3rd Ser. (1866) X. 108 On Wednesday there was at Accrington an extraordinary instance of the disgraceful practice of 'notchel crying'. **1882** *Lanc. Gloss.* 202 To cry 'notchel' is to give notice that a certain person or persons will not pay the debts of another person. **1889** *N. & Q.* 7th Ser. VIII. 268 He is thus said to 'notchel' her, and the advertisement is termed a 'notchel' notice.

Hence **ˈnotchel** *v.*

1841 HAMILTON *Nugæ Lit.* 356 When a man advertises that he is not answerable for certain debts of a partner, in life or in trade, he knotchells them. **1886** *Cheshire Gloss.* 241 When a man makes public announcement that he will not pay his wife's debts, she is said to be *notchelled*.

notcher (ˈnɒtʃə(r)). [f. NOTCH *v.*] **a.** One who notches; a scorer. **b.** An instrument for making notches.

c **1740** in *Daily News* 19 Oct. (1897) 7/2 The Bowler, The Striker, The Notcher [etc.]. **1879** *Organ Voicing & Tuning* 8 Tools for voicing and tuning... 1. The *notchers* of various sizes. **1895** C. SCOTT *Apple Orchards* 52 A deal table accommodated the notcher or scorer.

ˈnotchet. *rare*$^{-1}$. (Of obscure meaning.)

Cf. Suff. and Essex dial. *notchet*, an insignificant thing, a small quantity.

1636 ABP. WILLIAMS *Holy Table* (1637) 53 In this imperfect time, and uneven Notchets, His house with Minum's swarm'd, his head with Crotchets.

ˈnotchful. [f. NOTCH *sb.*] The quantity which can be contained in a notch.

1733 TULL *Horse-Hoeing Husb.* xxii. 331 An equal Number of Notchfuls of seed will be delivered thro' the Seed Passage at each Revolution of the Wheels.

notching (ˈnɒtʃɪŋ), *vbl. sb.* [f. NOTCH *v.*]

1. The action or process of making notches, *esp.* in carpentry as a method of joining timbers.

1611 COTGR., *Creneure*, a iagging, nicking, notching. **1825** J. NICHOLSON *Operat. Mechanic* 564 Notching admits two pieces to be joined at from one to four angles. **1847** SMEATON *Builder's Man.* 80 The carpenter usually connects his timbers either by notching, or by mortice and tenon. **1875** KNIGHT *Dict. Mech.* 1534/2 Halving, scarfing, and cauking are forms of notching, and form a lap-joint.

2. A notch or notch-like incision.

1842 GWILT *Encycl. Arch.* 1008 *Notching*, a hollow cut from one of the faces of a piece of timber, generally made rectangular in section. **1849** MURCHISON *Siluria* ix. 201 The galleries thus formed falling in, and producing furrow-like markings, with or without transverse notchings.

3. A method of planting seedling trees in which a slit is made in the earth to take the roots of the plant. Also *attrib.*

1847 J. BROWN *Forester* iii. 85 He [*sc.* the superintendent] must examine almost each tree as it is put into the ground, whether it may be done by the pitting or notching system. **1851** *Ibid.* (ed. 2) iii. 237 The method of planting termed notching, or slitting, is done with the common spade or planting mattock. **1891** W. SCHLICH *Man. Forestry* II. ii. 126 Notching..differs from planting with a peg in the shape of the planting hole, which is that of a notch. *Ibid.*, The notching spade is wedge-shaped. **1930** *Forestry* IV. 18 Notching. The idea behind this type of planting is to..make an opening quickly which is of sufficient size to take in the roots of small plants. **1953** H. L. EDLIN *Forester's Handbk.* ix. 145 A proper straight notching spade..has no 'crank' between handle and blade. **1967** C. E. HART *Practical Forestry* (ed. 2) iv. 63 The most usual method [of planting] is notching with a spade or a mattock.

4. A type of pruning in which twigs are partially cut to stimulate the growth of a bud lower down the twig.

1913 J. C. NEWSHAM *Propagation & Pruning* 23 Notching is used to force the development of particular buds, the notch being made in the bark and young wood immediately above the selected bud. **1916** L. H. BAILEY *Pruning-Manual* v. 127 Notching into the wood above a bud tends to produce strong growth from that bud. **1972** G. E. BROWN *Pruning of Trees* ii. 24 'Notching'..is carried out during the dormant season, when a notch is cut about 10 to 15 mm. above the bud, completely removing a wedge-shaped piece. **1974** R. GROUNDS *Practical Pruning* iii. 29 The lowest branches resulting from the first year's notching are pulled down and tied at the horizontal.

notchy (ˈnɒtʃɪ), *a.* [f. NOTCH *sb.* + -Y^{1}.]

1. Having notches or indentations.

1850 ALLINGHAM *Poems, To the Cicada*, Scraping to your heart's desire Dusky sides with notchy feet. **1883** MISS BROUGHTON *Belinda* III. 152 The Langdale Pikes have just shaken the rain-clouds off their notchy crests.

2. Of a manual gear-changing mechanism: difficult to use because the lever has to be moved accurately (as if into a narrow notch).

1967 *Autocar* 28 Dec. 20/2 The gear change is rather notchy, which is somewhat typical. **1972** *Drive* Spring 150/2 Short, precise movements..are features of the four-speed gearbox, though the lever has a slightly notchy feeling. **1975** *Daily Tel.* 16 Apr. 12/6 The short gear lever is a trifle notchy in operation although I always find this preferable to vague sloppiness.

note, *sb.*[1] *Obs.* exc. *north. dial.* Forms: 1 notu, (1) 2–5, 9 note, 5 noote; 4–5 not, 4 notte, 5 nott; 5 noytt, 5, 7 noyt, 9 noit. [OE. *notu* fem. = MDu. *note* (cf. MDu. *not*, ON. *not* neut.), f. the weak grade of the series *neut-*, *naut-*, *nut-*: see NAIT *sb.* and *v.*[1], NEAT *sb.*, and NOWT.

In later ME. the word is most common in alliterative verse; in the *Wars Alex.* it occurs at least a score of times in a variety of senses. In some passages it appears to have no very definite meaning.]

1. Use, usefulness, profit, advantage.

c **893** K. ÆLFRED *Oros.* I. x. 48 Hit ær þiosan ȝenoȝ æmittiȝ læȝ.., & ȝe his nane note ne hæfdon. *c* **960** *Rule St. Benet* (Schröer) 11 He bið ȝewitnod swa swa ȝymeleas hyrde, ȝif se hyredes ealdor.. to lytele note & nytwyrðnesse on his heorde angyt. *a* **1250** *Owl & Night.* 557 Is in þe eni oþer note, Bute þu hauest schille þrote? *c* **1290** *St. Katherine* 51 in *S. Eng. Leg.* I. 93 We schulle betere i-leue alle men, and more it wole beo note. **13..** *Seuyn Sag.* (W.) 992 For here bolt is sone i-schote, More to harm than to note. **1338** R. BRUNNE *Chron.* (1810) 169 God gif þam grace to spede, With douhty fo, to note, whan þei com to dede. *a* **1425** *Cursor M.* 22883 (Trin.), Owe we here of to fecche resoun How he doþ alle þinge to note [*v.r.* nait]. *a* **1450** MYRC 1484 Hast þow ouer-holde corne or ote, Or oþer þynge þat come neuer to note?

b. (One's) good, benefit, or profit.

a **1240** *Ureisun* in *O.E. Hom.* I. 195 Ihesu cristes blode, þet for ure note was i-sched oðere rode. *a* **1250** *Owl & Night.* 330 Ich do god mid mine þrote, And warni men to hore note. *c* **1300** *Cursor M.* 21772 Sco þat fand quar it was hid,.. And til vr note nu has it broght. **1340** *Ayenb.* 159 Huanne þe man zekþ his oȝene note in al þet he deþ.

c. *to do note*, to do good.

13.. *Coer de Lion* 2651 Stones that deden never note, Grounde they never whete, no grote. *c* **1325** *Chron. Eng.* 434 in Ritson *Metr. Rom.* II. 288 Ethelwolf.. dude ys lond lute note. *c* **1425** *Cast. Persev.* 2730 þou mayst purchase þer-with bothe ponde & parke, & do þer-with mekyl note. *c* **1440** *Jacob's Well* 197 þin handyl is all to schort, þi schouyl is noȝt worthe. þou doost no note.

d. *in note*, in use.

c **1400** *Destr. Troy* 792 Ho raught hym a ring with a riche stone,.. Eneas it name & in note hade. *c* **1440** *York Myst.* xxxvi. 383 A graue.. þat neuer was in noote, it is newe.

e. *dial.* The milk given by a cow; the period of giving milk; the condition of a cow when giving, or beginning to give, milk after calving.

a **1728** KENNETT in *MS. Lansd.* 1033 fol. 272b, *Noyt*, a cow's milk for one year. W.R. Yorksh. where they hire out a cow for a summer at so much a *Noyt*. **1847** in HALLIW., *Note*,.. the time during which a cow is in milk. *North.* **1875** in *Antrim & Down Gloss.* (1880) 73 A Kerry cow,.. at her note in May. **1880–** in dial. glossaries (Cumb., Yks., Lanc., Chesh.).

2. Office; employment, occupation, or work, as properly pertaining or assigned to a person. Also, way of acting, practice.

c **960** *Rule St. Benet* (Schröer) 63 Ne ræden ȝebroðru, ne ne singen.. ac ða syn ȝecorene to ðære note. *c* **1000** ÆLFRIC *Gen.* xl. 13 Æfter þam Pharao.. ȝeset þe to þære ylcan note. **1303** R. BRUNNE *Handl. Synne* 963 Y swore.. þat y wlde nat.. halewe þys day of my note. *c* **1386** CHAUCER *Reeve's T.* 148 This meller goth agayn, and no word seyde, But doth his note,.. Til that her corn was fair and wel i-grounde. *c* **1450** *St. Cuthbert* (Surtees) 8056 þarfore prior turgote þe bischope preferd to þis note. **1513** DOUGLAS *Æneis* VI. iv. 26 Vtheris, quhilk wer ordanit for sic notis, The warme new blude keppit in coup and peis.

b. Work, as occupying one for or at a particular time; temporary occupation or employment.

c **1325** *Metr. Hom.* 61 Of thair not yet standes merk, In Babilony the tour yet standes. **13..** *E.E. Allit. P.* B. 1233 ȝet nolde neuer nabugo þis ilke note leue, Er he hade tuyred þis toun & torne hit to grounde. *c* **1400** *Destr. Troy* 284 Mony noble for þe nonest to þe note yode,.. To this Journey with Jason. *c* **1460** *How the Goode Wif* 103 Hazl. *E.P.P.* I. 187 Loke what note is moste nede for to done.

1883 *Almondbury Gloss.* 92 'What noit are ye at?' = 'What are you doing?'

c. Work of a specified kind.

c **1400** *Sege Jerus.* 800 Myche of masonus note þey marden þat tyme. **1419** *Surtees Misc.* (1890) 15 The wryght note of a gutter betwix the newe house.. and the hall.

d. A piece of work.

13.. *St. Erkenwolde* 38 in Horstm. *Altengl. Leg.* (1881) 267 þe temple.. was.. A noble note for þe nones & new werke hit hatte. **13..** *E.E. Allit. P.* A. 921 In Iudee hit is þat noble note [*sc.* Jerusalem].

3. A matter, affair, or circumstance; a thing.

a **1350** *St. Lucy* 199 in Horstm. *Altengl. Leg.* (1881) 19 One of his men wightly ȝode To venge his lord of þis lang note. *a* **1375** *Lay Folks Mass Bk.* App. IV. 551 Hit is a nedful note to neuen. *a* **1400–50** *Alexander* 125 As many Besandis on his bake as he bere miȝt, And oþire necessari notis as nedis to his craftis. *c* **1470** *Gol. & Gaw.* 506 'Quhat nedis', said Spinagrus, 'sic notis to nevin'?

1883 *Almondbury Gloss.* 92 'We sud be at the same noit as before,' *i.e.* in the same position, or difficulty.

b. In phrase ***new note*(*s*)**.

13.. *Evang. Nicod.* 77 in Herrig *Archiv.* LIII. 393 Vs noyes gretely þir notes new. **13..** *E.E. Allit. P.* A. 155 þenne nwe note me com on honde þat meued my mynde ay more & more. *c* **1400** *Rowland & O.* 49 Now come tham newe note one hande And wondirfull hasty tythande. *c* **1470** *Gol. & Gaw.* 501 Thoght I suld fynd thame new notis for this ix yeir.

4. The tenor or purport *of* a letter. *rare*$^{-1}$.

a **1400–50** *Alexander* 1719 Now sall I neuen vs here next þe note of his lettir.

note (nəʊt), *sb.*[2] Also 3–4 (6 *Sc.*) not (7 *Sc.* notte), 4 noot, 5 noote, *Sc.* noyt, 6 *Sc.* noit, 6–7 noate, 7 noat. [a. OF. *note* (12th c.), ad. L. *nota*, a mark. Cf. It., Sp., Pg. *nota*.]

I. 1. a. A written character or sign, expressing the pitch and duration of a musical sound.

c **1300** *Learning Music* in *Rel. Ant.* I. 292 Summe notes arn shorte and somme a long noke, Somme kroken a-weyward als a fleshoke. *c* **1440** *Promp. Parv.* 359/1 Noote, of songe yn a boke, *nota*. **1597** T. MORLEY *Introd. Mus.* 11 Euery small note of a Ligature descending being a square note is a long. **1609** DOULAND *Ornith. Microl.* 6 Now *Notes* is that by which the highnes, or lownes of a Song is expressed. **1662** PLAYFORD *Skill Mus.* I. x, This swifter Triple Time is sometimes prick'd in Black Notes, which Black Note is of the same Measure with the Minim. **1716** HEARNE *Collect.* (O.H.S.) V. 277 He hath got an old MS. with Musical Notes. **1762–71** H. WALPOLE *Vertue's Anecd. Paint.* (1786) II. 206 His own portrait done by himself with a pallet and pencils in his hand, and musical notes on a scrip of paper. **1848** RIMBAULT *Pianoforte* 11 Two notes are obtained without the assistance of ledger-lines, by merely placing one below and the other above the staff. **1893** DUFF *Early Printed Bks.* 139 Higden's *Polycronicon*, the first English book containing musical notes.

b. A key of a pianoforte or similar instrument.

1848 RIMBAULT *Pianoforte* 67 One is kept in motion by repeatedly striking the same note. **1884** F. M. CRAWFORD *Rom. Singer* I. 6 Two of the notes are dumb.

fig. **1899** J. SMITH *Chr. Charac.* 172 Instinctively we discern in others a dumb note,.. a moral insensitiveness, which awakens a sense of alarm.

2. a. A single tone of definite pitch, such as is produced by a musical instrument or by the human voice in singing.

c **1300** *Learning Music* in *Rel. Ant.* I. 292 Thu holdest nowt a note, by God! in riht ton... Thu tuchest nowt the notes, thu bites hem on sonder. **1340** *Ayenb.* 105 Ine þise zonge byeþ zeue notes. **1390** GOWER *Conf.* III. 90 Nou scharpe notes and nou softe, Nou hihe notes and nou lowe, As be the gamme a man mai knowe. **1526** *Pilgr. Perf.* (W. de W. 1531) 158 Not clipping the syllables,.. not chauntyng nor brekynge your notes. **1590** SHAKS. *Mids. N.* V. i. 405 First rehearse this song by roate To each word a warbling note. **1611** BIBLE *Wisd.* xix. 18 As in a Psaltery notes change the name of the tune, and yet are alwayes sounds. **1662** PLAYFORD *Skill Mus.* I. i, Those below Gam-ut are called double Notes. **1753** HOGARTH *Anal. Beauty* ii. 16 The ear is as much offended with one even continued note. **1762** FRANKLIN *Exp. Electr.* (1769) 30 It often happens that two [glasses] of the same size differ a note or half a note in tone. **1824** W. IRVING *T. Trav.* I. 47 She even hummed an air, and did not make a single false note. **1887** BOWEN *Virg. Æneid* VI. 646 Their Thracian priest.. Chants them the air with the seven sweet notes of his musical scales.

fig. **1885** *Harper's Mag.* Apr. 696/2 The gardens and orchards.. strike.. joyous notes of color.

b. With reference to the song, or other musical utterance, of birds. (Cf. 3 b.)

1393 LANGL. *P. Pl.* C. XI. 65 Vnder lynde in a launde lenede ich a stounde, To lithen here laies and here loueliche notes. *c* **1430** LYDG. *Min. Poems* (Percy Soc.) 157 The yelwe swan.. Ageyn his dethe melodyously syngyng His fatal notys. *c* **1450** HOLLAND *Howlat* 716 Thar notis anone.. War of Mary the myld. **1570** *Satir. Poems Reform.* XV. 35 Thow luifsum Lark & gay Goldspink,.. Lat be ȝour heuinly noitis. **1591** SHAKS. *Two Gent.* V. iv. 5 Here can I.. to the Nightingales complaining Notes Tune my distresses. **1613–16** W. BROWNE *Brit. Past.* I. iv. 72 Or to the groues, where birds.. Sit sweetly tuning of their noates together. **1738** *Gentl. Mag.* VIII. 596/2 Happy Bird,.. You alone her heart could move With sweetest Notes of tender Love. **1774** GOLDSM. *Nat. Hist.* (1776) V. 324 A region where the birds excel rather in the beauty of their plumage than the sweetness of their notes. **1810** SCOTT *Lady of L.* III. ii, In answer coo'd the cushat dove Her notes of peace, and rest, and love. **1875** NEWTON in *Encycl. Brit.* III. 770/2 The notes to which we have.. hearkened with rapt admiration are changed to a guttural croak.

3. a. A strain of music, a melody, a tune, a song. In later use only *poet.*

c **1275** LAY. 6999 Blaþgabarat was king ihote Of alle manere note. *a* **1300** *Cursor M.* 7407 Dauid cuth on sere-kin note; Bath he cuth on harpe and rote. *c* **1305** *St. Dunstan* 165 in *E.E.P.* (1862) 39 Kirieleyson, christeleyson, was þe murie note and song. **1390** GOWER *Conf.* I. 39 He song, that he the bestes wilde Made of his note tame and milde. **1493** *Festivall* (W. de W. 1515) 90b, Two yonge men began masse w^t a solempne note. **1560** DAUS tr. *Sleidane's Comm.* 233 He made it also in metre, & set a note to it veryе consonant to the argument. **1599** B. JONSON *Cynthia's Rev.* IV. i, I made this ditty, and the note to it. **1635** PAGITT *Christianogr.* I. iii. (1636) 131 If it be some high or Festivall day:.. 'We praise thee O God', is sung with a more solemne and curious note. **1667** MILTON *P.L.* IV. 683 Celestial voices.. responsive each to others note Singing thir great Creator. **1750** GRAY *Elegy* 40 Through the long-drawn aisle and fretted vault The pealing anthem swells the note of praise.

b. The musical song or call of a bird. (Cf. 2 b.)

c **1330** *Amis & Amil.* 536 She herd the foules gret and smale, The swete note of the nightingale. **1500–20** DUNBAR *Poems* xxii. 17 The pyet with hir pretty cot Fenȝeis to sing the nychtingalis not. **1590** SHAKS. *Mids. N.* III. i. 135 The plainsong Cuckow gray; Whose note full many a man doth marke. **1667** MILTON *P.L.* III. 40 The wakeful Bird.. in shadiest Covert hid Tunes her nocturnal Note. **1742** GRAY *On Spring* i, The Attic warbler pours her throat, Responsive to the cuckoo's note. **1800–24** CAMPBELL *Poems, Field Flowers* ii, The deep mellow crush of the wood-pigeon's note. **1846** DICKENS *Cricket on Hearth* i, A Cuckoo looked out of a trap-door in the Palace, and gave note six times.

†**c.** In phr. ***to say, sing*, etc., *by note*.** *Obs.*

1436 *E.E. Wills* (1882) 106, xx s' to sey be note the dirige. *c* **1485** *Digby Myst.* (1882) III. 1223 Ower servyse be note lett vs syng. *a* **1548** HALL *Chron., Hen. VIII*, 82b, The sayd lorde Cardinal sang an high and solempne masse by note before the two kynges and quenes. **1762** CHURCHILL *Rosciad* Poems 1767 I. 46 And, in six months, my dog shall howl by note.

4. A cry, call, or sound, *esp.* that made by a bird or fowl.

a **1300** *Cursor M.* 22467 Childer in moder wamb to lij, Witin þair wambs sal þai cri, Wit hei not and lude steuen. **1573** *Satir. Poems Reform.* xxxix. 144, I saw thame fane To cry 'Peccaui' with the waithman noit. **1593** SHAKS. *2 Hen. VI*, III. ii. 40 Came he right now to sing a Rauens Note, Whose dismall tune bereft my Vitall powres. *a* **1682** SIR T. BROWNE *Tracts* (1683) 105 From the proper note it is called an Hoopebird with us. **1693** WARDER *True Amazons* (1713) 63 With a piteous and discontented Note, searching for their Queen. **1719** DE FOE *Crusoe* I. (Globe) 53 Fowls of many Sorts,.. crying every one according to his usual Note. **1782** COWPER *Jackdaw* i, There is a bird who.. by the hoarseness of his note Might be suppos'd a crow. **1845** *P. Parley's Ann.* VI. 36 [The bullfinch] has a wild hooping note. **1866** HATFIELD *Notices Doncaster* I. 86 The note of the carrion crow.., a note-call of danger.

5. a. In transferred applications.

1483 CAXTON *G. de la Tour* (1868) 183 She wold neuer here ne understand the noote and wordes of none, sauf one tyme that a knyghte prayd her. **1599** SHAKS. *Hen. V*, IV. Prol. 14 The Armourers.., With busie Hammers closing Riuets vp, Giue dreadfull note of preparation. **1702** C. MATHER *Magn. Chr.* III. iii. (1853) I. 306 The gentry at the table were at their old notes. **1839** CARLYLE *Chartism* (1842) 49 The terror and horror they inspire is but the note of preparation for the truth they are to teach. **1849** MACAULAY *Hist. Eng.* IV. I. 492 Roger Lestrange.. sounded the note of war in the Observator. **1877** 'H. A. PAGE' *De Quincey* I. viii. 151 We can catch clearly enough the note of extreme, almost austere self-dependence.

b. ***to change* (*one's*) *note***: To alter (one's) way of speaking or thinking. (Cf. F. *changer de note*.)

1633 G. HERBERT *Temple, Joseph's Coat* 3 Sorrow hath chang'd its note. **1680** *Obs. on 'Curse Ye Meroz'* 7 Do you imagine such a Fool would not think it high time to change Note and Coat? **1734** tr. *Rollin's Anc. Hist.* III. VII. 449 Finding that the more he declined the command the more they pressed him to accept it, he changed his note. **1778** SHERIDAN *Camp.* I. i, Here he comes.—Now you'll change your note. **1873** DIXON *Two Queens* XV. vi. III. 161 Tournay won, these Spanish allies had begun to change their note.

c. In perfumery, one of the basic components of the fragrance of a perfume which give it its character.

1905 F. W. BURBIDGE *Bk. of Scented Garden* 34 Dr Piesse goes so far as to say that one false note amongst odours will destroy the whole harmony of the chord, just as in music or in colour. **1945** E. SAGARIN *Science & Art of Perfumery* xii. 145 The odors were like sounds.. and a scale could be created going from the first or lowest note, the heavy smell, to the last or highest note, the sharp smell. **1954** A. J. KRAJKEMAN tr. *Jellinek's Pract. Mod. Perfumery* IV. 180 Honey-like odours, combining a sweet-floral with an animal note. **1960** A. ELLIS *Essence of Beauty* xii. 142 The characteristic a discerning and discriminating user looks for in a perfume.. is what the perfumer calls '*the soft odour note*'. **1970** *Daily Tel.* 16 Dec. 11/6 The top notes are the lightest and most volatile. **1973** E. MAPLE *Magic of Perfume* vi. 51 There has long existed in perfumers' language a system of 'musical notation' in which the constituents of perfume are accorded 'top notes', 'middle notes' and 'bass notes'.

II. †**6.** A name or distinctive appellation. *Obs.*

1390 GOWER *Conf.* II. 16 A knave child.. which was after hote Paphus, of whom yit hath the note A certein yle, which Paphos Men clepe.

7. a. A mark, sign, token, or indication *of* some quality, condition, or fact, or from which something may be inferred; a characteristic or distinguishing feature.

Common from *c* 1575 to 1690, and again in recent use (from *c* 1865).

c **1374** CHAUCER *Boeth.* V. met. iii. (1868) 159 Wherfore eschaufiþ it so.. to fynden þilke notes of soþe y-couered. **1547–64** BAULDWIN *Mor. Philos.* (Palfr.) 111 Patience & perseuerance are two proper notes; whereby Gods children are truly known from hypocrites. *a* **1568** ASCHAM *Scholem.* (Arb.) 37 The most speciall notes of a good witte for learning in a childe [etc.]. **1607** TOPSELL *Four-f. Beasts* 435 Both kindes haue vnder their tailes a double note of passage. **1628** T. SPENCER *Logick* 288 That Axiome is probable which seemes so to all.. by certaine frequent notes, and cleerenes. **1696** WHISTON *The. Earth* IV. (1722) 346 'Tis a plain Note of the Vileness of our present State. **1738** WARBURTON *Div. Legat.* I. Ded. p. xxxii, To shew how certain Notes they are of the Temper of Mind I charge upon you. **1794** PALEY *Evid.* II. vii. (1817) 185 Between the letters.. of St. Paul.. and his history in the Acts of the Apostles, there exist many notes of correspondency. **1846** KEBLE *Lyra Innoc.* (1873) 12 The welcome notes of fatherhood. **1891** *Speaker* 2 May 532/2 These are the notes of the 'Neo-paganism', which began a good hundred years ago.

b. *Theol.* One of certain characteristics by which the true Church may be known; a sign or proof of genuine origin, authority, and practice.

1555 L. SAUNDERS in Coverdale *Lett. Martyrs* (1564) 187 Besydes these outward notes and tokens declaryng y^t we be the true church. **1563** *Homilies* II. xvi. (1859) 462 The true Church.. hath always three notes or marks whereby it is known; pure and sound doctrine, the Sacraments ministered according to Christ's holy institution, and the right use of ecclesiastical discipline. **1656** BRAMHALL *Replic.* i. 3 Other notes of the Church which did not please us so well, as Antiquity, and Uniuersality, and Splendour. **1749** WESLEY *Wks.* (1872) X. 88 How comes subjection to the Pope to be.. an essential note of the Church? **1841** J. H. NEWMAN *Lett.* (1891) II. 354 Many persons are doubtful whether we have the notes of the true Church upon us. **1864** —— *Apol.* v. 198, I do not wish it supposed, that I considered the note of Catholicity really to belong to Rome [etc.].

transf. **1871** R. H. HUTTON *Ess.* I. 337 To have a compact statement of the whole gist of Christianity is the principal 'note' of the Common-Sense Church.

8. a. A stigma, reproach. Const. *of*.

In common use from *c* 1570 to 1650; now *rare*.

1531 ELYOT *Gov.* (1580) 80 Augustus,..only for playing at dice,..sustaineth in hystories a note of reproche. **1570-6** LAMBARDE *Peramb. Kent* (1826) 323 Whatsoever note of infamie we heeretofore may have contracted. **1635** R. N. tr. *Camden's Hist. Eliz.* I. 17 Amongst all men he underwent the note of cruelty. **1669** DRYDEN *Tyrannic Love* Pref., My outward Conversation..shall never be justly tax'd with the Note of Atheism or Prophaneness.

1849 MACAULAY *Hist. Eng.* v. I. 568 A crime on which divine and human laws have justly set a peculiar note of infamy. **1865** PUSEY *Truth Eng. Ch.* 130 To leave those who disbelieved it free from the note of heresy.

b. The mark of censure used by the Roman censors.

1614 RALEIGH *Hist. World* v. iii. §13. 422 Neither was the note of the Censors at this time (as otherwise it had used to be) hurtful onely in reputation.

†**c.** An object of censure. *Obs. rare*⁻¹.

1563 FOXE *A. & M.* 59/2 Better it were to sustaine pouerty with praise, than in greate promotions to be a common note to al men.

9. An objective sign, or visible token, which serves to identify or distinguish some person or thing, or to denote some circumstance or fact in connexion therewith.

Pretty common from *c* 1580 to 1680; now *rare*.

1577-87 HOLINSHED *Scot. Chron.* (1806) II. 148 A red lion (the peculiar note of the kingdom of Scotland). **1583** STUBBES *Anat. Abus.* II. (1882) 110 So the other notes of apparell..may make a difference, and distinguish them from others of the laitie abroad. **1618** BOLTON *Florus* I. xviii. (1636) 54 Having first cast away his ensignes or notes of a King. **1683** RAY *Corr.* (1848) 134 Those notes of having flat feet..argue it to belong to the genus of Colymbi. **1899** *Allbutt's Syst. Med.* VIII. 865 The 'note' of scabies is the burrow; and in this the parasite must be sought.

10. a. A sign or character (other than a letter) used in writing or printing; a mark *of* interrogation, etc. (Also *fig.*) ***note of interrogation***: see INTERROGATION 2 b.

1529 MORE *Dyaloge* IV. Wks. 286/1, I haue laid you the places ready with ryshes betwene the leaues and notes marked in the margentes where the matter is touched. **1611** SHAKS. *Wint. T.* v. ii. 12 The changes I perceiued in the King, and Camillo, were very Notes of admiration. **1636** B. JONSON *Eng. Gram.* Wks. 1816 IX. 345 If a sentence be with an interrogation, we use this note (?). **1668** WILKINS *Real Char.* III. xi. 365 There should be some Note or Mark to express when a Vowel is to be used long. **1748** J. MASON *Elocution* 23 There are four more Notes or Distinctions of Pause, viz. a Parenthesis [etc.]. **1795** L. MURRAY *Eng. Gram.* 169 A note of interrogation is used at the end of an interrogative sentence. **1859** [see ADMIRATION 5]. **1899** *Allbutt's Syst. Med.* VIII. 775 Bald patches with note of exclamation hairs. *Ibid.* 856 The short hairs..are shaped like a note of exclamation (!).

†**b.** A mark on a flower or leaf. *Obs. rare.*

1578 LYTE *Dodoens* 206 These be not those Hyacinthes wherein the notes or mourning markes are printed. **1691** RAY *Creation* (1714) 113 The signatures of Plants or the Notes impressed upon them as indices of their vertues.

†**11.** A (Hebrew) particle. *Obs. rare.*

1607 TOPSELL *Four-f. Beasts* (1658) 339 The Hebrew notes cannot admit such a version or exposition. *c* **1620** A. HUME *Brit. Tongue* II. v, This difference we declyne, not as doth the latines and greekes, be terminationes, but with noates, after the maner of the hebrues, quhilk they cal particles. *a* **1653** GOUGE *Comm. Heb.* ii. 9 The passage may be brought in with discretive notes,..'though'..'yet'.

III. 12. *Law.* **a.** An abstract of essential particulars relating to transfer of land by process of FINE, which was engrossed and placed on record.

1483 *Act 1 Rich. III*, c. 7 §1 Notes and Fines levied in the King's Courts..should be openly and solemnly read. **1581** *Act 23 Eliz.* c. 3 §1 The Concord, Note and Foot of every such Fine. **1594** WEST *2nd Pt. Symbol.* §58 The notes of all writs whereupon fines are to be levied. **1670** BLOUNT *Law Dict.* s.v., Note of a fine..is a Brief of a Fine made by the Chirographer, before it be engrossed. **1766** BLACKSTONE *Comm.* II. xxi. 351 The note of a fine: which is only..an abstract of the writ of covenant, and the concord; naming the parties, the parcels of land, and the agreement.

b. In *Sc. Law* applied to various forms of legal records and memoranda.

1560 ROLLAND *Crt. Venus* IV. 292 Scho..thairupon tuik notis and Instrumentis. **1825** *Act 6 Geo. IV*, c. 120 §9 A short and concise Note, drawn and signed by Counsel, of the Pleas in Law on which the Action or Defence is to be maintained. **1838** W. BELL *Dict. Law Scot.* 679 The term note is also applied to various incidental applications, the occasions for which it would be difficult to enumerate. **1868-88** [see RECLAIMING *vbl. sb.* b].

13. a. A brief record or abstract of facts written down for the purpose of assisting the memory, or to serve as a basis for a more complete or full statement; also *transf.*, a recollection or mental impression of something. (Usually *pl.*)

1548 PATTEN *Exped. Scotl.* Peroration P ij b, The which indede I had not so perfitly written in my notes. **1595** SHAKS. *John* v. ii. 5 That..they and we, perusing ore these notes May know wherefore we tooke the Sacrament. **1617** MORYSON *Itin.* I. 287, I find in my notes that at Lasagna I changed a silver crowne for eight and twenty batzen. **1695** WOODWARD *Nat. Hist. Earth* I. (1723) 4 And 'tis out of these Notes that my Observations are compiled. **1817** W. SELWYN *Law Nisi Prius* (ed. 4) II. 798 Where the agreement is to be performed upon a contingency,..there a note in writing is not necessary. **1854** CHR. WORDSW. *Misc.* (1879) I. 95 A brief account of my impression was published anonymously under the title of 'Notes at Paris'. **1885** *Law Rep. 29 Chanc. Div.* 543 There is merely a short note of what he decided.

b. In phr. ***to make,*** or ***take, a note*** or ***notes.***

1548 PATTEN *Exped. Scotl.* Ded., Hauying in these last warres againste Scotlande..made notes of actes thear done. **1591** SHAKS. *Two Gent.* II. vii. 84 Goe with me to my chamber To take a note of what I stand in need of. **1641** SIR S. D'EWES in Forster *Gr. Remonstr.* 124, I drew out againe my pen and ink, and took notes. **1726** SWIFT *Gulliver* II. vi, The King heard the whole.., frequently taking Notes of what I spoke. **1789** BURNS *Capt. Grose* i, A chield's amang you taking notes. **1837** SOUTHEY *Lett.* (1856) IV. 538 He has only his memory to trust to, never having made any notes. **1848** DICKENS *Dombey* xv, When found, make a note of. **1875** JOWETT *Plato* (ed. 2) IV. 234, I took notes.., which I afterwards filled up at leisure.

c. ***to compare notes***: see COMPARE *v.*¹ 2 b.

d. A brief memorandum made to serve as a help in discoursing on any subject. (Chiefly *pl.*)

1693 *Humours Town* 19 'Tis as necessary as Notes to the Parson in the Pulpit. **1719** SWIFT *Lett. to Young Clergym.* Wks. 1751 V. 15 My frequent hearing of Foreigners, who never make Use of Notes, may have added to my Disgust. **1796** PEGGE *Anonym.* (1809) 139 They call a Clergyman's Sermon, what he preaches from, his Notes; because formerly it was written in characters, or short-hand, usually called Notes. **1872** FROUDE *Short Stud.* I. 2 He spoke for more than an hour without a note.

14. a. An explanatory or critical annotation or comment appended to a passage in a writing or book.

1560 DAUS tr. *Sleidane's Comm.* 40 b, This writing dyd Luther translate into the vulgare toungue, & set to his notes in the margente. **1618** BOLTON *Florus* To Rdr., The words ..are for the most part explanatory of the Authors meaning, supplying marginall notes. **1653** MILTON *Hirelings* Wks. 1851 V. 369 The entire Scripture translated into English with plenty of Notes. **1714** in Wodrow *Corr.* (1843) II. 8 A new edition of Homer's Odyssey,..with Gronovius' notes. **1771** LUCKOMBE *Hist. Printing* 260 The Parallel is another Sign which serves for a Reference, and is fit to be used either for side or bottom Notes. **1809** LAMB *Let. to Coleridge* 7 June, I found two other volumes.., the *Arcadia*, and *Daniel*, enriched with manuscript notes. **1841-** [see FOOTNOTE]. **1878** R. HOLT *Ormulum* I. p. v, In this new edition the Editor..has revised, and added somewhat to, the Notes.

†**b.** An observation deserving of notice or remembrance; an interesting or noteworthy remark.

1577 GOOGE *Heresbach's Husb.* (1586) 24 b, There is also another necessarie note, to have the seede from strange grounde, and from the woorse to the better. **1601** SHAKS. *Twel. N.* III. iv. 168 A good note, that keepes you from the blow of yᵉ Law. **1642-4** VICARS *God in Mount* 203 To give thee but one note more concerning this fight.

15. A brief statement of particulars or of some fact; †a bill or account.

1587 *Galway Arch.* in *10th Rep. Hist. MSS. Comm.* App. V. 444 A trewe noate and bill of accompt. **1590** SHAKS. *Com. Err.* IV. i. 27 Here's a note How much your Chaine weighs to the vtmost charect. **1597** —— *2 Hen. IV*, v. i. 19 Heere is now the Smithes note, for Shooing, And Plough-Irons. **1602** DEKKER *Satirom.* Wks. 1873 I. 188 Flash, where's the note of the guestes you have invited? **1660** F. BROOKE tr. *Le Blanc's Trav.* 48 Then I produced the..notes, that witnessed the discharging of the excises and customes. **1715** HEARNE *Collect.* (O.H.S.) V. 128 This Morning preached.. Dr. Potter... Mr. Taylor of Xᵗ. Ch. was put in the Note, there having been a Mistake in delivering the Moneo. **1732** *Acc. Workhouses* 175 Keep the tradesmen's notes upon a file. **1895** *19th Cent.* Aug. 337 That little document is a note of the box-office receipts for the evening.

16. a. A short letter or written communication of an informal kind.

1594 SHAKS. *Rich. III*, v. iii. 41 Giue him from me, this most needfull Note. **1603** —— *Meas. for M.* IV. ii. 106 My Lord has sent you this note, And by mee this further charge. **1624** in *Cosin's Corr.* (Surtees) I. 37, I received your note from Fetherston. I thank you for your pains. **1687** A. LOVELL tr. *Thevenot's Trav.* I. d, I shall Answer, Sir, in as few words as I can, the Note you did me the Honour to write to me. **1776** *Trial of Nundocomar* 61/2 Did you send a verbal or a written message? I wrote a note. **1796-7** JANE AUSTEN *Pride & Prej.* xxvi. (1813) 130 Not a note, not a line did I receive in the mean time. **1846** DICKENS *Battle of Life* i, He sent them on, with a pencilled note to me. **1891** A. H. CRAUFURD *Gen. Craufurd's Light Div.* 6 Six little notes addressed to the brothers Craufurd.

ellipt. **1892** *Phot. Ann.* II. 62 Get a piece of stiff paper (thick note does well), twist it into a sugar-loaf shape.

b. A formal diplomatic communication.

1796 BURKE *Regic. Peace* i. Wks. VIII. 120 Nothing can be more proper or more manly than the state publication called a note on this proceeding. **1848** W. H. KELLY tr. *Blanc's Hist. Ten Yrs.* I. 473 M. de Talleyrand..warmly adopted the project, and promised to present a note to the British government in its favour. **1863** KINGLAKE *Crimea* (1876) I. iii. 50 The Porte..acknowledged the validity of the Latin claims in a formal note.

17. †**a.** A signed receipt or voucher. *Obs. rare.*

a **1700** EVELYN *Diary* 21 Apr. 1644, Two reasonable faire publiq Libraries whence one may borrow a booke to one's chamber, giving but a note under hand. **1722** DE FOE *Col. Jack* (1840) 60 When he had paid in all the money..he.. stayed..to take notes..for what he had paid. **1739** LADY M. W. MONTAGU *Lett.* III. 9 The Borromean library, where all strangers have..liberty, on giving a note for it, to take any printed book home with them.

b. A written promise to pay a certain sum at a specified time. (Cf. next.)

1683 *Lond. Gaz.* No. 1862/8 A Note under the Hand of John Swettaple, Goldsmith,..for Ninety nine Pounds Ten Shillings, paid to Edward Callender or Bearer. **1712** ARBUTHNOT *John Bull* I. xvi, His Note will go farther than my Bond. **1798** W. HUTTON *Life* 33, I..paid one hundred guineas down, and gave my note six months after date, for the remainder. **1806** SURR *Winter in Lond.* III. 152, I shall give her a note at a month after date for fifty or a hundred pounds. **1879** PENTECOST *Vol. of Bk.* vi. (1882) 43 A man's note is only current..because the man is good.

c. More fully ***note of hand.*** (Cf. PROMISSORY *a.*)

1727-38 CHAMBERS *Cycl.* s.v. *Note*, In which sense we say, a promissory note, a note under hand,..&c. **1766** BLACKSTONE *Comm.* II. xxx. 467 Promissory notes, or notes of hand, are a plain and direct engagement in writing, to pay a sum specified at the time therein limited to a person therein named, or sometimes to his order, or often to the bearer at large. **1809** R. LANGFORD *Introd. Trade* 12 Notes of Hand under one pound are void. **1867** TROLLOPE *Chron. Barset* xxxvii, She can have my note-of-hand for it all at fourteen days.

18. a. A bank-note, or similar promissory note passing current as money.

1696 LUTTRELL *Brief Rel.* (1857) IV. 79 The said bank have resolved to take for subscriptions the bank of England's notes. **1728** SWIFT *Intelligencer* No. 19 He gave notes instead of money (from twopence to twenty shillings) which passed current in all shops where meat or drink was sold. **1806-7** J. BERESFORD *Miseries Hum. Life* (1826) IV. xiii, You have involuntarily confided your..uncounted cash and notes to the care of the public. **1834** MARRYAT *P. Simple* ii, Change for a one-pound note. **1856** MRS. CARLYLE *Lett.* II. 302 The five-pound note I sent you.

b. *Australia* (and *Sc.*). A bank-note worth £1; the amount of a pound sterling.

1864 J. ROGERS *New Rush* II. 28 A note's so very trifling, it's no sooner changed than gone; For it is but twenty shillings. **1875** WOOD & LAPHAM *Waiting for Mail* 39 Even at half fifty notes a week You ought to have made a pile.

IV. 19. a. Distinction, mark, importance; reputation, fame. Esp. in phr. ***of*** (***good, bad,*** etc.) ***note.***

1538 BALE *Thre Lawes* 293 Thynges of slendre note. **1601** SHAKS. *All's Well* v. iii. 14 The yong Lord Did to his Maiesty..Offence of mighty note. **1610** HOLLAND *Camden's Brit.* (1637) 463 A towne of good note in these dayes for making of clothes. **1698** FRYER *Acc. E. India & P.* 92 Their Windows, except some few of the highest Note, are usually folding Doors. **1708** J. CHAMBERLAYNE *St. Gt. Brit.* I. I. iii. (1710) 5 It contains..12 Market-Towns: The chief in note are Reading,..Abington [etc.]. **1745** P. THOMAS *Jrnl. Anson's Voy.* 5 *note*, The same..is the frequent Repast even of those of better Note. **1788** PRIESTLEY *Lect. Hist.* IV. xxi. 172 Polybius..was of the first note in his age as a soldier, statesman, and philosopher. **1838** MACAULAY *Let. to Napier* 22 July, As if he were a young writer struggling into note. **1873** DIXON *Two Queens* I. ii. I. 11 Had he died at sixty years of age, he might have left behind him an obscure and blameless note.

b. ***of note,*** of distinction or eminence; notable.

1588 SHAKS. *L.L.L.* III. i. 25 These betraie nice wenches .., and make them men of note. **1611** BIBLE *Transl. Pref.* ¶ 2 As oft as we do anything of note or consequence. **1667** PRIMATT *City & C. Build.* 94 A Platform for a House in a high Street, or Lane of Note. **1710** STEELE *Tatler* No. 135 ¶ 1 All the Philosophers of Note in Greece. **1780** HARRIS *Philol. Enq.* Wks. (1841) 390 Among the Romans, the first critic of note was Cicero. **1840** DICKENS *Barn. Rudge* xlviii, The fluttering of a banner caught the eye, and became a circumstance of note. **1877** MRS. OLIPHANT *Makers Flor.* x. 254 Five noble citizens of Florence, all men of note and weight.

20. a. Notice, regard, or attention.

1598 BACON *Ess., Of Ceremonies* (Arb.) 24 Smal matters winne great commendation: because they are continually in vse and in note. *a* **1635** NAUNTON *Fragm. Reg.* (Arb.) 56 The factions of the Court, which were all his times strong, and in every mans note. *a* **1641** FINETT *For. Ambass.* 10 The Ambassador..kept himselfe all this while quiet without.. thrusting for publique Note. **1789** COWPER *Tiroc.* 641 To.. commend, With designation of the finger's end, Its various parts to his attentive note. *c* **1810** HOGG *May of Moril Glen* I, The virgin cast on him a look,..As on some things below her note. **1886** *Law Q. Rev.* Oct. 484 The manner in which these statutes were interpreted is worthy of note.

b. In phr. ***to take note of.***

1596 SHAKS. *Merch. Ven.* v. i. 120 Giue order to my seruants, that they take No note at all of our being absent hence. **1601** —— *All's Well* I. iii. 195 My loue hath in't a bond Where of the world takes note. **1852** THACKERAY *Esmond* II. xi, No one took note of me. **1863** E. V. NEALE *Anal. Th. & Nat.* 15 We select from the multitude what we want.., and take no note of the rest.

c. Knowledge, information; intimation. *rare.*

1598 BACON *Ess., of Suitors* (Arb.) 44 If intelligence of the matter coulde not otherwise haue beene had but by him, aduantage be not taken of the note. **1606** SHAKS. *Tr. & Cr.* IV. i. 43 Rouse him, and giue him note of our approach. **1610** —— *Temp.* II. i. 248 She that from Naples Can haue no note, vnlesse the Sun were post.

1835 W. IRVING *Tour Prairies* vii, A streaming flight of wild geese..gave note of the waning year.

V. 21. *attrib.* and *Comb.*, as (sense 1) ***note-head, -value***; (sense 2) ***note-singing***; ***note-spinning*** vbl. sb. and ppl. adj.; (sense 13) ***note-block, -gatherer, -maker, -pad, -taker, -writer***; ***note-taking***; (sense 16) ***note-sized*** adj., ***-wise*** adv., ***-writing*** (also as *adj.*); (sense 18) ***note-case, -issue, -palming***; **note-broker** *U.S.*, a broker who deals in promissory notes and bills of exchange; **note-cluster**, several neighbouring notes played simultaneously; **notehead paper**, business notepaper having a printed heading; **note-holder**, a holder of notes (sense 17) issued by a business company or the like for temporary financing; **note-layer** (sense 18), a petty thief who operates a short-change swindle; **note-row, -series** = *tone-row* (TONE *sb.* 11).

1927 R. A. FREEMAN *Certain Dr. Thorndyke* II. xiv. 207 Jotting down on a *note-block a few brief memoranda. **1870** W. W. FOWLER *10 Yrs. Wall St.* 226 This man..is an English Jew, who has gone into the business of a *note broker. **1929** *Encycl. Brit.* IV. 233/1 Bill-brokers are practically unknown in the United States; their general analogue is the note-broker. **1838** DICKENS *O. Twist* ix, Placing a snuff-box in one pocket of his trousers, a *note-case in the other. **1934** C. LAMBERT *Music Ho!* v. 330 Van Dieren's attitude towards harmony is more indicative of future developments than the '*note clusters' of Henry Cowell. **1965** *New Statesman* 24 Sept. 458/3 A younger composer like Peter Sculthorpe attempts to enter the heart of the Australian experience by way of a static technique of cumulative ostinati and note-clusters that is more Asiatic than occidental. **1637** DOW *Answ. to Burton* 120 His *note-gatherers in the gallery. **1946** H. FOSS in A. L. Bacharach *Brit. Mus. of our Time* iv. 78 Warlock wrote with exquisite precision:..the shape of the *note-heads, the uprights, the binds and ties, were of enormous interest to him. **1974** G. READ *Music Notation* v. 63 The note-head..is somewhat oval in shape, and is either open (or 'white'..) or closed ('black'..). **1909** *Westm. Gaz.* 20 May 7/2 The..*notehead paper of a London firm of stock, share, and bond dealers. **1927** *Daily Tel.* 21 June 2/3 Shareholders were prepared for unfavourable figures by the necessity for an arrangement regarding..the rights of the *note-holders. **1968** *Globe & Mail* (Toronto) 13 Jan. B. 1/2 Fraudulent financial statements and a false prospectus were means used..to defraud 8,500 noteholders of Prudential Finance Corp. Ltd. of $20-million. **1893** *Times* 27 Apr. 9/5 The privilege of *note issue enjoyed by the Scotch banks. **1928** *Note-layer [see CREEP *sb.* 1 d]. **1938** D. CASTLE *Do Your Own Time* viii. 83 They boasted of having been knock-off gees, gow peddlers, ..note layers, and torpedo men. **1950** H. E. GOLDIN *Dict. Amer. Underworld Lingo* 146/1 The note-layer usually works with an accomplice. **1638** BAKER tr. *Balzac's Lett.* (vol. II.) 61 Erecting as it were Trophees of like passages, after the fashion of our *Note-Makers now adayes. **1738** *Gentl. Mag.* VIII. 634 Any Critick or Note-maker. **1922** A. BENNETT *Lilian* I. iv. 41 She repeated the number, even writing it on her *note pad. **1961** *Encounter* Apr. 29/2 He asked me for one of my notepads. **1975** D. BAGLEY *Snow Tiger* xi. 95 Smithers consulted his note-pad. **1900** WEYMAN *Sophia* iii, Until you are away from here I'll answer there shall be no *note palming. **1955** *Oxf. Compan. Mus.* (ed. 9) 698/1 *Note-row... This is a rigid method of composition introduced by Schönberg... All the twelve notes of the octave are employed in every composition, and all the notes are treated in such a way as to enjoy an equal footing. **1961** *Listener* 12 Oct. 578/3 He spoke of his contrapuntal technique, of note rows, their combinations and inversions. **1947** *Penguin Music Mag.* Dec. 20 'Twelve-tone technique', in which the twelve notes of the chromatic scale are used in an order known as a '*note-series', which remains the same throughout the work. **1962** *Times* 19 Oct. 18/6 The American group admit to working from a note-series. **1896** *Musical Herald* 1 Feb. 41/1 Thousands of teachers waste time in *note-singing practice. **1908** E. M. SNEYD-KYNNERSLEY *H.M.I.* xxiv. 288 The clergy encouraged note-singing for the sake of their choirs. **1870** *Routledge's Every Boy's Ann.* June Suppl. 12 A small *note-sized envelope. **1946** H. FOSS in A. L. Bacharach *Brit. Music of our Time* iv. 67 He [*sc.* 'Peter Warlock'] was no devotee of *note-spinning, of blowing up frog-ideas into bull-like proportions. **1961** *Listener* 20 Apr. 717/3 The ideas in the other two movements are of an altogether lower standard and there is some tiresome note-spinning. **1970** *Times* (Sat. Suppl.) 18 Apr. p. iii/5, I confess to finding it rather like late, not very strongly motivated, note-spinning Schumann. **1886** T. HARDY *Mayor Casterbr.* xxviii, Henchard being no *note-taker himself. **1935** *Essays & Studies* XX. 123 All these matters can be conscientiously taught to the plodding note-taker and be redelivered at examinations. **1961** *Sunday Express* 29 Jan. 9/6 Police note-takers filled four foolscap pages. **1496–7** *Rec. St. Mary at Hill* (1904) 224 Furst, paid at the *Note takyng of the Endentour of comnandes, ij d. **1862** THORNBURY *Turner* II. 134 That vast tenacious memory, which no note-taking habits could weaken. **1954** J. MASTERS *Bhowani Junction* II. xii. 107 They didn't want me for any more note-taking. **1955** H. ROTH *Sleeper* xi. 92 The stilted feeling that note-taking causes in some interviewees. **1975** *Times* 5 July 2/5 Jurors..were often required to perform fantastic feats of attention and memory..without the aid of note-taking. **1915** *Musical Quarterly* I. 191 An Indian [*sc.* North American Indian] can give short *note-values corresponding to eighth or sixteenth notes with perfect distinctness. **1917** H. JAMES *Middle Years* iv. 46 Whereas the smartness and newness beyond the sea supposedly disavowed the low, they did so but thinly and vainly, falling markedly short of the high; which the little boxed and boiled Albany attained to some effect of,..just by having its so thoroughly appreciable note-value in a scheme of manners. **1944** W. APEL *Harvard Dict. Mus.* 497/2 The illustration shows the note values with their American terminology. **1955** G. ABRAHAM in H. van Thal *Fanfare for E. Newman* ii. 10 The first two bars were originally written as four, in double note-values. **1963** *Listener* 17 Jan. 141/2 It [*sc.* the basic five-note figure] is repeated eight times in succession, with progressively lengthening note-values. **1703** *Rules of Civility* 177 If we be desir'd to..write *Notewise, that is to say, without Sir, and the great Space at the top [of the letter], we must comply. **1836–48** B. D. WALSH *Aristoph.* 394 *note*, Some of the Greek *note-writers call him a composer of tragedies. **1814** JANE AUSTEN *Mansfield Park* II. xiii. 291 Quite unpractised in such sort of *note-writing. **1826** MISS MITFORD *Village* Ser. II. (1863) 274 The closetings, the note-writings, the whisperings. **1967** G. KELLY in *Coast to Coast 1965–66* 101 He became the victim of their gum-chewing, note-writing, hair-combing inattention.

†**note**, *sb.*[3] *Obs.* (Prob. var. of NUT *sb.*, here applied to the uropygial gland.)

1486 *Bk. St. Albans* a vj, Youre hawke..fetcheth moystour like oyle at hir taill,..and strikyth the federis of hir wynges throw her beke, and it is calde the note, than as she fetchis the oyle. [Hence Guillim (1632) and Holme (1688).]

note, obs. f. NUT; dial. variant of NOWT.

†**note**, *a. Obs. rare.* (Meaning doubtful.)

Perh. properly an attributive use of NOTE *sb.*[1], employed mainly for alliteration. L. *nōtus* has also been suggested.

13.. *Gaw. & Gr. Knt.* 2092 Now nar ȝe not fer fro þat note place. *a* **1400–50** *Alexander* 1227 Arystes..noyed of þare note-men at þe nete kepid. *Ibid.* 4870 Fra þens oure note men be northe nymes þaim þe way.

†**note**, *v.*[1] *Obs.* Forms: α. 1 notian, 3 notien, 4 notye. β. 3 noten, 4 notun (6 *Sc.* noyt, noit, not), 4–5 (6 *Sc.*), note. [OE. *notian*, f. *notu* NOTE *sb.*[1] Cf. Icel. *nota.*]

1. *trans.* To use, to make use of (something).

α. *c* **888** K. ÆLFRED *Boeth.* xviii. §1 Eall moncynn & ealle netenu ne notigað nawer neah feorðan dæles þisse eorðan. *c* **960** *Rule St. Benet* (Schröer) 52 ðif he furðon þurh þa ȝebedu ȝehæled ne bið, notiȝe þonne se abbod cyrfes. *c* **1200** *Trin. Coll. Hom.* 189 Hereð nu to wiche fihte we oȝen þis strengðe notien. *a* **1250** *Owl & Night.* 1033 þar men habbeþ milde mod, Ich noti mid hom mine þrote. *c* **1315** SHOREHAM *Poems* I. 2198 In fourme of bred and eke of wyn, þat we hyt notye scholde. **1393** LANGL. *P. Pl.* C. XVIII. 101 Tyliers.. tolden here maystres By þe seed þat þei sewe what þei shoulde notye.

β. *a* **1000** *Colloq. Ælfric* in Wr.-Wülcker 100 Se treow-wyrhta seȝð, hwilc eower ne notaþ cræfte minon. *c* **1200** ORMIN 12228 Swa þatt tu nohht ne notesst itt At naness kinness nede. *c* **1250** *Gen. & Ex.* 3144 So mikil hird so it noten mai. **13..** *Cursor M.* 23763 (Gött.), If we will note on þaim vr might, Certes þai er feld in flight. *c* **1330** R. BRUNNE *Chron. Wace* (Rolls) 2403 Folyly hold we þis meyne þus, þat mykel þyng al day notes. *c* **1400** *Destr. Troy* 402 Of nygramansi ynogh to note when she liket. *c* **1440** *Promp. Parv.* 359/2 Notun, or vsyn, *utor.* **1513** DOUGLAS *Æneis* XIII. vi. 64 The agit Drances with curage hoit Begowth the first hys toung for to noit. *c* **1560** A. SCOTT *Poems* (S.T.S.) i. 221 Noblest natour, nurice to nurtour, not This dull indyte.

2. *intr.* To make use *of* (something). *rare*⁻¹.

c **1220** *Bestiary* 612 No golsipe is hem minde, til he noten of a gres, ðe name is mandragores.

note (nəʊt), *v.*[2] Also 3 notien, 3, 6–7 noat(e, 4 (6 *Sc.*) not, 6 notte, noth (*Sc.* noit). [ad. OF. *noter*, *notter*, ad. L. *notāre*, f. *nota* NOTE *sb.*[1]]

I. 1. a. *trans.* To observe or mark carefully; to give heed or attention to; to notice closely.

a **1225** *Ancr. R.* 158 Her beoð, in þeos wordes, two eadie wordes to noten. *c* **1375** *Sc. Leg. Saints* xxxviii. (*Adrian*) 43 þe king..notyt wel..þe ansuere þat ilkane mad. *a* **1400–50** *Alexander* 5655 Now sall I neuyn ȝow þe names, note ȝe þe wordis. **1483** CAXTON *Cato* g j, Euery man ought to note and reteyne them in their mynde and wytte. *a* **1533** LD. BERNERS *Gold. Bk. M. Aurel.* (1546) L viij b, It is a thyng well to be noted, howe all good and yll heartes are applied. **1596** DRAYTON *Legends* ii. 400 My Paths by Spyes he diligently noted. **1630** *R. Johnson's Kingd. & Commw.* 144 Of both these Forces of horse and foot of France, you are to note this which followeth. **1697** DRYDEN *Virg. Georg.* III. 162 His Age and Courage weigh: Nor those alone, But note his Father's Virtues and his own. **1774** BURKE *Corr.* (1844) I. 516, I received your lordship's letter, and as the merchants say, note the contents. **1791** MRS. RADCLIFFE *Rom. Forest* ii, I took special care to note how the trees stood. **1850** MCCOSH *Div. Govt.* II. ii. (1874) 162 This is a circumstance worthy of being noted. **1878** HUXLEY *Physiogr.* 79 It may be well to note the characters of the two constituents.

absol. **1605** B. JONSON *Volpone* II. i, I haue some generall notions; I do loue To note, and to obserue.

b. To take notice of; to observe, perceive.

c **1315** SHOREHAM I. 60 þat he so wel ypeawed be, þat alle men hit noteþe. *c* **1386** CHAUCER *Pars. T.* ¶336 If ther hadde be no synne in clothing, Crist wolde not so soone have notid and spoke of the clothing of thilke riche man in the gospel. *c* **1400** LOVE *Bonavent. Mirr.* xxxiii. (B.N.C. MS.) lf. 73 In þis processe of þe gospelle..we mowe noten and vnderstonde many faire þinges. **1526** *Pilgr. Perf.* (W. de W. 1531) 11 b, In the whiche mercyfull liberalite, I note the superaboundant goodnes of god. **1582** STANYHURST *Æneis* II. (Arb.) 68, I noted on suddeyn the goast of verye Creüsa. **1632** J. HAYWARD tr. *Biondi's Eromena* 19 The slave noting his master all alone, presented himselfe before him. **1658** JER. TAYLOR in *12th Rep. Hist. MSS. Comm.* App. V. 5 If ever you have noted or heard of any overtures of unkindnesse betweene them. **1712** HEARNE *Collect.* (O.H.S.) III. 373, I told him I had noted it before. **1821–22** SHELLEY *Chas. I*, II. 456 Have you not noted that the Fool of late Has lost his careless mirth? **1874** GREEN *Short Hist.* iv. §4. 192 Such severances as we note in the thirteenth century of the cloth-merchant from the tailor.

2. To mention separately or specially among other items or matters committed to writing.

c **1380** WYCLIF *Sel. Wks.* II. 345 Poul notiþ first þis word. *Ibid.*, Poul notiþ, as trewe men shulden, ech variynge of Goddis word. **1390** GOWER *Conf.* II. 172 Nereïdes that thei ben hote, The Nimphes whiche that thei note To regne upon the stremes salte. *c* **1450** *Godstow Reg.* (1905) 273 The forsaid acre of lond, with all the mede and xviij. d. of yerely rent afore-noted. **1563** FULKE *Meteors* (1640) 16 Generally it is noted of all Historiographers, that after the appearing of Comets, most commonly follow great..calamities. **1641** J. JACKSON *True Evang. T.* iii. 185 Which thing the Evangelist notes as one of the criticall passages of his Passion. **1692** RAY *Creation* I. (1704) 150 They not being able, as I noted before, to see them at that distance. **1721** DE FOE *Mem. Cavalier* (1840) 123, I shall only note this. **1873** HELPS *Anim. & Mast.* i. (1875) 11, I must just note that Bastiah's censure does not apply to England as much as to France.

3. a. To set down in writing; to put down as a memorandum; †to write, indite.

a **1400–50** *Alexander* 2795 To Nostanda on next þus notis he a lettir. **1535** COVERDALE *Isa.* xxx. 8 Write them this in their tables, and note it in a booke. **1591** SHAKS. *1 Hen. VI*, II. iv. 101 Ile note you in my Booke of Memorie. **1663** GERBIER *Counsel* 25 He ought also to note in his book the materials. **1697** *C'tess D'Aunoy's Trav.* (1706) 114, I contented myself to note only on my Table-Book these Lines. **1806** PIKE *Sources Mississ.* (1810) App. 51 Lieut. Wilkinson..carries with him a..sketch of the route, noting the streams, hills, &c. that we crossed. **1834** SIR H. TAYLOR *Artevelde* I. I. ix, 'Twere well to note him on your list. **1868** MORRIS *Earthly Par.* (1870) I. I. 342 At the King's command A clerk that day did note it every whit.

b. So with *down.*

1669 STURMY *Mariner's Mag.* IV. xvii. 205 If there be any Current, you may..allow for it, and note it down. **1695–6** T. SMITH in *Lett. Lit. Men* (Camden) 239 Additions and alterations..which I have noted down. **1754** SHERLOCK *Disc.* (1759) I. vii. 225 Things noted down in God's Book. **1784** COWPER *Task* VI. 899 Thy prophets..noting down The features of the last degen'rate times. **1836–7** DICKENS *Sk. Boz, Scenes* viii, A hard-featured old man..was intently perusing a lengthy will..and slily noting down some brief memorandum of the bequests contained in it.

†**4.** To set down as having a certain (good or bad) character. *Obs.*

1526 *Pilgr. Perf.* (W. de W. 1531) 65 Or els bycause they wolde be noted outwardly relygyous. **1533** CRANMER *Misc. Writ.* (Parker Soc.) 250 If I had not, or would not so have done, I might right well have been noted negligent. **1573** L. LLOYD *Marrow of Hist.* (1653) 105 In divers autheurs and places, this prince is noted a glutton and drunkard.

II. †**5. a.** To denote, or signify (something). *Obs.*

a **1300** *Cursor M.* 25204 Wit þis word 'in heuen', us es Noted sothfast buxumnes. **1399** LANGL. *Rich. Redeles* IV. 54 þan satte summe as siphre doth in awgrym, þat noteth a place and no þing availith. **1559** *Mirr. Mag.* (1563) X viij, Both sence and names do note them very nere. **1579** LYLY *Euphues* (Arb.) 38 A woman..hauing one hande in his pocket as noting hir theft. **1644** BULWER *Chirol.* 168 The coyners of the Hieroglyphiques introduce this gesture to note Taciturnity. **1697** DRYDEN *Virg. Georg.* III. 442 The Shepherd knows it well; and calls by Name Hippomanes, to note the Mother's Flame. **1755** JOHNSON s.v. *Ling*, The termination notes commonly diminution; as Kitling [etc.].

†**b.** To point at, indicate by pointing. *Obs.*

1517 TORKINGTON *Pilgr.* (1884) 3 The Fynger of Seynt John Baptiste whych he notyd or shewyd crist Jhu whanne he seyd Ecce Agnus Dei. **1581** J. BELL *Haddon's Answ. Osor.* 249 Doth he herein not note you excellently (Osorius) and (as it were) poynt at you with the finger?

c. To indicate; †to point *out*, set or show *forth.*

1521 WARHAM in Ellis *Orig. Lett.* Ser. III. I. 242 My lorde of London to note out..all other suche names of writers.. as they perceyve to be erroneous. **1565** COOPER *Thesaurus* Pref., I haue thought it good by examples to note vnto them, what fruit & commodity they may take therof. **1607** TOPSELL *Four-f. Beasts* (1658) 63 The Turks use in their greatest feasts..to roast or seethe an Ox whole,..to note forth their plenty. **1646** P. BULKELEY *Gospel Covt.* IV. 337 To note out the property and nature of that faith. **1697** DRYDEN *Virg. Georg.* III. 252 Distinguish all betimes, with branding Fire; To note the Tribe, the Lineage, and the Sire. **1812** WOODHOUSE *Astron.* ix. 61 A sidereal clock will note that time. **1813** SHELLEY *Q. Mab* IV. 67 Black ashes note where their proud city stood.

6. a. To mark (a book, words, etc.) with a musical score. *rare.* Also *absol.*

c **1440** LYDG. *Hors, Shepe & G.* 184 Men plukke stalkes out of my weengis tweyn, Somme to portraye, somme to noote & write. *c* **1440** *Promp. Parv.* 359/2 Notun songe, *noto.* **1592** SHAKS. *Rom. & Jul.* IV. v. 122, I will carie no Crochets, Ile Re you, Ile Fa you, do you note me? *Mus.* And you Re vs, and Fa vs, you Note vs. **1755** JOHNSON, *Note*, to set down the notes of a tune. **1850** HELMORE *Accomp. Harmonies to Hymnal Noted* Pref. 2 The English Words Noted, for the use of all who sing. **1866** ROGERS *Agric. & Prices* I. xv. 285 The payments made at Oxford in the year 1308 for noting an antiphonary. **1897** *Musical Herald* 1 June 189/1 They organise vocal music competitions, but they have no sight-singing, and no noting music by ear.

†**b.** To mark; to distinguish by a mark. *Obs.*

1490 CAXTON *Eneydos* vi. 24 The fenyces fonde to note wyth rede colour or ynke firste the sayd lettres. **1559** W. CUNNINGHAM *Cosmogr. Glasse* 129 Draw arkes in every of the divisions,..and note the hiest Arke next with G.H. *a* **1568** ASCHAM *Scholem.* (Arb.) 152 Whan Varros name.. was brought in a schedule vnto him, to be noted to death, he tooke his penne and wrote his warrant of sauegard. **1604** E. G[RIMSTONE] *D'Acosta's Hist. Indies* VI. xxvi. 488 Every order of these Knightes had his lodging in the pallace noted with their markes. **1641** J. JACKSON *True Evang. T.* I. 71 It is sufficient to note these things with an obeliske. **1725** WATTS *Logic* (ed. 2) 75 What Remarks you find there worthy of your riper Observation, you may note them with a marginal Star.

c. *to note a bill* (see quots.).

1727–38 CHAMBERS *Cycl.* s.v., *To note a bill*, is when a public notary goes as a witness, or takes notice, that a merchant will not accept or pay it. **1809** R. LANGFORD *Introd. Trade* 133 Noting a bill, the customary form executed by a notary when a bill is not honoured. **1835** *Penny Cycl.* IV. 403/1 Inland bills..are merely noted for non-acceptance, which itself also is a useless form.

d. To annotate; to write notes in.

1809 LAMB *Let. to Coleridge* 7 June, I wish every book I have were so noted. **1844** DISRAELI *Coningsby* IV. v, Nibbing their pens, noting their memorandum-books. **1885** *Law Times* LXXVIII. 356/1 Decided cases bearing upon the matter..have been..noted where a note seemed necessary.

†**7. a.** To affix to (one) the stigma or accusation *of* some fault, etc. *Obs.*

1412–20 LYDG. *Chron. Troy* II. vi, I might..merked be And noted eke of wilfull nycetye To folylye to voyde away my grace. **1513** DOUGLAS *Æneis* XIII. iii. 135 Bot thai sal nocht behald the with sik lak.., Ne note the of na cowardys in thar mynd. **1579** LYLY *Euphues* (Arb.) 125 If the mother be noted of incontinencie, or the father of vice. **1653** ASHWELL *Fides Apost.* 244 None have either denied the Author, or defamed the Creed, but such whom the Church hath noted of Heresy. **1680** DRYDEN *Ovid's Epist.* Ess. (Ker) I. 232 The Julias who were both noted of incontinency.

†**b.** To mark or brand *with* some disgrace or defect. *Obs.*

1565 COOPER *Thesaurus* s.v. *Aspergo*, To be in suspicion, and noted with infamy. **1568** GRAFTON *Chron.* II. 739 Lest he peradventure should be noted with the spot of Nigardship. **1615** WALSAL *Life Christ* (1622) B 2 Can wee once imagine, that Christs bodie..was euer..enfeebled with infirmitie, or noted with deformitie? **1652** GAULE *Magastrom.* 265 The children marry publikly, and by the law are noted with no reproach for it.

†**c.** To stigmatize for some reason. *Obs.*

1542 UDALL *Erasm. Apoph.* 279 Notyng Sylla, that the same had purchaced yᵉ said office by gevyng greate giftes. 1548 UDALL, etc. *Erasm. Par. Matt.* v. 43 No man shall note her as an aduoutresse. 1575 FENTON *Gold. Epist.* (1582) 62 Also you note me, that in saying of service, I am very long. 1601 SHAKS. *Jul. C.* IV. iii. 2 You haue condemn'd, and noted Lucius Pella For taking Bribes heere of the Sardians.

III. 8. *intr.* To produce musical notes; to practise singing (cf. RECORD *v.* 2). *rare.*

1430–40 LYDG. *Daunce Machabre, Bochas* (1554) 224/2 O thou minstrall that can so note and pipe Vnto folke for to done pleasaunce.

1906 *Westm. Gaz.* 27 Mar. 2/1 The thrush and the blackbird fluted in the wood, noting for their coming songs.

†**note, n'ote, no'te,** *v.*³ 'could not', a misuse of *note* NOT *v.*'know(s) not'. *Obs.*

1590 SPENSER *F.Q.* II. vii. 39 Mammon was much displeasd, yet no'te he chuse But bear the rigour. ?1630 QUARLES *Hymn to God* Wks. (Grosart) II. 27 And euery minute's time ten ages were, To chaunt forth all thy praise it no'te auaile. 1642 H. MORE *Song of Soul* I. III. 22 The fiercest but of Ram no'te make them fall.

†**note,** variant of *nort* NURT *v.*

1674 RAY *N.C. Words* 34 To Note: to push, strike or goar with the horn as a Bull or Ram.

'note-book. [f. NOTE *sb.*² + BOOK.] A book reserved for or containing notes or memoranda.

1579 W. FULKE *Heskins's Parl.* 401 His note booke serued him no further. 1601 SHAKS. *Jul. C.* IV. iii. 98 All his faults obseru'd, Set in a Note-booke, learn'd, and con'd by roate. 1642 H. MORE *Song of Soul* II. iii. II. 47 We..Make that our note-book, there our choisest notions write. 1831 MRS. DAVY in Lockhart *Scott* (1839) X. 136, I thought the day.. so white a one as to mark it especially in a little note book. 1882 PEBODY *Eng. Journalism* xxiii. 184 The correspondent ..has returned with his note-books full of sketches and information which..may be of the highest service.

noted ('nəʊtɪd), *ppl. a.* [f. NOTE *v.*² + -ED¹.]

1. That is specially noticed, observed, or marked; hence, distinguished, celebrated, famous.

a. In predicative use.

13.. *E.E. Allit. P.* B. 1651 So was noted þe note of nabugo-de-nozar [etc.]. 1412–20 LYDG. *Chron. Troy* I. vi, Throughout the worlde noted ouer all, In euery land spoke of in special. 1500–20 DUNBAR *Poems* lxxvii. 5 He [= high] nottit is thy name of nobilnes. 1532–3 *Act 24 Hen. VIII,* c. 2 In times past [they] haue in al outwarde partes bene noted to haue had the most substanciall coloured wollen clothes. 1581 MULCASTER *Positions* xxxvii. (1887) 150 There be three kindes of gouernment most noted among all writers. 1607 FLETCHER *Wom. Hater* II. i, We shall find out the truth more easilie, Some other way lesse noted. 1653 WALTON *Angler* iv. 94 There be also of lob-worms, some called squirel-tails, ..which are noted to be the best.

b. Const. *for* something.

1596 SHAKS. *Tam. Shr.* III. ii. 14 He was a franticke foole, ..And to be noted for a merry man; Hee'll wooe a thousand. 1622 FLETCHER *Prophetess* I. iii, She is a holy Druid, A woman noted for that faith [etc.]. 1669 PEPYS *Diary* 10 May, Creed..tells me he hears how fine my horses and coach are, and advises me to avoid being noted for it. 1709 *Tatler* No. 75 ¶5 The Butler, who was noted for round Shoulders, and a Roman nose. 1789 BURNS *The Whistle* x, The board of Glenriddel.., So noted for drowning of sorrow and care. 1874 GREEN *Short Hist.* iii. §7. 148 He was noted for his scant indulgence in meat, drink, or sleep.

c. In attributive use.

The superl. *notedst* is not uncommon in the 17th c.

1596 SHAKS. *1 Hen. IV,* I. ii. 202, I haue Cases of Buckram for the nonce, to immaske our noted outward garments. 1623 COCKERAM I. s.v. *Clymactericall,* The most dangerous and notedst climactericall yeere. 1662 STILLINGFL. *Orig. Sacræ* III. ii. §17 To run through the noted Phænomena of the Universe. 1736 POPE *Let. to Swift* 25 Mar., He is the most noted, and most deserving man, in the whole profession of Chirurgery. 1822 SCOTT *Nigel* xviii, Old Trapbois, the noted usurer of Whitefriars. 1828 —— *F.M. Perth* iv, He was far too noted a person to venture to go entirely unarmed. 1855 MACAULAY *Hist. Eng.* xv. III. 605 That evening Clarendon, and several other noted Jacobites, were lodged in the Tower.

2. Provided with a musical score; having musical notation.

1849 ROCK *Ch. of Fathers* II. 202 The Antiphoner—from the noted and illuminated leaves of which they were chanting. 1881 BRADSHAW in Cox & Hope *Chron. All Saints, Derby* App. 231 One or more of the *Antiphonaria* were..noted Breviaries, containing the whole Breviary Service, only with musical notation to the choral parts.

Hence **'notedness.** *rare*⁻¹.

1661 BOYLE *Style of Script.* 186 Supposing..that the Prophane Aspirer should be so Lucky..as to attain the so Criminally courted Notednesse.

'notedly, *adv.* [f. prec. + -LY².] In a noted manner; markedly; especially, particularly.

1603 SHAKS. *Meas. for M.* v. i. 335 *Luc.* Do you remember what you said of the Duke? *Duk.* Most notedly Sir. 1797 *Hist.* in *Ann. Reg.* 99/1 His principles were notedly republican. *a* 1835 MᶜCULLOCH *Attributes* (1843) III. 25 An instinct..which compels us notedly to enquire into human plans. 1864 *Intellect. Observer* No. 34. 272 Many friends —notedly Lord Overstone. 1884 BLACK *Judith Shakespeare* i, She came of a quite notedly handsome family.

†**'noteful,** *a.*¹ *Obs.* Also 4 notful. [f. NOTE *sb.*¹ + -FUL.] Useful, beneficial, serviceable.

a 1300 *Cursor M.* 8473 Cantica [is] a noteful bok in haly writte. *a* 1340 HAMPOLE *Psalter* i. 4 It sall be noteful lerand þe way till heuen. *c* 1391 CHAUCER *Astrol.* Prol., Tables of dignetis of planetes & other noteful thingez.

Hence †**'notefulhead,** usefulness. *Obs. rare*⁻¹.

a 1300 *E.E. Psalter* xxix. 11 What notfulhede in mi blode es Whils I dounga in wemmednes?

'noteful, *a.*² *rare.* [f. NOTE *sb.*² or *v.*² + -FUL.]

†a. Worthy of note. *Obs.* b. Observant.

a. 1644 DIGBY *Nat. Bodies* xxiii. 207 Out of the remembrance of such notefull and artificiall Masterpeeces, to frame a modell in their fancies that shall reade this.

b. 1882 MISS BRADDON *Mt. Royal* I. v. 134 Christabel, noteful of every change,..saw how much more healthy a tinge cheek and brow had taken.

notefy, obs. f. NOTIFY.

note-hach(e, -hatch, obs. ff. NUTHATCH.

note-herd, var. of NOWT-HERD.

'notekin. *rare.* [f. NOTE *sb.*²] A little note.

1866 CARLYLE *Reminis.* (1881) II. 243 Should not I collect her fine notekins and reposit them here? 1896 *Westm. Gaz.* 19 Sept. 3/2 Here is a 'notekin', eminently Carlylean.

noteless ('nəʊtlɪs), *a.* [f. NOTE *sb.*² + -LESS.]

1. Devoid of note; unmarked, undistinguished, unnoticed.

a 1616 BEAUM. & FL. *Bonduca* II. i, Whose virtues..Must not be lost in mists and fogs of people, Noteless, and out of name. 1630 DEKKER *2nd Pt. Honest Wh.* Wks. 1873 II. 154 Let her walke Saint-like, notelesse, and vnknowne. 1786 BURNS *A Bard's Epitaph* ii, Is there a bard of rustic song, Who, noteless, steals the crouds among. 1814 SCOTT *Ld. Isles* III. iv, In hurry of the night, 'Scaped noteless, and without remark, Two strangers. 1878 STANFORD *Symb. Christ* ix. 250 Some noteless action may be the germ of a power that shall spread through all the earth.

2. Unmusical, unharmonious; voiceless.

1721 D'URFEY *Two Queens of Brentford* I. ii, The Bagpipe with its Squeak and Drone, Or Parish-Clerk, with noteless Tone, Are Owls to us Sweet Singers. 1820 BYRON *Juan* IV. lxxxvii, An ignorant, noteless, timeless, tuneless fellow. 1826 *Blackw. Mag.* XX. 405 A little brown noteless bird starts from among our feet.

Hence **'notelessly** *adv.*; **'notelessness.**

1830 R. CHAMBERS *Life Jas. I,* II. iii. 209 Clouds..decline notelessly..beneath the horizon. *Ibid.* x. 258 His life was spent in its usual tranquillity and notelessness. 1854 *Chamb. Jrnl.* I. 305, I at least do not pass notelessly.

notelet ('nəʊtlɪt). [f. NOTE *sb.*² + -LET.]

1. A short note or communication.

1824 LAMB *Lett., To Barton* (1837) II. 155, I am sure I cannot fill a letter,..but you expect something and shall have a notelet. 1857 *Chamb. Jrnl.* VII. 404, I want you to insinuate my notelet into her bouquet. 1884 *Stationery Trade Rev.* Sept. 213/2 As there was no space for addressing these notelets after they were folded [etc.].

attrib. 1880 DISRAELI *Endym.* II. 332 Quires of letter paper and note paper and notelet paper from despatches of state to billet-doux.

2. A short annotation or statement.

1887 *N. & Q.* 7th Ser. IV. 245/1 This notelet has been written because I know not that the fact herein narrated is generally known.

3. A folded card or sheet of paper on which a note may be written, having a picture or design on the face of the first leaf.

1955 *Stationery Trade Ref. Bk.* 71/1 Macniven & Cameron Ltd...manufacturers of social and gift stationery. 189/1 Notelets Products. Macniven & Cameron Ltd. 1971 *Countryman* Autumn 205/2 (Advt.), S.A.E. brings our list of Christmas gifts, cards, notelets, calendars for country lovers. 1972 *Stationery Trade Rev.* Aug. 39/2 Many of the Waverley gift stationery boxes also includes [*sic*] Notelets.

notemeg, -muge, -mygge, obs. ff. NUTMEG.

'note-paper. [f. NOTE *sb.*² 16 + PAPER *sb.*] Paper of the various sizes and qualities now generally used for correspondence.

1849 MRS. CARLYLE *Lett.* II. 68 A piece of black bordered note-paper. 1862 *Catal. Internat. Exhib., Brit.* II. §5127 Mourning note papers and envelopes. 1875 HELPS *Soc. Press.* xvi. 228, I folded up the sheet of notepaper, [and] put it in an envelope.

noter ('nəʊtə(r)). [f. NOTE *v.*² + -ER¹.

An OE. *notere* occurs as a gloss to L. *notarius* (Napier *O.E. Glosses* i. 2846).]

†1. A writer of the musical score in MSS.

1491 in L. Toulmin Smith *York Myst.* Introd. p. xxxix, Tixt-wryters, luminers, noters, turners, and florisschers.

2. One who takes or writes notes.

1589 J. RIDER *Bibl. Schol.,* A breefe noter of the contentes of bookes, *eclogarius.* 1611 COTGR., *Remarquer,* a marker, or noter of things. 1755 JOHNSON, *Noter,* he who takes notice. 1849 *N. & Q.* 1st Ser. I. 13 John Aubrey, the most noted Querist, if not the Querist noter of all English antiquaries.

3. An annotator or commentator. *rare.*

1644 LAUD *Wks.* (1854) IV. 334 The beast is primarily the Roman empire, in the judgment of the Geneva noters. 1655 FULLER *Ch. Hist.* VII. 397 His Notes as the Noter, got perfection with His age.

4. One who notes a protested bill. *rare*⁻¹.

1849 DE QUINCEY *Eng. Mail Coach* Select. 1854 IV. 297 You are made unhappy—if noters and protesters are the sort of wretches whose..shadows darken the house of life.

†**'noterer.** *Obs. rare.* [f. L. *notār-ius,* or OF. *notier* + -ER¹.] A notary.

c 1380 *Antecrist* in Todd *Three Treat. Wyclif* (1851) 125 But take we heede..to þe popes noterers, parsones & vikers, & prestis, monkes [etc.]. 14.. *Nom.* in Wr.-Wülcker 681 *Hic notarius,* a noterer.

†**noterly,** var. of NOTOURLY *adv.*

1513 DOUGLAS *Æneis* XII. i. 88 Now of our recent blude, as noterly kend is, The flude of Tibir waxis hait agane.

'note-shaver. *U.S. slang.* [f. NOTE *sb.*²] A promoter of bogus financial companies; a usurer.

1816 *Massachusetts Spy* 4 Sept. (Th.), We have too many note-shavers; too many gentlemen. 1851 HAWTHORNE *Ho. Sev. Gables* xviii, The wrinkled note-shaver will have taken his railroad trip in vain. 1880 'OUIDA' *Moths* I. 194 His father 'd always been thought one of the biggest note-shavers in New York City. 1905 D. G. PHILLIPS *Plum Tree* 11 But my clients were poor, and poor pay, and slow pay. Nobody was doing well but the note-shavers. 1911 R. D. SAUNDERS *Col. Todhunter* viii. 113 Old Eph Tucker was a note-shaver long before he was a politician, and he's got note-shavin' in his blood bigger'n a mule. 1942 BERREY & VAN DEN BARK *Amer. Thes. Slang* ix. 520 *Shaver, note shaver,* a discounter of notes at an exorbitant rate.

'note-shaving. *U.S. slang.* [f. prec.] The profession of a note-shaver; the making of an excessive profit on the discounting of notes.

1828 *Yankee* (Portland, Maine) I. 52/1 [By] the system of note-shaving that prevails here..the industrious and active are held in a state of bondage to the more wealthy and more lazy. 1855 P. T. BARNUM *Life* 138 Had I termed the deed an extortion or note-shaving..the verdict might have been different—but I had called the act 'usury'. 1902 W. N. HARBEN *Abner Daniel* 38 He began to utilize this captial in 'note shaving', and other methods of turning over money for a handsome profit. 1911 [see NOTE-SHAVER].

‖**notes inégales** (nɔts inegal), *pl. Mus.* [Fr., lit. 'unequal notes'.] In Baroque music, notes performed by convention in a rhythm different from that shown in the score.

1927 *Grove's Dict. Mus.* (ed. 3) II. 708/2 To avoid all uncertainity, authors frequently make use of the expression *notes égales* or *notes inégales.* 1954 *Ibid.* (ed. 5) IV. 479/2 In common 4-4 time semi-quavers or quavers but not crotchets or minims are eligible as 'notes inégales'. 1965 *Times* 9 July 16 Chief among these 'errors' is the convention of *notes inégales,* which decreed that with certain specified or understood exceptions, pairs of stepwise quavers (or, in some time-signatures, semiquavers) were to be played unevenly, the first note rather longer than the second. 1970 *Sat. Rev.* 31 Oct. 55 Mr. Weaver shows a commendable awareness of performance practice, even though scholars are not unanimous—namely the *notes inégales* in the finale of No. 3 where he adjusts the left hand to the triplet meter in the right. 1972 *Times* 22 Nov. 11/5 A sound knowledge of the more ticklish stylistic points to be observed, *notes inégales,* for instance in music from Couperin's Ninth Suite. 1975 *Times Lit. Suppl.* 9 May 503/4 (Advt.), Notes on ornamentation, bowing, *notes inégales,* and other performance problems.

note-taker, -taking: see NOTE *sb.*² 21.

note-tre, obs. form of NUT-TREE.

‖**note verbale** (nɔt vɛrbal). [Fr., lit. 'verbal note'.] An unsigned diplomatic note, of the nature of a memorandum, which is written in the third person.

1855 E. GRENVILLE MURRAY *Embassies & Foreign Courts* xvii. 264 Certain diplomatic worthies invented a double-faced document called a *note verbale,* or summary of conversation. These notes are unsigned. Their object is merely to refresh the diplomatic memory... They are supposed..to combine all the advantages of writing and conversation. 1911 *Encycl. Brit.* XIX. 823/2 The so-called *notes verbales* are unsigned, and are merely of the nature of memoranda (of conversations, &c.). 1917 E. SATOW *Guide to Diplomatic Practice* vii. 75 As not many *Notes Verbales* are to be met with in print, it seems worth while to reproduce it here. 1939 H. NICOLSON *Diplomacy* x. 246 *Note verbale.* This is a type of communication which is less formal than a signed Note and more formal than a memorandum. It is unsigned, but it is customary that it should contain at the end some conventional expression of courtesy. It is, in fact, merely the addition of this polite tag which differentiates it from the mémoire. 1955 *Times* 20 May 8/1 Among the papers now issued by the secretariat is a *note verbale* from the permanent delegation of the United Kingdom to the United Nations. 1970 R. G. FELTHAM *Diplomatic Handbk.* iv. 42 The Note Verbale is not common, but it is used to clarify or confirm points raised in a previous conversation or to list items which one could not expect to be recalled precisely. 1973 I. M. SINCLAIR *Vienna Convention on Law of Treaties* ii. 36 The conference decided otherwise, no doubt influenced by the growing practice of constituting treaties by an exchange of unsigned *notes verbales.*

noteworthy ('nəʊtwɜːðɪ), *a.* [f. NOTE *sb.*² + WORTHY *a.*] Worthy of attention, observation, or notice; remarkable.

1552 in *Vicary's Anat.* (1888) App. XVI. 304 To note..the somme and content of euerye article..that shall appiere noteworthie. 1596 HARINGTON *Metam. Ajax* (1814) 60 Is it not a custom when a prince hath spoken anything noteworthy, to say he hath delivered it majestically? 1639 FULLER *Holy War* III. xii. 128 Saladine by his intelligencers was certified of every noteworthy passage in the English armie. 1855 BROWNING *One Word More* xvi, What, there's nothing in the moon note-worthy? 1878 GLADSTONE *Prim. Homer* 68 In this prayer there is a noteworthy absence of what may be termed pagan elements.

Hence **'noteworthily** *adv.*; **'noteworthiness.**

1886 *Athenæum* 23 Jan. 144/1 This fine..taste prevails in half the later drawings before us—noteworthily in the beautiful design for the Laureate's 'Edward Gray'. 1887 *Old Man's Favour* III. iii, She was aware of the noteworthiness of the apparently simple occurrence.

† **noteye.** *Obs. rare*⁻¹. [app. f. *note* NUT.] A dish consisting of various ingredients, garnished and flavoured with nuts.

c **1430** *Two Cookery-bks.* 31 Noteye... Take smal notys & breke hem; take þe kyrnellys & make hem whyte,..plante þer-with þin mete & serue forth.

not-go (ˈnɒtgəʊ), *a. Engin.* [f. NOT *adv.* + GO *v.*] Designating (part of) a gauge so made that it will not enter, or will not admit, an object whose dimensions are within a designated limit.

1917 *Proc. Inst. Mech. Engin.* Jan. 58 Those gauges that were considered right might be put into one lot..the tests being made solely by 'go' and 'not go' check gauges. **1951** [see GO *a.* 1]. **1964** S. CRAWFORD *Basic Engin. Processes* xiv. 296 The 'Not-Go' end is of such a size that it will not enter the hole when the hole is up to the highest limit.

noth, obs. Sc. variant of NOUGHT.

nothagge, -hak, obs. forms of NUTHATCH.

† **ˈnothal**, *a. Obs. rare.* [f. L. *nothus*, Gr. νόθος spurious + -AL¹.] Spurious, not authentic.

1716 M. DAVIES *Athen. Brit.* II. 372 All his other Didactick, Parænetick, and Nothal Writings. *Ibid.* III. *Diss. Physick* 33 There be likewise some nothal Tracts ascrib'd to old Melampos.

† **nothe.** *Obs. rare.* [Of obscure origin.] *to let to nothe*, to let alone, neglect.

c **1315** SHOREHAM *Poems* I. 1799 Ac ȝef þer were ryȝt treuþyng,..To soþe, Hy scholde aȝen to þe spousyng, And lete al þat to noþe. *Ibid.* IV. 293 For ȝef he let to noþe.., Ich segge hym wel to soþe [etc.].

not-headed: see NOT *a.* 1 b.

† **notheless**, *adv. Obs.* Forms: 1 **no þy læs**, 2–5 **noþeles(s**, (3 **-las**, 4 ? **noþo-**), 3 **noðeles, -las**, 3–4 **notheles**, 7 **nothlesse**. [f. OE. *nó* NO *adv.*²; in later use perh. also a variant of NATHELESS.] Nevertheless.

c **888** K. ÆLFRED *Boeth.* xvi. §4 Ond þeah betwuh þyllecum unrihtum wæs him no þy læs underþeod eall þes middangeard. *c* **1175** *Lamb. Hom.* 23 Noþeles oðerhwile þu suneȝest mid summe of þisse limen ofter þenne þu scoldest. *c* **1205** LAY. 141 þare quene hit of-þouhte; noþeles heo hit þolede. *a* **1250** *Owl & Night.* 1297 Ac noþeles heo hur vnderstod. **1338** R. BRUNNE *Chron.* (1810) 97 In couenant of pes,..Bituex þam noþeles a skrite enselid & writen. *c* **1380** WYCLIF *Sel. Wks.* III. 396 And noþoles God techis to swere by hym in nede. *c* **1400** tr. *Secreta Secret., Gov. Lordsh.* 60 And noþeles of wynd comys diuers perils and lettynges. **1606** HOLLAND *Sueton.* 148 Yet might hee bee heard nothlesse of them that stoode a farre off.

notheme, obs. variant of NOTAMY.

† **nothemo**, *adv. Obs.* In 3 **no þe mo, noþemo.** [f. OE. *nó* NO *adv.*²; cf. NATHEMO(RE.] Never the more.

c **1275** LAY. 4627 Ne we neote no þe mo, þoh we speke wid houre fon. *c* **1290** *Beket* 61 in *S. Eng. Leg.* I. 108 Heo ne couþe no-þing conteini hire ne speken no þe mo. **1297** R. GLOUC. (Rolls) 4445 Lucye ne wilnede noþemo no þing somoche alonde As to fiȝte mid a such kniȝt.

nother, obs. variant of NETHER *a.*

ˈnother, *pron.*¹ and *a.*¹ *Obs.* exc. *dial.* Also 4 **noiþer**, 4–5 **noþer** (4 **-ere**, 5 **-ir, -ire**), 5 **noder, -yr, nothire, -yr(e**, 5–6 *Sc.* **nothir.** [var. of OTHER, with *n* transferred from the article: see N 3.]

1. *a nother*, an other. (See also ANOTHER.)

a **1300** *Cursor M.* 3390 Of hir he had a sun madan And a noiþer hight madian. *c* **1380** WYCLIF *Wks.* (1880) 50 A noþer symple frere þat nys not so gret flaterere. *c* **1440** *Alph. Tales* 193 And a noþer tyme he had with hym a monk. *c* **1450** HOLLAND *Howlat* 36, I haue mekle matir..Of ane nothir sentence. **1523** FITZHERB. *Husb.* §2 In Buckyngham-shyre, are plowes made of an nother maner. **1559** AYLMER *Harborowe* E 4, Of Paul I shal speak of at a nother time. **1608** D. PRICE *Chr. War* 26 To establish true religion in one kingdome, to confirme it in a nother. **1782** in *N.W. Linc. Gloss.* (1877) 181 New wheel and a nother mending.

2. *no nother*, none other, no other.

c **1320** *Sir. Tristr.* 1852 Hastow no noþer þing? *c* **1375** *Sc. Leg. Saints* xxxv. (*Thaddæus*) 138 Quhare þu Is, & in na nothyre place I-wyse. *c* **1440** *Alph. Tales* 245 It was no noder to giff to mynstrals bod for to offyr to fendis. *c* **1470** HENRY *Wallace* VIII. 906 Thocht he wes best, no nothir lak we nocht. **1523** LD. BERNERS *Froiss.* I. ccclix. 582 They shulde haue no nother trust in him, but that he wolde be their Enemy. **1557** N. T. (Genev.) *Mark* ix. 29 This kynd can by no nother meanes come forth, but by prayer.

b. *no notherways* or *-wise*, no otherwise.

c **1375** *Sc. Leg. Saints* i. (*Peter*) 511 It, þat we ȝarne, sal fall ws, and na nothirwais. *c* **1440** *Alph. Tales* 482 On a tyme hym happend to tell þaim, and he cuthe no noderways tell, & he cuthe say none oder bod þus. **1465** *Paston Lett.* II. 251 They derst no otherwysse don for ferre.

3. *the notheren*, repr. OE. *ðam óðrum.*

c **1315** SHOREHAM I. 1225 Ase broþeren, For to seruy ine godes house Byfore alle þe noþeren. *Ibid.* 1227 To segge hys 'leuy' an englysch, 'Fram þe noþeren ytake'.

ˈnother, *pron.*² and *a.*² *Obs.* exc. *dial.* Forms: 1 **nóðer**, 2 **noðer**, 3 **neoðer**, 4 **noþer**, 4–6 (9 *dial.*) **nother** (4 **-ir**, 9 *dial.* **noather**); 4 **noiþer, noither**, 5 **noythere.** [f. *ne* NE + **óðer*, contracted form of **óhwæðer*, as *áðer* is of *áhwæðer*: cf. NOUTHER.]

A. *pron.* Neither of two persons or things.

a. With genitive or pers. pron. preceding.

c **897** K. ÆLFRED *Gregory's Past. Care* li. 399 Ne fornime incer noðer oðer eft wið butan geðafunge. **1297** R. GLOUC. (Rolls) 4884 þat hor noþer nadde noþing, þat to oþeres wille nas. *c* **1330** *Amis & Amil.* 852 Y seighe it meself this ich day, ..Your noither it may forsake. **1393** LANGL. *P. Pl.* C. XI. 273 Here noþer loueþ oþere.

b. Followed by *of* (dial. *on*), or without const.

c **1200** *Trin. Coll. Hom.* 165 Nis nower non trewðe for nis þe gist siker of þe husebonde, ne noðer of oðer. **1297** R. GLOUC. (Rolls) 8702 Noþer of is breþerin, þo is fader was ded, Nas nei him bote he one. *c* **1320** *Sir. Tristr.* 3233 Noiþer of ous nil spare Erl, baroun no kniȝt. *c* **1450** *Mirour Saluacioun* (Roxb.) 18 A prest and eft a Dekene come by... But noythere of them myght hele this ilke sore wounded man. **1551** TURNER *Herbal* I. (1568) 93 And nother of bothe grow oute of the grounde. **1854–** in *Eng. Dial. Dict.* (s.v. *Nowther*), in forms *nother, noather.*

c. Preceded by *never* (later *ner, nere*).

c **1205** LAY. 30834 For nauer neoðer nalde..þat þe king hit wusten. *c* **1385** CHAUCER *L.G.W.* Prol. 192 (Fairf.), I nam withholden yit with never nother. **1540** MORYSINE *Vives' Introd. to Wysd.* C v, That god alone aprove our inwarde and outwarde actis, though men alow ner nother. **1565** CALFHILL *Answ. Martiall* (1846) 73 Whereof there is nere nother commanded, but forbidden.

d. Preceded by *neither* (or *nether*).

c **1500** *Chaucer's L.G.W.* Prol. 192 (Trin.), I am wytholde yet with neyther nother. **1529** MORE *Dyaloge* I. Wks. 155/1 Of which twayne ye woulde in the beginning admit neither nother. **1589** *Marprelate Epit.* (1843) 48, I wad counsell them, if they wad be ruled bai me, to be nether nother. **1612** T. JAMES *Jesuits Downefall* 71, I could wish that all such.. would consent to beleeue nether nother.

B. *adj.* Neither. (Usually *neither nother.*)

1297 R. GLOUC. (Rolls) 4561 Vor þer ne bileuede in noþer syde non heymon vnneþe. *Ibid.* 6221 Noþer partye ne miȝte þe maistrie al biȝite. **1387** TREVISA *Higden* (Rolls) III. 201 By neuere noþer weie I schal paye þe þat þou axest. **1530** FRITH *Disput. Purgat.* (1829) 195 Neither nother text serveth any whit for purgatory. **1533** MORE *Apol.* 180 There are fewe or none good in neyther nother parte. **1640** BROME *Sparagus Gard.* IV. v, No sir, we come with no zick intendment on neither nother zide.

ˈnother, *adv.*¹ and *conj. Obs.* exc. *dial.* Forms: α. 3 **noðer, neoðer**, 3–5 **noþer** (4 **notþer**, 5 **noþire, -eir**), 4–5 **nothyr(e**, 5–6 *Sc.* **-ire**, 5 **-ur**, 3– **nother** (9 *dial.* **noather, nuther**). β. 4 **noiþer, noither, noyther.** γ. 4 **nodur**, 5–6 *Sc.* **noder** (5 **-ir, -yr**), 6 **nolder**, 8 **nodder.** [f. as prec.: cf. NATHER *conj.* and OFris. *noder*, var. of *nouder* NOUTHER.]

† **1.** = NEITHER A. 1. (Followed by *ne, na, no, nor*, and in early use frequently with another negative.) *Obs.*

α. *c* **1205** LAY. 16736 Ne mihte þer na man neoðer [*c* **1275** noþer] ute no ingan. *a* **1250** *Owl & Night.* 465 Vor he nys noþer yep ne wis. *a* **1300** *Cursor M.* 5857 Noþer I knau him þat yee sai, Ne i ne wil lat þe folk a-wai. **1390** GOWER *Conf.* II. 44 Thei merveille how such a wiht..Desireth nother Mariage Ne yit the love of paramours. *c* **1450** *Merlin* 87 This childe..nys nother youre ne myn by reson. **1523** CROMWELL in Merriman *Life & Lett.* I. 34 They dare not trye hyt by the sworde, nother with us, nor with the saide Emparours Subiectes. **1596** DALRYMPLE tr. *Leslie's Hist. Scot.* VIII. 58 Bot that nother the king nor cuntrie mycht cum to skaith. **1867** WAUGH *Home Life Factory Folk* xxi. 185 Hoo's noather feyther nor mother. **1873** SPILLING *Molly Miggs' Trip* (1903) 9 But that's nuther here nor there.

β. *a* **1300** *Cursor M.* 7303 Yee ar to fraward wit to dele, For noiþer ar ȝe war ne wise. **1377** LANGL. *P. Pl.* B. XII. 209 It were noyther resoun ne riȝt to rewarde hem bothe aliche.

γ. *c* **1375** *Sc. Leg. Saints* iv. (*James*) 70 Philet..mycht ster noder hand na fete. *c* **1471** *Pol. Poems* (Rolls) II. 271 The wynde, the water spareth nodyr pryynce ne kyng. **1533** GAU *Richt Vay* 105 Bot alace thay wil noder prech thair self nay ȝeit suffer oders quhilk wald prech. **1574** in Littlejohn *Aberd. Sheriff Crt.* (1904) 261 Syme is noder persewar nor Moir defender in this present caus of Cognitioune.

† **b.** = NEITHER A. 2. *Obs.*

1531 TINDALE *Expos. 1 John* (1537) 36 We..loue you all alyke, nother loue we one more and another lesse. **1547** RECORDE *Uryne* 3 Nother is it so easy a thing..to translate well. **1561** HOLLYBUSH *Hom. Apoth.* 31 b, He is hevy and waketh much, nother can rest in one place.

† **2.** *nother ... nother*, neither ... nor. *Obs.*

c **1275** LAY. 22853 Ne sal him noþer go vore gold noþer garisome. **1398** TREVISA *Barth. De P.R.* XVI. viii. (Bodl. MS.), Wiþout þis siluer noþer golde noþer copre maye be ouere gilte. *c* **1400** *Apol. Loll.* 50 Noiþer in biggings, noiþer in liȝts, noiþer in instruments. **1496** *Somerset Med. Wills* (1901) 340, 12 shepe nother of the best nother of the worste. **1530** RASTELL *Bk. Purgat.* II. i, Nother by exhortacyon.. nother by..punysshment..nor other thynge. **1551** TURNER *Herbal* I. (1568) 84 It hath nother seedes like vnto marrishe mallowe, nother may a man make roopes of it.

† **3.** = NOR. (Usually with preceding negative.)

1377 LANGL. *P. Pl.* B. IV. 130 Bere no siluer ouer see.., golde noither siluer. *c* **1386** CHAUCER *Knt.'s T.* 512 No man couthe knowe His speche nother his vois, though men it herde. *a* **1400–50** *Alexander* 1372 [He] band hire..bigly to-gedire, with þat scho flisch noþer fayle, fyue score aunkirs. **1474** in *10th Rep. Hist. MSS. Comm.* App. V. 311 That no manere man nor woman procure nother take away no childe. *a* **1529** SKELTON *Ware the Hauke* 196 Nor yet dronken Bacus; Nother Olibrius, Nor Dionisyus. **1581** J. BELL *Haddon's Answ. Osor.* 80 b, Nor in eating and drinking nother in chambring and wantonnesse.

4. = NEITHER A. 3.

c **1350** *Will. Palerne* 722 Mi-self knowe ich nouȝt mi ken ne mi kontre noiþer. **1362** LANGL. *P. Pl.* A. IX. 111 Was no pride on his apparail ne no pouert noþer. *a* **1400–50** *Alexander* 402 'Be noȝt a-bayste', quod þe berne, 'ne a-bleyd nothire'. *c* **1489** CAXTON *Sonnes of Aymon* ix. 222 'I shall never sette foote there'. 'Nor I nother', sayd Richarde. **1560** DAUS tr. *Sleidane's Comm.* 234 When that wolde take no place nother. **1561** HOLLYBUSH *Hom. Apoth.* 3 If ye can not have the same nother, then take [etc.].

1840 HALIBURTON *Clockm.* Ser. III. v, It don't seem to hang very well together nother. **1841** *Gaskel's Comic Songs* 48 (E.D.D.), Nay, I cannot do that nother. **1886–** in dial. glossaries (Kent, Surrey, Berks, Som.), usually in form *nuther.*

† **b.** With preceding negative inferred. *Obs.*⁻¹

1508 DUNBAR *Tua Mariit Wemen* 358 Thus the scorne and the scaith scapit he nothir.

† **ˈnother**, *adv.*² *Obs.* In 4–5 **noþer**, 5 *Sc.* **nothir.** [app. for NOWER *adv.*, after prec. Cf. NOUTHER *adv.*²] Nowhere. Usually in comb. † **nother-where.**

a **1300** *Cursor M.* 3495 For-þi ne was he noþer quar sent Bot to þe huse ai tok he tent. *Ibid.* 17556 In israel er hei felles; þar es he soth and noþer elles. *c* **1375** *Sc. Leg. Saints* xli. (*Agnes*) 63 Seknes had he nothir-quhare, bot in his hart he had sic care. *a* **1400–50** *Alexander* 993 (Dubl.), There is no region ne realm..Ne noþer-whare no nacion bot sall my name lowte.

ˈnother, colloq. var. ANOTHER *a.*, *pron.*

1934 D. MACKAIL *Summer Leaves* x. 341 'How long have you got here?'..''Nother month, I expect.' **1935** in Z. N. Hurston *Mules & Men* (1970) 20 People told one 'nother that God was talking in de mountains. **1972** 'L. EGAN' *Paper Chase* (1973) xii. 195 'Nother little bit of the thing just occurred to me. **1973** H. MCCLOY *Change of Heart* iv. 39 'Nother cup of coffee, gramps?

nothing (ˈnʌθɪŋ), *sb.* and *adv.* Forms: α. 1–2 **nán**, 1–6 **na-** (6–8 *Sc.* **nai-**, 6 **nay-**, 8–9 **nae-**), 3 **nað-**, 4 **nat-**. β. 3 **none** (3, 5 **non**), 3– **no-** (4–5 **noo-**, 6 **noa-**); also 1 **-þinc**, 4 **-thinc**, 5 **-thynk**, 7 **-think**; 1–5 **-þing** (3 **-e**), 3 **-ðing**, 4 **-thinge**, 4–6 **-thyng(e**, 5 **-thyngge, -tyng**; 9 *dial.* **nothin', -en.** [f. NO *a.* + THING. In ME. written indifferently as one word or as two.]

A. *sb.* **I.** Not any (material or immaterial) thing; nought.

1. a. In ordinary uses and constructions.

In OE. and ME. frequently accompanied by another negative, as still in vulgar and dialect speech.

α. *c* **888** K. ÆLFRED *Boeth.* xxvi. §1 Nis nan þing soðre þonne þæt ðu segst. *c* **1000** *Ags. Gosp.* John xvi. 23 On þam dæge ge ne biddað me nanes þinges. *c* **1200** *Vices & Virtues* 43 Ðat he ðarof ne forleas naþing ðe godd him hadde betaht. *a* **1225** *Leg. Kath.* 225 Ne ne mei na þing wiðstonden his wille. *a* **1300** *Cursor M.* 560 He has it wroght..for-þi es nathing him sua dere. *c* **1375** *Sc. Leg. Saints* xii. (*Matthias*) 343, I na-thynge spek forthire her of his lowynge. **1456** SIR G. HAYE *Law Arms* (S.T.S.) 175 He mysdois nocht in nathing. *c* **1475** *Rauf Coilȝear* 506 Thow fand me fechand nathing that followit to feid. **1508** KENNEDIE *Flyting w. Dunbar* 390 That successione..has na thing ado now with the deuile. **1567** *Satir. Poems Reform.* vi. 107 Leif nathing that belangis to the Paip. **1596** DALRYMPLE tr. *Leslie's Hist. Scot.* Prol. 63 Of the fishes, how copious thair thay ar, I neid to say naything. **1725** RAMSAY *Gentle Sheph.* II. iii, Keep naithing up,—ye naithing have to fear. **1786** BURNS *Holy Fair* xxv, Lasses that hae naething!

β. *a* **1225** *Ancr. R.* 120 No þing þet heo deð nis Gode licwurðe ne icweme. *c* **1250** *Gen. & Ex.* 1126 Ðat water is so deades driuen, Non ðing ne mai ðor-inne liuen. **1297** R. GLOUC. (Rolls) 2086 So moche poer him com to, þat him ne miȝte no þing atstonde. *c* **1380** WYCLIF *Wks.* (1880) 42 Freris schulle no þing apropre to hem self, neiþer hous ne place ne ony oþer þing. **1390** GOWER *Conf.* I. 72 Thanne out of his place he crepte So stille that sche nothing herde. *c* **1450** *Cron. Eng.* ccxv. (Caxton, 1480) 202 So they slewe hir lord that no thynge was perceyued. **1548–9** (Mar.) *Bk. Com. Prayer*, Collect 4 Trin., Without whom nothyng is strong, nothing is holy. **1560** DAUS tr. *Sleidane's Comm.* 118 b, Nothing escapeth their handes. **1601** R. JOHNSON *Kingd. & Commw.* (1603) 151 He..bestoweth vppon them some other reward, and many times nothing at all. **1671** MILTON *Samson* 1721 Nothing is here for tears, nothing to wail Or knock the breast. **1733** SWIFT *Corr.* Wks. 1841 II. 694 He asks nothing; and thinks, like a philosopher, that he wants nothing. **1794** PALEY *Evid.* (1825) II. 304 He..omitted nothing that was prescribed by the law. **1827** SOUTHEY *Penins. War* II. 4 Nothing which skill and expense could effect had been spared. **1864** BRYCE *Holy Rom. Emp.* vi. (1875) 85 From the Byzantine Empire..nothing could be hoped.

b. Followed by a positive adj.

c **1205** LAY. 3014 Ah heo ne seide naþing soð, no more þenne hiire suster. **1548** GESTE *Pr. Masse* 7478 Nothing grevouse at al, nothing holy at al. **1560** DAUS tr. *Sleidane's Comm.* 262 Therfore did we nothing in this warre contrary to our dutie. **1610** SHAKS. *Temp.* I. ii. 457 Ther's nothing ill can dwell in such a Temple. **1652** SPARKE *Prim. Devot.* (1663) 442 There being in them nothing either petitory or gratulatory. **1697** DRYDEN *Virg. Georg.* III. 70 Without thee nothing lofty can I sing. **1861** J. NICHOL in *Mem.* (1896) 95 Remember the proverb, 'Nothing great is easy'. **1892** *Chamb. Jrnl.* Oct. 636/2 Apsley Villa was nothing surprisingly grand.

c. In proverbs and proverbial expressions.

1546 J. HEYWOOD *Prov.* (1867) 39 Whereas nothing is, the kynge must lose his ryght. **1562** —— *Prov. & Epigr.* (1867) 141 Where nothing is, a little thyng doth ease. Where al thyng is, nothyng can fully please. **1573** TUSSER *Husb.* (1878) 48 This Prouerbe.., that nothing who practiseth nothing shall haue. **1602** BRETON *Wonders* Wks. (Grosart) II. 9/2 With that the young man replyed: oh sir, nothing venter, nothing haue. **1614** COCKS in *Cal. Col. P., E. Indies* 342 As the saying is, nothing seek nothing find. **1668** SEDLEY *Mulberry Gard.* III. ii, Who ever caught any thing with a naked hook? Nothing venture, nothing win. *a* **1704** T. BROWN *To Author of Address* in *Collect. of Poems* 97 Thou know'st the Proverb: Nothing due for naught. **1885** *Cent. Mag.* XXIX. 186/2 'Nothing venture, nothing have', Betty replied saucily.

d. Denoting mental inferiority.

a **1754** FIELDING *Essay on Nothing* iii, A fellow, whom all the world knew to have Nothing in him.

e. Denoting absence of religious belief.

1855 J. H. NEWMAN *Callista* ii, There were a vast many persons who ought to be Catholics, but were heretics, or nothing at all. **1891** L. FALCONER *Mlle. Ixe* i, Foreign governesses, in my opinion,..are always either Roman Catholics or nothing.

f. As *adj.* or *interj.* Not at all; in no respect. *colloq.* (orig. *U.S.*).

1883 G. W. PECK *Mirth for Million* 325 'You are pretty rough on the old man..after he has..given you nice presents.' 'Nice presents nothin. All I got was a "Come to Jesus" Christmas card.' **1888** [see NOPE *adv.*]. **1899** A. NICHOLAS *Idyl of Wabash* 175 'My account—nothing!' was her scornful ejaculation. **1899** B. TARKINGTON *Gentleman from Indiana* i. 10 'But you only wait—' The editor smiled sadly. 'Wait nothing. Don't threaten, man.' **1911** H. QUICK *Yellowstone Nights* xi. 288 Stop nothing! Federal injunction won't do it. **1922** M. B. HOUSTON *Witch-man* xviii. 238 'He could have found it, of course.'..'Found it, nothing. I saw other things he'd taken.' **1925** WODEHOUSE *Sam the Sudden* xiii. 93 'Two million smackers it's going to get him,' retorted Dolly. 'Two million smackers nothing! The stuff's hidden in a place where he'd never think of looking in two million years.' **1946** K. TENNANT *Lost Haven* (1968) ii. 43 'How about the spooks?'.. 'Spooks nothing.' **1966** A. E. LINDOP *I start Counting* xxii. 275 Grandad said, poor little mite nothing. The man that gave her a lift told the police she'd done her best to seduce him. **1969** R. RENDELL *Best Man to Die* xii. 117 'Did you wait for him?' 'Wait, nothing!' said Cullam hotly. 'Why would I?' **1972** D. LEES *Zodiac* 46 'Francs?' 'Francs nothing—pounds.' **1974** T. BARLING *Shooter Man* iii. 23 'It just slipped out.' 'Slipped nothing. You couldn't resist.'

g. ***as slick as nothing at all***: very promptly or quickly, 'in the twinkling of an eye'. *rare.*

1884 'MARK TWAIN' *Huck. Finn* xl. 410 Done it just as slick as nothing at all.

h. ***with*** (or ***having***) ***nothing on***, wearing no clothes, undressed, naked.

1719 DEFOE *Robinson Crusoe* 62, I stripp'd..having nothing on but a Chequer'd Shirt, and a Pair of Linnen Drawers. **1908** KIPLING *Let.* in C. E. Carrington *Rudyard Kipling* (1955) xvi. 399, I cannot help blushing when I am rung-up by women—with nothing on but spectacles and a bath-towel. **1971** E. PAUL *Reluctant Cloak & Dagger Man* xi. 137 We always swam here with nothing on.

i. ***nothing doing***: see DO *v.* 34c.

j. ***like nothing on earth***: strange, ugly, wretched, etc., in a superlative degree.

1923 A. CHRISTIE *Murder on Links* xxvi. 286 She looked like nothing on God's earth. **1927** W. E. COLLINSON *Contemp. Eng.* 117 To look or feel like nothing on earth (*very bad*). **1974** M. G. EBERHART *Danger Money* (1975) iv. 39 'What's he like?' 'Nothing on earth... I wouldn't trust him with a nickel.'

k. ***there is nothing*** (***much***) ***in it***: there is no important feature of interest or value in something; there is no significant difference between two things, etc.

1927 *Observer* 18 Dec. 19/3 The first round there was nothing much in it. In the second round Angus..punched Mansfield round the ring. **1950** PARTRIDGE *Dict. Clichés* (ed. 4) 156 *Nothing in it*, esp., *there's nothing*...(there is no appreciable—or important—difference): c. 20.

l. ***to have nothing on*** (someone): to be no match for (someone). See HAVE *v.* 14h.

2. a. With dependent genitive: No part, share, etc., *of* some thing (or person).

c **1000** in Assmann *Ags. Hom.* (1889) XVIII. 48 Þa ne ȝefredde he naþinc þæs brynes for þam miclan luste. *a* **1122** *O.E. Chron.* (Laud MS.) an. 1096, Se wæs Papa ȝehaten þeah þe he þæs setles naþing næfde on Rome. *a* **1200** *Moral Ode* 98 in *O.E. Hom.* I. 165 Nabbeð hi naþing forȝeten of al þet ho [ere] iseȝen. *a* **1300** *Cursor M.* 2543 O prai wald abram nathing haue. *c* **1375** *Sc. Leg. Saints* xxxiv. (*Pelagia*) 23 Wantande nathing of bewte, þat in a woman suld fundyn be. *c* **1400** *Destr. Troy* 13215 Of Nigromansy ynogh nothing hom lakked. **1540–1** ELYOT *Image Gov.* 31 Ye nothyng haue appayred of the imperyall maiesttee. **1585** T. WASHINGTON tr. *Nicholay's Voy.* I. vii. 6 Finding nothyng of that they sought for. **1610** SHAKS. *Temp.* I. ii. 399 Nothing of him that doth fade. **1671** MILTON *Samson* 374 Nothing of all these evils hath befall'n me But justly. **1711** STEELE *Spect.* No. 43 ¶8 We were in nothing of the Secret. **1722** DE FOE *Col. Jack* (1840) 172, I..began..with nothing; that is to say, I had nothing of stock. **1768** GOLDSM. in *Boswell*, Johnson..has nothing of the bear but his skin. **1872** HOLMES *Poet Breakf.-t.* vi. (1906) 137 There was no atmosphere in it, nothing of the light that never was.

b. Const. *of* with adjective. Now *rare.*

Prob. after F. *rien de* (*nouveau*, etc.).

1645 CHAS. I *Wks.* (1662) 316, I..have nothing of new to direct you in. **1662** EVELYN *Chalcogr.* 11 That there might be nothing of deficient as to our Institution. *a* **1700** DRYDEN (J.), Yet had his aspect nothing of severe. **1829** LANDOR *Imag. Conv.*, *Barrow & Newton* Wks. 1853 I. 482/2 Nothing of excellent is to be done by felicity. **1870** SWINBURNE *Ess. & Stud.* (1875) 12 Nothing of common is there, nothing of theatrical.

3. a. Denoting comparative insignificance or unimportance: A thing (or person) not worth reckoning, considering, or mentioning.

1382 WYCLIF *Matt.* xxiii. 16 Who euere shal swere by the temple of God, no thing is [**1388** it is no thing]. **1390** GOWER *Conf.* I. 340 For who that is of man no king, The remenant is as no thing. *c* **1500** *Melusine* 120 For if..I were taken of our enmyes, of my lyf is nothing. *a* **1548** HALL *Chron.*, *K. Hen. VIII* 230b, Yᵉ same night..fel a smal raine, nothyng to speak of. **1597** SHAKS. *2 Hen. IV*, IV. iii. 123 So, that skill in the Weapon is nothing, without Sack. **1611** —— *Wint. T.* IV. ii. 44 A man (they say) that from very nothing..is growne into an vnspeakable estate. **1632** LITHGOW *Trav.* III. 88 It was nothing to see euery day foure or fiue men killed in the streetes. **1705** STANHOPE *Paraphr.* II. 274 We..falsely imagine we are Something when in Truth we are Nothing. **1837** J. H. NEWMAN *Par. Serm.* (ed. 3) I. iii. 31 Knowledge is nothing compared with doing. **1883** HOWELLS *Woman's Reason* xii, He would be nothing without her.

†b. In phr. ***thing***, ***man***, etc., ***of nothing***. *Obs.*

Prob. after F. *homme*, etc., *de rien*, or L. *nihili*.

1583 GOLDING *Calvin on Deut.* xv. 89 The daunger that wee bee scaped out of seemeth to be a thing of nothing. **1591** SAVILE *Tacitus, Hist.* I. 35 Vitellius, a man of nothing,..drunck at noone-day and heauy with surfet. *a* **1628** PRESTON *Breastpl. Love, Effect. Faith* (1631) 145 Looke upon them as trifles, as matters of nothing.

c. As *adj.* in trivial use: of no account, insignificant, meaningless, insipid, dull; (of a dress, etc.) discreet, elegantly unobtrusive.

1961 *Time* (Atlantic ed.) 18 Aug. 60 All these beautiful people with nothing faces. **1964** 'E. MCBAIN' *Axe* vi. 118 This is a *nothing* game, you dig? A buck, two bucks a time, that's all. **1965** *Vogue* Aug. 43/2 Little 'nothing' sweaters and shirts for wearing with suits. **1967** W. MURRAY *Sweet Ride* iv. 46 It was a nothing place, just a few booths and a counter. **1969** P. KAVANAGH *Such Men are Dangerous* (1971) ii. 30 The characters..were all hung up on trivia, little nothing problems in their careers and marriages. **1971** *Sunday Times* (Colour Suppl.) 23 May 53/1 A girl in one of those 'nothing' dresses with the Quant signature written all over it. **1972** P. DICKINSON *Lizard in Cup* vi. 97 It's a nothing thing, like I said... But drugs aren't a nothing thing, no.

4. *Arith.* That which is not any number, and possesses neither quantity nor value; the figure or character representing this; NOUGHT. Also *fig.*

c **1425** *Crafte of Nombryng* (1897) 25 Multiplye 2 be a o, it wol be nothyng. [**1605** SHAKS. *Lear* I. iv. 213 Now thou art an O without a figure, I am better then thou art now, I am a Foole, thou art nothing.] **1743** EMERSON *Fluxions* 6 Consequently *o* will be nothing, and therefore all the Terms wherein it is found will be nothing. **1812** WOODHOUSE *Astron.* xxii. 236 The equation between the two periods at which it is successively nothing. **1850** MCCOSH *Div. Govt.* (1852) 486 The whole would be like multiplying nothing by nothing—the result would still be nothing.

5. a. That which is non-existent. Also personified.

to dance on nothing: see DANCE *v.* 3b.

1535 COVERDALE *Job* xxvi. 7 He stretcheth out yᵉ north ouer the emptie, & hangeth yᵉ earth vpon nothinge. **1587** GOLDING *De Mornay* ii. (1592) 23 God, to shew vs that he made all of nothing, hath left a certeine inclination in his Creatures, whereby they tend naturally to nothing. **1633** G. HERBERT *Temple, Dotage* i, Embroider'd lyes, nothing between two dishes; These are the pleasures here. **1692** BENTLEY *Boyle Lect.* ii. 52 Mere nothing being never able to produce anything at all. **1701** NORRIS *Ideal World* I. ii. 74, I thought it had been a..maxim all the world over, that nothing could have no properties or relations. **1790** BURKE *Fr. Rev.* Wks. V. 332 It is here that your modern legislators have gone deep into the negative series, and sunk even below their own nothing. **1828** CARLYLE *Misc.* (1857) I. 120 An emissary of the primeval Nothing. **1862** H. SPENCER *First Princ.* II. iv. §3 (1875) 177 Nothing cannot become an object of consciousness.

pers. **1648** J. BEAUMONT *Psyche* VII. ccxcviii, A mortal Life is but an handsom fiction Nothing well-drest, a flattering Contradiction. **1656** COWLEY *Pindar. Odes, Life & Fame* i, Oh Life, thou Nothings younger Brother! *a* **1708** BEVERIDGE *Priv. Th.* I. (1730) 73 It is as easy for Him to..send me back into my mother Nothing.

b. Denoting extinction or destruction.

1590 SHAKS. *Mids. N.* V. i. 315 *Dem.* No Die, but an ace for him; for he is but one. *Lis.* Less then an ace man. For he is dead, he is nothing. **1613** —— *Hen. VIII*, III. ii. 208 So lookes the chafed Lyon Vpon the daring Huntsman that has gall'd him: Then makes him nothing. **1812** BYRON *And thou art dead* ii, To me there needs no stone to tell, 'Tis Nothing that I loved so well.

c. ***to nothing***, denoting the final point, stage, or state of the process of destruction, dissolution, etc.

1600 E. BLOUNT tr. *Conestaggio* 22 Which made euery man suppose that after the expence of much mony, it would vanish to nothing. **1655** M. CASAUBON *Enthus.* iii. (1656) 169 Through continuall contemplation..having reduced his body to almost nothing. **1671** MILTON *P.R.* III. 389 Much instrument of war Long in preparing, soon to nothing brought. **1731–8** SWIFT *Pol. Conversat.* Introd. 3 The Conversation falls and drops to nothing. **1774** MITFORD *Ess. Harmony Lang.* 35 The vowel-sound..is nearly of the same kind, but degenerated to almost nothing. **1875** KINGLAKE *Crimea* vi. xii. V. 248 The parapet..dwarfed down to nothing. **1887** MORRIS *Odyss.* XII. 46 Dead men rotting to nothing.

6. With *a* and *pl.*

a. A non-existent, a comparatively insignificant or worthless, thing; a trifling event.

1607 SHAKS. *Cor.* II. ii. 81 To heare my Nothings monster'd. **1644** DIGBY *Nat. Bodies* Concl. 449 Seeking for that, which if they had found, were but a nothing of a nothing in respect of true beatitude. **1698** FRYER *Acc. E. India & P.* 181 A Bundle of Nonsensical Fortuitous Atoms conjoined into a Hodg-Podge of confused Nothings. **1723** SWIFT *Stella at Woodpark* Wks. 1751 X. 47 A Supper worthy of herself, Five Nothings in five Plates of Delph. **1782** MISS BURNEY *Cecilia* VII. ix, She then proceeded..to relate the little nothings that had passed since the winter. **1821** SHELLEY *Adonais* xxxix, 'Tis we, who..strike with our spirit's knife Invulnerable nothings. **1850** MONCKTON MILNES in *Life* (1891) I. x. 444 The little nothings of occupied life leave a man no time for his duty. **1898** HENLEY *Lond. Types, Hawker*, Hawking in either hand Some artful nothing made of twine and tin.

b. A trivial or trifling remark.

1601 SHAKS. *All's Well* II. i. 95 Thus he his speciall nothing euer prologues. **1654** WHITLOCK *Zootomia* 320 Mistresses that must have each day two or three Houres spent in speaking to them Nothings. **1709** POPE *Ess. Crit.* 326 Such labour'd nothings, in so strange a style, Amaze th' unlearn'd. **1797** LAMB *Let. to Coleridge* in *Final Mem.* iii. 25 You are very good to submit to be pleased with reading my nothings. **1824** BYRON *Juan* XV. lxxviii, To his gay nothings, nothing was replied. **1894** MRS. H. WARD *Marcella* I. 181 A few nothings had passed between them as to the weather.

c. A person of no note; a nobody.

1611 SHAKS. *Cymb.* III. iv. 135 That harsh, noble, simple nothing: That Cloten. **1681–4** J. SCOTT *Chr. Life* 81 In the presence of God we shall be Nothings. **17..** RAMSAY *To Duncan Forbes* x, Strutting naethings are despis'd. **1826** DISRAELI *Viv. Grey* III. iv, The nameless nothings that are always lounging about the country mansions of the great. **1879** FROUDE *Cæsar* xii. 163 Metellus and..Afranius, who had been chosen consuls for the year 60, were mere nothings.

d. ***a new nothing***, a worthless novelty. Now *dial.* (see quot. 1854).

1641 WILKINS *Mercury* Pref. (1707) 5 Fresh Heresies (New-nothings) still appear. **1653** JER. TAYLOR *Serm. for Year* Ep. Ded., No man ought to be offended, that Sermons are not like curious Inquiries after New-nothings, but pursuances of Old Truths. **1820** T. L. PEACOCK *Misc.* Wks. 1875 III. 330 Commonplace, which at length becomes thoroughly wearisome, even to the most indefatigable readers of the newest new nothings. **1854** MISS BAKER *Northampt. Gloss.* II. 52 If you'll be good children, I'll bring you all a new-nothing to hang on your sleeves, *i.e.* nothing at all.

e. ***no nothing***, nothing at all. *colloq.*

1835 J. F. COOPER *Monikins* III. iv. 93 In this happy land, there was no registration, no passports, 'no nothin'—as Mr. Poke pointedly expressed it. **1884** *Harper's Mag.* Mar. 516/2 There is no store, no post-office, no sidewalked street,—no nothing. **1905** KIPLING *Actions & Reactions* (1909) 8 'No roads, no nothing!' said Sophie. **1948** H. L. MENCKEN *Amer. Lang.* Suppl. II. ix. 392 There may not be no nothing. **1968** *Washington Post* 21 Sept. A. 12/1 His [*sc.* Wallace's] appeal is to racial animosity, no-nothing policies.

†7. = NOTHINGNESS. *Obs. rare.*

1611 SHAKS. *Wint. T.* IV. iv. 626 No hearing, no feeling, but my Sirs Song, and admiring the Nothing of it. **1630** LENNARD tr. *Charron's Wisd.* I. xxxvii. (1670) 121 To make man feel his own evil, his infirmity, his nothing. **1682** SIR T. BROWNE *Chr. Mor.* (1756) 122 He will experimentally find the emptiness of all things, and the nothing of what is past.

II. In various collocations and phrases.

nothing less, see LESS *a.* 7b and *adv.* 3. ***almost nothing***, see ALMOST *adv.* 3. ***neck or nothing***, see NECK *sb.*[1] 8.

8. Followed by a limiting particle.

a. ***nothing else*** (***but*** or ***than***): see ELSE *adv.* 1.

a **1300** *Cursor M.* 13471 Þis he said..To fand him and nathing elles. **1390** GOWER *Conf.* I. 198 Sche wolde him nothing elles sein Bot of her name. **1523** LD. BERNERS *Froiss.* I. clxix. 206 And they had neuer done nothynge els, I was bounde to rewarde theym. **1560** DAUS tr. *Sleidane's Comm.* 123b, In suche also as concerned religion and nothyng els. **1653** MILTON *Ps.* iv. 12 Things false and vain and nothing else but lies? **1756** TOLDERVY *Hist. 2 Orphans* I. 123 Have you nothing else to do but cleaning the books? *a* **1774** GOLDSM. *Surv. Exp. Philos.* (1776) I. 187 The followers of Newton say, that this power is nothing else but that of attraction. **1804–6** SYD. SMITH *Mor. Philos.* (1850) 172 If I can point out the cause.., I see nothing else which I have to do. **1869** MARTINEAU *Ess.* II. 42 Sin is nothing else than moral evil.

b. ***nothing but*** (or ***except***): see BUT *conj.* 4b.

c **1380** WYCLIF *Sel. Wks.* I. 94 Love we God..and drede we noo þing but hym. *c* **1400** *Sir Perc.* 714 He had nothynge to bere But his sadille and his gere. *a* **1533** FRITH *Disput. Purgat.* (1829) 102 That their words are nothing but even their own imagination. **1594** T. B. *La Primaud. Fr. Acad.* II. 529 Beastes thinke of nothing but that which they beholde. **1635** HEYLIN *Sabbath* I. (1636) 77 Having almost nothing but what they borrowed of the Egyptians. **1663** BOYLE *Usef. Exp. Nat. Philos.* I. i. 3 Nothing but Mens inbred fondnesse for the Object it converses with. **1711** BUDGELL *Spect.* No. 161 ¶7 The Prizes were generally nothing but a Crown of Cypress or Parsley. **1751** JOHNSON *Rambler* No. 175 ¶2 Nothing but the desert or the cell can exclude it from notice. *c* **1838** W. H. MURRAY in M. R. Booth *Eng. Plays of 19th Cent.* (1973) IV. 160 Mark me: no amendments, no conferences—I'll have '*the* bill, the *whole* bill, and *nothing* but the bill'. **1849** MACAULAY *Hist. Eng.* i. I. 141 It had been fruitful of nothing but disputes. **1884** *Encycl. Brit.* XVII. 701/2 Witnesses are sworn: 'The evidence you shall give..shall be the truth, the whole truth, and nothing but the truth. So', &c. **1886** FROUDE *Oceana* 140 When doing nothing except wandering in the shade of the wood. **1934** J. G. BRANDON *One-Minute Murder* iv. 32 As far as that poor devil's concerned..it's accident and nothing but. **1973** *Black World* June 30 A poet ain't nothin' but a bird.

ellipt. **1607** SHAKS. *Cor.* IV. v. 234 This peace is nothing, but to rust Iron, encrease Taylors [etc.].

(*b*) Also used to typify theorizing which attempts to reduce, simplify, or explain concepts in such a way that they seem to accord with the theory propounded; so ***the nothing-but***; also ***nothing-but-ism***, ***nothing-buttery***.

1923 R. H. THOULESS *Introd. Psychol. Relig.* x. 129 The essential requirement of this theory is that it should be shown that religion contains nothing but elements of this kind, and this is exactly what Mr Schroeder makes no attempt at all to prove. **1935** *Mind* XLIV. 91 Jung's formulation..is the antithesis of '*nothing-but*'-ism. **1937** A. HUXLEY *Ends & Means* xiv. 257 All who advance theories of mind containing the word 'nothing but', tend to involve themselves in this kind of contradiction. The very fact that they formulate theories which they believe to have general validity..constitutes in itself a sufficient denial of the validity of 'nothing-but' judgments concerning the nature of the mind. **1951** M. LOWRY *Let.* 25 Aug. (1967) 252 You might call it pseudo-Freud and the philosophy of the 'nothingbut'. **1961** *Mind* LXX. 100 There is much else in the literary idiom of nature-philosophy: *nothing-buttery*, for example, always part of the minor symptomatology of the bogus. 'Love is..nothing more, and nothing less, than [etc.]'.

c. After *did* or *done*, formerly followed by pa. t. or pa. pple., now usually by infinitive.

[*c* **1386** CHAUCER *Merch. T.* 682, I wol hym visite, Haue I no thyng but rested me a lite.] **1485** CAXTON *Paris & V.*

(1868) 61 The doulphyn dyd nothyng, nyȝt ne day, but admoneshed hys doughter. **1512** *Helyas* in Thoms *Prose Rom.* (1827) 76, vi. children, to whome they did nothing but tooke away theyr chaines. **1554-5** RIDLEY *Wks.* (Parker Soc.) 14, I haue..done nothing else but digged a pit. **1671** H. M. tr. *Erasm. Colloq.* 542 If I had done nothing else herein but trifled. **1686** tr. *Chardin's Trav. Persia* 165 We did nothing but ascend.

d. ***one has,*** or ***there is, nothing for it but,*** denoting absence of any alternative course. (Cf. FOR *prep.* 13 c.)

1742 RICHARDSON *Pamela* III. 78 So that between one and t'other, a poor Girl has nothing for it, but a few Weeks Courtship. **1792** *Elvina* I. 74 They were prepared to banter me, so I had nothing for it but downright impudence. **1843** F. E. PAGET *Pageant* 121 There was nothing for it but to submit with a good grace. **1875** RUSKIN *Fors Clav.* lv. 196 Hansli had nothing for it but to obey.

e. ***nothing, if not..,*** above everything.

1604 SHAKS. *Oth.* II. i. 120 O, gentle Lady, do not put me too't, For I am nothing, if not Criticall. **1876** J. PARKER *Paracl.* I. ii. 175 Christianity is nothing, if not spiritual. **1881** H. JAMES *Portrait Lady* xxxv, He was never precipitate; he was nothing if not discreet.

9. ***for nothing***: †**a.** By no means; on no account; for no consideration. *Obs.*

c **1275** LAY. 12419 He ne mihte for noþing Melga i-finde. *a* **1300** *Cursor M.* 11149 Of hir ne wald he for nathing, Lai of hordome mistruing. *c* **1385** CHAUCER *L.G.W.* 1853 *Lucrece*, Y wol not haue noo forgyft for no-thinge. *c* **1420** *Palladius on Husb.* XII. 275 They growe vnnethe in sad lond or rubrik, And for no thing the cley [they] may not vse. *c* **1450** LOVELICH *Merlin* 2562 And it be so,..thanne wolde j that ȝe hym slowen for non thing. **1581** MARBECK *Bk. Notes* 258 But there present he would not bee for nothing.

b. In vain, to no purpose.

1560 DAUS tr. *Sleidane's Comm.* 80 Leste they shoulde appeere to haue commen thyther for nothyng. **1872** HOLMES *Poet Breakf.-t.* vi. (1906) 130 That old Lawgiver wasn't learned in all the wisdom of the Egyptians for nothing.

c. For no reason; causelessly.

1590 SHAKS. *Com. Err.* IV. iv. 130 Will you be bound for nothing? **1600** —— *A.Y.L.* IV. i. 154, I will weepe for nothing, like Diana in the Fountaine. **1642** FULLER *Holy & Prof. St.* III. viii. 169 He who will be angry for any thing, will be angry for nothing.

d. Without payment or cost; free, gratuitously.

1610 SHAKS. *Temp.* III. ii. 154 A braue kingdome.., Where I shall haue my Musicke for nothing. **1662** J. DAVIES tr. *Mandelslo's Trav.* 132 Provisions in these parts, are so plentiful, that the Inhabitants..sell them in a manner for nothing. **1693** DRYDEN *Disc. Satire* Ess. (ed. Ker) II. 90 To do any thing for nothing, was not his Maxim. **1742** FIELDING *J. Andrews* I. xv, Loving the public well enough to give them a sermon or a dose of physic for nothing. **1886** D. C. MURRAY *Cynic Fortune* xii, There was not a woman of them who would not have done his clear-starching for nothing.

10. ***nothing to***: **a.** Of no consequence *to* one.

1584 COGAN *Haven Health* l. (1636) 64 What Rusticks doe, or may doe without hinderance of their health, is nothing to Students. **1686** tr. *Chardin's Coronat. Solyman* 90 The Townsmen made answer, 'twas nothing to them if there were such a Famine in the City. **1885** 'M. RUTHERFORD' *M. Rutherford's Deliverance* iv. 65 She had learned that she was nothing specially to him. **1947** E. O'NEILL *Iceman Cometh* I. 79 He's nothing to you—or to me, either. *Ibid.* II. 105 The good old Cause means nothing to you any more.

b. Insignificant or worthless compared *to* some other person or thing.

1591 SHAKS. *Two Gent.* II. iv. 165 All I can is nothing, To her, whose worth, make other worthies nothing. **1639** W. C. *Italian Convert* Ep. Ded. 3 But all this is nothing to that which they both suffered for their conscience. **1697** R. COLLIER *Ess.* I. (1703) 169 A new way of extracting the spirit of happiness; the Chymistry of a bee is nothing to it. **1793** GOUVR. MORRIS Sparks' *Life & Writ.* (1832) I. 415 Our old Congress was nothing to this Convention. **1877** SPURGEON *Serm.* XXIII. 77 Self is an unpleasant object for study. Anatomy is nothing to it.

c. ***there's nothing to it***: it is very easy to do; there is no difficulty involved.

1934 E. O'NEILL *Ah, Wilderness!* I. 21 There (*with a grin*). I know there's nothing to it, anyway. **1951** H. WOUK *Caine Mutiny* viii. 77 There's nothing to it, really, except making damn sure none of your watch-standers sit down or fall asleep standing up. **1953** F. STARK *Coast of Incense* iv. 232, I am puzzled when asked what makes my style, for there is nothing to it except a natural ear for cadence and the wish to get the meaning right. **1963** 'S. WOODS' *Taste of Fears* i. 13 'There's nothing to it if you're quick, or so I'm told,' he added. **1971** D. EDEN *Afternoon Walk* vii. 83 'You used to automatic drive?' 'Yes.' 'Then there's nothing to it.' **1974** *Country Life* 14 Feb. 322/1, I mentioned that I was spending the following night at a Japanese inn. He assured me that there was nothing to it.

11. ***to make nothing of***: **a.** To make light of.

Usually with gerund; for the earlier const. with infinitive, see MAKE *v.*¹ 51 c.

1632 SHERWOOD, To make nothing of, *desestimer.* **1711** ADDISON *Spect.* No. 57 ¶3 She..makes nothing of leaping over a Six-bar Gate. **1821** *Examiner* 732/2 He made nothing of eating burning coals. **1838** S. PARKER *Explor. Tour* (1846) 28 The river makes nothing of washing away banks and islands. **1850** W. SCORESBY *Cheever's Whalem. Adv.* vi. (1859) 80 This forced trial of hydropathy is, indeed, so common an occurrence that whalemen make nothing of it.

b. (With *can.*) To be unable to accomplish anything; to fail to comprehend or solve.

1687 A. LOVELL tr. *Thevenot's Trav.* I. 229 They boarded her again the third time, but could make nothing on't. **1852** FROUDE *Ess., Eng. Forgotten Worthies* (1906) 67 They could make nothing..of his odd ironical answers. **1865** DICKENS *Mut. Fr.* IV. xii, Bella could make nothing of it but that John was in the right.

12. ***to come to nothing***: to have no effect or result; to break down, fail.

1568 GRAFTON *Chron.* II. 233 This voyage..came to nothing. **1625** K. LONG tr. *Barclay's Argenis* V. x. (1636) 645 Her promises came to nothing. **1719** DE FOE *Crusoe* I. (Globe) 203 All my Fancies and Schemes came to nothing. **1796-7** MISS AUSTEN *Pride & Prej.* v. (1813) 15 It may all come to nothing. **1814** —— *Mansf. Park* (1847) 172 His falling in love with Julia had come to nothing.

13. ***to have nothing to do with*** (a thing or person): see DO *v.* 33 d. Also *ellipt.*

1605 SHAKS. *Lear* II. ii. 37 Away, I haue nothing to do with thee. **1715** DE FOE *Fam. Instruct.* I. iv. (1841) I. 86 I'll have nothing to do with it. **1830** *Fraser's Mag.* I. 203 It has nothing to do with the purpose. **1835** F. W. FABER *Lett.* (1869) 39 God caters for tomorrow; we have nothing to do with it. **1892** *Punch* 16 Jan. 41/2 'A Wife's Secret' (nothing to do with the old play of that name).

14. **a.** ***all to nothing***: to the fullest extent.

1742 RICHARDSON *Pamela* IV. 53 And has carry'd his Point all to nothing, as the Racing Gentlemen say. **1797** MRS. A. M. BENNETT *Beggar Girl* (1813) I. 161 Why a voyage to India was all to nothing a better venture than marriage. *a* **1818** M. G. LEWIS *Jrnl. W. Ind.* (1834) 67 The most beautiful tree, or, rather, group of trees, all to nothing, is the Bamboo.

b. With *beat.* (Also simply *to nothing.*)

1760-72 H. BROOKE *Fool of Qual.* (1809) III. 88 Christians ..beat us all to nothing in honour and humanity. **1784** R. BAGE *Barham Downs* II. 263 If the Gods had made you poetical I should have beat Swift's Sacharissa all to nothing. **1819** *Metropolis* I. 173 Our Opera..and our balls at Almack's beat them to nothing.

15. ***nothing off*** (see quot. 1846). *Naut.*

1846 A. YOUNG *Naut. Dict.* s.v. *Near*, *Nothing off!* is an order not to let her fall off from the wind. *c* **1860** H. STUART *Seaman's Catech.* 41 What is the meaning of 'nothing off'? Keeping the ship close to the wind without shaking the sails.

16. ***nothing to write*** (or ***cable, wire***) ***home about,*** denoting something that is unworthy of comment, unremarkable or mediocre. *slang* (orig. *Forces*').

1917 W. MUIR *Observations of Orderly* 227 Miserable conditions.., bad accommodation, doubtful food..these, in the lingo of our now much-travelled and stoical troops, are 'nothing to write home about'. **1937** AUDEN & MACNEICE *Lett. from Iceland* iv. 38 Fare from Hull to any-where in Iceland, £4 10s. plus 5 kr. a day for food. The latter is nothing to write home about but eatable. **1942** BERREY & VAN DEN BARK *Amer. Thes. Slang* i. 33 Fair to middling,.. nothing to..shout about, nothing to wire *or* write home about.

III. *attrib.* and *Comb.*

17. **a.** Attrib., as ***nothing-case, -creature, -gift.***

1611 SHAKS. *Cymb.* III. vi. 86 That nothing-guift of differing Multitudes. **1647** JESSEY (*title*), The Exceeding Riches of Grace Advanced by the Spirit of Grace, in an Empty Nothing Creature. **1700** C. NESSE *Antid. Armin.* (1827) 107 Unconverted men are nothing-creatures. **1847** ALB. SMITH *Stuck-up People* (ed. 4) 22 Cups, and saucers, and miniatures; inkstands,..and *papier-mâché* nothing-cases.

b. Objective, as *nothing-do, -doing, -saying,* etc.

1629 T. ADAMS *Barren Tree* Wks. 966 What innumerable Swarmes of nothing-does beleaguer this Citie! **1633** —— *Exp. 2 Peter* ii. 10. 729 Droves of beggars, profest cyphers, nothing-does that swarme about this Citie. **1667** DENHAM *Direct. Paint.* IV. iii. 2 The mad shout Of a poor nothing-understanding Rout. **1773** MRS. GRANT *Lett. fr. Mts.* (1807) I. v. 47 The incursions of these nothing-doing people. **1811** JANE AUSTEN *Lett.* (1884) II. 83 His usual nothing-meaning, harmless, heartless civility. *a* **1817** —— *Persuasion* (1818) IV. viii. 160 After a period of nothing-saying amongst the party.

c. In various phrases used attributively, or as the basis of a noun or adjective.

1778 *Learning at a Loss* I. 79 That Kind of Ennuyant Nothing-to-do-ishness which is worse than all the Rest. **1794** COLERIDGE *Lett.* (1895) 72 Gloucester is a nothing-to-be-said-about town. **1812** COLMAN *Br. Grins, Two Parsons* lxxxv, These practical, nothing-so-easy jokers. **1828** *Lights & Shades* I. 210 Let him be bound apprentice to a nothing-to-do man. **1878** H. WRIGHT *Mental Trav.* 143 An abyss of commonplace or nothing-in-lifeism. **1888** 'R. BOLDREWOOD' *Robbery under Arms* 126 One of those nothing-particular-looking old chaps. **1906** *All-Story Mag.* (U.S.) Aug. 593/1 The nothing-doingness of things in general outside the office. **1924** R. GRAVES *Mock Beggar Hall* 16 A formless lumpish, nothing-in-particular. **1924** D. H. LAWRENCE *England, My England* 98 They passed an agreeable, casual, nothing-in-particular evening.

B. *adv.* Not at all, in no way.

1. **a.** Qualifying a verb.

α. *a* **1122** *O.E. Chron.* (Laud MS.) an. 1070, þa munecas ..beaden heom grið, ac hi na rohten na þing. *c* **1205** LAY. 22048 þat no bið he for þan watere naððing idracched. *a* **1300** *Cursor M.* 12245 Na thinc can i him discreue, For sagh i neuer nan suilk mi liue. *c* **1470** *Gol. & Gaw.* 117 To prise hym forthir to pray, It helpis na thing. *c* **1475** *Rauf Coilȝear* 561 Thow trowis nathing thir taillis that I am telland. **1567** *Reg. Privy Council Scot.* I. 573 The proffeitt quhilk na thing belangit to thame. *a* **1585** MONTGOMERIE *Cherrie & Slae* 289 Quhilk profitis nathing at the lenth.

β. **1297** R. GLOUC. (Rolls) 982 Vor þing þat woneþ & noþing wexþ, sone it worþ ido. *c* **1330** *Arth. & Merl.* 5154 (Kölbing), His scheld perced Gvinbating, Ac his strong hauberk no þing. **1393** LANGL. *P. Pl.* C. IX. 214 Hit is no þyng for loue thei labour þus faste. *c* **1440** *Alph. Tales* 455 All way þai war nothyng lukid after. **1483** CAXTON *G. de la Tour* C ij, Hir lord her husbond was no thing plesid that she went so gladly. *a* **1533** LD. BERNERS *Golden Bk. M. Aurel.* (1546) B ij, I praise nothyng the knowlege of myne auncesters. **1597** T. MORLEY *Introd. Mus.* 95 You blamed my beginning, yet haue you altred it nothing. **1615** A. STAFFORD *Heavenly Dog* 68 Though this be the most terrible of deaths..yet it shall nothing appale me. **1666** M. M. *Solomon's Prescr.* 83 Perhaps thou art one that think'st thyself safe, and that this nothing belongs to thee. **1702** *English Theophrastus* 164 Naked lessons and precepts have nothing the force that Images and Parables have upon our minds. **1788** PRIESTLEY *Lect. Hist.* v. lxii. 307 An aristocracy however differs nothing from a despotism. **1829** LANDOR *Imag. Conv., Marvel & Bp. Parker* Wks. 1853 II. 107/1 They often infect those who ailed nothing. **1867** DK. ARGYLL *Reign of Law* ii. (1871) 58 It helps us nothing in such a difficulty, to say that [etc.].

†**b.** ***to make nothing,*** not to pertain or be of consequence *to,* not to tell *for* or *against* (a person or thing).

After L. *nihil facere* or F. *ne..faire rien.*

1551 ROBINSON tr. *More's Utopia* II. vi. (1895) 205 It maketh nothing to thys matter, whether yow saye that sickenes is a griefe, or that in sickenes is griefe. **1560** DAUS *Sleidane's Comm.* 424 b, That maketh nothing for the matter saith he, for he beareth witnes of him self. **1687** MIÉGE *Gt. Fr. Dict.* II. s.v., It makes nothing against me, *cela ne fait rien contre moi.* **1690** LOCKE *Hum. Underst.* I. iii. §3 But this makes nothing for Innate Characters on the Mind. **1727** BOYER *Eng.-Fr. Dict.* s.v. *Make*, It makes nothing to me, ..*Cela..ne me regarde point.*

2. **a.** Qualifying an adj. or adv. Now *arch.*

a **1050** *Wærferth's Gregory's Dial.* 114 Wyrc þin worc, & ne beo þu nan þing sari. *a* **1290** *St. Dunstan* 122 in *S. Eng. Leg.* I. 23 Hit ne þhouhte him no-þing long. **1315** SHOREHAM I. 891 Myd sucher sorȝe schryfte, man, Wel stylle, and no þyng loude. ? **1370** *Robt. Cicyle* 56 The crowne semyth the no thyng welle. *c* **1450** *Merlin* 18 She is nothynge gilty. *c* **1485** *Digby Myst.* (1882) III. 1981 Now of hyr goyng I am nothyng glad. **1503** HAWES *Examp. Virt.* IX. 163 For she was horned and no thynge cleere. **1597** GERARDE *Herbal* I. vii. 8 [It] is nothing rough in handling. **1632** LITHGOW *Trav.* X. 495 The Wooll..is nothing inferiour to that of..Spaine. **1667** MILTON *P.L.* IX. 1039 Her hand he seis'd, and to a shadie bank..He led her nothing loath. **1808** SCOTT *Marm.* II. iv, She loved to see her maids obey, Yet nothing stern was she in cell. **1867** MYERS *St. Paul* (1898) 21 Nothing disdainful of the Virgin's womb.

b. With adjs. or advs. preceded by *so.*

a **1466** *Paston Lett.* II. 264 For I wys she ys no thyng so sadde as I wold she wer. **1526** *Pilgr. Perf.* (W. de W. 1531) 153 b, Theyr syght is duske or dymme, & nothynge so clere as is the syght of the contemplatyue persone. **1576** FLEMING *Panopl. Epist.* 78 My calamities seeme nothing so many in comparison of your great miseries. **1620** E. BLOUNT *Horæ Subs.* 317 A passion that can be mastered, is nothing so dangerous as one that cannot. **1644** EVELYN *Diary* 24 Sept., Some bathes of medicinal waters,..but nothing so neately wall'd & adorn'd as ours in Som'erset-shire. **1712** HEARNE *Collect.* III. 413 He was nothing so learned and judicious a Man as he is represented to have been. **1826** E. IRVING *Babylon* III. I. 169 The insight which was given to Daniel.. was nothing so minute and particular as that which was given to the apostle John.

c. Followed by *the* and a comparative.

1547 HOOPER *Declar. Christ* x. Wks. (Parker Soc.) 76 An infidel may receive the external sign of baptism and yet no Christian man nothing the rather. **1559** W. CUNNINGHAM *Cosmogr. Glasse* 116 So shall the example be the more familiar, and your paines nothing the greater. **1592** GREENE *Conny Catch.* To Young Gentl., I haue eaten Spanishe Mirabolanes, and yet am nothing the more metamorphosed. *a* **1662** HEYLIN *Laud* (1671) 129 More recent were the Puritans, but nothing the less dangerous. **1829** SOUTHEY *Sir T. More* (1831) II. 18 The bird was nothing the worse for what it had undergone.

3. **a.** ***nothing like,*** in various uses. Cf. LIKE *a.* 2.

c **1412** HOCCLEVE *De Reg. Princ.* 3023 Hir woys was.. nothyng lyke a mannys voise in soun. **1547** BOORDE *Introd. Knowl.* 133 Not of that effycacyte as is spoken of, nor nothing like. **1560** DAUS tr. *Sleidane's Comm.* 43 b, Not so much credit to be given unto them, nothing like, as to the scripture. **1782** ELIZ. BLOWER *G. Bateman* III. 111 [She sits her horse] nothing like so well as you used to do. **1815** *Zeluca* I. 194 Nothing like so excellent as your epigrammatic translation. **1868** THIRLWALL *Lett.* (1881) II. 130 Our frost ..seems to have been nothing like so severe as it has been in France or Italy.

b. ***nothing near.*** Cf. NEAR *adv.* 6.

1581 G. PETTIE tr. *Guazzo's Civ. Conv.* (1586) I. 5 b, Your courteous good will maketh you go beyond the trueth,.. which commeth nothing neere to that you spake of. **1609** BIBLE (Douay) *Ezek.* xlviii. Comm., The terrestrial citie of Jerusalem..was nothing nere so large. **1642** ROGERS *Naaman* 59 This was no great state (nothing neere Naamans). **1712** J. JAMES tr. *Le Blond's Gardening* 25 Not much inferior to the other, but nothing near so large. *a* **1797** BURKE (Webster), The influence of reason in producing our passions is nothing near so extensive as is commonly believed.

c. ***nothing so,*** in various uses.

1515 BARCLAY *Egloges* ii. (1570) B iv b/2 But many fooles thinke it is nothing so. **1576** FLEMING *Panopl. Epist.* 275 As if Democritus had bene outragious indeede: who was nothing so. **1600** J. PORY tr. *Leo's Africa* III. 139 In the spring-time it is nothing so. **1642** JER. TAYLOR *God's Judgem.* I. xxiii. 91 When some replyed, That the soules of men were immortall..hee..swore, that he thought it nothing so. **1701** GREW *Cosmol. Sacra* IV. iv. 189 Some may think of Jael that..she was no better than a Trapanning Hussy. But nothing so. **1874** LOWELL *Agassiz* IV. ii, Our social monotone of level days, Might make our best seem banishment; But it was nothing so.

4. ***nothing worth,*** of no value. Now *rare.*

Perh. partly an inversion of *worth nothing.*

1535 COVERDALE *Job* xxiv. 25 Who wil then reproue me as a lyar, & saye yᵗ my wordes are nothinge worth? **1587** GOLDING *De Mornay* xviii. 288 Who knoweth not that thing to be nothing worth, that is given for nought? **1619** R. WESTE *Bk. of Demeanor* 116 in *Babees Bk.* 295 To belch or bulch..Commendeth manners to be base, most foule and nothing worth. **1654** FULLER *Triana* ii. (1664) 180 Mustard is nothing worth unless it bite. **1727** MATHER *Yng. Man's Comp.* 70 Some Rich Men over-valued, tho' nothing worth. **1833** COLERIDGE *Table-t.* 16 Feb., My Devil was to be, like

Goethe's, the universal humorist, who should make all things vain and nothing worth. **1833** TENNYSON *Two Voices* 331 A life of nothings, nothing-worth.

absol. **1580** HOLLYBAND *Treas. Fr. Tong, Vn poltron*, a nothing worth, a slouthfull person.

Hence **'nothing** *v.*, to reduce to nothing. **'nothingist**, a nihilist. **'nothingizing**, reduction to nothing, obliteration. **'nothingless** *a.*, insignificant; non-existent. **'nothingly** *sb.*, a cipher; *a.*, of no value or effect. **nothing'ology**, the study or science of nothing. **nothing'ousian** (see quot.). **'nothingy** *a.*, of no worth or importance.

1652 BENLOWES *Theoph.* VII. xv, Their Spiritual Natures would be *nothing'd quite. **1648** W. BROWNE tr. *Le Foy's Polexander* II. 339 'Tis an abasement; (Madam) 'tis an humiliation; 'Tis such a prodigious *nothinging of your selfe. **1890** *Daily News* 17 Jan. 4/8 Thus Bazaroff becomes the first 'Nihilist' or '*Nothingist'. *c* **1830** COLERIDGE in *Blackw. Mag.* Jan. (1882) 111 It is a discontinuing in descent, and a *nothingising of the female. **1822** MRS. SHELLEY *Let.* 20 Dec., I have nothing else except my *nothingless self to talk about. **1856** DOVE *Logic Chr. Faith* v. i. 278 The solar system would sink into a nothingless relation to us. **1814** D'ARBLAY *Wanderer* I. v, That *nothingly, Ireton, has nearly shrugged his shoulders out of joint. **1833** *New Monthly Mag.* XXXVIII. 158 How vain, how nothingly is the groaning and struggling, and the Truth and the Virtue of the world! **1803** FESSENDEN *Terrible Tract.* I. (ed. 2) 18 *note*, Sublime discoveries with abstruse sciences of insect-ology, mite-ology and *nothing-ology. **1811** *Spirit Public Jrnls.* XV. 325 What new prospects arise for adventurers in nothingology. **1791** in Parr *Wks.* (1828) VII. 93 You are a Parousian, . . and my clergy are *Nothingousians, for they have no notion at all about the matter. **1801** EARL MALMESBURY *Diaries & Corr.* IV. 36 It would be very strange if such *nothingy men were to stand in the way of so great a measure. **1834** GREVILLE *Mem.* (1875) III. xxii. 55 Parliament had opened the day before, with a long nothingy (a word I have coined) speech from the throne.

nothing'arian, *sb.* and *a.* [f. NOTHING *sb.*]

A. *sb.* **1.** One who holds no religious belief.

1789 MORSE *Amer. Geogr.* 206 There is a considerable number of the people who . . are, as to religion, Nothingarians. **1815** J. MASON in B. P. Smith *Hist. Dartmouth Coll.* (1878) 95 This comprises . . most of the Baptists and Methodists, and all the nothingarians. **1845** T. W. COIT *Puritanism* 433 The taxes of all the stragglers, nothingarians, and infidels, went there. **1880** *Echo* 20 Aug. 2/5 Are the consecrated churchyards . . to be desecrated . . to indulge the whim of a few nothingarians and unbelievers?

2. = NIHILIST 2. *rare*$^{-1}$.

1820 LADY GRANVILLE *Lett.* (1894) I. 171 Sir Robert Wilson . . says he can bear anything but those nothingarians.

B. *adj.* Having no definite aim or purpose.

1889 *Open Court* 3 Jan. II. 1393/2 The blessed leisure of wealth was not to him the occasion of a nothingarian dilettantism, of idleness, . . pleasure, or ambition.

Hence **nothing'arianism**, absence of any religious belief or political creed.

1872 J. GRANT *Newspaper Press* III. 282 Conservative, Independent, or Neutral, which last word is but another name for Nothingarianism. **1894** BARING GOULD *Deserts S. France* I. 102 The losses of the Catholics are into Nothingarianism.

'nothingism. [f. as prec. + -ISM.]

1. A triviality, a trifle.

1742 LADY M. W. MONTAGU *Lett.* II. 189 It is surprising what nothingisms make a figure in polite conversation. **1864** *Realm* 13 Apr. 2 The article is one of those sensational nothingisms—a sample of that sensationalism *des riens*, as the French have it.

2. = NIHILISM I.

1809–10 COLERIDGE *Friend* (1818) I. 275 The whole groundwork of Rousseau's Philosophy ends in a mere Nothingism. **1884** *19th Cent.* Mar. 505 The attempted religion of Spiritism has lost one after another every resource of a real religion, until . . it ends in a religion of Nothingism.

3. = NIHILISM 2.

1890 *Daily News* 17 Jan. 4/8 The Nihilists, . . as 'nothingism' seemed of somewhat kindred meaning with destruction, simply filched from Bazaroff his good name.

'nothingness. [f. as prec. + -NESS.]

1. Non-existence; that which is non-existent.

a **1631** DONNE *Nocturnall* Poems (1654) 36 His art did expresse A quintessence even from nothingnesse. **1690** BAXTER *Kingd. Christ* ii. (1691) 30 Here we have Anihilation and Nothingness in themselves. **1797** LAMB *Let. to Coleridge* 10 Jan., My letter is full of nothingness. I talk of nothing. **1831** CARLYLE *Sart. Res.* I. i, The immeasurable circumambient realm of Nothingness and Night! **1866** ALGER *Solit. Nat. & Man* IV. 251 He sees man suspended between the two abysses of infinity and nothingness. **1884** *19th Cent.* Mar. 500 Its sole dogma is the infinity of Nothingness.

b. The condition of being non-existent.

Common in 19th cent., esp. in phrases *to sink, fade*, etc., *into nothingness*.

1809 IRVING *Knickerb.* VII. xiii. (1849) 449 Each has returned to its primeval nothingness. **1875** M^{c}LAREN *Serm.* 2nd Ser. i. 18 It must . . be done by Faith, whose rod disenchants them into their native nothingness, and then it is blessed. **1894** JESSOPP *Rand. Roam.* i. 3 How beautiful plans do fade into nothingness.

c. Cessation of consciousness or of life.

1813 BYRON *Giaour* iii, The first dark day of nothingness. **1816** —— *Let. to Murray* 30 Sept., A sort of grey giddiness first, then nothingness. **1818** SHELLEY *Rosal. & Helen* 403 They themselves were weaned each one . . even from the thirst Of death, and nothingness, and rest.

2. The worthlessness or vanity *of* something.

1646 H. LAWRENCE *Comm. Angells* 150 By the foolishnesse, that is, by the Nothingnesse, of Preaching hee saves them that beleeve. **1693** G. FIRMIN *Rev. Davis's Vind.* i. 10 Why should a Man look after anothers Righteousness, till he see the nothingness of his own? **1724** *Lond. Gaz.* No. 6240/3 Sensible . . of the Nothingness of this World and the Vanity of its Grandeurs. **1771** SMOLLETT *Humph. Cl.* II. ii. 14 June, A sarment upon the nothingness of good works . . was preached. **1822** BYRON *Juan* VII. vi, Must I restrain me, through the fear of strife, From holding up the nothingness of life? **1867** LEWES *Hist. Philos.* (ed. 3) I. 43 Which first called men's attention to the nothingness of knowledge. **1884** W. S. LILLY in *Contemp. Rev.* Feb. 257 This self-renunciation . . founded itself upon the vanity and nothingness of what was given up.

b. That which has no value; the condition of being worthless.

1654 WHITLOCK *Zootomia* 251 A whole Dictionary where-of would hold forth but Muchnesse of Nothingnesse. **1743** H. WALPOLE *Lett.* (1903) I. 376 My letters are now at their *ne plus ultra* of nothingness. **1800** COLERIDGE *Piccolom.* I. iv, Mere bustling nothingness, where the soul is not. **1863** KINGLAKE *Crimea* (1877) II. vi. 54 The political conversation between the booted Czar and the men of peace was sheer nothingness. **1880** 'OUIDA' *Moths* II. 384 What a confession of internal nothingness.

3. Utter insignificance or unimportance.

a **1652** J. SMITH *Sel. Disc.* ix. (1821) 419 Triumphing in nothing more than in his own nothingness, and in the allness of the Divinity. *a* **1672** STERRY *Freed. Will* (1675) 142 The nothingness of the Creature prevailing in the absence of the Divine beams. **1721** R. KEITH tr. *T. à Kempis, Solil. Soul* xxii. 291 Accept however the Sacrifice of my Humility, my Poverty, and my Nothingness. **1749** LAVINGTON *Enthus. Meth. & Papists* (1820) 51 She sunk down to the centre of her own nothingness. **1821–30** LD. COCKBURN *Mem.* 80, I entered the Faculty of Advocates; and with a feeling of nothingness paced the Outer House. **1874** SYMONDS *Sk. Italy & Greece* (1898) I. i. 9 Many . . have found a deep peace in the sense of their own nothingness.

4. A non-existent thing; a state of non-existence or worthlessness; a thing of no value, etc.

1652 BENLOWES *Theoph.* II. vi, Soul, Th' Architect of Wonders blesse Whose All-creating Word embirth'd a Nothingnesse. **1660** tr. *Paracelsus' Archidoxis* I. VII. 110 A Specifical Corrosive . . wholly Consumes Metals even to a nothingness. **1748** HARTLEY *Observ. Man* I. iv. §3. 460 They . . afterwards fix a positive Nothingness and Worthlessness upon them. **1751** SMOLLETT *Per. Pic.* xxxix, A nothingness of conversation which he could never attain. **1884** *Lotze's Metaph.* 235 Just as little could that which separates them and makes them diverge be a mere nothingness when compared to the space . . itself.

pl. **1680** *Refl. on Late Libel* 33 Though he . . speak hard Words, and new Words, or . . cries Incomes, Outgoings, &c. which are indeed Nothingnesses. **1826** SOUTHEY *Lett.* (1856) IV. 1 The follies and impertinencies and nothingnesses with which I am pestered. **1879** BARING-GOULD *Germany* I. 324 The professors . . do not waste the hour of lecture with verbose nothingnesses.

nothofagus (nɒθəʊ'feɪgəs). [mod.L. (K. L. Blume *Museum Botanicum Lugduno-Batavum* (1850) I. 307). f. Gr. νόθος false + φηγός beech tree.] An evergreen or deciduous tree of the genus so called, belonging to the family Fagaceæ and native to Australasia and South America; also called southern beech.

1914 W. J. BEAN *Trees & Shrubs Hardy in Brit. Isles* II. 100 Of the Nothofagus group of beeches, this [sc. *N. Moorei*] has the largest leaves of any cultivated out-of-doors in this country. **1956** *Handbk. Hardwoods* (Forest Prod. Res. Lab.) 76 *Nothofagus* is the beech of the southern hemisphere. **1961** *Times* 18 July 11/7 The dark and light greens of the nothofagus forest. **1974** R. L. FOX *Variations on Garden* 138 Foresters are beginning to realize the merits of a cousin of the beech tree called nothofagus... These southern beeches grow wild in New Zealand and South America... Their leaves are small, like a small beech or hornbeam, and their autumn colouring is most remarkable: each leaf changes individually to its own shade of orange, red, brown or plain green.

nothomorph ('nɒθəʊmɔːf). *Bot.* [f. Gr. νόθος cross-bred + μορφή form.] A plant produced by hybridization.

1939 R. MELVILLE in *Proc. Linn. Soc.* CLI. 158, I therefore propose the term nothomorph (nothomorphus = hybrid form) for all hybrid forms of sexual origin, whether F_1 segregates or back-crosses. **1949** *Jrnl. R. Hort. Soc.* LXXIV. 43 This original seedling and its vegetatively produced offspring may . . be the product of hybridization, i.e. a nothomorph. **1953** *Rep. Proc. 7th Internat. Bot. Congr. 1950* XII. 544/2 These forms are recognized as nothomorphs; when desirable they may be designated by an epithet preceded by the binary name of the group and the term nothomorph. **1963** DAVIS & HEYWOOD *Princ. Angiosperm Taxonomy* xiv. 482 The term nothomorph can be used to distinguish different derivatives of hybridisation between the same species.

no-'thoroughfare. A way, lane, etc., from which there is no exit at one end; a cul-de-sac.

The notice *No Thoroughfare* is freq. put up at the entrance to such places; also in streets temporarily closed, or ways not open to the public.

1809 MALKIN *Gil Blas* II. iii. ¶1, I was on my way to No Thoroughfare. **1843** DICKENS *Mart. Chuz.* ix, In the throats and maws of dark no-thoroughfares. **1870** J. H. NEWMAN *Gram. of Assent* II. vii. 211 A host of like questions . . must be deliberately put aside, . . as (so to speak) no-thoroughfares, having no outlet themselves [etc.].

attrib. **1815** SIMOND *Tour Gt. Brit.* II. 259 One of those no-thoroughfare lanes or courts.

nothosaur ('nɒθəʊsɔː(r)). *Palæont.* [f. mod.L. name of suborder *Nothosauria*, f. generic name NOTHOSAURUS (Georg, Graf von Münster 1834, in *Neues Jahrb. f. Min.* 525).] An extinct marine reptile belonging to the suborder Nothosauria, known from Triassic fossil remains in Europe.

1933 A. S. ROMER *Vertebr. Paleont.* vii. 153 A nothosaur in which this pterygoid union had not been quite completed would make an ideal plesiosaur ancestor. **1962** *New Scientist* 5 July 34/2 Some of the nothosaurs seem to have been very lightly built, others larger and more sturdy. They all had fairly long, flexible necks and long jaws with many pointed teeth. They must have caught their food in the shallow waters . . paddling along with their stubby webbed feet. **1971** *Nature* 15 Jan. 172/1 In a great many aquatic and marine reptiles, past and present, ichthyosaurs, placodonts, nothosaurs, . . the external nares are just in front of the eyes.

notho'saurian, *a. Palæont.* [f. next + -IAN.] Resembling the Nothosaurus.

1893 *Proc. Zoological Soc.* 616 Mr. G. A. Boulenger . . read a paper 'On a Nothosaurian Reptile . . apparently referable to *Lariosaurus*'.

nothosaurus (nɒθəʊ'sɔːrəs). *Palæont.* [f. Gr. νόθος spurious + σαῦρος lizard.] A fossil saurian belonging to the Triassic epoch.

1845 R. CHAMBERS *Vestiges Nat. Hist. Creation* (ed. 4) 99 Other reptiles there were—nothosaurus and rhynchosaurus—of lacertian or lizard-like character. **1870** NICHOLSON *Man. Zool.* (1875) 492 Of the other genera of the Sauropterygia, Simosaurus and Nothosaurus are from the Trias, and are chiefly characteristic of . . the Muschelkalk.

no-thought: see NO *a.* 5 e.

no-throw. [f. NO *a.* + THROW *sb.*[2]] In various games or sports, a throw disallowed because it does not comply with the rules.

1959 *Times* 14 Sept. 3/2 Ellis . . won the hammer . . with his second throw . . , thereafter having four no-throws. **1964** A. WYKES *Gambling* iii. 62 The bettors place their money on whether the coins will land as two heads or two tails; a head and a tail is a 'no-throw'. **1967** WARD & WATTS *Athletics* xii. 115 *Major fault 9*: point [of javelin] not coming down—no mark is made, hence there is a 'No throw'.

notht, obs. Sc. variant of NOUGHT.

not-I, not-me. [f. NOT *adv.* 14 d + I, ME *pers. prons.*] That from which the subjective or personal is excluded.

1846 J. D. MORELL *Hist. View Philos.* I. 59 In the same manner as *the me* implies the notion of a *not-me* from which it is distinguished . . so the notion of the limited and the finite implies the correlative one of the unlimited and the infinite. **1854** A. G. HENDERSON tr. *Cousin's Philos. of Kant* vii. 179 The me . . could only become cognizant of the not-me by means of the faculties it possesses. **1895** tr. *M. Nordau's Degeneration* III. i. 245 It has . . jumped to the conclusion that the 'I' has actually no knowledge of a 'not-I', of an external world. *Ibid.*, These wise men repeated, in a tone of conviction, the doctrine of the non-existence of the 'not-I'. **1917** D. H. LAWRENCE *Look! We have come Through!* 147, I suppose ultimately, she is all beyond me, She is all not-me, ultimately. **1950** A. HUXLEY *Themes & Variations* i. 114 Not the hyper-organic 'I', still less the divine not-I, which transcends the ego and is its ground. **1953** S. SPENDER *Creative Element* ii. 54 He [*sc.* Rimbaud] was attempting to remove the barrier which divides subject from object, the 'I' from the 'not I'. **1953** H. L. SULLIVAN *Interpersonal Theory of Psychiatry* x. 162 The personification of not-me is . . very emphatically encountered by people who are having a severe schizophrenic episode. **1965** *Listener* 4 Nov. 691/2 We are accustomed to distinguish so sharply between 'I' and 'not-I' and between 'now' and 'not-now' that any blurring of the dichotomy may seem unnatural to us. **1974** A. PLANT in M. Fordham et al. *Technique in Jungian Analysis* II. 215 The analyst can be of use by letting the patient experience him as a 'not-me' possession.

notice ('nəʊtɪs), *sb.* Also 5 **notyce**, 6 **notize**. [a. F. *notice* (14th c.), ad. L. *nōtitia* (whence also It. *notizia*, Sp. and Pg. *noticia*), f. *nōtus* known.]

1. a. Intimation, information, intelligence, warning. Also with *pl.*, and *transf.* (quot. 1741).

1483 *Cal. Proc. Chanc. Q. Eliz.* (1830) Pref. 72 Byfore any knowlegge or notyce therof made or yeven to . . Robert Scrope. **1599** SHAKS. *Hen. V*, IV. vii. 122 Bring me iust notice of the numbers dead. **1653** WALTON *Angler* To Rdr. 2 Of these . . I thought fit to give thee this notice. **1671** MILTON *Samson* 1536 A little stay will bring some notice hither. **1710** STEELE *Tatler* No. 173 ¶2 His Epistles and Satires are full of proper Notices for the Conduct of Life in a Court. **1741** RICHARDSON *Pamela* (1824) I. xxxii. 313 My lord . . , being a little tender in his feet, from a gouty notice, walked very slowly. **1847** TENNYSON *Princ.* vii. 234 Notice of a change in the dark world Was lispt about the acacias. **1859** —— *Geraint* 149 Before him came a forester . . with notice of a hart . . First seen that day.

b. In phr. *to give* (and *to have*) *notice*.

1582 STANYHURST *Æneis* III. (Arb.) 85 Shee wyl geeue notice to the streight of al Italye dwellers. **1588** SHAKS. *L.L.L.* II. i. 81 Nauar had notice of your faire approach. **1617** MORYSON *Itin.* I. 37 Promising rewards . . to any man [who] should give them notice when any such passed. **1695** WOODWARD *Nat. Hist. Earth* I. (1723) 4 Wheresoever I had Notice of any considerable natural Spelunca . . I forthwith had recourse thereunto. **1719–20** SWIFT *To Yng. Clergym.* Wks. 1751 V. 5 Allow him with the utmost Freedom to give you notice of whatever he shall find amiss either in your voice or gesture. **1847** MARRYAT *Childr. N. Forest* xx, He knew the dogs would give notice of the approach of any one.

c. *at short notice*, with little time for action or preparation. So *at ten minutes' notice*, etc.

1784 COWPER *Task* IV. 136 Gath'ring, at short notice, in one group The family dispers'd. **1839** DICKENS *Let.* 25 July (1965) I. 569 There is *always* a bed for you at five minutes' notice. **1864** G. A. SALA in *Daily Tel.* 20 July, One of those tremendous gales..which spring up at ten minutes' notice. 1875 Higginson *Hist. U.S.* xxxi. 295 All these..had to be bought..at very short notice.

d. A sign, placard, etc., conveying some intimation or intelligence.

1805 Wordsw. *Waggoner* I. 81 Some shining notice will be there, Of open house and ready fare. 1822 Shelley *To Jane, Invitation* 29, I leave this notice on my door For each accustomed visitor. 1834 *West India Sketch Bk.* I. 28 At the Exchange, where thou wilt find notices of vessels.. according to the ports or places.

2. a. Formal intimation or warning of something.

1594 Shaks. *Rich. III*, III. v. 108 (Q.), Now will I in..to giue notice, that no manner of person..haue recourse vnto the Princes. *a*1641 Bp. Mountagu *Acts & Mon.* (1642) 401 It was done with sound of Trumpet,..as Players with us use to give notice of a Play. 1650 *Cal. St. P., Dom. Ser.* (1876) 540 Masters of the letter packet boat, Not to carry any male passengers to France or Flanders until further notice. 1711 Swift *Lett.* (1767) III. 167 Cairnes's clerks..said, they had received no notice of it. 1770 Langhorne *Plutarch* (1879) I. 79/2 A herald went before, who gave notice to the people to keep holiday. 1818 Cruise *Digest* (ed. 2) III. 451 Where the trust was destroyed by a conveyance to a purchaser, without notice. 1853 Mrs. Carlyle *Lett.* II. 240, I had the lease of the house, and the notice to quit lying at my disposal. 1896 *Act 59 & 60 Vict.* c. 36 §2 Public notice of any order made under this Act shall be given in the manner required.

b. An intimation by one of the parties to an agreement that it is to terminate at a specified time, *esp.* with reference to quitting a house, lodgings, or employment.

1765 Earl of Malmesbury *Let.* 16 Sept. (1870) I. 129 It is 150 florins, or fourteen guineas, a-year; but I am to try it first, and may, at any time after, quit it by giving six weeks' notice. 1836 Dickens *Let.* 5 Nov. (1965) I. 191, I have deemed it right to beg you to accept my notice from to-day. 1837 —— *Pickw.* xxvi, All I've come about, is just..to give my governor's notice. 1844 —— *Mart. Chuz.* x, All I've got to say to you, Mrs. Todgers, is,—a week's notice from next Saturday. 1887 Sims *Mary Jane's Mem.* 299 The girl was under notice.

c. An announcement read to a church congregation (freq. *pl.*).

1855 F. Procter *Hist. Bk. Com. Prayer* II. iii. 322 The correct interpretation concerning notices to be given in church. *a*1870 'Mark Twain' *Let.* in C. Clemens *My Father* (1931) i. 11 The local minister had read sixteen 'notices' of Sunday-school and Bible-class and church and sewing-society and other meetings. 1967 *Alternative Services* (*Second Series*): *An Order for Holy Communion* 4 Banns of Marriage and other notices may then be published, if they have not been published before the service.

†**3.** Knowledge. *Obs.*

*c*1586 C'tess Pembroke *Ps.* LXXIX. iv, O kindle there thy furies flame, Where lives no notice of thy name. 1602 Marston *Antonio's Rev.* v. i, The Florence Prince (Drawne by firme notice of the Dukes black deeds) Is made a partner in conspiracie. 1631 Weever *Anc. Funeral Mon.* 382 Many Chantries, Chappels [etc.], more then I haue notice of, were erected..within the spacious vast Fabricke of this Episcopall Chaire. 1726 Shelvocke *Voy. round World* 28 Being very ready to assist me with his advice, and notice of the state of affairs.

†**4.** A notion or idea. *Obs.*

1654 Jer. Taylor *Real Pres.* §11 That unreasonable thing, which all the natural and congenite notices of men cry down. 1665 Glanvill *Scepsis Sci.* Addr. p. vii, Improving the minds of Men in solid and useful notices of things. 1696 Stillingfl. *12 Serm.* iv. 142 The virtuous heathens,.. according to those short and obscure notices which they had of God. 1784 Cowper *Tiroc.* 199 Our early notices of truth, disgrac'd, Soon lose their credit, and are all effac'd.

5. a. Heed, cognizance, note, attention.

1597 Hooker *Eccl. Pol.* v. xlix. §2 As farre as any dutie of ours dependeth vpon the notize of their condition. 1605 Shaks. *Lear* II. iv. 252 To no more Will I giue place or notice. 1665 Sir T. Herbert *Trav.* (1677) 333 Give me leave therefore to name some Fruit may be worth the notice. 1769 Burke *Late St. Nation* Wks. II. 82 The author speaks ..or her debt, as a thing scarcely worthy of notice. 1784 Cowper *Task* v. 257 They soon grow drunk With gazing, when they see an able man Step forth to notice. 1874 Geo. Eliot *Coll. Breakf.-P.* 269 If you turn away From narrow notice how the scent of gold Has guided sense of damning heresy. 1885 *Law Times Rep.* LIII. 61/2 He had no reason to give particular notice to what lights the *I.C.U.* was showing.

b. One's cognizance or observation.

1607 Shaks. *Cor.* II. iii. 166 To my poore vnworthy notice, He mock'd vs, when he begg'd our Voyces. 1679 Dryden *Limberham* I. i, For fear that Name shou'd bring me to the notice of my Father. 1742 Fielding *J. Andrews* I. xv, Nor is the meanest thief below, or the greatest hero above, thy notice. 1784 Johnson in *Boswell* 2 Aug., Wherever I turn, the dead or the dying meet my notice. 1819 Shelley *Cenci* IV. iv. 86 A gold-inwoven robe..Betrayed them to our notice. 1895 *Law Times Rep.* LXXIII. 651/1 Keeping back that which there was a duty to bring specifically to the notice of the underwriters.

†**c.** An act of observation. *Obs. rare*$^{-1}$.

1625 Fletcher & Shirley *Nt. Walker* II. i, I saw the old Lady, ere she went to bed, Put up her plate..In a small long chest... *Lurc.* 'Twas a good notice.

†**d.** *for notice sake*, in order to be noticed. *Obs.*

1632 Lithgow *Trav.* I. 41 The Iewes..in Rome, weare red, and yellow hats for notice sake, to distinguish them from others.

6. a. *to take notice*, to give heed, bestow attention. Const. *of* the person or thing; also *that, how.*

1592 Shaks. *Ven. & Ad.* 341 Taking no notice that she is so nigh. 1597 Hooker *Eccl. Pol.* v. lxxii. §11 After notize taken how the Montanists held these additions to be supplements of the Gospell. 1638 Junius *Paint. Ancients* 24 Our mind shall never take notice of anything the eyes doe see. 1662 Stillingfl. *Orig. Sacræ* I. vi. §2 To which purpose the Testimony of Varro in Censorinus is generally taken notice of. 1711 Addison *Spect.* No. 39 ¶5 Men in Ordinary Discourse very often speak Iambicks, without taking notice of it. 1779 Sheridan *Critic* II. ii, But isn't it odd they never were taken notice of, not even by the commander-in-chief? 1868 Tennyson *Lucretius* 8 Yet often ..the master took Small notice. 1895 Maartens *My Lady Nobody* 345 Somebody tried the lock. Ursula took no notice.

b. *spec.* of babies: To show signs of intelligent observation.

1846 Dickens *Cricket on Hearth* i, Two months and three da-ays!.. Takes notice in a way quite won-der-ful! 1895 Maartens *My Lady Nobody* 309 'He is beginning to take notice', said Ursula... 'Don't you see how he opens and shuts his little fingers?'

†**7.** *to take notice to* (one), to point out, mention specially. *Obs.*

1660 Boyle *New Exp. Phys. Mech.* xxxvi. 283 The haste I was in..made me forget to take notice to you of a Problem that occurr'd to my thoughts. 1718 Lady M. W. Montagu *Lett.* II. 79, I cannot forbear taking notice to you of a mistake of Gemelli. 1765 H. Walpole *Otranto* iv, I took notice of it to Bianca, even before I saw him in armour. 1787 Earl Malmesbury *Diaries & Corr.* II. 345 He took again notice to both these Ministers. 1807 Southey *Espriella's Lett.* I. 100 He took notice to one of them, that the lad.. appeared very sickly and delicate.

8. a. A brief mention in writing; *spec.* in modern use, a paragraph or article on a newly published book, a review. Also, a review of a play or any public entertainment.

1835 Dickens *Let.* 23 Nov. (1965) I. 97, If I take a cab and put off writing my notice 'till we return, I can easily manage it. I shall come straight from the Theatre. 1841 Arnold in *Life & Corr.* (1844) II. x. 298, I thank you very much for your notices of my lecture. 1847 L. Hunt *Men, Wom. & Bks.* II. xi. 277 Pepys, not very consistently with some of his notices of the Doctor, complains that he did all the work. 1872 Holmes *Poet Breakf.-t.* vi. (1906) 132 Before you write that brilliant notice of some..book of verses. 1952 Granville *Dict. Theatrical Terms* 123 *Notice*, the newspaper critique following a first-night performance. 1959 N. Marsh *False Scent* (1960) ii. 76 'She's playing Eliza Doolittle,' Gantry remarked. 'Of course. Nice notices,' Marchant murmured.

b. *pl.* Notes of astronomical observations.

1861 J. Nichol in *Mem.* (1896) 88 You are popping your kind old head in at the stand 'to take the notices'.

9. *Comb.*, as ***notice-shunning, -taker, -taking, -worthy.***

1817 Coleridge *Biogr. Lit.* (Bohn) 20 In the days of our shy and *notice-shunning grandfathers! 1663 Spencer *Prodigies* (1665) 374 God's Rod hath a voice.., and it becomes us to be his *notice-takers. 1614 Jackson *Creed* III. 45 To smother their guilt, and preuent all *notice taking of their impietie. 1673 Ray *Journ. Low C.* 39 A handsome Building.., which we thought not unworthy the notice-taking. 1816 Scott *Old Mort.* xxxviii, Though ye are no blind, ye are no sae notice-taking as I am. 1856 Froude *Hist. Eng.* (1858) II. vii. 182 An illustration, very *notice-worthy, of the temper which was working in the country.

b. Special Comb. **notice paper**, a parliamentary paper giving the current day's proceedings.

1844 T. E. May *Law, Privileges Parliament* viii. 166 Any member [of the House of Commons] may propose a question... But in order to give the House due notice of his intention, he is required to state the form of his motion on a previous day, and to have it entered in the Order Book or Notice Paper. 1884 E. W. Hamilton *Diary* 3 Apr. (1972) II. 588 After the unprecedent[ed] number of questions had been disposed of (no less than 73 being on the Notice paper) ..Sir S. Northcote moved the adjournment of the House. 1956 P. & G. Ford *Guide to Parliamentary Papers* I. i. 3 The White Paper (Notice Paper)..contains certain portions of the Blue Paper and relates to the current day's sittings.

notice ('nəʊtɪs), *v.* Also 5 notyse, 6 notise, 7 notize. [f. the sb.]

Not much used before the middle of the 18th cent., after which it became common in American use, and was also mentioned as a Scotticism:—

1787 Beattie *Scoticisms* 59 *Narrate*, and *to notice*, have of late been used by some Eng. writers; but it is better to avoid them. 1789 Franklin *Wks.* (1888) X. 177 During my late absence in France, I find that several other new words have been introduced into our parliamentary language; for example, I find a verb formed from the substantive *notice*: I should not have noticed this [etc.].

†**1.** *trans.* To notify, intimate. *Obs.*

*c*1450 Lovelich *Merlin* 2812 The deth of the rede dragown Schal notyse ful gret Significaciown. *Ibid.* 6900 Alle the clergyse there anon thorwgh the rewm dyde notyse thus son. *c*1525 in Ellis *Orig. Lett.* Ser. III. II. 5 If it be ment that we shuld notise unto theis people where thoffence hathe bene committed. 1541 *Act 33 Hen. VIII*, c. 21 Some of his counsaile..ought shortly after to notice the same vnto him. 1627 Sclater *Exp. 2 Thess.* (1629) 305 This noticeth that we loue Gods children.., when all that are such, are entertained into our loue.

2. a. To make mention of; to remark upon; to refer to, speak of (something observed).

1611 T. Howard in *Harington's Nugæ Ant.* (1804) I. 396 That his eyes are fire, his tail is Berenice's locks, and a few more such fancies worthy your noticing.

1748 Miss C. Talbot in *Lett. Miss Carter & Miss Talbot* (1809) I. 296 Remember..in your answer not to notice this latter part of mine. 1766 *Lond. Chron.* 27–30 Dec. 631/3 Mr. Garrick's judicious alteration of this Play has been already noticed in a former number. 1800 *Med. Jrnl.* IV. 380 The Communications which have been received, shall be noticed as soon as possible. 1827 D. Johnson *Ind. Field Sports* 251, I hope, if properly noticed,..that the heads of Government will take it into consideration. 1838 J. H. Newman *Lett.* (1891) II. 263 His formal noticing the faults made them important.

b. To point out, make mention of, *to* one.

1627 Sclater *Exp. 2 Thess.* (1632) 289 Pauls noting or notizing them to the Congregation is not excommunication complete. 1718 De Foe in Lee *Life* (1869) I. Introd. 13 This ..I thought myself obliged to notice to you. 1793 Jefferson *Writ.* (1859) IV. 59 It has been thought better that I should notice to you its very exceptionable nature. 1866 Mrs. Gaskell *Wives & Daughters* lviii. (1867) 559 She looked so much better that Sir Charles noticed it to Lady Harriet.

3. a. To take notice of; to observe, perceive. Also *absol.* (cf. notice *sb.* 6 b).

1757 *Amer. Mag.* Dec. 118/1 Be it previously noticed that this observation is only applicable to a false taste in building. 1762 *Pennsylv. Arch.* (1853) IV. 88, I was in the house.., and did not notice any of the above circumstances. 1781 Cowper *Charity* 207 The wretch that works and weeps without relief, Has one that notices his silent grief. 1818 Shelley *Rosal. & Helen* 525 Nor noticed I where joyously Sate my two younger babes at play. 1860 Tyndall *Glac.* I. xxvii. 207, I could notice a turbidity gathering in the air. 1894 *Woman at Home* II. 437 Notice a latitudinal crease in the left sleeve.

absol. 1899 *Allbutt's Syst. Med.* VII. 820 A third [child] 'did not notice' for some weeks. A fourth 'did not notice at the time of head-retraction'.

b. colloq. phr. ***not so as you'd notice***: not to a noticeable degree.

1937 A. Christie *Murder in Mews* iii. 172 '*He* was fond of *you*?' 'Not so that you'd notice it..he rather resented my existence.' 1938 N. Marsh *Artists in Crime* (1954) xvi. 216 Garcia's not innocent, dear, not so's you'd notice it. 1966 'N. Blake' *Morning after Death* xiii. 198 'Was Chester interested?' 'Not so as you'd notice.' 1970 W. J. Burley *To kill a Cat* xi. 189 'Any luck?' 'Not so's you'd notice.'

c. *intr.* To be seen, to show, to be noticeable.

1961 Y. Olsson *On Syntax Eng. Verb* vii. 177, I have mended the hole now. I don't think it notices.

4. To treat (a person) with some degree of attention, favour, or politeness; to recognize or acknowledge (one).

1746 H. Walpole *Lett.* (1891) II. 24 The Venetian ambassadress..is the only woman he has yet noticed. 1775 *N. Eng. Hist. & Gen. Reg.* (1864) XIX. 135, I was much Oblig'd to them for their good wishes and Opinion; in short, no Person could possibly be more Notic'd than myself. *a*1817 Jane Austen *Persuasion* i, Mr. Elliot had..shown himself as unsolicitous of being longer noticed by the family. 1857 Mrs. Gore *Two Aristocr.* III. 245 But of course, my dear, you did not *notice* such people?

5. †**a.** To notify (one) *of* a thing. *Obs. rare.*

1775 Trumbull in Sparks *Corr. Amer. Rev.* (1853) I. 31 Whether these are the same ships your Excellency noticed us of, remains uncertain.

b. To serve with a notice; to give notice to.

1850 *Tait's Mag.* XVII. 561/1 The widow was regularly noticed to quit at the ensuing term. 1862 Trollope *Orley F.* i, On these fields Mr. Dockwrath expended some money.., and when noticed to give them up.., expressed himself terribly aggrieved. 1880 *Daily News* 18 Dec. 5/3 The men, about forty in number, were 'noticed' on Friday.

6. *refl.* To take (oneself) *out of* something by giving the requisite notice.

1881 Chaplin in *Daily News* 24 Mar. 2/1 The clauses of the Act of 1875 which gave power to landlords and tenants to 'notice' themselves out of it.

7. To write a review or 'notice' of a book, play, etc.

1854 *Punch* 15 July 20/1 The reporter who 'noticed' the diplomatists. 1859 G. H. Lewes *Let.* 5 Feb. in *Geo. Eliot Lett.* (1954) III. 10 Perhaps also you will send the 'Times' should that 'publication' notice the carpenter [sc. *Adam Bede*].

Hence **'noticing** *ppl. a.*, observant, wide awake.

1843 Carlyle *Past & Pres.* I. (1858) 118 A brisk-eyed, noticing youth and novice. 1903 E. Wharton *Sanctuary* II. i. 79 You know she's an uncommonly noticing person, and little things tell with her. 1905 J. C. Lincoln *Partners of Tide* ii. 20 Bradley, being what his late 'Uncle Solon' had called a 'noticin' boy', remembered Captain Titcomb's hint. 1940 R. Postgate *Verdict of Twelve* i. 12 Father was not 'noticing'; Mother was, and what's more would twist your arm till you screamed if you sulked and wouldn't answer. 1959 A. Christie *Cat among Pigeons* xx. 205 She's not what I'd call a noticing kind of child.

noticea'bility. [f. next + -ity.] **a.** That which is noticeable. **b.** The quality, state, or fact of being noticeable.

1897 *Pall Mall Mag.* Jan. 112 These little noticeabilities are just what mankind has to suffer under. 1926 Fowler *Mod. Eng. Usage* 639 The reader will perhaps conclude that its noticeability is not a grace.

noticeable ('nəʊtɪsəb(ə)l), *a.* [f. notice *v.*]

1. Worthy or deserving of notice.

1796 Morse *Amer. Geogr.* I. 191 Many [trees] probably equally noticeable with those enumerated. 1802 Wordsw. *Stanzas Thomson's Cast. Indolence* v, A noticeable Man with large grey eyes, And a pale face. 1828 Southey *Ess.* (1832) II. 411 The concluding clause is noticeable. 1878 Grosart in *H. More's Poems* 208 It has been my aim to register every noticeable word.

2. Capable of being noticed or observed.

1809 *Mem. Amer. Acad. Arts & Sci.* III. 248 The moon's limb exhibited very little of that rough or serrated appearance, which was so noticeable in 1806. 1849 Lytton *Caxtons* VIII. iv, Traces..of a constitutional love of show.. were noticeable: but one by one they disappeared. 1869 Tyndall *Notes Lect. Light* §188 A slight extension of their images upon the retina becomes noticeable. 1882 Howells in *Longm. Mag.* I. 53 It is in the country that this waste..is most sorrowfully noticeable.

ˈnoticeably, *adv.* [f. prec. + -LY^2.] In a noticeable manner or degree; remarkably.

1855 OGILVIE *Suppl.* **1856** MRS. BROWNING *Aur. Leigh* v. 670 Good Sir Blaise's brow is high And noticeably narrow. **1872** MINTO *Eng. Prose Lit.* 6 A sentence, so constructed, as to be noticeably loose.

ˈnotice-board. [f. NOTICE *sb.*] A board bearing a notice, or on which notices are commonly fixed.

1854 DICKENS *Hard T.* II. viii, They will be punished with the utmost rigor of the laws, as notice-boards observe. **1874** MICKLETHWAITE *Mod. Par. Churches* 220 Notice boards cannot be too simple. **1887** *Spectator* 26 Mar. 415/1 We were confronted by a notice-board threatening vengeance on trespassers.

ˈnoticer. *rare*$^{-1}$. [f. NOTICE *v.*] One who, or that which, gives notice or intimation.

1751 WARBURTON *Pope's Wks.* V. 253 So that the station of a Professor is only a kind of legal Noticer to inform us where the shattered bulk of Learning lies at anchor.

notice-taker, -taking: see NOTICE *sb.*

ˈnotifiable, *a.* [f. NOTIFY *v.* + -ABLE.] That should be notified to some authority.

1889 *Lancet* II. 565/2 Diseases..differentiated into notifiable and non-notifiable. **1898** *Westm. Gaz.* 11 Oct. 2/3 Steps are being taken..to make consumption a notifiable disease.

†**notificate,** *v. Obs. rare*$^{-1}$. [See next and -ATE.] *trans.* To denote.

1654 Z. COKE *Logick* 10 A good division should be commodious, and apt to notificate the whole.

notification (ˌnəʊtɪfɪˈkeɪʃən). Also 4 **-acioun.** [a. F. *notification* (13–14th c., = It. *notificazione*, Sp. *-acion*), or ad. med.L. *nōtificātiōn-em*, f. L. *nōtificāre*: see NOTIFY *v.* and -ATION.]

1. The action of notifying or making known; an intimation, a notice.

c **1374** CHAUCER *Boeth.* v. met. iii. (1868) 159 To knowen þilke notificaciouns [L. *notas*] þat ben yhidd vndir þe couertours of soþe. **1472–75** *Rolls of Parlt.* VI. 159/1 Within half yere after notification to hym therof to be made. **1540** *Act 32 Hen. VIII*, c. 48 The sayd constable shal make relacion and notification therof to the Kinges maiestie. **1627** DONNE *Serm.* v. 46 The Name of God is the Notification of God. **1669** HOLDER *Elem. Speech* 4 Four or Five Torches.. elevated or depressed out of their Order..may by agreement give great variety of Notifications. **1748** H. WALPOLE *Lett.* (1846) II. 224 This seems to have been a very unnecessary notification. **1791** BURKE *Th. Fr. Aff.* Wks. VII. 10 The second notification was that of the king's acceptance of the new constitution. **1812** WELLINGTON in Gurw. *Desp.* (1837) IX. 143, I have not seen any official notification of this appointment. **1866** CRUMP *Banking* ix. 179 A notification was published partially suspending cash payments. **1871** MARKBY *Elem. Law* §5 Very rarely notifications in the form of commands are issued by the rulers of a political society.

†**2.** The action of taking notice. *Obs. rare*$^{-1}$.

1659 in *Burton's Diary* (1828) IV. 333 This is a matter of that consequence, that it ought not to be passed by without your notification.

†**notificative,** *a. Obs. rare*$^{-1}$. [Cf. F. *notificatif, -ive.*] Designative.

1652 G. COLLIER *Vind. Sabbath* (1656) 9 The seventh.. being notificative of a particular day.

ˈnotified, *ppl. a.* Now *dial.* [f. NOTIFY *v.* + -ED^1.] Celebrated, notorious, well known.

1535 STEWART *Cron. Scot.* I. 35 In all land wes notifeit his name. **1570** *Satir. Poems Reform.* x. 402 Ane false tratour, sa knawin and notifeit. **1610** HEALEY *St. Aug. Citie of God* XXII. viii. 831 Paul and Palladia came to vs, being notified by their miseries in many other places. **1763** *Wilkes' Corr.* (1805) II. 33 The notified John Wilkes, esq. arrived here last night. **1796** *Look before You Leap* (ed. 2) 91 These are chiefly the great body of inhabitants who at present crowd this notified place. **1855** [ROBINSON] *Whitby Gloss.* s.v., 'He was a notified man in his day,' renowned in his lifetime.

ˈnotifier. [f. next + -ER^1. Cf. OF. *notifieur.*] One who or that which notifies.

1738 W. WILSON *Def. Ref. Princ.* (1769) I. i. 36 The Church..is a public keeper and notifier of the truth. **1741** T. MORGAN *Physico-Theol.* iv. §8. 143 As if they [*sc.* words] were natural, necessary Signs of Ideas, or Notifiers of Things. **1900** *Lancet* 2 June 1634/1 Whether the case notified occurred in the course of the notifier's private practice.

notify (ˈnəʊtɪfaɪ), *v.* Forms: 4–7 **notifie** (4–5 **-fye,** 5 **-ffie**); 4–6 **notefie** (5–6 **-fy**); 5–6 **notyfie** (5 **-fy**); 6– **notify.** [ad. F. *notifier*, †*notefier* (13–14th c.), = Sp. and Pg. *notificar*, It. *notificare*, ad. L. *nōtificāre*, f. *nōtus* known.]

†**1.** *trans.* To take note of, observe, notice. *Obs.*

c **1374** CHAUCER *Troylus* II. 1591 Herde al this thynge Criseyde wel inough, And every word gan for to notifie. *c* **1485** *Digby Myst.* (1882) II. 22 Saule ys my name, I wyll that ye notyfy. **1509** BARCLAY *Shyp Folys* (1570) 132 So hangeth on his shoulders his pipe continually, Whereby men may his lewdenes notifye. **1598** SHAKS. *Merry W.* II. ii. 85 She giues you to notifie, that her husband will be absence from his house, betweene ten and eleuen. **1678** R. RUSSELL tr. *Geber* III. II. I. i. 143 Therefore we will first notifie the Principles.

2. To make known, publish, proclaim; to intimate, give notice of, announce.

c **1386** CHAUCER *Man of Law's T.* 158 And notefied is thurghout the toun, That every wight..Schulde preye Crist. **1390** GOWER *Conf.* I. 254 Which notefied was be bulle To holi cherche. **1433** *Rolls of Parlt.* IV. 425/1 The whiche offre and agrement..[was] notified and communed to all the Lordes. **1490** CAXTON *Eneydos* viii. 34 [They] notefyden vnto the quene, how the sayd kyng had requyred her in maryage. **1542** HENRY VIII *Decl.* 192 We haue thought good to notify vnto the world his doinges and behauour. **1598** BARRET *Theor. Warres* IV. iii. 110 The ensignes and Lieutenants to giue and notifie the orders and commandes. **1641** *Nicholas P.* (Camden) I. 5 To notify throughout their circuits his Majesties greate grace and goodnesse to his people [etc.]. **1691** LUTTRELL *Brief Rel.* (1857) II. 205 A memorial to the states general, notifyeing to them that the queen of Englands fleet is ready to putt to sea. **1724** A. COLLINS *Gr. Chr. Relig.* 10 The Assembly..order'd Letters to be written to notify the same to all concern'd. **1757** BURKE *Abridgem. Eng. Hist.* Wks. X. 316 His nobility, whom he had assembled to notify this resolution to them. **1849** MACAULAY *Hist. Eng.* iv. I. 457 The king therefore notified to the country his intention of holding a parliament. **1863** H. COX *Instit.* III. viii. 714 *note*, The appointment..was merely notified to him by a letter from a Secretary of State.

refl. **1718** *Freethinker* No. 25 ¶17 In paying a Visit, the Visiter was obliged to notify himself by a set Form.

absol. **1604** SHAKS. *Oth.* III. i. 31 If she will stirre hither, I shall seeme to notifie vnto her. **1889** *Leeds Mercury* 15 Aug. 8/5 She was too ill to notify.

†**b.** *intr.* To give intimation *of* something. *Obs.*

1509 HAWES *Past. Pleas.* xix. (Percy Soc.) 89 All that, madame, was to me certyfyde By good dame Fame,..Whan she to me of you well notyfide. *a* **1548** HALL *Chron., K. Hen. VII* 58 He sent dyuerse postes too notefie to hys grace of Kynge Philippes landynge.

†**3.** To indicate, denote. *Obs.*

c **1386** CHAUCER *Pars. T.* ¶356 Yet notifien they, in hir array of attire, licourousness and pride. **1542** UDALL *Erasm. Apoph.* 84 Notifiyng in myne opinion, a manne to be ferre unmeete for all good occupacions. **1627** SPEED *England* xl. §7 All distinguished and notified from the rest by the wearing of purple garments. *a* **1661** FULLER *Worthies* (1840) I. xxi. 82 Some persons in our work are notified by all of these indications. *a* **1727** NEWTON *Chronol. Amended* ii. (1728) 240 Their design was to notify the distraction of Egypt.

4. To give notice to; to inform.

Common in American use from the end of the 17th c.

1440 in *Wars Eng. in France* (Rolls) II. 589 If any of thappointementis..be brokyn..and the king..certified and notifiede therof. **1652** WADSWORTH tr. *Sandoval's Civ. Wars Spain* 169 The Frier..notified and commanded them ..to go with them to Tordesillas. **1697** *Boston Rec.* (1881) VII. 226 The Selectmen are to be notified thereof that they may be present. **1716** J. WINTHROP in *Mass. Hist. Collect.* V. 324, I am notify'd by the County Sheriff..to answer before you to a very wrong complaint. **1781** S. PETERS *Hist. Connect.* 352 All parties, who had causes depending in any court, were to be duly notified by the Governor's proclamation. **1843** CUSTINE *Empire Czar* I. 107 Peter notified him, through his first minister, that he was to attend the ceremony. **1883** L. OLIPHANT *Altiora Peto* I. 66 The asphalt..resounded with the clatter of the hoofs which notified the concierge..that Baron Grandesella's family and luggage were on the point of arrival.

5. To write notes to; to annotate. *rare*$^{-1}$.

1830 SCOTT *Jrnl.* 27 Dec., I took up the Magnum, and began to notify the romance called *Woodstock.*

Hence **ˈnotifying** *vbl. sb.* and *ppl. a.*

1591 PERCIVALL *Sp. Dict.*, *Notificacion*, notifying. **1611** FLORIO, *Notificatione*, a notifying, a publishing. **1680** BAXTER *Answ. Stillingfl.* xvi. 32 Are these notifying Terms for a Definition?

no-time. [f. NO *a.* + TIME *sb.*] A time which does not exist (*poet.*); a very short time (*U.S. local*).

a **1918** W. OWEN *Poems* (1931) 69 And in the happy no-time of his sleeping Death took him by the heart. **1942** W. FAULKNER *Go Down, Moses* 224 After a no-time he returned. **1943** D. GASCOYNE *Poems 1937–1942* 22 Black was the No-time at the heart Of Time (the frameless mirror's back). **1963** [see NO-PLACE *sb.*].

†**ˈnoting,** *vbl. sb.*^{1} *Obs.* [f. NOTE *v.*^{1}] Using.

13.. *E.E. Allit. P.* B. 1354 In notyng of nwe metes & of nice gettes, Al was þe mynde of þat man.

ˈnoting, *vbl. sb.*^{2} [f. NOTE *v.*^{2}] The action of the vb., in various senses.

c **1440** *Promp. Parv.* 359/2 Notynge, *notacio.* *c* **1500** in *Antiq. Rep.* (1809) IV. 408 Thou maist be judged by a crochet of wronge notynge in thy presumcion. **1570** T. NORTON in *Udall's Royster D.* (1847) p. xli, Partly to shunne publike noting, partely for better hearkening. **1607** HIERON *Wks.* I. 302 There must be..a diligent noting how the preaching of the word fitteth the particulars of Christs fulnesse to the soules particular wants. **1645** MILTON *Tetrach.* Wks. 1851 IV. 151 Many things..not ordinary, nor unworth the noting. **1817** J. SCOTT *Paris Revis.* (ed. 4) 311 A careful noting of indirect and circumstantial evidence. **1860** *Merc. Mar. Mag.* VII. 157 A coble has been stationed opposite the..Quay, for the hailing and noting of vessels.

attrib. **1576** FLEMING *Panopl. Epist.* 257 Take into your handes againe your noting tables. **1591** PERCIVALL *Sp. Dict.*, *Cartapacio*, a noting booke, a noting paper.

b. *spec.* (See quots. and NOTE *v.*^{2} 6 c.)

1843–56 BOUVIER *Law Dict.* (ed. 6) II. 246 The noting is not indispensable, it being only a part of the protest. **1849** C. G. ADDISON *Contracts* xxiii. (ed. 2) 1100 Noting is a minute made on the bill by the officer at the time of the refusal to accept and is the preparatory step to protest.

†**notiˈometer.** *Obs. rare*$^{-1}$. [f. Gr. νότιος wet + -METER.] (See quot.)

1730 CHAMBERLAYNE *Relig. Philos.* II. xix. §xlvi, The making of Hygrometers or Notiometers, or those Machines by which we measure the Moisture of the Air.

notion (ˈnəʊʃən). [ad. L. *nōtiōn-em*, f. *nōt-*, ppl. stem of *nōscĕre* to know: see -TION. Hence also F. *notion* (1653), It. *nozione*, Sp. *nocion*, Pg. *noçao.*]

I. 1. a. A general concept under which a particular thing or person is comprehended or classed; a term expressive of such a concept. Chiefly with *under.*

1567 MAPLET *Gr. Forest* 8 b, We haue beene occasioned, and shall be hereafter to vse it as the generaltie or notion of the name and stock in these kindes. **1641–2** in Clarendon *Hist. Reb.* v. §99 Neither House had Presented them [the Malignant Party] to his Majesty, under such a Notion, as he might well understand, whom they intended. **1655** FULLER *Ch. Hist.* IX. 192 No Spaniard setting foot on English ground, under other notion then a prisoner. **1678** CUDWORTH *Intell. Syst.* 324 One and the same Deity, was worshipped under Several Names and Notions, according to its Several Powers and Vertues.

1864 BOWEN *Logic* v. 138 When we bring an object under a notion, that is, when we predicate of it that it belongs to such a class.

b. *under the notion of*, under the concept, category, designation, or name *of* something.

1655 FULLER *Ch. Hist.* IX. 52 These opposite parties,.. concurring in doctrine, under the generall notion of Protestants. **1665** BOYLE *Occas. Refl.* (1848) 61 The consideration of the pruning of Trees, under the Notion of *that which wounds them.* **1704** SWIFT *T. Tub* Apol. §3 Under the Notion of Prejudices, he knew to what dangerous Heights some Men have proceeded. **1764** *Mem. G. Psalmanazar* 147, I travelled several hundred leagues.. under the notion of a Japanese converted to Christianity. **1836** J. GILBERT *Chr. Atonem.* i. (1852) 17 It must be some other than the rule of perfection itself under the notion of law.

†**c.** A character, relation, form, etc., in which anything is conceived, mentioned, or exists. *Obs.*

a **1631** DONNE *Six Serm.* (1634) i. 26 He is received by me in the severall notions of Father, Sonne, and holy Ghost. **1650** FULLER *Pisgah* II. ii. 75 A fair City, whereof frequent mention in Scripture, but in no other notion, but only as the Eastern boundary of Canaan. *Ibid.* xiii. 274 Angels in the shape of men, Christ in the notion of an angel. **1651** BAXTER *Inf. Bapt.* 47 It is the same thing in another notion.

†**2.** The connotation or meaning *of* a term. *Obs.*

a **1643** LD. FALKLAND *Infallib.* (1646) 59 *Probable* being more than *credible* in the ordinary notion of the words. **1662** STILLINGFL. *Orig. Sacræ* II. v. §5 This being then the chief notion of a Prophet. **1713** BENTLEY *Freethinking* I. §31. 152 For pray, what is the Notion of the word Canon?

†**3.** A phrase or term. *Obs. rare.*

The Winchester use of *notion* may be a survival of this.

1655 VAUGHAN *Silex Scint.* I. Pref. (1858) 3 This Kingdom hath abounded with those ingenious persons which in the late notion are termed Wits. **1657** TRAPP *Comm. Ps.* iii. 2 [Selah] The Greek maketh it only a Musical Notion.

II. 4. An idea or concept.

a. In philosophical use. ***first*** and ***second notions*** (see quots. 1852 and 1864). ***general notion*** (see GENERAL *a.* 5 c).

1605 B. JONSON *Volpone* II. i, I haue some generall notions; I do loue To note, and to obserue. **1615** CROOKE *Body of Man* 502 This..alone maketh the differences of Images as wee call them or Abstracted Notions. **1690** LOCKE *Hum. Und.* III. v. §12 Essences of the Species of mix'd Modes are by a more particular Name call'd Notions. **1725** WATTS *Logic* 246 It is very useful to have some general principles of truth settled in the mind... These may be called first notions, or fundamental principles. **1785** REID *Intell. Powers* v. v. Wks. (1846) 403 The words notion and conception, in their proper and most common sense, signify the act and operation of the mind in conceiving an object. **1852** SIR W. HAMILTON *Discuss.* 139 *note*, A first notion is the concept of a thing as it exists of itself... A second notion is the concept, not of an object as it is in reality, but of the mode under which it is thought by the mind. **1864** BOWEN *Logic* iv. 70 A second intention or notion is a Concept which denotes first intentions in their relation, not to the things denoted, but to each other.

b. In general use. Freq. const. *of.*

1643 SIR T. BROWNE *Relig. Med.* II. §1 Charity, without which Faith is a meer notion, and of no existence. *c* **1680** BEVERIDGE *Serm.* (1729) I. 279 That you may be able to form such an idea or notion of it. **1760** JOHNSON *Idler* No. 100 ¶8 Her notion of a joke is not very delicate. **1781** COWPER *Truth* 424 His books well trimm'd..teach him notions splendid as themselves. **1821** SCOTT *Kenilw.* xi, Wayland Smith..had a good notion of horse diseases. **1837** DICKENS *Pickw.* li, 'Not a bad notion that, Sam', said Mr. Bob Sawyer approvingly. **1873** BLACK *Pr. Thule* xx. 330 The notion of my marrying her is absurd.

c. With a negative, or virtual negative.

1704–5 *Pennsylv. Hist. Soc. Mem.* IX. 365, I never had the least notion of thy mortgaging the quit-rents. **1706** E. WARD *Wooden World Diss.* (1708) 106 He has no more Notion of Navigation than an African of Snow. **1719** DE FOE *Crusoe* II. (Globe) 346 He had no Thoughts, no Notion of its being me. **1856** FROUDE *Hist. Eng.* (1858) I. iii. 221 Little notion, indeed, could the bishops have possessed of the position in which they were standing. **1878** *Masque of Poets* 181 How he first Learned of the complication, I've no notion.

d. ***notion-writing*** = IDEOGRAPHY.

1863 SUMMERS *Hdbk. Chinese* Introd. p. xviii, Notion-writing..is independent of any given language and conveys its meaning to the understanding immediately through the eye.

5. †**a.** Understanding, mind, intellect. *Obs.*

1605 SHAKS. *Lear* I. iv. 245 Either his Notion weakens, his Discernings Are Lethargied. **1605** —— *Macb.* III. i. 83 All things else, that might To halfe a Soule, and to a Notion craz'd, Say, Thus did Banquo. **1649** J. TAYLOR *Gt. Exemp.*

Sect. vii. §5 Whether it were..by increase of notion or experience, it is certain the promotions of the holy Child were great. **1667** MILTON *P.L.* VII. 179 The Acts of God..Cannot without process of speech be told, So told as earthly notion can receave.

†**b.** Conception, imagination, fancy. *Obs.*

1647 N. BACON *Disc. Govt. Eng.* Advt. (1739) p. iii, Ambition hath done much..to bring forth Absolute Monarchy out of the Womb of Notion. **1671** GLANVILL *Further Disc. Stubbe* 11, I spake of the Natural Philosophers, and their Methods, which were made up of Notion, and ministred to everlasting Disputes.

6. An idea, view, opinion, theory, or belief, held by one or more persons.

1603 HOLLAND *Plutarch* 1087 See how these Philosophers mainteine ordinary custome, and teach according to common notions. **1628** DOUGHTY *Serm. Schismes* 23 Agrippa among others his foppish notions perswades vs [etc.]. **1697** [C. LESLIE] *Snake in Grass* (ed. 2) 12 It will be very hard..to make Sense of the Quaker Notion of the Light within. **1710** NORRIS *Chr. Prud.* viii. 372 That Notion of the Schools, of Sins being an Aversion from God. **1777** BRAND *Pop. Antiq.* Gen. Pref. p. vii, Seemingly trivial Reasons assigned for the beginning..of this or that Notion or Ceremony. **1857** MAURICE *Ep. St. John* ix. 135 It is not a new notion..that the history of the world is divided into certain great periods. **1871** FREEMAN *Norm. Conq.* (1876) IV. xviii. 134 It is further remarkable as showing that the notion of succession through females was already beginning to be entertained.

Comb. **1873** M. ARNOLD *Lit. & Dogma* (1876) 333 A piece of metaphysical notion-building. *Ibid.* 360 To read between the lines of a notion-work is absurd, for it is of the essence of a notion-work not to need it.

7. a. An inclination, disposition, or desire, to do something specified; a fancy for something. Usu. const. *of* with gerund, or *to* with inf.

1746 H. WALPOLE *Lett.* (1857) II. 33, I have no notion of going to anybody's house, and have the servants look on the arms of the chaise to find out one's name. **1774** D. JONES *Jrnl.* (1865) 100 It would have been otherwise, if I had come last fall, while they were in the notion of it. **1776** J. VERRIEUL *Let.* 17 Apr. in F. Chase *Hist. Dartmouth Coll.* (1891) I. vi. 347 Ther was Ten Regt ordert to march for Newyoark, and I toock a notion to go with them. **1807** GASS *Jrnl.* 225 The Indian..said he had a notion to cross the mountains with us. **1825** COBBETT *Rur. Rides* 436 The Gloucestershire people have no notion of dying with hunger. **1891** C. ROBERTS *Adrift Amer.* 207 After being here for a week, I took a notion to leave, and accordingly did so.

b. *north.* and *Sc.* A fancy or affection for one of the other sex.

1789 *Shepherd's Wedding* 14 (E.D.D.), I hae lang, altho' I didna tell, Had a strang notion o' the lass mysel'. **1824** MACTAGGART *Gallovid. Encycl.* 226 In the regular routine of a matrimonial transaction; first, taking the notion; secondly, courting. **1864** TENNYSON *Aylmer's Field* 271 The boy might get a notion into him; The girl might be entangled ere she knew.

8. A product of invention. *rare.*

a **1700** EVELYN *Diary* (1872) I. 211 Machines for flying in the air, and other wonderful notions. *a* **1765** YOUNG (Cent.), And robes, and notions framed in foreign looms.

9. *U.S.* **a.** *pl.* Articles or wares of various kinds forming a miscellaneous cargo.

1805 SOUTHEY in *Ann. Rev.* III. 31 The Americans.., finding no longer a market there for their lumber cargoes, or notions, as they call them. **1834** MARRYAT *P. Simple* (1863) 325 Her cargo consisted of what the Americans called notions; that is, in English, an assorted cargo. **1840** R. H. DANA *Bef. Mast* xxxv. 133 A cargo of fresh provisions, mules, tin bake-pans and other notions.

b. *pl.* Small wares, *esp.* cheap useful articles of some ingenious design. Now *spec.* in haberdashery.

Also freq. *Yankee notions*: see YANKEE *a.*

1803 F. ASBURY *Jrnl.* (1821) III. 106 How would it tell to the South, that priests were among the notions of Yankee traffick? **1830** GALT *Lawrie T.* III. xiv. (1849) 130 Mr. Hoskins and his wife with a great cargo of wares and other notions in their wagons, arrived. **1842** MRS. CLAVERS *Forest Life* II. 166 Can I suit ye to-day, ma'am? I've all sorts o' notions. **1876** C. D. WARNER *Winter Nile* xii. 157 The artisans work up ostrich feathers into a variety of 'notions'. **1913** F. H. BURNETT *T. Tembaron* xx. 264 The young lady from the notion counter (those wonderful shops!). **1964** *McCall's Sewing* ii. 22 While making a list of the fabrics and trims needed, check the 'Notions' section to see what notions are needed. *Ibid.* 30/2 *Notions*, all dressmaking supplies that are used in the construction of a garment: thread, zippers, tape, buttons, etc. **1965** 'L. EGAN' *Detective's Due* (1966) iv. 39 Varallo and Katz were led past Notions, Gift Cards and Cameras, to a counter in the center of the store.

c. *attrib.*, as ***notion-counter***, ***-peddler*** (or ***-pedlar***), ***-peddling***, ***-seller***, ***-store***, ***-vessel***.

1894 S. FISKE *Holiday Stories* (1900) 152, I went to the store..and recognised her..at the *notion counter. **1932** L. C. DOUGLAS *Forgive our Trespasses* (1937) i. 1 The steel-bowed spectacles that had been her mother's, had of a *notion peddler for two dozen eggs & a pound of butter. **1809** 'D. KNICKERBOCKER' *Hist. N.Y.* I. IV. iii. 214 He swore that he would have nothing more to do with such a squatting, bundling, guessing,..*notion-peddling crew. **1839** *Chemung* (N.Y.) *Democrat* 17 Apr. (Th.), A '*notion seller' was offering Yankee clocks, &c. **1830** GALT *Lawrie T.* III. x. (1849) 116 A small seed and *notion store. **1861** *Macm. Mag.* Feb. 273 A Yankee grocery or a Yankee 'notion store' is an epitome of almost every thing. **1867** SMYTH *Sailor's Word-bk.* 501 A *notion-vessel on the west coast of America is a perfect bazaar.

Hence **'notion** *v.*, to divide into several notions.

1641 J. JACKSON *True Evang. T.* i. 8, I have therefore notioned and cast the Text according to the number of the verses, into three plain and conspicuous members.

†**'notional**, *sb. Obs. rare.* [ad. med.L. **nōtiōnāle*, neut. of *nōtiōnālis*: see next.]

1. A divine attribute. (See quot.)

a **1533** FRITH *Disput. Purgat.* (1829) 131 If he make one Notional in God greater than another, (by this word Notional, which the schoolmen use, I would you should understand the goodness, wisdom, power, justice, and mercy of God, &c.) then shall he..imagine that one Notional subdueth another.

2. A mere supposition or idea.

1653 R. G. tr. *Bacon's Hist. Winds* 277 We shall finde ill determined notionalls, phantasms, and imaginary things, and Axioms daily to be amended. **1666** *Phil. Trans.* I. 325 Philosophy, which searches out the real Productions of Nature.., does manifest the Divine Glory more, than the Notionals of the Gentiles.

notional ('nəʊʃənəl), *a.* Also 6–7 **-all.** [ad. med.L. *nōtiōnālis*: see NOTION and -AL[1]. So obs. F. *notional*, *-el* (Godef.), It. *notionale*, Sp. and Pg. *nocional*.]

1. a. Of knowledge, etc.: Purely speculative; not based upon fact or demonstration.

1597 HOOKER *Eccl. Pol.* v. lxxxi. (1611) 442 Whatsoever we may..write in our bookes through a notionall conceipt of things needfull. **1626** BACON *Sylva* §836 They are to be set aside, being but Notional, and ill Limited; and Definite Axiomes are to be drawn out of Measured Instances. **1677** GALE *Crt. Gentiles* IV. Proem. 3 Philosophie considered in its Particular Ideas, is either Notional or Real. **1680** BOYLE *Exper. Chem. Princ.* Pref. 9, I have a very differing esteem of the Notionall and of the Practicall part of Chymistry. **1730** CHAMBERLAYNE *Relig. Philos.* Pref. p. xx, People may be very well experienced in these Ideal or Notional Sciences, and yet be Masters of very little Knowledge, in Things that actually exist. **1771** WESLEY *Wks.* (1872) V. 213 It is not a barely notional or speculative faith. **1831** WHEWELL in Todhunter *Acct. Writ.* (1876) II. 115 A popular exposition of the matter applied mainly to moral, political, and other notional sciences. **1873** M. ARNOLD *Lit. & Dogma* (1876) 280 A notional work as distinguished from an experimental work.

†**b.** Of persons: Given to abstract or fanciful speculation; holding merely speculative views.

1664 POWER *Exp. Philos.* III. 193 The old Dogmatists and Notional Speculators. **1671** BOHUN *Wind* 170 The impertinence of those Notionall men, that enquire no further, but declare, That [etc.]. **1710** STEELE *Tatler* No. 125 ¶3, I would not be thought altogether notional in what I have to say, and pass only for a Projector in Morality. **1732** BERKELEY *Alciphr.* v. §33 Airy, notional men, enthusiasts [etc.]. **1772** WESLEY *Jrnl.* 12 Aug., I preached at Salop, and spake strong words, to the amazement of many notional believers.

c. *Economics.* Of a figure, profit, etc.: speculative, hypothetical; for the purposes of a particular interpretation or theory.

1958 *Spectator* 8 Aug. 204/3 The profit attributable to Iraq is the notional one which the oil companies regard as economic. **1960** *Economist* 15 Oct. 278/1 Costs per ton of storage, mainly notional interest charges, were put at roughly £5 for lead and zinc. **1964** *Financial Times* 3 Mar. 15/6 The formula for calculating this standard price has been drawn up so that it would leave the Corporation with a notional profit of £1·8 m. before tax. **1972** *Accountant* 17 Aug. 197/1 A company..will be able to obtain relief..on a notional figure.

2. Of things, relations, etc.: Existing only in thought; not real or actually existent; imaginary.

1629 GAULE *Holy Madn.* 138 Meere notionall is their [gems] value; which is in the Opinion, not in the Thing. **1655–87** H. MORE *App. Antid.* (1712) 199 Distance is no Physical affection of any thing, but only Notional. **1710** BERKELEY *Princ. Hum. Knowl.* §34 All things that exist, exist only in the mind, that is, they are purely notional. **1748** RICHARDSON *Clarissa* (1811) II. 81 As it is founded generally upon mere notional excellencies. **1817** COLERIDGE *Biog. Lit.* I. xii. 247 No wonder, that..he..bewilders himself in the pursuit of notional phantoms. **1841** D'ISRAELI *Amen. Lit.* (1867) 639 Her Majesty seems to have remunerated empty phrases by providing notional places. **1858** BUSHNELL *Serm. New Life* 94 It is a mind dealing with notions or notional truths.

3. (See quot. 1806.)

1794 PIOZZI *Synon.* II. 5 In notional and ideal Madness, particularly the first, many symptoms are only cunningly suppressed. **1806** T. ARNOLD *Insanity* I. 56 Notional Insanity is that state of mind in which a person..perceives external objects as they really exist..; yet conceives such notions of the powers, properties [etc.], of things and persons,..as appear obviously..erroneous or unreasonable.

4. *U.S.* Of persons: **a.** Inclined to think.

1823 COOPER *Pioneers* ix, I'm glad if the Judge is pleased; but I'm notional that you'll find the sa'ce overdone.

b. Fanciful; full of fancies, whims, or caprices.

1791 *Gazette of U.S.* (N.Y.) 9 Feb. (Th.), If a man is a little odd in his ways, his friends say he is a notional creature, or full of notions... Love is the most notional passion. **1859** BARTLETT *Dict. Amer.* (ed. 2), *Notional*, fanciful, whimsical. Applied to persons; as, 'He's a very notional man'. **1881** HOWELLS *Dr. Breen's Practice* ix, She's been a little notional, she's had her head addled by women's talk. **1894** *Outing* XXIV. 96/2 He did think he would have to get the room cleaned and whitewashed, as his wife was rather notional.

5. Of the nature of, pertaining or relating to, a notion or idea. (See quots.)

1861 *National Rev.* Oct. 379 The various modifications of time..are expressed by the notional words themselves, not by distinct words. **1870** J. H. NEWMAN *Gram. Assent* I. i. 7 There are propositions, in which one or both of the terms are common nouns, as standing for what is abstract... These I shall call notional propositions, and the apprehension with which we infer or assent to them, notional. *Ibid.* iv. 72 In Notional Assent as well as in inferring, the mind contemplates its own creations instead of things.

6. *Gram.* Used (orig. by Jespersen) in relation to the semantic content, real or apparent, of grammatical forms and categories; of a word: carrying full meaning, not merely grammatical; of a verb: principal, main, not auxiliary.

1924 O. JESPERSEN *Philos. Gram.* iii. 56 Our examples of gender and sex will make it clear that the relations between the syntactic and notional categories will often present a similar kind of network to that noticed between formal and syntactic categories. **1933** —— *Syst. Gram.* 20 In 'he happened to fall' the notional subject is a nexus 'he..to fall'. **1942** PARTRIDGE *Usage & Abusage* 148/2 Jespersen's *The Philosophy of Grammar*..urges us to consider all words..in their three aspects, form, syntactic function, and 'natural or logical meaning'; this third aspect he calls 'notional'. **1957** R. W. ZANDVOORT *Handbk. Eng. Gram.* I. v. 64 The opposite of 'auxiliary' is 'notional verb', 'principal verb', or 'verb of full meaning'. **1966** M. PEI *Gloss. Linguistic Terminol.* 182 *Notional word*, a word that carries a full meaning ('he *has* luck' vs. 'he *has* gone'). **1971** P. J. LUCAS in *Archivum Linguisticum* II. 19 There is a considerable degree of overlap (in Capgrave's *Chronicle*) between the notional signs on the one hand, and, between the grammatical signs on the other, but there is no overlap between primarily notional and primarily grammatical signs.

notionalist ('nəʊʃənəlɪst). [f. prec. + -IST.] A speculative thinker; a theorist.

a **1677** MANTON *Serm. Ps. cxix.* cvi. 100 A young practiser hath more understanding than an ancient notionalist. **1716** M. DAVIES *Athen. Brit.* III. Diss. Physick 25 The Counterfeit Jew-Physical Notionalists be Pseudo-Salmon, Pseudo-Maria [etc.]. **1831** *Edin. Rev.* LIII. 529 No notionalist..can be so practically insane, as to see an abstract right or wrong in any particular combination of political powers.

†**notio'nality.** *Obs.* [f. as prec. + -ITY.]

1. The fact, state, or condition of being notional; a notional or imaginary thing.

1653 H. MORE *Conj. Cabbal.* 58 For multifarious Notionality and Inconstancy of life and knowledge, are certain signs that a man is in the night. **1665** GLANVILL *Def. Van. Dogm.* 66 Whether the notionality and obscurity of the Aristotelian method it self do not give occasion to the endless babble. **1705** GOODMAN *Wint. Even. Conf.* III. 18 True and manly religion is..not a lukewarm notionality,.. but is lively, vigorous, and sparkling.

2. A notion or category. *rare*[−1].

1651 BIGGS *New Disp.* ¶287 Under the notionality of *Potables* is not to be understood here, jusculous sorbitions.

'notionally, *adv.* [f. as prec. + -LY[2].] In a notional fashion; speculatively, theoretically.

1643 T. GOODWIN *Aggravation Sin* 74 They have learnt it from..observations of Gods dealings with themselves or others, and not onely from the word notionally. **1698** NORRIS *Pract. Disc.* IV. 65 When we talk of Religion we should..discourse of it not Notionally and Speculatively,.. but Cordially and Spiritually. **1752** LAW *Spirit Love* I. (1816) 9 The Schools have..shown us how to conceive them as notionally distinguished from one another. **1771** BURROW *Reports* III. 1609 In the Country, Leases at Will, in the strict legal Notion of a Lease at Will,..exist only notionally. **1868** BUSHNELL *Serm. Living Subj.* 58 Something notional or notionally affirmed.

'notionalness. *rare*[−0]. [f. as prec. + -NESS.] 'Imaginariness' (Bailey, 1730).

'notionary, *a.* [f. NOTION *sb.* + -ARY.] = NOTIONAL *a.*

1646 E. F[ISHER] *Marrow Mod. Div.* 172 If our friend do content himself with a meere Gospell knowledge, in a notionary way. **1675** OGILBY *Brit.* Pref. 1 The Tracing of Notionary Roads upon imperfect Charts. **1700** ROWE *Amb. Step-Moth.* III. ii, He'll be convinc'd that only Fools would lose A Crown for notionary Principles. **1822** *Blackw. Mag.* XII. 491 It is but a notionary cause, a mere opinion.

'notionate, *a. Sc.* and *U.S.* [f. NOTION *sb.* + -ATE[2]; cf. *opinionate.*] Full of notions, fanciful; also, headstrong, obstinate.

1859 BARTLETT *Dict. Amer.* (ed. 2), *Notionate*, fanciful, whimsical. **1871** W. ALEXANDER *Johnny Gibb* (1873) 197 He was a 'notionate' old fellow the elder Mains of Yawal, and would be obeyed. **1896** HOWELLS *Idyls in Drab* 119 That young woman has made you blame yourself for nothin'. You're perfectly notionate about it.

†**'notionate**, *v. Obs. rare*[−1]. [f. NOTION *sb.* + -ATE[3].] *trans.* To devise or originate by process of thought.

1661 R. BURNEY *Κέρδιστον Δῶρον* 5 I take in all things, Heavenly and earthly within my breast; I form them with essence, and stamp them with existence, I notionate their seed and kernell, their quintessence and effluxes.

'notionist. Now *rare.* [f. NOTION *sb.* + -IST.]

1. One who holds extravagant religious opinions. Esp. ***high notionist.*** Now *arch.*

1652 R. SANDERS *Balm* 138 A step higher then the quaintest Notionists of our times desire to be brought. **1653** G. FOX *Jrnl. Life*, etc. I. 108 The Pastor of the Baptists (being an high Notionist and a flashy Man) came to me. **1697** G. KEITH *2nd Narr. Proc. Turner's Hall* 13 In this he agrees with the Ranters and other vain Notionists. *a* **1720** SEWEL *Hist. Quakers* (1795) I. II. 103 A high notionist, and rich in words. **1869** *Contemp. Rev.* XI. 451 How the bold youth did stand up against the high notionist!

2. One who forms notions of things.

1825 LAMB *Let. to Barton* in *Final Mem.* viii. 259 The whimsies of such a half-baked notionist as I am.

ˈnotionless, *a.* [f. NOTION *sb.* + -LESS.] Destitute of any notion or idea.
1814 *New Brit. Theatre* I. 529 The notionless words of the intellectual masters and misses. **1825** ESTHER HEWLETT *Cottage Comf.* vi. 41 Quite helpless and notionless in common things.

ˈnotionless, *adv. rare*⁻¹. [f. as prec.] Not in a notional manner; with certainty.
1607 J. DAVIES *Summa Totalis* Wks. (Grosart) I. 23/1 Yet, Creatures onely know in that degree; But God knowes (Notionlesse) Essentially.

†**ˈnotist.** *Obs. rare*⁻¹. [f. NOTE *v.*² + -IST.] A commentator or annotator.
1670 MILTON *Hist. Eng.* III. 123 Nennius or his notist avers that Artur was called Mab-Uther, that is to say, a cruel Son, for the fierseness that men saw in him of a Child.

notitia (nəʊˈtɪʃ(ɪ)ə). [a. L. *nōtitia* knowledge, f. *nōtus* known.]
†**1.** Literary particulars. *Obs. rare*⁻¹.
1700-1 HEARNE in Wood *Life* (1848) 332 This ingenious retired and modest person helped him very much in the notitia of divers modern authors.
2. An account or list; now *spec.* a register or list of ecclesiastical sees or districts.
1797 *Encycl. Brit.* (ed. 3) II. 186/1 We have also a *notitia* of all the Arabian physicians by Fabricius. **1843** C. INNES in *Reg. Episc. Glasg.* I. p. xviii, It is a memoir or *notitia*, which ..is much less common with us than in the religious houses abroad. **1850** NEALE *East. Ch.* Pref. p. xiv, I procured..an official notitia of the Sees which belong to the Coptic Communion in Egypt. *Ibid.*, The modern notitia of Antioch was drawn up in 1844.

†**noˈtition.** *Obs.* Also 5-6 **noticion, -ycion, -cyon.** [a. OF. *noticion* (Godef.): cf. prec. and -ITION.] Knowledge, information, intelligence.
c **1485** *Digby Myst.* (1882) II. 12 Whoo lyst to rede the booke.., ther shall he haue the very notycyon. **1494** FABYAN *Chron.* VII. 494 Whan noticion of this great outrage and ryot came vnto the Kynge. **1513** BRADSHAW *St. Werburge* I. 2230 In presence of the pryor.., Whiche pryor of this mater had best notycyon. **1547** BOORDE *Brev. Health* cxii. 42 b, By the egestion the Physicion in sycke persons hath a great noticion and knowledge of mans infirmyties.

Notkerian (nɒtˈkɪərɪən), *a.* [See def. and -IAN.] Composed or originated by Notker Balbulus (†912), a monk of St. Gall in Switzerland.
1881 *Encycl. Brit.* XII. 583/2 Numerous examples..of the 'proses', properly so called, of the Notkerian type. **1901** *Chambers's Encycl.* VI. 46/2 Sequences, or as we now call them hymns, ..known as Notkerian Sequences.

not-life. [NOT *adv.* 14 d.] Inanimate matter, esp. as contrasted with that which contains life. So **not-living** *a.* and *sb.*
1869 T. H. HUXLEY in *Fortn. Rev.* 1 Feb. 140 The assumption of the existence in the living matter of a something which has no representative or correlative in the not living matter which gave rise to it. **1895** *Churchman* No. 185. 251 Science..affirms that not-life can never under existing conditions produce life. **1943** J. S. HUXLEY *Evolutionary Ethics* i. 7 The scientific study of change, of becoming, of the production of novelty, whether of life from not-life, of a baby from an ovum. **1953** MASSINGHAM & HYAMS *Prophecy of Famine* iii. 57 The harmony..between the living creature..and the not-living habitat itself. *Ibid.* viii. 169 A short-circuiting of the life-cycle in terms of not-life. **1964** GOULD & KOLB *Dict. Social Sci.* 607/1 Birth rituals..signifying the separation of the infant from the world of the dead (or not-living) and his aggregation to that of the living.

not-me: see NOT-I.

notmugge, -myg(ge, obs. variants of NUTMEG.

not-ness. *rare.* [f. NOT *adv.* + -NESS.] The quality or state of not accepting something; something negative.
1933 DYLAN THOMAS *Let.* Sept. (1966) 21 Your 'not-ness' alone is worth all the superlatives at my command. **1945** H. MILLER *Air-Conditioned Nightmare* 12 It was something negative, some not-ness of some kind or other.

noto- (ˈnəʊtəʊ), combining form of Gr. νῶτον back, employed in a certain number of scientific terms, the most usual of which are given below.
Various others, app. never actually current, are given by Mayne, as *notographous, -nectideous, -podous, -pterygious.*

notoˈbranchiate, *a.* [See prec. and BRANCHIATE *a.*] Having dorsal branchiæ or gills.
1870 H. A. NICHOLSON *Man. Zool.* (1875) 220 From the position of the branchiæ, the members of this order are often spoken of as the 'Dorsibranchiate' (or more properly 'Notobranchiate') Annelides.
So **notoˈbranchious** *a.* (Mayne, 1857.)

notochord (ˈnəʊtəkɔːd). *Biol.* [f. NOTO- + CHORD. So F. *notochorde, -corde.*] A cartilaginous band or rod forming the primitive basis of the spinal column in vertebrates. Also *Comb.*
1848 OWEN *Arch. & Homol. Vertebr. Skel.* 86 An extremely delicate fibrous band,..inclosed by a membranous sheath, is the primitive basis, called 'notochord'. **1870** ROLLESTON *Anim. Life* p. lxix, A cylindrical fibro-cartilaginous sheath surrounding the cylindrical notochord. **1879** tr. *Haeckel's Evol. Man* I. xiii. 418 The Amphioxus is enclosed in a firm membranous covering, the notochord-sheath. **1888** ROLLESTON & JACKSON *Anim. Life* 757 A notochord-like axis of modified endoderm cells.

notoˈchordal, *a. Biol.* [f. prec. + -AL¹. So F. *notocordal.*]
1. Of the nature of a notochord.
1866 OWEN *Anat. Vert.* I. 7 Endo-skeleton membrano-cartilaginous and notochordal. **1878** A. H. GREEN, etc. *Coal* iv. 121 A third point of importance..is the notochordal vertebral column.
2. Of or pertaining to the notochord.
1872 HUMPHRY *Myology* 105 The membranous septa extend from the skin down to the notochordal sheath and blend with it. **1887** E. D. COPE *Orig. Fittest* 332 It also shows that the vertebræ have passed from a notochordal state.

Notogæa (nəʊtəˈdʒiːə). [f. Gr. νότος south wind + γαῖα earth, land.] A large zoological region, comprising the Australian, New Zealand, and Neotropical regions.
1868 HUXLEY in *Proc. Zool. Soc.* 315 If the great frontier line is latitudinal.., and divides a north world from a south world, we must speak of *Arctogæa* and *Notogæa* rather than of Neogæa and Palæogæa as the primary distributional areæ. **1893** NEWTON *Dict. Birds* 314 Brigading, if he so please, the first three as Notogæa, and the last three as Arctogæa.
Hence **Notoˈgæal, Notoˈgæan, Notoˈgæic,** *adjs.*
1879 NEWTON in *Encycl. Brit.* IX. 192/1 The existence of but very few [finches] in the Notogæan hemisphere can as yet be regarded as certain. **1896** LYDEKKER *Geogr. Hist. Mammals* 28 The Notogæic realm may..be taken as the first of the three primary zoological divisions of the globe.

†**notoire,** *a. Obs. rare.* Also 5 **-oyre.** [a. F. *notoire*, ad. med.L. *nōtōrius* notorious. Cf. NOTOUR *a.*] Notorious, evident.
a **1470** TIPTOFT *Tulle on Old Age* (Caxton, 1481) h iv, It is clere and notoire in what place al the other thynges goen. *c* **1477** CAXTON *Jason* 72 b, Hit is among yow euydent and notoyre that ye shall not take in pacience my correccion.
Hence †**notoirly** *adv.*, notoriously. *Obs.*
1409-10 *Proc. Privy Council* (1834) I. 323 As it is notoirly knowen and he hym selfe as trewe knyghte may noght witheseye it. **1470-85** MALORY *Arthur* Pref. 1 For it is notoyrly knowen thorugh the vnyuersal world.

notonecta (nəʊtəˈnɛktə). *Ent.* Also 7-8 as *pl.*, with *sing.* **-nectum.** [mod.L., f. NOTO- + Gr. νήκτης swimmer.] A species of water-beetle which swims on its back; the boat-fly.
1658 ROWLAND tr. *Moufet's Theat. Ins.* II. xxxviii, Of the Notonectum. *Ibid.*, We call some Insects of the water Notonecta, which do not swim upon their bellies, as the rest do. **1706** in PHILLIPS (ed. Kersey), *Notonecta*, certain Water-Insects, ..always swimming on their Backs. **1752** J. HILL *Hist. Anim.* 63 The rostrum or snout of the Notonecta is inflected. *Ibid.*, The grey Notonecta.., the little Boat-fly. **1774** GOLDSM. *Nat. Hist.* (1790) VII. 359 The Common Water Fly..is by some called *Notonecta.* **1855** *Orr's Circ. Sci., Org. Nat.* II. 351 Hence the *Notonecta*..is generally known as the *boat-fly.* **1887** *Amer. Naturalist* XXI. 578 The *Notonecta* can, in an emergency, avail itself of a method of purifying its supply of air.

notoˈpodial, *a. Biol.* [f. next.] Pertaining to, of the nature of, a notopodium.
1877 HUXLEY *Anat. Inv. Anim.* v. 229 The neuropodial is very much longer than the notopodial aciculum. **1888** ROLLESTON & JACKSON *Anim. Life* 607 Small branches.. develope a head with large eyes and long notopodial sexual setæ.

notoˈpodium. *Biol.* [mod.L., f. NOTO- + Gr. ποδίον, dim. of πούς foot.] The upper or dorsal branch of a parapodium.
1870 H. A. NICHOLSON *Man. Zool.* 160 An upper process, called the 'notopodium' or 'dorsal oar'. **1877** HUXLEY *Anat. Inv. Anim.* v. 229 In the young state of Polynöe, the notopodium is as large as the neuropodium.

†**notorely,** var. of NOTOIRLY or NOTORILY *adv.*
1502 *Ord. Crysten Men* (W. de W. 1506) IV. xxi, Unto synners notorely knowen & open.

notoriety (nəʊtəˈraɪətɪ). [a. F. *notoriété* (= It. *notorietà*, Sp. *-edad*, Pg. *-edade*), or ad. med.L. *nōtōrietas*, f. *nōtōrius* NOTORIOUS *a.*; cf. *dubiety, nimiety*, etc.]
1. The state or character of being notorious; the fact of being publicly or commonly known.
1592 [cited by Nashe, *Four Lett. Confut.* Wks. (Grosart) II. 263, as one of Gabriel Harvey's words]. **1637-50** Row *Hist. Kirk* (Wodrow Soc.) 28 Upon the notorietie of a great and haynous fact,..the transgressor to be secluded fra the communion. **1660** JER. TAYLOR *Duct. Dubit.* III. iii. rule 6 §2 But this thing is evident by notoriety of fact. *a* **1683** OWEN *Holy Sp.* (1693) 195 The joynt Participation of the same Gift by all, and the Notoriety of the matter thereon. **1749** FIELDING *Tom Jones* (1775) II. 5 The credit of the former [historians] is by common notoriety supported for a long time. **1771** *Junius Lett.* lxv. (1788) 338 The truth of which you dare not deny, because it is of public notoriety. **1824** W. IRVING *T. Trav.* I. 4 He has become a character of considerable notoriety in two or three country towns. **1849** MACAULAY *Hist. Eng.* ii. I. 237 He had been raised..to notoriety such as has for low and bad minds all the attractions of glory. **1873** FARRAR *Fam. Speech* ii. 47 It is now a matter of simple notoriety that not merely in sounds and letters [etc.].
Comb. **1891** *Spectator* 18 Apr. 534/1 Some of them may be notoriety-hunters.
†**2.** A notorious thing or fact. *Obs. rare*⁻¹.
1745 H. WALPOLE *Lett.* (1846) II. 52 Letters from Holland speak of it as a notoriety.
3. A well-known or celebrated person.
1837 THACKERAY *Ravenswing* ii, He knew..all the actors, all the 'notorieties' of the town. **1840** CARLYLE *Heroes* (1858) 283 We cannot but see..that it was against his will he ever became a notoriety. **1884** *Athenæum* 21 June 786/2 The Bonaparte family and the heroes or notorieties of the French Revolution.

noˈtorify, *v. nonce-wd.* [f. NOTORI-OUS *a.* + -FY.] *trans.* To make notorious.
a **1871** DE MORGAN *Budget Parad.* (1872) 32 Mr. James Smith, of Liverpool—hereinafter notorified.

†**notorily,** *adv. Obs. rare.* [f. NOTORY *a.* + -LY².] Notoriously.
1455 *Paston Lett.* I. 363 The seyd Fastolf lent to the voyage.., as it is notorily knowen,..C li. **1475** *Bk. Noblesse* (Roxb.) 8 It is notorily and openly knowen thoroughe alle Cristen Royaumes. **1512** *Helyas* in Thoms *Prose Rom.* (1828) III. 39 It is of trouthe notorily..that my wife.. during hir viage hath be delivered of .vii. litle whelpes.

notorious (nəʊˈtɔərɪəs), *a.*¹ Also 6 **-iouse, -ius.** [ad. med.L. *nōtōrius* (cf. late L. *nōtōria* fem., *nōtōrium* neut., intelligence, information, etc.), f. *nōtus* known: see -ORY. So It., Sp., and Pg. *notorio*, F. *notoire*: cf. NOTOIR, NOTORY, NOTOUR.]
1. Of facts: Well known; commonly or generally known; forming a matter of common knowledge.
1555 EDEN *Dec. W. Ind.* (Arb.) 198 His courage was such and his factes so notorious. *a* **1586** SIDNEY *Ps.* XX. iii, Lett him [God] notorious make, That in good part he did thy offrings take. **1621** BP. MOUNTAGU *Diatribæ* 567 Why were not other Examples brought into practice, as notorious as that of Abraham paying Tithes? **1686** CLAGETT 17 *Serm.* (1699) App. 15 These testimonies were too notorious and publick to be gainsaid. **1705** STANHOPE *Paraphr.* II. 407 That Every one is bound..to..keep within his own Property..is too notorious to need a Proof. **1758** JOHNSON *Idler* No. 10 ¶6 Men..who deny the most notorious facts. **1779** SHERIDAN *Critic* I. i, My power with the managers is pretty notorious. **1856** FROUDE *Hist. Eng.* (1858) I. iii. 241 The House of Commons had stated their complaints in the form of special notorious facts. **1866** LIDDON *Bampton Lect.* vii. (1875) 391 The worship of Christ by the early Christians was a living and notorious practice.
b. In phr. *it is notorious that.*
a **1738** SWIFT *Misc.* (J.), Although it be notorious that they do not receive the third penny of the real value. **1756** LUCAS *Ess. Waters* III. 116 It is notorious that the former never parts with it's acid. **1809** W. IRVING *Knickerb.* I. v. (1849) 63 It is notorious, that the savages knew nothing of agriculture. **1849** MACAULAY *Hist. Eng.* vii. II. 262 It was notorious that loyal and able men had been turned out of office in England merely for being Protestants. **1883** *Manch. Exam.* 29 Oct. 5/2 That the army, at least the more active spirits within it, were discontented was notorious.
2. Of places, persons, etc.: Well or widely known (now *rare*); †famous.
1555 EDEN *Dec. W. Ind.* (Arb.) 346 A famous and notorious place amonge the Indians. **1588** *Marprel. Epist.* (Arb.) 40 Manie of you..are men verie notorious for their learning and preaching. **1610** HOLLAND *Camden's Brit.* Auth. to Rdr., I purposed to mention only such [towns and castles] as were most notorious. **1614** PURCHAS *Pilgrimage* (ed. 2) 44 Of Cham is the name Chemmis in Ægypt; and Ammon the Idoll and Oracle so notorious.
1865 GROTE *Plato* I. 136 Where was the person to be found, notorious and accessible, who could say [etc.].
b. Such as is or may be generally, openly, or publicly known. Now *rare.*
1584 D. FENNER *Def. Ministers* (1587) 125 Their liues are not put to notorious and publike examination. **1622** BACON *Hen. VII* (1876) 28 That Edward Plantagenet..should be, in the most public and notorious manner,..shewed unto the people. **1669-70** MARVELL *Corr.* Wks. (Grosart) II. 308 Either by confession of the party, or oath of witnesses, or by notorious evidence. **1715** *Lond. Gaz.* No. 5455/1 The Clerks of the Peace are to keep Parchment Books or Rolls at some notorious Place. **1724** *Ibid.* No. 6257/3 All..Sheriffs..are.. required to keep Parchment Books..at some notorious Place in the County. **1818** HALLAM *Mid. Ages* (1872) I. 251 This formality was by degrees..deemed essential to render them authentic and notorious. **1863** COX *Instit.* III. v. 647 The Privy Council, whom the law recognized as the sworn and notorious Councillors of the Crown.
†**3.** Conspicuous; obvious, evident. *Obs.*
1608 TOPSELL *Serpents* (1658) 639 The elder sort..very notorious and goodly to see to in regard of their gravity, hoariness, and anciency. *Ibid.* 785 If it did represent any notorious and manifest colour, they would..take heed of such traps aforehand. **1609** BIBLE (Douay) *Levit.* xxvi. 1 Neither shal you erect titles, nor set a notorious stone in your land, for to adore it. *a* **1677** BARROW *Serm.* (1683) II. ii. 22 That God hath an especial regard to men will thence also become notorious. **1704** RAY *Creation* (ed. 4) II. 278 The failing in any of these would cause Irregularity in the Body ..such as would be very notorious. **1770** *Amherst Rec.* (1884) 49/2 To Chose a Comittee to Visit the boundaries of the town and renew such as are Destroyed and make them Notorious.
4. Used attributively with designations of persons which imply evil or wickedness: Well known, noted (as being of this kind).
1548-9 (Mar.) *Bk. Comm. Prayer* Offices 31 Suche persones as were notorious synners. **1574** *Reg. Privy Council Scot.* II. 395 Declarit tratouris and notorius rebellis. **1614** RALEIGH *Hist. World* I. (1634) 163 Ninus was the first notorious sacrificer to Idols. **1687** A. LOVELL tr. *Thevenot's Trav.* II. 23 These Arabs are notorious Robbers. **1755** YOUNG *Centaur* ii. Wks. 1757 IV. 151 This will excuse my indignation at two notorious offenders. **1785** BURKE *Wks.* IV. 312 Sending that notorious incendiary to the Court of the nabob of Arcot. **1844** H. H. WILSON *Brit. India* II. 434 His subjects, many of whom were notorious robbers. **1884**

PAE *Eustace* xix, I know where some of the most notorious smugglers reside.

b. Similarly of deeds, facts, etc.

1561 WINȜET *Tractates* Wks. (S.T.S.) I. 11 Preseruing.. thy bewtifull body and saule fra al spot of notorius cryme. **1590** SHAKS. *Com. Err.* IV. i. 84, I shall haue Law in Ephesus, To your notorious shame, I doubt it not. *a* **1631** DONNE *Serm.* viii. 82 To proceed in those pious works, which with so notorious falshood they deny. **1673** CAVE *Prim. Chr.* III. v. 359 Striking them dead upon the place for their notorious couzenage and gross hypocrisie. **1729** LAW *Serious C.* ii. (1732) 17 Do but now find the reason why the generality of men live in this notorious vice. **1807** *Med. Jrnl.* XVII. 341 His mean subterfuge renders him more contemptible than his notorious untruth. **1839** JAMES *Louis XIV*, III. 310 Charles's notorious breach of his most solemn engagement.

†**c.** Quasi-*adv.* Notoriously. *Obs.* $rare^{-1}$.

1607 *Stat.* in *Hist. Wakefield Sch.* (1892) 62 Notorious negligent in the execution of the office of a Governour.

5. Noted *for* some bad practice, quality, etc.; unfavourably known; well known on account of something which is not generally approved of or admired. **a.** Of persons.

1603 DRAYTON *Bar. Wars* v. xxix, Such Men these had, to Mischiefe wholly bent, In Villainie notorious for their skill. **1609** B. JONSON *Sil. Wom.* IV. ii, You notorious stinkardly beareward. **1693** CONGREVE in *Dryden's Juvenal* xi. (1726) 162 Rutilus is so notorious grown, That he's the Common Theme of all the Town. **1718** *Free-thinker* No. 87. 226 A Fifth may be notorious for some scandalous Practice, or vicious Habits. **1837** THIRLWALL *Greece* IV. xxxii. 270 Socrates.. became one of the most conspicuous and notorious persons in Athens. **1880** W. DAY *Racehorse in Training* xvi. 156 The celebrated, or as some may be inclined to call her, the notorious, Lady Elizabeth.

b. Of actions, qualities, facts, etc.

1579 G. HARVEY *Letter-bk.* (Camden) 61 Dislikinge, murmuring,.. quippinge notorious or auricular iybinge. **1590** SIR J. SMYTH *Disc. Weapons* Ded. 12 b, To bring to passe.. such notorious and deformed effectes amongst the English Nation. **1653** VAUX tr. *Godeau's St. Paul* 45 The Emperor Tiberius succeeded Augustus, and made his Reign notorious by all.. cruelties. *a* **1721** SHEFFIELD (Dk. Buckhm.) *Wks.* (1753) I. 244 Should our mistakes be never so notorious, You'll have the joy of being more censorious. **1794** PALEY *Evidences* (1825) II. 116 These books were perfectly notorious. **1853** KANE *Grinnell Exp.* vii. (1856) 51 Melville Bay, notorious in the annals of the whalers for its many disasters. **1877** FROUDE *Short Stud.* (1883) IV. I. v. 54 The influences by which the papal court was determined were already too grossly notorious.

†**6.** Discreditable, disgraceful *to* one. *Obs.*$^{-1}$

1666 WOOD *Life* (O.H.S.) II. 96 Wheras it [the pox] was notorious formerly to those that had it, it is now soe common .. that they glory of it.

†**no'torious**, *a.*[2] *Obs.* $rare^{-1}$. = NOTORY *a.*[2]

1652 GAULE *Magastrom.* 191 And now (it is agreed among themselves) their art shall no more be called the notorious.

notoriously (nəʊˈtɔərɪəslɪ), *adv.* [-LY[2].]

1. In a notorious manner; as a matter of common knowledge; recognizedly, admittedly.

1512 *Act 4 Hen. VIII.* c. 19 Preamble, It ys openly and notoryously knowen unto all persones of Cristes Religion. *c* **1555** HARPSFIELD *Divorce Hen. VIII* (Camden) 87 The first part.. is by common consent of all the interpreters of Scripture notoriously true. **1650** FULLER *Pisgah* I. vii. 19 Their abode is notoriously known to have been in, and about Jebus or Jerusalem. **1698** FRYER *Acc. E. India & P.* 220 That Promontory.. being most notoriously Sandy. **1751** *Narr. Of H.M.S. Wager* 126 There was a weekly Intercourse notoriously carried on over Land between the Places. **1788** BURKE *Sp. agst. W. Hastings* Wks. XII. 254 His ministers (who are notoriously known [to be] under his absolute command). **1818** COBBETT *Pol. Reg.* XXXIII. 104 Let us confine ourselves to notoriously public transactions. **1881** *Sat. Rev.* LII. 570 The notoriously cleanly living of the vegetarian inhabitants of Western Africa.

b. In unfavourable sense.

1581 PETTIE tr. *Guazzo's Civ. Conv.* (1586) I. 45 The infamous, and those which are notoriouslie naught. **1615** G. SANDYS *Trav.* 73 He is of no bloudy disposition, nor otherwise notoriously vicious. **1677** HORNECK *Gt. Law Consid.* iv. (1704) 234 A man, that had notoriously betrayed his trust. **1729** BERKELEY *Serm.* Wks. 1871 IV. 639 Men of notoriously wicked lives. **1839** JAMES *Louis XIV*, II. 399 He was, in short, notoriously faithless and interested. **1849** MACAULAY *Hist. Eng.* vi. II. 47 His title had notoriously been purchased by his wife's dishonor and his own. **1877** FREEMAN *Norm. Conq.* II. App. 705 His only references are to Domesday and the notoriously spurious charter.

†**2.** Manifestly, evidently, obviously. *Obs.*

1589 PUTTENHAM *Eng. Poesie* II. xiv. (Arb.) 139 For euermore this word [alás] is accented vpon the last, and that lowdly and notoriously. **1603** HOLLAND *Plutarch Mor.* 1035 Farre is he off, from being contradictory and repugnant to himselfe so notoriously. **1645** MILTON *Colast.* Wks. 1851 IV. 345 His very first page notoriously bewraies him. **1690** BAXTER *Kingd. Christ* (1691) ii. 33 The distance between Christs Rising and his Coming to Judgment are so notoriously revealed.

notoriousness (nəʊˈtɔərɪəsnɪs). [f. as prec. + -NESS.] The fact of being notorious; notoriety.

1607 *Stat.* in *Hist. Wakefield Sch.* (1892) 58 Upon the notoriousnes of the fact of misdemeanour. **1649** ROBERTS *Clavis Bibl.* 533 The notoriousnesse of their offences. **1706** in PHILLIPS (ed. Kersey), and in later Dicts.

†**no'tority**, obs. variant of NOTORIETY.

c **1555** HARPSFIELD *Divorce Hen. VIII* (Camden) 37 The notoritie of the manifest and open justice of our cause.

notorly, variant of NOTOURLY *adv.*

notornis (nəʊˈtɔːnɪs). *Ornith.* [mod.L. (R. Owen 1848, in *Proc. Zool. Soc.* 2), f. Gr. νότος south + ὄρνις bird.] A flightless New Zealand bird of the genus so called, which includes the single species *Notornis mantelli*, belonging to the family Rallidæ, and distinguished by blue-green plumage and pink bill and legs; = MOHO[1], TAKAHE.

The bird was believed to be extinct until Dr. G. B. Orbell rediscovered it in a mountain valley near Lake Te Anau in November 1948.

1848 OWEN in *Proc. Zool. Soc.* 8 The *Notornis* is a large modified form of the same natural family of the *Grallæ* as the *Porphyrio* and *Brachypteryx*. **1850** MANTELL *Ibid.* 209 Notice of the discovery.., in the Middle Island of New Zealand, of a living specimen of the Notornis, a bird of the Rail family. **1870** H. A. NICHOLSON *Man. Zool.* (1875) 527 The *Notornis* is much larger than the ordinary Coots, and.. the wings are so rudimentary as to be useless for flight. **1882** *Trans. N.Z. Inst.* XIV. 253 It has always been acknowledged that Notornis is a degenerate rail. **1930** W. R. B. OLIVER *N.Z. Birds* 350 Suspecting that it was a Notornis, Connor took it to the station where he carefully skinned it, preserving both the skin and the bones. **1950** *Discovery* July 217/2 The news of the discovery of *Notornis* was announced on the following day—November 21 [1948]. **1962** J. FRAME *Edge of Alphabet* xii. 74 There's a valley of the notornis, the flightless bird. **1970** *Notornis* XVII. 67 This encounter [with a Takahe] was approximately 12 km from the closed Notornis area.

†**'notory**, *a.*[1] *Obs.* Also -ie, -ye. [ad. med.L. *nōtōrius* or F. *notoire.*] Notorious.

1399 *Rolls of Parlt.* III. 424/1 Hem thoght hem so trewe and so notorie and knowen. **1430** *Ibid.* V. 417/1 For many notorye and evident resons. **1490** in *10th Rep. Hist. MSS. Comm.* App. V. 322 If the trespasse be not notory, the plaintif shall prove the trespasse. **1528** ROY *Rede me* (Arb.) 104 He did some faulte gretly notory. **1603** COKE in Howell *St. Trials* II. 1 [Raleigh] the notoriest Traitor that ever came to the bar.

†**'notory**, *a.*[2] *Obs. rare.* = NOTARY *a.*[2]

1652 GAULE *Magastrom.* 190 Whether the art called the art notorie had even been so notorious, but for magick and astrologie? **1657** TURNER (*title*), Ars Notoria, or the Notory Art of Solomon, showing the Cabbalistical Key of Magical Operations,.. and the Art of Memory.

'notostome. *Biol.* [f. NOTO- + Gr. στόμα mouth.] A supposed 'dorsal mouth' in some early vertebrate and pre-vertebrate forms.

1887 E. D. COPE *Orig. Fittest* 323 The valve of the dorsal mouth, or notostome, is broken.

'notothere. *Palæont.* [Anglicized f. mod.L. *notothérium*, f. Gr. νότος south + θηρίον beast.] An extinct marsupial of great size found in post-tertiary formations.

1881 *Times* 28 Jan. 3/4 Nototheres of the size of the ox.

no-touch (nəʊˈtʌtʃ), *a. Med.* [f. NO *a* + TOUCH *sb.*] Applied to a method of dressing wounds in an environment that is not aseptic in which no one is allowed to touch either the wound or its dressings.

1944 *Med. Res. Council Special Rep. Ser.* No. 249. 24 'No-touch' technique, and dry instruments are used throughout. **1950** *Lancet* 18 Feb. 294/1 A no-touch technique was used for all wounds; this was not a theatre technique, but comprised the exclusive use of sterile instruments and dressing swabs. **1961** R. HARE *Bacteriol. & Immunity* v. 74 For most wounds, a method of dressing known as the 'no-touch' (or 'non-touch') technique is the method of choice.

notour ('notər), *a. Sc.* Also 6–7 notoure, 7 notor, -ure, 7–8 nottour. [ad. med.L. *nōtōrius* or F. *notoire.*] Well known, notorious. (Now only as a legal archaism in ***notour bankrupt.***)

1456 SIR G. HAYE *Law Arms* (S.T.S.) 173 It is notour thing that he had maid that promess throu fors and violence. **1563–4** *Reg. Privy Council Scot.* I. 272 Althocht the deid be notour and certane to the said Colene. **1571** in Spottiswood *Hist. Ch. Scot.* v. (1677) 254 For.. other considerations notour to the whole Estates. **1637–50** ROW *Hist. Kirk* (Wodrow Soc.) 304 That he was a vyld filthie bellie-god beast is notoure to all. **1678** SIR G. MACKENZIE *Crim. Laws Scot.* I. xvii. §3 (1699) 87 Our Law divides Adultery, in that which is notour Adultery, and single Adultery. **1696** *Lond. Gaz.* No. 3225/3 Act declaring Nottour Bankrupt. **1711** *Country-man's Lett. to Curat* 38 This is so notour a piece of History, that no Man ever denied it. **1772** *Weekly Mag.* 16 Apr. 74/2 The story of Provost Crichton of Sanquhar was also a most nottour story in that town. **1830** GALT *Lawrie T.* IV. v. (1849) 161 To scald his lips in other folks' kail was the most notour thing in the settlement. **1886** *Act 49 & 50 Vict.* c. 29 §1 Any act whereby he becomes notour bankrupt.

†**'notourly**, *adv. Sc. Obs.* Also 6–7 -lie, 7 -urely, -orlie. [f. prec. + -LY[2].] Notoriously or generally *known.*

1533 BELLENDEN *Livy* App. I. (S.T.S.) II. 285 The ancient gabynis.., to quham þir materis war maist notourly knawin. **1570** BUCHANAN *Chamæleon* Wks. (S.T.S.) 44 It is notourlie knawin bayth in Ingland and Scotland. **1637–50** ROW *Hist. Kirk* (Wodrow Soc.) 288 It was informed also, and notourely knowen, that whoever got of that accursed thing.. did neither thryve nor prosper. **1671** [R. MACWARD] *True Nonconf.* 66 Their frequent and continual intimations .. are notourly known. **1711** *Country-man's Lett. to Curat* 5 The Famous act of the six articles in the Year, 1539, is notourly known. [**1759** ROBERTSON *Hist. Scot.* VIII. Wks. 1813 II. 44 He was not notourly known during his life to be an accomplice in the crime.]

not-out, *a.* and *sb. Cricket.* The phrase 'not out' (see OUT *adv.* 19c.) used attributively to designate a batsman (his score, etc.) whose innings either are unfinished or are ended only by his side going out. Also as *sb.*: (*a*) A batsman who is 'not out'; (*b*) a 'not out' innings. Also *transf.*

1860 *Baily's Monthly Mag.* Sept. 426 We were most pleased with the two 'not-out' innings of 15 and 12 played by Mr. C. D. Marsham. **1869** *Ibid.* July 22 On the Tuesday the two not outs resumed their innings. **1891** *Daily News* 15 July 3/7 The professional from Oldham.. increased his not-out score of 60 to 124. **1895** *Ibid.* 26 Aug. 7/1 Not only did he take all the ten wickets, but the not-out man was missed from his bowling. **1898** *Field* 11 June 873/1 At the outset Troup and Townsend, the not-outs, were very slow. **1898** *Westm. Gaz.* 8 Sept. 7/3 His not-out innings realised 112 runs out of a total of 206. **1900** W. J. FORD *Cricketer on Cricket* 140 Last year.. in 56 innings he had an average of over 30, with only one not-out to help him. **1960** *Times* 14 June 16/2 With the aid of a number of not-outs Statham's batting average for England.. is more than 30. **1974** *Daily Tel.* 12 June 34/4/ Graves added a not-out 55 at a run a minute.

not-pated: see NOT *a.* 1 b.

not-quite, *a.* and *adv.* [f. NOT *adv.* 10 + QUITE *adv.*] **A.** *adj.* Almost, not wholly; *spec.* (*a*) not wholly committed or involved; (*b*) not wholly acceptable or respectable. Also as *sb.*

1920 D. H. LAWRENCE *Let.* 28 May (1962) I. 632 There is always a kind of half-measure, half-length, 'not quite' feeling about. **1948** L. MACNEICE *Holes in Sky* 39 He spelled out True and Good, With their interleaving of half-truths and not-quites. **1955** N. MARSH *Scales of Justice* xii. 236 Kitty, over-painted, knowledgeable, fantastically 'Not-quite'. **1961** M. BEADLE *These Ruins are Inhabited* (1963) vii. 96 We awoke on Sunday to not-quite-fog. **1962** *Punch* 15 Aug. 241/3 Marriage by special licence will be Not Quite. **1968** 'HAN SUYIN' *Birdless Summer* 281 The 'half-caste'. The Anglo-Indian, the chi-chi, the not-quite.

B. *adv.* Nearly, almost.

1940 W. FAULKNER *Hamlet* I. i. 20 The other [face] pumping up and down with metronome-like regularity to the wheel's not-quite-musical complaint. **1944** AUDEN *Sea & Mirror* in *For Time Being* iii. 30 The notable absence of the slightest shiver or not-quite-inhibited sneeze. **1975** M. BABSON *There must be Some Mistake* xiii. 93 Karen and Jill exchanged glances of not-quite-mock despair.

no-'trumper. [f. next + ER[1].] A no-trump call, or a hand on which a no-trump bid is or can be made; a person who makes a no-trump call.

1899 A. DUNN *Bridge* 29 As the dealer's hand is not worth a single trick, a light 'no-trumper' means absolute ruin. **1906** W. DALTON *'Saturday' Bridge* 42 Both of the hands quoted above are sound No Trumpers. **1929** M. C. WORK *Compl. Contract Bridge* ii. 12 In deciding whether to advance the No Trump.. the no trumper's partner uses the same count.

no trump(s), *phr. Bridge.* Also no-trump, notrump. [f. NO *a.* 1, 6 + TRUMP *sb.*[2]] **1.** *ellipt.* A call which provides for the playing of a hand without a trump suit; the play at bridge without trumps; also with preceding number (as ***three no trumps***), referring to the number of tricks (above six). Also *fig.*

1899 A. DUNN *Bridge* 19 The dealer should declare 'no trumps' when he holds four aces. **1902** *Encycl. Brit.* XXVI. 370/2 With an established black suit of 5 or 6 cards the dealer should declare no-trump if he has another suit protected. **1904** J. B. ELWELL *Adv. Bridge* 236 It is the rule at 'no-trump' to return partner's suit with your highest card. **1910** *Blackw. Mag.* Dec. 809/2 Nine times out of ten it is No Trumps, but sometimes the class element creeps in. **1929** M. C. WORK *Compl. Contract Bridge* ii. 9 He may overcall a No Trump with a suit-bid, or overcall a suit-bid with another suit or No Trump. **1933** [see BID *v.* 3c]. **1952** PHILLIPS & REESE *Bridge with Mr. Playbetter* iv. 20 Mrs. Rougenoir responded One No Trump. This was a good bid on her part. **1965** *Listener* 20 May 758/2 West has a minimum strong No Trump in terms of high cards. **1969** A. TRUSCOTT *Gt. Bridge Scandal* xx. 237 Schapiro opened this hand with a non-vulnerable weak notrump. **1974** *Country Life* 16 May 1239/3 You have to find a way to make Three No Trumps.

2. *attrib.* Made or played without a trump suit; of or pertaining to such a call.

1902 *Encycl. Brit.* XXVI. 369/2 If in a no-trump hand the partners conjointly hold 3 aces, they score 30 for honours. *Ibid.*, Each trick above 6 counts.. 12 in a no-trump declaration. **1906** W. DALTON'S *'Saturday' Bridge* 41 This is an undoubted No Trump call for the dealer. **1931** G. F. HERVEY *Headlights on Contract Bridge* viii. 69 When the dealer has made an initial No-Trump bid and second hand has passed, the third hand has three courses open to him. **1973** REESE & DORMER *Compl. Bk. Bridge* v. 71 The partner of the notrump bidder.. is able to judge the combined assets at once and can often select the final contract with his first call. **1975** *Way to Play* 90 In 'no trump' games, the four aces are honors. *Ibid.*, A no trump call ranks above all suits.

not-seeing, *vbl. sb. Literary.* [f. NOT *sb.* C 1 + SEEING *vbl. sb.*] The state of not seeing.

a **1930** D. H. LAWRENCE *Last Poems* (1932) 250 In not-looking, and in not-seeing Comes a new strength. **1932** W. FAULKNER *Light in August* (1933) viii. 177 In the notseeing and the hardknowing as though in a cave he seemed to see a diminishing row of suavely shaped urns. **1963** *Listener* 10 Jan. 71/2 To the not-seeing of the flat surface of Renaissance painting Abstract Art opposes the not-seeing of figures or patterns.

not-self. [f. NOT *adv.* 14 d + SELF.] That which is other than self; something different from the conscious self; the non-ego. So **not-'selfness**.

1839 SIR W. HAMILTON *Discuss.* (1852) 192 This *not-self* or *non-ego*. **1867** LEWES *Hist. Philos.* (ed. 3) II. 154, I am conscious of all that passes within myself; but I am not conscious of what passes in not-self. **1872** *Dublin Rev.* July 145 A philosophy that shall confirm the existence of an independent Not-Self. **1876** GEO. ELIOT *Dan. Der.* xxxii, Our self is a not-self for whose sake we become virtuous. **1901** J. MCTAGGART *Stud. Hegelian Cosmol.* ix. 277 But I mean that the characteristic which experience possesses of being not-self—its 'not-selfness', if the barbarism is permissible,—will always remain as an external and alien element. **1927** J. S. HUXLEY *Relig. without Revelation* viii. 285 The objective outer world and the subjective un-self-organised parts of the mind are usually interwoven in what is felt as 'not-self'. **1949** D. L. SAYERS tr. *Dante's Divine Comedy* I. 68 That experience of the Not-self—which, by arousing his adoring love, has become for him the God-bearing image. **1958** *Times Lit. Suppl.* 10 Oct. 581/1 Reality for him belongs exclusively to the Atman, the one impersonal Self or not-Self with which we can, and should, identify ourselves by shedding all that is personal, desirous and therefore fatally separatist in ourselves. **1960** C. DAY LEWIS *Buried Day* i. 25 His proper concern is with the object to be created—an object which, however much of himself goes into it, must end up as not-self.

†nott, obs. variant of KNOT *sb.*[2]

1768 *Ann. Reg.* I. 170 The bill of fare at the king of Denmark's table was as follows:..Ortolans, Pheasants, Notts.

nott, variant of NOT *v.*[1], *v.*[2], and *adv.*

†notted, *a. Obs.* [f. NOT *v.*[1] + -ED[1].]

1. Without horns; hornless.

1591 PERCIVALL *Sp. Dict.*, *Mocha*, without hornes, notted. **1630** DRAYTON *Muses Elys.* ii. Wks. 1753 IV. 1456, I have a lamb..Of the right kind, it is notted.

2. Shaven, shorn; cut short.

1576 FLEMING tr. *Caius' Dogs* (1880) 17 The water Spaniell [is]..powlde & notted from the shoulders to the hinder-most legges. **1599** *Life Sir T. More* in Wordsw. *Eccl. Biog.* (1853) II. 107 Once I thought to have gone to my death, notted, as I was wont to wear it [the beard].

transf. **1650** FULLER *Pisgah* 365 Many..cut down all top-masts from the ship of Christs Church..and make her close notted to the very keel.

3. Of wheat: Smooth; not bearded.

1603 OWEN *Pembrokeshire* (1892) I. 60 Bearded and notted wheate, as the husbands term it. *a* **1661** FULLER *Worthies, Middlesex* 189 The Mildew.., which sticketh on notted or pollard Wheat.

notte-tree, obs. form of NUT-TREE.

nott-head, -pated: see NOT *a.* 1 b.

not the less, *adv.* Also *Sc.* 5–6 **nochtþeles(e**, 6 **-theles(s**. [See the separate words, and cf. NA-, NE-, NOTHELESS. The Sc. forms properly belong to NOUGHT *adv.*] Nevertheless; nonetheless.

α. *c* **1375** *Sc. Leg. Saints* i. (*Peter*) 605 þe quhilk petir nocht-þe-lese Conuertit. *Ibid.* xv. (*Barnabas*) 137 Debonare wes he nocht-þe-les. **1533** BELLENDEN *Livy* I. vi. (S.T.S.) I. 38 Nochtþeles, þe cumpany of horsmen..was Impediment. **1596** DALRYMPLE tr. *Leslie's Hist. Scot.* Prol. 14 Carik nochttheless hes ane monasterie called Croce Regal.

β. **1535** COVERDALE *Dan.* v. 17 Yet not thelesse, I wil rede the wrytynge. **1567** *Gude & Godlie B.* (S.T.S.) 41 Bot not the les, Abraham this answer maid. **1637–50** ROW *Hist. Kirk* (Wodrow Soc.) 301 Nottheles, the Bishops being so preferred to high places [etc.]. **1639** SPOTTISWOOD *Hist. Ch. Scot.* VII. (1677) 519 Nottheless going on in his wonted course, he sent his base Son..into the Country.

1839 KEMBLE *Resid. Georgia* (1863) 11 They are free from the chain,..but they are not the less under a ban. *a* **1869** CONINGTON *Misc. Writ.* I. 213 It is determined, not the less, by the causes which were appointed [etc.].

not-'thereness. [f. NOT *adv.* + THERE *adv.* + -NESS.] The state of being absent or preoccupied.

1934 A. HUXLEY *Beyond Mexique Bay* 261 There is something profoundly horrifying in this immense, indefinite not-thereness of the Mexican scene. **1950** —— *Themes & Variations* 86 Rushing from one soirée to another in a strange state of alienation and not-thereness.

Nottingham ('nɒtɪŋəm; also locally 'nɒtɪŋgəm). The name of a city in the Midlands of England, used *attrib.* to denote: **a.** Any of a variety of articles made or found there; something originating there.

1708 in *Bagford Ballads* (1877) I. II. 389 With Nottingham Ale At every Meal. **1748** M. W. MONTAGU *Let.* 18 Aug. (1966) II. 410 If you would order me six dozen of Nottingham ale..it would be very acceptable. **1851** J. PYCROFT *Cricket Field* vii. 151 Practise each kind of cut..and the Nottingham forward cut, with left leg over. **1866** 'CAPT. CRAWLEY' *Cricket* 29 If the ball is far-pitched, carry the left foot across the front of the wicket..and hit the ball on to the ground in a direction between point and mid-wicket. This is the 'Forward Cut', or 'Nottingham Drive'. **1869** J. C. PATTESON *Let.* 24 Nov. in C. M. Yonge *Life J. C. Patteson* (1874) II. xi. 392 Nottingham drill, good towelling, huckaback, &c., ought to be worthwhile to send out. **1931** *Star* 8 May 8/3 She [*sc.* the housewife] would be even more annoyed if we were to prove to her that she had been burning Nottingham Top Hard for years to her satisfaction. **1963** *Homes & Gardens* May 81/3 The pink Nottingham brickwork for the outside walls. **1973** *Country Life* 29 Nov. 1798/2 The pale creamy-grey of the Nottingham stone of which the house is built.

b. Nottingham catchfly, a white-flowered, perennial herb, *Silene nutans*, of the family Caryophyllaceæ, distinguished by the soft hair on its leaves and stems and the stickiness of the upper part of the plant.

[**1690** J. RAY *Synopsis Methodica Stirpium Britannicarum* 140 *Lychnis sylvestris alba*... Wild white Catchfly. On the walls of Nottingham-Castle, and thereabout; shewn us first by Tho. Willsel.] **1762** W. HUDSON *Flora Anglica* 165 Nottingham catchfly. Habitat in pratis montosis. On the walls of Nottingham-castle, and thereabout. **1852** A. PRATT *Wild Flowers* I. 158 No less fragrant are the flowers of one variety of the Nottingham Catchfly. **1960** *Oxf. Bk. Wild Flowers* 72/2 Nottingham Catchfly is a rare plant of dry, stony places and sea cliffs in England and Wales. **1963** W. BLUNT *Of Flowers & Village* 106 Fresh seed of the Nottingham catchfly (*Silene nutans*) germinates better in the dark.

c. A type of stoneware produced at Nottingham until the end of the eighteenth century.

1855 E. ACTON *Mod. Cookery* (rev. ed.) xii. 243 Fill a brown upright Nottingham jar with alternate layers of mutton..potatoes, and ..onions. **1957** MANKOWITZ & HAGGAR *Conc. Encycl. Eng. Pott. & Porc.* 167/1 Examples of Nottingham stoneware may be seen in the Victoria and Albert Museum. **1960** H. HAYWARD *Antique Collecting* 200/2 *Nottingham earthenware*, pottery made in Nottingham from the 13th cent. and its production continued along characteristic lines until about 1800. The manufactories making Nottingham wares are unidentified. **1973** *Times* 25 Aug. 12/4 The Nottingham bear jugs and owl jugs, weirdly modelled, are particularly sought after.

d. A type of machine-made flat lace originally produced at Nottingham (also ***N. net***).

1859 GEO. ELIOT *Adam Bede* I. ix. 182 Hetty's dreams were all of luxuries: to sit in a carpeted parlour..to have Nottingham lace round the top of her gown. **1881** C. C. HARRISON *Woman's Handiwork* III. 187 Nottingham lace is now sold in excellent block patterns. *Ibid.* 188 Edgings of the common Nottingham antique lace at eight to ten cents a yard. **1919** T. WRIGHT *Romance of Lace Pillow* xv. 213 The low prices at which machine lace could be sold caused great consternation among the Bucks workers. 'Nottingham Net' followed by 'Urling's Figured Imitations'. **1921** *Daily Colonist* (Victoria, B.C.) 5 Oct. 7/7, 50 Pairs of Nottingham Lace Curtains at $1.95 a Pair. **1939** O. LANCASTER *Homes Sweet Homes* 60 Small tight-shut windows, the light from which is further dimmed by a barrage of Nottingham lace. **1963** *Times* 5 June 17/2 The future of Byard Manufacturing, the Nottingham lace and textile manufacturers, was plunged into even greater obscurity yesterday by the announcement of yet another offer for the company. **1967** *Guardian* 3 July 4 Some of us still think of machine-made lace as 'Nottingham' and equate it with soot-soiled curtains in back streets. **1969** *New Yorker* 29 Nov. 55/1 Her denigratory glance travelled from the plush tablecloth to the Nottingham-lace curtains.

e. *Nottingham white* (see quot. 1969).

1883 J. W. MOLLETT *Illustr. Dict. Art & Archeol.* 227/2 *Nottingham white*, white lead. **1897** *Sears, Roebuck Catal.* 360/3 Colors for Artists... New Blue, Nottingham White, Olive Lake [etc.]. **1934** H. HILER *Notes on Technique of Painting* ii. 91 White lead..also called flake-white,.. Nottingham white, [etc.]. **1969** R. MAYER *Dict. Art Terms & Techniques* 263/2 *Nottingham white*, an obsolete name for white lead, used in England during the 19th century.

f. A style of fishing; also, a type of reel (see quots.).

1900 A. E. T. WATSON *Young Sportsman* 22 The principle of the Nottingham men was the travelling tackle, or 'long corking'... The special tackle for this is a long and supple rod, upright rings, a Nottingham reel without check or complications..and quill or cork float. **1939** 'G. ORWELL' *Coming up for Air* II. iv. 87, I could give you all the details about gut-substitute and gimp and Limerick hooks..and Nottingham reels. **1963** *Newnes Encycl. Angling* 156/1 Nottingham reel, a reel made in wood instead of the usual brass. *Ibid.* 156/2 The tackle used in Nottingham-style fishing is heavier than that generally adopted in the Sheffield style.

g. Nottingham (one club) system *Bridge*, a system originating at Nottingham.

1954 M. BURNS (*title*) The Nottingham club system of contract bridge. **1959** *Listener* 8 Jan. 84/2 In this town our convention is the Nottingham One Club. **1959** REESE & DORMER *Bridge Player's Dict.* 154 Of the many one-club systems that were popular in the early days of contract, one of the few that have survived in Britain and America is the Nottingham system. **1959** *Listener* 31 Dec. 1178/2 The Skegness pair were convincing, using the Nottingham One Club system. **1964** *Official Encycl. Bridge* 385/1 *Nottingham Club*, a system popular in the English Midlands.

†'notty, *sb.*, obs. var. of *anotto*, ANATTA.

1707 SLOANE *Jamaica* (1725) II. 54 Notty has the same qualities with Saffron. *Ibid.*, Notty is added to chocolate to colour it.

†'notty, *a.* var. of *noppy* NAPPY *a.*[2]

1420–22 LYDG. *Thebes* 110 (MS. Laud 557), After soper slepe will do non ill... Stronge notti [*altered to* noppy] ale will make you to rowte.

‖**notum** ('nəʊtəm). [mod.L., ad. Gr. νῶτον back.] The dorsal part of the thorax in insects.

1877 HUXLEY *Anat. Inv. Anim.* vii. 404 A distinct median sclerite, the sternum, may be observed; and a much larger tergal piece, the notum.

Notus ('nəʊtəs). *rare.* [L. *Notus*, Gr. Νότος.] The south wind.

c **1374** CHAUCER *Boeth.* II. Met. vi. (1868) 55 And eke Nero gouernede alle þe poeples þat þe violent wynde Nothus scorchiþ. **1667** MILTON *P.L.* x. 702 Notus and Afer black with thundrous Clouds from Serraliona.

†notwithstand, obs. var. of next.

1596 RALEIGH *Discov. Gviana* Ep. Ded. 3 It appeareth notwithstand that I made no other brauado of going to sea. **1609** SKENE *Reg. Maj.* 60 Proces sall proceid against him, notwithstand of his minoritie.

notwith'standing, *prep.*, *adv.*, and *conj.* Also 4–5 **-stonding(e**, **-yng(e**. [f. NOT *adv.* + pres. pple. of WITHSTAND *v.*, after med.L. *non obstante*, OF. *non obstant*.] **A.** *prep.* In spite of.

Properly the same construction as in 2, differing only in the order of the words.

c **1380** WYCLIF *Sel. Wks.* III. 434 And notwiþstondynge þis, Crists Chirche shulde live, ʒif alle siche prelats wanteden þerinne. *c* **1402** LYDG. *Compl. Bl. Knt.* 333 Notwithstanding his manhood and his might, Love unto him did full great unright. *c* **1460** FORTESCUE *Abs. & Lim. Mon.* iv. (1885) 117 He dothe wronge, nothwithstondynge the said lawe declared by the prophete. **1568** GRAFTON *Chron.* II. 651 Notwith-standyng gentle aduertisement to them geuen,..they remayned still in one obstinate minde. **1591** SHAKS. *Two Gent.* IV. ii. 12 Notwithstanding all her sodaine quips. **1625** BACON *Ess.*, *Nobility* (Arb.) 191 Wee see the Switzers last well, notwithstanding their Diuersitie of Religion. **1662** STILLINGFL. *Orig. Sacræ* I. ii. §4 It might be the old famous Tyre still, notwithstanding what Sanchoniathon speaks. **1766** GOLDSM. *Vic. W.* xxxii, But notwithstanding this, it is impossible to describe our good humour. *a* **1806** FOX *Jas. II* (1808) 214 Thomas Archer, a clergyman.., was executed, nothwithstanding many applications in his favour. **1888** BURGON *Lives 12 Gd. Men* II. x. 258 Notwithstanding the engrossing labours of the Hall..[he] was..a thoughtful and laborious student in Divinity.

b. *Sc.* In spite *of* something.

1639 SPOTTISWOOD *Hist. Ch. Scot.* v. (1677) 251 The Factions at home, notwithstanding of the Abstinence, were not idle. **1653** BAILLIE *Dissuas. Vind.* (1655) 16 Acts of most hearty communion, nothwithstanding of some avowed differences. **1697** [C. LESLIE] *Snake in Grass* (ed. 2) 117 Not-withstanding of this high Value they put upon themselves, ..See how Jealous they are [etc.]. *c* **1817** HOGG *Tales & Sk.* III. 66 Notwithstanding of his..remonstrances. **1844** H. STEPHENS *Bk. Farm* II. 404 Notwithstanding of this common opinion, a loss of a small portion of time..may have a material effect upon some future operations.

2. Following *this*, *that*, or a sb., in a syntactical relation corresponding to the ablative absolute in Latin. Also † ***not that withstanding***.

1490 CAXTON *Eneydos* vi. 23 This notwystondyng, alwaye they be in awayte. *c* **1500** *Melusine* 208 She was abasshed of the grete honour.., not that withstandyng she ansuerd in this manere. *c* **1555** HARPSFIELD *Divorce Hen. VIII* (Camden Soc.) 179 But, her worthiness notwithstanding, and that he had a fair daughter by her, he..was wonderfully tormented in conscience. **1593** SHAKS. *Rich. II*, II. i. 260 He hath not monie for these Irish warres: (His burthenous taxations notwithstanding). *a* **1640** MASSINGER, etc. *Old Law* III. ii, These notwithstanding, His hair and wrinkles will betray his age.

1844 *Act 7 & 8 Vict.* c. 32 §26 Any other Act to the contrary notwithstanding. **1857** G. LAWRENCE *Guy Liv.* iii, Hunting three days a week, which he persisted in doing, all lectures and regulations notwithstanding.

†b. As a quasi-*sb. rare*[−1].

1689 *Consid. conc. Succession* 28 We may easily perceive that it binds Men to Allegiance (not indefinitely, but) with a Notwithstanding to the pretended Authority of the Pope.

B. *adv.* Nevertheless, still, yet.

c **1440** *Alph. Tales* 8 Not-with-stondyng, afor his bruther was abbott, he was a wurthie merchand. *c* **1450** *Merlin* 235 Not-with-stondinge, I sey not [etc.]. **1530** TINDALE *Doctr. Treat.* (Parker Soc.) 480 Notwithstanding yet, when Paul wrote the epistle to the Colossians, Mark was with him. **1551** T. WILSON *Logike* (1580) 88 The people of Crete are liers,..yet Epimenides maie be excepted, and be a true manne of his worde notwithstandyng. **1585** T. WASHINGTON tr. *Nicholay's Voy.* I. xi. 13 Borasques.. proceed not out of the West, notwithstanding do often happen in Winter. **1606** G. W[OODCOCKE] *Hist. Ivstine* XXIX. 100 Yet notwithstanding he promised to send friendly succours. **1651** HOBBES *Leviath.* II. xix. 95 Their King was notwithstanding never considered as their Representative. **1736** BUTLER *Anal.* I. vii. Wks. 1874 I. 134 Were these assertions true, yet the government of the world might be just and good notwithstanding. **1769** GOLDSM. *Hist. Rome* (1786) II. 494 Julian..was, notwithstanding, a very good and a very valiant prince. **1813** SOUTHEY *Nelson* II. 22 The father..declared he saw that it would come to pass notwithstanding. **1875** THIRLWALL *Lett.* (1881) I. 393 It can matter little that the rite is notwithstanding a real sacrament.

C. *conj.* Although.

c **1449** PECOCK *Repr.* III. xii. 355 Thei bileeueden it and witnessen it, not withstonding Pope Damasis wroot the contrarie to Ierom. **1502** *Lett. Rich. III & Hen. VII* (Rolls) II. 111 Notwithstanding your grace had commaundid us to retorne, yet we..wold be content to make here abode. **1565** STAPLETON tr. *Bede's Hist. Ch. Eng.* 155 He returned home, notwithstanding the bisshop offred him lodginge. **1596** DANETT tr. *Comines* (1614) 243 That the Duke of Lorrain had no right thereto, notwithstanding others maintained the contrary. **1613** PURCHAS *Pilgrimage* (1614) 745 [He] would needes goe on shore.., notwithstanding some advised and intreated him the contrary. **1676** *Doctrine of Devils* 170 Notwithstanding they knew the Laws, Customes, and Statutes, of the Nation. **1765** GOLDSM. *Ess.* xxiv. Misc. Wks. 1837 I. 323 Notwithstanding he had set his features to the semblance of a smile, I could perceive he was out of humour. **1786** tr. *Beckford's Vathek* (1868) 16 The Caliph, notwithstanding the table had been thirty times covered, found himself incommoded by the voraciousness of his guest. **1829** WORDSW. *Prose Wks.* (1876) I. 264 Notwithstanding objections may lie against some parts of her Liturgy,..her doctrines are exclusively scriptural. **1859** LANG *Wand. India* 409 Notwithstanding it was enlivened by several exciting incidents,..I was very glad when it was over.

b. Followed by *that* with dependent clause.

1584 COGAN *Haven Health* (1636) 176 Milke, notwithstanding that it seemeth to be wholly of one substance, yet it is compact, or made of three severall substances. **1596** DANETT tr. *Comines* (1614) 125

Notwithstanding that it were once burned by the D. of Burgundie.
1820 W. IRVING *Sk. Bk.* (1821) I. 149 He [James I of Scotland] was detained prisoner by Henry IV, notwithstanding that a truce existed between the two countries. **1855** PUSEY *Doctr. Real Pres.* iii. (1859) 329 The Church has ever worshipped our Lord truly and spiritually present in the Sacrament, notwithstanding that.. His Human nature is at the Right Hand of God in Heaven.

notycyon, -yfy, obs. ff. NOTITION, NOTIFY.

notye, var. of NOTE *v.*[1]

nou, obs. f. NOW.

nouacion, noualty, nouasse, obs. ff. NOVATION, NOVELTY, NOVICE.

Nouba, var. NUBA.

nouch, orig. form of OUCH, clasp, and var. of NUCHE *Obs.*

†**nouch.** *Obs. rare.* [Of obscure origin.] A projection or projecting part.
Holme also uses *noches* in a similar sense (III. ix. 393/1).
1688 HOLME *Armoury* I. 32/1 Imbattleing stands equally proportioned on both sides, with the nouches contrary one to the other: as if they were Strong Staves put throw a peece of Timber. *Ibid.* III. xiv. (Roxb.) 8/2 The parts of a Flesh pott... The feet, three nouches on which the pot standeth.

noucin, variant of NOWCIN, need. *Obs.*

†**'noudy,** obs. Sc. variant of NODDY *sb.*[2]
c **1700** in Maidment *Scot. Pasquils* (1868) 331 For preaching, for drinking, for playing at noudy, Bannocks of bear meal, cakes of croudy. *Ibid.*, They preach well, feast well, and play well at noudy.

‖**noué,** *a. rare*⁻¹. [F. *noué*, pa. pple. of *nouer* to knot.] = NOWED *a.*
1761 *Brit. Mag.* II. 76 On a wreath, a snake noué, proper.

noueis, nouel, nouell, -eltie, Nouembre, obs. ff. NOVICE, NAVEL, NOVEL(TY), NOVEMBER.

‖**nougat** ('nu:gɑ:). Also nogat. [F. *nougat*, a. Prov. *nougat*, = Sp. and Pg. *nogada*, *nogado*:—Romanic **nucātum*, f. L. *nuc-*, *nux* nut.] A sweetmeat composed principally of sugar and almonds, or other varieties of nuts.
1827 JARRIN *Ital. Confectioner* (ed. 3) 24 Cake Nogat, This nogat may be made in moulds, or square pieces. **1846** *French Domest. Cookery* 235 When you make a nougat of large dimensions, put in the almonds a few at a time. **1853** SOYER *Pantroph.* 285 That learned and exquisite mixture now designated under the name of Nougat.

nougatine (nu:gə'ti:n). [f. NOUGAT + -INE[1].] A form of nougat freq. covered with chocolate.
1894 E. SKUSE *Compl. Confectioner* 58 Nougatines. 4 lbs. Ground Almonds. 7 lbs. Castor Sugar. **1897** *Sears, Roebuck Catal.* 7/2 Almond Nougatines. **1916** *Daily Colonist* (Victoria, B.C.) 21 July 14/5 (Advt.), Chocolate Fig Nougatines. *c* **1938** *Fortnum & Mason Price List* 8/1 Chocolate Nougatine Batons—per lb. 5/-.

'nough (nʌf). An aphetic form of ENOUGH; phr. ***'nough said***: used to emphasize and conclude a statement. Cf. NUFF.
1839 *Philadelphia Gaz.* 12 Nov. 2/1 N.S.M.J., 'nough said 'mong gentlemen. **1903** K. D. WIGGIN *Rebecca* ii. 24 L.D.M. was talented 'nough to *get* Reely's money, but M.D.L. would 'a' ben practical 'nough to have *kep*' it. **1934** *Amer. Speech* IX. 319/2 *'Nough said.* Implies the ending of all discussion by acceptance of proposition or challenge. **1944** C. HIMES *Cotton gonna kill me Yet* in *Black on Black* (1973) 197 Ain't got sense 'nough to be mad. **1973** *Amer. Speech 1970* XLV. 76 Sure 'nough is.

nought (nɔ:t), *sb.*, *a.*, and *adv.* Forms: α. 1-3 nowiht, 1 -wuht, 3 -wyht, -wiþt (-wist, -whit). β. 1-4 noht (3 *Orm.* nohht), 3-4 nohut; 3-5 (6-9 *Sc.*) nocht; 3-4 nogt, 3-6 noght (4-5 -te); 3-5 noʒt (4 noeʒt), 4-5 noʒte (4 -the); 3 noþt, 6 *Sc.* notht, 4 (6 *Sc.*) noth; 3 noh, 4 nogh, 6-7 *Sc.* noch. γ. 3-5 nouht, 5 nowhte, 6 (9) *Sc.* noucht; 3-6 nouʒt (4 -th), 4-5 nouʒte (4 -the), nowʒte; 3- nought (5 nougt, nough), 5-6 noughte (5 now-); 3 nouthe, 4 nouþe, 4-5 nouth, 5 nowth(e. δ. 3 nowit, -wyt, 2-4 (8 *dial.*) nout, 5-7 noute, 3-5 (9 *dial.*) nowt. [OE. *nówiht*, *-wuht*, f. *ne* NE + *ówiht*, var. of *áwiht*: see AUGHT and NAUGHT.
Parallel formations to OE. *náwiht*, *nówiht* appear in OS. *nêowiht*, *niowiht*, OHG. *nêowiht*, *nio-*, *niewiht*, *nieht* (G. *nicht*), and with the guttural dropped in OHG. *niewet*, *niet*, MDu. *niewet*, *nieut*, *niet*, OFris. *nawet*, *nauet*, *naut*. A simpler form occurs in OHG. *niwiht*, *-weht* (Goth. *ne waihts*, OE. *ne..wiht*).]

A. *sb.* **1.** Nothing. (Now only literary.)
α. *c* **825** *Vesp. Psalter* xxxiii. 10 Ondredað dryhten.. forðon nowiht wonu bið ðæm ondredendum hine. *c* **897** K. ÆLFRED tr. *Gregory's Past. C.* 389 Sien ða hæbbendan swelce hie nowiht hæbben. *c* **950** *Lindisf. Gosp.* Matt. x. 26 Nowiht forðon [is] ʒedeʒled þæt ne se unwriʒen. *c* **1200** *Moral Ode* 152 (Trin. Coll. MS.), þan he biðohte an helle fur þat nowiht ne mai quenche. *c* **1275** LAY. 3182 Ich þe segge soþ riht, ne sal ʒeo habbe no wiþt.
β. *c* **888** K. ÆLFRED tr. *Boethius* vii. §1 þonne nis þe noht swiðor þonne ðæt þæt þu forloren hæfst þa woruldsælða. *c* **900** tr. *Bæda's Hist.* I. xxvii. (1890) 80 þæm besmitenum.. noht bið clæne. **971** *Blickl. Hom.* 147 Næfde heo noht on hire buton þæt an. *c* **1128** *O.E. Chron.* (Laud MS.) an. 1128, þa hi þider comon ða ne was hit noht buton læsunge. *c* **1200** ORMIN 18749, & nohht nass wrohht wiþþutenn himm Off all þatt iss summ shaffte. *c* **1250** *Lutel soth Serm.* 6 in *O.E. Misc.* 186 Wel we witen alle þaʒ ich eou noʒt ne telle. **13..** *E.E. Allit. P.* A. 520 No mon byddez vus do ryʒt noʒt. **1390** GOWER *Conf.* I. 24 Al was in to pouldre broght, And so forth torned into noght. *c* **1440** *Generydes* 144 For his plesur trowly ther lakkyd noght. **1456** SIR G. HAYE *Law Arms* (S.T.S.) 161 [He] can nocht ellis do bot sitt on the felde. **1567** *Satir. Poems Reform.* iv. 181 In earth.. sen nocht is permanent. *a* **1585** MONTGOMERIE *Cherrie & Slae* 149 Quhat gif.. it coist thee nocht Bot randring it againe? **1611** SIR W. MURE *Elegie* Wks. (S.T.S.) I. 15 Nocht els bot cruell Cupid's ire my martyrdome constrainis. *c* **1650** —— *Ps.* cxix. 20 Besyde Thy judgements noght, no time, contents. **1724** RAMSAY *Vision* vi, Let nocht thy hairt affray. **1791** BURNS *Lament Earl Glencairn* iii, But nocht in all revolving time Can gladness bring again to me.
γ. *c* **1300** *K. Alis.* (Weber) 3767 Tho that up the water fyghtis, Yet neotith nought of this knyghtis. **1389** in *Eng. Gilds* (1870) 7 ʒif any brother deye, þat haþ nouʒt of his owne to be beried withe. **1393** LANGL. *P. Pl.* C. I. 210 Bote soffren and sigge nouht, and so is the beste. *c* **1440** *Promp. Parv.* 359/2 Nowhte (nowth, K).., *nichil.* **1484** CAXTON *Fables of Alfonce* ix, I promysed to the nought at al. **1529** RASTELL *Pastyme* (1811) 52 He dyd noughte but made his kyn ryche of the goodys of the church. **1562** J. HEYWOOD *Prov. & Epigr.* (1867) 38 He that hath right nought, right nought shall possesse. **1600** J. PORY tr. *Leo's Africa* III. 187 Besides barly-bread the inhabitants haue nought to liue on. **1665** S. PATRICK *Parab. Pilgr.* 80, I am nought, I have nought, I desire nought. **1718** HICKES & NELSON *J. Kettlewell* II. lvii. 178 The whole Course of his Ministry was nought else but an Uniform Obedience. **1781** COWPER *Anti-Thelyphth.* 182 She whisper'd still that he had nought to fear. **1836** KINGSLEY *Lett.* (1878) I. 33 She loved all living things, and nought harmed her. **1860** TYNDALL *Glac.* I. viii. 267 Nought remains to mark the huge moraine, but a strip of dirt. **1872** HOLLAND *Marble Prophecy* 46 Then dream that nought so real comes in dreams.
δ. *a* **1200** *Moral Ode* 292 (Egerton MS.), Heom nas nout of godes bode ne of godes hese. **1362** LANGL. *P. Pl.* A. VI. 119 'No', quaþ an Apeward, 'for nout þat I knowe'. *c* **1450** *Gesta Rom.* (1879) 107 þe drynk is noute elles but passion. *c* **1485** *Promp. Parv.* (S) 359/2 Nowte, *nichil.*
1741-3 WESLEY *Jrnl.* (1749) 89 She cares not, if she never look in a book. She minds *nout* but play. **1827-30** T. WILSON *Pitman's Pay* (1843) 13, I want for nowt that she can gie me. **1864** TENNYSON *North. Farmer* I. i, Thourt nowt o' a noorse. **1913** [see BLEEDER 3]. **1963** *Times* 11 Mar. 3/6 The verdict was just, anyway, for Yorkshire took their chances like men who seldom get 'owt for nowt', and were better disciplined on a day that demanded it. **1975** *Daily Tel.* 13 Dec. 9/1 There's nowt else possible in this weather.

2. a. Nothing; nonentity. Now *rare* or *Obs.*
c **1200** ORMIN 12009 Forr I þe shop off nohht. *c* **1300** *Cursor M.* 345 He þat mad al thing o noght. **1388** WYCLIF *Ps.* xxxii[i]. 9 He comaundide, and thingis weren maad of nouʒt. **1500-20** DUNBAR *Poems* xlvi. 44 God.. That him of nocht wrocht lyk his awin figour. **1567** *Gude & Godlie B.* (S.T.S.) 131 O Lord, quhilk wrocht all thingis of nocht. **1635** SWAN *Spec. M.* i. §1 (1643) 4 All this All did once of nought begin. **1642** H. MORE *Song Soul* II. I. III. vii, To their ancient Nought their empty selves betake. *a* **1711** KEN *Hymnarium* Poet. Wks. 1721 II. 43 The boundless Gulf betwixt Eternal Nought and Being fix'd.
b. *Arith.* = NOTHING *sb.* 4.
c **1430** *Art Nombryng* 18 þat wel be noʒt, for a o is noʒt. And twyes noʒt is but noʒt. **1588** A. KING tr. *Canisius' Catech.* p. vi, Giff nocht restis, ye divisor 19. sall be it. **1788** JEFFERSON *Writ.* (1859) II. 464 The honor of their nation has been calculated at nought. **1884** tr. *Lotze's Logic* 269 The proportion $p\alpha : p\beta = b$: *a* must always subsist; therefore *m* cannot be nought.
c. ***to be nought***: (see NAUGHT *sb.* 1 e). *rare.*
1565 *Kyng Darius* (Brandl) 747 Come away, and be nought a whyle. **1573** *New Custom* I. ii, With all my harte and a vengeance, come up and be nought.
d. A score of no points in a game.
1862 *Lillywhite's Cricket Scores* I. 354 It is certainly curious that Beldham should have made two noughts in this contest. **1876** *Haygarth's Cricket Scores* V. 165 Thirty-three noughts were obtained in the match.

3. a. In phr. ***to bring, come, go,*** etc., ***to nought.***
β. *c* **1200** ORMIN 10960 þæraffterr warrþ itt efft to nohht. **1297** R. GLOUC. (Rolls) 5466 þe contreye folc com mid gret route & driue hom al to noʒte. **13..** *Cursor M.* 22172 (Edin.), To bring þe cristin men to nochte. **13..** *Gaw. & Gr. Knt.* 680 So had better haf ben þen britned to noʒt. **1596** DALRYMPLE tr. *Leslie's Hist. Scot.* II. 157 The maiestie of the Romane Impire.. almaist was cum to nocht. **1888** *Scot. Serm.* in *Brit. Workm.* XXXIV. 19 Sae the precious seed cam' tae nocht ava.
γ. *c* **1290** *S. Eng. Leg.* I. 1 Alle þe heþene men þat neiʒ him were, sone he dude to nouʒte. *a* **1400** HYLTON *Scala Perf.* (W. de W. 1494) II. xlv, Spoylleth hym and renteth hym all to nought. **1470-85** MALORY *Arthur* XX. xix. 831 They shalle by processe brynge vs alle to noughte. **1526** TINDALE *1 Cor.* ii. 6 Wisdom of this worlde.. (which goeth to nought). **1577** B. GOOGE *Heresbach's Husb.* I. (1586) 31 b, Yf it be sowed thicke, it comes to nought. **1602** CAREW *Cornwall* 84 All which.. is now growne to nought or nought. *c* **1680** BEVERIDGE *Serm.* (1729) II. 301 Carried away by the next wind that blows and so comes to nought. **1781** COWPER *Conversat.* 403 Recov'ring.. The faculties that seem'd reduc'd to nought. **1869** BROWNING *Ring & Bk.* VII. 902 All human plans and projects come to nought. **1871** FREEMAN *Norm. Conq.* (1876) IV. xviii. 186 Zeal and courage.. brought to nought by.. cowardice.
†**b.** ***to call to nought*** (see NAUGHT *sb.* 1 d). *Obs.*
1738-9 MRS. PENDARVES *Let.* in Mrs. Delany *Life & Corr.* (1861) I. 37 The duchess of Portland.. calls herself all to nought for having been so long in her debt.

4. †**a.** In *gen. sing.* Of no value. *Obs. rare*⁻¹.
c **1205** LAY. 13947 Eoure godes ne beoð nohtes, in helle heo niðer liggeð.
†**b.** ***nought worth***, worth nothing, of no value.
a **1225** *Leg. Kath.* 343 Hwa walde ileuen þis, þet is as noht wurð. *c* **1380** WYCLIF *Sel. Wks.* III. 367 Men sey þat oþer newe ordiris and reulis ben noeʒt worth. *c* **1380** *Abbey Holy Ghost* in *Hampole's Wks.* (1896) I. 323 No werkes þat we wyrke are noghte worthe to god nor spedfull till oure sawles. **1456** SIR G. HAYE *Law Arms* (S.T.S.) 182 It passis his power, and tharfore the obligacioun is nocht worth. **1568** GRAFTON *Chron.* II. 109 That neither Rome can shew any such graunt,.. and if they could it were right nought worth. **1587** GOLDING *De Mornay* xviii. (1592) 288 That thing.. that is giuen for nought, and by such as are nought worth. *c* **1610** BEN JONSON *Barriers* Wks. (1616) 929 Mirrors, though deckt with diamants, are nought worth, If the like formes of things they set not forth.
†**c.** ***a thing of nought***, a mere nothing. *Obs.*
c **1425** LYDG. *Assembly of Gods* 2050 Hit was but a whew, A dreme, a fantasy, and a thyng of nought. **1551** ROBINSON tr. *More's Utopia* I. (1895) 53 They be constrayned to sell it for a thyng of nought. **1587** GOLDING *De Mornay* x. (1592) 137 Seeing that a thing of nought is able to doe so much. **1611** BIBLE *Isa.* xxix. 21 That.. turne aside the iust for a thing of nought. **1743** BLAIR *The Grave* 739 Shrunk to a thing of nought.

5. ***for nought.*** †**a.** ? Nevertheless. *Obs.*⁻¹.
1297 R. GLOUC. (Rolls) 1442 þis romeins were vor noʒt ouercome atte laste.
†**b.** In vain, to no purpose. *Obs.*
c **1290** *St. Kenelm* 101 in *S. Eng. Leg.* I. 348 þo þe luþere quene þat i-sai þat hit was al for nouʒt [etc.]. *a* **1300** *Cursor M.* 7298 'Sir', þai said, 'þou sais for noght'. *c* **1385** CHAUCER *L.G.W.* 2206 *Ariadne*, But all for nought, his wey he is gon. **1430-40** LYDG. *Bochas* IX. xxxi. (1554) 32 b, But al for nought they were so indurate. *c* **1477** CAXTON *Jason* 58 Yet they sent unto the king.., but that was for nought. **1513** DOUGLAS *Æneis* XI. xi. 106 For nocht scho was desyrt with mony a man, And moderis feill.. Desyrit hyr thair gude douchter, in vane. **1596** DALRYMPLE tr. *Leslie's Hist. Scot.* IV. 244 Colman & Finnan oft had admonised him, bot in vane, and al for no^t.
†**c.** Without payment or recompense; gratis.
1535 COVERDALE *Gen.* xxix. 15 Because thou art my brother, shalt thou therfore serue me for nought? **1562** J. HEYWOOD *Prov. & Epigr.* (1867) 138 As good to play for nought, as to woorke for nought. **1671** MILTON *Samson* 1215 To thir Masters gave me up for nought. *a* **1770** JORTIN *Serm.* (1771) I. iv. 65 He would eat no man's bread for nought. **1784** COWPER *Task* I. 675 We travel far, 'tis true, but not for nought; And must be brib'd [etc.].
d. For no reason, without good cause. *rare.*
1607 NORDEN *Surv. Dial.* III. 84 It is spacious in circuit, ..and beareth not the name for nought, for the Manner is faire.

6. ***to set at nought***: to despise, defy, scorn, disregard. So †***to put to nought***; ***to give nought of*** (see GIVE *v.* 9 d).
a **1340** HAMPOLE *Ps.* ix. 33 Halymen sall be despisid þan, and sett att noght. *c* **1375** *Cursor M.* 14459 (Fairf.), Alle þat .. þe iewes sette atte noʒt. *c* **1400** MAUNDEV. (Roxb.) xxxii. 144 All erthely thingez þai sette at noʒt. **1500-20** DUNBAR *Poems* lxxxiv. 5 Setand at nocht God nor manis blame. *Ibid.* xliv. 9 Wo wirth the fruct wald put the tre to nocht. **1534** WHITINTON *Tullyes Offyces* III. (1540) 148 What shal I say of them that setteth all honest and iust thinges at nouʒt? **1634** MILTON *Comus* 444 The huntress Dian.. set at nought The frivolous bolt of Cupid. *a* **1720** SEWEL *Hist. Quakers* (1795) I. IV. 247 The protector.. would have given him audience, had not others set him at nought. **1850** MARSDEN *Early Purit.* (1853) 40 Had she not set at nought the wishes of such men as Jewel, Grindal, Horn, and Parker.

7. With *a* and *pl.* **a.** A thing or person of no worth or value; a mere nothing.
a **1300** *Cursor M.* 16990 Again þe pine he for me drou, bot als a noght it were. *a* **1400-50** *Alexander* 1742 Slike a nekard as þi-selfe, a noʒt of all othire. *c* **1400** *26 Pol. Poems* 21 þis world is a fayre nouʒt, A false lemman. *c* **1560** A. SCOTT *Poems* (S.T.S.) xxxv. 17 Sall non be so off nochtis, no! Quhilk bene of cursit kind. *c* **1590** GREENE *Fr. Bacon* iii, We .. Come to buy needlesse noughts to make vs fine. **1595** SPENSER *Col. Clout* 718 Like bladders blowen up with wynd, That being prickt do vanish into noughts.
†**b.** *pl.* in predicative or adverbial use. *Obs. rare.*
1561 WINʒET *Tractates* Wks. (S.T.S.) I. 21 Quhilk auctoritie geue ʒe esteme as nochtis, be reasoun it wes geuin to ʒow.. be ane papiste bischope. **1589** GREENE *Menaphon* (Arb.) 89 Repentant thoughts Of daies ill spent, for that which profits noughts.
c. *Arith.* A cipher. ***noughts and crosses***: see OUGHT *sb.*[3]
a **1660** HAMMOND *Serm.* Wks. 1684 IV. 379 A defect in the power of numbering, that discerns no difference between Ciphers and Millions, but only that the noughts are a little the blacker. **1718, 1801** [see CIPHER *sb.* 1]. **1839-52** BAILEY *Festus* 11 The spheres themselves are but as shining noughts Upon the mantle of the night impearled. **1889** *Spectator* 26 Oct., A majority so elected is but a series of noughts intended to elevate the power of one. **1894** K. GRAHAME *Pagan P.* 140 True, noughts-and-crosses might be indulged in.

8. a. Low estate and poverty. *rare*⁻¹.
c **1400** *Brut* (E.E.T.S.) 216 A Knyght þat þe Erl had brouʒt vp of nouʒt.
b. Worthless character or conduct.
c **1400** *26 Pol. Poems* 27 ʒe, þouʒ þou be of feble fame, Bere good visage, þy nouʒt aspye. **1586** A. DAY *Eng. Secretary* II. (1625) 31 To relieve such an one.. in bringing him from nought to ought. **1622** W. WHATELY *Gods Husb.* II. 136 We shall grow worse and worse, euen from ought to nought, as the Prouerbe speaketh. **1651** C. CARTWRIGHT *Cert. Relig.* I. 4 Else you'll fall from nought to worse, from thence to nothing.
†**c.** ***to do nought***, to do wrong. ***to play the nought***, to act immorally. *Obs.*
1538 STARKEY *England* I. i. 6, I wyl not yet say.. that therin they dyd vtturly nought. **1565** *Child Marriages* 129 The said Thomas Grenehalgh had plaid the nought with the said Jone, in the house of the said Margaret, her mother.

9. *Comb.*, as ***nought-availing, -fearing, -worth.***

1589 NASHE *Anat. Absurd.* Wks. (Grosart) I. 44 Least he ..make a nought worth peeble his Jewell. **1591** FLORIO *2nd Fruites* 127 A counterfaite, lazie, and nought-worth seruant. *a* **1591** H. SMITH *Wks.* (1867) II. 237 These nought-fearing fellows, these high-stomached men, .. are brought down by danger. **1613** DRUMM. OF HAWTH. *Cypress Grove* Wks. (1711) 118 With unprofitable and nought-availing Stubbornness.

B. *adj.* [Cf. NAUGHT *a.*, which is the more usual form.]

†**1. a.** Of material things: Bad in condition or in their own kind. *Obs.*

1387 TREVISA *Higden* (Rolls) I. 51 As a sore membre þat is nouȝt from membres þat beeþ hole and sounde. **1402** HOCCLEVE *Lett. Cupid* 321 The soyl ys noght, ther may no trouthe growe! **1496** *Fysshynge w. Angle* (1883) 32 Whan they ben in a slough or elles deed thenne ben they nought. *c* **1540** *Plumpton Corr.* (Camden) 239 The cofer wherin your said court rowles lieth is nought & the lock therof not worth a pene. **1577** B. GOOGE *Heresbach's Husb.* I. (1586) 44 With continuall bearing of Hey, it hath growen to be mossie and nought. **1611** BIBLE *2 Kings* ii. 19 The water is nought, and the ground barren. **1693** EVELYN *De la Quint. Compl. Gard.* I. 38 All that is nought in the Ground must of necessity be removed. **1704** SWIFT *Batt. Bks.* Misc. (1711) 237 'Tis too plain, the Materials are nought. **1728** E. SMITH *Compl. Housew.* (1750) 5 If [the egg is] muddy or cloudy, and the yolk broken, it is nought.

†**b.** Of actions, etc.: Bad, wicked. *Obs.*

a **1425** *Cursor M.* 14459 (Trin.), Alle þat he wiþ loue hem souȝt þe iewes entent was euer nouȝt. **1481** CAXTON *Myrr.* III. xxi. 181 That synne is nought, ffor as moche as it is voyde and disgarnysshed of all goodnes. **1531** ELYOT *Gov.* (1580) 180 If the purpose be noughte he can not.. hope to obtain it. **1598** GRENEWEY *Tacitus, Ann.* VI. ix. (1622) 134 A people not vnderstanding what is good, nor hauing a care of that which is nought. **1607** J. DAVIES *Summa Totalis* vi. Wks. (Grosart) I. 5/2 Hate, Anger, and the like, in vs are nought, But in thee good, and iust.

†**c.** Immoral, vicious. *Obs.*

1388–9 in *Wyclif's Sel. Wks.* III. 488 þo hoore-hows þat alle men knowen is nouȝt. **1513** MORE *Rich. III* (1883) 53 She was nought of her body. **1526** *Pilgr. Perf.* (W. de W. 1531) 30 b, Many dyd myracles that were nought of lyuyng, as the enchauntours of Pharao. **1550** BALE *Eng. Votaries* I. (1560) 96 Callynge them all that nought was.

2. Good for nothing, worthless, useless.

c **1400** *Apol. Loll.* 28 þat is no power, but fals pride, & presumid, & onli in name, & as to ȝend & effect is nowȝt. **1483** *Vulgaria* 33 Thow kunnest me no thanke, therfore thow art nought to do fore. *c* **1535** M. NISBET *Prol. Rom.* (S.T.S.) III. 347 That ande all lyk argumentes ar nocht. **1550** CROWLEY *Epigr.* 1410 A wryter of thynges nought and vayne. **1615** BRATHWAIT *Strappado* (1878) 132 Thou mun not blush, nor colour change for ought, Though th' plea thou hast in hand be nere so nought. **1658** A. FOX tr. *Würtz' Surg.* II. i. 47 Experience, that great Teacher, tels us to be nought, at all times to undertake for health. **1790** *Borrowdale Lett.* (1821) 14 Hees fearful nowt I racken.

†**3.** Injurious *to*, bad *for*, a thing or person. Also without const. *Obs.*

1532 HERVET *Xenophon Œcon.* (1768) 2, I do not accompte that amonge a mans.. goodes, that is nought and hurtful vnto him. **1578** LYTE *Dodoens* 639 Garlyke is hurtfull and nought for cholerique people. **1658** A. FOX tr. *Würtz' Surg.* II. i. 49 A Surgeon.. may easily know.. what is good or nought for the Wound. **1690** CHILD *Disc. Trade* (1698) 111, I conclude.. that all restrictions of trade are nought, and consequently that no company.. can be for publick good.

4. *at nought feet*: in *Aeronaut.*, very close to the ground, just above the ground.

1945 *Aeroplane Spotter* 20 Sept. 218/1 Other note-worthy flying displays were given by the Messenger I, showing off its manœuvrability at nought feet. **1949** F. MACLEAN *Eastern Approaches* III. vi. 372 A large three-engined German flying boat.. scared the life out of our cook by skimming past our house at what is known by the R.A.F. as 'nought feet'. **1960** *Observer* 17 Jan. 9/6 If there were an emergency at 'nought feet' the airmen could not afford the precious seconds needed to jettison the cockpit canopy normally.

C. *adv.* [Orig. the accusative of the *sb.*]

1. To no extent; in no way; not at all.

c **825** *Vesp. Psalter* lxxxviii. 23 Nowiht fromað se fiond in him. **971** *Blickl. Hom.* 119 Hie seoþþan.. him nowiht fore ne ondredon. *a* **1225** *Leg. Kath.* 2103 'Alle þine þreates ne drede ich', quoð ha, 'riht noht'. *a* **1250** *Prov. Ælfred* 284 in *O.E. Misc.* 120 þeyh heo wel wolde, ne may heo hi nowiht welde. *c* **1275** LAY. 25632 Ne dorste þar no cniht to vuele hit teorne no wiht. **1381** in *Wyclif's Sel. Wks.* III. 500 Bodely etyng ne profites nouth to soule. **1413** *Pilgr. Sowle* (Caxton) v. i. (1859) 68 Me semyd that wonder lytel or nought my peynes were abredged. **1503** HAWES *Examp. Virt.* IX. 168 Where I am poore and sette by nought. **1568** TILNEY *Disc. Mariage* B iv b, But vertues are laide aside, and nought accounted off. **1590** SPENSER *F.Q.* II. iv. 7 As a blindfold Bull, at randon fares, And where he hits nought knowes, and whom he hurts nought cares.

1828 *Sporting Mag.* XXI. 232 'It matters nout', as the Yorkshire men have it. **1870** MORRIS *Earthly Par.* II. III. 127 Never complaining; resting nought, And yet scarce asking what he sought. **1887** —— *Odyss.* XI. 363 Odysseus, nought do we deem thee.. To be a cheat.

†**2.** = NOT *adv.* *Obs.*

β. *c* **825** *Vesp. Psalter* xlii. 1 Doem mec, god, & toscad intingan minne of ðeode noht haliȝre. *c* **897** K. ÆLFRED *Gregory's Past. C.* xxxi. 206 Næron ȝe noht æmettiȝe, ðeah ȝe wel ne dyden. **971** *Blickl. Hom.* 171 Ne þurfan ȝe noht besorȝian hwæt ȝe sprecan. *c* **1131** *O.E. Chron.* (Laud MS.) an. 1131, On þa tun þa wæs tenn ploȝes.. ne belæf þær noht an. *c* **1200** ORMIN 11343 Nohht ne maȝȝ þe mann Bi bræd all ane libbenn. *c* **1250** *Kent. Serm.* in *O.E. Misc.* 29 Ha niste nocht þe miracle, ac þo serganz wel hit wiste. *a* **1300** *Cursor M.* 15315 Noth fete allan, bot hefd and hand. *c* **1340** HAMPOLE *Pr. Consc.* 605 Man when he is til worshepe broght Right understandyng has he noght. *c* **1400** *Laud Troy Bk.* 5903 He that wil not whan he may, When he wolde, he getis it noght. **1473** WARKW. *Chron.* (Camden) 2 Thei durst noȝt come neghe the castelle. **1533** GAU *Richt Vay* 4 Thay.. suld noth be slayne. *Ibid.* 14 Thay yat bannis or wil notht heir thaime. **1571** *Satir. Poems Reform.* xxvi. 5 ȝe neid nocht for to feir The craft.. of man. **1615** SIR W. MURE *Misc. Poems* xiii. Wks. (S.T.S.) I. 31 Bereft of breath, ȝit nocht from lyfe depoised. [**1724** RAMSAY *Vision* xiii, It's nocht fit an mortal man Should ken all I can tell.]

Comb. **1569** *Reg. Privy Council Scot.* II. 17 The absence and noc[h]t comperance of the saidis personis.

γ. *c* **1275** *Passion our Lord* 36 in *O.E. Misc.* 38 He nuste nouht þat he wes boþe god and mon. *c* **1315** SHOREHAM I. 1835 Ine þe weddynge ne gaynet nouȝt þaȝ þon þe oþer byswyke. **1390** GOWER *Conf.* I. 3 The cause whi it changeth so It needeth nought to specifie. **1411** *Rolls of Parlt.* III. 650/1 The sayd Robert wold nouht graunte that he had submytted hym in that mater. *c* **1470** HARDING *Chron.* Pref. p. vi, He wolde nought suffre I had such waryson.

δ. *c* **1205** LAY. 298 þat bearn nas nowit feie. *a* **1225** *Ancr. R.* 28 ȝif þu ne const nout ðesne, seie summe oðer of ðe creoiz. *a* **1300** *Vox & Wolf* 153 in Hazl. *E.P.P.* I. 63 Ne beth nout ȝet thre daies a-go. **1388–9** in *Wyclif's Sel. Wks.* III. 479 If ȝee wil nout do þis riȝtwisenes. *a* **1400** *Pol. Rel. & L. Poems* 259, I am þi broþer, be nout in wer; be nout agast. **1475** *Paston Lett.* III. 123 Robard Clere.. told me that he was nowt payd of the mony that.. was borowd of hys modyr.

†**3.** In the phrases ***nought (for) than, for thi, for that***, nevertheless. Also NOUGHTWITHSTANDING.

c **1250** *Kent. Serm.* in *O.E. Misc.* 36 Nocht for þan.. ne solde no-man targi for to wende to godalmichti. **1297** R. GLOUC. (Rolls) 4015 þe king clupede noȝt uor þan is conseil sone. **13..** *Cursor M.* 8345 (Gött.), Bot noght for-þi ne tald he noght þe bod-word. *c* **1375** *Sc. Leg. Saints* iii. (*Andrew*) 465 Nocht-þane, bot þu consent to me, .. I sal ger mene þe crucify. **1413** *Pilgr. Sowle* (Caxton) II. lvii. (1859) 56 But nought for thy, blessid be his grace. **1422** tr. *Secreta Secret., Priv. Priv.* 225 And noght for that they bene moste febill of body. *Ibid.* 239 In tymes.. al þe body of man is hote, and noȝth for than the stomake is colde. **1456** SIR G. HAYE *Law Arms* (S.T.S.) 107 And ȝit, nocht than thai graunt that the Emperour is temporale lord.

†**nought**, *v.* *Obs. rare.* [f. prec.]

1. *trans.* To set (one) at nought.

a **1400–50** *Alexander* 753 'For þou has noȝtid me now, Nicollas', he sayd, 'I swere þe' [etc.]. *c* **1440** *Promp. Parv.* 360/1 Nowtun, or syettyn at nowhte.., *vilipendo.*

2. *refl.* To efface (oneself).

a **1400** HYLTON *Scala Perf.* II. xx. (Bodl. MS.) lf. 114 And soþeli vnto a soule kan felabli þoruȝ grace nouȝten him silf.. he is not perfytli meke. *c* **1450** tr. *De Imitatione* III. xlvii. 118 Yf þou coudist parfitly nouȝt [L. *annihilare*] þiself & voide þiself from all loue of creatures.

†**'noughtihood.** *Obs. rare*⁻¹. [f. NOUGHTY *a.* + -HOOD.] Wickedness.

1536 *Pilgrim's T.* 303 in Thynne *Animadv.* (1875) 85 Fyndis in hell full of dissention, dothe extoll ther awn noghtihod aboue all that is called god.

†**'noughtily**, *adv.* *Obs. rare.* [f. as prec. + -LY[2].] Badly; in a bad or evil manner.

c **1550** CHEKE *Matt.* xxi. 41 He wil destroie.. y^ees^ noughti men noughtili. *a* **1569** KINGESMYLL *Confl. w. Satan* (1578) 6 They were noughtily done though they seemed never so good. **1597** A. M. tr. *Guillemeau's Fr. Chirurg.* 55/1 A heade noughtilye formed.

†**'noughtiness.** *Obs. rare.* [f. as prec. + -NESS.] **a.** Nothingness, worthlessness, vileness. **b.** Badness, wickedness.

c **1425** tr. *T. à Kempis' Consol.* III. ix, Al maner estimacion, be it neuer so litel, shal be drouned in þe valey of my nouȝtines [L. *nihileitas*]. **1526** *Pilgr. Perf.* (W. de W. 1531) 270 b, The more they se theyr owne noughtynesse, and thinketh themselfe more and more vyle. **1551** TURNER *Herbal* I. (1568) 38 It may be the noughtines of the place may wonderfully minish the operation of the herbe. **1577** B. GOOGE *Heresbach's Husb.* I. (1586) 15 It is very necessarie for them sometimes to recreate them selues, so that.. they geue not them selues to noughtinesse.

†**'noughting**, *sb.* *Obs. rare*⁻¹. [f. NOUGHT *sb.* + -ING[3].] A worthless or insignificant person.

c **1440** MYRC *Festial* (E.E.T.S.) 201 Mony a byge and a strong I haue ouercom, and now suche a noȝtyng haþe getyn þe maystry, and putte me vndyr her fote.

†**'noughting**, *vbl. sb.* *Obs.* [f. NOUGHT *v.* + -ING[1].] Depreciation, scorn; effacement.

a **1225** *Ancr. R.* 426 Hwon his blowinge ne geineð nout, þeonne bringeð he up sum luðer word, oðer sum nouhtunge hwar þuruh heo to-hurteð eiðer urommard oðer. *c* **1230** *Hali Meid.* 9 [Thou shalt] se ofte beon imaket arm of an eðeliche mon.. for noht oðer nohtunge. *a* **1400** HYLTON *Scala Perf.* (W. de W. 1494) II. xxvi, And casten hemself downe vnder god by noughtynge of hemself. **1926** A. E. TAYLOR *Plato* ix. 225 The 'noughting' and remaking of the soul is the greatest business of life.

†**'noughtly**, *adv.* *Obs. rare.* Also 1 nohtlice, 4 noght-, 6 noughtely. [f. NOUGHT *a.* + -LY[2].] **a.** Wickedly, wrongly. **b.** Badly, poorly.

c **825** *Vesp. Psalter* xxxvi. 8–9 Blin from eorre & forlet hatheortnisse; ne elna ðu þætte nohtlice ðu doe. Forðon ða nohtlice doð biað abreotte. *c* **1400** *Cursor M.* 27574 (Cott. Galba), Of þam we suld noghtly late, for of þaire gude werkes noght we wate. **1502** *Ord. Crysten Men* (W. de W. 1506) IV. vi, Moche better is it to examyn one or two unto saluacyon, than twenty and foure noughtelye. **1551** TURNER *Herbal* 143 It is not harde to be digested, if it be not corrupted before. And that chanceth vnto it when it is noughtely dressed. **1594** WEST *2nd Pt. Symbol.* §163 Whereby his mind is corrupted and made worse to do or attempt anything noughtly.

†**noughtwithstanding** (nocht-, noght-, nouȝt, etc.), obs. var. of NOTWITHSTANDING.

c **1360** in Horstm. *Altengl. Leg.* (1881) 11 Noght-withstanding þat he was ȝing, He chastyd his flesch with fasting. **1386** *Rolls of Parlt.* III. 225/1 Noughtwithstondyng the same fredam or fraunchise, Nichol Brembre.. was chosen Mair. **1413** *Pilgr. Sowle* (Caxton) I. xx. (1859) 21 Ne woldest thou neuer byleue, nouȝtwithstandynge that I haue put al my power. **1426** *Paston Lett.* I. 25 Nought with stondyng that I herde nevere of this matier.., yet I made an appell. **1533** BELLENDEN *Livy* II. xiii. (S.T.S.) I. 179 The small pepill, nochtwithstanding þat þis valerius was create dictator [etc.]. **1596** DALRYMPLE tr. *Leslie's Hist. Scot.* Prol. 5 The are nochtwithstanding [is] sumthing thiker, and mae cloudes.

'noughty, *a.* *Obs.* exc. *Sc.* Forms: 4 noȝt-, 5–6 nowght-, nought-, 6 *Sc.* nochth-, 7– *Sc.* nocht-, 4– noughty; also 5–6 -i, 6 -ie, -ye. [f. NOUGHT *sb.* + -Y: cf. NAUGHTY *a.*]

†**1.** Of actions, etc.: Bad, immoral, wicked. *Obs.*

13.. *E.E. Allit. P.* B. 1359 Hit is not innoghe to þe nice al noȝty þink [= thing] vse, Bot if alle þe worlde wyt his wykked dedes. **1450–80** tr. *Secreta Secret.* 14 Leue þe noughti lyf of bestis that euyr lyve in filthis. **1533** MORE *Debell. Salem* i. Wks. 931/2 Of many noughti thinges I touch there but a fewe, and suche as were in no wise to be dissembled. **1541** *Act 33 Hen. VIII*, c. 21 §1 A woman, whiche was priuie to hir noughtie life before. **1603** J. DAVIES (Heref.) *Microcos.* xxxv. Wks. (Grosart) I. 26/2 Sin, noughty Nothing that mak'st all things nought.

†**2.** Of persons: Abject, worthless, vile, bad.

c **1395** *Plowman's Tale* III. 1097 And they were noughty, foule, and horowe, To worship god men wolde wlate. **1461** *Paston Lett.* II. 26 Be ware howe ye ryd or go, for nowgty and evyll desposyd felacheps. **1477** EARL RIVERS (Caxton) *Dictes* 24 Yf he geue by wil to noughty folkis.. it puteth aweye the courage of his goode seruauntis. *a* **1529** SKELTON *Agst. Scottes* 56 Ye for to sende such a citacion, It shameth all your noughty nacion. **1563** GOOGE *Eglogs* vii. (Arb.) 79 Let noughtye men saye what they lyst to the[e].

Comb. **1553** T. WILSON *Rhet.* (1580) 121 It is a folie to suffer the fome of a horse, or the strikyng of his foote, and not abide any thyng that a foole doeth, or a noughtie disposed fellowe speaketh.

†**b.** ***noughty pack*** = NAUGHTY PACK. *Obs.*

1526 *Pilgr. Perf.* (W. de W. 1531) 37 b, Al though they be wretched lyuers & noughty packes amonge. **1553** T. WILSON *Rhet.* (1580) 140 Euery one thinketh it a better and a meter deede, to punishe noughtie packes, then to scoffe at their euill demeanour.

3. Of things: **a.** Good for nothing; worthless or of little worth; also in mod. *Sc.*, insignificant, trifling.

1508 FISHER *7 Penit. Ps.* cii. Wks. (1876) 198 Syth he hath gyuen vnto this noughty worlde so many grete pleasures. **1551** TURNER *Herbal* 141 That whiche is.. sharpe or rough or darke and full of asshes.. is greuous and noughty. **1655** *Sess. Rec. Lesmahagow, Ann.* viii. (1864) 128 Ye Session taking into y^r^ consideration that Mr Thomas' school has been very nochtie. **1835** WEBSTER *Rhymes* 203 When he lifts his mole-like een, With a nochty nose between. **1882** W. ALEXANDER *Ain Folk* 101 The farmers did not wish to have a Highland cow, and the coupers who passed sneered at it as a 'nochty beastie'.

†**b.** In bad condition; of a bad kind. *Obs.*

1541 COPLAND *Guydon's Quest. Chirurg.* O ij b, They that .. be rotten, and founde in noughty waters be daungerous. **1578** LYTE *Dodoens* 361 The same put into the holes of corrupt and noughtie teeth, swageth the tooth-ache. **1657** S. PURCHAS *Pol. Flying-Ins.* II. 296 They may not after build upon a rotten, noughty, or weake foundation.

nouȝwhere, obs. f. NOWHERE.

nouh, ought not: see OWE *v.*

nouice, -iciat, obs. ff. NOVICE, -ICIATE.

‖**nouille** (nuj). [Fr.] = NOODLE *sb.*[2] Usu. in *pl.* Also (in *sing.*) *attrib.*, as ***nouille paste***.

1845 E. ACTON *Mod. Cookery* i. 6 (*heading*) To make nouilles;.. Wet, with the yolks of four eggs, as much fine, dry, and sifted flour as will make them into a firm but very smooth paste. *Ibid.* 13 Make into nouille paste the yolks of four fresh eggs. **1938** *Times Lit. Suppl.* 9 July p. iii/1 Excursions to Soho to buy the authentic *nouilles* and the right kind of cheeses. **1960** *Good Housek. Cookery Bk.* (rev. ed.) 266/1 (*heading*) Noodles (Nouilles).

nouite(e, obs. ff. NOVITY.

nouke, noul, obs. ff. NOOK, NOLL.

†**nould**, would not: see NILL *v.* *Obs.*

1579 SPENSER *Sheph. Cal.* Feb. 192 The good man noulde stay his leasure. **1596** DANETT tr. *Comines* Ep. Ded. (1614) p. iii, Would I nould I, to the presse the booke must go. **1642** H. MORE *Song Soul* I. I. xxxviii, Then they.. desired, That he nould break this happy union. [**1742** SHENSTONE *Schoolmistr.* xv, Simple faith.. That nould on wooden image place her creed.]

noule, noult, obs. forms of NOLL, NOLT.

noumber, -bre, -bur, obs. ff. NUMBER *sb.*

noumbles, -buls, obs. ff. NUMBLES.

noumbrable, -brary, obs. ff. NUMBERABLE, -BRARY.

noumeite ('nu:mi:aɪt). *Min.* Also **noumeaite, numeite.** [From its locality, *Noumea* in New Caledonia.] A variety of garnierite.

1874 *Sidney Herald* 29 Sept., Noumeite. **1881** *Nature* XXV. 45 Some minerals from New Caledonia, including the nickel-bearing Noumeaite. **1894** *Min. Mag.* V. 193 The Oregon nickel is found in two varieties.., Garnierite and Noumeite.

noumenal ('nu:mənəl, 'naʊ-), *a.* [f. NOUMEN-ON + -AL[1]. So F. *nouménal*.] Relating to, consisting of, noumena; that can only be apprehended by intuition; not phenomenal.

1803 *Edin. Rev.* I. 262 Himself, however, the sole exception in nature, he knows in objective noumenal reality. **1830** COLERIDGE *Lett.* (1895) 755 Some other term must be used as the antithet to phenomenal, perhaps noumenal. **1862** SPENCER *First Princ.* II. iii. §46 (1875) 159 Contrasting it with a noumenal existence which we imagine. *a* **1881** A. BARRATT *Phys. Metempiric* (1883) 25 The extension of a noumenal fact beyond the limits of our own individual noumenon.

Hence **noume'nality**; **'noumenalize** *v.*

1872 *Contemp. Rev.* XX. 822 He phenomenalizes the old Ding-an-sich merely to noumenalize the Concepts and the law of Contradiction. *a* **1881** BARRATT *Phys. Metempiric* (1883) 36 'Outside' losing its former meaning of externality in space and acquiring the new meaning of Noumenality.

noumenalism ('nu:mənəlɪz(ə)m, 'naʊ-). [f. NOUMENAL *a.* + -ISM.] = NOUMENISM.

1902 *Encycl. Brit.* XXX. 679/2 Fechner regarded every composite body as the appearance of a spirit;..This noumenalism would not do for Lewes. **1926** J. E. TURNER *Theory Direct Realism* 22 Noumenalism, meaning by this term that the character and existence of the real physical world are essentially different from and independent of the existence and attributes of sensed content.

noumenalist ('nu:mənəlɪst, 'naʊ-). [f. as prec. + -IST.] A believer in noumenalism. Also *attrib.* or as *adj.*

1904 G. S. FULLERTON *Syst. Metaphysics* v. 88 The hypostatized abstractions of the noumenalist and the neo-Kantian. **1925** J. E. TURNER *Theory Direct Realism* 8 The term 'Direct' is intended to imply further the complete absence of any representative or noumenalist factors in the process and object of perception.

'noumenally, *adv.* [f. NOUMENAL *a.* + -LY[2].] In a noumenal aspect; as regards noumena.

1858 SPENCER *Ess.* I. 27 That we can comprehend such cause noumenally considered is not to be supposed. **1882** *Athenæum* 27 May 664/1 Kant had made the will phenomenally determined, but noumenally free.

'noumenism. *nonce-wd.* [f. next + -ISM.] A philosophical system dealing with, or based on, noumena.

1865 J. GROTE *Explor. Philos.* I. 182 All this is entirely different from the notion of an unknowable noumenism with which phænomenism (as I here on purpose write it) is contrasted.

noumenon ('nu:mənɒn, 'naʊ-). *Metaph.* Pl. **noumena.** [ad. Gr. νοούμενον, neut. of the pres. pple. pass. of νοεῖν to apprehend, conceive; introduced by Kant in contrast to *phenomenon*.] In the philosophy of Kant: An object of purely intellectual intuition, devoid of all phenomenal attributes.

1796 F. A. NITSCH *Gen. View Kant's Princ. concerning Man* 118 The conception we have of the world of Noumena, contains no knowledge of that world, but is a mere conception of demarkation [i.e. *Grenzbegriff*, or limiting concept]. **1798** W. TAYLOR in *Monthly Rev.* XXV. 585 The phænomena of beauty, with respect to him [*sc.* Kant], rank among the noumena. **1803** *Edin. Rev.* I. 267 We will admit to the transcendentalist his solitary noumenon and its separate functions. **1867** LEWES *Hist. Philos.* (ed. 3) II. 485 The peculiar merit of his doctrine is held to be that he distinguishes Phenomena from things in themselves, or Noumena. **1877** CAIRD *Philos. Kant* II. xiii. 498 In a negative sense, a noumenon would be an object not given in sensuous perception; in a positive sense, a noumenon would be an object given in a non-sensuous, i.e. an intellectual perception. **1967** *Listener* 27 July 123/3 It was a revelation, a vision of the noumenon..and I fear that—for quite a long time—we will glory in the sensuous bliss of it all and become uncritical of the human content.

noumer, obs. form of NUMBER.

noumeracioun, obs. form of NUMERATION.

†**noumpere.** *Obs.* Forms: 4–5 **nounper, -pier;** 4 **noumpere,** 5 **nowmper(e, -powre;** 4 **nompere, -peyr.** [a. OF. *nonper, nomper*, f. *non-* NON- + *per, pair* PEER.] The original form of UMPIRE.

1362 LANGL. *P. Pl.* A. v. 181 Til Robyn þe Ropere weore ..nempned for a noumpere þat no de-bat neore. *a* **1420** BIBLE (Wycl.) IV. 302 And while thei stryuen thus, the apostil putte him bitwene as a mene, distruynge alle her qwestiouns, as a good noumpere. **1424** *Paston Lett.* I. 14 The decree and jugement of a nounpier to be chosen by the same arbitrores. **1435** *Plumpton Corr.* (Camden) p. li, That the said award & ordinance of the said Nowmper be made be the feast of the Nativity. *c* **1440** *Promp. Parv.* 360 Nowmpere, or owmpere,..*arbiter, sequester*.

noun (naʊn). *Gram.* Forms: 4–7 **nowne** (7 **nown**), 6–7 **noune,** 7– **noun.** [a. AF. *noun*, OF. *nun, num, non, nom*:—L. *nōmen* name.]

1. a. A word used as the name or designation of a person or thing (cf. sense 2). In older grammars also including the adjective (cf. sense 3) and occas. the pronoun.

1398 TREVISA *Barth. De. P.R.* VIII. xxviii. (Bodl. MS.), Lux and lumen is liȝt in Englissche, butt in latine is difference bitwene þilke twey nownes. *c* **1430** *Art Nombryng* 19 And tweyn nombres schal be tokenyde be a nowne. **1483** *Cath. Angl.* 257/1 A Nowne, *nomen*. **1530** BAYNTON in Palsgr. Introd. p. xiii, Be it nowne, verbe, adverbe, or any other parte of speche. **1586** W. WEBBE *Eng. Poetrie* (Arb.) 63 Placing the verbe out of his order, and too farre behinde the nowne. *c* **1620** A. HUME *Brit. Tongue* (1865) 27 A personal word is a noun or a verb. A noun is a word of one person with gender and case. **1651** HOBBES *Leviath.* III. xxxvi. 222 A part of Speech, such as Grammarians call a Nown. **1725** WATTS *Logic* I. vi. §8 It would be very ridiculous..to divide a book..into nouns and pronouns. **1784** COWPER *Tiroc.* 619 No nourishment to feed his growing mind, But conjugated verbs and nouns declin'd? **1844** EMERSON *Nature, Language*, Children and savages use only nouns or names of things, which they convert into verbs. **1894** LINDSAY *Latin Lang.* 369 The proneness of nouns to take a new gender by analogy of a noun which had a similar termination.

†**b.** An adjective. *Obs. rare.*

1657 C. HOOLE *Rudim. Lat. Gram.* 99 Nouns of the Comparative and Superlative degree, being put partitively .., require a Genitive case.

c. *attrib.* and *Comb.* ***noun-adjunct, -complement, -compound, -equivalent, -group, -modifier, phrase, -stem; noun-forming, -like*** adjs.; **noun-adjective** *a.*, of or pertaining to the relationship between a noun and an adjective.

1963 *Times Lit. Suppl.* 22 Mar. 193/4 The English *noun-adjective relationship..as in 'church'—'ecclesiastical'. **1962** H. A. GLEASON in Householder & Saporta *Probl. Lexicogr.* 93 Among the nouns is a considerable subclass including, *United States*,.. *Hague*,... These are..always preceded by *the* except in *noun-adjunct position. **1964** C. BARBER *Ling. Change Present-Day Eng.* v. 121 The tendency of *economy* used as noun-adjunct to develop the meaning of 'large'... The largest packet is frequently called 'economy size'. **1963** F. T. VISSER *Hist. Syntax Eng. Lang.* I. iv. 624 The adoption of numerous French verbs which were construed with *à* before a *noun-complement. **1966** *English Studies* XLVII. 51 Concerning the noun-complement the author discusses two points. **1914** L. BLOOMFIELD in C. F. Hockett *Leonard Bloomfield Anthol.* (1970) 67 Any one who reads Brugmann's section on *noun-compounds..will be impressed by the endless deviations..of composition-stems from independent words. **1965** J. E. CROSS in *English Studies* XLVI. 108 Such noun-compounds having *wulf* as the second element are used simply of warriors to express the idea that they are anxious to fight and kill. **1935** *Jrnl. Eng. & Gmc. Philol.* XXXIV. 416 All that the primaries.. have in common is their noun character; it would be simpler and clearer to call them nouns and *noun-equivalents. **1954** PEI & GAYNOR *Dict. Ling.* 149 *Noun-equivalent*, a word (pronoun, participle, adjective) or group of words used in the sense and function of a noun. **1963** F. T. VISSER *Hist. Syntax Eng. Lang.* I. iv. 410 The direct object might be defined as the (pro)noun or noun-equivalent not preceded by a preposition. **1875** WHITNEY *Life Lang.* vii. 123 There are *noun-forming suffixes. **1871** EARLE *Philol. Eng. Tongue* (1887) 305 All the words which we shall include in the *noun-group are essentially presentive. **1935** G. K. ZIPF *Psycho-Biol. of Lang.* (1936) v. 31 Not all languages make, say, *noun-like and verb-like distinctions. **1958** C. F. HOCKETT *Course Mod. Ling.* xxvi. 222 A few stems which show no inflection show syntactical behavior so nounlike that we class them as nouns. **1971** D. CRYSTAL *Ling.* 92 We may have isolated a few noun-like words. **1955** QUIRK & WRENN *Old Eng. Gram.* iii. 68 (*heading*) *Noun modifiers and pronouns. *Ibid.* iv. 109 An example of a common noun-modifier is *and*——, which has the force of 'opposite' or 'corresponding to'. **1958** W. N. FRANCIS *Struct. Amer. Eng.* vi. 298 Nouns appear very frequently as heads of structures of modification. The modifiers in such structures may belong to any of the four parts of speech... The most common noun-modifier is the adjective. **1964** C. BARBER *Ling. Change Present-Day Eng.* vii. 147 In the phrase *an old grey stone wall*,.. we have the headword *wall* and as noun-modifiers the adjectives *old* and *grey*. **1951** *Mind* LX. 425 A *noun-phrase used predicatively. **1965** N. CHOMSKY *Aspects of Theory of Syntax* ii. 63 *Frighten the boy* is a Verb Phrase ..consisting of the Verb..*frighten* and the Noun Phrase ..*the boy*. **1973** *Amer. Speech* 1970 XLV. 133 The grammatical transformation..operates so as to convert the noun phrase that follows the verb into the derived subject. **1935** G. K. ZIPF *Psycho-Biol. of Lang.* (1936) iv. 166 The number of different *verb-stems* and *noun-stems* which enter into compounds far surpasses the number of available prefixes which may be used in compounds. **1957** R. W. ZANDVOORT *Handbk. Eng. Gram.* IX. i. 278 Sometimes combinations of genitive + noun and of noun-stem + noun exist side by side: *a large schoolboy hand*. **1973** *Archivum Linguisticum* IV. 37 The premiss that a noun-stem has an inherent gender.

2. ***noun substantive*** = sense 1. Cf. SUBSTANTIVE.

1509 HAWES *Past. Pleas.* v. (Percy Soc.) 24 A nowne substantyve Might stand wythout helpe of an adjectyve. **1530** PALSGR. *Introd.* 24 Nownes substantives have thre chefe accidentes, gender, nombre, and parson. **1612** BRINSLEY *Lud. Lit.* 133 If the childe but knowe his word to be like any of the examples of a Nown Substantiue,..he knoweth it to be a Nown Substantiue. **1696** LORIMER *Rem. Goodwin's Disc.* ix. 179 The one halfe of it, the Nown Substantive, *Law*, is expresly in Scripture. **1779** SHERIDAN *Critic* II. ii, You have trope, figure, and metaphor, as plenty as noun-substantives. **1832** MARRYAT *N. Forster* xxi, There is no talking with noun substantives only. **1843** *Proc. Philol. Soc.* I. 63 The institution of nouns substantive, would probably be one of the first steps towards the formation of language.

fig. **1705** HICKERINGILL *Priest-cr.* IV. (1721) 215 The true Church of England..is a Noun-substantive that can stand by it self. **1741** *Pol. Ballads* (1860) II. 267 So I by myself can Noun Substantive stand, Impose on my Owners, and save my own Land.

3. ***noun adjective*** = ADJECTIVE B. Also *fig.*

1530 PALSGR. *Introd.* 27 Nownes adjectives have..thre chefe accidentes, gendre, nombre, and comparation. **1608** BRETON *Div. Consid.* Wks. (Grosart) II. 18/1 Naked and feeble like a nowne adiectiue that cannot stand alone. **1668** WILKINS *Real Charact.* III. i. §7 The true genuine sense of a Noun Adjective..imports this general notion, of Pertaining to. **1705** HICKERINGILL *Priest-cr.* I. (1721) 36 Christian Government is a Noun-Adjective, and cannot stand by it self, without such Adjutants. **1786** H. TOOKE *Purley* II. vi, What is an Adjective? I dare not call it Noun Adjective. **1876** KENNEDY *Pub. Sch. Lat. Gram.* (ed. 4) §15. **1930** W. EMPSON *Seven Types Ambiguity* viii. 300 Here we have the English language..given particular meaning by noun-adjectives in apposition.

attrib. and *Comb.* *a* **1628** F. GREVIL *Life Sidney* (1907) 107 The Nown-adjective-natured Princes, and subjects of this time. *Ibid.* 166 The Noune adjective nature of this superstitious Princesse.

Hence **'nouning** *vbl. sb.*, using words as nouns; **'nounless** *a.*, having no nouns; **'nounship,** status as a noun. *nonce-wds.*

1757 MRS. GRIFFITH *Lett. Henry & Frances* (1767) IV. 60 As to the Nouning and Verbing, which he so heavily charged you with. **1858** J. ROBERTSON *Poems* 80 The eternal, unambiguous speech, The nounless, verbless tongue. **1890** *Cassell's Fam. Mag.* Apr. 315/2 The parent noun, *while*, whose nounship is denied by some grammarians.., can only get employment as an adverb.

nounal ('naʊnəl), *a.* [f. prec. + -AL[1].] Of the nature or quality of a noun. Also, of an author's style: containing many nouns.

1871 EARLE *Philol. Eng. Tongue* vii. 261 When verbs are presentive, they are so precisely in proportion to the amount of nounal stuff that is mixed up in their constitution. **1883** J. W. F. ROGERS *Gram. & Logic* 65 A phrase formed of *to* and an infinitive noun may be either Nounal, Adjectival or Adverbial. *Ibid.* 67 Nounal Phrase. **1952** *Scrutiny* XVIII. IV. 306 That same test on Milton generally bears out her observation that Milton is predominantly nounal and adjectival in the sense of described scenery rather than re-enacted experience. **1961** R. B. LONG *Sentence & its Part* xiii. 292 The demonstratives have very considerable nounal use. *This* is fun... Who's *that*?

So **'nounally** *adv.*, as a noun.

1871 EARLE *Philol. Eng. Tongue* iv. 182 The sporting world employs the word nounally. **1961** R. B. LONG *Sentence & its Parts* xiii. 292. But demonstratives used nounally of people can be emotional also. *That's* a good fellow.

nounbre, noune, obs. ff. NUMBER, OWN *a.*

nounce, nouns, obs. varr. of OUNCE *sb.*[1]

'nounism. *rare.* [f. NOUN + -ISM.] In an author's style: a marked preference for nouns.

1904 G. S. HALL *Adolescence* II. xvi. 467 Adjectivism, adverbism, and nounism, or marked disposition to multiply one or more of the above classes of words.

'nounize, *v. rare.* [f. NOUN + -IZE.] *trans.* To make into a noun.

1871 J. EARLE *Philol. Eng. Tongue* 190, 2 Henry IV, iv. I. 71 *there* (nounized).

'nounness. [f. NOUN + -NESS.] The quality or nature of a noun.

1971 D. CRYSTAL *Linguistics* 124 We might arrive at an explicit notion of nounness. **1971** R. FOWLER in *Archivum Linguisticum* II. 143 A Pronoun..represents features proper to *N* (gender, noun-ness, [etc.]).

‖**nounou** ('nu:nu:). [Fr.] A child's name for a nurse; a wet nurse.

1894 G. DU MAURIER *Trilby* II. VI. 208 In the formal dusty gardens were the same pioupious and zouzous still walking with the same nounous. *Ibid.*, Nounou——a wet-nurse with a pretty ribboned cap and long streamers. **1900** *Glasgow Herald* 17 July 4 He was in the charge of a nou-nou (wet nurse). **1930** *Observer* 23 Feb. 12/1 The 'nou-nous' which it was naturally the chief object of the 'piou-pious' of that period to dazzle. **1951** M. SHARP *Lise Lillywhite* i. 9 A sea-sick *nounou*.

†**nouns.** *Obs.* Also 6 **nownes,** 7–8 **nowns,** 7 **nounz.** A perversion of *wounds* (see GOD *sb.* 14 a) used as an oath: cf. ZOUNDS. In early examples in the fuller forms ***Cock's*** and ***Od's nouns.***

a **1553** UDALL *Royster D.* I. iv, Kock's nownes, what meanest thou man? tut, a whistle. **1598** SHAKS. *Merry W.* IV. i. 25, I thought there had bin one Number more, because they say od's-Nownes. ? **1608** *Merry Devil of Edmonton* Hazl. *Dodsley* X. 225 Nouns! there's fire i' th' tail on't. **1675** T. DUFFETT *Mock Tempest* I. i, Nounz, stir about, or I'le beat thy brains out with my Bottle. **1709** *Rambling Fuddle-Cups* 13 But, Nouns, if the Rake-hell continues thus loose [etc.]. **1790** R. TYLER *Contrast* v. i. (1887) 93, I can't laugh for the blood and nowns of me. [**1822** SCOTT *Nigel* ii, Nouns, man, the Whitehall gateways were planned by the great Holbein.]

b. With punning allusion to NOUN.

1607 WILKINS *Mis. Enforced Marriage* 111, But nouns, pronouns and participles! where be these rogues here?

'nouny, *a. rare.* [f. NOUN + -Y[1].] Having or using many nouns; having the nature of a noun.

1926 FOWLER *Mod. Eng. Usage* 654 It is as an unfailing sign of a nouny abstract style that a cluster of *-ion* words is chiefly to be dreaded.

So **'nouniness,** the state or quality of a noun.

1973 *Ann. N.Y. Acad. Sci.* CCXI. 170 Degrees of adjectiveness, degrees of nouniness.

noup (nu:p). Also **noop.** [a. ON. *núpr* (*gnúpr*).] A steep and lofty headland. (Occurs in Orkney and Shetland place-names.)

1822 SCOTT *Pirate* xix, By stack and by skerry, by noup, and by voe.

nour, var. of NOWER, nowhere.

nource, -cery, obs. ff. NURSE, -SERY.

†**nourice**, *sb. Obs.* Forms: α. 3, 6–7 nurice (6 -rice), 4 -yse, 5–6 -ys, 6 *Sc.* -is(s, 5 -ess, 6 *Sc.* -eis, nwreis. β. 3–6 norice, 4 -iche, 4–6 -yce, 4 -isse, 4–6 -ise, 4–5 -yse, 5 -ys(s(e, -e(i)s. γ. 4, 6– nourice, 5–6 -yce, -ysse, 6 -ise; 4 nowrise, -ys; 8 nooriss. [a. OF. *nurice, -isce, nor(r)ice, noriche, nour(r)ice*, = Prov. *noir-, nuirissa*, Catal. *nudrissa*, Sp. *nod-, nudriza*:—late L. *nūtrīcia*, fem. of *nūtrīcius*, f. *nūtrīc-em, nūtrix*, f. *nūtrīre* to nourish. L. *nūtrīcem* is represented by It. *nut-, not-, nud-, nodrice*, Sp. *nut-, nodriz*. Cf. NOURISH *sb.* and NURSE *sb.*] A nurse. Also *attrib.* in *nourice-fee, -milk*.

α. *a* **1225** *Ancr. R.* 82 Heo makeð of hire tunge cradel to þes deofles bearn, & rockeð hit ȝeorneliche ase nurice. *c* **1230** *Hali Meid.* 37 Þah þu riche beo, & nurice habbe. *c* **1375** *Sc. Leg. Saints* xxvii. (*Machor*) 47 He tuk þe child hym til, & gat a nuryse gud in hy. **1440** *Alph. Tales* 216 He tuke ane offrand hym selfe and gaff vnto þer nuress. **1515** *Acc. Ld. High Treas. Scot.* V. 10 Bocht..for my lord duke's nurys, to be hir ane goune. **1596** DALRYMPLE tr. *Leslie's Hist. Scot.* II. 146 Eder..be the ingine and the industrie of his nurice was preseruet. *c* **1620** A. HUME *Brit. Tongue* (1865) 19 Nurice, from nutrix, quhilk the south calles nurse, not without a falt both in sound and symbol.

β. *c* **1290** *St. Lucy* 61 in *S. Eng. Leg.* I. 102 He wende to seinte lucies norice. **1340** *Ayenb.* 60 þe blonderes byeþ þe dyeules noriches, þet his children yeueþ zouke. **1387** TREVISA *Higden* (Rolls) III. 449 Þis Clitus his suster was Alisaundre his norise. **1413** *Pilgr. Sowle* (Caxton, 1483) v. iii. 93 That blysful lady Mary was very moder and noryce of Ihesu goddes sone. **1483** CAXTON *Gold. Leg.* 44/2 Thenne they lete her goo and her noryce wyth her. **1541** ELYOT *Cast. Helthe* II. xxv. 40 b, Their noryces shall perceyve what dygesteth welle. **1568** GRAFTON *Chron.* II. 196 By meane of a false Norice, he was stollen out of his Cradell.

γ. *c* **1375** *Sc. Leg. Saints* xxvi. (*Nicholas*) 40 Na one fryday bot anys wald he þe nowrys suk. **1483** CAXTON *Gold. Leg.* 251/2 One named Concordia Nouryce of Ypolyte answerd for them alle. **1530** PALSGR. 577/2 She is worthy to be a nouryce, she can handell a chylde dayntely. **1599** JAS. I *Basilikon Doron* (1603) 45 Drinking in with their very nouris-milke that their honor stood in committing three points of iniquitie. **1600** HOLLAND *Livy* III. xlviii. 120 To enquire of her nourice the truth of this matter. **1768** ROSS *Helenore* (1812) 68 Then sud she gae frae head to foot in silk; Wi' castings rare, and a gueed nooriss-fee, To nurse the king of Elfin's heir.

b. In figurative uses.

β. *c* **1386** CHAUCER *Pars. T.* ¶874 Slepyng long in grete quyete is eke a grete Norice to lecherie. *c* **1412** HOCCLEVE *De Reg. Princ.* 4813 Loue is norice of welþe and of gladnesse. *a* **1548** HALL *Chron., Edw. IV* 245 b, The not deliuery of the same should be the norice and continuer of warre and hostilitie. **1550** J. COKE *Eng. & Fr. Herald.* §1 (1877) 55 Idlenes, norise of vyces.

γ. **1502** *Ord. Crysten Men* (W. de W. 1506) II. v. 92 Charyte is..moder and nouryce and yᵉ lyght of these other vertues. **1576** GASCOIGNE *Steele Gl.* (Arb.) 60 Gold, which is..The neast of strife, and nourice of debate. **1609** HOLLAND *Amm. Marcell.* xx. viii. 156 But putting aside flatterie, the very nourice of vices, set your mind upon iustice. **1612** SELDEN *Illustr. Drayton's Poly-olb.* A iij b, That most learned Nourice of Antiquitie..Mr. Camden.

Hence †'**nourice** *v.*, to nurse. †'**nouriceship**, the office of a nurse. *Obs.*

1588 GREENE *Perimedes* H j b, The Syren Venus nourist in hir lap Faire Adon. **1818** SCOTT *Br. Lamm.* iii, 'What is her connection with the former proprietor's family?' 'O, it was something of a nourice-ship, I believe'.

†'**nouricery**. *Obs. rare.* Forms: 4 noricerie, 5 norysrye, 7 *Sc.* nouricerie. [f. *norice, norys* NOURICE *sb.* + -RY. Cf. mod.F. *nourricerie*.]

1. A nursery for children.

c **1330** *Amis & Amil.* 2258 The douke wel fast gan aspie The kays of the noricerie. *c* **1440** *Promp. Parv.* 358/2 Norysrye, where yonge chyldur arn kept.

2. A nursery for plants.

1684–9 *Glamis Bk. Record* (S.H.S.) 34 The whole bounds of the kitchen yeard and nouricerie below the house.

†'**nourish**, *sb. Obs.* Forms: α. 4 **nurishe**, 5 -isch(e. β. 4–5 nory(s)she, 5–6 -ishe, 5 -ysch, -isch(e, -yhs. γ. 5 nourysshe, 6 nourish. [var. of *nurice, norice* NOURICE *sb.* Cf. next.] A nurse. Also *fig.*

α. **1382** WYCLIF *Hos.* xi. 3 And Y as a nurishe..bare hem in myn armys. *c* **1449** PECOCK *Repr.* II. xii. 219 Euen as a nurisch or a modir is not bounde forto alwey and for euere fede her children. *a* **1585** MONTGOMERIE *Misc. Poems* xlviii. 47 Thair tender babis, ȝit on the nurish knee, Tane by the feet and cast into the see. **1600** BIRREL *Diary* 2 July, Her nurische was brunt at the same tyme, at 4 houres in the morneing.

attrib. **1483** *Cath. Angl.* 257/2 A nurische house.

β. **1382** WYCLIF *Gen.* xxiv. 59 Thanne thei leten hir, and Delbora, hir noryshe. *c* **1400** *Rule St. Benet* (Prose) 121 Idylnesse, þe norisshe of al synnes. **1480** *Robt. Devyll* 151 in Hazl. *E.P.P.* I. 225 When that he shoulde soucke, The noryshe nypples..byte he woulde. **1559** W. CUNNINGHAM *Cosmogr. Glasse* 43 Th' Earth..is called the..norishe of lyuing creatures, the foundation of all buildinges.

γ. **1480** CAXTON *Trevisa's Higden* I. xxii. (1527) 18 b, Auctours tellen that..Grece..is lady of kyngdomes, Nourysshe of knyghthode. **1502** *Ord. Crysten Men* (W. de W. 1506) IV. xix. 218 Yf fader or moder or nourysshe, stoppe the breth of a lytell chylde. **1563** SHUTE *Archit.* B j b, A certaine maiden, after whose burial her nourishe (who lamented much her death) [etc.]. **1591** SHAKS. *1 Hen. VI*, I. i. 50 Our Ile be made a Nourish of salt Teares.

nourish ('nʌrɪʃ), *v.* Forms: α. 3 norisi, 4 -ici, -issi, -isy, -ysy; 3 norischei, 4 -ischi; 4 norice, -isse, -ysse, 6 -esse, 4–5 noris, 4 -ijs; 3 norichce, 4 -iche, 3–5 -ische, 4–5 -issche, -ysche, 5 -yssch, 5–6 -ysshe, 6 -yshe; 4–6 norisshe, 5–6 -ishe, 6– 7 -ish (6 norrish). β. 4, 5–6 *Sc.*, nuris (*Sc.* 5 nwris, 6 nurys, nureis, nvreis), 6 nurris; 4–5 nurische, 4 (6 *Sc.*), -ishe, 5 -yche, -ysh, 6 -ys(s)ch; 5–6 nurrish(e, -ysh(e. γ. 5 nouryssche, -isshe, 5–6 -ysshe (6 nowr-), 6 -yshe, 6– nourish. [ad. OF. *noris(s)-, nuris(s)-*, etc., lengthened stem of *norir, nurir, nourir*, etc. (later *nourrir*), = It. *nodrire, nudrire, nutrire*, Sp. *nutrir* (*nudrir, nodrir*), Pg. *nutrir*:—L. *nūtrīre* to feed, foster, cherish, etc. See also NORSH *v.* and NURSH *v.*]

I. †**1.** *trans.* To bring up, rear, nurture (a child or young person). *Obs.*

α. *c* **1290** *St. John* 372 in *S. Eng. Leg.* I. 413 Þis bischop nam þis Ioliue man, and ladde hom to is inne, And norichcede him softe and wel. *c* **1330** R. BRUNNE *Chron. Wace* (Rolls) 6997 He dide hym norice at Wynchestre, And ȝald hym monk in þat same estre. **1382** WYCLIF *1 Tim.* v. 10 If she norische sones, if she resseyue pore men to herbore. *c* **1450** *St. Cuthbert* (Surtees) 2516 He noryscht me þan In Mailros mynster many ȝere. **1523** LD. BERNERS *Froiss.* I. cccxiv. 482 He..left the yonger [daughter] styll in Englande, wheras she had been brought vp and norisshed. **1581** HAMILTON *Tract.* in *Cath. Tract.* (S.T.S.) 75 Hou tenderlie all his forbeiris var norishit in the bosome of the Catholik kirk.

absol. *c* **1290** *St. Dunstan* 22 in *S. Eng. Leg.* I. 20 Þo þis child was i-bore,..huy leten hit do to Glastingburi, to norischi and to fede. *a* **1340** HAMPOLE *Psalter* xxvi. 16 He takis me to norysch and to rewle, as fadire and modire. *c* **1489** CAXTON *Blanchardyn* 12 Blanchardyn, the chylde, was taken in to the handes of a right noble lady of the lande for to norysshe and bryngen vp.

β. *c* **1340** HAMPOLE *Pr. Consc.* 4198 He sal be lered,..And nurist and mast conversand In þe cite of Bethsayda. *c* **1400** MAUNDEV. (Roxb.) xiii. 55 He þis antecriste sall be nuríscht in Bethsaida. **1538** STARKEY *England* I. i. 3 Syns you haue byn of your cuntrey so wel nuryschyd and brought vp. **1596** DALRYMPLE tr. *Leslie's Hist. Scot.* VIII. 111 An Inglis-man..susteinit sumpteouslie, and with gret cost nurist, and brocht vp.

γ. **1483** CAXTON *G. de la Tour* F vij, One [child] that a good man..made to be nouryssbed secretely. **1585** T. WASHINGTON tr. *Nicholay's Voy.* II. xviii. 51 b, Yong children..are there nourished, instructed, and exercised. **1611** BIBLE *Ecclus.* xvii. 18 Whom being his first borne, hee nourisheth with discipline. *a* **1618** RALEIGH *Mahomet* (1637) 88 And as his child amongst his children nourished, with whom shee lived.

†**b.** Const. *in* (some condition, pursuit, etc.).

1375 BARBOUR *Bruce* XIX. 164 His men ar worthyn all sa wicht For lang vsage of gret fechting, That has beyne norist in sic thing. **1456** SIR G. HAYE *Law Arms* (S.T.S.) 68 Faderis..quhilk norist thair barnis ay the mare in vicis. **1604** E. G[RIMSTONE] *D'Acosta's Hist. Indies* VI. x. 452 Men of great agilitie,..whome they did nourish in this exercise of running from their youth.

†**c.** To cherish (a person). *Obs.*

c **1380** WYCLIF *Wks.* (1880) 43 For ȝif a modir norscheþ & loueþ here fleschly child, wiþ hou mychel more diligence schal on loue & norische his gostly broþer. **1535** COVERDALE *1 Kings* i. 4 She was a very fayre damsell, and noryshed yᵉ kynge, and serued him. *c* **1560** A. SCOTT *Poems* (S.T.S.) xv. 22 My lady..Wᵗin myne armes I nureiss on the nycht.

†**2.** To bring up or rear (animals). *Obs.*

c **1290** *St. Michael* 267 in *S. Eng. Leg.* I. 307 He fierde ase doth a port-doggue, I-norischet in port-toun. **1375** BARBOUR *Bruce* VI. 487 Sum men sais ȝeit that the kyng As a strecour hym nwrist had. **1422** tr. *Secreta Secret., Priv. Priv.* 225 Amonge al bestis that bene nuryshid..by witte of man, the femalis bene moste mekyste. **1496** *Fysshynge w. Angle* (1883) 37 Ye shall besye yourselfe to nouryssh the game in all that ye maye. **1553** EDEN *Treat. Newe Ind.* (Arb.) 27 In whose honoure he nourisheth a ramme al that yeare. **1604** E. G[RIMSTONE] tr. *D'Acosta's Hist. Indies* III. ix. 144 Such as nourish silkewormes, have great care to shut their windowes, whenas the South-west windes do blow.

†**3.** To grow, or allow (one's hair) to grow. *Obs.*

1382 WYCLIF *1 Cor.* xi. 15 But if a womman norische long heer, it is glorie to hir. **1603** KNOLLES *Hist. Turks* (1621) 235 Which [hair] his mother comming of the race of Sampson..willed him to nourish. **1615** G. SANDYS *Trav.* 3 They nourish onely a locke of haire on the crowne of their heads. **1712–4** POPE *Rape Lock* II. 20 This Nymph, to the destruction of mankind, Nourish'd two Locks, which graceful hung behind In equal curls. **1807** ROBINSON *Archæol. Græca* IV. vii. 364 The soldiers of the cavalry..were forbidden by a law to nourish their hair and to live delicately.

†**4.** To promote the growth of, to tend or cultivate (plants or trees). *Obs.*

1523 FITZHERB. *Husb.* §130 In many places bothe the lordes, freeholders and tenauntes at wyll, sette suche wethyes, and popelers, in marsshe grounde, to nouryssbe wodde. **1555** EDEN *Decades* (Arb.) 32 They sowe and norysshe the seades of melons with greate diligence. **1669** J. WORLIDGE *Syst. Agric.* (1681) 46 Although Turneps be usually nourisht in Gardens, and be properly Garden-Plants. **1727** A. HAMILTON *New Acc. E. Ind.* II. xxxix. 82 There is little Corn or Pulse grows in this Country but what is nourisht in Gardens. **1792** BURNS *My Tocher's the Jewel* 5 It's a' for the apple he'll nourish the tree.

II. †**5. a.** Of a female: To feed (a young animal or child) with milk from the breast; to suckle; to nurse or rear in this way. *Obs.*

a **1300** *Cursor M.* 12337 Be þat water side Lai a leoness..Norisand hir quelpes. **1377** LANGL. *P. Pl.* B. xv. 459 For as þe cow þorw kynde mylke þe calf norisseth til an oxe. *c* **1450** *Merlin* 15 Therfore was the moder suffred to norishe it tell it was x monthes of age. **1470–85** MALORY *Arthur* I. iii–v. 39 So sir Ectors wyf nouryssbed hym with her owne pappe. **1551** ROBINSON *More's Utopia* II. v. (1895) 163 The chylde that is nouryshed euer after taketh hys nource for his owne naturall mother.

absol. **1382** WYCLIF *Matt.* xxiv. 19 Forsoth wo to wymmen with childe and noryschinge in tho dayes.

b. To sustain (a person or living organism) with food or proper nutriment.

1340 *Ayenb.* 154 His bodi..huich he ssel zuo norissi. *c* **1380** WYCLIF *Sel. Wks.* I. 376 Þis modir haþ conseyved Crist, and norisiþ Crist wiþinne hir. **1422** tr. *Secreta Secret., Priv. Priv.* 237 Thegh the body may not alway endure, hit may endure longe tyme, yf the kynde of man be Well y-noryschid. **1432–50** tr. *Higden* (Rolls) III. 43 Faustulus..toke the ij. childer awey from that beste, noryschenge theyme in his flocke of bestes with herbes, gresse, and suche other þinges. **1538** STARKEY *England* I. ii. 56 The multytude of pepul..plentuously nuryschyd wyth abundance of al thyngys. **1585** T. WASHINGTON tr. *Nicholay's Voy.* I. xviii. 21 Palm trees: of the fruit of which trees, the more part of the inhabitants..are nourished. **1651** HOBBES *Leviath.* II. xxiv, Naturall Bloud..circulating, nourisheth by the way, every Member of the Body of Man. **1837** EMERSON *Amer. Schol.* Wks. (Bohn) II. 179 The human body can be nourished on any food. **1871** T. R. JONES *Anim. Kingd.* (ed. 4) 709 Being hatched internally, the offspring are nourished in receptacles provided for the purpose.

fig. *c* **1400** *Apol. Loll.* 92 Þat sche schuld growe to þe feiþ, norischid wiþ miraclis, as we watteren plantis til þey han ben rotid. **1548–9** (Mar.) *Bk. Com. Prayer*, Collect 7 Trinity, Increase in us true religion, norishe us with all goodnes. **1820** SHELLEY *Ode to Naples* 139 An hundred tribes nourished on strange religions And lawless slaveries. **1843** PRESCOTT *Mexico* VII. ii, Men of unblemished purity of life, nourished with the learning of the cloister.

c. To supply (a thing) with whatever is necessary to promote its growth or formation, or to maintain it in proper condition.

c **1380** WYCLIF *Sel. Wks.* I. 96 As wete somers nurishen siche tares. *c* **1400** MAUNDEV. (Roxb.) xvii. 79 Þai [diamonds] er nurischt with dew of heuen. **1471** RIPLEY *Comp. Alch.* VI. xx. in Ashm. (1652) 166 Mineralls be nurryshyd by mynystracyon Of Moysture radycall, whych theyr begynnyng was. **1542** BOORDE *Dyetary* x. (1870) 254 It doth reioyce all the powers of man, and doth nowrysshe them. *a* **1586** SIDNEY *Ps.* I. ii, Like a freshly planted tree,..Whose braunches faile not timelie fruite to nourish. **1604** E. G[RIMSTONE] tr. *D'Acosta's Hist. Indies* III. xxi. 188 Yet this mist is wonderfull profitable to bring forth grasse, and to raise vp and nourish the seede. **1667** MILTON *P.L.* v. 183 Aire, and ye Elements.., that..mix And nourish all things. **1765** DICKSON *Agric.* 13 That plants are actually nourished by earth; that they are also nourished by water. **1784** COWPER *Task* VI. 36 Threat'ning at once and nourishing the plant. **1834** McMURTRIE *Cuvier's Anim. Kingd.* 7 They also nourish the solids by the interposition of their particles. **1872** TYNDALL *Forms of Water* 95 Were you to stand upon the mountain slopes which nourish the glacier [etc.].

d. *Glove-making.* = FEED *v.* 6 e.

1884 *Health Exhib. Catal.* 38 The skins..are then put into a mixture of water, flour, yelk of eggs, alum, and salt..to be 'nourished'. **1884** *Pall Mall G.* 16 May 4/1 After it [the kid-skin] has been unhaired, dressed, nourished, staked.

6. To provide with food or sustenance; to maintain, support. Now *rare*. **a.** Of places.

c **1400** MAUNDEV. (Roxb.) xii. 50 It bringes furth ne nurischez na qwikk thing. **1495** *Trevisa's Barth. De P.R.* XIV. liv. 487 Some dyches ben full of water and therin is fysshe nouryssbyd and..wormes of dyuers kynde. **1538** STARKEY *England* I. iii. 72 Wher as befor tyme hath byn nuryschyd much gud and Chrystyan pepul, now you schal fynd no thyng maynteynyd but wyld and brute bestys. **1585** T. WASHINGTON tr. *Nicholay's Voy.* I. xii. 14 [The country] nourisheth & pastoureth in the valley a great number of oxen. **1634** SIR T. HERBERT *Trav.* 23 Of these Iles Chromroe..nourishes a people treacherous and least sociable. **1697** DRYDEN *Virg. Georg.* II. 208 Our Land is from the Rage of Tygers freed, Nor nourishes the Lyon's angry Seed.

transf. **1820** SHELLEY *Hymn Merc.* xcvi, Cattle which the mighty Mother mild Nourishes in her bosom.

b. Of persons.

1432–50 tr. *Higden* (Rolls) VIII. 7 The seide kynge..was movede to leve that faste and to norische a c. poore men that day. *c* **1500** *Melusine* 111 Counseylle the pouere wydowes, nouryssbe or doo to be noryssbed the pouere orphenyns. **1581** G. PETTIE tr. *Guazzo's Civ. Conv.* (1586) II. 105 b, With one Art onely, I nourish my selfe, my wife, and children. **1611** BIBLE *Gen.* xlv. 11 And thou shalt dwell in the land of Goshen.., And there wil I nourish thee.

fig. *c* **1645** HOWELL *Lett.* II. xv, Egmont and Horn were nourish'd still with hopes, until Philip II had prepar'd an army. **1847** YEOWELL *Anc. Brit. Ch.* (ed. 2) v. 48 He publicly protected and nourished the church in Britain.

7. *absol.* To afford nourishment. *Obs.*

c **1400** *Lanfranc's Cirurg.* 210 Nyȝ þe brayn, or in ony place nyȝ þe herte, or nyȝ ony lyme þat norischeth. **1541** ELYOT *Cast. Helthe* II. xi. 29 The greattest loues do norishe moste faste, for as muche as the fyre hath not exhausted the moisture of them. **1577** B. GOOGE *Heresbach's Husb.* III. (1586) 146 Sheepes Milke is sweeter, and nourisheth more. **1626** BACON *Sylva* §45 As Graines and Roots nourish more, than the Leaues. **1667** MILTON *P.L.* v. 325 Save what by frugal storing firmness gains To nourish, and superfluous moist consumes.

†**8.** *intr.* To receive nourishment; to be fed.

1595 T. EDWARDS *Narcissus* L'Envoy v, By his toile we do nourish And by him are inlarg'd. **1626** BACON *Sylva* §544 By the Coldnesse of the Ground,..the Plants nourish lesse. *Ibid.* §602 Plants doe nourish; Inanimate Bodies doe not; They have an Accretion, but no Alimentation.

III. 9. To promote or foster (a feeling, habit, condition, state of things, etc.) in or among persons.

α. *c* **1290** *Beket* 1840 in *S. Eng. Leg.* I. 159 In faire Manere [they] beden him..to norisi loue with is felawes. *c* **1315** SHOREHAM III. 275 Glotenye..norysseþ lecherye, Ase fer, þe brondes hote. **1377** LANGL. *P. Pl.* B. XVI. 33 It nourissheth nice siȝtes and some tyme wordes. **1432–50** tr. *Higden* (Rolls) I. 165 Takenge a multitude of yonge men..and lxxx. virgynes to norysche multiplicacion. *c* **1477** CAXTON *Jason* 71, I praye yow that ye norisshe pees and concorde togeder. **1529** MORE *Dyaloge* I. Wks. 120/1 Men reken that the clergie is glad to fauour theis waies, & to norishe this superisticion. **1607** SHAKS. *Cor.* III. i. 117, I say they norisht disobedience; fed the ruin of the State.

β. **1456** SIR G. HAYE *Law Arms* (S.T.S.) 117 He that procuris, or artis, or nurisis discordis, rumouris, or mortall fedis. **1560** DAUS tr. *Sleidane's Comm.* 194 b, He did what he coulde, to nurryshe stryfe in religion. **1596** DALRYMPLE tr. *Leslie's Hist. Scot.* IV. 255 He fande out the way to nurishe peace with his nychtbouris.

γ. **1594** KYD *Cornelia* V. 400 Their souldiers (sent to nowrish vp those warrs). **1617** MORYSON *Itin.* I. 87 Here to nourish acquaintance, they spend an houre in discourses. **1665** DRYDEN *Ind. Emp.* I. ii, Ill does he represent the Powers above, who nourishes Debate, not preaches Love. **1837** CHANNING *Temperance* Wks. (1881) 128 Freedom nourishes self-respect.

b. To foster, cherish, or nurse (a feeling) in one's own heart or mind.

1560 BIBLE (Genev.) *Ecclus.* xxviii. 5 If he that is but flesh nourishe hatred, [and aske pardone of God,] who wil intreate for his sinnes? *a* **1586** SIDNEY *Ps.* XXXVII. i, [No] envy in thy bosome nourish. *a* **1639** WOTTON *Reliq.* (1651) 58 Whether the frenzy was norish'd in the warm brest of yong men. **1642** ROGERS *Naaman* 14 That wee nourish not a cavilling heart against God in this behalfe. **1709** PRIOR *Despairing Sheph.* i, And wand'ring thro' the lonely Rocks, He nourish'd endless Woe. **1781** COWPER *Retirement* 603 Thus some retire to nourish hopeless woe. **1828** SCOTT *F.M. Perth* ii, To think that Catharine Glover nourished the private wish to retire from the world. **1879** FROUDE *Cæsar* xv. 242 Clodius..nourishing an implacable hate against Cicero.

†**c.** To support, give ground for. *Obs.*

1719 DE FOE *Crusoe* I. (Globe) 228, I could find nothing to nourish my Suspicion.

10. To maintain, encourage, strengthen (one's heart, mind, etc.) in or with something.

c **1374** CHAUCER *Boeth.* III. met. vi. (1868) 79 Than is þer no forlyued wyȝht but ȝif he norisse his corage vnto vices. **1450–1530** *Myrr. Our Ladye* I This holy relygion, which as a mother noryssheth youre soulles in grace. **1555** EDEN *Decades* (Arb.) 49 The mynde of man..is nuryssheed with knowleage. **1651** HOBBES *Leviath.* I. xi. 49 It [frugality] weakeneth their Endeavour, which is to be nourished and kept in vigor by Reward. **1817** JAS. MILL *Brit. Ind.* II. v. v. 536 A man, who nourished his spirit with the contemplation of ancient heroes. **1859** WHITTIER *Joseph Sturge* 81 His zeal seemed nourished by failure and by fall.

†**11.** To provide for or supply (one's wants).

c **1560** A. SCOTT *Poems* (S.T.S.) xxvi. 57 Thay wald men nvreist all thair neidis.

'nourishable, *a.* [f. prec. + -ABLE. Cf. OF. *norrissable* (Godef.).]

†**1.** Capable of affording nourishment; nutritive, nutritious. (Common in 17th c.) *Obs.*

1496 *Fysshynge w. Angle* (1883) 2 And yf he woll be dyetyd mesurably..he must..ete nourishable [*a* **1450** norysching] meetes and dyffyable also. **1565** SPARKE *Hawkins Voy.* (Hakluyt Soc.) 57 It maketh also good beuerage sodden in water, and nourishable. **1589** FLEMING *Virg. Georg.* II. 26 Then is the soile but thin, And fitter yeeld it is for beasts and nourishable vines. **1612** T. TAYLOR *Comm. Titus* i. 13 Let the food be nourishable, hungry Elias stands not vpon it, whether an Angel or a rauen serue it. **1635** SWAN *Spec. M.* (1670) 458 The fruits of the Earth were much more nourishable and healthful before the Flood than afterwards. **1721** BRADLEY *Philos. Acc. Wks. Nat.* 178 The Fall of great Rains may wash down Insects and other nourishable Matter into it.

2. Capable of being nourished; susceptive of nourishment.

1545 RAYNOLD *Byrth Mankynde* 41 From whense agayne it is attracted into all partes nouryssshable of the infant. **1654** EARL MONM. tr. *Bentivoglio's Wars Flanders* 87 He had no money to maintain it [his army], nor was it any longer nourishable by rapine. **1662** J. CHANDLER *Van Helmont's Oriat.* 219 There are as many stomacks, as there are members nourishable. **1701** GREW *Cosmol. Sacra* I. v. 28 Its more ready adhesion to all the nourishable Parts. **1876** G. MEREDITH *Lett.* (1912) I. 269 The dear heart of him so frankly nourishable by flattery that [etc.].

†**'nourishant,** *a. Obs. rare.* In 5 norisch-, norisshaunt. [ad. OF. *norissant* (mod.F. *nourrissant*), pres. pple. of *norir*: see NOURISH *v.* and -ANT.] Nourishing.

c **1400** *Lanfranc's Cirurg.* 76 Whanne þou art siker from apostyme & swellinge, it is good to ȝeue norischaunt [*v.r.* norysschande] metis. **1450–80** tr. *Secreta Secret.* 23 Whan the body is smalle and drie, smale metis are goode and norisshaunt.

nourished ('nʌrɪʃt), *ppl. a.* [f. NOURISH *v.*]

†**1.** ***well-nourished***, well brought-up or educated. *Obs.*

a **1330** *Syr Degarre* 275 Hit was a fair child, & a bold, Wel i-norisschet, god & hende. *c* **1386** CHAUCER *Reeve's T.* 28 For Symkyn wolde no wyf, as he sayde, But sche were wel i-norissched and a mayde. *c* **1400** *Destr. Troy* 3978 Ecuba, the onest & onerable qwene, Was..Alse sad in þe syens as semyt for a lady, Wele norisshed þerwith.

2. Provided with nutriment or nourishment. Also ***well-nourished***, well-fed.

c **1400** *Lanfranc's Cirurg.* 81 Þis oynement is clepid litargirum nutritum;..take of þilke litarge norischid .vij. parties [etc.]. **1567** *Gude & Godlie B.* (S.T.S.) 105 With hurklit hude ouer a weill nureist neck. **1727–46** THOMSON *Summer* 1737 Hence thro' her nourish'd powers.., She springs aloft.

†**b.** ***nourished brother***, foster-brother. *Obs.*[−1]

1470–85 MALORY *Arthur* I. iii–v. 41 Syre Ector..rode vnto the Iustes, & with hym rode syr kaynus his sone & yong Arthur that was hys nourisshed broder.

nourisher ('nʌrɪʃə(r)). Forms: *α.* 5 norischer, -yschere (-are), -yssher, -eshoure, 6 -issher, -ysher, 6–7 norisher. *β.* 6 *Sc.* nurisare, -issar, -isear. *γ.* 6 nouryssher, 6– nourisher. [f. NOURISH *v.* + -ER[1]. Cf. OF. *norissere*, *nouriseur*, etc. (mod.F. *nourrisseur*).]

1. One who or that which nourishes.

α. **1413** *Pilgr. Sowle* (Caxton, 1483) v. xiv. 109 Good wyl is approprid to the holy ghoost as to the very noryssher and keper. *c* **1440** *Jacob's Well* 189 For almes-dede is noryschere & makere redy þe weye to god. **1533** J. HEYWOOD *Play of Wether* 1223 (Brandl), Of every thynge, I se, you are norysher. **1589** COOPER *Admon.* 226 Whome hee hath appointed as fosterers and norishers of his church.

β. **1561** WINȜET *First Tract.* Wks. (S.T.S.) I. 7 The inventaris, nurissaris, and simoniacall merchandis of the samyn mischeif. **1581** *Reg. Privy Council Scot.* III. 384 The makers and nurissaris of trouble and disorder.

γ. **1526** R. WHYTFORD *Martiloge* (1893) 43 Saynt Ioseph was nouryssher & bringer up of our sauyour Chryst. **1586** T. B. *La Primaud. Fr. Acad.* I. (1594) 685 Amongst such nourishers of our miseries this proverbe is rife. **1641** J. JACKSON *True Evang. T.* I. 38 The Clergy, as the fomenters and nourishers of the religion. **1667** MILTON *P.L.* v. 398 These bounties which our Nourisher..hath caus'd The Earth to yeild. **1768–74** TUCKER *Lt. Nat.* (1834) II. 553 Pleasure..is the greatest nourisher of indolence and indulgence. **1808** LAMB *Charac. Dram. Writ.* Wks. 528 The nourisher and the destroyer of hopeful wits.

2. A thing which affords nourishment; a nourishing agent. Also const. *of.*

1528 PAYNELL *Salerne's Regim.* F iv, Wyne that is redde.. and claret..are moche greatter nourishers than other wynes. **1577** B. GOOGE *Heresbach's Husb.* III. (1586) 146 The greatest nourisher is womans milke. **1651** FRENCH *Distill.* v. 110 He may finde out, how great a nourisher, and restorative Wheat is. **1676** GREW *Anat. Pl., Anat. Leaves* I. vi. §4 Most Bodies which abound with Salt, are the greatest Nourishers of Plants. **1742** RICHARDSON *Pamela* IV. 318 Sound Sleep is one of the greatest Nourishers in Nature. **1865** *Englishm. Mag.* Sept. 200 As a nourisher of the body, it [*sc.* water] is certainly entitled to rank as a food.

†**'nourishery,** obs. variant of NURSERY.

1572 HULOET, Nourisherie, *gynæceum.*

†**nourish-father.** *Obs.*[−1] A foster-father.

1619 SIR J. SEMPILL *Sacrilege Handl.* Ded., To the Most Noble, and truly sacred Prince; Defender of Christ's Faith, and Nourish-father of his Church, James.

nourishing ('nʌrɪʃɪŋ), *vbl. sb.* [f. NOURISH *v.*]

1. The action of the verb, in various senses.

α. **1297** R. GLOUC. (Rolls) 4900 Þis children were wel ȝonge ysend..to gode norrissinge. *c* **1386** CHAUCER *Pars. T.* ¶274 Eueryech of vs hath..occasion to be tempted of þe norisshyng of synne. *c* **1440** *Gesta Rom.* xxvi. 98 He ordeynid for fostering & noreshing of this childe iij. norisis. **1525** LD. BERNERS *Froiss.* II. ciii. [xcix.] 299, I thynke they shall be skrymysshed withall, for that is the lyfe and norysshynge of men of warre and their passetyme. **1560** BP. PILKINGTON *Expos. Aggeus* (1562) 91 Norishing is defined of the physicions [etc.].

β. *c* **1440** *Alph. Tales* I Ye spend full wele your nurysshyng ..þat of men makis bestis. **1477** *Exch. Rolls Scot.* VIII. 403 *note*, For the service..done in the nurysing of oure said derrest sone. **1538** STARKEY *England* I. ii. 36 The lake of necessarys, for nuryschyng and clothyng of the body. **1609** SKENE *Reg. Maj.* II. 23 b, Nvrisching of peace and love.

γ. **1470–85** MALORY *Arthur* I. iii–v. 38 He will put his owne child to nourisshynge to another woman. **1526** *Pilgr. Perf.* (W. de W. 1531) 201 b, She wrought naturally as other mothers doth to his nourysshynge & conseruacyon. **1615** G. SANDYS *Trav.* 213 The people about Sidon are greatly giuen to the nourishing of cattell. **1680** FILMER *Patriarcha* ii. §4 A law..acquitted the son from nourishing of his father. **1765** DICKSON *Agric.* 30 The nourishing of plants by water, is an evidence that salt and oil are parts of their food. **1855** PUSEY *Doctr. Real Pres.* Note Q 260 The earliest Fathers..speak also of the natural power of nourishing, as still existing in the consecrated elements.

†**2.** That which nourishes; nourishment, nutriment. *Obs.*

c **1290** *St. Michael* 740 in *S. Eng. Leg.* I. 320 Ase it were a-manere lijf þat sent norischingue To þe limes. *c* **1374** CHAUCER *Boeth.* III. pr. xi. (1868) 97 They drawen alle hyr norysshynges by hyr rootes. *c* **1450** *De Imitatione* III. xxx. 100 Lo! mete, drinke, cloþe... Graunte me to use suche norisshinges temperatly. **1541** ELYOT *Cast. Helthe* 16 Biefe of Englande to Englysshemen, whiche are in helth, bringeth stronge nouryshynge. *a* **1623** R. HILL *Pathw. Piety* I. 190 But so much of each as may give nourishing and cheering to my body.

nourishing ('nʌrɪʃɪŋ), *ppl. a.* [f. NOURISH *v.*] That nourishes, in senses of the verb; giving or affording nourishment.

1398 TREVISA *Barth. De P.R.* XVII. clxix. (Bodl. MS.), In fatte londe & wele dunged growiþ fatte whete..& is more norisschinge þan is þe whete þᵗ growiþ in lene londe. *a* **1450** *Fysshynge w. Angle* (1883) 2 He must..ete norysching metes & defyabul. **1541** COPLAND *Guydon's Quest.* G iij, A pyt wherin the nourysshynge blode commynge fro the liuer is dygered. **1607** TOPSELL *Four-f. Beasts* (1658) 369 A good house-keeper, and charitable nourishing man. **1668** STEELE *Husbandm. Calling* viii. (1672) 219 Covetousness is the nourishing root of all evil. **1725** DE FOE *Voy. round World* (1840) 251 The grass more strengthening and nourishing for the cattle. **1793** BEDDOES *Calculus*, etc. 248 Oils, fat, sugar, alcohol, and other substances, which have a great affinity to oxygene, are very nourishing. **1861** FLOR. NIGHTINGALE *Nursing* (ed. 2) 52 The nourishing power of milk..is very much undervalued.

Hence **'nourishingly** *adv.*

1891 MEREDITH *One of our Conq.* III. viii. 158 His flattery of his girl..restored her broken feeling of personal value; it permeated her nourishingly.

nourishment ('nʌrɪʃmənt). Forms: 5 norysshe-, norysch-, 6 norish(e-; 6 nuryshe-, nurrish-, 6 *Sc.* nurish-; 6 nouryssh-, 6– nourish-. [ad. OF. *nor-*, *nur-*, *nour(r)issement*; see NOURISH *v.* and -MENT.]

1. That which nourishes or sustains; aliment, sustenance, food. Also *fig.* or *transf.*

1413 *Pilgr. Sowle* (Caxton, 1483) IV. xxxiv. 82 The wombe oweth to dispense to all the membres norysshement. **1526** *Pilgr. Perf.* (W. de W. 1531) 202 Takynge refeccyon & nourysshment of her blessed body. **1570–6** LAMBARDE *Peramb. Kent* (1826) 228 It is verie likely, that the Towne of Feversham received the chiefe nourishment of hir increase from the Religious house. **1651** HOBBES *Leviath.* II. xxiv. 130 Distribution of the Nourishment, to the severall Members of the Common-wealth. **1697** DRYDEN *Virg. Georg.* II. 590 No Dressing they require..; The Soil it self due Nourishment supplies. **1728** YOUNG *Odes to King* xxx, At his proud foot The sea..Immortal nourishment supplies. **1781** COWPER *Conversat.* 672 'Tis narrow, selfish, arrogant, and draws Its sordid nourishment from man's applause. **1850** LYNCH *Theoph. Trinal* ii. 29 He may see.. the bird visiting her young with nourishment. **1886** RUSKIN *Præterita* I. 415 The Idler and Rambler did..contain more substantial literary nourishment than could be..packed into so portable compass.

2. The action, process, or fact of nourishing.

c **1485** *Digby Myst.* (1882) II. 335 Take yow sum coumforth for your bodyes noryschment. **1596** SPENSER *F.Q.* VI. ix. 20 Nature, which doth litle need Of forreine helpes to lifes due nourishment. **1597** HOOKER *Eccl. Pol.* v. lxvii. §1 No dead thing is capable of nourishment. **1790** BURKE *Fr. Rev.* Wks. V. 431 The Paris, upon whose nourishment..such immense sums..have been expended. **1819** SHELLEY *Mask Anarchy* 167 So that ye for them are made Loom, and plough, and sword,..bent To their defence and nourishment. **1872** YEATS *Growth Comm.* 293 Internal conditions necessary for the nourishment of shipping and trade.

†**3.** Nutritive quality or property. *Obs. rare*[−1].

1555 EDEN *Decades* (Arb.) 104 Wylde frutes whiche they eate, beinge of muche better nooryshement then maste. **1620** VENNER *Via Recta* iii. 52 The faculties of nourishments attributed vnto Beefe.

4. *spec.* The treatment of leather with some substance to keep it soft or pliant.

1897 C. T. DAVIS *Manuf. Leather* (ed. 2) xlii. 596 For the nourishment of fine glacé leather, yolk of eggs is..used.

'nouriture. Now *rare* or *Obs.* Forms: *α.* 4–6 noriture (5 -tur), 5 nore-, norry-, 6 nory-, norriture. *β.* 6 nurry-, nurriture (-tor, -tour), 6–7 nuriture. *γ.* 5 nowry-, 6 noury-, 5–9 nouriture (6 -tour). *δ.* 6–9 nourriture. [a. OF. *norreture*, *noureture*, etc. (mod.F. *nourriture*): cf. late L. *nūtrītūra*, f. *nūtrīre* to nourish.]

1. Nourishment, sustenance, food.

α. *c* **1374** CHAUCER *Troylus* IV. 768 How shold a plaunte, or lyves creature, Lyve withouten his kynde noriture? **1387–8** T. USK *Test. Love* I. i. (Skeat) I. 34 How shulde the ground, without kyndly noriture, bringen forth any frutes? **1483** CAXTON *Gold. Leg.* 364 b/1 She sawe wel that she myght not haue..the noreture of holy scrypture. **1565** CALFHILL *Answ. Martiall* (1846) 72 In the first proposition,..the necessity of Sacraments and of noriture, to be compared together.

β. **1548** GESTE *Pr. Masse* 75 The verye ghostely nurryture and foode bothe of our bodyes and soules. **1581** MULCASTER *Positions* vi. (1887) 47 For inward bestowing of nurriture, and maintenaunce of life. **1632** LITHGOW *Trav.* IV. 165 The Turkes..consume the wealth of the people they ouercome, leauing them destitute of nuriture.

γ. **1483** CAXTON *Gold. Leg.* 423 b/1 They took theyr refeccion or food of nouriture dyuyne. **1561** T. NORTON *Calvin's Inst.* II. 73 To cal it a certain nouriture, that allureth ..to sinne. **1581** MARBECK *Book of Notes* 1062 The whole and perfect spiritual nouritour, which we haue by the.. bloud of Jesus Christ. **1607** J. NORDEN *Surv. Dial.* v. 189 So will the weedes..beginne to wither, as they are depriued of their nouriture. **1664** EVELYN *Kal. Hort.* (1729) 228 The Consumption of that inspiriting balsamick Nouriture, by reason of dry Heat. **1713** *Guardian* No. 171, I put nothing in it but what is clean and wholsom nouriture. **1743** H. WALPOLE *Lett.* (1903) I. 372, I have contracted a most religious veneration for your spiritual nouriture. **1845** T. COOPER *Purgatory Suicides* (1877) 52 Thou feddst the mind and heart with virtue's nouriture.

δ. **1581** G. PETTIE tr. *Guazzo's Civ. Conv.* III. (1586) 143 If wee should make mention of this first Nourriture [etc.]. *c* **1645** HOWELL *Lett.* I. xxv, I think if you saw me, you would hardly know me, such nourriture this deep Sanguin Alicant Grape gives. **1654–66** EARL ORRERY *Parthen.* (1676) 228 Water of so excellent a quality, that its Nourriture was Iron. **1737** *Common Sense* I. 198 The gold, no doubt,..may be exchanged for convenient Necessaries, and a comfortable Nourriture. **1800** MME. D'ARBLAY *Lett.* 27 Apr., All sorts of nourriture or clothing seem to rise [in price]..without any adequate cause. [**1848** BORRER *Campaign Kabylie* vi. 92 Receiving their nourriture from the hand of the Most High.]

†**2.** Nurture, upbringing. *Obs.*

c **1400** *Beryn* 841 A wyff like to his parage; For noriture & connyng, bewte, & parentyne. **1470–85** MALORY *Arthur* 6 Of the byrthe of kyng arthur and of his nouryture. **1527** *Inv. Wardr. Henry Fitzroy* (1855) 44 By example of good education, as well in noryture as good lernyng. **1590** SPENSER *F.Q.* I. ix. 5 He had charge my discipline to frame, And Tutors nouriture to oversee. **1647** N. BACON *Disc. Govt. Eng.* I. lxiv. (1739) 129 The Child of a King, that by good nouriture might prove a wise and just King.

Hence †**'nouritured** *ppl. a.*, brought up, nurtured; †**'nourituring** *vbl. sb.*, upbringing. *Obs.*

c **1500** *Melusine* 259 She that was wel nourrytured held her two children tofore geffray. **1555** WATREMAN *Fardle Facions* II. vii. 158 For their nourituryng and trainyng in good maners, thei haue appoincted them masters.

nourne, variant of NURN *v. Obs.*

nour-quar: see NOWER.

†'**nourry**, *sb. Obs. rare*⁻¹. [ad. F. *nourri*, pa. pple. of *nourrir* to nourish. Cf. NOORIE.] A foster-child.
1526 SIR R. WINGFIELD *Let. to Wolsey* (MS. Cott. Galba B. ix. 19), [The Earl of Hochstrat] beinge oon of the lorde Scheevyrs chieff nourrys.

†'**nourry**, *v. Obs. rare*⁻¹. [ad. F. *nourrir* to nourish. Cf. NORY *v.*] *trans.* To nourish.
1603 KNOLLES *Hist. Turks* (Nares), And nourried with the same milke of infidelitie that their prince was.

nourse, noursell, -sle, noursling, obs. ff. NURSE, -SLE, -LING.

nourt, var. of NURT *v.*

nourtoure, -ture, obs. ff. NURTURE.

nourwhare: see NOWER.

nouryce, -ysse, obs. ff. NOURICE.

nourysshe, obs. f. NOURISH.

‖**nous** (naʊs). Also 8-9 nouse, 9 nowse. [a. Gr. νοῦς, Attic contracted form of νόος mind.]
1. *Greek Philos.* Mind, intellect.
1678 CUDWORTH *Intell. Syst.* I. iv. 406 An Immovable and Standing Nous or Intellect, which was properly the Demiurgus, or Architectonick Framer of the whole World. **1768-74** TUCKER *Lt. Nat.* (1834) II. 197 They conceived of the Word as something analogous to the Nous or second Hypostasis of Plato. **1884** *Encycl. Brit.* XVII. 336/1 What Plotinus understands by the nous is the highest sphere accessible to the human mind.., and, along with that, pure thought itself.
2. *colloq.* or *slang.* Intelligence, common sense, gumption. (Common from 19th cent.)
Sometimes written in Greek letters: ——
[**1729** POPE *Dunc.* IV. 244 Thine is the genuine head of many a house, And much Divinity without a Νοῦς. **1797** R. POLWHELE *Old Engl. Gentl.* 87 Turning to the signs with keener νοῦς Foretold the future fortunes of his house. **1819** BYRON *Juan* II. cxxx, Because the good old man had so much νοῦς.]
1706 BAYNARD *Cold Baths* II. 306 A Demo-brain'd Doctor of more Note than Nous. *c* **1790** WOLCOT (P. Pindar) *Lousiad* II. Wks. 1816 I. 158 Oh! aid, as lofty Homer says, my *nouse*, To sing sublime the Monarch and the Louse! **1819** SIR G. JACKSON *Diaries & Lett.* (1873) I. 89 They would not send Oakeley. He has no nouse. **1847** FR. A. KEMBLE *Later Life* III. 282, I think his doing so exhibits considerable nous in a brute. **1884** *Graphic* 8 Nov. 494/3, I am glad that my people had the nous to show you into a room where there was a fire. **1927** F. B. YOUNG *Portrait of Clare* 509 'Upon my soul, Clare,' Aunt Cathie declared, 'I thought you had more nous.' **1928** GALSWORTHY *Swan Song* I. ii. 12 They've got no more *nous* than a tom-cat. **1930** R. CAMPBELL *Adamastor* 26 Had Creswell, Smuts or Hertzog half his nous, There would be far more goats on the Karroo And far less in the Senate and the House. **1945** R. HARGREAVES *Enemy at Gate* 291 Nothing compensated for ignorance or lack of *nous* in a leader. **1946** [see COMMON *sb.*¹ 16]. **1956** [see BACKWOODS b]. **1959** [see CAN *sb.*¹ 1 f]. **1972** *Daily Tel.* 8 Dec. 14/6, I do know how easy it would be for anyone with a camera and a little nous to film 'The Breakdown of Life' in Britain. **1973** *Times* 22 Feb. 25/1 If we had had a bit of *nous* we'd have probably discovered this earlier. **1975** *Daily Tel.* 29 Jan. 17 The City, extraordinary as it may sound, has very limited political nous.
attrib. **1823** *Grose's Dict. Vulgar T.* (Egan), Nous Box, the head.
Hence **nous(e**, *v.* (see quot.). *rare.*
1859 *Slang Dict.* 69 Nouse, to understand or comprehend.

‖**nous autres** (nuz otr). [Fr., lit. 'we others'.] The personal pronoun *we*, somewhat stressed or emphasized.
1860 C. LEVER *Day's Ride* in *All Year Round* III. 470/1 We were, in fact, henceforth 'nous autres'. **1870** J. C. PATTESON *Let.* 9 Dec. in C. M. Yonge *Life J. C. Patteson* (1874) II. xii. 472 We fail to understand him, *nous autres* I mean, outside the sanctuary. **1911** E. M. CLOWES *On Wallaby* v. 140 It gave us a nasty lumpy feeling in our throats—*nous autres* who had nobody to come and see us.

nousel, nousle, varr. of NUZZLE *v.*¹ and *v.*²

noust (naʊst, nuːst). *Sc. dial.* Also †newst, noost, †nowst. [ad. Norw. dial. *naust(r)*, *nøst*, f. ON. *naust* boat-shed, dock.] 'The place in which a boat is hauled up, gen. a scooped-out trench at the edge of a beach surrounded by a shallow wall of stones, a boat-stance in gen.' (Sc. Nat. Dict.) Also *fig.*
The pronunc. (naʊst) is used in Orkney, (nuːst) in Shetland.
1613 *Court Bk. Orkney & Shetland* (1967) 76 William Ewinsone..found her lying..beneath the boat nowst in Wytfoord. *a* **1693** T. BROWN *Diary* (1898) 63 Ther wes a great boat blowen owt of the Newst at the Air. **1869** J. T. REID *Art Rambles* 41 Down to the boat-noust the trio hirpled. **1894** L. J. NICOLSON *Songs of Thule* 79 My fecht is owre wi' wind an' wave Da Noost is noo da quiet grave. **1922** *Glasgow Herald* 22 July 86 Her bow could be seen in the 'noust'. *Ibid.*, In the afternoon at ebb tide they went down to take the boats out of the 'nousts'. **1931** J. NICOLSON *Tales* 55 When a boat was taken from its 'noost', and put into the water, the bow had to be turned 'sun-gaets'. **1956** C. M. COSTIE *Benjie's Bodle* 7 Jamie Peace sitting at the noust sorting his creels. **1971** G. M. BROWN *Fishermen with Ploughs* 69 He coughed his way to the noust And launched the *Belle*.

‖**nous verrons** (nu vɛrɔ̃). [Fr.] We shall see; it remains to be seen.
1764 H. WALPOLE *Lett.* (1857) IV. 262 *Nous verrons*—the temptation [to go to Paris] is strong, but [etc.]. **1840** DICKENS *Let.* ?9 Sept. (1969) II. 125, I have opened the second volume with Kit; and I saw..on looking out at sea an affecting thing that I can do with him bye and bye. Nous verrons. **1861** G. MEREDITH *Let.* 17 May (1970) I. 81, I think it will be my best book as yet... *Nous verrons.* **1889** E. C. DOWSON *Let.* 21 Feb. (1967) 39, I don't feel much like matinizing at the moment mais *nous verrons.* **1951** A. HUXLEY *Let.* 23 Dec. (1969) 639, I may collaborate on a film about Gandhi..but feel a little hesitant, in view of the precarious condition of my eyes... *Nous verrons.*

nout, obs. form of NOUGHT, NOWT.

nouþe, variant of NOWTHE *adv. Obs.*

†**noutheless**, *adv. Obs.* Also now-. [perh. for *nouȝ(t)þeles*, f. *nouȝt* NOUGHT.] Nevertheless.
1340-70 *Alex. & Dind.* 816 But nouþeles anon riht anied in his herte, Sone sente he again his sel & his lettrus. **13..** *E.E. Allit. P.* A. 889 Nowþe-lese non was neuer so quoynt ..þat of þat songe myȝt synge a poynt.

nouther, nowther, *pron.*, *a.*, *adv.*¹, and *conj.* Now *dial.* Forms: α. 1, 3 nowðer, 3 *Orm.* nowwþerr, 4-5 nowþer, 4-6 nowþir (5 -ire), 5-9 nowther (5 -ere, -re, 5-6 -ir); 5 nowdyr(e, 5-6 (9) nowder, -ir. β. 3 nouðer, 2-5 nouþer, 4-5 -ir, 4 -ur, 2-9 nouther, 4-6 -ir (5 -ire); 4 (9) nouder. [OE. *nowðer* (= OFris. *nouder*), contracted form of *nóhwæðer* (= OFris. *noweder*), f. *ne* NE + *ó* O *adv.* + *hwæðer* WHETHER. Cf. NAUTHER and NOTHER.]
A. †**1.** *pron.* Neither (of two persons or things). Also ***nether nouther*** (quot. 1401). *Obs.*
896 in Birch *Cartul. Sax.* II. 217 He næfre ne heora nowðer hine bereafian wolde ðære mæstreddene. **1154** *O.E. Chron.* (Laud MS.) an. 1140, þe king & Randolf eorl.. treuthes fæston ðæt her nouþer sculde be suiken other. *c* **1200** ORMIN 12872 Þatt nowwþerr þeȝȝre nohht ne laȝȝ I nane depe sinness. *a* **1225** *Ancr. R.* 52 Auh toten vt wiðuten vuel ne mei nouðer of ou. *c* **1340** HAMPOLE *Pr. Consc.* 1842 Nouther of þam wald other forga Swa mykel lof es bytwen þam twa. **1401** *Pol. Poems* (Rolls) II. 95 As I wene the Holigost appreveth nether nouther. **1456** SIR G. HAYE *Law Arms* (S.T.S.) 52 Nouthir of the parties had power to stryke a strake. **1483** *Cath. Angl.* 256/2 Nowdyr, *neuter.* **1596** DALRYMPLE tr. *Leslie's Hist. Scot.* I. 98 Quhen baith ar present, thay ar seine in nouther of thame to delyte mekle.
†**2.** *adj.* Neither. Also ***neither nouther.*** *Obs.*
c **1374** CHAUCER *Boeth.* v. metr. iii. (1868) 160 He nis in neiþer nouþir habit, for he not nat alle ne he hap nat alle for-ȝeten. **1390** GOWER *Conf.* II. 77 Sche which oure Eldemoder is, The Erthe, bothe that and this Receiveth and alich devoureth, That sche to nouther part favoureth.
B. *adv.*¹ and *conj.*
1. = NEITHER A. 1 (followed by *ne*, *na*, *nor*, etc.).
α. *c* **1200** ORMIN 3124 Forr birrþ me nowwþerr hellpenn þe To lif, ne to þe sawle. *c* **1250** *Doomsday* 33 in *O.E. Misc.* 164 Ne schulen heo nowðer fiȝte mid schelde ne mid spere. *a* **1340** HAMPOLE *Psalter* (1884) 498 Whaim þou nowþer delyuers fra syn na fra hell. **1390** GOWER *Conf.* I. 125 Ther halp him nowther swerd ne scheld. *c* **1420** *Chron. Vilod.* 3202 Þat he myȝt nowther se ny go. **1477** *Paston Lett.* III. 211 They arn nowthir redyn nor corayd... Whyte wol not a tende hem, nowdyr for Peris ner for me. *c* **1560** A. SCOTT *Poems* (S.T.S.) xxv. 21 My hairt, tak nowdir pane nor wa. *a* **1585** MONTGOMERIE *Cherrie & Slae* 1143 For nowther rigour nor for reuth. **1684** *Yorkshire Dialogue* (E.D.S.) 448 But nowther th' Why nor Filly we will sell. **1719** HAMILTON *Epist.* I. i. in Ramsay *Poems* (1760) 96 There's nowther highlandman nor lawlan [etc.]. **1804** R. ANDERSON *Cumbld. Ball.* 79, I nowther heed house, lan, or siller. **1888** MRS. H. WARD *R. Elsmere* I. ii, I can mak' nowt o' ya', nowder back nor edge.
β. **1154** *O.E. Chron.* (Laud MS.) an. 1137, Ne for-baren hi nouther circe ne cyrce iærd. *a* **1225** *Ancr. R.* 44 Mid him ne schule ȝe nouðer uerslen ne singen. *a* **1310** in Wright *Lyric P.* xxxvii. 102 When thou shalt deȝe, ner thou nost nouther day ne nyht. **1390** GOWER *Conf.* I. 206 For he was nouther ther ne hiere. *c* **1450** LYDG. *Secrees* 1148 With Oute moysture..Comyth nouthir flour nor greyn. **1470-85** MALORY *Arthur* XIX. iii. 775 Spare not thy hors..nouther for water neyther for lond. **1530** PALSGR. 688/2 It never ceaseth nouther daye nor nyght. **1567** *Gude & Godlie B.* (S.T.S.) 110 Thay haif a mouth can nouther say nor sing. **1724** RAMSAY *Tea-t. Misc.* (1733) I. 29 We have nouther pot nor pan. **1865** in *Eng. Dial. Dict.*
†**b.** = NOR. *Obs. rare.*
a **1225** *Leg. Kath.* 1703 þe neauer ne linneð nowðer ne lesseð. **1534** CROMWELL in Merriman *Life & Lett.* (1902) I. 375 Ye tried out nothing of her falshed, nouther..entended to do. **1596** DALRYMPLE tr. *Leslie's Hist. Scot.* IX. 260 For nowther was he ouer lang,..nouther ouer schort. *Ibid.*, Nouther was this done without cause.
2. = NEITHER A. 3.
c **1200** ORMIN 10216 Forr hellepitt niss næfre full, Ne grediȝnesse nowwþerr. *c* **1400** *Destr. Troy* 1930 We loue noght his lede, ne his land nowþer.
1826 SCOTT *Jrnl.* 4 Feb., As the boatswain said, one can't dance always *nowther.*

†**nouther**, *adv.*² *Obs.* In 4 nouþer, 4-5 nouthir. [app. an alteration of NOWER *adv.*, by confusion with prec. Cf. NOTHER *adv.*²] Nowhere. Usually in comb. **nouther-where.**
13.. *Cursor M.* 17556 (Gött.), þar es he soth and nouþer ellis. *Ibid.* 18604 His bodi here, his gast was þar, His goddhede wanted nouþer-quar. *Ibid.* 23819 Ouþer here or nouþer-quar ellis. **1375** BARBOUR *Bruce* VI. 522 The kyng.. Till thame, and nouthir ellis-quhar, Had ey. *a* **1400-50** *Alexander* 993 (Ashm.), þare is na region na rewme..Ne nouthire-quare na nacion [etc.].
So †**nouther-whither**, nowhither. *Obs. rare*⁻¹.
1338 R. BRUNNE *Chron.* (1810) 257 We se nouþer whidere þou may haf sikerer weie.

†**nou'thetical**, *a. Obs. rare*⁻¹. [f. Gr. νουθετικ-ός.] Monitory, warning.
a **1652** J. SMITH *Sel. Disc.* VI. iii. (1821) 199 The general difference between prophetical dreams and those that are merely nouthetical or monitory,..Philo Jud. in his Tract περὶ τοῦ θεοπέμπτους εἶναι ὀνείρους..hath at large laid down.

nouveau art (ˌnuːvəʊ 'ɑːt) = *art nouveau.*
1911 G. B. SHAW *Lett. to Granville Barker* 11 Jan. (1956) 170 Olivier's new poet-earthquake [*sic*] palace of reinforced concrete is a masterpiece of *nouveau* art. *a* **1946** J. M. KEYNES 'Dr Melchior' in *Two Memoirs* (1949) 35 The raised pattern of the *nouveau art* wall-paper. **1947** E. TAYLOR *View of Harbour* (1954) xi. 159 A picture of Our Lord carrying a *nouveau*-art lantern.

‖**nouveau pauvre** (nuvo povr). Pl. **nouveaux pauvres.** Also fem. **nouvelle pauvre** (*rare*). [Fr., after next.] A person who has recently become poor. Also (with hyphen) *attrib.* or as *adj.*, newly impoverished.
1965 *Punch* 27 Oct. 619/1 Maigret, holidaying with his wife in a small Normandy fishing port, is summoned to the home of a morally rotten, nouveau-pauvre family where a maid has died of arsenic poisoning after swallowing her mistress's sleeping draught. **1970** *Time* 3 Aug. 49 One of every four Americans 65 or over lives at or below 'the poverty line'. Some of these 5,000,000 old people were poor to begin with, but most are bewildered and bitter *nouveaux pauvres*, their savings and fixed incomes devoured by spiraling property taxes and other forms of inflation. **1975** *Country Life* 13 Feb. 413/1 Nouveau-pauvre? Could you do with an extra bedroom? **1975** *Harpers & Queen* May 101 Crisis for coiffeurs... Some of the *nouvelles pauvres* are clamouring for Brillo-pad mouse, the new colour and the new texture.

‖**nouveau riche** (nuvo riʃ). Pl. **nouveaux riches.** Also fem. **nouvelle riche** (*rare*). [Fr.] One who has recently attained to wealth; usu. with connotation of ostentation or vulgar show. Also *attrib.* or as *adj.*
1813 M. EDGEWORTH *Let.* 6 Apr. (1971) 15 Larry the footboy and Mrs. Rafferty's dinner are nothing to what has been seen at the dinners of les nouveaux riches at Liverpool and Manchester. **1828** LYTTON *Pelham* I. xxiii. 193 You never pass by the white and modern mansion of a *nouveau riche.* **1838** W. H. PRESCOTT *Hist. Reign Ferdinand & Isabella* III. II. xxvi. 560 This same *nouveau riche* used to serve gold dust, says Herrera, instead of salt, at his entertainments. **1853** C. M. YONGE *Heir of Redclyffe* II. xvii. 278 His manner became so dry and repellent that visitors went away moralizing on the absurdity of *nouveau riches* taking so much state on them. **1863** 'OUIDA' *Strathmore* (1865) I. vi. 96 She was a *nouvelle riche*, and brought him money. **1899** E. WHARTON *Greater Inclination* 187 She had none of the *nouveau riche* prudery which classes poverty with the nude in art. **1936** F. CLUNE *Roaming round Darling* vi. 58 The hovels they occupy are made of mud, except a few palaces of their *nouveaux riches.* **1957** A. E. COPPARD *It's Me, O Lord!* iii. 37 Modern upstarts such as the piano are as inelegant as *nouveaux riches* in a cathedral. **1957** *New Yorker* 2 Nov. 76/1 The elder members of the two families..are..rather crudely drawn caricatures of the *nouveau riche.* **1959** G. SAVAGE *Antique Collector's Handbk.* 238 The industrializing process which started in the 1750s had gained considerable ground by the end of the century, and the Napoleonic Wars, by creating a *nouveau riche* class, succeeded in debasing taste to an extremely low level. **1966** R. ELLISON in A. Chapman *New Black Voices* (1972) 404 Some of the *nouveau riche* oilmen who were members of the club. **1972** T. ARONSON *Queen Victoria & Bonapartes* ix. 111 The society of the Second Empire—the courtesans, the financiers, the foreign adventurers, the *nouveaux riches.*

‖**nouveau roman** (nuvo rɔmɑ̃). [Fr., lit. new novel.] 'A type of novel developed chiefly in France in the 1960's by such writers as Alain Robbe-Grillet, Michel Butor, Marguerite Duras, and Claude Mauriac, characterized by lack of moral, social, or psychological comment and by precise descriptions that suggest the mental state of the person experiencing or seeing them.' (C. L. Barnhart et al. *Dict. New Eng.* (1973).)
1961 *Listener* 24 Aug. 289/1 *The Key*..reads very like something young and French: it has the soberness of the *nouveau roman.* **1962** *Times* 13 Dec. 14/3 The *nouveau roman* is already a bit *vieux jeu* in France. **1965** *Harper's Mag.* July 112 The characters are many and the story jumps from one to another, often (in the manner of the *nouveau roman*) with no names other than 'he' or 'the boy' to tell you whose episode it is. **1965** *New Society* 12 Aug. 26/3 The author obviously owes a big debt both to Beckett and to the French exponents of the *nouveau roman*, with their insistent emphasis on the depiction of physical detail and visual objectivity. **1967** *Listener* 23 Mar. 391/3 One of the most successful recent attempts, for instance, is to be found in a novel by one of Robbe-Grillet's fellow-practitioners of the *nouveau roman*, Michel Butor's *Passing Time*, which combines a narrative giving us the hero's present experience and a diary containing his experiences of several months

before. **1974** *Times Lit. Suppl.* 25 Jan. 69/2 The sources of Mr Gordon's off-the-peg technique are fairly clear: some Kafka; the Burroughs scissors; but mostly the *nouveau roman*. The novel, so this modish dogma asserts, is a 'vision of things', and the universe no more than the sum of his author's sensations.

‖**nouvelle** (nuvɛl). [Fr.] A short piece of fictitious narrative, freq. one dealing with a single situation or a single aspect of a character or characters.

1680 H. SAVILE *Let.* 24 Feb. in W. D. Cooper *Savile Corr.* (1858) 140 Disposed to those kind of books you mention of *nouvell's* and other *entretiens* of folly and levity. [**1717** M. W. MONTAGU *Let.* 1 Jan. (1965) I. 293 Would you have me write novelles like the Countess of D'Aunois?] **1887** *Athenæum* 1 Jan. 10/2 M. de Maupassant's 'Petite Roque', a collection of *nouvelles* written with his usual cleverness. **1917** G. SAINTSBURY *Hist. Fr. Novel* I. iv. 88 The faults of long-windedness, of otiose padding, of unnecessary episodes, etc., are almost mechanically or mathematically impossible in the *nouvelle*. **1935** S. SPENDER *Destructive Element* 48 Many other of the stories of this period, especially what he [*sc.* Henry James] called the 'nouvelles', as distinct from the short stories which are more in the nature of the anecdote. **1959** *Times Lit. Suppl.* 27 Mar. 182/1 *Mademoiselle B*—is a *nouvelle* in a recognizable style (it reads as if it had been intelligently translated from the French) and a familiar convention. **1975** *Times* 5 Apr. 5/7 What we learnt from Henry James to call a *nouvelle*, which I take to be a fictional narrative longer than a long short-story and shorter than a short novel.

‖**nouvelle cuisine** (ˌnuːvɛl kwɪˈziːn). [Fr., = 'new cooking'.] A style of (esp. French) cooking that avoids traditional rich sauces and emphasizes the freshness of the ingredients and attractive presentation.

1975 *Harpers & Queen* June 124/1 Certainly the French National Digestive System should be functioning more comfortably these days, thanks to the influence of La Nouvelle Cuisine Française. *Ibid.* The devoted journal of La Nouvelle Cuisine Française is the monthly food magazine *Le Nouveau Guide Gault-Millau*. **1977** *Bon Appétit* May 24/1 Theoretically, *la nouvelle cuisine*.. aims at producing clear, fresh flavors and light textures instead of self-defeating richness. **1978** *Esquire* 23 May 69/3 Gault and Millau claim to have invented in 1974 the now familiar term 'la nouvelle cuisine', a cooking style that is 'light, imaginative, modern'. **1978** CONRAN & HOBHOUSE tr. *Guerard's Cuisine Gourmande* 9 These three-star chefs have between them changed French cooking radically. The new style.. which they have developed together over the years is called Nouvelle Cuisine, and its principles are that food should have a 'lyrical lightness'. **1980** C. CONRAN in Conran & Sharman tr. *Nouvelle Cuisine Jean & Pierre Troisgros* 10 They went to work for the family godfather of the nouvelle cuisine, Fernand Point, whose restaurant.. was.. the Mecca of all serious eaters. **1982** J. GRIGSON *Fruit Bk.* 167 Even manuals of *nouvelle cuisine*, in which fruit is put to new savoury uses, neglect the gooseberry. **1986** S. ORBACH *Hunger Strike* iii. 57 The relative simplicity of nouvelle cuisine has seriously challenged the hegemony of French bourgeois cookery.

nouvelles. *rare.* [a. F. *nouvelles*, later form of *novelles*: see NOVEL *sb.* 1.] News.

c **1500** *Melusine* 166 The pucelle was so joyous of these nouuelles that she had neuer in her natural lyf so grete joye. **1548** *Compl. Scot.* 119 Dauid said to the ȝoung man that brocht the nouuelles. **1894** E. DOWSON *Let.* 30 July (1967) 307 Write and give me your nouvelles.

nouvellette, variant of NOVELETTE, after F. *nouvelle*.

1824 *Blackw. Mag.* XV. 835 As novels and nouvellettes go at present, the story is not particularly valuable. **1872** HARDWICK *Trad. Lanc.* 128 The tales might, perhaps with propriety, be termed *nouvelletes*, or little novels.

‖**nouvelle vague** (nuvɛl vag). [Fr., f. *nouvelle* (fem.) new + *vague* wave.] A new movement or trend; *spec.* one in film-making originating in France in the late 1950s; also applied to other arts; also *attrib.*

1959 *Times* 4 Sept. 5/4 It is a film made by one of the old guard rather than by a member of the *nouvelle vague*. **1960** *Times* 1 Nov. 16/4 The film is in no important sense *nouvelle vague*. **1962** *John o' London's* 19 Apr. 371/2 If no clique, trend, *avant garde* or *nouvelle vague* has yet arisen to claim the creative heritage of social change, perhaps it is because the upheaval is still with us. **1962** *Movie* Sept. 34/1 *Paris Nous Appartient* is arguably the most important Nouvelle Vague film to date. **1965** *Philos. Rev.* LXXIV. 53 The *nouvelle vague* of mathematics teachers. **1973** 'E. MCBAIN' *Let's hear It* xiv. 209 Teddy normally enjoyed films, except when she was submitted to the excesses of a sadistic *nouvelle vague* camera. **1974** *Times* 26 Apr. 16/3 In terms of chronology the celebrated *nouvelle vague* of the late Fifties must by now be reckoned the old guard.

nouzle, obs. form of NUZZLE *v.*

nov, obs. form of NEW *a.*; NOW *adv.*

Nov., abbreviation of NOVEMBER.

‖**nova** (ˈnəʊvə). Pl. **novæ** (ˈnəʊviː). [L. *nova*, fem. sing. of *novus* new.]

†**1.** (See quot.) *Obs. rare*⁻⁰.

1688 HOLME *Armoury* III. xxii. (Roxb.) 274/1 Sorts of Tobacco: Pig taile, is a very small wreath or roll tobacco..: Nova, the thickest wreath.

2. *Astr.* A new star or nebula. In mod. use, a star that suddenly increases in brightness by several magnitudes and then, after a period of maximum brightness lasting from a few days to several years, decreases to its former brightness over a much longer period.

Now distinguished from a SUPERNOVA.

1877 G. F. CHAMBERS *Astron.* 918 Nova; a word introduced by Sir J. Herschel to signify a star or nebula not previously recorded. **1899** *Daily News* 22 Apr. 8/6 The appearance of a Nova was recorded on the plates... The appearances of Novæ have given rise to many theories as to their origin. **1927** H. N. RUSSELL et al. *Astronomy* II. xxii. 777 The brightest stars ever recorded have been novæ. Nova B Cassiopeiæ, known as 'Tycho's star', which appeared in November, 1572, was for some days as bright as Venus at her best (visible in the daytime), and then gradually waned. **1939** *Nature* 15 July 122/2 Some of these extra-galactic novæ have a brightness equal to nearly 100 million suns... In 1934 Baade and Zwicky suggested that these extremely bright objects were not ordinary novæ, but presented a class by themselves—the class of super-novæ. **1955** *Sci. News Let.* 9 July 31/1 Because of a sudden break-down of the normally stable energy conditions in its interior, a nova abruptly flares up to thousands of times its normal brightness, so that a star never before visible from the earth bursts into brilliance. **1956** R. A. LYTTLETON *Mod. Universe* v. 167 Every year on the average about a score of stars within our own galaxy undergo this catastrophic development and become what are termed novae. **1968** *Times* 2 Dec. 17/2 Most of the X-ray sources are located in the Milky Way and some of them have been identified with old novae—stars that flared brightly a long time ago and are now fading.

nováčekite (nəʊˈvɑːtʃəkaɪt). *Min.* Also **novacekite**. [f. the name of Radim *Nováček* (see quot. 1951) + -ITE¹.] A hydrated oxide and arsenate of magnesium and uranium, $Mg(UO_2)_2(AsO_4)_2.12H_2O$, which is a member of the autunite group and is found as yellow, tetragonal crystals.

1951 C. FRONDEL in *Amer. Mineralogist* XXXVI. 682 In the course of examination of a small suite of secondary uranium minerals from Schneeberg, Saxony,..two specimens were found of a mineral that has proved to be a new hydrated magnesium uranyl arsenate member of the autunite group. The name novacekite is proposed for this species after the Czech mineralogist Radim Nováček (1905—1942), who made important contributions to the knowledge of the mineralogy of uranium. **1956** *Ibid.* XLI. 152 (*heading*) Novacekite from the Wichita Mountains, Oklahoma. **1965** G. J. WILLIAMS *Econ. Geol. N.Z.* xiii. 206/2 The novacekite-like secondary uranium mineral is consistent with the presence of arsenopyrite. **1971** *Mineral. Abstr.* XXII. 226/2 Localities are mentioned for.. nováčekite, especially in NE Brazil.

Novachord (ˈnəʊvəkɔːd). Also **novachord**. [f. L. *nova* new + CHORD *sb.*²] Name of an electronic musical instrument of the organ family.

1940 *Chamber's Techn. Dict.* 584/1 *Novachord*, an electronic musical instrument using a single keyboard, sustaining and swell pedals. **1944** W. APEL *Harvard Dict. Mus.* 237/1 The *Novachord*, a six-octave, single-manual instrument which.. resembles the spinet in form, employs a purely electronic tone-generating system. **1952** B. ULANOV *Hist. Jazz in Amer.* (1958) xxiii. 324 He made Shearing-like records with rhythm section and Novachord. **1955** L. FEATHER *Encycl. Jazz* (1956) 111 LPs: Bruns. 58048 (trio & Terry Gibbs);.. Dec. 5297 (novachord, w. Hampton). **1970** *Oxf. Compan. Mus.* (ed. 10) 325/1 Akin to oscillating valve organs is the *Novachord*, a domestic six-octave keyboard instrument giving fourteen different tonal qualities.

novaculite (nəʊˈvækjʊlaɪt). *Min.* [f. L. *novacula* a razor + -ITE¹ 2 b.] A hard argillaceous slate used for hones. Also *attrib.*

1796 KIRWAN *Elem. Min.* (ed. 2) I. 238 Novaculite. Turkey hone. *Ibid.* 356 Novaculite Porphyry. **1802** ACERBI *Trav.* II. 276 If the novaculite of Kirwan were meant, it should be referred to the argillaceous genus. **1863** DANA *Man. Geol.* 322 In Arkansas, the novaculite used extensively for hones.. occur[s] in beds referred to this [Millstone soil] epoch. **1882** GEIKIE *Text-bk. Geol.* II. II. §6. 122 Whet-slate, novaculite, hone-stone, an exceedingly hard fine-grained siliceous rock.

novákite (nəʊˈvɑːkaɪt). *Min.* Also **novakite**. [ad. G. *novákit* (Johan & Hak 1959, in *Chem. der Erde* XX. 49), f. the name of Jiří *Novák*, 20th-cent. Czechoslovakian mineralogist: see -ITE¹.] A tetragonal arsenide of copper, Cu_4As_3, found at Černy Důl, Czechoslovakia, which is steel-grey on fresh fracture but becomes almost black on exposure to air.

1959 *Amer. Mineralogist* XLIV. 1321 From the powder pattern, novakite is tetragonal.. and.. pseudocubic. **1961** *Mineral. Abstr.* XV. 292/2 Novakite occurs (with chalcocite and löllingite) as impregnations in carbonate rocks in Cu-Co-As ores. **1970** *Amer. Mineralogist* LV. 1084 (*caption*) Polished surface of kutinaite.. intergrown with novákite.. and calcite.

‖**novalia** (nəʊˈveɪlɪə). [L., pl. of *novāle*, f. *novus* new.] Lands newly brought under cultivation.

1838 W. BELL *Dict. Law Scot.* 681 By the canon law, the prescription of tithes did not extend to those of novalia, or newly improved lands. **1896** *Mem. St. Giles, Durham* (Surtees) p. xx, The tithes of all novalia.

†**no'vality.** *Obs. rare*⁻¹. [a. OF. *novalité* = med.L. *novalitas*, f. *novalis* new.] Novelty.

a **1450** *Knt. de la Tour* (1868) 62 No wise woman aught to be hasty to take upon the new noualitees of array.

†'**novalty.** *Obs. rare.* [Cf. prec. and OF. *novaleté*.] Novelty.

1585 *Reg. Privy Council Scot.* IV. 17 The graunting of this pretendit commissioun is ane novaltie. **1630** PRYNNE *Anti-Armin.* 258 The Articles of Lambheth contain in them no noualties.

†**No'vangle.** *Obs. rare*⁻¹. [Cf. next.] A New Englander.

1652 H. L'ESTRANGE *Amer. no Jewes* 68, I like not the word *Novangles*;.. the word *Novangles* in English is too prostitute and subject.. to the abuse of the Author's meaning, and to be exchanged and spoken Newfangles.

No'vanglian, *a.* and *sb.* [f. *Nov(a) Anglia*, Latinized name of New England.] **A.** *adj.* Of or pertaining to New England. **B.** *sb.* = prec.

1679 *New Eng. Hist. Reg.* (1850) IV. 130 Nov-Anglian Heroes universall call, Did Constitute him major Generall. **1752** MACSPARRAN *Amer. Dissect.* (1753) 31 The Novanglians in general, the Rhode-Islanders in particular. *Ibid.* 42 The Novanglian Clergy of our Church. **1813** J. ADAMS *Wks.* (1856) X. 49 Correspondences,.. Virginian and Novanglian, English and French. **1860** B. TAYLOR *At Home & Abroad* Ser. II. (1888) 339, I must say, I rather admire this stolid self-reliance and Novanglian assumption.

†**novantique,** *a. Obs. rare*⁻¹. [f. L. *nov-us* new + ANTIQUE.] = New-old (see NEW *a.* 10 a).

a **1688** CUDWORTH *Immut. Mor.* (1731) 62 The Assertors of this Novantique Philosophy.

novargent (nəʊˈvɑːdʒənt). [f. L. *nov-um* new + *argent-um* silver.] (See quot.)

1856 *Orr's Circ. Sci., Pract. Chem.* 65 A 'novargent' solution for re-silvering old plated goods.

Nova Scotian (nəʊvə ˈskəʊʃ(ɪ)ən), *sb.* and *a.*

A. *sb.* A native or inhabitant of the province of Nova Scotia in Eastern Canada.

1867 B. MURDOCH *Hist. Nova Scotia* III. xxxix. 536 Captain Stewart.. assured them he was a Nova Scotian in temperament. **1879** *Rep. of Nova Scotia Hist. Soc.* I. 28 As Nova Scotians, the duty of the moment.. is to garner up the materials of Provincial History before they perish. **1913** B. WILSON *Nova Scotia* (ed. 2) iii. 29 Cherishing of the memory of their worthy forerunners is perhaps the most marked characteristic of Nova Scotians today. **1968** *Globe & Mail* (Toronto) 13 Feb. 3/2 A Nova Scotian, he is the only declared candidate from the Atlantic provinces. **1971** E. JONES in J. Spencer *Eng. Lang. W. Afr.* 67 The Sierra Leone settlement consisted of the following groups of people: The Black Poor, the Maroons and Nova Scotians, and the West African recaptives.

B. *adj.* Of or pertaining to Nova Scotia.

1866 B. MURDOCH *Hist. Nova Scotia* II. p. iii, By almost imperceptible degrees the people acquire habits, sentiments and pursuits suited to the land in which they live.. and thus the Nova Scotian character is gradually developed. **1869** *Bradshaw's Railway Manual* XXI. 390 The Nova Scotian Government secured the passage of an Act to authorize the extension of the trunk line. **1902** W. JAMES *Var. Relig. Exper.* viii. 173 The autobiography of Henry Alline, the Nova Scotian evangelist. **1969** in Halpert & Story *Christmas Mumming in Newfoundland* 24 South coast Newfoundlanders.. manned a substantial part of the Nova Scotian.. deep-sea fishing fleets.

novate (nəʊˈveɪt), *v. rare.* [f. ppl. stem of L. *novāre* to make new, etc., f. *novus* new.] *trans.* To replace by something new; *spec.* in (Roman) law, to replace by a new obligation, debt, etc.

1611 SPEED *Hist. Gt. Brit.* IX. xxiv. §55 And if that Peace doth make *nouationem*, then the forfeiture of your right.. is wiped away, nouated and cleansed by this Peace. **1875** POSTE *Gaius* xv, Non-statutory actions.. have no power at civil law of consuming or novating a right of action. **1880** MUIRHEAD *Gaius* 552 It.. might be employed even when the obligation novated was only a natural one.

absol. **1876** *Law Rep.* 5 Chanc. Div. 261 There can be no novation without an intention to novate on the part of the creditor.

†**novateur.** *Obs. rare*⁻¹. [a. F. *novateur* (16th c.).] = NOVATOR.

1600 HAMILTON in *Cath. Tract.* (S.T.S.) 225 To reid the scriptures corruptit be the fals translations of thir nouateurs.

Novatian (nəʊˈveɪʃ(ɪ)ən), *sb.* and *a.* Also 5 **Nouacian**. [ad. late L. *Novātiān-ī* (pl.), f. *Novātiān-us* (see def.).]

A. *sb.* A member of the sect founded by Novatianus, a Roman presbyter in the middle of the third century (see quots.). Chiefly *pl.*

'Novatian has sometimes been confounded with his contemporary Novatus, a Carthaginian presbyter, who held similar views' (*Encycl. Brit.* XVII. 604/1).

c **1449** PECOCK *Repr.* v. iii. 499 The sect of Nouacianys, whiche helden that if eny man falle oonys fro the feith, that he schal neuere haue ther of forȝeunes. **1546** HOOPER *Early Writ.* (Parker Soc.) 169 One Meletius.. said that every sin committed was irremissible, as the Novatians and Catharenes say. **1581** HAMILTON in *Cath. Tract.* (S.T.S.) 75 He socht the iugement of Agelius, albeit he vas ane Nouatian of the contrare faction. **1638** CHILLINGW. *Relig. Prot.* I. vi. §49. 368 The Novatians, excepting their peculiar error, of denying reconciliation to those that fell in persecution, held other things in common with Catholiques. **1685** STILLINGFL. *Orig. Brit.* iii. 94 If any among the Novatians returned to the Church,.. their Ordination seems to be allowed. **1740** N. LARDNER *Credib. Gosp. Hist.* II. xlvii. Wks. 1788 III. 218 The Novatians are said to have condemned second marriages as unlawful and sinful. **1788** GIBBON *Decl. & F.* xlvii. IV. 547 Cyril auspiciously opened his reign by oppressing the Novatians, the most innocent and harmless of the sectaries. **1869** LECKY *Europ. Mor.* II. 109 The Montanists and the Novatians surpassed and stimulated the private penances of the orthodox.

B. *adj.* Of or pertaining to Novatianus or the sect of Novatians.

1630 PRYNNE *Lame Giles* 12 The Novatian Catherist. **1651** BAXTER *Inf. Bapt.* 310 The Novatian error bred such a fear in men of sinning after baptism, that at last multitudes delayed it. **1670** G. H. *Hist. Cardinals* I. III. 84 Which was the Foundation of the Novatian Schism. **1740** N. LARDNER *Credib. Gosp. Hist.* II. xlvii. Wks. 1788 III. 223 There is no ground for thinking the African Novatus the first author of the Novatian rigid principle. **1875** LIGHTFOOT *Comm. Col.* 98 [Phrygia] was the foster mother of Novatian rigorism.

Novatianism (nəʊˈveɪʃ(ɪ)ənɪz(ə)m). [f. prec. + -ISM.] The doctrine or tenets of the Novatians.

1574 WHITGIFT *Def. Aunsw.* i. Wks. 1851 I. 174 That very perfection of an outward platform..is one step to Novatianism. *a* **1656** BP. HALL *Rem. Wks.* (1660) 303, I do not tell you that this author is wont to be impeached of Novatianisme. **1740** N. LARDNER *Credib. Gosp. Hist.* II. xliii. Wks. 1788 III. 69 The same letter.., where Dionysius informs Stephen of the peace of the eastern churches with regard to Novatianism. **1854** MILMAN *Lat. Chr.* I. 50 Cyprian had grounds..for his fears of Novatianism.

Novatianist (nəʊˈveɪʃ(ɪ)ənɪst). [f. as prec. + -IST.] A Novatian. Also *attrib.*

1597 HOOKER *Eccl. Pol.* v. lxii. §6. 324 The Baptisme which Nouatianists gaue, stood firme. **1707** POTTER *Ch. Govt.* v. (1845) 210 To encourage the Novatianists to return to the church. **1874** ROBERTSON *Hist. Chr. Ch.* (ed. 6) I. 170 The Novatianists assumed the name of Cathari, or Puritans. **1876** PLUMMER tr. *Döllinger Hippolytus & Callistus* ii. 61 The Novatianist sect still existed in the poet's home in North Spain.

novation (nəʊˈveɪʃən). Also 6–7 nouation (6 -cion), 6 *Sc.* novatioun, nowation. [ad. L. *novātiōn-em*, n. of action f. *novāre*: see NOVATE *v.* So F. *novation*, Sp. *novacion*, It. *novazione*.]

1. The introduction of something new; a change, an innovation.

Common in Sc. use from *c* 1560 to 1650. Now *rare.*

1533 BELLENDEN *Livy* IV. ii. (S.T.S.) II. 54 In þe nixt petitioun we desire na novatiouns nor new materis. **1561–2** *Reg. Privy Council Scot.* I. 266 Gif ony suddane alteratioun or novatioun be preissit or attemptit. **1607** J. NORDEN *Surv. Dial.* I. 22, I like not nouations and new deuices that our forefathers haue not seene or done. *a* **1670** SPALDING *Troub. Chas. I* (1850) 47 Their inbringing of novations within the church, such as rotchets.., the book of ordination [etc.]. **1806** W. TAYLOR in *Monthly Mag.* XXI. 492 These schemes of novation deserve a deliberate discussion. **1830** —— *Hist. Surv. Germ. Poetry* I. 121 In all the Gothic dialects rime is a novation.

†**b.** A revolution. *Obs. rare*$^{-1}$.

1607 CHAPMAN *Bussy d' Ambois* Plays 1873 II. 134 What newes? Strange ones, and fit for a Nouation.

†**2.** Alteration, renewal. *Obs. rare.*

1549 COVERDALE, etc. *Erasm. Par. 2 Pet.* ii. 20 Like as the mutacion chaunced, what tyme they loked not for it.., euen so shall the nouacion happen. **1635** PERSON *Varieties* I. 8 At the last conflagration it [the heaven] shall suffer a change and novation, but no dissolution.

3. *Law.* The substitution of a new debtor, creditor, contract, etc., in place of an old one.

1682 SCARLETT *Exchanges* 341 Here is a relinquishing the first Debtor, and a taking of another in his stead, which is a Novation, which doth alwayes extinguish the first Contract. **1726** AYLIFFE *Parergon* 445 When a Prescription,..a Novation, Payment of Debt..and the like are propounded in Judgment. **1838** BELL *Dict. Law Scot.* 681 *Novation.* See *Innovation.* **1876** *Law Rep.* 5 *Chanc. Div.* 259 In all three cases there has been a complete novation, and a substitution of new debtors in the place of the old. **1891** *Times* 28 Feb. 8/4 There was a novation of contract as soon as the company was incorporated.

noˈvative, *a. rare*$^{-1}$. [See prec. and -ATIVE.] Of the nature of novation.

1875 POSTE *Gaius* III. 447 Gaius attributes a Novative power not only to Litis contestatio, but also to Judgment.

†**novato.** *Obs. rare.* Some kind of fabric.

1623 J. TAYLOR (Water P.) *Praise Hempseed* Wks. III. 64/2 Rash, Taffata, Paropa, and Nouato, Shagge, Fillizetta, Damaske and Mockado. **1668** KIRKMAN *Eng. Rogue* II. (1871) II. 114 Now to hear them muster up the names of their stuffs,..there's your Parragon, Burragon,..Novato, Pinckanilly [etc.].

novator (nəʊˈveɪtə(r)). [ad. L. *novātor*, agent-n. f. *novāre*: see NOVATE *v.*] An innovator.

1644 BP. MAXWELL *Prerog. Chr. Kings* v. 59 He knew not these differencies these novators have coyned and forged upon the Anvell of their owne braines. **1659** T. PECKE *Parnassi Puerp.* 93 Antiquarians and Novators. [**1870** BURTON *Hist. Scot.* VI. lxviii. 415 Half a century afterwards the Brownist separatists or novators were a considerable body.]

novatory, *a. rare*$^{-1}$. [See NOVATE *v.* and -ORY.] Novative.

1880 MUIRHEAD *Gaius* III. §176 But the rule is different if my novatory stipulation be with a slave.

‖**novatrix.** [L. *novātrix*: see NOVATOR and -TRIX.] A female renewer.

1866 J. B. ROSE tr. *Ovid's Met.* 442 Nature the novatrix remoulds the frame.

†**novaturient,** *a. Obs. rare.* [f. *novāt-*, ppl. stem of L. *novāre* + -URIENT.] Desiring changes or alterations.

1679 PETTY in Ld. E. Fitzmaurice *Life* (1895) 244 The novaturient world is gaping here after the like alterations for Ireland.

novel (ˈnɒvəl), *sb.* Forms: *pl.* 5 nouellys, 5–6 -ellis, 6–7 -elles (5 -eles), -ells, 5–7 nouels; 6 *Sc.* nowellis; 5–6 novellis (6 *Sc.* -allis), 6 -elles, 7 -ells, 5–8 novels; *sing.* 6–7 nouell, 7– novel. [In senses 1 and 2, a. OF. *novelle* (*-ele, nuvele*, etc.; mod.F. *nouvelle*), = It. *novella*, fem.:—L. *novella* neut. plur. of *novellus*, f. *novus* new: see NOVEL *a.* The original stress was on the second syllable. In sense 3, ultimately from It. *novella*, Sp. *novela*, whence also F. *nouvelle*. In sense 4, ad. late L. *novella* (sc. *constitutio*), usually in pl. *novellæ*.]

†**1.** Something new; a novelty. *Obs.*

In early use always *pl.*, and freq. implying sense 2.

c **1460** *Towneley Myst.* xviii. 188 Whens euer this barne may be That shewys thise novels new? **1533** BELLENDEN *Livy* I. xix. (S.T.S.) I. 110 To be consultit with þame of certane novellis & haisty materis. **1579** SPENSER *Sheph. Cal.* Feb. 95 To nought more..my mind is bent Then to heare nouells of his deuise. **1591** SYLVESTER *Du Bartas* I. ii. 233 Who loving novels, full of affectation, Receive the Manners of each other Nation. **1613** HEYWOOD *Braz. Age* II. ii, Do you wonder..To see this Prince lye dead? Why that's no nouell, All men must dye. **1695** CONGREVE *Love for L.* III. iii, Perhaps I might..have introduc'd an Amour of my own, in Conversation, by way of Novel. **1703** T. N. *City & C. Purchaser* 57 Such Men will not..be..perswaded to a more compleat way..because it is a Novel to them. **1719** J. T. PHILLIPPS tr. *Thirty-four Confer.* p. xvi, That..no ancient Indian Apostolical Monuments might remain in those Parts to reflect Reproach upon Romish Novels.

Comb. **1596** LODGE *Wits Miserie* 13 His name is Superfluous Inuention, or as some tearme him Novel-monger or Fashions.

†**2.** **a.** *pl.* News, tidings. *Obs.*

c **1475** *Partenay* 45 Erle amerye..thes nouels hurd at that entreual. **1561** AWDELAY *Frat. Vacab.* (1869) 14 Ready to bring his Maister Nouels and tidinges, whether they be true or false. **1635** PERSON *Varieties* IV. i. §9 Saluting the Antipodes, and bringing novells from their Courts and of their caballs. **1688** in Ellis *Orig. Lett.* Ser. II. IV. 115 An invention of them that love to feed the town with the Air of Novels. **1724** *Wodrow Corr.* (1843) III. 167 When you favour me with a line, I'll be glad to have your thoughts of it, with all your novels.

†**b.** *sing.* A piece of news. *Obs.*

1610 HEYWOOD *Gold. Age* IV. i, Discourse the nouell, Neptune. **1636** MASSINGER *Gt. Dk. Florence* I. ii, You.. promise, in your clear aspect, some novel That may delight us. **1728** FIELDING *Love in Several Masques* IV. iv, *Wisemore.* What novel's this? *Malvil.* Faith! it may be a pleasant one to you. **1736** HERVEY *Mem. Geo. II*, I. 430 They must know very little of the nature of Courts..who flatter themselves that the disgrace of one person..would be anything more than the novel of a fortnight.

3. **a.** (Chiefly in *pl.*) One of the tales or short stories contained in such works as the *Decameron* of Boccaccio, the *Heptameron* of Marguerite of Valois, etc.; a short story of this type.

1566 PAINTER *Pal. Pleas.* Ded., In these histories (which by another terme I call Nouelles) he described the liues..of great princes. **1578** in *Maitland Cl. Misc.* I. (1840) 7 The first buik of the novallis of Ronsard. **1621** BURTON *Anat. Mel.* IV. II. ii. (1624) 230 Such as the old womene tolde Psyche in Apuleius, Bocace Nouells, and the rest. **1674** EVELYN *Mem.* (1857) III. 245 Marguerite of Valois..whose novels are equal to those of the witty Boccaccio. **1697** DRYDEN *Æneid* Ded., Ess. (Ker) II. 155 The trifling novels, which Ariosto, and others, have inserted in their poems. **1700** —— *Pref. Fables* ibid. 248 Boccace..wrote novels in prose, and many works in verse. [**1834** MOTLEY *Corr.* (1889) I. iii. 35 Tieck's novels (which last are a set of exquisite little tales, novels in the original meaning of the word).]

b. A fictitious prose narrative or tale of considerable length (now usually one long enough to fill one or more volumes), in which characters and actions representative of the real life of past or present times are portrayed in a plot of more or less complexity.

In 17–18th c. freq. contrasted with a *romance*, as being shorter than this, and having more relation to real life.

The older pron. *noˈvel* was retained in Sc. till the 19th c. (See NOVELLE, and cf. Burns *Rob Mossgiel*, 'O leave novels, ye Mauchline belles.')

1639 J. S. *Clidamas* pref. sign. A2 *recto*, Here I present you with this little Novel..which though in it selfe it be nothing, yet..may prove something. **1643** MILTON *Divorce* I. vi. Wks. 1851 IV. 33 This is no mere amatorious novel. **1676** ETHEREDGE *Man of Mode* II. i, Leave your raillery, and tell us, is there any New Wit come forth, Songs or Novels? **1693** *Humours Town* 24 She seats herself, with some Novel or Play, in a very solitary posture. **1711** STEELE *Spect.* No. 254 ¶3, I am afraid thy Brains are a little disordered with Romances and Novels. **1769** WESLEY *Wks.* (1872) III. 357 Sure no Novel in the world can be more affecting, or more surprising, than this history. **1774** *Chesterfield's Lett.* I. 130 A Novel is a kind of abbreviation of a Romance. **1806–7** BERESFORD *Mis. Hum. Life* (1826) II. xxxi, A cargo of novels of their own choice with such titles as 'Delicate Sensibility'. **1867** TROLLOPE *Chron. Barset* I. xxxv. 311 [He] sat down over the fire with a volume of a novel. **1889** *Cornh. Mag.* Feb. 119 It's more like a novel than real life.

c. The particular type of literature which is constituted or exemplified by this class of fiction. (Formerly without article; now with *the*.)

1757 MRS. GRIFFITH *Lett. Henry & Frances* (1767) I. p. iii, I never read higher love-letters in my life, without the bombast of romance, or the levity of novel. **1766** FORDYCE *Serm. to Yng. Wom.* (1767) I. iv. 148 There seem to me.. very few, in the style of Novel, that you can read with safety. **1859** MASSON *Brit. Novelists* i. 2 The Novel, at its highest, is a prose Epic. **1871** *Spectator* 22 April 484 England has hardly received the honour she deserves as the birthplace of the modern novel.

d. A fiction, story, invention. *rare*$^{-1}$.

1762 FOOTE *Liar* III. Wks. 1799 I. 314 Your novels won't pass upon me.

4. *Roman Law.* A new decree or constitution, supplementary to the Codex, *esp.* one of those made by the Emperor Justinian. (Cf. NOVELL.)

1612 BREREWOOD *Lang. & Relig.* xv. 154 As appeareth in the novel of Leo Sophus, touching the order and precedence of metropolitans. **1672–5** COMBER *Comp. Temple* (1702) 223 The Codes and Novels of Justinian, Theodosius, and other Emperors in the East. **1715** BINGHAM *Orig. Eccles.* IV. 275 The Edict which that Council refers to, was another Novel of Justinian's. **1788** GIBBON *Decl. & F.* xliv. IV. 366 The nine collations, the legal standard of modern tribunals, consist of ninety-eight Novels. **1818** HALLAM *Mid. Ages* (1872) II. 149 By a novel of Valentinian III about 450. **1871** BRYCE *Holy Rom. Emp.* xv. (ed. 3) 248 Edicts issued by a Franconian or Swabian sovereign were inserted as Novels in the Corpus Juris, in the latest editions of which custom still allows them a place.

transf. **1695** J. EDWARDS *Perfect. Script.* 415 The sacred books of the New Testament, the Evangelical Novels, the new laws. **1885** tr. *Wellhansen's Proleg. Hist. of Israel* v. i. 159 A novel of the law (Exod. xxx. 15) raised it to half a shekel.

5. *attrib.* and *Comb.* (sense 3). **a.** in various uses.

1757 MRS. GRIFFITH *Lett. Henry & Frances* (1767) I. 174 *note*, This was her *Novel application [Ethelinda]. **1797** COLMAN *Br. Grins, Nightgown & Slippers* xviii, Stomacks are so cloyed with *novel-feeding. **1883** *19th Cent.* Feb. 288 They prefer penny fiction serials to being *novel-less. **1788** BURKE *Sp. agst. W. Hastings* Wks. XIII. 30 The false, idle, girlish, *novel-like morality of the world.. **1797** MRS. ROBINSON *Walsingham* III. 230 It was fresh from a modern *novel-mill, and strongly recommended by the reviewers. **1886** WILLIS & CLARK *Cambridge* III. 121 The Newspaper Room, the Music Room, and the *Novel Room. **1806** CUMBERLAND *Mem.* (1807) II. 256, I had no books but such as a circulating *novel-shop provided. **1801** SURR *Splendid Misery* I. 79 She blushed at the exposure of her *novel-sick passion. **1768–74** TUCKER *Lt. Nat.* (1834) I. 596 The new-loosened school-boy and *novel-studied girl.

b. Objective and obj. genitive.

1903 A. BENNETT *Truth about Author* xii. 150, I was almost bound to pander to the vulgar taste..in my short stories, but I had sworn solemnly that I would keep the *novel-form unsullied. **1967** A. BURGESS *Novel Now* ii. 27 In *The Waves*, whose poetic prose now reads very awkwardly, we seem to get as far away from the novel-form as possible. **1838** J. S. MILL in *Westm. Rev.* XXVIII. 439 He..fulfils with propriety the essential functions of a *novel-hero. **1768–74** TUCKER *Lt. Nat.* (1834) II. 612 Our *novel-hunters learn to despise all common prudence. *a* **1810** TANNAHILL *Poems* (1846) 60 In these *novel-huntin' days, There's nane but bairns can act our plays. **1948** F. R. LEAVIS *Great Tradition* iii. 138 He wrote..other 'American' classics. Not to speak of short-stories and things of less than *novel-length. **1972** E. ROUTLEY *Puritan Pleasures of Detective Story* vi. 72 [Austin] Freeman..was not stylist enough to sustain the technique through a story of full novel-length. **1866** *Cornh. Mag.* Jan. 13 There is little in either of these scenes..which the ordinary *novel-maker could 'seize'. **1850** KINGSLEY *Alt. Locke* vii, Quickened into prurient activity by the low, *novel-mongering press. **1841** THACKERAY *Men & Pictures* Wks. 1900 XIII. 377 A couple of instances from 'actual life', as the fashionable *novel-puffers say. **1775** BP. WATSON *Anecd.* (1817) 51, I hate the flimsy womanish eloquence of *novel readers. **1894** RALEIGH *Eng. Novel* ix. (1903) 256 Novelists have generally been insatiable novel-readers. **1921** P. LUBBOCK *Craft of Fiction* (1926) iii. 41 There is nothing more familiar to a novel-reader of today than the difficulty of discovering what the novel in his hand is about. **1789** A. SEWARD *Let.* 17 Aug. (1811) II. 319 The contemptible rage for *novel-reading, is a pernicious and deplorably prevalent taste. **1802** MRS. E. PARSONS *Myst. Visit* II. 172 Very unlike a novel-reading Miss. ?*c* **1810** *New Comic Songster* 20 She learnt it from novel reading, O. **1870** EMERSON *Soc. & Sol.* viii. 172 So much novel reading cannot leave the young men and maidens untouched. **1947** 'G. ORWELL' in *Tribune* 31 Jan. 8/1 Raymond Postgate, who was then editor, had asked me to do the *novel reviews from time to time. **1951** *Observer* 8 Apr. 7/4 *Novel-reviewers receive letters from readers asking why the books we choose to notice are all..'sad, bad and mad'. **1893** E. DOWSON *Let.* *c* 20 Sept. (1967) 292 The opinion of the average *novel-reviewing Le Gallienish animal. **1862** THACKERAY *Round. Papers, De Finibus*, Of all the *novel-spinners now extant. **1833** MACAULAY in Trevelyan *Life* (1876) I. 303 Have I nothing to do but to be your *novel-taster. **1832** CARLYLE *Misc.* (1857) III. 39 The distressed *Novelwright. **1873** W. S. MAYO *Never Again* xvii. 222 The chapter is the crowning mercy of novel-wrights. **1728** *Novel-writer [see NOVELIST 4]. **1814** SCOTT *Wav.* Pref. to ed. 3, A man..to whom the reputation of being a novel-writer might be prejudicial. **1883** W. BLACK *Shandon Bells* xxxii, You would have me allow..novel-writers to review other people's novels. **1818** LADY MORGAN *Autobiogr.* (1859) 44 He [Monk Lewis] was the founder of the dramatic school of *novel-writing. **1856** DE QUINCEY *Confess.* Wks. 1859 I. 216 *note*, The deluge of novel-writing talent..which has overflowed our literature.

novel (ˈnɒvəl), *a.* Also 5–6 nouel, 5–7 -ell, 7 novell. [a. OF. *novel* (mod.F. *nouvel, nouveau*), = Sp. and Pg. *novel*, It. *novello*:—L. *novell-um*, f. *nov-um* new: cf. prec. Not in common use till after 1600. See also NOVILE *a.*]

1. †**a.** New, young, fresh. *Obs. rare.*

c **1420** *Pallad. on Husb.* I. 209 A novel vyne vp gooth by diligence As fast as hit gooth doun by negligence. **1616** CHAPMAN *Homer's Hymn Hermes* 60 He strait assumed a novell voices note.

†**b.** Newly made or created. *Obs.*

c **1475** *Partenay* 694 The writyng sealled ful truly With the gret seal of thys Erle nouel. *Ibid.* 5397 For men had hym told off this strenght nouell. *c* **1650** *Don Bellianis* 22 One in a white armor like a novell knight.

†**c.** Newly acquired. *Obs. rare*$^{-1}$.

1586 MARLOWE *1st Pt. Tamburl.* II. v, Then shall we send to this triumphing King, And bid him battle for his novel crown?

†**d.** Recent; of recent origin. *Obs.*

novel disseisin: see DISSEISIN 1 b.

1641 'SMECTYMNUUS' *Answ.* (1653) 19 A Bishop..is but a Novell invention. *a* **1676** HALE *Prim. Orig. Man.* (1677) 163 But this seems to be but a novel Conceit. *a* **1727** NEWTON *Chronol. Amended* ii. (1728) 222 They..boast their antiquity, not knowing that they are novel, and lived not above eleven hundred years ago.

2. New; of a new kind or nature; strange; hitherto unknown.

c **1475** *Partenay* 2696, I thorughly know all thes nouell tidinges Full good and fair ben vnto vs. **1567** DRANT *Horace, Ep.* I. ii. Giij, If nouel woorkes had bene of greekes accompted of so could,..where now had bene these workes, which we call oulde? **1615** CROOKE *Body of Man* 321 Let himselfe see how farre this nouell speculation of his hath transported him. **1651** BAXTER *Inf. Bapt.* 345 My present purpose is..to manifest the concent of the learned to most that seemeth novel and singular. **1718** HICKES & NELSON *J. Kettlewell* II. xxxiv. 140 The Novel Fancies and Inventions of our Modern Humorists in Religion. **1782** PRIESTLEY *Corrupt. Chr.* II. VI. 38 This opinion..was bold and novel. **1832** R. & J. LANDER *Exped. Niger* III. xix. 162 It was something quite novel to see two large parties of people bartering commodities in this manner. **1870** L'ESTRANGE *Life Miss Mitford* I. vi. 169 A style of decoration more novel than elegant.

†**b.** ***novel assignment*** (see quots.). *Obs.*

1607 COWELL *Interpr.*, *Novel assignement*, is an assignement of time, Place, or such like, otherwise then as before it was assigned. **1696** PHILLIPS, *Novel assignment*, is where a Man brings Trespass for breaking his Close, and the Defendant justifies in a Place where no Trespass was done; but the Plaintiff assigns the Place where the Trespass was done. **1727–38** CHAMBERS *Cycl.*, *Novel assignment*, in an action of trespass, is an assignment of time, place, or the like, in a declaration, otherwise or more particularly than it was in the writ.

c. ***novel constitution***, = NOVEL *sb.* 4.

1726 AYLIFFE *Parergon* 135 By the Novel Constitutions, Burial may not be inhibited, or deny'd to any one.

†**'novelant.** *Obs.* Also **nouell-, novellant(e, novilant.** [ad. It. *novellante*, pres. pple. of *novellare* to relate news; orig. used in It. form.] A relater of current events; a newsmonger.

1602 *Archpriests' Controv.* II. 37 Which he deliuered vnto the nouellantes of Rome, to be spreaded amongst them. **1610** in Birch *Crt. & Times. Jas. I* (1849) I. 115 You need no better novellante than my lady, who was present at all. **1660** FULLER *Mixt Contempl.* (1841) 184, I know some who repair to such novelants on purpose to know what news is false by their reporting thereof. *a* **1661** —— *Worthies, Essex* I. (1662) 335 For things past he was a Perfect Historian; for things present, a Judicious Novilant.

noveldom ('nɒvəldəm). [f. NOVEL *sb.* 3 b + -DOM.] The world of novels; novels collectively.

1831 *Fraser's Mag.* III. 96 This being the state of Noveldom. **1854** THOREAU *Walden* iii. (1863) 114 Aspiring heroes of universal noveldom. **1887** *Pall Mall G.* 29 Sept. 3/1 The realists of noveldom.

nove'lese. [f. NOVEL *sb.* 3 b + -ESE: cf. *journalese*.] The style of language characteristic of inferior novels.

1900 *Pall Mall G.* 13 Jan. 3 The English is novelese, when it does not degenerate into sheer bad grammar.

nove'lesque, *a.* [f. as prec. + -ESQUE.] Characteristic of, in the manner of, a novel.

1883 *Academy* 15 Sept. 171/2 To look aghast at such novelesque treatment of an historical theme.

'novelet. Also **novellet.** [f. NOVEL *sb.* + -ET¹ or -LET: cf. next.]

†**1.** A little new book or pamphlet. *Obs. rare*⁻¹.

1592 G. HARVEY *Four Lett.* Wks. (Grosart) I. 215 Idle creatures, the only busy readers of such Nouellets.

2. = NOVELETTE 1.

1815 W. TAYLOR in *Monthly Rev.* LXXVII. 481 A translation from the German of some tales, or Novellets, of Pfeffel. **1844** *Camp of Refuge* Publishers' Introd., We do not offer our 'Old English Novelets' as Historical. We call them Novelets—or little novels.

novelette (nɒvə'lɛt). Also **novellette.** [f. NOVEL *sb.* 3 b + -ETTE; or ad. It. *novelletta*.]

1. A story of moderate length having the characteristics of a novel. Now freq. applied to a short romantic or sentimental novel of inferior quality.

1814 J. C. DUNLOP *Hist. Fiction* II. vii. 127 The endless variety of tales, or *Novelettes*,..which form so popular and so extensive a branch of Italian literature. **1820** MOORE *Mem.* (1853) III. 180 He has nearly finished a little novelette, a story, since he has been in Paris. **1847** H. MILLER *First Impr. Eng.* xiii. (1857) 221 The novelette and poem for the young lady, and the tale for the child. **1873** RUSKIN *Fors Clav.* xxx. 2 Among them were also many tiny novelettes. **1914** G. B. SHAW *Misalliance* 66 'You want to be the hero of a romance and to get into the papers... A son revenges his mother's shame. Villain weltering in his gore...' *The Man* 'Oh, rot! do you think I read novelettes?' **1919** W. S. MAUGHAM *Moon & Sixpence* xix. 161 If I am rhetorical it is because Stroeve was rhetorical. (Do we not know that man in moments of emotion expresses himself naturally in the terms of a novelette?) **1962** *Woman's Own* 3 Nov. 14/3 A ghost-lover..is a mixture of novelettes, and film stars, and pop singers, and a girl's inner yearnings as to what she thinks she wants in a man. **1965** R. PAULSON *Novelette before 1900* p. v, Novelette..designates a distinctive, yet certainly vague, genre; a narrative in prose that is longer than a short story and shorter than a novel... It lacks the diffuseness as well as the length of a novel, and it covers more ground as well as more space than its modern offspring, the short story. **1967** A. BURGESS *Novel Now* i. 16 We're unwilling to dignify books of, say, fifty thousand words and under with the title of novel, preferring to use the Italian term *novella* ('novelette' disparages not only length but content).

2. *Music* (see quot. 1893).

1893 tr. *Riemann's Dict. Mus.*, *Novelette*, a term probably first used by Schumann for pianoforte pieces of free form and containing a considerable number of themes. **1894** *Times* 24 Nov. 7/2 She played as her solos Schumann's novelette in E major [etc.].

Hence **nove'lettist**, a writer of novelettes; also **nove'letter.**

1883 D. C. MURRAY *Hearts* III. xxxii. 210 Novelists and novelettists, poets and poetasters, are thick about her. **1898** G. B. SHAW *Our Theatres in Nineties* (1932) III. 327 Mr Ogilvie is no mere twaddling novelettist. **1904** BEERBOHM *Around Theatres* (1953) 313 The plot of it was just that which even our worst novelettists have out-grown. **1955** *Times* 28 July 3/5 She was the novelettist of the repressions of a vanished social world.

nove'lettish, *a.* Also **noveletteish.** [f. NOVELETTE + -ISH¹.] Pertaining to or characteristic of a novelette.

1904 J. C. SNAITH *Broke of Covenden* xv. 222 Our dear stiff-backed..simple-minded, penny-noveletteish feudal baron. **1921** *Sat. Westm. Gaz.* 10 Sept. 15/2 The blue-eyed make-up of the novelettish débutante. **1940** *Illustr. London News* CXCVII. 98 What an incredible creature is Maxim de Winter himself, with his novelettish name and his novelettish riches and mansion. **1963** *Listener* 31 Jan. 217/1 The abortive seduction scene, with the couple's novelettish dialogue..was unfortunate enough. **1972** *Daily Tel.* 16 Nov. 10/4 The writing is uneven, often degenerating into the novelettish.

'novelish, *a.* [f. NOVEL *sb.* + -ISH.] Inclined to ideas characteristic of novels; somewhat resembling, or suggestive of, a novel.

1805 SOUTHEY in Robberds *Mem. W. Taylor* (1843) II. 103, I..should be apt to think her a little too novelish (it is a better word than romantic). **1840** DE QUINCEY in *Tait's Mag.* VII. 355 The place, spite of its slipshod novelish name,..was really simple and unpretending. **1892** SLADEN *Japs at Home* xviii, 'Wounded Pride,' though not very novelish, has a very interesting subject.

novelism ('nɒvəlɪz(ə)m). Also 7 **nouellisme, novellisme, novalism,** 7–8 **novellism.** [f. NOVEL *sb.* + -ISM: cf. F. *nouvellisme*, Sp. *novel-*, Pg. *novellismo*.]

†**1.** Innovation; novelty. *Obs.* (freq. in 17th c.).

1626 T. H[AWKINS] tr. *Caussin's Holy Crt.* 143 Those, which haue obtruded Nouellisme so disasterous..to Christendome. **1657** J. WATTS *Dipper Sprinkled* 92 The new upstart and out-staring novelisms of these later Ages. **1673** CAVE *Prim. Chr.* I. ii. 21 Obliquely reflecting on the novellism of Christianity. **1703** *Secret Policy Jansenists* 27 If he were but the least suspected of Novellism.

2. Novel-writing.

1828 *Blackw. Mag.* XXIV. 469 What a host of pens and printers have been pressed into the service of romance and novelism by the appearance of the Waverley Novels. **1849** *Fraser's Mag.* XL. 691 A mass of volumes,..all equally marked with the generic and unmistakeable character of novelism. **1881** *Spectator* 29 Oct. 1372 The ordinary level of what may be called novelism.

novelist ('nɒvəlɪst). Also 6 **noouelist,** 7– **nouell-,** 7–9 **novell-;** 7 **nouelist(e.** [f. NOVEL *sb.* + -IST: cf. F. *nouvelliste* (1620), It. and Pg. *novellista*, Sp. *novelista*.]

†**1.** An innovator, an introducer of something new; a favourer of novelty. *Obs.* (Very common in 17th c.)

1583 FOXE *A. & M.* (1634) III. 904 Had you rather hold with these Novelists, as with Calvin? **1589** G. HARVEY *Pierce's Super.* Wks. (Grosart) II. 208 All the grayer heads begin to be stale with these Noouellists. **1608** WILLET *Hexapla Exod.* 571 Augustine doth directly oppose himselfe to all such Dogmatistes and Nouelistes. **1690** LOCKE *Hum. Und.* IV. xix. (1695) 402 To have his Authority of forty years standing..over-turned by an upstart Novelist. **1725** tr. *Dupin's Eccl. Hist. 17th C.* VI. iii. 239 By this Faith he must not understand a simple Belief (with the Novelists).

†**2.** One who is inexperienced; a novice. *Obs.*⁻¹

1630 LENNARD tr. *Charron's Wisd.* II. vii. §18. 305 There is not any thing so easie that doth not hurt and hinder vs, if wee bee but nouelists therein.

†**3.** A newsmonger, news-carrier. *Obs.*

1706 *Lond. Gaz.* No. 4207/3 The Novelist; The Tale Bearer. **1710** STEELE *Tatler* No. 178 ¶2 My Contemporaries the Novelists have..a most happy Art in saying and unsaying. **1764** GOLDSM. *Hist. Eng.* (1771) III. 186 If we may credit the novelists of that time, the prince had already fixed his affections upon the French princess.

4. A writer of novels.

1728 MORGAN *Algiers* II. iii. 239 Such opportunities of gallantizing their Wives, as the French and other Novelists, I mean Novel-writers, would insinuate. **1766** FORDYCE *Serm. Yng. Wom.* (1767) I. iv. 155 With..Novelists..we may join the common herd of Play-writers. **1804** *Gentl. Mag.* LXXIV. 404 Many of our novellists..complain of the dullness of the market at home. **1849–50** ALISON *Hist. Europe* I. i. §22. 68 The graphic novelist, with historic truth, makes Norman Richard the leader of English chivalry. **1895** TYRRELL *Latin Poet.* 220 The Greek novelists actually turned their backs on the portraiture of character.

nove'listic, *a.* [f. NOVEL *sb.* 3 b + -ISTIC.] Pertaining to, characteristic of, novels.

1835 *Fraser's Mag.* XI. 596 It..is wrought out with more novelistic skill. **1850** *Tait's Mag.* XVII. 636/1 Any subject, political, literary, artistical, or novelistic. **1881** CLARK RUSSELL *Ocean Free-Lance* III. v. 170 The theatrical, poetical, and novelistic fresh-water mountebank.

Hence **nove'listically** *adv.*

1892 *Pall Mall G.* 25 May 3/2 The methods by which a more than novelistically beautiful hero escapes.

noveli'zation. [f. next + -ATION.] The process of novelizing; conversion into a novel.

1876 *Copyright Comm., Parl. P.* (1878) 156 The converse case, namely novelization of a drama, appears to stand on the same footing. **1897** *Mem. Copyright Bill* 2 A similar injury can be inflicted by the novelisation of dramas.

novelize ('nɒvəlaɪz), *v.* Also 7 **novellize.** [f. NOVEL *sb.* + -IZE.]

1. †**a.** *trans.* To bring into a new condition; to make new or novel. *Obs.*

1642 SIR E. DERING *Sp. on Relig.* vi. 21 Affections doe stand to be novellized by the mutability of the present times. **1660** HEYLIN *Hist. Quinquart.* III. 76 These opinions.. which are now novelized by the name of Arminianism.

refl. **1631** BRATHWAIT *Whimzies* 210 If hee travaile to novellize himselfe, and not to benefit his Country.

b. *intr.* To produce something new; to introduce novelty.

1823 *Blackw. Mag.* XIV. 546 Even on beaten subjects, however, ingenuity will find means to novelize.

2. a. *trans.* To convert into the form or style of a novel.

1828 SCOTT *F.M. Perth* Introd., You surely mean to novelize, or to dramatize if you will, this most singular of all tragedies? **1833** HERSCHEL *Ess.* (1857) 15 The desperate attempts to novelize history which the herd of Scott's imitators have put forth. **1890** *Athenæum* 303/1 In 'Judge Lynch' Mr. Jessop has 'novelized' a drama.

b. *intr.* To write novels. *rare.*

1889 G. B. SHAW *Let.* 31 Aug. (1965) 221 Some time ago I tried novelizing again. **1961** *Times Lit. Suppl.* 27 Jan. 62/2 Dr. Johnson would certainly not have wanted to bring women novelizing into his analogy about dogs standing on their hind legs—even women novelizing at sixteen.

Hence **'novelized** *ppl. a.*, **'novelizing** *vbl. sb.* and *ppl. a.*

1625 BP. MOUNTAGU *App. Cæsar* 60, I must confesse my dissent thorough and sincere from the Faction of novellizing Puritans. **1651** W. JANE Εικων Ακλαστος 156 Antiquitie.. condemnes their fantasticall, and presumptuous novelizing. **1682** SIR T. BROWNE *Chr. Mor.* (1756) 36 For the novelizing spirit of man lives by variety, and the new faces of things. **1825** *Blackw. Mag.* XVIII. 238 Its author never will shine in novelizing. **1850** T. A. TROLLOPE *Impress. Wand.* xvii. 266 It was a novelised version, by no means ill done.

novell, variant of NOVEL *sb.* 4.

1853 WHEWELL *Grotius* I. p. lxxv, Of the teachers of the Roman Law, there are three kinds; the first those whose works appear in the..laws called Novells. **1883** SHELDON *Rom. Law* 1 The period was long enough to admit of the promulgation of the Digest, the Institutes, the Code, and the Novells throughout Italy.

‖**novella** (nəʊ'vɛlə). [It.] A short narrative (as the stories of Boccaccio's *Decameron*), = NOVEL *sb.* 3; a short novel or long short-story.

1902 W. D. HOWELLS *Literature & Life* 116 Few modern fictions of the novel's dimensions..have the beauty of form many a novella embodies. **1911** *Encycl. Brit.* XIX. 834/2 After Bandello the decline of the Italian *novella* is evident. **1934** *Times Lit. Suppl.* 6 Dec. 868/1 A brilliant *novella* of life in a remote Welsh valley. **1957** *Ibid.* 30 Aug. 517/3 Why is any story of more than fifty pages now called 'a short novel' or 'novella'—have publishers invented a new literary category? **1958** *Ibid.* 15 Aug. 458/2 The novella is a simpler medieval form brought to perfection in the *Decameron*. Essentially the novella is an anecdote about people you know, or know of. **1959** *John o' London's* 17 Dec. 350/1 H. E. Bates has made the *novella*, which is more generally referred to as the 'long-short story' a form of fiction which is very much his own. **1974** *Times* 23 May 10/8 There are two novellas here, both written entirely in dialogue.

†**no'velle,** obs. variant of NOVEL *sb.* 3 b.

1830 GALT *Lawrie T.* IV. i. (1849) 142, I have seen such a journey as ours described in a novelle book.

†**'noveller.** *Obs.* [f. NOVEL *sb.* or *a.* + -ER¹.] An innovator; an introducer of new ideas. (Common in 17th c.)

1604 *Supplic. Masse Priests* §36 We yeeld our selves to be prophane Novellers, yea Heretikes. **1647** TRAPP *Comm. Phil.* xi. 29 Horrible is the contempt that is now cast upon the Ministry by our Novellers. **1679** C. NESSE *Antid. agst. Popery* 125 They do scornfully call us Novellers.

So †**'novelling** *ppl. a.*, innovating. *Obs. rare.*

1621 BP. MOUNTAGU *Diatribæ* 19 The surest and gainest way to confound oppositions, and stop the mouth for euer of all nouelling Schismaticks. *Ibid.* 212 What is any nouelling vpstart, that he should controll..their *dictata*?

†**novellery.** *Obs.* [a. OF. *novellerie*, var. of *novel(e)rie*, NOVELRY.] Novelty.

1390 GOWER *Conf.* II. 259 It is a wonder thing to hiere, Bot yit for the novellerie I thenke tellen a partie. **1401** *26 Pol. Poems* 11 Laweles nouellerye loke ȝe lete. *c* **1440** *Partonope* 3626 Thow hast he falle to novellerye.

†**novellity.** *Obs. rare.* [a. OF. *novellité*, or ad. late L. *novellitas* (Tertullian): see NOVEL *a.* and -ITY.] An unwonted act; novelty.

1456 SIR G. HAYE *Law Arms* (S.T.S.) 279 Kingis suld kepe that na man do till othir dishonour, schame, na vilany, na injure, na new novelliteis. **1617** COLLINS *Def. Bp. Ely* I. p. viii, Peters primacie opposed to Pauls nouellitie and iunioritie in the words of S. Cyprian.

†**'novellous**, *a.* *Obs. rare.* [f. NOVEL *sb.*] Inclined to novelty; of a novel nature or kind.
1619 SCLATER *Exp. 1 Thess.* (1630) 550 But why are we nouellous? **1627** —— *Exp. 2 Thess.* (1629) 138 We..may thinke that nouellous of which may be said, *Non fuit sic ab initio.*

novelly ('nɒvəlɪ), *adv. rare.* [f. NOVEL *a.* + -LY².] In a novel manner; by a novel method.
1821 *Examiner* 429/2 Attitudes novelly chosen. **1844** FONBLANQUE *Life* (1874) 437 What has been so novelly and eloquently written. **1888** *Scribner's Mag.* IV. 744 A peculiar phase of hereditary insanity..which I had treated novelly and successfully in the East.

'novelness. 'Novelty, newness' (Bailey, 1731).

†**'novelry.** *Obs.* Forms: 4-5 nouelrye (5 -ry), -rie, 4 -erie; 4-5 novelrye, -rie (5 *Sc.* -re), 4 (5 *Sc.*) nowelry. [a. OF. *novelrie, -erie*, f. *novel* NOVEL *a.*: see -RY, and cf. NOVELLERY.]
1. Novelty.
1303 R. BRUNNE *Handl. Synne* 3341 Gretly þey synne yn þer queyntyse þat nouelrye al day areyse. *c* **1374** CHAUCER *Troylus* II. 756 Either they be ful of jelosye, Or maystreful, or lovyn novelrye. **1406** HOCCLEVE *La Male Regle* 38 Me longed aftir nouelrie.
2. A novel thing or matter.
1375 BARBOUR *Bruce* XIX. 394 Twa novelreis that day thai saw. *c* **1380** WYCLIF *Sel. Wks.* II. 244 Siche men synnen ofte in novelryes of þe worlde. *c* **1430** *Pilgr. Lyf Manhode* I. xl. (1869) 24 There ye mowe, if ye wole, make nouelries ynowe. **1491** *Act 7 Hen. VII*, c. 15 Persones of evyll..disposicions joyed in rumor and rebellious novelries.

†**'noveltiness.** *Obs. rare*⁻¹. [f. NOVELTY + -NESS.] Novelty, newness.
1690 W. WALKER *Idiomat. Anglo-Lat.* 461 You will be taken with the noveltiness of it.

novelty ('nɒvəltɪ). Forms: 4-6 **nouelte(e**, 5 novel-, nofeltee, 6 *Sc.* nowelte; 5-7 **noveltie** (6-7 nouel-, 6 nouil-); 5 **nouelty**, 6- **novelty**. [a. OF. *novelté* (mod.F. *nouveauté*): see NOVEL *a.* and -TY.]
1. a. Something new or unusual; a novel thing or occurrence. Also ***the novelty***, the newest thing.
1382 WYCLIF *1 Tim.* vi. 20 Eschewinge curside noueltees of voyces. *c* **1386** CHAUCER *Clerk's T.* 1004 Thay were glad right for the novelté, To have a newe lady of her toun. *c* **1440** *Gesta Rom.* xlvii. 197 Of al maner thinges ande noveltees that wer in baldak, and not in lumbardye. *a* **1533** LD. BERNERS *Gold. Bk. M. Aurel.* (1546) B, The tyme is an inuenter of nouelties. **1585** T. WASHINGTON tr. *Nicholay's Voy.* Ep. Ded., The general profite and pleasure of..such as delight in nouelties. **1632** LITHGOW *Trav.* IX. 386 They are curious, and great louers of nouelties. **1667** MILTON *P.L.* x. 891 O why did God..create at last This noveltie on Earth? **1728** R. MORRIS *Ess. Anc. Archit.* 21 Blindly fond of every little Novelty offer'd to our view. **1793** SMEATON *Edystone L.* §241 The level platform we had then obtained being something of a novelty. **1835** W. IRVING *Tour Prairies* xx, The sight of the wild horse had been a great novelty. **1868** FREEMAN *Norm. Conq.* (1877) II. viii. 299 Such visits as these were, in England at least, altogether novelties. **1868** HOLME LEE *B. Godfrey* vii, They're *the novelty* quite, but chancy things to sell.
†**b.** A new matter, a recent event, as a subject of report or talk. (Usually in *pl.*) *Obs.*
1447 BOKENHAM *Lyvys Seyntys* (Roxb.) 58 Whan þis miracle abowte was blowe..Ful gret ioy was of þat nouelte. **1475** *Plumpton Corr.* (Camden) 31 Thomas can enforme you of novelties in this countrie better then I can writte. **1502** ATKYNSON tr. *De Imitatione* I. xx. 169 If thou haue delyte to here noueltise thou muste somtyme therof suffer trybulacyon of herte. *a* **1548** HALL *Chron., Hen. VI* 183 b, The duke of Yorke.., somewhat spurred and quickened with these noveltyes, retired backe. **1595** *Locrine* II. i, What uncouth novelties Bring'st thou unto our royal majesty?
c. An innovation, a novel proceeding.
1576 FLEMING *Panopl. Epist.* 55 The explication of causes which gaue originall to nouelties. **1678** WANLEY *Wonders Lit. World* v. ii. §87. 473/1 Mustapha, brother to Achmet, succeeded, which was a novelty never before heard of in this Kingdom. **1876** FREEMAN *Norm. Conq.* V. xxiv. 385 The days of King Eadward remained the standard, every departure from which was noticed as a novelty.
d. An often useless, but decorative or amusing, object which relies for its appeal on the newness of its design. Hence **novelty shop**.
1901 *Daily Colonist* (Victoria, B.C.) 19 Oct. 4/6 (Advt.), Sterling Silver Novelties. An English manufacturer's range of samples: no two pieces alike. Puff Boxes, Tooth Brush Boxes, Vases, Cigarette Cases, Match Boxes, Napkin Rings. **1911** *Woman's Home Companion* Apr. 28/3 This idea can be carried out to any extent by having quantities of things which are more or less novelties to sell. **1933** *Planning* I. XVI. 14 The climax to this orgy of designs is reached at Christmas-time when the shops are filled with 'novelties' that no customer would think of wanting for himself. **1972** *Guardian* 23 Dec. 1/1 A cracker-making contract..has been withdrawn because blue jokes were found with the paper hats and novelties. **1973** 'I. DRUMMOND' *Jaws of Watchdog* xi. 145 The only retailer who handled the macabre Belgian masks had a novelty shop in High Holborn.
2. a. Novel or unusual character *of* something.
1387 TREVISA *Higden* (Rolls) III. 67 For wonder of nouelte of þis doynge, me axede counsaille..of Appolyn. *a* **1548** HALL *Chron., Hen. IV* 2 b, Somwhat unquieted for the noveltie of the thyng. **1625** USHER (*title*), An Answer to a Challenge... Wherein..the Noveltie of the now Romish doctrine [is] plainely discovered. **1709** STEELE *Tatler* No. 46 ¶ 1 The Novelty of the History, and Manner of Life, of the Emperor Aurengezebe. **1765** BLACKSTONE *Comm.* I. 1 The novelty and the importance of the duty required. **1841** LANE *Arab. Nts.* I. 127 The novelty of these amusements interested me. **1860** TYNDALL *Glac.* I. ii. 23 The novelty of this day's experience may have rendered it impressive.
†**b.** Newness, freshness *of* a thing. *Obs. rare.*
1398 TREVISA *Barth. De P.R.* XII. ix. (Bodl. MS.), In here comynge þei boodeþ noueltee of tyme. **1614** RALEIGH *Hist. World* v. i. §4. 283 Some of the Syracusians..tooke armes against him, even in the noveltie of his Rule.
3. The quality or state of being novel; that which is novel, new, or hitherto unknown.
1484 CAXTON *Fables of Poge* iv, As by caas of nouelte he callyd the sayd yong man. *c* **1500** *Three Kings' Sons* 85 It thought them a cas of nouelte. **1581** MULCASTER *Positions* v. (1887) 29, I may..feare no note of noueltie, where nothing is but auncient. **1604** JAS. I *Counterbl. to Tobacco* (Arb.) 99 An inconsiderate and childish affectation of Noueltie. **1665** BOYLE *Occas. Refl.*, Disc. Med. II. i, That unexpectedness being the highest Degree of Novelty. **1728** R. MORRIS *Ess. Anc. Archit.* 21 Any thing which has the least appearance of Novelty. **1796** H. HUNTER tr. *St.-Pierre's Stud. Nat.* (1799) II. 16 To induce others to dive into this rich mine, with the additional value of novelty. **1824** J. H. NEWMAN *Hist. Sk.* (1873) II. II. viii. 276 Novelty in the speaker supplies the want of novelty in the matter. **1886** RUSKIN *Præterita* I. 238 Very early, indeed, I had found that novelty was soon exhausted.
personif. **1784** COWPER *Task* III. 54 Pleasure..leaning on the arm Of Novelty, her fickle frail support.
4. a. *attrib.* and *Comb.*, as ***novelty-affecting, -bit, -hunter*** (so ***-hunting***), ***-value***; **novelty number, song** (see quot. 1952).
1640 G. SANDYS *Christ's Passion* II. 246 The Novelty-affecting Multitude. **1784** *Bishopric Garland* (1810) 26 The next was Will Dunn, our painter, Who wanted a novelty-bit. **1926** FOWLER *Mod. Eng. Usage* 387/2 If each novelty-hunter struck out a line for himself, we could be content to register novelty-hunting as a useful outward sign of inward dullness, and leave such writers carefully alone. **1938** I. GOLDBERG *Wonder of Words* xviii. 372 We all know the novelty-hunter who uses his neologisms because he wishes to stun his reader. **1940** *Scrutiny* VIII. 397, I am thinking mostly of course of the hack of Tin Pan Alley and the ubiquitous and cynically named 'novelty' number. **1952** B. ULANOV *Hist. Jazz in Amer.* (1958) 352 *Novelty song:* a song that depends on some obvious contrivance for its appeal, such as a reorganized nursery rhyme..or an infectious sort of gibberish. **1955** L. FEATHER *Encycl. Jazz* (1956) 79 Novelty songs such as *Ol' Man Mose* and *Brother Bill* began to edge out the jazz material in his repertoire. **1959** *Times* (Suppl. Britain's Food) 9 Mar. p. vii/6 Novelty-value has its own appeal. **1968** 'J. CHRISTOPHER' *Pendulum* v. 42 The novelty value won't last.
b. Of fabrics, etc.: see quot. 1968.
1945 M. D. POTTER *Fiber to Fabric* iii. 51 Novelty yarns produce the attractive nubby effects seen in tweeds. **1950** *'Mercury' Dict. Textile Terms* 368/2 *Novelty suitings*, a name applied originally to plain homespun weaves with rough, irregular fillings of different colours, but now referring to all weaves, especially brocaded or jacquard effects. **1968** J. IRONSIDE *Fashion Alphabet* 94 *Novelty*, when used of fabrics this indicates that the material is made from more than one basic fibre and may be in an unusual weave. **1974** *Guardian* 26 Mar. 16/1, 12 leading French cloth manufacturers will be showing..jerseys, shirtings, novelty silks.

novem- ('nəʊvɛm), the L. numeral *novem* nine, used to form combs. with adjectives in *-ate*, as ***novemarticulate***, having nine joints.
1856-8 W. CLARK *Van der Hoeven's Zool.* I. 340 Antennæ novemarticulate, perfoliate. **1857** MAYNE *Expos. Lex.* 776 Novemcostate, -digitate, -lobate, -nervate.

November (nəʊ'vɛmbə(r)). Also 3, 5 **Nouembre**, 4-6 **Novembre**. Abbreviated **Nov.** [a. L. *November* (also *Novembris*, sc. *mensis*), f. *novem* nine. The ME. form was perh. ad. OF. *Novembre.*] The eleventh month of the year, containing 30 days.
[*c* **960** *Rule St. Benet* (Schröer) 32 Fram þan anȝinne þæs monðes, þe is nouember ȝehaten. *a* **1000** *Menologium* 196 þæs ofstum bringð..Blot-monað on tun,..Nouembris, niða bearnum eadiȝnesse.]
a **1225** *Leg. Kath.* 1414 þe þreottuðe dei Of Nouembres moneð. *c* **1290** *St. Michael* 103 in *S. Eng. Leg.* I. 302 Seint Miȝhel in nouembre hath ȝeot an-oþur dai. **1390** GOWER *Conf.* III. 124 That is Novembre which I meene, Whan that the lef hath lost his greene. **1481** CAXTON *Godfrey* 312 Enprynted the xx day of nouembre the yere a forsayd. **1594** BLUNDEVIL *Exerc.* III. I. xlv. (1636) 358 Thirty daies hath November, Aprill, Iune, and September. **1672-3** GREW *Anat. Plants* II. iii. (1682) 68 The Root of Dandelion being cut in November, seems to bleed both a Milk and a Lympha. **1784** COWPER *Task* III. 467 When now November dark Checks vegetation in the torpid plant. **1808** SCOTT *Marm.* Introd. i, November's sky is chill and drear, November's leaf is red and sear. **1897** OUIDA *Massarenes* xii, Our Aprils are considerably worse than our Novembers.
b. *attrib.* and *Comb.*, as ***November dawn, day, mist, tide.***
1820 SCOTT *Monast.* viii, A November mist overspread the little valley. *Ibid.* ix, The November day was well spent ere the Sub-Prior resumed his journey. **1864** TENNYSON *En. Ard.* 611 The chill November dawns and dewy-glooming downs. **1866** NEALE *Sequences & Hymns* 87 It was about November-tide.
c. As a moth-name: (see quots.).
1832 RENNIE *Butterfl. & Moths* 266 November, (*Harr.*) See Feathered Thorn [*Himera pennaria*]. November, (*Haw.*) See Autumn Border [*Oporabia dilutata*]. **1874** E. NEWMAN *Brit. Moths* 109 The November Moth [*Oporabia*] appears on the wing in November, and is common everywhere in England, Scotland, and Ireland.

Hence **No'vemberish** *a.*, **No'vemb(e)ry** *a.*, characteristic of November; dismal, gloomy.
1792 BURNS *Let.* Wks. (Globe) 516 Here I sit, altogether Novemberish, a d—d *mélange* of fretfulness and melancholy. **1840** MISS SEDGWICK *Lett. fr. Abroad* (1841) II. 32 It is cold, Novemberish, and raining. *a* **1864** HAWTHORNE *Amer. Note-bks.* (1879) II. 52 Unpleasant, Novembery days. **1870** *Daily News* 2 Nov., Weather still 'Novembry' in the extreme. **1939** *War Illustr.* 9 Dec. p. ii/2 We are approaching the shortest day, and the weather has been thoroughly Novemberish, in London especially. *a* **1945** E. R. EDDISON *Mezentian Gate* (1958) xxxvii. 193 Even in that Novemberish raw weather of her years, some strength of lost youth, some glory,..lived on.

no'vemdial, variant of NOVENDIAL.
1624 DARCIE *Birth Heresies* xviii. 74 As the ancient Romane Idolaters had recourse likewise to the Nouemdiall Masse, vpon any monstrous prodigies. **1793** A. MURPHY *Tacitus, Ann.* VI. v. *note*, Nothing different from a novemdial, or mourning-festival.

novemfid, *a. rare*⁻¹. [f. NOVEM-, after *bifid*, etc.] Cleft into nine divisions.
1785 MARTYN *Rousseau's Bot.* xxiv. (1794) 341 The exterior calyx..in Althæa is novemfid.

‖**novena** (nəʊ'viːnə). *R.C. Ch.* [med.L. *novēna*, f. *novem* nine.] A devotion consisting of special prayers or services on nine successive days.
1853 FABER *All for Jesus* Ded., Every month that went by, every feast, novena, octave, triduo. **1880** LITTLEDALE *Plain Reasons* xviii. 54 Litanies and novenas take up most of the time spent in church. **1889** *Cath. News* 23 Nov. 2/5 A Novena of Masses to Mary Immaculate.

novenary ('nɒvənərɪ), *a.* and *sb.* [ad. L. *novēnārius*, f. *novem* nine. So F. *novénaire*, It. and Sp. *novenario.*]
A. *adj.* Pertaining to, or consisting of, the number nine. *rare.*
1603 HOLLAND *Plutarch* Explan. Words, *Novenary* number, that is to say, Nine. **1609** C. BUTLER *Fem. Monar.* (1634) 31 The seven Novenary ranks from West to East. **1635** HEYWOOD *Hierarchie* IV. 208 Prime Muses of the Novenary stocke.
B. *sb.* **1.** An aggregate or set of nine.
1577-87 HOLINSHED *Chron.* I. 29/1 From Brute to the extinction of his posteritie..are 630 yeares, or 70 nouenaries. **1646** SIR T. BROWNE *Pseud. Ep.* 215 By these numbers..he implyeth Climactericall years, that is, septenaries, and novenaries set downe by the bare observation of numbers. **1653** H. MORE *Conject. Cabbal.* (1713) 146 We are not at all concerned in the Octonary and Novenary, they having no reference to any of the Days of the Creation.
2. = NOVENA.
1818 SOUTHEY in *Q. Rev.* XVIII. 10 A novenary or service of nine days was performed for him. **1855** KELLY tr. *Cervantes' Exempl. Novels* 119 To perform a novenary in the church of our Lady of Guadalupe.

no'vendial, *a.* and *sb. rare.* [ad. L. *novendiālis*, f. *novem* nine + *diēs* day; cf. NOVEMDIAL.]
A. *adj.* Lasting nine days.
1533 BELLENDEN *Livy* I. xii. (S.T.S.) I. 72 The Romanis ..Institute ane new sacrifice, callit in þai dais þe sacrifice nouendiall. **1600** HOLLAND *Livy* XXI. lxii. 429 For the raining of stones in Picenum, there was ordeined a Nouendial feast for nine dayes. [**1880** BREWER *Reader's Hdbk.*, A Novendial holiday, nine days set apart by the Romans in expiation of a shower of stones.]
B. *sb.* **a.** Religious solemnities or sacrifices lasting for nine days, observed by the Romans. **b.** A funeral ceremony held on the ninth day after the burial of the deceased person.
1600 HOLLAND *Livy* I. xxxi. 22 The Romanes..celebrated solemne publicke sacrifices for the space of nine daies, called a Novendiall. *a* **1719** ADDISON tr. *Petronius Arbiter* (1736) 129 Scissa kept a Novendial for his servant Misellus, whom he enfranchised after he was dead.
So †**no'vendinal** *a.*, taking place on the ninth day after the burial. *Obs. rare*⁻¹.
1598 GRENEWEY *Tacitus, Ann.* VI. i. (1622) 122 After a banket on the birth day of Augusta.., hee tearmed that a Nouendinall supper, or belonging to a mortuary.

novene, *sb.*, anglicized form of NOVENA.
1826 SOUTHEY in *Q. Rev.* XXXIII. 379 The nuns also performed a novene for her.

'novene, *a. rare*⁻¹. [ad. L. *novēn-us*, distrib. adj. f. *novem* nine.] Proceeding by nines.
1855 MILMAN *Lat. Chr.* VI. 405 The triple and novene division ran throughout, and connected..the mundane and supermundane Church.

†**no'vennal**, *a. Obs. rare*⁻¹. [Irreg. f. L. *novem* nine.] Consisting of nine.
1716 M. DAVIES *Athen. Brit.* II. To Rdr. 50 Of all that Novennal Number, of those Circæan Jesuitical Muses, Caussin is by far the worst Poet.

novennial (nəʊ'vɛnɪəl), *a.* [f. L. *novennis*, f. *novem* nine, and *annus* year.] Happening or recurring every ninth year.
1656 BLOUNT *Glossogr.*, *Novennial*, of nine years. **1697** POTTER *Antiq. Greece* I. ii. 10 To send a Novennial, or Septennial, or an Annual Tribute. *Ibid.* II. xx. 342 Δαφνηφορια, a novennial Festival, celebrated by the Bœotians.

novercal (nəʊ'vɜːkəl), *a.* Also 7 nouercall. [ad. L. *novercālis*, f. *noverca* stepmother.] Characteristic of, or resembling, a stepmother.

1623 COCKERAM *Eng. Dict.* I., *Nouercall*, belonging to a step-mother. **1646** BUCK *Rich. III* 41 Fortune..soone cald for the Principall and Interest from this Prince, to whom she was meerly Novercall. **1661** HICKERINGILL *Jamaica* 12 The Soil is so pregnant and fertile, that nature hath stor'd it in no niggardly nor novercal benevolence. **1713** DERHAM *Phys. Theol.* VII. vi. 392 It is a wonderfull Deviation, that some few families [of birds] only should do it in a more novercal way. **1767** W. BENNET *Let. to Parr* P.'s Wks. 1828 VII. 69 A firmer basis than either novercal rapacity would have designed, or novercal malice left you. **1831** *Blackw. Mag.* XXIX. 767 In compensation of this novercal usage, fortune has given him a long purse. **1868** BROWNING *Ring & Bk.* II. 490 Guido's old lady-mother Beatrice..Was recognised of true novercal type, Dragon and devil.

† **no'vercant**, *a. Obs. rare*$^{-1}$. [ad. pres. pple. of late L. *novercārī*, f. *noverca*: see prec.] Acting like a stepmother.

1472-3 *Rolls of Parlt.* VI. 8/2 To kepe in remembrance.. their noble Actes, pryncipally in execution of Justice, ayenst novercant Oblivion, ennemy to memorye.

† **'noverint.** *Obs.* [L. *nōverint*, 3rd plur. perf. subj. of *nōscĕre* to know, occurring in the opening phrase of writs, *noverint universi* 'let all men know'.]

1. The making of writs. *rare*$^{-1}$.

1589 NASHE *Pref. Greene's Menaphon* (Arb.) 9 It is a common practise now a daies amongst a sort of shifting companions..to leaue the trade of *Nouerint* whereto they were borne, and busie themselues with the indeuors of Art.

2. A writ.

1592 GREENE *Groat's Worth Wit* (1617) B j b, Yet was not the Father altogether vnlettered, for hee had good experience in a Nouerint. **1621** SANDERSON *Serm.* I. 203 Why doth he not in his bills and bonds and noverints, make it known to all men by those presents that he is an usurer? **1634** FORD *Perk. Warbeck* II. iii, As no indenture but has its counter-pane, no noverint but his condition or defeasance [etc.].

Comb. **1594** NASHE *Terrors Nt.* Ep. Ded., Wks. (Grosart) III. 214 Some vnskilfull pen-man or Nouerint-maker.

3. Applied to a scrivener.

1629 SHIRLEY *Wedding* III. i. 396 Sirra Nouerint.., ile set one a top of Paules to watch thee.

† **no'verk.** *Obs. rare*$^{-1}$. [ad. L. *noverca*.] A stepmother.

1535 STEWART *Cron. Scot.* II. 584 Edwardis bruther wes marterit of the new Be his noverk.

Novial ('nəʊvɪəl). [See quot. 1928[1].] Name of an artificial language created by Otto Jespersen in 1928 for use as an international auxiliary language. Hence **'Novialist**, a speaker of Novial; an advocate of Novial.

1928 O. JESPERSEN *International Language* I. 52 As such a scheme must have a name, I have called it NOVIAL = Nov(new) I.A.L., where I.A.L. stands for International Auxiliary Language. *Ibid.* II. 67 In Novial..we simplify the spelling in all words containing double letters in the national languages, from which the words are taken. *Ibid.* 137 N[ovial] therefore adopts both suffixes, but Novialists need not commit to memory which words take one and which the other ending. **1930** *S.P.E. Tract* XXXIV. 462 Novial will be suspiciously easy; keen Novialists will rattle it off together in the family circle. **1943** F. BODMER *Loom of Language* xi. 471 Novial departs from English usage in one particular. The dictionary form does the work of our past participle in compound past tenses. **1947** H. JACOB *Planned Auxiliary Lang.* iv. 83 Jespersen's Novial has many features which are advocated by the naturalistic school of interlinguists, the use of auxiliary verbs, the revised system of spelling, a certain number of flexional elements in indirect derivation, the abolition of so-called pleonastic endings, the plural form in *-s*. **1973** *Trans. Philol. Soc. 1972* 16 This work extended over many years and led eventually to the invention of his own auxiliary language, Novial. .. He came to think, later on, that he could have put that time to better use.

novice ('nɒvɪs). Forms: α. 4 **nouys**, 5 **novys**, **novise**, *Sc.* **nowis**, 6 **nouise**, **nou-**, **novesse**, 7 **nouasse**. β. 5 **nouyce**, 4, 6 **novyce**, 5–7 **nouice**, 6– **novice**. [a. OF. *novisse*, *novice*, = Sp. *novicio* masc., *novicia* fem., Pg. *noviço*, *-iça*, It. *novizio*, *-izia*, ad. L. *novīcius*, *-īcia*, f. *novus* new: see -ITIOUS[1].]

1. a. *Eccl.* One who has entered a religious house, and is under probation or trial, before taking the required vows; a candidate for admission into a religious order; a probationer.

α. **13..** *Metr. Hom.* (Vernon MS.) in Herrig's *Archiv* LVII. 278 In þis hous Nouys was I And aftur Monk ȝeres moni. *c* **1375** *Sc. Leg. Saints* XXX. (*Theodora*) 411 þane wes he tane & mad nowis & leryt sa. **1401** *Pol. Poems* (Rolls) II. 20 Why will ye not suffer your novises hear your councels in your chapter house? *c* **1440** *Promp. Parv.* 360/1 Nouyce, or novys, *novisius*. **1571** *Satir. Poems Reform.* xxviii. 53 Than twa ȝeiris Noueis..ȝond in Kiluinning my prentischip I past. **1589** WARNER *Alb. Eng.* v. xxvii. (1602) 133 The Lady Prioresse Did taunt the Nouasse bitterly.

β. *c* **1380** WYCLIF *Sel. Wks.* III. 397 Freris..bynden novycis to unknowen þing. *c* **1380** *Abbey Holy Ghost* in *Hampole's Wks.* (1895) I. 330 Honeste es maystresse of þe nouyce, and teches þam alle curtasye. **1530** PALSGR. 248/2 Novyce a newe relygious persone, *nouice*. **1560** DAUS tr. *Sleidane's Comm.* 156 b, We thinke mete, that all yong Novices..be presently removed from thence. **1603** SHAKS. *Meas. for M.* I. iv. 19 Can you so steed me, As bring me to the sight of Isabella, A Nouice of this place? **1663** H. COGAN tr. *Pinto's Trav.* iii. 5 Above four thousand Priests, besides a great Number of Novices. **1797** MRS. RADCLIFFE *Italian* viii, She was seated among the novices. **1849** JAMES *Woodman* ii, It was very different from the veil of the nun or even of the novice. **1859** JEPHSON *Brittany* xv. 246 He then assumes the dress of the Order, a cassock and bands, and becomes a novice.

b. A newly converted person.

1526 *Pilgr. Perf.* (W. de W. 1531) 35 In them that be nouices, newly conuerted to religyon. **1611** BIBLE *I Tim.* iii. 6 Not a nouice, lest being lifted vp with pride, hee fall into the condemnation of the deuill. **1649** JER. TAYLOR *Gt. Exemp.* III. Disc. xvi. 53 Christ's litle ones, that is such as are novices and babes in Christianity. **1879** FARRAR *St. Paul* (1883) 188 St. Paul was still a suspected novice.

2. An inexperienced person; one who is new to the circumstances in which he is placed; a beginner, tyro.

1432-50 tr. *Higden* (Rolls) IV. 61 That tyme alle the senate was but as a nouice. **1502** ATKYNSON tr. *De Imitatione* I. xxiii. 172 It were expedient that they were instructe as Nouices, begynners to growe in more perfyte vertues. **1579** LYLY *Euphues* (Arb.) 47 Such is the Nature of these nouises, that thinke to haue learning without labour, and treasure without trauaile. **1638** JUNIUS *Paint. Ancients* 30 Small profit the Novices of these Arts receive by meere Imitation. **1699** BENTLEY *Phal.* 94 Every Novice in Geography knows they were Maritime. **1726** SHELVOCKE *Voy. round World* 102 Though they came to us under the name of Veterans, [they] proved to be ignorant Novices. **1795** BURKE *Regic. Peace* Wks. VIII. 343 You are but novices in the art of naval resources. **1856** KANE *Arct. Expl.* II. x. 100 Refraction will deceive a novice on the ice. **1873** BROWNING *Red Cott. Nt.-cap* 109 As the haschisch-man Prepares a novice to receive his drug.

3. a. *attrib.* and *Comb.*, as ***novice life***, ***modesty***, ***time***, ***way***; ***novice-like*** adj.

1530 PALSGR. 248/2 Novyce tyme, *nouicerie*. **1671** MILTON *P.R.* III. 241 With novice modesty. **1689** HICKERINGILL *Ceremony Monger* Concl. iii, No Mortal ever did or can discharge it, but in this Novice way. **1842** MRS. CLAVERS *Forest Life* II. 56 Seymour, novice-like, was amusingly conscious. **1888** BERNARD *Fr. World to Cloister* ii, The cell in which my novice life was to be lived.

b. Appositive, as ***novice lover***, ***thief***, etc.; also ***novice hand***, ***heart***, ***thought***.

1605 SYLVESTER *Imposture* 338 A novice Thief. **1606** —— *Du Bartas* II. iv. *Magnificence* 836 These novice Lovers at their first arrive Are bashfull both. **1632** LITHGOW *Trav.* I. 19, I need no information of any Romane Nouice Traueller. **1654** VILVAIN *Chronography* Title-p., To lead the wandring steps of Novice Chronologers in a right cours. **1708** OZELL tr. *Boileau's Lutrin* 20 His Artless Novice-hand he lends. **1751** *Female Foundling* I. 78 But perhaps..my Novice-heart may be deceived. **1794** COLERIDGE *Relig. Musings* I. 108, I discipline my young and novice thought. **1811** W. R. SPENCER *Poems* Ded., Whene'er my novice hand presum'd To wake the chords of grief or glee. **1888** BERNARD *Fr. World to Cloister* ii, The novitiate..had its own special door and enclosure, with its own special novice porter.

c. In sense 'of the novices'.

1850 NEWMAN *Serm.* (1881) xii. 239 He acted as novice-master to the children of St. Dominic. **1898** *Dubl. Rev.* Apr. 356 When Clara was made novice-mistress he dedicated a small book to her.

d. Applied to animals entered in a competitive event which have not previously (or before a specified date) won other than very minor prizes; also a competition restricted to such animals.

1903 *Forest & Stream* 21 Feb. 151 (Cent. Suppl.), Novice dogs was a large class, 28 in all. **1909** *Daily Chron.* 19 June 7/6 'Canterbury Belle' headed the list in a fine show of novice hacks. **1962** D. FRANCIS *Dead Cert* iii. 26, I was riding him in novice hurdle races. **1969** [see CHASE *sb.*[1] 1 f]. **1975** *Country Life* 13 Nov. 1281/2 Brown Lad was a novice chaser last year... He is an absolutely top-class horse, and he stays three miles readily.

Hence **'novicehood**, the condition of a novice.

1748 RICHARDSON *Clarissa* (1811) III. 132, I encouraged and collected every thing of this sort that I had ever had from novicehood to maturity.

† **novicery.** *Obs. rare.* [a. OF. *novicerie*, *novisserie*: see NOVICE and -ERY.]

1. = NOVICIATE 3.

c **1400** *Rule St. Benet* (Prose) 142 And hir mastres sall haue hir to þe Nouycery, & infurme as religiun will.

2. = NOVICIATE 1.

c **1440** *Promp. Parv.* 360/1 Novysrye (nouycery), *noviciatus*. *a* **1470** H. PARKER *Dives & Pauper* (Pynson, 1493) IV. xx, If the religious were bounde to obey in al thynge, his professyon were al vncertein and vnassayed in his nouycery. *Ibid.*, In the yere of hys assaye in hys nouycery.

'noviceship. Also 8 noviship. [f. NOVICE.]

1. = NOVICIATE 1.

1639 S. DU VERGER tr. *Camus' Admir. Events* 266 Beeing as yet but in the beginning of his Noviceship. **1677** *Lond. Gaz.* No. 1247/1 Having passed his Noviceship, he celebrated High Mass on Friday last. **1763** *Brit. Mag.* IV. 467 Her year of noviceship was now expired. **1845** G. OLIVER *Biogr. Soc. Jesus* 97, I cannot discover where he made his noviceship. **1887** STANTON *Menology Eng. & Wales* 45 He..went to St. Omers to begin his noviceship with the Jesuits.

attrib. **1716** M. DAVIES *Athen. Brit.* III. *Diss. Dram.* 38 After..the Noviship-Exercises or Trials of the..Sincerity of his Christian Pretensions.

b. Initial stages; inexperience. *rare.*

1703 SAVAGE *Lett. Antients* ii. 10 You (yet in the very Noviceship of your Youth, tho robust and old in the Virtue of Faith). **1748** RICHARDSON *Clarissa* (1811) V. 297 If giddy fellows, or giddy girls, misbehave in a first marriage..from noviceship.

2. A Jesuit college where novices are trained.

1620 E. BLOUNT *Horæ Subs.* 380 That Garden of Cardinall Bandinoes, by the Nouiceship of the Iesuites. **1629** WADSWORTH *Pilgr.* vii. 74 The Iesuites haue a Colledge at Watton,..which they call their Nouiship for the nurturing of their young Iesuites. **1889** *Pall Mall G.* 10 July 21/1 Their cadets' training homes remind me of nothing so much as our noviceships.

noviciate, novitiate (nəʊ'vɪʃ(ɪ)ət). Also 7 nouitiat. [ad. F. *noviciat*, †*novitiat*, = Sp. and Pg. *noviciado*, It. *noviziato*, or med.L. *novitiatus*: see NOVICE and -ATE[1].]

1. The probationary period of a novice before finally taking religious vows.

1600 W. WATSON *Decacordon* (1602) 90 He sent him to Antwerpe to haue his Nouitiat by the Prouincial there. **1671** WOODHEAD *St. Teresa* II. vii. 50 Let them not admit them to make profession, if in the year of their Noviciate they find not [etc.]. **1757** BURKE *Abridg. Eng. Hist.* Wks. X. 188 None were admitted into this order but after a long and laborious novitiate. **1819** SCOTT *Ivanhoe* xxxvi, The aspirants after this holy Order wore during their noviciate the cast-off garments of the knights. **1884** TENNYSON *Becket* v. ii, Breaking already from thy noviciate To plunge into this bitter world again.

b. *transf.* and *fig.* The state or time of being a novice or beginner in anything; time of initiation, apprenticeship, or probation.

1610 DONNE *Pseudo-martyr* 6 But those..God doth ordinarily bring vp in a nouitiate, and Apprentisage of worldly Crosses. *a* **1716** SOUTH *Serm.* (1727) II. 179 He must have pass'd his Tyrocinium, or Novitiate, in Sinning, before he can come to this. **1723** SWIFT *Corr.* Wks. 1841 II. 565, I know no vows so solemn as those of friendship, and therefore a pretty long noviciate of acquaintance should.. precede them. **1791** BURKE *Th. French Aff.* Wks. 1842 I. 573 After they have passed the novitiate, those who take any sort of lead are placed in very lucrative offices. **1822-56** DE QUINCEY *Confess.* (1862) 189 The calamities of my novitiate in London had struck root. **1871** L. STEPHEN *Playgr. Eur.* II. iv. 319 Fix yourself for the period of your noviciate at one of the great Alpine centres of interest.

2. A novice in a religious order.

1655 FULLER *Ch. Hist.* IX. xvi. 92 These Colledges.. dispatch their ripe Noviciats for England. **1679** PRANCE *Add. Narrative* 40 The Ecclesiasticks..yearly receive young Students or Novitiates from hence. **1711** ADDISON *Spect.* No. 164 ¶7 The Abbess had been informed..of all that had passed between her Noviciate and Father Francis. **1775** JEBB *Corr.* (1894) 24 A preparatory sermon addressed entirely to the novitiate. **1817** JAS. MILL *Brit. India* I. II. ii. 114 The noviciates to the sacerdotal office are commanded to find their subsistence by begging. **1888** BERNARD *Fr. World to Cloister* ii, Former novitiates..had to make use of the floor as a seat.

b. A beginner, tyro; one who is new to anything.

a **1734** NORTH *Examen* I. ii. §11 (1740) 36 Scarce enough ..for a Novitiate as he was to acquire an ordinary Prattique of the cursory part of Business. **1793** J. WILLIAMS *Calm Exam.* 60 Political Noviciates rush into the Chamber of the third Estate. **1828** P. CUNNINGHAM *N.S. Wales* (ed. 3) II. 178 Such indeed as may frequently induce the desponding noviciate..to lament the hour in which he became a tiller of our untamed soils. **1849** *Escape fr. Toil* 13/1 The sincere noviciate..setting candidly and resolutely to the work will never give up, nor go back.

3. The quarters occupied by novices during their period of probation; a noviceship.

1626 L. OWEN *Spec. Jesuit.* (1629) 48 Their house of approbation or Nouiciat. **1687** A. LOVELL tr. *Thevenot's Trav.* I. 3 The Novitiate of the Jesuites stands upon a Hill higher than any place of the Town. **1704** *Collect. Voy.* (Churchill) III. 19/1 The Jesuites have also a Novitiate. **1761** *Ann. Reg.* I. 172 In the year 1710, there were [in France]..612 jesuits colleges,..59 noviciates. **1826** SOUTHEY *Vind. Eccl. Angl.* 449 When St. Francisco.., as Commissary for the Order in Spain, visited a noviciate. **1888** BERNARD *Fr. World to Cloister* ii, The novitiate was situated on the third floor at the top of the house.

transf. **1760-72** tr. *Juan & Ulloa's Voy.* (ed. 3) I. 223 The deserts of the mountains..were the noviciates, in which we were inured to the severe life we led.

4. *attrib.*, as ***noviciate chapel***, ***guide***, ***habit***, etc.

1704 *Collect. Voy.* (Churchill) III. 6/2 The Founder of our Novitiat-House. **1756-7** tr. *Keysler's Trav.* (1760) II. 52 The tomb..is in the novitiate chapel of the convent. **1789** *Trifler* No. 32. 408 The whole family, in which I passed my noviciate year. **1799** SHERIDAN *Pizarro* v. ii, The noviciate habit which you first beheld her in. **1840** *Penny Cycl.* XVI. 355/2 Persons who apply to enter the noviciate state. **1869** *Daily News* 6 Feb., The vow of poverty, as explained by the Noviciate Guide.

b. Appositive, as ***noviciate candidate***, etc.

1775 SHERIDAN *Art of Reading* 39 Such..as for a long time to baffle all the efforts of the noviciate tongue. **1788** tr. *Swedenborg's Wisd. Angels* IV. §341. 311 When they are opened a little, as is the Case when noviciate Devils enter. **1802** LAMB in *Athenæum* (1888) 4 Aug. 171/3 Now that.. Mr. Cooke is no longer a novitiate candidate for public favour. **1885** H. O. FORBES *Wandr. Archip.* 468 The noviciate gold-washer..accompanies the Dato to the river.

Hence **no'viciateship**.

a **1670** HACKET *Abp. Williams* I. (1692) 77 It was much that in his novitiatship in that house, he durst contradict such mighty ones in so tender a cause. **1835** LYTTON *Student*, *New Phædo* iii, The habit of thinking, by degrees, cures the faults of its novitiateship.

novici'ation. *rare*$^{-1}$. [See NOVICE and -ATION.] The admission of a novice.

1797 MRS. RADCLIFFE *Italian* xi, When this ceremony had concluded, another began, and he was told it was that of a noviciation.

†**novicie.** *Obs. rare*⁻¹. [f. NOVICE + -IE, -Y.] Inexperience.

1600 EDMONDS *Observ. Cæsar's Comm.* 43 How much an old experienced souldier..exceedeth the nouicie of such as are newly enrolled.

novilant, variant of NOVELANT *Obs.*

†**novile,** *a. Obs. rare.* [var. of NOVEL *a.*, after adjs. in -ILE.] Novel.

1586 WARNER *Alb. Eng.* I. iv. (1602) 12 This nouile Prize to gaine. **1676** WOOD *Jrnl.* in *Acc. Sev. Late Voy.* I. (1694) 145 Of late within this year or two some Novile Accidents happening [etc.].

‖**novillada** (noviˈʎada). [Sp.] A bullfight in which three-year-old bulls are fought by novice matadors.

1897 *Encycl. Sport* I. 152/2 Bulls for a *novillada* or second-rate bull-fight cost far less. **1932** E. HEMINGWAY *Death in Afternoon* ii. 23 At a novillada the spectator may see the mistakes of the bullfighters, and the penalties that these mistakes carry. **1955** K. TYNAN *Bull Fever* ii. 14 A matador's career..nowadays rarely exceeds ten years. Manolo González, who fought his first novillada in 1946 and retired rich in 1952, is a fair example. **1964** G. ERIK *Corrida* v. 21 He can become a novice matador..fighting three year old bulls with *picadors*. Such fights are known as '*corridas de novillos-toros*' or '*novilladas*'. **1967** MCCORMICK & MASCAREÑAS *Compl. Aficionado* iii. 78 They are walking back from a novillada.

‖**novillero** (noviˈʎero). [Sp.] An apprentice matador who has fought only in *novilladas*.

1921 L. FITZ-BARNARD *Fighting Sports* III. 166 They enter the troupe of some matador and serve an apprenticeship..; and as they improve become *novilleros*. **1932** E. HEMINGWAY *Death in Afternoon* xiii. 152 The novilleros you see killed are all victims of economics. **1955** K. TYNAN *Bull Fever* ii. 27 He took his doctorate at Seville in the spring of 1948, after a riotously successful career as novillero. **1969** *Telegraph* (Brisbane) 13 Jan. 8/1 This year could see him leaving the ranks of the novillero..and moving into the arenas of big bulls and big money. **1970** *Times* 4 May 8/7 He was the leading novillero in Spain in mid-season last year, but three bad gorings put him out of action.

‖**novillo** (noˈviʎo). [Sp.] A young bull; *spec.* a fighting bull not more than three years old.

1838 *Quarterly Rev.* LXII. 398 A calf, a 'novillo'—which true bull-fighters place on a par with a cow. **1846** R. FORD *Gatherings from Spain* xxi. 292 The villagers..amuse themselves with baiting *novillos*, or bull-youngsters—calves of one year old. **1925** E. HEMINGWAY *The Undefeated* in *This Quarter* II. 205 You can..kill two novillos... Whatever stuff they've got in the corrals. **1967** MCCORMICK & MASCAREÑAS *Compl. Aficionado* ii. 32 The neophyte..while gaining experience, faces not toros (four-year-olds and up) but novillos (three-year-olds).

noviˈlunar, *a. rare.* [f. late L. *novilūn-ium* (f. *novus* new + *lūna* moon), after LUNAR *a.*] Of or pertaining to the new moon.

1686 GOAD *Celest. Bodies* I. xii. 54 We shall see into the very Anatomy of the Novilunar Influence. *Ibid.* 55 The Novilunar Days in the Hyemal moiety of the year. **1710** *Brit. Apollo* No. 80. 1/2 Which Days..are supposed to be Novilunar. **1847** in WEBSTER.

†**novilune.** *Obs. rare*⁻¹. [ad. late L. *novilūnium* (see prec.).] The new moon.

1619 SIR J. SEMPILL *Sacrilege Handl.* 57 The Sabbaths thence deriued of seuen yeeres..: with their nouilunes.

‖**novio** (ˈnovjo). [Sp.] A boy friend, lover.

1920 *Chambers's Jrnl.* June 359/1 She has a novio, a sweetheart. **1929** J. LANGDON-DAVIES *Dancing Catalans* iii. 63 She had a 'novio', a bad young fisherman. **1950** G. BRENAN *Face of Spain* xii. 249 They trip gaily along with their *novio* by their side.

†ˈ**novist.** *Obs. rare.* [f. L. *nov-us* new.]

1. A novice, beginner.

1632 J. HAYWARD tr. *Biondi's Eromena* 13 Being but a Novist in that practise.

2. One given to novel opinions; an innovator.

1660 BONDE *Scut. Reg.* 339 He would be but a poor revenger..had the people, (as our Novists feign) not he, the sole disposing of the Militia. **1672** VENN *Milit. & Mar. Discipline* Ep. Ded., It was not to raise a dispute among the Novists.

noˈvitial, *a. rare.* [f. L. *novīti-us* (see next).] Of the nature of, characteristic of, a novice.

1778 [W. MARSHALL] *Minutes Agric., Digest* 7 Nor will a few Sketches..be useless to the Novitial Agriculturist. **1812** SOUTHEY *Omniana* II. 272 Not by a novitial fervour of devotion, but by long probation in a monastical kind of life.

†**noˈvitious,** *a. Obs.* [ad. L. *novītius*, f. *novus* new: see -ITIOUS¹.]

1. Having the character of novices.

1619 SCLATER *Exp. 1 Thess.* (1630) 484 Saith our Sauiour, iustifying his milder inpositions on his nouitious Disciples.

2. Of recent origin.

1659 PEARSON *Creed* (1839) 501 What is now taught by the Church of Rome is..a novitious interpretation. **1669** GALE *Crt. Gentiles* I. I. xii. 79 Those Letters, which the Jews now use.., are novitious, and of late original.

ˈ**novity.** Now *rare* or *Obs.* Forms: 6 nouite(e, 6–7 nouitie, 7 -ity; 5 novitee, 6 -ite, 6–7 -itie, 7– novity. [a. OF. *novité*, = It. *novita*, Sp. *novedad*, Pg. *novidade*, ad. L. *novitāt-em*, f. *novus* new: see -ITY.]

†**1.** An innovation; a novelty. *Obs.*

1460 *Anc. Cal. Rec. Dubl.* (1889) 307 Forasmuch as such novitees hath not be uset afor this time. **1545** JOYE *Exp. Dan.* vi. M iij b, This perillouse novite and mutacion put into his head. **1588** J. HARVEY *Disc. Probl.* 119 Two Eclipses in the space of one month, are no great strange nouities. **1654** VILVAIN *Theor. Theol.* i. 31 'Tis a witty novity, or castle in the air. **1692** S. PATRICK *Answ. Touchstone* 85 When Pope Gregory VII. adventured upon it, it was esteemed a Novity, not to say an Heresy.

2. Novelty; newness. (Common in 17th c.)

1569 J. SANFORD tr. *Agrippa's Van. Artes* 14 b, With a nouitee or straungnesse full of trifles. **1607** J. CARPENTER *Plaine Mans Plough* 105 This..is Christ, by whom we have a triple Nouitie or Newnesse. **1662** STILLINGFL. *Orig. Sacræ* III. ii. §2 Was it not a strong presumption of the Novity of the Universe? **1699** BENTLEY *Phal.* xiii. 393, I know the novity of these Epistles from the whole body and form of the work. **1823** LAMB *Ess., Amicus Redivivus*, That unmeaning assumption of eternal novity.

novmir, obs. form of NUMBER.

novobiocin (nəʊvəʊˈbaɪəsɪn). *Pharm.* [prob. f. as next + BIO- + -MY)CIN.] A weakly acidic tetracyclic phenol, $C_{31}H_{35}N_2O_{11}$, that is produced by certain actinomycetes of the genus *Streptomyces* and is used in treating infections with bacteria resistant to less toxic antibiotics; also, the sodium or calcium salt of this phenol, in which forms it is usually administered.

1956 *Antibiotics & Chemotherapy* VI. 195 It has been announced that by mutual agreement of The Upjohn Co. and of Merck & Co., Inc., the generic name of novobiocin would be used for the antibiotic previously called streptonivicin and cathomycin. **1961** *Lancet* 23 Sept. 688/2 Kanamycin..was changed to a combination of erythromycin..with novobiocin 500 mg. six-hourly. **1967** *Martindale's Extra Pharmacopoeia* (ed. 25) 990/1 The usefulness of novobiocin is limited by the frequent occurrence of side-effects. *Ibid.*, Novobiocin sodium is usually administered by mouth. **1972** *Jrnl. Pharmacy & Pharmacol.* XXIV. 972 Novobiocin..is used infrequently because micro-organisms rapidly develop resistance to it.

novocain (ˈnəʊvəʊkeɪn). *Pharm.* Also **novocaine**, and with capital initial. [f. *novo-*, comb. form of L. *novus* new + CO)CAIN(E.] A proprietary name for procaine.

1905 *Trade Marks Jrnl.* 22 Nov. 1450 Novocain... Chemical substances prepared for use in medicine and pharmacy. Farbwerke vorm. Meister Lucius & Brüning, Hoechst a/Main, Germany; manufacturers. **1910** *Practitioner* Feb. 255 For regional anaesthesia novocain has given good results. **1926** *Glasgow Herald* 25 Aug. 10 Mrs Mary Agnes Brown..died..following injections of cocaine hydrochlorate, which had been mistakenly administered instead of novocaine solution. **1952** MORIN & SMITH tr. *Herzog's Annapurna* xvi. 232 It meant injecting novocaine into the nerve ganglion. **1961** C. MCCULLERS *Clock without Hands* iii. 55 Poke, Doc's brother, just drew the tooth for me—with novocain and antibiotics. **1972** 'G. BLACK' *Bitter Tea* (1973) ix. 139, I sat like a man coming from dental extractions under Novocaine, given a time of numb reprieve before the pain flared.

Novocastrian (nəʊvəʊˈkæstrɪən), *sb.* and *a.* Also with lower-case initial. [f. L. *novo-* reduced form of *novum* new + *castr(um* castle + -IAN.] **A.** *sb.* A native or inhabitant of Newcastle upon Tyne. **B.** *adj.* Of or pertaining to Newcastle or its inhabitants.

1888 L. A. SMITH *Music of Waters* 123 They must have been scarcely as sensitive and refined as one would like to imagine the ancestors of the..Novocastrians. **1915** E. CORRI *30 Yrs. Boxing Ref.* 228, I had no friends in Newcastle when I arrived, but made many during that short visit, coming away with a tremendously high opinion of Novocastrian hospitality. **1949** H. L. HONEYMAN *Northumberland* I. vi. 104 Ralph Gardiner, a renegade Novocastrian and pupil of its Grammar School, settled at Chirton near Shields in 1650. **1959** E. L. MASCALL *Pi in High* 26 What coals to Novocastrians are, To Generals what caviare, To Hecubas what divers he's, Were mushrooms to Ozonides. **1969** C. GEESON *Northumberland & Durham Word Bk.* 4 Wilfred Whitten, the distinguished original editor of *John o' London's Weekly*, spoke of his native Novocastrian tongue as 'that abominable dialect'. **1973** I. CARR in B. S. Johnson *All Bull* 107 He quizzed me about distinguished novocastrian citizens. **1974** *Times* 29 Apr. 5/4 Mr. T. Dan Smith will be remembered as the man who changed the face of Newcastle upon Tyne... The pace and scale of the change have.. frightened Novocastrians.

‖**novodamus** (nəʊvəʊˈdeɪməs). *Sc. Law.* [L. (*de*) *novo damus* 'we grant anew'.] A charter containing a clause (also called 'of *novodamus*') by which the superior grants afresh the matters described in the dispositive clause.

1838 W. BELL *Dict. Law Scot.* 681 A charter of novodamus is accounted in law an original right, which imports a discharge of all prior burdens. **1857** J. PATERSON *Regality of Musselburgh* 26 A novodamus of the nether miln of Brunstain, to be holden of the Earl.

novolak (ˈnəʊvəʊlæk). Also **novolac.** [f. as NOVOCASTRIAN *sb.* and *a.* + (alteration of) LAC(QUER *sb.*] Any of a range of soluble, fusible resins formed by condensing formaldehyde with phenol using an acid catalyst, which are used extensively in varnishes.

1909 L. H. BAEKELAND in *Jrnl. Industr. & Engin. Chem.* Aug. 547/2 In order to simplify matters, I propose to call this substance *Novolak*. **1944** H. R. FLECK *Plastics: Sci. & Technol.* ix. 203 Such properties as the durability and hardness of the Novolac type of resin were obviously very desirable properties to have in a varnish. **1970** E. PARKES et al. in K. Strauss *Appl. Sci. in Casting of Metals* ix. 359 The novolac produced in this way, when cooled down, is a hard glass-like solid and may be ground for use in the manufacture of precoated sand by the hot-coating technique. **1973** *Materials & Technol.* VI. viii. 590 The prime use of moulding powders based on novolak resins is for the production of articles and components in the electrical engineering field.

†ˈ**novum.** *Obs.* [app. L. *novum*, neut. sing. of *novus* new.] An old game at dice played by five or six persons, the two principal throws being nine and five.

1588 SHAKS. *L.L.L.* v. ii. 547 Abate throw at Novum, and the whole world againe, Cannot pricke out fiue such. **1614** J. COOKE *Greene's Tu Quoque* D iij, Change your Game for dice, We are a full number for Nouum. **1616** J. LANE *Contn. Sqr's. T.* IV. 410 Yet these binn th'arpeies of the droopinge time, that all at novum settes, on fyve or nyne. **1621** J. TAYLOR (Water-P.) *Motto* D 4, At Nouum, Mumchance, Mischance (chuse ye which).

‖**novus homo** (ˈnəʊvəs ˈhɒməʊ). Pl. novi homines. [L., lit. 'new man'.] Orig. used in ancient Rome of the first man in a family to rise to a curule office; hence, a man who has recently risen to a position of importance from insignificance; an upstart.

1589 T. SMITH *Commonw. of Eng.* I. xx. 36 Those which were *noui homines*, were more allowed, for their vertues new and newly shewen, than the old smell of auncient race. **1764** SMOLLETT *Let.* 2 July in *Trav.* (1766) I. xvii. 280 Of these, three or four families are really respectable: the rest are *novi homines*, sprung from Bourgeois, who have saved a little money by their different occupations and raised themselves to the rank of noblesse by purchase. **1824** J. S. MILL in *Westm. Rev.* II. 391 The military leaders, being *novi homines*, were the great opponents of the aristocracy. **1956** A. TOYNBEE *Historian's Approach to Relig.* xvi. 211 All of which had to draw their diplomats from among *novi homines*. **1960** *Times* 17 Sept. 7/2 The competition of radical politicians—the *novi homines* of Africa—has weakened it [*sc.* the tribal system].

novy (ˈnəʊvɪ). Also **Novy**. Shortened colloq. form of Nova Scotia, used ellipt.: (*a*) a type of local boat; (*b*) a person from Nova Scotia.

1885 *Bull. U.S. Fish Comm.* V. 8 The boats used in the ordinary fishing [along the Labrador coast] are of two kinds; those called 'novies' or Nova Scotia boats, being long and narrow. **1897** KIPLING *Captains Courageous* vi. 138 'Git aout, you Novy!' To call a Gloucester man a Nova Scotian is not well received. **1942** BERREY & VAN DEN BARK *Amer. Thes. Slang* §385/5 *Novy*, a Nova Scotian. **1970** J. F. LEAVITT *Wake of Coasters* xvii. 165 In deep water parlance, Nova Scotia and New Brunswick vessels were usually spoken of as 'Bluenoses', but along the coast they were more frequently called 'Novies'.

novyl, obs. variant of NAVEL *sb.*

now (naʊ), *adv., conj., sb.*¹, and *a.* Forms: 1–4 nu, 1 nuu, 2–3 nv, 4 new, nw, 9 *Sc.* noo; 3–6 nou (4–5 -e), 3 no, 3–5 nov, 3– now, 4–6 nowe. [OE. *nú*; the same form occurs in all the older Teutonic languages, and corresponds to Skr. *nu*, *nú*, Gr. νυ, νῦν, L. *nunc*.]

I. *adv.* **1. a.** At the present time or moment.

Sometimes strengthened by *even, just,* or *right* (for examples see these words).

c **825** *Vesp. Ps.* xi. 6 Fore..ȝeamrunge ðearfena nu ic arisu, cwið dryhten. *c* **893** K. ÆLFRED *Oros.* II. v. 86 þonne næron naþer gode ne þa ne nu. **971** *Blickl. Hom.* 25 Wa eow þe nu hlihaþ, forþon ȝe eft wepað on ecnesse. *a* **1100** *Gerefa* in *Anglia* IX. 264 Fela ðinga ðe ic nu ȝenæmnian ne can. *c* **1200** ORMIN 2683 Ȝho iss nu & æfre beoþ Heȝhesst of alle shaffte. *c* **1250** *Gen. & Ex.* 3918 To lond moab druȝen he so, ðor nu is a burȝ, ierico. *a* **1300** *Cursor M.* 8094 Sir, sauued be þou nov and ai. *c* **1380** WYCLIF *Sel. Wks.* III. 24 In þe laste eelde þat now is, þat is clepid myddis of ȝeeris. *c* **1450** *Godstow Reg.* 549 Be hit knowe to them that be now and to come. **1475** *Paston Lett.* III. 130 Other labor that I have takyn on me nowe in to Fraunce warde. **1530** PALSGR. 423/2 Fyve pounde you have all redy receyved, but what is behynde nowe onpayed. **1559** W. CUNNINGHAM *Cosmogr. Glasse* 170 But now I will commit it to thy descretion and judgement. **1631** WEEVER *Anc. Funeral Mon.* 58 The..little Island, as then called Aualon, now Glastenbury. **1671** MILTON *P.R.* III. 95 Who names not now with honour patient Job? **1712** SWIFT *Jrnl. to Stella* 26 Mar., Now they don't distinguish between a cow and a Christian. **1784** COWPER *Task* v. 90 Neither grub, nor root, nor earth-nut, now Repays their labour more. **1802** MAR. EDGEWORTH *Moral T.* (1816) I. i. 2 My master is just going to dinner, and can't see anybody now. **1852** M. ARNOLD *Empedocles* II. (1906) 109 They will be our lords, as they are now. **1896** *Law Times* C. 408/1 The salary of a Chancery taxing master is now only £1500 a year.

b. Under the present circumstances; in view of these facts.

1508 KENNEDIE *Flyting w. Dunbar* 470 Thair is na schip that wil the now ressaue. **1592** SHAKS. *Ven. & Ad.* 249 Being mad before, how doth she now for wits? *Ibid.* 253 Now which way shall she turn? what shall she say? **1710** MRS. CENTLIVRE *Bickerstaff's Burying* I. i, I warrant you think to be an Ambral now. **1796** H. HUNTER tr. *St.-Pierre's Stud. Nat.* (1796) III. 140, I now plainly perceive the reason. **1854** MRS. STOWE *Uncle Tom's C.* v, I can believe anything now; I can believe now that you could sell little Harry.

c. Phr. ***now-it-can-be-told***, used *attrib.* to designate a book, story, etc., which reveals previously classified or unknown facts.

1932 *N.Y. Times Book Rev.* 7 Feb. 15/3 Colonel Reeve's book belongs in the now-it-can-be-told class—and he has a lot to tell. **1948** Q. WRIGHT in J. Towster *Political Power in* *the U.S.S.R.* p. ix, Correspondents..have produced books of the 'now-it-can-be-told' variety.

d. In colloq. expressions of the type —— *now* (*and*) —— *later*.

1965 N. Freeling *Criminal Conversation* I. vii. 44 Van der Valk the tally-boy; live now and pay later. **1970** *Guardian* 18 Mar. 19/2 Profit now and pay later. **1973** *P.O. Telephone Directory* (§101 London area A–D) 4/1 Telephone credit cards. Talk now—pay later.

2. In the time directly following on the present moment; immediately, forthwith.

c **1000** Ælfric *Saints' Lives* xxvi. 249 Nu ic sceall ʒeendian earmlicum deaþe. *c* **1290** *St. James* 29 in *S. Eng. Leg.* I. 34 'Nov,' he seide, 'we schullen i-seo ʒwat Iemes þe mai don here'. **1382** Wyclif *1 Sam.* ii. 16 Nay, forsothe nowe thow shalt ʒyue; ellis I shal tak bi forse. *a* **1400–50** *Alexander* 212 Now sall ʒe here How he kide him in þe courete. *c* **1450** Holland *Howlat* 151, I sall not ʒow richt now thar names in ane. **1503** Hawes *Examp. Virtue* Prol. ii, But at auenture I wyll now wryte. **1682** [see just *adv.* 7 c]. **1875** Jowett *Plato* (ed. 2) I. 333, I am in a hurry, and must go now. **1898** Flor. Montgomery *Tony* 11 The train would start now.

3. In the time directly preceding the present moment. Now only in *just now* or (*poet.*) *even now*. Also † *now* (*a*) *late*, *now of late*, recently.

c **888** K. Ælfred *Boeth.* v. §iii, Ymb þæt ilce þu ʒiddodest nu hwene ær. *c* **1055** *Byrhtferth's Handboc* in *Anglia* VIII. 298 Heo wunað on ælcum tacne swa we nu ʒerehton. *Ibid.* 304 þa þing þe we nu handledon. **1435** *Wars Eng. in France* (Rolls) II. 576 The king shulde take appointement offred now late unto hym at Arras. *c* **1440** *York Myst.* i. 43 þat lufly lorde..That vs thus mighty has made, þat nowe was righte noghte. **1533** Cromwell in Merriman *Life & Lett.* (1902) I. 353 Whose Auncestors of longe tyme hadd the same untill nowe of late. **1583** Golding *Calvin on Deut.* lxxxv. 522 If wee alleage It is not nowalate that this thing came vp. **1601** Dolman *La Primaud. Fr. Acad.* (1618) III. 673 As wee said euen now. **1633**- [see just *adv.* 7 b]. **1703**, **1820** [see even *adv.* 6 b]. **1881** Rossetti *House of Life* vi, Even now my lady's lips did play With these my lips such consonant interlude.

4. At this time; at the time spoken of or referred to.

1548 Udall, etc. *Erasm. Par. Acts* 58 For his mother, beeing now a widow, was a Iewe borne. **1592** Shaks. *Ven. & Ad.* 349 Now was she just before him as he sat. **1611** Bible *Mark* iv. 37 The waues beat into the ship, so that it was now full. **1697** Dryden *Virg. Georg.* III. 556 Swift Rivers are with sudden Ice constrain'd;..An Hostry now for Waggons. **1758** S. Hayward *Serm.* xvi. 496 What season more important than the hour of death? Every thing now conspires to fill the soul with gloom. **1795** W. Roscoe *Lorenzo de Medici* I. i. 57 Cosmo now approached the period of his mortal existence. **1845** Pattison *Ess.* (1889) I. 25 The assurance he had at first displayed was now succeeded by an air of embarrassment. **1874** Bancroft *Footpr. Time* viii. 201 The war was now practically concluded.

5. † **a.** *as now*, at this time, just now. *Obs.*

c **1386** [see as *adv.* 34]. **1390** Gower *Conf.* I. 60 Of thi wittes five I wole as now nomore schryve, Bot only of these ilke tuo. **1456** Sir G. Haye *Law Arms* (S.T.S.) 292 It is sufficiand ynouche to me to tell as now that [etc.]. *a* **1533** Ld. Berners *Huon* xliii. 144 Shew me for what cause ye haue as now sent for me. **1594** Marlowe & Nashe *Dido* I. i, Instruct us under what good heaven We breathe as now.

† **b.** *now by dawe*, = now-a-days. *Obs. rare.*

c **1327** *Pol. Songs* (Camden) 326 Everich man nu bi dawe may sen that thus hit is. *a* **1450** Myrc 5 So faren prestes now by dawe.

† **c.** *now about*, about this time. *Obs. rare.*

1713 S. Sewall *Diary* 11 June, Now about the Govr. procures a Letter to be written. **1721** *Ibid.* 23 Jan., Now about I gave his Excellency a Ring.

6. a. *now and again*, *anon*, † *eft*, † *now*, at one time and another, from time to time.

c **1386** Chaucer *Sqr.'s T.* 422 Eueremoore as she stood She swowneth now and now for lakke of blood. **1390** Gower *Conf.* I. 246 And in the Marches now and eft,..He wroghte such knihthode there. *c* **1420** *Pallad. on Husb.* I. 570 The seed of mirte..Lete yeue hem now & now for chaunge of mete. **1470–85** Malory *Arthur* VI. xviii. 211 Euer now and now came alle the Knyghtes home that sir Turquyn hadde prysoners. *a* **1641** Bp. Mountagu *Acts & Mon.* (1642) 171 God amongst the Pagans did,..now and anon, reveale the mysterie of Christ Jesus. **1884** Miss Braddon *Ishmael* III. x. 217 Seized now and again with that terrible cough of hers.

b. *now and* (also †*or*) *then*, occasionally, fitfully, intermittently, at intervals. †Also with *by*.

a **1533** Ld. Berners *Gold. Bk. M. Aurel.* (1546) O viij, Sometyme on the daie, and nowe and than by nyght, they would walke abrode. **1576** Fleming *Panopl. Epist.* 211 *marg.*, Familiar friends vse ieasting nowe and then, in their letters. **1621** I. C. in *T. Bedford's Sin unto Death* A j, The Apothecaries Glasse or Gally-pot..being emptied by now and then of a little. **1623** Byfield *Expos. Coloss.* II. v. 16 Tis not enough to doe good now or then, by flashes. **1663** Gerbier *Counsel* g 2 b, This manual doth both now and then proffer a word or two to cherish the Readers patience. **1711** Addison *Spect.* No. 130 ¶3 These Gypsies now and then foretold very strange things. **1761** Mrs. Sheridan *Sidney Bidulph* I. 14 The strictness of her notions..now-and-then gave a tincture of severity to her actions. **1802** Wordsw. '*When I have borne in Memory*', What wonder, if a Poet, now and then..Felt for thee as a Lover. **1890** *Spectator* 11 Oct. 474/2 She never took up, except by moments now and then, the legitimate side.

attrib. **1762** Lloyd *St. James's Mag.* 50 Such now-and-then negligences, incidental to all poems of length. **1775** S. J. Pratt *Liberal Opin.* lxxxvii. (1783) III. 147, I have set you down as a now-and-then friend.

c. So *every now and then* (or *again*).

1720 C'tess Cowper *Diary* (1864) 152 The King cast an angry Look that Way every now and then. **1769** Burke *Late St. Nation* Wks. II. 13 It is piteously doleful, nodding every now and then towards dulness. **1802** Beddoes *Hygëia* II. 42 A sentence which we physicians are doomed, every now and then, to hear. **1865** [see again 4 b]. **1868** F. E. Paget *Lucretia* 216 Still, except every now and then, at rare intervals, it was polished. **1883** [see every 1 f].

7. a. *now...now*, used to introduce antithetical clauses, phrases, or words.

a **1300** *Cursor M.* 24545 Nu i lig and no i stand, Bunden þus in balful band. **1390** Gower *Conf.* I. 23 Now hier now ther, now to now fro, Now up now down, this world goth so. *c* **1400** Maundev. (Roxb.) xiv. 65 Riȝt sodaynely es þare chaungeyng of þe aer, nowe grete calde and now grete hete. *c* **1491** *Chast. Goddes Chyld.* 21 Her thoughtes ben full chaungable now here now there, now so, now thus, like to winde. **1535** Coverdale *2 Sam.* xi. 25 The swerde consumeth now one now another. **1567** Maplet *Gr. Forest* 79 It is now abiding vpon the earth now in the waters. **1620** T. Granger *Div. Logike* 258 Now vsed in this sence, now in that. **1697** Dryden *Virg. Georg.* III. 171 The flying Chariot kindles in the Course: And now a-low; and now aloft they fly. **1741** Richardson *Pamela* I. 21 In this Quandary, now considering, now crying, and not knowing what to do, I pass'd the Time. **1808** Scott *Marm.* VI. xxvii, Now low, now high, The pennon sunk and rose. **1883** Stevenson *Silverado Sq.* 9 A great variety of oaks stood, now severally, now in a becoming grove.

b. So *now...then*, *now...and again*, etc.

1593 Shaks. *3 Hen. VI*, II. v. 10 Now, one [is] the better: then, another best. **1600** —— *A.Y.L.* III. ii. 437 Now weepe for him, then spit at him. **1634** Sir T. Herbert *Trav.* 5 [The weather is] so vncertaine, that now you shall haue a quiet breath and gale, and suddenly an vnexpected violent gust. **1667** Milton *P.L.* II. 634 Now [he] shaves with level wing the Deep, then soares. **1750** Johnson *Rambler* No. 60 ¶8 His walk was now quick, and again slow.

8. In phr. *now or never*.

1560 Daus tr. *Sleidane's Comm.* 442 b, Therfore thought they now, or els never, y^t God was on theyr side. **1593** Shaks. *2 Hen. VI*, III. i. 331 Now Yorke, or neuer, steele thy fearfull thoughts And change misdoubt to resolution. **1648** Crashaw *Steps to Temple* Poems (1904) 75 Now Lord, or never, they'l beleeve on thee. *a* **1658** Cleveland *Rustic Rampant* Wks. (1687) 459 Now or never for the Liberty of the Subject. **1709** Steele *Tatler* No. 38 ¶6 Now or never is the Time. **1855** Kingsley *Westw. Ho!* xix, 'Come off, now or never,' cried Amyas. **1860** Motley *Netherl.* IV. 170 Taking the ground that now or never was the time for driving the Spaniards..out of the Netherlands.

II. 9. a. In sentences expressing a command or request, with the purely temporal sense weakened or effaced. In later use also with ellipse of verb.

c **825** *Vesp. Ps.* ii. 7 And nu, cyningas, onʒeotað. *a* **900** Cynewulf *Crist* 243 Cum nu, siʒores weard,..& þine miltse her arfæst ywe. **971** *Blickl. Hom.* 19 Cleopian we nu in eglum mode & inneweardre heortan. *c* **1200** *Vices & Virtues* 17 Andswere me nu, þu un-ʒesælie saule. *c* **1275** *Passion Our Lord* 1 in *O.E. Misc.* 37 I-hereþ nv one lutele tale þat ich eu wille telle. *a* **1300** *Cursor M.* 11694 Rise vp, he said, and right þe nu. *a* **1400** *Pistill of Susan* 122 Aspieþ nou specialy þe ʒates bene sperde. *c* **1500** *Melusine* 251 Fayre lordes, now lightly on horsback. **1588** Shaks. *L.L.L.* II. i. 124 Now faire befall your maske. **1610** —— *Temp.* III. i. 15 Alas, now pray you Worke not so hard..; pray now rest your selfe. **1617** Fletcher *Mad Lover* IV. i, Now your Counsels, For I am at my wits end. **1735** Berkeley *Free-think. Mathem.* Wks. 1871 III. 316 Now, in the name of truth, I entreat you to tell what this moment is. *a* **1814** *Intrigues of a Day* III. i. in *New Brit. Theatre* I. 116 *Mrs. H.* Oh! I insist upon hearing. *Sir J.* Nay, now, my dear cousin. **1872** O. W. Holmes *Poet Breakf.-t.* vi, No humbug, now, about my boyhood! *Ibid.*, Come now, I don't believe [etc.]. **1893** Sir G. Chesney *Lesters* II. xxi, 'Now, Peter, behave yourself'; and again the threatening crop was raised.

b. So *now then*. (Freq. in mod. use.)

c **1000** *Ags. Ps.* (Thorpe) xxxiii. 8 Fandiað nu þonne; onʒite ʒe þæt Drihten is swyðe sefte. *c* **1485** *Digby Myst.* (1882) III. 1970 Now thanne, yower puer blyssyng gravnt vs tylle! *c* **1500** *Melusine* 238 Now thenne, noble Cousyne, seace your wepyng. **1611** Cotgr. s.v. *Or*, *Or ça*, now then, or goe to. *a* **1700** Dryden (J.), Now then be all thy weighty cares away. **1837** Dickens *Pickw.* xix, 'Keep your eyes open,' said Wardle...'Now then.' **1855** Kingsley *Westw. Ho!* xx, 'Now, then,' said Amyas, 'to breakfast'.

10. a. Used to introduce an important or noteworthy point in an argument or proof, or in a series of statements. Also † *now then*.

c **897** K. Ælfred *Gregory's Past. C.* xlix. 376 Nu ðonne,..nu is to onʒietonne æt hu micelre scylde ða bioð befangne. *c* **1000** Ælfric *Saints' Lives* xxvi. 272 Nu cwæð se halʒa Beda, þe ðas boc ʒedihte, þæt hit nan wundor nys. *a* **1240** *Sawles Warde* in *O.E. Hom.* I. 257 Nu is riht þenne þat we demen us seolf euer unmihtie to werien ant to witen us. **1340** *Ayenb.* 53 Nou behoueþ to habbe tuo mesures, ane little..and anoþre gode and large. **1426** Audelay *Poems* 4 Nou ʒif a woman maryd schal be, Anoon sche schal be boȝt and sold. **1525** in Ellis *Orig. Lett.* Ser. II. III. 75 Nowe, Sir, as God hathe endued your Grace with Christen couraige [etc.]. **1597** Hooker *Eccl. Pol.* v. xix. §2 Now the principal thing required in a witness is fidelity. **1600** Shaks. *A.Y.L.* III. iii. 26 Now if thou wert a Poet, I might haue some hope thou didst feigne. **1715** tr. *Gregory's Astron.* (1726) I. 498 Now, the Observation may be made very commodiously, after the following..Method. **1836** Dickens *Sk. Boz, Our Parish* vii, Now, this was bad enough, occurring as it did three times a week on the average, but this was not all. **1881** Jowett *Thucyd.* I. 150 Now the Acharnians are famous for their skill in slinging.

b. Inserted parenthetically, or at the end of a clause, with similar force.

c **888** K. Ælfred *Boeth.* xviii. §3 þeah he nu maran wilniʒe, he ne mæʒ furðum þæt forðbringan. *a* **1225** *Leg. Kath.* 977 þis is nu þe derfschipe of þi dusi onsware. *c* **1230** *Hali Meid.* 3 Hwat is nu þis lare þat tu nimest se deopliche? **13..** *Cursor M.* 3589 (Gött), Elde es nou a selcuth thing, For all it ʒernis þat er ʒing.

1749 Fielding *Tom Jones* v. vi, I am sure you cannot be in earnest now. **1760** Sarah Fielding *Ophelia* II. iii, There's a wise young woman, now! **1802** Mar. Edgeworth *Moral T.* (1816) I. xv. 130, I should be glad now..to employ you,..but [etc.].

11. Used elliptically in various ways, esp. at the beginning of a clause.

how now?: see how *adv.* 4 b.

c **1450** *Merlin* 501 'Now trewly,' seide she, 'that lady were nothinge wise'. **1579** Fulke *Heskins' Parl.* 75 Nowe to M. Heskins Collections. **1592** Lyly *Midas* IV. i, Now Nymphes, what say you? **1606** Shaks. *Tr. & Cr.* v. iii. 98 Doe you heare my Lord?..What now? **1653** Walton *Angler* ii, Now, now, Ringwood has him. **1680** Otway *Orphan* II. iv, Now by my Father's Soul, the Witch was honest. **1764** Foote *Mayor of G.* II. i, Now for it, Sneak; the enemy's at hand. **1774** M. Mackenzie *Maritime Surv.* 59 The Moment the Star touches the same Side of the Plumb-line as before, call out, Now. **1864** J. H. Newman *Apol.* i, And now as to Dr. Whately. I owe him a great deal. **1898** Doyle *Trag. Korosko* v, That very morning..how pleasant was life!..And now!

12. a. As *conj.* Since, seeing that; as...now.

c **888** K. Ælfred *Boeth.* xxx. §1 Forhwy þe haten dysiʒe men mid leasre stemne wuldor, nu ðu nane neart? **971** *Blickl. Hom.* 123 And nu þeos haliʒe tid englum þus healice ..to blisse wearþ, hwæt þonne [etc.]. **1377** Langl. *P. Pl.* B. v. 143 And now persones han parceyued that Freres parte with hem, þise possessioneres preche and depraue freres. *c* **1400** *Gamelyn* 232 Now I am older woxe, thou schalt me finde a more [shrew]. **1594** Marlowe & Nashe *Dido* III. i, *Æneas*. I understand, your highness sent for me. *Dido*. No; but, now thou art here, tell me. **1610** Shaks. *Temp.* III. iii. 15 Now they are oppress'd with trauaile, they..cannot vse such vigilance As when they are fresh. **1702** De Foe *Shortest Way w. Dissenters* 137 There are some People in the World, who now they are unpearcht,..begin with Æsop's Cock, to preach up Peace. **1889** 'R. Boldrewood' *Robbery under Arms* xli, We'd as good as got a free pardon.., now the police was away.

b. So *now that*.

1530 Palsgr. 645/1, I have notted my heed nowe that sommer is come. **1595** Shaks. *John* III. iv. 180 'Tis wonder-full, What may be wrought.., Now that their soules are topfull of offence. **1631** Gouge *God's Arrows* v. 406 Now that you have brought me forth..leave me not to shift for my selfe. **1676** Towerson *Decalogue* 383 There is not the same reason, now that the world is peopled [etc.]. **1844** Mrs. Browning *Drama of Exile* 30 Now that the fruit is plucked, ..I hold that Eden is impregnable. **1876** *World* V. 9 Is there no new field.., now that the schoolmaster is so fearfully and wonderfully abroad?

III. 13. a. With preps., as *by*, *ere*, *for*, *or*, *till*, *unto*, *now*.

c **825** *Vesp. Psalter* lxx. 17 Oð nu ic forðsecʒu wundur ðin. *c* **1200** Ormin 14066 And tu þe gode win till nu Aȝȝ hafesst hidd and haldenn. *a* **1300** *Cursor M.* 12800 Es þou helias halden til nu, Crist or prophet, quam to bu? *c* **1450** *Ibid.* 17785 (Laud), Ye wold nevir yt leve or now. *c* **1450** tr. *De Imitatione* I. xxiv. 35 If þou haddist lyued unto now in worshipes & lustes of þe worlde. *c* **1500** *Melusine* 121 But as for now I shall reste of hym and I shal retourne there. **1592** Shaks. *Ven. & Ad.* 1062 Her eyes are mad that they have wept till now. **1619** Fletcher *Mons. Thomas* I. iii, No word of visitation, as ye love me, And for now Ile leave ye. **1860** Thirlwall *Rem.* (1877) I. 395 Without this, she would have fallen ere now under the blows. **1885–94** R. Bridges *Eros. & Psyche* Feb. iv, She is not hence by now six miles at most.

b. *from now* (*forth*, *forthward*, *forward*).

a **1300** *Cursor M.* 3758 In dew and gress sere o þorth Sal be þi blissing fra no forth. *Ibid.* 10976 þou sal be dumb fra nu, Til þat he be born. *c* **1400** *Hampole's Wks.* I. 221 And þou sall lufe gastely ilk a mane, and flee fra now forthwarde to lufe fleschly. **1503** *Surtees Misc.* (1890) 30 John Mitteley & his heires frome now forthe shall wall up..the utter west syde of his swynstye. **1855** Kingsley *Westw. Ho!* xvi, I could live very well from now till Doomsday without [etc.]. **1890** *Spectator* 10 May 651/2 The Gladstonians could talk with ease on one line of one clause from now till Christmas.

14. a. As *sb.* The present time. Also *Comb.*

Gower uses *time now* in the same sense.

1390 Gower *Conf.* I. 32 To peise now with that beforn, The chaf is take for the corn. *Ibid.* III. 346 Ensamples thou hast many on Of now and ek of time gon. **1549** Strype *Eccl. Mem.* 431 The tyme is tourned: then was then and now is now. **1607** Shaks. *Timon* II. ii. 152 Though you heare now (too late), yet nowes a time. **1631** *Celestina* vii. 97 Now is now, and then is then; when time serves, we will follow your counsell. **1655** Fuller *Serm.* 29 Now is an atome, it will puzzle the skill of an angell to divide. **1854** Patmore *Angel in Ho.* I. II. x, Where Now and Then are no more twain. **1861** Angus *Serm.* 43 Base and profligate now-wasters. *Ibid.* 44 It is only a make-believe of happiness which does not dwell in now.

b. So with *the* or *this*.

1633 Ford *Broken Hrt.* IV. i, Now, uncle, now; this Now is now too late. **1685** Dryden *Threnodia* 28 With scarce a breathing space betwixt, This now becalmed, and perishing the next. **1713** Rowe *Jane Shore* III, This present now Some matters of the State detain our leisure. **1771** Wesley *Wks.* (1872) V. 392 Enjoy the very, very now, by enjoying Him 'whose years fail not'. **1820** Scott *Monast.* xxxii, It must be done this very *now*; or it may never be done. **1851** Brimley *Ess.* 183 Plant the great hereafter in the now.

15. a. A present point or moment of time.

1630 Drumm. of Hawth. *Flowers of Sion* Poems (1856) 179 Still is the same thy Day and Yesterday An undivided Now. **1692** Dryden *Eleonora* 306 We can scarcely say she died; For but a now did heaven and earth divide. **1751** Harris *Hermes* Wks. (1841) 146 If a point or now were extended, each of them would contain within itself infinite ..other nows. **1801** Southey *Thalaba* I. xxviii, Time is not here, nor days, nor months, nor years, An everlasting now of solitude! **1870** Emerson *Soc. & Solit.* Wks. (Bohn) III. 71 An everlasting Now reigns in nature.

b. With possessive pronouns.

a **1668** Sir W. Waller *Div. Medit.* (1839) 146 In this my day, or rather in this my now. *a* **1711** Ken *Preparatives* Poet. Wks. 1721 IV. 7, I oft made solemn vows To consecrate to God my Nows. *c* **1859** Lowell *Ode to Happiness* 49 Man ever with his Now at strife.

IV. *attrib.* and *Comb.* **16.** In attributive or adjectival use: Present; of the present time. (Very common in the 17th cent.)

1444 *Rolls of Parlt.* V. 75/1 The estate and possession of the saide nowe Maistur and Brethern. **1486** in Hearne *Collect.* (O.H.S.) I. 262 Dame Kateryn my now wief. **1565** *Child-Marriages* 136 John Olton decessid, father to the nowe plaintiff. **1586** WARNER *Alb. Eng.* III. xv, Thise Irish, sometime Spanish Scotts, of whence our now-Scotts bee. **1600** W. WATSON *Decacordon* (1602) 168 Their now surcease from calling this vsurpate authority in question. **1668** WILKINS *Real Char.* 3 The Latin..(of which the now French, Spanish, and Italian are several off-springs and derivations). *a* **1715** BURNET *Own Time* (1766) I. 357 His second son, the now Earl of Rochester. **1793** BURKE *Corr.* (1844) IV. 147 The dreadful treatment of the now king. **1824** BYRON *Def. Transf.* II. iii. 41 His now escape may furnish A future miracle. **1875** HANNAH W. SMITH *Secr. Happy Life* iv. 47 He has to come to the *now* belief, and say by faith, 'My sins are now forgiven'.

(*b*) Revived in adjectival use: modern, fashionable, up-to-date, 'with it'.

1963 *New Yorker* 8 June 72 A black crepe dress..a now-and-future shaping of pebbly acetate-and-rayon crepe. **1967** *Time* 7 Apr. 20 The more mature of the unmarried in the Now Generation say that, far from promoting promiscuity, the pills impose a sense of responsibility. **1967** *Listener* 2 Nov. 564/2 'Drag', of course, is very now (as the copy-writers are saying). **1968** *Sat. Rev.* (U.S.) 28 Dec. 18 *Bullitt*, I find, is completely typical of the 'now' look in American movies—a swift-moving, constantly shifting surface that suggests rather than reveals depths. **1970** G. GREER *Female Eunuch* 255 Even a poet as *now* as Dylan has two kinds of female character in his imagery. **1972** *Sat. Rev.* (U.S.) 27 May 18/2 Dig the now scene. **1973** E. BULLINS *Theme is Blackness* 167 Everybody in our integrated circle of mod people is with it, man. We're the Now Crowd.

17. *Comb.* **a.** With pa. pples., as ***now-accumulated, -borne, -cantoned, fallen, -forgotten, neglected***, etc.

1591 SYLVESTER *Du Bartas* I. ii. 845 When valiant Romans warr'd Victoriously, on the (now-Canton'd) Suisses. **1601** SHAKS. *All's Well* II. iii. 186 Whose Ceremonie Shall seeme expedient on the now borne briefe. **1617** A. NEWMAN *Pleas. Vis.* 20 Where may my now-lost honours be? **1725** POPE *Odyss.* XIII. 398 Whose now-neglected altars, in thy reign, Blush'd with the blood of sheep and oxen slain. **1785** A. SEWARD *Let.* 30 Mar. (1811) I. 53 Mr. Warton demonstrates, that the general plan of L'Allegro, Il Penseroso, was suggested to Milton by a now-forgotten work of one Burton. **1802–12** BENTHAM *Ration. Judic. Evid.* Wks. 1827 I. 583 The now-accumulated stock of experience. **1865** GOSSE *Land & Sea* (1874) 354 The position once borne by the now-fallen fronds. **1951** M. MCLUHAN *Mech. Bride* (1967) 132/2 Mere attacks on salesmanship are confusing.. when these now-forgotten assumptions are missed.

b. With pres. pples., as ***now-declining, -existing, -passing, -waning***; and vbl. sbs., as ***now-being***.

1612 DRAYTON *Poly-olb.* x. 252 Such immortall men As this now-waning world shall hardly heare agen. **1830** I. TAYLOR *Unitarianism* 81 The 'stolid fanaticism' of this now-passing time. **1845** DARWIN *Voy. Nat.* xiv. (1873) 297 A great bed of now-existing shells. **1854** CDL. WISEMAN *Fabiola* I. x, Looking at the now-declining moon. **1876** WHITNEY *Sights & Ins.* vi. 69 It is full of presence..of now-being.

c. With adjs., as ***now-big, -full, -Roman***, etc.

1625 [see NOVELTY *sb.* 2]. **1659** W. BROUGH *Sacred Principles* Title-p., The doctrine of the Church of England, as differing from the now-Roman. **1660** *Speech to Gen. Monk* 1 Faile not her now-bigg hopes. **1817** KEATINGE *Trav.* II. 96 The brightness of the now-full moon.

Hence **now** *v.*[1] (*nonce-use.*)

1647 WARD *Simp. Cobler* 52 Good Casuists would case it, and case it,..now it, and then it, punctually.

†**now**, *sb.*[2], obs. Sc. variant of NOLL.

15.. *Christs Kirk* xviii. in *Bann. MS.* 287 Thair durst nocht ten cum him to tak, So nowit he thair nowis. *a* **1585** POLWART *Flyting* 551 Athort his nitty now Ilke louse lyes linkand like a large lint bow. **1721** KELLY *Sc. Prov.* 133 He had need to have a heal Pow, That calls his Neighbour Nitty Know.

now, *v.*[1]: see NOW *adv.*

†**now**, *v.*[2] *Sc. Obs.*[−1] [Perh. a var. of *noll*: see Jam. and *E.D.D.*] *trans.* To beat, pummel.

15.. *Christs Kirk* xviii. [See prec.]

now, obs. Sc. form of NEW *a.*

nowackiite (nəʊ'vɑːkiːaɪt). *Min.* [f. the name of Werner *Nowacki* (b. 1909), Swiss crystallographer + -ITE[1].] A sulphide of copper, zinc, and arsenic, $Cu_6Zn_3As_4S_{12}$, found as grey or black rhombohedral crystals at Lengenbach, Switzerland.

1965 MARUMO & BURRI in *Chimia* XIX. 501/2 Our mineral, for which we—together with Mr. J. Imhof—suggest the name *nowackiite*, in honour of Professor Werner Nowacki (Bern). **1967** *Zeitschr. für Kristallogr.* CXXIV. 354 The structure determination of nowackiite was undertaken to determine the coordination around the As atoms in the mineral, and to clarify the structural relationship to the zincblende type.

now-a-day, *adv.* [f. NOW *adv.* Cf. next and ADAY.] = next.

1390 GOWER *Conf.* II. 89 Ther ben full manye now aday, That knowen litel what thei meene. *a* **1425** *Cursor M.* 702 (Trin.), þe sonne was þat tyme we say Seuen siþe briȝtere þen now aday. **1530** *Hickscorner* in Hazl. *Dodsley* I. 174 We all may say well-a-way for sin that is now-a-day. **1799** E. DU BOIS *Piece Family Biog.* II. 94 *Χρυσεα χαλχειων* won't do now-a-day. **1801** tr. *Gabrielli's Myst. Husb.* III. 47 To be sure great folks now-a-day look out for grand fortunes! **1837** WHITTOCK *Bk. Trades* (1842) 411 A very humble..branch of manufactures, receives several names, now a-day, according to the means used.

b. *attrib.*

? **1630** H. R. *Mythomystes* 13 The sore of our now-a-day Poets. **1819** W. TAYLOR in *Monthly Mag.* XLVII. 118 Horace addicted himself to verse-making (like our now-a-day rimesters). **1866** *Lyndesay's Monarche* (E.E.T.S.) 157 Now-a-day saints compared with those of old. **1898** BARING-GOULD *Old Eng. Home* iv. 84, I do not know much about the cupboards of nowaday folk.

c. As *sb.* The present time.

1886 J. R. REES *Divers. Bookworm* iii. 83 His delightful stand-still is refreshing if only to think of, in the bustling nowaday.

now-a-days, *adv.* [f. NOW *adv.* + ADAYS 2. Now freq. written without hyphens as one word.]

1. At the present day, in these times.

1362 LANGL. *P. Pl.* A. XI. 37 Lecherie and losengrie.. beoþ gamus nou A dayes. **1390** GOWER *Conf.* II. 291 As men mai finde nou adaies. *a* **1450** *Knt. de la Tour* (1868) 53 Men of these maners there be now a dayes to mani. **1474** CAXTON *Chesse* 30 The lawes nowadayes ben not executed but vpon the poure peple. *a* **1533** LD. BERNERS *Huon* lxxxi. 252 Now a dayes can not be founde trew frendes as were wont to be. **1583** STUBBES *Anat. Abus.* II. (1882) 19, I cannot but lament the small preferment now adaies that learning getteth in the world. **1611** BIBLE *1 Sam.* xxv. 10 There bee many seruants now a daies that breake away. **1658** A. FOX *Würtz' Surg.* II. Introd. 43 Yet have I not related all the abuses which are practised and committed now adayes. **1712** ADDISON *Spect.* No. 481 ¶4 Lacqueys were never so saucy and pragmatical, as they are now-a-days. **1766** FORDYCE *Serm. Yng. Wom.* (1767) I. vi. 226 We speak of good housewifery now a days. **1833** HT. MARTINEAU *Berkeley the Banker* I. i. 21 Guineas are scarce now-a-days. **1893** *Law Times* XCV. 248/1 The Crown has certain privileges which appear somewhat anomalous nowadays.

b. *attrib.*

1609 J. RAWLINSON *Fishermen* 32 Such indeed..is our now-adaies religion. **1897** *Westm. Gaz.* 2 Mar. 2/1 These nowadays parsons are just a set of fussing insurance agents.

c. As *sb.*

1645 MILTON *Tetrach.* 26 Not partly right and partly wrong,..as Divines of now adaies dare censure them. **1647** tr. *Maloezzi's Pourtract* 94 The Phisitians of now a dayes. **1852** HAWTHORNE *Wonder Bk.* (1879) 121 In the orchards of nowadays.

2. In variant forms ***now o'*** (†*of*, or †*on*) ***days***.

[**1390** GOWER *Conf.* II. 59 On daies nou The blinde god.. set the thinges in discord.] *c* **1400** MAUNDEV. (Roxb.) xxviii. 128 þis myracle..schuld stirre Cristen men to be mare deuote..þan þai er now on days. *c* **1440** *Alph. Tales* 16 Bod monkis er not so now o dayis. *Ibid.* 73 So it happens oft sithes now-of-dayes. **1535** STEWART *Cron. Scot.* II. 486 Men wald be..meikar als than now on dais tha ar. **1542** UDALL *Erasm. Apoph.* 223 Such as our princes & noble menne have nowe of dayes.

1819 *Metropolis* III. 81 No one comes to hear the play now o' days.

So **now-a-nights**.

1841 THOREAU *Let.* 21 July in *Corr.* (1958) 45 Now-a-nights I go on to the hill. **1847** FR. A. KEMBLE *Rec. Later Life* III. 289 Murray's Handbook..and the foreign 'Bradshaw'. These furnish my lullaby now-a-nights. **1920** M. BEERBOHM *And Even Now* 120 The Golden Drugget is not outspread nowanights across the high dark coast-road between Rapallo and Zoagli. **1939** JOYCE *Finnegans Wake* 15 And still nowanights and by nights of yore do all bold floras ..say only: Cull me ere I wilt to thee!

no waiting. Used (with hyphen) *attrib.* and *absol.* to designate an area, place, etc., where vehicles may not be parked.

1959 *Times* 8 Dec. 5/1 In streets where there is unilateral no-waiting, the signs only indicate the side of the road on which waiting is not allowed. **1963** M. LEVINSON *Taxi!* v. 66 A taxi-driver..must wait for..a passenger if he is asked to do so..although this law..is cancelled out by the no-waiting restrictions. **1969** *Morning Star* 18 Nov. 3 Mr Callaghan said the inquiries were about a car causing obstruction in a no-waiting area of Brixton. **1969** *Highway Code* 43 Along the edge of the Carriageway. No waiting..at times shown on nearby plates or on entry signs to controlled parking zones. **1970** O. NORTON *Dead on Prediction* ii. 22 They had painted yellow no-waiting lines all the way.

nowar(e, variants of NOWER, nowhere. *Obs.*

'**noway**, *adv.* Also 4 **na wai**, 6 *Sc.* **naway**, 5 **no wey(e**. [f. NO *a.* + WAY *sb.*] In no way or manner; not at all; by no means.

For the phrases *by, in, on no way*, see the sb.

a **1300** *Cursor M.* 22250 Ai quils þe frankis kinges es.., o rome..þe dignite Ne mai na wai al perist be. *a* **1425** *Ibid.* 9794 (Trin.), How miȝte þei mon of synne make clene? Certis no wey as hit is sene. **1573** TYRIE *Refut.* in *Cath. Tract.* (S.T.S.) 16 Quhilk ansuer as euerie man may sie is naway to the propos. **1581** LAMBARDE *Eiren.* I. xi. (1588) 64 No way better shall the Discretion of a Iustice of the Peace appeare. *a* **1648** LD. HERBERT *Hen. VIII* (1683) 340 He protested he was no way faulty in his Allegiance. **1685** BOYLE *Enq. Notion Nat.* 173 Divers no-way mortal excrescenses and ulcers in the throat. **1711** SHAFTESB. *Charac.* (1737) II. 58 The principle of self-love..being no-way moderated or restrain'd. **1760–2** GOLDSM. *Cit. World* xxii, His learning, his virtues,..were qualifications that no way served to recommend him. **1844** HERSCHEL *Ess.* (1857) 592 Cavendish..is therefore no way to blame for any misconception which may prevail. **1875** TENNYSON *Q. Mary* II. ii, I have lived a virgin, and I noway doubt But that with God's grace, I can live so still.

2. Usu. **no way.** In colloq. use: it is impossible, it can't be done.

1968–70 *Current Slang* (Univ. S. Dakota) III–IV. 86 Can we get out of the test? No Way! **1970** J. G. VERMANDEL *Dine with Devil* vii. 36 'No way I can do it any faster than that'. .. But Peter Angel was shaking his head. 'No way, sorry.' **1973** *Observer* 16 Dec. 40/1 A letter was dispatched to the Foreign Office asking HMG to foot the bill for any damage done—no way. **1973** *Chicago Sun-Times* 29 Dec. 25/1, I say Fred Astaire played a drunk in the made-for-TV movie 'The Over-the-Hill Gang Rides Again'. My brother says, 'No way.' Who is right? **1974** *Nature* 15 Feb. 420/2 Suppose then that an ingenious scribe..decided to use the very compound which wasn't used again for that purpose until about 1920? No way, says McCrone. **1975** *New Yorker* 20 Jan. 29/1 He said he wouldn't start up a gang today—no way.

'**noways**, *adv.* Forms: α. 3 **nanes**, 4 **nan-**, 4, 6 *Sc.* **na-**. β. 3 **nones**, 3, 5 **none**, 5– **no**. Also 3 **wei(e)s**, 4, 7 **waies**, 5–7 **wayes**, 4, 6–7 **wais**, 6 *Sc.* **wayis**, 4, 6– **ways**. [Orig. f. gen. sing. of NONE *a.* and WAY *sb.*; in later use only the second element retains its inflection.] = prec.

α. *c* **1205** LAY. 11216 He ne mihte nanes weies [*c* **1275** none weies] cumen to þissere kineriche. *c* **1230** *Hali Meid.* 28 Him ne mai ha nanes weis..neauer mare leosen. *a* **1300** *Cursor M.* 26224 þat mai nanwais elles be Bot men his opin penance see. *c* **1375** *Ibid.* 8742 (Fairf.), Quar-fore me þink..þe childe be na-ways done to ded. **1563** WINȜET *Four Scoir Thre Quest.* Wks. (S.T.S.) I. 67 Quhilk contrare our conscience.. we dar naways attempt. **1597** *Sc. Acts Jas. VI* (1814) 128 The samin lykwayes naways previt that..article of the said summondis.

β. *a* **1225** *Ancr. R.* 212 Nonesweis ne muwen heo loken þiderward. *c* **1275** [see above]. **13..** *Cursor M.* 17951 (Arundel), ȝit may he gete hit no wayes. *a* **1425** *Ibid.* 19652 (Trin.), Nouȝte he ete þo þre dayes, Ny siȝte saw he none wayes. *c* **1550** CHEKE *Matt.* ii. 6 Thou art no wais yᵉ lest among yᵉ Princes of Juda. **1648** GAGE *West Ind.* 17 No wayes fearfull of the naked Barbarians. **1656** H. PHILLIPS *Purch. Patt.* 114, I no wayes find fault therewith. **1702** *Pennsylv. Hist. Soc. Mem.* IX. 153 They were tied up and could noways appear. **1760–2** GOLDSM. *Cit. W.* lxviii, Age, however, has no ways impaired his usual health and vivacity. **1813** SOUTHEY *Nelson* I. 119 This was no ways imputable to the admiral. **1887** MᶜNEILL *Blawearie* 189 The situation.. he was noways loath to accept.

nowch(e, obs. forms of OUCH, clasp.

†'**nowcin.** *Obs.* Forms: 3 **nowcin** (neow-, 4 no-), 3–4 **noucine**. [ad. ON. *nauðsyn* need = MDu. *nootsin, noodzin*.] Hardship, distress.

a **1225** *St. Marher.* 1 His icorne þe deð dreheð for him, oðer eni nowcin. *a* **1225** *Leg. Kath.* 2395 In neode & in nowcin. *a* **1240** *Sawles Warde* in *O.E. Hom.* I. 261 Alles cunnes neowcins, ant eorðliche tintreohen. *a* **1300** *Cursor M.* 5372 He has saued me and mine Fra mikel nede, and fra noucine. *Ibid.* 5802, I wil þam bring of þair nocin.

nowd. *Sc.* Also **noud, knowd.** [Of obscure origin.] (See quots.)

1824 MACTAGGART *Encycl.*, *Nouds*, little fish, about the size of herring, with a horny skin, common in the Galloway seas. **1863** *Glasgow Her.* 15 Apr., The poor bird..had, in attempting to swallow a 'nowd', perished in the act. **1890** *Antrim & Down Gloss.*, *Nowd*, the grey gurnard.

nowder, variant of NOUTHER, neither.

nowe, obs. form of NEW *a.*

nowed, *a. Her.* [f. F. *noué* (see NOWY *a.*) + -ED[1].] Knotted; tied in a knot.

1572 BOSSEWELL *Armorie* II. 42 Their tayles forked, nowed, resignante. **1610** GUILLIM *Heraldry* III. xviii. (1611) 153 The field is Gules, an Adder Nowed. *Ibid.* IV. iii. 195 The long strings thereof..Nowed, buttoned, and tasselled. **1661** MORGAN *Sph. Gentry* I. iii. 38 An Escarbuncle of eight staves nowed and flowred Topaz. **1739** J. REYNOLDS *Her.* 9 Ednowain..bore Guls, three Snakes nowed, Azure. **1780** EDMONDSON *Heraldry* II. Gloss. s.v. *Per close*, Is that part of the garter that is buckled or nowed. **1850** W. D. COOPER *Hist. Winchelsea* 152 On the point a flying dragon..without legs, tail nowed. **1868** CUSSANS *Her.* (1893) 97 Serpents may be Nowed, twisted or knotted.

nowel[1] (nəʊ'ɛl). Also 5 **-elle**, 5–6, 9 **-ell**. [a. OF. *noel, nouel* (mod.F. *noël* NOEL), = Prov. *nadal, nadau*, Sp. and Pg. *natal*, It. *natale*:—L. *nātālem*, acc. sing. of *nātālis* NATAL *a.*]

1. A word shouted or sung as an expression of joy, originally to commemorate the birth of Christ. Now only as retained in old Christmas carols.

13.. *Gaw. & Gr. Knt.* 65 Loude crye was þer kest of clerkez & oþer, Nowel nayted o-newe, neuened ful ofte. *c* **1386** CHAUCER *Frankl. T.* 519 Biforn him stont the braun of toskid swyn, And nowel crieth every lusty man. *c* **1450** *Godstow Reg.* 13, I pray þe teche me, blessid Seynt sulpice, With þat holy virgyn Prisce, syng nowel. *c* **1450** in Halliw., Therefore let us alle syng nowelle;..And Cryst save mery Ynglond. *c* **1500** *Three Kings' Sons* 192 They cried with a high voice, 'Nowell!' clappyng their handes. *a* **1533** LD. BERNERS *Huon* cli. 578 The children rynnynge in the stretes cryenge nowell for ioye.

1887 in *N. & Q.* 7th Ser. III. 168 Nowel! nowel! nowel! Born is a king in Israel. *Ibid.* 291 The first Nowell the Angel did say Was to three poor shepherds. **1894** *Daily News* 8 Feb. 5/5 The child..had been taught the well-known Christmas carol entitled 'The First Nowell'.

†**2.** The feast of Christmas; Christmastide. *Obs.*

c **1450** LOVELICH *Merlin* 6870 ȝe vndirstondyn alle ful wel that now cometh the feste of nowel, jn whiche the goode Lord was bore. **1599** THYNNE *Animadv.* (1875) 40 Placinge ther Christemas, a parte of this tyme of Nowell, for all the tyme that Nowell conteynethe.

'nowel[2]. [Variant of NEWEL[1].]

†**1.** = NEWEL 1. *Obs.*

1365 [see NEWEL[1]]. **1388–9** in C. Welch *Tower Bridge* (1894) 71 Twenty great pieces of hard stone from Kent, called noweles. **1416–17** [see NEWEL[1]]. **1443** in Willis & Clark *Cambridge* (1886) I. 386 The same Thomas..and John shall ..make..xxxij Nowels... And they shal haue..for euery pece of the same Noweles iij. *s.* **1622** *Extr. Aberd. Reg.* (1848) II. 379 Sex scoir four peice of free aisler stanes.. thairof thrie scoir sevin peice long wark for lintellis and nowellis. **1688** HOLME *Armoury* III. 112/2 *Nowel*, ..the middle Pillar, or Post of a turning-stair.

2. *Founding.* (See quots. and cf. NIUELL.)

1864 WEBSTER, *Nowel*, the core or inner wall of a mold for casting large cylinders. **1879** *Encycl. Brit.* IX. 481/1 A hollow core of iron or brick.., and around it a layer of loam .., forming the 'nowel' or core.

nowel, obs. Sc. form of NOVEL *sb.*

†**nower**, *adv. Obs.* Forms: α. 3 **neower, neouwar, noware, nowor,** 3–4 **nowar,** 3–5 **nower** (5 **-ere**), 4 **nour(e,** 5 **nowr(e.** β. 3 **noȝwer,** 4 **noȝher,** 5 **nougher.** [Reduced form of ME. *nōhwer* NOWHERE *adv.*, or repr. OE. *nāwer* NAWER.] Nowhere.

α. *a* **1050** [see NOWHERE *adv.* 1 β]. *c* **1200** *Trin. Coll. Hom.* 165 *Nusquam tuta fides*..Nis nower non trewðe. *c* **1250** *Owl & Night.* 1168 Þu ne myht noware [*v.r.* nowar] atrute. **1297** R. GLOUC. (Rolls) 2506 Vairor womman nour aboute in none londe nas. *c* **1330** R. BRUNNE *Chron. Wace* (Rolls) 5083 Þey ne myghte nower [*v.r.* noure] about, Bot þorow hym, haue issue oute. *c* **1380** *Sir. Ferumb.* 415 Nowar nys founde non so wyȝt. *c* **1400** MAUNDEV. (Roxb.) xxviii. 128 Alssone come a thikke mirkness.., so þat þai myȝt nower go away.

β. *c* **1250** *Gen. & Exod.* 1271 He bad him maken siker pliȝt, ..Ðat ne sulde him noȝwer deren. **1382** WYCLIF *Wisd.* Prol., The booc of Wisdam anent Ebrues noȝher is. *c* **1412** HOCCLEEVE *De Reg. Princ.* 11 No richere man was nougher in no coost.

b. Qualifying *nigh* or *near*.

a **1225** *Leg. Kath.* 2094 Ne schaltu nower neh se lihtliche etsterten. *c* **1230** *Hali Meid.* 9 Nis hit nower neh gold al þat ter schineð. **1483** *Cath. Angl.* 256/2 Nowre nere, *longe minus, multum citra.*

c. In the combs. **nower-where, -whither.**

a **1300** *Cursor M.* 1082 His broiþer ded sua wend he dil, Pot he moght nourquar it hil. *Ibid.* 4959 For nour-quider mai we stere, þair will most we suffer here. *a* **1340** HAMPOLE *Psalter* xxxi. 13 That þe enmy fynde nourwhare inlate. *c* **1400** MAUNDEV. (Roxb.) xxxii. 147 Þare growez grete plentee of baume and nowere whare elles þat I couthe here off. *c* **1425** *Seven Sag.* (P.) 755 Thay ne durst nower ware goo. **1483** *Cath. Angl.* 256/2 Nowre whare, *nullicubi, nuspiam, nusquam.*

nowey, variant of NOWY *a.*

nowgar, obs. form of AUGER *sb.*[1]

'nowhat, *sb.* and *adv.* [f. NO *a.* + WHAT, on analogy of *somewhat*.]

†**A.** *sb.* Nothing. *Obs. rare*$^{-1}$.

1530 RASTELL *Bk. Purgat.* I. ii, There was evermore a thyng or nothyng, somwhat or nowhat.

B. *adv.* Not at all, not in the least.

1651 FULLER *Abel Rediv., Jerome* (1867) I. 31 The malice of his adversaries being no what abated in violence. **1867** TROLLOPE *Chron. Barset* II. 99 Many kisses,..of which she had been nowhat ashamed.

'nowhen, *adv. rare.* [f. NO *a.* + WHEN *adv.*] At no time, never.

a **1767** LYE *A.S. Dict., Na-hwanan,* No when. *Nunquam.* **1884** *Gosp. Divine Humanity* iii. 49 When was the beginning? Nowhen as regards universal existence.

'nowhence, *adv. rare.* [f. NO *a.* + WHENCE *adv.*] From no place. (Also with *from.*)

a **1767** LYE *A.S. Dict., Na-hwanan,* No whence. *Nusquam.* **1853** KINGSLEY *Hypatia* xxv, The homeless Universe falling..for ever from nowhence toward nowhither. **1890** MARTINEAU *Authority on Relig.* I. i. 20 Coming nowhence and going nowhither.

nowhere ('nəʊhwɛə(r)), *adv.* Forms: α. 1 **nahwær, -hwar,** 4 **naquer, -quhare;** 3 **nawhar,** 4–5 **nawher(e,** 5 **nay-where.** β. 1 **nohwær,** 2–3 **-hwer,** 3 **-hwere, -hwar(e;** 4 **noquar, -quer,** 5 **noqwere;** 3 **neowhær,** 3–5 **nowher,** 3–4 **-whar,** 4– **nowhere,** 6 **noo-, noewhere.** γ. 3 **nohwhar, noþware,** 4 **noghwhere;** 3 **nouhwar,** 4 **nouhewere, nouȝwher** (5 **-e**), 3 **nowhwere,** *Orm.* **nowwhar,** 5 **nowewhere.** [f. NO *adv.* + WHERE *adv.* Cf. NAWER and NOWER *adv.*]

1. a. In or at no place; not anywhere.

α. **971** *Blickl. Hom.* 59 Ealle þa ʒewitaþ swa swa wolcn,.., & ofer þæt nahwær eft ne æteowaþ. *c* **1000** ÆLFRIC *Gen.* xix. 17 Ne þu ne ætstande na hwar on þisum earde. *c* **1055** *Byrhtferth's Handboc* in *Anglia* VIII. 308 Þæt we nahwar ne gan of laȝe. *a* **1300** *Cursor M.* 16762 + 131 He miȝt not bere vp his hede, Ne nawhar it doun lay. **1393** LANGL. *P. Pl.* C. III. 227 He was nawher welcome for hus meny tales. *c* **1475** *Partenay* 1924 A man no better myght hit employ nay-where.

β. *a* **1050** *Gregory's Dial.* (1900) 127 'Hwær æton ʒe?' Hi him andswaredon & cwædon 'nohwær' [*v.r.* 'nower']. *c* **1175** *Lamb. Hom.* 113 He ne scal nohwer ortrowian bi godes fultum. *c* **1205** LAY. 8392 Nes hit nowher itald þat weore nowhar swa muchel mete [etc.]. *c* **1275** *Wom. Samaria* 44 in *O.E. Misc.* 85 No-hwere bute in þe temple. **13..** *Cursor M.* 6047 (Gött.), Men noquar ne miht se Griss on erde, ne lef on tre. **1387** TREVISA *Higden* (Rolls) V. 297 He..passed nowher his fader bondes. *c* **1400** *Destr. Troy* 12083 He denyet..þat noqwere he knew þat commly be keppet. **1490** CAXTON *Eneydos* iv. 20 The..bloode.. hath..yssued oute of my body, and nowher ellis. **1511** *Guylforde's Pilgr.* (Camden) 11, I trowe they haue noo where so stronge a place. **1603** DEKKER *Batchelors Banquet* (1882) 193 To auoid greater charges..he rests nowhere by the way. **1651** HOBBES *Leviath.* IV. xlvi. 371 Because the Universe is All, that which is no part of it, is Nothing; and consequently no where. **1711** ADDISON *Spect.* No. 163 ¶3 Theodosius..had left his Chamber about Midnight, and could no-where be found. **1797** MRS. RADCLIFFE *Italian* Prol., He was nowhere to be seen. **1822** SHELLEY *The Zucca* 22 Thou, whom, seen nowhere, I feel everywhere. **1875** JOWETT *Plato* (ed. 2) I. 441 There only, and nowhere else, he can find wisdom in her purity.

attrib. **1589** NASHE *Anat. Absurd.* Wks. (Grosart) I. 14 Those worne out impressions of the feyned no where acts, of Arthur of the rounde table. **1889** *Advance* (Chicago) 10 Jan., Had he arrived at his hotel in Detroit, instead of at a nowhere side-hill.

γ. *c* **1200** ORMIN 13073, I Crisstenndom mann findenn maȝȝ Hemm alle, & nowwhar elless. *a* **1225** *Leg. Kath.* 1306 Ne funde we nowhwer nan swa deope ilearet. **1362** LANGL. *P. Pl.* A. II. 193 He nas nouȝwher wel-come for his mony tales. **1390** GOWER *Conf.* III. 136 And that is noghwhere elles sene Of kinde with non other beste. *c* **1450** *Cursor M.* 17556 (Laud), In Israell bene grete fellis, There is he sothe and now-wher ellis.

b. To no place.

13.. *Cursor M.* 3495 (Gött.), For-þi was he noquer sent, Bot to þe hous ay tok he tent. **1484** CAXTON *Fables of Alfonce* xii, She myght not goo nowher. **1720** DE FOE *Capt. Singleton* (1906) 37 We were upon a voyage and no voyage, we were bound somewhere and nowhere. **1778** BURNEY *Evelina* xvi, I never go nowhere without him. **1861** MRS. CARLYLE *Lett.* III. 73 Mr. C. was minded to go nowhere this summer.

2. In no part or passage of a book, etc.; in no work or author. Also *Comb.*

a **1225** *Ancr. R.* 160 Nouhware ine holi write nis iwriten of hire speche. **1396–7** in *Eng. Hist. Rev.* (1907) XXII. 296 Þat is..nowhere ensample in holi scripture. **1594** HOOKER *Eccl. Pol.* II. vii. §2 Some men..have in their books and writings nowhere mentioned or taught that such things should be in the church. **1678–9** PRIDEAUX *Lett.* (Camden) 64 The original..of the Roman Empire is noe where better treated of then in this author. **1789** BELSHAM *Ess.* II. xxxvi. 281 This, however, is..no-where countenanced by Aristotle. **1870** ROGERS *Hist. Glean.* Ser. II. 77 This great writer..is nowhere a partisan. **1875** JOWETT *Plato* (ed. 2) III. 280 Sweet sauces are nowhere mentioned in Homer. **1889** R. B. ANDERSON tr. *Rydberg's Teut. Mythol.* 155 A new, nowhere-supported myth.

3. ***nowhere near*** or †***nigh***, not nearly, not by a long way. (Cf. NEAR *adv.*[2] 6, NIGH *adv.* 12 d.)

1413 *Pilgr. Sowle* (Caxton, 1483) v. xi. 101 Though the dede were nowhere nyghe soo greete, yett is hit a manere of resemblaunce. *c* **1449** PECOCK *Repr.* I. viii. 42 Into the contrarie parti is not had nouȝwhere nyȝ so probable.. euydencis. *Ibid.* II. xi. 208 Nowhere nyȝ alle men.

4. *slang.* **a.** ***to be nowhere***, to be badly beaten (in a race, contest, etc.); to be hopelessly distanced or out of the running. Freq. *transf.* (In common use from *c* 1850.)

1755 *Gentl. Mag.* XXV. 153 His powerful deep rate, by which all the horses that ran against him were no-where. **1826** *Sporting Mag.* XVII. 306 Many men were nowhere at the end. **1831** MACAULAY *Essay on Boswell's Life Johnson* in *Edin. Rev.* Sept. 16 Boswell is the first of biographers..and the rest nowhere. **1861** *Illustr. Lond. News* 7 Dec. 569/3 The first cow..was 'nowhere' at Birmingham. **1869** SEELEY *Lect. & Ess.* (1870) 22 In the Augustan age democracy was nowhere. **1895** *Athenæum* 14 Sept. 347/3 To the philologist and the student of English literature, it is Oxford first, the rest nowhere. **1928** C. A. NICHOLSON *Hell & Duchess* vi. 108 Don't imagine you have a fortune there. A hundred francs goes nowhere these days.

b. *U.S.* (See quot. 1859.)

1859 BARTLETT *Dict. Amer.* (ed. 2) 297 To be nowhere is to be at sea; to be utterly at a loss; to be ignorant. **1868** in De Vere *Americanisms* (1871), When he began to ask me questions about surgery, I was just nowhere, and I can't tell, to save my life, what I said to him.

5. a. As *sb.* A non-existent place; absence of all place.

1831 CARLYLE *Sart. Res.* II. v, How wilt thou..find that shorter North-west Passage to thy fair Spice-country of a Nowhere? **1872** BUSHNELL *Serm. Living Subj.* 167 It is now become as if all truth were gone out, and night and nowhere had the world.

b. A remote or inaccessible place; freq. in colloq. phr. ***the middle of nowhere***.

1908 *Dialect Notes* III. 312 *Forty miles from nowhere*, far from any civilized or settled section. **1951** E. COXHEAD *One Green Bottle* vii. 182 My uncle's farm is on the road to nowhere... They often don't see a new face for months on end. **1960** *Times* 21 Nov. (Canada Suppl.) p. xi/2 Hydro-Quebec is starting to move far up the Manicouagan, in the middle of nowhere. **1963** A. LUBBOCK *Austral. Roundabout* 30, I got going again pretty quickly as I didn't want to be caught by the storm in the middle of nowhere. **1967** MRS. L. B. JOHNSON *White House Diary* 7 July (1970) 544 The country was sparsely populated and it was surprising to come upon such an enormous church, out in nowhere. **1967** E. COUSINS *Death in Quiet Place* i. 10 'I never heard of Boling Green.' 'You wouldn't, old boy. Fag-end of nowhere, down a two-mile lane from the second-class road.'

c. A dull person, place, or thing. Passing into *adj.*: insignificant, unsatisfactory, dull; non-existent. In most contexts *slang.*

1940 L. MACNEICE *Last Ditch* 14 The here and there and nowhere birds. **1948** L. SPITZER *Linguistics & Literary History* i. 18 The priestess Bacbuc (whose ambiguous response: '*Trinc!*' is just a nowhere word). **1953** W. BURROUGHS *Junkie* x. 110 The others [*sc.* patients] were a beat, nowhere bunch of people. The type psychiatrists like. **1956** B. HOLIDAY *Lady sings Blues* (1958) viii. 82 A Rolls is built for pleasure... But it's nowhere for highballing a hundred and fifty miles to make a gig. **1959** 'F. NEWTON' *Jazz Scene* xii. 220 The hipster classifies..an undesirable state as *nowhere*. **1959** *Esquire* Nov. 70J *Nowhere*, the absolute of nothing. Example: That guy is nowhere. **1966** *Melody Maker* 7 May 5/2 We all thought it was the most nowhere record we'd made. **1970** *Globe & Mail* (Toronto) 26 Sept. 12/2 He wants to spread this physical act as a sign ..and then..see work expanding in the nowhere parish to merge with the national scene. **1974** *Ibid.* 14 Sept. 27/4 What you'll remember is the casual dreariness of the nowhere towns and the faded dreams of the guys who never managed to get out of them.

Hence **'nowhereness.**

1838 STERLING *Ess.* (1848) I. 150 A dateless no-whereness of the facts and topics. **1928** D. H. LAWRENCE *Let.* 15 Dec. (1932) 766 A ghastly slummy nowhereness—but France seems all like that. **1929** —— *Pansies* 105 We can but howl the lugubrious howl of idiots, The howl of the utterly lost Howling their nowhereness.

nowheres ('nəʊhwɛəz), *adv. U.S. dial.* = NOWHERE *adv.*

1884 'MARK TWAIN' *Huck. Finn* xli. 415, I hain't been nowheres. **1909** *Dialect Notes* III. 353 *Nowheres*, nowhere.

†**no while**, *adv. Obs. rare.* Also 4 **na quil(e, quyle.** [See WHILE.] For no space of time.

a **1300** *Cursor M.* 3124 He began to luf him sua þat he moght na quil him for-ga. **1470–85** MALORY *Arth.* x. xviii. 459 There with came Elyas and badde the Kynge yelde vp the castel, for ye maye not hold it no whyle.

no whit, *adv.* Also 7 **whitte,** *Sc.* **quhite.** [See WHIT *sb.*] Not at all, not the least.

1530 PALSGR. 862/1 No whyt nere done, *pas paracheué de beaucoup pres.* **1556** J. HEYWOOD *Spider & Fly* ii, That nowhit cared I what flie did know it. **1600** J. PORY tr. *Leo's Africa* VII. 294 His son, being no whit inferiour in valour & high courage vnto his father. **1644** DIGBY *Nat. Bodies* xxxvii. §3. 321 They are no whitte more extra-ordinary, then a fawkeners manning of a hawke. **1660** JER. TAYLOR *Duct. Dubit.* IV. i. rule 5 §16 He was very much the worse Man for it, but no whit the worse Painter.

1805 SCOTT *Last Minstr.* III. iv, But no whit weary did he seem. **1820** —— *Monast.* xvi, Considering the hardships of this..gallant knight, no whit mentioning or weighing those we ourselves have endured.

nowhither ('nəʊhwɪðə(r)), *adv.* Forms: 1 **nahwider,** 4 **-quiþer;** 1–3 **nohwider,** 2 **nowider,** 3 **-weder** (**nouhwuder**), 4 **-whyþer, -whider,** 5 **-whedyr,** 6– **-whither.** [f. NO *adv.* + WHITHER *adv.*] To no place; nowhere.

c **888** K. ÆLFRED *Boeth.* xxxvi. §6 Se bið meahteʒost þe to him cuman mæʒ, forðæm he nohwider ofer þæt cuman ne mæʒ. *c* **960** *Rule St. Benet* (Schröer, 1885) 137 Hy nahwider faraþ butan þæs abbodes ræde. *a* **1225** *Ancr. R.* 424 Nouhwuder elles ne go heo bute þider ase me sent hire. *a* **1300** *Body & Soul* 338 in *Map's Poems* (Camden), Helle houndes here I ʒelle.., ne may I noweder fro him fle. *c* **1375** *Canticum de Creatione* 54 in Hortsm. *Altengl. Leg.* (1878) 125 Wile ʒe nowhyþer gon To seken somwhat to oure fode. **1390** GOWER *Conf.* II. 144 Sche ne mai nowhider gon, Ne speke a word. **1471** *Paston Lett.* III. 7 Not to go owght to watyr, nor no whedyr ellys. **1542** UDALL *Erasm. Apoph.* 86 He came nowhither without bearyng his porcion of the shot for his repaste. **1611** BIBLE *2 Kings* v. 25 And hee said, Thy seruant went no whither. **1681** T. FLATMAN *Heraclitus Ridens* No. 4 (1713) I. 19, I can go no whither about my Vocation but you hunt me dry Foot I think. **1828–9** BENTHAM *Offic. Apt. Maximized, Militia* (1830) 9 But from whence, henceforward, is it to come? From no whither, unless it be in a fleet of steamboats. **1853** [see NOWHENCE]. **1872** SWINBURNE *Under Microscope* 1 The human intellect must still as of old go limping and blinking on its way no-whither. **1890** [see NOWHENCE].

Hence †**nowhitherward(s.** *Obs. rare.*

1154 *O.E. Chron.* (Laud MS.) an. 1137, He ne myhte nowider wardes ne sitten ne lien ne slepen. **13..** *Cursor M.* 4959 (Gött.), Naquiþer-war may we nu stire, þair will bihouis vs suffre here.

no-win, *a.* [f. NO *a.* + WIN *sb.*[1]] Of a contest or struggle: that cannot be won.

1962 *Economist* 30 June 1310/1 He recommended an agreement with the Russians—a 'no-win' approach, in fact, 'an accommodation with tyranny'. **1966** *Ibid.* 5 Nov. 565/1 Both attack Washington for a 'no-win war policy' in Vietnam. **1973** *Daily Colonist* (Victoria, B.C.) 24 July 5/3 So the trail of broken fixes has put Nixon in a no-win position.

nowise ('nəʊwaɪs, -z), *adv.* Forms: α. *Sc.* 5 **na-vis, -vyse,** 6 **-uyse, -vyis,** 5–6 **-wyse,** 6 **-wise.** β. 5 **no-wyse** (*Sc.* **-wis**), 7– **nowise.** [f. NO *a.* + WISE *sb.*] In no way or manner; not at all.

α. **1375** BARBOUR *Bruce* VI. 594 Ryn eftir hym,..And let hym na-vis pas ȝow fra. *c* **1375** *Sc. Leg. Saints* xli. (*Agnes*) 292 Þar bad stil amarentia, þat nawyse wald fra hyr grawe ga. **1581** BURNE *Disput.* in *Cath. Tract.* (S.T.S.) 131 The benediction..is nauyse practised in your deformet kirkis. **1598** *Sc. Acts Jas. VI* (1814) 173 His hienes subjectis..sall navyis pretend ony excuiss.

β. **14..** *Tundale's Vis.* 296 Þei mey no wyse from me þe lede. **1487** *Barbour's Bruce* IV. 214 Now may I no wis forthir ga. *a* **1677** BARROW *Serm.* Wks. 1687 I. 466 There-by no-wise to impair or obscure..the glories of his sovereign dignity. **1735** BERKELEY *Free-think. Mathem.* §24 Wks. 1871 III. 313 The smallness of the practical error nowise concerns it. **1761** HUME *Hist. Eng.* xlviii. III. 40 *note*, A prelate nowise complaisant to the court. **1818** COLEBROOKE *Import. Col. Corn* 154 It does nowise follow that ingenuity is unlikely to devise other means. **1884** *Law Rep.* 9 *App. Cases* 76 The exemption of the Crown..is nowise dependent upon the local or imperial character of the rate.

nowk, nowl(e, nowlt, obs. ff. NOOK, NOLL, NOWT.

nowmber, -bre, -byr, obs. ff. NUMBER.

nowmel, obs. f. NUMBLE.

nowmer, -yr, obs. ff. NUMBER.

nowmpere, -powre, variants of NOUMPERE *Obs.*

†**nown(e, n'own**, obs. variants of OWN *a.*, through wrong division of *myn own, thyn own*; afterwards used also with *your, her*, etc.

See also OWN *a.* 1 ε, and cf. NAIN *a.*

c **1400** *Song Roland* 639 Wit it thy nown werk. **1482** *Monk of Evesham* (Arb.) 44 Helpe me that for myn nowne propyr synnys am yn desperacyon. *a* **1553** UDALL *Royster D.* I. iii, Well sowed,.. And een as well knitte, my nowne Annot Alyface. **1622** BRETON *Strange News* Wks. (Grosart) II. 7/2 Fathers darling and mothers nowne childe. **1681** T. FLATMAN *Heraclitus Ridens* No. 45 (1713) II. 37 Upon further Examination, I found 'em to be the Ape's nown Poetry. **1762** *Gentl. Mag.* 288 Bussed with a smack her nown good man. **1790** R. TYLER *Contrast* I. i, Maria, like a good girl, to keep herself constant to her nown true-love, avoided company.

b. Used without preceding pron. or genitive. **1603** BRETON *Packet Mad Lett.* II. lx, Nowne Loue, and kinde soule, I thanke thee. **1673** DRYDEN *Marr. à la Mode* III. ii, And did I wrong n'own Rhodophil, with a false suspicion? **1691** SHADWELL *Scowerers* I. i, Some wise lecture from nown daddy.

nown(e, obs. ff. NOUN.

†**nowne**, obs. variant (see N 3) of OVEN.

c **1450** *Two Cookery Bks.* 73 Put hem into a Nowne til þei be a litull hard.

'nowness. [f. NOW *adv.*] The quality of being always present. Also, the quality of taking place in the present time.

1674 N. FAIRFAX *Bulk & Selv.* Contents, The Doctors objection against the Nowness of eternity answer'd. **1891** [see -NESS *suff.* 2 a]. **1926** *Spectator* 22 May 871/1 We enter upon a consideration of 'thenness' and nowness. **1928** A. S. EDDINGTON *Nature of Physical World* iii. 49 From this point of view the 'nowness' of an event is like a shadow cast by it into space. **1962** *Punch* 1 Aug. 153/2 Once the viewer has tasted.. This-is-actually-happening, or what we might.. describe as Nowness, he's going to waste no time in demanding it. **1973** *Sci. Amer.* Apr. 8/2 Nowness and Permanence. Thanks to the former, it is possible for an art historian to give at least an approximate date for its making.

nowns, variant of NOUNS.

nowpe, obs. variant of NOPE *sb.*

nowre, obs. form of HOUR; variant of NOWER.

†**nowse**, ? obs. variant of NOOSE *sb.*

1592 KYD *Sp. Trag.* IV. iv, See, here's a goodly nowse will hold them all.

nowsel, obs. form of NUZZLE *v.*[2]

nowst, var. NOUST.

nowt (naʊt). *Sc.* and *north. dial.* Forms: α. 3 *Orm.* nowwt, 5 nowyt, 6 nowit, nowlt, 5, 8–9 nowte, 5– nowt; 2, 5, 7 noute (3 neute), 6, 8–9 nout (9 knout). β. 5 naute, noyt, 6 noote, note. [a. ON. *naut* (Norw. *naut*, Sw. *nöt*, Da. *nöd-*), = OE. *néat* NEAT *sb.* See also NOLT.]

1. *pl.* Cattle, oxen.

α. *c* **1200** ORMIN 15558 He fand i þe temmple þær Well fele menn þatt saldenn þærinne baþe nowwt & shep. *c* **1375** *Sc. Leg. Saints* xl. (*Ninian*) 1121 Of nowt, schepe, hors and ky. *a* **1400–50** *Alexander* 3823 Camels and mules, And out of nounbre of nowte. *c* **1470** HENRY *Wallace* VIII. 1059 Bestiall, as hors and nowt. **1533** *Acc. Ld. H. Treas. Scot.* VI. 139 To deliver certane nowit and hors agane. **1565** *Wills & Invent. N.C.* (Surtees, 1835) 237 To Isabell Lysle my nece foure kye and foure yownge nowlt. **1596** DALRYMPLE tr. *Leslie's Hist. Scot.* Prol. 7 Grene bankes,.. quhilkes are verie conuenient to feid horse or nout. **1725** RAMSAY *Gentle Sheph.* I. i, Nine braw nowt were smoor'd. **1786** BURNS *Inventory* 37 Wee Davock hauds the nowt in fother. **1819** W. TENNANT *Papistry Storm'd* (1827) 109 Tossin' our heads.. Like Hannibal's fire-puttin' nowt. **1881** *Blackw. Mag.* Apr. 521 He rode to market to drive hard bargains over his 'nowt'.

β. *c* **1375** *Sc. Leg. Saints* l. (*Catherine*) 37 þe raryng & þe bere of noyt & schepe. *c* **1420** *Sir Amadace* (Camden) xxxiii, Hors and naute, shepe and sqwyne, A-way thay drafe and bare. **1525** *State P. Hen. VIII*, IV. 371 The said Erle hath also wonne thirty score noote,.. and many good horses. **1544** *Ld. Hertford's Raid* (1798) 14 A great nomber of cattel, bothe note and shepe.

2. a. *sing.* An ox, a bullock.

a **1400–50** *Alexander* 4744 Vmquile he noys as a nowte, as a nox quen he lawes. **1595** DUNCAN *App. Etym.* (E.D.S.) 71 *Mugio*, to rowt like a nowt. *c* **1620** A. HUME *Brit. Tongue* (1865) 27 A horse, an hundred horse; a noute, ten noute. **1875** W. MCILWRAITH *Guide Wigtownsh.* 137 Every day in the year a Galloway nowt was killed. **1883** J. MARTIN *Old Haddington* 103 He blew through a 'nout's' horn.

b. *transf.* A stupid, coarse, or clumsy person. **1806** BLACK *Falls of Clyde* 195 You ugly nowt! Swithe! frae my sight, ye filthy ragged cowt! **1898** CROCKETT *Standard Bearer* x, A great, strong, kindly, hard-driving 'nowt' of a man.

3. a. *attrib.* and *Comb.*, as *nowt-foot, -head, -horn*; *nowt-doctor, -man*; *nowt-beast, -market*, etc.

For further illustration see the *Eng. Dial. Dict.*

1657 in Holmes *Pontefract Bk. Entries* (1882) 54 Burroughe of Pontefract.. Nautmarkett. *a* **1685** SEMPILL *Blythsome Wedding* vii, Callour nout-feet in a plate. **17..** *Humble Beggar* in Herd *Sc. Songs* (1776) II. 29 A meikle nowt-horn to rout on had he. **1790** GROSE *Prov. Gloss.* Suppl., Nowt-foot oil. **1808** JAMIESON s.v., It is used in composition for an individual of the kind, as a *nowt-beast*. **1824** MACTAGGART *Encycl.* s.v. *Caumshell*, It is reduced by nowt doctors to a fine powder, and blown through the hollows of quills into cattles' eyes. **1862** *Luck of Ladysmede* I. 194 Out upon thee, nowt-head! hast no more sense than to leave the poor brutes out in a wild night like this? **1871** W. ALEXANDER *Johnny Gibb* (1873) 120 He had first visited the 'nowt market' at the top of the brae, and cheapened several stirks. **1883** *Longman's Mag.* Apr. 646 The cattle or 'nowt' man.. receives about twelve or thirteen shillings per week.

b. *nowt-geld*, a rent-payment in cattle, or a tax levied on cattle, formerly in use in the north of England. Cf. CORNAGE.

a **1180** in *Victoria Hist. Cumbld.* (1902) I. 316 *note*, Noverit paternitas vestra me dedisse.. Deo.. vi. vaccas in perpetuam elemosinam reddendas anno omni quo meum Noutegeld debuerit fieri. **1200** *Rotul. Chart.* (1837) 50/1 Danegeld, & neutegeld & horngeld. **1688** HICKES *Dict. Island.* s.v. *Gelld*, *Nowt-gelt*, tributum pro pecore solutum. **1825** BROCKETT *N.C. Gloss.*, Nout-geld, Neat-geld, cornage rent, originally paid in cattle—horn tax. **1872** E. W. ROBERTSON *Hist. Ess.* 134 Nowt-geld or Cornage appears both as an obligation and as a tenure.

c. *nowt-gowan*, (*a*) the Horse-gowan or Ox-eye Daisy; (*b*) the Corn-Marigold. *Sc.*

1844 H. STEPHENS *Bk. Farm* III. 943 The great white ox-eye, or nowt-gowan,.. and the yellow nowt-gowan.

nowt(h, dial. and obs. forms of NOUGHT.

†**'nowthe**, *adv. Obs.* Forms: 1 nuþa, 1–2 nuða, 2–3 nuþe, 3 nuðe, 3–4 nouþe (4 noþe), 3–5 nouthe, 3 nowþe, 5 nowthe; 3 nouþ, 4–5 nouth. [OE., f. *nú* NOW, and *þá, ðá* THO *adv.* In common use from *c* 1200 to 1400.] Now.

Beowulf 427 Ic þe nuða breȝo beorht-dena biddan wille ..þæt [etc.]. *c* **1000** ÆLFRIC *Hom.* I. 182 He astah up to heofenum, and þær sitt nuða mid his halȝum. *c* **1175** *Lamb. Hom.* 15 Ne scalt þu ȝelden vuel onȝein uuel nuða. *Ibid.* 25 Ic nuþe eow tellen wulle. *c* **1205** LAY. 29863 Lusteð nuðe alle Whæt ich sugge wulle. **1297** R. GLOUC. (Rolls) 4195 þat noble mayde.. þat ichabbe nouþe riȝt here ybured. *c* **1320** *Sir Beues* 3632 Goþ and wendeþ hennes nouþe. **1387** TREVISA *Higden* (Rolls) VI. 227 þe comyn fame telleþ þat he is at Durham nowþe, wiþ Seynt Cuthbert. *c* **1420** *Chron. Vilod.* 537 Cudberth of Dereham, he sayde, ychame þat telle þe nowthe of þis casse.

nowther, variant of NOUTHER.

'nowtherd. [f. NOWT *sb.*] = NEATHERD.

c **1330** *Newminster Cartul.* 259 Gylbertus dictus noutherd. *c* **1440** *Alph. Tales* 254 þe kyngis nowte-hard come home with his catell. *Ibid.*, þis nowterd & his wife. **1483** *Cath. Angl.* 257/1 A Nowthyrde, *armentareus*. **1530** PALSGR. 248/2 Noetherde or bulherde, *bovuier*. **1691** RAY *N.C. Words* (ed. 2), A Note-heard; a Neat-heard. **1818** HOGG *Brownie of Bodsbeck* viii, There was wee Willy the nout-herd. **1882** J. WALKER *Jaunt to Auld Reekie* 9 Across the rigs the nowtherd drags the rake.

attrib. **1641** BEST *Farm. Bks.* (Surtees) 119 Wee must pay noutheard-wages, and sesses, and layes; the noutheard-wages weare (for every beast) 2*d.*

Hence **'nowtherdship.** *rare.*

1592 in *Northumbld. Gloss.* (1894) s.v., Paid to Mr. Marmaduke Thirlekill.. for the nowtardshipp of this towne. **1596** in Welford *Hist. Newcastle* III. 96.

nowy ('naʊɪ), *a. Her.* Also 6 -ey. [ad. OF. *noé* (mod.F. *noué*), pa. pple. of *noer, nouer*:—L. *nōdāre*, f. *nōdus* knot.]

†**1.** = NOWED *a. Obs. rare*⁻¹.

1562 LEGH *Armory* 100 He beareth a Serpent nowey.

2. Having a small semicircular projection, *esp.* at the centre of a partition line, or (in a cross) at each of the points where the arms meet.

1562 LEGH *Armory* (1597) 35 Hee beareth Geules a Crosse nowye degraded fitche Argent. **1688** HOLME *Armoury* III. xv. (Roxb.) 30/2 He beareth Azure, an Anchor reuersed, the Nutt (or Nowy) in the middle of the Beame or Arme. **1868** CUSSANS *Her.* (1893) 48 The lines by which a shield is divided.. may assume any of the following forms: Engrailed, Invected,.. Nowy. *Ibid.* 62 The Cross Nowy has the angles formed by the conjunction of its limbs rounded outwards. All the varieties of the Cross may be Nowy or Quadrate.

b. *nowy quadrate.* (See quot. 1868.)

1868 CUSSANS *Her.* (1893) 62 The Cross Quadrate, or Nowy-Quadrate, has its centre square, instead of round. **1894** *Parker's Gloss. Her., Cross*, Nowy quadrate.. is applied when the projections appear to form a square.

So **'nowyed** *a.*, 'a term applied to a projection not in the centre of a cross but in one of its branches' (Cassell, 1886).

†**nowyr**, obs. form (see N 3) of HOUR.

a **1450** *Fysshynge w. Angle* (1883) 9 Let hyt boyle softly halfe a nowyr.

‖**nox**[1] (nɒks). [L.] Night. (Chiefly *poet.*)

1567 TURBERV. *Ovid's Ep.* Q viij, Forging dolefull plaints that Nox hath runne her race. *a* **1593** GREENE *Alphonsus* IV, Darksome Nox had spread about the earth Her blackish mantle. **1810** SIM in *Harp of Perthshire* (1893) 95 Nox had spread his sable sark Owre the Creation. **1844** CARLYLE *Let.* in *Westm. Gaz.* (1901) 12 Aug., All books ever written upon him.. belong to the realm of Nox and Erebus.

†**nox**[2], obs. form (see N 3) of OX.

a **1400–50** *Alexander* 4744 As a nox quen he lawes. *c* **1420** *Chron. Vilod.* 1912 Hurre thouȝt.. þat a nox went þreyȝe abouȝte alle þat. **1483** *Cath. Angl.* 49/1 A Buse for a noxe.

noxa ('nɒksə). *Med.* Pl. **noxæ**. [L., = 'hurt, damage'.] Anything harmful to the body.

1894 GOULD *Dict. Med.* 877/2 *Noxa*, an injurious principle; especially a pathogeneic microörganism, or other *materies morbi*. **1960** BLOOD & HENDERSON *Vet. Med.* I. iii. 44 The embryo.. does not react to noxa in the same way as the fœtus since no inflammation or leucocytosis develops. **1966** *Ann. N.Y. Acad. Sci.* CXXV. 884 What became obviously and inevitably clear.. was the extreme 'communicability' of a purely symbolic 'noxa' in working with patients in the valley of the shadow of death. **1971** *Nature* 2 July 18/2 Aspirin does not lessen pain in skin, elicited by noxious substances, but it does lessen pain in other sites, when elicited by similar noxae.

'noxal, *a. Civil Law.* [ad. L. *noxālis*, f. *noxa* hurt, damage.] Relating to damage or injury done by a person or animal belonging to another.

noxal action (see quots. 1775 and 1880). *noxal surrender*, the compensatory surrender to the plaintiff of the slave, animal, etc., by which the injury was done.

1605 DANIEL *Queen's Arcadia* III. i, I ouer-whelm My practise too with darknesse and strange words, With.. Codicilles, Acceptilations, Actions recissorie, Noxall, and Hypothecall. **1775** HALLIFAX *Rom. Law* (1795) 94 In case of an Offence committed by a Slave, and of Damage done by a Beast, the Master of the Slave and Owner of the Beast were liable to be convened, by what was called a Noxal Action. **1880** MUIRHEAD *Gaius* IV. §75 In respect of the wrong-doing of *filiifamilias* and slaves, as when they have committed theft say, or personal injury, noxal actions have been provided. **1903** JENKS in *Law Q. Rev.* Jan. 24 The practice of noxal surrender of animals prevailed in Flanders until the sixteenth century.

Hence **'noxally** *adv.*, by way of noxal surrender.

1880 MUIRHEAD *Gaius* I. §141 It is not for any long time that persons are detained in this condition,.. unless they have been mancipated noxally.

†**'noxial**, *a. Obs. rare.* In 6 -iall(e, -yall. [Irreg. f. L. *nox* + -IAL. Cf. obs. F. *noctial* (Godef.).] Nocturnal.

a **1500** *Pol., Rel., & L. Poems* (1866) 43 Whan Reste And slepe y shulde haue noxialle, As Requereth bothe nature and kynde. **1503** HAWES *Example Virtue* XII. ccxxxvii, Depryuynge the noxyall derkenes. *a* **1568** in *Dunbar's Poems* (S.T.S.) App. xi. 31 To the superne eternall regioun, Quhair noxiall skyis may mak no sogeorn.

noxious ('nɒkʃəs), *a.* Also 7 noctious. [ad. L. *noxius*, f. *noxa* hurt, damage.]

1. Injurious, hurtful, harmful; unwholesome.

1612 WOODALL *Surg. Mate* Wks. (1653) 387 The adjacent parts being freed from many noxious humours thereby. **1650** BULWER *Anthropomet.* 221 Many would have it an unprofitable excrement and of a noxious or hurtful quality. **1671** MILTON *P.R.* IV. 460 Being oft times noxious where they light On man, beast, plant. **1711** ADDISON *Spect.* No. 121 ¶1 That seeming Sagacity in Animals, which.. makes them naturally avoid whatever is noxious or unwholsome. **1752** HUME *Ess. & Treat.* (1777) I. 157 The body, full of noxious humours, feels the torment. **1837** M. DONOVAN *Dom. Econ.* II. 87 The liver is always given to the dogs, and that may possibly be the noxious part. **1880** HAUGHTON *Phys. Geogr.* IV. 190 It blows over the whole island steadily, a cold noxious wind.

†**2.** Guilty, criminal. *Obs. rare.*

1623 COCKERAM I, *Noxious*, guilty. **1652** GAULE *Magastrom.* 171 Whether Magicians and Astrologers be.. noxious or guilty of a diabolical compact and commerce. **1656** BRAMHALL *Replic.* iii. 130 No man or Society of men can be justly punished.. because they are noxious, unless they be noxious in the eye of the Law.

3. **noxious weed**, a weed growing on neglected land, esp., in Australia and New Zealand, one considered harmful to animals, which may be the subject of regulations governing attempts to control it.

1897 *Bull. Central Exper. Farm Dept. Agric.* (Canada) No. 28. 5 Under special circumstances some of our native wild plants may increase and become 'noxious weeds'. **1913** F. M. BAILEY *Comprehensive Catal. Queensland Plants* 259 Many of the species [of *Calotis*] are noxious weeds, but it would be impossible to get rid of them by Act of Parliament. **1923** R. MACAULAY *Told by an Idiot* III. 256 As to Ireland, a bill was passed to reduce her docks, thistles, and noxious weeds: no other bill. **1966** G. W. TURNER *Eng. Lang. Austral. & N.Z.* vii. 142 Inspectors call [on New Zealand farmers] to make sure.. that noxious weeds, weeds officially proscribed, are controlled. **1971** *Guardian* 12 Aug. 1/5 She is not opposed to the killing.. of clumps of noxious weeds like docks or thistles. **1973** *Stand. Encycl. S. Afr.* VIII. 103/2 A 'wild flower' is defined as a plant indigenous to the Republic of South Africa, except noxious weeds.

Hence **'noxiously** *adv.*, in a noxious manner; injuriously, perniciously.

1755 in JOHNSON. **1811** BYRON *Let. to Dallas* 21 Aug., A most decided atheist, indeed noxiously so. **1879** M. ARNOLD *Mixed Ess., Democracy* 24 That which operates noxiously in the one, may operate wholesomely in the other.

'noxiousness. [f. prec. + -NESS.] The quality or state of being noxious or injurious.

1654 H. L'ESTRANGE *Chas. I* (1655) 7 That there was any intrinsique noxiousnesse in it... I am yet to be convinced. **1691** T. H[ALE] *Acc. New Invent.* 42 This suggestion of the noxiousness of Lead to Iron-work. **1777** ROBERTSON *Hist. Amer.* VII. (1778) II. 338 The peculiar noxiousness of its climate has prevented Porto-bello from increasing in the same proportion. **1862** G. WILSON *Relig. Chem.* 29 Conferring the character of noxiousness to vegetable and animal life.

noy, *sb.*[1] *Obs.* (exc. *dial.*). Forms: α. 4 **nuy**, 4–5 **nuye**, 5 **nue**. β. 4 **noiȝe, noyȝe**, 4–5, 7 **noye**, 5 **noie**, 4–6 (9) **noy**. γ. 4 **niye**, 4–5 **nye**, 5 **ney**. [Aphetic form of *anuy, anoy* ANNOY *sb.*] Annoyance, trouble.

α. *c* **1320** *Cast. Love* 442 For pees bi-leueþ in no londe Wher þer is werre, nuy and onde. *c* **1340** HAMPOLE *Pr. Consc.* 3538 Thurgh nuyes and angers sere. **1422** tr. *Secreta Secret., Priv. Priv.* 140 Aftyr nves and dyssesis. *a* **1450** MYRC 120 Lest afterwarde hyt do the nuye.

β. **1338** R. BRUNNE *Chron.* (1810) 183 To slo doun & to stroye,..þei left for dede no noye. *c* **1380** WYCLIF *Sel. Wks.* I. 4 þis shall ever last wiþout irkyng or noye. **1436** *Libel Eng. Policy* in *Pol. Poems* (Rolls) II. 182 Wee shulde hem destroy, As prysoners wee shulde hem brynge to noy. **1490** CAXTON *Eneydos* xiv. 50 For alle debates to accorde..and to brynge alle noves atte an ende. **1536** BELLENDEN *Cron. Scot.* (1821) I. 138 Galdus, be noy of the woundis gottin in this last battall, was sa wery, that [etc.]. **1598** TOFTE *Alba* (1880) 27 Banisht from Mirth, and Bondslaue vnto Noy. **1611** FLORIO, *Noianza*, annoyance, noye, trouble. [**1819** W. TENNANT *Papistry Storm'd* (1827) 188 Whose shadows 'tween them and the sky Forebodit noucht but noy.]

γ. **13..** *E.E. Allit. P.* B. 1002 Alle naȝt so much niye hade no mon in his hert. *Ibid.* 1376 To neuen þe noumbre to much nye were. **14..** *Sir Beues* (C) 1965 þe patriark sawe his gret nye. *c* **1440** MYRC *Festial* (E.E.T.S.) 197 To don Thomas al þe nye and þe gref þat he cowth.

noy (nɔɪ), *sb.*[2] *Physics.* [repr. the pronunc. of the first part of *noise.*] A unit of perceived noisiness, defined so that the number of noys is proportional to the noisiness of a sound, and one noy is equal to the noisiness of a sound of specified bandwidth and intensity (see quot. 1959).

1959 K. D. KRYTER in *Jrnl. Acoustical Soc. Amer.* XXXI. 1424/1 The following..steps were taken in arriving at the procedure suggested for the calculation of the perceived noise kind of a sound: Step 1. First, the word 'noy' was coined for the units on the scale of perceived noisiness. The numerical value of 1 was assigned to the perceived noisiness of the band from 910–1090 cps of random noise at a sound pressure level of 40 db *re* 0·0002 μ bar. **1963** JERRARD & MCNEILL *Dict. Sci. Units* 96 The noisiness of a jet aircraft taking off is about 110 noys. **1970** R. D. FORD *Introd. Acoustics* vii. 138 The relationship between PN dB and noys is exactly the same as that between phons and sones. **1971** B. J. SMITH *Acoustics* ii. 29 Find the total noisiness N from $N = N_{max} + 0{\cdot}3(\Sigma N - N_{max})$ where N_{max} = highest noy value and ΣN = sum of the noy values in all octave bands.

noy, *v.* *Obs.* (exc. *dial.*). Forms: α. 4 **nuiȝe**, 4–5 **nuye**, 5 **nue, nve**. β. 4 **noyȝe, noȝe**, 4–7 **noye**, 4–6 **noie**, 4– **noy**. γ. 4–5 **nye**, 5 **ney**. [Aphetic form of *anuye, anoye* ANNOY *v.*; perhaps also partly repr. OF. *nuire, noire*:—pop. L. **nocēre*, L. *nocēre* to injure.]

1. *trans.* To annoy, trouble, vex, harass; to harm or injure.

α. *c* **1300** *Beket* 198 Aȝen the lithere conteccours that Nuyede him of his lyve. *c* **1340** HAMPOLE *Pr. Consc.* 1184 Many he nuyes and fon avayles. **1393** LANGL. *P. Pl.* C. IV. 437 An aunter hit nuyede me, non ende wol ich make. **1422** tr. *Secreta Secret., Priv. Priv.* 165 Yf harme is befall to any man,..hit me touchyth and nuyth.

β. *c* **1330** R. BRUNNE *Chron. Wace* (Rolls) 789 þanne fond he non þat hym noyed. *c* **1380** WYCLIF *Wks.* (1880) 307 þing þat moost noyeþ þis ship ben felle flodis of þis world. *c* **1400** *Destr. Troy* 2591 Hit meuys into mynd, & mekill me noyes. *c* **1470** HARDYNG *Chron.* VI. i, So stronge then was this generacion, None durst it noye. **1523** CROMWELL in Merriman *Life & Lett.* (1902) I. 37, I ymagyn with myself whiche wayes they myght take to noy our enemyes most. **1568** GRAFTON *Chron.* II. 623 The Citezens..manfully defended themselues, and sore noyed and hurt their enimies. **1602** J. DAVIES (Heref.), *Mirum in Modum* xxxiv, So violent each Sense her virtue bindes, And noyes, or ioyes the Mind in diuerse kindes.

1829 BROCKETT *N.C. Gloss.* (ed. 2), *Noy*, to vex, to trouble —to annoy. Not now in use, Dr. Johnson says. As a Northern word it is quite common.

γ. **13..** *E.E. Allit. P.* B. 1603 When nabugo-de-nozar was nyed in stoundes. **13..** *Gaw. & Gr. Knt.* 1575 With hym þen irked Alle þe burnez so bolde..To nye hym on-ferum. *a* **1400–50** *Alexander* 771 (Dubl.), þe nowmbre of sir nicholas it neyt me to rekyn. **1432–50** tr. *Higden* (Rolls) I. 407 But the infortuny of flesche nyouthe theim moche.

b. Used impersonally, and const. *with* or *at.*

a **1340** HAMPOLE *Psalter* cvi. 18 Thaim noyed with godis worde. *c* **1400** *Destr. Troy* 6613 þe lede vppon lyue leuyt he þen, And nolpit to another, þat hym noiet at.

2. *refl.* and *intr.* To vex oneself, to grieve.

c **1470** *Gol. & Gaw.* 823 Noy you noght at his note, that nobill is to nevin. **1535** STEWART *Cron. Scot.* II. 498 Ilk da by da he studeit moir and noyit. **1587** GROVE *Pelops & Hipp.* (1878) 13 The case of this my child, her selfe which noyeth so.

3. *absol.* To cause annoyance or harm.

c **1340** HAMPOLE *Pr. Consc.* 4395 þe devels þat er now bunden swa, þat þai may noght..nuye als mykel als þai walde. *c* **1400** tr. *Secreta Secret., Gov. Lordsh.* 76 Also it noyeth mekyl, to renne after mete, or ryde mekyll. **1432–50** tr. *Higden* (Rolls) VI. 49 Grawntynge to us the eytynge of flesche, that noyethe not. **1534** MORE *Treat. Passion* Wks. 1348/2 If nothing auaileth, but ouer that it sore noyeth and hurteth. **1573** TUSSER *Husb.* (1878) 19 He noieth, destroieth, and al to this drift, to strip his poore tenant.

b. Const. *to* a person.

c **1400** *Apol. Loll.* 5 If þe pope be..vnprofitable & slow in his dedis,..þat more noyeþ to him & alle oþer. *a* **1485** FORTESCUE *Wks.* (1869) 488 On the other side their inyquyte may noye to every man. **1512** *Helyas* in Thoms *Prose Rom.* (1828) III. 71 As he that had the grace of God with him to whom none may noy.

Hence **noyed** *ppl. a.*

1587 GROVE *Pelops & Hipp.* (1878) 26 Ther was not..a wight that felt such greefe as now I feele, or had such cause to wayle his noyed life.

‖**noyade** (nwajad), *sb.* [F., f. *noyer*:—L. *necāre* to put to death (in late L., to drown).] The execution of persons by drowning, as practised by Carrier at Nantes in 1794. Also *transf.* and *fig.*

1822 *Blackw. Mag.* XII. 13 They choked their rivers with their *noyades.* **1835** MACAULAY *Ess., Mackintosh's Hist. Revol.* (1897) 320 Then came..revolutionary tribunals, guillotinades, noyades, fusillades. **1878** SEELEY *Stein* I. 163 No guillotine was to be set up..; the Oder, Spree and Weichsel were to see no noyades.

transf. **1819** J. ADAMS *Lett.* Wks. 1850 II. 334 *note*, The Mohawks, who were concerned in the noyade of the tea in Boston harbor. **1899** E. WHARTON *Greater Inclination* iv. 126 He and she..were bound together in a *noyade* of passion that left them resisting yet clinging as they went down. **1955** AUDEN *Shield of Achilles* iii. 76 Some autumn night of delations and noyades.

Hence **noyade** *v.*, to put to death by drowning; also **noyading** *vbl. sb.*

1837 CARLYLE *Fr. Rev.* III. v. vi, Sounds of fusillading and noyading. **1839** —— *Chartism* v. 141 Lyons fusilladings, Nantes noyadings. **1844** TH. PARKER in Weiss *Life & Corr.* I. 225 The wretched Terrorists..guillotined, and noyaded, and mitrailled, I know not how many.

†**Noyals.** *Obs. rare.* [a. F. *noyales* (pl.), from the place of manufacture, *Noyal* in the department Ille-et-Vilaine.] (See quots.)

1662 *Irish Stat.* (1765) II. 410 Noyals canvas the hundred ells. **1721** C. KING *Brit. Merch.* I. 181, 17000 Hund. of Vitry and Noyals Canvas.

†'**noyance.** *Obs.* Also 4–6 **noyaunce**, 6 **noiance.** [Aphetic form of ANNOYANCE.]

1. A source of annoyance; a nuisance.

c **1330** R. BRUNNE *Chron. Wace* (Rolls) 3444 Longe lastede þat ilk distaunce, To þe breþere gret noyaunce. **1534** in W. H. Turner *Select. Rec. Oxford* (1880) 124 They..doe use to reforme all common noyaunces. **1577** B. GOOGE *Heresbach's Husb.* IV. (1586) 179 Whereby the winde..may dry vp all Cobwebbes, or such like noiances. **1639** G. DANIEL *Ecclus.* xliii. 55 Soe, for the Summer's Sun (noyance as great) A gentle Dew falls, to allay the heat. **1670** J. SMITH *Eng. Improv. Reviv'd* 99 That the distance of them be such, that every Tree be not a noyance..to his fellows.

2. The condition or fact of being annoyed, troubled, or harmed.

c **1400** *Brut* clxi. 180 Kyng Edward dede his diligence..to amende þe noyaunce of þe commune peple. **1494** *Act II Hen. VII*, c. 13 Preamble, The Price..[is] greatly enhansed here, to the Loss and Noyance of all the King's Subjects. **1502** *Ord. Crysten Men* (W. de W. 1506) II. vii. 102 Slouthe the whiche is an heuynesse and noyaunce to doo well. **1568** GRAFTON *Chron.* II. 165 Other coynes of mettall went among the people, to their great noyaunce.

3. The action of annoying or troubling; annoyance, molestation.

1431 *Eng. Gilds* (1870) 279 In disturblyng and noyaunce of the compenye. **1483** CAXTON *Gold. Leg.* 193/2 She was sore aferd leste he wold do to her ony gryef or noyance ayenst her avowe. **1523** LD. BERNERS *Froiss.* I. ccxix. 282 We shall go and do hym some noyaunce and domage. **1590** SPENSER *F.Q.* I. i. xxiii, A cloud of cumbrous gnattes doe him molest,..That from their noyance he no where can rest. [**1748** THOMSON *Cast. Indol.* I. vi, Whate'er smack'd of noyance, or unrest, Was far, far off expelled.]

So †'**noyancy.** *Obs. rare*[−1].

1414 *Rolls of Parlt.* IV. 59/1 Mischiefs that mighten.. turne to gret prejudice to the kyng, & noiancie to al the Reume.

†'**noyant**, *a.* *Obs.* [Aphetic f. OF. *anoyant*: cf. NOY *v.*] Injurious (to); causing annoyance.

c **1400** tr. *Secreta Secret., Gov. Lordsh.* 79 Drynkyng of cold water fastynge, byfore mete, ys noyant þe body. *c* **1460** ASHBY *Dicta Philos.* 699 Al suche thing noyant to your high estate Eschewe al wey. **1550** in Strype *Stow's Surv.* (1754) II. v. xxii. 421/1 Sea coal, Dust, Rushes or any other thing Noyant. **1582** in W. H. Turner *Select. Rec. Oxford* (1880) 422 Ordure, rubbysh, carreine, or any other thinge noyant.

‖**noyau** (nwajo). Also **noyeau.** [F., repr. earlier *noyal, noial, nuial*, etc.:—pop. L. **nucale*, f. L. *nuc-, nux* nut.] **1. a.** A liqueur made of brandy flavoured with the kernels of certain fruits.

1787 W. DYOTT *Diary* (1907) I. 38 We dined at half-past three and drank pretty freely till eight, when we had coffee, and after noyau, etc. **1797** CANNING *Rovers* II. ii, This cherry-bounce, this loved noyau, My drink for ever be. **1818** MOORE *Fudge Fam. Paris* 161 Your Noyeaus, Curaçoes, and the devil knows what. **1842** ORDERSON *Creoleana* xx. 245 You will..venture to sip the noyeau. **1882** *Cornh. Mag.* Jan. 86 A glass of noyau and still more cakes.

b. A type of sweetmeat related to nougat.

1913 C. MACKENZIE *Sinister St.* I. I. vii. 103 Richer boys emerged from the tuckshop, sucking gelatines and satin pralines and chocolate creams and raspberry noyau. **1963** —— *My Life & Times* II. 135 A small boy tried to make up his mind whether he would invest a penny in a bar of raspberry, or greengage, or apricot noyau... Noyau was a second-best to nougat.

2. *transf.* A nucleus (of people).

1965 *Listener* 27 May 792/1 They picked out, from the far from 'little' *noyau* of young, hopeful writers who had gathered around them, any Lucien de Rubempré..who came their way. **1966** R. ARDREY *Territorial Imperative* (1967) v. 167, I have taken from the French ethologist Jean-Jacques Petter the term '*noyau*' as a label for the society of inward antagonism.... It has seemed wise..to get..away.. from all those English words like 'community' or 'society' which inevitably bear connotations of co-operation. *Noyau* —meaning, roughly, a nucleus—is correct in that it implies a primitive evolutionary step towards societies characterized by mutual aid.

noych(e, obs. forms of OUCH, clasp.

†'**noyer.** *Obs.*[−1] [f. NOY *v.*] = ANNOYER.

1573 TUSSER *Husb.* (1878) 29 The north is a noyer to grasse of all suites, The east a destroyer to herbe and all fruites.

†'**noyful**, *a.* *Obs.* Forms: 4 **noiȝe-**, 4–6 **noye-** (5 **nuye-**), **noi-**, 4–7 **noyful**; also 4–5 **-fulle**, 5–7 **-full.** [f. NOY *sb.*[1] + -FUL.]

1. Annoying, troublesome, tiresome; also, harmful, hurtful, noxious.

1382 WYCLIF *Luke* xi. 7 Nyle thou be noyful to me. **1398** TREVISA *Barth. De P.R.* XI. iii. (Bodl. MS.), þe norþeren winde..is noifulle to ham þat haue tesike. **1435** *Coventry Leet Bk.* (E.E.T.S.) 3 Oct., As the mater of this bille is grevous & Nuyefull to the comen pepull. **1483** CAXTON *Gold. Leg.* 299b/1 Opene my woundes lest ony noyeful humour corrupte..the hyd passions. **1523** LD. BERNERS *Froiss.* I. ccclvi. 575 It is noyfull to me to recorde it. **1584** COGAN *Haven Health* ci. (1636) 100 Declaring their noyfull qualities in appeyring of nature. *a* **1618** J. DAVIES *Commend. Poems* Wks. (Grosart) II. 20/1 To be fore-pinde..In many a noyfull stoure of willing bale.

2. Annoyed, vexed. *rare.*

1387 TREVISA *Higden* (Rolls) V. 331 After sixe and twenty ȝere of Cerdicus his comyng, Arthur was wery and noyeful. *Ibid.* VI. 57 þe kyng of strange tonge was greved and noyful, ..and brouȝte yn anoþer [bishop] of his owne longage.

Hence †'**noyfully** *adv.*; '**noyfulness** *sb.* *Obs.*

1395 PURVEY *Remonstr.* (1851) 46 Settinge noiefully in thraldom that the holi scripture settith profitabli in fredom. **1398** TREVISA *Barth. De P.R.* VIII. xiii. (1495) 320 By nighnes of eyther sterre his noyfulnesse is tempred.

†'**noying**, *vbl. sb.* *Obs.* [f. NOY *v.* + -ING[1].] Annoyance, harm, injury.

1474 CAXTON *Chesse* (1883) 144 They ought to requyre theyr passage..wyth oute noynge and contencion. **1511** *Guylforde's Pilgr.* (Camden) 54 Saffely assuryd from noyeng of any beste. **1548–77** VICARY *Anat.* v. (1888) 37 The cause why he taketh that Pannicle, is to keepe him from noying.

†'**noying**, *ppl. a.* *Obs.* [-ING[2].] That annoys or vexes; vexatious; injurious.

a **1340** HAMPOLE *Psalter* i. 3 A tre þ[t] is profitabile til many & noyand til nane. **1398** TREVISA *Barth. De P.R.* X. vi. (Bodl. MS.), He..streyneþ and bindeþ nuyynge rennyng of rewmne. *c* **1440** *Gesta Rom.* xlviii. 217 Grace of withestondynge of noynge þynges. **1505** *Berwick Reg.* (Hist. MSS. Comm.) *Var. Collect.* I. 7 Defaultes..noynge and paynfull unto the Kinges lieges and all other strangers.

noyl, variant of NOIL.

†'**noyment.** *Obs.*[−1] [f. NOY *v.*] Annoyance.

1502 ARNOLDE *Chron.* (1811) 211 So that it be not to the noyment of any neybur.

noynyng, obs. variant of NOONING.

†'**noyous**, *a.* *Obs.* Forms: 4–5 **noyus**, 4–7 **-ous**, 5–6 **-ose**, 5 **-ows(e, -ose**, *Sc.* **-us**, 5–6 **noyes** (5 **-is**); 5 **noiose**, 5–6 **noious** (6 **-ouse**); 5 **nuous, nvous**, 6 **nuyouse.** [Aphetic form of *anoyous*, etc., ANNOYOUS *a.*] Causing annoyance; vexatious, troublesome, etc.

a **1340** HAMPOLE *Psalter* xxxvii. 15 Here noyus wordis and ȝeld not agayn. *c* **1374** CHAUCER *Troylus* III. 1504 (Harl.), Lat in ȝour herte no noyouse fantasie So crepe, þat it cause me to die. *c* **1400** *Lanfranc's Cirurg.* 55 þer is no þing more noious to a wounde. **1422** tr. *Secreta Secret., Priv. Priv.* 212 Profitable as an hors, nuous as a mows. **1470–85** MALORY *Arthur* XVII. viii. 701 That yeldyng, sayd they, shal be noyous to yow. **1533** MORE *Apol.* 86 b, Suche as are..euyle, and nought, and noyouse vnto the comen well. **1576** BAKER *Jewell of Health* 10 b, Howe noyous and hurtfull such a vapour and savour is. **1634** LEVETT *Ordering of Bees* 13 Those noyous and filthy things being taken away. **1675** HUYBERTS *Corner-Stone* 11 Divers medicines which at the first usage..were exclaimed against..as noyous and hurtful to the king's subjects.

Hence †'**noyously** *adv.* *Obs.*

1483 *Cath. Angl.* 256/1 Noyovsly, *nocue.* **1641** BAKER *Chron.* (1653) 359 Houndsditch..till that time, had lien very noyously to all travellers that way.

†**noyra**: see NEWRY. *Obs.*

1613 PURCHAS *Pilgrimage* v. xii. 429 As for fowles, they haue abundance of Parrots and Noyras, more pleasing in beautie, speech and other delights then the Parrot.

noys(e, obs. ff. NOISE, NOSE.

noysance, -ant, varr. of NOISANCE, -ANT.

noysom(e, -sum, obs. ff. NOISOME.

noyt, *v.* *Sc.* [Of obscure origin. In mod. use commonly written *knoit.*] To strike, rap.

15.. *Christs Kirk* xix. (Maitl. MS.), Thair durst na ten cum him to tak, Sa noytit he thair nowis.

nozel, variant of NUZZLE *v.*[2] *Obs.*

nozzel, obs. variant of NORSEL.

nozzer ('nɒzə(r)). *Naut. slang.* [Orig. uncertain: ? f. colloq. repr. of *No, sir*; but see quot. 1962.] A new recruit, a novice sailor.

1943 'TAFFRAIL' *White Ensigns* ii. 32 To make matters worse the 'nozzers', or novices, usually had their soap and water purloined by those who had been longer on board and knew the ropes. **1962** GRANVILLE *Dict. Sailors' Slang* 82/2

Nozzer, new entry boy at the training establishment, HMS *Ganges*... These boys have been called *nozzers*..since the establishment opened, because the petty officer in charge was nicknamed 'Nosey'.

nozzle ('nɒz(ə)l), *sb.* Forms: α. 7–9 **nosle, nosel,** 7–8 **nossel.** β. 7–9 **nozle,** 7–8 **nozel,** 8 **nozzel,** 8– **nozzle.** [f. NOSE *sb.* + -LE.]

1. A socket on a candlestick or sconce, for receiving the lower end of the candle; also, a part projecting from the socket (quot. 1608). Now *rare.*

α. **1608** WILLET *Hexapla Exod.* 593 Euery socket had *rostrum in vna parte*, a certaine nosle hanging out. **1657** W. COLES *Adam in Eden* cclix, In fashion like unto the Nossel of a wooden candlestick. **1714** *Lond. Gaz.* No. 5282/9 A Nosel for a Candle. **1847** HALLIW., The nosle of a candlestick is that part which holds the end of the candle.

β. **1682** WHELER *Journ. Greece* v. 398 A Stem, formed like a Nozel, or Socket of a Candlestick. **1741** ARBUTHNOT & POPE *Mem. Mart. Scriblerus* iii, A paultry old Sconce, with the nozzle broke off. *a* **1764** LLOYD *Candle & Snuffers* Poet. Wks. 1774 II. 133 A candle stuck in flaring state Within the nozel of French plate. **1791** *Ann. Reg., Chron.* 8 A pair of silver snuffers and stand, and two candlestick nozzles.

2. a. A small spout, mouthpiece, or projecting aperture; a short terminal pipe or part of a pipe, such as the nose of a pair of bellows, the muzzle of a gun-barrel, etc.

α. **1683** SALMON *Doron Med.* II. xx. 570 The Top thereof [a stove] may be firm Tin, with a nossel or pipe in it, like that of a pair of Bellows. **1702** SAVERY *Miner's Friend* 44 Taking away his Thumb, he by directing the Nosle to the Fire immediately extinguishes it. **1787** *Phil. Trans.* LXXVIII. 46 Icicles, adhering to the nosel of the cock.

β. **1684** tr. *Bonet's Merc. Compit.* III. 98 A Pipe being tied to the nozle of a pair of Bellows. **1764** *Mus. Rusticum* III. lxvii. 304 At every fathom distance there should be wooden nozels. **1825** J. NICHOLSON *Operat. Mechanic* 261 A wooden plug may be chained to the pump, betwixt the spouts or nozles. **1844** H. STEPHENS *Bk. Farm* II. 208 The nozzle that leads from the steam pipe is stopped with a wooden plug. **1894** CURZON *Probl. Far East* 246 Boards upon which are painted the nozzles of imaginary cannons.

b. Applied to various parts of a steam-engine, *esp.* the steam-port, or the part of the cylinder enclosing this, and the exhaust-pipe or the adjustable end of this. Also applied to similiar parts of other engines, e.g. turbines (for directing the fluid on to the rotor), internal-combustion engines (for injecting fuel into the carburettor or the combustion chamber), and jet engines (for increasing the speed of the ejected fluid).

1839 R. S. ROBINSON *Naut. Steam Eng.* 34 On one side of the cylinder, and cast with it, are two square projections called nosles, which enclose within them the steam ports. **1848** ALBAN *Steam Eng.* 257 *note*, By some mechanics these parts of the engine are called nozzles, a corruption of nose-holes. **1875** KNIGHT *Dict. Mech.* 1535/1. **1906** W. H. S. GARNETT *Turbines* I. v. 56 When it is required to reduce the power more rapidly..it is usual to deflect the nozzle so that the jet misses the buckets. **1912** *Motor Manual* (ed. 14) i. 10 When the suction of the engine occurs petrol issues through the nozzle, and an inrush of air..passes upwards, carrying the sprayed petrol with it, and thus forming the explosive mixture. **1946** [see AFTER-BURNING *vbl. sb.* 2]. **1949** G. P. SUTTON *Rocket Propulsion Elem.* i. 3 When a rocket unit operates, a chemical reaction occurs which generates high temperature, high pressure gases; these..are ejected through a nozzle. **1950** SKROTZKI & VOPAT *Steam & Gas Turbines* ix. 371 Mechanical spray nozzles for injecting fuel oil into combustion chambers. **1962** D. SLAYTON in *Into Orbit* 22 The job of keeping the capsule in its correct attitude during flight is taken care of by small jet nozzles fastened on the outside of the spacecraft. **1966** *Aviation Week & Space Technol.* 6 Dec. 24/1 A rocket engine with a conventional bell nozzle. **1971** B. SCHARF *Engin. & its Lang.* xiv. 207 In impulse turbines, the high pressure steam..expands through nozzles or guide blades shaped to form nozzles.

attrib. **1895** *Model Steam Eng.* 84 This is regulated by the size of the aperture at the nozzle end of the boiler.

3. *slang.* The nose.

1771 SMOLLETT *Humph. Cl.* 18 Apr., His..face was overshadowed by this tremendous nozzle. **1854** 'C. BEDE' *Verdant Green* II. iv. 31 That'll take the bark from your nozzle. **1863** SPEKE *Discov. Nile* 271 But Bombey, showing his nozzle rather flatter than usual, said 'No; I got this on account of your lies'.

4. A small nose or beak; a projecting part or end.

1850 GROTE *Greece* II. lx. VII. 408 Instead of having one single beak, the Corinthian ship might be said to have three nozzles. **1874** BEDFORD *Sailor's Pkt.-Bk.* v. 108 Each buoy, exclusive of the nozzle, is to be divided horizontally into four, and vertically into eight equal parts.

5. Special combs., as **nozzle-block** (see quot.); **nozzle-face** (see quot.); **nozzle-man,** a man in charge of the nozzle of the hose of a fire-engine, or that of a suction- or other pipe; **nozzle-pipe** = NOZZLE 2; **nozzle-plate** = *nozzle-face*; **nozzle-screw,** a nozzle having a screw-thread cut on it.

1875 KNIGHT *Dict. Mech.* 1535/1 *Nozzle-block, one in which two bellows-nozzles unite. **1846** A. YOUNG *Naut. Dict.* 298 Within the casing, at the top and bottom of the cylinder, are the two *nosle-faces, which are square plates of brass raised upon the cylinder, one round each of the steam-ports, for the valve-plates to slide upon. **1885** T. A. D. *Where Chineses Drive* 139 One of the rest acted as *nozzle-man to direct the jet. **1893** *Times* 10 July 13/6 There are to each such suction pipe, when in operation, one weigher, and one nozzle-man in the ship's hold and two boys. **1816** ACCUM *Chem. Tests* 245 If the flame have a cavity through it, the aperture of the *nozzle-pipe is too large. **1875** KNIGHT *Dict. Mech.* 1535/1 *Nozzle-plate, a seat for a slide-valve of a steam-engine. **1839** *Civil Eng. & Arch. Jrnl.* IV. 195/1 The aperture through which the *nozzle-screw is to pass.

Hence **'nozzle** *v. trans.*, to fit *with* something after the manner of a nozzle. **'nozzler** *slang*, a blow on the nose.

1866 J. B. ROSE *Virg. Ecl. & Georg.* 111 Some to the young the mother's teats forbid, And nozzle with sharp spikes the calf and kid. **1828** *Sporting Mag.* XXII. 198 In the ninth round Bob received a nozzler drawing claret.

nozzle, variant of NUZZLE *v.*[1]

n-p-n (ˌɛn,piː'ɛn). *Electronics.* Also **npn,** and in capitals. Designating a semiconductor device in which a *p*-type region is sandwiched between two *n*-type regions.

1951 W. SHOCKLEY et al. in *Physical Rev.* LXXXIII. 151/1 The *p-n-p* transistor has been discussed previously... In this article we shall consider..the *n-p-n* transistor. **1962** SIMPSON & RICHARDS *Physical Princ. Junction Transistors* iii. 46 In the manufacture of *n-p-n* grown-junction transistors, the *p*-type section is grown for a very short time to give a thin base layer. **1967** *Electronics* 6 Mar. 4/2 Transistors Types: PNP and NPN. **1969** J. J. SPARKES *Transistor Switching* v. 126 Using *npn* transistors, pulsed *R-S* flip-flops using three basic types of pulse steering are available.

†**npnam,** variant of *nam* MNAM *Obs.*

1362 LANGL. *P. Pl.* A. VII. 226 Seruus nequam hedde npnam, and for he nolde hit vsen [etc.].

‖**nritta** (n'rɪtə). Also **nrtta.** [Skr. *nṛitta* dance.] A type of 'pure', abstract Indian dance (quot. 1967).

1917 COOMARASWAMY & DUGGIRALA tr. *Mirror of Gesture* 14 Nṛtta is here dismissed with a merely negative definition, as the object of the Abhinaya Darpaṇa is to explain how to express by gesture definite themes. **1953** F. BOWERS *Dance in India* 24 Sanskrit has no single word for dance in our sense... *Nritta*..refers to dance pure and simple, unadulterated by meaning, interpretation gesture, or language. **1967** SINGHA & MASSEY *Indian Dances* 24 Nritta is the rhythmic movement of the body in dance... It visualizes and reproduces music and rhythm by means of abstract gestures of the body and hands... Nritta..is concerned solely with rhythmic movement in dancing and is therefore loosely termed 'pure dance'. **1967** CHUJOY & MANCHESTER *Dance Encycl.* 457/2 The repertoire of the Bharata Natya dancer includes nrtta, nrtya, and nautch. Nrtta is an abstact dance of pure lyricism; nrtya is an expressive dance, pantomimic in content; nautch is a combination of song and dance. **1971** *Femina* (Bombay) 30 Apr. 49/1 Kuchipudi is the regional variation of Bharata Natyam. Both share classical Carnatic music and the Nritta (pure dance) and Nritya (expressional dance) aspects.

‖**nritya** (n'rɪtjə). Also **nrtya.** [Skr. *nṛitya* dance, play.] A type of Indian dance through which ideas or emotions are expressed.

1875 MONIER WILLIAMS *Indian Wisdom* xv. 463 The root *naṭ* and the nouns *nāṭya* and *nāṭaka*, which are now applied to dramatic acting, are probably mere corruptions of *nṛit*, 'to dance', *nṛitya*, 'dancing'. **1917** COOMARASWAMY & DUGGIRALA tr. *Mirror of Gesture* 14 Nṛtya should be seen by a royal audience in the court of kings. **1953** F. BOWERS *Dance in India* 25 *Nritya*..refers to expression, interpretation, and gesticulation with meaning. In other words, dance when it conveys sense and ideas. **1967** SINGHA & MASSEY *Indian Dances* 24 Nritya is that element of the dance which 'suggests *ras* (sentiment) and *bhava* (mood)'. Both..are conveyed through facial expressions and appropriate gestures... The object of both natya and nritya..is to depict ideas, themes, moods and sentiments. **1967, 1971** [see NRITTA].

nshiego: see JOCKO.

Nsima, var. NZIMA.

nth: see N I. 4.

n-tuple: see -TUPLE.

n-type ('ɛntaɪp), *a. Physics.* [f. *N* (repr. *negative*) + TYPE *sb.*[1]] Applied to (a region in) a semiconductor in which electrical conduction is due chiefly to the movement of electrons. Opp. P-TYPE *a.*

1946 J. A. BECKER et al. in *Trans. Amer. Inst. Electr. Engin.* LXV. 714/1 The theoretical and experimental physicists have established that there are two types of electronic semiconductors which can be called *N* and *P* type, depending on whether the carriers are negative electrons or are equivalent to positive 'holes' in the filled energy band. *Ibid.* 715/1 *N*-type oxides, such as ZnO... *P*-type oxides, such as NiO. **1948** TORREY & WHITMAN *Crystal Rectifiers* iii. 49 A semiconductor that conducts principally by electrons in the nearly empty band is said to be an '*n*-type' semiconductor. **1962** SIMPSON & RICHARDS *Physical Princ. Junction Transistors* i. 8 If this type of impurity semiconduction is predominant the material is said to be an *n*-type extrinsic semiconductor, or simply of *n*-type. **1967** *Electronics* 6 Mar. 60/2 Light-sensitive diodes are produced by diffusing islands of boron into a substrate of n-type silicon.

‖**nu** (nuː), *int.* [Yiddish, f. Russ. *nu* well, well now.] An exclamation variously used to express interrogation, surprise, emphasis, doubt, etc.

1892 I. ZANGWILL *Childr. Ghetto* I. I. ii. 52 '*Nu*, Pesach, another glass of rum,' said Mr. Beleovitch genially. **1945** A. KOBER *Parm Me* 134 '*Nu*,' she said, 'is lust by you the tunk, you can't give a person a hello when you coming home?' **1967** C. POTOK *Chosen* vii. 139 'Nu,' Reb Saunders said, smiling, 'how should you not know that?' **1968** L. ROSTEN *Joys of Yiddish* 268 *Nu* is so very Yiddish an interjection that it has become the one word which can identify a Jew. **1970** L. M. FEINSILVER *Taste of Yiddish* ii. 155 Growing impatience makes for Nu-nu? and nu-nu-nu? **1971** D. MEIRING *Wall of Glass* xvii. 147 *Nu*? thought Geyra, So what?

nu, obs. form of NEW *a.* and NOW.

‖**nuance** (nɥɑ̃s, 'nuːɑ̃ːs, 'njuː-, -ɑːns), *sb.* [F. *nuance* shade of colour, etc., f. *nuer* to shade, f. *nue* cloud:—pop. L. **nuba* for classical L. *nūbēs*.]

1. A slight or delicate variation or difference in expression, feeling, opinion, etc.

1781 H. WALPOLE *Let. to C'tess Ossory* 4 Jan., The more expert one were at *nuances*, the more poetic one should be. **1846** H. GREVILLE *Diary* (1883) 165 The English and French difference on the Spanish question is considered as serious by people of every political *nuance*. **1873** SYMONDS *Grk. Poets* viii. 255 Much of the obscurity..arises from our having lost the finer *nuances* of Athenian feeling respecting the persons satirized in the old Comedy.

2. A shade of colour; a slight difference or variation in shade or tone.

1856–7 GEO. ELIOT *Sc. Clerical Life* II. iv, Whose face Nature seemed to have coloured in a hurry, and had no time to attend to *nuances*. **1879** A. J. C. HARE *Story Life* (1900) V. xx. 160 Her rooms were draped with every possible nuance of colour which can harmonise together.

3. A delicate gradation in musical expression.

1879 GROVE *Dict. Mus.* I. 171 Comparatively careless as to the right notes being played, but angry..at any failure in expression or nuance. **1885** *Athenæum* 7 Feb. 192/3 Some numbers were splendidly given... The *nuances* were also observed to a remarkable degree.

nuance ('nuːɑ̃ːs, 'njuː-, -ɑːns), *v.* [f. the sb.] *trans.* To give nuances to. Hence **'nuancing** *vbl. sb.*

1897 W. ARCHER *Theatr. World 1896* 94 Nor the elocutionary skill to give variety to a long speech, *nuancing* it, if I may say so, by means of his voice alone. **1959** M. SCHLAUCH *Eng. Lang. in Mod. Times* II. iii. 53 Some tendencies toward such nuancing may be detected in the late medieval distribution of *thou* and *ye* for the singular. **1973** P. A. ALLUM *Politics & Society in Post-War Naples* vi. 191 We can nuance this conclusion and reveal that in some communes the relation of the first to the fourth candidate was 2:1..; in other communes the difference between first and fourth was less than 1,000 votes out of 5,000. **1975** *Gramophone* Oct. 652/1 Take the Wagner piece.., and note the impassioned recitative, nuanced as by the human voice.

‖**nuancé** (nɥɑ̃se), *ppl. a.* [Fr.] = NUANCED *ppl. a.*

1963 *Times Lit. Suppl.* 1 Feb. 71/1 Life..was extremely *nuancé*. *Ibid.* 3 May 318/5 His answer is extremely *nuancé*. **1973** P. A. ALLUM *Politics & Society in Post-War Naples* vi. 181 Macciocchi's judgement in Amendola is more *nuancé*.

nuanced ('nuːɑ̃ːst, 'njuː-, -ɑːnst), *ppl. a.* [f. NUANCE *v.* + -ED[1].] Possessing or exhibiting delicate gradations in tone, expression, etc.

1920 [see BOSTONIAN *a.*]. **1965** *Listener* 21 Oct. 613/1 Marxists often distingush between 'Marxism' and 'vulgar Marxism'... The former is subtle, profound, nuanced,.. and dialectical. **1969** N. FREELING *Tsing-Boum* xi. 71 An immensely nuanced and confused double-think. **1971** *Daily Tel.* 23 Mar. 16/5 He brought a wealth of finely nuanced expression to the eloquently fashioned vocal line. **1972** *Language* XLVIII. 457 In a study devoted to discriminations among adverbs, one would expect a nuanced feeling for them, and to a large extent this is borne out.

nub (nʌb), *sb.*[1] Also 7, 9 **nubb.** [app. a variant of KNUB *sb.*]

†**1.** = KNUB *sb.* 3. *Obs. rare.*

1594 *Cecil Papers* (Hist. MSS. Comm.) IV. 574 Silk nubbs, 700 *li.* **1640** in Entick *London* (1766) II. 178 Silk nubs, or husks of silk. **1759** *Chron.* in *Ann. Reg.* 182 The duties now payable upon raw short silk or capiton, and silk nubs, or husks of silk, shall..cease.

2. A knob or protuberance; a lump.

Common in dialect use in various applications. '*Nub*, the neck' in the *Dict. Cant. Crew* (*a* 1700) may belong here, but cf. NUB *sb.*[2]

1727 BRADLEY *Fam. Dict.* s.v. *Garden fences*, That when the Tree is quite fixed, the Nub or Bottom of the Stem, above the Division of the Roots, may be rather above the Surface then even with it. **1760** *Boston Gaz.* 5 May 4/3 Strayed away,..a black Mare.., has..two small Nubs on the near Flank. **1859** BARTLETT *Dict. Amer.* (ed. 3) 297 *Nub*, a knob. **1864** WEBSTER, *Nub*, a jag, or snag; also a knob, a protuberance. **1866** *Fortn. Rev.* Jan. 617 People..have very feeble notions of the difficulty that every nub of coal represents. **1893** G. D. LESLIE *Lett. Marco* xxviii. 191 The ground is alive with little nubs and noses poking through.

3. The point or gist of a story or matter.

1834 S. SMITH *Sel. Lett. J. Downing* 205 That's pretty much the *nub* of the business. **1859** BARTLETT *Dict. Amer.* (ed. 3) 297 The nub of a story is the point or gist of it. **1889** 'MARK TWAIN' *Yankee at Crt. of K. Arthur* xvii. 176 When the nub was sprung, the assemblage let go with a horse-laugh. **1899** *Scribner's Mag.* XXV. 105/2 It's the nub of the whole matter. **1933** WODEHOUSE *Heavy Weather* viii. 166 'The problem..is, How the hell is one to get it away from the blighter?' 'Quite.' 'That is, as you might say, the nub?' **1963** *Guardian* 11 Mar. 13/6 Speaking on the election of vice-presidents, he came to the nub of the unrest among active athletes. **1974** *Times* 22 Oct. 14/6 The nub of the judges' difficulty lay in Lord Widgery's reference to the claim..that the judge had no authority in law to give a direction binding on the press.

†**nub,** *sb.*[2] *Obs. Cant.* [Cf. NUB *v.*[2]] The gallows.

a **1700** B. E. *Dict. Cant. Crew* s.v. *Glim*, As the Cull was Glimm'd, he gangs to the Nubb, [i.e.] if the Fellow has been Burnt in the Hand, he'll be Hang'd now.

nub, *v.*[1], var. of KNUB *v.* 2. (Cf. NUBBLE *v.*)
c **1610** *Grobiana's Nuptialls* (MS. Bodl. 30) lf. 24 b, I tooke him a polt of the pate... I nubb'd his noddle.

† **nub**, *v.*[2] *Obs. Cant.* [Cf. NUB *sb.*[2]] To hang (one) by the neck; to execute by hanging.
1673 R. HEAD *Cant. Acad.* 16 The other was (nub'd) hang'd, and the last (marrinated) transported. *Ibid.* 191 They are rub'd, Up to the Nubbing-Cheat, And there they're nubb'd. *a* **1754** FIELDING *Jonathan Wild* IV. ii, We shall be both nubbed together. I'faith, my dear, it almost makes me amends for being nubbed myself, to have the pleasure of seeing thee nubbed too.
Hence † '**nubbing** *vbl. sb.*, hanging.
a **1700** B. E. *Dict. Cant. Crew.*

Nuba ('nu:bə). Also **Nouba**. [See NUBIAN *a.* and *sb.*] The name of a group of peoples of southern Kordofan in the Sudan; a member of these peoples. Also *attrib.* or as *adj.*
1827 J. CONDER *Mod. Traveller: Egypt, Nubia, & Abyssinia* II. 242 The male Noubas, in Egypt as well as in Arabia, are preferred to all others for labour. **1884** *Encycl. Brit.* XVII. 316/2 Certainly none of the chief native races in Soudan.. Maba in Wadai, Nuba in the Nile valley.. can be considered as of pure Negro descent. **1910** *Ibid.* II. 51/2 The Nuba and Nuer [of the Upper Nile] worship the bull. **1911** *Ibid.* XV. 907/2 The Nubas have their own language, though the inhabitants of each hill have usually a different dialect... In the northern hills [of Kordofan] are communities of black people... They speak Arabic and are called Nuba Arabs. **1911** J. G. FRAZER *Golden Bough: Magic Art* (ed. 3) I. iii. 122 When a Nuba of north-eastern Africa goes to El Obeid for the first time, he tells his wife not to wash or oil herself. **1936** *Discovery* June 170/1 The Nubians (not to be confused with the Nuba of Kordofan). **1949** J. S. TRIMINGHAM *Islam in Sudan* i. 3 Here live the settled 'Arab' population of Kordofān, the Baqqāra cattle-breeding Arabs, the pastoral negroid Shilluk, and the pagan Nūba in the hills. **1962** OLIVER & FAGE *Short Hist. Afr.* iv. 47 The kingdom of the Nuba who are above upper Egypt. **1966** C. SWEENEY *Scurrying Bush* iii. 46 The Nuba of Kordofan.. say that it was the baboon that stole the *Kako's* (hyrax's) tail. **1970** *Man, Myth, & Magic* v. 138/3 Victorious Nuba wrestlers are awarded branches which are burnt; the wrestler covers himself with the ashes before the next fight. **1972** J. C. FARIS in Cunnison & James *Ess. Sudan Ethnogr.* i. 3 The Southeastern Nuba have suffered locally at the hands of a series of raiders and slavers for a long time.

nub-berry. *Sc. rare.* = NOOP[1].
1794 *Statist. Acc. Scotl.* XIII. 243 Upon the top of this hill, grows a small berry, commonly called the Nub Berry.

'**nubbin**. *U.S.* [f. NUB *sb.*[1]] A dwarfed or imperfect ear of maize. Also *transf.* and *fig.*, esp. something small or something that remains when the main part is worn away.
1692 in *Maryland Hist. Mag.* (1918) XIII. 209 Jones saw him buy one beaver skin.. for thirty ears and nubbins of corn. **1838** B. DRAKE *Tales & Sketches* 150 A handfull of salt and a few nubbins of corn. **1847** in WEBSTER. **1857** *Harper's Mag.* Feb. 399/2 They served me, at the 'American', with a little hard *nubbin* of steak. **1897** GEN. H. PORTER in *Cent. Mag.* Aug. 591 Well,.. that's the littlest nubbin I ever did see. **1904** H. F. DAY *Kin O'Ktaadn* 93 She'd squizzle all to nubbins a speech an hour long. **1910** 'O. HENRY' *Strictly Business* vi. 76 A red nubbin of corn. **1915** A. C. LAWSON in *Bull. Dept. Geol. Univ. Calif.* IX. III. 38 Broad alluvial embankments.. rise by a gentle slope to the summits of the ranges, where there are residual rock crests, or 'nubbins'. **1931** *Times Educ. Suppl.* 11 July 275/4 One may find 'nubbins'—hard, undeveloped, useless things—the result of non-fertilization. **1945** B. MACDONALD *Egg & I* (1946) I. iii. 45 Many of the trees bore nothing or merely two or three wizened nubbins. **1954** G. I. M. SWYER *Reprod. & Sex* App. I. 249 Shortly before puberty.. a small nubbin of tissue appears beneath the areola, converting it to a cone. **1954** DYLAN THOMAS *Quite Early One Morning* I. 56 The Telecinema.. blobs and nubbins and rubbery squirls receding. **1969** D. BAGLEY *Spoilers* i. 10 The lipstick was worn right down... Another lipstick worn to a nubbin.

'**nubbing-cheat**. *Cant.* [f. *nubbing* NUB *v.*[2] + CHEAT *sb.*[1] 3.] The gallows. Now only *arch.*
1673 R. HEAD *Cant. Acad.* 94 They are.. sent to the Nubbing cheat. **1745** FIELDING *Tom Jones* VIII. xii, 'I will shew you a way to empty the pocket of a queer cull, without any danger of the nubbing cheat.' 'Nubbing cheat,' cries Partridge, 'Pray, Sir, what is that?' 'Why that, Sir,' says the stranger, 'is a cant-phrase for the gallows.' **1826** SCOTT *Woodst.* xxxvi, We trine to the nubbing cheat to-morrow. **1834** AINSWORTH *Rookwood* (1864) 313, I fear Dick will scarce cheat the Nubbing-cheat this go. **1902** *Blackw. Mag.* May 704/2 They pay the last debt at the nubbing-cheat.
So † '**nubbing-cove**, the hangman; † '**nubbing-ken**, 'the Sessions-house'.
a **1700** B. E. *Dict. Cant. Crew.*

nubble ('nʌb(ə)l), *sb.* [dim. of NUB *sb.*[1] Cf. *knubble, knobble.*] A small knob or lump.
1818 J. BROWN *Psyche* 171 Counting the nubbles and the dints That form the cornice. *a* **1845** HOOD *To Henrietta* 23 That a *corne* is not the nubble that brings trouble to your toes. **1860** PIESSE *Lab. Chem. Wonders* 42 A nubble of iron .. dissolves in it like sugar does in water. **1897** KIPLING *Capt. Cour.* 14 A piece of dingy ticking full of lumps and nubbles.

† '**nubble**. variant of KNUBBLE *v.*
1676 *Verney Fam. Mem.* (1899) VII. 223 Sr Fr. [Vincent] ..beate him [Ld. Pembroke], threw him downe in ye kennell, nubbled him & dawb'd him daintily. **1725** N. BAILEY *Erasm. Colloq.* 462, I.. took him hold by the Hair with my left Hand, and nubbled him so well-favouredly with my Right, that you could see no Eyes he had for the Swellings.

'**nubbling**. *dial.* [f. NUB *sb.*[1] or NUBBLE *sb.*] A small lump of coal.
1825 LAMB *Refl. Pillory* in *Eliana* (1867) 141 Cinders are dear, gentlemen. This nubbling might have helped the pot boil. **1847** HALLIW., *Nubblings*, small coal. *Worc.* **1876-** in dial. glossaries (Oxf., Worc., Warw.).

'**nubbling-chit**, late var. of NUBBING-CHEAT.
1836 MAHONY *Reliq. Father Prout* ix. *Songs France* 269 When he came to the nubbling chit, He was tucked up so neat and so pretty. **1841** 'BON GAULTIER' in *Tait's Edin. Mag.* VIII. 223 The faking boy to the crap has gone, At the nubbling-chit you'll find him.

nubbly ('nʌblɪ), *a.* [f. NUBBLE *sb.* + -Y[1].]
1. Having numerous small protuberances; knobby, lumpy. (See also KNUBBLY.) Also *transf.* and *fig.*
1829 HOOD in *The Gem* 181 A large order was sent for nubbly sofas and crooked chairs. **1844** —— *Mrs. Barrage* Wks. 1862 VI. 345 Her nose nubbly and red as a rosebud. **1871** L. STEPHEN *Playgr. Eur.* (1894) vii. 156 Four of us were packed between a couple of nubbly rocks. **1882** BLACKMORE *Christowell* III. iii. 49 Ungainly, nubbly fruit it was.
Comb. **1879** F. W. ROBINSON *Coward Consc.* I. iv, A stout, nubbly-faced, white-haired man.
transf. **1864** *Daily Tel.* 27 Oct., By enduring the nubbly and poignant anguish of those flint-stones. **1958** *Economist* 8 Nov. 487/1 Labour had seemed in danger of becoming obsessed with the nubbly problems of publicity. **1963** *Times Lit. Suppl.* 8 Feb. 96/5 A nubbly and idiosyncratic style.
2. Having the form of small lumps.
1845 HOOD *The Storm*, Quick, some coal, some nubbly pieces. **1864** *Guardian* 21 Dec., Bright black nubbly antimony. **1894** FENN *Real Gold* 80, I hope it's going to be my luck to get just a few nubbly bits for myself.
3. Of cloth or fabric: rough-textured. Also as *sb.*
1935 *Amer. Speech* X. 192/1 A dress of *nubby* crepe may have *nubbly* knots. **1958** J. D. MACDONALD *Executioners* (1959) v. 72 She wore a green nubbly suit. **1964** *McCall's Sewing* i. 8/1 A pebbly crêpe will not noticeably add pounds, but a very rough, nubbly wool tweed may have a decided effect. **1972** *Daily Tel.* 20 Nov. 15 Janice is shopping.. for new fabrics.. and her mood is for nubblies, for lots of texture. **1973** J. BURROWS *Like an Evening Gone* iii. 39 A jacket of the same nubbly tweed material as the victim's skirt.
So '**nubby** *a.*
1876 LEVESON GOWER *Surrey Provinc.*, *Nubby*, cloddy, of land that breaks up in clods or lumps. **1935** [see NUBBLY *a.* 3]. **1938** *Times* 19 Jan. 17/2 The nubby type jacket to the waistline is worn with vivid coloured woollen frocks. **1967** *Boston Sunday Globe* 23 Apr. 24 (Advt.), An elegant new drapery in a nubby solid and open weave design. **1974** *Union* (S. Carolina) *Daily Times* 19 Apr. 5/3 Also, when washing acrylic sweaters, socks and other wash-and-wear things turn them inside out before washing and they do not get nubby and I think they wear longer.

‖**nubecula** (nju:'bi:kjʊ:lə). Pl. **-culae**. [L. *nūbēcula* little cloud, dark spot, dim. of *nūbēs* cloud. So F. *nubécule*.]
1. *Path.* **a.** A cloudy formation in urine.
1699 WOODWARD in *Phil. Trans.* XXI. 197 Large thin Masses, appearing like Nubeculæ, or Clouds in the Water. **1744** tr. *Boerhaave's Lect. The. Physic* III. 149 The Nubeculæ or Clouds proceed chiefly from the muriatic Salt. **1857-** in MAYNE *Expos. Lex.*, and later Dicts.
b. A speck or small cloud in the eye.
1727-38 CHAMBERS *Cycl.* s.v., The nubecula seems to arise from certain gross particles detained in the pores of the cornea, or swimming in the aqueous humour. **1758** J. S. *Le Dran's Observ. Surg.* (1771) Dictionary, *Leucoma*, a Disease of the Cornea, called also Albugo, Nubecula. **1859-** in WORCESTER and some later Dicts.
2. *Astron.* One or other of the Magellanic Clouds.
1842 *Penny Cycl.* XXII. 449/2 There is no account of the celebrated Nubeculæ (major and minor), two very large patches of Milky Way not far from the south pole. **1855** H. J. S. SMITH in *Oxford Ess.* 128 We can feel no absolutely insuperable difficulty in admitting, within the globe of Nubecula Major, of the presence of distinct stars as well as nebulae.

nubelus, obs. form of NUBILOUS.

nubia ('nju:bɪə). [Irreg. f. L. *nūbēs* cloud.] A soft fleecy wrap for the head and neck, worn by women.
1881 *Confessions of a frivolous Girl*, Emerging therefrom, five minutes later, in my nubia and snowy wrap. **1885** VAN VOORST *Without a Compass* 34 The bracelet of a lady.. became entangled in the nubia of Agnes.

Nubian ('nju:bɪən), *a.* and *sb.* [ad. med.L. *Nūbiān-us*, of f. med.L. *Nūbia*, f. L. *Nūbæ*, Gr. *Νοῦβαι*, the name of the people.]
A. *adj.* **1.** Pertaining or belonging to the country of Nubia.
1727-46 THOMSON *Summer* 819 Down the Nubian rocks ..he pours his urn. **1790** BRUCE *Trav.* IV. VIII. x. 523 What figure the Nubian breed would make in point of fleetness is very doubtful. **1845** *Encycl. Metrop.* XXII. 558/1 The Nubian language.. seems to bear no affinity to the Koptic or Ancient Egyptian. **1871** P. SMITH *Anc. Hist. East* vii. §12 (1881) 125 The Nubian eye, more elongated than the Egyptian, is still seen in the *Shangallas.*
2. In the specific names of certain animals.
1879 *Encycl. Brit.* X. 709/2 The Nubian Goat, which is met with in Nubia, Upper Egypt, and Abyssinia. **1881** *Trans. Zool. Soc.* II. 235 In the male Nubian Giraffes.. the posterior horns.. were less firmly attached to the skull than they were in the full-grown Cape Giraffes. **1896** tr. *Boas' Text-Bk. Zool.* 517 The Domestic Cat.. is probably a descendant of the Nubian Wild Cat.
B. *sb.* †**1.** *pl.* An Eastern sect of Christians.
c **1400** *Three Kings Cologne* 146 þes men be noȝt holde in so grete reuerence as þe Nubyans, for þei kepe noȝt þe feith so trewlich as þei do.
2. A native of Nubia; a Nubian slave.
1788 GIBBON *Decl. & F.* xlvii. IV. 562 A wandering tribe of the Blemmyes or Nubians invaded his solitary prison. **1813** BYRON *Giaour* xv, Such is the tale his Nubians tell. **1836** *Brit. Cycl. Lit., Hist.*, etc. III. 143/1 The Nubians.. have the thick lips.. of the negro race. **1884** *Encycl. Brit.* XVII. 611/2 Ethnologically the modern Nubians are therefore to be considered as a very mixed people.
3. A Nubian horse.
1790 BRUCE *Trav.* IV. VIII. x. 523 If beautiful and symmetrical parts, great size and strength,.. can promise anything for a stallion, the Nubian is.. the most eligible in the world.
4. The language spoken by the Nubians.
1855 LATHAM in *Trans. Philol. Soc.* 91 The languages spoken on the water-system of the Nile:—Coptic, Bishari, Nubian,.. Amharic, &c.
5. A kind of black dress-material.
1899 *Daily News* 8 Apr. 9/1 Some of the moirettes and the new Nubian make good substitutes. The latter is, however, only in black.

nubiferous (nju:'bɪfərəs), *a.* [f. L. *nūbifer*, f. L. *nūbēs* cloud: see -FEROUS.] Cloud-bringing.
1656 BLOUNT *Glossogr.*, *Nubiferous*, that brings or carries clouds, cloudy. **1829** T. HOOK *Bank to Barnes* 160 The wind blowing east-by-east, which is a most nubiferous quarter. **1862** HOLMES *Old Vol. Life* (1891) 65 But let us sit awhile with nubiferous, or, if I may coin a word, nepheligenous accompaniment.

'**nubiform**, *a. rare.* [f. as prec.: see -FORM.] Having the form of a cloud; cloud-like, vague.
1874 RUSKIN *Val D'Arno* (1886) 6 The more or less spectral, hooded, imaginative, and nubiform authority of the Pope and Church.

† '**nubilate**, *ppl. a. Obs. rare*$^{-1}$. [ad. pa. pple. of L. *nūbilāre*: see next.] Clouded.
c **1510** BARCLAY *Mirr. of Gd. Manners* (1570) B v, O howe oft hath hid truth and simple veritie Lurked vnder ymage of falshood nubilate.

nubilate ('nju:bɪleɪt), *v.* [f. ppl. stem of L. *nūbilāre*, f. *nūbila* (neut. pl.), f. *nūbēs* cloud.] *trans.* To cloud; to obscure; to render less clear or transparent.
a **1691** AUBREY *Wilts.* (MS. Royal Soc.) lf. 100 (Halliw.), About the beginning of March, 1660, I bought.. a Turkey-stone ring; it was then wholly serene; toward the end of the moneth it began to be nubilated. **1730** BAILEY (folio), *To Nubilate*, to make cloudy. **1801** W. TAYLOR in *Monthly Mag.* XI. 646 Reinhard's [perspicuity], strong as it is, has been somewhat nubilated in the school of Kant.
Hence **nubi'lation**, cloudiness. *rare*$^{-1}$.
1874 COUES *Birds N.W.* 613 Various degrees of this dusky nubilation approach in some specimens nearly to the uniform dusky below characterized.

nubile ('nju:bɪl), *a.*[1] [ad. L. *nūbilis*, f. *nūbere* to marry, or a. F. *nubile* (= It. *nubile*, Sp. and Pg. *nubil*).]
1. Of females: Marriageable; of an age or condition suitable for marriage.
a **1642** EGLISHAM *Forerunner of Revenge* 12 Buckinghams Neece was not yet Nubile in yeares. **1718** PRIOR *Solomon* I. 97 The Cowslip smiles, in brighter yellow dress'd, Than that which veils the nubile Virgin's Breast. **1789** *Charact.* in *Ann. Reg.* 18 They.. feed when they become nubile on a diet somewhat like forced-meat balls. **1849-52** *Todd's Cycl. Anat.* IV. 1340/2 Hindoo women would gradually come to consist of such as by constitution are early nubile. **1879** W. L. LINDSAY *Mind in Lower Anim.* 468 Preference or choice in the selection of mates by the nubile females.
fig. **1873** BROWNING *Red Cott. Nt.-cap* III. 708 On the day when Spring's green girlishness Grew nubile and she trembled into May.
2. Of age: Admitting of, suitable for, marriage.
1831 *Blackw. Mag.* XXIX. 425 The female slaves were, at a nubile age, as numerous as the males. **1889** J. M. DUNCAN *Clin. Lect. Dis. Wom.* xxi. (ed. 4) 170 Twenty to twenty-five years is the best nubile age of women.
3. Of women: sexually attractive.
1973 *Times* 8 Mar. 3/1 Some of the slimmest and most nubile girls in London, animadverted on by the Chancellor in his Budget statement, were on parade in London yesterday beneath the chandelier and haze of perfume of Christian Dior's thrice-repeated display of spring fashion. **1973** N. MAILER in *Atlantic Monthly* Aug. 52/2 A woman so sensitive and alive, so nubile as flesh and evanescent as a wisp of vapour. **1975** *New Society* 17 July 154/2 Most women of my acquaintance.. prefer the nubile bodies and erotic accessories of the female nudes. **1975** T. HEALD *Deadline* ii. 22 Waiting by the lift doors was a nubile blonde.

† **nubilé**, *a.*[2] *Her. Obs.* [a. obs. F. *nubilé*, pa. pple. of *nubiler*.] = NEBULÉ.
1661 MORGAN *Sph. Gentry* I. v. 54 The Martlet is the Honour point, the Nubile line is the exact Fess point, the Swan the exact Midde base.

nu'bility. [f. NUBILE *a.*[1] + -ITY: cf. F. *nubilité* (1750), It. *nubilita*, Sp. *nubilidad*.] Capability for marriage. (Properly on the part of females.)
1813 W. TAYLOR in *Monthly Rev.* LXXI. 131 When the age of nubility approached. **1857** BULLOCK tr. *Cazeaux's Midwifery* 82 Its first appearance.. constitutes one of the earliest signs of puberty or nubility. **1889** D. J. MATTHEWS *Clin. Lect. Dis. Wom.* xxi. (ed. 4) 169 The old and wisest counsels as to the nubility of men and women.

nubi'lose, *a. rare*$^{-0}$. [Cf. next.] 'Full of clouds, cloudy' (Bailey, folio, 1730).

nubilous ('nju:bɪləs), *a.* Now *rare*. Also 6 *Sc.* nubilus, **-elus**. [ad. late L. *nūbilōs-us*, or f. L. *nūbilus*, f. *nūbēs* cloud. Cf. It., Sp., and Pg. *nubiloso*, F. *nubileux*.]

1. a. Cloudy, foggy, misty. **b.** = NEBULOUS 2.

1535 STEWART *Cron. Scot.* II. 526 And all the lift baith dirk and nubelus, Perturbit wes with cloudis mervelus. **1536** BELLENDEN *Cron. Scot.* (1821) I. 139 The air was nubilus and donk. **1656** BLOUNT *Glossogr.*, *Nubilous*, full of clouds, cloudy, stormy, tempestuous. **1671** R. BOHUN *Wind* 223 The radiant, sanguine, pallid, nubilous, or other Appearances of the Sun. **1739** E. CARTER tr. *Algarotti Newton's Theory* (1742) I. 164 Some nubilous Stars, on being viewed with a Telescope, appear to be a Cluster of innumerable other Stars. **1820** *Examiner* 634/1 A nubilous atmosphere. **1823** *Ibid.* 186/2 A blue and nubilous sky.

2. *fig.* Obscure, indefinite.

1533 BELLENDEN *Livy* III. xiv. (S.T.S.) I. 302 To mak þe mater..sa dirk and nubilus, þat na thing salbe sene clerelie in it quhat suld be done. **1817** T. L. PEACOCK *Melincourt* xxxi, Pointing out innumerable images of singularly nubilous beauty. **1861** *N. Brit. Rev.* Nov. 382 The mass of the people..entertained the most vague and nubilous notions with regard to the state of the soul after death.

nu'bivagant, *a. rare*$^{-0}$. [f. L. *nūbivagus*.]

1656 BLOUNT *Glossogr.*, *Nubivagant*, passing through or among clouds.

‖**nubk**. [var. of *nabk*, *nebk* NEBBUK.] A spiny, evergreen shrub or tree of the genus *Zizyphus*, esp. *Z. spina-Christi*, belonging to the family Rhamnaceæ, native to north Africa and southwestern Asia and bearing edible fruit. Cf. ILB.

1873 TRISTRAM *Moab* xviii. 347 Under a thorny nubk-tree. **1874** FARRAR *Christ* II. lx. 381 *note*, The nubk..struck me..as being the most suitable for mockery and pain, since its leaves are bright and its thorns singularly strong. **1899** *Harper's Mag.* Feb. 359 Will the nubk grow on the grounds of the Temple? **1958** L. DURRELL *Mountolive* xvi. 304 He made his way..to the great *nubk* tree standing up starkly in its clearing. **1960** —— *Clea* I. iii. 57 The 'nubk' forms the great circular palisade of trees which encircles the Moslem Paradise.

nuca, obs. form of NUCHA.

nucal ('nju:kəl), *a.* [ad. late L. *nucālis*, f. *nuc-*, *nux* nut.] Of or pertaining to a nut.

1892 in *Syd. Soc. Lex.*

'nucament. *Bot. rare.* Also 7 *erron.* **nug-**. [ad. L. *nucāmentum* (Pliny), f. *nuc-*, *nux* nut.] An amentum, a catkin.

1633 JOHNSON *Gerarde's Herbal* III. xl. 1353 Of this sort [of pitch-tree] there is found another that..remaineth dwarfish, and it carries certaine little nugaments or catkins of the bignesse of a small nut. **1657** TOMLINSON *Renou's Disp.* 230 Leaves accuminated like nucaments. **1819** *Pantologia* VIII, *Nucament*, in botany, the same with ament.

,nucamen'taceous, *a. Bot.* [See prec. and -ACEOUS.] Resembling a small nut; having the hardness of a nut; also, indehiscent.

1830 LINDLEY *Nat. Syst. Bot.* 258 Fruit capsular, valvular, seldom indehiscent, somewhat nucamentaceous. **1845** —— *Sch. Bot.* vi. (1858) 107 Fruit nucamentaceous, composed of two or four nucules in a state of adhesion.

So **nuca'mentous** *a.* (Smart, 1840.)

†**nuce**, obs. variant of NOOSE *sb.* 1.

1688 HOLME *Armoury* III. 107/2 A particular Nuce of Pack-thrid. *Ibid.* xv. (Roxb.) 30/1 The nuce or eye of the cabell which holds the anchor is called the clinch.

nucellar (nju:'sɛlə(r)), *a. Bot.* [f. NUCELL(US + -AR[1].] Of, pertaining to, or involving the nucellus; derived from or produced in the nucellus.

1904 *Jrnl. R. Microsc. Soc.* 665 Two series of vascular bundles run in the ovule, and it is proved that the inner series, frequently described as 'nucellar', belong to the soft inner layer of the integument. **1949** DARLINGTON & MATHER *Elem. Genetics* 406 *Nucellar embryony*, a form of apomixis where the embryo arises directly from the nucellus. **1953** K. ESAU *Plant Anat.* xviii. 555 The nucellar epidermis is sometimes highly resistant and may proliferate into a nucellar cap with relatively thick walls. **1972** *Theoret. & Appl. Genetics* XLII. 314 (*heading*) Differentiation between nucellar and zygotic citrus seedlings by leaf shape.

‖**nucellus** (nju:'sɛləs). *Bot.* [mod.L., app. intended as a dim. of *nucleus*.] The essential part of an ovule, containing the embryo-sac.

1882 VINES tr. *Sachs' Bot.* 487 That part of the ovule in which the embryo-sac arises (the nucellus) must be considered the equivalent of the macrosporangium. **1887** BENTLEY *Man. Bot.* (ed. 5) 329, Fig. 738 Ovule of the Mistletoe..consisting of a naked nucellus.

'nuceous, *a. rare*$^{-0}$. [ad. L. *nuceus*, f. *nuc-*, *nux* nut.] 'Of or pertaining to a nut.'

1656 BLOUNT *Glossogr.* (Hence in later Dicts.)

‖**nucha** ('nju:kə). *Anat.* Also 5 **nuca**. [a. med.L. *nucha*, a. Arab. *nukhāʿ* spinal marrow. Hence also It., Sp., and Pg. *nuca*, F. *nuque* NUQUE: see also NUCHE, NUKE *sb.*[1]] †**a.** The spinal cord. *Obs.* **b.** The nape of the neck.

c **1400** *Lanfranc's Cirurg.* 24 Alle þe cordis þat comen of þe brayn & nucha [*v.r.* nuca]. *Ibid.* 29 þe senewe þat comeþ fro þe brayn & þe nucha [*v.r.* nuca]. **1576** NEWTON *Lemnie's Complex.* (1633) 194 They doe very well, which keepe their Nucha and nape of their neckes warme. **1661** LOVELL *Anim. & Min.* 50 The decoction of a Fox.., used as an embrocation to the nucha and paralytick part, helpeth the same. **1726** FREIND *Hist. Physick* II. 315 Those from the 6th and 7th pair, which arise from the brain and the *Nucha*, serve for its voluntary motion. **1768** PENNANT *Brit. Zool.* (1776) I. 139 Nucha, the hind part of the head. **1878** HAMILTON *Nerv. Dis.* 211 Rollet has used the cautery even in the last stages, applying it from the nucha to the sacrum, and with good effect.

nuchal ('nju:kəl), *a. Anat.* [f. prec. + -AL[1]. Cf. F., Sp., and Pg. *nucal*.] Of, belonging or pertaining to, the nucha or nape of the neck.

1835 KIRBY *Hab. & Inst. Anim.* I. x. 303 The wheel-animals in which Ehrenberg detected..a nuchal nervous collar. **1855** OWEN *Skel. & Teeth* 31 The nuchal ligament in the mole. **1888** ROLLESTON & JACKSON *Anim. Life* 468 The structure of the eyes on the nuchal tentacles.

†**nuche**. *Obs. rare.* Also 7 **nouch**. [a. obs. F. *nuche*, or ad. med.L. *nucha*.] = NUCHA.

1528 PAYNELL *Salerne's Regim.* B ij, The membres of flematike complexion, as the brayne and nuche. **1541** COPLAND *Guydon's Quest.* E ij, Demaunde. Is yᵉ nuche any party of yᵉ brayne? Answere. It semeth to be a party therof. **1601** HOLLAND *Pliny* II. 395 A liniment made of earth-wormes, if the nouch or chine of the necke and the shoulder blades bee annointed therewith [etc.].

nuche, obs. form of OUCH, clasp.

nuchthe'merinal, *a. rare*$^{-1}$. [f. Gr. νυχθημέρινος: see NYCHTHEMER(ON.] Lasting a night and a day; completed in twenty-four hours.

1677 R. CARY *Palæol. Chron.* I. i. 2 They came to hit upon the number of 360 Days in the first place, concluding..that in so many Nuchthemerinal Revolutions, the Sun came to the same τροπή,..where he was the Year before.

nuci- ('nju:sɪ), combining form of L. *nux*, *nucis*, nut, as in **nu'ciferous** *a.*, bearing nuts. **'nuciform** *a.* [= F. and Sp. *nuciforme*], nut-shaped. **'nucifrage**, the Nutcracker (*Cent. Dict.* 1890). **nu'cifragous** *a.*, given to cracking nuts (*ibid.*). †**'nuciprune**, a fruit having the character of nut and plum; hence †**nucipru'niferous** *a.*, bearing fruit of this kind. **nuci'tannic** *a.*, in *n. acid*, = **nuci'tannin** (see quot.). **nu'civorous** *a.* [= F. *nucivore*, Sp. *nucivoro*], nut-eating.

1668 WILKINS *Real Char.* II. 116 *Nuciferous trees, may be distinguished into such as are Europæan; conteining in one common husk One Nut [etc.]. **1688** HOLME *Armoury* II. 119/1 Nuciferous Trees..bear Fruit in hard husks. **1755** *Gentl. Mag.* XXV. 450 It is different from ours, being of the nuciferous kind. **1857** ASA GRAY *First Less. Bot.* (1866) 223 **Nuciform*, nut-shaped or nut-like. [Hence in **1864** WEBSTER and later Dicts.] **1677** GREW *Anat. Fruits* iii. §8. 185 A Walnut, is a *Nuciprune; or betwixt a Plum and a Nut. **1693** *Phil. Trans.* XVII. 621 That *Nucipruniferous, which in Barbados they call the Mastick-Tree. **1892** *Syd. Soc. Lex.*, **Nucitannic*, relating to a nut and to tannin. **1894** FOSTER *Med. Dict.*, *Nucitannic Acid*, a glucoside occurring in the episperm of walnuts. **1892** *Syd. Soc. Lex.*, **Nucitannin*, a peculiar form of tannin found by Phipson, along with gallic and ellagic acids, in the outer layer of the episperm of the walnut. **1835** KIRBY *Hab. & Inst. Anim.* II. xxiv. 514 The great majority [of Mammalians] are said to be granivorous, or *nucivorous, or even graminivorous.

nucin ('nju:sɪn). *Chem.* [f. L. *nuc-*, *nux* nut + -IN.] A crystalline substance obtained from green walnut-shells.

1885 in CASSELL. **1892** THORPE *Dict. Appl. Chem.* III. 100 Juglone.., Nucin, Regianin.

nuck. *rare*$^{-1}$. (See quot.)

1663 BAXTER *Div. Life* 83 The wants in the wheels of your watch are as useful to the motion as the nucks or solid parts.

nuck, var. KNUCK.

nuckelt, nuckle, variants of NEWCAL(D.

nuckle, obs. variant of KNUCKLE.

nuckler, variant of KNUCKLER, pickpocket.

1801 COL. HANGER *Life* I. 181 *note*, An adept in the art of frisking a ken, trapping a scamp, or hobbling a nuckler.

nucleal ('nju:klɪəl), *a.* [f. NUCLE-US + -AL[1]: cf. F. *nucléal*, Pg. *nucleal*.] Pertaining to, having the form or position of, a nucleus.

1840 in SMART. **1863** DANA *Man. Geol.* Introd. 1 The crystal..begins in a nucleal molecule. **1876** CHASE in *Philos. Mag.* I. 316 The upper nebular or vector radii vary as the $\frac{3}{2}$ powers of the orbital times; the lower nebular or nucleal radii, as the $\frac{1}{2}$ powers of the times. *Ibid.* 318 In the earliest stages of nucleal aggregation.

nucleant ('nju:klɪənt), *a.* and *sb.* [f. NUCLE(US *sb.* + -ANT[1].] **A.** *adj.* Forming a nucleus. *rare*$^{-1}$.

1953 S. BECKETT *Watt* 142 In his own vitals, nucleant, he knew them clasped.

B. *sb.* A particle that initiates nucleation; = NUCLEUS *sb.* 9.

1968 *Jrnl. Appl. Meteorol.* VII. 858/1 The relatively high base temperatures of the convective clouds makes [*sic*] it rather unlikely that their precipitation can be increased by the injection of ice nucleants. **1969** G. F. BOLLING in *Solidification* (Amer. Soc. Metals) (1971) xi. 364 The effective nucleants seem to be those active in the melt, in the sense of having been freshly formed in the melt.

nuclear ('nju:klɪə(r)), *a.* and *sb.* [f. NUCLE-US + -AR: cf. F. *nucléaire*, Pg. *nuclear*.]

A. *adj.*

1. a. Having the character or position of a nucleus; like a nucleus; constituting or forming a nucleus. Chiefly in *Biol.* and *Astron.*

(*a*) **1846** *Dubl. Q. Jrnl. Med. Sci.* II. 93 In place of a molecule of bone restored for one removed, we find cytoblasts, a nucleolated nuclear cell. **1861** H. MACMILLAN *Footn. fr. Nature* 31 Cells, containing granular matter arranged around a bright red nuclear body. **1888** ROLLESTON & JACKSON *Anim. Life* Introd. p. xxii, The nuclear membrane is dissolved in mitosis.

(*b*) **1851** NICHOL *Archit. Heav.* (ed. 9) 106 Who has well defined it generally as a nuclear centre. **1877** STARK in G. F. Chambers *Astron.* 57 There appeared a black, well-defined nuclear spot,..as large as Mercury. **1881** PROCTOR *Poet. Astron.* i. 40 Inferring that the nuclear parts of the sun are exceedingly dense.

(*c*) **1865** MANSFIELD *Salts* 120 The hydrocarbon is conjugated to the Oxygen of the nuclear or prostylobasic water. **1891** *Edin. Rev.* Oct. 336 A shaft was, at some remote epoch, sunk downward towards the expected nuclear hoard.

b. ***nuclear cataract***: (see quot.).

1878 T. BRYANT *Pract. Surg.* I. 365 Nuclear cataract..is characterised by the presence of a hard yellowish central portion or nucleus of varying size and density.

c. Central, cardinal; *spec.* in *Linguistics* and *Phonetics*, being or constituting a linguistic or phonetic nucleus.

1912 *Housemaster's Lett.* 91 You will forgive me if I tell you what I consider the nuclear fault underlying all this writing. **1940** H. G. WELLS *All Aboard for Ararat* ii. 82, I must look round to find those nuclear men who are needed to carry through the next revolution.

1941 *Language* XVII. 224 In the structure of the syllable vowels are nuclear, consonants marginal. **1949** E. A. NIDA *Morphol.* (ed. 2) 84 A nuclear structure consists of or contains the nucleus... In the word *formal* the nuclear element is *form-* and the peripheral element *-al*. *Ibid.* 118 There are a number of morphological classes represented by the nuclear immediate constituent. **1952** A. COHEN *Phonemes of English* 39 In general, independent nuclear words are first examined, i.e. words which do not carry morphological characteristics in the shape of phonemes and which do not show 'outer sandhi' (= external open juncture). **1962** A. C. GIMSON *Introd. Pronunc. Eng.* x. 245 In the sense that the nuclear syllable stands out from amongst its neighbours (both accented and unaccented syllables), the nucleus and its situation may be said to have a special contrastive function. **1966** G. N. LEECH *Eng. in Advertising* v. 48 The italicised portion represents a nuclear syllable. **1971** *Language* XLVII. 586 Linguists have long also recognized the existence of stress originating from phrasal structure: Chomsky and Halle call this the Nuclear Stress Rule. **1973** *Archivum Linguisticum* IV. 25 The different varieties of the same nuclear tone.

d. *Psychoanalysis.* Central to the development of the sexual components of the ego; pertaining to or being the emotional nucleus of a neurosis, esp. the Oedipus complex.

[**1913** C. G. JUNG in *17th Internat. Congr. Med.* XII. 67 The unconscious existence of manifold phantasies, which have their final root in the infantile past and turn around the so-called 'Kern-complex', or nucleus-complex, which may be qualified in male individuals as the Œdipus-complex and in females as the Electra-complex.] **1916** B. M. HINKLE tr. *Jung's Psychol. of Unconscious* II. iv. 195 Taken at the roots in the case of our patients, the 'nuclear complex' (Freud) reveals itself as the incest problem. **1925** A. & J. STRACHEY tr. *Freud's Case of Obsessional Neurosis* in *Coll. Papers* III. 345 The formation of that complex which deserves to be called the nuclear complex of the neuroses. It is the complex which comprises the child's earliest impulses, alike tender and hostile, towards its parents and brothers and sisters, after its curiosity has been awakened. **1939** E. GLOVER *Psycho-analysis* x. 74 Findings of this order give rise to the tenet that the Oedipus complex is the nuclear complex of the neurosis. **1968** —— *Birth of Ego* i. 11 My views on the theoretical concept of the ego, and in particular on the 'nuclear theory' of its development. *Ibid.* 17 If one were prepared not to stick too slavishly to the idea of a *fixed* nuclear system one could put the psychic situation of the Oedipus complex in clearer perspective.

e. ***nuclear family*** (Sociology): a term for the basic family unit or group, consisting normally of father, mother, and offspring.

1949 G. P. MURDOCK *Social Structure* i. 1 The first and most basic, called herewith the nuclear family, consists typically of a married man and woman with their offspring. **1963** A. HERON *Towards Quaker View of Sex* 56 This taboo is of social origin, designed to protect the basic unit of society—the 'nuclear' family—from disintegration. **1966** D. JENKINS *Educated Society* iii. 98 The extended, as distinct from the nuclear, family. **1971** *Guardian* 24 Mar. 11/6 If they get rid of the nuclear family there won't be grannies any more than there will be widows. **1973** *Times Lit. Suppl.* 29 June 736/1 This is a loose network of ordinary nuclear families.

2. Of or belonging to a nucleus or nuclei, esp. atomic nuclei; also, with or by (atomic) nuclei.

1880 PROCTOR *Rough Ways* 94 One of the first and most obvious effects of this more rapid nuclear contraction would be [etc.]. **1882** VINES tr. *Sachs' Bot.* 582 They [the synergidæ] are the product of a nuclear division and cell-formation. **1899** *Allbutt's Syst. Med.* VI. 811 Nuclear palsy is characterised by bilateral..atrophy of the tongue. *Ibid.* VII. 237 The diagnosis of acute nuclear from acute infra-nuclear lesions. **1914** *Engineering* 20 Nov. 607/2 A point raised by Professor Rutherford concerning the effective nuclear charge. 1920 L. Doncaster *Introd. Study Cytol.* ii. 17 It is from the chromatin that the bodies called chromosomes, which play a great part in nuclear division, are formed. 1929 *Physical Rev.* XXXIV. 1501 The new quantum number is associated with the nucleus intrinsically in the same way that *s* is associated with the electron, and because of its similar properties might be interpreted as a nuclear spin moment. 1933 *Discovery* Apr. 106/2 With this generator, it is hoped to produce currents of the order of 1 milliampere at 5 to 10 million volts, and to insert a large vacuum tube between the sphere and ground for nuclear bombardment. 1934 *Proc. Nat. Acad. Sci.* XX. 470 When certain substances are bombarded with deutons, many and varied nuclear reactions take place. 1935 *Discovery* May 150/1 The interpretation of atomic, molecular, and nuclear radiation. 1936 [see cyclotron]. 1945 H. D. Smyth *Gen. Acct. Devel. Atomic Energy Mil. Purposes* vi. 59 The pile was first operated..on December 2, 1942... This was the first time that human beings ever initiated a self-maintaining nuclear chain reaction. 1958 *Times Rev. Industry* Aug. 7/1 An article..on the nuclear bombardment of reactor metals ..is evidence of the valuable work now being done. 1961 G. R. Choppin *Exper. Nuclear Chem.* i. 4 Nuclear transformations are on the order of 10^5 to 10^6 more energetic than chemical reactions on an individual molecular or atomic basis. *Ibid.* iii. 27 Nuclear scattering is a more important factor for electrons that it is for heavy particles. 1963 *Oxf. Univ. Gaz.* 9 May 1183/2 The University has established a Professorship of Nuclear Structure in the Department of Nuclear Physics. 1966 C. R. Tottle *Sci. Engin. Materials* x. 235 The term nuclear cross-section is used to define the effective area that the target nucleus presents to the neutron as it moves through the lattice, on a statistical or probability basis. 1969 *Times* 20 Feb. 17/5 A single type of nuclear reaction in the sun is thought to bathe each square centimetre of the earth's surface with a flux of 10 million neutrinos every second. 1970 Ambrose & Easty *Cell Biol.* v. 161 During cell division in both plant and animal cells the nuclear membrane disappears.

b. ***nuclear energy*** or ***power***: = *atomic energy* (atomic *a.* and *sb.* A. 2 d). So ***nuclear-powered*** adj.

In quot. 1930, merely 'energy possessed by a nucleus'. [1926 D. H. Lawrence *Plumed Serpent* vii. 130 She was attracted, almost fascinated by the strange *nuclear* power of the men in the circle.] 1930 *Nature* 20 Dec. 953/2 When a nucleus passes from an excited state into a state of lower energy, two different processes may occur: either a γ-quantum is emitted or one of the extra-nuclear electrons [is] thrown out of the atom..; in this case we speak of internal conversion of nuclear energy. 1941 in M. Gowing *Britain & Atomic Energy* (1964) 431 The results..indicate that it should be possible to develop a nuclear energy machine on these lines. 1945 H. D. Smyth *Gen. Acct. Devel. Atomic Energy Mil. Purposes* xiii. 135 The possible uses of nuclear energy are not all destructive. *Ibid.*, There is no immediate prospect of running cars with nuclear power. 1945 [see sense 3 b]. 1948 *Time* 5 July 44/1 Since atomic fuel would have over two million times as much energy as gasoline, a 'nuclear-powered' plane could fly on and on. 1951 *Jane's Fighting Ships 1951–52* 6 The contract for the first nuclear-powered submarine has been awarded to the Electric Boat Co. 1958 *Daily Express* 11 Mar. 7/1 He was speaking on the hazards which arrive from the peaceful use of nuclear energy. 1962 H. D. Bush *Atomic & Nucl. Physics* vii. 137 For an isotope to be considered as a source of nuclear power, not only must fission be induced by neutrons of moderate energies but also the cross section must be reasonably high. 1970 *Daily Tel.* 30 June 4/8 A nuclear-powered cardiac pacemaker has been placed in an unidentified female patient in the second such operation in France.

c. Applied to research and fields of study concerned with the atomic nucleus (as ***nuclear chemistry, physics***) and to specialists in those fields (as ***nuclear physicist***).

1933 *Discovery* Jan. 31/2 Lord Rutherford of Nelson, to whom so much of what is best in modern nuclear physics is due. 1934 *Times* 12 Dec. 19/3 The new field of nuclear chemistry was opening up with great rapidity. 1935 *Discovery* Oct. 291/1 The nuclear chemist, Professor Aston prophesied, 'will transmute and synthesise atoms as his elder brother had done molecules'. 1936 N. Feather *Introd. Nucl. Physics* i. 2 The astronomer and modern physicist.. discard inconvenient powers of ten for ease in forming mental pictures... But they invite danger whenever they forget what they have discarded. To such danger the nuclear physicist is particularly liable. 1945 H. D. Smyth *Gen. Acct. Devel. Atomic Energy Mil. Purposes* 247 The first man-made atomic explosion, the outstanding achievement of nuclear science, was achieved at 5:30 a.m. of that day. 1947 *Sci. News* V. 158 The most recent development of all is the production of new elements and isotopes by bombardment of elements with neutrons or other particles, but this so-called nuclear chemistry..is really a branch of physics. 1948 *Nucleonics* June 2 Nuclear engineering, concerned with the design, construction, and operation of nuclear fission reactors. 1956 A. H. Compton *Atomic Quest* 5 The use of the cyclotron was of epochal importance in nuclear physics. *Ibid.* 7 Nuclear research as a subject for wartime study. 1956 *N.Y. Times* 23 July 6/5 The coming years will bring to mankind limitless ways in which this new nuclear science can advance human welfare. 1964 M. Gowing *Britain & Atomic Energy* i. 33 The sobriety of the notes and articles concealed an intense excitement amongst the nuclear scientists. *Ibid.* x. 282 Ideas whose problems were to preoccupy the nuclear engineers for many years to come. 1969 *Times* 25 Jan. 17/5 Gamma rays are a familiar form of radiation to nuclear physicists. 1970 *New Scientist* 29 Oct. 230/1 About five years ago, the University of London decided to set up the first and still the only department in the United Kingdom awarding a first degree in nuclear engineering. 1973 'D. Halliday' *Dolly & Starry Bird* xviii. 278 He had offered to help track down some rather worrying leaks from our brave nuclear physicist boys.

3. Pertaining to or employing nuclear energy. (In senses a and b opp. conventional *a.* 4 c.)

a. Employing nuclear energy as a source of propulsive power or electricity.

1945 *Engineering Jrnl.* XXVIII. 757/1 A large stationary power installation might be used for heat and motive power in the Arctic or Antarctic regions..where the difficulty of transporting other fuels..outweigh[s] the disadvantages and difficulties of operating and maintaining a nuclear power plant. 1955 *Tribune* 22 Apr. 4/2 Nuclear power stations are designed to be safe. 1956 *Jrnl. Brit. Interplanetary Soc.* XV. 235 The range between the energy concentrations of the typical chemical combustion rockets with moderate exhaust velocities and those of not yet realized true nuclear rockets. 1957 *Newsweek* 12 Aug. 65/2 Nuclear-power plants capable of driving jets, rockets, or even space ships tremendous distances are being developed. 1957 *Jane's Fighting Ships 1957–58* 7 Advances in nuclear propulsion enable submarines to remain submerged indefinitely. *Ibid.* 50 It was officially stated in the 1957–58 Navy estimates that progress is being made with the design of the nuclear submarine 'Dreadnought'. 1959 *Daily Tel.* 24 Feb. 11/8 The day has not yet arrived when nuclear ships can prove commercially much more attractive to ship owners than ships using conventional fuel. 1960 *Aeroplane* XCVIII. 772/2 During its development the first nuclear aircraft will inevitably have alternative chemical propulsion. 1961 *Daily Tel.* 4 Oct. 21/5 The United States plans to start flight test of nuclear rocket engines by 1967. 1968 *New Scientist* 18 Jan. 147/2 There are still no plans for a British nuclear ship, and now the Japanese are coming into the field. 1968 *Brit. Med. Bull.* XXIV. 260/2 It offers the possibility of biological monitoring of workers such as nuclear-power-station employees who are exposed to unusual environmental hazards. 1974 L. Deighton *Spy Story* xii. 118 He pointed down at the War Table... Ferdy had wiped out nuclear subs.

b. Of a weapon: deriving its destructive power from the rapid, uncontrolled release of nuclear energy.

1945 *Engineering Jrnl.* XXVIII. 752/1 In view of the source of the energy, the current terms 'atomic bomb' and 'atomic power' might well be replaced by the more exact terms 'nuclear bomb' and 'nuclear power'. 1948 *Nuclear Science Abstracts* 30 Sept. 265 Fourth, nuclear weapons have not reached their maximum size in the present type bomb. 1954 *Commonweal* 1 Oct. 621/2 It has been suggested that the nuclear warhead may be small enough to be fitted to an air-to-ground rocket. *Ibid.* 10 Dec. 279/2 The vocabulary of the nuclear age began to grow:..'nuclear device' vs. a deliverable weapon; [etc.]. 1955 [see deterrent *sb.*]. 1956 *Time* 25 June 34/3 Hopping off on his inspection of nuclear-weapons testing grounds at Eniwetok and Bikini. 1956 *Newsweek* 3 Sept. 17/2 A nuclear device can mean either hydrogen or atomic. 1957 *Observer* 28 July 6/4 To keep the British nuclear deterrent up to date on its present scale in relation to the Soviet defence will cost more and more each year. 1958 *Times Lit. Suppl.* 15 Aug. p. xxxviii/3 After all, scientists put their skill in making nuclear bombs at the service of those who believe in things; so why cannot artists act correspondingly? 1958 in *Ann. Reg. 1958* (1959) 519 The United States Government shall provide nuclear war-heads for the missiles transferred to the United Kingdom Government. 1965 H. Kahn *On Escalation* vi. 101 The U.S. should be willing to adopt the concept that the only purpose of nuclear weapons is to negate nuclear weapons... It should not try to get any 'positive' benefits from its nuclear weaponry. 1973 C. Bonington *Next Horizon* xxi. 283 The argument seemed settled, but then Don came on the air with the effect of a small nuclear weapon.

c. Of, pertaining to, possessing, or employing nuclear weapons; ***nuclear club***, the nations that possess nuclear weapons; ***to go nuclear***, to acquire nuclear weapons.

1954 *Commonweal* 30 Apr. 83 (*heading*) Nuclear war: a false dilemma. 1954 *Newsweek* 8 Nov. 30/1 Talk and thought in government circle about nuclear weapons still seems to be geared largely to the period during which we alone had the capacity to wage nuclear warfare. 1956 *Foreign Policy Bull.* 1 Jan. 59 (*heading*) Nuclear tests: psychological defeat for West. 1957 *Observer* 28 July 6/3 It does not take a very elaborate calculation to realise that our contribution to the strategic Anglo-American nuclear striking force must be very small. 1957 *Christian Science Monitor* 15 Aug. 1 *Nuclear club*, those nations which possess nuclear weapons. The only current members are the United States, Britain, and the Soviet Union. 1958 *Ann. Reg. 1957* 166 The risk of leaving no alternative save nuclear retaliation in the event of war. *Ibid.* 347 The resolution urged that the United Nations and the 'nuclear' Powers should immediately suspend all such tests. 1958 *New Statesman* 22 Feb. 218/1 The response to last Monday's inaugural meetings of the Campaign for Nuclear Disarmament suggests that it is becoming a focus for a real movement of opinion on this issue. 1958 *Economist* 22 Mar. 1006/1 The starting point of most current speeches made by the nuclear disarmers is that a hydrogen-bomb war would be an unspeakably terrible thing. 1958 *Spectator* 15 Aug. 211/2 It seems impossible to convince them that a nuclear war, should it come, will not be like that. 1959 *Daily Tel.* 27 Feb. 10 There was real anxiety lest what we should need for non-nuclear wars had been excessively cut down in favour of what is needed to deal with nuclear threats. *Ibid.* 23 Mar. 18 The rate of descent from the stratosphere of radio-active debris, including strontium 90, from nuclear explosions. 1960 *Spectator* 26 Aug. 303 The American nuclear umbrella is a myth. 1963 *Daily Tel.* 1 Feb. 22/2 The Soviet Union might threaten us with nuclear attack. *Ibid.*, A sort of last-ditch argument now being used by Conservatives under the heading of 'nuclear blackmail'. 1964 *Ann. Reg. 1963* 133 The nuclear test ban treaty.. symbolized their mutual determination to secure an abatement of the arms race. *Ibid.* 138 The treaty..did at least symbolize a new and welcome flexibility of outlook on the part of the leading nuclear Powers. 1964 M. Gowing *Britain & Atomic Energy* xiii. 346 Sir John Anderson's forebodings about a nuclear arms race between competing power blocs were not the result of his concern over the specific problem of the French. 1964 J. H. Rothschild *Tomorrow's Weapons* iii. 24 Nuclear warfare would include atomic (fission) bombs, shells, and mines, and hydrogen (fusion) bombs and missile warheads. 1965 H. Kahn *On Escalation* vi. 94 Alain Enthoven has described the nuclear threshold as follows: 'In efforts to limit violence, there is.. a recognizable, qualitative distinction that both combatants can recognize and agree upon if they want to.' *Ibid.* 98 As Soviet nuclear capability has grown, the Soviets have.. become less aggressive. *Ibid.* 297 A nuclear stalemate.. exists when the balance of central war forces is such that neither side is capable of making a disarming first strike. 1967 *Listener* 11 May 607/2 The decision of certain powers to go nuclear would have the effect of making endemic regional conflicts totally insoluble. 1970 [see go *v.* B. 44 a]. 1973 *Times* 22 Feb. 16/4 He was attacking the nuclear disarmers or some such, who had for a time been predicting that we would all be blown up or poisoned by the Bomb. *Ibid.* 9 Nov. 20/1 The nuclear umbrella is now demonstrably in shreds. 1974 *Sci. Amer.* July 46/1 India became the sixth member of the nuclear club on May 18 by carrying out what it called a 'peaceful nuclear explosion experiment using an implosion device'.

d. = atomic *a.* 2 f.

1954 *Commonweal* 10 Dec. 279/2 With that tragic event the facts of the nuclear age were spread out for all to see. 1960 Koestler *Lotus & Robot* 11 The first generation of the Nuclear Age seems to have found a like solace in Zen.

4. Special collocations: **nuclear atom**, (*a*) the concept of the atom as having the charges of one sign surrounding those of the opposite sign, which are regarded as concentrated in a much smaller central volume; (*b*) an elementary constituent of an atomic nucleus (*nonce-use*); **nuclear battery**, an electric battery that utilizes the separation of positive and negative charges accompanying radioactivity; **nuclear emulsion**, a fine-grained photographic emulsion specially designed for recording the tracks of sub-atomic particles in it; **nuclear force**, a force that acts between nucleons; now *spec.* the strong interaction; **nuclear fuel** = fuel *sb.* 3 d; so ***nuclear-fuelled*** adj.; **nuclear isomer** (see isomer 2); **nuclear magnetic resonance**, magnetic resonance (see resonance) exhibited by atomic nuclei; **nuclear magneton** (see magneton); **nuclear medicine**, the branch of medicine concerned with the use of radioactive substances in research, diagnosis, and treatment; **nuclear pile** = *nuclear reactor* (see also pile *sb.*[3]); **nuclear reactor**, an apparatus or structure in which fissile material can be made to undergo a controlled, self-sustaining nuclear reaction with the consequent release of energy; **nuclear sap** *Biol.* (see sap *sb.*[1]); **nuclear waste**, radioactive waste material from the reprocessing of spent nuclear fuel; **nuclear winter**, a period of extreme cold and devastation that has been conjectured to follow a nuclear war, caused by an atmospheric layer of smoke and dust particles shutting out the sun's rays. Also nuclear fission, nuclear fusion.

1922 A. D. Udden tr. *Bohr's Theory of Spectra* iii. i. 61 The conception of atomic structure which will form the basis of all the following remarks is the so-called *nuclear atom according to which an atom is assumed to consist of a nucleus surrounded by a number of electrons whose distances from one another and from the nucleus are very large compared to the dimensions of the particles themselves. 1936 *Discovery* Jan. 31/1 The quantum mechanical theory of the nuclear atom. 1938 Nuclear atom [see alpha 3 e]. 1961 Powell & Crasemann *Quantum Mech.* i. 14 A nuclear atom had already been considered mathematically by Nagaoka in 1904, but it was Rutherford's analysis that established this concept as an experimental fact. 1970 G. K. Woodgate *Elem. Atomic Struct.* i. 1 Bohr's theory of hydrogen, based on Rutherford's nuclear atom and incorporating the ideas of Planck, was the famous starting point for atomic structure. 1955 *Jrnl. Brit. Interplanetary Soc.* XIV. 85 The *nuclear battery, thermo-couples, photo-electric effects, etc., present further possibilities. 1962 Simpson & Richards *Physical Princ. Junction Transistors* iv. 74 'Nuclear batteries' in which the radiation consists of fast electrons from a β-emitter have also been built. 1949 H. Yagoda *Radioactive Measurements with Nucl. Emulsions* i. 6 These emulsions, intended for the registration of alpha-particle, proton, and fission-fragment tracks, are conveniently referred to as *Nuclear Emulsions. 1958 K. M. Hornsby tr. *Glafkides' Photogr. Chem.* I. xxiii. 409 Nuclear emulsions..have a very high concentration of silver bromide (80%), fine grain (0·1 to 0·5 μ), and are coated in very thick layers. 1966 *McGraw-Hill Encycl. Sci. & Technol.* IX. 584/2 Nuclear emulsion plates are important particle detectors for research in high-energy nuclear physics. 1935 *Sci. Abstr.* A. XXXIII. 2 (*heading*) Constitution of elementary particles and *nuclear forces. 1955 Friedman & Weisskopf in W. Pauli *Niels Bohr* 144 Our present difficulties in understanding the saturation of nuclear forces on the basis of the free nucleon-nucleon interaction speak in favour of some change in the internucleon potential when the nucleons are closely packed. 1972 *Sci. Amer.* Oct. 100/2 Although the nuclear force acts between all nucleons, whether they are protons or neutrons, it must overcome the disruptive influence of the electrical repulsion between the positive charges of the protons in the nucleus. 1946 *Scientific & Techn. Aspects of Control of Atomic Energy* (U.N. Dept. Public Information) i. 8 The *nuclear fuel provided by nature is uranium-235. 1948 Nuclear fuel [see fuel *sb.* 3 d]. 1970 *Daily Tel.* 4 Nov. 5 Russia is prepared to supply West Germany with enriched uranium as nuclear fuel for peaceful purposes. 1968 *Times* 18 Oct. 16/7 The element [*sc.* gadolinium] can be used in the design of *nuclear-fuelled batteries. 1942 *Physica* IX. 591 (*heading*) Negative result of an attempt to observe *nuclear magnetic resonance in solids. 1970 G. K. Woodgate *Elem. Atomic Struct.* ix. 174 Some of the most accurate values of nuclear moments have been obtained directly by nuclear magnetic resonance. **1952** (*periodical title*) The American journal of roentgenology, radium therapy and *nuclear medicine. **1975** *Univ. of London Bull.* Feb. 5/2 This University stands alone in the United Kingdom in having supported since 1961, in one of its medical schools, an academic department devoted solely to nuclear medicine. **1955** *Gloss. Terms Radiology* (*B.S.I.*) 17 *Nuclear pile. **1962** F. I. ORDWAY et al. *Basic Astronautics* xii. 497 The effects in general would be the same as those experienced by victims of an atomic bomb blast or an accident in a nuclear pile. **1964** M. GOWING *Britain & Atomic Energy* x. 284 Now the doctors..also appreciated the great usefulness of nuclear piles for medical and biological purposes. **1945** *Sci. Amer.* Nov. 285/3 The radiation emitted by present *nuclear reactors requires..heavy shielding. **1948** *Electronic Engin.* XX. 148 An atomic pile, or nuclear reactor, consists usually of an assembly of uranium metal in a pile of graphite. **1955** *Times* 16 July 6/4 The first atomic stations of the Central Electricity Authority will have two nuclear reactors each, together providing a net output of electricity of 100 to 200 megawatts. **1966** J. BETJEMAN *High & Low* 31 No nuclear reactors Bulge hideous on the downs. **1974** *Euro Spectra* Mar. 23/1 Problems connected with the widespread construction of nuclear power plants..in particular, the problems attendant upon the inevitable production of '*nuclear waste' which must be stored in safety for periods of hundreds or thousands of years. **1976** *Glasgow Herald* 26 Nov. 1/1 Environment secretary Peter Shore has delayed planning permission for the controversial £600m nuclear waste reprocessing facility at Windscale. **1986** *N.Y. Times Mag.* 11 May 24/2 Most high-level nuclear waste from the military is in liquid form. **1983** C. SAGAN in *Washington Post Parade* 30 Oct. 7/3 We considered a war in which a mere 100 megatons were exploded, less than one per-cent of the world arsenals, and only in low-yield airbursts over cities. This scenario, we found, would ignite thousands of fires, and the smoke from these fires alone would be enough to generate an epoch of cold and dark almost as severe as in the 5000-megaton case. The threshold for what Richard Turco has called The *Nuclear Winter is very low. **1983** R. P. TURCO et al. in *Science* 23 Dec. 1283 (*heading*) Nuclear winter: global consequences of multiple nuclear explosions. **1984** *Listener* 27 Sept. 5/1 Scientists have discussed the nuclear winter and published their results in the open scientific literature. *Ibid.* 5/2 The possibility of a nuclear winter was discovered almost by accident. **1986** *Times* 20 May 14/1 Downwind from Chernobyl, the first faint chill of a nuclear winter has caused..shivers of anxiety.

B. *ellipt.* as *sb.*

a. *Phonetics.* A nuclear word, sound, etc. Cf. NUCLEUS *sb.* 12.

1949 E. A. NIDA *Morphol.* (ed. 2) 84 There are single-morpheme nuclears, e.g. count, poet.., and multiple-morpheme nuclears, e.g. waiter, hunter.

b. A nuclear weapon. Also *Comb.*, as ***nuclear-armed, -free, -tipped***, adjs.

1957 *Time* 15 Apr. 29/1 The British decision to convert almost completely to nuclear-armed missles had deep meaning for all of the world. **1958** *New Statesman* 5 Apr. 423/1 The SPD are demanding in effect no nuclear weapons for the Bundeswehr, none for foreign troops stationed on German territory, and a nuclear-free zone in central Europe. **1959** *Economist* 14 Feb. 615/2 A nuclear-tipped anti-aircraft missile. **1962** *Listener* 29 Mar. 541/2 What difference does the presence of nuclear weapons make to the strategy and tactics of conventional war?..What is it that prevents either side from going to nuclears on the battlefield? **1964** *Ann. Reg. 1963* 73 The A.L.P. supported moves to establish a 'nuclear-free zone'. **1964** *Economist* 7 Mar. 892/1 Armed with nuclear-tipped missiles. **1972** *Daily Tel.* 2 May 16 The current Nato strategy is one of flexible response, implying that both sides will seek to put off firing nuclears until the last possible moment. **1975** *Nature* 27 Mar. 281/2 It is widely believed that the CIA failed to retrieve the two chief items it wanted—the nuclear-tipped missiles and code machines.

c. A nuclear-powered submarine.

1969 *New Scientist* 28 Aug. 420/2 One can imagine an enemy submarine lying in wait..to pick up the trail of one of our patrolling 'nuclears'. **1974** 'M. HEBDEN' *Pride of Dolphins* I. v. 50 'Would you say Nanjizel was a good submariner?' 'He'd done his stint in nuclears.'

nuclear fission. [f. NUCLEAR *a.* + FISSION.]

1. *Biol.* The division of a cell nucleus (cf. FISSION 2).

1889 *Jrnl. R. Microsc. Soc.* 728 (*heading*) Phenomena of indirect nuclear fission in inverting epithelia. **1960** L. PICKEN *Organization of Cells* vii. 295 The formation of a secondary [myotube] is prepared by nuclear fission, leading to the formation of a second linear series of nuclei.

2. *Nuclear Sci.* = FISSION 4.

1939 *Physical Rev.* LV. 418/2 As pointed out by Meitner and Frisch, the recent discovery..of the appearance of a radioactive barium isotope as the product of such transmutations offers evidence of a new type of nuclear reaction in which the nucleus divides into two nuclei of smaller charges and masses with release of an energy of more than a hundred million electron volts. The direct proof of the occurrence of this so-called nuclear fission was given by Frisch. **1945** H. D. SMYTH *Gen. Acct. Devel. Atomic Energy Mil. Purposes* i. 1 Such a conversion is observed in the phenomenon of nuclear fission of uranium. **1958** J. BETJEMAN *Coll. Poems* 230 Where Hodge sits down beside his wife And talks of Marx and nuclear fission With all a rustic's intuition. **1958** *Listener* 19 June 1005/1 Reactors operating by nuclear fission. **1971** *Sci. Amer.* June 24/3 Nuclear-fusion fuels such as deuterium and tritium liberate more energy per nucleon (neutron or proton) than nuclear-fission fuels. Unfortunately these hydrogen isotopes only burn efficiently at high temperature.

nuclear fusion. [f. NUCLEAR *a.* + FUSION.]

1. *Biol.* The fusion of cell nuclei.

1900 *Jrnl. R. Microsc. Soc.* 73 The generation in which the nuclear fusion occurs is probably in all cases degenerate. **1970** *Protoplasma* LXX. 292 Once the outer cell surfaces have joined and two nuclei are in a common cytoplasm, nuclear fusion nearly always seems to follow.

2. *Nuclear Sci.* = FUSION 3 d.

1952 [see FUSION 3 d]. **1959** *Ann. Reg. 1958* 137 The Secretary-General expressed the hope that progress would be made on..the potentiality of nuclear fusion to solve the world's energy problems. **1969** *New Scientist* 25 Sept. 640/1 The *Tokamak* machines..have formed the basis of the main Soviet research effort into achieving controlled nuclear fusion during the past few years. **1971** [see NUCLEAR FISSION 2].

nuclearist ('nju:klɪərɪst). [f. NUCLEAR *a.* 3 + -IST.] One who advocates the possession or use of nuclear weapons; a nation that possesses nuclear weapons. (See also quot. 1952.) So **'nuclearism** (see quot. 1970[1]).

1952 *Time* 26 May 73 In Venice last week, 13 Italian painters who call themselves 'spatialists' and 'nuclearists' gave their answer with an exhibit 'inspired by the atomic bomb'. The canvases were almost as explosive as the bomb itself: furious fireballs of bright colors and bold contrasts. **1962** *Times Lit. Suppl.* 7 Dec. 948/3 In the great debate on nuclear disarmament..the advantages of sober logic and clear thought have usually lain with the anti-unilateralists, sometimes called the nuclearists. **1964** *Listener* 6 Feb. 220/2 The inclusion of a number of uncommitted countries..has ..made of the Commonwealth a useful bridge,..a witness that even neutralists and a nuclearist can work closely together. **1969** *Bull. Atomic Sci.* June 39/2 The weapons.. become grotesque technological deities for a debased religion of nuclearism. **1970** *Atlantic Monthly* Oct. 106 The most extreme state of contemporary deformation is ..'nuclearism'. By this term I mean to suggest the passionate embrace of nuclear weapons as a solution to our anxieties..and as a means of restoring a lost sense of immortality. *Ibid.*, This deity is seen as an all-powerful force,..and the nuclear believer, or nuclearist, allies himself to that force.

nuclearize ('nju:klɪəraɪz), *v.* [f. NUCLEAR *a.* 3 + -IZE.] **1.** *trans.* To supply or equip (a nation) with nuclear weapons. So **ˌnucleari'zation.**

1960 *New Left Rev.* Nov.–Dec. 4/1 A generalised discontent with the prospects of a nuclearised Germany. *Ibid.* 8/1 The NEC is against the nuclearisation of West Germany. **1967** *Times* 20 Jan. 11/7 The difficulty of predicting the resolution of crises in advance, from the blockade of Berlin to the nuclearization of Cuba.

2. To render (a family, etc.) nuclear in character (see NUCLEAR *a.* 1 e). *rare.*

1972 P. LASLETT *Household & Family in Past Time* 55 The extent to which the domestic group has been 'nuclearised', that is, has lost extension and multiplicity.

nuclearly ('nju:klɪəlɪ), *adv.* [f. NUCLEAR *a.* + -LY[2].] In a nuclear manner (in quot. 1959, with nuclear weapons).

1959 *Listener* 17 Dec. 1062/1 The conventional forces, whether or not nuclearly armed, should be..reduced in the Soviet Union. **1966** J. E. BUSE in C. E. Bazell *In Memory of J. R. Firth* 56 Statives..also occur nuclearly in the verbal phrase.

nucleary ('nju:klɪərɪ), *a.* [f. NUCLE-US + -ARY.] Of the nature of a nucleus.

1847–9 *Todd's Cycl. Anat.* IV. 663/2 The so-called metacarpal bone of the thumb corresponds as to nucleary deposit with the first phalanx of the finger. **1881** *Nature* XXIV. 73 A slightly yellow, hyaline jelly, absolutely deprived of nucleary elements.

nuclease ('nju:klɪeɪz, -s). *Biochem.* [a. G. *nuclease*, f. *nucl-* (in *nucleoproteïd* nucleo-protein): see -ASE.

The Ger. word was coined by Emmerich and Löw 1899, in *Zeitschr. für Hygiene* XXXI. 10, but in a different sense (see quot. 1902); the present meaning originated with L. Iwanoff 1903, in *Zeitschr. für physiol. Chem.* XXXIX. 43.]

Any enzyme that catalyses the hydrolysis of polynucleotides or oligonucleotides into smaller units.

1902 VAUGHAN & NOVY *Cellular Toxins* (ed. 4) ix. 175 It is proposed that bacteriolytic enzymes be given the general name of nucleases, because they digest the nucleo-proteids of the bacterial cells. *Ibid.*, In their second paper Emmerich and Löw detail the methods which they have employed in the preparation of their nucleases and immuneproteids. **1903** *Jrnl. Chem. Soc.* LXXXIV. II. 679 Various fungi.. decompose nucleic acid with the liberation of phosphoric acid and purine bases; this appears to be a ferment action... The name *nuclease* is suggested for the enzyme responsible for the action. **1911** *Jrnl. Biol. Chem.* IX. 129 The term nuclease is usually understood to designate a ferment.. through whose agency nucleic acid is decomposed with the liberation of purine bases. **1949** H. W. FLOREY et al. *Antibiotics* I. i. 20 The active material was supposed to be an enzyme—it was even stated to be a nuclease. **1954** A. WHITE et al. *Princ. Biochem.* xx. 582 The intestinal mucosa is also believed to form nucleases which aid in the digestion of the high molecular weight nucleic acids and polynucleotides. **1970** R. W. MCGILVERY *Biochem.* xx. 481 The effect of the lysosomal nucleases is to cleave the molecule [of nucleic acid] into smaller polynucleotide fragments, with the liberation of only a few free nucleotides.

nucleate ('nju:klɪət), *a.* [ad. L. *nucleātus*, pa. pple. of *nucleāre* (see next): cf. F. *nucléé*, Pg. *nucleado.*] **a.** Having a nucleus; nucleated.

1864 in WEBSTER and later Dicts. **1962** R. P. LEVINE *Genetics* ix. 115 Gene recombination among the sexually reproducing nucleate organisms can occur as a result of both independent assortment and crossing over. **1972** *Nature* 28 Jan. 211/2 Cultures..of nucleate and enucleate sea urchin egg halves.

b. Applied to a kind of boiling process in which streams of bubbles rise from specific sites on a hot surface in the liquid and are recondensed in the surrounding liquid.

1938 *Trans. Amer. Inst. Chem. Engin.* XXXIII. 449 'Nucleate boiling' is what is ordinarily seen when a pan of water boils upon a stove. **1948** *Trans. Amer. Soc. Mech. Engin.* LXX. 372/1 The boiling was nucleate in the sense that the bubbles originated at favored spots on the metal surface. **1975** *Nature* 27 Mar. 322/2 This [*sc.* pulsation boiling] then progressively changes to nucleate boiling from the front of the sphere to the back.

nucleate ('nju:klɪeɪt), *v.* [f. L. *nucleāt-*, ppl. stem of *nucleāre* to become kernelly or hard, f. *nucleus* kernel, NUCLEUS.]

1. a. *trans.* To form (anything) into, to bring together as, a nucleus.

1864 WEBSTER, *Nucleate*, to gather, as about a nucleus or center. **1870** *Daily Tel.* 20 Aug., No doubt the plan of nucleating a second Grand Army at Châlons was a good one. **1871** FARRAR *Witn. Hist.* i. 36 Even then he must account for the intervention which nucleated the first particle of protoplasm.

b. To form nuclei in; to act as or provide a nucleus for.

1952 *Industr. & Engin. Chem.* June 1273/2 Such fluctuations [in local density] are occurring continuously but it is only under very special, almost critical, conditions that they become of sufficient magnitude to nucleate the phase for a transition to a more stable state. **1961** J. W. MULLIN *Crystallization* v. 109 Ethyl acetanilide can nucleate methyl acetanilide. **1969** D. K. ALLEN *Metall.* vii. 179 (*caption*) Bainite is nucleated by a ferrite crystal. **1972** *Physics Bull.* Nov. 656/1 They do predict static fatigue (since for example the probability of nucleating a crack of critical size increases with time). **1973** *Nature* 23 Nov. 212/2 Freezing nuclei are defined as particles capable of nucleating ice in supercooled water.

2. *intr.* To form a nucleus or nuclei; to gather or collect about a nucleus or nuclei. Hence **'nucleating** *ppl. a.* and *vbl. sb.*

1883 *American* VII. 152 Irresolvable nebulæ of nucleating and nucleated or resolvable nebulæ. **1948** *Jrnl. Colloid Sci.* III. 569 The rate of nucleation in the water drops on the metal plate is much larger than that in the water drops in a cloud, probably because of the nucleating effect of the surface of the plate and chance impurities. **1959** *Engineering* 30 Jan. 152/2 Many of the domains appeared to 'nucleate' at crystalline imperfections. **1961** J. W. MULLIN *Crystallization* v. 104 A saturated solution cannot nucleate spontaneously. **1961** *New Scientist* 28 Sept. 813/1 Nucleation is associated with the similarity in spacing between the lattices of the ice crystal and of the nucleating substance. **1969** P. G. SHEWMON *Transform. in Metals* vi. 210 If ferrite containing virtually no carbon..is to nucleate in a given region of austenite containing much more carbon, several changes must occur. **1969** G. F. BOLLING in *Solidification* (Amer. Soc. Metals) (1971) xi. 364 (*heading*) Inoculating, nucleating and alloying. **1974** F. D. RICHARDSON *Physical Chem. of Melts in Metallurgy* II. xii. 459 Small unfilled crevices in containers can act as nucleating sites for the evolution of gases from metals at very small supersaturation pressures. **1974** *Sci Amer.* Dec. 94/2 Inclusions can nucleate, multiply and grow dendritically just as the primary metallic phase does.

nucleate ('nju:klɪeɪt), *sb.* *Biochem.* [f. NUCLE(IC *a.* + -ATE[4].] Any salt of a nucleic acid.

1907 *Jrnl. Chem. Soc.* XCII. I. 266 In the estimation of purine bases, much smaller yields of guanine are obtained when the copper nucleate is hydrolysed instead of the free acid. **1952** *Jrnl. Biol. Chem.* CXCVIII. 85 They attributed this discrepancy to the formation of ion pairs between sodium ions and the phosphate residues of the nucleate.

nucleated ('nju:klɪeɪtɪd), *a.* [f. NUCLEATE *v.*]

1. Having a nucleus. (Chiefly *Biol.*; common from 1845, esp. in ***nucleated cell.***)

1845 *Zoologist* III. 955 The nucleated vesicle, the fundamental form of all organization. **1855** OWEN *Skel. & Teeth* 6 The appearance in it of numerous minute nucleated cells. **1880** BASTIAN *Brain* 40 The cell in this case is only a nucleated expansion of the fibre.

2. Clustered together, esp. of buildings in villages.

1897 *Eng. Hist. Rev.* Apr. 314 The Germanic nucleated village is distinguished from the isolated homestead. *Ibid.* Oct. 769 He draws a sharp distinction between the 'nucleated' villages of eastern and central England, and the 'hamletted' villages of the south-west. **1942** *Rep. Comm. Land Utilisation in Rural Areas* 11 in *Parl. Papers 1941–2* (Cmd. 6378) IV. 421 In other parts, especially where the community was organised under the feudal or manorial systems, nucleated settlements or villages are the rule. **1954** M. BERESFORD *Lost Villages* vii. 233 One such district is the plain of Lancashire. Here, at first blush, we might seem to have nothing but a countryside of compact, nucleated villages. **1970** N. CHADWICK *Celts* v. 125 Houses..were grouped together in small nucleated settlements. *Ibid.*, Most settlement sites, whether nucleated or individual, were enclosed.

nucle'ation. [f. NUCLEATE *v.*] **a.** The formation of nuclei, esp. by the aggregation of molecules into a new phase within a medium. **b.** The formation of something, esp. a crystal, droplet, or bubble, on or into a nucleus.

1861 H. MACMILLAN *Footn. fr. Nature* 243 Giving rise either by gemmation or nucleation to new plants. **1902** *Science* 31 Jan. 177/1 After nucleation the first dense fogs were vaguely annular during the first..exhaustions. **1906** S. S. LAURIE *Synthetica* I. iii. 39 A nucleation or involution or articulation or specific determination of Universal Being whereby an independent centre of actuality is constituted *in rerum natura.* **1906** H. T. BARNES *Ice Formation* iv. 106 An appropriate term, nucleation, might be applied to the formation of ice-crystals throughout the volume of the water, on nuclei supplied by fine particles of sand. **1933** H.

G. WELLS *Shape of Things to Come* II. §3. 147 What we now call social nucleation was failing; the grouping of human beings in families and working communities was not going on. *Ibid.* 158 This chaotic nucleation of human beings about gangs and organizations for frankly criminal purposes. **1941** DOAN & MAHLA *Princ. Physical Metallurgy* (ed. 2) vi. 224 In the transformation of a solid solution, such as austenite, the rate of nucleation is limited further by the rates of diffusion of the atoms forming the precipitate. **1950** *Engineering* 13 Jan. 36/2 If the gas concentration is fairly low and the nucleation of bubbles difficult. **1966** C. R. TOTTLE *Sci. Engin. Materials* vii. 167 In b.c.c. metals, some of which do show ductile failure, the nucleation of cavities occurs at piled-up dislocation sites. **1967** A. H. COTTRELL *Introd. Metallurgy* xii. 153 Many metallurgical processes occur by nucleation and growth, e.g. the formation of CO bubbles in a steel-making bath. *Ibid.* 154 When the probability of forming a nucleus is the same everywhere, the system is in a state suitable for homogeneous nucleation.

nucleator ('nju:klɪeɪtə(r)). [f. NUCLEAT(E *v.* + -OR.] A substance which provides nuclei.

1903 *Nature* 3 Dec. 103/1 Phosphorus as a nucleator suddenly bursts forth into maximum activity at about 13°. **1961** *New Scientist* 28 Sept. 813/1 Steroids can act as effective ice nucleators. **1965** *Ibid.* 4 Nov. 341/1 Glass-crystalline materials that are made from special glassy compositions containing crystal nucleators.

nuclei, pl. of NUCLEUS.

nucleic (nju:'kli:ɪk, -'eɪɪk, 'nju:klɪɪk), *a. Chem.* [f. NUCLE-US + -IC.] *nucleic acid*, any of the naturally occurring polynucleotides present in most cells (chiefly in the chromosomes and ribosomes), which either store genetic information or translate this into the structure of proteins; they fall into two distinct classes, deoxyribonucleic acid (DNA) and ribonucleic acid (RNA), each of which consists of long unbranched molecules of very high molecular weight and usu. occurs in combination with protein (nucleoprotein). [prob. tr. G. *nucleïnsäure* (R. Altmann 1889, in *Arch. für Anat. u. Physiol.* (*Physiol. Abth.*) 524).]

1892 *Jrnl. Chem. Soc.* LXII. 224 The preparation of nucleïc acid from nucleïn by Altmann..gives a further means of distinguishing between the two groups. **1893** *Brit. Med. Jrnl.* Mar. 573/1 Nucleic acid contains carbon [etc.]. **1896** *Allbutt's Syst. Med.* I. 165 Nuclein, which consists of an organic phosphorus-containing acid, termed nucleic acid, in combination with proteid. **1908** [see *glycoprotein* s.v. GLYCO-]. **1942** *Endeavour* I. 104/1 Nucleic acid renders a further invaluable service—it makes the chromosomes visible. **1958** *Listener* 31 July 165/1 The advances of organic chemistry in the last 100 years, advances culminating in the nucleic acid story, lately so much discussed. **1960** L. PICKEN *Organization of Cells* iv. 126 The Watson and Crick helical model of nucleic acid suggests that accurate replication of a unique serial order of nucleotides might readily occur if the two helical chains could be partially uncoiled, so that each might serve as a mould for a new chain. **1972** *Sci. Amer.* June 41/3 The only other compounds that are as important in living systems are the nucleic acids, which are the repository of genetic information and direct the synthesis of proteins.

nucle'iferous, *a. Bot.* [See -FEROUS.] Bearing a nucleus or nuclei.

1857 M. J. BERKELEY *Introd. Cryptogamic Bot.* 389 Apothecia closed or nucleiferous.

'nuclei,form, *a.* [See -FORM.] Having the form of a nucleus; of a rounded shape; esp. of the apothecia and spermogones of certain lichens.

1840 in SMART. **1882** *Encycl. Brit.* XIV. 554/1 It may be here observed that young disciform apothecia are more or less nucleiform. *Ibid.* 555/1 In form they [the spermogones] are nucleiform, round, or oblong.

nuclein ('nju:klɪɪn). *Chem.* Also **-ine**. [f. NUCLE-US + -IN[1], after G. *nuklein* or F. *nucléine*.] The principal constituent of cell-nuclei.

α. **1878** KINGZETT *Anim. Chem.* 278 Jaksch discovered in the brain the substance termed by Miescher 'nuclein'. **1888** ROLLESTON & JACKSON *Anim. Life* p. xxii, The nucleus of a cell..consists principally of a substance termed nuclein..or chromatin. **1899** *Allbutt's Syst. Med.* VI. 491 These chromatin particles are almost certainly identical with nuclein.
β. **1880** *Libr. Univ. Knowl.* VIII. 488 Glutine, elastine, and nucleine. **1887** A. M. BROWN *Anim. Alkaloids* 114 The Nucleine of the unhatched fecundated egg.

Hence **nucle'inic** *a.*, in ***nucleinic acid***, an organic acid rich in phosphorus which is a constituent of nuclein.

1896 *Allbutt's Syst. Med.* I. 90 From blood-serum a nuclein (or nucleinic acid) can be separated.

nucleo- ('nju:klɪəʊ), modern combining form of L. *nucleus*, used in a number of compounds, chiefly biological, as ***nucleo-albumin, -albuminous, -chylema, -chyme, -hyaloplasm, -idioplasm, -phosphoric, -proteid***, etc.; **,nucleo-cyto'plasmic** *a.*, existing or taking place between the nucleus and the cytoplasm; relating the nucleus to the cytoplasm (with respect to some property); **nucleo'genesis**, the formation of nuclei; *spec.* = *nucleosynthesis* below; **nucleo'histone** (also formerly **-'histon**) *Biochem.*, a nucleoprotein in which the protein component is a histone; **nucleo'protamine** *Biochem.*, any nucleoprotein in which the protein component is a protamine; †**nucleoproteid** *Biochem.* = NUCLEOPROTEIN; **nucleo'synthesis** *Astr.*, the cosmic formation of atoms more complicated than the hydrogen atom; hence **nucleosyn'thetic** *a.*

1892 *Syd. Soc. Lex.*, *Nucleo-albumins, compounds of nuclein and proteids, chiefly globulin, found in the protoplasm of cells and in bile. **1896** *Allbutt's Syst. Med.* I. 526 Gamaleia extracted poisonous substances from the bodies of the dead bacteria, which he classified as nucleins and nucleo-albumins. **1895** *Nucleo-albuminous [see *nucleo-histon*]. **1889** *Q. Jrnl. Microsc. Sci.* XXX. 211 To the nuclear sap which fills the spaces in the Nucleohyaloplasm he [Strasburger] gives the name *Nucleochylema. **1894** FOSTER *Med. Dict.*, **Nucleochyme*.., the more fluid, hyaline substance of a cell-nucleus. **1905** *Publ. Carnegie Inst. Washington* No. 37. 66 In order that the *nucleo-cytoplasmic equilibrium may be maintained, it [*sc.* the ascus] must be provided with an excess of nuclear material as compared with the other cells of the ascogenous hyphæ and the ascogonium. **1956** *Nature* 4 Feb. 236/2 The mean nucleo-cytoplasmic ratio was then measured by the method of Chalkley. **1968** H. HARRIS *Nucleus & Cytoplasm* p. vii, The object of this book..is to provide an introduction to some of the salient problems in the field of nucleo-cytoplasmic relationships. **1952** *Industr. & Engin. Chem.* June 1276/1 One of the more practical results of the theory of *nucleo-genesis is the explanation and the guidance..it has offered in preparing monodisperse colloids. **1955** *Nature* 16 July 130/2 If the assumptions..are valid,..all the radioactive elements with half-lives short compared to 4 × 10[8] yr. would have decayed in the time interval between nucleogenesis and the formation of the Earth. **1974** *Physics Bull.* Oct. 464/3 Nucleogenesis in stars. **1895** *Jrnl. Chem. Soc.* LXVIII. II. 52 The active agent in [blood] coagulation is regarded as a nucleo-albuminous substance, named *nucleo-histon. **1914** *Chem. Abstr.* VIII. 714 There is no reason to assume that nucleohistones contain any other but the genuine nucleic acid. **1964** G. H. HAGGIS et al. *Introd. Molecular Biol.* ix. 236 Nucleic acids carry a large net negative charge, and the protein and nucleic acid components of nucleoprotamines and nucleohistones are held together largely by electrostatic forces. **1888** *Nature* 1 Nov. 5/1 The author prefers to speak of the *nucleo-hyaloplasm with Schwarz, as Linin. **1892** *Syd. Soc. Lex.*, *Nucleohyaloplasm*.., applied by Strasburger to the hyaline ground substance in which chromatin spherules are embedded. *Ibid.*, **Nucleo-idioplasm*, the part of the nucleus which consists of Idioplasm. **1898** *Allbutt's Syst. Med.* V. 647 By some observers, other substances—gluten, leucin, *nucleo-phosphoric acid, guanin—have been found as abnormal bodies. **1929** *Chem. Abstr.* XXIII. 4724 (*heading*) The behavior of *nucleoprotamine and its components in animal metabolism. **1956** *Nature* 31 Mar. 603/1 The X-ray data indicate that the molecule [of DNA] has two grooves of unequal depths, and that in the nucleoprotamines the polypeptide chains lie inside these grooves. **1971** D. M. P. PHILLIPS *Histones & Nucleohistones* iii. 121 A conformation similar to the extended-chain form of protamine in nucleoprotamine could be present. **1886** *Jrnl. Chem. Soc.* L. 1051 The author [*sc.* E. Merck] calls '*nucleo-proteïds' substances which, when boiled with water under pressure or treated with acids, alkalis, or ferments, are resolved into nucleïn and albumin. **1914** M. DRUMMOND tr. *Haberlandt's Physiol. Plant Anat.* viii. 415 The reserve proteins include the various globulins, vitellins..and albumoses, also certain nucleoproteids. **1960** WASSERBURG, FOWLER, & HOYLE in *Physical Rev. Lett.* IV. 113/1 There is considerable uncertainty as to the exact time dependence of stellar evolution and *nucleosynthesis in the Galaxy. **1960** FOWLER & HOYLE in *Ann. Physics* X. 281 Type I supernovae were considered to be the only events rapid enough for nucleosynthesis. [*Note*] We use the term *nucleosynthesis* rather than *nucleogenesis* for good reason. We refer..to the synthesis of the elements beyond hydrogen from..the proton, and the neutron... We reserve genesis for the creation of matter-energy. **1963** E. ANDERS in Middlehurst & Kuiper *Moon, Meteorites & Comets* xiii. 458 A second model, involving continuous nucleosynthesis throughout the Galaxy, must be considered. **1965** *Ann. Rev. Astron. & Astrophysics* III. 227 Reynold's discovery was first interpreted as indicating a surprisingly short time-interval between the end of nucleosynthesis and the formation of the solar system. **1971** *Nature* 3 Sept. 39/2 It is now clear that while this effect is operating, a large amount of nucleosynthesis takes place early in the life of a galaxy. **1960** *Physical Rev. Lett.* IV. 113/1 The *nucleosynthetic processes during which iodine was made were instantaneous. **1973** *Physics Bull.* Nov. 652/1 This high percentage of helium apparently could not have been produced by the kind of nucleosynthetic processes currently occurring in stars.

'nucleobranch. *Zool.* Also **-branche**. [ad. F. *nucléobranche*: cf. prec. and BRANCHIÆ.] A mollusc of the order *Nucleobranchiata*; a Heteropod.

Some recent Dicts. also give the form as an *adj.*

1851 WOODWARD *Mollusca* I. 11 The nucleobranches and pteropods swim in the open sea. *Ibid.* 97 The nucleobranches are 'aberrant' gasteropods, having the foot thin and vertical. **1861** CARPENTER in *Rep. Smithsonian Instit.* 172 The Nucleobranchs have the gills in a tuft at the lower part of the back, sometimes protected by a shell.

So **nucleo'branchiate** *a.* (Cf. BRANCHIATE.)

1854 WOODWARD *Mollusca* II. 198 There are two families of nucleobranchiate mollusks.

nucleoid ('nju:klɪɔɪd), *a.* and *sb.* [f. NUCLE-US + -OID.] **A.** *adj.* Like a nucleus in form or appearance.

1855 in OGILVIE *Suppl.* **1880** BASTIAN *Brain* xxiii. 465 These are either mere nucleoid bodies or small angular cells. **1889** *Jrnl. R. Microsc. Soc.* 429 (*heading*) Nucleus or nucleoid bodies of schizomycetes.

B. *sb.* †**a.** [a. G. *nucleoïd* (M. Lavdowsky 1893, in *Zeitschr. für wiss. Mikrosk.* X. 8).] (See quots.) *Obs.*

Arnold (*Virchows Arch. für path. Anat. u. Physiol.* (1896) CXLV. 22) took over the term from Lavdowsky.

1905 GOULD *Dict. New Med. Terms* 383/2 *Nucleoid*, a term used by Arnold to designate the substance in the red corpuscles formed from the original nucleus. It is finely granular or fibrillar and is surrounded by a substance which Arnold calls paraplasm. **1913** O. C. GRUNER *Biol. Blood-Cells* 361 *Nucleoid*. Syn.: *nuclear rests, inclusion-body*. (*a*) A precipitation effect of hæmoglobin; (*b*) if basic, a special appearance of the basophile cell membrane. **1928** E. B. KRUMBHAAR in E. V. Cowdry *Special Cytol.* I. x. 307 In addition to the several bodies just mentioned, various artefacts can be produced [in erythrocytes] by standing, poor fixation, non-isotonic solutions, etc., termed 'nucleoids'.

b. [a. G. *nucleoid* (coined independently in this sense by G. Piekarski 1937, in *Arch. für Mikrobiol.* VIII. 438).] An organelle in bacteria and viruses functionally analogous to the cell nucleus of higher organisms.

1938 *Biol. Abstr.* XII. 1407/2 The author's [*sc.* G. Piekarski's] studies seem to show that the nucleoids which he observed in bacteria and sarcina are equivalent to cell nuclei. **1965** *Bacteriol. Rev.* XXIX. 277/1 The genetic material in bacterial cells forms structures which are called nucleoids... Although from the very beginning there was no doubt that these structures are nuclei with respect to their function.., their simple architecture and morphological appearance, which distinguish them from the type of nucleus present in higher organisms..make a special term desirable. **1970** *Nature* 31 Oct. 410/2 The RNA dependent activity resides in the nucleoid. **1971** *Ibid.* 30 Apr. 568 (*caption*) Cell from culture of *B*[*acillus*] *subtilis*... Two chromosomes appear as tightly packed 'nucleoids'. **1972** *Sci. Amer.* Jan. 29/2 The virion of the Rous sarcoma virus consists of a lipid-containing envelope.., an inner membrane and a nucleoid, or core, that contains the viral RNA and certain proteins.

nucleoid, var. NUCLOID.

nucleolar (nju:'kli:ələ(r), nju:kli:'əʊlə(r)), *a.* [f. NUCLEOL-US.] Of the nature of, pertaining to, a nucleolus.

1861 HULME tr. *Moquin-Tandon* II. vii. 407 One or two very small corpuscles, or nucleolar bodies, may sometimes be seen in the interior. **1890** *Spectator* 10 May, From every ovum, before metamorphosis begins, one or more masses of nucleolar matter, the so-called 'polar bodies', are extruded.

'nucleolate, *a.* [f. NUCLEOL-US + -ATE[2]: cf. F. *nucléolé*.] = next. (*Cent. Dict.* 1890.)

nucleolated ('nju:klɪəleɪtɪd), *a. Biol.* [f. as prec. + -ED[1].] Furnished with a nucleolus.

1846 [see NUCLEAR *a.* 1]. **1870** ROLLESTON *Anim. Life* 257 Showing..its nucleolated nucleus. **1879** *St. George's Hosp. Rep.* IX. 339 Their nuclei were large, oval, and nucleolated.

nucleole ('nju:klɪəʊl). *Biol.* [ad. L. *nucleolus*: cf. F. *nucléole*, Pg. *nucleolo*.] = NUCLEOLUS.

1864 WEBSTER, *Nucleole*, the nucleus within a nucleus; nucleolus. *Dana.* **1875** tr. *Schmidt's Desc. & Darwinism* 44 The nucleus is termed the germinal vesicle, and the nucleole the germinal spot.

'nucleolid. *Biol.* [-ID.] (See quot.)

1886 *Jrnl. R. Microsc. Soc.* Apr. 232 The typical nuclear network..is frequently exhibited: often complicated, however, by the presence of nucleolids or nucleolus-like bodies.

'nucleolin(e, *sb.* and *a. Biol.* [Cf. next.]

a. *sb.* = next. **b.** *adj.* Pertaining to, connected with, a nucleolinus.

1890 in *Cent. Dict.* **1905** MCCABE tr. *Haeckel's Evol. Man* I. 112 We find in many ova..a still further point within the germinal spot, a 'nucleolin', which goes by the name of the germinal point.

‖**nucleolinus** (nju:klɪə'laɪnəs). *Biol.* [mod.L., f. *nucleolus*.] The germinal point of a nucleolus.

1879 tr. *Haeckel's Evol. Man* I. 133 Within this germinal spot [nucleolus] is found yet another little point, a nucleolinus, which may be called the germinal point. **1895** *Atlantic Monthly* Feb. 192 The nucleus contains a nucleolinus within a nucleolus.

nucleolo- (nju:'kli:ələʊ), modern combining form of L. *nucleolus* (dim. of *nucleus*) a little nut; used in some biological compounds, as ***nucleolo-centrosome, -nucleated, -nucleolus, -nucleus***.

1892 *Syd. Soc. Lex.*, *Nucleolo-nucleated*, Erasmus Wilson's term for a cell, the nucleus of which contains one or more nucleoli. *Ibid.*, *Nucleolo-nucleus*, term applied by Mr. J. M. Macfarlane to a small body existing within the nucleolus of a cell. **1900** B. D. JACKSON *Gloss. Bot. Terms* 171/1 Nucleolo-Nucleolus, = Endonucleus. **1900** E. B. WILSON *The Cell* (ed. 2) 34 The nucleolus is shown..to be comparable with an attraction sphere or centrosome (nucleolo-centrosome).

nucleolonema (,nju:kli:əʊləʊ'ni:mə). *Cytology.* Pl. **-nemas, -nemata**. [a. Sp. *nucleolonema* (Estable & Sotelo 1951, in *Publicaciones Inst. de Invest. de Ciencias Biol.* I. 105), f. NUCLEOLO- + Gr. νῆμα thread.] (See quot. 1968.)

Quot. 1951 is from the authors' English translation of the summary of their Sp. paper.

[**1951** ESTABLE & SOTELO in *Publicaciones Instituto de Investigación de Ciencias Biol.* I. 123 Every true..nucleolus is made up of two different parts... The first one is always the most important, and on account of its filamentous structure we shall call it nucleoloneme. *Ibid.*, No cell having a nucleus lacks a nucleoloneme.] **1952** —— in *Stain Technol.* XXVII. 307 In a recent paper the authors have shown filamentous structures within the nucleolus of all cells. This structure was named the nucleolonema. **1955** *Jrnl. Biophysical & Biochem. Cytol.* I. 185 (*heading*) Note on nucleolonemata in human cultured cells. **1968** R. Rieger et al. *Gloss. Genetics & Cytogenetics* 316 As far as the ultrastructure of the n[ucleolus] is concerned, the early work was interpreted as indicating the presence of a coiled filament called the 'nucleolonema' (diameter 90–180 nm). Later this nucleolonema was found to consist of coarse granules of the size of ribosomes (diameter about 150 Å). **1973** *Jrnl. Invertebrate Path.* XXII. 405/2 The nucleolus was compact, without nucleolonema, and was completely surrounded by an electron-dense material, apparently chromatin.

'nucleolule. *Biol.* [f. NUCLEOLE + -ULE: cf. F. *nucléolule.*] 'A minute granule in the centre of a nucleolus' (*Syd. Soc. Lex.* 1892).

‖**nucleolus** (njuː'kliːələs, njuːkliː'əʊləs). *Biol.* Pl. -oli (-əlaɪ, -əʊlaɪ). [L. *nucleolus*, dim. of *nucleus.*] A small nucleus; *esp.* a minute rounded body within the nucleus of a cell in animal or vegetable substance; also, a paranucleus. Also *Comb.*

1845 Todd & Bowman *Phys. Anat.* I. 158 They usually contain some central granules or nucleoli. **1846** Day tr. *Simon's Anim. Chem.* II. 449 It contains a nucleus about the size of a nut,.. and in the centre of this is a nucleolus of the size of a large pea. **1870** H. A. Nicholson *Man. Zool.* 41 No differentiated organs of any kind beyond the nucleus and nucleolus exist. **1886** [see NUCLEOLID].

†**nucleon**[1] ('njuːklɪɒn). *Biochem. Obs.* [a. G. *nucleon* (M. Siegfried 1895, in *Ber. d. Deut. Chem. Ges.* XXVIII. 518), f. *nucle-ïn* (now *nuklein*) NUCLEIN + *pept-on* PEPTONE.] (See quots.)

1895 *Jrnl. Chem. Soc.* LXVIII. I. 314 The term *nucleon* is suggested for compounds, such as phosphorcarnic acid, which are allied to the nucleïns but contain peptone instead of albumin. **1905** W. H. Howell *Text-bk. Physiol.* ii. 60 The discoverer of nucleon has attributed to it a very great physiological importance, as a source of energy to the muscle, and as an efficient means of transportation of iron, calcium, [etc.]... It must be stated, however, that there still remains some doubt as to the chemical individuality of the nucleon or the nucleons. **1921** *Physiol. Abstr.* VI. 477 Nucleon is a mixture of which the chief constituent is denatured protein.

nucleon[2] ('njuːklɪɒn). *Nuclear Physics.* [f. NUCLE(US *sb.* + -ON[1].] †**a.** = PROTON 2. *Obs. rare.*

1923 D. Ll. Hammick tr. *Perrin's Atoms* (ed. 2) 223 If we represent the hydrogen nucleus or positive protoatom by *h* and the corpuscle or negative protoatom by *β* we may say that all matter is made up of protoatoms *h* and *β*... The negative protoatom may be called the corpuscle and the positive protoatom the nucleon. [*Note*] Suggested by P. Auger. *Proton* has also been proposed.

b. A proton or neutron; a sub-atomic particle of which these may be regarded as two distinct states, differing in the third component of isospin. [Orig. formed as *nuclon* (see quot. 1941).]

1939 F. J. Belinfante *Theory of Heavy Quanta* (Leiden Univ., thesis) 40 The interaction of the heavy quanta with the heavy particles (the proton-neutron, or 'nuclon', as we shall call it briefly). **1940** Pauli & Belinfante in *Physica* VII. 179 The particle that is a proton in its charged state and a neutron in its neutral state, we have called a nuclon. **1940** C. Møller in *Physical Rev.* LVIII. 1118/1 The strength of the couplings between the nuclons and the 'vector' and 'pseudoscalar' meson fields. [*Note*] Following the proposal of Belinfante.. we use the word nuclon as a common name for the nuclear constituents, the protons and neutrons. **1941** —— in *Ibid.* LIX. 323/2 Following the original proposal of Belinfante, the writer has.. used the word 'nuclon' as a common notation for.. neutrons and protons. In the meantime, however, it has been pointed out to me that, since the root of the word nucleus is 'nucle', the notation 'nucleon' would from a philological point of view be more appropriate. **1952** *Sci. News* XXIII. 28 It seems that each nucleon (a general name for either proton or neutron) cannot interact with all the other particles in the nucleus, but only with its neighbours. **1968** M. S. Livingston *Particle Physics* v. 97 With both protons bombarding a high-Z target, to create a nucleon-antinucleon pair.., the threshold kinetic energy must be 5·4 GeV. **1971** *New Scientist* 17 June 695/2 The questions arise why cosmic-ray nucleons or X-rays or ultraviolet photons should be produced in the centres of Seyfert galaxies.

nucleonic (njuːklɪ'ɒnɪk), *a.* [Partly f. prec. + -IC, partly a back-formation from next.] Of or pertaining to the nucleon or nucleonics.

1946 *Proc. Amer. Philos. Soc.* XC. 42/2 A second class of transformation.. comprises the nucleonic changes which occur in the atmosphere under cosmic-ray bombardment. **1947** *Nucleonics* Sept. 1/1 Nucleonic physics.. has come to be understood as the science of those changes in which there occurs a rearrangement, but no change, in the total number of nucleons present. Radioactivity, nuclear disintegration, nuclear fission, and nuclear synthesis are the processes comprehended by this science. **1947** *Electronics* Dec. 84/1 An important tool of nucleonic research is the mass spectrograph. **1955** J. A. Wheeler in W. Pauli *Niels Bohr* 163 Nuclear division calls forth a uniquely drastic kind of nucleonic re-arrangement. **1957** *Financial Times Ann. Rev. Brit. Industry* 35/5 Industrial applications.. developed in conjunction with the nucleonic instrument manufacturers. **1974** *Physics Bull.* Dec. 579/3 We have been aware for many years of the inadequacy of the neutrons and protons only approach for the simplest systems because there we have had good enough nucleonic wavefunctions to show up the deficiency of the nucleons only approach.

nucleonics (njuːklɪ'ɒnɪks), *sb. pl.* (const. as *sing.*). [Blend of NUCLEON[2] + ELECTRONICS.] The branch of science and technology concerned with nucleons and the atomic nucleus, esp. with the practical applications of nuclear phenomena and associated techniques.

1945 *Nature* 10 Nov. 549/1 If science is to be controlled on a national level, the Association [of Oak Ridge Scientists] believes that the inevitable armament competition will prevent science, especially 'nucleonics', from ever being free again. **1946** Z. Jeffries in *Chem. & Engin. News* 25 Jan. 186 'Nucleonics' is the generic name used to some extent within the Atomic Energy Project during the war and its use is now gaining in popularity... Since released atomic energy and certain other phenomena [are] derived from the nuclei of atoms and thus from the nucleons, it seems appropriate that the generic name should be 'nucleonics'. **1950** Glasstone *Sourcebk. Atomic Energy* iv. 94 The use of the word 'nucleonics'.. was proposed by Z. Jeffries in July 1944. **1952** *Electronic Engin.* XXIV. 533 The newer science of nucleonics is gradually leaving the nuclear physics research laboratory and finding applications aimed at producing greater productivity of our industrial processes. **1955** J. A. Wheeler in W. Pauli *Niels Bohr* 164 Looking back, one sees in nucleonics as in so many other parts of physics how much progress can be made on the basis of simple principles. **1959** *Times* 2 Jan. 2 Developments will range from high voltage transmission systems to nucleonics and computer design. **1966** *New Scientist* 15 Dec. 623/1 Nucleonics—Soldering in place the printed circuit of a geiger counter kit, designed to patent specification of the UK Atomic Energy Authority.

nucle'opetal, *a. rare*[−1]. [f. NUCLEO-, after *centripetal.*] Towards the nucleus.

1887 *Jrnl. Morphol.* I. 236 The change from a centripetal to a nucleopetal direction.

nucleophile ('njuːklɪəfaɪl). *Chem.* [f. NUCLEO- + -PHILE.] A nucleophilic reagent.

1953 C. K. Ingold *Struct. & Mech. Org. Chem.* v. 201 All bases are nucleophiles. **1959** Cram & Hammond *Org. Chem.* xvii. 395 Nucleophiles such as RS-, which owe much of their reactivity to high polarizability, tend to bring about substitution rather than elimination. **1971** *Nature* 5 Nov. 42/1 Any agent which.. can therefore react with nucleophiles in the cell, is a potential carcinogen.

nucleophilic (njuːklɪə'fɪlɪk), *a. Chem.* [f. NUCLEO- + -PHILIC.] **a.** Having an affinity for atomic nuclei, and so reacting at an electron-deficient bond or atom in a substrate; anionoid.

1933 C. K. Ingold in *Jrnl. Chem. Soc.* 1121 The terms *electrophilic* (electron-seeking) and *nucleophilic* (nucleus-seeking) are suggested in place of the adjectives anionoid and cationoid introduced by Lapworth. **1946** *Nature* 20 July 94/1 Those bimolecular and unimolecular substitutions in which a nucleophilic reagent displaces halogen as halide ion from an alkyl halide. **1968** R. O. C. Norman *Princ. Org. Synthesis* iv. 127 A thiol anion, RS-, although less basic than its oxygen analogue, RO-, is more strongly nucleophilic.

b. Of a reaction: brought about by a nucleophilic reagent.

1935 Hughes & Ingold in *Jrnl. Chem. Soc.* 245 According as this [*sc.* the substituting agent] is nucleophilic.. or electrophilic.., the reaction may be termed a 'nucleophilic' or 'electrophilic' substitution. **1946** *Nature* 20 July 94/1 That the polar effect is not absent in general from bimolecular nucleophilic substitutions is consistent with the result of exchanging the electron-releasing methyl substituents for electron-attracting groups. **1969** T. C. Thorstensen *Pract. Leather Technol.* vi. 91 Windus and Showell have reported the explanation of mechanism of unhairing as a nucleophilic displacement.

Hence **nucleo'philically** *adv.*, after the manner of a nucleophile; **,nucleophi'licity**, nucleophilic character.

1953 C. K. Ingold *Struct. & Mech. Org. Chem.* v. 201 Basicity.. is a special manifestation of nucleophilic character, or nucleophilicity, that is, affinity for atomic nuclei in general. **1970** J. E. Gearin in A. Burger *Medicinal Chem.* (ed. 3) II. xlvii. 1302/2 This group must be capable of attacking nucleophilically the carbon atom of the ester group of acetylcholine. **1971** C. J. Gray *Enzyme-catalysed Reactions* i. 21 The nucleophilicity of the small fluoride ion is higher in non-hydroxyl solvents where the solvation is less effective.

'nucleoplasm. *Biol.* [f. NUCLEO- + PLASM.] Nuclear protoplasm.

The precise application of the term has varied.

1889 Mivart in *Dubl. Rev.* Oct. 290 The first polar body extruded, he believes to consist of this superfluous nucleoplasm. **1893** A. M. Marshall *Vertebr. Embryol.* 4 The nucleus.. consists of an outer nuclear membrane, enclosing a clear coagulable fluid, the nucleoplasm.

Hence **nucleo'plasmic** *a.*

1890 in *Cent. Dict.* **1894** Foster *Med. Dict.* s.v. *Nucleolus*, Fine protoplasmic or nucleoplasmic fibrils.

'nucleoplast. *Biol.* [f. NUCLEO- + -PLAST.] A nucleoplasmic body.

1876 *Q. Jrnl. Microsc. Sci.* XVI. 154 The nucleoplast with the pseudo-nucleoli are thrown off.

Hence **nucleo'plastic** *a.*

1894 Foster *Med. Dict.*

nucleoprotein (njuːklɪə'prəʊtiːn). *Biochem.* [a. G. *nucleoproteïn* (E. Merck 1885, in *Patentschrift 35,724*), which was formerly rendered in Eng. as *nucleoproteid* (s.v. NUCLEO-): see PROTEIN.] A combination of a protein and a nucleic acid such as occurs in living organisms.

1907 *Practitioner* Oct. 588 From the nuclein and nucleoprotein, the purin bodies, are produced, such as hypoxanthin, xanthin, adenin, and uric acid. **1938** *Ann. Reg. 1937* 352 Tobacco mosaic virus is a nucleoprotein of special character. **1944** *Adv. Protein Chem.* I. 258 The simplest and perhaps best available definition of a nucleoprotein would be to designate as such any protein with which nucleic acid is associated. **1959** *Times* 12 June 15/6 Both genes.. and viruses are nucleo-proteins. **1970** *Sci. Amer.* Feb. 102 The constituents of the chromosomes—deoxyribonucleic acid (DNA) and nucleoproteins—do not absorb visible light readily.

nucleoside ('njuːklɪəsaɪd). *Biochem.* [ad. G. *nucleosid* (Levene & Jacobs 1909, in *Ber. d. Deut. Chem. Ges.* XLII. 2475), f. after *glucosid* GLUCOSIDE: see NUCLEO-.] Any compound in which a sugar (usu. ribose or deoxyribose) is linked glycosidically to a purine or pyrimidine base; *spec.* such a compound derived from a nucleic acid by hydrolysis. (See quot. 1973.)

1911 [see NUCLEOTIDE]. **1911** [see ADENOSINE]. **1931** Levene & Bass *Nucleic Acids* vi. 126 The name 'nucleoside' was assigned to the substances of this group for the reason that.. they contain sugar in a glucosidic union, and.. the substances linked to the sugars are nuclein bases. **1946** *Nature* 24 Aug. 275/2 Miss Mejbaum has found.. that the pentose contained in pyrimidine nucleotides (uridylic acid and cydidylic [*read* cytidylic] acid) and nucleosides (uridine) are not determined by her method. **1969** *New Scientist* 10 July 65/2 A nucleoside like adenosine or inosine. **1973** [see NUCLEOTIDE].

Hence **'nucleosidase** [-ASE], any enzyme which catalyses the hydrolysis of a nucleoside into its constituent base and sugar, or the reaction between a nucleoside and phosphate to yield a base and a sugar phosphate.

1911 Levene & Medigreceanu in *Jrnl. Biol. Chem.* IX. 396 Under the influence of mineral acids nucleosides are readily hydrolyzed into their components. The same cleavage can be brought about by the action of enzymes present in the plasma of most of the organs tested in that direction... Since this reaction is brought about by an enzyme different from the other nucleolytic enzymes, it may be proper to refer to it under the name of *Nucleosidase*. **1935** *Biochem. Jrnl.* XXIX. 1100 If adenine nucleosidase is present it must therefore be only in relatively small amounts. **1955** Chargaff & Davidson *Nucleic Acids* I. xv. 600 The enzymic cleavage of *N*-glycoside bonds of nucleic acid derivatives was first observed in nucleosides, and the term 'nucleosidases'.. is still used. In the current literature this name tends to be replaced by the designations 'nucleoside phosphorylases' and 'nucleoside hydrolases'.

nucleotide ('njuːklɪətaɪd). *Biochem.* [ad. G. *nucleotid* (Levene & Mandel 1908, in *Ber. d. Deut. Chem. Ges.* XLI. 1907): see NUCLEO- and -IDE.] Any compound in which a phosphate group is linked to the sugar of a nucleoside; *spec.* any of the compounds of this type obtained by the partial hydrolysis of a nucleic acid, which are the individual monomers of which such acids are composed. (See quot. 1973.)

1908 *Jrnl. Chem. Soc.* XCIV. I. 587 It is suggested that the nucleic acids are composed of simpler complexes, the nucleotides, each formed of phosphoric acid, a carbohydrate, and a base. **1911** *Jrnl. Biol. Chem.* IX. 66 It was demonstrated that the molecule of the complex nucleic acids is composed of nucleotides and these of phosphoric acid, carbohydrate and base linked to one another in the order here given... It is possible to detach from the complex either phosphoric acid alone, giving rise to a nucleoside, or a complex of carbohydrate and base. **1937** *Nature* 30 Oct. 745/2 The co-ferments now described as phosphopyridine nucleotides, the nature of which has been at last worked out. **1952** *Sci. News* XXIV. 33 The complete nucleic acid molecules are generally considered as being built up of nucleotides, linked through the hydroxyl (OH) groups of the sugar and the acid groups of the phosphoric acid. **1957** *Times* 1 Nov. 10/3 The award to Sir Alexander Todd.. of the Nobel prize for chemistry.. for his work on nucleotides and nucleotide enzymes. **1968** *Observer* (Colour Suppl.) 10 Mar. 15/1 The DNA molecule.. is a two-stranded helix. Each strand is built up of smaller molecules called nucleotides. *Ibid.* 15/2 There are only four kinds of nucleotide, each with a different chemical base. These bases are adenine, thymine, guanine and cytosine. **1971** J. Z. Young *Introd. Study Man* iii. 47 The symbols of the genetic code.. are the nucleotides arranged in the helical DNA molecules. **1973** Henderson & Paterson *Nucleotide Metabolism* p. xiv, The terms 'nucleoside' and 'nucleotide' in the strictest sense refer to N-glycosides, and phosphorylated N-glycosides, respectively, derived from nucleic acids. The term is now used, however, in several broader ways. Thus, adenosine triphosphate (ATP) is not derived from nucleic acids, but is quite legitimately a nucleotide through its relation to adenosine monophosphate (AMP), which is so derived. Other N-ribosides, such as nicotinamide mononucleotide (NMN), are called nucleotides only by extension and analogy, and nicotinamide-adenine dinucleotide (NAD^+), nicotinamide-adenine dinucleotide phosphate ($NADP^+$), etc., are called dinucleotides only by a similar process. Flavin mononucleotide (FMN) is a step still further removed, as it contains ribitol instead of ribose, and flavin-adenine dinucleotide similarly extends the meaning of dinucleotide. N-glycosides such as orotidylate (OMP) and adenylosuccinate are called nucleotides through their close relationship to the 'true' nucleotides. *Ibid.* i. 10 In animal cells, a few nucleotides with sugars other than ribose and deoxyribose are known.

Hence **'nucleotidase** [-ASE], any enzyme which catalyses the hydrolysis of a nucleotide to a nucleoside and phosphate.

1911 LEVENE & MEDIGRECEANU in *Jrnl. Biol. Chem.* IX. 395 The enzymes performing this cleavage [of nucleotides to phosphoric acid and carbohydrate-base complex] may be referred to as Nucleotidases. **1932** *Jrnl. Biol. Chem.* XCVI. 462 The optimal activity of the nucleotidase is at a pH > 11. **1970** R. W. MCGILVERY *Biochem.* xx. 481 The phosphate group of nucleotides is liberated by hydrolysis, catalyzed by nucleotidases.

nucleus ('nju:klɪəs), *sb.* Pl. **nuclei** ('nju:klɪaɪ) and **nucleuses.** [a. L. *nucleus* (*nuculeus*) kernel, inner part, f. *nucula* or *nuc-*, *nux* nut. So F. *nucleus*, It., Sp., and Pg. *nucleo*.]

I. 1. *Astr.* **a.** The more condensed portion of the head of a comet.

[**1704** J. HARRIS *Lex. Techn.* I. *Nucleus*..is by Hevelius and others used for the Head of a Comet.] **1708** WHISTON *The. Earth* (ed. 2) II. 76 The lowest part next the Nucleus, or Dense Body, seems to be Opake. **1766** *Phil. Trans.* LV. 310, I compared the nucleus of the comet with two new stars that were just by. **1837** J. F. COOPER *Europe* II. v. 99 The astronomers tell us that some of these comets have no visible nucleuses. **1868** LOCKYER *Elem. Astron.* §291 The brighter part of the comet is called the head, or coma, and sometimes the head contains a brighter portion still, called the nucleus.

fig. **1759** STERNE *Tr. Shandy* II. ix, Would not such a phenomenon..have been a subject of juster apprehension.. than the worst of Whiston's comets?—To say nothing of the Nucleus; that is, of Obadiah and the coach-horse.

b. A more condensed, usu. brighter, central part of a galaxy or nebula.

1784 W. HERSCHEL in *Phil. Trans. R. Soc.* LXXIV. 442, I have seen double and treble nebulæ, variously arranged; large ones with small, seeming attendants;..others of the cometic shape, with a seeming nucleus in the center. **1849** J. F. W. HERSCHEL *Outlines Astron.* xvii. 601 The nebula in Andromeda is visible to the naked eye... Mr. G. P. Bond, assistant at the observatory of Cambridge, U.S., describes and figures it as..very suddenly condensed at the nucleus almost to the semblance of a star. **1898** A. M. CLERKE et al. *Concise Knowledge Astron.* IV. vi. 534 The photograph shows both nuclei of the nebula to be stellar. **1955** *Sci. Amer.* May 48/3 Because of heavy dust clouds this nucleus [of the Milky Way] has not been observed visually or photographically; it was discovered by radio astronomy. **1970** *Sci. Jrnl.* Feb. 61/1 The emission line spectrum of a Seyfert nucleus is rather like that from typical hot clouds of gas such as the Orion Nebula.

†**2.** A supposed interior crust of the earth. *Obs.*

1715 tr. *Gregory's Astron.* I. I. §69. 144 He [Kepler] found it necessary to suppose an interior Crust (which might be like a Nucleus, in regard of the exterior). *Ibid.* 145 And within this Nucleus, or rather Crust, he is forced to suppose again another interior Nucleus. **1727** POPE *Mem. Mart. Scriblerus* I. xiv, A Proposal..to pierce the first crust or Nucleus of this our Earth, quite through, to the next Concentrical Sphere.

3. A central part or thing around which other parts or things are grouped, collected, or compacted; that which forms the centre or kernel of some aggregate or mass.

a. Of material (esp. more or less solid) things.

1762 *Phil. Trans.* LII. 470 The nucleus of the nearest light will appear whitest and brightest. **1764** *Ibid.* LIV. 42 The conical cavity and its nucleus are always proportioned to the bulk of the Belemnite. **1797** M. BAILLIE *Morbid Anat.* (1807) 306 Some extraneous body, which becomes the nucleus of the calculus. *Ibid.*, The nucleus which I have seen. **1826** S. COOPER *First Lines Surg.* (ed. 5) 66 Every portion of the gangrenous cellular membrane, nucleus, or core, [should be] extracted. **1878** HUXLEY *Physiogr.* xxi. 366 There may sometimes be detected a yet darker part [of a sun-spot] which is called the nucleus.

b. Of communities or groups of persons.

1798 W. HUTTON *Life* 120 About 700 individuals..were the nucleus of his colony of Georgia. **1853** MERIVALE *Rom. Repub.* v. (1867) 150 The few hundred families, which formed the original nucleus of her citizenship. **1868** BLUNT *Ref. Ch. Eng.* II. 95 A Protestant party which crystallized around the nucleus of antisacerdotalists.

attrib. **1904** *Westm. Gaz.* 10 Dec. 11/1 They will have a nucleus crew of two-fifths of their war complement. **1905** *Fortn. Rev.* 2 Jan. 15 The officers and men withdrawn.. from distant squadrons will be utilised as nucleus crews in the Reserve ships. **1914** C. F. TWENEY *Dict. Naval & Mil. Terms* 163 *Nucleus crew*, the essential members of a ship's crew, such as petty officers, gunners, etc., the crew being raised to full strength in case of mobilisation. **1926** in Fowler *Mod. Eng. Usage* 713/2 Ships with nucleus crews were not so efficient as ships fully manned. **1965** M. MORSE *Unattached* i. 57 The mood of each rehearsal..depended very much on the attitude of the nucleus group.

c. Of immaterial things.

1820 *Edin. Rev.* XXXIII. 314 The *nucleus* of fine thought is there. **1835** THIRLWALL *Greece* I. vi. 248 They manifestly formed the basis or nucleus of the epic cycle. **1876** GEO. ELIOT *Dan. Der.* li, Each nucleus of pain or pleasure.

d. Of places, buildings, etc.

1839 JAMES *Louis XIV*, I. 266 A town was the nucleus round which a province, a kingdom, an empire was gathered together. **1865** LECKY *Ration.* II. vi. 261 When a monastery was planted, it soon became the nucleus around which the inhabitants of the neighbourhood clustered. **1872** BAKER *Nile Trib.* v. 73 It formed a nucleus for the general gathering of the people with their flocks.

e. Of collections of things.

1866 *Cornh. Mag.* Nov. 575 There are little nuclei of future collections. **1875** J. H. BENNET *Shores Medit.* I. vii. 200 There is already a very fair collection of modern books in hand, as the nucleus of a library. *a* **1878** SCOTT *Lect. Archit.* (1879) I. 149 These may in their turn be made the nucleus round which detached..shafts may be grouped.

4. *Archæol.* A block of flint or other stone from which early implements have been made.

1869 LUBBOCK *Preh. Times* iv. 87 These 'livres de beurre' appear to have been the blocks or nuclei from which they were obtained. **1899** R. MUNRO *Preh. Scotl.* v. 143 Nuclei of obsidian have also been found in Greece.

II. 5. *Bot.* **a.** The kernel of a nut. Now *rare* or *Obs.*

1704 J. HARRIS *Lex. Techn.* I, *Nucleus* is the Edible part of the Kernel of any Nut, which is contained within the Skin of the Kernel; and in a larger sense is by Botanists used for any Fruit or Seed contained within an Husk or Shell. **1727–38** CHAMBERS *Cycl.* s.v. *Nut*, An hard cortex, or shell; which contains a softer edible nucleus, or kernel. **1785** MARTYN tr. *Rousseau's Bot.* (1794) 439 The fruit is a drupe containing a nut, with a furrowed shell, within which is a four-lobed irregularly furrowed nucleus. **1846–50** A. WOOD *Class-bk. Bot.* 490 White Walnut..; nucleus oblong, acuminate, deeply..furrowed.

b. The kernel of a seed (see quots.).

1829 CLINTON tr. *Richard's Elem. Bot.* (ed. 4) 387 The kernel or nucleus is the whole of the ripe and perfect seed contained in the cavity of the episperm. **1849** BALFOUR *Man. Bot.* §577 The seed..consists of a nucleus or kernel, and integuments. **1861** BENTLEY *Man. Bot.* 343 The nucleus of the seed may either consist of the embryo alone,..or of the embryo enclosed in albumen or perisperm.

c. The central part of an ovule.

1829 CLINTON tr. *Richard's Elem. Bot.* (ed. 4) 383 The nucleus contained within both the integuments of the ovule is a cellular body. **1832** LINDLEY *Introd. Bot.* I. ii. 155 The central part is a fleshy, pointed, pulpy mass, called the *nucleus* or *nucelle*. **1861** BENTLEY *Man. Bot.* 330 As development proceeds, a cavity is formed at or near the apex of the nucleus..in which the embryo..is developed.

d. In Lichens: (see quot. 1832).

1832 LINDLEY *Introd. Bot.* I. iii. 206 *Nucleus*, is the disk of the shield which contains the sporules and their cases. *Asci*, are tubes, in which the sporules are contained while in the nucleus. **1882** *Encycl. Brit.* XIV. 554/2 When the pyrenium quite covers the nucleus it is said to be entire.

e. In Fungi: (see quots.).

1832 LINDLEY *Introd. Bot.* I. iii. 209 *Nucleus*, is the central part of a perithecium. **1866** *Treas. Bot.* II, *Nucleus*,..the gelatinous mass of asci or spores which is found in the perithecia of *Sphæriæ* or the analogous fungi. **1875** COOKE & BERKELEY *Fungi* 79 Fruit consisting of sporidia,..contained in asci,..forming a hymenium or nucleus = Ascomycetes.

f. The hilum of a starch-granule.

1861 BENTLEY *Man. Bot.* 23 Starch granules, when fully formed, usually present a small rounded spot, which is commonly situated at one end..; this is called the *hilum* or *nucleus*.

6. a. The rudiments of the shell in certain molluscs.

1851 WOODWARD *Mollusca* I. 36 A rudimental shell.. which becomes the nucleus of the adult shell. **1866** R. TATE *British Mollusks* iii. 64 The operculum is horny with the nucleus lateral. **1889** NICHOLSON *Palæont.* (ed. 3) I. 682 In the Spiral Gastropods the embryonic shell, or 'nucleus', is placed at the apex of the permanent shell.

b. Any discrete mass of grey matter in the central nervous system.

The term is used in numerous English and mod.L. combs. distinguishing the various different nuclei.

1828 J. QUAIN *Elem. Anat.* x. 622 If a vertical section be made of one of the lobes of the cerebellum, in such a way as that two-thirds of its breadth shall lie external to the incision, an oval nucleus of grey substance (*corpus dentatum*, vel *rhomboideum*) will be exposed. **1856** *Ibid.* (ed. 6) II. 493 Another division passes directly up, its fibres embracing the olivary nucleus. **1875** *Encycl. Brit.* I. 878/1 The upper mass of grey matter projects into the lateral ventricle, and is called the intra-ventricular portion or nucleus caudatus. **1881** MIVART *Cat* 271 The third pair of nerves..arise deeply from a grey nucleus..close to the origin of the fourth nerve. **1896** CLELAND & MACKAY *Anat.* 614 The superior peduncles.. turn down..and reach the red nucleus. **1899** [see HYPOTHALAMUS]. **1968** PASSMORE & ROBSON *Compan. Med. Stud.* I. xix. 12/1 Masses of grey matter are called nuclei, some of which, e.g. the basal nuclei, are large and embedded in the depths of the brain. **1972** *Sci. Amer.* Dec. 73/1 A sensory pathway consists of peripheral sense organs and several clusters of nerve cells called nuclei. Sensory information is processed in several stages, so that each nucleus receives input from the preceding one, processes the input and sends an output to the next nucleus.

7. *Biol.* A cell organelle present in most of the cells of all organisms except the most primitive, usu. as a single subspherical structure, and consisting (except when undergoing division) of a membrane enclosing a ground substance (the nuclear sap) in which lie the chromosomes, one or more nucleoli, etc., and functioning as the repository of genetic information and as the director of metabolic and synthetic activity of the cell. Hence, by extension, applied by some writers to an organelle in some of the more primitive organisms, esp. bacteria, which is analogous in function but structurally simpler (cf. NUCLEOID *a.* B. b).

1831 R. BROWN in *Trans. Linn. Soc.* (1833) XVI. 710 This areola, or nucleus of the cell as perhaps it might be termed. **1842** CARPENTER *Hum. Phys.* §735. 618 At first having but one nucleus and afterwards presenting several; these nuclei ..it is probable..are to be regarded as cytoblasts. **1847–9** *Todd's Cycl. Anat.* IV. 120/2 No cell, or nucleus-stage having pre-existed. **1849** BALFOUR *Man. Bot.* §16 Each cell is found to contain, at some period of its existence, a small body, called a nucleus. **1857** *G. Bird's Urin. Deposits* (ed. 5) 362 A regularly organized body, consisting of a granular membrane enveloping transparent nuclei; being in fact a nucleated cell. **1861** BENTLEY *Man. Bot.* 18 Almost all young cells contain one or more bodies called Nuclei or Cytoblasts... In cells of the higher classes of plants the nucleus consists of a rounded or lenticular granular-looking body. **1880** BASTIAN *Brain* 35 Nerve cells are more or less granular bodies, each of which contains a large nucleus. **1882** VINES tr. *Sachs' Bot.* 551 In most Monocotyledons the large central nucleus divides, and two fresh nuclei make their appearance. **1888** ROLLESTON & JACKSON *Anim. Life* Introd. p. xxii, The nucleus is limited externally by a nuclear membrane. **1889** [see NUCLEOID *a.*]. **1962** *Brit. Med. Bull.* XVIII. 31/1 (*heading*) Morphology of the bacterial nucleus. **1965** [see NUCLEOID *sb.* b]. **1968** PASSMORE & ROBSON *Compan. Med. Stud.* I. xxvi. 2/1 The mature red [blood] cell..appears as a biconcave disc with no nucleus. **1970** AMBROSE & EASTY *Cell Biol.* v. 163 This may also explain how acridine dyes penetrate the nucleus without staining the cytoplasm.

8. *Chem.* An arrangement of atoms, esp. a ring structure, characteristic of a number of organic compounds.

1845 W. GREGORY *Outl. Chem.: Org. Chem.* 512 Laurent considers benzole as in some measure the fundamental compound, or nucleus, and calls it phene. **1886** E. F. SMITH tr. *V. von Richter's Chem. Carbon Compounds* 465 The azo-group, N=N, decomposes, each nitrogen atom remaining attached as NH_2 to a benzene nucleus. **1932** *Jrnl. Chem. Soc.* 1132 Table III summarises the effect of varying the nature of the side-chain halogen in the compounds with an unsubstituted phenyl nucleus. **1951** I. L. FINAR *Org. Chem.* x. 185 If *one* acetic acid nucleus is blocked off, the fragment required is ethyl chloroacetate. **1971** *Nature* 7 May 25/1 Many psychoto-mimetic substances possess an indole nucleus.

9. A particle on which crystals, droplets, or bubbles can form in a fluid.

1857 MILLER *Elem. Chem., Org.* ii. §1 (1862) 90 Small pieces of wood are then introduced to act as nuclei upon which the crystals of lactose are deposited. **1886** *Proc. R. Soc. Edin.* XIII. 79 If this were the case, no nucleus would be *absolutely* requisite for the formation either of liquid from vapour or of vapour from liquid. **1906** [see NUCLEATION]. **1939** *Q. Jrnl. R. Meteorol. Soc.* LXV. 411 If supersaturation is attained the fogs may thicken considerably owing to the deposition of water on the sea-salt nuclei. **1952** *Industr. & Engin. Chem.* June 1273/1 A nucleus in water-fog formation consists of about 80 water molecules. **1957** G. E. HUTCHINSON *Treat. Limnol.* I. ix. 583 In a free volume of water containing no minute masses of gas that can act as nuclei, an enormous excess tension is needed for bubble formation. **1967** [see NUCLEATION].

10. A small group of bees, including a queen, used as the foundation of a new colony.

1886 F. R. CHESHIRE *Bees & Bee-keeping* II. vii. 306 These small nuclei will sustain themselves, in average seasons. **1915** E. F. PHILLIPS *Beekeeping* iii. 39 A mere handful of bees (perhaps 200) may constitute a small colony (usually called a nucleus). **1952** H. MACE *Bee-Keeper's Handbk.* xxxiii. 154 Nucleus hives can be purchased or made, either to hold a single nucleus up to four combs, or two or more separate nuclei, separated by partitions. **1963** F. G. SMITH *Beekeeping* vii. 60 A nucleus is a very small colony of bees. It consists of a queen and up to four or six frames of brood and food, well covered with bees.

11. *Physics.* The positively charged central constituent of the atom, comprising nearly all its mass but occupying only a very small part of its volume and now known to be composed of protons and neutrons.

In Rutherford's 1911 paper called merely a 'central charge'. In the examples in the first paragraph *nucleus* is used for various speculative notions concerning the atom.

[**1844** FARADAY in *Phil. Mag.* XXIV. 141 If, in the ordinary view of atoms, we call the particle of matter away from the powers *a*, and the system of powers or forces in and around it *m*, then in Boscovitch's theory *a* disappears, or is a mere mathematical point... To my mind..the *a* or nucleus vanishes, and the substance consists of the powers or *m*. **1851** W. J. M. RANKINE in *Phil. Mag.* I. 443 The fundamental suppositions of the hypothesis of molecular vortices are the following:—*First.* That each atom of matter consists of a nucleus or central physical point enveloped by an elastic atmosphere, which is retained around it by attraction. *Ibid.*, If an indefinitely extended vibrating medium..consist of a system of atomic nuclei. **1900** *Rep. Brit. Assoc. Adv. Sci. 1900* 619 The material atom must be some kind of permanent nucleus that retains around itself an æthereal field of physical influence. *Ibid.*, If..the distances at which they [*sc.* atoms] are kept apart are large compared with the diameters of the atomic nuclei. **1903** O. LODGE *Mod. Views on Matter* 5 If the charge of electricity usually associated with a single monad atom of matter were concentrated on to a spherical nucleus one hundred-thousandth of an atom's dimension in diameter, it would thereby possess a mass about one-thousandth of that of the lightest atom known... Such a hypothetical concentrated unit of electricity it has become customary to call an 'electron'.]

1912 E. RUTHERFORD in *Phil. Mag.* XXIV. 461 In a previous paper [sc. *Phil. Mag.* (1911) XXI. 669] I have given reasons for believing that the atom consists of a positively charged nucleus of very small dimensions, surrounded by a distribution of electrons in rapid motion, possibly of rings of electrons rotating in one plane. **1919** *Conquest* I. I. 36/2 An atom is a sort of solar system in miniature, and comprises a central core or nucleus..and a number of particles, called corpuscles, circulating round the nucleus. **1942** J. D. STRANATHAN '*Particles' of Mod. Physics* xi. 417 The nucleus must be very small, not larger than 10^{-12} cm. **1955** C. G. DARWIN in W. Pauli *Niels Bohr* 6 In 1911 he [*sc.* Rutherford] tried the idea of a heavy central electric charge repelling the α-particle—it was I think several months before it was called the nucleus—and at once the whole theory of the nuclear atom emerged. **1962** H. D. BUSH *Atomic & Nuclear Physics* iii. 62 The hypothesis that every nucleus consisted of protons and neutrons, was first suggested by Heisenberg (1932).

12. a. *Phonetics.* The syllable of a word (spoken in isolation) that bears the primary

accent; in an utterance, the syllable or syllables given particular emphasis.
1922 H. E. PALMER *English Intonation* ii. 7 Each Tone-Group contains a Nucleus, which is the stressed syllable of the most prominent word in the Tone-Group. The nucleus corresponds to what is usually called sentence-stress. *Ibid.* 8 In Southern English there are four characteristic Nucleus Tones. **1924** —— *Gram. Spoken Eng.* 6 If..tonetic transcription is used, the syllable [ˈ] will be replaced by the appropriate nucleus-symbol. *Ibid.* 14 Instead of the rise taking place in the nucleus-syllable itself, it is distributed over the nucleus and tail. **1941** *Language* XVII. 224 The present study..will deal with junctures, stresses, and consonants only in summary, and then devote itself to the syllabic nuclei. **1942** *English Studies* XXIV. 157 In combinations of noun + adjective (like French master, black bird) the marking of the nucleus tone (i.e. the point at which the pitch begins to rise or fall) is an excellent device to bring home to students the two meanings such combinations may express. **1962** A. C. GIMSON *Introd. Pronunc. Eng.* x. 244 The primary accent (or accents) in a sentence is shown by initiating a change of pitch direction, with the nucleus (falling, rising, or a combination of the two) on the appropriate syllable of the word (or words) on which attention is particularly to be concentrated. **1962** S. STUBELIUS in F. Behre *Contrib. Eng. Syntax* 151 The main features of intonation, particularly whether the sentences studied had a falling or a rising end intonation (nucleus). **1973** *Archivum Linguisticum* IV. 21 Tonality, tonicity, and tone, which refer to the number of tone-groups, the location of the tonic, or nucleus, and the choice of tone used, respectively.

b. *Linguistics.* The main word or words in a combination, phrase, or sentence; also = KERNEL *sb.*[1] 8 b.
1934 [see DETERMINANT *a.* and *sb.* B. 2 c]. **1949** E. A. NIDA *Morphol.* (ed. 2) 83 The nucleus of a morphological construction consists of (1) a root or (2) a combination of roots... The nonnucleus is made up of nonroots. In the construction *boyishness* the element *boy* is the nucleus and *-ishness* constitutes the nonnucleus. **1961** R. B. LONG *Sentence & its Parts* i. 20 Isolates sometimes take adjunct modifiers, much as nucleuses do. *Ibid.* 497 *Nucleuses*, minimal sequences made up of subjects, predicators, and complements, or of such of these as occur... In *come in!* the nucleus is made up of the predicator *come* and the complement *in*. **1961** Y. OLSSON *Syntax Eng. Verb* iv. 77 The relationship between a group of nuclei (like *London*, etc.) and equivalent members of the paradigms based on them (like *London-er*, etc.) give rise to an expectancy which may or may not be met in the same way. **1968** J. LYONS *Introd. Theoretical Linguistics* viii. 334 The subject and the predicate together form the nucleus of the sentence.

Hence ˈ**nucleus** *v. trans.*, to make into a nucleus, to concentrate.
1899 KIPLING *Stalky* 252 They'd withdrawn all the troops they could, but I nucleused about forty Pathans.

nuclide (ˈnjuːklaɪd). *Nuclear Physics.* [f. NUCL(EUS *sb.* + *-ide* (f. Gr. εἶδος form, kind).] A particular kind of atom, as defined by the number of protons and the number of neutrons in the nucleus.
Synonymous with ISOTOPE in its broader sense, which the introduction of *nuclide* was intended to discourage in favour of the original stricter meaning of that word.
1947 T. P. KOHMAN in *Amer. Jrnl. Physics* XV. 356/2 There is at present no word in the English language to express the concept of a particular species of atom, differing from all others in the constitution of its nucleus... *Nuclear species* and the German *Kernsorte*..refer to nuclei rather than to atoms... In recent years the word *isotope* has come into use for this purpose, less by design than by default... Evidently a new word is required, and *nuclide* is proposed... The new word and its derivatives should be used in such expressions as 'stable nuclides'..and 'nuclidic weight'. **1955** R. D. EVANS *Atomic Nucleus* xvi. 522 Because it is the only naturally occurring nuclide which undergoes fission by slow neutrons, U^{235} has attained international fame even in lay circles. **1957** *Technology* June 139/3 β and γ ionization chambers for secondary standardisation of radioactive nuclides have been designed. **1961** G. R. CHOPPIN *Exper. Nuclear Chem.* 215 Na^{22}, Na^{23}, and Na^{24} are all isotopes of sodium... Na^{22} and C^{14} are nuclides but are not isotopic to each other. **1967** *Guardian* 17 May 3/2 There was less Strontium-90 and Caesium-137 in milk last year... Levels of both nuclides were lower than at any time since 1962. **1971** *Daily Colonist* (Victoria, B.C.) 9 July 9/3 The nuclear explosive was designed to reduce the amount of residual tritium, a radioactive nuclide.

Hence **nuclidic** (-ˈɪdɪk) *a.*
1947 [see above]. **1955** R. D. EVANS *Atomic Nucleus* xvi. 519 In order to identify the new artificial nuclides, it was logical and essential to utilize the usual nuclidic notation, for example, ${}_{83}Bi^{213}$. **1962** *Nature* 19 May 621/2 Modern methods make possible much more exact measurements of nuclidic masses. *Ibid.*, The atomic physicist is usually concerned with individual nuclidic species—the differences in their nuclear characteristics and the nuclear, as opposed to chemical, changes they undergo. **1973** J. YARWOOD *Atomic & Nuclear Physics* xv. 429 A useful method of correlating data about the nuclides is to plot a nuclidic chart of *N*, the number of neutrons in the nucleus, against *Z*, the atomic number.

nucloid (ˈnjuːklɔɪd). Also **nucleoid**. [f. NUCLEUS *sb.* + -OID.] (See quot. 1962.)
1908 *Westm. Gaz.* 31 July 1/3 (*heading*) 'Nucleoids' in naval manœuvres. *Ibid.* 2/2 The balance is still all on the side of the 'nucleoid' as against the newly commissioned ship. **1917** 'TAFFRAIL' *Sub* vii. 176 About June, came the summer manœuvres, when the crews of all the 'nucloids' were brought up to full strength. **1962** W. GRANVILLE *Dict. Sailors' Slang* 82/2 *Nucloid*, ship of the Reserve Fleet in peacetime, carrying a nucleus crew.

nuclon: see NUCLEON[2] b.

nucoline (ˈnjuːkəliːn). [f. L. *nuc-*, *nux* nut + *ol-eum* oil + -INE[5].] A kind of butter made from nuts; nut-butter.
1898 LEWKOWITSCH *Anal. Oils*, etc. (ed. 2) 541 'Vegetable butter,' 'Lactine,'..'Nucoline' is therefore practically neutral cocoa nut oil. **1906** *Westm. Gaz.* 18 May 4/2 'Nutter,' 'Nucoline,' and 'Nuttene'—all representing butter made from nuts.

†**nucquedah**, obs. variant of NAKHODA.
1698 FRYER *Acc. India & P.* 107 The Captain is called Nucquedah, the Boatswain Tindal.

‖**nuculanium** (njuːkjuːˈleɪnɪəm). *Bot.* [mod.L., irreg. f. L. *nucula* NUCULE.]
1. (See quots.)
1819 LINDLEY tr. *Richard's Fruits & Seeds* 86 *Nuculanium*; fruit whose fleshy pericarp forms several distinct nuts. **1829** CLINTON tr. *Richard's Elem. Bot.* (ed. 4) 430 The nuculanium is a fleshy fruit proceeding from a free ovary,..containing within it several small nuts, which bear the name nuculæ. **1887** BENTLEY *Man. Bot.* (ed. 5) 318 The Nuculanium..does not differ in any important characters from the berry, except in being superior.
2. A hard nut-like case in the interior of a fleshy fruit, enclosing several seeds.
1849 BALFOUR *Man. Bot.* §553 The covering of the cells [of the endocarp] is sometimes stony, as in the Medlar..and the Holly, forming what has been called a Nuculanium (*nucula*, a nut). **1876** *Encycl. Brit.* IV. 152/2 Some apply the term nuculanium to the Medlar.

nucule (ˈnjuːkjuːl). *Bot.* [a. F. *nucule*, ad. L. *nucula*, dim. of *nuc-*, *nux* nut.]
1. One of the seeds of a nuculanium; a nutlet; a small hard seed-like or nut-like fruit; a small stone or seed.
1819 LINDLEY tr. *Richard's Fruits & Seeds* 86 *Nucule*; each nut of a nuculanium. **1847** W. E. STEELE *Field Bot.* 137 Fruit a capsule or berry of 2 or 4 adhering nucules. **1879** A. GRAY *Struct. Bot.* (ed. 6) 298 Pyrenæ are not uncommonly in English descriptions called nutlets or nucules.
2. The female organ of reproduction in the cryptogamic tribe *Chara*.
1830 LINDLEY *Nat. Syst. Bot.* 325 Axillary nucules, formed of a few short tubes, twisted spirally around a centre. **1858** CARPENTER *Veg. Phys.* §776 The fructification of the Characeae is of two kinds, nucules, and globules. **1884** *Trans. Victoria Instit.* 86 The organ known as the nucule consists of an axial row of cells, which form a kind of crown at the summit.

nud, *v. rare.* [Of obscure origin: cf. NUDDLE *v.*] (See quots.)
1688 HOLME *Armoury* II. 176/2 Lamb bossing the Ewe, when it Nuds the Dug. **1887** *Chesh. Gloss.*, *Nud*, to butt with the head... The forward jerking motion with the head which calves make in sucking is called *nuddin'*.

nud, obs. form of NUDE.

†**nuˈdate**, *v. Obs. rare.* [f. ppl. stem of L. *nūdāre*.] *trans.* 'To make bare or naked' (Bailey, 1721). Hence **nuˈdated** *ppl. a.*
1688 HOLME *Armoury* II. 119/1 Such [trees] as are covered with thick or thin husks..are of three sorts, as..Nudated, or smooth thin husks.

†**nuˈdation.** *Obs.*—[0] [ad. L. *nūdātio*.] 'A making bare' (Blount *Glossogr.*, 1656).

nuddle (ˈnʌd(ə)l), *v.* Now *dial.* [Related to NUD *v.*: see -LE 3. Connexion with G. *nudeln*, to press, is very doubtful.]
1. *intr.* †**a.** To push with the nose; to press close to the ground in this way; to grovel. *Obs.*
1650 H. MORE *Enthus. Tri.*, *Obs.* (1656) 111 A pig in a poke, that grunting and nudling to get out, drove the yielding bag out of this corner and that corner. **1653** —— *Antid. Ath.* III. xi. (1662) 123 A thing in the shape of a Weasel came.., nudling along in the grass. *a* **1661** FULLER *Worthies, Hertfordsh.* II. (1662) 18 The People in this County,..taxed for covetousness, and their constant nudling on the Earth.
b. *dial.* To hang the head; to stoop in walking.
1828– in various dial. glossaries (Yks., Nhp., E. Anglia).
c. To nestle, to press close.
1854 MISS BAKER *Northampton Gloss.*
2. *trans.* †**a.** To beat, pummel. *Obs. rare.*
1640 RAWLINS *Rebellion* IV. i, I, I, Meder; the Divill Meder him, he has so nudled me.
b. To squeeze, press.
1875 *Whitby Gloss.*, *Nuddled*, as a parcel carried in the hand is apt to be squeezed out of shape. **1888** *Sheffield Gloss.*, *Nuddle*, to press wheat into the earth with a roller.
c. To rub with the nose.
1898 *Speaker* 5 Feb. 181 The mother nuddles him [*sc.* a lamb] with her nose.
Hence ˈ**nuddling** *ppl. a.* (Cf. NUD, NUDGEL.)
1640 J. GOWER *Ovids Festivalls* II. 34 She stands and fawns upon the nuddling twins And with her tongue licks o're their tender skins.

nuddock, obs. variant of NIDDICK.

nude (njuːd), *a.* and *sb.* Also 8 **nud.** [ad. L. *nūd-us*, whence also It. and Sp. *nudo*, Pg. and F. *nu*. In sense B. 2 the immediate source is the obs. F. form *nud*.]
A. *adj.* **1.** *Law.* **a.** Of statements, promises, etc.: Not formally attested or recorded.
1531 *Dial. on Laws Eng.* I. xii. 21 b, That euery man by a nude parol and by a bare auerment shulde auoyde an oblygacyon. **1532** *Ibid.* II. xxiii. 48 If a man seased of landes make a gyfte therof or graunte by a nude promyse. **1594** WEST *2nd Pt. Symbol.*, *Chancerie* §37 If by such nude averrments matters of record should be avoided. **1607** COWELL *Interpreter* s.v. *Mater*, Kitchin..saith, that nude mater is not of so high nature, as either a mater of Record or a Speciality. **1634** *Irish Act 10 Chas. I* Sess. II. c. 1 Preamble, Wills and testaments..made by nude parolx and words.
b. *nude contract* or *pact* (see quots.).
1532 *Dial. on Laws Eng.* II. xxiv. 49 A nude contracte is when a man maketh a bargayn, or a sale of his goodes or landes without any recompence appoynted for it. **1658** PHILLIPS, *Nude contract*, in Common-law, is a bare contract, or promise of any thing without assigning, or agreeing what another shall give. **1766** BLACKSTONE *Comm.* II. xxx. 445 Any degree of reciprocity will prevent the pact from being nude. **1875** POSTE *Gaius* III. (ed. 2) 361 A nude pact creates no (civil) obligation, but creates a defence.
c. Of persons, esp. *nude executor* (see quots.).
1590 SWINBURNE *Testaments* 176 If the testator giue his goods to one person, and make another executor: this executor is called Nude executor, for that he reapeth no commoditie by the testament. **1726** AYLIFFE *Parergon* 269 A nude Executor here mention'd is no more than an Executor in Trust. **1875** POSTE *Gaius* III. (ed. 2) 422 Including the nude or nominal proprietor.
†**2.** Naked, bare, mere, plain. *Obs.*
1551 CRANMER *Answ. Gardner* (1580) 10 Is therfore the whole vse of the bread..but a naked or nude and bare token? **1654** H. L'ESTRANGE *Chas. I* (1655) 89 Yet this could be.. but a nude conjecture. **1667** WATERHOUSE *Fire London* 34 A bare accident and a nude casualty.
3. a. Naked, bare; without covering or investment; devoid of furniture or decorations.
Given by Blount *Glossogr.* (1656), partly from Cotgrave, but app. not in actual use before the 19th c.
1866 *Treas. Bot.*, *Nude*,..bald from the total absence of hairs, or uncovered in consequence of the absence of any investing organs. **1867** LADY HERBERT *Cradle L.* iii. 85 A nude modern octagonal room. **1879** STEVENSON *Trav. Donkey* (1886) 74 A broad nude valley in Vivarais. **1897** *Allbutt's Syst. Med.* II. 1124 The bladders may..remain entirely nude and free in the peritoneal cavity. **1926** E. O'NEILL *Great God Brown* I. iii. 46, I am thy shorn, bald, nude sheep! **1928** *Oxford Poetry* 3 The pale, nude flowers That I Picked for you. **1952** E. O'NEILL *Moon for Misbegotten* I. 38 It is full of nude rocks. **1964** D. VARADAY *Gara-Yaka* xii. 102 (*caption*) Vultures like baubles on a nude tree.
Comb. **1881** *Gard. Chron.* XVI. 725 A west wall against which had been planted the nude-flowered Jasminum.
b. Of the human figure, or those parts of it which are usually clothed: Naked, unclothed, undraped. Also *fig.*
1845 *Punch* VIII. 247 A regret that Etty should content himself with merely painting from '*the nude Academy model*'. **1873** SYMONDS *Grk. Poets* viii. 237 Of all the Greeks, essentially a nude nation, Aristophanes is the most naked. **1879** H. PHILLIPS *Notes Coins* 1 The medals..bear..on their obverse the nude bust of that Empress. **1880** 'OUIDA' *Moths* I. 73 He was so used to seeing pretty nude feet at Trouville. **1974** *Publishers Weekly* 26 Aug. 250/3 A novel about a nude model who longs for true love.
c. Of a revue, show, photograph, etc.: involving or portraying nude, or lightly clad, figures (usu. female).
In quot. 1870 the actresses referred to were clothed in flesh-coloured tights.
1870 O. LOGAN *Before Footlights & Behind Scenes* xv. 128 Bringing upon stage that hideous disgrace known as the 'nude drama', which took its rise with the flimsy absurdity called the 'Black Crook'. **1947** *Amer. Speech* XXII. 171 America enthusiastically adopted the word..*nude drama*. **1957** J. OSBORNE *Entertainer* xiii. 86 Nude tableau, behind first act gauze. **1959** *Sunday Times* 16 Aug. 10/4 It is the later nude revue days of Collins's Music Hall. **1959** *Listener* 15 Jan. 132/3 The night-clubs in Calvin's city put on nude shows. *Ibid.* 6 Aug. 195/2 There are packed houses at nude revues. **1972** *Daily Tel.* 27 Nov. 17/6 An Italian magazine published nine pages of nude photographs of her last week.
4. As a colour, esp. of stockings, flesh-coloured.
1922 *Daily Mail* 18 Dec. 2 (Advt.), Ladies' Hose... Black, white,.. taupe, navy, nude, and all shades. **1926** GALSWORTHY *Silver Spoon* II. xii. 216 'Blue-stockings.' 'No, sir; they nearly all wear "nude".' **1931** M. DE LA ROCHE *Finch's Fortune* ix. 156 She had on..'nude' stockings. **1947** *Sun* (Baltimore) 10 Sept. 5 Nude and white in sizes 33 to 40. Corset Shop, third floor. **1973** *Philadelphia Inquirer* (Today Suppl.) 14 Oct. 17/3 (Advt.), Choose black, brown, navy or nude calfskin.
5. *Med.* Of a mouse: homozygous for a mutant gene which produces apparent hairlessness and (in most cases) a grossly hypoplastic thymus gland.
1966 S. P. FLANAGAN in *Genetical Res.* VIII. 295 [The hairless mutant was found by Dr. N. R. Grist of the Virus Laboratory, Ruchill Hospital, Glasgow... The name 'nude', symbol *nu*, has been adopted.] *Ibid.* 308 The majority of nude mice die of general body weakness within 2 weeks. **1974** *Nature* 20 Sept. 184/2 Nude mice have spread through the immunological world at a remarkable pace... The thymus abnormality leads to a marked deficiency in thymus-derived (T) lymphocytes and nude mice are rapidly replacing thymectomised mice as models of T cell deprivation and as a source of relatively pure B lymphocytes for *in vitro* studies. **1975** *Ibid.* 13 Mar. 140/2 (*heading*) Nude mice with normal thymus.
B. *sb.* **1. a.** A nude figure in painting or sculpture.
1708 *New View Lond.* II. 824/2 A *Nude* or *Nudity*, is a naked Figure painted or sculpted, without Drapery (or Cloathing). *a* **1849** H. COLERIDGE *Ess.* (1851) I. 205 Are not the greatest masters almost as much celebrated for their draperies as for their nudes? **1889** *Pall Mall G.* 9 May 3/2 We went round the Academy noticing the..pictures, and

dismissing..a certain number of nudes, babies, and portraits of nobodies.

b. A woman given to wearing very low-necked dresses. *rare*$^{-1}$.

1816 *Spirit Public Jrnls.* XIII. 273 As a link-boy was showing a certain fashionable nude, in Baker Street, out of her carriage [etc.].

2. a. With *the*. The undraped human figure; the representation of this in drawing, painting, or sculpture.

1760 D. WEBB *Enq. Beauties Painting* iv. 51 The result of this habit is evident, when our first artists come to design the nud. **1782** R. CUMBERLAND *Anecd. Painters* I. 56 Being most in the *nude*, their crime will in some people's judgment appear their recommendation. **1868** BROWNING *Ring & Bk.* I. 58 Modern chalk drawings, studies from the nude. **1887** F. M. CRAWFORD *Saracinesca* i, The French school had not [yet] demonstrated the startling distinction between the nude and the naked.

b. The condition of being undraped.

1856 MRS. BROWNING *Aur. Leigh* III. 710 Stands sublimely in the nude, as chaste As Medicean Venus. **1882** *Globe* 14 Dec. 5/5 They had seen him modelling..from Miss Felden, who stood in the nude as a model.

3. *Med.* A nude mouse.

1968 *Nature* 27 Jan. 371/1 (*heading*) Section of liver of an adult homozygote nude. **1974** *Ibid.* 20 Sept. 184/2 The T cell deficiency in nudes make them highly susceptible to infection (but apparently not to cancer) and they survive poorly in conventional animal houses.

Hence **'nudely** *adv.*, barely, simply, plainly; **'nudeness**, the state of being nude or undraped.

1627 DONNE *Serm.* lxxxi. Wks. 1839 IV. 10 Being crudely and nudely taken, not decocted and boiled up. **1882** OGILVIE, *Nudeness.* **1895** *Cent. Mag.* Aug. 494/2 Whether the nudeness itself outraged his sense of propriety.

nude, *v. rare.* [ad. L. *nūd-āre*, or f. NUDE *a.*]

† **1.** *trans.* To denude; to deprive or strip (one) *of* something. *Obs.*

1551-2 *Burgh Rec. Prestwick* (Maitl. Cl.) 62 The inquest ..ordains hym to be nwdyt of his fredome.

2. To strip, unclothe, make naked.

1845 T. COOPER *Purgat. Suicides* Wks. (1877) 30 They clothe with prudent mask The image from whose worship Man might swerve If nuded.

nudey, var. NUDIE.

nudge (nʌdʒ), *sb.* [f. the vb.] **1.** A slight push or poke given to another with the elbow. Also *fig.*

1836 MARRYAT *Midsh. Easy* xxii, Gascoigne gave Jack a nudge. **1847** ALB. SMITH *Chr. Tadpole* i, One of those pleasant nudges which funny men will inflict upon you. **1871** B. TAYLOR *Faust* (1875) II. I. iii. 25 Though with one [thou] wast wont to dance, Gav'st another nudge and glance. *fig.* **1865** LOWELL *Thoreau* Prose Wks. 1890 I. 366 The mental and moral nudge which he received from the writings of his..brave-spirited countryman. **1922** JOYCE *Ulysses* 631 Hynes wrote it with a nudge from Corny. **1950** *Sun* (Baltimore) 20 June 21/4 Didn't you like the comeback of Cardinal Manager Eddie Dyer when given a slight nudge over his club's loss of three straight. **1953** A. HUXLEY *Let.* 19 July (1969) 679 Your publishers..would send me proofs as soon as they became available. I have heard nothing... Would you be kind enough to give them a little nudge?

2. *nudge, nudge* (*wink, wink*, etc.): a catch-phrase from the British television comedy programme *Monty Python's Flying Circus* (see PYTHONESQUE *a.*), used to imply mischievously an insinuation or innuendo, esp. of a sexual or otherwise dubious nature.

1973 *Punch* 7 Feb. 178/1 We are largely informed about British public affairs by a hallowed process of nudge-nudge, wink-wink, Know-what-I-mean. **1977** *Club Tennis* Mar. 6/6 Senior lady players, in my experience (and I have some experience in that field, nudge, nudge), take very badly to being beaten by up-and-comings. **1977** *Daily Tel.* 23 Sept. 16/5 In the sketches there is a bit too much of the nudge-nudge, wink-wink approach. **1979** *Guardian* 24 May 11/7 Woman—a sexual object to be lusted after..whistled at on the silver screen and nudge nudge wink wink'd in every comedy series. **1981** P. INCHBALD *Tondo for Short* x. 109 Another good friend of ours, nudge nudge, wink wink, as the saying goes. **1985** T. HEALD *Red Herrings* iv. 115 He seemed to think I was running some sort of a brothel... He had one or two clients who..nudge, nudge, wink, wink, know what I mean.

nudge (nʌdʒ), *v.* [Of obscure origin: perh. related to Norw. dial. *nugga*, *nyggja*, to push, rub.]

1. *trans.* To touch or push (one) slightly with the elbow for the purpose of attracting attention. Also *transf.* and *fig.*

1675 HOBBES *Odyssey* (1677) 177 When a third part of the night was gone, I nudg'd Ulysses, who did next me lie. **1838** DICKENS *Nich. Nick.* vii, Squeers then nudged Mrs. Squeers to bring away the brandy bottle. **1860** HOLLAND *Miss Gilbert's Career* i, What wonder that Mrs. Bloomer and Mrs. Witton nudged each other? **1880** JEFFERIES *Hodge & M.* II. 28 She is partly deaf, and until nudged by her neighbours did not hear her husband's name.

transf. and *fig.* **1850** CARLYLE *Latter-d. Pamph.* i. 19 The inexorable Icebergs..will nudge you with most chaotic 'admonition'. **1877** G. H. LEWES *Let.* 27 Feb. in *Geo. Eliot's Lett.* (1956) VI. 345 He might still be induced to resume that idea if you thought fit to nudge his elbow a little. **1922** JOYCE *Ulysses* 63 Nudging the door open with his knee he carried the tray in. **1925** H. V. MORTON *Heart of London* (1926) 75 Watch the way a press of omnibuses..will edge and nudge a way with a mere inch between their mudguards. **1936** DYLAN THOMAS *Twenty-Five Poems* 9 Half The dear, daft time I take to nudge the sentence. **1971** *Times* 28 Aug. 10/1 A smarter, cleaner place undergoing the upheaval of architectural surgery, being nudged by bulldozers and demolition gangs from one century into the next. **1973** *Guardian* 10 Mar. 1/7 Governments would use their reserves..and nudge the price if it tended to drift out of line. **1975** *Physics Bull.* Apr. 162/1 The Science Research Council's attempts to nudge university research into areas more relevant to social and economic needs are meeting some resistance.

2. *intr.* To give a push or thrust. Also const. *up*, to move up by pushing.

1825 BROCKETT *N.C. Gloss.* s.v., What are ye nudging at? **1888** GOODE *Amer. Fishes* 109 In the surf the Drum nudges like the sheepshead when he first takes the bait. **1940** DYLAN THOMAS *Portrait of Artist as Young Dog* 7 The bar was full; two fat women in bright dresses sat near the door, one with a small, dark child on her knee; they saw Uncle Jim and nudged up on the bench.

Hence **'nudging** *vbl. sb.*; *ppl. a.* and *pres. pple.*, approaching, nearing, close to (used e.g. of someone's age).

1854 THOREAU *Walden* 97 We are not awakened by our Genius, but by the mechanical nudgings of some servitor. **1858** R. S. SURTEES *Ask Mamma* iii, Amid the nudging of outsiders, and staring of street-loungers. **1880** H. CONWAY *Called Back* 60 There were no nudgings and sly glances among our fellow passengers. **1889** FARRAR *Lives Fathers* II. xiv. 100 A gaping and nudging crowd. **1949** E. E. CUMMINGS *Let.* 23 Aug. (1969) 193 Now et comment The quote Oxford unquote Press registers alarm nudging horror. **1961** *Sunday Times* 30 Apr. 13/6 Nudging forty..Secombe knows where his ultimate responsibility lies. **1969** D. BARRON *Man who was There* ii. 30 Hughes was tough and nudging fifty. **1971** D. LEES *Rainbow Conspiracy* i. 17 The Manchester circulation is nudging the one and a half million a day mark. **1972** A. MACVICAR *Golden Venus Affair* i. 9, I was big, nudging six feet two. **1974** *Country Life* 25 Apr. 1012/2 A fuel gauge nudging zero.

† **'nudgel**, *v. Obs. rare*$^{-1}$. [Cf. NUD *v.* and NUDDLING *ppl. a.*] *intr.* To press, squeeze.

1603 HOLLAND *Plutarch's Mor.* 220 A nipple..ready for the little babe's mouth, about which to nuzzle and nudgell with its pretty lips it taketh pleasure.

nudger ('nʌdʒə(r)). [f. NUDGE *v.* + -ER^{1}.] **a.** One who nudges another or others.

1910 H. G. WELLS *Hist. Mr. Polly* vi. 177 A sprinkling of girls in gay hats from Miriam's place of business appeared in church, great nudgers all of them. *Ibid.* 178 A murmer from the nudgers announced the arrival of the bridal party. **1960** S. PLATH *Colossus* 35 Nudgers and shovers In spite of ourselves Our kind multiplies.

b. *dial.* A hat.

1903 *Eng. Dial. Dict.* IV. 309/2 *Nudger*,..a hat. **1966** *Sun* 10 June 4/2 He was the only one wearing a bowler, called a 'nudger'.

nudi- ('njuːdɪ), combining form of L. *nūd-us* NUDE *a.*, used in a number of compounds of which the more important are given below. Some others are given in recent Dictionaries, as ***nudicaudate***, having a hairless tail; ***nudicaul(ous***, having leafless stems; ***nudifolious***, having bare or smooth leaves; ***nudiped***, having naked feet; ***nudirostrate***, having a naked beak; etc.

nudi'brachiate, *a. Zool.* [f. NUDI- + BRACHIATE.] Of polyps: Having arms or tentacles which are not covered with cilia.

1847-9 *Todd's Cycl. Anat.* IV. 50/1 The Bryozoa.. exhibiting a much higher phase of organisation than any of the nudibrachiate races. *Ibid.*, In the nudibrachiate polypes.

nudibranch ('njuːdɪbræŋk). *Zool.* Also -branche. [ad. F. *nudibranche* (Cuvier): see NUDI- and BRANCHIÆ.] A mollusc of the order *Nudibranchiata*, having naked gills and no shell.

1844 ALLMAN in *Ann. & Mag. Nat. Hist.* (1845) XVI. 154 A small Nudibranchiate Gasteropod, which this naturalist [M. de Quatrefages] conceives himself justified in separating..from all previously characterized genera of Nudibranchs. **1851** WOODWARD *Mollusca* I. 36 The rudimentary shell of the nudibranchs is shed at an early age. **1862** KEARLEY *Links in Chain* vi. 136 One beautiful little Nudibranch common on our northern coasts.

b. *attrib.* or as *adj.* = NUDIBRANCHIATE.

1871 DARWIN *Desc. Man* II. ix. I. 32 Many of the nudibranch mollusca, or sea-slugs, are as brightly coloured as any shells. **1896** tr. *Boas' Text-Bk. Zool.* 303 The nudibranch larva is furnished with shell and operculum.

So **nudi'branchial** *a.*; **nudi'branchian.**

1839 *Penny Cycl.* XIV. 322/1 The third class, Gastropods, are divided into the following orders and suborders:—1. Nudibranchians. **1841** *Proc. Berw. Nat. Club* I. No. 9. 249 The naked nudibranchial mollusk alluded to.

nudi'branchiate, *a.* and *sb. Zool.* [See NUDI- and BRANCHIATE.] **a.** *adj.* Of molluscs: Having naked gills or branchiæ; belonging to the *Nudibranchiata*. **b.** *sb.* A mollusc of this order (Ogilvie, 1882).

1836-9 *Todd's Cycl. Anat.* II. 393/2 It is in the Nudibranchiate division..that the nervous centres exist in their most concentrated form. **1855** *Orr's Circ. Sci.*, *Org. Nature* II. 441 The Nudibranchiate Mollusks are distributed into three families. **1877** THOMSON *Voy. Challenger* I. iii. 194 Several of the nudibranchiate mollusca characteristic of the gulf-weed fauna.

nudie ('njuːdɪ). Also nudey. [f. NUDE *a.* and *sb.* + -IE.] A nude show; a nude person; a film, photograph, or magazine featuring nudity. Also *attrib.* or as *adj.*

1935 *Amer. Mercury* June 230/1 *Nudie*, nude show. **1939** *Amer. Speech* XIV. 4 A 'nudie' (nudist picture)..is 'cinemerotic'. **1942** BERREY & VAN DEN BARK *Amer. Thes. Slang* §509/24 '*Strip-tease*',..nudie. *Ibid.* §583/31 '*Strip-teaser*',..nudie. *Ibid.* §590/9 *Burlesque show*,..nudie. *Ibid.* §608/1 Bare skinema, nudie, nudie pic,..a nudist picture. **1964** *New Statesman* 21 Feb. 306/3 Trying to break away from nudies and naughties. **1967** *Punch* 4 Oct. 506/2 He had ..submitted Furd's photograph to several nudie magazines. **1968** *Wall St. Jrnl.* 24 Apr., Russ Meyer is king of the 'nudies'. But his influence on American moviemaking is not inconsiderable. **1970** K. PLATT *Pushbutton Butterfly* xiv. 161, I riffled the chromos. Nudies of Janet Sanders. **1971** R. PETRIE *Thorne in Flesh* vi. 84 Desmond Morris's 'Naked Ape'. Another case of a nudey dust-jacket selling a serious book. **1971** *Petticoat* 17 July 7/3 The nudie stills appear in sex magazines all over the world. **1972** *Guardian* 16 Feb. 13/1 Male nudie pin-ups. **1974** P. GZOWSKI *This Country* 197/1 That the nudies have such phenomenal mass-market circulations says something about our sexuality.

nudifi'cation. *rare*$^{-0}$. [See NUDI- and -FICATION.] 'A making naked' (Ogilvie, 1855).

† **nudi'fidian.** *Obs. rare.* [f. NUDI- after *nullifidian.*] One who holds that faith alone is sufficient for salvation.

1648 SYMMONS *Vindic.* 84 Saint James tells us of nudifidians..who say they have faith... The bare beleeving sort of Protestants perhaps they are. *a* **1653** T. ADAMS *Wks.* (1862) II. 280 A Christian must work; for no nudifidian, as well as no nullifidian, shall be admitted into heaven.

'nudified, *a. rare.* [See NUDI- and -FY.] Made or become bare.

1883 H. JAMES *Let.* 11 Jan. in R. B. Perry *Tht. & Char. of W. James* (1935) I. xxii. 388 This morning I went out to poor *nudified* and staring Cambridge [Massachusetts].

'nudifier. *rare*$^{-1}$. [See NUDI- and -FY.] One who strips himself of his clothes.

1880 *22nd Rep. Scotch Commiss. Lunacy* 129 One was a chronic maniac and a determined nudifier.

'nudiflor. *rare*$^{-1}$. [ad. L. type **nūdiflōrus*, f. NUDI- + *flōs*, *flōris* flower.] (See quot.)

1885 *Pall Mall Budget* 19 June 17/2 The original azalea was a nudiflor.., its flowers came out before its leaves.

† **nudil**, erroneous form of NODULE 1.

1657 TOMLINSON *Renou's Disp.* 180 Of Nudils or Penicils. [Hence in the *Physical Dict.* (1657), compiled mainly from this work.]

'nudish, *a.* [-ISH.] Somewhat nude.

1880 *Academy* 18 Dec. 447/2 The presence..of the nudish damsels, ill-drawn and foolishly smirking.

nudism ('njuːdɪz(ə)m). [f. NUDE *a.* and *sb.* + -ISM.] The cult and practice of going unclothed.

1929 *Time* 1 July 23/1 Made in Germany, imported to France, is the cult of Nudism, a mulligan stew of vegetarianism, physical culture and pagan worship. **1931** F. & M. MERRILL *Among Nudists* xv. 221 The Doctors Durville ..insist that France is not ready for nudism as is Germany. *Ibid.* xvi. 233 In spite of their [*sc.* the French bourgeoisie's] modesty on the subject, nudism is growing in France. **1935** *Punch* 19 June 721/1 'A real tent... Think of the saving. Hotel bills, nothing. Meals, practically nothing. Clothes, nothing whatever.' 'Pamela,' I said imploringly, 'not Nudism.' **1944** B. MALINOWSKI *Sci. Theory of Culture* v. 44 If we were to examine from this point of view any movement, such as..fundamentalism or nudism..we would see that in one and all we can register a certain agreement on the statement of a common purpose as between the members of the movement. **1973** *Guardian* 28 June 6/1 The principles of nudism.

nudist ('njuːdɪst). [f. NUDE *a.* and *sb.* + -IST.] An adherent of the cult of the nude; a person who advocates or practises going unclothed. Also *attrib.*

1929 *Time* 1 July 23/1 Much publicity has been given the Nudist colony on an island in the Seine near Paris. *Ibid.*, A U.S. parallel would be if elegant Editor Frank Crowninshield of *Vanity Fair* should suddenly appear as a vegetable-eating, hairy-chested Nudist. **1931** *John o' London's* 8 Aug. 620/2 The other members of the nudist colony were..entirely normal people. *Ibid.* 620/3 The nudists of France are pursued by the police, by the clergy, by the wit of Parisian cartoonists. **1932** *Daily Express* 28 June 1/7 Nudist camps have sprung up all over England in the past fortnight, in which happy families disport themselves in the warm sunshine. **1938** L. MACNEICE *I crossed Minch* I. vi. 85 The Devil's business fell as flat As a nudist camp or an opera hat. **1960** *Guardian* 6 Jan. 1/7 One father..regularly went off and joined a nudist colony. **1966** J. BALL *Cool Cottontail* iii. 22 Have you ever been in a nudist park before, doctor? **1973** G. MITCHELL *Murder of Busy Lizzie* xiii. 146 'Did you know..that there is a nudist colony on the island?'..'If nudists excite you, you're welcome to them.'

nudi'tarian, *a. rare.* [f. NUDIT-Y + *-arian.*] Advocating the study of the nude.

1867 *Contemp. Rev.* VI. 387 The high aim and motive.. enable the Nuditarian school to quote Cellini's dictum with emphatic confidence.

nudity ('njuːdɪtɪ). [a. F. *nudité* (= It. *nudita*), or ad. L. *nūditāt-em*, f. *nūd-us* NUDE: see -ITY.]

1. The condition or fact of being naked or nude; a nude or naked state. **a.** Of persons.

1611 COTGR., *Nudité*, nuditie, nakednesse. **1656** BLOUNT *Glossogr.*, *Nudity*, bareness, nakedness, want of any thing, poverty.

1807 tr. *Goede's Trav.* II. 106 Two elegant Cyprians..in all the fashionable nudity of French freedom. **1856** KANE *Arct. Expl.* II. i. 24 To bend forward exposes the back to partial nudity. **1872** SHIPLEY *Gloss. Eccl. Terms* 360 Picard, who..attempted to introduce nudity and other shameful practices.

fig. **1872** GEO. ELIOT *Middlem.* II. xx, Many souls in their young nudity are tumbled out among incongruities. **1892** *Athenæum* 4 June 739/2 The whole, if indiscreet in nudity of soul, is at least admirable in art.

b. Of things or places.

c **1890** H. JAMES *Little Tour* xxix, It may appear that I insist too much upon the nudity of the Provençal horizon... But it is an exquisite bareness. **1900** *Westm. Gaz.* 20 Mar. 4/3 In another [plate] the august nudity of Downing-street is made interesting.

2. A nude figure, *esp.* as represented in painting or sculpture.

1662 EVELYN *Chalcogr.* 45 Divers Nudities, and Clad Figures. **1682** SHADWELL *Medal Bayes* Epist., And a good Drawer, in that time, may observe enough to make a Nuditie of him. **1756–7** tr. *Keysler's Trav.* (1760) II. 40, I think the church is of all places the least proper for nudities. **1758** H. WALPOLE *Let. to Mann* 14 Apr. (1846) III. 349 He had, besides, a fine collection of drawings after nudities. **1858** HAWTHORNE *Fr. & It. Note-bks.* II. 5 Fat Graces and other plump nudities by Rubens. **1894** *Athenæum* 5 May 583/3 The charming nudity who forms the leading element..of this picture.

†**3.** *pl.* The privy parts when exposed. *Obs.*

1686 BURNET *Trav.* III. 174, I was much scandalized to see Statues with nudities here. **1703** MAUNDRELL *Journ. Jerus.* (1721) 95 They took Men with their heels upward, and hurry'd them about in such an undecent manner, as to expose their Nudities. **1769** E. BANCROFT *Guiana* 264 Pieces of India Salempores, with which they cover their nudities.

fig. **1742** YOUNG *Nt. Th.* VIII. 333 The man who shows his heart, Is hooted for his nudities, and scorn'd.

†**nudiustertian**, *a.* *Obs. rare*$^{-1}$. [f. L. *nudius tertius*.] Of the day before yesterday.

1647 WARD *Simp. Cobler* 26 When I heare a..Gentledame inquire..what [is] the nudiustertian fashion of the Court; I mean the very newest.

‖**nudnik** (ˈnʊdnɪk). *U.S.* Also **nudnick.** [Yiddish *nudnik*, f. Russ. *núdnyĭ* tedious, boring; see -NIK.] Someone who pesters, nags, or irritates; a bore. Also *attrib.*

1947 *New Republic* 14 Apr. 42 The patrons of New York's Ruban Bleu are as boorish a collection of *nudnicks* as ever assembled in a public place. **1949** *Amer. Fabrics* No. 9. 108 *Nudnick*, a bothersome customer. **1950** *Commentary* 10 Dec. 558/2 It makes no difference to me if these *nudniks* happen to be atheists. **1955** T. STURGEON in E. Crispin *Best SF Two* (1956) 141 You are a nowhere type, a *nudnick* type, *nothing*! **1961** *John o' London's* 28 Sept. 345/2 What a pair of nudniks they are. **1964** W. MARKFIELD *To Early Grave* (1965) i. 12 'Worrier. Pest. *Nudnick*.' She lashed out at him. **1968** P. DURST *Badge of Infamy* v. 39 Nudnik is a kind of insulting endearment—a sort of lovable nitwit. **1968** L. ROSTEN *Joys of Yiddish* 265 A *nudnik* is someone who *nudzhes* or pesters. **1972** *New York* 8 May 70/1 Too many of our nudnik moviegoers..dread the prospect of sharing their pleasures with the plain folks.

nue, obs. form of NEW *a.*

‖**nuée ardente** (nɥe ardɑ̃t). *Geol.* Pl. **nuées ardentes.** [Fr., lit. 'burning cloud'.

Introduced by A. Lacroix 1903, in *Compt. Rend.* CXXXVI. 874. In *La Montagne Pelée et ses Eruptions* (1904) 170 Lacroix says that he has since realised that the expression had earlier been used by the inhabitants of San Jorge in the Azores. He also says that by *ardent* he implies *brulant* 'burning' rather than *incandescent* 'glowing'. However the expression *nuée ardente* is usually rendered into English as 'glowing cloud' rather than 'burning cloud'.]

A hot, dense cloud of ash and fragmented lava suspended in a mass of gas, which typically is ejected laterally from the side of the dome of certain volcanoes (as Mount Pelée) and flows downhill at great speed like an avalanche. Also ellipt. **nuée.**

1904 A. HEILPRIN *Tower of Pelée* iv. 47 Professor Lacroix ..refers to a number of discharges of the *nuée ardente* breaking out laterally from the base of the obelisk surmounting the crater-cone. **1912** *Amer. Jrnl. Sci.* CLXXXIV. 413 The highly viscous lavas of andesitic and trachytic nature might explode subaërially..into gas and divided solid material, causing such effects as the 'Nuées Ardentes' of Mt. Pelée. **1935** *Publ. Carnegie Inst. Washington* No. 458. 85 They witnessed the series of three rapidly succeeding *nuées* of July 9, 1902. *Ibid.* 89 The ejections followed one another at such brief intervals as to form an unbroken procession of *nuées ardentes*. **1966** *Earth-Sci. Rev.* I. 158 Large acid sheets might have a nuée origin. **1969** *Nature* 29 Nov. 864/1 Natural terrestrial examples of fluidized systems include certain quicksands..and the volcanic eruptions known as *nuées ardentes*. **1969** BENNISON & WRIGHT *Geol. Hist. Brit. Isles* v. 94 The ignimbrites..are the product of nuées ardentes—the fiery cloud of lava and gas which occurs when lavas are silica rich and viscous. **1972** G. A. MACDONALD *Volcanoes* viii. 146 The cloud was the conspicuous feature and led Lacroix to give the name 'nuée ardente' (glowing cloud)... The name 'glowing cloud' seems, therefore, to give too much emphasis to a relatively minor feature, and many volcanologists today prefer to call the phenomenon a glowing avalanche.

†**nuel**, *a.* *Obs.* [OE. *niwol*, *neowol*, *nifol*, of obscure etym.] Prone, prostrate.

c **888** K. ÆLFRED *Boeth.* i. §1 He ȝefeoll niwol ofdune on þa flor. *c* **1000** ÆLFRIC *Josh.* vii. 10 Hwi list þu neowel on eorðan? *c* **1275** LAY. 16777 Octa..nuel feol to grunde bi-vore þis kinges fote.

nuel(l, obs. forms of NEWEL.

nuellry: see NEWELRY.

Nuer (ˈnuːə(r)). [Native name.] Name of an African people living in the south-eastern area of the Sudan; a member of this people; also, their language. Also *attrib.* or as *adj.*

1861 J. PETHERICK *Egypt, Soudan & Central Africa* xx. 362 We..made fast under two villages, which we found were inhabited by the Nouaer. **1873** E. E. FREWER tr. *Schweinfurth's Heart of Africa* I. iii. 118 We made a stop, and did some bartering with the Nueir... Here, in the heart of the Nueir population, in a district called Nyeng, we fixed our quarters. **1894** A. LEFÈVRE *Race & Lang.* v. 162 From the lakes of the Upper Nile to the Atlantic, the Negro dialects, properly so called, prevail: (1.) The Dinka group (Bari, Bongo, Chillouk, Nouer, etc.), the poorest of all, hardly issued from the mono-syllabic stage. **1923** C. H. STIGAND *(title)* A Nuer-English vocabulary. **1932** C. G. & B. Z. SELIGMAN *Pagan Tribes Nilotic Sudan* i. 13 The Nuer.. are tall, long-headed, very dark-skinned, and woolly-haired. *Ibid.* vi. 222 Every Nuer has a name given to him at birth by his father or other member of his family. **1940** E. E. EVANS-PRITCHARD *Nuer* iv. 184 Arab merchants..generally speak Nuer well. **1949** tr. *L. Homburger's Negro-African Langs.* iv. 89 In Nuer *ko* is used for 'we' distinct from *nè* 'I and thou' and *ne* 'we and you'. **1955** J. H. GREENBERG *Studies in African Linguistic Classification* 65 It is..probable that the *ti* plural demonstrative and relative of Nuer..is cognate with the *ti* possessive and relative of Bari. **1964** E. A. NIDA *Toward Sci. Transl.* iii. 51 The Nuers of the Sudan have a very highly specialized vocabulary relating to cattle.

nuff (nʌf). *colloq.* (orig. *U.S.*). Also **nuf, 'nuff.** [colloq. and dial. abbrev. of ENOUGH *a.*, *sb.*, and *adv.*; cf. 'NOUGH.] **1. a. nuff said**, an indication that nothing more need be said on a particular topic. Also ***nuf(f) ced, nuf(f) sed***, abbrev. *N.C.*, *N.S.*

1840 *Ninawah* (Peru, Ill.) *Gaz.* 20 June 2/3 'N.S. (Nuff said,)' whispered Mr. Fox. **1841** *Spirit of Times* 30 Oct. 409/1 'N.S., nuf sed', and up went *the soap*. **1873** HOTTEN *Slang Dict.* 235 *N.C.*, 'enough said', being the initials of *Nuf ced.* A certain theatrical manager spells, it is said, in this style. **1882** *Sydney Slang Dict.* 6/2 *N.C.*, '*Nuff Ced*', enough said. Thea. origin. **1892** J. C. DUVAL *Young Explorers* 151 'Nuf ced,' says Bill, 'you jess take care of your own har, and I'll see arter mine.' **1909** J. R. WARE *Passing Eng.* 184 *Nuf ced* (*From America*). Contraction of 'enough said'—absurdly spelt. Warning to say no more. Used in Liverpool chiefly. **1912** *Pedagogical Seminary* XIX. 97 [Expressions of] Negation and denial..'nuff said. **1942** N. BALCHIN *Darkness falls from Air* xiv. 234 'All right,' he said. ''Nuff said.' **1958** *Spectator* 30 May 677/2 Mr. Randall is one of the newer members; 'nuff said. **1965** M. SPARK *Mandelbaum Gate* vi. 164, I hope the food..is not unwholesome. How well I remember those weeks following your return from Spain... 'Nuff said'! **1971** J. AITKEN *Nightly Deadshade* v. 49 'He and Steinherz knew one another at university before they were here.' 'Nuff said, I suppose.

b. sure 'nuff, sho' nuff, sure enough; often used as an intensive or to give emphasis to a point. (This sense chiefly *U.S.*, esp. in representations of Black English.)

1880 J. C. HARRIS *Uncle Remus* (1881) vi. 31 Den Brer Fox grit his toof sho' nuff; he did, en he look mighty dumpy. **1887** C. W. CHESNUTT in *Atlantic Monthly* Aug. 257/1 Sho nuff, it rain de nex' day. **1898** J. D. BRAYSHAW *Slum Silhouettes* 150 An' sure 'nuff the nex' night arter, bang-bang comes a posty's knock at the door. **1921** E. O'NEILL *Emperor Jones* (1953) ii. 168 I'se done up sho' 'nuff. *Ibid.* 170 I'se gone lost de place sho' 'nuff. **1935** Z. N. HURSTON *Mules & Men* I. i. 26 Ole Massa begin to figger dat John musta seen somethin' sho nuff because John never had disobeyed him before. **1942** S. KENNEDY in B. A. Botkin *Treas. S. Folklore* (1949) III. ii. 511 Sho nuff there was the preacher's buggy. **1971** J. D. CARR *Deadly Hall* xvii. 200 He's sho' nuff in good shape and ought to thank you.

2. Various other uses (see quots.).

1890 BARRÈRE & LELAND *Dict. Slang* II. 91/2 *Nuff* (soldiers): to have one's *nuff*, means to have had more drink than is good for one, *i.e.*, enough. **1923** J. MANCHON *Le Slang* 208 *Nuff*,..abr. *enough*; *to have one's nuff*,..être plein, ivre. **1967** C. HIMES *Black on Black* (1973) 133 Go on, baby, you can be back in an hour with 'nuff bread so we can scoff. **1972** T. KENRICK *Tough One to Lose* xxi. 167 'Nuff outa you guys,' the big man called.

Nuffield (ˈnʌfiːld). The name of William Richard Morris, 1st Viscount *Nuffield* (1877–1963), founder of Morris Motors Ltd., used *attrib.* in **Nuffield Foundation**, a charitable trust set up by him to finance various schemes and organizations; hence *spec.* in *Educ.*, used *attrib.* and *absol.* in connection with the teaching methods and syllabuses advocated by the Nuffield Foundation since 1964, designed esp. for primary school level in mathematics, science, and French with the object of stimulating interest and individual thinking.

1943 *Times* 13 Feb. 4/4 Lord Nuffield has intimated his intention of founding forthwith a charitable trust, which will be known as 'The Nuffield Foundation'. **1946** *Nuffield Foundation First Report* 9 Early in 1943 Lord Nuffield established the Nuffield Foundation as a charitable trust and endowed it with Ordinary Stock Units in Morris Motors Ltd., to the value of £10,000,000. **1947** *Rep. Survey Comm. Old People* i. 1 The trustees of the Nuffield Foundation. **1952** C. P. BLACKER *Eugenics* 307 Some voluntary organizations, such as those embodied in the Nuffield Foundation, have performed semi-official functions, such as the regional hospital surveys conducted for the Ministry of Health during the war. **1964** *Times Educ. Suppl.* 21 Aug. 249/4 If we do get new syllabuses for our nationwide school examinations they will probably be Nuffield ones. *Ibid.* 20 Nov. 932/5 Members of the Nuffield teams will act as examiners. **1971** *Where* Nov. 332/1 The sort of problem, taken from the Nuffield materials, young secondary children would soon get to work on. **1972** E. ELIAS *Learning & Playing* v. 81 Your child's teacher may well be using the Nuffield 'guides', a series of booklets stressing..*how* to teach. *Ibid.* vii. 128 Like Nuffield maths..Nuffield science is being introduced into more and more junior schools. *Ibid.* 129 Nuffield French has spread to schools all over the country. **1975** *Physics Bull.* Dec. 532/3 When a school starts taking Nuffield (other than Nuffield physical science) it never appears to give up doing so.

nuffieldite (ˈnʌfiːldaɪt). *Min.* [f. the name of E. W. *Nuffield* (b. 1914), Canadian geologist + -ITE[1].] A sulphide of copper, lead, and bismuth, $Cu_4Pb_{10}Bi_{10}S_{27}$, found as steel-grey orthorhombic crystals at Lime Creek, British Columbia, Canada.

1968 P. W. KINGSTON in *Canad. Mineralogist* IX. 439 A second new sulphosalt mineral was discovered by R. M. Thompson... The new species is named nuffieldite in honour of E. W. Nuffield, who has made outstanding contributions to the understanding of many of the less well-known sulphosalt minerals. **1969** *Ibid.* X. 93 Because of the close similarity in physical properties of neyite, cosalite, aikinite, and nuffieldite, it was necessary to make numerous *x*-ray powder photographs to confirm the identity of the material used for analysis.

nuffin (ˈnʌfɪn). Also **nuffink.** [Repr. a colloq. or dial. pronunc. of NOTHING.] = NOTHING *sb.* and *adv.* in var. senses.

1877 GEO. ELIOT *Let.* 23 Nov. (1956) VI. 426 We have never seen Saturn's ring, nor Jupiter's moons—'nor nuffin'. **1897** [see DRIFT *sb.* 9]. **1898** J. D. BRAYSHAW *Slum Silhouettes* I If anyfink's wrong, yer won't get nuffink aht o' me. **1910** H. G. WELLS *Hist. Mr. Polly* ix. 316, I don't stick at nuffin. **1922** 'R. CROMPTON' *More William* (1924) i. 24, I can't do nuffink with the mincing machine gone. **1951** 'J. WYNDHAM' *Day of Triffids* (1956) ii. 46 On its [*sc.* the triffid's] origins the Russians, true to type, lay low and said nuffin. **1957** *Economist* 28 Sept. 1002/1 It is..very nearly impossible for an Opposition to lie low and say nuffin at a time like this. **1958** J. TOWNSEND *Young Devils* ii. 20 'Don't learn nuffin' in this school,' sneered another boy. **1971** G. SIMS *Deadhand* II. ii. 88 Albert Chevalier's adage: 'Wot's the good of hanyfink?—Why—nuffink!' **1974** 'A. GILBERT' *Nice Little Killing* ix. 119 We don't know nuffin about the dear departed.

†**nug**[1]. *Obs.* [Perh. the south-western dial. *nug* lump.] ***nugs of balm***, some distilled liquor.

1609 *Pimlyco* C iv b, Waters drawne by Distillations With medicinable Operations, As Rosa Solis, Aqua Vitæ, And Nugs of Balme, so quicke, and sprighty.

†**nug**[2]. *Obs. Cant.* (See quot.)

a **1700** B. E. *Dict. Cant. Crew*, *Nug*, a Word of Love, as, my Dear Nug, my Dear Love.

nugacious (njuːˈgeɪʃəs), *a.* Now *rare.* [f. L. *nūgāci-s*, *nūgax* trifling + -OUS.] Trivial, trifling, of no moment or importance.

1652 GAULE *Magastrom.* 57 On purpose to vend their nugacious fables and prestigious impostures with more esteem. *Ibid.* 189 These nugacious kinds of men. **1661** GLANVILL *Van. Dogm.* 165 'Tis these nugacious Disputations, that have been the great hinderance to.. Learning. **1829** SOUTHEY *Sir T. More* II. 61 Things as nugacious as the colour of a habit, or the shape of a cowl.

Hence **nuˈgaciousness** (Bailey, vol. II, 1727).

nugacity (njuːˈgæsɪtɪ). [ad. late L. *nūgācitas*, f. *nūgāci-s*, *nūgax*: see prec. and -ITY.]

1. Trifling, triviality, futility.

1593 BILSON *Govt. Christ's Ch.* 278 Ful of follie, nugacitie, error. **1607** HARINGTON in *Nugæ Ant.* (1804) II. 262 He knows such nugacitie becomes not his place. **1662** STILLINGFLEET *Orig. Sacræ* I. iv. §10 Strabo seems to accuse Herodotus much of nugacity. **1676** H. MORE *Remarks* 189 There is no nugacity at all in this.

1862 *Sat. Rev.* XIII. 719 Parr's general nugacity as an exegetical and polemical divine.

2. A trifling or frivolous idea.

1653 H. MORE *Conject. Cabbal.* (1713) 82 Such Arithmetical nugacities as are ordinarily recorded for his. **1668** —— *Div. Dial.* II. ii. (1713) 90 Such Nugacities as are exploded even by the Theologers themselves.

1818 COLERIDGE *Lit. Rem.* (1838) III. 179 To confute the whims and superstitious nugacities of these Sermons. **1829** SOUTHEY in *Q. Rev.* XXXIX. 111 Throat-choking.. nugacities of hyper-grammatical..absurdity.

‖**nugæ** (ˈnjuːdʒiː). [L.] *pl.* Trifles. *spec.* in phr. **nugæ difficiles** *Philos.*, matters of trifling importance over which a disproportionate amount of time may be taken owing to their difficulty.

1710 BERKELEY *Princ. Human Knowl.* 170 We may perhaps..look on all Inquiries about Numbers, only as so many *difficiles nugæ*, so far as they are not subservient to practise. **1822–34** *Good's Study Med.* (ed. 4) IV. 15 In all these attempts..there is a great deal that cannot but be regarded as philosophical nugæ. **1867** MILL *Inaug. Addr.* 39, I am often tempted to ask the favourites of nature and fortune, whether all the serious and important work of the world is done, that their time and energy can be spared for these *nugae difficiles*? **1890** W. JAMES *Princ. Psychol.* II. xxviii. 662 Such painstaking attempts..to prove all necessary judgments to be analytic..seem accordingly but *nugae difficiles*, and little better than wastes of ink and paper.

ˈnugal, *a.* *rare*$^{-0}$. [ad. L. *nūgāl-is*.]

1656 BLOUNT *Glossogr.*, *Nugal*, trifling, vain, of no force.

†**nuˈgality.** *Obs. rare*$^{-1}$. [ad. L. *nūgālitas*: cf. prec.] Frivolity, trifling.

1676 H. MORE *Remarks* 188 *Difficiles Nugæ*,..there may be some difficulty, yet there is no Nugality at all.

†**'nugament.** *Obs. rare.* [ad. L. *nūgāmenta* (neut. pl.).] A trifle, trifling opinion.

1623 COCKERAM *Eng. Dict.* I, *Nugament*, a bable, toy, or lie. **1716** M. DAVIES *Athen. Brit.* II. 431 Nothing but such quisquilian Nugaments.

†**nu'gation.** *Obs.* [ad. med.L. *nūgātio*, f. L. *nūgārī* to trifle. Cf. obs. F. *nugacion*, It. *nugazione*.] Trifling; speaking or acting in trifling manner; an instance of this.

1581 LAMBARDE *Eiren.* III. i. (1588) 318 Conveighing the Riotters unto the gaole: without which the arrest were but nugation. **1583** FULKE *Defence* i. (1843) 144 Then followeth that vain nugation which I have noted against Saunder. **1602** WARNER *Alb. Eng.* Epit. 350 Many impertinent digressions, and some meere nugations. **1626** BACON *Sylva* §836 As for the Received Opinion,..it is but Nugation. **1664** H. MORE *Myst. Iniq.* 309 If it were not determined to this sense it would rather be a Nugation..then an Interpretation.

nu'gator. *rare*$^{-0}$. [ad. L. *nūgātor*.]

1656 BLOUNT *Glossogr.*, *Nugator*, a trifler.

'nugatoriness. The fact of being nugatory.

1856 RUSKIN *Mod. Paint.* III. IV. xviii. §26. 328 An incapacity..quite unequalled, as far as I know, in human nugatoriness.

†**nuga'torious,** *a. Obs.*$^{-1}$ [-OUS.] = next.

1646 R. BAILLIE *Anabaptism* (1647) 44 The tenet of the Catholick Church concerning Angels and Devils..is nugatorious.

nugatory ('nju:gətərɪ), *a.* [ad. L. *nūgātōrius*, f. ppl. stem of *nūgārī* to trifle. Cf. It. and Sp. *nugatorio*, F. *nugatoire*.]

1. Trifling, of no value or importance, worthless.

1603 HOLLAND *Plutarch's Mor.* 1156 That we may not range too farre, nor use any superfluous and nugatory words. **1674** JEAKE *Arith. Surv.* (1696) 613 The Equation is either Nugatory or Impossible. **1692** BENTLEY *Boyle Lect.* iii. 106 Too much addicted to this nugatory Art. **1786** JEFFERSON *Writ.* (1859) I. 520, I have been obliged..to a nugatory interference, merely to prevent the affairs of the United States from standing still. **1791** W. MAXWELL in Boswell *Johnson* an. 1770, Lord Lyttelton's Dialogues he deemed a nugatory performance. **1841** D'ISRAELI *Amen. Lit.* (1867) 299 The diligence of the editor has not been wasted on trivial researches or nugatory commentaries. **1879** THOMSON & TAIT *Nat. Phil.* I. I. §81 Therefore the construction fails..and the theorem becomes nugatory.

2. Of no force, invalid; useless, futile, of no avail, inoperative.

1605 BACON *Adv. Learn.* II. vii. §5 Which assignation.. may seem to be nugatory and void. **1648** PRYNNE *Plea for Lords* 27 Which Act will be..void and nugatory. **1772** *Junius Lett.* Pref. (1788) 19 As the fact is usually admitted, ..the office of the petty jury is nugatory. **1786** tr. *Beckford's Vathek* (1868) 9 His reiterated attempts were all of them nugatory. **1838** PRESCOTT *Ferd. & Isab.* (1846) II. xvii. 128 Those provisions of the edict..were contrived so artfully as to be nearly nugatory. **1878** LECKY *Eng. in 18th C.* I. ii. 306 The law..was evaded and made almost nugatory.

nuggar ('nʌgə(r)). Also **nugger, -ur, noggur,** ?**negger.** [Native name.] A large boat, of very broad beam, used on the upper Nile for the transport of cargo, troops, etc.

1870 BAKER *Ismailïa* (1874) I. 173 We were hailed.. within the Bahr Giraffe, by two noggurs (vessels) in distress. **1875** GORDON in *G. in Centr. Africa* (1881) 91 We have taken nuggars down the Western Passage. **1884** COLBORNE *With Hicks Pasha in Soudan* 109 We brought two battalions up with us in nuggurs.

nugget ('nʌgɪt), *sb.* [App. a derivative of south-western dial. *nug*, a lump, a block, a rough unshapen mass, etc.]

1. a. A rough lump of native gold. Also *transf.*

1852 MUNDY *Antipodes* III. 322 Gold was not so plentiful as was anticipated,..nor were nuggets to be dug up..by the bushel. **1853** *Ann. Reg., Chron.* 86 Crawcour came on board, and asked me for the nuggets of gold. **1871** CARLYLE in Mrs. Carlyle *Lett.* I. 162 Californian nuggets versus jewels of Heaven itself. **1880** SUTHERLAND *Tales Goldfields* 86 When the nugget had been deposited on the floor of the banker's room, it was weighed.

transf. *a* **1859** T. DE QUINCEY *Coll. Writings* (1889) I. 412 The secret truth, that rarest of all 'nuggets'. **1859** JEPHSON *Brittany* xx. 344 Here and there a nugget of true poetry glitters among the clay. **1870** LOWELL *Study Wind.* 209 His quotations are always nuggets of the purest ore.

b. *attrib.* and *Comb.*, as ***nugget-fashion***; ***-hunter, -hunting, -testing.***

1857 RUSKIN *Pol. Econ. Art* 30 You dig him out as he lies nugget-fashion in the mountain stream. **1880** SUTHERLAND *Tales Goldfields* 80 That [occupation] which gold miners call nugget-hunting... To the nugget-hunter [etc.]. **1894** H. NISBET *Bush Girl's Romance* 9 Those fingers of yours are too sticky for nugget-testing in the dark.

2. A lump of anything.

1860 TENNENT *Story Guns* (1864) 244 Cast iron was found to crumble into harmless nuggets. **1891** PEARCE *Esther Pentreath* IV. i, Casy.., taking out the nugget of cake, held it timidly out to his rivals.

3. A small, compact, stocky animal or person; also, a runt. *Austral.*

1852 MUNDY *Antipodes* III. 322 The word nugget among farmers, signifies a small compact beast or runt. **1888** 'R. BOLDREWOOD' *Robbery under Arms* 14 We branded the little red heifer calf first—a fine fat six-months-old nugget. **1919** W. H. DOWNING *Digger Dial.* 36 *Nugget*, a short soldier. **1941** BAKER *Dict. Austral. Slang* 50 *Nugget*, a small, weedy horse or other animal. (2) A small stocky man.

'nugget, *v. Austral.* [f. prec.] *trans.* To appropriate (an unbranded calf).

1885 MRS. C. PRAED *Head Station* 239 Nobody would go there except after calves to nugget. **1893** —— *Outlaw & Lawmaker* II. 19 In the days of their nefarious practices, [they] probably 'nuggeted' a good many..calves up here.

'nuggeting, *vbl. sb.* [f. as prec.] The occupation of searching for nuggets.

1880 SILVER *Handbk. Austral.* 163 Nuggeting is a pleasant and profitable occupation,..when..the lumps are found a few feet only from the surface.

'nugget(t)y, *a.* [f. NUGGET *sb.* + -Y.]

1. Having the form of nuggets.

1859 *Chamb. Jrnl.* XI. 290 If the gold should turn out to be 'nuggety'. **1890** *Nature* 20 Mar. 465 The origin of nuggetty gold.

2. Rich in nuggets.

1870 *Pall Mall G.* 26 Aug. 4 A district which..has earned for itself the proud title of the 'Nuggety Diggings'.

3. *Austral.* and *N.Z.* Of horses or cattle: Stout, compact, thick-set. Used also of other animals, and of people.

1874 C. DE BOOS *Congewoi Correspondence* 141 He's just oner them short, square-built, nuggetty kinder fellers. **1887** *Daily News* 9 Apr. 5/4 The typical volunteer is gradually framing himself into a medium-sized, somewhat thickset, sturdy style of fellow, with a good chest measurement, firm on the pins, with the stamp on him of strength and hardihood—the sort of man..the Australians style 'nuggetty'. **1893** *Pall Mall G.* 28 Jan. 3/1 The light spring waggon, drawn by a pair of sleek, nuggetty cobs. **1926** 'J. DOONE' *Timely Tips for New Australians* (Gloss.) *Nuggetty*, short and sturdy. **1941** I. L. IDRIESS *Great Boomerang* vii. 52 Scowler was a square-faced, nuggety man, with a set scowl under a shock of hair. **1946** F. SARGESON *That Summer* 66 He wasn't a rangy specimen like me, no, he was nuggety. **1953** O. E. MIDDLETON in C. K. Stead *N.Z. Short Stories* (1966) 187 Belle was..more nuggety, but still powerful. She was short-haired..but had less white on the throat. **1969** O. WHITE *Under Iron Rainbow* 107 He was a nuggety little bloke and moved as if he could handle himself in a blue. **1971** *Sunday Times* (Johannesburg) 28 Mar. 21/1 The nuggety young Wits University scrumhalf will be in the Springbok team to tour Australia. **1971** *N.Z. Listener* 19 Apr. 56/5 One was a nuggetty bloke in a sou'-wester, oilskin slicker, and bowyangs.

†**'nugging-dress.** *Obs. Cant.* (See quot.)

a **1700** B. E. *Dict. Cant. Crew*, *Nugging-Dress*, an odd or particular way, out of the Fashion.

†**nuȝe, nuȝu,** *adv. Obs. rare.* [Cf. OE. *nú ȝén(a)*.] Now, even now.

c **1200** ORMIN 9961 Forr nuȝȝu wat he well all hu He shall all mannkinn demenn. *c* **1250** *Gen. & Ex.* 1328 Abraham ðat swerd ut-droȝ, And was redi to slon him nuȝe.

nughtsom: see MIGHTSOME.

nugi- ('nju:dʒɪ), combining form of L. *nūgæ*, occurring in a few words which have not obtained any currency, as **nugi'frivolous** *a.*, free for frivolous trifling; **'nugifying** *ppl. a.*, productive of mere trifling; **nugi'gerulous** *a.* [L. *nūgigerulus*], 'carrying trifles, toys, etc.' (Bailey, vol. II, 1727); **'nugilogue,** trifling talk; **nu'giperous** *a.*, ? inventing trifles.

1589 NASHE *Martin Marprelate* IV. Wks. (Grosart) I. 201 And now pretie youthes,..we shal haue some *nugifriulous leasure to talke with you. **1818** COLERIDGE *Lit. Rem.* (1838) III. 183 The stultifying, *nugifying effect of a blind and uncritical study of the Fathers. **1649** DANIEL *Trinarch.*, *Hen. V* cxxxviii, How ere the heapes Who Crowd to see, in Expectation fall To the Sweet *Nugilogues of Jacke, and Hall. **1647** WARD *Simpl. Cobler* 26 When I heare a *nugiperous Gentledame inquire What dresse the Queen is in [etc.].

nuik, Sc. form of NOOK *sb.*

†**'nuisable,** *a. Obs. rare*$^{-1}$. [a. OF. *nuys-, nuisable*.] = NUISIBLE.

1483 CAXTON *Gold. Leg.* 439/2 Ryght so is the body of our lord Jhesu cryste nuysable and lettyng to the synnars.

nuisance ('nju:səns). Forms: α. 5, 7–8 **nusance,** 5 **-aunce,** 7 **-ans, -anze, nuzance;** 6 **newsance.** β. 5 **nuisaunce, nuysance,** 7– **nuisance.** [a. OF. *nuisance, nusance*, etc., f. *nuis-, nuire* to hurt, harm: see -ANCE.]

1. Injury, hurt, harm, annoyance. (In later use only as implying sense 2 or 2 b.)

c **1410** HOCCLEVE *Mother of God* 21 Helpe me to weye Ageyn the feend!.. Keepe vs from his nusance. *c* **1412** —— *De Reg. Princ.* 810 To me thus longe walke, it doth nusance Vnto my crookid feeble lymes olde. **1512** *Nottingham Rec.* III. 339 To the gret hurtte of owre medo and newsance to vs all.

1776 E. TOPHAM *Lett. Edinb.* 9 The herb-women throw about the stalks of the bad vegetables to the great nuisance of the passengers. **1862** BURTON *Bk. Hunter* (1863) 106 Actions of damages for nuisance, trespass, or assault. **1888** *19th Cent.* Jan. 6 Declaring that cremation is a legal procedure, provided it be effected without nuisance to others.

2. a. Anything injurious or obnoxious to the community, or to the individual as a member of it (esp. as an owner or occupier of property), for which some legal remedy may be found.

α. **1464** *Rolls of Parlt.* V. 569/2 That if eny such nusaunce were made, that it shuld be beten down. **1495** *Act 11 Hen. VII*, c. 26 Preamble, Many greate nusances and offences [are] not presented. **1641** *Commons Rem.* in Chas. I. Wks. 1662 II. 60 The sale of pretended Nusanzes, as Buildings in and about London. **1691** T. H[ALE] *Acc. New Invent.* p. lxxxi, I find that a Nusance once erected may be abated by any Body. **1710** *Lond. Gaz.* No. 4768/1 All such Lotteries are..declared to be Common Nusances. **1721** *Modern Rep.* X. 336 The keeping of a gaming-house is an offence indictable at common law as a nusance. **1817** W. SELWYN *Law Nisi Prius* (ed. 4) II. 1044 If A. build an house so as to hang over the land of B., whereby the rain falls upon B.'s land, and injures it, B. may maintain an action against A. for this nusance.

β. **1638** POTTER in Chillingw. *Relig. Prot.* I. iv. §67. 228 Shall it bee a fault to straiten and encumber the Kings high way with publique nuisances? **1773** *Obs. State Poor* 59 In vain is there a power..in the magistrate, of removing in great measure a nuisance so flagrantly pernicious to the community. **1853** T. J. WHARTON *Pennsylv. Digest* (ed. 6) II. 361 Some actions which would otherwise be nuisances may be justified by necessity. **1896** *Law Times* C. 488/1 Calling upon him to repair the drain so as to abate the nuisance complained of.

Comb. **1853** URE *Dict. Arts* (ed. 4) II. 799 They..would not again return to the nuisance-creating system.

b. In more general use: Anything obnoxious or annoying to the community or individual by offensiveness of smell or appearance, by causing obstruction or damage, etc.

1661 EVELYN *Diary* 1 Oct., My book inveighing against the nuisance of the smoke of London. **1712** STEELE *Spect.* No. 430 ¶1 Whatsoever looks ill, and is offensive to the Sight; the worst Nusance of which kind [etc.]. **1756–7** tr. *Keysler's Trav.* (1760) II. 396 The lumber, old cloaths,.. and the herb-stalls, are a great nusance. **1774** GOLDSM. *Nat. Hist.* (1776) VI. 328 The annual inundation of these fish is so great, that they cover the shores in such quantities as to become a nuisance. **1807** SOUTHEY *Espriella's Lett.* (1814) II. 225 It is so frequent as to be quite a nuisance along the road. **1849** MACAULAY *Hist. Eng.* I. 312 The fox..was considered as a mere nuisance. **1864** C. GEIKIE *Life in Woods* iii. 54 But the pigs were not the only nuisance.

c. Applied to persons.

1695 CONGREVE *Love for L.* II. iii, I'll swear you are a nuisance to the neighbourhood.—What a bustle did you keep against the last invisible eclipse! *a* **1732** SWIFT *Serm.* Wks. 1841 II. 143/2 A wise man who does not assist with his counsels,..and a poor man with his labour, are perfect nuisances in a commonwealth. **1781** COWPER *Truth* 508 Seest thou yon harlot,..The worn-out nuisance of the public streets. **1816** SCOTT *Antiq.* iv, But here..he is a sort of privileged nuisance. **1859** SALA *Tw. round Clock* (1861) 154, I am an intolerable little nuisance. **1880** HAUGHTON *Phys. Geogr.* iv. 171 The Syrian highlanders..were a perpetual nuisance to the more powerful countries that surrounded them.

d. A highly obnoxious or troublesome practice, institution, state of things, etc.

1820 *Edin. Rev.* XXXIII. 350 The nuisance of monopoly completely put down. **1828** CARLYLE *Misc.* (1857) I. 163 In the eyes of Voltaire and his disciples, Religion was a superfluity, indeed a nuisance. **1865** MILL in *Morn. Star* 6 July, Of all the political nuisances of the day this is one which it most behoves everyone to make a stand against.

e. A source of annoyance; something personally unpleasant or disagreeable.

1831 LYTTON *Godolphin* viii, The other set,..who go little into parties, and vote balls a nuisance. **1865** TROLLOPE *Belton Est.* vii, The journey..was always a nuisance, and was more so now than usual. **1897** MARY KINGSLEY *W. Africa* 363 Neither de Ballay nor the steamer had arrived, and a very bitter nuisance this must have been.

f. In phr. ***to commit a nuisance.***

1863 *Harper's Mag.* Dec. 24/1 Commit no Nuisance. *a* **1922** T. S. ELIOT *Waste Land Drafts* (1971) 5 We'd just gone up the alley, a fly cop came along, Looking for trouble; committing a nuisance, he said. **1942** PARTRIDGE *Usage & Abusage* 122/1 Euphemism may be obtained by using an extremely vague phrase, as in *commit a nuisance*.

3. *attrib.* and *Comb.*, as ***nuisance action, aspect, candidate, tactics, tax;*** **nuisance ground** *Canad.*, a rubbish dump; **nuisance raid,** a wartime bomb attack intended only to inconvenience or disrupt the enemy; also **nuisance-bombing, -raider; nuisance value,** the value or importance of a person or thing arising from a capacity to be a nuisance.

1964 C. CHAPLIN *Autobiogr.* xxix. 499 It's nothing but a nuisance action, Charlie; all the same I want you to keep from being served a summons. **1941** *Scrutiny* X. 80 There is a certain savage heightening of his nuisance-aspect towards the end. **1940** *Times Weekly* 27 Nov. 6 The change in the enemy's air tactics from general nuisance bombing to concentrated attacks on more restricted targets. **1968** *Globe & Mail* (Toronto) 13 Feb. 7/6 The only apple carts that Mr. Trudeau could not upset are those of..the three nuisance candidates. **1889** in *Herald Mag.* (Calgary) (1961) 11 Jan. 8/6 A well-grounded complaint has been made..in reference to dumping of filth in to the old cellar holes along the main road..instead of taking it to the nuisance ground. **1970** J. H. GRAY *Boy from Winnipeg* 72 He had hauling contracts with the city that included carrying the manure from the city stables to the nuisance grounds. **1972** *Maclean's Mag.* (Toronto) Dec. 23/3 The town dump was known as the *nuisance grounds*, a phrase fraught with weird connotations, as though the effluvia of our lives was beneath contempt but at the same time was subtly threatening to the determined and sometimes hysterical propriety of our ways. **1942** *Hutchinson's Pict. Hist. of War* 18 Mar.–9 June 110 Some of the raids into enemy territory are merely nuisance raids to upset enemy nerves. **1943** *R.A.F. Jrnl.* Aug. 34 Cases of..nuisance raids by single rodents had been reported. **1944** *Ann. Reg. 1943* 341 The Germans..began a series of nuisance raids. **1944** *Daily Tel.* 11 July 1 German radio early to-day reported several nuisance raiders over the Berlin area. **1952** *Ann. Reg. 1951* 325 Government workers, forbidden..to strike, resorted to go-slow, work to rule, and other nuisance tactics. **1933** *Sun* (Baltimore) 4 July 6/6 (*heading*) Nuisance taxes help careerists. *Ibid.*, Authorities on taxation recently persuaded the State Legislature to abolish this tax as a nuisance, although its nuisance value was the chief reason for its existence. **1937** *Harper's Mag.* Jan. 846 If Hitler has a high nuisance value to France and England. **1958** A. HOCKING *Epitaph for Nurse* v. 82 To add to her other nuisance-values, Geraldine complained and made trouble from morning to night. **1961** P. W. BROOKS *Mod. Airliner* i. 22 'Nuisance value' of the aircraft to the general public on the ground (defined as the external overall noise level at climbing power at 650 ft.). **1972** *Guardian* 5 Jan. 4/6 Muskie's aides dismiss them airily as being no threat at all except for the nuisance value they may have in primaries.

Hence **'nuisancer**, one who causes a nuisance.

1769 BLACKSTONE *Comm.* IV. xvi. 223 The animadversion of the law upon eaves-droppers, nusancers, and incendiaries.

†**'nuisant**, *a. Obs. rare.* In 5, 7 **nusant**. [a. OF. *nuisant*, pres. pple. of *nuire*.] Harmful, hurtful; of the nature of a nuisance.

c **1400** tr. *Secreta Secret., Gov. Lordsh.* 86 Whenne þe nusant sterres loke noght aȝeyn. *Ibid.*, His remuynge fro nusant sterrys. **1676** *Grant of Ballastage to Trinity Ho.* 41 Anything that shall be prejudicial, nusant, or obnoxious, to any of our Palaces, Houses, or Buildings.

†**nuise**, *v. Obs. rare.* In 4 **nusy**. [a. OF. *nuisir*.] *intr.* To do injury.

c **1315** SHOREHAM I. 530 Þe fend hym-self him maky mey Wel dyuerse liknynges.. To nusy [*rime* vsy]. *Ibid.* 936 Senne ony-schryue wanne he uor-ȝet, Hys senne þer-be doubleþ To nusy [*rime* acusy].

†**'nuisible**, *a. Obs. rare.* [a. OF. *nuisible*, f. *nuisir* or *nuire* to harm.] Harmful, hurtful.

1490 CAXTON *Eneydos* xxi. 76 Neuer of me came euyll vnto them, nor no thyng that was to theym nuysible. *Ibid.* xxiv. 89 All thynges that ben cruell and nuysyble.

†**'nuisome**, *a. Obs. rare*$^{-1}$. [var. of NOISOME, after *nuisance*.] Annoying.

1738 BOLINGBROKE *Patriot King* II. 152 Whole swarms of little, nuisome, nameless insects will hum and buzz in every corner of the court.

‖**nuit blanche** (nɥi blɑ̃ʃ). [Fr., lit. 'white night'.] A sleepless night. Also *fig.*

1853 C. BRONTË *Villette* III. xli. 296 Leaving the radiant park and well-lit Haute-Ville (still well-lit, for this it seems was to be a 'nuit blanche' in Villette), I sought the dim lower quarter. **1904** W. STEVENS *Let.* 14 Feb. (1967) 69, I do *not* want my dreams—my castles, my hunts, my *nuits blanches.* **1923** D. H. LAWRENCE *Ladybird* 81 She had gone to sleep from the *nuit blanche* of her days. **1964** L. MEYNELL *More Deadly than Male* xiv. 244 He lay awake for the rest of the night. A *nuit blanche.*

Nuits (St. George(s (nɥi sɛ̃ ʒɔrʒ). [The name of the capital town of the Côte de Nuits, in the department of Côte d'Or, France.] A red wine of Burgundy, produced in the district of Nuits St. Georges.

1841 THACKERAY in *Fraser's Mag.* June 715/1 We had.. A bottle of nuits with the beef. **1875** [see BEAUNE]. **1914** G. K. CHESTERTON *Flying Inn* xvii. 196 A strictly vegetarian beverage which bears the noble and starry name of Nuits. **1946** G. MILLAR *Horned Pigeon* xvi. 236 We found Eugène and his wife celebrating.. with a bottle of Nuits St. Georges. **1966** B. E. WALLACE *Murder in Touraine* vi. 56 Rocky swirled his Nuits St. George slowly round the glass. **1967** A. LICHINE *Encycl. Wines* 383/2 Bouquet is also a Nuits characteristic, and the wines are sometimes quite pungent.

Nujol ('nju:dʒɒl). The proprietary name of a paraffin oil used as an emulsifying agent in pharmacy and for making mulls in infra-red spectroscopy.

1916 *Trade Marks Jrnl.* 16 Feb. 153 Nujol... Medicinal and curative preparations.. all being for human use. Standard Oil Company.., Bayonne, Hudson County, New Jersey, United States of America; manufacturers. **1923** W. CLAYTON *Theory of Emulsions* ii. 30 If a solution of KI be added to an emulsion of 'Nujol' in sodium oleate solution, prismatic colours are secured. **1943, 1948** [see MULL *v.*[1] 1 b]. **1956** [see MULL *sb.*[1] 2]. **1971** ROSENBLATT & DAVIS *Course in Org. Chem.* iii. 71 Nujol is only useful in regions not involving carbon-hydrogen vibrations. **1975** D. H. BURRIN in Williams & Wilson *Biologist's Guide to Princ. & Techniques Pract. Biochem.* v. 151 A Nujol mull, consisting of a fine paste of sample in liquid paraffin may be prepared.

nuk(e, obs. forms of NOOK.

†**nuke**, *sb.*[1] *Obs.* Also 6 **newke**. [var. of NUCHE and NUQUE.]

1. The spinal cord.

1541 COPLAND *Guydon's Quest. Chirurg.* D iv b, Holes.. by the whiche descendeth the nuke of the brayne.. tyll vnto the ende of the backe. **1543** TRAHERON *Vigo's Chirurg.* I. i. 2 The Nuke which is the mary of the backe bone.. is as it were a streame descendynge from the said partie. **1547** BOORDE *Brev. Health* cccixvii. 118 The synewes doth procede from the newke which is the mary of the backe.

2. The nape of the neck.

1562 BULLEIN *Bulwarke, Dial. Sorenes & Chir.* 22 b, Cold is an enemie to the.. braine, and nuke of the necke. **1634** T. JOHNSON tr. *Parey's Chirurg.* III. i. (1678) 55 The back-part of the neck called.. the nuke or nape. **1676** WISEMAN *Surg. Treat.* IV. iv. 282 Those on the left side were then swelled from the Nuke down that side of the Neck.

So †**nuke-bone**. *Obs. rare*$^{-0}$.

1611 COTGR., *Os basilaire*, the Nape, or Nuke-bone.

nuke (nju:k, U.S. nu:k), *sb.*[2] *slang* (chiefly *U.S.*). Also (*U.S.*) **nook**. Abbrev. of 'nuclear bomb, weapon,' etc.

1959 *N.Y. Times Mag.* 1 Feb. 46/3 Soon there may be 5-inch nuclear shells and portable Davy Crockett 'nukes' for the infantryman. **1960** *Time* 4 July 52/1 But the nuclear submarines—called 'nukes'—can cruise underwater for weeks at top speed. **1964** *Daily Mirror* 24 Aug. 4/5 The generals should be allowed to decide whether to use tactical nuclear weapons, or as the current ugly phrase has it: 'Where and when to put in the nooks.' **1967** *Word Study* Oct. 8/1, I heard a grim, affectionate diminutive: 'nook' (nŭk). 'If the bird is carrying nooks.' **1969** *Life* 29 Sept. 23/2 Once communities vied for nuclear power plants ('nukes') as passports to prosperity. **1971** J. BALL *First Team* (1972) xv. 224 'What is nukes?' the man asked. 'Nuclear specialists; no one else can handle this stuff.' **1973** *Publishers' Weekly* 14 May 44/1 They hijack a liner at sea and sink it with a baby nuke... He is given the job of detonating the big nuke.

Hence as *v. trans.*, to use nuclear weapons against; **'nuking** *vbl. sb.*

1967 *Look* 11 July 25, I remember in Saigon how disturbed General Westmoreland was after talking to a group of American editors.. who told him they favored 'nuking' (A-bombing) China. **1970** *New Yorker* 4 July 52 We have to get ready to nuke 'em to kingdom come. **1972** *S. China Morning Post* (Hong Kong) 29 Sept. 2/3 Dr. Strangelove nuked the Russians on his own authority. **1972** *Japan Times Weekly* 23 Dec. 4/2, I asked how he could be sure that the Soviet Union would nuke us if we nuked China. **1973** *Daily Tel.* (Colour Suppl.) 13 Apr. 40/1 'Nuked', for those unfamiliar with modern war-parlance, means to let off a nuclear bomb.

nul(e, will not, **nulde**, would not: see NILL *v.*

null, *sb.*[1] [a. F. *nulle*, It. *nulla*, fem. of F. *nul*, It. *nullo*: see NULL *a.* So G. *null(e*, †*nulla*, Sw. *nolla*; G. *null*, Du., Da. *nul*, Sw. *nol.*]

a. A cipher; a nought.

1605 BACON *Adv. Learn.* II. xvi. §6 The kinds of Cyphars (besides the simple cyphars with Changes, and intermixtures of Nulles and Nonsignificants) are many. *a* **1626** —— *War with Spain* (1629) 5 If part of the People or Estate be somewhat in the Election, you cannot make them Nulls or Cyphers in the.. Translation. **1691** T. H[ALE] *Acc. New Invent.* p. ix, An Unite was too much, and a Null too little.

b. *Cryptography.* (See quot. 1961.)

1915 J. BUCHAN *39 Steps* iii. 72 It was a numerical cypher, and by an elaborate system of experiments I had pretty well discovered what were the nulls and stops. **1961** SHULMAN & WEINTRAUB *Gloss. Cryptography, Null cipher*, a form of concealment in which most of the letters used in a text are nulls. *Nulls*, meaningless letters or numbers used in cryptograms for various purposes. **1968** 'S. JAY' *Sleepers can Kill* iv. 47 A very simple cypher, Mr. Connor, but it can of course be broken by frequency analysis... Don't forget to reverse and arrange in five letter groups, of course, with nulls to make the numbers up. **1972** *Sci. Amer.* Nov. 114/2 If this is intercepted and a translation demanded of the sender, he strikes out the symbols of the true text, explaining that they are what cryptographers today call 'nulls', meaningless symbols inserted only to make the cipher harder to break.

c. *Linguistics.* (See quots.)

The *attrib.* example properly belongs in sense 4 of the *adj.*

1964 E. BACH *Introd. Transformational Gram.* v. 110 Since Y and Z (as usual) include the possibility of null, the transformation will have the desired effect of producing all permutations of the terminal elements. **1968** *Amer. Speech* XLIII. 277 In treating *few* in 'few people' and *much* in 'much money' as pre-article forms, Roberts assumes the existence of an unarticulated determiner he calls *null.* **1968** R. T. HARMS *Introd. Phonological Theory* v. 44 If two obstruents occur initially, the first one is deleted. (Instead of 'null', the symbol 'ø' is sometimes used.) **1972** R. A. PALMATIER *Gloss. Eng. Transformational Gram.* 111 *Null*, lacking status as a morpheme or formative—that is, having no overt representation on any level of the grammar... *Null string*, an empty string—that is, no string at all.

null *sb.*[2], variant of KNURR.

1816 *Sporting Mag.* XLVIII. 178 The games most common at Newmarket were fives, spell and null, marbles [and] chuck-farthing.

null *sb.*[3], variant of KNURL *sb.* 1.

1875 KNIGHT *Dict. Mech.* 1535/2 By moving the lever up and down, the carriage is.. advanced the proper distance and the nulls or beads formed by the cutter.

null (nʌl), *a.* Also **nul**. [a. OF. *nul* masc., *nulle* fem., = It. *nullo*, *nulla*, Sp. *nulo*, *nula*, or ad. L. *nullus*, f. *ne* not + *ullus* any. So G. *null*, Du. *nul.*]

1. a. Void, of no legal or binding force; of no efficacy, invalid.

1563-7 BUCHANAN *Reform. St. Andros* Vernac. Writ. (S.T.S.) 16 Al thayr votis that tendis to continuation, to be nul. **1569** *Reg. Privy Council Scot.* II. 7 In caise the same titillis of the law be reduceable or may be declarit null. **1639** SIR T. STAFFORD in *Lismore Papers* Ser. II. (1888) IV. 66 There Late assemblie to be held null, the Kinge to appoint a new one. **1657** W. MORICE *Coena quasi Κοινή* §23. 231 To say expressly that all is Null which was done at Pyworthy. **1714** R. FIDDES *Pract. Disc.* II. 35 Their commands are originally null and of no force. **1765** BLACKSTONE *Comm.* I. xv. 425 If such consent from the father was wanting, the marriage was null. **1849** MACAULAY *Hist. Eng.* v. I. 582 The act of attainder.. would become superfluous at the very moment at which it ceased to be null. **1888** BRYCE *Amer. Commonw.* I. xxxiv. 524 The tribunal is disposed rather to support than to treat as null the act done.

b. In phrase ***null and void.***

1669 MARVELL *Corr.* Wks. (Grosart) II. 297 Prorogation makes all Bills, Votes, and Proceedings of this Session null and voyd. **1769** *Junius Lett.* xvi. (1788) 95 Any votes given to him are null and void. **1803** WELLINGTON in Gurw. *Desp.* (1835) II. 610, I yesterday gave notice.. that I should consider it null and void from the 27th instant. **1871** FREEMAN *Norm. Conq.* (1876) IV. xvii. 27 That all acts done by the authority of the usurper Harold were held to be null and void.

2. a. Of no value or importance; insignificant, ineffective.

1790 BURKE *French Rev.* Sel. Wks. II. 208 Here the principle of contribution.. is reprobated as null, and destructive to equality. **1803** MALTHUS *Popul.* (1817) III. 185 We take all possible pains to weaken and render null the ties of nature. **1842** KINGSLEY *Lett.* (1878) I. 79 Truth made practically null by modifying it to suit circumstances. **1880** KINGLAKE *Crimea* VI. ix. 304 Upon grounds thus weak, or, to speak more exactly, thus null he founded his charges.

b. Devoid of character, expression, or distinctive personality.

a **1850** MARG. FULLER *At Home & Abroad* (1860) 343 As to character, so null that everybody laughed. **1855** TENNYSON *Maud* I. II. 6 Faultily faultless, icily regular, splendidly null. **1889** H. F. WOOD *Englishm. Rue Caïn* i, The ordeal of lighting up that terribly null countenance.

3. Nothing; nil; non-existent.

1761 *Phil. Trans.* LII. 277 The effect of the other planets is either null or known. **1792** *Ibid.* LXXXII. 242 Atmospheric electricity has been.. variable..; sometimes quite null, then weak, or strong by turns. **1811** PINKERTON *Petral.* II. 486 Its influence on that element was absolutely null. **1834** McMURTRIE *Cuvier's Anim. Kingd.* 384 The internal lobe of the maxillæ null or very small. **1866** R. M. FERGUSON *Electr.* (1870) 15 The combined effect of the two terrestrial poles.. is thus null.

4. a. *spec.* in ***null belt, method, point*** (see quots.). Also more widely, esp. in *Math.*, with the sense: having, being, or associated with the value zero. ***null space***, a space composed of all quantities that are transformed into zero by some given transformation.

1809-10 COLERIDGE *Friend* (1818) III. 150 That confusion and formality are but the opposite poles of the same null-point? **1835** W. R. HAMILTON *Conjugate Functions* 23 The transition may be said to be null, or a null step, as producing no real alteration in the moment from which it is made. *Ibid.* 31 The standard or zero-moment A itself may be denoted by the complex symbol 0 + A, because it may be conceived as generated from itself by applying the null step 0. *Ibid.* 35 The null cardinal (or number none). **1851** NICHOL *Archit. Heav.* (ed. 9) 208 The centre of gravity and motion, being the mere point where all opposite tendencies find their balance—the system's null point. **1860** MAURY *Phys. Geogr.* xv. §640 This calm zone.. may be considered as a thermal adjustment—the dynamical null-belt—between the trade-winds of the two hemispheres. **1873** MAXWELL *Electr. & Magn.* (1881) I. 301 Methods of this kind, in which the thing to be observed is the non-existence of some phenomenon, are called *null* or *zero* methods. **1884** A. BUCHHEIM in *Phil. Mag.* XVIII. 459 A linear space of $(a-1)$ dimensions will be called an *a*-point... A matrix A of order *n* is considered as operating on the coordinates of the points of an *n*-point... If A is of nullity *a*, the equation $A(x_1 \ldots x_n) = 0$ is satisfied by all the points of a certain *a*-point, and conversely. I call this *a*-point the null space of A. **1885** *Proc. London Math. Soc.* XVI. 78 A point *x*, such that $\phi x = 0$, is called a null-point of [the matrix] ϕ. **1898** A. N. WHITEHEAD *Universal Algebra* I. II. iii. 25 Since in combination with any other element the null element 0 disappears, the symbolism may be rendered more convenient by writing $-a$ for $0-a$. **1922** E. H. NEVILLE *Prolegomena to Analytical Geom.* v. v. 303 An ordinary circle of radius zero is called a nul circle. **1926** H. BAGCHI *Course of Geom. Anal.* v. 263 The theorem.. prescribes a null value for a determinant having two coincident rows or columns. **1930** J. W. YOUNG *Projective Geom.* ix. 158 If *A* and *B* coincide, the vector *AB* is called the null vector and is denoted by 0. **1941** BIRKHOFF & MACLANE *Surv. Mod. Algebra* x. 268 The null-space of a linear transformation *T* is the set of all vectors ξ such that $\xi T = O$. The null-space of a matrix *A* is the set of all row matrices *X* which satisfy the homogeneous linear equations $XA = O$. **1954** H. GRIFFIN *Elem. Theory of Numbers* i. 8 A null element is an integer that divides only itself. *Ibid.*, Zero is the null element of the rational integers. **1956** R. H. ATKIN *Math. & Wave Mech.* iii. 76 As in all algebras we find it convenient to introduce two identity operators. These are called the unit operator (idem factor) and the nul operator (zero). **1961** SEIFERT & BROWN *Ballistic Missile & Space Vehicle Systems* xvii. 404 They [*sc.* gyroscopes].. operate as angular error detectors over a very small range around their reference or null positions. **1962** C. WEXLER *Analytic Geom.* v. 141 The plane cuts the cone merely in a point (the vertex), resulting in a null circle or a null ellipse. **1964** E. BACH *Introd. Transformational Gram.* ii. 14 Among the elements assumed to be available for each grammar.. there is one which plays a special role, namely, the null (unit or identity) element. It functions in the mathematical system underlying the representations of a grammatical theory as does zero in ordinary addition, or the digit 1 in ordinary multiplication. **1971** L. T. AGGER *Introd. Electricity* xviii. 326 Balance occurs with null, or zero, deflection of the pointer. **1971** C. W. CURTIS in Powell & Higman *Finite Simple Groups* iii. 171 *f* vanishes on the nullspace of *a*. **1971** J. Z. YOUNG *Introd. Study Man* xvi. 201 This ingeniously establishes the change in growth power by a nul method.

b. *Mech.* and *Geom.* ***null point*** [tr. G. *nullpunkt* (A. F. Möbius *Lehrb. d. Statik* (1837) I. vi. 144)], the point of intersection of all the null lines of a given wrench that lie in a given plane; ***null line***, a line about which the moment of a given wrench is zero; ***null plane*** [tr. G. *nullebene* (A. F. Möbius, *loc. cit.*)], the plane containing all the null lines of a given wrench that pass through a given point; ***null system***, a system of null points and their corresponding null planes.

1903 C. M. JESSOP *Treat. Line Complex* iii. 45 The distinction between the two spaces Σ and Σ' has now disappeared and we have a (1, 1) correspondence between the points and planes of space in which each point lies in its corresponding plane... Such a correspondence is called a null-system. The corresponding points and planes are called 'null-points' and 'null-planes'. **1911** *Encycl. Brit.* XVII. 967/1 In the 'Null-System' of A. F. Möbius (1790–1868), a line such that the moment of a given wrench about it is zero is called a null-line. **1942** Synge & Griffith *Princ. Mech.* x. 301 A rigid body is acted on by a force **F** at *O* and a couple **G**. *P* is an assigned point, with position vector **r** relative to *O*. Show that there is a single infinity of lines through *P* about which the force system has no moment; show that these lines lie in a plane... (The lines are called null lines, and the plane a null plane.) **1964** C. E. Springer *Geom. & Anal. Projective Spaces* x. 273 In a polar correlation with a skew-symmetric matrix, every point is incident with its corresponding plane. This type of correlation is called a null system, a designation used in the theory of statics as developed by Möbius.

c. *Math.* and *Logic.* Of a class or set: having no members. Of a propositional function or relation: always false; having the null class as its range.

1903 B. Russell *Princ. Math.* ii. 22 A propositional function is said to be null when it is false for all values of *x*; and the class of *x*'s satisfying the function is called the null-class, being in fact a class of no terms. **1906** W. H. & G. C. Young *Theory of Sets of Points* 288 The null-set..contains no point. **1932** Lewis & Langford *Symbolic Logic* vii. 208 The universal function is expressible as $p \vee \sim p$. The null-function is the negative of this. **1941** O. Helmer tr. *Tarski's Introd. Logic* v. 90 We have..in the calculus of relations two special relations, the universal relation $\vee$ and the null relation $\wedge$, the first of which holds between any two individuals, and the second between none. **1948** Ambrose & Lazerowitz *Fund. Symbolic Logic* x. 215 To say that a class is null, or empty, is the same as saying that there are no values satisfying its defining function. **1955** [see domain *sb.* 4 f]. **1956** A. Church *Introd. Math. Logic* (rev. ed.) I. 31 If the range is given,..there is only one null class. But, e.g., the range of the null class associated with the form sin x = 2 and the range of the null class associated with the form $\in < 0$ are not the same... We shall speak respectively of the 'null class of real numbers' and of the 'null class of positive real numbers'. **1966** S. Beer *Decision & Control* vi. 107 This does not matter; it simply means that the complementary set has no elements—and this is called a null set.

d. *Physics.* Existing between or joining points in space-time between which the interval is zero; ***null cone*** = *light cone* s.v. light *sb.* 16.

1928 *Phil. Mag.* V. 242 A null-surface is defined as an envelope of null-cones,..while the characteristic lines on a null-surface prove to be geodesic null-lines. *Ibid.*, The history of a light wave in space-time is a null-surface. **1942** Synge & Griffith *Princ. Mech.* xvi. 475 A null line represents the history of a flash of light traveling along the axis *Ox* of a Galilean frame. **1959** J. Aharoni *Special Theory of Relativity* i. 25 An interval *ds* between two events can be either real, zero, or imaginary... In the first case the interval is called space-like, in the second case a null-interval, and in the third case time-like. **1968** T. C. Bradbury *Theoret. Mech.* xiii. 589 If the four-vector joins *O* and *C*, then $r^2 - c^2t^2 = r'^2 - c^2t'^2 = 0$. Such a vector is a null vector. Events separated by null vectors can be joined by light signals; in fact, the light cone is frequently called the null cone. **1972** J. Ehlers et al. in L. O'Raifeartaigh *Gen. Relativity* iv. 75 In a normal hyperbolic Riemannian manifold, the distinction between the interior and exterior of the null cone N_p of a point p can locally be defined by means of the sign of the world function $\Omega(p, q)$, for q near p.

e. Statistics. ***null hypothesis***, a hypothesis that is the subject of a significance test, esp. the hypothesis that there is no difference between specified populations (any apparent difference being due to sampling or experimental error).

1935 R. A. Fisher *Design of Experiments* ii. 19 The two clases of results which are distinguished by our test of significance are..those which show a significant discrepancy from a certain hypothesis; namely, in this case, the hypothesis that the judgements given are in no way influenced by the order in which the ingredients have been added; and..results which show no significant discrepancy from this hypothesis. This hypothesis..is again characteristic of all experimentation... We may speak of this hypothesis as the 'null hypothesis', and it should be noted that the null hypothesis is never proved or established, but is possibly disproved, in the course of experimentation. **1973** *Jrnl. Genetic Psychol.* CXXIII. 86 The specific null hypotheses tested were as follows: 1. There were no differences in hostile press (fear of failure) score decreases between self-reinforcement, group therapy, and control groups. 2. Hostile press scores do not decrease significantly during the self-reinforcement condition. [Etc.] **1975** *Nature* 20 Feb. 607/1 The evidence..for positive selection directing the evolution of early vertebrate haemoglobin is supported by a χ^2 test, performed to test the null hypothesis that sites where mutations produced acquired crucial functions did not evolve at a different rate from all other sites.

5. Passing into *sb.*: A condition of no signal; also, a direction in which no radiation is detected or emitted. Freq. *attrib.*

1926 *Bell Syst. Techn. Jrnl.* V. 295 The number of lobes is, of course, equal to the number of null directions. **1931** *Proc. IRE* XXXI. 1426 The nulls and maxima..have been plotted in Fig. 16 for an element length of four wavelengths. *Ibid.* 1427 Figs. 15 and 16..give the null points. These are seen to be 0, 30, and 90 degrees in Fig. 15. **1931** Moyer & Wostrel *Radio Handbk.* xii. 601 A direct-current galvanometer, protected by a suitable shunt, is used as a null indicator. **1958** Condon & Odishaw *Handbk. Physics* iv. v. 66/2 Null determinations in d-c measurements are almost invariably made with a D'Arsonval-type galvanometer. **1962** *Newnes Conc. Encycl. Electr. Engin.* 94/2 The precision of a bridge measurement depends on the sensitivity of the null detector. **1968** M. Woodhouse *Rock Baby* xv. 150, I set up the loop of the D.F. set and plugged in the headset. When the signal came..I got a clear null a little west of due south. **1973** J. Hulbert *All About Navigating* vii. 96 It is much easier to pick out the softest point than the loudest point and so a null is used for direction finding. **1975** *Gramophone* Oct. 734/3 The many nulls and lobes beyond these angles are not too important, and are due to the interaction of the radiator with its housing and the corners of the cabinet.

null (nʌl), *v.*[1] [f. null *a.*, after *annul.* Cf. also OF. *nuller*, med.L. *nullare* (rare).]

†**1.** *trans.* To negative; to make negative. *Obs.*

c **1620** A. Hume *Brit. Tongue* (1865) 33 Not is an adverb, ..and in our tong followes the verb that it nulleth.

†**2. a.** To reduce to nothing; to destroy or efface completely. *Obs.* (freq. in 17th c.)

c **1645** Howell *Lett.* (1650) I. 384, I believe [not]..that she was able to null and extinguish the native languages she found in those places. *a* **1691** Boyle *Hist. Air* (1692) 69 These objections..do not really null or take away the possibility of the thing. **1702** S. Parker tr. *Cicero De Finibus* v. 356 In a manner to null and erase their very Being. **1722** De Foe *Col. Jack* (1840) 342 He does all he can to null or quash the story.

†**b.** To deny the validity of. *Obs. rare*$^{-1}$.

1656 Baxter *Reformed Partn.* 338, I speak not this against any Bishops that acknowledge the Presbyters to be true Pastors..but of them that null the Presbyters office.

3. To annul, cancel, make void. Also with *out.*

1643 *Richlieu's Epit.* in *Harl. Misc.* (Malh.) V. 333 Lest he should spare her, when she was dead, he nulled her last will. **1663–4** Marvell *Corr.* Wks. (Grosart) II. 139 They affirm that his.. Royal majesty..desired that the Privileges might be nulled. **1693** Norris *Pract. Disc.* (1711) III. 90 God forbid that such a Law should ever be null'd or made void. *a* **1716** Blackall *Wks.* (1723) I. 294 Because these Marriages had been made before the Law against them was given,..it was not reasonable that they would be nulled. **1757** Burke *Abridgm. Eng. Hist.* Wks. 1842 II. 584 The first election he nulled, because its irregularity was glaring. **1869** Doran *Table Traits* 384 A particular act of their worships.. nulled the proclamation. **1957** *Electronics* 1 Mar. 163 The receiver uses a shielded-loop antenna to null out main powerline noise. *Ibid.*, The atmospherics..are greater in amplitude than most of the peaks of the background hash after nulling the main source of powerline noise. **1971** *Sci. Amer.* Aug. 65/2 The harmonic signal is electronically processed and sent through the feedback winding to 'null out', or cancel, the ambient field within the sensor.

Hence **'nulling** *vbl. sb.*

1654 H. L'Estrange *Chas. I* (1655) 78 The unbilleting of Souldiers and nulling of Martiall Law in times of Peace. *a* **1687** H. More *Cont. Remark. Stories* 446 Which is a perfect dissolution or nulling of the True..Religion.

null, *v.*[2] [var. of *nurl*, knurl *v.*] *intr.* **a.** To make knurls. Hence **'nulling** *vbl. sb.*, the making of knurls; knurled work. **b.** Of a line: To kink.

1851 C. Cist *Sk. Cincinnati* xiii. 245 All kinds of turning used by cabinet makers, including nulling of every pattern, furnished at the shortest notice. **1890** in *Cent. Dict.* **1914** Eberlein & McClure *Pract. Bk. Period Furnit.* 63 Nulling, made up chiefly of beading, cabling and hollows, is often used to ornament the bulbous legs of Jacobean furniture. **1934** J. Gloag *Eng. Furnit.* v. 86 The edges of tables and desks were scalloped with nulling, heavily gilded. **1936** C. H. Hayward *Eng. Period Furnit.* ii. 33 The carved flutes partly filled with nullings are a feature that was used considerably in Elizabethan times. **1966** M. M. Pegler *Dict. Interior Design* 307 *Nulling*, a Jacobean wood-carving technique which produced an effect similar to repoussé or chased metalwork. The patterns were created by a series of small projections or recessions from the surface (like a boss or bead) of the wood.

'nulla. Also **nullah.** = nulla-nulla.

1881 *Gentl. Mag.* Jan. 69 The birds are so tame that the natives knock them down by hurling their nullahs. **1890** 'R. Boldrewood' *Col.-Reformer* (1891) 204 Hutkeeper at once seized his nulla in one hand.

nulla, variant of nullah.

'nullable, *a. rare*$^{-1}$. [f. null *v.* + -able.] Capable of being annulled.

a **1718** W. Penn *Tracts* Wks. 1727 I. 683 If that Fundamental which gives to the People a Power of Legislation be not nullable.

‖**nulla bona** ('nʌlə 'bəʊnə). [L., 'no goods'.] The return made by a sheriff upon an execution when the party has no goods to be distrained.

[**1713** Arbuthnot *John Bull* ii. xvi, For a Return of a *Non est invent.*, and *Nulla habet bona.*]

1807 *Amer. State P.* Misc. (1834) I. 675 (Stanf.), For return of nulla bona 25 cents. **1829** W. H. Maxwell *Stories Waterloo* (1856) 63 The sheriff returned a *non est inventus*... I ran him to execution, and got *nulla bona* on my return. **1885** *Law Times* LXXVIII. 109/1 The sheriff made a return of *nulla bona*, Cramond's execution..having swept all the goods away.

nullafidian, variant of nullifidian.

‖**nullah** ('nʌlə). *Anglo-Indian.* Also **nala, nulla.** [Hindī *nālā* brook, rivulet, ravine.] A river or stream; a watercourse, river-bed, ravine.

1776 Halhed *Code Gentoo Laws* 52 When the water fails in all the *Nullahs*. **1793** Hodges *Trav. India* 20 This road is crossed by several nullahs, some of which have ferry boats stationed at them. **1834** Medwin *Angler in Wales* II. 16 A nullah, broader and swifter than usual, cut off my communication with the budgerow. **1859** R. F. Burton *Centr. Afr.* in *Jrnl. Geogr. Soc.* XXIX. 206 Here and there are nullahs, with high stiff earthbanks for the passage of rain torrents. **1883** F. M. Crawford *Mr. Isaacs* x, We had just crossed a nullah in the forest, full from the recent rains. **1920** *Blackw. Mag.* Jan. 117/1 You feel him..open out again to his stride, or drop out into a sudden nala without a peck. **1933** *Discovery* June 204/1 The nalas and river beds were parched, awaiting the flood. **1963** T. Tullett *Inside Interpol* xiv. 184 After twenty minutes of careful tracking it led him to a *nala* (ditch) where he found the impression of the sole of a heavy boot. **1964** R. Perry *World of Tiger* i. 10 The tigers he shot were living in nullahs close to villages. **1972** I. Baker *Grave Doubt* vii. 90 Could it be because it was England and not some god-forsaken Afghan nullah?

attrib. **1869** E. A. Parkes *Pract. Hygiene* (ed. 3) 71 Marsh or nullah water full of vegetable debris.

‖**'nulla-'nulla.** Also **gnulla-, nullah-, nolla-.** [Native Australian.] A club of hard wood used as a weapon by the aborigines of Australia.

1838 T. L. Mitchell *Exped. E. Austral.* I. 350 Striking him on the back of the head with a nulla-nulla. **1863** Beveridge *Gatherings* 10 Wherein lay his Nullah-nullah. **1885** Mrs. C. Praed *Head Station* 176 The elder men beat their nulla-nullas, and waved their spears. **1890** Lumholtz *Cannibals* 72 The nolla-nolla or club, the warlike weapon of the Australian native most commonly in use.

nulle, will not: see nill *v.*

nulled, variant of knurled *ppl. a.*

1875 Knight *Dict. Mech.* 1535/1 *Nulled-work*, turned work resembling a series of beads strung on a rod.

†**'nuller.** *Obs. rare*$^{-1}$. [f. null *v.*[1] + -er[1].] One who annuls; a nullifier.

1650–87 H. More *Conject. Cabbal.* (1713) 240 Gross Idolaters, bold Nullers or Abrogators of the indispensable Laws of Christ.

nulli'bicity. *rare*$^{-1}$. [f. L. *nullibi* nowhere.] The condition of being nowhere existent. So **nulli'biety, nulli'bility.** Also **nulli'biquitous** *a.*, nowhere existing.

1822 Mrs. E. Nathan *Langreath* III. 290 They have succeeded so far as to render her [*sc.* Liberty] in a state of *nulibicity. **1668** Wilkins *Real Char.* ii. vii. §2. 188 Ubiquity, omnipresence, *Nullibiety. **1896** *Common Nietzsche's Wks.* XI. 38 Wagner's ubiquity and nullibiety. **1832** *Fraser's Mag.* VI. 483 Our mock-modest rulers..have almost persuaded themselves of the *nullibility of these houses. **1820** *Examiner* 632/2 Mr. Dadikey's *nullibiquitous hat and waistcoat.

†**'nullibism.** *Obs. rare.* [See next and -ism.] The doctrine of the nullibists.

1681 Glanvill *Sadducismus* 111 Dost thou hear, my Nullibist, what one of the..Symmists of that stupendious secret of Nullibism plainly professes?

'nullibist. Now *rare* or *Obs.* [f. L. *nullibi* nowhere + -ist.] One who affirms that a spirit or incorporeal being nowhere exists.

1662 H. More *Philos. Writ.* Pref. Gen., Scholia xxvii. (1712) 28 For what relates to the opinion of the Nullibists, I have abundantly demonstrated how wild a notion it is. **1681** Glanvill *Sadducismus* 100 Those other therefore because they so boldly affirm that a Spirit is Nullibi..have deservedly purchased to themselves the Name or Title of Nullibists. *a* **1763** Doddridge *Wks.* (1803) IV. 408 We must go into the scheme of the Nullibists, and affirm that God is no where. **1803** W. Taylor in *Monthly Mag.* XIV. 490 He may, consequentially, with respect to external beings, be a nullibist.

nullification (nʌlɪfɪ'keɪʃən). [ad. late L. *nullificātio*, f. *nullificāre*: see nullify and -ation.]

†**1.** Reduction to nothing. *Obs. rare.*

1630 Donne *Serm.* clviii. Wks. 1839 VI. 288 This is..the most deadly and peremptory Nullification of Man that we can consider.

2. a. The action of rendering null or of no effect.

1808 Bentham *Sc. Reform* 18 Principle of nullification; decision on grounds avowedly foreign to the merits. **1810** —— *Packing* (1821) 7 The most efficient instrument of injustice may be seen in the principle and practice of nullification. **1839** James *Louis XIV*, I. 66 His accession to the throne was ushered in by the nullification of his father's will. **1886** *Manch. Exam.* 17 Feb. 5/4 The nullification of elections by a partisan majority.

b. *U.S.* The action, on the part of a State legislature, of refusing to allow a general law to be enforced within the State. Also *attrib.*

1798 T. Jefferson *Writings* (1905) XVII. 386 Where powers are assumed which have not been delegated, a nullification of the act is the rightful remedy. **1830** *Massachusetts Spy* 22 Sept. (Th.), Nullification nullified. **1838** Ht. Martineau *Western Trav.* I. 244 Mr. Calhoun is as full as ever of his Nullification doctrines. **1859** Bartlett *Dict. Amer.* (ed. 2) 298 Nullification, in the case of South Carolina, was simply an act, or at least a threat of open rebellion. **1894** Fiske *Hist. Amer.* 270 The government of the United States has never acknowledged the right of nullification, or permitted any state to exercise it.

Hence **nullifi'cationist**; **'nullifi,cator.**

1862 Ludlow *Hist. U.S.* 135 The President..seemed almost a natural ally to the Nullificationists. **1833** *New Monthly Mag.* XXXVII. 358 The little distracted band of nullificators, as some of your journals call them.

nullifidian (nʌlɪ'fɪdɪən), *sb.* and *a.* Also 6 **nulla-**; 7 **-fidean.** [f. L. *nulli-*, comb. form of *nullus* no + *fidēs* faith.]

A. *sb.* **1.** One of no faith or religion; a sceptic in matters of religion.

1564–78 Bullein *Dial. agst. Pest.* (1888) 14 To be plain, I am a Nullafidian, and there are many of our secte. **1596** Harington *Metam. Apol.* Dd ij b, Then all sayd they would condemne mee as a neuter, or *nulli fidian*, except I gaue a better answere. **1637** GILLESPIE *Eng. Pop. Cerem.* Epist. A 2 The Atheisticall Nullifidian nothing regardeth the assoyling of Ecclesiasticall controversies. **1668** HOWE *Bless. Righteous* (1825) 157 Sure to be so a Solifidian is to be a nullifidian. **1775** HOWIE *Scots Worthies* Pref. (1871) p. xxx, Some sceptical nullifidian or other may be ready to object. **1816** SCOTT *Old Mort.* xxxi, In their eyes, a lukewarm Presbyterian was little better than a Prelatist, an anti-Covenanter, and a Nullifidian. **1826** —— *Woodst.* xv, In case thou shouldst holla for assistance, as yonder Nullifidian hath it.

2. *transf.* One who lacks faith; a disbeliever. **1668** KIRKMAN *Eng. Rogue* (1871) II. 57 The very Ale-house-keeper..was now grown such a Nullifidian that he would not believe us for small-beer. **1830** *Blackw. Mag.* XXVII. 533 Sir John Moore was professedly a nullifidian in Spanish energy and patriotism. **1872** GEO. ELIOT *Middlem.* I. iv, Celia was no longer the eternal cherub, but..a pink-and-white nullifidian.

B. *adj.* Having no faith or belief. **1627** FELTHAM *Resolves* II. xlvii. (1677) 253 A Solifidean-Christian is a Nullifidean-Pagan. **1816** SCOTT *Old Mort.* xxxi, I fear treachery to the host from this nullifidian Achan. **1885** SWINBURNE *Misc.* (1886) 175 The sceptic, or in the phrase of Wither's time the nullifidian Nott.

nullifier (ˈnʌlɪfaɪə(r)). [f. NULLIFY *v.* + -ER[1].]

1. One who nullifies; *spec.* in *U.S. Hist.*, one who maintained the right of any State to annul, within its own boundaries, laws passed in Congress. **1832** W. IRVING *Life & Lett.* (1866) III. 44 A member of the legislature, and one of the leaders of the nullifiers. **1844** EMERSON *New Eng. Reformers* Wks. (Bohn) I. 260 So the country is frequently affording..examples of..solitary nullifiers, who throw themselves on their reserved rights. **1894** FISKE *Hist. Amer.* 312 To the mixture of threat with persuasion the nullifiers yielded.

2. *transf.* (See quot.) **1859** BARTLETT *Dict. Amer.* (ed. 2) 298 *Nullifier*..was also applied to a sort of shoe, made like a decapitated boot, brought into fashion in the 'nullification' times.

†ˈ**nulliform**, *a. Obs. rare*⁻¹. [f. L. *nulli-*, *nullus* no + -FORM.] Having no proper form. Hence †**nulliˈformity**. *Obs. rare*⁻¹. *c* **1581** in *Grindal's Rem.* (Parker Soc.) 471 It was like that religion..would against his nature have proved milliform, yea, in continuance nulliform. **1644** HARDWICK in *Toleration Disapproved & Condemned* (1670) 26 We have undertaken..the establishment of Uniformity, and how can that stand with this Omniformitie, indeed Nulliformity, I understand not.

nullify (ˈnʌlɪfaɪ), *v.* [ad. late L. *nullificāre* (Tertullian), f. *nulli-*, *nullus* NULL *a.*: see -FY. So F. *nullifier.*]

1. *trans.* To render legally null and void; to annul, cancel. **1595** DANIEL *Civ. Wars* III. lxxxix, Which accusation was th' occasion, that His successour by order nullifies Many his Patents. **1607** R. C[AREW] tr. *Estienne's World of Wonders* 353 He nullified all the indulgences granted to the French. **1643** MARSHALL *Lett.* 22 The judgements of all other Courts are ratified or nullified by a Parliament. **1775** JOHNSON *Tax. no Tyr.* 38 By crossing the Atlantick he has not nullified his right. **1817** COBBETT *Wks.* XXXII. 360 Seeing that the act nullifies their previous engagement. **1825** *Gentl. Mag.* XCV. I. 501 This bequest being to the poor indefinitely, nullified his will. **1880** E. KIRKE *Life Garfield* 43 It was that act which South Carolina nullified and refused to allow to be executed within her borders.

absol. **1832** J. P. KENNEDY *Swallow Barn* I. xviii. 186 I'd be glad to know if we couldn't nullify. **1837** CALHOUN *Wks.* III. 57 The State of South Carolina..declared the act to be unconstitutional, and as such null and void. In a word, we nullified.

2. a. To make of no value, use, or efficacy; to reduce to nothingness; to efface completely. **1609** SIR E. HOBY *Let. to T. H[iggons]* 56 If Aërius..doe ioyne with the Primitiue Church, in nullifying oblations for the dead. **1642** J. EATON *Honey-c. Free Justif.* 373 If it heale not these,..is not Justification nullified, and made of no use? **1675** BROOKS *Gold. Key* Wks. 1867 V. 218 He hath weakened, yea, nullified and taken away sin. **1781** S. PETERS *Hist. Connecticut* 26 Enough, surely, has been said to nullify the Colonists' plea of having bought their lands of the Indians. **1809** *Med. Jrnl.* XXI. 509 These facts..could by no means subvert and nullify the very obvious and evident advantages. **1850** GROTE *Greece* II. lx. (1862) V. 288 The narrow dimensions of the harbour would have nullified her superiority at all times. **1876** FARRAR *St. Paul* (1883) 47 They had long learnt to nullify what they professed to defend.

b. With personal object. **1603** J. DAVIES *Microcos.* Wks. (Grosart) I. 43/1 If otherwise he should with them abide, They would through glory be quite nullified. **1625** B. JONSON *Staple of N.* IV. Interm. iv, I would haue..her Graces Herald to..nullifie him for no Gentleman. **1642** ROGERS *Naaman* 311 Absolutely unsubsisting in themselves, meerly nullified. **1702** C. MATHER *Magn. Chr.* III. I. (1852) 343 Thus content was he to be nullified, that the Lord might be magnified. **1849–50** ALISON *Hist. Europe* I. i. §63. 106 He not only brought the nobility to Paris, but he nullified them when there.

Hence ˈ**nullifying** *vbl. sb.* and *ppl. a.* **1647** WARD *Simp. Cobler* 50 Such usurpations are the Neronian nullifyings of Kingdomes. **1651** BAXTER *Inf. Bapt.* 226 The violating of the Covenant is not fitly called a nullifying of it. **1681** —— *Answ. Dodwell* iii. 22 Against even the Nullifying Canons. **1832** W. IRVING *Life & Lett.* (1866) III. 44, I dined with him at Governor Hamilton's, the nullifying Governor. **1852** HANNA *Mem. Dr. Chalmers* IV. xiii. 203 A nullifying edict..from the Civil Court.

‖**nullipara** (nʌˈlɪpərə). [mod.L., f. *nulli-* (cf. prec.) + *-para*, fem. of *-parus*: see -PAROUS.] A female who has never given birth to a child. **1872** T. G. THOMAS *Dis. Women* (ed. 3) 76 In a nullipara, or virgin, this is often produced. **1904** *Brit. Med. Jrnl.* 3 Dec. 83 The patient was a nullipara.

Hence **nulliˈparity**; **nuˈlliparous** *a.* **1859** *Todd's Cycl. Anat.* V. 624/2 The average dimensions of the virgin or nulliparous uterus. **1872** T. G. THOMAS *Dis. Women* (ed. 3) 127 Parturition is almost never met with in nulliparous women, except after removal of large tumors per vaginam. **1878** *Obstet. Trans.* (1879) XX. 173 Circumstances..in which proof of parity or nulliparity may turn out to be proof of innocence or guilt.

nulliplex (ˈnʌlɪplɛks), *a. Genetics.* [f. L. *nulli-*, *nullus* no + *-plex* as in SIMPLEX, DUPLEX *adjs.* etc.] Of a polyploid individual: having the dominant allele of any particular gene not represented. **1921** A. F. BLAKESLEE in *Amer. Naturalist* LV. 257 A Poinsettia plant may, to speak in terms of the dominant factor, be considered nulliplex with no dominant genes, or simplex, duplex or triplex with, respectively, 1, 2, or 3 dominant factors. **1929** *Jrnl. Genetics* XXI. 141 From previous results it has been assumed that 14/26 is triplex for *Y* and heterozygous for *I*, and that 'White Star' is nulliplex for *Y* and heterozygous for *I*. **1963** LEWIS & JOHN *Chromosome Marker* IV. iii. 327 On selfing, a tetraploid of this kind [*sc.* AAaa] will give not three types of offspring but five, namely AAAA (quadruplex), AAAa (triplex), AAaa (duplex), Aaaa (simplex) and aaaa (nulliplex). *Ibid.* 328 Thus, with chromatid segregation a triplex can produce nulliplex offspring.

nullipore (ˈnʌlɪpɔə(r)). [f. L. *nulli-*, *nullus* no + PORE *sb.*[1]] A form of marine vegetation having the power of secreting lime like the coral polyp. **1840** *Penny Cycl.* XVI. 363/1 In his system, the Nullipores are rejected from the place so long assigned them. **1860** MAURY *Phys. Geogr.* xiii. §560 Brilliant, rosy, or peach coloured Nullipores overgrow the decaying masses. **1882** GEIKIE *Geol. Sketches* 34 We pick up..broken whelks, nullipores, and corallines.

attrib. **1888** H. W. PARKER *Spirit Beauty* (1889) 20 Gorgon corals and nullipore sea-weeds.

‖**nulli secundus** (ˈnʌlɪ sɪˈkʌndəs), *adj. phr.* Also (applied to things) **nulli secundum**. [L.] Second to none. **1869** S. R. HOLE *Bk. about Roses* iv. 55 If Mr. Shirley Hibberd..can grow good Roses within four miles of the General Post-Office..it is quite certain that he would be *nulli secundus* with the full advantage of situation and soil. **1935** G. K. ZIPF *Psycho-Biol. Lang.* (1966) 75 The conventional Sanskrit alphabet is an amazingly accurate phonetic alphabet, practically *nulli secundum*. **1963** *Brewer's Dict. Phr. & Fable* 649/2 *Nulli secundus*,..the motto of the Coldstream Guards, which regiment is hence sometimes spoken of as the *Nulli Secundus Club*.

ˈ**nullism.** *rare*⁻¹. [f. NULL *a.* + -ISM.] Absence of distinctive character. **1831** CARLYLE in *Fraser's Mag.* III. 130 All critical guild-brethren now working diligently..in the calmer sphere of Vapidism or even Nullism.

nullisome (ˈnʌlɪsəʊm). *Cytology.* [f. L. *nulli-*, *nullus* no + -SOME[4].] A pair of homologous chromosomes lacking from a diploid chromosome complement; also, a nullisomic individual. **1944** *Genetics* XXIX. 233 Speltoidy..has been shown..frequently to be due to the effects of a particular monosome or its corresponding nullisome. *Ibid.* 234 Seventeen of the possible 21 different nullisomes in *Triticum vulgare* have now been obtained. **1968** [see next]. **1973** G. S. KHUSH *Cytogenetics Aneuploids* ix. 221 In wheat, a successful method was the test of the ability of a particular tetrasome to compensate for a particular nullisome.

nullisomic (nʌlɪˈsəʊmɪk), *a.* (*sb.*) *Cytology.* Also †**nullosomic**. [f. as prec. + *-somic*, after MONOSOMIC *a.* (*sb.*), etc.] Having or being a diploid chromosome complement in which one or more than one pair of homologous chromosomes is lacking. Hence as *sb.*, a nullisomic individual. **1932** *Genetics* XVII. 694 In the hybrid population the nullosomics were readily recognized. **1939** *Ibid.* XXIV. 510 Neither of the nullosomic plants set seeds. **1941** *Ibid.* XXVI. 167 (*heading*) Nullisomics in *Triticum vulgare.* **1944** *Ibid.* XXIX. 233 Some of these have been nullisomic types. **1968** R. RIEGER et al. *Gloss. Genetics & Cytogenetics* 319 Normally, nullisomics (or nullisomes) cannot survive in diploids. **1973** G. S. KHUSH *Cytogenetics Aneuploids* i. 3 Kihara (1924) and Winge (1924) were the first to report the nullisomic plants of wheat. *Ibid.* viii. 186 Some nullisomics of *Avena* may have normal viability.

nullity (ˈnʌlɪtɪ). [a. F. *nullité* (= It. *nullita*, Sp. *nulidad*), or med.L. *nullitas*: see NULL *a.* and -ITY.]

1. The fact of being legally null and void; invalidity. Also (with *a* and *pl.*), an instance of this; a fact or circumstance causing invalidity.

a. With reference to marriage. Also *attrib.* **1570** FOXE *A. & M.* (ed. 2) 1222/1 The Pope beyng minded..to geue sentence for the inualiditie and nullitie of the kyngs first pretensed matrimonie. **1613** SIR R. NAUNTON in *Buccleuch MSS.* (Hist. MSS. Comm.) I. 140 The nullity in the case of my Lord of Essex and his Lady. **1645** MILTON (title-p.), Tetrachordon, Expositions upon the four chief places in Scripture which treat of Marriage or Nullities in Marriage. **1707** tr. *Wks. C'tess D'Anois* (1715) 114 Omitting nothing that was necessary to be done, to prevent the starting of any Nullities in my Wedlock. **1765** BLACKSTONE *Comm.* I. 434 These disabilities..only make the marriage voidable, and not *ipso facto* void, until sentence of nullity be obtained. **1845** CAMPBELL *Chancellors* xxxiv. (1857) II. 85 They..introduced into it words respecting the original nullity of the King's first marriage. **1865** *Morn. Star* 3 Feb., This was a petition for nullity of marriage on the ground of imperfect publication of the banns. **1894** *Daily News* 26 July 9/1 The respondent not having entered an appearance or put in any defence in the nullity suit.

b. In general use. **1608** WILLET *Hexapla Exod.* 675 Notwithstanding this negligence there was no nullitie of Aarons consecration. **1637–50** ROW *Hist. Kirk* (Wodrow Soc.) 111 The nullitie of the former gift to be discussed als well by way of exception as action. *a* **1683** OWEN *Holy Sp.* (1693) 222 There would have been a Nullity in what they did. *a* **1715** BURNET *Own Time* (1766) I. 84 Which inferred a nullity on all their proceedings. **1776** J. ADAMS *Wks.* (1854) IX. 390 You have my hearty concurrence in telling the jury the nullity of acts of parliament. **1875** STUBBS *Const. Hist.* II. xiv. 142 The nullity of all proceedings taken in contravention of them.

†**2.** Nullification. *Obs. rare.* **1597** HOOKER *Eccl. Pol.* V. lxii. §13 Dissolutions and Nullities of things done are not onely not fauoured, but hated. *Ibid.* V. lxxxi. §3 A nullitie or frustration of all such acts. **1654** H. L'ESTRANGE *Chas. I* (1655) 155 The next day a Declinator and Protestation was presented..against the Assembly and containing a Nullity of it.

3. An act or thing which is null or invalid. **1624** GEE *New Shreds Old Snare* 17 The Consistories of our Bishops can doe no Acts but nullities against any of these. **1652** N. CULVERWEL *Treat.* I. vii. (1661) 49 They are not onely irregularities, but meer nullities. **1768** BLACKSTONE *Comm.* III. 246 This the temporal courts pay no regard to, and look upon a caveat as a mere nullity. **1818** CRUISE *Digest* (ed. 2) IV. 281 The last execution shall stand; the first being a mere nullity. **1849** MACAULAY *Hist. Eng.* ii. I. 178 The national sales, not having been confirmed by parliament, were regarded by the tribunals as nullities. **1891** *Law Times* XC. 462/1 The Court declared the deed a nullity.

4. The condition of being null or nought; a state of nothingness. **1589** G. HARVEY *Pierces Super.* Wks. (Grosart) II. 176 Euerlasting infamie, horrible damnation, & a most hideous nullity. **1620** T. GRANGER *Div. Logike* 112 For where there is no essence, or a thing depriued of essence, there is negation, or nullitie. **1649** JER. TAYLOR *Gt. Exemp.* Disc. ii. §11 Sometimes such..smaller indecencies are therefore pardoned and lessened almost to a nullity. **1715** BENTLEY *Serm.* xi. 376 The whole system of Nature must immediately..vanish into its primitive Nullity. **1791** COWPER *Yardley Oak* 88 Thy growth From almost nullity into a state Of matchless grandeur. **1848** W. H. KELLY tr. *L. Blanc's Hist. Ten Y.* I. 39 Had not the hundred days afforded proof of the political nullity of the elder Bourbons? **1873** M. ARNOLD *Lit. & Dogma* 285 The nullity of its deliverances, where..to bring it manifestly to book is impossible.

5. †**a.** A nought, a cipher. *Obs.* **1587** FLEMING *Cont. Holinshed* III. 1371/1 The cipher with the nullities and marks for names of princes and councillors. **1624** BEDELL *Lett.* xii. 161 If..you finde you haue taken manie nullities for signifying numbers,..correct the totall.

b. A mere nothing. *a* **1591** H. SMITH *Wks.* (1867) II. 448 The error..is great, but yet not such as doth make a nullity of our church. **1596** NASHE *Saffron Walden* Wks. (Grosart) III. 69 What the plausibilitie of Martin? A Nullitie; yea and a wofull Nullitie, and a piteous Nullitie. **1642** H. MORE *Song of Soul* II. i. IV. i, [I] them nigh blame of deep idolatrie That give so much to that slight nullitie. **1791** COWPER *Wks.* (1837) XV. 226 Such a mere nullity is time, to a creature to whom God gives a feeling heart. **1828** D'ISRAELI *Chas. I*, I. x. 287 Like many similar attempts..this predatory attack concluded in a nullity. **1860** MOTLEY *Netherl.* v. (1868) I. 137 His army was shrinking to a nullity.

c. Of persons: A nonentity. **1657** J. TRAPP *Comm. Job* xxx. 2 These Sanniones, in the text were, through idleness, meer nullities in the world. **1846** BROWNING *Lett.* (1899) I. 394 Such a miserable nullity, and husk of a man. **1874** BLACKIE *Self-Cult.* 30 In society the most accomplished man of mere professional skill is often a nullity.

6. *Math.* The number of columns of a matrix minus its rank; the dimension of the null space of a matrix or linear transformation (equal to the dimension of its domain minus that of its range). **1884** J. J. SYLVESTER in *Amer. Jrnl. Math.* VI. 274 The absolute zero for matrices of any order is the matrix all of whose elements are zero. It possesses so far as regards multiplication..the distinguishing property of the zero, viz. that when entering into composition with any other matrix..the product..is itself over again... This is the highest degree of nullity which any matrix can possess, and (regarded as an integer) will be called ω, the order of the matrix... In general..., if all the minors of order $\omega - i + 1$ vanish, but the minors of order $\omega - i$ do not all vanish, the nullity will be said to be i. **1941** BIRKHOFF & MACLANE *Survey Mod. Algebra* x. 268 Rank + nullity = Dimension of Domain. **1972** A. G. HOWSON *Handbk. Terms Algebra & Anal.* ix. 47 In the case of a homogeneous system, $Ax = 0$, the inverse image of 0, i.e. the set of solutions, is Ker(t)..which is a subspace of F^n..of dimension $n - r$, a number known as the nullity of t (or A).

ˈ**nulliverse.** [f. L. *nulli-*, *nullus* no, in contrast to *universe.*] A world devoid of any unifying principle or plan. **1847** WILKINSON tr. *Swedenborg's Outl. Infinite* Introd. 17 [He] made of the universe an incoherent nulliverse, a whirl of fleeting sequences, and a delirious 'chase of Pan'. **1882** W. JAMES in *Mind* 192 The world..is pure incoherence, a chaos, a nulliverse, to whose haphazard sway I will not truckle.

†**nullize**, *v. Obs. rare*⁻¹. [f. NULL *a.* + -IZE.] *trans.* To bring to nothing.

a **1618** SYLVESTER *Honour's Farewell* 82 Wks. (Grosart) II. 287 A lowly Fortune is of all despised: A lofty one, oft, of it selfe, nullized.

nullness (ˈnʌlnɪs). [f. NULL *a.* + -NESS.] The property or state of being null.

1949 E. BOWEN *Heat of Day* xvii. 301 The coming of winter to a stop had been most felt in the absolute nullness of night. **1959** *Proc. R. Soc.* A. CCLI. 521 The wave-like character will appear in the intrinsically *null* properties of these metrics... The nullness will become apparent from the physical properties of the metrics. **1967** *Punch* 22 Nov. 795/2 This feeling of organic injury is caused by..an utter nullness of non-taste, a denatured, defused..triviality.

ˈnullo. [a. It. *nullo*: see NULL *a.*] **1.** Now *Typog.* A nought, a cipher.

1598 FLORIO, *Cero*, Zero, a sipher of naught, a nullo. *a* **1640** JACKSON *Creed* x. Notes, Wks. IX. 271 To reckon it [*sc.* pleasure] not only as a nullo or cypher,..but as a mere vacuum or nothing. **1680** W. DE BRITAINE *Hum. Prud.* vi. (1686) 29, I am not much concerned if the Plebeian Heads take me for the Image of a Fly, a Nullo, a Cypher. **1824** J. JOHNSON *Typogr.* II. iv. 71 The nullo..may be used as a degree in geometrical works.

2. A type of bridge in which the object is to lose rather than gain tricks, or one in which tricks gained count against a player. Also *attrib.*

1914 *London Opinion* 7 Feb. 231/1 The new 'nullo' call at auction bridge is catching on... The Editor of the *Strand Magazine* intends publishing an article about 'nullos' in the March number. **1929** M. C. WORK *Compl. Contract Bridge* 241 *Nullos*, an unauthorized, and now obsolete, form of the game in which points were scored for losing instead of winning tricks. **1945** A. A. OSTROW *Compl. Card Player* 620 *Null* (*Nullo*): this is a declaration in which the bidder contracts not to win a single trick. **1972** H. PHILLIPS *Pop. Bk. Card Games* 373 Nullos is a form of Bridge for two which I have long recommended. *Ibid.* 375 Nullos with Contract scoring is an improvement on the original game, where the scoring and conditions are based on Auction.

nullubist, variant of NULLIBIST.

1668 *H. More's Div. Dial.* Publisher's Pref. A 3 That new fond Opinion of the Nullubists,..that God is no-where.

‖**nullus** (ˈnʌləs), *sb. rare*⁻¹. [L.] No one, nobody.

1929 D. H. LAWRENCE *Pansies* 100 My whole consciousness is cliché And I am null; I exist as an organism And a nullus.

nully (ˈnʌlɪ). *slang.* [? f. NULL *a.*; cf. *nullion* (Sc. Nat. Dict.) a stupid fellow.] A fool, a stupid person.

1973 BOYD & PARKES *Dark Number* iv. 45 You'll be a right nully if you don't mistrust all *polis* on sight. *Ibid.* vii. 78 He's a nully, a cipher. He contributes nothing. **1973** R. PARKES *Guardians* ii. 48 He's a sick, junked-up, pathetic old nully.

†**num**, abbreviation of NUMSKULL.

1807 W. IRVING *Salmag.* (1811) I. 67 *Mem.* All the New-Jersey lawyers *nums.*

†**num**, variant of *nome* NAME *v.*

a **1300** *Cursor M.* 9823 Þe stalworth godd man sal him num, Godd fader o werld es for to cum.

num, obs. pa. pple. of NIM *v.*

num, var. YUM. Cf. NUMMY-NUMMY.

1899 R. WHITEING *No. 5 John St.* ix. 86 Her handkerchief perfumes the whole room..to which Covey's frequent 'Num! num! num!' calls embarrassing attention. **1924** *Dialect Notes* V. 274 *Num, num, nummy, num* (humming or joy). **1961** W. SANSOM *Last Hours of Sandra Lee* vi. 112 Mouths ooed and nummed noises of appreciation.

numb (nʌm), *a.* (and *sb.*) Forms: (5 **nomyn,**) 5–6 **nome,** 6–8 **num,** 6–7 **numme, numbe,** 7 **numne,** 7– **numb.** [pa. pple. of NIM *v.*]

A. *adj.* **1. a.** Deprived of feeling, or of the power of movement, *esp.* through excessive cold. Also *transf.* and *fig.*

c **1440** *Promp. Parv.* 358/1 Nomyn, or take wythe þe palsye, *paraliticus.* *c* **1460** *Towneley Myst.* xxx. 111 There chachid I the crumpe, yit held I my grounde halfe nome. **1551** TURNER *Herbal* I. (1568) 9 Leopardes bayne layd to a scorpione maketh hyr utterly amased and num. **1577–82** BRETON *Toys of Idle Head* ix, My harte it selfe, is bitten so with frost, That all my sences now are waxed nome. **1607** ROWLANDS *Diogines Lanth.* D 2, I make them warme, That are both colde and numme. **1626** BACON *Sylva* §735 Leaning long upon any Part maketh it Numme, and as we call it, Asleep. **1674** N. FAIRFAX *Bulk & Selv.* 47 Were all seeing things sightless, there would be no colours..; all feelers numb, nothing handlesom. **1820** KEATS *Eve of St. Agnes* i, Numb were the Beadsman's fingers, while he told His rosary.

transf. and *fig.* *a* **1568** ASCHAM *Scholem.* (Arb.) 148 That their feete: be feete without ioyntes, that is to say, not distinct by trew quantitie of sillabes: And so, soch feete, be but numme..feete. **1610** *Histrio-mastix* I. 33 Musick shall feast the bounteous eares of Peace, Whil'st she inspires her numme conceipt with life. **1869** *Speaker* 7 Feb. 453/2 To foster that sense of history which is as active in that country as it is numb in our own. **1874** [see DOBBER[2]]. **1882** 'OUIDA' *Maremma* I. 209 Just now I grew blind and numb. **1892** P. H. EMERSON *Son of Fens* xxxii. 349 My old head fare as numb as a beetle. **1958** [see FEEL *sb.* 5]. **1970** H. E. ROBERTS *Third Ear* 10/2 *Numb*, dumb; stupid.

b. Helpless, incapable. ***numb hand***, an inexpert or clumsy person. *slang.*

1802 PALEY *Nat. Theol.* xix. (1819) 302 A snail, as it should seem, is the most numb and unprovided of all artificers. **1853** R. S. SURTEES *Sponge's Sp. Tour* xxxviii. 212 The fact is, that ladies'-maids are only numb hands in all that relates to hunting. **1866** *Punch* 27 Oct. 177 The Bradford writer is a 'numb hand'.

c. *Comb.*, as ***numb-cold, -footed, -handed.***

1605 *Tryall Chevalry* III. ii, But death hath layd his num-cold hand upon me. **1853** R. S. SURTEES *Sponge's Sp. Tour* xxiii. 123 You scandalous, hypocritical, rusty-booted, numb-handed son of a puffing corn-cutter. **1866** CARLYLE *Remin.* (1881) I. 272 A heavy, shortish, numb-footed man.

2. a. Of the nature of numbness.

1641 MILTON *Ch. Govt.* vi. Wks. 1851 III. 124 If to bring a num and chil stupidity of soul..be to keep away schisme, they keep away schisme indeed. **1836** SIR W. HAMILTON *Discuss.* (1852) 269 To induce that numb rigidity into our intellectual life. **1879** *St. George's Hosp. Rep.* IX. 795 The note on that day shows that there had been some smarting pain in the ear, and also a 'numb' feeling in it occasionally.

†**b.** ***numb palsy***, paralysis. *Obs.*

1642 ROGERS *Naaman* 35 What a numbe palsey, what a Laodicean temper..hath covered us over. **1709** STRYPE *Ann. Ref.* I. xliii. 434 He was taken with the numb palsy on one side. **1772** *Boston Gaz.* 2 Mar. 3/1 Last Friday died very sudden of the Numb-Palsey, Mrs. Mary Sigourney.

3. Causing numbness. *rare*⁻¹.

1594 SHAKS. *Rich. III*, II. i. 117 He..did giue himselfe (All thin and naked) to the numbe cold night.

B. *sb.* A cold which numbs fish.

1888 ARMSTRONG in Goode *Amer. Fishes* 119 When we have extremely cold and cloudy weather,..the Trout at the mouth of New River are benumbed... When these 'numbs' occur, it is generally known through this and the adjoining counties. *Ibid.*, There was a 'numb' in January, 1877, and another in the winter of 1879.

numb (nʌm), *v.* Also 7 **numme, numn, num.** [f. prec., or back-formation from NUMBED *ppl. a.*: cf. the earlier *benumb.*] *trans.* To make numb.

1602 MARSTON *Antonio's Rev.* IV. iv, I will live, Onely to numme some others cursed bloode With the dead palsie of like misery. **1645** N. DRAKE *Sieges Pontefract Castle* (Surtees) 27 The bullitt grased upon Captin Fluddes legg, and numned it a little. **1697** DRYDEN *Virg. Georg.* I. 401 Plough naked, Swain, and naked sow the Land, For lazy Winter nums the lab'ring Hand. **1742** GRAY *Eton* 89 Lo, Poverty,..That numbs the soul with icy hand. **1774** GOLDSM. *Nat. Hist.* (1776) VI. 266 The people..perceived, that the torpedo had actually numbed the dead fishes into life again. **1813** SCOTT *Rokeby* III. xxi, A silent mood Hath numb'd the current of his blood. **1875** JOWETT *Plato* (ed. 2) I. 413 Age numbs the sense of both worlds.

absol. **1610** MARKHAM *Masterp.* II. clxxiii. 487 Cicuta which wee call hemlocke..numbeth and astonieth.

numbat (ˈnʌmbæt). *Austral.* [Aboriginal name.] The banded anteater, *Myrmecobius fasciatus*, a small, rare marsupial native to south-western Australia.

1923 F. WOOD JONES *Mammals of South Australia* I. 123 To the aboriginals..it is known as the Numbat, and this name will be adopted here. **1942** C. BARRETT *On Wallaby* iii. 38, I trailed the numbat, in South-western Australia, taking the first photograph..of that little-known animal. **1962** *Times* 22 Nov. 24/2 The numbat, once thought to be extinct, cannot be kept in captivity. **1965** *Sunday Mail Mag.* (Brisbane) 4 Apr. 14/1 The numbat, or banded ant-eater, of South-west Australia..is about the size of a large rat with a coat of coarse, reddish brown fur... It also has a long bushy tail, something like the fox's brush. On the upper part of its body it has white or cream bands. *Ibid.* 14/2 Ants are ripped out of the wood with a flick of the numbat's long tongue... When eating the numbat makes a noise which sounds like 'Tut-tut'. If interrupted it makes a sound more like 'Churr!'.

numbed (nʌmd), *ppl. a.* Also 6–7 **numd,** 6–8 **nummed,** 7 **nu(m)m'd;** 6 **nombde,** 8 **numb'd.** [f. NUMB *a.*; cf. NUMB *v.* and *benumbed.*]

1. Deprived of feeling or power of movement, *esp.* through cold. Also *fig.* **a.** In predicative use. Also with *up.*

1553 BRENDE *Q. Curtius* S j, They were streighte wayes so nummed for colde, that they coulde not ryse agayne. **1577** GOOGE *Heresbach's Husb.* II. (1586) 68 b, You must shake of the Caterpillers in the morning,..when they be numbed. *a* **1601** ? MARSTON *Pasquil & Kath.* II. 235, I am almost dead, numb'd vp with feare. **1655** GURNALL *Chr. in Arm.* v. 195/1 Finding his hands nummed with cold he goes first to the fire. **1727** A. HAMILTON *New Acc. E. Indies* II. xxxix. 89 It grew first red by Inflammation, and then blue and nummed. **1768** SIR W. JONES *Solima* Poems (1777) 3 To warm the traveller, numb'd with winter's cold. **1860** TYNDALL *Glac.* I. xxv. 190, I was too intent upon my work to heed the cold much, but I was numbed. **1899** *Allbutt's Syst. Med.* VI. 586 The tip of the tongue and the lips felt numbed during cold weather.

b. In attributive use.

1596 SPENSER *F.Q.* VI. xi. 45 Like lyfull heat to nummed senses brought, And life to feele that long for death had sought. **1602** MARSTON *Antonio's Rev.* Prol., Drizling sleete Chilleth the wan bleak cheek of the numd earth. *a* **1659** LOVELACE *Poems* 50 I'm Ice; A nummed speaking clod, and mine own show, My Self congeal'd, a Man cut out in Snow. **1716** POPE *Iliad* VIII. 396 The Tendon burst beneath the pondrous Blow, And his numb'd Hand dismiss'd the useless Bow. **1842** MANNING *Serm.* (1848) I. 195 We are slowly recovering, anxiously chafing our numbed limbs to life. **1884** *Manch. Exam.* 4 June 5/2 The reform agitation first stirred his numbed faculties into the energies of a free and active manhood.

absol. *a* **1659** LOVELACE *Poems* 72 Fearing we Numm'd should be no Flagration. [He] Hath curled all his Fires in this one One.

†**2.** ***numbed palsy*** (see NUMB *a.* 2 b). *Obs.*⁻¹

1655 MOUFET & BENNET *Health's Improv.* 224 They cast ..Sophia Queen of Poland into a numb'd Palsie.

†**ˈnumbedness.** *Obs.* Also 7 **nummed-, numbd-.** [f. prec. + -NESS.] Numbness.

1600 HOLLAND *Livy* IX. iii. 313 Their bodies also were possessed as it were with a strange and extraordinarie nummednesse in their limmes. **1657** RAND tr. *Gassendi's Life Peiresc* II. 57 He could not rise.., by reason of the like numbedness of his thigh and foot. **1676** WISEMAN *Surgery* (J.), If the nerve be quite divided, the pain is little, only a kind of stupor or numbedness.

number (ˈnʌmbə(r)), *sb.* Forms: α. 3–5 **noumbre** (4–6 **-ber,** 5 **-bur**), 5 **nounbre;** 4–5 **nowmbre** (5 **-ber,** 5–6 **-bur**); 3–6 **nombre** (5–6 **-bur, -byr,** 5–7 **-ber**); 4 **numbur** (**-bir, -bere**), 4–6 **numbre,** 4– **number.** β. 4–5 **nowmyre,** 4 **-mir,** 5–6 **-mer(e,** 5 **noumer;** 4 **nomir** (6 **-er,** 6 *Sc.* **-mer**); 5–6 **nummer** (6 **-meir,** 6 *Sc.* **-mir**). [f. OF. *nombre, nonbre, numbre, numere*:—L. *numerum*, acc. sing. of *numerus*, a number. Cf. Du. *nommer*, G., Dan., Sw., Norw. *nummer.*]

I. 1. a. The precise sum or aggregate *of* any collection of individual things or persons.

α. **1297** R. GLOUC. (Rolls) 1397 As wel..Vor loue of þe panes as to wite þe noumbre of eche manne [*v.r.* þe menne]. *a* **1300** *Cursor M.* 503 Þe numbre þat out of heuen fell þo can na tung in erth noght tell. *c* **1340** HAMPOLE *Pr. Consc.* 7436 Þe noumbre of payns þat þare griefes Passes þe mens witt þat here liefes. *c* **1380** WYCLIF *Serm.* Sel. Wks. II. 139 Þis noumbre of fishis þat here weren taken, bitokeneþ þe noumbre of seintis. **1422** tr. *Secreta Secret., Priv. Priv.* 129 Xerses, kynge of Inde,..strongly gederid huge hostis of whych no man couth tell the nombyr. **1486** *Bk. St. Albans* e ij, The moore nombur than ywis, the gretter the beuy is. **1529** MORE *Suppl. Souls* Wks. 307/2 He sayth that then shall the number of sore and sick beggers decreace. **1593** SHAKS. *Rich. II*, I. iii. 210 Thy sad aspect, Hath from the number of his banish'd yeares Pluck'd foure away. **1667** MILTON *P.L.* III. 706 What created mind can comprehend Thir number. **1700** DRYDEN *Pref. Fables*, I found, by the number of my verses, that they began to swell into a little volume. **1796** SOUTHEY *Lett. fr. Spain* (1790) 441 The number of fools is infinite. *a* **1844** in Stephens *Bk. Farm* II. 71 The number of hurdles required for feeding sheep on turnips is [etc.]. **1891** E. PEACOCK *Narcissa Brendon* I. 114 The number of books was very large.

pl. **1597** SHAKS. *2 Hen. IV*, IV. i. 4 Send discoueerers forth, To know the numbers of our Enemies. *a* **1719** ADDISON (J.), There is but one gate for strangers to enter at, that it may be known what numbers of them are in the town. **1815** ELPHINSTONE *Acc. Caubul* (1842) II. 98 Their numbers are not less than thirty thousand families.

β. *c* **1400** MAUNDEV. (Roxb.) vi. 18 Þare was sum tyme fyue sowdanes after þe noumer of þe fyue kyngdomes. **1513** DOUGLAS *Æneis* XI. vii. 77 Of thar schippis the nummeir and maner. **1552** LYNDESAY *Monarche* 6229 Thow knew the nomer of predestinat, Quhome thow did call.

b. *pl.* The title of the fourth book in the Bible, the earlier part of which contains a census of the Israelites. †Also in *sing.*

c **1400** BIBLE (Wycl.) *Num.* Prol., This book clepid Numeri, that is to seie, the book of Noumbre. **1502** *Ord. Crysten Men* (W. de W. 1506) IV. xxi. X j b, The auncyent testament in the .xxv. chapitre of nombres. **1563** *Homilies* II. *Idolatry* iii. (1859) 175 As it is written in the book of Numbers, the twenty-third chapter, that there was *no idol in Jacob.* **1589** COOPER *Admon.* 127 In the Nombers, he that brake the Sabbath day, was stoned to death. **1649** ROBERTS *Clavis Bibl.* 52 Numbers,..so called because a great part of the Book, especially at the beginning, is spent in Numbring of the Tribes and Families of Israel. **1727–38** CHAMBERS *Cycl.* s.v. *Pentateuch*, The five books of Moses..; viz. Genesis,..Numbers, and Deuteronomy. **1840** *Penny Cycl.* XVII. 426/2 The book of Deuteronomy supposes the previous composition of Exodus, Leviticus, and Numbers. **1875** *Encycl. Brit.* III. 638/1 The Levitico-Elohistic document, which embraces most of the laws in Leviticus with large parts of Exodus and Numbers.

c. A census or enumeration *of* persons. *rare*⁻¹.

1831 BUTTRICK *Voy.* 33 Two gentlemen undertook to take a number of these people, and found it to be about twelve hundred.

2. a. A particular sum or aggregate of units, of a kind specified or implied in the context.

a **1300** *Cursor M.* 423 Þis numbre þat he ordend þan Suld be bath of angel and man. **1393** LANGL. *P. Pl.* C. XXIII. 255 In mesure god made alle manere þynges, And sette hit at a sertayn and at a syker numbre. **1595** SHAKS. *John* II. i. 347 Wee'l put thee downe, gainst whom these Armes wee beare, Or adde a royall number to the dead. **1822** SHELLEY *Faust* ii. 408 Quite a new piece, the last of seven, for 'tis The custom now to represent that number. **1861** F. METCALFE *Oxonian in Iceland* (1867) 166, 1200 people were invited to the Grave-ale, the greatest number that ever came to such a ceremony in Iceland.

b. In phr. ***the number of*** (so many).

1426 *Catal. Deeds P.R.O.* IV. 547 [He may] send who that he will undir the nowmbre of a dozen persons. **1470–85** MALORY *Arthur* XII. vii. 601 Whanne this crye was made vnto Ioyous yle drewe knyghtes to the nomber of fyue honderd. *c* **1530** LD. BERNERS *Arth. Lyt. Bryt.* 481 Al thys company were to the numbre of xv. thousande Knightes. **1582** N. LICHEFIELD tr. *Castanheda's Conq. E. Ind.* I. vii. 18 b, Where also then were in sight the number of twentie Moores skirmishing with their dartes.

3. a. A sum or total of abstract units.

golden number: see GOLDEN *a.* 6.

13.. *Cursor M.* 419 (Gött.), Þat suld be a numbre hale, And mani thousand to haue in tale. *a* **1380** in Horstm. *Altengl. Leg.* (1878) 63/1 Of þe mesures of figures and musek, And of alle þe noumbres ek. **1398** TREVISA *Barth. De P.R.* XIX. cxviii. (1495) 922 The seconde odde nombre, that is the nombre of fiue and hyghte Quinarius. *c* **1420** *York Myst.* xliv. 9 For parfite noumbre it is none, Off elleuen for to lere. **1570** BILLINGSLEY *Euclid* VII. def. 17. 186 When two numbers multiplying them selues..produce an other: the number produced is called a plaine or super-ficiall number. **1598** SHAKS. *Merry W.* v. i. 3, I hope good lucke lies in odde numbers. **1608** D. T. *Ess. Pol. & Mor.* 46 Themselues alone will be thought the Numbers, that giue a substantiall existence to the being of them all. **1667** MILTON *P.L.* VIII. 114 Distance inexpressible By Numbers that have name. **1753** CHAMBERS *Cycl. Suppl.* App. s.v., The figurate Numbers of any order may be found without computing those of the preceding orders. **1820** SHELLEY *Œd. Tyr.* I. 128 If you were to dream Of a particular number in the Lottery, You would not buy the ticket? **1859** B. SMITH *Arith. & Alg.* (ed. 6) 35 A Mixed Number is composed of a whole number and a fraction.

b. In *pl.* as a subject of study or science.

1377 LANGL. *P. Pl.* B. XIX. 234 Some to dyuyne and diuide, noumbres to kenne. *c* **1391** CHAUCER *Astrol.* Prol., I haue perceiued well by certeyne euidences thine abilite to lerne sciencez touchinge noumbres & proporcioums. **1693** PEPYS *Let. to Newton* 22 Nov., The late project..has almost extinguished..at all places of public conversation in this town, especially among men of numbers, every other talk. **1711** STEELE *Spect.* No. 174 ¶5 None of all these Things could be done by him without the Exercise of his Skill in Numbers. **1776** JOHNSON in *Boswell* 16 Mar., We may instance the science of numbers, which all minds are equally capable of attaining.

c. ***line of numbers***, Gunter's line.

1667 LEYBOURN (*title*), The Line of Proportion or Numbers, commonly called Gunter's Line, made easie. By which may be measured all manner of Superficies and Solids. **1688**, etc. [see GUNTER]. **1828** MOORE *Pract. Navig.* 91 The diff. of long. 419 on the line of numbers.

d. A symbol or figure, or collection of these, which represents graphically an arithmetical total; a ticket or label bearing such signs.

1837 DICKENS *Pickw.* ii, A strange specimen of the human race..with a brass label and number round his neck. **1854** *Orr's Circ. Sci., Math. Sci.* 5 Figures thus have..a value depending upon the places they occupy in a number. **1864** J. DONALDSON *Chr. Lit.* I. 214 The appeal to the Greek letters as numbers, is conclusive proof of the writer's habitual use of the Greek Scriptures.

e. *U.S. slang.* Usu. in *pl.* An illegal form of gambling in which bets are taken on the occurrence of numbers in a lottery or in the financial columns of a newspaper. Esp. in phr. ***to play the numbers***. Also called **numbers game, racket**. Cf. POLICY *sb.*[2] 1 c. Freq. *attrib.* and *Comb.*, as ***number(s)-man***; **numbers drop**, a session of such betting; **number(s)-runner**, one who collects the bets of those playing the numbers.

1897 ADE *Pink Marsh* 170 She tell Belle 'at she heah I like gin an' roll'e bones an' play numbehs. **1926** C. VAN VECHTEN *Nigger Heaven* 286 *Numbers*, a gambling game highly popular in contemporary Harlem. The winning numbers each day are derived from the New York Clearing House bank exchanges and balances..published in the newspapers. **1934** *Sun* (Baltimore) 25 Aug. 1/2 Hawkins.. identified himself as a 'pay-off man' in the 'numbers business'. **1935** *Time* 21 Jan. 45/1 In Danville, Va., operators of a 'numbers' game were bankrupt. **1949** E. E. BLANCHE *You can't Win* 70 The 'numbers' racket is known by different names in various sections of the country—The Numbers Policy, Clearing House, Butter and Eggs, and the Bug. **1950** H. E. GOLDIN *Dict. Amer. Underworld Lingo* 146 Number-man, anyone engaged in the policy numbers racket. **1958** S. ELLIN *Eighth Circle* (1959) II. v. 65 He was saying something about the numbers game... The *bolita*. **1958** R. ELLISON in A. Dundes *Mother Wit* (1973) 63/1 As a numbers runner he is a bringer of manna and a worker of miracles. **1959** *Times Lit. Suppl.* 16 Jan. 29/3 The 'numbers' do for Harlem what the pools do for Notting Hill Gate—and for that matter Knightsbridge as well—provide unsustaining nourishment for dreams. **1959** *Listener* 28 May 924/2, I wonder how many people now remember that prominent feature of American life in the 'thirties—the numbers racket. **1964** O. HARRINGTON in J. H. Clarke *Harlem* 90 One of the local numbers runners dug my cartoon and..nobody covers as much Harlem territory as the numbers man. **1965** 'MALCOLM X' *Autobiogr.* 52 Betting my dollar a day on the numbers. **1968** P. OLIVER *Screening Blues* iv. 134 The policy writers and numbers runners who took the bet by a rapid code of signals in the street or at the 'numbers drop' would urge them to play other numbers and at higher stakes. **1970** L. MERIWETHER *Daddy was Number Runner* 21 Mother played the numbers like everyone else in Harlem but she was scared about Daddy being a number runner. **1973** *Black Panther* 22 Sept. 8/3 A panel of prominent lawyers recommended last week that the District of Columbia legalize 'the numbers' racket. **1975** *New Yorker* 29 Sept. 54/3 She had met Delgado while she was selling numbers on the streets of the lower East Side.

f. *Austral.* and *N.Z.* Elementary arithmetic taught to children in primary school.

1922 *N.Z. Education Gaz.* 1 Dec. 137/1 Miss Caldwell has published a book entitled 'The Simplicity of Number', a copy of which, along with the apparatus, can..be obtained from her by teachers. **1963** B. PEARSON *Coal Flat* iv. 63 You'd best make sure of his reading and his number and see if he's good enough for this class.

4. a. The particular mark or symbol, having an arithmetical value, by which anything has a place assigned to it in a series.

c **1391** CHAUCER *Astrol.* I. §8 The nombres of the degres of tho signes ben writen in Augrim aboue. **1830** MARRYAT *King's Own* xxxix, A strange sail, who had not..shown her number. **1837** DICKENS *Pickw.* ii, Would any body believe as an informer 'ud go about in a man's cab, not only takin' down his number, but ev'ry word he says into the bargain? **1850** —— *Dav. Copp.* xix, Where does he sleep? What's his number? **1880** *Standard* 17 Dec., If anybody imagines that it is easy to 'take' a Policeman's 'number' he had better try the experiment. **1898** G. B. SHAW *Philanderer* in *Plays Unpleasant* III. 135 *Julia*... What is Dr Paramore's number in Savile Row? *Charteris.* Seventy-nine. **1908** E. F. BENSON *Blotting Bk.* i. 16, I saw one policeman trying to take my number. **1973** R. LEWIS *Blood Money* iv. 47 'Could it be the number of the hire-car he used?'..'It's a Leeds number.'

b. *Naut.* Of a ship: ***to make her number***, (*a*) to communicate by signal the figure by which she is registered; in later use also *transf.* in phr. ***to make one's number***, to report one's arrival, to report for duty, to pay a duty or courtesy call, to make oneself known, to make oneself acquainted (*colloq.*); (*b*) to obtain a good place on the shipping register.

1836 MARRYAT *Pirate* xvii, The Enterprise had made her number. **1861** J. LAMONT *Seasons with Sea-Horses* xviii. 293 We found that the 'Anna Louise' had only made her number twelve hours before us. **1880** *Daily Tel.* 14 Apr. 5/5 The good ship had a first-rate captain, a skilled crew, was well found and fitted, and she may 'make her number' yet. **1897** P. E. STEVENSON *Deep-Water Voyage* 29 We made our number, where from, where bound, and 'all well' to the steamer, which hoisted her pennant immediately. **1927** B. M. CHAMBERS *Salt Junk* xxx. 256 Almost every ship on her way to and from South America makes her number to the island [Fernando Noronha]. **1937** C. S. FORESTER *Happy Return* xxiv. 281 The *Lydia* made her number, and the sound of the salutes began to roll slowly round the bay. **1942** PARTRIDGE in *New Statesman* 1 Aug. 75/1 'To *make one's number*' is still slang; it may be used absolutely, as in 'As soon as I join my unit I must make my number at Brigade', or in reference to a person, as in 'I must lose no time in making my number with one of the Staff Officers at Division'—in short, to *contact* him... By the way, one 'makes one's number' with one's *opposite number*, a phrase taken over from civil life. **1945** 'N. SHUTE' *Most Secret* ix. 211 Captain (D.) was there to see them off; I made my number with him as representing V.A.C.O. and we stood chatting for a time. **1951** H. JORDAN *Islander* II. vii. 92 Jim brought his ketch.. alongside the *Islander* soon after breakfast and made his number to the master. **1955** E. WAUGH *Officers & Gentlemen* I. vi. 56 You go ahead and make your number with your CO. **1958** M. DICKENS *Man Overboard* xii. 192 Ben saw himself on Speech Day, making his number with mothers in garden-party hats. **1963** P. MCCUTCHAN *Man from Moscow* ix. 87 On arrival in Moscow..Shaw made his number at the W.I.O.C.A. office. **1965** B. SWEET-ESCOTT *Baker Street Irregular* vii. 224 We turned back and made our number with the navy there. **1974** D. SEAMAN *Bomb that could Lip-Read* xviii. 177 'Will you go to the conference site today?' 'Might as well make my number with the R.U.C.'

c. ***to lose the number of one's mess***, to die, to perish. So ***to settle*** etc., to cause one's death.

1834 MARRYAT *P. Simple* xxxiii, I have an idea that some of us will lose the number of our mess. **1867** SMYTH *Sailor's Word-bk.* 501 *Losing the number of the mess* is a phrase for dying suddenly; being killed or drowned. **1881** J. F. KEANE *Six Mths. in Meccah* 60 Fetching me one on the skull, that would have 'settled the number of my mess', but for the thickness of my too attractive head-dress.

d. With reference to a lottery number, or some other number by or with which one may be identified, as an army number, esp. in fig. phr. ***one's number is*** (or ***has gone***) ***up***, one is doomed (to die), one's time is come, one is 'done for'; ***one's number is on*** (something, esp. a bullet or shell), one is doomed (to die, or to a particular destiny). Cf. NAME *sb.* 1 g.

1806 C. LAMB *Let.* 25 Jan. in *Works* (1870) II. 89 Though this is a lottery to which none but G. Barnett would choose to trust his all, there is no harm just to call in at Despair's office for a friend, and see if *his* number is come up. **1899** C. ROOK *Hooligan Nights* iv. 56 You couldn't tallygraft to Billy no more. His number's up awright, wiv no error. **1914** *London Opinion* XL. 231/2 The late Patsey Cadogan, who left £100,000 when his number went up. **1915** 'BARTIMEUS' *Tall Ship* i. 11, I think our number's up, old thing. **1922** WODEHOUSE *Girl on Boat* xi. 181 Fate had dealt him a knock-out blow; his number was up. **1925** FRASER & GIBBONS *Soldier & Sailor Words* 163 *Name* (or *number*) *on, to have one's*, said of a bullet that hit a man; *i.e.*, that it was destined for him. **1929** *Mercury Story Bk.* 98 It was about midday that I first realised that his number was up. **1937** V. BARTLETT *This is my Life* xi. 188 The Director-General said that he would nevertheless like me to broadcast a short talk under my own name... My number was up. **1965** BROPHY & PARTRIDGE *Long Trail* 154 *Number on.* A fatalistic but consolatory superstition insisted that no man need fear any bullet or shell, however close it came, unless it *had his regimental number* (or his name and number) engraved on it. **1965** F. SARGESON *Memoirs of Peon* vi. 138 She was forgiven for insisting upon her husband's undertaking the labour which had unfortunately sent his number up. **1966** *Listener* 23 June 923/2 The endless stream of cars and lorries swept on, only momentarily slowed down when the number of one of them came up... It was the arbitrariness of accident. **1974** C. FREMLIN *By Horror Haunted* 15 I'm as safe here as ..any where..if it's got your number on it, you'll get it, no matter *where* you are! **1975** J. AIKEN *Voices in Empty House* xviii. 331 He'd got leukaemia. He knew his number was up.

e. In fig. use in phr. ***to get*** (***take, have***) ***someone's number***, to make a correct appraisal of someone's character, motives or intentions, to size someone up.

1853 DICKENS *Bleak Ho.* lvii. 550 Whenever a person proclaims to you 'In worldly matters I'm a child,'..that person is only a crying off from being held accountable, and ..you have got that person's number, and it's Number One. **1889** 'MARK TWAIN' *Yankee* xxxiv. 405 Let him go, for the present; I took his number, so to speak. *Ibid.* xxxv. 414 That was the sort of master we had. I took *his* number. **1912** C. MATHEWSON *Pitching in a Pinch* i. 4 'I've got your number now, Matty!' he shouted at me as he drew up at second base. **1920** W. HARD *Raymond Robins' Own Story* 190 To hurt Bolshevism you need at least to get its number. **1921** R. D. PAINE *Comr. Rolling Ocean* viii. 129 Do you remember the day before when he made that crack at you in front of Miss Crozier? I had his number right then. **1934** J. M. CAIN *Postman always rings Twice* ii. 15 She knew what I meant, and she knew I had her number. **1939** I. BAIRD *Waste Heritage* vi. 74 'Never mind who I am,' Matt said, 'I got your number anyway.' **1956** W. GRAHAM *Sleeping Partner* xiii. 111, I was trying to think of a verse all last night... I can't think who wrote it, but he rather got my number. **1970** G. JACKSON *Let.* 29 May in *Soledad Brother* (1971) 265 Big Brother. He is rather transparent. I have his number. **1975** *Times Lit. Suppl.* 21 Mar. 332/4 Field-Marshal Lord Montgomery..had [Augustus] John's number right away. 'Who is this chap?' he demanded to know. 'He drinks, he's dirty, and I know there are women in the background!'

f. A number assigned to a particular telephone (or group of telephones) which corresponds to the terminals of its line at the exchange and in modern systems is dialled by a caller in order to establish a connection with it and cause it to ring; ***number-unobtainable signal*** or ***tone***, a sound indicating to a caller that the number dialled is unobtainable for a reason other than its being engaged; similarly ***number-engaged signal***; ***wrong number***, a number obtained other than the one required by the caller.

1879 *Times* 8 Sept. 12/1 The person at No. 2 calls the attention of the attendant at the exchange by means of an electric bell. At the same moment a shutter on the switch-board falls and discloses the number of the applicant. *Ibid.*, So with any other numbers; they can be instantly connected or disconnected. **1884** *List of Subscribers* (London & Globe Telephone Co.) 4 Take telephones from hooks and speak at once, giving number of subscriber wanted. **1891** [see ENGAGED *ppl. a.* 3]. **1911** W. J. LOCKE *Glory of Clementina Wing* 324 She..took up the telephone and gave a number. **1930** WODEHOUSE *Very Good, Jeeves!* vi. 169 A woman has tossed my heart lightly away, but what of it?..The voice of Love seemed to call to me, but it was a wrong number. **1930** *Gloss. Terms Telegraphs & Telephones* (*B.S.I.*) 47/1 Number-unobtainable tone. **1932** E. BOWEN *To North* vi. 63 Markie, too well advised to encounter Cecilia over the wire, soon traced Emmeline to her number at Woburn Place. **1942** A. CHRISTIE *Body in Library* i. 12 Miss Marple's telephone rang... 'It must be,' Miss Marple decided, 'a wrong number.' **1959** H. HOBSON *Mission House Murder* xiv. 92 The phone..has been giving the number-engaged signal for over half an hour. **1965** MRS. L. B. JOHNSON *White House Diary* 3 June (1970) 283, I tried to reach him, or rather his wife, to no avail. The number didn't answer. **1969** 'D. RUTHERFORD' *Gilt-Edged Cockpit* viii. 148 He listened.. to the high whine of the 'number unobtainable' signal, knowing that she had left the receiver off. **1972** H. MACINNES *Message from Málaga* xii. 183 The telephone will ring... I shall..apologize for speaking to a wrong number. **1972** 'W. HAGGARD' *Protectors* iii. 38 Phone me at once... You know the number.

g. ***to lose one's number***, to make a gaffe, to lose stock. *rare.*

a **1936** KIPLING *Something of Myself* (1937) iv. 86 He produced a bottle of real Tokay, which I tasted, and lost my number badly by saying that it reminded me of some medicinal wine.

5. a. Prefixed to a numeral, as ***number two*** or *No.* 2 (see NO.), for the purpose of designating things or persons by the place assigned to them in an arithmetical series.

1390 GOWER *Conf.* III. 125 Of Signes in the nombre ellevene Aquarius hath take his place. **1677** MOXON *Mech. Exerc.* II. 20 The true square..as you were taught [in] Numb. 1..is a great ornament. **1707** MORTIMER *Husb.* (1721) I. 162 Sometimes the best Madder is worth eight or nine Pounds a hundred, and the Number *O* six Pound Ten Shillings. **1710** SWIFT *Jrnl. to Stella* 15 Sept., I forgot to mark my two former letters; but I remember this is number 3. **1836** DICKENS *Pickw.* x, Number twenty-two wants his boots. **1867** *Mabel's Progress* III. 5 It is hard to say..why this especial house should have been Number Nine at all, seeing there were to be but six houses in the row. **1890** 'R. BOLDREWOOD' *Col.-Reformer* (1891) 288 [We] are having a glass of champagne; will you join us?—it is 'number two'. **1930** E. H. YOUNG *Miss Mole* ix. 79 She sometimes saw No. 16 [*sc.* the person living at that house] trundling towards the back gate, she sometimes heard him calling in the cats at night. **1938** S. BECKETT *Murphy* v. 95 A staple recreation.. had been to wait at Walham Green for a nice number eleven [bus] and take it through the evening rush to Liverpool Street and back. **1970** Y. CARTER *Mr. Campion's Falcon* xii. 91 A shabby row of houses..[with] Queen Anne porches... Number Seven..had an intricate semi-circular fanlight.

b. ***number one***, one's self, one's own person and interests; esp. in ***to look after***, or ***take care of, number one***. (Cf. ONE 6 d.)

1704–5 T. PITT in Hedges *Diary* (Hakl. Soc.) III. 99 The Knight I doubt not, but 'tis very careful of number one, and looks no further. **1794** *Times* 21 Mar. in Ashton *Old Times* (1885) 306 Long had it [a cat] lived upon the fat of the land, in Charlotte St.,..where it took great care of Number one! **1829** MARRYAT *F. Mildmay* xix, We always take care of number one. **1830–** [see ONE 6 d]. **1850** THACKERAY *Pendennis* lvi, Almost every person,..as it seems to us, is occupied about Number One. **1892** *Newcastle Even. Chron.* 11 Jan. 4/4 They..were going to look after 'number one' in the future.

c. ***number ones***, ellipt. form of 'No. 1 dress', 'No. 1 suit' (also used), a best dress uniform worn esp. in the Navy.

1829 F. MARRYAT *F. Mildmay* II. 132 Each was dressed out in our No. 1 suits, in most exact and unquizzable uniform. **1914** 'BARTIMEUS' *Naval Occasions* xviii. 157 The 'Rig of the Day' was 'Number Ones'. **1947** *Landfall* I. 287 Hughes unpacked his kit to find his number ones badly crushed, and cursing, he went in search of an iron. **1950** A. P. HERBERT *Independent Member* lxi. 359 The queer-looking spectacled P.O., 'sculling about' in his No. 1's astern of the Field-Marshal. **1955** [see DOLL *v.*[2]]. **1968** J. LOCK *Lady Policeman* ix. 78 The PCs in their quaint, high-buttoned 'number one' uniforms look as though they have stepped out of a jaded print. **1972** *Police Rev.* 17 Nov. 1489/2 (*caption*) Probably the last Policemen ever to wear their 'number ones', the ceremonial dress of the Force which is probably being phased out at the end of the year.

d. *colloq.* **number one**, the finest quality, the best obtainable. As *attrib.* or *adj. phr.*, first-rate, 'tip-top'; leading, principal.

1839 *Spirit of Times* 29 June 195/1 He is the sole owner of the estate upon which the [race] track is located, and will, no doubt, do all he can to make it 'a number one' concern. **1843** F. Marryat *Trav. M. Violet* II. xi. 231 After having drained half-a-dozen cups of 'stiff, true, downright Yankee No. 1', we all of us took our blankets. **1846** *Swell's Night Guide* 40 This *sanctum-sanctorum* is..the number one of cribberies. **1848** J. T. Fields *Let.* 15 Aug. in *R. W. Griswold's Corresp.* (1898) 242, I have some beautiful poems by me by Mrs. Barnes... They are No. 1, full of passionate feeling and eminently worthy of a place. **1855** *Trans. Mich. Agric. Soc.* VI. 495 Wheat first-rate, peas, also, oats number one. **1871** E. Eggleston *Hoosier Schoolmaster* (1872) xv. 125 Seems to me it would be number one to have God help you. **1872** —— *End of World* xi. 78 This walk seems the shortest, when I'm in superfine, number-one comp'ny. *c* **1882** in R. Pearsall *Worm in Bud* (1969) ii. 43 Awfully rollicking, fearfully frollicking, Number one Masher of all. **1897** G. B. Shaw *Let.* 16 Apr. in *Ellen Terry & Shaw* (1931) 186, I have *all* the British rights of Arms and all but eleven No. 1 towns for You Never Can Tell. **1904** —— *Let.* 9 Sept. in *Ibid.* 414 The tour is on the cheapest scale..and the towns by no means all Number Ones. **1933** P. Godfrey *Back-Stage* xvi. 199 The No. 1 dates, such as Birmingham, Manchester, Liverpool, Glasgow, and Edinburgh, get the best companies. *Ibid.* 200 Actors on the No. 1's are the best paid. **1942** E. Paul *Narrow St.* xxiv. 212 The sluggish public began to scent the No. 1 scandal of the century. **1943** Koestler *Arrival & Departure* iv. 148, I could even point to a number of similarities between your No. 1 and our No. 1. **1944** *Living off Land* iv. 62 (*heading*) Panic as Enemy No. 1. **1955** W. Gaddis *Recognitions* iii. ii. 752 Look, what did Schmuck's number-one boy want over there, when you stopped and talked to them. **1957** A. Grimble *Return to Islands* iii. 58 He turned out to be a number-one boat-builder. **1968** *Globe & Mail* (Toronto) 3 Feb. 51/3 One small folded letter on blue paper bearing a 12-pence stamp will be the number one feature. **1969** C. Burke *God is Beautiful, Man* (1970) 80 And it don't really make no difference if you're one or two. 'Cause with God, you're always number one. **1971** *Flying* Apr. S7/1 Pilot briefing is the number-one item in the present FSS system. **1974** *Plain Dealer* (Cleveland, Ohio) 26 Oct. 3-D/1 Officials here expect a crowd of only 35,000 for the No. 1 team in the nation.

e. ***Number ten***, also ***No. 10***, in full No. 10 Downing Street, the London residence of the Prime Minister. Hence used allusively to denote the influence or opinions of the Prime Minister. Also *transf.*, as quot. 1972.

1880 *Leisure Hour* 383/2 Doubtless 'oblivious forgetfulness' would occur to any one who, having been created a peer of Parliament by a late occupant of No. 10, should happen to be seen by the fallen Minister. **1905** [see *No., N°.]. **1934** *Punch* 28 Mar. 345/1 The Muse at No. 10. 'It is rare to find a Prime Minister who is also a poet.'—*Press.* **1939** *Ibid.* 13 Sept. 284/2 The mystery deepened when the man did not enter No. 10 at all. **1958** L. Durrell *Mountolive* iv. 86 Even in the rain there was the usual little cluster of tourists and loungers outside the gates of Number Ten. **1961** I. Jefferies *It wasn't Me!* iii. 36 If academic opinion differs from that at No. 10 we go our own way. **1969** 'W. Haggard' *Doubtful Disciple* i. 1 The summons to Number Ten had knocked him flat. Under-Secretaries weren't called to the Prime Minister's house. **1972** *Guardian* 14 June 12/1 Now that Mr Suto is on the brink of retirement ..his wife feels she can lift the curtain on life at Japan's No. 10. **1974** *Daily Mail* 9/3 It was this which..put Edward Heath into Number 10.

f. ***number one***, a children's word or euphemism for 'urine'; similarly ***number two*** for 'fæces'.

1902 Farmer & Henley *Slang* V. 75/2 *Number one*, ..(nursery). Urination; also a chamber-pot. *Ibid.*, *Number two*,..(nursery). Evacuation. **1923** J. Manchon *Le Slang* 212 *I want to do number one*, je veux faire pipi. **1937** A. S. Neill *That Dreadful School* vii. 118 Our juniors have an interest in the Old English word for faeces. They use it a lot —the ones from polite homes do, I mean homes that talk of No. 2 and 'going to the House of Commons' (how appropriate a name!). **1938** I. Goldberg *Wonder of Words* vi. 108 The child is early taught to refer to his needs as 'number one' and 'number two'. **1949** F. Sargeson *I saw in my Dream* 15 You felt sick and told mother, and she felt your forehead and asked how long it was since you did number two. **1959** I. & P. Opie *Lore & Lang. Schoolch.* vi. 96 Dirty kangaroo, Sitting on the dustbin Doing his 'Number Two'. **1963** G. Greene *Sense of Reality* 47 'I want to do number one.' I blurted out... He called to Maria, 'The boy wants to piss. Fetch him the golden po.' **1967** A. Wilson *No Laughing Matter* ii. 70 This little ginger [kitten] is going to do a number one if we're not careful. **1971** M. McCarthy *Birds of America* 145 When I had done Number Two, you always washed them out yourself before sending them to the diaper service.

g. ***number two***: colloq. phr. (freq. attrib.), a provincial town (in contexts one not noted for its appreciation of the theatre); also, a person second in importance or rank to a head of a department, etc., a second in command.

1908 G. B. Shaw *Let.* 11 Aug. in *Lett. to G. Barker* (1956) 134 You might let her begin on a number two tour of it [*sc.* a play]. **1920** —— *Let.* 22 Dec. in *B. Shaw & Mrs. Campbell* (1952) 215 You yourself have held up the six big cities and kept poor Macdona wandering in the number twos. **1934** R. Ferguson *Celebrated Sequels* 180 My elocution..*has* been admired in such Number Two towns as Wigan. **1952** 'M. Innes' *Private View* xiv. 214 This fellow, Cadover, is your husband's Number Two? **1968** M. Woodhouse *Rock Baby* vii. 76 I'll introduce you to your Number Two... You'll need some help. **1970** *Guardian Weekly* 25 Apr. 17 Russia feels the understandable necessity to catch up in the arms race... It just does not pay to be number two. **1973** W. Fairchild *Swiss Arrangement* xiii. 173 'Lisa Kestler was in charge of the whole operation—right?' 'Right..Gray was her number two.' **1975** S. Johnson *Urbane Guerilla* ii. 103 Usually we don't bother with the no. 2 man.

h. Naval. ***number one***, a first lieutenant, esp. one who is second in command to the captain of a ship. Freq. as a form of address.

1909 J. R. Ware *Passing English* 184/2 *Number one*.., strictly naval for first lieutenant. **1916** 'Taffrail' *Stand By!* 120 'I'm sorry for him,' said No. One, lifting his glass with a grin. **1948** Partridge *Dict. Forces' Slang* 129 *Number one.* The sergeant in charge of a gun. (Army.) (2) The First Lieutenant. (Ward-room).

i. *Forces' slang.* ***number nine***, an aperient pill freq. prescribed as a cure-all for minor illnesses or doubtful symptoms (see quot. 1925).

1916 *Anzac Book* 110 And should my health appear to fail And appetite grow fine, My doctor hands me—not a bill, But just a Number 9. **1925** Fraser & Gibbons *Soldier & Sailor Words* 211 *Number nine...* The popular name for the Service aperient dose or pill. From its listed number, No. 9, in the Field Hospital Case of drugs. Being the Medical Officer's stock remedy in case of doubtful ailments, or suspected malingering, in the war the expression 'A No. 9' came to be used in all kinds of applications, more or less in jest. **1926** N. Lucas *London & its Criminals* xv. 181 They have one medicine in prison for all ills—from toothache to broken limbs, this is known to all old-timers as 'white mixture' and it corresponds to the 'number nines' of the Army. **1930** Brophy & Partridge *Songs & Slang Brit. Soldier* 161 The regimental Medical Officer..invariably gave him a standardized purgative pill, known as Number 9, and marked him down as *M.D.* i.e. medicine and duty.

6. a. A single (numbered) part or issue of a book or periodical. ***in numbers***, in a series of separate parts published at intervals.

1757 Foote *Author* i. Wks. 1799 I. 132 Master Clench.. has a folio a coming out in numbers. **1795** *Gentl. Mag.* 540/1 A good-natured friend, who shewed me the last number of the Critical Review. **1851** Mayhew *London Lab.* I. 290/1 He used to buy up all the old back numbers of the cheap periodicals. **1853** Mrs. Gaskell *Cranford* i, I consider it vulgar, and below the dignity of literature, to publish in numbers. **1884** *Athenæum* Dec. 773 In our number for December 27th we shall give a series of articles on the Continental Literature of the Year.

attrib. **1813** in *N. & Q.* 10th Ser. III. (1905) 66 Those subscribers..who choose to be accommodated with the Apocrypha may now be supplied by giving orders to the.. Number-men. **1827** Mackenzie *Hist. Newcastle* II. 729 Mr. M. Brown carried on the number business with great spirit. **1864** *Glasgow Her.* 11 Apr., Messrs. J. & J. Forsyth..beg to inform Dealers, Canvassers, and all others connected with the 'Number Trade', that they [etc.].

b. A person designated by a certain number.

1859 F. A. Griffiths *Artil. Man.* (1862) 196 The first seven numbers run up. *c* **1860** H. Stuart *Seaman's Catech.* 14 Order any two numbers to draw it out.

c. One of a collection of songs or poems.

1878 Stevenson *Inland Voy.* 119 There was a number in the hawker's collection called *Conscrits Français*, which may rank among the most dissuasive war-lyrics on record. **1894** *Westm. Gaz.* 21 Feb. 3/1 There are only 28 numbers in the little book, but none of them is quite insignificant, while many contain really memorable lines and stanzas.

d. A part or division of an opera, oratorio, etc.

1881 *Athenæum* 347/2 The best numbers of the work are, in our opinion, the duet for soprano and tenor..and the final chorus. **1891** *Guardian* 23 Sept. 1531 The names of the singers of all the solo numbers. **1897** *Yorksh. Post* 8 Mar. 4/5 A drawing-room recital of some of its numbers was given on Thursday.

e. An item in a programme of musical entertainment. Also, more loosely, any song or tune. Cf. senses 6c and d above.

1885 G. B. Shaw *How to become Musical Critic* (1960) 80 To tap their feet and wag their heads to the seductive swing of his numbers. **1900** E. E. Peake *Darlingtons* i. 2 After a rattling number by the band, a brief address by the Mayor, and another rattling number by the band, a neatly dressed, handsome man..advanced to the front of the platform. **1913** *Confessions of Dancing Girl* vi. 109 We had worked all the variety halls and cafés..and we had no novel 'numbers'. **1920** Wodehouse *Jill the Reckless* (1922) xi. 161 He's put over any amount of shows which would have flopped like dogs without him to stage the numbers. **1927** T. S. Eliot in *Newton's Seneca* (Tudor Translations) p. x, But the characters in a play of Seneca behave more like members of a minstrel troupe..rising in turn each to do his 'number'. **1933** P. Godfrey *Back-Stage* xiv. 173 A 'number' is any song or musical item in the programme, so named because every such item is numbered in rotation in the musical director's copy, and is always referred to by its cypher. **1948** *Penguin Music Mag.* Feb. 25 The B.B.C. could start..by putting some kind of check on the manner and matter of their inane songs—'numbers' I think they call them. **1958** *Publ. Amer. Dial. Soc.* xxx. 41 Words deeply engrained in the speech of the jazzman... Any tune is a 'number'. **1962** *Movie* Oct. 36/2 The garnish of musical numbers. **1973** J. Wainwright *Pride of Pigs* 175 It was a fine intro to a fine number. The style was traditional jazz.

f. *colloq.* A person or thing, esp. (i) an article of apparel.

1894 Somerville & 'Ross' *Real Charlotte* I. iii. 22 The shop windows..had progressed..to straw hats, tennis shoes, and coloured Summer Numbers. *c* **1900** in M. Johnson *Amer. Advertising* (1960), Indian panama horse hat. Last year our sales on this number were enormous, showing that this hat is no longer a fad. **1935** *Ladies' Home Jrnl.* Apr. 19/3 Deedee had swathed herself in an afternoon number and was happily emptying the last of my..perfume down her front. **1953** M. Steen *Anna Fitzalan* viii. 211 Petula Wimbleby's solution turned out to be an exquisite but throat-high 'little number' redeemed by lumps of jade. **1959** P. Bull *I know Face* ix. 149 The camel-hair number suffered most, as the majority of my friends wished to wear it. **1969** *Daily Tel.* 17 Jan. 17 Two of Mattli's best numbers were in impeccable white: a coat..and a wool suit.

(ii) A person, frequently with qualifying word; more usually, a woman. Cf. article *sb.* 14b.

1919 *Dialect Notes* V. 70 *Hot one, hot number*, used as a term of disgust. 'You're a hot one I must say.' New Mexico. **1924** H. C. Witwer in *Cosmopolitan* Apr. 70/1 Oh, she's beautiful enough!.. She's a snappy number with the skin you love to touch. **1936** L. C. Douglas *White Banners* xvi. 343 She's an odd number... I rather fancy she wears a hair shirt herself. **1938** R. C. Sherwood *Idiot's Delight* (ed. 2) 12 Bebe is a hard, harsh little number who shimmies. **1944** Auden *For Time Being* (1945) 10 And every gorgeous number may Be laid by anyone. **1950** R. Chandler *Trouble is my Business* i. 8 A girl. A red-headed number with bedroom eyes. **1955** W. Gaddis *Recognitions* ii. vii. 627 Have you seen a little blond number named Adeline? **1960** C. Watson *Bump in Night* xii. 122 The fellow was rather a dull number when you get down to a straight life story. **1968** J. Sangster *Touchfeather* ii. 17, I make do with three [men] ..my home number is just a nice guy who sells motor cars.

(iii) An occupation, job, assignment.

1948 Partridge *Dict. Forces' Slang* 129 *Number, quiet*, an easy job at sea or ashore. **1959** *N.Z. Listener* 24 July 5/1 A navigator's yeoman who had the cushy number of rubbing out old minefields and putting in new ones. **1968** *Listener* 19 Sept. 370/2 Transferred to what was described as a 'cushy number' with the Commandos. **1975** J. Wainwright *Square Dance* 187 He silently congratulated himself. It was a soft number, sitting here.

g. = denier[3] 4. Cf. count *sb.*[1] 2b.

1923 G. G. Denny *Fabrics* i. 31 Yarn count—a number given to yarn indicating its fineness, based upon number of yards per pound, more correctly called 'yarn number'. **1927** M. H. Avram *Rayon Industry* 516 There are many systems by which the 'number', 'size', or 'count' of yarns is expressed. *Ibid.*, The number..is..the weight of a standard unit skein or hank. **1928** V. Hottenroth *Artificial Silk* ix. 160 Before the silk is ready for sale or for treatment in the dye works, it must be sorted according to quality and number (that is, thickness of thread). **1931** D. L. Pellatt *Viscose Rayon Production* xi. 97 For 150-denier yarn..the number has risen from 18 to 21, 24, 27.

II. 7. a. The full tale or count of a collection, company, or class of persons. Also *pl.*

a **1300** *Cursor M.* 9416 Þat þis oxspring war o þat tale þat moght fulfill þe numbre hale..o þam þat fell. **1390** Gower *Conf.* III. 276 The nombre of Angles which was lore..He thoghte to restore. **1483** *Anc. Cal. Rec. Dubl.* (1889) 364 Suche persones as they thynketh lyable to full-fill the nombre of the xlviii. demi jures. *c* **1520** M. Nisbet *N.T., Acts* Prol., The novmer of the apostilis war fulfillit. **1597** Shaks. *2 Hen. IV*, iii. ii. 201 There is two more called then your number: You must haue but foure heere sir. **1667** Milton *P.L.* iii. 332 Hell, her numbers full, Thence-forth shall be for ever shut. **1859** Tennyson *Guinevere* 494 How sad it were for Arthur..To..miss the wonted number of my knights.

b. In contexts denoting inclusion in the particular company or collection of persons (or things) specified. Usu. *of, in,* or *to the number of* (etc.).

a **1300** *Cursor M.* 23875 He has us in his numbur tald, Als his scepe of his aun fald. *c* **1400** *Apol. Loll.* 56 If I were..of þe noumbre of bischoppis, I were of þe noumbre of men to be dampnid. **1470–85** Malory *Arthur* Pref. 1 Admytted.. in to the nombre of the ix beste & worthy of whome was fyrst the noble Arthur. **1533** Bellenden *Livy* i. i. (S.T.S.) I. 15 He was haldin be þe pepil for Iupiter Indiges, and ekit to þe nowmer of goddis. **1560** Daus tr. *Sleidane's Comm.* 197 So that men also of theyr religion might be admitted to be of that nombre. **1611** Bible *2 Cor.* x. 12 For we dare not make our selues of the number. **1667** Milton *P.L.* v. 840 But more illustrious made, since he the Head One of our number thus reduc't becomes. **1754** Chatham *Lett. to Nephew* iv. 25 Is gratitude in the number of a man's virtues? **1821** Shelley *Hellas* 17 Whose lover was of the number Who now keep That calm sleep Whence none may wake. **1852** Gladstone *Glean.* (1879) IV. 100 They would..rank as enemies of order, and be added to the number of those who are the unfortunate subjects of the Return.

†**c.** (As in prec.) The class or category *of* something. *Obs.*

1577 Googe *Heresbach's Husb.* i. (1586) 35 Columella countes it rather in the number of Fodder for cattell, then of Pulse for man. **1638** R. Baker tr. *Balzac's Lett.* (vol. III.) 103, I count not Amazons in the Number of women, but of Monsters and prodigees. **1690** Temple *Ess., Learning* Wks. 1720 I. 298 There are three, which I do not conceive well, how they can be brought into the Number of Sciences; which are, Chymistry, Philology, and Divinity. **1757** A. Cooper *Distiller* iii. lxiv. (1760) 261 Universally allowed to be a mineral Production of the Number of Bitumens.

d. The body or aggregate of persons specified.

1529 More *Dyaloge* iii. Wks. 205/2 Yᵉ church that is to witte the nombre & congregacion of good and right beleuyng folke. *a* **1562** G. Cavendish *Wolsey* (Ellis) 74 The Kyng..havyng abouyt his person,..beside the wonderfull nomber of nobyll men and gentilmen, iii great gards. **1600** Shaks. *A.Y.L.* v. iv. 178 Euery of this happie number That haue endur'd shrew'd daies, and nights with vs.

†**e.** Those forming a specified class; also, the multitude, the common herd. *Obs. rare.*

1578 Banister *Hist. Man* vii. 92 Casula;..the barbarous number, by the addition of one letter pronounce it Capsula. **1607** Shaks. *Cor.* iii. i. 72 By mingling them with vs, the honor'd Number. **1738** Pope *Epil. Sat.* ii. 111 The Number may be hang'd, but not be crown'd.

8. a. A (large, small, etc.) collection or company *of* persons or things.

c **1350** *Will. Palerne* 2300 A brem numbre of bestes. *c* **1400** Maundev. (Roxb.) xiii. 55 A grete noumer of þe childer of Israel ware slayne. *c* **1400** *Destr. Troy* 1173 A noumbur hoge Of Grekes were gedret. *c* **1475** *Partenay* 37 Ther was A Erle..Which of children had A huge noumbre gret. **1533** More *Debell. Salem* Wks. 1036/2 There is no smal nomber of suche erronious englishe bokes prynted. **1560** Daus tr. *Sleidane's Comm.* 192 b, An infinite nombre of grassehoppers came flieng into Germany. **1638** Junius *Paint. Ancients* 28 Among such a number of rich and artificiall monuments. **1678** J. Phillips tr. *Tavernier's Trav.* II. II. xxiv. 202 The Java Lords,..drawing their poyson'd Daggers, cry'd *a Mocca* upon the English, killing a great number of them. **1719** De Foe *Crusoe* I. (Globe) 53 There arose an innumerable Number of Fowls of many Sorts. **1743** J. Morris *Serm.* vii. 191 There is a great number of other passages of scripture, in which they must be understood of children. **1897** F. Hall in *Nation* LXIV. 396/2 A good number of them were, doubtless, brought across the ocean by British immigrants.

b. Without dependent genitive.

c **1400** *Destr. Troy* 8212 Agamynon the grete..With a noyus nowmbur, nait men of strenght. **1470–85** Malory *Arthur* xx. xx. 834 The noble knyghtes came oute of the Cyte by a grete nombre. **1535** Coverdale *Gen.* xxxiv. 30, I am but a small nombre: Yf they gather them selues now together against me, they shal slaye me. **1560** Daus tr. *Sleidane's Comm.* 130 Therfore were bookes brought thether in a wonderfull numbre. **1589** Cooper *Admon.* 120 Which dealing..cannot be without great offence of an infinite nomber. **1833** Cruse tr. *Eusebius* IV. iii. 130 This work is also preserved by a great number. **1895** *Pall Mall Mag.* Nov. 459 A considerable number are employed in..workshops.

9. a. A certain (usu. a large or considerable) company, collection, or aggregate *of* persons or things, not precisely reckoned or counted.

c **1380** Wyclif *Serm.* Sel. Wks. II. 309 In þe Chirche above in heven is a noumbre of greete seintis. *c* **1400** *Destr. Troy* 1147 Nestor with a nombur of noble men all. **1535** Coverdale *Acts* v. 36 There cleued vnto him a nombre of men, aboute a foure hundreth. **1580** Fulke *Retentive, Disc. Dang. Rock* 164 A number more of such principall heades of Christian learning. **1626** Bacon *Sylva* §567 Water-Lilly..hath a Root in the Ground; And so have a Number of other Herbs that grow in Ponds. **1795** Southey *Lett. fr. Spain* (1799) 8 A number of little forts are erected about the adjoining coast. **1807** G. Chalmers *Caledonia* I. II. vi. 282 The dates of both agree..in a number of their notices. **1860** S. Wilberforce *Sp. Missions* (1874) 338 He..kept himself by keeping a number of bees.

b. Without dependent genitive. Freq. = many persons (cf. 10 b).

1566 *Cott. Libr. Cal.* B 10 fol. 372 In this mean time there rose a nombre in the Court. **1594** Hooker *Eccl. Pol.* I. i. §2 Much..may seem to a number perhaps tedious, perhaps obscure. *Ibid.* x §2 After men began to grow to a number, the first thing we read they gave themselves unto was the tilling of the earth. **1833–6** J. H. Newman *Hist. Sk.* (1873) II. IV. ii. 382 The testimony of a number is more cogent than the testimony of two or three.

†**c.** Const. without *of*. *Obs. rare.*

1583 Babington *Commandm.* 245 With a number such mockes and diuelish tauntes. *Ibid.* 252 Vnto which and a number such other perswasions in the word the prophane writers..haue agreed. **1623** Breton *Souls Love* xxiii, A number plagues the Lord did further threaten.

10. a. *pl.* A (great, infinite, etc.) multitude or aggregate of persons or things.

c **1400** *Destr. Troy* 11139 What fortherit the fight of þo fell maidyns, Syn the grekes on hom gedrit in so gret nowmbers? *c* **1470** Henry *Wallace* VII. 1104 He chargyt thaim, with nowmeris mony ane Rycht weill beseyn, in Scotland for to ryd. **1573** L. Lloyd *Marrow of Hist.* (1653) 21 Xerxes,..whose infinite numbers of Navies covered the Ocean seas. **1600** Pory tr. *Leo's Africa* VI. 271 Here are infinite numbers of scorpions, but no flies at all. **1813** Wellington in Gurw. *Desp.* (1838) XI. 21 The French have lost immense numbers of men. **1847–9** *Todd's Cycl. Anat.* IV. 2/2 The numbers in which these creatures abound baffles all expression.

b. Many (persons, etc.).

1597 Hooker *Eccl. Pol.* v. lxviii. §6 Whereas none of them which were in the one could perish, numbers in the other are cast away. **1667** Milton *P.L.* XI. 480 A Lazar-house it seemd, wherein were laid Numbers of all diseas'd. **1709** Swift *Adv. Relig.* Wks. 1751 IV. 124 They might..be raised to as high a Perfection as Numbers are capable of receiving. **1760–2** Goldsm. *Cit. W.* lxxv, There are numbers in this city who live by writing new books. **1802** Mar. Edgeworth *Moral T.* (1816) I. viii. 57 Able to speak ..before numbers. **1861** F. Metcalfe *Oxonian in Iceland* (1867) 182 Numbers of fish kept rising at my grilse flies. **1866** S. Wilberforce *Sp. Missions* (1874) 261 It was a time when sermons were read by numbers, and admired by multitudes.

c. In contexts denoting superiority or power derived from numerical preponderance.

1638 Sir T. Herbert *Trav.* (ed. 2) 289, 1000 Persians were slaine and 20000 Turks; but by their numbers the Persians were forced to leave the field. **1761** Churchill *Night* 359 Can numbers then change Nature's stated laws? Can numbers make the worse the better cause? **1823** J. Marshall *Const. Opin.* (1839) 276 European policy, numbers and skill prevailed. **1861** F. Metcalfe *Oxonian in Iceland* (1867) 176 Coming to close quarters, they overpowered the foreigners by force of numbers. **1888** Bryce *Amer. Commw.* III. xcv. 325 This is in fact the essence of..popular government, and the justification for vesting powers in numbers.

III. 11. a. That aspect of things which is involved in considering them as separate units of which one or more may be taken or distinguished.

c **1305** *St. Edmund* 225 in *E.E.P.* (1862) 77 Arsmetrike is a lore þat of figours al is..& in [*read* of] numbre iwis. **1388** Wyclif *Pref. Ep. Jerome* vii, The mysteries of al the hool crafte of noumbre. *c* **1400** tr. *Secreta Secret., Gov. Lordsh.* 60 He hauys ordeyned by his wyt alle þinges yn euyn weight and certeyn nombre and ordre. *c* **1440** *Alph. Tales* 482 A chanon at was so symple & so vnconnyng þat he cuthe nott tell no maner of nowmer, nor tell whilk was od whilk was evyn. **1570** Billingsley *Euclid* VII. 183 Nomber compaseth all thinges, and is..the being and very essence of all thinges. **1623** Massinger *Dk. Milan* I. iii, This present journey, From whence it is all number to a cipher, I ne'er return with honour. **1667** Milton *P.L.* VIII. 38 Speed, to describe whose swiftness Number failes. **1690** Locke *Hum. Und.* II. xvi. (1695) 107 Our Idea of Infinity..seems to be nothing, but the infinity of Number. **1762** Kames *Elem. Crit.* (1774) II. 535 A child..perceives a difference between many and few; and that difference it is taught to call number. **1867** Dk. Argyll *Reign of Law* ii. 75 These laws of number and proportion pervade all Nature. **1884** tr. *Lotze's Logic* 189 That other saying.., that God has ordered everything by measure and number.

Comb. **1610** Heywood *Gold. Age* II. i, Shall I sweet Lady, adde vnto your grace, And but for number-sake supply that place?

fig. **1773** Foote *Bankrupt* II. Wks. 1799 II. 115, I..call'd him a citizen in the London Gazette,..Pass'd a few necessary notes to get him number and value, white-wash'd him, and sent him home.

†**b.** Geometrical figure. *Obs. rare.*

1398 Trevisa *Barth. De P.R.* XIX. cxxvi. (1495) 926 The nombre lineall begynnyth fro one and is wryte arowe and lyne vnto endlesse. *Ibid.*, The nombre superficiall is wryten not oonly in lengthe but also in brede as thre cornerde nombre and four cornerde and fyue cornerde and rounde.

†**c.** Proportion or comparison. *Obs. rare*$^{-1}$.

1387–8 T. Usk *Test. Love* I. viii. (Skeat) l. 119 It is a fayr lykenesse, a pees or oon grayn of whete, to a thousand shippes ful of corne charged! What nombre is betwene the oon and th' other?

d. *Phren.* The faculty of numbering or calculating.

1835 *Brit. Cycl., Arts & Sci.* II. 218/1 The organ of calculation or number (as it is sometimes called) is marked 28. **1865** *Chambers's Encycl.* VII. 516/2 *Number.*—The organ of this faculty is placed at the outer extremity of the eyebrows. **1885** *Encycl. Brit.* XVIII. 845/2 Number, on the external angular process of the frontal bone.

12. In phrases denoting that persons, things, etc., have not been, or cannot be, counted.

1297 R. Glouc. (Rolls) 8161 Folc of arabie, So muche þat þer nas non noumbre of hor compainye. **1393** Langl. *P. Pl.* C. XXIII. 269 ȝe wexeþ oute of numbre. *c* **1400** *Apol. Loll.* 5 He lediþ wiþ him self going bifore to helle peple wiþoutun nowmbre. *a* **1400–50** *Alexander* 1554 With prestis & with prelatis a pake out of nombre. **1483** Caxton *Gold. Leg.* 366 b/1 The holy poure ladyes whiche [thou] hast drawen to penaunce without nombre. **1534** Whitinton *Tullyes Offices* I. (1540) 28 Marathon, Salamyne, Plate,..and other out of nombre. **1667** Milton *P.L.* III. 346 A shout Loud as from numbers without number. **1751** Johnson *Rambler* No. 36 ⁋5 The sense of this universal pleasure has invited numbers without number to try their skill in pastoral performances. **1810** Bentham *Packing* (1821) 92 Persons out of number are amusing themselves with rendering what, I hope, appears to themselves, at least, good service to the country. **1892** *Law Times* XCII. 147/1 Times without number the courts in bankruptcy have been called upon to decide the question.

13. *in number*: **a.** In sum total; altogether. (Also †*by number*.)

c **1350** *Will. Palerne* 2289 Kene men of armes, twenty hundered & tvo trewli in numbre. **1382** Wyclif *2 Sam.* ii. 15 Thanne rysen and wenten twelue bi noumbre of Beniamyn. *c* **1400** *Rom. Rose* 5259 For tweyn in nombre is bet than three In every counsel and secree. **1423** Jas. I *Kingis Q.* xix, Goddis and sistris all, In nowmer ix., as bokis specifye. **1538** Starkey *England* II. i. 150 We schold not only haue the pepul incresyd in nombur, but also [etc.]. **1573** Tusser *Husb.* (1878) 107 These toppingly gests be in number but ten. **1615** Sandys *Trav.* 50 In number about thirtie or fortie thousand. **1667** Milton *P.L.* VI. 49 Equal in number to that Godless crew. **1789** Cowper *Catharina* 26 Though the pleasures of London exceed In number the days of the year. **1886** *Law Times* LXXXII. 94/1 A mortgage of the stock of sheep, about 6500 in number, on an Australian run.

†**b.** In numerical place or order. *Obs.*

c **1375** *Sc. Leg. Saints* xii. (*Matthias*) 3 Þe apostil sancte mathy, þat In nowmyr þe laste ves, In stad of þe tratour Iudas. **1561** Winȝet *Cert. Tractates* Wks. (S.T.S.) I. 2 Thre Questionis,..quhilkis ar in noumbre the xxxiii. xxxiiii. and xxxv. of The Four Score Thre Questionis.

†**c.** Together or along *with* others. *Obs.*$^{-1}$

c **1470** Henry *Wallace* IX. 874 Off this dispyt amendys I think to haiff, Or de thar for in nowmyr with the laiff.

†**14. a.** A (great) collection, etc. = sense 8. Also without *adj.* = sense 9. *Obs.*

a **1352** Minot *Poems* (ed. Hall) iii. 82 With grete noumber of smale botes. *a* **1400–50** *Alexander* 215 Þe mode kynge of Messedone with mekill nounbre..farne out of toune. **1456** Sir G. Haye *Law Arms* (S.T.S.) 53 He sawdit grete nowmer of men of armys. *a* **1533** Ld. Berners *Gold. Bk. M. Aurel.* (1546) B ij, There is greatte nombre of parcialities. **1601** Shaks. *Twel. N.* III. iii. 29 Belike you slew great number of his people. **1663** Gerbier *Counsel* f 1, Clovis..did coate number of Flour-de-lis. *Ibid.* g 2 b, Nor is this present Age void of number of Authors, who have written more on Architecture.

b. = sense 10. *rare.*

c **1400** Maundev. (Roxb.) xviii. 83 In bathe þir citez dwellez Cristen men..in grete noumer. **1485** *Surtees Misc.* (1888) 43 W[t] othre in grete nombre assembled ther. **1819** Shelley *Mask of Anarchy* xxxviii, Rise like Lions after slumber, In unvanquishable number.

c. = sense 10 c. *rare.*

1612 Bacon *Ess., Greatn. Kingd.* (Arb.) 472 Walled Towns,..Masse of treasure, Number in Armies.., are all but a Sheep in a Lions skin, except the..disposition of the people be militarie. **1625** *Ibid.* 473 Many are the Examples, of the great oddes between Number and Courage. **1667** Milton *P.L.* v. 899 Nor number, nor example with him wrought To swerve from truth.

IV. †**15.** Quantity, amount. *Obs. rare.*

13.. *E.E. Allit. P.* B. 1283 Þe golde of þe gazafylace to swyþe gret noumbre. *c* **1380** Wyclif *Sel. Wks.* III. 277 So þes worldly clerkis and religiouse taken huge noumbre of temperal goodis. **1477** Caxton *Jason* 76 b, And [they] promised them grete nombre of money if they might come and obteyn their entent. **1534** Whitinton *Tullyes Offices* III. (1540) 135 An honest man hath..brought a great nombre of wheate in the derth tyme. *a* **1670** Spalding *Troub. Chas. I* (1850) I. 347 The cordineris of both Abirdeins wes commandit..to give wp..the number of thair ledder, and to mak wp..thair portion of 20,000 pair of schois. **1720** *Humourist* 185, I have seen..one Man plowing with one Horse; which..saves a Number of Money.

16. *Gram.* The property in words of denoting that one, two, or more persons or things are spoken of; the special form of a word by which this is expressed.

1377 Langl. *P. Pl.* B. x. 237 Three propre persones ac nouȝt in plurel noumbre, For al is but on god. **1393** *Ibid.* C. IV. 349 In kynde and in case and in cours of noumbre. **1523** Fitzherb. *Surv.* 9 b, Where he sayth de molendinis, y[e] whiche is in the plurell nombre. **1530** Palsgr. *Introd.* 26 Of the gendre and nombre of the substantyve. **1591** Percivall *Sp. Dict.* B iij, There are two numbers, the singular speaking of one, the plurall of moe. **1636** B. Jonson *Eng. Gram.* vii, Of number that word is termed to be, which signifieth a number singular, or plural. **1738** *Gentl. Mag.* VIII. 182/2 The Plural Number of ὕδωρ is often made use of where a large Quantity of Water is designed to be expressed. ? **1751** Chatham *Lett. to his Nephew* i. 3, I will desire you..to write smoaks in the plural number, in the last line but one. **1824** L. Murray *Gram.* (ed. 5) I. 80 The singular number expresses but one object. **1872** Morris *Eng. Accidence* 93 The oldest English had the dual number only in the personal pronouns, which we no longer preserve.

17. Conformity, in verse or music, to a certain regular beat or measure; rhythm.

1477 Norton *Ord. Alch.* v. in Ashm. (1652) 81 Without true Number no Man trulie maie sing. **1553** T. Wilson *Rhet.* (1580) 163 He maie appere to keepe an uniformitie, and (as I might saie) a nomber in the vttering of his sentence. **1641** Hinde *J. Bruen* iii. 11 Mixt dancing of men and women, with light and lascivious gestures and actions, framed in number and measure to please a wanton eye. **1667** Milton *P.L.* IV. 687 With Heav'nly touch of instrumental sounds In full harmonic number joind.

18. *pl.* **a.** Musical periods or groups of notes.

1579 E. K. *Gloss. Spenser's Sheph. Cal.* Oct. 27 Plato and Pythagoras, held for opinion, that the mynd was made of a certaine harmonie and musicall nombers. **1598** Drayton *Heroic. Ep.* xv. 93 In Musickes Numbers my Voyce rose and fell. **1671** Milton *P.R.* IV. 255 The secret power Of harmony in tones and numbers hit By voice or hand. *c* **1690** Prior *To C'tess of Exeter Playing on Lute*, That with Your Numbers You our Zeal might raise. **1702** Rowe *Tamerl.* I. i, When some skilful Artist strikes the Strings The magick Numbers rouze our sleeping Passions. **1762** Sir W. Jones *Arcadia* Poems (1777) 117 Now on the flute with equal grace he play'd, And his soft numbers died along the shade. **1810** Scott *Lady of L.* I. Introd., Harp of the North! that..down the fitful breeze thy numbers flung. *a* **1839** Praed *Poems* (1864) II. 354 Pour again those holy numbers, Which thou warblest there alone.

b. Metrical periods or feet; hence, lines, verses.

1588 Shaks. *L.L.L.* IV. iii. 57, I feare these stubborn lines lack power to moue... These numbers will I teare, and write in prose. **1629** Davenant *Albovine* Ded., My Numbers I do not shew unto the publick Eye, with an ambition to be quickly known. **1667** Milton *P.L.* III. 38 Then feed on thoughts, that voluntarie move Harmonious numbers. **1709** Pope *Ess. Crit.* 337 But most by Numbers judge a Poet's song; And smooth or rough, with them is right or wrong. **1773** Mrs. Chapone *Improv. Mind* (1774) II. 167 Numbers and rhymes..being so easily learn'd by heart. **1824** L. Murray *Eng. Gram.* (ed. 5) I. 479 Our translators of the Bible, have often been happy in suiting their numbers to the subject. **1849** Macaulay *Hist. Eng.* vii. II. 202 Men were in no humour to be charmed by the transparent style and melodious numbers of the apostate.

†**c.** A subdivision of a line. *Obs. rare*$^{-1}$.

1797 *Monthly Mag.* III. 258 *note*, Whatever exceeded two times (a short syllable being estimated as half a time) was termed not a foot but a number.

19. *attrib.* and *Comb.*, as (sense 1) ***number-word***, ***-work***; (sense 3) ***number continuum***, ***series***, ***system***; (sense 6 a) ***number book***, ***-carrier***, ***man***; (sense 6 d) ***number opera***; **number-average** *Chem.*, an average of some parameter of the molecules of a mixture calculated as an arithmetic mean with each individual molecule contributing equally, regardless of size; **number board**, a board on which numbers are displayed; **number-cloth**, the cloth bearing a horse's number in a race; **number-cruncher** *colloq.*, a machine (or occas. a person) with the capacity for performing arithmetical operations of great complexity or length; so **number-crunching**; **number-form**, the shapes into which series of numbers are formed in the mental imagery of some people; **number line**, a graduated line used to illustrate simple numerical concepts and operations; **number-plate**, a plate bearing a number, esp. that on a registered vehicle; **number six**, (*a*) *U.S. colloq.*, a household medicinal remedy, so called from its place on the pharmaceutical list of its inventor, Samuel Thomson; (*b*) a curl having the shape of the figure six which is dressed on to the forehead; cf. *figure-six* adj. (FIGURE *sb.* 26); **number six nose**, a large fleshy nose, supposed to be similar in shape to the figure six; **number theory**, the branch of mathematics dealing with the properties and relationships of numbers, esp. the positive integers (cf. THEORY[1] 4 c); so **number-theoretic**, **-theoretical** *adjs.*; **number-theoretically** *adv.*; **number theorist**.

1935 Kraemer & Lansing in *Jrnl. Physical Chem.* XXXIX. 165 For heterogeneous materials, different methods for determining molecular weights give different 'average' values. Thus, it may be shown that freezing point, osmotic pressure, and end-group methods, when applied properly to an ideal mixture, result in an average value defined by the expression $M_n = 1/\Sigma\,(f_i/M_i)$ where f_i is the fractional weight of the constituent of molecular weight M_i in the mixture, and the summation is to be applied to all constituents present. This average may be designated as a '*number-average molecular weight'. **1955** *Jrnl. Polymer Sci.* XVII. 263 Number average degrees of polymerization are used to calculate the rates of initiation and transfer in vinyl polymerizations, and the extent of reaction in polycondensations. **1974** ALLEN & PATRICK *Kinetics & Mechanisms Polymerization Reactions* vii. 419 Until recent years determination of number-average molecular weights was a most imprecise measurement. **1938** G. H. SEWELL *Amateur Film-Making* v. 54 That [*sc.* numbering each shot] is done by exposing before each shot a *Number Board. **1961** K. REISZ *Technique Film Editing* (ed. 9) 281 Number board, board momentarily held before the camera and photographed at the beginning of a take, recording the title of the film, number of the take and scene, in order to facilitate identification for the editor. **1969** D. FRANCIS *Enquiry* I. i. 14 The Oxford Stewards had been elected for social reasons only..one of them couldn't read a number board at five paces. **1960** G. A. GLAISTER *Gloss. Bk.* 278 **Number books*, books published serially... Each part consisted of two or more sheets stitched together within blue-paper covers. **1963** *English Studies* XLIV. 149 But the kind of serialisation..(often called 'number books' or 'subscription books') was really the issue and sale of a book in separate fascicules..so that the purchaser could..collect the entire work and have it..bound if he so wished. **1919** M. BEER *Hist. Brit. Socialism* I. II. ii. 108 He was successively a *number-carrier, street bookseller, and editor of a democratic periodical. **1924** E. WALLACE *Educated Evans* vi. 131 Catskin was the one horse..that Educated Evans would have recognized without colours and *number-cloth. **1975** D. FRANCIS *High Stakes* i. 5 People..carrying out saddles and number cloths for the next steeplechase. **1903** *Number-continuum [see CONTINUUM]. **1966** *New Scientist* 29 Sept. 729/1 The Flowers report recommended the setting up of some 'regional centres' each with a large '*number-cruncher' to take the bulk-computing load off more local machines. **1971** *Ibid.* 3 June 572/3 Tools ranging from the slide rule to the number-cruncher. **1971** A. SAMPSON *New Anat. Britain* v. xxvi. 497 Kenneth Keith, a brusque number-cruncher who had come into banking from accountancy. **1971** *Sci. Amer.* Aug. 100 (Advt.), Here's a calculator that speaks your language. You can customize its keyboard, memory size, display, programs and peripherals to suit your *number-crunching tasks. **1883** F. GALTON *Inquiries into Human Faculty* 124 The character of the forms under which historical dates are visualised contrast strongly with the ordinary *Number-Forms. **1903** G. M. STRATTON *Experimental Psychol.* xiii. 253 A peculiarity of this same number-form..is that with the higher numbers the person changes his point of view. **1936** *Brit. Jrnl. Educ. Psychol.* VI. 60 The main object of the investigation..was to find if the presence of number forms is correlated to any significant degree with arithmetical ability. **1963** *Listener* 28 Mar. 547/1 Some people, whenever they think about numbers, picture them in a spatial arrangement... The experiences are called number forms. **1964** E. J. SWENSON *Teaching Arithm. to Children* v. 99/1 When *number lines are introduced to children, they should come in as a representation of a problem situation. **1968** MURPHY & KEMPF *New Math. made Simple* ii. 36 Since addition and subtraction are inverse operations, we expect subtraction to be associated with moving to the left on a number line. **1866** J. BLACKWOOD *Let.* 21 Dec. in *Geo. Eliot's Lett.* (1956) IV. 321 The '*Number Men', i.e. men who sell the weekly and monthly publications in large numbers. **1947** A. EINSTEIN *Music in Romantic Era* x. 117 Even a musician so retrospective as Louis Spohr could not help abandoning the *number-opera towards the end of his career. **1958** *Listener* 24 July 141/3 'Die Zaubergeige', for example, is a 'number opera' whose folkish tunes stem from popular Bavarian art. **1869** *Good Words* 1 Mar. 170/2 The white porcelain *number-plates upon the doors. **1901** *Motor-Car World* Apr. 74/1 We greatly fear that the number-plate is coming. **1911** *Chambers's Jrnl.* Dec. 831/1 White light to illumine the number-plate. **1973** P. EVANS *Bodyguard Man* viii. 67 He.. scooped up a handful of dirt from the roadside and rubbed it on to the rear number-plate until it became nearly illegible. **1975** *Drive* New Year 98/1 Numberplate collecting has always been a popular hobby in the USA. **1890** W. JAMES *Princ. Psychol.* II. xxviii. 653 Little by little in our minds the *number-series is formed. **1822** S. THOMSON *Narr. Life* 63, I began with him by giving medicine to correct and strengthen the system; bathed the wound with my rhumatic drops, or *No. 6. **1842** C. M. KIRKLAND *Forest Life* I. 71 We stick to thoroughwort,—balmony,—soot tea,—'number six',—and the like. **1909** *Bull. of Lloyd Library of Botany, Pharmacy & Materia Medica* 15 Thomson's *Compound Tincture of Myrrh and Capsicum* became celebrated as 'Number 6'. **1923** J. MANCHON *Le Slang* 271 *Number sixes*,..des accroche-cœur. **1966** J. S. COX *Illustr. Dict. Hairdressing & Wigmaking* 104/1 *Number sixes*, curls dressed onto the forehead. **1923** G. B. SHAW *Matter with Ireland* (1962) 260 Whereas my Irish nationality was formerly a valuable asset to me in England, I am now expected to apologize for it by men with wooly heads or *number six noses. **1932** —— *Adventures of Black Girl* 18 A dark man with wavy black hair, and a number six nose. **1924** R. M. OGDEN tr. *Koffka's Growth of Mind* v. 332 Max Wertheimer has investigated the kind of ideas employed by men who do not possess our developed *number-system, in tasks where we would use numbers. **1914** *Q. Jrnl. Pure & Applied Math.* XLV. 373 We begin by listing the analogues of the algebraic invariants and then supplement these with the necessary invariants peculiar to the *number-theoretic case. **1966** J. H. CADWELL *Topics Recr. Math.* xii. 133 The well-known ratio 22/7 shows that rational approximations have their uses. They are of considerable importance from a number-theoretic standpoint. **1968** A. M. TROPPER tr. *H. Meschkowski's Introd. Mod. Math.* viii. 178 There are still many unsolved *number theoretical problems. **1950** *Math. Tables & Other Aids to Computation* IV. 110 Something *number-theoretically significant may be occurring. **1929** *Bull. Amer. Math. Soc.* XXXV. 779 There is no *number-theorist who has not heard of 'Farey's series'. **1971** *Sci. Amer.* June 56/2 The pattern of occurrence of Mersenne numbers, Mersenne primes and perfect numbers continues to mystify number theorists. [**1798** A. M. LE GENDRE (*title*) Essai sur la théorie des nombres. **1811** P. BARLOW (*title*) An elementary investigation of the theory of numbers.] **1912** *Bull. Amer. Math. Soc.* XVIII. 335 The theory of determinants..in the nineteenth century came to permeate all branches of *number theory, algebra, [etc.]. **1939** USPENSKY & HEASLET *Elem. Number Theory* p. v, Instruction in elementary number theory is given in an ever-increasing number of American universities and colleges. **1948** O. ORE *Number Theory & its Hist.* v. 76 The study of these laws in the distribution of the primes falls in the field of analytic number theory. This particular domain of number theory..is considered to be technically one of the most difficult fields of mathematics. **1964** M. MCLUHAN *Understanding Media* (1967) xxxiii. 370 Arithmetic in grade three or nine, when taught in terms of number theory, symbolic logic, and cultural history, ceases to be mere practice in problems. **1924** R. M. OGDEN tr. *Koffka's Growth of Mind* v. 334 Many peoples use other *number-words in counting than the ones they use in naming sums. **1911** S. S. COLVIN *Learning Process* iii. 51 Much of it might function equally well for the reading habit, or the *number-work habit. **1962** *Listener* 15 Mar. 469/2 Earlier attempts to teach 'number work' are premature and cannot lead beyond the learning of meaningless rules.

number ('nʌmbə(r)), *v.* Forms: α. 3 noumbri (4 -bir, 5–6 -bre), 4–5 nowmbre (5 -ber, byr, -bur), 4–6 nombre (5 -brye, 6 -ber), 6–8 numbre (6 *Sc.* -bir), 6– number. β. 4 nomer, 5 (6 *Sc.*) nowmer (5 -on), 5 *Sc.* noumer, 6 *Sc.* novmer, nummer. [ad. OF. *nombrer*:—L. *numerāre* (cf. NUMERATE), f. *numerus* number.]

1. *trans.* To count, to ascertain the number of (individual things or persons).

α. **1297** R. GLOUC. (Rolls) 1399 Aboute ierusalem þis noumbringe he bigan As in þe middel of þe world to noumbri eche man. *a* **1340** HAMPOLE *Psalter* xxi. 17 Þai noumbird..all my banes. **1390** GOWER *Conf.* I. 218 It mihte noght be nombred, The folk which after was encombred Thurgh him. **1426** LYDG. *De Guil. Pilgr.* 19338 Thousandis mo than I kan nowmbre. **1470–85** MALORY *Arthur* XIII. xv. 633 Syr Galahad..sawe soo moche peple in the stretes that he myghte not nombre them. **1526** *Pilgr. Perf.* (W. de W. 1531) 254 His ioyntes were dissolued and losed, so that his bones myght be nombred. **1651** HOBBES *Leviath.* III. xlii. 290 The Principall Person of the Assembly, whose office was to number the Votes. **1671** MILTON *P.R.* III. 410 When thou stood'st up his Tempter to the pride Of numbring Israel. **1709** STEELE & ADDISON *Tatler* No. 81 ¶2 Prodigious Multitudes of People, which no Man could number. **1820** SHELLEY *Prometh. Unb.* IV. 420 Like a flock of sheep They pass before his eye, are numbered, and roll on! *a* **1862** BUCKLE *Misc. Wks.* (1872) I. 527 Mussulmans consider every attempt to number the people as a mark of great impiety.

absol. *c* **1430** *Freemasonry* (ed. Halliw. 1840) 571 Astronomy nombreth, my dere brother, Arsmetyk scheweth won thyng that ys another.

β. *c* **1375** *Sc. Leg. Saints* xliii. (*Cecilia*) 404 Þai ma nocht nomeryt be, þat resawit þis halynes. *c* **1440** *Promp. Parv.* 360/1 Nowmeron, *numero*. *c* **1440** *Alph. Tales* 293, I am þe aungell off God sent for to nowmer þi fute-steppis.

b. To ascertain the amount or quantity of (something). *rare.*

c **1420** LYDG. *Commend. Our Lady* 100 Whan that Gabriel With joy thee grette that may not be nombred. **1535** COVERDALE *Gen.* xli. 49 He left of nombrynge of it [corn], for it coude not be nombred. **1606** SHAKS. *Ant. & Cl.* III. ii. 17 Scribes, Bards, Poets, cannot Thinke, speake, cast, write, sing, number: hoo, His loue to Anthony.

†**c.** To compute, calculate, reckon, measure.

c **1394** *P. Pl. Crede* 178 Merkes of marchauntes y-medled bytwene, Mo þan twenty and two twyes y-noumbred. **1530** PALSGR. 644/2, I nombre, as an astronomer doth his thing by aulgorisme, *je calcule*. *Ibid.*, Have you nombred the distaunce bytwene the sonne and the moone? **1579** DIGGES *Stratiot.* 1 To number anye summe nothing else it is, but to declare the value of everie Figure placed. **1669** STURMY *Mariner's Mag.* IV. viii. 218 The half of the deg. and min. thus numbred together, will be the Elevation of the Pole. **1794** T. TAYLOR *Pausanias's Descr. Greece* III. 7, I was desirous of accurately numbering the interval of time from one Daedal festival to another.

2. To enumerate, to reckon *up*. Also *absol.*

? *a* **1400** *Morte Arth.* 2658 They are nowmerde fulle neghe, and namede in rollez, Sexty thowsande and tene. **1435** MISYN *Fire of Love* 97, I hope no þinge emonge all oþer þat may be nowmbyrde of clarkis þat may vs socur so mikyll ..als feruent lufe of þe godhede. **1470–85** MALORY *Arthur* XVIII. xviii. 757 Thenne syr Bors de ganys came..and he was nombred that he smote doune twenty knyghtes. **1590** MARLOWE *2nd Pt. Tamburl.* III. v, So from Arabia Desert.. Came forty thousand warlike foot and horse, Since last we number'd to your majesty. **1601** R. JOHNSON *Kingd. & Commw.* (1603) 26 The quantities of ladders, bridges, shot, powder, and other furnitures following so royall an armie, what pen can number? **1686** tr. *Chardin's Trav. Persia* 252 Relicks..among which they number up the Veronique. **1871** R. H. HUTTON *Ess.* (1877) I. 4 If..you numbered up the acts of trust.

†**b.** In *passive.* To be of a certain number; to amount *to*, or be equal *to*, in number. *Obs.*

14.. *Tundale's Vis.* 2220 He mad colagys and chyrchys mony That nomburd wer to foure and fourty. *c* **1470** *Gol. & Gaw.* 227 Thay drive on the da deir be dalis and doun, And of the nobillest be-name, noumerit of nyne. **1628** GAULE *Pract. The.* 43 Had I..Tongues and Lips numbred to those Hands of the Poets Briareus.

c. To fix the number of; to reduce to a definite number; to make few in number; to bring near to a close. (Chiefly in *passive.*)

1382 WYCLIF *Dan.* v. 26 God hath noumbride thi rewme, and fulfilled it. **1584** R. SCOT *Discov. Witchcr.* v. v. (1886) 79 Man..hath his daies numbred. **1593** SHAKS. *3 Hen. VI*, I. iv. 25 The Sands are numbred, that makes vp my Life. **1847** C. BRONTË *J. Eyre* xxv, The month of courtship had wasted, its very last hours were being numbered. **1869** TROLLOPE *He Knew*, etc. li. (1878) 281 The opinion became general that Miss Stanbury's days were numbered. **1883** *Daily Tel.* 10 Nov. 5/3 We are told by croakers that the days of fox-hunting are numbered in these sporting islands.

†**d.** To collect, up to a certain number. *Obs.*

1382 WYCLIF *2 Chron.* ii. 2 And he noumbrede seuenty thousand of men berynge in schulderis. **1533** BELLENDEN *Livy* II. xvii. (S.T.S.) I. 195 Quhen þir consulis war nowmerand þare legiouns,..Comperit afore þame ane huge pepill desiring peace. **1611** BIBLE *1 Kings* xx. 25 Number thee an armie, like the armie that thou hast lost.

3. To check, control, or verify the number of; to count or tell *over*. Also *absol.*

1535 COVERDALE *1 Sam.* xiv. 17 And whan they nombred, beholde, Ionathas & his wapen bearer was not there. **1632** MASSINGER *City Madam* v. iii, Let my brother number His beads devoutly! **1692** DRYDEN *Eleonora* 198 Anchises looked not with so pleased a face In numbering o'er his future Roman race. **1725** POPE *Odyss.* XIII. 262 Then on the sands he rang'd his wealthy store, The gold, the vests, the tripods, number'd o'er. **1784** COWPER *Task* v. 425 To wear out time in numb'ring to and fro The studs that thick emboss his iron door. **1813** SHELLEY *Q. Mab* IV. 241 Or thou delight'st In numbering o'er the myriads of thy slain.

†**b.** To count out or pay *down* (money). *Obs.*

1502 *Will of Heed* (Somerset Ho.), l[li] in Redy money nombred. **1671** MILTON *Samson* 1478 His ransom..shall willingly be paid And numberd down. **1725** *Portland Papers* (Hist. MSS. Comm.) VI. 140 The seller carries home to the merchant's house what goods they had bargained for, where he has immediately his money numbered down.

c. To apportion (one's days) with care.

1535 COVERDALE *Ps.* lxxxix. 5 O teach vs to nombre oure dayes, that we maye applie our hertes vnto wyszdome. **1665** BRATHWAIT *Comment. Two Tales* (1901) 97 The Remainder of his Hours henceforth to number his Daies. **1860** WARTER *Sea-board* II. 133 Days of this life's pilgrimage spared to me in mercy to number wisely.

†**d.** To appoint or allot *to* some fate. *Obs.*

1611 BIBLE *Isa.* lxv. 12 Therefore will I number you to the sword.

e. To portion out, to divide.

1887 MORRIS *Odyss.* x. 203 Then my well-greaved fellows I numbered into two companies.

4. To count, reckon, or class among certain persons or things. Chiefly const. *among*, *in*, or *with*.

1382 WYCLIF *Acts* i. 17 The which was noumbrid in vs, and gat the sort of this mynysterie. **1493** *Petronilla* 27 (Pynson), She was acceptyd so in the lordys sight To be noumbryd one of the maydyns fyue. **1548–9** (Mar.) *Bk. Com. Prayer*, *Te Deum*, Make them to be noumbred with thy sainctes. **1590** SHAKS. *Mids. N.* III. ii. 67 Henceforth be neuer numbred among men. **1624** MASSINGER *Bondman* IV. ii, Happy those times When lords..number'd Their servants almost equal with their sons. **1652** GAULE *Magastrom.* xxvi, To these dreamers we may number those who give a faith of divinity to the vaticinations of madmen. **1719** SWIFT *Let. Yng. Clergym.* Wks. 1751 V. 9 If..he be any where too obscure..it ought to be numbred among his Omissions. **1753** SMOLLETT *Cnt. Fathom* (1784) 12/1 An Englishwoman, who, after having been five times a widow in one campaign, was..numbered among the baggage of the allied army. **1817** SHELLEY *Rev. Islam* IX. xxix, Let sense and thought..be numbered not Among the things that are. **1884** *Manch. Exam.* 20 Feb. 4/7 The nation which is proud to number him among her sons.

b. *intr.* To rank or be included *with* (others).

1864 TENNYSON *Aylmer's Field* 663 And tho' thou numberest with the followers Of One who cried, 'Leave all and follow me'.

5. To assign or attach a number to (a thing); *spec.* to mark or distinguish by a numerical symbol.

1390 GOWER *Conf.* III. 122 Among the Signes upon heighte The Signe which is nombred eighte Is Scorpio. **1593** FALE *Art Dialling* 12 Number the residue of the lines in their place as they follow in order. **1651** HOBBES *Leviath.* IV. xlvi. 374 Men divide a Body in their thought, by numbring parts of it, and in numbring those parts number also the parts of the Place it filled. **1678** MOXON *Mech. Exer.* vi. §31. 100 These Inches are numbred from one end of the Rule to the other. **1836–7** DICKENS *Sk. Boz*, *Scenes* vii, Hackney-coaches.. were..plated and numbered by the wisdom of Parliament. **1849** MACAULAY *Hist. Eng.* iii. I. 360 The houses were not numbered. There would indeed have been little advantage in numbering them. **1877** *Act 40 & 41 Vict.* c. 60 §3 Every canal boat..shall be lettered, marked, and numbered in some conspicuous manner.

b. To set down in a numerical series.

1846 GROTE *Greece* I. xviii. (1862) I. 424 Kodrus is numbered as the last king of Athens.

6. To have lived, or to live (so many years).

1590 PEELE *Polyhymnia* 9 Thirty-three [years] she numbereth, in her throne, That long..I pray May number many to these thirty-three. **1601** SHAKS. *All's Well* IV. v. 86 Of as able bodie as when he number'd thirty. **1604** —— *Oth.* III. iv. 70 A Sybill that had numbred in the world The Sun to course two hundred compasses. **1791** COWPER *Yardley Oak* 3 My birth (Since which I number three-score winters past). **1850** TENNYSON *In Mem.* Concl. 9, Tho' I since then have number'd o'er Some thrice three years.

7. To include or comprise in a number; to have or comprise (so many things or persons).

c **1645** MILTON *Sonn.* xi, It walk'd the Town a while, Numbring good intellects; now seldom por'd on.

1867 THIRLWALL *Rem.* III. 450 It would show not only that the Anglican Communion numbered so many Bishops. **1872** YEATS *Growth Comm.* 91 Kafsah numbered in its environs..200 castles. **1881** FREEMAN *Venice* 323 It is said that..Otranto numbered twenty-two thousand inhabitants.

b. To equal, amount to (a specified sum).

1842 TENNYSON *Talking Oak* 80 When The maiden blossoms of her teens Could number five from ten. **1881** TYLOR *Anthropol.* i. 7 It appears that the distinct languages known number about a thousand. **1883** *Manch. Guard.* 22 Oct. 5/2 The crew and passengers numbered 33.

c. *intr.* To be equal in number *with.*

1833 TENNYSON *Two Voices* 330 A wife.. Whose troubles number with his days.

8. To issue (a book) in numbers. *rare*⁻¹.

1781 CRABBE *Library* 192 A folio-Number once a week; Bibles, with cuts and comments, thus go down; E'en light Voltaire is number'd through the town.

ˈnumberable, *a. rare.* Also 4 **noumberabile.** [f. NUMBER *v.* + -ABLE: cf. NUMBRABLE *a.*]

1. Capable of being numbered; numerable.

a **1340** HAMPOLE *Psalter* xxi. 17 Þai made noumberabile all my banes. **1611** COTGR., *Nombrable*, numberable, numerable. **1839** J. ROGERS *Antipopopr.* xvi. §3. 331 The blessings and graces of Holy Orders.. are fully numberable ..by none but priestly penetration.

†**2.** Numerous. *Obs. rare*⁻¹.

1596 DALRYMPLE tr. *Leslie's Hist. Scot.* x. 427 The Quene gatherit ane hoste numberable anuich with preparatione anuich to the weiris scho sent into scotland.

numbered (ˈnʌmbəd), *ppl. a.* [f. NUMBER *v.* + -ED.] **1. a.** Reckoned by number; enumerated, counted. **b.** Marked with a number.

1611 SHAKS. *Cymb.* I. vi. 36 The twinn'd Stones Vpon the number'd Beach. **1628** GAULE *Pract. The.* (1629) 402 This numbred while Christ passed not ouer idly. **1667** MILTON *P.L.* VIII. 19 An Atom, with the Firmament compar'd And all her numberd Starrs. *Ibid.* x. 576 To undergo This annual humbling certain number'd days. **1771** *Antiq. Sarisb., Lives Bps.* 149 They.. pillaged his house of every thing, and took 10,000 marks in numbered money. **1839** *Lett. fr. Madras* (1843) 281 In future I will keep numbered duplicates. **1895** *Trans. Bibl. Soc.* II. II. 112 The first use of numbered leaves ..by Arnold ter Hoernen.

2. *Comb.*, as **numbered account**, an account at a bank, esp. a Swiss bank, which is identified only by a number and does not bear the owner's name.

1963 'HAN SUYIN' *Four Faces* 31 He..had money salted away in a numbered account in Switzerland. **1968** J. BLACKBURN *Young Man from Lima* vi. 61 Numbered accounts in Swiss banks tell no tales. **1972** W. DAVIS *Money Talks* 136 Italian businessmen, who appreciate this more than most, often enter Switzerland with suitcases full of banknotes and open numbered accounts on the spot.

ˈnumberer. [f. NUMBER *v.* + -ER¹.] One who, or that which, numbers.

1594 BLUNDEVIL *Exerc.* I. vii. (1636) 21 The Numerator is as much to say as the numberer. **1611** BIBLE *Dan.* viii. 13 That certaine Saint [*marg.*, the numberer of secrets] which spake. **1693** J. EDWARDS *Author. O. & N. Test.* 52 Those transcribers of the Bible were called by the Jews Sopherim, i.e. numberers. **1848** L. HUNT *Town* iii. 115 He was numberer at Drury Lane Theatre, that is to say, the person who counted the number of people in the house. **1883** E. A. ABBOTT *Hints on Home Teaching* 98 Since the upper figure [*sc.* of a fraction] represents the number of the parts taken together it may be called the Numberer.

†**ˈnumberful,** *a. Obs. rare.* [f. NUMBER *sb.* + -FUL.] Numerous, multitudinous.

1594 CAREW *Huarte's Exam. Wits* xiv. (1596) 239 Salomon was chosen king and head of so great and numberfull a people, as that of Israell. **1653** WATERHOUSE *Apol. Learning* 50 About the year 700 great was the company of learned men of the English race; yea, so numberfull, that they upon the point excelled all Nations in learning.

ˈnumbering, *vbl. sb.* [f. NUMBER *v.* + -ING¹.] The action of the verb, in various senses.

1297 R. GLOUC. (Rolls) 1398 Aboute ierusalem þis noumbringe he bigan. **1382** WYCLIF *2 Chron.* ii. 17 Than Salomon noumbride alle the men comlyngis.. after the noumbrynge that Dauid, his fadir, noumbred. *c* **1430** *Art Nombryng* 1 And þis boke tretys þe Craft of Nombrynge, þe quych crafte is called also Algorym. **1497** *Naval Acc. Hen. VII* (1896) 83 Without other noumbryng or weying of the stuffes. **1557** RECORDE *Whetst.* b ij b, Measure is but the nombryng of the partes of lengthe, bredthe, or depthe. **1570** J. DEE *Math. Pref.* *j b, His Continuall Numbryng, of all things, is the Conseruation of them in being. **1638** SIR T. HERBERT *Trav.* (ed. 2) 150 Dancing wenches, Hocus Pocusses, and other Anticks past my numbring inobled the ceremony. **1669** STURMY *Mariner's Mag.* II. vi. 65 At every 5 Parts make a Point, for the ready numbering of the Divisions. **1860** TYNDALL *Glac.* II. x. 280 The numbering of the stakes.. commenced from the Chapeau-side of the glacier. **1885** *Manch. Exam.* 6 Mar. 5/4 The scientific thoroughness which marks the numbering of the people in European countries.

attrib. **1683** MOXON *Mech. Exerc., Printing* 267 The Numbring Rods of the Right Honourable John Lord Nepeer. **1860** *Knight's Eng. Cycl., Arts & Sci.* V. 995 *Numbering Machines*... Their work is that of numbering, or enumerating, and registering the results in some conspicuous way. **1875** KNIGHT *Dict. Mech.* 1536/1 The numbering-apparatus. *Ibid.*, Adjacent to the numbering-wheels.

So **ˈnumbering** *ppl. a.*

1576 GASCOIGNE *Steele Gl.* (Arb.) 77 That Numbring men, in all their euens and odds Do not forget, that only Vnitie. **1593** SHAKS. *Rich. II*, v. v. 50 For now hath Time made me his numbring clocke.

ˈnumberless, *a.* [f. NUMBER *sb.* + -LESS.]

1. Innumerable, countless, beyond computation.

1573 TWYNE *Æneid* XI. (1584) R b, The hugie heape of such as there lay slaine, Both numbrelesse, and honourlesse they burne. **1590** GREENE *Never too late* (1600) 68 Then should.. the furrowes in my face be numberlesse. **1624** GATAKER *Transubst.* 68 To bee in heaven, and in numberlesse places of the Earth. **1667** MILTON *P.L.* VII. 197 About his Chariot numberless were pour'd Cherub and Seraph. **1736** BUTLER *Anal.* Introd., Wks. 1874 I. 3 Number-less instances might be mentioned. **1782** PRIESTLEY *Corrupt. Chr.* II. IX. 189 The clergy exercised numberless cruelties. **1819** SHELLEY *Cyclops* 175 The cavern has recesses numberless. **1879** R. K. DOUGLAS *Confucianism* iii. 79 The 'Book of History' contains numberless references to them.

b. Used with *number(s).* (Freq. in 17th cent.)

1594 PEELE *Alcazar* IV. i, A number almost numberless. **1612** J. DAVIES *Muses Sacr.* Wks. (Grosart) II. 26/1 Cast, if thou canst, a Number numberlesse. **1638** SIR T. HERBERT *Trav.* (ed. 2) 181 Of all the trees I saw, none exceeded the Mulberies, for numberlesse numbers. *a* **1716** SOUTH *Serm.* (1744) VII. 60 What then will become of those numberless numbers of men?

2. Devoid of metrical numbers. *rare*⁻¹.

a **1658** CLEVELAND *Agst. Ale* iv, Saltless and galless be thy Curse, Numberless, rugged.

†**ˈnumberous,** *a. Obs.* [f. NUMBER *sb.* + -OUS: cf. NUMBROUS *a.*] Numerous.

1566 DRANT *Horace, Sat.* I. vii. D vij, So these same two, tongue puisaunte knyghts, with scoulding ginn the fyghte. The auditorye numberouse. *Ibid.* II. iii. F vij, This rule makes mad a noumberouse swarme Of subiects and of kinges. **1592** WYRLEY *Armorie* 156 Fore passed life I ouer canvassing Found my great sins exceeding numberous. *a* **1603** T. CARTWRIGHT *Confut. Rhem. N.T.* (1618) 26 A more honorable or more numberous senate.

†**ˈnumbersome,** *a. Obs.* [f. as prec. + -SOME.] Numerous.

a **1617** BAYNE *On Eph.* (1658) 109 The Church in Jerusalem did grow numbersome. **1628** PEMBLE *Salomons Recant.* 17 Numbersome heards of Cattell.

†**ˈnumbery,** *a. Obs.* [f. NUMBER *sb.* + -Y.]

1. Numerous, rich in numbers.

1591 SYLVESTER *Du Bartas* I. *Ivry* 25 So many, and so numb'ry Armies scatter'd. **1605** *Ibid.* II. *Lawe* 1320 Thy numbry Flocks in part shall barren be.

2. Poetical, metrical.

1598 SYLVESTER *Du Bartas* II. i. iv. *Handicrafts* 542 The tunes that his sweet numbery soule.. learn'd of the warbling Pole. *Ibid., Columnes* 719 Sacred Harmony, And Numb'ry Law, which did accompany Th' Almighty-most.

numb-fish. [f. NUMB *a.*] The Electric Ray or Torpedo, so called from the effect of the electric shocks emitted by it.

1711 *Brit. Apollo* No. 123. 1/2 A Fish called by Name a Nummfish. **1738** F. MOORE *Trav. Africa* 176 By this time I understood it was a Torpedo or Numbfish. **1774** *Phil. Trans.* LXIV. 467 The Torpedo, or Numb-fish, is by no means plenty in these parts. **1854** BADHAM *Halieut.* 78 The numb-fish (*narke*) applied alive over the temples in headache is mentioned by Galen as a specific for that complaint. **1867** *Chambers's Encycl.* IX. 488/2 The popular names Numb-fish, Cramp-fish, and Cramp Ray are given to torpedos by English fishermen.

numbhead (ˈnʌmhɛd). *U.S. colloq.* Also **numhead.** [f. NUMB *a.* + HEAD *sb.*¹, after NUMSKULL.] = NUMSKULL. So **ˈnumbheaded** *a.*

a **1852** F. M. WHITCHER *Widow Bedott Papers* (1856) x. 98 The old coot was so awful numbheaded I couldent beat anythin' into him. **1876** *Rep. Vermont Board Agric.* III. 624 The opinion too generally prevails that almost any numhead will do for a farm laborer. **1960** WENTWORTH & FLEXNER *Dict. Amer. Slang* 359/2 *Numb-head*, a stupid or dull person.

ˈnumbing, *vbl. sb.* [f. NUMB *v.* + -ING¹.] The action of making numb.

1598 SYLVESTER *Du Bartas* II. i. IV. *Handicrafts* 191 A flock of Muttons..(Whose freez-clad bodies feele not Winter's numming). **1875** WHITNEY *Life Lang.* xiv. 292 By the numbing of the single nerve of audition.

ˈnumbing, *ppl. a.* [f. NUMB *v.* + -ING².]

1. That numbs, or induces numbness. Also *fig.*

1634 MILTON *Comus* 853 She can unlock The clasping charm, and thaw the numming spell. **1699** GARTH *Dispens.* i. (1706) 6 The Poppy and each numming Plant dispense Their drowzy Virtue. **1716** POPE *Iliad* VII. 324 His slacken'd knees received the numbing stroke. **1774** GOLDSM. *Nat. Hist.* (1776) VI. 267 The numbing quality, which has acquired them the name of the torpedo. **1801** SOUTHEY *Thalaba* XII. xxi, Thalaba, with numbing force, Smites his raised arm, and rushes by. **1885** *Athenæum* 23 May 658/3 The numbing effect of sixth forms and university honours.

2. *numbing-fish* or *-eel*, = NUMB-FISH.

1748 *Anson's Voy.* II. xii. 362 We here.. met with that extraordinary fish called the Torpedo, or numbing fish. **1794** WOLCOT (P. Pindar) *Celebration* Wks. 1816 III. 8 Th' electric shock.. a man upon the black-brow'd rock Has oft experienc'd from the numbing eel.

Hence **ˈnumbingly** *adv.*

1768 *Woman of Honor* III. 108 Hardly possible to conceive any thing more.. numbingly stupid than their assembly-nights.

numbles (ˈnʌmb(ə)lz). Now only *arch.* Forms: α. 4 noubles (?), 4–6 **noumbles** (5 **-buls, nownbils**), 5 **nowm(b)elys**, 6 *Sc.* **nowmyllis.** β. 4, 6–7, 9 **numbles.** γ. 6–7 **noombles**, 5–6, 9 **nombles.** [a. OF. *numbles* (1239 in Du Cange), *nombles* pl. (Latinized as *numbli*, *numbuli*, and *numbilia*), loin of veal, fillet of beef or venison, chine of pork, app. for **lomble(s)* and repr. L. *lumbulus* (Pliny), dim. of *lumbus* loin. In Norman dial., *nombles* has the same sense as that usual in English. Variant forms are UMBLES and HUMBLE.] Certain of the inward parts of an animal (chiefly those of a deer) as used for food. Also, in early use, part of the back and loins of a hart.

α. *c* **1320** *Sir Tristr.* 491 Þe wombe oway he bare, þe noubles he ȝaf to mede. **13..** *Gaw. & Gr. Knt.* 1347 So ryde þay of by resoun bi þ e rygge bonez, Euenden to þe haunche, ..& hwen hit of þere, & þat þay neme for þe noumbles, bi nome as I trowe. *c* **1420** *Liber Cocorum* (1862) 10 Take þe noumbuls of þe veneson, In water and salt þo wasshe hom sone. *c* **1440** *Promp. Parv.* 360/1 Nowmelys of a beest (*K.* nowmbelys), *burbalia.* **1483** *Cath. Angl.* 256/2 Þe Nownbils of a dere,.. *pepinum.* **1508** *Burgh Rec. Edin.* (1869) I. 114 At thai sell nocht oppinly.. thair nolt heids, nowmyllis, nor interallis of thair flesche. **1530** PALSGR. 248/2 Noumbles of a dere or beest, *entrailles.*

β. **1333–4** *Durh. Acct. Rolls* 21 In.. iij paribus de Numbles. *c* **1500** *Wyl Bucke's Test.* (Halliw.) 60 Take the numbleis, and loke that they be clene. **1531** ELYOT *Gov.* III. vii. (1880) II. 253 His glorious harte, as it were numbles chopped in peaces. **1575** in Brand *Newcastle* (1789) II. 721 Of every purpose [= porpoise] to have the fynnes and the head and the numbles. **1613** PURCHAS *Pilgrimage* IV. vii. 371 Some, it is reported, lay a part of the Numbles on the fire. **1857** *Fraser's Mag.* LVI. 217 Commend us to a venison pudding, composed of the numbles and trimmings from the joints and breast.

attrib. **1822** T. L. PEACOCK *Maid Marian* 241 Robin helped him largely to numble-pie.. and the other dainties of his table.

γ. **14..** *Lat.-Eng. Voc.* in Wr.-Wülcker 569 *Burbilium*, nombles. *c* **1430** *Two Cookery-bks.* 10 Take þe Nombles of Venysoun, an cutte hem smal whyle þey ben raw. **1486** *Bk. St. Albans, Hawking* e vij b, The man to his mayster spekyth ..Off the nomblys of the hert that he wolde hym kith How mony endys ther shall be hem with inne. **1575** TURBERV. *Venerie* 129 You shall take the harts heart.. and rayse the Noombles from his fillets. **1688** HOLME *Armoury* II. 188/1 Noombles, or Umbles; the Hart or Bucks plucks, as Heart, Lights, Liver, with other appendices. **1820** SCOTT *Monast.* xvii, If you be so heavy, I will content me with the best.., and that's the haunch and the nombles.

ˈnumbly, *adv.* [f. NUMB *a.*] In a numb or torpid manner.

1895 'H. S. MERRIMAN' *Grey Lady* II. iv, Agatha was puzzling vaguely and numbly over the contradictions that come into human existence. **1897** CROCKETT *Lad's Love* xxiv, Her fingers fumbled numbly with the string.

numbness (ˈnʌmnɪs). Also 6 **nomme-**, 6–8 **num-**, 7 **numm-**. [f. NUMB *a.* + -NESS.] The state or condition of being numb. Also *fig.*

1571 GOLDING *Calvin on Ps.* lxxi. 15 If the innumerable multitude amend not both our nommenes and our coldnes. **1586** A. DAY *Eng. Secretary* I. (1625) 45 The man somewhat before his sicknesse grew into an extreame numnesse. **1643** MILTON *Divorce* I. ix. Wks. 1851 IV. 46 Disproportion, contrariety, or numnesse of mind may justly be divorc't. **1673** O. WALKER *Educ.* (1677) 71 A stagnation of humors, numnes of the joints, and dulnes in the brain. **1701** *Lond. Gaz.* No. 3714/4 Bruises, Strains, Numbness of any Part. **1753** *Scots Mag.* July 315/1 The nation sinks into the.. abyss of numbness, supineness, and indifference. **1820** KEATS *Ode to Nightingale* 1 My heart aches, and a drowsy numbness pains My sense. **1883** H. DRUMMOND *Nat. Law in Spir. W.* (ed. 2) 160 What is the creed of the Agnostic, but the confession of the spiritual numbness of humanity?

†**ˈnumbrable,** *a. Obs. rare.* In 4–5 **noumb-**. [a. OF. *nomb-, numbrable.*] = NUMBERABLE.

1382 WYCLIF *Ps.* xxi. 18 Thei dolue myn hondis and my feet; and ful noumbrable maden alle my bones. *c* **1400** tr. *Secreta Secret., Gov. Lordsh.* 104 No best, no thynge vegetable, no originale, no noumbrable,.. no non oþer þinge.

So **ˈnumbrableness.** *rare*⁻¹.

c **1705** BERKELEY in Fraser *Life* (1871) 427 The multitude of points, or feet, inches, &c., hinders not their numbrableness (i.e. hinders not their being numerable) in the least.

†**ˈnumbrary.** *Obs.* Also **noumb-, nomb-.** [Prob. ad. late L. *numerāria, -ārium*, fem. and neut. of *numerārius* NUMERARY.] Number; numeration, reckoning.

13.. *Cursor M.* 423 (Gött.), Þis numbrari [*Trin.* noumbrary] he ordeined þan, Suld be bath of angel and man. **1382** WYCLIF *Pref. Ep. Jerome* vii, Numeri forsothe, whether thei conteynen not the mysteries of al the hole craft of noumbrarie. *c* **1430** LYDG. *Min. Poems* (Percy Soc.) 11 And Arsmetryk, be castyng of nombrary, Chees Pyktegoras for her parte. **1430–40** —— *Bochas* II. xxv. (1554) 61 The numbrary Of thy reigning and of thy great substaunce.

†**ˈnumbrer.** *Obs. rare*⁻¹. In 4 **noumbrere.** [a. OF. *nombrere*, f. *nombrer.*] = NUMBERER.

1382 WYCLIF *Jer.* xxxiii. 13 Ȝit shul passe flockes, at the hond of the noumbrere, seith the Lord.

†**ˈnumbrous,** *a. Obs.* [f. NUMBER *sb.* + -OUS: cf. F. *nombreux* (1564) and NUMBEROUS.]

1. = NUMEROUS *a.*

a **1586** SIDNEY *Ps.* III. i, How many ones there be That all against poor me Their numbrous strength redouble? **1607** S. COLLINS *Serm.* (1608) 40 They need not, because so obuious; and they could not, because so numbrous. **1628** SIR W. MURE *Domesday* 869 Wks. (S.T.S.) I. 190 What Joyes (to view this numbrous host).

2. Exhibiting poetic numbers; rhythmical.

1581 SIDNEY *Apol. Poetrie* (Arb.) 28 The greatest part of Poets have apparelled their poeticall inuentions in that numbrous kinde of writing which is called verse. *c* **1615** SIR W. ALEXANDER in Drumm. of Hawth. *Wks.* (1711) 150 He numbrous Notes with measur'd Fury frames, Each Accent weigh'd, no Jarr in Sense, or Sound.

numbry, variant of NUMBERY *a. Obs.*

numbskull, obs. form of NUMSKULL.

'numby, *a. rare.* In 7–8 nummie, -y. [f. NUMB *a.* + -Y.] Numbed; somewhat numb.
1603 FLORIO *Montaigne* II. xvii. (1632) 363 My hands are so stiffe and nummie, that I can hardly write for my selfe. *a***1780** POTT *Chirurg. Wks.* (1790) III. 430 His legs and thighs were cold, and what he called nummy.

†**numcorn,** app. for *mun-*, MONGCORN.
1570 LEVINS *Manip.* 172 Numcorne, *trimestre hordeum.*

‖**numdah** ('nʌmdə). *Anglo-Ind.* [a. Urdū *namdā*, f. Pers. *namad* carpet, rug.] A kind of felt or coarse woollen cloth; a saddle-cloth or pad made of this. (See also NUMNAH.)
1876 VOYLE & STEVENSON *Milit. Dict.* 272/2. **1879** E. ARNOLD *Lt. Asia* IV. 105 On the steed he laid the numdah square, Fitted the saddle-cloth across, and set the saddle fair. **1903** *Blackw. Mag.* Sept. 374/2 The costume is completed by long riding boots of red and white numdah.

nume, obs. pa. t. of NIM *v.*

numelarien: see NUMMULARIAN.

numen ('nju:mən). [a. L. *nūmen* divine will, divinity, related to *nuĕre* to nod (assent).] Deity, divinity; divine or presiding power or spirit.
1628 FELTHAM *Resolves* II. xvi. 50 As if allowing them the name, they would conserue the Numen to themselues. **1634** SIR T. HERBERT *Trav.* 193 That what they first meet..they make their Numen and tutelary God for that day. **1662** H. MORE *Philos. Writ.* Pref. Gen. (1712) 9 For it is the same Numen in us that moves all things in some sort or other. **1711** SHAFTESB. *Charac.* (1737) III. Misc. II. ii. 65 They madly dote upon Matter, and devoutly worship it, as the only Numen. **1788** *Antiq.* in *Ann. Reg.* 120/2 Any local one whose numen and worship..was already established as local. **1874** J. FERGUSSON in *Contemp. Rev.* Oct. 765 In a cathedral town where all unite..in..adoring the sacred and historical numen of the place.

numen, obs. pa. pple. of NIM *v.*

numerable ('nju:mərəb(ə)l), *a.* [ad. L. *numerābilis*, f. *numerāre* to number. So It. *numerabile*, Sp. *-able*, Pg. *-avel.*]
1. Capable of being numbered.
1570 J. DEE *Math. Pref.* *j, The Glas of Creation, the Forme of Formes, the Exemplar Number of all thinges Numerable. **1629** J. COLE *Of Death* 107 That hee must dye, and that his dayes were numerable, nature taught him. **1665** SIR T. HERBERT *Trav.* (1677) 58 So numerous in Islands as they are scarce numerable. **1710** BERKELEY *Princ. Hum. Knowl.* §122 Particular numerable things. **1829** JAS. MILL *Hum. Mind* (1869) II. 137 Aristotle defines Time as.. Continuous Motion, considered as numerable and successive. **1865** GROTE *Plato* I. i. 10 By this..he did not mean simply that all things were numerable.
†**2.** Numerous. *Obs. rare*$^{-1}$.
1596 DALRYMPLE tr. *Leslie's Hist. Scot.* I. 14 A certane toune copious in citizenis and verie numerable.
Hence **numera'bility,** the quality of being numerable; **numerableness,** 'capableness of being numbred' (Bailey, vol. II, 1727).
1943 [see ABSTRACTABLE *a.*].

numeracy ('nju:mərəsi). [f. NUMERATE *a.*, after *literacy.*] The quality or state of being numerate; ability with or knowledge of numbers.
1959 *15 to 18: Rep. Cent. Advisory Council for Educ. (Eng.)* (Ministry of Educ.) I. xxv. 270 When we say that a scientist is 'illiterate', we mean that he is not well enough read to be able to communicate effectively with those who have had a literary education. When we say that a historian or a linguist is 'innumerate' we mean that he cannot even begin to understand what scientists and mathematicians are talking about... It is perhaps possible to distinguish two different aspects of numeracy that should concern the Sixth Former. **1960** *English* XIII. 44 A certain lack of 'numeracy' on the part of those trained in the Arts can make them a little purblind to the implications of figures such as these. **1960** *Rep. Proc. Conf. Univ. U.K.* 23 If scientific barbarians are to be given a veneer of literacy, and literary barbarians a veneer of numeracy, I suggest the proper apparatus for it is a lot of deep armchairs in an open access library. **1966** *Economist* 22 Jan. 310/2 The need for numeracy today is enormous. Business requires..people who..have grasped the principles of reducing a chaos of information to some kind of order. **1970** *Sci. Jrnl.* Feb. 73/2 The scientist does, however, possess the advantage of numeracy and can usually acquire quite easily the statistical and theoretical background to modern management techniques. **1972** *Daily Tel.* 22 Jan. 2/5 The plan must be welcomed for introducing pre-school children to reading, writing and numeracy.

numeraire ('nju:mərɛə(r)). *Econ.* Also **numéraire.** [ad. F. *numéraire.*] The function of money as a measure of value or unit of account; a standard for currency exchange rates.
1964 GOULD & KOLB *Dict. Soc. Sci.* 532/2 In a primitive society two knives might exchange for one calf. Often one good is singled out to serve as a *numeraire* or common measure for other goods, thus precious metals serve both as a good wanted for particular purposes and as a unit of value and exchange. **1965** J. L. HANSON *Dict. Econ. & Commerce* 302/1 *Numeraire*, a term sometimes used of the function of money as a measure of value. **1971** *New Yorker* 23 Oct. 118 The Bretton Woods agreement..established the dollar as the *numéraire*, or measuring rod, against which the value of other currencies was set. **1972** *National Westminster Bank Quarterly Rev.* May 21 Three points constitute the core of the Barber proposals [at the last IMF meetings]: a) That SDRs 'become the numeraire in terms of which parities are expressed and in relation to which currencies are revalued or devalued'. **1972** *Times* 27 Sept. 21/2 The use of Special Drawing Rights rather than the dollar as the effective numeraire in the new system is widely acceptable. **1973** *Times* 26 Jan. 17/6 It is the European currencies which have been adjusted against the dollar—the numeraire in the exchange system.

numeral ('nju:mərəl), *a.* and *sb.* [ad. late L. *numerālis* (Priscian), f. *numerus* number. So F. *numéral* (1474), Sp. and Pg. *numeral*, It. *-ale.*]
A. *adj.* **1.** Expressing or denoting number.
a. Of words, or parts of speech.
1530 PALSGR. 73 Adjectyves somtyme be formed..of theyr nownes numeralles. **1651** HOBBES *Gov. & Soc.* xviii. §4. 346 By calling to minde the order of those numerall words. **1824** L. MURRAY *Eng. Gram.* (ed. 5) I. 342 *One* is a numeral adjective, agreeing with its substantive 'remove'.
b. Of letters, figures, or other characters.
1577 T. KENDALL *Flowers of Epigr., Trifles* 17 b, A verse wherein the numerall letters shewe the yere of the Lorde. **1594** BLUNDEVIL *Exerc.* III. I. liv. (1636) 372 The houres of the night written..in common numerall letters. **1636** *Camden's Rem.* 355 Hee which set downe the nine numerall figures. **1690** LEYBOURN *Curs. Math.* 334 The Digits on the Left Side in Numeral Letters shew the several Roots. **1727–38** CHAMBERS *Cycl.* s.v. *Character*, Numeral characters are either letters; or figures, otherwise called digits. **1840** *Penny Cycl.* XVI. 366/2 Distinct numeral characters are found to have existed..among the Chinese, Indians, and Arabs.
2. Belonging or appertaining to number.
1607 *Schol. Disc. agst. Antichr.* I. i. 29 The first difference (forsooth) in our new Crosse is Numerall... It is not the same in number. **1646** SIR T. BROWNE *Pseud. Ep.* 377 Surely the conceit is numerall, and..relateth unto the number of ten. **1685** H. MORE *Illustr.* 293 Those letters, in their numeral value, make just 666. **1704** J. HARRIS *Lex. Techn.* I, *Numeral Algebra*, is that which makes use of Numbers instead of Letters of the Alphabet.
†**3.** Measured, rhythmic. *Obs. rare*$^{-1}$.
1610 HEALEY *St. Aug. Citie of God* (1620) 51 In the feasts of Cybele was much of this numerall musicke.
B. *sb.* **1.** A word expressing a number.
1530 PALSGR. 367 Annotacyons to knowe all maner sortes of numeralles in the Frenche tonge. **1591** PERCIVALL *Sp. Dict.* B iij, Of Primitiues the numerals are especially worth the noting. **1678** PHILLIPS s.v., Cardinal numerals, are those which express the number of things. **1872** MORRIS *Eng. Accid.* 110 Numbers may be considered under their divisions—Cardinal, Ordinal, and Indefinite Numerals.
2. A figure or character (or a group of these) denoting a number.
1686 R. H. *Obs. conc. Chinese Charac.* in *Misc. Curiosa* (1708) III. 219 Marks methodically disposed like Letters in a literal, or like Numbers in a Numeral. **1741** *Wilford's Mem. & Charac.* App. 43 The Figures direct to the Pages of the Book. The Numerals to those of the Appendix. **1758** *Gentl. Mag.* XXVIII. 56 The Roman numerals..are yet retained in use in some cases. **1842** DICKENS *Amer. Notes* (1850) 34/1 These boys are divided into four classes, each denoted by a numeral, worn on a badge upon the arm. **1884** *Encycl. Brit.* XVII. 625/2 The letters of the alphabet themselves came to be used as numerals.
transf. **1874** WHYTE-MELVILLE *Uncle John* xxi, It is hardly possible..to conceive how a man loses his own identity [in prison] when he becomes a numeral.
3. *Eccl.* (See quot.)
1853 ROCK *Ch. of Fathers* III. II. ii. 19 The 'numeral' was a calendar or directory which told the variations in the canonical hours and in the mass, caused by saints'-days and festivals.

†**nume'rality.** *Obs. rare.* [f. prec. + -ITY.] The quality of being numerical.
1646 SIR T. BROWNE *Pseud. Ep.* IV. xii. 214 Yet are they not appliable vnto precise numerality, nor strictly to be drawne vnto the rigid test of numbers. *a***1687** H. MORE *Answ. Psychopyrist* (1689) 134 There being Metaphysical Extension as well as Metaphysical Numerality.

†**'numerally,** *adv. Obs. rare.* [f. as prec. + -LY^2.] Numerically.
1646 SIR T. BROWNE *Pseud. Ep.* 377 Yet doe the blasts.. maintaine no certainty in their course: nor are they numerally feared by Navigators. **1691** BAXTER *Nat. Ch.* viii. 30 And no doubt but they may and must be divided Numerally and Notionally.

†**'numerant.** *Obs. rare*$^{-1}$. [ad. pres. pple. of L. *numerāre.*] One who numbers.
1655–60 T. STANLEY *Hist. Phil.* (1701) 249/2 Time being a numerate number, exists not without a numerant, which is the Soul.

numerary ('nju:mərərı), *a.* [ad. med.L. *numerārius* (in class. L. as sb.), f. *numerus* number: see -ARY. So It., Sp., and Pg. *numerario*, F. *numéraire* (1752).]
1. *Eccl.* Of a canon: Forming one of the regular number. (After med.L. *numerarius canonicus.*)
1726 AYLIFFE *Parergon* 139 A supernumerary Canon when he obtains a Prebend, ceases to be a supernumerary, and becomes a numerary Canon.
2. Of or pertaining to a number or numbers.
1742 HUME *Ess., Money* (1817) I. 285 It was always found, that the augmenting of the numerary value did not produce a proportional rise of the prices. **1788** PRIESTLEY *Lect. Hist.* III. xvi. 140 The numerary pound in the time of Charlemagne was twelve ounces of silver. **1818** R. P. KNIGHT *Inq. Symbolical Lang.* 9 In Greece and Macedonia ..the numerary division seems to have regulated the scale of coinage. **1867** SMYTH *Sailor's Word-bk.* 502 *Numerary* or *Marryat's Signals*, a useful code used by the mercantile marine, by an arrangement of flags from a cypher to units, and thence to thousands.

'numerate ('nju:mərət), *pa. pple.* and *ppl. a.* [ad. L. *numerāt-us*, pa. pple. of *numerāre* to number.] †**a.** Numbered; counted. *Obs.*
1432–50 tr. *Higden* (Rolls) III. 115 In the tyme of whom [807,000] citesynnes..were numerate in the cite of Rome. *a***1560** ROLLAND *Crt. Venus* IV. 226 Ten Mulȝeoun Of fine reid gold in hand weill numerait. **1580** *Exch. Rolls Scotl.* XXI. 545 In numerat money..the sowme of tua hundreth fourscoir aucht pundis. **1623** *Disposition Ratified* in Macfarlane *Genealog. Collect.* (1900) 114 The saids Earles paying in numerate Money..the Sum [etc.]. **1655–60** T. STANLEY *Hist. Phil.* (1701) 523/2 If the Monads are equal in number to all numerate things.
b. As *adj.* [f. L. *numerus* number + -ATE^2, after *literate.*] Acquainted with the basic principles of mathematics and science.
1959 *15 to 18: Rep. Cent. Advisory Council for Educ. (Eng.)* (Ministry of Educ.) I. xxv. 269 Little is done to make science specialists more 'literate' than they were when they left the Fifth Form and nothing to make arts specialists more 'numerate', if we may coin a word to represent the mirror image of literacy. **1960** [see ART *sb.* 7]. **1966** A. BATTERSBY *Math. in Management* i. 21 The aim of a good Sixth Form should be to send out into the world men and women who are both literate and numerate. **1967** *Times Rev. Industry* Mar. 103/2 (Advt.), Lecturer..in Management Science... Applicants should have a good honours degree..in a 'numerate' subject (e.g., engineering, mathematics, mathematical economics, physics, statistics). **1967** C. BERNERS-LEE in Wills & Yearsley *Handbk. Management Technol.* 1 It has become a commonplace of the day that we must all be numerate as well as literate. *Ibid.* 8 The ability to communicate easily with a computer is one which is greatly prized by all numerate professionals in the larger commercial and industrial organizations and in the universities. **1971** *Country Life* 20 May 1264/2 It has been my impression..that..children are much less literate and numerate than ever before.

'numerate, *v. rare.* [f. ppl. stem of L. *numerāre*: see prec.] *trans.* To number, reckon. Also *absol.* Hence **'numerated** *ppl. a.*
1721 in BAILEY. **1751** *Gentl. Mag.* XXI. 61/2 In this manner he numerates his long series of numbers. **1788** T. TAYLOR *Proclus* I. 15 (Disser.), So far as by a discursive operation of the soul, we numerate, we effect a particular quantum. **1862** LEWIS *Astron. Ancients* 240 The simple mode of numerating them in one series from the beginning to the end of the month. **1866** J. B. ROSE tr. *Ovid's Met.* 4 No brazen tables then affrighted swains With numerated penalties and pains.

numeration (nju:mə'reɪʃən). Also 5 **numeracion,** 6 **noumeracioun.** [ad. L. *numerātiōn-em*, n. of action f. *numerāre* to number. So F. *numération* (1484), Sp. *numeracion*, It. *-azione.*]
1. a. A method or process of numbering, reckoning, or computing.
1432–50 tr. *Higden* (Rolls) IV. 271 Men of the londe of Grece, that founde..a numeracion of yeres callede Olimpias. **1653** JER. TAYLOR *Serm. for Year* I. xi. 144 Every day of sorrow is a thousand years of comfort, multiplied with a never ceasing numeration. *a***1695** J. SCOTT *Chr. Life* (1747) III. 663 The intellectual Numerations do eternally testify the Trinity of the King. **1727–38** CHAMBERS *Cycl.* s.v., It being the law of the common numeration, that when you are arrived at ten, you begin again. **1837** WHEWELL *Hist. Induct. Sci.* (1857) I. 35 If..time is a numeration of motion.
b. Without article: Calculation; assignation of number to things.
1596 NASHE *Saffron Walden* Wks. III. 178 Lying by Addition and Numeration, making frayes..by Diuision. **1646** SIR T. BROWNE *Pseud. Ep.* VI. iii. 285 That starre is the terme of numeration, or point from whence we commence the account. **1648** T. BEAUMONT *Psyche* VII. xciii, In Seed Which past the shores of Numeration flows. **1690** LOCKE *Hum. Und.* II. xvi. §5 All Numeration being but still the adding of one Unit more, and giving to the whole..a new or distinct Name or Sign. **1831** CARLYLE *Sartor Res.* I. x, That progress of Science, which is to destroy Wonder, and in its stead substitute Mensuration and Numeration. **1867** G. MUSGRAVE *Nooks & Corners Old France* I. i. 34 The system of decimal numeration..facilitates this head-work.
2. The action, process, or result of ascertaining the number *of* people, etc.
1533 BELLENDEN *Livy* III. viii. (S.T.S.) I. 278 Þe nowmeration of pepill..was endit in þis ȝere. *a***1676** HALE *Prim. Orig. Man.* (1677) 231, I do not remember any Numeration of the People from this time till the time of King David. **1733** BERKELEY in Fraser *Life* (1871) vi. 207, I long for the numeration of Protestant and Popish families, which you tell me has been taken by the collectors. **1795** BURKE *Corr.* (1844) IV. 322 To make an exact numeration of the inhabitants of Ireland, distinguishing their religion. **1902** *Bible Student* Oct. 216 The twofold numeration of the people.
3. *Arith.* (See quots.)
1542 RECORDE *Gr. Artes* (1575) 42 Numeration, is that Arithmeticall skill, whereby we may..value, expresse and reade any Number or summe propounded. **1594** BLUNDEVIL *Exerc.* I. i. (1636) 1 What belongeth to Numeration? Two things, to know the shapes of the figures, and signification of their places. **1679** MOXON *Math. Dict.* 107 *Numeration*, the first of the five Vulgar Rules of Arithmetick, teaching to read truly any Sum or Number. **1798** HUTTON *Course Math.* (1806) I. 8 Numeration is the reading of any number in words that is proposed or set down in figures. **1859** B. SMITH *Arith. & Alg.* (ed. 6) 3 Numeration is the converse of Notation, being the art of expressing any number in words which is already given in figures.
b. *numeration table*, a table showing the value of figures according to their place in a system of notation.
1800 MAR. EDGEWORTH *Belinda* xx, His thousands and tens of thousands..pass the comprehension of the

numeration table. **1854** *Orr's Circ. Sci., Math. Sci.* 5 When the local values of these figures are written against them, it supplies what is..called the numeration table.

†**4.** Number. *Obs. rare.*

1646 Sir T. Browne *Pseud. Ep.* iii. v. 115 If we survey the totall set of animals, we may in their legs..observe an equality of length, and parity of numeration. **1674** Jeake *Arith.* (1696) 172 When Division is said to make a Sum less in numeration..: It is to be understood of Integers.

5. Enumeration *of* things. *rare*$^{-1}$.

1801 Strutt *Sports & Past.* iii. ii. 145 The numeration of the dresses appropriated to one of these plays.

'numerative, *a.* and *sb.* [f. numerate *v.*]

A. *adj.* Pertaining to numeration or numbering.

1788 T. Taylor *Proclus* I. 17 (Disser.), The numerative soul..gives form and subsistence to all her inherent numbers. **1840** *Penny Cycl.* XVI. 368/1 Our present numerative system is stated by writers to employ the words unit, ten, hundred [etc.]. **1889** R. K. Douglas *Chinese Man.* 40 The indefinite article is, when necessary, expressed by the first numeral.., with, in the case of persons or things, a numerative noun interposed between it and the substantive.

B. *sb. Gram.* (See quots.)

1863 Summers *Hdbk. Chinese* 47 Under the appositional relation we must also consider the very large class of nouns formed by the use of what have been called numeratives or classifiers... The Chinese, in conversation, extend the use of such words to every object; they say..'one handle fan' for *a fan*, 'one length road' for *a road*. **1889** R. K. Douglas *Chinese Man.* 64 These numeratives correspond to a certain extent to the use of such words as 'head', 'sail'.

numerator ('nju:məreɪtə(r)). [ad. late L. *numerātor*, agent-n. f. *numerāre* to number. So F. *numérateur* (1515), It. *numeratore*, Sp. *-ador.*]

1. *Arith.* †**a.** The word(s) or figure(s) by which the number of things or persons in question is denoted. *Obs.*

1542 Recorde *Gr. Artes* C j b, *Scholar.* What shall I call .CCiii. ioined before the myllions? *Master.* That is called the numeratour or valewer. **1674** Jeake *Arith.* (1696) 15 Thirty Men, here Men is the Contract Denominator, and Thirty the Numerator, or Valuer.

b. The number written above the line in a vulgar fraction, which shows how many of the specified parts of a unit are taken.

1575 *Recorde's Gr. Artes* ii. X ij b, Those two numbers whiche expresse a fraction, haue seuerall names. The ouermost which is aboue the line, is called the Numerator. **1594** Blundevil *Exerc.* i. vii. (1636) 20 Of how many parts doth a Fraction consist? Of two, that is the Numerator, and the Denominator. **1655** Bramhall *Agst. Hobbes* iii. Wks. 1844 IV. 385 Their rules of algebra and helcataim, their integers, and numerators. **1674** Jeake *Arith.* (1696) 41 As in 3/5 the Numerator is 3. **1706** W. Jones *Syn. Palmar. Matheseos* 84 To multiply the Numerator is to multiply the Fraction. **1797** *Encycl. Brit.* (ed. 3) II. 297/2 The division is completed by a vulgar fraction, whose numerator is the remainder. **1838** De Morgan *Ess. Probab.* 40 The process for finding the greatest common measure of the numerator and denominator. **1864** Bowen *Logic* xii. 406 The resulting fractions fall into a series, any one of which has for its numerator the sum of the two preceding numerators.

fig. **1763** tr. *Rousseau's Emilius* I. 7 Civilized man is only a relative unit, the numerator of a fraction, that depends on its denominator. **1831, 1893** [see denominator].

2. One who or that which numbers.

1675 G. R. tr. *Le Grand's Man without Passion* 202 It becomes the numerator of expected Treasures, but cares not to cast up what it hath in possession. **1739** Tonkin *Carew's Cornwall* (1811) 45 *note*, There is..a Numerator, whose business it is to set down the number of blocks coined every coinage. **1902** *Bible Student* Oct. 216 Here numerators are set apart to superintend the numeration in the different tribes.

numeric (nju:'mɛrɪk), *a.* and *sb.* [ad. mod.L. *numeric-us*, f. *numerus* number. So F. *numérique* (1697), It., Sp., and Pg. *numerico.*]

†**A.** *adj.* **1.** Identical. *Obs.*

1663 Butler *Hud.* i. iii. 461 This is the same numerick Crew Which we so lately did subdue. **1727** Swift *To Delany* Wks. 1751 VII. 236 Shew me the same numerick Flea, That bit your Neck but yesterday.

2. = numerical *a.* (and *sb.*) 1, esp. 1 e.

1949 E. C. Berkeley *Giant Brains* iv. 54 It will be reasonable to use numeric codes 0 to 9 in each column.. because..numeric codes can be sorted faster than alphabetic codes. **1955** [see alpha-numeric *a.*]. **1967** D. Wilson in Wills & Yearsley *Handbk. Management Technol.* 45 In addition to the usual numeric and alphabetic characters, a range of special characters can normally be included. **1972** *Computer Jrnl.* XV. 209/1 A monotonically increasing numeric value is associated with each partition or level of the tree. **1973** *Sci. Amer.* June 65/2 Instruments that make rapid, high-precision measurements demand numeric readouts, since analogue presentations cannot display the results in any simple way.

B. *sb.* (See quot. 1879.)

1879 Thomson & Tait *Nat. Phil.* I. i. §345 The term numeric has been recently introduced by Professor James Thomson to denote a number, or a proper fraction, or an improper fraction, or an incommensurable ratio. **1888** *Jrnl. Educ.* Dec. 573/2 When two numerics multiplied together give unity.., each is said to be the 'reciprocal' of the other.

numerical (nju:'mɛrɪkəl), *a.* (and *sb.*) [f. as prec. + -al^{1}.]

1. a. Pertaining or relating to number; of the nature of, according to, number; etc.

1628 Spencer *Logick* 112 Vnequals..cannot be one in numericall quantitie. **1656** Blount *Glossogr.* s.v. *Numerical*, As when we say a numerical difference, that is to say, the last difference, by which one individual thing is distinguished from one another. **1700** Gregory in *Collect.* (O.H.S.) I. 323 He supposeth one is pretty well acquainted with the numerical arithmetick. **1712** *Lond. Gaz.* No. 4952/4 An exact Table of the..Tickets in a Numerical Order..will be publish'd. **1782** Priestley *Corrupt. Chr.* I. i. 127 Joachim.. denied that.. nothing but a numerical or moral union was left. **1837** Whewell *Hist. Induct. Sci.* (1857) I. 47 He confounded..a numerical unit with a geometrical point. **1867** Dk. Argyll *Reign of Law* ii. (ed. 4) 73 All that we ever know is some numerical rule or measure according to which some unknown forces operate. **1881** Lubbock in *Nature* XXIV. 410/2 He obtained a numerical value of the mechanical equivalent of heat.

b. Of figures, etc.: Denoting a number.

1706 A. Bedford *Temple Mus.* vii. 153 The Numbers.. might have been writ in Numerical Letters. **1800** *Naval Chron.* III. 295 Jackson hoisted the horary and numerical signal. **1816** Bentham *Chrestom.* 184 A quantity, for the designation of which no more than one numerical figure..is employed. **1863** Max Müller *Chips* (1880) II. xxvi. 289 The Brahmans were the original inventors of those numerical symbols.

c. In respect of numbers.

1812 *Examiner* 24 Aug. 539/2 He would..state the numerical force of his own and the enemy's army. **1849** Grote *Greece* ii. l. (1862) IV. 379 Nikostratus..was not afraid of this numerical superiority. **1881** Westcott & Hort *Grk. N.T.* Introd. §53 The numerical authority of the two supposed witnesses against the third.

d. Of playing-cards: Bearing a certain number of distinguishing marks or 'pips'.

1816 Singer *Hist. Cards* 45 The numerical cards in each suit appear to have been ten in number.

e. Characterized by the use of ordinary figures expressive of number.

1840 *Penny Cycl.* XVI. 369/1 Numerical, as opposed to literal, in algebra, applies to an expression in which the coefficients of a letter are all numbers, and not letters. **1881** Burnside & Panton *The. Equations* (1886) 2 An equation is numerical or algebraical according as its coefficients are numbers or algebraical symbols.

f. Designated by a number instead of a name.

1872 Howells *Wedd. Journ.* (1892) 29 They turned into one of the numerical streets to cross to Broadway.

g. Special collocations: ***numerical analysis***: the branch of mathematics that deals with the development and use of numerical methods for solving problems (usu. ones too complicated for analytic methods); so ***numerical analyst***; ***numerical aperture***: a measure of the resolving power of a microscope objective (for a given wavelength), equal to the product of the refractive index of the medium in front of it and the sine of the semi-angle of the cone it subtends at the centre of the object; ***numerical control***: the use of numerical data stored on tape or punched cards to control automatically the movement and operations of machine tools and work-pieces.

[**1930** J. B. Scarborough (*title*) Numerical mathematical analysis.] **1946** *Ann. Computation Lab. Harvard Univ.* I. 338 (*heading*) Bibliography of numerical analysis. **1947** *Sci. News Let.* 27 Sept. 201/2 The National Bureau of Standards' new Institute of Numerical Analysis will feature high-speed electronic calculators. **1952** D. R. Hartree *Numerical Anal.* i. 2 The methods of numerical analysis.. have that degree of generality which entitles them to be considered part of mathematics. **1974** *Encycl. Brit. Macropædia* XIII. 390/1 The numerical solution of ordinary differential equations is one of the most important branches of numerical analysis because many physical problems lead to ordinary differential equations that cannot be solved analytically. **1956** F. B. Hildebrand *Introd. Numerical Anal.* i. 1 Generally the numerical analyst does not strive for exactness. **1878** *Jrnl. R. Microsc. Soc.* I. 19 The inner scale shows the air-angle, the outer scale the 'numerical aperture'. *Ibid.* 21 This quantity *a*, which Professor Abbe calls 'numerical aperture', gives an absolute definition of aperture..by which lenses of every kind are directly comparable. **1952** R. W. Ditchburn *Light* viii. 253 With a dry lens, the maximum value of the numerical aperture is 1·0, and values up to 0·95 have been obtained. Oil-immersion objectives with numerical apertures up to 1·65 have been constructed. *Ibid.*, Higher magnifications have been obtained using electron microscopes... The effective wave-length may be of the order of 0·1 Å., but the numerical aperture of models so far available is very low, being only of the order of 0·01. **1969** S. G. & H. Lipson *Optical Physics* ix. 278 The limit of resolution of the microscope..is equal to λ/numerical aperture. **1952** *Final Rep. Construction & Operation of Numerically Controlled Milling Machine* (Mass. Inst. Technol. Servomechanisms Lab.) 30 July 1 (AD 22241). Summary 1 A new technique of automatic machine-tool control..promises to simplify some of the manufacturing problems of medium and small run production often encountered in the aircraft industry. Called numerical control, this technique has been applied by M.I.T...to a milling machine controlled by a numerical code punched on paper tape. **1955** *IRE Trans. Industr. Electronics* II. 3 (*heading*) Numerical control of machine tools. *Ibid.* 5/1 The numerical control for this turret punch press uses the Remington-Rand 45 column tabulating card. **1966** *Economist* 2 July 56/1 What the two companies are claiming is that..numerical control is now suitable for mass production. *Ibid.* 57/1 There are 25 British companies producing machine tools for numerical control. **1971** H. C. Town *Design & Construction Machine Tools* vii. 159 With numerical control the instructions for the various phases of a cycle are transmitted by punched or magnetic tape inserted in a reader unit.

2. †**a.** Particular, individual. *Obs. rare.*

1643 Sir T. Browne *Relig. Med.* i. §33, I beleeve..that they [spirits] have knowledge not only of the specificall, but numericall formes of individuals. **1674** Hickman *Quinquart. Hist.* Ep. (ed. 2) A 3 b, I cannot comprehend.. how three Persons subsist in one numerical nature. **1699** Bentley *Phal.* 419 Every such Couple were the Numerical Halves, that made up one compleat Person in the former State.

†**b.** With *this* or *that* (passing into next). *Obs.*

1644 Bulwer *Chiron.* 89 Many of these Numericall postures of the Fingers are found in the statues of the Ancients. **1660** Boyle *New Exp. Phys. Mech.* xxix. 222 Though it be now divers years since this Numerical Liquor was prepared. **1702** Steele *Funeral* i. (1734) 25 Am I really Alive? Am I that Identical, that Numerical, that very same Lord Brumpton? **1720-21** *Lett. fr. Mist's Jrnl.* (1722) II. 248, I would gladly be informed if..Mr. William Tong..be that numerical Will Tong, who formerly kept a canting School in this City.

†**3. a.** With *same*: Individual, identical. *Obs.*

In common use from 1650 to 1700: see also numeric *a.*

1624 Burton *Anat. Mel.* i. iii. i. ii. (ed. 2) 165 As in a Riuer we swimme in the same place, though not in the same numericall water. **1662** Hibbert *Body Divinity* ii. 62 It was the very same numerical body which he had before. **1710** Norris *Chr. Prud.* vii. 305 The same Numerical Act cannot be well conceiv'd to govern itself.

†**b.** Similarly with *very*. *Obs.*

1650 Fuller *Pisgah* v. xix. 179 The Law of the Jews; probably that very numericall book..kept in the Temple. **1673** Dryden *Marr. à la Mode* ii. i, I may tell you,..this is that very numerical Lady, with whom I am in love. **1699** Bentley *Phal.* 213 The Writer of the Epistle has the very numerical words of Euripides. **1716** M. Davies *Athen. Brit.* II. 175 All the several Manuscripts of the Policraticon..are the very Numerical Book describ'd by Bale and Pitts.

†**4.** Metrical, rhythmical. *Obs. rare*$^{-1}$.

1749 *Power Numbers in Poet. Compositions* 4 What I intend then is a particular Examination of the numerical Structure both in Verse and Prose.

†**5.** *sb.* A number. *Obs. rare*$^{-1}$.

1766 Holwell *Princ. Anc. Bramins* vi. (1779) 121 The cause of the superstitious veneration paid by the Gentoos to the numericals one and three.

nu'merically, *adv.* [f. prec. + -ly^{2}.]

1. As regards number; with respect to number.

1628 T. Spencer *Logick* 66 Both of them are one numerically, because each of them haue a bodie, flesh, and bones. **1691** Baxter *Nat. Ch.* viii. 30 When the Subjects are various and really divided Numerically, there the Accidents are divers and divided. **1748** Hartley *Observ. Man* ii. i. §5. 30 We suppose other Beings generically the same and yet numerically different. **1794** G. Adams *Nat. & Exp. Philos.* III. xxv. 76 Something that is numerically one and undivided. **1850** 'Bat' *Cricket. Man.* 86 Numerically speaking, these rivals are upon a par. **1881** *19th Cent.* IX. 564 The community has never increased numerically except within itself.

†**b.** Used with *same* (or *one*) to emphasize the idea of identity. (Cf. prec. 3.) *Obs.*

1648 Jenkyn *Blind Guide* 58 May not the same thing numerically be the subject of accidents specifically different? **1678** Cudworth *Intell. Syst.* 46 According to this Hypothesis, the Souls of Animals could not be numerically the same throughout the whole space of their lives. **1710** [Bedford] *Vindic. Ch. Eng.* 64 If both those Subscriptions were made to numerically the same Articles. **1714** R. Fiddes *Pract. Disc.* ii. 79 The attributes of God..are numerically and entirely one with his essence.

2. By means of numbers.

1728 Earbery tr. *Burnet's St. Dead* II. 42 If it measures or divides space numerically, it cannot be a Spirit. **1774** *Phil. Trans.* LXIV. 386 These Indians cannot reckon numerically beyond six. **1802** *Ibid.* XCII. 96 Which value of π may be numerically computed. **1859** Darwin *Orig. Species* ii. (1873) 46, I have endeavoured to test this numerically by averages.

nu'mericalness. *rare*$^{-0}$. 'Individualness' (Bailey, vol. II, 1727).

†**numeri'cation.** *Obs. rare.* [f. numeric *a.* + -ation.] The action of making individual.

1694 R. Burthogge *Reason* 167 Since all Individuation.. is Numerication, and all Numeration arises from Division.

'numerist. *rare.* [f. L. *numer-us* number + -ist. Cf. Sp. *numerista.*] One who attaches importance to, or concerns himself with, numbers.

1646 Sir T. Browne *Pseud. Ep.* 217 We..should rather assigne a respective fatality unto each: which is concordant unto the doctrine of the numerists. **1658** —— *Garden Cyrus* Wks. (Bohn) II. 557 Which ancient Numerists made out by two and three, the first parity and imparity. **1827** Pollok *Course T.* ii. (1828) 55 The numerist, in calculations deep Grew gray.

†**'numero,** *sb.*^{1} *Obs.* [L., abl. sing. of *numerus* number. So It., Sp., and Pg. *numero*, F. *numéro.*]

1. A copy of a book.

1604 *Petit. Apol. Lay Cathol. to Jas. I* 17 The very originall Bible, the selfe same *numero* which S. Gregory sent in with our Apostle S. Augustine.

2. A numbered thing or article.

1649 Sir W. Dugdale in *Lett. Lit. Men* (Camden) 175 You shall herewith receive the 23 first numero's of the Bundell Chart. Antiq. **1727-38** Chambers *Cycl.* s.v. *Book*, Book of Numero's or Wares.

‖**numéro** (nymero), *sb.*^{2} [Fr.] Number. Also *transf.*

Quots. 1944 and 1958 reflect the Fr. sense 'une personne bizarre'.

1944 Auden *For Time Being* (1945) 118 George, you old numero, How did you get in the Army? **1958** L. Durrell *Mountolive* v. 107 Well, you can see what a *numéro* he is. **1961** *House & Garden* May 20/2 The chair he has designed. .. This heavy *numéro* seems very different from the essays in lightness with which Saarinen's name has hitherto been associated. **1973** *Sunday Times* 26 Aug. Katharine Schofield opens the second act with a *numéro* of great panache.

numerology (njuːməˈrɒlədʒɪ). [f. L. *numer(us* number + -OLOGY.] Divination by numbers; the study of the esoteric meaning of numbers.

1911 'SEPHARIAL' *Kabala of Numbers* I. iii. 25 A general consideration of the principles involved in the science of numerology. **1926** K. ADAMS *Numerology Up-to-Date* i. 11 In the science of Numerology each letter of the alphabet has a given number and each number has its special significance. **1935** *Punch* 21 Aug. 207/1 Next we come to numerology. One of the most vital factors in your life is the Science of Numbers. **1937** M. COVARRUBIAS *Island of Bali* (1972) ix. 312 For special occasions an offering, to be effective, must conform to certain specifications based on the influences that rule the day; the calendar, the cardinal directions, numerology and so forth. **1960** AUDEN *Homage to Clio* 30 The burly slave of ritual and a martyr To Numerology. **1962** *Times* 23 Feb. 5/1 Numerology is..a term of superiority or near-abuse applied by physicists to those of their colleagues, who, by playing with numbers hope to arrive at physical understanding. **1971** *Times Lit. Suppl.* 1 Oct. 1179/1 Numerology has even had some impact on poetry in its 'concrete' forms.

Hence **numeroˈlogical** *a.*, **numeroˈlogically** *adv.*; **numeˈrologist**, one who studies or is expert in numerology.

1923 C. W. CHEASLEY *Numerology* (rev. ed.) vi. 67 The final digit of the whole name—the Expression..has the greatest influence of all... When Numerologists use the term 'a number 2 person', 'a number 6 person', etc., it is this Expression number that should be implied. **1926** K. ADAMS *Numerology Up-to-Date* ix. 79 What are the numerological properties of 1? *Ibid.* viii. 74 Cities, numerologically speaking, are a most fascinating study. **1932** *Discovery* June 204/1 It is not only the number seven that possesses a peculiar significance for numerologists. **1952** G. SARTON *Hist. Sci.* I. xvii. 439 The regular solids..must each have some definite meaning... Plato bethought himself of the four elements; the fifth solid would then represent the whole universe. This patching up of the theory, plus the finding of a meaning for the superfluous solid, is typical of the analogies invented by numerologists and other mystical mathematicians. **1972** *Sci. Amer.* Feb. 101/1 Mel Stover, a Winnipeg numerologist, has pointed out that in Roman numerals 9 changes to 11 when turned over, but 9 in the binary system—1001—doesn't change at all. **1973** *Nature* 12 Oct. 313/1 Several dependent and independent numerological relations have been proposed. Dirac noticed that the ratio between the age of the Universe and the natural unit of time..is approximately equal to the ratio between the electrostatic and the gravitational force acting between two electrons. **1974** *Sci. Amer.* June 118/3 Anything numerologically interesting about Nixon and Watergate?

†**numerose**, *a. Obs. rare*⁻¹. [ad. L. *numerōsus.*] = NUMEROUS *a.* 5.

1704 HEARNE *Ductor Hist.* (1714) I. 421 All the Nations where Literature was early propagated have made use of numerose Style and chiming Rhimes.

numerosity (njuːməˈrɒsɪtɪ). [ad. late L. *numerōsitas*: see NUMEROUS and -ITY. So It. *numerosita*, Sp. *-idad*, Pg. *-idade.*]

1. The state of being numerous; condition in respect of number.

1611 SPEED *Hist. Gt. Brit.* IX. xx. §61. 971 Those Fences, which the possession of Majestie and numerositie of issue had for sundry ages cast about it. **1658** J. ROBINSON *Endoxa* v. 144 The variety and numerosity of these Characters, and Lineaments. *a* **1687** H. MORE *Answ. Psychopyrist* (1689) 126 The Vigour of the Body must be increased, according to the Numerosity of these actuating Spirits in it. **1812** G. CHALMERS *Dom. Econ. Gt. Brit.* 404 Inhabited by people of various principles, and of dissimilar numerosity. **1870** LOWELL *Study Wind.* 33 Marching in a circle with the cheap numerosity of a stage-army.

2. Rhythmic quality.

1589 PUTTENHAM *Eng. Poesie* II. v[i]. (Arb.) 91 This is called *rithmos* or numerositie, that is to say, a certaine flowing vtteraunce by slipper words and sillables. **1656** COWLEY *Misc.* Pref., Almost all their Sweetness and Numerosity..lies in a manner wholly at the Mercy of the Reader. **1774** MITFORD *Ess. Harmony Lang.* 89 Those..who in considering the numerosity of writings attend to quantity alone. *c* **1790** PARR *Educ.* Wks. 1828 II. 107 The numerosity of the sentence pleased the ear. **1869** WADHAM *Eng. Versification* 114 Melody is rather numerosity, a blending murmur, than one full concordance.

‖**numero uno** (ˈnumero ˈuno). [It.] 'Number one', the best or most important (person). (Cf. NUMBER *sb.* 5 d.)

1973 *Publishers Weekly* 25 June 71/1 Fred Carr, *numero uno* in the mutual fund game. **1973** *Philadelphia Inquirer* (Today Suppl.) 14 Oct. 24/1 (*caption*) 'Fat Rob'..may be *numero uno* in his neighborhood, but he doesn't have anything that compares with the paneled office of Reuben Maldonado, president of the Royal Javelins in New York's South Bronx. **1975** *Publishers Weekly* 14 Apr. 55/1 The sex goddess of the moment, who stays aloof from filmland's numero uno stud only to be misused by an intellectual French director.

numerous (ˈnjuːmərəs), *a.* [ad. L. *numerōsus*, f. *numerus* number: see -OUS. So F. *numereux*, It., Sp., and Pg. *numeroso.*]

1. Plentiful, abundant, copious; comprising many units, items, or separate things.

c **1586** C'TESS PEMBROKE *Ps.* LXXII. vii, Men shall passe The numerous grasse, Such store each town shall have. *a* **1634** RANDOLPH *Poems* (1638) 99 Two that have horns, that while they butting stand, Strike from their feet a cloud of numerous sand. **1665** SIR T. HERBERT *Trav.* (1677) 58 It abounds with Inhabitants... So numerous in Islands as they are scarce numerable. *a* **1693** *Urquhart's Rabelais* III. xlix. 398 This is a numerous Herb. **1711** STEELE *Spect.* No. 88 ¶1, I have contracted a numerous Acquaintance among the best Sort of People. **1792–3** GIBBON *Autobiogr.* (1897) 63 The free use of a numerous and learned library. **1796** SOUTHEY *Lett. fr. Spain* (1799) 416 In the colonies..the evil is, if possible, still more numerous. **1827** POLLOK *Course T.* VI. 36 Now behold the fair inhabitants..from numerous business turn. **1894** G. MOORE *Esther Waters* 125 That testy and perplexed look that comes of numerous business and many interruptions.

b. Consisting of many individuals.

1647 CLARENDON *Hist. Reb.* I. §18 He..exalted allmost all of his own numerous Family. **1667** MILTON *P.L.* I. 675 Thither wing'd with speed A numerous Brigad hasten'd. **1700** DRYDEN *Cymon & Iph.* 47 A Cyprian lord..with a numerous issue blest. **1778** JOHNSON in *Boswell* 11 Apr., Garrick had under him a numerous body of people. **1797** EARL MALMESBURY *Diaries & Corr.* III. 596 There is a numerous and safe army. **1829** SOUTHEY *Sir T. More* (1831) II. 297 That very numerous class who are left with-out instruction in their childhood. **1855** MACAULAY *Hist. Eng.* xv. III. 595 The commoners who had been summoned..formed a numerous assembly.

†**c.** Composed of many parts; extensive. *Obs.*

a **1661** FULLER *Worthies* (1840) III. 269 So numerous is the church, with its appendences,..that he can accommodate one clergyman, of all dignities and degrees,..in several chapels or vestries by themselves.

d. Coming from, pertaining to, large numbers.

1832 L. HUNT *Poems* 207 With thousand tiny hushings, like a swarm of atom bees..Or noise of numerous bliss from distant sphere. **1841** D'ISRAELI *Amen. Lit.* (1867) 368 How long has existed that numerous voice which we designate as 'Public Opinion'?

2. Many; of great number.

1622 MASSINGER & DEKKER *Virg. Mart.* II. iii. To be parted in their numerous shares. **1666** PEPYS *Diary* 23 July, Contriving presses to put my books up in; they now growing numerous. **1713** STEELE *Englishm.* No. 8. 48 Letters from Correspondents begin to be very numerous. **1781** COWPER *Hope* 546 Deem life a blessing with its numerous woes. **1826** SOUTHEY *Vind. Eccl. Angl.* 449 They are greatly more numerous, and much more frequented. **1860** TYNDALL *Glac.* II. xxv. 363 These shafts..are very numerous in the Unteraar glacier.

3. Containing or including many individuals; thronged, crowded, well-filled, etc. Also const. *of.*

c **1611** CHAPMAN *Iliad* To Rdr. p. liii, In this porch to his numerous fane Hear ancient oracles speak. **1681** H. NEVILE *Plato Rediv.* 61 Though every Tribe was very numerous of Inhabitants that lived in the City. **1704** N. N. tr. *Boccalini's Advts. fr. Parnass.* I. 149 A Colony thrust out of the fruitful Loyns of some numerous Country. **1829** SOUTHEY *Sir T. More* (1831) II. 140 Both Universities are already sufficiently numerous. **1831** MOORE *Mem.* (1856) VI. 214 The dinner.., from being so numerous, had all the ease of a *table d'hôte.*

†**b.** Copious, liberal. *Obs. rare*⁻¹.

1655 FULLER *Ch. Hist.* XI. 152 He delighted more to be numerous with many then ponderous with select quotations.

†**4.** That can be numbered; numerable. *Obs.*⁻¹

1638 SIR T. HERBERT *Trav.* (ed. 2) 160 Xerxes viewd the innumerable Army he had... At Salamys..his huge Armie melted away, and quickly became numerous.

5. Measured, rhythmic, harmonious, musical.

1589 PUTTENHAM *Eng. Poesie* I. iv. (Arb.) 24 The vtterance in prose is..nothing numerous, nor contriued into measures. **1611** J. DAVIES (Heref.) *Sco. Folly* Wks. (Grosart) II. 23 Or else would offer in Homerean fire, An heccatombe of numerous-plaints therefore. **1667** MILTON *P.L.* V. 150 Such prompt eloquence Flowd from thir lips, in Prose or numerous Verse. **1749** *Power & Harm. Prosaic Numbers* 4 Men grew excessively fond of the numerous Stile, and readily sacrificed the Strength and Energy of their Discourse to the Harmony and Cadence of their Language. **1778** HARRIS in *Boswell* 9 Apr., In my opinion, the chief excellence of our language is numerous prose. **1839** HALLAM *Hist. Lit.* II. vi. §28. 270 Blank verse..falling occasionally almost into numerous prose.

transf. **1613** CAMPION *Lord's Masque* Wks. 203 Their numerous feet May aptly in just measures meet. **1648** G. DANIEL *Eclog* v. 107 Jonson's numerous Soule (Now great as Pindar's) might these Gests enroll. **1661** BOYLE *Style of Script.* 244 Bays and laurel which his successful sword and numerous pen..gained him from victory and the muses.

ˈnumerously, *adv.* [f. prec. + -LY².]

1. In or by great numbers; abundantly.

1611 TOURNEUR *Ath. Trag.* I. i, They..may as numerously be multiplied. **1646** SIR T. BROWNE *Pseud. Ep.* 79 The Atomes or small particles will ascend most numerously unto it. **1673–4** GREW *Anat. Pl., Anat. Trunks* ii. §8 In standing, most numerously, in or near, the inner Margin of the Barque. **1779** H. WALPOLE *Wks.* (1846) VI. 47 You, who keep your-self so warm and so numerously clothed. **1822–34** *Good's Study Med.* (ed. 4) IV. 502 The box is numerously perforated at the bottom. **1849** MACAULAY *Hist. Eng.* vii. II. 225 Nor is there any reason to believe that any of these addresses was numerously signed. **1870** ROGERS *Hist. Glean.* Ser. II. 17 So numerously did students throng to the medieval university.

Comb. **1829** BENTHAM *Justice & Cod. Petit., Abr. Petit. Justice* 37 Another and more numerously-seated Westminster Hall judicatory. **1887** *Pall Mall G.* 6 Sept. 2/1 The same case of a numerously-daughtered paterfamilias.

2. Harmoniously, rhythmically. *rare*⁻¹.

1656 COWLEY *Misc., Elegie upon Anacreon*, The Smooth-pac'd Hours of ev'ry day Glided numerously away.

ˈnumerousness. [f. as prec. + -NESS.]

1. The state of being numerous; the condition of being many in number.

1631 T. POWELL *Tom of All Trades* 142 Numerousnes spoiles all. **1659** HAMMOND *On Ps.* lxxxvii. 1 In respect of the numerousness of eminent persons. **1741** BERKELEY *Wks.* (1871) IV. 274 You seem to think the numerousness of her sons an argument of her truth. **1782** MISS BURNEY *Cecilia* II. iv, The numerousness of splendid engagements, of which..every one was proud to boast. **1841** L. HUNT *Seer* II. (1864) 42 There are times when the numerousness may scatter the individual gusto. **1887** T. A. TROLLOPE *What I remember* I. xv. 311 English wanderers at that time earned the privilege since accorded to their numerousness.

2. Measured or rhythmic quality; regularity in measure or rhythm.

1712 ADDISON *Spect.* No. 357 ¶4 He has rather chosen to neglect the Numerousness of his Verse. **1727–38** CHAMBERS *Cycl.* s.v. *Numbers*, It contributes greatly to the numerousness of a period, to have it closed by magnificent and well-sounding words. **1839** *Blackw. Mag.* XLV. 135 The richness and numerousness of the harmony. **1893** *Nat. Obs.* 17 June 115/2 His own gorgeous appreciation of quality and numerousness in instrumentation.

‖**numerus clausus** (ˈnjuːmərəs ˈklaʊsəs). [L., lit. 'closed, or restricted, number'.] A fixed maximum number of entrants admissible to an academic institution.

1925 *Nation* (N.Y.) 8 Apr. 374 The *numerus clausus*, driven out of Russia, still keeps eager Jewish youth from the learning they crave in Poland, Hungary, and Rumania. **1959** D. D. RUNES *Conc. Dict. Judaism* 178 *Numerus clausus* (Latin), limited number of Jews admitted to schools of higher education; still operative in Soviet Union. **1960** *Encounter* June 46 Owing to the *numerus clausus* imposed in Russian universities, a very large number of the students present were Jews, compelled to come West in order to graduate. **1963** *Higher Educ.* (Cmnd. 2154) v. 38 Shortage of accommodation may effectively impose a *numerus clausus* in some disciplines.

†**ˈnumery.** *Obs.* Also -ye, -ie. [ad. L. *Numeri*, pl. of *numerus* number.] The book of Numbers.

c **1400** *Wyclif Bible* (1850) I. 363 Here endith Leuyticus, and here bigynneth Numery [*v.r.* Numeri]. **1534** MORE *Treat. Passion* Wks. 1301/1 As it appeareth in the .xi. chapiter of Numerye. **1562** LEGH *Armory* (1597) 52 This is a strong beast, as appeareth by that is spoken in Numery. **1574** J. JONES *Nat. Begin. Growing Things* 34 The booke of Exodus, of Numery, and of Iosua.

numhead, var. NUMBHEAD.

Numidian (njuːˈmɪdɪən), *sb.* and *a.* [f. L. *Numidia* the former name of a country in North Africa + -AN.] **a.** *sb.* A native or inhabitant of Numidia. **b.** *adj.* Of or belonging to Numidia. *spec.* **Numidian crane**, a grey and black crane, *Anthropoides virgo*, found in southern Europe, north Africa, and parts of Asia; = DEMOISELLE 2 a.

1600 HOLLAND tr. *Livy's Romane Hist.* XXIX. 731 Then the kingdome fell by descent, according to the custome and manner of the Numidians, unto Desalces the late kings brother. *Ibid.* XXX. 752 They would enlarge and set at libertie all the Numidian captives that lay in prison at Rome. **1614** A. GORGES tr. *Lucans Pharsalia* IV. 156 The vagrant fierce Numidæans. **1697** DRYDEN *Æneid* IV. 57 And fierce Numidians there your Frontiers bound. **1757** A. BUTLER *Lives Saints* III. 3 Certain false Numidian zealots. *Ibid.* 4 Seventy bishops, chiefly Numidians. **1766** [see DEMOISELLE 2 a]. **1836** N. ISAACS *Trav. E. Afr.* II. xvii. 324 The wild sort [of birds] are easily obtained... The Crane (Numidion [*sic*] or Demoiselle), Baleari or Crowned Crane..are common. *c* **1876** E. DICKINSON *Poems* (1955) III. 956 The Butterfly's Numidian Gown With spots of Burnish roasted on Is proof against the Sun. **1893** A. NEWTON *Dict. Birds* 111 In Europe, besides the *G*[*rus*] *communis* already mentioned, we have as an inhabitant that which is generally known as the Numidian Crane or Demoiselle..distinguished from every other by its long white ear-tufts. **1905** T. HODGKIN in L. Creighton *Life & Lett. T. Hodgkin* (1917) xi. 229, I wish I had come to this Numidian land when I was younger... Our Numidians long held Rome at bay. **1906** KIPLING *Puck of Pook's Hill* 147 'Was your nurse a—a Romaness too?' 'No, a Numidian... A dear, fat, brown thing.' **1921** *Edin. Rev.* July 105 A Numidian, riding bareback and stirrupless, is throwing a lasso at a wild ass. **1957** *Encycl. Brit.* XVI. 615/1 Numidians were divided into two great tribes, the Massyli on the east, and the Massaesyli on the west... At the end of the [second Punic] war,..the Numidian kingdom surrounded Carthage except towards the sea.

ˈnuminal, *a. rare.* [f. L. *nūmin-*, stem of *nūmen* NUMEN + -AL¹.] Divine.

1652 FELTHAM *Low Countries* (1677) 56 Their wisdom is not indeed Heroic or Numinal,..but rather narrow and restrictive. **1927** *Contemp. Rev.* Mar. 352 Rudolf Otto in his *Idea of the Holy*, accords to music a place upon the 'wholly other' or 'numinal' of religion.

‖**numinosum** (njuːmɪˈnəʊzəm). [ad. G. *numinose* the numinous.] = NUMINOUS *sb.*

1938 C. G. JUNG *Psychol. & Relig.* i. 4 Religion, as the Latin word denotes, is a careful and scrupulous observation of what Rudolf Otto aptly termed the 'numinosum'. **1950** *Brit. Jrnl. Psychol.* XL. 235 Modern psychology, with its exploration of complexes, has touched upon a taboo laid by ego-consciousness on the psychic 'numinosum' and 'tremendum'. **1973** J. SINGER *Boundaries of Soul* v. 123 Many religious practices and performances seem to be carried out for the sole purpose of calling forth the power of the *numinosum* at will by invocation, incantation, sacrifice [etc.].

numinous (ˈnjuːmɪnəs), *a.* [f. as NUMINAL *a.*: see -OUS.] Of or pertaining to a numen; divine, spiritual, revealing or suggesting the presence of a god; inspiring awe and reverence. Also *absol.* or as *sb.*

1647 WARD *Simp. Cobler* 66 The Will of a King is very numinous; it hath a kinde of vast universality in it. **1864** R.

S. Hawker *Quest of Sangraal* 17 An Orient Cruse, Fulfill'd, and running o'er, with Numynous Light. **1923** J. W. Harvey tr. *R. Otto's Idea of Holy* ii. 6 For this purpose I adopt a word coined from the Latin *numen*. *Omen* has given us *ominous*, and there is no reason why from *numen* we should not similarly form a word '*numinous*'. I shall speak.. of a unique 'numinous' category of value and of a definitely 'numinous' state of mind. *Ibid.* iii. 11 The numinous is thus felt as objective and outside the self. **1934** W. Temple *Nature, Man & God* i. 23 What Otto speaks of as the '*Mysterium tremendum*', the quality in the object of religion which he describes as 'Numinous', is just that before which we do not reason but bow. **1941** G. G. Scholem *Major Trends in Jewish Mysticism* 59 The key-word of the numinous, the *Kedushah*, the trishagion from Isaiah vi, 3, in which the ecstasy of the mystic culminates: holy, holy, holy is the Lord of Hosts. **1951** J. L. Adams tr. *Tillich's Protestant Era* p. xxxix, Protestants..often are unaware of the numinous power inherent in genuine symbols. **1957** *Times Lit. Suppl.* 11 Oct. 602/5 He now urges us..to transfer finally our more numinous speculations from the altar to the earth, to the observable universe and to all its children. **1962** *Listener* 17 May, Simple English exchanges that caught the suburban yet numinous quality of the original French. **1967** G. Steiner *Lang. & Silence* 62, I want to draw attention to..the recurrent acknowledgement by poets..that music *is* the deeper, more numinous code, that language..aspires to the condition of music. **1969** *New Scientist* 17 Apr. 114/1 There is a growing revolt of young people against what they call materialism..because they want to take seriously the experience of the inner life—in particular, experience of the 'numinous' and of 'immortal longings'. **1972** *Times Lit. Suppl.* 31 Mar. 365/4 Homer reveals the world of gods as well as the world of men, both in epic verse, and this difference from later, more numinous writers has many consequences. **1972** S. W. Sykes in Cox & Dyson *20th-Cent. Mind* II. vi. 154 [Rudolf] Otto defined numinous as the non-rational mystery behind religion, which is both awesome and fascinating. It is, he asserted, the permanent and essential feature of all religion, including Christianity.

Hence **numi'nosity**, **'numinousness**, the condition or state of being numinous; also †**numinously** *adv.*

1650 B. *Discollim.* 26 They shall prove such Jupiters as to fall a thundring and lightning so numinously over our heads. **1932** R. A. Knox *Broadcast Minds* iv. 70 What is the proper object around which the idea of 'numinousness' ought to cling? **1936** *Essays & Stud.* XXI. 132 The poet's own religious fervour, mysticism, or (if you will) poetic 'numinosity'. **1951** *Theology* LIV. 233 Somehow he manages again and again to take from the Gospel its fascination, its haunting power over the imagination, its numinosity. **1962** *Listener* 29 Nov. 940/1 Nelly, the hag, the witch, the personification of Corvey's incipient madness, lost some of her numinousness in being acted out. **1963** *Times* 29 May 11/5 If the Church is to be preserved from degenerating into a nondescript club of nebulous numinosity. **1969** E. C. Whitmont *Symbolic Quest* vii. 126 The energy which is withdrawn from the external world remains focussed exclusively upon the unconscious primitive image with its archaic numinosity.

†**numis'marian**, *a. Obs.* = numismatic.

1716 M. Davies *Athen. Brit.* III. 74 The same Medal-Pyramids were presently prop'd up and enlarg'd by the following Numismarian-Pioneers in chief.

numismatic (njuːmɪz'mætɪk), *a.* and *sb.* [ad. F. *numismatique* (1579), = It., Sp., and Pg. *numismatico*, f. L. *numismat-*, stem of *numisma*, *nomisma*, a. Gr. *νόμισμα* current coin, f. *νομίζειν* to have in use.] **A.** *adj.*

1. Of, pertaining or relating to, coins or coinage.

1792 *Gentl. Mag.* LXII. i. 51 A numismatic History of France was among the *desiderata* of her national history. **1804** *Ibid.* LXXIV. ii. 1102 In order to settle these numismatic difficulties. **1839** James *Louis XIV*, III. 196 Under their care the numismatic art was carried to a very high degree of perfection. **1882** A. J. C. Hare in *Gd. Words* Mar. 185 She lives only by numismatic record.

2. Consisting of coins.

1851 D. Wilson *Preh. Ann.* iii. ii. (1863) II. 62 The numismatic treasures including an almost unbroken series of imperial coins from Augustus to Diocletian. **1868** Stephens *Runic Mon.* II. 879 A meaning in harmony with a whole class of numismatic remains.

B. *sb. pl.* The study of coins and medals, esp. from an archæological or historical standpoint.

1829–32 in Webster. **1850** Leitch tr. *C. O. Müller's Anc. Art* §317 (ed. 2) 366 Numismatics..is, in the main, an auxiliary to the knowledge of the trade and mutual intercourse of the ancients. **1876** Mathews *Coinage* Introd. p. iii, Numismatics..might be considered as a branch of Archæology, were its inquiries confined to the coins of bygone days.

So †**numis'matical** *a.*, numismatic. *Obs.*$^{-1}$ **numis'matically** *adv.*, as regards numismatics. **numisma'tician**, a numismatist.

1716 M. Davies *Athen. Brit.* III. 73 Of all the Sorts and Kinds of Writers and Writings, Great Britain has produc'd the fewest of Medal-Tracts and Numismatical Collectors. **1881** *Daily Tel.* 8 Mar., The national money of Britain is neither clipped, nor unduly worn, nor debased in value. It is numismatically splendid. **1883** *St. James's Gaz.* 20 Feb. 5 About the last place where a numismatician would expect to find a valuable gold coin.

numismatist (njuː'mɪzmætɪst). [ad. F. *numismatiste*: see prec. and -ist.] One who has a special interest in numismatics; a student of coins.

1799 *Gentl. Mag.* LXIX. ii. 1172 A deception attempted to be played off upon numismatists. **1839** *Penny Cycl.* XV. 52/2 Numismatists have usually given the name of medals to those coins that have been struck..for particular purposes. **1879** C. R. Low *Jrnl. Gen. Abbott* ii. 164 Captain Abbott, who was a keen numismatist, and had an excellent collection of coins.

numisma'tography. *rare.* [= F. *numismatographie*, Sp. *-grafia*, Pg. and mod.L. *-graphia*: see -graphy.] The systematic description of coins; the descriptive part of numismatics.

1853 Humphrey *Coin Coll. Man.* xvi. 180 Our term numismatics, numismatography, &c., &c., by which the science of the study of coins is known, we also receive from the Romans.

numisma'tologist. [Cf. next and -ologist.] A numismatist.

1835 Burnes *Trav. Bokhara* (ed. 2) III. 379 Taking impressions and drawings of it..for the..satisfaction of numismatologists. **1859** W. H. Gregory *Egypt* II. 130 Naturalist, archæologist, numismatologist; in short, something of everything.

numisma'tology. [-ology.] The science of numismatics.

1815 Southey in *Q. Rev.* XII. 519 At a very early age, Barré had formed a taste for numismatology. **1839** *Gentl. Mag.* Sept. 316/2 The General..turned his attention to numismatology. **1856** Smyth *Roman Fam. Coins* 276 The numismatology of Europe has been so bitterly degraded.

†**numm.** *Obs. rare*$^{-1}$. [a. F. *numme*, ad. L. *nummus*.] A coin.

1694 Motteux *Rabelais* v. Ep. Pantagruel's Lymosin, Large heaps of Numms to fill your largest Coffers.

nummary ('nʌmərɪ), *a.* [ad. L. *nummārius*, f. *nummus* a coin.]

1. Pertaining or relating to money or coinage.

1660 Waterhouse *Arms & Arm.* 31 They allowed none participants with them on ordinary and nummary accounts. **1740** W. Douglass *Disc. Curr. Brit. Plant. Amer.* 5 All over Europe for many Ages preceding the 14th Century, the nummary Pound, and the Ponderal or Pound Weight of Silver were the same. **1810** G. Chalmers *Caledonia* II. i. 37 Alexander III followed the nummary example of Alexander I. **1817** Ruding *Ann. Coinage* (1840) I. 112 He is of opinion that they borrowed their money pound from the Greeks, and their nummary language from the Romans. **1837** *Penny Cycl.* VII. 329/2 It was then, as it still is, the 240th part of the nummary pound.

2. Dealing with, occupied with, coins or money.

1695 Kennett *Par. Antiq.* iv. 12 Nummary Authors observe, that a Castle or wall'd City was the pourtraicture of a Roman Colony. **1807–8** Syd. Smyth *P. Plymley's Lett.* Wks. 1859 II. 168/2 Indignity to George Rose would be felt by the smallest nummary gentleman in the king's employ.

numme, obs. f. numb.

nummen, pa. pple. of nim *sb.*[1] to take. *Obs.*

nummer, obs. f. number.

nummet ('nʌmɪt). *dial.* Also nommit, -et. [Corruption of noonmeat; cf. nammet and nummock.] A light meal or luncheon.

1825 Jennings *Obs. Dial. W. Eng.*, *Nummet*, a short meal between breakfast and dinner; nunchion. **1850** Collins *Gower Dial.* in *Trans. Phil. Soc.* IV. 222 *Nommet*, a luncheon of bread, cheese, &c.—not a regular meal. **1892** O'Neill *Devonshire Idyls* 110 Fore-bit and Breakfast, Rear-bit and Dinner; Nummit and Crummit, And a bit after Supper.

nummi-, combining form of L. *nummus* coin, as †**nummi-amorous** *a.*, fond of or loving money. **nummi-cultivate** *v.*, to encourage or assist with money or payment; so **nummi-cultivated** *ppl. a.* and **nummi-culture**. **nummiform** *a.*, shaped like a coin (*Cent. Dict.* 1890).

1650 B. *Discollim.* 28, I could demonstrate it to be.. Versipellous, Centireligious, Nummiamorous. **1860** Reade *8th Commandm.* 250 The dagger stroke that slew Marloe in his twenty-ninth year, struck down a heaven born and nummi-cultivated genius. *Ibid.* 265 If this Anglo-Saxon [Shakespeare] had not been nummicultivated by the theatre. *Ibid.*, Under example, stimulus, and nummi-culture.

nummie, numming: see numby, numbing.

nummion ('nuːmɪɒn) Usu. in pl. **nummia** (-ɪə). [ad. Gr. *νουμ(μ)ίον*, dim. of *νοῦμμος* coin.] A Byzantine copper coin, equal to one fortieth of a follis.

1908, 1962 [see follis]. **1970** *Ashmolean Mus. Rep. Visitors 1969* 40 The earliest in a series of Byzantine accessions is a scarce 33-nummia coin of Justinian I. **1973** P. D. Whitting *Byzantine Coins* vii. 89 The copper nummia in their thousands were too small to have any recognizable value in themselves and could only circulate on a basis of public confidence.

†**'nummist.** *Obs. rare*$^{-1}$. [f. L. *numm-us* + -ist.] Numismatist.

1703 Hickes in *Thoresby Corr.* II. 36 This gentleman,.. so particularly a great nummist, as famous as any..for his knowledge of coins.

nummock, variant of nummet.

1875 *Sat. Rev.* 3 Aug. 140/1 Our whortle-gatherers..sit down for their 'nummock' of bread and whortleberries, washed down by..water.

†**numms.** *Obs. Cant.* (See quots.)

a **1700** B. E. *Dict. Cant. Crew*, *Numms*, a Sham, or Collar Shirt, to hide the t'other when Dirty. **1755** Deane Swift *Ess. on Swift* 273 The wearing of numms, or scraps of linen to cover dirty shirts.

nummular ('nʌmjʊlə(r)), *a.* [f. L. *nummul-us*, dim. of *nummus* coin, piece of money + -ar[2].]

1. Of or pertaining to money.

1731 in Bailey (vol. II). Hence in Johnson, etc.

2. *Path.* Coin-shaped, *esp.* of sputa.

1846 Brittan tr. *Malgaigne's Man. Oper. Surg.* 15 All these [cauteries] may be very well reduced to three. The oval, octagonal, and nummular. **1879** *St. George's Hosp. Rep.* IX. 166 The sputum was frothy on admission, but subsequently became nummular. **1899** *Allbutt's Syst. Med.* VIII. 553 Spots intermediate in size between the guttate and nummular.

†**nummu'larian.** *Obs. rare*$^{-1}$. [f. L. *nummulārius*, f. *nummulus*.] A money-changer.

c **1450** *Mirour Saluacioun* (Roxb.) 58 He ouerthrewe the bordes & shedde the monee of the Numelariens.

nummulary ('nʌmjʊlərɪ), *a.* [See nummular *a.* and -ary[1].] Nummary.

1767 W. Clarke *Connexion Coins* 283 The Romans applied all their nummulary language to such real coins as were struck within that empire. *Ibid.* 483 The Roman nummulary pound was one quarter less than that by which this payment was adjusted. **1817** Ruding *Ann. Coinage* (1840) I. 205 The nummulary Talent, which was in common use by the Greeks, and according to which the Anglo-Saxons rated their greater fines, that is, by multiples of sixty Pounds. **1838** *Encycl. Brit.* (ed. 7) XVI. 514/2 The twelfth part of the nummulary Saxon pound, and the fifteenth of the commercial. **1871** C. Davies *Metric Syst.* iii. 92 The identity of the nummulary weight and of the standard silver coin..was first defaced by Edward I himself.

'nummulated, *ppl. a. Path.* [f. L. *nummul-us.*] Coin-shaped, nummular.

1873 F. T. Roberts *Handbk. Med.* 419 Sometimes they [*sc.* sputa] are very tenacious..and may form distinct 'nummulated' masses. **1876** Bristowe *Th. & Pract. Med.* (1878) 367 The sputa which yield this odour are generally distinctly purulent, occasionally nummulated.

nummuline ('nʌmjʊlaɪn), *a.* and *sb. Geol.* [f. as prec. + -ine[1].] **A.** *adj.* Nummulitic.

1865 Carpenter in *Intellect. Obs.* May 291 These tubuli, as in the existing representatives of the Nummuline series, usually run parallel to each other. **1875** Dawson *Dawn of Life* vii. 185 The nummuline-layer..unmistakably occurs in cracks or fissures, both in Canadian and Connemara ophite.

B. *sb.* A nummulite.

1879 Carpenter in *Encycl. Brit.* IX. 384/2 The same irregularities in the grouping of the tubuli that..we find in recent Nummulines.

nummulite ('nʌmjʊlaɪt). *Zool.* [f. L. *nummul-us*, dim. of *nummus* coin + -ite[1] 2.] A genus of fossil foraminiferous cephalopods belonging to the order *Polythalamia*, found abundantly in the Tertiary strata; an individual of this genus.

1811 Pinkerton *Petral.* I. 453 The nummulites, or porpites, occur in the limestone of Egypt and of France. **1839** *Civil Eng. & Arch. Jrnl.* II. 148/2 In the freshwater rocks of the Isle of Wight we find the nummulite. **1868** W. S. O. tr. *Figuier's Ocean World* iv. 79 The greater part of the Egyptian pyramids is only an aggregation of Nummulites. **1884** *Leisure Hour* Apr. 236/2 Immense numbers of disc-like shells of protozoa, the Nummulites.

attrib. **1873** Dawson *Earth & Man* x. 241 The Nummulite Limestone was undoubtedly oceanic.

nummulitic (nʌmjʊ'lɪtɪk), *a. Geol.* [f. prec. + -ic.] Containing, or formed of, nummulites.

1833 Lyell *Princ. Geol.* III. 185 Secondary rocks, composed in great part of grey and greenish sandstone and conglomerate, with some thick beds of nummulitic limestone. **1863** Dana *Man. Geol.* 523 They [the pyramids] are largely Nummulitic, many beds consisting almost wholly of ..Nummulites. **1882** Geikie *Text-bk. Geol.* vi. iv. 837 The early Tertiary or nummulitic sea was upheaved into a succession of giant mountains.

'nummy-'nummy. An exclamation of pleasure; = yummy-yummy. Cf. num.

1929 E. Bowen *Last September* vi. 62 'Nummy-nummy,' she said, pointing out the raspberries.

numnah ('nʌmnə). [var. of numdah.] A thick cloth or felt; a saddle-cloth; a pad placed under a saddle to prevent soreness.

1859 F. A. Griffiths *Artil. Man.* (1862) 157 The bridles are laid over the cantles,..numnah or blanket over all. **1873** in Champion & Wilton *Saddles & Sore Backs* 31 Far superior to the numnah at present in use, or the leather numnah or pad. **1891** *Field* 7 Mar. p. xiv/3 Sponge-lined patent numnahs for the prevention of sore backs.

attrib. **1893** *Baily's Mag.* May 261/2, I crept into my numnah bag, where I was soon quite snug.

numness, obs. form of numbness.

num-num (nʊm'nʊm). *S. Afr.* Also nam-nam, noem-noem. [Afrikaans, perh. f. Hottentot or Nama name.] A spiny, evergreen shrub or small tree of the genus *Carissa*, belonging to the family Apocynaceæ and bearing fragrant white flowers; also, the edible red or purple fruit of a plant of this kind. Cf. *Natal plum* (Natal *sb.*[2] 2).

1822 W. J. Burchell *Trav. Interior S. Afr.* I. x. 192 The Hottentots call this shrub 'Num'num (or Noomnoom, agreeably to English orthography), each syllable preceded by a guttural clap of the tongue. **1897** S. J. Du Toit *Rhodesia* iv. 32 Various kinds of sweet-grass and small shrubs, varied with very good large bush and trees, as ..'noem noem', 'quarri', [etc.]. **1926** O. Schreiner *From Man to Man* iii. 113 The nam-nams and jasmine shrubs made a thick wall on either side. [*Note*] A shrub with a small edible berry (also 'num-num'). **1951** R. Campbell *Light on Dark Horse* ix. 127 It was the sort of scrub which reminds one of an enormous roll of vegetable barbed wire, composed chiefly of num-num and wait-a-bit thorn. **1972** Palmer & Pitman *Trees S. Afr.* III. 1899 The species [of *Carissa*] are usually known as num-nums. *Ibid.* 1903 Although the Karoo num-num is most often a bush it can grow into a small tree 3·5 m high with a round, much-branched, immensely dense and twiggy evergreen crown.

numori, var. nomoli.

†**nump(s.** *Obs.* Also 8 **numphs**. [Of obscure origin.] A silly or stupid person. (Used chiefly in jocular address.)

1611 Beaum. & Fl. *Kt. Burning P.* II. ii, *Hum.* What do you think I am? *Jasp.* An arrant noddy... *Luce.* Fare-wel, my pretty Nump, I am very sorry I cannot bear thee company. **1673** Bp. S. Parker *Repr. Reh. Transp.* 85 These are villainous Engines indeed; but take heart, Numps! **1709** *Brit. Apollo* No. 56. 3/1 Alas! poor Numphs, thy Jobbernole Seems scarce informed by a Soul. ?**1730** *Royal Remarks* 37 Many Fools.., poetical Numpses.

numparel(l, obs. or dial. ff. nonpareil.

ˈ**numquid**. *rare*⁻¹. [L. *numquid*, used to introduce a question.] An inquisitive person.

1833 *Blackw. Mag.* XXXIV. 675 The barber's shop is the everlasting resort and solace of the numquids of the turban.

numskull (ˈnʌmskʌl). Forms: α. 8–9 **numbskull**; **numpscull, -skull**. β. 8–9 **numscull** (8 **-scul, -scal**), 8– **numskull** (8 **-skul**). [f. numb *a.* + skull *sb.*]

1. A dull-witted or stupid person; a blockhead, thickhead, dolt.

α. **1724** Swift *Let. to Wood* Wks. 1841 II. 50, I remember not to have known a greater numbskull than thou art. **1773** Goldsm. *Stoops to Conq.* II. i, You numbskulls! and so while ..you are quarrelling for places the guests must be starved. **1800** *Sporting Mag.* XVI. 284 I'm not so great a fool..as that great numpscull Jack! **1834** M. Scott *Tom Cringle* xvi, Why will not the numbskulls confine their infernal dullness to them. **1839** Landor *Andrea of Hungary* 84 I've swum two nights And days together upon Baian wine..; 'twould swamp that leaky nump-skull.

β. **1728** Vanbr. & Cib. *Prov. Husb.* I. ii, Thou art a numscul I see already. **1756** *Gentl. Mag.* XXVI. 490 If he's a fool, and like a numskul chuses To consort with those weedling jades, the Muses. **1807–8** W. Irving *Salmag.* (1824) 130 Every modern numskull, who takes hold of a subject he knows nothing about. **1867** Trollope *Chron. Barset* II. lxxiii. 295 He considered them to be numskulls, and little better than idiots.

attrib. and *Comb.* **1814** Hill *Let. to Carlyle* 9 May, Ever varying the scene with wit and mirth, while honest Peter must hold on in one numskull track to all eternity. **1828** Southey *Ep. to A. Cunningham*, An honest fellow of the numskull race;..a very goose.

2. The head, pate, noddle, *esp.* that of a dull or stupid person.

1717 Prior *Alma* I. 127 Or Toes, or Fingers, in this Case, Of Num-scull's Self shou'd take the Place. **1738** *Gentl. Mag.* VIII. 197/2 Their Children..having at their Birth Numsculls, like those obtain'd by Art by their Parents. **1742** Fielding *J. Andrews* III. xii, The nonsensical dictates of his own numscull. *a* **1818** M. G. Lewis *Jrnl. W. Ind.* (1834) 37 He never could squeeze his great numskull into it. **1842** Lover *Handy Andy* iii, Confound your numskull! I didn't say a word about ink. **1850** T. A. Trollope *Impress. Wand.* xiii. 210 Tell them what you will, they shake their wise numskulls when you have done.

Hence ˈ**numskullism**, stupidity.

1806 Anna Seward *Lett.* (1811) VI. 268 His reminiscences familiarize us with the interior of the court of George the First and Second, and display, in full light, the numskullism of both those regal personages.

numskulled (ˈnʌmskʌld), *a.* [f. prec. + -ed².] Dull- or slow-witted; stupid.

1706 E. Ward *Wooden World Diss.* (1708) 12 His Proxy, some numb-skull'd Officer, whom he most esteems. **1712** Arbuthnot *John Bull* I. xii, That Clod-pated, Numskull'd, Ninny-hammer of yours. **1881** Duffield *Don Quixote* II. 361 Is it possible that your worship is so numskulled and so lacking in brains?

Hence num'**skulledness**.

1885 *Sat. Rev.* 28 Nov. 717 The practitioners of this black art..carried it out with at least a heroic consistency of numskulledness.

†ˈ**numskully**, *adv. Obs.* [f. as prec. + -ly².] In the manner of a numskull; stupidly.

1708 *Brit. Apollo* No. 88. 3/2 You answer Questions so Numscully.

nun (nʌn), *sb.*¹ Forms: α. 1–7 **nunne**, 5 **nune**, 4– **nun** (5 **nunn**, *Sc.* **nwn**). β. 3–6 **nonne**, 5–6 **none** (5 **nonn**, 6 **noone**). [OE. *nunne*, = OHG. *nunna* (MHG. and mod.G. dial. *nunne*), ON. and (M)Sw. *nunna*; also ME. *nonne* (prob. a. OFr. *nonne*), = MDu. *nonne* (Du. *non*), MSw. *nonna*, Da. and G. *nonne*. The ultimate source is eccl. L. *nonna*, fem. of *nonnus* monk (in late Gr. *νόννα, νόννος*), originally a title given to elderly persons, whence It. *nonno*, *nonna* grandfather, grandmother, Sicilian *nunnu*, *nunna* father, mother, Sard. *nonnu*, *nonna* godfather, godmother.]

1. A woman devoted to a religious life under certain vows; usually, one who has vowed poverty, chastity, and obedience, and who lives in a convent under a certain rule, as in the Roman Catholic and Greek Churches.

α. *c* **900** tr. *Bæda's Hist.* IV. xxiii. (1890) 340 Wæs in þæm seolfan mynstre sumu haliȝu nunne. *c* **1000** Ælfric in Assmann *Ags. Hom.* (1889) III. 368 Synd swa þeah þa wudewan..to nunnan ȝehadode. *a* **1122** *O.E. Chron.* (Laud MS.) an. 963, He macode þær twa abbotrice, an of muneca, oðer of nunna. *a* **1225** *Ancr. R.* 316 Ich am on ancre, a nunne,..a meiden. *c* **1275** *Sinners beware* 169 in *O.E. Misc.* 77 Mvnekes and Nunnen þat heom wyte ne kunnen From sucche lecherye Heo schule to helle cume. *a* **1300** *Cursor M.* 29284 Qua smites..munk, or frer, nun, or chanun,..he is cursd. *c* **1380** *Sir Ferumb.* 62 Saue nunnes sloȝ he sykerly þe relygyous þat þar war. *c* **1430** Lydg. *Min. Poems* (Percy Soc.) 200 Rympled liche a nunnys veylle. *c* **1440** *Promp. Parv.* 360/2 Nune, womann of relygione, *monialis, monacha*. **1538** Starkey *England* II. i. 148 Monkys, frerys,..and nunnys, of the wych..ther ys no smal nombur. **1594** Shaks. *Rich. III*, IV. iv. 201 For my Daughters..They shall be praying Nunnes, not weeping Queenes. **1613** May *Decl. Est. Clothing* iv. 19 Then do they punish the clothier for that fault as the Frier whipt the Nun with a Fox taile. **1671** Woodhead *St. Teresa* II. xxvi. 166 There was no perswading her to be a Quire-Nun, but a Lay-Sister. **1715** De Foe *Fam. Instruct.* I. iv. (1841) I. 78 Does my mother think to make a nun of me? **1797** Mrs. Radcliffe *Italian* xi, Vivaldi perceived a procession of nuns approaching from a distant aisle. **1838** Lytton *Calderon* iii, You may well look surprised, when actresses turn nuns. **1880** 'Ouida' *Moths* I. 107 It seems to me you are shut up like a nun.

β. *c* **1290** *S. Eng. Leg.* I. 18 A Nonne þare was of on Abbeie. *c* **1330** R. Brunne *Chron. Wace* (Rolls) 8029 Scho ys nonne of relygion At Seint Petres kirke of þis toun. **1377** Langl. *P. Pl.* B. v. 153, I haue an aunte to nonne and an abbesse bothe. **1420** *E.E. Wills* (1882) 54, I will þat þᵉ nonne þat kepid me in my seknes haue ij nobles. **1481** Caxton *Reynard* (Arb.) 28 A lytel besyde the waye..stode a cloyster of black nonnes. **1491** —— *Vitas Patr.* (W. de W. 1495) II. 305 She is my nonne & yours & he named her so; bycause they named in lyke wyse the deuoute virgynes in that regyon. **1523** Ld. Berners *Froiss.* I. clv. 187 Noones, hauynge no reuenewes aboue x.li. shall pay nothynge. *c* **1550** Bale *K. Johan* (Camden) 2 Monkes, Chanons & nones in dyvers coloure and shappe. **1594** Willobie *Avisa* xlii, She is no Saynt, She is no Nonne.

b. A priestess or votaress of some pagan deity.

c **893** K. Ælfred *Oros.* IV. iv. 162 On ðære ilcan tide Caperronie wæs hatenu heora goda nunne. *a* **1400–50** *Alexander* 2179 (Dubl.), Zacora hym sayd, a semlych Nonn, þar was none oþer answer. *a* **1547** Surrey *Æneid* IV. 389 And whisketh through the town like Bachus nunne. **1598** Drayton *Heroic. Ep.* xiii. 175 Like one of Bacchus raging frantike Nunnes. **1608** Topsell *Serpents* (1658) 765 The Nuns that keep the fire of Vesta are their lives. **1647** Clarendon *Hist. Rebell.* VI. §42 How much more Christian was that Athenian Nun in Plutarch. **1698** Houghton *Husb.* (ed. Bradley, 1727) II. 365 The law of the twelve tables prohibited all but the Emperor and Vestal Nuns to be bury'd within the city [Rome].

c. *transf.* A courtesan.

1770 Foote *Lame Lover* I. Wks. 1799 II. 60 An abbess, well known about town, with a smart little nun in her suite. **1825** C. Westmacott *Eng. Spy* I. 167 The nuns of St. Clements.

2. The name of various birds: **a.** The Blue Titmouse, *Parus cæruleus*.

1589 Higins tr. *Junius' Nomenclator* 60 *Parus minor*, a little titmouse, called a Nunne, because his heade is filletted as it were Nunlike. **1678** Ray *Willughby's Ornith.* 262 The blue Titmouse or Nun: *Parus cæruleus*. **1774** G. White *Selborne* xli, The blue titmouse, or nun, is a great frequenter of houses, and a general devourer. **1843** *Zoologist* I. 215 Looking cautiously through a crevice, I saw a nun actively engaged in ferreting out the small white grub. **1903** *Daily Graphic* 31 Jan. 11/1 During the winter you generally see the tomtit..in his character of 'the nun'.

b. The Smew, *Mergus albellus*. [So G. *nonne*.]

1666 Merrett *Pinax* 183 *Nun* est avis aquatica querquedula paulo minor, Rostrum ei rotundum [etc.]. **1674** Ray *Coll. Words, Water Fowl* 95 This hath no English name known to me, unless it be that which Dr. Merret in his *Pinax* calls by the name of Nun: The Germans call it the White Nun. **1709** *Phil. Trans.* XXVI. 466 *Mergus major cirratus*, the Smew, or White Nun. **1768** Pennant *Brit. Zool.* II. 438. **1817** T. Forster *Nat. Hist. Swallow-tribe* (ed. 6) 93 *Mergus albellus*, Smew.., white Nun, Lough-diver. **1894** Newton *Dict. Birds* 646 *Nun*.., the adult male Smew, from his delicate white and black plumage.

c. A variety of the domestic pigeon.

1725 Bradley *Fam. Dict.* s.v. *Pigeon*, There are indeed many sorts of pigeons such as Helmets, Nuns, Tumblers, Barbs. **1735** J. Moore *Columbarium* 48 The Nun..is a bird somewhat larger than a Jacobine, her Plumage is very particular, and she seems to take her Name from it. **1868** *Boy's Own Bk.* 359 The Nun..attracts notice from the pleasing contrast in its feathers; its head is almost covered with a veil of white feathers, which gives it its name.

d. = nun-bird. (*Cent. Dict.* 1890.)

3. A species of Venus-shell. *rare*⁻¹.

1681 Grew *Musæum* I. vi. i. 138 Many of this sort, striated, are found, saith Mr. Lyster, near Hartle-pool in the County of Durham, where the People call them Nuns.

4. A species of moth.

1832 Rennie *Butterfl. & M.* 96 The Nun... Wings one inch one-twelfth. **1890** *Pall Mall G.* 14 Aug. 4/3 The devastating moth, known as the 'nun', has made its appearance in north and west Germany.

†**5.** (See damsel 4.) *Obs.*

6. *attrib.* and *Comb.* **a.** Appositive, as ***nun-novice, -portress, -princess, -sister***, etc.

c **900** Wærferth tr. *Gregory's Dial.* 30 Be þære nunfæmnan, þe bat þone leahtric. *c* **1400** *Rule St. Benet* (Prose) 147 Efter þis sal þat nun nouece stand stil befor þe auter. **1768** Baretti *Mann. & Customs Italy* II. 21 To get out of the convent at night by the connivance of the nun-portress. **1879** J. D. Long *Æneid* I. 304 Till the nun-princess Ilia Bear unto Mars two children at a birth. **1892** *Daily News* 20 Oct. 5/7 To crown their sorrows, another nun-sister..had sunk under an attack of typhus.

b. Miscellaneous: as ***nun-looking, -nature***, etc.

1817 J. Scott *Paris Revisit.* (ed. 4) 90 These black eyes..took additional charms from the nun-looking wimple. **1824** Scott *Redgauntlet* ch. xvi, The place they live in was some sort of nun-shop long ago. **1863** Kingsley in *Reader* Oct. 507 Theirs is the true nun-nature. **1872** Howells *Wedd. Journ.* (1892) 268 Soft nun-voices speaking French through grated doors.

c. In genitive combs., as **nun's cloth**, a thin woollen stuff; **nun's cotton** = *nun's thread*; **nun's fiddle** (see quot.); †**nun's flesh**, a cold or ascetic temperament; **nun's thread**, a fine white sewing-cotton, such as is used by nuns; **nun's veiling**, a thin dress-stuff.

1884 *Cassell's Mag.* Mar. 246/1 *Nun's cloths are also now printed in chintz patterns. **1903** Hughes *Mus. Guide* 213 **Nun's-fiddle*, marine trumpet. **1672** Dryden *Assignation* I. i, They that look for *Nuns flesh in me shall be mistaken. **1731–8** Swift *Polite Conv.* i, I'll be sworn Miss has not an Inch of Nun's Flesh about her. **1796** Windham *Sp.* (1812) I. 304 With no haste to privation of their own comforts, with not one bit of Nun's flesh about them. **1815** *Zeluca* III. 234 Lady Floray couldn't have been much of a girl when she did marry—if she was engaged eight years, she must have had a little nun's flesh about her. **1766** W. Gordon *Gen. Counting-ho.* 322, 1 small box *nuns thread. **1844** G. Dodd *Textile Manuf.* iv. 140 The making of sewing-thread, known by the names of 'ounce-thread' and 'nun's-thread'. **1883** *Truth* 31 May 747/1 Lady Florence Maxwell's toilette was of cream *nun's veiling.

†**nun**, *sb.*² *Obs. rare.* [Perh. the same as prec.] A child's top. Also **nun-gig**.

1598 Florio, *Turbine*, a toppe, gigge or nunne that children plaie with, a whirlegigge. **1611** Cotgr., *Sabot*, a Top, Gig, or Nunne to whip, or play with. **1615** Markham *Country Contentm.* I. (1635) ii. 11 There be other Anglers which make their Corks [for floats] in the fashion of a Nun-gigge, small at both ends, and bigge in the middest.

nun, *v. rare*⁻¹. [f. nun *sb.*¹] *trans.* To confine or shut *up* as in a nunnery.

1753–4 Richardson *Grandison* (1766) V. 45, I will have you to town, and nun you up with Aunt Nell.

‖ˈ**nunatak**. [Eskimo: introduced by Nordenskiöld.] A peak of rock appearing above the surface of the inland ice in Greenland. Also applied to similar mountains in other regions.

The Swedish plural *nunatakker* has sometimes been used in English works.

1877 *Q. Jrnl. Geol. Soc.* XXXIII. 145 At Kangerdlugssuak, where the mountains are lofty and the sides of the fjords steep, there are three Nunataks..equalling the height of the neighbouring land; but above the Inland Ice of Disko..the Nunataks are lower Knolls. **1882** J. D. Whitney *Climatic Changes* 303 Camp was made..at the foot of a nunatak, the summit of which was 4,960 feet above the sea-level. **1888** *Times* 20 Nov. 9/5 The 'nunataks' which rise like skeletons above the frozen waste. **1900** *Nation* 15 Nov. 391/3 The visible land is in the form of nunataks, or of sea-cliffs, with talus beaches here and there. **1921** E. R. G. R. Evans *South with Scott* xiv. 190 Mount Hope is a nunatak of granite, about 2,800 feet in height. **1959** *Times* 9 Jan. 11/6 *Antarctic Findings*... At Shackleton Base..we lacked..solid ground. Some nunataks could be seen over 20 miles away to the east, near Vahsel Bay. **1963** 'G. Carr' *Lewker in Norway* vi. 129 The only light..had turned snow-hummocks into far-off mountains and ricky *nunataks* into boulders.

nun-bird. *Ornith.* [f. nun *sb.*¹] A South American puff-bird of the genus *Monacha*.

1881 Sclater *Jacamars & Puff-birds* 146 The White-winged Nunbird [*Monacha nigra*] was one of the first South American birds known to scientific naturalists. *Ibid.* 153 The Peruvian White-faced Nunbird seems to be an abundant and generally distributed species in Upper Amazonia. *Ibid.* 158 *Monacha pallescens*, the Pale Nunbird.

nun-buoy. *Naut.* [Cf. nun *sb.*², quot. 1615.] A buoy of circular shape in the middle and tapering towards each end.

1703 Dampier *Voy.* III. I. 149 The Tide..runs very swift here, so that our Nun-buoy would not bear above the Water to be seen. **1769** Falconer *Dict. Marine* (1780) s.v. *Buoy*, *Nun-Buoys*, are shaped like the middle frustum of two cones, abutting upon one common base. **1816** *Specif. Fouleton's Patent* No. 4040, The term nun buoy is applied generally to that description of buoy which is fastened by a rope to a ship's anchor by which you may know where the anchor lies. **1875** Bedford *Sailor's Pkt.-Bk.* v. (ed. 2) 136 Wrecks will still continue to be marked by green nun-buoys.

nunc, nunk, nunks, familiar forms of nuncle. Cf nunky.

1841 *Comic Almanack* Dec. 48 Come, nunks, one game at Blindman's-buff. **1876** Geo. Eliot *Dan. Der.* I. II. xvi. 311 His uncle or 'Nunc', as Sir Hugo had taught him to say. **1884** C. M. Yonge *Armourer's Prentices* I. 142 Should you know this nunks of yours? **1915** A. Bennett *These Twain* (1916) II. xiii. 259 'Here's Nunks!' exclaimed George. **1919** C. Orr *Glorious Things* xxiii. 279 The very night old Nunk was away.

‖**nunc di'mittis**. [L., the first words of the Song of Simeon in Luke ii. 29.]

1. The canticle beginning with these words.

1552 *Bk. Com. Prayer, Evening Pr.* Rubric, After that, (*Nunc dimittis*) in Englishe, as foloweth. **1625** Bacon *Ess.*,

On Death, The sweetest Canticle is, *Nunc dimittis*; when a Man hath obtained worthy Ends, and Expectations. **1872** A. DE VERE *Leg. St. Patrick, St. P. & Impostor*, Those Elders twain With hands upraised..sang the 'Nunc Dimittis'.

b. Hence *to sing* (*one's*) *nunc dimittis*, to declare oneself willing or delighted to depart from life or from some occupation.

1642 NETHERSOLE *Consid. upon Affairs* 8, I should.. cheerfully sing my *Nunc dimittis*. **1776** J. ADAMS *Wks.* (1854) IX. 391 When these things are once completed, I shall..sing my *nunc dimittis*, return to my farm [etc.]. **1825** HAN. MORE in W. Roberts *Mem.* (1834) IV. 257 If I could see the abolition of the slavery..in the West Indies..I could sing my *nunc dimittis* with joy. **1859** DARWIN *Life & Lett.* (1887) II. 232, I am now contented, and can sing my 'nunc dimittis'.

2. Permission to depart; departure, dismissal.

1654 *Wotton's Lett.* I. 120 (Stanf.), Yet my good Lord, at least procure me of my Lord the King a *Nunc dimittis*, leave to depart. **1699** 'MISAURUS' *Honour of Gout* in *Harl. Misc.* (1809) II. 44 He tells the decumbent a long story of the pains and misery of life, in order to make his *nunc dimittis* go down the easier. **1829** *Edin. Rev.* XLIX. 218 We shall now bow our heads to the *nunc dimittis*, come when it may.

†**nunce.** *Obs.* Also 7 nonce. [Anglicized form of NUNCIO or *nuncius* NUNTIUS, or a. F. *nonce.*] = NUNCIO.

1566 in Keith *Hist. Ch. Scot.* App. II. 135 Hir Majestie can nocht be empescheit with ony Besines concerning the Nunce. **1596** DALRYMPLE tr. *Leslie's Hist. Scot.* x. 420 Pelleuæi.. was the Papes nunce. **1611** SPEED *Hist. Gt. Brit.* IX. viii. §44. 498 Two Nunces from the Pope..meete him at Northampton. **1686** WAKE *Expos. Doctr. Ch. Eng.* p. xxxv, The Faculty of Divinity, at the Command of the Nonce,.. censured his Propositions.

‖**nunchaku** (nun'tʃaku). [Jap., f. Okinawa dialect.] Esp. in *pl.*, two hardwood sticks joined together by a strap, etc., as a defensive weapon.

1970 *Guardian Weekly* 2 May 11 The radical taste tends.. to nunchakus, which go back more than 500 years. They were..invented by Japanese peasants for self-defence when metal weapons were forbidden to all but the Samurai. **1973** *Express* (Trinidad & Tobago) 27 Apr. 31/3 The experts will give exhibitions in kobudo (weaponery) displaying their martial skill with the sai, nunchaku stick, bow, sword and daggers. **1975** *Globe & Mail* (Toronto) 17 Jan. 4/1 The proper name is nunchaku sticks. They are made of two sticks of hardwood joined together at one end by a chain, leather or rope.

nuncheon ('nʌnʃən). Now *dial.* Forms: α. 4 **nonechenche, nonschonches,** 5 **-senches;** *Sc.* 4 **noynsankys,** 5–6 **none-, nunschank(i)s.** β. 5 **noonchyns, -shyns, nonsiens,** 6 **nunchings,** 6–7 **nuncions** (7 **-chions**), **-tions.** γ. 5 **noneshyne,** 8–9 **noonchin(e;** 7, 9 **noonshun.** δ. 6–7 (9) **nonchion;** 6 **nuntion,** 7 **-cian;** 6– **nunchion,** 7– **nuncheon,** 9 *dial.* **nunchen, -chin(g), -chun, -shon.** [ME. *nōn(e)shench*, f. *nōn*(*e* NOON + *shench* (OE. *scenc*) draught, cup. Until the 17th cent. usually in forms with final *s*. In mod. western and south-western dialect the shorter form *nunch* is also current: cf. *luncheon* and *lunch.*] A slight refreshment of liquor, etc., originally taken in the afternoon; a light refreshment taken between meals; a lunch.

α. **1353** in Riley *Mem. London* 265 Nonechenche. **1375–6** *Abingdon Abbey Acc.* (1892) 28 Vnde liberantur Conuentui, pro eorum nonschonches,..j panis et j lagena ceruisie. **1394** *Reg. Nigrum Aberbrothoc* (Bann. Club) 43 That day that he wyrkis he sal haf a penny til his noynsankys. **1422–3** in *Gentl. Mag.* (1830) C. II. 592 It'm to ij Carpenters be j day to eche of hem, with her Nonsenches. **1491** *St. Giles Charters* (1859) p. xx, To haif bot thair noneschanks allanerly after-none. **1529** *Burgh Rec. Stirling* (1887) I. 35 Haiffand ilk werk day ane half hour afor nyne houris afor none to his disjone, and ane othir half hour afor four houris eftyr none to his nunschankis. **1536** in Jervise *Mem. Angus & Mearns* (1885) I. 298 Na tyme of license of dennar nor noneshankis.

β. **1422–3** in *Gentl. Mag.* (1830) C. II. 592 It'm to on Robert Dawber for his dawbyng be vij dayes,..with his noonchyns. **1426–7** *Rec. St. Mary at Hill* (1904) 64, ij carpenters with her nonsiens. **1591** PERCIVALL *Sp. Dict.*, *Merenda*,..an afternoones nuncions or drinking, a beuer. **1592** NASHE *P. Penilesse* (1842) 57 Then a set breakfast, then dinner, then afternoones nunchings, a supper, and a rere supper. **1622** MABBE tr. *Aleman's Guzman d'Alf.* 276 Which being both put together would not make up together a reasonable nunchions. **1649** *Wandering Jew* in Halliw. *Bk. Charac.* (1857) 24 In one of these pipes is my mornings draught,..in a third, my after-noons nuntions.

γ. *a* **1500** *Egerton MS.* 2108 lf. 57 b, To vij. other laborers .., every man, iij.*d.* and for noneshyne, iv.*d.* **1613–16** W. BROWNE *Brit. Past.* II. i, Harvest-folkes..On sheafes of corne were at their noonshuns close. **1772** GRAVES *Spir. Quix.* (1783) III. 14 They took a comfortable noonchine together. **1808** JANE AUSTEN *Lett.* (1884) I. 353 Immediately after the noonshine which succeeded their arrival a party set off for Buckwell. **1875** *Whitby Gloss.* s.v., It was n't a dinner, it was only a bit of a noonshun. **1880** MISS YONGE *Love & Life* I. 36, I will give you some bread and cheese and gingerbread for noonchin.

δ. **1580** HOLLYBAND *Treas. Fr. Tong, Le Gouster*,..an afternoones banket, an onchion. *a* **1591** H. SMITH *Wks.* (1867) I. 56 Is there nothing in the sacrament but bread and wine, like an hungry nuncion? **1603** HARSNET *Pop. Impost.* xxiii. 158 Perverting the Nature of the Holy Communion, to a private Nunchion for a priest alone. **1611** COTGR., *Collation de Moyne*, a Monks nuncheon; as much as another man eats at a large meale. **1694** *Urquhart's Rabelais* IV. xlvi, Some say there is..no Dinner like a Lawyer's, no Afternoon's Nunchion like a Vintner's. **1734** FIELDING *Old Man taught Wisd.* Wks. 1784 III. 126, I don't eat a great deal, unless it be at breakfast..and afternoon's nunchion. **1790** T. PRYCE *Voc. Cornish, Croust*, an afternoon's nuncheon. **1822** SCOTT *Nigel* ii, I came to get my four-hours' nunchion from you. **1858** HUGHES *Scour. White Horse* 61 A long table was laid out for luncheon, or nunching as the boots..called it. **1893** *Wiltsh. Gloss.* App. 198 About Salisbury Nuncheon is between 10 and 10.30 a.m., and again at 4 p.m., and is a very small meal.

nunciate ('nʌnʃ(ı)eıt), *sb.*[1] [Irreg. f. L. *nuncius* or *nunciāre*, perh. after *legate.*] One who or that which announces; a messenger, nuntius.

1596 W. SMITH *Chloris* (1877) 4 Vouchsafe to reade these lines.., Nuntiates of wo with sorrow being clad. **1762** HOOLE *Tasso* XI. viii, All the nunciates of th' ethereal reign, Who testified the glorious death to man. **1851** C. L. SMITH tr. *Tasso* I. lxix, Do thou, my nunciate,..Dispose him in my name to what imparts vantage to us and him.

'**nunciate**, *sb.*[2] [ad. It. *nunziato*, †*nuntiato*: see NUNCIO and -ATE[1] a.] Nunciature.

1882–3 SCHAFF *Encycl. Relig. Knowl.* 2273 Carlo Borromeo..established a nunciate in Switzerland.

†'**nunciate**, *v. Obs. rare*$^{-1}$. (See quot.)

1708 *Brit. Apollo* No. 7. 3/1 This Court had resolv'd to send thither Monsieur Aldobrandin without being Nunciated, or having a Brief for Nuncio.

†**nunci'ation.** *Obs.* [ad. L. *nunciātiōn-em*, n. of action f. *nunciāre*, *nuntiāre* to announce. So Sp. *nunciacion*, It. *nunziazione.*] The action of announcing; annunciation.

c **1450** *Cursor M.* 11001 (Laud), The nunciacion Of Cryst that broght vs alle pardoun. **1620** T. GRANGER *Div. Logike* 3 Nunciation, that is, telling, or reporting. **1633** T. ADAMS *Exp. 2 Pet.* i. 13 There is no nunciation of the Gospel, how-soever there may be a proclamation of Judgment. **1649** *Argts. upon Writ of Habeas Corpus* 19 Our case is by the Nunciation of many.

nunciative ('nʌnʃ(ı)ətıv), *a. rare.* [f. L. *nunciāt-*, ppl. stem of *nunciāre* (see prec.) + -IVE.] Conveying a message or messages; making announcements.

1653 BAXTER *Chr. Concord* xviii. B 2, The Ministeriall power being not compulsive,..but Nunciative, Swasory, and directive. *a* **1901** F. W. H. MYERS *Hum. Personality* (1903) II. 88 They are all of them message-bearing or nunciative automatisms.

So †'**nunciatory** *a. Obs. rare.*

1576 FLEMING *Panopl. Epist.* To Rdr., For of letters there be sundrie sortes [*Marg.* Nunciatorie, Lamentatorie, Consolatorie]. **1586** A. DAY *Eng. Secretary* II. (1625) 59 A Letter Nunciatorie from a sonne to his father or friends touching his being in service.

nunciature ('nʌnʃ(ı)ətjʊə(r)). Also 7 **nuntiature.** [ad. It. *nunziatura* (= Sp. and Pg. *nunciatura*, F. *nonciature*), f. *nunzio* NUNCIO.]

1. The representation of the Pope at a foreign court by his nuncio; the office of nuncio.

1652 EARL MONM. tr. *Bentivoglio's Hist. Relat.* 51 All Affairs of Religion which occur in those Kingdoms, fall likewise under the same Nuntiature. **1670–98** LASSELS *Voy. Italy* I. 12 They are good for Nunciatures, Embassies, and State employments. **1710** *Lond. Gaz.* No. 4775/2 The Pope's Nuncio was lodged in the palace of the nunciature. **1768** *Ann. Reg., Hist. Europe* 9/1 It was also resolved..to suppress the jurisdiction of the Nunciature. **1858** tr. *Life Xavier* 44 Xavier replied that however vile such services might appear they would not degrade the dignity of the Nunciature. **1887** *Pall Mall G.* 11 July 7/1 The time has not arrived..for establishing anything resembling a nunciature or apostolic delegation in London.

2. The period during which a given person holds the office of papal nuncio.

1662 J. BARGRAVE *Pope Alex. VII* (1867) 106 Some [churches] remaining without pastors all the time of his nuntiature. **1670** G. H. *Hist. Cardinals* II. III. 186 He had been..pleas'd with his proceedings during his Nuntiature. **1706** tr. *Dupin's Eccl. Hist. 16th C.* II. v. 121 A History.. which he wrote during his Nunciature in Spain. **1818** *Gentl. Mag.* LXXXVIII. II. 127 The Pope..sent him to the Court of Spain, during which Nunciature he was promoted to the purple. **1896** VIZETELLY tr. *Zola's Rome* 28 First Leo's religious education at Rome, then his brief nunciature at Brussels.

nuncio ('nʌnʃıəʊ). Also 6– **nuntio.** [a. earlier It. *nuncio*, *nuntio* (now *nunzio*), = Sp. and Pg. *nuncio*:—L. *nuncius*, *nuntius* messenger.]

1. A permanent official representative of the Roman See at a foreign court.

α. **1528** in Ellis *Orig. Lett.* Ser. III. II. 103 His Holines morover sent to his Nuncio a Copie of a lettre sent from the Nuncio in Hungaria. **1577** HARRISON *Descr. Eng.* ii. in *Holinshed* I. 143 The pope understanding what he was by his Nuncio here in England. **1655** FULLER *Ch. Hist.* III. 63 A Nuncio differed from a Legate, almost as a Lieger from an extraordinary Ambassadour. **1700** TYRRELL *Hist. Eng.* II. 858 The Pope had sent his Nuncios all over Europe. **1759** ROBERTSON *Hist. Scot.* I. IV. 293 She now resolved to allow a nuncio from the pope publicly to enter her dominions. **1827** HALLAM *Const. Hist.* iii. (1876) I. 115 The nuncio received a message at Brussels, that he must not enter the kingdom. **1866** ROGERS *Agric. & Prices* I. ix. 155 Contributions for the maintenance of cardinals, foreign bishops, and nuncios.

β. **1586** J. HOOKER *Hist. Irel.* in *Holinshed* II. 169/1 Two friers, whose gownes were too long for them to follow the earle and the popes nuntio. **1617** MORYSON *Itin.* I. 81 The Inquisitors of Religion..: namely the Popes Nuntio, and the Patriarke. *a* **1648** LD. HERBERT *Autobiog.* (1886) 236 The Pope's nuntio, the Emperor's ambassador,..and others. *a* **1715** BURNET *Own Time* (1766) II. 57 In dangerous practices with the Pope's Nuntio. **1762–71** H. WALPOLE *Vertue's Anecd. Paint.* (1786) III. 216 In the service of cardinal Dada, the pope's nuntio. **1823** LINGARD *Hist. Eng.* VI. 139 Leo sent to the court, as nuntio for religious matters, Girolamo Aleandri, prefect of the Vatican library.

2. One who bears a message; a messenger.

1601 SHAKS. *Twel. N.* I. iv. 28 She will attend it better in thy youth, Then in a Nuntio's of more graue aspect. **1644** *10th Rep. Hist. MSS. Comm.* App. IV. 70 Having so opportune a nuncio I could not let pass without presenting a few lines unto you. **1710** *Pol. Ballads* (1860) II. 95 The godly Lay-Five..By me their sure nuncio do send you this greeting.

fig. **1617** WITHER *Fidelia, Juvenilia* (1633) 447, I had not now been forced to have sent Those lines for Nuncios of my discontent. **1672** SIR T. BROWNE *Let. Friend* § 2 Some secret sense or intimation by dreams,..airy nuncios [etc.]. **1777** BRAND *Pop. Antiq.* 92 Swallows..were honoured antiently as the Nuncios of the Spring.

3. *Hist.* A member of the Polish diet.

1684 *Scanderbeg Redivivus* ii. 22 Now this distinct Body of Nuntio's..is a Ballance to the Senators. **1753** *Scots Mag.* Jan. 3/1 The nuncios of a general diet of Poland were chosen in August last. **1773** *Ann. Reg.* 39 Fifty of the Nuncios still opposing it to fifty-two who voted for it. **1831** SIR J. SINCLAIR *Corr.* II. 293 About two-thirds of the Nuncios wore the Polish dress. **1848** W. H. KELLY tr. *L. Blanc's Hist. Ten Y.* I. 482 All the nuncios rose as one man, and shouted, 'To the ramparts!'

Hence †'**nuncioship**, †'**nunciotist**.

1652 EARL MONM. tr. *Bentivoglio's Hist. Relat.* 51 For that the Church-men which are in those parts are under the same Nuntioship. **1673** *Conf. betw. Protestants & Papist* 25 Many Nunciotist Provincials of Regular Orders, and Abbots also.

nuncion, obs. form of NUNCHEON.

nuncius ('nʌnʃ(ı)əs). *rare.* [a. L. *nuncius*: cf. NUNTIUS.] A messenger.

1613–16 W. BROWNE *Brit. Past.* I. i, The Nuncius of peace, the seely Dove. ? **1633** COWLEY *Dream of Elysium* 89 Th' watchfull Bird, true Nuncius of the Light, Straight crow'd. **1848** LYTTON *Harold* III. ii, He stretched forth his sceptre, and motioning to his chamberlain, bade him introduce the nuncius.

nuncle, variant of UNCLE with transferred *n* (see N 3 b). Now *dial.* (Cf. NUNKY and NUNC, NUNK, NUNKS.)

c **1589** *Theses Martinianæ* 2 To my nunckle Canturburie. **1599** PORTER *Angry Wom. Abingd.* (Percy Soc.) 132, I should be glad To haue myselfe called nunckle, and thou dad. **1605** SHAKS. *Lear* I. iv. 170 Nuncle, giue me an egge. **1663** DRYDEN *Wild Gallant* III. i, Alas, alas, poor nuncle! **1710** *Brit. Apollo* No. 89. 3/2 Why Nuncle Hermes, this is very odd. **1760** FOOTE *Minor* II. Wks. 1799 I. 252 Oh, a proof of my respect, dear nuncle. **1838–** in *Eng. Dial. Dict.*

Hence †'**nuncle** *v. Obs. rare*$^{-1}$.

a **1676** *Roxb. Ball.* (1895) VIII. 203 She still'd her mother's tongue,..Nuncl'd her Mam.

‖**nunc stans.** [L. *nunc* now + *stans* pres. pple. of *stāre* to stand.] The eternal timeless 'now' presumed, as an attribute of God, to be co-existent with Time.

1651 HOBBES *Leviathan* xlvi. 374 But they will teach us that Eternity is the Standing still of the Present Time, a *Nunc-stans* (as the Schools call it;) which neither they, nor any else understand. **1678** CUDWORTH *Intell. Syst.* 645 *Nunc-stans*, or a Standing Now of Eternity. **1733** A. BAXTER *Enquiry Human Soul* viii. 376 The distinction of past and future vanishes with respect to such a Mind; and the expression *nunc stans* will appear to have propriety. **1854** H. L. MANSEL *Lett.* (1873) 119 Augustine, and the Schoolmen after him,..speaking of Eternity as a *nunc stans*. **1896** W. CALDWELL *Schopenhauer's System* viii. 393 In willing the world is at once an eternal process and an eternal stationary thing—a *nunc stans*—at the same time. **1946** J. LAIRD *Philos. Incursions Eng. Lit.* vi. 96 On a few occasions..Wordsworth described the specious *nunc stans* of mystical ecstasy; its apparent arrest of time itself. **1958** E. HELLER *Ironic German* vi. 241 Thomas Mann was..well prepared for 'the mystery of the revolving sphere' by Schopenhauer's philosophy of the eternal *nunc stans* which resides at the centre of the illusory motion of Time. **1967** P. MERLAN in *Cambr. Hist. Later Greek & Early Medieval Philos.* 100 A supreme god.. lives in the *aiôn* which can also be characterized as a *nunc stans*.

†'**nuncupate,** *pa. pple. Obs. rare*$^{-1}$. In 6 num-. [ad. L. *nuncupāt-us*: see next.] Called.

a **1548** HALL *Chron. Edw. IV* 248 b, We beyng called reasonable creatures,..be more worthy to be numcupate, and demed persones vnresonable.

nuncupate ('nʌnkju:peıt), *v.* [f. ppl. stem of L. *nuncupāre* to name, declare.]

†**1.** *trans.* To name, designate. *Obs. rare.*

1609 HOLLAND *Amm. Marcell.* XXII. ii. 189 By the last words he spake he nuncupated him successor in his imperiall throne. **1656** BLOUNT *Glossogr.*, *Nuncupate*, to name, to call by some name; also to pronounce, tell by name or rehearse.

†**2.** To express (a vow) in words. *Obs.*

1606 HOLLAND *Sueton.* 83 The vowes..he commanded his colleague Tiberivs to nuncupate and pronounce. **1635** JACKSON *Creed* VIII. xxii. Wks. VIII. 69 They nuncupate this their solemn vow unto the Lord our God. **1788** BURKE *Sp. agst. W. Hastings* Wks. XV. 32 They do here..make this solemn declaration, and nuncupate this deliberate vow.

3. To declare (a will) orally.

a **1677** BARROW *Pope's Supremacy* v. § 7 But how doth that Will appear?..in what Registers is it extant? in whose presence did he nuncupate it? **1880** MUIRHEAD *Gaius* II. 109 Although they may neither have provided the number of witnesses.., nor nuncupated their will, they do not the less test validly.

†**4.** To dedicate (a work) *to* some one. *Obs.*

1550 VERON tr. *Zwinglius' Short Pathw.* Ded., Which small worke I doo moste humblye dedicate, offer, and nuncupate vnto your ryghte worshipfull maistershippe. **1637** BASTWICK *Litany* I. 1 [It] was one of the principall causes of this nuncupating my Letany to your Ladiship. **1656** EVELYN *Mem.* (1857) III. 82 You should on my advice have nuncupated this handsome monument of your skill and dexterity to some great one.

Hence **'nuncupating** *vbl. sb.*

1679 PULLER *Moder. Ch. Eng.* (1843) 152 Our Church.. nowhere.. alloweth nuncupating of vows, or offering sacrifices to Saints.

nuncupation (nʌnkjuː'peɪʃən). Also 4 -acion. [ad. L. *nuncupātiōn-em*, n. of action f. *nuncupāre*: see prec. and -ATION. So F. *nuncupation* (16th c.), Sp. *nuncupacion.*]

† **1.** The action of naming or designating. *Obs.*

1387-8 T. USK *Test. Love* I. ix. (Skeat) I. 119 But images ben goddes by nuncupacion. **1616** BULLOKAR *Eng. Expos.*, *Nuncupation*, a naming. **1619** SIR J. SEMPILL *Sacrilege Handl.* 84 Heere then was but a Nuncupation, a Fundation of Priest-hood. *a* **1670** HACKET *Cent. Serm.* (1675) 102 What they have, it is by entitling and nuncupation.

† **2.** The solemn expression *of* a vow. *Obs.*

1615 JACKSON *Creed* v. xxxi. Wks. IV. 276 Of this internal adoration.. they make intercession or nuncupation of vows essential parts. **1678** CUDWORTH *Intell. Syst.* I. iv. §14. 259 He being frequently thus stiled in their solemn Nuncupations of Vows.. Jupiter Father.

3. The oral declaration of a will.

1726 AYLIFFE *Parergon* 520 When a Codicil is not made by Nuncupation, but solemnly and in writing. **1880** MUIRHEAD *Ulpian* xx. §9 The mancipation of the *familia* or estate, and the nuncupation of the testament.

nuncupative ('nʌnkjuːpeɪtɪv, nʌn'kjuːpətɪv), *a.* (and *sb.*) [ad. late and med.L. *nuncupātīv-us*: see NUNCUPATE *v.* and -IVE. So F. *nuncupatif* (1354); It., Sp., and Pg. *nuncupativo.*]

1. Of wills: Oral, not written.

After med.L. *testamentum nuncupativum* (Du Cange).

1546 *Knaresb. Wills* (Surtees) I. 50 John Oxennarde of Bramley made his nuncupatyve will before Ric. Pullen, sen^r^. **1590** SWINBURNE *Testaments* 23 The appointing of an executor, (without the which there can be no testament at all, neither written nor nuncupatiue). **1634** C. DOWNING *State Eccl. Kingd.* 51 By the Nuncupative will of his sacred predecessour, who then adopted him. **1651** G. W. tr. *Cowell's Inst.* 118 Lands cannot be given by a Nuncupative will. **1726** AYLIFFE *Parergon* 142 This Cancelling.. is suppos'd to be extended to those Testaments Nuncupative, that are afterwards reduced to Writing. **1754** ERSKINE *Princ. Sc. Law* (1809) 473 Probation by witnesses is admitted to the extent of L. 100 Scots, in payments, nuncupative legacies, and verbal agreements. **1818** CRUISE *Digest* (ed. 2) VI. 60 It is not sufficient that it be put into writing after his death, being first declared by words only; for then it is but a nuncupative will. **1883** *American* VI. 270 Soldiers and sailors, however, when on service may make nuncupative wills.

transf. **1660** JER. TAYLOR *Duct. Dubit.* II. iii. rule 14 §32 Nuncupative records are like diagrams in sand, and figures efformed in air.

† **b.** *sb.* An oral decree. *Obs. rare*$^{-1}$.

1698 FRYER *Acc. E. India & P.* 367 As in Nuncupatives the irrevocable Decrees and Commands of the Emperor stand firm, so his Determinations in the Written Law are as Authentick.

† **2.** Nominal; so-called. *Obs. rare.*

a **1548** HALL *Chron., Hen. VII* 39 b, He determined rather to retourne with his assured gaine then to tary the nuncupative dukes.. uncerteine victory. *a* **1670** HACKET *Cent. Serm.* (1675) 101 The princes of the people are Nuncupative Gods in Scripture.

3. Denoting nuncupation; designative. *rare.*

a **1619** FOTHERBY *Atheom.* I. vi. §2 (1622) 41 That nuncupatiue tittle, wherewith both Heathens and Christians haue honoured their Oathes. **1817** G. S. FABER *Eight Dissert.* (1845) II. 275 We may.. anticipate, among the Pelasgi also, a similar nuncupative reference to the same ancient city of Nimrod. **1828** MIDDLETON *Grk. Article* 43 Nouns preceded by Verbs or Participles Substantive or Nuncupative.

Hence **nuncupatively** *adv.*

1657 W. MORICE *Coena quasi Κοινὴ* vi. 312 The Idols of the Gentiles were called Gods, nuncupatively or ironically. **1767** tr. *Voltaire's Ignorant Philosopher* xxiii. 46 He [God] exists essentially, participatively and nuncupatively.

† **nuncupatory**, *a. Obs.* [Cf. prec. and -ORY. So Sp. and Pg. *nuncupatorio*, obs. F. *-atoire.*]

1. Nuncupative, oral, verbal.

a **1603** T. CARTWRIGHT *Confut. Rhem. N.T.* (1618) 463 Lest they should here cavill at the word *Testament*,.. to make it as well nuncupatory and unwritten, as written. **1638** FEATLY *Strict. Lyndom.* II. 121 They refuse the triall, pretending I know not what nuncupatory will by word of mouth. **1691** WOOD *Ath. Oxon.* I. 485 By his nuncupatory Will, which he spake on the 14. day of the same month. **1704** SWIFT *T. Tub* II. Wks. 1751 I. 55 You are to be informed, that of Wills *duo sunt genera*, Nuncupatory and Scriptory.

2. Dedicatory.

1654 JER. TAYLOR *Real Pres.* 76 As the Archbishop of Cæsarea.. hath enumerated them in his nuncupatory Epistle to Pope Sixtus Quintus. **1679** EVELYN *Sylva* (ed. 3) To Rdr., The many Nuncupatory Epistles to be seen in the fronts of so many learned Volumes.

nundinal ('nʌndɪnəl), *a.* (and *sb.*) [ad. L. *nundināl-is*, f. *nundinæ* NUNDINE. So F. *nundinal.*] Pertaining to a fair or market; connected with the Roman nundines.

nundinal letter, a letter of the alphabet (A to H) attached to each day of the Roman nundinal period.

1656 in BLOUNT *Glossogr.* **1721** in BAILEY. **1727-38** CHAMBERS *Cycl.* s.v., The letter D will be the nundinal letter of the year following. **1839** J. TAYLOR *Poems & Transl.* 183 Nundinal or Market Days. **1862** LEWIS *Astron. of Ancients* 56 The nundinal or eight-day period of Rome.

b. *sb.* A nundinal letter.

1727-38 CHAMBERS *Cycl.* s.v., These nundinals bear a very great resemblance to the dominical letters, which return every eight days, as the nundinals did every nine.

So † **'nundinary** *a.* [L. *nundinārius.*] *Obs.*

1656 in BLOUNT *Glossogr.* **1762** tr. *Busching's Syst. Geogr.* I. Pref. p. xviii, The commercial or nundinary measures being, for the most part, less than the mean.

† **nundinate**, *v.* [L. *nundinārī.*] (See quot.)

1623 COCKERAM I, *Nundinate*, to buy and sell, as at faires.

nundi'nation. [ad. L. *nundinātiōn-em*, n. of action f. *nundinārī*, f. *nundinæ* NUNDINE.] Traffic, trade, buying and selling; sale.

1623 COCKERAM I, *Nundination*, a buying and selling. **1635** SWAN *Spec. M.* ii. §3 (1643) 33 In regard that the nundinations and things of that nature appertained to the Jubilee. **1642** DRUMM. OF HAWTH. *Skiamachia* Wks. (1711) 199 Ye are.. approvers of purgatory, of.. transubstantiation, nundination of pardons. **1684** H. MORE *Answ.* 282 This Vision of the Prince of Tyre is taken Notice of in *Synopsis Prophetica*, for a Prediction of Ecclesiastical Nundinations.

1840 I. TAYLOR *Ancient Chr.* (1842) II. vi. 141 The nundination of indulgences and the oecumenic authority of the pope.. are the characteristics of popery.

† **nundinative**, *a. Obs. rare*$^{-1}$. [See next and -ATIVE.] Nundinal.

1631 R. BYFIELD *Doctr. Sabb.* 81 Macrobius saith, there are foure kindes of publike holy-dayes.., Stative, Conceptive, Imperative, and nundinative.

nundine ('nʌndaɪn). Also *pl.* [ad. L. *nundinæ* fem. pl., f. *novem* nine + *diēs* day.] Among the ancient Romans, a market-day held every eighth (by Roman reckoning, ninth) day.

1533 BELLENDEN *Livy* III. xi. (S.T.S.) I. 292 Now war þe commites proclamit to be haldin þe thrid day eftir þe nundinis for creatioun of þir ten men.

1853 *Fraser's Mag.* XLVII. 289 The præfect.. had threatened to bring the case, on the next Nundines, before the sitting ædile. **1891** FARRAR *Dark & Dawn* (1893) 249 The meeting was fixed to take place on the next nundine.

b. A recurring period of eight days.

1860 HESSEY *Sunday* 385 Even after Constantine's time nundines as well as weeks were in use.

nune, Sc. form of NOON.

nunefar, obs. variant of NENUPHAR.

† **nun-fish.** *Obs.* A kind of shell-fish.

1661 LOVELL *Hist. Anim. & Min.* 234 *Nun-fishes*.. are a wholesome and delicate meate, as any periwinckle... Their face is white, their head covered with a black vaile like the nuns of Saint Bridgets Order, so had the name.

nun-gig: see NUN *sb.*[2]

'nunhood. [f. NUN *sb.*[1] + -HOOD.] The state of being a nun.

1812 COLERIDGE in *Lit. Rem.* (1839) IV. 69 She at length resolved on nunhood because she thought it could not be much worse than Purgatory. **1890** *Eng. Illustr. Mag.* Dec. 261 Her fifty-two years' nunhood.

† **'nunka.** *Obs.* Also nuncka. = next.

1589 [? LYLY] *Pappe w. Hatchet* C iij, The babie comes in with Nunka, Neame, and Dad. **1589** NASHE *Mart. Marprelate* IV. Wks. (Grosart) I. 173 He requireth in scorne, of his Nunkaes.., whether they haue not closelie murdered the Gentleman.

nunky ('nʌŋkɪ). Also nunkie. **1.** Familiar form of NUNCLE. Cf. NUNC, NUNK, NUNKS.

1798 CHARLOTTE SMITH *Yng. Philos.* I. 101, I only repeat what I have heard, that old nunky looks upon you as still belonging to him. **1815** *Zeluca* III. 232 Nunky pays for all. **1840** HOOD *Up Rhine* 4 When the qualm is over,.. Nunky, Nevy and Watch go on as usual. **1870** MISS BRIDGMAN *R. Lynne* II. v. 102, I saw.. how rich your dutiful old nunky had cut up. **1969** 'A. GILBERT' *Missing from Home* vi. 86 We don't even know she had an uncle... And if it was seven o'clock.. she was running it pretty fine if she was going for a drive with Nunkie. **1973** *Times Lit. Suppl.* 30 Nov. 1472/2 She was A. J. Balfour's favourite niece... 'Nunky' died in 1930.

2. *slang.* A pawnbroker. Cf. UNCLE *sb.* 3.

1921 *Daily Colonist* (Victoria, B.C.) 5 Apr. 13/5 If you happen to want a ten-dollar bill and trot round the corner to 'nunky'; why, that's really not quite done, my dear fellow. **1937** in PARTRIDGE *Dict. Slang.*

'nunlet. *Ornith.* [f. NUN *sb.*[1] + -LET.] A South American puff-bird of the genus *Nonnula.*

1899 A. H. EVANS *Birds* 447 The Nunlets.. are distributed from Panama to Peru and Brazil; they are brown above and ferruginous beneath, with a little white.

'nun-like, *adv.* and *a.* [f. NUN *sb.*[1]]

A. *adv.* After the fashion of a nun.

1589 [see NUN *sb.*[1] 2 a]. **1755** in Dodsley *Coll. Poems* III. 275 She.. Most nun-like mourns.

B. *adj.* Resembling (that of) a nun.

1611 COTGR. s.v. *Nonnette*, She seemes to weare a Nunne-like fillet about her head. **1626** PURCHAS *Pilgrimage* v. i. (ed. 4) 480 The like was done by their Nun-like women.

1865 ALLINGHAM *50 Mod. Poems, Southwell Park* II. 118 The well-fended nunlike child. **1870** MISS BRIDGMAN *R. Lynne* II. xii. 255 The usual nunlike simplicity of her dress.

nunmor: see etym. note to NO MORE.

nunnated, *a.* (See quot. and next.)

1841 LADY EGERTON in C. Forster *Mon. Assyria* (1859) 339 Being the very title nunnated (that is marked with the final n) now borne by the Chief of the Sheraunee Affghans.

nunnation (nʌ'neɪʃən). Also nunation. [ad. mod.L. *nunnātiōn-em*, f. *nūn* the Arabic name of the letter *n.*]

1. The addition of a final *n* in the declension of Arabic nouns, denoted by doubling the vowel sign.

1776 J. RICHARDSON *Arab. Gram.* 2 The nunnation is seldom sounded, excepting in the pompous or solemn style of reading. *Ibid.* 12 The final ا adds nothing to the sound when the nunnation is pronounced. **1874** SAYCE *Compar. Philol.* v. 187 The natives of Harar.. use a postfixed '-n', which seems a relic of a primitive nunnation. **1883** *Encycl. Brit.* XV. 473/1 The *on* in Madabron apparently represents the Arabic nunation.

2. A similar addition of *n* in Middle English nouns, etc.

1838 GUEST *Hist. Eng. Rhythms* II. 111 One of its [the language of Layamon] most striking peculiarities is its nunnation, if we may be allowed to use a term already familiar to the scholar. **1844** *Proc. Philol. Soc.* I. 261 Nouns of the *n* declension often took the nunnation in the nominative in place of the usual vowel-ending. **1866** G. STEPHENS *Runic Mon.* I. 26 This Northumbrian form.. is clearly a separately developt local dialectic 'nunnation'.

nunnery ('nʌnərɪ). Forms: α. 3-7 nonnerie, 3-5 -erye, 4, 6 nonery, 6 noonery. β. 4, 7 nunnerie, 5 nvnnerye, 6- nunnery (7 nunery). [Prob. ad. AF. *nonnerie, f. *nonne* NUN *sb.*[1]: see -ERY. Cf. F. *nonnerie* (Littré).]

1. A place of residence for a body or community of nuns; a building in which nuns live under religious rule and discipline; a convent.

α. *c* **1275** LAY. 15642 Nou was Merlyn his moder.. in one nonnerie munechene ihoded. *c* **1290** *S. Eng. Leg.* I. 91/148 And al þis compaygnie I-burede weren in Coloyne, in one Nonnerie. *c* **1330** R. BRUNNE *Chron. Wace* (Rolls) 14225 Scheo ȝald hure til þat nonnerye, & tok þe veil for hure folye. *c* **1386** CHAUCER *Reeve's T.* 48 For hir kynreed and hir nortelrye, That sche had lerned in a nonnerye. *c* **1425** *Hampole's Psalter* Metr. Pref. 28 Þar it lyȝt in cheyn bondes in þe same nonery. **1470-85** MALORY *Arthur* XXI. ix. 854 Atte last he cam to a nonnerye. **1523** LD. BERNERS *Froiss.* I. cxxv. 151 The kyng of Englande was at Poissoy, and lay in the nonery there. *c* **1612** *Women Saints* 55 Her sister St. Etheldred.. founder of that Nonnerie.

β. *c* **1305** *Land Cokayne* 147 An oþer abbei is þerbi For soth a gret fair nunnerie. **1483** *Cath. Angl.* 257/1 A Nvnnerye, *cenobium.* **1571** A. JENKINSON *Voy. & Trav.* (Hakl. Soc.) I. 137 Not farre from the said Castle was a Nunnery of sumptuous building. **1602** SHAKS. *Ham.* III. i. 122 Get thee to a Nunnerie. *Ibid.* 132 Goe thy wayes to a Nunnery. **1648** GAGE *West Ind.* 58 This man alone built a Nunery of Franciscan Nuns. *a* **1699** LADY HALKETT *Autobiog.* (Camden) 15 That there was a nunery in Holland for those of the Protestant religion. **1707** LADY M. W. MONTAGU *Lett.* II. xlvii. 43 Her relations.. would certainly confine her to a nunnery for the rest of her days. **1756-7** tr. *Keysler's Trav.* (1760) II. 229 There are boards placed before most of the windows, like those in a great many nunneries. **1841** ELPHINSTONE *Hist. Ind.* I. 201 Nunneries for women seem also, at one time, to have been general. **1886** *Pall Mall G.* 17 July 5/2 To the south-east we may see the ruins of Sopwell nunnery.

fig. **1634** HABINGTON *Castara* I. (Arb.) 18 Yee blushing Virgins [*sc.* roses] happie are In the chaste Nunn'ry of her brests. **1652** CRASHAW *Elegy Mr. Stanninow*, Whose nest Was in the modest Nunnery of his brest.

attrib. **1859** TENNYSON *Guinev.* 225 O little maid, shut in by nunnery walls. **1884** J. HALL *Christian Home* 113 When no safety could be hoped for California girls but in nunnery schools.

b. *transf.* A house of ill fame.

1593 NASHE *Christ's T.* 79 b, [To] some one Gentleman generally acquainted, they giue.. free priuiledge thence-forward in theyr Nunnery, to procure them frequentance. **1617** FLETCHER *Mad Lover* IV. ii, Theres an old Nunnerie at hand. What's that? A bawdy-house. **17..** (*title-p.*), The Complete London Spy, or Disclosures of the Transactions in and around London and Westminster Coffee houses, Nunneries, Night Houses, Taverns, Bagnios, etc.

† **2.** The institution of conventual life for women; nunship. *Obs.*

1650 FULLER *Pisgah* II. iii. §11. 95 *marg.*, Nicolas Lyra *in locum*, with most Roman commentators since his time, in hope to found Nunnery thereupon. **1679** PRANCE *Add. Narrative* 11 English Gentlewomen,.. who have a mind to take the Vail of Nunnery upon them.

† **b.** Nun-like chastity. *Obs. rare*$^{-1}$.

1654 GAYTON *Pleas. Notes* II. vi. 60 Marcelas speech is a pure defence of resolv'd virginity, vow'd Nunnery [etc.].

3. A company of nuns. (In quots. *fig.*)

1651 CLEVELAND *Poems* 1 Not the fair Abbess of the skies, With all her Nunnery of eyes. **1715** ADDISON *Freeholder* No. 15 (1751) 88 A Fan which has on it a Nunnery of lively black-ey'd Vestals.

† **'nunnify**, *v. Obs. rare.* [f. NUN *sb.*[1]] *trans.* To make a nun of (one).

1624 J. GEE *New Shreds of Old Snare* 7 They determined to set her packing beyond the Seas, there to be Nunnified. **1640** SHIRLEY *Imposture* I. ii, Do not you find it? They Have nunnified her.

'nunnish, *a.* [f. NUN *sb.*[1]] Pertaining to, characteristic of, a nun; nun-like.

1570 FOXE *A. & M.* (ed. 2) 178/2 Three daughters of Merwaldus.. entred the profession and vow of Nunnish virginitie. **1654** WHITLOCK *Zootomia* 203 The Nunnish, or Monastick life. **1891** TUCKLEY *Under the Queen* 242 These women have a nunnish look.

Hence †**'nunnishness**. *Obs.*$^{-1}$

1570 FOXE *A. & M.* (ed. 2) 319 Elysabeth the nonne, who for her holy nonnyshenes was canonised of the..church.

nunny bag ('nʌnɪ bæg). *Newfoundland.* Also nonny bag. [f. Eng. dial. *noony* meal at noon + BAG *sb.*] A kind of haversack, often made of sealskin.

1842 J. B. JUKES *Excursions in Newfoundland* II. 146 Having determined to return, we hung up in the tilt a 'nunny bag' full of bread. **1895** *Dialect Notes* I. 380 *Nunny bag*, lunch bag; usually made of a piece of sealskin, and used by sealers when they go off for a day. **1919** W. T. GRENFELL *Labrador Doctor* 90 Our sealers carry dry oatmeal and sugar in their 'nonny bags', which, mixed with snow, assuage their thirst and hunger as well. **1925** *Dialect Notes* V. 337 *Nonny bag*, a small knapsack to carry out on the ice; ditty bag. **1944** H. WENTWORTH *Amer. Dial. Dict.* 419/1 *Nunny bag*, a lunch bag, usually of sealskin. **1961** *Maclean's Mag.* 28 Jan. 47/2 He clawed through his nunny-bag till he found a bit of oatmeal.

†**nunon**, *adv. Obs. rare*$^{-1}$. [app. f. *nu* NOW + ANON.] In a short time; presently.

a **1225** *Ancr. R.* 270 Ich chulle gon nu slepen & arisen nunon, & don cwicluker þen nu þet ich schulde don nu.

†**'nunry**. *Obs.* Forms: α. 5 nonrie, 5–6 nonry, 6 nonrye, nondry. β. 4–6 nunrye, 5–7 nunry (5 nvn-), 6 -ri(e. [f. NUN *sb.*[1] Cf. NUNNERY and -RY.] A nunnery. Also *attrib.*

α. *c* **1440** *Alph. Tales* 320 On a day sho come vnto þe nonrie yate. *c* **1450** *St. Cuthbert* (Surtees) 8139 Thare he made an Nonry. *a* **1548** HALL *Chron., Hen. VIII* 258 b, Hadington toune with the Friers and Nonry. **1550** BALE *Eng. Votaries* I. 42 Both men and women dwellyng to-gyther sell by sell (as the maner was than of all Nondryes in England).

β. **1389** *Eng. Gilds* (1870) 43 To ye nunrye of Carrowe. *c* **1425** *Hampole's Psalter* Metr. Pref. 29 In ȝork shyre þis nvnry ys. **1538–9** WRIOTHESLEY *Chron.* (Camden) I. 93 In this moneth the nunrye of St. Helins..was suppressed. **1577–87** HOLINSHED *Chron.* III. 963/1 The same daie was Haddington burnt, with a great nunrie and house of friers there. **1629** MAXWELL tr. *Herodian* (1635) 299 He violently tooke out of Vestaes sacred nunry at Rome a Vestall Virgin. **1639** DRUMM. OF HAWTH. *Consid. to Parl.* Wks. (1711) 186 That all Bishops Houses, Concierges, Abbays, and Nunries, be made Places to entertain Souldiers.

'nunship. [f. NUN *sb.*[1]] The condition of being a nun.

1624 J. GEE *Foot out of Snare* 61 There appeared in her some passion incompatible with Nunship. **1672** DRYDEN *Assignation* III. i, Lay by your Nun-ship for an Hour or two, and come amongst us in Disguise. **1904** F. HARRISON *Theophano* ix. 82 The two younger princesses..would not accept the obligation of nunship.

'nunter. In carriage-building: (see quot.).

1794 W. FELTON *Carriages* (1801) I. 49 The nunters are two pieces of timber fixed under the block, and tenoned in the Axletree bed.

'nunting, *a. dial.* [Of obscure origin.] Awkward, ungainly, stunted.

1836 W. D. COOPER *Sussex Gloss., Nunting*, awkward looking. **1848** J. H. NEWMAN *Loss & Gain* (1853) 78 The dilapidated deformed church with..its uncouth pews, its low nunting table, its forlorn vestry. **1854** MISS BAKER *Northampt. Gloss.* s.v., A small unbecoming bonnet would be called 'a nunting little thing'.

nuntio, variant of NUNCIO *sb.*[1]

nuntion, obs. form of NUNCHEON.

‖**nuntius** ('nʌnʃ(ɪ)əs). Pl. nuntii (-ʃɪaɪ). [L.; cf. NUNCIUS.] A messenger; a member of the Polish diet; a papal nuncio.

1605 BACON *Adv. Learn.* II. xii. §1 The imagination is an Agent or Nuntius. **1606** MARSTON *Fawne* I. ii, An excellent nuntius. **1713** *Lond. Gaz.* No. 5093/2 The Chamber of the Nuntii or Deputies, sat upon that Matter. **1885** *Encycl. Brit.* XIX. 288/1 The nuntii..were the deputies returned by the various districts of the palatinates. **1903** *Contemp. Rev.* Mar. 410 The papal nuntius presses every lever and turns every screw.

‖**nuoc mam** (nwɒk mɑːm). [Vietnamese.] A spicy Vietnamese fish sauce.

1919 *Experiment Station Record* (U.S. Dept. Agric.) July 66 Analyses of nuoc-mam (a product similar to soy sauce) and other sauces are reported. **1920** *Ibid.* Oct. 458 Nuoc-mam..the Indochinese fish sauce.., has been successfully condensed for transportation and use by the Indochinese soldiers in France. **1935** M. MORPHY *Recipes of All Nations* 782 A small teaspoon of nuoc-man, a typically Annamese condiment which is used in practically all their dishes. **1969** I. KEMP *Brit. G.I. in Vietnam* iv. 77 The staple Vietnamese diet of rice with fish and *nuoc mam*—'Vietnamese national sauce', they would explain, chuckling among themselves—made from rotten fish and sea water. **1970** *Harper's Mag.* July 83 Bits of rice and *nuoc-mam* are what they're used to. **1972** *Times* 25 Mar. 11 There is nothing in either Chinese or French cooking that exactly corresponds with the Vietnamese thin sauce or relish called nuôc mam formed..from the liquor of decomposing fish.

†**nup**. *Obs. rare*$^{-1}$. (Cf. NUPSON.)

1607 *Lingua* II. i, Tis he [Phantastes] indeede, the vilest nup; yet the foole loues mee exceedinglie.

Nupe ('nuːpeɪ), *a.* and *sb.*[1] Also 9 Nufi, Nupé, Nyffee. [f. the name of a former kingdom at the junction of the Niger and Benue rivers in West Africa.] **A.** *adj.* Of, pertaining to, or designating a Negro people of central Nigeria, or their language. **B.** *sb.* **a.** The Nupe people; a member of this people. **b.** The language of this people, which belongs to the Kura division of the Sudanic language family.

1829 H. CLAPPERTON *Jrnl. 2nd Exped. to Interior of Afr.* i. 25 He hoped that we should settle the war with the Nyffee people and the Fellatah. **1841** J. F. SCHÖN *Jrnl.* 14 Sept. (1842) 119 The Nufi Language is spoken to a considerable distance, even beyond Rabba. **1883** R. N. CUST *Sk. Mod. Lang. Afr.* I. xi. 228 At Lokója, at the confluence, Nupé is the principal language, though others are spoken. **1885** J. S. KINGSLEY *Standard Nat. Hist.* VI. 320 We meet the Ibo language on the lower course of the Niger, and the Nupe from the Benne up. *Ibid.* 321 The Nupe..are genuine negroes in complexion and form of face, and indisputably one of the best-formed tribes in Africa. **1888** G. T. BETTANY *World's Inhabitants* vi. 614 Gando..includes the territory of the Nupe negroes. **1892** A. F. MOCKLER-FERRYMAN *Up Niger* xiii. 151 The Mohammedan Nupe lives the life of a man-about-town. **1932** J. CARY *Aissa Saved* iv. 24 The new town on the waterside, inhabited by Hausas, Nupes, Yorubas, the mixed population of a harbour. **1942** S. F. NADEL *Black Byzantium* iii. 27 The Nupe have only one work for kinship, *dengi*, which defines relationship in the widest as well as in a more restricted sense. *Ibid.* vi. 70 The people in the capital regard the Nupe spoken in the districts and on the borders of the country as an inferior brand. **1974** *African Encycl.* 375/2 The Nupe people live in valleys of the middle Niger and Kaduna rivers in Nigeria... They are famous for their work in glass, silver, bronze, and brass.

N.U.P.E., NUPE[2] ('njuːpɪ). Also **Nupe**. [Acronym f. the initial letters of *N*ational *U*nion of *P*ublic *E*mployees.] The name of a British trade union for manual, clerical, and professional employees of local authorities (until 1928, the National Union of Corporation Workers).

1931 *Public Employees Jrnl.* Sept. 1 (*figure*) N.U.P.E. **1932** *Ibid.* Mar. 21/1 (*heading*) Why N.U.P.E. is winning its way every day. **1940** *Hammer* (Ewell Branch NUPE) II. 2 A special meeting of N.U.P.E. members and non-unionists. **1955** W. W. CRAIK *Bryn Robert & Nat. Union Public Employees* iii. 45 The history of NUPE from its earliest years is the history of a trade union confining its membership and its service to public employees. **1976** H. WILSON *Governance of Britain* iv. 86 On 20 May I met a deputation consisting of the Royal Colleges of Midwives and Nursing, the Association of Nurse Administrators, the National Union of Public Employees (NUPE), [etc.]. **1985** *Financial Times* 12 Oct. 6/2 An item in his curriculum vitae states baldly: 'Organiser in all Nupe strikes from 1978'.

nuphar ('njuːfə(r)). [a. med. or mod.L. *nuphar*, ad. Arab.-Pers. *nūfar*, a reduced form of *nīlūfar* or *nīnūfar* NENUPHAR.] The yellow water-lily (*Nymphæa lutea*).

1845 FABER *Rosary* 33 Stripes of yellow nuphar drawn In random lines across the lawn. **1857** —— *Sir Lancelot* (ed. 2) 7 With yellow flag-flowers..And dimpling globes of nuphar netted o'er. **1897** *Outing* XXIX. 562/2 The idyllic little streams, carpeted with nuphars, swathed in reeds.

nuplex ('njuːplɛks). [f. NU(CLEAR *a.* + COM)PLEX *sb.*] A combined agricultural and industrial complex built around a nuclear reactor as the source of all power and providing employment for a large number of people.

1968 *Courier-Mail* (Brisbane) 27 Aug. 4/1 Mr. Seaborg [Chairman of the U.S. Atomic Energy Commission] defined the 'nuplex' as 'a giant agro-industrial complex built around nuclear reactors'. **1970** *New Scientist* 8 Oct. 89/3 One such investigation is into nuclear farms for the Middle East: half-million-acre 'nuplexes' with a reactor desalinating seawater for irrigation..and manufacturing fertilizer on the spot.

nuppence ('nʌpəns). *slang.* [Modelled on *tuppence*.] No money.

1886 *Longman's Mag.* VII. 551 The Americans can get our books, and do get them, and republish them and give us nothing—that awful minus quantity, nuppence! **1964** *Observer* 20 Sept. 27/7 Living on nuppence. **1973** *Times Lit. Suppl.* 30 Mar. 347/4 For the appreciation of the novel, this information matters little more than nuppence.

†**'nupson**. *Obs.* A simpleton, a fool.

1598 B. JONSON *Ev. Man in Hum.* IV. vi, O that I were so happy, as to light on a nupson, now, of this Justice's novice. **1607** *Lingua* V. xviii, Phantastes is a foolish transparent gull, a miere fanatick nupson, in my immagination not worthie to sit as a Iudges assistant. **1616** B. JONSON *Devil an Ass* II. ii, Who hauing match'd with such a Nupson.., will yet..defraud the poore Gentleman.

nuptial ('nʌpʃəl), *a.* and *sb.* Also 5 nupcyalle. [a. F. *nuptial* (†*nupcial*, = Sp. and Pg. *nupcial*, It. *nuziale*), or ad. L. *nuptiālis*, f. *nuptiæ* wedding, f. *nupt-*, *nubĕre* to wed.]

A. *adj.* **1.** Of or pertaining to marriage or the marriage ceremony. Also *fig.*

1490 CAXTON *Eneydos* xv. 56 The goddesse Iuno, quene and patronesse of the commocyons nupcyalle. **1581** E. CAMPION in *Conferences* II. (1584) L ij, He that had not the nuptial garment, maketh this claime to be the sonne of God. **1589** PUTTENHAM *Eng. Poesie* I. xxiii. (Arb.) 61 Those to celebrate marriages were called songs nuptiall or Epithalamies. **1632** LITHGOW *Trav.* IV. 154 Now I come to their nuptiall rites, their custome and manner of marriage is thus. **1671** MILTON *Samson* 1194, I chose a Wife,..And in your City held my Nuptial Feast. **1751** JOHNSON *Rambler* No. 182 ⁋9 She..at last fixed the nuptial day. **1796** MORSE *Amer. Geogr.* II. 44 The priest chants the nuptial benediction. **1836** THIRLWALL *Greece* II. 125 The nuptial ceremony, the feast, and the funeral, would have appeared spiritless..without this accompaniment. **1891** J. ADAM (*title*), The Nuptial Number of Plato.

†**b.** ***nuptial father***, one who represents the bride's father at a wedding. *Obs.*

1748 RICHARDSON *Clarissa* IV. l. 306 My letter of invitation to my Lord M. to be her Nuptial-father. **1802** MRS. J. WEST *Infidel Father* II. 52 He officiated as the nuptial father. **1804** EUGENIA DE ACTON *Tale without Title* III. 135 Mr. and Miss Webster, her intended nuptial father and bride-maid.

c. ***nuptial plumage***, the special plumage of birds during the breeding season.

1840 *Penny Cycl.* XVIII. 280/1 Old Male and Female [Plover] in summer or nuptial plumage.

†**2.** Married, wedded. *Obs. rare.*

1615 CHAPMAN *Odyss.* I. 664 Love's equal flame To her he felt, as to his nuptial dame. **1642** C. VERNON *Consid. Exch.* 52 The nuptiall Queens of this Realme, participating so much in the Regality of the Crowne.

B. *sb.* **1.** Marriage, wedding. (Usually in *pl.*)

pl. *c* **1555** HARPSFIELD *Divorce Hen. VIII* (Camden) 245 St. Hierome & St. Gregorie that will not call our ladie's marriage nuptialls. **1599** B. JONSON *Cynthia's Rev.* V. ii, Accommodate to the nuptials of my scholar's 'haviour to the lady Courtship. **1624** HEYWOOD *Gunaik.* VI. 282 Shee was by her father compelled to a second nuptialls with King Cephordus. **1709** STEELE *Tatler* No. 82 ⁋3 Soon after their Nuptials, the Bridegroom was obliged to go into a Foreign Country. **1791** MRS. RADCLIFFE *Rom. Forest* I Their nuptials had been celebrated under the auspices of an approving..world. **1840** THIRLWALL *Greece* lv. VII. 77 The nuptials were solemnised according to Persian usage. **1876** GLADSTONE *Glean.* (1879) II. 325 The nuptials of women of rank with clergymen of average station.

sing. **1590** SHAKS. *Mids. N.* I. i. 125, I must imploy you in some businesse against our nuptiall. **1611** —— *Wint. T.* IV. iv. 406 Me-thinkes a Father Is, at the Nuptiall of his sonne, a guest That best becomes the Table. **1654–66** EARL ORRERY *Parthen.* (1676) 614 The Nuptial was no sooner celebrated, than he repented it. **1721** RAMSAY *Content* 214 Rare she appears, unless on some fine day She grace a nuptial, but soon hastes away. **1891** MERIVALE & MARZIALS *Thackeray* 27 Her own paltering..has brought about that ill-omened nuptial.

†**2.** Matrimony. *Obs. rare*$^{-1}$.

c **1620** Z. BOYD *Zion's Flowers* (1855) 84 Who in chast nuptialls shall lead their life.

Hence **'nuptial** *v.*, to speak of (a wedding); to marry. Also **'nuptialist**. (See quot.) *rare*$^{-0}$.

1656 BLOUNT *Glossogr., Nuptialist*, a Bride or Wife; or a Bridegroom or Husband; Also one that makes Marriages. **1887** BROWNING *Parleyings* II. vi, Nuptial me no such nuptials! **1893** A. AUSTIN *Betrothal Ode* in *Standard* 5 May 5/3 For, though Love betrothes you, must Sovereign Duty nuptial you.

nuptiality (nʌpʃɪ'ælɪtɪ). [f. NUPTIAL.]

1. *pl.* A couple about to be married. *rare*$^{-1}$.

1759 WALPOLE *Let. to G. Montague* 26 Apr., My Nuptialities dined here yesterday. The wedding is fixed for the 15th.

2. *pl.* Nuptial ceremonies.

1863 COWDEN CLARKE *Shaks. Char.* iv. 96 The classic stateliness of Theseus and Hypolita, with their sedate and lofty nuptialities, form..a splendid frame to the picture.

3. Conjugial virtues or character.

1789 WALPOLE *Let. to Miss M. Berry* 19 July, In France, where nuptiality is not the virtue most in request. **1879** MEREDITH *Egoist* II. ii. 34 Innocent of the Bacchic nuptiality of the allusion.

4. The frequency or incidence of marriage within a population.

1902 *Encycl. Brit.* XXXI. 839/1 Nuptiality and Fecundity.—In connexion with the subject of natural increase may be mentioned the tendency of a people towards marriage, and the average fertility of each union. **1949** *Population Studies* II. 356 The relations between male and female nuptiality in general. **1966** E. A. WRIGLEY *Introd. Eng. Hist. Demogr.* iv. 111 The demographic mechanisms which produced changes in population totals—the interplay of nuptiality, fertility and mortality. **1973** *Times* 12 Dec. 2/3 Although nuptiality was higher than ever, mean family size for couples..had dropped.

'nuptialize, *v. rare*$^{-1}$. [f. as prec. + -IZE.] *refl.* To get married.

1857 *Gambler's Dream* III. 255 Hunchback cannot, I am sure, have yet nuptialized himself, for no woman would have him without the money.

'nuptialling. *rare*$^{-1}$. [f. as prec. + -ING[1].] *pl.* Nuptials.

1600 *Newe Metamorphosis* XII. 249 b, The Catalogue of ancient Brittish Kinges: Prince Henries deathe: Elizas Nuptiallinges.

nuptially ('nʌpʃəlɪ), *adv.* [-LY[2].] As regards marriage; with respect to marriage or the marriage ceremony. (*Cent. Dict.* 1890.)

nuque (nyk). *rare.* [a. F. *nuque*: see NUKE *sb.*[1] and NUCHE.]

1. The nape of the neck.

1578 LYTE *Dodoens* 310 If it be applied to the nuque or nape of the necke, it restoreth the speache. **1886** GUILLEMARD *Cruise Marchesa* II. 186 The latter is a fine bird,..a curious tawny patch upon the nuque.

2. (See quot.)

1884 *Western Daily Press* 29 May 3/7 A new device of the hairdresser, called a nuque.

nuragh ('nʊəræg). Forms: α. *pl.* nuraggi(s), noraghe, nuraghe. β. nurhag, n(o)uragh.

[Sardinian dialect.] A massive stone tower of ancient date, of a type peculiar to Sardinia.

α. **1828** CAPT. SMYTH *Pres. St. Sardinia* 4 The very singular remains strewed over Sardinia..called Nuraggis... They are strong buildings, in the form of a truncated cone, composed of masses of stone..arranged in layers. **1866** BRANDE & COX *Dict. Sci.*, etc. II. 679/2 The noraghe are generally built upon a circular or elliptical plan. **1889** C. EDWARDES *Sardinia & Sardes* 175, I have already described the nuraghe as a number of circular towers. **1905** *Athenæum* 29 July 137/3 The dolmens, nuraghe, beehive tombs, &c., all round the basin of the Mediterranean.

β. **1875** *Encycl. Brit.* II. 384/1 The design of the 'nurhags'..has greatly puzzled archæologists. **1893** *Athenæum* 2 Sept. 328/1 Like the Sardinian nuragh, the talayot is essentially a vaulted tower of extra-massive proportions.

nurce, -ling, -ry, obs. ff. NURSE, NURSLING, NURSERY.

nurd, var. NERD.

nure-, obs. Sc. f. NEW-YEAR.

nureis, -ice, is, obs. ff. NOURICE.

Nuremberg ('nju:rəmbɜ:g). Also (erron.) -burg. [G. *Nürnberg.*] The name of a city in southern Germany. **1.** Used *attrib.* to designate a type of porcelain manufactured in Nuremberg.

1617 F. MORYSON *Itinerary* III. II. iii. 80 The Germans export..*Nurnberg* wares (so they call small wares.) **1863** W. CHAFFERS *Marks Pott. & Porc.* 105 *Nuremburg*, there are two plates of the XVIIIth Century in the Sèvres Museum; one in imitation of Faenza, the other an allegory of Luther. **1925** B. RACKHAM tr. *Hannover's Pott. & Porc.* I. iv. 355 Chinese motives..are not wanting in Nuremberg faïence in the first and best period. But at an early stage they give way to plant ornament, in which a feather-like leaf..is a constantly-recurring element. **1960** R. G. HAGGAR *Conc. Encycl. Cont. Pott. & Porc.* 331/1 Two personalities are connected with Nuremberg *faïence* in the sixteenth century, Oswald Reinhard, and Augustin Hirsvogel. **1974** *Country Life* 6 June 1411/3 The architectural detail is executed in scagliola and the walls are clad in Nuremburg tiles.

b. ***Nuremberg egg***, a type of watch (see quot. 1960).

[**1895** H. L. NELTHROPP *Catal. Collection of Clocks* 2 Nuremberg egg-shaped watch, metal and silver case.] **1960** H. HAYWARD *Antique Coll.* 201/1 *Nuremberg egg*, a misnomer applied to early South German watches. Arose from the misreading and mistranslation of 'Uhrlein' into 'Eierlein' (little clocks into little eggs). These early watches were usually drum shaped.

2. Used *attrib.* to designate a connection with the German National Socialist Party with which the city was associated, as **Nuremberg Laws**, laws promulgated in 1935 barring Jews from German citizenship and forbidding intermarriage between 'Aryans' and Jews; **Nuremberg rally**, one of the mass meetings of the German National Socialist Party which were held annually at Nuremberg from 1933 to 1938; **Nuremberg trial(s)**, a series of trials of former Nazi leaders for alleged war crimes and crimes against humanity presided over by an International Military Tribunal formed from the victorious Allied Powers and held in Nuremberg in 1945–6 (also ellipt. as *Nuremberg*).

1937 JANOWSKY & FAGEN *Internat. Aspects German Racial Policies* ii. 106 Even the official commentary on the Nuremberg laws..concluded that the German Jews were a racial (voelkische), though not a national minority. **1945** H. NICOLSON *Diary* 4 June (1968) III. 64 Smuts recalled the decision... 'It..shows..the value of Nuremberg. Had we shot Jodl at sight, that precious piece of evidence would never have been obtained.' **1945** *Daily Mail* 19 Nov. 2/3 All day today Lord Justice Lawrence and Mr. Justice Birkett have been discussing..the arguments for and against postponement of the Nuremberg trials. **1946** M. BELGION *Epitaph on Nuremberg* 12 The argument rested on the plea..that justice was going to be done. Of this argument the official explanation of the Nuremberg trial consisted. **1952** A. BULLOCK *Hitler* II. vii. 347 The Nuremberg rallies held every year in September were masterpieces of theatrical art, with the most carefully devised effects. **1963** *Guardian* 25 Feb. 8/1 Towards the end of the Stalin era a Soviet brand of anti-Semitism had undoubtedly reached very dangerous proportions..even if it was never codified in a Soviet version of the 'Nuremberg Laws'. **1969** W. CARR *Hist. of Germany 1815–1945* xiv. 405 Hitler's violent speech at the Nuremburg party rally. **1970** *Guardian* 20 Nov. 12/6 Ever since Vietnam got big, Nuremberg has been injected into the national argument... The Nuremberg precedents demand that..American high commanders ought to be tried for war crimes. **1971** M. MCCARTHY *Birds of America* 110 Under the Nuremberg Laws, he would have counted as a Jew, while in Israel he would count as a Christian, since what mattered to them was your mother. **1974** *Times* 14 Feb. 16/7 Thank heavens we don't do it like the Tories. Their adulation is reminiscent of a Nuremberg rally.

Nuremberger ('nju:rəmbɜ:gə(r)). [f. NUREMBERG + -ER[1].] A native or inhabitant of Nuremberg, Germany.

1673 J. RAY *Observations Journey Low-Countries* 112 Aldtdorf, a little walled Town and an University belonging to the Nurenbergers. **1894** S. WEYMAN *My Lady Rotha* xxxi. 349 Deserting a friend because the Nurembergers frowned upon him. **1946** H. NICOLSON *Diary* 1 May (1968) III. 62 If I were a Nuremberger I should feel nothing but undying hatred for those who had destroyed my lovely city.

nuris(ch, -ishe, obs. ff. NOURISH.

nurling, var. of KNURLING.

'nurly, *a.* [var. of KNURLY *a.*] (See quots.)

1806 FESSENDEN *Orig. Poems* 136 He's tall, like swamp cedar,..But shrub-oak was never so nurly. *Note*, A yankeyism for knotty, or gnarled. **1859** BARTLETT *Dict. Amer.* (ed. 2) 298 *Nurly*, a corrupt pronunciation and orthography of gnarly, *i.e.* gnarled. **1871** DE VERE *Americanisms* 620 Persons..are said to be nurly when they are ill-tempered and cross-grained.

†**nurn,** *v. Obs.* Also no(u)rne. [Of obscure origin; peculiar to the Gawain poet.]

1. a. *trans.* To utter, say.

13.. *E.E. Allit. P.* B. 65 An oþer nayed also & nurned þis cawse. *Ibid.* 669 'Now innoghe hit is not so' þenne nurned þe dryȝtyn. **13..** *St. Erkenwolde* 101 in Horstm. *Altengl. Leg.* (1881) 152 þer is no lede opone lyfe..may..his nome ne his note nourne of one speche.

b. *intr.* To speak, discourse.

13.. *Gaw. & Gr. Knt.* 1661 He nolde not for his nurture nurne hir a-ȝaynez. *Ibid.* 1669 þer þay dronken, & dalten, & demed eft nwe, To norne on þe same note.

2. *trans.* To ask or request; to urge or press.

13.. *E.E. Allit. P.* B. 803, I norne yow bot for on nyȝt neȝe me to lenge. **13..** *Gaw. & Gr. Knt.* 1771 þat prynce of pris ..Nurned hym so neȝe þe þred, þat nede hym bi-houed [etc.].

3. To offer, proffer.

13.. *Gaw. & Gr. Knt.* 1823, I wil no giftez for gode..; I haf none yow to norne, ne noȝt wyl I take.

nurr, variant of KNUR(R.

nurrice, obs. form of NOURICE.

†**'nurrior.** *Obs. rare*[−1]. [f. OF. *nurr-ir* to nourish: cf. next.] Foster-father.

1487 *Rolls of Parlt.* VI. 406/2 Our old Servaunt and well beloved nurriour.

†**'nurry.** *Obs.* Also nurrye, nurri, nurre(e; nury(e. [a. OF. *nurri*, pa. pple. of *nurrir*: cf. NORRY and NOURRY.]

1. Foster-child, nursling.

a **1374** CHAUCER *Boeth.* III. pr. ix. (1868) 86 O my nurry, quod she, by þis oppinioun..I seye þat þou art blisful. **1387** TREVISA *Higden* (Rolls) VII. 139 Sche putte hir nurri, whiche sche had brouȝt with hir out of Engelond, for to fiȝte aȝenst þe accuser. ? *a* **1400** *Morte Arth.* 689 Thowe arte my neuewe fulle nere, my nurree of olde. ? *a* **1500** *Chester Pl.* (E.E.T.S.) IV. 154, I have noe childe, fowle ne fayre, Safe my Nurry, to be my heyre.

2. Fosterer, upbringer.

c **1450** *St. Cuthbert* (Surtees) 605 þe bischop cuthbert nurry, When he saw þat he suld dy,.. Betaght cuthbert to his cuyr.

nurse (nɜ:s), *sb.*[1] Forms: α. 4–6 nors(e, 5–6 norce, 6 norsse. β. 4– nurse, 6 nurs(se, 6– 7 nurce. γ. 6 nourse, 6–7 nource. [Reduced form of ME. *norice, nurice* NOURICE.]

1. a. A woman employed to suckle, and otherwise attend to, an infant; also, one who has general care and charge of a young child or children.

The two applications of the word are more precisely expressed by WET NURSE and DRY NURSE. In ordinary use the latter is now the more usual sense.

α. *a* **1387** TREVISA *Higden* (Rolls) VI. 401 þanne þe norse [*v.r.* nors] brouȝt forþ þe childe. *c* **1400** *Destr. Troy* 8484 Two sonnes hade þat semly,..þat were bothe at the brest of the bright norse. **1470** *Anc. Cal. Rec. Dubl.* (1889) 339 Noo Irisshe hostler, Irisshe nors, Irisshe hokester. **1529** MORE *Dyaloge* I. Wks. 124/2 For possible it wer that..a riche mannes norce bringe home her owne chylde for her maisters. **1551** BIBLE (Mathew) *Gen.* xxiv. 59 So they let Rebecca their syster go with her norse.

transf. c **1420** *Pallad. on Husb.* I. 658 But xxx daies olde, They [peafowl] with their norce into the feld be tolde.

β. *a* **1420** BIBLE (Wycl.) *Gen.* xxiv. 59 Therfor they delyueriden hir, and hir nurse. **1535** COVERDALE *Exod.* ii. 7 Shal I go, and call the a nurse of the Hebrues wemen, to nurse yᵉ the childe? **1587** GOLDING *De Mornay* xi. (1592) 158 Thou playest the babe, which thinkes his Nurce does him wrong when she kemes his head. **1607** S. HIERON *Wks.* I. 179 The loue of fathers toward their children,..of nurces to the sucklings. **1700** DRYDEN *Cock & Fox* 335 The nurse's legends are for truths receiv'd. **1781** COWPER *Conversat.* 242 What neither yields us profit nor delight Is like a nurse's lullaby at night. **1818** SHELLEY *Rosal. & Helen* 347 A sleep more deep..Than a baby's rocked on its nurse's knee. **1878** MEREDITH *Teeth* 15 The nurse's age should not be far from that of the mother, and her confinement should have taken place at about the same time.

γ. **1546** PHAER *Bk. Childr.* (1553) Tij, Ye must be well aduised in taking of a nource. *a* **1553** UDALL *Royster D.* I. iii, Nourse, medle you with your spyndle and your whirle. **1606** HOLLAND *Sueton.* 80 Being by his nource laide in the evening within a Cradell in swadling bands, beneath uppon a lowe floure. **1642** [see NURSERY 1 c].

b. *transf.* One who takes care of, looks after, or advises another.

c **1425** *Cast. Persev.* 862 in *Macro Plays* 103 What..art þou þe wers þou brekyste Goddys heste? Do after me! I am þi nors. **1613** G. ABBOT *Expos. Jonah* 3 That woman, who was..a nurce to that reuerend man Elias, in the time of bitter famine. **1812** *Ann. Reg., Gen. Hist.* 6 He 'ridiculed the idea of such a man..being sent on an expedition with a nurse to superintend him'. **1867** SMYTH *Sailor's Word-bk.* 502 *Nurse*, an able first lieutenant, who in former times had charge of a young boy-captain of interest, but possessing no knowledge for command.

c. That which supplies nutriment to something.

c **1420** *Pallad. on Husb.* IV. 35 Mold anoon on euery side hit hepith. This roote & molde as nors & moder kepeth. **1650** CHARLETON tr. *Van Helmont's Paradoxes* 114 But red French Wines, unlesse nourisht by their Lees, (which for this effect, Vintners call, the Mother, or Nurse of Claret) dissolve their owne Tincture.

d. *fig.* That which nourishes or fosters some quality, condition, etc.

1526 *Pilgr. Perf.* (W. de W. 1531) 81 b, Obedyence..is the helth of faythfull soules, the nurse of all vertue. **1591** SHAKS. *Two Gent.* III. i. 243 Time is the Nurse, and breeder of all good. **1610** GUILLIM *Heraldry* IV. vi. 201 Agriculture.. being the chiefe Nourice of mans life. **1642** GAUDEN *Three Serm.* 66 Truth and justice the mother and nurse of Peace. **1764** GOLDSM. *Trav.* 356 The land of scholars, and the nurse of arms. **1817** SHELLEY *Rev. Islam* IX. xiii, Fear, The nurse of Vengeance, bade him wait the event. **1873** TRISTRAM *Moab* xvi. 300 Gently sloping valleys, the mothers and nurses of the ravines which plough the bowels of the rocks.

2. a. ***at nurse***, in the care or charge of a nurse. Also with *take* (cf. next).

1557 *Order of Hospitalls* F v, Whether the same Childe be ..in the House, or at Nurse. **1570** FOXE *A. & M.* (ed. 2) 930/2 This Richard Hune had a child at nourse in Midlesex. **1711** *Lond. Gaz.* No. 4929/4 An Infant then at Nurse. **1796** *Hist. Ned Evans* I. 66 A new born son, who was said to have also died at nurse. *a* **1845** [see NURTURESHIP]. **1866** W. COLLINS *Armadale* III. xv. II. 110 A woman who took in children at nurse.

b. ***to put to nurse***, to commit to the care of a nurse. Usually with *out*, denoting removal of the child from its proper home. Also *fig.*

1593 SHAKS. *2 Hen. VI*, IV. ii. 150 The elder of them being put to nurse, Was..stolne away. **1602** MARSTON *Antonio's Rev.* IV. ii, As some weake breasted dame Giveth her infant, puts it out to nurse. *a* **1658** CLEVELAND *Wks.* (1687) 18 Can Wedlock know so great a Curse, As putting Husbands out To nurse? **1776** JOHNSON in *Boswell* 26 Mar., There is nothing against which an old man should be so much upon his guard as putting himself to nurse. **1837** DICKENS *Pickw.* xxii, I should very much like to see your mother-in-law born again. Wouldn't I put her out to nurse! **1847** C. BRONTË *J. Eyre* xxi, He would send for the baby, though I entreated him rather to put it out to nurse and pay for its maintenance.

c. *fig.* Of estates in the hands of trustees.

1771 SMOLLETT *Humph. Cl.* I. 5 May, He has..put his estate to nurse. **1800** MRS. HERVEY *Mourtray Fam.* III. 134 His estate of 1200*l.* a year went to nurse; and a small allowance from his creditors..remained for the maintenance of his family. **1824** *Hist. Gaming* 10 In trust for H.R.H., as the lawyers have it, but which the fashionable world call 'being at nurse'. **1875** J. GRANT *One of the* '600' viii. 65 His father..died in time to let the estates go to nurse during the present man's minority.

3. a. A person, generally a woman, who attends or waits upon the sick; now *esp.* one properly trained for this purpose.

1590 SHAKS. *Com. Err.* V. i. 98, I will attend my husband, be his nurse, Diet his sicknesse, for it is my Office. **1766** ENTICK *London* IV. 382, 19 sisters, 19 nurses. **1784** COWPER *Task* I. 89 The nurse sleeps sweetly, hired to watch the sick. **1809** *Med. Jrnl.* XXI. 183 He returned the vessel to the nurse, after he had swallowed some of the fluid. **1843** ABDY *Water Cure* 178 A young man, delirious in the small pox, when his nurse was asleep, jumped out of bed. **1876** BRISTOWE *Th. & Pract. Med.* (1878) 232 Nurses and medical attendants seldom..take the disease from patients under their charge.

b. Prefixed as a title to the name of one qualified to nurse, esp. in a hospital; used as a mode of address to such a person.

1702 J. MORDAUNT *Let.* in E. Hamilton *Mordaunts* (1965) ii. 33, I did not doubt but that you would have great trouble in parting wth Nurse Lucas. **1791** F. BURNEY *Let.* 12 Sept. (1972) I. 65 Less than an hour compleated the whole business without any help excepting Nurse Whittons. **1874** [see SOUL *sb.* 14 a]. **1940** A. CHRISTIE *Sad Cypress* I. i. 21 'Do you think she's really good-looking, Nurse?' Nurse Hopkins said: 'Difficult to tell what these girls really look like under their make-up!' **1955** 'A. GILBERT' *Is she Dead Too?* vi. 116 I'll be sending Nurse Wilson along. **1975** P. D. JAMES *Black Tower* iv. 100 They made the bed together, Nurse Rainer flicking the sheets into place and neatly mitring each corner.

c. Without article in reference to the nurse in charge of a patient.

1766 [see *home-baked* (HOME *sb.*[1] 14 i)]. **1914** G. B. SHAW *Misalliance* 68 Is anything the matter, John? Nurse says she heard you calling me a quarter of an hour ago. **1937** J. BETJEMAN *Continual Dew* 25 Nurse looked at the silent bedstead.

4. *Forestry.* A tree set in a plantation to protect smaller or newly planted ones from wind or cold.

1788 *Trans. Soc. Arts* VI. 10, I only consider them [Scotch firs] as nurses to my other trees. **1827** STEUART *Planter's G.* (1828) 224 These had been introduced merely as nurses to the deciduous Trees. **1833** HT. MARTINEAU *Brooke Farm* v. 62 Half the larches are to remain for timber trees; the other half are nurses, and will be thinned out. **1966** *Times* 21 Apr. 16/6 Scots pines were commonly planted as nurses to oak. **1973** *Country Life* 6 Dec. 1928/1 Larch has been..used..as a nurse with hardwoods and alone.

5. *Entom.* A sexually imperfect member of a community of bees, ants, etc., upon whom devolves the care of the young brood; a worker.

1818 KIRBY & SP. *Entomol.* xxvii. (ed. 2) II. 500 The workers, termed by Huber *nourrices*, or *petites abeilles* (nurses), upon whom..the principal labours of the hive devolve. **1835** *Penny Cycl.* IV. 155/2 The large-sized workers..make cells of a larger diameter than those made by the nurses. **1860** *Chambers's Encycl.* I. 801/2 It is supposed by many naturalists, that some of the working-bees are exclusively wax-workers, some nurses, &c.

attrib. **1818** KIRBY & SP. *Entomol.* xv. (ed. 3) I. 493 The nurse-bees..do secrete wax, but in very small quantities.

1831 *Insect Misc.* (L.E.K.) x. 239 The males [of aphides] being..excluded from the nurse-boxes in which the females were isolated. **1834** *Penny Cycl.* II. 60/1 A sort of barren females,..variously termed neuters, workers, or nurse-ants.

6. *Zool.* An individual in the asexual stage of metagenesis.

1845 Busk tr. *Steenstrup's Altern. Generations* 24, I shall.. designate them by the short name of *Ammen* (*altrices, nurses* or *foster-parents*). *Ibid.*, All of which become..polypiform 'nurses', which nourish the Medusæ-larvæ from their bodies. **1871** T. R. Jones *Anim. Kingd.* (ed. 4) 160 The stomach, for instance, in the full-grown 'parent nurses' is longer and wider than in any even of the youngest 'nurses'. **1888** Rolleston & Jackson *Anim. Life* 446 The ovum in both Salpa and Doliolum produces the nurse.

attrib. **1845** Busk tr. *Steenstrup's Altern. Generations* 89 *note*, A confounding of 'nurse'-germs and Cercaria-germs may occur very readily. **1888** Rolleston & Jackson *Anim. Life* 445 Sexual organs are absent, or at least atrophied, in the nurse forms of Salpa and Doliolum.

7. *Brewing.* (See quot.)

1880 *Spon's Encycl. Manuf.* II. 407 The somewhat clumsy expedient of immersing in the wort casks filled with hot or cold water was employed for the purpose of accelerating or retarding the fermentation. The casks so used were termed 'nurses', and are still used in some breweries.

8. *attrib.* and *Comb.*, as ***nurse-book, -clout, -companion, -girl, -like, -secretary***, etc.; also **nurse-cell**, any cell whose function appears to be to assist another cell, esp. an ovum, in some way; **nurse cloth**, a plain-weave cotton fabric used for nurses' uniforms; **nurse-crop**, a crop planted to protect others; cf. 4 above and nurse-tree; **nurse-frog**, the obstetrical toad, the male of which carries the eggs till hatched.

1557 *Order of Hospitalls* F v, You shall kepe a Booke of all the Nurses which keep any of the said Children..and the same shall yow call the *Nurse-Booke; thereby to shew how many children every Nurse hath. **1896** E. B. Wilson *Cell* iii. 114 In all these cases it is doubtful whether the *nurse-cells are sister-cells of the egg which have sacrificed their own development for the sake of their companions, or whether they have had a distinct origin from a very early period. **1964** Bishop & Surgenor *Red Blood Cell* viii. 324 These authors present electron micrographs which depict erythroblastic islands in the bone marrow, in which a central reticulum cell (nurse cell) is surrounded by a ring of erythroblasts. **1967** *Jrnl. Cell Sci.* II. 613 Extensive nuclear fusion has been described in the trophocytes (nurse cells) in the ovaries of the milkweed bug *Oncopeltus*. **1907** *Harrods Catal.* 1407 Cotton dresses, in good quality *Nurse Cloth. **1932** D. C. Minter *Mod. Needlecraft* 248/2 *Book Carrier*..Blue nurse cloth, hessian or heavy Russian crash. **1596** Nashe *Saffron Walden* Ep. Ded., To rush in bluntly with thy washing-bowle and thy *nurse-cloutes vnder thy cloake. **1908** B. Harraden *Interplay* 210 Dr. Edgar can no doubt find you a *nurse-companion. **1973** A. Christie *Postern of Fate* III. ii. 132 She was a kind of nurse-companion with Mrs. Beddingfield. **1938** *U.S. Dept. Agric. Yearbk.* 409 Wheat is a good *nurse crop for the clover and grass. **1955** *Archit. Rev.* CXVII. 249 Even in hardwood country they [*sc.* conifers] are often required as nurse-crops to the deciduous trees. **1971** *Country Life* 4 Nov. 1237/1 Shall it [*sc.* seeding] be in spring or mid-August, under a nurse crop or without? **1847** C. Brontë *Jane Eyre* III. iii. 98, I will be a servant, a *nurse-girl, if I can be no better. **1871** Mrs. H. Wood *Dene Hollow* xii, They have a fresh nursegirl, too. Polly had to send away the other. **1953** D. Lessing *Five* i. 16 There was a little black nurse-girl seated on one of the logs, under a big tree, with a white child in her arms. **1896** *Edin. Rev.* Apr. 480 To make himself personally acquainted with the *nurse-land of the poet. **1611** Shaks. *Cymb.* v. v. 88 Neuer Master had A Page..So feate, so *Nurse-like. **1845** Busk tr. *Steenstrup's Altern. Generations* 89 *note*, They are developed from germ-granules in other 'nurse'-like animals. **1605** Camden *Rem.* 114 From Nicknames or *Nursenames came these..Bill for William, Clem for Clement. **1664** Walton *Angler* xx. (ed. 4) 243 If you put them..into a *nurse-pond, or feeding pond,..then no care is to be taken whether there be most Male or Female Carps. **1950** *Nurse-secretary [see appointment 4]. **1610** Holland *Camden's Brit.* I. 382 Sir Thomas Bodley..a most worthy *Nource-sonne of this University. **1878** Browning *Poets Croisic* iii, That old *nurse-taught game.

nurse (nɜːs), *sb.*[2] Also 5 nusse, 6 ?nuse. [Perh. a variant of huss, with *n* from the article (see N 3); the later form is assimilated to prec.] **a.** A dog-fish or shark (of various species).

1499 *Promp. Parv.* (Pynson) 361/1 Nusse fisshe. **1598** Hakluyt *Voy.* I. 283 There we gate a great Nuse, which Nuses were there [near Nova Zembla] so plentie, that they would scarcely suffer any other fish to come neere the hookes. **1699** Dampier *Voy.* II. II. 25 The Fish near the Island are Sharks, Sword Fishes and Nurses... The Nurse is just like a Shark, only its skin is rougher. **1711** C. Lockyer *Acct. Trade India* 279 Small parcels of shark's fins, nurses skins and tariands very reasonable. **1782** P. H. Bruce *Mem.* 424 They make plenty of oil from the nurses,..and a beneficial whale fishery might be established here. **1851** P. H. Gosse *Nat. in Jamaica* 243 The Nurse is of a dull brown hue on the upper parts, without spots.

b. So ***nurse-fish, -shark***; also **nurse-hound**, a name used for several dog-fish, esp. the large-spotted dog-fish, *Scyliorhinus stellaris*.

c **1682** J. Collins *Salt & Fishery* 83 Their [*sc.* the Icelanders'] Bread is also another sort of Fish, called Hokettle, or the *Nurse-Fish, which hath a sharp Ridge on his Back that cuts asunder Fishery-Tackle. **1848** *Zoologist* VI. 1973 Larger Spotted Dog, *S*[*cyllium*] *catulus*,..commonly called '*nurse-hound'. **1877** *Encycl. Brit.* VII. 332/1 The Small-spotted Dog-fish..and the Large-spotted or Nurse Hound ..are also known as ground-sharks. **1921** *Nature* 29 Dec. 585/1 The spur-dog and nurse-hound are viviparous. **1922** *Ibid.* 12 Jan. 55/2 Mr. E. Ford writes to inform us that the term 'nurse-hound' is applied at Plymouth to *Scyliorhinus stellaris*, which is not viviparous. We understand from the writer of our article that confusion has arisen from the fact that the name 'nurse-hound' is also used by fishermen in his district to refer to *Mustelus vulgaris*, which is viviparous. **1959** A. Hardy *Fish & Fisheries* ix. 179 The rough hound and the nurse hound are both spotted with dark spots.. upon a lighter ground. **1967** [see huss *sb.*]. **1969** A. Wheeler *Fishes Brit. Is. & NW. Europe* 44/1 The nurse hound is most common on rough, even rocky ground and it may be found within the algal zone close inshore, although it is most common in deeper water. **1972** [see huss *sb.*]. **1851** P. H. Gosse *Nat. in Jamaica* 241 The *nurse shark. **1879** Goode *Anim. Res. & Fish. U.S.* 69 *Ginglymostoma cirratum*.. Nurse Shark.—Tropical Atlantic.

nurse (nɜːs), *v.* Forms: 6–7 nource, -se, 6– nurse (7 -ce). [Later form of nursh *v.*, by assimilation to nurse *sb.*[1]]

1. a. Of a woman: To suckle, and otherwise attend to, or simply to take care or charge of (an infant). Cf. nurse *sb.*[1]

1535 Coverdale *Exod.* ii. 9 Take this childe, and nurse it for me... The woman toke the childe, and nursed it. **1546** Phaer *Bk. Childr.* T ij, So is it..comly for the own mother to nource her own childe. **1600** Pory tr. *Leo's Africa* 55 The women would not willingly nurse their owne children, but caused them to be suckled by goates. *c* **1620** Moryson *Itin.* IV. v. i. 458 The mothers..nurse not their owne Children, but send them forth (as in England) to be nursed in the Country. *c* **1670** Wood *Life* (O.H.S.) I. 44 As she nursed his 3 elder brothers, so she nursed him. **1717** Addison tr. *Ovid's Met.* III. Wks. 1721 I. 206 The Niseans, in their dark abode, Nurs'd secretly with milk the thriving God. **1756–7** tr. *Keysler's Trav.* (1760) II. 51 His parents..sent their son to be nursed in the village of Settignano. **1827** *Perils & Captivity* (Constable's Misc.) 19 My mother was then nursing my youngest sister. **1864** Tennyson *En. Ard.* 150 Annie..Nursing the sickly babe, her latest-born. **1896** *Allbutt's Syst. Med.* I. 413 So many mothers are unable to nurse their babies that a large proportion of infants have to be brought up by other means.

b. *intr.* To give suck; to act as wet-nurse.

1789 W. Buchan *Dom. Med.* (1790) 34 One of the most common faults of those who nurse for hire, is to dose children with stupefactives. **1843** R. J. Graves *Syst. Clin. Med.* xxiii. 290 When such persons begin to nurse, you should watch the effect of this new drain on the system. **1851** Carpenter *Man. Phys.* (ed. 2) 316 That which may be superfluous is..eliminated by the Liver, the Sebaceous follicles of the Skin, and, in the female when nursing, by the Mammary glands.

c. *intr.* To take the breast.

1893 Davis & Keating *Mother & Child* xxiii. 74 A sore or cracked nipple may bleed when the infant nurses. **1897** *Trans. Amer. Pediatric Soc.* IX. 40 The child seemed languid, and would not nurse. **1938** M. K. Rawlings *Yearling* xi. 98 The fawn nuzzled her full udders and began to nurse. **1946** M. C. Self *Horseman's Encycl.* 289 It is important that the foal nurse as soon as he is strong enough to stand. **1963** M. McCarthy *Group* x. 223 If they gave him a second drink of water, he might not nurse properly when feeding time finally came. **1972** *Sci. Amer.* Dec. 18/2 After the fifth week..the kittens are able to pursue her around the cage until they can get hold of a nipple, after which the mother allows them to nurse.

2. In *passive.* **a.** To be reared or brought up in a certain place.

1526 Tindale *Luke* iv. 16 He cam to nazareth where he was noursed. **1566** Painter *Pal. Pleas.* Ded. I. 5 A man.. rather fostred in the bosome of Bellona, than nourced in Kentish soile. **1590** Nashe *Pasquil's Apol.* I. C, Manie excellent learned wits, and religious mindes, are nursed there. **1637** Milton *Lycidas* 23 For we were nurst upon the self-same hill, Fed the same flock. **1820** Shelley *Prometh. Unb.* III. iii. 99 Like sister-antelopes..Nursed among lilies near a brimming stream. **1830** Tennyson *Ode to Memory* iv, Thou wert not nursed by the waterfall Which ever sounds and shines.

b. To be brought up under certain conditions, *in* a certain environment, etc.

1601 B. Jonson *Poetaster* v. i, True borne and nurst with all the Sciences. **1634** Milton *Comus* 34 His fair off-spring nurs't in Princely lore, Are coming to attend their Fathers state. **1775** Sheridan *Duenna* III. iii, There is a chilling air around poverty, that often kills affection, that was not nursed in it. **1796** Coleridge *Sibyl. Leaves, Ode to Georgiana*, O Lady, nursed in pomp and pleasure! Whence learnt you that heroic measure? **1818** Shelley *Rosal. & Helen* 869 The fierce savage, nursed in hate.

3. a. To foster, tend, cherish, take care of (a thing); to promote the growth or development of.

a **1542** Wyatt in *Tottel's Misc.* (Arb.) 62 Why shoulde such spite be nursed then in thy thought! **1562** J. Heywood *Prov. & Epigr.* (1867) 70 God graunt the head and bodie both twoo To nourse eche other, better then they doo. **1603** Shaks. *Meas. for M.* III. i. 15 All th' accommodations that thou bearst, Are nurst by basenesse. **1679** *Establ. Test* 15 Our Neighbors may..Nurse this Mitre till it shall devour the Crown. **1704** *Lond. Gaz.* No. 4068/3 Your Majesty so carefully Nurses our Establish'd Church. **1781** Cowper *Table-T.* 69 To nurse with tender care the thriving arts. **1784** —— *Task* IV. 383 The few small embers left she nurses well. **1834** Lytton *Pompeii* III. ii, The land we live in yet nurses mysterious terror. **1859** Gen. P. Thompson *Audi Alt.* xcviii. II. 86 The version of their telegraphic message.. is just such as a man would use who wanted to nurse a duel.

b. To supply (plants) with warmth or moisture; to tend or cultivate carefully.

1594 Kyd *Cornelia* III. iii, Let fayre Nylus (wont to nurse your Corne) Couer your Land with Toades and Crocadils. **1633** Milton *Arcades* 46, I..live in Oak'n bowr, To nurse the Saplings tall. **1655** T. Moufet & Bennet *Health's Improv.* (1746) 325 The Bohemians have Turneps as red outwardly as Blood..; they are counted so restorative and dainty, that the Emperor himself nurseth them in his Garden. **1781** Cowper *Charity* 573 True charity, a plant divinely nurs'd,..Thrives against hope. **1794** Mrs. Radcliffe *Myst. Udolpho* viii, Her favourite plants, St. Aubert had taught her to nurse. **1813** Marshall *Gardening* xiv. (ed. 5) 190 The pots are to be nursed and preserved moderately warm. **1871** R. Ellis tr. *Catullus* lxii. 41 A flower..Strok'd by the breeze, by the sun nurs'd sturdily.

c. To manage (land) carefully or economically.

1745 *Season. Adv. Protestants* 17 Protestants, who..have swarmed into many Stocks, built Houses,..and nursed the Land. **1790** *Bystander* 346 The young lord's estate was what they call nursed by his steward, during the time his lordship was a minor. **1815** Scott *Guy M.* ii, He nursed what property was yet left to him.

d. To foster or cherish (a feeling, etc.) in one's own heart.

a **1763** Shenstone *Elegies* xiii. 23 Say, shall we nurse the rage, assist the storm? **1791** Burke *Th. French Aff.* Wks. 1842 I. 573 Very great discontents every where prevail. But they only produce misery to those who nurse them at home. **1827** Scott *Jrnl.* 10 July, I had nursed the idea that he had been hasty in his resignation. **1866** Alger *Solit. Nat. & Man* IV. 225 In this profound retreat..he nursed and sang his love for Laura. **1879** Dixon *Windsor* II. 82 He could nurse his injuries for many years.

e. To assist or cause (a thing) to develop *into* a certain form, or *to* a certain size.

1775 Johnson *Tax. no Tyr.* 4 Whose kindness was employed to nurse them into mischief. **1800** T. Moore *Anacreon* xlvi. 22 Little infant fruits we see Nursing into luxury! **1860** Tyndall *Glac.* I. xxiv. 353 In this way crystals can be nursed to an enormous size. **1868** E. Edwards *Ralegh* I. xiii. 248 Men..who fancied it to be their interest..to nurse the embers of the old enmity into a flame. **1933** P. Godfrey *Back-Stage* ix. 131 A good play which does not catch on at once may sometimes be 'nursed' to genuine success. **1936** *Discovery* May 164/1 If two climbers can be 'nursed' to that height the victory [over Everest] may at last be won. **1942** *Tee Emm* (Air Ministry) II. 72 The instructor is, therefore, less able to..nurse each individual into efficiency.

4. To bring or rear *up* with care.

1603 Shaks. *Meas. for M.* IV. ii. 134 *Duke.* What is that Barnardine..? *Pro.* A Bohemian borne: But here nurst vp & bred. **1629** Parkinson (*title*), Paradisi..; or a Garden of all sorts of pleasant flowers which our English ayre will permitt to be noursed vp. **1676** Marvell *Mr. Smirke* I iij b, No Christian Emperor did more make it his business to Nurse up the Church. **1719** De Foe *Crusoe* I. (Globe) 164, I was loth..to have them all [*sc.* goats] to nurse up over again. **1790** *Trans. Soc. Arts* VIII. 5 One row of Scotch firs, in order to nurse up the Oaks.

5. a. To wait upon, attend to (a person who is ill).

1736 Swift *Let. to Pope* 22 Apr., Nothing..could hinder me from waiting on you at Twickenham, and nursing you to Paris. **1782** Johnson in *Boswell* 21 Mar., This season I have been almost wholly employed in nursing myself. **1837** Ht. Martineau *Soc. Amer.* 154 They will utterly neglect a sick parent or husband; while they will nurse a white mistress with much ostentation. **1881** *Encycl. Brit.* XII. 305/2 The arrangements for nursing the sick have greatly improved in recent times.

b. To try to cure (an illness or injury) by taking care of oneself. Also, to take or drive *away* by nursing.

1778 F. Burney *Evelina* I. xix. 129 She had a bad cold, and chose to nurse it. **1785** in T. Hutchinson *Diary* II. 417 Tell her it is of great importance to her to nurse her cold. **1813** Lady Burghersh *Lett.* (1893) 26 My cold..has returned, and I am nursing it before I sail again. **1854** Monckton Milnes *Life* (1891) I. xi. 497, I am nursing an influenza which came on the evening I got here. **1885–94** R. Bridges *Eros & Psyche* Oct. 17 But sleep, the gracious pursuivant of toil, Came swiftly down, and nursed away her care. **1951** *N.Y. Times* 11 Dec., The..pilot was safely at his home.. nursing only a slight scratch on his nose.

c. *intr.* To perform the duties of a sick-nurse.

1861 Flor. Nightingale *Nursing* (ed. 2) 5 Other bad arrangements often make it impossible to nurse.

6. a. To clasp (the knee, etc.) in one's hands.

1849 C. Bronte *Shirley* xxvii, With nonchalant air, and left foot nursed on his right knee. **1873** Black *Pr. Thule* vi. 86 A gentleman..was sitting on the grass, nursing his knees.

b. To hold caressingly or carefully, as a nurse does a child, *esp.* in the arms or on the lap.

1850 Ht. Martineau *Hist. Peace* v. viii. II. 338 The Premier might now have less leisure..for blowing feathers, and nursing sofa cushions. **1852** Dickens *Bleak Ho.* xxx, Then Caddy hung upon her father, and nursed his cheek against hers as if he were some poor dull child in pain. **1887** 'Edna Lyall' *Knt. Errant* xi, They..drove home again, Francesca nursing a Dying Gladiator in terra-cotta.

c. To sit close to, as if taking care of.

1857 Hughes *Tom Brown* iv, And there he found his father nursing a bright fire.

d. With a drink as object: to consume slowly, holding the glass in the hand between sips.

1942 *Sun* (Baltimore) 5 Oct. 13/4 They buy several drinks in the bar, then they come in to catch the floor show, and nurse one drink along. **1962** K. Orvis *Damned & Destroyed* xiii. 88 'Don't nurse this—drink it!' I said. She gulped the straight whisky gratefully. **1964** B. Malamud *Idiots First* 70 Cronin, pretty much contented, had had one drink to her two, and he was nursing his first when she asked for a third. **1974** R. B. Parker *God save Child* (1975) xix. 134 A thin black man..was nursing a brandy glass at..the bar.

7. *slang.* **a.** (See quots.) *rare*⁻⁰.

1796 *Grose's Dict. Vulg. Tongue* (ed. 3), *Nurse*, to cheat; as, They nursed him out of it. **1859** *Slang Dict.* 69 *Nurse* to cheat, or swindle; trustees are said to nurse property, i.e. gradually eat it up themselves.

b. To keep close to (a rival omnibus) in such a way as to prevent it from getting a fair share of passengers (esp. as in quot. 1859).

1858 *Morning Chron.* 8 Mar. (Cassell), The cause of the delay was that the defendant was waiting to nurse one of their omnibuses. **1859** *Slang Dict.* 69 Two omnibuses are placed on the road to nurse, or oppose each opposition 'buss', one before, the other behind. **1882** *Standard* 28 Feb. 3/8 The Defendant had 'nursed' one of the Company's cars from Chancery-lane to Charing Cross.

c. To impede (a horse) in a race, by surrounding it with other and slower ones.

1893 P. H. EMERSON *Signor Lippo* xvi. 75 Some of 'em wanted to 'nurse' me, but I managed to give the mare a touch of the spur, and she flew out.

8. a. To keep in touch with or influence (a constituency) in order to obtain votes.

1869 *Latest News* 17 Oct., To 'nurse' the borough cost him £500 a year at least. **1888** BRYCE *Amer. Commw.* (1890) I. xix. 262 An ambitious congressman is therefore forced to think..of his re-nomination, and to secure it..by sedulously 'nursing' the constituency during the vacations.

b. To assist (a business house) so as to prevent its bankruptcy.

1890 *Daily News* 29 Dec. 2/2 The tendency to 'nurse' financial houses has grown to a striking extent.

9. *Billiards.* To keep (the balls) close to one another in order to enable a prolonged series of cannons to be made.

1869 BUCK *Roberts on Billiards* 27 When Tieman was 200 points ahead, and sure of a great break, he 'nursed' the balls until 70 had been scored. **1896** BROADFOOT *Billiards* 28 His [Cook's] beautiful delicacy of touch was more striking than ever, and he 'nursed' the balls with even more than his old skill.

Hence **'nursed** *ppl. a.*

1859 *Slang Dict.* 69 The central or nursed buss has very little chance, unless it happens to be a favourite with the public. **1899** *Allbutt's Syst. Med.* VIII. 667 In carefully nursed children it is generally observed in the first two months.

'nurse-child. [NURSE *sb.*[1]] A child in relation to its nurse; a foster-child.

1560 BECON *New Catech.* Wks. 1564 I. 537b, Can the nurses instill any goodnes into the tender brestes of their nurse children, when they themselues haue learned none? **1587** GOLDING *De Mornay* xii. (1592) 184 After the same maner dealeth the Nurce with her Nurcechild. **1626** T. H[AWKINS] tr. *Caussin's Holy Crt.* 70 She..made her litle Nurse-child superlatiuely inheritour of her vices. **1681** W. ROBERTSON *Phraseol. Gen.* (1693) 329 A nurse-child; or one that sucketh the same milk. **1769** JOHNSON in *Croker's Boswell* (1831) II. 94 If we had..given her a nurse-child to tend, her life would have been saved. **1815** *Paris Chit-Chat* (1816) II. 18 Each nurse has her bed placed between two cradles, one for her own, and the other for the nurse-child. **1866** *Routledge's Mag. for Boys* July 408 Norwood was a dreadful place for nurse-children never being called for at one time.

fig. **1622** J. DAVIES *Hymns* vii, Sweet Nurse-child of the Springs young Hours. **1823** LAMB *Elia, Witches & other Night-fears*, From his little midnight pillow this nurse-child of optimism will start at shapes.

'nursedom. [NURSE *sb.*[1]] An organized system of nurses; the ways of nurses.

1881 in Ld. Tennyson *Mem. Tennyson* (1897) II. 499 *note*, Another of the London hospitals is in danger of entering upon a career of rampant nursedom. **1883** *Pall Mall G.* 26 Sept. 3/2 A pernicious device of antiquated nursedom.

†**'nurse-father.** *Obs.* [f. NURSE *sb.*[1] or *v.* Cf. *nursing-father.*] A foster-father. Chiefly *fig.*

1564 *Brief Exam.* **iiij, Kynges shalbe thy Nursefathers. **1608** JAS. I in *3rd Rep. Hist. MSS. Comm.* 414/1 We doe acknowledge ourselves in duty to God bound to be a nurse-father of his Church. **1644** MAXWELL *Prerog. Chr. Kings* 11, I pray you consider what encouragement is it for Kings and Monarchs to become Nurse-fathers of the Reformed Church. **1714** FORTESCUE-ALAND *Fortescue's Abs. & Lim. Mon.* 123 The verb *bajulando*, to carry in one's arms, as the Nurse-Fathers used to do the children that were put to them to nurse.

†**'nurse-fellow.** *Obs. rare.* A foster-brother.

1526 TINDALE *Acts* xiii. 1 Menahen Herode the tetrarkes norsfelowe. [Also in Coverdale.]

†**'nurse-garden.** *Obs.* [f. NURSE *sb.*[1] or *v.*] A nursery for plants. Also *fig.*

1565 COOPER *Thesaurus, Seminarium*, a place where plantes be set to be removed; a nourse garden. **1601** HOLLAND *Pliny* I. 510 Concerning seminaries and nourse-gardens, Nature hath shewed vs the reason and maner thereof. **1610** —— *Camden's Brit.* I. 429 Queene Elizabeth converted it..into a Seminary and nurse-garden of the Church. **1657** AUSTEN *Fruit Trees* I. 66.

nurse-hound: see NURSE *sb.*[2] b.

†**'nurse-keeper.** A sick-nurse. Also *fig.*

1602 HERRING *Anat.* 4 Chattering Char-women and Nurs-keepers. **1653** JER. TAYLOR *Serm. for Year* I. viii. 101 When the heart of Man is..tended by those Nurse-Keepers of the Soul, it is not easie for a man to wander. **1656** W. COLES *Art of Simpling* 92 Democritus, when he lay a dying, heard his Nurse-keeper complaine. **1724** *Lond. Gaz.* No. 6250/11 Mary Easton,..Widow and Nursekeeper. **1781** C. JOHNSTON *Hist. J. Juniper* II. 243, I was turned out in the condition you see by my nurse-keeper.

'nursekin, -let. [NURSE *sb.*[1]] A little nurse.

1862 THACKERAY *Adventures of Philip* xxxiv, Mrs. Char went down Thornhaugh Street..with Betsy the nursekin and baby in the new cloak. **1894** *Argosy* Jan. 39 She had in occasionally a nurselet who had not yet flowered into full dignity.

'nurse-maid. [NURSE *sb.*[1]] **a.** A young woman employed as maid to attend to little children.

1657 *Rutland MSS.* (Hist. MSS. Comm.) IV. 539 To Lord Burley for the nurse maids 7s. 6d. **1785** MRS. FLETCHER in Wesley *Serm.* lvii. Wks. 1811 IX. 28 He was reproved by his nurse maid. **1801** *Med. Jrnl.* V. 109 The nurse-maid, and two children of my friend,..were inoculated for the Cow-pox. **1836–7** DICKENS *Sk. Boz, Tales* iv, Nurse-maids displayed their charms to the greatest possible advantage; and their sweet little charges ran up and down. **1885** *Harper's Mag.* Mar. 566/2 This bright girl who had at present eclipsed..the prettiest nurse-maids.

b. *slang.* (See quot.)

1943 C. H. WARD-JACKSON *Piece of Cake* 44 *Nursemaid*, a long-distance fighter escort for bombers.

Hence **'nurse-maid** *v.*, to tend and care for (a person) as a nurse-maid does her charge; also with non-personal object; **'nurse-maiding** *vbl. sb.*

1921 *Glasgow Herald* 19 Apr. 8 He had to be nurse-maided and chaperoned to his meals, his bath, and his bed. **1924** 'J. SUTHERLAND' *Circle of Stars* iv. 40 'I really don't need the nurse-maiding you think I ought to have,' Gloria said impatiently. **1935** C. S. FORESTER *African Queen* iv. 87 That engine..was greased and cleaned and nurse-maided. **1960** *Times* 5 Apr. 14/6 The kroomen from the African mainland who nursemaided us. **1967** *Economist* 27 May 896/1 By..telling the UN force it could stop nursemaiding his country, President Nasser had scored a clear political success in the Arab world. **1973** 'A. YORK' *Captivator* ii. 32 Nursemaiding princesses..is not really in my line.

'nurse-mother. Now *rare.* [f. NURSE *sb.*[1] or *v.* Cf. *nursing-mother.*] A foster-mother.

1579 TOMSON *Calvin's Serm. Tim.* 137/2 When Iesus Christe shall be come, Princes must be protectours of Christianitie, and Queenes must be nurse mothers. **1610** HOLLAND *Camden's Brit.* I. 383 Thus much briefely of my deare nourse-mother, Oxford.

1896 *Daily News* 8 Jan. 2/4 The Coroner expressed great surprise that the..authorities should send these children to 'nurse mothers' who were not duly registered.

'nurse-plant. [NURSE *sb.*[1] or *v.*]

†**1.** A seedling plant. *Obs. rare*$^{-1}$.

1601 HOLLAND *Pliny* I. 523 The Broom loueth to be set of Nource-plants, comming of seed, in dry and light grounds.

2. A plant which nourishes a parasite.

1857 HENFREY *Bot.* §40 When the radicle sprouts, it drives its way through the rind of the nurse-plant until it reaches the cambium-layer. *Ibid.*, Beneath the bark of the nurse-plant. **1882** *Gard. Chron.* XVII. 20 They cannot be very exacting as to the species of nurse-plant.

'nurser. [f. NURSE *v.* + -ER[1].] One who or that which nurses, fosters, or encourages.

1388 WYCLIF *Isa.* xlix. 23 And kingis schulen be thi nurseris, and quenys schulen be thi nursis. **1591** SHAKS. *1 Hen. VI*, IV. vii. 46 See where he lyes inherced in the armes Of the most bloody Nursser of his harmes. **1651** FEATLY in Fuller *Abel Rediv.* 485 Colledges..ought to be as nursers for choyce plants to be set and nourished there for a while. **1719** D'URFEY *Pills* (1872) III. 7 The Nurser of Subjects, bold Britain's chief Meat. **1825** HONE *Every-day Bk.* I. 1138 The early nursers and improvers of our art. **1888** CUSHING *Blacksmith of Voe* III. 34 If old Abel was..a nurser of wrath, he would probably object.

nursery ('nɜːsərɪ). Forms: 4–5 **norcery**, 5 **norserye** (6 -ie), 6–7 **nourcery; nurcery** (6 -ie); 6–7 **nursserye** (-ie), 5– **nursery** (6 -ye, 6–7 -ie). [prob. ad. AF. ***noricerie**, f. *norice* NOURICE: see -ERY, and cf. NOURICERY.]

†**1. a.** Fosterage, upbringing, breeding; nursing. ***at nursery***, at nurse. *Obs.*

a **1400** *Chron. R. Glouc.* (MS. C) 8938 Vor þis Mold was þe wule heo was ȝong to norcery ido In þe abbeye of rameseye. **1430–40** LYDG. *Bochas* VII. ii. (1554) 166 One of his children, being at norcery,..Of aventure, or they could it espye, His Knightes slough. *a* **1460** *Lybeaus Disc.* (Kaluza) 960 Elene, þe messengere, Semeþ but a lavendere Of her norserie. **1605** SHAKS. *Lear* I. i. 126, I lou'd her most, and thought to set my rest On her kind nursery. **1653** H. WHISTLER *Upshot Inf. Baptisme* 69 Allaying the tedious nights, and carefull daies of Nursery. *a* **1671** CASAUBON *Treat. Spirits* (1672) 199 Two brothers preserved by the milk and nursery of a she-wolf.

†**b.** Relationship by having acted as nurse or foster-mother to one. *Obs. rare*$^{-1}$.

c **1613** *Cond. People Anglesey* (1860) 17 An old impudent drabb..that can alleadge either kindred, alliance, nurserie, or some affinity or other, with all men.

†**c.** That which is nursed; a nursling. *Obs. rare.*

1642 FULLER *Holy & Prof. St.* II. xv. 106 The thriving of the nourcery is the best argument to prove the skill and care of the nource. **1650** —— *Pisgah* II. viii. 177 A jolly dame.., as appears by the well battling of the plump boy her nursery.

2. a. The place or apartment which is given up to infants and young children with their nurse.

1499 *Promp. Parv.* (Pynson), Norcery, where yonge children be kepte, *brephotropheum*. **1532** HERVET tr. *Xenophon's Œconomy* (1768) 40, I shewed her the nourcery and the womens lodgyng, diuided from the mens lodgyng. **1577** tr. *Bullinger's Decades* (1592) 156 For there is mention made of nourceries for children. **1611** SHAKS. *Cymb.* I. i. 59 He had two Sonnes..[who] from their Nursery Were stolne. **1641** J. JACKSON *True Evang. T.* II. 162 Are wee the Lambs and Kids of Gods fold,..the Babes of his Nursery? **1720** SWIFT *Mod. Educ.* Wks. 1751 V. 52 He is taught from the Nursery, that he must inherit a great Estate. **1784** COWPER *Tiroc.* 117 Our parents..wisely store the nurs'ry by degrees With wholesome learning. **1803** *Med. Jrnl.* IX. 529 Female domestics, and the inhabitants of the nursery, seldom escaped its influence. **1882** MISS BRADDON *Mt. Royal* III. i. 17 Christabel carried him back to the nursery.

†**b.** (See quot.) *Obs. rare*$^{-0}$.

1611 COTGR., *Chambre des femmes*, a Nurserie, or priuat roome onely for women.

3. a. A practice, institution, etc., in or by which something is fostered or developed.

1509 BARCLAY *Shyp of Folys* (1570) 115 What els is daunsing but euen a nurcery..to purchase and mayntayne In yonge heartes the vile sinne of ribawdry? **1583** BABINGTON *Commandm.* 193 [Cloisters] became as we wel know dens of drones, and nurceries of vngodlinesse. **1604** T. WRIGHT *Passions* I. iv. 19 Passions..be the nurcery of vices, and pathway to all wickednesse. **1654** WHITLOCK *Zootomia* 235 The Press..is Truths Armory, The Bank of Knowledge, and Nursery of Religion. **1725** BERKELEY *Proposal* Wks. 1871 III. 217 Until a nursery of learning for the education of the natives be founded. **1780** BURKE *Œcon. Reform* Wks. 1842 I. 234 That all subordinate treasuries, as the nurseries of mismanagement,..ought to be dissolved. **1846** KEBLE *Serm.* xiii. (1848) 322 The other calamities..have been a great field and nursery for saintly hope. **1894** H. DRUMMOND *Ascent Man* 383 Family Life, the first and last nursery of the higher sympathies.

b. A place, sphere, etc., in which people are trained or educated; a school *of*, or *for*, certain professions, etc.

1581 MULCASTER *Positions* xli. (1887) 255 This colledge for teachers, might proue an excellent nurserie for good schoolemaisters. **1596** SPENSER *State Irel.* Wks. (Globe) 678/1 This keeping of cowes is of it selfe a verye idle life, and a fitt nurserye of a theefe. *a* **1618** RALEIGH *Remains* (1661) 198 A continual Nursery for breeding and encreasing our Mariners. **1654** WHITLOCK *Zootomia* 95 In this Nursery..of Charlatans, or Mountebanks (as Doctor Primrose justly calleth England). **1701** W. WOTTON *Hist. Rome* 455 The Equestrian Order was the proper Nursery of the Senate. **1715** M. DAVIES *Athen. Brit.* I. 18 The College of St. Mary the Virgin, a Nursery belonging then unto the Canon Regulars of the Order of St. Austin at Oxford. **1777** PRIESTLEY *Phil. Necess.* Ded. p. ix, This world, we see, is an admirable nursery for great minds. **1839** THIRLWALL *Greece* li. VI. 258 His little kingdom was now chiefly valuable to him as a nursery of soldiers. **1876** FREEMAN *Norm. Conq.* V. 135 Under William Rufus the Chancery became a nursery of clever and unscrupulous churchmen.

†**c.** A theatre established in London for the training of young players. *Obs.*

1664 PEPYS *Diary* 2 Aug., Tom Killigrew..is setting up a nursery; that is, is going to build a house in Moorefields, wherein he will have common plays acted. **1672** VILLIERS (Dk. Buckm.) *Rehearsal* II. ii. (Arb.) 55, I am resolv'd, hereafter, to bend all my thoughts for the service of the Nursery, and mump your proud Players, I gad. *a* **1683** OLDHAM *Satyr* Poems (1684) 179 Then slighted by the very Nursery, May'st thou at last be forc'd to starve, like me.

d. An establishment for training promising young players of a particular sport.

1950 W. HAMMOND *Cricketers' School* viii. 80 Yorkshire does not run the usual cricket Nursery that a team like Middlesex maintains. **1954** F. C. AVIS *Boxing Ref. Dict.* 76 *Nursery*, a club in which boxing talent is developed. **1961** —— *Sportsman's Gloss.* 36/1 *Nursery*, a junior club taken under the wing of a bigger club to which talented nursery players graduate. **1962** G. SCOTT in B. Glanville *Footballer's Compan.* 447 It seemed that lads who had been taken from the 'nursery' clubs by the slag heaps and the pits had weak heads for success.

4. a. A plot or piece of ground in which young plants or trees are reared until fit for transplantation; †a collection of such plants. Now usually a piece of ground of considerable extent in which the plants or trees are reared for sale; a nursery-garden.

1565 COOPER *Thesaurus, Nutrix*, a nourcerie or place where men plante and graffe trees or hearbes, to thende afterward to remoue them. **1568** WITHALS *Dict.* 24b/1 A norserie, or place wherein groweth, or be kepte to increase yonge vines or trees, *seminarium*. **1622** BONOEIL *Art Making Silke* 34 How to prepare the seed of Mulbery trees to make a Nurcery. **1664** EVELYN *Kal. Hort.* (1729) 191 Set up your Traps for Vermine; especially in your Nurseries of Kernels and Stones. **1712** J. JAMES tr. *Le Blond's Gardening* 178 The Seed and young Plants you set in a Nursery. **1751** JOHNSON *Rambler* No. 112 ⁋3 A plant transplanted to northern nurseries. **1808** *Phil. Trans.* XCVIII. 315 A nursery of apple trees. **1860** HOGG *Fruit Man.* Pref., A Manual of Fruits which..included most of the varieties found in nurseries and private gardens.

transf. **1797** *Encycl. Brit.* (ed. 3) III. 549/2 Whoever has a turn for making experiments..will find it much easier..to preserve and raise nurseries of the common ones [sorts of yeast], than to devise mixtures of others.

b. In figurative context.

1606 SHAKS. *Tr. & Cr.* I. iii. 319 The seeded Pride That hath to this maturity blowne vp..must or now be cropt, Or shedding breed a Nursery of like euil. **1653** BAXTER *Peace Consc.* Ep. Ded., When Satan hath a design to burn up those Nurseries, you are watering God's plants. **1719–20** SWIFT *Let. to Yng. Clergym.* Wks. 1751 V. 22 Extracts of Theological and Moral Sentences..intended for Materials, or Nurseries to stock future Sermons. **1820** WORDSW. *Misc. Sonn.* III. ii, Ye sacred Nurseries of blooming Youth! **1877** SPARROW *Serm.* xvi. 207 This world was meant to be only a nursery for the garden of the Lord of heaven.

c. Grass-land left uncut in summer, to serve as winter feed. *rare*$^{-1}$.

1780 A. YOUNG *Tour Irel.* II. 86 The winter food..is to keep bottom lands through the summer, which they call a nursery, to which they bring the cattle down from the mountains when the weather becomes severe.

5. a. A place which breeds or supports animals.

1661 HICKERINGILL *Jamaica* 13 Nor are the Woods a more Plentiful Nursery for the Hoggs then the Savana's are for the Beeves and wild Cattel. **1689** LOCKE *Govt.* I. vi. (Rtldg.) 56 The dens of lions and nurseries of wolves.

b. In pisciculture, a pond or place in which the young fry are reared.

1771 *Phil. Trans.* LXI. 320 The nurseries are the second kind of ponds intended for the bringing up the young fry. **1837** DONOVAN *Dom. Econ.* II. 197 There ought in fact to be three ponds, a spawning pond, a nursery, and a pond for adult fish. **1868** PEARD *Water-farm.* v. 61 The instinct which carries the fish to the highest tributaries teaches us the importance of improving and creating such nurseries.

c. Of ants, etc.: The cells or chambers in which the larval and nymphal insects attain maturity.

1797 *Encycl. Brit.* (ed. 3) XVIII. 387/1 The most striking parts of these structures are, the royal apartments, the nurseries. **1816** KIRBY & SP. *Entomol.* xvii. (1818) II. 33 The office of..conveying the eggs when laid to what Smeathman calls the nurseries. **1830** *Insect Architecture* (L.E.K.) xvi. 296 When the nest [of ants] is in the infant state, the nurseries are close to the royal chambers.

d. A place or part in which any form of animal life is developed.

1871 T. R. JONES *Anim. Kingd.* (ed. 5) 93 The swimming-bell is converted into a chamber or nursery in which the embryo passes through its early stages of development. **1899** *Allbutt's Syst. Med.* VIII. 762 The persistence of dry seborrhœa on the scalp appears to convert that part into a nursery of various kinds of microbes.

6. A race for two-year-old horses.

1883 *Daily Tel.* 26 Oct. (Cassell), Winning three nurseries off the reel.

7. *Billiards.* (See quots.) Also *attrib.*

1869 BUCK *Roberts on Billiards* 135 *Nursery*, when the three balls are within an inch or two of one another, and a long score is likely. **1885** *Billiards Simplified* (1889) 125 To play for a series of cannons, moving the balls as little as possible, such series being called 'a nursery of cannons'. **1893** *Westm. Gaz.* 17 May 5/2 He seems to depend almost entirely on nursery cannons, with little taste for hazards.

8. *attrib.* and *Comb.* **a.** In a sense 2, as ***nursery bathroom, bedroom, -book, chair, child, -door, fender, food, -governess, meal, -rhyme, -song, story, supper, -tale***, etc. **nursery-girl**, a nursery-maid; **nursery language**, a stylized form of language used in addressing small children; **nursery word**, a non-standard word used by a child or by an adult to address a child.

1949 'J. TEY' *Brat Farrar* xii. 94 You can have the *nursery bathroom all to yourself, but *do* go slow on the hot water, will you? **1941** T. S. ELIOT *Dry Salvages* i. 7 His [*sc.* the river's] rhythm was present in the *nursery bedroom. **1818** KEATS *Let.* 23 Jan. (1958) I. 210, I was at Hunt's the other day, and he surprised me with a real authenticated Lock of *Milton's Hair.* I know you would like what I wrote thereon—so here it is—*as they say of a Sheep in a *Nursery Book.* **1870** EMERSON *Soc. & Solit.* x. 205 The very nursery-books, the ballads which delight boys. **1739** G. OGLE *Gualtherus & Griselda* 106 Vain talk for Children! *Nursery Cant of Sprites! **1869** C. L. EASTLAKE *Hints on Household Taste* (ed. 2) viii. 191 The rush-bottomed '*nursery' chairs, of which the wood-work is stained black, with low seats and high backs..are still to be bought in the East of London. **1896** *Heal & Son Catal.* 153 Nursery Chair, low cane seat and high back. **1817** JANE AUSTEN *Let.* 13 Mar. (1952) 484 When Caroline was sent to School some years, *Miss Bell* was still retained, though the others were then mere *Nursery Children. **1973** *Guardian* 22 May 13/1 Nanny's pride, the nursery child, ringletted, smocked and sashed, is no more. **1875** TENNYSON *Q. Mary* II. ii, The *nursery-cocker'd child will jeer at aught That may seem strange beyond his nursery. **1718** PRIOR *Hans Carvel* vii, The Devil..stands before the *Nurs'ry Doors, To take the naughty Boy that roars. **1796** BP. WATSON *Apol. Bible* x. (1799) 379 They presently get rid of their *nursery faith, and are seldom sedulous in the acquisition of another. **1907** *Yesterday's Shopping* (1969) 177/1 *Nursery Fenders... Brass top, japanned diamond wire work, black bottom plate. **1913** C. MACKENZIE *Sinister St.* I, I. i. 10 Round the fire was a nursery fender on which hung perpetually various cloths and clothes and blankets and sheets. **1926–7** *Army & Navy Stores Catal.* 275/2 Nursery fender, with..brass top. ⅜ in. mesh..30 in. high with 12 in. return ends. **1949** A. CHRISTIE *Crooked House* v. 29 Proper wholesome *nursery food—not those queer spiced rice dishes. **1965** D. FRANCIS *Odds Against* vi. 84 A tiny service lift used long ago to take nursery food to top floor children. **1861** C. M. YONGE *Stokesley Secret* xii. 193 She..suspected Rhoda, the little *nursery-girl, who was quite a child, and had not long been in the house. **1873** —— *Pillars of House* I. v. 96 Why, you might as well turn nursery-girl at once. **1820** M. WILMOT *Let.* 4 May (1935) 60 The loss of a most valuable little french *Nursery Governess. **1835** ELIZ. NAPIER (*title*), The Nursery Governess. **1884** J. HALL *Christ. Home* 58 Family arrangements will have to be different where nursery-governesses and tutors are called in. **1742** RICHARDSON *Pamela* IV. 320 What *Nursery Impertinencies are these, to trouble a Man with! **1845** F. A. KEMBLE *Let.* 8 Dec. in *Rec. Later Life* (1882) III. 95 In *nursery language, I *peacified* the good old lady to the best of my ability. **1925** O. JESPERSEN *Mankind, Nation & Individual* vii. 145 Another dialect used with regard to the person addressed is that more or less affected nursery-language which many mothers and nurses..use with small children—where 'stomach' is 'tum-tum', 'horse' is 'gee-gee', 'thank-you' is 'ta' etc. **1968** *Trans. Philol. Soc.* 107 The special structures and lexical items employed by adults when talking to young children, which we can conveniently group together under the label of *Nursery Language.* **1677** *Compl. Servant-Maid* Title-p., Chamber-maid, Cook-maid, *Nursery-maid, Dairy-maid. **1799** UNDERWOOD *Diseases Children* (ed. 4) III. 102 Nursery-maids are often indiscreet in keeping them too long in the air at a time. **1869** CLARIDGE *Cold Water Cure* 39 At a spring the nursery-maid asked me if she might give the child water. **1942** M. B. LOWNDES *Let.* 15 Apr. (1971) 229 Many people..live in their country houses with relations, children, and so on. I know of one where there are three sets of *nursery meals! **1953** H. NICOLSON *Diary* 6 May (1968) III. 240 Dull nursery meals—beef, mutton, and milk-puddings. **1832** A. FONBLANQUE *England under Seven Admins.* (1837) II. 304 The man of Thessaly, famed for wondrous wisdom in *nursery rhymes, who, having scratched his eyes out by jumping into one hedge, jumped into another to scratch them in again. **1841** HALLIWELL *Nursery Rhymes* (1843) 1 The traditional Nursery Rhymes of England commence with a legendary satire on King Cole. **1972** (*title*) The bedtime book of 365 nursery rhymes. *c* **1820** S. ROGERS *Italy* (1839) 201 Singing the *nursery-song he learnt so soon. **1927** W. E. COLLINSON *Contemporary Eng.* 9, I mention these nursery-songs. **1971** A. MIZENER *Saddest Story* xxvi. 358 Ford led them in a round dance on the [Avignon] bridge to the tune of the nursery song. **1834** G. CRABBE JR. *Life of Rev. George Crabbe* in *Poetical Works & Life of Crabbe* I. x. 304 Little tales, as nearly resembling those which had delighted his own infancy as modern systems permit..the German *Nursery Stories. **1848** THACKERAY *Van. Fair* xxv. 219 It was as in the old nursery-story, when the stick forgot to beat the dog. **1966** B. IRESON (*title*) The Faber book of nursery stories. **1857** C. M. YONGE *Dynevor Terrace* II. xii. 186 She often comes down after our dinner to find something for the *nursery supper. **1971** J. DRUMMOND *Farewell Party* xxi. 117, I was given a huge nursery supper by old Bertha. **1741** RICHARDSON *Pamela* IV. lxiv. 451 You desired me to send you a little Specimen of my **Nursery Tales* and *Stories*, with which..I entertain ..my little Boys. **1822** SCOTT in *Lockhart* (1839) VII. 7 It was to me a nursery-tale, often told by Mrs. Margaret Swinton. **1871** FROUDE in *Devon Assoc. Trans.* IV. 21 Legends grew as nursery tales grow now. **1888** KIPLING *Story of Gadsbys* 4 *Miss T*... Won't you have some eggs? *Captain G*... Eggs! (*Aside.*) Oh Hades! She must have a *nursery-tea at this hour. **1939** T. S. ELIOT *Family Reunion* I. i. 17 Harry must often have remembered Wishwood—The nursery tea, the school holiday. **1958** M. STEWART *Nine Coaches Waiting* iii. 33 A little pantry with an electric stove for making nursery tea. **1790** COWPER *Mother's Picture* 30, I,..turning from my *nurs'ry window, drew A long, long sigh. **1828** MISS MITFORD *Village* Ser. III. (1863) 31 A certain..Sophy, who died..by falling out of the nursery-window. **1933** L. BLOOMFIELD *Language* ix. 157 In English almost any doubled syllable may be used, in almost any meaning, as a *nursery-word. **1957** R. W. ZANDVOORT *Handbk. Eng. Gram.* IX. i. 287 Many of them are nursery words... *Georgy-Porgy, piggie-wiggie, tootsy-wootsies* (feet), etc.

b. In sense 4, as ***nursery-bed, -garden, -gardener, -ground, -monger, -tree.***

1719 LONDON & WISE *Compl. Gard.* 215 To place them near together afterward in another *Nursery-Bed, and cover them up with long Litter. **1880** C. R. MARKHAM *Peruv. Bark* x. 398 A large number of seedlings were raised in nursery-beds and in the propagating-house during 1872. **1757** *Phil. Trans.* L. 434 Most of the plants in the *nursery-gardens about London. **1887** MOLONEY *Forest. W. Afr.* 70 The establishment of Botanic Stations, Model Farms, or Nursery-gardens. **1766** *Compl. Farmer* s.v. *Nursery* 5 R 3/2 All good *nursery-gardeners shift and change their land, from time to time. **1859** *Edin. Rev.* CIX. 302/1 There are the florists and nursery-gardeners,—not infrequently quakers. **1789** MRS. PIOZZI *Journ. France* I. 335 They were watering ..., just as we do in a *nursery-ground about London. **1868** *Rep. U.S. Commissioner Agric.* (1869) 252 Suitable for vegetable and flower gardens, and nursery grounds. **1693** EVELYN *De La Quint. Compl. Gard.* I. 139 With the hazard of incurring the displeasure of a great many of our *Nursery Mongers. **1707** MORTIMER *Husb.* (1721) II. 40 They are manag'd like other *Nursery Trees, and may, when they are big enough, be planted out for Walks or other occasions.

c. In sense 3, as ***nursery education***; **nursery class**, a class attached to a primary or other school for the education of children usu. between the ages of three and five years; **nursery nurse**, a person trained to care for babies and young children; so **nursery nursing**; **nursery school**, a school for children usu. between the ages of two and five years; also *attrib.* and *fig.*; so **nursery schooling; nursery slope** *Skiing*, a gentle slope considered most suitable for beginners; also in extended uses (see quots.).

1921 *Act 11 & 12 Geo. V* c. 51 §21 Supplying..nursery schools (which expression shall include nursery classes) for children over two or under five years of age. **1943** *Educational Reconstruction* 5 A certain number of children enter..nursery classes attached to infants' schools, at an earlier age on a voluntary basis. **1970** J. & P. KENT *Nursery Schools for All* II. iv. 94 Nursery classes are..defined..as 'a class mainly for children who have attained the age of three years but not the age of five years', and which is part of a primary school for infants or juniors. **1938** P. E. CUSDEN *English Nursery School* xvii. 257 The general provision of facilities for nursery education. **1969** *Guardian* 17 Jan. 9/2 Under the new Urban Aid Scheme £3 million are promised for more nursery education. **1974** *Ibid.* 24 Jan. 13/2 Mrs. Thatcher has announced a programme of expanding nursery education. **1947** A. B. MEERING *Handbk. for Nursery Nurses* 1 The Nursery Nurse who prefers the care of individual children..may become a nanny in a private family. **1967** V. C. JONES in P. J. Cunningham *Nursery Nursing* 13 Nursery nurses..care for the young child in its earliest and most impressionable years. **1972** *Guardian* 30 Aug. 11/3 The nanny or nursery nurse of today is trained in child care... Norland..describes nursery nursing as a growing profession. **1973** E. LEMARCHAND *Let or Hindrance* ii. 16 She was in training as a nursery nurse, and had one more year to go. **1835** D. W. WEBBER *Let.* in I. Butler *Eldest Brother* (1973) I. ii. 29 It was..in the year 1765 that Lord Wellesley was brought to school... It was quite a nursery school... As a kind of Preparatory School it was in great Fashion. **1891** MICHAELIS & MOORE tr. *Froebel's Lett.* 30 He [*sc.* Froebel] thinks of christening it 'Nursery School for Little Children' or 'Self-teaching Institution'. **1918** *Act 8 & 9 Geo. V.* c. 39 The Board shall have regard to the adequacy of the provision of nursery schools for the area. **1958** *Economist* 24 Oct. 303/1 His [*sc.* Gaitskell's] back-benchers still belong to the nursery school of political manœuvre. **1967** O. WYND *Walk Softly* iii. 33 A nursery-school teacher who has happily dedicated a whole life to very young minds. **1970** J. & P. KENT *Nursery Schools for All* I. i. 28 From that time the nursery school problem assumed the distinctive character which it still has today. **1974** *Times* 14 Oct. 4/1 Nursery school grants rejected by councils. Mrs. Thatcher introduced a £34m programme in 1971..to make nursery schooling available to half the three to five age group by 1980. **1924** K. FURSE *Ski-Running* p. vi, Every beginner should be content to devote two or three of his first days to the Nursery slopes. **1924** W. LE QUEUX *Crystal Claw* i. 21 She had been three times before to winter sports, and had long passed the period when she practiced her 'telemarks' and 'stemmings' on the 'nursery slopes'. **1943** HUNT & PRINGLE *Service Slang* 47 *Nursery slopes*, the easy targets allotted to beginners on bombing tests. **1959** *Daily Mail* 14 Oct. 12/6 If you do not limber up before you go [skiing] you may find your second or third day on the nursery slopes surprisingly painful. **1972** M. YORKE *Silent Witness* ii. 12 The lifts, and even the cable-car.., had stopped... Only the two short drags on the nursery slopes were working. **1975** *Daily Tel.* 15 Jan. 13 (*caption*) An early flight [in hang-gliding] lasting about 45 seconds down a nursery slope, straight into wind.

Hence **'nursery** *v.*, to rear or tend with care. **'nurserydom**, nurseries taken collectively. **'nurseryful**, the fill of a nursery.

1885–94 R. BRIDGES *Eros & Psyche* Mar. i, The land.. Where grave Demeter nurseried her wheat. **1886** H. F. LESTER *Under two Fig Trees* 195 He was multitudinously a married man having a nurseryful of children. **1892** *Daily News* 14 May 2/1 They are little suited to the ways of English nurserydom.

'nurseryman. [f. prec.] One who owns, or works in, a nursery for plants.

1672 *Phil. Trans.* VII. 5050 A peculiar way of grafting, much used by some of the best Nursery-men about London. **1719** LONDON & WISE *Compl. Gard.* p. v, Gentlemen who send for the best Sorts of Fruit-Trees from a Nursery-man, or Gardener. **1793** *Trans. Soc. Arts* V. 163 Three modes of raising Mulberry-trees, to which we are directed by Nursery-men. **1824** LOUDON *Encycl. Gard.* (ed. 2) 890 Ample lists..may be had from all the principal nurserymen. **1856** DELAMER *Fl. Gard.* (1861) 2 You may order to any reasonable extent of the country nurserymen.

'nurse-tend, *v.* [Back-formation on NURSE-TENDER or -TENDING.]

1. *trans.* To tend (a person) as a sick-nurse does.

1792 *Elvina* II. 85 They would not have any violent objection to nurse-tend each other. **1858** MORRIS *Welland River* 230, I pray you, nurse-tend me, my knight, Whiles that I have my breath.

2. *intr.* To act or serve as a sick-nurse.

1863 MRS. GASKELL *Sylvia's Lovers* (ed. 2) I. 233 Sylvie shall go play hersen; she's been nurse-tending long enough. **1888** *Quiver* May 492/1 She has done nothing but nurse-tend ever since she married that old man.

'nurse-tender. [NURSE *sb.*[1]] One who tends a sick person; a sick-nurse.

Still current in Ireland, and in south-western dial.

1789 CHARLOTTE SMITH *Ethelinde* (1814) IV. 181 Mr. Montgomery was glad of an excuse to play the nurse-tender. **1842** LOVER *Handy Andy* ii, Mrs. O'Grady was near the bed of the sick man as the nurse-tender entered. **1855** THACKERAY *Newcomes* lix, The world is full of Miss Nightingales, and we sick and wounded in our private Scutaris, have countless nurse-tenders. **1872** *Routledge's Ev. Boy's Ann.* 4/2 She was a born nurse tender, as they call sick-room attendants in..Ireland.

So **'nurse-tending** *vbl. sb.*, the tending or nursing of the sick. (Cf. NURSE-TEND *v.*)

1771 MRS. GRIFFITH *Hist. Lady Barton* II. 264, I..am therefore inclined to elevate the office of nurse-tending, by placing it amongst our rational pleasures. **1792** *Elvina* II. 85 Her talents for nurse-tending. **1888** *Quiver* May 492/1 All the nurse-tending Annette has done.

'nurse-tree. [NURSE *sb.*[1]]

1. A tree planted to protect others.

1805 R. W. DICKSON *Pract. Agric.* II. 1089 In mixed plantations the nurse trees should be first gradually thinned out. **1891** FERNOW *What is Forestry?* 17 Where..the mother or nurse trees are removed, a thicket of young beeches has replaced the old growth. **1902** B. E. FERNOW *Economics of Forestry* vii. 175 When the latter [*sc.* the young crop] has come up, the nurse trees are gradually removed to give the young seedlings the required light. **1953** H. L. EDLIN *Forester's Handbk.* v. 75 Frost-tender trees should never be planted in frost-hollows without the protection of a hardier nurse-tree. **1971** E. HYAMS *Capability Brown* I. v. 49 He [*sc.* Brown] used some conifers as nurse trees.

2. A tree supporting a parasitic plant.

1857 HENFREY *Bot.* §40 The full-grown plant appears rootless, and like a branch or graft upon the nurse-tree.

'nursey. Also nursie. A child's pet-form of NURSE *sb.*[1] 1.

a **1814** *Way to win her* I. ii. in *New Brit. Theatre* II. 407 Nursey, did you see the fine dancing-master who called to give me a lesson yesterday. **1860** G. H. LEWES *Let.* 17 Mar. in *Geo. Eliot's Lett.* (1954) III. 274, I went to see Nursie, who will 'keep house' while I am away. **1889** *Pall Mall G.* 17 Dec. 3/2 Nursey, you will not take Dorothy away when it is quite dark, will you? **1918** A. BENNETT *Roll-Call* II. i. 220 Nursey's sunshade was undiscoverable. **1968** 'D. SHANNON' *Kill with Kindness* xiii. 210 He was nursie's favorite—he could coax money out of her. **1973** R. ADAMS *Watership Down* (ed. 2) xvii. 94 You risk the life of one of the best rabbits we've got, just to play nursey while you go wandering about like a moon-struck field-mouse.

†**nursh,** *sb. Obs. rare*[−1]. [Reduced form of NOURISH *sb.* Cf. next and NORSH *sb.*] A nurse.

a **1420** BIBLE (Wycl.) *Hos.* xi. 3 And Y as a nursche of Effraym bare hem in myn armes.

†**nursh,** *v. Obs.* Also **nursch, nurch.** [Reduced form of *nurish* NOURISH *v.* Cf. NORSH *v.*] *trans.* To nurse, rear, nourish.

c **1380** WYCLIF *Wks.* (1880) 421 Stronge & idil men, þat ben nurschid in þe fendis nest to be an oost aȝenus crist. **1387** TREVISA *Higden* (Rolls) VII. 195 A chowȝe þat sche hadde nursched delicately, chatered more lowde þan it was wonte. **1422** tr. *Secreta Secret., Priv. Priv.* 245 Good Swete wyne..nurshyth the body.

So †'**nursher**; '**nurshing**; '**nurshment**.

1382 WYCLIF *Isa.* xxx. 33 His nurshemens [**1388** the nurschyngis therof] deep and spred, fyr and myche wode. *Ibid.* xlix. 23 And kingis shul be thi nursheres, and queenes thi nurses. **1422** tr. *Secreta Secret., Priv. Priv.* 248 Lytill mette that is not nurshynge.

'**nursing**, *vbl. sb.* [f. NURSE *v.* + -ING[1].]

1. a. The action of the verb, in various senses.

c **1532** DU WES *Introd. Fr.* in *Palsgr.* 1061 Nother more nor lesse may nat the soule..contynewe without her propre norsinge. **1579** LYLY *Euphues* (Arb.) 128 Neither can [she] conceive the like pleasure in noursing as the mother doth. **1611** SHAKS. *Cymb.* v. v. 322 First pay me for the Nursing of thy Sonnes. **1671** J. WEBSTER *Metallogr.* i. 7 Moses after his nursing was brought to Pharaoh's daughter. **1727** *Philip Quarll* (1816) 27 With careful nursing, I quite recovered him. **1770–4** A. HUNTER *Georg. Ess.* (1803) I. 510 Nursing causes a luxuriant growth in this hardy mountainous tree. **1867** BAKER *Nile Trib.* iii. 64 This most necessary ammunition required much nursing during a long exploration. **1883** *Athenæum* 27 Jan. 119/1 A money-lender's 'nursing' of a small seaside constituency.

b. The profession of a nurse (NURSE *sb.*[1] 3); the duties of a nurse.

1860 F. NIGHTINGALE *Notes on Nursing* 6, I use the word nursing for want of a better. *Ibid.* 72 She [*sc.* the writer].. honestly believes that the perfection of surgical nursing may be seen practised by the old-fashioned 'sister' of a London hospital. **1889** O'NEILL & BARNETT *Our Nurses* i. 2 It is commonly and justly coming to be held that nursing in all its branches is a career for educated women. **1937** E. C. PEARCE (*title*) A general textbook of nursing. **1955** *Oxf. Jun. Encycl.* XI. 333/2 Florence Nightingale was the real founder of the modern profession of nursing. **1970** K. K. GUINÉE *Professional Nurse* i. 6 The teacher of nursing carefully selects learning experiences in the clinical area.

2. *attrib.*, as ***nursing-bottle, -chair***, etc.; (sense 1 b) ***nursing-training***.

1827 HONE *Every-day Bk.* 16 Nov. II. 1546 'Aunt Shakerly'..placed Mr. Hood's baby cousin in the nursing-chair. **1837** *Penny Cycl.* VII. 26/2 Females for the most part with nursing pouches. **1839** *Saturday Mag.* Feb. 70, 3000 bees..will be enough to do the nursing-work of the hive. **1861** MRS. BEETON *Bk. Househ. Managem.* 1041 Many kinds of nursing-bottles have been lately invented, and some mounted with India-rubber nipples. **1897** P. WARUNG *Tales Old Regime* 148 Appointment to a nursing post would be an indulgence the woman does not merit. **1914** W. OWEN *Let.* 29 Oct. (1967) 291 The Nursing Training is capital for you. **1944** A. SETON *Dragonwyck* i. 4 She unbuttoned her bodice, snatched up the hungry baby, and settled on the low nursing chair. **1971** *Country Life* 22 July (Suppl.) 32b/2 (Advt.), A Wm. IV nursing chair of hammock shape upholstered in deeply buttoned Havana brown leather.

b. Designating garments designed to facilitate the breast-feeding of a baby, as ***nursing basque, bra, brassière, corset***.

1939 M. B. PICKEN *Lang. Fashion* 104/3 *Nursing basque*, basque with buttoned closings, one on each side of the front. **1969** *Sears, Roebuck Catal.* Spring/Summer 362/2 Finest nylon lace nursing bra... Easy-open clasp lets you hold baby as you open cups. **1950** HEATON & DAYNES *Feeding Mothers & Babies* II. 55 A nursing brassière..should have a waterproof lining. **1895** *Montgomery Ward Catal.* 309/2 Dr. Strong's Tricora Nursing Corset has proved a great comfort to mothers.

c. Special Combs., as **nursing home**, (*a*) a small, private institution where the sick are cared for; also *attrib.*; (*b*) a place where certain qualities are nurtured.

1896 *Allbutt's Syst. Med.* I. 681 He was removed to a nursing-home. **1938** L. P. SMITH *Unforgotten Years* vi. 149 Her barrister husband insisted..that I should be transferred without delay to what was, in his opinion, the only nursing home of reasonable thought and noble ambition—in fact, to Balliol College. **1951** [see CLINIC *sb.*[2] 2]. **1959** T. S. ELIOT *Elder Statesman* II. 45 We've studied to avoid Anything like a nursing-home atmosphere.

'**nursing**, *ppl. a.* [f. NURSE *v.* + -ING[2].]

1. That nurses, or tends like a nurse.

a. ***nursing-father***, a foster-father.

1535 COVERDALE *Isa.* xlix. 23 For kinges shalbe thy noursinge fathers, and Quenes shalbe thy noursinge mothers. **1611** BIBLE *Transl. Pref.* ¶1 Those noursing fathers and mothers that withdraw..liuelyhood and support. **1641** HINDE *J. Bruen* xxviii. 89 So that this Parish hath cause for ever, to acknowledge him a nursing father of Religion amongst them. **1703** KELSEY *Serm.* 246 The Empire turned Christian, and became a Nursing-Father to the Infancy of the Church. **1827** KEBLE *Chr. Y., St. Barnabas*, 'Twixt Prayer and watchful Love his heart dividing; A nursing-father day and night. **1889** JESSOPP *Coming of Friars* vi. 274 The friars were to some extent nursing fathers of the University.

b. ***nursing-mother***, (*a*) a foster-mother; (*b*) a woman who is breast-feeding her own baby.

1535, 1611 [see above]. **1728** POPE *Dunc.* I. 256 A Nursing-mother born to rock the throne! **1731** *Pol. Ballads* (1860) II. 230 Of Arian and of Orthodox Alike the nursing-mother. **1806** D. WORDSWORTH *Let.* 23 July in *Lett. William & Dorothy Wordsworth* (1969) II. 60 She thinks herself quite well, but *I* do not think she is as yet as strong as she ought to be for a nursing mother. **1855** WINTHROP *Sargent Braddock's Exped.* 19 Under its ancient lords, this nursing-mother of privateers would be powerful..in that part of the world. **1873** HAMERTON *Intell. Life* I. iii. 16 In the lands of the vine—the plant is looked upon as a nursing-mother. **1897** G. TUCKER *Mother, Baby & Nursery* 96 It becomes the first duty of the nursing mother to take care of herself. **1926** M. A. VON ARNIM *Introd. to Sally* ix. 154 Good job I ain't a nursin' mother..or the lady'd turn my milk sour. **1950** E. PANTIN *Mod. Mothercraft* i. 19 The health of a nursing mother affects the quality of her milk. **1970** J. DE BAIRACLI-LEVY *Natural Rearing of Children* iii. 28 It is an error to say that a nursing mother must take milk from animals to increase her own milk. **1974** A. HUXLEY *Plant & Planet* xxviii. 328 Nursing mothers in the United States have so much DDT in their milk that, to quote a scientific humorist, 'in strict terms of federal law, it is illegal for them to carry their busts..across one state line to another'.

c. In general use.

1671 MILTON *Samson* 924 My redoubl'd love and care With nursing diligence..May ever tend about thee to old age. **1708** J. PHILIPS *Cyder* II. 62 Ev'n afflictive Birch.. distills A limpid Current from her wounded Bark, Profuse of nursing Sap. **1785** BURKE *Nabob of Arcot's Debts* Wks. IV. 264 Does any one of you think that England..would, under such a nursing attendance, so rapidly..recover? **1812** *Examiner* 4 May 282/2 The figures of a nursing and a waiting girl. **1840** F. MARRYATT *Olla Podr.* III. 4 He would soon have him in command of a fine frigate, with a good nursing first lieutenant. **1866** SHUCKARD *Brit. Bees* 356 They are nurtured by nursing-workers just like them. **1887** BENTLEY *Man. Bot.* (ed. 5) 146 The first leaves which are developed are called cotyledons..or nursing leaves.

2. That is being nursed. *rare*[−1].

1860 J. BROWN *Rab & F., Let. to J. Cairns* (1906) 246 One woman..had a nursing baby in her arms.

Hence '**nursingly** *adv.*

1865 RUSKIN *Sesame* I. 69 Whether it ought not piously to save, and nursingly cherish, the lives of its murderers.

nursle ('nɜːs(ə)l), *v.* Also 6, 8 **noursle**. [var. of *nousle* NUZZLE *v.*[2], assimilated to NURSE *v.*

In modernized reprints of 16th century works *nursle* is sometimes substituted for *nusle, nousle*, etc.]

1. *trans.* = NUZZLE *v.*[2] 2.

1596 SPENSER *F.Q.* VI. iv. 35 Whether ye list him traine in chevalry, Or noursle up in lore of learn'd Philosophy. *a* **1656** BP. HALL *Rem. Wks.* (1660) 30 The poor seduced souls of forraign subjects, that have been invincibly noursled up in ignorance and superstition.

1860 MOTLEY *Netherl.* II. x. 77 The lewd sinner, nursled in revolutions, had detected the secret policy. **1899** GARDINER *Cromwell* 48 Nursled as we are under a regime of religious liberty.

2. To nurse, foster, cherish.

a **1652** BROME *Eng. Moor* III. iii, To have a Bastard of so many years Nursled i' th' Countrey. **1746** W. THOMPSON *Hymn to May* xxxi. 4 Whose bosom..Flows out to noursle innocence distrest. **1829** POE *Al Aaraaf*, The wave that sparkled there, And nursled the young mountain in its lair.

nursling, nurseling ('nɜːslɪŋ). Also 6–7 **nurce-**, 6, 8 **nours-**, and 6 **-lynge**. [f. NURSE *sb.* + -LING.]

1. The object of a nurse's care; an infant or child in relation to its nurse.

1607 EARL STIRLING *J. Cæsar* v. Chor., The nurceling of a Wolfe o're men did raigne. **1671** MILTON *Samson* 633, I was his nursling once and choice delight. **1693** DRYDEN *Persius* II. 75 A Body made of Brass the Crone demands For her lov'd Nursling. **1784** COWPER *Task* II. 771 Now, blame we most the nurslings or the nurse? **1814** SCOTT *Ld. of Isles* I. vii, She..knew her nursling's heart In the vain pomp took little part. **1858** CARLYLE *Fredk. Gt.* IV. i. I. (1865) 275 She saw now her little nurseling grown to be a brilliant man and King. **1899** *Allbutt's Syst. Med.* VIII. 872 Mothers and wet-nurses suffering from the disease..infecting their nurslings.

b. *transf.* of persons, in various applications.

1557 *More's Wks.* 1456, I haue been now almost this fourtie yeares, not a geaste, but a continuall nurslynge in maister Bonuice house. **1601** HOLLAND *Pliny* I. 159 Thou that standest so much vpon Fortunes fauors,..taking thy self not to be a foster-child and nurceling of hers, but a naturall son. **1664** H. MORE *Myst. Iniq., Apol.* 542 A limited indulgence..to their weak but sincere Nurselings [in religion]. **1733** TICKELL *Her Majesty's Rebuilding* 23 Thy Nurslings, ancient Dome! to virtue form'd. **1748** THOMSON *Cast. Indol.* II. xxi, Where Isis many a famous noursling breeds. **1817** COLERIDGE *Biog. Lit.* i. (Bohn) 6 These nurslings of improved pedagogy are taught to dispute and decide. **1845** S. AUSTIN *Ranke's Hist. Ref.* I. 515 Charles V was the child and nursling of that Burgundian court. **1872** A. DE VERE *Legends St. Patrick, St. Patrick & Armagh Cathedral*, Men of might, Fierce men, the battle's nurslings.

c. *transf.* of things.

1591 SPENSER *Virg. Gnat* 282 A litle noursling of the humid ayre, A Gnat. **1608** SYLVESTER *Du Bartas* II. *Colonies* 256 Each Hive supplying new-com Colonies (Heav'n's tender Nurcelings) to those fragrant mountains. **1656** CULPEPPER *Eng. Physic. Enlarged* 116 The last [*sc.* garden Gromel] is a Nursling in the Gardens of the curious. **1697** DRYDEN *Virg. Georg.* II. 500 Upward while they shoot in open Air, Indulge their Childhood, and the Nurselings spare. **1750** JOHNSON *Rambler* No. 74 ¶12 Peevishness..is much oftener..the child of vanity, and nursling of ignorance. **1835** I. TAYLOR *Spir. Despot.* IV. 174 The inevitable product of evil times—the child of oppression, and the nurseling of persecution. **1874** GEO. ELIOT *Coll. Breakf.-P.* 44 The daily nurslings of creative light.

2. *attrib.*, as ***nursling babe, boat, child, imp***.

1793 WORDSW. *Descrip. Sketches* 176 A nursling babe her only comforter. **1818** SHELLEY *Rosal. & Helen* 590, I am weak like a nursling child. **1860** HOLMES *Prof. Breakf.-t.* xi, Nursling imps addict themselves..to these little excrescences. **1884** *Daily News* 6 Sept. 5/7 Many sailors still argue for the old system of the nurseling boat carried by the great ship.

nursrow-tree. [f. dial. *nurs-, nuss-, noss-row* the harvest-shrew.] A tree vulgarly supposed to be efficacious in curing swollen cattle, through having one or more shrew-mice confined in it.

1686 PLOT *Staffordsh.* 222 To make any tree..a Nursrow-tree, they catch one or more of these mice,..and having bored a hole.., they put the mice in [etc.].

†**nurt**, *v. Obs.* Also 6 **nourt**, 7 **nort**. [Of obscure origin; given by Ray as *note*.] *intr.* To push or butt with the horns.

1555 W. WATREMAN *Fardle Facions* App. 341 The Neate that nourteth with the horne shall the owner kille. **1573** TUSSER *Husb.* (1878) 55 Curst cattel that nurteth, poore wennel soon hurteth. **1601** HOLLAND *Pliny* I. 206 One while [he sets his hornes] streight forward to offend, other whiles bending byas, as he hath reason to nort or push toward, or avoid his enemie.

†**nurth.** *Obs.* In 3 **nurð, nurhð.** [Of obscure origin.] Noise, din.

a **1225** *Leg. Kath.* 140 Ha iherde a swuch nurð towart te awariede maumetes temple. *c* **1230** *Hali Meid.* 31 His laðliche nurð & his untohe bere makeð þe to agrisen. *a* **1240** *Sawles Warde* in *O.E. Hom.* I. 247 We mahen ifelen hare nurhð [*v.r.* nurð] & hare untohe bere.

†'**nurturable**, *a. Obs. rare*[−1]. [f. NURTURE *v.* + -ABLE.] Capable of nourishing.

1579 W. WILKINSON *Confut. Fam. Love* Biiij, Blasphemyng the Catholique Church of Rome, and rentyng the consent and nurturable sustenance of the same.

nurtural ('nɜːtjʊərəl), *a.* [f. NURTUR(E *sb.* + -AL.] Of, belonging to, or due to nurture; usually designating characteristics, etc., which can be attributed to training, environment, or the like, and are not natural or inherited.

1889 *Jrnl. Anthrop. Inst.* XIX. 78 The problem of determining purely 'racial characteristics' will be considerably simplified if we can in this way determine what may be described in contradistinction as 'nurtural characteristics'. **1922** W. R. INGE *Outspoken Ess.* 2nd Ser. 257 Professor Pearson has tabulated a long list of natural characters, and another long list of nurtural characters. **1922** *Edin. Rev.* July 47 Religion is the strongest of nurtural influences.

nurturance ('nɜːtjʊərəns). *Psychol.* [f. NURTUR(E *v.* + -ANCE.] Emotional and physical nourishment and care.

1938 H. A. MURRAY *Explorations in Personality* ii. 83 *Nurturance*,..to nourish, aid or protect... To express sympathy. To 'mother' a child. **1957** E. R. HILGARD *Introd. Psychol.* (ed. 2) vi. 134/2 Scales were designed to get at nurturance (i.e., the mother's care in feeding). **1964** COFER & APPLEY *Motivation* xiv. 719 Someone else may help or sympathize with him, that is, he may receive nurturance from another. **1973** *Jrnl. Genetic Psychol.* June 185 A wide spectrum of 15 personality dimensions (e.g. need achievement, nurturance, dominance, aggression). **1974** *Nature* 9 Aug. 466/1 Warm and outgoing students (high on nurturance) also display a more favourable attitude.

nurturant ('nɜːtjʊərənt), *a. Psychol.* [f. as prec. + -ANT[1].] Caring or nourishing (emotionally or physically); exhibiting or pertaining to nurturance.

1938 H. A. MURRAY *Explorations in Personality* iii. 181 The succorance drive seeks a nurturant O and the nurturant drive seeks a succorant O. **1951** R. R. SEARS in Parsons & Shils *Toward General Theory of Action* 471 The nurturant mother. **1973** *Jrnl. Genetic Psychol.* Mar. 37 Psychopaths.. saw their fathers as having been less nurturant toward them and as having given them less praise. **1973** S. FISHER *Fem. Orgasm* iv. 108 Femininity is associated with being nurturant and 'nice'.

nurture ('nɜːtjʊə(r)), *sb.* Forms: 4–6 **nortour(e, -tur(e**, 5–6 **norter**; 5–7 **nourtoure**, 6–7 **-ture**; 4– **nurture** (5 *Sc.* **nwr-**), 5–6 **-tur, -tour(e.** [a. OF. *nourture, nurture*, var. of *noure-, nourriture*: see NOURITURE.]

1. Breeding, upbringing, training, education (received or possessed by one). Now *rare*.

c **1330** R. BRUNNE *Chron. Wace* (Rolls) 4295 Vs wondreþ at ȝowre nurture of pris. ? *a* **1366** CHAUCER *Rom. Rose* 179 Ful foule and cherlysshe semed she,..And litel coude of norture. **1422** tr. *Secreta Secret., Priv. Priv.* 122 He was of hey nourtoure, wel prowed and I-lernyd of al Sciencis. **1470–85** MALORY *Arthur* VIII. iii. 276 He sente yonge Trystram..in to Fraunce to lerne the langage and nurture and dedes of armes. *a* **1533** LD. BERNERS *Gold. Bk. M. Aurel.* (1546) C iij b, His father in his youthe had taught him good nurture. **1573** TUSSER *Husb.* (1878) 26 The greatest preferment that childe we can giue, is learning and nurture, to traine him to liue. **1607** *Statute* in *Hist. Wakefield School* (1892) 60 The general course of Religion and good nurture in the scollers of this schole. **1644** MILTON *Educ.* 3 To drive our dullest and laziest youth..from the infinite desire of such a happy nurture.

1813 SCOTT *Rokeby* VI. xv, He bred him in their nurture wild. **1867** PARKMAN *Jesuits in N. Amer.* ix. (1875) 99 Both were of noble birth and gentle nurture.

†**b.** Moral training or discipline. *Obs.*

1526 TINDALE *Eph.* vi. 4 Brynge them uppe with the norter and informacion off the Lorde. **1535** COVERDALE *Ecclus.* xviii. Contents, God suffreth longe, rebuketh and teacheth all soch as wil receaue nurtoure. **1611** BIBLE *Wisd.* iii. 11 Who so despiseth wisedome, and nurture, he is miserable. **1637** RUTHERFORD *Lett.* (1862) I. xcviii. 251 Yet I get my meat from Christ with nurture.

2. That which nourishes; nourishment, food.

1398 TREVISA *Barth. De P.R.* XIX. xxxii. (Bodl. MS.), Swetnes is þe propre sauour & norture ȝif it is stedefaste.. in þe membres. *c* **1407** LYDG. *Reson & Sens.* 1630 Iuno.. bisyly dide hir cure To yive him mylke to hys norture. **1596** SPENSER *Hymn Hon. Love* 39 Your lovers feeble eyes you feed, But sterve their harts that needeth nourture most. **1671** MILTON *Samson* 362 For this did the Angel twice descend? for this Ordain'd thy nurture holy, as of a Plant? **1818** BYRON *Ch. Har.* IV. cxlix, Where..from the heart we took Our first and sweetest nurture. **1880** BLACKMORE *Mary Anerley* xl, He fed him well, and nourished himself, and took nurture for the road.

Comb. **1777** POTTER *Æschylus* 319 These crisped locks, Once sacred to the nurture-giving stream Of Inachus.

3. The bringing-up or rearing *of* some one; tutelage; fostering care.

1676 W. ALLEN *Addr. Nonconf.* 44 Whom God put under the nurture of believing Parents, or Tutors. 1727 POPE, etc. *Art of Sinking* xvi, That to prevent unmarried Actresses making away with their Infants, a competent Provision be allowed for the Nurture of them. c1775 BURKE *Addr. Colonists N. Amer.* Wks. IX. 213 Under the paternal care and nurture of a protecting Parliament. 1784 COWPER *Task* II. 779 Things so sacred as a nation's trust, The nurture of her youth, her dearest pledge. 1818 CRUISE *Digest* (ed. 2) III. 372 If guardian by nurture make a lease by indenture to one, being under the title of the infant. 1875 MANNING *Mission H. Ghost* ix. 230 Even in the lower animals there is a certain love, and care, a nurture in the parent towards its offspring.

nurture (ˈnɜːtjʊə(r)), *v.* Also 5, 7 norture, 5–6 nurtur (6 -ter, -tor, -tour), 6–7 nourture (6 -ter, -toure). [f. prec.]

1. *trans.* To feed or nourish; to support and bring up to maturity; to rear. Also *fig.* (cf. 2).

c1430 LYDG. *Min. Poems* (Percy Soc.) 41 But also pleyne was his bedde at the morwe, As at even so was he nortured wele. c1440 *Alph. Tales* 437 He knew it & had compassion þeroff, & garte name it & nurtur it. c1450 LOVELICH *Grail* xxxv. 216 His Eldest sone .. was put into thike partye For to Norture. 1575 TURBERV. *Trag. Tales* (1837) 161 By his Grandsyre nourisht up And nurtred from a boye. 1715 BENTLEY *Serm.* (J.), They suppose mother earth to be a great animal, and to have nurtured up her young offspring with a conscious tenderness. 1815 SHELLEY *Alastor* 68 By solemn vision, and bright silver dream, His infancy was nurtured. 1828 LYTTON *Disowned* iii, The woman who nurtured me as my mother was rather capricious than kind. 1872 O. W. HOLMES *Poet Breakf.-t.* viii, He was not nurtured by the best of mothers.

refl. c1511 *1st Eng. Bk. Amer.* Introd. (Arb.) 32/2 All the other byrdes .. gyue them mete & drinke to the tyme that the[y] can flee & nurter them selfe. 1820 SHELLEY *Œd. Tyr.* I. 356 That very Rat, who, like the Pontic tyrant, Nurtures himself on poison.

b. *transf.* To foster, cherish.

1828 MACAULAY *Ess., Hallam* (1851) I. 57 Sprung from brutal passion, nurtured by selfish policy, the Reformation in England [etc.]. 1847 H. MILLER *Test. Rocks* iii. (1857) 115 It has been said that they nurture infidel propensities. 1872 BLACK *Adv. Phaeton* xxi. 298 The Lieutenant began to nurture a secret affection for Scotland.

2. To bring up, train, educate.

1526 TINDALE *Titus* ii. 4 That they nurter the yonge wemen for to love their husbandes. 1579 NORTHBROOKE *Dicing* (1843) 11 A child .. In tender yeares brought vp In vertues schoole, and nurtred wel. 1639 ROUSE *Heav. Univ.* viii. (1702) 106 He will delight to teach and nurture thee. 1652 BP. HALL *Eloquence* p. xiv, We ought to nurture our souls to greatnesse. 1774 BURKE *Sp. Amer. Tax.* Wks. 1842 I. 164 Persons who are nurtured in office do admirably well as long as things go on in their common order. 1784 COWPER *Task* II. 532 My man of morals, nurtur'd in the shades Of Academus—is this false or true? 1817 SHELLEY *Rev. Islam* I. xxxvii, Before A woman's heart beat in my virgin breast, It had been nurtured in divinest lore. 1863 GEO. ELIOT *Romola* I. xi, He had been nurtured in contempt for the tales of priests.

†**b.** To discipline, chasten. *Obs.*

1528 TINDALE *Doctr. Treat.* (Parker Soc.) 136 God laid him where he could neither see sun nor moon .., to nurture him, .. and to teach him God's ways. 1535 COVERDALE *1 Kings* xii. 11. a1564 BECON *Commpl. H. Script.* Wks. II. III. 93 They verely for a fewe daies nurtred vs after their own pleasure; But he nurtreth vs for our profit. 1609 BIBLE (Douay) *Prov.* xiii. 24 He that spareth the rod, hateth his childe; but he that loveth him doth instantly nurture him. 1636 RUTHERFORD *Lett.* (1862) I. lxx. 182 You have had your own large share of troubles ..; but it saith your Father counteth you not a bastard; full-begotten bairns are nurtured.

†**c.** To wean (one) *from* something. *Obs. rare*⁻¹.

1621 SANDERSON *Serm.* I. 172 As a fatherly correction and chastisement, to nurture us from some past sin.

ˈnurtured, *ppl. a.* [f. prec. + -ED¹.] Trained, educated. Chiefly in ***evil-, ill-, well-nurtured.***

a1400–50 *Alexander* 3177 A ix score of new geere of nurtrid maydens. c1475 *Babees Bk.* 119 Als to the worlde better [boon] in noo degre Mihte yee desire thanne nurtred forto be. 1599 *George-a-Greene* Greene's Wks. (Grosart) 1229 Nay, good my Liege, ill nurtur'd we were, then. 1611 BIBLE *Ecclus.* xxii. 3 An euill nurtured sonne is the dishonour of his father. *Ibid.* xxxi. 19 A very litle is sufficient for a man well nurtured. 1612 DEKKER *If it be not Good* Wks. 1873 II. 281 How dar'st thou mock vs, thou ill nurtur'd slaue? 1781 COWPER *Table-T.* 634 A well-nurtur'd train Of abler votaries. 1854 G. GREENWOOD *Haps & Mishaps* 60 Revealing the .. hell of ferocity in their blood-nurtured natures. 1887 *Murray's Mag.* I. 558 His India-nurtured blood felt comforted by the warmth.

ˈnurtureless. *rare*⁻¹. [f. NURTURE *sb.* + -LESS.] Without nurture or nourishment.

1835 TALFOURD *Ion* II. i, Who perish not alone, but in their fall Break the far-spreading tendrils that they feed, And leave them nurtureless.

ˈnurturer. [f. NURTURE *v.* + -ER¹.] One who nurtures or trains.

1796 *Hist. Ned Evans* II. 253 Mrs. Waldron could not behold the nurturers of her grandson without the tenderest emotions. 1826 *Blackw. Mag.* XX. 491 These are under the conduct of the great Nurturer. 1875 JOWETT *Plato* (ed. 2) III. 62 Subjects who in other States are termed slaves, are by us termed nurturers and paymasters.

ˈnurtureship. [-SHIP.] Upbringing.

a1845 HOOD *The Desert-Born* 95 Like an infant changed at nurse By fairies, you have undergone a nurtureship perverse.

ˈnurturing, *vbl. sb.* [f. NURTURE *v.* + -ING¹.] The action of the verb, in various senses.

1535 COVERDALE *Job* xxxvi. 10 He with punyshinge and nurturinge off them .., warneth them to leaue of from their wickednesse. 1578 *Chr. Prayers, Priv. Pr.* (Parker Soc.) 534 We acknowledge thy fatherly nurturing of us. 1629 WADSWORTH *Pilgr.* vii. 74 The Iesuites haue a Colledge .. for the nurturing of their young Iesuites. 1843 LYTTON *Last Bar.* IV. v, Well-a-day, my lord, my nurturing was somewhat neglected in the province.

ˈnurturing, *ppl. a.* [-ING².] That nurtures.

1875 JOWETT *Plato* (ed. 2) III. 664 Blood, being the nurturing principle of the flesh. 1883 SWINBURNE *Cent. Roundels* 47 Each mother's nurturing breast Feeds a flower of bliss.

†**nurvil.** *Obs. rare*⁻⁰. [var. of NYRVYL, agreeing in vowel with Norw. dial. *nurv* masc., *nurva* fem.; perhaps represented by mod. dial. *knurl.*] A dwarfish person.

1499 *Promp. Parv.* (Pynson), Nuruyll, dwerfe.

nurye, variant of NURRY *Obs.*

nurysch, obs. f. NOURISH *v.*

nusance, -anze, -auns, obs. ff. NUISANCE.

nuse, obs. f. NURSE *sb.*²

nushed, *pa. pple. dial.* (See quot.)

1674–91 RAY *S. & E.C. Words, Nush'd*, starved, in the bringing up.

nusle, var. of NUZZLE *v.*²

Nusranee, Nusrani: see NASRANI.

nusse, obs. form of NURSE *sb.*²

nussel, var. of NUZZLE *v.*²

Nusselt (ˈnʊsəlt). [the name of E. K. Wilhelm *Nusselt* (1882–1957), German engineer.] ***Nusselt number***, a dimensionless parameter used in calculations of the heat transfer between a moving fluid and a solid, equivalent to hD/k, where h is the rate of heat loss per unit area per degree difference in temperature between the body and its surroundings, D is a characteristic length of the body, and k is the thermal conductivity of the fluid.

1933 W. H. MCADAMS *Heat Transmission* iv. 96 hD/k... Nusselt number. 1958 CONDON & ODISHAW *Handbk. Physics* III. ii. 35/1 For low speeds the Nusselt number is a function of the Reynolds number, the Prandtl (or Péclet) number, and the Grashof number... In the case of forced convection, for which gravitational effects are insignificant, the Nusselt number is a function only of the Reynolds number and of the Prandtl number. In natural (free) convection the Nusselt number is a function only of the Grashof number and of the Prandtl number. 1974 J. R. WELTY *Engin. Heat Transfer* v. 265 Heat Transfer for Cylinders in Crossflow... At higher Reynolds numbers .. the Nusselt number experiences two sudden increases, one at the separation point and one where the boundary layer undergoes a transition from laminar to turbulent flow.

ˈnussierite. *Min.* [See first quot.] A variety of pyromorphite.

1836–41 BRANDE *Chem.* (ed. 5) 843 Baruel has described a double phosphate of lead and lime from the mine of Nussiere, near Beaujeu, in the department of Rhone: he has called it Nussierite. 1846 *Penny Cycl.* Suppl. II. 308/2 *Nussierite*, Occurs in crystals, which are almost lenticular... Colour yellow, greyish or greenish.

nussle, var. of NUZZLE *v.*²

nustaleek, var. NASTALIK.

nuste, var. of NIST *v. Obs.*

nustle, obs. f. NUZZLE *v.*¹

nusy: see NUISE *v.*

nut (nʌt), *sb.*¹ Forms: α. 1 hnutu (*pl.* hnyte, hnite, nyte), 2–4, 6 nute (3 nouthe). β. 3–5 note (4 nhote), 5 noote. γ. 4–6 nott(e, 5–6 not. δ. 4–6 nutte, 5–8 nutt, 6– nut (8–9 *Sc.* nit). [Common Teut.: OE. *hnutu* fem. = MDu. *note, nuete* (Du. *noot, neut*), and *not*, MLG. *note, not*, ON. *hnot* (Norw. *not*, Sw. *nöt*, Da. *nöd*), OHG. *(h)nuȥ* (G. *nuss*). The stem **hnut-*:—pre-Teut. **knud-*, is related to that of OIr. *cnū*, Gael. *cnù, cnò*, Welsh *cneuen* (pl. *cnau*) nut.]

I. 1. a. A fruit which consists of a hard or leathery (indehiscent) shell enclosing an edible kernel; the kernel itself.

For the many specific names of nuts, and of other fruits or vegetable products to which the name is loosely applied (as *earth-nut, pea-nut*), see the distinguishing word.

α. c875 *Erfurt Gloss.* 15 Abilina, hnutu. c975 *Rushw. Gosp.* Matt. vii. 16 Ah he somniȝaþ .. of gorstum ficos *vel* nyte? c1000 *Sax. Leechd.* III. 134 Pinhnutena cyrnles, & amigdalas, & oþera hnutena cyrnlu. c1175 *Lamb. Hom.* 79 Me brekeð þe nute for to habbene þene curnel. c1265 *Voc. Plants* in Wr.-Wülcker 557 *Auellane, petite noiz*, litel nute. a1300 *Cursor M.* 18833 His hare [was] like to þe nute brun, Quen it for ripnes fals dun. c1590 MONTGOMERIE *Sonn.* xlvi. 8 Lat sie vho first my wedfie wins; For I will wed ane apple and a nute [*rime* shute].

β. c1290 *Beket* 1191 in *S. Eng. Leg.* I. 140 Deinteþes to him brouȝte, Applene, & peoren, and notes also. 13.. *K. Alis.* 5193 It wil al fruyt ete, Applen, noten, reisyns, and whete. 1387 TREVISA *Higden* (Rolls) VII. 129 Þe duke bouȝte notes wiþ þe whiche he seþe his mete and vitailles. c1440 *Gesta Rom.* lvi. 373 Þe ape wil gladly Ete the kyrnell of the note, for it is swete. 1486 *Bk. St. Albans* b iij b, Wete a morcell of flesh therin, the mowntenaunce of a Note.

γ. c1380 WYCLIF *Wks.* (1880) 12 A fewe peris, appelis or nottis. 1398 TREVISA *Barth. De P.R.* XVII. cviii. (Bodl. MS.), The nutte tre hatte Nux & so þe notte also. c1425 *Voc.* in Wr.-Wülcker 647 *Hec nux*, .. notte. 1486 *Bk. St. Albans* c v, Pellettis of the grettenes of a Not. *Ibid.* f vij, A Clustre of Nottis. c1532 DU WES *Introd. Fr.* in *Palsgr.* 912 Small nottes, *noisettes*.

δ. c1400 MAUNDEV. (Roxb.) xxix. 131 Treesse berand garioflez and nute mugez and grete nuttez of Inde. c1450 *Mirour Saluacioun* (Roxb.) 59 Thai callid figes, Razines and Nuttes and apples collibies. 1526 *Pilgr. Perf.* (W. de W. 1531) 5 b, As the shale of the nut to be broken that he may fede of the cornell. 1594 CAREW *Huarte's Exam. Wits* xiv. (1596) 258 He hath his haire coloured like a nut full ripe. 1642 FULLER *Holy & Prof. St.* III. xvii. 196 Worldly riches, like nuts, teare many clothes in getting them. 1671 SALMON *Syn. Med.* III. xxii. 413 *Haslenut tree*, the nut is pectoral. 1732 ARBUTHNOT *Rules of Diet* in *Aliments*, etc. I. 257 Such as abound with a soft Oil, .. as most sorts of Nuts. 1784 COWPER *Task* I. 315 The beech of oily nuts Prolific. 1828 SCOTT *F.M. Perth* xiii, My Lord of Rothsay, who .. was cracking nuts with a strolling musician. 1864 TENNYSON *En. Ard.* 556 Soft fruitage, mighty nuts, and nourishing roots.

b. As a symbol of something of trifling value.

c1300 *Havelok* 419 He ne yaf a note of his oþes. *Ibid.* 1332 Nouth þe worth of one nouthe [= nute]. 1340 *Ayenb.* 143 Ne prosperite ne aduersete of þe wordle hi ne prazeþ ane nhote.

†**c.** One of the seeds in a pine-cone. *Obs.*

c1000 *Sax. Leechd.* I. 250 Ðenim .. cyrnlu of pintrywenum hnutum. 1611 COTGR., *Noix de pin*, .. the nut, or fruit of the Pine-apple. 1727 BRADLEY *Fam. Dict.* s.v. *Fir tree*, The Kernels and Nuts, which may be got out of their Cones and Clogs.

†**d.** The stone of a peach or date. *Obs. rare.*

1600 PORY tr. *Leo's Africa* III. 207 Their peaches they cut into fower quarters, and casting away the nuts or stones, they drie them in the sunne. *Ibid.* VI. 269 They feede their goates with the nuts or stones of their dates beaten to powder, whereby they grow exceeding fat.

†**e.** The fruit of the cocoa-tree. *Obs.*

1707 FUNNELL *Voy.* v. 89 The Nut or Kernel .. ripens in a great Husk, wherein are sometimes 30, nay 40 cocoas. 1711 *Spect.* Advt. (1891) 903 Chocolate all Nut 2*s.* 6*d.* and 3*s.* with sugar 1*s.* 8*d.*

f. Pl. *vulg.* The testicles. Also in various vulgar phrases.

1915 *Dialect Notes* IV. 186 *Nut*, in *pl.* testicles. 1922 JOYCE *Ulysses* 467 How's the nuts? .. Off side. Curiously they are on the right. Heavier I suppose. 1955 W. GADDIS *Recognitions* II. vii. 630 The lady lost her nuts, Anselm said to no one. He mumbled,—That's the world we live in, the ladies wear the nuts. 1969 B. MALCOLM in A. Chapman *New Black Voices* (1972) 385 Easy way out To hate the white man .. for Kicking my papa in the nuts. 1970 C. MAJOR *Dict. Afro-Amer. Slang* 58 *Get (one's) nuts off*, sexual release, implies ejaculation more than orgasm. 1970 E. BULLINS *Theme is Blackness* (1973) 167 Screwin' my best white friend's black wife makes me feel even better. Makes me get my nuts off. 1973 R. BUSBY *Pattern of Violence* v. 79 Russell got a boot in the nuts. 1974 J. WAINWRIGHT *Evidence I shall Give* xxi. 102 He was working his nuts off.

†**2.** A cup formed from the shell of a coconut mounted in metal; also, one made of other materials to resemble this. *Obs.* (See also 4 c.)

1337 in Riley *Mem. Lond.* (1868) 200 One cup called 'note', with a foot and cover of silver, value 30*s.* 1427 *Will of Esturmy* (Somerset Ho.), Vnum note de dogean cum coopertario. 1479 *Paston Lett.* III. 272 A blak notte standing of silver and gilt, with a kover to the same. 1520 SIR R. ELYOT *Will* in Elyot *Gov.* (1883) App. A, ii playn bolles of silver .., ii nuttes garnysshed with silver and gilt. c1580 in *Archæol.* (1840) XXVIII. 132 A drynkinge nutte of sylver, worth about twentie pounds. [1828 SCOTT *F.M. Perth* xvi, Tender him the nut once more.]

3. In various proverbial and allusive contexts. (For *deaf nut* see DEAF *a.* 6 b.) Phr. ***for nuts,*** in neg. contexts: at all.

1562 J. HEYWOOD *Prov. & Epigr.* (1867) 20 She is lost with an apple, and woon with a nut. 1647 COWLEY *Mistr.*, *The Tree* ii, With Art as strange, as Homer in the Nut, Love in my Heart has Volumes put. 1660 HOWELL *Eng. Prov.* 15 He may be gott by an Apple, and lost by a Nutt. 1722 WOLLASTON *Relig. Nat.* viii. 161 They, who are not, or but lately, past their nuts, cannot be supposed to have any extent of knowledge. 1843 LONGF. *Sp. Stud.* I. iv, Very little meat and a great deal of tablecloth... And more noise than nuts. 1895 W. PETT RIDGE *Minor Dialogues* 82 An' the eldest gal *she* thinks she can play, and, if you'll believe me, she carn't play for nuts. 1899 *Times* 25 Oct. 5/3 They can't shoot for nuts; go ahead. 1934 A. THIRKELL *Wild Strawberries* xi. 237 That Miss Stevenson can't play for nuts.

4. In allusions to the difficulty of cracking hard-shelled nuts: **a.** A question difficult to answer, or a problem hard to solve.

1545 ELYOT *Def. Gd. Wom.* B iv b, Nowe knacke me that nut, maister Candidus. 1589 *Hay any Work* (1844) 33 Like you any of these Nuts, John Canterbury? 1655 FULLER *Hist. Cambr.* (1840) 95 Why was this Hall first visited? .. But the nut is not worth the cracking. 1705 HICKERINGILL *Priest-cr.* IV. (1721) 236 Here's Nuts enough to employ their Teeth, .. but .. before they crack them they will break their Brains. 1801 HUNTINGTON *God the Guard. of Poor* Ded. p. iii, Those providences which appear rather out of the common line are hard nuts in the mouth of a weak believer. 1858–61 J. BROWN *Horæ Subs.* (1863) 17 He especially liked his mental nuts. 1886 STEVENSON *Dr. Jekyll* i, It was a nut to crack for many, what these two could see in each other.

b. A matter or undertaking difficult to accomplish; a person hard to deal with or conciliate.

1662–7 COWLEY *Of Plants* Wks. (Grosart) II. 276/1 'Tis time that you these childish Sports forsake, Hymen for you has other Nuts to crack. **1745** FRANKLIN *Lett.* Wks. 1887 II. 16 Fortified towns are hard nuts to crack; and your teeth have not been accustomed to it. **1866** *Illustr. Lond. N.* 9 June 549 Spain has.. got some of her teeth broken in the attempt to crack a nut that was too hard for them. **1888** J. PAYN *Myst. Mirbridge* xxi, You will find Robert Morris a hard nut to crack.

c. (See quots. and sense 2.)

1828 SCOTT *F.M. Perth* xvi, A huge calabash full of sack was offered to the lips of the supplicant, while this prince of revellers exhorted him,—'Crack me this nut, and do it handsomely'. **1889** *N. & Q.* 7th Ser. VIII. 437 When a fresh guest arrived he was met by the laird, who made him 'crack a nut', that is, drink a silver-mounted cocoanut-shell full of claret.

5. a. ***nuts to*** (a person): A source of pleasure or delight to one. Now *slang*.

1617 FLETCHER *Mad Lover* v. iv, But they are needful mischiefs, And such are Nuts to me. **1672** MARVELL *Reh. Transp.* I. 56 This story would have been Nuts to Mother Midnight. **1705** in W. S. Perry *Hist. Coll. Amer. Col. Ch.* I. 147 Pray remember that our divisions will be nuts to the adversaries of the Church. **1768–74** TUCKER *Lt. Nat.* (1834) II. 484 Mischief is said to be nuts to some folks. **1805** *Naval Chron.* XIII. 11 This was Nuts to many of them whose purses could afford it. **1840** R. H. DANA *Bef. Mast* xxv, This was nuts to us, for we liked to have a Spaniard wet with salt water. **1891** F. R. STOCKTON *House Martha* 208 To see me here would be simply nuts to her.

b. (See NUT *v.* 2, quot. 1812.)

6. ***to be*** (***dead***) ***nuts on*** or ***upon***, to set great store upon, to be devoted to, fond of, or delighted with (a person or thing). *slang*. Also const. *about*.

1785 GROSE *Dict. Vulgar T.* s.v. *Well-hung*, The blowen was nutts upon the Kiddey because he is well-hung. **1812** J. H. VAUX *Flash Dict.* s.v., A man who is much gratified with any bargain he has made,.. will express his self-satisfaction .. by declaring that he is, or was, quite nuts upon himself. **1862** *Punch* 29 Mar. 127/1 Johnny and Georgy were nuts on their pet.., and tabled their money freely. **1873** W. BLACK *Pr. Thule* xi. 168 My aunt is awful nuts on Marcus Aurelius. **1894** ASTLEY *50 Yrs. Life* I. 152 He wasn't dead nuts on meeting with them. **1920** S. LEWIS *Main Street* xxiii. 280 Carrie's nuts about this Russian revolution. **1945** E. WAUGH *Brideshead Revisited* I. vii. 177, I was still nuts about Rex. **1975** *New Yorker* 21 Apr. 39/1 You're nuts about me, right?

7. a. *slang*. The head (of a person).

1846 *Swell's Night Guide* 76 Why, she's getting groggy on her pins, and if you don't pipe rumbo, she'll go prat over nut (head over heels). **1852** J. LABERN *Pop. Comic Song Bk.* 76 But vun chap flung a bunch of turnips, which nearly split Dick's nut in two. **1858** MAYHEW *Paved w. Gold* II. xii. 189 The first round was soon terminated, for Jack got a 'cracker on his nut'. **1894** CLARK RUSSELL *Good Ship Mohock* II. 19 Let that chap there be ready with his cutlass to job me over the nut on my showing myself.

b. ***off one's nut***, out of one's mind, insane. (See also quot. 1860.)

1860 *Slang Dict.* (ed. 2) 182 To be 'off one's nut', to be in liquor. **1873** MISS BRADDON *Str. & Pilgr.* II. iii. 178 There are the men who go off their nuts by the time they're worth a million or so. **1893** *Fam. Herald* 68/2 But is the master off his nut that he has her down here to stay?

c. *pl.* (as *adj.*): insane, crazy, 'off one's head'.

1846 *Swell's Night Guide* 75 Vhy, Owen.. you knows it's no use of me being nuts, ven the donna's only nut crackers. **1914** JACKSON & HELLYER *Vocab. Criminal Slang* 62 Nuts,.. As an adjective and adverb it signifies daft, mentally deranged. **1928** C. SANDBURG in *Amer. Mercury* Oct. 154 There was a screw loose somewhere in him, he had a kink and he was a Crank, he was nuts and belonged in a booby hatch. **1953** [see GEE *int.*[2]]. **1969** I. & P. OPIE *Children's Games* ii. 76 The person was.. looney, nuts, a nit.

d. Phr. ***to do one's*** (or ***the***) ***nut***, to become angry, lose one's head; to be worked up about something; to be crazy.

1919 W. H. DOWNING *Digger Dialects* 20 *Do the nut*, lose one's head. **1936** J. CURTIS *Gilt Kid* 231 The jane'd be bound to think he had done his nut. **1956** [see CHOKED *ppl. a.* 2]. **1957** J. OSBORNE *Entertainer* xiii. 86 I'm doing me nut up here. **1958** F. NORMAN *Bang to Rights* III. 92 The twirl would do his nut and give up. **1959** P. BULL *I know Face* xi. 199, I would be doing my 'nut' and my probable swansong for Auntie BBC. **1960** *News Chron.* 16 Feb. 6/5 Been doing his nut about little Barbara for months, he had. **1961** J. STROUD *Touch & Go* xv. 155 He's nearly done his nut over this daughter of his. **1972** J. BROWN *Chancer* v. 68, I thought what Grace would say, that she'd do her nut maybe. But she didn't blink an eyelid.

e. *Pl.* Used as a derisive retort: nonsense, rubbish; I defy you. Freq. const. *to*.

1931 M. E. GILMAN *Sob Sister* 267 Nuts! You'll forget Nick the minute you smell your freedom. **1934** J. O'HARA *Appointment in Samarra* iv. 86 'Nuts to you, sister,' he said. **1936** *New Yorker* 18 Jan. 20 With a hay-nonny-nonny and a nuts to you. **1938** J. CURTIS *They drive by Night* ix. 109 A feather shopping bag lay on a table. He stepped across towards it. As he stepped his golf-clubs rattled. Aw, nuts to that dog barking. **1946** WODEHOUSE *Joy in Morning* II. xii. 91 'If you think I've got the force of character to come back with a *nolle prosequi*—' 'With a what?' 'One of Jeeves' gags. It means roughly "Nuts to you!"' **1974** D. FRANCIS *Knock Down* ii. 25 'I'll give you a hundred.' 'Nuts.' 'A hundred and fifty.'

f. ***the nuts***, an excellent person or thing. *U.S. slang*.

1932 *Amer. Speech* VII. 334 *The nuts*, denotes superlative quality. **1949** W. STEVENS *Let.* 9 Sept. (1967) 647 At the Museum of Modern Art they cultivate the idea that everything is the nuts. **1955** W. GADDIS *Recognitions* II. vii. 634 Get a little cross with mirrors in it, that would be the nuts if you want to suffer your way.

8. a. Applied disparagingly to persons.

1887 FENN *Master of Ceremonies* vii, He is a close old nut. **1896** *Harper's Mag.* XCIII. 150/2 'Who's the old nut walking with your father-in-law?' 'He's my clerk'.

b. A certain type of Australian (see quots.).

1882 A. J. BOYD *Old Colonials* 60 What is a Nut?.. Imagine a long, lank, lantern-jawed, whiskerless, colonial youth. *Ibid.* 65 He is a bully, a low, coarse, blasphemous blackguard—what is termed a regular colonial Nut.

c. A madman; a crank. *slang* (orig. *U.S.*).

1903 R. L. MCCARDELL *Conversat. of Chorus Girl* 15 'Circus Joe'.. worked the nuts on the edge of the crowd. **1914** JACKSON & HELLYER *Vocab. Criminal Slang* 62 *Nut*, commonly current in all circles when the meaning is 'loco'. **1919** [see BUGHOUSE *sb.* 1]. **1931** D. RUNYON *Guys & Dolls* (1932) 213, I am commencing to think this Count Saro is some kind of a nut, and is only speaking through his hat. **1936** K. MACKENZIE *Living Rough* xv. 216 We're sure a pair of nuts riding the outside over the hump this time of the year. **1960** H. PINTER *Room* 118 You're not only a nut, you're a blind nut and you can get out the way you came. **1966** T. PYNCHON *Crying of Lot 49* v. 107 Why worry, she worried; Nefastis is a nut, forget it, a sincere nut. **1973** *Nation Rev.* (Melbourne) 31 Aug. 1444/1 The Worker Student Alliance, a bunch of nuts in Melbourne.

9. *slang*. A fashionable or showy young man of affected elegance; a 'young blood', fop, or masher. Cf. NUTTY *a.* 4 and KNUT.

1904 in *N. & Q.* (1913) 26 July 78/1 I'm one of the nuts, one of the nibs. **1913** *Punch* 12 Feb. 115/1 Spring socks will be black and Spring ties a quiet blue. A strike of nuts is expected at any moment. **1915** KIPLING in *Nash's & Pall Mall Mag.* Oct. 131/2 Winchmore, the youngest, was more on the lines of a conventional nut. **1920** W. J. LOCKE *House of Baltazar* xvii. 205 I've a jolly good mind to set him up regardless, like a pre-war nut—with solid silver boot-trees and the rest to correspond. **1920** R. MACAULAY *Potterism* I. iv. 44 He always looked the same, calm, unruffled, tidy, the exquisite nut. **1923** *Other Lands* Oct. 3/3 The last named continue to be marks of the 'nut'.

II. 10. A small metal projection upon a spindle (of a clock, etc.) furnished with teeth, and engaging in a cog-wheel; a small spur-wheel.

1426–7 in *Archæologia* (1857) XXXVII. 25 Thomas Clock-maker received 7s. for amending of the note and spindle. **1567** in *Antiquary* (1888) Apr. 169 For makyng a nutte for the dyall, iij*d*. **1648** WILKINS *Math. Magic* I. xx. (1707) 82 Let us imagine every Wheel in this following Figure to have a hundred Teeth in it, and every Nut ten. **1677** MOXON *Mech. Exerc.* iii. 45 Before a revolution of the Wheel be perform'd, it would go off from the length of the Teeth of the Nut. **1775** ASH, *Nut*, a small protuberance with indentures answering to the teeth of a wheel. **1825** J. NICHOLSON *Operat. Mechanic* 130 A spur nut *a*, and a bevelled nut *b*;.. the nut *a* works into the spur-wheel.

†11. A projection from the lock of a crossbow, serving to detain the string until released by the trigger. *Obs.*

1528 PAYNELL *Salerne's Regim.* Q ij b, The iij nutte, that is, the nutte of the crosse bowe, is dethe, for the crosse bowe sleethe men. **1578** *Lanc. Wills* (Chetham Soc.) II. 59 My crossebowe wth out the nutte. **1611** COTGR., *La noix d'vne arbaleste*, the nut of a crossebow. **1674** tr. *Scheffer's Lapland* 98 They.. draw the string up to the nut made of bone in the handle, with an iron hook they wear at their girdle.

12. a. A small block of wood, iron, etc., pierced, and wormed with a female screw; used to make a bolt fast, or to allow of its adjustment. Also *fig*.

Cf. *nottes.. et escrûues* in a Lille document of 1597 cited by Godefroi, s.v. *Nottet*.

1611 COTGR., *Couplot de bois*, a woodden sole, or Nut for a Scrue; the foot of a Scrue. **1677** MOXON *Mech. Exerc.* i. 5 The Nut or Screw Box hath also a square Worm, and is brazed into the round Box. **1735** J. PRICE *Stone-Br. Thames* 7 Iron Hooks should be let into their Flanks, and screw'd into Nuts. **1815** J. SMITH *Panorama Sci. & Art* I. 62 A screw with a button head, tightened at the back with a nut. **1894** BOTTONE *Electr. Instr.* 173 The nut, of course, works against the springs... When the nut is loosened the spring causes G to rise. **1911** *Rep. Labour & Social Conditions in Germany* (Tariff Reform League) III. 39 When we get our nuts screwed a little tighter we shall be able to look after our own industries and mind our own business. **1973** 'J. PATRICK' *Glasgow Gang Observed* x. 88 Asked why so few boys over twenty remained in the Fleet [gang], Tim replied: 'They used tae be in it but they've screwed the nut.' *Ibid.* 235 *Screw*, as in '*screw the nut*', to become sensible, to 'get wise' to oneself, to pull oneself together.

b. The portion of a wooden printing-press in which the screw plays.

1642 *Ordin. Lords & Comm. Prohib. Print.* 6 The Printers Nuts and Spindles which they find so employed. **1683** MOXON *Mech. Exerc., Printing* xi. ¶1 To preserve the Worms of the Spindle and Nut from wearing each other out the faster. **1824** J. JOHNSON *Typogr.* II. 507 The brass nut in which the screw of the spindle works. **1841** *Penny Cycl.* XXI. 111/1 In the upper cross-bar or head.. a nut is firmly secured. The screw works up and down in this nut.

c. The contrivance at the lower end of a violin-bow, or any similar instrument, by which the horse-hair may be relaxed or tightened.

1662 PLAYFORD *Skill Mus.* II. (1674) 101 Hold the Bow betwixt the ends of your Thumb and your Forefinger, an Inch below the Nut. **1836** DUBOURG *Violin* ix. (1878) 280 So regulated as to cause the nearest approach made by the stick to the hair to be exactly in the middle, between the head and the nut. **1884** HERON-ALLEN *Violin-making* 93 A bow.. with a properly constructed head and nut to receive the hair.

d. *fig.* in phr. (***the***) ***nuts and bolts***, the practical, basic elements, or the mechanics, of a situation or thing. Freq. *attrib.*

1960 *Times* 9 Feb. 11/4 When we talk about technicians—the 'nuts-and-bolts boys'—we are all right there. **1967** *Observer* 30 Apr. 11/8 A.. keen-eyed Army colonel.. talks to you about 'the nuts and bolts' of the programme. **1971** *Times* 10 June 16/6 His preference was for journalism. He learnt the nuts and bolts of his profession with the Montreal *Gazette*. **1972** *Guardian* 10 June 11/7 Most of some hundreds of recommendations in the action plan and its annexe, where the nuts and bolts are, will go through. **1973** T. ALLBEURY *Choice of Enemies* xvii. 83 There are two kinds of security that we cover... A bit of cigarette ash on a magnetic tape could screw up a whole pay-roll.. but.. that's pretty well a nuts and bolts area for us. We know it inside out. **1974** *Times* 22 Feb. 14 The electors are not to be despised for this conspicuous lack of interest in the nuts and bolts of politics. **1974** *Socialist Worker* 7 Dec. 9/6 There was also a tendency to go very easy on replies to those delegates who urged the conference to adopt a fuller and finer programme rather than discuss the nuts and bolts of trying to build in the real world.

13. *Naut.* A part of a ship's anchor (see quots.).

1627 CAPT. SMITH *Seaman's Gram.* vii. 29 At the head of the Shanke there is a hole.., and in it a Ring, wherein is the Nut to which there is fast fixed a Stocke of wood crossing the Flookes. **1688** HOLME *Armoury* III. xv. (Roxb.) 29/1 The nutt, the round part under the eye, to which the stock is fixt. **1769** FALCONER *Dict. Marine* (1780), *Nuts of the anchor*, two little prominencies, appearing like short square bars of iron, fixed across the upper part of the anchor-shank, to secure the stock thereof in it's place. **1867** SMYTH *Sailor's Word-bk.* 502 *Nuts*, two projections either raised or welded on the square part of the shank [etc.].

14. a. (See quot. 1876.)

1698 *Phil. Trans.* XX. 80 The Frets are nearer to one another toward the Bridge, and wider toward the Nut or Head of a Viol. **1771** *Encycl. Brit.* III. 323/2 An equal division of a string between either the nut and bridge, or stop and bridge. **1876** STAINER & BARRETT *Dict. Mus. Terms* 316 *Nut*, the fixed bridge formed by a slight prominence or ridge at the upper end of the strings of instruments of the violin and guitar family.

b. ***to make the nut***: (see quot.).

1899 *Allbutt's Syst. Med.* VIII. 12 The violoncello players .. who seek to get high-pitched notes from their instruments by shortening the strings by violent pressure with the outside of the phalangeal joint of the left thumb, while the fingers are engaged in stopping the string lower down (a manœuvre known as 'making the nut').

15. The central part of a potter's wheel.

1735 *Dict. Polygraph.* s.v. *Pottery*, The potters wheel consists principally in the nut, which is a beam or axis, whose foot or pivot plays perpendicularly on a free-stone sole or bottom.

III. †16. The glans penis. *Obs.*

1577 tr. *Bullinger's Decades* (1592) 358 There is a skinne which doth.. couer.. the nut or foreparte of a mannes yarde. **1611** COTGR., *Pennache de mer*.. at one end resembles a feather, and th' vncouered nut of a mans yard at th' other. **1687** A. LOVELL tr. *Thevenot's Trav.* I. 42 After they have cut off the fore-skin, [they] slit with their nails the skin also that covers the nut. **1758** J. S. tr. *Le Dran's Observ. Surg.* (1771) Dictionary, *Balanus*, the Glands or Nut of the Yard.

†17. a. = POPE'S EYE. *Obs.*

1611 COTGR., *Oeil de Iudas*, the Nut, or Fryers peece of a Leg of Mutton. **1682** GIBSON *Anat.* IV. (1697) App., A gland which we.. call in sheep the Nut or Pope's eye.

†b. A small knob (of meat). *Obs. rare*$^{-1}$.

1769 J. SKEAT *Art Cookery* 12 A sham Tortoise... is made of a calf's liver. There is a small nut of liver that hangs to it, which serves for the head.

c. *dial.* The pancreas; also, part of the caul.

c **1816** *Yng. Woman's Companion* 2 The liver, lights, heart, nut, and milt. **1893** P. H. EMERSON *Eng. Lagoons* xvii. 76 Jim .. had bought a pig's fry... I ate of all parts—the 'nut' and the 'mint'.. were really good. *Ibid.*, The apron (omentum), that's nice..; but the kell, that's the thing, and the nut of that is the sweetest part of all.

18. *pl.* Coal in small lumps.

1870 *Eng. Mech.* 18 Feb. 563/3 We have been using silkstone nuts. **1883** GRESLEY *Gloss. Coal-mining* 175 *Nuts*, small lumps of coal which will pass through a screen the bars of which vary in width apart between ½ inch and 2½ inches.

19. A small rounded biscuit or cake. Only in *doughnut*, *gingerbread* or *spice nut*, q.v.

20. *U.S. slang*. The amount of money required for a venture; overhead costs. Hence *transf.*, any sum of money.

1912 A. H. LEWIS *Apaches N.Y.* 201 Every day I'm open puts me fifty dollars on th' nut. **1914** JACKSON & HELLYER *Vocab. Criminal Slang* 62 *Nut*,.. used by grafters whose operations involve an investment to signify an expense incurred in connection with a venture. **1933** *Sun* (Baltimore) 28 Jan. 16/4 The difficulty of 'making the nut', the term applied to accumulating the rental charge due each night to the owner of the cab. **1935** *Amer. Mercury* June 230/1 *Nut*, concession charges for booking a joint; expenses. **1936** *Amer. Speech* XI. 219 He [*sc.* the producer] decides that in order to open the show a certain amount of money will be necessary. This amount is the production *nut*. **1948** *Sun* (Baltimore) 7 Aug. 9/2 In any event the 'nut' will be close to $400,000, counting fighters, rent and promotional expenses. **1955** *Publ. Amer. Dial. Soc.* XXIV. 37 Recreation, such as gambling.. and other cultural pursuits dear to the hearts of pickpockets, will cost extra... All this is counted as *nut*.. and anything they make over and above this they consider income. **1956** H. GOLD *Man who was not with It* (1965) xviii. 159, I was getting a nut of cash, and it felt good. **1962** J. B. PRIESTLEY *Margin Released* vi. 202 In the Thirties, when we could produce *Laburnum Grove*.. for about £800.. the weekly running costs—the 'get-out' or 'nut'—were round about the same figure, theatre and all. **1970** *Daily Tel.* 27 Apr. 3 New York police have their own secret slang to deal with their illegal business... 'Nut' is a cash bribe. **1972** *Publishers' Weekly* 14 Feb. 60/1 He submitted a strong script that led Fox to substitute color film and wide screen for black-and-white and the conventional small-screen ratio, and to raise the nut to $400,000.

IV. *attrib.* and *Comb.*

21. Attributive: **a.** In sense 1, as ***nut-bunch, -bush, -flower, -fruit, -garden, -grove***, etc.; (sense 8 c), as ***nut alley, -doctor, -farm***.

1935 A. J. POLLOCK *Underworld Speaks* 81/2 *Nut alley, prison insane ward. **1877** HORTON in Moloney *Forestry W. Afr.* (1887) 38 The *nut bunches are cut down from the trees. **1483** *Cath. Angl.* 257/2 A *Nutte buske, *corvletum*. **1955** A. HUXLEY *Let.* 7 May (1969) 742 Next week.. I go to Atlantic City to attend the Psychiatrists' Assn. meeting... I shall arrange to meet the boys on my return from the *nut-doctors. *a* **1940** F. SCOTT FITZGERALD *Last Tycoon* (1949) i. 12 Some mystic.. spouting tripe that'd land him on a *nut-farm anywhere outside of California. **1648** HEXHAM II, *Note-bloemen*, *Nut-flowers. **1850** MRS. BROWNING *Poems* II. 262 They listen For.. *nut-fruit falling from the trees. **1535** COVERDALE *Song. Sol.* vi. 11, I wente downe in to the *nutt garden, to se what grew by the brokes. **1872** CALVERLEY *Fly Leaves* (1903) 27 In the *nutgroves of Morocco. *c* **1000** *Sax. Leechd.* II. 34 Ʒenim *hnutcyrnla & hwæte corn. **1398** TREVISA *Barth. De P.R.* XVII. cviii. (Bodl. MS.), Wtin is þe notte curnel þt is sauorie & ful swete. **1460–70** *Bk. Quintessence* 23 Putte þerine.. note-kirnelis, fyn triacle, radisch. **1530** PALSGR. 254/1 Pyll of a nutte curnell. **1681** GREW *Musæum* II. §i. i. 200 A small Orbicular Fruit, as it seems, of the *Nut-kind. **1816** KIRBY & SP. *Entomol.* xxv. (1818) II. 416 The beetle to which the *nut-maggot is transformed. **1765** *Museum Rust.* III. 285 In the *nut season fences are pulled in pieces for the fruit by all the boys and girls in the neighbourhood. **1648** HEXHAM II, *Een Note-booste*, a *Nut-skin or Husk. **1845** DISRAELI *Sybil* (1863) 135 He cut my eyelid open once with a *nut-stick. **1886** W. J. TUCKER *E. Europe* 367 The fourth course was a *nut tart, very large, very rich, very sweet. **1496** *Fysshynge w. Angle* (1883) 29 The bayte that bredith on an oke, and the *notworme.

b. In sense 12, as ***nut-frame, -iron, -key, -sling***.

1711 W. SUTHERLAND *Shipbuilder's Assist.* 153 Nut-slings of the Guns. **1825** J. NICHOLSON *Operat. Mechanic* 443 The nut-frame should carry three flat pieces of wood or iron. *Ibid.* 338 Scrap or nut-iron, consisting of old nails, screws, nuts, and pieces of that description. **1844** H. STEPHENS *Bk. Farm* I. 425 The head and handle are forged in one piece.., the latter part being formed into a nut-key.

c. In sense 18, as ***nut-coal, -slack***.

1869 MRS. WHITNEY *We Girls* vi. (1873) 129 A sprinkle of small, shiny nut-coal. **1870** *Eng. Mech.* 18 Mar. 661/2 Coke (made.. of nut-slack riddled).

22. a. Objective and obj. genitive, as ***nut-catcher, -eater, -gathering, -seller***. Also ***nut-bearing, -grown, -questing***.

1877 L. H. MORGAN *Anc. Society* (1907) I. ii. 20 In fruit and *nut-bearing forests under a tropical sun, we are accustomed.. to regard our progenitors as having commenced their existence. **1952** A. G. L. HELLYER *Sanders' Encycl. Gardening* (ed. 22) 130 Corylus (Cob-nut; Filbert)... Hardy deciduous nut-bearing shrubs. **1746** MRS. CARTER in Pennington *Life* (1808) I. 105 My fellow *nut-catcher and I have another wood in reserve where we hope for better success. **1883** D. COOK *P. Foster's Daughter* i, He seeks the *nut-eater. **1876** H. H. THOMAS *Mem. D. Thomas* i. 4 Delighting in country rambles, in *nut-gathering and bathing. **1809** CAMPBELL *Gert. Wyom.* I. iii, And playful squirrel on his *nut-grown tree. **1922** JOYCE *Ulysses* 535 Who left his *nutquesting classmates to seek our shade? **1648** HEXHAM II, *Een note-menger*, a *Nut-seller.

b. Similative, as ***nut-deaf, -grey, -like, -sweet***.

1828 *Blackw. Mag.* XXIII. 806 Old men are our aversion, so *nut-deaf are they, so sand-blind. **1797** *Encycl. Brit.* (ed. 3) VI. 220/2 To give an example of the manner of producing these colours we shall take the *nut-grey. **1830** LINDLEY *Nat. Syst. Bot.* 181 Seeds *nut-like. **1874** A. GRAY *Less. Bot.* 469 The 2 nut-like seeds partly sunk in excavations at the base of the scale. **1586** BRIGHT *Melanch.* xviii. 110 For of it selfe [the blood] being *nutsweete or milke-sweete, by this heate becommeth sugar or hony sweete.

23. Special combs.: †**nut-beam**, a nut-tree; †**nut-boy**, a boy who gathers nuts; †**nut-breaker** = NUT-CRACKER 3 b; **nut-butter**, a substitute for butter obtained from the oil of nuts; **nut (milk) chocolate**, (milk) chocolate containing nuts; **nut college** *U.S. slang* = *nut-house* (below); **nut-cut**, *slang* (see quot.); **nut cutlet**, a portion of meat-substitute made from nuts and various other ingredients and shaped like a cutlet; **nut factory** *U.S. slang*, = *nut-house* (below); **nut food**, food prepared from nuts; so **nut-fooder**; †**nut-head**, the plant Tormentil, which has nut-like seeds; **nut-house** *slang*, a mental hospital; †**nut-housing**, a nutshell; **nut-meat**, the kernel of a nut; **nut-Monday**, the first Monday in August, locally observed as a holiday; †**nut-mouse**, the dormouse; †**nut-mussel** (?); **nut-palm**, an Australian palm (*Cycas media*) which bears edible nuts; †**nut-penny** (cf. *nut-silver*); **nut-pine**, one of several species of pine producing edible seeds, native to south-western North America and the Rocky Mountains; †**nut-plum** (see quot. 1601); **nut runner**, a power tool for tightening nuts; **nut-rush**, a kind of sedge with nut-like seeds; †**nut-silver**, a yearly payment formerly customary in Northumberland; **nut-steak**, a portion of meat-substitute made from nuts and shaped like a steak; **nut-wood**, ? walnut wood.

c **1000** *Sax. Leechd.* II. 42 *Hnutbeames rinde seaw.. drype on eare. **1412–13** *Abingdon Rolls* (Camden) 75 Et de vs de j notebem vendito in Gardino hoc anno. **1653** DOROTHY OSBORNE *Lett.* (1903) 29 She wears twenty strung upon a ribbon, like the *nut boys play withal. **1778** PENNANT *Tour Wales* (1883) I. 29 Excepting the Caryocatactes or *nut-breaker, I do not recollect any very uncommon bird to have visited this parish. **1907** *Nut-butter [see s.v. NUCOLINE]. **1908** *Westm. Gaz.* 5 Aug. 2/3 Vegetarians cannot expect to be allowed to call their butter-substitute 'nut butter' when other people's butter-substitutes are called 'margarine'. **1918** C. A. MITCHELL *Edible Oils & Fats* ix. 117 Deodorised coconut oil is used in the preparation of both margarine and 'nut butter'. **1961** C. LOEWENFELD tr. *Bircher's Eating your Way to Health* II. iii. 246 Nut butter is a good and easily digested substitute for those who do not like, or should not have, butter. **1971** J. HEWITT *N.Y. Times Natural Foods* xv. 393 *Nut butter spread*... Place the nuts, sunflower seeds, kernels and seeds in an electric blender and blend until fine. **1975** *Times* 14 Feb. 9/7 They bake daily... They also make various nut butters. **1918–19** *T. Eaton & Co. Catal.* Fall & Winter 385/2 Eaton's *Nut Milk Chocolate... Each bar made from fine chocolate, milk and *nuts. **1926–7** *Army & Navy Stores Catal.* 54/1 Chocolate ..Nut (¼ lb. pkts.). **1932** R. LEHMANN *Invitation to Waltz* III. vi. 215, I preferred to spend the afternoon on the schoolroom sofa reading *East Lynne* and eating nut-milk chocolate. **1936** 'J. TEY' *Shilling for Candles* xi. 128 'Nut or plain?' 'What?' 'The chocolate.' **1955** M. ALLINGHAM *Beckoning Lady* xvi. 228 Offering Westy half a bar of nut chocolate. **1960** *Sunday Express* 25 Dec. 13/3 When nut milk chocolate was 2d. a bar. **1931** *Amer. Speech* VII. 111 **Nut college*, an insane asylum. **1951** in Wentworth & Flexner *Dict. Amer. Slang* (1960) 360/2 He has been recalled by the nut college to join Napoleon.. and Shakespeare, inventing paper dolls! **1874** *Slang Dict.* 239 **Nut-cut*, roguish, mischievous. **1908** F. A. GEORGE *Vegetarian Cookery* ix. 113 **Nut cutlets*... Make into cutlet shapes. Egg and crumb. Fry in deep fat. **1925** D. H. LAWRENCE *Let.* ? 17 Dec. (1962) II. 871 So Sonya will never cook us another goose, only marmite pie and nut-cutlet. **1959** 'M. INNES' *Hare sitting Up* II. vi. 112 Didn't I say something about Burgundy? Capital with nut cutlets. **1965** J. B. PRIESTLEY *Lost Empires* II. ii. 115 Mr Foster-Jones makes Health Foods... He's probably brought a case of date sandwiches and nut cutlets with him. **1973** *Times* 10 Apr. 14/1 You can no longer get nut cutlets... What you get instead now are nut rissoles. **1915** *Recruiter's Bull.* (U.S. Marine Corps., N.Y.) Oct. 15/1 It would have been impossible to have found a man any other place than a '*nut-factory' who would voluntarily have told the commanding officer that he was a deserter. **1929** J. CALLAHAN *Man's Grim Justice* xiii. 156 They should have been in the 'nut factory'.. the insane department. **1939** J. H. CHASE *No Orchids for Miss Blandish* i. 33 Johnnie was a rummy... Drink had rotted him, and he was only two jumps ahead of the nut-factory. **1905** *Vegetarian Messenger* Apr. 105, I will send any readers who wish for it an address where *nut-foods can be had guaranteed free of pea-nuts. **1917** N. DOUGLAS *South Wind* x. 142 He will be an anti-vivisectionist, a *nut-fooder, costume-maniac.., or a spiritualist into the bargain. *c* **1265** *Voc. Plants* in Wr.-Wülcker 557 *Turmentine*, i. *nutehede. **1929** *Amer. Speech* IV. 343 **Nut House*, an insane asylum. **1936** 'P. QUENTIN' *Puzzle for Fools* i. 6 It wasn't a sanatorium really. It was just an expensive nuthouse for people like me who had lost control. **1953** W. BURROUGHS *Junkie* (1972) 10, I decided I was not going to like the Army and copped out on my nut-house record... The nut-house doctors had never heard of Van Gogh. **1958** 'N. BLAKE' *Penknife in my Heart* iii. 42 Miriam drives you into the nut-house. **1973** 'H. HOWARD' *Highway to Murder* xi. 141 Supposing the plan succeeded and his wife got stuck away in a nut-house? **1974** *Radio Times* 24 Oct. 11/2 Clothing for the Government, prisons and nut-'ouses—what is it they call 'em now? **1483** *Cath. Angl.* 257/2 A *Nutte husynge, *nucleus*. **1913** A. B. EMERSON *R. Fielding at Snow Camp* 102 The three boys stuck to their work.. until there was a great bowl of *nutmeats. **1967** *Economist* 9 Sept. 892/1 Kukui nut-meat burning gently in a shell. **1974** *Aiken* (S. Carolina) *Standard* 22 Apr. 8-A/5 The Viennese desserts called Torten are sometimes made with finely ground nut-meats without the inclusion of any flour. **1867** *Q. Rev.* CXXII. 380 '*Nut-Monday' is still a great occasion in Kendal. **1607** TOPSELL *Four-f. Beasts* (1658) 423 Of the *Nut-mouse, Hasel-mouse, or Filbird-mouse. **1705** PETIVER in *Phil. Trans.* XXV. 1954 *Chama Carolina*... This Shell resembles our *Nut-Muscle. **1889** J. H. MAIDEN *Usef. Native Pl.* 21 '*Nut Palm.'.. Employed by the aborigines as food. An excellent farina is obtained from it. **1702** in J. C. Hodgson *Hist. Northumbld.* (1904) VII. 316 The rent called *Nutt pennys. **1845** J. C. FRÉMONT *Rep. Expl. Exped. Rocky Mountains* 221 A pine tree.. which Dr. Torrey has described as a new species, under the name of *pinus monophyllus*; in popular language, it might be called the *nut pine. **1851** MAYNE REID *Scalp Hunt.* xxvi. 190 We cachéd them [the horses] in a thicket of nut-pine. **1872** RAYMOND *Mines & Mining* 11 The Cuyanne Mountain is thickly covered with nut-pine timber. **1896** C. H. SHINN *Story of the Mine* 63 The nut-pine trees were soon cut down. **1949** COLLINGWOOD & BRUSH *Knowing your Trees* 18/1 This is one of four nut pines of the Southwest. **1969** T. H. EVERETT *Living Trees of World* 50/2 The piñon or Mexican stone pine (*P. cembroides*) is small and spreading and, like its variety *P. c. edulis*, the nut pine, produces delicious edible seeds or 'nuts'. Both are natives of the southwestern United States and Mexico, the nut pine extending north to Wyoming. **1601** HOLLAND *Pliny* I. 437 Those plums.. that are graffed in Nut-tree stocks.. retain the face and forme still of the mother graffe, but they get the taste of the stock where-in they are set..: of them both they carry the name, and are called *nut-plums. **1611** FLORIO, *Nocipruna*, the Nut-plumbe. **1958** R. M. BARNES *Motion & Time Study* (ed. 4) xvii. 288 The multiple-spindle air-operated *nut runner.. is used to tighten all five wheel nuts at once. **1966** *Engineers' Digest* Dec. 97/2 Suitable for light duties and often employed with power screwdrivers and nutrunners, another type of torque limiting device utilizes a spring-loaded steel ball. **1874** A. GRAY *Less. Bot.* 570 *Scleria*, *Nut-Rush. **1569** in J. C. Hodgson *Hist. Northumbld.* (1904) VII. 306 All the tenants pay yearly by ancient custom.. *Nutsylver. **1908** *Daily Chron.* 2 Sept. 3/4 High thinking is still nourished upon the banana and the *nut-steak. **1922** JOYCE *Ulysses* 163 Why do they call that thing they gave me nutsteak? Nutarians, Fruitarians. To give you the idea you are eating rumpsteak. **1966** K. GILES *Provenance of Death* iv. 103 The man.. is a vegetarian... He had a nut steak. **1701** WOLLEY *Jrnl. New York* (1860) 52 They had Needles of Wood, for which *Nut-wood was esteemed best. **1898** *Daily News* 15 Feb. 9/6 Tenders are also invited.. for the delivery of 6,000 rough nut-wood stocks for carbines.

24. Passing into *adj.* Stupid, insane (cf. senses 7, 8, and 21 a).

1919 *Sci. Amer.* 23 Aug. 184/1 Other ideas, no more revolutionary and no more absurd from the standpoint of entrenched orthodoxy, never graduate from the 'nut' class. **1922** U. SINCLAIR *They call me Carpenter* xix. 66, I just want to know where he got his nut ideas. **1922** S. LEWIS *Babbitt* ii. 17 Ever since somebody slipped up and let you out of college.. you been pulling these nut conversations about what-nots and so-on-and-so-forths. **1966** T. PYNCHON *Crying of Lot 49* iii. 48 'You one of these right-wing nut outfits?' inquired the diplomatic Metzger.

†**nut**, *sb.*² *Obs.* [OE. *nyt*.] Use, worth.

c **1205** LAY. 13428 A he seide þat Bruttes neoren noht to nuttes, ah he seide þat þa Peohtes weoren gode cnihtes.

†**nut**, *a. Obs.* Also 4 neȝt. [OE. *nyt*. The form *neȝt* is for *net*, riming with *pet*, pit.] Useful.

c **1205** LAY. 9470 Wel is þe man nut þe sæhtnesse wurcheð. *c* **1315** SHOREHAM IV. 136 Ine felþe þou schelt lygge, þou ert nauȝt elles neȝt.

nut (nʌt), *v.* [f. NUT *sb.*¹]

1. *intr.* To seek for, or gather, nuts; *esp.* in phr. ***to go (a) nutting***.

1604 DEKKER *Honest Wh.* Wks. 1873 II. 84 Whither gad you? A nutting forsooth. *c* **1670** WOOD *Life* (O.H.S.) I. 176 A. W. went to angle with William Staine of Mert. coll. to Wheately bridge and nutted in Shotover by the way. **1693** LUTTRELL *Brief Rel.* (1857) III. 197 Last week 3 clippers were taken in the very act in a wood.., being discovered by a boy a nutting. **1824** MRS. CAMERON *Marten & his Scholars* vii. 45 A set of wild chaps ticed me.. to go a-nutting with them. **1855** MACAULAY *Hist. Eng.* xxi. IV. 624 A schoolboy who goes nutting in the wood of a neighbour. **1879** 'E. GARRETT' *House by Works* I. 47 When he and I used to go nutting in Culstead.

2. *trans.* To curry favour with, to court (a person). *slang.* (Cf. NUT *sb.*¹ 6.)

1812 J. H. VAUX *Flash Dict.*, *Nut*, to please a person by any little act of assiduity, by a present, or by flattering words, is called *nutting* him; as the present, &c., by which you have gratified them is termed a *nut*. **1823** *Grose's Dict. Vulgar T.* (Egan) s.v. *Nuts*, The cove's nutting the blowen; the man is trying to please the girl.

3. *slang.* **a.** To think, to use one's head. Freq. const. *out*, also *up*. (Cf. NUT *sb.*¹ 7.)

1919 W. H. DOWNING *Digger Dialects* 36 *Nut it out*, think it out. **1925** FRASER & GIBBONS *Soldier & Sailor Words* 213 *Nut out, to*, to think over. Consider. To use one's head. **1951** D. STIVENS *Jimmy Brockett* 168, I did a bit of hard nutting over my plans for trotting. **1953** K. TENNANT *Joyful Condemned* iv. 38 Just nut that out. **1962** A. UPFIELD *Will of Tribe* xix. 180, I asked him how he nutted up the idea. **1965** M. SHADBOLT *Among Cinders* xiii. 112, I haven't nutted out what I'm going to say about the poultry. **1971** R. DENTRY *Encounter at Kharmel* (1973) v. 81 I've been nutting the whole thing out... There's no future in it for you.

b. To butt with the head; to hit a blow on the head. Also '**nutting** *vbl. sb.*

1937 PARTRIDGE *Dict. Slang* 575/1 *Nut*,.. to punch on the head. **1963** T. & P. MORRIS *Pentonville* xi. 241 Few prison fights are conducted in accordance with Queensberry Rules; fists, heads (for the painful infliction of injury to the opponent's nose by 'nutting'), teeth and nails may be used at any time. **1966** D. SKIRROW *It won't get you Anywhere* xiv. 61, I shot my head backwards in time to miss the nutting that was coming... The tearaway special nowadays is to hug tight, rupture his kidneys and nut him hard. **1971** J. MANDELKAU *Buttons* xiii. 145 He took it off and as I was getting out of mine he nutted me in the head.

Nut, var. NAT *sb.*²

nutant (ˈnjuːtənt), *a.* [ad. L. *nūtant-em*, pres. pple. of *nūtāre* to nod. So F. *nutant*, Sp. and Pg. *nutante*.] Drooping, pendent. Also *Comb.*

1751 J. HILL *Hist. Plants* 371 The great nutant-flowered Lilium, called the great Martagon. **1797** *Encycl. Brit.* (ed. 3) III. 442/1 *Nutant*, nodding, having the point turned outward. **1819** SAMOUELLE *Entomol. Compend.* 212 Head nutant, forming an obtuse angle with the thorax. **1853** G. JOHNSTON *Nat. Hist. E. Bord.* I. 42 The ripe capsules are generally erect, but sometimes nutant.

nutarian (nʌˈtɛərɪən). [f. after *vegetarian*.] A vegetarian whose diet is based on nut products.

1914 *Chambers's Eng. Dict.* Suppl. 1281/2 *Nutarian*, one who lives on nuts.—Also adj. (From *Nut*, in imitation of *Vegetarian*.) **1922** [see *nut-steak* s.v. NUT *sb.*¹ 23].

nu'tate, *v.* [f. ppl. stem of L. *nūtāre*: cf. NUTANT *a.*] *intr.* To undergo or exhibit nutation. Hence **nu'tating** *ppl. a.*

1880 C. & F. DARWIN *Movem. Pl.* 99 He has shewn in the case of certain seedlings, whose tips are bent downwards (or which nutate), that [etc.]. **1881** *Spectator* 8 Jan. 51 That side of the nutating stem.. faces the north throughout the movement. **1897** WILLIS *Fl. Pl. & Ferns* I. 174 The nutating tip of a twining stem. **1898** S. H. VIVES *Elem. Text-bk. Bot.* iii. 211 All growing members nutate in a more or less marked manner. **1921** J. SMALL *Textbk. Bot.* xvii. 221 In the mature plant the top three internodes of the stem turn or nutate in a circle. **1943** R. C. BINDER *Fluid Mech.* viii. 107 The nutating-disk meter or wobble-plate meter.. is frequently used to meter the water supply for domestic use. **1948** C. E. INGALLS in S. N. Van Voorhis *Microwave Receivers* xv. 380 Tracking in azimuth and elevation is made possible by the use of a nutating antenna. A fixed paraboloidal reflector is combined with a dipole, which is caused to move in a small circular orbit about the focus of the reflector, to give a radiation pattern in the form of a beam that traces out a small cone. **1950** H. GOLDSTEIN *Class.*

Mech. v. 168 It is not the regular precession encountered in force-free motion, for as the figure axis goes around it nods up and down..—the top nutates. **1965** BELL & COOMBE tr. *Strasburger's Textbk. Bot.* 390 A nutating shoot. **1969** R. SKINNER *Mech.* iv. 469 The top continues to spin about its axis of symmetry, while this axis rotates, or precesses, about a vertical axis. All the while, this axis [of symmetry] nods up and down, or nutates, as it precesses.

nutation (nju:ˈteɪʃən). [ad. L. *nūtātiōn-em*, noun of action f. *nūtāre* to nod. So F. *nutation*, It. *nutazione*, Sp. *nutacion*.]

1. The action of nodding the head; an instance of this. Also *transf.*

1612 COTTA *Disc. Dang. Pract. Phys.* I. v. 42 The nutation and staggering of nature doth make warie proceeding. **1656** BLOUNT *Glossogr.*, *Nutation*, nodding, as one doth when he sits sleeping. **1728** POPE *Dunc.* II. 409 So from the mid-most the nutation spreads Round, and more round, o'er all the sea of heads. **1859** J. G. SAXE *Poems, Richard of Gloster*, Ugly relations Who'll be very apt to disturb your nutations By unpleasant allusions, and rude observations! **1897** *Allbutt's Syst. Med.* III. 78 The cervical vertebræ are usually attacked first; a difficulty is felt in rotation and nutation.

2. a. *Astr.* A slight oscillation of the earth's axis; now *spec.* that by which the pole of the equator would describe a small ellipse in about 19 years, and which actually renders its motion round the pole of the ecliptic (see PRECESSION) wavy instead of purely circular.

1715 tr. *Gregory's Astron.* (1726) I. 502 Another Nutation arising from another Cause may produce all this diversity in the distance of the Pole-Star from the Pole. **1748** BRADLEY in *Phil. Trans.* XLV. 13 This apparent Motion, in both those Stars, might proceed from a Nutation in the Earth's Axis. *Ibid.* 15 The Changes which I had observed, both in the annual Precession and Nutation. **1789** E. DARWIN *Bot. Gard.* II. (1791) 63 Marking her solar and sidereal day, Her slow nutation, and her varying clime. **1842** *Penny Cycl.* XXII. 448/1 A large number of stars..have a slight apparent motion not attributable either to precession or nutation. **1882** R. PROCTOR in *Knowledge* 220 A more perfect method of illustrating the precession of the equinoxes or the earth's reeling, and also the nutation (or nodding, still to be described).

b. The oscillation of a top in spinning.

1879 THOMSON & TAIT *Nat. Phil.* I. I. §107 If a Troughton's top be placed on its pivot in any inclined position, and then spun off with very great angular velocity about its axis of figure, the nutation will be insensible.

c. Movement (as of a beam or aerial) by which an axis is made to describe a cone. (Analogous to the precession of a spinning top rather than its nutation.)

1947 *Bell Syst. Techn. Jrnl.* XXVI. 307 The axis of the beam was rotated in an orbit by 'nutation' about the mechanical axis of the antenna. **1966** *McGraw-Hill Encycl. Sci. & Technol.* XI. 204/2 Either the feed or the reflector whirls rapidly in a manner that causes the beam axis to describe a circular cone; this motion of the beam axis is called nutation.

3. Curvature in the stem of a growing plant.

1789 E. DARWIN *Bot. Gard.* II. (1791) 19 The sun flower follows the course of the sun by nutation, not by twisting its stem. **1816** KEITH *Phys. Bot.* II. 447 Such flowers are designated by the appellation of Heliotropes, on account of their following the course of the sun; and the movement they thus exhibit is denominated their nutation. **1880** C. & F. DARWIN *Movem. Pl.* 1 The stem of a climbing plant, which bends successively to all points of the compass, so that the tip revolves. This movement has been called by Sachs 'revolving nutation'.

nutational (nju:ˈteɪʃənəl), *a.* [f. NUTATION + -AL.] Of or pertaining to nutation.

1881 W. D. HAY *300 Years Hence* viii. 152 The precessional and nutational movements of the earth. **1959** VAN LEAR & LASSEN in Puckett & Ramo *Guided Missile Engin.* x. 275 If the gyro is started up with the inner gimbal initially inclined to the plane perpendicular to the outer gimbal, there is first a transitory nutational bobbing around. **1965** BELL & COOMBE tr. *Strasburger's Textbk. Bot.* 361 In both kinds of movement the mechanical cause may be either a difference in growth rates on the two sides of an organ (nutational movements) or differential changes in the turgor of the cells (variational movements).

ˈnut-bone. Now *rare.* [f. NUT *sb.*[1]] One of the sesamoid bones in the foot of a horse. Also applied to the navicular bone.

1615 CROOKE *Body of Man* 973 Pliny calles them *ossa orbiculata* round or nut-bones. **1766** *Compl. Farmer* s.v. *Shoeing*, Thus the cannon-bone presses on the pastern, this on the coronary, the coronary upon the coffin, or foot-bone, and upon the nut-bone. **1816** BLAINE *Vet. Art* 74 Anterior extremities. Z. Navicular or nutbone.

ˈnut-brown, *a.* (and *sb.*) [f. NUT *sb.*[1] Cf. Sw. *nötbrun*, Da. *nöddebrun*, G. *nussbraun*.]

1. Of the colour of a ripe hazel-nut; brown as a nut; of a warm reddish-brown colour.

a. Of hair or complexion, or of animals.

a **1300** *Cursor M.* 18846 Berd and hefd of a heu ware, Nute brun als i tald yow are. **1575** GASCOIGNE *Herbes* Wks. (Grosart) I. 356 A louely nutbrowne face is best of all. **1723** *Lond. Gaz.* No. 6154/4 One Nut-brown Mare. **1823** BYRON *Island* II. vii, The sun-born blood..threw O'er her clear nut-brown skin a lucid hue. **1823** —— *Juan* XIII. lxxv, Ah, nut-brown partridges! *a* **1855** C. BRONTE *Professor* ix, Her hair was nut-brown.

b. Of girls, in respect of complexion.

a **1500** *Nutbrowne Maide* viii. in *Arnolde's Chron.* (1502) fol. 75 b, Shal neuer be sayd the Nutbrowne mayd was to her loue vnkind. **1579** LYLY *Euphues* (Arb.) 115 If she be well sette, then call hir a Bosse,..if Nut broune, as blacke as a coale. **1611** COTGR., s.v. *Fille*, The nut-browne lasse for mirth and neatnesse doth surpasse. **1637** MASSINGER *Guardian* I. i, My tenants' nut-brown daughters, wholesome girls. **1728** POPE *Dunc.* II. 337 Shown him by the Nut-brown maids, A branch of Styx here rises from the Shades. **1820** SCOTT *Monast.* xv, The attention which was paid to every word that he uttered by the nut-brown Mysie. **1895** *Daily News* 20 Mar. 7/1 For the nut-brown maids, who strike the happy medium between dark and fair, there is a large choice of gentle tints.

absol. **1800** MRS. HERVEY *Mourtray Fam.* I. 228 Well, and what of that, my pretty nut-brown?

c. Of things, *esp.* ale.

1586 A. DAY *Eng. Secretary* I. (1625) 110 The nut-broun Colour of Seller-Ale in a frosty morning. **1608** DEKKER *Belman of Lond.* Wks. (Grosart) III. 78 Nut-browne round trenchers lay in good order. *a* **1668** DAVENANT *News fr. Plimouth* III. i, Good Nutbrowne-Ale and Tost. **1770** GOLDSM. *Des. Vill.* 221 Low lies that house where nut-brown draughts inspir'd.

†d. Of a sword. (Cf. BROWN *a.* 4.) *Obs.*

16.. *Robin Hood and Beggar* in Child *Ballads* III. 157/1 The beggar he had a mickle long staffe, And Robin had a nut-brown sword. **1674** BUTLER *Hud.* I. ii. 797 When his nut-brown sword was out, Courageously he laid about.

†e. *fig.* Rustic. *Obs. rare*$^{-1}$.

1648 HERRICK *Hesp.*, *Sweet Country Life* 60 Thy Nut-browne mirth, thy Russet wit.

2. *absol.* as *sb.* **a.** Ale. (Cf. 1 c.)

1828 SCOTT *F.M. Perth* ii, Thou shalt have a cup of the nut-brown for thyself, my boy. **1867** BRIERLEY *Marlocks* 121, I began to have doubts whether the parson would have cared to leave the 'nut-brown'.

b. A brown colour like that of nuts.

1883 *Harper's Mag.* Apr. 772 Her hair was of a soft nut-brown. **1896** *Daily News* 12 Sept. 6/2 Deep nutbrowns and the red of the robin's breast are skilfully combined.

ˈnutburger. Also **nutberger.** [f. NUT *sb.*[1] 1 + BURGER.] A meat-substitute made from nuts, formed into a cake, and usu. served between the two halves of a toasted bun; also, a hamburger topped with nuts. Also *attrib.*

1934 M. WESEEN *Dict. Amer. Slang* XIX. 291 *Nutberger*, a hamburger sprinkled with nuts. **1939** A. HUXLEY *After Many a Summer* I. i. 6 Drive In For Nutbergers—whatever they were. **1942** *Amer. Speech* XVII. 132/2 *Nutbergers* are on sale in California. **1948** E. WAUGH *Loved One* 120 Dennis ..followed her to a nutburger counter. *Ibid.*, D'you know, this is the first time I've ever eaten a nutburger? **1959** *Listener* 24 Sept. 497/2 It is ready to try anything, from Mormonism to nutburgers. **1973** *Guardian* 17 Mar. 13/1 Thrifty high-protein meat substitutes..soyabeanburgers and nutburgers and fishwiches.

ˈnut-cake. [NUT *sb.*[1] 1.] **a.** *U.S.* A doughnut or fried cake. **b.** A cake containing nuts.

a **1800** *Spirit of Farmer's Museum* (1801) 235 Heap the nut-cakes, fried in butter. **1823** J. F. COOPER *Pioneers* ix, The four corners were garnished with plates of cake. On one was piled certain curiously twisted and complicated figures called 'nut-cakes'. **1844** *Knickerbocker* XXIV. 483 Reflection..was interrupted by the appearance..of 'nut-cakes and cider'. **1857** *Quinland* I. II. ii. 34 By the way, Hepsy, make us some 'nut-cakes', and bring us the cider. **1873** M. HOLLEY *My Opinions* (1891) 251 Where is the rich happy woman that wouldn't give a nutcake to a sick beggar? **1889** R. T. COOKE *Steadfast* xviii. 198 Who ever heard tell of puttin' a reason and a bit of citron into the middle of a riz nut-cake before 'twas fried? **1957** G. MANN *Bk. Cakes* 157 *Nut Cake*... Put into a shallow greased tin and spread the nut covering over the cake. **1966** W. I. KAUFMAN *Nut Cookery Bk.* 65 *Nut cake*... Fold in walnuts, stirring as little as possible... Bake in a moderate oven.

ˈnut-case. *colloq.* [f. NUT *sb.*[1] (cf. 8 c) + CASE *sb.*[2]] A crazy person; a madman.

1959 *Punch* 21 Oct. 337/2, I couldn't get anyone to talk about it openly. The way they clammed up you'd have thought I was a spy or a nut-case. **1965** A. PRIOR *Interrogators* iii. 28 He knew the nut-cases, the convicted sexual offenders. **1969** *Listener* 24 Apr. 586/2 You nut-case, you ought to be locked up. **1973** BOYD & PARKES *Dark Number* v. 57 They were all shams... She was a nutcase really.

ˈnut-crack. [f. NUT *sb.*[1]]

1. = NUT-CRACKER 1. Now *rare* or *Obs.*

1570 LEVINS *Manip.* 5 Nutcracke, *nucifrangium*. **1681** *Reply to 'Mischief of Impositions'* 4 They can find in their hearts to play with Nut-cracks and Hobby-horses. **1682** SOUTHERNE *Loyal Brother* v. Wks. 1721 I. 59 Indeed a nutcrack, or some such conceited Hyroglyphical Engine does well in the hand of a magistrate. **1793** ANNA SEWARD *Lett.* (1811) III. 266 A mouth that will be nut-cracks at 60. **1806** J. Tomlinson *Doncaster* (1887) 257 For 16 pairs of nut-cracks to mansion house.

2. ***Nut-crack Night***, Hallowe'en.

1777 BRAND *Pop. Antiq.* App. 344 From the Custom of flinging [nuts]..into the Fire, it has doubtless had its vulgar Name of Nutcrack-Night. **1825** BROCKETT *N.C. Gloss.*

ˈnut-cracker. Also **nutcracker** (esp. in sense 3 b). [f. NUT *sb.*[1] Cf. Du. *note(n)kraker*.]

1. a. An instrument used for the purpose of breaking the shells of nuts. Also, and now usually, (***a pair of***) ***nut-crackers***.

sing. **1548** ELYOT *Nucifrangibulum*,..a nut cracker. **1650** B. *Discolliminium* 14 He was fain at length to make a Nutcracker of it. **1673** *S'too him Bayes* 16 A sword..which was as like a nut-cracker for it crack'd men clad in steel. **1710** STEELE *Tatler* No. 115 ¶1 He had once actually laid aside his [Punch's] Head for a Nut-cracker. **1844** DICKENS *Mart. Chuz.* ii, After the manner of a toy nut-cracker.

pl. **1634** MASSINGER *Very Woman* III. ii, A thousand iron mills Can be heard no further than a pair of nut-crackers. **1736** SWIFT *Corr.* Wks. 1841 II. 779, I shall send..a fine pair of Cavan nut-crackers to save her white teeth. **1772** FOOTE *Nabob* III. Wks. 1799 II. 314 A pair of nut-crackers presented by Harry the Eighth to Anna Bullen. **1815** J. SMITH *Panorama Sci. & Art* I. 298 A pair of bellows, nut-crackers, &c. are composed of two levers of the second kind. **1879** F. W. ROBINSON *Coward Conscience* I. viii, You need not hammer away on the table with the nut-crackers any longer.

†b. *Cant.* (See quot.) *Obs.*

a **1700** B. E. *Dict. Cant. Crew*, *Nut-crackers*, a Pillory. The Cull lookt through the Nut-crackers.

c. Used *attrib.* and *Comb.* to describe the appearance of nose and chin which is produced by the want of teeth.

c **1700** T. BROWN *Wks.* (1708) III. 22 Hollow cheeks,.. nut-cracker chin that almost meets her nose. **1818** W. WILBERFORCE in S. Wilberforce *Life* xxiii. (1868) 380 She is a toothless, nutcracker jawed old woman, but quite upright and active. **1859** LD. LYTTON *Wanderer* (ed. 2) 292 That gin-drinking hag, with her nut-cracker face. **1891** 'J. S. WINTER' *Mrs. Bob* 272 A..bunch of bones, with a nut-cracker nose and chin.

†2. One who cracks nuts; a common spectator at the theatre. *Obs.*

1601 B. JONSON *Poetaster* I. ii, Sirrah, you, nut-cracker, goe your waies to him agaiue, and tell him I must ha' money, I. **1625** —— *Staple of N.* Prol. Crt., Schollers, that can iudge, and faire report The sense they heare, aboue the vulgar sort Of Nut-crackers, that onely come for sight.

3. †a. The cardinal grosbeak. *Obs. rare.*

1688 HOLME *Armoury* II. 242/2 The Virginian Nightingale..is called the Nut-craker, because it loves to feed on Kernels.

b. A brown corvine bird (*Nucifraga caryocatactes*), common in various parts of Europe, but rarely seen in Britain.

The English and Latin names are translations of G. *nussbrecher*.

1758 G. EDWARDS *Glean. Nat. Hist.* I. 63 The Nut-Cracker. This bird..is about the size of our jack-daw. **1768** PENNANT *Brit. Zool.* (1776) II. 531 Nutcracker; the specimen we took our description from is the only one we ever heard was shot in these kingdoms. **1802** MONTAGU *Ornith. Dict.* (1831) 339 The Nutcracker is said to lay up a store of acorns and nuts for winter. **1840** *Cuvier's Anim. Kingd.* 204 The Nutcrackers..have both mandibles equally pointed, straight, and without curvature. **1894** NEWTON *Dict. Birds* 646 The Nutcracker breeds very early in the year, long before the snows are melted.

Comb. **1853** WOOD *Nat. Hist.* 270 The Nutcracker Crow ..is about the size of a jackdaw, but its form is more slender.

4. As a book-title. (Cf. NUT *sb.*[1] 4 a.)

1751 'F. FOOT' (*title*), The Nut-Cracker: Containing an agreeable Variety of well-season'd Jests, Epigrams, Epitaphs, &c.

5. Nutcracker Man, a nickname for the fossil hominid, *Australopithecus robustus* (or *A. boisei*), the maker of the oldest stone tools known, esp. the specimen discovered by L. S. B. and M. D. Leakey at Olduvai, Tanzania, in 1959; similar remains, including the characteristic large premolar teeth, have also been found in South Africa.

1959 *Times* 4 Sept. 8/4 He [*sc.* L. S. B. Leakey] has named the species *Zinjanthropus Boisei*... The nickname given by Dr. Leakey to the world's oldest man is 'Nutcracker Man' because of the tremendously developed teeth. **1961** *New Scientist* 26 Oct. 221 Not only is *Zinjanthropus* or Nutcracker Man 'unquestionably' human but some of his fairly distant ancestors were human as well. **1962** *Listener* 5 Apr. 589/1 Dr. Leakey's famous 'nutcracker man' Zinjanthropus (which has now been dated as having lived over 1,000,000 years ago). **1972** S. CUPITT tr. *Wendt's From Ape to Adam* iv. 228 He [*sc.* Robert Broom] found the remains of an australopithecine equipped with a particularly powerful jaw and truly nutcracker-like teeth... These 'Nutcracker men' even had a small sagittal crest on their skulls. *Ibid.* 232 At first Leakey thought that this ancient Oldowan ancestor of ours was very different from the South African 'Nutcracker man', despite his powerful back teeth. **1974** WASHBURN & MOORE *Ape into Man* iv. 107 The huge molars..could have cracked nuts, and the Leakeys sometimes liked to call their discovery 'nutcracker man'.

Hence **ˈnutcracker** *v.*; **ˈnutcrackery** *a.*

1861 DICKENS *Gt. Expect.* xxxiii, Are infants to be nut-crackered into their tombs? *Ibid.*, Babies are to be nut-crackered dead. **1868** MISS BRADDON *Birds of Prey* I. i, An old lady who had been seen to arrive in a brougham, especially weird and nutcrackery of aspect.

ˈnut-cracking, *ppl. a.* [f. NUT *sb.*[1]] That cracks nuts; constructed so as to crack nuts.

1828 *Lights & Shades* I. 203 Nut-cracking human heads, and wax dolls with moveable eyes. **1842** *Penny Cycl.* XXII. 399/2 The type..intermediate between the tree-nesting and nut-cracking squirrels on the one hand and the burrowing and frugivorous *Tamias* on the other.

ˈnut-cut, *a. India.* [Hind. *naṭkhaṭ*.] Roguish. Also as *sb.*, a rogue, rascal.

1848 J. H. STOCQUELER *Oriental Interpreter* 175/2 *Nut-cut*, roguish, mischievous. A term of reproach, good-naturedly applied in India to *vauriens*. **1901** KIPLING *Kim.* iv. 107 'That is a *nut-cut* (rogue),' she said. 'All police-constables are *nut-cuts*; but the police-wallahs are the worst.'

†nute (also **nuten, -eth**), for *ne wite* know not: cf. NETE, NITEN, and NOT *v.*[2] *Obs.*

c **950** *Lindisf. Gosp.* Matt. xxi. 27 [Hia] ȝeondueardon ðæm hælende [and] cuedon, 'nutu we' [*c* **1000** we nyton, *Hatton* nyten]. *c* **1175** *Lamb. Hom.* 75 Alle ȝe kunnen..ower credo, þeh ȝe nuten nawiht alle hwat hit seið. *a* **1225** *Ancr. R.* 194 Þe oðre, þauh we habben ham ofte, we nuteð ham nout. *a* **1250** *Owl & Night.* 1010 Hi drinkeþ milc and wei þar to Hi nute elles wat hi do. *c* **1300** *St. Brandan* 286 This bred that we eteth nou we Nuteth whanne hit is.

† **'nutelness.** *Obs.* *rare*$^{-1}$. [repr. OE. **nytolnesse*, f. *ne* NE + *witol* knowing.] Ignorance.

c **1200** *Trin. Coll. Hom.* 73 Nutelnesse leteð þe mannes shrifte þe ne wot neure hwanne he sineȝeð, and swiche ben alle þo þe ne wilen listen lorspel.

'nut-gall. [f. NUT *sb.*[1] + GALL *sb.*[3]] A gall produced upon the Dyer's Oak (*Quercus infectoria*), used especially as a dye-stuff.

1595 DUNCAN *App. Etymol.* (E.D.S.) 69 *Galla*, a nutgall, or a sowters last. **1646** SIR T. BROWNE *Pseud. Ep.* 336 In this composition wee use only Nut-galles, that is an excrescence from the Oake. **1670–1** NARBOROUGH *Jrnl.* in *Acc. Sev. Late Voy.* I. (1694) 40 Small Nut-galls growing on the Bushes. **1716** CHEYNE *Phil. Princ. Nat. Relig.* I. 250 This we evidently see in Nutgals, and the other Excrescences of the Leaves of Vegetables. **1807** T. THOMSON *Chem.* (ed. 3) II. 351 Deyeux found, that a French pound of nutgalls required 96 French pints of water. **1870** YEATS *Nat. Hist. Comm.* 236 We receive nut-galls from Turkey, Greece, .. Hungary, and Sclavonia.

'nut-grass. [f. NUT *sb.*[1] + GRASS *sb.*] A small sedge of the genus *Cyperus*, esp. *C. rotundus*, whose roots form small nut-like tubers.

1775 B. ROMANS *Conc. Nat. Hist. Florida* 129 In Carolina it [sc. *herbe au cheval*] is called nutt grass from a nutt found at its root. **1830** LINDLEY *Nat. Syst. Bot.* 306 Cyperus Hydra is said by Dr. Hamilton to be a pest to the sugar-cane plantations of the West India Islands... The planters call it Nut Grass. **1857** A. GRAY *First Less. Bot.* (1866) 43 Tubers are produced, like those of the Nut-grass of the Southern States .. and of the Jerusalem Artichoke. **1860** DARLINGTON *Amer. Weeds*, etc. 359 *C. phymatodes*, 'Nut Grass' of Florida. *Ibid.* 360 *Hydra Cyperus*, 'Nut-grass' of S. Carolina. **1894** J. M. COULTER *Bot. W. Texas* III. 463 *Cyperus rotundus*... From the South Atlantic and Gulf States to the Texan coast... Often called 'nut grass'. **1903** 'S. RUDD' *Our New Selection* iv. 36 Nothing but burr and thistle and nut-grass grew. **1944** *Living off Land* ii. 42 The little bulbs of the onion weed (or nut grass). **1965** *Austral. Encycl.* VIII. 68/1 The latter species [sc. *Cyperus rotundus*], known as 'nut grass', is widely spread in warmer parts of the world (including Australia) and is a serious weed pest—probably the worst in areas where rice is extensively cultivated.

nuthatch ('nʌthætʃ). Forms: 4–5 **note-**, 5–6 **not-**; 5 **nutte-**, 5– **nut-**. Also 4 **-hache**, 5 **-hach**, 7 **-hatch** (9 **hatchet**); 5 **-hak(e**, **-hage**, 6 **-hagge**. [f. NUT *sb.*[1] The second element is connected with HACK *v.*[1], HAG *v.*[1], and HATCH *v.*[2], but the precise development of the forms is obscure.] A small creeping bird belonging to the genus *Sitta*, so named from the peculiar way in which it breaks nuts in order to feed on the kernel. The common British species is *S. cæsia*.

c **1340** *Nominale* (Skeat) 796 Wyldegos and notehache. **14..** *Lat.-Eng. Voc.* in Wr.-Wülcker 598 *Nucifragus*, a notehach. **14..** *Nom.* ibid. 702 *Hic ficedula*, a nuthage. *c* **1440** *Promp. Parv.* 359/1 Nothak, byrde, *picus*. ? *c* **1475** *Sqr. lowe Degre* 55 The nuthake with her notes newe. **1530** PALSGR. 248/2 Nothagge, a byrde, *jaye*.

1668 WILKINS *Real Char.* II. v. §4. 147 To the second sort of the Woodpecker kind, those other Birds may be reduced, which are .. called Nuthatch. **1678** RAY *Willughby's Ornith.* 142 The Nuthatch or Nutjobber. **1752** HILL *Hist. Anim.* 503 *Sitta*, the Nuthatch; it is frequent with us. **1768** PENNANT *Brit. Zool.* I. 185 The nuthatch weighs near an ounce. **1799** SOUTHEY *The Filbert* Wks. (1845) 164/1 Him may the Nut-hatch, piercing with strong bill, Unwittingly destroy. **1802** MONTAGU *Ornith. Dict.* (1831) 341 The Nuthatch is more expert in climbing than the wood-pecker. **1854** *Orr's Circ. Sci.*, *Org. Nat.* I. 150 The nut-hatch utters a loud call, which may be heard at a considerable distance, resembling *grew, deck, deck*. **1894** NEWTON *Dict. Birds* 648 Corsica has a Nuthatch peculiar to itself and remarkable for its black crown.

† **'nuthen,** *adv. Obs. rare.* In 3 **nuþen, nuðen.** [f. *nu* NOW + THEN. Cf. NOWTHE.] Now.

a **1225** *St. Marher.* 21 For þi deorewurðe nome ich habbe idrohen nowcin ant nume deað nuðen. *c* **1275** *Wom. Samaria* 56 in *O.E. Misc.* 85 Þe king þat wurþ, and nuþen is, and euer yete was.

nuther, dial. variant of NOTHER *conj.*

nuthin ('nʌθɪn). Repr. of a colloq. pronunc. of NOTHING *sb.*

1925 E. O'NEILL *Desire under Elms* I. 69 Oceans o' trouble an' nuthin' but wuk fur reward. **1968** R. CLAPPERTON *No News on Monday* vi. 73 Course I never said nuthin'. **1968** A. DIMENT *Bang Bang Birds* x. 181 Don't you cats know nuthin' about acid? **1971** *Black World* Oct. 64/2 So I don't say nuthin'. **1973** 'J. PATRICK' *Glasgow Gang Observed* v. 51 Ah *hate* somewan in a company who disnae say nuthin'.

'nut-hook. Also 4 **nutthocke.** [f. NUT *sb.*[1] + HOOK *sb.*[1]] A hooked stick used by persons when nutting, in order to pull down the branches of the trees. Also *fig.*

? *a* **1500** *Chester Pl., Adoration Sheph.* (E.E.T.S.) 157 To pull downe peares, appells, and plomes .. I geue thie here my nvtthocke. **1618** HOLYDAY *Marriages Arts* III. vi, I will make this Verse like a Nut-hooke, like a Nut-hooke—and then pull downe—pull down the Moone with it. **1631** DEKKER *Match me in Lond.* I. C 2 b, She's the Kings nut-hooke .., that when any Filbert-tree is ripe, puls down the brauest bowes to his hand. **1724** STUKELY in Hone *Everyday Bk.* (1825) I. 717 The family reaching them victuals with the nut-hook.

† **b.** Applied to a beadle, constable, etc. *Obs.*

1597 SHAKS. *2 Hen. IV*, v. iv. 8 Nut-hooke, nut-hooke, you Lye. **1598** —— *Merry W.* I. i. 171, I will say marry trap with you, if you runne the nut-hooks humor on me. *a* **1658** CLEVELAND *Count. Com. Man* Poems (1677) 99 A Sequestratour! He is the Devil's Nut-hook, the Sign with him is always in the Clutches.

'nutjobber. Now *dial.* [f. NUT *sb.*[1] + JOBBER *sb.*[1]] = NUTHATCH.

1544 TURNER *Avium Præcip.* I 3, *Sitta, Anglicè* a nut iobber. **1580** HOLLYBAND *Treas. Fr. Tong, Grimpereau*, a little bird making warre against the Egle, as Robin red brest, some do call that birde a nut iobber. **1655** MOUFET & BENNET *Health's Improv.* (1746) 185 The little Pyet, which we call a Nutjobber. **1678** [see NUTHATCH]. **1713** *Phil. Trans.* XXVIII. 170 The Nut-hatch, or Nut-jobber, is not frequently to be met with in the South. **1840** *Penny Cycl.* XVI. 372/1 *Sitta Europæa*, the Common Nuthatch, or Nutjobber. **1885** SWAINSON *Prov. Names Birds* 35 Nut-hatch, .. Nutjobber (Berks).

'nutlet. [f. NUT *sb.*[1] + -LET.] A small nut.

1856 A. GRAY *Man. Bot.* (1860) 319 A deeply 4-lobed ovary .., which forms in fruit 4 little seed-like nutlets. **1873** MOGGERIDGE *Harvesting Ants*, etc. 18 In this manner .. entire calyces, containing the nutlets of Calaminth, are gathered. **1899** C. REID *Orig. Brit. Flora* 135 The small size of its nutlets having caused it to be overlooked till specially searched for.

nutmeg ('nʌtmɛg). Forms: *α.* 4 **notemugge** (5 **not-**), 4–5 **-mug(e** (4 **notte-**), 5 **noot-, notmoge**; 4–5 **nutemug(e**, 5 **nutmuge, -muke**, 9 *dial.* **-mug**, *Sc.* **netmug.** *β.* 5 **not(e)mygge, notmyg**; 6 **nutmygge, -migge (nutte-), -mig.** *γ.* 6 **not(e)meg; nutte-, nutmegge, nutmege**, 6– **nutmeg**, 9 *Sc.* **nitmeg.** [A partial translation of OF. or AF. **nois mugue* or *muge* (f. *nois* nut, and *mugue*, *muge* musk), an unrecorded variant of the common OF. *nois mug(u)ede*, *mug(u)ete*, *muguette*, *musguette*, also *muscade*, *muscate* (mod.F. *noix muscade*), = Prov. *notz muscada*, Sp. *nuez moscada*, It. *noce moscada*, med.L. *nux muscāta*, f. late L. *muscus* MUSK. The common Romanic type is directly represented by MDu. *note muscate* (Du. *muskaatnoot*), MHG. *muscâtnuȥ* (G. *-nuss*), Sw. *muskotnöt*, Da. *muskatnöd*.]

1. a. A hard aromatic seed, of spheroidal form and about an inch in length, obtained from the fruit of an evergreen tree (*Myristica fragrans* or *officinalis*) indigenous to the Molucca and other East Indian islands, and largely used as a spice and in medicine.

Inferior kinds are also obtained from other species of *Myristicaceæ* in various parts of the world; and with distinguishing epithets, as *American*, *Brazilian*, *Peruvian*, the name is occasionally applied to the produce of trees belonging to other genera.

α. **13..** *K. Alis.* 6792 Notemugge, and the sedewale, On heom smullith. *c* **1386** CHAUCER *Sir Thopas* 52 The licorys and the cetewale, And many a clow gilofre, And notemuge to put in ale. *c* **1400** MAUNDEV. (Roxb.) xxi. 94 Clowes, canell, nutemuges, macez... Þe macez er þe huskes of þe nutemug. *c* **1440** *Anc. Cookery* in *Househ. Ordin.* (1790) 473 Take clowes, maces, spikenarde, nutmukes. **1483** *Cath. Angl.* 257/2 A Nut muge, *nux muscata*. **1877** *Holderness Gloss.*, *Nutmug*, a nutmeg.

β. ? *a* **1366** CHAUCER *Rom. Rose* 1361 Trees there were gret foisoun, That baren notes in her sesoun, Such as men notemygges calle. *c* **1440** *Promp. Parv.* 359/2 Notemygge, *nux muscata*. **1481** CAXTON *Myrr.* II. x. 90 Other trees there growe .. that bere notemygges. **1541** ELYOT *Cast. Helthe* 27 b, Nutmigges with their swete odour comforte and dissolue. **1544** PHAER *Regim. Lyfe* (1553) B viij b, Ye must vse euery daye to eate Nuttemigges. **1570** LEVINS *Manip.* 119 A Nutmig, *nux myristica*.

γ. *c* **1515** *Test Ebor.* (Surtees) V. 68 For notmegys j*d.* **1542** BOORDE *Dyetary* xxii. (1870) 287 Nutmeges be good for them the whiche haue colde in theyr hed. **1578** LYTE *Dodoens* 221 The rootes are like a couple of Nutmegges. **1620** VENNER *Via Recta* ii. 44 Take .. of Nutmegs and Cynamon of each halfe an ounce. **1688** HOLME *Armoury* II. 77/2 The Nutmeg hath the middle broad, the ends sharp and bending like a waved leaf. **1731–8** SWIFT *Pol. Conversat.* 97 If you carry a Nutmeg in your Pocket, you'll certainly be marry'd to an old Man. **1768** *Med. Observ. & Inq.* (ed. 2) IV. 3 The bigness of a nutmeg of a digestive .. was mixed with the former poultice. **1849** BALFOUR *Man. Bot.* §996 It is said that a single tree will yield on an average about six pounds of nutmegs. **1870** YEATS *Nat. Hist. Comm.* 144 The mace and the nutmeg are both valuable spices.

b. ***wooden nutmeg***, anything false or fraudulent; a fraud, cheat, deception. *U.S.*

The story to which the phrase alludes is related by Haliburton ('Sam Slick') in the *Clockmaker* (1836) Ser. I. viii. See also *Nutmeg State* in 5 below.

1830 GALT *Lawrie T.* II. i, 'I reckon, Squire Lawrie,' said he [a Vermont farmer], 'is a puffing of a parley voo, but I sells no wooden nutmegs'. **1871** DE VERE *Americanisms* 620 In the press and Congress wooden nutmegs have to answer for forged telegrams, political tricks, and falsified election-returns.

2. a. ***nutmeg-tree***, the tree (see above) which produces the nutmeg.

1594 BLUNDEVIL *Exerc.* v. xi. (1636) 554 The Nutmegge tree groweth in the Ile of Bada, and differeth not much from the Peach tree. **1681** GREW *Musæum* IV. §iii. 376 The Nutmeg-Tree: Together with a Branch of the same after the life. **1712** tr. *Pomet's Hist. Drugs* I. 127 These Isles are so stock'd with Nutmeg-Trees, that it is almost incredible. **1779** FORREST *Voy. N. Guinea* 106 Went again to Long Island, in quest of the nutmeg tree. **1861** BENTLEY *Man. Bot.* 633 The Nutmeg tree bears pear-shaped fruits, commonly about the size of an ordinary peach.

b. ***nutmeg-grater*** (see GRATER[1] I).

1695 CONGREVE *Love for L.* II. iii, About a little nutmeg-grater, which she had forgot in the caudlecup. **1705** *Lond. Gaz.* No. 4154/4 Stolen .., a Nutmeg-Grater. **1806–7** J. BERESFORD *Miseries Hum. Life* IX. lvii, Just as if you were swallowing a nutmeg-grater three and a half yards long. **1847** *Nat. Cycl.* II. 882 Plates of iron perforated .. so as to resemble a nutmeg-grater.

Comb. **1899** *Allbutt's Syst. Med.* VIII. 664 Conical projections, which give almost a nutmeg-grater-like sensation to the hand when passed over it.

3. Employed as a distinguishing name for varieties of apples, pears, peaches, etc.

1664 EVELYN *Kal. Hort.* July 70 Fruits in Prime, .. Peaches, Nutmeg, Isabella, Persian. *Ibid.* Aug. 72 Plums, .. White Nutmeg, late Pear-plum. **1731** MILLER *Gard. Dict.* s.v. *Persica*, The White Nutmeg .. is the first ripe Peach. *Ibid.*, The Red Nutmeg is .. somewhat larger than the white. **1766** *Compl. Farmer* s.v. *Peach-tree* 5 Y 1/1 The white nutmeg peach, this is ripe in July. 2. The red nutmeg, this ripens about the beginning of August. **1822** J. WOODS *2 Yrs. Res. Eng. Prairie Illinois* 307 There are many sorts of sweet melons... I have only noticed musk, of a large size; and nutmeg, a smaller one. **1860** HOGG *Fruit Man.* 5 Cockle Pippin (Nutmeg Pippin). *Ibid.* 168 Bezi de Caissoy .. (Nutmeg; .. Winter Poplin).

4. a. Used to denote colour or appearance.

c **1610** MIDDLETON, etc. *Widow* II. i, He in the nutmeg-colour'd band. **1687** *Lond. Gaz.* No. 2218/4 A new fashionable Suit near a Nutmeg colour. **1689** *Ibid.* No. 2422/4 Stolen .., a well shaped Nutmeg grey Stone Nag. **1745** *Daily Advertiser* 28 Sept. 4/1 Two Mares, one a Roan or Nutmeg colour'd Mare. **1865** *Morn. Star* 22 Feb., Liver very large and of nutmeg appearance. **1876** BRISTOWE *Th. & Pract. Med.* (1878) 797 The liver may consequently present something of the nutmeg character.

b. ***nutmeg liver***, a diseased condition of the liver, also called *red atrophy*. (Cf. NUTMEGGY.)

1876 BRISTOWE *Th. & Pract. Med.* (1878) 742 The simple induration and congestion which constitute the 'nutmeg liver' may have the same effect. **1897** *Allbutt's Syst. Med.* IV. 121 Sometimes the liver was nutmeg.

5. Misc. combs., as ***nutmeg boletus***, ***butter***, ***oil***, ***plantation***, ***rock***, ***trade***, ***tribe***; **nutmeg-apple**, the fruit of the nutmeg-tree, containing the mace and nutmeg; **nutmeg-bird**, **-cowrie**, **-finch**, **-flower**, **-pigeon**, **State**, **-wood** (see quots.); **nutmeg hickory**, a species of hickory, *Carya myristicæformis*, bearing a fruit resembling a nutmeg and found in southern North America.

1871 KINGSLEY *At Last* v, Here and there a *nutmeg-apple has split, and shows within the delicate crimson caul of mace. **1888** NEWTON in *Encycl. Brit.* XXIV. 463 *Nutmeg-birds. **1894** —— *Dict. Birds* 648 *Nutmeg bird*, the dealers' name in common use for *Munia punctulata*, but apparently of somewhat recent origin. **1899** A. H. EVANS *Birds* 577 *M*[*unia*] *punctulata*, the Cowry- or Nutmeg-bird, is brown with white streaks above and spots below. **1819** *Pantologia* VIII. s.v. *Myristica*, The soil on which any large quantity of this is deposited shoots forth very speedily a *nutmeg-boletus, or mushroom. **1857** MILLER *Elem. Chem.*, *Org.* (1862) 260 Palm oil, *nutmeg butter, and cocoa-nut oil, each contain a different solid fatty acid. **1884** *Encycl. Brit.* XVII. 666/2 Nutmeg butter is a solid fatty substance of a reddish-brown colour, obtained by grinding the refuse nutmegs to a fine powder. **1815** BURROW *Conchol.* 198 *Cypræa Arabica*, *Nutmeg Cowry. **1881** *Proc. Zool. Soc.* 1002 *Nutmeg-Finch (Munia undulata). **1846–50** A. WOOD *Class-bk. Bot.* 149 *N*[*igella*] *Sativa*, *Nutmeg Flower .., From Egypt. **1810** F. A. MICHAUX *Hist. Arbres Forestiers de l'Amérique Septentrionale* I. 21 *Nutmeg hickory nut .., nom donné par moi. **1832** D. J. BROWNE *Sylva Amer.* 177 This species .. bears the name of Nutmeg Hickory from the resemblance of its fruits to that of the nutmeg. **1901** C. T. MOHR *Plant Life Alabama* 101 The nutmeg hickory, when full grown, resembles the shagbark hickory in its pale, shreddy bark. **1951** *Dict. Gardening* (R. Hort. Soc.) I. 404/2 Nutmeg Hickory. Tree 80 to 100 ft., shoots covered with yellowish, glossy scales... Nut ovoid, sweet, its shell hard and furrowed like a nutmeg. **1849** tr. *Mulder's Chem. Veg. & Anim. Phys.* 818 The greater number of fats .. may therefore in this respect be compared with the stearopt of *nutmeg oil, $C^{16} H^{16} O^{5}$. **1891** THORPE *Dict. Appl. Chem.* II. 712 Nutmeg-oil (syn. Oil of Mace) .. is extracted by bruising the fruit and submitting the paste to the action of steam. **1895** LYDDEKER *Royal Nat. Hist.* IV. 368 The *Nutmeg-pigeon (*Carpophaga ænea*) common in the Indo-Burmese countries, Ceylon, and the Andamans. This bird .. lives on fruit, especially the wild nutmeg. *Ibid.* 369 The white nutmeg pigeon .. is a handsome species found in the Philippine Islands [etc.]. **1800** *Asiat. Ann. Reg.* 217/2 The general idleness, and consequent neglect of the *nut-meg plantations. **1864** TENNYSON *Voyage* 40 Where those long swells of breaker sweep The *nutmeg rocks and isles of clove. **1859** BARTLETT *Dict. Amer.* (ed. 2) 298 **Nutmeg State*, a nickname given to the State of Connecticut, in allusion to the story that wooden nutmegs are there manufactured for exportation. **1819** *Pantologia* VIII. s.v. *Myristica*, The chief *nutmeg trade lies at Ceylon. **1830** LINDLEY *Introd. Bot.* 23 *Myristiceæ*, the *Nutmeg Tribe. **1866** *Treas. Bot.*, **Nutmeg-wood*, the wood of the Palmyra palm, *Borassus flabelliformis*.

'nutmegged, *a.* [f. prec. + -ED[2].]

1. Flavoured with nutmeg.

1743 *Lond. & Country Brew.* IV. (ed. 2) 305 Bake a Rye Loaf well nutmegg'd of two pence price. **1770** WARTON *Oxford Newsman's Verses*, Your hospitable board With cold sirloin is amply stor'd, And old October, nutmeg'd nice.

2. *Path.* Affected with red atrophy.

1879 *St. George's Hosp. Rep.* IX. 149 Liver nutmegged. Apoplectic patches in the lungs.

So **'nutmeggy** *a.*

1843 SIR T. WATSON *Princ. & Pract. Physic* II. lxxv. 519 Again and again have I met with the nutmeggy liver, strongly marked. **1871** *Ibid.* (ed. 5) II. lxix. 670 What used to be called the 'nutmeggy' liver, is simply the result of congestion of its blood-vessels. **1928** *Daily Express* 17 Feb.

4 Luscious prunes with a creamy, nutmeggy rice pudding. **1971** *Daily Tel.* 17 Apr. 7 A large proportion of the bed could be occupied by.. Cherry Pic, which has a warm nutty, almost 'nutmeggy' scent, spicy and yet sweet.

'nut-oil. [Cf. Du. *nootolie* (MDu. *noit-*), Sw. *nötolja*, G. *nussöl*.] Oil obtained from nut-kernels, esp. those of the hazel and walnut, largely used in the manufacture of paints, varnishes, etc.

1664 EVELYN *Sylva* 95 For this [polishing] Lin-seed, or the sweeter Nut-oyl does the effect best. **1807** T. THOMSON *Chem.* (ed. 3) II. 445 Nut-oil has been found preferable to all other oils for printers ink. **1839** URE *Dict. Arts* 897 *Nut oil*, is at first greenish coloured, but becomes pale yellow by time. **1873** SPON *Workshop Rec.* Ser. I. 102/1 Nut oil is more uncertain in its qualities than either linseed or poppy oil.

†**nutrate.** *Obs. rare.* = NUTRATIVE b.

The form may orig. be due to copying from a French text which had *nutratis* for *nutratifs*.

1548–77 VICARY *Anat.* viii. (1888) 62 The Midriffe was ordeyned..[to] diuide the spirituals from the nutrates. *Ibid.*, The malicious fumes reared vp from the nutrates.

†**'nutrative,** obs. variant of NUTRITIVE *a.*

1536 BELLENDEN *Chron. Scot.*, *Vertue & Vice* vii, Ane plesand meid, Quhaire flora maid the tender blewmys to speid Throw kindlie dew and humouris nutratiue. **1562** BULLEIN *Bulwarke, Bk. Simples* 14 b, If they be swete thei be partly nutrative, and warme the bodie.

b. *sb.* in *pl.* The organs which supply nourishment to the body. (Cf. NUTRATE.)

1548–77 VICARY *Anat.* viii. (1888) 64 They were ordeyned..that they shuld defend yᵉ nutratiues outwardly.

nutria ('njuːtrɪə). [a. Sp. *nutria* otter, also *lutria* = F. *loutre*, It. *lontra*:—L. *lutra*.] The skin or fur of the coypu of South America. Hence also, a mid-brown colour such as that of the nutria fur.

1836 W. IRVING *Astoria* III. 278 Nutria, Vicunia, Chinchilla and a few deer skins. **1837** *Penny Cycl.* VIII. 125/2 The skins..are imported into Great Britain..under the name of Neutria or Nutria skins. **1897** *Sears, Roebuck Catal.* 234/1 Ranch Hats... Colors, light nutria or tan. **1902** *Brit. Med. Jrnl.* 377 The shorter finer hairs in the fur of the rabbit, hare, musk rat, nutria [etc.]. **1923** *Daily Mail* 26 Mar. 6 Colours: Gold, Grey,..Nutria, Putty. **1949** *Brit. Colour Council Dict. Colours Int. Decoration* III. 19/1 *Nutria*, a colour selected in consultation with expert furriers and standardized by B.C.C. in 1934.

nutri'bility. *rare.* [See next and -ITY.] Capacity of receiving nutriment.

1684 T. BURNET *The. Earth* II. iv. 206 That disposition whereby they are capable of receiving nourishment, which we may call Nutribility. *Ibid.* 207 The Nutribility of the Body depends upon a certain temperament in the parts.

†**'nutrible,** *a.* *rare*⁻¹. [ad. late L. *nūtrībilis*, f. *nūtrīre*: see -IBLE.] Nutritious.

1607 TOPSELL *Four-f. Beasts* (1658) 525 Swines flesh also is lesse excremental.., and therefore more nutrible.

†**nutri'cation.** *Obs. rare.* [ad. late L. *nūtrīcātiōn-em*, noun of action f. *nūtrīcāre* to nourish.] Nourishment.

1623 COCKERAM I, *Nutrication*, nourishing. **1646** SIR T. BROWNE *Pseud. Ep.* 158 Beside the teeth, the tongue of this animall is a second argument to overthrow this airie nutrication. **1657** TOMLINSON *Renou's Disp.* 494 Animals..tend..to the nutrication of our bodies.

nutrice. *rare.* [ad. L. *nūtrīcem*, *nūtrix*: see NOURICE.] Nurse.

1547 J. HARRISON *Exhort. Scottes* 232 Of me your mother, your nutryce, and your bringer vp. **1880** *Times* 19 Aug. 4 Indicative of the character of the goddess as the nutrice of all the created nature.

nutriceptor ('njuːtrɪsɛptə(r)). *Immunol.* [f. *nutri-* (in *nutrient*, *nutrition*, etc., or L. *nūtrīment-um*, etc.) + RE)CEPTOR.] (See quot. 1926.)

1911 *Jrnl. Amer. Med. Assoc.* 7 Oct. 1210/2 According to Ehrlich's view, when a parasite becomes refractory to an immune serum it does so by developing new groups of receptors..these receptors being the same receptors as combine with the food materials, and hence called 'nutriceptors'. **1926** R. J. E. SCOTT *Gould's Med. Dict.* 907/2 *Nutriceptors*, Ehrlich's name for receptors which react with foodstuffs more or less exclusively, and which therefore serve the nutrition of the cell. **1932** [see CHEMOCEPTOR].

nutricious, obs. form of NUTRITIOUS.

nutrient ('njuːtrɪənt), *a.* and *sb.* [ad. L. *nūtrient-em*, pres. pple. of *nūtrīre* to nourish.]

A. *adj.* **1.** Serving as nourishment; possessing nutrimental qualities.

1661 LOVELL *Hist. Anim. & Min.* 374 A tumour..caused by humours carried out with the nutrient bloud. **1825** *Blackw. Mag.* XVII. 532 They both did hang On the same breast, and drew the nutrient stream From the same fount. **1844** *Proc. Berw. Nat. Club* II. No. 12. 108 The old tree [is] thus bereft of its few remaining drops of nutrient aliment. **1876** BRISTOWE *Th. & Pract. Med.* (1878) 79 Do the decaying tissues attract them to themselves from the blood or extra-vascular nutrient fluid?

2. Conveying or providing nourishment.

1650 BULWER *Anthropomet.* 171 By how much the Practique intellect is more noble then the Nutrient soul. **1798** ABERNETHY in *Phil. Trans.* LXXXVIII. 106 The plethoric state of the nutrient vessels of the heart. **1804** —— *Surg. Obs.* 28 Some principal nutrient artery will afterwards be met with. **1861** J. R. GREENE *Man. Anim. Kingd.*, *Cœlent.* 222 The little yet known of the development of the nutrient apparatus in the *Ctenophora*.

B. *sb.* **1.** A nutritious substance.

1828–32 in WEBSTER. **1880** *Med. Temp. Jrnl.* July 174 It is not always that nutrients can be taken in sufficient quantity. **1899** *Bull. Div. Veg. Physiol. & Path.* (U.S. Dept. Agric.) XVIII. 6 We can accept it as an indisputable fact that mineral matters found in plants also are real nutrients for them. **1903** H. SNYDER *Chem. Plant & Anima Life* xxxvi. 344 A balanced ration is one which contains a sufficient amount of nutrients from a variety of foods to meet the requirements of the animal. **1924** *Bot. Gaz.* LXXXVII. 121 (*heading*) Absorption of nutrients from sub-soil in relation to crop yield. **1974** *Encycl. Brit. Macropædia* XIII. 403/2 Carbon dioxide (CO_2) and water (H_2O)..are important nutrients for all organisms. *Ibid.* 407/2 Lists of nutrients—both organic and inorganic—required by plants and animals. *Ibid.*, Essential nutrients include many amino acids, some fatty acids, many vitamins, and some minerals and trace elements.

2. Comb. ***nutrient-poor***, ***-rich*** adjs.

1946 *Nature* 21 Sept. 421/2 In the nutrient-rich waters of the Thames type, a burst of algal growth may sometimes cease before any serious depletion of the mineral nutrient in the water has apparently taken place. **1955** *New Biol.* XVIII. 115 *N. alba* occupies a wide range of waters in the British Isles, from the oligotrophic, or nutrient-poor, peat-bottomed moorland lakes in Scotland and Ireland, to the eutrophic, or nutrient-rich, fen-lodes and broads of East Anglia. **1967** *Oceanogr. & Marine Biol.* V. 108 Massive upward displacement of nutrient-rich water on to the shelf may occur a few times in a century.

nutrify ('njuːtrɪfaɪ), *v.* [f. L. *nūtr-īre* to nourish + -(I)FY.] **a.** *trans.* To nourish. Also *fig.* **b.** *intr.* To supply nutriment.

1509 HAWES *Past. Pleas.* xvi. (Percy Soc.) 73 In which the golde is truely nutryfyde. *Ibid.* xx. 95 His propre death him selfe he nutrifyed. **1542** BOORDE *Dyetary* xi. (1870) 259 The whiche haue ben nourisshed or nutryfyde with suche breade. **1595** CHAPMAN *Banq. Sence* (1639) 3 And with fit foode her Plants did nutrifie. *c* **1645** HOWELL *Lett.* (1655) II. lv. 71 The wine..doth not only breed good bloud, but it nutrifieth also. **1879** *Expositor* IX. 83 That which in one quietly and pleasantly nutrifies, in another deranges and defiles.

nutriment ('njuːtrɪmənt). [ad. L. *nūtrīment-um*, f. *nūtrīre* to nourish: see -MENT. So F. *nutriment*, It. and Sp. *nutri-*, *nudrimento*.]

1. That which nourishes; food, nourishment; nourishing food.

1541 ELYOT *Cast. Helthe* 38 b, Than must be withdrawen and minished some parte of that nutriment. **1558** BP. WATSON *Sev. Sacram.* vii. 36 Our dayly and special nutrimentes of breade and wyne. *a* **1610** HEALEY *Cebes* (1636) 134 Now hee..purgeth away the causes and nutriment of the maladie. **1667** MILTON *P.L.* v. 496 From these corporal nutriments perhaps Your bodies may at last turn all to Spirit. **1724–5** SWIFT *Rec. to restore Stella's Youth*, The Nutriment will from within Round all your Body plump your Skin. **1795** BURKE *On Scarcity* Wks. VII. 384 It is impossible that he should continue that abundant nutriment. **1855** BAIN *Senses & Int.* I. ii. §24 The action of the nutriment supplied to the body.

b. Without article.

1607 TOPSELL *Four-f. Beasts* (1658) 358 All hard things which are dissolved with difficulty, do retain their force of nutriment longer. **1667** MILTON *P.L.* VII. 408 Or in thir Pearlie shells at ease, attend Moist nutriment. **1751** JOHNSON *Rambler* No. 85 ¶5 Observing the proportion between nutriment and labour, and keeping the body in a healthy state. **1821** BYRON *Sardanap.* I. ii, They banqueted upon your gods, And died for lack of further nutriment. **1881** MIVART *Cat* 22 It..both helps to keep the body warm and serves as a store of nutriment.

c. In figurative applications.

1612 ROWLANDS *Knave of Harts* (Hunterian Cl.) 29, I feede on euils, they are my nutriment. **1624** GATAKER *Transubst.* 160 The bread and wine themselves are signes of spirituall nutriment, not nutrition. **1726** SWIFT *Stella's Birthday*, Is not Virtue in Mankind The Nutriment, that feeds the Mind? **1791** COWPER *Four Ages* 36 Myst'ries are food for angels; they digest With ease, and find them nutriment. **1849** ROBERTSON *Serm.* Ser. I. ii. (1866) 22 In the soil of the heart is found all the nutriment of spiritual life. **1873** DIXON *Two Queens* I. i. I. 2 To feel that Homer and Thucydides might yield them richer nutriment than any of their Lives of Saints.

†**2.** The act of nourishing or fostering. *Obs.*⁻¹

1535 CROMWELL in Merriman *Life & Lett.* (1902) I. 437 The contynuaunce and nutryment of discorde and trouble amonge the kings subieetts.

nutrimental (njuːtrɪ'mɛntəl), *a.* [ad. late L. *nūtrīmentāl-is*: see prec. and -AL¹.] Having the qualities of nutriment or food; nutritious, nourishing; also, conveying nourishment.

1483 CAXTON *Gold. Leg.* 231/3 Thre thynges ben founden in seed germynyng, that is to wete, natural hete, humour nutrimental, and reson of seed. **1495** *Trevisa's Barth. De P.R.* XVII. xx, The humoure nutrimentall of boxe is full gleymy and cleuynge togyders. **1548–77** VICARY *Anat.* ii. (1888) 21 The Veyne is a vessel of blood nutrimental. **1578** BANISTER *Hist. Man.* I. 22 Their holes likewise..give entraunce..to the nutrimentall vesselles. **1656** RIDGLEY *Pract. Physick* 301 It may be made from nutrimental Juyce, thickned and hardned. *c* **1682** J. COLLINS *Salt & Fishery* 68 It..consumes the goodness or nutrimental part of the Meat. **1747** HARVEY *Medit. & Contemp.* (1818) 367 His bounty covers the fields with a profusion of nutrimental treasure. **1828** *Blackw. Mag.* XXIII. 589 Mutton broth, that exquisite, assuaging, nutrimental luxury. **1901** *Law Jrnl.* 15 June 314/1 Certain nutrimental combinations have to be plainly labelled..by the seller.

†**nutrimented,** *a.* *Obs. rare.* [Cf. prec. and -ED¹.] With *well*: Well-bred.

1590 GREENE *Orl. Fur.* (1599) 13 Come hither my well nutrimented knaue, whom takest thou me to be? **1594** ? GREENE *Selimus* Wks. (Grosart) XIV. 267 A good well nutrimented lad.

†**nutrimentive,** *a.* *Obs.* [f. NUTRIMENT + -IVE.] = NUTRIMENTAL.

1610 W. FOLKINGHAM *Art of Survey* I. x. 24 It pinguifies the soyle, and imparts to the seede some secret nutrimentiue power. **1633** T. NASH *Quaternio* 45 The chyle, and what part thereof is nutrimentiue. **1683** TRYON *Way to Health* 197 It must be confessed that the Nutrimentive Quality is contained in the fine Flour.

†**nutrite,** *v.* *Obs. rare*⁻¹. [f. ppl. stem of L. *nūtrīre*.] *trans.* (See NUTRITION I c.)

1657 TOMLINSON *Renou's Disp.* 703 Lithargie should be levigated in Oyl, and nutrited on a slow fire.

†**nu'tritial,** *a.* *Obs. rare.* [f. L. *nūtrīti-us*: see -AL¹.] Connected with nursing or rearing.

1616 CHAPMAN *Homer's Hymn Diana* 2 Diana..had nutritiall rights With her borne-Brother, the farr-shooting Sunn. **1650** BULWER *Anthropomet.* 83 These Nutritial Eunuches did conform the Nose..with Leaden Plates.

nutrition (njuː'trɪʃən). [ad. L. type **nūtrītiōn-em*, noun of action f. *nūtrīre* to nourish. So F. *nutrition*, Sp. *nutricion*, It. *nutrizione*.]

1. a. The action or process of supplying, or of receiving, nourishment.

1615 CROOKE *Body of Man* 727 The bowels are mostwhat alike in all, both for Nutrition, Generation, Life and Sense. **1682** GREW *Anat. Pl.* Introd. 3 All these being formed, by continual Nutrition still to be increased. **1704** F. FULLER *Med. Gymn.* (1711) 24 That the Spirits..are concern'd in Nutrition is plain enough. **1803** MALTHUS *Popul.* IV. i. (1806) II. 304 The kind of food, and the mode of preparing it, best suited to the purposes of nutrition. **1845** DAY tr. *Simon's Anim. Chem.* I. 161 The metamorphosis of the plasma during the nutrition of every form of tissue. **1896** *Allbutt's Syst. Med.* I. 178 Nutrition and functional activity are interdependent, the two falling off together.

b. In figurative uses.

1551 CRANMER *Answ. Gardiner* 42 Our spiritual generation and our spiritual nutrition be..obscure and hyd vnto vs. **1624** GATAKER *Transubst.* 160 The spirituall nutrition of soules living by grace. **1651** HOBBES *Leviath.* II. xxiv. 127 The Nutrition of a Common-wealth consisteth, in the Plenty, and Distribution of Materials conducing to Life. **1879** *Fortn. Rev.* Nov. 687 The self-preservative instinct of humanity rejects such art as does not contribute to its intellectual nutrition and moral sustenance.

†**c.** (See quot., and cf. NUTRITE *v.*) *Obs. rare.*

1612 WOODALL *Surg. Mate* Wks. (1653) 273 *Nutrition* is the permission of humidity by little and little, for the alteration of the quality of the medicament. **1727–38** [see NUTRITUM].

2. That which nourishes; food, nutriment.

1603 HOLLAND *Plutarch's Mor.* 671 Any thing that hath the nature of the superfluity or excrement of nutrition. *c* **1611** CHAPMAN *Iliad* XIII. 298 Aiax..to none alive will yeeld..whose life takes Ceres nutritions. **1732** POPE *Ess. Man* II. 64 Fix'd like a plant on his peculiar spot, To draw nutrition, propagate, and rot. **1758** J. WOOD *Suppl. to Treat. Farriery* 25 A Putrefaction of the stagnated Juices, whence the Parts are essentially deprived of all manner of Nutrition. **1868** PEARD *Water-farm.* ix. 97 These articles of nutrition materially assist the growth of the infant brood. **1894** H. DRUMMOND *Ascent Man* 272 Chemistry is devoting itself to the experiment of manufacturing nutrition.

Hence **nu'tritional** *a.*; **nu'tritionally** *adv.*; **nu'tritionary** *a.*

a **1852** MACGILLIVRAY *Nat. Hist. of Dee Side* (1855) 462 That general condition of nutritionary activity, which is produced by the development of the reproductive powers of the system. **1869** E. A. PARKES *Pract. Hygiene* (ed. 3) 493 That these acids are most important nutritional agents no one can doubt. **1878** T. BRYANT *Pract. Surg.* I. 558 Incapable of further growth or nutritional change. **1890** *Cent. Dict.*, Nutritionally. **1922** *Sci. Amer.* July 42/3 A diet may furnish a sufficient amount of protein, fat, carbohydrates, salts and vitamins and yet fail to promote growth or sustain well-being unless the quality of protein is nutritionally adequate. **1949** M. MEAD *Male & Female* x. 215 Foods all of which are suitable nutritionally. **1972** *Which?* Sept. 263/2 Nutritionally, there is not much difference between dairy and non-dairy [ice cream].

nutritionalist (njuː'trɪʃənəlɪst). [f. NUTRITIONAL *a.* + -IST.] = next.

1956 *Nature* 24 Mar. 565/2 The importance of close co-operation between chemists, pharmacologists, biochemists and nutritionalists in this field cannot be over-emphasized. **1971** *Islander* (Victoria, B.C.) 9 May 14/3 Steers a clear course through conflicting nutritionalists' claims to a reasonable assessment of the nation's dietary practices.

nutritionist (njuː'trɪʃənɪst). [f. NUTRITION + -IST.] One who studies, or is knowledgeable about, food and nutrition, esp. of humans.

1926 *University of State of N.Y. Bull. to Schools* June 261/2 Dentists, dental hygienists and nutritionists, when employed, are required to assist the medical inspector. **1936** *Nature* 31 Oct. 744/2 That highly trained specialist, the nutritionist—who, to be competent, must needs use the methods not only of chemistry and physics but also those of the various biological sciences. **1959** *New Biol.* XXX. 106 Animal nutritionists also have considered the possibility that traces of boron may be required in the vertebrate diet. **1969** *Daily Tel.* 21 Nov. 17/1 Until recently, nutritionists and health experts focused their attention on expectant mothers, babies and adolescents. **1973** *Nature* 27 Apr. 593/2 Few nutritionists are interested in the problems of old age.

nutritious (nju:'trɪʃəs), *a.* Also 8–9 **nutricious** (*rare*), 8 **-ceous.** [ad. L. *nūtrītius, nūtrīcius*, f. *nūtrīc-, nūtrīx* nurse: see -ITIOUS[1]. So It., Sp., and Pg. *nutricio*.]

1. Serving as nourishment; capable of supplying nutriment.

1665 *Phil. Trans.* I. 75 Whether there be a Nervous and Nutritious Juice? **1679** RUSDEN *Further Discov. Bees* 51 They gather nutritious or augmentative matter. **1708** J. PHILIPS *Cyder* II. 192 O, may'st thou often see Thy furrows whiten'd by the woolly rain Nutriceous. **1781** COWPER *Retirem.* 43 Draining its nutritious pow'rs to feed Their noxious growth. **1819** BYRON *Juan* II. xcix, Which..to their mind Proved even still a more nutritious matter. **1841** LANE *Arab. Nts.* I. 58 As dates are very nutritious,..they are an excellent article of provision for travellers. **1871** NAPHEYS *Prev. & Cure Dis.* I. ii. 60 Salt meat is one-third less nutritious than fresh.

b. *transf.* Of taste.

1862 DARWIN *Orchids* v. 220 This cavity does not secrete nectar, but its walls are thick and fleshy, and have a slightly sweet nutritious taste.

2. Conveying nourishment. *rare.*

1741 MONRO *Anat. Nerves* (ed. 3) 130 The Holes for the Passage of the nutritious Vessels of these Bones are very conspicuous. **1831** R. KNOX *Cloquet's Anat.* 688 One of them..enters the nutritious canal of that bone.

Hence **nu'tritiously** *adv.*; **nu'tritiousness**, 'nourishing quality' (Bailey, vol. II, 1727).

1753 TORRIANO *Midwifery* 12 As if it was designed nutritiously by Nature to assist the Child. **1831** *Fraser's Mag.* III. 406 How generous must be the vegetation of the affections when nutritiously manured by..hospitality! **1877** *Encycl. Brit.* VII. 201 The nutritiousness of food depends on digestibility and concentration.

nutritive ('nju:trɪtɪv), *a.* and *sb.* Also 5–6 **nutrytive** (5 **-tiff, -tyf**), 5 **nutritiff, -tyf**; 6–7 **nutritiue.** [a. F. *nutritif, -ive*, = Sp., Pg., and It. *nutritivo*, ad. med.L. *nūtrītīv-us*, f. ppl. stem of *nūtrīre* to nourish: see -IVE.]

A. *adj.* **1.** Having the property of nourishing; nutritious, nutrimental.

c **1430** LYDG. *Min. Poems* (Percy Soc.) 195 Which sesoun is to flewme nutritiff. *c* **1440** —— *Hors, Shepe & G.* 376 Holsom is moton:..Ful nutritiff aftir a gret accesse. **1491** CAXTON *Vitas Patr.* (W. de W. 1495) I. xl. 60 The physycyens counseylled her that she sholde ete metes more nutrytyf. **1566** DRANT *Horace, Sat.* I. iv. G viij, Egges longe and whyte be nutritiue muche better then the rounde. **1601** HOLLAND *Pliny* II. 567 The broth of Limpins, Muscles, Cockles and Wilkes, is verie nutritive, and maketh them fat that use it. **1667** *Phil. Trans.* II. 513 The Humours..in all Animals are Nutritive. **1704** F. FULLER *Med. Gymn.* (1711) 85, I had reason to believe it did in some Measure prove Nutritive. **1748** HARTLEY *Observ. Man* I. iii. §2. 342 We infer that the Bread before us is nutritive and wholesome. **1842** COMBE *Digestion* 63 Both the chyle and the venous blood are converted into red, arterial, or nutritive blood. **1881** TYNDALL *Ess. Floating Matter Air* 215 In the case of very nutritive infusions..the interval ought to be shorter.

fig. **1654** JER. TAYLOR *Real Pres.* 61 He is nutritive in all the ways of spiritual manducation. **1868** BROWNING *Ring & Bk.* IX. 19 Throughout our city nutritive of arts.

2. Of, pertaining to, or concerned in, nutrition.

c **1400** tr. *Secreta Secret., Gov. Lordsh.* 96 Of strengthe nutrityf, and infirmatyf, and sustantyf. **1546** LANGLEY tr. *Pol. Verg. de Invent.* I. iii. 5 The Riuer Nilus..hath in it selfe naturally a certain power nutrytiue. **1650** BULWER *Anthropomet.* 171 Admonishing us of alition, and the work of the Nutritive Faculty. **1658** MANTON *Expos. Jude* ii, Life hath a nutritive appetite joined with it. *a* **1716** SOUTH *Serm.* (1744) IX. ii. 44 The hidden nutritive power of the Divine Benediction being withheld. **1756** BURKE *Subl. & B.* Introd., The qualities which they possess for nutritive or medicinal purposes. **1849** BALFOUR *Man. Bot.* §43 These Compound Organs may be divided into Nutritive, or those concerned in the nourishment of the plant. **1871** T. R. JONES *Anim. Kingd.* (ed. 4) 79 The circular marginal canal into which the nutritive tubes, radiating from the stomach, empty themselves. **1894** H. DRUMMOND *Ascent Man* 326 Defective nutritive conditions produce males.

3. Giving or providing nourishment.

a **1548** HALL *Chron., Rich. III* 55 b, Suche as made warre for the welthe and tuycyon of ther awne naturall and nutritive countrey. **1603** HOLLAND *Plutarch's Mor.* 1304 The Stoicks..holde that the generative and nutritive Spirit, is Bacchus. **1667** FLAVEL *Saint Indeed* (1754) 40 He was pitied by a Lord of Italy, who..wished him to be more careful and nutritive of his person. **1881** LANKESTER in *Encycl. Brit.* XII. 554/2 In the *Siphonophora*, in addition to nutritive (hydriform) persons and generative (medusiform) persons, there may be rows of swimming-bells.

B. *sb.* A nourishing article of food.

a **1440** BURGH *Cato* 617 Reffressheth you with this holsom diete... To your persone me thynkith it ful meete For to receyue such a nutrytiue. **1601** HOLLAND *Pliny* II. Index. **1638** RAWLEY tr. *Bacon's Life & Death* (1650) 50 Things alike in Substance, to the Body of Man, are, Nutritives; Fat Fleshes. **1699** BURNET *39 Art.* xxv. 283 An abstinence which is made up with other delicious and inflaming Nutritives. **1896** *Allbutt's Syst. Med.* I. 414 All are found in some respects to be faulty as nutritives.

Hence **'nutritively** *adv.*; **'nutritiveness.**

1727 BAILEY (vol. II.), Nutritiveness. **1847** in WEBSTER. **1856** *Orr's Circ. Sci., Pract. Chem.* 341 Pigeons and fowls, however, surpass beef in nutritiveness. **1889** *Harper's Mag.* June 60/2 He had been eating nutritively of the tree of artistic knowledge.

†**nutritor.** *Obs. rare*[−1]. [a. L. *nūtrītor*, agent-noun f. *nūtrīre.*] Nourisher.

1677 GALE *Crt. Gentiles* IV. 449 Creator and Vivificator and Nutritor of althings that are under him.

'nutritory, *a.* [ad. late L. *nūtrītōri-us*: see -ORY.] Concerned in or pertaining to nutrition.

1883 *Harper's Mag.* June 125/1 A class of ailments which may be described as general nutritory perversions.

†**nu'tritum.** *Obs. rare.* [L. *nūtrītum*, neut. pa. pple. of *nūtrīre.*] (See quots.)

1727–38 CHAMBERS *Cycl.*, *Nutritum*, in pharmacy, is a denomination given to a desiccative, cooling unguent, prepared by the agitation and nutrition of litharge of gold with oil and vinegar, or the juice of solanum, in a mortar. **1741** *Compl. Fam. Piece* I. i. 81 Add..as much Oil of Elder as will serve to reduce the Mixture into the Form of a Nutritum or Ointment.

†**'nutriture.** *Obs.* [ad. late L. *nūtrītūra*, f. ppl. stem of *nūtrīre*: see -URE. So It. *nut-, nud-, nodritura.*]

1. Nourishment, nutrition.

1557 NORTH *Gueuara's Diall Pr.* (1619) 698/2 [The trees] instead of meate receave into them for nutriture the heate of the Sunne. **1567** *Reg. Privy Council Scot.* I. 515 Na thing requisite for his nutriture..and preservatioun salbe foryot. **1601** HOLLAND *Pliny* XVIII. xvii, The root is contented with lesse nutriture. **1666** G. HARVEY *Morb. Ang.* xx. (1672) 248 Nature..rather hungers for a greater supply of nutriture. **1740** CHEYNE *Regimen* p. ii, The Supply and Nutriture of the Fluids and Solids must pass..through them.

b. Condition as to nourishment. *rare*[−1].

1620 VENNER *Via Recta* iii. 51 If it be of the age betweene one and two moneths, and competently fat, then it is of an excellent temperament, and nutriture.

2. Fostering; careful rearing or bringing up.

1577 HARRISON *Desc. Brit.* II. xx. in *Holinshed* 210 Their continuall nutriture and cherishing of such homeborne and forren simples. **1671** PANTON *Spec. Juv.* 282 Leave them a stock of Vertue and good Nutriture to set up withall in the World. **1684** BUNYAN *Pilgr.* II. 158 Besides, here they shall be sure to haue good Nutriture and Admonition.

†**'nutrix.** *Obs. rare.* [L.] Nurse, rearer.

1432–50 tr. *Higden* (Rolls) I. 147 Cappadocia is a region nutrix of horses. *Ibid.* 273 The cite callede Parisius floryschethe there, the nutrix of vertu.

†**nutrure.** *Obs. rare*[−1]. = NUTRITURE.

a **1400** *Stockholm Med. MS.* ii. 960 in *Anglia* XVIII. 330 It drywyth awey fowle nutrures, And distroith venym.

'nutshell, *sb.* Forms: 3 **nutescale, -scell**; 4 **noteschale, -schell, notscel**; 6 **nut(te)shale**, 5 **nutschell**, 6 **-shel**; 6 **nutte-**, 6–7 **nutt-**, 7– **nutshell.** [f. NUT *sb.*[1] + SHALE *sb.*, SHELL *sb.* Cf. MDu. *noot-, notescale, no(o)tscael* (Kilian *notschaele*), MSw. *notskal* (Sw. *nötskal*; Da. *nöddeskal*), MHG. *nuȥschal* (G. *nussschale*).]

1. The hard exterior covering within which the kernel of a nut is enclosed.

c **1205** LAY. 29265 Þa bi-sohte he nute-scalen and lette þe curneles ut draȝen. **1387** TREVISA *Higden* (Rolls) IV. 141 He wroot alle þe gestes of Troye sotelliche, as it myȝte be closed in a note schale. *c* **1450** HOLLAND *Howlat* 788 [He could make] Nobillis of nut schellis, and siluer of sand. **1562** TURNER *Herbal* (1568) 133 Yf nutt shelles be burnt and made lyke asshes. **1577** *F. de Lisle's Legendarie* I viij, His sonne Henrie, yet more meete to play with nutshales, then to handle a sword. **1610** SHAKS. *Temp.* I. i. 50 I'le warrant him for drowning, though the Ship were no stronger then a Nutt-shell. **1687** SETTLE *Refl. Dryden* 6 For who believes that one Magot waits for the Nutshel another has left. **1771** SMOLLETT *Humph. Cl.* (1815) 110 We embarked..in a wherry, so light and slender, that we looked like so many fairies sailing in a nut-shell. **1832** MARRYAT *N. Forster* iii, He swam nut-shells in a puddle. **1870** MISS BRIDGMAN *R. Lynne* I. iv. 47 Miniature fleets of nutshells.

†**b.** = NUT *sb.* 2. *Obs. rare*[−1].

c **1530** in Gutch *Coll. Cur.* II. 299 Item twoo Nutte Shells wheche I dyd receive amongst the Plate that came from Sent Albonnes, poiss. vij oz.

2. As an example of something without value.

a **1300** *Cursor M.* 23828 Þair spede es noght a nute-scell [*Edinb.* Þam sped noht worþe a not-scel]. **1390** GOWER *Conf.* II. 20 Bot al nys worth a note schale. *a* **1529** SKELTON *Agst. Venemous Tongues* Wks. 1843 I. 135 All is not worth a couple of nut shalis. *a* **1618** RALEIGH *Apology* 21 Mr. Candish.., when he was without hope,..met a ship.., a thousand pounds to a Nutshell. **1687** R. L'ESTRANGE *Answ. Dissenter* 26 'Tis the World to a Nut-shell, if he be one of That Party, that he is likewise One of Those Managers. **1697** COLLIER *Ess. Mor. Subj.* I. (1703) 115 Dont stake your life against a nutshell.

b. As an example of something extremely small in size or scanty in amount.

1602 SHAKS. *Ham.* II. ii. 260 O God, I could be bounded in a nutshell, and count my selfe a King of infinite space. **1675** TRAHERNE *Chr. Ethics* 442 A magnanimous soul is alwaies awake. The whole globe of the earth is but a nut-shell in comparison of its enjoyments. **1786** COWPER *Priv. Corresp.* (1824) II. 72 As soon as breakfast is over, I retire to my nutshell of a summer-house. **1822** SCOTT *Nigel* xxiii, Sufficient single beer, old Pillory—and, as I take it, brewed at the rate of a nutshell of malt to a butt of Thames. **1846** DICKENS *Cricket on Hearth* ii, A little cracked nutshell of a wooden house. **1861** ALEXANDER *Gosp. Jesus Christ* xv. 202 Seeing..the world reduced to a nutshell and our own house or village swelled into a world.

3. In allusions to the copy of Homer's *Iliad* mentioned by Pliny (*Nat. Hist.* VII. xxi) which was small enough to be enclosed in the shell of a nut.

1579 GOSSON *Sch. Abuse* (Arb.) 16 The whole worlde is drawen in a mappe; Homers Iliades in a nutte shel. **1704** SWIFT *T. Tub* vii, I have sometimes heard of an Iliad in a Nut-shell. **1843** CARLYLE *Past & Pres.* (1858) 137 It is an Iliad in a nutshell. **1865** *Times* 29 Apr., A whole Iliad of finance in a comparative nutshell. **1881** *Dr. Gheist, An Autobiog. fr. Midlands* 143 In short, it is the iliad of the controversy in a nutshell.

4. In phrases denoting great condensation, brevity, or limitation.

1693 W. FREKE *Sel. Ess.* i. 8 Can we reduce the school-men to a Nut-shell? **1760** *Phil. Trans.* LII. 67 The ground-work I present would lie in a nut-shell. **1840** DICKENS *Barn. Rudge* xxix, The simplest thing in the world. It lies in a nut-shell. **1852** MISS YONGE *Cameos* (1877) I. xxi. 149 The difference was said to lie in a nutshell, but..Becket was inflexible. **1870** J. H. NEWMAN *Gram. Assent.* II. viii. 300 A great complex argument, which..cannot by any ingenuity ..be packed into a nutshell.

b. With *in.* In a few words; in a brief or condensed statement.

1831 T. L. PEACOCK *Crotchet Castle* ii, There, sir, is political economy in a nutshell. **1841** THACKERAY *Sec. Funeral Napoleon* ii, In a nutshell, you have the whole matter. **1879** BROWNING *Ned Bratts* 210 You have my history in a nutshell.

5. *attrib.*, as ***nutshell brain, sort, truth.***

1704 *New Pract. Piety* 38 Metaphysical Speculations of Nutshell Brains. **1852** J. H. NEWMAN *Scope Univ. Educ.* Pref. p. xxvi, Extemporizing his lucid views, leading ideas, and nutshell truths for the breakfast-table. **1872** BLACK *Adv. Phaeton* xxiii, The padded uniform may enclose a nutshell sort of heart.

Hence **'nutshell** *v.*, to sum up in a few words; to state concisely.

1883 'MARK TWAIN' *Life on Mississippi* lviii. 570 The clerk nut-shelled the contrast between the former time and the present. **1892** *Nat. Observer* 17 Dec. 107/2 To add that the hour-glass or Victorian type of figures vies with the high-waisted or Empire is to nutshell the extreme ideals of the moment. **1900** *Speaker* 14 Apr. 45/1 He thus nutshells the tragic fate of the Stuarts.

nutsy ('nʌtsɪ), *a. colloq.* Also **nutsey.** [f. *nuts* (NUT *sb.*[1] 7 c) + -Y[1].] Crazy, insane.

a **1941** F. SCOTT FITZGERALD *Tender is Night* (rev. ed., 1953) III. viii. 175 A boy..she thought was pretty nutsey. **1942** BERREY & VAN DEN BARK *Amer. Thes. Slang* §152/5 *Insane*; *crazy*,..nutsy. **1962** *Guardian* 27 Aug. 5/3 Gee, it was nutsy. **1964** W. MARKFIELD *To Early Grave* (1965) x. 169 Take a train, you nutsy you!

'nuttallite. *Min.* [See quot. 1824.] A white or brown silicate of aluminium and calcium, occurring in Massachusetts.

1824 BROOKE in *Ann. Phil.* VII. 367, I have therefore named it Nuttallite, out of respect to the gentleman who first brought it to this country. **1840** *Penny Cycl.* XVI. 374/2 *Nuttalite*, a mineral which occurs crystallized. Primary form a square prism. **1896** CHESTER *Dict. Min.* 191.

†**nutte,** *v. Obs.* [OE. *nyttian*, = OHG. *nuȥȥôn* (G. *nutzen*); cf. OHG. *nuȥȥan* (G. *nützen*), MDu. *nutten*, MSw. *nytja* (Sw. *nyttja*, Da. *nytte*) to use, be of use, ON. *nytja* to milk.] *trans.* To use, make use of. (See also NITTE.)

c **1000** *Sax. Leechd.* II. 184 Þises þu nytta ȝe on æfenne ȝe on underne. *c* **1200** *Trin. Coll. Hom.* 23 He binam him alle þe mihte þe he hadde nutted fram þe biginninge of þe worelde. *a* **1225** *St. Marher.* 1 Alle cristene men..swa ȝef ha nutteð hare nome haueð yernet þe lif þe echeliche ilesteð. *a* **1225** *Ancr. R.* 370 Bute þe on was iwuned, uor his kolde mawe uorto nutten hote spices.

'nutted, *a.* [f. NUT *sb.*[1] + -ED[2].]

1. Provided with, fastened by, a nut. Also *fig.*

1688 HOLME *Armoury* III. xv. (Roxb.) 30/2 An anchor reuersed, sans stock, the Arme nutted and edged. **1825** J. NICHOLSON *Operat. Mechanic* 563 The ends of the abutments are also made of iron, screwed, or nutted, at each of the ends. **1830** *Examiner* 308/2 All her feelings..seem to have been screwed down and nutted. **1885** *Bazaar* 30 Mar. 1272/3 Bicycle, U rim, nutted spokes.

2. Abounding in, prolific of, nuts. *rare*[−1].

1859 WHITTIER *Kenoza Lake* 14 The nutted woods we wandered through.

nutter[1] ('nʌtə(r)). [f. NUT *sb.*[1] or *v.* + -ER[1].] One who gathers nuts.

1483 *Cath. Angl.* 257/2 A Nutter, *nuclearius.* **1826** in Cobbett *Rur. Rides* (1885) II. 95, I had some talk with some of these nutters. **1864** TENNYSON *En. Ard.* 8 And a hazlewood, By autumn nutters haunted.

'Nutter[2]. Also **nutter.** [f. NUT *sb.*[1] I + BUT)TER *sb.*[1]] The proprietary name of a substitute for butter made from the oil of nuts; nut-butter.

1906 *Westm. Gaz.* 18 May 4/2 'Nutter', 'Nucoline', and 'Nuttene' —all representing butter made from nuts. **1909** H. G. WELLS *Ann Veronica* vii. §3 Fruitarian refreshments —chestnut sandwiches buttered with nutter, and so forth. **1915** BARNETT *Let.* 2 May (1915) 127 One [*sc.* a trench mortar]..fires a cylindrical thing like a *Nutter* tin. **1920** *Trade Marks Jrnl.* 19 May 971 Nutter... Fats used in cooking. Mapleton's Nut Food Company, Limited,.. Liverpool; food manufacturers. **1926–7** *Army & Navy Stores Catal.* 67/1 Nutter—the ideal cooking fat. **1958** *Catal. County Stores* (Taunton) June 29 Vegetarian foods.. Cooking Fat, Nutter lb. 2/1. **1974** R. B. PARKER *God save Child* (1975) xi. 81 Dolly Bartlett got a package of Nutter Butter cookies from the cabinet.

'nutter[3]. *slang.* [f. NUT *sb.*[1] 8 c + -ER[1].] An insane person; a violent and deranged person. Occas. used in weaker sense: an eccentric person.

1958 F. NORMAN *Bang to Rights* I. 36 The reason for this is to find out wether [*sic*] or not you are a nutter. **1960** *Observer* 24 July 24/7 Sally is, at first sight, one of those romantic schizoids, a near nutter. **1963** 'A. GARVE' *Sea Monks* ii. 66 Reckon we'd be nutters to try it now. *Ibid.* v.

135, I reckon Chris was right, Rosie—King's a nutter. I reckon he'll go on killin' till there ain't no one left. **1963** [see BARM *sb.*[2] 3]. **1965** A. PRIOR *Interrogators* xi. 200 A lot of 'em are nutters, I reckon. **1968** J. LOCK *Lady Policeman* v. 43 The term 'nutter' was invariably used though not meant unkindly and included all types from the eccentric (a bit of a nutter) to the raving lunatic (a right nutter). **1972** R. QUILTY *Tenth Session* 7 You could make out on the tipping lark—all those rich nutters.

nuttery ('nʌtərɪ). [f. NUT *sb.*[1] + -ERY.]

1. A place in which nut-trees grow.

1824 MISS MITFORD *Village* Ser. I. (1863) 50 In another moment he has mounted the bank, and is in the midst of the nuttery. **1932** H. NICOLSON *Diary* 20 Mar. (1966) 113 What would be good.. would be to put the end of the main nuttery walk at the end of a main vista.

2. A place in which nuts are stored.

1881 *Graphic* 15 Oct. 402/1 Busy rats, who carry off and also establish a nuttery. **1882** *Cent. Mag.* XXV. 300 They [mice] generally have a well-filled granary or nuttery.

3. *slang.* A mental hospital.

1931 'D. STIFF' *Milk & Honey Route* vi. 62 Should the sociotechnic social worker be convinced that you are not normal she will have you bound for a nuttery before sunset. **1950** H. E. GOLDIN *Dict. Amer. Underworld Lingo* 147/2 *Nuttery*, an institution for the criminally insane or for mentally defective delinquents.

nuttiness ('nʌtɪnɪs). [f. NUTTY *a.* + -NESS.] The quality or state of being nutty (in various senses).

1865 R. D. BLACKMORE *Cradock Nowell* (1866) xv. 137 In the height of summer, [his colour was] a dappled bay; towards the autumnal equinox, a tendency to nuttiness. **1884** *Sat. Rev.* 8 Mar. 321/2 The six essays.. have the 'nuttiness' of age about them. **1916** E. V. LUCAS *Vermilion Box* 27 All his nuttiness has gone. You remember how his hair used to be swept right back from his forehead with lovely comb marks in it. **1926** E. O'NEILL *Great God Brown* 20 And I know damn well, underneath your nuttiness, you're gone on her. **1965** H. GOLD *Man who was not with It* xv. 128 It's the nuttiness of the mark and his fist in his palm. **1965** *Listener* 24 June 951/2 Scientists.. regard these same assumptions as 'nuttiness from an amateur'.

†**nutting**, *sb. Obs. rare*[-1]. (See quot.)

1606 *Wily Beguiled* C iv b, Sweet Pegge.., comely Pegge, my nutting, my sweeting, my Love, my Doue.

'nutting, *vbl. sb.* [f. NUT *v.* + -ING[1].]

1. The action of gathering nuts.

1824 MISS MITFORD *Village* Ser. I. (1863) 50 Manage it how you may, nutting is scrambling work. **1861** GEO. ELIOT *Silas M.* i. 2 Who would often leave off their nutting or bird's-nesting to peep in at the window of the stone cottage. **1884** *Harper's Mag.* Sept. 615/2 Ozias found Prudy doing anything but nutting.

2. *slang.* See NUT *v.* 3 b.

3. *attrib.*, as ***nutting-crook, -stick, -time***, etc.

1723 *Case of Edw. Collins* 8 In nutting-time.. he spent the Sundays.. in his woods. **1799** WORDSW. *Nutting* 7 A nutting-crook in hand. *a* **1849** H. COLERIDGE *Ess.* (1851) II. 350 Let no one make his nutting-stick like a pastoral staff. **1867** *Englishwom. Dom. Mag.* Sept. 475 Nutting day is still kept up as a rural holiday in September. **1873** 'SUSAN COOLIDGE' *What Katy Did at Sch.* x. 174 The other day we had a nutting picnic.

'nutting, *ppl. a.* [Cf. prec.] Nut-gathering.

1821 CLARE *Vill. Minstr.* I. 88 Now a scene of rural glee, With many a nutting swain and maid.

'nuttish, *a.*[1] [f. NUT *sb.*[1]] Nut-like.

1893 *Sat. Rev.* 11 Mar. 258/1 They ought to live entirely upon nuts, or, failing nuts, such food as is most nuttish in its nature.

'nuttish, *a.*[2] [f. NUT *sb.*[1] 8 c.] Characteristic or suggestive of a crank or a crazy person.

1909 *Punch* 24 Mar. 208/3 He indulged in a variety of eccentricities. I can imagine nothing more nuttish.

'nut-tree. [f. NUT *sb.*[1] + TREE *sb.*] A tree that bears nuts; *esp.* the hazel (*Corylus Avellana*).

1390 GOWER *Conf.* II. 30 Phillis in the same throwe Was schape into a Notetre. *c* **1400** MAUNDEV. (1839) xxviii. 289 There ben Note Trees, that beren Notes all grete as a Mannes Hed. **1483** *Cath. Angl.* 257/2 Nuttre, *corulus.* **1567** MAPLET *Gr. Forest* 53 b, The Nut tree may be called and that very aptlie, an iniurious and vnquiet neighbour. **1598** W. PHILLIP tr. *Linschoten* 8 Therein growe many Indian palmes or nut trees. **1662** J. DAVIES tr. *Mandelslo's Trav.* (1669) 119 The Mangas grow on Trees not much unlike our Nut-trees. **1726** LEONI *Alberti's Archit.* I. 27/1 The Nut Tree.. is extremely tractable, and good for.. Boards or Planks. **1839–40** W. IRVING *Wolfert's Roost* (1855) 35 The squirrel, from his nut-tree, would gaze at me for an instant, with sparkling eye.

attrib. **1601** HOLLAND *Pliny* I. 437 Those plums.. that are graffed in Nut-tree stocks. **1706** PHILLIPS (ed. Kersey), *Nuciprunum*, a Plum grafted on a Nut-tree Stock. **1882** W. F. KIRBY *Europ. Butterflies & M.* (1903) Plate lv, *Nepticula Microtheriella*—Nut-tree Pigmy.

nutty ('nʌtɪ), *a.* [f. NUT *sb.*[1] + -Y[1].]

1. Abounding in, or productive of, nuts.

1662–7 COWLEY *Of Plants* Wks. (Grosart) II. 276/1 The Hazel.., upon whose nutty Top A Squirrel sits. **1859** SALA *Tw. Round Clock* (1861) 271 Barcelona (which nutty seaport I have never visited). **1870** MISS BROUGHTON *Red as Rose* I. 268 The nutty, briary hedgerows.

2. a. Nut-like; having a taste like nuts.

1836–41 BRANDE *Chem.* (ed. 5) 1132 Fine olive oil is extremely bland and tasteless, or at least has only a slight nutty flavour. **1853** WOLFF *Pict. Sp. Life* 38 Next comes *orchata de chufas*, white creamy nutty liquid, soothing the soul. **1879** JEFFERIES *Wild Life in S. Co.* 211 Their flavour when taken from the bush is sweet, juicy, 'nutty'.

b. Pleasant, rich, full of zest or flavour.

1823 *New Monthly Mag.* VIII. 498 Supper, drink, and nutty mirth succeeded. **1894** *Current Hist.* IV. 475 It has, too, Mr. Blackmore's characteristic, leisurely, nutty humor in abundance.

c. *slang.* Spicy or piquant in interest.

1894 SALA *London up to Date* 329 The case, he incidentally adds, promises to be a 'nutty' one.

d. nutty slack, coal slack in small lumps or nuts (see NUT *sb.*[1] 18). Also *fig.*

1953 *New Yorker* 31 Jan. 58/2 The low-grade small coal appetizingly known as 'nutty slack',.. gives off far less appetizing fumes and dirt. **1953** *Truth* 13 Feb. 165 Durham Dilemma. We can't buy Nutty Slack. **1959** I. & P. OPIE *Lore & Lang. Schoolch.* ix. 163 Stew, a not infrequent component of school dinners, is.. in Croydon, 'nutty slack'. After an inapt term coined by the Ministry of Fuel (1952) for a poor quality coal, obtainable off the ration. The nuts were few and far between.

3. *slang.* **a.** Amorous, fond; enthusiastic. Usu. const. *upon* (a person).

1821 EGAN *Life in London* I. 223 The Hon. Tom Dashall .. was getting.. rather nutty in that quarter of the globe. **1823** *Grose's Dict. Vulgar T.* (Egan) s.v. *Nuts*, A person who conceives a strong inclination for another of the opposite sex, is said to be quite nutty, or nuts upon him or her. **1828** *Sporting Mag.* XXII. 174 The Strand-lane and Lambeth men became quite nutty upon their brethren, and offered to back them at any odds. **1840** *Fraser's Mag.* XXII. 583 Being so nutty upon one another.

b. Queer; not right in the head. Also in phr. ***nutty as a fruit-cake.***

1898 S. CRANE in *Cosmopolitan* Dec. 169/1 'What's the matter with that feller?' asked Martin. 'Nutty,' said the man. **1901** *Pall Mall G.* 27 May 6/2 Patterson declared that Philbrook was 'nutty' in regard to the question of fraud, and that he was crazy over the idea that everybody opposed to him was dishonest. **1935** G. & S. LORIMER *Heart Specialist* vi. 163 ' Listen, Alix, you're as nutty as a fruitcake,' I said .. 'If I were you I'd have more sense.' **1955** P. WILDEBLOOD *Against Law* 104 He's as nutty as a fruit-cake. **1960** H. PINTER *Caretaker* III. 77 He's nutty, he's half way gone. **1963** *Daily Mirror* 6 Nov. 2/3 You have to be a real sour square not to love the nutty, noisy, happy, handsome Beatles. **1967** WODEHOUSE *Company for Henry* v. 84 'He doesn't strike me as unbalanced.' 'On his special subject he's as nutty as a fruit cake.' **1972** C. WESTON *Poor, Poor Ophelia* (1973) xxxii. 207 Jesus, you and your nutty imagination! **1974** *Author* Spring 26 Yeats was a great poet and a fascinating critic, but if he had been hired to give a year's course of lectures on the development of English poetry his performance would have been extremely nutty.

c. Of jazz or popular music: see quots.

1955 L. FEATHER *Encycl. Jazz* x. 347 *Nutty*,.. great, exceptional. **1959** 'F. NEWTON' *Jazz Scene* 290 The modern .. fashion of using terms taken from mental derangement for praise (*crazy, insane, nutty*).

4. *slang.* Smart, spruce.

1823 BYRON *Juan* XI. xix, Black-eyed Sal (his blowing), So prime, so swell, so nutty, and so knowing. **1834** AINSWORTH *Rookwood* III. v. II. 346 But my nuttiest blowen, one fine day,.. To the beaks did her fancy man betray. **1839** REYNOLDS *Pickw. Abroad* xxvi. 224 And the beak wore his nuttiest wig.

5. *Comb.*, as ***nutty-brown, -flavoured, -looking.***

1828 *Sporting Mag.* XXIII. 33 Master Tommy, who by the bye is a devilish nutty looking lad. **1861** THACKERAY *Four Georges* iv. (1862) 185 One of Truefitt's best nutty-brown wigs. **1874** GARROD & BAXTER *Mat. Med.* 251 With a clear cinnamon-brown seed-coat, and a bland, sweetish, nutty-flavoured kernel.

†**'nutual**, *a. Obs. rare.* [f. L. *nūtus* nod, gesture.] Expressed merely by a gesture.

1607 *Scholast. Disc. agst. Antichrist* I. iii. 160 Bellarmine .. teacheth that besides mentall and vocall prayer, the Crosse is a Nutuall prayer by him selfe. *Ibid.* 161 So then the nutuall prayer of the Crosse wanteth inward deuotion.

'nut-weevil. *Ent.* [f. NUT *sb.*[1] + WEEVIL. Cf. Sw. *nötvifvel.*] A small beetle (*Balaninus nucum*), which deposits its eggs in green hazel- and filbert-nuts.

1802 BINGLEY *Anim. Biogr.* (1813) III. 134 The Nut Weevil.. is produced from the white grub that we often find living in the interior of the hazel nut. **1838** *Penny Cycl.* X. 269/2 Great quantities of filberts are rendered useless by being attacked by the nut-weevil. **1863** J. G. WOOD *Illustr. Nat. Hist.* III. 475 The maggots that are so frequently found in nuts.. are the larvæ of the Nut weevil.

nuwa(u)b, variants of NAWAB, nabob.

nuwe, obs. form of NEW *a.*

‖**nux vomica** (nʌks 'vɒmɪkə). [med.L. f. *nux* nut + fem. of **vomicus*, f. *vomĕre* to vomit.]

1. The seed contained in the pulpy fruit of an East Indian tree (*Strychnos Nux-vomica*), from which the poison strychnia is obtained.

1578 LANGHAM *Gard. Health* 437 Nvx vomica either alone or with salt, causeth a strong vomite. **1584** R. SCOT *Discov. Witchcr.* XIII. xiii. (1886) 252 Into whom he had thrust a dramme of *Nux vomica*, or some other such poison. **1656** EARL MONM. tr. *Boccalini's Advts. fr. Parnass.* II. xc. (1674) 244 The Arsnick, and Nux Vomica of those torturing plaisters. **1693** *Phil. Trans.* XVII. 763 The Publisher gives us 4 sorts of *Caniram*, all a-kin to the *Nux Vomica* of our Shops. **1711** *Lond. Gaz.* No. 4845/4, 2 Bales qt. each 5 C. of Nux Vomica. **1778** *R. James' Diss. Fevers* (ed. 8) 48 Cutting in small pieces some of the crow fig, commonly called *nux vomica*. **1822–34** *Good's Study Med.* (ed. 4) I. 627 The nux vomica and Ignatius's bean.. combine, with an intense bitter, a most active narcotic virtue. **1860** PIESSE *Lab. Chem. Wonders* 63 The fearful and fatal powers of nux-vomica have rendered it well known throughout the world. **1879** *St. George's Hosp. Rep.* IX. 157 She was in hospital for eleven weeks, under treatment by nux vomica and valerian.

attrib. **1861** BENTLEY *Man. Bot.* 591 The Koochla tree produces Nux Vomica seeds, so well known for their powerfully poisonous effects. **1866** *Treas. Bot.* 1106/1 The alkaloid.. had been derived from nux-vomica bark. *Ibid.*, The wood of the nux-vomica tree is hard and very bitter.

2. The tree producing the nux-vomica seeds.

1876 HARLEY *Mat. Med.* (ed. 6) 511 Nux-vomica, is a small tree, with a crooked stem, and corymbs of greenish white flowers. **1879** *Cassell's Techn. Educ.* II. 66 Strychnine .. is procured from the bruised seeds of the *nux vomica*, which are imported from.. Ceylon.

Hence **nux-'vomicize** *v.*, to adulterate by infusing nux vomica.

1866 BLACKMORE *Cradock Nowell* xlviii, Stuff.. which the publicans nux vomicize up to proof.

nuysible, -yble, obs. forms of NUISIBLE.

nuzzer: see NAZAR.

'nuzzing, *vbl. sb.* [Imitative.] The noise made by the camel.

a **1693** *Urquhart's Rabelais* III. xiii, The barking of curs, bawling of Mastiffs,.. nuzzing of Camels.

'nuzzle, *sb. rare.* [f. next.] An act of nuzzling; a rub with the nose.

a **1890** *Mind in Nature* I. 142 (Cent.), Horses, cows, deer, and dogs even, nuzzle each other; but then a nuzzle, being performed with the nose, is not a kiss.

nuzzle ('nʌz(ə)l), *v.*[1] Forms: *α.* 5 **nosele**, 6 **nosyll**, 6, 8 **nosle**, 9 **nozzle**. *β.* 6–7 **nousle**. *γ.* 6–7 **nusle**, 7–8 **nussle** (6 **nuszle**), 7 **nuzzel**, 7–8 **nuzle**, 6– **nuzzle**. [f. NOSE *sb.* + -LE 3; perh. originally suggested by the adv. NOSELING, but cf. Du. *neuzelen* (Kilian *neuselen*), G. *nus(s)eln*, *nüs(s)eln*, *nös(s)eln*, Sw. dial. *nössla* to poke with the nose, to snuffle, to speak through the nose. For the variation in the forms cf. next.]

I. *intr.* †**1.** To bring the nose towards the ground; to grovel. *Obs. rare.*

c **1425** *St. Elizabeth of Spalbeck* in *Anglia* VIII. 109/2 Sche noseles downe forwarde and wonderly crokes her body.

2. To burrow or dig with the nose; to thrust the nose into the ground or anything lying on it.

1530 PALSGR. 645/1, I nosyll, as a swyne dothe in the yerth with her groyne, *je fouille du museau.* **1575** TURBERV. *Venerie* 156 The male pigges.. will nouzle and turne up the grounde tenne or twelve paces further of.. than the females do. **1595** SPENSER *Col. Clout* 763 In pleasures wastefull well.. like moldwarps nousling still they lurke. **1600** SURFLET *Countrie Farme* VII. xxviii. 854 The wilde bore.. willingly followeth one furrowe, nusling all along the ridge vntill he come to the ende of it. **1622** MABBE tr. *Aleman's Guzman d' Alf.* II. 51 This Bore one of the Groomes found Nuzzling in the litter, .. turning it all topsie-turvy. **1707** tr. *Wks. C'tess D'Anois* (1715) 440 She trotted away grunting and nuzling with her Snout. **1790** BURKE *Fr. Rev.* 347 It was not made to entice the smell of a mole, nuzzling and burying himself in his mother earth. **1814** SCOTT *Wav.* lxiv, Davie all this while lay with his nose almost in the fire, nuzzling among the ashes. **1866** J. B. ROSE tr. *Ovid's Met.* 61 Mingling with steers and nuzzling in the grass. **1889** T. HARDY *Mayor Casterbr.* v, Like sows nuzzling for acorns.

b. In *fig.* use, with *along*.

1713 ARBUTHNOT *John Bull* II[1]. vii, Sir Roger shook his Ears, and nuzled along, well-satisfied within himself that he was doing a charitable Work.

3. To poke or push with the nose *in* or *into* something. Also *fig.*

1592 SHAKS. *Ven. & Ad.* 1115 And nousling in his flanke the louing swine Sheath'd vnaware the tuske in his soft groine. **1682** N. O. *Boileau's Lutrin* IV. 305 A heavy Abbey Lubber! Whose Head was always nuzzling in the Cubber'd! **1750** SOAME JENYNS *Mod. Fine Lady* Wks. 1790 I. 73 Th' embroider'd colonel flatters with a sneer, And the cropt ensign nuzzles in her ear. **1812** W. TENNANT *Anster F.* II. viii, The bev'rage wherein fiddlers like to nuzzle. **1847** YOUATT *Horse* vii. 150 If a pail of good gruel is placed within his reach, how will he nuzzle in it. **1899** *Pall Mall Mag.* Feb. 262 'Hut, you beast!' he added,.. when the mare nuzzled into his neck.

b. To keep the nose pressing *at* or *about*, to press or rub the nose *against*, something.

With *against* the sense approximates to 4 b.

1603 [see NUDGEL *v.*]. **1657** G. THORNLEY *Daphnis & Chloe* 125 The Lambs riggle and nussle at their dugs. **1726** SWIFT *Gulliver* IV. ii, Carrying them on their Backs, nuzzling with their Face against the Mother's Shoulders. **1855** STEPHENS *Bk. Farm* (ed. 2) I. 654/1 Every pig takes its own place, and nuzzles at the udder with the teat held in the mouth. **1855** KINGSLEY *Westw. Ho!* xviii, [The sharks] are nuzzling already at my toes! **1892** KIPLING *Barrack-r. Ballads, East & West* 65 The red mare ran to the Colonel's son, and nuzzled against his breast.

transf. **1894** R. LE GALLIENNE *Prose Fancies* 188, I could see the boat nuzzling up against the pier.

c. Of dogs: To snuff or poke with the nose.

1806–7 J. BERESFORD *Miseries Hum. Life* II. xix, A large bulldog.. who keeps up a stifled growl with his muzzle nuzzling about your calf. **1834** SIR H. TAYLOR *Artevelde* II. IV. iv, Sanxere Came nuzzling like a dog to find some flesh Whereon to fix. **1879** BROWNING *Ivan Ivanovitch* 183 Nuzzling now with snout, Now ripping, tooth and claw.

d. To poke with the fingers. *rare.*

1806–7 J. BERESFORD *Miseries Hum. Life* XII. xxvii, The dull.. sound.. in your ears.. which all your tweaking, nuzzling, and rummaging at them, serves only to increase. **1860** O. W. HOLMES *Prof. Breakf.-t.* viii, [The Professor] feels thorax and arm, and nuzzles round among muscles as those horrid old women poke their fingers into the salt-meat on the provision-stalls.

4. To nestle, to lie snug in bed, etc.
1601 Weever *Mirr. Mart.* B iij b, Twixt the sheete and pillow I nuzled in, joyn'd knees and chin together. **1654** Gayton *Pleas. Notes* iv. viii. 217 At Cock-crowing he takes his bed, and there nuzzles till Hesperus cramps him by the toes. **1685** Cotton tr. *Montaigne* III. 450 Was not this to nustle and settle himself to sleep at greater ease? **1878** Jefferies *Gamekeeper at H.* 2 The ferret is a shivery creature, and likes nothing so well as to nozzle down in a coat-pocket with a little hay.
fig. **1597** J. Payne *Royal Exch.* 14 The Lord saw cowldnes and backwardnes in religion, by nuszling to depely in the world. **1648** J. Beaumont *Psyche* xx. ccx, Th' abstrusest things Which in the Mind's dark Temper nuzling lie, By you exposed are to every eye. *a* **1658** Cleveland *The Times* 48 Wks. (1687) 240 Thus Tyranny's a stately Palace, where Ambition sweats to climb and nustle there.

b. To nestle on or close to some part of a person. Also *refl.*
1611 A. Stafford *Niobe dissolv'd* 199 [Wisdom] nuzzleth her selfe in his bosom, cherisheth his soule. **1637** Heywood *Pleas. Dial.* v. Wks. 1874 VI. 201 Will your rest Seeme sweeter, if I nuzzle on your brest? *a* **1652** Brome *Novella* iii. i, To Kisse the hand,.. and then embrace, Then nuzzle in the Elizium of your bosome! **17..** Henley *Mirope* in Galt *Rothelan* (1824) iii. iv, That artless homage, Which the fond infant to his mother paid, Smiling and nuzzling, hanging to her bosom. **1752** F. Coventry *Pompey the Little* (ed. 3) 135 In this agreeable situation nuzzling behind the back of a lousy drab. *a* **1849** H. Coleridge *Poems* (1850) II. 270 Free to nuzzle and to nest In the sweet valley of her breast. **1894** Hall Caine *Manxman* 14 Pete nuzzled up to Philip's side.

c. To lie, or otherwise associate, close *together*, or *with* another. Also *fig.*
1708 *Brit. Apollo* No. 104. 3/1 He was nuzzled together with a Doxy. **1719** D'Urfey *Pills* (1872) IV. 322 No Pigs in a Stye.. E'er nussled so close, Or more amourous together. **1742** Jarvis *Don Quix.* i. iv. xlvi, If she were so, she would not be nuzzling at every turn and in every corner with a certain person in the company. **1883** *Sat. Review* 15 Dec. 752 The theory which bids the greatest of all kingdoms huddle and nuzzle with the trumpery republics of yesterday.

II. *trans.* **5. a.** To root *up* with the nose or snout; to push *aside* with the nose. *rare.*
1613 *Answ. Uncasing of Machiavel* G j b, Swine eats the flowres, then nusles vp the roote. **1628** Wither *Brit. Rememb.* viii. 1105 Gods herbs of grace To nouzle up; his Vineyard to deface. **1764** *Nat. Hist.* in *Ann. Reg.* 87/2 The sheep industriously nosled it aside to bite a blade.

b. To touch or rub with the nose.
1812 W. Tennant *Anster F.* iii. xxxvii, Nuzzling the nasty ground obsequiously. **1883** *Longman's Mag.* Dec. 200 The vicious animal.. began to 'nuzzle' me with his nose and prehensile upper lip. **1891** Kipling *Light that Failed* (1900) 16 Twenty whale-boats were nuzzling a sand-bank.

6. To thrust in (the nose or head).
1594 Nashe *Unfort. Trav.* 59 The Dogge nusling his nose vnder the necke of the Deare. **1683** *Phil. Trans.* XIII. 133 It nuzzles its head so deep in the coats of the intestines. **1860** *All Year Round* No. 37. 258 Some of the wretches were nuzzling their gory heads in the scooped-out stomach. **1892** Symonds *Life in Swiss Highl.* vi. 132 Six stalwart horses.. nuzzling their noses to the brimful stalls.

7. 'To put a ring into the nose, as of a hog' (Ogilvie, 1850).

Hence **'nuzzling** *ppl. a.*
1596 Spenser *F.Q.* iv. xi. 32 Mole, that like a nousling Mole doth make His way still under ground, till Thamis he overtake.

nuzzle ('nʌz(ə)l), *v.*[2] Now *rare.* Forms: α. 6 **nosyll, -el (6–7 -ell), nossel, noz(z)el, nozle.** β. 6 **nowsel, nousel(l, 6–7 nousle, nouzle, nouzel(l.** γ. 6 **noosell (6–7 -el), noozel, noozle.** δ. 6 **nusell, 6–7 nussel, nus(s)le.** ε. 6–7 **nuz(z)el, -ell, nuzle, 6– nuzzle.** [Of obscure origin. The identity of the forms with those of the prec. verb make it possible that this also is f. nose *sb.*, but the connexion of sense is not clear. In sense 2 the word had great vogue from about 1530 to 1650.]

†**1.** *trans.* To accustom (a dog or hawk) to attack other animals or birds. *Obs.*
1530 Palsgr. 645/1, I nosyll a yonge thing, I bolden it fyrst to do, or enterprise a thynge, where afore it wanteth boldnesse, *Je apprime.* I have nosylled my yonge dogge to daye at a beare, he is made for ever. **1575** Turberv. *Faulconrie* 126 If you woulde nousel or enter a haggarde, then do not enter hir or sette hir in bloude upon a yong praye or inure hir thereto. **1618** Latham *Falconry* (1633) 96 Let her kill some two or three more..; it will so nuzzell her, as that shee wil not after misse the wilde Rooke or any other thing. **1688** Holme *Armoury* ii. xi. 239/2 *Nowsell*, to entize or inure the Hawk to love to fly at her Prey.

†**2.** To train, educate, nurture (a person) *in* some opinion, habit, etc. Freq. with *up*. *Obs.*
α. **1519** Horman *Vulg.* 86 It were more a vauntage.. that yonge childrens wyttis were other wyse sette a warke than nossel them in suche errour. **1545** Brinklow *Compl.* 60 Thus for lukers sake the greasy canonistes nosel the peple in idolatory. *a* **1600** Hooker *Answ. Travers' Suppl.* §26, I take no ioy in striuing, I haue not beene nozled or trayned vp in it.
β. **1532** More *Confut. Tindale* Wks. 587/1 Some be so sore nowseled in the false heresies,.. yt finally thei die therin. **1579** J. Stubbes *Gaping Gulf* D j, Her father will nousell her in hys own religion. **1612** T. James *Corrupt. Script.* iv. 98 To humor their Nouices, and nousle them vp in this fond conceit. **1655** Fuller *Ch. Hist.* vii. 374 The infirmities of people, long nouzled in ignorance and superstition, and incapable of a sudden.. alteration.
γ. *c* **1540** tr. *Pol. Verg. Eng. Hist.* (Camden) I. 214 The Danes.. weare all readie nooseled in the sweetenesse of the soyle. **1591** Savile *Tacitus, Hist.* iv. lxxii. 225 To noosell his souldiers in licentiousness and cruelty. **1606** J. Carpenter *Solomon's Solace* xxviii. 118 The man which hath beene long nooseled vp in vices, will.. onely with much adoe leaue them.
δ. **1553** Bale *Vocacyon* in *Harl. Misc.* (Malh.) I. 337 Thus were the people nusled vp from their yowth, in calling vpon dead men, and ymages. **1583** Stubbes *Anat. Abus.* i. (1879) 54 Thei must needs be a nice and curious people who are thus nusseled up in such daintie attyre. **1652–62** Heylin *Cosmogr.* iii. (1682) 202 Natural Indians, nusled in Paganism. **1686** W. de Britaine *Hum. Prud.* iii. 12 The ends of the Common People, if nusled up in Factious Liberty, are much different from the Designs of Soveraign Princes.
ε. **1587** Holinshed *Chron.* III. 1225/2 Being an English-man by birth, and from his infancie.. nuzled in papistrie. **1598** Barret *Theor. Warres* v. i. 169 One that had bene nuzled vp in warre euen from a child. **1642** J. Ball *Answ. to Can* ii. 18 The ordaining of ignorant ministers.. the meanes to nuzzle people in ignorance. **1669** W. Simpson *Hydrol. Chym.* 213 The people may no longer be nuzzled up in the expectation.

†**b.** *refl.* (Const. as prec.) *Obs.*
1548 Udall, etc. *Erasm. Par. John* xi. 79 Wherein we haue long tyme nusseled our selues. **1579** Tomson *Calvin's Serm. Tim.* 88/1 He that will cherishe and nousell vp him selfe in wickednesse. **1607** Hieron *Wks.* I. 80 The diuell helping them forward with many shifts to nouzell themselues in ignorance. **1642** Rogers *Naaman* 49 Doubtlesse he meanes they shall nuzzle up themselves in a dead senselesse estate. *Ibid.* 140 That they might nouzle up themselves the more unsuspectedly in their secret uncleannesse.

†**c.** With other constructions (esp. *with*). *Obs.*
1530 Tindale *Pract. Prelates* H ij, His mynde was to.. kepe him without a wife that.. he might haue bene noselled and entangled with hores. **1548** Patten *Exped. Scot.* c vij b, Nooseld of my nurce neuer too be spare of spech. *a* **1591** H. Smith *Serm.* (1637) 228 They are so nousled to the world and acquainted with sinne. **1621** Burton *Anat. Mel.* iii. i. i. ii. (1651) 655 Possessed with blinde zeal, and nusled with superstition. **1689** Hickeringill *Modest Inquiries* ii. 11 Bigotted and Nuzled to maintain Priest-Craft. **1692** Wagstaffe *Vindicæ Carol.* x. 74 The London and Westminster Pulpits.. nuzzled the People into a resisting the King.

†**3.** To bring up, rear, train, educate. *Obs.*
1558 Warde tr. *Alexis' Secr.* To Rdr., Yet haue I alwaies been noseled vp by a certaine ambition and vainglorie. **1568** Skinner tr. *Montanus' Inquisit.* 82 b, So that hauing such store both of bookes and maisters to instruct them, they began to nosell their whole couent. **1600** Holland *Livy* iii. lii. 123 To flesh the Commons, and to nuzzle them up, and acquaint them with exercising crueltie upon the Nobles. **1615** Brathwait *Strappado* (1878) 150 What Saint is she, That.. Nusles my damned Atheist, makes him curse Nature and fortune? **1645** *Procl. conc. Bk. Com. Pr.* 5 The Common-Prayer was a meanes to nuzzle up a non-preaching and ignorant Ministry.

†**b.** To impose upon, deceive. *Obs. rare.*
c **1680** Hickeringill *Whiggism* i. Wks. 1716 I. 23 Can a few Renegadoes, or Papists think to nuzzle the most glorious Isle and City of the Universe? **1705** —— *Priest-cr.* iv. (1721) 205 Therefore you are a Pack of nonsensical Bigots, to be nuzled so easily by Priest-craft.

4. To nurse, to cherish fondly; to provide with a snug place of rest (cf. nuzzle *v.*[1] 4).
1581 Mulcaster *Positions* vi. (1887) 47 All those offices, wherunto our bodie serueth naturally,.. must be cherished and nusled. **1602** Marston *Antonio's Rev.* Prol., Being hugged in the armes, And nuzzled twixt the breastes of happinesse. **1607** Walkington *Opt. Glass* iv. 46 We nusle Serpents in our own bosom.. till they sting us to death. **1652** Crashaw *Mary Magdalene* Wks. (1904) 260 The deaw no more will sleep Nuzzel'd in the lilly's neck. **1854** *Fraser's Mag.* XLIX. 212 As thirsty bees that sup Nuzzled within a noonday lily's cup. **1891** Hall Caine *Scapegoat* xi, Why had he been.. fondling and nuzzling and coddling them [= fancies]?

Hence **'nuzzled** *ppl. a.*; **'nuzzling** *vbl. sb.*; also †**'nuzzling** *sb.*, nursling.
1586 Leicester *Corresp.* (Camden) 338 The count Morrice was there.. and young Mr. Hatton, for his first nuselinge. **1593** *Bacchus Bountie* in *Harl. Misc.* (1809) II. 264 Fragrantlie fuming vp.. into the nosetrills of all his nosled nouises. **1638** Drumm. of Hawth. *Irene* Wks. (1711) 164 These few Miles of Ground, which bred and intertain'd thy Nuslings young.

nwyn, variant of new *v. Obs.*

ny, variant of nye; obs. f. nigh *a.*

†**ny,** obs. variant of ne *conj.*[1], nor.
c **1425** *Cursor M.* 7361 (Trin.), Nor his sones ny him I knowe. *a* **1450** Myrc 48 In honeste clothes thow moste gon, Baselard ny bawdryke were þow non.

†**ny,** variant of ne *conj.*[2], than. *Obs.*
c **1420** *Chron. Vilod.* 4140 Of hurre hurt he toke nomore hede Ny þaw he hadde y-hade no harme.

nyala ('njɑːlə). [Native name in Tsonga and Venda languages.] A large, gregarious antelope, *Tragelaphus angasi*, or the closely related species, *T. buxtoni*, occurring in parts of southern Africa; the male is greyish-brown with several white stripes and spiral, black horns, the female is reddish-brown and hornless; = inyala. Also *attrib.*
1899 [see harnessed *ppl. a.* 4]. **1915** *Chambers's Jrnl.* Nov. 702/1 The horns of this antelope.. approximate more to those of the nyala, one of the largest of the bushbucks. **1931** *Discovery* Feb. 61/1 It [*sc.* the nyala] is one of the few forest-frequenting antelopes, and there cannot be many hundreds left in the jungles of Zululand and Southern Nyasaland. **1947** J. Stevenson-Hamilton *Wild Life S. Afr.* xv. 109 Along the Pafuri River in the nyala bush they have become accustomed to motor traffic. **1964** *Punch* 2 Sept. 359/3 Shooting a nyala. **1975** *Country Life* 20 Feb. 444/3 A visit to.. these [South African] reserves is always rewarded with views of zebra, nyala, impala, duiker, waterbuck.

nyam, *sb.* and *v.* Also **nyam-nyam.** See yam *v.* and *sb.*[3]

Nyanja ('njændʒə), *sb.* and *a.* Also **Manganja, Anyanja.** [f. Bantu *nyanja* lake + *ma-* tribal prefix, or *a-* plural prefix.] **A.** *sb.* **a.** The name of a Bantu people found in Malawi. **b.** A member of this people. **c.** The Bantu language spoken by this people. **B.** *attrib.* or as *adj.* Of or pertaining to the Nyanja people or their language.
1865 D. & C. Livingstone *Narr. Expedition Zambesi* v. 108 The Manganja generally live in villages, each of which has its own headman. *Ibid.* 123 The practice of bathing.. we afterwards found to be common in other parts of the Manganja country. **1892** D. C. Scott (*title*) A cyclopaedic dictionary of the Mang'anja Language spoken in British Central Africa. **1902** H. Barnes *Nyanja-English Vocab.* p. ii, The vocabulary is primarily intended to help people to understand the Nyanja that they hear or read, and not to make up Nyanja to inflict on wandering natives. **1914** J. B. Keble in *Oxf. Survey Brit. Empire* III. x. 243 The Anyanja are a large and important group... They inhabit the western and south-western shores of Lake Nyasa and the Shiré Highlands. **1924** A. Werner in G. Lagden *Native Races of Empire* iii. 88 A Nyanja man, if addressed in Yao or Konde, would probably not understand... But a Nyanja and a Tumbuka might understand each other. **1930** A. Hetherwick *Dict. Nyanja Lang.* p. v, Not only in Nyasaland itself, but also in Northern and Southern Rhodesia.. Mang'anja, or, as it is now called, Nyanja, has come to occupy the place of a lingua franca. **1966** C. G. Seligman *Races of Africa* (ed. 4) ix. 148 The spirits of dead Nyanja chiefs.. are specially appealed to for rain. **1974** *Encycl. Brit. Macropædia* XI. 361/2 Nine main groups are historically associated with modern Malawi—the Chewa, Nyanja, Lomwe, Yao, Tumbuka, Sena, Tonga, Ngone, and Ngonde.

†**nyas,** *sb.* (and *a.*) *Obs.* Forms: 5 **nyesse,** 6 **niesse, niass(e, nyasse, 6–7 nias, 7 niaise, nias, nyas.** [See eyas.]
1. A young hawk, an eyas.
1495 *Act 11 Hen. VII*, c. 17 Any Hauke of the brede of Englond called Nyesse, gossehauke, tassel,.. or faucon. **1575** Turberv. *Faulconrie* 103 Whither they bee sorehawkes mowed or Nyesse, yet are they of sundrye natures.
b. *attrib.* or *adj.* Also *transf.*
1611 Cotgr. s.v. *Niard*, *Faulcon niard*, a Nias Faulcon. **1617** Minsheu *Ductor*, A Nias Hawke. **1636** *Fasciculus Florum* 48, I on my Table set.. Capons, Lamb, Veal, and daintiest Fowl,.. Then like a Nyas-dragon on them fly.
2. Applied allusively to persons.
1576 Pettie *Pallace* 82 If they.. knowe him to be a Niesse, which wyl neuer away, then they make hym flee. **1581** —— *Guazzo's Civ. Conv.* iii. (1586) 136 Ther is no man such a Niasse, but that continuall bobbes and repulses wil make him soare away. **1589** Greene *Tullies Loue* Wks. (Grosart) VII. 167 If shee be so ramage let hir flye, and seeke for a Niess that may prooue more gentle. **1616** B. Jonson *Devil an Ass* i. vi, Laught at, sweet bird? is that the scruple? Come, come, Thou art a Niaise [*marg.* A Niaise is a young Hawke, tane crying out of the nest].

Nyassa (naɪ'æsə, nj-). Also **Nyasa. a.** Name of a people in Malawi. **b.** A member of this people. Also *attrib.* or as *adj.*
1849 C. Pickering *Races of Man* ix. 197 The *N'yasa*, who inhabit the islands and perhaps the further shores of the Great Lake, seemed to be the most distant tribe known at Zanzibar. **1883** R. N. Cust *Sk. Mod. Lang. Afr.* II. xii. 330 Rebman.. employed.. a slave, whom he imagined to be a Swahili, but he overheard him speaking a totally different language, and upon inquiry he proved to be a Wa-Nyassa. **1887** A. C. Madan *Kiungani* ii. 30 We had never seen a single European in my time... They are called in the Nyasa language 'wan'tu oyela' meaning 'white man'. **1912** C. T. Domingo *Let.* 17 Mar. in Shepperson & Price *Independent African* (1958) Plate 11 (betw. pp. 158 and 159) It may take sometimes [*sic*] to possess jewels of Independance [*sic*] among *we* [*sic*] the Nyassas. Yours, lovely. For Africa. **1959** *Listener* 24 Sept. 471/1 A Nyasa is hardly thought to be a man until he has gone off to work for some years in the Johannesburg gold-mines.

nyce, obs. form of niece, nice *a.*

nycebecetur, -byceter: see nicebecetur.

nyceling: see niceling.

†**nycette.** *Obs. rare.* Also 5 **nyzett,** 6 **nysett,** ? **niced.** [Of obscure origin.] 'A breastcloth; a light wrapper for the bosom, or neck' (Halliwell, s.v. *Niced*).
1499 in *Somerset Med. Wills* (1901) 385 [My best kerchief called a] 'Nyzett'. **1508** *Will of Hampton* (Somerset Ho.), ij newe aprons, ij kercheffes & ij nycettes. **1530** *Wilts. Wills* (1890) 155 My best carchyve, my best apron, my best nycette.

Nycholaite, -ayte: see Nicolaite *Obs.*

†**nychomet.** *Obs.*[−1] [ad. *onichimata* of the Latin text.] Onyx.
a **1400–50** *Alexander* 3671 Sum was smeth smaragdyns & oþire small gemmes, And new nychometis nemellus endentid.

nycht(e, obs. Sc. forms of nigh *v.*, night.

nychtbur, -bour, obs. Sc. ff. neighbour.

nychtertaill, Sc. var. of nightertale *Obs.*

'nychthemer, anglicized form of NYCHTHEMERON.

1837 WHEWELL *Hist. Induct. Sci.* (1857) I. 150 The solar days (or rather the *nycthemers*, compounded of a night and a day), would be unequal.

nychthemeral (nɪk'θiːmərəl), *a.* Also **nycthemeral.** [f. NYCHTHEMER(ON + -AL.] Occurring with a variation that matches that of night and day.

1907 *Nature* 17 Jan. 287/2 The regulation of the nychthemeral cycle of temperature and its inversion in the aged. **1967** *Oceanogr. & Marine Biol.* V. 495 These nycthemeral changes of the gas tension in the different levels of water. **1974** *Nature* 13 Sept. 143/2 These animals have a nychthemeral variation of less than 2° C.

‖**nychthemeron** (nɪk'θiːmərɒn). Also **nycth-.** [a. Gr. νυχθήμερον, neut. of νυχθήμερος lasting for a day and a night, f. νύξ, νυκτ- night + ἡμέρα day.] A period of twenty-four hours, consisting of a day and a night.

1682 H. MORE *Annot. Glanvill's Lux O.* 115 Onely the shadowy Vale of the Night will be cast over them once in a Nycthemeron. **1727–38** CHAMBERS *Cycl.* s.v. *Gout*, About two or three o'clock in the morning (the space of a nychthemeron from its access). **1882** MORTON *Heroes Sci., Astron.* 51 Tables of the prosthapheresis and nychthemeron are given. **1882** *Nature* XXVI. 79/2 The year was regarded by them as an extended nycthemeron.

nychtingale, obs. Sc. form of NIGHTINGALE.

nycitee, obs. form of NICETY.

nycker, obs. form of NICKER *sb.*[1]

Nycolait, variant of NICOLAITE *Obs.*

nycromancye, -mansy, obs. forms of NECROMANCY.

nyctalope ('nɪktələʊp), *sb.* and *a.* [ad. Gr. νυκτάλωψ, -άλωπος NYCTALOPS. Cf. F. and Pg. *nyctalope*, Sp. *nictalope*.]

A. *sb.* One affected with nyctalopia.

Found only in the plural, which may be intended for the classical plural (nɪktə'ləʊpiːz) of NYCTALOPS.

1601 HOLLAND *Pliny* XXVIII. xi, Since as be dim-sighted and see little or nothing toward night (whome the Greeks call Nyctalopes). **1754** *Med. Observ. & Inq.* (1776) I. xiii. 119 Of the Nyctalopes of the Ancients. **1764** *W. India Dis.* 61 Neither do any of the Nyctalopes complain of head-achs. **1838** *Penny Cycl.* XII. 114/2 In the 2nd book of his 'Prædicta', he [Hippocrates] says, 'We call those nyctalopes who see by night'.

B. *adj.* Having the power of seeing by night.

1847–9 *Todd's Cycl. Anat.* IV. 219/1 This great development in a nyctalope animal is an interesting fact.

‖**nyctalopia** (nɪktə'ləʊpɪə). *Path.* Also 9 **nycht-.** [late L. *nyctalopia* (Isidore, with variant *nyctalmos*), a. Gr. *νυκταλωπία, f. νυκτάλωψ, f. νύξ, νυκτ- night + ἀλα-ός blind + ὤψ eye: cf. the rare forms ἀλαωπός and ἀλαῶπις blind. So Sp. *nictalopia*, F. *nyctalopie*.

The term νυκτάλωψ was used by Galen and other writers in its proper sense of 'blind by night', but was afterwards erroneously taken to mean 'seeing by night' (as if simply from νύξ and ὤψ). The confusion resulting from this mistake has also extended to the converse term HEMERALOPIA.]

a. Night-blindness; recurrent dimness or loss of vision after sunset, generally produced by exposure to a strong light. **b.** Inability to see clearly except by night; night-vision, day-blindness.

1684 BRIGGS in *Phil. Trans.* XIV. 563 The case now mention'd..is call'd by later Writers *Nyctalopia.* **1693** tr. *Blancard's Phys. Dict.* (ed. 2), *Nyctalopia*, Two-fold; the first is a Dimness of Sight in the Night, or in dark Places, without any Impediment in the Light: The other is a Dimness in the Light, and clear Sight in the Night, or in Shades. **1764** *W. India Dis.* 60 Of the Nyctalopia. I never saw the Hemeralopia in the West-Indies; but the night-blindness I have seen there. **1803** W. HEBERDEN *Comment.* lxvi. (1806) 328 A blindness will also come and go..unlike the nychtalopia, which returns every night. **1814–** [see HEMERALOPIA]. **1880** J. W. LEGG *Bile* 379 Xanthopsy and nyctalopia are thought by some to be very bad signs. **1899** *Allbutt's Syst. Med.* VIII. 708 Nystagmus, nyctalopia, and nictitation also, are always present.

transf. **1841** LATHAM *Engl. Lang.* I. vii. 98 To those writers ..I apply the term Nyctalopia (the power of seeing best in the dark), applied by a writer in one of the periodicals to similar Etymologists.

nycta'lopic, *a. Path.* [See prec. and -IC. So F. *nyctalopique*.] Of the nature of, affected with, nyctalopia.

1868 COLLINGWOOD *Rambles Naturalist* xviii. 310 This singular nyctalopic affection [*sc.* moon-blindness]. **1880** *Libr. Univ. Knowl.* X. 757 Albinos are frequently nyctalopic. **1898** *Allbutt's Syst. Med.* V. 597 If one eye of a nyctalopic patient be bandaged this eye will recover.

‖**nyctalops** ('nɪktəlɒps). *rare.* Also 7 **nycti-.** [L. *nyctalops* (Pliny), a. Gr. νυκτάλωψ: see NYCTALOPIA and NYCTALOPE.]

†**1.** Nyctalopia. *Obs.*

1661 LOVELL *Hist. Anim. & Min.* 105 The gall cureth the weft in the eye, and nyctalops. *Ibid.* 169 Some use the parts dissected to weake joynts, others against the nyctilops. **1727–38** CHAMBERS *Cycl.*, *Nyctalopia*, or *Nyctalops*, a disease which prevents the seeing by day, not by night.

2. One affected with nyctalopia.

1818 TODD, *Nyctalops*, one who sees best in the night. **1828–32** WEBSTER, *Nyctalops*, one who loses his sight as night comes on, and remains blind until morning.

nyctalopy ('nɪktələʊpɪ). Also 7 -ie. [Anglicized form of NYCTALOPIA.] Nyctalopia.

1661 LOVELL *Hist. Anim. & Min.* 110 The liver cureth the nyctalopie, the eyes being washed with the decoction. **1818** TODD, *Nyctalopy*, a disease or indisposition of the eye, in which a person sees better by night than by day. **1879** LEWIS & SHORT *Lat. Dict.*, *Nyctalopia*, the disease of one who cannot see in the twilight, nyctalopy.

'nycterin(e, *sb.* and *a. Zool.* [f. mod.L. *Nycteris* + -INE.] **a.** *sb.* A bat of the genus *Nycteris.* **b.** *adj.* Belonging or related to the genus *Nycteris.*

1840 *Cuvier's Anim. Kingd.* 73 The Nycterins have the forehead furrowed by a longitudinal groove.

nycthemer(on, variant of NYCHTHEMER(ON.

nycti- ('nɪktɪ), repr. Gr. νυκτι-, a combining form (properly locative) of νυκτ-, νύξ night, used in a few scientific terms, chiefly zoological, as ***nyctiardea***, the nycticorax; ***Nycticebus***, a genus including the slow-paced lemur; ***nyctipithecus***, a night-monkey; ***nyctisaura***, a nocturnal lizard. Adjectival derivatives from these, as ***nycticebine***, ***nyctipithecine***, ***nyctisaurian***, are given in some recent Dictionaries.

‖**nycticorax** (nɪk'tɪkəræks). *Ornith.* [L. *nycticorax*, a. Gr. νυκτικόραξ, f. νύξ, νυκτι- night + κόραξ raven.] The night-heron (formerly also called the night-raven).

1688 HOLME *Armoury* II. 255/1 He beareth Argent, a Nycticorax his Head couped Sable. **1753** CHAMBERS *Cycl. Suppl.*, *Nycticorax*, in zoology, the name of a bird called in English the night raven. It is of the heron kind. **1838** BP. M. RUSSELL *Hist. Anc. & Mod. Egypt* (1853) V. 148 The image ..of a nycticorax..[became] the sign of *M.*

nyctilops: see NYCTALOPS.

nyctinastic (nɪktɪ'næstɪk), *a. Bot.* [a. G. *nyctinastisch* (W. Pfeffer *Pflanzenphysiologie* (ed. 2, 1904) II. xii. 476): see NYCTI- and NASTIC *a.*] Of the movements of flowers or leaves, caused by a regular cycle of changes in light and temperature. So **nycti'nastism, 'nyctinasty,** movement of this kind. Cf. NYCTITROPIC *a.*, NYCTITROPISM.

1906 A. J. EWART tr. *Pfeffer's Physiol. Plants* III. ii. 97 Since the term 'tropism' is reserved for curvatures produced by unilateral stimuli, it becomes necessary to change the term 'nyctitropic' used by Darwin..into that of 'nyctinastic'. *Ibid.* 101 There is no reason for restricting the term nyctinastic to pronounced sleep-movements. **1921** J. SMALL *Textbk. Bot.* xxvi. 378 Nyctitropism or Nyctinastism includes the opening and closing of flowers.., also the rising and falling of leaves..in response to the stimulation of changes in temperature and light. **1936** J. B. HILL et al. *Botany* ix. 228 Certain leaves as well as flowers may fold up at night. These so-called 'sleep movements' of plants, brought about by the alternation of night and day, are the most common nasties and are termed nyctinasties. **1968** *New Scientist* 26 Dec. 717/1 The closing of the leaves..in fact, happens after the transfer of the plants to darkness—a so-called nyctinastic or 'sleep' movement.

nyctitropic (nɪktɪ'trɒpɪk), *a. Bot.* [f. NYCTI- + Gr. τρόπος turn; cf. *geotropic*, *heliotropic*.] Turning in a certain direction at night. So **nyctitropism.** (See quots.)

1880 C. & F. DARWIN *Movem. Pl.* 281 Nyctitropism and nyctitropic, i.e. night-turning, may be applied both to leaves and flowers,..but it would be best to confine the term to leaves. *Ibid.* 298 No movement deserves to be called nyctitropic, unless it has been acquired for the sake of lessening radiation. **1885** GOODALL *Physiol. Bot.* (1892) 411 When leaves which naturally assume nyctitropic positions are pinned.., serious injuries result.

nycto- ('nɪktəʊ), repr. Gr. νυκτο-, combining form of νυκτ-, νύξ night, used in a few scientific terms, as ***Nyctophilus***, a genus of bats (hence ***nyctophilet***, a bat of this genus); ***nyctophobia***, fear of the night or of darkness; ***nyctophonia***, loss of voice during the day; ***nyctotyphlosis***, night-blindness.

1840 *Cuvier's Anim. Kingd.* 73 The Nyctophilets..are, according to Temminck, somewhat intermediate to the Rhinol[o]phines and the next genus of Nycterins.

nyctograph ('nɪktəgrɑːf, -æ-). [f. NYCTO- + -GRAPH.] A device invented by 'Lewis Carroll' with which one can record one's ideas at night, in the dark, or when not fully awake.

1891 'L. CARROLL' *Diary* 24 Sept. (1953) II. xiv. 486 Today I conceived the idea of having a series of *squares*, cut out in card, and devising an alphabet, of which each letter could be made of lines along the edges of the squares, and dots at the corners... I shall call it 'The Typhlograph'. (24/10/91. Instead of 'typhlograph' I have adopted 'Nyctograph' at the suggestion of Warner). **1898** S. D. COLLINGWOOD *Life & Lett. L. Carroll* vii. 295 In 1891 he conceived the device..and he named it the 'Typhlograph', but, at the suggestion of one of his brother-students, this was subsequently changed into 'Nyctograph'. **1930** W. DE LA MARE *Eighteen-Eighties* 236 He invented..poetical acrostics and the nyctograph. **1959** R. THOMSON *Psychol. Thinking* x. 198 Lewis Carroll derived so much from this source [*sc.* hypnagogic imagery] that he invented a peculiar instrument, the 'nyctograph', to enable him to jot down ideas without fully waking up.

nycy, obs. form of NICE *a.*

†**nyd-bedrip.** *Obs. rare.* (See NEED *sb.* 15 and BEDRIP.)

a **1300** in Spelman *Gloss.* (1664) s.v., Alicia Frere..debet ..cariare fenam ad 3 Nydbedripes in autumpno... Jo. Iverton debet..invenire 1 hominem per 3 dies ad Nydbedripes ad metendum.

nydder, obs. Sc. variant of NITHER *v.*

nydeote, nydyote, variants of NIDIOT.

nye. Now *dial.* Also 5 **neye,** 7 **ny,** 9 **ni.** [ad. OF. *ni*, *ny* (mod.F. *nid*):—L. *nīdus* nest.] A brood (of pheasants). Cf. EYE *sb.*[2]

c **1470** *Hors, Shepe, & G.* (Roxb.) 30 A neye of fesantes. **1486** *Bk. St. Albans* f vj, A Nye of Fesaunttys. **1688** HOLME *Armoury* II. 310/2. **1818** TODD, *Nye of pheasants*, a brood of pheasants: So an eye is sometimes called. **1853–** in various dial. glossaries (Essex, Sussex, Hants, Berks, Warw., Worc., etc.).

†**nye,** variant of NEYE, eye. *Obs.*

1602 DEKKER *Satirom.* G 2 b, And there stucke a nose and two nyes in his pate. **1624** DAVENPORT *City Night-c.* I. ii, Sweet chick, I come to take leave of thee: finger in nye already! **1681** T. FLATMAN *Heraclitus Ridens* No. 39 (1713) I. 255 As like one of your Smithfield Lions, as ever he can peke out of his Nyes.

nye, obs. f. NEIGH, NIGH, NINE; var. of NOY *v. Obs.*

nyef(f)e, obs. ff. NEIF.

nyegh, nyeȝ, obs. ff. NIGH.

nyen, obs. f. NINE.

nyend, obs. f. NINTH.

nyentene, -tethe, obs. ff. NINETEEN(TH.

nyesse, variant of NYAS *Obs.*

nyeþe, obs. f. NINTH.

†**nyf,** var. NIF, for *ne if*, if not, unless. *Obs.*

13.. *E.E. Allit. P.* B. 424 Nyf oure lorde hade ben her lodez-mon, hem had lumpen harde.

nyfel, -fil, -fle, -fyl, obs. ff. NIFLE.

nyfte, var. of NIFT *Obs.*

nygard(e, -art, -erd(e, nyggard(e, etc., obs. ff. NIGGARD.

nygghe, nyȝghe, obs. ff. NIGH.

nyggish, -yshe, varr. of NIGGISH *a. Obs.*

nyggoun, var. of NIGON *Obs.*

nyghbur, obs. f. NEIGHBOUR.

†**nyȝe,** variant of NY = *ne*, nor. *Obs.*

c **1420** *Chron. Vilod.* 1834 In..bode, flessh, nyȝe bone.

nyȝe, obs. f. NIGH, NINE.

nyȝeþe, obs. f. NINTH.

nyght(e, obs. ff. NIGH, NIGHT; var. of NIFT *Obs.*

nyghtertale, etc., **nyghtyngale,** obs. ff. NIGHTERTALE, NIGHTINGALE.

†**nygot,** error for *yngot*, INGOT.

1579–80 NORTH *Plutarch* 458 In his triumphe were caried ..of siluer nygots, fiue thousand..pounde weight.

nygo(u)n, varr. of NIGON *Obs.*

nygramancy, etc., obs. ff. NECROMANCY.

nygro, variant of NIGRO *Obs.*

nygromancer, etc., obs. ff. NECROMANCER.

nygun, variant of NIGON *Obs.*

nygyshe, variant of NIGGISH *a. Obs.*

nyhe, obs. f. NIGH.

nyht, obs. f. NIGHT.

nyhtingale, obs. f. NIGHTINGALE.

†**'nying,** *vbl. sb. Obs.*[−1] [Cf. NE *v.*] Denial.

c **1450** *Mirour Saluacioun* (Roxb.) 106 The threfald nying be Petere.

nyit, var. of NITE *v. Obs.*

nyk, var. of NICK *v.*[1] *Obs.*

nyke, obs. f. NICK *sb.*[1]

nyker, obs. f. NICKER *sb.*[1]

† **nykin.** *Obs.* [Of obscure origin.] A term of endearment.

1693 CONGREVE *Old Bach.* IV. i, *Lætitia*, I hope my dearest Jewel is not going to leave me. Are you Nykin? *Fondle-wife*, Go naughty Nykin, you don't love me. *Ibid.* iv, Now my dear Nyken.

nykke, variant of NICK *v.*[1] *Obs.*

† **nykle,** variant (see N 3) of ICKLE *sb.*, icicle. *Obs.*

a **1450** *Medulla* in *Promp. Parv.* 259 *note*, *Stiria est gutta fluens, vel cadens congelata*, a nykle.

nykyr, obs. f. NICKER *sb.*[1]

nyl(e, obs. ff. NILL *v.*

nyld, obs. var. of NEEDLE.

† **nyle.** *Obs.*[−1] [a. F. *nielle*:—L. *nebula*.] A fog or mist.

1481 CAXTON *Godfrey* xlv. 85 This londe..is ful..of lakes and mareys that a grete nyle sourdeth euery day.

† **nylet.** *Obs. rare*[−1]. (Of uncertain meaning.) Printed *niset* (cf. NYSOT) in Hazlitt's *Dodsley* II. 22.

1554 *Interlude of Youth* B iij, A lytell pretye nylet, Ye be well nise, God wote; Ye be a lytell prety pye.

Nylex ('naɪlɛks). A proprietary name of nylon.

1957 *Official Gazette* (U.S. Patent Office) 3 Sept. TM 3/2 Polymers, Inc...*Nylex* for extruded synthetic fibres, particularly adapted for use as brush bristles. **1967** E. A. GOLLSCHEWSKY in *Coast to Coast 1965–66* 88 She sank into a patio chair of plaited nylex. **1969** *Guardian* 7 Jan. 7/2 For dinghy sailors, showerproof clothes in Nylex, lightweight and very strong, are..sufficient.

nylghau ('nɪlgɔː). Forms: 8 **nyl-gau**, 8–9 **nyl-ghau**, 9 **nyl ghau**, **nylghau**; 8 **neel-gaw**, 9 **neelghau**; **nilgau**, **nilghau**. [a. Pers. *nīlgāw*, f. *nīl* blue + *gāw* ox, cow. See also NILGAI.] A large short-horned Indian antelope, the adult male of which is of a bluish- or iron-grey colour, and has a tuft of hair on the throat.

1770 HUNTER in *Phil. Trans.* LXI. 171 The male Nyl-ghau struck my imagination with being of a middle stature, between black cattle and deer. **1794** *Sporting Mag.* III. 121 The nyl-ghau, with the quickness of lightning, darted against the wood work. **1800** *Asiatic Ann. Reg.* 285/2 His activity and courage in the attack of the boar, the neel-gaw ..and of the tiger. **1824** HEBER *Jrnl.* xv. (1844) I. 214/1 There are not only neelghaus,..but some noble red-deer in this park. **1855** *Orr's Circ. Sci., Org. Nat.* III. 442 The Nyl Ghau has frequently been brought to this country, and breeds pretty freely in confinement. **1887** L. OLIPHANT *Episodes Adventure* 163, I shot my first and only blue bull or nylgau.

† **nyll,** obs. form (see N 3) of ILL *a.*

1575 LANEHAM *Let.* (1871) 130 Haue ye..slaunderd any man or woman, & browght them in a nyll name?

nyll(e, obs. ff. NILL *sb.*[1], *sb.*[2], and *v.*

nylon ('naɪlɒn). Also **Nylon**. [Invented word, with *-on* suggested by *rayon*, *cotton*.

There is no evidence to support the derivations freq. given for this word in popular sources. Cf. the following quot.: **1940** *Women's Wear Daily* 9 Feb. 22 The du Pont letter, written by John W. Eckelberry, covers the general status of nylon as follows: 'The word is a generic word coined by the du Pont Co. It is not a registered name or trademark... We wish to emphasize the following additional points: First, that the letters n-y-l-o-n have absolutely no significance, etymologically or otherwise... Because the names of two textile fibers in common use—namely 'cotton' and 'rayon', end with letters 'on'..it was felt that a word ending in 'on' might be desirable. A number of words..were rejected because it was found they were not sufficiently distinct from words found in the dictionary, or in lists of classified trademarks. After much deliberation, the term 'nylon' was finally adopted.']

1. Any of the thermoplastics that are wholly synthetic polyamides with a straight-chain molecular structure, many of which are tough, lightweight, and resistant to heat and chemicals, may be produced as filaments, bristles, or sheets and as moulded objects, and are widely used for textile fabrics and industrially; *esp.* nylon 66, made from adipic acid and hexamethylene-diamine.

1938 *N.Y. Times* 28 Oct. 34/3 'Nylon' is a generic name, coined by the du Pont chemists, to designate all materials defined scientifically as 'synthetic fiber-forming polymeric amides having a protein-like chemical structure; derivable from coal, air and water, or other substances, and characterized by extreme toughness and strength and the peculiar ability to be formed into fibers and into various shapes, such as bristles and sheets'. **1940** *Times* 21 Mar. 5/5 Imperial Chemical Industries, Limited, announce that progress is being made in the erection of three factories for the manufacture of nylon in England. **1942** *Industr. & Engin. Chem.* Jan. 56/2 After polymerization, the molten nylon is extruded as a ribbon onto a chilled roll. **1943** *Chem. Abstr.* XXXVII. 3947 A description of the manuf. of No. 66 Nylon (as the most important nylon). **1950** R. W. MONCRIEFF *Artificial Fibres* xvii. 206 '610' nylon may be preferred to '66', for use as bristles. **1955** *Sci. News Let.* 2 Apr. 217/2 The new, tempered form of nylon, named Nylon 8 by the Du Pont Co., is a liquid. It can be molded into fuel tanks, pipes, gaskets and seals. **1958** D. E. FLOYD *Polyamide Resins* i. 4 Nylon-6,10 means that the diamine contained 6 carbon atoms and the dibasic acid contained 10 carbon atoms. **1963** H. R. CLAUSER *Encycl. Engin. Materials* 451/1 Nylons resist electrolytic corrosion, hydrolysis, fungi, bacteria and most chemicals. **1964** *Which?* Aug. 253/2 There are a number of different nylons used in textiles. *Ibid.*, Fabrics made from nylon tend to attract dirt. **1964** N. G. CLARK *Mod. Org. Chem.* xvii. 361 The most famous example of this is nylon 66 (popularly known as Nylon), which is straight chain polyamide constructed from two six-carbon components. **1972** J. WREN-LEWIS in Cox & Dyson *20th-Cent. Mind* II. ix. 279 In modern chemical jargon the term 'nylon' refers, not to any one specific material but to any macromolecular material made by interacting dibasic acids with diamines: such materials are sometimes also called polyamides. **1973** *Sci. Amer.* July 42/3 Today the matrix in glass-reinforced composites may be either a thermoset plastic, such as polyester,..or any of a number of thermoplastic resins, such as nylon, polyethylene or polystyrene.

2. *pl.* Nylon stockings.

1940 *Woman* (U.S.) V. II. 68 Dunk your nylons in rich suds of neutral soap. **1948** *Daily Mail* 21 Apr. 1/2 The two cases were opened by Customs officers. Both were full of nylons and powder compacts. **1951** M. MCLUHAN *Mech. Bride* (1967) 33/1 Food and nylons..are consumed and promoted with moral fervor. **1957** J. BRAINE *Room at Top* vii. 72 High heels and nylons. **1965** *N.Y. Times* 16 May VI. 80/2 By 1964, silk and rayon stockings were almost unknown in the United States, while production of nylons had risen to 83,900,000 dozen pairs. **1966** J. BETJEMAN *High & Low* 67 Encase your legs in nylons, Bestride your hills with pylons, O age without a soul.

3. Fabric or cloth made from nylon yarn.

1940 *Jrnl. R. Aeronaut. Soc.* XLIV. 312 Possible use of synthetic textile Nylon as a parachute material. **1945** *Times* 6 Nov. 4/4 Arrangements are being made for the conversion into clothing and other goods of 26,000,000 yards of nylon, cotton and celanese which will become available from finished parachutes surrendered by the services as surplus. **1958** *Woman's Own* 5 Feb. 37/3 (Advt.), Nighties, blouses, slips, underwear in silk, nylon, rayon, 'Terylene', chiffon.. keep their soft sheen and filmy finery. **1967** E. SHORT *Embroidery & Fabric Collage* iii. 81 Appliqué in more net, or in nylon, organdie, etc., would give weight and definition to the design.

II. 4. *attrib.* or as *adj.* Made or consisting of nylon.

1939 *Industrial Fibres Rev.* III. 167/1 The first considerable use of 'Nylon' yarn will be in the full-fashioned hose trade where silk is at present the raw material. **1941** *Jrnl. R. Aeronaut. Soc.* XLV. 219 Fabrics manufactured of Nylon artificial fibre, a coal derivative.., has [*sic*] been.. compared with pure silk, as a possible substitute for the latter, for use in the manufacture of parachutes. **1941** *Jrnl. Amer. Med. Assoc.* 4 Oct. 1221/1 One of the principal reasons why Nylon stockings have achieved popularity is the fact that they are more 'sheer' than silk stockings. **1951** *Good Housek. Home Encycl.* 29/2 Nylon brushes are available in a variety of colours. **1958** *New Statesman* 28 June 831/1 Men who had nylon shirts and terylene suits before those fabrics got into Marks and Spencer's. **1958** L. VAN DER POST *Lost World of Kalahari* ix. 209 We had to make our home under a nylon tarpaulin stretched taut between our Land-Rovers. **1961** *Lancet* 22 July 206/2 Nylon film as a wrapping material for sterilisation. **1968** *Bodl. Libr. Rec.* VIII. 61 It runs on four 4-inch nylon wheels fitted with roller bearings. **1973** 'E. PETERS' *City of Gold & Shadows* iv. 65 In a nylon jersey house-gown..she could not possibly be anyone but Mrs. Paviour.

b. (See quots.)

1955 *Caribbean Q.* IV. II. 103 Nylon, pronounced 'nilô' or 'dilô' has come to signify anything new, different, and better. The new ice house in Soufriere advertises 'nylon' ice, and nylon starch and nylon peanuts can be had, the latter being candies shaped like peanuts. **1967** CASSIDY & LE PAGE *Dict. Jamaican Eng.* 326/2 *Nylon road*, any new very smooth asphalt-surfaced road—much smoother than the average Jamaican road. (From about 1958, FGC.)

5. General attrib.

1942 *Industr. & Engin. Chem.* Jan. 58/2 The nylon industry is only in its infancy. **1951** *Economist* 22 Sept. 686/1 Nylon output is now running at an annual rate of 100 million pounds. **1953** K. H. INDERFURTH *Nylon Technol.* 11 Du Pont's third nylon plant. **1963** H. R. CLAUSER *Encycl. Engin. Materials* 452/1 Tubing and rod stock manufacture, plus the coating of wire and cable, are the major forms of nylon extrusion.

6. *Comb.* **a.** Instrumental, as ***nylon-covered***, ***-faced*** adjs. **b.** Parasynthetic, as ***nylon-bristled***, ***-geared***, ***-legged***, ***-tipped*** adjs.

1954 H. R. MAUERSBERGER in *Matthews's Textile Fibers* (ed. 6) xviii. 946 Nylon-bristled toothbrushes. **1960** *Farmer & Stockbreeder* 29 Mar. 75/3 The pump..incorporates nylon-covered steel rollers to push the milk round. **1967** *Jane's Surface Skimmer Systems 1967–68* 25/1 Propulsion fans are driven by nylon-faced toothed rubber timing belts. **1961** *Listener* 5 Oct. 498/2 Nylon-geared egg beaters. **1954** J. BETJEMAN *Few Late Chrysanthemums* 74 And country girls with lips and nails vermilion Wait, nylon-legged, to straddle on the pillion. **1966** *Melody Maker* 23 July 10/4 His [drum] sticks are..Autocrat nylon-tipped and Japanese Star 7a.

7. Special comb.: **nylon (stocking) dermatitis**, dermatitis caused by the dye of nylon stockings; **nylon salt**, a salt formed by the reaction of hexamethylenediamine (or another diamine) with adipic acid (or another dibasic acid), which is polymerized to give nylon.

1954 H. R. MAUERSBERGER in *Matthews's Textile Fibers* (ed. 6) xviii. 961 Any references to 'nylon dermatitis'..are distinct misnomers. **1964** *Listener* 26 Mar. 520/1 Nylon dermatitis and bunions are related to fashions of dress. **1945** *Industr. Fibres & By-Products* VII. 53/2 The nylon salt solution is..ready to be made into new nylon polymer. **1958** D. E. FLOYD *Polyamide Resins* iv. 54 Nylon salts may be formed in water or aqueous alcohol solution and are crystallized from aqueous alcohol or alcohol itself. They are usually soluble in water, but insoluble in alcohol, acetone, ether, or hydrocarbons. **1964** J. G. COOK *Your Guide to Plastics* 239 Hexamethylene diamine and adipic acid are reacted together to form a salt, hexamethylene diammonium adipate, or 'nylon salt'. *Ibid.* 240 Hexamethylene diamine and sebacic acid are combined to form nylon 6:10 salt, or hexamethylene diammonium sebacate. **1947** *Jrnl. Investigative Dermatol.* IX. 207 All the subjects suffering from nylon stocking dermatitis were hypersensitive to azodyes used in the manufacture of the stockings. **1957** *Year Bk. Dermatol. & Syphilol.* 117 Nylon stocking dermatitis results from sensitivity to the dye.

nyloned ('naɪlɒnd), *a.* [f. prec. + -ED[2].] Clad in nylons.

1952 B. MALAMUD *Natural* (1963) 16 Her nyloned legs made Roy's pulses dance. **1959** *Times Lit. Suppl.* 9 Oct. 573/3 Also making the voyage are a group of American girls ..normal, nyloned, streamlined, wide-eyed, cynical and destructive. **1962** *Economist* 31 Mar. 1240/1 The men are well shod, the women well nyloned. **1963** G. FREEMAN *Campaign* iv. 69 Lady Andover's knees emerging, pinkly nyloned, from under her black coat. **1975** I. MURDOCH *Word Child* 195, I looked down, inspecting a nyloned ankle and a smart..high-heeled shoe.

nylt: see NILL *v.*

nym, var. of NIM *v.*

nymbil, nymble, nymill, obs. ff. NIMBLE *a.*

nym(m)e, variants of NIM *v.*

nymph (nɪmf), *sb.* Forms: 4–7 **nimphe**, 6–7 **nymphe**, 7 **nimph**, 6– **nymph**. [a. F. *nymphe* (OF. *nimphe*), ad. L. *nympha*: see NYMPHA.]

1. a. *Myth.* One of a numerous class of semi-divine beings, imagined as beautiful maidens inhabiting the sea, rivers, fountains, hills, woods, or trees, and frequently introduced by the poets as attendants on a superior deity.

Special names for the various kinds of nymphs existed in Greek, and most of these have been employed in English, as *dryad*, *hamadryad*, *naiad*, *Nereid*, *oceanid*, *oread*.

1390 GOWER *Conf.* I. 306, I rede Of thilke Nimphe which Laar hihte. *Ibid.* II. 336 With the Nimphes ek also Upon the spring of freisshe welles Sche schop to duelle. **1412–20** LYDG. *Chron. Troy* II. 2580 With hir nimphes, Iuno cam be-hynde. *c* **1500** *Melusine* 15 Ye shuld shortly haue ben out of the handes of the Nymphes & of the fairees. **1567** MAPLET *Gr. Forest* 54 Neptunes Daughter a Nymph, fleeing from Priapus, was turned into this tree. **1634** MILTON *Comus* 824 There is a gentle Nymph not farr from hence, That with moist curb sways the smooth Severn stream. **1717** LADY M. W. MONTAGU *Lett.* I. xxxvii. 145 Her fair maids..put me in mind of the pictures of the ancient nymphs. **1791** COWPER *Iliad* XVIII. 63 Nor alone Came these, but every ocean-nymph beside. **1835** THIRLWALL *Greece* vi. I. 200 Where flocks and herds of the Sun were tended by the nymphs. **1869** TOZER *Highl. Turkey* II. 308 By night they appear, and, like all the nymphs of ancient times, amuse themselves with graceful dances.

b. *transf.* A stream, river.

1591 SYLVESTER *Du Bartas* I. vi. 656 Kennet,..Her Silver Nymphs (almost) directly leading To meet her Mistress (the great Thames) at Reading. *a* **1649** DRUMM. OF HAWTH. *Fam. Ep.* Wks. (1711) 156 Having to these Seas of Joy..added this small Brook or Nymph of mine. **1889** GRETTON *Memory's Harkback* 291 If the wandering nymph, Vaga, instead of flowing zigzag from Hereford to Ross, would but have meandered down this valley.

c. A ship.

1876 R. F. BURTON *Gorilla L.* II. 15, I transferred myself on board H.M. Steamship 'Zebra', one of the nymphs of the British navy.

2. a. *poet.* A young and beautiful woman; hence, a maiden, damsel.

1584 LODGE *Forbonius & Prisceria* 32 O Nimph of beauties train, The onely cause and easer of my paine. **1590** SHAKS. *Mids. N.* IV. i. 124 But soft, what nimphs are these? *Egeus.* My Lord, this is my daughter heere asleepe. *c* **1616** SIR W. MURE *Miscell. Poems* xv. 19 Then happie nimph, quhoise spreit in peace repoises. **1682** DRYDEN *To Duchess York* 12 But now the illustrious nymph, returned again, Brings every grace triumphant in her train. **1703** ROWE *Fair Penit.* I. i, I hastily took leave and left the Nymph. **1768–74** TUCKER *Lt. Nat.* (1834) II. 574 They expect to find a faithful nymph or swain in whatever their fancy sets upon. **1821** BYRON *Sardanap.* I. ii, Fair nymphs, who deign To share the soft hours of Sardanapalus. *a* **1839** PRAED *Poems* (1864) I. 326 And when the little Nymph had done, Said 'Thank you, Love;—I'll write another!'

b. In euphemistic or jocular use. (Chiefly in phrases.)

1632 LITHGOW *Trav.* I. 27 These vermillion Nymphs.. would oft runne races, skipping like wanton Lambes. **1751** F. COVENTRY *Pompey the Little* 96 His Master..sold him a second time to a Nymph of Billingsgate for a Pennyworth of Oysters. **1833** W. TOLMIE *Jrnl.* 28 Mar. (1963) 133 Nymphs of the pavé numerous (in Honolulu). **1859** *Slang Dict.* 69 *Nymph of the Pave*, a girl of the town. **1902** FARMER & HENLEY *Slang* V. 81 *Nymph of darkness* (or *the pavement*),.. a prostitute. **1942** BERREY & VAN DEN BARK *Amer. Thes. Slang* §507/2 Prostitute..Nymph du pave. **1964** 'W. HAGGARD' *Antagonists* vii. 71 Counsellor of Embassy living with fellow-travelling nymph.... They'd do most things to muffle that one. **1965** 'S. HARVESTER' *Assassins Road* xvii. 180 He had been pretty sure she was a nymph. **1968** R. STOUT *Father Hunt* (1969) xiii. 157 She was a nymph. She was a goddam tart.

c. A type of fashionable woman under the Directory in France.

1898 LADY M. LOYD tr. *O. Uzanne's Fashion in Paris* i. 14 The Nymph and the Merveilleuse—those types of a period of deep corruption and open libertinage.

3. a. An insect in that stage of development which intervenes between the larva and the imago; a pupa.

1577 B. GOOGE *Heresbach's Husb.* IV. (1586) 185 b, The other common sort, when they begin to haue fashion, are called nimphes. **1609** C. BUTLER *Fem. Mon.* (1634) 28 The young weak nymphs falling in those shady places..are in danger to be chilled. **1658** ROWLAND tr. *Moufet's Theat. Ins.* 898 At length they grow to be Nymphs, *i.e.* little Bees, but without wings. **1747** GOULD *Eng. Ants* 44 They are called Nymphs in allusion to Brides, because when they leave this State, they are often arrayed in Gayety and Splendour. **1797** *Encycl. Brit.* (ed. 3) III. 123/1 The hive is cleared of every egg, maggot, or nymph. **1834** MCMURTRIE *Cuvier's Anim. Kingd.* 415 The nymphs of the large species leave the water altogether. **1895** D. SHARP *Insects* I. 420 The mouth of the nymph bears a remarkable structure called the mask.

attrib. **1753** CHAMBERS *Cycl. Suppl.* s.v., This is properly the nymph state.

b. A fishing fly made in imitation of the aquatic larval form of may-flies, insects of the order Ephemeroptera.

1910 G. E. M. SKUES *Minor Tactics of Chalk Stream* iv. 32, I had tied some nymphs of appropriate colour of body. **1922** R. C. BRIDGETT *Dry-fly Fishing* i. 17 The place of honour [as a lure] is occupied by the artificial nymph. **1973** *Shooting Times & Country Mag.* 7 July 13/3 There were virtually no rising fish to be seen and I decided to plod on with the nymph.

†**4.** *pl. Anat.* = NYMPHA 2. *Obs. rare.*

1615 CROOKE *Body of Man* 239 The two smaller clefts.. between the Nymphes, the two Nymphes themselues.

5. *Conch.* = NYMPHA 3.

1839 *Penny Cycl.* XIV. 319/1 Shell often gaping a little at the lateral extremities... Nymphs..gaping outwards.

6. *attrib.* and *Comb.*, as ***nymph-fishing, -land, -mother, -queen, -song; nymph-haunted, -less, -pink, -prompted, -strong*** adjs.

1598 SYLVESTER *Du Bartas* II. ii. *Babylon* 71 The rowling ridges Of Nymph-strong floods. **1605** *Ibid.* iii. *Lawe* 982 Nymph-prompted Numa, or the Spartan's Lord. **1812** BYRON *Ch. Har.* II. xxix, While thus of both bereft, the nymph-queen [Calypso] doubly sigh'd. **1835** WILLIS *Pencillings* xxxviii. I. 257 The lovely nymph-mother of Ganymede. **1881** O. WILDE *Poems* 69 Blue nymph-haunted seas. **1887** BOWEN *Virg. Ecl.* ix. 19 Who was to chant to us stories of Nymph-land, blossom and flower. **1891** *Bazaar* 20 Feb. 264/3 Ivory-white, nymph-pink, blue, and heliotrope. **1930** E. BLUNDEN *Summer's Fancy* 15 When nymph-songs echoed on the blossomed breeze. **1932** *Times Lit. Suppl.* 5 May 374/2 The delicate art of nymph-fishing. **1939** W. B. YEATS *On Boiler* 28 Nymph-haunted or Fury-haunted wood. **1948** C. DAY LEWIS *Poems 1943–47* 19 Otherwise the forest was silent: birdless; nymphless. **1972** *Shooting Times & Country Mag.* 1 July 15/2 The Club rules permit only dry fly and nymph fishing until the end of July.

nymph (nɪmf), *v.* [f. the sb., sense 3.] Of fish, esp. trout: to feed upon insect larvæ near the surface of the water. So **'nymphing** *ppl. a.*

1963 O. KITE in C. F. Walker *Compl. Fly-fisher* iv. 140 A nymphing trout..can be seen making little movements, lifting slightly in the water from time to time. **1972** *Shooting Times & Country Mag.* 24 June 15/2 In the sheltered bay we saw the odd fish nymphing.

‖**nympha** ('nɪmfə). Pl. nymphæ ('nɪmfiː); 7 nympha's. [L., a. Gr. νύμφη bride, nymph.]

1. = NYMPH *sb.* 3.

1601 HOLLAND *Pliny* I. 318 The rest of the multitude, when they begin to take some shape, are called Nymphæ. **1670** *Phil. Trans.* V. 2100 All mine being of a late Hatch, and none of them yet turned into *Nympha's* (which is the word of Art for the *Aurelia* of a Bee). **1740** CHEYNE *Regimen* 155 The different Shapes of seminal Animalculs, Eggs, Nymphæ and young Insects. **1816** KIRBY & SP. *Entomol.* iii. (1818) I. 66 To these Aristotle originally gave the name of *nymphæ*. **1875** HOUGHTON *Brit. Insects* 56 When the nympha is ready to undergo its transformation, it creeps up the stem of some water plant.

attrib. **1713** DERHAM *Phys.-Theol.* IV. xiv. (1714) 251 Sufficient Food and Nourishment in all their Nympha-State, in which they need Food. **1816** KIRBY & SP. *Entomol.* xvi. (1818) II. 16 They arrived at their full growth, and threw off their nympha-state by casting their outward skin.

2. *pl. Anat.* The labia minora of the vulva, situated within the labia majora.

1693 tr. *Blancard's Phys. Dict.* (ed. 2), *Nymphæ*, little pieces of Flesh in a Woman's Secrets. **1754** SMELLIE *Midwifery* (1764) I. 92 From the lower part of the Clitoris the Nymphæ rising spread outwards and downwards. **1843** R. J. GRAVES *Clin. Med.* xxvi. 329 The internal wall of the nymphæ. **1863** tr. *Waitz' Introd. Anthropol.* I. 106 Adams reports that in Dahomey the nymphæ are artificially elongated.

3. *pl. Conch.* (See quot.)

1835–6 *Todd's Cycl. Anat.* I. 710/1 There are other parts ..destined for the implantation of the ligament when it is external; to these parts the name of *nymphæ* is given. These form two callosities more or less prominent, which are seen along the posterior and superior edge of the shell.

‖**nymphæa** (nɪm'fiːə). Also nymphea. [L., ad. Gr. νυμφαία, fem. of νυμφαῖος sacred to the nymphs. So F. *nymphæa, nymphéa*, Sp. and It. *ninfea*.] The common white or yellow water-lily; a genus of aquatic plants including these and other species.

1562 TURNER *Herbal* II. (1568) 66 The roote of the whyte Nymphea is black,..of the yellow..whyte. **1601** HOLLAND *Pliny* II. 222 Nenuphar is called in Greeke Nymphæa. **1673** RAY *Journ. Low C.* (1693) II. 97 Their Alterative Physick consists of Coolers, and Anodyns, as Nymphæa, Poppy, Endive. **1741** *Compl. Fam.-Piece* II. iii. 374 In the Water Tubs, the yellow Nymphea or Water Lilly. **1796** H. HUNTER tr. *St.-Pierre's Stud. Nat.* (1799) II. 113 The yellow roses of the nymphæa, which float on lakes. **1851** MADDEN *Shrines & Sepul.* I. 178 Pools of water covered with nymphæas. **1882** *Garden* 14 Jan. 20/2 In many of the stagnant ponds was a small yellow Nymphæa, the leaves of which are used as a pickle by the Japanese.

Comb. **1855** MISS PRATT *Flower. Pl.* IV. 13 Nymphæa-like Villarsia... This is a most elegant water-plant.

‖**nymphæum, -eum** (nɪm'fiːəm). *Archæol.* Pl. -æa, -ea. [L. *nymphæum, -ēum*, ad. Gr. νυμφαῖον, -εῖον temple or shrine of the nymphs, neut. of νυμφαῖος, -εῖος sacred to the nymphs, f. νύμφη NYMPH *sb.* So F. *nymphéum*.] A grotto or shrine of the nymphs; a building, or part of one, designed to represent this.

1770 tr. *Mme. du Bocage Lett.* II. 203 The temple, the spring, the nympheum, the bason of the Romans. **1850** LEITCH tr. *C. O. Müller's Anc. Art* § 150 (ed. 2) 125 The mass of the population in the great cities was cared for by the erection of theatres, probably also thermæ and nymphæa. *c***1890** H. JAMES *Little Tour* xxviii. (1900) 189 A small Roman ruin, which is known as a temple of Diana, but was more apparently a *nymphæum*.

†**nymphal**, *sb.*[1] *Obs.* Also nimphall. [ad. L. *nymphāl-is* belonging to nymphs: see NYMPH *sb.* and -AL[1].] **a.** A meeting or gathering of nymphs. **b.** Used by Drayton as the name of each division of his *Muses' Elysium*.

1622 DRAYTON *Poly-olb.* xx. 4 He that doth of sea the powerful trident weld, His Tritons made proclaim, a Nymphall to be held In honour of himself. **1630** —— *Muses' Elys.*, Nymphal i, This Nimphall of delight doth treat, Choice beauties, and proportions meet.

nymphal ('nɪmfəl), *a.* (and *sb.*[2]) [f. as prec.]

A. *adj.* **1.** Belonging to a nymph; consisting of nymphs.

1656 BLOUNT *Glossogr.*, *Nymphal*, of or belonging to a Nymph or Bride; Nymph-like. **1842** *Fraser's Mag.* XXVI. 79 Thou glory of the Nymphal train.

2. Of the nature of, pertaining to, a pupa.

1864 HOUGHTON in *Intellect. Observ.* Oct. 150 Not a particle of food has she [a may-fly] tasted since she left her nymphal state. **1884** MICHAEL *Brit. Oribatidæ* 22 Whether it was a mature or simply a nymphal form.

3. Including or belonging to the water-plants related to *Nymphæa*.

Lindley's ***nymphal alliance*** included the natural orders *Nymphæaceæ, Cabombaceæ*, and *Nelumbiaceæ*.

1846 LINDLEY *Veget. Kingd.* 408 *Nymphales.* The Nymphal Alliance. *Ibid.* 409 Nymphal Exogens, with a many-celled fruit and dissepimental placentæ.

B. *sb.*[2] **1.** [ad. F. *nymphale*.] A name for a class of butterflies.

1797 *Encycl. Brit.* (ed. 3) XIII. 721/1 Mr. Barbut has divided them [*sc.* butterflies] into four sections... 4. The nymphals, whose wings are denticulated.

2. A plant belonging to the nymphal alliance.

1846 LINDLEY *Veget. Kingd.* 408 To distinguish Nymphals with certainty from all those Orders with which they are here associated.

nymphalid ('nɪmfəlɪd), *a.* and *sb.* [ad. mod. L. *nymphalis, -idis*, f. *nympha* NYMPH *sb.*]

a. *adj.* Belonging to the family *Nymphalidæ*. **b.** *sb.* A butterfly belonging to this family.

1895 *Athenæum* 23 Nov. 722/1 He showed the changes in mimetic forms in a single genus of nymphalid butterflies. **1897** BLES tr. *Brunner's Coloration Ins.* 2/2 Very striking is the appearance of..a Nymphalid from Mexico.

nymphean (nɪm'fiːən). *a.* [f. Gr. νυμφαῖ-ος of or belonging to a nymph + -AN. Cf. F. *nymphéen*.] Of or belonging to a nymph or nymphs; nymph-like.

*a***1758** DYER *Ruins of Rome* Poems (1761) 42 Flow'ry bow'rs they seek,..Or cool Nymphean grots. **1816** G. S. FABER *Orig. Pagan Idol.* III. 219 The description of the cavern is taken from the nymphean grotto and its subterraneous stream. **1874** T. HARDY *Far fr. Mad. Crowd* I. iii. 27 Without throwing a Nymphean tissue over a milk-maid. **1881** CABLE *Mme. Delphine* ii, The cultivation of.. nymphean grace and beauty.

Nymphenburg ('nɪmfənbɜːg). The name of a former village in Bavaria, now a suburb of Munich, used *attrib.* to designate pottery manufactured there from 1761.

1863 W. CHAFFERS *Marks Pott. & Porc.* 183 Nymphenburg. Another form of the arms of Bavaria, also impressed on the ware. **1869** C. SCHREIBER *Jrnl.* 4 & 5 July (1911) I. 26 A small Nymphenburg vase mounted, £1. **1881** *Ibid.* 16 Nov. II. 374 Our only purchase was a Nymphenburg shell piece..signed and dated C.H.Z. 1771. **1882** 'OUIDA' *Bimbi* 50 A little pale-faced chit of a damsel in white Nymphenburg china. **1910** *Encycl. Brit.* V. 751/1 His Nymphenburg figures are as highly esteemed as those he modelled at Höchst. **1960** *House & Garden* Oct. 112/1 A collection of Nymphenburg equestrian statuettes. **1971** L. A. BOGER *Dict. World Pott. & Porc.* 247 (*caption*) Nymphenburg figure.

nymphet ('nɪmfɪt). [f. NYMPH *sb.* + -ET[1].]

a. A young or little nymph.

1612 DRAYTON *Poly-olb.* xi. Argt., Of the Nymphets sporting there In Wyrrall, and in Delamere. **1616** DRUMM. OF HAWTH. *Poems* 2 Whose names shall now make ring The echoes? of whom shall the nymphets sing? **1855** SINGLETON *Virgil* I. 60 Who could the nymphets sing?

b. A nymph-like or sexually attractive young girl.

1955 V. NABOKOV *Lolita* (1959) I. v. 18 Between the age limits of nine and fourteen there occur maidens who, to certain bewitched travellers, twice or many times older than they, reveal their true nature which is not human, but nymphic (that is, demoniac); and these chosen creatures I propose to designate as 'nymphets'. **1959** *Listener* 8 Jan. 63/2 A whole chorus of what the author of *Lolita* calls 'nymphets'. **1959** *Daily Mail* 31 Jan. 4/4 He is in the thick of an affair with an idealised nymphet of 20. **1963** *Spectator* 15 Feb. 199 Two nymphets visit him together, he orders them both into his bed. **1971** *Southerly* XXXI. 12 She is.. at her first appearance a shameless nymphet of thirteen already *indifferent* to the number of boys who have enjoyed her favours. **1973** J. DI MONA *Last Man at Arlington* (1974) 51 Most of the 'sales executives' had turned out to be eighteen- and nineteen-year-old nymphets.

c. *attrib.* and *Comb.* in sense b.

1959 *Spectator* 25 Sept. 406/1 Their 'baby doll' outfits had the nymphet look which has been in fashion this summer. **1960** *Spectator* 3 June 804/1 Seems to have convinced herself that..every nymphet gesture..can be repeated again and again with ever-increasing success. **1960** *Encounter* June 86/2 The hero..bails out a nymphet-loving painter. **1971** *Daily Tel.* 27 May 8/4 Mother, a randy alcoholic; father, a seedy, nymphet-chasing Peter Pan.

nymphic ('nɪmfɪk), *a. rare*$^{-0}$. [f. NYMPH *sb.* + -IC.] Of or belonging to (the) nymphs.

1890 in *Cent. Dict.*

'nymphical, *a. rare.* [f. as prec. + -AL[1].] Characteristic of or belonging to nymphs.

1793 T. TAYLOR *Orat. Julian* 93 *note*, The sun produces angelical, dæmoniacal, heroical, and nymphical powers. **1822** —— *Apuleius* I. 320 *note*, Many essences, different from each other, such as dæmoniacal, heroical, nymphical.

nymphid ('nɪmfɪd). *rare.* [-ID.] A nymph.

1866 J. B. ROSE tr. *Ovid's Met.* 127 Born was he Of Ganges, and the nymphid Lymnatè. *Ibid.* 264 Thither Dryope..To offer garlands to the nymphids went.

nymphine ('nɪmfaɪn), *a.* [f. NYMPH *sb.* + -INE[1].] Nymphal.

1806 tr. *Huber's New Obs. Bees* (1808) 87 The worms [bees]..died before passing into their nymphine state.

nymphiparous (nɪm'fɪpərəs), *a. Ent.* [f. NYMPH *sb.* + -(I)PAROUS.] Of insects: Producing nymphæ or pupæ.

1835 KIRBY *Hab. & Inst. Anim.* II. xx. 324 Those two-winged insects called pupiparous or nymphiparous. **1844** H. STEPHENS *Bk. Farm* III. 874 This peculiarity has caused the Hippoboscidæ to be termed nymphiparous or pupiparous insects.

nymphish ('nɪmfɪʃ), *a.* [f. NYMPH *sb.* + -ISH[1].]

1. Of or belonging to, consisting of, nymphs.

1578 T. PROCTER *Gorg. Gallery* P ij b, Embouldned with your Nimphish ayde. **1605** DRAYTON *Man in the Moone* 428 He followes Phœbe, that him safely brings..unto the nymphish Bowres. **1630** —— *Muses' Elys.*, Nymphal ix, The nymphish crew Thrust in amongst them thronging.

2. Nymph-like, bewitching.

1789 MRS. PIOZZI *Journ. France* I. 306 A pretty perking air, which is infinitely nymphish and smart.

nymph-like, *a.* and *adv.* [f. NYMPH *sb.* + -LIKE.]

A. *adj.* Resembling (that of) a nymph; graceful, beautiful.

*a***1586** SIDNEY *Arcadia* (1622) 51 Young Philoclea appeared in her nimph-like apparell. **1621** QUARLES *Argalus & P.* I. Wks. (Grosart) III. 248/1, I saw..thy Nymph-like haire Loosely dishevel'd. **1667** MILTON *P.L.* IX. 452 If chance with Nymphlike step fair Virgin pass. **1718** *Free-thinker* No. 94 ¶3 There were, amongst them, a great Number of Nymph-like Genies. **1791** CHARLOTTE SMITH *Celestina* (ed. 2) I. 126 Her nymphlike and graceful form. **1822** W. IRVING *Bracebr. Hall* (1890) 136 Contemplating the door half open, and the nymph-like form within. **1886** BRET HARTE *Snowbound* 134 There was a quaint nymph-like contour to her figure.

B. *adv.* In the manner of a nymph. *rare.*

1611 FLORIO, *Nimfarsi*,..to spruce or Nimph-like dresse himselfe.

'nymphlin. *rare*$^{-1}$. [f. NYMPH *sb.* + *-lin* for -LING[1].] A little nymph.

1773 R. GRAVES *Euphrosyne* (1776) 38 Well-pleas'd she sees her infant train Of nymphlins sporting on the plain.

'nymphly, *adv. rare*$^{-1}$. [f. NYMPH *sb.* + -LY[2].] In the manner of nymphs.

1632 LITHGOW *Trav.* x. 440 Diana; and her Allabaster Nymphly-portrayed trayne.

nympho ('nɪmfəʊ), colloq. abbrev. of NYMPHOMANIAC *a.* and *sb.*

1935 [see DIPSO]. **1954** D. SCHWARTZ in *Avon Bk. Mod. Writing* II. 129 Some girls at school said that Phoebe was a nympho. **1958** A. WILSON *Middle Age of Mrs Eliot* 232 'That Cynthia Robertson's a bit nympho,' he announced in worldly tones. **1959** 'J. BELL' *Easy Prey* x. 106 Red-haired bitch... Distinctly nympho. **1960** 'R. EAST' *Kingston Black* xiv. 140 Tim Askew, degenerate turkey farmer, had pulled the trigger on the Danish nympho. **1973** 'E. PETERS' *City of Gold & Shadows* xiii. 208 She was a sex-nut-case, a virgin nympho who couldn't stand being mauled but couldn't help asking for it.

nym'phoidal, *a. rare.* [f. NYMPH-ÆA + -OIDAL.] Resembling those of the Nymphæa.

1819 LINDLEY tr. *Richard's Fruits & Seeds* 63 In considering..the nymphoidal characters of *Nelumbium*.

nympholepsy ('nɪmfəlɛpsɪ). [f. next, after *epilepsy*.] A state of rapture supposed to be inspired in men by nymphs; hence, an ecstasy or frenzy of emotion, esp. that inspired by something unattainable.

1775 R. CHANDLER *Trav. Greece* (1825) II. 191 Nympholepsy is characterised as a phrensy, which arose from having beheld them [the nymphs]. **1818** BYRON *Ch. Har.* IV. cxv, A young Aurora of the air, The nympholepsy of some fond despair. **1831** LYTTON *Godolphin* xx, The most common disease to genius is nympholepsy—the saddening for a spirit that the world knows not. **1839** De Quincey *Recoll. Lakes* Wks. 1862 II. 32 He languished with a sort of despairing nympholepsy after intellectual pleasures. **1888** *Times* 21 Aug. 8/4, I have not been reduced to a state of nympholepsy by any of the beauty that I have been privileged to behold. **1955** V. Nabokov *Lolita* (1958) I. 174 The science of nympholepsy is a precise science. Actual contact would do it in one second flat. An interspace of a millimeter would do it in ten. **1974** *Times Lit. Suppl.* 8 Feb. 122/3 His congenital nympholepsy for slender girls with thin arms.

So ‖**nympho'lepsia**.

1885 F. B. Van Voorst *Without a Compass* 13 The poor dreamer hurried on by the nympholepsia of the ideal.

nympholept ('nɪmfəlɛpt), *sb.* and *a.* [ad. Gr. νυμφόληπτ-ος caught by nymphs, f. νύμφη nymph + λαμβάνειν to take.]

A. *sb.* One who is inspired by a violent enthusiasm, especially by a passion for an unattainable ideal.

1813 J. C. Hobhouse *Journey* (ed. 2) 405 He became a nympholept; and furnished another tale, to be..adorned by the fancy of the poet. **1855** Mrs. Browning *Lett.* (1897) II. 201 We are all nympholepts in running after our ideals—and none more than yourself, indeed! **1884** A. Birrell *Obiter Dicta* Ser. I. 117 Those who pursue Truth as by a divine compulsion, and who can be likened only to the nympholepts of old.

b. Const. *of*.

1835 Lytton *Rienzi* VII. v, The very nympholept of Freedom, yet of Power— of Knowledge, yet of Religion! **1884** A. Birrell *Obiter Dicta* Ser. I. 118 The nympholepts of Truth are profoundly interesting figures in..history.

B. *adj.* Inspired by such enthusiasm.

1902 *Athenæum* 19 July 91/1 The lyric cry of nympholept modernity.

nympho'leptic, *a.* [f. prec. + -ic.]

1. Relating to or dealing with nympholepsy.

1818 Shelley *Lett.* (1882) 38, I hope your nympholeptic tale is not abandoned. **1895** *Athenæum* 21 Sept. 382/1 Writers and publishers of nympholeptic stories.

2. Affected by nympholepsy; enraptured, entranced.

1844 Mrs. Browning *Lady Geraldine's Courtship* viii, Nymphs of mountain, not of valley, we are wont to call the Muses, And in nympholeptic climbing, poets pass from mount to star. **1881** *Heptalogia* 45 To the skirts of contemplation, cramped with nympholeptic weight.

nym'phology. *rare*$^{-1}$. [f. nymph *sb.* + -(o)logy.] That branch of knowledge which treats of nymphs. Hence **nympho'logical** *a.* *rare*.

1836 *New Monthly Mag.* XLVII. 96 Egle (brightness) is a celebrated name in nymphology. **1953** R. Graves *Poems* 4 Confess, what elegant square or lumpish hamlet Lives free from nymphological disquiet?

‖**nymphomania** (nɪmfə'meɪnɪə). *Path.* [f. Gr. νύμφη bride, nymph *sb.* + μανία madness.] A feminine disease characterized by morbid and uncontrollable sexual desire.

1775 E. S. Wilmot tr. de Bienville (*title*) Nymphomania, or, a dissertation concerning the furor uterinus. **1800** tr. *Cullen's Nosology* (1820) 230 Melancholia..(c) With vehement love, without satyriasis or nymphomania. **1860** Tanner *Pregnancy* xi. 435 In a few rare cases, the attack has degenerated into nymphomania. **1876** D. Ferrier *Functions Brain* 122 The girl..in whom the cerebellum was absent suffered from nymphomania. **1905** Moussu & Dollar *Dis. Cattle* vii. iv. 562 Nymphomania may be considered as almost invariably the result of a genital lesion. **1962** C. Allen *Textbk. Psychosexual Disorders* v. xvi. 306 Since writers..have become fascinated with the concept of nymphomania..it might be as well here to state that it is clinically very rare. **1967** L. W. van den Heever tr. *Heidrich & Renk's Dis. Mammary Glands Domestic Anim.* v. 48/1 In nymphomania the cysts should be ruptured when possible and chorionic gonadotropin..administered subcutaneously or intracystally to prevent recrudescence.

Hence **nympho'maniac** (and **-manic**) *a.*, of or belonging to nymphomania; *sb.*, one suffering from nymphomania; also **nymphoma'niacal** *a.*

1861 J. Millar *Hints on Insanity* 40 Though nymphomanic symptoms are constantly present when young females are insane. **1867** Maudsley *Physiol. Mind* 285 She, ..though ultimately married, was a regular nymphomaniac. **1899** *Allbutt's Syst. Med.* VIII. 279 The furious nymphomaniac who embraces every man she can get at. **1900** *Lancet* 24 Mar. 866/2 It is practised upon mares..which have nymphomaniac tendencies. **1906** J. Joyce *Let.* 13 Nov. (1966) II. 193 Cosgrave [was sure] that I would become a nymphomaniac. **1923** *Physiol. Rev.* III. 338 The writer has examined a section..of an ovary of a nymphomaniac cow. **1923** A. Huxley *Antic Hay* xx. 287 When I call my lover a nymphomaniacal dog, she runs the penknife into my arm. **1932** Gaiger & Davies *Vet. Pathol. & Bacteriol.* III. xxxv. 513 The presence of nymphomaniac cysts is always accompanied by sterility, even though the cysts are confined to one ovary. **1949** 'J. Tey' *Brat Farrar* xxiii. 208 Pawning his life to a nymphomaniacal moron. **1967** L. W. van den Heever tr. *Heidrich & Renk's Dis. Mammary Glands Domestic Anim.* iii. 34/2 Protracted nymphomaniacal estrus associated with relaxation of the pelvic ligaments, vaginal prolapse, nervousness and aggressiveness is commonly encountered. **1969** C. Allen *Textbk. Psychosexual Disorders* (ed. 2) v. xvi. 356 Nymphomaniacs who have a compulsion due to brain lesions, hormonal imbalance or other physical abnormalities. **1973** R. Hayes *Hungarian Game* viii. 59 From different sources I'd heard that she was nymphomaniacal or homosexual or frigid.

‖**nymphon** ('nɪmfɒn). *Zool.* [a. Gr. νυμφών bride-chamber, f. νύμφη bride, nymph *sb.*] A species of sea-spider.

1855 *Orr's Circ. Sci., Org. Nat.* II. 317 Podosomata..are all marine; some of them, like the *Nymphon*, being found amongst stones and sea-weeds on the beach. **1855** Kingsley *Glaucus* (1878) 80 A little black sea-spider, a Nymphon, who ..carries his needful stomach in long branches, packed inside his legs.

nymphotomy (nɪm'fɒtəmɪ). *Surg.* [a. mod.L. *nymphotomia*, f. Gr. νύμφη (see nympha 2) + -τομία (see -tomy).] Excision of the nymphæ.

1704 in J. Harris *Lex. Techn.* I. **1892** in *Syd. Soc. Lex.*

nymyl, obs. f. nimble *a.*

nymyos, obs. f. nimious *a.*

nyn, obs. f. nine.

†**nyn**, variant of ny = *ne*, nor. *Obs. rare.*

c **1425** *Cast. Persev.* 875 in *Macro Plays* 103, I schal neuere begger bede mete nyn drynke. *c* **1450** *Cov. Myst.* (Shaks. Soc.) 84 My herte is not hevyed on lofte, Nyn myn Eyn be not lokynge abowte.

nyncetie: see nincety-fincety.

†**nynche**, obs. form (see N 3) of inch.

a **1400–50** *Alexander* 3675 And þe thinnest was a nynche thicke quen þai ware þurȝe persed.

nynde, obs. f. ninth.

nyne, etc., obs. f. nine, etc.

nyngkiling, obs. f. inkling.

nynmurder, obs. f. nine-murder.

†**nynnat**, for *ne nat*, know not. *Obs.*

1553 *Respublica* v. vii. 28 (Brandl), Masse, but I nynnat. *Ibid.* v. x. 10 Marye, but I ninnat.

Nynorsk ('njuːnɔːsk). Also **nynorsk, Ny Norsk.** [Norw., f. *ny* new + *norsk* Norwegian.] The official name by which Landsmål is now known. Cf. Landsmål.

1937 E. I. Haugen *Beginning Norwegian* 5 Ivar Aasen (1813–1896) conceived the idea that if one studied the most 'genuine' native dialects..one might create a form of Norwegian equivalent to what the national language would have been had Norway never been united with Denmark... He called it *landsmål*, a name by which it is still commonly known (though *nynorsk* is now official). **1952** B. Berulfsen in *Norseman* X. 187 In 1929 official action changed the names Landsmål to *Nynorsk* and Riksmål to *Bokmål*. **1966** E. I. Haugen *Lang. Conflict & Lang. Planning* vi. 257 The choice given in the proposed ballot was between 'natural Riksmål, Nynorsk, and official Bokmål'. **1971** *Computers & Humanities* V. 205 The data bank of the project, which covers both *bokmaal* and *nynorsk*, is intended to assist various types of linguistic projects in the future. **1975** *Scottish Rev.* I. 22 The 'Landsmaal', the distinctively Norwegian language that in the 70s of last century a group of writers were endeavouring to institute as the literary language of Norway as distinct from the usual Dano-Norwegian, an attempt which has developed into the 'Ny Norsk' (New Norwegian), in which a number of works are written now.

nynt(e, nynten(e, nyntie, obs. ff. ninth, nineteen, ninety.

†**nyny**, obs. variant of ninny[1] or [2].

1687 Cotton *Poet. Wks.* (1765) 55 This Cupid was a little Tiny Cogging, Lying, Peevish Nyny.

Nyon ('niːɔn). The name of a commune in Switzerland, used *attrib.* and *absol.* to designate pottery manufactured there from *c* 1780.

1869 C. Schreiber *Jrnl.* 10 May (1911) I. 2 A very fine service of Nyon, dinner and dessert. **1910** E. Dillon *Porcelain & how to collect It* xii. 181 The only distinctive mark of Nyon is a fish painted in blue under the glaze. **1960** H. Hayward *Antique Coll.* 202/1 *Nyon porcelain*, a factory was founded at Nyon, near Geneva in 1780... Current French fashions were closely adhered to and many of the wares bear floral decoration.

nypa, nyper, obs. ff. nipa.

nype, to nip: see nipe *v.*[2]

nypil, obs. f. nipple.

nypt(e, varr. of nift *Obs.*

†**nyrvyl.** *Obs. rare*$^{-0}$. [Of Scand. origin, agreeing in sense with Norw. dial. *nyrv(e* neut., *nyrva* masc., and in form with Icel. *nyrfill* miser: see also nurvil. In mod. dial. represented by *nirl*.] A dwarfish person.

c **1440** *Promp. Parv.* 357/1 Nyrvyl, or lytyl manne, *pusillus, nanus.*

nys, obs. form of nice *a.*; variant of nis *sb.*

†**nys**, variant of nis, is not. *Obs.*

c **1000** Ælfric *Saints' Lives* xxvi. 273 Hit nan wundor nys. *c* **1160** *Hatton Gosp.* John v. 10 Hit ys reste-daiȝ; nys þe alyfed þæt þu þin bed bere. *a* **1250** *Owl & Night.* 465 Vor he nys noþer yep ne wis. **13..** *E.E. Allit. P.* A. 951 Ierusalem..nys to yow no more to mene, Bot cete of god. ? *a* **1366** Chaucer *Rom. Rose* 333 In world nys wight so hard of herte..That nolde have had of hir pite. *c* **1420** *Chron. Vilod.* 3184 Botȝyff seynt Woltrude hurre þe rather holpe he nys bot dedde. *c* **1489** Caxton *Blanchardyn* xxxv. 133 Ther nys so grete sorowe, but that it may be forgoton at the laste. *a* **1529** Skelton *Balettys* Wks. 1843 I. 26 There nys thynge that I court so fayne. **1579** Spenser *Sheph. Cal.* May 144 Thou findest faulte where nys to be found.

nyse, obs. f. neeze *v.*, nice *a.*

nysebecetur: see nicebecetur.

nysete(e, obs. ff. nicety.

nysett, var. of nycette *Obs.*

nysing, obs. f. neezing.

†**nysot.** *Obs. rare.* [? ad. OF. *nicet* (fem. *nicette*), a dim. form of nice *a.*] A wanton girl.

1526 Skelton *Magnyf.* 1244 Where I spy a nysot gay, That wyll syt ydyll all the day [etc.].

nyss, obs. Sc. f. nice *a.*

nyssa ('nɪsə). [mod.L. (J. F. Gronovius in Linnæus *Systema Naturæ* (1735)), f. *Nysa* the name of a water nymph, in allusion to the swamp habitat of some species.] A deciduous tree of the genus so called, belonging to the family Nyssaceæ and native to North America and Asia, esp. the American species *Nyssa sylvatica*, the tupelo.

1886 G. Nicholson *Illustr. Dict. Gardening* II. 461/1 Nyssas thrive best in low, damp, moist situations, such as peat swamps. **1901** L. H. Bailey *Cycl. Amer. Hort.* III. 1109/2 Nyssas are trees or shrubs with petiolate, usually entire leaves and small flowers borne in short racemes or dense heads. **1961** *Amateur Gardening* 23 Sept. 3/3 The tulip tree..and the nyssa in the Long Walk to the Pagoda.. are among the tallest trees in the Garden [at Kew]. **1962** *Times* 24 Dec. 11/1 No exotics means..no *Nyssas.*

nyssete, obs. Sc. f. nicety.

nyst, obs. f. nest; var. of nist.

nystagmic (nɪ'stægmɪk), *a.* [f. nystagm-us. Cf. F. *nystagmique*.] Of the nature of nystagmus. So **ny'stagmiform** *a.*, **ny'stagmoid** *a.*

1878 A. M. Hamilton *Nerv. Dis.* 85 The eyeballs may be sometimes slightly agitated by a feeble movement of a nystagmic character. **1899** *Brit. Med. Jrnl.* May 1077 Nystagmiform movements of the eyes. **1899** *Allbutt's Syst. Med.* VII. 68 Such phenomena we are in the habit of calling 'nystagmoid' jerks or movements.

‖**nystagmus** (nɪ'stægməs). *Path.* [mod.L., ad. Gr. νυσταγμός nodding, drowsiness, f. νυστάζειν to nod, to be sleepy.]

†**1.** (See quot.) *Obs.*

1822 Good *Study Med.* III. 238 Habitual squinting... The first of these varieties constitutes the Nystagmus of Dr. Plenck.

2. An involuntary oscillation of the eyeball, usually lateral, but sometimes rotatory or vertical, especially common among miners. Also *Comb.*

1869 *Eng. Mech.* 10 Dec. 294/3 One very curious affection of the muscles of the eye..deserves notice,..—Nystagmus. .. The motion of the ball..is ceaseless, as if the eye was making vain endeavours to glimpse the light. **1879** Harlan *Eyesight* viii. 111 An affection noticed in miners, and called 'miner's nystagmus', in which..the eyes continually oscillate. **1899** *Allbutt's Syst. Med.* VII. 89 In addition to tremors, there may be nystagmus-like twitchings of the eyeball.

nystatin ('naɪstətɪn). *Pharm.* [f. the name of New York State, U.S.A., where it was developed + -in[1].] A yellow antifungal substance, $C_{46}H_{77}NO_{19}$, that is produced by the growth of the bacterium *Streptomyces noursei* and is used locally in the treatment of moniliasis, esp. when caused by *Candida albicans*, and of anal and vaginal infections.

1952 *Arch. Pediatrics* LXIX. 414 Hazen et al. have shown that an antibiotic called fungicidin, Nystatin®, has inhibited coccidioides immitis spherules at 6·25 micrograms per milliliter. [*The name* Nystatin *is not in fact registered as a trade mark at the U.S. Patent Office.*] **1953** *Science* 29 May 609/2 The senior authors [*sc.* Brown & Hazen] have given the name Nystatin to their product fungicidin. It is being manufactured by E. R. Squibb and Sons under this name. **1962** E. O. Morris in Hawthorn & Leitch *Recent Adv. Food Sci.* I. 33 Yeasts appear to be particularly troublesome and it has been suggested that these organisms may be inhibited by the use of nystatin. **1974** R. N. Richards *Venereal Dis.* 104/1 The diagnosis of monilia was made and she responded well to the insertion of nystatin tablets in her vagina twice daily.

†**nyster**, for *ne ys þer*, there is not. *Obs.*

c **1330** R. Brunne *Chron. Wace* (Rolls) 15723 No lond nyster ferrere west, þer þe sonne goþ to rest.

nyt, obs. f. net, nit; variant of nite *v.* *Obs.*

nyte, obs. f. nit; variant of nite *v.* *Obs.*

†**nyte**, *a.* or *adv.* (Meaning uncertain.)

a **1560** Rolland *Crt. Venus* III. 229 The May Thisbe wald tine hir self sa nyte, Caus Pyramus away and deid was quite.

†**nytel**, *v. Obs. rare*$^{-1}$. [Of obscure origin.] *intr*. ? To be busy in a trifling manner.
13.. *E.E. Allit. P.* B. 888 þay lest [= failed] of lotez logging any lysoun [= trace] to fynde, Bot nyteled þer alle the nyȝt for noȝt at þe last.

nyth, obs. f. NIGHT; var. of NITH(E.

nyþe, obs. f. NINTH; var. of NITH(E.

nyþe-, nythemest, varr. of NETHEMEST *Obs.*

nyþer(e, nyðer(e: see NETHER *a.* and *adv.*; NITHER *v.*

nythertale, var. of NIGHTERTALE *Obs.*

nythyng(e, obs. ff. NITHING.

nytte, obs. f. NIT.

nytyngale, obs. f. NIGHTINGALE.

nyuck, var. YU(C)K.

nyuel, var. of NIVEL *v. Obs.*

nyumyum ('njʌ'mjʌm). *rare*$^{-1}$. = YUM-YUM.
1922 JOYCE *Ulysses* 159 O, that's nyumyum.

nywe, obs. f. NEW *a.*

Nzima (n'zi:mə). Also **Nsima, Nzema.** The name of an African language spoken in Ghana.
1911 F. W. H. MIGEOD *Lang. W. Afr.* I. vii. 179 In Nsima (Zema) there is also a suffix, but it appears that there exists also initial change, the same as in Twi. **1945** I. C. WARD *Rep. Investigation Gold Coast Lang. Probl.* 61 Nzema.. appears to be a strong admixture of two language groups, the Fante branch of the Akan language and some other group lying to the west. **1971** L. A. BOADI in J. Spencer *Eng. Lang. W. Afr.* 49 The indigenous languages [of the Gold Coast],.. are still used and are, in many cases, deliberately cultivated; no less than six of them—Akan, Gã, Ewe, Nzima, Dagbani and Hausa—are regularly heard on the radio. **1975** *Archivum Linguisticum* VI. 2 In certain environments Nzema and Ahanta *k* alternates with *g*.

O

O (əʊ), the fifteenth letter of the alphabet in English and other modern languages, and the fourth vowel letter. O was the fourteenth letter in the ancient Roman alphabet, corresponding in form and value to the ancient Greek *O*, derived from the sixteenth letter of the Phœnician and ancient Semitic alphabet, ○, ◇, ▽, (Heb. ע), called *ʿain*, i.e. 'eye'. The latter represented a peculiar articulation or consonant, the 'glottal catch' (modern Arabic ع, ع), a sound unknown to Greek, in which the symbol was appropriated to the vowel *o* (which the sound of Semitic *ʿain* in conjunction with *a* may have somewhat resembled). In early Greek, *O* was used for both short and long *o*; subsequently a new symbol *Ω*, *ω* (*O méga*, 'great O'), was added to the alphabet to distinguish long open *ō*; the original *O o* (now known as *O micrón*, 'little O') being then restricted to short *o*. From Greek times downward, this letter has regularly represented some variety or varieties of the 'mid-back-round' (or labial) vowel of Bell's Visible Speech scale. On account of its intermediate position, this vowel is (like *e*) liable to considerable variations of quality; and many languages distinguish, as practically different vowels, 'close' (or 'narrow') (o), and 'open' (or 'wide') (ɔ); the former tending to approach, and at length to pass into, the still closer sounds (ʊ), (u); the latter tending to fall into the still opener (ɒ).

In OE., short *o* and long *ó* were etymologically and phonetically distinct. Short *o* was originally both close and open. Short close *o* was normally derived from an original *u*, as in OE. *oxa* ox, Skr. *ukshán*, OE. *dohtor*, Gr. θυγάτηρ, Indo-European **dhughətḗr*. Short open *o* normally represented an earlier *a* before a nasal, as in OE. *on*, Goth. *ana*, Gr. ἀνά. This OE. *o* from *a*(*n*) is often distinguished for etymological purposes as *ǫ*. OE. long *ó* corresponded generally to Com. Teut. long *ō*, in which were combined Indo-European *ō* and *ā*, as in OE. *bóc* beech, OTeut. **bôkâ*, Dor.Gr. φᾱγος, L. *fāgus*; OE. *flód*, Goth. *flôdus*, Gr. πλωτός swimming. Long *ó* also arose out of a lengthening of short open *ǫ* from *a*(*n*), with *n* absorbed, as in *tóð* tooth, OTeut. **tanþ-*, Indo-Eur. **dont-*; *hón* to hang, OHG. and Goth. *hāhan* from OTeut. **haŋh-*, χaŋχ-. Long *ó* was prob. originally both close and open, but in late OE. it must, from its subsequent history, have been close. In unstressed syllables, *o* was the ordinary OE. representative of the obscure vowel (ə); and in this capacity it often varied with *a*, *e*, *u*.

In the Middle English period the distinction between open and close short *o* is no longer discernible; and the vowel was apparently always open *o* before a consonant in the accented syllable. Of long *ō* ME. had two distinct sounds, open and close. Open *ō* was the normal representative (in midland and southern speech) of OE. long *á* (or lengthened *a*), which passed through the sound of (ɒː) to that of (ɔː), being sometimes written in the 13th c. *oa*, but, eventually, simply *o*, or *oo*: thus OE. *máre*, *nán*, *ald* (*eald*), ME. *moare*, *noan* (1257), *more*, *non*, *old*. It often represented long *ō* derived from Fr. or L., or arose out of an earlier short *o* in an open syllable, as OE. *hopa*, ME. *hōpe*. ME. close *ō* represented OE. *ó*. This *ō* must have been a very close sound, for about the end of the ME. or beginning of the mod.Eng. period it passed into the sound of (uː), usually with the spelling *oo*, though sometimes with the simple *o* spelling, as in the words *do*, *to*, *lose*. ME. open *ō* either continued into mod.Eng. as *o* (bone, ore, hope), or was, from 16th c., written *oa* (oak, oar, coal); but in sound it became at length close and quasi-diphthongal (ou) (now in southern British pronunciation usually (əʊ)), except before *r*, where it remains open (ɔə) (now usually (ɔː)). In the 13th c., *o* began to be written in certain cases for *u*, esp. before *m*, *n*, *u* (= *v*), as in some, son, loue (= love), OE. *sum*, *sunu*, *lufu*. This, which has largely survived into mod.E., was merely a *graphic*, not a *phonetic*, change.

The normal sound of short *o* is now (ɒ), low-back-round; but it frequently stands for (ʌ), as in son, doth, or (ɜː), as in word; and in unaccented syllables sinks to (ə), as in nation. When original short *o* comes before *r* final, or *r* + consonant, as in or, for, corn, sort, it is now lengthened into the corresponding long sound (ɔː) (ɔː(r), fɔː(r), kɔːn, sɔːt). A still more recent lengthening of *ŏ* often took place during the 19th century in southern English before certain consonants, as in cross, off, moth, soft; having never become general in standard English, it is here recorded as a variant (ɔː) in the pronunciation of those words it affected.

The normal sound of long *ō*, as in no, toe, bone, is the quasi- or imperfect diphthong (əʊ); but before *r*, as in bore, choral, story, the sound is that of the open quasi-diphthong (ɔə). In London and the south of England, this *ō*, esp. when *r* follows in the same syllable, as in ore, worn, porter, is usually identified with the (ɔː) mentioned above as arising from ME. short *o* before *r*. This is not the case, however, in the educated speech of the country as a whole, nor in America, and the sounds are still separated by most orthoepists (see Ellis, *E.E. Pronunciation*, I. 94–95), and in dictionaries generally; they are distinguished in this dictionary, as in boarder, border ('bɔədə(r)), ('bɔːdə(r)), mourn, morn (mɔən), (mɔːn).

Hence, in modern English, the normal sounds of *o* are

1. (əʊ) in no, bone (nəʊ, bəʊn)
2. (ɔə) " ore, glory (ɔə(r), 'glɔərɪ)
3. (ɔː) " or, north (ɔː(r), nɔːθ)
4. (ɒ) " rob, got (rɒb, gɒt)

Exceptional sounds, due to special causes, and normally spelt otherwise, are

5. (uː/ʊ) in to do (tʊ duː)
6. (ʌ) " son, other (sʌn, 'ʌðə(r))
7. (ɜː) " word, worthy (wɜːd, 'wɜːðɪ)

No. 1 is also represented by *oa*, *oe* (final), *ou*, *ow*, *oh*, rarely *oo*; as in load, hoe, soul, low, *oh*, brooch.

No. 2, by *oa*, *ou*, *ow*, rarely *oo*; as in boar, pour, Gower, door, floor. In broad, *oa* has the sound (ɔː).

The combination *oo* now normally represents long (uː), diphthongal (ʊə), short (ʊ), as in moon, moor, good; exceptionally, it has the sound of 'short u' (ʌ), as in blood, flood, or of 'long o' = Nos. 1 and 2 above.

Oi, *oy*, normally represent a true diphthong (ɔɪ), as boil, boy; or an imperfect triphthong, as in Moir (mɔɪə(r)).

Ou, *ow*, also normally represent a diphthong (aʊ), as in out, house, now, or an imperfect triphthong, as in hour (aʊə). But *ou* has also various other sounds, as in soup, tour, through, you; soul, pour; brought, cough, enough; in unstressed final syllables it is commonly (ə), as in favour, pious.

In unaccented syllables, all the sounds of *o* are liable to shortening and obscuration, and tend to sink to (ə), as in tobacco, anatomy, dilatory, sailor, comfort, cannot , parrot, notion, random.

The change of OE. *á* to *ō* in ME. was a characteristic of the southern and midland dialects, and thus of Standard English. But the northern dialects retained *a*, the presence of which instead of *o*, as in *stane*, *hame*, *mare* = *stone*, *home*, *more*, is one of the most distinctive features of northern English and Scotch. In later times this *a* is often written *ai*, or *ae*, and narrowed to *ea*, *e*, *ee* (ɛː, eː, ɪə, iː). The change of OE. *ó* to (uː, ʊ), is also proper to Standard English and its related dialects, the sound having become in Scotch one akin to German *ö* and *ü*, or Fr. *eu* and *u*. This, like the English (uː, ʊ) sound, is often written *oo*, but more distinctively *u* or *ui*, as in Eng. good, Sc. good, gude, guid. The northern dialects also retain the earlier (uː) for English (aʊ); this is often written in Scotch, as in ME., *ou*, *ow*; but in modern times sometimes *oo*, as in *coo*, *aboot* = *cow*, *about*.

The fancy, frequent in authors of the 16th and 17th c., that the shape of the letter O represented the rounded form of the mouth in forming the sound, is seen from the history of the letter to be without foundation in fact.

1. a. The letter. (In quot. *c* 1460 = the Greek *Omega*.) The pl. appears as *O*s, O's, *o*s, o's (oes).

O per se, the letter O forming by itself a word, as in the interjection O! (Cf. ***a per se***, ***I per se***.)

c **1000** ÆLFRIC *Gram.* iii. (Z.) 5 Of ðam [stafum] syndon fif *vocales*, þæt synd clypiendlice: *a*, *e*, *i*, *o*, *u*. *c* **1460** *Towneley Myst.* i. 1 Ego sum alpha et o, I am the first, the last also. **1492** RYMAN *Poems* lvii. 3 in *Archiv Stud. neu. Spr.* LXXXIX. 222 Heven and erthe rounde like an O. **1530** PALSGR. 6 O in the frenche tong hath two diuers maners of soundynges. **1612** DEKKER (*title*) O per se O, or a newe Cryer of Lanthorne and Candle Light. **1711** STEELE *Spect.* No. 168 ¶ 5 Whipped . . for writing an O for an A, or an A for an O. **1814** CARY *Dante's Inf.* XXIV. 98 Far more quickly than e'er pen Wrote O or I, he kindled, burn'd and chang'd.

Comb. **1900** *Daily News* 20 Oct. 6/4 The whole superstructure is supported . . by A and O shaped trestles.

b. The sound of the letter, the vowel-sound *o*.

1842 TENNYSON *Epic* 50 Mouthing out his hollow oes and aes. **1867** A. J. ELLIS *E.E. Pronunc.* I. iii. 94 What sounds of *o* exist. They are all round vowels, that is, the action of the lips with a tolerably round opening is necessary.

2. Used, like the other letters, to indicate serial order and distinguish things in a series, as the 'quires' or sheets of a book, the parts of a figure, the companies of a military force, the batteries of the Royal Artillery, the different MSS. of a work, etc.

3. In *Logic*, the symbol of a particular negative.

1551 T. WILSON *Logike* G vij b, I dothe signifie a particular affirmatiue. O doth signifie a particular negatiue. **1552**, **1620** [see I (the letter) 4]. **1870** JEVONS *Elem. Logic* viii. (1875) 67 A proposition of this kind is generally to be classed rather as O than I.

4. In *Chem.* O is the symbol for Oxygen.

5. [orig. denoting absence: cf. O *sb.*[1]] In *Hæmatology*, designating absence of the A and B agglutinogens of the ABO blood group system; hence (and now usu.) used to designate the blood group of individuals lacking these two agglutinogens; also, more widely, used to designate the allele involved in determining this blood group.

1926 LANDSTEINER & WITT in *Jrnl. Immunol.* XI. 242 It has been pointed out by one of the writers . . that the isoagglutinin reactions of human blood can be possibly explained by the simple assumption of only two different agglutinogens and agglutinins. Designating these by α and β, and the agglutinogens by A and B, the following symbols are obtained for the blood groups: I–α, β; II A, β; III B, α; IV A, B–; if we include the factors A^1 and α^1 in the scheme, and if O and o signify the absence of agglutinogens or agglutinins, then the signs are: I O α, β, α^1; II A, β, and A, A^1, β; III B, α, α^1; IV A, B, o. **1927** [see A II. 7]. **1929** L. H. SNYDER *Blood Grouping* i. 3 To try to obviate the confusion still existing from a reversal of groups I and IV in the two systems, a new system of nomenclature, based on the agglutinophyllic [*sic*] capacity of the cells, has been suggested. In this system, Jansky's group IV is known as *AB*, having the two agglutinogens A and B. Group III, containing agglutinogen B, is known as group *B*, group II as group *A*, and group I, containing neither agglutinogen, as group *O*. **1948** C. C. STURGIS *Hematol.* xxiii. 825 These characteristics in the erythrocytes may be present singly or together, or they can be absent. If the absence of these isogglutinable substances is designated as O, then there are four possibilities: namely, groups, O, A, B, and AB. **1958** J. B. MIALE *Lab. Med.: Hematol.* vi. 319 The O gene, when carried by both chromosomes, determines phenotype O. **1966** *Listener* 6 Oct. 493/1 Mr and Mrs H's blood was found to belong to group O, while Clive's blood was found to belong to group A2. **1968** PASSMORE & ROBSON *Compan. Med. Stud.* I. xxvi. 17/1 Every person has a pair of chromosomes each of which carries the A, B or O gene. **1969** J. H. GREEN *Basic Clin. Physiol.* vi. 34/2 The remainder of the population (46 per cent.) have neither A nor B on their red cells, and they are said to be Group O.

6. O is an abbreviation, **a.** for some Christian names, as *Octavia*, *Oliver*, *Olivia*, *Oswald*, *Oswyn*. **b.** for 'old', as in **O.A.P.**, old age pensioner; (also formerly old age pension); **OE.**, Old English, **OF.**, Old French, **OHG.**, Old High German, **ON.**, Old Norse, etc.; **O.P.**, old prices (see d); **O.S.**, old style; **O.T.**, Old Testament; and frequently in public school abbreviations, as **O.E.**, Old Etonian, **O.W.**, Old Wellingtonian, and the like. **c.** for 'Order', as in **D.S.O.**, Distinguished Service Order; **O.B.E.**, (Officer of the) Order of the British Empire; **O.D.C.**, Order of Discalced Carmelites; **O.M.**, Order of Merit; also by metonymy, a member of this Order; **O.M.I.** (see quot. 1907); **O.P.**, Order of Preachers; **O.S.A.**, Order of Saint Augustine; **O.S.B.**, Order of Saint Benedict; **O.S.F.(C.)**, Order of Saint Francis (, Capuchin), etc.

1708 J. KERSEY *Dict. Anglo-Britannicum* Pref., *O.F.*, Old French. **1710** *Lond. Gaz.* No. 4785/2 The 14th of the last Month, O.S. **1724** *Ibid.* No. 6301/1 Stockholm, August 19, O.S. **1864** R. MORRIS *Early Eng. Allit. Poems* p. xxxvi, The preposition *from* never occurs in the following poems; it is replaced by *fro* (Northumbrian *fra*, O.N. *frá*). **1868** —— *Old Eng. Homilies* I. p. lvi, In Gothic we find plural forms in *-a*, as *worda*, &c., which are certainly older than the O.E. forms word, &c. *Ibid.* 312 Cp. the O.N. *lât, læti.* **1884** *N.E.D.*, s.v. *a* adj.¹, O.E. **1884** *N.E.D.*, s.v. *a* adv., O.H.G., O.N. **1887** W. W. Skeat *Princ. Eng. Etymol.* 1st Ser. x. 172 The G. *trieb* (drove) is a modern form. The O.H.G. was *dreib* or *treib.* **1891** *Ibid.* 2nd ser. iii. 43 Lat. *u*..was sometimes long, as in Lat. *nūllum*, and sometimes short, as in Lat. *mŭltum*; and was developed accordingly. Hence O.F. *nul* (nyl) and *moult* (mult). **1892** Westcott *Gospel of Life* 198 The record of the Fall is not unquestionably noticed once in the later books of the O.T. **1901** *Scotsman* 15 Mar. 8/2 Grateful if friends of O.W.'s..would communicate with him at Wellington College. **1901** G. Frankau *Eton Echoes* 48 Or pass to hear them say with eyes askance 'The siding ass! Suppose he's some O.E.' **1912** R. W. Chambers *Widsith* 191 Kluge has pointed out that this form of the name corresponds to the O.N. *Atli*, as against the M.H.G. *Etzel*, O.H.G. *Ezzilo.* **1914** C. Mackenzie *Sinister St.* II. iii. i. 516 Come and have coffee with me after hall. One or two O.E.'s are coming in, but you won't mind? **1927** *Englische Studien* 10 Nov. 81 ON. *lífr* occurs in Norwegian river-names. **1934** M. K. Pope *From Lat. to Mod. Fr.* ii. xi. 172 In educated Parisian speech the denasalisation of O.F. *ã* appears to have begun in the later sixteenth century. **1936** J. Buchan *Island of Sheep* vi. 112 He wore white linen breeches, a smartly cut flannel coat, and an O.E. tie. **1940** W. O. Ross *M. E. Sermons* p. xxix, *S* appears very rarely for OE. *sc.* **1942** Partridge *Dict. Abbrev.* 70/1 *O.A.P.*, Old Age Pension(s). **1959** P. Bull *I know Face* x. 186 The O.A.P.s were very angry indeed, at not only having to witness *Waiting for Godot*, but also having to pay twelve pennies for the privilege. **1959** M. Schlauch *Eng. Lang. in Mod. Times* i. 29 The [pronoun] forms which sprang from the OE and ON datives later assumed the function of accusatives as well. **1970** B. M. H. Strang *Hist. English* iv. 274 A few native formations are calques on OF prepositions. **1972** M. L. Samuels *Linguistic Evol.* ii. 25 One of the best known of irreversible consonant-changes is that of voiceless plosives to fricatives or affricates, as in.. OHG [p, t, k] > [pf, ts, kx]. **1972** E. J. Dobson *Eng. Text of Ancrene Riwle* p. cxlix, OE (ON) *ā* is normally spelt *o.* **1973** 'B. Graeme' *Two & Two* xiv. 139 'What about the Rexalls?' 'Apart from being O.A.P.s, I know nothing.' **1973** *Listener* 7 June 777/1 Tony sports an OE tie. **1976** *Evening Post* (Nottingham) 15 Dec. 19/7 (Advt.), Gamston Kennels (Est 1926)..Pedigree puppies..Labradors, O.E. sheepdogs, Pekes, Poodles.

1798 J. Milnes *Life Challoner* 32 That zealous orthodox prelate..whose loss we at the present moment deplore, the Right Reverend Bishop Walmesley, O.S.B. *Ibid.*, Another person for whom he had deservedly the greatest respect and regard was the Rev. Pacificus Baker, O.S.F. **1839** *Dublin Rev.* May 556 English sermons were delivered by the Rev. Dr. Wiseman, F. Hughes, O.S.F., and the Rev. Messrs. McGill and Kyan. **1865** *Cath. Directory* p. lxii, Rev. F. Lawrence (Praxmarer), O.S.F.C. **1891** *Cath. Times* 6 Mar. 2/7 Very Rev. Dr Keane, O.P. **1903** *Who's Who* 760 Keppel, Hon. Sir Harry, G.C.B.; cr. 1857; O.M. **1907** *Cath. Encycl.* I. 28/1 *O.M.I.*, Oblati Mariæ Immaculatæ—Oblate Fathers of Mary Immaculate. *Ibid.*, *O.P.*, Ordo Prædicatorum—Dominicans. *Ibid.*, *O.S.A.*, Ordo (Eremitarum) Sancti Augustini—Augustinians. **1917** O.B.E. [see M.B.E. s.v. M 5]. **1922** Joyce *Ulysses* 312 Amongst the clergy present were..the rev. P. J. Cleary, O.S.F.; the rev. L. J. Hickey, O.P.; the very rev. Fr. Nicholas, O.S.F.C.; the very rev. B. Gorman, O.D.C.;..the rev. T. Brangan, O.S.A.;..the rev. B. R. Slattery, O.M.I.; [etc.]. **1923** *Cornh. Mag.* June 765 A Captain and an O.B.E. **1937** B. Jarrett *Eng. Dominicans* (rev. ed.) 186 Consecrated Bishop of Tiberiopolis by Pope Benedict XIII, O.P. **1955** *Times* 9 Aug. 4/7 A person of the highest character, who served with distinction in both world wars and received the O.B.E. **1955** *Essays in Crit.* V. 430 Od's life, need an O.M. swear to the truth of an epigram? **1955** 'D. Knowles' *Relig. Orders in Eng.* II. 390/1 Ashbourne, Thomas, OSA. **1957** *Oxf. Dict. Chr. Ch.* 235/1 In England and Ireland they [*sc.* the Capuchins] sign O.S.F.C. ('Ordinis Sancti Francisci Capuccinorum'). **1963** I. Wilkes *Brit. Init. & Abbrev.* 82/1 *ODC*, Order of Discalced Carmelites, 41, Kensington Church Street, London, W.8. **1969** I. & P. Opie *Children's Games* p. xvi, We have also to thank Father Damian Webb O.S.B. **1972** *Bookseller* 2 Dec. 2543 (Advt.), Sister Mary Joyce O.P.

d. In other combinations: as **O. and M.**, organization and methods; **OAO** *Forces' slang*, one and only; **OAO**, orbiting astronomical observatory; **O.A.S.**, on active service; **O.A.S.**, Organisation de l'Armée Secrète, an organization opposed to Algerian independence from France; **O.A.S.**, Organization of American States; **O.A.U.**, Organization of African Unity; **OB**, obstetrics, obstetric, or obstetrician (*U.S.*); **OB**, order of battle; **O.B.**, outside broadcast; **O.B.U.**, One Big Union; **O.C.**, officer commanding; **OCR**, optical character recognition; **O.C.T.U.**, officer cadet(s') training unit; also **Octu** ('ɒktuː); **O.D.** (*U.S.*) officer of the day; olive drab; **O.D.**, ordinary seaman; **O.D.**, Ordnance datum; **OD**, organization development; **O.D.**, **o.d.**, outside diameter; **O.D.** *slang* (orig. *U.S.*), overdose; so as *v. intr.*, to take an overdose; **O.D.'d**, overdosed, dead of an overdose; **O.D.V.** *joc.*, eau-de-vie; **O.E.C.D.**, Organization for Economic Co-operation and Development; **O.E.D.**, Oxford English Dictionary; **O.E.E.C.**, Organization for European Economic Co-operation; **O.E.O.** (*U.S.*), Office of Economic Opportunity; **OGO**, orbiting geophysical observatory; **O.H.C.**, **ohc.**, overhead camshaft; **O.H.M.S.**, on His (or Her) Majesty's Service; **O.H.V.**, **o.h.v.**, overhead valve; **O level**, Ordinary level (of the General Certificate of Education examination); hence ***O leveller***; **O.N.C.**, Ordinary National Certificate; **o.n.o.**, or near(est) offer; **O.O.W.**, Officer of the Watch; **O.P.**, (*a*) 'old price', 'old prices', referring to the demonstrations at Covent Garden Theatre, London, in 1809, against the proposed new tariff of prices; (*b*) (also o.p.) 'opposite the prompter side' in a theatre; (*c*) 'over-proof'; (*d*) (also o.p., *o.p.*) in Bookseller's Catalogues, 'out of print'; (*e*) observation post (also ***O. Pip***); **OPEC** ('əʊpɛk), Organization of Petroleum-Exporting Countries; **O.P.M.**, other people's money (*U.S. slang*); **O.P.M.**, output per man; **O.R.**, **OR**, operational research; **O.R.**, other ranks; **O.R.T.F.**, Office de Radiodiffusion-Télévision Française, formerly the state television and radio service of France; **O.S.**, ordinary seaman; **O.S.**, Ordnance Survey; **O.S.**, outsize; **OSHA**, Occupational Safety and Health Act (or Administration) (*U.S.*); **OSO**, orbiting solar observatory; **OSO**, Ordnance Survey Office; **O.S.S.** (*U.S.*), Office of Strategic Services; **OTB**, off-track betting (*U.S.*); **O.T.C.**, Officers' Training Corps; **O.T.C.**, Organization for Trade Co-operation; **OTC**, over the counter; **O.T.U.**, Operational Training Unit; **O.U.**, Open University; **O.U.D.S.**, Oxford University Dramatic Society; cf. also Ouds; **O.V.R.A.** [see quot. 1961], the secret police of Fascist Italy. See also O.K. *a.*, *sb.*, and *v.*

1958 *Daily Mail* 3 July 4/3 Modern business techniques using 'work study' and the '*O. and M.' treatment (Organisation and Methods), can prove 'a considerable help to us in the hospitals'. **1965** *New Statesman* 7 May 707/2 An O & M survey should swiftly be initiated to decide what dead wood needs to be cut out. **1971** K. Gottschalk in B. de Ferranti *Living with Computer* v. 46 Groups concerned with efficiency in the office are sometimes called organization and methods (O & M) groups. **1936** *Nat. Geogr. Mag.* June 778/2 Or she may be the *OAO—the One and Only. **1967** *Everybody's Mag.* (Austral.) 18 Jan. 36/2 In each war, a new vocabulary is created. Today, in Vietnam, Australians are again catching up on American Army slang. .. All would refer to a special girlfriend as their OAO—one and only. Probably, the OAO was met on skirt patrol. **1962** F. I. Ordway et al. *Basic Astronautics* iv. 119 An *OAO is seen in Fig. 4.2. **1971** *McGraw-Hill Yearbk. Sci. & Technol.* 300 Although the first OAO malfunctioned, the second one (launched on Dec. 7, 1968) has..produced a wealth of important new astronomical data. **1928** Blunden *Undertones of War* 178, I remember your superscriptions, '*O.A.S.' and 'B.E.F.'. **1962** *Listener* 4 Jan. 10/2 An *O.A.S. bomb. **1963** *Times* 14 Mar. 16/2 Algeria at the period when O.A.S. terrorism was at its height. **1973** C. Egleton *Seven Days to Killing* vii. 78 He was an Algerian colonist..and the French police had long been satisfied that he had never been connected with the OAS. **1949** *Ann. Organization Amer. States* I. No. 1. (title-page), Charter of the *OAS. **1972** *Buenos Aires Herald* 3 Feb. 7/6 The juridical commission of the Organization of American States (OAS) has condemned the sending of British troops to Honduras. **1974** *Greenville* (S. Carolina) *News* 22 Apr. 3/5 Kissinger was asked why he had not mentioned Cuba in a speech Saturday to the Organization of American States (OAS) meeting in Atlanta. **1964** *Ann. Reg. 1963* 322 Organisation of African Unity (*O.A.U.). Established at Conference of African Heads of State at Addis Ababa, 22–26 May 1963. **1971** *Sunday Nation* (Nairobi) 11 Apr. 7/1 The announcement had little to do with any assumed prevailing trends among members of the OAU. **1944** Dorland & Miller *Med. Dict.* (ed. 20) 1005/1 **O.B.*, abbreviation for *obstetrics.* **1967** *Boston Globe* 21 May 9/3 Sitting in an office for an OB check. *Ibid.* 9/4 A two hour wait in the OB's office. **1972** *Daily Colonist* (Victoria, B.C.) 29 Feb. 2/1 My last checkup with my OB doctor revealed a fibroid tumor. **1946** Chandler & Robb *Front-Line Intelligence* xii. 137 *O/B (Order of Battle) is a military science whose mission is to determine: (1) How strong the enemy is, [etc.]. **1950** *Tactics & Techniques Infantry* (U.S.) II. ii. 312 The order of battle (OB) team. **1971** *Combat Intelligence* (U.S. Dept. Army, Field Manual 30-5) vii. 7-1 Order of battle (OB) is the identification, strength, command structure, and disposition of the personnel, units, and equipment of any military force. **1975** tr. *Melchior's Sleeper Agent* (1976) III. 192 He'd sent him on to the Corps OB team, to see if there was anything in the latest Order of Battle book. **1927** *B.B.C. Handbk. 1928* 143/1 Outside Broadcast Features... Every *O.B. of the simplest..nature necessitates the provision of two complete telephone line circuits..between the site of the performance and the Station Control Room. **1960** *Punch* 17 Feb. 251/1 Oh, I agree, it's [television is] splendid for sport and O.B.s. **1971** R. Busby *Deadlock* xiii. 200 You'd think he was the bloody big white chief instead of an OB technician. **1919** *Camp Worker* (Vancouver) 17 May 5/3 At Medicine Hat the Federated Railway Trades have unanimously endorsed the *O.B.U. **1931** 'D. Stiff' *Milk & Honey Route* 210 *O.B.U.*, One Big Union. The ideal of the soap boxers. **1977** *Guardian Weekly* 11 Sept. 10/2 The Industrial Workers of the World... In Canada its counterpart was called the OBU, One Big Union..an attempt to prevent divisions in the labour movement by creating a single trade union. **1904** *N.Y. World Mag.* 1 May 6/5 '*O.C.' is the officer in charge. **1917** F. M. Ford *Let.* 19 Feb. (1965) 84 It suits me better to write: 'O.C. Canadous will detail a fatigue party of 1 NCO & 10 men at 4:30 a.m.' **1928** T. E. Lawrence *Let.* 2 May (1938) 600 Also [you will inherit] my copyrights which now no longer include *Revolt in the Desert*: but you will be O.C. *The Seven Pillars.* **1967** G. F. Fiennes *I tried to run a Railway* iii. 25 He had been a gunner himself and had warned the O.C. of the 15 inch crew. **1966** *Computer Jrnl.* IX. 224/2 We decided to experiment to see what limitations, if any, *O.C.R. would place on our stationery design. **1970** *Brit. Printer* July 57/1 The alphabet itself does not have any practical OCR use at all. **1942** E. Waugh *Put out More Flags* ii. 121 '*O.C.T.U. candidates,' said the company sergeant-major. **1972** D. McLachlan *No Case for Crown* iv. 56 He reminded me sometimes of a sergeant who gave me hell in my O.C.T.U. **1929** *Papers Mich. Acad. Sci., Arts & Lett.* X. 311 **O.D.*, I, the officer of the day; II, olive drab. **1966** *Sunday Times* (Colour Suppl.) 4 Dec. 73/2 GI Jargon *OD*, officer of the day, or olive drab (both the colour and the uniforms themselves, e.g. 'I'm wearing my ODs tonight'). **1915** *Recruiter's Bull.* (U.S.) June 17/2 Two *O.D. shirts you next slip in, A pair of shoes goes in between. **1975** tr. *Melchior's Sleeper Agent* (1976) III. 173 He was clad only in his OD shorts and undershirt. **1916** 'Taffrail' *Pincher Martin* i. 7 'Strumbles,' he said, ''ere's another *O.D. come to join your mess.' **1962** Granville *Dict. Sailors' Slang* 83/1 *O.D.* Naval colloquialism for ordinary seaman. *OS* or *Ord* is the official abbreviation. **1926** J. Malcolm *Agric. Surveying* v. 123 The datum adopted in the Ordnance Survey of Great Britain, denoted by the letters *O.D., was what was considered in 1844 to be mean sea level at Liverpool... The new datum is mean sea level at Newlyn. **1956** *Railway Mag.* Mar. 185/2 The top of the wall at the Barmouth end is 35 ft. above Ordnance Datum, dropping to 28 ft. above O.D. at the slipway. **1972** L. Alcock *By South Cadbury* ii. 25 Roughly one quarter of the hill-top, lying above four hundred and ninety feet O.D., forms a broad summit ridge. **1972** *Times* 5 June 22/6 *OD. not infrequently causes strong reactions among managers. **1976** Blake & Mouton (*title*) Diary of an OD man. **1930** Walker & Crocker *Piping Handbk.* iv. 293 In sizes 14 in. and upward pipe is designated by its outside diameter (*O.D.) and the wall thickness is specified. **1963** H. R. Clauser *Encycl. Engin. Materials* 120/1 Non-ferrous castings are produced commercially in o.d.'s ranging from about 1 in. to 6 ft. **1967** *Electronics* 6 Mar. 15/2 (Advt.), The screw-on has an OD of only ⅛ inch with a mated length of only one inch. **1960** R. G. Reisner *Jazz Titans* 162 **O.D.*, an overdose of narcotics. **1971** *Black World* Apr. 38/1 A truly brilliant Black filmmaker goes into his grave at 24..an O.D. takes him, he loses a battle of several years—the 'stuff' wins. **1972** *Telegraph* (Brisbane) 17 Oct. 70/6 A fatal dosage of drugs —*O.D.* (*successful overdose*). **1970** S. O'Callaghan *Drug Addiction in Britain* xii. 151 Diana has O.D.'d and she's dead. **1969** R. De Sola *Abbrev. Dict.* (rev. ed.) 196/1 **Od'd*, overdosed (dope addict). **1973** *Black World* Aug. 55/1 The garbage collectors found Little Prez in the alley near Sixtrey, OD'd away, layin' there cool and stiff. **1839** *Picayune* (New Orleans) in *Spirit of Times* (N.Y.) 5 Oct. 368/3 Why, that in French, is nothing but *O.D.V. **1886** H. Baumann *Londinismen* 124/1 *O.D.V.*,..Branntwein, Spiritus. **1965** *Acronyms & Initialisms Dict.* (Gale Research Co.) 530 *ODV*, taken from pronunciation of French eau-de-vie and used to refer to brandy. **1960** *Times* 25 Nov. 10/7 The 20 members of *O.E.C.D. are the 18 full members of O.E.E.C., together with the United States and Canada. **1971** *Power Farming* Mar. 15/1 European standards, issued by the Organization for Economic Co-operation and Development (O.E.C.D.) and the European Committee of Associations of Manufacturers of Agricultural Machinery (C.E.M.A.). **1898** Morris *Austral English* p. xviii, The practice of the '*O.E.D.' has been followed in this respect. **1962** *New Yorker* 10 Mar. 132/2 The compositor..who began setting type for the O.E.D. in 1884 and was still at it when the last volume came off the presses in 1928. **1973** *Daily Tel.* 20 Oct. 11/5 The word *hoax*..at present connotes more of the mischief than of the humour mentioned in the O.E.D.'s leisurely definition. **1976** *Times* 15 Apr. 13/8 'Fanatical', in the strict OED sense of the word, is surely..appropriate.. to describe those serried ranks. **1948** *News Chron.* 13 Sept. 1/2 The job they were doing had been given them by *O.E.E.C. **1964** *Listener* 13 Aug. 222/2, I was nearly four years chairman of what was then called the O.E.E.C. **1965** *Economist* 17 Apr. 297/1 The testimony of..the head of the Office of Economic Opportunity, revived the emotions of last year, when Congress established the *OEO. **1974** *Black Panther* 16 Mar. 4/3 Congressman Dellums is co-sponsor of a tax reform measure that will work to the same end and has fought to save the programs that were funded through the Office of Economic Opportunity (OEO). **1961** *Sat. Rev.* (U.S.) 6 May 71/3 (Advt.), Each spacecraft in the *OGO series will be capable of carrying up to 50 selected scientific experiments in a single flight. **1969** *Times* 4 June 5/1 The satellite being prepared for launch tomorrow..is the sixth and last of Orbiting Geophysical Observatories (OGO). **1974** *McGraw-Hill Yearbk. Sci. & Technol.* 346/2 Figure 2 shows an altitude-density profile through the plasmasphere measured by the *Ogo 5* satellite. **1932** *O.H.C. [see O.H.V. below]. **1954** P. H. Smith *Design & Tuning of Competition Engines* iv. 57 The merits of the double o.h.c. arrangement lie mainly in the substitution of rotary for reciprocating motion right up to the valves. **1977** *Drive* Sept.–Oct. 113/1 *Ohc*, overhead camshaft. **1895** *Brewer's Dict. Phr. & Fable* (new ed.) 904/2 **O.H.M.S.*, On His (or Her) Majesty's Service. **1907** *Yesterday's Shopping* (1969) 338/2 In accordance with the provisions of the Post Office Protection Acts, Envelopes with 'O.H.M.S.' or 'On His Majesty's Service', will only be supplied to those persons who have authority to use them. **1952** L. Durrell *Spirit of Place* (1969) 115, I think one or two white lined notebooks, official Foreign Office Stationery labelled OHMS. **1972** P. Cleife *Slick & Dead* i. i. 17 Nearly all the flying I've done has been O.H.M.S. I don't think I go much on civil operations. **1932** F. J. Camm *Motor Car Upkeep* i. 15 (*caption*) Three common types of Valve Gear: Side-by-side, overhead valve (*O.H.V.), operated by rocker, and overhead valves (O.H.C.), operated by camshaft. **1958** *Engineering* 28 Feb. 265/1 It is a two-door all-steel saloon of unit construction with..a flat twin air-cooled o.h.v. 600 c.c. four-stroke engine. **1968** Burdett & Ellis *Motor Vehicle Mechanics' Course* II. v. 102 The filling of the cylinder is much improved by this design, particularly where the O.H.V. is placed towards the other side of the chamber. **1949** *Joint Matric. Board Exam. for G.C.E. 1951* 6 If a language is to be specially approved..at the *O level. **1959** *Times* 3 June 8/1 O level in any subject was 'very O'. **1974** *Times* 6 July 21/3 (Advt.), Expense account—plus £25 for an 'O' level man 17–22. **1961** *Listener* 26 Oct. 659/2 The £6-odd offered (per week) by banks and post offices, etc., to sixteen-year-old '*O' levellers. **1949** *Educ. in 1948*, 44 (*caption*) in *Parl. Papers 1948–9* (Cmd. 7724) XIV. 345 *O.N.C. **1962** in H. O. Beecheno *Introd. Business Stud.* p. iii, Mr. Beecheno has written a comprehensive introduction to the commercial world. It is intended particularly for the ONC and HNC student. **1977** P. Carter *Under Goliath* xv. 79 'Our Billy got the G.C.E.,' I said. '*And* the O.N.C. He is going in for the Higher National now.' **1958** *Listener* 6 Nov. 732/1 'O.o.o' means 'one owner only', whereas '*o.n.o.' means 'or near offer'. **1973** *Country Gentlemen's Mag.* Mar. 183/1 Coffee set, thirteen pieces, £5 o.n.o. plus postage. **1977** *Drive*

Sept.–Oct. 113/1 *Ono*, or nearest offer. **1923** *Man. Seamanship* (Admiralty) II. ii. 48 Any man discovering a fire ..is to send a message to the *O.O.W. immediately. **1958** *Spectator* 1 Aug. 169/3, I hear that the archaic and old-fashioned Officer of the Watch (briefly, OOW) is to be changed to Period Progress and Procedure Organiser and Overseer. **1815** BYRON *Let. to Moore* 12 June, Which will end in an *O.P. combustion. **1825** HONE *Every-day Bk.* I. 603 Perry's firemen, who nightly assisted John Kemble's 'What d'ye want' during the 'O.P. row' at Covent-garden theatre. **1876** W. H. POLLOCK *Drama* in *Contemp. Rev.* June 72 The disturbance was hardly less than that of the O.P. riots in England. **1790** T. WILKINSON *Mem.* II. 226 So, on their not complying with my expectations and proposals, we parted with mutual disdain, rage, and anger at *O.P. and P.S. **1836–9** DICKENS *Sk. Boz, Scenes* xiii, That gentleman ..lounging behind the stage-box on the O.P. side. **1892** *Pall Mall G.* 5 Dec. 3/1 [They] occupied the box next the stage on the o.p. side. **1919** WODEHOUSE *My Man Jeeves* 45 Lady Malvern was a hearty..female,..measuring about six feet from the *O.P. to the Prompt Side. **1933** O.P. [see FLOOD *sb.* 7]. **1874** WALCH *Head over Heels* (Tasmania) 21 Old Mills soon took to tasting *O.P. rum in pints and gills. *Ibid.* 42 'Pshaw', cried Sandy (Clan MacTavish) In his beautiful O.P. Scotch. **1859** G. SIMPSON *Let.* 19 Nov. in *Geo. Eliot Lett.* (1954) III. 209 He says you tell him Clerical Scenes is *O.P. **1921** A. BENNETT *Let.* 4 Sept. (1966) I. 296 It seems to me that..*The Old Wives' Tale* ought not to be o.p. **1916** F. M. FORD *Let.* 23 Aug. (1965) 69 George V..really was in some danger. At least he was in an *O.P. that was being shelled fairly heavily. **1972** L. LAMB *Picture Frame* ii. 20 Gerry's no fool, but we don't think our o.p. has been rumbled. **1960** *Times* 15 Sept. 11/4 The conference adopted the (Iraq) proposal to establish an 'Organization of Petroleum-Exporting Countries'... The five participating states are founder-members of *O.P.E.C. **1975** *Petroleum Economist* Aug. 282/1 For eighteen months the problem of OPEC's surplus oil revenues has occupied the minds of western statesmen, bankers and economists. **1916** *War Illustr.* 7 Oct. 185/1 A French '*O-Pip' in the Hills. **1919** J. MASEFIELD *Battle of Somme* 88 Some of them were quite good trees, and we had an O. Pip in one of them (artillery observation post). **1943** HUNT & PRINGLE *Service Slang* 49 *O pip*, an Observation Post of the Field Artillery. ['Pip' stood for 'P' in the services' phonetic alphabet.] **1901** 'J. FLYNT' *World of Graft* IV. 169 It cost me nothing to play the game, because I played it with *O.P.M. (other people's money). **1969** *Time* 15 Aug. 60 No institution manages more 'O.P.M.', or Other People's Money, than Manhattan's 116-year-old United States Trust Co. **1946** J. JEWKES in *Manch. Sch. Econ. & Social Stud.* XIV. 4 Of two industries that with the higher *O.P.M. is not necessarily the more efficient. *Ibid.* 5 O.P.M. may always be increased by installing new machinery but it may be the quickest way to the bankruptcy court. **1969** *New Scientist* 5 June 543 The UK with much higher R & D spending..had only a third of Japan's growth in output per man (OPM) employed. **1953** *Operational Research Q.* IV. 72 The evolution of *O.R...is reflected by the number of publications. **1960** *Times* 17 Mar. 2/7 We shall require evidence of experience in either O.R. or cybernetics. **1964** T. W. MCRAE *Impact of Computers on Accounting* v. 118 A good number of O.R. problems can be solved by using nothing more powerful than a desk calculator. **1969** J. ARGENTI *Managem. Techniques* 107 Courses on OR designed for managers. **1942** PARTRIDGE *Dict. Abbrev.* 72/1 *O.R., other ranks, i.e. ranks other than officers. **1947** J. BERTRAM *Shadow of War* VII. ii. 217 The heavy work in the camp was done by N.C.O.s and O.R.s., known as 'camp-employed'. **1967** J. PORTER *Chinks in Curtain* xv. 147, I..tried to invoke the officer/O.R. relationship. **1964** *Economist* 30 May 945/2 The new [French] broadcasting service will be called *ORTF, *Office de Radiodiffusion Télévision Française*. **1969** *Listener* 27 Mar. 410/2 The ORTF is never happier than with the state visit to Paris of the President of some French-speaking African statelet. **1977** *Rep. Comm. Future of Broadcasting* ii. 15 In France, years of feuding between government and broadcasters led in 1974 to the dissolution of the ORTF. **1894** *Gloss. Terms Evidence R. Comm. Labour* 60/1 in *Parl. Papers 1893–4* (C. 7063) XXXVIII. 411, **O.S.*, an abbreviation for 'ordinary seaman'. **1908** *Army & Navy Gaz.* 7 Nov. 1066/1 The two marines, a stoker, and an O.S. caged like rats in a trap. **1914** C. F. TWENEY *Dict. Naval & Mil. Terms* 164 *O.S.*, Ordinary Seaman; one who has undergone training as a ship's boy, but who is not fully qualified as a seaman. **1962** *O.S. [see O.D. above]. **1962** *Punch* 10 Oct. 534/3 A good submarine forest, marked on the OS map. **1971** A. HUNTER *Gently at Gallop* ii. 20 At the summit of the rise..stood an O.S. triangulation pedestal. **1907** *Yesterday's Shopping* (1969) 768/1 *O.S. Night Dresses... O.S. Chemises. **1927** *Daily Express* 3 Nov. 7 Forty inches at the hips would be O.S. A woman with 60 inches at the hips would be O.O.S., or extra outsize. **1973** *Country Gentlemen's Mag.* Mar. 184/1 For sale owing to loss of weight, full length O.S. evening dress, deep mauve velvet ..will accept £15. **1971** *New Acronyms & Initialisms* (Gale Research Co.) 56/1 **OSHA*, Occupational Safety and Health Act (1970). *OSHA*, Occupational Safety and Health Administration (Department of Labor). **1975** V. BUSH (*title*) Safety in the construction industry: OSHA. **1976** G. & H. MATWES (*title*) A retailer's guide to OSHA. **1938** *Times* 2 Feb. 18/1 He could say that it would launch the *O.S.O. on a new programme. **1962** *Daily Tel.* 8 Mar. 19/6 Yesterday the American National Aeronautics and Space Administration launched..the first of a new series of satellites, the orbiting solar observatories. The first was called OSO-1. **1971** *McGraw-Hill Yearbk. Sci. & Technol.* 301 Each OSO contains instruments that monitor the UV and x-ray radiation emitted by the entire solar disk. **1943** *Newsweek* 25 Jan. 26/2 *OSS is the planning agency in psychological warfare for the Joint Chiefs of Staff. **1972** K. BENTON *Spy in Chancery* viii. 83 We were together in Italy at the end of the war. I was in the OSS and he'd switched over to MI 6. **1964** *Horsemen's Jrnl.* Jan. 69/2 The political sponsors of the bill have figures and plans on how to 'cut-up' the tax dollar taken through *O.T.B. **1971** *New Yorker* 31 July 65 Seems that the OTB computers that are linked with those at the race track developed a colic or something, and wagers at the fourteen shops around town had to be recorded manually. **1975** *Ibid.* 16 June 101/2 The OTB shops around town took in $2,442,589, of which $1,649,591 was bet on the Belmont. **1909** *Captain* XXI. p. xiv/1 Senior Divisions of the *O.T.C. **1974** 'M. INNES' *Mysterious Commission* xiv. 124 He had also done rather well in what, during his public-school days, had still been called the O.T.C. **1955** *Times* 12 Aug. 8/6 The United States Congress rose without voting on President Eisenhower's proposal for entry into the *O.T.C., and it cannot now be dealt with until next year. **1965** *Acronyms & Initialisms Dict.* (Gale Research Co.) 543 **OTC*, over-the-counter (Pharmacy). **1968** *Wall Street Jrnl.* 1 May 24/3 (*heading*) Bunker Ramo to make an automated system for O-T-C quotations. **1972** *N.Y. Law Jrnl.* 10 Oct. 3/1 The information required..to permit a broker to quote an OTC security. **1974** M. C. GERALD *Pharmacol.* ii. 20 Nonprescription (over-the-counter, OTC) sleep-facilitating products. **1976** *National Observer* (U.S.) 4 Sept. 1/3 Fourteen prescription remedies —mostly antihistamines—be sold as nonprescription, over-the-counter (OTC) drugs. **1986** *Times* 5 June 15/8 The OTC market is an informal listing of companies whose shares are traded on screens directly between stockbrokers' offices. **1942** *R.A.F. Jrnl.* 3 Oct. 31 At last *O.T.U. and the introduction to real aircraft. **1966** GURNETT & KYTE *Cassell's Dict. Abbrev.* 163/1 *O.T.U.*, Operational Training Unit. **1969** *Guardian* 23 July 9/3 Milton Keynes, seat of the *OU from September. **1975** *Times* 28 Aug. 12/5 The OU campus seems to have a strangely insular attitude... Town and gown seldom mix. **1886** *Oxford Tatler* 15 May 35/2 No one will be surprised to hear the *O.U.D.S. does not intend to put another play on the stage this term. **1959** *Oxf. Univ. Gaz.* 9 Mar. 740/2 An O.U.D.S. producer might be a clear bet for the B.B.C., a bridge and chess expert for data-processing. **1976** J. COOPER *Harriet* ii. 18 She'd seen him.. in the OUDS production of *Cat on a Hot Tin Roof*. **1930** *Times* 4 Dec. 15/3 All these arrests are said to have been made by the '*O.V.R.A.', a special section of the police, dependent directly on the Ministry of the Interior. These letters are supposed in some quarters to stand for 'Organizzazione di Vigilanza Riservata sulle Associazione', whereas other persons explain the last two initials as standing for 'Repressione di Anti-Fascismo'. **1941** W. GRAHAM *Night Journey* viii. 98 Supposing the Gestapo cut their agreement with Bonini and communicate with the O.V.R.A. **1958** *Listener* 21 Aug. 278/3 The O.V.R.A. (or Italian secret police) was by no means incompetent. **1961** C. F. DELZELL *Mussolini's Enemies* i. 41 The first of these sections was the OVRA, established late in 1927 as a 'special inspectorate' with headquarters in Milan, but soon extended throughout the country. The precise meaning of the initials is still uncertain, according to the knowledgeable Guido Leto, who headed the dread agency from 1938 until 1943. [Note] Three interpretations have been suggested: Organizzazione di Vigilanza e Repressione dell'Antifascismo ('Organization for Vigilance and Repression of Anti-Fascism'); Organo di Vigilanza dei Reati Antistatali ('Organ of Vigilance for Anti-State Crimes'); and Opera Volontaria di Repressione Antifascista ('Voluntary Agency for Anti-Fascist Repression').

e. In *Chem.* *o-* (usu. italic) signifies *ortho-* (ORTHO- 2 b).

1889 G. M'GOWAN tr. *Bernthsen's Text-bk. Org. Chem.* xvi. 310 Thus, *o*-diamido-benzene is that one which results from the reduction of *o*-dinitro-benzene. **1926** A. DAVIDSON *Intermediates for Dyestuffs* v. 109 *o*-Tolidine is used in making azo dyes of the same types as those derived from benzidine. **1968** R. O. C. NORMAN *Princ. Org. Synthesis* xi. 387 The use as a protective group is illustrated by the synthesis of *o*-nitroaniline. **1971** [see *m-* s.v. M 5].

7. Used with reference to the shape of the letter, as ***O-ring***, a gasket (usu. in the form of a ring) with a circular cross-section.

1955 J. YARWOOD *High Vacuum Technique* (ed. 3) i. 60 In many ways, the best solution is the 'o' ring gasket made of rubber or, preferably, oil-resisting neoprene cord, of circular cross-section. **1959** H. BARNES *Oceanogr. & Marine Biol.* iv. 182 The sphere [*sc.* the Deep Sea Benthograph] has five openings, the largest of which is a 15-in. diameter access door closed by a cast steel plate bolted in place and sealed by two neoprene O-rings. **1971** C. M. BLOW *Rubber Technol. & Manuf.* x. 443 The O-ring is very widely used, though some designers prefer the rectangular, D, or delta sections. **1975** G. ANDERSON *Coring* iv. 77 The pycnometer has a breech-locked lid which utilizes an 'O' ring for pressure sealing.

O (əʊ), *sb.*[1] [From resemblance in shape to the letter O: see prec.]

1. The Arabic zero or cipher o; hence, a cipher, a mere nothing.

1605 SHAKS. *Lear* I. iv. 212 Now thou art an O without a figure, I am better then thou art now; I am a Foole, thou art nothing. **1649** MILTON *Eikon.* xxvii. Wks. (1851) 513 To be ..cast away like so many Naughts in Arithmetick, unless it be to turne the O of thir insignificance into a lamentation with the people. **1863** J. THOMSON *Sunday at Hampstead* ix. 24 The ring is round, Life naught, the world an O.

2. a. (Pl. 7 **oaes, oos,** 7– **oes.**) Anything round, as a circle, round spot, orb. Also *Comb.*

Giotto's O, the perfect circle which the Italian painter Giotto is said to have thrown off free hand.

1588 SHAKS. *L.L.L.* v. ii. 45 O that your face were full of Oes. **1590** —— *Mids. N.* III. ii. 188 Faire Helena; who more engilds the night, Then all yon fierie oes, and eies of light. **1599** —— *Hen. V*, I. Chorus 13 Or may we cramme Within this Wooden O, the very Caskes That did affright the Ayre of Agincourt. **1838** CARLYLE *Misc. Ess., Scott.* (1872) VI. 68 There is..the free dash of a master's hand 'round as the O of Giotto' [cf. note]. *Ibid.* 72 It was..necessary that these works should be produced rapidly; and, round or not, be thrown off like Giotto's O. **1864** BROWNING *Confessions* vii, Their eyes might strain And stretch themselves to Oes. **1865** LE FANU *Guy Dev.* I. xiii. 169 His lips severed themselves unconsciously into a small *o*. **1869** RUSKIN *Queen of the Air* iii. 168, I saw..that the practical teaching of the masters of Art was summed by the O of Giotto. **1883** G. HAY *Round about the Round O*, The round O. A name given by seamen to a St. Catherine wheel window, 12 ft. in diameter, in the gable of the south transept of the ruined Abbey of Arbroath.

attrib. **1884** *Illustr. Lond. News* Christm. No. 19/1 Beady eyes and an O mouth. **1917** 'H. H. RICHARDSON' *Fortunes R. Mahony* III. iii. 196 He stood o-mouthed and absent-minded.

†**b.** *spec.* (*pl.*) Small circular spangles used to ornament dress in the 17th c. *Obs.*

1611 COTGR., *Parpillottes*, Spangles, or Oes. **1613** CHAPMAN *Masque of Inns of Court* Plays 1873 III. 94 A vaile of net lawne, enbrodered with Oos and Spangl'd. **1625** BACON *Ess., Masques* (Arb.) 540 Oes, or Spangs, as they are of no great Cost, so they are of most Glory. **1683** CHALKHILL *Thealma & Cl.* 75 Here and there gold Oaes 'mong Pearls she strew.

3. Name of one of several gauges of track in model railways: specifically 32 mm.; so ***O gauge***. Also ***OO***, 16½ mm., ***OOO***, 10 mm., etc.

1905 W. IVES *Something for Boys* 3 *Rails, crossings, switches*, with automatic lock action. No. O gauge, 1⅜ in. **1922** *Everyday Science* Nov. 441/1 (*heading*) No. OO gauge model 'table' railways. *Ibid.*, I am pleased to see that a small gauge, i.e., 'oo' gauge, railway, is to be placed on the market shortly. **1924** H. GREENLY *Model Railways* i. 3 A plan is given of Mr. H. L. Stevens' No. O gauge railway. *Ibid.* vi. 103 *No. OO Gauge 'Table' Railways.*—This standard gauge has been recently introduced by the writer..to provide for those who are limited in space to that of an ordinary dining-room table... The actual gauge is 16 mm. (⅝ in.). **1932** P. BLOOMFIELD *Imaginary Worlds* ii. 34 Pretending..that our O gauge railway round the nursery floor is really the line taken by the 'Flying Scotsman'. **1967** C. J. FREEZER *Model Railway Terminol.* 3, O. Gauge: 32 mm. Scale: 7 mm. Limited commercial support, but..in a flourishing condition. *Ibid.*, OO. Gauge: 16·5 mm. Scale: 4 mm. The most popular gauge in Britain. Fully supported commercially with ample selection of models.

O', O, *sb.*[2] The Irish word *ó, ua*, OIr. *au*, 'descendant', used as a prefix of Irish patronymic surnames, as *O'Connell, O'Connor, O'Neil*. Hence, a person whose surname begins with *O'*, a member of an ancient Irish family.

1730 FIELDING *Tom Thumb* I. iii, Ireland her O's, her Mac's let Scotland boast. **1887** P. GILLMORE *Hunter's Arcadia*, An Irishman who claims his direct descent from Finn McCoul, or some king whose name begins with an 'O' or 'Mc'.

See also *o*, obs. f. OY *sb. Sc.*, grandchild, nephew.

O, *sb.*[3]: see O *int.*

†**o, oo,** *numeral adj. Obs.* The reduced form of *ôn, oon* [:—OE. *án*], ONE, used in ME., southern and midl., before a consonant. The earlier form was *a* (which also continued in the north): see A *adj.*[1] and ONE.

[*c* **1200** *Trin. Coll. Hom.* 39 Ure drihten drof fele deules togedere ut of a man.] *c* **1205** LAY. 3660 Ʒef o man hit wille breke. *a* **1225** *Ancr. R.* 308 Þet o man beo uor one þinge twien idemed. **1362** LANGL. *P. Pl.* A. II. 96 At oo ȝeris ende whan ȝe reken schul. *c* **1386** CHAUCER *Merch. T.* 91 O [*v.r.* Oo] flessh they been, and o flessh as I gesse Hath but oon [*v.r.* on] herte, in wele and in distresse. *c* **1425** *Seven Sag.* (P.) 2807 O day a town he fande. *c* **1489** CAXTON *Sonnes of Aymon* iii. 113 He rood soo longe oo daye after a nother. *Ibid.* vi. 146 Reynawde..drew hym a lityll atte oo side.

†**o, oe,** *v. Obs. rare.* Pa. pple. oed. [f. O *sb.*[1] 2 b.] *trans.* To spangle, to decorate with small circular disks of tinsel.

1627–77 FELTHAM *Resolves* I. xx. 36 Divinity..will cast a far more radiant lustre,..than the Stage presents us with, though oe'd and spangled in their gawdiest tyre.

†**o, oo,** *adv. Obs.* Forms: (1–3 **a**), 3–5 **o, oo,** (4–5 **ho**). [The form taken regularly in ME. by OE. *á*, which remained in the north, till both forms were replaced by the cognate AY from Norse. See A *adv.* and AY.] Ay, ever, always.

c **1200** *Trin. Coll. Hom.* 7 Witeð ȝe..into þat eche fir on helle and wunieð þar ô and ô abuten ende. *c* **1250** *Gen. & Ex.* 111 Ful o life ðe lested oo. *c* **1325** *Deo Gracias* 4 in *E.E.P.* (1862) 128 Leeue me wel hit lasteþ o. *c* **1420** *Chron. Vilod.* st. 503 Dwelle þu shalt þere for evere and ho. *a* **1425** *Cursor M.* 19091 (Trin.) Of oure eldres þat han bene o [*earlier MSS.* a, aa]. ? *a* **1500** *Chester Pl.* xiii. 463 A! lord, honored be thou oo, That us hath saved from muche woe.

o, o' (əʊ, ə), *prep.*[1] [Worn down or apocopate form of ON *prep.*, used in ME. before a consonant; sometimes also, in mod. dial., before a vowel: cf. A *prep.*[1]] = ON *prep.*, in its various senses and uses; in early use including 'in'.

†**a.** in ME.

The ME. literary use appears to have ceased *c* 1400.

a **1200** *Moral Ode* 27 Al to loma ich habbe igult a werke and o worde. *c* **1200** *Trin. Coll. Hom.* 67 Ete nu leinte mete, and enes o dai. *a* **1225** *Ancr. R.* 212 Biholdeð o luft & asquint. *c* **1230** *Hali Meid.* 17 Leccherie o meidenhad.. weorreð o þis wise. *a* **1240** *Ureisun* in *Cott. Hom.* 189 Ase [he] stod o rode. *a* **1240** *Sawles Warde* ibid. 249 Lest sum for-truste him, ant feole o slepe. *a* **1300** *Cursor M.* 6749 (Cott.) If..þe dede be don o night [*Fairf.* on niȝt]. *Ibid.* 28861 Criand o crist wit-vten steuen. *a* **1340** HAMPOLE *Psalter* i. 1 Pestilens is an euyl rechand o lenght and bred. *c* **1400** MAUNDEV. (1839) xxvi. 269 Of suche Lyouns as ben o this half. *c* **1400** *Destr. Troy* 3145 O nowise may we wyn þat woman to gete. *a* **1400–50** *Alexander* 4055 Neuire to dee ..bot euire dure o lyue.

†**b.** In ME., frequently joined in writing to the following word, or hyphened to it by editors. *Obs.*

In early times this was esp. the case when it was followed by *þe, þis, þat*, or by words with which it combined to form an adv. or quasi-adv., now usually formed with *a-*, as *o-bak, o-bout, o-boven, o-drey, o-ferre, o-length, o-live, o-loft, o-lufte, o-slepe*, etc. The more important of these will be found as main words, in A- or O-.

c **1220** *Bestiary* 673 Oðe wise ðat ic haue ȝie seid. *c* **1300** *Havelok* 2311 That dide [he] hem o-boke swere. *Ibid.* 2505 The mere.. Skabbed and ful iuele o-bone. *a* **1340** HAMPOLE *Psalter* xxv. 1 Depart me fro ille men in body, for we are fere otwyn in soul. *Ibid.* xxxvii. 12 þai þat ware biside me stode olenght.

c. In modern Eng., *o'* is frequent in Shaks. and later dramatists, esp. in *o' th'* for 'on the' (cf. *i' th'* = in the). It also occurs in some archaic or traditional phrases or collocations, and dialectally.

In *o' nights*, and the like, though representing ME. *on* (*on nyȝtes*), it is often associated with *o'* = *of* (cf. *of a night*).

1598 SHAKS. *Merry W.* I. i. 40 Ha; o' my life, if I were yong againe, the sword should end it. **1600** —— *A.Y.L.* IV. i. 48 Cupid hath clapt him oth' shoulder. **1610** —— *Temp.* I. i. 43 A poxe o' your throat, you bawling.. Dog. **1613** —— *Hen. VIII*, V. iv. 71 Mercy o' me. [Cf. *Merry W.* III. i. 22, *John* IV. i. 12.] **1647** R. STAPYLTON *Juvenal* 283 Whose parts oth stage he lately play'd. **1675** HOBBES *Odyss.* (1677) 154 O'th' tenth at night the gods brought me to land. **1775** SHERIDAN *Rivals* III. iii, Tender! ay, and prophane too, o' my conscience. *Ibid.* IV. iii, Being knocked o' the head by-and-by. **1887** A. BIRRELL *Obiter Dicta* Ser. II. 119 He did not always go home o' nights. **1890** W. A. WALLACE *Only a Sister* 88 He went to church twice o' Sundays.

d. = A *prep.*[1] 10.

1850 JAMES *Headsman* III. vi. 357 O' Heaven's sake, thy glass of kirschwasser!

o, o' (əʊ, ə), *prep.*[2] [Worn down or apocopate form of *of*, used before a cons., and sometimes in dial. before a vowel also: cf. A *prep.*[2]] = OF in its various uses. Now *Obs.* exc. as in b.

In ME. sometimes joined to the following word.

a **1300** *Cursor M.* 7116 His wijf fader and moder he gaue O þis hony at ete þe laue. *Ibid.* 10701 It cums o will. *c* **1400** *Apol. Loll.* 13 Wan it is don onli up on comyn form o lawe. *a* **1400-50** *Alexander* 2898 ȝit has þe floum, as I fynde, a forelange obrede. *c* **1460** *Towneley Myst.* XII. 292 Iesus onazorus [= of Nazareth]. **1567** *Gude & Godly Bal.* (S.T.S.) 158 Of [*ed.* 1578 O] pure lufe & meir mercy Myne awin Sone downe I send.

b. In form *o'*, still used *dial.*, *colloq.*, and in some traditional phrases and locutions; esp., *What's o' clock? six o' clock*; also in *John o' Groats, Jack o' lantern, Will o' the wisp, Tom o' Bedlam*, etc.

Formerly in many others, as *Inns o' Court, man o' war, Isle o' Wight*, but in these *of* is now usually written, even when *o'* is familiarly pronounced. The contracted form is common in the dramatists in familiar phraseology, and is occasional in modern poets; it is usual in the representation of dialectal or vulgar speech.

1591 SHAKS. *Two Gent.* I. ii. 83 Best sing it to the tune of Light O Loue. **1593** —— *2 Hen. VI*, I. i. 186 More like a Souldier then a man o' th' church. **1600** —— *A.Y.L.* III. ii. 318 You should aske me what time o' day. **1610** —— *Temp.* I. ii. 123 In lieu o' th' premises. **1676** HOBBES *Iliad* I. 163 The greatest part o' th' gain. **1713** S. PYCROFT *Brief Enq. Free-thinking* 26 The two Universities have been constantly traduc'd o' late. **1803** TANNAHILL *Soldier's Return* 43 Ye hinna the ambition o a moose. **1864** TENNYSON *North. Farmer* I. ii, Naw soort o' koind o' use to saäy the things that a do. **1868** BROWNING *Ring & Bk.* I. 24 Just a spirt O' the proper fiery acid. *Ibid.* I. 46 The basement-ledge O' the pedestal.

†**o**, *prep.*[3] *Obs.* [Worn down form of *oð*, OE. *oððe*, before *þ* or *th*: cf. A *prep.*[3]] In the early ME. phr. *o that*, until that.

c **1300** *Harrow. Hell* 128 Thou shalt buen in bondes ay O that come domes day. *c* **1320** *Cast. Love* 152 O þat of hem to weren at-sprong þe noumbre of þe soule þ[t] fro heuene felle.

O (əʊ), *int.* (*sb.*[1], *v.*) [A natural (or what now seems a natural) exclamation, expressive of feeling. OE. had neither *ó!*, nor *á!* (which would have phonetically given ME. *ô!*). Not in OHG., or early ON.; in Goth., prob. from Greek; in MHG. and later (Christian) Norse, prob. from Latin. In early ME. 12th c., app. from L. (or ? Fr.); but often varying with *A!*, esp. in northern writers. Wyclif has *O* (or *A*) only when *O* is in the Vulgate. In OE., Lat. *O* was rendered by *lá* or *éalá*.]

1. Standing before a sb. in the vocative relation.

c **1205** LAY. 17126 O Aurilie þe king, þu fræinest me a sellic þing. *a* **1225** *Leg. Kath.* 1453 O mihti meiden! O witti wummon!.. O schene nebschaft & schape se swiðe semlich. *a* **1225** *Ancr. R.* 54 O mine leoue sustren, hwu Eue haueð monie douhtren þe uoluweð hore moder. *a* **1300** *Sarmun* xxxii. in *E.E.P.* (1862) 4 O sinful man wo worþ þi rede whan al þis wrech sal be for þe. **1340** *Ayenb.* 93 O god, hou is nou grat þe mochelhede of þine zuetnesse. **1382** WYCLIF *Ps.* cxvii[i]. 25 O! Lord [Vulg. *O domine*] mac me saf, O! Lord, weel be thou welsum [*most MS. in both places* A!]. *c* **1386** CHAUCER *Knt.'s T.* 1439 O chaste goddesse of the wodes grene. **1535** COVERDALE *Ps.* lix. [lx.] 1 O God thou y[t] hast cast vs out [WYCLIF God, thou hast put vs abac]. **1563-87** FOXE *A. & M.* (1596) 73/1 We are, ô emperor, your souldiors. **1611** BIBLE *Ps.* cxlvii. 12 Praise the Lord, O Ierusalem: praise thy God, O Zion. **1742** H. CAREY *Loyal Song* ii, O Lord, our God, arise! Scatter our enemies. **1796** H. HUNTER tr. *St. Pierre's Stud. Nat.* (1799) I. 430 O Eternal! Have mercy upon me, because I am passing away: O Infinite! because I am but a speck. **1850** TENNYSON *In Mem.* IV. 5 O heart, how fares it with thee now?

2. In other connexions, or without construction, expressing, according to intonation, various emotions, as appeal, entreaty, surprise, pain, lament, etc.

In this use, in 17th and 18th c., often written OH (q.v.); but this form is now usual only when the exclamation is quite detached from what follows (see OH); *O* being used with an imperative, optative, or exclamatory sentence or phrase, as in *O take me back again! O would I were there! O that I might see him! O for another glimpse of it! O the pity of it! O dear me! O dear! O me!*; often also in *O yes, O no, O indeed, O really*, and the like.

c **1175** *Lamb. Hom.* 21 O, seið þus þe boc, wei þet he eure hit wule iþenche in his þonke. *a* **1225** *Ancr. R.* 246 O muchel is, he seið, þe mihte of schir & of clene bone. *Ibid.* 280 O, þouhte ure Louerd þet al þis biheold, I schal don [etc.]. **13..** *E.E. Allit. P.* B. 861 O. O! my frendez so fre, your fare is to strange. **1388** WYCLIF *Rom.* xi. 33 O! the heiȝnesse of the ritchessis of the wisdom and of the kunnyng of God [**1382** A! **1526** TINDALE, etc. O]. **1450-1530** *Myrr. our Ladye* 91 Thys hympne begynneth wyth O... here yt meanyth praysynge and meruelynge, as when a man seyth or heryth a thynge that ys ryghte meruaylous, he sayeth.. O. what ys thys, or such other. **1526** *Pilgr. Perf.* (W. de W. 1531) 7 b, O, who wolde not be there? **1535** COVERDALE *Ps.* liv. [lv.] 6 O that I had wynges like a doue. *a* **1610** HEALEY *Epictetus* (1636) 46 Woe is mee! O mee most wretched man! **1611** HEYWOOD *Gold. Age* II. i. Wks. 1874 III. 23 Whence (ô whence ye Gods) Are all yon grones? **1667** MILTON *P.L.* IV. 715 Pandora, whom the Gods Endowd with all their gifts, and O too like In sad event. *a* **1748** WATTS *Improv. Mind* (1801) 325 But O! how exceedingly difficult it is. **1766** GOLDSM. *Vic. W.* xxii, O misery! 'Where', cried I, 'where are my little ones?' **1792** BURNS '*What can a Yng. Lassie*' iii, O, dool on the day I met wi' an auld man! **1816** SCOTT *Antiq.* xxxi, O dear, my poor Steenie, the pride o' my very heart. **1833** HT. MARTINEAU *Berkeley the Banker* I. i. 22 O no, Enoch protested; it was.. quite out of the question. **1837** —— *Soc. Amer.* III. 48 O, but we all live beyond our incomes. **1842** TENNYSON '*Break, break*' iii, O for the touch of a vanish'd hand. **1850** —— *In Mem.* xxxv, O me, what profits it to put An idle case? **1865** WHITMAN *Manhattan Arming* iv, It's O for a manly life in the camp!

3. In ballads (chiefly Sc.) added after the rime-word at the end of a line. App. identical in origin with A *int.*[4], as in the Shakespearian 'the stile-a', 'a mile-a', the *a* being at length treated as *int.*

In quot. 1859, from the usage of street cries.

1724-7 RAMSAY *The Mill-O* iv, O! the mill, mill-O, and the kill, kill-O, and the cogging of the wheel-O,.. And round wi' a soger reel-O! *a* **1775** *The Barrin' o' the door, O!*, It fell about the Martinmas time, An' a gay time it was than, O! [*rime* pan, O!]. **1781** BURNS *My Nanie, O* i, Behind yon hills where Stinchar flows, 'Mang moors an' mosses many, O; The wintry sun the day has clos'd, And I'll awa to Nanie, O. *a* **1810** TANNAHILL '*Gloomy winter's now awa*' 3 The mavis sings fu' cheery O [*rimes* dearie O, weary O]. **1830-83** R. E. WARBURTON *Hunt. Songs* xxvii. (ed. 7) 81 Stags in the forest lie, hares in the valley-o! **1859** SALA *Gas-light & D.* xvi. 177 The shows at Saville House remained alive O!

B. as *sb.* **1.** The interjection considered as a word. So **O me, O dear**, etc.

1609 B. JONSON *Case Altered* v. i, O me no O's, but hear. **1646** CRASHAW *Sosp. d'Her.* xxv, A desperate O me! drew from his deep breast. **1833-6** J. EAGLES *Sketcher* (1856) 18 They are not Virgil's Fortunati, with an O and an if, '*sua si bona norint*'. **1849** THACKERAY *Pendennis* xxxvii, Many O's of admiration.

2. pl. *O's of Advent*, the seven Advent Anthems sung on the days next preceding Christmas Eve, each containing a separate invocation to Christ beginning with *O*, as *O Sapientia* (O Wisdom), *O Adonai*, etc.

O's of St. Bridget or *Fifteen O's*, fifteen meditations on the Passion of Christ, composed by St. Bridget, each beginning with *O Jesu*, or a similar invocation.

1531 *Hore bte. Marie Virg.* 65 b, Thys be the xv. oos the whych the holy virgyn saint brigitta was [wonte] to say dayly befor the holy roode. **1547** *Homilies* I. *Good Wks.* III. (1859) 62 Other kinds of papistical superstitions and abuses, as of Beads, of Lady Psalters and Rosaries, of Fifteen Os. **1729** JACOB *Law Dict.* s.v. **1885** *Catholic Dict.* (ed. 3) 13/2 The seven greater antiphons or anthems.. called the O's of Advent. **1896** *Fortn. Rev.* LIX. 131 These feasts were called O's, because at vespers on these days the anthems all began with O.

-o, *suffix*[1] of combining forms of words. On the analogy of Greek combinations (in which the combining stem usually ended in *-o*, as thematic vowel or its representative, or as an addition to a consonant stem), and their adaptations and imitations in Latin, late and mediæval, like *Syrophœnix, Gallograeci, Gallohispani, Anglosaxonicus*, etc., *-o-* has come to be, in modern Latin and in English, the usual connecting vowel in combinations, not merely in ethnic names as *Anglo-Saxon, Anglo-Indian, Indo-European*, etc., but in scientific terms generally; it is affixed, not only to terms of Greek origin, but also to those derived from Latin (Latin compounds of which would have been formed with the L. connecting or reduced thematic vowel, *-i*), especially when compounds are wanted with a sense that Latin composition, even if possible, would not warrant, but which would be authorized by the principles of Greek composition. Such are *concavo-, convexo-, cymbo-, dolicho-, oblongo-, ovato-; chloro-, iodo-; cirrho-, cumulo-; occipito-, pneumo-; dramatico-, economico-, historico-, politico-; joco-, serio-*; etc.

1. The primary and etymological function of a combining form in *-o* is to qualify adverbially the adj. to which it is prefixed; as, in Gr., λευκό-χλωρος 'whitely green', pale green; mod.L. *ovato-cordatus* 'ovately heart-shaped', cordate with ovate modification; *Anglo-Norman*, Norman as modified in England. Such a comb. is, as it were, the adj. with adverbial qualification, belonging to a sb. with adj. qualification; thus, as to the qualified sb. *steady industry* (adj. + sb.) the corresponding qualified adj. is *steadily industrious* (adv. + adj.), so to *political economy* the corresponding adj. is *politico-economic*. Lord Campbell has used *lego-literary* in the sense 'pertaining to legal literature'.

2. But the use of these forms has been extended, so as to express, as by a kind of abbreviation, almost any manner of relation between the two components. *Anglo-French*, originally 'French of an English sort', 'French as established or spoken in England', is sometimes taken with the converse meaning of 'English settled in France', and commonly with that of 'English in alliance, conjunction, or partnership with French'; so *Franco-German* may even mean 'French in conflict with German', *Græco-Latin* 'common to Greek and Latin'; *pneumo-gastric*, 'communicating with both lungs and stomach'; *occipito-frontal*, 'reaching from occiput to forehead', or connecting these parts; *occipito-temporo-parietal*, 'including the occipital, temporal, and parietal (lobes of the brain)'; *gramino-carnivorous*, 'feeding on grass as well as flesh'.

3. This *-o* is used also, on Greek analogies, in word-formation. From its regular appearance before certain suffixal elements, as *-cracy, -graphy, -logy, -meter*, it tends to be treated practically as a part of these elements; hence, such expressions as 'the *bureau-ocracy, shop-ocracy, trade-ocracy*, and other *-ocracies*', 'a professor of all the *-ologies*,' 'the last new *-ology*,' 'galvanometers, lactometers, and other *-ometers* without number'.

-o, *suffix*[2]. Perh. connected with O *int.* 3 and reinforced by the final syllable of abbrev. forms such as COMPO, HIPPO, PHOTO, etc. The use of the suffix is widespread in English-speaking countries but nowhere more so than in Australia (e.g. *afto*, ARVO, COMMO, etc.).

a. Forming colloq. or slang equivalents added as a final syllable to (*a*) shortened forms of sbs., as AGGRO, AMMO, BEANO, COMBO, COMPO[2], METHO[1], etc.; (*b*) sbs., as BOYO, BUCKO, KIDDO, etc.; (*c*) adjs., as CHEAPO, *deado*.

1967 J. BURKE *Till Death us do Part* ii. 31 You can buy that cheapo, cos no one wants it. **1969** *It* 13-25 June 16/2 Hustle the bread from whatever source you can... If all the above sounds like too much aggro don't.. go and.. run your benefit event in conjunction with an existing club. *Ibid.* 10-23 Oct. 10/1 At the moment kids are split up into different subcultural groups which have been driven by the system into a permanent state of aggro with each other. **1969** *Daily Mail* 8 Nov. 8/3 How do we get past him, man? Like he might start some agro. **1970** *Observer* 11 Jan. 28/2 Hippies and aggro-boys may look collectively and individually startling, pretty or repulsive according to tribal loyalty. **1973** A. HUNTER *Gently French* iii. 29, I gets hold of the bastard and tries to pull him up. Then I sees he's bloody deado. **1973** M. AMIS *Rachel Papers* 65 It wasn't day-to-day aggro, nor the drooped, guilty, somehow sexless disgruntlement I had seen overtake many relationships. **1977** 'E. CRISPIN' *Glimpses of Moon* xi. 215 It was possible to judge.. that his aggro was strictly verbal.

b. Forming personal (chiefly occupational) sbs. from non-personal sbs., as BOTTLE-O(H, MILKO, WINO, etc.

c. Forming sbs. from adjs., as PINKO, WEIRDO, etc.

d. As a meaningless ending in other words, as BILLY-O, *good-o*, CHEERIO, *right*(*y*)*o*, etc.

oacombe, obs. form of OAKUM.

oad, oade, obs. forms of WOAD, ODE.

oaes, pl. of O *sb.*[1] 2.

oaf[1] (əʊf). Also 7-8 **oph**, 8 **oaph**. *Pl.* **oafs** (also 9 **oaves**). [A phonetic variant of AUF, earlier *aulf*: see also OUPH.] An elf's child, a goblin child, a supposed changeling left by the elves or fairies; hence, a misbegotten, deformed, or idiot child; a half-wit, fool, dolt, booby, as being by inference a changeling.

1625 FLETCHER & SHIRLEY *Nt. Walker* I. iv, Free us both from the fear of breeding fools And ophs, got by this shadow. **1638** FORD *Fancies* IV. i, I am.. an oaf, a simple alcatote, an innocent. **1693** SHADWELL *Volunteers* II. i, Be gone you saucy Oafe. **1702** DE FOE *Good Advice to Ladies* 110 Every word he spoke was like an Oph. **1708** *Brit. Apollo* No. 68. 3/1 Pray under what Name must the Bubbl'd Oaph pass? **1710** STEELE *Tatler* No. 248 ¶8 Marriages.. between the most accomplished Women, and the veriest Oafs. **1826** SCOTT *Woodst.* xii, Those terrified oafs, who take fright at every puff of wind. **1858** BAILEY *Age* 22 What oaves we must appear.

b. *Comb.*, as *oaf-rocked* adj.

1855 ROBINSON *Whitby Gloss.*, *Oaf-rock'd*, fool-born, of mentally weak from the cradle; spoiled by early indulgence.

Hence **'oafdom**, state of being an oaf, stupidity.

1883 AUSTIN DOBSON *O W. Idylls, Une Marquise* 34 Grown contented in our oafdom.

oaf². Abbrev. of OFAY. *U.S.*

1941 J. SMILEY *Hash House Lingo* 40 *Oaf*, white person (used by negroes).

oafish ('əʊfɪʃ), *a.* Also 8 auf-, awf-. [f. OAF¹ + -ISH¹.] Of the nature of an oaf, dull-witted, stupid, loutish.

1610 *Selden's Eng. Janus* Pref., An idle oafish affront. *a* **1700** B. E. *Dict. Cant. Crew*, *Oafish*, Silly. *a* **1734** NORTH *Exam.* I. ii. §153 Can he think that his Readers are so awfish as to imagine [etc.]? **1896** MRS. H. WARD *Sir G. Tressady* 157 She's got that oafish lad.. hung round her neck.

Hence **'oafishness**, stupidity and awkwardness.

1727 BAILEY, Vol. II, *Oafishness*, foolishness. **1890** *Sat. Rev.* 19 Apr. 475/1 The whole is ruined by the oafishness of Stockmann.

'oafishly, *adv.* [f. OAFISH *a.* + -LY².] In an oafish or stupid manner.

1876 F. K. ROBINSON *Gloss. Whitby* 134/1 *Oafishly*, *oafly*, absurdly; foolishly. **1908** A. S. M. HUTCHINSON *Once aboard Lugger* I. vii. 38 The driver becomes temporarily idiot—stands us oafishly silent. **1958** P. KEMP *No Colours or Crest* vii. 137, I stared back oafishly at him from under the brim of my hat.

oafo ('əʊfəʊ). *slang.* [f. OAF + -O².] A lout or hooligan. Also *attrib.*

1959 C. MACINNES *Absolute Beginners* 39, I eyed the oafo. *Ibid.* 184 The oafo lot went off laughing. **1962** R. COOK *Crust on its Uppers* i. 25 The middle classes.. the working classes.. not to mention the oafos.

oagar, -er, oagle, obs. ff. AUGER *sb.*¹, OGLE.

oak (əʊk). Forms: α. 1 ác (*plur.* ǽc), 3 ooc, 3–5 ok, (4 oek), 4–6 ook, (5–6 ooke), 4–7 oke, (5 hoke, a noke, 5–6 hooke), 6– oak, (*dial.* 6 oyke, woke, 6– woak, 7 yoake). β. *north.* and *Sc.* 5– ake, 6– aik, (5 a nak(e, ayk, 6 eike, 9 *dial.* yek, yak. [Com. Teut.: OE. *ác* fem. (pl. *ǽc*, gen. sing. **ǽc*, *áce*, dat. sing. *ǽc*, *ác*) = OFris. *êk*, ODu. *eik* (MDu. *eike*, *êke*, MLG. *êk*, *êke*, Flem. *eeke*, Du. *eik* masc.), OHG. *eih* (MHG. *eich*, Ger. *eiche*), ON. *eik* (in Icel. = 'tree', Norw. *eik*, *ek* Sw. *ek* 'oak', Da. *eeg*, *eg*):—OTeut. **aiks*, a fem. consonantal stem; ulterior relations obscure.]

1. a. The name of a well-known British and European forest tree, *Quercus Robur* (under which botanists now distinguish two subspecies, *Q. pedunculata* and *Q. sessiliflora*, DURMAST), noted for its timber, and bearing a fruit or species of mast called the ACORN; thence extended to all species of *Quercus*, trees or shrubs; the common species in N. America being *Q. alba*, the white oak, and *Q. macrocarpa*, the bur oak: see b.

α. **749** *Charter* in Kemble *Cod. Dipl.* V. 48 Of coferan treowe on ða bradan ac; of ðæræ [*MS.* ðara] bradan æc on stuteres hylle niðeweardе. *c* **1000** ÆLFRIC *Hom.* II. 150 Hire hyrdeman.. sume ac astah. *c* **1000** *Sax. Leechd* II. 98 Wipig rinde, & geongre ace. *c* **1250** *Gen. & Ex.* 1873 Diep he is dalf under an ooc. **1297** R. GLOUC. (Rolls) 510 A gret ok he wolde braide adoun, as it a smal ȝerd were. *c* **1374** CHAUCER *Boeth.* II. met. v. 35 (Camb. MS.), To slakyn hyr hungyr at euen with accornes of Okes. **1387** TREVISA *Higden* (Rolls) II. 85 Barkschire, þat haþ þat name of a baar ook þat is in þe forest of Wyndesore. **1398** —— *Barth. De P.R.* XVII. cxxxiv. (1495) 690 The hoke.. is a tree that bredyth maste. *c* **1420** *Avow. Arth.* xv, As he neghet bi a noke. *c* **1440** *Promp. Parv.* 363/1 Oke, tre, *Quercus*, *ylex*. **1506** *Will of Chamberlen* (Somerset Ho.), Vnder the grete hooke. **1539** TAVERNER *Erasm. Prov.* (1545) 66 If thou wylte begge an ooke of thy frende, aske twenty or an hundreth ookes. **1577** B. GOOGE *Heresbach's Husb.* (1586) 101 The first place of right belongeth to the oak. **1598** SHAKS. *Merry W.* IV. iv. 42 Marry this is our deuise, That Falstaffe at that Oake shall meete with vs. *Ibid.* V. v. 79 Our Dance of Custome, round about the Oke Of Herne the Hunter, let vs not forget. **1611** COTGR., *Charmoye*, a groue of Yoakes. **1784** COWPER *Task* I. 313 Lord of the woods, the long-surviving oak. **1842** SELBY *Brit. Forest Trees* (L.), Of the various North-American oaks, many are distinguished for the beauty of their foliage [etc.]. **1846** J. BAXTER *Libr. Pract. Agric.* II. 168 There are above forty different species of oak introduced into Great Britain. **1855** LONGF. *Hiaw.* XII. 93 On their pathway.. Lay an oak, by storms uprooted. **1859** W. S. COLEMAN *Woodlands* (1866) 5 The majestic Oak, the Monarch of the forest. **1887** T. HARDY *Woodlanders* III. i. 6 Hardly knowing a beech from a woak.

β. *c* **1400** MAUNDEV. (Roxb.) ix. 35 A tree of ake. **14..** *Med. Receipts* in *Rel. Ant.* I. 54 Tak everferne that waxes on the ake. **14..** *Nom.* in Wr.-Wülcker 716/7 *Hec quercus*,.. a nak. *c* **1470** HENRY *Wallace* v. 821 Wallace retorned besyd a burly ayk. **1513** DOUGLAS *Æneis* XII. Prol. 167 Endlang the hedgeis thyk, and on rank akis. *c* **1560** A. SCOTT *Poems* (S.T.S.) ii. 7 Nor Hercules, that aikkis vprent, And dang the devill of hell. **1562** TURNER *Herbal* II. 109 Quercus.. is called.. in yᵉ North countre an Eike tre... An acorn or an Eykorn, that is yᵉ corne or fruit of an Eike. **1801** MACNEILL *Poems, Waes o' War* 63 Auld chesnut, ake, and yew-tree. **1804** R. ANDERSON *Cumberld. Ball.* 83 O, Matthew! they've cutten the yeks and the eshes, That grew owre anent the kurk waw! **1855** ROBINSON *Whitby Gloss.*, Yak.

b. With defining adjective, applied to other species of *Quercus*, which are very numerous.

black or **dyer's oak**, *Q. tinctoria* = QUERCITRON; **blue oak**, **mountain white oak**, *Q. Douglassii* of California; **bur**, **mossy-cup**, or **overcup oak**, *Q. macrocarpa* of N. America; **chestnut oak**, *Q. sessiliflora*, and in N. America, *Q. Prinus* and other species having leaves like the chestnut; **cork oak**, *Q. Suber*, a native of southern Europe and northern Africa, the bark of which furnishes cork; **evergreen** or **holm oak** (also †*oak-holm*) = ILEX; **Italian oak**, *Q. Æsculus* of southern Europe, having edible acorns; **kermes-oak**, *Q. coccifera*, in which the kermes insect lives; **live oak**, a name given to several N. American species, but especially *Q. virens*; **scarlet oak**, *Q. coccinea* of N. America, so called from the colour of its foliage in autumn; **turkey oak**, *Q. Cerris* of southern Europe; the name is also given in America to *Q. Catesbæi*; **weeping oak**, *Q. lobata* of Western U.S.; **white oak**, *Q. alba*, a large American tree, sometimes called in England *Quebec oak*; also applied locally to other species, as, on the Pacific slope, to *Q. Garriana* and three others. **oak of Bashan**: see quot. 1892.

1727–41 CHAMBERS *Cycl.* s.v. *Kermes*.. Found adhering to the bark on the stem and branches of a sort of scarlet oak.. growing in Spain [etc.]. **1765** J. BARTRAM *Jrnl.* 25 Dec. in Stork *Acc. E. Florida* (1766) 5 Many live oak-trees grew upon it. **1766** STORK *Acc. E. Florida* 44 The live oak (so called from being an evergreen) is tougher, and of a better grain than the English oak. *Ibid.* 45 The chestnut oak, very little known in other parts of America, is very common in Florida. **1785** MARTYN *Rousseau's Bot.* xxviii. (1794) 437 Ilex or Evergreen Oak has oblong-ovate leaves.. continuing all the year. **1832** *Planting* 115 (U.K.S.) The Turkey oak, *Quercus cerris*, was introduced into England in 1739. **1841** *Penny Cycl.* XIX. 213/2 The timber of the Turkey oak is beautifully mottled, in consequence of the abundance of its silver grain. **1858** HOGG *Veg. Kingd.* 696 The acorns of *Q. esculus*, or Italian Oak, have somewhat prickly cups, and are long, slender, and esculent. **1861** HULME tr. *Moquin-Tandon* II. III. v. 150 The Aleppo Gall.. is found on the Dyer's Oak, *Quercus Infectoria*. **1887** BOURDILLON tr. *Aucassin & Nicolette* 122 She took many a lily head, With the bushy kermes-oak shoot. **1892** AGNES CLERKE *Fam. Stud. Homer* vi. 152 The species of oak at present dominant both in Greece and the Troad is the 'oak of Bashan', *Quercus ægilops*.

2. In English versions of the Bible, used also to render Heb. *ēlāh*, and one or two related words, now generally considered, since Gesenius, to mean the terebinth tree.

Five Heb. words have been rendered 'oak'; of which only two, *allōn* and *allāh*, are held to have certainly this meaning. The word *ēlāh* is in the LXX and Vulg. sometimes rendered τερέβινθος -μινθος, *terebinthus*, but in neither case regularly; Wyclif follows the Vulgate; the 16–17th c. versions have regularly 'oak'; the Revised Version has 'terebinth' in Isa. vi. 13 (1611 teil tree), Hos. iv. 13 (1611 elm), but elsewhere retains 'oak' with 'or *terebinth*' in the margin.

1382 WYCLIF *2 Sam.* xviii. 9 Whanne the muyle wente yn vndur a thik ook [Vulg. *quercum*, LXX δρυός, *R.V. margin*, or terebinth] and a greet, the heed of hym [1388 Absolon] cleuyd to the ook. —— *Isa.* i. 30 Whan ȝee shul ben as an oek [1388 ook, Vulg. *quercus*, LXX τερέβινθος], the leues fallende doun. **1535** COVERDALE *Gen.* xxxv. 4 He buried them vnder an Oke [LXX τερέβινθον, Vulg. *terebinthum*, WYCLIF theribynte, *R.V. marg.* or terebinth].

3. a. With qualification, applied to trees or plants in some way resembling the oak: esp. **dwarf oak**, **ground oak**, various species of *Teucrium*; **oak of Cappadocia**, *Ambrosia maritima*; **oak of Jerusalem** or **Paradise**, *Chenopodium Botrys*, having leaves jagged like those of an oak; **poison oak**, name for species of Sumach, esp. *Rhus Toxicodendron*.

1551 TURNER *Herbal* I. G j, Oke of Hierusalem is an herbe all yelow and all full of branches and spred abrode. **1578** LYTE *Dodoens* II. lxxiii. 243 It is called in English Oke of Hierusalem and of some Oke of Paradise... The Oke of Paradise is hoate and dry in the second degree. **1597** GERARDE *Herbal* 950 Leaues deepely cut or iagged, very much resembling the leafe of an Oke, which hath caused our English women to call it Okes of Ierusalem. *Ibid.* 951 Oke of Cappadocia is called.. in Latine *Ambrosia*. **1611** COTGR., *Ambrosie*, Ambrosia; also, the hearbe called Oke of Cappadocia; and another, called Oke of Ierusalem. **1760** J. LEE *Introd. Bot.* App. 320 Oak, Dwarf, *Teucrium*. Oak of Cappadocia, *Ambrosia*. Oak of Jerusalem, *Chenopodium*. **1766** J. BARTRAM *Jrnl.* 20 Jan. 43 Rising ground producing.. bay and water-oak, then ground-oak, chamaerops. **1805** A. WILSON in *Poems & Lit. Prose* (1876) II. 144 Waving reeds and scrubby ground-oak grew Where stores and taverns now arrest the view. **1858** MAYNE *Expos. Lex.*, *Poison-oak*,.. the sumach. **1883** STEVENSON *Silverado Sq.* (1886) 20 An abominable shrub or weed, called poison-oak, whose very neighbourhood is venomous to some. *a* **1887** M. S. G. NICHOLS in *Health Manual* xv. 188 Domestic Remedies—tea made of tanzy, oak of Jerusalem [etc.].

b. In Australia, applied to trees of the genus *Casuarina* ('Native Oak'), species of which are locally distinguished as ***bull-***, ***desert-***, ***river-***, ***swamp-oak***, etc. (cf. SHE-OAK); in New Zealand to species of *Alectryon* and *Knightia*.

1802 J. FLEMING in *Hist. Rec. Port Phillip* (1879) 22 (Morris) The land is.. thin of timber, consisting of gum, oak, Banksia, and thorn. **1838** T. L. MITCHELL *Exped. E. Austral.* (1839) I. 38 (ibid.) The dense, umbrageous foliage of the *casuarina*, or 'river-oak' of the colonists. **1862** KENDALL *Poems* 56 The wail in the native oak. **1885** HOOD *Land of Fern* 53 The sighing of the native oak Which the light wind whispered through. **1892** A. SUTHERLAND *Geog. Brit. Col.* 27 (Morris) A peculiar class of trees, called.. *Casuarina*, is popularly known as oaks, 'swamp-oaks', 'forest-oaks', 'she-oaks', and so forth, although the trees are not the least like oaks. **1896** B. SPENCER in *Rep. Horn Exped.* I. 49 We had now come into the region of the 'Desert Oak' (*Casuarina Decaisneania*).

4. a. The wood or timber of the oak. Hence, allusively, in phrases referring to its hardness and enduring qualities. ***heart of oak***: see HEART *sb.* 19.

c **1400** MAUNDEV. (1839) xviii. 190 Makynge Houses and Schippes of Oke. **1480** CAXTON *Chron. Eng.* ccxxiii. 220 Grete staues of fyne oke. **1575** *Richmond Wills* (1853) 255, Ij long burds of oyke. **1604** SHAKS. *Oth.* III. iii. 210 To seele her Father's eyes vp, close as Oake. **1664** EVELYN *Sylva* iii. §17 (1670) 26 Men had indeed hearts of Oak. **1693** *Apol. Clergy Scot.* 26 Taught better manners than to venture upon this man of Oak and Horehead. **1801** CAMPBELL *Ye Mariners of Eng.* iii, With thunders from her native oak She quells the floods below. **1849** JAMES *Woodman* ii, The tables, the chairs, the cupboard.. were all of old oak. **1860** TENNENT *Story Guns* (1864) 224 A far ruder shock.. to the confidence traditionally reposed in British oak. **1876** *Whitby Gloss.* s.v., A bit o' brave aud yak. **1888** *Glasgow Herald* 12 Oct. 4/6 A piece of finely selected English oak.

b. Timber of oak as the material of a ship.

a **1000** *Runes* xxv. 4 (Gr.) Garsecg fandað, Hwæðer ac hæbbe æðele treowe. **1763–5** CHURCHILL *Gotham* I. 260 The English Oak, which, dead, commands the flood. **1782** COWPER *Charity* 23 When Cook.. Steered Britain's oak into a world unknown.

c. *Univ. colloq.* An oaken door; esp. in phr. ***to sport one's oak***, to shut the outer door of one's rooms as a sign that one is engaged.

1785 GROSE *Dict. Vulg. Tongue* s.v., To sport oak; to shut the outward door of a student's room at college. *c* **1803** C. K. SHARPE *New Oxford Guide* ii. in *Mem.* (1888) I. 18 And sporting of oaks they call shutting of doors. **1810** SHELLEY in Hogg *Life* (1858) I. 93 Then the oak is such a blessing. **1827** *Sporting Mag.* XXI. 75 Having in the middle of the night nailed up his oak. **1861** HUGHES *Tom Brown at Oxf.* i. (1889) 7 A great.. outer door, my oak, which I sport when I go out or want to be quiet. **1890** BESANT *Demoniac* i. 18 Your oak was sported and you were not at home to anybody.

5. a. The leaves of the oak, *esp.* as worn in a chaplet or garland.

c **1386** CHAUCER *Knt.'s T.* 1432 A coroune of a grene ook cerial Vp on hir heed. **1587** GOLDING *De Mornay* xii. 166 The Garlond of Oke, he giueth.. to such as.. first.. enter the breach. **1607** SHAKS. *Cor.* I. iii. 16 To a cruell Warre I sent him, from whence he return'd, his browes bound with Oake. **1772** PRIESTLEY *Inst. Relig.* (1782) I. 384 Our custom of wearing oak on the twenty-ninth of May.

b. A shade of brown like that of the oak-leaf when opening.

1888 *Lady* 25 Oct. 378/1 [Gloves] in the new and beautiful shades of brown, chocolate, oak, tans, and black.

6. *dial.* The suit of clubs in cards. (= Ger. *Eicheln*, the suit bearing the figures of acorns.)

1847–78 HALLIWELL, *Oak*,.. the club at cards. *West.* **1886** ELWORTHY *W. Som. Word-bk.*, *Oaks*, the suit of clubs in cards.. 'Oaks be trumps, Mr. Hosegood'.

7. *the Oaks*: a race for three-year-old fillies, founded in 1779, and run at Epsom on the Friday after the Derby.

So called from an estate near Epsom.

1844 W. H. MAXWELL *Sports & Adv. Scotl.* xxxix. (1855) 305 what care I about Oaks or Derbys? **1864** *Racing Cal.* 131 Renewals of the Oaks stakes for 50 sovereigns each. **1870** BLAINE *Encycl. Rur. Sports* §1317 The stakes run for in the Oaks have recently rivalled in amount those of the Derby, and sometimes surpassed them.

8. *attrib.* and *Comb.* **a.** simple attrib. (often = OAKEN *a.*), as ***oak bough***, ***floor***, ***forest***, ***grove***, ***leaf*** (whence ***oak-leaved*** adj.), ***roofing***, ***sapling***, ***-scroll***, ***set***, ***table***, ***-thicket***, ***timber***, ***wreath***. **b.** objective, as ***oak-cleaving*** adj. **c.** instrumental, as ***oak-beamed***, ***-boarded***, ***clad***, ***-crested***, ***-crowned***, ***framed***, ***-timbered***, ***-wainscoted*** adjs. **d.** similative, etc., as ***oak-brown***, ***-like***, ***-pale***, ***-trunked*** adjs.

1796 C. MARSHALL *Garden.* vi. (1813) 82 Let *Oak-acorns be thrown into water and those only used which sink quickly. **1759** BROWN *Compl. Farmer* 21 Rub it over with oil or *oak-asnes. **1886** W. J. TUCKER *E. Europe* 33 A low, *oak-beamed room. **1897** BARING-GOULD in *Mag. Art* Sept. 270 The broad oak staircase gave access to a great gallery, *oak-boarded. **1895** *Daily News* 5 Feb. 6/6 Another corduroy dress is *oak-brown. *a* **1748** THOMSON *Hymn Solitude* 43 From Norwood's *oak-clad hill. **1605** SHAKS. *Lear* III. ii. 5 Vaunt-curriors of *Oake-cleauing Thunder-bolts. **1897** *Outing* (U.S.) XXIX. 438/1 This *oak-covered tract is a mile in width. **1747** COLLINS *Passions* 74 The *oak-crown'd Sisters and their chaste-eyed Queen. **1750** T. WARTON *Ode* vii. 4 Yonder oak-crown'd airy steep. **1789** J. PILKINGTON *View Derbysh.* I. 369 For polishing.. *oak floors and furniture. **1859** W. S. COLEMAN *Woodlands* (1866) 8 Covered with *oak-forests. **1953** E. SIMON *Past Masters* I. 47 On the walls.. two *oak-framed prints. **1977** *Times* 15 Oct. 8/2 The house.. had.. an oak-framed porch. **1535** COVERDALE *Gen.* xiii. 18 So Abram remoued his tent and wente and dwelt in yᵉ *Okegroue of Mamre. **1766** J. BARTRAM *Jrnl.* 31 Jan. in Stork *Acc. E. Florida* 56 Cypress-swamps and *oak-hammocks alternately mixed with pine-land. **1389** in *Eng. Gilds* (1870) 117 A garlond of *hoke Lewes. **1768–74** TUCKER *Lt. Nat.* (1834) II. 77 The little fly sits boring the oak-leaf. **1855** LONGF. *Hiaw.* XII. 118 As brown and withered as an oak-leaf is in Winter. **1856** MISS PRATT *Flower. Pl.* IV. 275 *Oak-leaved Goosefoot. **1883** S. B. PARSONS in *Harper's Mag.* Apr. 726/2 The oak-leaved hydrangea. **1883** STEVENSON *Treas. Isl.* III. xiv, A long thicket of these *oak-like trees. **1922** JOYCE *Ulysses* 6 His fair *oakpale hair stirring slightly. **1840** DICKENS *Barn. Rudge* i, A certain *oak-panelled room with a deep bay window. **1888** MISS BRADDON *Fatal Three* I. v, The chief characteristic of the interior was the *oak-panelling. **1815** SCOTT *Guy M.* xlii, What was called the great *oak-parlour, a long room, panelled with well-varnished wainscot. **1499** *Promp. Parv.* 363/2 (Pynson) *Oke plante, *Ornus*. **1787** HAWKINS *Life Johnson* 491 It was an oak-plant of a tremendous size. **1663** GERBIER *Counsel* 66 *Oake Roofing raysing pieces eight Inches one way. **1853** A. Smith *Life Drama* II. 21 At the *oak-roots I've seen full many a flower. **1882** *Garden* 14 Oct. 335/1 The *Oak root gall..is formed by Andricus noduli. **1826** Scott in *Croker Papers* (1884) I. xi. 318 A set-to with *oak saplings. **1874** G. M. Hopkins *Jrnls. & Papers* (1959) 245 A beautiful spray-off of the dead *oak-scrolls. **1523** Fitzherb. *Husb.* §124 Set thy *oke settes and thy asshe .x. or .xii fote asonder. **1822** in Cobbett *Rur. Rides* I. 83 Genuine *oak-soil: a bottom of yellow clay. **1890** J. G. Frazer *Gold. Bough* II. iv. 364 The King of the Wood must have been a personification of the *oak-spirit. **1653** *N. Riding Rec.* V. 151 [Indictment for unjustly taking away an] *oak-stoop. **1798** Coleridge *Anc. Mar.* VII. ii, The rotted old *Oak-stump. **1846–7** Thoreau *Walden* (1957) 186 Pine woods and *oak-thickets. **1767** A. Young *Farmer's Lett. to People* 157 Complaints of the decay of *oak timber. **1934** Dylan Thomas *Let.* 21 Sept. (1966) 268 No One more welcome than the *oak-trunked maestro—. **1885** G. Allen *Babylon* v, In the *oak-wainscoted study. **1801** Macneill *Poems, May-day* 21 This *oak-waving mountain would ward winter's blast. **1879** Froude *Cæsar* 93 He..won the *oak wreath, the Victoria Cross of the Roman army.

9. Special combs.: **oak-bark**, the bark of the oak, used in tanning, and as an astringent; **oak barren** *U.S.*: see quot. 1889; **oak-beauty**, a beautiful geometrid moth (*Biston* or *Amphidasis prodromaria*), the larva of which feeds on the oak; **oak-beetle**: see quot.; †**oak-berry**, a berry-like gall found on the oak; **oak-boy**, a member of a body of insurgents in Ireland in 1763, who rose against forced labour on the roads and the exaction of tithes; their badge was a sprig of oak worn in the hat; **oak-button** = *oak-gall*; **oak cist, coffin** (see quot. 1957); **oak-egger (moth)**: see EGGER; **oak-fig**, a gall, somewhat resembling a fig, produced on twigs of white oak in the United States by *Cynips forticornis*; **oak flat** *U.S.*, a level expanse of ground bearing a growth of oaks; **oak-fly**, a fly used by anglers; **oak-frog**, a small light-coloured toad of North America, frequenting oak-openings; **oak-gall**, a gall or excrescence produced on various species of oak by the punctures of various gall-flies; *spec.* a nut-gall or gall-nut used in making ink; †**oak-holm** = HOLM-OAK; **oak hook-tip**, a moth (*Platypteryx hamula*) inhabiting oak-woods; **oak-lappet**, a moth (*Gastropacha quercifolia*) the wings of which resemble a dried oak-leaf; **oakleaf braid** (see quots.); **oakleaf jar** (see quot. 1960); **oak-leather**, a fungus found on old oaks and somewhat resembling white kid-leather; †**oak-lungs**, a kind of lichen (*Sticta pulmonacea*), lungwort (*obs.*); **oak-mast**: see quot.; **oak moss**, the lichen *Evernia prunastri* or one closely related to it, often found growing on oak trees and used to produce an aromatic extract; also the extract itself; also *attrib.*; **oak-moth**, a moth (*Tortrix viridiana*) living on oaks; †**oak-nut**, an excrescence found on the oak; **oak-opening**, *U.S.*, an opening or thinly wooded space in an oak-forest (Webster, 1864); **oak-pest**, an insect (*Phylloxera rileyi*) which infests oaks in the United States; **oak-plum**, a plum-shaped gall produced on the acorns of the black and red oaks in U.S. by the gall-fly *Cynips quercus-prunus*; **oak-potato**, a potato-shaped gall produced on the twigs of white oaks in U.S. by the gall-fly *Cynips quercus-batatas*; **oak-pruner** *U.S.*, a longicorn beetle *Elaphidion villosum*, the larva of which mines down the centre of hardwood twigs, causing them to snap; now usually called the twig pruner; **oak room**, an oak-panelled room; **oak-spangle**, a kind of flattened fungus-like gall, occurring on the lower side of oak-leaves; **oak towel** *slang* (see quot.); **oak-truffle**, a truffle growing among the roots of oaks; **oak-wart**, an oak-gall; **oak-water**, a medicine made of oak-bark; **oak-web** *dial.*, a cockchafer; **oak wilt** *U.S.*, a disease of oaks and certain other trees produced by the fungus *Ceratocystis fagacearum*, which causes the wilting and death of foliage and eventually kills affected trees; **oak-worm**, a worm that lives on the oak; **oak yard** *U.S.*, an enclosure in which oaks are grown.

1666 J. Davies *Hist. Caribby Isl.* 62 As hard as *Oak-bark. **1811** A. T. Thomson *Lond. Disp.* (1818) 332 Oak bark is inodorous, has a rough astringent taste. **1859** W. S. Coleman *Woodlands* 16 A decoction of Oak-bark has..been used..in modern medicine. **1811** *Weekly Reg.* 12 Oct. 101/2 Our *oak barrens and underwooded plains may be profitably applied to sheep. **1835** W. Irving *Tour Prairies* 144 The soil of these 'oak barrens' is loose and unsound, being little better, at times, than a mere quick-sand. **1889** Farmer *Americanisms, Oak barrens*, scrubby oak brush, the stunted growth of which indicates an extreme poverty of soil. **1832** J. Rennie *Consp. Butterfl. & M.* 104 The *Oak Beauty..appears in March or April... Rather scarce. **1854** A. Adams, etc. *Man. Nat. Hist.* 191 *Oak-Beetles (*Eucnemidæ*)... Living in decayed oak-trees. **1626** *Oak-berries [see *oak-nut*]. **1776** R. Twiss *Tour Irel.* 143 Insurgents, who wore oak-leaves in their hats, and called themselves *Oak-boys. **1780** A. Young *Tour Irel.* I. 168 The oak boys and steel boys had their rise in the increase of rents. **1882** Lecky *Eng. in 18th C.* IV. xvi. 345 The Oakboys appear to have first risen against the Road Act. **1937** E. V. Gordon tr. *Shetelig & Falk's Scand. Archaeol.* 146 Of similar type is the other well-known form of Norse bronze-age grave, the '*oak cist', a coffin made from a thick trunk of oak, split and hollowed out. **1968** G. Jones *Hist. Vikings* I. i. 19 The tannin of the 'oak cists' of Denmark, the very flesh and fell of the wearers. **1937** E. V. Gordon tr. *Shetelig & Falk's Scand. Archaeol.* 147 The complete picture of this personal equipment is obtained from the *oak coffins mentioned earlier. **1957** T. C. Lethbridge *Gogmagog* viii. 132 Occasionally in Britain and more frequently in Denmark human bodies are found buried in what are known as 'oak coffins'. These are not coffins in the ordinary sense; but are large sections of tree trunks, split lengthwise and hollowed out to contain the body. **1964** W. L. Goodman *Hist. Woodworking Tools* 10 The remarkable wooden folding stool found with an oak-coffin burial at Guldhoj in Jutland. *a* **1816** B. Hawkins *Sk. Creek Country* (1848) 29 *Oak flats, red and post oak,..on its left side. **1849** E. Chamberlain *Indiana Gazetteer* (ed. 3) 381 Beech and oak flats, which are adapted only to grass. **1651** T. Barker *Art of Angling* (1653) 6 The *Oake-Flie is to bee had on the butt of an Oake or an Ash..it is a brownish Flie. **1653** Walton *Angler* v. 115 You may make the Oak-flie with an Orange tawny and black ground, and the brown of a Mallards feather for the wings. **1787** Best *Angling* (ed. 2) 114 The Oakfly comes on about the sixteenth of May, and continues on till about a week in June... It is bred in oak-apples. **1867** F. Francis *Angling* vi. (1880) 221 The Oak Fly, called also the cannon fly, the down-hill or down-looker. **1768–74** Tucker *Lt. Nat.* (1834) II. 91 Gums, *oak-galls, and variegated leaves [are] the distempers of plants. **1838** Loudon *Arboretum* III. 1726 Oak-galls..much in demand for the manufacture of ink and for dyeing black. **1601** Holland *Pliny* II. 177 The Scarlet graine growing upon the *Oke-holm. **1954** *N. & Q.* June 273/1 **Oakleaf braid.*—This is the black braid supplied for hats of senior police officials and also used by St. John Ambulance. **1957** *Textile Terms & Definitions* (Textile Inst.) (ed. 3) 70 *Oakleaf braid*, a woven narrow fabric having a conventional oakleaf and acorn and border Jacquard design, now always black... It is used as a hatband for officials such as Police Inspectors. **1903** H. Wallis (*title*) *Oak-leaf Jars: A fifteenth century Italian Ware showing Moresco Influence. **1960** R. G. Haggar *Conc. Encycl. Cont. Pott. & Porc.* 334/1 *Oak-leaf jars*, Tuscan fifteenth century maiolica drug pots painted with an oak-like..leaf decoration. **1754** Watson *Agaric* in *Phil. Trans.* XLVIII. 812 Mr. Ray..says, that this Fungus ..is found upon putrid oaks in Ireland, where it is called *oak-leather. **1750** E. Smith *Compl. Housewife* (ed. 14) 295 Take of *oak-lungs, French moss, and maiden-hair, of each a handful. **1758** *Phil. Trans.* L. 682 The *muscus pulmonarius officinarum*, tree-lung-wort, or oak-lungs. **1849** E. Chamberlain *Indiana Gazetteer* (ed. 3) 17 *Oak and beech mast is found in such quantities as to contribute largely both to feeding and fattening hogs. **1859** W. S. Coleman *Woodlands* (1866) 7 These acorns or oak-mast as they are collectively called. **1921** A. L. Smith *Lichens* x. 418 French perfumers extract an excellent perfume from *Evernia prunastri*..known as 'Mousse des Chênes' (*Oak moss), and it appears that the plants which grow on oak contain more perfume than those which live on other trees. **1921** *Times Lit. Suppl.* 25 Aug. 542/4 The oak-moss lichen is used as a basis for perfumes, the thallus on being soaked in spirit yielding a sweet and persistent odour. **1966** J. S. Cox *Illustr. Dict. Hairdressing* 104/2 Oak Moss Resin. Obtained from tree lichens, especially oak; used in perfumery. **1967** M. E. Hale *Biol. Lichens* iv. 59 These 'oak mosses' accumulated silicon, phosphorus, magnesium, iron and aluminium to a significant degree. **1975** F. Kennett *Hist. Perfume* vii. 148 The main ingredients of it [*sc.* Poudre de Chypre] are oakmoss (extracted from a species of lichen and still commonly used in perfumery, by the name *mousse de chêne*), rose-water, musk, civet, and a little sandalwood. **1868** Wood *Homes without H.* xiv. 295 One of the most common among the Leaf-rollers is the pretty *Oak Moth. **1626** Bacon *Sylva* §635 Besides its acorns, it beareth galls, Oak-apples, *oak-nuts which are inflammable, and oak-berries. **1830** J. M'Call in *Wisconsin State Hist. Soc. Coll.* (1892) XII. 185 From that up, on the right bank, it is *oak openings. **1833** C. F. Hoffman *Winter in West* (1835) I. 142 At a sudden turning of the path, I came at once upon the 'oak openings'. **1835** W. Irving *Tour Prairies* 77 (Bartlett) We ascended the hills, taking a course through the oak-openings. **1839** C. M. Kirkland *New Home* xx. 133 The 'grubs' present a most formidable hindrance to all gardening efforts in the 'oak-openings'. **1848** J. F. Cooper *Oak Openings* I. i. 10 Giving their appellation to this particular species of native forest, under the name of 'Oak Openings'. **1882** *Econ. Geol. Illinois* II. vi. 104 There is an intermediate district occupied by oak-openings. **1970** *Daily Progress* (Charlottesville, Va.) 24 May 4/1 Trees and shrubs grew along the streams, on wooded knolls or ridges, and in occasional 'oak openings'. **1819** *Mass. Agric. Repository & Jrnl.* V. 308 From the effect of its labours, it may be called the *oak pruner. **1838** *Mass. Zool. Survey Rep.* 92 The oak-pruner, so named by Prof. Peck, inhabits the white and black oaks. **1862** *Rep. Comm. Patents: Agric. 1861* (U.S. Dept. Agric.) 615 The black and white oak trees are infested with..the 'Oak-pruner'. **1899** D. Sharp in *Cambr. Nat. Hist.* VI. v. 286 *Elaphidion villosum* is called the oak-pruner in North America. **1884** Cooke *Struct. Bot.* xxxvi. 105. **1849** Thackeray *Pendennis* I. xxiii. 213 On the other side [of the hall] the *oak room. **1922** Joyce *Ulysses* 154 In the supper room or oakroom of the mansion house. **1971** D. Francis *Bonecrack* iii. 34 The account books..are in the oak room. **1851** *Zoologist* IX. 3309 Oak-leaves, with galls, commonly known as '*oak-spangles', attached. **1859** W. S. Coleman *Woodlands* (1862) 14 The pretty 'Oak-spangles'..were formerly considered to be parasitic fungi, but are now ascertained to be the work of gall-flies. **1889** Farmer *Americanisms* 396/1 **Oak towel*..a stout oaken stick. There is an allusion here to 'wiping' or 'dressing one down'. **1874** Cooke *Fungi* 114 In Vaucluse..seedling oaks have been reared, and with them, what have been termed *oak-truffles. **1864** Browning *Caliban upon Setebos* 51 The pie..That pricks deep into *oakwarts for a worm. **1523** Fitzherb. *Husb.* §87 It appereth at his nosethryll lyke *oke-water. **1771** Gallet in *Phil. Trans.* LXII. 351 This county was so infested with cock chaffers or *oakwebs, that in many parishes they eat every green thing, but elder. **1880** *W. Cornw. Gloss.*, *Oak-web*, a May-bee; the cock-chafer. **1942** *Bull. Wisconsin Agric. Exper. Stat.* No. 455. 75/1 *Oak wilt, a disease now ravaging many fine Southern Wisconsin woodlots, is caused by a certain fungus. *Ibid.* 76/1 Thus far there is no way of controlling oak wilt. **1944** B. W. Henry et al. in *Phytopathology* XXXIV. 163 The present paper presents evidence on the significance, symptoms, and cause of a disease called oak wilt. **1957** J. M. Haller *Tree Care* ix. 148 The oak wilt came into prominence about seven years ago, spreading rapidly through the midwestern states. **1959** P. P. Pirone *Tree Maintenance* (ed. 3) xvi. 346 The oak wilt fungus appears to be most infectious early in the growing season. **1969** *New Scientist* 28 Aug. 430/2 They inoculate the weed oaks with the organism that causes oakwilt disease, *Ceratocystis fagacearum*. **1653** Walton *Angler* iv. 95 The dock-worm, the *oake-worm, the gilt-tail, and too many to name. **1835** R. M. Bird *Hawks of Hawk-Hollow* II. v. 52 His father..had suddenly checked his horse at the entrance of the little *oak-yard.

oak, oakam, obs. forms of YOKE, OAKUM.

oak-apple (ˈəʊkˌæp(ə)l). **1.** A globular form of oak-gall; *spec.* the bright-coloured spongy gall formed on the leaf-bud of the common British oak.

14.. *Nom.* in Wr.-Wülcker 716/9 *Hec galla*, a nake appylle. **1486** *Bk. St. Albans* B vj b, Take..oke appilles and make Iuce of theym. **1578** Lyte *Dodoens* VI. lxviii. 745 The Oke apples do grow in sommer, and do begin to fall in September. **1753** Chambers *Cycl. Supp.* s.v., If the oak apple..be found full of worms..it bodes, if not a plague, yet an unhealthy year. **1818** Keats *Enaym.* I. 276 Silvery oak-apples, and fir-cones brown. **1874** Lubbock *Orig. & Met. Ins.* i. 10 The oak supports several kinds of gallflies, one produces the well known oak-apple.

2. In Australia, the young cone of the She-oak.

1889 J. H. Maiden *Useful Native Pl.* 15 (Morris) Children chew the young cones [of Casuarina], which they call 'oak-apples'.

3. *attrib.*, as **oak-apple day**, the 29th of May, the day of the Restoration of Charles II, when oak-apples or oak-leaves have been worn in memory of his hiding from his pursuers in an oak, on the 6th of September, 1651.

1807–8 Syd. Smith *Plymley's Let.* Wks. 1859 II. 80/1 He does not say whether this is a loyal procession, like Oak-apple Day. **1859** W. S. Coleman *Woodlands* (1862) 14 Oak-apples, so much in vogue on the 'Twenty-ninth of May, Oak-Apple Day', are also excrescences of this nature.

†**ˈoaked**, *a.* *Obs. rare.* Hard like oak; oaken.

1591 Sylvester *Du Bartas* I. iv. 47 Under the oaked bark.

oaken (ˈəʊkən), *a.* [f. OAK + -EN[4].]

1. Made of the wood of the oak. (Now often replaced by 'oak' used *attrib.*, OAK 8 a.)

13.. *K. Alis.* 6415 The face of heom is playn, and hard, Al so hit weore an oken bord. **1390–1** *Earl Derby's Exp.* (Camden) 157 Pro xiij oken sparrez, iiijs. *xd.* **1495** *Naval Acc. Hen. VII* (1896) 154 Oken plankes. **1616** Surfl. & Markh. *Country Farme* 335 Stake well with strong Oaken stakes. **1703** Moxon *Mech. Exerc.* 173 An Oaken plank. *c* **1820** S. Rogers *Italy* (1830) 112 An oaken chest, half eaten by the worm. **1864** Mrs. Gatty *Parables fr. Nat.* Ser. IV. 148 The chancel, where there were carved oaken screens. *fig.* **1577** Harrison *England* II. xxii. [xvi.] (1877) I. 337 When our houses were builded of willow, then had we oken men. **1887** G. Meredith *Ballads & P.* 23 And lo, the man of oaken head, He fled his land.

†**2.** Of, pertaining to, or forming part of the oak. *Obs.* or *arch.* (replaced by 'oak' used *attrib.*).

a **1450** *Fysshynge w. Angle* (1883) 29 The bayte on þe slothorn & on the oken leyf. **1544** Phaer *Regim. Lyfe* (1553) H vj b, The water of oken buddes..dronken in redde wine. **1561** Hollybush *Hom. Apoth.* 2 Take leaves of oken tre. **1579** Langham *Gard. Health* (1633) 528 A good handfull of oken barke. **1669** Worlidge *Syst. Agric.* (1681) 90 The Acorns, or Oaken-Mast. **1691** T. H[ale] *Acc. New Invent.* p. xviii, Oaken Trees..and..Oaken Timber. **1697** Dryden *Virg. Georg.* I. 200 Jove..shook from Oaken Leaves the liquid Gold. **1804** J. Grahame *Sabbath* 245 Massy oaken trunks Half-buried lie.

3. Formed of oak leaves or twigs. *arch.*

1605 Shaks. *Cor.* II. i. 188 Menenius, hee comes the third time home with the Oaken Garland. **1697** Dryden *Virg. Georg.* I. 480 Let the lab'ring Hind With Oaken Wreaths his hollow Temples bind. **1762** Falconer *Shipwr.* I. 879 Around her head an oaken wreath was seen. **1880** C. R. Markham *Peruv. Bark* 76 A Knight of the Netherlands Lion, and Commander of the Order of the Oaken Crown.

4. Consisting of oak trees. *arch.* and *poetic.*

a **1638** Mede *Wks.* (1672) 65 How this..Oaken-holt of Sichem is said here in my Text to have been in,..or by, the Sanctuary of the Lord. **1702** C. Mather *Magn. Chr.* IV. I. (1852) 16 The Druids..chose oaken retirements for their studies. **1832** Tennyson *Eleanore* 10 With breezes from our oaken glades. **1881** Rossetti *Ballads & Sonn.* 30 Like the struck fawn in the oakenshaw. **1903** A. E. Housman 'The Oracles' in *Venture* I. 39 When winds were in the oakenshaws.

5. *Comb.*, as *oaken-beamed*, *-panelled* adjs.; **oaken-pin**, a name for a hard kind of apple; **oaken-tenant**: see quot. 1619.

1619 Sir J. Sempill *Sacrilege Handl.* 82 Leui was vnder the Law, as a tenent at will, remoueable: Melchisedec, and Christs Ministery, as Freeholders: Oaken-tenants. **1707–12** Mortimer *Husb.* (J.), Oakenpin, so called from its hardness, is a lasting fruit. **1741** *Compl. Fam.-Piece* II. iii. 377 Apples [June] Oaken Pin,..Golden Russet. **1863** Hawthorne *Our Old Home* (1879) 215 Vast college-halls, high-windowed, oaken-panelled. **1900** *Westm. Gaz.* 24 Feb. 2/1 The low-ceiled, oaken-beamed parlour.

oaker, obs. form of OCHRE.

'oakery. *U.S. rare.* [f. OAK + -ERY.] An oak yard.

1838 C. GILMAN *Recoll. Southern Matron* xxx. 213 Turning suddenly, he bounded over the fence into papa's oakery.

oak-fern. [A transl. of L. *dryopteris*, Gr. δρυοπτερίς (Diosc.), said to be applied to a fern growing on the trunks of oaks or other trees; but employed by Linnæus as the name of a species of *Polypodium* (*P. Dryopteris*), the Smooth Three-branched Polypody (not the ancient δρυοπτερίς).]

†**1.** Variously applied by the early herbalists to the Common Polypody (which grows on the trunks of trees), and to several other ferns.

These include *Nephrodium Thelypteris*, *Cystopteris fragilis*, *Asplenium Adiantum-nigrum* (identified by Fraas with the Greek δρυοπτερίς), and *Polypodium calcareum*.

1548 TURNER *Names of Herbes* 35, I haue founde it in bushe rootes ofte tymes in Germany, it may be called in englishe petie Ferne, or okeferne. *c* **1550** LLOYD *Treas. Health* (1585) Lv, An old cocke filled with oke ferne or walferne. **1578** LYTE *Dodoens* III. lxii. 403 This herbe is called..in Englishe Polypodie, Wall Ferne, and Oke Ferne. *Ibid.* 404 *Dryopteris candida*, White Oke Ferne [= *Cystopteris*]. *Dryopteris nigra*, Blacke Oke Ferne [= *Asplenium Adiantum-nigrum*]. **1707** *Curios. in Husb. & Gard.* 58 The Moderns have discover'd that Oak-fern has seed.

2. Now applied by collectors to *Polypodium Dryopteris* of Linnæus.

1844 NEWMAN *Hist. Brit. Ferns* (ed. 2) 128 The name of Oak Fern, derived from *Dryopteris*, appears as inapplicable as that of Beech Fern..and is adopted in deference to the opinions of others. **1855** T. MOORE *Nature printed Ferns* Plate v, The smooth three-branched Polypody, or Oak fern. **1882** THOMSON in *Proc. Berw. Nat. Club* IX. No. 4. 449 The oak-fern..showed exquisitely fine fronds.

oakham, obs. variant of OAKUM.

'oakiness. [f. OAKY *a.*] The quality of being oaky.

1863 'G. HAMILTON' *Gala-Days* 128 [In] the English Church..there is a general tone of oakiness, solid, substantial, sincere.

oak land, oak-land. Chiefly *U.S.* [OAK 8.] Land bearing a growth of oak-trees.

c **1658** in *Early Rec. Lancaster, Mass.* (1884) 271 There is another peice of upland..Sum part pine Land & partly oak Land. *Ibid.*, Sum part of it [is]..oake land. **1737** J. WESLEY *Jrnl.* 2 Dec. (1909) I. 401 The land is of four sorts—pine-barren, oak-land, swamp, and marsh. **1751** J. BARTRAM *Observ. Trav. Pennsylv.* etc. 21 A steep hill..the soil middling oak land. **1811** *Weekly Reg.* 28 Dec. 302/1 It was a piece of dry oak land. **1837** W. JENKINS *Ohio Gazetteer* 187 The soil of Franklin is, what is generally called oak land, being a mixture of clay, sand and gravel. **1849** E. CHAMBERLAIN *Indiana Gazetteer* (ed. 3) 209 The oak land is more extensive than the beech. **1850** MRS. BROWNING *Lament Adonis* iv, The mountains above, and the oaklands below.

oaklet ('əʊklɪt). [f. OAK + -LET.] A small or young oak-tree.

1871 TYNDALL *Fragm. Sc.* (1879) II. xi. 242 On the ground near the tree little oaklets were successfully fighting for life. **1872** W. CORY *Lett. & Jrnls.* (1897) 288 Straggling acacias and oaklets.

oakling ('əʊklɪŋ). [f. OAK + -LING.] A young or small oak; an oak sapling.

1664 EVELYN *Sylva* (1776) 11 Oaklings, young beeches, Ash and some others, spring from the self-sown Mast and Keys. **1754** RICHARDSON *Grandison* (1781) II. xxiv. 232 He would plant an oakling for every oak he cut down. **1833** *Q. Rev.* 521 The oakling withers beneath the shadow of the oak.

oak-tree ('əʊk,triː). = OAK 1.

a **1000** *Wife's Complaint* 28 (in *Cod. Exon.* lf. 115 a) Heht mec mon wunian on wuda bearwe Under actreo in þam eorðscræfe. *Ibid.* 36. **1530** PALSGR. 249/1 Oke tree, *chesne.* **1535** COVERDALE *Isa.* i. 29 Ashamed of the oketrees wherein ye haue so delited. **1609** SKENE *Reg. Maj., Forest Laws* c. 12. 12 Gif the forestar finds anie man..heueand dune ane aik trie. **1821** CLARE *Vill. Minstr.* I. 112 The oak tree gnarl'd and notch'd. **1841** CARLYLE *Pref. to Emerson's Ess.*, The smallest living acorn is fit to be the parent of oaktrees without end.

attrib. **1888** STEVENSON *Black Arrow* 172 The heart misgave her [the ship] in her oak-tree ribs.

†**b. oak-tree clay**, W. Smith's name for the Wealden Clay: from the oak forests of the Weald.

1816 W. SMITH *Strata Ident.* Pt. II. 11 The Oak-tree Clay also may be mistaken or confounded with the Brick Earth, which in several parts produces good oak.

oakum ('əʊkəm). Forms: 1 **acumba, æcumbe,** 5 **okom(e, okcome, okem,** 6 **okym, ocom, occam,** 6–7 **ocam,** 6–8 **okam, ockam,** 7 **ocum, oc(c)ome, ocham, oacombe, okeham, okame,** 7–8 **oakam, -ham, ockham, okum,** 7– **oakum.** [OE. *ácumbe* fem. or neut., *ácumba, ácuma* masc., var. of *æ̆cumbe, æ̆cuma*, pl. *-an*, lit. off-combings = OHG. *âchambi*, MHG. *âkambe, âkamp* neut., f. *æ-, â-* privative, 'away', 'off', + *camb-* stem of *cęmban*, KEMB, to comb.]

†**1.** The coarse part of the flax separated in hackling; hards, tow; also, clippings, trimmings, shreds. *Obs.*

c **1000** *Sax. Leechd.* II. 22 Afyl ða wunde, & mid acumban besweðe. *Ibid.* 80 Sealf eft, medowyrt acumban. *c* **1000** ÆLFRIC *Voc.* in Wr.-Wülcker 152/15 *Stuppa*, æcumbe. *a* **1100** *Aldhelm Gloss.* I. 3293 (Napier 88/1) *Putamina*, acumba. *Ibid.* 2. 187 Acuman.

2. Loose fibre, obtained by untwisting and picking old rope; used in caulking ships' seams, in stopping up leaks, and sometimes in dressing wounds. The picking of it as an employment of convicts and inmates of workhouses, which was formerly common, has now fallen into disuse.

1481–90 *Howard Househ. Bks.* (Roxb.) 24 Item, for pich and okom viij. d. **1485** in *Cely Papers* (1900) 182 Item a stone okem, *vd.* **1486** *Naval Acc. Hen. VII* (1896) 18 Pitche tarre okum and other stuffe. **1495** *Ibid.* 164 Okome bought & spent abought Calkyng. **1577** NORTHBROOKE *Dicing* (1843) 81 Many of them..may..tose okam. **1599** HAKLUYT *Voy.* II. II. 104 Calked with the huskes of Cocos shels beaten, whereof they make Occam. **1617** J. LANE *Cont. Sqr.'s T.* 242 With tallowe, boild pitch, okeham, tarr, bedipps. **1622** R. HAWKINS *Voy. S. Sea* 155 Peeces of a junke or rope, chopped very small, and..tozed all as oacombe. **1630** J. TAYLOR (Water P.) *Praise Hempseed* Wks. III. 66/2 Ships, Barks, Hoyes, Drumlers, Craires, Boats, all would sink But for the Ocum caulked in every chink. **1666** DRYDEN *Ann. Mirab.* cxlvi, Some drive old Okum through each seam and rift. **1666** PEPYS *Diary* 4 June, Who should it be but Mr. Daniel, all muffled up,..and his right eye stopped with oakum? **1706** PHILLIPS, *Oakam, Ockam*, or *Okum*, (a Sea-Term). **1733** P. LINDSAY *Interest Scot.* 23 Easy Labour at first, such as picking of Wool or Cotton, teasing of Ockam. **1769** FALCONER *Dict. Marine* (1789) Aa a iij b, Black oakum..is made of tarred ropes. **1840** R. H. DANA *Bef. Mast* xxvi. 87 Picking oakum, until we got enough to caulk the ship all over. **1876** *Clin. Soc. Trans.* IX. 59 An oakum poultice is kept applied.

3. *attrib.* and *Comb.*, as ***oakum-ball, -boy, -chisel; oakum-headed, -whiskered*** adjs.

1701 *Enq. Inconven. Pub. Elections* 17 A sufficient Number of Setts of Oakham Balls. **1805** *Naval Chron.* XIII. 243 From the first Officer to the lowest Oakum-boy [at Dockyard]. **1865** DICKENS *Mut. Fr.* II. xiii, The oakum-headed, oakum-whiskered man.

oak-wood ('əʊk,wʊd).

1. The wood or timber of the oak. **b.** Growing oak-timber; oak-trees.

1504 *Plumpton Corr.* (Camden) 188 They have sold oke wood at Nesfeld. **1801** MACNEILL *Mayday* 15 The cliffs crown'd with oakwood. **1890** FRAZER *Gold. Bough* II. iv. 293 The needfire was..kindled by the friction of oak-wood.

2. A wood or forest of oaks.

1823 in Cobbett *Rur. Rides* (1885) I. 287 Land, great part of which consists of oak-woods. **1856** STANLEY *Sinai & Pal.* ii. (1858) 144 On the table-lands of Gilead are the thick oak-woods of Bashan. **1881** VERN. LEE *Belcaro* vii. 194 Among the undulating fields and oakwoods.

oaky ('əʊkɪ), *a.* [f. OAK + -Y.]

1. Resembling oak; strong, firm, hard. Also ***oaky-looking*** adj.

1631 *Celestina* xxi. 198 Better..in that my more strong and oaky age, then in this my weake and feeble declining. *a* **1656** BP. HALL *Estate Chr.* Wks. 1837 V. 261 The oaky, rocky, flinty hearts of men turned into flesh. **1921** D. H. LAWRENCE *Sea & Sardinia* 165 Curious slim oaky-looking trees.

2. Abounding in oaks.

a **1816** B. HAWKINS *Sk. Creek Country* (1848) 62 The good land spreads out for four or five miles on both sides of the creek, with oaky woods. *a* **1849** BEDDOES *Lines Written in Switzerland* Poems 213 What silence drear in England's oaky forest.

-oan (əʊən, 'əʊən), *suffix. Min.* [f. *-o* (in FERRO-, -OUS c, as against FERRI-, -IC 1 b) + -I)AN 2.] Used like -IAN 2, but denoting a lower valency than that suffix (see quot.).

1930 [see -IAN 2].

oaph, obs. form of OAF[1].

oar (ɔə(r)), *sb.* Forms: α. 1 **ár,** acc. **áre,** 3–7 **ore,** (5 **hore, oyre),** 4–6 **oore,** 6–8 **oare,** 6– **oar,** (6 **oer, owre,** 6–7 **ower).** β. *north.* 3–6 **ar, are,** 5–6 **ayr(e, air(e,** 7 **aer.** [OE. *ár* str. fem. cognate with ON. *ár, ǫr* (Sw. *år, åra*, Da., Norw. *aare*):—OTeut. **airā*: perh. radically akin to Gr. ἐρ- in ἐρέτης rower, ἐρετμός oar.]

1. a. A long wooden lever used to propel a boat, consisting of a stout pole, widened and flattened at one end into a blade, to press against the water as a fulcrum.

A small oar, a pair of which is used by one rower, is called a *scull.* Large ship oars are called *sweeps.* Oars are sometimes used for steering, as in whale-boats.

α. *a* **900** *O.E. Chron.* an. 897 Sume hæfdon .lx. ara. *c* **1000** *Gnomic Verses* 188 (Gr.) Drugað his ar on borde. *c* **1290** *S. Eng. Leg.* I. 472/347 Huy drowen op seil and ore. *c* **1330** R. BRUNNE *Chron. Wace* (Rolls) 12059 Ancres, ores, redy to hande. *c* **1385** CHAUCER *L.G.W.* 2308 *Philomene*, The oris pullyn forth the vessel faste. **1387** TREVISA *Higden* (Rolls) IV. 183 An hondred schippes and þritty, wiþ seilles and wiþ oores. **1486** *Naval Acc. Hen. VII* (1896) 14 A Cokke of xiiij ores. **1493** *Newminster Cartul.* (1878) 195 A cobyll wt ij oyres. **1496** *Naval Acc. Hen. VII* (1896) 167 Orys for the mayne Bote. *c* **1500** *Melusine* xxiv. 177 [He] rowed in hys galyote with eyght hores. **1539** TAVERNER *Erasm. Prov.* (1552) 11 He ought to holde the oore yt hathe lerned it. **1540** in Marsden *Sel. Pl. Crt. Adm.* (1894) I. 99 John Pope toke hold of on of the owers and stept in my bote. **1555** EDEN *Decades* 157 Without oers..they were caried awaye by the vyolence of the water. **1582** STANYHURST *Æneis* I. (Arb.) 21 The oars are cleene splintred. **1623** BINGHAM *Xenophon* 83 They had also a ship of fiftie owers. **1624** CAPT. SMITH *Virginia* I. 3 To bring our Ores into the house. **1632** J. HAYWARD tr. *Biondi's Eromena* 11 A bastard Galley of three and thirty banks with sixe men to an oare, he armed her. **1659** D. PELL *Impr. Sea* 14 They must first take a turn at the Oar, before they come either to the Helm or Stern. **1799** CHARNOCK in *Naval Chron.* I. 132 In the modern galleys,..the oars..are forty-four feet long. **1863** FR. A. KEMBLE *Resid. in Georgia* 36 Pulling an oar across the stream.

β. **13..** *Sir Tristr.* 354 His maister þan þai fand A bot and an are. **1375** BARBOUR *Bruce* III. 576 Sum went till ster, and sum till ar. *c* **1425** WYNTOUN *Cron.* II. viii. 73 Sum of þame þai slewe rycht þare Wytht arys. *c* **1470** HENRY *Wallace* VII. 1067 A hundreth schippys, that ruthyr bur and ayr. **1549** *Compl. Scot.* vi. 42 The galliasse pat furtht..ane hundredtht aris on euerye syde. **1572** *Satir. Poems Reform.* xxxi. 102 Intil a bait vpon Lochlowmond, But boddum, air, or Ruther. **1609** SKENE *Reg. Maj.* 144 (*Stat. Gild* c. 22) Before the ship ly on dry land, and put forth ane aer.

b. In reference to slaves or condemned criminals compelled to row in galleys: see GALLEY *sb.* 1.

1711 *Lond. Gaz.* No. 4942/1 To condemn Criminals..to the Oar. **1715** NELSON *Addr. Pers. Qual.* 24 The Anguish and Smart that flows from Your Sins chain you to the Oar.

2. *fig.* Anything that serves, like an oar, as a means of propulsion in the water (or *transf.* the air).

c **1586** C'TESS PEMBROKE *Ps.* LXVIII. iv, [The dove] That glides with feathered oare through wavy sky. **1599** SHAKS. *Much Ado* III. i. 27 To see the fish Cut with her golden ores the siluer streame. **1615** CHAPMAN *Odyss.* XII. 628 And there row'd off with owers of my hands. **1658** SIR T. BROWNE *Gard. Cyrus* iii. 55 The Oars or finny feet of Water-Fowl. **1834** MEDWIN *Angler in Wales* II. 16 With my gun therefore raised in my left hand, and making an oar of my right, I endeavoured to cross over. **1871** G. MACDONALD *A Book of Dreams* II. I. ii, She [a swan] comes..With stroke of swarthy oar.

3. *transf.* **a.** A rowing boat. ***pair of oars***, a boat rowed by two men. (In quot. 1611 including the rowers.)

1611 [TARLTON] *Jests* (1628) A iij b, Tarlton..caused a paire of Oares to tend him, who, at night, called on him to be gone. **1632** SHERWOOD, A pair of oares, *petite nacelle, ou bateau long ramé par deux hommes, ayans chascun deux avirons.* **1634–5** BRERETON *Trav.* (Chatham Soc.) 80 To take ..a pair of oars to Greenwitch. **1665** PEPYS *Diary* 13 July, There being no oars to carry me, I was fain to call a skuller. *a* **1674** CLARENDON *Hist. Reb.* XI. §20 He..went into a pair of Oars that was ready. **1758** *Descr. Thames* 269 Tilt-boats, Wherries, Oars, or Scullars.

b. An oarsman. ***first oars***, the man who rows stroke; *fig.* one who takes the first place.

1749 H. WALPOLE *Lett. H. Mann* (1846) II. 265 Legge, who..was next oars. **1774** C. DIBDIN *Song, Jolly Young Waterman*, He was always first oars when the fine city ladies In a party to Ranelagh went, or Vauxhall. **1861** HUGHES *Tom Brown at Oxf.* i, One of the best oars in the University boat. *Ibid.* iv, I heard he was a capital oar at Eton.

4. A stick, pole, or paddle, with which anything is stirred; *esp.* in *Brewing*, one with which the mash is stirred in the tun.

1743 *Lond. & Country Brew.* III. (ed. 2) 187 A second Person stirs it with an Oar or Paddle, as it runs out of the Sack. **1842** MRS. DODS *Cook's Man.* 447 The interstices between the spars or rounds of the oar allow the mash to be shaken through. **1850** *Nat. Encycl.* XI. 595/1 The perfect solution of the sugar is aided by stirring with long poles or oars.

5. Phrases. **a.** ***to have an oar in every man's boat*** (***barge***), etc., to have a hand in every one's business or affairs; so, ***to put one's oar in another man's boat, to put in one's oar***, etc. Also, ***to get, shove,*** etc., ***one's oar in.*** The primary sense is 'to interfere, to be (or become) meddlesome'. **b.** ***to rest*** (***lie***) ***on one's oars***, to lean on the handles of one's oars and thereby raise them horizontally out of the water; *fig.* to suspend one's efforts, take things easy. **c.** ***to have,*** (***take,*** etc.) ***the labouring oar***: see LABOURING *ppl. a.* 4.

a. 1543 UDALL *Erasm. Apoph.* II. 180 In eche mannes bote, would he haue an ore. **1653** H. COGAN tr. *Pinto's Trav.* xxv. 95 One of ours..who would needs have an oar in our talk, told him [etc.]. **1630** R. BRATHWAIT *Eng. Gentleman* i. 11 Youth..putting his oare in every mans boat. **1706** [E. WARD] *Wooden World Dissected* (1708) 64 He's sure to have an Oar in other Mens Concerns. **1731** C. COFFEY *Devil to Pay* I. ii. 12, I will govern my own House without your putting in an Oar. *c* **1779** R. CUMBERLAND in *Lett. Lit. Men* (Camden) 412 Whilst I have such a friend to act for me, why should I put in my oar? **1809** MALKIN *Gil Blas* I. vii. ¶1, I ..put in my oar whenever I thought I could say a good thing. **1886** BESANT *Childr. Gibeon* II. xxx, Now, don't you put your oar in, young woman. You'd best stand out of the way, you had! **1890** BARRÈRE & LELAND *Dict. Slang* II. 92/2 '*To shove in an oar*', to intermeddle, or give an opinion unasked. **1908** J. H. SHINN *Pioneers Arkansas* xxxii. 258 The idea is always to do the other fellow before he does you, and if he does get his oar in first, come back with remark called for brevity, 'The Retort Courteous'. **1916** 'TAFFRAIL' *Pincher Martin* vii. 109 'It ain't fit an' proper fur gals o' your age to go abart unpertected like.'..'And who asked you to put your oar in, Mister Billings?' **1946** K. TENNANT *Lost Haven* (1947) xiv. 224 He would probably go on talking all the morning, if a bloke didn't put in his oar. *Ibid.* 226 Look here, Dip. You're shoving in your oar, so I'll just tell you what I'm up against. **1968** J. R. ACKERLY *My Father & Myself* ix. 87 One who preferred to stand outside of life and observe it not (as he would have phrased it) to 'put one's oar in'. **1977** *Film & Television Technician* Mar. 5/1 The more that the workers stick their oar into the administration of actual film production the more they will weaken their strength in negotiation for the improvement of wages and terms of employment. **1978** J. ANDERSON *Angel of Death* i.

6 Senior police officers couldn't go around saying things like that... He'd better get his oar in first.

b. **1726** Shelvocke *Voy. round World* (1757) 271 They lay upon their oars for some time, in spite of all I could do to make them keep their way. **1784** R. Putnam in M. Cutler *Life*, etc. (1888) I. 175 Many of them are unable to lie long on their oars, waiting the decision of Congress on our petition. **1836** Marryat *Midsh. Easy* xiii, Mr. Sawbridge immediately ordered the boats to lie upon their oars. **1836** Lady Granville *Lett.* Oct. (1894) II. 215 We shall be able .. to rest on our oars for a long time. **1887** *Athenæum* 16 Apr. 520/3 The managers of the usual autumn gathering of paintings .. will rest on their oars.

6. *attrib.* and *Comb.*: simple attrib., as ***oar-band***, ***-bench***, ***-blade***, ***-leather***, ***-roll***, ***-song***, ***-stroke***, ***-thong***, ***-tie***, ***-timber***, ***-work***; objective, instrumental, etc., as ***oar-breaker***, ***-maker***; ***oar-finned***, ***-footed***, ***-like***, ***-loving*** adjs.; **oar-fish**, a name for fishes of the family *Regalecidæ*, esp. *Regalecus Banksii*, from their compressed oar-like bodies; **oar-helm**, an oar used as a helm; **oar-lop** (see LOP); now *obs.*, a lop-eared rabbit with its ears sticking out at right angles to its head; (the form *oar-lap* appears to be an error arising from the misprint in the source of quot. 1868); **oar-peg** = *oar-thole*; **oar-port** = OAR-HOLE; **oar-propeller** (see quot.); **oar-rudder**, an oar used as a rudder; **oar-thole**, a thole-pin.

1841 Faraday in B. Jones *Life* (1870) II. 151 We broke the *oar-band; we were blown back and sideways. **1888** T. Watts *Burden Armada* in *Athenæum* 18 Aug. 224/2 *Oar-benches gleam with smoking glaives. **1849** Grote *Greece* II. xli. V. 179 The *oar-blades were broken by collision. **1897** *Archæologia* V. 392 An ancient Irish oar-blade of black oak found at Toome Bar. **1643** Denham *Cooper's H.* 307 So toward a Ship the *oare-fin'd Gallies ply. **1860** J. Richardson *Yarrell's Hist. Brit. Fishes* (2nd Suppl.) 27 (*heading*) Banks's *oar-fish. **1880** A. C. L. G. Günther *Introd. Study Fishes* II. 522 They [sc. *Regalecus* species] are frequently called .. 'Oar-fishes', from their two ventral fins, which have a dilatation at their extremity not unlike the blade of an oar. **1925** J. T. Jenkins *Fishes Brit. Isles* 120 The name Oar-fish is derived from the presence of the two pelvic fins, which are .. something like the blade of an oar. **1959** A. Hardy *Open Sea* II. iv. 76 The oar-fish *Regalecus glesne* .. is world-wide in distribution... It is the largest of the so-called ribbon-fish and .. it looks almost like one's idea of the mythical sea-serpent. **1972** *N.Z. News* 31 May 3/2 Two small boys rowing their boat in the Otago Harbour .. bumped into a comparatively rare oar fish, 10 feet long and weighing about 100 pounds... Only about a dozen of the species, Regalecus pacificus, have been washed up on the New Zealand coast in the past 100 years. Oar fish are a deep-water variety. **1846** Worcester, **Oar-footed*, having feet used as oars. *Burnet.* **1883** A. R. Colquhoun *Across Chrysê* I. xvi. 90 By means of a huge *oar-helm worked over the bow. **1836–48** B. D. Walsh *Aristoph.* 54 *note*, The *oar-leather was a strap by which the oar was fastened to the rowlock. **1835–6** Todd *Cycl. Anat.* I. 269/2 Their *oar-like feet. **1887** J. F. Keane *Three Years Wand.* I. ii. 34 A true sea-snake, with flattened oar-like tail. **1854** 'E. S. Delamer' *Pigeons & Rabbits* 136 The *Oar-lop is the next stage of deflection, when the ears extend horizontally outwards on each side, forming a line that is more or less straight, giving the idea of a pair of oars which a waterman is resting out of the water. **1868** [see LOP *sb.*[7]]. **1872** C. Rayson *Rabbits* III. xiii. 71 The 'oar-lop' .. is not fit for exhibition purposes. **1912** G. A. Townsend *Pract. Rabbit Keeping* vii. 62 If both ears stood out from the head at right angles, the rabbit was an 'Oar Lop'. **1933** F. L. Washburn *Rabbit Bk.* (ed. 2) ii. 55 The term 'oar-lop' was used to express the condition where the ears are horizontal. **1866** Blackie *Homer & Iliad* I. 93 All the *oar-loving Paphians honour the sceptre of Mentes. **1863** P. Barry *Dockyard Econ.* 111 Eighteenth in order stand the *oar-makers' shops. **1874** *Athenæum* 10 Oct. 477/3 All galleys .. had their *oar-ports placed obliquely above each other in horizontal rows. **1875** Knight *Dict. Mech.*, **Oar-propeller*, a device to imitate by machinery the action of sculling. **1845** Stocqueler *Handbk. Brit. India* (1854) 189 Native boats .. their strange *oar-rudders far-projecting. **1775** Johnson *West. Isl.*, *Raasay*, There is now an *oar-song used by the Hebrideans. **1875** Knight *Dict. Mech.*, **Oar-swivel*, a pivotal device for an oar on the gunwale. **1889** P. B. Du Chaillu *Viking Age* I. xii. 223 The *oar-tholes were loosened from the gunwale. **1886** Corbett *Fall of Asgard* II. 148 There was no such *oar-work done in the whole fleet.

oar (ɔə(r)), *v.* [f. prec. sb.]

1. *trans.* To propel with or as with oars; to row. Also *transf.* and *fig.*

1610 Shaks. *Temp.* II. i. 118 He .. oared Himselfe with his good armes in lusty stroke To th'shore. **1725** Pope *Odyss.* XVI. 247 And what blessed hands have oared thee on the way? **1818** Shelley *Rev. Islam* VII. xxvii, The eagle .. Oaring with rosy feet its silver boat. **1842** Tennyson *To E.L.* iv. **1883** J. Hawthorne *Dust* II. 340 Many boats .. oared by the jolly young watermen.

2. *intr.* To row; to advance, as if propelled by oars.

1647 Trapp *Comm. 1 Thess.* iv. 11 Not oaring in other mens boats nor medling in other mens bishopricks. [Cf. OAR *sb.* 6 a.] **1725** Pope *Odyss.* XII. 526 Sudden I dropt amidst the flashing main .. And oar'd with laboring arms along the flood. **1816** Southey *Poets' Pilgrim.* I. 27 A swan kept oaring near with upraised eye. **1885–94** R. Bridges *Eros & Psyche* Sept. vii, Till, oaring here and there, the queen he found.

b. *transf.*, with *it*: To swim.

1894 K. Grahame *Pagan Papers* 136 A golden carp of fattest build, I oared it in translucent waters.

3. *trans.* To make (one's way) as with oars.

1801 Southey *Thalaba* XI. vi, Now oaring with slow wing her upward way. *a* **1851** D. M. Moir *Poems, Remembered Beauty*, Graceful as the swan Oaring its way athwart a summer lake. **1863** W. W. Story *Roba di R.* I. vii. 182 Stately white swans oaring their way with rosy feet.

4. To strike (the water) as with oars, to traverse as by rowing.

1773–83 Hoole *Orl. Fur.* XI. 260 The Paladin .. oar'd with nervous limbs The billowy brine.

5. To move (one's hands, etc.) like oars.

1882 Jefferies *Bevis* I. ix. 148 He put his flat hands together, pushed them out, and oared them round as he had often done on land.

oar, oare, obs. forms of ORE *sb.*

oarage ('ɔərɪdʒ). [f. OAR *sb.* + -AGE.]

1. The action of oars, rowing; movement of limbs like that of oars.

1762 *Gentl. Mag.* 544 Hands that with even oarage part and meet. **1872** Blackie *Lays Highl.* 7 They oared with gentle oarage From the dear-loved oaks of Derry. **1888** E. Warre in Woodgate *Boating* 3 The first man .. who essayed the oarage of his arms and legs.

2. Apparatus or fittings of the nature of oars; outfit of oars; rowing apparatus.

1828 J. Bailey *Facciolati's Lex.*, *Remigium*, all that part of a ship's furniture which is connected with the rowing of it, or (as might be said) the *oarage*. **1855** Singleton *Virgil* I. 240 He plies along the Empyrean vast On th' oarage of his wings. **1865** Swinburne *Poems & Ball.*, *At Eleusis* 172 Like scaled oarage of a keen thin fish In seawater. **1887** Bowen *Virg. Æneid* v. 280 So with her oarage crippled, the ship makes slowly her way.

oared (ɔəd), *a.* [f. OAR *sb.* + -ED[2].] Provided with oars; also in parasynthetic combinations, as ***four-oared***, ***six-oared***.

1748 *Anson's Voy.* II. vi. 191 The eighteen oared barge. **1772–84** Cook *Voy.* (1790) I. 18 A ten-oared boat filled with soldiers approached. **1847** *Illustr. Lond. News* 10 July 23/2 Trial races for the classification of oared boats. **1866** Neale *Sequences & Hymns* 41 Where shall go no oared galley. **1884** [Hamilton] *Jaunt in a Junk* ii. 18 At a pace which speedily put oared pursuit out of the question.

oar-hole ('ɔəhəʊl). Also 5 **arehole**. The hole in the side of a galley, etc. through which an oar passes.

14.. *Nom.* in Wr.-Wülcker 737/32 *Hoc columber*, a are-hole. **1436** *Pol. Poems* (Rolls) II. 197 Eche of them an ore toke in hande, At *ore-holes viij., as I understonde. **1648–78** Hexham *Dutch Dict.*, *Riem-gaten*, *Roey-gaten*, the Oar-holes to put out the Oars. **1880** Wallace *Ben-Hur* III. ii, Each oar-hole was a vent through which the labourer .. had plenty of sweet air.

oarie, obs. form of ORY.

oario- (əʊ'ɛərɪəʊ, əʊɛərɪ'ɒ), combining form of Gr. ᾠάριον little egg, taken in sense of L. *ōvārium* ovary, found in a few rarely used terms of Pathology, etc., instead of the more usual OVARIO-. Examples are: **o'ariocele** [Gr. κήλη tumour], hernia or tumour of the ovary. **oari'opathy** [see -PATHY], disease of the ovary; hence **oario'pathic** *a.*, pertaining to oariopathy. **oari'otomy** [Gr. τομή cutting], excision of the ovary, ovariotomy. So also **oaritis** (əʊə'raɪtɪs) [see -ITIS], inflammation of the ovary, ovaritis; hence **oaritic** (əʊə'rɪtɪk) *a.*, pertaining to oaritis.

1857 Mayne *Expos. Lex.* [*has* Oariocele, Oariopathic, Oariopathy, Oaritic, Oaritis]. **1892** *Syd. Soc. Lex.*, *Oariotomy*, same as *Ovariotomy*.

oarless ('ɔəlɪs), *a.* [f. OAR *sb.* + -LESS.] Having no oar or oars; undisturbed by oars.

1591 Sylvester *Du Bartas* I. ii. 27 Mast-less, oar-less, and from Harbour far. **1813** Byron *Br. Abydos* II. xxvi, A broken torch, an oarless boat. **1882** Tennyson *To Virgil* v, Summers of the snakeless meadow, unlaborious earth and oarless sea.

oarlock ('ɔəlɒk). Forms: 1 **árloc**, 5 **orlok**, 7 **orelock**, 9 **oar-lock**. [OE. *árloc*, f. *ár* oar + *loc* lock, closure, enclosure. Cf. also ROWLOCK.] A notch or fork in which the oar of a boat plays; a rowlock. Also *attrib.* in ***oarlock seat***.

a **1100** *Ags. Voc.* in Wr.-Wülcker 288/6 *Columbaria*, arlocu. *a* **1419** *Liber Albus* (Rolls) I. 235 Le bate qe nage deinz orlok, .. paiera i denier. *Ibid.* 237 Une petite nief ove orlokes. *Ibid.* 239 De qualibet navi in qua navigatur infra orlokes. *Ibid.* 375 Si navigat in horlok, unum denarium. **1657** Howell *Londinop.* 85 Euery little Ship with orelocks [paid] a peny. **1874** J. W. Long *Amer. Wild-Fowl Shooting* 85 Both may row, if two sets of oarlock-seats are provided. **1880** N. H. Bishop *Sneak-Box* 218, I heard in the distance the sound of oars moving in the oar-locks.

'oarman. *rare.* [f. as prec. + MAN.] = next.

1608 D. T[uvill] *Ess. Pol. & Mor.* 56 Like vnto our Ower-men, looke one way, and row another. *a* **1619** Fotherby *Atheom.* II. xi. §4 (1622) 317 The Oare-men, and Rowers of her Barge. **1725** Dudley in *Phil. Trans.* XXXIII. 263 [They] carry six Men, *viz.* the Harponeer in the Fore-part of the Boat, four Oar-men, and the Steers-man. **1818** Milman *Samor* 173 The homage fawn'd By her fair handmaids, and her oarmen gay.

oarsman ('ɔəzmən). [f. *oar's*, possessive of OAR + MAN; formerly *oarman*: see prec.] A 'man of the oar'; one who uses oars; a rower.

1811 *Weekly Reg.* I. XIV. 245/1 They certainly possess great dexterity as oarsmen. **1824** W. Irving *T. Trav.* I. 328, I was one of the most expert oarsmen that rowed on the Isis. **1871** R. Ellis *Catullus* lxiv. 13 Scarcely the wave foamed white to the reckless harrow of oarsmen. **1891** A. J. Foster *Ouse* 208 Sandy's Cut is well known to Cambridge oarsmen.

Hence **'oarsmanship**, the art of rowing.

1873 *Daily News* 18 Feb. 5/6 The apparent decline of good oarsmanship on the Isis. **1882** *Standard* 16 Sept. 3/6 The amateur oarsmanship of the London Clubs.

'oarswoman. [f. as prec. + WOMAN.] A woman who rows.

1882 J. Payn *Kit* iii, You are a first-rate oarswoman. **1895** *Lady* 12 Sept., To distinguish herself as an oarswoman.

oarweed, variant of OREWEED.

oary ('ɔərɪ), *a.* [f. OAR *sb.* + -Y.]

1. a. Of the nature, or having the function of, an oar or oars; oar-like. **b.** Furnished with oars; oared.

1667 Milton *P.L.* VII. 440 The Swan with Arched neck .. proudly Rowes Her state with Oarie feet. **1791** Cowper *Iliad* II. 198 All launch their oary barks into the flood. **1832** J. Austin *Sel. Grk. Choric Poet.*, *Æschylus' Agam.* 53 So, when bereaved the vultures ply Their oary wings athwart the sky. **1871** R. Ellis *Catullus* lxvi. 53 Came and shook thro' heaven his pennons oary before me.

2. *Comb.* (parasynthetic), as ***oary-footed***, ***-winged***, having oary feet, wings.

1872 Geo. Eliot *Middlem.* Prel. (1878) 3 Here and there a cygnet .. never finds the living stream in fellowship with its own oary-footed kind. **1871** R. Ellis *Catullus* iv. 4 Oary-wing'd alike To fleet beyond them, or to scud beneath a sail.

oas(e, obs. forms of OOZE *sb.*

oasis (əʊ'eɪsɪs, 'əʊəsɪs). Pl. **oases** (-iːz). [a. L. *oasis*, a. Gr. ὄασις (Herod.), app. of Egyptian origin: cf. Coptic *ouahe* (whence Egyptian Arab. *wāh*) dwelling-place, oasis, f. *ouih* to dwell.

As to the quantity of the *a* in Gr. and L. there appears to be no direct evidence; but the tradition of the schools, and the preponderance of English usage, as well as the practice of the poets, make it long, *o'āsis*; so also, Ger. and Sp. *o'āsis*, It. *o'āsi*. The pronunciation *'ōăsis* is however used by many, esp. in Scotland and U.S.]

A name of the fertile spots in the Libyan desert; hence *gen.* A fertile spot in the midst of a desert.

1613 Purchas *Pilgrimage* VII. i. 549 But were no lesse injurious to Oasis, and other Roman subjects. **1684** tr. *Zosimus's Hist.* v. 321 Now this Oasis was a sad barren place, from whence no Man could ever return who was once carry'd into it. **1731** Chandler tr. *Limborch's Hist. Inquis.* I. 17 They banished them into great Hoasis, a country in Egypt. **1816** J. Scott *Vis. Paris* (ed. 5) 239 Near it is a model of the pyramids .. accompanied by an oasis with its grove of palms, and a caravan of camels. **1838** *Econ. Vegetation* 158 The garniture of the oases, or 'isles of the desert'. **1841** Elphinstone *Hist. Ind.* I. 3 A waste of sand, in which are oases of different size and fertility. **1877** A. B. Edwards *Up Nile* vii. 171 A little oasis of date palms indicating the presence of a spring.

fig. **1800–24** Campbell *Poems, to Sir F. Burdett* iii, England could not stand A lone oasis in the desert ground Of Europe's slavery. **1842** Tennyson *E. Morris* 3 My one Oasis in the dust and drouth Of city life! **1868** E. Edwards *Ralegh* I. xxv. 609 The one pleasant oasis amidst the dreary memories of a voyage.

Hence (irreg.) **o'asal, oa'sitic**, *adjs.*, pertaining to, of the nature of, or resembling an oasis.

1888 W. Boyd in *Cambridge* (Mass.) *Press* 15 Sept., Castle Hill looks like an oasal mountain in the midst of a desert of low sand-hills. **1896** *Pop. Sci. Monthly* Feb. 465 Over-crowding of animal life in these oasitic areas.

oast (əʊst). Forms: α. 1 **ást**, (4 **a nost**), 4–9 **ost**, 4–7 **host(e**, 6 **oste**, 7 **oost**, 8 **oust**, 6– **oast**. β. 5 **est**, 7 **east**, **eest**. [OE. *ást*, corresp. to MLG. *eist*, Du. *eest*, formerly also *eist*:—OTeut. **aisto-z* from **aiđto-z*, f. root *aidh*, weak grade *idh*, *iđ*, *aiđ* (Skr. *idh*) to burn, whence also OE. *ád*, OHG. *eit* blazing pile, funeral pyre, and, outside Teut., L. *ædes*, OLat. *aidis* hearth, house, *æstus* heat, *æstās* summer, Gr. αἶθος heat, Irish *aedh* heat. *Oast* is the native form; *est*, *eest*, *east*, introduced from Flanders.]

1. † **a.** *orig.* = KILN. **b.** Later, A kiln for drying malt or hops, now *spec.* for drying hops.

c **1050** *Suppl. Ælfric's Voc.* in Wr.-Wülcker 185/30 *Siccatorium*, cyln, *uel* ast. **1380** *Anc. Deeds C.* 364 (Pub. Rec. Office), [Grant by John Haddele of a cottage, &c. to Peter atte Hacche, near] 'les lymhostes'. ? *c* **1390** *Form of Cury* in Warner *Antiq. Culin.* 4 Take benes and dry hem in a nost or in an ovene. *c* **1420** *Pallad. on Husb.* I. 457 Wel derk & fer from ostis, bath & stable. **1577** B. Googe *Heresbach's Husb.* (1586) 9 b, A Brewhouse with an Oast for drying of Malt. **1669** Worlidge *Syst. Agric.* (1681) 150 To contain .. the hair of your Oost or Kiln, or a Blanket tacked round the same about the edges. **1710** *Act 9 Anne* c. 13. §8 No Person .. shall .. make use of any Oust Storehouse or other Place or of any Kiln for curing or keeping of Hops. **1805** R. W. Dickson *Pract. Agric.* (1807) II. 242 It is necessary to keep the oast or kiln constantly at work. **1881** Whitehead *Hops* 24 Oasts and other buildings must be built.

2. *Comb.* **oast-cloth, oast-haire** (see quot. 1861); **oast-house**, a building containing a kiln for drying hops; also the whole structure composing a kiln.

1410 in Rogers *Agric. & Prices* III. 546/2 *Hoste cloth. **1462** *Ibid.* 556/2 Ostcloth. **1669** Worlidge *Syst. Agric.* (1681) 153 On this Bed, without any Oost-cloth, lay your Hops by Basket-fulls. **1861** *Illustr. Times* 5 Oct. 221 Covered with the oastcloth, a sort of haircloth blanket, on which the hops are laid to dry. **1668** *Canterb. Marriage Licences* (MS.), Robert Joy of S. Peter in Thanet, *hosthair weaver. **1677** Plot *Oxfordsh.* 252 The square above, immediatly supporting the Oast-hair and the Mault. **1764** *Museum Rusticum* I. 3 These pokes [of hops] are .. carried ..

to the *oust-house, where the hops are to be dried. **1882** K. Lee *West. Wildfl.* I. 140 He passed to a rick-yard and oast-house beyond.

oast, oastess(e, obs. forms of HOST, HOSTESS *sb.*

oastler, oastman, obs. ff. OSTLER, HOASTMAN.

oasy, obs. form of OOZY *a.*

oat (əʊt), *sb.* Usually in pl. **oats** (əʊts). Forms: *sing.* 1 **áte, ǽte,** 4–7 **ote,** (5 **hote**), 6–7 **oate,** 6– *Sc.* **ait,** 7 *dial.* **eat,** 8– **oat.** *pl.* α. 1 **átan,** 3 **aten,** 3–4 **oten,** 4 **ooten,** 5 **otyn.** β. 4–7 **otes,** 5 **otys, otis,** (**hotys**), 5–6 **ootes, -is,** 6 **ottes,** (**wot(t)es**), 6–7 **oates,** 6– **oats;** *Sc.* 5 **atis, etes, aitis, aittes,** 8– **aits.** [OE. *áte*, pl. *átan*, wk. fem., not found in the cognate langs., and of obscure origin. The general Teutonic name is OTeut. **haƀron-* and its representatives: see HAVER.

Oat differs from other names of cereals, ancient or modern, as *wheat, barley* (*bigg, beer*), *rye, rice, maize, millet*, and from its own synonym *haver*, in that, while these are (like *dust, sand, snow*), names of *substances* or *things in the mass*, the collective form of which is singular, they having in ordinary language no plural, *oat* is an individual singular, the collective or mass sense of which has to be expressed by the plural, e.g. 'Is the crop rye or oats?', 'wheat, barley, and oats are cereals'. Comparing this with *beans, peasen, potatoes*, and other names of similar grammatical form, it may be inferred that primarily *oat* was not the plant or its produce in the mass, but denoted an individual grain; cf. *groat* with its collective pl. *groats*. This may point to oats being eaten originally in the grains, not, like wheat and barley, in the form of meal or flour. But the scanty early evidence is not sufficient to show this.]

1. a. *pl.* The grains of a hardy cereal (see sense 2) forming an important article of food in many countries for men and also a chief food of horses; usually collectively, as a species of grain.

c **1000** *Sax. Leechd.* II. 84 ȝenim bean mela oþþe ætena, oððe beres. ? *a* **1100** *Ibid.* III. 292 Nim atena gratan. *c* **1126** *O.E. Chron.* anno 1124 (Laud. MS.) Man sælde.. þæt acer sæd aten, þæt is feower sed læpas to feower scillingas. *c* **1205** Lay. 29256 Þer biforen he gon ȝeoten draf and chaf and aten. *a* **1225** *Ancr. R.* 312 Me nimeð et vuel dettur oten uor hweate. **1362** Langl. *P. Pl.* A. iv. 45 A tayle of Ten quarter oten. **1393** *Ibid.* C. ix. 306 A fewe croddes and creyme, and a cake of otes. *c* **1500** *Melusine* xxi. 127 That ootis shuld be gyuen to the horses. **1508** Dunbar *Flyting w. Kennedie* 133 Thow skaffis and beggis mair beir and aitis. *c* **1530** *Househ. Acc. Hampton Crt.* in Law *Hampton C.* (1885) I. 367, 4 boshells of wotes at 4^{d}. the boshell. **1601** F. Tate *Househ. Ord. Edw. II* (1876) 14 Hay and otes, litter and shoing and other necessaries for iiij horses. **1732** Arbuthnot *Rules of Diet* in *Ailments*, etc. I. 251 Oats, cleansing, resolving, and pectoral. **1857** Eliza Acton *Eng. Bread-Bk.* I. vi. 75 In the south of England oats are not employed for bread, but only for feeding horses. **1900** *Westm. Gaz.* 15 Nov. 2/1 With.. two camp kettles and packets of tea and Quaker Oats.. we made a great feast of tea and porridge.

b. *sing.* A single grain of oats. *rare.*

1677 Grew *Anat. Fruits* III. i. § 11 A Cluster of other little Bags, about the bigness of an Oate. **1780** A. Young *Tour Irel.* I. 288 Nor would the horses touch an oat, while they could get carrots.

2. The cereal plant *Avena sativa*, which yields this grain, cultivated in numerous varieties in all cool climates. **a.** Usually in *pl.*, collectively, as a crop.

1303 R. Brunne *Handl. Synne* 10110 Whete corne wyl nat prykke, As otes dowun, or barlykke. *c* **1425** *Voc.* in Wr.-Wülcker 664/13 *Hec auena*, otys. **1523** Fitzherb. *Husb.* § 14 There be .iii. maner of otes, that is to saye, redde otes, blacke otes, and roughe otes. **1578** Lyte *Dodoens* IV. xiii. 467 The pilde Otes are sowen in the gardens of Herboristes. **1610** Shaks. *Temp.* IV. 61 Ceres.. thy riche Leas of Wheate, Rye, Barley, Fetches, Oates and Pease. **1671** H. M. tr. *Erasm. Colloq.* 181 Nor do they sell it [hay] much cheaper than oats itself. **1786** Burns *Sc. Drink* iii, Let.. Aits set up their awnie horn. **1843** J. A. Smith *Product. Farming* (ed. 2) 105 Upon the same field which will yield only one harvest of wheat, two successive crops of barley may be raised, and three of oats.

b. The singular, *oat*, is used either to individualize the plant or a particular variety or sort, or to denote a single plant (but this would ordinarily be called an *oat-plant*).

1398 Trevisa *Barth. De P.R.* XVII. xvii. (Tollem. MS.) Ote is an herbe, and þe seed þerof acordeþ to use of men and of hors. *c* **1440** *Promp. Parv.* 372/2 Ote, or havur corne, *Avena*. **1620** Venner *Via Recta* ii. 40 It receiueth a singular cooling qualitie from the Oate. **1741** *Compl. Fam.-Piece* III. 423 There are two sorts, the white or Polish Oat.. and the black Oat. **1879** *Cassell's Techn. Educ.* I. 17 The oat is the hardiest of all cereal plants.

3. *sing.* and *collect. pl.* Applied to wild species of *Avena* (called also *oat-grass*), several of which are indigenous to the British Isles; esp. the **wild oat**, *Avena fatua*, a tall grass resembling the cultivated oat (of which it is perhaps the wild original), a frequent weed in cornfields, and noted for its long twisted awn, which makes an excellent hygrometer; **false oat**, the Oat-like Grass, *Arrhenatherum*.

a **700** *Epinal Gloss.* 599 *Lolium*, atae. *a* **1100** *Gloss.* in Wr.-Wülcker 480/28 *Zizania*, atan, oððe lasor. *c* **1475** *Pict. Voc.* ibid. 785/13 *Hec avicula*, wild hote. **1551** Turner *Herbal* I. E vj, Ther are ij. kyndes of otes: the one is called in English comonly, otes: and the other.. wild otes. **1578** Lyte *Dodoens* IV. xiii. 467 Also there is a barren Ote, of some called the purre Otes, of others wilde Otes.. The Purwottes or wilde Otes, commeth vp in many places amongst wheate and without sowing. **1697** Dryden *Virg. Georg.* I. 229 And oats unblest, and darnel domineers. **1785** Martyn *Rousseau's Bot.* xiii. (1794) 141 Bearded Oat grass, vulgarly called Wild Oats. **1806** Galpine *Brit. Bot.* 40 Wild oat or haver. **1835** Hooker *Brit. Flora* 53 *A. fatua*, wild Oat.. *A. strigosa*, bristle-pointed Oat.

attrib. **1676** *Phil. Trans.* XI. 651 The commodiousness of this kind of Hygroscope in comparison of those made of wild Oat-beards. *a* **1774** Goldsm. *Surv. Exp. Philos.* (1776) II. 30 An easier and still a cheaper [hygrometer].. may be made by a wild oat-beard, which lengthens with dry weather and contracts with moisture.

4. a. Phr. ***to sow one's wild oats***: to commit youthful excesses or follies; to spend early life in dissipation or dissolute courses (usually implying subsequent reform). (In reference to the folly and mischief of sowing wild oats instead of good grain.)

1576 Newton *Lemnie's Complex.* II. 99 That wilfull and vnruly age, which lacketh rypenes and discretion, and (as wee saye) hath not sowed all theyr wyeld Oates. **1583** T. Watson *Centurie of Love* lxxxvii, I finde that all my wildest Oates are sowne. **1604** Dekker *Honest Wh.* Wks. 1873 II. 9 You ha travelled enough now.. to sowe your wilde oates. **1720** De Foe *Capt. Singleton* ix. (1840) 169 Thus ended my first harvest of wild oats. **1849** Robertson *Serm.* Ser. I. vii. (1866) 125 A leniency which often talks thus:.. A young man must sow his wild oats and reform. **1892** *Pall Mall G.* 12 Nov. 2/3 The wild oats, fully sown, are a veritable road to ruin.

†**b.** Hence ***wild oats***, a name for a dissipated or dissolute young fellow; a 'wild' young man. *Obs.*

a **1564** Becon *Nosegay* Wks. (1843) 204 The foolish desire of certain light brains and wild oats, which are altogether given to newfangleness. **1602** *How Chuse Good Wife* (N.), Well, go to, wild oats! spendthrift! prodigal! **1605** *Lond. Prodigal* II. i, For this wild oats here, young Flowerdale, I will not judge.

c. *attrib.* Pertaining to the 'sowing of wild oats'.

1881 *Pop. Sci. Monthly* XIX. 153 Girls, it seems, have to pass through a millinery climacteric, as their brothers through a wild-oats period.

d. ***to feel one's oats***, to be lively; to feel important, to display one's self-importance. *colloq.* (orig. *U.S.*).

1831 *Boston Even. Transcript* 22 Dec. 1/1 Whether the pony felt his oats,.. He took a frightful canter. **1833** A. Lawrence *Diary & Corr.* (1855) 126 We both 'feel our oats' and our youth. **1843** T. C. Haliburton *Attaché* 1st Ser. II. 157 You know that, and you feel your oats, too, as well as any one. **1869** P. T. Barnum *Struggles & Triumphs* i. 33 My father.. installed me as clerk in this country store. Of course I 'felt my oats'. **1897** C. M. Flandrau *Harvard Episodes* 85, I suppose he was feeling his oats when he captained his class eleven. **1959** *Listener* 5 Nov. 770/1 The new influences and pressures within a colony that was 'feeling its oats'. **1971** D. Lees *Rainbow Conspiracy* i. 17 The Manchester circulation is nudging the one and a half million a day mark and they are beginning to feel their oats.

e. ***off one's oats*** colloq., off one's food.

1890 Kipling in *Lippincott's Monthly Mag.* Aug. 254 I'm a bit restless and off my oats. **1898** *Bulletin* (Sydney) 17 Dec. (Red Page), The horse is a power in Australia, and a few choice expressions spring from horses.. *out of collar* aptly describes out of work; *off his oats*, sickness or state of offishness. **1930** Wodehouse *Very Good, Jeeves!* iv. 98 The poor kid, who's quite off her oats about him. **1949** D. M. Davin *Roads from Home* II. ii. 99 What's the matter, John? Off your oats this morning? **1977** J. Fleming *Every Inch a Lady* I. i. 5 It's not like to put me off me oats.. but it's been a nasty day.

f. ***one's oats***, sexual gratification. *slang.*

1923 J. Manchon *Le Slang* 209 *To have one's oats*, faire des bêtises avec une femme, courir la gueuse. **1941** Baker *Austral. Slang* 50 *Oats from* (*a woman*), *get one's*, to coit with a woman. **1961** X. Herbert *Soldiers' Women* 265 There's nothing makes a hot-shot sheik like that so mad as being asked to pay for his oats. **1965** W. Dick *Bunch of Ratbags* 188, I was kissing her excitedly and passionately. You're doin' O.K., Cookie, you're gonna get your oats tonight for sure, I thought to myself. **1968** A. Diment *Bang Bang Birds* v. 65 Despite her lovely body it was her face that had me hooked... I like to watch something pretty.. when collecting my oats. **1976** P. Hill *Hunters* vii. 90 She wouldn't let you have your oats... You wanted to go to bed with her.. she wouldn't have it. **1978** J. Wainwright *Jury People* xxxvi. 108 This wife he was lumbered with. Okay —he loved her... But, even *he* wanted his oats, occasionally. He was human.

5. *transf.* (*poetic*). A pipe made of an oaten straw, as a pastoral instrument of music. [After L. *avena*.]

1637 Milton *Lycidas* 88 That strain I heard was of a higher mood: But now my Oate proceeds. **1648** Herrick *Hesper.*, *Beucolick*, That thou shalt swear, my pipe do's raigne Over thine oat, as soveraigne. *a* **1876** M. Collins *Greek Idyl* iv. Poems (1886) 82 While an old shepherd with his oat Pipes to the autumn breezes.

6. oats and chaff *Rhyming slang*, a footpath.

1857 'Ducange Anglicus' *Vulgar Tongue* 14 *Oats and chaff*,.. footpath. **1935** A. J. Pollock *Underworld Speaks* 82/1 *Oats and chaff*, footpath.

7. *Comb.* **a.** General combinations: simple attrib., as ***oat-beard*** (see BEARD *sb.* 6), ***-bran, -dust, -grain, -hull*** (see HULL *sb.*[1] 1), ***-husk, -stalk, -straw, stubble***; made from oat-grains, as ***oat-ale, -beer, -bread, -flour, -groats, -malt***; containing or carrying oats, as ***oat-bag, -cart, -field***; objective and obj. gen., as ***oat-bruiser, -consumer, -eater, -importer, -sheller, -tying***; ***oat-bearing, -growing, -producing*** adjs.; instrumental, as ***oat(s)-fed*** adj.; similative, as ***oat-shaped*** adj.

1693 *Humours Town* 5, I had rather a' been drinking *Oat-Ale at a Cake-house. **1886** C. E. Doble *Hearne's Collect.* (O.H.S.) II. 449 A draught of oat-ale. **1851** A. O. Hall *Manhattaner* 5 It was a modest commercial plain.. with.. bits of machinery, and ploughs, and *oat bags, and hay bales. **1882** Rogers *Agric. & Prices* III. 565/4, 2 canvas *oat bags at /3½. **1676**, *a* **1774** *Oat-beard [see sense 3]. **1893** Dk. Argyll *Unseen Found. Soc.* xi. 337 Piece of *oat-bearing land. **1705** Hearne *Collect.* 13 Oct. (O.H.S.) I. 55 He mentions Malt & *Oat Beer. **1900** *Daily News* 26 Apr. 5/6 Porridge made from *oat-bran husks. **1579** Langham *Gard. Health* (1633) 456 *Otebread nourisheth but little, and is not very agreable to mankind. **1780** A. Young *Tour Irel.* I. 213 Their diet is milk, potatoes, and oat bread. **1822–34** *Good's Study Med.* (ed. 4) I. 216 Attached to toast and water, which he made with oat-bread boiled in the water. **1898** *Daily News* 8 Feb. 3/5, I saw a bean crusher, a chaff cutter and an *oat bruiser. **1812** Col. Hawker *Diary* (1893) I. 45 We observed his people at *oat cart. **1805** Forsyth *Beauties Scotl.* III. 348 *Oat-dust from the mill.. makes part of the mixture. *a* **1668** Davenant *Vacation Lond.* Poems (1673) 291 And white *Oate-eater that does dwell; In Stable small at Sign of Bell. **1870** Miss Broughton *Red as Rose* I. 190 A young *oats-fed mare. **1900** *Daily News* 4 May 5/4 A glance at these rations shows the important part which *oat flour plays in all of them. **1881** Darwin *Veg. Mould* ii. 115 In one of the chambers there was a decayed *oat-grain, with its husk. *c* **1420** *Liber Cocorum* (1862) 20 Bray þen with wyne, With *ote grotis, and whyte brede eke. **1892** E. Reeves *Homeward Bound* 82 Invercargill.. is our chief *oat-growing country. **1607** Markham *Caval.* v. (1617) 11 A fewe Pease or Beanes mixt with *oate-hulls, which are taken from oates when you make Oate-meale. **1830** M. Donovan *Dom. Econ.* I. 253 The worts were allowed to filter through the stratum of *oat-husks and heath. **1707** Mortimer *Husb.* (J.), In Kent they brew with one half *oatmalt and the other half barleymalt. **1893** Dk. Argyll *Unseen Found. Soc.* xi. 337 *Oat-producing acres. **1845** *Athenæum* 1 Mar. 222 The *oat-shaped or nucleated body. **1879** *St. George's Hosp. Rep.* IX. 372 Stone.. very small and flat, about ½ inch long, oat-shaped. **1897** *Outing* (U.S.) XXIX. 554/1 Black oat-shaped worms. **1723** *Lond. Gaz.* No. 6222/10 Robert Wadford, late of Preston.. *Oat-Shiller. **1887** Bowen *Virg. Ecl.* v. 34 The unfruitful darnel, the *oatstalks barren. *a* **1650** D. Calderwood *Hist. Kirk* (1842–9) VI. 27 A scheaffe of *oat straw was sold for fourtie shillings in Edinburgh. **1850** *Rep. Comm. Patents: Agric. 1849* (U.S. Dept. Agric.) 380 Getting no other food in winter but a scanty supply of oat-straw. **1859** A. Cary *Pict. Country Life* i. 7 [He] lay.. with a bundle of oat-straw for his pillow. **1884** T. Speedy *Sport Highl.* iii. 29 Their bed.. should consist of clean oat-straw. **1807** Vancouver *Agric. Devon* (1813) 168 The *oat-stubbles are cleaned immediately after harvest.

b. Special combinations: **oat burner** *N. Amer. colloq.*, a horse; **oat cell** *Med.*, a small oval cell with little cytoplasm and an oval, densely staining nucleus which is characteristic of a type of carcinoma of the lung (formerly regarded as a sarcoma); freq. *attrib.* in ***oat-cell carcinoma, tumour***, etc.; hence **oat-celled** *a.*, containing such cells; **oat-fowl**, a local name of the Snow Bunting; **oat-grass**, a grass of the genus *Avena*; sometimes also applied to those of some allied genera, as *Arrhenatherum, Bromus*; **oat-hair**, the hairs or villi of the grain of the oat; **oat-hay** = *oaten hay*: see OATEN 3; **oatland**, land on which oats are grown; **oat-like** *a.*, like or resembling an oat; **oat-like grass**, *Arrhenatherum avenaceum*, considered by Linnæus an *Avena*; **oat-mill**, a mill for grinding oats (in quot. 1837 humorously applied to a horse's mouth); †**oatmonger**, a dealer in oats; **oat(s opera** = OATER; **oat-pipe, oat-reed**, a musical instrument made of an oat-straw; **oat-ridder**, a sieve or riddle for sifting oats; **oat-seed**, †(*a*) the season for sowing oats (*obs.*); (*b*) the seed or grain of the oat; hence ***oat-seed bird***, a local name of the Grey Wagtail; **oat-stone** (see quot.); **oat-thistle**, Turner's name for the cotton-thistle, *Onopordum Acanthium*.

1941 *Sun* (Baltimore) 21 July 11/4 There isn't a galloper in the lot who can say 'I'm the boss', so your milkman's *oat burner might do just as well as any of 'em. **1952** *Daily News* (N.Y.) 20 Aug. C 11/4 When the time comes.. that even an oat-burner must sport a tax stamp on its stem or stern. **1973** B. Broadfoot *Ten Lost Years* v. 50 Them oatburners never broke down. **1903** W. S. L. Barlow *Elem. Path. Anat. & Histol.* I. ix. 190 (*heading*) *Oat cell Sarcoma. **1926** *Jrnl. Path. & Bacteriol.* XXIX. 244 In obvious carcinomata of the lung 'oat cells' have been found in addition to the more readily recognisable carcinoma cells. **1956** Mayer & Maier *Pulmonary Carcinoma* iv. 96 Among anaplastic tumors belong the 'oat cell' carcinomas, called 'reserve cell' by some. **1957** A. I. Spriggs *Cytol. of Effusions* vi. 24 One of the most characteristic types of malignant cell is the oat-cell, so named after its appearance in histological sections. **1966** Wright & Symmers *Systemic Path.* I. x. 418/1 The finding of tubules in 'oat-cell' tumours.. should not affect the histological diagnosis. **1972** *Brit. Jrnl. Dis. Chest* LXVI. 164 Oat cell carcinomas have a more sinister prognosis. **1926** *Jrnl. Path. & Bacteriol.* XXIX. 244 The so-called '*oat-celled Sarcoma' of the posterior mediastinum is a medullary carcinoma of the bronchi. **1948** R. A. Willis *Path. Tumours* xix. 369 'Oat-celled' or spindle-celled structure.. is common in bronchial carcinoma. **1793** *Statist. Acc. Scot.* VII. 461 A small bird, rather less than a sparrow, resorts here in winter.. and is called by the people here *oat-fowls, because they prey on the oats. **1885** Swainson *Prov. Names Birds* 72 Snow bunting.. Oatfowl. **1742** Cole *Eng.-Lat. Dict.*, *Oat-gavel, *avenae vectigales*. **1578** Lyte *Dodoens* IV. xlvi. 505 Bycause of the likenesse it hath with Otes.. we may call it in Englishe, Hauer, or *Ote grasse. **1760** J. Lee *Introd. Bot.* App. 320 Oat-grass, *Bromus*. **1832** Tennyson *May Queen* II. vii, The summer airs blow cool On the oat-grass and the sword-grass, and the bulrush in the pool. **1866**

Treas. Bot. 93 The tall Oat-grass, *A[rrhenatherum] avenaceum*..in many instances forms a very considerable portion of good meadows and pastures. **1847** Wilson *Rural Cycl.* I. 623 Other kinds of intestinal calculi..consist principally of the filamentous portion of the grain of oats..and are sometimes known by the popular designation of *oat-hair calculi. **1892** *Cradock* (S. Afr.) *Register* 4 Mar. 2 *Oathay, ℔ 100 lbs., 3*s.* 6*d.* to 5*s.* 6*d.* **1899** *Daily News* 30 June 5/3 [see oaten 3]. **1706** Phillips, *Oat-thistle* or **Oatland-thistle*. **1821** Clare *Vill. Minstr.* II. 104 Multitudes of crowding beans; And flighty oatlands of a lighter hue. **1835** Hooker *Brit. Flora* I. 42 *Arrhenatherum*, *Oat-like grass. **1686** Plot *Staffordsh.* 337, I was shewed an *Oat-Mill, that husk't the Oats and winnow'd them, and then ground them to meal. **1837–40** Haliburton *Clockm.* (1862) 497 Hold up your old oatmill, and see if you can snuff the stable at minister's. **1327** in Riley *Mem.* (1868) 167 Denis le *Otemonger. **1942** Berrey & Van den Bark *Amer. Thes. Slang* §608/9 *Western picture*,..*oats opera. **1947** *Richmond* (Virginia) *Times-Dispatch* 2 May 10/1 Roy Rogers, Gene Autry and other oat opera stars. **1586** W. Webbe *Eng. Poetrie* (Arb.) 73 All in a fine *oate pipe these sweete songs lustilie chaunting. **1513** Douglas *Æneis* I. Prol. 511, I the ylk wmquhile that in the small *ait reid Tonit my sang. **1743** *Lond. & Country Brew.* IV. (ed. 2) 254 Some Maltsters, to improve the small Sort of Welch Coal, sift it thro' an *Oat-Ridder. **1637–50** J. Row *Hist. Kirk* (1842) p. xxv, The journay was farr, and it wes the haitt of thair *eat-seid. **1900** *Daily News* 4 July 5/6 Distribution of oatseeds for stable forage. **1864** Atkinson *Prov. Names Birds*, **Oat-seed-bird*, Ray's wagtail. **1885** Swainson *Prov. Names Birds* 44 Grey wagtail (*Motacilla melanope*)..Oat seed bird (Yorkshire). **1897** *Allbutt's Syst. Med.* III. 855 These concretions comprise the '*oat-stones' or avenoliths, which are composed of the indigestible fragments of oatmeal. **1548** Turner *Names of Herbes* 8 Acanthium..maye be called in englishe *otethistle, because the seedes are lyke vnto rough otes.

oat (əʊt), *v.* *U.S.* [f. prec. sb.: cf. corn *v.* 6.] *trans.* To feed (a horse) with oats. Also *absol.*

1732 B. Lynde *Diary* 9 May (1880) 26 Next morning..dined at Hampton;..thence to Greenland, where oated, and for 2 horses and drink, 2*s.* **1741** *Ibid.* 27 Oct. 121 Breakfasted and oated our 3 horses, at Deacon Tucker's. **1751** *MacSparran Diary* (1899) 51 Got up early, set out, oated at Peirce's. **1770** J. Adams *Diary* Wks. 1850 II. 240 Oated my horse at Newbury. **1787** M. Cutler in *Life*, etc. (1888) I. 290 Stopped at a miserable hut of a tavern and oated my horse. **1788** *Ibid.* 402 Made a stage at Jennison's..only to oat. *Ibid.*, After oating, we went on to Martin's. **1855** P. T. Barnum *Life* 70 Old 'Bob' was duly oated and watered.

oat-cake. [f. oat *sb.* + cake *sb.* 1 a.] A 'cake' made of oatmeal; = cake *sb.* 1 b.

[**1599** Shaks. *Much Ado* III. i. 11 Hugh *Ote-cake sir, or George Sea-coale.] *a* **1640** Peacham (J.), A blue stone they make haver or oatcakes upon. **1813** Sir H. Davy *Agric. Chem.* (1814) 151 The Derbyshire Miners in winter, prefer oat cakes to wheaten bread; finding that this kind of nourishment enables them to support their strength, and perform their labour better. **1865** Mrs. Carlyle *Lett.* III. 291 Mr. C. eats it to his oat-cakes. **1886** Ruskin *Præterita* I. xi. 358 With an oat-cake and butter—for I was always a gourmand.

oaten ('əʊt(ə)n), *a.* (*sb.*) [f. oat *sb.* + -en[4]. In first quot. perh. the gen. pl. of oat = OE. *átena*.]

1. Composed of the grain of oats, or of oatmeal.

c **1420** *Liber Cocorum* (1862) 47 Take porke, wele þou hit sethe With otene grotes. **1523** Ld. Berners *Froiss.* I. xviii. 24 They lacked oten meale to make cakes withall. **1610** Holland *Camden's Brit.* I. 537 They did eate..oten bread. **1832** *Veg. Subst. Food* 72 Oaten cakes..are much used in Lancashire.

2. Made of the straw or stem of an oat.

1579 Spenser *Sheph. Cal.* Jan. 72 [He] broke his oaten pype. **1589** Greene *Menaphon* (Arb.) 52 Tune on my pipe the praises of my Loue, And midst thy oaten harmonie recount How faire she is. **1637** Milton *Lycidas* 32 The Rural ditties..Temper'd to th' Oaten Flute. **1746** Collins *Ode Evening* 1 Aught of oaten stop, or pastoral song. **1809** W. Irving *Knickerb.* II. iv. (1849) 101 Oh! sweet Theocritus! had I thine oaten reed.

3. Of or belonging to the oat as a plant. *oaten hay*: see quot. 1899.

1588 Shaks. *L.L.L.* v. ii. 913 When Shepheards pipe on Oaten strawes. **1601** Holland *Pliny* I. 146 Drawing it in with an oaten straw. **1891** E. Kinglake *Australian at H.* 141 The farmers grow their maize and their oaten hay and sell it, and are comfortably off. **1899** *Daily News* 30 June 5/3 There has recently been some demand in Australia for 'oaten hay', for English race horses. Oaten hay, or as it is called in Cape Colony 'oat hay'..consists of oat sheaves with the oats not thrashed out of them.

†**4.** Abounding in oats; oat-producing. *rare.*

1640 Parkinson *Theat. Bot.* 958 The Oaten land or Muske Thistle. *c* **1648–50** Brathwait *Barnabees Jrnl.* IV. Kj, Thence to oaten Ouston fruitfull.

B. *sb.* An oaten pipe: see 2 above.

1825 *New Monthly Mag.* XIV. II. 469 Which, when as the oaten spoke, From their green dreams aye awoke.

oater ('əʊtə(r)). Chiefly *U.S.* = *horse opera.*

1951 Green & Laurie *Show Biz* 570/1 *Oater*, Western film. **1961** A. Berkman *Singers' Gloss. Show Business* 64 *Oater*, Western film. **1969** M. Pei *Words in Sheep's Clothing* (1970) iii. 22 'Western'..along with its synonyms, 'horse opera', 'oater'. **1975** *Radio Times* 10 Jan. 10/1 Borden (*Red River*) Chase wrote this expansive oater [sc. *Lone Star*] for Clark Gable.

oater, obs. form of otter.

oath (əʊθ), *sb.* Pl. **oaths** (əʊðz). Forms: 1–4 **áð, áþ,** (1 **háð**), 2–4 **oð, oþ,** 3 **æð, oað, othþ,** (**hoþ**), 4–5 **ooþ,** 4–6 **ooth,** (5 -**e**), 4–7 **oth, -e,** (6 **oith, oethe**), 7– **oath,** (*dial.* 5 **wothe, woothe**); also *β.* *north.* and *Sc.* 4 **ath, aithe, aythe,** 4–5 **athe, ayth,** (5 **haith,** 6 **eith,** 7 **eath**), 5–9 **aith.** [Com. Teut.: OE. *áþ* str. masc., = OFris. *êth, êd*, OS. *êð* (MDu. *eet, eed-*, Du. *eed*, MLG. LG. *êd*), OHG. *eid* (MHG. *eit, eid-*, Ger. *eid*), ON. *eiðr* (Sw. *ed*, Da. *eed*), Goth. *aiþs*:—OTeut. **aiþo-z*:—pre-Teut. **óitos*, cf. OIr. *oeth.*]

1. a. A solemn or formal appeal to God (or to a deity or something held in reverence or regard), in witness of the truth of a statement, or the binding character of a promise or undertaking; an act of swearing; a statement or promise corroborated by such an appeal, or the form of words in which such a statement or promise is made.

to take (an) oath: to utter, or bind oneself by, an oath; to swear: also ***to make (an) oath***, and in earlier use ***to swear an oath***. † ***to take an oath of (a person)***: to cause (him) to swear; to administer, or be witness to, an oath (*obs.*). ***on*** or ***upon oath***: under the obligation of an oath; as having made an oath. ***under oath***, on or upon oath.

Beowulf 1107 (Z.) Að wæs ʒeæfned. *c* **1000** *Ags. Gosp.* Matt. xiv. 7 Ða behet he mid aðe, hyre to syllenne swa hwæt swa heo hyne bæde. *a* **1123** *O.E. Chron.* an. 1101 Þis mid aðe ʒefestnodan. **1297** R. Glouc. (Rolls) 6108 Nou adde heyemen of þe lond..deop oþ ysuore, Wiþ him to holde treweliche, & breke þo hor oþ. *a* **1300** *Cursor M.* 1618 Be his right hand he suar his ath. *c* **1300** *Seyn Julian* 25 Ihote icham alle cristenemen, to deðe do yp myn oþe. *c* **1420** *Chron. Vilod.* st. 292 Wt owte ony wothe. *c* **1449** Pecock *Repr.* III. xi. 344 Bi ooth and so bi avisement. *c* **1450** *Merlin* 140 Whan the two kynges hadde take the oth of these two. **1482** *Monk of Evesham* (Arb.) 96 He..bade hem with grete instaunce and wothys that the nexte nyghte..the lampys afore seyd schuld be lyghtynde. **1511** in W. H. Turner *Select. Rec. Oxford* (1880) 3 John Husscher wyll take a othe a pon a boke. **1526** *Pilgr. Perf.* (W. de W. 1531) 92 Prelates to whome they haue bounde themselfe by othe, promesse or vowe. *a* **1533** Ld. Berners *Huon* xcv. 310 Themperour hath so made his oth and promyse & hath sworne by his crowne imperyall. **1593** Shaks. *Rich. II*, I. iii. 14 Speake truly on thy knighthood, and thine oath. —— *Lucr.* Argt., She, first taking an oath of them for her revenge, revealed the actor. **1599** —— *Hen. V*, v. ii. 399 My Lord of Burgundy wee'le take your Oath..for suretie of our Leagues. **1601** —— *All's Well* v. iii. 185 Aske him vpon his oath, if hee do's thinke [etc.]. **1651** Hobbes *Leviath.* (1839) 179 Which swearing, or oath, is a form of speech, added to a promise; by which he that promiseth, signifieth, that unless he perform, he renounceth the mercy of his God, or calleth to him for vengeance on himself. **1712** [see under *prep.* 14 b]. **1764** Burn *Poor Laws* 253 The administring of an oath to witnesses by justices of the peace. **1818** Jas. Mill *Brit. India* II. v. ii. 374 He declined examination upon oath. **1848** Dickens *Dombey* iv, I could take my oath he said son. **1849** Macaulay *Hist. Eng.* x. II. 653 The new oaths were sent down to the Commons. **1851** R. Glisan *Jrnl. Army Life* (1874) viii. 83 He was then under oath not to drink for six months. **1861** G. Meredith *Evan Harrington* xliii. (1886) 481 Rose..made oath to her soul she would rescue him.

β. *a* **1300** *Cursor M.* 27666 And gain sum þai suare þair ath [*v.r.* mak ane athe] For to do him melle and lath. *c* **1340** Hampole *Prose Tr.* 10 Here es forbodene athe with-owttene cheson. **1375** Barbour *Bruce* IX. 540 Sum of the men of the Cuntre Com till his pess and maid him ath. **1552** Abp. Hamilton *Catech.* (1884) 61 The first conditioun requirit to ane lauchful eith is verite or truth. **1609** Skene *Reg. Maj.* 13 To make ane aith before ane Judge. **1785** Burns *Death & Dr. Hornbook* 147 I'm free to tak my aith.

b. Loosely applied to an asseveration in the form of an oath, but not involving a reference to God or anything sacred.

1600 Shaks. *A.Y.L.* IV. i. 192–3. **1808** Scott *Marm.* v. xi, She..laughed, and blushed, and oft did say Her pretty oath, by Yea and Nay, She could not, would not, durst not play!

c. ***my*** (*colonial*, etc.) ***oath***, a mild expletive or exclamation: yes! of course! upon my word! *Austral.* and *N.Z. slang.*

1859 H. Kingsley *Recoll. G. Hamlyn* II. vi. 94 'You're not fit company for any man except the hangman,' said Tom,..'Oh my —— (colonial oath!)' said the other; 'oh my —— cabbage tree!' **1895** J. Kirby *Old Times in Bush* x. 143 The snake..made a hoop of hisself, and then, my oath, he did go. **1896** H. Lawson *While Billy Boils* 203 (*title*) His colonial oath. *Ibid.*, 'My oath!' he replied... 'My blooming oath!' **1899** *Bulletin* (Sydney) 25 Feb. (Red Page), I don't mean the variety whose conversation consists of expectoration and 'Yer' or 'My — oath'. **1916** J. B. Cooper *Coo-oo-ee* i. 11 Ain't that like a woman with a man? My oath it is! I know 'em. **1925** H. H. Cook *Far Flung* 12 'Perhaps ye'll square up?'..'My oath!' cried the debtor. **1928** 'Brent of Bin Bin' *Up Country* xv. 255 'My — Colonial oath!' echoed Erroll. **1941** *Coast to Coast 1941* 45 'Who said I was going to give you a quid anyway?' 'You did.' ' My oath I didn't.' **1946** E. G. Webber *Johnny Enzed in Italy* 36 'All this us der merry laugh gives, no?' I said. 'My oath!' said the Bloke. 'My colonial oath!' **1952** M. Tripp *Faith is Windsock* i. 7 'Pay twenties and twenty-ones.' 'My oath!' Bergen threw his cards (a king and a six) face down on the table. **1969** *Melbourne Truth* 12 July 3/4 Whitton, with his ear close to the receiver, listened to the reply. It was: 'My bloody oath I will.' **1974** N. Marsh *Black as he's Painted* iii. 73 'And that's when your headache really sets in, is it, Fred?' 'My oath! Well, take a look at it.' **1977** J. Wainwright *Do Nothin'* xi. 185 My oath—those couple of hours were some session.

2. Such an appeal made lightly in ordinary speech in corroboration of a statement, etc.; a careless use of the name of God or Christ, or of something sacred, in asseveration or imprecation, or a formula of words involving this (often with suppression or perversion of the sacred name, and becoming at length practically meaningless, or a mere expression of anger, surprise, or other strong feeling): an act of profane swearing; a curse.

c **1175** *Lamb. Hom.* 11 Ne haue þu þines drihtenes nome in nane aða ne in nane idel speche. *a* **1225** *Ancr. R.* 198 Blasphemie..þet swereð greate oðes, oðer bitterliche kurseð, oðer mis-seið bi God, oðer bi his haluwen. **1362** Langl. *P. Pl.* A. v. 177 Þer weoren oþes an hep, hose þat hit herde. *a* **1420** Hoccleve *De Reg. Princ.* 629 Þe former of euery creature Dismembred y with oþes grete, and rente Lyme for lyme. **1550** Crowley *Epigr.* 697 The wycked othes, and the times myspent. **1606** Dekker *Sev. Sinnes* II. (Arb.) 21 Oathes are Crutches, vpon whych Lyes..go, and neede no other pasport... Oathes are wounds that a man stabs into himselfe. **1796** H. Hunter tr. *St.-Pierre's Stud. Nat.* (1799) II. 511 Every street of the city rings with the horrible oaths of their drivers. **1837** Lytton *E. Maltrav.* (1851) 8 He closed the window with an oath. **1898** D. C. Murray *Tales* 209 Oaths are the flash-notes of speech.

3. With qualifying words, as Bible *oath*, bodily *oath*, book *oath*, corporal *oath*, *oath of abjuration*, *of allegiance*, *of office*, *of supremacy*, etc. ***great oath***: an oath of special solemnity, or (in sense 2) of special emphasis or profanity; the form of oath held by the swearer, or considered at the time, most sacred.

a **1225** [see 2]. *c* **1330** R. Brunne *Chron.* (1810) 75 Þerfor William þe kyng..suore a grete othe, þat he suld neuer spare Noiþer lefe no lothe northeren, what so þei ware. **13..** *K. Alis.* 4575 (Bodl. MS.) Now he..haþ yswore his grete ooþ þat he ne shal twies seen þe sonne Er he hym haue þe forte ywonne. **1389** in Sir W. Fraser *Wemyss of W.* (1888) II. 24 Til there thyngys..lelily and fermly to be fulfyllyt..bath the partys fornemmyt, the haly wangelis twechyt, the gret ath bodylyke has sworn. *c* **1425** Wyntoun *Cron.* IX. xx. 1961 He swore the great aith bodely. *c* **1440** *Promp. Parv.* 210/2 Grete oothe, *jusjurandum.* **1530** Palsgr. 495 He hath constrayned me..by a boke othe (*par mon serment sur ung liure*). *c* **1565** Lindesay (Pitscottie) *Chron. Scot.* (1899) I. 41 The chanceleir suore be his great aith and hailie sacrament thair was..no wther..that he faworit sa weill. **1589** Cooper *Admonit.* 32 Thomas Orwin..himselfe hath vpon his booke oath denied, that he euer printed [the books]. **1606** *Proc. agst. late Traitors* 6 Should receive several corporall othes upon the holy Evangelists. **1609** Skene *Reg. Maj.* 12 Twelue loyall men..sall be chosen; quha sall sweare the great eath in presence of the parties, that they sall declare quhilk of them hes best richt. **1771** E. Long *Trial of Dog 'Porter'* in Hone *Every-day Bk.* II. 204 I'm ready to take my bible oath on't. **1777** G. Clinton in Sparks *Corr. Amer. Rev.* (1853) I. 415 To attend at Kingston, and take the oath of office in consequence of my late appointment. **1842** S. Lover *Handy Andy* xii, I dhruv him to Squire Egan's, I'll take my book oath. **1849** Macaulay *Hist. Eng.* iv. I. 504 A law..imposed severe penalties on every person who refused to take the oath of supremacy when required to do so.

4. *transf.* A person by whom, or thing by which, one swears. *rare.*

c **1825** Beddoes *Poems, Torrismond* I. iii, If thou art..The admiration, oath, and patron saint, Of frivolous revellers.

5. *attrib.* and *Comb.*, as ***oath-parole***, ***-pledge***, ***-rite***; ***oath-breaker***, ***-breaking***, ***-keeper***, ***-making***, ***-sanctioner***, ***-taker***, ***-taking***; ***oath-bound***, ***-despising***, ***-detesting*** adjs.; **oath-helper** = compurgator 1 b; hence ***oath-helping*** vbl. sb.; **oath-sick** *a.*, fastidious about oaths, having an objection to take an oath; **oath-worthy** *a. arch.*, worthy of credit on oath, worthy to be sworn by.

1890 *Pall Mall G.* 23 Oct. 6/3 An open organization and not *oath-bound, except in the case of the council. **1894** *Cath. News* 27 Oct. 3/2 Freemasonry is an oath-bound body. **1939** W. B. Yeats *Last Poems* 8 That all are oath-bound men. **1601** Dent *Pathw. Heaven* 148 Blasphemers and *oath-breakers. *a* **1973** J. R. R. Tolkien *Silmarillion* (1977) ix. 83 For so sworn, good or evil, an oath may not be broken, and it shall pursue oathkeeper and oathbreaker to the world's end. **1596** Shaks. *1 Hen. IV*, v. ii. 38, I told him gently..Of his *Oath-breaking. **1826** Hor. Smith *Tor Hill* (1838) III. 8 The depositions of his *oath-despising retainers. **1786** Burns *Earnest Cry & Prayer* xiii, Dempster, a true blue Scot I'se warran'; Thee, *aith-detesting, chaste Kilkerran. **1891** *Oath-helper [used s.v. compurgator 1 b]. **1902** *Encycl. Brit.* XXVIII. 331/1 One of the two litigants must prove his case, by his body in battle,..or by an oath with oath-helpers. **1943** F. M. Stenton *Anglo-Saxon Eng.* ix. 312 It is probable that in the earliest time a man's 'oath-helpers' had been chosen exclusively from among his kin. *Ibid.* 313 Ine of Wessex orders that every person accused of homicide, whatever his status, must include at least one man of high rank among his oath-helpers. **1970** Foote & Wilson *Viking Achievement* xi. 375 After the man accused had made his statement on oath, then each of his oath-helpers swore that they believed his oath to be honest. **1973** A. Harding *Law Courts Med. Eng.* 25 The Normans let the parties fight an actual physical battle, but the Anglo-Saxons preferred trial by ordeal or by *oath-helping. *a* **1973** *Oath-keeper [see *oath-breaker* above]. **1553** Grimalde *Cicero's Offices* III. (1558) 160 In an *othe-makinge, not what the feare but what the vertue of it is, ought to be considered. *a* **1661** Fuller *Worthies* II. (1662) 189 What *Oath-office is kept in London; I know not. **1900** *Daily Tel.* 11 Aug. 7/2 These spies and breakers of *oath-paroles. **1884** *Congregationalist* June 465 The sacramental solemnity, the *oath-pledge against evil. *a* **1634** Chapman (J.), All the *oath-rites said, I have ascended her adorned bed. **1846** Grote *Greece* (1869) I. 8 Zeus..conferred upon Styx the majestic distinction of being the Horkos, or *oath-sanctioner of the Gods. *a* **1716** South *Twelve Serm.* (1717) IV. 219 A scrupulous *Oath-sick Conscience. **1818** Cobbett *Pol. Reg.* XXXIII. 49 The Magistrates, who co-operated with this hirer of *oath-takers. **1897** Mary Kingsley *W. Africa* 465 Oath-takers being sadly prone to kiss their thumb, as it were. **1458** *Waterf. Arch.* in *10th Rep. Hist. MSS. Comm.* App. v. 299 That no man..be recevid unto the franches..of the said citie save only for the same crafte that he usith at his *othe takyng. **1960** *News Chron.* 9 July 1/3 The Mau Mau oath-taking ceremonies. **1961** *Guardian* 29 Mar. 2/1 Recent reports of Mau-Mau oath-taking in Kenya. **1882** BOSWORTH-TOLLER *Anglo-Sax. Dict.* s.v. *āþ-wyrþe*, Gif he āþwyrþe biþ, 'if he be *oath-worthy', *Laws of Ine* 46. **1886** CORBETT *Fall of Asgard* II. 170 By all that we of old have deemed holy and oathworthy.

Hence **oathed** (in comb.) *a.*, furnished with oaths; 'oathful *a.*, full of oaths; '**oathlet**, a small or petty oath.

1828 J. WILSON in *Blackw. Mag.* XXIV. 296 Cursing and swearing in triumph in a *many-oathed language. **1887** SIMPSON *Golf* x. 171 An earnest *oathful desire for victory. **1835** *Blackw. Mag.* XXXVIII. 270 A tiny tart *oathlet.

oath (əʊθ, əʊð), *v. rare.* Forms: 4 athe, 6 othe, 7– oath, oathe. [f. OATH *sb.*]

†**1.** *trans.* To impose an oath upon, put to one's oath, conjure. *Obs.*

13.. *Evang. Nicod.* 1141 in Herrig *Archiv* LIII. 412 Bi gret god we yhow athe [L. *conjurantes eos*]. *Ibid.* 1699 We war athed full nere [L. *coniurati sumus*].

2. *intr.* (or with *obj. cl.*) To utter an oath or oaths, to swear. Also *to oath it.*

a **1617** P. BAYNE *Lect.* (1634) 167 They carry their sinne in their fore-head, braving men, oathing it. **1627–47** FELTHAM *Resolves* I. xix. 67 'Tis easy to know a beginning swearer.. He oathes it, as a cowardly fencer plays. **1851** R. F. BURTON *Goa* 309 Complainant swears that he was not paid; witness oathes by the sun that he was. **1900** *Longm. Mag.* Nov. 72 Some of the soldiers..laughed and oathed in evident glee.

3. *trans.* To take to oath, swear by.

1740 T. CONNOR in *Gentl. Mag.* 461/2, I do oath the holy seven [i.e. sacraments], His soul's with Patrick now in heaven.

4. To address or call with oaths.

1834 *Tait's Mag.* I. 41 Some lusty carter is heard oathing a bit of the blood patrician. **1853** S. G. OSBORNE in Visc. Ingestre *Meliora* II. 11 The dogs..kept up growls of defiance, till their owners oathed them into order.

Hence '**oathing** *vbl. sb.* Also *attrib.*

1680 I. C. *Vind. Oaths* (ed. 2) 19 If there be no oathing or swearing, there can be no for-swearing. **1681** HICKERINGILL *Sin Man-catching* Wks. 1716 I. 186 These Men-catchers lay their Snares and their Oathing-Gins to catch them. **1961** *Guardian* 12 May 5/5, I don't attribute the oathing to the party. *Ibid.* 7 June 11/4 The oathing ceremonies at Meru last month when more than a thousand people took an undisclosed oath. **1969** *Daily Tel.* 9 Sept. 20/6 To a Christian, secret oathing is repugnant and unacceptable. *Ibid.*, Secret oathing ceremonies.

oathable ('əʊθəb(ə)l), *a. rare*⁻¹. In 7 **othable.** [f. OATH *sb.* or *v.* + -ABLE.] Capable of taking an oath; fit or able to be sworn; oath-worthy.

1607 SHAKS. *Timon* IV. iii. 135 You are not Othable, Although I know you'l sweare, terribly sweare.

oatmeal ('əʊtmi:l). Forms: see OAT and MEAL.

1. a. Meal made from oats.

c **1420** *Liber Cocorum* (1862) 14 Take almondes unblanchid..Put ote-mele to. **1422** tr. *Secreta Secret., Priv. Priv.* 244 A man Sholde ette mettis of colde and moisti complexcion,..as..Potage of oot-mell. **1523** LD. BERNERS *Froiss.* I. xvii. 19 Behynde the saddyl, they [the Scottis] wyll haue a lytle sacke full of ootemele. **1535** COVERDALE *Prov.* xxvii. 22 Though thou shuldest bray a foole with a pestell in a morter like otemeell. **1683** TRYON *Way to Health* 29 Oatmeal is to be accounted the best of all Flour. **1776** ADAM SMITH *W.N.* I. xi. I. (1869) I. 171 The common people in Scotland..are fed with oat-meal. **1813** J. THOMSON *Lect. Inflam.* 333 Poultices..formed of oat-meal. **1873** KINGSLEY *Lett.* (1878) II. 417 For growing children, oatmeal is invaluable.

†**b.** Proverb. *Obs.*

1542 UDALL *Erasm. Apoph.* (1877) 329 Leosthenes had perswaded the citee of Athenes to make warre, beeyng set agog to thinke all the worlde otemele. **1615** SWETNAM *Arraignm. Wom.* iii, The worlde is not all made of ote-meale, nor all is not golde that glisters. **1673** *Vinegar & Must.* Wedn. Lect., You think..that all the world is oat-meal.

c. Short for oatmeal porridge.

1891 in *Cent. Dict.*

†**2.** *pl.* A name for a set of riotous or profligate young men early in the 17th century. *Obs. slang.*

'No trace of this odd appellation has yet been found except that the author of a ludicrous pamphlet has taken the name of Oliver Oat-meale' (Nares *Gloss.* 1822).

1624 FORD *Sun's Darling* I. i, Do mad prank with Roaring boys and oatmeals.

3. A greyish-fawn colour resembling that of oatmeal. Also *attrib.* or as *adj.*

1927 *Daily Express* 2 May 7 Colours: Beige, Oatmeal, [etc.]. **1935** A. CHRISTIE *Three Act Tragedy* III. ix. 188 The room..had walls of a rather drab oatmeal colour. **1939–40** *Army & Navy Stores Catal.* 636/2 All wool flannels... Oatmeal Shade. **1951** 'C. CARNAC' *It's her own Funeral* i. 10 The dark panelling made a good background to her oatmeal suit. **1951** *Catal. of Exhibits, South Bank Exhib., Festival of Britain* 58/2 Women's oatmeal glacé gloves. **1960** *House & Garden* May 61/2 Settee..covered in oatmeal tweed. **1961** *Guardian* 1 Feb. 7/5 Colours were pale green, oatmeal, navy. **1963** *Times* 27 Feb. 12/5 Contrasting cravats of silk or organza set off soft oatmeal or sand tones, pale *tilleul* greens, navy, black, off-white. **1970** [see KINGFISHER 3]. **1973** 'R. MACLEOD' *Burial in Portugal* iii. 69 An oatmeal sports coat.

4. *attrib.* and *Comb.*, as ***oatmeal bread, flummery, groats, gruel, man, mill, porridge, stout; oatmeal-chewer, -eater, -maker***; also applied *attrib.* to cloth of a minutely speckled pattern suggestive of oatmeal, as ***oatmeal frieze, serge***, etc.; **oatmeal mush** *U.S.*, porridge made with oatmeal; **oatmeal soap**, soap containing oatmeal as a mild abrasive.

1943 A. SIMON *Conc. Encycl. Gastron.* IV. 83/1 *Oatmeal bread. **1974** R. B. PARKER *God save Child* (1975) xii. 86 He put a plate of sliced turkey..and a loaf of oatmeal bread on the table. **1712** STEELE *Spect.* No. 431 ¶3, I desire you would find out some Name for these craving Damsels,.. Trash-eaters, *Oatmeal-chewers, Pipe-champers, Chalk-lickers [etc.]. **1886** *Ripon Chron.* 4 Sept. 2/6 New *Oatmeal Cloths, in plain and fancy cream. **1885** *Pall Mall G.* 28 Jan. 9/1 Dresses of *oatmeal cream, with bonnets to match. **1767** A. CAMPBELL *Lexiph.* 38 Professions..of everlasting amity, past now between the Cow-killer and *Oat-meal-eater. **1778** MRS. RAFFALD *Eng. Housekpr.* 204 To make *Oatmeal Flummery. **1594** LYLY *Moth. Bomb.* in *O. Pl.* (1814) I. 278 You *oatmeal-groat you were acquainted with this plot. **1611** *Closet for Ladies & Gentlew.* 134 Oatemeale grotes soked in vineger. **1579** LANGHAM *Gard. Health* (1633) 457 Throat squincy..vse *Otemeale grewell well sifted. **1599** *Canterbury Marriage Licences* (MS.), Thomas Jones ..*Otmellmaker. **1720** *Lond. Gaz.* No. 5882/3 Thomas Cozens,..Oatmeal maker. **1649** BLITHE *Eng. Improv. Impr.* (1653) 102 For these Crops, being but of Oates, I could have had five pound an Acre, being offered it by an *Oat-meal man. **1883** H. P. SPOFFORD in *Harper's Mag.* Aug. 465/1 You've been the means of starving me..on *oatmeal mush. **1903** S. CLAPIN *New Dict. Amer.* 291 Oatmeal-mush. **1812** *Examiner* 24 Aug. 533/2 Oatmeal boiled in water (*oatmeal porridge). **1890–91** *T. Eaton & Co. Catal.* Fall & Winter 42 Colgate's soaps—*oatmeal, [etc.]. **1897** *Sears, Roebuck Catal.* 19/1 (*heading*) 'Oat Meal' Toilet Soap. *c* **1938** *Fortnum & Mason Price List* 54/1 Soaps... Violet Oatmeal. **1977** *Honey* Nov. 55/2 Friction cleaning is most effective on blackheads... You can use Boots No 7. very mild oatmeal and lavender soap 89p. **1926–7** *Army & Navy Stores Catal.* 64/1 *Oatmeal Stout (recommended for its tonic properties) doz. 9/-. **1976** J. B. HILTON *Gamekeeper's Gallows* iii. 26 If he wins, he always takes it [*sc.* a rabbit] a bottle of oatmeal stout home.

oaty ('əʊtɪ), *a. rare.* [f. OAT + -Y.] Of the nature of, or full of oats, †esp. of wild oats.

1603 OWEN *Pembrokeshire* vii. (1891) 55 Verye fruitfull for corne especciallie barlie, but it is accounted oatie and not soe fine as that of the other partes. *Ibid.*, The negligence of husbandmen in sowinge of bad and oatie seade. **1611** COTGR., *Avenier*, oatie, belonging to oats.

Oaxacan (əʊæk'sɑ:kən), *a.* [f. *Oaxaca* (see below) + -AN.] Of or pertaining to the southern Mexican state of Oaxaca.

1934 A. HUXLEY *Beyond Mexique Bay* 263 Our Oaxacan friend, Don Manuel, invited us one evening to join this endless procession. **1977** *Dædalus* Summer 88 This early Oaxacan elite was distinctly less sophisticated than the Olmec aristocracy of the neighboring Mexican Gulf Coast country.

oaze, oazy, obs. forms of OOZE, OOZY.

†**ob**, *sb.*¹ *Obs.* [From *ob.*, abbreviation of *objection*, used in conjunction with *sol.* = *solution*, in old books of divinity.] In phr. ***ob(s) and sol(s)*** = objection(s) and solution(s); scholastic or subtle disputation. Hence †**ob-and-soller** *Obs. nonce-wd.*, a scholastic or subtle disputant.

1588 *Marprel. Epist.* (Arb.) 11 Very skilfull in the learning of ob and Sol. **1621** BURTON *Anat. Mel.* III. iv. I. iii. (1651) 675 A thousand idle questions, nice distinctions, subtleties, Obs and Sols. *c* **1660** *Loyal Songs* (1731) II. 217 Whilst he should give us Sol's and Ob's, He brings us in some simple bobs. **1678** BUTLER *Hud.* III. ii. 1242 To pass for Deep and Learned Scholars; Although but Paltry, Ob and Sollers.

†**ob**, *sb.*² *Obs.* [a. Heb. *ōb(h* necromancer.] A wizard, magician, sorcerer, ventriloquist.

1659 GAUDEN *Tears Ch.* III. xxii. 336 They peep and mutter, like Obs and Pythons, whispering as out of the earth and their bellies.

ob (ɒb). A representation of a pronunciation of the word OF *prep.*, supposed to occur esp. in the speech of American Blacks.

1839 *Bentley's Misc.* VI. 263 He said de Queen ob Sheba wab a dark lady, may be bery dark. **1846** *Negro Singer's Own Bk.* 5, I am glad ob it, for my part. *Ibid.* 23 One day just at de set ob sun,..When de work war did an done. *Ibid.* 29, I tell you ob a scrape I had wid a gal. **1848** S. C. FOSTER *Old Uncle Ned (song)* 3 He had no wool on de top ob de head. **1851** —— *Ring de Banjo (song)* 4 Den come again, Susanna, By de gas-light ob de moon; We'll tum de old piano When de banjo's out ob tune. **1882** *Judge* (N.Y.) 30 Dec. 10/3 Money am de root ob all ebil. **1891** C. TOWNSEND *Negro Minstrels* 22 He..drank a gallon ob tangle foot. **1893** M. A. OWEN *Voodoo Tales* 168 Hit am er powdeh mek outen de same hef' ob snails an' lizuhds. **1893** K. MACKAY *Out Back* (ed. 2) III. viii. 288 'Any fella longa tribe ob my sister, Queen Victoria, friend longa mine,' replied the black-fellow. **1895** BANKS & SMILEY in A. Dundes *Mother Wit* (1973) 256/2 Three bottles sittin' in de road, one ob dem full. **1950** R. AMES in *Ibid.* 492/2 In de fork ob de branch. **1974** R. B. PARKER *Godwulf Manuscript* vii. 55 Ah is a member ob de press, baby.

†**ob.**, abbreviation of OBOLUS, formerly used to denote a halfpenny.

1442 in Willis & Clark *Cambridge* (1886) I. 387, xvj Skaynys of grete packethrede..at ob a pec'; in al viij*d*. **1463** *Bury Wills* (Camden) 30 To reseyve an ob..fore here offryng. *c* **1550** *Disc. Common Weal Eng.* (1893) 42 His hen at a peny, his chiken at ob. **1596** SHAKS. *1 Hen. IV*, II. iv. 590 Item, Sacke, two Gallons. v.s. viii.*d*... Item, Bread. ob. *Prince.* O monstrous, but one halfe penny-worth of Bread to this intollerable deale of Sacke? **1631** WEEVER *Anc. Fun. Mon.* 238 The Hospitall of Saint Iames was..valued at the suppression to 32.*l.* 2.*s.* 1*d.* ob.

ob., abbrev. of L. *obiit*, died; used before the date of a person's death.

1890 BARRÈRE & LELAND *Dict. Slang* II. 93/1 *Ob* (Winchester College), for *obit.* **1952** D. BALSDON *Freshman's Folly* iii. 141 The highly complexioned countenance of the Reverend Nathaniel Blunt, S.T.P., ob. 1782. **1978** C. JONES et al. *Study of Liturgy* II. I. vii. 57 *The Apostolic Tradition*, ascribed by many scholars to Hippolytus, the schismatic bishop of Rome (ob. A.D. 236, 237?).

ob-, *pref.* The Lat. prep. *ob* 'in the direction of, towards, against, in the way of, in front of, in view of, on account of'. In combination with vbs. and their derivatives, the *b* is assimilated to certain consonants, becoming *oc-* before *c-*, *of-* before *f-*, *op-* before *p-*, and app. *o-* before *m-* (in *omittĕre*). In combination it has the following senses: a. In the direction of, towards; facing, in front of; as *obvertĕre* to turn towards, *obœdīre* to listen to. b. Against, in opposition, as *occurrĕre* to run against, *oppōnĕre* to place against; often merely implying the injurious or objectionable character of an action. c. Upon or over; down upon, down; as *obdūcĕre* to draw upon or over, *obligāre* to bind down, *occidĕre* to fall down. d. Completely; sometimes pleonastic, as *obdulcāre* to sweeten (completely), *obdūrāre* to harden greatly; often with a colouring of sense a.

In English use, *ob-* (*oc-*, *of-*, *op-*, *o-*) occurs.

1. In combinations already formed in Latin in the senses above-mentioned; rarely in words formed in Eng. itself on Latin elements; e.g. **a.** *obedience*, *obversion*; **b.** *object*, *occur*, *opponent*, *opposite*; **c.** *obduce*, *occident*; **d.** *obdulcorate*, *obdurate.*

2. In mod. scientific Latin, and hence in Eng., in Botany, etc., *ob-* is prefixed to adjs. in the sense 'inversely', or 'in the opposite direction'; e.g. *obcordātus* (Linnæus), *obcordate*, i.e. cordate with the base or broad end presented; *obovate*, ovate or egg-shaped with the wider end presented; *obtriangular*, triangular with the apex downward. See below OBCLAVATE to OBTURBINATE.

This is not an ancient L. use, where *ob-* was rarely combined with an adj., the chief example being *oblongus* OBLONG, which could hardly be in sense the model for these words. Apparently the prefix represents the *ob-* of the adv. *obversè* OBVERSELY, and is an abridged representation of that word.

oba ('ɒbə). *W. Afr.* Also **obba.** [Yoruba.] The title of the ruler of the ancient West African kingdom of Benin, now part of Nigeria, whose power used to be absolute. Now revived as the title of a local chief.

1903 H. L. ROTH *Great Benin* xi. 118 The Obba kindly promised to send a messenger round with orders. **1906** R. E. DENNETT *At Back of Black Man's Mind* xvii. 175 The OBA's throne or chair was placed on a platform of mud three steps above the ordinary level of the ground. **1926** P. A. TALBOT *Peoples S. Nigeria* I. iv. 155 The land of Southern Nigeria, including the kingdom of Benin, was discovered by Ruy de Sequeira. The Portuguese were presented by the Obba with ..carved wooden platters. **1936** J. U. EGHAREVBA *Short Hist. Benin* i. 8 The oracle declared..the senior wife of the Oba, to be the cause. **1957** W. M. HAILEY *Afr. Survey* (rev. ed.) ii. 35 The Yoruba kingdoms in Nigeria were..highly centralized... The rulers, generally known as Obas, were traditionally sacred persons. **1967** W. SOYINKA *Kongi's Harvest* 4 When an Oba stops the procession And squats on the wayside, It's on an urgent matter. **1972** R. N. HENDERSON *King in Every Man* I. ii. 43 The first king or oba, Eweka I, whose regalia came from the Yoruba city of Ife. **1975** *Times* 16 July 77/5 A massive Benin bronze head of an oba. **1976** *Nigerian Herald* 20 July 4/5 The Deji suggested that a law should be made by the federal military government to leave the selection and appointment of obas and chiefs to those who were versed in the custom culture of the community concerned as a means to curb chieftaincy wranglings in the country. **1976** *Sunday Times* (Lagos) 1 Aug. 24/3 It is the turn of this ruling house to provide an Oba for the town.

†**ob'acerate**, *v. Obs. rare.* [f. ppl. stem of L. *obacerāre* to contradict. (Derived according to some Lat. grammarians from *acus, acer-* chaff.)] Hence †**obace'ration**, a stopping one's mouth.

1656 BLOUNT *Glossogr.*, *Obacerate*, to stop ones mouth, that he cannot tell out his tale. **1658** PHILLIPS, *Obaceration.*

obaie, obs. form of OBEY.

†**obak**, obs. form of ABACK: cf. O *prep.*¹

1435 MISYN *Fire of Love* 3 All þinges putt o-bak. *c* **1450** *St. Cuthbert* (Surtees) 5084 His pryde was put obak.

obambulate (ɒ'bæmbjʊleɪt), *v. rare.* [f. ppl. stem of L. *obambulāre*, f. *ob-* (OB-) + *ambulare* to walk.] *intr.* To walk about; to wander hither and thither.

1614–15 BOYS *Wks.* (1622) 597 Soules departed..doe not obambulate and wander vp and downe, but remaine in places of happinesse or vnhappinesse. **1633** EARL MANCH. *Al Mondo* (1636) 100 In the interim the Soule doth not wander and obambulate. **1694** MOTTEUX *Rabelais* v. (1737) 231 We..must still obambulate, Sequacious of the Court.

So **obambu'lation**, walking to and fro; **ob'ambulatory** *a.*, habitually walking about, itinerant.

1600 O. E. (M. SUTCLIFFE) *Repl. Libel* v. 100 Their stationarie obambulations about the limits of parishes. **1610** BOYS *Wks.* (1622) 375 Their obambulations of spirits and apparitions of dead men. **1818** J. BROWN *Psyche* 107 Obambulation much befriends The point for which a man contends. **1855** CHAMIER *My Travels* III. i. 16 Many obambulatory merchants of such wares.

‖**obang** (ˈəʊbæŋ). Also 7 **oeban.** [Jap. *ô-ban*, f. *ô* great + *ban* (a. Chinese *fan*) sheet, division: cf. KOBANG.] A gold coin formerly current in Japan, of an oblong form rounded at the corners, and equal in value to ten kobangs.

1662 J. DAVIES tr. *Mandelslo's Trav.* II. (1669) 147 A thousand *Oebans* of Gold, which amount to forty seven thousand *Thayls*, or crowns. **1863** *Reader* 21 Nov. 595 The half-obang is almost literally an obang, which is elliptic in form, cut in half. **1890** *Daily News* 11 Oct. 5/4 The next in size to this unwieldy coin is the Japanese 'obang', which weighs rather more than two ounces and a half, about equal to ten English sovereigns.

Obanian (əʊˈbeɪnɪən), *a. Archæol.* [f. the name of the Scottish burgh of *Oban*, Strathclyde (formerly Argyllshire).] Applied to a culture of the mesolithic period for which most evidence is found in the neighbourhood of Oban. Also as *sb.*, the Obanian culture or a person living in this culture.

1942 H. L. MOVIUS *Irish Stone Age* II. iii. 180 With the changing environment certain new forms were evolved to meet the new needs, but lack of flint or other easily worked rocks hampered cultural progress. It is proposed to call this culture the *Obanian*, after the type site in Argyllshire. *Ibid.*, The Obanian was discovered in 1879 by Symington Grieve (1883) at Caisteal-nan-Gillean, a large kitchen-midden 150 feet in diameter on the Island of Oronsay, Argyllshire. *Ibid.*, At Caisteal-nan-Gillean a large series of stone, bone and antler implements was found, typical of the Obanian culture. **1957** V. G. CHILDE *Dawn European Civilization* (ed. 6) i. 5 On the south-west coast of Scotland..the industry..is distinctive enough to be regarded as a new culture, 'the Obanian', not certainly descended from the French Azilian. **1958** *Proc. Soc. Antiquaries Scot.* LXXXIX. 91 (*heading*) Notes on the Obanian with special reference to antler- and bone-work. **1959** *Chambers's Encycl.* V. 452/1 The contents of the middens show that the Obanians hunted red and roe deer [etc.]. **1963** *Field Archaeol.* (Ordnance Survey) (ed. 4) 24 The Obanians are found on the west coast and in the islands. **1963** E. S. WOOD *Collins Field Guide Archaeol.* iv. 52 The old description of the Obanian culture, based on hunting, and on fish and molluscs, as a movement of the mesolithic people called Azilian, from south-west Europe, no longer holds. **1970** BRAY & TRUMP *Dict. Archaeol.* 165/1 *Obanian culture*... The sites are rock-shelters, and also shell middens on post-glacial raised beaches. The way of life was adapted to coastal conditions. Flintwork is scarce, but diagnostic tools include barbed spears and stone limpet-picks.

†**ob'armate**, *v. Obs. rare*$^{-0}$. [f. ppl. stem of L. *obarmāre* to arm against.] *trans.* To arm (Cockeram, 1623). Hence †**obar'mation**, an arming (Ibid.).

1658 PHILLIPS, *Obarmation*, an arming against.

‖**o'barni, o'barne.** *Obs.* [Russ. *obvarnyi*, scalded, prepared by scalding.] In full, ***mead obarni***, i.e. 'scalded mead', a drink used in Russia, and known in England *c* 1600.

1598 HAKLUYT *Voy.* I. 461 One veather of sodden mead called *Obarni*. **1609** *Pimlyco* C iv b, With spiced Meades.. As Meade Obarne, and Meade Cherunck. **1616** B. JONSON *Devil an Ass* I. i, Chimney-sweepers [Are got] To their tobacco, and strong-waters, Hum, Meath, and Obarni.

obay(e, obbet, -it, -yt, obs. forms of OBEY, OBIT.

obba, var. OBA.

obbley, variant of OBLEY *Obs.*

‖**obbligato** (obbliˈgato, ɒblɪˈgɑːtəʊ), *a.* (*sb.*) *Mus.* Often **obligato**. [a. It. *obbligato*, formerly *obligato*, obliged, obligatory.]

A. *adj.* Indispensable; that cannot be omitted: applied to a part essential to the completeness of a composition (or to the instrument on which such a part is played); esp. to an accompaniment having an independent value. (Opposed to *ad libitum*.) Also *transf.* indispensable; forced, compulsory.

[**1724** *Explic. For. Wds. in Mus. Bks.* 50 *Obligata* Necessary, Expressly, or on Purpose. **1730–6** BAILEY (folio), *Obligati*, signifies for, or on purpose, or necessary; as *doi violin obligati*, on purpose for two violins.] **1794** MATHIAS *Purs. Lit.* (1798) 342 And with Raimondi's fire, and warlike art, Play'd some French General's *obligato* part. **1821** COL. HAWKER *Diary* (1893) I. 234 He added an obbligato accompaniment of a large hand-bell. **1861** GEO. ELIOT *Let.* 13 Apr. (1954) III. 405 Don't think about reading Silas Marner, just because it is come out. I hate obligato reading and obligato talk about my books. **1878** E. J. HOPKINS in Grove *Dict. Mus.* I. 20 An accompaniment may be either 'Ad libitum' or 'Obligato'.. It is said to be Obligato when.. it forms an integral part of the composition.

B. *sb.* An obbligato part or accompaniment. Also *transf.*

1845 E. HOLMES *Mozart* 276 The scena and rondo, *Non temer*, with pianoforte *obligato*. **1861** *Times* 26 Aug., He has furnished a sort of 'obbligato', or independent part. **1888** KIPLING *Departmental Ditties* (ed. 3) 58 A Wagner *obbligato*, *scherzo*, double-hand *staccato*, Played..by the clacking tonga-bar. **1921** G. HOPKINS *City in Foreground* i. 15 He took the easiest way, which was to supply a gentle *obbligato* to the inspired melody of his companion's speech. **1955** *Times* 21 May 6/5 Lady Megan..was wreathed in smiles and her chuckle was a frequent obbligato. **1972** A. ROUDYBUSH *Sybaritic Death* (1974) ix. 82 Her complaints.. formed a sort of obbligato to their drive.

obbo (ˈɒbəʊ). *slang.* Also **obo.** [Abbrev. of OBSERVATION: cf. -O^{2}]. Observation, esp. in police work. In military use *ellipt.* for *observation balloon.*

1925 FRASER & GIBBONS *Soldier & Sailor Words* 212 *Obbo*, observation balloon. **1933** C. E. LEACH *On Top of Underworld* 9, I am still 'on the trail', like you, and my thoughts hark back to the long weary days and nights of 'obbo' (observation) and shadowing. **1940** PARTRIDGE *Slang* 192 An observation balloon is an *obbo* or a *sausage*. **1968** BUSBY & HOLTHAM *Main Line Kill* vi. 68 Now I got a fix on the place I got to do some obo first. Get the lie of the land. **1972** 'B. GRAEME' *Tomorrow's Yesterday* xi. 117 We're keeping a man, suspected of robbery..under obbo. **1973** D. LEES *Rape of Quiet Town* iv. 68, I went to keep obbo for a bit.

obbraid, corrupt form of UPBRAID.

†**obcæcate**, *a. Obs.* Also 6 obse-, 6–7 obce-. [ad. L. *obcæcāt-us*, pa. pple. of *obcæcāre* or *occæcāre* to blind, f. *ob-* (OB- 1 b) + *cæcāre* to blind, *cæcus* blind. See also OCCÆCATE *v.*] Blinded; blind; destitute of mental or spiritual vision. So †**obcæcated** (-cec-) *a.*, in same sense; †**obcæcation** (-cec-), blinded condition; mental or spiritual blindness.

a **1568** A. KID in *Bannatyne MS.* (1875) 263/40 And prince of iustice the verry image suld be, The quhilk but vertew is blind and obsecat. **1579** FULKE *Heskins' Parl.* 121 His obsecate and blind enemies. **1627–77** FELTHAM *Resolves* II. lxiii. 293 Neither was their obduration nor their obcecation less. *a* **1631** DONNE *Serm.* V. 125 A heavy blindness and obcæcation. **1641** *Family of Love* in *Harl. Misc.* (Malham) IV. 447 Let not us persuade ourselves.. that our great god Cupid is obcecated. **1696** EVELYN in *Bentley's Corr.* (1842) I. 115 The fillets, with which the Iunto's eyes are banded..to represent their Obcæcation.

obcess, obs. (erron.) form of OBSESS.

obclavate (ɒbˈkleɪvət), *a. Nat. Hist.* [See OB- 2.] Inversely clavate; club-shaped with the thickened part at the base.

1857 in MAYNE *Expos. Lex.*

obclude, var. OCCLUDE *v.*

obcompressed (ɒbkəmˈprɛst), *a. Nat. Hist.* [See OB- 2.] Compressed or flattened in the opposite of the usual direction: see quots.

1857 MAYNE *Expos. Lex.*, *Obcompressus, Bot.* Applied by H. Cassini to the ovary and seeds of the *Synantheræ* [= *Compositæ*], when their greater diameter is from right to left, as in the *Coreopsis*: obcompressed. **1892** *Syd. Soc. Lex.*, *Obcompressed*, flattened anteriorly.

obconic (ɒbˈkɒnɪk), *a. Nat. Hist.* = next.

1819 SAMOUELLE *Entomol. Compend.* 153 *Broscus*..labial palpi with their fourth joint obconic. **1847** HARDY in *Proc. Berw. Nat. Club* II. No. 5. 235 Antennæ..clavate, second and third joints obconic.

obconical (ɒbˈkɒnɪkəl), *a.* Chiefly *Nat. Hist.* [See OB- 2.] Inversely conical; of the form of a cone with the base upward or outward.

1806 GALPINE *Brit. Bot.* 1 *Salicornia*... Joints compressed, emarginate; internodes obconical. **1828** STARK *Elem. Nat. Hist.* II. 298 Antennæ with obconical joints. **1872** OLIVER *Elem. Bot.* II. 133 Carpels..immersed in a large, obconical receptacle.

obcordate (ɒbˈkɔːdət), *a. Nat. Hist.* [See OB- 2.] Inversely cordate; heart-shaped, with the apex serving as base or point of attachment.

1775 J. JENKINSON *Gen. & Specif. Descr. Br. Pl.* Gloss., *Obcordate*, heart-shaped with the *apex* downwards. **1819** SAMOUELLE *Entomol. Compend.* 153 Thorax obcordate, its base very narrow or pedunculated. **1896** EDMONDS *Bot. for Beginners* vi. 42 In the Wood Sorrel we have an obcordate, or inversely heart-shaped leaf.

So **ob'cordiform** *a.* = prec.

1857 in MAYNE *Expos. Lex.* **1892** in *Syd. Soc. Lex.*

obcuneate (ɒbˈkjuːniːət), *a. Nat. Hist.* [See OB- 2.] Inversely cuneate; wedge-shaped, with the thin end at the base of the organ or part.

1870 HOOKER *Stud. Flora* 166 Segments of submerged leaves obcuneate. *Ibid.* 346 Bracts of fruiting catkins broadly obcuneate.

obcurrent, obs. variant of OCCURRENT.

obdeltoid (ɒbˈdɛltɔɪd), *a. Nat. Hist.* [See OB- 2.] Inversely deltoid; of a triangular form, with the apex downward, or at the base of the organ or part.

1891 in *Cent. Dict.*

obdiplostemonous (ɒbdɪpləʊˈstiːmənəs), *a. Bot.* [See OB- 2.] Diplostemonous with the disposition of the two stamen-whorls reversed; having the stamens of the outer whorl opposite to, and those of the inner whorl alternate with, the petals. Hence **obdiplo'stemony**, the condition of being obdiplostemonous.

1880 GRAY *Struct. Bot.* vi. §3. 198 It..occurs that the antipetalous stamens are more or less exterior in insertion, and then the carpels, when isomerous, are alternate with the inner and antisepalous stamens, and therefore opposite the petals... This arrangement takes the name of Obdiplostemony. **1882** *Nature* 7 Dec. 126 The..curious 'obdiplostemonous' arrangement in the..genus *Platytheca*. **1888** HENSLOW *Origin Floral Struct.* xx. 189 In..most.. genera..obdiplostemony..is..due to the petaline whorl of filaments being, so to say, thrust outside the level of the calycine whorl by the protruding..bases of the carpels.

obdormition (ɒbdɔːˈmɪʃən). [ad. L. *obdormītiōn-em*, n. of action from *obdormīre* to fall asleep, f. *ob-* (OB- 1 d) + *dormīre* to sleep.]

†**1.** A falling asleep, or the condition of being asleep. *Obs. rare*$^{-1}$.

1634 BP. HALL *Contempl., N.T.* IV. xxxii, A peaceable obdormition in thy bed of ease and honour.

2. Numbness of a limb, etc. due to pressure on a nerve; the condition of being 'asleep'. *rare*$^{-0}$.

1857 in MAYNE *Expos. Lex.* **1886** in THOMAS *Med. Dict.*

†**ob'duce**, *v. Obs.* [ad. L. *obdūc-ĕre* to draw over, cover over, f. *ob-* (OB- 1 c) + *ducĕre* to lead, draw.]

1. *trans.* To cover, envelop.

1657 TOMLINSON *Renou's Disp.* 223 This plant is.. obduced on every side with long strait..leaves. **1709** BLAIR in *Phil. Trans.* XXVII. 71 A certain Crust..obducing the Cutis. *Ibid.* 118 Cellules..obduc'd with a thin Membrane.

2. To draw or put over as a covering.

a **1677** HALE *Prim. Orig. Man.* I. ii. 65 A Cortex that is obduced over the Cutis, as in Elephants.

ob'duct, *v.* [f. L. *obduct-*, ppl. stem of *obdūcĕre*: see prec.; cf. INDUCT.] †**1.** *trans.* = prec. 1. *Obs.*

1623 COCKERAM, *Obduct*, to couer. **1646** SIR T. BROWNE *Pseud. Ep.* IV. v. 188 When the Liver is..so obducted and covered with thick skins, that it cannot diffuse its virtue.

2. *Geol.* To cause to undergo obduction. Hence **ob'ducted** *ppl. a.*

1971 R. G. COLEMAN in *Jrnl. Geophysical Res.* LXXVI. 1216/2 Parts of the oceanic crust have been overthrust (obducted) onto thin continental edges. **1974** *Nature* 1 Mar. 38/2 The ophiolites of west Newfoundland and the Burlington Peninsula represent obducted oceanic lithosphere. *Ibid.* 20 Sept. 259/1 With the development of actual collision between continental blocks a period of tectogenesis and orogenesis (uplift) results in F_3 flexuring of the subducted lithosphere, slivers of which are consequently overthrust (obducted) on to the 'active' continental block.

ob'duction. [ad. L. *obductiōn-em*, n. of action f. *obdūcĕre*: see OBDUCE.] †**1.** The action of covering or enveloping. *Obs.*

In quot. 1609 repr. L. *obductio* of the Vulgate, tr. Gr. ἐπαγωγή of the LXX., variously explained in the versions. **1578** BANISTER *Hist. Man* I. 34 A strong Ligament within the ioynt..beside the outward obductions, and clothynges with Ligamentes. **1609** BIBLE (Douay) *Ecclus.* ii. 2 Make no hast in the time of obduction. **1623** COCKERAM, *Obduction*, a couering. **1656** BLOUNT *Glossogr.*, *Obduction*, a covering or laying over.

2. *Geol.* The movement of a lithospheric plate sideways and upwards over the margin of an adjacent plate.

1971 R. G. COLEMAN in *Jrnl. Geophysical Res.* LXXVI. 1216/2 According to Davies.., the ophiolites represent a slab of oceanic crust and mantle emplaced in Cretaceous or Eocene time by overthrusting (obduction) oceanic crust onto the continental crust. **1972** *Rep. 24th Internat. Geol. Congr.* III. 409 The obduction zone is..an upthrust of the oceanic crust and mantle..mostly of a marginal sea (small ocean basin). **1972** *Nature* 31 Mar. 222/2 The Alpine orogeny culminated with the collision between the continental plates of Eurasia and Africa and was probably preceded by subduction or obduction of the Tethyan plate along the European continental margin. **1975** *Ibid.* 20 Feb. 615/2 Ophiolite emplacement is integrally associated with plate subduction, either by the accretion of oceanic crust on to the wall of the upper plate (in oceanic trenches) or by the bodily thrusting (obduction) of the oceanic crust on to a continental margin.

†**ob'dulcorate**, *v. Obs. rare.* [f. OB- 1 d + late L. *dulcōrāre* to sweeten, f. *dulcōr-em* sweetness, f. *dulc-is* sweet: cf. L. *obdulcāre*.] *trans.* To sweeten.

1657 TOMLINSON *Renou's Disp.* 36 Such medicaments are obdulcorated with cordial electuaries.

obduracy (ˈɒbdjʊrəsɪ, əbˈdjʊərəsɪ). [f. OBDURATE: see -ACY 3, and cf. late L. *obdūrātio*.] The state or quality of being obdurate.

1. Stubbornness, obstinacy; obstinate hardness of heart, relentlessness; persistence in evil.

1597 SHAKS. *2 Hen. IV*, II. ii. 50 Thou think'st me as farre in the Diuels Booke, as thou, and Falstaffe, for obduracie and persistencie. **1670** G. H. *Hist. Cardinals* II. II. 161 He is so constant in his resolutions, that it passes almost to obduracy. **1720** WELTON *Suffer. Son of God* II. xvi. 436 To break the Obduracy of my Harden'd and ungrateful Heart. **1855** MILMAN *Lat. Chr.* (1864) I. II. iv. 238 If Rome at times was courted with promising submission, at others it was opposed with inflexible obduracy.

2. The state of being physically hardened. *rare.*

1822–34 *Good's Study Med.* (ed. 4) IV. 514 They [caruncles] are found to acquire the obduracy of a rigid scirrhus.

obdurate ('ɒbdjʊrət, əb'djʊərət), *a.* [ad. L. *obdūrāt-us* hardened, hardened in heart, pa. pple. of *obdūrāre*: see next.]

1. a. Hardened in wickedness or sin; persistently impenitent; stubbornly resisting, or insensible to, moral influence.

c 1440 *Jacob's Well* 126 þei be so obdurate in here coueytise. 1558 Bp. Watson *Sev. Sacram.* xvi. 98 What obdurate vnkindness is this, not to recognise these so great benefites. 1667 Milton *P.L.* vi. 790 What..Wonders move th' obdurate to relent? 1720 Welton *Suffer. Son of God* I. iv. 76 Mollifie and Soften the Hardness of my Obdurate Heart. 1830 Scott *Demonol.* x. 366 The obdurate conscience of the old sinner.

absol. as *sb.* 1830 W. Phillips *Mt. Sinai* iv. 177 Beholding ..With righteous wrath such obdurates.

b. Hardened, or hardening oneself, against persuasion, entreaty, the sentiment of pity, etc.; stubborn, obstinate, unyielding, inflexible, relentless, hard-hearted, inexorable.

1586 Marlowe *1st Pt. Tamburl.* v. i, If humble suits or imprecations..Might have entreated your obdurate breasts. 1593 Shaks. *3 Hen. VI*, i. iv. 142 Women are soft, milde, pittifull, and flexible; Thou, sterne, obdurate, flintie, rough, remorselesse. 1692 Dryden *St. Euremont's Ess.* 187 The miserable condition of old King Priam touches the most obdurate Soul. 1751 Johnson *Rambler* No. 171 ¶8 To supplicate obdurate brutality, was hopeless. 1818 Shelley *Rev. Islam* iv. ix, But custom maketh blind and obdurate The loftiest hearts. 1840 Barham *Ingol. Leg.*, *Look at Clock* xix, Why the fair was obdurate None knows,—to be sure it Was said she was setting her cap at the Curate. 1866 Mrs. H. Wood *St. Martin's Eve* xxv. (1874) 311 She was compelled to be more obdurate than even her father had been.

c. *fig.* of things.

1727 Swift *Let. Eng. Tongue* Wks. 1755 II. i. 188 They have joined the most obdurate consonants without one intervening vowel. 1804 Abernethy *Surg. Obs.* 69 This obdurate and destructive disease. 1814 Cary *Dante, Inf.* xxxiii, We all were silent. Ah, obdurate earth! 1840 Dickens *Old C. Shop* xl, Said Kit, hammering stoutly at an obdurate nail.

†**2.** Physically hardened or hard. *Obs.*

1597 A. M. tr. *Guillemeau's Fr. Chirurg.* 10/2 The fissures are filled vp with some obdurate substance and callositye. *c* 1600 Norden *Spec. Brit., Cornw.* (1728) 11 Tynn..the owre thereof beyng an obdurate stone spred in the veynes of the mountaynes. 1743 tr. *Heister's Surg.* 394 Attended with an obdurate Callus. 1784 Cowper *Task* i. 52 Well-tann'd hides, Obdurate and unyielding.

b. *transf.* Harsh or disagreeable to the senses. *Obs. rare.*

1647 H. More *Song of Soul* i. ii. cxxiii, I mean not Natures harsh obdurate light.

obdurate ('ɒbdjʊreɪt, əb'djʊəreɪt), *v.* [f. obdurate *a.*, or L. *obdūrāt-*, ppl. stem of *obdūrāre* to harden, harden in heart, f. *ob-* (ob- 1 b) + *dūrāre* to harden.]

1. *trans.* To make obdurate, to harden in wickedness, or against moral influence, entreaty, etc.; to make stubborn or obstinate; to harden the heart of, make relentless or pitiless.

a 1540 Barnes *Wks.* (1573) 279/2 The holy Ghost sayth, I will obdurate the hart of Pharao. 1605 J. Dove *Confut. Atheism* 1 [They] haue so hardned and obdurated them selues, that they haue no sence or feeling. 1651 Howell *Venice* 44 She [Venice] is obdurated with the same kind of vigor and vertu as old Rome. 1662 Petty *Taxes* 58 Most of the punishments..are but shame..which shame for ever after obdurates the offender. 1710 [see obdurated below]. 1860 Pusey *Min. Proph.* 84 Not..from God, dooming to perdition, reprobating, obdurating, damning, but from man ..obduring or hardening himself in sin.

2. To harden physically. *Obs. rare.*

1597 [see obdurated below]. 1599 A. M. tr. *Gabelhouer's Bk. Physicke* 4/2 Sprede it on two papers..and in the night it will obdurate itselfe. 1657 Tomlinson *Renou's Disp.* 10 So as either too much to obdurate or mollify.

†**3.** *intr.* To become hard. *Obs. rare.*

1659 D. Pell *Impr. Sea* 263 This tree brings forth blossomes, first white, then green, afterwards red, and then obdurates, from whence come the cloves.

Hence **'obdurated** *ppl. a.*

1597 A. M. tr. *Guillemeau's Fr. Chirurg.* 20/2 The debilest syde of the obdurated liver or milte. 1599 —— tr. *Gabelhouer's Bk. Physicke* 248/2 When as a woman getteth an obduratede Breste. 1710 *Acc. Last Distemp. Tom Whigg* ii. 55 Our Young, and not yet Obdurated Kitt Catt. 1874 Pusey *Lent. Serm.* 442 The obstinacy of an obdurated will.

obdurately (see the adj.), *adv.* [f. obdurate *a.* + -ly².] In an obdurate manner; stubbornly; relentlessly.

a 1711 Ken *Hymnotheo* Poet. Wks. III. 33 Israel, grown obdurately profane. 1838 Dickens *Nich. Nick.* xv, Still Mr. Lillyvick, regardless of the siren, cried obdurately [etc.]. 1865 Trollope *Belton Est.* x. 115 Shut your doors obdurately against [them].

obdurateness (see the adj.). [f. as prec. + -ness.] The state or quality or being obdurate.

1. = obduracy 1.

1618 Gainsford *Perk. Warbeck* in *Select. fr. Harl. Misc.* (1793) 74 If the duchess continued in her obdurateness, and would not desist from her feminine rages, and terrible prosecutions. 1708 *Brit. Apollo* No. 23. 3/1 With fervent heat m' obdurateness he blames. 1720 Welton *Suffer. Son of God* II. xix. 532 How often have I felt this Obdurateness of Heart within!

2. = obduracy 2. *rare.*

1597 A. M. tr. *Guillemeau's Fr. Chirurg.* 44/1 [Bandages] must be softe..because through the obduratnes therof, they might hurte that parte. 1657 Tomlinson *Renou's Disp.* 146 It presently acquired a stony obdurateness.

obduration (ɒbdjʊ'reɪʃən). [ad. L. *obdūrātiōn-em* hardening, n. of action from *obdūrāre* to harden.] The action or fact of hardening, or condition of being hardened.

1. A hardening, or condition of being hardened, in sin or wickedness; a making or becoming stubborn, obstinate, or insensible to moral influence; *rarely*, a becoming, or condition of having become, relentless or insensible to entreaty (quots. 1494, 1526).

1494 Fabyan *Chron.* vii. 553 Than the Gaunteners supprysyd with more obduracion of herte agayn theyr prynce, made theym a capytayne namyd Phylyp Artyuele. 1526 *Pilgr. Perf.* (W. de W. 1531) 90 b, Obduracion or vnpitefulnes. 1585 Parsons *Chr. Exerc.* ii. vi. 367 This.. was the obduration of Pharao. 1647 M. Hudson *Div. Right Govt.* i. ii. 7 God doth work..upon the will, either by way of Obduration, or by way of Mollification and conversion. 1728 Ramsay *General Mistake* 20 Obduration follows public shame. 1778 Bp. Lowth *Isaiah* Notes (ed. 12) 182 The obduration of the Jews of that age. 1882–3 Schaff *Encycl. Relig. Knowl.* III. 1740/1 Falling under that judgment of obduration of which Isaiah speaks.

2. Physical hardening. *rare.*

1654 Gayton *Pleas. Notes* iii. vii. 113 The obduration of his Posteriors,..almost petrified by continuall hardnings upon his Asses bare backe. 1822–34 *Good's Study Med.* (ed. 4) IV. 231 As the distension and obduration increase.

†**obdu'ratious**, *a. Obs. rare*⁻¹. [f. obduration: see -ious.] Characterized by or showing obduration; obdurate.

1672 Baxter *Bagshaw's Scand.* i. 4, I had been guilty of an obdurateous self-saving, and perfidious silence.

†**obdure** (əb'djʊə(r)), *a. Obs.* (exc. *arch.*) [f. ob- 1 b + *dūr-us* hard: after L. *obdūrāre*: see next.]

1. = obdurate *a.* 1.

1608 Heywood *Lucrece* iv. ii. Wks. 1874 V. 219 My doors the day time to my friends are free, But in the night the obdure gates are lesse kinde. 1639 G. Daniel *Ecclus.* xvi. 45 Hee made obdure the heart of yᵉ proud King Pharoh. 1655 Heywood & Rowley *Fortune by Land & Sea* i. ii. Wks. 1874 VI. 375 The boy's inflexible, and I obdure. 1844 Mrs. Browning *Sonn.*, *Meaning of the Look*, When thy deathly need is obdurest [*later edd.* dreariest].

2. = obdurate *a.* 2.

1624 Quarles *Sion's Sonn.* xxiv. 1632 —— *Div. Fancies* ii. xiv. (1660) 54 Gods sacred Word is like the Lamp of Day, Which softens wax, but makes obdure the clay.

Hence †**ob'durely** *adv.*; †**ob'dureness**.

1624 Heywood *Gunaik.* i. 55 The fates For her obdurenesse turn'd her into stone. 1634 Bp. Hall *Contempl.*, *N.T.* iv. *Christ Betrayed*, Oh the sottishnesse and obdurenesse of this sonne of perdition! 1848 Lytton *K. Arthur* ix. civ, The morsels least obdurely tough.

obdure (əb'djʊə(r)), *v.* Now *rare* or *Obs.* [ad. L. *obdūrā-re* to harden, to render or become hard; f. *ob-* (ob- 1 b) + *dūrāre* to harden, f. *dūr-us* hard.]

1. *trans.* = obdurate *v.* 1. (In quots. 1640 in good sense: To strengthen, fortify, 'steel'.)

1598 Yong *Diana* 24 Now mollifie thy dire Hardnes and brest of thine so much obdured. 1633 Heywood *Eng. Trav.* v. Wks. 1874 IV. 90 Hath..sinne so obdur'd thy heart? 1640 Bp. Hall *Chr. Moder.* (Ward) 20/1 We may not so obdure ourselves as to be like the Spartan boys, who would not so much as change a countenance at their beating. *Ibid.* 23/2 It concerns a wise man to obdure himself against these weak fears. 1678 R. Barclay *Apol. Quakers* v. §18. 153 God seems..to have obdur'd their Hearts, to force them unto great Sins. 1860 [see obdurate *v.* 1].

†**2.** To harden physically; = obdurate *v.* 2.

1624 Heywood *Gunaik.* i. 55 A dragon they espie Obdur'd to stone. 1665 Sir T. Herbert *Trav.* (1677) 112 Brick..hardned by the Sun, which makes them..no less solid and usefull than those the Fire obdures.

†**3.** *intr.* **a.** To become hard. **b.** To become or remain obdurate; to persist stubbornly. *Obs.*

1609 Heywood *Brit. Troy* vi. ii, Sencelesse of good as stones they soone obdure. 1641 'Smectymnuus' *Answ.* Post. (1653) 88 Becket obdures, denies that the..Courts have authoritie to judge him. *c* 1750 Shenstone *Ruin'd Abbey* 213 Resolute in wrongs the priest obdur'd.

Hence †**ob'during** *vbl. sb.*

1643 Milton *Divorce* ii. xx, He..would little perplex his thought for the obduring of nine hundred and ninety such as will dayly take worse liberties.

obdured (əb'djʊəd, *poet.* əb'djʊərɪd), *ppl. a.* Now *rare* or *Obs.* [pa. pple. of prec. vb., after L. *obdūrātus* obdurated.]

1. = obdurate *a.* 1.

1585 Jas. I. *Ess. Poesie* (Arb.) 53 To ignorants obdurde, quhair wilful errour lyis. *a* 1619 Fotherby *Atheom.* i. xv. §2 (1622) 154 A notable mirrour of obdured vngodlinesse. 1649 Bp. Hall *Cases Consc.* iii. ix. (1654) 252 Denouncing judgement to the unbeleeving and obdured sinner. 1667 Milton *P.L.* ii. 568 Arm th' obdured brest With stubborn patience as with triple steel. 1830 Carlyle *Richter* in *Misc. Ess.* (1872) III. 40 A man with such obdured Stoicism like triple steel round his breast.

†**2.** = obdurate *a.* 2. *rare.*

1619 H. Hutton *Follie's Anat.* (Percy Soc.) 9, I could.. Reade them a lecture should their vice imprint With sable lines in the obdured flint.

Hence †**ob'duredness**, obdurateness.

1633 Bp. Hall *Hard Texts, N.T.* 183 With further obduredness of heart. *a* 1656 —— *Specialities Life* Rem. Wks. (1660) 13 The obduredness and hopeless condition of that man. 1652 Urquhart *Jewel* Wks. (1834) 180 Their implacable obduredness, and unreclaimability of nature.

†**ob'durity.** *Obs. rare.* [f. obdure *a.* + -ity: cf. durity.] Hardness: obduracy.

c 1600 Norden *Spec. Brit., Cornw.* (1728) 18 A stone called a Moar-stone... Notwithstanding their naturall obduritie, the Countrie people haue a deuice to cleeue them. 1653 F. G. tr. *Scuderi's Artamenes* (1655) IV. viii. ii. 113 When you discover any obdurity or inhumanity in her. 1657 Tomlinson *Renou's Disp.* 116 Because of their obdurity and density they preserve the strength of those medicaments.

obe (əʊb). *Gr. Hist.* [ad. Gr. *ὠβά*.] A village or district in ancient Laconia; a subdivision of an original *φυλή* or clan.

1835 Thirlwall *Greece* viii. I. 315 An obe, which originally signified a village or district. *a* 1873 Lytton *Pausanias* iv. v, The divisions or obes acknowledged by the State.

‖**obeah** ('əʊbiːə), **obi** ('əʊbɪ). Also 8 obia, 9 obea, obeeyah. [A West Africa word: cf. Efik *ubio*, 'a thing, or mixture of things, put in the ground, as a charm to cause sickness or death; the Obeah of the West Indies' (Goldie *Dict. of Efik* 1874). With the senses cf. those of juju. 'Also the base of Twi ɔ-*bayifó*, witch, wizard, sorcerer (more literally sorcery-man, "obeah-man", since *-fó* means *person*).' (Cassidy & Le Page *Dict. Jamaican Eng.* 1967).]

1. An amulet, charm, or fetish used by Negroes for magical purposes.

1796 Stedman *Surinam* II. xx. 89 A superstitious *obia* or amulet tied about his neck. *Ibid.* (1813) II. xxix. 360 To whom he sells his obias or amulets, in order to make them invulnerable.

2. A kind of pretended sorcery or witchcraft practised by the Negroes in Africa, a form of which survives in the West Indies and neighbouring countries.

1760 *Jrnls. Assembly Jamaica* 16 Dec. (1798) V. 245/1 The engrossed bill to remedy the evils arising from irregular assemblies of slaves..and for preventing the practice of *obeah*. 1764 Grainger *Sugar Cane* iv. 381 In Obia, all the sons of sable Afric trust. 1802 Mar. Edgeworth *Grateful Negro* (1832) 246 *note*, Strict investigation..has..been made after the professors of Obi. *a* 1818 M. G. Lewis *Jrnl. W. Ind.* (1834) 94 The belief in Obeah is now greatly weakened. 1823 T. Roughley *Jamaica Planter's Guide* ii. 83 Perhaps the horrid and abominable practice of Obea is carried on, dismembering and disabling one another. 1889 H. J. Bell *Obeah*; *Witchcraft in W. Indies* i. 9 Before the emancipation..the practice of Obeah was rampant in all the West Indian Colonies. 1889 *Pall Mall G.*, The awful mysteries of Obeeyah (*vulgo* Obi) and the powers possessed by the Obeeyah women of those days, were sufficiently known to all the slave-traders of the West Coast. 1930 J. J. Williams *Hebrewisms W. Afr.* 17 The word Obeah itself is really the Ashanti Obayifo, a witch or rather more properly, ..a wizard, being derived from bayi, sorcery. 1934 J. Rhys *Voy. in Dark* iii. iv. 192 Anne Chewett used to say that it's haunted and obeah—she had been in gaol for obeah. 1934 *Times Lit. Suppl.* 19 July 502/4 On the subject of obia (which a Jamaican negro will never mention) they are quite unreserved. 1954 *Caribbean Q.* III. i. 5 Obeah has been prohibited by law, and is always spoken of with a laugh; but the laughter is..never sneering. 1957 *Times Lit. Suppl.* 2 May 237/3 You have also to reckon with *obeah* (in the shape of a mongrel puppy) with the other candidate Preacher, who wickedly distorts the slogan 'Vote Harbans or Die'. 1963 G. J. McCall in A. Dundes *Mother Wit* (1973) 420/1 'Hoodoo' ..corresponding to *vodun* ('voodoo') and *obeah* in Haiti.

3. *attrib.* and *Comb.*, as **obeah** (or *obi*) **-man, -woman**, one who practises obeah, a Negro sorcerer or sorceress.

1764 Grainger *Sugar Cane* iv. 370 *note*, The negro-conjurers or obia-men as they are called. *a* 1818 M. G. Lewis *Jrnl. W. Ind.* (1834) 237 Adam, the reputed Obeah-man. 1840 Marryat *Poor Jack* xli, She..had always been considered as an Obi woman. 1886 Grant Allen *In all Shades* xxviii. (1887) 200 His mouldy obeah mummery of loose alligators' teeth and..little human knuckle-bones. 1917 *Chambers's Jrnl.* Apr. 248/1 No treasure was found, and the Obeahman had disappeared just when he was most wanted to counsel and guide. 1934 J. Rhys *Voy. in Dark* iii. iv. 192 Obeah-women who dig up dead people. 1970 J. Brown *Un-Melting Pot* vii. 99 Though St Lucia is 92 per cent Catholic,..obeah beliefs and practices still pervade its whole fabric of life. 1973 *Sunday Express* (Trinidad & Tobago) 1 Apr. (Suppl.) 12/2 Sometimes they would visit Rattan, the famed obeah man..and ask him to cast a good spell on them. 1974 *Practitioner* Dec. 848 An Obeahman or Obeahwoman may also be consulted about social matters, including a child's education.

Hence **'obeah, 'obi,** *v. trans.*, to bewitch by obeah, put under a spell; **'obeahism (obeoism, obeism, obiism)**, the practice of or belief in obeah.

a 1818 M. G. Lewis *Jrnl. W. Ind.* (1834) 134 Edward had Obeahed him. 1836 E. Howard *R. Reefer* xlviii, Such superstitious nonsense as Obeoism. 1866 Beckford Davis in *Rep. R. Comm. Jamaica* 521 Obeahism..is the art of poisoning, combined with the art of imposing upon the credulity of ignorant people by a pretence of witchcraft. 1874 Sir S. D. Scott *To Jamaica* xiii. 231 Belief in witchcraft, under the name of Obeism and Myalism. 1895 H. J. Bell in Stoddart *Cruising Caribbees* xi. 89 'Missis, I'm Obeahed, I know I'll go dead'. 1902 *Chambers's Jrnl.* Feb. 82/1 The vitality of *obeahism* is surprising. 1949 *Caribbean Q.* I. ii. 45 Mr. Waugh manages to feature an immigrant London crooner..and an obeahed French colonial official, in his treatment of..St. Lucia, Dominica, and Martinique.

1972 *Guardian* 6 Dec. 13/1 Obeahism, the Jamaican form of voodooism..that originated in Haiti.

obeche (əʊˈbiːtʃiː). [Bini name in Nigeria.] A large West African tree, *Triplochiton scleroxylon*, of the family Sterculiaceæ, found in lowland forests; also its light-coloured timber. Also *attrib.*

1908 H. N. Thompson in *Kew Bull.* 195 'Satinwood', 'Obeche'... At the Liverpool Market..it was classified as Satinwood... It is a very common tree. **1934** *Jrnl. R. Aeronaut Soc.* XXXVIII. 56 One of the most remarkable instances of clean fracture is in the West African Obeche... This wood is relatively new to commerce, and is being used ..for motor-body work. **1956** *Handbk. Hardwoods* (Forest Prod. Res. Lab.) 171 Obeche grows to a height of 150 ft... Obeche is nearly white to pale straw in colour with no clear distinction between sapwood and heartwood. **1958** *Archit. Rev.* CXXIV. 41/1 The wall is of a natural obeche timber. **1965** W. Soyinka *Road* 27 And high class timber kid. High class. Golden walnut. Obeche. Iron-wood. **1971** *Country Life* 1 Apr. 731/2 My obeche wood decoys have been admired a great deal in the five or six years since I made them. **1972** *Timber Trades Jrnl.* 13 May 47/2 Among the species displayed by Lathams were two hardwoods—guarea and obeche—which were comparatively unknown at the time [*sc.* 1925].

obeche, var. OBEISH *Obs.*, to obey.

†**obˈedible**, *a. Obs. rare*$^{-1}$. [f. L. *obēdī-re* to obey: see -BLE, -IBLE. Cf. OF. *obéissable* obedient, docile.] Capable of obedience; docile.

1622 Bp. Hall *Contempl. N.T.* III. *Christ amg. Gergesens*, Spirits..may be made most sensible of paine, and by the obedible submission of their created nature, wrought upon immediately by their appointed tortures.

obedience (əʊˈbiːdɪəns). Also 4-5 -iens(e, 4-6 -yence, 5 -yans; 4 obyd-, 6 obœdience. [a. F. *obédience* (12th c. in Littré), ad. L. *obēdientia*, n. of quality f. *obēdient-em* OBEDIENT: see -ENCE. With senses 2-4 cf. med.L. *obēdientia* in Du Cange.]

1. a. The action or practice of obeying; the fact or character of being obedient; submission to the rule or authority of another; compliance with or performance of a command, law, or the like; the action of doing what one is bidden.

a **1225** *Ancr. R.* 6 Vor neod one, als..obedience of hire bischope, oðer of hire herre. **1340** *Ayenb.* 140 Of boȝsamnesse..þe milde bouȝþ gledliche,..uor þe loue þet he heþ to þe obedience. *c* **1380** Wyclif *Wks.* (1880) 9 For feyned obydience to synful mannus tradicions. **1484** Caxton *Fables of Æsop* II. ix, Vndone and lost for faulte of obedyence. **1563** Winȝet *Four Scoir Thre Quest.* Wks. 1888 I. 59 For our humil and dew obœdience vnto our lauchful Souerane. **1602** Fulbecke *1st Pt. Parall.* Introd. 2 To bee brought vppe in the obedience of Lawes. **1638** Sir T. Herbert *Trav.* (ed. 2) 19 They traine their cattell to such obedience, as with a Call or Whistle..a great Heard will follow them like dogges. **1754** Edwards *Freed. Will* III. iv. (1762) 160 Obedience..is the submitting and yielding of the Will of one, to the Will of another. **1825** Jefferson *Autobiog.* Wks. 1859 I. 3 The King's Council..held their places at will, and were in most humble obedience to that will. **1838** Dickens *Nich. Nick.* xxi, In obedience to this request the qualifications were all gone through again. **1874** Morley *Compromise* (1886) 65 Superstition, blind obedience to custom, and the other substitutes for a right and independent use of the mind.

b. *fig.* The action or fact of yielding to some actuating force or agency: see OBEY *v.* 1 d. Usually in phr. *in obedience to.*

1671 L. Addison *W. Barbary* 102 They remove from one place to another, in obedience to their fickle Humors and cogent Necessities. *Mod.* A heavy body falls to the ground in obedience to the law of gravitation. The *s* becomes *r* in obedience to Verner's law.

c. ***passive obedience.*** (*a*) (Opposed to *active* obedience) an obedience in which the subject allows himself to be treated according to the will of another; or in which he suffers without remonstrance or resistance. (*b*) Unqualified obedience or submission to authority, whether the commands be reasonable or unreasonable, lawful or unlawful.

1656 Bramhall *Replic.* vi. 231 Whether a power to reform abuses and inconveniences be necessary to a King, to which all his Subjects owe at least passive obedience. *a* **1708** Beveridge *Thes. Theol.* (1711) III. 328 As by Christ's passive obedience we are freed from the guilt of sin, so by His active obedience we are invested with righteousness. **1712** Berkeley (*title*) Passive Obedience; or, the Christian Doctrine of not resisting the Supreme Power, proved and vindicated, upon the Principles of the Law of Nature. **1808** Moore *Poet. Wks.* II. 16 The churchman's opiate draught, Of passive prone obedience. **1827** Hallam *Const. Hist.* (1857) II. xi. 330 The doctrine of passive obedience had now crept from the homilies into the statute-book.

2. a. The fact or position of being obeyed, or of having others subject to one; command, authority, rule, dominion. (Now chiefly of ecclesiastical authority, esp. that of the Church of Rome.)

c **1200** *Vices & Virtues* 7 Sume læteð wel of hem seluen ..ȝif he bie of heiȝe menstre, oðer ȝif he hafð sum hei obedience. **1393** Langl. *P. Pl.* C. x. 220 Holy churche hoteþ alle manere puple Vnder obedience to bee and buxum to þe lawe. *a* **1400-50** *Alexander* 1965 All þe gracieux goddez þat þe ground viseten, All er vndir my obedience, dredles I telle. **1555** Eden *Decades* 27 We are determyned noo longer to bee vnder yowre obedience. **1642** tr. *Perkins' Prof. Bk.* xi. §754. 330 C D is a Monke professed under the obedience of the same Abbot. **1655** Fuller *Ch. Hist.* IX. ii. §24 To abjure the authority and obedience of the Bishop of Rome. **1827** Hallam *Const. Hist.* (1876) III. xvi. 214 The prospect of reducing Spain to the archduke's obedience. **1874** Green *Short Hist.* vii. §2. 356 The two Houses decided..to return to the obedience of the Papal See.

b. *transf.* A sphere of authority; a realm, district, or body of persons subject to some rule, esp. ecclesiastical; a dominion.

1635 Pagitt *Christianogr.* I. iii. (1636) 125 Christians..of the Patriarch of Constantinoples obedience. **1832** tr. *Sismondi's Ital. Rep.* ix. 209 On the 7th of July, the assembled cardinals of the two 'obediences' named in their place a third, Alexander V. **1876** Freeman *Norm. Conq.* V. xxii. 20 All the English land-owners within William's obedience. **1878** Stubbs *Medieval & Mod. Hist.* viii. (1900) 184 The Armenian Church..was so far schismatic as not to be integrally a portion of either Roman or Byzantine obedience.

3. A salutation expressive of submission or reverence; a bow or curtsy; = OBEISANCE 3. Now *arch.* and *dial.* ***to make (one's) obedience***, med.L. *obedientiam facere*.

1503 Dunbar *Thistle & Rose* 76 To hir [Dame Nature] thair makar to mak obediens, Full law inclynnand with all dew reuerens. **1604** Drayton *Owle* 1151 The poore Owle (his Obedience done) Thus to his Liege Lord reverently begun. **1661** Evelyn *Diary* 22 Apr., After obedience on their several approches to ye throne. **1800** Helena Wells *Constantia Neville* III. xxix. 193 'Be sure to bring your music books', he cried, as I made my obedience. **1885** 'J. S. Winter' *In Quarters* vi. 105 A..nurse..who rose and made her obedience when he entered.

4. In a monastic or conventual establishment: Any office, official position, or duty, under the abbot or superior; the particular office or duty of any inmate of a convent; also, the cell, room, or place appertaining or appropriate to a particular office; = med.L. *obedientia* (see Du Cange).

1727-41 Chambers *Cycl.* s.v., Obedience, *Obedientia*, is sometimes used in the canon law, for an office, or the administration of it... *Obedientia* was used in the general, for every thing that was enjoined the monks, by the abbot. .. In a more restrained sense [it] was applied to the farm belonging to the abbey, to which the monks were sent,.. either to look after the farm, or collect the rents. **1815** Mary Schimmelpenninck *Demol. Monast. Pt. Royal* III. 51 All the obediences..were put into..disorder. Obedience is the name given to those rooms containing the materials for the different kinds of works in which nuns are employed... There were a great many of these obediences at Port Royal, as for example, obediences for the linen, the robery, the mattresses, the bedding, the furniture, the drugs, the apothecary's shop. **1882** Ogilvie (Annandale), *Obedience*.. 3..(*b*) A written precept or other formal instrument by which a superior in a religious order communicates to one of his subjects any special precept or instruction. **1891** *Cent. Dict.*, *Obedience*..4. *Eccles*... (*b*) In Roman Catholic monasteries, any ecclesiastical and official position, with the estate and profits belonging to it, which is subordinate to the abbot's jurisdiction.

5. obedience class, test, trial, a competition designed to test a dog's obedience; **obedience training**, the process of teaching a dog to obey orders; hence (as a back-formation) **obedience-train** *v.*

1930 E. C. Ash *Practical Dog Bk.* ii. 21 Obedience classes are held at Cruft's Show, and are always an occasion of considerable interest. **1936** J. Z. Rine *Dog Owner's Manual* xii. 195 We see these blue ribbon dogs carrying off prizes also in obedience tests. **1961** J. Holmes (*title*) Obedience training for dogs. **1971** 'L. Egan' *Malicious Mischief* (1972) i. 15 'If your dog had been obedience-trained he would not have been stolen so easily... An obedience-trained dog is impossible to steal or poison.'..'Obedience training? What does that mean?' **1945** C. L. B. Hubbard *Observer's Bk. Dogs* 105 The breed [*sc.* the Monkey Terrier] is surprisingly intelligent and..should do well in Obedience Trials. **1971** 'L. Egan' *Malicious Mischief* (1972) iii. 40 Most of the big bench shows have obedience trials.

†**oˈbediencer.** *Obs.* [f. OBEDIENCE + -ER: cf. F. *obédiencier.*] = OBEDIENTIARY *sb.*

c **1380** Wyclif *Sel. Wks.* III. 27 As oure prelatis wiþ her obedienseers and her lyvyng dispisen þe mekenes and þe povert of Crist. **1393** Langl. *P. Pl.* C. vi. 91 Bote he be obediencer to pryour oþer to mynstre. **1529** More *Dyaloge* I. Wks. 157/1 God willed the woman to be subiecte and obediencer of man. **1535** *Act 27 Hen. VIII*, c. 28 §15 The abbottes or pryours to whome thei be obedyencers. **1721** *St. German's Doctor & Stud.* 284 All that the Obediencer hath is the Superior's. [**1892** Kirk *Abingdon Acc.* p. xi, We might ..use 'obediencer'.]

obedienciarie, obs. form of OBEDIENTIARY.

oˈbediency. *rare.* [ad. L. *obēdientia*: see OBEDIENCE and -ENCY.] = OBEDIENCE 1.

1614 R. Tailor *Hog hath lost Pearl* v. in Hazl. *Dodsley* XI. 486 Great Crœsus' shadow may dispose of me To what he pleaseth. *Light.* So speaks obediency. **1800** Coleridge *Piccolom.* v. ii, The holy habit of obediency.

obedient (əʊˈbiːdɪənt), *a.* (*sb.*) Also 4-6 -yent, 5-6 -iente, 5 obeydyand, 6 obœdient. [a. OF. *obédient* (11th c. in Godef.), ad. L. *obēdient-em*, pr. pple. of *obēdire* to OBEY.]

A. *adj.* **1. a.** That obeys or is willing to obey; submissive to the will of a superior; complying with or carrying out a command or commands; doing what one is bidden; subservient; dutiful.

a **1225** *Ancr. R.* 424 Boðe beon obedient to hore dame in alle þinges, bute ine sunne one. **1382** Wyclif *2 Cor.* ii. 9 That I knowe..wher in alle thingis ȝe ben obedyent. **14..** *Tundale's Vis.* 1944 Lovyd ay God..And to hym ever obeydyand were. **1535** Coverdale *Ps.* civ. [cv.] 28 They were not obedient vnto his worde. **1632** J. Hayward tr. *Biondi's Eromena* 158 The obedient executor of your commands. **1667** Milton *P.L.* xii. 246 Such delight hath God in Men Obedient to his Will. **1715** De Foe *Fam. Instruct.* (1841) I. Introd. 1 To be made obedient to what they have already learnt. **1828** Scott *F.M. Perth* x, He lacks the homage and obedient affection which the poorest yeoman receives from his family. **1833** Alison *Hist. Europe* (1849-53) I. iv. §123. 561 The armed force..is essentially obedient—it acts, but should never deliberate. **1875** Jowett *Plato* (ed. 2) III. 702 They were obedient to the laws.

†**b.** Owning, or subject to, the rule of another as sovereign or superior; subject. *Obs.*

1340 Hampole *Pr. Consc.* 4072 Ne fra þan sal na man be bughsome, Ne obedient to þe kirk of Rome. *c* **1400** Maundev. (1839) iii. 16 Contreys that ben obedyent to the Emperour. *c* **1440** *Gesta Rom.* i. 5 (Harl. MS.) A spirit obediente to a new guernaunce. *c* **1511** *1st Eng. Bk. Amer.* (Arb.) Introd. 30/2 [It] is not obedient to the chyrch of Rome.

c. Conventionally used as an expression of respect or courtesy, esp. at leave-taking, or in the conclusion of a letter; in phr. ***your obedient servant***.

a **1548** Hall *Chron. Hen. VIII* 137 This subscribed by your humble and obedient sonne Frances. **1681** in Ellis *Orig. Lett.* Ser. II. IV. 66, I am so entirely myself as being, Sir, Your most obedient and most devoted servant, Z. Isham. **1777** Sheridan *Sch. Scand.* I. i, *Snake*..Mr. Surface, your most obedient. (*Exit.*) *Jos.* Mr. Snake, your most obedient. **1781** Cowper *Truth* 212 Reduce his wages, or get rid of her, Tom quits you, with—'Your most obedient, Sir'. **1885** *Times* 24 Nov. 10/4 You will greatly oblige, Sir, Your obedient servant.

†**2.** *Astrol.* Said of certain signs of the zodiac, etc.: Subject; see OBEY *v.* 5. *Obs.*

1390 Gower *Conf.* III. 132 Which [the star Botercadent] of his kinde obedient Is to Mercurie and to Venus. *c* **1391** Chaucer *Astrol.* II. §28 Thise crokede signes ben obedient to the signes þat ben of riht Assencioun.

†**3.** Yielding to desires or wishes; compliant. *Obs.*

1362 Langl. *P. Pl.* A. xi. 188 Obedient as breþeren and sustren to oþere. **1497** Bp. Alcock *Mons Perfect.* C ij b/1 Yf we be obedyent unto our hedes, god is obedient unto our prayers.

4. *fig.* (chiefly of things or involuntary agents): Moving or yielding as actuated or affected by something else.

1398 Trevisa *Barth. De P. R.* xvi. lxxiv. (Bodl. MS.) He findeþ mater more able and obedient to his worchinge þe more noble impression he prenteþ þerein. **1551** T. Wilson *Logike* (1580) 43 b, Other efficient causes that are obedient, are but instrumentes of doyng, as Hatchettes, Hammers. **1590** Shaks. *Com. Err.* I. i. 87 My wife and I..floating.. obedient to the streame, Was carried towards Corinth, as we thought. **1726** Leoni tr. *Alberti's Archit.* I. 27/1 The Ash is accounted very obedient in all manner of Works. **1857** Buckle *Civiliz.* I. vii. 344 Soldiers live upon an element much more obedient to man.

5. obedient plant = PHYSOSTEGIA.

1948 F. Perry *Herbaceous Border* v. 103 *P*[*hysostegia*] *virginiana*, sometimes known as the Obedient Plant because the individual sage-like blossoms on the flower spikes may be moved from side to side and remain as placed. **1971** J. Raven *Botanist's Garden* xi. 201 A curious plant, of better value perhaps for the entertainment it affords children than for beauty, called the obedient plant or *Physostegia virginiana*.

†**B.** *sb.* One who is obedient or subject to authority; a subordinate: see quots. *Obs.*

1626 C. Potter tr. *Father Paul's Hist.* II. 81 Apt to condemne and reprehend any action whatsoeuer, if it were not done with their knowledge and counsell, as also to iustifie all the actions of their Obedients. **1662** Ray *Three Itin.* II. 159 Here [Glasgow] are most commonly about forty students of the first year, which they call obedients.

obediential (əʊbiːdɪˈɛnʃəl), *a.* (*sb.*) [ad. med.L. *obēdientiāl-is*, f. *obēdientia* OBEDIENCE: see -AL[1] 2; cf. F. *obédientiel* (1636 in Hatz.-Darm.).]

1. Of, pertaining to, of the nature of, or characterized by obedience. (Common in 17th c., chiefly *Theol.*; now *rare* or *Obs.* in *gen.* sense.)

1619 Sanderson *Serm.* (1657) 15 Which..distinction of Doctrinall and Obedientiall Necessity..is..sufficient to clear all doubts in this point. **1645** Rutherford *Tryal & Tri. Faith* xxv. (1845) 371 Every being..hath a power obediential to hear what God saith, and do it. *a* **1677** Hale *Prim. Orig. Man.* I. i. 38 There is no Power in the World but owes..an obediential subjection to the Lord of Nature. **1755** S. Walker *Serm.* i, An obediential Spirit..is the only Qualification for happiness in us. **1825** Culbertson *Lect. Revel.* vi. 77 The obediential sufferings and death of Christ.

2. *Sc. Law.* (See quots.).

1693 Stair *Institutes* I. iii. §3 (ed. 2) 20 Obediential Obligations are these, which are put upon men by the will of God, not by their own will, and so are most Natural, as introduced by the Law of Nature. **1773** Erskine *Inst. Law Scot.* III. i. §9. 414 These are called by Lord Stair *obediential* or *natural obligations*, in opposition to *conventional*. **1832** Austin *Jurispr.* (1879) II. 945.

†**B.** *sb.* (See quot.) *Obs. rare*$^{-0}$.

1674 Blount *Glossogr.* (ed. 4), *Obedientials*, those that execute an Office under Superiours, and with obedience to their commands.

Hence **obediˈentially** *adv.*, in the way of obedience; **obediˈentialness**, a relation of obedience.

1640 Gauden *The Love*, etc. (1641) 12 No men or minds are more obedientially disposed to an heroick patience. **1651** J. F[reake] *Agrippa's Occ. Philos.* 28 Which obedientialness ..is such as our bodies to our souls. *a* **1708** Beveridge *Thes.*

Theol. (1710) II. 275 To do..works of charity to the poor, obedientially to God's command.

obedi'entiar. *rare.* [See -AR².] = next, A. 2.
1892 KIRK (*title*) Accounts of the Obedientiars of Abingdon Abbey.

obedientiary (əʊbiːdɪ'ɛnʃərɪ), *sb.* and *a.* Also 6 -enci-, -ency-. [ad. med.L. *obēdientiāri-us*, adj. and sb., f. *obēdientia* OBEDIENCE: see -ARY.]

A. *sb.* † **1.** A person practising obedience, or in a position of subjection; one owning allegiance; a subject; a liegeman. *Obs.*

c **1540** BP. OF BANGOR in Ellis *Orig. Lett.* Ser. III. II. 151, I, your verye humble obediencyarye, most mekelye besechithe your Grace. **1563–87** FOXE *A. & M.* (1596) 694/1 The great prelates and fat doctors, and other obedienciaries of the Romish sea. **1603** STOW *Surv.* (1842) 204/1 In respect of the whole realm, London is but..a subject and no free estate, an obediencīary and no place endowed with..absolute power.

2. A member of a conventual establishment charged with any duty or 'obedience'; the holder of any office in a monastery, under the abbot or superior. (See OBEDIENCE 4.)

1794 W. TINDAL *Hist. Evesham* 94 The prior, sub prior, the third prior, and other obedientiaries of the order. **1886** *Athenæum* 3 July 14/1 In the case in point the convent in its corporate capacity stood to the obedientiary in the relation of owner of the fee. **1897** E. L. TAUNTON *Eng. Black Monks* I. 57 These payments were often assigned to divers officers of the abbey, obedientiaries as they were called.

attrib. **1892** KITCHIN (*title*) Obedientiary Rolls of St. Swithun's, Winchester.

† **B.** *adj.* Practising or professing obedience; owning allegiance; subject. *Obs.*

1700 J. BROME *Trav. Eng., Scot.*, etc. iii. (1707) 300 John ..yielded his Realm Tributary, and himself an obedientiary Vassal to the Bishop of Rome.

obediently (əʊ'biːdɪəntlɪ), *adv.* [f. OBEDIENT + -LY².] In an obedient manner; in or with obedience; submissively, dutifully.

1398 TREVISA *Barth. De P.R.* II. x. (1495) b vj b/1 Sedes make hemselfe subget to god obedyently, & not compellyd but by very fredom. *a* **1557** MRS. M. BASSET tr. *More's Treat. Passion* Wks. 1365/2 Yf we..be readye obediently to folowe hys most blessed will. **1642** MILTON *Apol. Smect.* ii. Wks. (1851) 284 Reason..conducting without error those that give themselves obediently to be led accordingly. **1748** RICHARDSON *Clarissa* (1811) II. xxiii. 152 You are so obediently principled. **1818** SHELLEY *Rev. Islam* x. v, Obediently they came, Like sheep. **1885** *Manch. Exam.* 18 Feb. 6/1 To submit obediently to the powers that be.

† **o'bedientness.** *Obs. rare.* [f. as prec. + -NESS.] The quality of being obedient; obedience.

1571 GOLDING *Calvin on Ps.* xxx. 5 With how redy obedientness he submitted his backe to Gods rod. **1583** —— *Calvin on Deut.* iii. 13 A true tryal of their obedientnesse.

obeiance, -auns, obs. forms of OBEYANCE.

obeie, obs. form of OBEY, *v.*

obeisance (əʊ'beɪsəns). Forms: 4- obeis-; 4-8 obeys-; also 4 obeish-, 5 obeyssh-, obeiss-, obayss-, (obeyes-, obecy-, obbeis-, obeisi-), 5-6 obeyss-, 7 obays-; 4- -ance, 4-6 -aunce, 5-6 -ans. See also the aphetic BEISANCE. [a. F. *obéissance* (13th c. in Littré), f. *obéissant*, pr. pple. of *obéir* to OBEY: see -ANCE. *Obéissance* had the same relation to *obéissant* that L. *obēdientia* had to *obēdient-em*. With senses 2-4, cf. med.L. *obēdientia* in Du Cange.]

† **1.** The action or fact of obeying; = OBEDIENCE 1.

c **1374** CHAUCER *Compl. Mars* 47 He bynt him to perpetuall obeisaunce. **1382** WYCLIF *1 Sam.* xv. 22 Betre is obeishaunce [1388 obedience] than slayn sacrificis. *a* **1450** *Knt. de la Tour* (1868) 26 Alle women..be not of the obeisaunce that a merchauntez wiff was. **1553** LADY JANE GREY in Ellis *Orig. Lett.* Ser. I. II. 186 To remayne fast in your obeysaunce and duetie to the imperiall Crowne of this Realme. **1660** SHARROCK *Vegetables* Ep. ded., A testimony of my obeysance and humble submission to your judgment.

† **2.** *the obeisance* (of any one), the obedience which he claims; hence, Authority, rule, command, sway: = OBEDIENCE 2. *Obs.*

c **1385** CHAUCER *L.G.W.* 587 *Cleopatra*, To conqueryn regnys and honour Vn to the toun of rome..To han the worlde vn-to hyre obeysaunce. *c* **1440** *Generydes* 6630 Sette the lande in rewle..hole to be..vnder his obeysaunce. *a* **1533** LD. BERNERS *Gold. Bk. M. Aurel.* (1546) E ij, The realme of Acaye submytted his..proude heade, to the sweete obeysaunce of the empyre. **1664** *Floddan F.* I. 5 To bring that Land to his obeysance.

† **b.** The sphere within which any one rules; a district under the rule or jurisdiction (of some one), a dominion; = OBEDIENCE 2 b. *Obs.*

1419 J. DE ASSHETON in Ellis *Orig. Lett.* Ser. II. I. 73 The Abbot..has sent for safe condute for to come to ȝour obeysshans. **1467** *Waterf. Arch.* in *10th Rep. Hist. MSS. Comm.* App. v. 305 No manere alient, borne out of thobeysaunce of the Kyng of Inglande. **1493** HEN. VII in *Four C. Eng. Lett.* (Camden) 9 The Flemmings and other of the archduke's obeissaunce. **1569** T. NORTON in Strype *Ann. Ref.* (1709) I. lv. 561 The country round about within her obeisance. **1616** R. C. *Times Whistle* ii. 701 The Iewes, together with their Palestine, Which he by force will conquer, and confine To his obeisance.

3. A bodily act or gesture expressive of submission or respect (almost always, A bending or prostration of the body in token of this); a respectful salutation; a bow or curtsy: = OBEDIENCE 3. Often in phr. *to do, make, pay obeisance*, in med.L. *obedientiam facere*. (The chief current sense, but almost restricted to literary use, and often with an archaic tinge.)

(In F., Godefroy has one 16th c. example of *obéissance* = *révérence, salut*, but no OF. examples. The sense is not in Cotgr., Littré, or Hatz.-Darm.)

c **1385** CHAUCER *L.G.W.* 1268 *Dido*, And can so wel don alle hise obeysauncis And waytyn hire at festis and at dauncis. **1484** CAXTON *Fables of Æsop* II. i, They approched to theyr kynge for to make obeyssaunce vnto hym. *a* **1555** LATIMER *Serm. & Rem.* (1845) 150 A gentleman that brought the cup, in making obeisance, the cover fell to the ground. **1610** G. FLETCHER *Christ's Vict.* II. xvii, He lowted low With prone obeysance. **1640** in Rushw. *Hist. Coll.* III. (1692) I. 124 He made a low Obeysance. *c* **1710** CELIA FIENNES *Diary* (1888) 69 They shewed us the wearing of ye pavement with ye obeisance of his votarys. **1765** H. WALPOLE *Otranto* iii. (1798) 49 The herald made three obeisances. *c* **1850** *Arab. Nts.* (Rtldg.) 448 The young merchant made his obeisance, by throwing himself with his face to the ground. **1855** PRESCOTT *Philip II*, I. I. iv. 46 The Spanish prince was welcomed..by a goodly company of English lords, assembled to pay him their obeisance.

4. In more general sense: Respectfulness of manner or bearing, deference; respect such as is or may be shown by bending the body; homage, submission. Often in phr. *to do, make, pay obeisance*, fig., = to 'do homage', submit, show reverence or respect. (In mod. use regarded as *fig.* from 3.)

c **1385** CHAUCER *L.G.W.* 1375 *Hypsip.*, Thyne feynede trouthe..With thyn obeysaunce and humble cheere. *c* **1450** HOLLAND *Howlat* 870 Quhom thai ressaif with reuerens, And bowsome obeysance. *c* **1530** *Crt. of Love* 46 Love arted me to do myn observaunce To his astate, and doon him obeysaunce. **1711** STEELE *Spect.* No. 167 ¶3 A Throne to which conquered Nations yielded Obeysance. *a* **1716** SOUTH *Serm.* VIII. vi. (1744) 164 The eye must do obeisance to the window, and discourse submit to sensation. **1865** SEELEY *Ecce Homo* I. (1868) 6 He [John the Baptist] did obeisance to the royalty of inward happiness.

† **5.** Alleged term for a company of servants. *Obs.*

1486 *Bk. St. Albans* F vj b, An obeisians of seruauntis.

o'beisancy. *rare.* [See -ANCY.] = prec.
1846 WORCESTER cites POLLOK.

† **o'beisand, obeysand,** *a. Obs.* [A northern form in which F. *obéissant*, OBEISANT receives the northern participial ending -AND¹, and thus becomes in form the pr. pple. of *obeis* OBEISH *v.*] = OBEISANT, OBEDIENT.

1375 BARBOUR *Bruce* VIII. 10 That land He maid till him all obeysand. *c* **1500** *Lancelot* 642 He..makith al obeisand to his honde, That nocht is left wnconquest in that lond. *a* **1568** in *Bannatyne Poems* (1873) 104/28 He..ordanit all at thy command to be, And thow to be obeysand to his lawis.

obeisant (əʊ'beɪsənt), *a.* (*sb.*) Forms: 3-8 obeysant, 4-6 -aunt, obeissant, -aunt, 5 obeyssant, -aunt, (obeyssiant, obeiceant), 4- obeisant; also 4-5 obeisch-, obesch-, 5 obeyshaunt. [a. F. *obéissant*, pr. pple. of *obéir*:—L. *obēdīre* to OBEY: see -ANT.]

† **1.** = OBEDIENT 1. *Obs.* exc. as in 2.

1297 R. GLOUC. (Rolls) 10355 þat þou to god & to holichirche obeysant were. *c* **1380** WYCLIF *Wks.* (1880) 277 þat clerkis be meke & obeschaunt to worldly lordis. **1382** —— *Exod.* xxiv. 7 We shulen be obeysaunt. **1450–80** tr. *Secreta Secret.* 4 He..found hem more lowly and obeyshaunt to him than any othir were. **1475** *Bk. Noblesse* (Roxb.) 3 Your verray true obeisaunt subjectis. **1546** *Supplic. Commons* (E.E.T.S.) 76 We, your..most obeisant leage people. **1570** *Satir. Poems Reform.* xiii. 164 Be obeysant to God and mans Lawis.

† **b.** Subject; = OBEDIENT 1 b. *Obs.*

c **1400** MAUNDEV. (1839) xxv. 263 Many ben obeyssant to the greate Chane. **1485** CAXTON *Trevisa's Higden* II. viii. (1527) 66 [He] made them all longe and be obeyssaunt to yᵉ kyngdome of Rome. **1536** BELLENDEN *Cron. Scot.* (1821) I. 78 Al regionis circulit with the occeane sees, ar obeysant to Romane lawis. **1609** HOLLAND *Amm. Marcell.* XXXI. vii. 410 They..joyned themselves unto him, as duetiful and obeisant allyes.

† **c.** Compliant: = OBEDIENT 3. *Obs.*

c **1400** MAUNDEV. (Roxb.) xi. 41 þat þai schuld..be obeischaunt to myne askynges.

d. *fig.* = OBEDIENT 4. *Obs.* or *arch.*

1430–40 LYDG. *Bochas* VII. iv. (1554) 167 b, Of heauenly cours the disposicion Is obeysaunt and subiect to reason. **1818** MILMAN *Samor* 178 The bark obeisant to its dashing oars.

2. Showing respect or deference, deferential; humbly or servilely obedient, obsequious.

1642 ROGERS *Naaman* 99 If Eglon an heathen King, hearing of a charge from God was so obeysant, as to come off his throne, and worship God. **1725** RAMSAY *Gentle Sheph.* IV. ii, Obeysant servants, honour, wealth, and ease. **1855** MILMAN *Lat. Chr.* (1864) V. IX. viii. 414 They were commanded to be the obeisant executioners of punishments ..of which they did not admit the justice. **1878** *Masque Poets* 27 The obeisant slaves would bring rare cups.

b. Doing obeisance; offering homage; bowing.

1900 *Expositor* Jan. 77 Joseph dreams of obeisant sheaf and obeisant star.

† **B.** *sb.* One who is obedient, an obedient servant, one under authority, a subordinate. *Obs.*

1475 *Bk. Noblesse* (Roxb.) 30 In defaute of largesse to youre obeissauntes. **1600** W. WATSON *Decacordon* (1602) 110 A distinction betwixt a Iesuit commandant, and a Iesuit obeisant.

† **o'beisantly,** *adv. Obs.* [f. prec. + -LY².] In an obeisant manner; obediently; deferentially; with an obeisance.

c **1400** *Lay Folks Mass Bk.* App. iii. 126 þerfore schulde he ..obeschauntely seye to hym þus. **1507** *Justes June* 103 in Hazl. *E.P.P.* II. 124 By the kynge they past And obeysauntly doune theyr heedes they cast. **1555** ABP. PARKER *Ps.* lxiii. 175 Obeysantly To lyft my handes. **1902** *Westm. Gaz.* 2 July 2/3, I..came in turn Of him myself obeisantly to learn.

† **o'beish, o'beis,** *v. Obs.* Forms: 4 obeshe, obeche, obeishe, obeiche, 4-5 obeische, obesche, 5 obeisshe, obeysche, obeysshe; 4-5 obes, obeis, obeyse, 5 obeisse, obeise. [a. F. *obéiss-*, lengthened stem of *obéir* to OBEY (formally corresponding to a L. inchoative type **obēdīsc-*). As to constructions cf. OBEY.]

1. a. *trans.* (or *intr.* with *dat.*) = OBEY *v.* 1.

a **1400–50** *Alexander* 2694 ȝour satrapers, your souerraynte with seruice obeysshyng. *c* **1400** tr. *Secreta Secret., Gov. Lordsh.* 57 To loue, honoure, obeisse, and doute þe kynge. **1483** CAXTON *G. de la Tour* F iv b, Ye ought to..obeysshe and bere hym honour.

b. *intr.* with *to*: = OBEY *v.* 2.

1375 BARBOUR *Bruce* IX. 303 The north cuntre, that hwmylly Obeysit till his senȝory. *c* **1380** WYCLIF *Serm.* Sel. Wks. I. 82 Men moten more obeishe to God þan to man. *c* **1449** PECOCK *Repr.* IV. i. 420 Poul witnessith the same,.. Seiyng thus, Servauntis, obeische ȝe to fleischli lordis. *c* **1500** *Lancelot* 2134 To ȝhour command, god will, y sal obes.

c. *refl.* = OBEY *v.* 4.

c **1400** tr. *Secreta Secret., Gov. Lordsh.* 50 Whenne..þat his subgitz of oon accord obeisse hem to his lordschipe.

2. *trans.* (or *intr.* with simple *dat.*) To do obeisance to, bow to: = OBEY *v.* 6.

13.. *E.E. Allit. P.* A. 885 Byfore godez chayere, & þe fowre bestez þat hym obes. *Ibid.* B. 745 þen Abraham obeched hym & loȝly him þonkkez. *a* **1400–50** *Alexander* 1620 þan Permeon..askis at him swythe..Qui he obeschid so lawe and bende þe bischop of iewis?

† **o'beishing, o'beising,** *vbl. sb. Obs.* [f. prec. + -ING¹.] OBEDIENCE, OBEISANCE; homage.

c **1400** *Rom. Rose* 3380 For seruice and obeissing. **1450–70** *Golagros & Gaw.* 1322 Heir mak I yow obeising, As liege lord of landis.

† **o'beishing, o'beising,** *ppl. a. Obs.* [f. as prec. + -ING²: cf. OBEISAND, the northern equivalent.] = OBEDIENT, OBEISANT.

c **1380** WYCLIF *Serm.* Sel. Wks. I. 53 Whan al his wittis and alle his strengþis ben obeishinge to resoun. *c* **1385** CHAUCER *L.G.W.* 1266 *Dido*, That feynyth hym so trewe & obeysynge. **1483** CAXTON *G. de la Tour* D vj b, Al tho that.. hadde be obeisshyng to his commaundements.

obeism: see OBEAH.

obele, -ey, obs. forms of OBLEY.

obelia (əʊ'biːlɪə). [mod.L. (Peron & Lesueur 1809, in *Ann. du Muséum d'Hist. Nat.* XIV. 355), f. Gr. ὀβελ-ός + -IA¹.] A marine colony-forming coelenterate of the genus so called, belonging to the class Hydrozoa.

1868 T. HINCKS *Hist. Brit. Hydroid Zoophytes* I. 148 Some of his [*sc.* Edward Forbes's] species are only various stages of one and the same *Obelia*. **1897** PARKER & HASWELL *Text-bk. Zool.* I. iv. 118 Obelia is a common zoophyte occurring in the form of a delicate, whitish or light brown, almost fur-like growth on the wooden piles of piers and wharfs. **1927** HALDANE & HUXLEY *Animal Biol.* ix. 179 If an ordinary hydroid polyp like Obelia be kept in the laboratory, the hydranths, or separate organized individuals of the colony, will (unless the water is well aerated artificially) show a curious series of changes. **1974** A. SILVERSTEIN *Biol. Sciences* 178/2 *Obelia*, a typical colonial coelenterate, has a number of specialized feeding polyps and reproductive polyps, growing in a branchlike arrangement.

‖ **obelion** (əʊ'biːlɪən). *Anat.* [ad. F. *obélion* (P. Broca 1875, in *Bull. de la Soc. d'Anthrop. de Paris* X. 356), f. Gr. ὀβελιαῖος sagittal (given in Broca's paper as ὀβελαῖος): see -ION².] (See quots.)

1878 BARTLEY tr. *Topinard's Anthrop.* II. ii. 234 Obelion.. the region situated between the two parietal foramina, where the sagittal suture becomes simple, which is generally at its fourth posterior fifth. **1892** *Syd. Soc. Lex.*, *Obelion*, the point of a line stretching between the two parietal foramina where the sagittal suture becomes simple and where its closure generally commences, about four fifths of its length from the front of the suture.

Hence **o'beliac** *a.*, pertaining to the obelion; **o'belial** *a.*

1890 H. ALLEN *Clin. Study Skull* 52 The parietal foramina lie on the sides and serve as guides to this the obelial portion.

obeliscal (ɒbɪ'lɪskəl), *a.* Also obeliskal. [f. L. *obelisc-us* OBELISK + -AL¹.] Of or pertaining to an obelisk; of the nature of an obelisk.

1763 STUKELEY *Palæogr. Sacra* 16 In the open temples of the Druids, they had an obeliscal stone, set upright. **1837**

O'BRIEN *Phœnic. Irel.* xxxiv. (ed. 2) 321 *note*, A pyramidial or obeliscal stone, six or seven feet in height, is said to have stood in the centre. **1880** *Times* 6 Nov. 4/5 The obeliscal character.. between the legs and the lower half of the spear must denote 'king'.

obe'liscar, *a. rare.* [f. as prec. + -AR, after an analogical L. *obeliscāris.] = prec.

1837 *Fraser's Mag.* XVI. 629 Confirmed by the obeliscar inscriptions. *Ibid.*, The obeliscar sculptures.

obeliscoid (ɒbɪ'lɪskɔɪd), *a.* [f. OBELISK + -OID.] Resembling an obelisk in form; obelisk-shaped; obeliscal.

1877 W. R. COOPER *Short Hist. Egypt. Obelisks* v. 25 An obeliscoid monolith originally erected by Osirtesen. **1901** A. J. EVANS in *Jrnl. Hellenic Stud.* XXI. 173 The obeliskoid pillar of the Cretan ring.

†**obelisco'lychny.** *Obs. rare.* [a. F. *obeliscolychnie* (Rabelais), ad. Gr. ὀβελισκολύχνιον, a spit used (by soldiers) as a lamp-holder, f. ὀβελίσκος small spit + λυχνίον lamp-stand.] A lighthouse; a light-bearer.

1694 MOTTEUX *Rabelais* IV. xxii, I see a Light on an *Obeliscolychny*. *Ibid.* v. xxxiii, We were conducted.. by those Obeliscolychnys, Military-Guards of the Port, with high-crown'd Hats.

obelisk ('ɒbɪlɪsk), *sb.* (*a.*) Also 6–7 -iske, 7 -isck, 7–8 -isque, -isc. [ad. L. *obelisc-us* small spit, obelisk, a. Gr. ὀβελίσκος dim. of ὀβελός spit, pointed pillar. In F. *obélisque* (1537 in Hatz.-Darm.).]

A. *sb.* **1. a.** A tapering shaft or column of stone, square or rectangular in section, and usually monolithic and finished with a pyramidal apex; a type of monument specifically characteristic of ancient Egypt.

[**1549** THOMAS *Hist. Italie* (1561) 33 Obeliscus is a stone that beyng broade and squere at the foote ascendeth proporcionallye to a sharpe poincte.] **1569** J. SANFORD tr. *Agrippa's Van. Artes* 127 The Spaniardes raised up so many Obeliskes about the sepulcre of the deade, as he had slaine enimies. **1613** PURCHAS *Pilgrimage* VI. ii. 471 Obelisks;.. their Pillars of one stone, fashioned like a needle. **1648** J. RAYMOND *Il Merc. Ital.* 78 The Obelisque which.. is held to be the biggest of one stone.. that ever came into Rome. **1695** E. BERNARD *Voy. Aleppo to Tadmor* in *Misc. Cur.* (1708) III. 95 A very tall and stately Obelisk or Pillar, consisting of seven large Stones, besides its Capital. **1735** J. PRICE *Stone-Br. Thames* 5 Stone Obelisques for Lamps. **1869** RAWLINSON *Anc. Hist.* 3 Historical events.. recorded.. sometimes on obelisks or pillars.

†**b.** Loosely applied to a column or pillar of any form; in quot. 1698 app. a minaret. *Obs.*

1587 FLEMING *Contn. Holinshed* III. 1340/1 Two obeliskes or round spires, and betweene them a triumphall arch. **1698** FRYER *Acc. E. India & P.* 368 At constant Hours the superior Clergy.. from their Obelisks.. call to the People to Pray.

c. A natural formation resembling an obelisk, as a lofty sharp-pointed mountain peak.

1845 DARWIN *Voy. Nat.* i. (1852) 11 At St. Helena.. some pinnacles of a nearly similar figure.. had been formed by the injection of melted rock into yielding strata, which had thus formed the moulds for these gigantic obelisks. **1860** TYNDALL *Glac.* I. xv. 102 The dark and the stern obelisk of the Matterhorn. **1886** SHELDON tr. *Flaubert's Salammbô* 2 An avenue of cypress trees formed a double colonnade of green obelisks.

2. A straight horizontal stroke, either simple (–), or with a dot above and one below (÷), used in ancient manuscripts to point out a spurious, corrupt, doubtful, or superfluous word or passage (= OBELUS, Gr. ὀβελος); in modern use applied to the mark † used in printing for marginal references, foot-notes, etc. (= DAGGER *sb.*[1] 8). *double obelisk*, the double dagger (‡).

1583 FULKE *Defence* (1843) 25 Whatsoever is not found in the canon of the Jews.. St. Jerome did thrust through with a spit or obelisk, as not worthy to be received. **1641** J. JACKSON *True Evang. T.* I. 71 It is sufficient to note these things with an obeliske; They are dead tenets. *a* **1711** GREW (J.), Having compared it [the Septuagint] with the Hebrew, and noted by asterisks what was defective, and by obelisks what redundant. **1727** W. MATHER *Yng. Man's Comp.* 38 *Obelisk*, is a mark of Reference to the Margin, thus, †. **1864** *Sat. Rev.* 9 July 60 Learned commentators.. may transfix it with their 'obelisk' of condemnation as spurious.

†**3.** As rendering of Gr. ὀβελίσκος a spit. *Obs.*

1622 PEACHAM *Compl. Gent.* xii. (1634) 116 Obolus (because it carryed the forme of a spit or obelisque so called) was the sixth part of a dram.

4. *Comb.*

1813 *Gentl. Mag.* LXXXIII. 336/1 Obelisk-turned pinnacles. **1855** *Cornwall* 63 Obelisk-like rocks. **1901** *Scotsman* 12 Mar. 4/8 A magnificent obelisk-shaped pillar-stone.

B. as *adj.* Obelisk-shaped, obeliscal. *rare.*

1638 SIR T. HERBERT *Trav.* (ed. 2) 146 Consisting of Figures, obelisk, triangular, and pyramidall. **1922** JOYCE *Ulysses* 45 Their pushedback chairs, my obelisk valise, around a board of abandoned platters.

obe'liskine, *a. nonce-wd.* [irreg. f. prec. + -INE[1].] Pertaining to or resembling an obelisk; obeliscal.

1818 SHELLEY *Pr. Wks.* (1888) III. 51 Cypress groves whose obeliskine forms of intense green pierce the grey shadow of the wintry hill.

obelize ('ɒbɪlaɪz), *v.* Also 9 *erron.* obolize. [ad. Gr. ὀβελίζ-ειν to mark with a critical obelus: see OBELUS and -IZE.] *trans.* To mark (a word or passage) with an obelus or obelisk; to condemn as spurious or corrupt.

[**1611** CORYAT *Crudities* Ep. to Rdr. bij b, Such seuere Aristarches as are wont ὀβελίζειν.] **1656** BLOUNT *Glossogr.*, *Obelise*,.. to make a long stroke in writing, to signifie somewhat to be put out. **1830** DE QUINCEY in *Blackw. Mag.* XXVIII. 672 A suitable dictionary.. distinguishes the gold and silver words, and obolizes the base Brummagem copper coinage. **1837** WHEELWRIGHT tr. *Aristophanes* I. 200 *note*, These and the three following verses were, according to the Scholiast, obelized by the illustrious grammarians. **1876** GLADSTONE *Homeric Synchr.* 216 The line *Od.* II. 631, obelised as spurious.

So '**obelism** [Gr. ὀβελισμός, f. ὀβελίζειν to obelize], the action of marking as spurious.

1860 D. COLERIDGE in *Trans. Philol. Soc.* 156 The office of a Dictionary.. is eminently regulative... It separates the spurious from the genuine, either.. in the way of exclusion, .. or by careful obelism.

‖**obelus** ('ɒbɪləs). Pl. obeli (-laɪ). [L. *obelus* spit, critical obelus, a. Gr. ὀβελός spit, obelisk, critical mark.] = OBELISK 2.

1382 WYCLIF *2 Chron.* Prol. ad fin., Than wher euer ȝe seen.. obelus ouerturned, that is, a ȝerde, is sette before, there is betokened what the seuenty remenours addeden.. and in Ebrue volumes it is not rad. **1833** SIR W. HAMILTON *Discuss.* (1853) 140 They stand likewise without an obelus in Dr. Gaisford's respectable edition of the *Florilegium*. **1846** TRENCH *Mirac.* xv. (1862) 251 In other MSS... the obelus which hints suspicion, or the asterisk which marks rejection, is attached to it. **1889** FARRAR *Lives Fathers* II. xvi. 351 To amend the Latin version.. with asterisks and obeli.

obely, -ley, obs. forms of OBLEY.

obeophone ('əʊbɪəʊfəʊn). [first element uncertain + -PHONE.] A type of orchestrina (ORCHESTRINA a) (see quot. 1927). (*Disused.*)

1927 H. E. WORTHAM *O. Browning* xiii. 234 For the performance of chamber music he possessed a number of *orchestrine di camera*, familiarly known as 'obeophones', which represented the wood-wind, or even supplemented the strings. **1940** V. WOOLF *Roger Fry* ii. 49 The host himself pedalled away at the obeophone.

†**ob'equitate**, *v. Obs. rare*[−0]. [f. ppl. stem of L. *obequitāre* to ride towards, or up to, f. *ob-* (OB- 1) + *equitāre* to ride.] Hence †**obequi'tation**.

1623 COCKERAM, *Obequitate*, to ride about. **1658** PHILLIPS, *Obequitation*, a riding about. **1694** MOTTEUX *Rabelais* v. (1737) 231 Cruciated.. With an indesinent Obequitation.

oberek (əʊ'berɪk). [Polish.] A lively Polish dance in triple time, related to the mazurka.

1938 *Oxf. Compan. Mus.* 624/2 *Oberek*, a type of Polish dance. **1952** H. WOLSKA *Dances of Poland* 33 Oberek. *Region*—Mazovia.. *Character*—Gay and vigorous. *Formation*—Couple Dance. **1958** [see KRAKOWIAK]. **1976** *Times* 23 July 11/3 The Mazowsze Song and Dance Company from Poland.. whirl through oberek and mazurka, polka and Krakowiak.

†**obe'rration.** *Obs. rare*[−0]. [n. of action of L. *oberrāre* to wander about.]

1658 PHILLIPS, *Oberration*, a straying, or wandring about [not in edd. 1696–1706]. **1721–1800** BAILEY, *Oberration*, a wandering up and down.

obertas (əʊ'beətəs). Also obertass. [Polish.] = OBEREK.

1889 GROVE *Dict. Mus.* IV. 733/1 *Obertas*, this is described in the 'Encyklopedyja Powszechna'.. as the most popular of Polish national dances. **1895** L. GROVE et al. *Dancing* vii. 234 The *Obertas*, one of the most popular of national dances, is a variation of the *Mazur*. **1938** *Oxf. Compan. Mus.* 270/1 It [*sc.* a drabant] began with a solemn march and then changed to an Obertass. **1944** W. APEL *Harvard Dict. Mus.* 500/1 Chopin's Mazurka op. 56, no. 2 is in the character of an obertas. **1954** *Grove's Dict. Mus.* (ed. 5) V. 641/2 The Obertas or Oberek.

obese (əʊ'biːs), *a.* [ad. L. *obēs-us* that has eaten itself fat, stout, plump, pa. pple. of *obedĕre* to eat away, f. *ob-* (OB- 1) + *edĕre* to eat.

Rare before 19th c.; in Johnson without quot.]

Very fat or fleshy; exceedingly corpulent.

1651 BIGGS *New Disp.* ¶251 More obese and plethorick bodies. **1654** GAYTON *Pleas. Notes* I. iii. 8 One said of an Over-Obese Priest that he was a great Arminian; grant, quoth a second, that he be an Arminian, I'll swear he is the greatest that ever I saw. **1822** T. TAYLOR *Apuleius* 316 A back obese, and animated breast. **1848** C. BRONTË *J. Eyre* iv. (1857) 30 A woman of robust frame, square shouldered,.. and though stout, not obese. **1864** F. OAKELEY *Hist. Notes* 85 An obese octavo, extending to six hundred closely printed pages.

b. *Entom.* (See quot.)

1826 KIRBY & SP. *Entomol.* IV. 260 *Obese*.. Unnaturally enlarged and distended, as if from disease or too much food.

Hence **o'besely** *adv.*; **o'beseness** (= next).

1653 GAUDEN *Hierasp.* 560 The fatnesse of Monkes, and the obeseness of Abbots. **1654** R. CODRINGTON tr. *Iustine* xxxviii. 456 He.. was.. short in stature, and by the obeseness of his strutting belly, more like unto a Beast then to a man. **1820** MOORE *Fables* v. 79 Her fat locusts, like a cloud Of pluralists, obesely lowering. **1891** G. MEREDITH *One of our Conq.* I. ix. 151 Obeseness is the most sensitive of our ailments.

obesity (əʊ'besɪtɪ, -'biːsɪtɪ). [ad. L. *obēsitās*, f. *obēs-us* OBESE: cf. F. *obésité*.] The condition of being obese; excessive fatness or corpulence.

1611 COTGR., *Obesité*, obesitie. **1620** VENNER *Via Recta* Introd. 12 Those that feare obesity, that is, would not waxe grosse. **1728** POPE *Dunc.* I. Notes (1736) 110 He may justly be called a martyr to obesity. **1847** J. WILSON *Chr. North* (1857) I. 156 The cattle.. eat themselves up.. into obesity. *fig.* **1812** W. TAYLOR in *Monthly Rev.* LXVIII. 254 Many writers have perished of literary obesity. **1876** FAIRBAIRN *Strauss* II. in *Contemp. Rev.* June 138 A religion as well as a man may perish through obesity.

[**obesse, obess**, app. mispr. for *chesse*, CHESS.

1626 SIR CH. CORNWALLIS *Dis. Pr. Henry* (1641) 17 Yet would [he] sometimes play at Obesse at Biliors and at Cards. [Reprinted in *Harl. Misc.*; thence in Halliwell, etc.]

obet(e, obs. forms of OBIT.

‖**obex** ('əʊbeks). [L. *obex, obic-em* barrier, bolt, f. *obicĕre* to cast in front of, f. *ob-* (OB- 1 a) + *jacĕre* to cast.]

1. An impediment, an obstacle. Now *rare* or *Obs.*

1611 CORYAT *Crudities* 442 That he might object the same as an obex or barre for repulsing the violent inuasion of the Batavians. **1681** FLAVEL *Meth. Grace* xix. 337 The great obex or bar to our enjoyment of God, is.. removed by the death of Christ. **1874** *Chron. Convocation* 29 Apr. 126 If this Lower House should interpose any obex or bar.

2. *Anat.* A small plate of white nervous substance sometimes occurring in the membrane forming the roof of the fourth ventricle of the brain, over the point of the *calamus scriptorius*, and filling the angle between the diverging *funiculi graciles*. *Syd. Soc. Lex.* (1892).

obey (əʊ'beɪ), *v.* Forms: 3–6 obeie, 4–7 obeye, (5 obbey(e, abeyȝe, abey), 5–6 obay(e, obaie, (6 abeye, abaye), 5– obey. [ME. *obei-en*, a. F. *obéir*:—L. *obēdīre*, orig. *obœdīre* to give ear, hearken, obey f. *ob-* (OB- 1 a) + *audīre* to hear. Certain parts of the F. verb (e.g. pr. pple. *obéiss-ant*, 3 pl. pres. *ils obéiss-ent*) have the lengthened stem *obéiss-* (L. type **obēdīsc-ĕre*), whence the Eng. secondary verb OBEISH, OBEIS, as well as OBEISANCE, etc.

F. *obéir*, like L. *obēdīre*, is an intransitive verb, construed with a dative pronoun, or the prep. *à*: *je lui obéis*; *nous obéissons au roi, aux lois.* When the vb. was taken into Eng., the dative and accusative were already levelled under the common object case, or objective; hence, the Eng. construction was either with a simple object, representing the dative, or with the preposition *to*, the vb. being thus syntactically, either trans. or intr. in the same sense. The const. with *to* has now become obsolete, and that with the simple object survived; an intrans. use, e.g. 'to obey is better than sacrifice', is now felt as an absolute use of the transitive. The trans. construction is here taken first, but it is to be remembered that the object was orig. a dative.]

1. *trans.* (orig. *intr.* with *dat. object*).

a. To comply with, or perform, the bidding of; to do what one is commanded by (a person); to submit to the rule or authority of, to be obedient to. (In quot. 1631, To comply with or accede to the request of: cf. OBEDIENT 3.)

c **1290** *S. Eng. Leg.* I. 76/179 For-to obeien is souereins: he wende forth. *c* **1391** CHAUCER *Astrol.* Prol., God save the kyng & alle that him feyth bereth & obeieth. *c* **1470** HENRY *Wallace* VI. 793 Fra Gamlis peth the land obeyt him haill, Til Ur wattir. **1523** LD. BERNERS *Froiss.* I. viii. 6 They wolde all.. abeye her and her sonne Edward, as they were bounde to do. **1529** S. FISH *Supplic. Beggars* 11 The highe powers shuld be alweys obeid. *a* **1631** DONNE *Lett., To Sir H. Goodere* (1651) 203, I cannot obey you, if you go to morrow to Parsons-green. **1638** SIR T. HERBERT *Trav.* (ed. 2) 25 It lately obeyed a Queen rectrix.. but now submits to a King. **1697** DRYDEN *Virg. Georg.* III. 184 The Lapithæ.. taught the Steed.. T' obey the Rider. **1794** MRS. RADCLIFFE *Myst. Udolpho* xliv, You shall be obeyed, my lord. **1842** TENNYSON *Dora* 57, I have obey'd my uncle until now.

b. To comply with, perform (a command, etc.).

c **1400** *Destr. Troy* 506 Chethes.. Bade his doughter come doune.. And sho obeit his bone, & of boure come. *a* **1533** LD. BERNERS *Huon* lxi. 212 We are redy to obey your commaundementes. **1578** TIMME *Caluine on Gen.* 255 How reverently His Word was to be obeied. **1667** MILTON *P.L.* VI. 185 Let mee serve.. God.. and his Divine Behests obey. **1762** GOLDSM. *Cit. W.* xlvi, The ladies obeying the summons, came up in a group. **1891** E. PEACOCK *N. Brendon* I. 60 Brendon obeyed orders.

c. To submit to, subject oneself to; to act in accordance with (a principle, authority, etc.). Now *rare* or *arch.*

a **1400–50** *Alexander* 3983 Latt þan þine erlis and þine erd myne empire obeyi. **1539** BIBLE (Great) *Rom.* ii. 8 Vnto them that are rebelles, and that do not obey the trueth, but folowe vnrighteousnes [**1611** doe not obey the trueth, but obey vnrighteousnes]. **1667** MILTON *P.L.* ix. 351 What obeyes Reason, is free. **1733** POPE *Ess. Man* III. 213 Virtue .. The same which in a Sire the Sons obey'd.

d. *fig.* (chiefly of things or involuntary agents): To act according to, or as compelled by (a thing, agency, force, impulse, etc.); to be actuated by.

1598 SHAKS. *Merry W.* III. iii. 204 His dissolute disease will scarse obey this medicine. **1646** J. HALL *Horæ Vac.* 146 He..that can make his hand obey the judgement of his eye. **1729** BUTLER *Serm.* Wks. 1874 II. Pref. 14 Brutes obey their instincts. **1813** BYRON *Corsair* I. xvii, He marks how well the ship her helm obeys. **1871** B. STEWART *Heat* (ed. 2) §67 A perfect gas obeys Gay Lussac's law.

†**e.** *to obey obedience*, to render obedience due.

1426 AUDELAY *Poems* 11 Thai most obey obedyans that thai be bounden to. *Ibid.* 17 And obey obedyans and kepe observans.

f. Naut. phr. ***obey orders, if (though) you break owners***, obey orders, even when they are wrong.

1840 R. H. DANA *Two Yrs. before Mast* xvii. 92 It almost broke our poor darky's heart when he heard that Bess [a pet pig] was to be taken ashore... 'Obey orders, if you break owners!' said he..and lent a hand to get her over the side. **1849** H. MELVILLE *Redburn* I. vi. 57 The motto is, 'Obey orders, though you break owners'. **1915** J. E. PATTERSON *Epistles from Deep Seas* xiv. 300 There was the unwritten shipboard law: 'Obey orders, even if you break owners.' **1924** R. CLEMENTS *Gipsy of Horn* iii. 50 What could be sounder than 'Obey orders, if you break owners'—meaning, do as you're told, even if you know it's wrong.

†**2.** *intr.* To be obedient *to* or *unto*: **a.** a person: = 1 a. *Obs.*

1382 WYCLIF *1 Macc.* ii. 19 If alle folkis obeien to the kyng Antiochus,..Y and my sonys, and my bretheren shuln obeie to the lawe of oure fadris. *a* **1450** *Knt. de la Tour* (1868) 86 To obeye beter to her husbonde. **1523** LD. BERNERS *Froiss.* I. xxxiv. 48 The Emperour..commaunded..that..all..his subgiettes shulde obey to the kyng of England. *Ibid.* lxvii. 89 The most part of the contrey hath obeyed vnto him. **1611** BIBLE *Rom.* vi. 16 To whom yee yeeld your selues seruants to obey, his seruants ye are to whom ye obey. **1651** tr. *De-las-Coveras' Don Fenise* 86 His conductresse prayed him to stay a little, to whom he obeyed.

†**b.** a command, etc.: = 1 b. *Obs.*

1382 [see a]. **1424** *Paston Lett.* I. 14 [They] schuld stonde and obeye to the ordinaunce. *c* **1530** *Spirituall Counsayle* E v, Make me alwaye to obey to thy commaundementes. **1584** R. SCOT *Discov. Witchcr.* xv. viii. (1886) 335, I conjure thee..that thou doo obey to my words. **1667** MILTON *P.L.* I. 337 To their Generals Voyce they soon obeyd.

†**c.** a principle, authority, etc.: = 1 c. *Obs.*

c **1374** CHAUCER *Boeth.* I. pr. v. 15 (Camb. MS.) It ys a soueraigne fredom to ben gouernyd by the brydul of hym and obeye to hys Iustyce. *c* **1449** PECOCK *Repr.* 70 As the Romeyns obeieden to the open resoun and reproof which Seint Poul made. **1526** TINDALE *Rom.* i. 5 Thatt all gentiles shulde obeye to the fayth which is in his name. **1604** HIERON *Wks.* I. 476 To obey from the heart vnto the forme of doctrine, wherevnto thou..art..deliuered.

†**d.** *fig.* = 1 d. *Obs.*

c **1385** CHAUCER *L.G.W.* Prol. 90 As an harpe obeieth to the hond. *c* **1430** *Pilgr. Lyf Manhode* I. cxxii. (1869) 65 Whan he sygh þat his body..wolde not obeye to him. *c* **1566** J. ALDAY tr. *Boaystuau's Theat. World* T ij b, So that his spirites..was constrained to obey to the harmony that proceeded from the instrument. **1604** E. G. tr. *D'Acosta's Hist. Indies* III. xix. 181 For that all obeys to golde and silver.

3. *absol.* **a.** To do what one is commanded; to submit; to be obedient. (An original intrans. use, but now regarded as absol. use of sense 1.)

1390 GOWER *Conf.* I. 28 Ther myhte nothing contrevaille, Bot every contre most obeie. **1508** KENNEDIE *Flyting w. Dunbar* 42 Obey and ceis the play that thow pretendis. **1610** SHAKS. *Temp.* I. ii. 38 Obey, and be attentiue. **1667** MILTON *P.L.* XII. 126 Him God..voutsafes To call by Vision..hee straight obeys. **1733** POPE *Ess. Man* III. 196 Thus let the wiser make the rest obey. **1842** TENNYSON *Two Voices* 244 Will he obey when one commands? **1847** —— *Princess* v. 440 Man to command and woman to obey.

b. *fig.* Of a thing.

1567 MAPLET *Gr. Forest* 12 Adamant..draweth it [iron] to it, and this last followeth and obeyeth. **1667** MILTON *P.L.* VII. 453 The Earth obey'd, and..teem'd at a Birth Innumerous living Creatures. *Ibid.* VIII. 272 To speak I tri'd ..My Tongue obey'd.

†**4.** *refl.* [= F. *s'obéir*]. To submit oneself *to* or *unto*; = 2. In quot. *c* 1440[3], to comply with or accede *to* (a request). Also *trans.* To submit, subject (one's will) *to*. *Obs.*

a **1400–50** *Alexander* 2837 Obey þe to þe baratour. *c* **1420** *Chron. Vilod.* 3458 þey a-beyȝedone hem no-thyng to þe kyngus hest. *c* **1440** *Jacob's Well* 268 Obeye þe to þi god & to his comaundmentys. *Ibid.* 269 Obeye þi wyll to þi goddys wyll. *Ibid.* 270 Seynt gregorie seyth, ȝif we be obedyent to oure prelatys & curatys, god schal obeye hym to oure prayerys. *c* **1450** *Merlin* 104 Wele ye Than obbey yow to this eleccion? **1477** EARL RIVERS (Caxton) *Dictes* 6 b, Humble and obeye yourself to your kyng.

5. *intr. Astrol.* Said of certain signs of the zodiac in relation to others (called *commanding* or *sovereign* signs), or of planets when in such signs: see quots. (See also OBEDIENT 2.)

c **1391** CHAUCER *Astrol.* ii. §28 Gemini obeieth to Cancer, and taurus to leo, [etc.]... And thus euermo 2 signes that ben illike fer fro the heued of capricorne, obeien euerich of hem til other. **1696** PHILLIPS (ed. 5), *Obeying Signs*, the Southern, or six last Signs of the Zodiack are so called. **1819** WILSON *Dict. Astrol.*, *Northern signs*..are also called commanding signs, because planets in them are said to command, and those in the opposite signs to obey.

†**6.** (*with various constructions*). To do obeisance to, salute respectfully, bow to. *Obs.*

1390 GOWER *Conf.* III. 210 With that hire oghne lord cam nyh And is to themperour obeied. *c* **1430** *Syr Gener.* 6268 Whan he come to his presence, He obeid him with grete reuerence. *a* **1450** *Knt. de la Tour* (1868) 150 Fulle goodly thei reuerenced and obeyed eche to other as louyng cosynes and parentys. *c* **1475** *Babees Bk.* 85 At euery tyme obeye vnto youre lorde Whenne yee answere. *a* **1650** *Sir Lambewell* 577 in Furniv. *Percy Folio* I. 162 She..obayd her to the King soe hend, & tooke leaue away to wend.

Hence **o'beyed** *ppl. a.*, **o'beying** *vbl. sb.* and *ppl. a.*: also **o'beyingly** *adv.*

c **1489** CAXTON *Sonnes of Aymon* xxvi. 550, I sawe that.. ye were obeyeng to me. **1607** HIERON *Wks.* I. 308 The willing obeying of the Lord. **1654–66** EARL ORRERY *Parthen.* (1676) 536 Arsaces had given an obeyed command. **1656** *Artif. Handsom.* 52 They are servings and obeyings of it. **1843** CARLYLE *Past & Pr.* II. ix, To learn obeying is the fundamental art of governing. **1864** WEBSTER, *Obeyingly.*

†**obey**, *sb. Obs. rare.* [f. prec. vb.] = OBEDIENCE 2. In phr. *at his obey* = at his command.

1584 R. SCOT *Discov. Witchcr.* xv. ii. (1886) 316 Six and twentie legions are at his obeie and commandement.

obeyable (əʊˈbeɪəb(ə)l), *a. rare.* [f. OBEY *v.* + -ABLE.] That can, or should, be obeyed.

1676 M. CLIFFORD *Hum. Reason* in *Phenix* (1708) II. 550 No Authority is obeyable or believable in it self, without farther examination. **1894** *Season* X. No. 9. 36/2 The tenth commandment appears to me fairly obeyable.

o'beyance. [f. OBEY *v.* + -ANCE: cf. next.] Obedience; obeisance, homage.

a **1400–50** *Alexander* 5106 To ȝour honoure with obeyaunce me ane I comaunde. **1422** tr. *Secreta Secret., Priv. Priv.* 131 Than shalte thow fynde Frendis wythout Fayle, obeiance in al thynge. **1460** CAPGRAVE *Chron.* (Rolls) 171 In vhech letter he mad a new obeiauns to the Kyng. **1921** C. E. MULFORD *Bar-20 Three* x. 118 The obeyance of the order might possibly be accepted by the crowd as grounds for justification. **1939** JOYCE *Finnegans Wake* III. 540 Obeyance from the townsmen spills felixity by the toun. **1950** *Tablet* 9 Dec. 504/1 Erecting pointed arches in blind obeyance of mechanical efficiency.

†**o'beyand**, *a. north. Obs.* [The pr. pple. of OBEY *v.*, treated as identical with OBEYANT.] Obeying, obedient.

c **1400** MAUNDEV. (Roxb.) iii. 9 þai er noȝt obeyand to þe kirke of Rome. *Ibid.* xvii. 78 Til hir þai er all obeyand. **1450–70** *Golagros & Gaw.* 1217 Now wil I be obeyand.

†**o'beyant**, *a. Obs.* [f. OBEY *v.* + -ANT[1]: not in Fr.] Obedient.

c **1400** MAUNDEV. (Roxb.) xxvi. 124 Will ȝe be obeyaunt vnto my comaundementes? **1422** tr. *Secreta Secret., Priv. Priv.* 123 Al thay shal be to yow obeyaunt. *Ibid.* 135 That he be..subiecte and obeyaunte to the laue of god.

obeyer (əʊˈbeɪə(r)). [f. OBEY *v.* + -ER[1].] One who obeys.

1551 T. WILSON *Logike* 44 The captaine is the efficient commaunder, the soldiour the efficient obei[e]r. **1680** BAXTER *Cath. Commun.* (1684) 28 You should have distinguished..the evil of the Law and Law-maker from the evil of the Obeyer. **1777** BURKE *Corr.* (1844) II. 201 A true obeyer of the laws. **1867** EMERSON *Lett. & Soc. Aims* vii. 177 Newton the philosopher, the perceiver, and obeyer of truth.

obeysa(u)nce, -a(u)nt, obs. ff. OBEISANCE, -ANT.

obeysche, -eyse, -eysshe, var. OBEISH.

†**ob'firm**, *v. Obs.* [ad. L. *obfirmā-re* (also *offirmāre*), to render firm or steadfast; refl., to persevere in, persist, be obstinate; f. *ob-* (OB- 1 b) + *firmāre* to strengthen, *firm-us* strong, FIRM.] *trans.* To make firm (in bad sense); to confirm (*in* an evil course, erroneous opinion, etc.); to make stubborn or obstinate; to harden.

1563–87 FOXE *A. & M.* (1684) II. 110 An obstinate and stubborn person, obfirmed in his own opinion. **1612** T. TAYLOR *Comm. Titus* iii. 3 In some subiects the will is confirmed and free to nothing but good... In some..the will is obfirmed and hardened in euill. **1629** BURTON *Babel no Bethel* Epist. to Cholmley 8 You haue..obdurated and obfirmed the hearts of Recusants. **1686** H. MORE *Disc. Real Pres.* 20 To obfirm or harden us in our unbelief of.. Transubstantiation.

Hence †**ob'firmed** *ppl. a.*, confirmed in evil, hardened, stubborn, obdurate.

1597 J. KING *On Jonas* (1618) 182 An obstinate, obfirmed minde against the commandement of God. **1634** BP. HALL *Contempl., N.T.* IV. *Christ Betrayed*, The obfirmed traitor knows his way to the high-priests hall, and to the garden. **1637** —— *Rem. Prophanenesse* II. xi. 153 The obfirmed soule will hold out.

†**ob'firmate**, *v. Obs. rare.* [f. ppl. stem of L. *obfirmāre*: see prec.] = OBFIRM *v.*

1616 R. SHELDON *Mirac. Antichr.* 327 They..doe obfirmate and make obstinate their mindes for the constant suffering of death.

†**obfir'mation.** *Obs.* [ad. med.L. *obfirmātiōn-em* (Du Cange), n. of action from L. *obfirmāre*: see OBFIRM.] The action of confirming or state of being confirmed in evil; stubborness, obduracy.

1592 tr. *Junius on Rev.* ix. 20 An impenitent obfirmation of the ungodly in their impiety. **1612** W. SCLATER *Ministers Portion* 43 Begetting..either a loathnesse to bee informed, or obfirmation against all perswasions. **1656** H. MORE *Enthus. Tri.* (1712) 41 A Spartan obfirmation of Mind, back'd with the sense of shame. **1665** JER. TAYLOR *Unum Necess.* ii. §2 The obfirmation and obstinacy of mind by which they shut their eyes against that light.

ob'fuscate, *ppl. a.* Now *rare* or *Obs.* [ad. L. *obfuscāt-us* (also *offuscātus*), pa. pple. of *obfuscāre*: see next. Cf. the later variant OFFUSCATE.] Darkened, obscured, obfuscated (*lit.* and *fig.*).

1531 ELYOT *Gov.* II. vii, The vertues beynge in a cruell persone be..obfuscate or hyd. **1535** STEWART *Cron. Scot.* III. 173 Obfuscat wes thair honour and thair name. **1600** E. BLOUNT *Hosp. Inc. Fooles* 25 Their disturbed braine.. obfuscate understanding. **1621** BURTON *Anat. Mel.* III. ii. III. iv. (1651) 482 A very obfuscate and obscure sight. **1888** *Pall Mall G.* 14 Feb. 11/2 Even the Tories, in their stupid and obfuscate way, are conscious of the fact.

obfuscate (əbˈfʌskeɪt, ˈɒbfʌskeɪt), *v.* [f. L. *obfuscāt-*, ppl. stem of *obfuscāre* to darken, obscure, f. *ob-* (OB- 1 b) + *fuscāre* to darken, *fuscus* dark. See also the later form OFFUSCATE.]

1. *trans.* To darken, obscure (physically); to deprive of light or brightness; to overshadow or eclipse; to make dark or dusky. Now *rare.*

1650 EARLE MONM. tr. *Senault's Man bec. Guilty* 336 [That] a constellation which was in all things inferiour to the Sun, should obfuscate his beauties. **1725** BRADLEY *Fam. Dict.* s.v. *Garden*, A Garden should not be obfuscated or darkened. **1734** EAMES in *Phil. Trans.* XXXVIII. 255 Atmospheres..so dense..as may suffice to obfuscate..the Light of the Star. *a* **1834** LAMB *In re Squirrels* Misc. Wks. (1871) 421 Rather more obfuscated than your fruit of Seville.

†**2.** *fig.* To darken or obscure to the mind or intellectual perception; to deprive of clearness, render obscure; to deprive of lustre or glory, throw into the shade. *Obs.*

1536 *Act 28 Hen. VIII*, c. 10 The..usurped auctorite of ..the pope.. which did obfuscate and wrest goddes holy word. **1623** HEXHAM *Tongue-Combat* 94 To obfuscate truth, and cause men to..beleeue lyes. **1628** PRYNNE *Love-lockes* 53 Ecclipsing, obfuscating, and deprauing that naturall and liuely Beauty. **1702** ECHARD *Eccl. Hist.* (1710) 474 To obfuscate the brightness of the Gospel.

3. To deprive of clearness of perception: **a.** to dim (the sight); **b.** to darken, obscure (the understanding, judgement, etc.); to darken the understanding of (a person), stupefy, bewilder.

1577 PATERICKE tr. *Gentillet* (1602) 33 Love of ones selfe obfuscateth and blindeth judgement. **1656** W. COLES *Art of Simpling* xxxii. 115 If his sight be obfuscated and dull. **1729** BERKELEY *Serm.* Wks. 1871 IV. 632 Curb..every passion, each whereof inebriates and obfuscates no less than drink or meat. *a* **1862** THOREAU *Yankee in Canada* iii. (1866) 43 The process, not of enlightening, but of obfuscating the mind. **1893** VIZETELLY *Glances back* I. xii. 239 He was obfuscated with brandy and water.

Hence **obfuscated** *ppl. a.*

1620 VENNER *Via Recta* Introd. 6 The Inhabitants..haue turbid and obfuscated spirits. **1792** A. YOUNG *Trav. France* 195 The houses are of an ugly obfuscated brick. **1876** J. WEISS *Wit, Hum. & Shaks.* iii. 79 An obfuscated person who was feeling around in vain to recover his carpet-bag.

obfuscation (ɒbfʌˈskeɪʃən). [ad. L. *obfuscātiōn-em*, n. of action from *obfuscāre*: see prec. Cf. also OFFUSCATION.]

1. The action of obfuscating, or condition of being obfuscated; darkening, obscuration:

a. physical, or of the sight (see prec. 1, 3 a).

1608 TOPSELL *Serpents* 214 It [the bite of the serpent Pelias] bringeth obfuscation or dimnesse to the eyes. **1794–6** E. DARWIN *Zoon.* (1801) I. 28 In cataracts and obfuscations of the cornea. **1881** E. W. GOSSE in *Fortn. Rev.* June 692 Mr. W...has in this instance [in a portrait] given the poet a sort of obfuscation which is not entirely satisfactory.

b. of an object of perception or thought.

1656 JEANES *Mixt. Schol. Div.* 61 This morall corruption and obfuscation of the soules immortality by worldly mindednesse. **1660** WATERHOUSE *Arms & Arm.* 77 Which variation causing much obfuscation in History. **1886** BYNNER *A. Surriage* xxix. 341 The obfuscation is studied.

c. of the understanding, etc.: Stupefaction, bewilderment (see prec. 3 b).

1621 BURTON *Anat. Mel.* I. iii. II. iv. (1651) 202 Care, sorrow, and anxiety, obfuscation of spirits. **1837** *Old Commodore* I. 31 That obfuscation..with which he was always afflicted on shore. **1878** DODS *Mohammed, Buddha & Christ* i. 26 His conscience was in a state of obfuscation.

2. *transf.* Something that darkens, or obscures.

1660 H. MORE *Myst. Godl.* x. xii. 526 Quite rid of all pretended Traditions and whatever obfuscations and entanglements of humane Invention. **1881** J. OWEN *Even. w. Skeptics* viii. II. 142 Too often theologians, like..cuttle-fish, escape pursuit by enveloping themselves in their self-raised obfuscations.

ob'fuscity (ɒbˈfʌsɪtɪ). *rare*[−1]. [f. *obfusc-ous*: see -ITY.] Obfuscated condition, obfuscation.

1832 J. WILSON in *Blackw. Mag.* XXXII. 711 A brutal state of mental obfuscity.

obfuscous (ɒbˈfʌskəs), *a. rare*[−1]. [f. L. type **obfusc-us* (f. *ob-*, OB- 1 + *fusc-us* dark) + -OUS. Cf. OF. *obfusque, offusque*, It. *offusco*: see OFFUSC.] Dark in colour or aspect, dusky.

1822–34 *Good's Study Med.* (ed. 4) IV. 450 The term is [*khh*] (cecha).., and it immediately imports obfuscous, or over-cast with shade or smoke.

†**ob'fusk**, *v. Obs.* Also 6 -ke, 6–8 -que. [a. OF. *obfusquer*, also *offusquer*, ad. L. *ob-*, *offuscāre* to darken. See also OFFUSQUE.] = OBFUSCATE *v.*
1490 CAXTON *Eneydos* xi. 41 All my entendement is obfusked, endullyd and rauysshed. *c* **1540** BOORDE *The boke for to Lerne* C iij b, It doth obfuske and doth obnebulat the memorie. **1549** *Compl. Scot.* vi. 56 The interpositione of the mune..empeschis and obfusquis the beymis of the soune fra our sycht. *a* **1751** BOLINGBROKE *Fragm. Ess.* v. Wks. 1754 V. 68 A superfluous glare not only tires, but obfusques, the intellectual sight.

†**ob'ganiate**, *v. Obs. rare*$^{-0}$. [irreg. f. L. *obgannīre* (also *ogg-*) to yelp or growl at + -ATE[3].]
1623 COCKERAM, *Obganiate*, to trouble one with often repeating of one thing.

‖**obi**[1], **obia**, **obi-man**, **-woman**: see OBEAH.

‖**obi**[2] ('əʊbɪ). [Japanese *ōbi* belt.] A brightly coloured sash worn round the waist by Japanese women and children.
1878 LADY BRASSEY *Voy. Sunbeam* xx. 335 They [Japanese children] wore gay embroidered *obis*, or large sashes. **1893** SIR E. ARNOLD in *Graphic* 15 Apr. 412/3 The *obi* [may be] a spendid piece of figured satin.

‖**obi**[3] ('əʊbɪ). *W. Afr.* [Igbo.] In Nigeria, a native hut.
1931 *Discovery* May 154/1 The more important natives have what is called an *obi* house, which is practically a shrine to the family gods and ancestors. **1937** C. K. MEEK *Law & Authority in Nigerian Tribe* iii. 62 It [*sc.* a wooden pillar] is fixed inside the householder's *obi* (entrance hut) facing outwards. **1958** C. ACHEBE *Things fall Apart* ix. 69 'Where do you sleep with your wife, in your *obi* or in her own hut?' asked the medicine-man. **1962** —— in F. Ademola *Reflections* 24 Their grand-father..was waiting in his Obi when his grand-children arrived.

‖**obi**[4] ('əʊbɪ). *W. Afr.* Also Obi. [Ibo: see quot. 1958.] A king of the Onitsha people of Nigeria.
1937 C. K. MEEK *Law & Authority in Nigerian Tribe* x. 219 At Onitsha it was a capital offence for any one to have sexual relations with a wife of the Obi. **1958** J. S. COLEMAN *Nigeria* i. 28 The *obi* (an Ibo term—of likely Yoruba origin—for king or chief) was appointed by the Oba of Benin. **1973** *Times Lit. Suppl.* 9 Mar. 258/3 It is these sons who today are trying to rediscover..their ancient customs and, in particular, those relating to the office of King (Obi) of Onitsha.

obia: see OBEAH.

Obie ('əʊbɪ). *U.S. Theatr.* [repr. pronunc. of *OB*, colloq. abbrev. OFF-BROADWAY *a.* and *sb.*] One of a number of annual awards for off-Broadway experimental theatre productions. Also *attrib.*
1967 *National Observer* (U.S.) 10 Apr. 20/1 Last year several 'Obies', the prize theater awards normally reserved for the stalwarts of Off-Broadway, were given to OOB [*sc.* off-off-Broadway] veterans, among them actor Kevin O'Connor and playwright Sam Shepard. **1970** *Time* 12 Jan. 37 Meanwhile he was acting (six Broadway shows, 25 off-Broadway), collecting two Obies for off-Broadway performances, [etc.]. **1972** *Village Voice* (N.Y.) 1 June 54/2 Sharon Thie's play with its Open Theatre performers, including Sharon Gans (Obie winner for her performance as November). **1973** *Black World* Apr. 20/2 The next Proscenium production of Black significance was Derek Walcott's Obie Award-winning *Dream on Monkey Mountain.*

obimbricate (ɒ'bɪmbrɪkət), *a. Bot.* [See OB- 2.] Imbricate, with the scales decreasing in length from without inwards, as the involucre in some *Compositæ*.
1857 MAYNE *Expos. Lex.*, *Obimbricatus*, that which is imbricated contrariwise; applied by H. Cassini to the scales of the *periclinium*..when..those of the interior rows are progressively shorter than those of the external: obimbricate. **1892** in *Syd. Soc. Lex.*

obit ('ɒbɪt, 'əʊbɪt), *sb. Obs.* exc. *Hist.* Forms: 4–6 obyt, 4–7 obite, (5–6 abit), 5–7 obitt, 5–7 (9 *arch.*) obyte, 6 obytt, obete, obbit, -yt, -et, -ett(e, (obijt, 6–9 obiit), 7 obet, 5- obit. [a. OF. *obit* (Wace 11th c.) = Sp. *óbito*, Pg. and It. *obito*, ad. L. *obit-us* a going down, setting, death, f. *obīre* to go down, perish, die, f. *ob-* (OB- 1 c) + *īre* to go. The frequent *obiit* was perh. due to identification with L. *obiit* 'he died'.]

†**1. a.** Departure from life, death, decease (of a particular person). *Obs.*
(In quot. 1694 a humorously pedantic imitation of Latin.) *c* **1375** *Sc. Leg. Saints* xxxiv. (*Pelagia*) 357 þe obyt be-tyd of hyre þe aucht day of octobre. *c* **1425** *Orolog. Sapient* v. in *Anglia* X. 365/19 To þat ende þat þou haue a blessid obyte. **1502** ARNOLDE *Chron.* (1811) 215 Abyde she in the chief hous and mansion of her husbond by xl. daies aftir the obyte of her husbond. **1625** USSHER *Answ. Jesuit* 189 The anniversarie commemoration of the obite of Oswald. **1694** MOTTEUX *Rabelais* v. (1737) 232 These Times denote Morbs to the Sane, and Obits to th' Ægrote.

b. A record or notice of a person's death, or of the date of it; an obituary notice. In mod. *colloq.* (esp. *journalists*') use usu. regarded as an abbrev. of OBITUARY *sb.*
1459 *Test. Ebor.* (Surtees) II. 227 Another olde Messe boke..in the which ar titled of olde tyme the Obitts of the auncetors..of the said Sir Thomas. **1535** BOORDE *Let.* in *Introd. Knowl.* (1870) Forew. 57 þe sayd reuerend faþer hath sentt to yow þe obytt off hys predycessor. **1673** WOOD *Life* June (O.H.S.) II. 265 Hutton told me his obit was in the Gazet. **1691** —— *Ath. Oxon.* I. 415 A Latine Manuscript containing the obits and characters of many eminent Benedictines. **1874** *Athenæum* 12 Sept. 353 The sub-editor of a New York daily newspaper wrote to me begging me to send him the proper materials for the construction of an obit. He said it was the custom of his journal to keep obits in readiness. **1899** C. PLUMMER *Two Saxon Chrons. Parallel* II. p. lxiv, Then comes a period, 893–958, during which E and F are almost barren, containing only a few obits, [etc.]. **1901** FARMER & HENLEY *Slang* (1902) V. 85/1 *Obit*..(journalists') an obituary notice. **1935** *Atlantic Monthly* Jan. 43 (*title*) Obit for E. Harris. **1953** *N.Y. Times* 9 Aug. 8/3 This is not the obit page. **1957** D. BETHURUM *Homilies of Wulfstan* 64 Wulfstan's obit is marked in MS Hatton 113, in an Ely calendar, and in the E and F *Chronicle*, 1023. **1964** W. R. NASH *How Newspapers Work* iv. 74 The 'obits'..are revised at regular intervals. **1972** *Daily Tel.* (Colour Suppl.) 11 Aug. 5/1 The obituarists polish their obits. **1975** B. MEGGS *Matter of Paradise* (1976) IV. iv. 96 Doc had been given a very nice obit coverage on page 42.

2. †**a.** A ceremony or office performed at the burial of a deceased person; funeral rites, obsequies. (Also in *pl.*) *Obs.*
c **1400** *Destr. Troy* 5357 Honour me with obit as ogh myn astate. **1525** LD. BERNERS *Froiss.* II. xliii. 141 When the kynges obyte was done, the comons of Lysbone..wente to the cathedral chyrche. **1556** *Chron. Gr. Friars* (Camden) 96 The xxvij. of June [1555] was kept the obijt of the kynges grandhame, with a goodly herse as ever was sene. **1660** OGILBY *Iliad* xxiv. (*end*), Thus Hectors Obits celebrated were. **1708** *Termes de la Ley* 449 b, *Obit* is a Funeral solemnity or office for the dead, most commonly performed at the Funeral when the Corps lies in the Church uninterred.

b. A ceremony or office (usually a mass) performed in commemoration of, or on behalf of the soul of, a deceased person (esp. a founder or benefactor of some institution) on the anniversary or other mind-day of his death; a yearly (or other) memorial service. *Obs.* exc. *Hist.*
c **1400** *Apol. Loll.* 103 If þei vow þem to hold an abit, or oþer ritis. **1408** *E.E. Wills* (1882) 15 My obytis, that ys for to sayn, my ȝerys mynde. **1494** FABYAN *Will* in *Chron.* Pref. 7, I will, that by the terme of .ix. years after my decesse be kept an obite wtin the parisshe churche of seynt Benet Fynk. **1562** A. SCOTT *New Year's Gift* 91 With owklie abitis to augment þair rentalis. *a* **1670** HACKET *Abp. Williams* I. (1693) 215 Obits, Dirges, Masses are not said for nothing. **1732** NEAL *Hist. Purit.* I. 42 Some preached against the lawfulness of Soul Masses and Obits. **1851** W. WHITE *Hist. Staffordsh.* 498 Ralph Lord Basset..died in 1389, and for the yearly keeping of his obit, gave 200 marks to the altar of St. Nicholas.

†**c.** A gift or offering made at or for such an office, or in commemoration of a deceased person.
1522 *Wills & Inv. N.C.* (Surtees 1835) 106, I will that myne Executor make an obbet of xxs at my twelfmonth day. **1566** *Eng. Ch. Furniture* (Peacock 1866) 103 An obbett geven to ye sayd chirch by John Cod..off the valew of three schillynges and fowre pence by yere to have bene bestowed off the pore..in bred.

†**3.** The setting of a heavenly body. *Obs. rare.*
1686 GOAD *Celest. Bodies* I. xii. 53 The Rises and Obits of the Planets.

4. *attrib.* and *Comb.* (in senses 2 a and 2 b), as ***obit book, day, feast, gift, rite, silver, song, Sunday***.
1520 *Lanc. Wills* II. 7 To kepe myne obete days and to pray for me. **1558** PHAER *Æneid* VII. S ij b, When her obyt ryghtes were ended all, And tombe vpreysyd. **1565** GOLDING *Ovid's Met.* XII. (1593) 286 Hold here an obit-gift he said. **1587** —— *De Mornay* xxii. 339 (As Tertullian saieth) the Obit-feast differeth not from Iupiters feast. **1609** J. DAVIES *Holy Roode* (1878) 27/1 Of sad sighes, they make their Obiit-Song. **1725** Obit book [see OBITUARY A. 1]. **1897** *Daily News* 27 Sept. 5/2 Yesterday being 'Obiit Sunday' Bp. Barry preached a special sermon at St. George's Chapel, Windsor.

†**obit**, *a. Obs. rare.* In 5 obitte. [ad. L. *obit-us*, pa. pple. of *obīre*: see prec.] Departed, deceased, dead.
c **1440** *York Myst.* xxxvii. 269 þai [prophets] saide þat I [Jesus] schulde be obitte, To hell þat I schulde entre in, And saue my seruauntis fro þat pitte.

†**'obital**, *a.* and *sb. Obs.* [f. OBIT *sb.* + -AL[1]: the etymological form from L. *obitu-s* is OBITUAL.]
A. *adj.* Recording or commemorating a death or deaths, or the celebration of obits (see prec. 2 b).
1690 WOOD *Life* (O.H.S.) III. 330 May 10..alderman Thomas Fifield died. [Entered] in obital book. **1691** —— *Ath. Oxon.* I. 415 This obital book..I have in my little Library. **1694** —— *Life* 10 July (O.H.S.) III. 460 Edward Wells..spoke a speech in praise of Dr. John Fell (being his obitall day). **1715** M. DAVIES *Athen. Brit.* I. 121 The White-Book, or Obital-Book of that Church.

B. *sb.* A record or register of deaths, or of obit-days; an obituary.
1691 WOOD *Ath. Oxon.* I. 415 This English obital was pen'd by another Benedictine.

†**obi'taneously**, *adv. nonce-wd.* [f. *obitaneous adj. (irreg. f. L. *obiter* (see next) + *-aneous*, as in *instantaneous, momentaneous*, etc.) + -LY[2].] By the way, in passing: = next, A.
a **1834** COLERIDGE *Confess. Enq. Spir.* ii. (1840) 18 That such a Doctrine..should be left thus faintly, thus obscurely, and, if I may so say, obitaneously, declared.

obiter ('ɒbɪtə(r)), *adv.*, *a.*, and *sb.* [L. *obiter* adv., orig. two words, *ob iter*, by the way.]

A. *adv.* **a.** By the way, in passing, incidentally.
1573 G. HARVEY *Letter-bk.* (Camden) 9 Al this was spokin obiter at the table. **1626** BACON *Sylva* §166 The Communication of Sounds..hath been touched *obiter* in the Majoration of Sounds. **1716** M. DAVIES *Athen. Brit.* II. 209 [He] never thought worth his while to mention his Life nor Writings, not so much as obiter or occasionally. **1841** J. H. NEWMAN *Tamworth Reading Room* in *Discuss. & Argts.* (1872) 262 Sir Robert does obiter talk of improved modes of draining. **1886** SIR C. BOWEN in *Law Rep.* 34 Chanc. Div. 37 The present Master of the Rolls..expressed *obiter* an opinion..with which..I cannot agree.

b. *esp.* in the phr. **obiter dictum** [L., (a thing) said by the way]: in *Law*, An expression of opinion on a matter of law, given by a judge in court in the course of either argument or judgement, but not forming an essential part of the reasons determining the decision, and therefore not of binding authority; hence *gen.* Anything said by the way, an incidental statement or remark.
1812 *Edin. Rev.* XIX. 302 It was more of an *obiter dictum* than of a point ruled. **1831** *Ibid.* LIV. 289 The *obiter dictum* of a judge or two. **1865** FARRAR *Chapt. Lang.* i. (1878) 8 The supposed revelation of language from the obiter dictum of an *auctoris aliud agentis*. *a* **1884** in A. Birrell *Obiter Dicta* title-p., An *obiter dictum*, in the language of the law, is a gratuitous opinion, an individual impertinence which, whether it be wise or foolish, right or wrong, bindeth none—not even the lips that utter it.

B. quasi-*adj.* (after *obiter dictum*). Made or uttered by the way; incidental.
1767 LD. MANSFIELD in *Burrow's Rep.* IV. 2068 That is an *obiter* saying only; and not a resolution or determination of the Court. **1769** BURROW *Ibid.* 2294 Mr. Justice Willes..declared, that he should give no *obiter* opinion about personal property..being liable to be rated. **1891** SIR R. WEBSTER in *Daily News* 21 Apr. 3/2 The obiter observations said to have been made by magistrates' clerks. **1957** G. SCHWARZENBERGER *Internat. Law* (ed. 3) I. xxiv. 437 The Commission's observations..were strictly *obiter dicta*. As, however, the reformulation of Article 18..followed the line taken in this Award, the view expressed by the Commission, though *obiter*, deserves not to pass unnoticed. **1959** 'W. HAGGARD' *Venetian Blind* ii. 24 Mr Justice Downderry refused an injunction. He did more. He made it very clear that his remarks were *obiter*, but he was exquisitely acidulous.

C. *sb.* Something said, done, or occurring by the way; an incidental matter. Also, an *obiter dictum.*
1607 WALKINGTON *Opt. Glass* 160 In so little a toy vnlesse there were obiters, what would be worthy vewing? **1650** FULLER *Pisgah* II. iv. 109 Each parenthesis of our Saviours motion is full of heavenly matter, and his *obiter* more to the purpose, than our *iter*. **1927** *Daily Tel.* 19 July 9/2 Lord Justice Scrutton recalled a recent obiter by Mr. Justice Eve to the effect that [etc.].

†**'obiterly**, *adv. Obs. rare*$^{-1}$. [irreg. f. L. *obiter* (see prec.) + -LY[2].] = prec., A.
1605 VERSTEGAN *Dec. Intell.* iii. (1628) 82, I haue hitherto spoken as I yet intend to speake (except obiterly).

obitual (əʊ'bɪtjʊəl), *a.* and *sb. rare.* [f. L. *obitu-s* OBIT + -AL[1]: cf. *habitual.*]
A. *adj.* = OBITAL A. (In quot. 1887 in reference to an obituary notice.)
1706 PHILLIPS, *Obituary*, a Calendar, or Register-Book, in which the Friers in a Monastery enter'd the Obits, or Obitual Days of their Founders and Benefactors. **1887** *Harper's Mag.* Dec. 146/1 The *Bassoon* [a newspaper] was so tearfully obitual. **1893** *Nation* (N.Y.) 30 Nov. 406/3 Obitual days constitute an important, distinctive, and ever recurrent feature in the proceedings of our national Legislature.
B. *sb.* = OBITAL B, OBITUARY A. 1.
1812 J. BRADY *Clav. Calend.* (1815) 202 The avaricious priests registered in their Obituals those persons who purchased such remembrance.

obituarian (əʊˌbɪtjuː'ɛərɪən). *U.S.* [f. OBITUARY + -IAN.] = OBITUARIST.
1909 in *Cent. Dict.* Suppl. II. 882/3 There is one characteristic story to be told about Robert Louis Stevenson which his obituarians have missed, probably because they knew nothing about it. **1971** *Sat. Rev.* (U.S.) 6 Nov. 44/3 Alden Whitman is the obituarian for The New York Times.

obituarist (əʊ'bɪtjʊərɪst). [f. OBITUARY + -IST: cf. *botanist.*] The writer of an obituary notice.
1792 *Childr. Thespis* 183 When the tomb claims his limbs shall the Obituarists say, Where's now his successor, so brilliant—so gay. **1871** M. COLLINS *Mrq. & Merch.* II. 262 The obituarists of Charles Dickens have some of them felt bound to defend him against the charge of being vulgar. **1905** M. BEERBOHM *Around Theatres* (1953) 399 The obituarists seem hardly to do justice to the intensely interesting personality of Irving in private life. **1930** A. HUXLEY *Brief Candles* 4 'Metaphysically and artistically a cretin.' 'The obituarist doesn't seem to be of your opinion.' **1961** P. FLEMING *Bayonets to Lhasa* 295 'The man' wrote one of his obituarists 'was greater than his message.' **1972** [see OBIT *sb.* 1 b]. **1974** *Punch* 3 Apr. 550/3 He joins the staff of this magazine as assistant obituarist. **1978** P. SUTCLIFFE *Oxf. Univ. Press* III. iii. 82 When he died in 1904 *The Times* obituarist attributed his failure to write in later life to the fact that he was unmethodical.

So **o'bituarize** *v. intr.*, to write an obituary notice; also *trans.*
1891 *Sat. Rev.* 17 Oct. 437/2 The enormously difficult task of 'obituarizing' with appropriateness on a departed enemy of their country. **1969** *Observer* 21 Dec. 28/2 Stand by for a barrage of TV programmes obituarising the Sixties.

1972 *Times Lit. Suppl.* 31 Mar. 352/2 Evelyn Waugh, obituarizing Duggan, wrote [etc.].

obituary (əʊˈbɪtjʊərɪ), *sb.* and *a.* [ad. med.L. *obituāri-us* adj. and sb., f. *obitu-s*: see OBIT and -ARY. Cf. F. *obituaire* (1690 in Hatz.-Darm.).]

A. *sb.* **1.** A register of deaths, or of obit-days.

1706 [see OBITUAL A]. **1725** HEARNE *R. Brunne* Pref. 25 *margin*, The Obituaries, or Obit Books of Bridlington. *Ibid.* 26 As may appear even from the Obituaries, or Obit Books. **1952** *Latin Litutg. MSS.* (Exhib. Guide, Bodl. Libr.) 35 *Obituary* (and martyrology) Secular; cathedral of St. Ethelbert, Hereford; mid-14th century.

2. A record or announcement of a death or deaths, esp. in a newspaper; usually comprising a brief biographical sketch of the deceased.

1738 BIRCH *Life Milton* M.'s Wks. 1738 I. 59 He died at his House in Bunhill-Row Novemer 15th, according to Mr. Richard Smith, his Neighbour, in his Obituary. **1792** BURNS *Let. to Mrs. Dunlop* 6 Dec., I scarcely look over the obituary of a newspaper, that I do not see some names that I have known. **1875** J. H. BENNET *Winter Medit.* I. vi. 161 The cold east winds of the spring, which yearly fill the obituaries. **1885** *Glasgow News* 31 Dec. 6/1 The obituary of the year is somewhat heavy.

B. *adj.* Relating to or recording a death (usually with a biographical sketch of the deceased).

1828 WEBSTER, *Obituary, a.* relating to the decease of a person or persons; as, an obituary notice. **1885** *19th Cent.* 269 His Lordship has given obituary notices of them in his blue book of 1883. **1900** G. C. BRODRICK *Mem. & Impr.* 157 If he could have written his own obituary memoir.

Hence **oˈbituarily** *adv.*, 'in the manner of an obituary' (Webster, 1864).

1889 G. B. SHAW *London Music 1888–89* (1937) 61 Madame Ilma de Murska is dead; and an ungrateful world is describing her obituarily as a person remarkable for a compass that extended to F in alt. **1902** *Westm. Gaz.* 1 Aug. 1/3 Whatever may happen 'obituarily' or otherwise..to the organisation and officials making these 'distributions', they have not ceased. **1974** *Daily Tel.* (Colour Suppl.) 22 Feb. 7/3 Perhaps the generation of the Seventies, will be willing to accept the notion of dressing the deceased (obituarily) in the same garments he wore in life, gravy stains and all.

object (ˈɒbdʒɪkt), *sb.* [Partly sb. use of OBJECT *ppl. a.*: cf. Lat. *objecta* pl. things objected, charges, accusations; but in philosophical and derived senses, ad. med. Schol. L. *objectum* (Duns Scotus *a* 1308, Prantl III. 208), lit. thing thrown before or presented to (the mind or thought); cf. OF. *object* (Oresme, 14th c.), now *objet.* In branch II rendering L. *objectu-s* , and so in origin a distinct word.]

I. From L. *objectum*, pl. *objecta*.

†**1.** A statement thrown in or introduced in opposition; an objection. *Obs.*

c **1380** WYCLIF *Sel. Wks.* I. 343 It is liȝt to assoile objectis aȝens þis. *Ibid.* II. 74 How Crist answeride to objectis of false Jewis. **1617** MINSHEU *Ductor*, An object or obiection.

†**2.** Something 'thrown' or put in the way, so as to interrupt or obstruct the course of a person or thing; an obstacle, a hindrance. *Obs.*

c **1450** tr. *De Imitatione* III. lxii. 144 þy frailte wherof þou hast experience in many smale obiectes & contrariousnes. *a* **1564** BECON *Comp. Lord's Supp. & Mass* in *Prayers*, etc. (1844) 380 The massmonger prateth and babbleth that the sacraments of the new law..to him that putteth not an object or let (I use the school-men's words), that is to say, to him that hath no actual purpose of deadly sin..give grace, righteousness, forgiveness of sins, the Holy Ghost.

3. a. Something placed before the eyes, or presented to the sight or other sense; an individual thing seen or perceived, or that may be seen or perceived; a material thing; *spec.* the thing or body of which an observation is made, or an image produced, by means of an optical instrument, or in drawing or perspective.

1398 TREVISA *Barth. De P.R.* III. xvi. (1495) d iv/1 þe obiecte of the eye is all þ^t may be seen, & al þ^t maye be herde is obiect to the heryng. **1567** MAPLET *Gr. Forest* 79 That the earth..should give to the nose obiecte so swete Or minister scent so strong. **1588** SHAKS. *L.L.L.* II. i. 70 His eye begets occasion for his wit, For euery obiect that the one doth catch, The other turnes to a mirth-mouing iest. **1613** PURCHAS *Pilgrimage* (1614) 829 Both Land and Water feasting varietie of senses with varietie of objects. **1736** BUTLER *Anal.* I. v. Wks. 1874 I. 93 Children, from their very birth, are daily growing acquainted with the objects about them. **1821** CRAIG *Lect. Drawing* iii. 183 To represent your object in the state of appearance which it has by its light and shadow. **1834** MEDWIN *Angler in Wales* I. 160 The torch's glare gave horrible indistinctness to objects. **1845** M. PATTISON *Ess.* (1889) I. 19 Several persons..producing different objects of value, declared that they had been given to them by the bishop. **1877** G. MACDONALD *Marquis of Lossie* xxviii, [The painter] looking up and finding no object in the focus of his eyes.

b. Something which on being seen excites a particular emotion, as admiration, horror, disdain, commiseration, amusement; a sight, spectacle, gazing-stock; formerly sometimes, an object (sense 4) of pity or relief, an afflicted person, sufferer; in colloq. use, a person or thing of pitiable or ridiculous aspect, a gazing-stock, 'guy', 'fright', 'sight'.

1588 GREENE *Perimedes* 43 Women are more glorious obiects. **1605** SHAKS. *Lear* v. iii. 238 Produce the bodies... Seest thou this obiect, Kent? **1607** —— *Timon* IV. iii. 122 Sweare against Obiects, Put Armour on thine eares, and on thine eyes. **1671** MILTON *Samson* 568 To sit idle on the houshold hearth,..to visitants a gaze, Or pitied object. **1740** BUTLER *Serm. Pub. Occas.* ii. *note*, Some poor objects will be sent thither in hopes of relief. **1826** in Hone *Every-day Bk.* II. 620 That their apprentices..were..rendered objects for the remainder of their lives. **1878** BESANT & RICE *Celia's Arb.* xxxvi. (1887) 260 The children are..breaking out again, in a way dreadful to look at. Forty-six is nothing but an Object—an Object—from insufficiency of diet.

c. *object of art* = *objet d'art* (OBJET 3). Also ***object of art and virtu*** (see sense 3 d and cf. OBJET 6).

1862 E. HALL *Diary* 5 June in O. A. Sherrard *Two Victorian Girls* (1966) 294 Went..to a private view of objects of art at South Kensington..the Wedgwood ware exquisite. **1863** MRS. GASKELL *Dark Night's Work* x. 180 The beautiful pictures and other objects of art in the house. **1879** C. SCHREIBER *Jrnl.* 6 Dec. (1911) II. 250 As an object of art, it is vile, but in an antiquarian point of view, most curious. **1894** G. DU MAURIER *Trilby* I. I. 66 I've brought you these objects of art and virtu to make the peace with you. **1918** A. BENNETT *Roll Call* I. viii. 152 The perfunctory accents in which she had catalogued her objects of art. **1925** CONRAD *Suspense* II. ii. 96 Cosmo looked at it with appreciation, as if it had been an object of art. **1973** W. JUST *Congressman who loved Flaubert* 119 The columnist treated Caroline as a singular object of art, a serene and delicate event.

d. ***object of virtu*** (see VIRTU, VERTU 1 c).

1914 A. HUXLEY *Let.* 13 May (1969) 59, I hope things at Eastbourne are more or less settled now... I gather that 27 will fairly burst with bits of objects of vertu and utility. **1970** S. J. PERELMAN *Baby, it's Cold Inside* 54 The objects of virtu rifled from a hundred auction rooms. **1971** *Daily Tel.* 11 May 10/5 The sale, of miniatures and objects of vertu brought £15,919. **1974** *Ibid.* 9 May 6/8 The sale of miniatures, gold watches, enamels and objects of vertu, totalled £37,294.

4. That to which action, thought, or feeling is directed; the thing (or person) to which something is done, or upon or about which something acts or operates (= *materia circa quem* in Scholastic philosophy). Const. *of* (the action, etc. or agent).

c **1586** C'TESS PEMBROKE *Ps.* CIX. x, Want and woe my life their object make. **1611** TOURNEUR *Ath. Trag.* v. i. Wks. 1878 I. 137 My wisedome that has beene The obiect of men's admiration. **1676** M. CLIFFORD *Hum. Reason* in *Phenix* (1708) II. 547 Matters that concern Religion..being ..a part of the Understanding's Object as much [as]..any other. **1697** LOCKE *Lett. to Stillingfleet* Wks. (Bohn) II. 340 Ideas are..the immediate objects of our minds in thinking. **1773** *Observ. State Poor* 47 He..will be deemed a proper object of public charity. **1845** M. PATTISON *Ess.* (1889) I. 27 The volume..which had formed the object of his study. **1853** J. H. NEWMAN *Hist. Sk.* (1873) II. I. iv. 170 To substitute objects of sense for objects of imagination.

5. a. The end to which effort is directed; the thing aimed at; that which one endeavours to attain or carry out; purpose, end, aim. ***the object of the exercise***: see EXERCISE *sb.* 8 h.

[Cf. Thomas Aquinas *Summa contra Gentes* I. lxxii, Objectum voluntatis est finis.]

1597 SHAKS. *2 Hen. IV*, IV. v. 67 How quickly Nature falls into reuolt, When Gold becomes her Obiect? **1665** SIR T. HERBERT *Trav.* (1677) 169 A Traveller is not to imagine pleasure his object. **1736** BUTLER *Anal.* I. iii. 85 Rendering public good an object and end to every member of the society. **1780** BENTHAM *Princ. Legisl.* xvi. §8 The first object ..is to prevent..all sorts of offences. **1821** D. STEWART *Progr. Philos.* II. iv. (1858) 317 The profession of Bayle.. made it an object to him to turn to account even the sweepings of his study. **1832** HT. MARTINEAU *Hill & Valley* iv. 52 Blast furnaces and forges serve no object but that for which they were erected. **1875** JOWETT *Plato* (ed. 2) I. 129 When you have heard the object of our visit.

b. ***no object***, not a thing aimed at or regarded as important to obtain. Freq. also used of distance, expense, etc., not taken into account or forming no obstacle.

See C. T. Onions in *S.P.E. Tract* (1930) XXXVI. 531–4. **1782** *Morning Herald* 20 May 4/2 (Advt.), A Gentle-woman..wishes to superintend the family of a single Gentleman or Lady..and salary will be no object. **1796** *Deb. Congress U.S.* 7 Apr. (1849) 878/2 Enjoying..unexampled prosperity,..the expense of completing the frigates could be no object to the country. **1800** *Morning Herald* 4 Jan. 4/2 (Advt.), Wanted, in Chatham-place or New Bridge-street, a roomy convenient House... Rent no object, if the house is agreeable. **1855** *Poultry Chron.* III. 67/2 Where every convenience is obtainable, and expense no object. *a* **1864** R. S. SURTEES *Mr. F. Romford's Hounds* (1865) i. 4 Money! Money would be no object to him! He'd give anything for a good horse! **1871** *English Mechanic* 20 Jan. 431/1 The colour of the solder is no object, as the joint will be hidden. **1873** J. H. BEADLE *Undevel. West* xxxv. 762 With one team to each family (time being no object to such people) it cost them nothing to move. **1886** *Encycl. Brit.* XX. 228/1 Only those travel who travel by necessity, or to whom money is no object. **1891** MRS. J. H. RIDDELL *Mad Tour* 3 The time when distance was, as the advertisements say, 'no object'. **1909** 'O. HENRY' *Roads of Destiny* iv. 62 She..gave her *a la carte* to fit me out—money no object. **1916** G. B. SHAW *Pygmalion* I. 116 *I'm* going home in a taxi... Eightpence aint no object to me, Charlie. **1926** A. BENNETT *Lord Raingo* II. lxxii. 326 'I'm thinking of going back to town now, sir.. Unless of course you'd like me to stay.' 'No object in staying,' Sam murmured, as if in disgust. **1930** *London Mercury* Nov. 45 Distance being no object.. scenes in Siam can be..transmitted. **1956** B. HOLIDAY *Lady sings Blues* (1973) xiv. 121 We looked for the best private sanatorium around. Money was no object. **1964** R. BRADDON *Year Angry Rabbit* xii. 109 Each side, having already bankrupted itself to finance this war, declared that money was no object.

6. *Metaph.* A thing or being of which one thinks or has cognition, as correlative to the thinking or knowing *subject*; something external, or regarded as external, to the mind; the non-ego as related to, or distinguished from, the ego; also extended to include states of the ego, or of consciousness, as thought of or mentally perceived. (Cf. OBJECTIVE A. 2 b.)

[**1513** DOUGLAS *Æneis* I. Prol. 379 *Obiectum* and *subiectum* ..termes tua, Quhilkis ar..rife amange clerkis in scule.] **1651** HOBBES *Leviath.* I. i, [The thoughts of men] are every one of them a representation or appearance of some quality or other accident of a body without us; which is called an Object. *a* **1670** RUST *Disc. Truth* (1682) 193 Concerning the truth of things, or Truth in the object. **1762** KAMES *Elem. Crit.* (1833) 471 Every thing we perceive or are conscious of, whether a being or a quality,..is with respect to the percipient termed an object. **1829** SIR W. HAMILTON *Disc., Philos. Unconditioned* Notes 5 The exact distinction of subject and object was first made by the schoolmen... These correlative terms correspond to the first and most important distinction in philosophy; they embody the original antithesis in consciousness of self and not-self. **1856** FERRIER *Inst. Metaph.* XXII. ix. (ed. 2) 393 The constitution of the synthesis of all cognition is..subject and object, the word *object* being used in the most general sense in which it can be employed to signify any thing, or thought, or state of mind whatsoever, of which any intelligence may be cognisant. **1860** MANSEL *Proleg. Log.* i. (ed. 2) 7 Every state of consciousness necessarily implies two elements at least; a conscious subject, and an object of which he is conscious.

7. *Gram.* A substantive word, phrase, or clause, immediately dependent on, or 'governed by', a verb, as expressing, in the case of a verb of action, the person or thing to which the action is directed, or on which it is exerted. Also, the word dependent on or 'governed by' a preposition, indicating that to which the preposition expresses a relation.

direct object of a verb: the word, etc., denoting that which is directly affected by the action (commonly expressed by the accusative, or case of direction *to*, in Latin and other languages); the word 'governed' by a transitive verb. So ***indirect object*** of a (transitive or intransitive) verb (commonly expressed by the dative case in Latin, etc.): see INDIRECT 3 c. ***object clause***, a clause or subordinate sentence forming the object of a verb, as in 'we know (that) he is alive'. Also ***object-case*** = ACCUSATIVE *a.* 1; ***object complement***, a word, usu. a noun or adjective, which complements the object of a verb, expressing the state or condition of the object at the time of, or resulting from, the action; cf. *objective complement*; ***object-pronoun***, a pronoun, esp. a relative pronoun, which is the object of a verb or which introduces an object clause.

[**1727–41** CHAMBERS *Cycl.* s.v. *Verb*, Verb Neuter, is that which signifies an action that has no particular object whereon to fall; but which, of itself, takes up the whole idea of the action.] *a* **1729** CLARKE (J.), The accusative after a verb transitive, or a sentence in room thereof, is called, by grammarians, the object of the verb. [**1824** L. MURRAY *Eng. Gram.* (ed. 5) I. 267 Verbs neuter do not act upon, or govern, nouns and pronouns... They are, therefore, not followed by an objective case, specifying the object of an action.] **1853** C. MARCEL *Lang. as Means Ment. Cult.* II. 26 The word denoting this complement of the action [of a transitive verb] is called *object*. **1870** W. W. GOODWIN *Elem. Greek Gram.* III. 167 Object clauses depending on verbs signifying *to strive for, to care for, to effect*, regularly take the future indicative after both primary and secondary tenses. **1877** WHITNEY *Essent. Eng. Gram.* iii. 32 We speak of both verbs and prepositions as governing in the objective the word that is their object. **1879** ROBY *Lat. Gram.* IV. viii. §1122 Some verbs have..two direct objects, one being a person, the other a thing. *Ibid.* ix. §1132 Not unfrequently..the indirect object in Latin corresponds to the direct object in English. **1881** MASON *Eng. Gram.* (ed. 24) §369 The Direct Object denotes—(*a*) the Passive Object, or that which suffers or receives the action denoted by the verb... (*b*) The Factitive Object, or that which is the product of the action. **1885** Object clause [used s.v. ASK *v.* 5 a]. **1904** C. T. ONIONS *Adv. Eng. Syntax* 92 The large majority of verbs took the Accusative as Object, and thus there was a tendency for the Accusative to become the universal Object-case. **1906** G. R. CARPENTER *Eng. Gram.* ii. 25 An object complement is a noun or adjective completing the meaning of a transitive verb. **1927** E. A. SONNENSCHEIN *Soil of Grammar* 10 There is no ambiguity in sentences like the following, though the object-case has the same *form* as the subject-case: 'the lion beat the unicorn'. **1957** R. W. ZANDVOORT *Handbk. Eng. Gram.* III. vi. 165 *What*..may introduce a subject clause, an object clause. **1960** T. F. MUSTANOJA *M.E. Syntax* I. 205 Non-expression of the object-pronoun in a relative clause has not been attested in OE. **1963** F. T. VISSER *Hist. Syntax Eng. Lang.* I. iv. 550 Since these added adjectives or nouns do not affect the meaning of the verb, but are merely adjuncts to the object the term 'object complement' or 'objective complement'..seems preferable to the appellation 'predicative adjunct'. **1964** *English Studies* XLV. 386 The rapidly developing 'periphrastic genitive', in which object-case pronouns *h-r* and *h-m* (after *of*) contrasted. **1966** *Ibid.* XLVII. 55 Of special importance is the absence of the relative object-pronoun (e.g. *The spirits I have raised* abandon me), one of the most frequent idioms in coll. English. *Ibid.* 253 A third argument against calling the *that*-clause an object clause is that it lacks the noun characteristic of forming prepositional adjuncts.

II. [= L. *objectu-s* (*u*-stem), = OBJECTION 3, 4.]

†**8.** The fact of throwing itself or being thrown in the way; interposition, obstruction; = OBJECTION 3. *Obs. rare.*

1555 EDEN *Decades W. Ind.* III. vi. 118 Those waters shulde bee turned aboute by the obiecte or resystaunce of that lande [tr. Petrus Martyr d'Anghiera *Unde credunt eas aquas obiectu magnæ telluris circumagi*].

†**9.** The presentation (of something) to the eye or perception; = OBJECTION 4. *Obs.*

1606 Shaks. *Tr. & Cr.* II. ii. 41 Reason flyes the obiect of all harme. **1607** —— *Cor.* I. i. 21 The obiect of our misery, is as an inuentory to particularize their abundance. *c* **1616** Chapman *Batrachom.* 15 He aduancing..past all the rest arose In glorious obiect.

III. 10. *attrib.* and *Comb.*, as ***object-carrier***, ***-end***, etc.; ***object-directed*** adj. (so ***object-directedness***); **object-ball** (*Billiards*, *Croquet*, etc.), the ball which the player endeavours to strike with his own ball; **object chart**, a chart for use in object lessons; **object choice** *Psychol.*, something external to the ego chosen as a desirable object; **object code** *Computing*, code produced by a compiler or assembler; **object-finder**, a contrivance for registering the position of an object on a mounted microscopic slide, so as to find it again; **object-lens** = object-glass; **object-lesson**, a lesson in which instruction is conveyed by actual examination of a material object; *fig.* something that furnishes instruction by exemplifying some principle in a concrete form; **object libido** *Psychoanal.*, that part of psychic energy which is directed to objects other than the ego; **object love**, love for something external to the ego or self; **object-object** (*Metaph.*): see quot.; **object-plate** (*Microscopy*), the plate upon which the object to be examined is placed (but used by Power as = object-glass); **object program** *Computers*, a program into which some other program is translated by an assembler or compiler; cf. object language 3; **object-relation, -relationship** *Psychol.*, a relationship felt, or the emotional energy directed, by the self or ego towards a chosen object; also *attrib.*; **object-soul**, a soul believed to animate a material object; **object-speculum** (after *object-glass*), the mirror in a reflecting telescope which receives and reflects the rays proceeding from the object; **object-staff** (*Surveying*), a levelling-staff; **object-subject**, (*Metaph.*): see quot.; **object-system**, the system of teaching by object-lessons; **object-teaching**, teaching by means of object-lessons; **object-white** *Billiards*, the white object-ball; **object word**, a word which designates an object or material thing; *spec.* in the theories of Bertrand Russell, a word the meaning of which can be learnt independently of the rest of the linguistic system; **object-world**, the world external to the self, apprehended through the objects in it. See also object-glass, object-matter.

1856 'Crawley' *Billiards* (1859) 17 The *object ball is the ball struck at with your own. **1891** *Graphic* 2 May 486/2 Tom Taylor got the object-balls jammed in one of the corner pockets, and..made a break of 1467. **1879** Rutley *Stud. Rocks* vii. 50 A well-fitted sliding *object-carrier. **1872** *Rep. Indian Affairs 1871* (U.S.) 306 A new and original series of '*object charts' gotten up expressly for the Indians of Oregon by myself. **1920** *Internat. Jrnl. Psycho-Anal.* I. 137 Such motivation of the homosexual *object-choice must be by no means uncommon. **1948** M. Klein *Contrib. Psycho-Anal.* 121 His homosexual object choice at the narcissistic level. **1965** P. L. Giovacchini in B. L. Greene *Psychother. Marital Disharmony* 43 The spouse, representing a heterosexual object choice, would ideally be associated with ego transactions. **1961** *Communications Assoc. Computing Machinery* IV. 70/1 An intermediate language is being used for the *object code of the compiling routines being developed at Berkeley. **1977** in C. S. French *Computer Sci.* (1980) 351 This is a load-and-go compiler, reading source code from a deck of punched cards and writing object code directly into core storage. **1985** *Personal Computer World* Feb. 160/2 The object code produced by the compiler can be saved to tape along with the relevant runtimes, allowing programs to stand alone. **1960** W. V. Quine *Word & Object* vii. 239 Some of us are carried away by the *object-directed pattern of our thinking. **1973** *Jrnl. Genetic Psychol.* CXXII. 264 Six categories of object-directed behavior. **1963** A. Kenny *Action, Emotion & Will* 195 How..can Brentano say that *object-directedness is peculiar to psychological phenomena? **1793** Wollaston in *Phil. Trans.* LXXXIII. 145 From the eye-end to the *object-end of the telescope. **1831** Brewster *Nat. Magic* iv. (1833) 79 So that the figure on the glass is at the proper distance from the *object lens. **1831** C. Mayo *Lessons on Objects* Pref. 9 The miscellaneous *object lessons were abandoned. **1881** 'Mark Twain' *Prince & Pauper* xii. 115 In the times of which we are writing, the Bridge furnished 'object lessons' in English history. **1896** A. H. Beavan *Marlbor. Ho.* xii. 210 Unhappy Charles! for all time, object-lesson of lost opportunities. **1936** N. Streatfeild *Ballet Shoes* xi. 180 It was an object lesson she might remember always. **1977** *Early Music* July 401/3 Saul Novak gives an object-lesson in linear analysis for early music. **1920** *Internat. Jrnl. Psycho-Anal.* I. 170 Paraphrenia differs from the psychoneuroses in that the *object-libido is re-converted into ego-libido. **1933** A. A. Brill in S. Lorand *Psycho-Anal. Today* 108 We thus distinguish an ego libido and an object libido. **1955** J. Strachey et al. tr. *Freud's Compl. Psychol. Wks.* XVIII. 257 The transformation of object-libido into narcissism necessarily carried along with it a certain degree of desexualization. **1964** H. Hartmann *Ess. Ego Psychol.* x. 185 It has sometimes been said..that the loss of object libido destroys the repressions. **1918** E. Jones *Papers on Psycho-Anal.* (ed. 2) xviii. 332 The transference.. like every '*object love', has its deepest root in the repressed parent-complex. **1924** J. Riviere et al. tr. *Freud's Coll. Papers* II. 83 The sexual instinct passes on from auto-erotism to object-love. **1938** *Times Lit. Suppl.* 26 Feb. 132/4 The stage of 'object-love', when the moral superego takes charge and the ego is no longer coercive but submissive. **1968** A. H. Modell (*title*) Object love and reality. **1836–7** Sir W. Hamilton *Metaph.* xlii. (1859) II. 432 An object known..may either be the quality of some-thing different from the ego; or it may be a modification of the ego or subject itself. In the former case the object, which may be called..the *object-object, is given as some-thing different from the percipient subject. **1664** Power *Exp. Philos.* 38 If you let her keep upon the lower side of your glass-*object-plate. **1667** E. King in *Phil. Trans.* II. 426 Lay it on the object-plate of a good Microscope. **1959** M. H. Wrubel *Primer of Programming* vi. 128 At the end of the assembly or translation phase.., the programmer is presented with a machine-language deck [of cards] called the '*object program'. **1970** O. Dopping *Computers & Data Processing* xix. 304 In the most common systems for automatic coding, the translation from source program to object program is done in a separate computer run, called the compilation run. **1968** L. Breger in J. Marmor *Mod. Psychoanal.* 47 The concept of '*object relation' (that is, the idea that there is a fixed quantity of energy in a more or less closed system, so that if libido is 'invested' in one object it is 'unavailable' for other purposes). **1968** R. & G. Blanck *Marriage & Pers. Devel.* vi. 70 Persons on the need-gratifying level of object relations can change partners..readily. **1970** *Jrnl. Analytical Psychol.* XV. I. 7 True object relations are the goal of our efforts towards insight into our emotions. **1926** *Brit. Jrnl. Med. Psychol.* VI. 292 The hetero-sexual stage, which is the most complete form of allo-erotic *object relationship. **1946** *Internat. Jrnl. Psycho-Anal.* XXVII. 31/2 From the point of view of object-relationship psychology, explicit pleasure-seeking represents a deterioration of behaviour. **1974** K. Lambert in M. Fordham et al. *Technique in Jungian Analysis* III. 312 This annuls the 'object relationship' between the patient and the analyst. **1875** A. C. O. Lonie in *Encycl. Brit.* II. 56/2 The doctrine of *object-souls..becomes the origin of Fetichism and idolatry. **1781** Herschel in *Phil. Trans.* LXXII. 96 The *object-speculum or object-glass of a telescope. **1867** Lewes *Hist. Philos.* (ed. 3) II. 484 Pure thought and pure matter are unknown quantities, to be reached by no equation. The thought is necessarily and universally subject-object; matter is necessarily, and to us universally, *object-subject. Thought is only called into existence under appropriate conditions; and in the objective stimulus, the object and subject are merged, as acid and base are merged in the salt. **1869** C. L. Brace *New West* vi. 75 The improvement which we have sought so much to bring before the public in New York..—the '*Object System'—has already been adopted here. **1878** *Harper's Mag.* Mar. 607/2 This school is too large for strictly Kindergarten Teaching; but the 'object system'..was the one adopted. **1860** H. Barnard (*title*) *Object teaching and oral lessons on social science and common things. **1945** C. V. Good *Dict. Educ.* 411/2 *Teaching, object*, a method of elementary-school teaching derived from the work of Pestalozzi in Europe and introduced into the United States at the Westfield, Massachusetts, State Teachers' College in 1848 and at Oswego, New York, in 1861. **1904** Mannock & Mussabini *Billiards Expounded* I. iii. 97 To enable the object-ball to go on to the baulk cushion and return up by the *object-white. **1907** *Westm. Gaz.* 19 June 7/2 He got the red ball against the top cushion,..and..the object-white against the side cushion. **1914** L. Bloomfield *Introd. Study Lang.* iv. 111 The explicit predication of quality or action is impossible for languages in which every word expresses an object... In these languages the sentence consists of one or more *object-words. **1940** B. Russell *Inquiry into Meaning & Truth* 80 'Object words' are defined, logically, as words having meaning in isolation, and, psychologically, as words which have been learnt without its being necessary to have previously learnt any other words. **1953** *Mind* LXII. 10 Harm has been done by the well-meaning distinction between object words and logical words... An object word such as 'table'..has meaning in isolation from other words. **1954** E. Branth tr. *H. Spang-Hanssen's Recent Theories Nature of Lang. Sign* in *Travaux du Cercle Ling. de Copenhague* IX. 75 Even in the presence of an object, an object-word will only have an extremely vague 'meaning' if it did not—through its oppositions—concentrate its meaning on a particular 'property' in the object. **1964** E. A. Nida *Toward Sci. Transl.* iv. 62 Basically there are four principal functional classes of lexical symbols: object words, event words, abstracts, and relationals. **1880** G. M. Hopkins *Sermons & Devotional Writings* (1959) II. i. 127 Part of this world of objects, this *object-world, is also part of the very self in question. **1904** W. James *Coll. Ess. & Rev.* (1920) 446 There is..no account of the fact (which I assume the writers to believe in) that different subjects share a common object-world. **1934** W. Temple *Nature, Man & God* I. vi. 135 That discussion will be primarily concerned neither with the inner life of mind, conceived as separate from environment, nor with the object-world which mind apprehends and contemplates, but with the interrelation of these two. **1948** M. Klein *Contrib. Psycho-Anal.* 313 By being internalized, people, things, situations and happenings..cannot be verified by the means of perception which are available in connection with the tangible and palpable object-world. **1964** Gould & Kolb *Dict. Social Sci.* 313/2 Our understanding and its object-world.

†**ob'ject**, *ppl. a. Obs.* [ad. L. *object-us*, pa. pple. of *objicĕre* (*obicĕre*) to throw towards or against, to place in front of, expose, f. *ob-* (ob- 1 a) + *jacĕre* to throw, place. In use app. before the formation of object *v.*, of which it afterwards functioned as the pa. pple. until displaced in that use by *objected*.]

1. Thrown or put in the way, interposed, exposed; placed before one's eyes, presented to the view or perception; exposed (to injury or any influence, or to sight).

c **1374** Chaucer *Boeth.* v. pr. v. 130 (Camb. MS.) þe qualites of bodies þat ben obiecte fro with-owte-forþe moeuen..the Instrumentz of the wittes. *c* **1420** *Pallad. on Husb.* IV. 763 Colde Blastis, sumthing obiect, ek from hem holde. **1538** Leland *Itin.* V. 99 An Abbay..standing very blekely and object to al Wynddes. *a* **1592** H. Smith *Wks.* (1867) II. 333 The text is plain, and object to every man's capacity. **1608** Willet *Hexapla Exod.* 801 Sensible things which are obiect to the eye. **1650** Sir W. Mure *Cry Blood* 411 To refine His Gold, and purge away the object Ore.

b. Situated in front of, or over against, something else; opposite; also *fig.* opposed, contrary.

a **1541** Wyatt *Song of Topas* Poet. Wks. (1861) 151 The one [pole] we see alway, the other stands object Against the same. **1601** Holland *Pliny* I. 71 [An island] vpon the Calabrian coast before Brundusium; by the obiect site whereof the hauen is made. **1603** H. Chettle *Eng. Mourn. Garm.* E, [The Puritans] though they be vtterly object to the Romanistes; yet haue they more..Saints among them than are in the Romish Kalendar. **1613** R. Cawdrey *Table Alph.* (ed. 3), *Obiect*, laide, or set against.

2. Objected, brought as an objection, charged (*against* a person). With *at* = charged with something, accused: cf. object *v.* 5.

1485 *Surtees Misc.* (1888) 43 No thing probable object ayenst the same by the said craft. **1504** Atkynson tr. *De Imitatione* III. lxii. 254 Lytell thynges obiecte agaynst the. *a* **1529** Skelton *Col. Cloute* 796 Bachelers in that facultie.. Shall not be objecte at by me.

object (əb'dʒɛkt), *v.* [f. L. *object-*, ppl. stem of *objicĕre* (*obicĕre*) to throw against, etc.: see prec. It may also partly represent the L. frequentative *objectāre*. OF. has a solitary instance of *objeter* in 1298; but the current *objecter* began as *objetter* in 14th c. For earlier use of *object* as pa. pple., see prec.]

†**1. a.** *trans.* To put over against or in the way of something else; to place so as to meet or intercept something: to expose *to*. *Obs.* or *arch.*

1578 Banister *Hist. Man* VIII. 102 A certeine soft sinew ..[is] obiected to the holes transuersely. **1646** Sir T. Browne *Pseud. Ep.* 334 Every one of these doe blacke the bodies objected unto them. **1654** R. Codrington tr. *Iustine* xv. 240 He commanded him to be objected to a hungry and an enraged Lyon. **1673–4** Grew *Anat. Trunks* I. ii. §33 A very white..piece of Ashwood..objected to a proper Light. **1813–21** Bentham *Wks.* (1843) VIII. 205 This body.. stands objected, i.e. cast before, that other body which moves. **1850** Neale *Med. Hymns* (1867) 195 From what point the wind his course On the tower directeth, To that point the cock his head Manfully objecteth.

†**b.** To place so as to interrupt or hinder the course of a person or thing; to put in the way or interpose, as an obstacle or hindrance to progress, or a defence from attack. *Obs.* or *arch.*

1548 Bodrugan [Adams] *Epit. King's Title* Aij, To deliuer vs from the perill obiected. **1563** *Homilies* II. *Idolatry* III. (1859) 253 To object to the weake..such stumbling-blocks. *c* **1611** Chapman *Iliad* IV. 208 My girdle, curets doubled here, and my most trusted plate, Objected all 'twixt me and death. **1725** Pope *Odyss.* VII. 54 Pallas to their eyes The mist objected. **1814** Southey *Roderick* xxv, The Goth objects His shield, and on its rim received the edge.

†**c.** To expose *to* danger or evil of any kind. *Obs.*

c **1520** Barclay tr. *Sallust* 7 He concluded with hymselfe to obiect hym to daunger and peryll of warre. **1533** Bellenden *Livy* IV. (1822) 331 Quhy wald thay object him aganis sa hie dangere and perrellis. **1566** Painter *Pal. Pleas.* I. 105 Obiecting himselfe to the daunger wherein he was likely to be overwhelmed. *a* **1677** Barrow *Serm.* Wks. 1716 II. 307 All these afflictions..they knowingly did object themselves to.

†**2.** To place (something) before the eyes or other organs of sense, or the mind; to present or offer to the sight, perception, understanding, etc. *Obs.* or *arch.*

1534 More *Comf. agst. Trib.* III. Wks. 1249/1 The bodily senses, moued by such thinges..as are outwardly thorowe sensible worldly thinges offred & obiected vnto them. **1586** T. B. *La Primaud. Fr. Acad.* I. 22 Concupiscence.. apprehendeth whatsoever phantasie and sence obiect unto it. *a* **1661** Fuller *Worthies* (1840) III. 400 Whose temperance was of proof against any meat objected to his appetite. *a* **1677** Hale *Prim. Orig. Man.* I. i. 2 As the Objects of Light or Colour are objected to the Eye when it is open. **1720** Welton *Suffer. Son of God* I. Pref. 89 The Mysterious Work, objected to his contemplation. **1826** K. Digby *Broadst. Hon.* (1829) I. *Godefridus* 182 Religion.. convinces man that there are other things in heaven and earth besides those which are objected to his senses.

†**3.** To present or offer in discourse or argument; to bring forward as a reason, ground, or instance; to adduce. *Obs.* or *arch.*

1536 *Act 28 Hen. VIII*, c. 7 §12 Such questions..as shalbe obiected to them. **1584** R. Scot *Discov. Witchcr.* v. vii. (1886) 82 For the maintenance of witches transportations, they object the words of the Gospell, where the divell is said to take up Christ. **1634** Canne *Necess. Separ.* (1849) 232 Augustine was of mind, that councils, bishops, &c., ought not to be objected for trial of controversies, but the holy scriptures only. **1704** Swift *T. Tub* Apol., He has never yet found it in that discourse, nor has heard it objected by any body else. **1849** W. Fitzgerald tr. *Whitaker's Disput.* 67 What church is it whose example they object to us as an argument?

4. To bring forward or state in opposition; to adduce as a reason against something; to urge as an objection (*to*, *unto*, *against*). **a.** with simple obj.

c **1400** *Apol. Loll.* 33 For obieccouns & sophims þat men may mak & obiect. **1513–14** *Act 5 Hen. VIII*, c. 1 If the same persons..obiecte or allege any cause why he shall not soo doo. **1630** Prynne *Anti-Armin.* 165 The self-same Scriptures that are here obiected against us. **1754** Richardson *Grandison* (1781) III. xx. 184 They objected the more obvious difficulties in relation to religion, and my country. **1830** H. N. COLERIDGE *Grk. Poets* (1834) 352 Bryant objects this very circumstance to the authenticity of the Iliad. **1855** MILMAN *Lat. Chr.* (1864) II. IV. vii. 372 Its adversaries objected the absence of all the great Patriarchs.

b. with object clause. Also with direct speech.

1559 BP. SCOT in Strype *Ann. Ref.* (1824) I. II. App. vii. 411 It wilbe objectid against me, that as this place dothe make against the supremacye of princes, so dothe it not make for the primacye of saint Peter. **1613** PURCHAS *Pilgrimage* (1614) 23 But some object, This is to slacken him running, rather then to incite. **1685** LUTTRELL *Brief Rel.* (1857) I. 365 Objecting how unlikely it was. **1736** BUTLER *Anal.* I. iii. 70 If it is objected that good actions..are often punished. **1818** CRUISE *Digest* (ed. 2) II. 404 It hath been objected, that this relates only to the preservation of the legal estate of the use, and not to the timber or mines. **1972** D. BLOODWORTH *Any Number can Play* xvi. 154 'But it would have been..a pointed piece of skin,' objected Green. **1974** *Listener* 3 Oct. 423/2 Mr Johnston objected: 'But we already have..a shop stewards' movement.'

5. To bring as a charge against any one; to attribute to any one as a fault or crime; to lay to one's charge, cast in one's teeth, accuse one of, reproach one with. Const. *to*, *against* (†*upon*, indirect obj.) **a.** with simple obj. *arch.*

1469 *Paston Lett.* II. 338 Charging yow..to appear afore the said Lords of our Councell..there to answere to such thinges as..by them shall be laid and objected against yow. **1526** *Pilgr. Perf.* (W. de W. 1531) 10 Yf euer thou dyd ony notable synne..he wyll obiecte it to the, and cast it in thy nose. **1541** R. COPLAND *Galyen's Terapeut.* 2 E ij, The which thyng we do obiect them. *a* **1648** LD. HERBERT *Hen. VIII* (1683) 66 They were committed to diuers Prisons, for Crimes objected against them. **1656** HOBBES *Lib., Necess.*, etc. (1841) 116 When God afflicted Job, he did object no sin to him. **1761-2** HUME *Hist. Eng.* (1806) IV. lvii. 363 This subtlety, which has been frequently objected to Charles. **1844** LINGARD *Anglo-Sax. Ch.* (1858) II. x. 83 This hypocrisy was invisible to the contemporaries of those to whom it is objected.

b. with object clause.

1587 HOLINSHED *Chron., Scot.* II. 259 Those taunts which the Frenchmen laid upon them, obiecting that the greedinesse of wine and vittles had brought them ouer into that countrie. **1658** SIR T. BROWNE *Hydriot.* i. (1736) 13 It was obviously objected upon Christians, that they condemned the Practice of Burning. **1711** STEELE *Spect.* No. 95 ¶6, I have heard it objected against that Piece, that its Instructions are not of general use. **1833-6** J. EAGLES *The Sketcher* (1856) 18, I once heard a person object to Gaspar Poussin, that there was too much in his pictures.

†**6.** *trans.* To impute, attribute (*to*). (A weakening of prec. sense.) *Obs.*

1613 PURCHAS *Pilgrimage* (1614) 120 They were so scrupulous concerning the Moone, that Clemens Alexand. ..objects the worship therof unto them. **1734** FIELDING *Univ. Gallant* II. i, Do you object my care of your reputation to want of fondness? **1776** BURNEY *Hist. Mus.* (1789) I. 342 Homer who celebrates the Greeks for their long hair and Achilles for his skill on the harp, makes Hector in this place object them both to Paris.

7. a. *intr.* To state an objection or adverse reason; now often in weakened sense: To express or feel disapproval, to disapprove.

1430-50 tr. *Higden* (Rolls) VII. 157 But peraventure ye obiecte, and say hit longethe not to a preste to schedde bloode; I graunte þerto; but [etc.]. **1526** *Pilgr. Perf.* (W. de W. 1531) 173 b, The vntreatable irefull persone wyll obiect & saye [etc.]. **1560** J. DAUS tr. *Sleidane's Comm.* 58 b, Vnto such as will question and obiect what shall we then do? **1865** DICKENS *Mut. Fr.* IV. xvi, Then it is the lady as formerly objected? *Mod.* I think I'll have a smoke, if you don't object.

b. with *to* (sometimes *against*, rarely *at*) or *inf.*: To bring forward a reason against; to state, and maintain by argument, one's disagreement with or disapproval of; now usually in weakened sense: To express, or merely to feel, disapproval of; to have an objection *to*, disapprove of, dislike. (The prevailing current sense.)

1513 MORE *Rich. III*, Wks. 60/1 Ye kinges mother obiected openly against his mariage. **1678** RYMER *Trag. last Age* 8 Those who object against reason, are the Fanaticks in Poetry. **1735** POPE *Donne Sat.* IV. 117 His Patience I provoke, Mistake, confound, object at all he spoke. **1758** *Ann. Reg.* 98/2 The doctor objected against fifteen, and the council for the crown against three. **1775** SHERIDAN *Rivals* II. i, 'Tis more unreasonable in you to object to a lady you know nothing of. **1839** KEIGHTLEY *Hist. Eng.* II. 68 He objected to this as a harsh measure. **1865** DICKENS *Mut. Fr.* IV. xii, Would the lady object to my lighting the pair of candles? **1869** J. MARTINEAU *Ess.* II. 176 We object to the argument on scientific grounds. **1885** *Manch. Exam.* 6 Nov. 5/3 They objected to be actors in a farce.

†**c.** *intr.* To bring a charge or accusation. *Obs.*

1611 BIBLE *Acts* xxiv. 19 Who ought to haue beene here before thee, and obiect, if they had ought against me.

Hence **ob'jecting** *vbl. sb.* and *ppl. a.*

1552 HULOET, Obiectinge, *obiectus, obiectio.* **1886** MRS. LYNN LINTON *Paston Carew* III. ii. 32 Petrarca had..praised Yetta Carew with dangerous fervency to his objecting Laura.

objectable (əbˈdʒɛktəb(ə)l), *a.* Also 8 *erron.* -ible. [f. OBJECT *v.* + -ABLE.]

1. That may be objected, or urged as an objection, chargeable (*against* or *to*). ? *Obs.*

1656 *Artif. Handsom.* 145 As for that depravednesse of mind..it is as objectable against all those things. *Ibid.* 173 Nothing of consequence was objectable to Christ. **1667** *Decay Chr. Piety* vi. ¶7 There are but two objections..and these are usually objectable to one sin as well as to another.

2. That may be objected to, objectionable.

1775-83 S. J. PRATT *Liberal Opin.* I. 120, I have ventured to assert that [etc.]... Objectible as this may seem, I must take upon me..to push the point farther. **1776** —— *Pupil of Pleasure* II. 109, I will not, Delia, distress you. I see nothing at present objectible. **1885** *Eng. Illustr. Mag.* III. 230 As for marriage..(the lady not objectable, and an addition of fortune attending) I have no unconquerable aversion to it.

ob'jectant. [f. OBJECT *v.* + -ANT[1]. Cf. F. *objectant* pr. pple.] One who or that which objects or objectifies. In recent use as a legal term in the U.S.

1625 GILL *Sacr. Philos.* II. 145 If the Father [had been incarnate], then the fountaine of the Deitie should become not the objectant, or being which understandeth, but onely the object understood. **1972** *N.Y. Law Jrnl.* 22 Aug. 6/4 The proponent or the objectant seeks an examination of the adverse party before trial. **1973** *Ibid.* 19 July 13/5 In view of the failure of the objectant to proceed with this matter, his objections are denied.

objectation (ɒbdʒɪkˈteɪʃən). *rare.* [Noun of action from L. *objectāre* to OBJECT: cf. L. *objectātio* reproach.] The action of objecting or making objections. So **objectative** (əbˈdʒɛktətɪv), *a.*, given to objecting, fond of making objections; †**objectator** (*obs. rare*$^{-0}$), an objector.

1656 BLOUNT *Glossogr.*, *Objectator* (Lat.), he that reproacheth or lays to ones charge. **1873** HELPS *Anim. & Mast.* vi. (1875) 146 If he is only objectative and Ellesmerian. **1886** STUBBS *Lect. Med. & Mod. Hist.* vii. 143 Knotty questions..are discussed..without strife or objectation.

objected (əbˈdʒɛktɪd), *ppl. a.* [f. OBJECT *v.*]

†**1.** Placed over against or opposite; presented to the view or perception. *Obs.* or *arch.*

1606 N. BAXTER *Man Created* in Farr *S.P. Jas. I* (1848) 238 The forehead kept obiected phantasie, The hinder part reteyneth memorie. **1668** HOWE *Bless. Righteous* (1825) 30 This objected or exhibited glory is two-fold. **1713** C'TESS WINCHELSEA *Misc. Poems* 86 A Dream, a vision..Hangs on my pensive Heart, and bears it down More than the weight of an objected Crown. **1848** R. I. WILBERFORCE *Doctr. Incarnation* xiv. (1852) 414 The inspiration of Scripture..as the imparted record of objected truth.

†**2.** Adduced in argument, esp. against something; urged as an objection. *Obs.* or *arch.*

1641 MILTON *Prel. Episc.* Wks. (1851) 89 To alledge for Images the ancient Fathers, Dionysius, and this our objected Irenæus. **1669** W. HOLDER *Elem. Speech* 119 The former part of this objected difficulty.

objectee (ɒbdʒɪkˈtiː). [f. OBJECT *v.* + -EE.] A person objected to; one against whom an objection is made.

1861 *Even. Star* 4 Oct., The Revising Barrister remarked that..the production of the stamped duplicate was merely evidence that the notice had been sent to the objectee. The signature of the objector must be proved. **1884** *Pall Mall G.* 19 Sept. 8/2 The word..could refer only to the place of abode of the objectee at the time the objection was made.

object-glass (ˈɒbdʒɪktglɑːs, -æ-). [OBJECT *sb.* 3.] The lens or combination of lenses in a telescope, microscope, or other optical instrument, which is situated nearest to the object, and thus receives the rays of light directly from it. (Cf. EYE-GLASS 4.)

1665 R. HOOKE *Microgr.* ii. 4, I..plac'd it between the Object-glass and the light. **1784** HERSCHEL in *Phil. Trans.* LXXV. 44 Turning or unscrewing the object-glass or speculum a little. **1829** *Nat. Philos.* I. *Optics* x. 27 (U.K.S.) The triple achromatic object-glass..consists of..a concave flint glass lens placed between two convex lenses of crown glass. **1839** G. BIRD *Nat. Phil.* 390 The magnifying power of these telescopes is found by dividing the focal length of the object-glass by that of the eye-glass.

objectifiable (əbˈdʒɛktɪˌfaɪəb(ə)l), *a.* [f. OBJECTIFY *v.* + -ABLE.] That is capable of being objectified.

1925 C. D. BROAD *Mind & its Place* vi. 306 To be 'epistemologically objectifiable' means to be capable of corresponding to the epistemological object of some referential situation.

objectification (əbˌdʒɛktɪfɪˈkeɪʃən). [n. of action from OBJECTIFY: see -FICATION.] The action of objectifying, or condition of being objectified; an instance of this, an external thing in which an idea, principle, etc. is expressed concretely.

1836-7 SIR W. HAMILTON *Metaph.* xlii. (1870) II. 432 This discrimination of self from self,—this objectification,—is the quality which constitutes the essential peculiarity of Cognition. **1883** HALDANE & KEMP tr. *Schopenhauer's World as Will & Idea* I. II. 121 (*heading*) The objectification of the will. **1900** STODDARD *Evol. Eng. Novel* 78 These mystic symbols are like the weird sisters in 'Macbeth'; they are the objectification of mystery. **1927** A. N. WHITEHEAD *Symbolism* (1928) i. 30 Thus 'objectification' itself is an abstraction. **1931** W. R. B. GIBSON tr. *Husserl's Ideas* II. ii. 123 Thanks to this objectification we find facing us in the natural setting..not natural things merely, but values and practical objects of every kind. **1963** J. MACQUARRIE *Twentieth-Century Relig. Thought* xii. 203 Berdyaev goes further..in his antipathy to objectification, which he identifies with the fall of man. **1971** E. B. ASHTON tr. *Jaspers's Philos.* III. i. 8 Metaphysical objectifications of transcendence.

objectifier (əbˈdʒɛktɪˌfaɪə(r)). [f. OBJECTIFY *v.* + -ER[1].] That which objectifies or makes objective.

1956 J. D. MABBOTT in H. D. Lewis *Contemp. Brit. Philos.* (ser. 3) 307 Morality has to be sustained by conviction and conviction is a great objectifier.

objectify (əbˈdʒɛktɪfaɪ), *v.* [f. med.L. *object-um* OBJECT *sb.* + -FY; after L. type **objectificāre*.] *trans.* To make into, or present as, an object, esp. as an object of sense; to render objective; to express in an external or concrete form.

1836-7 SIR W. HAMILTON *Metaph.* xlii. (1870) II. 432 Consciousness..projects, as it were, this subjective phænomenon from itself,—views it at a distance,—in a word, objectifies it. **1856** DOVE *Logic Chr. Faith* I. ii. 70 In the latter [case] we objectify knowledge. **1880** W. WALLACE in *Encycl. Brit.* XI. 620/2 The theory of the mind as objectified in the institutions of law, the family, and the state, is discussed in the 'Philosophy of Right'.

Hence **ob'jectified** *ppl. a.*, **ob'jectifying** *vbl. sb.* and *ppl. a.*

1868 *Contemp. Rev.* VIII. 612 Morality..is a certain state of mind viewed in relation to certain objectified objects of a wider consciousness. **1883** A. BARRATT *Phys. Metempiric* 73 Considered as impressed..it is a phenomenon, and..becomes through the inner objectifying process worked up into an external object or event. **1892** TRAILL in *19th Cent.* Dec. 964 The objectifying faculty became..weakened. **1927** A. N. WHITEHEAD *Symbolism* (1928) i. 30 No actual thing is 'objectified' in its 'formal' completeness. **1931** W. R. B. GIBSON tr. *Husserl's Ideas* II. ii. 122 The intentional object first becomes an apprehended object through a distinctively 'objectifying' turn of thought. **1940** S. C. PEPPER in P. A. Schilpp *Philos. Santayana* 229 The expression of moral and political greatness, however, is the satisfaction of interests quite different from objectified pleasure. **1977** R. WILLIAMS *Marxism & Lit.* II. ii. 86 Here society is the objectified (unconscious and unwilled) general process.

objection (əbˈdʒɛkʃən). [a. F. *objection* (12-13th c. in Hatz.-Darm.), ad. L. *objectiōn-em* a throwing before, upbraiding, reproach, objection, n. of action f. *objicĕre* to OBJECT.]

1. a. The action of objecting, or stating something in opposition to a person or thing; **b.** That which is objected, a statement made in opposition; †a charge or accusation against a person (*obs.*); an adverse reason, argument, or contention (*spec.* in *Horse Racing*). Now often in weakened sense: An expression, or merely a feeling, of disapproval, disagreement, or dislike (esp. in phr. ***to have an*** (or ***no***) ***objection***). ***to take objection***: to bring forward a reason against something, or merely to state one's disapproval of or disagreement with it; to object. **c.** A document in which an objection is stated.

c **1380** WYCLIF *Sel. Wks.* II. 198 Here ben many objecciouns þat þes wordis of Crist ben false. **1387** TREVISA *Higden* (Rolls) VII. 157 Peraventure þere is an objectioun, it falleþ nouȝt a preost þat he schede blood. **1432-50** tr. *Higden* (Rolls) I. 379 An obieccion was made..to the bischoppe..how so mony seyntes myȝhte be in that londe, and alle confessores and noo martir. **1513-14** *Act 5 Hen. VIII*, c. 1 A convenyent peremptorie day to prove hys objeccion and allegacion. **1613** SHAKS. *Hen. VIII*, III. ii. 307 Speake on, Sir; I dare your worst objections. **1691** T. HALE *Acc. New Invent.* 40 To which nothing is so much as pretended to, in Objection by the Officers. **1736** BUTLER *Anal.* II. viii. 383 The objections which may be made against arguing from the Analogy of Nature. **1813** *Sk. Character* (ed. 2) I. 190 If Lucy had no objection to him, I admire her for letting him see it. **1866** DK. ARGYLL *Reign Law* (1871) 426 *note*, Mr. Mahaffy ..has taken objection to the breadth of meaning I have given ..to the word 'motive'. **1875** JOWETT *Plato* (ed. 2) I. 281, I have no objection to join with you in the enquiry. *Ibid.* IV. 239 A serious objection which may be urged against this doctrine. **1898** *Encycl. Sport* II. 228/1 All disputes, objections, and appeals referred to or brought before the Stewards of the Jockey Club for their decision, shall be decided by the three Stewards. **1930** *Daily Express* 6 Oct. 17/6 An objection to Kippit Lore on behalf of Ferry Maid was overruled. **1977** 'J. LE CARRÉ' *Hon. Schoolboy* vii. 165 Objection!.. Where's the Stewards..? That horse was pulled!

†**2.** *transf.* or *fig.* An adverse action, an assault.

a **1450** *Mankind* (Brandl) 824 þe ineuetabyll obieccione of my gostly enmy. **1526** *Pilgr. Perf.* (W. de W. 1531) 79 They have..suffred actually or in dede many obieccions & iniuryes innocently. *a* **1586** SIDNEY *Arcadia* I. 23 The parts either not armed, or weakly armed..should have bin sharpely visited, but that the answer was as quicke as the objection.

†**3. a.** The action of throwing, or condition of being thrown, in the way, or so as to intercept something else; interposition. *Obs.*

1549 *Compl. Scot.* vi. 56 The mune is in eclips be the obiectione of the eird. *c* **1611** CHAPMAN *Iliad* xx. 323 His worst shall be withstood With sole objection of myself.

†**b.** The condition of there being something in the way; hindrance, obstruction. *Obs.*

a **1667** JER. TAYLOR in Spurgeon *Treas. Dav.* Ps. lxxxv. 13 Our way is troublesome, obscure, full of objection and danger.

†**4.** Presentation to the view or to the mind, or that which is so presented; representation; offer.

1554 W. PRAT *Africa* E ij b, By that representacion they be warned of the mortall condicion by one of the sayd obiections, and by the other of the passion of Iesus Christ. **1596** *Edward III*, II. ii. 123 Art thou come To speak the more than heavenly word of yea, To my objection in thy beauteous love? **1649** JER. TAYLOR *Gt. Exemp.* xv. §18 Which Prediction he made, that they might not be scandalized at the sadness of objection of the Passion, but be confirmed in their belief.

objectionable (əb'dʒɛkʃənəb(ə)l), *a.* (*sb.*) [f. prec. + -ABLE.] Open to objection; that may be objected to; against which an adverse reason may be urged; now often in weakened sense: Exciting disapproval or dislike, unacceptable, disagreeable, unpleasant.

1781 COWPER *Lett.* Wks. 1837 XV. 110 It does not appear to me that the expression is objectionable: it is plain, indeed, but not bald. **1851** CARPENTER *Man. Phys.* (ed. 2) 571 It is ..not unfrequently termed the ganglionic system... But this term is objectionable, as leading to a supposed analogy between this system and the general nervous system of Invertebrata. **1856** MISS MULOCK *J. Halifax* ii, But all this was highly objectionable to Jael. **1881** LADY HERBERT *Edith* 31 People about them..of a very objectionable kind. **1881** FENN *Off to the Wilds* xxii. 156 The crocodiles are most objectionable beasts.

B. as *sb.* An objectionable person or thing.

1884 *Blackw. Mag.* Mar. 295/2 We consign our own 'objectionables' to Jericho. **1886** R. KIPLING *Departm. Ditties*, etc. (1899) 117 The whiskified Objectionable, Unclean, abominable, out-at-heels.

Hence **objectiona'bility** = next; also something objectionable; **ob'jectionableness**, the quality of being objectionable; **ob'jectionably** *adv.*, in an objectionable manner.

1865 *Pall Mall G.* 27 Mar. 3/1 What possible objectionabilities may the practice of riding to hounds lead to? **1856** RUSKIN *Mod. Paint.* III. IV. xiii. §25 Expressive of general objectionableness and unpleasantness. **1892** E. REEVES *Homeward Bound* 322 One of the objectionably placed churches in the Alhambra precincts.

ob'jectional, *a.* [f. OBJECTION + -AL[1].]

1. Of the nature of, or involving, objection.

1651 C. CARTWRIGHT *Cert. Relig.* I. 42 No more prejudiciall or objectionall..then the disputations in the Schools. **1827** AIKMAN *Hist. Scot.* IV. x. 348 The objectional acts of his Majesty.

2. Open to objection, objectionable.

1799 MRS. JANE WEST *Tale of Times* III. 138 Interpreters ..have substituted a sort of gay licentiousness in the place of the objectional grossness. **1845** *Blackw. Mag.* LVII. 725 A weak solution..may not be very objectional. **1897** HUGHES *Mediterranean Malta Fever* i. 8 The name *micrococcus Melitensis*..has not the same objectional characters.

ob'jectioner. *rare*$^{-1}$. [See -ER.] = next.

1799 WASHINGTON *Lett.* Writ. 1893 XIV. 177 The testimony of Generals Lincoln, Knox, Brooks, Jackson, and others..would be a counterpoise to the objectioners.

ob'jectionist. *rare.* [f. OBJECTION + -IST.] One who offers an objection; an objector.

1607 WALKINGTON *Opt. Glass* 91 To shend it from all the ..stabadoes of any..objectionist. **1836–7** SIR W. HAMILTON *Metaph.* xli. (1870) II. 423 So far our objectionist.

ob'jectist. *rare.* 'One versed in the objective philosophy or doctrine' (Worcester 1846, citing *Eclectic Rev.*).

ob'jectivate, *v.* [f. OBJECTIVE *a.* + -ATE. Cf. F. *objectiver* (neologism in Littré).] *trans.* To render objective; = OBJECTIFY.

1873 *Contemp. Rev.* XXI. 447 Knowledge or perception is an effect of the objectivating will.

ob,jecti'vation. [n. of action from prec.: so in mod.F., neologism in Littré.] The action of making objective, or an instance of this; = OBJECTIFICATION.

1873 *Contemp. Rev.* XXI. 447 The degree of 'objectivation of Will' in phenomena is what divides them into kinds. **1886** W. S. LILLY *Chapt. Europ. Hist.* II. 199 The objectivation of the principles of '89. **1894** A. LANG *Cock Lane* 217 Objectivations of ideas or images, consciously or unconsciously present to the mind.

objective (əb'dʒɛktɪv), *a.* and *sb.* [ad. Schol. L. *objectīv-us* (a 1300, in adv. *objectīvē* in Duns Scotus *Qu. de Anima* 17, 14), f. *objectus* ppl. a., *objectum* sb.; F. *objectif, -ive* (represented by the adv. *objectivement*, 15th c. in Hatz.-Darm.).]

A. *adj.* †**1.** *Philos.* **a.** Pertaining or considered in relation to its object; constituting, or belonging to, an object of action, thought, or feeling (as distinguished from the exercise of these); 'material', as opposed to *subjective* or 'formal' (in the old sense of these words). *Obs.*

1620 BRENT tr. *Sarpi's Hist. Counc. Trent* VIII. 799 [He] added, that, where they were dedicated,..a worship did belong vnto them, besides the adoration due vnto the Saint worshipped in them, calling this adoration Relatiue, and the other Obiectiue. **1645** RUTHERFORD *Tryal and Tri. Faith* vii. (1845) 85 Christ himself, the objective happiness, is far above a created and formal beatitude, which issueth from him. **1675** TRAHERNE *Chr. Ethics* 16 Objective happiness is all the goodness that is fit to be enjoyed either in God or in His creatures: while formal happiness is an active enjoyment of all objects by contemplation and love, attended with full complacency in all their perfections.

†**b.** Of or pertaining to the object or end as the cause of action; ***objective cause*** = final cause: see CAUSE *sb.* 4 b, 5. *Obs.*

1626 J. YATES *Ibis ad Cæsarem* II. 25 God,..who doth..by a most sweet influence, and not by any coactiue violence, nor yet only by obiectiue allurements,..turne the wils of men at his pleasure. **1678** CUDWORTH *Intell. Syst.* I. iii. 170 Aristotle's first mover is not properly the efficient, but only the final and objective cause, of the heavenly motions.

2. *Philos.* Used of the existence or nature of a thing *as an object of consciousness* (as distinguished from an existence or nature termed *subjective*).

The Scholastic Philosophy made the distinction between what belongs to things subjectively (*subjectīvē*), or as they are 'in themselves', and what belongs to them objectively (*objectīvē*), as they are presented to consciousness. In later times the custom of considering the perceiving or thinking consciousness as pre-eminently 'the subject' brought about a different use of these words, which now prevails in philosophical language. According to this, what is considered as belonging to the perceiving or thinking self is called *subjective*, and what is considered as independent of the perceiving or thinking self is called in contrast *objective*. As to this transition of use (which primarily concerns the word *subjective*, and affects *objective* as its antithesis) resulting in what is almost an exchange of sense between the two adjectives, see HAMILTON *Reid's Wks.* 806 note, R. L. NETTLESHIP *Philos. Lect. & Remains* I. 193.

†**a.** Opposed to *subjective* in the older sense = 'in itself': Existing as an object of consciousness as distinct from having any real existence; considered only as presented to the mind (not as it is, or may be, in itself or its own nature). *Obs.*

[*c* **1325** OCCAM *Sent.* I, Dict. 2, qu. 8 E, Universale non est aliquid reale habens esse subiectivum nec in anima nec extra animam, sed tantum habet esse obiectivum in anima et est quoddam fictum habens esse tale in esse obiectivo, quale habet res extra in esse subiectivo.]

1647 JER. TAYLOR *Lib. Proph.* 133 This confession was the objective foundation of faith; and Christ and his Apostles, the subjective. **1659** PEARSON *Creed* ii. (1839) 168 'In the beginning was the Word'; there *was* must signify an actual existence; and if so, why in the next sentence ('the Word was with God') shall the same verb signify an objective being only? **1727–41** CHAMBERS *Cycl.*, *Objective*..is used in the schools in speaking of a thing which exists no otherwise than as an object known. The esse, or existence of such thing is said to be objective. **1744** BERKELEY *Siris* §292 Natural phænomena are only natural appearances. They are, therefore, such as we see and perceive them: Their real and objective natures are, therefore, the same.

b. Opposed to *subjective* in the modern sense: That is or belongs to what is presented to consciousness, as opposed to the consciousness itself; that is the object of perception or thought, as distinct from the perceiving or thinking subject; hence, that is, or has the character of being, a 'thing' external to the mind; real.

This sense is occasional in writers of the later 17th and early 18th c. (the early examples being more or less transitional); but its current use appears to be derived from Kant, and to appear in Eng. subsequently to 1790, and chiefly after 1817 (see quot. from Coleridge).

1647 J. CARDELL *Serm.* (1648) 15 We do not say, That God doth infuse any positive, objective malice or wickedness into the hearts of men. **1662** STILLINGFL. *Orig. Sacr.* III. i. §3 The Idea may be considered in regard of its Objective Reality, or as it represents some outward object. *Ibid.*, Wee are apt to imagine such a Power in the understanding, whereby it may form Idea's of such things which have no objective reality at all. **1724** WATTS *Logic* II. ii. §8 Objective certainty, is when the proposition is certainly true in itself; and subjective, when we are certain of the truth of it. The one is in things, the other is in our minds. **1793** *Monthly Rev.* XI. 498 Have the objects..in fact a real objective existence, independent of our mode of perceiving them? **1817** COLERIDGE *Biog. Lit.* I. x. 160 The very words *objective* and *subjective* of such constant recurrence in the schools of yore, I have ventured to re-introduce. **1853** HAMILTON *Discuss.*, *Philos. Unconditioned 5 note*, In the philosophy of mind, subjective denotes what is referred to the thinking subject, the Ego; objective what belongs to the object of thought, the Non-Ego. **1856** DE QUINCEY *Confess.* Wks. V. 265 *note*, *Objective*: This word, so nearly unintelligible in 1821, so intensely scholastic, and, consequently, when surrounded by familiar and vernacular words, so apparently pedantic, yet, on the other hand, so indispensable to accurate thinking, and to wide thinking, has since 1821 become too common to need any apology. **1861** MILL *Utilit.* 43 A person who sees in moral obligation..an objective reality belonging to the province of 'Things in themselves'. **1879** FARRAR *St. Paul* I. 372 This [Christ's resurrection] was an historic objective fact.

3. *transf.* (from 2 b) **a.** Of a person, a writing, work of art, etc.: Dealing with, or laying stress upon, that which is external to the mind; treating of outward things or events, rather than inward thoughts or feelings; regarding or representing things from an objective standpoint. (Occas., after mod. Ger. *objektiv*: Treating a subject so as to exhibit the actual facts, not coloured by the feelings or opinions of the writer.)

1838 J. S. MILL in *London & Westm. Rev.* Aug. 496 An essentially *objective* people, like those of Northern and Central Italy. **1855** FITZJ. STEPHEN in *Camb. Ess.* 190 The book [Robinson Crusoe]..is, to use a much-abused word, eminently objective; that is, the circumstances are drawn from a real study of things as they are, and not in order to exemplify the workings of a particular habit of mind. **1878** GLADSTONE *Prim. Homer* xiii. 153 Of all poets he [Homer] is the most objective, and the least speculative. **1888** BRYCE *Amer. Commw.* II. lxxv. 619 To complete the survey of the actualities of party politics by stating in a purely positive, or as the Germans say 'objective', way, what the Americans think about..their system. **1899** LECKY *Map of Life* ii. 8 English character on both sides of the Atlantic is an eminently objective one—a character in which thoughts, interests, and emotions are most habitually thrown on that which is without. **1967** H. ARENDT *Orig. Totalitarianism* (new ed.) xii. 423 The Jews in Nazi Germany or the descendants of the former ruling classes in Soviet Russia were not really suspected of any hostile action; they had been declared 'objective' enemies of the regime in accordance with its ideology.

b. *Med.* Applied to symptoms 'observed by the practitioner, in distinction from those which are only felt by the patient' (*Syd. Soc. Lex.* 1892).

1877 ROBERTS *Handbk. Med.* (ed. 3) I. 19 The actual clinical phenomena observed, especially those of an objective character. **1898** *Allbutt's Syst. Med.* V. 871 He manifests the subjective and objective signs of valvular disease.

4. With *to*: That is the object of sensation or thought; that is presented or exposed as an object, perceived, apprehended, etc. In *Metaph.* Related as object to subject (see OBJECT *sb.* 6).

1762 GIBBON *Misc. Wks.* (1814) IV. 148 Operations, which are made objective to sense by the means of speech, gesture and action. **1837** *New Monthly Mag.* L. 535 The inhabitants of this hostel were seldom 'objective' to the garish eye of day. **1841** MYERS *Cath. Th.* IV. §13. 251 The Supreme Creator has..so separated Himself from His creation as to make it objective to Himself.

5. *Perspective.* That is, or belongs to, the object of which the delineation is required.

1706 PHILLIPS, *Line Objective* (in Perspect.), is the Line of an Object; from whence the Appearance is sought for in the Draught or Picture. **1727–41** CHAMBERS *Cycl.* s.v. *Line*, *Objective Line*, in perspective, is any line drawn on the geometrical plane, whose representation is sought for in the draught, or picture. *Ibid.* s.v. *Plane*, *Objective Plane*, in perspective, is any plane situate in the horizontal plane, whose representation in perspective is required. *Ibid.* s.v. *Perspective*, To exhibit the perspective appearance, *h*, of an objective point, H.

6. Applied to the lens or combination of lenses in an optical instrument which is nearest to the object (***objective glass***; now commonly called *object-glass*, or simply *objective*).

1753 SHORT in *Phil. Trans.* XLVIII. 165 An heliometer; which is an instrument, consisting of two objective glasses, for measuring the diameters of the planets. **1762** MATY *ibid.* LII. 375 The objective-glass of my 9 feet telescope. **1837** GORING & PRITCHARD *Microgr.* 154 So far as the objective part of the instrument is concerned.

7. *Gram.* **a.** Expressing or denoting the object of an action; *spec.* applied to that case of mod.Eng. in which a substantive or pronoun stands when it is the object of a verb, or is governed by a preposition, with which it forms an attributive or advb. phrase (see OBJECT *sb.* 7); also to the relation of such noun or pronoun to such verb or preposition.

The accusative and dative of earlier Eng. (as well as the instrumental, locative, and ablative of prehistoric times) are merged in mod.Eng. in the objective, which in personal and relative pronouns is distinct in form from the nominative, but in sbs. and other pronominal words is identical with the nominative.

1763 LOWTH *Eng. Gram.* (ed. 2) 32 A Case, which follows the Verb Active, or the Preposition..answers to the Oblique Cases in Latin; and may be properly enough called the Objective Case. **1824** L. MURRAY *Eng. Gram.* (ed. 5) I. 86 There seems to be great propriety in admitting a case in English substantives, which shall serve to denote the objects of active verbs and of prepositions; and which is, therefore, properly termed the *objective case*. *Ibid.* 268 Part of a sentence..may be said to be in the objective case, or to be put objectively, governed by the active verb... Sentences or phrases under this circumstance, may be termed objective sentences or phrases. **1879** ROBY *Lat. Gram.* IV. xi. §1312 [Genitive denoting] Object of action implied in substantives and adjectives. (Objective genitive.) **1881** MASON *Eng. Gram.* (ed. 24) §368 When a verb, participle, or gerund denotes an action which is directed towards some object, the word denoting that object stands in the objective relation to the verb, participle, or gerund.

b. ***objective complement*** = *object complement* (OBJECT *sb.* 7).

1870 C. P. MASON *Eng. Gram.* (ed. 14) 127 When the verb is transitive, and in the active voice, the complement of the predicate stands in the attributive relation to the object of the verb; as, 'He dyed the cloth red.'.. This kind of complement may be termed the *Objective Complement*, inasmuch as it is closely connected with the object of the verb. **1897** CLARKE & MULLER *Class Bk. Eng. Gram.* 219 The name *Objective Complement* would be applied by some Grammarians [to 'captain' in the sentence 'They elected *James captain*']. **1945** M. M. BRYANT *Functional Eng. Gram.* xii. 132 In 'They made him chairman'..the second complement is called an objective complement. *Ibid.*, In the sentence 'The frost turned the leaves red', the objective complement is of a somewhat different nature, since here the word *red* is an adjective rather than a noun. **1963** [see OBJECT *sb.* 7].

8. ***objective point***: orig. *Mil.* the point towards which the advance of troops is directed; hence *gen.* the point aimed at.

1864 *Daily Tel.* 18 Oct., In acquiring possession of Atlanta the Federals have gained a great..advantage. It is the objective point to which their western campaign was directed. **1865** *Spectator* 4 Feb. 117 No light as to his next 'objective point', as the slang phrase goes, has yet been gained. **1890** *Times* 27 Dec. 9/1 When the railway is extended to Mafeking, the objective point in Mashona-land is stil 800 miles from the base. **1893** EARL DUNMORE *Pamirs* II. 338 The city of Meshed being my objective point.

9. Characterized by objecting; that states objections: cf. OBJECTIVELY 4.

1814 W. TAYLOR in *Monthly Mag.* XXXVIII. 34 Let us examine Mr. Pilgrim's objective argument. **1833** HT. MARTINEAU *Brooke Farm* i. 14 'And what says Sergeant

Rayne?' 'He too is of the objective school, sir'. 'And were his objections listened to?'

B. *sb.* (elliptical uses of the adj.)

1. Short for *objective glass* (see A. 6): the object-glass of an optical instrument.

1835 LINDLEY *Introd. Bot.* (1848) I. 17, I commonly make use, in important investigations, of the three strongest of Plössl's objectives. **1879** NEWCOMB & HOLDEN *Astron.* 61 The construction of the achromatic objective. **1889** *Nature* 31 Oct. 648 An objective which can be adjusted to work as either a photographic or visual objective.

2. *Gram.* Short for *objective case*: see A. 7.

1861 ANGUS *Handbk. Eng. Tongue* 275 Objective with Passive Verb. **1881** MASON *Eng. Gram.* (ed. 24) §80 *note*, The fact that pronouns still distinguish the Objective from the Nominative..compels us to recognize three cases in English.

3. Short for *objective point* (see A. 8); also *fig.* something aimed at, an object or end.

1881 BURNIE *Mem. Thomas* 152 At Johnstown, one objective was the Cambrian Works. **1882** *Times* 10 Feb., Servian Railways..have been for years past the objective of innumerable financial attempts. **1882** *Standard* 14 July, The objective must be Cairo,..the most useful strategical point. **1894** *Dublin Rev.* Apr. 391 The king had for his objective the divorce, and contingently the religious policy.. subsequently engrafted upon it.

4. Something objective or external to the mind.

1884 *Chr. Commw.* 20 Mar. 536/2 The value and attraction of the externals and objectives.

5. *attrib.*, as **objective function**, in linear programming, the function that it is desired to maximize or minimize.

1949 *Econometrica* XVII. 207 The optimum feasible program is that feasible program which maximizes a specified linear objective function. **1958** RILEY & GASS *Linear Programming* i. 5 The linear-programming problem has a linear function of the variables to aid in choosing a solution to the problem. This linear combination of the variables, called the objective function, must be optimized by the selected solution. **1969** D. C. HAGUE *Managerial Econ.* I. i. 16 We shall find that the aim of the business is set out in what is called an objective function—a name which indicates its purpose exactly.

objective correlative. [f. OBJECTIVE *a.* 2 b + CORRELATIVE *sb.* 1.] Term applied by T. S. Eliot to the technique in art of representing or evoking a particular emotion by the presentation of physical symbols of it, as surroundings, situations, sets of objects, etc., which become indicative of that emotion and are associated with it.

[**1850** W. ALLSTON *Lect. Art, & Poems* 16 No possible modification in the degrees or proportion of these elements [*sc.* air, earth, heat, water] can change the specific form of a plant... So, too, is the external world to the mind; which needs, also, as the condition of its manifestation, its objective correlative.] **1919** T. S. ELIOT in *Athenæum* 26 Sept. 941/1 The only way of expressing emotion in the form of art is by finding an 'objective correlative'; in other words, a set of objects, a situation, a chain of events which shall be the formula of that *particular* emotion; such that when the external facts, which must terminate in sensory experience, are given, the emotion is immediately evoked. **1946** *Sewanee Rev.* LIV. 301 In that Eliot proposes the objective correlative, 'he accepts with the vast majority of his contemporaries the modern dogma that the artist is primarily concerned with emotion'. **1947** T. S. ELIOT *Milton* 7 Two or three phrases of my coinage—like 'objective correlative'—which have had a success in the world astonishing to their author. **1951** H. KENNER *Poetry E. Pound* viii. 66 It is easy to see why the objective correlative, the image as sensory equivalent of an emotion, the Aristotelian equation of a poem with an action, and Eliot's claim that emotions the poet has never experienced will serve his turn as well as familiar ones, should seem in such eyes impossibly muddle-headed. **1955** D. DAVIE *Articulate Energy* vii. 86 The use of the objective correlative, the invention of a fable or an 'unreal' landscape. **1957** WIMSATT & BROOKS *Lit. Crit.* 676 A realization that Winters' conception of poetry, like Eliot's, is ultimately 'dramatic' need not impugn the useful distinction between motive (the reason for an emotion) and objective correlative (the symbol of an emotion). **1962** T. P. DUNNING in Davis & Wrenn *Eng. & Medieval Stud.* 168 The pagan element of the story is superbly handled by Chaucer as an essential feature of his *inventum*, or objective correlative. **1963** N. FRYE *Romanticism Reconsidered* 3 Some belief of which Romantic poetry is supposed to form the objective correlative. **1964** J. B. LEISHMAN *Rilke's New Poems* 9 An essentially expounding poet..might still be continuously engaged in a search for ever new 'objective correlatives' for old and unchanged convictions. **1966** K. AMIS *Anti-Death League* II. 176 This communicability..can work via an outward symbol or artefact, so that state-of-mind produces object which in turn produces state-of-mind. There are obvious analogies here with aesthetic theory, in particular with Eliot's notion of the objective correlative. **1971** *Times Lit. Suppl.* 31 Dec. 1629/4 In all these poems the objective correlative was utterly unsatisfactory from any partisan political point of view.

objectively (əb'dʒɛktɪvlɪ), *adv.* [f. OBJECTIVE *a.* + -LY².] In an objective manner or relation: in senses 1-3 opposed to *subjectively* in various senses.

†**1. a.** In relation to its object; as to the object of the action. *Obs.*

1624 BP. MOUNTAGU *New Gagg* 133 Cyril restrayneth ..'thou shalt not covet or desire', unto one particular Act, objectively, the not-lusting after or desiring of a Woman. **1631** J. BURGES *Answ. Rejoined* Pref. 36 The people.. worshipped God and the King: the ceremonie was materially the same; but objectively different; one Civill, the other Sacred. **1673** H. MORE *App. Antid. Idol.* 17 He must ..bow towards the Cherubins objectively, and not meerly circumstantially. **1698** NORRIS *Pract. Disc.* (1707) IV. 167 That love whereby a man loves God, taking the Term objectively.

†**b.** By means of, or in the way of, an 'objective cause'; by the attraction of some object or end. (See OBJECTIVE 1 b.) *Obs.*

1675 BROOKS *Gold. Key* Wks. 1867 V. 164 Some think that Christ by his hunger did objectively allure Satan to tempt him, that so he might overcome him. **1678** CUDWORTH *Intell. Syst.* I. iii. 170 That which it self being moved, (objectively, or by Appetite and Desire of the First Good) moveth other things.

†**2.** As an object of consciousness, as presented to or perceived by the mind (not as it is in itself).

a **1617** P. BAYNE *Lect.* (1634) 315 Not from any inward habit..but from some external suavities objectively apprehended. **1642** W. PRICE *Serm.* 19 Our Creed is objectively called our faith. **1646** SIR T. BROWNE *Pseud. Ep.* 120 The Basilisk..receiveth the rayes of his Antipathy and venemous emissions which objectively move his sense. **1662** STILLINGFL. *Orig. Sacr.* III. i. §3 The Divine Intellect doth understand things by their Idea's, which are..the things themselves as they are objectively represented to the understanding. **1682** H. MORE *Annot. Glanvill's Lux O.* 177 As existent objectively, not really. **1727-41** CHAMBERS *Cycl.* s.v. *Objective*, A thing is said to exist objectively, *objectivè*, when it exists no otherwise than in being known; or by being an object of the mind.

3. As an object of consciousness, in distinction from the mind or conscious subject; in relation to what is external to the mind; externally, really, in actual outward fact.

1796 [see SUBJECTIVELY *adv.* 4]. **1798** A. F. M. WILLICH *Elem. Critical Philos.* 6 Our knowledge is called objectively true, in so far as objects must be perceived by every other being, in the same manner in which we represent them to ourselves. **1817** W. TAYLOR in *Monthly Rev.* LXXXIII. 461 The manner in which the thing becomes a phænomenon.. is explicable only subjectively, not objectively. **1832** AUSTIN *Jurispr.* (1879) II. xlii. 737 In the language of Kant, that exists objectively which lies without the understanding or which the understanding knows by looking beyond itself. **1855** H. SPENCER *Princ. Psychol.* (1872) I. I. vi. 122 What is objectively a nervous action and subjectively a feeling. **1879** *Gd. Words* 30 Any miracle..ascribed to our Lord was objectively real.

†**4.** By way of objection or adverse reason. *Obs.*

1593 R. HARVEY *Philad.* 40 Hee allowed his fathers lawes for his time, lesse any man should objectiuely quarrell with him. **1642** SIR E. DERING *Sp. on Relig.* 149 Let me here by way of anticipation prevent that which will else come in objectively upon me.

5. *Gram.* In the objective case or relation.

[Cf. quot. 1698 in sense 1.] **1824** [see OBJECTIVE A. 7]. **1881** MASON *Eng. Gram.* (ed. 24) Index, Possessive case..used objectively, 72.

ob'jectiveness. [f. as prec. + -NESS.] The quality or character of being objective; the quality of presenting itself as an object of sense (quot. 1677); existence as an object external to the mind; (of a person, work of art, etc.) the character of dealing with or representing outward things rather than inward feelings.

a **1677** HALE *Prim. Orig. Man.* I. i. 1 Is there such a motion or objectiveness of external Bodies which produceth light or colour..? the Faculty of Sight is fitted to receive that impression or objectiveness, and that objectiveness fitted and accomodate to that Faculty. *a* **1834** COLERIDGE *Confess. Enq. Spir.* vii. (1840) 93 No man..can recognize his own inward experiences in such writings, and not find an objectiveness, a confirming and assuring outwardness, and all the main characters of reality, reflected therefrom on the spirit. **1856** FROUDE *Hist. Eng.* (1858) I. v. 391 The healthy objectiveness of an old English Chronicler is no longer possible for us. **1881** LE CONTE *Sight* 13 In smell, there is an equal commingling of subjectiveness and objectiveness.

ob'jectivism. [f. OBJECTIVE *a.* + -ISM.]

a. The tendency to lay stress upon what is objective or external to the mind; the philosophical doctrine that knowledge of the non-ego is prior in sequence and importance to that of the ego; the character (in a work of art, etc.) of being objective. So **ob'jectivist**, one who holds or advocates the doctrine of objectivism (also *attrib.*); **objecti'vistic** *a.*, characterized by objectivism.

1854 GEO. ELIOT tr. *Feuerbach's Essence Christianity* xxi. 203 Belief in revelation is the culminating point of religious objectivism. *Ibid.* xxiii. 224 Religious objectivism has two passives, two modes in which God is thought. **1872** W. G. WARD in *Dublin Rev.* Jan. 71 It is a favourite argument of Mr. Mill's, that objectivism keeps moral science in a stationary state. *Ibid.*, Objectivists hold as strongly as phenomenists, that the morality of actions is importantly affected by their consequences. **1876** MIVART *Less. fr. Nat.* 24 The dogmas which the objectivist philosophy enunciates. **1883** EDERSHEIM *Life Messiah* (1886) I. 208 True religion is ever objectivistic, sensuous subjectivistic. **1954** *Mind* LXIII. 265 'Objectivism'..is so ambiguous that there are very few ethical theories which cannot claim to be in some sense 'objectivist'. **1966** tr. *Kotarbinski's Gnosiology* ii. 68 The gap within idealist views between objectivism and subjectivism. **1972** PICCONE & HANSEN tr. *Paci's Function of Sci.* ii. 27 According to Husserl the struggle between objectivism and transcendentalism gives us the 'meaning' of the history of the modern spirit.

b. A derogatory term used in communist theory to describe an objective attitude towards existing conditions and acceptance of working within their limitations, as opposed to the concern for changing them according to revolutionary theories. So **ob'jectivist**.

1933 T. B. H. BRAMELD *Philos. Approach to Communism* xi. 156 An objectivism which tends to deny the significance of conscious men. **1957** R. N. C. HUNT *Guide to Communist Jargon* 99 Objectivism is thus the opposite of 'party-mindedness', and is a serious offence. **1960** tr. *Lenin's Coll. Wks.* I. 401 The objectivist speaks of 'insurmountable historical tendencies'; the materialist speaks of the class which 'directs' the given economic system. **1972** tr. *Marx et al. On Hist. Materialism* 708 [Editor's note] He [*sc.* Lenin] exposed their attempts to devoid Marxism of its revolutionary content and showed that their views were based on bourgeois objectivism which justified capitalism and glossed over class contradictions.

objectivity (ɒbdʒɪk'tɪvɪtɪ). [mod. f. med.L. *objectīv-us*: see -ITY. Cf. F. *objectivité* (1878 in *Dict. Acad.*).] The quality or character of being objective; external reality; objectiveness.

1803 *Edin. Rev.* I. 258 In both these views it [philosophy] has relation only to their objectivity. [**1812** SOUTHEY *Omniana* I. 220 A confusion of (what the Schoolmen would have called) Objectivety and Subjectivety.] **1848** J. H. NEWMAN *Loss & Gain* III. vi. (1858) 311, I am not denying ..the objectivity of revelation. **1851** CARLYLE *Sterling* II. ii. (1872) 96 The principle of this difference..seems to be that well-known one of the predominant objectivity of the Pagan mind. **1884** F. TEMPLE *Relat. Relig. & Sc.* i. (1885) 16 Kant appears to have no escape from assigning this objectivity of space to delusion. **1950** W. H. BARBER tr. *Jolivet's Introd. Kierkegaard* III. ii. 98 'Objectivity', whose idolatrous worship has been propagated by the modern nationalists, might equally well be defined as 'positivity'. **1957** R. MAY et al. *Existence* i. 25 He [*sc.* Kierkegaard] was convinced not only that the goal of 'pure objectivity' is impossible but that even if it were possible it would be undesirable. **1966** K. HARTMANN *Sartre's Ontology* i. 7 Thus, the phenomena would cease to be moments of myself and would take on 'objectivity'. **1969** R. STRACHAN tr. *Malet's Thought R. Bultmann* i. 19 In its objectivity the other is only an extension of myself.

objectivization (əb,dʒɛktɪvaɪ'zeɪʃən). [n. of action from OBJECTIVIZE *v.*: see -ATION.] The action or condition of making or becoming objective; an instance of this; something external in which an idea, principle, etc., is expressed concretely.

1929 [see EXPRESSIONISM]. **1944** S. PUTNAM tr. *E. da Cunha's Rebellion in Backlands* ii. 144 It [*sc.* Canudos] was the objectivization of a tremendous insanity. **1965** D. A. LOWRIE tr. *Berdyaev's Christian Existentialism* ii. 33 The objectivization of the criterion of truth usually means that that is transferred to another's consciousness and conscience. **1969** W. GLEN-DOEPEL tr. *Metz's Theol. of World* III. 126 The de-privatization and de-existentialization, or, to put it positively, the 'new objectivization' of the Christian message. **1970** R. J. HOLLINGDALE tr. *Schopenhauer's Ess. & Aphorisms* 59 The will's objectivization.

objectivize (əb'dʒɛktɪvaɪz), *v.* [f. OBJECTIVE *a.* + -IZE.] *trans.* To render objective; to objectify. Hence **ob'jectivized** *ppl. a.*

1856 MASSON *Ess., The. Poetry* 432 Goethe's theory of poetical or creative literature was, that it is nothing else than the moods of its practitioners objectivized as they rise. **1874** BUSHNELL *Forgiveness & Law* Introd. 12, I..accounted for the word as one by which the disciple objectivizes his own feelings. **1899** *Westm. Gaz.* 8 June 3/1 The tendency to externalise and objectivise spiritual things. **1965** D. A. LOWRIE tr. *Berdyaev's Christian Existentialism* ii. 34 Objectivized knowledge in all its levels is withdrawn from the existential subject, that is from man.

objectivo- (ɒbdʒɪk'taɪvəʊ), used as combining form of OBJECTIVE *a.*, in **objectivo-objective** *a.*, of the nature of an object-object; **objectivo-subjective** *a.*, of the nature of an object-subject.

1836-7 SIR W. HAMILTON *Metaph.* xxxix. (1859) II. 385 The cognition..is Objective, or rather Objectivo-Objective, when held to consist in an immediate perception of the power or efficacy of causes in the external and internal worlds; and Subjective, or rather Objectivo-Subjective, when viewed as given in a self-consciousness alone of the power or efficacy of our own volitions.

objectize ('ɒbdʒɪktaɪz), *v.* [f. OBJECT *sb.* + -IZE.] *trans.* To make into an object, render objective, objectify. So **objecti'zation**, the action of making (something) an object of thought.

1668 WILKINS *Real Char.* II. ix. 227 Actions of the Understanding and Judgment..in the first Objectization of a thing: or the reflexive Thought about it. **1817** COLERIDGE *Biog. Lit.* xii. (1882) 134 The intelligence in the one tends to objectize itself, and in the other to know itself in the object. **1838** *Blackw. Mag.* XLIII. 193 Man objectises himself as 'the human mind'.

object language. [OBJECT *sb.* + LANGUAGE *sb.*]

1. A language described or analysed in terms of another language (known as the metalanguage).

1935 *Mind* XLIV. 501 Formal syntax requires a language of which it is the syntax. This language is called the 'object-language' (*Objektsprache*) in distinction from the syntax language. **1937** A. SMEATON tr. *Carnap's Logical Syntax of Lang.* 4 We are concerned with two languages: in the first place with the language which is the object of our investigation—we shall call this the *object-language*—and, secondly, with the language in which we speak *about* the syntactical forms of the object-language. **1946** C. MORRIS *Signs, Lang. & Behavior* 179 So if we talked about French in English, French would be the object language and

English the metalanguage. **1947** A. J. AYER *Thinking & Meaning* 26, I am using English in a twofold aspect, as an object-language and as a meta-language in which I speak about the object-language. **1947** R. CARNAP *Meaning & Necessity* i. 4 In order to speak *about* any *object language*..we need a *metalanguage*. **1965** B. MATES *Elem. Logic* ii. 36 In the case of a Greek grammar written in English, Greek is the object-language and English is the metalanguage. **1977** J. LYONS *Semantics* I. i. 10 We may say that the language being described is the object-language and the language which is used to make the descriptive statements is the metalanguage.

2. In the theories of Bertrand Russell: a language consisting only of words having meaning in isolation.

1940 B. RUSSELL *Inquiry into Meaning & Truth* iv. 63 There must..be a language of lowest type... I shall call this sometimes the 'object-language', sometimes the 'primary language'. **1954** E. BRANTH tr. *H. Spang-Hanssen's Recent Theories Nature of Lang. Sign* in *Travaux du Cercle Ling. de Copenhague* IX. 76 Object-words form an object-language, which is the primary language in a language hierarchy. **1963** J. LYONS *Structural Semantics* iv. 54, I do not accept..that there is a basic 'object-language', the elements of which are learnt in isolation and to which the rest of the vocabulary can be reduced.

3. *Computers.* A language into which a program is translated by an assembler or compiler. Cf. *object program* (OBJECT *sb.* 10).

1961 LEEDS & WEINBERG *Computer Programming Fund.* ii. 49 Just as in language translation, a type of dictionary is employed in translating from the source language to the object language. **1970** P. M. SHERMAN *Techniques Computer Programming* vi. 109 The result of the translation process is an object program in an object language or machine language.

objectless ('ɒbdʒɪktlɪs), *a.* [f. OBJECT *sb.* + -LESS.] Devoid of an object or objects.

1. Having no object to which it is directed; not relative to something else as an object.

1805 SOUTHEY *Madoc* I. III, His eyes..Fix'd lifelessly, or objectless they roll'd. **1868** G. MACDONALD *Seaboard Parish* I. xv. 224 Her eyes..had an infinite objectless outlook.

b. *esp.* Having no object or end in view; aimless, purposeless.

1818 *Blackw. Mag.* III. 294 The dull and objectless mode of life adopted by too many of our nobility. **1846** TRENCH *Mirac.* Introd. (1862) 51 They must not be aimless and objectless, fantastic freaks of power. **1879** JULIAN HAWTHORNE *Laughing Mill*, etc. 36, I set off on an objectless tramp.

2. Devoid of (visible) objects; presenting no object to the view.

1820 *Blackw. Mag.* VII. 263 As we were obliged to keep the glasses up, our drive for several miles was objectless and dreary. **1860** GOSSE *Rom. Nat. Hist.* 199 We trace the same bird far up in the solitudes of the sky, breaking into view out of the objectless expanse.

Hence **'objectlessly** *adv.*; **'objectlessness.**

1859 R. F. BURTON *Centr. Afr.* in *Jrnl. Geog. Soc.* XXIX. 55 They lie..objectlessly, needlessly, when fact would be more profitable than falsehood. **1862** F. HALL *Hindu Philos. Syst.* 284 The doctrine of the objectlessness of Brahma's so-called cognition. **1869** W. M. ROSSETTI *Mem. Shelley* p. lxxxii, The objectlessness of inventing such a tale.

object-lesson: see under OBJECT *sb.* 10.

objectly ('ɒbdʒɪktlɪ), *adv.* [f. OBJECT *sb.* + -LY².] Objectively.

1925 *Blackw. Mag.* Dec. 786/1 He saw himself objectly as a felon with the mark of Cain.

object-matter. [f. OBJECT *ppl. a.* + MATTER.]

†**1.** (Properly two words: see OBJECT *ppl. a.* 1.) Matter presented to view, or to be employed as an instrument or means to some end. *Obs.*

1652 GAULE *Magastrom.* 60 The object matter or signall means of divining (by things in heaven, or on earth).

2. The matter that is the object of some action or study; the matter dealt with or treated. (Usually coincident in sense with the more common *subject-matter*.)

1836–7 SIR W. HAMILTON *Metaph.* (1877) I. iii. 51 The first and second [definitions] define philosophy from its object-matter;—that which it is about. **1860** MANSEL *Proleg. Log.* iii. 93 To think actually we must think about something; this something, the object-matter of thought,..must in the first instance be supplied through..the senses. **1884** tr. *Lotze's Logic* 28 A synthesis in which the..requirement would be completely satisfied in regard to any given object-matter.

'objectness. [f. OBJECT *sb.* + -NESS.] The state or quality of being objective or perceptible.

1933 *Mind* XLII. 510 This second relation..is a relation neither to the material object nor to 'objectness'. **1973** J. ELSOM *Erotic Theatre* ix. 179 The laws concerning static nakedness exactly illustrated the idea of 'objectness'. **1975** *Russ. Rev.* (N.Y.) XXXIV. 272 In futurism, in cubism, space is almost always cultivated, but its form, being connected with objectness, does not convey, even to the imagination, the presence of world space; its space is limited by the space which is shared by the things on the earth.

objector (əb'dʒɛktə(r)). Also 7 -er, -our. [f. OBJECT *v.* + -OR, the form being coincident with that of the L. agent-n. from *objicĕre* to OBJECT. But the Eng. form in *-er* has also been used: cf. *rejecter*.] One who objects or makes an objection; one who brings forward a reason or argument against something, or expresses disapproval of or disagreement with it.

1640 BP. HALL *Episc.* II. vi. 119 Let me put the Objector in minde that [etc.]. **1645** MILTON *Tetrach.* Wks. 1738 I. 235 (*Deut.* xxiv. 1) If these objecters might be the judges of human frailty. **1654** WHITLOCK *Zootomia* 496, I..feare not the half-witted Objectours that I may meet with. **1722** WOLLASTON *Relig. Nat.* iv. 62 Another question, supposed ..to be proposed by an objector. **1861** [see OBJECTEE]. **1883** FROUDE *Short Stud.* IV. II. iv. 215 Expressions..qualified to satisfy objectors. **1899** *Whitaker's Alm.* 400/1 A conscientious objector to vaccination can..escape all penalties.

†**ob'jectual**, *a. Obs.* [f. L. *objectu-s* a throwing against, an object + -AL¹.] Of the nature of an object; that is the object of some action, or that which is aimed at; that is a material or external object; objective.

1606 *Proc. agst. late Traitors* 339 Without any other point or scope objectual to move unto. **1624** T. ADAMS *Temple* Wks. 1861 II. 296 Concerning the material temple, external or objectual idols.

‖**objet** (ɔbʒɛ). [Fr., = object.]

1. An object which is displayed as an ornament.

1857 A. MATHEWS *Tea-Table Talk* I. 98 Every part of it [*sc.* the house] abounded in pretty things—*objets*, as they are sometimes called, which her visitors were strictly forbidden to touch. **1960** *Good Housekeeping* Feb. 60/2 For some people a collection is worthwhile only if the pieces are rare. ..For others, the pleasure lies, quite simply, in possessing a number of more ordinary *objets* which intrigue, amuse or otherwise delight the owner. **1970** V. C. CLINTON-BADDELEY *No Case for Police* vii. 136 All those lamentable *objets* on the window-sills. **1973** *Listener* 6 Sept. 319/3 The sights and textures of bourgeois existence: the plush, the antimacassars, the *objets* in the home and in the shops.

2. One who is the object of (someone's) attentions or affection. Cf. OBJECT *sb.* 4. *rare.*

1847 THACKERAY *Van. Fair* (1848) xv. 132 Find out who is the *objet*, Briggs. I'll set him up in a shop. **1877** L. W. M. LOCKHART *Mine is Thine* (1878) II. xviii. 33 He..protested, ..against being 'swindled' into further association with the *objet aimé* for the present.

3. ***objet d'art*** (ɔbʒɛ dar), a small artistic object; a curio; a precious and finely worked ornament. Also *transf.* Also ***objet d'art et de vertu*** (see sense 6 below and VIRTU, VERTU 1 c). Cf. *object of art (and virtu)* (OBJECT *sb.* 3 c).

1865 'OUIDA' *Strathmore* II. xx. 236 Cachemires, sables, flowers, objets d'art, were scattered over it. **1866** MRS. GASKELL *Wives & Daughters* II. x. 98 The various little tables, loaded with 'objets d'art' (as Mrs. Gibson delighted to call them) with which the drawing room was crowded. **1872** C. SCHREIBER *Jrnl.* 27 Mar. (1911) I. 145 We were surprised..to find a house containing 3 rooms entirely hung with pictures, in which were a few unimportant objets d'art. **1883** E. W. HAMILTON *Diary* 29 Jan. (1972) II. 395 Mentmore..certainly is a gorgeous place, full of *objets d'art* and choice articles of furniture. **1913** W. LAWRENCE *Let.* 14 Oct. in T. E. Lawrence *Lett.* (1938) 159 Great collectors of objets d'art. **1921** M. CORELLI *Secret Power* xxii. 267 The ceremony..has become a mere show of dressed-up manikins and womenkins, many of the latter being mere *objets d'art*,—stands for the display of millinery. **1931** *N. & Q.* 5 Sept. 175/1, I should be much obliged for any notes of the mention of platinum—as *objet d'art*, precious possession, gift, jewel or the like—in literature. **1939** O. LANCASTER *Homes Sweet Homes* 38 *Objets d'art et de vertu* had been collected by rich men since the end of the seventeenth century. **1940** N. MARSH *Surfeit of Lampreys* (1941) v. 72 The jewellery and *objets-d'art* idea seemed a capital one. **1955** *Times* 27 May 14/3, I have seen him start from his chair and literally explode from the room, scattering priceless *objets d'art* to right and left. **1965** A. NICOL *Truly Married Woman* 17 He turned over the pages with the hopeless air of a connoisseur examining an objet d'art. **1973** G. SIMS *Hunters Point* xiii. 119 Buchanan knew nothing of fine wines or *objets d'art* but he considered himself a connoisseur of loneliness. **1974** K. CLARK *Another Part of Wood* vi. 257 At Portland Place they [*sc.* the author's children] were hidden away at the top of the house and brought down to be exhibited as *objets d'art* to our friends.

4. ***objet de luxe*** (see DE LUXE *adj. phr.*), an especially fine or sumptuous article of value, a luxury article.

1881 C. C. HARRISON *Woman's Handiwork* III. 149 This was chiefly for the chambers of royal palaces—screens, then as now, being *objets de luxe* in the literal sense. **1934** *Burlington Mag.* Sept. 125/2 Cabinets and boxes covered with tortoise-shell veneer..are among the many 'objets de luxe' brought from India to Europe and now found in old collections. **1941** [see BÆTYL]. **1956** K. CLARK *Nude* i. 8 A few *objets de luxe*, like the Veroli Casket. **1976** *Times Lit. Suppl.* 12 Mar. 290/2 To trace the changing fortunes of Ruritanian royalty, through the dispersal of their Fabergé objets de luxe.

5. ***objet trouvé*** (lit. 'found object', pl. ***objets trouvés***), an object found or picked up at random and presented as a rarity or a work of art. Also *transf.* and *fig.*

1937 AUDEN & MACNEICE *Lett. from Iceland* xvii. 243 The Surrealists shall have J. A. Smith as an Objet Trouvé in disguise. **1940** GRAVES & HODGE *Long Week-End* xx. 352 The similarity between '*objets trouvés*'..and the neo-Victorian knick-knack collecting habit. **1956** M. LASKI in *Pick of Today's Short Stories* VII. 121 *Collages* were countered by *montages*, *objets trouvés* by *objets faits*. **1959** P. & L. MURRAY *Dict. Art & Artists* 112 *Found object* (*objet trouvé*), in Surrealist theory an object of any kind, such as a shell found on a walk, can be a work of art; and such 'Found Objects' have been exhibited. **1962** *Listener* 6 Sept. 350/2 He was far ahead of his time. In the eighteen-nineties he was working on *objets trouvés*, in his case coals from his fire. **1967** L. DEIGHTON *Expensive Place* v. 34 An *objet trouvé* is a piece of driftwood or a fine stone—it's something in which an artist has found and seen otherwise unnoticed beauty. **1970** *New Yorker* 17 Oct. 159/2 Mr. Berio allows that he has treated the Mahler movement as an *objet trouvé*. **1973** *Guardian* 17 Oct. 7/8 The City's food... Among *objets trouvés* were a screw in a cheese and tomato roll, a brass rivet in a Chelsea bun. **1974** *Sunday Times* 14 July 28/2 He [*sc.* Lord Goodman] plonked himself down, a volunteer *objet-trouvé*, and was given a studiously informal treatment.

6. ***objet de vertu*** (or ***virtu***), a spurious transl. into French of *object of virtu* (see VIRTU, VERTU 1 c), after *objet d'art* above. (The required meaning of *vertu* does not exist in French.) Also in phr. ***objet d'art et de vertu.***

1939 [see sense 3 above]. **1947** M. MCCARTHY in *Partisan Rev.* XIV. 63 Lady Windermere's fan becomes an *objet de virtu* as powerful as Desdemona's handkerchief. **1954** 'N. BLAKE' *Whisper in Gloom* II. x. 139 Mr. Borch was in search of information rather than *objets de vertu*. **1961** *Connoisseur* Dec. p. xlvi, *Objets de Vertu* and fine Works of Art. **1974** *Times* 7 Dec. 14/7 His main interests are *objets de vertu* and antique weapons.

objicient (əb'dʒɪʃ(ɪ)ənt). [ad. L. *objicient-em*, pr. pple. of *objicĕre* to OBJECT.] One who objects, an objector; an opponent of a motion or proposition.

1864 in WEBSTER. **18..** OGILVIE cites CDL. WISEMAN. **1894** *Month* June 223 With the commentary of the objicient's character, antecedents, and circumstances. **1896** R. F. CLARKE in *19th Cent.* Aug. 221 (Train. of Jesuit), The 'objicients' do their best to hunt out difficulties which may puzzle the exponent of the truth, who is called the 'defendent'.

objuration (ɒbdʒʊ'reɪʃən). *rare.* [n. of action from L. *objūrāre* to OBJURE.] The action of binding by oath, or of solemnly charging or entreating as if under oath.

a **1557** *Diurn. Occurr.* (Banatyne Club) 15 Objuratioun of the fauouraris of Mertene Lutar, in the abbay of Haly rudhous. **1623** COCKERAM II, A *Binding* by oath, Exorcisme, Obiuration. **1812** SCOTT *Let. to Southey* 4 June in *Lockhart*, I wrote..begging him..for the remembrance of his father ..and by every objuration I could think of.

objure (əb'dʒʊə(r)), *v. rare.* [ad. L. *objūrāre* to bind by an oath, f. *ob-* (OB- 1) + *jūrāre* to swear. Cf. obs. F. *objurer* (1460 in Godef.).]

1. *trans.* To bind by, or charge under oath.

1613 R. CAWDREY *Table Alph.*, *Obiure*, binde by oath.

2. *intr.* To utter an oath, to swear.

1830 *Fraser's Mag.* II. 178 As the people only laughed at him, he cried the..more vehemently; nay, at last, began objuring, foaming, imprecating.

objurgate (ɒb'dʒɜːgeɪt, 'ɒbdʒɜːgeɪt), *v.* [f. L. *objurgāt-*, ppl. stem of *objurgāre* to chide, rebuke, f. *ob-* (OB- 1) + *jurgāre* to quarrel, scold.]

trans. To rebuke severely; to chide, scold.

1616 BULLOKAR *Eng. Expos.*, *Obiurgate*, to chide, to reprooue sharpely. **1856** R. A. VAUGHAN *Mystics* (1860) I. 242 Violently had he objurgated that wretch of a groom. **1873** TRISTRAM *Moab* v. 90 The old man..objurgated his son.

b. *absol.* or *intr.*

1642 JER. TAYLOR *Episc.* xiv. 76 Command, but not objurgate. **1837** CARLYLE *Fr. Rev.* II. v. vii, This poor Legislative..cannot act; can only objurgate and perorate. **1870** SWINBURNE *Ess. & Stud.* (1875) 269 Coleridge wails, appeals, deprecates, objurgates.

Hence **objurgated** *ppl. a.*, **objurgating** *vbl. sb.* and *ppl. a.*

1864 *Sat. Rev.* XVIII. 445/2 Objurgating impotence has always been a legitimate subject for ridicule. **1887** A. BIRRELL *Obiter Dicta* Ser. II. 54 A history of thought during this objurgated period. **1893** *Times* 16 Mar. 9/4 All the hypo-critical whining and objurgating in the world will not alter their determination.

objurgation (ɒbdʒɜː'geɪʃən). [ad. L. *objurgātiōn-em*, n. of action from *objurgāre*: see prec. Cf. F. *objurgation* (15–16th c. in Godefroy).] The action, or an act, of objurgating; a sharp or severe rebuke; chiding, scolding.

1550 HOOPER *Serm. Jonas* i. Wks. (Parker Soc.) 445 The fourth part [of the book of Jonah] containeth an objurgation and rebuke of God. **1653** A. WILSON *Jas. I*, 108 He handled him roughly, with objurgations. **1828** MISS MITFORD *Village* Ser. III. (1863) 54 A smart young sailor..by no means insensible to female objurgation or indifferent to female charms. **1875** KINGLAKE *Crimea* (1877) V. i. 366 The angry objurgations of officers.

objurgative (əb'dʒɜːgətɪv), *a.* [f. L. *objurgāt-*, ppl. stem of *objurgāre* to OBJURGATE + -IVE.] = next. Hence **ob'jurgatively** *adv.*

1854 'MARION HARLAND' (Mary Hawes) *Alone* xvii, The driver's objurgative eloquence. **1897** BARING-GOULD *Bladys* xxii. 260 They expressed their disapproval..loudly and objurgatively.

objurgatory (əb'dʒɜːgətərɪ), *a.* [ad. L. *objurgātōri-us* reproachful, f. *objurgātōr-em*, agent-n. from *objurgāre* to OBJURGATE: see -ORY. Cf. F. *objurgatoire* (Cotgr.).] Having the character of scolding or chiding; conveying or uttering an objurgation or sharp rebuke.

1576 FLEMING *Panopl. Epist.* Epit. B iv b, Dehortatorie, Obiurgatorie, Petitorie. **1603** HOLLAND *Plutarch's Mor.* 116

Touched to the quicke by some objurgatorie reprehension. *c* **1645** Howell *Lett.* (1650) I. 1 Letters..commonly..are either narratory, objurgatory, consolatory, monitory, or congratulatory. **1794** Paley *Evid.* II. iv. (1800) II. 110 The objurgatory question of the Pharisees. **1859** Geo. Eliot *A. Bede* vi, Remarkable for the facility with which she could relapse from her official objurgatory tone to one of fondness.

Hence **ob'jurgatorily** *adv.*, in the way of objurgation, chidingly.

1659 D. Pell *Impr. Sea* 490 May I not objurgatorily speak it? **1882** W. G. Ward *Ess. Philos. Theism* (1884) II. 150 We are not wishing to speak objurgatorily but only to express our meaning, when we say [etc.].

oblanceolate (ɒˈblɑːnsiːəleɪt, -æ-), *a. Bot.* [See ob- 2.] Inversely lanceolate; shaped like a lance-head with the more tapering end at the base.

1850 Dana *Geol.* App. i. 715 The younger [leaves] are quite narrow oblanceolate. **1872** Oliver *Elem. Bot.* II. 203 Common Primrose..A perennial herb, with oblanceolate.. radical leaves.

‖**oblast** (ˈoblast). [Russ.] A second-order administrative subdivision in Imperial Russia and the U.S.S.R.; a Russian province or region. Also *attrib.* Cf. kray.

1886 *Encycl. Brit.* XXI. 69/2 *Oblasts*, or provinces. **1911** *Ibid.* XXIII. 875/2 For purposes of provincial administration Russia is divided into 78 governments (*guberniya*), 18 provinces (*oblast*) and 1 district (*okrug*). **1934** Webster s.v. *Soviet*, They [*sc.* the soviets]..send deputies to the higher soviet congresses: *volosts* (rural district), ..*oblasts* (regional), and the congresses of the constituent republics. **1936** *Nature* 23 May 843/1 They [*sc.* the soviets] in their turn send delegates to the rayons, above which are the oblasts. **1938**, etc. [see kray]. **1951** *Ann. Reg. 1950* 202 The unsatisfactory condition of agriculture in the *oblast* was attributed to organizational deficiencies... N. S. Patolichev ..had spent the previous two years in the comparatively obscure post of *oblast* party Secretary. **1955** *Times* 23 Aug. 6/3 Every credit is given to those oblast and individual state and collective farms which fulfil..the plan. **1964** *New Statesman* 6 Mar. 353/1 Interference at the district level by agricultural departments of the town or village council has been superseded by 'guidance' at the *oblast* (regional) level. **1964** *Economist* 13 June 1264/2 The first oil was struck in the Tyumen oblast only in 1960. **1976** *Survey* Spring 57 He embarked on a successful career in party administration, attaining the rank of *oblast* First Secretary.

‖**oblat.** *Obs.* [F., ad. L. *oblāt-us.*] = oblate *sb.*[1]; also, a disabled soldier placed by the king in a monastery to be there maintained.

[**1656** Blount *Glossogr.*, *Oblat* (Fr.), a Souldier, who, grown impotent or maimed in Service, hath maintenance or the benefit of a Monks place assigned him in an Abbey; Also the means or place of a Monk, or such Souldier.] **1693** tr. *Emilianne's Hist. Monast. Ord.* xvii. 179 These Oblats have no Votes in the Chapter. **1706** Phillips, *Oblats of St. Jerom*, a Congregation of Secular Priests in Italy, founded by St. Charles Borromeo. So **1721**- in Bailey.

‖**oblata** (ɒˈbleɪtə), *sb. pl. Law.* [L., neut. pl. of *oblātus*, used absol.: see oblate *sb.*[1]] See quot. 1670. (In quot. 1761, erron. pl. *oblatas.*)

1658 Fanshawe *Pract. Exchequer Crt.* 78 (*Heading*) Oblata or old Debts. He maketh *oblata* the next title of the Charge of the Sheriff. **1670** Blount *Law Dict.*, *Oblata*,..in the Exchequer it signifies old Debts, brought, as it were together from precedent years, and put to the present Sheriff's charge... Also Gifts or Oblations made to the King by any of his Subjects; which were..entered in the Fine Rolls under the Title *Oblata*; and, if not paid, estreated, and put in charge to the Sheriffs. **1761** Hume *Hist. Eng.* I. App. ii. 257 Fines, amerciaments, and oblatas. **1848** in Wharton *Law Lex.*

oblate (ˈɒbleɪt, ɒˈbleɪt), *sb.*[1] [ad. med.L. *oblāt-us*, sb. use of pa. pple. of L. *offerre* to offer.] A person devoted to a monastery or to religious work.

spec. **a.** A child dedicated by his or her parents to a monastic life and placed in a monastery to be trained. **b.** One who has devoted himself and his property to the service of a monastery in which he lives as a lay brother. **c.** A member of a congregation of secular priests or a community of women devoted to some special work, as ***Oblate of St. Charles***, a priest of the order of St. Charles Borromeo, etc. Also *attrib.*, as ***Oblate Father***.

1864 (*title*) The Complete Works of St. John of the Cross. .. Edited by the Oblate Fathers of Saint Charles. **1865** *Morn. Star* 9 May, Dr. Manning..was also chief of an order called the Oblates of St. Charles Borromeo. **1880** C. E. Norton *Church-build. Mid. Ages* 151 One Master Guccio and his wife, Mina, who had given themselves as 'oblates', with all their property to the church [at Siena]. **1889** —— in *Harper's Mag.* Oct. 768/2 Born of humble parents, who offered him in his early youth, as an oblate at the altar of St.-Denis, he had been bred in the schools of the abbey.

oblate (ˈɒbleɪt), *sb.*[2] [ad. L. *oblāta*: see above.] *attrib.* in ***oblate roll***, an exchequer roll containing a record of the oblata.

1875 Stubbs *Const. Hist.* I. xiii. 598 The Pipe Rolls of Henry II are supplemented under John by Oblate, Liberate, and Mise Rolls.

oblate (ɒˈbleɪt, ˈɒbleɪt), *a. Geom.* [ad. med. or mod.L. *oblātus*, f. *ob-* (ob- 1 b or ? 2) + *lātus* in L. *prōlātus* lengthened out.] Flattened at the poles: said of a spheroid produced by the revolution of an ellipse about its shorter axis. Opposed to *prolate*.

1705 Cheyne *Phil. Princ. Relig.* I. (1715) 56 By this Gravitation, Bodies on this Globe will press towards its Center, tho' not exactly thither neither, by reason of the oblate spheroidical Figure of the Earth. **1774** Goldsm. *Nat. Hist.* (1776) I. 33 The earth..in its figure, which, from being round, was now become oblate. **1778** *Phil. Surv. S. Irel.* 10 An oblate dome. **1831** Brewster *Newton* (1855) I. xii. 324 The figure of the earth is an oblate spheroid. **1852** Dana *Crust.* II. 1026 A large oblate lens-shaped cornea.

Hence **oblately** *adv.*, in an oblate manner; **oblateness**, the quality or fact of being oblate.

1753 N. Torriano *Midwifry* 16 The Womb..becomes above the Neck oblately [*printed* ablately] spheroidical. **1787** Roy in *Phil. Trans.* LXXVII. 202 Seven ellipsoids of different degrees of oblateness. **1871** Rollwyn *Astron. Simpl.* xx. 235 Centrifugal force would satisfactorily explain this spheroidal oblateness. **1880** Gray *Struct. Bot.* (ed. 6) 417/2 *Kidney-shaped*, crescentic with the ends rounded; very oblately cordate.

†**o'blate**, *v. Obs. rare.* Pa. t. and pple. oblated; also 6 *Sc.* oblait. [f. L. *oblāt-*, ppl. stem of *offerre* to offer; cf. *refer, relate.*] *trans.* To offer.

a **1548** Hall *Chron., Hen. VI* 166 b, To render the citie upon reasonable condicions, to them by the French kyng sent and oblated. **1560** Rolland *Crt. Venus* I. 150 Ane goldin Ball, the quhilk himself oblait To Venus.

b. To offer as an oblation.

1872 O. Shipley *Gloss. Eccl. Terms* s.v. *Oblation*, According to the Roman use, the elements were separately oblated, which in England was followed by York, whilst the other two uses, of Sarum and Hereford, oblated both together.

oblation (əˈbleɪʃən). [a. OF. *oblation, -cion* offering, a sacrifice, a kind of impost, ad. late L. *oblātiōn-em* offering, presenting, gift, in eccl. L. sacrifice, n. of action f. *offerre* to offer.] The action of offering; an offering.

I. In religious or ecclesiastical senses.

1. The action of solemnly offering or presenting something to God or to a deity; the offering of a sacrifice, of thanksgiving, or of religious devotion.

1412-20 Lydg. *Chron. Troy* II. xiii, He..quit him manly in his oblacions And ful deuoutly in his orysons. **14..** in *Tundale's Vis.* (1843) 95 He was called Cryst for this entent For he for mon schuld make oblacyon. **1535** Coverdale *Ps.* xxvi[i]. 6 Therfore will I offre in his dwellinge, the oblacion of thankes geuynge. **1548** Latimer *Serm. Plough* Wks. I. 74 What other oblation have we to make but of obedience, of good living, of good works, and of helping our neighbours? **1548-9** *Bk. Com. Prayer, Commun. Serv., Prayer of Consecration.* **1628** Wither *Brit. Rememb.* I. 1645 Oblations of true thankes, and love. **1641** J. Jackson *True Evang. T.* II. 98 The Oxe..is an holy creature, being one of the beasts for oblation, and sacrifice. **1695** Locke *Reas. Chr.* (R.), This oblation of an heart, fixed with dependence on..him, is the most acceptable tribute we can pay him. **1734** tr. *Rollin's Anc. Hist.* I. Pref. (1827) 35 By the oblation of the most precious of the spoils. **1755** Young *Centaur* i. Wks. 1757 IV. 112 [Faith] is a submission of our understandings, an oblation of our idolized reason, to God. **1772** Fletcher *Logica Genev.* 228 Free will to good is founded upon free-grace, and general free grace upon the perfect oblation which Christ made upon the cross. **1865** J. H. Ingraham *Pillar of Fire* (1872) 179 This beautiful temple was erected ..by Amenophis I, for the purpose of sacrifices and oblations.

2. The action of offering or presenting the elements of bread and wine to God in the Eucharist; also, the whole office of the Eucharist.

The Eucharistic service of the Roman Catholic Church, contains two oblations: the offertory or anticipatory oblation, in which the unconsecrated bread and wine are offered, and the ***great oblation***, in which the consecrated elements are presented as sacramentally the body and blood of Christ (forming the second part of the prayer of consecration).

c **1450** Langforde *Medit. ghostly Exerc.* (Bodl. MS. A. Wood 17 lf. 10), At ye offertory when ye prest doith taik ye Chalice and holde yt vp and formys ye Oblatyon. **1529** More *Suppl. Soulys* Wks. 327/2 By the sacred oblacion of that holy sacrament offred for the in the masse. **1651** C. Cartwright *Cert. Relig.* I. 135 They doe not admit Eucharists, and oblations, because they doe not confesse the Eucharist. **1660** Jer. Taylor *Worthy Commun.* i. §1. 21 These men.. enumerate many glories of the Holy Sacrament..calling it ..the paschal oblation. **1706** Hearne *Collect.* 27 Jan. (O.H.S.) I. 171 The Oblation or Sacrifice of Bread and Wine before Consecration. **1866** Neale *Sequences & Hymns* 213 Morning by morning the Great Oblation is made in our temple. **1885** *Cath. Dict.* (ed. 3) 616/1 The great oblation of Christ's body and blood must be carefully distinguished from the Offertory or anticipatory oblation of bread and wine.

3. That which is offered or presented to God or to a deity; an offering, sacrifice; a victim.

[*c* **1430** Lydg. *Vertue of the Masse* (MS. Harl. 2251. lf. 182 b) Whan a man offrithe to god his hert Richest oblacion.] **1561** T. Norton *Calvin's Inst.* III. 210 Forasmuch as he alone is the Lambe of God, he also alone is ye oblation for sinnes. **1611** Bible *Lev.* vii. 29 Hee..shall bring his oblation vnto the Lord. **1678** Dryden & Lee *Œdipus* II. i, Hear me, gods!.. I stand up an oblation, To meet your swiftest and severest anger. **1788** Gibbon *Decl. & F.* l. (ed. Milman) V. 19 The life of a man is the most precious oblation to deprecate a public calamity. **1811** Heber *Hymn, 'Brightest & best'* iv, Vainly we offer each ample oblation; Vainly with gifts would his favour secure. **1828** Macaulay *Ess., Hallam* (1887) 56 To lay all their oblations on the shrine of St. Thomas.

†**b.** *transf.* A person sacrificed on any account; a victim. *Obs.*

1594 Daniel *Cleopatra* IV. 996 Here to be made th' oblation for his feares. **1613** Hayward *Norm. Kings* 91 Many Innocents were made the oblations of his ambitious feares.

4. The presentation of something to God for the services of the Church, the maintenance of its ministers, the relief of the poor, or other pious uses; that which is so presented. **b.** A donation or bequest of property. **c.** A customary offering made on certain occasions, especially in connexion with the Eucharist.

1455 *Rolls of Parlt.* V. 304/2 Pensions, Portions, Tithes, Oblations,..ne noon othir thynge to the seid Priories.. belongyng. **1547** *Injunctions* in *Cranmer's Misc. Writ.* (Parker Soc.) 503 Which chest you shall set and fasten near unto the high altar, to the intent the parishioners should put into it their oblation and alms for their poor neighbours. *a* **1548** Hall *Chron., Edw. IV* 200 b, The whole Province of Yorke, gave yerely to this Hospitall certain measures of corne: in maner as an oblacion of the first fruites of their newe grayne. **1597** Hooker *Eccl. Pol.* v. lxxiv. §4 The name of Oblations applyed not onely here to those small and petite payments which yet are a part of the Ministers right, but also generally giuen vnto all such allowances as serue for their needfull maintenance, is both ancient and conuenient... Nothing..more proper then to giue the name of Oblations to such payments, in token that wee offer vnto him whatsoeuer his Ministers receiue. **1635** Pagitt *Christianogr.* 211 Churches..and their Livings were dedicated unto God..by the solemne vow and oblation of the Founders. **1645** Hammond *View New Direct.* i. §38 Many portions of Scripture are by the Liturgie designed to be read to stir up & quicken this bounty, and those of three sorts, some belonging to good works in general, others to almes-deeds, others to oblations. **1662** *Bk. Com. Prayer, Commun. Serv., Prayer Ch. Militant*, We humbly beseech thee most mercifully (to accept our alms and oblations). *Margin*, If there be no alms or oblations, then shall the words (of accepting our alms and oblations) be left out unsaid. **1706** Phillips, *Funeral Oblations*,..to atone for the Neglects or Defaults of the deceased Party in paying Tithes, or other Ecclesiastical Dues. **1845** Stephen *Comm. Laws Eng.* (1874) II. 740 Those fees and dues which go by the name of surplice fees..and Easter offerings, and mortuaries: all which are mentioned generally in our books by the name of *oblations*. **1885** *Cath. Dict.* (ed. 3) 616/1 The oblations of bread and wine by the faithful began to fall into disuse about the year 1000. [See Bp. Dowden 'Our Alms and Oblations' in *Jrnl. Theol. Studies* April 1900.]

II. In general senses.

†**5.** The action of offering or presenting: **a.** of a gift, esp. in token of respect or honour; also, a gift so offered. *Obs.*

1595 Markham *Sir R. Grinvile* (Arb.) 43 Ill limn'd memorials of divinest rage, I offer as oblations. **1605** Bacon *Adv. Learn.* I. To the King §1, I thought it more respectiue to make choyce of some oblation, which might..referre to the..excellencie of your individuall person. **1689** *Tryal Bps.* Pref. 2 To your illustrious Highness therefore the Oblation of these Sheets..is most justly due.

†**b.** of an opportunity, inducement, or the like. *Obs. rare*[-1].

1678 Gale *Crt. Gentiles* III. 76 The permission and laxation of the reins to Satan, the oblation of occasions and irritaments.

c. (In Roman law) of an amount due.

[**1880-1900** Holland *Jurispr.* (ed. 9) xii. 300 'Tender', 'oblatio', of the precise amount due, followed by 'payment into court'..either extinguishes or suspends the debt.]

†**6.** A present or gratuity. *Obs.*

1433 *Waterf. Arch.* in *10th Rep. Hist. MSS. Comm.* App. v. 296 Herafter no man sholde have none oblationes except the sierjaunt and bakere.

†**7.** A subsidy or tax; a gift to the king. (Cf. oblata.) *Obs.*

1613 Purchas *Pilgrimage* (1614) 132 This Poll-money.. other Authors mention these Oblations of the Iewes to their Treasurie yearely. **1656** Blount *Glossogr.*, *Oblation*,..an aid or Subsidy money. **1668** Prynne *Aurum Reginæ* 103 Queen-gold was payd for every Fine and Oblation amounting to 10 Marks and upwards.

o'blational, *a.* [f. prec. + -al[1].] Of or pertaining to an oblation; of the nature of an oblation.

1867 M. Patterson in *Ess. Relig. & Lit.* Ser. II. (1867) 499 The words..bear one and the same sacrificial or oblational meaning. **1876** S. Manning *Land of Pharaohs* 113 Those long oblational processions to the sacred shrines.

o'blationary, *sb.* and *a. Eccl.* [ad. med.L. *oblātiōnāri-us*, f. late L. *oblātiōn-em* oblation.]

a. *sb.* One who receives the oblations at the celebration of the Eucharist. **b.** *adj.* Having the function of receiving the oblations.

1872 O. Shipley *Gloss. Eccl. Terms* s.v. *Acolyte*, 4 [Acolytes] Oblationary who received the oblations. **1893** *Month* July 362 Two other subdeacons and an acolyte in an alb, with an oblationary to make way for them.

o'blationer. [f. oblation + -er[1].]

†**1.** One who makes an oblation or offering. *Obs.*

1593 Nashe *Christ's T.* (1613) 44 The..profuse sacrificatory expences of ful-hand oblationers. **1660** H. More *Myst. Godl.* VIII. xiv. 423 He..presents himself an Oblationer before the Almighty.

2. = oblationary *sb.* (*Cent. Dict.* 1891.)

oblatory (ˈɒblətərɪ), *a.* [f. L. *oblāt-*, ppl. stem of *offerre* to offer: see -ory.] Pertaining to oblations or offerings.

1611 Speed *Hist. Gt. Brit.* x. i. (1623) 1254 Masses and oblatory Sacrifices. *a* **1638** Mede *Wks.* (1672) 293 Our Prayer for the whole state of Christ's Church is yet Oblatory ..and in the very beginning thereof we desire Almighty God to accept our Alms and to receive our Prayers. **1659** H. L'Estrange *Alliance Div. Off.* (Lib. Anglo-Cath. Theol.)

274 Plain it is that our Church intended a double offering —one eleemosynary, alms for the poor—another oblatory, for the maintenance of the clergy. **1717** COLLIER in Lathbury *Nonjurors* 280 The Oblatory Prayer goes upon this ground, that the Holy Eucharist is a proper sacrifice. **1835** T. STAPLETON in *Archæologia* XXVI. 343 The Queen's oblatory coin of the same value of seven-pence. **1882** T. F. SIMMONS *Alms and Oblations* 6 This prayer is in substitution of the oblatory portion of the prayer for the Church Militant.

†**o'blatrant**, *a. Obs. rare*$^{-1}$. [ad. L. *oblātrānt-em*, pr. pple. of *oblātrā-re* to rail or carp at, f. *ob-* (OB- 1 b) + *lātrāre* to bark.] Railing, reviling.
1601 B. JONSON *Poetaster* v. iii, Hor. *Barmy froth, puffie, inflate, turgidous* and *ventosity* are come up. *Tib.* O terrible windy words... *Hor.* Here's a deal; *oblatrant, furibund, fatuate, strenuous*. *Cæs.* Now all's come up, I trow. What a tumult he had in his belly.

†**o'blatrate**, *v. Obs. rare*$^{-0}$. [f. L. *oblātrāt-*, ppl. stem of *oblātrāre*: see prec.]
1623 COCKERAM, *Oblatrate*, to barke or rayle against one.

†**obla'tration**. *Obs.* [ad. late L. *oblātrātiōn-em*, n. of action f. *oblātrāre*: see OBLATRANT.] Barking at a person, railing, scolding.
c **1560** CHURCHYARD *(title)* A Playn and Fynall Confutation of Cammell's corlyke Oblatracion. **16..** BP. HALL *Serm. to Lds.* (R.), The apostle feares none of these currish oblatrations. **1661** J. S[TEPHENS] *Procurations* To Rdr., He that feareth oblatration must not travel.

oble, obs. form of OBLEY.

†**o'blect**, *v. Obs. rare.* [ad. L. *oblectāre* to delight: cf. obs. F. *oblecter* (Cotgr.).] *trans.* = next.
1555 ABP. PARKER *Ps.* cxix. 356 Obtaynd I haue: thy witnesses in iust fee simple state Oblected so.

†**o'blectate**, *v. Obs. rare.* [f. L. *oblectāt-*, ppl. stem of *oblectāre* to delight, f. *ob-* (OB- 1 d) + *lactāre*, freq. of *lacĕre* to entice.] *trans.* To delight, please, rejoice.
1611 COTGR., *Oblecter*, to oblectate, reioyce, delight. **1620** VENNER *Via Recta* vi. 102 Mixt sauces..to oblectate the pallate. *Ibid.* (1650) 17 Nothing doth more oblectate the heart. **1621** *Ibid., Tobacco* 405 That which adorns the back or oblectate[s] the palat and throat.

†**oblec'tation**. *Obs.* [ad. L. *oblectātiōn-em*, n. of action f. *oblectāre*: see prec.] Delight, pleasure, enjoyment.
1508 FISHER *7 Penit. Ps.* vi. Wks. (1876) 18 Yf euery oblectacyon of synne shall be done away by wepynge. **1596** BELL *Surv. Popery* I. I. xvi. 64 Whatever bringeth corporall oblectation. **1669** WORLIDGE *Syst. Agric.* (1681) 214 Pleasant Hills, or shadowie Vallies, delightful Meadows, or other the like Oblectations. **1832** LYTTON *Eugene A.* v. viii, Furnishing great oblectation unto his neighbors.

oble(e)ge, -leis(h, -lesse, obs. ff. OBLIGE.

†**o'blesion**. *Obs. rare*$^{-0}$. [a. obs. F. *oblésion* (in Cotgr. *obloesion* 'sore hurt,..great harme'), ad. late L. *oblæsiōn-em*, n. of action f. **oblædĕre*, f. *ob-* (OB- 1 b) + *lædĕre*, to hurt, injure.] Hurt, injury.
1656 BLOUNT *Glossogr.*, *Oblesion*, an hurting or annoying. **1721–1800** BAILEY, *Oblesion*, an Injury done to any Part. **1857** in MAYNE *Expos. Lex.*

†**oblest**, corrupt f. ARBALEST: cf. next.
1780 T. SINGLETON *Inv. Properties of Theatre* in *N. & Q.* 5th Ser. (1876) VI. 64/2 Shilock's Knife and Sheath 0. 0. 9 Twelve Oblests for Coronation 0. 12. 0.

†**'oblester**, obs. var. *ar-, al-, awblaster*, ARBALESTER *sb.*[1]
1487 *Barbour's Bruce* XVII. 236 (Camb. MS.) He had vith him..oblesteris [*MS. Edinb.* awblasteris].

obley ('ɒblɪ). Also 4 ub(b)le, ubli, obele, 4–5 oble, 5 ubly, obly(e, obeley, -ly, (oblys), 6 obleye, (obbley), 7 oublie; also 5 oblete, 7 oblett. [ME., a. OF. *oublee, ublee, o(u)bleie, oblie*, etc., mod.F. *oublie*:—eccl. L. *oblāta*, sb. from fem. pa. pple. of *offerre* to offer. Med.L. had also *obliga, obleta*, and other forms fashioned on or influenced by OF. The forms *oblete, oblett*, show med.L. influence. Cf. Ger. *oblate* wafer.]
†**1.** An offering, oblation, sacrifice. *Obs.*
a **1340** HAMPOLE *Psalter* l. 20 Þan þou sall accept þe sacrifice of rightwisnes, obles, & offrandis [*oblaciones & holocausta*].
2. A little cake of bread, usually thin, flat, and circular, and stamped with a cross, an Agnus Dei, or the letters IHS, prepared for consecration in the celebration of the Eucharist; a wafer. Now *Hist.*
1303 R. BRUNNE *Handl. Synne* 10044 Whan þe vble was on þe autere leyde, And þe prest þe wrdes hade seyde. **13..** *Metr. Hom.* (Vernon MS.) in Herrig *Archiv* LVII. 281 In his hond bret full he beere Of bernynge Obeleis a paniere. **1387** TREVISA tr. *Higden* (Rolls) VIII. 9 Anon þey brouȝte an obley þat was i-sacred [*eucharistiam consecratam*]. *c* **1450** *St. Cuthbert* (Surtees) 7060 Þe parte of þe oble he saw blak as any pyk. *c* **1509** *Devyse Coron. Hen. VIII* in Maskell *Mon. Rit.* III. p. lv. *note*, The kyng shall offre an obbley of brede ..with the whiche obleye after consecrate, the king shall be howseld. **1881** T. E. BRIDGETT *Hist. Holy Eucharist* I. 169 Very detailed instructions were given..on the preparation of the ofletes or obleys. **1898** J. T. FOWLER *Durh. Cath.* 58 An oven that was used for baking the obleys, or altar-bread.
†**3.** A thin cake of pastry; a wafer. (Cf. F. *oublie.*) *Obs.*
c **1420** *Liber Cocorum* (1862) 22 Take obles and wafrons.. Close hom in dysshes fare and wele. **14..** *Noble Bk. Cookry* (Napier, 1882) 114 Tak obleys or waiffurs and couche them in a platter. **1616** SURFL. & MARKH. *Country Farme* 585 The kinde of Wafers called Oublies, are made with Honey in stead of Sugar.
†**4.** (See quot.) *Obs.*
1688 R. HOLME *Armoury* II. 21/1 Obletts are certain pieces of Mony having the stamp of J.H.S. coined thereon..in Value it was worth our Penny Farthing.
5. *Comb.*, as *obley-maker*; **obley-irons**, irons between the plates of which wafers were baked, wafer-irons.
1346–7 *Durham Acc. Rolls* (Surtees) 118 Et in j par de vblihirnes..3s. 2d. *c* **1430** *Pilgr. Lyf Manhode* I. lxix. (1869) 41 Bi the doore of an obley makere. *a* **1440** *Liber de diversis medicinis* in *MS. Lincoln A* i. 17 lf. 291 (Halliw.) Mak paste, and bake it in oble-yryns..and after ete the obletes.

oblick, oblicque, obs. ff. OBLIQUE, OBLOQUY.

oblidge, -lie(d)ge, -liesh, obs. ff. OBLIGE.

‖**oblietjie** (ɔ'blici). *S. Afr.* Also **oubl(i)etje.** [Afrikaans, f. F. *oublie* wafer (see OBLEY) + *-tjie* (dim. ending).] A type of wafer-thin teacake.
1890 *Hilda's Where is it? of Recipes* (ed. 2) 243 See also 'obletjes', Scones and Cakes, Puffs and Sandwiches. **1904** *Ibid.* (new ed.) 153 (Pettman), *Obletjes* (or *Oubliès*). An old-fashioned recipe for tea cakes brought to the Cape by the French refugees. **1912** *Northern News* 27 Aug. (Pettman), The one word I feel sure of is *oublietje*, that delicious, crisp, wafer-like pastry to be invariably found at bazaars in the districts settled by the Huguenots. **1947** *Cape Times* 26 Apr. 14/4 The old South African confectionery oblietjies, which the King so much enjoyed. **1947** L. G. GREEN *Tavern of Seas* viii. 65 She also served the rolled wafer tea cakes called oblietjies, made with cinnamon and white wine—a Huguenot contribution to Cape cookery. **1950** M. MASSON *Birds of Passage* vii. 69 The cook they employed..would turn out a number of delicious local confections which included wafer thin teacakes, known as oublietjes.

obligable ('ɒblɪgəb(ə)l), *a. rare*$^{-1}$. [ad. L. type **obligābil-is*, f. *obligāre* to OBLIGE: see -ABLE.] Capable of being brought under an obligation.
1860 EMERSON *Cond. Life* vii. (1861) 162 One man can come under obligations on which you can rely,—is obligable; and another is not.

'obligancy. *rare.* [f. next: see -ANCY. Cf. med.L. *obligāntia* (Du Cange).] Obligatory quality or character.
1826 CARLYLE *Notebook* 7 Dec. in Froude *Life* I. xx. 372 Whence..comes..the obligancy of this utility.

obligant ('ɒblɪgənt), *a.* and *sb.* [ad. L. *obligānt-em*, pr. pple. of *obligāre* to OBLIGE.]
†**A.** *adj.* That obliges or binds, obligatory. *Obs.*
1624 F. WHITE *Repl. Fisher* 525 Fit to be done, but not obligant. *Ibid.*, All the Precepts thereof are perpetually obligant.
B. *sb. Sc. Law.* One who binds himself, or is legally bound, to pay or perform something.
1754 ERSKINE *Princ. Sc. Law* (1809) 328 One of several obligants of this sort, who pays the whole debt, or fulfils the obligation, is entitled to a proportional relief against the rest. **1821–30** LD. COCKBURN *Mem.* vi. (1874) 330 The other obligants withdrew their names from the bond. **1861** W. BELL *Dict. Law Scot.* 596/2 The debtor, whom the English term the obligor, is in Scotland termed the obligant or granter. **1882** *Times* 28 Jan. 11/2, £25,658 has been paid to creditors by other obligants.

obligate ('ɒblɪgət), *ppl. a.* [ad. L. *obligāt-us*, pa. pple. of *obligāre* to OBLIGE.]
†**1.** Bound by oath, law, or duty; obliged. *Obs.*
1432–50 tr. *Higden* (Rolls) V. 185 A man obligate [**1387** TREVISA þat hadde obleged hym self] to the deville for þe luffe of a mayde. **1538–9** *Instr. Hen. VIII, Visit. Monast.* (1886) 22 That they be in no case..obligate to the same.
2. *Biol.* That is of necessity such. ***obligate parasite***, an organism of necessity parasitical.
1887 GARNSEY tr. *De Bary's Morph. & Biol. Fungi* vii. 356 Obligate parasites, that is, species to which a parasitic life is indispensable for the attainment of their full development. **1890** B. A. WHITELEGGE *Hygiene & Pub. Health* x. 227 Parasites..found to grow under any known conditions as saprophytes are distinguished as 'obligate' parasites.

obligate ('ɒblɪgeɪt), *v.* [f. L. *obligāt-*, ppl. stem of *obligāre* to OBLIGE.]
†**1.** *trans.* To bind round, fasten up. *Obs.*
c **1600** *Timon* III. v, Let it be lawfull for me..to ligate and obligate your eares with my words.
†**2.** *fig.* To bind, connect, attach. *Obs.*
1547 HOOPER *Declar. Christ* xi. Wks. (Parker Soc.) 84 Therefore is not the interpretation of the scripture obligated unto an ordinary power, nor to the most part.
3. To bind (a person) by a moral or legal tie.
a. To put under moral obligation, to oblige. Chiefly in *pass.*: To be bound or compelled. In later use chiefly *dial.* and *U.S. colloq.*
1668 in *Athenæum* (1894) 2 June 710/1 My station obligates me to render service with obedience to her commands. **1764** FOOTE *Mayor of G.* I. Wks. 1799 I. 171 Sir, I am obligated to leave you. **1768–74** TUCKER *Lt. Nat.* (1834) II. 308 The more ties wherewith we are obligated to any, the nearer he stands in proximity to us. **1859** W. ANDERSON *Disc.* (1860) 308 You are not only warranted but obligated to vindicate yourself. **1888** 'C. E. CRADDOCK' *Despot of Broomsedge Cove* 146 The parson..was 'obligated' to go down to the Settlement. **1900** S. R. CROCKETT *Little Anna Mark* xl. 340 When she came to New Milns she was obligated to go to the Scots kirk with Sir James.
b. To bind by law.
1755 MAGENS *Insurances* II. 109 If a Master sells his Ship, the new Master and Sailors shall not be obligated to each other. **1879** *Standard* 15 Dec. (D.), The Royal Princes.. having been properly obligated, were invested as Knights of the Temple and Malta. **1888** in Bryce *Amer. Commw.* II. App. 673 Every contract..by which a debtor is obligated to pay any tax.
†**4.** To make (a thing) a security; to pledge, pawn, mortgage; cf. OBLIGE *v.* 3 a. *Obs.*
1541 in R. G. Marsden *Sel. Pl. Crt. Adm.* (1894) I. 107 The..capitayn..hath full power..to bynd and obligate.. the shipp with her frayghte. **1774** BP. HALLIFAX *Anal. Rom. Law* (1795) 87 Actio Serviana..for the recovery of goods, obligated by the Hirer, as a security for his Rent. **1890** E. JOHNSON *Rise Christendom* 57 Which things..we forbid to be alienated and obligated, except for the sake of the redemption of captives.
5. a. = OBLIGE *v.* 6, 7. (Not now in good use.) In later use chiefly *dial.* and *U.S. colloq.*
1692 SOUTH *12 Serm.* (1697) I. 503 While the Courteous person thinks that he is obligating and doing such an one a kindness, the Proud person..accounts him to be only paying a debt. **1726** G. ROBERTS *Four Years Voy.* 159 Yet, said they, we are more obligated to St. Antonio, because it was he that directed the Portuguese..to this Island. **1810** SHELLEY *Lett.* Pr. Wks. 1880 III. 333, I am much obligated by the trouble you have taken to fit it for the press. **1882** *Nature* XXV. 453/2 For which all scientific men will feel deeply obligated. **1898** J. MACMANUS *Bend of Road* 73 I'll be happy to obligate ye. **1919** F. HURST *Humoresque* 226 She thought maybe..I'd go over to her place for Wednesday-night supper for a change. You know how a girl like Clara gets to feeling obligated. **1955** C. MCCULLERS in *Mademoiselle* Nov. 134/1 'I can't stay but just a minute,' John said. 'I'm obligated to sell those tickets. I have to eat and run.' **1963** *PMLA* LXXVIII. IV. ii. 11/1 Many of them felt obligated to turn out teaching materials as a kind of *quid pro quo* for their $350 stipend. **1970** N. ARMSTRONG et al. *First on Moon* ix. 212 The foreman..has to side with his mechanics because he is obligated to a schedule. **1975** *N.Y. Times* 29 Nov. 26/1 President Ford is obligated early next month to report to Congress on the 'progress' of negotiations looking toward a Cyprus settlement.
b. To render (conduct, etc.) obligatory.
1879 G. MACDONALD *P. Faber* I. xvii. 219 The purpose justified an interest in him beyond what gratitude obligated.
Hence **'obligated** *ppl. a.*
1741 RICHARDSON *Pamela* II. 72 Your so much obligated Pamela. **1813** T. BUSBY tr. *Lucretius* I. III. Comm. p. xxx, If ..the only obligated difference..be its subjection to mortality.

obligately ('ɒblɪgətlɪ), *adv. Biol.* [f. OBLIGATE *ppl. a.* + -LY[2].] Out of necessity, because restricted to such a mode of life or such environmental conditions.
1952 [see SAPROBE]. **1955** *New Biol.* XVIII. 54 These nitrogen-fixing bacteria were found to differ strikingly in that *Clostridium* is obligately anaerobic, i.e. able to grow only in the absence of oxygen. **1967** *Oceanogr. & Marine Biol.* V. 194 An obligately psychrophilic marine bacterium. **1971** [see HALOPHILIC *a.*]. **1974** *Nature* 18 Oct. 574/2 Whether a symbiotic association is mutualistic or obligately parasitic.

obligation (ɒblɪ'geɪʃən). [a. OF. *obligation, -acion* (1235 in Godef. *Compl.*), ad. L. *obligātiōn-em* an engaging or pledging, a binding agreement or bond; rarely lit., a binding; fig., an entangling, ensnaring; n. of action f. *obligāre* to OBLIGE.]
1. The action of binding oneself by oath, promise, or contract to do or forbear something; an agreement whereby one person is bound to another, or two or more persons are mutually bound; also, that to which one binds oneself, a formal promise.
1297 R. GLOUC. (Rolls) 8042 Þe king..bed him..to him to gloucestre wende And made him obligacion & ostage him gan sende þat he ssolde to him come al sauf. *c* **1330** R. BRUNNE *Chron.* (1810) 134 He with scrite & oth mad obligacion, þat for leue no loth..Suld werre on him begynne. **1426** LYDG. *De Guil. Pilgr.* 23758 Iustly, this condicioun is worth an obligacioun. **1526** *Pilgr. Perf.* (W. de W. 1531) 8 b, Of the obligacyon made bytwene god and us. **1634** SIR T. HERBERT *Trav.* 30 As well to discharge themselves, from their obligation as to give satisfaction unto the people. **1879** G. BARNETT SMITH *W. E. Gladstone* (ed. 2) I. vi. 169 A valid obligation could not be made with the Court of Rome without communication with the Pope himself.
2. *Law.* An agreement, enforceable by law, whereby a person or persons become bound to the payment of a sum of money or other performance; the document containing such an agreement; *esp.* in Eng. Law, a written contract or bond under seal containing a penalty with a condition annexed. Also, the right created or liability incurred by such an agreement, document, or bond.
1382 WYCLIF *Luke* xvi. 6 And he seide to him, Taak thin obligacioun, and sitte doon, and wryt fyfti. **1431** in *Eng. Gilds* (1870) 276, ij. sufficient plegges, bowndyn w[t] hem in a symple [*v.r.* syngyll] obligacion, for to make a trewe delyueraunce of swiche goodys as thei receyue. **1538** FITZHERB. *Just. Peas* 91 b, Till he be bounde by obligacion to the kynges use, in such some as..shal be thought

resonable. **1615** BEDWELL *Arab. Trudg.* Talby, A peece of parchment, not any whit bigger then an ordinary.. obligation. **1786** BURKE *Sp. agst. W. Hastings* Wks. XII. 260 He had made a temporary seizure of the profits.. for the re-payment of which he gave his bonds and obligations. **1818** JAS. MILL *Brit. Ind.* II. v. viii. 668 Security.. for the discharge of the obligations which the Company held upon the government of Oude. **1883** *Wharton's Law Lex.* (ed. 7) 105/1 A bond is called single when it is without a penalty, and an obligation when it contains a penalty, which is generally double the amount of the principal sum secured.

3. Moral or legal constraint, or constraining force or influence; the condition of being morally or legally obliged or bound; a moral or legal tie binding to some performance; the binding power of a law, moral precept, duty, contract, etc.

of obligation, obligatory. *day* or *holiday of obligation*, a day on which every one is obliged to abstain from work and to attend divine service.

1602 SHAKS. *Ham.* I. ii. 91 Bound In filiall Obligation, for some terme To do obsequious Sorrow. **1638** BAKER tr. *Balzac's Lett.* (vol. II.) 47 There is no obligation to follow them in their opinions. **1689** POPPLE tr. *Locke's 1st Let. Toleration*, L.'s Wks. 1727 II. 247 'Hear O Israel', sufficiently restrains the Obligation of the Law of Moses only to that People. **1701** GREW *Cosm. Sacra* IV. ii. §54 And Numa appointed an Oath unto the Romans, say Plutarch and Livy, as the chiefest Obligation unto Faith and Truth. **1732** BERKELEY *Alciphr.* I. §13 They took great pains to strengthen the obligations to virtue. **1780** BURKE *Sp. Bristol bef. Elect.* Wks. III. 371 What obligation lay on me to be popular? **1849** MACAULAY *Hist. Eng.* ii. I. 172 He had a strong sense of moral and religious obligation. **1885** LITTLEDALE in *Encycl. Brit.* XIX. 93/1 The Mohammedan pilgrimages.. consist.. of two main classes, which may be distinguished conveniently by Latin theological terms, as those of 'obligation' and those of 'devotion'. There is properly only one Moslem pilgrimage of obligation, that to Mecca. **1885** *Cath. Dict.* (ed. 3) 564/2 All bishops and priests with cure of souls are bound to say Mass for their people on Sundays and holidays of obligation.

b. Without moral or legal reference: The fact of being logically or customarily obligatory.

1664 J. WEBB *Stone-Heng* (1725) 67 So many other Obligations induce us to grant the being of Porticoes there. **1896** A. J. HIPKINS *Pianoforte* 44 Setting the military bands aside as forming a province ruled by its own law, the French pitch yet remains as appertaining to preference and not obligation.

4. Action, or an act, to which one is morally or legally obliged; that which one is bound to do; one's bounden duty, or a particular duty. Sometimes with the further notion of coercion: An enforced or burdensome task or charge.

1605 SHAKS. *Lear* II. iv. 144, I cannot thinke my Sister in the least Would faile her Obligation. *a* **1704** T. BROWN *Praise Drunkenness* Wks. 1730 I. 36 The first linger away their lives in perpetual drudgery, in slavery and obligations. **1728** MORGAN *Algiers* II. iv. 270 Thus died this valorous cavalier, for his Faith and for his Prince, as is the obligation of every gentleman of Honour and Character. **1857** TOULMIN SMITH *Parish* 64 If he have not fulfilled his obligations in one respect, he cannot rightly claim his prerogatives in the other. **1875** BRYCE *Holy Rom. Emp.* ix. (ed. 5) 148 He released the Polish dukes from the obligation of tribute.

5. a. The fact or condition of being indebted to a person for a benefit or service received; a debt of gratitude.

1632 J. HAYWARD tr. *Biondi's Eromena* 47 She.. might not see him, to acknowledge the obligation shee owed him. **1751** JOHNSON *Rambler* No. 87 ¶9 They return benefits,.. because obligation is a pain. **1847** MARRYAT *Childr. N. Forest* x, You have no right to put her under an obligation. **1881** SHORTHOUSE *J. Inglesant* (1882) I. xvii. 305 Inglesant returned a courteous message expressive of his obligation for her extraordinary generosity.

b. A benefit or service for which gratitude is due, a kindness done or received.

1618 EARL OF SUFFOLK in *Fortesc. Papers* (Camden) 51 Which I wyll ever acknowledg to you for a great oblygation. **1775** SHERIDAN *Rivals* v. iii, Captain, give me your hand; an affront handsomely acknowledged becomes an obligation. **1821** LAMB *Elia* Ser. I. *Valentine's Day*, When a kindly face greets us, though but passing by,.. we should feel it as an obligation.

†**c.** Obligingness, civility. *Obs. rare.*

1664 PEPYS *Diary* 4 June, To make him civill, and to command in words of great obligation to his officers and men.

†**6.** Legal liability. Cf. OBLIGE *v.* 5. *Obs.*

1676 HALE *Contempl.* I. 93 As an imputed sin drew with it the obligation unto punishment. **1758** S. HAYWARD *Serm.* i. 5 Guilt is an obligation to punishment on account of Sin.

†**7.** A binding, fastening, or connecting; a connexion, link. *Obs. rare.*

1646 SIR T. BROWNE *Pseud. Ep.* 240 Yet is there one link and common connexion, one generall ligament, and necessary obligation of all whatever unto God.

†**8.** A bond by which one is held captive. *rare.*

1582 N. T. (Rhem.) *Acts* viii. 23, I see thou art in the gall of bitternes and the obligation [Vulg. *obligatione*] of iniquitie.

9. *Comb.*, as *obligation-maker*.

1678 CUDWORTH *Intell. Syst.* Contents (I. v. 895) These artificial Justice-makers and Obligation-makers.

obli'gational, *a. rare*⁻¹. [f. prec. + -AL¹.] Of the nature of, or pertaining to an obligation.

1887 E. GURNEY *Tertium Quid* I. 294 Whether the axiom, when this latter obligational form is given to it, ceases to be scientific, is perhaps no more than a verbal question.

obli'gationary, *a.* [f. as prec. + -ARY¹.] Pertaining to a legal obligation or bond.

1880 MUIRHEAD *Gaius* Digest 565 She was entitled to alienate her *res nec mancipi*, amongst which obligationary claims were included.

obligative ('ɒblɪgətɪv), *a.* [f. L. *obligāt-*, ppl. stem of *obligāre* to OBLIGE + -IVE.]

1. Imposing obligation; obligatory.

1596 BELL *Surv. Popery* III. ii. 240 Or give power obligative unto them. **1622** MABBE tr. *Aleman's Guzman d'Alf.* II. 242 Bills and answers.. processiue, justificatiue, obligatiue.. renunciatiue, and infinite other the like. **1875** POSTE *Gaius* I. (ed. 2) 73 Contract in the narrower sense may.. be distinguished as an obligative contract.

2. *Gram.* Of a verb form, mood, etc.: implying obligation. Hence as *sb.*

1877 W. D. WHITNEY *Essent. Eng. Gram.* v. 122 With *must* and *ought (to)* we make forms which may be called *obligative*, 'implying obligation': thus, *I must give, I ought to give.* **1968** J. LYONS *Introd. Theoret. Linguistics* vii. 309 The distinction between the 'obligative' and the 'inferential' sense associated with the auxiliary verb *must* in English is neutralized in a non-part sentence like *He must come regularly. Ibid.*, There is a further distinction within the 'obligative' in English, which has to do with the acceptance or fulfilment of the obligation. **1974** W. P. LEHMANN *Proto-Indo-Europ. Syntax* iv. 105 The PIE subjunctive may resemble in meaning an obligative. *Ibid.* 131 In time the obligative meaning of the subjunctive came to be subsidiary to its function of indicating subordination.

Hence '**obligativeness**, obligatoriness.

1678 NORRIS *Coll. Misc.* (1699) 165 The Obligativeness and Reasonableness of the Institution. **1831** R. SHARP *Lett. & Ess.* (1834) 150 The obligativeness of moral conduct.

obligato, variant of OBBLIGATO.

obligator ('ɒblɪgeɪtə(r)). *rare.* [a. med.L. *obligātor*, agent-n. f. *obligāre* to OBLIGE.]

1. *Law.* One who binds himself; = OBLIGOR.

a **1625** SIR H. FINCH *Law* (1636) 294 So if two be bound in an obligation to a fem sole, and after she taketh one of the obligators to husband, the whole dutie is extinct.

2. One who confers an obligation; = OBLIGER 2.

1798 *Sporting Mag.* XI. 42 He was thus interrupted by the sagacious obligator.

†**obliga'torious**, *a. Obs. rare.* [f. as next + -OUS.] Obligatory.

1602 FULBECKE *2nd Pt. Parall.* 28 It is on both sides obligatorious.

obligatory (ə'blɪ-, 'ɒblɪgətərɪ), *a.* [ad. late L. *obligātōri-us*, f. ppl. stem of *obligāre* to OBLIGE: see -ORY.]

1. Imposing obligation, binding in law or on the conscience; of the nature of an obligation; that must be done or practised. Const. *on, upon* (†*to*, †*of*).

1502 *Ord. Crysten Men* (W. de W. 1506) III. i. 140 Also it is a thynge obligatorye. *a* **1626** BACON (J.), Whether it be not obligatory to Christian princes. **1655** FULLER *Ch. Hist.* III. i. §14 This his confirmation of King Edward's Laws was.. but a personal act.. and no whit obligatory of his posterity. **1661** BOYLE *Style of Script.* (1675) 132 Many things enacted in the Old Testament.. which are not now.. obligatory on us Christians. **1702** ECHARD *Eccl. Hist.* (1710) 10 They were not obligatory to other nations. **1795** BURKE *Regic. Peace* i. Wks. VIII. 185 There are situations.. in which, therefore, these duties are obligatory. **1875** JOWETT *Plato* (ed. 2) I. 478 The obligatory and containing power of the good is as nothing. **1888** *Times* (weekly ed.) 6 Apr. 16/4 A Royal decree.. making it obligatory on managers of theatres in Madrid to light those buildings by electricity.

2. Creating or constituting an obligation; esp. in *writing* (*bill*, etc.) *obligatory* = OBLIGATION 2.

1456 SIR G. HAYE *Law Arms* (S.T.S) 182 Suppos the Capitane, wald obliss him be his lettres obligatoris. **1480** CAXTON *Chron. Eng.* clxii, As the strengthe of the letter oblygatorye wytnessyd. *a* **1548** HALL *Chron., Edw. IV* 246 A sufficient instrument obligatorie.. for the.. contentacion of the same money. **1644** BULWER *Chirol.* 108 In all obligatory bargaines and pledges. **1666** J. DAVIES *Hist. Caribby Isls* 200 They commonly deliver obligatory acts to their Masters,.. by which writings they oblige themselves to serve them.. three years. **1691** BOYLE *Will* Wks. 1772 I. Life 160 Whereas my servant John Warr is indebted unto me in the sum of 50*l*. by bond or bill obligatory. **1776** *Trial of Nundocomar* 23/2, I never heard of his putting his seal to obligatory papers, on which money was to be received. **1892** *Daily News* 30 July 5/3 The Judge decided that the fact that the document was not 'under seal', removed it from the legal definition of a 'writing obligatory'.

3. *Biol.* = OBLIGATE *ppl. a.* 2.

1896 *Allbutt's Syst. Med.* I. 513 Obligatory aerobes, which must be supplied with oxygen. **1898** *Ibid.* V. 166 If this observation should be confirmed, the tubercle bacillus could no longer be considered an obligatory parasite.

Hence **obligatorily** *adv.*, in an obligatory manner, so as to be obligatory; **obligatoriness**, the quality or fact of being obligatory.

1563–87 FOXE *A. & M.* (1596) 230 Being bound obligatorilie, both for himselfe and his successors. **1650** R. HOLLINGWORTH *Exerc. Usurped Powers* 28 The obligatorinesse of the Oaths and Covenant. **1755** JOHNSON, *Indissolubly*.. 2 For ever obligatorily. **1879** FARRAR *St. Paul* I. 419 The obligatoriness of circumcision had at that time been less seriously impugned. **1942** PARTRIDGE *Usage & Abusage* 346/2 *Vari-coloured* and *variegated* are, the first obligatorily, the second preferably, to be used of or in reference to colour. **1961** *Amer. Speech* XXXVI. iii. 163 Postnominal modifiers can be shifted out beyond the noun obligatorily. **1975** T. P. WHITNEY tr. *Solzhenitsyn's Gulag Archipel.* II. III. i. 15 Camps for forced labor were obligatorily created.

oblige (ə'blaɪdʒ), *v.* Forms: α. 3 obligi, 4 -lege, 4–5 -liche, 5 -lyge, 6 -leege, 7 -lidge, -liege, (-ligue), 8 -liedge, -leadg; 3- oblige. β. 3–5 (-7 *Sc.*) oblisch, 4–5 -lissh, -lyssh, 4 (6–7 *Sc.*) -lish, 5 -lesche, (obblish), 7 *Sc.* obliesh, -leish. γ. *Sc.* 4–5 oblise, 4–6 -lis, -lys, 5–6 -lyss, 5–7 -liss, 6 -leiss, -leas, -lesse, -las, 6–7 -leis. [a. OF. *obliger, -ier* (1267 in Hatz.-Darm.) to bind by oath or promise, pledge, render liable (also refl.), ad. L. *obligāre* to bind or tie around, bind up, bind by an oath, promise, or moral or legal tie, render liable, pledge, mortgage, impede, restrain, f. *ob-* towards + *ligāre* to tie, bind. Formerly pronounced (ə'bliːdʒ) after Fr.]

I. 1. *trans.* To bind (a person) by an oath, promise, contract, or any moral or legal tie (*to* a person or a course, or *to do* a thing); to put under an obligation or engagement, to engage. Now only in *Law*.

1297 R. GLOUC. (Rolls) 7995 Þo adde william vr king.. to him vaste iobliged [*v.r.* oblisched] Þe king of scotlond. *c* **1400** *Apol. Loll.* 41 See Þei Þat Þei oblesche no man to Þer maner of pouert. *a* **1548** HALL *Chron., Hen. VII* 2 All menne were perdoned.. which would.. by othe be obliged truly to serve and obeye hym. *a* **1657** R. LOVEDAY *Lett.* (1663) 275, I inclos'd the Note.. in a Letter to my Brother, and oblig'd him to be very careful in sending it. **1690** LOCKE *Govt.* II. vi. §73 It has been commonly suppos'd, That a Father could oblige his Posterity to that Government, of which he himself was a Subject. **1759** JOHNSON *Rasselas* viii, My father had obliged me to the improvement of my stock, not by a promise.. but by a penalty which I was at liberty to incur. **1880** MUIRHEAD *Gaius* III. §104 Slaves.. cannot be obliged to any.. person. *Ibid.* §137 In *nomina*, while one, by making an entry to the other's debit, lays him under an obligation, it is only the latter that is obliged.

2. a. *refl.* To bind oneself by an oath, promise, or contract (*to* a person, *to* a course or *to do* something, †*that* something shall be done); to come under an obligation, to pledge, engage oneself.

1297 R. GLOUC. (Rolls) 2161 Hii hom wolde obligi & sikernesse vinde gode To bere hom clene hor truage. *c* **1375** *Sc. Leg. Saints* xxxiii. (*George*) 503 Þane sais Þe wich: 'gyf I ne ma Ourcum his craft.. I oblise me.. Bat ransoninge to thole dede'. **1405** *Rolls of Parlt.* III. 605/2 We.. oblyssyng us, by thys presentes,.. to fulfill all maner accordez. *a* **1575** *Diurn. Occurr.* (Bannatyne Club) 308 We obleiss ws, and promeiss that.. the said abstinence of weir.. sall continew. **1609** W. M. *Man in Moone* (1849) 37 Having plighted your faith and solemnly obliged yourselfe unto an husband. **1664** MARVELL *Corr.* Wks. 1872–5 II. 154 The time for which he had obliged himself being expired. **1721** in T. W. Marsh *Early Friends* iii. (1886) 29 We Desire John Croker to take his place and.. we doe obleadg our selves to give him 40 shili. **1890** *Pall Mall G.* 9 Sept. 7/3 In gratitude for the bequest of Preston, the town council obliged themselves to his son to build that aisle to his memory.

†**b.** *intr.* (for *refl.*) *Sc. Obs.*

1501 DOUGLAS *Pal. Hon.* II. xxvi, I obleis be my hand, He sall obserue in all pointis ȝour behest. **1567** in Row *Hist. Kirk* (1842) 34 That these præsent oblishes to reforme themselves. **1634** *Ibid.* 374 We.. undersubscryve, and oblishes and promises to obey the wholl contents of the said letter.

†**3.** *trans.* **a.** To make (lands, property, a possession) a guarantee or security for the discharge of a promise or debt; to pledge, pawn, or mortgage. Also *fig.*, to pledge (one's life, honour, etc.). *Obs.*

1297 R. GLOUC. (Rolls) 6771 Þe emperour of rome to him.. Obligede [*v.r.* obleged] bi his messagers alle Þing Þat was his. **1388** WYCLIF *Prov.* xxii. 26 Nyle thou be with hem that oblischen [1382 ficche doun] her hondis, and that proferen hem silf borewis for dettis. **1395** PURVEY *Remonstr.* (1851) 81 King Jon oblisshide his rewme of Ingelond and his lordshipe of Ireland in a thousand mark, to be paied yeer bi yeer. **1474** CAXTON *Chesse* 131 Yf thou wylt oblyge thy sowle to me ayenst my hors I wyl playe wyth the. **1675** MARVELL *Corr.* Wks. 1872–5 II. 449 The gentlemen.. were ordered to oblige each their honour, not to take any resentment. **1700** TYRRELL *Hist. Eng.* II. 928 [He] forbid all the Prelates.. to oblige their Lay-Fees to the See of Rome. **1750** BEAWES *Lex Mercat.* (1752) 113 The ship is tacitly obliged for their wages.

†**b.** To agree to as obligatory. *Obs. rare.*

1513 DOUGLAS *Æneis* XIII. iii. 83 The haly promys and the bandis gent Of pece and concord oblisit and sworn.

4. a. Of an oath, promise, law, command, etc.: To bind (a person); to make (one) morally or legally bound to some action or conduct, or *to do* something; also, *to* a person (*obs.* exc. in *Law*).

c **1380** WYCLIF *Sel. Wks.* III. 70 Siþin gode deedis, in Goddis myraclis, oblischen men moore to serve God. *a* **1548** HALL *Chron., Hen. VII* 28 b, The statutes and ordinaunces.. dothe not oblige and bynde them to that case, but in certayne poyntes. **1589** R. BRUCE *Serm.* (1843) 28 The command oblishes you to obey. **1649** W. BALL *Power of Kings* 8 As the Kings Oath tieth and obligeth Him to the People, certainly the Peoples Oath tieth and obligeth them to the King. **1741** WATTS *Improv. Mind* I. i. (1801) 15 Christianity so much the more obliges us.. to invoke the assistance of the true God. **1865** W. G. PALGRAVE *Arabia* I. 449 The names of those whom vicinity obliges to attendance are read over morning and evening.

b. With simple obj.: To bind, to be binding on (a person, conscience). Also *absol.*

c **1400** *Apol. Loll.* 101 Four þingis are requirid to ilk vowe þat oblischiþ. **1643** PRYNNE *Sov. Power Parlt.* I. (ed. 2) 47 Yet these Lawes would no wayes obliege them, unlesse they voluntarily consented and submitted to them in Parliament. **1673** MARVELL *Reh. Transp.* II. 241 You say they are no Laws unless they oblige the Conscience. **1722** WOLLASTON *Relig. Nat.* vii. 153 Two inconsistent laws cannot both oblige.

c. *pass. to be obliged*: to be bound by a legal or moral tie.

c **1375** *Sc. Leg. Saints* xxxviii. (*Adrian*) 165 He wes obliste til his wyfe To speke with hir in-to his lyfe. **1484** CAXTON *Fables of Alfonce* ix, I promysed to the nought at al, in the presence of whom I am oblyged or bound. **1552** ABP. HAMILTON *Catech.* (1884) 43 We ar oblissit to lufe God. **1609** SKENE *Reg. Maj.* 5 b (*Stat. Will.* c. 19), The wyfe is nocht oblisched to accuse hir husband. **1672** CAVE *Prim. Chr.* III. i. (1673) 268 That Duty and Respect, wherein we stand obliged to others. **1709** STRYPE *Ann. Ref.* I. xxi. 244 Martyr excused his coming, partly because he was obliged to the city and church of Zurick. **1810** HORSLEY *Serm.* (1811) 439 Thus it should seem that Christians are clearly obliged to the observance of a Sabbath.

II. 5. †**a.** *trans.* To make (any one) subject or liable *to* a bond, penalty, or the like. *Obs.*

1340 *Ayenb.* 113 Þe zenuolle be one zenne dyadlich .. is y-obliged to zuo ane greate gauelinge. *c* **1386** CHAUCER *Pars. T.* ¶773 This cursed synne anoyeth greuousliche hem that it haunten And first to hire soule, for he obligeth it to synne and to peyne of deeth. **1533** GAU *Richt Vay* 105 Quhen Adam sinnit he oblist hime self and al his offspring to the eternal deid. **1649** JER. TAYLOR *Gt. Exemp.* Pref. §14 It is to be inquired how these became laws; obliging us to sin, if we transgress.

b. *refl.* To render oneself liable to punishment, to involve oneself in guilt. (Lat. *sē obligāre*.) Now only in *Civil Law*.

1382 WYCLIF *Prov.* xiii. 13 Who bacbiteth to any thing, he oblisheth hymself in to the time to come. **1880** MUIRHEAD *Gaius* III. §208 Most agree that, as theft depends upon intent, such a child can only oblige himself in respect of it when he is close upon puberty.

III. 6. a. *trans.* To bind or make indebted (†*to* oneself) by conferring a benefit or kindness; to gratify *with* or *by doing* something; to do a service to, confer a favour on; †to be of service to, to benefit (*obs.*).

1567 TUBERV. *Ovid's Ep.* 71 And oblige mee unto thee by this boone. *a* **1610** HEALEY *Theophrastus* (1636) 83 If any man be oblig'd, he will command him to remember the favour. **1615** G. SANDYS *Trav.* 2 Here take oh Zani this ring of gold, and by giuing it to the sea, oblige it vnto thee. **1626** T. H[AWKINS] *Caussin's Holy Crt.* 38 Pliny .. pronounceth .. That the greatest diuinity is to see a mortall man oblige his like. **1670** COTTON *Espernon* I. II. 60 That her Family had oblig'd Hungary with a Queen, and France with a Gaston de Foix. **1775** SHERIDAN *Rivals* v. iii, O pray, Faulkland, fight to oblige Sir Lucius. **1840** DICKENS *Barn. Rudge* xv, Oblige me with the milk. **1885** SIR W. V. FIELD in *Law Rep. 15 Queen's Bench Div.* 413 The customer requested the appellant, to oblige her, to send the loaves home with other goods she had purchased.

b. Said of the service, kindness, etc.

1638 BAKER tr. *Balzac's Lett.* (vol. II.) 85 If this tendernesse proceeded from a soft effeminate spirit, yet it would .. oblige me infinitely unto you. **1685** BAXTER *Paraphr. N.T.*, *Rom.* xvi. 3–4 The .. helping an eminent Minister, may oblige many Churches. **1769** SIR J. SINCLAIR *Corr.* (1831) II. 439 Your early attention to this application, will much oblige, Sir, your very faithful and obedient servant.

c. *absol.* To confer a favour; *esp.* to favour a company (with some performance). *colloq.*

1735 POPE *Prol. Sat.* 208 So obliging, that he ne'er oblig'd [*rime* besieg'd]. **1865** DICKENS *Mut. Fr.* III. vi, Sir, would you obleege with the snuffers. **1888** *Pall Mall G.* 16 Nov. 7/1 To-night, Mr. Grossmith .. and all the talents will oblige. **1897** tr. *Balzac's Cousin Pons* 12 He 'obliged' at the pianoforte. **1899** *Westm. Gaz.* 15 Apr. 2/1 A chairman was elected, obliged with a song, and then called upon a member of the company. When gents were shy, or dry, or both, professional talent obliged.

d. *intr.* and *trans.* To act as a charwoman (for); to provide with domestic help. *euphem.*

1933 D. C. PEEL *Life's Enchanted Cup* xix. 259 The mother took in washing and went out to 'oblige' and earned roughly 22s. a week and some of her food. **1937** E. GARNETT *Family from One End St.* i. 13 She occasionally did odd work to 'oblige' Mrs. Theobald, the Vicar's wife. **1958** J. CANNAN *And be a Villain* iii. 51 I'm not in service. I oblige by the hour. **1963** A. LUBBOCK *Austral. Roundabout* 165 Twice a week a lady came to 'oblige' in the house. **1972** 'A. ARMSTRONG' *One Jump Ahead* i. 8 A bachelor who .. paid well and wasn't too fussy .. was a far better proposition than some others she had 'obliged'.

7. *pass.* To be bound *to* a person by ties of gratitude; to owe or feel gratitude; to be indebted *to* a person (or thing) *for* something. Now said only in reference to small services, esp. in making an acknowledgement or request; also, formally, where there is no real indebtedness, as in ordering goods from a tradesman, etc.

a **1548** HALL *Chron., Hen. VII* 39 Yf yt chaunce me by your ayde .. to recover .. I .. shalbe so muche obliged and bounde unto you. **1619** WOTTON *Let.* in *Eng. & Germ.* (Camden) 49 For the foresaid resolution in youre Ma[tie] ymplying .. the good of so manie of your freindes, they held themselves eternally obliged. **1692** BENTLEY *Boyle Lect.* viii. 295 To those Hills we are obliged for all our Metals. **1726** G. ROBERTS *Four Years Voy.* 53, I told them, I was very much obliged to them for their Good-will. **1791** *Gentl. Mag.* 32/2 The republick of letters is infinitely obliged to M. Coste for the pains he has taken. **1836** MACAULAY in Trevelyan *Life* I. vi. 453 There is an oversight in the article on Bacon, which I shall be much obliged to you to correct.

†**8.** *trans.* In looser sense: To gratify, please, attract, charm. *Obs.*

1635–56 [see OBLIGING *ppl. a.* 2 b]. **1673** S. C. *Art of Complaisance* 8 Without which it is impossible to oblige in conversation. **1679** G. R. tr. *Boyatuau's Theat. World* Ded. 2 Perceiving many things in it which did oblige my fancy. **1709** SWIFT *Tritical Ess.*, It was reasonable to suppose, you would be very much obliged with any thing, that was new.

IV. 9. *trans.* To constrain, esp. by moral or legal force or influence; to force, compel.

a. *to do* something.

1632 J. HAYWARD tr. *Biondi's Eromena* 91, I will obey you (my Lord) for all things oblige me so to doe. **1715** DE FOE *Fam. Instruct.* I. iii. (1841) I. 64 From this time I resolve to oblige all my family to serve God. **1776** *Trial of Nundocomar* 23/2 He is so weak that he has been obliged to be held up by people when he came out of the house. **1808** PIKE *Sources Mississ.* III. 215, I will give you a certificate from under my hand of my having obliged you to march. **1896** T. F. TOUT *Edw. I*, iv. 83 The royal officials committed so many misdeeds that the king on his return was obliged to make a stern example.

b. *to* a course of action, etc.

1654 tr. *Scudery's Curia Pol.* 66 See here the reasons which obliged this illustrious Prince to his resolution, and the true Motives of so glorious an action. **1722** DE FOE *Plague* 153 Self-preservation obliged the people to these severities. **1875** HOWELLS *Foregone Concl.* 129 It is flattering to a man to be indispensable to a woman so long as he is not obliged to it.

†**c.** To restrain *from* action, etc. *Obs.*

c **1661** *Marq. Argyle's Last Will* in *Harl. Misc.* (1746) VIII. 29/1 [Argyle] being .. to oblige from the Rebellion then on Foot, created a Marquis. **1709** J. JOHNSON *Clergym. Vade M.* II. p. lxxi, To oblige the delinquent from the exercise of his function.

10. To render imperative; to necessitate.

1638 SIR T. HERBERT *Trav.* (ed. 2) 82 In some sort to oblige their dependance upon his acts and fortunes. **1742** RICHARDSON *Pamela* III. 60 Policy .. obliged from the dear Gentleman this Frankness and Acknowlegement. **1866** *Cornh. Mag.* Dec. 734 The custom of the Elizabethan theatre obliged this double authorship.

V. †**11.** *trans.* To fasten or attach closely; to bind, tie up. *Obs.*

1656 STANLEY *Hist. Philos.* VIII. (1701) 333/1 Touching is a Spirit extended from the Hegemonick part to the Superficies, so that it perceiveth that which is obliged to it. **1718** MOTTEUX *Quix.* II. xvi. (1865) 293 As soon as Maritornes had fastened him, she .. left him so strongly obliged, that it was impossible he should disengage himself.

†**12.** To fetter, ensnare. *Obs.*

a **1340** HAMPOLE *Psalter* xix. 9 Þai ere obligid and þai fell. **1382** WYCLIF *Ps.* xix. 9 Thei ben oblisht, and fellen.

†**o'blige**, *sb. Obs. rare*$^{-1}$. In 7 obliege. [f. prec. vb.] Obligation.

1611 SPEED *Hist. Gt. Brit.* IX. xvii. §31. 858 Whether he did it in policy .. or else of duety of obliege .. is vncertaine.

oblige, obs. form of OBLIGEE.

†**obli'geant**, *a. Obs.* [a. F. *obligeant* (ɔbliʒɑ̃), pr. pple. of *obliger* to OBLIGE.] Obliging.

1654 tr. *Scudery's Curia Pol.* 81 Reputed the most civill and obligeant Prince of all the world. *a* **1734** NORTH *Exam.* I. iii. §103 (1740) 193 It is prodigious that a Parcel of .. Lyes .. shall be thus tenderly treated in the soft and obligeant style of Superstructures and subsequent Additions.

obliged (ə'blaɪdʒd), *ppl. a.* [-ED[1].]

1. Bound by law, duty, or any moral tie, esp. one of gratitude; under obligation; freq. in phr. *obliged servant*, used in signing a letter, etc.

1604 R. CAWDREY *Table Alph.*, *Obliged*, bound or beholden. **1612** JAS. I, *Declar. Conradus Vorstius* Ded., To the Honour of our Lord and Saviour Jesus Christ, by His most obliged servant, James, by the Grace of God, King [etc.]. **1650** JER. TAYLOR *Holy Living* iii. §4 (1727) 184 A Prayer to be said by Masters of Families, Curates, Tutors, or other obliged Persons. **1764** REID *Inquiry* Ded., Your Lordship's most obliged and most devoted Servant. **1862** THACKERAY *Let.* 1 May in *Athenæum* (1918) 20 June 800/2 Believe me Your obliged faithful Servt. W. M. Thackeray.

2. †**a.** Rendered binding or obligatory, bounden (*obs.*). **b.** Compelled, necessitated.

1659 HAMMOND *On Ps.* lxvi. 1 It is the obliged duty of all. **1891** STEVENSON & OSBOURNE *Wrecker* xii, Every spoke of the wheel a rash but an obliged experiment.

†**3.** Pledged. *Obs.*

1596 SHAKS. *Merch. V.* II. vi. 7 O ten times faster Venus Pidgions flye To steale loues bonds new made, then they are wont To keepe obliged faith vnforfaited.

Hence **o'bligedly** (-ɪdlɪ) *adv.*, in an obliged manner; **o'bligedness** (-ɪdnɪs), the condition or fact of being obliged.

1659 D. PELL *Impr. Sea* b v, A little monument of that great respect I oblidgedly, and deservedly bear you. **1662** J. BARGRAVE *Pope Alex. VII* (1867) 10 He was .. the chief author of the election of Innocent X[th], who carrieth himself to this prince most affectionately, obligedly, and in way of gratitude. **1687** BOYLE *Martyrd. Theodora* xi. (1703) 150 Looks, wherein both gratitude and obligedness displayed themselves. **1853** TENNYSON in *Mem. J. Nichol* (1896) 121 Renewing my thanks to all,—I remain, my dear Sir, yours obligedly, A. Tennyson.

obligee (ɒblɪ'dʒiː). Also 6 oblyge, -lige. [f. OBLIGE *v.*: see -EE.]

1. *Law.* One to whom another is bound by contract; the person to whom a bond is given. (Correlative to *obligor*.)

1574 tr. *Littleton's Tenures* 104 b, If y[e] oblyge .. release to the obligor al actions. *a* **1625** SIR H. FINCH *Law* (1636) 61 So vpon condition that the Obligee shall bring to the Obligors shop (being a tailor) three yards of cloth which shall be shapen, and the Obligor to make the Obligee a gowne of it: the Obligor must shape it. **1767** BLACKSTONE *Comm.* II. xx. 341 If the condition .. becomes impossible by .. the act of the obligee himself, there the penalty of the obligation is saved. **1841** S. WARREN *Ten Thousand a Year* XVII, The obligee of the bond .. was Mr. Tittlebat Titmouse.

†**b.** One who undertakes an obligation. *Obs.*

1590 SWINBURNE *Testaments* 261–2 No more to be accounted a testament .. then .. the draught of an obligation is to be accounted for an obligation before it be sealed and deliuered by the oblige as his acte and deede. **1689** *Def. Liberty agst. Tyrants* 144 Can the bankrumpting of one of the Obligees quit the rest of their ingagement?

2. One who is under obligation on account of benefits or kindnesses received.

1610 W. FOLKINGHAM *Art of Survey* Ep. Ded. 1 Presidents of worthy witts and particular Obligees to eminent Patrons. **1682** VILLIERS (Dk. Buckhm.) *Chances* Wks. (1714) 172, I am so highly your Obligee for the manner of your Enquiries. **1827** LYTTON *Pelham* xxiii, If you wish to please, you will find it wiser to receive—solicit even—favours, than to accord them; for the vanity of the obliger is always flattered—that of the obligee rarely.

obligement (ə'blaɪdʒmənt). Also 6–7 *Sc.* oblis-, obleis-. [f. OBLIGE *v.* + -MENT.]

1. The fact of obliging or binding oneself by formal promise or contract; a contract, covenant; = OBLIGATION 2. *Obs.* exc. in *Civil Law*.

1584 *Sc. Acts Jas. VI* (1814) III. 325/2 Conforme to thair oblismentis and contractis respectiue maid w[t] the said Colonell thairvpoun. **1612** W. PARKES *Curtaine-Dr.* (1876) 38 What man dare trust his friend .. yea almost vpon the surest obligement that may be deuiesed or drawne? **1671** *True Nonconf.* 207 If he confirme the samine by an Oath, the force and vertue thereof doth also reach all the off-spring, concerned in the obligement. **1832** in Penney *Linlithgowshire* 192 With obligements by the baillies of Queensferry to him, obliging themselves to remove therefrom when desired. **1880** MUIRHEAD *Gaius* I. §192 As regards alienation or obligement.

2. Obligation (moral or legal); obligation for benefits or kindnesses received; a kindness, favour.

1611 SPEED *Hist. Gt. Brit.* IX. viii. §12. 538 Finding hee had not the sway hee .. thought hee deserued (by obligement of his first Agency about the Crowne). **1664** DRYDEN *Rival Ladies* II. i, This I would endure, And more, to cancel my obligements to him. **1721** CIBBER *Com. Lovers* III, Yet I have some Obligements to him: He teaches me new Airs on the Guitarre. **1828** LAMB in *Blackw. Mag.* XXIV. 773 All my leisure .. Would not express a tythe of the obligements I every hour incur. *Mod.* (*Sc.*) 'It would be a great obligement if you would, etc.'

†**b.** Attachment (by affection or regard). *Obs.*

1647 N. BACON *Disc. Govt. Eng.* I. ii, The deep obligement of the people unto these their Rabbies, in a devotion beyond the reach of other Nations.

†**c.** A bond of union; a tie. *Obs.*

1627 *Taking of Saint Esprit* in *Harl. Misc.* (Malh.) III. 548 Those obligements which bind them to that nation.

†**3.** Compulsion, constraint. *Obs. rare.*

1641 MILTON *Reform.* I. (1851) 2 Urgently pretending a necessity, and obligement of joyning the body in a formall reverence.

†**o'bligence.** *Obs. rare*$^{-1}$. [ad. F. *obligeance*, f. *obliger* to OBLIGE: see -ENCE, -ANCE; cf. med.L. *obligāntia*.] Obligation.

1610 W. FOLKINGHAM *Art of Survey* To Rdr. 2 They now slight their Lords and amoundre their Obligence.

obliger (ə'blaɪdʒə(r)). [f. OBLIGE *v.* + -ER[1].] One who obliges.

1. One who binds another to the performance of a contract, law, or duty; one who imposes obligation. (†In early quots., One to whom another is bound: = OBLIGEE 1.)

1650 HOBBES *De Corp. Pol.* 16 Universally .. all obligations are determinable at the Will of the Obliger. **1651** —— *Govt. & Soc.* ii. §13. 27, I call him the Obliger to whom any one is tyed, and the Obliged him who is tyed. **1651** G. W. tr. *Cowel's Inst.* 175 If the Covenanter thinketh and supposeth one thing and the Obliger another, the Covenant is no more valid then [etc.]. **1738** WARBURTON *Div. Legat.* I. 45 Obligation, in general, necessarily implies an Obliger. *a* **1822** SHELLEY *Pr. Wks.* (1888) II. 197 There can be no obligation without an obliger. **1895** *Edin. Rev.* July 219 Obligation implies at least two terms—the obliged and the obliger.

2. a. One who confers an obligation or favour.

1634 W. TIRWHYT tr. *Balzac's Lett.* (vol. I.) 111 You are so gracious an obliger, that it doth even augment the value of your bounty. **1748** RICHARDSON *Clarissa* (1811) II. ii. 15 Shall it be said, that fear makes us more gentle obligers than love? **1893** K. GRAHAME *Pagan Ess.* 69 Some unfortunate allusion shall pain the delicate feelings of the obliger.

b. One who obliges (sense 6 d); a charwoman. *euphem.*

1959 T. GIRTIN *Unnatural Break* 107, I thought that it was a bit odd the tea-things not being cleared away. I mean that looks as if they hadn't got an obliger. **1960** P. COLERIDGE *Running Footsteps* 63, I was agreeably surprised to be confronted by an elderly obliger, trailing a floor-mop.

oblight, variant of OBLITE *v.*, to forget. *Obs.*

obliging (ə'blaɪdʒɪŋ), *vbl. sb.* [f. OBLIGE *v.* + -ING[1].] The action of the vb. OBLIGE, in its various senses; obligation. (Now only *gerundial.*)

c **1380** WYCLIF *Sel. Wks.* III. 431 It is greet oblishyng to be bonde to perpetual kepyng of siche maner signes. *c* **1470** HENRYSON *Mor. Fab.* x. (*Fox & Wolf*) vii, 'Gaif I my hand or oblissing?' said he, 'Or haif ye writ or witnes for to schaw?' **1563** WINȜET *Four Scoir Thre Quest.* Wks. 1888 I. 60 He labouris to fulfill his oblising. **1676** *Phil. Trans.* XI. Ded., Nations..contending..who shall excel the other in the most beneficial obligings of Mankind.

obliging (əˈblaɪdʒɪŋ), *ppl. a.* [f. as prec. + -ING².] That obliges.

1. That imposes obligation; binding in law or morality; obligatory. Now *rare.*

1638 CHILLINGW. *Relig. Prot.* I. iii. §54. 161 Whether the Decree of a Councell, without the Popes confirmation, be such an obliging proposall. **1678** J. BROWN *Life of Faith* II. ix. (1824) 238 The ceremonial law was not obliging. **1748** G. WHITE *Serm.* (MS.), Yet the Second [Commandment] 'Thou shalt love thy neighbour as thyself' is..as necessary and obliging. [**1875** E. WHITE *Life in Christ* II. x. (1878) 99 The all-obliging commandment of the Supreme.]

2. Of persons, their disposition, etc.: That confers or is willing to confer kindnesses; ready to do services or favours or show polite attention; complaisant, courteous, civil, accommodating.

1632 J. HAYWARD tr. *Biondi's Eromena* 86 You being the obliging, I must consequently needs be the obliged unto you. **1665** SIR T. HERBERT *Trav.* (1677) 305 Of a very gentle and obliging Nature. **1772** MISS WILKES in *Wilkes's Corr.* (1805) IV. 102 My uncle Heaton was so obliging as to call here yesterday. **1834** MEDWIN *Angler in Wales* I. 65 The inn ..was clean and comfortable..and the landlady civil and obliging. *a* **1859** MACAULAY *Hist. Eng.* xxiii. V. 81 Keppel had a sweet and obliging temper.

b. Of actions, words, etc.: Courteous, civil, polite; †gratifying, pleasing (*obs.*).

1635-56 COWLEY *Davideis* III. 931 All that was done, or said; the Grief, Hope, Fears, His troubled Joys, and her obliging Tears. **1652** SIR E. NICHOLAS in *N. Papers* (Camden) 293 His Majesty's gracious letter..was not only most welcome but very obliging. *a* **1713** ELLWOOD *Autobiog.* (1765) 193 The Endowments of her Mind were every way extraordinary and highly obliging. **1781** COWPER *Lett.* Wks. 1837 XV. 67 My principal design is to thank you..for your obliging present. **1854** J. S. C. ABBOTT *Napoleon* (1855) II. vii. 112 He spoke some obliging words to Gen. Cohorn on the feat of gallantry he had displayed.

oˈbligingly, *adv.* [f. prec. + -LY².] In an obliging manner, so as to oblige. **a.** In a binding manner, so as to impose obligation; so as to force or constrain. **b.** So as to confer a favour or gratification; courteously, with kindly manner.

1654-66 EARL ORRERY *Parthen.* (1676) 603 Torments, which my resolution is so obligingly ready to confer on me. **1663** BOYLE *Usef. Exp. Nat. Philos.* I. ii. 23 The Resident's arrival being obligingly suspended till the palace was made ready to entertain him. **1678** CUDWORTH *Intell. Syst.* I. v. 897 Something unjust or unlawful, which therefore cannot be obligingly commanded by any authority whatsoever. **1741** MIDDLETON *Cicero* II. vii. 5 Nothing..could be said more obligingly either in his words or manner. **1848** C. BRONTE *J. Eyre* x, She obligingly consented to act as mediatrix.

oˈbligingness. [f. as prec. + -NESS.] The quality of being obliging. **a.** Binding quality or character, obligatoriness. **b.** Readiness to oblige by doing a service or favour; complaisance, courtesy; kindness.

1638 LD. DIGBY *Lett.* (1651) 5 It is an inconvenience drawn upon you by your excess of favour and obligingness. **1648** LD. FAIRFAX, etc. *Remonstr.* 34 These Declarations.. will remaine..perpetuall witnesses against the validity there-of, or any obligingnesse to them. **1790** MAD. D'ARBLAY *Diary* Aug., She is always happy when permitted to show her native obligingness. **1814** JANE AUSTEN *Mansf. Park* I. vii. 55 She played with the greatest obligingness. **1891** G. J. HOLYOAKE in *Voice* (N.Y.) 12 Nov., This obligingness and accessibility is more rare in monarchical England than it is in republican America.

obligor (ˈɒblɪgɔː(r)). *Law.* Also 6-7 -our, 8 -eor (-ˌdʒɔː(r)). [f. OBLIGE *v.* + -OR.] One who binds himself to another by contract; the person who gives a bond or obligation. (Correlative with *obligee.*)

1541 *Act 33 Hen. VIII,* c. 39 §80 If any manours..be..in the season and possession of.. persones, other then the obligour or obligours. **1574, 1625** [see OBLIGEE 1]. **1628** COKE *On Litt.* 212 If the Obligor or Lessor pay a lesser summe..and the Obligee or Feoffee receiueth it, this is a good satisfaction. **1755** MAGENS *Insurances* II. 56 We, Don J. B. Garravin..as principal Debtor, and Obligeor; and Don J. B. Molinari, as Security..acknowledge that we owe..to Dona M. del Duque, three Thousand Dollars. **1818** CRUISE *Digest* (ed. 2) IV. 465 It was more convenient that the counsellor should give his advice to the obligee, than to the obligor. **1879** TOURGEE *Fool's Err.* xx. (1880) 113 The obligor, in his indefinite promise to pay, had vanished.

†**b.** = OBLIGER 1. *Obs. rare.*

1660 R. COKE *Justice Vind.* 7 Now here let any man see.. whether our Author does not make obedience to consist, on the obligors part, in conformity to a delegate and subordinate power of their own making.

obligulate (ɒˈblɪgjʊlət), *a. Bot.* [See OB- 2.] Applied to a ligulate floret of a composite flower, having the ligula on the inner instead of the outer side.

1857 in MAYNE *Expos. Lex.* **1892** *Syd. Soc. Lex.*, *Obligulate,* Cassini's term for a floret of a composite plant when there is a small ligula on the inner side, as in *Zœgea.*

†**oˈbligurate,** *v. Obs. rare*⁻⁰. [irreg.: see next.]

1623 COCKERAM, *Obligurate,* to spend in belly-cheere.

†**obligure,** *v. Obs. rare*⁻⁰. [ad. L. *obligūrī-re,* f. *ob* (OB- 1) + *ligūrīre* to be dainty, lick, lick up.]

1623 COCKERAM II, To Banquet, *Obligure.*

oblike, obs. form of OBLIQUE *a.*

†**obliˈmation.** *Obs. rare.* [n. of action from next.] Covering or stopping up with mud or slime; silting up.

1656 BLOUNT *Glossogr.*, *Oblimation,* a dawbing or covering over with mud or soft clay. **1691** T. H[ALE] *Acc. New Invent.* p. lxiv, Harbours..destroy'd by Oblimation or Sullage.

†**oˈblime,** *v. Obs. rare*⁻⁰. [ad. L. *oblīmāre* to cover with mud or slime, f. *ob-* (OB- 1 b) + *līmāre,* f. *līmus* mud, slime.]

1623 COCKERAM, *Oblime,* to couer with clay.

†**obliquangled,** obs. form of *oblique-angled.*

1688 J. S. *Fortification* 5 Obliquangled [Parallelograms] are such as have oblique angles.

obliquangular (ɒblɪˈkwæŋgjʊlə(r)), *a.* [f. mod.L. *oblīquangul-us* (f. *oblīqu-us* OBLIQUE + *angulus* ANGLE) + -AR¹.] Oblique-angled.

1686 PLOT *Staffordsh.* 176 Hexaedra of equal obliquangular sides. **1812** SIR H. DAVY *Chem. Philos.* 196 The rays of light in passing through obliquangular crystalline bodies, follow different laws. **1857** MAYNE *Expos. Lex.* s.v. *Obliquangulus,* A quadrangular, obliquangular prism.

†**obliˈquangulous,** *a. Obs. rare*⁻¹. [f. as prec. + -OUS.] = prec.

1680 T. LAWSON *Mite into Treas.* 33 The Feats and Terms of this Art, their Points,..their Lines, Parralels,..Triangle, Rectangulous, Obliquangulous [etc.].

†**obliquate,** *ppl. a. Obs. rare*⁻¹. [ad. L. *oblīquāt-us,* pa. pple. of *oblīquāre*: see OBLIQUE *v.*] Bent to one side; twisted obliquely.

1578 BANISTER *Hist. Man* v. 69 So that the stomach might be lesse obliquate or crooked.

†**obliquate,** *v. Obs. rare.* [f. L. *oblīquāt-,* ppl. stem of *oblīquāre*: see OBLIQUE *v.* and -ATE³.] *trans.* To bend aside, twist obliquely.

a **1670** HACKET *Abp. Williams* II. (1692) 145 Shall these crooked rules obliquate those loyal maxims which are so strait in St. Paul? *a* **1703** WALLIS *Serm.* (1791) 128 They represent God's simplicity obliquated and refracted by reason of many inadequate conceptions.

†**obliˈquation.** *Obs.* [ad. L. *oblīquātiōn-em,* n. of action f. *oblīquāre*: see prec.] A bending aside or in an oblique direction; a twisting awry.

a **1648** LD. HERBERT *Hen. VIII* (1683) 394 That some such obliquation of Religion hath hap'ned. **1658** SIR T. BROWNE *Gard. Cyrus* iii. 56 The right and transverse fibres are decussated by the oblick fibres, and so must frame a Reticulate and Quincuncial Figure by their Obliquations. **1677** GALE *Crt. Gentiles* IV. 109 Obliquations or crooked ways. **1822** T. TAYLOR *Apuleius* XI. 271, I..passed through the crowd..with a gradual obliquation of my body.

oblique (əˈbliːk, -ˈlaɪk), *a.* (*sb.*) Also 5 oblyke, 5-7 -like, 7 -lick. [ad. L. *oblīqu-us,* f. *ob-* pref. + an element *līqu-, līc-* (cf. *licinus* bent upward): cf. F. *oblique* (13-14th c. in Godef.).]

A. *adj.* **1. a.** Having a slanting or sloping direction or position; declining from the upright or vertical, or from the horizontal; lying aslant; diverging from a given straight line or course.

oblique pianoforte: see quot. 1880.

1432-50 tr. *Higden* (Rolls) II. 207 The stappes þer [in sowthe parte of Ethioppe] be oblike and contrarious [*ubi obliqua et pæne contraria fiunt vestigia*] to theyme whiche dwelle..vnder that pole artike. **1603** B. JONSON *Jas. I.'s Entertainm.*, She [Anna] fills the year, And knits the oblique scarf that girts the sphere. **1626** BACON *Sylva* §139 Hunter's Horns..are sometimes made straight, and not Oblique. **1697** DRYDEN *Virg. Georg.* IV. 420 Four Windows are contriv'd, that strike To the four Winds oppos'd their Beams oblique. **1713** STEELE *Guard.* No. 20 ¶2 The oblique glance with which hatred doth always see things. **1781** GIBBON *Decl. & F.* xviii. II. 120 Advancing their whole wing of cavalry in an oblique line. **1842** TENNYSON *Two Voices* 193 If straight thy track, or if oblique [*rimes* strike, like], Thou know'st not. **1860** TYNDALL *Glac.* I. ii. 17 My shadow was oblique to the river. **1875** KNIGHT *Dict. Mech.*, *Oblique Arch*..also called a *skew-arch.* **1880** A. J. HIPKINS in Grove *Dict. Mus.* II. 486/1 *Oblique Piano,* a cottage pianoforte the strings of which are disposed diagonally, instead of vertically as is usual in upright instruments.

b. quasi-*adv.* = OBLIQUELY 1.

1667 MILTON *P.L.* x. 671 They with labour push'd Oblique the Centric Globe. **1796** *Instr. & Reg. Cavalry* (1813) 88 If the column halts oblique..to the new line, the divisions will proportionally wheel so as [etc.].

2. Specific uses.

a. *Geom.* Of a line, a plane figure, or surface: Inclined at some angle other than a right angle. Of an angle (less than two right angles): Either greater or less than a right angle. Of a solid, as a cone, cylinder, or prism: Having its axis not perpendicular to the plane of its base.

oblique hyperbola, a hyperbola the asymptotes of which are not at right angles to one another.

1571 DIGGES *Pantom.* III. i. Qj, Of Solides called Prismata, there are two kindes, the one directe or vpright.. the other oblique or declining, whose Paralelogrammes are obliquely situate on their bases. **1695** ALINGHAM *Geom. Epit.* 7 An Oblique Angle, is either Acute or Obtuse. **1709** J. WARD *Introd. Math.* IV. i. (1734) 362 A Scalene, or Oblique Cone. **1727-41** CHAMBERS *Cycl.*, *Oblique Planes,* in dialing, are such as recline from the zenith, or incline toward the horizon. **1826** DISRAELI *Viv. Grey* VI. i, His Highness held the bottle at an oblique angle with the chandelier. **1837** BREWSTER *Magnet.* 177 A position more or less oblique to the plane of the paper.

b. *Astron.* ***oblique sphere,*** the celestial or terrestrial sphere when its axis is oblique to the horizon of the place; which it is at any part of the earth's surface except the poles and the equator. ***oblique ascension, descension***: see ASCENSION 3, DESCENSION 5. ***oblique horizon,*** †***climate,*** one which is oblique to the celestial equator.

1503 *Kalender of Shepherdes* I ij, They the qwych dwellys other placys bot wnder the eqwynoxyal they haue thayr oryzon oblyk. **1594** BLUNDEVIL *Exerc.* II. (1636) 116 If the declination be Southward, then adde the ascentionall difference unto the right ascention, and the sum shall be the oblique ascention. *Ibid.* III. I. xvii. 313 When is it said to be an oblique Horizon, and therby to make an oblique Spheare? **1669** WORLIDGE *Syst. Agric.* (1681) 293 In such Countries where the seasons and variations of weather more exactly followed the Cœlestial Configurations, than in these more oblique Climates. **1726** tr. *Gregory's Astron.* I. 223 In an Oblique Sphere, where the Horizon..cuts the Equator.. at oblique Angles; neither of them passes through the Poles of the other. **1854** TOMLINSON tr. *Arago's Astron.* 37 The circles described by the stars are inclined to the horizon; whence this position of the sphere derives its name of oblique.

c. *Anat.* Having a direction parallel neither to the long axis of the body or limb, nor to its transverse section; said esp. of certain muscles; also of various lines, ridges, ligaments, etc.

oblique processes of the vertebræ: = ZYGAPOPHYSES.

1615 CROOKE *Body of Man* 801 If each Muscle worke by it selfe, then the oblique descendent drawes the haunch obliquely to his owne side..the oblique ascendent leadeth the chest obliquely to the haunches. **1658** SIR T. BROWNE *Gard. Cyrus* iii. 55 Wherein according to common Anatomy the right and transverse fibres are decussated, by the oblick fibres. **1741** MONRO *Anat. Bones* (ed. 3) 168 The two inferior oblique Processes of each Vertebra. **1838** *Penny Cycl.* X. 141/1 When the oblique muscles act together with force, they hold the eye-ball firmly against the lids and to the nasal side of the orbit.

d. *Bot.* Of a leaf: Having unequal sides, inequilateral; see also quot. 1776.

1776 J. LEE *Introd. Bot.* (1788) 206 *Oblique,* when the Base of the Leaf looks towards Heaven, and the Apex or Tip towards the Horizon; as in *Protea* and *Fritillaria.* **1835** HOOKER *Brit. Flora* 145 *Ulmus major*..leaves ovato-acuminate, very oblique at the base. **1857** HENFREY *Elem. Bot.* 53 *Oblique,* is applied to leaves where the portions on either side of the midrib are unequal, as in the Begonias.

e. *Cryst.* = MONOCLINIC.

1878 GURNEY *Crystallogr.* 37 Crystals of..the Oblique or Monoclinic System.

f. *Naut.* ***oblique sailing.*** (See quots.)

1706 PHILLIPS, *Oblique Sailing* (among Sea-men), is when a Ship runs upon some Rhumb, between any of the four Cardinal Points, and makes an Oblique Angle with the Meridian. **1867** SMYTH *Sailor's Word-bk.*, *Oblique Sailing,* is the reduction of the position of the ship from the various courses made good, oblique to the meridian or parallel of latitude.

g. ***oblique perspective***: see PERSPECTIVE.

3. *fig.* **a.** Not taking the straight or direct course to the end in view; not going straight to the point; indirectly stated or expressed; indirect.

1432-50 tr. *Higden* (Rolls) IV. 407 The office of a poete is to transmute those thynges whiche be doen truly in to other similitudes in oblike figuraciones with pulcritude. **1606** SHAKS. *Tr. & Cr.* v. i. 60 The primatiue Statue, and oblique memoriall of Cuckolds. **1618** in Gutch *Coll. Cur.* II. 423 His pleading Innocency was an oblique taxing of the Justice of the Realms upon him. **1735** BOLINGBROKE *On Parties* Ded. (1738) 27 Innuendo's, and Parallels, and oblique Meanings. **1778** JOHNSON in *Boswell* 25 Apr., All censure of a man's self is oblique praise. **1818** JAS. MILL *Brit. India* II. IV. vii. 255 Good reasons existed for precluding the Governor from such oblique channels of gain. **1876** MOZLEY *Univ. Serm.* vi. 134 The language of oblique and indirect expression. **1883** FROUDE *Short Stud.* IV. I. iv. 45 Oblique accusations..were raised against him.

b. Of an end, result, etc.: Indirectly aimed at; resulting or arising indirectly.

1528 FOX *Let. to Gardiner* in Strype *Eccl. Mem.* (1721) I. App. xxvi. 80 Wherby may arise..oblique dammage or prejudice to the see apostolique. **1630** DRAYTON *Muses' Elys.* iii. Poems (1810) 453/2 For that the love we bear our friends..Hath in it certain oblique ends. **1711** ADDISON *Spect.* No. 59 ¶4 Not..for any oblique Reason..but purely for the sake of being Witty. **1825-80** JAMIESON s.v. *Hirst,* This is only an oblique sense.

4. Deviating from right conduct or thought; morally or mentally one-sided or perverse.

1576 FLEMING *Panopl. Epist.* 82 Albeit he follow an oblique and crooked opinion. **1677** GALE *Crt. Gentiles* IV. 182 Oblique regard to private interests doth subvert and over-throw them [Republics]. *a* **1770** JORTIN *Serm.* (1771) I. vii. 128 There are persons to be found..who grow rich and great..by various oblique and scandalous ways. **1837-9** HALLAM *Hist. Lit.* III. ii. §80 (1855) II. 464 It is..seldom discussed with all the temper and freedom from oblique views which the subject demands.

5. *Gram.* **a.** ***oblique case***, any case except the nominative and vocative (or sometimes, except the nominative, vocative, and accusative): see CASE *sb.*[1] 9. **b.** Of speech or narration: Put in a reported form, with consequent change of person and tense: = INDIRECT 3 b (L. *oratio obliqua*).

1530 PALSGR. Introd. 30 Pronownes.. have but thre cases, nominatyve, accusatyve and oblique, as, *je, me, moy*. *a* **1568** ASCHAM *Scholem.* II. (Arb.) 158 Salust [hath] *Multis sibi quisque imperium petentibus.* I beleue, the best Grammarien in England can scarse giue a good reule, why *quisque* the nominatiue case.. is so thrust vp amongest so many oblique cases. **1678** PHILLIPS (ed. 4), *Oblique Cases* in Grammar, are most properly the Genitive, the Dative, and Ablative; however, some will have all Oblique but the Nominative. **1860** J. C. JEAFFRESON *Bk. Doctors* II. 17 We have adopted the oblique narration instead of his form, which uses the first person. **1868** GLADSTONE *Juv. Mundi* v. (1870) 169 He is mentioned six times in oblique cases.. and five times in the nominative. **1882** FARRAR *Early Chr.* II. 385 There is scarcely a single oblique sentence throughout St. John's Gospel.

6. *Mus.* ***oblique motion***: see quots. (Opp. to *similar* and *contrary*.)

1811 BUSBY *Dict. Mus.* (ed. 3), *Oblique Motion*, that motion of the parts of a composition in which one voice or instrument repeats the same note, while another, by ascending or descending, recedes from or approaches it. **1875** OUSELEY *Harmony* i. 11 Oblique motion is when one part remains without moving while another ascends or descends.

7. *Comb.*, as ***oblique-angled, -angular, -leaved*** adjs.

1594 BLUNDEVIL *Exerc.* II. (1636) 119 If they have right sides, such Triangles are eyther right angled Triangles, or oblique angled Triangles. **1744** PARSONS in *Phil. Trans.* XLIII. 26 An oblique-angular Parallelogram. **1851** RICHARDSON *Geol.* v. 88 An oblique-angled parallelogram. **1854** HOOKER *Himal. Jrnls.* I. ii. 28 An oblique-leaved fig climbs the other trees.

B. absol. as *sb.* (usually elliptical).

1. An oblique muscle: see A. 2 c. Also in L. form ***obliquus*** (sc. ***musculus***), pl. ***-i***, as ***obliquus (abdominis) ascendens***; ***obliquus capitis inferior***; ***obliquus oculi inferior***, etc.

1800 *Phil. Trans.* XC. 9 The obliquus,.. the antagonist of the tensor muscle. **1838** *Penny Cycl.* X. 141/1 If the pupil be inclined either way, to the nose or to the temple, the inferior oblique increases that inclination. **1869** H. USSHER in *Eng. Mech.* 10 Dec. 294/3 A rolling or oblique motion [of the eye] is provided for by two.. muscles called obliques.

2. *Geom.* An oblique figure: see 2 a above.

a **1608** SIR F. VERE *Comm.* 124 A piece of ground.. stretched out in the form of a geometrical oblique or oblong.

3. = *oblique case* (see OBLIQUE *a.* 5).

1695 WHEELER *Royal Gram. Reformed* vii. 26 *Qui* standing alone as a personal Relative is Englished *who* in the Nominatives, and *whom* in the Obliques. **1939** *Language* XV. 81 The obliques regularly have -äs. **1961** R. B. LONG *Sentence & its Parts* 494 Obliques such as the *insist* of *she insists on paying*.

4. *Photogr.* A photograph taken at an oblique angle.

1942 *R.A.F. Jrnl.* 27 June 10 The second photograph is an earlier oblique of a similar type of *Sperrbrecher*. **1955** E. WAUGH *Officers & Gentlemen* II. i. 158 Guy, have you still got those obliques of 'Badger'?.. Bung 'em back to GHQ. **1958** C. B. SMITH *Evidence in Camera* i. 19 The other two [cameras]—one on either side—were at an angle to take obliques. **1970** M. KELLY *Spinifex* ii. 48 Oosterman bracing the Newman cine-camera, F.245 aimed for obliques.

5. An oblique line, *spec.* a sloping virgule.

1961 in WEBSTER. **1965** W. S. ALLEN *Vox Latina* 9 Phonemic symbols.. are conventionally set between obliques, e.g. /t/. **1973** A. H. SOMMERSTEIN *Sound Pattern Anc. Greek* i. 7, I follow the practice of Chomsky and Halle, who say.. that they use obliques 'for representations in which the features are functioning as classificatory devices'.

oblique (ə'bli:k, -'laɪk), *v.* [a. F. *obliquer* to march in an oblique direction, rarely, to make oblique, f. *oblique* adj.; cf. L. *oblīqu-āre*, trans., to make crooked, turn or bend aside, in med.L. intr., to go aside or astray, It. *obliquare* 'to crooke, to make crooked' (Florio).]

†1. *trans.* To turn askew or in a sidelong direction. *Obs.*

1775 SHERIDAN *Rivals* IV. iii, When her love-eye was fixed on me, t'other, her eye of duty, was finely obliqued.

2. *intr.* To advance obliquely or in a slanting direction, esp. (*Mil.*) by making a half-face to the right or left and then marching forward.

1796 *Instr. & Reg. Cavalry* (1813) 104 The leader of the head division orders his second sub-division, Left incline, March! on which it briskly obliques to the left. **1827** AIKMAN tr. *Buchanan's Hist. Scot.* II. xv. l. 368 They gradually obliqued from the direct ascent. **1857** MAYNE REID *War-Trail* xlii, Savage and Saxon were now obliquing towards each other. **1865** *Star* 3 Feb., General Curtis went into the assault under instructions from General Ames.. to oblique to the right.

b. Of a line, etc.: To slant or slope at an angle.

1814 SCOTT *Wav.* xi, He.. achieved a communication with his plate by projecting his person towards it in a line which obliqued from the bottom of his spine.

obliquely (ə'bli:klɪ), *adv.* [f. OBLIQUE *a.* + -LY[2].] In an oblique manner.

1. In a slanting or sidelong direction or position; with deviation from the straight line or direct course; diagonally, or so as to make an oblique angle; aslant, slantwise.

1571 [see OBLIQUE *a.* 2 a]. **1594** BLUNDEVIL *Exerc.* III. I. xxxi. (1636) 340 According as any portion of the Ecliptique riseth or setteth rightly or obliquely. **1615** [see OBLIQUE *a.* 2 c]. **1634** PEACHAM *Gentl. Exerc.* I. x. 33 The beames of the Sunne comming oblikely or sideway. **1660** R. COKE *Justice Vind.* 10 The nearer the radii are reflected to right angles, the hotter it is: and the more obliquely they are reflected, the colder it is. **1725** POPE *Odyss.* IX. 441 His neck obliquely o'er his shoulders hung. **1860** TYNDALL *Glac.* I. xvii. 120 Ramsay and myself crossed the mountains obliquely.

2. *fig.* In a way that is not direct or straightforward; by suggestion or implication; indirectly; with deviation from the point; †evasively; not straightforwardly, dishonestly, unfairly (*obs.*).

1601 BP. W. BARLOW *Defence* 181 The scripture.. worketh in vs faith, not obliquely, hoouerly, and ambiguously. **1646** TRAPP *Comm. John* ix. 20 They answer obliquely and over-warily. **1771** BURKE *Let. to Bp. Chester* Corr. 1844 I. 291, I shall think myself happy, if the subject of my defence.. may be obliquely and accidentally the means of undeceiving you. **1816** 'QUIZ' *Grand Master* v. *Argt.*, In fact, the reader, very likely, Will find some truths, tho' told obliquely. **1881** H. JAMES *Portr. Lady* xxi, They approached each other obliquely, as it were, and they addressed each other by implication.

b. In or by oblique oration. (See OBLIQUE *a.* 5 b.)

1824 L. MURRAY *Eng. Gram.* (ed. 5) I. 415 When a quotation is brought in obliquely after a comma, a capital is unnecessary.

o'bliqueness. [f. OBLIQUE *a.* + -NESS.] The quality of being oblique or slanting, obliquity.

1611 COTGR., *Biaiseure*, slopenesse, byasnesse, obliquenesse, or obliquitie. **1727** in BAILEY vol. II. **1755** in JOHNSON. **1869** *Daily News* 1 July, Windows of aggravating obliqueness, which prevent your seeing any object in them properly. **1877** MORLEY *Crit. Misc.* Ser. II. 288 Controversies.. marked by obliqueness, evasiveness, a shiftiness of issue.

†obliquiangular, obs. var. OBLIQUANGULAR.

1635 GELLIBRAND *Variation Magn. Needle* 12 The obliquiangular sphæricall Triangle.

†o'bliquid, *ppl. a. Obs.* [app. for *obliqued*, from OBLIQUE *v.*: cf. OBLIQUATE *a.*] Directed obliquely.

a **1599** SPENSER *F.Q.* VII. vii. 54 That vertue.. Is checkt and changed from his nature trew, By others opposition or obliquid view.

†obliquie, ? *a.* Prob. a misprint for *oblique*.

1607 SHAKS. *Timon* IV. iii. 18 All's obliquie [*later edd.* All is oblique]: There's nothing leuell in our cursed Natures But direct villanie.

obliquitous (ə'blɪkwɪtəs), *a.* [f. OBLIQUIT-Y + -OUS: cf. *felicitous, iniquitous*.] Characterized by obliquity; morally or mentally perverse.

1864 S. P. DAY in *Athenæum* No. 1937. 779/2 Morally obliquitous to the distinction of *meum* and *tuum*. **1884** RUSKIN *Art of Eng.* iv. 136 They will not.. be disposed.. to ascribe to the obliquitous nation that of simplicity of mind.

obliquity (ə'blɪkwɪtɪ). [a. F. *obliquité* (Oresme 14th c.), ad. L. *oblīquitāt-em*, n. of quality f. *oblīqu-us*: see OBLIQUE and -ITY.]

1. The quality of being oblique; inclination at other than a right angle to any straight line or plane; degree or extent of such inclination.

obliquity of the ecliptic, the inclination of the plane of the ecliptic to that of the equator.

1551 RECORDE *Cast. Knowl.* (1556) 248 A thyrde diuersitye is.. the obliquitie of the Horizonte. **1625** N. CARPENTER *Geog. Del.* I. v. (1635) 114 By reason of the obliquity of the Eclipticke line. **1667** MILTON *P.L.* VIII. 132 Several Sphears.. Mov'd contrarie with thwart obliquities. **1739** LABELYE *Short Acc. Piers Westm. Bridge* 3 The Stream of the Tide.. will pass thro' the Arches without any sensible Obliquity. **1794** G. ADAMS *Nat. & Exp. Philos.* II. xv. 161 The rays undergo no alteration, because they have no obliquity of incidence. **1871** DARWIN *Desc. Man* II. xix. 344 The obliquity of the eye, which is proper to the Chinese and Japanese, is exaggerated in their pictures.

b. *Bot.* Of a leaf: Inequilateral quality.

1872 OLIVER *Elem. Bot.* II. 152 Observe the obliquity of the base of the leaf-blade, characteristic of the Lime.

2. *fig.* Divergence from moral rectitude, sound thinking, or right practice; moral or mental perversity or aberration; an instance of this, a delinquency, a fault, an error.

c **1422** HOCCLEVE *Jonathas* Moral, By the ryng þat is rownd We shul vndirstande feith which is rownd, withouten obliquitee or crookidnesse. **1551** CRANMER *Answ. Gardiner* I. Wks. (Parker Soc.) I. 19 Your book is so full of crafts, sleights, shifts, obliquities, and manifest untruths. **1627** DONNE *Serm.* xxviii. 283 The perversnesse and obliquity of my will. **1759** STERNE *Tr. Shandy* I. iii, A most unaccountable obliquity, (as he call'd it) in my manner of setting up my top, and justifying the principles upon which I had done it. **1844** GLADSTONE *Glean.* V. xxxvi. 109 Mr. Ward evinces the same thorough one-sidedness and obliquity of judgment.

†3. Deviation from any rule or order. *rare.*

1646 H. LAWRENCE *Comm. Angels* 87 Let us, therefore,.. learne the rule from the obliquity, as well as the obliquity from the rule. **1751** JOHNSON *Rambler* No. 127 ¶3 Far the greater part.. deviate at first into slight obliquities.

†4. Deviation from directness in action, conduct, or speech; a way or method that is not direct or straightforward. *Obs.*

a **1619** FOTHERBY *Atheom.* I. xii. §6 (1622) 135 We may behold, euen in the Atheists, by a kinde of obliquity, diuers manifest foote-stepps, and acknowledgments of a Diuinity. **1751** JOHNSON *Rambler* No. 149 ¶9 The insolence of benefaction terminates not in negative rudeness or obliquities of insult. I am often told in express terms of the miseries from which charity has snatched me. **1818** JAS. MILL *Brit. India* II. IV. iv. 134 The obliquities of Eastern negotiation wore out the temper of Lally.

†5. *Gram.* Case-inflexion, declension. *Obs.*

1668 WILKINS *Real Char.* IV. vi. 446 'Tis capable of that kind of Obliquity by prefixing Prepositions, which is commonly stiled variation by Cases.

o'bliquo-, comb. form of L. *obliqu-us* OBLIQUE *a.* = obliquely-, oblique and ——. (See -O *suffix*[1].)

1852 DANA *Crust.* II. 866 Palm obliquo-transverse,.. and having a tooth near base of finger.

†o'bliquous, *a. Obs. rare.* [f. L. *oblīqu-us* OBLIQUE + -OUS.] = OBLIQUE.

1614 SIR A. GORGES tr. *Lucan* I. 33 Through the aire did flying passe Obliquous streames, like torches bright. **1757** *Herald* No. 7 (1758) I. 106 A contempt, which speedily matures into obliquous hatred.

oblis(e, -lis(c)h, -liss, obs. forms of OBLIGE.

oblisk, obs. variant of OBELISK.

†oblite, *ppl. a. Obs. rare*[−1]. [ad. L. *oblit-us*, pa. pple. of *oblinĕre*: see OBLITE *v.*[2]] Dim, as if partly blotted out; indistinct, obscure.

1650 FULLER *Pisgah* II. v. 132 But obscure and oblite mention is made of those water-works.

†o'blite, *v.*[1] *Obs.* Also **oblight.** [f. L. *oblīt-*, ppl. stem of *oblīv-isc-ī* to forget.] To forget.

1547 *Richmond Wills* (Surtees) 64 Item, I give to the hye alter for oblited thiethes a newe altare clothe. *c* **1560** PRESTON *Cambyses* in Hazl. *Dodsley* IV. 238 Then nought oblight my message given.

†oblite, *v.*[2] *Obs. rare*[−1]. [f. L. *oblit-*, ppl. stem of *oblinĕre* to smear over, f. *ob-* (OB- 1 c) + *linĕre* to smear.] *trans.* To smear over, daub.

1657 TOMLINSON *Renou's Disp.* 282 A little bottle oblited with wax.

obliterate (ə'blɪtərət), *ppl. a.* [ad. L. *oblit(t)erāt-us*, pa. pple. of *oblit(t)erāre*: see next.]

1. Blotted out; effaced; cancelled; obliterated. Now only *poet.* **a.** Construed as *pa. pple.*

1598 in Row *Hist. Kirk* (1842) 190 It is concluded that all those greevances be obliterat and buried. **1613** JACKSON *Creed* II. xvii. §1 The Prints of Moses footsteps, almost obliterate and ouergrown by the sloth and negligence of former times. **1647** H. MORE *Song of Soul* II. ii. III. xi, A name.. through time almost obliterate. **1834** LD. HOUGHTON *Mem. Many Scenes, Mod. Greece* (1844) 67 History records a time (Though in the splendour of the after-light Nearly obliterate).

b. Construed as *adj.*

a **1631** DONNE in *Select.* (1840) 16 Impouerished and forgotten, and obliterate families. **1647** WARD *Simp. Cobler* 34 It may maintain.. a legible possession against an obliterate Claime. **1737** BRACKEN *Farriery Impr.* (1757) II. 106 Parts of their Bodies become obliterate and defaced. **1860** HEAVYSEGE *Ct. Filippo* 35 Dwindled doubtful to obliterate shade.

2. *Ent.* (See quot.)

1826 KIRBY & SP. *Entomol.* IV. 292 *Obliterate*, when the borders of spots fade into the general ground-colour; and when elevations and depressions, &c. are so little raised or sunk from the general surface, as to be almost erased.

obliterate (ə'blɪtəreɪt), *v.* [f. L. *oblit(t)erāt-*, ppl. stem of *oblit(t)erāre* to strike or blot out, erase, blot out of remembrance (rare in lit. sense), f. *ob-* (OB- 1 b) + *lit(t)era* anything written, a letter. Cf. F. *oblitérer* (15–16th c.).]

1. *trans.* To blot out (anything written, figured, or imprinted) so as to leave no distinct traces; to erase, delete, efface.

1611 SPEED *Hist. Gt. Brit.* VI. xxvi. §6. 120 The Senate.. decreed that his name should bee obliterated out of all monuments in Rome. **1701** GREW *Cosm. Sacra* II. iii. 43 When we forget Things.. the Impressions are obliterated. **1843** LYTTON *Last Bar.* I. iv, The colours were half obliterated by time and damp. **1863** BURTON *Bk. Hunter* 44 As he did not obliterate the original matter, the printer was rather puzzled.

b. To cause to disappear, to efface (anything visible or perceived by the senses).

1607 TOPSELL *Four-f. Beasts* (1658) 120 The fragrancy of every green herb yeeldeth such a savour as doth not a little obliterate and oversway the savour of the beast. **1833–6** J. EAGLES *Sketcher* (1856) 355 The snow, obliterating the very ground on which you stood sketching. **1848** W. H. BARTLETT *Egypt to Pal.* v. (1879) 99 Everything upon the lower levels of the Nile must gradually or rapidly be obliterated by its inundations. **1878** HUXLEY *Physiogr.* 195 New cones being thrown up at one time and old ones being obliterated at another.

2. To efface, wipe out (a mental impression, memory, or feeling); to do away the

remembrance or sense of; to do away with, destroy (qualities, characteristics, etc.).

1600 W. WATSON *Decacordon* (1602) 224 To obliterate, eradicate, and vtterly extinguish the name of Bishops. **1605** BACON *Adv. Learn.* I. vi. §14 He designed to obliterate and extinguish the memory of heathen antiquity and authors. **1734** tr. *Rollin's Anc. Hist.* (1827) VI. xv. xiv. 229 It entirely obliterates the glory of all his other actions. **1881** WESTCOTT & HORT *Grk. N.T.* Introd. §8 The professional training of scribes can rarely obliterate individual differences.

3. *Phys.* and *Path.* To efface, close up, or otherwise destroy for its special purpose (esp. a duct or passage, the cavity of which disappears by contraction and adhesion of the walls). Also *intr.* for *refl.*

1813 J. THOMSON *Lect. Inflam.* 417 Consequently a less extent of surface in the new parts is wanted to obliterate, or fill up this cavity, than what formerly filled it. **1828** D. LE MARCHANT *Rep. Claims Barony of Gardner* 164 The neck of the womb gradually obliterates. **1835–6** TODD *Cycl. Anat.* I. 641/2 The umbilical vessels [are] obliterated at the navel after.. pulmonic respiration is established. **1841–71** T. R. JONES *Anim. Kingd.* (ed. 4) 528 Ultimately the communication between the parent [ascidian] and the young individual becomes obliterated.

Hence **o'bliterated** *ppl. a.*; **o'bliterating** *vbl. sb.* and *ppl. a.*

1611 COTGR., *Obliteré*, obliterated. **1677** GILPIN *Demonol.* (1867) 144 His power seems to extend to the obliterating of principles. **1694** SALMON *Bate's Dispens.* (1713) 453/2 Stirring up the latent or almost obliterated ferment of Life. **1863** BURTON *Bk. Hunter* 3 An obliterated manuscript written over again is called a palimpsest. **1882** STEVENSON *New Arab. Nts.* (1884) 123 [They] showed their common-place and obliterated countenances. **1892** LD. LYTTON *King Poppy* iv. 254 Down fell an obliterating blot. *Mod.* An obliterating stamp for cancelling postage stamps.

o'bliteratingly, *adv.* [f. OBLITERATING *ppl. a.* + -LY².] In an obliterating manner; so as to obliterate.

1904 H. G. WELLS *Food of Gods* I. iii. 56 He scarcely remembers the leap he must have made.. so obliteratingly hot and swift did his impressions rush upon him.

obliteration (əblɪtə'reɪʃən). [ad. late L. *oblit(t)erātiōn-em*, n. of action f. *oblit(t)erāre* to OBLITERATE: cf. F. *oblitération* (1787 in Hatz.-Darm.).]

1. The action of obliterating or fact of being obliterated; erasure; effacement; extinction.

1658 PHILLIPS, *Obliteration*, a blotting out, a cancelling or abolishing. **1670** in Somers *Tracts* I. 30 This.. is of so odious a Condition, as pity it is, there cannot be a total Obliteration of it. **1793** BEDDOES *Demonstr. Evid.* 96 Cause, from being the name of a particular object, has become, in consequence of the obliteration of that original signification, a remarkable abbreviation in language. **1830** LYELL *Princ. Geol.* I. 223 The examination of almost all valleys in mountainous districts affords abundant proofs of the obliteration of a series of lakes. **1858** LD. ST. LEONARDS *Handy Bk. Prop. Law* xviii. 143 If the obliteration is effectual, of course the disposition in the will as it originally stood cannot be made out.

(*b*) *attrib.*, as ***obliteration bombing***: heavy bombing intended to destroy a target completely.

1943 *Spectator* 24 Sept. 289/2 (*heading*) 'Obliteration' bombing. *Ibid.* 8 Oct. 337/2 The question of 'obliteration bombing'.. raises more difficulties than Mr. Johnstone envisages. **1944** *Sat. Rev. Lit.* (U.S.) 8 Apr. 14/1 Vera Brittain, has become the spearhead of a movement.. directed against the mass air attacks of enemy cities, which she describes as 'obliteration bombings'. **1945** L. MUMFORD *City Devel.* (1946) 173 This failure would still be serious.. even if obliteration bombing had not been practised.

2. *Phys.* and *Path.* The disappearance or extinction, in regard to its original purpose, of a structure, vessel, cavity, etc., e.g. of a duct through adhesion of the walls.

1857 MAYNE *Expos. Lex.* 784/2 Obliteration. **1875** H. C. WOOD *Therap.* (1879) 402 Iodine has been very largely employed by injection into serous cysts.. for the purpose of exciting inflammation and causing obliteration of their cavity. **1876** *Trans. Clinical Soc.* IX. 117 The curative effect in aortic aneurism of obliteration of the carotid artery. **1884** BOWER & SCOTT *De Bary's Phaner.* 542 The obliteration of the sieve-tubes begins in the oldest external zones of the cortex, and advances.. in the centripetal direction.

obliterative (ə'blɪtərətɪv), *a.* [f. as OBLITERATE *v.* + -IVE.] **1. a.** Having the quality of obliterating; tending to obliterate.

1802–12 BENTHAM *Ration. Judic. Evid.* (1827) III. 50 Forgery is susceptible of one main distinction—into fabricative and obliterative. **1858** *National Rev.* Oct. 342 If the education and lives of women have been so utterly obliterative of such important qualities [etc.].

b. *Phys.* and *Path.* (See OBLITERATION 2.)

1899 *Allbutt's Syst. Med.* VI. 301 Specimen of obliterative endarteritis.

2. *Zool.* ***obliterative coloration, shading*** = COUNTERSHADING.

1909 [see COUNTERSHADING]. **1926** W. P. PYCRAFT *Camouflage in Nature* vi. 66 This type of coloration he [*sc.* A. H. Thayer] designated 'obliterative coloration'. **1940** H. B. COTT *Adaptive Coloration in Animals* I. iii. 39 The appearance of obliterative shading can be.. reproduced by means of patterns.. rather than by the more usual method of graded ground colour. **1964** A. L. THOMSON *New Dict. Birds* 139/2 Graded coloration, ranging from darkest on the back to lightest on the under parts, neutralises relief and thus renders the solid body as an apparently flat surface. Obliterative shading forms a basis for the coloration of nearly all cryptic birds, whether or not they carry a super-imposed pattern.

obliterator (ə'blɪtəreɪtə(r)). [f. OBLITERATE *v.* + -OR¹.] One who or a thing which obliterates.

1895 HARDY *Jude* I. i. 7 In place of it a tall new building.. had been erected.. by a certain obliterator of historic records. **1900** *Pall Mall Gaz.* 18 Apr. 3/2 Fire was an obliterator of evil deeds more sure than any other.

obliterature. = OBLITERATION.

1711 G. HICKES *Two Treat. Christ. Priesth.* (1847) II. 50 A perfect obliterature of all injuries.

†**o'blive,** *v. Obs. rare*⁻¹. [f. stem of L. *oblīvisc-ī* to forget.] *trans.* To forget.

c **1500** *Proverbs* in *Antiq. Rep.* (1809) IV. 407 He that hath an ere oblyving, and febill stomake of affexion.

†**o'blivial,** *a. Obs. rare*⁻⁰. [f. L. *oblīvi-um* OBLIVION + -AL¹.]

1721 BAILEY, *Oblivial*, causing Oblivion.

oblivi'ality. *rare.* [f. OBLIVIAL *a.* + -ITY.] Liability to be forgotten.

1905 E. F. BENSON *Image in Sand* i. 5 You certainly did not [meet him], or you would remember. Mr. Henderson has absolutely none of the quality of obliviality.

†**o'bliviance.** *Obs. rare*⁻¹. In 6 oblyuyaunce. [f. L. type **obliviā-re*: see OBLIVIATE and -ANCE. (Cf. OF. *oubliance*.)] Oblivion.

1503 HAWES *Examp. Virt.* XII. vii, Ye neuer cast me in oblyuyaunce.

†**o'bliviancy.** *Obs. rare*⁻¹. = prec.

1820 *Examiner* No. 663. 820/1 Extravagancies which, as he observed of 'the immortal names of Wellington and Nelson', can never 'be cast into the shade of obliviancy'.

†**o'bliviate,** *v. Obs. rare.* [f. L. type **oblīviā-re*, f. *oblīvi-um* = *oblīvio*, OBLIVION: see -ATE³ 7.] *trans.* To forget, commit to oblivion.

1661 in *Typographer* (1790) 19, I will not obliviate the Right Hon. and late Lord Governour of Berwicke. **1791** MRS. RADCLIFFE *Rom. Forest* III. xxii. 288 She withdrew.. and tried to obliviate her anxieties in sleep. **1835–40** HALIBURTON *Clockm.* xxii. (1862) 103 They obliviated their arrand and left her.

oblivion (ə'blɪvɪən), *sb.* [a. OF. *oblivion* (*c* 1245 in Godef.), ad. L. *oblīviōn-em* forgetfulness, state of being forgotten, f. vb.-stem *oblīv-*, found in inceptive deponent *oblīv-iscī* to forget; f. *ob-* (OB- 1 b) + **līv-*: cf. *līvēre* to be black and blue, *līvid-us* black and blue, dark.]

1. a. The state or fact of forgetting or having forgotten; forgetfulness.

1390 GOWER *Conf.* II. 23 Which Ring bar of Oblivion The name. **1432–50** tr. *Higden* (Rolls) I. 197 There be þer ij. welles also, of whom oon inducethe memory, that other obliuion. **1602** MARSTON *Antonio's Rev.* IV. iii, Make us drinke Lethe by your queint conceipts; That for two daies oblivion smother griefe. **1770** GOLDSMITH *Des. Vill.* 242 Thither no more the peasant shall repair To sweet oblivion of his daily care. **1873** HAMERTON *Intell. Life* I. iv. (1875) 24 Your soul had become deaf in sleep's oblivion.

b. Forgetfulness as resulting from inattention or carelessness; heedlessness, disregard.

?*c* **1470** G. ASHBY *Policy Prince* 637 Take this lesson to noon obliuion. **1526** *Pilgr. Perf.* (W. de W. 1531) 80 b, By obliuion or forgetynge of my selfe. *a* **1700** DRYDEN (J.), Among our crimes oblivion may be set; But 'tis our king's perfection to forget. **1850** CARLYLE *Latter-d. Pamph.* ii. (1872) 43 The deep oblivion of the Law of Right and Wrong.. is by no means beautiful. **1895** *Forum* (N.Y.) Feb. 674 Oblivion of this fact is the root of the wasteful opposition to prison labor and imported labor.

c. Intentional overlooking, esp. of political offences. ***Act*** or ***Bill of Oblivion***, an act or bill granting a general pardon for political offences.

In *Eng. Hist.* the term is specifically applied to the Acts of 1660 and 1690, exempting those who had taken arms or acted against Charles II and William III respectively from the penal consequences of their former deeds.

1612 NORTH *Plutarch, Thrasyb.* 1233 A law that no man should be called in question nor troubled for things that were past.. called Amnestia, or law of obliuion. **1647** CLARENDON *Hist. Reb.* II. §49 The Armies were to be disbanded: an Act of Oblivion passed. **1654** tr. *Scudery's Curia Pol.* 98 The oblivion of injuries is an Act every way as noble as revenge. **1793** BURKE *Rem. Policy Allies* Wks. 1842 I. 603 A valuable friend.. asked me what I thought of acts of general indemnity and oblivion, as a means of settling France. **1804** WELLINGTON in Gurw. *Desp.* (1837) III. 400 There shall be a mutual oblivion and pardon of all injuries on both sides. **1855** MACAULAY *Hist. Eng.* xiv. III. 398 William.. expressed his hope that a bill of general pardon and oblivion would be.. presented for his sanction.

2. a. The state or condition of being forgotten. (Hence many phrases and fig. expressions.)

c **1425** LYDG. *Assembly of Gods* 1337 Your names shalbe put to oblyuyone. **1447** BOKENHAM *Seyntys* (Roxb.) 2 To.. Throwyn it [a book] in the angle of oblyvyoun. *a* **1548** HALL *Chron.* Pref. (1809) 6 Buried in the poke of oblivion. **1555** EDEN *Decades* Ded. (Arb.) 63 Drowned in the whirle-poole of obliuion. **1594** SHAKS. *Rich. III*, III. vii. 129 The swallowing Gulfe Of darke Forgetfulnesse, and deepe Obliuion. **1697** EVELYN *Numism.* Introd. 2 Men have sought Immortality and Freedom from Oblivion, by Marbles, Statues, Trophies. **1769** *Junius Lett.* i. 6 A question.. which ought to have been buried in oblivion. **1810** D. STEWART *Philos. Ess.* iii. 117 In England.. this doctrine has sunk into complete oblivion. **1858** HAWTHORNE *Fr. & It. Jrnls.* II. 38 Let him pass into the garret of oblivion, where many things as good, or better, are piled away. **1912** GALSWORTHY *Inn of Tranquility* 128 Hand-wrought bronze sconces and a band of metal bordering, all blackened with oblivion.

†**b.** *transf.* A thing forgotten. *Obs.*

1598 YONG *Diana* 75 Minds change from that they wont to bee, Obliuions doe reuiue againe.

3. *attrib.*, as ***oblivion point, power***.

1865 DICKENS *Mut. Fr.* III. vii, To lower himself to oblivion-point. **1871** MACDUFF *Mem. Patmos* vii. 90 If first convictions are suffered to die away, the world's oblivion-power does its work.

Hence †**o'blivion** *v. Obs.*, to put into oblivion; **o'blivionist**, one who holds a theory of, or favours, oblivion.

1658–9 *Burton's Diary* (1828) III. 210, I wish there were an act to oblivion all these things. **1878** T. SINCLAIR *Mount* 22 The oblivionists do not clearly see the whole truth here.

o'blivionize, *v.* [f. OBLIVION *sb.* + -IZE.] *trans.* To consign to oblivion.

1593 NASHE *Christ's T.* (1613) 46 Let thy deepe entring Dart obliuionize their memories. **1603** DEKKER *Grissil* (Shaks. Soc.) 21, I will oblivionize my love to the Welsh widow. **1790** MAD. D'ARBLAY *Diary* 30 May, I am perpetually preparing myself for perceiving his thoughts about me oblivionised. **1892** *Echo* 2 Apr. 2/3 A conquest.. misrepresented or oblivionised by leaders of the Opposition.

oblivious (ə'blɪvɪəs), *a.* [ad. L. *oblīviōs-us* forgetful, producing forgetfulness, f. *oblīviōn-em* or *oblīvium* OBLIVION: see -OUS.]

1. That forgets or is given to forgetting; forgetful; unmindful. Const. *of*.

a **1450** *Mankind* (Brandl) 866 ȝe were obliuyous of my doctrine. **1581** J. BELL *Haddon's Answ. Osor.* 430 Gods memory is not so oblivious, that it can so soone forgett this covenaunt. **1697** LOCKE *2nd Vind. Reas. Chr.* 213 (Seager) What shall we say to such an oblivious author? **1780** BURKE *Econ. Ref.* Wks. III. 261 The slow formality of an oblivious and drowsy exchequer. **1860** TYNDALL *Glac.* I. xvi. 107 Happily for him, he was soon oblivious of this.

b. Unaware or unconscious of. Const. *of* or (esp.) *to*. Formerly regarded as *erron.*

[See *Daily News*, 18 Apr. 1899. 6/6.]

a **1862** BUCKLE *Civiliz.* (1869) III. v. 341 He was so little given to observation as to be frequently oblivious of what was passing around him. [**1880** MRS. FORRESTER *Roy & Viola* I. 74 The obliviousness of lovers to anything but themselves is truly amusing.] **1926** W. DE LA MARE *Connoisseur* 173 Above them, as if entirely oblivious to their ranting, a glazed King Edward VII stared stolidly out of a Christmas lithograph. **1960** C. DAY LEWIS *Buried Day* v. 84, I stayed indoors all day for several days, oblivious to the damp heat of Falmouth.., re-living battles I had never fought. **1970** *Daily Tel.* (Colour Suppl.) 17 Apr. 54/3 For a man who has lived here all his life Makinen is oddly oblivious to the city's history.

2. Of or pertaining to forgetfulness; attended by or associated with oblivion.

1563 B. GOOGE *Eglogs* (Arb.) 74 In deepe obliuious grounde. **1605** SHAKS. *Macb.* v. iii. 43 Some sweet Obliuious Antidote. **1667** MILTON *P.L.* I. 266 Wherfore let we then our faithful friends,.. Lye thus astonisht on th' oblivious Pool? **1794** MRS. PIOZZI *Synon.* II. 306 A full but gentle river glides slowly.. into a dark oblivious lake. **1821** LAMB *Elia* Ser. I. *My relations*, Consigned to the oblivious lumber-room.

†**3.** Forgotten. *Obs. rare.*

1535–6 in *Southwell Visit.* (1891) 140 Item I geve to sir James lee, vicar of caunton, for oblivious tithes and other, iijs. iiijd. **1813** H. & J. SMITH *Rej. Addr., Cui Bono* iv, His life a flash, his memory a dream, Oblivious down he drops in Lethe's stream.

o'bliviously, *adv.* [f. prec. + -LY².] In an oblivious manner, forgetfully; with oblivion.

a **1548** HALL *Chron., Rich. III* 29 Obliviouslie forgettynge, and littell consyderyng, that [etc.]. **1623** J. TAYLOR (Water P.) *Wks.* (1630) II. 243/2 What great pitty was it, that the.. memories of them [Pharaoh's chariots] had not beene obliuiously swallowed in that Egyptian downfall. **1812** *Examiner* 11 May 303/1 Before the public act.. so obliviously by past sacrifices of blood and treasure. **1870** *Even. Standard* 29 Oct., Those who are so obliviously generous to France in the hour of her misfortunes.

o'bliviousness. [f. as prec. + -NESS.] The state or quality of being oblivious; forgetfulness.

1533 FRITH *Answ. Bp. Rochester* Wks. (1829) 185, I wonder what obliviousness is come upon him. **1542** BOORDE *Dyetary* viii. (1870) 244 Immoderate slepe.. induceth and causeth oblyuyousnes. **1727** in BAILEY vol. II. **1850** MERIVALE *Hist. Rom. Emp.* (1865) VI. l. 147 This imputation of extraordinary weakness and obliviousness. **1887** T. HARDY *Woodlanders* vii. 49 Memories revived after an interval of obliviousness.

obliviscence (ɒblɪ'vɪsəns). [f. L. *oblīviscent-em*, pr. pple. of *oblīviscī* to forget: see -ENCE, and cf. obs. F. *obliviscence* (*c* 1420).] The fact of forgetting or state of having forgotten; forgetfulness.

1774 *Nat. Hist.* in *Ann. Reg.* 120/2 He had returned to life.. with a total obliviscence of every past transaction. **1832** *Boston Herald* 22 May 3/6 It would take a volume to record his obliviscences. **1877** JEVONS in *Mind* VI. 198 His mind has probably sifted out the facts and rejected the unimportant ones by the law of obliviscence.

obliviscible (ɒblɪ'vɪsɪb(ə)l), *a.* [f. L. *oblīvisci* to forget + -IBLE.] Able or likely to be forgotten.

1905 *N.Y. Times* 12 Aug. II. 526/4 The sonnets he [*sc.* Swinburne] wrote about those poets, so obliviscible, excepting by himself.

‖**o'blivium.** *Obs.* [L. *oblīvium* = *oblīvio* oblivion.] = OBLIVION; forgetfulness.

1699 EVELYN *Acetaria* 54 [Parsley] was of old, we read, never brought to the Table at all, as sacred to *Oblivium* and the *Defunct*.

†**'oblivy.** *Obs.* [ad. L. *oblīvi-um*: see prec. (Perh. refash. from OF. *oublie, oubliee.*)] Oblivion.

c **1475** *Partenay* 3798 Your sone Fromount in obliuy put ay. **1513** DOUGLAS *Æneis* VI. Prol. 4 Lethe, Cochite, the wateris of oblivie. **1550** J. COKE *Eng. & Fr. Heralds* §125 (1877) 96 Who..ought not to be put in oblyvie.

†**'oblocate,** *v. Obs. rare*—⁰. [f. L. *oblocāt-*, ppl. stem of (post-cl.) *oblocāre*, f. *ob-* (OB- 1 a) + *locāre* to let out on hire: see LOCATE.] *trans.* To let out on hire. So †**oblo'cation.**

1623 COCKERAM, *Oblocate*, to set out to hire. *Oblocation*, a setting out to hire.

†**oblo'cution.** *Obs.* [a. OF. *oblocution* (1352 in Godef.), ad. late L. *oblocūtiōn-em* contradiction, n. of action f. L. *obloquī*: see OBLOQUY.]

1. Evil-speaking, obloquy, slander.

1432-50 tr. *Higden* (Rolls) VI. 73 The kynge..askede forȝifenesse, promisenge that he wolde not use oblocucion after that in that parte. *c* **1450** tr. *De Imitatione* III. xli. 111 For þe loue of god þou owist to suffre all þinges..wronges, oblocucions, reprehensions. **1526** *Pilgr. Perf.* (W. de W. 1531) 93 Preuy backbytynge..is whan one..secretely speketh oblocucyon or euyll of theyr neyghbour. **1731** BAILEY, *Oblocution*, obloquy, ill Report.

2. Bad locution or utterance, bad delivery.

c **1450** *Cov. Myst.* viii. (Shaks. Soc.) 70 Cryst conserve.. the personys here pleand, that the pronunciacion Of here sentens to be seyd mote be sad and sure, And that non oblocucyon make this matere obscure.

†**oblo'cutor.** *Obs.* Also 7 -quutor. [a. L. *oblocūtor*, *-quūtor*, agent-n. f. *obloquī*: see OBLOQUY.] A gainsayer, contradictor; a detractor, slanderer.

1603 HARSNET *Pop. Impost.* xxii. 147 To stop the mouthe of all carping obloquutors. **1656** in BLOUNT *Glossogr.*

Oblomov, Oblomoff ('ɒbləʊmɒf). The name of a character in Ivan Goncharov's novel 'Oblomov' (1855), represented as inactive, weak-willed, and procrastinating: used allusively. Hence **Oblomovism** (ɒb'ləʊməʊvɪz(ə)m, 'ɒbləʊməvɪz(ə)m), conduct resembling that of Oblomov; sluggishness, inertia.

1902 *Encycl. Brit.* XXIX. 29/2 Dobroluboff said of it, '.. something of Oblomoff is to be found in every one of us'. Peesareff..declared that 'Oblomoffism'..'is an illness fostered by the nature of the Slavonic character and the life of Russian society.' **1924** *Psyche* V. 55 This type of introversion..is known in Russia as 'Oblomovism'. **1925** I. A. RICHARDS *Princ. Lit. Crit.* vii. 52 Most people in the same day are Bonaparte and Oblomov by turns. **1942** *Penguin New Writing* XII. 62 Thompson had been sinking towards semi-starvation, I to the insidious Oblomovism of the country. **1957** A. G. MEYER *Leninism* ix. 214 Oblomovism —the behavior of Oblomov, pathetic hero of Goncharov's novel of the same name, who prefers to contemplate and discuss the universe, including his own predicament, instead of taking an active part in solving his problems and participating in life. **1970** *Harper's Mag.* Oct. 44 Friends hint there may be a touch of Oblomovism combined with whatever real ills his aging flesh may be heir to.

oblong ('ɒblɒŋ), *a.* and *sb.* [ad. L. *oblong-us* somewhat long, longish, (later) oblong; f. *ob-* + *longus* LONG. Cf. F. *oblong* (Cotgr.).

The exact force of the prefix in *oblongus* is obscure: there is no analogous word in Latin.]

A. *adj.* **1.** Elongated in one direction (usually as a deviation from an exact square or circular form); having the chief axis considerably longer than the transverse diameter; *spec.* in *Geom.*, Rectangular with the adjacent sides unequal.

†***oblong marrow***, the medulla oblongata (*obs.*). ***oblong spheroid***, a prolate spheroid.

c **1420** *Pallad. on Husb.* I. 1098 Make pipis..The cellis square oblonge, as x in breede As for xv in lengthe, is out to sprede. **1611** COTGR., *Oblong*, oblong, somewhat long. **1657** S. PURCHAS *Pol. Flying-Ins.* 4 [The Bee's] shape is little, brown, bowing, oblong. **1658** SIR T. BROWNE *Gard. Cyrus* ii. 119 The beds of the Ancients were different from ours.. being framed ob-long. **1706** PHILLIPS, *Oblong*,..of a Figure, inclining to long, longish, or somewhat long. **1774** GOLDSM. *Nat. Hist.* (1776) VI. 384 The egg..though round when in the body, yet becomes much more oblong than those of fowls, upon being excluded. **1777** W. DALRYMPLE *Trav. Sp. & Port.* lvi, An antient wall with towers, forming a kind of oblong square. **1801** *Encycl. Brit.* (ed. 3) Suppl. II. 305/1 *Oblong spheroid*..is formed by an ellipse revolved about its longer or transverse axis; in contradistinction from the *oblate spheroid*. **1834** MRS. SOMERVILLE *Connex. Phys. Sc.* xiii. (1849) 104 The waters thus attracted by the moon would assume the form of an oblong spheroid. **1853** KANE *Grinnell Exp.* iii. (1856) 27 It was in shape an oblong cube.

b. *Bot.* and *Ent.* (See quots.)

1753 CHAMBERS *Cycl. Supp.* s.v. *Leaf, Oblong Leaf*, one the length of which is many times equal to its breadth, and the extremities of which are both too narrow to form segments of circles. **1776** J. LEE *Introd. Bot.* Explan. Terms 383 *Oblongum*, oblong, twice the Length of its Breadth. **1826** KIRBY & SP. *Entomol.* IV. 261 *Oblong*, having the longitudinal diameter more than twice the length of the transverse, and the ends varying, or rounded. **1861** MISS PRATT *Flower. Pl.* VI. 171 *Oblong Woodsia*... Frond lanceolate or oblong, pinnate, hairy beneath.

c. Of a sheet of paper, page, book, picture, panel, postage stamp, etc.: Rectangular, with the breadth greater than the height: as an ***oblong octavo***, opposed to an *ordinary* or *upright octavo*.

1888 in JACOBI *Printers' Vocab.* 89. **1898** *Kegan Paul's List of Publications*, Sizes of Books..the breadth being greater than the height—the size is described as 'oblong' 8vo., 'oblong' 4to. &c.

†**2.** *fig.* Disproportionately long, drawn out. *Obs. nonce-use.*

1643 P. BALES *Oratio Dom.* 12 Their prayers are oblong and tedious, for they are..sometimes..three houres long.

3. *Comb.* (*Bot.*) in definitions of form, implying an oblong modification of another shape; as ***oblong-acuminate, -cordate, -elliptic, -hastate, -ovate, -wedgeshaped***, etc., adjs.; also ***oblong-leaved*** adj.

1769 ELLIS in *Phil. Trans.* LIX. 139 *note*, Little oblong-oval seed vessels. **1776-96** WITHERING *Brit. Plants* (ed. 3) III. 138 Leafits..obtusely oval, or oblong-wedgeshaped. **1822-34** *Good's Study Med.* (ed. 4) I. 630 The three species of cinchona used officinally..the lance-leaved,..heart-leaved,..and oblong-leaved. **1847** W. E. STEELE *Field Bot.* 9 Lower leaves oblong-lanceolate. *Ibid.* 196 Fruit oblong-obovate. *Ibid.* 199 Fruit patent, oblong-acuminate. *Ibid.* 203 Barren spikes..oblong-cylindrical. **1870** HOOKER *Stud. Flora* 34 Radical leaves oblong-rhomboid or ovate not cordate. *Ibid.* 198 Leaves oblong-cordate. *Ibid.* 316 Leaves more oblong-hastate. *Ibid.* 353 Spikes oblong-pyramidal.

B. *sb.* An oblong figure, or something having an oblong form; *spec.* in *Geom.*, A rectangle of greater length than breadth.

a **1608** SIR F. VERE *Comm.* 124 Stretched out in the form of a geometrical oblique or oblong. **1664** H. MORE *Myst. Iniq.* xvii. 60 Stoop to divide clay or dirt into squares or oblongs. **1787** M. CUTLER in *Life, Jrnls. & Corr.* (1888) I. 330 Were the ends increased..I should prefer an oblong to a square. **1849** GROTE *Greece* II. lxx. (1862) VI. 256 Xenophon then moved..that the march should be in a hollow oblong, with the baggage in the centre. **1890** PROCTOR *Other Worlds* ii. 38 Each image would also be a horizontally-placed oblong.

Hence **'oblongness.** *rare*—⁰.

1727 BAILEY vol. II, *Oblongness*, oblong Form, or the being of the Form of a long Square.

oblongatal (ɒblɒŋ'geɪtəl), *a.* [f. mod.L. *oblongāt-us* (as in *medulla oblongāta*), pa. pple. of *oblongāre* to prolong, f. L. *oblongus* OBLONG + -AL[1].] Of or pertaining to the medulla oblongata, the hindmost segment of the brain.

1885 A. H. BUCK *Handbk. Med. Sc.* VIII. 124 *Funiculus gracilis*, the oblongatal continuation of the myelic dorsomesal..column.

oblongated ('ɒblɒŋgeɪtɪd), *ppl. a.* [f. as prec. + -ED[1].] Prolonged; in ***oblongated marrow***, the medulla oblongata.

1822-34 *Good's Study Med.* (ed. 4) III. 2 The cerebrum, or brain, properly so called, the cerebrel, or little brain, and the oblongated marrow.

oblongish ('ɒblɒŋɪʃ), *a. rare.* [f. OBLONG *a.* + -ISH.] Somewhat oblong.

1693 EVELYN *De la Quint. Orange-Trees* vi. 12 Though they sometimes make little Round ones, and other [cases for trees] Oblongish. **1750** tr. *Leonardus' Mirr. Stones* 73 A round oblongish figure of the bigness of a midling nut. **1786** *Families of Plants* I. 78 Anthers oblongish.

oblongitude (ɒ'blɒndʒɪtju:d). *rare.* [f. OBLONG after *longitude.*] Oblong form. Hence **oblongi'tudinal** *a.*, having an oblong form.

1739 ELIZ. CARTER tr. *Algarotti on Newton's Theory* (1742) II. 26 This Oblongitude of the solar Image. **1892** *Pall Mall G.* 1 Oct. 4/3 Mr. Gladstone..sat in the curve of an oblongitudinal segment, as our correspondent's informant described the Premier's situation.

'oblongly, *adv. rare.* [f. OBLONG *a.* + -LY[2].] In an oblong manner or form.

1650 BULWER *Anthropomet.* Pref., Like a Ball of wax, oblongly spread. *a* **1742** CHEYNE (J.), Had the globe..been either spherical, or oblongly spheroidical.

o'blongo-, used in *Bot.* as combining form of *oblong* adj. in sense 'with oblong extension' = OBLONG *a.* 3, as ***oblongo-cylindrical, -elliptic, -fusiform, -lanceolate, -ovoid*** adjs.

1775 W. JENKINSON *Descr. Br. Pl.* Gloss., *Oblongo-ovate*, partly oblong, but rather more of an oval. **1846** BERKELEY in *Proc. Berw. Nat. Club* II. No. 14. 191 The sporidia..are regularly oblongo-elliptic. **1847** W. E. STEELE *Field Bot.* 149 Leaves oblongo-lanceolate. **1871** LEIGHTON *Lichenflora* 37 Oblong or oblongo-ovoid.

o'bloquial, *a. rare.* [f. as next + -AL[1]: cf. *colloquial.*] Of or pertaining to obloquy.

1790 J. WILLIAMS *Shrove Tuesday* 24 Obloquial arrows seldom whiz around, But from that quiver Error hangs— behind.

obloquious (ɒ'bləʊkwɪəs), *a. rare.* [f. L. *obloqui-um* OBLOQUY + -OUS.] Characterized by obloquy or evil-speaking; bringing reproach or disgrace.

1611 COTGR., *Mesdisant*, reproachfull, detractiue, obloquious. *a* **1635** NAUNTON *Fragm. Reg.* (Arb.) 16 Emulations, which are apt to rise and vent in obloquious acrimony. **1698** FRYER *Acc. E. India & P.* 193 After many obloquious Salutes she put this Affront on him.

†**o'bloquity.** *Obs. rare.* [irreg. f. L. *obloquī* or *obloquium* (see next) + -ITY.] Opposition or contradiction in speech or writing.

1620 BRENT tr. *Sarpi's Hist. Counc. Trent* VIII. 792 To doe it by way of narration, or by obliquity [*later edd.* oblo-] of wordes. **1624** F. WHITE *Repl. Fisher* 363 A line or sentence cannot escape these Critickes, if there appeare obloquitie, or antipathie to their inueterate forgeries.

obloquy ('ɒbləkwɪ). Also 5-6 obliqui, -lyquy, 6 -licque, -loqui, -ye, 6-7 -ie. [ad. late L. *obloqui-um* contradiction, f. *obloquī* to speak against, gainsay, contradict, f. *ob-* (OB- 1 b) + *loquī* to speak. (The early spelling *obliq-* may have arisen through confusion with *oblique.*)]

1. Evil-speaking directed against a person or thing; abuse, detraction, calumny, slander. †Formerly also with *an* and *pl.*, An abusive or calumnious speech or utterance (*obs.*).

1460 CAPGRAVE *Chron.* 281 In this tyme cam oute a bulle ..which revokid alle the graces that had be graunted..of whech ros mech slaundir and obliqui ageyn the Cherch. **1502** ATKYNSON tr. *De Imitatione* III. xl. 229 Infyrmytes, & iniurye, oblyquies & repreues..these thynges helpe to purches vertues. **1591** SHAKS. *1 Hen. VI*, II. v. 49 He..did vpbrayd me with my Fathers death; Which obloquie set barres before my tongue. **1673** *True Worsh. God* p. ii, I shall not much concern my self with the obloquies of such men. **1777** WATSON *Philip II* (1839) 375 It would be prudent perhaps not to expose himself again to the obloquy of his detractors. **1867** SMILES *Huguenots Eng.* viii. (1880) 137 They had to..hold their convictions in the face of obloquy, opposition.

b. Abuse or detraction as it affects the person spoken against; the condition of being spoken against; evil fame, bad repute; reproach, disgrace.

1469 *Paston Lett.* II. 380 They that be abut yow be in obloquy of all men. **1494** FABYAN *Chron.* VII. 618 All was ruled by the quene & her counsayll..to the great maugre & oblyquy of the quene. **1513** MORE in Grafton *Chron.* (1568) II. 767 From the great obloquy that he was in so late before, he was..in so great trust that..he was made [etc.] **1602** MARSTON *Antonio's Rev.* IV. iii, The just revenge Upon the author of thy obloquies. **1647** CLARENDON *Hist. Reb.* VII. §337 And undergo the perpetual obloquy of having lost a Kingdom.

†**2.** *transf.* A cause, occasion, or object of detraction or reproach; a reproach, a disgrace. *Obs.*

1589 NASHE *Anat. Absurd.* 39 To shew what an obloquie these impudent incipients in Arts are vnto Art. **1601** SHAKS. *All's Well* IV. ii. 44 An honour longing to our house,.. Which were the greatest obloquie i' the world, In me to loose. **1621** BURTON *Anat. Mel.* II. iii. VII. (1651) 356, I have been..arraigned and condemned, I am a common obloquy.

†**obluc'tation.** *Obs.* [ad. late L. *obluctātiōn-em*, n. of action f. L. *obluctārī*, f. *ob-* (OB- 1 b) + *luctārī* to wrestle, struggle.] Striving or struggling against something; resistance, opposition.

1615 CROOKE *Body of Man* 400 These muscles partly by yeelding and giuing ground, partly by obluctation or opposition do secure the Membrane from being torne. *a* **1619** FOTHERBY *Atheom.* I. xii. §2 (1622) 125 To vse that artificiall obluctation, and facing out of the matter.

oblyge, -lys, oblyke, obs. ff. OBLIGE, OBLIQUE.

†**obmiss,** *v. Obs. rare.* In 5 obmysse, 6 obmyse. [f. L. *obmiss-*, ppl. stem of *obmitt-ĕre*, late spelling of *omittĕre* to OMIT.] = next.

1490 CAXTON *Eneydos* xxviii. 110 To haue obmyssed for to dyscute som of the condycyons and euyll operacyons of the cursed proserpyne. **1541** R. COPLAND *Galyen's Terapeut.* 2 E iv, Where they haue estemed that it shulde be superflue to recyte, they haue obmysed and left some.

†**obmit,** *v. Obs. rare.* [ad. L. *obmittĕre*: see prec.] *trans.* To leave out, omit.

1541 R. COPLAND *Galyen's Terapeut.* 2 E iv, Obmyttyng and leauyng the seconde. **1547** BOORDE *Introd. Knowl.* xx. 173 The whyche I do thinke better to obmyt, and to leue vnwryten. **1684** *Col. Rec. Pennsylv.* I. 107 To continue These words, writing [etc.]..Speaking to be Obmitted.

†**obmurmu'ration,** *Obs.* [ad. L. *obmurmurātiōn-em*, n. of action from *obmurmurāre* to murmur against, f. *ob-* (OB- 1 b) + *murmurāre* to MURMUR.] A murmuring against something. So †**ob'murmuring** *vbl. sb.* [f. **obmurmur* vb.].

1604 TOOKER *Fabrique Ch.* 120 Their envie and obmurmuration. **1647** H. MORE *Song of Soul* II. II. x, Maugre all th' obmurmurings of sense. **1648** J. GOODWIN *Right & Might* 26 Religious men breake out of the way of.. truth, with the renitency and obmurmuration of their judgements and consciences.

obmutescence (ɒbmju:'tɛsəns). [f. L. *obmūtēscĕre* to become dumb or mute (f. *ob-* (OB- 1 b) + *mūtēscĕre* to grow mute) + -ENCE.] A becoming (wilfully) mute, speechless, or dumb; the action of obstinately remaining mute.

1646 SIR T. BROWNE *Pseud. Ep.* III. viii. 122 A vehement fear which naturally produceth obmutescence. **1794** PALEY *Evid.* II. ii. (1817) 59 The obmutescence, the gloom and mortification of religious orders. **1827** *Blackw. Mag.* XXII. 488 Subject to habitual and invincible obmutescence.

So **obmu'tescent** *a.*, remaining mute.

1876 G. MEREDITH *Beauch. Career* I. iv. 61 [He] pummelled the obmutescent mass, to the confusion of a conceivable epic.

obnebulate (ɒbˈnɛbjuːleɪt), *v. rare.* [f. OB- 1 c + L. *nebula* mist, fog + -ATE³: cf. OBNUBILATE *v.*] *trans.* To obscure as with a mist; to befog, cloud.

c **1540** BOORDE *The boke for to Lerne* C iij b, It doth obfuske and doth obnebulat the memorie. **1547** —— *Brev. Health* CCX. 72 b, Colde reume .. doth obnebulate a mans memorye. **1834** H. O'BRIEN *R. Towers Irel.* 120 So punctilious was their regard to euphony, they scrupled not to cancel, or otherwise obnebulate the essential .. letters of the primitive words.

† **obˈnection.** *Obs. rare*⁻⁰. [n. of action f. L. *obnectĕre*, f. *ob-* (OB- 1 a) + *nectĕre* to tie.]

1656 BLOUNT *Glossogr.*, *Obnection*, a fast knitting, as in marriage.

† **obˈnixely,** *adv. Obs. rare*⁻¹. [f. after L. *obnixē* adv., strenuously (f. *obnix-us*, pa. pple. of *obnītī* to struggle or strive against): see -LY².] Earnestly, strenuously.

1641 E. CODRINGTON *Let. to Sir E. Dering* 24 May in *Proc. in Kent* (Camden) 50 Most humbly and most obnixely I must beseach both them and you.

† **obˈnixiously,** *adv. Obs. rare*⁻¹. [irreg. f. L. *obnixē* (see prec.) + -OUS + -LY².] = prec.

1632 LITHGOW *Trav.* x. 450 At the sight of each new Moone [they] bequeath their Cattell to her protection, obnixiously imploring the pale Lady of the night, that shee will leaue their Bestiall in as good plight, as shee found them.

obnounce (ɒbˈnaʊns), *v. Rom. Antiq.* [ad. L. *obnuntiāre*, f. *ob-* (OB- 1 b) + *nuntiāre* to tell.] *intr.* Of a Roman magistrate: To announce an unfavourable omen (and thus prevent, stop, or render void, some public transaction).

1741 MIDDLETON *Cicero* I. vi. 424 Milo .. was always at hand to inhibit his proceedings, by *obnouncing*, as it was called, or declaring that he was taking the auspices on that day. **1853** MERIVALE *Rom. Rep.* ix. (1867) 266 The people .. offered him, his colleague in vain obnouncing, the provinces of the Cisalpine and Illyricum.

obnoxiety (ɒbnɒkˈsaɪɪtɪ). *rare.* [f. L. *obnoxius* OBNOXIOUS + *-ety*: see -ITY.] The state of being obnoxious or liable *to* something; liability.

1656 BLOUNT *Glossogr.*, *Obnoxiety*, obnoxiousness; liableness to danger, punishment, or to the lash. **1839** J. ROGERS *Antipopopr.* III. iii. 155 Obnoxiety to the ridicule .. of man.

obnoxious (əbˈnɒkʃəs), *a.* [f. L. *obnoxiōs-us*, f. *obnoxi-us* exposed to harm, subject, liable, f. *ob-* (OB- 1 a, b) + *noxa* hurt, injury; cf. *noxius* hurtful, injurious, NOXIOUS.]

1. Exposed to (actual or possible) harm; subject or liable to injury or evil of any kind.

a. With *to*: Liable, subject, exposed, open (*to* anything harmful, or undesirable; also, by extension, *to* any kind of influence or agency). Formerly the prevailing use; now less frequent than 6.

1597 HOOKER *Eccl. Pol.* v. lxxxi. §13 Whom .. they would .. make obnoxious to what punishment themselves list. **1621** BURTON *Anat. Mel.* I. i. III. ii, The finest wits .. are before other obnoxious to it [melancholy]. **1658** EVELYN *Fr. Gard.* (1675) 93 Cover them with fern or straw, to secure them from the frosts, to which they are obnoxious. **1665** GLANVILL *Scepsis Sci.* xiii. 75 Being .. thus obnoxious to fallacy in our apprehensions. **1682** BUNYAN *Holy War* (Cassell) 208 The town of Mansoul .. now lies obnoxious to its foes. **1712** ADDISON *Spect.* No. 441 ⁋2 We are obnoxious to so many Accidents. **1754** SHERLOCK *Disc.* (1759) I. i. 45 They render themselves obnoxious to the Justice of God. **1810** SOUTHEY *Kehama* XIV. xiv, That corporeal shape alike to pain Obnoxious as to pleasure. **1847** GROTE *Greece* II. liv. (1862) IV. 565 Obnoxious to general dislike. **1891** *Law Times* XCI. 406/2 A similar case, and is obnoxious to similar criticism.

†**b.** With *inf.* Liable. *Obs.*

1610 DONNE *Pseudo-martyr* 118 Our corruption now is more obnoxious and apter to admitte and inuite such poysonous ingredients. **1643** ABP. WILLIAMS *Let.* in Carte *Collect. Lett.* (1735) 254 His Majestie .. soe obnoxious to be shaken and removed by variety of councills out of any settled resolution. *a* **1677** HALE *Contempl.* II. 49 The time of Youth is most Obnoxious to forget God. *a* **1734** NORTH *Lives* (1826) II. 72 They .. were obnoxious to be taken up by every peevish sheriff or magistrate.

†**c.** *simply.* Liable or exposed to harm. *rare.*

a **1631** DONNE *Progr. Soul* in *Poems* (1633) 265 Thinke but how poore thou wast, how obnoxious, Whom a small lumpe of flesh could poyson thus. **1682** *Enq. Elect. Sheriffs* 1 Were it not for the discharge of my duty .. I should not so far expose and lay myself obnoxious, as I foresee I shall do.

†**2.** Liable to punishment or censure; guilty, blameworthy, reprehensible. *Obs.*

1604 R. CAWDREY *Table Alph.*, *Obnoxious*, subiect to danger, faultie. **1610** DONNE *Pseudo-martyr* 353 The Doctrines of the Keyes .. and all the ceremonies, which were the most obnoxious matters. **1642** *Vind. of King* p. ii, It could make that obnoxious, which till this Parliament no man could ever call a fault. **1719** DE FOE *Crusoe* II. xiii, Our .. persons were not obnoxious. *a* **1774** GOLDSM. *Misc. Writ.* (ed. Prior) I. 535 A late work has appeared to us highly obnoxious in this respect.

†**3.** Subject to the rule, power, or authority of another; answerable, amenable (*to* some authority); dependent, subject; hence, submissive, obsequious, deferential. Const. *to. Obs.*

1581 SAVILE *Tacitus, Hist.* II. xix. (1604) 80 The Generals being obnoxious, and not daring to prohibit it. *Ibid.* xxxvii. (1591) 75 One .. of their owne creation, and therefore wholly obnoxious to them. **1658** CLEVELAND *Rustick Ramp.* Wks. (1687) 437 That Kings are only the Tenants of Heaven, obnoxious to God alone. **1659** B. HARRIS *Parival's Iron Age* 119 Hans-Towns, .. partly .. free; and partly Provincial, and obnoxious. *a* **1695** WOOD *Life* (O.H.S.) I. 397 Most of them .. being sneaking and obnoxious, they did run rather with the temper of the Warden than stand against him. **1722** WOLLASTON *Relig. Nat.* v. 77 An existence that is not dependent upon or obnoxious to any other. **1754** A. MURPHY *Gray's Inn Jrnl.* No. 72 Whether they are not obnoxious to the Association for preserving the Game.

†**4.** With *to*: Exposed to the (physical) action or influence of; liable to be affected by; open to.

1628 LE GRYS tr. *Barclay's Argenis* 56 That thinne substance, which by its own lenitie is obnoxious to whateuer presseth it. **1665** *Surv. Aff. Netherl.* 122 West-Friezland .. lyeth Eastward obnoxious to Westphalen in High-Germany, N. and W. to the main Ocean. **1666** DRYDEN *Ann. Mirab.* cclviii, The most in fields like herded beasts lie down, To dews obnoxious. **1671** EVELYN *Mem.* (1857) III. 235 They are obnoxious to sense, and fall under our cognisance.

¶**5.** *erron.* (by confusion with *noxious*): Hurtful, injurious. *Obs.*

1612 WOODALL *Surg. Mate* Wks. (1653) 368 Cold aire in time of sweating is obnoxious and dangerous. **1638** SIR T. HERBERT *Trav.* (ed. 2) 323 Crocodile .. the most obnoxious of sea monsters. **1646** J. HALL *Horæ Vac.* 81 Unseasonable times of study are very obnoxious, as after meales. **1683** SALMON *Doron Med.* II. 587 Powerful in extirpating all obnoctious tumors.

6. That is an object of aversion or dislike; offensive, objectionable, odious, highly disagreeable; sometimes with more active force: Giving offence, acting objectionably. (Cf. 2 and 5.) The chief current use, app. affected by association with *noxious*. Const. *to*.

1675 WOOD *Life* 3 July (O.H.S.) II. 318 A very obnoxious person; an ill neighbour; and given much to law sutes with any. **1680** in Somers *Tracts* I. 110 To make them lothsome and obnoxious to the People. **1789** BELSHAM *Ess.* I. iii. 53 Strickland .. had the presumption to move the obnoxious bill. **1841** E. FITZGERALD *Lett.* (1889) I. 69 Carlyle .. is becoming very obnoxious now that he has become popular. **1857** BUCKLE *Civiliz.* I. vii. 449 They did not dare to publish a work if its author were obnoxious to the Court. **1866** G. MACDONALD *Ann. Q. Neighb.* xi. (1878) 216 Thumb-marks I find very obnoxious.

obˈnoxiously, *adv.* [f. prec. + -LY².] In an obnoxious manner (in any sense of the adj.).

1625 K. LONG tr. *Barclay's Argenis* III. iv. 161 They seldome come to a pitcht Field: their dangers are little or soddaine, for they are obnoxiously pacified [*obnoxie placantur*; see prec. 3]. **1755** JOHNSON, *Obnoxiously*, in a state of subjection; in the state of one liable to punishment. **1828** WEBSTER, *Obnoxiously*. [1.] In a state of subjection or liability. 2. Reprehensibly; odiously; offensively. *Mod.* He behaved most obnoxiously.

obˈnoxiousness. [f. as prec. + -NESS.] The quality or state of being obnoxious.

1. Liability to injury, evil, etc.: see OBNOXIOUS 1. Const. *to, unto.*

1652 BP. HALL *Invis. World* I. v, Their deadly machinations and our miserable obnoxiousness. **1654** WARREN *Unbelievers* 48 An obnoxiousnesse unto punishment. *a* **1677** BARROW *Serm.* Wks. 1716 I. 166 Sensible of our own obnoxiousness to the like slips and falls. **1729** STACKHOUSE *Body Divin.* IV. i. §2 (1776) II. 419 Our obnoxiousness to the severity of his laws. **1871** MARKBY *Elem. Law* §148 Duty or obligation is .. sometimes described as obnoxiousness to a sanction.

†**2.** Liability to punishment or censure; guilt, blameworthiness. *Obs.*

1610 DONNE *Pseudo-martyr* 269 Bellarmine .. delt herein with more obnoxiousnesse and lesse excuse then Binius. *a* **1661** FULLER *Worthies, Dorsetshire* I. (1662) 289 Considering his own Obnoxiousness for so rash a fact, he .. procured his pardon at Court. **1704** M. HENRY *Communicant's Comp.* x, Considering .. our unworthiness and obnoxiousness.

3. Offensiveness, objectionableness, odiousness.

1828 WEBSTER s.v., The obnoxiousness of the law rendered the legislature unpopular. **1851** GALLENGA *Italy* i. 26 They could not drive the Austrians from Lombardy, but gave them palpable hints of their obnoxiousness there.

obnoxity (əbˈnɒksɪtɪ). [f. as OBNOXIOUS *a.* + -ITY.] An obnoxious, objectionable, or offensive person or thing; an object of aversion.

1924 LAWRENCE & SKINNER *Boy in Bush* xx. 282 The parlour was the coolest place for the meat. Esau shifted the red obnoxity, wire cover and all, to the top of a cupboard. *c* **1925** D. H. LAWRENCE *Virgin & Gipsy* (1930) iii. 38 That widow of a knighted doctor, a harmless person indeed, had become an obnoxity in their lives.

† **obˈnubilate,** *ppl. a. Obs.* [ad. L. *obnūbilāt-us*, pa. pple. of *obnūbilāre*: see next.] Covered or darkened as with a cloud; overclouded; obscured.

1560 ROLLAND *Crt. Venus* I. 246 In hir net thow art obnubilate. **1610** HEALEY *St. Aug. Citie of God* XIX. iv. 758 The reason and sence are both besotted and obnubilate. **1630** J. TAYLOR (Water P.) *Epigr.* xxxvi. Wks. II. 266/1 Mans vnderstanding's so obnubilate.

obnubilate (ɒbˈnjuːbɪleɪt), *v.* [f. L. *obnūbilāt-*, ppl. stem of *obnūbilāre* to cover with clouds or fog. Cf. F. *obnubiler*, OF. *obnubler* (12th c. in Godef.).] *trans.* To darken, dim, cover, or hide with or as with a cloud; to overcloud; to obscure (*lit.* and *fig.*).

1583 STUBBES *Anat. Abus.* I. (1879) 78 As mystes and exhalations .. obnubilate and darken the beames of the Sun. **1616** R. C. *Times' Whistle* Cert. Poems (1871) 135 Your false intent faire wordes obnubilate. **1621** BURTON *Anat. Mel.* I. iii. II. ii, So doth this melancholy vapour obnubilate the mind. **1686** GOAD *Celest. Bodies* II. iv. 196 Clouds obnubilating the Face of Heaven shall skreen the Sun from us. **1768–74** TUCKER *Lt. Nat.* (1834) I. 461 Until they raise a dust which obnubilates that better light. **1838** J. P. KENNEDY *Rob of Bowl* x. (1860) 93 Your smokers [are] obnubilated in their own clouds.

Hence **obˈnubilated** *ppl. a.*

1658 [see ADIAPHANOUS *a.*]. **1830** R. CHAMBERS *Life Jas. I*, I. ix. 246 He found his mind in that obnubilated state. **1839** RAYMOND in *New Monthly Mag.* LV. 514 Some narration of 'himself and times', whereby his obnubilated patronymic might transpire to the fullest content. **1939** E. POUND *Let.* 7 Nov. (1971) 330, I loathe and always have loathed Indian art... Obnubilated, short curves, muddle, jungle, etc.

obnubilation (ɒbnjuːbɪˈleɪʃən). [n. of action from OBNUBILATE *v.* Cf. OF. *obnubilation* (15th c. in Godef.).] The action of darkening or fact of being darkened as with a cloud; obscuration.

1610 J. HEALEY *St. Aug. Citie of God* III. xv. 128 Neither can the Moone be eclipsed but .. in her farthest posture from the sunne: then is she prostitute to obnubilation. **1653** WATERHOUSE *Apol. Learn.* 175 Their obnubilation of bodies coruscant. **1819** *Hermit in London* II. 133 Fog and sunshine, obnubilation and light.

b. *spec.* Obscuration or clouding of the mind or faculties. See also quot. 1892.

1753 RUTTY *Diary* 17 Dec. in Boswell *Johnson* an. 1777, An hypochondriack obnubilation from wind and indigestion. **1803** BEDDOES *Hygeia* IX. 198 Dimness or *obnubilation* of sight. **1888** *Amer. Jrnl. Psychol.* I. 519 The patient lost consciousness for several hours, and afterwards lay for several days in a state of torpor or obnubilation. **1892** *Syd. Soc. Lex.*, *Obnubilation*, a dazzling of the eyes without giddiness, so that objects seem to be seen through a cloud, as in threatened fainting.

† **obˈnubilous,** *a. Obs. rare*⁻¹. [f. L. *obnūbil-us* overclouded (f. *ob-* (OB- 1 c) + *nūbilum* cloudy sky, cloud) + -OUS. Cf. OF. *obnuble* in same sense.] Overclouded; cloudy, indistinct.

1432–50 tr. *Higden* (Rolls) I. 9 The obnubilous and clowdy processe of this mater.

obˈnunciate, *v. rare*⁻⁰. [f. ppl. stem of L. *obnunciāre*: see OBNOUNCE.] = OBNOUNCE. So **obnunciˈation.**

1623 COCKERAM II, To Tell ill newes, *Obnunciate*; a Telling thereof, *Obnunciation*. **1656** BLOUNT *Glossogr.* s.v., *Obnunciation*, .. as the ancient Romans were wont to dissolve their Assemblies (which dissolution they called obnunciation) when soever any evil token was seen or heard, either by the Magistrate or Augur.

‖**obo** (ˈəʊbəʊ). [Native word.] In Mongolia, a ritual cairn of stones.

Quot. 1923 may be a different word.

1923 G. COLLINS *Valley of Eyes Unseen* 58 The *obo* consists of slabs of slate .. inscribed all over with Tibetan characters. **1934** H. HASLUND *Tents in Mongolia* vi. 59 We passed by two colossal heaps of stones, which the caravan men called *obos*. *Ibid.*, The two obo were .. erected at the point where the caravan route crosses the boundary between Inner and Outer Mongolia. **1936** P. FLEMING *News from Tartary* v. 134 There were also prayer flags and a good many *obos*, which are cairns of stones with a wide range of superstitious significance. **1970** C. R. BAWDEN in L. Ligeti *Mongolian Studies* 65 The worship of the mountains and *obos* (ritual cairns).

obo, var. OBBO.

oboe (ˈəʊbəʊ, formerly also ˈəʊbɔɪ, ‖ˈoboe), *sb.* [a. It. *oboe* (ˈoboe), adapted spelling of F. *hautbois*: see HAUTBOY.]

1. A wooden double-reed wind-instrument, forming the treble to the bassoon: = HAUTBOY, 1.

[**1724** *Explic. For. Wds. in Mus. Bks.* 51 *Oboe*, or *Oboy*, is a Hautboy, or Hoboy. **1796** PEGGE *Anonym.* (1809) 105 *Hoboy*. The name of this instrument is from the French *Hautbois*; and not from the Italian *Oboe*... *Oboe* has no meaning, as the French name has.] **1794** MRS. RADCLIFFE *Myst. Udolpho* i, With the tender accents of his oboe. **1840** HOOD *Up the Rhine* 244 They played upon fiddles, oboes, &c. **1879** GEO. ELIOT *Theo. Such* ix. 160 The trumpet breaking in on the flute, and the oboë confounding both.

attrib. and *Comb.* **1881** J. T. SLUGG *Remin. Manch.* xxvi. 298 Gregory, violinist; Hughes, oboe player.

2. Name of a reed-stop in an organ, with metal pipes, giving a penetrating tone.

[*c* **1700**, **1829**: see HAUTBOY 1 c.] **1834** *Specif. Organ York Minster* in Grove *Dict. Mus.* I. 600 Swell Organ... 42. Horn. 43. Trumpet. 44. Oboe.

3. (With capital initial.) The name of a radar system for guiding military aircraft in which two ground stations interrogate a transponder in the aircraft to identify it and determine its position, which information is then transmitted to the aircraft. Also *attrib.* and *Comb.*

1945 *Daily Mirror* 15 Aug. 4/2 Next came 'Gee', the bombing beam which guided our radar-equipped bombers on to their targets, and the even more accurate 'Oboe'. **1946** *R.A.F. Jrnl.* May 169 'Oboe'-controlled Mosquito aircraft were assigned to the marking of targets. **1947** CROWTHER & WHIDDINGTON *Science at War* I. 59 The Oboe pathfinders started later and were faster... The pathfinder was under Oboe control, while approaching the target, for about ten minutes. **1974** *Encycl. Brit. Macropædia* XV. 371/1 The extreme accuracy of Oboe, H, or Shoran was not needed for guiding a plane between airfields on a friendly mission.

oboe ('əubəu), *v. rare.* [f. the sb.] *trans.* To sound in the tone of an oboe.

1923 A. HUXLEY *Antic Hay* i. 8 Like an oboe, Mr. Pelvey intoned: 'The Lord be with you.'..those words, good Lord! that Mr. Pelvey was oboeing out of existence.

‖**oboe da caccia** ('oboe da 'kattʃia). Also oboe di caccia. Pl. oboi. [It., lit. 'hunting oboe'.] An old form of oboe, a fifth lower in pitch than the ordinary instrument. Cf. TENOROON.

1876 STAINER & BARRETT *Dict. Mus. Terms* 317/2 The oboe d'amore, which was also called *oboe luonga*, produced a delicate and sweet tone, while the *oboe da caccia* corresponded to the tenoroon oboe, or corno inglese. **1880** GROVE *Dict. Mus.* II. 489/1 Two important movements..in Haydn's Stabat mater are scored for two oboi di caccia obligati. **1938** *Oxf. Compan. Mus.* 627/1 Bach does not make much sole use of the normal hautboy... The oboe d'amore and the oboe da caccia were the instruments to which he gave a solo position in his cantatas, &c. **1963** *Listener* 21 Mar. 532/2 No oboi da caccia in *Qui tollis.*

‖**oboe d'amore** ('oboe da'more). Pl. oboes, oboi. [It., lit. 'oboe of love'.] An old form of oboe with a pitch a minor third below that of the ordinary oboe.

1876 [see prec.]. **1885** G. B. SHAW *How to become Mus. Critic* (1960) 62 The renovation of the obsolete *oboe d'amore* (love-hautboy)..proved very successful. **1930** [see FLÛTE-À-BEC]. **1962** *Listener* 27 Dec. 1109/2 Oboe d'amore and two bassoons. **1976** *Gramophone* July 199/3 Scored only for strings and two oboi d'amore, it has some of the most remarkable writing in all Bach's church cantatas.

†**o-bofe**, obs. form of ABOVE.

a **1400–50** *Alexander* 4912 A blewe bleaut o-bofe brad him al ouire.

oboist ('əubəuɪst). [f. OBO-E + -IST.] A performer on the oboe.

1863 HUSK in *N. & Q.* 3rd Ser. III. 415 The oboists of the last generation using reeds of very large dimensions. **1882** E. J. C. MORTON *Heroes Sc., Astron.* 273 The future astronomer [Herschel] was oboeist in the band of the guards at Hanover.

obol ('ɒbɒl). Also 8 obole. [ad. L. *obol-us*, a. Gr. ὀβολός.] = OBOLUS 1.

a **1670** HACKET *Abp. Williams* I. (1693) 225 The Romans says Plutarch, allowed Nine Obols, or Fifteen Pence a day to him that was sent Abroad upon a publick Treaty. **1771** RAPER in *Phil. Trans.* LXI. 469 The current coin of Athens, was the silver Drachm, which they divided into 6 Oboles. **1820** T. MITCHELL *Aristoph.* I. 75 A man That hath not one small obol in his purse. **1875** BROWNING *Aristoph. Apol.* 1374 To stuff the mouth Of dikast with the due three-obol fee.

obolary, *a. nonce-wd.* [f. L. *obol-us* + -ARY.] That contributes an obolus; or, Possessing only oboli or small coins, impecunious.

1820 LAMB *Elia* Ser. I. *Two Races Men*, Distance..as vast ..as subsisted between the Augustan Majesty, and the poorest obolary Jew that paid it tribute-pittance at Jerusalem.

†**obolate.** *Obs.* [ad. med.L. *obolāta* (*terræ*), f. *obol-us*: see -ATE[1] 2 (= It. *-ata*, Pr. *-ada*, F. *-ée*).] A portion of land assumed to be worth a halfpenny a year.

1610 W. FOLKINGHAM *Art of Survey* II. vii. 58 Quantities of Land taking their denominations from our vsual Coine; as Fardingdeales, Obolates, Denariates, Solidates, Librates. *Ibid.* 59 Then must the Obolat be ½ Acre, the Denariat an Acre, the Solidat 12. acres.

obole ('ɒbəʊl). [a. F. *obole* (13th c. in Littré), ad. L. *obolus*: see OBOLUS.]

1. A small French coin orig. of silver, later of billon, in use from 10th to 15th c.; also called *maille* = ½ a denier.

1656 BLOUNT *Glossogr.*, *Obole* (*obolus*), a Coyn, variable according to the Country, with us it is an halfpenny. **1830** [E. HAWKINS] *Anglo-Fr. Coinage* 47 The obole or half denier of Henry the Second.

†**2.** = OBOLUS 3. *Obs.*

1601 HOLLAND *Pliny* II. 36 An obole or half a scruple. **1656** BLOUNT *Glossogr.*, *Obole*... Also a halfpenny weight, twelve grains among Apothecaries, and fourteen among Mintmen and Goldsmiths.

†'**obolet.** *Obs. rare*[−1]. [f. OBOL + -ET[1] dim.] = OBOLUS 3.

1727 W. MATHER *Yng. Man's Comp.* 399 These are reduced into Drachms, Scruples, Obolets, Carats and Grains.

obolite ('ɒbəlaɪt). *Palæont.* [f. L. *obol-us* + -ITE.] A fossil shell of the genus *Obolus.* ***obolite-grit***, a name for the Silurian formation containing these.

1859 OWEN in *Encycl. Brit.* (ed. 8) XVII. 105/1 Obolite grit. **1865** PAGE *Handbk. Geol. Terms*, *Obolus*, a genus of bivalves belonging to the Lingula family, and characterised by their orbicular, smooth, calcareo-corneous, sub-equivalve shells... There are several species occurring in the Silurians of Northern Europe; hence the 'obolite grit' of Sweden and Russia.

obolize, erron. form of OBELIZE.

‖**obolus** ('ɒbələs). Pl. oboli (-aɪ). [L. *obolus*, a. Gr. ὀβολός.]

1. A silver (in later times bronze) coin of ancient Greece, of the value of ⅙ of a drachma.

1579–80 NORTH *Plutarch* (1612) 455 Small peeces of mony ..called Oboli, whereof sixe made a Drachma. **1702** ADDISON *Dial. Medals* Wks. 1854 I. 258 An *as* or an *obolus* may carry an higher price than a *denarius* or a drachma. **1838** THIRLWALL *Greece* IV. 243 The pay for attendance in the Assembly was raised from one obolus to three. **1851** WILLMOTT *Pleas. Lit.* xvii. (1857) 86 Belesarius asking an obolus is more touching than a blind sailor who lost his sight before the mast.

2. Applied to the French OBOLE, and to other coins, mostly of small value, formerly current in Europe; also used allusively for any small coin.

In the Middle Ages there were *oboli* of gold, silver, and copper: see Du Cange s.v.

In English monetary reckoning formerly used for a half-penny, and abbreviated *ob.*; see OB., and cf. DENARIUS ¶.

1761 H. WALPOLE *Lett. to Mann* 28 Dec., Their East India bonds did not fall an obolus under par. **1849** W. IRVING *Mahomet* xxxiv. (1853) 152 The boor, who knew nothing of jewels, demanded four silver *oboli*, or drachms. **1856** MRS. BROWNING *Aur. Leigh* IV. 209 We women should..not throw back an obolus inscribed With Cæsar's image lightly. **1861** *Morn. Post* 22 Nov., The obolus of St. Peter continues to supply the Government of his Holiness with ample means of providing for the pecuniary exigencies of the State. **1868** GEO. ELIOT *Sp. Gipsy* I. 78 Cheapen it meanly to an obolus. **1893** BITHELL *Counting-Ho. Dict.* s.v., In the Ionian Islands, before the introduction of the system of the French Monetary Convention, the Obolus was 1-100th part of the Ionian Dollar, worth ½*d.* English.

†**3.** *Apothecaries' Weight.* A weight of 10 grains, or half a scruple. *Obs.*

[**1398** TREVISA *Barth. De P.R.* XIX. cxxx. (1495) nn iij/2 The leest parte of weyghte hyghte Calculus and the fourth parte of weyghte Obulus.] **1634** T. JOHNSON *Parey's Chirurg.* XXVI. xxi. (1678) 642 Ten grains of these [barley corns] make an Obolus. **1661** LOVELL *Hist. Anim. & Min.* 22 The fabrile glue..3 Oboli being drunk with hot Water help the spitting of bloud.

4. *Palæont.* A genus of fossil brachiopods, with smooth orbicular bivalve shells, found in the Silurian rocks in Russia and elsewhere.

1859 *Encycl. Brit.* (ed. 8) XVII. 105/1. **1865** [see OBOLITE].

‖**obosom** (əʊ'bəʊsəm). 9 b-. Pl. abosom. [Ashanti.] In the religious system of the Ashanti peoples of Ghana, a general name for any of the many gods inferior to the Supreme Being.

1853 B. CRUICKSHANK *Eighteen Yrs. on Gold Coast* II. vi. 129 From the Souman, or idol of individuals, we come to the Boossum of a family or town, which frequently has no material representation. This..does not so much represent the god of an individual as a family god, or, more universally still, the god of a people. **1887** A. B. ELLIS *Tshi-Speaking Peoples of Gold Coast* ii. 18 They [*sc.* the local deities] are very numerous... The general name for these deities is *Bohsūm.* **1916** R. S. RATTRAY *Ashanti Proverbs* i. 30 A *sumān* would seem to derive its power from the *abosom*, just as the *ọbosom* in turn gains its own from *Onyankọ̄pọn.* **1923** —— *Ashanti* ii. 54 The great *obosom* (god) of all Ashanti is the Tano River, from which are derived countless of 'his children' as lesser *abosom*... Tano is considered as the 'son of the Supreme God'. **1960** M. J. FIELD *Search for Security* I. ii. 47 The Supreme God (called *Onyame* in Ashanti) is aloof... The *abosom* are the active, approachable executives of the Supreme God. The *abosom* are popularly referred to as 'the little gods', but each one is treated, in daily practice, as though he were omnipotent, omniscient and omnipresent. **1970** P. OLIVER *Savannah Syncopators* 30 The occasions which I was privileged to attend, culminating in a cult or 'fetish' dance for a local *obosom*, or protective spirit, were simple and moving.

oboue(n, obout, obs. ff. ABOVE, ABOUT.

oboval (ɒb'əʊvəl), *a. Nat. Hist.* = next.

1857 in MAYNE *Expos. Lex.* **1892** in *Syd. Soc. Lex.*

obovate (ɒb'əʊvət), *a. Nat. Hist.* [OB- 2.] Inversely ovate; egg-shaped with the broader end upmost or forward.

1785 MARTYN *Rousseau's Bot.* xxxii. (1794) 494 Apple-form Bryum has large spherical heads; and in the Pear-form species they are obovate. **1826** KIRBY & SP. *Entomol.* III. xxx. 157 The figure..in those [larvae] of the water-beetles ..approaches to an obovate shape. **1877–84** F. E. HULME *Wild Fl.* p. vi, Stem-leaves obovate, having petioles.

b. In comb. with another adj., denoting a form intermediate between the obovate and some other, as ***obovate-cuneate, -lanceolate, -oblong, -spathulate.***

1845 LINDLEY *Sch. Bot.* v. (1858) 56 Leaflets oblong, or obovate-cuneate. **1870** HOOKER *Stud. Flora* 196 Bellis perennis..leaves obovate-spathulate. *Ibid.* 324 Viscum album,..leaves obovate-lanceolate obuse. *Ibid.* 460 Asplenium Ruta-muraria..pinnæ 3–7 obovate-cuneate.

obovatifolious (ɒbəʊ,veɪtɪ'fəʊlɪəs), *a. Bot.* [f. mod.L. *obovātifoli-us* (f. *obovāt-us* OBOVATE + *folium* leaf) + -OUS.] Having obovate leaves.

1857 in MAYNE *Expos. Lex.*

obo'vato-, used as combining form of mod.L. *obovātus* OBOVATE, as in **obovato-lanceolate** (= *obovate-lanceolate*), **obovato-retuse** *adjs.*

1806 GALPINE *Brit. Bot.* No. 163 L[eaves] obovato-lanceolate. **1839** HARDY in *Proc. Berw. Nat. Club* I. 209 Leaflets obovato-retuse.

obovoid (ɒb'əʊvɔɪd), *a. Nat. Hist.* [OB- 2.] Somewhat egg-shaped, with the broader end upward or outward; somewhat obovate.

1819 G. SAMOUELLE *Entomol. Compend.* 276 Antennæ inserted near the mouth, the first joint obovoid. **1870** HOOKER *Stud. Flora* 361 Cypripedium Calceolus..lip.. obovoid.

oboy. *U.S.* = BOY *sb.*[1] 9.

1963 T. PYNCHON *V.* xvi. 429 'Oboy, oboy,' said Fat Clyde wearily. **1966** —— *Crying of Lot 49* vi. 181 Oboy... they'd call her names, proclaim her..as a redistributionist and pinko.

obprobrious, etc., obs. ff. OPPROBRIOUS, etc.

obpyramidal (ɒbpɪ'ræmɪdəl), *a. Nat. Hist.* [OB- 2.] Inversely pyramidal; of the form of an inverted pyramid.

1870 HOOKER *Stud. Flora* 210 Fruit obpyramidal.

obpyriform (ɒb'pɪrɪfɔːm), *a. Nat. Hist.* [OB- 2.] Inversely pyriform; pear-shaped, with the thicker end at the base.

1870 HOOKER *Stud. Flora* 408 Carex teretiuscula... Fruit obpyriform.

obraid, obrayde, obreide, corrupt ff. UPBRAID *v.*: cf. ABRAID *v.*[2]

obregge, obs. erron. form of ABRIDGE.

1444 *Rolls Parlt.* V. 124.

obreption (ɒ'brɛpʃən). [ad. L. *obreptiōn-em* a creeping or stealing upon, n. of action from *obrēp-ĕre* to creep up to, steal upon, f. *ob-* (OB- 1 a) + *rēpĕre* to creep. Cf. F. *obreption* (1457 *orrepcion* in Godef.).]

1. The obtaining or trying to obtain something by craft or deceit, *spec.* in *Eccl.* and *Sc. Law*, of a dispensation, gift, etc. by false statement. (Opp. to *subreption*, obtaining by suppression of truth.)

1611 COTGR., *Obreption*, an obreption; the creeping, or stealing to a thing by craftie meanes. **1623** COCKERAM, *Obreption*, a getting of things by craft. **1706** tr. *Dupin's Eccl. Hist. 16th C.* II. IV. xviii. 269 Dispensations..shall be invalid; if the Ordinaries..shall not first take..Cognizance of them, to see whether there is no Subreption or Obreption in their Petitions or Requests. **1752** MCDOUALL *Inst. Law Scot.* II. III. i. 259 Checks against subreption or obreption, *i.e.* their being obtained by concealing the truth, or expressing a falshood. **1894** *Month* Mar. 391 If in a petition for a dispensation, there is a narrative or statement which is false, there is said to be obreption.

†**2.** A creeping or stealing upon one unawares.

1642 CUDWORTH *Serm. 1 Cor.* xv. 57 in *Disc. Lord's Supp.*, etc. (1676) 81 Sudden incursions and obreptions, sins of mere ignorance and inadvertency. **1656** H. MORE *Enthus. Tri.* (1712) 3 The like obreptions or unavoidable importunities of Thoughts, which offer or force themselves upon the Mind.

obreptitious (ɒbrɛp'tɪʃəs), *a.* [f. L. *obreptīcius* (f. *obrept-us*, pa. pple. of *obrēp-ĕre*) + OUS: see -ITIOUS[1].] Characterized by obreption (see prec.); containing a false statement made for the sake of obtaining something. Hence **obrep'titiously** *adv.*

1611 COTGR., *Obreptice*, obreptitious, stollen, foisted in. **1658** PHILLIPS, *Obreption*, a creeping, or stealing upon by craft; whence obreptitious, *i.* stollen upon by crafty means. **1732** *Hist. Litteraria* IV. 295 An obreptitious and surreptitious Version. **1875** MANNING in *Contemp. Rev.* Dec. 18 The Archbishop, believing the Bull to be obreptitious..would not publish it. **1890** T. E. BRIDGETT *Blund. & Forg.* 18 Perhaps the rescript..was obtained obreptitiously or subreptitiously.

O'Brienism (əʊ'braɪənɪz(ə)m). [f. the name of William *O'Brien*, Irish patriot (1852–1928) + -ISM.] The conduct or anti-union policy of William O'Brien, esp. in the British Parliament about 1900 and 1901. **O''Brienite**, a supporter of William O'Brien.

1889 *Globe & Traveller* 18 Feb. 1/2 (*heading*) O'Brienism. **1900** *Westm. Gaz.* 22 Oct. 2/2 Mr. Redmond accepts..the new situation caused by the triumph of the O'Brienites and the defeat of the Healyites. *Ibid.* 24 Dec. 3/1 O'Brienism is an equivalent term for constitutional anarchy. **1911** *Q. Rev.* July 241 The realists come from the north, east, and south, the strongholds of Unionism and O'Brienism.

†**obrize.** *Obs.* Also obryze; obrison, -zon. [ad. L. *obryza*, *obryzum* (*aurum*) = Gr. ὄβρυζον (χρυσίον), tried or standard gold, in 16th c. F. *obrisé* (*or*). Cf. L. *obrussa* the testing of gold by fire, test, proof, touchstone.] In ***obrize gold***, also **(*gold-*)*obrizon***: Pure or refined gold; fine gold.

1430–40 LYDG. *Bochas* VII. viii. (1554) 172b, Iupiter reygned, put out his father clene Chaunged obrison into siluer shene. **1629** MAXWELL tr. *Herodian* (1635) 312 His Vessells, even of basest Vse, were of Obryze Gold. **1658** W. BURTON *Itin. Anton.* 158 A most fortunate jewel to Britain, better worth being but Copper, then obrize Gold. **1658**

PHILLIPS, *Obrizum* [**1706** *Obryzum*] q. *Ophirizum*, fine gold, gold of Ophir. **1670** (*title*) The Golden Calf.. In which is handled The.. Wonder of Nature, in Transmuting Metals; viz. How the intire Substance of Lead, was in one Moment Transmuted into Gold-Obrizon.

†**obrode**, obs. form of ABROAD.
1377 LANGL. *P. Pl.* B. v. 140 And sithen þei blosmed obrode.

obrogate ('ɒbrəgeɪt), *v. rare.* [f. ppl. stem of L. *obrogāre* partly to repeal a law by passing a new one, f. *ob-* (OB- 1 b) + *rogāre* to ask, supplicate, propose a law, introduce a bill.] **a.** To repeal (a law) by passing a new one. †**b.** (See quot. 1656.) So **obro'gation**.
1656 BLOUNT *Glossogr.*, *Obrogate*, to check or interrupt one in his tale, to gainsay. To abrogate [*sic*, *ed.* 1674 obrogate] a Law, is to proclaim a contrary Law, for taking away the former. **1658** PHILLIPS, *Obrogation*, an interrupting, or hindring, also a gain-saying. **1893** A. H. GREENIDGE in *Class. Rev.* Oct. 348/2 An act of parliament had been passed which was in direct conflict with a charter: .. and *ipso facto* the clause in this charter was obrogated. But we need not be surprised if the conservative party refused to admit this obrogation.

obrotund (ɒbrəʊ'tʌnd), *a.* [f. L. *ob-* + *rotund-us* round, after L. *oblong-us* oblong.] Of a rounded form, but longer in one direction than in the other; somewhat round.
1650 BULWER *Anthropomet.* vi. (1653) 110 In Sumatra, they have Eyes, obrotund, of green colour. **1892** *Syd. Soc. Lex.*, *Obrotund*, somewhat round.

†**obround**, *a. Obs.* [f. *ob-* + ROUND.] = prec.
1668 WILKINS *Real Char.* II. iv. 68 Of one single bulb or several, whether Obround, Compressed, Oblong, Coated or Scaly. **1688** R. HOLME *Armoury* II. 374/1 Obround [is] a round that is longer one way than another.

obruchevite (ɒ'bruːtʃəvaɪt). *Min.* [ad. Russ. *obruchevit*, f. the name of V. A. *Obruchev* (1863–1956), Russian geologist: see -ITE[1].] A mineral containing appreciable proportions of yttrium and uranium that was orig. regarded as a member of the pyrochlore group (see quot. 1977).
1955 *Internat. Conf. Peaceful Uses Atomic Energy* (United Nations) *U.S.S.R.: Sci. & Techn. Exhib.* 9 These classes of minerals include.. obruchevite. **1959** *Mineral. Abstr.* XIV. 54/1 In 1945 E. I. Nefedov discovered in a pegmatite vein in the Alakuztti region (N.W. Karelia) a peculiar metamict tantalo-niobate, which he classed with ellsworthite. In 1949 A. A. Beus after a study of this mineral called it obruchevite in honour of V. A. Obruchev... Obruchevite replaces albite and infills cracks in quartz. It occurs in association with garnet and other minerals as nests and irregular masses up to 5 cm. in diameter. **1966** Z. LERMAN tr. *Vlasov's Geochem. & Mineral. Rare Elements* II. 509 The mode of occurrence of obruchevite and its mineral paragenesis show that it forms during the latest stages of the replacement process. **1977** *Amer. Mineralogist* LXII. 407/1 [Report of the Subcommittee on Pyrochlore Nomenclature of the IMA Commission on New Minerals and Mineral Names.] Synonyms, doubtful and discredited names, and species not belonging to the pyrochlore group... *Obruchevite* (Kalita, 1957) is a name later shown to have been given to two different species (Gorzhevskaya and Sidorenko, 1969). One of these, brown obruchevite, after heating to 700°C, crystallized to the samiresite S phase... The other, black obruchevite, was subsequently renamed yttropyrochlore (Kupriyanova, 1970, unpublished). The Soviet Union's Commission of New Minerals (KNM) and Mineralogical Terminology have recommended the name *yttropyrochlore* replace this type of *obruchevite*.

†**o'brumpent**, *a. Obs. rare*$^{-0}$. [f. (reputed) L. *obrumpěre*, f. *ob-* (OB- 1 d) + *rumpěre* to break.]
1656 BLOUNT *Glossogr.*, *Obrumpent*, breaking or bursting.

†**o'brute**, *v. Obs. rare.* [f. L. *obrūt-*, ppl. stem of *obru-ěre* to overwhelm, bury; f. *ob-* (OB- 1 c) + *ru-ěre* to fall, rush down.] *trans.* To overwhelm, bury; to cover over.
1541 BECON *News out of Heaven* in *Early Wks.* (1843) 57 If ye seriously consider the misery wherewith ye were obruted and overwhelmed before. **1657** TOMLINSON *Renou's Disp.* 72 Obruted with dung after they were put into a new pot.

obs, slang abbrev. OBSERVATION. Cf. OBBO.
1943 *R.A.F. Jrnl.* Aug. 32 The Met. Officer has sent his obs through each hour in the usual way. **1970** O. NORTON *Dead on Prediction* v. 99 Hurry up. I'm keeping obs.

†**ob'salutate**, *v. Obs. rare*$^{-0}$. [f. ppl. stem of L. *obsalūtāre* to offer to salute, f. *ob-* (OB- 1 a) + *salūtāre* to salute.]
1623 COCKERAM, *Obsalutate*, to offer to salute. [**1644** Ridiculed in *Vindex Anglicus* 5, 6.]

†**ob'saturate**, *v. Obs. rare*$^{-0}$. [f. ppl. stem of L. *obsaturāre* to sate, cloy, f. *ob-* (OB- 1 b) + *saturāre* to fill.]
1623 COCKERAM, *Obsaturate*, to fill too much, to giue a man his fill.

obscene (əb'siːn), *a.* [ad. L. *obscēnus*, *obscænus* adverse, inauspicious, ill-omened; transf. abominable, disgusting, filthy, indecent: of doubtful etymology. Perh. immed. after F. *obscène* (1560 in Godef. *Compl.*).]

1. Offensive to the senses, or to taste or refinement; disgusting, repulsive, filthy, foul, abominable, loathsome.
1593 SHAKS. *Rich. II*, IV. i. 131 That in a Christian Climate, Soules refin'de Should shew so heynous, black, obscene a deed. **1664** H. MORE *Myst. Iniq.* ii. 5 Sorcerers.. are shut with obscene Dogs out of the holy City. **1725** POPE *Odyss.* xx. 263 In rags obscene decreed to roam. **1845** MRS. JAMESON *Mem. Early It. Paint.* II. 13 Hideous reptiles, as adders, lizards, toads,.. and other crawling and flying obscene and obnoxious things. **1869** RUSKIN *Q. of Air* iii. 178 The bright Wandel, divine of waters as Castaly, is filled .. with old shoes, obscene crockery, and ashes. **1875** 'MARK TWAIN' *Sk. New & Old* 148 The obscene Tumble-Bug. **1915** A. HUXLEY *Let.* 1 Feb. (1969) 65 Practically speaking, Sligger and myself are the only two possible people left alive in Oxford; even the few possibilities of last term have now vanished, leaving only a sort of obscene riff-raff. **1923** A. BENNETT *Riceyman Steps* I. x. 44 The three-story houses (with areas and basements) were all alike... The fronts of the door-steps were green with vegetable growth... The areas, except one or two, were obscene. The Square.. was merely decrepit, foul and slatternly. **1936** 'N. BLAKE' *Thou Shell of Death* i. 7 The shop windows, too, are piled with that diversity of obscene knick-knacks which nothing but the spirit of universal goodwill could surely tolerate. **1974** 'J. GRAHAM' *Bloody Passage* i. 19 Vietnam was the most obscene episode of the century. **1974** *Greenville* (S. Carolina) *News* 23 Apr. 1/8 Energy officials have already predicted that first-quarter oil profits will be 'embarrassingly high' or 'whoppers'. Sen. Henry Jackson, D-Wash., has said they'll be 'almost obscene'. **1974** *Observer* 1 Sept. 1/7 The result.. was another defeat for the image of football. In six hours of running skirmishes, 55 people were arrested; but what was particularly obscene was the mindlessness of the 3,000 or 4,000 youths who took part. **1977** *Time* 19 Dec. 19/2 Something in the very robustness of Germany's economy seemed to the terrorists and their sympathizers profoundly obscene.

2. Offensive to modesty or decency; expressing or suggesting unchaste or lustful ideas; impure, indecent, lewd. †*obscene parts*, privy parts (*obs.*).
1598 MARSTON *Pygmal.* xxxviii. 133 Be not obsceane though wanton in thy rimes. *a* **1656** BP. HALL *Rem. Wks.* (1660) 102 [He] lets his tongue loose to obscene and filthy Communication. **1667** MILTON *P.L.* I. 405 Chemos, th' obscene dread of Moabs Sons. **1698** FRYER *Acc. E. India & P.* 39 On the Walls.. were obscene Images. **1724** WATTS *Logic* I. iv. §3 Words that were once chaste, by frequent use grow obscene and uncleanly. **1725** POPE *Odyss.* XII. 115 Her [Scylla's] parts obscene the raging billows hide. **1825** MACAULAY *Ess.*, *Milton* (1851) I. 13 The rabble of Comus.. reeling in obscene dances. **1899** *Athenæum* 14 Apr. 475/2 Our later writers are saucy rather than obscene. **1959** *Act 7 & 8 Eliz. II* c. 66 § 1 An article shall be deemed to be obscene if its effect.. is, if taken as a whole, such as to tend to deprave and corrupt persons who are likely.. to read, see or hear the matter contained or embodied in it. **1964** *Daily Tel.* 11 Dec. 26/2 Appeal Court judges ruled.. that not only sex, but drug addiction, made a book obscene and depraved. **1972** *N.Y. Law Jrnl.* 31 Oct. 14/9 U.S.A. v. Various Articles of Obscene Merchandise.

†**3.** Ill-omened, inauspicious. (A Latinism.) *Obs.*
1635–56 COWLEY *Davideis* II. 818 The trembling Serpents close and silent lye The Birds obscene far from his Passage fly. **1833–6** J. EAGLES *Sketcher* (1856) 170 Evil-boding fowl, and bats obscene.

obscenely (əb'siːnlɪ), *adv.* [f. prec. + -LY[2].] In an obscene manner: **a.** Repulsively, loathsomely; **b.** Indecently, lewdly.
1588 SHAKS. *L.L.L.* IV. i. 145 Most inconie vulgar wit, When it comes so smoothly off, so obscenely, as it were, so fit. **1642** MILTON *Apol. Smect.* ii, The masoreths.. gave us this insulse rule out of their Talmud, that all words which in the law are writ obscenely, must be changd to more civil words. **1710** *Tatler* No. 259 ¶3 For speaking obscenely to the Lady Penelope Touchwood. **1740** C. PITT *Æneid* XII. 855 Then on a lofty beam, the matron ty'd The noose dishonest, and obscenely dy'd. **1922** F. SCOTT FITZGERALD *Beautiful & Damned* II. i. 157 This cowardice sprang out, became almost obscenely evident, then faded. **1964** R. CHURCH *Voyage Home* viii. 178 In those uncrowded years.. England was less obscenely populated. **1974** *Times* 9 Apr. 14/3 Broadmoor's forbidding buildings are obscenely overcrowded.

obsceneness (əb'siːnnɪs). [f. as prec. + -NESS.] The quality of being obscene; obscenity.
a **1637** B. JONSON *Discov.* Wks. (Rtldg.) 757/2 Herein is seen [the] elegance and propriety [of words], when we use them fitly,.. as when we.. escape obsceneness, and gain in the grace and property which helps significance. *a* **1700** DRYDEN (J.), Fables.. free from any note of infamy or obsceneness.

obscenity (əb'sɛnɪtɪ). [ad. L. *obscēnitās*, f. *obscēn-us* OBSCENE: perh. immed. ad. F. *obscénité* (1511 in Hatz.-Darm.).] Obscene quality or character: **a.** Impurity, indecency, lewdness (esp. of language); in *pl.* obscene words or matters.
1608 WILLET *Hexapla Exod.* 831 In many of their.. idoll seruices.. they vsed much obscenitie. **1643** MILTON *Divorce* II. iv, Worse.. then the worst obscenities of heathen superstition. **1709** POPE *Ess. Crit.* 530 No pardon vile Obscenity should find Tho' wit and art conspire to move your mind. **1829** SCOTT *Demonol.* vii. 208 The.. grossest obscenities ever impressed on paper. **1893** *Ch. Times* 6 Oct. 995/3 Pictures of foul obscenity not to be surpassed in Pompeii. **1971** J. TREVELYAN in *Mind & Mental Health* Winter 6/1 My own inclination is to apply the word 'pornography' to written or visual material concerned solely with sex, and the word 'obscenity' as a more general term covering pornography and also other things, especially violence. This view was held by D. H. Lawrence who suggested that obscenity was a matter of personal opinion, whereas pornography was something specific; he defined it as making sex dirty for money. **1972** *Police Rev.* 1 Dec. 1557/1 Mr. Chuter Ede.. asked the Commissioner whether the Yard's obscenity squad—as it was then— were judges of literature and art?

b. Foulness, loathsomeness; in *pl.* foul acts, dirty work.
a **1618** SYLVESTER *Tobacco Battered* 712 Consuming more, in their Obscure Obscænity, On Smoak and Smock, with their appendent Vanity, Then their brave Elders did, when they maintain'd Honour at home, and forrain Glory gain'd. **1621** BURTON *Anat. Mel.* II. iii. III. (1651) 323 Dishes.. nastily dressed by slovenly cooks, that after their obscenities, never wash their bawdy hands. **1807** C. BUCHANAN in *Academy* (1876) 21 Oct. 410/1 One of the victims.. was a well-made young man... He danced for a while before the idol [Juggernaut],.. then rushing suddenly to the wheels he shed his blood under the tower of obscenity. **1940** *Times* 19 Apr. 7/2 What one American newspaper stigmatizes as the 'obscenity' of the attack upon Norway. **1970** *Times* 21 Mar. 3/1 The obscenity of racial hatred has been vigorously propagated over the last few years. **1975** *New Yorker* 25 Aug. 31/3 We had said 'so long' to the U.S.A., had bade farewell to.. the obscenity of American life in our time. **1977** 'E. MCBAIN' *Long Time no See* xiii. 217 One-third of all the homicides committed in this city involved a victim and a murderer who didn't even *know* each other... Perfect strangers.. locked in the ultimate intimate obscenity.

†**ob'scenous**, *a. Obs.* [f. L. *obscēn-us* + -OUS.] = OBSCENE. Hence †**ob'scenously** *adv.*, †**ob'scenousness**.
1591 HARINGTON *Orl. Fur.* Pref. ¶7 In all Ariosto.. there is not a word of ribaldry or obscenousnesse. **1604** T. WRIGHT *Passions* VI. 333 Obscenous and naughty Bookes. **1606** WARNER *Alb. Eng.* XIV. To Rdr. (1612) 332 Their Literature obscenously So suteth to Scurrilitie.

obscura camera = *camera obscura*, CAMERA 4.
1706 in PHILLIPS.

ob'scurancy. *rare.* [f. next: see -ANCY.] The quality of being obscurant.
1825 *Edin. Rev.* XLII. 479 The time will certainly come when that power [Prussia] will repent that she ever sided with Barbarism, Obscurancy, and Despotism. **1970** *Nature* 1 Nov. 448/2 Throughout these early years, *Nature* offered its 'leadership' support against obscurancy and obstruction in high places.

obscurant (ɒb'skjʊərənt), *sb.* and *a.* [= Ger. *obscurant* (18th c.), f. L. *obscūrānt-*, pr. pple. of *obscūrāre* to darken, obscure: cf. mod.F. *obscurant* (Littré).]

A. *sb.* One who obscures; one who strives to prevent inquiry, enlightenment or reform.
1799 W. TAYLOR in *Monthly Mag.* VIII. 597 On their adversaries they endeavour to impose the names of *Finsterlinge*, *Obscurants*, or *Bedarkeners*. **1809–10** COLERIDGE *Friend* (1818) II. 153, I will venture to appeal to these self-obscurants whose faith dwells in the Land of the Shadow of Darkness. **1831** SIR W. HAMILTON *Discuss.* (1852) 211 The obscurants of that venerable seminary resisted only the more strenuously every effort at a reform within Cologne itself. **1900** E. CLODD in *Literary Guide* 1 Nov. 164/2 Here.. the battle between the psychological evolutionist and the theological obscurant still rages.

B. *adj.* That obscures or darkens; of or belonging to an obscurant: see A.
1878 GROSART *Introd. to H. More's Poems* 46/1 Recondite and obscurant speculation. **1879** G. MEREDITH *Egoist* I. v. 67 All around, she was yielding her hand to partners—obscurant males whose touch leaves a stain.

obscu'rantic, *a.* [f. OBSCURANT *sb.* and *a.* + -IC.] Opposed to enquiry or enlightenment. So **obscu'ranticism** = OBSCURANTISM. Also **obscuran'tistic** *a.*
1926 *Contemp. Rev.* Nov. 661 The book.. is full of warnings which sometimes are obvious and sometimes obscurantic. **1927** *Ibid.* Feb. 208 It would not be a work of truth or of love, but of well-meaning though mischievous obscuranticism. **1934** *Amer. Speech* IX. 278/1 The moralists .. are in reality ensuring that the minds of the young will develop into the same welter of obscurantistic obsessions as their own. **1941** F. MATTHIESSEN *Amer. Renaissance* XIV. iv. 653 Where Hawthorne's criticism runs no risk of being obscurantistic is in his portrait of Hollingsworth.

obscurantism (ɒb'skjʊərəntɪz(ə)m, ˌɒbskjʊə'rænt-). [f. OBSCURANT *sb.* and *a.* + -ISM: = Ger. *obscurantismus* (18th c.); in mod.F. *obscurantisme* (Littré).] The practice or principles of an obscurant; opposition to inquiry or enlightenment.
1834 GEN. P. THOMPSON *Exerc.* III. 4 When the clergy complain.. of the little influence they possess.. the hereditary 'obscurantism' of their caste is.. at once the reason and the defence. **1838–48** [see next]. **1860** MARSH *Lect. Eng. Lang.* 8 Continental liberty is threatened.. now by Muscovite barbarism, and now by pontifical obscurantism. **1883** *American* VII. 3 A victory of obscurantism and ignorance over enlightenment and progress.

obscurantist (ɒb'skjʊərəntɪst, ˌɒbskjʊə'rænt-), *sb.* and *a.* [f. as prec. + -IST.]

A. *sb.* One who opposes the progress of intellectual enlightenment.
1838–48 HARE *Guesses* (1874) 501 People have been sounding the alarm for many years past all over Europe

against what they call *obscurantism* and *obscurantists. Ibid.*, The true obscurantists are the passions, the prejudices, the blinding delusions of our nature, warpt by evil habits and self-indulgence; the real obscurantism is bigotry, in all its forms, which are many, and even opposite. **1858** GEN. P. THOMPSON *Audi Alt.* II. lxvii. 5 The obstacles thrown in the way of Education by the English Obscurantists.

B. *adj.* Of, pertaining to, or of the nature of an obscurantist; opposed to enlightenment.

1850 KINGSLEY *Alt. Locke* xvii, You working men complain of the clergy for being bigoted and obscurantist, and hating the cause of the people. **1882** GOLDW. SMITH in *19th Cent.* July 6 A priesthood as absolute and as obscurantist as the Druids.

†'obscurate, *ppl. a. Obs.* [ad. L. *obscūrāt-us*, pa. pple. of *obscūrāre* to obscure.] Obscured; darkened.

1471 RIPLEY *Comp. Alch.* v. xii. in Ashm. (1652) 151 The Son in hys uprysyng obscurate Shalbe. **1560** ROLLAND *Crt. Venus* II. 395 Except four houris the sone is obscurate.

obscuration (ˌɒbskjʊəˈreɪʃən). [ad. L. *obscūrātiōn-em*, n. of action f. *obscūrāre* to obscure. So mod.F. *obscuration* (Littré).]

1. The action of obscuring, darkening, or clouding over; the hiding or putting out of sight; obscured or dimmed state or condition; in *Astron.*, occultation, eclipse.

1471 RIPLEY *Comp. Alch.* Rec. in Ashm. (1652) 187 Then forth into the North procede by obscuratyon; Of the Red Man and hys Whyte Wyfe callyd Eclypsation. **1559** W. CUNNINGHAM *Cosmogr. Glasse* 103 If the time in the beginning of her obscuration be more, then that which I have heare placed. **1603** HOLLAND *Plutarch's Mor.* 1307 The obscuration or ecclipse of the Sunne. *a* **1715** BURNET (J.), As to the sun and moon, their obscuration or change of colour happens commonly before the eruption of a fiery mountain. **1816** PLAYFAIR *Nat. Phil.* (1819) II. 139 The moments..determine the beginning, the greatest obscuration, and the end of the eclipse. *a* **1852** MACGILLIVRAY *Nat. Hist. Dee Side* (1855) 178 Here, in the wood,..there is no continuous obscuration of the sky by the foliage.

transf. **1864** LOWELL *Biglow P.* II. Poet. Wks. (1879) 238 Our old dramatists are full of such obscurations..of the *th*, making *whe'r* of *whether*. **1884** *New Eng. Dict.* Introd. 24 By writing these [the original vowels] with the mark of obscuration, we are enabled to indicate at once the theoretical and the actual pronunciation. **1904** *Rep. Joint Comm. Phonetic Eng. Alphabet* (U.S.) ii. 12 In unstressed syllables the sounds undergo a change which, in the lack of a better name, may be called 'obscuration'. The quality and extent of this obscuration vary somewhat with the style of the discourse, the idiosyncrasy of the speaker and the nature of the neighboring consonants. **1935** J. S. KENYON *Amer. Pronunc.* (ed. 6) 101 Not all of these pairs of stressed and stressless vowels represent the same historical stage of obscuration of the unaccented vowel. **1962** A. C. GIMSON *Introd. Pronunc. Eng.* vii. 142 As a general rule, weak accent in OE led to the obscuration of short vowels and the shortening of long vowels.

2. *fig.* The darkening or dimming of intellectual light, of the mental vision or understanding, of the sense of words, of truth, etc.

1611 CORYAT *Crudities* 551 Not to the obscuration but the illustration of Gods glory. **1791** BOSWELL *Johnson* iii, To Johnson, whose supreme enjoyment was the exercise of his reason, the disturbance or obscuration of that faculty was the evil most to be dreaded. **1879** M. D. CONWAY *Demonol.* II. IV. xxix. 438 The obscuration of religion is superstition.

†ob'scurative, *a. Obs. rare*⁻¹. [f. L. *obscūrāt-*, ppl. stem of *obscūrāre* to obscure: see -IVE.] Tending or serving to obscure or render dark.

1664 H. MORE *Myst. Iniq.* 234 Antichronismus is an obscurative Scheme in Prophecy which sets down one measure of time for another; as a Week for Seven years.

obscure (əbˈskjʊə(r)), *a.* (*sb.*) [a. OF. *obscur* (14th c.), earlier *oscur* (12th c.) = It. *oscuro*, Sp., Pg. *obscuro*:—L. *obscūr-us*, f. *ob-* (OB- 1 c) + *scur-*, f. root *scu-*, Skr. *sku-* to cover; cf. L. *scū-tum* shield, Gr. σκευή attire, covering, σκῦτος hide.]

A. *adj.* **1. a.** Devoid of or deficient in light; dark, dim; hence, gloomy, dismal.

c **1400** *Rom. Rose* 5348 Love is right of sich nature; Now is fair, and now obscure,..And whylom dim, and whylom clere. *c* **1477** CAXTON *Jason* 19 b, Ha-a- obscure and derke night wherfore endurest thou so long. **1483** —— *G. de la Tour* E vij b, Put in a pryson which was right derke and obscure. **1596** SHAKS. *Merch. V.* II. vii. 51 Is't like that Lead containes her?..it were too grose To rib her seare-cloth in the obscure graue. **1611** BIBLE *Prov.* xx. 20 Who so curseth his father or his mother, his lampe shall be put out in obscure darkenesse. **1703** MAUNDRELL *Journ. Jerus.* (1732) 27 Their Chappel is large but obscure. **1799** COWPER *Castaway* 1 Obscurest night involved the sky. **1853** KANE *Grinnell Exp.* xliii. (1856) 396 The day misty and obscure.

b. ***obscure rays***, the dark or invisible heat-rays of the solar spectrum.

[**1794** J. HUTTON *Philos. Light*, etc. 44 Here is therefore a species of light which we may term obscure. **1860** TYNDALL *Glac.* II. i. 229 Rays which are obscure to some are luminous to others.] **1863** —— *Heat* 262 These incandescent coal-points emit an abundance of obscure rays—of rays of pure heat, which have no illuminating power. **1873** W. LEES *Acoustics* III. vii. 125 Most sources of heat emit heat rays, which are partly luminous and partly obscure.

†c. *fig.* Intellectually dark; unenlightened. *Obs.*

1588 FRAUNCE *Lawiers Log.* I. i. 2 The obscure head-pieces of one or two loytering Friers. **1596** BACON *Max. & Uses Com. Law* Ded., The more ignorant and obscure time undertooke to correct the more learned and flourishing.

2. Of, pertaining to, or frequenting the darkness; enveloped in darkness, and so eluding sight.

1605 SHAKS. *Macb.* II. iii. 65 The obscure Bird clamor'd the liue-long Night. **1667** MILTON *P.L.* II. 132 Thir Legions ..with obscure wing Scout farr and wide into the Realm of night. *Ibid.* IX. 159 Wrapt in mist Of midnight vapor, glide obscure, and prie In every Bush. *a* **1670** SPALDING *Troub. Chas. I* (1851) II. 468 In effect, we had no certainty quhair he went, he wes so obscure. **1882** G. F. ARMSTRONG *Garl. fr. Greece, Last Sortie* 268 There we mocked the keen pursuer's eye, And moved obscure in noiseless solitude.

3. Of colour or hue: Approaching black, dark, sombre; in later use, dingy, dull, not bright.

1490 CAXTON *Eneydos* xxii. 79 The holy waters dedicate to the sacryfice became blacke and obscure. **1604** E. G[RIMSTONE] *D'Acosta's Hist. Indies* VII. vii. 513 The which divided it selfe into two streames, whereof the one was of a very obscure azure. **1632** J. HAYWARD tr. *Biondi's Eromena* 54 Hang'd all over with blacke Arras... So as amongst all these obscure colours, there was not any whit discernable. **1650** BULWER *Anthropomet.* 167 It is an ill omen..if their nails decline to a livid or obscure colour. **1662** MERRETT tr. *Neri's Art of Glass* lviii, An obscure Yellow. **1725** BRADLEY *Fam. Dict.* s.v. *Presage*, If the new Moon has obscure Horns, and that the upper Horn is obscurer than the lower, it will rain in the Wane of the Moon. **1819** G. SAMOUELLE *Entomol. Compend.* 136 Wings partly obscure, partly diaphanous. **1826** KIRBY & SP. *Entomol.* IV. 284 *Obscure*,..a surface which reflects the light but little. **1890** A. R. WALLACE *Darwinism* 11 An obscure colour may render concealment more easy for some.

4. a. Without clearness of form or outline; indistinct; undefined; hardly perceptible to the eye; faint, 'light'.

1593 FALE *Dialling* 45 Draw an obscure or light line from A. to B. **1669** STURMY *Mariner's Mag.* v. (1684) 16 You must rule your Paper or Parchment with an obscure Meridian Line, and Parallel Lines. **1676** *Lond. Gaz.* No. 1115/4 The Nag hath two obscure flesh Brands on his Buttocks. **1751** JOHNSON *Rambler* No. 160 ¶2 What is distant is in itself obscure, and, when we have no wish to see it, easily escapes our notice. **1828** STARK *Elem. Nat. Hist.* II. 341 Wings slightly tinted with brown, and the nerves obscure. **1834** MRS. SOMERVILLE *Connex. Phys. Sc.* iv. (1849) 34 The satellites eclipse Jupiter, sometimes passing like obscure spots across his surface.

b. With reference to other senses: Indistinctly perceived, felt, or heard; indistinct. *spec.* of a vowel sound, weak and centralized; reduced.

[**1568** T. SMITH *De Recta et Emendata Linguæ Anglicæ Scriptione Dialogus* 14 Si Galli suum habent fœmininum obscurum, siue fuscum *e*, quod in fine dictionis positum, propè nihil sonat, auditur tamen, & apud illos est frequentissimum, nostræ linguæ prorsus incognitum.] **1597** A. M. tr. *Guillemeau's Fr. Chirurg.* 4/1 He hath a smalle, feeble, and obscure pulse. *a* **1637** B. JONSON *Eng. Gram.* iii, E..where it endeth, and soundeth obscure and faintly. [**1653** J. WALLIS *Grammatica Linguæ Anglicanæ* i. 6 Eodem loci..formatur Gallorum *e* fœmininum; sono nempe obscuro. *Ibid.* 7 Ibidem etiam... Sonatur *ò*, vel *ŭ*, obscurum.] **1656** RIDGLEY *Pract. Physic* 220 An obscure voice. **1665** O. PRICE *Vocal Organ* B3ᵛ The ,*e*, is twofold. 1. Clear; as in let... 2. Obscure, onely when *e* is short before *r*, as in her, liberty, brother, father, merchant. *Ibid.* B4 The short ŭ, and obscure *ò*, are formed in the throat, yet narrower then *è*. **1695** *Writing Scholar's Compan.* x. 36, o, is obscure, like (oo) or short (u)..before (m) as, *come* [etc.]. **1791** WALKER *Eng. Dict., Pronunciation* 23 Nothing tends more to tarnish and vulgarize the pronunciation than this short and obscure sound of the unaccented *u*. **1874** SWEET *Eng. Sounds* 63 The change of the old *u* into ə was fully established in the Transition period..Wallis calls it an obscure sound. **1884** *New Eng. Dict.* Introd. 24 In the Vowels, ordinary (or short) quantity is unmarked..obscure quality by (◡). **1892** W. W. SKEAT *Primer Eng. Etymol.* ii. 25 In the A.S. *Dūn-stān*..the *ā* has been shortened, and is now obscure. **1904** *Rep. Joint Comm. Phonetic Eng. Alphabet* (U.S.) iii. 30 The obscure [ə] is the goal to which the most of the other vowels tend when not supported by the stress. **1909** O. JESPERSEN *Mod. Eng. Gram.* I. ix. 249 Portuguese short *a* is an obscure vowel. **1924** J. S. KENYON *Amer. Pronunc.* 107 Naturalness..is gained only by observing the normal relation between strest and unstrest syllables, distinct and obscure vowels. **1967** J. D. O'CONNOR *Better Eng. Pronunc.* v. 106 In initial position, as in..*attempt*,.. *account*,..*observe*, you must again keep it very short and

5. Of a place: Not readily seen or discovered; hidden, retired, secret; remote from observation.

1484 CAXTON *Fables of Alfonce* i, He anone toke hym secretely in to his hows, and ledde hym in to a sure and obscure place. *c* **1500** *Melusine* 328 He departed & went by a waye obscure tyl he fond a feld. **1588** SHAKS. *Tit. A.* II. iii. 77 Why are you sequestred from all your traine?.. And wandred hither to an obscure plot. **1660** BLOUNT *Boscobel* 23 Penderel had conveyed Him into the obscurest part of it [a coppice]. **1796** BURKE *Let. Noble Ld.* Wks. VIII. 6 They pursue, even such as me, into the obscurest retreats, and haul them before their revolutionary tribunals. **1832** LYTTON *Eugene A.* I. iii, I also keep arms even in this obscure and safe retreat.

6. a. Inconspicuous, undistinguished, unnoticed.

1555 EDEN *Decades* 312 Great thynges procede & increase of smaul & obscure begynnynges. **1664** POWER *Exp. Philos.* I. 60 If you take Nature at the rise..in her rudimental and obscure beginnings. **1715** DE FOE *Fam. Instruct.* (1841) I. Introd. 5 The scene of this little action is not laid very remote, or the circumstance obscure. *a* **1854** H. REED *Lect. Eng. Hist.* v. (1876) 14 The small and obscure beginnings of great political institutions.

b. Of persons, their station, descent, etc.: Not illustrious or noted; unknown to fame; humble, lowly, mean.

a **1548** HALL *Chron., Hen. VII*, 33 The yonge man..was discended of a basse and obscure parentage. **1555** EDEN *Decades* To Rdr. (Arb.) 49 It had byn better for hym to haue byn obscure & vnknowen. **1662** WOOD *Life* Nov. (O.H.S.) I. 462 Died a little better than in an obscure condition. **1713** STEELE *Englishm.* No. 10. 69 Be obscure and innocent, rather than conspicuous and guilty. **1750** GRAY *Elegy* 30 Let not Ambition mock their useful toil, Their homely joys, and destiny obscure. **1878** J. P. HOPPS *Jesus* vi. 25 Jesus called poor fishermen, sorrowful sinners, obscure working-men, neglected children.

7. *fig.* **a.** Not manifest to the mind or understanding; imperfectly known or understood; not clear or plain; hidden, doubtful, vague, uncertain.

1432–50 tr. *Higden* (Rolls) II. 55 There be other names of cities founde in cronicles obscure to the intellecte. **1484** CAXTON *Fables of Alfonce* iii, Of a sentence gyuen upon a derke and obscure cause. **1596** DRAYTON *Legends* i. 96 And brought the most obscurest Things to light. **1632** J. HAYWARD tr. *Biondi's Eromena* 16 The King of Corsica, who gave no obscure signes of enmity. **1667** MILTON *P.L.* VIII. 192 Not to know at large of things remote From use, obscure and suttle. **1732** ARBUTHNOT *Rules of Diet* 315 To know the Cause and seat of this Disease, which is often obscure. **1830** LYELL *Princ. Geol.* I. 261 Yet geologists have presumed to resort to a nascent order of things..to explain every obscure phenomenon. **1878** HUXLEY *Physiogr.* 65 The origin of hail is still obscure.

b. Of words, statements, explanations, meanings: Not perspicuous; not clearly expressed; hard to understand. Also, of a speaker or writer.

1495 *Act 11 Hen. VII*, c. 8 Which acte..is so obscure derke and diffuse that the true entent of the makers therof cannot perfitely be undrestond. **1553** T. WILSON *Rhet.* 61 b, In seekyng to be short be not obscure. **1573–80** BARET *Alv.* O 11 A darke, obscure and crabbed style. **1651** HOBBES *Leviath.* IV. xliv. 339 Some of the obscurer places of the New Testament. **1794** PALEY *Evid.* (1825) II. 265 This discourse was obscure. **1865** GROTE *Plato* I. i. 27 Herakleitus of Ephesus, known throughout antiquity by the denomination of the Obscure. **1878** R. W. DALE *Lect. Preach.* viii. 230 If there are sentences which are at all obscure.

B. *sb.* **1.** Obscurity, darkness; the 'outer darkness'.

1667 MILTON *P.L.* II. 406 Who shall..through the palpable obscure find out His uncouth way. **1725** POPE *Odyss.* XIX. 458 Cautious in th' obscure he hop'd to fly The curious search of Euryclea's eye. **1812** S. ROGERS *Voy. Columbus* XII. 12 In his progress thro' the dread obscure. **1820** LAMB *Elia* Ser. I. *Oxf. in Vac.*, As though a palpable obscure had dimmed the face of things.

2. Indistinctness of outline or colour.

1792 A. YOUNG *Trav. France* (1889) 30 An animated.. mass of infinitely varied parts—melting gradually into the distant obscure. *a* **1839** PRAED *Poems* (1864) II. 353 And, in the calm obscure of even, All things and colours fade.

3. *Painting. pl.* The 'shades' of a picture.

1814 W. TAYLOR in *Monthly Mag.* XXXVIII. 213 Distance progressively the light, and you will weaken both the clears and the obscures.

obscure (əbˈskjʊə(r)), *v.* [f. OBSCURE *a.*, or the corresp. L. *obscūrā-re* to obscure, darken, OF. *obscurer*, earlier *oscurer*; cf. It. *oscurare* to darken.]

1. a. *trans.* To make obscure or dark, to involve in darkness; to darken; to deprive of light or brightness; to dim.

1432–50 tr. *Higden* (Rolls) VII. 411 That kynge dreamed that..the bloode of hym obscurede and hidde the sonne. *a* **1547** SURREY *Æneid* ii. (1557) C iij b, The cloude..Whoes moisture doth obscure allthinges about. **1592** SHAKS. *Ven. & Ad.* 728 Now of this dark night I perceive the reason: Cynthia for shame obscures her silver shine. **1651** HOBBES *Leviath.* I. ii. 5 The light of the Sun obscureth the light of the Starres. **1703** POPE *Winter* 30 See gloomy clouds obscure the cheerful day! **1781** COWPER *Hope* 534 Amazed that shadows should obscure the sight Of one whose birth was in a land of light. **1853** LYTTON *My Novel* III. xxii, The cuttle-fish, that by obscuring the water sails from its enemy.

b. *intr.* (for *refl.*) To become dark.

1500–20 DUNBAR *Poems* lxxii. 84 The erde did trimmill, the stanis claif, The sone obscurit of his licht.

c. *transf. trans.* To make obscure in quality of sound, etc.; *spec.* to articulate (a vowel) in a weaker, more centralized position.

a **1637** JONSON *Eng. Gram.* (1640) I. iii. 36 Where it [*sc.* e] endeth a last Syllable,..it either soundeth flat... Or, it passeth away obscur'd, like the faint *i.* as in these, *Written.. divel*, &c. *a* **1790** B. FRANKLIN *Autobiogr.* in *Writings* (1905) I. 358, I found his voice distinct till I came near Front Street, when some noise in that street obscur'd it. **1873** J. A. H. MURRAY *Dial. S. Counties Scot.* 132 In other positions the vowel sounds are dulled or obscured to such an extent that they lose their original quality and fall into the obscure *ě* described. **1884** *New Eng. Dict.* Introd. 24 In modern English speech, vowels are regularly obscured in syllables that have neither primary nor subordinate stress, especially in those that follow the main stress. **1924** J. S. KENYON *Amer. Pronunc.* 108 The student should rid himself of a common misconception; namely, that the obscuring of certain consonants and vowels owing to lack of stress on syllables or words is the result of a corruption of good English. **1934** *S.P.E. Tract* XXXIX. 621 'Short *e*'. This is rarely raised to [*i*], and never, except before *-r*, obscured to [ə]. **1934** S. ROBERTSON *Devel. Mod. Eng.* (1936) vii. 230 Obscuring and loss of formerly distinctive vowel sounds, and dropping of consonants in phonetically difficult combinations.., are both to be found in Old English. **1935** J. S. KENYON *Amer. Pronunc.* (ed. 6) 90 The vowels of unaccented syllables have gradually become obscured to a sound quite different in resonance, or quality, from what they had formerly been. **1962** A. C. GIMSON *Introd.*

Pronunc. Eng. vi. 80 Vowels under weak accent are increasingly obscured to [ə] or [ɪ], or are elided.

2. To dim or lessen the lustre or glory of; 'to put in the shade'; to overshadow or outshine.

1548 LATIMER *Serm. Ploughers* (Arb.) 30 To deface and obscure Godes glory. 1591 SHAKS. *1 Hen. VI*, v. iv. 22 You haue suborn'd this man Of purpose, to obscure my Noble birth. 1781 J. MOORE *View Soc. It.* (1790) II. lxviii. 327 His liberality..obscured the glory of all who had preceded him in the office. 1819 SHELLEY *Cenci* III. i. 102 That faith no agony shall obscure in me. 1874 GREEN *Short Hist.* iii. §4. 129 As yet..the fortunes of the University [of Oxford] were obscured by the glories of Paris.

3. a. To cover or hide from view; to conceal.

1606 G. W[OODCOCKE] *Hist. Ivstine* XXXIV. 112 He lay hoping to obscure himselfe in an vnfrequented and desolate place. 1632 LITHGOW *Trav.* v. 210 Blood-thirsty Arabians, who in holes, caues, and bushes, lie obs[c]ured, waiting for ..Trauellers. 1678 MRS. BEHN *Sir P. Fancy* II. i, What shall I do? 'tis too late to obscure myself. 1697 DAMPIER *Voy.* I. 70, I have lain obscured in the evening near..where they resort, and..have kill'd 14 of them. 1767 *Cries of Blood* 22 They plac'd me below..and obscur'd me with boards. 1810 SCOTT *Lady of L.* III. iv, His grisled beard and matted hair Obscured a visage of despair. 1866 G. MACDONALD *Ann. Q. Neighb.* xxxii. (1878) 548 The moon was now quite obscured.

†**b.** *intr.* (for *refl.*) To hide oneself. *Obs.*

1603 PETOWE in Farr *S.P. Jas. I* (1848) 105 When you might see all pleasures shun the light, And love obscuer, at Eliza's fall. 1623 FLETCHER & ROWLEY *Maid in Mill* IV. ii, How! there's bad tidings: I must obscure and hear it. 1632 SHIRLEY *Changes* IV. i, Here Ile obscure. [Withdrawes.]

4. To conceal from knowledge or observation; to keep secret the identity of; to keep dark; to disguise. Also *refl.* †**a.** Of persons. *Obs.*

c 1530 L. COX *Rhet.* (1899) 88, I wolde that they wolde set the penne to the paper, and by their industry obscure my rude ignoraunce. 1599 SHAKS. *Hen. V*, I. i. 63 The Prince obscur'd his Contemplation Vnder the Veyle of Wildnesse. 1614 RALEIGH *Hist. World* II. (1634) 405 David..fled thence ..to Achis,..Prince of Geth: where to obscure himselfe, he was forc't to counterfeit both simplicitie and distraction.

b. Of things.

1757 FOOTE *Author* I. Wks. 1799 I. 143 Ay, Robin, there's no obscuring extraordinary talents. 1821 SHELLEY *Epipsych.* 33 Thou Mirror In whom..All shapes look glorious which thou gazest on! Ay, even the dim words which obscure thee now Flash, lightning-like, with unaccustomed glow.

5. To render dim or vague to the understanding; to render unintelligible. †*to obscure oneself from*, to render one's meaning obscure to (*obs.*).

1584 in Spottiswood *Hist. Ch. Scot.* VI. (1677) 331 He at first obscured himself from me, and would not be plain. 1613 PURCHAS *Pilgrimage* (1614) 129 To obscure, rather than illustrate, that which is so..plainly there expressed. 1751 JOHNSON *Rambler* No. 156 ¶2 The evidence [is] obscured by inaccurate argumentation. 1840 MILL *Diss. & Disc.* (1875) I. 409 This language..serves not to elucidate, but to disguise and obscure. 1875 OUSELEY *Mus. Form* xii. 57 It [the fugue form for choruses] should be freely adopted whenever it does not too much obscure the sense of the words.

Hence **ob'scuring** *vbl. sb.* and *ppl. a.*

1602 MARSTON *Antonio's Rev.* II. iv, Under the hatches of obscuring earth. 1611 COTGR., *Obscurcissement*, an obscuring, darkening, dimming, ouercasting, ouershadowing. 1697 DAMPIER *Voy.* I. 494 This obscuring of the Sun [by clouds] at noon, is commonly sudden. 1750 tr. *Leonardus' Mirr. Stones* 128 The star..is hid with obscuring clouds. 1873 J. A. H. MURRAY *Dial. S. Counties Scot.* 133 To indicate this obscuring of unaccented vowels. 1885 *Athenæum* 26 Sept. 398/2 The relations between Eve and her brother, little Tom, until the premature obscuring of that bright young piece of manhood.

obscured (əb'skjʊəd, *poet.* -rɪd), *ppl. a.* [-ED¹.]

1. Made obscure; darkened, dimmed; hidden from the sight or perception; fallen into obscurity.

1590 SHAKS. *Com. Err.* I. i. 67 What obscured light the heauens did grant. 1598 —— *Merry W.* v. iii. 15 They are all couch'd in a pit hard by Hernes Oake, with obscur'd Lights. 1763 EDWARDS in *Phil. Trans.* LIII. 229 Reflections of obscured things in air, when reflected from the water. 1891 T. HARDY *Tess* (1900) 19/1 Pages of works devoted to extinct, half-extinct, obscured, and ruined families.

2. *Phonetics.* Of a vowel sound: having a neutral, centralized articulation; weakened; reduced.

1925 G. P. KRAPP *Eng. Lang. in Amer.* II. 250 Difficulty was expressed in disposing of this unstressed and obscured vowel. 1934 M. K. POPE *From Latin to Mod. French* v. 119 The obscured neutral vowel in use in Modern English is buccal and central, the one in Modern French is a slightly rounded front sound. 1935 J. S. KENYON *Amer. Pronunc.* (ed. 6) 90 The same spelling is kept for the obscured vowel that was used to spell it before it became obscured. 1962 A. C. GIMSON *Introd. Pronunc. Eng.* vii. 120 As the great variety of spellings indicates, /ə/ may represent the reduced (obscured, 'schwa') form of any vowel or diphthong in an unaccented position.

Hence **ob'scuredly** (-rɪdlɪ), *adv.*

1628 GAULE *Pract. The.* (1629) 402 This numbred while [the forty days between resurrection and ascension] Christ passed not..obscuredly; but appeared oft. *a* 1641 BP. MOUNTAGU *Acts & Mon.* (1642) 346 This continued among Pagans..though obscuredly.

obscurely (əb'skjʊəlɪ), *adv.* [f. OBSCURE *a.* + -LY².] In an obscure way, manner, or degree.

1. a. Darkly; dimly, dully; not brightly or luminously. **b.** So as to be indistinct to the sight or other sense; dimly, indistinctly. **c.** With a dark, sombre, or dingy colour; dully.

c 1596 JOHNSON *Seven Champions* II. vii. (1852) 194 They stood obscurely behind the trees. 1620 ROWLANDS *Night Raven* 28 A night..obscurely darke, or Moone light cleere. 1632 J. HAYWARD tr. *Biondi's Eromena* 54 Torches, which (though of pure white wax) were yet all artificially made obscurely browne. *a* 1839 PRAED *Poems* (1864) II. 420 There my Whole, obscurely bright, Still shows his little lamp by night. 1845 DARWIN *Voy. Nat.* xxi. (1873) 498 It is composed of obscurely-stratified hard sandstone. 1871 —— *Desc. Man* II. xii. 25 The young are obscurely tinted. 1871 ROBY *Lat. Gram.* I. Pref. 73 In English we are in the habit of changing, or pronouncing obscurely, short vowels in unaccented syllables.

2. *fig.* With obscurity of meaning, expression, or exposition; not plainly or clearly.

1527 R. THORNE in Hakluyt *Voy.* (1589) 253 It [a map] cannot be but obscurely set out. 1563 WINȜET *Four Scoir Thre Quest.* Wks. 1888 I. 107 Quhy hef ȝe setfurth the said pennance sa obscuirlie? 1632 J. HAYWARD tr. *Biondi's Eromena* 48 By your absence have I obscurely ghessed, and by your letters clearely understood of the strange resolution. 1797–1803 FOSTER in *Life & Corr.* (1846) I. 195 To reveal, though obscurely. 1838 DICKENS *Nich. Nick.* lv, She even went so far as to hint obscurely at an attachment.

3. In obscurity; inconspicuously.

1592 GREENE *Groat's W. Wit* (1617) 8 You will bee accounted..a peasant, if ye liue thus obscurelie. 1691 WOOD *Ath. Oxon.* I. 260 Most Poets dye poor, and consequently obscurely. 1762–71 H. WALPOLE *Vertue's Anecd. Paint.* (1786) III. 223 He lived obscurely in Knave's-acre, in partnership with a house-painter. 1876 BROWNING *St. Martin's S.* v, Though corpses rot obscurely, Ghosts escape.

ob'scurement. *rare.* [f. OBSCURE *v.* + -MENT.] = OBSCURATION; production of obscurity.

1658 R. FRANCK *North. Mem.* (1821) 282 The standard royal was advanced by Charles the First..not far from the obscurements of Mortimer's Hole. *a* 1703 POMFRET *Dies Noviss.* Poems (1790) 139 Now bolder fires appear, And o'er the palpable obscurement sport, Glaring and gay as falling Lucifer. 1834 *Fraser's Mag.* X. 659 There is a noble vein of poetry..which shines through all the obscurement of translation.

ob'scureness. Now *rare.* [f. OBSCURE *a.* + -NESS.] The quality or condition of being OBSCURE (in various senses); = OBSCURITY.

1509 BARCLAY *Shyp of Folys* (1570) 53 To knowe of Logike..For by argument it maketh euident Muche obscurenes. 1555 EDEN *Decades* 129 The obscurenesse of the caue into the which he was farre entered. 1570 BILLINGSLEY *Euclid* x. xviii. 247 The difficulty and obscurenes of this booke. 1605 BACON *Adv. Learn.* I. iii. §2 The privateness or obscureness..of life of contemplative men. 1727 BRADLEY *Fam. Dict.* s.v. *Draught horse*, If you discover some Spot, Obscureness, or Whiteness therein. 1754 EDWARDS *Freed. Will* IV. viii. 247 The Imperfection of our manner of conceiving of Things, and the Obscureness of Language. 1873 M. ARNOLD *Lit. & Dogma* (1876) 82 The characters of humility, obscureness, and depression, were commonly attributed to the Jewish Messiah.

ob'scurer. *rare.* [f. OBSCURE *v.* + -ER¹.] One who or that which obscures.

1630 LORD *Banians & Persees* 24 A waster and obscurer of such louelynesse. 1869 *Daily News* 23 Nov., It was fortunate that we were not dependent for illumination on these patent obscurers.

†**ob'scurify,** *v. Obs. rare.* [f. L. *obscūr-us* OBSCURE *a.* + -FY: cf. obs. F. *obscurifier* (Scarron 1650).] *trans.* To render obscure; to hide.

1622 WITHER *Mistr. Philar.* in Arb. *Garner* IV. 367 Not that I..wish obscurified Her matchless Beauty. 1826 BENTHAM in *Westm. Rev.* VI. 494 Misapplication of any one of the three obscurified terms—*trust, use,* and *confidence*.

ob'scuringly, *adv.* [-LY².] In an obscuring manner; so as to obscure.

1902 *New Liberal Rev.* Aug. 317 The Celtic fringes hang obscuringly over our eyes, as fringes do under befeathered hats in the Old Kent Road.

ob'scurism. *rare.* [f. OBSCURE *a.* + -ISM.] = OBSCURANTISM.

1841 *Fraser's Mag.* XXIII. 142 We have objected to the theological obscurism of blind submission which some are preaching as a cure for the evils of the day. *Ibid.*, To maintain that obscurism in religious doctrine.

obscurist (əb'skjʊərɪst). [f. OBSCURE *a.* or *v.* + -IST.] = OBSCURANTIST *sb.*

1925 *Chambers's Jrnl.* Mar. 196/1 He is no faddist or eccentric, no obscurist of any kind, but one who catches at charms in human life and paints them.

obscurity (əb'skjʊərɪtɪ). Also 5 obscurete(e, -itee, 5–6 obscurte, 6–7 -itie. [a. F. *obscurité* (1305 in Hatz.-Darm.), also in OF. *obscurté, oscurté*, ad. L. *obscūrität-em*, f. *obscūr-us* OBSCURE *a.*: see -ITY.] The quality or condition of being obscure.

1. Absence of light (total or partial); darkness; dimness, dullness; *concr.* a dark place.

1481 CAXTON *Myrr.* II. xxv. 118 This thynge is the clowde, But it hath not so moche obscurete that it taketh fro vs the clernes of the day. *c* 1500 *Melusine* 22 None obscurte or darknes was seen about it. 1611 BIBLE *Isa.* lix. 9 We waite for light, but behold obscuritie. 1791 MRS. RADCLIFFE *Rom. Forest* i, The obscurity of the dawn confined his views. 1853 KANE *Grinnell Exp.* xlvii. (1856) 444 A strange, palpable obscurity..gradually wrapped itself over every thing. 1854 J. S. C. ABBOTT *Napoleon* (1855) II. xx. 377 Caulaincourt.. galloped in the deep obscurity by another route to Paris.

2. The quality or condition of being unknown, inconspicuous, or insignificant.

1619 DRAYTON *Idea* x, Thy gifts thou in obscurity dost waste. 1659 B. HARRIS *Parival's Iron Age* 237 A certain Fellow of the very dregs of the People, who had dyed in the obscurity of his birth, had not this furious revolt..elevated him. 1730–46 THOMSON *Autumn* 1023 The sigh for suffering Worth Lost in obscurity. 1873 HAMERTON *Intell. Life* x. iii. (1875) 349 The greater number have to remain in positions of obscurity.

b. An obscure or unknown person.

1822 *Athenæum* 14 Jan. 51/2 Herr Zart goes through the whole number of obscurities from Leibnitz to Kant. 1890 B. L. GILDERSLEEVE *Ess. & Stud.* 306, I left them all and married this poor, young obscurity.

3. The quality or condition of not being clearly known or comprehended.

1474 CAXTON *Chesse* 109 The thought is enuoluped in obscurete and vnder the clowdes. 1603 HOLLAND *Plutarch's Mor.* 62 In Philosophie, where at the first there seemeth.. to be some strangenesse, obscuritie, and I wot not what barrennesse. 1674 in *Essex Papers* (Camden) I. 232, I must confess I have ever bin uneasy to finde things in so much obscurity. 1813 J. THOMSON *Lect. Inflam.* 503 To remove any part of the obscurity which prevails with regard to the nature and progress of mortification. 1876 HUMPHREYS *Coin-Coll. Man.* ii. 7 The precise date of the origin of coined money is lost in obscurity.

4. Lack of perspicuity in language; uncertainty of meaning; unintelligibleness.

1538 STARKEY *England* II. i. 145 Al obscuryte and darkenes both in wrytyng and in al communycatyon sprynging therof. 1602 CAMPION *Eng. Poesy* Wks. (Bullen) 231 There is no writing too brief that, without obscurity, comprehends the intent of the writer. 1751 JOHNSON *Rambler* No. 169 ¶13 One of the most pernicious effects of haste is obscurity. 1870 SWINBURNE *Ess. & Stud.* (1875) 273 Real and offensive obscurity comes merely of inadequate thought embodied in inadequate language.

b. An obscure point; an unintelligible, or not clearly intelligible, speech or passage.

1398 TREVISA *Barth. De P.R.* I. (1495) 3 Desyrous to vnderstonde the obscuretees or derknesse of holy scriptures. 1729 BUTLER *Serm.* Pref., But even obscurities arising from other causes than the abstruseness of the argument may not be always inexcusable. 1875 JOWETT *Plato* (ed. 2) III. 43 The obscurities of early Greek poets arose necessarily out of the state of language.

†**ob'scurous,** *a. Obs. rare*⁻¹. [f. L. *obscūr-us* OBSCURE + -OUS.] Dark, gloomy, obscure.

1491 CAXTON *Vitas Patrum* (W. de W. 1495) I. xlviii. 91 b/2 A countree where the sonne ne the mone dyde not shyne, but there were derke tenebrees and obscurous.

‖**obscurum per obscurius** (ɒb'skjʊərəm pɜː(r) ɒb'skjʊərɪəs), *phr.* [Late L., lit. the unclear (explained) by means of the more unclear.] An unclear argument or proposition (expressed) in terms of one that is even less clear; such an explanation. (Cf. IGNOTUM PER IGNOTIUS.)

[1616 W. CLERK *Withals's Dict. Eng. & Lat.* (rev. ed.) 574 *Obscurum per obscurius.* I am as wise as I was before.] 1892 C. A. M. FENNELL *Stanford Dict.* 580/1 *Obscūrum per obscūrius*, phr.: Late Lat.: the obscure by the more obscure. 1949 K. DAVIS *Human Society* viii. 202 At its best it was an explanation *obscurum per obscurius.* 1952 G. SARTON *Hist. Sci.* I. viii. 200 Herodotus..was already combining Pythagorean ideas with Egyptian, Orphic, and Bacchic ones, and he mixed up the story of Pythagoras with that of Zalmoxis, thus explaining *obscurum per obscurius.* 1959 *Listener* 8 Jan. 58/1 Alexander's attempt to describe certain other relations in nature on the analogy of this may seem like an attempt to explain *obscurum per obscurius.*

obsecate, erron. form of OBCÆCATE.

obsecrate ('ɒbsɪkreɪt), *v. rare, pedantic.* [f. L. *obsecrāt-*, ppl. stem of *obsecrāre* to beseech, entreat (prop. in the name or for the sake of something sacred), f. *ob* on account of + *sacrāre* to make sacred, f. *sacer, sacr-* sacred.] *trans.* To entreat earnestly, as in the name of something sacred; to beseech, supplicate (a person); to beg (a thing).

1597 A. M. tr. *Guillemeau's Fr. Chirurg.* *v, I most humblely obsecrate all men to receave gratefully this my laboure. 1601 MUNDAY & CHETTLE *Downf. Robt. Earl Huntington* II. ii. in Hazl. *Dodsley* VIII. 135 [*Ralph, bombastically*] I obsecrate ye with all courtesy..you would vouch or deign to proceed. 1767 CAMPBELL *Lexiph.* 113 [*in ridicule*] I obsecrate you, Mr. Doctor, to concede me leave of absence. 1818 SCOTT *Rob Roy* xxxi, Andrew Fairservice employed his lungs in obsecrating a share of Dougal's protection.

obsecration (ɒbsɪ'kreɪʃən). [ad. L. *obsecrātiōn-em*, n. of action f. *obsecrāre* to OBSECRATE: perh. immed. a. F. *obsécration* (13th c. in Godef.).]

1. Earnest entreaty, supplication; sometimes in orig. L. sense, Entreaty made in the name of the deity or some sacred thing.

1382 WYCLIF *Ps.* cxlii[i]. 1 Lord..parceyue myn obsecracioun [Vulg. *obsecrationem*]. —— *Prov.* xviii. 23 With obsecraciouns speketh the pore man. 1482 *Monk of Evesham* (Arb.) 25 For hys enmyes..he made meruailous prayers and obsecracyons. 1577 tr. *Bullinger's Decades* (1592) 914 In inuocation or petition we comprehend obsecration, which is a more vehement praier. *a* 1699 STILLINGFLEET (J.), That these were comprehended under the sacra, is manifest from the old form of obsecration. 1854 FABER *Growth in Holiness* xv. (1872) 275 Obsecration is the adding of some motive or adjuration to our demands [in prayer]. 1883 STEVENSON *Silverado Sq.* iii. (1886) 17 Behold the analyst..raising hands in obsecration, attesting god Lycœus.

b. *Rhet.* (See quots.)

1609 R. BARNERD *Faithf. Sheph.* 67 Obsecration; this is making of request to the Hearers..intreating the auditory to yeeld some thing for their good. **1837** *Encycl. Brit.* (ed. 7) XVI. 319/1 *Obsecration*, in *Rhetoric*, a figure by which the orator implores the assistance of God or man.

2. *spec.* One of the suffrages or prayers of the Litany introduced by the word 'by' (L. *per*).

1877 E. DANIEL *Prayerbook* 172 The Obsecrations which commence at ver. 11 are prayers for deliverance from sin and its consequences. **1890** MRS. PENNY *Caste & Creed* II. v. 133 He began the Litany..he selected certain of the obsecrations.

Hence **obse'crationary** *a.* = next.

1829 T. HOOK *Bank to Barnes* 76 The obsecrationary objurgation is beautiful.

†**obsecratory**, *a. Obs. rare.* [f. L. ppl. stem *obsecrāt-* (see above), or *obsecrātor* beseecher: see -ORY.] Characterized by obsecration.

1624 BP. HALL *Peace Maker* §26 (R.) That gracious and obsecratory charge of the blessed Apostle of the Gentiles.

ob'sede, *v. rare.* [a. F. *obséder* (16–17th c.), ad. L. *obsidēre*: cf. POSSEDE *v.*] *trans.* = OBSESS *v.* Hence **ob'seding** *ppl. a.*

1885 R. L. & F. STEVENSON *Dynamiter* 132 Half a minute ..and he would be free..from his obseding lodger. **1892** *Pall Mall G.* 21 Nov. 2/2 The Devil sugared over in a basket of fruit..obsedes the body of a Bavarian boy.

†**ob'seek**, *v. Obs. rare*$^{-1}$. [app. f. L. *ob-* (OB- 1 a) + SEEK *v.*, through association with L. *obsequī*: see next.] *trans.* To seek to obtain.

1646 J. BENBRIGGE *Vsura Acc.* 28 None but famous.. persons were wont to obseeke that Office of Censorship.

†**ob'seque**, *v. Obs. rare.* [ad. L. *obsequī*: see OBSEQUY[1].] *trans.* To comply with, yield to, obey.

1720 J. JOHNSON *Can. Eng. Ch.* lxx, If he formerly obsequed the Devil thro' Effeminacy, now let him fast by Way of Retaliation.

obseque, variant of OBSEQUY[1] *Obs.*

'obsequence. Now *rare.* [ad. L. *obsequentia*, f. *obsequent-em* OBSEQUENT.] Compliance, complaisance, obsequiousness.

1603 HOLLAND *Plutarch's Mor.* 1153 More force of law, than voluntary obsequence. **1622** CALDERWOOD *Course Conformity* 47 Insinuating them by flatterie and obsequence into the princes favour. **1884** D. G. MITCHELL *Bound Together* ii. 43 The monarch was charmed..not less by the splendor of his work than by his grave courtly obsequence [*sic*].

†**'obsequent**, *a.*[1] *Obs.* [ad. L. *obsequent-em* compliant, yielding, etc., pr. pple. of *obsequī*: cf. obs. F. *obsequent*, and see OBSEQUY[1].] Compliant, yielding, obedient.

1520 WHITINTON *Vulg.* (1527) 38 b, Benyuolent, lyberall, obsequent. **1543** *Necess. Doctr.* N ij b, The greate parte of the lerned men that were there, were..obsequente to the pleasure and wyll of the bysshoppes of Rome. **1601** HOLLAND *Pliny* Pref., The tongue in an Englishman's head is framed so flexible and obsequent, that it can pronounce naturally any other language. *a* **1619** FOTHERBY *Atheom.* II. i. §6 (1622) 181 Plyant, and obsequent to his pleasure.

obsequent ('ɒbsɪkwənt, ɒb'siːkwənt), *a.*[2] *Geomorphol.* [f. OB- + *-sequent* in CONSEQUENT, SUBSEQUENT *adjs.*] Of a stream, stream valley, or drainage pattern: having a course or character opposite to that of a consequent stream, stream valley, or drainage pattern, i.e. against the direction of dip of the strata. Hence as *sb.*, an obsequent stream.

1895 W. M. DAVIS in *Geogr. Jrnl.* V. 134 Its escarpment face sheds short, back-flowing streams into the longitudinal subsequent valley that has been developed along the weak underlying stratum: and, even at the risk of multiplying terms unduly, I would suggest that these streams be called obsequent, as their direction is opposed to that of the initial consequent streams. *Ibid.* 145 Such obsequents are represented by the Ousel and Ivel farther east. **1902** H. J. MACKINDER *Britain & Brit. Seas* 121 The Little Ouse of East Anglia is also an obsequent. **1954** W. D. THORNBURY *Princ. Geomorphol.* v. 114 Obsequent valleys drain in a direction opposite to the original consequent valleys. **1968** R. W. FAIRBRIDGE *Encycl. Geomorphol.* 288/2 (*caption*) Evolution of subsequent (plus obsequent and resequent) drainage system. *Ibid.* 1187/1 Obsequents were originally defined as streams having a direction opposite to that of the consequent streams in their vicinity. Usually, however, the term is interpreted to mean merely a stream flowing against the direction of dip.

b. Of a fault-line scarp or a related feature: having (as a result of differential erosion) a relief the reverse of that originally produced by the faulting.

1913 W. M. DAVIS in *Bull. Geol. Soc. Amer.* XXIV. 198 If it descends toward the relatively uplifted side, as must be the case when weaker rocks occur on that side, it may be called an obsequent scarp. **1954** W. D. THORNBURY *Princ. Geomorphol.* x. 260 If..the erosional topography is opposite to the original fault-produced topography, the mountain blocks would be obsequent tilt block mountains, the basins would be obsequent tilt block valleys, and the bounding scarps would be obsequent fault-line scarps. **1970** R. J. SMALL *Study of Landforms* iii. 103 An 'obsequent' fault-line scarp faces in the opposite direction to the original fault-scarp.

obsequial (əb'siːkwɪəl), *a.* [f. OBSEQUY[2] + -AL.] Of or pertaining to funeral obsequies.

a **1693** URQUHART *Rabelais* III. xxiii. 185 Funerary and Obsequial Festivals. **1844** H. H. WILSON *Brit. India* I. 467 To perform the obsequial rites. **1851** S. JUDD *Margaret* II. i. (1871) 172 Parson Welles, as the last obsequial act..thanked the people for their kindness..to the dead and the living.

ob'sequian, *a. Ancient Hist. rare.* [f. L. *obsequi-um* + -AN.] Of or pertaining to the *Obsequium*; see quot.

1788 GIBBON *Decl. & F.* lii. V. 398 The troops, who, in the new language of the empire, were styled of the *Obsequian Theme*. (*Note.* In the division of the *Themes*, or provinces described by Constantine Porphyrogenitus..the *Obsequium*, a Latin appellation of the army and palace, was the fourth in the public order.)

obsequies: see OBSEQUY[2].

obsequi'osity. [ad. med.L. *obsequiōsitās* (DuC.) f. *obsequiōsus*: see next and -ITY.] Obsequiousness.

1885 H. JAMES *Little Tour* xxix. 186 His application will be accompanied with the forms of a considerable obsequiosity, and in this case his request will be granted as civilly as it has been made.

obsequious (əb'siːkwɪəs), *a.* [ad. L. *obsequiōs-us* compliant, obedient, f. *obsequium* OBSEQUY[1]: cf. F. *obsequieux, -euse* (15–16th c. in Hatz.-Darm.).]

1. Compliant with the will or wishes of another, esp. of a superior; prompt to serve, please, or follow directions; obedient; dutiful. Now *rare*.

a **1450** *Mankind* (Brandl 1898) 4 Owur obsequyouse seruyce to hym xulde be aplyede. **1530** TINDALE *Pract. Prelates* Wks. (1573) 368/1 Was no man so obsequyous and seruiceable. **1598** SHAKS. *Merry W.* IV. ii. 2, I see you are obsequious in your loue. **1667** MILTON *P.L.* VI. 10 Light issues forth, and at the other dore Obsequious darkness enters. *a* **1703** BURKITT *On N.T.*, *Mark* xi. 6 The most unruly and untrained creatures become obsequious to Christ. *a* **1859** MACAULAY *Hist. Eng.* xxiii. V. 2. An army may be so constituted as to be..efficient against an enemy, and yet obsequious to the civil magistrate.

†**b.** Through association with OBSEQUY[2]: Dutiful in performing funeral obsequies or manifesting regard for the dead; proper to obsequies. *Obs.*

1588 SHAKS. *Tit. A.* v. iii. 152 Stand all aloofe, but Vnkle draw you neere, To shed obsequious teares vpon this Trunke. **1602** —— *Ham.* I. ii. 92 The Suruiuer bound In filiall Obligation..To do obsequious Sorrow. *c* **1674** *Inscr. Kingswood Ch.* in *Gentl. Mag.* LXX. I. 39/1 In memory of his deere Father..His obsequious son Richard Webb set up this monument.

2. Unduly or servilely compliant; ignobly submissive; manifesting or characterized by servile complaisance; fawning, cringing, sycophantic.

1602 MARSTON *Ant. & Mel.* I. Wks. 1856 I. 11 With most obsequious sleek-brow'd intertain. **1670** MARVELL *Corr.* Wks. 1872–5 II. 351 The House was thin and obsequious. **1720** SWIFT *Fates Clergymen*, He had now acquired a low, obsequious, aukward bow. **1848** DICKENS *Dombey* i, Following him out, with most obsequious politeness.

Comb. **1889** R. BRYDALL *Art Scot.* vii. 131 The timid, insignificant, and obsequious-looking pock-pitted youth.

†**b.** *transf.* of a plant: 'Creeping'. *Obs.*

1657 TOMLINSON *Renou's Disp.* 268 Its root emits many crass, obsequious branches.

ob'sequiously, *adv.* [f. prec. + -LY[2].] In an obsequious manner; †with ready compliance or eagerness to serve or please, dutifully (*obs.*); with undue submission, deference, or complaisance; in a servile, fawning, or abject way.

1599 MARSTON *Sco. Villanie* I. iv. 191 To day, to day, implore obsequiously: Trust not to morrowes will. **1623** BINGHAM *Xenophon* 21 What friends soeuer he chose..he vsed most obsequiously. **1701** DE FOE *True-born Eng.* 53 No subjects more obsequiously obey. **1736** SHENSTONE *To a Lady* 7 Oct., When theatres for you the scenes forgo, And the box bows, obsequiously low. **1866** GEO. ELIOT *F. Holt* xi. (1868) 122 'Won't you please to walk into the parlour, sir?' said Chubb, obsequiously.

†**b.** With dutiful performance of funeral obsequies or due tokens of regard for the dead; in the manner of a mourner. (Cf. OBSEQUIOUS 1 b.) *Obs.*

1594 SHAKS. *Rich. III*, I. ii. 3 Whil'st I a-while obsequiously lament Th' vntimely fall of Vertuous Lancaster. **1608** R. JOHNSON *Seven Champions* 60 There obsequiously to offer up unto the angry destinies many a bitter sighe and teare.

ob'sequiousness. [f. as prec. + -NESS.] The quality of being obsequious; obsequious conduct. **a.** Ready compliance or obedience; eagerness to serve or please; dutiful service. Now *rare* or *Obs.*

1447 BOKENHAM *Seyntys* (Roxb.) 157 In al this tyme wych so besyly She shewyd this meke obsequyousnesse. **1548** UDALL, etc. *Erasm. Par. John* xii. 82 This womans obsequiousnesse and benefite towardes me. **1638** RAWLEY tr. *Bacon's Life & Death* (1650) 14 A singular good Mother, and Wife; And yet, no lesse Famous, for her Libertie, than Obsequiousnesse towards her Husband. **1767** LEWIS *Statius* x. 923 *note*, In order to win her Affections by his Obsequiousness.

b. Servile submission or complaisance; servility.

1613 SHERLEY *Trav. Persia* 107 According to the corrupt condition of all Courts, in which the loue of obsequiousnesse to the Prince..is more power-able then the feare to do ill. **1727–38** GAY *Fables* II. iii. 23 With what obsequiousness they bend, to what vile actions condescend. **1877** BLACK *Green Past.* xxx. (1878) 240 The obseqiousness..that marks the relations between the waiter..and the guest at an hotel.

ob'sequity. *rare*$^{-1}$. [irreg. f. OBSEQUI-OUS + -ITY.] Obsequiousness.

1892 *Cornh. Mag.* June 586 He saluted the Provincial with a nervous obsequity which was unpleasant to look upon.

†**'obsequy**[1]. *Obs.* Also 6 obseque, 6–7 obsequie. [ad. L. *obsequi-um* compliance, complaisance, obedience, in pl. acts of compliance, f. *obsequī* to follow or comply with, f. *ob-* (OB- 1 a) + *sequī* to follow. Partly a. obs. F. *obseque* 'obéissance' (*a* 1420 in Godef.).] Ready compliance with the will or pleasure of another, esp. of a superior; deferential service; obsequiousness.

1432–50 tr. *Higden* (Rolls) II. 219 Bestes and other creatures, whiche were create..to the obsequy of subieccion [*ad obsequium subjectionis*]. *Ibid.* III. 35 Ligurgus ȝafe lawes ..movenge peple to the obsequy of princes. **1483** CAXTON *Gold. Leg.* 333 b/1 He gaf fyrst to his neyghbour his power in aydynge and obsequyes. *c* **1550** *Disc. Common Weal Eng.* (1893) 111, I owe him not only obeysaunce but also the obseque I can. **1652** EARL MONM. tr. *Bentivoglio's Hist. Relat.* 39 Very great is the obsequie which the whole People shew unto him. [*a* **1677** HALE *Prim. Orig. Man.* IV. ii. 308 We find every Command of the Divine Will..answered by an immediate *obsequium* in the created Matter.]

b. Ritual services, rites. *rare.*

1550 BALE *Apol.* 30 Appoynted to the ceremoniall obsequyes in the howse of God. **1605** CHAPMAN *All Fooles* Plays 1873 I. 127 You enioye a husband and may freely Performe all obsequies you desire to loue.

obsequy[2]; now always in pl. **obsequies** ('ɒbsɪkwɪz). Forms: *sing.* 5 obseque, 5–6 -qui, -quye, (6 oseque), 6–8 obsequie, 5–8 -quy; *pl.* 4– obsequies, (6 -cuyce). [a. AF. *obsequie* (also OF., 1316 in Godef.), = usual OF. *obsèque* (*osèque*, etc., 12th c.), pl. *obsèques*, ad. med.L. *obsequiæ*, acc. pl. *obsequiās*.

A solitary and doubtful instance of late L. *obsequiās* (otherwise read *exsequiās*) occurs in an inscription. Late or Med.L. *obsequiæ* appears to have arisen through mixture of *exsequiæ* funeral rites, and *obsequium* dutiful service; see these words in Du Cange, and cf. EXEQUY.]

Funeral rites or ceremonies; a funeral. †Formerly sometimes including commemorative rites or services (performed at the grave of the deceased or elsewhere), or denoting these alone. †**a.** *sing. Obs.*

c **1475** *Partenay* 2332 His funerall obseque to-morn we do. **1535** *MS.* (*Sotheby's Constable Cat.* Oct. 1899), Here folowythe the Oseque and intierment of the Right highe and excelent Prences Lade Kateryn. **1558** *Richmond Wills* (Surtees) 111, I will that my executors..shall maik one obsequi yerely for my soull in the place whear I am buried. **1599** HAKLUYT *Voy.* II. II. 86 Nor the seuenth day onely, but the seuenth moneth and yeere, within their owne houses they renue this obsequie. **1671** MILTON *Samson* 1732 To fetch him hence, and solemnly attend With silent obsequie and funeral train Home to his Fathers house. **1705** *Luctus Brit.* 2 Without some Mournful Pomp and Obsequie.

b. *pl.*

c **1386** CHAUCER *Knt.'s T.* 135 To the ladyes he restored agayn The bones of hir housbondes that weren slayn To doon obsequies as was tho the gyse. **1483** CAXTON *Gold. Leg.* 192/1 The mayde..kepte hym in vygylles wyth lyghtes and in deuyne obsequyes as long as she lyued. *c* **1530** LD. BERNERS *Arth. Lyt. Bryt.* (1814) 36 The kynge..caused her obsecuyce to be done ryght solempnely in the chirche. **1588** SHAKS. *Tit. A.* I. i. 160 Loe at this Tombe my tributarie teares, I render for my Bretherens Obsequies. **1670** DRYDEN *Conq. Granada* V. i, See perform'd their Fun'ral Obsequies. **1746** SMOLLETT *Reproof* 143 At Peter's obsequies I sung no dirge. **1877** GLADSTONE *Glean.* IV. xxxv. 364 We thus provide the Sultan with abundant funds for splendid obsequies.

†**'obserate**, *v. Obs. rare*$^{-0}$. [f. L. *obserāt-*, ppl. stem of *obserāre*, f. *ob-* (OB- 1 d) + *sera* bolt.] *trans.* To bolt, to lock up. Hence †**obse'ration**.

1623 COCKERAM, *Obserate.* **1658** PHILLIPS, *Obserration* [**1678** *Obseration*].

observa'bility. [f. OBSERVABLE *a.* + -ITY.] The quality of being observable; observable character or state; capacity for being seen.

1934 *Philos. Rev.* XLIII. 137 The simplest case of verifiability—observability at will. **1944** *Mind* LIII. 220 The new positivist principle..does not say anything at all about the observability or non-observability of the facts asserted or denied in P. **1956** E. H. HUTTEN *Lang. Mod. Physics* iv. 154 A numerical limit to the observability of microscopic events. **1968** R. A. LYTTLETON *Mysteries Solar Syst.* iv. 120 It may happen that two periods of observability occur as different parts of its path on opposite sides of perihelion bring the comet into the night sky. **1974** *Nature* 8 Feb. 352/2 It has been argued that the observability of the scattered waves is closely related to the presence of a caustic. **1974** M. HESSE *Struct. Sci. Inference* i. 9 Most accounts of the observation language were dependent on circular definitions of observability and its cognates.

observable (əbˈzɜːvəb(ə)l), *a.* and *sb.* [ad. L. *observābil-is*, f. *observāre* to OBSERVE: see -ABLE, and cf. F. *observable* (*c* 1500 in Godef.).]

A. *adj.* **1.** That must or may be observed, attended to, or kept.

1608 T. MORTON *Preamb. Encount.* 51 Obseruable for perpetuall remembrance. **1609** BIBLE (Douay) *Exod.* xii. 42 This is the observable night of our Lord. **1879** H. SPENCER *Princ. Sociol.* §348 Forms observable in social intercourse.

2. That may be observed or taken notice of; noticeable; perceptible.

1646 SIR T. BROWNE *Pseud. Ep.* 101 As the head may be disturbed by the skin, it may the same way be relieved; as is observable in balneations. **1711** ADDISON *Spect.* No. 256 ¶3 Any little Slip is more conspicuous and observable in his Conduct than in another's. **1823** H. J. BROOKE *Introd. Crystallogr.* 33 The regularity and symmetry observable in the forms of crystallized bodies. **1874** GREEN *Short Hist.* viii. §1. 455 A marked change in public sentiment became at once observable.

3. Worthy of observation, notice, or mention; noteworthy. †Formerly in stronger sense: Remarkable, notable.

1609 SIR E. HOBY *Let. to Mr. T. H.* 8 The Naturalistes, amongst manie other obseruable relations, record this of the *Struthio*. **1611** SPEED *Hist. Gt. Brit.* VI. xxxi. §5. 130 A man of so obseruable composednesse, as that he had bin neuer seene to laugh. **1667** PEPYS *Diary* 25 July, Hogg is..the most observable embezzler that ever was known. **1775** JOHNSON *Western Isl., Inch Kenneth*, We met with nothing very observable. **1789** BRAND *Hist. Newcastle* I. 495 There is an observable old chair in the vestry of this church. **1828** D'ISRAELI *Chas. I*, II. x. 244 A very observable incident in the history of Charles. **1884** SIR R. BAGGALLAY in *Law Rep.* 27 Chanc. Div. 108 It is observable that the application must be made on sufficient ground on affidavit or otherwise.

B. *sb.* †**1.** A noteworthy thing, fact, or circumstance. Chiefly in *pl. Obs.*

1639 FULLER *Holy War* xix. (1647) 30 Asher entertaineth us with these observables. **1663** PEPYS *Diary* 27 Feb., Among other observables we drank the King's health out of a gilt cup given by King Henry VIII to this Company. **1713** DERHAM *Phys.-Theol.* x. i. 447 Another Observable in the Fibers of the Leaf, is their orderly Position. **1746** G. ADAMS *Micrograph.* xxix. (1747) 102 (The Snail.) This slow paced slimy Animal hath many curious Observables. **1822** SOUTHEY *Lett.* (1856) III. 364 Among other observables, it ought to be noticed that she has peculiar names for her domestic implements.

2. a. A thing that may be observed or noticed; something that can be perceived more or less directly; something that is knowable through the senses.

1660 H. MORE *Myst. Godl.* III. vi. 70 Apparent as well from what they write of his birth and amours, as from other observables in his Image. **1954** A. J. AYER *Philos. Ess.* i. 9 It may be left open what situations are to count as being observable; whether, for example, we are to treat such objects as electrons as being directly accessible to observation, or only such common-sense objects as chairs and tables, or only sense-data. Whatever decision may be taken..we are..likely to be left with some descriptive expressions which do not signify observables. **1959** *Listener* 1 Oct. 520/1 According to Dingle, the observables of a science must be potentially observable 'by all normal people'. **1963** J. LYONS *Structural Semantics* i. 1 We must reject any theory of semantics the terms of which neither refer to observables nor are reducible to observables. **1964** *Philos.* XXXIX. 262 If one supposes observables to be ontologically fundamental then models appear gratuitous. **1965** P. CAWS *Philos. of Sci.* viii. 52 The concepts which science borrows from the knowledge and experience of ordinary men..yield principally substantive and adjectival constructs directly linked to perception. Constructs having this direct link will be called observables. **1968** J. J. C. SMART *Between Sci. & Philos.* v. 143 The instrumentalist.. would agree with the operationist in holding that in science no statements are made about entities other than macroscopic observables.

b. *Physics.* A quantity that can (in principle) be measured.

1930 P. A. M. DIRAC *Princ. Quantum Mech.* ii. 25 In quantum mechanics it is more convenient to deal with something that refers to one particular time instead of to all times, analogous to the value of a classical variable at a particular instant of time. We shall call such a quantity an observable. **1955** W. PAULI *Niels Bohr* 38 All physical observables are represented by Hermitian operators. **1966** C. G. HEMPEL *Philos. of Nat. Sci.* vi. 74 These wave-lengths are not observables in the ordinary sense of the word. **1974** H. CLARK *First Course Quantum Mech.* iii. 54 In quantum mechanics..not all the observables of a system can be measured simultaneously. If some observable is measured, this act of measurement may disturb the system and change the value of some other observable... The disturbance in a classical system..can in principle be allowed for exactly but not in quantum physics. **1975** *Nature* 31 Jan. 315/1 Body temperature, enzyme activity, leaf movement, neural firing, mitotic index or other convenient observables typically persist in regular up and down periods of about 24-h, even in ostensibly constant conditions.

†**3.** A point to be observed or attended to. *rare.*

1703 T. N. *City & C. Purchaser* 50 Of Observables in Buying and Laying Bricks.

Hence **obˈservably** *adv.*, noticeably, perceptibly, †notably; **obˈservableness**, the quality or fact of being observable.

1646 SIR T. BROWNE *Pseud. Ep.* 313 It grew observably shallower in his dayes. **1727** BAILEY vol. II, *Observableness*, fitness, easiness, or worthiness to be observed. **1840** CARLYLE *Heroes* i. (1858) 188 A primary law of human nature, still everywhere observably at work.

†**obˈserval.** *Obs.* [f. OBSERVE *v.* + -AL[1] 5.] The action of observing; observation; observance.

a **1734** NORTH *Exam.* III. x. (1740) 659 The full Force of the Libel will not appear without a previous Observal of what has been said of them. **1765** J. BROWN *Chr. Jrnl.* (1814) 291 The outward observal was partly remembered.

observance (əbˈzɜːvəns). Also 3–6 **-aunce**, (5 **obcerv-**), 5 **-ans**, **-auns**, (6 **-anss**). [a. F. *observance* (*c* 1250 in Godefroy), ad. L. *observāntia* regard, attention, notice; respect, reverence; keeping or following of a law, custom, etc.; in late L., religious worship, f. *observānt-em*, pr. pple. of *observāre* to OBSERVE.]

I. 1. The action or practice of observing, keeping, or paying attention to (a law, command, duty, ceremony, set time, or anything prescribed or fixed); due regard to (a custom, practice, rule, method, or any principle of action). Const. *of*, †*to*.

1390 GOWER *Conf.* III. 142 Fyf pointz, whiche he hath under-take To kepe and holde in observance. **1500–20** DUNBAR *Poems* xlv. 15 Thus I gife our the obseruanss Of luvis cure. **1596** SPENSER *F.Q.* VI. v. 35 In streight obseruaunce of religious vow. **1602** SHAKS. *Ham.* I. iv. 16 It is a Custome More honour'd in the breach, then the obseruance. **1649** MILTON *Eikon.* ix. 85 Under the colour of a blind and litteral observance to an oath. **1754** RICHARDSON *Grandison* IV. x. 78 Your own reason..shall..direct your observances of my advice. **1785** PALEY *Mor. Philos.* v. viii. (1827) 94/2 To comply with the religious observance of Sunday. **1841** LANE *Arab. Nts.* I. 70 The observance of this festival..continues three or four days. **1856** KANE *Arct. Expl.* II. viii. 89 The safety of the whole company exacts the sternest observance of discipline.

b. The keeping of a prescribed ritual; the performance of customary worship or ceremony.

c **1380** WYCLIF *Sel. Wks.* III. 432 ȝif observaunce in lyves of fadris profytede to many men..neverþelees it wer a pur open folye to make herof a rewle for al and for ever. *c* **1386** CHAUCER *Knt.'s T.* 642 For to doon his obseruaunce to May. **1500–20** DUNBAR *Poems* x. 27 Do ȝour obseruance devyne To him that is of kingis King. **1605** BACON *Adv. Learn.* I. To the King §1 Dayly sacrifices, and free will offerings: the one proceeding vpon ordinarie obseruance [L. *ex rituali cultu*]; the other vppon a devout cheerefulnesse. **1700** DRYDEN *Pal. & Arc.* I. 175 To do the observance due to sprightly May. **1813** H. & J. SMITH *Rej. Addr.* iii. 34 The scenes of Shakspeare and our bards of old, With due observance splendidly unfold. **1874** GREEN *Short Hist.* viii. §5. 509 The King's first acts were directed rather to points of outer observance.

2. An act performed in accordance with prescribed usage, esp. one of religious or ceremonial character; a practice which is customarily observed, customary rite or ceremony, custom; †something which has to be observed; an ordinance, rule, or obligatory practice (*obs.*).

a **1225** *Ancr. R.* 24 Heo voleweð her, ase in oþre obseruaunces, muchel of ure ordre. *c* **1391** CHAUCER *Astrol.* II. §4 Theise ben obseruauncez of iudicial matiere & rytes of paiens. *c* **1400** *Beryn* 3982 Thurh oute all our marchis it is the observaunce. *c* **1430** *Pilgr. Lyf Manhode* IV. xxix. (1869) 191 She is bounden and bounden ayen; fretted with obseruaunces. **1540–1** ELYOT *Image Gov.* 101 They all confessed..that suche landes as they had, were seruile, as for the whiche they were bounden to certayn obseruances. **1588** SHAKS. *L.L.L.* I. i. 36 There are other strict obseruances: As not to see a woman in that terme, .. And one day in a weeke to touch no foode. **1729** BUTLER *Serm. Balaam* Wks. 1874 II. 90 Superstitious observances..will not..mend matters with us. **1861** WRIGHT *Ess. Archæol.* II. xxi. 170 Almost all the fine arts derived their origin..from religious ceremonies and observances.

b. An ordinance to be observed; *esp.* the rule, or one of the regulations, of a religious order; *spec.* of the Observants or stricter Franciscans.

1382 WYCLIF *1 Chron.* xxiii. 32 And kepe thei the obseruauncis [*observationes*] of the tabernacle. —— *Ezek.* xliv. 8 ȝe han putte keepers of myn obseruaunces in my sayntuarie to ȝour self. **1387** TREVISA *Higden* (Rolls) VII. 401 Þese ben þe observaunces þat semeþ hard in þat [Cistercian] ordour: þei schal were no manere furres [etc.]. *c* **1450** *St. Cuthbert* (Surtees) 1401 Þe same obseruance þar þai auysed Before at mailrose þan had þai vsed. **1502** ARNOLDE *Chron.* (1811) 156 There he ded make friers of yᵉ obseruancis. **1706** tr. *Dupin's Eccl. Hist. 16th C.* II. IV. xi. 440 The Franciscans were divided into Conventual Friars and Friars of the strict Observance. **1834** *Encycl. Brit.* (ed. 7) X. 221/1 Two large bodies, comprehending the whole Franciscan order, which subsist to this day; namely, the *conventual brethren*, and the *brethren of the observance*.

c. *transf.* A company of religious persons observing some rule, or belonging to some order; also, their convent or place of habitation. *rare.*

1486 *Bk. St. Albans* F vij, An obseruans of herimytes. **1876** BROWNING *Pacchiarotto* xvii. 14 Lately was coffered A corpse in its sepulchre, situate By St. John's Observance.

II. 3. The observing of due respect or deference to a person; respectful or courteous attention, dutiful service. (Rarely const. *of*.) *arch.*

c **1374** CHAUCER *Anel. & Arc.* 218 Who-so truest is.. That ..dothe her obseruance Alwey to oon and chaungeth for no newe. **1423** JAS. I *Kingis Q.* cxxiii, Quhare Is becummyn,.. The besy awayte, the hertly obseruance, That quhilum was amongis thame so ryf? *a* **1548** HALL *Chron., Hen. VII*, 27 Of his bounden duetie and obseruaunce, which he ought to the kyng hys master. **1647** PRINCE CHARLES LEWIS in Ellis *Orig. Lett.* Ser. II. III. 334, I will never forget the personal respect and observance I doe owe you. **1741** MIDDLETON *Cicero* II. viii. 230 He attached himself very early to the observance of Cicero. **1859** TENNYSON *Geraint & Enid* 48 He compass'd her with sweet observances And worship.

III. †**4.** Observant care, heed. *Obs.*

c **1386** CHAUCER *Pars. T.* ¶673 The Auaricious man.. dooth moore obseruance in kepynge of his tresor than..to seruice of Ihesu crist. *c* **1449** PECOCK *Repr.* 226 The consideracioun and the observaunce Awaite and diligence which is to be had in such Mater. **1602** SHAKS. *Ham.* III. ii. 21 Sute the Action to the Word, the Word to the Action, with this speciall obseruance: That you ore-stop not the modestie of Nature. **1660** SHARROCK *Vegetables* 119 This observance is absolutely necessary to Damask roses.

5. The action of paying attention (to what is said), of observing or noticing (what is done); notice; watching: = OBSERVATION 5.

1600 SHAKS. *A.Y.L.* III. ii. 247 Take a taste of my finding him, and rellish it with good obseruance. **1602** MARSTON *Ant. & Mel.* I. Wks. 1856 I. 15 Vouchsafe me, then, your hush't observances. **1634** MASSINGER *Very Wom.* v. i, I passed, And pried, in every place, without observance. **1732** NEAL *Hist. Purit.* I. 22 The Popish party..put him upon a nice observance of her carriage. **1859** RUSKIN *Two Paths* iv. 156 Consider how much intellect was needed in the architect, and how much observance of nature.

observancy (əbˈzɜːvənsɪ). [ad. L. *observāntia*, or directly f. OBSERVANT: see -ANCY.]

1. The quality of being observant or observing; †the action of observing, observation (*obs.*).

1567 MAPLET *Gr. Forest* 80 Aristotle by observauncy had, much commendeth their flight. **1605** DANIEL *Queen's Arcadia* Wks. (1717) 152 Living here under the awful Hand Of Discipline and strict Observancy. **1871** CARLYLE in *Mrs. C.'s Lett.* I. 121 Shrewdness, accurate observancy.

2. Respectful or obsequious attention. *arch.*

1601 J. WHEELER *Treat. Comm.* Ded. A ij b, The dewtifull Observancie, and Promptitude, which the said Companie alwayes shewed towardes your.. Fathers seruice. **1616** R. C. *Times' Whistle* vi. 2829 A supple knee, And oyly mouth and much observancie. **1671** L. ADDISON *West Barbary* 114 To please their husbands, to whom they are taught by their Alcoran to bear a dutiful observancy. **1868** BROWNING *Ring & Bk.* IV. 939 How bend him To such observancy of beck and call.

†**3.** Observance of forms, rules, or ceremonies; a rule to be observed. *Obs. rare.*

1609 DANIEL *Civ. Wars* VIII. xcvii, Which they enjoy more naturall and free, Than can great Pow'rs, chain'd with Observancy. **1628** VENNER *Baths of Bathe* (1650) 261 By his clinical and unnecessary observancies.

4. A house of the Observant order.

1876 BROWNING *Pacchiarotto* xix. 9 A convent of monks, the Observancy.

‖**obserˈvandum.** *rare.* Pl. **-a** (erron. **-as**). [L., = (thing) to be observed.] Something to be observed or noted.

1704 SWIFT *T. Tub* vii, Those judicious Collectors of bright parts, flowers, and Observandas. *Ibid.* Concl., The issues of my Observanda begin to grow too large for the receipts.

observant (əbˈzɜːvənt), *a.* and *sb.* [a. F. *observant* (formerly as sb.), pr. pple. of *observer* to OBSERVE.]

A. *adj.* **1. a.** Attentive in observing a law, custom, principle, or anything prescribed or fixed; careful to perform or practise duly. Const. *of* (†*to*).

1608 TOPSELL *Serpents* (1658) 720 Thinking, by this devotion (..in this observant manner) to pacifie the wrath of God. **1632** J. HAYWARD tr. *Biondi's Eromena* 24 When custome hath brought a thing to become..honour, whosoever is not observant and obedient thereto, is dishonored. **1701** W. WOTTON *Hist. Rome, Marcus* i. 19 Exactly observant of Sincerity and Truth. **1829** LYTTON *Disowned* xi, [She was] very observant of the little niceties of phrase and manner. **1834** MEDWIN *Angler in Wales* II. 332 Conscientiously observant of contracts.

b. Acting in accordance with the precepts of behaviour associated with a particular religion, esp. Judaism.

1902 *Daily Chron.* 2 Oct. 7/1 To-day observant Jews throughout the world celebrate the commencement of their New Year. *Ibid.* Even the less observant..hasten to the Synagogue to-day to listen to the mystic sound of the Ram's Horn trumpets. **1905** *Westm. Gaz.* 25 Mar. 3/2 Someone will be suggesting [giving up] linen collars next—in which case the really Lenten-observant man will look like nothing so much as a burglar. **1972** C. POTOK *My Name is Asher Lev* i. 36 The stores that were run by observant Jews were all closed on Shabbos. **1975** *Times Lit. Suppl.* 21 Nov. 1392/5 An observant Jew..declined to join a prominent Berlin literary club because he would eat only kosher food.

†**2.** Showing respect, honour, or deference; dutifully regardful; considerately attentive; assiduous in service; obsequious. Const. *of*, *to*. *Obs.*

1604 R. CAWDREY *Table Alph.*, *Obseruant*, dutifull, full of diligent seruice. **1605** BACON *Adv. Learn.* I. To the King §2 Beholding you not with the inquisitive eye of presumption ..but with the observant eye of duty and admiration. *a* **1713** ELLWOOD *Autobiog.* (1714) 170 Yet this..made them a little the more observant to me. **1725** POPE *Odyss.* I. 342 Observant of the Gods, and sternly just. **1743** POCOCKE *Descr. East* I. IV. ii. 167 They are in the hands of very kind masters, and are as observant of them.

3. Carefully particular about a matter; heedful.

1627 HAKEWILL *Apol.* IV. vii. §6. 358 Of their weight they were so curious and observant, that they had them weighed many times at their very tables. **1691** T. H[ALE] *Acc. New Invent.* 22 The Dutch.. are equally observant with us, in the sheathing their Rudder Irons. *a* **1774** GOLDSM. *Hist. Greece* II. 118 To be scrupulously observant to avoid offending the prince. **1891** LOUNSBURY *Stud. Chaucer* I. iii. 232 The very difficulty of getting a correct copy at the hands of the scribe must have had a tendency to make the author..more observant about the character of his own original.

4. That takes notice; attentive in marking or noting; quick to notice or perceive. Const. *of* (†*on*).

1602 SHAKS. *Ham.* I. i. 71 This same strict and most obseruant Watch. **1649** JER. TAYLOR *Gt. Exemp.* I. Ad Sect. vi. §9 The active Piety of a credulous, a pious and less observant age. *a* **1661** FULLER *Worthies* (1840) III. 434 A most accomplished gentleman, and an observant traveller. **1725** POPE *Odyss.* I. 5 Wand'ring from clime to clime, observant stray'd. **1801** ELIZ. HELME *St. Margaret's Cave* (1819) I. xvii. 205 Cautiously observant on all that passed. **1824** BYRON *Juan* XV. xv, Observant of the foibles of the crowd. **1866** GEO. ELIOT *F. Holt* v. (1868) 53 Felix Holt, when he entered, was not in an observant mood.

¶**5.** *catachr.* Observable. *Obs.*

1615 BRATHWAIT *Strappado* (1878) 201 Onely such things as most obseruant were,..I thought to shadow briefely. **1623** AILESBURY *Serm.* 14 Foure things in Christ to us are very observant. **1653** BINNING *Serm.* (1845) 245, I wish we could have this image of ingratitude always observant to our eyes.

B. *sb.* †**1.** One who observes a law or anything prescribed or fixed. Const. *of*. *Obs.*

With the pl. *observance* (= OF. *observans*) in first quot., cf. *inhabitance*, early pl. of *inhabitant* sb., ACCIDENCE, etc.

c **1470** G. ASHBY *Policy Prince* 560 Muche more rather to be obseruance Of cristen lawe we shulde yeve attendance. **1593** NASHE *Christ's T.* 79 b, Our Lawes.. allow no rewarde to theyr temperate obseruants. **1613** PURCHAS *Pilgrimage* (1614) 150 Suidas calleth them observants of the Lawe.

2. *spec.* A member of that branch of the order of Franciscan friars which observes the strict rule, as restored at the beginning of the 15th cent.; the other branch being the Conventuals. Also *attrib.* and *appos.*, as ***Observant Friars***, ***Friars Observants***.

1474 CAXTON *Chesse* III. ii. E vij b, Religyous men as monkes freres chanons obseruantes. **1502** *Privy Purse Exp. Eliz. of York* (1830) 56 The Fryers Observauntes at Grenewiche. **1693** tr. *Emilianne's Hist. Monast. Ord.* xvi. 172 They were called Minors of the Observants. *a* **1746** LEWIS in Gutch *Coll. Cur.* II. 196 Frier Forest, one of the Observant Friers. **1856** FROUDE *Hist. Eng.* II. 220 The houses of the Observants at Canterbury and Greenwich.. were repressed. **1889** *Athenæum* 29 June 820/3 The Observant Order was..suppressed before all the others.

†**3.** A dutiful or attentive servant or follower; an obsequious attendant. *Obs.*

1605 SHAKS. *Lear* II. ii. 109 Twenty silly-ducking obseruants, That stretch their duties nicely. **1613** PURCHAS *Pilgrimage* (1614) 810 For the Festiuall of this Gaine-god,.. the Merchants, his deuoted and faithfull obseruants,.. bought a slaue..to represent that Idol. **1617** *Janua Ling.* Ded., Presented by..your highnesses most humblest obseruant I.B.P.

Hence **ob'servantly** *adv.*, in an observant manner, attentively, heedfully; †with dutiful service; †**ob'servantness**, the quality of being observant.

a **1653** W. GOUGE in Spurgeon *Treas. Dav.* Ps. cxvi. 6 Read observantly the histories of the Gospel. **1660** F. BROOKE tr. *Le Blanc's Trav.* 363 The whole multitude.. observantly return to the Temple. **1727** BAILEY vol. II, *Observantness*, regardfulness, respectfulness. **1817** FOSTER in *Life & Corr.* (1846) I. cvi. 467 He had observantly traversed the scenes.

†**obser'vantially**, *adv.* *Obs.* *rare.* [f. **observantial* adj. (f. L. *observāntia* observance + -AL[1]) + -LY[2].] With careful observance.

1652 GAULE *Magastrom.* 170 In that regard [he] seems very observantially to submit not only to stars and planetary constellations, but to plants, &c.

Observantine (əb'zɜːvəntɪn), *sb.* (*a.*) Also 7 **-in.** [a. F. *Observantin* (*c* 1575 in Godef.), f. OBSERVANT: see -INE[1].] = OBSERVANT B. 2. Also *attrib.* or as *adj.*

1646 EARL MONM. tr. *Biondi's Civil Warres* IX. 235 He built three Monasteries for the Conventuall Friers of Saint Francis order, and three for the Observantines. *a* **1773** A. BUTLER *Lives Saints* (1779) IV. 208 He [*sc.* St. James of Sclavonia] embraced with great fervour the humble and penitential state of a lay-brother among the Observantin Franciscan friars at Bitecto, a small town nine miles from Bari. **1838** PRESCOTT *Ferd. & Is.* (1846) II. v. 348 He selected for this purpose the Observantines of the Franciscan order. **1930** F. J. EBLE tr. *Grisar's Martin Luther* ii. 51 The vicar..jeopardized the canonical and disciplinary autonomy of the Observantine monasteries entrusted to his care. **1932** *Times Lit. Suppl.* 9 June 425/2 A fifteenth-century bard who joined the order at the time when the Observantine reform was making great headway in Ireland.

Observantist = OBSERVANT, OBSERVANTINE.
In some recent Dicts.

†**'observate**, *ppl. a.* *Obs.* *rare*$^{-1}$. [ad. L. *observāt-us*, pa. pple. of *observāre*.] = OBSERVED.

1652 GAULE *Magastrom.* 103 No appropriate, causate, and observate experiment.

†**'observate**, *v.* *Obs.* *rare*$^{-1}$. [f. L. *observāt-*, ppl. stem of *observāre*.] *trans.* = OBSERVE *v.*

1652 GAULE *Magastrom.* 187 Whether chiromancy or palmestry..may not be accounted for a mistresse in observating and ominating magick and astrologie?

†**obser'vatical**, *a.* *Obs.* *rare*$^{-1}$. [irreg. f. L. *observāt-us* observation + -ICAL.] Of or pertaining to (scientific) observation; observational.

1703 T. S. *Art's Improv.* p. iv, A Compleat Experimental, and Observatical History, will be of great use to Anticipate the loss of many rare and useful Experiments, Inventions and Arts.

observation (ɒbzə'veɪʃən). Also 4 **-cioun**, 6 **-cion**. [ad. L. *observātiōn-em*, n. of action f. *observāre* to OBSERVE: cf. F. *observation* (1200 in Godef. *Compl.*).] The action of observing; the fact observed.

1. The action or practice of observing a law, covenant, set day, or anything prescribed or fixed; practical adherence to a custom, usage, or rule: = OBSERVANCE 1. Const. *of*, †*to*. Now *rare* or *Obs.*

1535 *Act 27 Hen. VIII*, c. 11 §10 This present act..shall ..binde euery officer.. to thobservacion thereof. **1551** ROBINSON tr. *More's Utop.* II. ix. (1895) 279 Diuinations of vayne superstition, which in other countreys be in greate obseruation. **1581** MARBECK *Bk. of Notes* 254 Affirming that Circumcision was necessarie & the observation of the Lawe. **1656–7** *Burton's Diary* (1828) I. 310 An Act for the better observation of the Lord's day, read the first time. **1782** *Hist. Eur.* in *Ann. Reg.* 11/2 An inviolable observation of public faith. **1809–10** COLERIDGE *Friend* (1818) I. 298 The faithful observation of a contract. **1825** MACAULAY *Ess.*, *Milton* ¶ 5 The observation of the Sabbath.

2. That which is observed or practised: = OBSERVANCE 2.

1382 WYCLIF *Neh.* xii. 44 [45] Thei kepten the obseruacioun of their God, and the besinesse of clensing [*observationem Dei sui & observationem expiationis*]. **1540** *Act 32 Hen. VIII*, c. 26 The laufull rites ceremonies and obseruacions of goddes seruice. **1633** BP. HALL *Hard Texts*, *N.T.* 272 Circumcision and the rest of those legal observations. **1656** BRAMHALL *Replic.* vi. 241 To persist in an old observation when..the end for which the observation was made, calleth upon us for an alteration, is not obedience but obstinacie. *a* **1718** PENN *Let. to Young Convicted* Wks. 1782 I. 76 Will-performances and external observations. **1911** W. J. LOCKE *Glory of Clementina Wing* xxii. 277 The daily calls to inquire after her health and happiness had grown to be a sacred observation.

†**3.** Regard, respect, honour; respectful or courteous attention: = OBSERVANCE 3. *Obs.*

1644 QUARLES *Barnabas & B.* (1851) 55 A countenance that is revered breeds fear and observation. **1721** STRYPE *Eccl. Mem.* I. xlv. 339 They continued in their loving and friendly observation of his Majesty.

†**4.** Observant care, heed: = OBSERVANCE 4. *Obs.*

1610 SHAKS. *Temp.* III. iii. 87 So with good life, And obseruation strange, my meaner ministers Their seuerall kindes haue done. **1672–3** SIR C. LYTTELTON in *Hatton Corr.* (Camden) 104, I have at this time more than an ordinary observation how I behave myself.

5. a. The action or an act of paying attention, marking, or noticing; the fact of being noticed; notice, remark; perception: = OBSERVANCE 5.

1557 N. T. (Genev.) *Luke* xvii. 20 The kingdome of God commeth not with obseruation. **1588** SHAKS. *L.L.L.* III. i. 28 *Brag.* How hast thou purchased this experience? *Boy* By my penne of obseruation. **1646** J. HALL *Horæ Vac.* 46 Some lurking vice, which fled ones owne observation, and had not been hinted by..friends. **1702** *Eng. Theophrast.* 41, I made a thousand observations during this short journey, that fully confirmed me in this Opinion. **1791** MRS. RADCLIFFE *Rom. Forest* i, They were..in less danger of observation. **1863** KINGSLEY *Lett.* (1878) II. 161 The first thing for a boy to learn, after obedience and morality, is a habit of observation.

b. The faculty or habit of observing or taking notice.

1605 BACON *Adv. Learn.* II. v. §3 Men of narrow observation. **1627–77** FELTHAM *Resolves* I. xxviii. 48 He is thought one of too prying an observation. **1860** HAWTHORNE *Marb. Faun* (ed. Tauchn.) II. viii. 92 The statue had life and observation in it.

c. Inspection of, or attention to, presages or omens; an act of augury or divination. (Now only as in general sense.)

1605 BACON *Adv. Learn.* II. xi. §2 [Experimental divination] for the most part is superstitious; such as were the heathen observations upon the inspection of sacrifices, the flight of birds, the swarming of bees. **1620** MELTON *Astrolog.* 61 The viperous generation of Negromancy, which are Idolatry, Diuination, and vaine obseruation. **1718** *Freethinker* No. 62 ¶ 14 The bare Observation of Omens was not sufficient: It was likewise necessary to Accept them.

d. *Mil.* The watching of a fortress, of an enemy's movements, etc. ***army*** (***corps***, etc.) ***of observation***, a force employed in watching an army of the enemy, so as to be ready to check their movements.

1836 ALISON *Europe* (1849–50) V. xxxi. § 87. 374 No less than thirty thousand being in observation or garrison.

†**e.** ***of observation***, worthy to be observed; noteworthy, notable. *Obs.*

a **1635** NAUNTON *Fragm. Reg.* (Arb.) 40 It is of further observation that my Lord of Essex (after Leicester's decease)..loved him not in sincerity. **1665** *Sir T. Roe's Voy. E. Ind.* in G. Havers *P. della Valle's Trav.* 364 There is one great and fair Tree growing in that Soil, of special observation. **1679** LD. FINCH in *Buccleuch MSS.* (Hist. MSS. Comm.) I. 330 The case being of great consequence to the public, and of great observation.

6. a. The action or an act of observing scientifically; *esp.* the careful watching and noting of a phenomenon in regard to its cause or effect, or of phenomena in regard to their mutual relations, these being observed as they occur in nature (and so opposed to *experiment*); also, the record of this.

1559 W. CUNNINGHAM *Cosmogr. Glasse* 161 What be th' observations of this neadle, by whiche you affirme that it doth not exactlye poynte Northe and Southe? **1605** BACON *Adv. Learn* I. v. §7 Gilbertus our countryman hath made a philosophy out of the observations of a loadstone. **1665** HOOKE *Microgr.* Pref. b, The Science of Nature has been already too long made only a work of the..Fancy; It is now high time that it should return to..Observations. **1695** WOODWARD *Nat. Hist. Earth* I. 1 Observations are the only sure Grounds whereon to build a lasting and substantial Philosophy. **1704** HEARNE *Duct. Hist.* (1714) I. 398 Aristotle having requested his Nephew Calisthenes to..send him an account of their earliest Observations, it appear'd..that they amounted no higher than 1903 Years before that time. **1816** PLAYFAIR *Nat. Phil.* II. 261 The result of these investigations..agrees nearly with observation. **1843** MILL *Logic* III. vii. §4 (1856) I. 417 Observation..without experiment.. can ascertain sequences and co-existences, but cannot prove causation. **1860** TYNDALL *Glac.* I. xvi. 94, I halted, to check the observations already made. **1879** THOMSON & TAIT *Nat. Phil.* I. I. §371 Isothermal Lines, Lines of Equal Dip..and a host of other data and phenomena..are thus deducible from Observation merely.

b. *spec.* The taking of the altitude of the sun (or other heavenly body) by means of an astronomical instrument, in order to find the latitude or longitude; the result obtained.

to work an observation, to ascertain the latitude or longitude by means of calculations based on a measurement of the sun's altitude.

1559 W. CUNNINGHAM *Cosmogr. Glasse* 136 Longitudes and Latitudes..require longe and diligent observation. **1669** STURMY *Mariner's Mag.* II. 82, I have shewed you how to take an Observation by the Fore-Staff. The next thing.. will be to shew you how to work your Observation. **1719** DE FOE *Crusoe* I. ii. I..learned how to..take an observation. **1882** FLOYER *Unexpl. Baluchistan* 396, I got capital observations, both of sun for longitude, and Polaris for latitude.

7. Observed truth or fact: something learned by observing; a rule or maxim gathered from experience. Now *rare.*

1600 SHAKS. *A.Y.L.* II. vii. 41 In his braine..He hath strange places cram'd With obseruation, the which he vents In mangled formes. **1604** E. G[RIMSTONE] tr. *D'Acosta's Hist. Indies* III. iv. 131 The Mariners hold it for a certaine rule and observation, that within the Tropickes continually raine Easterly windes. **1719** SWIFT *To a Young Clergyman*, There is one observation, which I never knew to fail. **1793** C. MARSHALL *Garden.* xviii. (1813) 112 It may prove an observation of some use, that trees and shrubs raised from seed grow the largest.

8. An utterance as to something observed; a remark in speech or writing in reference to something.

1593 SHAKS. *3 Hen. VI*, II. vi. 108 Tut, that's a foolish obseruation. **1605** BACON *Adv. Learn* II. ii. §2 A scattered history of those actions..with politic discourse and observation thereupon. **1790** PALEY *Horæ Paul.* Rom. i. 8 The first passage..upon which a good deal of observation will be founded. **1803** *Med. Jrnl.* X. 129 The annexed letter contains some Observations on the late Influenza. **1848** DICKENS *Dombey* ii, Mrs. Chick made this impressive observation in the drawing-room.

†**9.** An object of attention or notice. *rare.*

1736 BUTLER *Anal.* II. vii, Insomuch that this one nation should continue to be the observation and the wonder of all the world.

10. *attrib.*, as ***observation balloon***, ***cell***, ***deck***, ***duty***, ***gallery***, ***hole***, ***platform***, ***post***, ***room***, ***terrace***, ***vehicle***, ***window***, etc.; ***observation-based*** adj.; (in Philos.) ***observation basis***, ***report***, ***term*** (see quots.); **observation-car**, an open railway carriage, or one with glass sides; **observation-mine**, a mine (originally) fired from an observing station; **observation officer** = OBSERVER 4 b; **observation-sentence** *Philos.*, in a scientific theory, a sentence that reports, or directly relates to, observed phenomena (opp. *theoretical sentence*); **observation-statement**, an observation-sentence, or the utterance of one; **observation ward** (see quot. 1927).

1909 *London Mag.* Sept. 15/2 He made numerous ascents in captive *observation balloons. **1917** F. STARK *Let.* 16 Oct. (1974) I. 49 We had a great time.., going to call on a Major ..who looks after the observation balloons in this sector. **1950** *Gloss. Aeronaut. Terms* (*B.S.I.*) I. 46 *Observation balloon*, a balloon fitted with a basket or car to carry passengers. **1965** *Language* XLI. 212 The value of *observation-based description. **1965** P. CAWS *Philos. of Sci.* xxiv. 182 The *observation basis must consist of carefully formulated protocol sentences. **1872** *Harper's Mag.* May 876/1 You look out of the open '*observation car' as you sweep down from a height of 7000 feet. **1880** 'E. LEATHES' *Actor Abroad* 177 An observation car, which is roomy, comfortable, and roofless is attached to the end of the train on leaving Sacramento. **1894** J. DALE *Round the World* 308 An 'observation' car, made for the purpose of seeing the scenery. **1936** WODEHOUSE *Laughing Gas* ii. 17 These observation cars, in case you don't know, are where the guard's van is on an English train. **1973** *Guardian* 17 Mar. 14/4 The 'Rheingold' from Basle to Amsterdam..has a vista-dome observation car. **1898** *Westm. Gaz.* 1 Oct. 7/1 The deceased..was placed in an *observation cell, being visited every quarter of an hour. The door would not be opened every time, but he would look through the observation place in the door. **1951** A. C. CLARKE *Sands of Mars* iii. 21 He..hurried out to the *observation deck, wondering what happened to Earth overnight. **1976** E. P. BENSON *Bulls of Ronda* vii. 51 Rafael Durán stood on the observation deck of the airport, watching the plane. 1951 *Observation gallery [see LINER sb.² 8c]. 1898 Westm. Gaz. 1 Oct. 7/1 Through the *observation hole in the door it was impossible to see the left-hand corner of the cell. 1886 Pall Mall G. 19 Aug. 10/1 '*Observation mines' are now automatically fired by a most ingenious method. 1904 Daily Chron. 22 June 9/3 The aim of the Japs..was deadly true, and the *observation officers were able to see, through their field-glasses, men falling in every direction. 1922 Observation officer [see flying officer s.v. FLYING vbl. sb. 3]. 1974 Times 23 Jan. 16/8 [Mr Arthur Harold Stevens] won the MC in 1916 for great courage under fire as an observation officer. 1906 F. LYNDE Quickening 29 At the rear of the string of Pullmans was a private car, with a deep *observation platform. 1943 J. S. HUXLEY TVA xv. 127 The operation building for the navigation lock..contains control machinery.., and observation platform. 1957 D. ROBINS Noble One x. 103 She could imagine him climbing up the ladders to the observation platforms on the tree tops. 1909 Westm. Gaz. 17 Sept. 3/1 The way of this little bird is to sit on its *observation post. 1914 Daily Express 28 Sept. 4/5 The damage to the cathedral was the inevitable result of the French using the cathedral as an observation post. 1937 KOESTLER Spanish Testament II. 276 At eight the prisoners came out into the courtyard again, and I took up my observation post. 1959 Listener 26 Mar. 553/1 In the extreme, as in modern totalitarianism, all 'observation posts' are available only to the duly qualified. 1974 K. ROYCE Trap Spider vii. 124, I could see the entrance... I had as good an observation post as any. 1964 Amer. Philos. Q. I. 251/1 The *observation report can be a singular statement that contradicts the law. 1974 M. HESSE Struct. Sci. Inference i. 35 The 'meaning' of observation reports is 'theory-laden'. 1970 Guardian 14 Feb. 8/2 *Observation rooms for looking down into the studios. 1936 R. CARNAP in Philos. of Sci. III. 429 My testing of any sentence..refers back ultimately to my own *observation-sentences. 1940 A. J. AYER Found. Empirical Knowl. ii. 86 Some observation-sentence should be derivable. 1964 I. SCHEFFLER Anat. Inquiry 135 Their vocabulary was appropriate, enabling derivation from observation-sentences. 1970 W. V. QUINE Philos. of Logic i. 5 Usually observation sentences are..individually responsive to observation. This is what distinguishes observation sentences from theoretical sentences. 1946 A. J. AYER Lang., Truth & Logic (ed. 2) 11 My principle..I shall restate here..using the phrase '*observation-statement' in place of 'experiential proposition', to designate a statement 'which records an actual or possible observation'. 1951 Mind LX. 19 Such observation statements as 'The hydrogen-oxygen mixture in this glass vessel when ignited changed into water vapour'. 1961 E. NAGEL Struct. of Sci. xi. 348 Singular statements that either formulate the outcome of observations..or describe the overt procedures ..we shall call..'observation statements'. 1966 Philos. XLI. 260 Various views..were held about observation-statements. 1965 P. CAWS Philos. of Sci. xi. 78 Terms which name percepts we have agreed to call *observation terms, since they refer to what is directly observed. 1974 M. HESSE Struct. Sci. Inference i. 10 The allegedly clear and distinct character of the observation terms. 1968 N.Y. City (Michelin Tire Corp.) 129 An *observation terrace..offers a splendid view of the airport. 1897 Daily News 21 July 6/5 A revolving *observation tower was opened at Great Yarmouth on Monday. 1972 Police Rev. 10 Nov. 1444/1 They merge into almost any background—and for this reason they are the colours selected for Police *observation vehicles. 1927 W. E. COLLINSON Contemp. Eng. 58 If there is doubt as to the presence of the disease in the patient when in hospital, he may be put in an *observation ward. 1961 C. COCKBURN View from West i. 7 This ward..had..been built ..probably as an observation ward for children. 1897 KIPLING Capt. Cour. ix. 193 The secretary and typewriter sat together..by the plate-glass *observation window at the rear end. 1974 P. DICKINSON Poison Oracle i. 7 Wesley Morris stared at Dinah [sc. an ape] through the observation window.

obser'vational, a. [f. prec. + -AL¹.]

1. Of or pertaining to observation or taking notice.

1854 Fraser's Mag. L. 344 Means of furthering the education of the young, and displaying the observational powers of the mature. 1885 Brit. Almanac Comp. 7 The observational tact and largeness of a disciplined imagination and eye.

2. Of or pertaining to scientific observation.

1834 CHALMERS Bridgewater Treat. II. ii. II. 191 At the commencement of this observational process. 1856 DOVE Logic Chr. Faith v. i. 248 We have in astronomic Science.. the observational element. 1880 Nature XXI. 207 Materials for observational and experimental research.

Hence **obser'vationally** adv., by means of observation; with regard to observation.

1893 HUXLEY in Westm. Gaz. 29 Dec. 4/3 A profound distrust of all long chains of deductive reasoning,..unless the links could be experimentally or observationally tested. 1930 A. S. EDDINGTON Rotation of Galaxy 13 The effect on the apparent angular motion..remains always on the verge of what is detectable observationally. 1964 Philos. Rev. LXXIII. 203 We cannot observationally verify the speaker's claims. 1976 Nature 26 Feb. 628/2 Observationally one requires better high resolution, far-infrared and molecular maps and a near-infrared search for the dust-enshrouded protostars in the H II regions before the vastly complex physics and mechanics of these birthplaces of stars can be understood fully.

obser'vationalism. [f. prec. + -ISM.] The theory that all knowledge is based on observation. Also, the doctrine that observation, rather than theory, is the basis of science. Hence **obser'vationalist** a. (sb.), adhering to observationalism; practising observational as opp. to theoretical work; also, one who adheres to observationalism. Also **observatio'nality**, closeness to the level of observation; non-theoreticality.

1888 CALDERWOOD Lecture Edin. Univ. 24 Oct. Observationalism..sought an explanation of existence in the facts of existence themselves. 1951 Mind LX. 44 The inductive account of scientific method, which is an alternative way of stating observationalism, postulated..the cautious generalization which must not go beyond the data. Ibid. 46 A consequence of observationalist presuppositions. 1960 W. V. QUINE Word & Object 42 We may speak of degrees of observationality. 1966 Philos. XLI. 360 Opposition to dogmatic observationalism should not develop into dogmatic anti-observationalism. 1973 Sci. Amer. May 12/3 Sclater..writes that McKenzie 'is the theoretician and I am the observationalist'.

observative (əb'zɜːvətɪv), a. [f. L. observāt-, ppl. stem of observāre to OBSERVE + -IVE.]

1. Of or pertaining to observation; given to observation, observant, attentive, heedful. Now rare.

1611 SPEED Hist. Gt. Brit. IX. xx. §70. 977 Let vs heare in this point the obseruatiue Knight. 1649 J. H. Motion to Parl. Adv. Learn. 37 Observative mindes might have.. variety of formes whereupon to work. 1892 Amer. Ann. Deaf XXXVII. 167 [She] took an observative and practical course at the Illinois Institution.

†2. Worthy of observation; observable. Obs. rare.

1608 TOPSELL Serpents (1658) 627 By the Serpent in holy Writ, are many observative significations.

†**'observator.** Obs. Also 6-7 -our. [ad. F. observateur (1495 in Godef. Compl.), ad. L. observātor, agent-n. f. observāre to OBSERVE. Earlier stress observa'tour, ob'servator, obser'vator.]

1. One who observes a law, command, or rule: = OBSERVER 1.

1502 Ord. Crysten Men (W. de W. 1506) II. iii. 89 Good & faythfull crysten people and true obseruatours of the commaundementes. Ibid. viii. 107 The observytour of this commaundement. 1663 GERBIER Counsel 61 A constant observator of the three chief Principles of Building.

2. One who marks, notes, or makes observations. Formerly a frequent name for a newspaper or pamphlet, and often applied to the editor or writer: = OBSERVER 3.

1642 View Print. Bk. int. Observat. 3 Prentices and Porters are below our Observator. 1682 SIR T. BROWNE Chr. Mor. III. §10 To thoughtful Observators the whole World is a Phylactery. 1708 SWIFT Sacram. Test Wks. 1755 II. I. 123 The archbishop of Dublin..whom you tamely suffer to be abused..by that paultry rascal of an observator. 1786 A. GIB Sacr. Contempl. 448 It is quite another sort of world that the Essayer and his friend the Observator are for.

b. One who 'observes' by way of divination: cf. OBSERVE v. 6b.

1652 GAULE Magastrom. 287 Two genethliacall astrologers, and so precise observatours as that they calculated the births of the very brute beasts in their families.

c. One who keeps watch over or looks after something; a monitor.

1611 COTGR., Observateur,..an obseruator, monitor, bill-keeper, in Schooles. 1658 SIR T. BROWNE Hydriot. v. 26 The Provincial Guardians, or tutelary observators. 1706 PHILLIPS, Observator,..a Monitor in a School.

3. One who makes scientific observations, esp. in astronomy: = OBSERVER 4.

1664 POWER Exp. Philos. III. 166 The Observators nominated [to make observations in magnetical variation]. 1765 WESLEY Wks. (1872) XIII. 398 Our best observators could never find the parallax of the sun to be above eleven seconds. 1776 Court & City Reg. 164/2 Astronomical Observator, Rev. N. Maskelyne. 1798 J. HORNSBY Introd. Bradley's Astron. Observ. i, The office of Astronomical Observator at the Observatory of Greenwich.

4. One who makes a verbal observation: = OBSERVER 5.

1660 JER. TAYLOR Duct. Dubit. II. ii. rule 3 §26 Which is well noted by the observator upon the mythologies of Natalis Comes. 1693 DRYDEN Juvenal x. (1697) 270 She may be handsom, yet be Chaste, you say; Good Observator, not so fast away.

5. A case or receptacle for the host, serving the purpose of a monstrance.

1560 Burgh Rec. Peebles (1872) 262 Ane obseruatour of irne to the ewcharist.

observa'torial, a. rare⁻¹. [f. as OBSERVATORY a. + -AL¹.] Of or belonging to a (scientific) observer; of the nature of an observatory.

1816 FABER Orig. Pagan Idol. I. II. ii. 355 With respect to Cader-Idris,..the gigantic astronomer Idris, whose observatorial chair it is feigned to have been.

observatory (əb'zɜːvətərɪ), sb. [Corresponds to a L. type *observātōri-um, neut. sb. from *observātōrius adj., and to mod.F. observatoire: cf. next, and see -ORY.]

1. A building or place set apart for, and furnished with instruments for making, observations of natural phenomena; esp., for astronomical, meteorological, or magnetic observations.

1676 EVELYN Diary 10 Sept., Mr. Flamstead the learned astrologer..whom his majesty had establish'd in the new Observatorie in Greenewich Park. 1795 [see OBSERVER 4]. 1872 YEATS Hist. Comm. 409 Magnetic observatories have been established in England, other parts of Europe, and the United States. 1899 Whitaker's Alm. 618 The Ben Nevis Observatory was to have ceased work..in October of this year [1898]. Ibid. The Magnetic Observatory at Toronto has been abandoned, and the magnets at the U.S. Naval Observatory have been rendered useless by the electric railways passing near.

2. A position affording an extensive view; a building erected to command a wide view.

1695 LD. PRESTON Boeth. IV. 196 He looks about him from the high Observatory of his Providence. 1809 KENDALL Trav. III. lxxiv. 153 A building called the observatory, a name by which..we are..to understand..a marine signal house. 1855 SINGLETON Virgil I. 321 Misenus gives A sign from his observatory high. 1860 EMERSON Cond. Life, Behaviour Wks. (Bohn) II. 383 The birds have ..the advantage by their wings of a higher observatory.

3. (nonce-use.) A place of observation.

1882 STEVENSON New Arab. Nts. (1884) 39 The observatory was blinded, a wardrobe having been drawn in front of it upon the other side. 1886 —— Kidnapped 296, I could hear the noise of a window gently thrust up, and knew that my uncle had come to his observatory.

ob'servatory, a. [f. L. observātōr-em, or observāt-, ppl. stem of observāre to OBSERVE: see -ORY.] Of or pertaining to scientific observation.

1864 Athenæum 15 Oct. 493 The system of bar hives, the very best for observatory purposes..is ignored. 1884 C. R. MARKHAM in Pall Mall G. 20 Aug. 1/2 The observatory work will be valuable, by supplementing the series taken on board her Majesty's ship Discovery.

†**obser'vatrix.** Obs. rare⁻¹. [L. fem. of OBSERVATOR.] A female observer.

1653 R. SANDERS Physiogn. a ij b, Of which, Physick her self (like a diligent hand-maid) is a continual observatrix.

observe (əb'zɜːv), v. [a. F. observer (10th c. in Godef. Compl.), ad. L. observāre to watch, look towards, look to, attend to, pay attention to, guard, keep; f. ob- (OB- 1 a) + servāre to watch, look at, guard, keep.]

I. To attend to in practice; to keep; to follow.

1. trans. To pay practical attention or regard to (a law, command, custom, practice, covenant, set time, or anything prescribed or fixed); to adhere to or abide by in practice: = KEEP v 11.

1390 GOWER Conf. III. 233 That bothe kinde schal be served And ek the lawe of god observed. 1484 CAXTON Fables of Æsop II. ix, Good Children ought to obserue and kepe euer the comaundements of theyr good parents. 1526 TINDALE Matt. xxiii. 3 Whatsoever they byd you observe, that observe and do. 1613 PURCHAS Pilgrimage (1614) 709 They..observe Circumcision. 1781 J. MOORE View Soc. It. (1790) II. lxii. 222, I shall observe your prohibition not to refer you to any medical book. 1884 A. R. PENNINGTON Wiclif ix. 298 They declared that neither faith nor promise was to be observed to the detriment of the Catholic Church.

b. To adhere to, follow (a method, rule, or principle of action).

a 1548 HALL Chron., Hen. VII 4 So that..he observyng the regyment that amongest the people was devysed could.. avoyde the..malyce of the sweate. 1669 STURMY Mariner's Mag. IV. 189 If you will seriously observe these short Directions..you shall never have your Expectation deceived. 1733 BERKELEY Th. Vision §38 Wks. 1871 I. 387 In considering the Theory of Vision, I observed a certain known method. 1739 C. LABELYE Short Acc. Piers Westm. Br. 60 A Precaution, which good Engineers often observe in the Foundation of Ramparts. 1870 JEVONS Elem. Logic xv. 129 In ordinary writing and speaking this rule is seldom observed.

2. To hold or keep to, to follow (a manner of life or conduct, a habit); to continue to hold, maintain, retain (a quality, state, or condition): = KEEP v. 23.

c 1386 CHAUCER Pars. T. ⁋873 Thise maner of wommen þat obseruen chaastitee most be clene in herte. 1497 BP. ALCOCK Mons Perfect. C iij, True religyous men obseruynge theyr obedyence. 1513 MORE Rich. III (1883) 1 Brigette, whiche..professed and obserued a religious life in Dertforde. 1613 PURCHAS Pilgrimage (1614) 540 A care to observe humanitie and pietie. 1716 ADDISON Freeholder No. 18 ⁋4 The present government..will so far observe this kind of Conduct, as to reduce [etc.]. 1843 LEFEVRE Life Trav. Phys. II. II. vii. 260 The people observe a dead silence. 1853 J. H. NEWMAN Hist. Sk. (1873) II. I. iii. 134 Othman observed the life of a Turcoman, till he became a conqueror.

†b. To follow the practice, be in the habit, 'use' (to do something). Obs.

1641 HINDE J. Bruen xxix. 90 Against S. Andrews day.. I observed (saith he) many yeares together, to invite two or three..preachers. 1743 Lond. & Country Brew. IV. (ed. 2) 271 Another who used to brew his strong Drink by only one Mashing,..observed to thrust down a good Handful of fresh Hops just over the Tapwhips.

3. To celebrate duly, to solemnize in the prescribed way (a religious rite, ceremony, fast, festival, etc.): = KEEP v. 12.

1526 TINDALE Gal. iv. 10 Ye observe the dayes and monethes and tymes and yeres. 1590 SHAKS. Mids. N. IV. i. 189 No doubt they rose vp early, to observe The right of May. 1611 BIBLE Exod. xii. 17 Ye shall obserue the feast of unleavened bread. 1613 PURCHAS Pilgrimage (1614) 348 The day wherein he overthrew Seleucus, was solemnely observed every yeare amongst them. 1770 LANGHORNE Plutarch (1879) I. 12/1 A chariot race at Veii..was observed as usual. 1833 R. CHOATE Addresses (1878) 16 A score of Indian tribes..observed the rites of that bloody and horrible Paganism which formed their only religion. Mod. Christmas is now observed in Scotland much more than formerly.

II. †4. To treat with attention or regard. Obs.

†a. *gen.* To show regard for, respect, defer to. *Obs. rare.*

c1386 CHAUCER *Prioress' T.* 179 This Prouost dooth the Iewes for to sterue That of this mordre wiste.. He nolde no swich cursednesse obserue, Yuele shal he haue þat yuele wol deserue.

†b. To show respectful or courteous attention to (a person); to treat with ceremonious respect or reverence; to worship, honour; to court; to humour, gratify. *Obs.*

1599 DAVIES *Astrea* xvi, No spirit but takes thee for her queen, And thinks she must observe thee. 1601 SHAKS. *Jul. C.* IV. iii. 45 Must I obserue you? Must I stand and crouch Vnder your Testie Humour? 1613 PURCHAS *Pilgrimage* (1614) 821 They which dwell on this River observe an Idoll of great note. 1754 RICHARDSON *Grandison* VII. xix. 107 Clementina loves to be punctiliously observed.

III. To attend to with the mind; to mark; to perceive.

†5. To give heed to (a point); to take care *that* something be done, or *to do* something. *Obs.*

1526 *Pilgr. Perf.* (W. de W. 1531) 8 Foure thynges be necessary to be vnderstande & obserued of all them that entendeth to trauayle the same. a1548 HALL *Chron., Hen VII* 4 One poynte diligently..is to be obserued and attended, that he never put..foote out of ye bed. 1611 BIBLE *Deut.* vi. 25 It shall be our righteousnes, if we obserue to doe all these Commandements. 1703 *Rules Civility* 41 You must ..observe to take a worse Seat than his Lordship. 1707 FUNNELL *Voy.* 164 Observe that you come not too near the Cape. 1793 SMEATON *Edystone L.* §97, I took off..the most remarkable points,..observing to have one at each end..of each step.

6. To regard with attention; to watch; †to watch over, look after (*obs.*).

1567 *Gude & Godlie B.* (S.T.S.) 98 The wickit dois obserue the Innocent, To seik to slay him with cruell intent. 1601 SHAKS. *All's Well* II. i. 46 Say to him I liue, and obserue his reports for me. 1685 BAXTER *Paraphr. N.T., Acts* xv. 36 Converted Souls and planted Churches, must be further visited, observed and watered. 1717 tr. *Frezier's Voy.* 65, I observ'd them attentively..and did not..see one smiling Countenance among them. 1861 M. PATTISON *Ess.* (1889) I. 36 Edward..requires his ambassador to observe the young prince, and to inform himself of his character and disposition. 1884 *Punch* 5 Apr. 160/2, I fancy I was being 'observed', as they say on the Stage.

b. *spec.* To regard with attention by way of augury or divination; to inspect for purposes of divination; to watch or take note of (presages or omens), L. *observare* or *servare cælum, sidera, motus stellarum*, etc.: cf. OBSERVATION 5 c.

c1391 CHAUCER *Astrol.* II. §4 The assendent..is a thing which þat thise Astrologiens gretly obseruen. 1513 MORE *Rich. III* (1883) 49 Yet hath it [the stumbling of one's horse] ben, of an olde rite and custome, obserued as a token.. notably foregoing some great misfortune. 1611 BIBLE *Lev.* xix. 26 Neither shall ye vse inchantment, nor obserue times. 1613 PURCHAS *Pilgrimage* (1614) 675 Which are great Witches, and observe entrals of sacrificed Beastes. 1718 *Free-thinker* No. 62 ¶3 As for the Occasions, upon which the Ancients had Recourse to Presages..it was judged requisite to observe Them, more especially, in Entring upon any Undertaking.

c. *Mil.* To watch (a fortress, the enemy's movements, etc.); also *absol.* or *intr.*

[1611 BIBLE *2 Sam.* xi. 16 When Joab observed the city.] 1799 FLOYD in Owen *Mrq. Wellesley's Desp.* (1877) 122, I was observing, with three regiments of cavalry, between the right flank of Colonel Wellesley and the left of General Harris. 1813 *Examiner* 3 May 274/2 The fortress..is.. observed by some parties of Cossacks. 1836 ALISON *Europe* (1849–50) V. xxvii. §78. 67 Froelich, with six thousand men, observed Coni. 1853 STOCQUELER *Mil. Encycl.* s.v., *To observe the motions of an enemy* is to keep a good look out by means of intelligent and steady spies or scouts.

d. *absol.* or *intr.* To make observations.

1604 SHAKS. *Oth.* III. iii. 240 Set on thy wife to obserue. 1760–72 H. BROOKE *Fool of Qual.* (1809) III. 138 You have seen and observed upon many courts of late. 1791 BURKE *To Member Nat. Assembly* Wks. VI. 32 He has not observed on the nature of vanity who does not know that it is omnivorous.

†7. *trans.* To watch for in order to take advantage of (a proper time, an opportunity). *Obs.*

1540–1 ELYOT *Image Gov.* 17 Obseruing the tyme, he by little and little withdrewe hym into suche places. *Ibid.* 92 Good diligence in obseruing the oportunity of tyme in sowyng & planting. 1560 DAUS tr. *Sleidane's Comm.* 109 The byshop..for this cause made the league, obseruing the occasion of tyme. a1642 SIR W. MONSON *Naval Tracts* v. (1704) 467/2 They must observe the Spring-Tides to come over the Barr.

8. To take notice of, to be conscious of seeing (a thing or fact); to notice, remark, perceive, see.

1560 DAUS tr. *Sleidane's Comm.* 285 The Sunne loked pale and dimme,..And this was not observed in Germany only, but also in Fraunce and England. 1634 SIR. T. HERBERT *Trav.* 223 King Henry..observing simplicitie in the Messengers delivery. 1736 BUTLER *Anal.* I. ii. Wks. 1874 I. 35 This every one observes to be the general course of things. 1775 SHERIDAN *Rivals* II. i, I observe you have got an odd kind of a new method of swearing. 1793 COWPER *Let.* 6 Sept., Hearing the hall-clock, I observed a great difference between that and ours. 1833–6 J. EAGLES *Sketcher* (1856) 200, I am not, observe, here saying one is preferable to another.

absol. 1605 BACON *Adv. Learn.* II. x. §4 If men will intend to observe, they shall find much worthy to observe. 1783 BLAIR *Rhet.* x. I. 200 We remark, in the way of attention, in order to remember; we observe, in the way of examination, in order to judge.

†b. To pay attention to (a person, i.e. to what he says); to mark. *Obs.*

1775 SHERIDAN *Rivals* I. ii, *Mrs. Mal.* Observe me, Sir Anthony. I would by no means wish a daughter of mine to be a progeny of learning.

9. To take notice of scientifically; *esp.* to examine (phenomena) as they are presented to the senses, without the aid of experiment; to perceive or learn by scientific inspection. (Cf. OBSERVATION 6.)

1559 W. CUNNINGHAM *Cosmogr. Glasse* 162, I can with my ..Quadrant, obserue the height of the sonne, and sterre, vntill that he come to the meridian. 1605 BACON *Adv. Learn.* II. x. §5 As for..impostumations,..they ought to have been exactly observed by multitude of anatomies. 1669 STURMY *Mariner's Mag.* III. 126 You must observe with your Instrument the Angle CBA, and measure the Distance. 1704 HEARNE *Duct. Hist.* (1714) I. 398 The Chaldæans.. said they had begun to observe the Stars 470000 years before Alexander's Expedition thither. 1849 MACAULAY *Hist. Eng.* iii. I. 372 The Marquess of Worcester had recently observed the expansive power of moisture rarefied by heat. 1871 B. STEWART *Heat* §63 Adding this to the height of the barometer which was observed at the same moment.

absol. 1879 THOMSON & TAIT *Nat. Phil.* I. I. §369 When, as in astronomy, we endeavour to ascertain these causes by simply watching their effects, we *observe*; when, as in our laboratories, we interfere arbitrarily with the causes or circumstances of a phenomenon, we are said to *experiment*.

b. *spec.* To make an observation (see OBSERVATION 6 b) in order to determine the altitude of (the sun or other heavenly body), to ascertain (the latitude or longitude), etc.; also *absol.* or *intr.*

[1559: see 9.] 1627 CAPT. SMITH *Seaman's Gram.* ix. 42 Obserue the height, that is, at twelue a clocke to take the height of the Sunne. 1669 STURMY *Mariner's Mag.* II. 78 The Mariner's Cross-Staff..by which we observe the Celestial Lights. 1761 DUNN in *Phil. Trans.* LII. 185 In taking altitudes, I always observe, when the sun, or other celestial body, is as near the prime vertical, or east and west azimuth, as possible. 1854 BARTLETT *Mex. Boundary* I. xvi. 373 Lieutenant Whipple observed here, and found the latitude to be 32°08′43″, longitude 109°24′33″.

IV. 10. To say by way of remark; to remark or mention in speech or writing.

1605 BACON *Adv. Learn* II. xxv. §24 Your Majesty doth excellently well observe, that witchcraft is the height of idolatry. 1646 J. HALL *Horæ Vac.* 172 Tis handsomely observed, that the maine of other Religions never gained by Christianity. 1709 ATTERBURY *Serm. Luke* x. 32 in *Serm.* (1726) II. 243 His Compassion and Benignity towards little Children is observ'd by all the Evangelists. 1716 ADDISON *Free-holder* No. 22 ¶2 My Fellow-Traveller, upon this, observed to me, there had been no good Weather since the Revolution. 1833 HT. MARTINEAU *Charmed Sea* i. 3 'You will not cross the testy sea to-night', observed one of the peasants. 1839 THIRLWALL *Greece* VI. lii. 319 The king.. observed that on a fine theme it was no hard task to speak well.

b. *absol.*, or *intr.* with *on* or *upon*: To make a remark or observation, to comment (on).

1613 PURCHAS *Pilgrimage* (1614) 120 Scaliger thus obserueth concerning the Iewish yeare. The Iewes (saith he) use [etc.]. 1665 SIR T. HERBERT *Trav.* (1677) 23 Not only the surface but the inward bowels of the Earth (as Sir Fran. Bacon observes). 1717 *Col. Rec. Pennsylv.* III. 39 It was moved that they should be read, for the members of Council to observe upon them. 1827 R. H. FROUDE *Rem.* (1838) I. 453, I will make my meals as simple as I can, without being observed on. 1883 SIR N. LINDLEY in *Law Rep.* 11 Queen's Bench Div. 527 These matters I thought it necessary to observe upon.

¶11. *catachr.* To keep, preserve; to retain. *Obs.*

c1420 *Pallad. on Husb.* IV. 332 Summen..With water mynge vryne observed longe. 1577 HANMER *Anc. Eccl. Hist.* 71 The fatherly affection of Rome, which..your bishop not onely obserued but augmented. 1596 DALRYMPLE tr. *Leslie's Hist. Scot.* II. 131 Thir armes we knawe evir his eftircumeris to haue obseruet.

Hence **observed** (-ˈzɜːvd), *ppl. a.*; **obˈservedly** (-ɪdlɪ) *adv.*, notably.

1602 SHAKS. *Ham.* III. i. 162 The glasse of Fashion, and the mould of Forme, Th' obseru'd of all Obseruers. 1615 CHAPMAN *Odyss.* VI. 112 Up to coach then goes Th' observed maid. 1669 STURMY *Mariner's Mag.* IV. 157 When the Dead Latitude differs from the Observed Latitude. 1860 TYNDALL *Glac.* Pref., To refer the observed phenomena to their physical causes. 1891 C. C. COE in *Relig. & Life* ii. 52 Science, and observedly the science of geology, has freed us.

obˈserve, *sb.* [f. OBSERVE *v.*]

†1. = OBSERVATION 5, 6, 7. *Obs.*

1686 GOAD *Celest. Bodies* I. iv. 14 Some that shoot without aim, may abandon these Observes for superstitions. 1830 GALT *Lawrie T.* III. i. (1849) 145 The Squire, and I, could scale the river, and make observes.

2. A verbal observation, a remark. *Sc.*

1711 *Countrey-Man's Lett. to Curat* 77 The observe of a certain Polititian, that *mundus regitur a stultis* holding generally true. 1738 W. WILSON *Def. Ref. Princ. Ch. Scot.* (1769) I. 34, I shall first offer a few observes concerning the Church. 1886 STEVENSON *Kidnapped* xii. 110 'And that's a good observe, David', said Alan. 1893 CROCKETT *Stickit Minister* 73 A most uncalled for observe.

†3. *Sc.* A division of a sermon.

1833 W. L. MACKENZIE *Sk. Canada & U.S.* 8, I went to hear Doctor McLeod, a steadfast Presbyterian of the old school. There..the discourse is divided and subdivided into heads and observes in true covenanting fashion.

observer (əbˈzɜːvə(r)). Also 6 -ar, 7 -or. [f. OBSERVE *v.* + -ER¹. Cf. OF. *observeur* (Godef. in sense 1).]

1. One who observes or keeps a law, rule, custom, practice, method, or anything prescribed or fixed.

1555 EDEN *Decades* 258 A diligente obseruer of his accustomed religion. 1660 R. COKE *Power & Subj.* 256 A devout observor of the government, rites, and ceremonies of the Church of England. 1721 G. ROUSSILLON tr. *Vertot's Rev. Portug.* 84 Suppos'd to be a conceal'd observer of the Jewish law. 1748 RICHARDSON *Clarissa* (1811) II. xxxiii. 241, I am such an observer of method, that I can go [etc.]. 1880 WALLACE *Ben-Hur* IV. xv, They were..rigorous observers of the Law as found in the books of Moses.

†2. One who shows respect, deference or dutiful attention; an obsequious follower. *Obs.*

1601 SIR. W. CORNWALLIS *Disc. Seneca* (1631) 38 The soul cherished and observed, recompenseth her observer. 1613 CHAPMAN *Rev. Bussy D'Ambois* IV. Hij, His iust contempt of Iesters, Parasites, Seruile obseruers. 1633 MASSINGER *Guardian* I. ii, You are my gracious patroness and supportress, And I your poor observer.

3. a. One who watches, marks, or takes notice. (A frequent title of newspapers.)

1581 MULCASTER *Positions* xxxix. (1887) 214 His observer, whom he [Plato] alloweth to go abroad to see fashions. 1601 SHAKS. *Jul. C.* I. ii. 202 He is a great Obseruer, and he lookes Quite through the Deeds of men. 1772 PRIESTLEY *Inst. Relig.* (1782) I. 24 This is the conclusion of a superficial observer. 1860 TYNDALL *Glac.* I. xx. 140 This completes the glorious circuit within the observer's view. 1866 WHIPPLE *Character* 238 Hawthorne is one of those true observers who concentrate in observation every power of their minds.

b. One who observes presages or omens: see OBSERVE *v.* 6 b.

1588 PARKE tr. *Mendoza's Hist. China* 348 They were great Agorismers or obseruers of times..if they..meete with a Cayman or lyzarde..they know it to be a signe of euill fortune. 1611 BIBLE *Deut.* xviii. 10 An obseruer of times, or an inchanter, or a witch. 1698 FRYER *Acc. E. India & P.* 193 Strict Observers of Omens.

c. A person who observes without participating; *spec.* (*a*) one who attends a conference, display, etc., to note the proceedings; (*b*) one posted to an area of conflict to note events, supervise a cease-fire, etc.; also *attrib.*, as ***observer force, group***.

1925 A. TOYNBEE *Survey Internat. Affairs 1920–23* 10 Several meetings were attended by an American observer. 1949 *Ann. Reg. 1948* 292 The U.N. Balkans Commission.. sent observers to watch the fighting there. 1958 *Observer* 10 Aug. 4/6 Any measures.., in addition to the original observer group, which would serve to ensure the territorial integrity and political independence of Lebanon. 1962 *Rep. Comm. Broadcasting 1960* 188 in *Parl. Papers 1961–2* (Cmnd. 1753) IX. 259 The three advertising organisations which now appoint one representative and one observer to the Committee formerly appointed two representatives each. 1970 *Guardian* 13 Jan. 9/8 The French and the Pope have already called for a new observer force. 1977 *Times* 9 Dec. 1/3 Sir David attended the inquest in Pretoria as an independent observer at the invitation of the Association of Law Societies of South Africa.

4. a. One who observes phenomena scientifically; one who makes observations in a particular science; sometimes the official title of the person in charge of an observatory.

1795 *Proc. Board of Longitude* 6 June 11 *note*, The.. Astronomical Observer at the new Observatory, founded by the Trustees of the Radcliffe money. 1805 *Med. Jrnl.* XIV. 563 It has been, and is still my intention..to confine the present survey to original observers of the disease. 1859 DARWIN *Orig. Spec.* ii. (1873) 46, I have..consulted some sagacious and experienced observers. 1871 B. STEWART *Heat* (ed. 2) §40 Dilatations obtained after this method by different observers. 1891 *Dict. Nat. Biog.* XXVII. 373 Immediately on his [Hornsby's] appointment in 1772 as the first Radcliffe Observer [at Oxford], he laid the foundation-stone of the present observatory.

b. One whose duty it is to make military observations; *esp.* (*a*) a member of an artillery group trained to identify the target; (*b*) a person trained to notice and identify aircraft, or carried in an aeroplane (†or other aircraft) to note the enemy's position, etc.; *spec.* as a rank in an air force; also *attrib.*, as ***observer company, corps, flight, officer***.

[1854 C. TOMLINSON *Cycl. Useful Arts* I. 16/1 Scarcely had the observer reached the height of 3,000 feet, than he observed..a thin vapour.] 1870 tr. *F. Marion's Wonderful Balloon Ascents* III. iv. 215 The soldiers of the enemy, all who saw the observer watching them.., came to the idea that they could do nothing without being seen. 1903 *Heavy Artill. Training* 36 If the target is not visible from the guns or ground quite close to them,..two observers are required. 1906 *Strand Mag.* May 515/1 The first of these was Mr. E. T. Fetch, accompanied by Mr. Krarup as observer, on a twelve-horse-power single cylinder Packard car. 1910 *Blackw. Mag.* Feb. 209/1 The service of an aeroplane, especially if..it could carry a military observer as well as the pilot, would be invaluable. 1914 *Field Artill. Training* ix. 325 The observer, having located the position of the target and conveyed the information to the artillery commander.. receives from him the signal 'Observe for line'. 1914 *Daily Express* 28 Aug. 2/6 (*heading*) Observer flights. 1916 H. BARBER *Aeroplane Speaks* 50 Quickly the Observer climbs into his seat in front of the Pilot. 1928 C. F. S. GAMBLE *Story N. Sea Air Station* xiii. 226 During this year [1916] the rank of Observer Officer was created. 1932 *Flight* 22 July 677/2 It is very necessary to see, at least once a year, how the Observer Corps is functioning. 1940 *War Illustr.* 5 Jan. p. ii/3 Parker..was a Group Commander in the Observer Companies of the Royal Defence Corps, which was founded in 1916. **1954** P. K. KEMP *Fleet Air Arm* 52 During 1916, the Admiralty opened a special school for training observers and instituted a new rank of Observer Officer. **1977** J. CLEARY *High Road to China* i. 26 The Bristol Fighter.. carried two guns, one fired straight ahead by the pilot and the other able to be fired in a complete circle by the observer.

c. Used *attrib.* with reference to the effect of subjective factors on the accuracy or veracity of scientific observations.

1959 *Times Lit. Suppl.* 31 July 441/2 Proper consideration of evidence, allowance for observer-error, the clarification of language as a communicative medium—these..are the barriers which stand between us and the irrational abyss. **1970** G. GREER *Female Eunuch* 90 It takes another psychiatrist to explain to her the function of observer bias. **1971** *Brit. Med. Bull.* XXVII. 6/1 Observer variability has also been shown to be a significant factor in errors in blood-pressure readings. *Ibid.* 8/1 There was little evidence to suggest variation between observers or observer bias.

5. One who makes a verbal observation or remark.

1724 SWIFT *Drapier's Lett.* Wks. 1755 V. II. 93 The maxim of common observers, that those who meddle in matters out of their calling, will have reason to repent.

Hence **ob'servership**, the office or position of Observer (sense 4 a above).

1839 J. B. MOZLEY *Lett.* 3 Apr. (1885) 90 Johnson of Magdalen Hall is standing for the place of Radcliffe Observer, vacant by Rigaud's death..any one can stand for the Observership, whereas it must be an M.A. for the other [*sc.* the Professorship].

†**ob'servicer.** *Obs. rare*⁻¹. [A hybrid form mixing up *observer* and *service.*] = OBSERVER 2.

1625 SHIRLEY *Love-tricks* III. v, I am your humble observicer, and wish you all cumulations of prosperity.

observing (əb'zɜːvɪŋ), *vbl. sb.* [f. OBSERVE *v.* + -ING[1].] The action of the vb. OBSERVE; observance; observation.

1526 *Pilgr. Perf.* (W. de W. 1531) 55 b, The vse and obseruynge of the x commaundementes. **1613** PURCHAS *Pilgrimage* (1614) 12 The swiftnesse of the heavens wheele, which even in the moment of observing is past observing. **1719** DE FOE *Crusoe* II. iv, I leave observing, and return to the story. **1887** *Athenæum* 12 Mar. 356/1 An amateur beginner in astronomical observing.

attrib. **1884** *Pall Mall G.* 27 May 11/1 The person in charge of the observing station.

observing (əb'zɜːvɪŋ), *ppl. a.* [-ING[2].]

1. That observes or takes notice; quick to notice, observant; engaged in scientific observation.

1628 tr. *Camden's Hist. Eliz.* IV. (1688) 654 If any Credit may be given to..the more observing men. **1704** J. TRAPP *Abra-Mulé* II. i. 447 Her Beauty could not 'scape th' observing Eyes Of some. **1898** *Daily News* 15 Feb. 8/4, I do not believe that a single member of the whole observing party ever doubted the possibility..of a cloudy day.

†**b.** Note-taking. *Obs.*

c **1720** HEARNE in *Wood's Life* (1848) App. iii. 337 Mr. Wood was afterwards expell'd the common room, and his company avoyded as an observing person. **1775** SHERIDAN *Rivals* I. ii, She has a most observing thumb; and..cherishes her nails for the convenience of making marginal notes.

†**2.** Compliant, obsequious. *Obs.*

1606 SHAKS. *Tr. & Cr.* II. iii. 137 [They] vnder write in an obseruing kinde His humorous predominance.

Hence **ob'servingly** *adv.*, in an observing manner, observantly.

1599 SHAKS. *Hen. V.* IV. i. 5 There is some soule of goodnesse in things euill, Would men obseruingly distill it out. **1828** FR. A. KEMBLE in *Rec. Girlhood* (1878) I. viii. 222, I have seen and heard observingly. **1889** A. E. BARR *Feet of Clay* xii. 233 His father listened patiently and observingly.

ob'servist. *nonce-wd.* [f. OBSERVE *v.* + -IST.] One who makes observation his business.

1827 CARLYLE *Germ. Rom.* II. 13 He is no mere observist and compiler.

obsess (əb'sɛs), *v.* Also 6 *erron.* obcess. [f. L. *obsess-*, ppl. stem of *obsidēre* to sit at or opposite to, sit down before, besiege, occupy, possess, f. *ob-* (OB- I a, b) + *sedēre* to sit. Cf. obs. F. *obsesser* (16th c. in Godef.).

The word appears to have become obsolete early in 18th c, and to have been revived in 19th: cf. OBSESSION.]

†**1.** *trans.* To sit down before (a fortress, the enemy); to besiege, invest. *Obs.*

1503 in Ellis *Orig. Lett.* Ser. I. I. 53 Parties so to be besegied, troubled, or obsessed by the said Turke. **1534** WHITINTON *Tullyes Offices* II. (1540) 97 These that be besyeged or obcessed of their enemyes. **1647** WHARTON *Bellum Hybern.* Wks. (1683) 254 The People of that Country shall be obsessed, or besieged, they shall not dare to go out of their Towns.

2. Of an evil spirit: To beset, assail, or harass (a person); to haunt; to move or actuate from without.

1540–1 ELYOT *Image Gov.* 54 b, I omyt to speake of the confession of dyuels, which..were cast out of people, which were obsessed. **1616** BULLOKAR *Eng. Expos.* s.v., A man is said to be obsest, when an euill spirit followeth him, troubling him at diuers times and seeking opportunity to enter into him. **1718** BP. HUTCHINSON *Witchcraft* 70 The Spirits obsess, haunt and dog them. **1827–45** SIR H. TAYLOR *Isaac Comnenus* II. iv, Which saint is most powerful for freeing the demoniacs? *Exorcist.* That is..according as they are obsessed or possessed.

3. *transf.* To beset, assail, or harass like a besieging force or an evil spirit; in modern use *esp.* to haunt and trouble as a 'fixed idea'.

1531 ELYOT *Gov.* II. iv, Where maiestie approcheth to excesse, and the mynde is obsessed with inordinat glorie. **1648** *Petit. East. Assoc.* 28 You are..Army-pinion'd and obsessed with Sectaries. **1885** F. W. H. MYERS in *Fortn. Rev.* XXXVIII. 643 The subject..felt the hypnotiser's will obsessing him. **1894** *Speaker* 28 Apr. 480/2 The extent to which political problems are obsessing men's minds. **1899** HOWELLS in *Literature* 3 June 578 The spirit of war seems to have obsessed our periodical literature.

Hence **obsessed** (-'sɛst) *ppl. a.*; **ob'sessing** *vbl. sb.* and *ppl. a.*

1623 COCKERAM, *Obsest*, one possesst with a spirit. **1665** NEEDHAM *Med. Medicinæ* 409 To the obsessing and distressing of those two most noble Vital Instruments of the Body. **1845** G. OLIVER *Coll. Biog. Soc. Jesus* 75 His fame for dispossessing obsessed persons becoming notorious.

†**ob'sess,** *sb. Obs. rare*⁻¹. [f. prec. vb., or L. type **obsessus.*] An investment, siege, blockade.

1694 MOTTEUX *Rabelais* v. 250 Obsesses [F. *obsidion*], Storms and Fights Sanguinolent.

obsession (əb'sɛʃən). [ad. L. *obsessiōn-em*, n. of action f. *obsidēre* to OBSESS: cf. F. *obsession* (1690 in Hatz.-Darm.).]

†**1.** The action of besieging; investment, siege.

1513 MORE *Richard III* in Hall *Chron.* (1809) 408 They which were in the castell..sent also to the Earle of Richemonde to advertise hym of their sodeine obsession. **1638** PENKETHMAN *Artach.* K iv b, Famine, occasioned through the Enemies obsession, or strict siege.

2. The hostile action of the devil or an evil spirit besetting any one; actuation by the devil or an evil spirit from without; the fact of being thus beset or actuated.

1605 B. JONSON *Volpone* v. xii, Graue fathers, he is possest ..nay if there be possession, And obsession, he has both. *a* **1641** BP. MOUNTAGU *Acts & Mon.* (1642) 190 To give them up to the power of Satan..to possesse, and really inhabite them, or by obsession to move, actuate and enspire them. **1696** AUBREY *Misc.* 156 Her fits and obsessions seem to be greater, for she Scrieches in a most Hellish tone. **1871** TYLOR *Prim. Cult.* II. 113 These cases belong rather to obsession than possession, the spirits not actually inhabiting the bodies, but hanging or hovering about them.

3. *transf.* **a.** The action of any influence, notion, or 'fixed idea', which persistently assails or vexes, esp. so as to discompose the mind.

1680 R. L'ESTRANGE *Mem. Lib. Press & Pulpit* 27 Never was any Nation..under such an Obsession [*printed* Ab-] of Credulity and Blindness. **1852** *Fraser's Mag.* XLV. 248 Beset..by foreign, by back-stairs, and domestic influences, by obsessions at home and abroad. **1893** H. CRACKANTHORPE *Wreckage* 99 The thought of death began to haunt him till it became a constant obsession. **1901** G. B. SHAW *Three Plays for Puritans* Pref. p. xvii, The English novelist, like the starving tramp who can think of nothing but his hunger, seems to be unable to escape from the obsession of sex. **1908** YEATS & GREGORY *Unicorn from Stars* II. 56 There is another kind of inspiration, or rather an obsession or possession. **1916** G. B. SHAW *Androcles & Lion* Pref. p. lxxviii, The mass of mankind..are concerned almost to obsession with sex. **1922** JOYCE *Ulysses* 130 The Roman, like the Englishman who follows in his footsteps, brought to every new shore on which he set his foot..only his cloacal obsession.

b. *Psychol.* An idea or image that repeatedly intrudes upon the mind of a person against his will and is usually distressing (in psychoanalytic theory attributed to the subconscious effect of a repressed emotion or experience).

1901 C. A. MERCIER *Psychol.* 368 Obsessions are extremely varied in character. **1913** E. JONES *Papers on Psycho-Anal.* v. 126 Twenty years ago Janet separated obsessions and phobias under the title of 'psychasthenia'. **1924** J. RIVIERE et al. tr. *Freud's Coll. Papers* I. vii. 129 Two components are found in every obsession: (1) an idea that forces itself upon the patient: (2) an associated emotional state. **1958** M. ARGYLE *Relig. Behaviour* xii. 165 The similarities and differences between rituals and obsessions. **1976** SMYTHIES & CORBETT *Psychiatry* vi. 82 If we see some particularly horrible disaster, most people find it very hard to get it 'out of their minds'. An image of horror keeps coming back unwanted and the person has to struggle to get it out of consciousness. More trivial examples are tunes that keep running through one's head or fears that one might forget one's lines in a play... These are examples of mild obsessions—unwanted thoughts and images that crowd into consciousness in spite of all attempts to keep them out.

obsessional (əb'sɛʃən(ə)l), *a.* [f. prec. + -AL.]

1. Of or pertaining to obsession or to a siege; obsidional.

1857 *National Mag.* II. 304 Pieces of obsessional, or siege money issued by private individuals.

2. a. Characterized by or caused by an obsession (sense 3).

1909 *Cent. Dict.* Suppl., *Obsessional*.., pertaining to or of the nature of obsession. **1913** E. JONES *Papers on Psycho-Anal.* v. 126 Krafft-Ebing maintained the independence of obsessional states. **1940** *Mind* XLIX. 370 Thus with obsessional duties, 'I must go and make sure I have turned out the lights, turned off the taps,..made sure of security'. **1952** V. GOLLANCZ *My Dear Timothy* i. 11 Breathless delight in ease and comfort, and an obsessional drive not merely to work but..'to work extra'. **1954** M. FORTES in E. E. Evans-Pritchard *Inst. Primitive Society* vii. 89 There are the individuals with obsessional and paranoiac fears whose fantasies about themselves..sound like morbid caricatures of primitive beliefs. **1973** R. LEWIS *Of Singular Purpose* vi. 139 There was only one word to describe Paul Mercereau's interest in Van Rijk. It was obsessional.

b. *obsessional neurosis*: in psychoanalytic theory, a psychoneurosis in which obsessional thoughts resulting from a regression of the libido lead to neurotic or compulsive behaviour. So ***obsessional neurotic***, a person suffering from an obsessional neurosis.

1918 E. JONES *Papers on Psycho-Anal.* (ed. 2) xxx. 515 A detailed study of the obsessional neurosis. **1924** J. RIVIERE et al. tr. *Freud's Coll. Papers* I. viii. 153 Hysteria's close association with the female sex and..the preference of the male for the obsessional neurosis. **1926** [see ISOLATION 2 b]. **1939** E. GLOVER *Psycho-Anal.* II. x. 78 The obsessional neurotic, like the hysteric, recognizes the irrationality of his symptoms. **1942** [see DE-EMOTIONALIZE *v.*]. **1968** C. RYCROFT *Crit. Dict. Psychoanal.* 103 According to classical theory, the psychopathology of obsessional neurosis centres round regression to the anal-sadistic stage.

ob'sessional, *sb.* [f. the adj.] Someone whose personality is dominated by an obsession.

1928 [see DIDDUMS]. **1945** *Brit. Jrnl. Psychol.* XXXV. 41 As a group, the obsessionals are distinctly more intelligent than the others. **1963** *Listener* 14 Mar. 474/3 The *soi-disant* realist was really just a neurotic old obsessional with an eye for detail. **1972** E. K. LEDERMANN *Existential Neurosis* ii. 13 Obsessionals and reactive depressives showed high sedation thresholds. **1978** P. PORTER *Cost of Seriousness* 43 Dangerous modes In all weather when obsessionals walk To a favourite spur above the land.

obsessionally (əb'sɛʃənəlɪ), *adv.* [f. OBSESSIONAL *a.* + -LY[2].] In an obsessional manner.

1961 J. DAWSON *Ha-Ha* vi. 126, I noticed the cracks between each board, and followed each one, uneasily, obsessionally, till it ran into the wall. **1961** *John o' London's* 12 Oct. 407/2 He *cares* for the theatre; passionately, obsessionally. **1966** P. GREEN tr. *Escarpit's Novel Computer* viii. 102 Fermigier never suspected a thing, though he was an obsessionally jealous man by nature. **1973** A. ROY *Sable Night* xvi. 167 The two men..had their attention almost obsessionally occupied.

obsessionist (əb'sɛʃənɪst). [f. OBSESSION + -IST.] One who is obsessed, or subject to obsession, by a fixed idea.

1921 *Glasgow Herald* 24 June 8/4 The canards of the anti-waste obsessionists. **1928** *Daily Express* 6 Dec. 10/5, I once sat in a train for five hours opposite an obsessionist, who played chess with himself on a miniature board.

obsessive (əb'sɛsɪv), *a.* [f. OBSESS *v.* 3 + -IVE.] Of or pertaining to obsession; liable to obsess; obsessing. So as *sb.*, a person characterized by obsessive behaviour.

1911 I. H. CORIAT *Abnormal Psychol.* II. vi. 281 One of the most common of these obsessive states is what is known as the obsession of self-consciousness. **1918** A. E. DAVIS *Hypnotism* I. 46 A frequent cause of..obsessive thoughts, is the feeling of shame or regret arising out of bad habits. **1926** J. I. SUTTIE tr. *Ferenczi's Further Contrib. Theory & Technique Psycho-Anal.* xviii. 232 The individual suffering from obsessive ideas is really substituting thought for action. **1966** *Listener* 17 Mar. 414/1 Of the medical obsessives I particularly liked Maurice Denham as Bloomfield Bonington. **1969** N. W. PIRIE *Food Resources* iii. 104 In 1939 many of us argued that protein supplies would be the main problem in feeding Britain in war-time. We were stigmatized as obsessives. **1973** T. & R. MILLON *Abnormal Behav.* (1974) III. xiii. 296 Obsessive thoughts are intrusive ideas which the person cannot block from consciousness. **1975** R. HILL *April Shroud* xii. 154 'I've got some rushes here. You want to see them?' Like all obsessives, he could not doubt the answer.

b. *obsessive-compulsive* adj. *Psychol.*, applied to a disorder in which an obsession results in the compulsion to perform repeatedly meaningless acts; also *fig.*; so as *sb.*, a person whose compulsive behaviour is due to obsessive thoughts.

1927 HENDERSON & GILLESPIE *Text-bk. Psychiatry* xiv. 399 'Obsessive-compulsive' state is applied to a..condition in which the preoccupation issues in motor acts of an apparently trifling or meaningless kind. **1941** S. H. KRAINES *Therapy Neuroses & Psychoses* i. 26 Hysteria and obsessive-compulsive neurosis in which states symbolic symptoms are more common. **1960** *Cambr. Rev.* 7 May 509/1 Of 100 severe reactions among students..the schizophrenic were the most frequent (34)... There were..7 obsessive-compulsives. **1965** *New Statesman* 24 Sept. 426/1 [Ronald] Reagan has been associated with the obsessive-compulsive faction of the Republican right. **1970** *Jrnl. Gen. Psychol.* LXXXII. 175 Schizophrenics, obsessive-compulsives, and depressed persons have a high level of health anxiety.

obsessively (əb'sɛsɪvlɪ), *adv.* [f. OBSESSIVE *a.* + -LY[2].] In an obsessive manner; insistently, beyond reason.

1949 M. MEAD *Male & Female* xv. 296 The picture can be obsessively elaborated. **1969** *Sunday Times* 2 Nov. 51/3 Expressions of a mind almost obsessively in pursuit of unification. **1971** *Physics Bull.* June 332/3 Each side..can select instances which demonstrate its point and..can obsessively ignore others which demonstrate the opposite. **1977** P. DICKINSON *Walking Dead* IV. i. 252 The Captain continued to flick obsessively at the wheel.

ob'sessiveness. [f. as prec. + -NESS.] The quality of being obsessive.

1961 in WEBSTER. **1966** *Listener* 8 Sept. 366/3 Mr Storey portrayed very accurately that brand of obsessiveness which salesmen call enthusiasm.

†**ob'sessor.** *Obs. rare*⁻¹. [a. L. *obsessor*, agent-n. from *obsidēre* to OBSESS.] A haunting or familiar spirit.

1652 GAULE *Magastrom.* 179 How many magicians,.. have had their..obsessors, their consiliaries, and auxiliaries.

† **ob'sibilate,** *v. Obs. rare*$^{-0}$. [f. ppl. stem of L. *obsibilāre*, f. *ob-* (OB-) + *sibilāre* to hiss, whistle.] (See quot.) Hence † **obsibi'lation.**

1656 BLOUNT *Glossogr.*, *Obsibilate*, to make a whistling noise, as Trees stirred with winds. **1658** PHILLIPS, *Obsibilation*, a hissing against.

† **ob'side,** *v. Obs. rare.* [ad. L. *obsidē-re*: see OBSESS.] *trans.* To beset, invest, surround, encompass. So † **'obsident** *a.* [ad. L. *obsidēnt-em* pr. pple.], investing, encompassing.

1695 BAYNARD in *Phil. Trans.* XIX. 19 Though the proper Coats of the Veins and Arteries seem to be indolent in themselves, yet those thin Membranes which obside them are most exquisite of Sense. **1706** —— in Sir J. Floyer *Hot & Cold Bath.* II. 313 The degrees of heat pressing on, or obsiding the Body. **1644** DIGBY *Nat. Bodies* xvi. (1658) 178 Fire.. is so easily overcome by any obsident body when it is dilated.

obsidian (əb'sɪdɪən). *Min.* [In current form ad. erron. L. *obsidiān-us*, in edd. of Pliny for *obsiānus*; so called from its resemblance to a stone found in Ethiopia by one *Obsius* (erron. *Obsidius*). In F. *obsidiane, -enne* (1752 in Dict. Trévoux).

The erroneous *Obsidius, obsidianus*, occur in the earliest printed edd. of Pliny; but *Obsius, obsianus*, came down through the mediæval writers on Natural History.]

A dark-coloured vitreous lava or volcanic rock, of varying composition, resembling common bottle-glass; volcanic glass.

[**1398** TREVISA *Barth. De P.R.* XVI. xcix. (MS. Bodl. lf. 184/2), þe stone osianus is irekned amonge glas, and þis is somtyme grene somtyme blacke & clere & briȝt. **1601** HOLLAND *Pliny* II. 598 There may be ranged among the kinds of glasses, those which they call Obsidiana, for that they carry some resemblance of that stone, which one Obsidius found in Æthyopia. **1661** LOVELL *Hist. Anim. & Min.* 79 The Obsidianus [represents] a Shaddow. **1750** tr. *Leonardus' Mirr. Stones* 216 Obsius, or Obsianus, is of a black transparent Colour in the Likeness of Glass.] **1796** KIRWAN *Elem. Min.* (ed. 2) I. 264 Obsidian.. is found in Hungary, inhering in gneiss, and disintegrated granite. **1811** PINKERTON *Petral.* II. 310 Black or blue obsidian. **1837** W. IRVING *Capt. Bonneville* II. 197 Their weapons were bows and arrows; the latter tipped with obsidian. **1868** DANA *Min.* (ed. 5) 359 Any lava will become glassy, and thus make obsidian, by rapid cooling. **1885–94** R. BRIDGES *Eros & Psyche* Jan. ix, A pyx.. of dark obsidian's rarest green.

b. Also *obsidian stone* (*lapis Obsi*(*di*)*anus*).

[**1601** HOLLAND *Pliny* II. 629 As touching the stone Obsidianus, I haue written sufficiently.] **1656** BLOUNT *Glossogr.*, *Obsidian Stone*, a precious stone, mentioned in Pliny. **1686** PLOT *Staffordsh.* 126 The Obsidian stone. **1715** tr. *Pancirollus' Rerum Mem.* I. I. iii. 10 Obsidian Stones are black, but very shining. *a* **1822** SHELLEY *Pr. Wks.* (1880) III 72 A remarkable figure of Sleep as a winged child.. sleeping on its great half unfolded wing of black obsidian stone.

c. *attrib.* and *Comb.*

1796 KIRWAN *Elem. Min.* (ed. 2) I. 352 Obsidian Porphyry. Black, or greyish black. **1861** TYLOR *Anahuac* iv. 97 Obsidian-headed arrows. **1863** BARING-GOULD *Iceland* 213 It is an obsidian mountain, it looks like a mountain of broken glass bottles. **1872** *Athenæum* 21 Dec. 813/1 Obsidian knives, and flakes.. reminding one of the Mexican examples in the British Museum. *Ibid.*, The so-called flint flakes of Marathon are, in reality, obsidian flakes.

obsidianite (əb'sɪdɪənaɪt). *Geol.* [f. OBSIDIAN + -ITE[1].] = TEKTITE.

1898 R. H. WALCOTT in *Proc. R. Soc. Victoria* XI. 23 As long as this uncertainty exists, some other name would be more appropriate, and I suggest and will refer to them in this paper as 'obsidianites'. **1909** [see AUSTRALITE]. **1933** *Nature* 28 Jan. 117/1 Small, curiously shaped pieces of.. glass have long been known from certain regions, and have been called moldavites from the Moldau River in Bohemia..; australites or obsidianites from Australia; [etc.]. **1963** J. A. O'KEEFE *Tektites* i. 1 Earlier writers referred to tektites as obsidianites.

† **ob'sidion.** *Obs. rare.* [a. OF. *obsidion* (14th c. in Godef.), ad. L. *obsidiōn-em* siege f. *obsidēre*: see OBSESS *v.*] Siege; state of being besieged.

c **1450** *Mirour Saluacioun* 2578 At the last fadere of mercyes.. Piely beheld the disese of oure obsidionne.

obsidional (əb'sɪdɪənəl), *a.* [ad. L. *obsidiōnāl-is*, f. *obsidiōn-em* siege; see prec. Cf. F. *obsidional* (15th c. in Godef.).]

1. Of or pertaining to a siege; esp. in ***obsidional crown*** (***coronet, garland, wreath***), tr. L. *corōna obsidiōnālis*, a wreath of grass or weeds conferred as a mark of honour upon a Roman general who raised a siege. ***obsidional coins***, coins struck in a besieged city to supply the want of current coins.

1542 UDALL *Erasm. Apoph.* 255 *Corona obsidionalis*, a garlande obsidionall. **1546** LANGLEY *Pol. Verg. de Invent.* II, xi. 55 b, Obsidionall croune yt was worne of him that deliuered a citee besieged & was made of Grasse. **1601** HOLLAND *Pliny* I. 117 Scipio syrnamed Æmilianus, was honoured with an Obsidionall Coronet in Africk.. for sauing three cohorts besieged. **1741** MIDDLETON *Cicero* II. xii. 577 An Obsidional Crown; which though made onely of the common grass,.. was esteemed the noblest reward of military glory. **1809** *Q. Rev.* I. 127 The obsidional coinage of Charles the first. **1884** H. FRITH tr. *Daryl's Pub. Life Eng.*. 43 The idea of sending obsidional letters by balloons.

2. *fig.* **a.** Besetting, obsidious. **b.** *nonce-use.* Apt to bore people by staying too long.

1826 SCOTT *Jrnl.* 3 Apr., My dear Chief, whom I love very much, though a little obsidional or so, remains till three. **1879** *World* 26 Nov. 12/1 The obsidional disease of suspicion which great public sufferings are apt to develop.

obsidionary (əb'sɪdɪənərɪ), *a.* [f. as prec. + -ARY.] = prec. 1.

1885 W. CHAFFERS in *N. & Q.* 6th Ser. XI. 94 These obsidionary Ormond coins may be called scarce.

obsidious (əb'sɪdɪəs), *a. rare.* [f. L. *obsidi-um* siege (f. *obsidēre*: see OBSESS *v.*) + -OUS.] Besieging; besetting.

1615 T. ADAMS *Myst. Bedlam* Wks. 1861 I. 261 It is safe from all obsidious or insidious oppugnations, from the reach of fraud or violence. **1900** *Daily Chron.* 3 Oct. 3/2 The struggle of the heroine.. against her own sex-imposed, obsidious desire to comply, to yield.

† **ob'sigillate,** *v. Obs. rare*$^{-0}$. [f. L. *ob-* (OB-) + late L. *sigillāre* to seal; after L. *obsignāre*: see next.] *trans.* To seal up. So † **obsigi'llation.**

1623 COCKERAM, *Obsigillate*, to hide, or seale. **1658** PHILLIPS, *Obsigillation*, a sealing up.

† **ob'sign,** *v.* [ad. L. *obsignāre* to seal up, f. *ob-* (OB- 1 c) + *signāre* to mark, seal, SIGN.] = next.

1554 BRADFORD *Wks.* (Parker Soc.) I. 395 The sacrament of his body and blood, whereby he doth.. give and obsign unto us himself wholly. **1658** J. ROBINSON *Eudoxa* v. 36 No spirituall transaction, though obsigned with a Religious Oath. **1670** BAXTER *Cure Ch.-Div.* 51 The Sacramental obsigning and investing sign.

† **ob'signate,** *v. Obs.* [f. ppl. stem of L. *obsignāre*: see prec.] *trans.* To seal: to mark as with a seal; to ratify or confirm formally, as by sealing.

1653 R. SANDERS *Physiogn.* 275 Moles, with which nature hath obsignated the parts of the body. *a* **1677** BARROW *Exp. Decal.* Wks. 1831 VII. 44 Keeping the Sabbath did obsignate the covenant made with the children of Israel.

obsignation (ɒbsɪg'neɪʃən). Now *rare.* [ad. L. *obsignātiōn-em*, n. of action from *obsignāre*: see OBSIGN *v.*] The action of sealing.

1. Formal ratification or confirmation of something, as by sealing.

a **1568** COVERDALE *Carrying of Christ's Cross* x. Wks. II. 267 This is a sacrament,.. in this.. we receive of God obsignation and full certificate of Christ's body broken for our sins, and his blood shed for our iniquities. **1633** BP. HALL *Hard Texts, N.T.* 102 His subscription to, and obsignation of his divine Truth. **1691** NORRIS *Pract. Disc.* 162 That Obsignation.. whereby the Spirit it self is said to bear Witness with our Spirit. **1859** *Sat. Rev.* 305/2 This obsignation can.. only be understood by adepts and experts in M. Comte's cerebral theory.

† **2.** The action of sealing up; a fastening or restraining as with a seal. *Obs. rare.*

1653 GATAKER *Vind. Annot. Jer.* 161 The word of *obsignation* or *sealing up*, hath.. a manifest notion of restraint. **1679** HARBY *Key Script.* ii. 35 The Book was sealed in a Figure; not that there was any evident obsignation upon, or great obscurity in, the sacred Oracles.

obsignatory (əb'sɪgnətərɪ), *a.* Now *rare.* [f. L. *obsignātor* a sealer, or *obsignāt-*, ppl. stem of *obsignāre* to OBSIGN: see -ORY.] Having the function of, or pertaining to, obsignation; ratifying or confirming as with a seal.

1630 S. WARD in *Ussher's Lett.* (1686) 438 Most of our Divines do make.. all Sacraments to be meerly Obsignatory Signs. **1693** R. FLEMING *Disc. Earthquakes* 121 No Contemplation can speak the Power of that Evidence.. when in an obsignatory way this is given unto the Soul. **1890** *Guardian* 26 Mar. 512 What may be called the 'obsignatory' view of sacramental operation.

Hence **ob'signatorily** *adv.*

1630 W. BEDELL in *Ussher's Lett.* (1686) 445 If you will aver that Baptism washes away otherwise than sacramentally, that is, obsignatorily original Sin.

† **ob'sist,** *v. Obs.* [ad. L. *obsist-ĕre* to stand against, f. *ob-* (OB- 1 b) + *sistĕre* to stand: cf. OF. *obsister* (15th c. in Godef.).] *trans.* To stand against, oppose, resist.

1432–50 tr. *Higden* (Rolls) VII. 177 The kynge.. callede.. Siwardus erle of Northumbrelonde, to obsiste Godewinus the erle. *a* **1548** HALL *Chron., Hen. VII*, 1 To obsist the first likely mischiefe he sent [etc.]. **1632** I. L. *Womens Rights* 327 Sutors come euerie day, who can obsist them?

So † **ob'sistent** [ad. L. *obsistent-em* pr. pple.], something that resists; in quot., an antidote.

1657 TOMLINSON *Renou's Disp.* 641 Precious-stones, and many more obsistents to poyson.

† **'obsited,** *pa. pple. Obs. rare*$^{-1}$. [f. L. *obsit-us*, pa. pple. of *obserĕre* to set with, cover with (f. *ob-* (OB- 1 c) + *serĕre* to set) + -ED[1].] Covered thickly as if sprinkled *with* something; studded, beset.

1657 TOMLINSON *Renou's Disp.* 457 Two horns.. obsited with many tubercles.

obsolesce (ɒbsəʊ'lɛs), *v. rare.* [ad. L. *obsolēscĕre* to grow old, decay, fall into disuse, inchoative form of **obsolēre*, f. *ob-* (OB- 1 b) + *solēre* to be accustomed, to use.] *intr.* To be obsolescent; to grow obsolete; to fall into disuse.

1873 F. HALL *Mod. Eng.* vii. 266 Intermediate between the English which I have been treating of, and English of recent emergence, stands that which is obsolescing. **1934** G. B. SHAW *On Rocks* 160 The lists of crimes and penalties will obsolesce like the doctors' lists of diseases and medicines. **1950** *N.Y. Times* 12 Nov. 96/2 (Advt.), New New a thousand times New (we'd rather die than obsolesce). **1975** *Amer. Speech 1972* XLVII. 261 *Exolinguistics* has never become a standard term in either linguistics or anthropology, but it has persisted in both periodicals and books for twenty years, and it refuses to obsolesce.

obsolescence (ɒbsəʊ'lɛsəns). [f. as OBSOLESCENT: see -ENCE.]

1. a. The process of gradually falling into disuse or growing out of date; the becoming obsolete.

a **1828** CROMBIE is cited in Webster. **1869** M. PATTISON *Introd. Pope's Ess. Man* 16 The same process of obsolescence is gradually affecting.. parts of Pope's poems. **1891** LOUNSBURY *Stud. Chaucer* III. vii. 110 He recognized the obsolescence of his language, if not its obsoleteness.

b. *spec.* of machinery or similar assets. Also *attrib.* See also *planned obsolescence*.

1887 GARCKE & FELLS *Factory Accounts* v. 93 This increased production may be due to certain parts being of a more permanent type than others and added to stock with less risk of obsolescence. **1913** R. J. PORTERS *Pitman's Dict. Book-Keeping* 330 Any loss sustained through obsolescence is charged to Profit and Loss. **1930** *Economist* 25 Jan. 163/2 In steelworks the question of obsolescence and the need for replacement of plant depend, partly, on the present condition of the plant and partly [etc.]. **1930** HUTCHINSON & LOVELL *Short Dict. Legal Terms* 87 *Obsolescence.* Where machinery is lessened in value not by mere usage or lapse of time, but by the fact that improved machinery is being brought into use, then this lessened value is termed obsolescence as distinguished from depreciation. **1957** CLARK & GOTTFRIED *University Dict. Business & Finance* 245/1 *Obsolescence*, with respect to an asset, the loss in value brought about through improvements in technology, changes in public taste, or a falling off in demand. **1959** JOWITT *Dict. Eng. Law* II. 1257/2 *Obsolescence allowance*, a charge allowed in determining profits for taxation purposes [etc.]. **1962** [see *built-in* (*b*) s.v. BUILT *ppl. a.* 1 b]. **1966** *New Statesman* 28 Jan. 140/2 We have set up an obsolescence reserve of £1,500,000.

2. *Biol.* **a.** The gradual disappearance or atrophy of an organ or part, esp. in the history of a species, and as a consequence of disuse.

1852 DANA *Crust.* II. 1024 By the obsolescence of the articulation *b* and the last segment becoming obsolete. **1876** BRISTOWE *Th. & Pract. Med.* (1878) 460 An occasional sequela of the obsolescence of scattered miliary tubercles. **1883** G. ALLEN in *Knowledge* 20 July 33/2 All parts which are seldom or never exercised tend to atrophy or obsolescence.

b. Nearly complete effacement of a mark, spot, etc., e.g. on the wing of an insect.

1877 COUES & ALLEN *N. Amer. Rod.* 291 The black spot at the tip of the ear varies greatly in extent in different specimens, in some being reduced almost to obsolescence.

obsolescent (ɒbsəʊ'lɛsənt), *a.* [ad. L. *obsolēscent-em*, pr. pple. of *obsolēscĕre*: see OBSOLESCE *v.*]

1. Becoming obsolete; going out of use or date.

1755 JOHNSON s.v. *Hereout*, All the words compounded of *here* and a preposition, except *hereafter*, are obsolete, or obsolescent. **1863** KIRK *Chas. Bold* II. 82 The stronghold of obsolescent opinions and decaying sects. **1880** PLUMPTRE *Comm. Luke* 381 'They were instant'. The adjective is almost passing into the list of obsolescent words. **1894** JOS. WRIGHT *Appeal Eng. Dial. Dict.* 3 In another generation the obsolescent will have become obsolete.

2. *Biol.* Gradually disappearing; imperfectly or slightly developed; said of an organ structure, or mark, which was formerly, in the life of the individual or the species, or is still in cognate species, fully developed or well-marked.

1846 DANA *Zooph.* iv. (1848) 80 The Echinopores are other examples of prominent polyps, and obsolescent striæ to the coralla. **1879** G. ALLEN *Colour Sense* iii. 26 The Law of Parsimony, whereby all unnecessary organs become gradually obsolescent. **1892** *Syd. Soc. Lex.*, *Obsolescent*,.. applied to such a thing as a tubercle in the lung which is shrinking and becoming the seat of calcareous infiltration. **1897** *Allbutt's Syst. Med.* II. 11 The fibroid patches.. are a form of what is called retrograde or obsolescent tubercles.

Hence **obso'lescently** *adv.* (cf. 2 above).

1846 DANA *Zooph.* (1848) 320 Polyps obsolescently tentaculate.

obso'lescing, *ppl. a.* [f. OBSOLESCE *v.* + -ING[2].] That is becoming obsolete.

1916 E. V. LUCAS *Cloud & Silver* 71 The Mayor.. still clung to the steadily obsolescing topper. **1953** *Sun* (Baltimore) 23 Oct. 2/7 This sort of conversion [of gun turrets] is, in fact, under way, with other heavy 'obsolescing' types.

obsolete ('ɒbsəliːt), *a.* (*sb.*) Also 6–7 -let. [ad. L. *obsolēt-us* grown old, worn out, pa. pple. of *obsolēscĕre*, or rather its primitive **obsolēre*: see OBSOLESCE. So mod.F. *obsolète* (Littré).]

1. That is no longer practised or used; fallen into disuse; of a discarded type or fashion; disused, out of date.

1579 E. K. in *Spenser's Sheph. Cal.* Ep. Ded., Such olde and obsolete wordes are most vsed of country folke. **1598** BARCKLEY *Felic. Man* (1631) 635 A faithfull friend is hard to be found; the bare name onely remaineth; the thing is obsolete and growne out of use. **1663** *Flagellum, or O. Cromwell* (1672) 158 Though many pretty stories shall happily be told of this obsolete Princess. **1780** HARRIS *Philol. Enq.* (1841) 391 Of things obsolete, the names became obsolete also. *a* **1847** MRS. SHERWOOD *Lady of Manor* I. ix. 366 Two female servants, whose prim and obsolete appearance were perfectly consistent with the venerable aspect of the place of their habitation. **1875** STUBBS *Const. Hist.* II. xvii. 521 Another ancient impost was now becoming obsolete. **1884** H. ARNOLD FORSTER in *Pall Mall G.* 14 Aug. 2/1 On the Pacific station..we have one obsolete ironclad, the *Swiftsure.*

2. Worn out; effaced through wearing down, atrophy, or degeneration.

1832 G. DOWNES *Lett. Cont. Countries* I. 351 The so-called Tomb of Nero. It is embellished with carving, and bears a nearly obsolete inscription. **1843** SIR T. WATSON *Lect. Phys.* lvi. (L.), A puckering of the surface indicates that beneath it there is probably a shrunken or obsolete vomica. **1851** GOSSE *Nat. in Jamaica* 51 After a while, the cliff becomes gradually obsolete, and the beach of coral sand reappears. **1897** *Allbutt's Syst. Med.* II. 34 Cases of obsolete tubercle found in cancer..examined post-mortem.

3. *Biol.* Indistinct; not clearly or sharply marked; very imperfectly developed, hardly perceptible. Usually implying the absence or rudimentary development of a character which is distinct in other individuals, or in allied species.

1760 J. LEE *Introd. Bot.* II. xxxiii. (1765) 160 *Carthamus,* with an obsolete crown to the seeds. **1785** MARTYN *Rousseau's Bot.* xxvii. (1794) 418 The middle lobe obsolete or so small as to be obscure. **1807** J. E. SMITH *Phys. Bot.* 377 *Dorstenia,* with its obsolete flowers, devoid of all beauty. **1826** KIRBY & SP. *Entomol.* IV. 293 *Obsolete,*..when a spot, tubercle, punctum, &c. is scarcely discoverable... This term is often employed where one sex, kindred species, or genera, want, or nearly so, a character which is conspicuous in the other sex, or in the species or genus to which they are most closely allied. **1864** F. O. MORRIS *Nests & Eggs Brit. Birds* I. 69 They [eggs of Long-tailed Tit] are sometimes entirely white, or with the spots almost obsolete.

B. *absol.* or *sb.* One who or that which is out of date or has fallen into disuse.

1748 RICHARDSON *Clarissa* (1811) II. 17 We bandied it about among twenty of us as an obsolete. **1885** *Pall Mall G.* 13 Oct. 4/2 Seniority is the rule of all the services..which fills the army with martinets, the navy with tubs,..the State generally with the amiable obsoletes. **1900** *Daily Express* 28 June 4/4 Bringing out Obsoletes [the war-ships Sultan, Dreadnought, and Superb].

obsolete ('ɒbsəliːt), *v.* Now chiefly *N. Amer.* [f. OBSOLETE *a.*, or f. L. *obsolēt-*, ppl. stem of **obsolēre, obsolēscěre*: see OBSOLESCE.] *trans.* To render or account obsolete; to discard, or practise no longer, as being out of date; to disuse.

1640 in Rushw. *Hist. Coll.* III. (1692) I. 133 But when Religion is innovated,..our modern Laws already obsoleted [etc.]. **1718** J. CHAMBERLAYNE *Relig. Philos.* Ded., We are not to be justified in obsoleting so many of our Words and Phrases. **1873** F. HALL *Mod. Eng.* vii. 261 *note,* And here I may mention sennight, for 'week', only recently obsoleted. **1944** *Amer. Speech* XIX. 234/1 A number of new laws and regulations..will almost certainly obsolete anything we might have given you during the past couple of months. **1945** in *Amer. Speech* (1948) XXIII. 70/1 The pressure of today's events has obsoleted many filing systems. **1960** [see PRE-TEEN *a.*]. **1961** *Flight* 3 Feb. 154/3, I have read Sir Percy Hunting's paper... It is competent, commendable stuff, marred only by the inclusion of..some Americanisms... For example: obsoleting, envisioned, peppercorn rentals, fiscal, transportation. **1967** *Technology Week* 23 Jan. 100/1 (Advt.), The new gas turbine engine that's out to obsolete the diesel. **1972** *Fortune* Jan. 52/3 Increasing emphasis upon service and repair of existing equipment, rather than mindlessly obsoleting it. **1975** *Sci. Amer.* Feb. 39/1 (Advt.), Our precoated sheet failed to obsolete the glass TLC plate. **1975** *Listener* 11 Dec. 788/2 (American speaker) News reporting on the hour or the half-hour—when only part of the earlier news had been obsoleted—meant a great deal of repetition. **1977** *Islander* (Victoria, B.C.) 1 May 13/1 Wire is being obsoleted in communication today.

Hence **'obsoleted** *ppl. a.*; **'obsoleting** *vbl. sb.*

1657 W. MORICE *Coena quasi Κοινή* Def. ii. 41 Fettering themselves with an oath..to the disparagement and obsoleting of the Scriptures. **1680** BOLRON *Papist's Oath Secrecy* in *Select. fr. Harl. Misc.* (1793) 452 The care of gaining souls became..obsoleted.

obsoletely ('ɒbsəliːtlɪ), *adv.* [f. OBSOLETE *a.* + -LY[2].] In an obsolete manner or degree.

1810 *Encycl. Lond.* I. 683/1 Calycled andromeda..leaves oval, scaly-dotted, obsoletely serrulate. **1845** LINDLEY *Sch. Bot.* iv. (1858) 27 Stem obsoletely angular. **1867** C. J. BOYLE *Far Away* xv. 180 The obsoletely famous representation of 'Rocket time at Vauxhall'. **1889** B. NICHOLSON in *Athenæum* 27 July 139/3 Words obsolete or obsoletely spelled.

obsoleteness ('ɒbsəliːtnɪs). [f. as prec. + -NESS.] The state or condition of being obsolete.

1613 JACKSON *Creed* II. xv. §6 The decay of Dialects, obsoletenesse of phrase..might breed some difficultie vnto posteritie. **1756** JOHNSON *Propos. Print. Shaks.* Wks. 1787 IX. 233 The reader is therefore embarrassed at once with dead and with foreign languages, with obsoleteness and innovation. **1884** SEELEY in *Contemp. Rev.* Oct. 505 We are startled at the obsoleteness of the opinions he expresses.

obsoletion (ɒbsəʊ'liːʃən). *rare.* [f. L. *obsolēt-us* OBSOLETE: see -ION[1].] The action of becoming or condition of being obsolete.

1804 MITFORD *Inquiry* 140 Words and phrases..verging ..toward obsoletion. *Ibid.* 170 Provincial dialects, still spoken, tho now fast going into obsoletion. **1817** KEATS *Lett.* Wks. 1889 III. 98 Lamentation on the obsoletion of Christmas gambols and pastimes.

obsoletism ('ɒbsəliːtɪz(ə)m). [f. OBSOLETE *a.* (or its L. source) + -ISM.]

1. An obsolete term, phrase, custom, or the like.

1799 G. E. GRIFFITHS in Robberds *Mem. W. Taylor* I. 198 Neither defying by bold neologisms, nor offending by tasteless obsoletisms. **1873** F. HALL *Mod. Eng.* vii. 276 In these..obsoletisms..is comprised everything,..at all savouring, as to language, of any days but our own.

2. The condition of being obsolete; obsoleteness.

1824 *New Monthly Mag.* XII. 222 The former editions presented a great drawback upon the reader's pleasure in the old orthography, and the obsoletism of many of the expressions. **1852** E. V. RIPPINGILLE (*title*) Obsoletism in Art, a Reply to Ruskin in his defence of Pre-Raphaelitism. **1873** C. W. BARDSLEY *Eng. Surnames* 408 *note,* Our Authorized Version still preserves the 'meteyard' from obsoletism.

obsolute, obsolution, obsolve, obs. erron. ff. ABSOLUTE, ABSOLUTION, ABSOLVE.

†**obso'nation.** *Obs. rare*[—0]. [ad. L. *obsōnātiōn-em* catering, n. of action f. *obsōnāre*: see next.] A feasting (Cockeram, 1623).

†**'obsonator.** *Obs. rare.* Also ops-. [a. L. *obsōnātor*, agent-n. f. *obsōnāre* to cater, purvey, treat, feast, f. L. *obsōnium* (*ops-*), a. Gr. ὀψώνιον provisions, viands.] A caterer or manciple.

[**1582** in Fowler *Hist. C.C.C.* (O.H.S.) 452 *note,* This John Middleton occurs..as Obsonator or Manciple, 1582.] **1656** BLOUNT *Glossogr., Opsonator,* a buyer or purveyor of meats.

†**ob'sorb,** *v. Obs. rare*[—1]. [ad. L. *obsorbēre* (poetical) to sup or drink up, gulp down, f. *ob-* (OB- 1 c) + *sorbēre* to suck in.] *trans.* To absorb.

1684 T. BURNET *The. Earth* II. 224 The earth and all its dependances are obsorpt into a mass of fire.

ob'sorbent, *a.* and *sb. rare.* [ad. L. *obsorbēnt-em*, pr. pple. of *obsorbēre*: see prec.]

a. *adj.* Imbibing, absorbent. **b.** *sb.* An absorbing substance.

1747 tr. *Astruc's Fevers* 303 To these cordials may be added obsorbents.

†**ob'sorption.** *Obs. rare.* [n. of action f. L. *obsorbēre, obsorpt-*: see OBSORB.] Swallowing up; absorption.

c **1600** NORDEN *Spec. Brit., Cornwall* (1728) 3 The Rockes ..had they bene of a more earthy or tender substance coulde not have so long prevented Cornwalls utter obsorption. *Ibid.* 42 Manie deuises they vse to preuent the obsorption of the churche [by drifting sand]. [*Printed* obsorpation *in both cases.*] **1693** *Phil. Trans.* XVII. 801 There would succeed other Emanations and Regenerations, and other succeeding Destructions and Obsorptions.

obstacle ('ɒbstək(ə)l), *sb.* Forms: 4–5 ost-, obstakil, -kyl, -kele, 5–6 -kell, 6 -cul, 4– obstacle. [a. OF. *obstacle*, earlier *ostacle*, *ostancle* (13th c. in Godef.), ad. L. *obstācul-um*, f. *obstāre* to withstand, resist]

1. Something that stands in the way and obstructs progress; a hindrance, impediment, obstruction.

a **1340** HAMPOLE *Psalter* xvii. 32, I sall ouerpasse þe wall þat is obstakil of synn. *c* **1386** CHAUCER *Frankl. T.* 572 And whan he knew þat ther was noon obstacle. **1434** MISYN *Mend. Life* 107 Violence he doys to all his lettars, & all ostakyls he byrstis to-gidyr. **1489** CAXTON *Faytes of A.* I. xxiii. 72 Maken an obstakell that on the baksyde they be not enuahysshed. *Ibid.* II. xiv. 118 They made hourdeys or obstacles full thykke of thornes. **1538** STARKEY *England* II. i. 148 Seyng that matrymony ys the only or chefe mean polytyke..we must..study to take away al obstaculys and lettys wych we fynd therto. **1691** T. H[ALE] *Acc. New Invent.* p. c, The Obstacle the course of the Tide meets with by London-bridge. **1709** STEELE *Tatler* No. 55 ¶1 He should remove the Obstacle which prevented the Use of his Sight. **1845** DARWIN *Voy. Nat.* vii. (1879) 131 The great table-land presents an obstacle to the migration of species. **1860** TYNDALL *Glac.* I. vii. 52 A glacier..when released from one opposing obstacle will be checked by another.

†**2.** Resistance, opposition, objection: in phr. ***to make obstacle***, to offer opposition. *Obs.*

c **1400** MAUNDEV. (1839) xxi. 226 Whan the Chane saghe that thei made non obstacle to performen his commandement thanne he thoughte wel that he myghte trusten in hem. **1489** *Barbour's Bruce* XVI. 260 (Edin. MS.) Throw all the land planly thai raid, Thai fand nane that thaim obstakill maid. **1632** LITHGOW *Trav.* III. 126 The French men making obstacle to pay that which I had giuen.

3. *Comb.*, as **obstacle course** (see quot. 1961); also *transf.* and *fig.*; **obstacle-race**, a race in which natural or artificial impediments have to be surmounted; also *transf.*

1961 WEBSTER s.v., *Obstacle course n,* a military training area filled with obstacles (as hurdles, fences, walls, ditches) that must be surmounted. **1973** *Black Panther* 31 Mar. 14/3 Could you describe some of the more known programs used in 'boot camp' such as the obstacle course and the firing range? **1976** J. WAINWRIGHT *Who goes Next?* 145 As an obstacle course the yard was a nothing. **1977** *New Yorker* 27 June 26/1 Then he picked two miracles attributed..to Neumann..and started them over what Father Litz called the Vatican obstacle course. **1869** *Sporting Life* 17 Mar. 4/2 Among the races on the [Thames Club] programme was one of a character entirely new to the athletic world, viz. an 'Obstacle Race'. [Mr. Walter Rye (late Hon. Sec. Lond. Athl. C.) informs us that this was the occasion of the introduction of the term, he having then invented it.] **1875** *Cliftonian* (Cl. Coll. Mag.) IV. 74 Obstacle Race... This race was two lengths, over two and under one obstacle placed across the bath. **1888** H. POTTINGER in *Fortn. Rev.* Jan. 93 For some time he [the elk] becomes engaged in a terrible obstacle-race and makes little progress.

Hence **'obstacle** *a.* (*obs.* except *dial.*), obstinate, stubborn; †**'obstacleness**, obstinacy.

1536 *Will of S. Humbell* (Somerset Ho.), Yf they or any of them be obstakell & roune away. **1548** UDALL, etc. *Erasm. Par. Mark* ix. 63 b, O faythlesse nacion..Howe long shall I ..striue with youre vnfaythfull obstaclenesse? **1591** SHAKS. *1 Hen. VI*, v. iv. 17 Fye Ione, that thou wilt be so obstacle.

'obstacle, *v. rare.* [a. obs. F. *obstacle-r* (16th c. and in Cotgr.), f. *obstacle* sb.] **a.** *trans.* To place obstacles or difficulties in the way of. **b.** *intr.* (*Mil.*) To erect obstacles to impede the progress of the enemy. Hence **'obstacling** *vbl. sb.*

1656 S. H. *Gold. Law* 18 Let not the passions of..love or hate obstacle ingenious judgement. *Ibid.* 64 Solomon also oppress the People so,..as it obstacled his son Rehoboams Kinging. **1882** *Daily News* 30 Aug. 3/5 The day for obstacling has also been changed..to give the men [engineers] a change from pick and shovel work. **1889** ELLEN V. TALBOT *Diary of Ann Page* in *Voice* (N.Y.) 24 Oct., Alack! that our pleasant friendship..should have been so soon obstacled.

†**ob'staculous,** *a. Obs. rare.* [f. L. *obstācul-um* OBSTACLE + -OUS.] Of the nature of an obstacle.

a **1643** J. SHUTE *Judgm. & Mercy* v. (1645) 105 Though many things obstaculous to them lye in the way, and confront them, and be impediments to them. **1657** W. MORICE *Coena quasi κοινὴ* Def. xxi. 213 They stand obstaculous in their way, who stand not for Presbytery.

obstain(e, obs. erroneous forms of ABSTAIN.

†**'obstance.** *Obs. rare*[—1]. [a. F. *obstance* (15th c. in Godef.) resistance, opposition, ad. L. *obstāntia*: see next and -ANCE.] *prop.* Opposition, resistance; but in quot. used erron. for 'substance'.

c **1340** HAMPOLE *Prose Tr.* 18 þe obstance of þis felynge lyes in þe lufe of Ihesu whilke es fedde and lyghtenede by swilke maner of sanges.

†**'obstancy.** *Obs. rare*[—1]. [ad. L. *obstāntia*, in med. L. 'juridical opposition' (Du Cange), f. *obstānt-em*: see next and -ANCY.] Opposing quality or effect.

1609 B. JONSON *Sil. Wom.* v. iii, After marriage it is of no obstancie.

†**'obstant,** *a. Obs.* [ad. L. *obstānt-em*, pr. pple. of *obstāre* to stand against, f. *ob-* (OB- 1 b) + *stāre* to stand.] Standing against; resisting, opposing.

1513 DOUGLAS *Æneis* XII. ix. 99 That nother scheild nor obstant plait of steyll This cativis breist hes helpit neuir a deill. *a* **1592** GREENE *Selimus* Prol., Like a sea or high resurging floud, All obstant lets, downe with his fury fling. **1623** COCKERAM, *Obstant,* resisting.

Hence †**'obstantly** *adv.*, resistingly.

1562 in Strype *Ann. Ref.* (1709) I. xxx. 302 If any person ..be thereof lawfully convicted..and will obstantly stand in the same.

obstetric (əb'stɛtrɪk), *a.* [ad. mod.L. *obstetric-us*, for L. *obstetrīci-us*, f. *obstetrix*, *-trīc-em* midwife. Association with words having the suffix *-ic* has led to the formation of such derivatives as *obstetrical*, *obstetrist*, etc.] Of or pertaining to a midwife or accoucheur, or to midwifery as a branch of medical practice.

1742 POPE *Dunciad* IV. 394 There all the Learn'd shall at the labour stand, And Douglas lend his soft, obstetric hand. *c* **1750** SHENSTONE *To the Virtuosi* vii, Tis you protect their pregnant hour;..Exerting your obstetric pow'r. **1793** R. RAWLINS (*title*) A Dissertation on the Structure of the Obstetric Forceps. **1799** *Med. Jrnl.* II. 453 The obstetric art ..began to emerge from its barbarity during the sixteenth century. **1862** BURTON *Bk. Hunter* (1863) 260 Paul of Ægina, the father of obstetric surgery. **1878** T. BRYANT *Pract. Surg.* I. 607 In obstetric works cases are recorded.

obstetrical (əb'stɛtrɪkəl), *a.* [f. as prec. + -AL[1].] = prec. ***obstetrical toad***, the nurse-frog, *Alytes obstetricans* (*Century Dict.* 1891).

1775 in ASH. **1776** PENNANT *Zool.* III. 17 They spawn like frogs; but what is singular, the male affords the female obstetrical aid [etc.]. **1855** RAMSBOTHAM *Obstetr. Med.* 2 Peculiarities, which, in an obstetrical point of view, as well as anatomically, are worthy of consideration. *Ibid.* 13 Of much interest to the obstetrical student. **1876** BRISTOWE *Th. & Pract. Med.* (1878) 273 In surgical and obstetrical practice.

fig. **1822** BYRON *Let. to Scott* 4 May, Mr. Murray has several things of mine in his obstetrical hands.

Hence **ob'stetrically** *adv.*

1759 STERNE *Tr. Shandy* II. xi, Art thou aware, that..a daughter of Lucina is put obstetrically over thy head?

†**ob'stetricate,** *v. Obs.* [f. ppl. stem of L. *obstetricāre*, f. *obstetric-em* midwife.]

1. *intr.* To act as midwife; to aid in childbirth. Also *fig.*

1623 COCKERAM, *Obstetricate,* to play the Midwife. **1652** SANCROFT *Mod. Policies, Colasterion,* Tis pitty that such a Sacred thing should be..made to obstetricate to rebellious irregular designes. **1664** EVELYN *Sylva* 53 Some advise us to break the Shells of Pines to facilitate their delivery, and I have essay'd it; but to my loss; Nature does obstetricate, and do that office of her self when it is the best season. **1809** *Edin. Rev.* XIII. 458 Russia..will probably..obstetricate at the birth of those affiliated kingdoms that are to be extracted from the bowels of the Austrian monarchy.

2. *trans.* To bring to the birth; to help the delivery of. Chiefly *fig.*

1651 in *Hartlib's Legacy* (1655) 237 Though you were not the parent of this husbandry, yet you were the hand that did obstetricate and give it birth which else had been strangled in a private hand. **1655** GURNALL *Chr. in Arm.* (1669) 405/2 Prayer hath had the name of old for its excellent usefulness to obstetricate mercies. **1671** *True Nonconf.* 261 He.. neither needeth a Set-form, to obstetricat his expression, nor therein confineth himself to it.

† obstetri'cation. *Obs. rare.* [n. of action from prec.] The action or office of a midwife or accoucheur; delivery.

a **1615** DONNE *Βιαθανατος* (1644) 78 Assemblies..for the delivery and obstetrication of those children of naturall law. **1644** BP. HALL *Free Prisoner* §8 There he must lye in an uncouth posture..till..hee shall be by an helpfull obstetrication drawn forth into the larger prison of the world.

† ob'stetricatory, *a. Obs. rare.* [f. as OBSTETRICATE *v.*: see -ORY.] Of or pertaining to the office of a midwife.

1640 J. DYKE *Worthy Commun.* To Rdr., Which..made me..afford my obstetricatory assistance to this Posthumous Infant.

obstetrician (ɒbstɪ'trɪʃən). [f. L. *obstetrīcia* midwifery + -AN.] One skilled in obstetrics or midwifery; an accoucheur.

1828 in WEBSTER citing *Med. Repos.* **1828** M. RYAN *Man. Midwif.* p. v, It may be necessary to say a few words apologetic, for my adoption of the word obstetrician. **1879** *Cassell's Techn. Educ.* IV. 119/1 Obstetricians may oppose it, but I believe our patients themselves will force the use of it on the profession.

† obste'tricious, *a. Obs.* [f. L. *obstetrīci-us* pertaining to a midwife + -OUS.] Of or pertaining to a midwife; = OBSTETRIC.

c **1645** HOWELL *Lett.* III. ix, He doth the obstetritious Office of a Midwife. **1678** CUDWORTH *Intell. Syst.* I. v. 693 Yet is all humane teaching but maieutical or obstetricious. *a* **1688** —— *Immut. Mor.* IV. i. (1731) 137 An Aporetical and Obstetricious Method.

obstetri'cography. *rare.* [f. OBSTETRIC + -(O)GRAPHY.] The scientific description of midwifery.

1828 M. RYAN *Man. Midwif.* 104 The next part of obstetricography, I have named geneseology.

ob'stetrics. [In form, pl. of OBSTETRIC: see -IC 2.] The branch of medical practice which deals with parturition, and its antecedents and sequels; the practice of midwifery; obstetric art.

1819 *Pantologia, Obstetrics*, the doctrines or practice of midwifery... Employed in a larger signification than midwifery in its usual sense. **1872** F. G. THOMAS *Dis. Women* 34 In the Talmud are found evidences of a great deal of knowledge concerning the Cæsarean section and other subjects in obstetrics.

ob'stetricy. *rare.* [ad. L. *obstetrīcia* midwifery.] Midwifery; the practice of obstetrics.

1841 M. RYAN (*title*) Illustrations to Obstetricy and Midwifery. **1857** *Tait's Mag.* XXIV. 161 Has chloroform at operations—at even those common ones of dentistry and obstetricy—..not completely silenced the 'hypnotists'?

ob'stetrist. *rare*$^{-1}$. [irreg. f. OBSTETRIC + -IST, for **obstetricist*.] An obstetrician or accoucheur.

18.. R. BARNES *Dis. Women* xxxvi. (Cent.), The same consummate obstetrist..insisted upon the rule, now generally adopted, of not removing the placenta if it in any degree adhere. **1892** in *Syd. Soc. Lex.*

‖**obstetrix** (ɒb'stɛtrɪks). *rare*$^{-1}$. [L. *obstetrix, -stitrix, -trīcem*, midwife, f. *obstāre*, or *obsistĕre*, ppl. stem *obstit-*, to stand or place oneself in front of or opposite to, f. *ob-* (OB- 1 a,b) + *stāre, sistĕre* to stand.] A midwife.

1839 I. TAYLOR *Anc. Chr.* I. 73 The report of the obstetrix. *a* **1885** BP. HANNINGTON in *Life* xix. (1887) 322 A dash of the obstetrix would be exceedingly useful...could not a little [experience] be gained before coming out?

obsti'nacious, *a. rare*$^{-1}$. [irreg. f. next + -OUS.] Of an obstinate nature.

1830 GALT *Lawrie T.* II. v. (1849) 55, I have myself obstinacious objections.

obstinacy ('ɒbstɪnəsɪ). [ad. med.L. *obstinātia* (Du Cange), f. *obstināt-us* OBSTINATE: see -ACY.]

1. The quality or condition of being obstinate; inflexibility of temper or purpose; pertinacity, obduracy, stubbornness; persistency. Rarely in neutral or good sense.

1390 GOWER *Conf.* II. 117 He hath with him Obstinacie. *c* **1491** *Chast. Goddes Chyld.* 46 Some haue fallen in to obstynacy whiche men haue ben so harde of hert that of malice they will not be repentaunte. **1555** EDEN *Decades* 19 The cause wherof was..theyr owne obstinacie and frowardnes. **1603** KNOLLES *Hist. Turks* (1638) 23 In this desperat conflict, fought with wonderful obstinacie of mind, many fel on both sides. **1643** SIR T. BROWNE *Relig. Med.* I. §25 Obstinacy in a bad cause, is but constancy in a good. **1769** ROBERTSON *Chas. V*, XI. Wks. 1826 IV. 367 [He] adhered to his own opinion with his usual obstinacy. **1872** DARWIN *Emotions* ix. 238 The habitual and firm closure of the mouth would thus come to show decision of character; and decision readily passes into obstinacy.

b. with *an* and *pl.* An act or instance of this.

1628 WITHER *Brit. Rememb.* v. 1788 Their obstinacies, and in all their sin. **1651** HOBBES *Leviath.* IV. xlvii. 383 They induce simple men into an obstinacy against the Laws. **1840** CARLYLE *Heroes* vi. (1872) 60/1 Cromwell's..Speech..to his third Parliament, in similar rebuke for their pedantries and obstinacies.

2. Of a disease: Stubborn or unyielding nature; continued resistance to treatment.

1808 *Med. Jrnl.* XIX. 183 This has been partly owing to the obstinacy of the disease.

obstinance ('ɒbstɪnəns). *rare.* [ad. med.L. *obstinantia* (Du Cange) f. *obstinānt-em*: see OBSTINANT and -ANCE.] Stubborn or self-willed persistence; obstinacy.

1432-50 tr. *Higden* (Rolls) VII. 371 [He] was correcte and reprovede moche of an holy man, Wilsius by name, for his obstinaunce or obstinacion. *c* **1489** *Plumpton Corr.* (Camden) 60 And he will not, I intend to shew his obstynance to the King. **1893** C. T. LUSTED *Stud., Poets* 33 [He] called me a fool for my obstinance.

'obstinancy. *rare.* [ad. L. *obstinantia*: see prec. and -ANCY.] = prec.

1614 SIR R. DUDLEY in *Fortesc. Papers* (Camden) 12 *note*, These natures, I doubte, in time may growe to a bad obstinancie. **1649** *Alcoran* 189 Such as dispute with obstinancy against the Faith. **1748** RICHARDSON *Clarissa* II. xxxiii, Such a sweetness here, and such an obstinancy there. **1894** B. THOMSON *Diversions of Prime Minister* xiii. 213 The steadfastness of their followers was obstinancy under the lash of persecution.

† 'obstinant. *Obs. rare*$^{-1}$. [ad. L. *obstinānt-em*, pr. pple. of *obstināre* (F. *obstiner*) to persist: see -ANT.] = OBSTINATE *sb.*

1581 STYWARD *Mart. Discipl.* II. 137 His speaking.. increaseth the obstinants to fight.

obstinate ('ɒbstɪnət), *a.* (*sb.*) [ad. L. *obstināt-us* determined, stubborn, pa. pple. of *obstināre* (derivative form of *obstāre*) to persist.]

1. Pertinacious or stubborn in adhering to one's own course; not yielding to argument, persuasion, or entreaty; inflexible, headstrong, self-willed. Rarely in neutral or good sense.

a **1340** HAMPOLE *Psalter* cxlii. 14 þou sall lose þe deuyl & all obstynate men. **1388** WYCLIF *Gen.* xlix. 7 Curside be the woodnesse of hem, for it is obstynat. **1463** *Bury Wills* (Camden) 24 And he be obstinat or froward I wil he haue noon of all. *c* **1510** BARCLAY *Mirr. Gd. Manners* (1570) G v, On obstinate dullardes waste not thy wit and brayne. **1512** *Act 4 Hen. VIII*, c. 19 *Preamble*, Erronyously defendyng & maynteynyng his seid obstynate opynyons agayne the unitye of the holye Churche. *a* **1680** BUTLER *Rem.* (1759) II. 422 The obstinate Man does not hold Opinions, but they hold him. **1717** LADY M. W. MONTAGU *Let. to C'tess Mar* 30 Jan., It yielded..after an obstinate defence. **1855** MILMAN *Lat. Chr.* (1864) IV. VII. iv. 144 His obstinate humility resisted their flattering importunities.

2. Unyielding, stiff, rigid; *spec.* of a disease, etc., not yielding readily to treatment; refractory, stubborn.

1638 RAWLEY tr. *Bacon's Life & Death* (1651) 7 Boots, grown hard and obstinate with age. *a* **1682** SIR T. BROWNE *Tracts* 115 This may probably destroy that obstinate disease. **1784** JOHNSON *Let. to Mrs. Thrale* 9 Feb., I have been forced to sit up many nights by an obstinate sleeplessness. **1871** NAPHEYS *Prev. & Cure Dis.* III. xii. 1048 An obstinate diarrhœa sometimes sets in. **1891** S. C. SCRIVENER *Our Fields & Cities* 13 The Nottinghamshire clays—obstinate red clay, good for bricks and oak trees.

† 3. Reluctant. *Obs. rare.*

a **1754** W. HAMILTON *To the Countess* etc., Sincere and equal to thy neighbour's fame, How swift to praise, how obstinate to blame.

B. *sb.* A stubborn or inflexible person.

1502 *Ord. Crysten Men* (W. de W. 1506) III. iii. 152 Promptynge correccyon..unto obstinates and perseuerynge theyr malyce. **1561** T. NORTON *Calvin's Inst.* Pref., Out of the bosome of these heretikes, rebelles, and obstinates. **1623** T. SCOTT *God & the King* (1633) 6 These obstinates be of two sorts..The Dogmaticall obstinates are such as erre in judgement. **1781** JUSTAMOND *Priv. Life Lewis XV*, I. 67 There were, as the Regent called them, some obstinates, that is to say, persons who could not persuade themselves, that paper was of greater value than money.

obstinate ('ɒbstɪneɪt), *v.* Now *rare.* [f. L. *obstināt-*, ppl. stem of *obstināre*: see prec. and -ATE³.] *trans.* To render obstinate; to cause to persist stubbornly. Also *refl.* (= F. *s'obstiner*).

c **1420** *Chron. Vilod.* st. 1245 þey ben obstynatyde so meche in covetyse. **1588** E. AGGAS tr. *Disc. pres. Est. France* 31 Being no great likelihood that the Suitzers woulde obstinate themselues against such great forces. *a* **1603** T. CARTWRIGHT *Confut. Rhem. N.T.* (1618) 536 One that hath obstinated himselfe against the Church. *a* **1648** LD. HERBERT *Hen. VIII* (1683) 133 These Abuses and Grievances..being published, Luther became more obstinated. **1864** LOWELL *Fireside Trav.* 308 If he still obstinates himself, he is finished by being made to measure one of the marble *putti*, which look like rather stoutish babies, and are found to be six feet.

obstinately ('ɒbstɪnətlɪ), *adv.* [f. OBSTINATE *a.* + -LY².] In an obstinate manner; stubbornly; pertinaciously.

c **1380** WYCLIF *Wks.* (1880) 376 If þu wilt not bileue effectualy cristis wordis..þan þu wilfully and obstynatly forsakist crist vttirly. **1555** EDEN *Decades* 91 Cruell and seuere to such as obstinatly withstande them. **1684** BOYLE *Porousn. Anim. & Solid Bod.* vii. 113 The obstinately adhering Odour. **1697** DRYDEN *Virg. Georg.* IV. 127 Unknowing how to fly, And obstinately bent to win or dye. **1744** MITCHELL in *Phil. Trans.* XLIII. 143 Obstinately chronical Maladies. **1855** MACAULAY *Hist. Eng.* xii. III. 207 In a few hours it was known that Londonderry held out as obstinately as ever. **1875** B. MEADOWS *Clin. Observ.* 35 Bowels..often obstinately confined.

'obstinateness. [f. as prec. + -NESS.] The quality of being obstinate; obstinacy.

1391 in Foxe *A. & M.* (1596) 434 Whom against yᵉ obstinatenesse of the said William Swinderby, we thought good to receiue, and did receiue. **1673** KIRKMAN *Unlucky Citizen* 228 Being much concerned that so brave a Gentleman should be lost by his own obstinateness.

† obsti'nation. *Obs.* Also 4-5 -cioun. [a. F. *obstination* (13th c. in Littré), ad. L. *obstinātiōn-em* determination, resolution, n. of action f. *obstināre*: see OBSTINATE *a.*] = OBSTINACY.

a **1340** HAMPOLE *Psalter* xiii. 5, And sithen þaim graues in obstynacioun. *c* **1440** *Jacob's Well* 294 Obstynacyoun in euyl doyng. **1549** *Compl. Scot.* xvi. 139 Al the insurrectionis.. hes procedit of the ignorance & obstinatione of the comount pepil. **1680** HICKES *Spir. Popery* 42 The incurable obstination of the Presbyterian Party in Schism against the Episcopal Church. *a* **1711** KEN *Anodynes* Poet. Wks. 1721 III. 401 Yet still with Obstination I, To win the Battle restless try. **1829** I. TAYLOR *Enthus.* x. 273 The obstination of the human mind in adhering to the worse, even when the better is presented to its choice.

obstinative, *sb.* An obstinate tendency.

1561 T. HOBY tr. *Castiglioni's Courtyer* (1577) I. D ij b, And of these errors there are diuers other causes and among other the obstinatiues of princes.

† 'obstined, *a. Obs. rare*$^{-1}$. [f. after L. *obstinātus* or F. *obstiné*, f. L. *obstināre*: see OBSTINATE *v.* and -ED¹.] Made obstinate or persistent.

1606 SYLVESTER *Du Bartas* II. iv. II. *Magnificence* 1274 You..Whose spirits, self-obstin'd in old musty Error, Repulse the Truth.

† 'obstipate, *v. Obs. rare.* [f. L. *obstīpāt-*, ppl. stem of L. type **obstīpāre*, f. *ob-* (OB- 1 b) + *stīpāre* to press together, pack: see next.] *trans.* To block or stop up; to stuff up; *absol.* to produce constipation.

1656 BLOUNT *Glossogr., Obstipate*, to stop chinks. **1657** R. CARPENTER *Astrol.* 9 An impediment in the medium, as being obstipated. **1702** FULLER *Pharmacopœia Extemporanea* (1730) 241 A Chartaceous Hydrogala.. edulcorates, incrassates, obstipates.

obstipation (ɒbstɪ'peɪʃən). [ad. L. *obstīpātiōn-em*, n. of action f. **obstīpāre*: see prec.] The action of blocking or stopping up. In *Med.*: see quot. 1880.

1597 LOWE *Chirurg.* (1634) 88 The cure consisteth..in purgations, dyet, and bleeding, which may be observed also in the time of the obstipation. **1658** PHILLIPS, *Obstipation*, a stopping up. **1783** *Phil. Trans.* LXXIII. 237 [They] produce an obstipation, which ends either in an abscess of the abdomen..or becomes fatal to the animal. **1880** A. FLINT *Princ. Med.* (ed. 5) 532 The term obstipation has been already defined to denote a greater amount of difficulty than constipation, that is, obstruction of the bowels, either as a functional disorder or dependent on various lesions.

† obstrepency. *Obs. rare*$^{-0}$. [f. L. *obstrepent-em*, pr. pple. of *obstrepĕre* to make a noise against, shout at: see -ENCY.]

1623 COCKERAM II, Noyse, *Obstrepency*.

† ob'streperate, *v. Obs. rare*$^{-1}$. [f. L. *obstreper-us* (see OBSTREPEROUS) + -ATE³ 7.] *intr.* To make a noise or clamour.

1765 STERNE *Tr. Shandy* VII. xxii, Thump—thump— obstreperated the abbess..with the end of her goldheaded cane against the bottom of the calash.

obstreperous (əb'strɛpərəs), *a.* Also 7 os-; (humorous or illiterate, chiefly in sense 2) 8 ab-, obstrepolous, -ulous, 8-9 obstropalous, -olous, -ulous, 9 obstreperlous. [f. L. *obstreper-us* clamorous (f. *obstrep-ĕre* to make a noise against, shout at, oppose noisily or troublesomely) + -OUS.]

1. Characterized by great noise or outcry, esp. in opposition; clamorous, noisy; vociferous.

Quot. 1922 is *ellipt.* for 'obstreperous mouth'.

c **1600** *Timon* I. ii. (1842) 6 Proceed'st thou still with thy ostreperous noyse. **1603** B. JONSON *Sejanus* v. iii, They [ravens] sate all night, Beating the ayre with their obstreperous beakes. *a* **1661** FULLER *Worthies* (1840) II. 211 He..was very obstreperous in arguing the case for transubstantiation. **1748** SMOLLETT *Rod. Rand.* viii. (1804) 41, I heard him very obstropulous in his sleep. **1751** JOHNSON *Rambler* No. 89 ¶11 The most careless and obstreperous merriment. **1824** J. WIGHT *Mornings at Bow St.* 155 They were forthwith conveyed to the watch-house, and there they conducted themselves so '*obstropolously*', that the constable of the night found it necessary to have them put down below. **1856** R. A. VAUGHAN *Mystics* (1860) II. 51 The obstreperous rhetoricians will plague me with their big words. **1875** EMERSON *Lett. & Soc. Aims* v. 131 Obstreperous roarings of the throat. **1922** JOYCE *Ulysses* 420 Hark! Shut your obstropolos.

2. Resisting control, management, advice, etc., in a noisy manner; turbulent or unruly in behaviour, esp. in resistance.

1657 [see OBSTREPEROUSNESS]. **1727** *Philip Quarll* 105 Fearing she would grow obstrepulous, they each of 'em took hold of one of her Arms. **1773** GOLDSM. *Stoops to Conq.* III, I'm sure you did not treat Miss Hardcastle..in this obstropalous manner. **1806** SURR *Winter in Lond.* (ed. 3) III. 5 You have been quite obstropulous; no getting any food into your mouth but by force. **1827** SCOTT *Diary* 2 Oct. in *Lockhart*, We dined at Wooler, where an obstreperous horse retarded us for an hour at least. **1874** BURNAND *My time* i. 4 Generally having my own way..and becoming remarkably obstreperous when thwarted. **1881** *Macm. Mag.* Nov. 40 The most obstreperous and unmanageable of all young merlins.

obstreperously (əb'strɛpərəslı), *adv.* [f. prec. + -LY^2.] In an obstreperous or clamorous manner; noisily; with loud unruliness.

1615 CROOKE *Body of Man* 243 The Peripatetians obstreperously deny the Testicles this power of procreation of seede. **1655** FULLER *Ch. Hist.* x. ii. §42 The catholics..at the two first behaved themselves so obstreperously, that some of them were forced to be gagged, before they would be quiet. **1750** JOHNSON *Rambler* No. 12 ¶6 Upon this, they all laughed so obstreperously, that I took the opportunity of sneaking off in the tumult. **1809** W. IRVING *Knickerb.* (1861) I. 544 Its vigilant defenders..were one and all snoring most obstreperously at their posts.

obstreperousness (ɒb'strɛpərəsnıs). [f. as prec. + -NESS.] The quality of being obstreperous; vociferousness, clamour, noisy behaviour; now *esp.* noisy and unruly resistance to control.

1655 FULLER *Ch. Hist.* VIII. i. §18 Things not being methodized with Scholasticall Formality, but managed with tumultuous Obstreperousnesse. **1657** REEVE *God's Plea* 37 This finding fault with God's actions, is called an obstreperousnesse against the Almighty. **1691** WOOD *Ath. Oxon.* II. 450 A numerous crowd..seemed to be hugely taken and enamour'd with his obstreperousness and undecent cants. **1865** MRS. WHITNEY *Gayworthys* xxxiv. (1879) 330 Comporting herself with the utmost self assertion and obstreperousness.

†**ob'strict,** *ppl. a. Obs. rare*$^{-1}$. [ad. L. *obstrict-us* bound, obliged, pa. pple. of *obstringĕre*: see OBSTRINGE.] Morally bound; bounden; obliged.

1527 *St. Papers Hen. VIII*, I. 252 His good brother; to whom he recogniseth hym self to be somoche indebted and obstricte.

obstriction (əb'strıkʃən). [ad. med.L. *obstrictiōn-em* obligation (Du Cange), n. of action f. *obstringĕre*: see OBSTRINGE.] The state of being morally or legally bound; obligation.

1671 MILTON *Samson* 312 [God] hath full right to exempt Whom so it pleases him by choice From National obstriction. *a* **1734** NORTH *Exam.* II. iv. §11 (1740) 237 The Priests..by their Conversation, and more by their religious Obstrictions, influence their Party.

†**ob'strictive,** *a. Obs. rare*$^{-1}$. [f. L. *obstrict-*, ppl. stem of *obstringĕre*: see OBSTRICT and -IVE.]

1642 *Animadv. Observator's Notes* 4 The same obligation of Iustice and Honour is as strong upon Kings, (and hath ever beene held more powerfull and obstrictive in them, then in any state mannaged by a Community).

†**ob'strigillate,** *v. Obs. rare*$^{-0}$. [ad. L. *obstrigillāt-*, ppl. stem of *obstrigillāre* to hinder, oppose, derivative of *obstringĕre*: see OBSTRINGE.] *trans.* To oppose or resist. Hence †**obstrigi'llation**, opposition.

1623 COCKERAM I, *Obstrigilate*, to resist. *Ibid.* II, *A resisting*, Obstrigillation, Oppugnation. **1656** in BLOUNT.

†**ob'stringe,** *v. Obs. rare.* [ad. L. *obstringĕre*, f. *ob-* (OB- I c) + *stringĕre* to tie, bind.] *trans.* To put under obligation; to bind.

1528 *Ambass. Let. to Wolsey* in Strype *Eccl. Mem.* (1822) I. II. App. xxiii. 66 He and the see was and is obstringed and bound to your Grace. **1660** tr. *Amyraldus' Treat. conc. Relig.* III. vi. 453 It was never lookt upon as unjust or strange, for those who are obstring'd one to another by those bonds to partake in the punishment of their Relatives.

obstropalous, -olous, -ulous, etc., illiterate variants of OBSTREPEROUS.

obstruct (əb'strʌkt), *v.* [f. L. *obstruct-*, ppl. stem of *obstruĕre* to build against, to block up, f. *ob-* (OB- I b) + *struĕre* to pile, build.]

1. *trans.* To block, close up, or fill (a way or passage) with obstacles or impediments; to render impassable or difficult of passage.

1611 COTGR., *Oppiler*, to stop, obstruct, shut up. **1651** HOBBES *Leviath.* II. xxix. 172 Wind in the head that obstructeth the roots of the Nerves. **1667** MILTON *P.L.* x. 637 Both Sin, and Death, and yawning Grave at last, Through Chaos hurld, obstruct the mouth of Hell, For ever, and seal up his ravenous Jawes. **1703** MAUNDRELL *Journ. Jerus.* (1732) 76 The door is now so obstructed with Stones. **1796** H. HUNTER tr. *St.-Pierre's Stud. Nat.* (1799) III. 103 Rolling stones, which now obstruct these roads as well as mar the greatest part of the surface of this island. **1834** LYTTON *Pompeii* IV. vii, 'Rise..thou obstructest the way'. **1845** BUDD. *Dis. Liver* 68 The common duct was much compressed and obstructed by enlargement and hardening of the pancreas.

absol. **1689** *Col. Rec. Pennsylv.* I. 264 But what then obstructed I am not certaine.

2. a. To interrupt, render difficult, or retard the passage or progress of; to impede, hinder, or retard (a person or thing in its motion).

1655 H. VAUGHAN *Silex Scint.* L'Envoy, Sin..quickly will Turn in, if not obstructed still. **1688** in Ellis *Orig. Lett.* Ser. II. IV. 134 The Wind..we believe obstructs the coming of any letters from Holland, and keeps back the Dutch fleet. **1768** BEATTIE *Minstr.* I. xlix, If but a cloud obstruct the solar ray. **1789** W. BUCHAN *Dom. Med.* (1790) 79 These, by obstructing the free current of air..render such places damp and unwholesome. **1821** CRAIG *Lect. Drawing*, etc. v. 259 If..the particles of air can obstruct and reflect light. **1845** S. AUSTIN *Ranke's Hist. Ref.* III. 507 They did not even take the trouble to obstruct his passage over the river.

b. Cricket. ***obstructing the field*** (formerly, ***the ball***): an expression used to denote the manner of dismissal of a batsman who, in the umpire's opinion, wilfully hindered a fieldsman or interfered with the ball in order to avoid being caught, stumped, etc.

1877 C. BOX *Eng. Game Cricket* 456 Obstructing the Ball.—A man may be given out, but seldom is on such an account. **1905** *Laws of Cricket* §26 The striker is out..if under pretence of running, or otherwise, either of the batsmen wilfully prevent a ball from being caught;—'Obstructing the field'. **1912** A. A. LILLEY *Twenty-Four Years Cricket* v. 57 As the ball struck it [*sc.* the bat] and fell to the ground, I pushed it further along with my bat, and Wheeler..gave me out. The point upon which he gave his decision was for obstructing the field.

c. In various games: to impede (a player) in a manner which constitutes an offence.

1895 H. F. BATTERSBY *Hockey* vii. 131 A player shall not run in between his opponent and the ball so as to obstruct him. **1953** *Association Football* ('Know the Game' Series) 33/2 If an opponent is obstructing a player, the player may charge him. **1969** *F.A. Guide to Laws of Game* 144 He is obstructing or interfering with an opponent. **1974** *Rules of Game* 163/3 An indirect free kick is awarded..for intentionally obstructing an opponent while not attempting to play the ball, in order to prevent him reaching it.

3. *fig.* To stand in the way of, or persistently oppose the progress or course of (proceedings, or a person or thing in a purpose or action); to hinder, impede, retard, delay, withstand, stop. ***to obstruct process*** (in *Law*): to commit the punishable offence of intentionally hindering the officers of the law in the execution of their duties.

1647 CLARENDON *Hist. Reb.* I. §63 A Servant..the prejudice to whose Person exceedingly obstructed all overtures made in Parliament for his service. **1649** MILTON *Eikon.* ix, To expect that their voting or not voting should obstruct the Commons. **1665** WALTON *Life Hooker* in *H.'s Wks.* (1888) I. 36 She was like an untamed heifer, that would not be ruled by God's people, but obstructed his discipline. **1738** *Col. Rec. Pennsylv.* IV. 284 The said Officers were obstructed in the lawful Discharge of their Duty. **1766** GOLDSM. *Vic. W.* xxviii, I don't know if it be just thus to obstruct the union of man and wife. **1772** *Jacob's Law Dict.* (ed. 9) s.v. *Process*, Obstructing the execution of lawful process, is an offence against publick justice. **1853** A. PRENTICE *Hist. Anti-Corn-Law League* I. viii. 112 Many..had come to obstruct the proceedings. **1858** FROUDE *Hist. Eng.* III. xiv. 212 He had obstructed good subjects, who would have done their duty, had he allowed them.

4. To come in the way of, interrupt, shut out (the sight or view of).

1717 tr. *Frezier's Voy.* 49 The next Morning..a thick Fog obstructing our Sight, we weigh'd, to go up thither. **1807** J. BARLOW *Columb.* III. 144 And hills above them still obstruct the skies. **1859** GEO. ELIOT *A. Bede* ii, On the..north western side, there was nothing to obstruct the view.

Hence **ob'structing,** *vbl. sb.* and *ppl. a.*; **ob'structingly** *adv.*, so as to obstruct.

1649 MILTON *Eikon.* xxvii, This is mischief without remedy, a stifling and obstructing evill that hath no vent. **1817** COBBETT *Pol. Reg.* XXXII. 37 One of the crimes..was the obstructing of petitions. **1889** 'ANNIE THOMAS' *That Other Woman* III. vi. 96 Two or three obstructingly stout bodies sat in their way. **1897** *Allbutt's Syst. Med.* III. 794 The obstructing agent may be..a peritoneal adhesion by which a loop of bowel is snared.

[**'obstruct,** *sb.*, conjectural emendation, by Warburton, of *abstract* in the following passage (but not otherwise known):

1606 SHAKS. *Ant. & Cl.* III. vi. 61 His pardon for returne. Which soone he granted, being an abstract 'tweene his Lust and him.]

obstructed (əb'strʌktıd), *ppl. a.* [f. OBSTRUCT *v.* + -ED^1.] Blocked up, stopped up, hindered, impeded: see the vb.

1611 COTGR., *Oppilé*, obstructed, stopped, shut vp. *a* **1658** CLEVELAND *General Eclipse*, As an obstructed fountain's head Cuts the entail off from the streams And brooks are disinherited. **1747** WESLEY *Prim. Physic* (1762) p. xxii, Obstructed Perspiration, vulgarly called Catching Cold. **1749** JOHNSON *Irene* III. iii, If e'r thy youth has..felt th' impatience of obstructed love. **1878** T. BRYANT *Pract. Surg.* I. 650 The symptoms of an obstructed hernia, as of obstructed intestine, are not very definite.

b. *Med.* Having a functional obstruction.

1662 R. MATHEW *Unl. Alch.* 94 One Maid..being obstructed about five or six years, insomuch as she grew very diseased.

Hence **ob'structedly** *adv.*, with obstruction.

1656 DUCHESS NEWCASTLE *Nature's Picture* XI. Epistle, Others in one discourse speak..weakly or obstructedly.

obstructer, variant of OBSTRUCTOR.

obstruction (əb'strʌkʃən). [ad. L. *obstructiōn-em*, n. of action f. *obstruĕre* to OBSTRUCT. Cf. F. *obstruction* (1540 in Godef. *Compl.*).] The action of obstructing; that in which this is embodied.

1. The action of blocking up a way or passage with an obstacle or impediment; the rendering impassable; the condition of being so blocked; frequently in reference to passages, organs, or functions of the body: *esp.* the ill-condition produced by constipation of the bowels. ***cold obstruction*** (also *fig.*), stoppage or cessation of the vital functions; the condition of the body in death.

1533 MORE *Apol.* xxii. Wks. 882/2 A diete as thinne as Galiene deuiseth for hym that hath an obstruccion in his liuer. **1601** SHAKS. *Twel. N.* III. iv. 22 This does make some obstruction in the blood: This crosse-gartering. **1603** —— *Meas. for M.* III. i. 119 To die,..To lie in cold obstruction, and to rot, This sensible warme motion, to become A kneaded clod. **1791** *Gentl. Mag.* 22/2 Where deafness proceeds from an obstruction of the auditory duct, by wax. **1813** BYRON *Giaour* iii, Where cold Obstruction's apathy Appals the gazing mourner's heart. **1844** DUFTON *Deafness* 75 The most efficient local means of treating..obstruction of the Eustachian tube. **1876** LOWELL *Among my Bks.* Ser. II. 157 The cold obstruction of two centuries thaws, and the stream of speech..seeks out its old windings. **1877** ROBERTS *Handbk. Med.* I. 30 Accumulations of fluid in the interior of hollow organs, as the result of obstruction at an orifice.

2. a. The action of hindering or rendering difficult the passage or progress of a person or thing; the fact of standing in the way; the shutting out of light by interposition.

1601 SHAKS. *Twel. N.* IV. ii. 43 *Clo.* Why it hath bay Windowes transparant as baricadoes,..and yet complainest thou of obstruction? **1755** YOUNG *Centaur* vi. Wks. 1757 IV. 269 Souls suffer no separation from obstruction of matter, or distance of place. **1841** ELPHINSTONE *Hist. Ind.* II. 413 He advanced without further obstruction to the capital.

b. *spec.* in *Law.*

1908 *Encycl. Laws Eng.* (ed. 2) X. 116 *Obstruction.* This term is used in law mainly in two senses: (1) Interference with public or private rights or easements, particularly of light, way, navigation, or watercourse; (2) interference with officers of justice in the execution of their duty. **1910** *Daily Chron.* 18 Sept. 1/7 The conviction of two men for obstructing the police. After the evidence of two witnesses denying the statements made by the policemen when the obstruction charge was being considered, [etc.]. **1933** P. MACDONALD *Mystery of Dead Police* v. 41 My car's outside Savarin's... There's a bobby by it. He wants me for obstruction.

c. *spec.* as an offence in various games.

1923 H. E. HASLAM *How to play Hockey* xiii. 81 Turning on the ball incurs a penalty on the score of obstruction. **1935** *Encycl. Sports* 521/2 Charging and Obstruction... A player who is not running for the ball must not charge or obstruct an opponent not holding the ball. **1950** *Men's Hockey* ('Know the Game' Series) 18/1 A penalty bully is awarded ..[for] a bad case of obstruction in front of goal. **1953** *Association Football* ('Know the Game' Series) 33/1 Should the obstruction take the form of a personal foul..then the foul is penalised by a direct free kick. **1969** *F.A. Guide to Laws of Game* 197 Indirect free-kick for obstruction. **1974** *Rules of Game* 163/2 A direct free kick..is awarded for the following intentional fouls..: charging from behind (unless the opponent is guilty of obstruction).

3. *fig.* The hindering or stopping of the course, performance, or doing of anything; *spec.* the persistent attempt to stop the progress of business in any meeting or legislative assembly, e.g. in the House of Commons.

1656 STANLEY *Hist. Philos.* IV. (1701) 144/1 To one who asked him what folly is, he said, the obstruction of Knowledge. **1674** TEMPLE *Let. to Coventry* Wks. 1731 II. 300, I am confident..that an Obstruction of the Peace will not arise from hence. **1698** FRYER *Acc. E. India & P.* 78 The general obstruction of Trade, occasioned by the War. **1741** MIDDLETON *Cicero* I. v. 381 This obstruction given to Cicero's return. **1772** *Jacob's Law Dict.* (ed. 9) s.v. *Process*, An obstruction of an arrest upon criminal process. **1845** MCCULLOCH *Taxation* I. i. (1852) 59 A project of this sort is liable to much obstruction from the difficulties in the way of fixing the primary or original valuation. **1879** M. ARNOLD *Ess., Irish Cathol.* 99 The obstruction offered by the Irish members in Parliament is really an expression of this uncontrollable antipathy. **1880** MCCARTHY *Own Times* IV. lix. 313 Its progress [the Ballot Bill of 1871] was delayed by that practice of talking against time which has more recently become famous under the name of obstruction. **1893** *Daily News* 26 Jan. 5/2 Mr. Gladstone..defined obstruction as resisting the will of the House otherwise than by argument.

4. Anything that stops or blocks a way or passage; that which hinders or prevents passage or progress; an obstructing obstacle.

a. physical.

1597 SHAKS. *2 Hen. IV*, IV. i. 65 To..purge th' obstructions, which begin to stop Our very Veines of Life. **1732** ARBUTHNOT *Rules of Diet* 301 And remove the Obstruction. **1836** W. IRVING *Astoria* I. 162 The turbulence and rapidity of the current..gave the voyagers intimation that they were approaching the great obstructions of the river. **1850** CHUBB *Locks & Keys* 10 The forms of these moveable obstructions to the bolt, in locks of modern date, are of course various. **1875** KNIGHT *Dict. Mech.* 1705/1 The cow-catcher, or frame in front of an engine, to push obstructions from the rails.

b. immaterial.

1601 SHAKS. *Twel. N.* II. v. 129 Why this [sentence] is euident to any formall capacitie. There is no obstruction in this. **1697** DAMPIER *Voy.* 507 Their designs meeting with such delays and obstructions, they many of them grew weary of it. **1810** R. HALL *Wks.* (1841) V. 182 Guilt is a legal obstruction to an approach to God. **1876** MOZLEY *Univ. Serm.* ix. (1877) 194 The great obstruction to generosity in our nature is jealousy.

5. *attrib.* and *Comb.*, **obstruction-guard**, a bar, etc. fixed in front of a railway-engine to remove an obstruction from the rails; **obstruction light** *Aeronaut.* (see quot. 1960).

1897 *Allbutt's Syst. Med.* III. 874 When once the obstruction symptoms have become definite. **1898** *Daily News* 25 Mar. 3/5 A rail chair had been placed on the rails. The impact was so severe as to smash the obstruction guard in front of the engine. **1934** *Jrnl. R. Aeronaut. Soc.* XXXVIII. 728 The Air Ministry specified the number and type of obstruction lights which had to be fitted to each mast. **1960** *Guide Civil Land Aerodrome Lighting* (*B.S.I.*) 9 *Obstruction light*, a light indicating the presence of an obstruction.

ob'structionary, *a. rare.* [f. OBSTRUCTION + -ARY^1.] Tending or disposed to obstruct.

1934 W. DE LA MARE *Froward Child* 13 He was not always too anxious as to what kind of self was being so obstructionary. **1975** *New Yorker* 27 Oct. 77/1 There were rules, not of Herr Kautz's making, that guaranteed us a coeducational clubroom and occasional dances, but he was always around in a silently obstructionary manner, operating the turntable, serving the punch, watching.

ob'structionism. [f. OBSTRUCTION + -ISM.] The practice of systematic obstruction, as in a legislative body.

1879 *Pall Mall Budget* 12 Sept., If obstructionism were to become extinct immediately, it would not have passed away without leaving a lasting..impression upon the character of the English House of Commons. **1941** W. S. CHURCHILL *Second World War* (1950) III. 752 Please report to me any signs of obstructionism. **1955** *Times* 9 Aug. 11/4 Obstructionism is a game two can play. What is required to solve the difficulty is sincerity on both sides. **1964** S. BRITTAN *Treasury under Tories* ii. 61 He would not dream of indulging in the narrow-minded obstructionism of some of his predecessors. **1977** *Time* 5 Sept. 35/1 O'Neill made it clear to Georgia's crusty John Flynt, chairman of the ethics committee, that neither he nor Jaworski would tolerate any obstructionism.

obstructionist (əbˈstrʌkʃənɪst). *sb.* (and *a.*) [f. as prec. + -IST.] One who advocates or systematically practises obstruction, esp. in reference to the proceedings of a legislative body. Also *attrib.* or as *adj.*

1846 R. BELL *Canning* 341 Luckily there is always an obstructionist in the House of Commons..to start up with an objection by way of rider to the very climax of unanimity. **1862** *Westm. Rev.* Jan. 60 Obstructionists make heretics, and heretics make obstructionists. **1879** *Pall Mall Budget* 12 Sept., The mischief which obstructionist impunity has already worked. **1882** *Tribune* (N.Y.) 5 Apr., It is hard to see what motive could have influenced the Democrats to act as obstructionists in this matter. **1882** GODKIN in *19th Cent.* Aug. 187 The scenes of disorder prepared by the Irish obstructionists last winter. **1934** C. LAMBERT *Music Ho!* IV. 242 They were..obstructionist rather than constructionist. **1965** [see FILIBUSTER *sb.* 4]. **1966** M. R. D. FOOT *SOE in France* ii. 11 Petty obstructionists of this kind lay about SOE's path all its life, and some have pursued it since its winding-up. **1975** *New Yorker* 26 May 94/2 The late nineteen-forties, when another President got himself returned to office by blaming nearly everything that was wrong with the country on an obstructionist Congress controlled by the opposing party.

obstructive (əbˈstrʌktɪv), *a.* (*sb.*) [f. L. *obstruct-*, ppl. stem (see OBSTRUCT *v.*) + -IVE: cf. F. *obstructif, -ive* (1690 in Hatz.-Darm.).]

1. Having the quality of obstructing; tending to obstruct; causing impediment. Const. *of, to.*

1611 COTGR., *Oppilatif*, oppilatiue, obstructiue, stopping. **1637–50** ROW *Hist. Kirk* (1842) 204 The King..knowing how obstructiue it would proue to his purpose, sent for Bishop Blackburne. *c* **1695** J. MILLER *Descr. New York* (1843) 12 Things..either wanting or obstructive to the happiness of New York. **1712** PRIDEAUX *Direct. Ch.-wardens* (ed. 4) 68 Nothing is to be permitted there which shall be.. obstructive of it [divine service]. **1717** *Poem Birthday K. George I*, Far from thy Brows, obstructive Slumbers shake. **1859** MILL *Diss. & Disc.* II. *French Rev. in 1848.* 402 Suppose it [a second Chamber] constituted in a manner, of all others, least calculated to render it an obstructive body. **1865** M. ARNOLD *Ess. Crit.* ii. (1875) 59 Academies may be said to be obstructive to energy and inventive genius. **1866** GEO. ELIOT *F. Holt* II. xxx. 227 This angry haste..might some day.. be obstructive of his own work. **1881** MISS YONGE *Lads & Lasses Langley* iii. 128 That obstructive old aunt insisted on dusting Mr. O'Toole's parlour herself.

2. Of, pertaining to, or of the nature of obstruction of the bowels or of any bodily duct or passage.

1620 VENNER *Via Recta* v. 89 It..abstergeth obstructiue humours in the stomacke. **1876** BRISTOWE *Th. & Pract. Med.* (1878) 531 Obstructive and regurgitant disease of the aortic and mitral orifices. **1897** *Allbutt's Syst. Med.* IV. 67 The coloration of skin in these cases is usually not so deep as that found in ordinary obstructive jaundice. *Ibid.* 395 Obstructive suppression may forbid the exit of the urine.. after it has been completely formed by the kidneys.

B. *sb.* **1.** An obstructive agent, instrument, or force; a hindrance.

1642 JER. TAYLOR *Episc.* (1647) 4 Episcopacy..was instituted as an obstructive to the diffusion of Schisme and Heresy. **1654** HAMMOND *Fundam.* xiii. 120 The second obstructive..is that of the Fiduciarie. **1860** TYNDALL *Glac.* I. xxvii. 218 The leading mule..proved a mere obstructive.

2. One who obstructs or retards progress in legislation, education, parliamentary business, etc.

1856 R. A. VAUGHAN *Mystics* (1860) II. VIII. ii. 41 He must stand condemned..as one of the obstructives of his day. **1856** EMERSON *Eng. Traits, The 'Times'* Wks. (Bohn) II. 116 The people are familiarized with the reason of reform, and, one by one, take away every argument of the obstructives. **1879** SALA in *Daily Tel.* 28 June, A meddlesome and intolerant body of political obstructives who called themselves the Constitutional Association. *a* **1884** M. PATTISON *Mem.* (1885) 239 Every Oxford man was a Liberal, even those whom nature had palpably destined for obstructives.

Hence **ob'structively** *adv.*, so as to obstruct; **ob'structivism**, the system or practice of being obstructive.

1863 MELVILLE BELL *Princ. Speech* 190 Gradually raising the point of the tongue..till it comes upon the palate obstructively, and so forms the letter D. **1870** DICKENS *E. Drood* iii, Fragments of old wall [etc.]..have got incongruously or obstructively built into many of its houses and gardens. **1885** *Academy* 19 Dec. 407/2 A fusion of fanatical obstructivism with official corruption.

ob'structiveness. [f. prec. + -NESS.] Obstructive quality or practice.

1727 in BAILEY vol. II. **1856** FROUDE *Hist. Eng.* (1858) II. vi. 4 In..nominations to the religious houses, the superiors ..residing abroad had equal facilities for obstructiveness. **1884** *Spectator* 12 July 904/2 The mischievous obstructiveness of the House of Lords.

obstructor (əbˈstrʌktə(r)). Also 7 -our, 7–9 -er. [agent-n. on L. type, f. *obstruĕre* to OBSTRUCT: cf. *constructor, instructor.*] One who or that which obstructs, stands in the way of, or impedes; a hinderer; an opponent of progress.

1649 J. GOODWIN (*title*) The Obstructours of Justice. **1665** WALTON *Life Hooker* in *H.'s Wks.* (1888) I. 34 The common people became so fanatic, as to believe the bishops to be Antichrist, and the only obstructors of God's Discipline. **1672** W. DE BRITAINE *Dutch Usurp.* 33 The Hollanders are the great Supplanters of Trade, and Obstructers of Commerce. **1755** JOHNSON, *Obstructer*, one that hinders or opposes. **1884** *Manch. Exam.* 22 May 5/1 [He] had chosen to turn himself into a deliberate obstructor of Irish measures.

obstruent (ˈɒbstru:ənt), *a.* and *sb.* [ad. L. *obstruent-em*, pr. pple. of *obstru-ĕre* to OBSTRUCT.]

A. *adj.* Obstructing; *Med.* closing up the ducts or passages of the body: cf. DEOBSTRUENT.

1755 JOHNSON, *Obstruent*, hindering, blocking up. **1827** W. G. S. *Exc. Vill. Curate* 132 If you subject me to such obstruent interruptions as these. **1857** MAYNE *Expos. Lex.*, *Obstruens*, shutting or closing up; applied to medicines: obstruent. **1892** in *Syd. Soc. Lex.* **1945** R. HARGREAVES *Enemy at Gate* 27 Cold, flabby, capricious, obstruent, and quite femininely vindictive, he was a creature of almost supernal selfishness, timidity and irresolution. **1973** J. WAINWRIGHT *Pride of Pigs* 70 The object of the exercise was to demolish any obstruent bushel likely to get in the way of *his* particular light.

B. *sb.* **a.** Something that obstructs, an obstruction. **b.** *Med.* A medicine which closes the orifices of ducts or vessels, or the natural passages of the body.

1669 W. SIMPSON *Hydrol. Chym.* 32 Vitiated by such an obstructive coagulative salt according to the strength and degree of the obstruent. **1888** A. S. WILSON *Lyric Hopeless Love* lxix, Some obstruent to clear away. **1892** in *Syd. Soc. Lex.*

c. *Phonetics.* Also *erron.* **obstruant.** A fricative or plosive speech sound. Also *attrib.* and *Comb.*

1942 *Language* XVIII. 13 The first member of a cluster of two obstruents (stop or spirant) is voiceless. **1952** W. P. LEHMANN *Proto-Indo-European Phonol.* ii. 7 We then arrive at three classes of phonemes: 1. those which may not function as syllabics will be called obstruents. **1955** C. F. HOCKETT *Man. Phonol.* 97 A number of obstruent systems include no symmetric set at all. **1956** J. WHATMOUGH *Language* iii. 36 Sounds which are partially or completely stopped at some point—between the larynx and the lips (these are known as obstruents), e.g. *p:k*, or *f:χ*. **1962** *Word* XVIII. 312 Post-vocalic consonants cluster in exactly the opposite direction, right to left, with privilege of occurrence of more than one consonant from an obstruent group, as many as three lenes or four fortes, but never a lenis after a fortis. **1963** ERVIN & MILLER in J. A. Fishman *Readings Sociol. of Lang.* (1968) 71 Vowel distinctions are learned first. The order of acquisition for the remaining features is: (*a*) vowels *vs.* consonants; (*b*) sonorants *vs.* articulated obstruants [etc.]. **1965** N. CHOMSKY *Aspects of Theory of Syntax* iv. 168 If the second consonant is a liquid, the first must be an obstruent. **1969** *Language* XLV. 248 We may symbolize the elements involved as C (any obstruent), R (any 'resonant' or semivowel) and V (any vowel). **1970** *Canad. Jrnl. Linguistics* XV. 122 Two examples [of persistent rule] are the well known devoicing of the final obstruents in German..and the loss of final /n/ in Livonian. **1973** A. H. SOMMERSTEIN *Sound Pattern Anc. Greek* ii. 26 The derivation of [n] from /nt/ is by Obstruent Dropping. **1975** *Language* LI. 528, I observed that the alternation between distinctively paired obstruents such as [p-b, t-d, k-g] had to be stated as a morphophonemic regularity. **1977** *Trans. Philol. Soc.* 1975 4 It is clear that a certain class of obstruent-final stems has the property of having inflected forms where the stem-final obstruents differ in voicing from those in the simplex forms.

†**ob'struse**, *a.*, erron. form of ABSTRUSE (formerly frequent, after *obstrūsus*, false reading in L.).

1604 T. WRIGHT *Passions* v. §2. 168 In such an obstruse difficultie, he that speaketh most apparently and probably, saith the best. **1683** MOXON *Mech. Exerc., Printing* 367 Obstruce Words and Phrases. *a* **1734** NORTH *Exam.* I. ii. §18 (1740) 39 If we sink..to his more obstruse Reaches.

obstupefacient (-ˈfeɪʃɪənt), *a.* [ad. L. *obstupefacient-em*, pr. pple. of *obstupefacĕre*: see below and -ENT.] Stupefying; in *Med.* = narcotic.

1857 in MAYNE *Expos. Lex.* **1892** in *Syd. Soc. Lex.*

†**ob'stupefact**, *a.* (*sb.*) *Obs. rare*$^{-1}$. [ad. L. *obstupefact-us*, pa. pple. of *obstupefac-ĕre*: see next.] Stupefied, stupid; as *sb.* a stupid person.

1601 B. JONSON *Poetaster* v. iii, *Hor.* How now, Crispinus? *Crisp.* O.—obstupefact. *Tib.* Nay, that we all are.

†**obstupe'faction.** *Obs. rare.* [n. of action f. *obstupefacĕre* to render senseless, f. *ob-* (OB- 1 b, d) + *stupefacĕre* to make stupid.] The fact or condition of being stupefied; stupefaction.

1625 JACKSON *Creed* v. xi. § 1 That obstupefaction wherein our souls..are miserably drenched by their delapse into these bodily sinks of corruption. **1664** H. MORE *Myst. Iniq.* 436 Whether those..doe it..rather in a kind of confusion and obstupefaction of mind out of fear and suspicion.

†**obstupe'factive**, *a.* *Obs. rare*$^{-1}$. [f. L. *obstupefact-* (see prec.) + -IVE.] Tending to stupefy.

a **1633** ABP. ABBOT (J.), The force of it is obstupefactive, and no other.

obstupefy (əbˈstju:pɪfaɪ), *v.* [f. L. *obstupefacĕre* (see above), after STUPEFY.] *trans.* To stupefy, esp. mentally.

1613 JACKSON *Creed* I. xii. § 1 So had the diuels..sought to work wonders about the Egyptian idols, which did obstupifie the people. **1660** H. MORE *Myst. Godliness* IV. i. 138 Some Lethargical or obstupifying disease. **1708** *Brit. Apollo* No. 36. 2/1 To Paradigmatize and..explain all obstupifying Quiddities. **1889** C. PRITCHARD *Occas. Th. Astron.* 167 You cannot obstupefy such a man.

†**obstu'pescence.** *Obs. rare.* [f. L. *obstupēscent-em*, pr. pple. of *obstupēscĕre* (*obstipēscĕre*) to become stupefied: see -ENCE.] The condition of being in a stupor.

1597 A. M. tr. *Guillemeau's Fr. Chirurg.* 52 b/2 The obstupescence and feare wherwith the..faynte-harted are often-times taken. **1857** MAYNE *Expos. Lex.*, *Obstupescentia*, old term for..that state when the patient remains still, with open eyes, as if astonished, and neither moves or speaks: obstupescence. **1892** in *Syd. Soc. Lex.*

†**'obstuprate**, *v. Obs. rare*$^{-1}$. [f. ppl. stem of L. *obstuprāre*, f. *ob-* (OB- 1 b) + *stuprāre* to ravish.] *trans.* To ravish; = CONSTUPRATE.

1658 BROMHALL *Treat. Specters* IV. 265 Snatching a ring from her father that did obstuprate her, delivered it to her Nurse.

†**ob'surd**, *v. Obs. trans.* To make dull of hearing, deafen.

1639 J. WELLES *Soules Progr.* 109 Old age..dimmed with blindness, obsurded with deafenes.

obtain (əbˈteɪn), *v.* Forms: 5–6 ob-, op-, -teyne, -tayne, -teigne, -teygne, (5 optyne), 6 obtaigne, opteine, (*Sc.* obtene, obtine, optene), 6–7 obteine, -taine, (optain(e, 7 *Sc.* obtean), 6– obtain. [ME. *obteine, -teyne, -tene*, a. F. *obten-ir* (14th c. in Littré), ad. L. *obtinēre*, f. *ob-* (OB- 1 b) + *tenēre* to hold, keep. Cf. CONTAIN.]

1. *trans.* To come into the possession or enjoyment of (something) by one's own effort, or by request; to procure or gain, as the result of purpose and effort; hence, generally, to acquire, get.

c **1425** LYDG. *Assembly of Gods* 2085 And so the vyctory shall ye obteyne. **1432–50** tr. *Higden* (Rolls) I. 291 Men of Norway..saylenge from Denmarke, opteynede and inhabite that grownde, callenge hit Normandy. **1490** CAXTON *Eneydos* x. 40 [Eneas] opteyned her grace for to soiourne. **1526** TINDALE *Matt.* v. 7 Blessed are the mercifull: for they shall obteyne mercy. **1548–9** (Mar.) *Bk. Com. Prayer* Coll. 23rd Sund. aft. Trin., Graunt that those thynges which we aske faithfully we maye obteine effectually. **1651** HOBBES *Leviath.* II. xxvii. 154 Obtaining Pardon by Mony, or other rewards. **1756** C. LUCAS *Ess. Waters* III. 278 Gilded shillings..had obtained the name of Bath guineas. **1800** tr. *Lagrange's Chem.* I. 223 The precipitate obtained is sulphite of barytes. **1860** TYNDALL *Glac.* I. xx. 138, I climbed..to obtain a general view of the surrounding scene. **1890** MERCIER *Sanity & Insanity* x. 261 The process of obtaining a livelihood.

b. With *obj. cl.* expressing what is granted in answer to a request. Now *rare* or *Obs.*

1432–50 tr. *Higden* (Rolls) V. 397 Opteynynge unnethe of God that þe sawles of the monastery scholde be salvede. **1460** CAPGRAVE *Chron.* 235 The abbot opteyned that there schuld no prioure longing to Seynt Albonne..be compelled for to gadere the dymes to the King. *a* **1648** LD. HERBERT *Hen. VIII* (1683) 318 They obtained that Francisco Sforza should be admitted to the Emperors prescence. **1737** WHISTON *Josephus Hist.* I. xvi. §7 Macheras..earnestly begged and obtained that he would be reconciled. **1844** KINGLAKE *Eothen* 101, I obtained that all of them..should sit at the table.

†**c.** With *inf. obj.* expressing what is got *from*, *of* a person; = to prevail upon. *Obs.*

1681 DRYDEN *Abs. & Achit.* To Rdr., I could not obtain from myself to show Absalom unfortunate. **1742** RICHARDSON *Pamela* III. 227 The Gentlemen..obtained of Miss to play several Tunes on the Spinnet. **1751** *Female Foundling* I. 172 It was with Difficulty..I had obtained from myself to have this Conversation.

d. *absol.* (Cf. 4.)

1526 TINDALE *1 Cor.* ix. 24 So runne that ye maye obtayne. **1599** B. JONSON *Cynthia's Rev.* I. Wks. (Rtldg.) 73/1 *Echo*..Vouchsafe me, I may do him these last rites... *Mer.* Thou dost obtain. **1854** WHITTIER *Hermit of the Thebaid* iii, The simple heart, that freely asks In love, obtains.

†**2. a.** With *pa. pple.* as *compl.* To procure something to be done: = GET *v.* 28 a. **b.** With *inf.* as *compl.* To induce, prevail upon (a person) *to do* something: = GET *v.* 30. *Obs. rare.*

1425 *Paston Lett.* I. 21 Sir John Paston..hath optyned me condempnyd to hym in ccc[vij] marcz. **1592** *Nobody & Someb.* 595 in Simpson *Sch. Shaks.* (1878) I. 300 He..will not be obtaind To take upon him this Realmes government.

†**3.** To gain, win (a battle or other contest).

a **1470** TIPTOFT *Cæsar* i. (1530) 2 All the battels which he obteynyd in France. **1615** G. SANDYS *Trav.* I. 4 That memorable Sea-battell there obtained against the Turk. *a* **1649** WINTHROP *Hist. New Eng.* (1853) II. 142, I might have obtained the cause I had in hand.

4. *intr.* To win the victory, gain the day, prevail; to succeed, prosper. *Obs.* or *arch.*

c **1425** LYDG. *Assembly of Gods* 1311 When olde Attropos had seen and herde..How Vertew had opteynyd. *c* **1440** *Gesta Rom.* I. xxxiv. 134 Pes, herynge..that mercy, hir sistre, myght not opteyne ne prevayle in hir purpose. **1526** R. WHYTFORD *Martiloge* (1893) 74 For whose eleccyon was a sysme, but he obteyned, and well ruled. **1642** MILTON *Apol. Smect.* Wks. (1847) 79/2 Too credulous is the confuter, if he think to obtain with me. **1701** SWIFT *Contests Nobles & Comm. Athens & Rome* iii, This, though it failed at present, yet afterwards obtained. **1847** TENNYSON *Princ.* VII. 56 Less prosperously the second suit obtain'd.

5. To attain to, get as far as, reach, gain.

†**a.** *intr.* with *to*, *unto*: To get to. *Obs.*

1477 EARL RIVERS (Caxton) *Dictes* 37 Aske forgeueness..of god, and in thy self so doyng, thou mayest opteyne vnto hys grace. **1555** EDEN *Decades* To Rdr. (Arb.) 51 Salomon..obteyned by his nauigations to Ophir. **1581** SIDNEY *Apol. Poetrie* (Arb.) 34 The Poets haue obtained to the..top of their profession. **1625** BACON *Ess., Simulation* (Arb.) 507 If a Man cannot obtaine to that Iudgment.

b. *trans.* To attain, reach, gain. *Obs.* or *arch.*

1589 HAKLUYT *Voy.* 817 His consorts, whereof one..hath not long since obtayned his port. **1733** P. SHAW tr. *Bacon's De Sap. Vet.* iii. Expl., Philos. Wks. I. 561 The End is seldom obtained. **1774** GOLDSM. *Nat. Hist.* (1776) IV. 316 If once the lama obtains the rocky precipice. **1830** SCOTT *Demonol.* (1831) 384 The vivacity of fancy..dies within us when we obtain the age of manhood.

†**c.** with *inf.* To attain or come *to be*, *to do*, etc.; to get opportunity, permission, ability, etc. *to do* something; to succeed in doing something. *Obs.*

1526 SKELTON *Magnyf.* 1815, I trust we shall optaine To do you servyce. *a* **1586** SIDNEY *Arcadia* (1622) 35 Clitophon by vehement importunitie obtained to goe with him. *a* **1688** CUDWORTH *Immut. Mor.* (1731) 117 The weaker Murmurs..cannot obtain to be heard. **1703** MAUNDRELL *Journ. Jerus.* (1732) 7 It was not without much importunity that we obtain'd to have the use of a dry part of the House.

†**6.** To hold; to possess; to occupy. [A Latin sense.] *Obs.*

1482 *Monk of Evesham* (Arb.) 92 To haue and opteyne hem yn my lappe or holde hem in my harmys. *c* **1530** LD. BERNERS *Arth. Lyt. Bryt.* (1814) 458 Who shal kepe and obtaine this countre after vs, syth that Arthur..is deed. **1671** MILTON *P.R.* I. 87 He who obtains the Monarchy of Heav'n. **1710** BERKELEY *Princ. Human Knowl.* I. §121 Varying the signification of each figure [in Arabic notation] according to the place it obtains.

7. *intr.* To prevail; to be prevalent, customary, or established; to be in force or in vogue; to hold good, have place, subsist, exist. [? Allied to 4 or 6.]

1618 HALES *Gold. Rem.* II. (1673) 66 Their opinions have now obtained for a hundred years. **1640** BP. HALL *Humb. Remonstr.* 17 That forme of Episcopall Government, which hath hitherto obtained in the Church. **1732** BERKELEY *Alciphr.* v. §13 A practice..which obtains only among the idle part of the nation. **1764** REID *Inquiry* i. §3 Laws of nature which universally obtain. **1842** GROVE *Corr. Phys. Forces* 75 Static equilibrium, such..as that which obtains in the two arms of a balance. **1890** LD. ESHER in *Law Times Rep.* LXIII. 731/2 The new mode, which now obtains, of drafting Acts of Parliament so as to legislate by incorporating other Acts of Parliament.

†**b.** *pass.* = prec. sense. *Obs. rare.*

1529 MORE *Dyaloge* IV. Wks. 283/1 Which thing had vndoubtedly neuer been obteined among yͤ people..if god had not broughte it vp hymselfe. **1565** JEWEL *Repl. Harding* (1611) 410 Him, that is the Priest, or Elder, he calleth the Sacrificer..And the same word, Sacrificer, is now obteined by Custome.

Hence **ob'tained** *ppl. a.*, **ob'taining** *vbl. sb.*

1495 *Act 11 Hen. VII*, c. 53 *Preamble*, Your moost victorius opteynyng agayns Richard. **1539** J. FOSTER in Ellis *Orig. Lett.* Ser. I. II. 112 For the optaynyng of hys gracyous pardon. *a* **1548** HALL *Chron., Hen. VII*, 4 In the very begynnyng of his newe obteyned reigne. *a* **1691** BOYLE *Hist. Air* (1692) 19 Whether these obtained substances ought to be looked upon as true air. **1875** WHITNEY *Life Lang.* ii. 23 The advantage won by the mind in the obtaining of a language.

obtainability (əbˌteɪnəˈbɪlɪtɪ). [f. OBTAINABLE *a.*: see -ITY.] The quality or state of being obtainable; capability of being obtained.

1932 H. H. PRICE *Perception* vii. 177 The existence or obtainability of the other sense-data. **1933** *Mind* XLII. 294, I fail to distinguish these merely entertained and probably false (in any case unverifiable) propositions as to the present and simultaneous actuality of the, as yet, unsensed sense, from that believed and probably true one as to their successive obtainability. **1971** *Analysis* XXXII. 55 The obtainability of the conditional.

obtainable (əbˈteɪnəb(ə)l), *a.* [f. OBTAIN *v.* + -ABLE.] That may be obtained or got; procurable.

1617 HIERON *Wks.* II. 198 We see which is the onely ioy; we see it is obtaineable. **1794** G. ADAMS *Nat. & Exp. Philos.* III. xxxi. 285 Effects..by no means obtainable by the moving force immediately applied. **1879** PROCTOR *Pleas. Ways Sc.* i. 4 At all obtainable temperatures, and under all obtainable conditions of pressure.

obtainal (əbˈteɪnəl). *rare.* [f. as prec. + -AL[1].] = OBTAINMENT.

1803 W. TAYLOR in *Ann. Rev.* I. 355 That commerce..which is carried on with the richest nation..is most favourable to the obtainal of capital. **1869** *Daily News* 20 Mar., The obtainal of a supplementary charter, to enable the University [of London] to grant certificates of proficiency to women. **1883** *Pall Mall G.* 22 June 2/2 The concentration of all efforts on the obtainal of high prices for landlords selling their estates.

ob'tainance. *rare.* [f. as prec. + -ANCE.] = OBTAINMENT.

1846 H. W. TORRENS *Rem. Mil. Hist.* 110 The great and only resource for the obtainance of victory.

obtainer (əbˈteɪnə(r)). [f. as prec. + -ER[1].] One who obtains; a gainer, winner; a getter.

1540 in R. G. Marsden *Sel. Pl. Crt. Adm.* (1894) I. 96 The obtayner therof owyth by the said custom..to be preferryd *omnibus aliis creditoribus.* *a* **1548** HALL *Chron., Hen. VII*, 26 b, The more renowmed is the glory, and the fame more immortall of the vanquisher and obteyner. **1651** N. BACON *Disc. Govt. Eng.* II. vi. (1739) 32 All obtainers of provisions in the Court at Rome. **1755** JOHNSON, *Obtainer*, he who obtains. **1861** COSMO INNES *Sk. Early Scotch Hist.* 259 The obtainer of the Papal and Royal privileges for the University.

ob'taining, *ppl. a.* [f. OBTAIN *v.* + -ING[2].] That obtains; winning; prevailing, prevalent (*obs.*).

1682 T. FLATMAN *Heraclitus Ridens* No. 77 (1713) II. 224 The Word Confirmation..in the Grammatical and most obtaining sense, signifies a strengthening or corroborating. **1803** MARY CHARLTON *Wife & Mistress* I. 191 A charming creature, who sings like an angel, and will be very obtaining..when she gets amongst them! *Ibid.* IV. 121 The result of the experiment will very shortly..prove it,..I believe it is on the eve of becoming very obtaining.

obtainment (əbˈteɪnmənt). [f. as prec. + -MENT.] The action of obtaining or getting.

1571 GOLDING *Calvin on Ps.* li. 12 For obteynment of forgivenesse of his sinnes. **1677** GALE *Crt. Gentiles* II. IV. 33 Every one is delighted in the obtainement of what he loves. **1802-12** BENTHAM *Ration. Judic. Evid.* (1827) I. 224 A species of fraudulent obtainment, the punishment of which consisted of transportation for three years. **1884** H. SPENCER in *Contemp. Rev.* July 39 Nutrition presupposes obtainment of food.

b. Something obtained.

1829 E. JESSE *Jrnl. Naturalist* 55 Grants from manorial lords for permission thus to feed them [swine] were recorded with care as valuable obtainments.

obtalmia, obs. form of OPHTHALMIA.

obtect (əbˈtɛkt), *a. Entom. rare*$^{-0}$. [ad. L. *obtect-us* covered over: see next.] = next.

In mod. Diets.

obtected (əbˈtɛktɪd), *ppl. a. Entom.* [f. L. *obtect-us*, pa. pple. of *obtegĕre* to cover over + -ED.]

a. Covered by a neighbouring part, as the hemielytra of some *Hemiptera* by the enlarged scutellum. **b.** Applied to the form of pupa characteristic of the *Lepidoptera*, in which the limbs, etc. of the future insect are indistinctly discernible through the outer covering (opp. to *coarctate*); in later use sometimes extended to all pupæ in which the whole body and limbs are enclosed in a horny case (including *coarctate*). Also said of the metamorphosis in which such pupæ occur.

1816 KIRBY & SP. *Entomol.* (1843) I. 52 Those of all lepidopterous insects..by Linné are denominated obtected pupæ. **1826** *Ibid.* IV. 335 Obtected (*Obtecta*). When the Hemelytra are covered by a scutelliform mesothorax. *Ibid.* 431 Metamorphosis incomplete. Metamorphosis obtected. **1888** ROLLESTON & JACKSON *Anim. Life* 152 The obtected pupa is either angular, as in the majority of *Lepidoptera* with club-shaped antennæ..or it is conical, as in *Sphinx*.

obtectovenose (əbˌtɛktəʊviːˈnəʊs), *a. Bot.* [f. L. *obtect-us* covered over, veiled + *vēnōsus* VENOUS, f. *vēna* vein.] Applied to a leaf having the principal and longitudinal veins connected by simple cross-veins.

1866 LINDLEY in *Treas. Bot.*

obtemper (əbˈtɛmpə(r)), *v.* [a. F. *obtempér-er* (14th c. in Hatz.-Darm.) ad. L. *obtemperāre* to obey, f. *ob-* (OB- 1 a) + *temperāre* to qualify, temper, to restrain oneself.]

1. To comply with, yield to, submit to, obey; now only in *Sc. Law*, to obey (a judgement or order of a court). **a.** *trans.*

c **1489** CAXTON *Blanchardyn* xxv. 93 But for to obtempre youre request, for this tyme I graunte hym his lyf. **1535** STEWART *Cron. Scot.* II. 12 The lordis..wald nocht obtemper his command. **1637-50** ROW *Hist. Kirk* (1842) 59 Being asked, if he would obtemper and obey the Act of the Assemblie. **1728** *Wodrow Corr.* (1843) III. 402 Refusing to obtemper the Acts of Assembly. **1884** *Edinburgh Courant* 12 Mar. 3/2 Lord Adam..granted decree of Absolvitor, pursuer having failed to obtemper Lord Fraser's order.

†**b.** *intr.* with *to*: To be obedient. *Obs.*

1491 CAXTON *Vitas Patr.* (W. de W. 1495) II. 185 b/1 To theyr wycked wylles..to obtempre or be agreable. **1536** BELLENDEN *Cron. Scot.* (1821) II. 91 Kinnatil, devotely obtemperand to Sanct Colme, randerit his saule to God. **1584** HUDSON *Du Bartas' Judith* Ded., The fervent desire I had to obtemper vnto your Majesties commandement.

†**2.** *trans.* To temper, restrain. *Obs. rare.*

1535 STEWART *Cron. Scot.* II. 94 Thir tuo kingis wald nocht heir thair desyre, Nor ȝit no way obtemper wald thair ire.

†**obtemperate,** *ppl. a. Obs.* Also 6-7 *Sc.* -at. [ad. L. *obtemperāt-us*, pa. pple. of *obtemperāre*: see prec.] **a.** as *adj.* Obedient, submissive. **b.** as *Sc. pa. pple.* of next: Obeyed, complied with.

1432-50 tr. *Higden* (Rolls) II. 213 The body scholde be..obtemperate [*Trev.* buxom] to the sawle. **1533** BELLENDEN *Livy* I. (1822) 51 Ye wald sone have obtemperat, and obeyit my chargis. **1676** ROW *Contn. Blair's Autobiog.* xii. (1848) 446 Others who had not obtemperat the act.

obtemperate (əbˈtɛmpəreɪt), *v.* [f. L. *obtemperāt-*, ppl. stem of *obtemperāre*: see OBTEMPER.]

1. = OBTEMPER I. **a.** *trans.*

1432-50 tr. *Higden* (Rolls) VII. 219 Duke Harolde, thenkynge better to obtemperate and favoure the cuntre raþer then the private profite of his broþer. **1611** COTGR., *Obtemperer*, to obtemperate, obey. **1653** A. WILSON *Jas. I*, 104 The King had fit Instruments..that could fit and obtemperate the Kings humour. **1766** W. GORDON *Gen. Counting-ho.* 340 When the order given is obtemperated by acceptance. **1865** *Blackw. Mag.* Sept. 343 After a violent quarrel the guides obtemperated his commands.

b. *intr.* with *to*: To be obedient.

c **1532** DU WES *Introd. Fr.* in Palsgr. 1036 Desiryng..to obtemperate to his pleasur & affection. **1884** A. A. WATTS *Life Alaric Watts* I. 33 To this suggestion he flatly declined to obtemperate. **1889** *Sat. Rev.* 20 July 64/1 The Marxists refused to obtemperate to any such demand.

†**2.** = OBTEMPER 2. *Sc. Obs. rare.*

1560 ROLLAND *Crt. Venus* III. 283 Quhairfoir we wald that ȝe obtemperat ȝour will with wit, and ȝour mind mitigat.

So †**ob'temperance,** †**obtempe'ration.** *Obs.*

1623 COCKERAM, *Obtemporance*, obeying. **1611** COTGR., *Obtemperation*, obtemperation, obedience. **1658** PHILLIPS, *Obtemperation*, an obeying, a yielding obedience.

†**ob'tend,** *v. Obs.* [ad. L. *obtend-ĕre* to spread in front of, f. *ob-* (OB- 1 a) + *tendĕre* to stretch.]

1. *trans.* To put forward as a statement, reason, etc.; to pretend, allege, maintain.

1573 *Satir. Poems Reform.* xl. 33 The force of men gif ony will obtend, Kinred, or friends to be ane gaird maist strang, All is bot vane. **1609** HUME *Admonit.* in *Wodrow Soc. Misc.* 574 Ye obtende also the releif of the Kirk. **1700** DRYDEN *Iliad* I. 161 Obtending heav'n for whate'er ills befal.

2. To hold out; to present in opposition; to oppose.

1697 DRYDEN *Æneid* x. 126 And for a Man obtend an empty Cloud. **1725** POPE *Odyss.* XXII. 88 Draw forth your swords, And to his shafts obtend these ample boards.

obtenebrate (əbˈtɛnɪbreɪt), *v.* [f. L. *obtenebrāt-*, ppl. stem of *obtenebrāre* to darken, f. *ob-* (OB- 1 a, b) + *tenebrāre* to make dark, *tenebræ* darkness.] *trans.* To cast a shadow over; to overshadow, shade, darken.

1611 COTGR., *Obtenebrer*, to obtenebrate, obscure, darken. **1626** AILESBURY *Passion-serm.* 29 In Mount Calvary all is obtenebrated. **1649** BULWER *Pathomyot.* I. vi. 35 Rationation, which should direct and moderate the phansie, is more obtenebrated. **1819** H. BUSK *Vestriad* I. 518 Clouds obtenebrate the solar light.

obtene'bration. [ad. late L. *obtenebrātiōn-em*, n. of action from *obtenebrāre*: see prec.] The action of overshadowing, or condition of being overshadowed; darkening.

1626 BACON *Sylva* §725 In every Megrim, or Vertigo, there is an Obtenebration joyned with a Semblance of Turning Round. **1669** GALE *Crt. Gentiles* I. III. x. 99 The Obtenebration of the Sun, Moon, Stars, and Light. **1881** E. M. BODDY *Hist. Salt* ii. 25 The dense obtenebration with which the object is surrounded.

†**ob'tenebrize,** *v.* [See -IZE.] = OBTENEBRATE.

1653 W. SCLATER *2nd Fun. Serm.* (1654) 13 The Beauty of the Saints is much obtenebrized and obscured.

†**ob'tension.** *Obs. rare*$^{-0}$. [n. of action from L. *obtendĕre* to OBTEND: cf. *extension*; the L. form was *obtentio*.] The action of obtending.

1755 in JOHNSON. (No quotation.)

†**ob'tent,** *sb. Obs.* [a. OF. *obtent* (in phr. *pour obtent de* out of regard to), ad. L. *obtent-us* a spreading before, pretext, pretence, f. ppl. stem of *obtendĕre* to OBTEND.] Purpose, intent.

1430-50 tr. *Higden* (Rolls) V. 53 Origenes..did gelde hym selfe..for the obtente and wille of chastite.

†**ob'tent,** *ppl. a. Obs.* [ad. L. *obtent-us*, pa. pple. of *obtinēre* to OBTAIN.] Obtained, procured.

1432-50 tr. *Higden* Harl. Contin. (Rolls) VIII. 463 Absente..withowte licence obtente off theire prelates.

obtention (əbˈtɛnʃən). [a. F. *obtention* (1525 in Godef.), n. of action from *obtenir*, L. *obtinēre*, *obtent-* to OBTAIN: cf. *detention*, *retention*.] The action of obtaining; obtainment.

1624 F. WHITE *Repl. Fisher* 521 The Fathers..speake of obtention and impetration. **1711** *Light to Blind* in *10th Rep. Hist. MSS. Comm.* App. v. 148 Not satisfied with the obtention of those little advanced posts. **1790** WOLCOTT (P.

Pindar) *Ep. to Sylv. Urban* Wks. 1812 II. 272 *note*, Interest made for the obtention of this Honour. **1815** MAD. D'ARBLAY *Diary* (1876) IV. 311 He aspired at its obtention, a word I make for my passing convenience. **1886** *Athenæum* 19 June 811/2 Their obtention of capitulations with the empire.

obtest (əbˈtɛst), *v.* [ad. L. *obtestā-rī* to call to witness, to protest by, f. *ob* on account of + *testārī* to bear witness, call upon as witness. Cf. OF. *obtester* (*c* 1350 in Godef.).]

1. *trans.* To call upon in the name or for the sake of something sacred, to charge solemnly, adjure; to beg earnestly, beseech, entreat, implore, supplicate (a person *that*..., or *to do* something).

a **1548** HALL *Chron.* (1809) 447 He earnestly obtested desyred and prayed him that he would..send some one. **1637** RUTHERFORD *Lett.* (1862) I. 345, I beseech and obtest you in the Lord to make conscience of rash and passionate oaths. **1725** POPE *Odyss.* XII. 436 Thus obtesting heav'n I mourn'd aloud. **1819** SCOTT *Leg. Montrose* xviii, Several other Chiefs..conjured and obtested their Chieftain to leave them..to the leading of Ardenvohr and Auchenbreck. *a* **1847** MACVEY NAPIER *Sel. Corr.* (1879) 68 To obtest you to secrecy by every form of conjuration.

†**b.** To beg earnestly for, beseech, entreat, implore (a thing). *Obs. rare.*

1577 NORTHBROOKE *Dicing* (1843) 6, I humblie obtest your friendlie countenance. **1697** DRYDEN *Æneid* XI. 151 Now suppliants..Obtest his clemency.

2. To call (the Deity, etc.) to witness; to appeal to in confirmation of a statement. *rare.*

1651 BIGGS *New Disp.* ¶7, I may safely obtest the highest. **1761-2** HUME *Hist. Eng.* (1806) IV. lix. 420 He obtested heaven and earth that his devoted attachment to the parliament had rendered him so odious in the army, that [etc.].

3. *intr.* or *absol.*, or with dependent clause: **a.** To make earnest supplication or entreaty; **b.** To call heaven to witness, to protest.

1650 BAXTER *Saints' R.* IV. iii. (1662) 656 He in vain obtested with them, that they should take in good part, what was delivered with a good intention. **1665** MANLEY *Grotius' Low C. Warres* 697 She obtested, that being a Woman, and so both by Sex and Fortune, exempt from troubles, and as she her self believed, maintaining no false Opinion [etc.]. **1667** WATERHOUSE *Fire Lond.* 173 Whose primitive Reformers..if they could be raised up now to hear them, would obtest against them. **1725** POPE *Odyss.* XVII. 281 Eumæus heav'd His hands obtesting. **1826** J. R. BEST *Four Yrs. France* 87, I detest, or obtest, against all revolutions. **1837** CARLYLE *Fr. Rev.* III. VII. v, Deputies, putting forth head, obtest, conjure.

Hence **obˈtesting** *ppl. a.*

1597 J. KING *On Jonas* (1618) 19 Whom he had..chidden, with so fatherly a spirit, and such obtesting protestations. **1837** CARLYLE *Fr. Rev.* III. VII. v, Obtesting Deputies obtest vainly.

†**obtestate**, *v. Obs. rare.* [f. ppl. stem of L. *obtestārī*: see prec.] = prec.

1613 R. CAWDREY *Table Alph.* (ed. 3), *Obtestate*, humbly to beseech, or to call to witnesse. **1632** VICARS tr. *Virgil* IV. 108 Readie to die, the Gods she obtestates.

obtestation (ɒbtɛˈsteɪʃən). [ad. L. *obtestātiōn-em*, n. of action from *obtestārī* to OBTEST: cf. OF. *obtestation* (15th c. in Godef.).] The action or an act of obtesting.

1. A charging or beseeching by some sacred name; solemn adjuration, entreaty, or supplication.

1531 ELYOT *Gov.* II. xii, With whiche wordes, obtestations, and teares,..Titus constrayned..brought furthe with great difficultie his wordes in this wyse. **1575-85** ABP. SANDYS *Serm.* (1841) 92 The apostle,..with a most vehement spirit, and most earnest obtestation, doth here exhort the Philippians. *a* **1677** MANTON *Serm. 2 Thess.* i. Wks. 1871 III. 5 By way of adjuration or obtestation. **1705** STANHOPE *Paraphr.* II. 107 Observe..their doleful Accents and Obtestations and..learn..at once to beg, and how to beg a Pardon. **1850** MERIVALE *Rom. Emp.* (1865) VI. xlvii. 12 The gaolers..consigned [them], in spite of their cries and obtestations, to the hands of the executioner.

2. The action of calling (the Deity, etc.) to witness; a solemn appeal or asseveration in confirmation of a statement; protestation.

a **1555** RIDLEY *Wks.* (Parker Soc.) 84 Note what a solemn obtestation God useth. **1589** PUTTENHAM *Eng. Poesie* III. xix. (Arb.) 221 By way of..obtestation or taking God and the world to witnes. **1678** CUDWORTH *Intell. Syst.* I. iv. §14. 261 That Form of Obtestation..by Jupiter and the Gods. **1814** SCOTT *Ess., Drama* (1874) 144 Frequent prayers and obtestations of the Deity. **1837** CARLYLE *Fr. Rev.* II. i. viii, They made oath and obtestation to stand faithfully by one another.

†**obˈtexed**, *ppl. a. Obs. rare*$^{-0}$. [f. L. *obtexĕre* to weave over.]

1623 COCKERAM, *Obtexed*, weaued.

obtick, obs. form of OPTIC.

†**obˈtortion.** *Obs. rare.* [ad. L. *obtortiōn-em*, n. of action from *obtorquē-re* to twist awry, f. *ob-* (OB- 1 b) + *torquēre* to twist.] A twisting, distortion, wresting, perversion.

a **1656** BP. HALL *Pref. Revel. Unrevealed*, Those strange obtortions of some particular prophecies to private interests.

†**obˈtractuous**, *a. Obs. rare*$^{-1}$. [Erroneously f. L. *obtrectātu-s*, f. *obtrectāre*: see next and -OUS.] Slanderous, calumnious.

1537 in W. H. Turner *Select. Rec. Oxford* 141 [He] seid, How sey you, syrs? with obtractuouse words.

†**obˈtrect**, *v. Obs.* Also obtract. [ad. L. *obtrectāre* to disparage, detract from, f. *ob-* (OB- 1 b) + *tractāre* to drag, haul.] *trans.* To detract from; to disparage, decry.

1596 J. TRUSSELL *Pref. Poem* in *Southwell's Tri. Death*, Sith then the worke is worthie of your view, Obtract not him which for your good it pend. **1612** T. TAYLOR *Comm. Titus* iii. 2 When men will speake their pleasure of men absent, obtrecting and detracting from them. **1617** MIDDLETON & ROWLEY *Fair Q.* IV. i, Thou dost obtrect my flesh and blood.

†**obtrecˈtation.** *Obs.* Also -tract-. [ad. L. *obtrectātiōn-em*, n. of action from *obtrectāre*: see prec. Cf. F. *obtrectation* (14th c. in Godef.).] Detraction, disparagement, slander, calumny.

1563-83 FOXE *A. & M.* 693/1 Charging also the Prelates and Priests for their slandrous obtrectations, and vndeserued contumelies. **1608** WILLET *Hexapla Exod.* 418 Priuie slaundering, and obtrectation of them that are absent. **1677** PLOT *Oxfordsh.* 223 [Lydiate] defended it against the obtractations of Joseph Scaliger. **1700** ASTRY tr. *Saavedra-Faxardo* I. 103 Obtrectation is a sign of Liberty in a Commonwealth.

†**ˈobtrectator.** *Obs.* [a. L. *obtrectātor*, agent-n. f. *obtrectāre*: see OBTRECT. Cf. F. *obtrectateur* (15th c. in Godef.).] A traducer, detractor.

1432-50 tr. *Higden* (Rolls) III. 255 The grete Pompeius.. was not perseuerante for drede of obtrectatores [*metu obtrectatorum*]. *a* **1670** HACKET *Abp. Williams* I. (1692) 95 Some were..a great deal more laborious in their cure than their obtrectators. **1679** L. ADDISON *1st St. Mahumedism* 87 That they be no obtrectators, or given to Calumny and Back-biting.

†**obˈtrector.** *Obs. rare*$^{-1}$. [For *obtrecter*, f. OBTRECT *v.*, the suffix being assimilated to the L. *-or* of agent-nouns, as in *corrector*.] = prec.

1563-83 FOXE *A. & M.* 302/2 They as wicked confederatours were..obtrectours of hys worthy laud and fame.

obtriangular (ɒbtraɪˈæŋgjʊlə(r)), *a. Nat. Hist.* [OB- 2.] Triangular in form, with the apex downwards, or at the base of the organ or part.

1826 KIRBY & SP. *Entomol.* III. xxxii. 324 The fourth joint is very large and obtriangular.

obtrigonal (ɒbˈtrɪgənəl), *a. Nat. Hist.* [OB- 2.] = prec. Also **obˈtrigonate** *a.*

1819 G. SAMOUELLE *Entomol. Compend.* 193 Opatrum.. maxillary palpi with their last joint obtrigonate. **1856-8** W. CLARK *Van der Hoeven's Zool.* I. 323 Antennæ moderate, third joint..obtrigonal. *Ibid.* 672 Shell oblong, oval or obtrigonal.

†**obˈtrite**, *a. Obs. rare*$^{-0}$. [ad. L. *obtrītus*, pa. pple. of *obterĕre* to bruise, crush.] Worn, bruised; trodden under foot (Blount *Glossogr.* 1656). Hence †**obˈtrition**, 'a bruising, or wearing away against anything' (Phillips, 1658).

obtrude (əbˈtruːd), *v.* [ad. L. *obtrūd-ĕre*, f. *ob-* (OB- 1 b) + *trūdĕre* to thrust.]

1. *trans.* To thrust forth; to eject, push out. Also *refl.*

1613 R. CAWDREY *Table Alph.* (ed. 3), *Obtrude*, thrust with violence. **1648** EARL RUTLAND in *12th Rep. Hist. MSS. Comm.* App. v. 3 Reasons why I ought not to be obtruded from my house at Belvoir. **1764** DUNN in *Phil. Trans.* LIV. 115, I thought I saw a little dull tremulous vibration obtrude itself on the limb of the Sun. **1813** *Examiner* 15 Mar. 165/2 He..ripped him open, and the bowels obtruded themselves.

2. To thrust forward forcibly or unduly; to thrust (a matter, a person, his presence, etc.) *upon* any one. Const. *on, upon, into* (†*to, unto*).

c **1555** HARPSFIELD *Divorce Hen. VIII* (Camden) 86 To reject such definitions as by most wise..men have been delivered unto us, and to obtrude to us other, partly their own. *a* **1592** H. SMITH *Wks.* (1867) II. 431 As for their traditions, which they cannot prove, but obtrude unto us without testimony of Scriptures, let us contemn them. **1654** BRAMHALL *Just Vind.* i. (1661) 2 To attempt..to obtrude any forrein Jurisdiction upon us. *a* **1661** FULLER *Worthies* (1840) I. 362 A man of low birth and high pride, obtruded on them..by the king for their general. **1791** PAINE *Rights of Man* (ed. 4) 79 Who, then, art thou,..that obtrudest thine insignificance between the soul of man and its Maker? **1840** THIRLWALL *Greece* VII. lvi. 185 Advice was obtruded on him. **1876** HOLLAND *Sev. Oaks* xvii. 257 She asked Mr. Balfour if she could have the liberty to obtrude a matter of business upon him. **1878** GLADSTONE *Prim. Homer* xiii. 142 With Homer the maker's mark never obtrudes the maker, or places him between the reader and the theme.

b. *refl.*

1754 EDWARDS *Freed. Will* IV. vii. 242 A Diversity and Order of distinct Parts..does as naturally obtrude itself on our Imagination, in one Case as the other. **1817** *Parl. Deb.* 756 Mr. Blake said, it was with much diffidence he obtruded himself again upon the attention of the House. **1847** MASKELL *Mon. Rit.* III. 86 *note*, Subordinate officials, who ..obtruded themselves into matters beyond their office.

c. *intr.* (for *refl.*). To be or become obtrusive; to intrude, force oneself.

1579 FENTON *Guicciard.* I. (1599) 7 To remember..with what wrongs and iniuries the familie of Aragon had obtruded upon his father. **1670** G. H. *Hist. Cardinals* III. I. 232 With his instances and importunity, he seem'd in some measure to obtrude upon the Colledge. *a* **1745** SWIFT *Will. II*, Lett. 1768 IV. 269 Either by not thinking of religion at all; or, if it will obtrude, by putting it out of countenance. **1844** R. H. DANA *Changes of Home* xlix, A little farther! Let us not obtrude Upon her sorrows' holy solitude.

Hence **obˈtruded** *ppl. a.*, **obˈtruding** *vbl. sb.*

1649 MILTON *Eikon.* xv. Wks. (1851) 451 The greatest part of Protestants were against him and his obtruded settlement. **1659** BP. WALTON *Consid. Considered* 151 Here is no obtruding of any Various Reading out of a MS. which is not. **1879** FARRAR *St. Paul* (1883) 134 He could crush by passion and energy such obtruding fancies.

obˈtruder. [f. prec. + -ER[1].] One who obtrudes or thrusts forward in an importunate or unwelcome manner.

1638 *Penit. Conf.* vii. (1657) 144 Hath caused the busie obtruders thereof to be suspected. **1664** H. MORE *Myst. Iniq.* i. 3 They are Teachers, Abettors, or Obtruders of such practices or principles upon pretence of Religion. **1879** T. P. O'CONNOR *Ld. Beaconsfield* 197 The rude and calculating obtruder of self forces you to his wishes.

obˈtruncate, *ppl. a.* [ad. L. *obtruncāt-us*, pa. pple. of *obtruncāre*: see next.] Cut short.

1805 *London Cries* 34 Those props, on which the knees obtruncate stand, That crutch ill-wielded in the widow'd hand.

obtruncate (əbˈtrʌŋkeɪt), *v.* [f. ppl. stem of L. *obtruncāre* to cut off, lop away, f. *ob-* (OB- 1 b, c) + *truncāre* to cut off, maim.] *trans.* To cut or lop off the head or top of; to top, decapitate. Hence **obˈtruncated** *ppl. a.*, **obtrunˈcation**.

1623 COCKERAM, *Obtruncate*, to cut off ones head. *Obtruncation*, a cutting off. **1657** TOMLINSON *Renou's Disp.* 465 The Female [Viper] satiated with pleasure obtruncates the male. **1762** STERNE *Tr. Shandy* V. iii, The proudest pyramid of them all..has lost its apex, and stands obtruncated in the traveller's horizon. **1863** HAWTHORNE *Our Old Home* I. 66 Rustic chairs..ponderously fashioned out of the stumps of obtruncated trees.

ˈobtrunˌcator. *rare.* [Agent-n. in L. form from L. *obtruncāre*: see prec.] One who cuts off.

a **1864** LANDOR in *Athenæum* (1889) 23 Nov. 707/3 The English King..obtruncator of conjugal heads.

obtrusion (əbˈtruːʒən). [f. L. *obtrūsiōn-em*, n. of action f. *obtrūdĕre* to OBTRUDE.] The action of obtruding.

1. The forcible pushing or thrusting (of anything) into any space or place, or against anything else.

1847 LEWES *Hist. Philos.* (1867) II. 362 Stimulated into motion by the obtrusions of surrounding bodies. **1875** KINGLAKE *Crimea* V. i. (1877) 225 Liprandi's obtrusion of troops in the direction of the..Heights.

2. The importunate obtruding or thrusting of some one or something (upon one, or upon one's attention); also *concr.* something thus thrust upon one.

1641 'SMECTYMNUUS' *Answ.* vii. (1653) 34 The Obtrusion of a Bishop upon the Church of Alexandria without the.. vote of the Clergie or People is Condemned by Athanasius. **1649** MILTON *Eikon.* xi. Wks. (1851) 417 Those violent and merciless obtrusions which for almost twenty yeares he had bin forcing upon tender consciences by all sorts of Persecution. **1751** JOHNSON *Rambler* No. 103 ¶7 Disturbed by the obtrusion of new ideas. **1865** *Cornh. Mag.* XI. 491 The obtrusion of these topics upon persons not conversant with professional technicalities.

b. The forcing of oneself or one's company upon any one.

1579 FENTON *Guicciard.* XVI. (1599) 763 He was at last made Pope..notwithstanding the many obtrusions and emulations of the most auncient Cardinals. **1834** G. BENNETT *Wand. N.S.W.* II. viii, On the approach of danger, or on the obtrusion of strangers. **1858** HOGG *Life Shelley* II. 343 There was no end of obtrusion: the word intrusion is not strong enough.

obtrusive (əbˈtruːsɪv), *a.* [f. L. *obtrūs-*, ppl. stem of *obtrūdĕre* to OBTRUDE + -IVE.]

1. Projecting so as to be in the way.

1842 T. MARTIN *My Namesake* in *Fraser's Mag.* Dec., Bang went my haunch against an obtrusive angle of my bed.

2. Characterized by forcibly thrusting (oneself, one's opinions, etc.) into notice or prominence; forward; unduly prominent.

1667 MILTON *P.L.* VIII. 504 Not obvious, not obtrusive, but retir'd, The more desirable. **1798** MALTHUS *Popul.* (1817) II. 246 Human institutions appear to be, and..often are, the obvious and obtrusive causes of much mischief to society. **1840** MALCOM *Trav.* 47/1 The beggars..are seldom obtrusive, but a donation to one will bring several upon you. **1872** MINTO *Eng. Prose Lit.* II. i. 227 An obtrusive profession of his faith.

obtrusively (əbˈtruːsɪvlɪ), *adv.* [f. prec. + -LY[2].] In an obtrusive manner; so as to obtrude.

1817 COLERIDGE *Biog. Lit.* I. x. 191, I have seen gross intolerance shewn in support of tolerance; sectarian antipathy most obtrusively displayed. **1849** MACAULAY *Hist. Eng.* x. II. 646 His advice was never asked, and, when obtrusively and importunately offered, was coldly received. **1853** C. BRONTË *Villette* vii, One or two gentlemen glanced at me occasionally, but none stared obtrusively. **1875** *Cornh. Mag.* Jan. 78 The 'Vision of Sir Launfal'..is perhaps rather too obtrusively didactic.

obtrusiveness (əbˈtruːsɪvnɪs). [f. as prec. + -NESS.] The quality of being obtrusive.

a **1817** JANE AUSTEN *Persuasion* (1818) IV. x. 213 He stood, as opposed to Captain Wentworth, in all his own unwelcome obtrusiveness. **1825** J. Neal *Bro. Jonathan* II. 142 Religion, or truth could never appear, without a look of absurdity..or obtrusiveness. **1863** Woolner *My Beautiful Lady* 19 We thread a copse where frequent brambles' spray With loose obtrusiveness from side roots stray. **1881** *Athenæum* 21 May 681/3 He complains of..the obtrusiveness of the natives, and more especially of the women.

† **obtu'mescence.** *Obs. rare*⁻¹. [f. L. *ob-* + *tumēsc-ĕre* to swell up: see -ENCE.] A swelling up; swollen condition.

1657 Tomlinson *Renou's Disp.* 236 It abates its durity and obtumescence.

obtund (əb'tʌnd), *v.* [ad. L. *obtund-ĕre* to beat against, blunt, dull, f. *ob-* (OB- 1 b) + *tundĕre* to beat. Cf. obs. F. *obtondre, -tundre* (*a* 1500 in Godef.).] *trans.* To blunt, deaden, dull, deprive of sharpness or vigour, render obtuse (the senses or faculties, physical qualities of things, etc.). Chiefly in medical use.

c **1400** *Lanfranc's Cirurg.* 83 Colde þingis whiche.. obtunden or casten bacħ þe scharpnes of þe same vlcus. **1471** Ripley *Comp. Alch.* Pref. in Ashm. (1652) 121 Whose Luminos Bemes obtundyth our speculation. **1620** Venner *Via Recta* viii. 164 Nothing..doth so greatly obtunde and weaken the natiue heate..as a fastidious fulnesse of the stomacke. **1664** H. More *Myst. Iniq.* 347 This passage, if there had been any force in the former, does quite obtund it. **1710** T. Fuller *Pharm. Extemp.* 36 Crayfish, Crabs and Lobsters..obtund the acidity of Vinegar it self. **1750** Johnson *Rambler* No. 78 ⁋4 No man can at pleasure obtund or invigorate his senses. *a* **1836** D. M'Nicoll *Inquiry Stage* Wks. (1837) 120 The moral sensibility of the character is.. obtunded. **1872** Cohen *Dis. Throat* 271 The sense of smell is obtunded.

† **b.** To deafen, din (the ears). *Obs. rare.*

1645 [see OBTUNDING below]. **1694** Motteux *Rabelais* v. (1737) 231 I'll not too many Verbs effund, Nor with our Ills your Auricles obtund.

Hence **ob'tunding** *ppl. a.*, deadening, deafening.

1645 Milton *Colast.* Wks. (1851) 363 John-a-Noaks and John-a-Stiles..have fill'd our Law-books with the obtunding story of their suits and trials. **1684** tr. *Bonet's Merc. Compit.* III. 85 The Heart-burn..is rather to be corrected with obtunding and alterative Medicines. **1895** *Scotsman* 11/6 Obtunding or anaesthetic properties.

obtundent (əb'tʌndənt), *a.* and *sb. Med.* [ad. L. *obtundent-em*, pr. pple. of *obtundĕre* to OBTUND.] **a.** *adj.* Having the property of dulling sensibility. **b.** *sb.* A substance used to dull sensibility or allay irritation; a demulcent.

[**1753** Chambers *Cycl. Supp.*, *Obtundentia*, a word used by some authors to express such medicines as are given to obtund, or edulcorate the acrimony of the humors.] **1842** Brande *Dict. Sci.*, *&c.*, *Obtundents*, mucilaginous, oily and other bland medicines, supposed to sheathe the parts from acrimony, and to blunt that of certain morbid secretions. **1864** Webster cites Forsyth. **1891** *Cent. Dict.*, *Obtundent*, I. *a.* Dulling; blunting. **1898** H. H. Burchard *Text-bk. Dental Path. & Therapeutics* VII. 538 Under the head of obtundents are included those agents which are applied locally to benumb the terminals of sensory nerves. **1908** J. D. Patterson in C. N. Johnson *Text-bk. Operative Dentistry* xxviii. 460 Obtundents. For the purpose of obtunding, many preparations have been advocated and many methods advised. **1930** W. H. O. McGehee *Text-bk. Operative Dentistry* xxiv. 700 An Obtundent Paste devised by Doctor J. Lewis Blass..used with splendid results. **1961** MacDougall & Nixon *Guide to Dental Therapeutics* viii. 115 When drugs are applied locally to relieve pain, they are referred to as local anaesthetics or obtundents.

† **ob'turant,** *ppl. a. Her. Obs. rare.* [a. F. *obturant*, pr. pple. of *obturer*, ad. L. *obtūrāre* to stop up.] Stopping, closing. (Const. as pple.)

1572 Bossewell *Armorie* II. 62 b, The field is Gules, an Aspe obturant her eares d'Or.

† **ob'turate,** *a. Obs. rare.* [ad. L. *obtūrāt-us*, pa. pple. of *obtūrāre*: see next.] Stopped up; *fig.* impervious.

c **1560** *Phylogamus* in *Skelton's Wks.* (1843) I. p. cxvi, O poet rare and recent..Obtused and obturate, Obumbylate, obdurate.

obturate (əb'tjʊəreɪt, 'ɒbtjʊ-), *v.* [f. ppl. stem of L. *obtūrāre* to stop up, in F. *obturer*.] *trans.* To stop up, close, obstruct. Hence **obturated** *ppl. a.*; **obturating** *ppl. a.* (*spec.* in *Gunnery*: see OBTURATOR 2 b).

1657 Tomlinson *Renou's Disp.* 683 In a..Boccia well obturated, that nothing may expire. **1736** Amyand in *Phil. Trans.* XXXIX. 334 As oft as this..Pin..did not exactly obturate the Aperture. **1859** Farrar *Julian Home* 260 His ears were so obturated with vanity. **1876** tr. *Wagner's Gen. Pathol.* 192 The canals traversing the thrombus..re-establish the circulation through the obturated vein. **1884** S. V. Benet in *Rep. Chief of Ordnance* 18 (Cent.), Three forms of an obturating primer have been manufactured recently at the Frankfort arsenal.

obturation (ɒbtjʊə'reɪʃən). [ad. L. *obtūrātiōn-em*, n. of action from *obtūrāre* to stop up: cf. F. *obturation* (15–16th c. in Hatz.-Darm.).] The action of stopping up; obstruction of an opening or channel; *spec.* in *Gunnery* (cf. next, 2 b).

1610 Barrough *Meth. Physick* III. xxxviii. (1639) 162 About the beginning of obturation and stopping, the urine is..little in quantity. **1611** Cotgr., *Amafrose*, blindnesse caused by the obturation of the Opticke sinew. **1634** Bp. Hall *Contempl.*, *N.T.* IV. ii, Some are deaf by an outward obturation. **1880** *Daily Tel.* 31 Dec. 2/6 The sealing of the breech, or obturation, as it is called, is effected by an expanding steel cap on the face of the breech-screw.

obturator ('ɒbtjʊəreɪtə(r)). [a. med.L. *obtūrātor*, agent-n. from *obtūrāre*: see prec.; in F. *obturateur* (*c* 1550 in Paré).] Something that stops up.

1. *Anat.* (almost always *attrib.*). Name of a membrane (**obturator membrane**, or **obturator ligament**) which closes the thyroid foramen; applied also to structures connected with this, as **obturator artery**, a branch of the internal iliac artery, supplying the obturator and other muscles of the thigh; **obturator canal**, a funnel-shaped opening in the obturator membrane, through which the obturator vessels and nerves pass; **obturator foramen**, another name for the thyroid foramen, a large opening in the os innominatum, representing the division between the ischium and pubis; **obturator muscles**, two muscles (*o. externus* and *o. internus*) serving for rotation and other movements of the thigh; **obturator nerve**, a branch of the lumbar plexus, having twigs distributed to the hip and knee joints and various muscles of the thigh; **obturator vein**, a branch of the internal iliac vein, accompanying the obturator artery.

1727–41 Chambers *Cycl.*, *Obturator*, in anatomy, a name given to two muscles of the thigh..covering up the foramen or aperture between the os pubis and the hip-bone. **1741** Monro *Anat. Nerves* (ed. 3) 211 The obturator Muscles. **1753** Chambers *Cycl. Supp.*, *Obturator ligament*, is one of the proper ligaments of the ossa innominata, and fills up the great foramen ovale. **1827** Abernethy *Surg. Wks.* II. 218 The anterior crural and obturator nerves. **1842** E. Wilson *Anat. Vade M.* (ed. 2) 110 The Obturator ligament or Membrane is a tendino-fibrous Membrane stretched across the obturator foramen. **1872** Humphry *Myology* 20 The internal obturator.

2. An artificial device for stopping an opening; *spec.* **a.** *Surg.* A plate or other contrivance for closing an opening of the body, esp. an abnormal opening, as in cleft palate. **b.** *Gunnery.* A cap, pad, or the like, used for preventing the escape of gas through a joint or hole, esp. through the breech of a cannon in firing; a gas-check. **c.** A shutter of a photographic camera. Also *attrib.*

1876 *Trans. Clinical Soc.* IX. 125 Mr. Sewill..made for me an obturator according to the following plan:—A small plate was made to accurately fit the roof of the mouth [etc.]. .. Immediately after the obturator was applied, the patient could articulate the letters *s* and *z* to perfection—sounds which she was quite unable to make before. **1887** *Brit. Jrnl. Photog.* 24 June 399/1 A new obturator or instantaneous shutter. **1891** *Cent. Dict.* s.v., A Broadwell ring, a Freire obturator, a De Bange obturator, or an Armstrong gas-check. **1894** *Times* 10 Oct. 5/1 The Chinese received the severest punishment while..struggling..to replace obturator rings.

ob'turatory, *a. rare.* [f. as prec.: see -ORY.] Serving to close or stop up. † *obturatory muscles* = *obturator muscles*: see prec. 1.

1719 *Glossogr. Anglicana Nova* (ed. 2), *Obturatory Muscles*, some of those that bend the Thigh.

† **ob'turb,** *v. Obs. rare*⁻⁰. [ad. L. *obturbāre* to make turbid.] (See quot.) So † **obtur'bation** [L. *obturbātio*].

1623 Cockeram, *Obturbe*, to trouble. *Obturbation*, a troubling.

obturbinate (ɒb'tɜːbɪnət), *a. Nat. Hist.* [OB- 2.] Inversely turbinate; having the form of a top with the peg upwards. Also **ob'turbinated** *a.*

1857 Mayne *Expos. Lex.* 787/1 *Obturbinated*. **1892** *Syd. Soc. Lex.*, *Obturbinate*.

obtusangular (ɒbtjuː'sæŋgjʊlə(r)), *a.* Now *rare* or *Obs.* [f. L. *obtūs-us* OBTUSE + ANGULAR.] = *obtuse-angled*: see OBTUSE *a.* 5. Also † **obtu'sangulous** *a. Obs.*

1680 T. Lawson *Mite into Treas.* 33 Terms of this Art,.. Rectangulous, Obliquangulous, Obtusangulous. **1706** Phillips, *Obtusangular*. **1732** Berkeley *Alciphr.* VII. §5 Triangles..are denominated..obtusangular, acutangular, or rectangular. **1826** Kirby & Sp. *Entomol.* III. xxxv. 570 A transverse obtusangular band.

obtuse (əb'tjuːs), *a.* [ad. L. *obtūs-us* dulled, blunt, pa. pple. of *obtundĕre* to OBTUND. Cf. F. *obtus, -use* (1542 in Hatz.-Darm.).] Blunt (in various senses): opp. to *acute*.

1. *lit.* Of a blunt form; not sharp or pointed: *esp.* in *Nat. Hist.* of parts or organs of animals or plants. The opposite of *acute*.

1589 Puttenham *Eng. Poesie* II. xi[i]. (Arb.) 114 Such shape as might not be sharpe..to passe as an angle, nor so large or obtuse as might not essay some issue out with one part moe then other as the rounde. **1657** S. Purchas *Pol. Flying-Ins.* 6 Their tails are somewhat sharp (the Drones more obtuse). **1660** Boyle *New Exp. Phys. Mech.* xxxix. 322 An Oval Glass..with a short Neck at the obtuser end. **1753** Chambers *Cycl. Supp.* s.v. *Leaf*, *Obtuse Leaf*, one terminated by the segment of a circle. **1767** Gooch *Treat. Wounds* I. 237 A blow with an obtuse weapon. **1845** Lindley *Sch. Bot.* i. (1858) 10 Leaves are *obtuse*, or *acute*, in the ordinary sense of those words. **1877–84** Hulme *Wild Fl.* p. viii, Spur stout, and obtuse.

2. *Geom.* Of a plane angle: Greater than a right angle; exceeding 90°.

obtuse bisectrix: the line bisecting an obtuse angle, e.g. between the optic axes of a crystal. *obtuse cone*: a cone of which the section by a plane through the axis has an obtuse angle at the vertex. *obtuse hyperbola*: a hyperbola lying within the obtuse angles between its asymptotes.

1570 Billingsley *Euclid* I. def. x. 3 An obtuse angle is that which is greater then a right angle. **1633** P. Fletcher *Purple Isl.* III. xxi, Into two obtuser angles bended. **1701** Grew *Cosm. Sacra* II. v. §18 All Salts are Angular; with Obtuse, Right, or Acute Angles. **1879** Wright *Anim. Life* 6 This bone forms an obtuse angle with the pelvis.

3. *fig.* Not acutely affecting the senses; indistinctly felt or perceived; dull.

1620 Venner *Via Recta* ii. 31 The wine..carrieth the same, which otherwise is of an obtuse operation, vnto all the parts [of the body]. **1726** Swift *To a Lady*, Bastings heavy, dry, obtuse. **1790** Crawford in *Phil. Trans.* LXXX. 426, I ..felt an obtuse pain..in my stomach. **1897** *Allbutt's Syst. Med.* IV. 126 Pain, sharp or obtuse.

4. Not acutely sensitive or perceptive; dull in feeling or intellect, or exhibiting such dullness; stupid, insensible. (In quot. 1606, Rough, unpolished: = BLUNT *a.* 4.)

1509 Hawes *Past. Pleas.* XIII. (Percy Soc.) 113, I am but yonge, it is to me obtuse Of these maters to presume to endyte. **1602** Marston *Antonio's Rev.* I. iii. Wks. 1856 I. 79, I scorne to retort the obtuse jeast of a foole. **1606** Warner *Alb. Eng.* XVI. civ. (1612) 408 Obtuse in phrase. **1667** Milton *P.L.* XI. 541 Thy Senses then Obtuse, all taste of pleasure must foregoe. **1829** Scott *Anne of G.* ii, Obtuse in his understanding, but kind and faithful in his disposition. **1885** Mathilde Blind *Tarantella* I. xi. 121 We were too obtuse to understand their peculiar way of manifesting it.

5. *Comb.*, as **obtuse-angled**, having an obtuse angle or angles (also **obtuse-angular** *rare*⁻⁰); also in *Nat. Hist.*, with another adj., expressing a combination of forms, as **obtuse-ellipsoid**.

1660 Barrow *Euclid* I. Def. xxvii, An Amblygonium, or obtuse-angled Triangle, is that which has one angle obtuse. **1706** Phillips, *Obtuse-angled Cone*. **1878** A. H. Green, etc. *Coal* iv. 146 The two types of fin-structure are sometimes distinguished as obtuse-lobate and acute-lobate. **1882** Ogilvie, *Obtuse-angular*, having obtuse angles.

† **obtuse,** *v. Obs. rare*⁻¹. In 7 *erron.* obtuce. [f. OBTUSE *a.*] *trans.* To blunt, to dull.

1618 Hornby *Sco. Drunk.* (1859) 11 Bacchus, thou god of all ebriety Which dost obtuce and blunt the edge of wit.

† **ob'tused,** *ppl. a. Obs. rare.* [f. prec., or f. L. *obtusus* OBTUSE *a.* + -ED¹.] Blunted, blunt, dull; = OBTUSE *a.* 1 and 4.

c **1560** [see OBTURATE *a.*]. **1578** Banister *Hist. Man* I. 26 This obtused corner, is..called the seate or foundation of the shoulder blade. **1664** Power *Exp. Philos.* I. 16 Mites in Cheese..seem'd oval and obtus'd towards the tail.

obtusely (əb'tjuːslɪ), *adv.* [f. OBTUSE *a.* + -LY².] In an obtuse manner or degree (*lit.* or *fig.*); bluntly; dully; stupidly.

1611 Cotgr., *Obtusement*, obtusely, dully, bluntly. **1765** Gray *Let.* in *Poems* (1775) 295 The arches are pointed, though very obtusely. **1822–34** *Good's Study Med.* (ed. 4) II. 46 The bubonous tumour is..obtusely painful. **1851–6** Woodward *Mollusca* 266 Valves obtusely keeled. **1863** Cowden Clarke *Shaks. Char.* xiv. 360 They are as obtusely blind as earth-worms.

obtuseness (əb'tjuːsnɪs). [f. as prec. + -NESS.] The quality of being obtuse, bluntness, want of sharpness; usually in *fig.* sense: Dullness of feeling, apprehension, etc.; defective sensibility, stupidity.

1648 Jenkyn *Blind Guide* iv. 104 The obtusenesse of the distinction. **1761** Sterne *Tr. Shandy* III. xl. (Jod.), Nor did this arise from any insensibility, or obtuseness of his intellectual parts. **1890** H. Ellis *Criminal* iii. 119 Gustatory obtuseness.

obtusi- (əb'tjuːsɪ), combining form of L. *obtūsus* OBTUSE, as in † **ob'tusiangle** *a. Obs.*, obtuse-angled; and in some rarely used terms of *Natural Hist.*, as **ob'tusifid** *a.* [mod.L. *obtūsifidus*, after *bifidus* BIFID, etc.], divided into obtuse segments; **obtusi'folious** *a.* [mod.L. *obtūsifolius*, f. *folium* leaf: see -OUS], having obtuse leaves; **obtusi'lingual** *a.* [L. *lingua* tongue], having an obtuse labium, as the bees of the division *Obtusilingues*; **obtu'silobus** *a.* [mod.L. *obtūsilobus*], having obtuse lobes; **obtusi'pennate** *a.* [mod.L. *obtūsipennis*: see -ATE²], having obtuse wings; **obtusi'rostrate** *a.* [mod.L. *obtūsirostris*], having an obtuse beak. (Mayne *Expos. Lex.* 1857, and *Cent. Dict.*)

1571 Digges *Pantom.* I. Elem. B iij, An Obtusiangle Triangle hath one obtuse angle. *Ibid.* II. iii. M j, The Area of this Obtusiangle Isoscheles.

† **obtusion** (əb'tjuːʒən). *Obs.* [ad. L. *obtūsiōn-em*, n. of action from *obtundĕre* to OBTUND.] The action of blunting or dulling, or the condition of being blunted or dulled.

1605 Z. Jones *Loyer's Specters* 56 The deception of the sight, and the obtusion of the other senses. *a* **1657** Harvey (J.), Obtusion of the senses, internal and external.

obtusity (əb'tjuːsɪtɪ). [ad. med.L. *obtūsitās*, f. *obtūs-us* OBTUSE: see -ITY. Cf. OF. *obtusité* (15th c. in Godef.).] The quality of being obtuse, obtuseness; dullness, insensibility, stupidity.

1823 Scott *Fam. Lett.* 11 Jan. (1894) II. xix. 165 What a terrible thing..obtusity of sight would be to me. *a* **1849** Poe *Dickens* Wks. 1864 III. 480 His combined conceit and obtusity. **1892** *Monist* II. 314 A lack of moral sense is often accompanied with an obtusity of the sense-organs.

Ob-Ugrian (ɒb'uːgrɪən). [f. *Ob*, the name of a Siberian river + UGRIAN *a.* and *sb.*] A Finno-Ugric linguistic group of Siberia related to Hungarian. So **Ob-Ugric** *a.* and *sb.*
1933 L. BLOOMFIELD *Language* iv. 68 *Ob-Ugrian*, consisting of *Ostyak*.. and *Vogule*. **1954** PEI & GAYNOR *Dict. Linguistics* 151 *Ob-Ugrian*, a language group (consisting of Ostyak and Vogul) which with Hungarian constitutes the Ugric branch of the Finno-Ugric (or Uralic) sub-family of the Ural-Altaic family of languages. **1955** B. COLLINDER *Fenno-Ugric Vocab.* p. xi, Vogul, Ostyak, and Hungarian are called Ugric languages; vg and os are called Ob-Ugric. *Ibid.* p. xiv, I made up my mind to quote even such words as occur only in Ugric and Permian, nay, even in Ob-Ugric and Permian. **1975** G. F. CUSHING tr. *Hajdu's Finno-Ugrian Lang. & Peoples* iii. 119 Ob-Ugrian is the collective name for the languages and peoples known as Vogul (Man'si) and Ostyak (Chanti).

†**o'bumber**, *v. Obs.* Also 5–6 -bre. [a. OF. *obumbre-r*, *obombre-r* (14th c. in Hatz.-Darm.), ad. Lat. *obumbra-re*: see OBUMBRATE.]
1. *trans.* To overshadow; to shade, obscure.
c **1420** *Pallad. on Husb.* XII. 13 For cloddis wol ther germinacioun Obumbre from the coold, & wel defende. [*c* **1420** LYDG. *Balade Commend. Our Lady* 102 Or half the blisse who coude write or tell, Whan the Holy Ghost to thee was obumbred.] *c* **1470** HARDING *Chron.* CCXXIII. i, His shadowe so obumbred all England. *c* **1510** BARCLAY *Mirr. Gd. Manners* (1570) Bj, Many thinges be hid and.. with obscure knowledge obumbred. *c* **1550** R. BIESTON *Bayte Fortune* Bj, And death.. at last him doth obumbre.
2. *intr.* To cast or make a shadow.
a **1568** in *Bannatyne MS.* 109/26 The vertew of the Holie Gaist devyne Within thy wame sall obvmbir and schyne.

†**o'bumbilate**, *a. Obs. rare*$^{-1}$. In 6 -ylate. [? a scribal error for *obnubilate*: the OF. instance of *obumbler* in Godef. is a misreading of *obnubler*: see -ATE^{2}.] Obscure.
c **1560** [see OBTURATE *a.*].

†**o'bumbilate**, *v. Obs. rare*$^{-1}$. [f. as prec.: see -ATE^{3}.] *trans.* To obscure, obnubilate.
a **1711** KEN *Edmund* Poet. Wks. 1721 II. 86 To chill, unhinge, obumbilate his Heart.

obumbrant (ɒ'bʌmbrənt), *a. Entom.* [ad. L. *obumbrānt-em*, pr. pple. of *obumbrā-re*: see OBUMBRATE.] Overshadowing; *spec.*: see quot.
1826 KIRBY & SP. *Entomol.* IV. 332 *Scutellum*.. *Obumbrant*, when it overhangs the metathorax.

obumbrate (ɒ'bʌmbrət), *a. rare.* [ad. L. *obumbrāt-us*, pa. pple. of *obumbrāre* to overshadow: see next.] †**a.** Overshadowed, darkened. *Obs.* **b.** *Entom.* Concealed under some overhanging part, as the abdomen in some spiders.
1513 DOUGLAS *Æneis* XII. Prol. 66 Wod and forest obumbrat with thar bewis. **1599** R. LINCHE *Fount. Anc. Fict.* A a ij, In some obumbrate thicket let us dwell. **1632** LITHGOW *Trav.* I. 42 To haue Mecenas praise This light obumbrat, Arthur courts the North. **1826** KIRBY & SP. *Entomol.* IV. 351 *Abdomen*.. *Obumbrate*, when it is overshadowed by the trunk and concealed under it.

obumbrate (ɒ'bʌmbreɪt), *v.* Now *rare.* [f. L. *obumbrāt-*, ppl. stem of *obumbrā-re* to overshadow, to shade, f. *ob-* (OB- 1 c) + *umbrā-re* to shade.]
1. *trans.* To overshadow; to shade, darken; to obscure. *lit.* and *fig.*
1526 *Pilgr. Perf.* (W. de W. 1531) 181 Whome the holy goost did obumbrate or shadowe.. with his presence and grace. **1632** LITHGOW *Trav.* x. 432 To obumbrate the true light of the Gospell. **1654** tr. *Scudery's Curia Pol.* 29 Aspiring Ramparts which obumbrate the Adriatique Sea. **1755** SMOLLETT *Quix.* II. IV. xvi, Madam Diana having taken a trip to the Antipodes, and left our mountains obumbrated, and our vallies obscured. *a* **1778** T. GENT *Life* 192 An action that for a while seemed to obumbrate the glories of Caesar. **1834** SOUTHEY *Doctor* v. (1862) 17 That awful wig which accompanies Dr. Parr.. that portentous head which is thus formidably obumbrated.
¶**2.** Misused for ADUMBRATE, to shadow forth.
1632 LITHGOW *Trav.* v. 174 More cleare then the force of policie can obumbrate their wicked deuices. **1741** WARBURTON *Div. Legat.* II. 556 The promises and denunciations.. obumbrated a future state of rewards and punishments. **1824** STEWARD in *Blackw. Mag.* XV. 42, I rather take her to be obscurely obumbrated as the *Ilia nimium querens*.
Hence **ob'umbrated** *ppl. a.*, overclouded.
1592 R. D. *Hypnerotomachia* 3 My eyes before used to such obumbrated darkenes. **1751** SMOLLETT *Per. Pic.* IV. xcii, Their countenances had begun to be a little obumbrated.

obumbration (ɒbʌm'breɪʃən). Now *rare.* [ad. L. *obumbrātiōn-em*, n. of action f. *obumbrā-re*: see prec. Cf. obs. F. *obumbration* (16th c. in Godef.).]
1. The action of overshadowing or condition of being overshadowed.
c **1420** *Pallad. on Husb.* IX. 18 The feruent ire of Phebus to declyne With obumbracioun. **1533** MORE *Answ. Poysoned Bk.* Wks. 1068 His body was in the blessed virgin his mother by the heauenly obumbracion of yᵉ holy ghost. **1647** M. HUDSON *Div. Right Govt.* Introd. 10 His production.. supernaturall and Mysticall, by an incomprehensible Obumbration of the Holy Ghost. **1819** H. BUSK *Dessert* 894 Partial eclipse.. Brighter the dish from casual obumbration. **1846** G. S. FABER *Lett. Tractar. Secess.* 101.
¶**2.** Misused for ADUMBRATION, a shadowing forth.
a **1631** DONNE *Serm.* xxxix. 385 That delineation, that obumbration of God, which the Creatures of God exhibit to us. *a* **1670** HACKET *Cent. Serm.* (1675) 975 In the dark glass of typical Obumbrations.

ob'umbratory, *a. rare.* [f. L. *obumbrāt-*, ppl. stem of *obumbrāre* to OBUMBRATE: see -ORY.] Having the quality of obumbrating or darkening.
1799 in *Spirit Pub. Jrnls.* II. 322 The nebulose or obumbratory style. By the assistance of this.. a plain subject is obscured.

†**o'buncous**, *a. Obs. rare*$^{-0}$. [f. L. *obunc-us* bent in, crooked (f. *ob-* (OB- 1 d) + *uncus* hooked, crooked, curved) + -OUS.] 'Very crooked' (Blount *Glossogr.* 1656).
Hence in PHILLIPS, COLES, ASH, and mod. Dicts.

†**obun'dation**. *Obs. rare*$^{-0}$. [f. L. *obundātiōn-em*, noun of action f. *obundāre* to overflow.] 'A flowing against' (Blount *Glossogr.* 1656).

‖**obus** (ɔbyz). [F. *obus* (1697 in Hatz.-Darm.), ad. Ger. *haubitze*: see HOWITZ.] A howitzer shell.
1871 *Daily News* 26 May, The clean white streets [of Paris] were bestrewn with the *débris* of shrapnel and obus. **1895** tr. *Let. Napoleon III* 2 Sept. 1870 in *Westm. Gaz.* 11 Feb., All the while the obuses rained down heavily upon this agglomeration of human heads.

obvallate (ɒb'vælət), *a. Nat. Hist.* [ad. L. *obvallāt-us*, pa. pple. of *obvallāre*: see next.] Walled up; surrounded as by a rampart.
1846 DANA *Zooph.* (1848) 497 This species.. differs in its obvallate cells. **1857** MAYNE *Expos. Lex.*, *Obvallātus*,.. applied to opposed leaves when they are disposed by spiral pairs, so that these cut or cross themselves at an acute angle, as the *Globulea obvallata*: obvallate.

†**ob'vallate**, *v. Obs. rare*$^{-1}$. [f. L. *obvallāt-*, ppl. stem of *obvallā-re* to surround with a wall, f. *ob-* (OB- 1 a) + *vallāre* to intrench.] *trans.* To surround with, or as with, a wall or entrenchment.
1623 COCKERAM, *Obuallate*, to compasse about with a trench. **1657** TOMLINSON *Renou's Disp.* 284 Which it obvallates with pricks supernally devolved.
Hence †**obva'llation**. *Obs. rare*$^{-0}$.
1658 PHILLIPS, *Obvallation*, an invironing or encompassing with a trench.

†**ob'varicate**, *v. Obs. rare*$^{-0}$. [f. L. type **obvāricāre*, repr. by *obvāricātor* one who obstructs another in his way (Paul. ex Fest.).] (See quot.) Hence †**obvari'cation**. *Obs. rare*$^{-0}$.
1623 COCKERAM, *Obuaricate*, to stop one of his passage. **1658** PHILLIPS, *Obvarication*, a hindring any in their passage.

obvelation (ɒbvɪ'leɪʃən). *rare.* [n. of action from L. *obvēlāre*: see next.] A veiling over, a hiding or concealing.
1664 H. MORE *Synopsis Proph.* 350 The title might have been more properly the obvelation or obscuration then the revelation. **1874** SPURGEON *Treas. Dav.* Ps. xcvii. 2 Every revelation of God must also be an obvelation.

†**ob'vele**, *v. Obs. rare.* [ad. L. *obvēlāre* to cover over, hide, conceal, f. *ob-* (OB- 1 c) + *vēlāre* to cover, veil.] *trans.* To wrap up, veil, cover.
1654 VILVAIN *Theol. Treat.* i. 23 This mixt mungrel action obveled in a mist of words.

†**ob'vene**, *v. Obs. rare.* [ad. L. *obvenīre* to come in the way of, to happen to, also, to prevent, f. *ob-* (OB- 1 b) + *venīre* to come: cf. F. *obvenir* (1369 in Godef.).] *intr.* To occur, befall, happen.
1654 VILVAIN *Theol. Treat.* vi. 179 What is reveled to John by word of mouth, how things shal obvene.

†**ob'vent**, *v. Obs. rare.* [f. L. *obvent-*, ppl. stem of *obveni-re*: see prec.] *trans.* To prevent, frustrate.
1599 HAKLUYT *Voy.* II. I. 181 We do require to obuent these harmes. **1643** PRYNNE *Sov. Power Parlt.* II. 70 To obvent the malice of such felons.

obvention (əb'vɛnʃən). [a. F. *obvention* (13th c. in Godef.), or ad. L. *obventiōn-em* revenue, n. of action f. *obvenīre*: see above.] That which comes to one incidentally; in *Eccl. Law*, an incoming fee or revenue, esp. one of an occasional or incidental character.
1459 *Rolls of Parlt.* V. 365/2 All.. Portions, Pensions, Dymes, Oblations, Obventions, and other Emolumentes and Profites. **1495** *Act 11 Hen. VII*, c. 44 §6 Tythes oblacions obvencions advousons. **1635** PAGITT *Christianogr.* III. (1636) 44 You shall finde these Oblations and Obventions to be of great value. **1655** FULLER *Ch. Hist.* v. iii. §50 Here we speak not of the accidentals, as Legacies.. and other Casualties, and Obventions. **1794** W. TINDAL *Hist. Evesham* 97 To the priorship belong all Obventions or fees under common seal. **1859** R. F. BURTON *Centr. Afr.* in *Jrnl. Geog. Soc.* XXIX. 344 These men.. receive as obventions and spiritual fees sheep and goats, cattle and provisions.

†**ob'versant**, *a. Obs.* [ad. L. *obversānt-em*, pr. pple. of *obversārī* to take position over against, to appear, f. *obversus* OBVERSE.] Standing over against, opposite, contrary; also, placed in front of; hence, familiar, well-known.
1579 TWYNE *Phisicke agst. Fort.* I. x. 10 Errour is obuersant vnto vertue, & contrary vnto it. *a* **1622** BACON *Let. to Sir H. Savill* in *Resuscitatio* (1661) 228 Example.. transformeth the Will of Man into the Similitude of that which is most obversant and familiar towards it. *a* **1754** J. MCLAURIN *Serm. & Ess.* (1755) 306 Our obligations to love and honour God are.. always obversant to our view and continually before our eyes.

obverse (see below), *a.* and *sb.* [ad. L. *obversus*, pa. pple. of *obvertĕre* to OBVERT.
Single instances of the adj. and sb. are known in 17th c.; otherwise the word is not exemplified till end of 18th c.; neither Johnson nor Todd has it, though giving *obversant*; under *reverse*, of coins, Chambers *Cycl.* (1727–41) and Johnson, in speaking of the other side, do not use *obverse*; both adj. and sb. are in Webster 1828.]
A. *adj.* ('ɒbvɜːs, ɒb'vɜːs).
1. Turned towards or against; opposite.
a **1656** USSHER *Ann.* (1658) 876 They fought.. until Carrhenes having overcome his obverse wing, wheeled about with a circumference and came upon the back of his enemies. **1840** S. R. TICKELL in *Jrnl. Asiat. Soc.* IX. 706 The obverse manners of the Oorias.
2. Of a figure: Narrower at the base or point of attachment than at the apex or top; *spec.* in *Nat. Hist.*, a general term comprising the various forms severally called *obconic*, *obcordate*, *oblanceolate*, *obovate*, etc. Also in *Comb.* = obversely, OB- 2, as ***obverse-lunate***.
1826 KIRBY & SP. *Entomol.* III. xxxiv. 508 When there are three of these organs [stemmata] they are arranged in an obverse triangle in a space behind the antennæ. *Ibid.* IV. 299 *Obverse*.. When an object is viewed with its head towards you. **1866** *Treas. Bot.* 799/2 *Obverse*, the same as *Ob. Obverse-lunate*, inversely crescent-shaped. **1875** KNIGHT *Dict. Mech.* 1543/2 An obverse tool has the smaller end towards the haft or stock.
3. Answering to something else as its counterpart.
1875 POSTE *Gaius* IV. (ed. 2) 443 To every mode of obligation there is an obverse mode of liberation. **1881** A. AUSTIN in *Macm. Mag.* XLIII. 401, I felt sure I should come to the other side of the shield, the obverse hollows of all this embossed and.. somewhat turgid appreciation.
4. *Logic.* Of a proposition: obtained from another proposition by the process of obversion.
1870 A. BAIN *Logic* I. 110 To each of the four Propositional Forms.. there is an obverse form. **1917** J. WELTON *Groundwork of Logic* v. 79 In no case is there any loss in the range of application in the obverse proposition.
B. *sb.* ('ɒbvɜːs).
1. That side of a coin, medal, seal, etc., on which the head or principal design is struck; the opposite of *reverse*. Also *attrib.*
1658 SIR T. BROWNE *Hydriot.* 16 Silver peeces.. with a rude head upon the obverse,.. and an ill formed horse on the reverse. **1797** *Encycl. Brit.* (ed. 3) XI. 41/1 On the obverse of this piece there are portraits of Francis and Mary, face to face. **1823** CRABB *Technol. Dict.*, *Reverse*, the back side of a medal, as opposed to the obverse. **1837** *Penny Cycl.* VII. 330/2 The noble.. The obverse represents the king standing in a vessel. **1864** BOUTELL *Her. Hist. & Pop.* xxiv. 401 The equestrian figures of the obverse of the Great Seals. **1895** *Proclam. Bronze Coinage* 11 May, Every Penny should have for the obverse impression Our Effigy with the Inscription 'Victoria' [etc.].
2. a. The face or side of anything intended to be presented to view; *front* as opposed to *back*.
1831 CARLYLE *Sart. Res.* I. x, In looking at the fair tapestry of human life.. he dwells not on the obverse alone, but here chiefly on the reverse. **1847** EMERSON *Repr. Men, Montaigne* Wks. (Bohn) I. 335 Nothing so thin, but has these two faces; and, when the observer has seen the obverse, he turns it over to see the reverse.
b. *fig.* The counterpart of any fact or truth.
1862 W. M. ROSSETTI in *Fraser's Mag.* Aug. 199 To say No, and stick to it, is a necessary obverse of the power of saying Yes to some purpose. **1862** W. W. STORY *Roba di R.* xv. (1864) 325 Here you have the two sides—the science of medicine, and its obverse, the practice of witchcraft. **1874** H. R. REYNOLDS *John Bapt.* viii. 512 Sin cannot be explained away as a mistake, as an illusion, as the obverse of good.
3. *Logic.* A proposition obtained as the result of obversion.
1870 A. BAIN *Logic* I. 110 No men are gods. The obverse is.. all men are no-gods. **1896** [see OBVERSION 2].

obversely (əb'vɜːslɪ), *adv.* [f. prec. + -LY^{2}. In Nat. Hist. after mod.L. *obversè*.] In an obverse form or manner; with an adj. of shape = OB- 2.
1752 SIR J. HILL *Hist. Anim.* 565 The tailed Vespertilio, with a foliated and obversely cordated nose. **1753** CHAMBERS *Cycl. Supp.* s.v. *Leaf*, *Obversely ovated Leaf*,.. a leaf of the same figure with the ovated leaf, only fixed to the petiole by its smaller end. *Ibid.* Botany Tab. 2, Leaves.. Obversely-cordated. **1849** JOHNSTON in *Proc. Berw. Nat. Club* II. No. 7. 368 An obversely conoid elongated vesicle. **1869** *Jas. Mill's Hum. Mind* II. xxiii. 324 *note*, And obversely, if a person acts [etc.].

obversion (əb'vɜːʃən). [ad. L. *obversiōn-em*, n. of action from *obvertĕre* to OBVERT.]

1. The action of turning towards some person or thing.

1864 in WEBSTER.

2. *Logic.* A form of immediate inference in which, by changing the quality, from one proposition another is inferred, having a contradictory predicate. Also called PERMUTATION.

1870 A. BAIN *Logic* I. 110 In affirming one thing, we must be prepared to deny the opposite: 'the road is level', 'it is not inclined', are not two facts, but the same fact from its other side. This process is named *Obversion*. **18..** BAIN *Educ. as Sc.* in *Cycl. Sci.* (U.S.) I. 539 The most searching equivalence of verbal forms is Obversion, or the stating of a fact from its other side. **1896** J. WELTON *Man. Logic* (ed. 2) I. III. iii. 251 Obversion is a change in the quality of a predication made of any given subject, whilst the import of the judgment remains unchanged. The original proposition is called the Obvertend, and that which is inferred from it is termed the Obverse.

3. The formation of an obverse or counterpart.

1892 *Daily News* 3 Sept. 3/3 There is no need..to insist that in the matter of mind, this distinct obversion should exist, which nature demands not.

obvert (əb'vɜːt), *v.* [ad. L. *obvert-ĕre* to turn towards or against, f. *ob-* (OB- 1 a, b) + *vertĕre* to turn.]

†**1.** *trans.* To turn (something) towards; to place fronting. *Obs.*

1623 COCKERAM, *Obuert*, to turne against one. **1646** SIR T. BROWNE *Pseud. Ep.* VI. vii. 309 The rooms of cænation in the Summer, he obverts unto the Winter ascent, that is, South-East. **1686** GOAD *Celest. Bodies* I. xv. 95 The Lunar Light being obverted towards us..in the Quadrates. **1781** WESLEY *Wks.* (1872) IV. 211 If the northern hemisphere be obverted to the sun longer than the southern.

†**2.** To turn (a thing) in a contrary direction.

1646 SIR T. BROWNE *Pseud. Ep.* 60 If wee place a Needle touched at the foote of tongues or andirons, it will obvert or turne aside its lyllie or North point, and conforme its cuspis or South extreme unto the andiron. **1657** TOMLINSON *Renou's Disp.* 131 That the manner of preparation and mixtion be not obverted thereby.

3. *Logic.* To change the quality of (a proposition) in the way of OBVERSION.

1870 A. BAIN *Logic* I. 110 Obvert the predicate, and prefix the sign of negation. **1896** J. WELTON *Man. Logic* (ed. 2) I. III. iii. 251 The one simple rule for obverting any proposition:—Negative the predicate and change the quality, but leave the quantity unaltered.

Hence **ob'verted** *ppl. a.*

1664 EVELYN *Sylva* (1679) 20 Place to warm south, or the obverted pole. **1870** A. BAIN *Logic* I. 115 These obverted forms are Particular Affirmatives, and are therefore converted simply. **1896** J. WELTON *Man. Logic* (ed. 2) I. III. iii. 249 The corresponding forms with negative predicates are termed the Obverted Converse, the Obverted Contrapositive, and the Obverted Inverse.

obvertend ('ɒbvəˌtɛnd). *Logic.* [ad. L. *obvertend-us*, gerundive of *obvertĕre*: see OBVERT *v.*] The proposition to be obverted.

1886 P. K. RAY *Text-bk. Deductive Logic* (ed. 2) III. ii. 129 The given proposition may be called the *Obvertend*. **1896** [see OBVERSION 2].

†**'obviate,** *ppl. a. Obs. rare*⁻¹. [ad. L. *obviāt-us*, pa. pple. of *obviāre*: see next.] = OBVIATED.

1671 *True Nonconf.* 12 This is already obviat by the Lord's own determination.

obviate ('ɒbvɪeɪt), *v.* [f. L. *obviāt-*, ppl. stem of *obviāre* to meet, withstand, oppose, prevent, f. *ob* against + *via* way. Cf. F. *obvier* (14th c., Godef.).]

†**1.** *trans.* To meet, encounter; hence, to withstand, oppose (a person or thing). *Obs.*

1600–9 ROWLANDS *Knaue of Clubbes* 37 As on the way I Itinerated, A Rurall person I Obuiated, Interogating times Transitation. **1654** EARL MONM. tr. *Bentivoglio's Warrs of Flanders* 326 [He] advanced suddenly with..300 Foot to obviat him. **1695** J. EDWARDS *Perfect. Script.* Ded., You obviated their folly..with a profound wisdom. **1702** J. LOGAN in *Pa. Hist. Soc. Mem.* IX. 84 To obviate those three unworthy charges..I have taken all proper courses.

2. To meet and dispose of or do away with (a thing); to clear out of the way; to prevent by anticipatory measures.

1598 YONG *Diana* 338 So did she obuiate this doubt with a sudden remedie. **1656** CROMWELL *Sp.* 17 Sept. in *Carlyle*, That I might..advise with you about the remedies and means to obviate these dangers. **1692** BENTLEY *Boyle Lect.* 243 [This] will obviate and preclude the most considerable objections of our adversaries. **1751** JOHNSON *Rambler* No. 148 ⁋11 But how has he obviated the inconveniences of old age? **1804** LD. ELLENBOROUGH in *East's Rep.* V. 254 The defect..cannot..be obviated in the manner suggested. **1868** ROGERS *Pol. Econ.* iv. (1876) 38 The risk of transporting money from one country to another has been obviated by the use of..Bills of Exchange.

†**b.** To anticipate, forestall. *Obs.*

1712 ADDISON *Spect.* No. 367 ⁋4 If I do not take care to obviate some of my witty Readers, they will be apt to tell me, that my Paper..is still beneficial [etc.].

†**3.** To lie in the way between. *Obs. rare.*

1705 SCARBURGH *Euclid* 8 A Strait line is That, All whose intermediar Parts do obviate the Extreams.

obviation (ɒbvɪ'eɪʃən). [ad. L. *obviātiōn-em*, n. of action f. *obviāre* to OBVIATE. Cf. OF. *obviacion, -tion* (14th c. in Godef.).]

1. The action of obviating or preventing, prevention.

c **1400** *Lanfranc's Cirurg.* 100 A surgian muste þanne be bisy..wiþ obuiacioun defendinge þe lyme, þat noon of þe iij causis tofore seid ne come nouȝt into þe wounde. **1683** E. HOOKER *Pref. Pordage's Mystic Div.* 64 By waie..of obviation, prævention, præoccupation, and anticipation. **1890** *Times* 20 June 5/1 The obviation of all cause of quarrel between Germany and England is..an object of great price.

2. The use, in some American Indian languages, of the obviative (see next).

1927 L. BLOOMFIELD in *Internat. Jrnl. Amer. Linguistics* IV. 191 Although obviation is confined to animate nouns.., verbs have obviative forms also for inanimate actors. **1974** P. H. VOORHIS *Introd. Kickapoo Lang.* 45 A noun and a pronoun agreeing with it in gender, number, and obviation are used to form statements of the identity of the noun and pronoun. **1976** *Language* LII. 519 Obviation is analysed as a dimension of contrast within the 3rd person.

obviative ('ɒbvɪətɪv, -eɪtɪv). [ad. F. *obviatif*, f. OBVIATE *v.* + -IVE.] A grammatical category of the Algonquian family of N. Amer. Indian languages that marks a third person as subordinate to another, animate, third person in a given context. Also, a similar category in certain other languages. Also *attrib.* or as *adj.*

[**1866** J. A. CUOQ *Études Philologiques sur Quelques Langues Sauvages de L'Amérique* I. ii. 43 *De L'Obviatif.* Quand dans une phrase, se *rencontrent* deux 3èmes personnes de première classe, l'une *sujet* et l'autre régime de la phrase, la personne-régime se met à *l'obviatif*. *Ibid.*, Si le nom de la personne *dominante* se trouve exprimé, on le met à l'obviatif simple.] **1877** *Trans. Amer. Philol. Assoc. 1876* VII. 150 When two nouns (or a noun and a pronoun) in the third person are introduced in the same sentence, one as a subject and the other as the object of a verb, the latter takes the *obviative*—or second third-personal-form. **1899** *Proc. Amer. Philos. Soc.* XXXVIII. 186 In *pōhē gūnūl* and the following word, we have the ending *-ūl* of the obviative, or accus[ative] of the third person, which appears in all the Algic idioms. **1922** L. BLOOMFIELD in *Amer. Jrnl. Philol.* XLIII. 276 He arrived at no clear statement of such features as the 'obviative' (the peculiar subsidiary third person of Algonquian grammar). **1927** —— in *Amer. Speech* II. 438/2 In inflection, Menomini, like the other Algonquian languages, has an *obviative* form for subsidiary third persons. **1958** *Archivum Linguisticum* X. II. 171 Distinction ..of Proximate and Obviative, a common Algonquian distinction. **1965** *Canad. Jrnl. Linguistics* X. 80 The use of the obviative in Kutenai. **1976** *Language* LII. 519 The 3rd person in Cree includes two dimensions of contrast: proximate/obviative and animate/inanimate.

obvious ('ɒbvɪəs), *a.* [f. L. *obvi-us* in the way, meeting, obvious (f. *ob* against + *via* way) + -OUS.]

1. Lying or standing in the way; placed in front of, or over against; fronting. *Obs.* or *arch.*

1603 DRAYTON *Bar. Warres* VI. ci, No more rejoycing in the obvious Light. **1609** C. BUTLER *Fem. Mon.* i. (1623) B iv, They [the horns of the bee] serue to giue warning in the darke..of any obuious thing quicke or dead that might offend her. **1635** SWAN *Spec. M.* (1670) 96 As in a broken looking-glass, every part will show the shadow of that face which is obvious to it. **1654** H. L'ESTRANGE *Chas. I* (1655) 3 Paris being obvious to him, and in his way to Spain, he delaid there one day. **1705** J. PHILIPS *Splendid Shilling* 80 So her disembowell'd web Arachne..spreads, Obvious to vagrant flies. **1744** AKENSIDE *Pleas. Imag.* II. 116 They strike In different lines the gazer's obvious eye. **1814** CARY *Dante* (Chandos Cl.) 238 From her..The appellation of that star, which views Now obvious, and now averse, the sun.

†**2.** Exposed or open *to* (action or influence); liable. *Obs.*

1601 DANIEL *Civ. Wars* (1609) VI. cii, Such as obvious unto hatred are. **1647** LILLY *Chr. Astrol.* clx. 672 It renders the Native obvious to many discommodities. **1669** WORLIDGE *Syst. Agric.* (1681) 169 If your Garden be obvious to the cold winds. **1710** STEELE *Tatler* No. 244 ⁋7 The Pendant is so obvious to Ridicule. **1760–72** H. BROOKE *Fool of Qual.* (1809) III. 13 She was artless, and obvious to seduction.

†**3.** Coming in one's way, met with; frequently met with or found; commonly occurring. *Obs.*

1586 W. WEBBE *Eng. Poetrie* (Arb.) 26 The Latinists, which are of greatest fame and most obuious among vs. **1638** SIR T. HERBERT *Trav.* (ed. 2) 25 Suffer me..to tell you of a fish or 2, which in these seas were obvious. **1695** WOODWARD *Nat. Hist. Earth* I. (1723) 9 The next Quarry, or Chalk-pit ..these are so ready and obvious in almost all Places. **1760–72** H. BROOKE *Fool of Qual.* (1809) III. 100 Though your women were as obvious to my walks as yonder pavement.

4. a. Plain and open to the eye or mind, clearly perceptible, perfectly evident or manifest; palpable.

1635 QUARLES *Embl.* II. xi. (1718) 105 My floor is not so flat, so fine, And has more obvious rubs than thine. **1651** HOBBES *Govt. & Soc.* iii. §31. 56 Things present are obvious to the sense, things to come to our Reason only. **1692** BENTLEY *Boyle Lect.* ix. 328 Racked and wrested from its obvious meaning. **1726** LEONI tr. *Alberti's Archit.* I. 31/2 If you make it in Winter, it is obvious that the Frost will crack it. **1793** BURKE *Obs. Conduct Minority* Wks. 1842 I. 627 It appears obvious to me, that one or the other of those two great men, that is, Mr. Pitt or Mr. Fox, must be minister. **1805** EUGENIA DI ACTON *Nuns of Desert* I. 68 A small palisade, not obvious to the sight. **1858** BUCKLE *Civiliz.* (1873) II. viii. 491 His predecessors in this matter had neglected their obvious duty.

b. *Zool.* Plainly distinguishable, clearly visible, evident, as ***an obvious marking*** or ***stripe***: opposed to *obscure*.

c. quasi-sb., ***the obvious***: something which is obvious; plain or manifest inferences, remarks, details, facts, etc.

1903 K. D. WIGGIN *Rebecca* (1904) i. 10 Their steadfast gaze..had the effect of looking directly through the obvious to something beyond. **1919** M. K. BRADBY *Psycho-Anal.* xiii. 175 The work of the artist who consciously and deliberately descends to the obvious..is uninteresting. **1976** G. MCDONALD *Confess, Fletch* (1977) iii. 19 You do the obvious and stop in at the first singles bar you come to.

obviously ('ɒbvɪəslɪ), *adv.* [f. prec. + -LY².]

†**1.** By the way, in passing, incidentally. *Obs.*

1627–77 FELTHAM *Resolves* II. xlviii. 254 He that hath inspection therein but by the by and obviously.

2. In a clearly perceptible manner, evidently, plainly, manifestly.

1638 SIR T. HERBERT *Trav.* (ed. 2) 304 Texts of holy Writ obviously writ or painted. **1668** HALE *Pref. Rolle's Abridgm.* b ij, Other matters more obviously deducible by Argumentation. **1748** *Anson's Voy.* III. i. 302 The other two Islands were obviously enough incapable of furnishing us with any assistance. **1872** BLACK *Adv. Phaeton* iii, Arthur.. was obviously in a bad temper.

obviousness ('ɒbvɪəsnɪs). [f. as prec. + -NESS.]

†**1.** The state or condition of being exposed or open *to*; openness, exposure, liability. *Obs.*

1669 WORLIDGE *Syst. Agric.* (1681) 169 According to the height of the Pole, nature of the ground, and obviousness to Winds. *a* **1677** HALE *Prim. Orig. Man.* IV. viii. 362 In respect of its vicinity and obviousness to Observation. **1841** TRENCH *Parables* xxviii. (1864) 467 The obviousness of the widow [in the East]..to all manner of oppressions and wrongs.

2. The quality of being clearly perceptible; the state or condition of being easily seen or understood; plainness or openness to the eye or mind.

1671 J. WEBSTER *Metallogr.* i. 17 Where obviousness and easiness are awanting to know the subject. **1704** NORRIS *Ideal World* II. iii. 158 Some are thought to write clearly merely through the easiness and obviousness of their matter. **1864** BOWEN *Logic* x. 338 Omitting nothing on account of its seeming triviality and obviousness. **1885** *Law Times* LXXVIII. 209/2 It has been remarked, with equal truth and obviousness, that [etc.].

†**ob'viscate,** *v. Obs. rare.* [f. L. *ob-* (OB- 1 b) + *viscāre* to smear.] *trans.* To smear over; to smooth as with a slimy coating; to mollify.

1684 tr. *Bonet's Merc. Compit.* XIX. 833 Sweet things.. obviscate and blunt its saline Acrimony. **1710** T. FULLER *Pharm. Extemp.* 35 It..obviscates, and mollifies and restrains their [fermenting particles of the blood] impetuous Torrent in the small Canals.

†**'obvolate,** *v. Obs. rare*⁻⁰. [f. L. *ob-* (OB- 1 b) + *volāre* to fly.] (See quot.) So †**obvo'lation.**

1656 BLOUNT *Glossogr.*, *Obvolate*, to flie against. **1658** PHILLIPS, *Obvolation*, a flying against.

obvolute ('ɒbvəl(j)uːt), *a. Bot.* [ad. L. *obvolūt-us*, pa. pple. of *obvolvĕre*: see next.] (See quots.)

1760 J. LEE *Introd. Bot.* III. xvi. (1765) 207 *Obvolute*, rowled against each other; when their respective Margins alternately embrace the strait Margin of the opposite Leaf. **1835** LINDLEY *Introd. Bot.* (1848) II. 374. **1870** BENTLEY *Man. Bot.* (ed. 2) 143 If the half of one conduplicate leaf receives in its fold the half of another folded in the same manner, the vernation is half equitant or obvolute. **1880** GRAY *Struct. Bot.* 139.

obvolution (ɒbvə'l(j)uːʃən). *rare.* [ad. L. *obvolūtiōn-em* a wrapping round, enveloping, n. of action f. *obvolvĕre*: see OBVOLVE.] The wrapping or folding of a bandage round a limb; also, †a fold, twist, or turn (of something coiled).

1578 BANISTER *Hist. Man* VI. 87 In..their foldes, wrethes obuolutions, and Glandules, so much seede is conteined. **1649** BULWER *Pathomyot.* II. x. 234 Although the Tongue may seeme a Muscle because of its wrested obvolutions and implications..yet it is not. **1857** MAYNE *Expos. Lex.*, *Obvolutio*,..applied to the employment of bandages that are wrapped round any limb: obvolution.

obvolutive ('ɒbvəl(j)uːtɪv), *a.* [f. L. *obvolūt-*, ppl. stem of *obvolvĕre* (see OBVOLUTE) + -IVE.] = OBVOLUTE *a.*

1886 in THOMAS *Med. Dict.*

obvolve (əb'vɒlv), *v. rare.* [f. L. *obvolvĕre* to wrap round, f. *ob-* (OB- 1 c) + *volvĕre* to roll.]

1. *trans.* To wrap round, muffle up; to disguise.

1623 COCKERAM, *Obuolue*, to fold round about. **1635** HEYWOOD *Hierarch.* VIII. 497 The doubtfull Oracles..all things obvolved leaue. **1651** BIGGS *New Disp.* ⁋288 Obvolved with an alien and feavorish odour. **1657** TOMLINSON *Renou's Disp.* 116 Pill masse..must be obvolved in fine leather.

†**2.** To cause to roll round or revolve. *Obs.*

1649 BULWER *Pathomyot.* II. v. 176 His [the Muscle's] Chords..with a kind of circular motion obvolve or roll the Eye to the greater Angle.

Hence **ob'volving** *ppl. a.*, wrapping round; *spec.* in *Entom.* (see quots.).

1826 KIRBY & SP. *Entomol.* IV. 328 Prothorax.. Obvolving, when there are neither ora nor suture to separate it from the antepectus. *Ibid.* 334 Elytra.. Obvolving, when their epipleuræ cover a considerable portion of the sides of the alitrunk.

obvolvent (əb'vɒlvənt), *a.* [ad. L. *obvolvent-em*, pr. pple. of *obvolvĕre*: see prec.] Wrapping or folding round; obvolving: see quot.

1857 MAYNE *Expos. Lex.*, *Obvolvens*.. Folding about; wrapping round; applied to remedies.. which act by affording mechanical support, as bandages, etc.: obvolvent.

obyte, -ytt, obs. forms of OBIT.

oc, var. AC *Obs.*, but; ME. pa. t. of ACHE *v.*

‖**oca** ('əʊkə); Also 9 occa. Also oka. [Sp. *oca*, a. Peruvian *occa*: cf. Gonçalez *Vocab.* 1608, 262 'Occa, cierta rayz llamada assi'.] A name of two South American species of *Oxalis*, *O. crenata* and *O. tuberosa*, cultivated for their tubers, which resemble potatoes; the former also for its acid leaf-stalks.

1604 E. G[RIMSTONE] *D'Acosta's Hist. Indies* IV. xviii. 261 The Papas and Ocas be the chiefe for nourishment and substance. **1688** SIR P. RYCAUT tr. *Garcilasso's Peru* VIII. xii, There is another sort which they [Peruvians] call Oca, of a very pleasant taste; it is long, and thick as a man's little finger. **1760–72** tr. *Juan & Ulloa's Voy.* (ed. 3) I. 283. **1842** PRICHARD *Nat. Hist. Man* 431 In the hot plains, they planted maize, and the occa, or oxalis. **1880** C. R. MARKHAM *Peruv. Bark* 113 Rows of Indian girls.. were sitting in the plaza before their little heaps of *chuñus*, ocas, potatoes, and other provisions. **1885** W. MILLER tr. *Vilmorin-Andrieux's Veget. Garden* 355 The Oka-plant is easily propagated from the tubers. **1950** *N.Z. Jrnl. Agric.* May 471/3 The oka plant.., a native of Peru,.. produces tubers which can be used as vegetables. **1966** *New Scientist* 9 June 643/1 Quinoa, papalisa, oka and isaño are plants [in Bolivia] which produce crops with higher nutritive value and protein content than wheat, maize and rice. **1972** Y. LOVELOCK *Vegetable Bk.* 221 The young leaves and flowers of the Spanish-American *oca* .. are used in soups and as a pot-herb, and the flowers serve as a kind of vinegar substitute in salads. It is cultivated, however, for the sake of its egg-sized tubers, which are an important staple in Mexico and the Andean states.

ocam, obs. form of OAKUM.

ocarina (ɒkə'riːnə). [f. It. *oca* goose (in ref. to its shape) + -INA[1].] A simple kind of musical instrument consisting of a somewhat egg-shaped terra-cotta body with a whistle-like mouthpiece and finger-holes; its notes are soft and sonorous, but it has little compass; it is made in several sizes to produce variety of tone.

[**1876** STAINER & BARRETT *Dict. Mus. T.*, *Ocarine (It.)*, a series of seven musical instruments made of terra cotta, pierced with small holes, invented by a company of performers calling themselves the Mountaineers of the Apennines.] **1877** *Patent Specif. T. Zach* No. 1020 A musical wind instrument.. preferably formed of clay, and then baked or burnt; it is to be called the 'Ocarina'. **1883** *Gd. Words* 132 Ducks and geese, which are to the loudest.. Cochin China, what an ocarina is to a flageolet. **1893** *Nation* (N.Y.) 16 Feb. 129/3 A single player with fife or ocarina.

occacion, obs. f. OCCASION; var. OCCATION *Obs.*

occæan, obs. form of OCEAN.

†**oc'cæcate**, *v. Obs.* Also -cec-. [f. L. *occæcāt-*, ppl. stem of *occæcāre* or *obcæcāre* to blind, f. *ob-* (OB- 1 b) + *cæcāre*, f. *cæcus* blind: cf. OBCÆCATE *a.*

The form in *occ-* is more in accordance with L. analogies; but that in *obc-* appears to have been more frequent in med.L. as well as in Eng. derivatives.]

trans. To blind. Hence †**oc'cæcated** *ppl. a.*

1661 K. W. *Conf. Charac.*, *Gd. Old Cause* (1860) 60 Like an occæcated Tobit. **1664** H. MORE *Synopsis Proph.* 532 Whereas God is said.. to occæcate the Jews, or deceive the prophets, it is to be understood of the permission of these things.

†**occæ'cation**. *Obs.* Also -cec-: see also OBCÆCATION. [ad. late L. *occæcātiōn-em*, n. of action f. L. *occæcāre*: see prec.] The action of blinding; a blinded condition.

1608–11 BP. HALL *Occas. Medit.* §57 It is an addition to the misery of this inward occæcation, that it is ever joyned with a secure confidence. **1691** tr. *Emilianne's Frauds Rom. Monks* (ed. 3) 137 O stupendous occæcation.

†'**occallated**, *ppl. a. Obs. rare*[−0]. [f. L. *occallāt-us* having a hard skin, callous, pa. pple. of **occallāre* (f. *ob-* (OB- 1 b) + *callum* hard skin) + -ED[1].] (See quot.) Hence †**occa'llation**.

1623 COCKERAM, *Occallated*, brawnie, hard. **1658** PHILLIPS, *Occallation*, a making hard like brawn.

occam, obs. form of OAKUM.

Occamism ('ɒkəmɪz(ə)m). [f. name *Occam* or *Ockham* + -ISM.] The doctrine or system of the English scholastic philosopher, William of Occam, who lived in the first half of the 14th c., called in later times the 'Invincible Doctor'.

Occam was a pupil of Duns Scotus, but rejected and opposed the Realism of his master, forming a new speculative sect who revived the tenets of Nominalism. He maintained that general ideas have no objective reality out of the mind, but are merely a product of abstraction. His teachings prepared the way for the overthrow of scholasticism.

Hence '**Occamist**, '**Occamite**, a disciple or follower of Occam; **Occa'mistic** *a.*

1579 FULKE *Ref. Rastel* 752 Brawlings between the Thomists, and Scotists, Albertists, Occamists. **1657** BAXTER *Winding-sheet Pop.* §14 They differ in many hundred points, as the writings of the Schoolmen, the Thomists, and Scotists, and Ockamists.. do declare. **1837–9** HALLAM *Hist. Lit.* I. iii. §69 Masters of arts were bound by oath never to teach Ockhamism. **1874** J. H. BLUNT *Dict. Sects*, *Occamites*, the school of English Nominalists, or rather the revivers of Nominalism, who followed William of Occham's lead in the first half of the fourteenth century, and whose opposition to Realism brought about the decline of scholastic philosophy.

Occam's razor: see RAZOR *sb.* 1 b.

occamy ('ɒkəmɪ). Forms: 6 ochamie, ockamie, occam, 8 ochimy, 8–9 ockamy, occamy, (ockumy). [A corrupt form of *alcomye*, *alcamy*, ALCHEMY.] A metallic composition imitating silver: cf. ALCHEMY 3. Also *attrib.* and *fig.*

1596 NASHE *Saffron Walden* N ij b, A tongue of copper or ochamie (meerely counterfetting silver) such as organe pipes and serjeants maces are made of. **1713** STEELE *Guard.* No. 26 ¶1 This thimble and an occamy spoon. **1755** JOHNSON, *Ochimy*, a mixed base metal. **1857** SIR F. PALGRAVE *Norm. & Eng.* II. 839 The dawning spirit of conventional honour gilding the ockamy shield of Chivalry. **1864** *N. & Q.* 3rd Ser. V. 410 This occamy of ridicule elaborated by three of the verbal alchemists of the day.

occar, obs. form of OCHRE, OCKER.

†**o'ccase**. *Obs. rare.* [ad. L. *occās-us* a falling, going down, setting, f. ppl. stem of *occidĕre* to fall down, f. *ob-* (OB- 1 a) + *cadĕre* to fall.] Falling, fall.

1609 HEYWOOD *Brit. Troy* v. xciv, He lights in Lemnos, nor can Vulcan die By this occase. **1657** TOMLINSON *Renou's Disp.* 323 A small.. seed.. follows upon the occase of its flowers.

occasion (ə'keɪʒən), *sb.*[1] Also 4–5 -ioun, -youn, 5 -ione, 5–6 -yon(e, (5 -cion, 6 -cyon, -tyon, 6–7 -tion). [ad. L. *occāsiōn-em* falling (of things) towards (each other), juncture, opportunity, motive, reason, pretext, in late L. also cause; n. of action f. *occidĕre* (see prec.); in F. *occasion* (12–13th c. in Hatz.-Darm.) a learned form, which at length displaced the popularly descended OF. *ocheison*, *ochison*, *ochoison*, north. Fr. *okeson*, *okison*, *ocaison*, etc., also OF. *achais-*, *acheis-*, *aches-*, *achis-un*, *-on*, etc., *an-*, *encheison*, etc., 'occasion, cause, reason, motive, accusation, accident, circumstance', whence the ME. forms ACHESOUN, ANCHESOUN, ENCHEASON, CHESOUN.]

I. 1. a. A falling together or juncture of circumstances favourable or suitable to an end or purpose, or admitting of something being done or effected; an opportunity. †In early use *esp.* in pregnant sense, Opportunity of attacking, of fault-finding, or of giving or taking offence; a 'handle' against a person. *to take occasion*, to take advantage of an opportunity (to do something). *to rise to the occasion*: see RISE *v.* 15 b.

1382 WYCLIF *2 Kings* v. 7 Takith heed and seeth, that occasiouns [Vulg. *occasiones*] he sechith aȝeyns me. —— *2 Cor.* xi. 12 That that I do, and I schal do, that I kitte awey the occasioun of hem, that wolen occasioun. **1484** CAXTON *Fables of Æsop* I. iv, Men.. sekynge occasion to doo some harme and dommage to the good. **1526** *Pilgr. Perf.* (W. de W. 1531) 17 b, All this he dyd to gyue vs an occasyon of reuerent familiarite. **1538** STARKEY *Dialogue England* I. i. 24 Let not occasyon slyppe. **1561** T. NORTON *Calvin's Inst.* II. 143 Of which wordes the Apostle toke occasion to make this comparison. **1613** PURCHAS *Pilgrimage* (1614) 345 Till fitter occasion of revenge offered it selfe. **1660** PEPYS *Diary* 6 Dec., I took occasion to go up and to bed in a pet. **1703** J. LOGAN in *Pa. Hist. Soc. Mem.* IX. 230 We take all possible care to avoid giving occasions. **1779** J. MOORE *View Soc. Fr.* (1789) I. i. 2, I now seize the first occasion of communicating the whole to you. **1799** HARRIS in Owen *Mrq. Wellesley's Desp.* (1877) 117 Colonel Wellesley's division turning the right flank of the enemy, gave occasion to General Floyd.. to disperse a cutchery of infantry. **1825** BENTHAM *Ration. Rew.* 244 A prime minister has not so many occasions for acquiring information respecting farming as a farmer. **1875** JOWETT *Plato* (ed. 2) III. 597 Here.. we may take occasion to correct an error which occurred at p. 582. **1879** FROUDE *Cæsar* ix. 103 Occasions of war had been caught at with rich communities.

b. Personified as a female bald behind; esp. in *to take occasion by the forelock*: see FORELOCK *sb.*[2] 2.

c **1592** MARLOWE *Jew of Malta* v. ii, Begin betimes; occasion's bald behind. **1606** BRYSKETT *Civ. Life* 9 If he may once lay hold vpon that locke, which, men say, Occasion hath growing on her forehead, being bald behind. **1671** MILTON *P.R.* III. 173 Zeal and duty are not slow, But on Occasions forelock watchful wait. **1819** SHELLEY *Cenci* v. i, We can escape even now, So we take fleet occasion by the hair. **1851** TENNYSON *To the Queen* 31 To take Occasion by the hand.

2. a. A juncture or condition of things, an occurrence, fact, or consideration, affording ground for an action or a state of mind or feeling; a reason, ground; also, in pregnant sense, good or adequate reason: = CAUSE *sb.* 3, 3 b.

†*occasion why* = 'reason why'; cf. *cause why*, CAUSE *sb.* 3 c. †*evil occasion*, inducement to sin, 'offence', 'stumbling-block' (= Gr. σκάνδαλον in N.T.).

c **1385** CHAUCER *L.G.W.* 994 *Dido*, And shortly tolde al the occasion Why Dido come in-to that Region. **1489** CAXTON *Faytes of A.* I. vii. 17 Be not moeued for lytyl occasion. **1523** LD. BERNERS *Froiss.* I. cxxxvii. 164 Tyll nowe there was none occasion why. **1526** TINDALE *Matt.* xviii. 7 Wo be unto the world because of evill occasions. *Ibid.* 8 Yff thy honde or thy fote geve the occasion of evyll. **1594** *La Primaud. Fr. Acad.* II. 3 We shall at the least giue them occasion to thinke more seriously of their error. **1613** R. HILL *Pathw. Piety* Pref., If ever people.. had occasion to praise God, we are they. **1634** SIR T. HERBERT *Trav.* 35 By degrees, upon small occasion he beheaded and strangled most of them. **1714** SWIFT *Pres. St. Aff.* Wks. 1755 II. I. 210 What occasions the ministry may have given for this coldness. **1748** RICHARDSON *Clarissa* (1811) I. xxxvii. 278, I beg your pardon.. for having given you occasion to remind me of the date of your last. **1763** J. BROWN *Poetry & Mus.* vii. 141 One of the first Efforts of a growing Politeness is to avoid all Occasions of Offence. **1843** DICKENS *Christmas Carol* ii, The occasion of its using.. a great extinguisher for a cap.

†**b.** A pretext; an excuse. *Obs.*

1388 WYCLIF *Phil.* i. 18 The while on al maner, ethir bi occasioun [L. *per occasionem*], ethir bi treuthe, Crist is schewid. **1444** *Rolls of Parlt.* V. 110/1 That none of the saide officers.. be occasion or under colour of her Offices take none other thing. **1596** SPENSER *F.Q.* IV. x. 13 Delay,.. Whose manner was all passengers to stay And entertaine with her occasions sly. **1649** MILTON *Eikon.* iv. Wks. (1847) 286 All this.. was but a mere colour and occasion taken of his resolved absence from the parliament.

3. a. An occurrence leading to some result; hence, generally, That which produces an effect: = CAUSE *sb.* 1. Const. *of*, †*that*. *to give occasion to*, to give rise to, to occasion.

1382 WYCLIF *Josh.* xxii. 25 Bi this occasioun ȝoure sones shulen turne awey oure sones fro the dreed of the Lord. *c* **1402** LYDG. *Compl. Bl. Knt.* 165 Thought & seknesse were occasioun That he thus lay in lamentacioun. **1560** DAUS tr. *Sleidane's Comm.* 49 b, Heresies.. to the reproch of Christ, .. or the which may be an occasion of sedition. **1669** MARVELL *Let. Mayor of Hull* Wks. 1776 I. 112 The crowd of business.. obliging us to sit both forenoon and afternoon,.. which indeed is the occasion that I have the less vigor left at night. **1728** NEWTON *Chronol. Amended* ii. 205 The expulsion of the Shepherds by the Kings of Thebais was the occasion that the Philistines were so numerous in the days of Saul. **1751** JOHNSON *Rambler* No. 141 ¶10 A mistake which had given occasion to a burst of merriment. **1859** TENNYSON *Geraint* 235 A little vext at losing of the hunt, A little at the vile occasion.

b. Something that contributes to produce an effect, by providing the opportunity for the efficient cause to operate; a subsidiary or incidental cause. Distinguished from *cause* = 'efficient cause' (CAUSE *sb.* 5).

[**1551** T. WILSON *Logike* I. I iij, Those causes, that are fetched farre of, and beeyng but halfe causes, partly and by the waye, geue onely the occasion.] **1605** BACON *Adv. Learn.* II. x. §3 It [medicine] considereth causes of diseases, with the occasions or impulsions. *c* **1705** BERKELEY *Common-pl. Bk.* in Fraser *Life* (1871) 430 What means Cause as distinguish'd from Occasion? Nothing but a being which wills, when the effect follows the volition. **1854** DE QUINCEY *Autobiog. Sk.*, *Coleridge* II. 224 Such were the causes; but the immediate occasion of his departure.. was the favourable opportunity.. of migrating in a pleasant way. **1860** MANSEL *Proleg. Log.* ix. 301 Experience furnishes if not the cause at least the occasion of every object of our cognition. **1871** MARKBY *Elem. Law* §433 The injury to the individual.. though it is never the cause of the action of a Court of Law is the occasion of it.

c. A person who causes or brings about something; *esp.* one who does so incidentally.

a **1548** HALL *Chron.*, *Hen. VII* 37 He suspected y[t] Geralde erle of Kyldare.. was the cause and occasion y[t] he had no succoures nor ayde sent to him. **1605** VERSTEGAN *Dec. Intell.* vi. (1628) 185 The Queene of English blood royal, was occasion that the depressed English nation was raised againe vnto honor and credit. **1680** *Establ. Test* 39 He will not forget those who have been the occasions.. of cruelty. **1711** STEELE *Spect.* No. 136 ¶3 He was the Occasion that the Muscovites kept their Fire in so soldier-like a manner. **1814** SOUTHEY *Roderick* XXIV. 255 Vain hope—if all the evil was ordained.. And we the poor occasion.

†**d.** The action of causing or occasioning. Also *transf.*, that which is caused or occasioned.

a **1533** LD. BERNERS *Huon* 531 He made his complayntis, how by the occasyon of duke Huon of Burdeaux, he had loste .iiii. of his nephues. **1560** DAUS tr. *Sleidane's Comm.* 276 They saye it is to be imputed, partly to their owne errour, partly to the occasion of others. **1598** B. JONSON *Ev. Man in Hum.* IV. viii, Without adjection of your Assistance or Occasion. **1600** SHAKS. *A.Y.L.* IV. i. 178 O that woman that cannot make her fault her husbands occasion, let her neuer nurse her childe her selfe.

†**4.** That which gives rise to discussion or consideration; the subject treated or debated. *Obs.*

1615 LATHAM *Falconry* (1633) 91 In the forepart of this book I haue written more at large vpon the same occasion. **1618** BP. LLANDAFF *Let. to Abp. Canterb.* in Hales *Gold. Rem.*, Since this time the Synod hath been somewhat warmed; for before we were held with small occasions. **1651** *Fuller's Abel Rediv.*, *Melancthon* (1867) I. 279 Telling them that in a general council all occasions, defendings, opinions and judgments ought to be free.

II. 5. a. A juncture of circumstances requiring or calling for action; necessity or need arising from circumstances. Const. *for* (†*of*) or *inf.*

1576 FLEMING *Panopl. Epist.* 278 Tell me (good friende) what occasion constrained you, to seeke accesse hether?

1596 SHAKS. *1 Hen. IV*, III. ii. 74 When he had occasion to be seene, He was but as the Cuckow is in Iune, Heard, not regarded. **1607** —— *Timon* III. i. 19 Hauing great and instant occasion to vse fiftie Talents. **1697** DAMPIER *Voy.* I. 110, 5000 packs of flower, for a reserve, if we should have occasion of any. **1712** ADDISON *Spect.* No. 439 ¶3 There will be no Occasion for him. **1762–71** H. WALPOLE *Vertue's Anecd. Paint.* (1786) II. 235 Having frequent occasion to make use of enamel. **1802** MAR. EDGEWORTH *Moral T.* (1816) I. xv. 129 The corrector..scarcely had occasion to alter a word. **1884** *Illustr. Lond. News* 27 Sept. 291/2 There is no occasion to call in the magicians, and the astrologers. **1885** *Law Times* LXXIX. 130/1 Every lawyer who has had occasion to thread the labyrinth of the statutes under which London is governed.

†**b.** A particular, esp. a personal, need, want, or requirement. Chiefly in *pl.* = needs, requirements. *Obs.*

1596 SHAKS. *Merch. V.* I. i. 139 My purse, my person, my extreamest meanes Lye all vnlock'd to your occasions. **1665** SIR T. HERBERT *Trav.* (1677) 174 Seeing the People cut them into many sluces, and divert the stream to serve their occasions. **1740** J. CLARKE *Educ. Youth* (ed. 3) 171 The Latin Tongue wants Words to answer a great many of our modern Occasions. **1752** FIELDING *Amelia* III. vii, He had not a shilling left to spare from his own occasions. **1795** NELSON 19 July in Nicolas *Disp.* (1845) II. 57 A total deprivation of sight for every common occasion in life is the consequence of the loss of part of the crystal of my right eye. **1806–7** J. BERESFORD *Miseries Hum. Life* (1826) v. Concl., I hope you can contrive to suit them to my occasions.

†**6. a.** That which one has need to do; necessary business; a matter, piece of business, business engagement. Chiefly in *pl.*, Affairs, business. *Obs.*

1594 NASHE *Unfort. Trav.* 28 No interpleading was there of opposite occasions. **1607** *Statutes* in *Hist. Wakefield Gram. Sch.* (1892) 57 Sucche as..have occasion with the governours. **1609** *N. Riding Rec.* (1884) I. 173 They going about their occasions. **1636** EARL OF MANCHESTER in *Buccleuch MSS.* (Hist. MSS. Comm.) I. 276 My occasions are so many as I know not whether they will give me any leave to see the country this summer. **1679** G. R. tr. *Boyatuau's Theat. World* I. 41 They employed themselves about their lawful occasions. *a* **1713** ELLWOOD *Autobiog.* (1714) 70 You are discharged, and may take your Liberty, to go about your Occasions. **1783** NELSON 28 Oct. in Nicolas *Disp.* (1845) I. 83 Six months leave of absence, to go to Lisle, in France, on my private occasions. **1840** BARHAM *Ingol. Leg.*, *Leech of Folkest.*, Betake thy self to thy lawful occasions.

b. *pl.* Necessities of nature. *Obs.*

1698 FRYER *Acc. E. India & P.* 156 Where they do all occasions, leaving their Excrements there. **1755** SMOLLETT *Quix.* IV. xx, My master Don Quixote..eats, drinks, and does his occasions like other men. **1789** M. MADAN tr. *Persius* (1795) 38 *note*, It was unlawful to do their occasions or to make water in any sacred place.

III. †**7. a.** A juncture of circumstances (in itself); the falling out or happening of anything; a casual occurrence; an event, incident, circumstance. *Obs.*

1534 ELYOT *Doctr. Princes* 9 b, Dooe thou nothyng in furie, sens other men knowe what time and occasion is meetest for the. **1602** SIR R. BOYLE *Diary* in *Lismore Papers* Ser. II. (1887) I. 41 Since my last hear is growne no occasion worthy the advertising. *a* **1649** WINTHROP *New Eng.* (1853) II. 368 There fell out at this time a very sad occasion.

b. *gen.* The falling out or happening of things or events; the course of events or circumstances. *Obs.*

1595 SHAKS. *John* IV. ii. 125 With-hold thy speed, dreadfull Occasion: O make a league with me, 'till I haue pleas'd My discontented Peeres. **1597** —— *2 Hen. IV*, IV. i. 72 Wee see which way the Streame of Time doth runne, And are enforc'd from our most quiet there, By the rough Torrent of Occasion.

8. A particular casual occurrence or juncture; a case of something happening; the time, or one of the times, at which something happens; a particular time marked by some occurrence or by its special character. †Formerly sometimes in more general sense, A case, an instance.

1568 GRAFTON *Chron.* II. 116 Hearyng the king upon an occasion to talke of breade. **1573** J. SANDFORD *Hours Recreat.* (1576) 121 When there were deade at Milan..certayne noble..yong men, Alciato made upon that occasion..these wittie verses. **1588** SHAKS. *L.L.L.* v. ii. 143 Vpon the next occasion that we meete. **1693** EVELYN *De la Quint. Compl. Gard.* I. 37 It ought to have a Ballustre with some Steps to come down into that Garden, which is an Ornament to be wish'd for in such Occasions. **1707** *Curios. in Husb. & Gard.* 145 Thus argues Boyle in several Occasions. **1748** HARTLEY *Observ. Man* I. ii. 218 These Muscles drawing the Eye out on eminent Occasions. **1781** COWPER *Friendship* 148 Sometimes occasion brings to light Our friend's defect long hid from sight. **1834** MEDWIN *Angler in Wales* II. 24 Till that occasion, I never had known what terror really was. **1883** *Athenæum* 8 Sept. 305/1 An article of his appearing on the occasion of the death of Gogol. *Mod.* On the occasion of her marriage with Mr. ——.

9. An event or function of some special kind.

a. A religious function or ceremonial; in Scotland, a Communion service; the annual, half-yearly, or quarterly sacramental season. *arch.* or *Obs.*

1789 A. WILSON *Poems & Lit. Prose* I. (1876) 29 It has been our custom, on the Tuesday's night after our Occasion, to be hearty over a pint. **1803** A. PRINGLE *Serm. & Lett.* (1840) 190 Our autumn occasions had been good times to many. **1844** *Sage's Wks.* I. 368 *note*, They [servants] were to be allowed to attend a certain number of fairs and occasions or sacraments during the year. **1892** C. G. MCCRIE *Worship Presbyt. Scot.* 311 The administration of the Lord's Supper upon what are styled 'occasions'. **1900** CHARLOTTE HANBURY in *Autobiog.* (1901) xv. 224 When the Home-going is, I want to say..'by desire'—no flowers;..Also I would much wish a Church of England occasion.

b. A special ceremony or celebration; a 'function'; an 'event'. Chiefly *colloq.*

1860 EMERSON *Cond. Life*, *Culture* Wks. (Bohn) II. 374 Keep the town for occasions, but the habits should be formed to retirement. **1870** DICKENS *E. Drood* iii, These occasions seem to go off tolerably well without me, Pussy. *Mod.* It was a great occasion.

IV. *Phrases* and *Comb.* **10.** †**a.** ***by occasion of***, through the (incidental) operation or agency of; by reason of; on account of; because of. ***by occasion that***, for the reason that, because. *Obs.*

1429 *Rolls of Parlt.* IV. 346/2 Be occasion of the seide diversite. *c* **1450** tr. *De Imitatione* I. xvi. 18 What euery man verily is, best is shewid by occasion of aduersite. *c* **1460** FORTESCUE *Abs. & Lim. Mon.* ix. (1885) 129 We haue also sene..somme off the kynges subgettes gyff hym bataill, by occasion þat thair livelod and offices were þe grettest off þe lande. **1560** DAUS tr. *Sleidane's Comm.* 466 The Archebyshops of Mentz, Trevers and Collon by occasion of the bathes met that tyme together. **1613** PURCHAS *Pilgrimage* (1614) 124 They which by occasion of iournying or uncleannesse could not now celebrate the Passeover. **1667** PEPYS *Diary* 15 May, The wrong the credit of this office has received by this rogue's occasion.

b. †***by occasion***, by chance, casually, incidentally (*obs.*). ***on*** or ***upon occasion*** (†***by occasions***), as occasion or opportunity arises; now and then, occasionally. ***on*** or ***upon*** (†***by***) ***occasion of***, in casual or incidental connexion with.

1560 DAUS tr. *Sleidane's Comm.* 378 A few daies after, Iohn Sleidane, by occasion of talke spake of the same to the Emperours Ambassadour. **1562** COOPER *Answ. Priv. Masse* (1850) 46 One of the copies of this answer by occasion..lighted into my hands. *c* **1585** R. BROWNE *Answ. Cartwright* 3 The prayers may be..left off by occasions: as when the Minister is to preach. **1590** SHAKS. *Mids. N.* III. i. 150 Nay, I can gleeke vpon occasion. *a* **1649** WINTHROP *Hist. New Eng.* (1853) II. 26 Mr. Peter by occasion preached one Lord's day. **1665** SIR T. HERBERT *Trav.* (1677) 24 Petty Islands..which..environ, and in a sort defend her upon occasion. **1711** STEELE *Spect.* No. 136 ¶3 Upon occasion of the mention of the Battle of Pultowa, I could not forbear giving an Account [etc.]. **1844** LINGARD *Anglo-Sax. Ch.* (1858) I. App. K. 369 On occasion of these grants it may not be amiss to add a few remarks. **1884** W. E. NORRIS *Thirlby Hall* ix, She could be extremely generous upon occasion.

11. ***for*** (***on***, ***upon***) ***one's occasion***, on one's account, for one's sake.

1656 BRAMHALL *Replic.* v. 221 Had they not reason to wellcome them..who were come only upon their occasion? **1856** EMERSON *Eng. Traits* iii. 41 The traveller..reads quietly the *Times* newspaper, which..seems to have machinized the rest of the world for his occasion. **1860** PUSEY *Min. Proph.* 388 Whoso amendeth not on occasion of others, others shall be amended on occasion of him.

12. *Comb.*, as ***occasion-giver***.

1568 GRAFTON *Chron.* II. 113 Stephen..which had bene the occasion geuer of all the tumults.

†**o'ccasion**, *sb.*[2] *Obs. rare.* [ad. L. *occāsiōn-em* (see prec.), taken as n. of action of *occidĕre* in sense 'to go down, set', for which the actual L. word was *occāsus*.] Setting (of the sun).

1533 BELLENDEN *Livy* I. (1822) 87 Ane litil afore the occasioun of the son. *Ibid.* 171 Now was the sonne fast tending to his occasion.

occasion (əˈkeɪʒən), *v.* [f. OCCASION *sb.*[1]; = F. *occasionner* to cause, occasion (15th c. in Godef. *Compl.*); cf. OF. *occasioner* to pick a quarrel with, to accuse; med.L. *occāsiōnāre* to burden with occasional taxes.]

†**1.** *trans.* To give occasion to (a person); to induce by affording an opportunity or a ground; to urge or impel by circumstances; also, to do this habitually; hence, to habituate, accustom.

a. to a course of action. *Obs.*

1530 *Proper Dyaloge* in *Rede me*, etc. (Arb.) 134 By the meanes wherof I & suche other..are occasioned to theft or murder. **1545** UDALL *Erasm. Par. Luke* xix. 156 This is thy daie, in whiche thou art occasioned to emendemente. *a* **1555** LATIMER *Serm. & Rem.* (1845) 243 That ye..do..the best that you can to occasion your parishioners to peace. **1684** I. MATHER *Remark. Provid.* i. (1890) 4 My children..poor souls, whom I had occasioned to such an end in their tender years, when as they could scarce be sensible of death.

†**b.** *to do* something (passing into 2 b). *Obs.*

1538 COVERDALE *N. Test.* Ded., Such ignorant bodies..shall through this small labour be occasioned to attain unto more knowledge. **1563** *Homilies* II. *Fasting* (1859) 294 Fasting was one of the meanes whereby Almighty God was occasioned to alter the thing which hee had purposed concerning Ahab. **1590** RECORDE, etc. *Gr. Artes* (1640) 405 To occasion you to study the better, I will leave this doubt wholly to your owne search. **1678** CUDWORTH *Intell. Syst.* I. iv. §13. 225 Aristotle..was not occasioned to do that..because it was a Doctrine then Generally Received, but only because he had a mind, odiously to impute such a thing to the Pythagoreans.

2. To be the occasion or cause of (something); to give ground for, give rise to, cause, bring about, esp. in an incidental or subsidiary manner (cf. OCCASION *sb.*[1] 3 b).

a. With simple obj. (Sometimes also with indirect personal obj.)

1596 SPENSER *F.Q.* VI. i. 12 My haplesse case Is not occasioned through my misdesert. **1632** J. HAYWARD tr. *Biondi's Eromena* 147 Either too light, or too free feeding hath occasioned you this dreame. **1665** PEPYS *Diary* 2 Jan., I occasioned much mirth with a ballet I brought with me. **1736** BUTLER *Anal.* I. iv. Wks. 1874 I. 76 Any course of action which will probably occasion them greater temporal inconvenience. **1796** MORSE *Amer. Geog.* I. 170 Its spray rises a great height in the air, occasioning a thick cloud of vapours. **1863** FR. A. KEMBLE *Resid. in Georgia* 70, I saw an advertisement which occasioned me much thought. **1875** JOWETT *Plato* (ed. 2) V. 166 He whose folly is occasioned by his own jealousy..is to suffer more heavily.

b. With *obj.* and *inf.*: To cause (a person or thing) *to be* or *to do* something; in *pass.* To be caused or constrained by circumstances.

1610 BOYS *Wks.* (1630) 413, I am occasioned here to meet a peeuish and vncharitable people. **1717** tr. *Frezier's Voy.* 77 When any Man happens to have a violent Fall, which occasions him to bleed at the Nose. **1802** MAR. EDGEWORTH *Moral T.* (1816) I. xiv. 109 This occasioned him to be much in the shop. **1849** GROTE *Greece* II. lv. (1862) V. 53 It occasioned them to make indignant remonstrance.

†**c.** To give (one) reason to go, to take (one).

1653 WALTON *Angler* i. 2, I have stretch'd my legs up Tottenham Hil to overtake you, hoping your businesse may occasion you towards Ware.

†**3.** To employ for one's occasions or needs, to make use of. *Obs. rare*[−1].

1632 SPELMAN *Hist. Sacrilege* (1698) 202, I know a Merchantman..that bought the Contents of two noble Libraries for 40*s.* a piece..this stuff hath he occasioned instead of Grey Paper by the space of more than these ten Years [*A quot. from Bale, who has* occupyed].

†**4.** The pa. pple. was formerly used to introduce the cause or occasion of a preceding fact; ***occasioned by***, in consequence of. *Obs.*

1634 SIR T. HERBERT *Trav.* 47 [The ship] sunke and was swallowed by the Sands, occasioned by a hole, neglected by the Carpenter. *Ibid.* 185 Some of which..were drowned, unable to swim to shore occasioned by age, and violent course of the Sea. **1657** R. LIGON *Barbadoes* (1673) 27 Our locks too..will rust in the wards..and all this occasion'd by the moistness of the Air. **1725** DE FOE *Voy. round World* (1840) 117 The Indians' dwellings..were all at a distance from the river, occasioned..by the rivers overflowing the flat grounds near its banks.

Hence **o'ccasioning** *vbl. sb.* and *ppl. a.*

1632 *Star Chamb. Cases* (Camden) 144 Mr Broughton and Mr Young were both to be sentenced, the one for makinge the disturbance, and the other for occasioning of it. **1683** *Brit. Spec.* 188 An easy Excise..upon such Commodities, as naturally tend to the occasioning of Pride, Idleness, Luxury. **1817** COLERIDGE *Biog. Lit.* 50 He admits five agents, or occasioning causes.

o'ccasionable, *a. rare.* [f. OCCASION *v.* + -ABLE.] Capable of being occasioned or caused; likely to be occasioned.

a **1677** BARROW *Serm.* Wks. 1686 III. xiii. 143 This Practice will fence us against immoderate displeasure occasionable by mens hard opinions.

occasional (əˈkeɪʒənəl), *a.* (*sb.*) [f. OCCASION *sb.*[1] + -AL[1]; cf. late L. *occāsiōnāliter* as occasion arises, F. *occasionnel* (1718 in *Dict. Acad.*).]

A. *adj.* †**1.** That happens or arises casually or incidentally; casual. *Obs.*

1568 GRAFTON *Chron.* II. 109 The stealyng of their Apples, and their other occasionall dammages. **1654** EARL MONM. tr. *Bentivoglio's Warrs of Flanders* 362 He said..that the tumults..might be caused by some occasional confusion.

2. a. Happening or operating on some particular occasion; limited to specific occasions; arising out of, required by, or made for, the occasion.

occasional conformity, *conformist*: see CONFORMITY 3, CONFORMIST 2; †*occasional bill* = Occasional Conformity Bill. *occasional cause* combines the meanings 'operating on a particular occasion' and 'serving as an occasion or secondary cause': see quots. under sense 4, and cf. OCCASIONALISM.

a **1631** DONNE in *Select.* (1840) 27 For other occasional points, the Church had need of a continual assistance of the Spirit of God. **1661** HEYLIN *Hist. Ref.* II. 35 The sacrifice of Noah as it was remarkable, so it was occasional. **1677** W. HUBBARD *Narrative* I. (1865) 247 By his occasional going from the Sermon, being forced thereunto by the Extremity of the Toothach. **1711** SWIFT *Lett.* III. 265 They say the Occasional bill is brought to-day into the house of lords. **1776** ADAM SMITH *W.N.* II. ii. (1869) I. 306 Gold and silver which he would otherwise have been obliged to keep by him for answering occasional demands. **1790** BURKE *Fr. Rev.* 301 The vice of the ancient democracies..was, that they ruled..by occasional decrees, *psephismata*. **1825** BENTHAM *Ration. Rew.* 5 With regard to rewards, the most important division is into occasional and permanent.

b. Of a speech, literary composition, religious service, etc.: Produced on, or intended for, a special occasion. Hence ***occasional speaker***, ***writer***, etc., one who delivers occasional speeches or writes occasional verses, pamphlets, etc.

1687 DRYDEN *Hind & P.* II. 339 Yet all those letters were not writ to all, Nor first intended, but occasional Their absent sermons. **1701** *Stanley's Hist. Philos.* Biog. 4 Their Doctrines, Letters, Occasional Speeches. **1779–81** JOHNSON *L.P.*, *Dryden* Wks. II. 389 In an occasional performance no height of excellence can be expected. **1829** H. C. ROBINSON *Diary* 13 Aug. (1967) 102 [Goethe] remarked..that *occasional* poems are among the best poems when the poet takes care to retain all the spirit of the occasion. **1834** G. CRABBE JUN. in *Poet. Wks. G. Crabbe* I. i. 15 His father took in a periodical work..which contained, at the end of each number, a sheet of 'occasional poetry'. **1849** MACAULAY *Hist. Eng.* x. II. 642 It..sustains, better perhaps than any occasional service which has been framed during two centuries, a comparison with..the Book of Common

Prayer. **1883** *Manch. Guard.* 22 Oct. 5/4 Some of his verses are purely occasional and have no claim to stability. **1891** F. LOCKER-LAMPSON *Lyra Elegantiarum* (rev. ed.) p. x, In his [*sc.* the Editor's] judgment Occasional Verse should be short, graceful, refined, and fanciful, not seldom distinguished by chastened sentiment, and often playful. **1894** *Westm. Gaz.* 5 Mar. 3/1 He is..one of the very best occasional speakers in England. No one is quicker at seizing the spirit of an occasion. **1932** CHADWICK & KERSHAW *Growth of Lit.* I. 25 Both poems [sc. *Deor* and *Widsith*]..contain passages describing what purport to be personal experiences of the authors, and which—at least in the case of *Deor*—approximate to 'occasional' poetry. **1965** M. SPARK *Mandelbaum Gate* i. 11 He..had before the war published a volume of his own occasional verses. **1976** S. HYNES *Auden Generation* v. 140 Lehmann's *The Noise of History* and Spender's *Vienna..are* occasional: like..'Easter 1916' and Auden's elegy on Yeats—they mythologize history.

c. Of an article of use, building, piece of furniture, etc.: Made or constructed for the occasion; adapted for use on special occasions.

1749 J. CLELAND *Mem. Woman Pleasure* II. 91 Mrs. Cole had prepar'd my spark and me an occasional field-bed, to which we retired. **1760–72** H. BROOKE *Fool of Qual.* (1809) III. 84 [We bored] a large hole in the side of our ship..for which we had an occasional plug prepared. **1771** SMOLLETT *Humph. Cl.* III. 25 At night, half a dozen occasional beds are ranged..along the wall. **1813** *Chron.* in *Ann. Reg.* 51 The occasional saloon was singularly novel and beautiful. **1857** DICKENS & COLLINS *Lazy Tour* i. in *Househ. Words* 3 Oct. 316/1 A little round occasional table in a window. **1875** *Carpentry and Join.* 115 A loo, or occasional table. **1897** *Westm. Gaz.* 21 June 7/1 The chair that the Queen sat in during the service was a Chippendale occasional Spanish mahogany chair.

d. Of persons: Acting or employed for the occasion or on particular occasions.

1759 *Ann. Reg.* 140 That the occasional proctors take all possible care that order..be observed. **1771** in *Priv. Lett. Ld. Malmesbury* (1870) I. 233 An occasional maid of Louisa's, who supplies the place of her own when she is absent with Gertrude. **1785** PALEY *Mor. Philos.* (1818) II. 430 Loose ranks of occasional and newly-levied troops. *a* **1859** MACAULAY *Hist. Eng.* xxiii. V. 14 The occasional soldier is no match for the professional soldier.

3. Happening as an occasion presents itself, but without certainty or regularity; taking place, occurring, or met with now and then.

1630 [implied in OCCASIONALLY 3]. *a* **1715** BURNET (J.), According to many occasional reflections dispersed in other places of Scripture concerning it [the flood]. **1828** WEBSTER s.v., We make occasional remarks on the events of the age. **1849** MACAULAY *Hist. Eng.* iii. I. 293 In spite of the occasional murmurs of the Commons. **1865** LIVINGSTONE *Zambesi* v. 108 With the exception of an occasional leopard, there are no beasts of prey to disturb domestic animals. **1878** L. P. MEREDITH *Teeth* 65 The human teeth have doubtless been subject through all time to occasional disease. **1881** J. RUSSELL *Haigs* v. 105 An occasional raid upon his neighbour's moveables.

4. Constituting or serving as the occasion or incidental cause; rarely const. *of.* ***occasional cause*** (*Metaph.*), (*a*) a secondary cause whereby or whereupon the primary or efficient cause comes into operation; (*b*) in the Cartesian philosophy: see OCCASIONALISM.

1646 SIR T. BROWNE *Pseud. Ep.* (J.), The ground or occasional origin hereof. **1662** J. CHANDLER *Van Helmont's Oriat.* 119 Second, partaking causes, also free mediating con-causes, and occasionall ones accompanying them: over all which..God is..the totall, immediate, and independent cause. **1727–41** CHAMBERS *Cycl.* s.v. *Cause*, The motions..of the soul and body, are only *Occasional Causes* of what passes in the one or the other. *a* **1850** ROSSETTI *Dante & Circ.* I. (1874) 124 Deem thou nothing else occasional Of my long silence. **1854** FERRIER *Inst. Metaph.* 476 The Cartesian doctrine of occasional, as distinguished from efficient causes. **1892** *Daily News* 24 Mar. 5/7 The 'occasional' question—using the adjective in the metaphysical sense—is a question about wages.

B. *sb.* †**1.** An occasional speech or writing. (Chiefly *pl.*) *Obs.*

1655 FULLER *Ch. Hist.* XI. x. §87 Hereat Mr. Dod..fell into a pertinent and seasonable discourse (as more better at occasionals). **1682** LD. NORTH (*title*) Light in the Way to Paradise, with other occasionals.

2. *colloq.* An occasional workman, etc. (cf. CASUAL B. 3).

1867 'MARK TWAIN' *Lett. to Publishers* (1967) 13, I am on the N.Y. Tribune staff here as an 'occasional', among other things. **1892** *Pall Mall G.* 6 Apr. 2/2 There is no way of meeting both cases at once except by discriminating between the regulars and the occasionals. **1908** *Westm. Gaz.* 10 Dec. 6/1 (*heading*) Oxford University v. Oxford Occasionals. **1977** 'J. LE CARRÉ' *Hon. Schoolboy* v. 112 He never got round to blowing [*sc.* betraying] the Occasionals ..the Occasionals were filed..in a separate archive.

Hence **o'ccasionalness** (Bailey vol. II, 1727).

occasionalism (əˈkeɪʒənəlɪz(ə)m). [f. prec. + -ISM, after G. *occasionalismus.*] The doctrine of the Cartesian philosopher Geulincx which accounted for the interaction of mind and matter by supposing that on occasion of every volition God produces a corresponding movement of the body and on occasion of every affection of the body a corresponding idea; mind and body thus standing to one another in the relation of occasional causes.

1842 in BRANDE *Dict. Sci.* etc. **1867** J. H. STIRLING tr. *Schwegler's Hist. Philos.* (ed. 9) 167 The philosophy of Malebranche..in its single leading thought that we see and know all things in God, demonstrates itself to be, like the occasionalism of Geulinx, a special attempt to overcome the dualism of the Cartesian philosophy on its own principles and under its own presuppositions. **1884** tr. *Lotze's Metaph.* 114 The first assumption would only have led back to the embarrassments of Occasionalism.

occasionalist (əˈkeɪʒənəlɪst). [See -IST.]

†**1.** An occasional conformist. *Obs.*

1705 *Char. of a Smoker* in *Harl. Misc.* (1808) XI. 30 He..makes an interest against the Occasional bill, because he is a sort of an occasionalist himself.

2. One who holds the doctrine of Occasionalism.

1776 BURKE *Corr., Let. to John Bourke* (1844) II. 112 Our love to the occasionalist, but not server of occasions. **1838** *Blackw. Mag.* XLIV. 234 From Aristotle, down through his scholastic followers, past the occasionalists and pre-established harmonists. **1879** HUXLEY *Hume* ix. 166 The successors of Descartes either found themselves obliged, with the Occasionalists, to call in the aid of the Deity, or [etc.].

attrib. **1891** *Athenæum* 10 Jan. 55/2 It contains..much information about the great Occasionalist thinker [Geulincx].

Hence **oˌccasionaˈlistic** *a.*, of or pertaining to Occasionalists or Occasionalism.

1884 MERZ *Leibniz* I. v. 100 He admits its advance on the ..occasionalistic theory of Descartes.

occasionality (əˌkeɪʒəˈnælɪtɪ). [f. OCCASIONAL + -ITY.] The quality or fact of being occasional (in various senses); esp. of being prepared, composed, or 'got up' for the occasion.

1767 A. CAMPBELL *Lexiph.* (ed. 2) 48 He was disgusted at ..the occasionality and ambitiousness of her dress. *a* **1822** SHELLEY in Bagehot *Lit. Stud.* (1879) I. 76 From the occasionality of its impulses, it will often seem silly. **1837–9** HALLAM *Hist. Lit.* I. viii. §44 From their occasionality or want of merit, far the greater part have perished.

occasionally (əˈkeɪʒənəlɪ), *adv.* [f. OCCASIONAL + -LY². Cf. L. *occāsiōnāliter*, F. *occasionnellement.*]

†**1.** By chance, casually, accidentally. *Obs.*

1622 *Relat. Eng. Plant. Plymouth* in Arber *Pilgrim Fathers* (1897) 446 The house was fired occasionally by a spark that flew into the thatch. **1654** GATAKER *Disc. Apol.* 64 Casting mine eye occasionallie on this Varlet's Postscript, I chanced to light..on the Allegations of two Autors. **1718** ATTERBURY *Serm.* (1737) III. 191 He appeared to them..sometimes at places where he had before appointed to meet them, sometimes occasionally, as they were travelling on the way.

2. On, for, or with a view to, some particular occasion; on certain particular occasions; when occasion arises. *Obs.* exc. *dial.*

a **1632** G. HERBERT *Priest to Temple* xxvii, He..intermingles some mirth in his discourses occasionally, according to the pulse of the hearer. **1678** CUDWORTH *Intell. Syst.* I. iv. §22. 393 Philo hereupon, occasionally cites this Remarkable Testimony of Philolaus the Pythagorean. **1756** JOHNSON *Life Browne* Wks. IV. 592 A treatise which seems to have been occasionally written. **1776** G. SEMPLE *Building in Water* 18 The Rods were in three Pieces..which screwed together occasionally. *a* **1791** WESLEY *Dress* v. i. Wks. 1822 IX. 48 Our Saviour once occasionally said, 'Behold they who wear gorgeous apparel are in kings' courts'. **1881** *Leic. Gloss., Occasionally*, upon occasion arising; if necessary.

†**b.** On the occasion of something else happening or being done, incidentally. *Obs.*

1657 HEYLIN *Hist. Ref.* I. 20 Whose Fortunes and Estates have been occasionally and collaterally confirmed in Parliament. *Ibid.* 24 Reformations which were made occasionally in that faulty Church. **1667** MILTON *P.L.* VIII. 556 As one intended first, not after made Occasionally. **1684** *Scanderbeg Rediv.* iii. 25 *heading*, Wherein occasionally is given a Brief Account of the Reign of King Casimir.

3. Now and then, at times, sometimes.

1630 BRATHWAIT *Eng. Gentlem.* 449 Such as these..shall wee occasionally encounter withall, in our readings. **1751** PALTOCK *Peter Wilkins* (1884) II. xvii. 188 To sweep round the whole country, and take all the towns in our way, and occasionally enter the middle parts, as the towns lay commodious. **1814** D. STEWART *Hum. Mind* II. i. §3. 89 All of these writers have..been occasionally misled in their speculations. **1884** PAE *Eustace* 7 Occasionally..his eye..had rested on the motionless form of a salmon-fisher.

†**o'ccasionarily**, *adv. Obs. rare.* [f. as next + -LY².] (From something) as the 'occasional cause'.

c **1449** PECOCK *Repr.* II. iv. 158 The yuelis whiche occasionarili comen out fro the having..of profitable craftis. *Ibid.* III. xi. 340 Which comen occasionarili oonli bi it.

†**o'ccasionary**, *a. Obs. rare*⁻¹. [f. OCCASION *sb.*¹ + -ARY.] Occasional, made for particular occasions.

1702 FARQUHAR (*title*) Love and Business: In a Collection of Occasionary Verse and Epistolary Prose.

†**o'ccasionate**, *ppl. a. Obs.* Also 5 **-at.** [ad. med.L. *occāsiōnāt-us*, pa. pple. of *occāsiōnāre*, f. *occāsiōn-em* OCCASION.] **a.** Occasioned, brought about. **b.** = OCCASIONAL 4.

1471 RIPLEY *Comp. Alch.* III. xvi. in Ashm. (1652) 143 Fyre occasionat we call Innaturall. *Ibid.* xvii, By help of fyre Occasionate. **1657** G. STARKEY *Helmont's Vind.* 73 Its efficient and continent causes, the material and occasionate.

†**o'ccasionate**, *v. Obs.* [f. med.L. *occāsiōnāt-*, ppl. stem of *occāsiōnāre*: see prec.] *trans.* = OCCASION *v.* 1, 2.

1545 RAYNOLD *Byrth Mankynde* Prol. Bj, It doth occationat any man to be the moore prompt, redy, and wyllyng to take payne, when he is assuryd..of the proffet, pourpoose, and fruict therof commynge. **1570** LEVINS *Manip.* 42/6 To Occasionate, *occasionare.* **1596** H. CLAPHAM *Briefe Bible* II. 234 Who desires not onely to do good my selfe, but also to occasionate your good by others. **1640** QUARLES *Enchiridion* (1641) II. xl, If therefore thou doe evill, thereby to occasionate a Good, thou laist a bad foundation for a good building. **1647** H. MORE *Song of Soul* II. iii. I. xxxiv, The lowest may occasionate much ill.

†**o'ccasionately**, *adv. Obs. rare*⁻¹. [f. OCCASIONATE *ppl. a.* + -LY².] In a manner brought about by some occasion or secondary cause.

1609 BP. W. BARLOW *Answ. Nameless Cath.* 135 Not intentionately from the Subiect, but occasionately by the vice of the Obiect.

†**o'ccasionative**, *a. Obs.* [f. as OCCASIONATE *v.* + -IVE.] Serving as occasion or cause, esp. as incidental cause. Hence †**o'ccasionatively** *adv.*, in an occasionative manner.

1526 *Pilgr. Perf.* (W. de W. 1531) 165 Eyther immediatly or mediatly,..directly or indirectly, principally or occasionatyuely. **1655** tr. *Sanderson's Promissory Oaths* iii. §11. 85 As they may be impeditive of good, or causative, or at the least (for we may use such words) occasionative, of evill. *a* **1693** URQUHART *Rabelais* III. xxiii. 193 In these..things..there may be somewhat occasionative of the..Yell.

occasioned (əˈkeɪʒənd), *ppl. a.* [f. OCCASION *sb.*¹ and *v.* + -ED.] **a.** Caused, brought about, esp. indirectly; †having a ground or reason (*obs.*). †**b.** Accustomed (*obs.*).

1576 NEWTON *Lemnie's Complex.* (1633) 221 The merry convocation being dissolved..[they] have eftsoones returned to their old nature, wonted manners, and occasioned gravity. **1631** R. H. *Arraignm. Whole Creature* x. §1. 78 Though he abstained from all pleasant bread..in his occasioned humiliation, for one and twenty dayes.

Hence †**o'ccasionedly** *adv.*, with occasion or cause, with ground or reason.

1631 R. H. *Arraignm. Whole Creature* vii. 53 Whom at last you will occasionedly curse. *Ibid.* xii. §4. 135 Wee occasionedly exclaime on these Impostors.

o'ccasioner. Now *rare.* [f. OCCASION *v.* + -ER¹.] One who or that which occasions.

1494 FABYAN *Chron.* VII. 368 He..commaunded..to endyte all suche persones as were occacyoners and executours of that dede. **1539** TAVERNER *Erasm. Prov.* (1545) 12 b, Certayne philosophers..plucked oute theyr owne eyes, bycause they were the occasioners and prouokers of all euyll affections and lustes. *a* **1656** HALES *Gold. Rem.* I. (1673) 109 Those things that were occasioners of his sin. **1682** SCARLETT *Exchanges* 286 The Acceptant, as the wilfull occasioner thereof, is obliged to make good all the loss. ? *a* **1800** *Jamie Douglas* vii. in Child *Ballads* VII. cciv. F. (1890) 98/1 Thou wast the first occasioner Of parting my gay lord and me.

†**o'ccasionet.** *Obs. nonce-wd.* [f. OCCASION *sb.* + -ET¹.] A small occasion.

1592 G. HARVEY *Pierce's Super.* (1593) 68 It is a Courtly feate, to snatch the least occasionet of aduantage, with a nimble dexteritie.

o'ccasionless, *a. rare.* Without occasion.

1631 R. BYFIELD *Doctr. Sabb.* 194 Who disperseth his..conceits upon an occasion occasionlesse.

†**o'ccasive**, *a. Obs. rare.* [ad. late L. *occāsīv-us*, f. *occās-*, ppl. stem of *occidĕre* to go down, set: see -IVE.] Pertaining to the setting sun, western.

1802 O. GREGORY *Astron.* 81 Amplitude is..either north and south, or ortive and occasive.

†**o'ccation.** *Obs. rare.* Also 5 -cioun. [ad. L. *occātiōn-em*, n. of action f. *occāre* to harrow.] Harrowing.

c **1420** *Pallad. on Husb.* XII. 11 Summen seyn the benes satioun In placis coold is best to fructifie, On hem yf me do noon occasioun [*Bodl. MS.* occacioun]. **1706** PHILLIPS, *Occation*, a harrowing or breaking of clods.

†**'occatory**, *a. Obs. rare*⁻¹. [ad. L. *occātōri-us*, f. ppl. stem of *occāre* to harrow: see -ORY.] Of or pertaining to harrowing.

1651 BIGGS *New Disp.* ¶297 Occatory operations.

occean, occian, obs. variants of OCEAN.

occecation, var. OCCÆCATION, blinding. *Obs.*

†**oc'cide**, *v. Obs. humorous nonce-wd.* [ad. L. *occīdĕre* to cut down, kill.] *trans.* To kill.

1694 MOTTEUX *Rabelais* v. (1737) 232 One Hebdomad wou'd..occide us.

Occident (ˈɒksɪdənt), *sb.* and *a.* Chiefly *poet.* and rhet. Also 5 **occydent, occidente, occedente, -entt.** See also OCCIENT. [a. F. *occident* (12th c. in Godef. *Compl.*), ad. L. *occident-em* setting, sunset, the west, orig. pr. pple. of *occidĕre* to fall towards, go down, set, f. *ob-* (OB- 1 a) + *cadĕre* to fall. Opposed in all uses to ORIENT.]

A. *sb.* **1.** That quarter or region of the sky in which the sun and other heavenly bodies set, or the corresponding quarter or region of the earth; the west. Now *rare.*

c **1386** CHAUCER *Man of Law's T.* 199 O firste moeuyng crueel firmament..that..hurlest al from Est til Occident. *a* **1420** HOCCLEVE *De Reg. Princ.* 4056 With þi riȝt honde, thow þe orient Shuldest han touchid..And with þi lift honde, eke þe occident. **1483** CAXTON *Gold. Leg.* 387 b/1 The sonne mone sterres and planettes..moeue fro thoryent to thoccidente. **1593** SHAKS. *Rich. II*, III. iii. 67 His [the sun's] bright passage to the Occident. **1607** ROWLANDS *Guy Earl Warw.* 38 Ere Phœbus in the Occident decline. **1632** LITHGOW *Trav.* VII. 320 Towards the occident, it ioyneth with the great Lake. **1753** CHAMBERS *Cycl. Supp.* s.v., *Equinoctial Occident*, that point of horizon where the sun sets, when entering aries, or libra. *Estival Occident*, that point of the horizon where the sun sets at his entrance into the sign cancer, when the days are longest. *Hybernal Occident*, that point of the horizon where the sun sets, when entering the sign of capricorn; at which time, the days, with us, are shortest.

2. That part of the earth's surface situated to the west of some recognized part; western countries, the West; i.e. originally, the countries of Western Europe or of the Western Empire, or of Europe as opposed to Asia and the Orient; also, in mod. use, a poetic appellation of America or the Western Hemisphere.

1390 GOWER *Conf.* III. 104 Ther ben of londis fele In occident. **1477** EARL RIVERS (Caxton) *Dictes* 97 In two yeres he [Alexander] sought alle thorient and occident. **1552** LYNDESAY *Monarche* 4265 All Princis of the Occident Ar tyll his grace obedient. **1588** A. KING tr. *Canisius' Catech.* 81 Greik and latin, Orient and Occident dois bear irrefragabl testimonie yat thair can na exception be maid. **1689** *Def. Liberty agst. Tyrants* 155 Constantine and Licinius governed the Empire together, the one in the Orient, the other in the Occident. **1871** JOAQUIN MILLER *Songs of Sierras, Tall Alcalde* (1872) 197 Thou Italy of the Occident!

†**B.** *adj.* Situated in the west, western, occidental.

1513 DOUGLAS *Æneis* VII. Prol. 25 Mars occident, retrograide in his speir. **1535** STEWART *Cron. Scot.* I. 3 In Iona yle within the occident se. *Ibid.* II. 695 The Ylis in the occident se.

'occident, *v. nonce-wd.* [f. prec., after ORIENT *v.*] *trans.* To turn or direct towards the west; to place (a church) with the chancel at the western end.

1896 IRENE PETRIE in *Life* xii. (1900) 269 The Bishop.. came to the west or rather the east door, as the Church is occidented.

occidental (ɒksɪ'dɛntəl), *a.* and *sb.* [a. F. *occidental* (14th c. in Littré), ad. L. *occidentāl-is* western, f. *occident-em*: see OCCIDENT and -AL[1]. Opposed in all uses to ORIENTAL, but less used.]

A. *adj.* **1.** Belonging to, situated in, or directed towards, that part or region of the heavens in which the sun sets; of or in the west, western, westerly; *spec.* in *Astrol.* said of a planet when seen after sunset, or when in the western part of the sky.

c **1391** CHAUCER *Astrol.* I. §5 The remenant of this lyne.. is cleped the west lyne, or the lyne occidentale. **1594** BLUNDEVIL *Exerc.* III. II. xx. (1636) 416 Their shadow is.. sometime orientall, and sometime occidentall. **1601** SHAKS. *All's Well* II. i. 166 Ere twice in murke and occidentall dampe Moist Hesperus hath quench'd her sleepy Lampe. **1647** LILLY *Chr. Astrol.* xix. 114 To be Occidentall is to be seen above the Horizon, or to set after the ☉ is downe. **1794** SULLIVAN *View Nat.* II. 411 On the oriental and occidental halves of the enlightened hemisphere of that planet. **1807** J. BARLOW *Columb.* I. 154 Which..hail'd thee first in occidental day.

fig. **1611** BIBLE *Transl. Ded.*, Vpon the setting of that bright Occidentall Starre, Queene Elizabeth of most happy memory. [With allusion to 2.]

2. Belonging to, found in, or characteristic of, western countries or regions of the earth (i.e. usually, those west of Asia; also formerly, Western Europe or Christendom; occas., America or the Western Hemisphere); belonging to or situated in the West; Western. Also, of, belonging to, or characteristic of, the western United States.

1553 BECON *Reliques of Rome* (1563) 140* The Occidentall or weast churches thorow out all Europe. **1581** MARBECK *Bk. of Notes* 243 This constitution..was neuer..receiued in the vniuersall Church, but onelie in this our Occidentall Church. **1589** PUTTENHAM *Eng. Poesie* I. vii. (Arb.) 28 Learned men, who wrote about the time of Charlemaines raigne in the Empire Occidentall. **1659** BP. WALTON *Consid. Considered* 127 The Oriental and Occidental Jews. **1727** BRADLEY *Fam. Dict.* s.v. *Corn*, The Smell is not so disagreeable as that of the occidental Civet. **1809** E. A. KENDALL *Travels Northern Parts U.S.* II. 28 Among the natural forest-trees, are the button-wood or occidental plane, the spruce-fir and the locust-tree. **1846** *Knickerbocker* XXVII. 471 'I.L. of this vicinity,' writes an occidental correspondent, 'had carried the knife for a long time.' **1862** DANA *Man. Geol.* 584 Both the oriental and occidental Continents. **1933** E. C. JAEGER *Calif. Deserts* v. 57 The occidental harvester (*P[ogonomyrmex] occidentalis*) is a large, reddish ant building conspicuous mounds of pebbles.

3. Applied to precious stones of inferior value and brilliancy, as opposed to ORIENTAL *a.* 4: see quot. 1747.

1747 DINGLEY in *Phil. Trans.* XLIV. 505 There are some of an inferior Class and Beauty... These are commonly called by Jewellers Occidental Stones: They are mostly the Produce of Europe..and are so named, in Opposition to those of a higher Class, which are always accounted Oriental, and supposed to be only produced in the more Eastern Parts of our Continent. **1796** KIRWAN *Elem. Min.* (ed. 2) I. 254 Occidental Topaz..Exposed to a moderate heat..is said to become red, and then becomes ruby of Brazil. *Ibid.* 256 Occidental or Brazilian Sapphire. **1860** C. W. KING *Antique Gems* i. (1866) 43 These occidental stones are of a deep, rich hue, but have very little brilliancy.

B. *sb.* (Often with capital initial.)

1. †**a.** A western country or region. *Obs.* **b.** A native or inhabitant of the West.

1587 HOLINSHED *Descr. Brit.* I. x. in *Chron.* I. 39/1 The Iles that lie about the north coast of..Scotland..are either occidentals, the west Iles [etc.]. **1857** W. M. THOMSON *Land & Book* ix. 115 That comparative inactivity which distinguishes Orientals from Occidentals. **1875** LOWELL *Spenser* Pr. Wks. 1890 IV. 282 For us Occidentals he has a kindly prophetic word.

2. An artificial language, based chiefly on the Romance languages, invented by E. J. de Wahl (1867–1948), an Estonian, in 1922.

1926 *Encycl. Brit.* III. 906/2 Mr. E. de Wahl..finally produced Occidental, 'comprehensible at first sight to 10,000,000 educated Europeans without preliminary study'. To write or speak it is less easy than to read it, variety being dearly bought by the introduction of irregularities. **1928** O. JESPERSEN *Internat. Lang.* I. 26, I have read articles and received letters, chiefly in Ido, but also in Esperanto and Occidental, written from not a few countries. **1934** S. ROBERTSON *Devel. Mod. Eng.* (1936) iv. 89 Jespersen now feels that there are enough points of similarity among the leading projects looking toward an international language—including Esperanto,..Occidental, and his own creation, Novial—to justify the hope that a single adequate International Auxiliary Language will some day emerge. **1949** M. PEI *Story of Language* (1952) VI. iii. 441 The twentieth century has continued the tradition [of creating artificial languages], with..Occidental.., Monding, and a host of others.

occi'dentalism. [f. prec. + -ISM.] Occidental quality, style, character, or spirit; the customs, institutions, characteristics, ways of thinking, etc. of Western nations.

1839 *Blackw. Mag.* XLVI. 105 The Sultan Mahmoud and his Turkish subjects..have no taste for..the occidentalism, the journalism, the budgetism, the parliamentaryism of the 19th Century. **1855** MILMAN *Lat. Chr.* (1864) IX. XIV. v. 204 There is a..confusion of uncongenial elements, of Orientalism and Occidentalism, in the language [ecclesiastical Latin]. **1890** *Athenæum* 15 Feb. 206/2 The curious transition from Orientalism to Occidentalism, of which contemporary Japan is the theatre.

occi'dentalist. [f. as prec. + -IST.] **a.** One who favours or advocates Western customs, modes of thought, etc. **b.** One who studies the languages and institutions of Western nations.

1877 D. M. WALLACE *Russia* xvi. 258 The literary society of Moscow was divided into two hostile camps—the Slavophils and the Occidentalists. **1890** J. RHYS in *Academy* 10 May 321/2 How was I, a benighted occidentalist, to know [etc.].

c. One who advocates or uses the artificial language called Occidental.

1946 H. JACOB *On Choice of Common Lang.* iii. 40 The Occidentalists were the most critical.

occiden'tality. [f. as prec. + -ITY.] Occidental quality or state.

1. The state of being in the western part of the sky, or of being visible after sunset, as a planet.

1647 LILLY *Chr. Astrol.* xix. 114 Their [Mercury's & Venus'] occidentality [is] when they are in more degrees of the Signe the ☉ is in, or in the next subsequent. **1731** *Gentl. Mag.* I. 145 Their [the Planets'] Orientality or Occidentality in respect of the Sun.

2. Western style or character; with *pl.* a Western (i.e., in quot., American) trait or peculiarity.

1873 W. S. MAYO *Never Again* 6 His occidentalities had for her the charm of novelty.

occi'dentalize, *v.* [f. as prec. + -IZE.] *trans.* To render occidental; to conform to or imbue with Western ideas or characteristics. Hence **occi'dentalized, occi'dentalizing** *ppl. adjs.*; also **occi,dentali'zation.**

1870 O. W. HOLMES *Mechanism in Th. & Mor.* (1888) 113 To occidentalise and modernise the Asiatic modes of Thought which have come down to us. **1878** *Fraser's Mag.* XVII. 62 The Occidentalised natives dressed in coats and trousers. **1888** *Athenæum* 14 July 59/2 In Indo-China, in China, and in Japan the same process of occidentalization may be seen in operation. **1893** F. ADAMS *New Egypt* 13 The result of his Occidentalising taste, at once so crude and so rudimentary. **1895** *Daily News* 1 Oct. 6/3 Mr. Hearn..loves the old Japanese people more than..their modern 'occidentalizing' descendants.

occi'dentally, *adv.* [f. as prec. + -LY[2].] In an occidental manner or situation; in the west; in a Western (e.g. American) fashion.

1833 G. S. FABER *Recapit. Apostasy* 119 The occidentally extinct apostasy of Paganism. **1861** R. F. BURTON *City of Saints*, The 'all-fired red-bellied varmints'—I speak, oh reader! occidentally.

†**oc'cidual,** *a. Obs. rare.* [ad. L. *occiduāl-is* western, f. *occidu-us* going down (f. *occidĕre*): see -AL[1].] Going down, setting; pertaining to the setting of a heavenly body. Also †**oc'ciduous** *a. rare.*

1635 GELLIBRAND *Variation Magn. Needle* 5 The Amplitude Ortive or Occiduall of the Sunne. **1656** BLOUNT *Glossogr.*, *Occiduous*, that goeth down, that will decay. *a* **1711** KEN *Edmund* Poet. Wks. 1721 II. 340 To brighten his occiduous Rays. **1727–41** CHAMBERS *Cycl.* s.v. *Amplitude*, Amplitude is of two kinds; eastern, or ortive; and western, or occiduous.

†**'occient.** *Obs.* Also 5 occyent. [a. OF. *occien(t)*, 14th c. in Godef.:—L. *occident-em.*] = OCCIDENT *sb.*

c **1460** *Launfal* 281 Her fadyr was kyng of fayrye, Of occient fer and nyghe. **1481** CAXTON *Godfrey* xxiii. 55 Themperour demanded of hym of thestate of his peple, and of other barons of thoccyent.

occipital (ək'sɪpɪtəl), *a.* (*sb.*) [ad. late or med.L. *occipitāl-is*, f. *occiput, occipit-*: see OCCIPUT and -AL[1]. So F. *occipital* (1546 in Hatz.-Darm.).]

1. Belonging to, or situated in or on, the occiput or back part of the head. Chiefly *Anat.*, in names of parts having this position, as ***occipital artery, bone, condyle, foramen*** or ***hole, muscle, nerve, protuberance, sinus, vein,*** etc.

1541 R. COPLAND *Guydon's Quest. Chirurg.* D iv b, The seconde bone of the heade in the hyndre parte is called Occipitall. **1597** A. M. tr. *Guillemeau's Fr. Chirurg.* 9/3 A blowe in the occipitalle parte of the heade. **1679** in Hickes *Spir. Popery* 58 Insomuch that the whole Occipital bone was shattered all in pieces. **1759** STERNE *Tr. Shandy* II. xix, In the cellulæ of the occipital parts of the cerebellum. **1826** KIRBY & SP. *Entomol.* III. xxix. 115 The head is armed with three occipital spines. **1831** R. KNOX *Cloquet's Anat.* 99 The occipital hole may be considered as being the commencement of the spinal canal. **1840** G. V. ELLIS *Anat.* 3 The occipital artery is the large trunk which occupies the occipital region of the head, with the branches of the great occipital nerve. **1872** NICHOLSON *Palæont.* 302 In the Amphibians..and in the Mammals, there are two 'occipital condyles', by which the skull is jointed to the neck. **1892** *Syd. Soc. Lex.*, *O[ccipital] bone*, a somewhat rhomboidal.. bone forming the lower and back part of the head, by means of which the cranium is attached to the spine, and affording a communication between the two cavities by a large aperture, the *Foramen magnum*... *O[ccipital] foramen*, the *Foramen magnum*. *Ibid.*, *O[ccipital] muscle*, the hinder part of the occipito-frontalis muscle; it is flat and thin..[and] expands over the outer side of the occiput.

2. Having a large occiput; having the back of the head more developed than the front.

1873 M. ARNOLD *Lit. & Dogma* (1876) 290 A poor ill-endowed Semite, belonging to the occipital races.

B. *sb.* **a.** The occipital bone. **b.** The occipital muscle. **c.** *pl.* A pair of occipital plates on the head of some serpents.

1758 J. S. *Le Dran's Observ. Surg.* (1771) 64 The Foramen of the Occipital. **1861** BUSK in *Nat. Hist. Rev.* Apr., The superior semicircular ridges of the occipital.

Hence **oc'cipitally** *adv.*, as regards the occiput; in the region or direction of the hindhead.

Mod. Skull occipitally well developed.

†**occi'pitial,** *a. Obs. rare.* Also 6 -issial. [f. L. *occipiti-um* (see next) + -AL[1].] = OCCIPITAL.

1548–77 VICARY *Anat.* iii. (1888) 27 The Coronal bone, in ..the middest of the head..meteth with the seconde bone called Occipissial. **1650** BULWER *Anthropomet.* 15 That which we call the Occipitial Line..is drawn from the top of the Head to the first Vertebre of the Neck.

‖**occi'pitium.** *Obs. rare.* [L., = *occiput*, and more used.] = OCCIPUT.

1650 BULWER *Anthropomet.* 16 If that of the Occipitium transgresse its bounds, the Head is acuminate. **1706** PHILLIPS, *Occiput* or *Occipitium*.

occipito- (ək,sɪpɪtəʊ), before a vowel sometimes occipit-, used in *Anat.* as combining form of OCCIPUT, in adjs. expressing a relation or connexion between the occiput and another part, and denominating a ligament, muscle, measurement, etc.; as

occipito-'angular (see quot. 1890). **occipito-an'terior**, denoting that form of vertex presentation in child-birth in which the occiput is directed away from the sacrum of the mother. **o,ccipito-at'lantal, -'atloid**, pertaining to the occiput and the atlas vertebra. **occipito-'axial, -'axoid**, pertaining to the occiput and the axis vertebra. **occipito-'frontal**, pertaining to, or extending between, the back of the head and the forehead; also *ellipt.* as *sb.*, the ***occipito-frontal muscle*** or ***occipitofrontalis***, the large flat muscle of the scalp, composed of the occipital and frontal muscles with the epicranial aponeurosis connecting them. **occipito-'hyoid**, pertaining to the occiput and the hyoid bone. **occipito-'mastoid**, pertaining to the occiput and the mastoid process. **occipito-'mental** [L. *mentum* chin], pertaining to the occiput and the chin, extending between these points. **occipito-'otic** [Gr. οὖς, ὠτ- ear], pertaining to the occiput and the ear. **occipito-pa'rietal**, pertaining to the occipital and parietal bones. **occipito-po'sterior**, denoting that form of vertex presentation in child-birth in which the occiput is directed towards the sacrum of the mother. **occipitor'bicular**, connecting the occiput with an orbicular muscle. **occipito-'scapular**, pertaining to the occiput and the scapula or shoulder-blade. **occipito-'sphenoid, -sphe'noidal**, pertaining to the occipital and sphenoidal bones. **occipito-'temporal**, pertaining to the occipital and temporal bones.

1890 *Cent. Dict.*, **Occipito-angular*, pertaining to or common to the occipital lobe and the angular convolution. **1898** Occipito-angular [see CORTICIPETAL *a.*]. **1831** C. D. MEIGS tr. *Velpeau's Elem. Treat. Midwifery* v. 290 The English accoucheurs..bestow the title of natural labour only upon the *occipito-anterior position, while according to them, the occipito-posterior position belongs to the class of preternatural labour. **1974** PASSMORE & ROBSON *Compan. Med. Stud.* III. 11/1 (*caption*) Vertex presentation, left occipito-anterior position, well flexed. **1831** R. KNOX *Cloquet's Anat.* 178 Anterior *Occipito-Atlantal Ligament. *Ibid.* 103 Another ligament named the *occipito-axoid. [**1746** PARSONS in *Phil. Trans.* XLIV. 8 The Office of the *Occipito-Frontalis is to pull the Skin of the Head backward, drawing up the Eye-brows.] **1811** HOOPER *Med.*

Dict., *Occipito-frontalis*..Occipito-frontal of Dumas. **1857** BULLOCK *Cazeaux' Midwif.* 220 The occipito-frontal extends from the occipital protuberance to the frontal boss. **1892** *Syd. Soc. Lex.*, **Occipito-hyoid muscle*, an occasional muscle arising from the occipital bone and inserted into the hyoid bone. **1855** HOLDEN *Hum. Osteol.* (1878) 114 The '*occipito-mastoid suture'..connects the occipital with the mastoid portion of the temporal bone. **1857** BULLOCK *Cazeaux' Midwif.* 221 The greatest circumference of the head corresponds with the *occipito-mental diameter. **1875** HUXLEY in *Encycl. Brit.* I. 761/1 The squamosal..is..somewhat loosely united with the frontal and parietal and with the complex *occipito-otic bone. **1892** *Syd. Soc. Lex.*, **Occipito-parietal index*, the relation between the transverse diameter of the skull and the distance from one asterion to the other, the former being taken at 100. **1831** *Occipito-posterior [see *occipito-anterior* above]. **1971** *Brit. Med. Bull.* XXVII. 49/1 Impaired performance was associated with toxaemia, occipitoposterior presentation and delivery in an ambulance. **1854** OWEN in *Circ. Sc.*, *Organ. Nat.* I. 232 An *occipito-sphenoidal bone..formed..by the coalescence of the basioccipital with the basisphenoid.

occiput ('ɒksɪpʌt). Chiefly *Anat.* [L. *occiput* back of head, f. *ob-* against + *caput* head: in F. *occiput* (1372 in Hatz.-Darm.).] The back or hinder part of the head.

[**1398** TREVISA *Barth. De. P.R.* v. iv. (1495) 108 The occiput, the nolle, is the hynder parte of the heed.] **1602** *2nd Pt. Return fr. Parnass.* II. i. 516 Your occiput. I meane your head peece. *c* **1645** HOWELL *Lett.* II. xvii, Expedition is the life of action, otherwise Time may shew his bald occiput, and shake his posteriors at them in derision. **1699** *Phil. Trans.* XXI. 400 Ruffians, who first by a Blow on the Occiput knockt him to the Ground. **1826** KIRBY & SP. *Entomol.* III. 365 *Occiput* (the Occiput). The back part of the head when it is vertical, or nearly so, to its point of junction with the trunk. **1881** MIVART *Cat* 81 The straight but inclined line of the occiput.

b. The occipital bone of the skull.

1578 BANISTER *Hist. Man* Proem B iv, The first Vertebre inseparably growne to Occiput. **1836** SIR G. HEAD *Home Tour* 263 It was but half a skull,..the occiput had entirely disappeared. **1865** LUBBOCK *Preh. Times* xiv. (1869) 506 The American skulls are characterised by a flattened occiput.

†**oc'cise**, *v.* *Obs.* *rare*⁻¹. [f. L. *occīs-*, ppl. stem of *occīd-ĕre* to cut down, kill. Cf. *excise*, *incise*.] *trans.* To kill, slay.

1560 ROLLAND *Crt. Venus* III. 268 Acteon quhome that ȝe gart occise With his awin doggis.

†**oc'cision.** *Obs.* [a. F. *occision* (11th c. in Littré), ad. L. *occīsiōn-em*, n. of action from *occīd-ĕre* to kill, slay.] Killing, slaying (esp. of a number of people, as in battle); slaughter.

1375 BARBOUR *Bruce* XIV. 220 The richt nobil Erll..Maid sic a slauchtir in the toune, And swa felloune occisioune. *c* **1430** *Pilgr. Lyf Manhode* II. cl. (1869) 135 Homicidye it is cleped..and occisioun. **1491** CAXTON *Vitas Patr.* (W. de W. 1495) v. xiv. 344 a/2 The horryble occysyon whiche thou haste commysed. **1536** BELLENDEN *Cron. Scot.* (1821) II. 354 The place quhare maist occision and slauchter wes of Danis. **1594** ? GREENE *Selimus* Wks. 1881–3 XIV. 287 Why stand I still, and rather do not flie The great occision which the victors make. *a* **1677** HALE *Hist. Placit. Cor.* xlii. (1736) I. 496 This kind of occision of a man according to the laws of the kingdom and in execution thereof ought not to be numbred in the rank of crimes.

Occitan ('ɒksɪtən, ‖ɔksitɑ̃). [Fr.]

a. Old Provençal, the *langue d'Oc*. **b.** Modern Provençal; *spec.* (see quot. 1974). Also *attrib.* or as *adj.* Also **Occitanian** (ɒksɪ'teɪnɪən) *sb.* and *a.*

1940 M. BELGION tr. *de Rougemont's Passion & Society* II. vi. 90 The whole of the Occitanian, Petrarchian, and Dantesque lyric has but a single theme—love. **1957** *Archivum Linguisticum* IX. II. 107 *Uniō* thrives in French, the adjoining fringe of Occitanian, and France-Provençal. **1960** [see LANGUEDOCIAN *a.* and *sb.*]. **1961** P. GREEN tr. *Oldenbourg's Massacre at Montségur* i. 18 Languedoc itself, the area where the Occitan dialect was spoken, was not a major Power. **1964** G. PRICE in *Archivum Linguisticum* XVI. 34 In the twelfth and thirteenth centuries, Occitan—or Provençal, as it is more usually known—was one of the major European literary languages. *Ibid.*, The whole Occitan-speaking area, from the Alps to the Pyrenees. **1970** *Times Lit. Suppl.* 8 Jan. 40/2 Occitanian or Provençal (raised again to the status of a literary language by the efforts of the Felibrige). **1971** P. WOLFF *Western Languages* v. 147 The years around 1100 also show the sudden appearance of lyrical poetry in Occitan, first made known in written form by the Duke troubadour William of Aquitaine (1071–1127). **1972** W. B. LOCKWOOD *Panorama Indo-European Lang.* 33 Provençal survives today in certain rural localities... Provençal is sometimes termed Occitan... **1974** R. A. HALL *External Hist. Romance Lang.* 26 Modern Provençal has had two main standard varieties: i. That of the lower Rhône valley and the French Riviera.., often called 'Mistralien'... ii. 'Occitan', a somewhat different variety with its base in the usage of Languedoc. Much, but not all, of the difference between 'Mistralien' and 'Occitan' lies in orthographical details.

occlude (ə'klu:d), *v.* Chiefly in scientific use. Also (*rare*) **obclude**. [ad. L. *oc-*, *obclūd-ĕre* to shut up, f. *ob-* (OB- 1 b, c) + *claudĕre* to close. Cf. mod.F. *occlure*.]

1. *trans.* To shut or stop up so as to prevent anything from passing in, out, or through; to obstruct (a passage); to close (a vessel or opening).

1597 A. M. tr. *Guillemeau's Fr. Chirurg.* 26/2 An vlceratione wherbye her throate was allmost occluded and stopped. **1646** SIR T. BROWNE *Pseud. Ep.* II. vi. 97 Ginger is the root of..an herbaceous plant..which..they take up, and..role it up in earth, whereby occluding the pores, they conserve the naturall humidity. **1670** MAYNWARING *Vita Sana* vii. 85 Exercise opens the Pores..which otherwise by too much rest are occluded and shut up. *a* **1850** CALHOUN *Wks.* (1874) II. 105 There was scarcely a port in Europe, which..was not occluded to British commerce. **1854** J. SCOFFERN in *Orr's Circ. Sc.*, *Chem.* 303 Occlude either end of the..tube with a..bung. **1880** M. MACKENZIE *Dis. Throat & Nose* I. 86 To produce suffocation by occluding the larynx. **1894** *Proc. Zool. Soc.* 434 Only about half the iris is visible, and even some part of the lens is obcluded.

2. a. To prevent the passage of (a thing) by placing something in the way; to shut in, out, or off; to inclose or exclude. Also, to cover or hide; *spec.* to cover (an eye) so as to block its sight.

1623 COCKERAM, *Occlude*, to shut out. **1657** TOMLINSON *Renou's Disp.* 60 Medicaments are occluded in some convenient vessel. **1879** STEVENSON *Trav. Cevennes* 102 The lights alternately occluded and revealed. **1909** H. G. WELLS *Tono-Bungay* I. ii. 74 In the middle was the brown coffin end,..half occluded by the vicar's Oxford hood. **1921** *Amer. Jrnl. Ophthalm.* IV. 239/1 The choice of the eye to be covered is usually determined by finding out which eye the patient uses for pointing or aiming at a distant object, and occluding the other, or if one eye is defective, by occluding that. **1932** *Ibid.* XV. 321/1 The nondominant eye is occluded by having its spectacle lens replaced..by a black patch. **1963** HIRSCH & WICK *Vision of Children* (1964) vii. 223 For suppression or for amblyopia with central (foveal) fixation, the preferred eye is usually occluded (direct occlusion). **1975** *Nature* 6 Feb. 406/1 During early childhood amblyopia can be cured by simple treatments such as by occluding the good eye for a period.

b. *Chem.* Of certain metals and other solids: To absorb and retain (gases) within their substance.

1866 T. GRAHAM in *Phil. Trans.* CLVI. 423 (21 June) It may be allowed to speak of this [power to absorb hydrogen at a red heat, and to retain that gas] as a power to *occlude* (to shut up) hydrogen, and the result as the *occlusion* of hydrogen by platinum. *Ibid.* 424 One volume of spongy platinum appears capable of occluding 1·48 vol. hydrogen. **1880** *Athenæum* No. 2748. 828 This Metal [Aluminium] occludes Hydrogen. **1881** C. W. SIEMENS in *Nature* XXIII. 327 These gases are partly occluded or absorbed within the coal. **1884** *Cassell's Fam. Mag.* Apr. 319/1 Hydrogen gas should be occluded in one of the platinum plates.

3. *intr.* *Dentistry.* Of a tooth: to come into contact with a tooth or teeth of the other set.

1888 E. S. TALBOT *Irregularities of Teeth* I. v. 64 When the first permanent molars in both jaws have erupted so that they occlude, this will prevent forward progression. *Ibid.* 65 The anterior teeth do not occlude, and when the jaws are closed quite a space is observed. **1913** A. HOPEWELL-SMITH *Introd. Dental. Anat. & Physiol.* xi. 233 The teeth in Man do not..occlude by means of their cusps, but by a perfect system of interdigitation. **1974** GEIGER & HIRSCHFELD *Minor Tooth Movement* (ed. 3) ii. 41 The mesiobuccal cusp of the maxillary first molar occludes with the buccal groove of the mandibular first molar in centric occlusion.

4. *trans.* *Chem.* To carry (a substance) out of solution by occlusion (sense 5); to trap within growing crystals of a precipitate.

1920 *Chem. Abstr.* XIV. 3030 Ca and Mg compds. are occluded in the pptn. of Fe‴ by NH_4OH. **1929** L. P. HAMMETT *Solutions of Electrolytes* I. iii. 40 Cadmium sulfide carries down or occludes barium sulfide, although the latter is a very soluble substance. **1930** W. T. HALL *Textbk. Quantitative Analysis* xi. 141 If the barium sulfate adsorbs or occludes ferric sulfate, the latter will lose SO_3 upon ignition. **1950** KOLTHOFF & SANDELL *Textbk. Quantitative Inorg. Analysis* (rev. ed.) viii. 111 If the incorporated material fits in the crystal lattice of the precipitate (host crystal), it is occluded in the form of *mixed* crystals or a solid solution. **1952** DIEHL & SMITH *Quantitative Analysis* ii. 33 Precipitates that occlude the mother liquor seriously should be dissolved and reprecipitated under such conditions that little foreign material..is present in the solution.

5. *intr.* *Meteorol.* Of a front or frontal system: to undergo occlusion (sense 7).

1940 N. SHAW *Forecasting Weather* (ed. 3) xxviii. 583 There is a further supply of warm air available to provide a warm sector in the new formation, which runs through a life-history..and in due course occludes. **1955** W. J. SAUCIER *Princ. Meteorol. Analysis* ix. 270/1 The front occludes further, and meantime the cyclonic circulation becomes larger and more symmetric. **1969** S. PETTERSSEN *Introd. Meteorol.* (ed. 3) xiii. 212 During the further development, the cold front overtakes the warm front and the system is said to occlude.

Hence **o'ccluded** *ppl. a.*, *spec.* in *Meteorol.*, applied to a front or frontal system in which a cold front has caught up with a warm front; **o'ccluding** *ppl. a.*

1802 PALEY *Nat. Theol.* xvi. §4 (1819) 249 The opening of this occluded mouth. **1866** T. GRAHAM in *Phil. Trans.* CLVI. 424 (21 June) The volume of occluded hydrogen is much larger than in the fused platinum. **1882** PROCTOR *Fam. Sc. Stud.* 52 Some meteors carry many times their own volume of occluded gas. **1899** *Allbutt's Syst. Med.* VI. 179 These veins may contain..occluding thrombi. **1922** BJERKNES & SOLBERG in *Geofysiske Publikationer* III. I. 4 The remaining part of the warm sector near the centre also disappears fairly soon, so that the cyclone on the ground only consists of cold air... For this type we have chosen the name 'occluded cyclones'. **1934** D. BRUNT *Physical & Dynamical Meteorol.* xviii. 324 When a depression has become occluded, the cold front trails behind the depression. **1941** B. HAURWITZ *Dynamic Meteorol.* xv. 315 In this situation the occluded cyclone can increase its kinetic energy again. **1955** [see OCCLUSION 7]. **1970** F. W. COLE *Introd. Meteorol.* xii. 266 If an occluded front is well advanced in development, the warm-front portion may have little or no effect on the ensuing weather.

occludent (ə'klu:dənt), *a.* and *sb.* [ad. L. *occlūdent-em*, pr. pple. of *occlūd-ĕre* to OCCLUDE.]

a. *adj.* Having the property or function of occluding. **b.** *sb.* Something having this property.

1762 STERNE *Tr. Shandy* V. xl, The radical heat and moisture..may be preserved..by consubstantials, impriments, and occludents. [BACON *Hist. Vitæ & Mortis* Canon xxvi, Per Consubstantialia, Imprimentia, & Occludentia.] **1864** WEBSTER, *Occludent*, serving to close, shutting up. **1877** HUXLEY *Anat. Inv. Anim.* vi. 299 On the inner side of the occludent margin of its scutum.

occluder (ə'klu:də(r)). *Ophthalm.* [f. OCCLUD(E *v.* + -ER[1].] Any device designed to occlude an eye.

1930 *Brit. Jrnl. Ophthalm.* XIV. 520 Many varieties of occluder..have been devised. **1949** S. DUKE-ELDER *Text-bk. Ophthalm.* IV. xlv. 3917 For older children who can be trusted not to peep round it, a simple occluder of metal..or rubber..may be attached to the spectacles... These should be replaced by strapping on a tie-on occluder during the night. **1974** *Nature* 11 Oct. 506/2 One eye was centred on a projection perimeter (the other eye was always covered with a plasticine occluder).

occlusal (ə'klu:səl), *a.* *Dentistry.* [f. L. *occlūs-*, ppl. stem of *occlūd-ere* to OCCLUDE + -AL.] Of, pertaining to, or involved in occlusion (sense 3); *spec.* applied to the surface of a tooth that comes into contact with a tooth in the other jaw in occlusion.

1897 S. H. GUILDFORD in E. C. Kirk *Amer. Text-bk. Operative Dentistry* vi. 142 Cavities upon the occlusal surface are very accessible and in full view. *Ibid.* 143 The occlusal surface of an upper first or second molar presents two points liable to decay. **1939** I. HIRSCHFELD *Toothbrush* i. 2 (*caption*) Mandible of Australian aboriginal, showing advanced occlusal wear. **1951** J. M. SCHWEITZER *Oral Rehabilitation* xxxi. 623 The question of whether natural teeth should have flat occlusal surfaces..or occlusal surfaces that have cusps. **1974** P. E. DAWSON (*title*) Evaluation, diagnosis, and treatment of occlusal problems.

Hence **o'cclusally** *adv.*, from or on an occlusal surface.

1912 B. E. LISCHER *Princ. & Methods Orthodontics* xiii. 202 An arm extended from the alignment wire..is made from an ordinary tube hook and prevented from dropping occlusally, or being forced gingivally, by flattening the alignment wire with a file along its lingual surface. **1946** TYLMAN & PEYTON *Acrylics* xvi. 408/2 Inlay wax is then added occlusally to the thin casting, the occlusal plane is determined, and finally the occlusal surfaces and contour are carved in the wax. **1969** *Gloss. Terms Dentistry* (*B.S.I.*) 72 *Occlusally approaching clasp*, a clasp originating on the occlusal side of the survey line and terminating in the infra-bulge area.

occluse (ə'klu:s), *a.* [ad. L. *occlūs-us*, pa. pple. of *occlūd-ĕre* to OCCLUDE.] Occluded; stopped up, closed; shut up, enclosed.

1669 HOLDER *Elem. Speech* 78 The Italians..make the Occluse Appulse, especially the Gingival, softer than we do. **1857** MAYNE *Expos. Lex.*, *Occlusus*,..applied to the florets of the fig shut up in the fleshy receptacle or fruit: occluse.

occlusion (ə'klu:ʒən). [ad. L. **occlūsiōn-em*, n. of action from *occlūd-ĕre*, *occlūs-*: see OCCLUDE. So mod.F. *occlusion* (1808 in Hatz.-Darm.).]

1. The action of occluding or fact of being occluded; stopping up, closing. (Chiefly scientific.)

c **1645** HOWELL *Lett.* I. III. xxix, By the constriction and occlusion of the orifice of the Matrix. **1746** PARSONS in *Phil. Trans.* XLIV. 14 To explain the Manner of the Occlusion of the Eye. **1786** H. LEE in Sparks *Corr. Amer. Rev.* (1853) IV. 137 In agreeing to the occlusion of the navigation of the Mississippi. **1876** tr. *Wagner's Gen. Pathol.* (ed. 6) 165 Anæmia occurs from contraction or occlusion of arteries.

2. *Chem.* The retention of gases in the pores of metals or other substances.

1866 T. GRAHAM in *Phil. Trans.* CLVI. 423 [see OCCLUDE 2 b]. *Ibid.* 426 The occlusion of hydrogen by palladium. **1871** ROSCOE *Elem. Chem.* 186 The fact that red-hot platinum and iron are porous for hydrogen may be explained by the absorption (or occlusion) of this gas on the one side of the metallic tube or plate and its evaporation at the other side.

3. *Dentistry.* The position assumed by the two sets of teeth relative to each other when the mouth is closed; the state of having the jaws closed and the teeth in contact.

1880 N. W. KINGSLEY *Treat. Oral Deformities* xxi. 525 In extreme pain (except in cases where the patient is suffering from periodontitis, when the occlusion of the jaws intensifies the suffering), the teeth are brought together with great force. **1904** V. H. JACKSON *Orthodontia & Orthopædia of Face* 198 The opening of the bite in any manner with apparatus, if continued for a considerable time, is likely to prove detrimental to the occlusion. **1962** BLAKE & TROTT *Periodontology* xv. 156 In the European it is usual to find that during lateral movements to either side molar and pre-molar teeth of one side remain in occlusion, while contact is completely lost on the other side. **1974** HARTY & ROBERTS *Restorative Procedures Practising Dentist* xii. 167 It is very important that the occlusion is studied and corrected before any fixed or removable prosthesis is made.

4. *Phonetics.* The act of closing, or the period of closure of, the breath passage during the articulation of an orally-released consonant, or of the mouth passage during the articulation of a nasal consonant.

1906 *Mod. Lang. Rev.* I. iv. 346 'Occlusion', was, if I remember aright, used by Wilkins in the seventeenth century, but this hardly justifies the employment of such a pedantic term instead of 'stoppage', 'closure', or 'stop'. **1926** *Germanic Rev.* I. i. 58 Here, 'occlusion' in the glottis does not mean glottal stop, but the partial occlusion in the articulation of voice sounds. **1935** J. S. Kenyon *Amer. Pronunc.* (ed. 6) 51 This initial contact for any sound that has contact is called the closure, or occlusion, and the end of the contact is called the opening, or release. **1943** *Amer. Speech* XVIII. 39 In pronouncing such phrases as 'Hello, Pete!'.. a British speaker ordinarily articulates the vowel of the final syllable, lifts his tongue to make the closure for the final consonant (applosion), holds it there from eight to twelve hundredths of a second (occlusion), and then breaks the closure with a sharp downward snap of the tongue which produces a clear 'pop' (explosion). **1966** B. Trnka *Phonol. Analysis Present-Day Stand. Eng.* (rev. ed.) ii. 11 In producing *l*, the tip of the tongue forms an occlusion against the alveolar ridge.

5. *Chem.* A kind of co-precipitation (see quots.); the trapping of foreign material by growing crystals of a precipitate.

1920 *Chem. Abstr.* XIV. 3029 (*heading*) The occlusion of lime and magnesia by ferric oxide. **1929** L. P. Hammett *Solutions of Electrolytes* i. iii. 40 Analytical separations are.. never quite as satisfactory..because of the existence of occlusion. **1932** [see co-precipitation]. **1942** W. Rieman et al. *Quantitative Analysis* (ed. 2) xvii. 244 The phenomenon [*sc.* coprecipitation] has also been called contamination, inclusion, occlusion, and adsorption. The last two terms should not be used as synonyms for coprecipitation because they denote certain mechanisms that apply to some but not all cases of coprecipitation. **1947** *Jrnl. Chem. Education* XXIV. 597/1 The term *occlusion* has been used to refer to contamination of a precipitate by the incorporation into the body of it during its formation of foreign substances whether or not the latter give rise to mixed crystal formation (solid solution)... It has been used to include both solid solution phenomena and contamination of the precipitate by adsorption..; it has been used to indicate contamination by basic salts and other substances not adsorbed and not in solid solution..; and I have heard a noted analytical chemist reserve the term to indicate the contamination of a precipitate by mechanically trapped solute or solvent ions or molecules. No doubt one could locate other senses in which *occlusion* has been used; the term is almost omnivorous. **1966** E. M. Rattenbury *Introd. Titrimetric & Gravimetric Anal.* vii. 146 Sometimes water or mother liquor is imprisoned by occlusion. **1969** E. S. Gilreath *Elem. Quantitative Chem.* x. 138 Occlusion is a form of coprecipitation in which impurities are enclosed..within the lattice structure of a crystalline precipitate. *Ibid.*, Contamination by occlusion..can produce serious errors in gravimetric analysis.

6. *Ophthalm.* The covering of an eye so as to block its sight.

1920 *Brit. Jrnl. Ophthalm.* IV. 146 (*heading*) The influence of prolonged monocular occlusion in revealing errors of the muscle balance. **1973** *Nature* 26 Jan. 288/2 The technique of monocular occlusion has long been used by ophthalmologists in the therapeutic treatment of such conditions as strabismus (squint) and amblyopia.

7. *Meteorol.* The overtaking of the warm front of a depression by the cold front, so that the body of warm air between them is forced upwards off the earth's surface by two wedges of cold air; also, the occluded front so formed.

1922 Bjerknes & Solberg in *Geofysiske Publikationer* III. i. 6 No boundary surface results when both branches meet during the occlusion of the cyclone. *Ibid.*, The occlusion then assumes the character of a cold front with a rather narrow rain zone. **1934** D. Brunt *Physical & Dynamical Meteorol.* xviii. 311 The occlusion begins at the centre, where the cold front has a shorter path to cover before overtaking the warm front. *Ibid.*, There will still be a warm sector in the upper air for some time after occlusion has taken place at the surface. **1941** B. Haurwitz *Dynamic Meteorol.* xv. 314 The part of the front where the cold front has caught up is called the occlusion. **1944** Hewson & Longley *Meteorol. Theoret. & Appl.* xvi. 277 The rate of occlusion in several types of frontal depressions may be discussed qualitatively. **1955** W. J. Saucier *Princ. Meteorol. Analysis* ix. 270/1 The cold front overtakes the warm front, resulting in an occluded front (or occlusion). **1974** *Encycl. Brit. Macropædia* V. 394/2 There still is a belt of thick cloud and rain along the line of the old occlusion.

occlusive (əˈkluːsɪv), *a.* and *sb.* [f. L. *occlūs-*, ppl. stem of *occlūd-ĕre* to occlude + -ive.]

A. *adj.* Having the function of occluding or closing. Also, characterized by occlusion.

1888 R. Park in *Medical News* (Philad.) LIII. 117 The wounds..closed with an antiseptic, occlusive dressing. **1961** *Lancet* 22 July 192/1 Of three techniques for treating the stump [of the umbilicus]—standard non-occlusive spirit technique, antibiotic or antiseptic non-occlusive technique, and occlusive technique with or without antibiotics—they showed the last to be the most reliable and the most effective. **1972** *Where* May/June 135/2 The sheath, the various occlusive caps, even chemical contraceptives do provide some barrier to the spread of germs from one person to another. **1974** Passmore & Robson *Compan. Med. Stud.* III. xvii. 16/2 The most important cause of occlusive arterial disease is atherosclerosis.

B. *sb. Phonetics.* A consonant sound produced with stoppage of breath by the organs of speech; a stop with suppression of the explosive sound.

1902 [see affricate *v.*]. **1943** *Amer. Speech* XVIII. 39 The only audible expression of the final consonant..is the cutting-off of the preceding vowel sound by the raising of the tongue to make the closure... The explosive stop here becomes what may most conveniently be termed a simple occlusive. **1976** *Archivum Linguisticum* VII. 183 He cannot add $^*H_3$ and a third series of guttural occlusives to the number of fallen consonantal phonemes he has postulated.

occluso- (əˈkluːsəʊ), comb. form of occlusal *a.* or occlusion (sense 3), as in **occluso-cerˈvical, occlusoˈgingival** *adjs.*

1923 Dorland *Med. Dict.* (ed. 12) 755/1 Occluso-cervical. **1962** J. E. H. Fowler *Heinemann Mod. Dict. Dental Students* 182/1 *Occlusocervical*, relating to the occlusal surface and the neck of a tooth. **1940** J. Osborne *Dental Mech.* xii. 136 The brush should be run in an occluso-gingival direction. **1963** C. R. Cowell et al. *Inlays, Crowns, & Bridges* iii. 14 Measuring the occlusogingival depth on the side of the tooth.

occlusor (əˈkluːsə(r)). [agent-n. in L. form, from *occlūdĕre* to occlude.] Something that occludes or closes; chiefly in *Anat.* a structure which closes an opening. Also *attrib.*, as ***occlusor apparatus, muscle.***

1877 Huxley *Anat. Inv. Anim.* vii. 438 The vocal organ of the Fly would thus appear to be a modification of the occlusor apparatus of the stigmata. **1878** Bell *Gegenbaur's Comp. Anat.* 355 They form a defensive organ for the eye by the possession of occlusor muscles.

occoast, occoy, obs. or erron. ff. accost, accoy.

occome, occorne, occour, obs. ff. oakum, acorn, ocker.

occra, -ro, var. okra.

†**oˈccrustate,** *v. Obs.* [f. med. or mod.L. type **occrustāre, -tāt-*, f. *ob-* (ob- 1 c) + *crustāre* to crust.] *trans.* To enclose in a crust, to encrust; *fig.* to harden, render obdurate.

1653 H. More *Conject. Cabbal.* (1713) 240 To arm and occrustate themselves in this devilish Apostasy. **1681** —— *Exp. Dan.* Pref. 101 These deceivers, who are sealed and occrustated in the trade of their impieties.

occular, -ate, obs. forms of ocular, -ate.

†**occulˈcation.** *Obs. rare*$^{-0}$. [n. of action from L. *ob-, occulcāre* to trample down, f. *ob-* (ob- 1 c) + *calcāre* to tread.]

1656 Blount *Glossogr.*, *Occulcation*, a treading on or spurning.

occult (əˈkʌlt, ˈɒkʌlt), *a.* (*sb.*) [ad. L. *occult-us*, pa. pple. of *occul-ĕre* to cover over, hide, conceal, f. *ob-, oc-* (ob- 1 c) + **cel-ĕre* (= OIr. *cel-im*, OTeut. *hel-an*, hele *v.*[1]); cf. L. *cēlāre* to hide. OF. *occult* (12th c.) app. did not enter Eng.]

A. *adj.* Hidden (*lit.* and *fig.*).

1. a. Hidden (from sight); concealed (by something interposed); not exposed to view. Now *rare* or *Obs.*

1567 Maplet *Gr. Forest* Pref. A vij b, Mettalles..are nothing else but the earths hid and occult Plants. **1635** Swan *Spec. M.* vi. § 2 (1643) 188 It joyneth it self unto other seas..through some occult passages under ground. **1671** Grew *Anat. Plants* i. i. §13 The lesser of the two said Appendents lies occult between the two Lobes of the Bean. **1795** T. Maurice *Hindostan* (1820) I. i. vii. 214 The stars of the hydra..became occult when the sun rose. **1850** Rossetti *Blessed Damozel* xiv, We two will stand beside that shrine, Occult, withheld, untrod.

b. Applied to a line drawn in the construction of a figure, but not forming part of the finished figure; also to a dotted line. ? *Obs.*

1669 Sturmy *Mariner's Mag.* iv. 205 In the Latitude of 13 *deg.* 10 *min.* I draw..an occult Parallel, and reckon.. towards the West: I draw by that Longitude an occult Meridian. **1688** R. Holme *Armoury* iii. 139/2 *Occult* or *White Line*; is a Line drawn out by points or pricks. **1703** Moxon *Mech. Exerc.* 324 Describe an occult Arch. **1731** W. Halfpenny *Perspective* 2 Draw the Occult Lines EA, = EB. **1823** P. Nicholson *Pract. Build.* 559 Occult arcs, or such as are to be rubbed out again.

c. *Med.* Of a disease or bodily process: †inexplicable, obscure; unaccompanied by any readily discernible signs or symptoms; ***occult blood***, blood abnormally present in some material (esp. fæces) but too scanty to be readily recognized; so ***occult bleeding*** [tr. G. *okkulte(magen)blutung* (I. Boas 1901, in *Deutsch. med. Wochenschr.* 16 May 315/2)].

[**1690** S. Blanckaert *Lexicon Novum Medicum* 450 *Occulti morbi*... Angl. Hiden disease.] **1809** R. Carmichael *Ess. Effects of Carbonate upon Cancer* iv. 292 Three of these lucky people had occult cancers of the breast, and a fourth had an occult cancer of the lip. **1820** R. Hooper *Lexicon Medicum* (ed. 4) 623/2 *Occult quality*, a term that has been much used by writers that had not clear ideas of what they undertook to explain; and which served therefore only for a cover to their ignorance. **1854** W. E. Swaine tr. *Rokitausky's Man. Path. Anat.* I. ix. 260 This process takes place either in the depths of the growth,..as so-termed occult cancer; or upon the free surface of the body or of a mucous cavity, as so-called apert or open cancer. **1872** D. C. Black *On Functional Dis. Renal Organs* ii. 108 The condition to which Dr. Barnes has applied the term occult menstruation... Owing to the imperforate condition of the hymen, the menstrual flux accumulates in the *cul de sac*.. formed by the upper portion of the vagina. **1904** *Progressive Med.* IV. 24 Occult blood is constantly found in cancer of the gastrointestinal tract. *Ibid.*, Occult bleeding in the cases of ulcer was most frequently observed when the patient had recently complained of pain in the stomach. **1905** G. R. Butler *Diagnostics of Internal Med.* (ed. 2) i. xii. 147 'Occult' blood is a term applied to blood in the fæces (or stomach contents) which is in such small quantity that it can not be recognised by the eye, or is so altered as not to be identified by the microscope. **1936** E. N. Chamberlain *Symptoms & Signs Clin. Med.* xii. 387 The most important chemical test applicable in the clinic room is that for occult blood. **1961** R. D. Baker *Essent. Path.* xvii. 458 Occult carcinoma of the prostate is a frequent finding at autopsy in persons who have died from other causes. **1962** *Lancet* 1 Dec. 1145/1 Orthotoluidine sampling of these motions was strongly positive for occult blood. **1973** *Q. Jrnl. Med.* XLII. 125 (*heading*) Occult rickets and osteomalacia amongst the Asian immigrant population. **1973** *Lancet* 4 Aug. 262/1 Occult bleeding in the alimentary tract.

2. Not disclosed or divulged, privy, secret; kept secret; communicated only to the initiated.

1533 Bellenden *Livy* i. (1822) 62 Began to rise ilk day occult slauchteris and cruelteis in his ciete. **1654** H. L'Estrange *Chas. I* (1655) 60 By occult interests of State. **1673** Ray *Journ. Low C., Milan* 255 These suffrages are all occult, that is, given by putting of balls into balloting-boxes. **1741** Middleton *Cicero* I. vi. 457 Ancient and occult sacrifices were polluted. **1841** D'Israeli *Amen. Lit.* (1867) 203 Printing remained..a secret and occult art. **1885–94** R. Bridges *Eros & Psyche* July iii, Of their plots occult [they] Sat whispering on their beds.

3. a. Not apprehended, or not apprehensible, by the mind; beyond the range of understanding or of ordinary knowledge; recondite, mysterious.

1545 Boorde *Pronost.* To Rdr. in *Introd. Knowl.* (1870) Forewords 25 To pronostycate any mater of the occulte iugements of god. **1665** Glanvill *Scepsis Sci.* iv. 20 Some secret Art of the Soul, which to us is utterly occult, and without the ken of our Intellects. **1751** Johnson *Rambler* No. 160 ¶8 Some have..an occult power of stealing upon the affections. **1830** Herschel *Stud. Nat. Phil.* i. iii. 39 If.. the essential qualities..be really occult, or incapable of being expressed in any form intelligible to our understandings.

b. Not affecting, or traceable by, the senses; imperceptible. Now *rare* or merged in prec.

1650 Bulwer *Anthropomet.* 170 The dissipation of those things which constitute our body, being occult and a thing which escapes the reach of our senses. **1743** *Lond. & Country Brew.* iv. (ed. 2) 297 There..ensues an occult Commotion upon first mixing it (tho' apparent enough soon after). **1876** Birch *Rede Lect. Egypt* 20 Amen at Thebes, the occult or unseen God hidden in the powers and operations of nature.

c. Applied in early science or natural philosophy to physical qualities not manifest to direct observation but discoverable only by experiment, or to those whose nature was unknown or unexplained; latent; also *transf.* treating of such qualities, experimental. *Obs.* exc. *Hist.* or as merged in 3 a.

a **1652** J. Smith *Sel. Disc.* x. iii. (1856) 473 Those natural antipathies..being nothing else but occult qualities, or natural instincts. **1662** Stillingfl. *Orig. Sacr.* iii. ii. §14 It will be the least of all pardonable in the exploders of substantiall forms and occult qualities, when the Origine of the whole world is resolved into an occult quality which gives motion to Atoms. **1671** J. Webster *Metallogr.* ii. 26 Others experimentally knew something in this occult Science. **1704** Newton *Optics* (J.), The Aristotelians give the name of occult qualities..to such qualities..as they supposed to lie hid in bodies, and to be the unknown causes of manifest effects. **1717** J. Keill *Anim. Oecon.* (1738) 52 How the Blood came first by its Motion..I leave to be determined by the occult Philosophers. **1727** De Foe *Syst. Magic* i. ii. (1840) 58 Occult powers, known in Nature, but unknown and unseen by vulgar heads and eyes. **1831** Brewster *Newton* (1855) II. xv. 60 He accuses him of reviving the occult qualities of the schools.

4. Of the nature of or pertaining to those ancient and mediæval reputed sciences (or their modern representatives) held to involve the knowledge or use of agencies of a secret and mysterious nature (as magic, alchemy, astrology, theosophy, and the like); also *transf.* treating of or versed in these; magical, mystical.

a **1633** Austin *Medit.* (1635) 249 Much vertue and power is attributed to these..by the Occult Philosophers. **1651** J. F[reake] (*title*) Three books of Occult Philosophy, written by Henry Cornelius Agrippa..Translated out of the Latin into the English Tongue. **1711** Shaftesb. *Charac.* (1737) III. ii. i. 53 From this Parent-Country of occult Sciences.. he was presum'd..to have learnt..judicial Astrology. **1832** W. Irving *Alhambra* I. 216 A beetle of baked clay, covered with Arabic inscriptions, which was pronounced a prodigious amulet of occult virtues. **1851** D. Wilson *Preh. Ann.* (1863) II. iv. iii. 257 A charm, or occult sign. **1884** H. Jennings *Phallicism* xiii. 133 An assertion of the occult philosophers.

†**B.** *sb.* Something hidden or secret. *Obs. rare.*

1656 S. H. *Gold. Law* 70 Its Natures, and not Names; its occults, and not occulars, entitle to the title King.

occult (əˈkʌlt), *v.* [ad. L. *occultā-re* to hide, conceal, freq. of *occulĕre*: see occult *a.* Cf. mod.F. *occulter* (Littré).] **a.** *trans.* To hide, conceal; to cut off from view by interposing some other body; also *fig.* Now chiefly in scientific or technical use (see b and occulting below; cf. *eclipse*).

1527 Andrew *Brunswyke's Distyll. Waters* B ij b, The same water occulteth and hydeth the pymples..in the face. **1597** A. M. tr. *Guillemeau's Fr. Chirurg.* xvii b/1 The vise which is occultede in the end of the handle. **1830** *Fraser's Mag.* I. 745 Knowing where the cat was occulted. **1870** Proctor *Other Worlds* vi. 152 The sun is occulted in the forenoon and afternoon but free from eclipse in the middle of the day. **1887** Rossetti *Keats* viii. 153 Nor was his personality by any means occulted. **1957** A. MacNab *Bulls of Iberia* vi. 61 In both the *gaonera* and the *mariposa* the man's body is fully exposed in front of the bull's face, and not occulted by the cloth lure. **1977** 'E. Crispin' *Glimpses of Moon* v. 76 The platform for the legs competition..had a wooden screen designed to occult the competitors from the groin upwards.

b. *spec.* in *Astron.* said of one heavenly body (as the moon, or a planet) hiding another (as a star, or a satellite) from view, by passing in front of it.

1764 Maskelyne in *Phil. Trans.* LIV. 391 The Virgin's spike was occulted by the ☽ this night. **1872** Proctor *Ess. Astron.* iii. 43 The epochs when the moon occults stars or when Jupiter's satellites are eclipsed or occulted.

c. *intr.* Of a lighthouse light: to be cut off from view as part of its cycle of light and dark.

1880, 1892 [implied in occulting *ppl. a.*]. **1902** *Encycl. Brit.* XXVI. 464/1 The light occults every ten seconds,.. the occultations being actuated by a double valve arrangement. **1964** J. Masters *Trial at Monomoy* i. 15 Close on the north the lighthouse tower edged into the view... That light occulted every four seconds.

Hence **o'cculted** *ppl. a.*, hidden, concealed; **o'cculter**, an apparatus for occulting lights; **o'cculting** *ppl. a.*, that occults; *spec.* in lighthouses, applied to a light cut off from view for a few seconds at regular intervals.

1597 A. M. tr. *Guillemeau's Fr. Chirurg.* 34/2 The occulted are soe called, because we noe wher externally espye them. **1602** Shaks. *Ham.* iii. ii. 85 If his occulted guilt, Do not it selfe vnkennell in one speech. **1880** *Trinity House Advt.* 30 Apr., During..June, 1880, the light at the North Foreland will be made occulting. That is to say, it will, once in every Half-minute, suddenly disappear for Five Seconds, and then as suddenly reappear at full power. **1892** *Strand Mag.* IV. 351/2 The occulting light..may be seen long after the tower itself is lost to view. **1902** *Encycl. Brit.* XXX. 256/1 This light shows, instead of one prolonged flash at intervals of one minute, as would be produced by the apparatus in the absence of a gas occulter, a group of short flashes.

occultation (ɒkəl'teɪʃən). [ad. L. *occultātiōn-em*, n. of action from *occultāre*: see prec. Cf. F. *occultation* in *Astron.* (*a* 1500 in Godef. *Compl.*).] The action of occulting or fact of being occulted.

1. Hiding, concealment (*obs.* in *gen.* sense); the fact of being cut off from view by something interposed. Now only scientific or technical: see also 2.

1432–50 tr. *Higden* (Rolls) III. 177 Suche occultacion other hidenge of kynges myȝhte be welle in the londe off Persides. **1582** N. Test. (Rhem.) p. xxvi, St. Augustine saith..In the Old Testament there is the occultation of the Newe; and in the New Testament there is the manifestation of the Old. **1678** Cudworth *Intell. Syst.* i. iv. §32. 508 Ignorantly attributing the Passions of Fruits, (their Appearances and Occultations) to the Gods..that preside over them. **1760–72** tr. *Juan & Ulloa's Voy.* (ed. 3) I. 444 At its occultation behind the Panecello its light was very faint. **1882** *Standard* 31 Mar. 1/3 The Light will be under occultation three times in quick succession every Minute.

2. *Astron.* †**a.** The disappearance of a star in the sun's rays when in an apparent position near that of the sun. *Obs.* **b.** The concealment of one heavenly body by another passing between it and the observer, as of a star or planet by the moon, or of a satellite by its primary planet. (Also, the concealment of a heavenly body behind the body of the earth; so in *circle of perpetual occultation*, for which see circle *sb.* 2 a.)

Commonly applied only in those cases in which the occulting body is of much greater apparent magnitude than that occulted; the (partial or total) concealment of the sun by the moon is called an *eclipse*. In the case of Jupiter's satellites, an *eclipse* takes place when a satellite passes into the planet's shadow, an *occultation* when it passes behind the planet's disk.

1551 Recorde *Cast. Knowl.* (1556) 196 When anye starre is so nyghe vnto the Son that the Sonne doothe take awaye or hyde the lyghte of it, it oughte to bee called the Hydynge or occultation of that starre, and not the settynge of that starre. **1613** Jackson *Creed* i. xxx. §6 The eleuation of the pole..doth giue vs the degrees of the others occultation. **1669** Flamstead in *Phil. Trans.* IV. 1102 In this Occultation,..the Center of the Moon passes very near the Star. **1827** Whately *Logic* (1837) 294 Those who.. registered the times of occultation of Jupiter's satellites. **1856** Kane *Arct. Expl.* I. xiii. 148 We had an occultation of Saturn at 2 A.M.

c. *fig.* Disappearance from view or notice.

1825 Jeffrey *Ess.* (1846) II. 199 The re-appearance of such an author after those long periods of occultation. **1840** Hood *Kilmansegg, Marriage* xxvii, To cloud the face of the honeymoon With a dismal occultation! **1892** A. Birrell *Res Judic.* vi. 206 The prospect of the coming occultation of personally disagreeable authors.

occultism (ə'kʌltɪz(ə)m, 'ɒkʌlt-). [f. occult *a.* + -ism.] The doctrine, principles, or practice of 'occult' science (magic, theosophy, etc.: see occult *a.* 4); mysticism.

1881 A. P. Sinnett *Occult World* (1883) 3 It is chiefly in the East that occultism is still kept up—in India and in adjacent countries. **1886** *St. James's Gaz.* 25 Sept. 6/1 Occultism was, indeed, a necessary concomitant of polytheism. **1895** *Thinker* VII. 541 Occultism deals with forces of nature not generally known.

occultist (ə'kʌltɪst, 'ɒkʌlt-). [f. as prec. + -ist.] One versed in, or believing in, occultism; a mystic. Also *attrib.*

1881 A. P. Sinnett *Occult World* (1883) 12 The occultists have been a race apart from an earlier period than we can fathom. **1886** *Forum* (N.Y.) Mar. 43 Our occultists and mystics had various..explanations of the higher significance of the sacred cross. **1902** *Encycl. Brit.* XXX. 275/1 Cabalistic, occultist, Indian, and modern spiritualistic ideas and formulas. **1977** R. L. Wolff *Gains & Losses* iv. 316 Charles Maurice Davies['s]..book *The Great Secret* (1896) ..was published anonymously. His occultist leanings were, however, well known.

Hence **occul'tistic** *a.*

1898 A. McMillan *Portentous Prophets* I. (Heading).

occultly (ə'kʌltlɪ), *adv.* [f. occult *a.* + -ly[2].] In an occult or hidden manner; secretly, privily; imperceptibly, latently; mysteriously, mystically.

1641 French *Distill.* v. (1651) 108 The humidity of the water hath the humidity of the salt laid up occultly in it. **1659** B. Harris *Parival's Iron Age* 272 The affairs of the last Assembly were conducted there so occultly. **1793** T. Taylor *Hymns* in *Sallust* etc. 162 Thy dreadful shield, in mystic fables fam'd, Occultly signifies the power untam'd. **1842** Mrs. Browning *Lett.* Sept. (1897) I. 109 To believe that philosophic thinking, like music, is involved, however occultly, in high ideality of any kind. **1895** *Westm. Gaz.* 14 Feb. 2/1 She [Madame Blavatsky]..assured her compatriot that before ever he appeared she knew occultly that he was being 'drawn towards her'.

o'ccultness. [f. as prec. + -ness.] The quality or state of being occult.

1727 Bailey vol. II, *Occultness*, hiddenness, concealedness. **1755** in Johnson. **1875** Masson *Wordsw.*, etc. 280 Consisting in a certain unusual degree of richness.. exquisiteness..occultness, grandeur, or passionateness.

occupable, *a. rare.* Capable of being occupied.

1851 Whewell *Grotius* I. 256 In things which are properly no-one's, two things are occupable; the lordship, and the ownership.

occupance ('ɒkjʊpəns). [f. occupant: see -ance.] = next, 1; *spec.* in *Geogr.*, the inhabiting and modification of an area by man.

1814 Scott *Diary* 4 Aug. in *Lockhart*, The chief stress is laid upon occupance. **1880** Mrs. Fetherstonhaugh *Alan Dering* II. x. 138 Lady Ruthven herself was in occupance of the pretty mansion. **1932** *Sci. Monthly* XXXV. 266/1 France..is strikingly an aggregation of '*pays*', each of which has its distinctive character stamped upon every aspect of the natural environment and upon every form of human occupance thereof. **1934** *Ann. Assoc. Amer. Geogr.* XXIV. 81 Occupance is..defined as the process of occupying or living in an area, and the transformations of the initial landscape which result. *Ibid.*, Occupance refers not only to ..economic activities but also to other activities..such as the construction of buildings, roads, and so on. The word includes also the results as well as the process of living in an area. **1974** F. Emery *Oxfordsh. Landscape* i. 35 People who could cultivate the land with digging-sticks in order to grow cereals, covering the ground..with a 'slash-and-burn' or shifting occupance of the kind we still meet today in certain forest environments.

occupancy ('ɒkjʊpənsɪ). [as prec.: see -ancy.]

1. a. The condition of being an occupant; the fact of occupying; the act of taking, or fact of holding, actual possession, esp. of land (*spec.* in *Law*, the taking possession of something not belonging to any one, as constituting a title to it); actual holding of or residence in a place; = occupation 1, 2.

1596 Bacon *Use of Law, Property in Land* i, An estate for another man's life by occupancy, may at this time be gotten by entry. **1643** Prynne *Sov. Power Parlt.* i. (ed. 2) 100 A thing which in its owne nature is not capable of an Occupancy, nor seisible by any. **1767** Blackstone *Comm.* II. xvi. 258 Occupancy is the taking possession of those things, which before belonged to nobody. This..is the true ground and foundation of all property. **1774** Jefferson *Autobiog.* App., Wks. 1859 I. 140 Each individual of the Society may appropriate to himself such lands as he finds vacant, and occupancy will give him title. **1861** M. Pattison *Ess.* (1889) I. 39 The occupancy of the English throne..by the line of Hanover. **1884** *Law Rep.* 27 Chanc. Div. 633 That..he should take a larger house for their joint occupancy.

attrib. **1883** *19th Cent.* Sept. 435 The rent payable by an occupancy tenant. *Ibid.* 436 Ryots..entitled to occupancy rights. **1883** *Manch. Exam.* 7 Nov. 5/3 The innovation of an occupancy franchise for the counties.

b. *concr.* A place occupied.

1864 Carlyle *Fredk. Gt.* xvii. v. IV. 562 *note*, The Saxon 'Camp' or Occupancy.

2. The fact of occupying or taking up (space).

1833 N. Arnott *Physics* (ed. 5) II. 3 Such expansion or occupancy of space by a small quantity of matter. **1875** Lyell *Princ. Geol.* II. iii. xlii. 439 The first..tend, by the mere occupancy of space, to exclude other species.

3. a. The state of being occupied or busy; = occupation 4.

1826 *New Monthly Mag.* XVI. 127 A train of reflections.. which his former state of professional occupancy had tended to exclude. **1843** J. Clason *Serm.* xvii. 295 We see heaven represented as a place of busy occupancy.

b. *Teleph.* The proportion of the time during which a circuit or device is handling calls.

1933 *Post Office Electr. Engineers' Jrnl.* XXVI. 269 (*caption*) Probabilities *P* for a delay exceeding *t* holding times when there are *n* switches with occupancy *a*. **1960** R. Syski *Introd. Congestion Theory Teleph. Syst.* i. 10 The traffic carried (or handled) refers to the changing patterns of occupancy conditions in the group. *Ibid.* vi. 365 The limit in (*4.6*) exists provided the traffic intensity ('occupancy')..is less than unity.

c. The proportion of accommodation occupied or used.

1974 *Economist* 7 Sept. 51 The 'France' has had a 77 per cent occupancy rate on the North Atlantic run and a 91 per cent rate on winter cruises. **1975** *Daily Tel.* 11 Dec. 9/6 If airlines did not overbook, planes would go out 40 per cent. full instead of the 70 per cent. occupancy needed to give a profit. **1977** *Daily Tel.* 2 Dec. 10/7 Hotels in large towns outside London experienced a similar increased occupancy this year. **1977** *Time* 19 Dec. 61/3 The 27,400-acre complex ..sports three Disney hotels, with an occupancy rate of about 97%.

†**'occupand**, *pr. pple. Sc. Obs.* [corresp. to F. *occupant*, L. *occupānt-em*, with Sc. ppl. ending -and[1].] Occupying.

1567 *Satir. Poems Reform.* ii. 2 It is not aneuch ye pure King is deid, Bot ye mischant murtheraris occupand his steid.

occupant ('ɒkjʊpənt). [ad. L. *occupānt-em*, pr. pple. of *occupāre* to occupy, perh. immed. a. F. *occupant* (15th c. in Hatz.-Darm.).]

1. A person occupying or holding in actual possession (property, esp. land, or an office or position); one who occupies, resides in, or is at the time in (a place); an occupier.

1622 Bp. Hall *Contempl., N.T.* iii. iv, One room is left void for a future occupant. **1652–62** Heylin *Cosmogr.* iii. (1673) 211/1 Retaining a third part of the profits to himself, and leaving two thirds to the Occupants. **1767** Blackstone *Comm.* II. i. 10 The most universal and effectual way of abandoning property, is by the death of the occupant. **1823** J. Marshall *Const. Opin.* (1839) 264 [The Indians] were admitted to be the rightful occupants of the soil. **1867** Smiles *Huguenots Eng.* v. (1880) 84 The sacrilegious occupant of the English throne. **1883** R. S. Wright in *Law Times Rep.* L. 273/2 The voter was the occupant of two rooms only in the house.

b. *Law.* One who takes possession of something having no owner, and so establishes a title to it.

1596 Bacon *Use of Law, Property in Lands* iv. §2 This land [goeth]..to the party that first entereth; and he is called an occupant. **1650** Bp. Hall *Balm Gil.* 195 Whose shall those things be?..perhaps a strangers, perhaps (as in case of undisposed Lands) the occupants. **1767** Blackstone *Comm.* II. xvi. 259 Belonging therefore to nobody..the law left it open to be seised and appropriated by the first person that could enter upon it..under the name of an occupant. **1844–75** Williams *Real Prop.* (ed. 11) i. 20 The person who had so entered was called a general occupant.

†**2.** A prostitute. (Cf. occupy 8.) *Obs.*

1599 Marston *Sco. Villanie* Prol. 166 Whose sences some damn'd Occupant bereaues. *Ibid.* ii. vii. 206 He with his Occupant, Are cling'd so close, like deaw-worms in the morne That he'le not stir.

†**'occupate**, *ppl. a. Obs.* [ad. L. *occupāt-us*, pa. pple. of *occupāre* to occupy.] Occupied, taken into and held in possession.

1605 Bacon *Adv. Learn.* ii. Concl., Those parts..not constantly occupate, or not well conuerted by the labour of man. **1618** *Decl. Demeanour Raleigh* 25 The Territories, occupate and possest by the Spaniards. **1860** Kingsley *Misc.* I. 82.

†**'occupate**, *v. Obs.* [f. L. *occupāt-*, ppl. stem of *occupāre* to occupy: cf. F. *occuper*.] = occupy. Hence †**'occupated** *ppl. a.*

1547 Boorde *Brev. Health* ccxxxv. 80 An universal sicknes doth occupate all the partes of a mans body. **1659** B. Harris *Parival's Iron Age* 104 The Imperialists departed out of Holstein, and all the other occupated places. *Ibid.* 160 The Lands which had been occupated, or seized on by the Swedes. **1697** J. Sergeant *Solid Philos.* 176 If they be not Penetrated, one of them must necessarily drive the other out of the Space it occupates.

‖**occupatio** (ɒkjʊ'peɪʃɪəʊ, -'pɑːtɪəʊ). *Rhet.* [L. (see occupation).] = preterition 3.

1586 [see paralipsis]. **1928** C. S. Baldwin *Medieval Rhetoric & Poetic* x. 296 The rehearsal of all the conventionally appropriate *loci* of description at the funeral of Arcite (A2919–2966) sounds to modern ears impatient, if not sarcastic. But, after all, the whole long passage is the 'colour' *occupatio* (præteritio). The shorter *occupatio* in the Squire's Tale (F63–75) suggests sarcasm less by itself than in its connection with lines 32–40 and 401–408. **1933** F. N. Robinson *Compl. Wks. Chaucer* 772/2 It should be added that the rhetorical figure here employed—the refusal to describe or narrate, technically known as 'occupatio'—is very common with Chaucer. **1957** C. Muscatine *Chaucer & French Tradition* vi. 177 Though Chaucer omits a great deal of the tale originally told by Boccaccio in the *Teseida*, he frequently resorts to the rhetorical device of *occupatio* to summarize in detail events or descriptions in such a way as to shorten the story without lessening weight and impressiveness. **1968** J. A. W. Bennett *Chaucer's Bk. of Fame* ii. 94 But the didactic bird is not to be thwarted utterly, and launches..into an *occupatio* summarizing the lore in Ovid's *Fasti* that would have enabled the poet to identify such constellations as Lyra, Gemini, and the Pleiades. **1975** *Times Lit. Suppl.* 28 Feb. 213/4 'Do not describe the total horror, the full degree of despair that rushes into your head, your brain and emotions...', and so on. The device used to be known as *occupatio*.

occupation (ɒkjʊ'peɪʃən). [a. F. *occupation* (12th c. in Hatz.-Darm.), Anglo-F. *ocupacioun* (1292 in sense 1): ad. L. *occupātiōn-em* seizing, taking possession, employment, n. of action from *occupā-re* to seize, occupy.] The action of occupying or condition of being occupied, or that in which this action is embodied (in senses of the verb).

1. a. The action of taking possession, esp. of a place or of land; seizure, as by military conquest, etc.; entrance upon possession.

[**1292** BRITTON II. ii. §3 Terre ou autre heritage dount nul n'est en seysine, et..tote autre chose guerpie, demoraunt hors de chescuni seysine, des queles choses homme se pora purchacer par ocupacioun.] **1552** HULOET, Occupation as deprehension, *Catalepsis.* **1624** BACON *Consid. War with Spain*, I speak not of matches or unions; but of arms, occupations, invasions. **1628** COKE *On Litt.* I. 249 b, Occupation..signifieth a putting out of a mans Freehold in time of warre, and it is all one with a disseisin in time of peace. **1659** B. HARRIS *Parival's Iron Age* 372 Wars begun, and carried on..for the.. occupation, or seazure of Countries. **1767** BLACKSTONE *Comm.* II. xxv. (1830) 393 Occupation, that is, hiving or including them, gives the property in bees. **1893** TRAILL *Soc. Eng.* Introd. 48 Its inhabitants must have possessed the art of working in metals before the Roman occupation.

b. *spec.*, by Germany and her allies during the war of 1939–45; usu., the period during which a country was held by German, etc., troops, or the state of being held by such troops.

1940 A. HUXLEY *Let.* 7 July (1969) 455 Jehanne was out of Paris during the occupation. **1957** *Times Lit. Suppl.* 27 Dec. 783/3 The particular man whose life has been conditioned by the hot North African sun and the cold chill of the Occupation. **1972** *Guardian* 9 Sept. 12/4 The programme is ..divided into three parts... There is life under the occupation..as drawn from experience in occupied Europe.

2. a. Actual holding or possession, esp. of a place or of land; rarely, also, of an office or position; tenure; occupancy.

army of occupation, an army left to occupy a newly conquered country or region until the conclusion of hostilities or establishment of a settled government.

1387 TREVISA *Higden* (Rolls) VII. 305 Forto begile þe occupacioun of þe pope. *c* **1475** *Crabhouse Reg.* (1889) 59 The viij yere of the ocupacion of the same Jane, Prioresse. **1574** tr. *Littleton's Tenures* 4 Suche thinges as a man may have a manuell occupacion, possession, or resceyte. **1652** NEEDHAM tr. *Selden's Mare Cl.* 196 If to such a corporal occupation, as this, wee add also, that they excluded others from the Sea. **1791** W. JESSOP *Rep. River Witham* 12 A Swivel-bridge over the Witham for the occupation of the common. **1842** ALISON *Hist. Europe* xcv. §24 Maintaining the army of occupation. **1870** FREEMAN *Norm. Conq.* I. App. AA. 621 Owners of lands then in monastic occupation. **1872** E. W. ROBERTSON *Hist. Ess.* 160 The Irish peasant..has.. confounded the occupation with the ownership of the land. *Mod.* During his occupation of the house and land.

b. A piece of land occupied by a tenant; a holding. (*local.* Cf. OCCUPYING *vbl. sb.* 2.)

1792 A. YOUNG *Trav. France* 411 These small occupations are a real loss of labour;..people are fed upon them, whose time is worth little or nothing. **1807** VANCOUVER *Agric. Devon* (1813) 108 The occupations fluctuate between 30*l.* and 120*l.* per annum. **1879** T. H. S. ESCOTT *England* I. 59 Held by tenantry whose occupations range from 100 to 500 acres each.

3. The taking up of space or time. *rare.*

1460–70 *Bk. Quintessence* 6 Wherby ȝe may make oure quinte essence wiþoute cost or traueile, and withoute occupacioun and lesynge of tyme. **1815** JANE AUSTEN *Emma* I. x, Stooping down in complete occupation of the foot-path.

4. a. The being occupied or employed with, or engaged in something; that in which one is engaged; employment, business. †***to have in occupation***, to be occupied or busied with. *Obs.*

a **1340** HAMPOLE *Psalter* cxviii[i] . 47 My thoght & myn occupacioun sall be in þi wordis. *a* **1420** HOCCLEVE *De Reg. Princ.* 281 Som man, for lak of occupacioun, Museþ forþer þanne his wyt may strecche. *c* **1510** MORE *Picus* Wks. 14/2 Vse them both, aswel studie as worldly occupacion. **1523** FITZHERB. *Husb.* §23 It is not conuenient, to haue hey and corne bothe in occupation at one tyme. **1776** GIBBON *Decl. & F.* xiii. I. 394 Minds, long exercised in business..in the loss of power..principally regret the want of occupation. **1833–6** J. EAGLES *Sketcher* (1856) 347 By the intense occupation of his mind. **1868** FREEMAN *Norm. Conq.* II. vii. 78 Harold and Swend..by their invasion..gave him full occupation throughout the year.

b. with *pl.* A particular action or course of action in which one is engaged, esp. habitually or statedly; an employment, business, calling.

c **1340** HAMPOLE *Prose Tr.* 3 Dos a-waye coryous and vayne ocupacyons. *c* **1386** CHAUCER *Melib.* ¶625 He that is ydel, and casteth hym to no bisynesse ne occupacion. *a* **1450** *Knt. de la Tour* (1868) 7 Thenke not on none other worldly ocupaciones. **1467** in *Eng. Gilds* (1870) 388 Doynge hur office & occupacion. **1513** in W. H. Turner *Select. Rec. Oxford* 10 The craft or occupation of brewers. **1589** *Pappe w. Hatchet* D ij b, Though he bee but a cobler by occupation. **1604** SHAKS. *Oth.* III. iii. 357 Farewell: Othello's Occupation's gone. **1791** BURKE *Th. French Aff.* Wks. 1842 I. 579 Condorcet..is a man of another sort of birth, fashion, and occupation from Brissot. **1868** RUSKIN *Arrows of Chace* (1880) II. 193 The character of men depends more on their occupations than on any teaching we can give them.

†c. *spec.* Mechanical or mercantile employment; handicraft; trade. *Obs.*

1530 *Proper Dialogue* 167 in *Rede me*, etc. (Arb.) 138 Artificers & men of occupacion. **1576** FLEMING *Panopl. Epist.* 364 Take awaye learning from among men, and how shall trades mechanical, occupations (I meane) be maintained? **1607** SHAKS. *Cor.* IV. vi. 97 You that stood so much Vpon the voyce of occupation and The breath of Garlicke-eaters.

†5. Use, employment (*of* a thing). *Obs.*

1388 WYCLIF *2 Macc.* iv. 14 In occupaciouns of a disch [*gloss* ether pleying with a ledun disch]. **1494** FABYAN *Chron.* VI. clxx. 165 Churches and temples they tourned to vse of stables, and other vyle occupacyons. **1552** HULOET, Occupation or vse, *vsus.* **1582** *Reg. Gild Corp. Chr. York* (1872) 233 *note*, My wyfe..shall have the occupacion of the said silver spoones duringe hir lyfe. **1703** MOXON *Mech. Exerc.* 136 Renders the whole Floor firm enough for all common Occupation.

†6. The exercising (*of* any business or office); exercise, discharge. *Obs.*

1432 *Paston Lett.* I. 32 Excercise and occupacion of the Kinges service. **1459** *Rolls of Parlt.* V. 367/2 To recovere the seid penaltees for eny occupation of their seid office for the premisses. **1483** *Gild of the Bakers, Exeter* in *Eng. Gilds* 336 Yn occupacyon of the said crafte.

7. *attrib.*, as **occupation bridge**, a bridge for the use of the occupiers of the land, *e.g.* one connecting parts of a farm, etc., separated by a canal or railway; **occupation centre**, an establishment where occupational therapy is practised or where the mentally handicapped are trained or employed; **occupation disease**, an occupational disease; **occupation franchise**, the right to vote at parliamentary elections as a tenant or occupier; **occupation neurosis** *Med.*, a painful and disabling spasm affecting muscles used more than normally because of the person's occupation; **occupation number** *Physics*, the number of particles in a system that are in any given state; **occupation road**, a private road for the use of the occupiers of the land. Also, in military uses, as ***occupation army, forces, troops***; in archæological use, as ***occupation floor, layer, level, scatter, site.***

1918 E. S. FARROW *Dict. Mil. Terms* 414 Occupation Army, an army that remains in possession of a newly conquered country, retaining it as a kind of hostage, until peace is signed and the war indemnity paid. **1976** T. ALLBEURY *Only Good German* xiv. 100 A goon on each staircase and the lift doors padlocked... It's like an occupation army. **1837** WHITTOCK, etc. *Bk. Trades* (1842) 207 The occupation bridge, at Rotterdam,..consists of two separate segments. **1878** F. S. WILLIAMS *Midl. Railw.* 509 Soon after..we come to an occupation bridge. **1940** FRAZER & STALLYBRASS *Text-bk. Public Health* (ed. 10) xix. 440 If the home conditions are good and the defective's condition is suitable he may attend at an occupation centre where simple occupational training can be given. **1958** [see *day-hospital* s.v. DAY *sb.* 23 a]. **1965** PETERS & KINNAIRD *Health Services Admin.* vii. 255 The [Education] Authorities establish training and occupation centres for the lower grades of the mentally handicapped who cannot take education in ordinary educational subjects. **1900** DORLAND *Med. Dict.* 209/1 Occupation-disease. **1901** *Brit. Med. Jrnl.* 17 Aug. 405/1 (*heading*) The medical profession and the control of occupation diseases. **1930** F. B. YOUNG *Jim Redlake* III. iii. 326 Overcrowding, short commons, adulterated food, occupation diseases—they're all just words in a newspaper. **1959** J. D. CLARK *Prehist. S. Afr.* plate 4 (*caption*) Handaxes, cleavers, and waste flakes of evolved Chelles-Acheul culture on occupation floors. **1971** W. TUCKER *This Witch* ii. 20 The native beer was vile... The occupation forces did their drinking elsewhere. **1884** GLADSTONE *Sp.* 28 Feb., There were four occupation franchises in boroughs. One of them was 10*l.* clear yearly value, and the other three were the lodger, the household, and the service franchise. **1895** *Westm. Gaz.* 15 Jan. 4/3 No sufficient allowance was made for tenant's improvements, nor for his occupation interest in his holding. **1953** R. J. C. ATKINSON *Field Archaeol.* (ed. 2) i. 39 The chief use of such detectors is in the excavation of graves and occupation-layers in which metal objects may be expected to occur. **1935** *Discovery* Nov. 343/1 Further excavations..have brought to light older occupation-levels and hearth-marks. **1888** W. R. GOWERS *Man. Dis. Nervous Syst.* II. v. 656 The term 'occupation neuroses', adopted from the German ('Beschaftigungs-neurosen'), is a convenient designation for a group of maladies in which certain symptoms are excited by the attempt to perform some often-repeated muscular action, commonly one that is involved in the occupation of the sufferer... The most frequent symptom is spasm. **1911** *Jrnl. Nerv. & Mental Dis.* XXXVIII. 107 An occupation neurosis is literally a fatigue cramp, and is characterized by spasms of muscles concerned in special movements, and brought on whenever these special movements, such as writing, are attempted. **1958** SYKES & BELL tr. *Landau & Lifshitz' Quantum Mech.* ix. 215 Let us seek to construct a mathematical formalism in which the occupation numbers ..of the states (and not the co-ordinates of the particles) play the part of independent variables. **1974** G. REECE tr. *Hund's Hist. Quantum Theory* xiii. 180 Jordan was thus entitled to express his hope of a quantum wave theory of matter in which the numbers of particles would be the occupation numbers *N*, of the discrete quantum wave states. **1852** WIGGINS *Embanking* 132 Making the requisite occupation roads. **1954** S. PIGGOTT *Neolithic Cultures* ix. 271 The occupation-scatter of small sherds and flints. **1939** *Oxoniensa* IV. 6 The region between Oxford and Northampton is notoriously, but probably deceptively, barren of occupation-sites. **1948** *N.Y. Jrnl. American* (Sunday Mail ed.) 9 May 1/7 Police and U.S. occupation troops are prepared for bloodshed. **1975** R. L. DUNCAN *Dragons at Gate* (1976) iv. 32 On the day of the surrender, before the Occupation troops could arrive, Takaeshi..set out into Tokyo Bay, and blew himself up.

Hence †**occu'pationer**, one engaged in an occupation (*obs.*); **occu'pationist**, one who advocates or favours occupation (sense 1); **occu'pationless** *a.*, having no occupation, unoccupied, idle.

1592 G. HARVEY *Pierce's Super.* (1593) 190 Let the braue enginer,..maruelous Vulcanist, and euery Mercuriall *occupationer..be respected. **1892** *Glasgow Herald* 12 Feb. 6/3 No more a permanent *occupationist [of Egypt] now than he was an immediate evacuationist some years ago. **1890** *Temple Bar Mag.* Nov. 314 To sit *occupationless, vaguely waiting.

occupational (ɒkjʊ'peɪʃən(ə)l), *a.* [f. prec. + -AL[1].] Of or belonging to an occupation or occupations (sense 4 b); ***occupational disease***, (a) disease to which a particular occupation renders a person especially liable; also *joc.*; ***occupational hazard, risk***, a risk accepted as part of a particular occupation; also *joc.*; ***occupational therapy***, an activity, mental or physical, prescribed as an aid to recovery from disease or injury or for mental patients; so ***occupational therapist***, someone skilled in supervising or trained to supervise such activity.

1850 HAWTHORNE *Amer. Note-bks.* (1883) 387 She sews, not like a lady, but with an occupational air. **1862** R. H. PATTERSON *Ess. Hist. & Art* 146 An amount of physical, mental, and occupational variety such as he will meet with nowhere else in the world. **1901** *Brit. Med. Jrnl.* 17 Aug. 412/2 A number of valuable papers upon occupational diseases. **1915** G. E. BARTON in *Trained Nurse & Hospital Rev.* Mar. 138 (*heading*) Occupational therapy. **1919** —— (*title*) Teaching the sick; a manual of occupational therapy and re-education. **1919** J. L. GARVIN *Econ. Found. Peace* 328 These occupational federations acted independently of each other. **1922** *Jrnl. Mental Sci.* LXVIII. 192 The *personnel* comprises a chief and five assistant trained occupational therapists. **1923** *Ibid.* LXIX. 126 The occupational centre or 'curative workshop' serves more or less as a proving ground. **1926** B. WEBB *My Apprenticeship* iii. 129 Personal vanity..was an 'occupational disease' of entertaining and being entertained. **1934** H. C. WARREN *Dict. Psychol.* 184/2 *Occupational hierarchy*, the serial arrangement of occupational groups according to average intelligence. **1937** *Discovery* May 144/1 The excavation..showed a mound that had already been abandoned by 1500 B.C., and 20 occupational levels below it. **1944** M. LASKI *Love on Supertax* iv. 52 You're insured against occupational risks. **1949** W. L. WARNER in M. Fortes *Social Struct.* 4 Interviews ..are taken from informants..from several occupational groups. **1951** R. FIRTH *Elem. Social Organiz.* iv. 138 A worker's choice of employment is guided by his wife's attitude to the conditions of his work, its cleanliness, occupational risks, or security. **1952** 'VIGILANS' *Chamber of Horrors* 94 *Occupational hazard*, a risk necessarily run in one's work. **1956** S. GIBBONS *Here be Dragons* xvii. 235, I don't think I shall marry if I'm asked. There's too much occupational risk. **1956** B. GOOLDEN *At Foot of Hills* ix. 202 Are you the young man who wants to see over the occupational therapy department? **1959** *Listener* 15 Oct. 614/1 Exile has been regarded as an occupational hazard for poets in particular ever since Plato denied them rights of citizenship in his republic. *Ibid.* 10 Dec. 1041/3 As a museum man himself, Mr. Baxandall will be aware of..that occupational disease of his profession which might be called 'collector's greediness'. **1959** B. WOOTTON *Social Sci. & Social Path.* ii. 48 Whether, on balance, prisoners are likely to exalt or to debase their occupational level is anybody's guess. **1971** *Times* 6 Sept. 7/8 The Department of Employment has occupational guidance services throughout the country. **1973** *Times* 13 Jan. 19/7 Occupational pension scheme is one established by an employer for the benefit of his employees, and wholly paid for by him and (frequently, but not necessarily) his employees. *Ibid.* 1 June 24/1 (Advt.), For further information please contact the Head Occupational Therapist. **1974** *Encycl. Brit. Micropædia* VII. 470/2 Occupational therapy provides not only training in daily living activities but also aids that make eating, dressing, and toilet less fatiguing for the sick or elderly. **1974** PASSMORE & ROBSON *Compan. Med. Stud.* III. 76/1 Asbestos has become an increasingly important occupational hazard. *Ibid.*, This led to a false sense of security about occupational disease in coal mining until 1920.

Hence **occu'pationally** *adv.*

1952 C. P. BLACKER *Eugenics* vii. 141 That there existed a group of occupationally unstable persons who are in continuous receipt of public assistance had been well recognized since the time of Charles Booth. **1971** D. CRYSTAL *Linguistics* 132 Do they occur in certain occupationally restricted uses of language only, such as journalese? **1973** *Daily Tel.* 18 Aug. 8/1 The Council, sitting in Star Chamber, publicly ordered anyone not occupationally resident in London to leave the City forthwith.

occu'pationalism. [-ISM.] Occupational character or conduct; professionalism.

1927 E. BARKER *National Character* iv. 96 It is true that a new and qualifying factor has been added to the national temper by the growth of occupationalism.

occupative ('ɒkjʊpətɪv), *a. rare.* [f. L. *occupāt-*, ppl. stem of *occupāre* + -IVE: cf. F. *occupatif* (15th c. in Godef.).] Characterized by occupying or being occupied; in *Law*, held by a tenure based upon occupation (see OCCUPATION 1).

1656 BLOUNT *Glossogr.* s.v., An *Occupative Field*, is that which, being deserted by its proper owner, or tiller, is possessed by another. **1894** *Spectator* 24 Feb. 269 The saying of the Neapolitan Carracioli—'The throne of Russia is not hereditary or elective, but occupative'.

occupiable ('ɒkjʊpaɪəb(ə)l), *a. rare.* [f. OCCUPY + -ABLE.] Capable of being occupied.

1865 *Pall Mall G.* 20 Sept. 3/2 There are points..where a man on an elevation, and with a glass, can nearly see across Canada—across, that is, the occupied, probably the occupiable portion of it.

occupied ('ɒkjʊpaɪd), *ppl. a.* [f. OCCUPY + -ED[1].] Taken possession of; held in possession, dwelt in; taken up, filled up; busied, engaged, employed: see the verb. Esp. of countries held by Germany and her allies during the war of

1939–45; of parts of countries under military occupation.

1483 *Cath. Angl.* 258/1 Occupyed, *occupatus.* **1535** Coverdale *Isa.* xxxii. 14 The palaces..shal be broken, and the greatly occupide cities desolate. **1884** Sir R. Rawlinson in *Pall Mall G.* 9 July 1/2 Eastern peoples..are to this day bad sanitarians; there occupied sites are foul. **1897** *Daily News* 10 Dec. 5/2 A mortality..greater than that of occupied males generally. **1940** R. W. B. Clarke *Britain's Blockade* 7 The division of France into 'occupied' and 'non-occupied' territory is nothing more than a device to relieve the Germans of the administrative difficulties created by the millions of refugees, [etc.]. **1940** A. Huxley *Let.* 9 Oct. (1969) 459 There is practically no communication between occupied France and the USA. **1941** *Times Lit. Suppl.* 18 Oct. 514/1 (*heading*) In occupied Belgium. **1965** M. Spark *Mandelbaum Gate* vii. 280 'So far as I know she's still in Israel—' Joe Ramdez clapped his hands over his ears... 'Occupied Palestine,' Freddy said with deference. **1973** L. Snelling *Heresy* i. i. 8 In Paris, capital of Occupied France, in the abnormally hot summer of nineteen-forty.

occupier ('ɒkjʊpaɪə(r)). Also 5 -our. [f. as prec. + -er[1], or weakening of AF. *occupiour.*] One who occupies, in various senses.

1. One who takes, or (more usually) holds, possession; the person who holds or is in actual possession *of* (a piece of property, esp. a house or land, or a place, position, or office); a holder, occupant.

[**1381** *Act 5 Rich. II,* Stat. i. c. 9 Occupiours des biens.. de diverses persones. *Ibid.* c. 10 Occupiours des biens ou terre tenantz.] **1387–8** T. Usk *Test. Love* ii. v. (Skeat) I. 63 Fairnesse of fieldes, ne of habitacions,..maie not bee rekened as riches, that are thine owne, for if thei be bad, it is great sclander and villanie to the occupier. **1450** *Rolls of Parlt.* V. 186/1 By the handes of the Fermours, Collectours or Occupiours, of the said subsidie and ulnage. **1494** Fabyan *Chron.* vi. cxlix. 137 He had ben occupyer of a kynges rome by y[e] name only x. yeres. *a* **1618** Raleigh (J.), If the title of occupiers be good in a land unpeopled, why should it be bad accounted in a country peopled thinly? **1698** Fryer *Acc. E. India & P.* 52 [The] Prince..in all India is sole Proprietor of Lands; allowing the Occupiers no more than a bare Subsistence. **1753** *Scots Mag.* Feb. 92/2 Some occupier of the premisses. **1863** Fawcett *Pol. Econ.* xi. vii. (1876) 616 The local rates fall with the greatest severity upon the occupiers of houses.

†**b.** A dweller, resident (*in* a place). *Obs.*

1545 Brinklow *Complaynt* 43 b, To euery citie acording to the nomber of the occupyers in the same.

†**2.** One who uses, employs, or deals in (something); one who practises or follows (a specified calling or occupation). *Obs.*

1537 Cromwell *Let. to M. Throgmorton* in Froude *Hist. Eng.* xiv. III. 45 A merchant & occupier of all deceits. **1548** Gest *Pr. Masse* in H. G. Dugdale *Life* App. i. (1840) 71 He wold..delyver it [the one talent] to the well occupyers of the fyve. **1577** B. Googe *Heresbach's Husb.* i. (1586) 4 b, All my Auncestours were occupiers of husbandry. **1611** Bible *Ezek.* xxvii. 27 The occupiers of thy merchandise.

†**b.** *esp.* One who employs money or goods in trading; a trader, dealer, merchant. *Obs.*

1509 Barclay *Shyp of Folys* (1570) 211 All occupiers almost suche gile deuise In euery chaffer. **1535** Coverdale *Ezek.* xxvii. 25 Thy maryners, thy shipmasters,..thy occupiers (that brought the thinges necessary). **1581** Marbeck *Bk. of Notes* 1134 When they have given out their money unto occupiers and merchaunt men. **1611** Barry *Ram Alley* ii. in Hazl. *Dodsley* X. 308 He will..Lie faster than ten city occupiers Or cunning tradesmen.

†**occupise.** *Obs. rare*[−1]. [Some kind of erroneous deriv. of occupy *v.*] ? Occupation; or ? things 'occupied' or held.

c **1478** *Plumpton Corr.* 38 They all not having any kow or kalves, or any other guds whearby they might live, nor any other occupise.

occupy ('ɒkjʊpaɪ), *v.* Also 4–6 ocupie, -ye, (5 -y), 4–7 occupie, 5–6 -ye, (4 occipie, 6 occypye; 4 okupie, 5 okepye, -paey; okew-, oky-, ocopy; hokewepye; 6 hocupy, *pa. pple.* okepyde); *pa. t.* and *pple.* 4 ocupid, 4–6 -yd, 6 ocuped, *Sc.* occupeit. [irreg. f. OF. *occuper*, ad. L. *occupāre* to seize (by force), take possession of, get hold of, take up, occupy, employ, invest (money); f. *oc-, ob-* (ob- 1 b) + stem *cap-* in *capĕre* to take, seize. The final *-ie, -ye, -y* of the English word, found in the vb. and its inflexions and derivatives (*occupier*, etc.) at their earliest appearance *c* 1340, are not explicable from the F. *occup-er, occup-ant, occupe*, etc., and their origin has not been ascertained. It is possible that the change took place in AFr., in which Act 5. Rich. II has *occupiours, occupiers* = occupiers: but this may be from Eng.]

†**1.** *trans.* To take possession of, take for one's own use, seize. *Obs.* in *gen.* sense: see b.

a **1340** Hampole *Psalter* xvii. 6 *Preoccupauerunt me laquei mortis*..bifore occupid has me þe snares of ded. *c* **1350** in *Leg. Rood* (1871) 64 All þi lims on ilka side Witht sorows sal be ocupide. **1463** in *Bury Wills* (Camden) 36, I beqwethe to Thomas Heighaum the yonger my tablys of ivory... And if he wil not ocupye hem I bequethe the seid tablees to..his wyf. *a* **1548** Hall *Chron., Hen. VII*, 60 Also dyed..the kynges chiefe chamberleyn, whose office Charles.. occupied and enioyed. **1553** Brende *Q. Curtius* ix. 4 Some occupied dartes, some speares, and other axes, and..leaped to and fro to their cartes. **1614** Raleigh *Hist. World* v. i. §2. (1634) 268 Which done, they occupied the Citie, Lands, Goods, and Wiues of those, whom they had murdered.

b. *spec.* To take possession of (a place) by settling in it, or by military conquest, etc.; to enter upon the possession and holding of.

1375 Barbour *Bruce* i. 98 Throw his mycht till occupy Landis, þat war till him marcheand. **1494** Fabyan *Chron.* v. xciv. 69 A Saxon named Ella..slewe many Brytons,..and after occupyed that Countre. *a* **1548** Hall *Chron., Hen. VII*, 25 b, That he would invade or occupie the territory of hys enemies. **1810** in Picton *L'pool Munic. Rec.* (1886) II. 372 The finishing, compleating and occupying..the building. **1849** Macaulay *Hist. Eng.* x. II. 582 The Dutch had occupied Chelsea and Kensington. **1855** *Ibid.* xviii. IV. 205 Glencoe was to be occupied by troops.

c. *intr.* or *absol.* To take possession. *rare.*

c **1400** *Destr. Troy* 5329 My fos were so fell..þat þai occupiet ouer all, euyn as hom list. **1862** Mrs. Norton *Lady of La Garaye* Prol., Creatures that dwell alone Occupy boldly.

2. *trans.* To hold possession of; to have in one's possession or power; to hold (a position or office).

c **1380** Wyclif *Wks.* (1880) 384 As þe baron or þe knyȝte occupieþ & gouerneþ his baronrye or his knyȝtte. ? *a* **1400** *Morte Arth.* 278 Belyne and Bremyne, and Bawdewyne the thyrde, They ocupyede þe empyre aughte score wynnttyrs. **1560** Daus tr. *Sleidane's Comm.* 380 You who occupie the chiefest places amongest the States of the Empire. **1568** Grafton *Chron.* II. 194 The Turkes and infidels which to that day had kept and occupied the same Isle [Rhodes]. **1784** Cowper *Tiroc.* 414 Least qualified..To occupy a sacred, awful post. **1845** M. Pattison *Ess.* (1889) I. 14 Gregory.. occupied the see of Tours twenty-three years. *Ibid.* 18 The ..inferior Franks..posted themselves, fully armed,..under the portico, occupying all the entrances. **1883** *Law Times* 20 Oct. 410/2 A married woman is now to occupy the same position as her Saxon ancestress.

b. To reside in and use (a place) as its tenant, or regular inhabitant; to tenant.

c **1400** Maundev. (Roxb.) xxiv. 109 He..occupies þe same land þat he was lorde off. **1489** *Act 4 Hen. VII*, c. 19 If any such owner or owners..take kepe & occupy any such house or houses & lands in his or their own hands. **1767** Blackstone *Comm.* II. i. 7 By constantly occupying the same individual spot, the fruits of the earth were consumed. **1853** J. H. Newman *Hist. Sk.* (1873) II. i. i. 2 This tract.. is at present occupied by civilized communities. **1881** J. Russell *Haigs* 5 Bemersyde House..has been occupied by the Haigs for more than seven centuries.

†**c.** *intr.* or *absol.* To hold possession or office; to dwell, reside; to stay, abide. *Obs.*

c **1425** Lydg. *Assembly of Gods* 1372 Where Vertew occupyeth must nedys well grow. **1483** Caxton *Gold. Leg.* 337/1 He..ordeyned an holy man to occupye in his place. **1523** Fitzherb. *Surv.* Prol., The names of the lordes and tenauntes that occupy. **1535** Coverdale *Matt.* xvii. 21 Whyle they occupied in Galile Iesus sayde vnto them [etc.].

3. *trans.* To take up, use up, fill (space or time); also in weakened sense, To be situated or stationed in, to be in or at (a place or position).

1340 Hampole *Pr. Consc.* 3025 It may occupy na stede. **1382** Wyclif *Luke* xiii. 7 Kitt it doun, wherto occupieth it the erthe? *c* **1386** Chaucer *Sqr.'s T.* 56 Thanne wolde it occupie a someres day. *c* **1400** *Three Kings Cologne* 27 Þei come so late and all placys were ocupied with pilgrymes and oþir men. *a* **1548** Hall *Chron., Hen. VII*, 11 b, Lyke a cypher in algorisme that is ioyned to no figure but onely occupieth a place. *c* **1566** J. Alday tr. *Boaystuau's Theat. World* S vij b, If we should rehearse and declare all the singularities..I should occupy a large volume. **1651** Hobbes *Leviath.* iii. xxxiv. 207 The Word Body..signifieth that which..occupyeth some certain room. **1839** G. Bird *Nat. Philos.* 369 The black cross disappearing, and leaving white spaces in the place it previously occupied. **1865** R. W. Dale *Jew. Temp.* xvi. 173, I shall not occupy your time with any description of the form of the sanctuary. **1875** Jowett *Plato* I. 399 The voyage..has occupied thirty days.

4. To employ, busy, engage (a person, or the mind, attention, etc.). Often in *pass.*; also *refl.*

c **1340** Hampole *Prose Tr.* 17 If þou se any mane gastely ocupiede ffalle in any of þise synnes. **1377** Langl. *P. Pl.* B. v. 409, I am occupied eche day, haliday and other, With ydel tales atte ale. **1413** *Pilgr. Sowle* (Caxton) i. xxi. (1859) 22 He occupyed my wyttes with other thynges. *c* **1489** Caxton *Sonnes of Aymon* xxviii. 578 Many stones..ynoughe for to ocupye at ones all the masons that were there. **1555** Eden *Decades* 136 They occupyed them selues in the searchinge of particular tractes and coastes. **1604** E. G[rimstone] *D'Acosta's Hist. Indies* iii. i. 117 Then shall he truly occupie himselfe in the studie of Philosophie. **1781** Cowper *Conversation* 57 Whatever subject occupy discourse. **1795** Burke *Corr.* IV. 330 It..would have occupied the attention of all companies. **1860** Tyndall *Glac.* i. xvi. 105, I occupied myself with my instruments. **1875** Jowett *Plato* (ed. 2) I. 80 Every one who is occupied with public affairs.

†**5.** To make use of, use (a thing). *Obs.*

c **1425** Lydg. *Assembly of Gods* 1935 As though that he wolde Hys darte haue occupyed. **1483** Caxton *Cato* B iij b, In makyng and ocupyeng false dyse. **1523** Fitzherb. *Husb.* §1 Than is the ploughe the moste necessaryest instrumente than an husbande can occupy. **1581** Marbeck *Bk. of Notes* 34 When the night is past..why should we occupie anie longer a candle. **1584** Cogan *Haven Health* (1636) 113 When you will occupie more or lesse, you may put in sugar and sit it over the fire, untill it boyle. **1774** C. Keith *Farmer's Ha'*, Lasses, occupy your wheel.

†**b.** *intr.* with *of.* *Obs.*

1558 Warde tr. *Alexis' Secr.* (1580) 52 b, Occupie alwaies of this Sope, when you will washe your heade. *Ibid.* (1568) 94 b, At every time that you wyll occupye of it, styrre it well.

†**6.** *trans.* To employ oneself in, engage in, practise, perform, carry on; to follow or ply as one's business or occupation. *Obs.*

? *c* **1400** in *Hist. & Antiq. Masonry* 28 Hit is called Effraym, and there was sciens of Gemetry and masonri fyrst occupied. **1465** *Paston Lett.* II. 182 Leve wylfullnesse whyche men sey ye occupye to excessifly. **1524** in *Vicary's Anat.* (1888) App. iii. 157 Iniunccion ys geuen to the seyd Roys, that he shall no more occupie Phisik. **1535** Coverdale *Ps.* cvi[i.] 23 They that go downe to the see in shippes, & occupie their busynesse in greate waters. **1581** W. Stafford *Exam. Compl.* ii. (1876) 48 Therefore men wil the gladder occupy husbandry.

†**b.** *intr.* To be busy or employed (in some capacity); to exercise one's craft or function; to practise; to do business, to work. *Obs.*

c **1425** Lydg. *Assembly of Gods* 450 Ye seelyd my patent, yeuyng me full power soo to occupy. **1512** *Act 3 Hen. VIII*, c. 11 To exercise and occupie as a Phisicion. **1576** *Lichfield Gilds* (E.E.T.S.) 27 Admytted..to occupie as a master, Iourney-man, or servaunte within the said Cittie. **1618** N. Field *Amends Ladies* A j, I do entertain you. How do you occupy? What can you use? **1653** Urquhart *Rabelais* i. vii, The Seamsters (when the point of their needles was broken) began to work and occupie with the tail.

†**7.** *trans.* To employ (money or capital) in trading; to lay out, invest, put out to interest, trade with; to deal in. [L. *occupare pecuniam.*]

1526 *Pilgr. Perf.* (W. de W. 1531) 28 b, This rychesse he hath gyuen to vs as a stocke to occupy. **1560** Daus tr. *Sleidane's Comm.* 118 He commaunded that the talentes received should be occupied that they might be made gainfull. **1581** Marbeck *Bk. of Notes* 1075 Wee be commaunded to occupie our Lords money, and not to hide it. **1602** Fulbecke *1st Pt. Parall.* 29 If two Merchantes occupie their goods and merchandise in common to their common profite, the one of them may haue a writ of accompt against his companion. **1611** Bible *Ezek.* xxvii. 9. **1773** Johnson *Let. to Mrs. Thrale* 17 May, Upon ten thousand pounds diligently occupied, they may live in great plenty.

†**b.** *intr.* To trade, deal. *Obs.*

1525 Ld. Berners *Froiss.* II. cxi. [cvii.] 318 Berthaulte of Malygnes..occupyeth to Damas, to Cayre, and to Alexandre. **1534** Tindale *Luke* xix. 13 Occupye tyll I come [*R.V.* Trade ye herewith]. **1581** Marbeck *Bk. of Notes* 653 [He] gained much by occupieng with the Iewes and Christians. **1650** Fuller *Pisgah* ii. v. 129 Such as occupied in her fairs with all precious stones.

†**8.** *trans.* and *intr.* To deal with or have to do with sexually; to cohabit. *Obs.*

[Cf. L. *occupare amplexu*, Ovid F. iii. 509; but perh. of Eng. origin.]

[**1432–50** tr. *Higden* (Rolls) III. 47 Men of Lacedemonia ..fatigate and wery thro the compleyntes of theire wifes beenge at home, made a decre and ordinaunce that thei scholde occupye [Trevisa, take; Higd. *pluribus uti viris*] mony men, thenkenge the nowmbre of men to be encreasede by that.] *c* **1520** in *Laneham's Let.* (1871) Introd. 130 To make hyme [your husband] lystear to occupye with youe. **1546** Bale *Eng. Votaries* i. (1550) 56 b, As king Edwine.. occupyed Alfgiua his concubine. **1632** Rowley *Wom. Never Vexed* iii. i. in Hazl. *Dodsley* XII. 137 Being partners, they did occupy long together before they were married. **1660** Hexham, *Genooten een Vrouw*, To Lie with, or to Occupie a woman.

[*Note.* The disuse of this verb in the 17th and most of the 18th c. is notable. Against 194 quots. for 16th c., we have for 17th only 8, outside the Bible of 1611 (where it occurs 10 times), and for 18th c. only 10, all of its last 33 years. The verb occurs only twice (equivocally) in Shaks., is entirely absent from the Concordances to Milton and Pope, is not used by Gray; all Johnson's quots., exc. 2, are from the Bible of 1611. It was again freely used by Cowper (13 instances in Concordance). This avoidance appears to have been due to its vulgar employment in sense 8; cf. **1597** Shaks. *2 Hen. IV*, ii. iv. 161 (Qo. 1600) A captaine? Gods light these villaines wil make the word as odious as the word occupy, which was an excellent good worde before it was il sorted. *a* **1637** B. Jonson *Discov., De Stylo* (1640) 112 Many, out of their owne obscene Apprehensions, refuse proper and fit words; as *occupie, nature*, and the like.]

'**occupying**, *vbl. sb.* Now *rare* exc. as gerund. [f. prec. + -ing[1].] The action of the verb occupy, or that in which this action is embodied.

1. The taking or holding possession.

1472–3 *Rolls of Parlt.* VI. 28/1 That no persone be charged..for any entre or occupyenge of the said Lordshippes, Londes, Tenementez or othur premisses.

†**2.** A piece of land occupied or held; a holding.

c **1449** Pecock *Repr.* v. xiii. 554 The same bildingis and her occupiyngis. **1577** Harrison *England* ii. xiii. (1877) i. 259 In the woodland countries..they [houses] stand scattered abroad, each one dwelling in the midst of his owne occupieng.

b. Residence in a place as its tenant. Chiefly *attrib.*

1884 Gladstone *Sp.* 28 Feb., The proportion of occupying franchises..to the property franchises. **1884** *Daily News* 24 Sept. 6/2 His views on peasant proprietary and occupying ownership.

3. The action of engaging or busying, or fact of being engaged in or busy about something; †that which occupies one, or in which one is engaged; occupation, business; trade, traffic.

c **1380** Wyclif *Wks.* (1880) 104 Þei suffren cristene soulis be stranglid wiþ woluys of helle þorouȝ here doumbnesse and occupiynge aboute þe world. **1548** *Act 2 & 3 Edw. VI*, c. 13 §11 Anye parishe..uppon..þe Sea costes, the commodities and occupyinge whereof consisteth chieflye in fysshinge. **1582** N. T. (Rhem.) *Luke* xix. 15 How much every man had gained by occupying. **1588** J. Mellis *Briefe Instr.* B viij, A butcher might sell you..all the felles, hides and tallowe growing and comming by his occupying.

†**b.** Carrying on, practice (*of* something). *Obs.*

1547 *Nottingham Rec.* IV. 92 For okypying of comyn skowddyng [scolding]. **1550** Bale *Apol.* 42 A full exercysed craftesman in that occupyeng of mischefe.

†**4.** Using, use, employment (see also prec. 8).

1535 Coverdale *Num.* iv. 26 The altare and their cordes and all that belongeth to their occupienge. **1540** Hyrde tr. *Vives' Instr. Chr. Wom.* U vj, By hir diligence & occupying of wooll, hir house shal lack nothing. **1544** STALBRIDGE *Epistle* 22b, From the fylthy occupying of an harlot he cometh strayght to the Aultre. **1579** GOSSON *Apol. Sch. Abuse* (Arb.) 72 Iron with much occupiying, is worne too naught.

ˈoccupying, *ppl. a.* [f. as prec. + -ING[2].] That occupies (see the verb); usually, That actually holds or resides in (a place or piece of land). **occupying power**, a state whose army occupies (part of) a foreign country; used *spec.* with ref. to the occupation of Germany after the war of 1939–45.

1552 HULOET, Occupyinge, *occupans.* **1780** A. YOUNG *Tour Irel.* II. 141 The occupying tenants have from 15 to 100 acres. **1887** J. BALL *Nat. in S. Amer.* ii. 57 To protect the occupying army from this danger. **1887** *Spectator* 16 Apr. 532/1 The extinction of great landlords and the creation of occupying owners. **1946** *Ann. Reg. 1945* 452/1 (Index) Germany,.. Legislation by occupying powers. **1959** *Observer* 22 Mar. 1/2 Nuclear weapons..would be in the hands of the occupying Powers and never pass into German control. **1965** A. J. P. TAYLOR *Eng. Hist. 1914–45* xvi. 594 The Allied leaders..reached agreement of a kind over the reparations which each of the occupying Powers could exact from its zone of Germany. **1975** J. CLEARY *Safe House* i. 26 The need to show the Occupying Powers that..they were not going to favour Nazis and ex-Nazis.

occur (əˈkɜː(r)), *v.* Also 6–7 occurre, 7 occurr. Inflexions occurred, occurring. [ad. L. *occurrĕre* to run to meet, run against, befall, present itself, occur, f. *oc-, ob-* (OB- 1 a, b) + *curr-ĕre* to run. Cf. obs. F. *occurrer, occurrir* to present itself, happen (16th c. in Godef.).]

†**1.** *intr.* To run to meet a person, to run up (to the spot); to run against something or against each other, to meet, encounter. *Obs.*

1596 DALRYMPLE tr. *Leslie's Hist. Scot.* II. 173 The Scottis ..brekis in ower the nerrest prouince,..Trebellie occuris in al haist. **1620** SHELTON *Quix.* III. ii. I. 117 She was of a charitable nature..and did therefore presently occur to cure Don Quixote. **1692** BENTLEY *Boyle Lect.* vii. 235 The whole multitude might freely move..with very little occurring or interfering. **1695** WOODWARD *Nat. Hist. Earth* (1723) 200 Such of those Corpuscles, as happen'd to occur or meet together.

†**b.** With prepositions: To meet *with*, encounter; to happen or light *upon*; to make resistance *against*, resist, oppose; to reply *to*, meet in argument (an adverse statement or contention); to prove adverse *to*, to stop the way of. *Obs.*

1527 *St. Papers Hen. VIII*, I. 233 The Frenche King was determyned that I should occurre, encountre, and mete with hym at Amyas. **1566** PAINTER *Pal. Pleas.* I. Ded. 2 Viewing in him great plenty of straung Histories,..I occurred upon some which I deemed most worthy the prouulgation. **1588** D. ROGERS in Ellis *Orig. Lett.* Ser. II. III. 153 How by a league they might..occurre against the daungerous practises of the papistes. **1660** PEARSON *No Necess. Ref. Ch. Eng.* 7 To leave nothing unanswered.. I shall endeavour to occurre to all Particulars which may seem to inferre the Doubtfulnesse of the Doctrine. **1692** BENTLEY *Boyle Lect.* 117 To this last subterfuge of the mechanical atheists we can occurr several ways. *Ibid.* 138 Bodies..have..a certain and determinate motion according to..the resistance of the bodies they occurr with. **1738** *Hist. Crt. Excheq.* vi. 113 No time occurs to the King.

†**c.** *trans.* (by ellipsis of prep.: see b.) To meet, encounter; to oppose, resist. *Obs.* (In quot. 1767 humorously pedantic.)

a **1548** HALL *Chron., Hen. VI*, 160b, That the citezens.. might occurre their enemies, and releve their frendes. **1577–87** HOLINSHED *Chron.* III. 1058/1 To occurre all inconueniences whatsoeuer. **1652** GAULE *Magastrom.* 146 Fate may..easily be occurred and prevented. **1767** A. CAMPBELL *Lexiph.* (ed. 2) 1 Most happily occurred, my very benevolent convivial associate.

2. *intr.* To present itself; to be met with or found, to 'turn up', or appear (*in* some place, class of things, course of action, etc.).

1538 CROMWELL *Let. to Sir T. Wyatt* 22 Feb. (R.), As soon as any opportunity shall occur for the same. **1563–7** BUCHANAN *Reform. St. Andros* Wks. (1892) 8 Other thyngis ..to be doin as commodite and tyme occurris. **1605** CAMDEN *Rem.* 60 That name doth often occurre in olde evidences. **1763** DODSLEY *Leasowes* ¶2 The first object that occurs is a ..ruinated wall. **1818** CRUISE *Digest* (ed. 2) IV. 470 The variety of cases that may occur in practice. **1823** H. J. BROOKE *Introd. Crystallogr.* 250 The different classes of primary forms in which irregular secondary forms occur. **1851** GOSSE *Nat. in Jamaica* 103 About fourteen species have occurred to me. *a* **1864** HAWTHORNE *Amer. Note-bks.* (1879) I. 131 Marble also occurs here. *Mod.* The wild tulip is said to occur in chalk-pits.

b. To present itself to thought, come into one's mind. Const. *to*; in mod. use often with *it* as subject, referring to a following clause or phrase.

1626 BACON *Sylva* §401 There doth not occurre to me, at this present, any use thereof, for profit. **1711** ADDISON *Spect.* No. 105 ¶3 Such Reflexions as occurred to me upon that Subject. **1809** MALKIN *Gil Blas* v. i. ¶22 It could not but occur to me that you would be agreeably surprised. **1833–6** J. EAGLES *Sketcher* (1856) 86 A picture occurs to my recollection. **1875** JOWETT *Plato* (ed. 2) III. 5 New ideas occur to him in the act of writing. *Mod.* It did not occur to me to mention it.

3. To present itself in the course of events; to happen, befall, take place as an event or incident.

1549 *Compl. Scot.* i The vniuersal pestilens and mortalite, that hes occurit mercyles amang the pepil. **1582** ABP. HAMILTON *Catech.* (1884) 4 All variance and discentioun that occurris or may apperandly occure. *a* **1680** BUTLER *Rem.* (1759) I. 13 It is uncertain, when Such Wonders will occur agen. **1835** URE *Philos. Manuf.* 402 It is almost impossible for an accident to occur. **1862** TROLLOPE *Orley F.* xiv. 112 To Mrs. Orme she told all that had occurred. **1891** W. J. DAWSON *Redempt. E. Strahan* vi. 106 Repentance was not a thing which occurred and was done with.

4. *Eccl.* (See quot., and cf. CONCUR 2 e.)

1863 NEALE *Ess. Liturgiol.* 109 One Festival *occurs* with another when the two feasts fall on the same day.

Hence **occurring** (əˈkɜːrɪŋ), *ppl. a.* (now *rare*).

1637 GILLESPIE *Eng. Pop. Cerem.* I. vii. 23 Fasts which are appointed for ocurring causes. **1682** T. FLATMAN *Heraclitus Ridens* No. 82 (1713) II. 249 To suggest the most occurring and probable Conjectures.

occur, occure: see OCKER, OCHRE.

occurrence (əˈkʌrəns). [prob. f. OCCURRENT: (see -ENCE); but cf. med.L. *occurrentia* (Du Cange), F. *occurrence* (*c* 1475 in Godef. *Compl.*).]

†**1.** An incidental meeting or encounter. *rare.*

1607 TOPSELL *Four-f. Beasts* (1658) 366 When Androcles was..cast in among these savage beasts, the lion..came toward him softly.. so the man began to know him, and both of them to congratulate each other in that their imprisoned occurrence.

2. The fact of occurring, *i.e.* of presenting itself, being found or met with, turning up, or of happening, taking place.

1725 WATTS *Logic* II. v, Things of the most frequent Occurrence. *a* **1748** WATTS (J.), Voyages detain the mind by the perpetual occurrence and expectation of something new. **1860** TYNDALL *Glac.* II. vii. 261 A number of facts of common occurrence. **1866** ROGERS *Agric. & Prices* I. xxiv. 607 Evidence of the occurrence of that fish on the Kentish coast. **1880** GEIKIE *Phys. Geog.* iv. §24. 249 Landslips are of frequent occurrence. **1897** *Westm. Gaz.* 2 Nov. 3/2 A bird whose occurrences in England can be counted on one hand.

3. That which occurs or is met with, or presents itself, formerly sometimes with the sense of opposition; now with *an* and *pl.*: Something that occurs, happens, or takes place; an event, incident. (= OCCURRENT B. 1, the earlier word for this.)

1539 CROMWELL *Let. to Wyatt* 13 Feb. (R.), Here we have no notable news and occurrences. **1601** SHAKS. *Twel. N.* v. i. 264 All the occurrence of my fortune since Hath beene betweene this Lady, and this Lord. **1623** BINGHAM *Xenophon* 109 While we march, let Timasion with the horse scout before..giuing aduertisement of all occurrence. **1652** NEEDHAM tr. *Selden's Mare Cl.* 3 What Occurrences seem to oppose the Dominion of Sea and what Arguments are wont to bee made against it. **1711** STEELE *Spect.* No. 96 ¶8 The chief Occurrences of my Life. **1719** YOUNG *Revenge* v. ii, The fix'd and noble mind Turns all occurrence to its own advantage. **1773** GOLDSM. *Stoops to Conq.* I. i, Trust to occurrences for success. **1884** tr. *Lotze's Metaph.* 239 The relation in which empty Time stands to the occurrences which fall within it.

4. *Eccl.* (See OCCUR 4; cf. CONCURRENCE 2 b.)

1863 NEALE *Ess. Liturgiol.* 109 These are all the occurrences, etc. which take place during this year. **1879, 1889** [see CONCURRENCE 2 b].

5. *attrib.*, as **occurrence(s book**, a record of events kept at a police station, drawn from the diaries of police officers.

1929 J. MOYLAN *Scotland Yard* vi. 138 Occurrence Books are kept at all stations, so that there may be a complete daily record of all occurrences, etc., at the station or within the area assigned to it. **1955** M. GILBERT *Sky High* v. 72 Everything that a policeman hears, sees and does goes down in the Occurrences Book. **1966** L. SOUTHWORTH *Felon in Disguise* xi. 158 The Inspector was about to complete his Occurrence Book entries. **1972** M. GILBERT *Body of Girl* xi. 103 It would have been in the Occurrence Book... Where are the 'O' books kept?

†**oˈccurrencer.** *Obs. rare*[−1]. [See -ER[1].] One who narrates occurrences; a newsmonger.

c **1680** *Fears & Jealousies Ceas'd* 2 The Shams of an Occurrencer, or..the base and detestable Artifices of the French Politicians.

oˈccurrency. *rare.* [f. next: see -ENCY.]

†**a.** = OCCURRENCE 3. *Obs.*

1656 SANDERSON *Serm.* (1689) 512 Discoursing..on the occurrency of the times. **1683** D. A. *Art Converse* 21 A suddain anger upon all occurrencies. *Ibid.* 36 To laugh on every slight occurrency.

b. = OCCURRENCE 2.

1935 G. K. ZIFF *Psycho-Biol. of Lang.* (1936) 289 Relative frequency of occurrency of meaning. **1967** *Oceanogr. & Marine Biol.* V. 283 Most of the clusters defined by joint occurrency of species have a given geographical distribution.

occurrent (əˈkʌrənt), *a.* and *sb.* Now *rare.* Also 6 occorent, 6–7 **occurrant, -ente,** (7 **obcurrent**). [prob. a. F. *occurrent, -ant* (1475 in Godef. *Compl.*), ad. L. *occurrent-em*, pr. pple. of *occurrĕre* to OCCUR.] **A.** *adj.*

1. That occurs, presents itself, or happens; occurring; current (at a time or place). Sometimes *spec.* That presents itself casually or by the way, incidental.

1535 E. HARVEL in Ellis *Orig. Lett.* Ser. II. II. 71, I have writen..advising yow of soche newis as hath ben occorent. *c* **1555** HARPSFIELD *Divorce Hen. VIII* (Camden) 171 The manifold examples whereof be in stories occurrent. **1601** HOLLAND *Pliny* I. 161 Many other accidents and occurrent obiects. **1632** LITHGOW *Trav.* I. 7, I..being young, and within minority, in that occurrent time. **1653** *Nissena* 65 Four thousand Talents should be by them disburst towards the occurrent affairs. **1654** EARL MONM. tr. *Bentivoglio's Warrs Flanders* 266 To treat with the Duke..upon the obcurrent necessities of the League. **1655** DIGGES *Compl. Ambass.* 21, I..make you partaker of such brutes as are here occurrent. **1822** T. TAYLOR *Apuleius, Philos. Plato* I. 337 Something unstable and occurrent is accustomed to intervene in things which were undertaken with counsel and meditation. **1860** I. TAYLOR *Spir. Hebr. Poetry* (1873) 91 [Words] which are technical or geographical,..and which are rarely occurrent in literature.

†**2.** Liable to encounter (something); exposed or obnoxious *to.* *Obs. rare.*

1566 PAINTER *Pal. Pleas.* I. 26 It is not meete for them to be your gouernours, that be subiect and occurrant to enuie and reproch.

B. *sb.*

1. Something that occurs, presents itself, or meets one (formerly sometimes in an adverse way); an event: = OCCURRENCE 3. (Common in 16th and 17th c.; now *Obs.* or a rare archaism.)

1538 FOX in Pocock *Rec. Ref.* I. 141, I wrote two letters unto you..ascertaining you of my arrival and other occurrents there. **1563–87** FOXE *A. & M.* (1596) 260/1 The King..thought to haue a staie by the cardinall against all occurrents. **1602** SHAKS. *Ham.* v. ii. 368 So tell him with the occurrents more and lesse, Which haue solicited. **1611** BIBLE *1 Kings* v. 4 There is neither aduersary, nor euill occurrent. **1648** GAGE *West Ind.* title-p., Divers Occurrents and Dangers that did befal in the said Journey. **1704** in B. Church *Hist. Philip's War* (1867) II. 145 Acquaint me of your proceedings and all occurrents. **1873** H. ROGERS *Orig. Bible* vi. (1875) 216 Receiving impressions from every new occurrent.

†**b.** *transf.* A narration of what has happened; *pl.* news. *Obs.*

a **1577** SIR T. SMITH *Commw. Eng.* (1633) 97 Such letters or occurrents as be sent to himselfe. **1596** DANETT tr. *Comines* (1614) 158 The occurrents he had already receiued of the Almains arriuall. **1655** DIGGES *Compl. Ambass.* 222 For Italian news, I refer your Honor to these inclosed Occurrents.

†**2.** A person or thing that meets, encounters, or runs against one. *Obs.*

1592 R. D. *Hypnerotomachia* 2, I resolved..to get out, that I might the better eschew such suspected occurrents. **1607** WALKINGTON *Opt. Glass* xiii. 139 Another..foole.. thought his..buttockes were made of brittle glasse; wherefore he shunned all occurrents. **1615** CROOKE *Body of Man* 582 If it had beene made of a thicke and solide bone, it ..would not haue yeelded to outward occurrents.

†**occurˈsation.** *Obs. rare*[−1]. [ad. L. *occursātiōn-em*, n. of action from *occursāre* to run to meet, freq. of *occurr-ĕre* to OCCUR.] = OCCURSION.

1615 CROOKE *Body of Man* 84 The skinne..is nearer to the occursation or confluence of outward obiects.

†**oˈccurse.** *Obs.* [ad. L. *occursu-s* meeting, n. of action from *occurr-ĕre* to OCCUR.] Meeting.

1621 BURTON *Anat. Mel.* I. iii. II. i, A suddaine accident, occurse, or meeting. **1647** LILLY *Chr. Astrol.* clvi. 653 Consideration had to the house in which the occurse doth happen. **1692** BENTLEY *Boyle Lect.* ii. (1693) 25 This mutual Occurse, this Pulsion and Repercussion of Atoms.

†**oˈccursion.** *Obs.* [ad. L. *occursiōn-em*, n. of action from *occurr-ĕre* to OCCUR.] The action, or an act, of running against something; attack; encounter; collision.

1533 BELLENDEN *Livy* IV. (1822) 351 Grete occursiounis war maid be Veanis in the Romane landis. *a* **1656** USSHER *Ann.* VI. (1658) 459 [He] would not so much have dreaded the sudden occursion of any wild beast. **1678** CUDWORTH *Intell. Syst.* I. ii. §22. 97 The mutual Occursions and Rencounters of Atoms. **1741** SHORT in *Phil. Trans.* XLI. 626 Running or dancing with sudden Occursions and Mixtures, like the Auroræ Boreales.

†**oˈccursive,** *a. Obs.* [f. L. *occurs-*, ppl. stem of *occurrĕre* to OCCUR + -IVE.] Such as may present itself, or be met with by the way. Hence †**oˈccursively** *adv.*, by the way.

1592 R. D. *Hypnerotomachia* 65b, Wipe out of thy remembrance all forepassed griefes, occursive troubles. **1592** G. HARVEY *Four Lett.* iii, Some of them occursively presented themselves in stationers shops. —— *Pierce's Super.* 202 The emperour Charles the fiftes army passing through Rome, occursively sacked the city.

occyan, occyent, occysion: see OCEAN, OCCIENT, OCCISION.

ocean (ˈəʊʃən), *sb.* (*a.*) Forms: 3–6 occean, -ian, (4 oxian, 4–5 occion(e, occyon, 5 -an), 4–6 occeane, 5–6 -iane, 6 -æan, ocian, -eane, -yane, 6– ocean. [a. F. *océan* (*occean* 12th c. in Littré), ad. L. *ōcean-us*, f. Gr. ὠκεανός, orig. the great stream or river (cf. ῥόος Ὠκεανοῖο, Ὠκεανόςποταμός, in Homer) supposed to encompass the disk of the earth, and personified as 'the god of the great primeval water', the son of Uranus and Gaia, and husband of Tethys; hence, the great outer sea, as opposed to the Mediterranean.]

1. The vast body of water on the surface of the globe, which surrounds the land; the main or great sea. (Down to *c* 1650, commonly *ocean* sea; before 1400 also *sea ocean, sea of ocean* = L. *mare oceanum* (Cæsar *Bell. Gall.* II. vii, Tacitus *Hist.* IV. xii); OF. *mer oceane, ocianne, occeanne mer*, where *oceane* was adj. fem. qualifying *mer*; and *ocean*-may sometimes have been viewed as an adj. in Eng.)

In early times, when only the one great mass of land, the Eastern hemisphere, with its islands, was known, the ocean was the Great Outer Sea of boundless extent, everywhere surrounding the land, as opposed to the Mediterranean and other inland seas.

(*a*) *c* **1290** *St. Brandan* 16 in *S. Eng. Leg.* I. 220 In þe mochele se of Occean [*MS. Harl.* 2277 occian] as ore louerd þe hath i-send. *c* **1374** CHAUCER *Boeth.* IV. met. vi. 111 (Camb. MS.) The same sterre vrsa..ne coueytith nat to deeyn his flaumbes in the see of the occian. **1398** TREVISA *Barth. De P.R.* VIII. xxviii. (Tollem. MS.), þe sonne was faste by þe see of occian [L. *juxta mare oceanum*]. *c* **1400** MAUNDEV. (1839) xiii. 143 Toward the see Occyan in Inde. **1483** CAXTON *Gold. Leg.* 412 b/2 The hete of thoccean see threwe them to the refudge. **1545** BRINKLOW *Compl.* 45, I thynck it is as well possyble for the ocyane se to be without water. **1652** EARL MONM. tr. *Bentivoglio's Hist. Relat.* 1 These Provinces are inviron'd..by the Ocean Sea. **1744** OZEL tr. *Brantome's Sp. Rhodomontades* 38 The King had given Orders to the Great Ocean-Sea. **1847** MARY HOWITT *Ballads* 71 The ocean-sea doth moan and moan Like an uneasy sprite.

(*b*) *a* **1300** *Cursor M.* 11395 A folk ferr and first vncuth, Wonnand be þe est occean [*v.rr.* occyon, -eane, -ione]. **1340–70** *Alex. & Dind.* 533 þat þou miht ouur oxian, wiþ þin ost saile. **1490** CAXTON *Eneydos* xxiii. 84 About the lymytes of the grete see that men calle occeane in the marches or the sonne goynge-vnder. **1591** SPENSER *Ruins of Time* 541 For from the one he could to th' other coast, Stretch his strong thighes, and th' Occæan ouerstride. **1635** SWAN *Spec. M.* vi. §2 (1643) 187 The ocean, is that generall collection of all waters, which environeth the world on every side. **1713** YOUNG *Last Day* I. 34 See how earth smiles, and hear old ocean roar. **1801** CAMPBELL *Ye Mariners of Eng.* ii, The deck it was their field of fame, And Ocean was their grave. **1834** *Nat. Philos.* III. *Phys. Geog.* 2/1 (U.K.S.) The Ocean is spread over nearly seven-tenths of the globe.

2. One of the main areas or regions into which this body of water is divided geographically.

These divisions are partly natural, through the intervention of portions of land, partly arbitrary for geographical convenience. It is usual to reckon five of them, the *Atlantic, Pacific, Indian, Arctic*, and *Antarctic Oceans*, of which the first two are sometimes subdivided into Northern and Southern. But the Pacific, Indian, and Antarctic really form one great ocean, the 'South Sea'; of which the Atlantic and Arctic again form a smaller prolongation, divided from the larger basin only by an imaginary line drawn between the southern points of Africa and America. The name *ocean* was formerly given to smaller portions of some of these; the North Sea has still the synonym *German Ocean*.

1387 TREVISA *Higden* (Rolls) I. 53 þere þe see of occean of Athlant brekeþ out [**1432–50** (Harl. MS.) the occean Atlantyke]. **1601** HOLLAND *Pliny* I. 51 The Spanish Atlantick Ocean. **1684** tr. *Eutropius* VI. 96 He marched a Conquerour even to the British Ocean. **1727–41** CHAMBERS *Cycl.* s.v., According to Maty, the ocean may be commodiously divided into *superior* or *upper*, and *inferior* or *lower*. *Upper Ocean* which the Ancients called the *exterior*, as environing all the known parts of the world... *Inferior* or *American Ocean*..which washes the coast of America; unknown in great measure, at least, to the Ancients. **1730–6** BAILEY (folio) s.v. *Ocean*, Hyperborean Ocean..Pacifick Ocean..South Ocean. **1814** SCOTT *Jrnl. Voy. Lighth. Yacht* 9 Aug., As the Atlantic and German Oceans unite at this point, a frightful tide runs here. **1827** LD. KING in *Hansard* 28 Mar. (1828) XVII. 112 It was as feasible to bring about such an event..as it was to attempt to 'bottle off the Atlantic ocean'. **1828** J. H. MOORE *Pract. Navig.* (ed. 20) 54 That part of the North Atlantic Ocean lying between Europe and America is frequently called the Western Ocean. **1880** GEIKIE *Phys. Geog.* i. §5. 35 Though the sea is one continuous liquid mass, it has been for the sake of convenience in description divided into different areas, termed oceans.

3. *transf.* and *fig.* **a.** An immense or boundless expanse of anything; *hyperbolically*, a very great or indefinite quantity. Also *pl.*, lots *of*.

1590 SPENSER *F.Q.* II. ii. 22 A Beare and Tygre being met ..on Lybicke Ocean wide. **1591** SHAKS. *Two Gent.* II. vii. 69 A thousand oathes, an Ocean of his teares,..Warrant me welcome to my Protheus. **1642** SIR T. STAFFORD in *Lismore Papers* Ser. II. (1888) V. 82, I am now plung'd into an ocean of troubles. **1649** J. H. *Motion to Parl. Adv. Learn.* 26 Then are they..with their paper-barks committed to the great Ocean of Learning. *a* **1711** KEN *Edmund* Poet. Wks. 1721 II. 167 Oceans of Sweetness overflow'd the Shore, And yet his thirsty Spirit long'd for more. **1812** BRACKENRIDGE *Views of Louisiana* (1814) 110 To the left, we behold the ocean of prairie, with islets at intervals. **1827** KEBLE *Chr. Y., Evening* xiv, Till in the ocean of Thy love We lose ourselves in Heaven above. **1834** MRS. SOMERVILLE *Connex. Phys. Sc.* xxvi. (1849) 273 The ocean of light and heat perpetually flowing from the sun. **1840** *Spirit of Times* 25 Apr. 85/3 The leader of this predatory band had oceans of money which he looked to when he sat down, and then crammed his greasy wallet back into his pocket. **1849** MACAULAY *Hist. Eng.* iii. I. 338 Ale flowed in oceans for the populace. **1886** H. BAUMANN *Londinismen* 123/2 He's got oceans o' money. **1926** *Amer. Mercury* Dec. 465/1 She is a flaming flamboyant blonde with oceans of stuff. **1952** M. LASKI *Village* ii. 36 Poor People's children..had oceans of pocket-money because Poor People didn't understand the value of money.

b. Phr. *ocean of being*.

1652 N. CULVERWEL *Worth of Souls* in *Lt. Nature* [II]. 201 All beings they are within the souls Horizon... It can take in the several drops of Being, and it can take in much of the Ocean of Being. **1690** LOCKE *Essay Hum. Und.* I. i. 3 We let loose our thoughts into the vast ocean of Being. **1931** G. F. STOUT *Mind & Matter* 14 Knowledge of this type..leaves us adrift on the ocean of being, with oars indeed, but without rudder or compass.

4. *attrib.* and *Comb.* **a.** simple attrib. (often hyphened): of or pertaining to the ocean in its natural and physical relations, as ***ocean arm, bed, -blue, bottom, brim, cave, cliff, current, -deep, depth, -flood, floor, foam, fowl, front, -green, ice, isle, level, main, monster, nymph, rock, roll, -side, storm, tide, water, wave***, etc.; connected with the ocean in its commercial, political, or social aspects, as ***ocean-inn*** (nonce-wd.), ***line, liner, port, postage, power, scout, -song, steamer, war, warrior***, etc.

1871 R. ELLIS *Catullus* iv. 9 Propontis, or the gusty Pontic *Ocean-arm. **1637** MILTON *Lycidas* 168 So sinks the day-star in the *Ocean bed. **1842** W. C. BRYANT *Child's Funeral* in *Fountain* 62 Flowers of the morning—red, or *ocean-blue. **1936** *Times* 6 Jan. 11/3 It is in a number of good colours, including ocean-blue. **1886** A. WINCHELL *Walks Geol. Field* 197 There must have been an *ocean-bottom for the very first sediments to rest on. **1667** MILTON *P.L.* v. 140 The Sun..yet hov'ring o're the *Ocean brim. **1808** SCOTT *Marm.* I. xxix, To fair St. Andrews bound, Within the *ocean-cave to pray. **1847** MARY HOWITT *Ballads* 346 Every bird that builds a nest on *ocean-cliffs is mine. **1856** KANE *Arct. Expl.* I. xxiii. 339 The influence which *ocean-currents may exert on the temperature. **1878** HUXLEY *Physiogr.* 173 The direction of the great ocean currents. **1926** J. PEDERSEN *Israel* I. II. 463 He is overwhelmed by the surges of death..and desires to be pulled up from the *tᵉhōmōth* of the earth, its *ocean-deep. **1966** 'J. HACKSTON' *Father clears Out* 43 His diving-dress would enable a diver to go down to the very depths of the ocean-deep. **1884–92** J. TAIT *Mind in Matter* 39 He knew that the work of death goes on in *ocean-depths as elsewhere. *a* **1957** R. CAMPBELL tr. *F. Garcia Lorca's He died of Love* in *Coll. Poems* (1960) III. 78 The *ocean-flood of perjured oaths Was thundering. **1820** SHELLEY *Ode to Liberty* v, in *Prometh. Unb.* 211 The *ocean-floors Pave it. **1884** R. BRIDGES *Prometheus* 5 This variegated ocean-floor of the air. **1968** *Times* 3 Oct. 13/3 The ocean floor is spreading out from the Mid-Atlantic Ridge at a rate of between one and three centimetres a year. **1974** L. DEIGHTON *Spy Story* xix. 202 The ship sank to the ocean floor. **1818** SHELLEY *Rosalind & H.* 1092 Frankincense, Whose smoke, wool-white as *ocean foam, Hung in dense flocks. **1864** TENNYSON *En. Arden* 584 The myriad shriek of wheeling *ocean-fowl. **1934** WEBSTER, *Ocean front. **1963** *New Yorker* 8 June 104 Your own ocean-front cottages. **1975** R. L. SIMON *Wild Turkey* (1976) xxii. 159 We headed ..onto the street by the pier... We were alone on the ocean front. **1922** JOYCE *Ulysses* 253 By bronze, by gold, in *oceangreen of shadow. **1976** *Yorkshire Even. Press* 9 Dec. 20/2 (Advt.), 1973 L 144 saloon de luxe, ocean green, black trim, two bar, wing mirrors, push button radio. **1667** MILTON *P.L.* IV. 354 The Sun..hasting now with prone carreer To th' *Ocean Iles. **1851** H. MELVILLE *Moby Dick* II. ii. 7 His casual stopping-places and *ocean-inns, so to speak. **1900** *Whitaker's Almanack* 713 *heading*, A Review of the Earliest Steamboats and *Ocean Lines. **1939** T. S. ELIOT *Family Reunion* I. i. 41 These *ocean liners With all their swimming baths and gymnasiums. **1964** M. MCLUHAN *Understanding Media* II. x. 94 People used to say that an ocean liner might as well be a hotel in a big city. **1974** W. GARNER *Big Enough Wreath* 154 Like a power-boat brought under the bows of an ocean liner. **1600** W. WATSON *Decacordon* (1602) 237 Tossed to and fro vpon the *Ocean maine. **1819** SHELLEY *Cyclops* 243 Calypso and the glaucous *ocean Nymphs. **1851** A. LAWRENCE *Offic. Desp. to Daniel Webster*, A large reduction on the *ocean-postage between the two countries. **1885** TENNYSON *The Fleet* ii, His Isle, the mightiest *Ocean-power on earth. **1824** J. BOWRING *Batav. Anthol.* 61 Sterner than the *ocean-rock That stands unmoved by tempest shock. **1872** SYMONDS *Introd. Stud. Dante* 230 Dante's Rime..has no Homeric *ocean-roll. **1813** WALKER *Poems* 146 (Jod.) Tidings of war and death I bring, The *Ocean-scout replied. **1934** WEBSTER, *Oceanside. **1962** J. D. MACDONALD *Girl, Gold Watch & Everything* vi. 71 These [rooms] interconnect so this whole oceanside can be turned into a big suite. **1975** *Sat. Rev.* (U.S.) 3 May 62/3 Immaculate oceanside apartments. **1922** JOYCE *Ulysses* 261 Lips that..hummed..the *oceansong. **1861** W. FAIRBAIRN *Addr. Brit. Assoc.*, The large *ocean steamers..abundantly show what can be done with iron. **1768** BEATTIE *Minstr.* I. xxxviii, The hollow murmur of the *ocean-tide. **1827** KEBLE *Chr. Y., 1st S. Advent*, Some majestic cloud, That o'er wild scenes of *ocean-war Holds its still course in Heaven afar. **1801** CAMPBELL *Ye Mariners of Eng.* iv, Then, then, ye *Ocean-warriors! Our song and feast shall flow To the fame of your name. **1775** ROMANS *Florida* App. 65 If in the morning you find yourself in *ocean water, run SW by S for the Matancas. **1590** SPENSER *F.Q.* II. x. 5 The *ocean waues. **1667** MILTON *P.L.* III. 539 Where bounds were set To darkness, such as bound the Ocean wave.

b. instrumental and locative, as ***ocean-born, -compassed, -flooded, -flowing, -girdled, -going, -guarded, -rocked, -severed, -skirted, -smelling, -sundered*** adjs.; ***ocean-farer, -flyer, -goer***; similative, as ***ocean-wide*** adj.; objective, as ***ocean-cleaving, -dividing*** adjs.

1886 A. WINCHELL *Walks Geol. Field* 197 We must look on all these rocks as *ocean-born. *a* **1926** R. CAMPBELL *Golden Shower* in *Coll. Poems* (1957) II. 21 The *ocean-cleaving whale. **1885** H. O. FORBES *Nat. Wand. E. Archip.* 112 The most *ocean-compassed speck. **1954** W. FAULKNER *Fable* 232 The mutual rage and fear of the three *ocean-dividing nations themselves. *a* **1806** K. WHITE *Christiad* I. xxvi, The spirit that commands The *ocean-farer's life. **1878** B. TAYLOR *Deukalion* III. i. 95 The *ocean-flooded throats Of headland caverns. **1922** JOYCE *Ulysses* 656 Confluent *oceanflowing rivers with their tributaries and transoceanic currents. **1884** *Pall Mall G.* 15 Aug. 4/1 The procession of steamers of all sorts and conditions,..spick-and-span *ocean-goers, graceful yachts, and ugly barges, is never ending. **1885** *Whitaker's Almanack* 450/2 Lines of steamships..omitted..because they do not fall within the category of '*ocean-going' ships. **1838** MISS PARDOE *River & Desert* II. 45 As the day-god sank to his *ocean-rest. **1895** STEAD in *Westm. Gaz.* 4 Sept. 3/3 The *ocean-severed members of the Anglo-Saxon race. **1864** TENNYSON *En. Arden* 94 Enoch's ocean-spoil In *ocean-smelling osier. **1863** W. PHILLIPS *Speeches* i. 4 No matter whether the line ..be an imaginary one or *ocean-wide.

c. Special combs., as **ocean-basin**, the depression of the earth's surface in which an ocean lies; **ocean-crown** (*rhet.*) the imaginary symbol of the sovereignty of the seas; **ocean-fountain** (*rhet.*), the source of the waters of the ocean; **ocean god**, a marine deity, esp. the Roman Neptune; **ocean greyhound**, a rhetorical appellation of a swift ocean steamer; **ocean-king** = *ocean-god*; also, the monarch of an island or maritime region; **ocean-lane**, a lane or track across the ocean; esp. a track prescribed for ocean steamers; **oceanless** *a.* (*nonce-wd.*) devoid of or lacking an ocean; **ocean-line** (only Melville) = *ocean-lane*; **ocean-palace** (*rhet.*), a sumptuously fitted and furnished ocean passenger-steamer; **ocean pipe-fish**, a pipe-fish, *Entelurus æquoreus*, found in oceanic waters of north-western Europe; = *snake pipe-fish* (SNAKE *sb.* 12 b); **ocean-river, ocean-stream**, the great stream anciently supposed to encompass the earth (see sense 1); **ocean-sea** (see sense 1); **ocean spray** *N. Amer.*, a shrub of western North America, *Holodiscus discolor*, of the family Rosaceæ, sometimes included in the genus *Spiræa*, and distinguished by curving branches bearing large panicles of small white flowers; **ocean tramp** (see quots.); **ocean-trout** (U.S.), the menhaden (*Cent. Dict.* 1891); **ocean wave**, rhyming slang for 'shave'.

1886 *Act 49 & 50 Vict.* c. 26. Sched. B. II. Class 4. (9) The expedition of Her Majesty's ship 'Challenger'..to investigate the physical and biological conditions of the great *ocean basins. **1861** W. F. COLLIER *Hist. Eng. Lit.* 150 When Britain began to take her first steps towards winning that *ocean-crown which she now so proudly wears. **1671** *True Non-conf.* 3 All our gloryings..ought to be carried back to, concentred in, and swallowed up of the *Ocean-fountain, whence they proceed. **1819** SHELLEY *Cyclops* 24 The one-eyed children of the *Ocean God, The man-destroying Cyclopses. **1891** *Daily Chron.* 24 Mar. (Farmer), An unarmoured cruiser, a 'commerce destroyer'..capable of catching any of the great *ocean greyhounds. **1913** F. H. BURNETT *T. Tembarom* xl. 519 An ocean greyhound had landed the pair at the dock. **1967** *Economist* 23 Sept. 1109/1 Ironically, the airlines which once had only speed to offer against the one-time ocean greyhounds, can now anticipate the lounges, cinemas, etc., which until the jumbo jets get going remain one of the few prerogatives of the ocean liners. **1725** POPE *Odyss.* XI. 161 A threefold offering to his altar bring..and hail the *Ocean-King. **1819** SHELLEY *Cyclops* 266 Great offspring of the ocean-king. **1842** TENNYSON *Voyage* 19 How oft we saw the Sun retire,..Fall from his *Ocean-lane of fire, And sleep beneath his pillar'd light! **1941** T. S. ELIOT *Dry Salvages* ii. 9 We cannot think of a time that is *oceanless. **1851** H. MELVILLE *Moby Dick* II. ii. 5 The sperm whales..mostly swim in *veins*, as they are called; continuing their way along a given *ocean-line with ..undeviating exactitude. **1900** E. C. BRODRICK *Mem. & Impr.* 60 The so-called *ocean-palaces which now crowd the Atlantic, the Mediterranean [etc.]. **1865** J. COUCH *Hist. Fishes Brit. Islands* IV. 358, I have possessed a male of the acknowledged *Ocean Pipefish which in length measured twenty-six inches. **1925** J. T. JENKINS *Fishes Brit. Isles* 372/2 Ocean pipefish. **1906** *Contrib. U.S. Nat. Herbarium* XI. 330 Schizonotus discolor... *Ocean spray. **1940** *Oregon: End of Trail* 20 In the spring and early summer..sweet syringa, ocean spray, and Douglas spirea form streamside thickets of riotous blossom. **1971** *Islander* (Victoria, B.C.) 28 Mar. 12/2 A rod made from a seasoned spirea (ocean spray), a common shrub around Victoria. **1667** MILTON *P.L.* I. 202 That Sea-beast Leviathan, which God of all his works Created hugest that swim th' *Ocean stream. **1891** *Labour Commission Gloss.*, *Ocean Tramps or Tramp Steamers, a nautical term applied to all seagoing steamships (outside the regular liners, *i.e.* not confined to one particular trade) which earn their freight solely by cargo-carrying to all or any parts of the world. **1899** *Daily News* 9 Jan. 6/1 Ocean tramps or cargo boats, jerry-built, run up by contract. **1928** M. C. SHARPE *Chicago May* 287/2 *Ocean waves [sic], shave. **1934** *John o' London's Weekly* 9 June 353/1, I 'as my ocean wave an' when I've got my mince-pie properly open I goes down the apples and pears.

Hence (*nonce-wds.*) **'oceaned** *a.*, provided with an ocean or oceans; **'oceaner**, †(*a*) one of an oceanic race; (*b*) an ocean-going vessel; **'oceanet**, a small ocean; **'oceanful**, as much as an ocean contains, an immense quantity; **'oceanly** *adv.*, in a manner like that of the ocean.

1853 ALEX. SMITH *Poems* Sonn. i, A porter is a porter though his load Be the *oceaned world. **1658** HARRINGTON *Oceana* 43 This an Army of *Oceaners in their own Country ..will never bear. **1879** W. WHITMAN *Specimen Days* (1882–3) 136 The proud, steady, noiseless cleaving of the grand oceaner down the bay. **1681** COTTON *Wond. Peak* (ed. 4) 26 Three minutes space To highest mark this *oceanet does raise. **1883** STEVENSON *Silverado Sq.* (1886) 34 It [the air] came pouring over these green slopes by the *oceanful. **1835** CLARE *Rural Muse* 167 The chill air comes around me *oceanly.

Oceana (əʊʃiːˈeɪnə). The name of Harrington's ideal state, applied by J. A. Froude to the British Maritime Empire.

[**1656** J. HARRINGTON (*title*) The Common-Wealth of Oceana.] **1886** J. A. FROUDE *Oceana* 395 If Oceana is to be hereafter governed by a federal parliament, such a parliament will grow when the time is ripe for it. **1889** J. MILNE *Romance of Pro-Consul* ix. 87 He was being set to the straightening-out of some twist in Oceana, to the healing of a sore which threatened one of her limbs.

oceanarium (əʊʃiːəˈnɛərɪəm). orig. *U.S.* Pl. -ia. [f. OCEAN *sb.* (*a.*) + *-arium*, after AQUARIUM.] An establishment having a pool in which large sea-creatures can be kept and observed, esp. for public entertainment.

1944 E. B. MARKS *They All had Glamour* 440 The aquarium of other days is now slated to be the oceanarium. **1955** *Sci. News Let.* 2 Apr. 211 (*caption*) A puzzled fisherman hauled the strange fish in in his shad net off the northern coast of Florida and it was identified by scientists at the oceanarium at Marineland, Fla. **1962** *Times* 15 Feb. 15/5 This is the usual training manœuvre for any type of animal in circuses and in oceanaria. **1972** *Village Voice* (N.Y.) 1 June 21/5 In exploiting the killer whale for the amusement of the crowds, the oceanarium people exploded two myths about Shamu's sisters and brothers of the sea. **1977** *Time* 4 July 28/3 In San Diego, 55 miles from Disneyland, is Sea World, the best-planned, best-stocked oceanarium in the U.S.

oceanaut (ˈəʊʃiːənɔːt). [f. OCEAN *sb.* (*a.*) + *-naut*, after AQUANAUT.] One who lives for a period at the bottom of the sea in an underwater 'house'.

1962 *Daily Tel.* 7 Sept. 1/5 This cylinder will be pierced in the middle by a large chimney, through which our two oceanauts will pass. **1967** *Ibid.* 30 Jan. 10/6 Cousteau looks forward to training oceanauts for completely new tasks like servicing and even laying deep underwater pipe lines for oil companies, as well as carrying out research on the almost unknown marine life found at such depths.

Oceania (əʊʃiːˈeɪnɪə). [mod.L., ad. F. *Océanie* (Malte Brun, *c* 1812), f. L. *ōcean-us*, after *Asia*, *Polynesia*, and other names of parts of the world.] A general name for the islands of the Pacific and its adjacent seas.

1849 *Syst. Univ. Geog.* 967 Oceanica or Oceania..this name has been employed by the French geographers and adopted by those of other nations. **1857** *Chambers' Inform.* II. 296/1 Oceania..naturally divides itself into three great sections—Malaysia, Australasia, and Polynesia. **1858** *Penny Cycl.* 2nd Supp. 470/2 *Oceania*, a name given by Balbi and other French geographers to a fifth division of the earth. **1860** FARRAR *Orig. Lang.* 167 In Oceania it has been asserted that nearly every island or group of islands possesses a speech which barely offers any affinity with that of the neighbouring groups.

Oceanian (əʊʃiːˈeɪnɪən), *a.* and *sb.* [ad. F. *océanien* (cf. quot. 1831), f. *océan* OCEAN.]

A. *adj.* Of or pertaining to the Pacific Ocean and its islands, or to Oceania generally.

1831 *Westm. Rev.* Jan. 19 Of the various races into which the population of the innumerable islands scattered through the vast extent of the Pacific Ocean have been divided, the first..is that termed by M. Lesson *The Oceanian* [in *Hist. Nat. de l'Homme*]. *Ibid.*, Attributing a high degree of beauty to the Oceanian women. **1899** *Westm. Gaz.* 9 Jan. 5/1 [From the *Gaulois*] The loss which she [Great Britain] would suffer by the eventful dislocation of her American and Oceanian possessions.

B. *sb.* A native of Oceania; a Polynesian.

1831 *Westm. Rev.* Jan. 19 The Oceanians are..superior in beauty of form and features, to the other races inhabiting the South Sea islands. **1861** HULME tr. *Moquin-Tandon* I. iv. 26 The Malays or Oceanians.

oceanic (əʊʃiːˈænɪk), *a.* [ad. med. or mod.L. *ōceanic-us*, f. *ōceanus* OCEAN: cf. F. *océanique* (1548 in Hatz.-Darm., also in Cotgr. 1611) and -IC.]

1. a. Of or pertaining to, situated or living in or by, the ocean; flowing into the ocean.

1656 [see OCEANINE]. **1755** in JOHNSON. **1772–84** COOK *Voy.* (1790) VI. 2116 Gulls, petrels, and other oceanic birds. **1830** LYELL *Princ. Geol.* I. 244 The population of all oceanic deltas are particularly exposed to suffer by such catastrophes. **1834** MRS. SOMERVILLE *Connex. Phys. Sc.* xv. (1849) 135 The Gulf-stream and other oceanic rivers. **1851–6** WOODWARD *Mollusca* 12 The oceanic-snail, and multitudes of other floating molluscs, pass their lives on the open sea. **1859** DARWIN *Orig. Spec.* iv. (1873) 82 An oceanic island at first sight seems to have been highly favourable for the production of new species. **1869** RAWLINSON *Anc. Hist.* 12 The rivers of the circumjacent plains are..oceanic, i.e. they mingle themselves with the waters of the great deep. **1880** W. B. CARPENTER in *19th Cent.* No. 38. 596 The proper oceanic area is a portion of the crust of the earth..depressed with tolerable uniformity some thousands of feet below the land area.

b. Pertaining to or inhabiting those regions of the open sea beyond the edge of a continental shelf.

1877 H. N. MOSELEY in *Q. Jrnl. Microsc. Sci.* XVII. 24 The present oceanic form is placed in the genus Stylochus on account of the position of the tentacles. **1902** *Encycl. Brit.* XXXIII. 936/2 The majority of the oceanic epiplankton appears to be stenothermal. **1909** [see *holoplankton* s.v. HOLO-]. **1942** H. U. SVERDRUP et al. *Oceans* viii. 278 The oceanic province has an upper lighted zone and a lower dark zone. **1953** E. PALMER tr. *Ekman's Zoogeogr. Sea* xiv. 312 The coastal organisms..are termed neritic and they are contrasted with the open-sea organisms; the latter are often called simply oceanic, but this term is less exact. **1974** LUCAS & CRITCH *Life in Oceans* i. 24 The pelagic division is divided into the region inshore of the continental edge, known as the 'neritic province', and the remainder, called the 'oceanic province'. In the oceanic province some aspects of the environment may change with level.

2. a. Of the nature of an ocean, ocean-like; of immense extent or magnitude; vast.

a **1834** COLERIDGE *Notes Eng. Divines* (1853) I. 209 His reading had been oceanic. **1834** —— *Table-t.* 15 Mar., The body and substance of his [Shakspere's] works came out of the unfathomable depths of his own oceanic mind. **1977** *Language* LIII. 391 One must at all times bear in mind, however, that this [*sc.* the philosophy of history] is a field of oceanic proportions.

b. *oceanic feeling*: a phrase used in a communication with Freud by R. Rolland (1866–1944), French writer and philosopher, in describing the longing for something vast and eternal of which he and others felt aware, and which he suggested as a possible source of religious feelings, but Freud interpreted as probably the nostalgia of the psyche for the ego-completeness of infancy; so *oceanic longing*.

1930 J. RIVIERE tr. *Freud's Civilization & its Discontents* i. 8 It is a feeling which he would like to call a sensation of 'eternity', a feeling as of something limitless, unbounded, something 'oceanic'... I cannot discover this 'oceanic' feeling in myself. *Ibid.* 21 The 'oceanic' feeling, which I suppose seeks to reinstate limitless narcissism... I can imagine that the oceanic feeling could become connected with religion later on. **1944** O. FENICHEL in *Psychoanal. Rev.* XXXI. 145 The masochist behaves masochistically because he has an oceanic longing for being united with a greater unity. **1949** KOESTLER *Insight & Outlook* xiii. 194 The general occurrence of the oceanic feeling, of the tendency towards cosmic self-transcendence, is a fact. **1967** *Philos. Rev.* LXXVI. 207 Correlates..may be lacking when we come to the experiencing of oceanic feelings. **1971** P. BALOGH *Freud* x. 109 The feeling described by Romain Rolland of being mystically identified with the universe Freud called an oceanic feeling.

3. Of or pertaining to Oceania; = OCEANIAN A.

1842 PRICHARD *Nat. Hist. Man* 332 The Oceanic race, is, on the other hand, the most beautiful..of all the nations who inhabit the isles of the Great Southern Ocean. **1857** *Chambers' Inform.* II. 296/1 The native inhabitants of all these islands..forming the Oceanic section of the Mongolidæ in Dr. Latham's classification. **1937** *Discovery* Oct. 303/2 The origins of the Oceanic peoples and the remarkable affinities of culture between them and the Naga tribes of Assam. **1971** L. A. BOGER *Dict. World Pott. & Porc.* 248/1 In a general sense Oceanic pottery is primarily a woman's craft. **1974** S. MARCUS *Minding the Store* (1975) xiv. 288 They then proceeded to duplicate the same systematic approach to pre-Columbian terracottas and Oceanic sculpture.

4. Of a climate: influenced by proximity to a large body of water and hence having a relatively small diurnal and annual range of temperature and relatively great precipitation.

1877 A. GEIKIE *Elem. Lessons Physical Geogr.* v. 351 An insular or oceanic climate is one where the difference between summer and winter temperature is reduced to a minimum, and where there is a copious supply of moisture from the large water-surface. **1902** *Encycl. Brit.* XXX. 710/2 A globe whose surface is dotted with land and water, so uniformly intermixed that there can be no chance for the existence of distinct areas of continental and oceanic climates. **1922** W. G. KENDREW *Climates of Continents* xxix. 215 The east of the British Isles has a continental rather than oceanic rainfall régime. **1957** G. E. HUTCHINSON *Treat. Limnol.* I. vii. 443 The distinction between oceanic and continental climatic regimes. **1974** *Encycl. Brit. Macropædia* IV. 726/1 The differences between oceanic (or maritime) and continental climates, though operative in all latitudes, are most apparent in middle latitudes.

Oceanica (əʊʃɪˈænɪkə). [mod.L., ad. F. *Océanique*, earlier form of *Océanie*.] = OCEANIA.

1832 LYELL *Princ. Geol.* II. 296 An area in eastern Oceanica, studded with minute islands. **1842** PRICHARD *Nat. Hist. Man* 326 The human inhabitants of Oceanica divide themselves into three groups. **1849** [see OCEANIA].

oceanicity (əʊʃiːəˈnɪsɪtɪ). [f. OCEANIC *a.* + -ITY.] The extent to which a particular climate is oceanic; the state of being or having an oceanic climate.

1946 *Proc. Prehist. Soc.* XII. 3 Conditions of lesser oceanicity such as are encountered for instance in the great central plain of Ireland. **1950** *Jrnl. Ecol.* XXXVIII. 335 A. Mann (1929) suggested using as a measure of the degree of oceanicity of climates an index of hygrothermy. **1950** F. E. ZEUNER *Dating Past* (ed. 2) 394 The Theory relies on periods of increased and decreased oceanicity of the climate coupled with favourable physiographic conditions. **1974** *Nature* 17 May 211/1 The term 'oceanicity' traditionally has conveyed to ecologists the impression of a climate with a low amplitude fluctuation in seasonal temperature and a high annual precipitation.

Oceanid (əʊˈsiːənɪd). Plur. -ids, and in Gr.-L. form ‖**Oceanides** (əʊsiːˈænɪdiːz). [ad. Gr. ὠκεανίς, pl. -ιδες, F. *Océanide* (1732 in *Dict. Trévoux*).]

1. In Greek mythology, A nymph of the ocean, one of the daughters of Oceanus and Tethys.

1869 LIDDELL & SCOTT *Gr. Lex.*, Ὠκεανός, Oceanus..sire of Thetis..and of all the Oceanids. **1890** *Athenæum* 28 Apr. 578 The white Oceanids flash to and fro with noiseless gliding. **1897** *Westm. Gaz.* 12 Jan. 2/1 Hearing in the gentle play of the waves round the promontory the song of the Sirens or the Oceanides.

2. in *pl.* A term applied to marine mollusca, as distinguished from *Naiades* or 'Fresh-water shells'.

†**o'ceanine**, *a. Obs. rare.* [f. L. *ocean-us* + -INE[1].]

1656 BLOUNT *Glossogr.*, *Oceanick*, *Oceanine*, belonging to the Ocean or Main Sea. **1658** in PHILLIPS.

oceanite (ˈəʊʃiːənaɪt). *Petrogr.* [ad. F. *océanite* (A. Lacroix *Minéral. de Madagascar* (1923) III. iii. 49), f. *océan* OCEAN *sb.* (*a.*), from the abundance of the rock on islands in the Pacific + *-ite* -ITE[1].] Any of various basalts which are very rich in olivine.

[**1923** *Mineral. Abstr.* II. 146 New rock-names are doréite, kivite, and océanite.] **1926** G. W. TYRRELL *Princ. Petrol.* vi. 131 (*caption*) Oceanite (ultrabasic olivine-rich 'basalt'). **1967** HESS & POLDERVAART *Basalts* I. 201 An increase in olivine and clinopyroxene in the alkali basalts (at the expense of plagioclase) leads to the development of melanocratic lavas (alkaline picrite-basalts, 'oceanites', and ankaramites). **1971** *Nature* 8 Oct. 406/2 The area includes both aa and pahoehoe lava flows which are olivine basalt, basalt, or oceanite in composition.

oceanity (əʊʃiːˈænɪtɪ). [ad. G. *oceanität* (W. Zenker *Der thermische Aufbau d. Klimate* (1895) II. 122): see OCEAN *sb.* (*a.*) + -ITY.] = OCEANICITY.

1922 [see CONTINENTALITY]. **1924** *Geogr. Jrnl.* LXIV. 43 A station near the coast will thus show marked 'continentality' or 'oceanity' of climate, according as the prevailing wind is from the land or from the sea. **1944** V. CONRAD *Methods in Climatol.* xvii. 195 It is always better to speak of continentality than of 'oceanity'. **1959** R. E. HUSCHKE *Gloss. Meteorol.* 402 *Oceanity*, same as oceanicity.

oceanization (əʊʃiːənaɪˈzeɪʃən). *Geol.* [f. OCEAN *sb.* (*a.*) + -IZATION.] The conversion of continental crust into the much thinner and petrologically distinct oceanic crust.

1960 *Jrnl. Geophysical Res.* LXV. 4128/2 We must do our best to find an explanation of this 'oceanization' of the earth's crust. **1961** *Jrnl. Geol.* LXIX. 653/1 The statement that the 'sial' may be transformed into oceanic crust which leads to the 'oceanization' of a certain part of the earth's surface seems to be quite reasonable. **1973** *Nature* 22 June 434/1 Subsidence being attributed variously to crustal warping associated with orogenic compression, subscrustal erosion, oceanization (and that very recently). **1975** *Ibid.* 6 Feb. 396/2 The Soviet tectonician Belousov has gone so far as to invoke extensive 'oceanisation' of continental crust to account for the ocean basins.

oceanographer (əʊʃiːəˈnɒgrəfə(r)). [f. OCEANOGRAPHY + -ER[1], after *geographer*, etc.] One who studies or is versed in oceanography.

1886 W. DITTMAR in *Encycl. Brit.* XXI. 613/2 One of the foremost duties of observing oceanographers. **1896** *Daily News* 5 Sept. 5/3 The Scottish oceanographer, Dr. John Murray, and the French Admiral Duperré, were elected honorary presidents.

oceanographic (əʊʃiːˌænəʊˈgræfɪk), *a.* [f. as prec. + -IC, after *geographic*, etc.] Of or pertaining to oceanography; thalassographic.

1893 *Athenæum* 20 May 641/1 An abstract of Admiral Makaroff's little work on oceanographic researches. **1899** *Pop. Sci. Monthly* LV. 575 The foundation stone of an oceanographic museum..was laid.

oceanographical (əʊʃɪˌænəʊˈgræfɪkəl), *a.* [f. as prec. + -AL[1].] Relating to, or dealing with, oceanography.

1895 *Daily News* 14 Sept. 3/2 The Section was left free to follow Mr. H. N. Dickson in his oceanographical research in the North Sea. **1900** *Pop. Sci. Monthly* Mar. 620 One of the most important scientific enterprises..was the German oceanographical expedition.

Hence **oceano'graphically** *adv.*, as regards oceanography.

1883 DITTMAR in *Proc. Philos. Soc. Glasgow* XVI. 56 Oceanographically speaking, the *salinity* [of the waters] is a function of geographic position, depth and time.

oceanography (əʊʃɪəˈnɒgrəfɪ). [A mod. formation (Ger. *oceanographie*), f. Gr. ὠκεανός ocean, on the pattern of *geography*, *hydrography*, etc. (*Océanographie* was used in Fr. in 1584 (Godefroy *Compl.*), but did not then survive.)]

The science dealing with the physical and biological properties and phenomena of the ocean. Cf. OCEANOLOGY.

1859 M. F. MAURY *Physical Geogr. Sea* (rev. ed.) xx. 330 'Text-book of Oceanography for the Use of the Imperial Naval Academy', by Dr. August Jilek, Vienna, 1857. **1883** DITTMAR in *Proc. Philos. Soc. Glasgow* XVI. 56 An interesting German book on Oceanography, which has lately come out. **1884** *Athenæum* 23 Aug. 242/3 Prof. Dittmar contrives to discuss incidentally a number of questions of the deepest interest in connexion with oceanography. **1900** *Dublin Rev.* Jan. 158 Oceanography dates only from the commencement of the *Challenger* investigations. **1931** H. B. BIGELOW *Oceanogr.* i. 8 The other [factor] is the growth of an economic demand that oceanography afford practical assistance to the sea fisheries. **1955** *Sci. News Let.* 27 Aug. 142/1 Explorers of the ocean depths have been turning up so many new peaks, ridges, basins, sea-mounts and other underwater landmarks that naming them all has become a major problem in the flourishing science of oceanography. **1970** D. A. ROSS *Introd. Oceanogr.* i. 3 Most oceanographers have divided oceanography into four main parts: (1) chemical oceanography; (2) biological oceanography; (3) physical oceanography; and (4) marine geology and geophysics. **1977** *Times Lit. Suppl.* 18 Nov. 1348/3 The only basic research programmes in which he was closely involved were..for high-energy physics, materials research and oceanography.

oceanological (əʊʃiːənəˈlɒdʒɪkəl), *a.* [f. OCEANOLOGY: see -LOGICAL.] Of or pertaining to oceanology.

1969 *New Scientist* 20 Feb. 382/1 A final element in oceanological development..is the promised White Paper. **1970** R. BARTON *Oceanology Today* vii. 187 Cooperation in oceanological endeavor is not confined to agreement between nations as to who owns what. **1975** *Nature* 2 Oct. 353/1 This will include atmospheric sounding, the investigation of deep-level ice cores.., oceanological investigation in the Drake Straits, [etc.].

oceanologist (əʊʃiːəˈnɒlədʒɪst). [f. as prec. + -IST.] An expert or specialist in oceanology.

1954 *Deep-Sea Research* II. 86 Any oceanologist could conceive an ideal plan, but when the problem of money is introduced, restrictions are needed. **1972** *Daily Tel.* 22 Mar. 7 (*caption*) The Russian research ship Professor Subov, 6,681 tons, which is making a three-day visit to London... The crew and team of oceanologists and meteorologists spent the day sightseeing.

oceaˈnology. [f. Gr. ὠκεανός OCEAN + -λογία discourse; after *geology*, etc.] = OCEANOGRAPHY (Webster 1864.) In mod. use freq. given a broader meaning than *oceanography* (see quots. 1969[1], 1973).

1898 *Ann. Rep. Board of Regents Smithsonian Inst. 1896* 295 This brings us to the equally important question of oceanology, which should comprise a complete knowledge not only of the surface currents in the Arctic seas, but also surface and deep-sea temperatures, [etc.]. **1955** *Deep-Sea Research* II. 247 The use of the words 'Oceanology' and 'Oceanologist' was well and truly pondered in days past. Today they are little used save in Russia. **1956** *Ibid.* IV. 68 In 1949 the R/V *Vitjaz* of the Institute of Oceanology of the Academy of Sciences of the U.S.S.R. started its investigations. **1969** *Nature* 1 Mar. 804/2 A brief explanation is required of the word 'oceanology'... In the early days it was often used synonymously with 'oceanography' to mean marine science... It is now often used to mean marine technology, and although it has no precise definition, is usually taken to exclude conventional naval architecture. [**1969** *Ibid.* 13 Dec. 1049/2 Much of what passes for oceanography is nothing more than the straightforward use of the sea for such things as fishing and transport.] **1970** R. BARTON *Oceanology Today* i. 12 The project becomes even more valuable when looked at in terms of the lessons.. that will be learned across the whole field of oceanology, from offshore oil exploration to physiological research in diving. **1973** HICKLING & BROWN *Seas & Oceans* p. viii, Sea or ocean science is nowadays called *oceanography*, or by an even newer word, *oceanology*, coined in the 1960s. Some like to differentiate between the use of these terms, using *oceanography* to describe the more academic aspects of ocean science, and *oceanology* to describe modern ocean technology, including the political, legal, financial and economic aspects of the seas and oceans.

†**oˈceanous,** *a. Obs. rare*[-0]. [f. L. *ocean-us* + -OUS.] Of or pertaining to the ocean (Bailey 1730–1800; in early edd. stressed *oceˈanous*).

oceanward, -wards (ˈəʊʃənwəd, -wədz), *adv.* (*a.*) [See -WARD and -WARDS.] Towards or in the direction of the ocean.

1855 BAILEY *Mystic* 7 Swift as eagle pouncing, drops Oceanwards. **1870** MORRIS *Earthly Par.* I. I. 11 Therefore my gold shall buy us Bordeaux swords And Bordeaux wine as we go oceanwards. **1891** *Chamb. Jrnl.* 14 Feb. 112/2 For centuries oceanward it has flowed on.

b. as *adj.* (only in form *-ward*).

Mod. The oceanward view is better than the landward.

ˈoceanways, *adv. rare.* [See -WAYS.] = next.

a **1649** DRUMM. OF HAWTH. *Poems* Wks. (1711) 4 Vast solitary mountains, pleasant plains, Embroidered meads, that ocean-ways you reach.

oceanwise (ˈəʊʃənwaɪz), *adv.* [See -WISE.] By way of the ocean.

1878 PERRY *Pol. Econ.* 556 All this was designed.. to keep the carrying trade, both coastwise and oceanwise to American bottoms.

ocellar (əʊˈsɛlə(r)), *a.* [f. L. *ocell-us* + -AR[1].]

1. Of or pertaining to the ocelli or small simple eyes of insects or other Arthropoda.

1891 *Cent. Dict.*, *Ocellar triangle*, a three-sided space, sharply defined in many insects, on which the ocelli are placed.

2. In *Petrography*, Applied (after Rosenbusch 1887) to that structure of rocks in which minute individual components of one mineral are arranged in radiating aggregations round another mineral.

(Many authors regard the 'ocellar' structure as simply a variety of the 'centric' structure of Becke, 1878).

1889 JUDD in *Q. Jrnl. Geol. Soc.* May 176 The structures which specially distinguish these granophyric rocks are.. the centric or ocellar structure.. and the drusy or miarolitic structures.

ocellary, *a.* [f. as prec. + -ARY.] = OCELLAR 1.

ocellary plates, same as *intergenital plates* (*Syd. Soc. Lex.* 1892). *ocellary segments* or *rings* (*Entom.*), supposed primary segments of the preoral region, of which the ocelli are viewed as representing the jointed appendages.

1864 WEBSTER, *Ocellary*, pertaining to ocelli.

ocellate (ˈɒsɪlət, əʊˈsɛlət), *a.* [ad. L. *ocellāt-us* having little eyes, f. *ocellus* eyelet: see -ATE[2].] = next.

1857 MAYNE *Expos. Lex.* 788/2 Marked by spots imitating the pupil of the eye.. ocellate. **1870** A. R. WALLACE *Nat. Select.* iv. 181 A group of pale-coloured butterflies, more or less adorned with ocellate spots. **1892** in *Syd. Soc. Lex.*

ocellated (ˈɒsɪleɪtɪd), *a.* [f. as prec. + -ED[1].]

1. Marked or ornamented with an ocellus or ocelli; having eye-like spots.

1713 DERHAM *Phys. Theol.* VIII. vi. 416 A very beautiful reddish ocellated [butterfly] lays its.. black Offspring.. on the Leaves of Nettles. **1864** P. L. SCLATER *Guide Zool. Gard.* 18 This gorgeous scheme of decoration may be observed as occurring also in the Ocellated Turkey of Honduras. **1870** GILLMORE *Reptiles & Birds* iii. 111 In the Ocellated Lizard, the upper part of the body is green, variegated, spotted, and reticulated or ocellated with black.

2. Formed like a small eye; said of a small round spot surrounded by a ring of a different colour.

1828 STARK *Elem. Nat. Hist.* I. 428 Body.. brown above, white below.. marked by whitish ocellated spots. **1870** HOOKER *Stud. Flora* 266 Digitalis purpurea.. corolla.. purple, speckled with ocellated spots.

oceˈllation. *rare.* [f. L. *ocellāt-us* OCELLATE: see -ATION.] An eye-shaped marking.

1846 DANA *Zooph.* (1848) 151 The tentacles.. marked with ashy ocellations near their base.

ocelli-, combining form of L. *ocellus* eyelet, used in forming terms of *Zoology* and *Botany*, as **ocellicyst** (əʊˈsɛlɪsɪst), the rudimentary eye or visual spot of Hydrozoa; hence **ocelliˈcystic** *a.*; **ocelliferous** (ɒsɪˈlɪfərəs) *a.*, bearing an ocellus or ocelli, ocellated; **oˈcelliform** *a.*, having the form of an ocellus or little eye; **ocelligerous** (ɒsɪˈlɪdʒərəs) *a.* = *ocelliferous* (*Cent. Dict.*).

1844 GOODSIR in *Proc. Berw. Nat. Club* II. No. 12. 114 It is.. dilated, and gives attachment.. dorsally to the ocelliferous tubercle. **1856–8** W. CLARK *Van der Hoeven's Zool.* I. 202 With two ocelliform points.

‖**ocellus** (əʊˈsɛləs). Pl. ocelli (-aɪ). [L. *ocellus* little eye, dim. of *oculus* eye.]

1. A little eye or eyelet; *spec.* **a.** One of the simple, as distinct from the compound, eyes of insects and some other Arthropoda, etc.; a stemma. **b.** The simple or rudimentary eye or visual spot of Mollusca, Hydrozoa, and other animals. **c.** One of the facets or segments of a compound eye. (Nearly always used in *pl.*)

1819 G. SAMOUELLE *Entomol. Compend.* 273 Ocelli or stemmata not distinct. **1828** STARK *Elem. Nat. Hist.* II. 319 Longilabra.. Two ocelli; antennæ always filiform. **1863** BATES *Nat. Amazon* I. 31 They [the workers among the Saiiba ants] have in the middle of the forehead a twin ocellus, or simple eye, of quite different structure from the ordinary compound eyes, on the sides of the head. **1869** H. USSHER in *Eng. Mech.* 3 Dec. 271/3 Catch your fly.. and with a lens you will see his ocular organ divided into numerous facets or ocelli. **1879** LUBBOCK *Sci. Lect.* iii. 88 In most ants.. There are generally three ocelli arranged in a triangle on the top of their heads, and on each side a large compound eye. **1879** G. ALLEN *Colour Sense* iii. 27 The simplest form in which they [visual organs] occur is that of the ocelli among naked-eyed Medusæ.

2. A coloured spot surrounded by a ring or rings of different colour, as found on some feathers, butterflies' wings, etc.; an eye-like spot, an eyelet.

1826 KIRBY & SP. *Entomol.* IV. 286 *Ocellus*, an eye-like spot in the Wings of many Lepidoptera, consisting of annuli of different colours, inclosing a central spot or pupil. **1871** DARWIN *Desc. Man* I. xi. 397 The lower surface is magnificently ornamented by an ocellus of cobalt-blue. *Ibid.* II. xiv. 132. **1879** *Cassell's Techn. Educ.* IV. 39/2 A clear ocellus in each of the four wings.

oceloid (ˈəʊsɪlɔɪd), *a. Zool. rare.* [f. *ocel(ot)* see next + -OID.] Resembling or akin to the ocelot: applied to a group of American spotted *Felidæ*.

1891 in *Cent. Dict.*

ocelot (ˈəʊsɪlɒt, ˈɒs-). [a. F. *ocelot*, abridged by Buffon from the Mexican name *tlalocelotl* (Hernandez), f. *tlalli* field + *ocelotl* tiger, jaguar. By thus dropping the qualifying element, Buffon took the Mexican name of the jaguar as the appellation of another feline beast. (Cf. Simeon *Dict. Langue Nahuatl* 1885.)] A leopard-like feline quadruped (*Felis pardalis*) of Central and South America, about three feet in length; the prevailing colour is grey, beautifully marked with numerous elongated fawn spots edged with black; the under parts are white or whitish with black markings; also called tiger-cat, leopard-cat.

1774 GOLDSM. *Nat. Hist.* II. 148 The catamountain which is the Ocelot of Mr. Buffon. **1851** MAYNE REID *Scalp Hunters* lviii. 434 Have you seen the captive ocelot?

och (ɒx), *int. Irish* and *Sc.* Also oche. [Ir. and Gael. *och.*] An exclamation of surprise, regret, or sorrow; ah! oh! also *och how!* alas!

1528 *Rede me* (Arb.) 59 Och, there is nether duke ne barone.. But they are constrayned to croutche, Before this butcherly sloutche. **1567** *King Henry's Murder* in *St. Papers Scot.* (P.R.O.) XIII. No. 47 His sorry song was Oche, and Wallaway. **1572** *Lament. Lady Scotl.* 401 in *Satir. Poems Reform.* I. 239 Och, Lord (quod he) now gif me patience. **1821** GALT *Ann. Parish* xiv. 140 But och how! this was the last happy summer that we had for many a year in the parish. **1838** J. GRANT *Sk. Lond.* 62 Och! by the mother that bore me, but that's just the thing for him. **1890** W. A. WALLACE *Only a Sister* 338 Och! lausy me! What's in the taking now, dearie?

ocha, variant of OKE, Turkish weight.

ocham, ochamie, obs. ff. OAKUM, OCCAMY.

ochane, obs. form of *ochone*, OHONE.

†**oche,** *v. Obs. rare.* [a. OF. *oschier*, *ocher*, to notch, nick, cut a deep notch in (12th c. in Godef.), app. = Pr. *auscar*, Cat. *oscar*:—L. **absecāre* to cut off or away: see Körting.] *trans.* To cut as with a blow; to lop.

? *a* **1400** *Morte Arth.* 2565 An alet enamelde he oches in sondire. *Ibid.* 4246 Swappes of þe swerde hande.. Ane inche fro þe elbow, he ochede it in sondyre.

oche, var. HOCKEY[3].

ocher, ocherous, ochery: see OCHRE, OCHROUS, OCHRY.

ochidore. (See quot., which appears to be the only authority for the word.)

1861 C. KINGSLEY *Westward Ho* ii, 'O! the ochidore! look to the blue ochidore! Who've put ochidore to maister's pole?' It was too true: neatly inserted between his neck, and his collar as he stooped forward, was a large live shore-crab, holding on tight with both hands. (It does not appear whence Kingsley got this name. One old fisherman, still alive at Clovelly, remembers that Kingsley so called the Spider-crab *Maya Squinado* (not the Shore-crab): but he never heard any one else do so.—Letter from Rev. T. L. Simkin, Rector of Clovelly, 10 Dec. 1901.)

†**ochiern.** *Sc. Hist.* Also 7 ochern, 9 ogtiern, oget-theyrn. [Phonetic reduction of Gael. *òigthighearna* young lord (*òg* young, *tighearna* lord).] 'A young lord, the son of a chief' (Macleod and Dewar).

1609 SKENE *Reg. Maj.* 73 Item, the ma[r]chet of the dochter of ane Thane, or Ochiern, twa kye, or twelue schillings. *Ibid.* 17 b (*Stat. Alex.* 11, c. 15), The king allanerlie sall haue the vnlaw: that is, of ane Thane, six kye, and ane zoung kow; of ane Ochiern, fivetene zowes, or sex schillings. **1614** SELDEN *Titles Hon.* 286 The Cro and the Kelchyn of them were both alike, as the Merchet of a Thanes daughter and an Ochern's... Where Earles, Earles sonnes, Thanes, Ochierns and the like are distinguisht by their Croes, the name of Baron occurrs not. **1860** C. INNES *Scot. in Mid. Ages* vi. 181 The nephew of a thane, or an oget-theyrn, was estimated at forty-four cows. **1872** E. W. ROBERTSON *Hist. Ess.* 140 The thane, his son, and the ogtiern of the laws of the Scots and Brets.. corresponding with the knight, his son, and the holder in knight's fee.

ochimy, obs. form of OCCAMY.

‖**ochlesis** (ɒˈkliːsɪs). [a. Gr. ὄχλησις disturbance, f. ὀχλεῖν to move, disturb, f. ὄχλος crowd, throng.] The condition of unhealthiness produced by the crowding of a number of persons under one roof. So **oˈchletic** *a.* [cf. Gr. ὀχλητικός, F. *ochlétique*], pertaining to, or affected by ochlesis: cf. OCHLOTIC.

1857 in MAYNE *Expos. Lex.* **1892** in *Syd. Soc. Lex.*

ochlocracy (ɒˈklɒkrəsɪ). Also 6–7 -tie, -ty, -cie, -sie. [a. F. *ochlocratie* (1568 in Hatz.-Darm.), a. Gr. ὀχλοκρατία mob-rule, f. ὄχλο-ς a crowd + -κρατία rule, authority: see -CRACY. Also in 16th c. in the Latin form *ochlocratia*.] Government by the mob or lowest of the people; mob-rule.

1584 J. STOCKWOOD *Serm.* C ij b, Ochlocratia, such a state, as in which the rude and rusticall people moderate all thinges after their own luste. **1594** R. ASHLEY tr. *Loys le Roy* 16 b, There followeth a Democratie; by the outrages, and iniquities whereof, is againe erected the Ochlocratie. **1632** C. DOWNING *St. Eccl. of Kingd.* (1634) 16 If it begin to degenerate into an Ochlocratie. **1697** POTTER *Antiq. Greece* I. iv. (1715) 16 Pericles.. brought in a confus'd Ochlocracie, whereby the Populace, and basest of the Rabble obtain'd as great a share in the Government, as Persons of the Highest Birth and Quality. **1791** MACKINTOSH *Vind. Gallicæ* Wks. 1846 III. 103 The authority of a corrupt and tumultuous populace has indeed.. been regarded rather as an ochlocracy than a democracy,—as the despotism of the rabble, not the dominion of the people. **1888** BRYCE *Amer. Commw.* III. v. xcv. 337 The commonest of the old charges against democracy was that it passed into ochlocracy.

ochlocrat (ˈɒkləkræt). [f. prec. after *aristocrat*, etc.: see -CRAT.] An advocate or partisan of ochlocracy.

1880 E. MYERS *Æschylus* in E. Abbott *Hellenica* 7 One which no democrat, who is not a mere ochlocrat, need repudiate. **1886** SIR F. DOYLE *Remin.* 73 A charge brought by the ochlocrats at present in power.

ochlocratic (ɒkləʊˈkrætɪk), *a.* [f. as prec.: cf. F. *ochlocratique* (Littré).] Of, pertaining to, of the nature of, or upholding ochlocracy.

1835 T. WALKER *Original* i. (1887) 9 By the ochlocratic principle, I mean the principle of mob government, or government by too large masses. **1873** GREG *Enigmas Life* 46 Ochlocratic institutions (those giving political power to the mere masses, the numerical majority).

ochlocratical (ɒkləʊˈkrætɪkəl), *a.* [f. as prec. + -AL[1].] = prec.

1659 *Quaeries Propos. Officers Armie to Parlt.* 7 What.. priviledge have you.. to prevent that most Tyrannical inconveniency; having once not onely admitted, but made and Authorized the tentation toward ochlocratical trouble and oppression? **1835** T. WALKER *Original* i. (1887) 9 It becomes in practice either oligarchical or ochlocratical.

Hence **ochloˈcratically** *adv.* (Webster 1864.)

† **ochlo'cratoric**, *a. Obs. rare*⁻¹. [f. Gr. ὄχλο-ς crowd, multitude, populace + -κράτωρ ruler + -IC.] Of or pertaining to a ruler of the multitude.
1647 R. BAILLIE *Anabaptism* Ep., A body of new Laws, a mould of a new Ochlocratorick government.

ochlophobia (ɒklɒ'fəʊbɪə). [f. Gr. ὄχλο-ς crowd + -PHOBIA: see OCHLOPHOBIST.] A morbid aversion to crowds. Hence **ochlo'phobic** *a.*
1894 GOULD *Dict. Med.* 884/2 Ochlophobia. **1929** C. CONNOLLY *Let.* Nov. in *Romantic Friendship* (1975) 330, I have had ochlophobia lately. **1976** R. PERRY *One Good Death* x. 157 [He] preferred to work in greater privacy. It could even be that he was ochlophobic like Toller, the Austrian killer.

ochlophobist (ɒ'klɒfəbɪst). *rare.* [f. Gr. ὄχλος crowd, mob + -φοβος -fearing + -IST.] One who has an aversion to a crowd.
1867 *Blackw. Mag.* July 42 The Easter trip of two ochlophobists. **1882** *Daily News* 5 Dec. 5/1 The ochlophobist..has but a hard life in London just now.

ochlospecies ('ɒkləʊ,spiːsiːz, -,spiːʃiːz). *Taxonomy.* [f. as OCHLOPHOBIA + SPECIES.] (See quot. 1967.)
1962 F. WHITE in D. Nichols *Taxon. & Geogr.* 79 Such species cannot be satisfactorily subdivided and could conveniently be distinguished from monotypic and polytypic species by calling them *ochlo*-species. **1967** *Gardens' Bull.* XXII. 6 White has coined the useful and appropriate term ochlospecies for species showing a complex reticulate pattern of variation. **1972** G. T. PRANCE in *Flora Neotropica* IX. 109 *Licania heteromorpha* is a good example of an ochlospecies.

ochlotic (ɒ'klɒtɪk), *a.* [irreg. f. Gr. ὄχλος a throng: the etymological form is OCHLETIC.] Of, belonging to, or caused by ochlesis.
1884 *Syd. Soc. Lex.*, *Fever, ochlotic*, Laycock's term for Typhus fever. **1896** *Allbutt's Syst. Med.* I. 868 These speculations..have concerned themselves with every possible influence—cosmic, sidereal, telluric, climatic, septic, ochlotic [etc.]—to account for cholera visitations.

ochone: see OHONE.

ochopetalous (ɒkəʊ'pɛtələs), *a. Bot. rare.* [f. Gr. ὀχός holding, capacious + PETAL *sb.* + -OUS.] 'Having broad and ample petals.'
1857 in MAYNE *Expos. Lex.* **1892** in *Syd. Soc. Lex.*

ochra, variant of OKRA.

ochraceous (əʊ'kreɪʃəs), *a.* [f. L. *ōchra* OCHRE + -ACEOUS. Cf. mod.L. *ōchrāceus*, mod.F. *ochracé* (Littré).]
1. Of the nature of ochre; = OCHREOUS 1.
1776 *Phil. Trans.* LXVI. 524 Whole banks of ocraceous minerals. **1789** MILLS *ibid.* LXXX. 96 A vein of blue shistus ..not far from which is an ochraceous earth, and much bog iron ore. **1869** PHILLIPS *Vesuv.* iv. 135 The deposit is covered by gray cellular lava, with a rough ochraceous, slaggy base.
2. Of the colour of ochre; = OCHREOUS 2.
1776 PENNANT *Zool.* II. 570 The head and neck cinereous, mixed with ochraceous yellow. **1874** COOKE *Fungi* (1875) 117 Fungi exhibit an almost endless variety of colour, from white through ochraceous to all tints of brown, until nearly black. **1876** PAGE *Adv. Text-bk. Geol.* xviii. 339 These sands, however, are not uniformly green, but partake of ochraceous and yellow tints.

Ochrana, var. OKHRANA.

ochre, ocher ('əʊkə(r)), *sb.* Forms: 5–9 oker, 6–8 oaker, 7– ochre, 9 *U.S.* ocher, (also 5 ocur, okyr, ockere, 6 occur, okur, 6–7 occar, 7 ocre, 8 okre, 9 ocker). [a. F. *ocre* (1307 in Hatz.-Darm.), ad. L. *ōchra* (Pliny), a. Gr. ὤχρα yellow ochre, f. ὠχρός pale yellow.]
1. a. A native earth, or class of earths, consisting of a mixture of hydrated oxide of iron with varying proportions of clay in a state of impalpable subdivision; varying in colour from light yellow to deep orange or brown. The ochres are extensively used as pigments; particular kinds are known as ***brown, red, white, yellow, Oxford ochre***, etc.
[**1398** TREVISA *Barth. De P.R.* XIX. xxxi. (1495) 878 Ocra bredyth in the ylonde Topasion there Sandaracha is founde and is somtyme made of Ocra.] **1481–90** *Howard Househ. Bks.* (Roxb.) 202 Item, in yelu okyr x. lb. *c* **1485** *E.E. Misc.* (Warton Club) 76 To temper ockere, grynd hit with gume and water. **1487–8** in Willis & Clark *Cambridge* (1886) I. 412, v li de colore fuluo sc. oker. **1591** SPENSER *Ruins of Time* 204 All is but fained, and with oaker dide. **1601** HOLLAND *Pliny* XXXIII. xiii. II. 485 As touching Ochre or Sil, it is exceeding hard to bee reduced into powder. **1605** TIMME *Quersit.* I. xiii. 53 The sulphur in vitriol is easily discerned by a certaine red ocre. **1688** R. HOLME *Armoury* II. 39/1 Of earth are several sorts, as..Marle, Clay, Occar. **1787** W. WILLIAMS *Mechanic of Oil Colours* 46 Brown oaker..may be made from yellow oaker. **1808** A. PARSONS *Trav.* xiii. 277 A cow..was led through the streets followed by all the Banyans, with their cloaths, face, and hands daubed over with yellow oker. **1809** KENDALL *Trav.* II. li. 190 The white ochre is a mere deposit of testaceous exuviae. **1839** URE *Dict. Arts* s.v., Native red ochre is called red chalk and reddle in England. It is an intimate mixture of clay and red iron ochre. **1854** T. H. FIELDING *Painting in Oil & Wat. Col.* (ed. 5) 179 Yellow Ochre is..sometimes called Oxford Ochre, being abundant in that neighbourhood.

b. As a pigment; also the colour of this; esp. a pale brownish yellow: cf. 4.
c **1440** *Promp. Parv.* 362/1 Ocur, colure. **1530** PALSGR. 249/1 Occur, reed colour, *ocre*. **1871** C. GIBBON *Lack of Gold* i, To match the yellow ochre of the cottage interior walls.

2. Applied to the earthy pulverulent oxides of other metals, as ***antimony, bismuth, chrome, molybdic, tantalic, tungstic ochre.***
1863–72 WATTS *Dict. Chem.* I. 324 Tetroxide of Antimony ..found native, as Cervantite or Antimony-ochre. *Ibid.* 504 Trioxide of Bismuth..occurs native, as bismuth-ochre. **1868** DANA *Min.* (ed. 5) 185 Bismite, Oxyd of Bismuth, Bismuth Ochre... Molybdite. Molybdena or Molybdic Ochre, Molybdic Acid. *Ibid.* 186 Tungstite. Tungstic Ochre. *Ibid.* 188 A tantalic ochre occurs on crystals of tantalite at Pennikoja..color brownish, lustre vitreous. *Ibid.* 510 Chrome Ochre, a clayey material, containing some oxyd of chrome.

3. *slang.* Applied to money, in allusion to the colour of gold coin.
1854 DICKENS *Hard T.* I. vi, Pay your ochre at the doors and take it out. **1890** *Punch* 22 Feb. (Farmer), If I was flush of the ochre, I tell yer I'd make the thing hum.

4. *attrib.* and *Comb.*, as ***ochre bed, pit***; of the colour of ochre, as ***ochre bank, bloom, colour, dye, face, pigment, wash***; ***ochre-coloured, -brown, -red, -yellow*** adjs.; **ochre-grave** (see quot.); also *attrib.*; **ochreman** († **okerman**), a man who works or deals in ochre, a colourman.
c **1586** C'TESS PEMBROKE *Ps.* CVI. ix, The *oker bancks their passage did inclose. **1808** WOLCOTT (P. Pindar) *One more Peep at R. Acad.* Wks. 1812 V. 379 Welcome, sweet Miss in *ochre bloom. **1894** R. B. SHARPE *Handbk. Birds Gt. Brit.* 34 Forehead and sides of face dull *ochre-brown. **1578** LYTE *Dodoens* II. xlvi. 204 Flowers..of a fainte or *Ochre colour yellowe. **1828** STARK *Elem. Nat. Hist.* I. 194 Great-horned Owl. Body variegated and waved with black and ochre colour. **1877** RAYMOND *Statist. Mines & Mining* 261 The ore, an *ocher-colored earth, is found evenly deposited upon a hill-side. **1868** J. A. B. *Meta* II. iii. 27 Then see, dear reader, 'fore your eyes The savage in his *ochre dyes. **1634** S. R. *Noble Soldier* II. i. in Bullen *O. Pl.* (1882) I. 277 You Don with th' *oaker face. **1928** PEAKE & FLEURE *Steppe & Sown* 20 In the early type of kurgan are found skeletons.. buried in a contracted position, the bones covered with red ochre. These..are now known as the *ochre-graves. *Ibid.* 26 The ochre-grave folk. **1957** V. G. CHILDE *Dawn Europ. Civilization* (ed. 6) ix. 149 *(heading)* The Ochre Grave Cultures of the Pontic Steppes. *Ibid.* 157 The beginnings of the Ochre Grave culture should go back well into the third millenium. **1592** NASHE *P. Penilesse* (ed. 2) 13 Their lips are as lauishly red, as if they vsed to kisse an *okerman euery morning. **1547** *Life Abp. Canterb.* To Rdr. E vb, That by this *oker marking he may knowe his owne sheepe. **1898** P. MANSON *Trop. Diseases* iv. 93 In such sections it is seen that the *ochre pigment is no longer in minute grains. **1839** URE *Dict. Arts* 894 A section of the *ochre pits at Shotover Hill, near Oxford. **1882** *Garden* 15 July 52/2 A pretty cut-leaved annual species..with *ochre-red flowers. **1847** J. WILSON *Chr. North* (1857) I. 159 The walls are sordid in the streaked *ochre-wash. **1899** *Ochre yellow [see *hæmochromatosis* s.v. HÆMO-, HEMO-]. **1952** A. G. L. HELLYER *Sanders' Encycl. Gardening* (ed. 22) 121 *Dayana*, ochre-yellow, lip white and brown.

ochre, ocher ('əʊkə(r)), *v.* [f. prec. sb.] *trans.* To colour, mark, or rub with ochre. Chiefly in *pa. pple.*
1608 DAY *Law Trickes* IV. i. (1881) 51 Where you see a face newly okered tis a signe ther's traffique. **1650** BULWER *Anthropomet.* 165 Their arms and thighs Oakred, and dyed with red..and yellow. **1844** *N. Brit. Rev.* I. 177 With horse-hair wig and ochred cheeks. **1878** J. GUTHRIE *Heroes of Faith* 51 The ochred skin of the savage.
Hence **ochreing** ('əʊkərɪŋ), *vbl. sb.*
1896 *Daily News* 9 Dec. 5/1 The yellow ochreing of the Southdowns has been practised for some time.

ochre, variant of OKRA.

ochreish ('əʊkərɪʃ), *a.* [f. OCHRE *sb.* + -ISH¹.] = OCHREOUS 1 and 2.
1859 R. F. BURTON *Centr. Afr.* in *Jrnl. Geog. Soc.* XXIX. 438 Blood-coloured fragments of ochreish earth. **1875** M. G. PEARSE *Daniel Quorm* 2 You met men dressed in suits of flannel stained a dull ochreish red.

ochreo-, combining form of OCHREOUS, as in *ochreo-ferreous, -stalactitical, -testaceous* adjs.
a **1728** WOODWARD *Fossils* I. (1729) I. 235 The Ochreo-ferreous Ætitæ. **1802** PLAYFAIR *Illustr. Hutton. Th.* 459 These remains are found in..what the Abbé Fortis calls an ocreo-stalactitical earth. **1847** HARDY in *Proc. Berw. Nat. Club* II. No. 5. 251 The shoulders and reflexed margins ochreo-testaceous.

ochreous ('əʊkrɪəs), *a.* [f. mod.L. *ōchre-us* ochry + -OUS: cf. *aqueous, cupreous, ligneous*, etc.]
1. Of the nature of, containing, or abounding in ochre.
a **1728** WOODWARD *Fossils* (1729) II. 99 A dusky, yellowish, ochreous Earth... Ochreous Earth, of a red Colour, somewhat approaching a Pink. **1822** IMISON *Sc. & Art* II. 417 Raw umbre is a native ochreous earth, of a light brown. **1858** GEIKIE *Hist. Boulder* xi. 222 The red ochreous matter with which the water was charged.
2. Of the colour of ochre; *spec.* of a light brownish yellow.
1750 RUTTY in *Phil. Trans.* LI. 471 It exhibited ochreous and green grumes. **1846** RUSKIN *Mod. Paint.* (1848) I. II. III. iv. §2. 242 A brown, bricky, ochreous tone, never bright. **1854** HOOKER *Himal. Jrnls.* I. ii. 28 Two species, one ochreous brown. **1900** *Trans. Highld. & Agric. Soc.* 304 The front wings are ochreous-white with a number of black spots dotted over them.

ochrey, variant of OCHRY *a.*

ochro, variant of OKRA, an esculent plant.

ochro- (əʊkrəʊ), comb. form of Gr. ὤχρα, ὠχρός (OCHRE), employed in various technical terms, to indicate a pale-yellow or ochreous condition, as **ochro'carpous** *a.* (*Bot.*), yellow-fruited; **ochro'leucous** *a.* [Gr. ὠχρόλευκος], yellowish-white (Mayne *Expos. Lex.* 1857); **ochro'pyra, -'typhus**, yellow fever (Mayne, and *Syd. Soc. Lex.* 1892).
1880 GRAY *Struct. Bot.* 422/1 *Ochroleucous*, yellowish-white or between white and yellow. **1882** E. TUCKERMAN *N. Amer. Lichens* 253 An ochrocarpious form occurs commonly in Sweden.

ochroid ('əʊkrɔɪd), *a.* [ad. Gr. ὠχροειδής pale-yellow-looking.] Pale-yellowish.
1897 *Allbutt's Syst. Med.* II. 91 There are two varieties of the disease, the one characterised by the presence of brownish or yellowish white particles, like fish roe (the pale or ochroid form). **1898** P. MANSON *Trop. Dis.* xxxvii. 572 Thus we have the white or ochroid, the black or melanoid, and the red forms of mycetoma.

† **ochroite** ('əʊkrəʊaɪt). *Min. Obs.* [Named 1804 (*Ochroit*) by Klaproth, f. Gr. ὤχρα OCHRE: see -ITE¹.] A synonym of CERITE.
[**1804** *Nicholson's Jrnl.* VIII. 207 (heading) Chemical Examination of the Ochroites, a Mineral..containing a new Earth.] **1866–72** WATTS *Dict. Chem.* IV. 170 *Ochroite*, an impure cerite mixed with quartz, analysed by Klaproth.

ochrolite ('əʊkrəlaɪt). [Named 1889, f. Gr. ὠχρός pale yellow + λίθος stone (see -LITE).] Chloro-antimonite of lead found in small crystals of a sulphur-yellow colour.
1889 *Amer. Jrnl. Sc.* XXXVII. 500 Ochrolite..occurs in tabular orthorhombic crystals.

ochronosis (əʊkrə'nəʊsɪs). *Path.* [mod.L. (R. Virchow 1866, in *Arch. f. path. Anat. u. Physiol.* XXXVII. 218), f. Gr. ὠχρός pale yellow + νόσος disease + -OSIS.] An abnormal brown pigmentation of tissue, notably cartilage, esp. when a symptom of the metabolic disorder alkaptonuria and resulting from the accumulation of polymerized homogentisic acid.
1867 *Half-Yearly Abstr. Med. Sci.* LXV. 28 Virchow proposes to call this affection ochronosis. **1876** tr. *Wagner's Gen. Pathol.* (ed. 6) 315 Virchow describes as ochronosis a peculiar black coloration of almost all the cartilages and ligaments of the..joints of the synovial membranes. **1906** *Lancet* 6 Jan. 26/1 The urine of his patient.., who had the blackening of cartilages which constitutes ochronosis, was brown when passed. **1948** W. A. D. ANDERSON *Path.* iv. 88 Phenol poisoning, due to absorption of phenol from surgical dressings, has been reported to cause a pigmentation similar to ochronosis. **1962** C. A. CLARKE *Genetics for Clinician* xiii. 156 Alkaptonuria... In addition to the urinary abnormality ..there is pigmentation of cartilage and ligaments (ochronosis). **1970** *Nature* 21 Nov. 770/1 Adults with alcaptonuria develop a destructive arthritis secondary to the deposition of a melanin-like pigment in their connective tissues, especially skin, tendon and cartilage (ochronosis).
Hence **ochro'notic** *a* [-OTIC].
1922 *Arch. Internal Med.* XXIX. 737 Hanseman observed diffuse and granular ochronotic pigment in the tissues. **1961** *Arthritis & Rheumatism* IV. 137 *(heading)* Studies on the pathogenesis of ochronotic arthropathy.

ochrous ('əʊkrəs), *a.* Also 9 (*U.S.*) ocherous. [f. OCHRE, or L. *ōchra* + -OUS: cf. *herba, herbōsus*. The spelling *ocherous* is not on L. analogies.]
1. = OCHREOUS 1.
1757 WALKER in *Phil. Trans.* L. 125 All chalybeat waters separate their ochrous parts, when exposed some time to the air. **1802** *Trans. Soc. Arts* XX. 224 The ochrous earth of iron, commonly called red ochre. **1806** WEBSTER, *Ocherous*, ..like or containing ocher. **1822** IMISON *Sc. & Art* II. 416 Raw Terra Sienna is a native ochrous earth brought from Italy. **1828** WEBSTER s.v. *Ocherous matter*, an ocherous color. **1869** *Rep. Comm. Agric. 1868* (U.S. Dept. Agric.) 427 The pasture..hardening in some such manner as 'hard-pan' forms in ocherous soil. **1885** *Century Mag.* XXX. 819 The red ocherous soil of their steep sides.
2. = OCHREOUS 2.
1877 PATMORE *Unknown Eros* (1890) 21 Many a haggard stair Ochrous with ancient stains.

ochry, ochery ('əʊkrɪ, 'əʊkərɪ), *a.* Also 6 ocrie, 8–9 ochrey. [f. OCHRE, *ocher* + -Y: cf. *fibry, miry, gory, fiery*.]
1. Of the colour of ochre; = OCHREOUS 2.
1567 MAPLET *Gr. Forest* 27 b, Some Ocrie or yellow as the Mariegold. **1755** *Phil. Trans.* XLIX. 297 Stone of a pale ochrey colour. **1766** *Ibid.* LVI. 13 Of a rusty ochry color. **1837** *Blackw. Mag.* XLII. 333 Foreign arid and ochery hills. **1862** THORNBURY *Turner* I. 393 Wafts of mist, ochry sails. **1885** *Harper's Mag.* Dec. 70/2 This bright ochery remnant re-appears on the hickory beyond. **1891** NISBET *Colonial Tramp* I. 13 Rocks rose-purple, ruddy and ochrey.
2. Of the nature of ochre; = OCHREOUS 1.
a **1728** WOODWARD *Fossils* (R.), This is conveyed about by the water; as we find in earthy, ochrey, and other loose matter. **1763** W. LEWIS *Comm. Phil.-Techn.* 349 Precipitating the iron nearly in the same ochery state. **1825** J. NICHOLSON *Operat. Mechanic* 753 Umber, Cologne earth, and different ochry argillaceous earths.

ocht, ochymy, ocian, obs. forms of AUGHT, OUGHT, OCCAMY, OCEAN.

ociositie, ocious, obs. ff. OTIOSITY, OTIOUS.

†**o'civity.** *Obs. rare*. [ad. F. *oisiveté*, after assumed L. type **ōcīvitās*, f. **ōcīvus*, f. *ōcium* for *ōtium* ease. (The Fr. word really goes back through OF. *oisdif*, *wisdif*, to a pop. L. *ōciōtīv-us* (= **ōtiōtīvus*) substituted for *ōtiōsus*: see OTIOSE, OTIOUS.)] Sloth, laziness.

1550 HOOPER *Godly Confess.* E vij b, We owe vnto our selues the exchuyng and auoydyng of Idlenes and ociuitie.

-ock, *suffix*, forming diminutives. A few examples of dimin. *-oc*, *-uc*, appear in OE., as *bealloc* ballock, *bulluc* bullock. In mod.Eng., the chief instance of the dim. suffix is *hillock* (found already in Wyclif); but other examples occur in the dialects, esp. in Sc., e.g. *bittock*, *lassock*, *queock* or *queyock*, *whilock*, *wyfock*, also proper names as *Bessock*, *Jamock*, *Kittock*: see Jamieson s.v. *-oc*, *-ock*. Several names of animals, esp. birds and fishes, have the same ending, and are prob. orig. diminutive; among these are OE. *cranoc*, *cornoc* (dim. of *cran*), crane; *ruddoc* (*read* red) redbreast, ruddock; cf. the modern (some ME.) *dunnock*, *haddock*, *girrock*, *paddock*, *piddock*, *pinnock*, *pollock*, *puttock*; also, as names of things, *buttock*, *hattock*, *tussock*. In other words (some of which, as *bannock*, *hassock*, *mattock*, go back to OE.) *-ock* appears to be of different origin.

ockam, obs. form of OAKUM.

ockamie, -y, variants of OCCAMY *Obs.*

ocke, variant of AC *Obs.*, but.

†**'ocker, 'oker,** *sb.*[1] *Obs.* Forms: 3–6 oker, -ir, 4 okyre, -ur, ocre, 4–5 ocur, okere, 5 okoure, -yr, occar, -ure, 5–6 -our, 6 -ur, okker, -ir, ockar, 6–7 ocker. [ME. *oker*, a. ON. *okr* increase of money, usury (Sw. *ocker*, Da. *okker*), corresp. to OE. *wócor* increase, fruit, offspring, OLG. **wôker* (OFris. *wôker*, MLG. *wôker*, MDu. and Du. *woeker*), OHG. *wuchhar* (MHG. *wuocher*, Ger. *wucher*), Goth. *wôkr-s* increase, usury (= Gr. τόκος); f. a root *wak-*, pre-Teut. *wog-*, perh. ultimately related to *aug-* in L. *augēre*, Goth. *aukan* to add, and to Teut. *wahs-*, wax, grow.] The lending of money at interest, usury. (Usually referred to as a crime or sin.)

a **1225** *Ancr. R.* 202 Þe Vox of ȝiscunge haueð þeos hweolpes: Tricherie,..Simonie, Gauel, Oker. *a* **1300** *E.E. Psalter* xiv. 5 Ne his silver til okir [WYCLIF vsure] noght is givande. *a* **1340** HAMPOLE *Psalter* liv. 11 In thaim failis not okire, for thai aske mare in all thyngis than thai gif. *c* **1375** *Sc. Leg. Saints, Adrian* 114 For þe tyme cumis quhene nane Sal gyfte na ȝet ocre be tane. **14..** *Tundale's Vis.* 53 Throw ocur wold he sylver leyn For nyne schyllyng he wold have ten. *a* **1450** MYRC *Par. Pr.* 372 Vsure and okere þat beth al on. **1533** BELLENDEN *Livy* II. (1822) 140 This dett that he wes awand be non payment was ay duplyit on him be usure and okkir. **1609** BIBLE (Douay) *Prov.* xxviii. 8 He that heapeth together riches by usuries and ocker. **1609** SKENE *Reg. Maj.* 47 b, Gif he receaves back againe mair nor he gaue; he commits vsurie and ocker. *a* **1651** CALDERWOOD *Hist. Kirk* (Wodrow Soc.) III. 14 Did wickedly receive some gaines and filthy Ocker.

ocker ('ɒkə(r)), *sb.*[2] *Austral. slang.* Also **Ocker.** [The name of a character in a series of Australian television sketches by Ron Frazer: used earlier as a colloquial variant of names like *Oscar* and *O'Connor*.] A rough, uncultivated, or aggressively boorish Australian. Also *attrib.* or as *adj.*

[**1959**: see NAUGHTY *sb.* 2.] **1971** G. JOHNSTON *Cartload of Clay* 71 The big man would be a good player, a vigorous clubman, a hearty participant in the companionship of the club bar. He was a type Julian had sometimes talked to him about, what the boy called an 'Ocker'. **1973** *Sunday Sun* (Brisbane) 1 July 21/5 His cigarette commercials were the next step in his career. And once again the ocker image worked wonders. **1973** *Nation Rev.* (Melbourne) 24–30 Aug. 1430/4 (Advt.), Sydney Femme, 27, bored by ozzie ockers and oedipal neurotics, desires to develop dynamic dalliance with..male human beings. **1974** *Sydney Morning Herald* 24 Apr. 6 That image, of the RSL itself as a sabre-rattling élitist organisation with an over-privileged influence on governments, and of RSL members themselves as beer-swilling, 'pokey-playing' Ockers, has, executives believe, faded if not totally evaporated. **1975** *TV Times* (Austral.) 12 Apr. 10 The cult of the ocker is sweeping Australia. **1976** *Telegraph* (Brisbane) 30 July 42/1 It is no use telling Australians to wake up; it is not in the ocker character.

Hence **'ockerdom,** ockers collectively. Also **'ockerism,** over-assertive boorishness, uncultivated behaviour.

1974 P. PORTER in *Australian* 5 Oct. 13 The new Australian boorishness is known as Ockerism, from a slob-like character called Ocker in a television series, the embodiment of oafish, blinkered self-satisfaction. **1975** M. HARRIS in *Ibid.* 18 Jan. 18 The resurgence of an aggressive Australian ockerdom was coincident with the first election of the Whitlam Government and the discovery of a 'new nationalism'. **1977** *Sunday Times* 23 Jan. 30/8 It is seen as a defeat for the spirit of ockerism (that is, being blatantly Australian).

†**'ocker, 'oker,** *v. Obs.* Forms: see OCKER *sb.*[1] [f. OCKER, OKER *sb.*[1]: cf. Sw. *ockra* to practise usury.]

1. *intr.* Of money: To grow with, or as with, the addition of interest.

a **1225** *Ancr. R.* 326 Þe pine, þet okereð euere: vor sunne is þes deofles feih þet he ȝiueð to gauel, & to okere of pine.

2. *intr.* To take usury; to lend at interest.

c **1380** WYCLIF *Serm.* Sel. Wks. I. 260 God okuriþ not wiþ man but ȝif God make þe encrees. **1382** —— *Deut.* xxviii. 12 Thow shalt okyr to many folkis, and thi self shal not borwe to oker of eny man.

3. *trans.* To increase (money) by usury; to put out to interest.

1303 R. BRUNNE *Handl. Synne* 2621 A neyȝt, when men hadde here reste He okerede pens yn hys cheste. *c* **1380** WYCLIF *Serm.* Sel. Wks. I. 259 Whi ȝavest þou not my moneie to þe table, to be occurid?

Hence †**'ockering, 'okering,** *vbl. sb.*, the taking of interest, usury.

a **1300** *Cursor M.* 6796 If þat þou lenis ani thing, þow ask it noght wit occiring [*v.r.* okering]. **1303** R. BRUNNE *Handl. Synne* 2465 Okeryng ys on many manere, Mo þan y kan telle now here. *a* **1340** HAMPOLE *Psalter* lxxi. 14 Of okerynge & wickednes he sal by þe saules of þaim.

ockere, obs. form of OCHRE.

†**'ockerer, 'okerer.** *Obs.* [f. OCKER *sb.*[1] or *v.* + -ER[1]: chiefly of northern, and finally Sc. use.] One who takes interest for the loan of money; a usurer. (Commonly referred to as a criminal or heinous sinner.)

a **1300** *Cursor M.* 14034 (Cott.) A man quilum was wont Penis for to lene vm-stunt, þis man he was an okerer [*Fairf.* okrure]. *a* **1340** HAMPOLE *Ps.* cviii. 10 [cix. 11] The okyrere ransake all his substaunce. *c* **1440** *Gesta Rom.* I. xxi. 71 (Harl.) He [the rook] betokenyth okerers and false merchauntz. *c* **1460** *Towneley Myst.* xxx. 297 Of beggars and okerars and lufars of symonee. **1552** LYNDESAY *Monarche* 5728 Fornicatoris, and Ockararis. **1591** JAS. I. *Furies, Poet. Exerc.* 1440 The treasures gathered by the paines..sore, Of their forebeers occurrars. **1609** SKENE *Reg. Maj.* 40 All the gudes and geir perteining to ane ockerer, quhither he deceis testat or vntestat, perteins to the King. **1699** in E. W. Dunbar *Soc. Life Moray* (1865) 31 Under the certificating of being pursued as Occurrers or Userers.

ockham, ockro, ockster: see OAKUM, OKRA, OXTER.

Ockham's razor: see RAZOR *sb.* 1 b.

o'clock (ə'klɒk), *adv.* **a.** See CLOCK *sb.*[1] 3 d.

b. *transf.* Used, in various contexts specifying direction, esp. with reference to the target in shooting, to give bearings corresponding to the positions of the numerals on a clock face, from the standpoint of one facing twelve o'clock. (Cf. quot. 1797 s.v. CLOCK *sb.*[1] 4.)

1904 W. WINANS *Hints on Revolver Shooting* iv. 33 When the hind sight comes to the level of your eyes.., the front sight will be seen through the middle of the 'U' pointed at the bottom of the bull's-eye, the top of the front sight just touching it at 'six o'clock'. **1913** A. G. FULTON *Notes on Rifle Shooting* 15 If the bull can be seen without much difficulty a 6 o'clock aim is probably the best. **1918** E. S. FARROW *Dict. Mil. Terms* 415 *O'clock*, a term employed to indicate, by means of the divisions on the dial of the clock, the location of a hit on the target or the direction from which the wind may be blowing, as a 7 o'clock, 4 or 5 o'clock wind. **1932** J. A. BARLOW *Elements of Rifle Shooting* iv. 47 Allowances for a constant strength of wind blowing from a varying o'clock, vary according to the length of the perpendicular drawn from the hour on the clock face to the 6–12 o'clock diameter. **1943** C. H. WARD-JACKSON *Piece of Cake* 44 *O'clock.* Used thus, 'Ten bandits at 6 o'clock' means ten enemy aircraft immediately below the recipient of the message. **1948** A. M. TAYLOR *Lang. World War II* (rev. ed.) 141 *O'clock*, term used largely by fliers in designating directions, e.g. 'twelve o'clock' indicates straight ahead; 'three o'clock' directly to the right, etc. **1967** B. KNOX *Blacklight* ii. 48 The lamp continued. 'They say we have it at about our ten o'clock sir.' **1970** M. KELLY *Spinifex* vii. 119 'Black rock. Eight o'clock. One hundred metres!' He'd instinctively ranged artillery in another war. **1972** *National Observer* (U.S.) 27 May 19/1 He says the hands should grasp the wheel at 3 and 9 o'clock. **1973** *Country Life* 25 Oct. 1292/1 From its position at twelve o'clock, the dog begins the critical 'lift'.

ocom, ocopy, ocorn, obs. ff. OAKUM, OCCUPY, ACORN.

ocote (ə'kəʊteɪ). [Amer. Sp., f. Nahuatl *ocotl* torch.] A resinous Mexican pine, *Pinus montezumæ*, or its wood; also = PITCH PINE. Also *attrib.*

[**1858** G. GORDON *Pinetum* 211 It [sc. *Pinus teocote*] is the 'de'ocote' or 'Pino de'ocote' (candle wood) of the Mexicans. **1861** E. B. TYLOR *Anahuac* 336/2 *Ocote* (Aztec, *ocotl*), a pine-tree, pine-torch.] **1908** H. GADOW *Through Southern Mexico* iii. 50 The forest consists mainly of the long-leaved *Pinus liophylla* and the 'ocote' or *Pinus montezumae*, which much resembles our Scotch fir. **1926** D. H. LAWRENCE *Plumed Serp.* vii. 129 The boy..sat apart watching the two ocote torches. **1927** —— *Mornings in Mexico* 10 There is a resinous smell of ocote wood. **1938** *Amer. Speech* XIII. 113 The name [*ocotillo*] is a derivative of Mexican-Spanish *ocote*, a word also applied to pitch-pines or the wood they yield.

ocotillo (əʊkəʊ'tiːjəʊ). *U.S.* Also **ocetilla, ocochilla, ocotilla.** [Amer. Sp., dim. of OCOTE.] A spiny shrub, *Fouquiera splendens*, of the family Fouquieraceæ, native to the south-western United States and Mexico and bearing narrow, inconspicuous leaves and panicles of red flowers. Also *attrib.*

1856 in *Dict. Americanisms*, Aside from the grass, there is a shrub called the..*Ocetilla.* **1864** *Harper's Mag.* Nov. 697/2 Passing through some dense thickets of mesquit and ocochilla, the struggling family found themselves at the foot of a rocky bluff. **1883** *Ibid.* Mar. 491/1 The houses consist of a frame-work of cottonwood or ocotilla wattles. *Ibid.* 502/2 The ocotilla is simply a wattle of sticks..waiting to be cut down and turned into palings. **1893** *Nation* (N.Y.) 7 Sept. 169/3 Walking-sticks made of the porous ocotillo cactus. **1915** L. H. BAILEY *Stand. Cycl. Hort.* III. 1271/1 Ocotillo..is a conspicuous object in the deserts from Texas westward,..the rod-like stiff canes looking like lifeless sticks in dry weather and in its season crowned with masses of showy bloom. **1948** *Natural Hist.* Apr. 181 The Ocotillo is frankly red, adding its flaming tips to every dry stick that looked dead a week ago. **1966** MRS. L. B. JOHNSON *White House Diary* 3 Apr. (1970) 381 The ocotillo..looks like about a dozen long coach whips stuck into the ground, spraying out in a weeping fashion. **1976** *San Antonio* (Texas) *Express-News* 27 Nov. 1B/5 'You know the *ocotillo*,' Ben said, pointing out the cactus that looks like five or six spiny, 10-foot pieces of rope snaking up into the air.

ocra, ocraceous, obs. ff. OKRA, OCHRACEOUS.

-ocracy, the suffix *-cracy*, with the combining **-o** (orig. taken from the stem of the prec. element): as *sb.*, any form of government or domination to which a word in *-ocracy* can be applied. So **-ocrat.** See -CRACY, -CRAT.

1831 C. C. F. GREVILLE *Mem.* (1874) II. xiii. 112 It has elicited a strong Conservative demonstration, and proved that out of the rabble-ocracy (for everything is in *ocracy* now) his power is anything but unlimited. **1834** *Tait's Mag.* I. 180/1 The trade-ocracy and bureauocracy must now..prepare themselves to defer to the opinion of the men of hardened hands. **1894** *Speaker* 14 July 40/2 [To] erect the great pillar of human brotherhood on the ruins of all the 'ocracies'. **1894** G. B. SHAW in *Fortn. Rev.* Apr. 489 Social-Democracy, like all other '-ocracies', will have a great deal more trouble with its idle and worthless members than with its able ones. **1928** —— *Intelligent Woman's Guide Socialism* xliii. 166 If it be still necessary to call the rich an ocracy of any kind, they must be called a plutocracy. **1963** F. W. FREY in L. W. Pye *Communications & Political Devel.* xvii. 299 Movement towards 'democracy'..or whatever one's preferred..'ocracy' happens to be.

ocre, obs. form of OCHRE; var. OCKER *Obs.*

‖**ocrea** ('ɒkrɪə). Erron. **ochrea.** *Pl.* **-æ.** [L. *ocrea* a greave or legging, worn by foot-soldiers, hunters, and country people.] **a.** *Bot.* (*a*) A sheath or tube round a stem or stalk formed by the lateral cohesion of two or more stipules; (*b*) The thin sheath surrounding the seta in mosses.

b. *Zool.* An investing part or growth similar to this; the 'boot' of a bird (see OCREATE *a.* 2).

1830 LINDLEY *Nat. Syst. Bot.* 169 The cohesion of the scarious stipulæ into a sheath, technically called an ochrea, or boot, is sufficient to distinguish Polygoneæ from all other plants. **1835** —— *Introd. Bot.* (1848) I. 308 When stipules surround the stem of a plant they become an ochrea. **1863** BERKELEY *Brit. Mosses* Gloss. 312 *Ocrea*, a little sheath sometimes investing the base of the fruitstalk, distinct from the vaginula.

Hence **ocre'aceous** *a.*, *Bot.*, of the nature or form of an ocrea.

1878 MASTERS *Henfrey's Bot.* 329 The..plants of this order may be distinguished by the peculiar ocreaceous stipules.

ocreate ('ɒkrɪːət), *a.* Erron. **ochreate.** [f. as prec. + -ATE[2].]

1. Wearing or furnished with an *ocrea*, greave, or legging; booted.

2. *Ornith.* Booted: having the tarsal envelope fused into a continuous ocrea or boot, as in Sundevall's group of Birds, *Ocreatæ*, containing the thrushes, nightingales, redbreasts, etc.

3. *Bot.* Having the stipules united by cohesion into a sheath surrounding the stem.

1830 LINDLEY *Nat. Syst. Bot.* 169 Apetalous dicotyledons, with..ochreate stipulæ. **1880** GRAY *Struct. Bot.* iii. §4 (ed. 6) 106 Sheathing stipules, like those of Polygonum, are said to be ochreate, or (better) ocreate.

†**'ocreated,** *a. Obs.* [-ED[1].] = prec. 1; booted.

a **1661** FULLER *Worthies, Norwich* II. (1662) 275 A Scholar undertook..to address himself ocreated unto the Vice-Chancellour.

ocreo-, ocrie: see OCHREO-, OCHRY.

ocro, variant of OKRA, an esculent plant.

oct-, form of OCTA- and OCTO-, used before a vowel, as in OCTACTINAL, OCTARTICULATE, *octammonio-*, see OCTA- b.

oct., abbrev. of OCTAVO, OCTOBER.

octa- ('ɒktə), Gr. ὀκτα-, comb. form of ὀκτώ eight, with which it varies in some words. Most of the English derivatives of *octa-* appear in their places as main words; the following are of minor importance: **octachronous** (-'ækrənəs) *a. Pros.* [Gr. χρόνος time] = *octasemic*. **octacolic** (-'kɒlɪk) *a. Pros.* [COLON[2]], consisting of eight cola. **octaphonic** (-ˈfɒnɪk) *a. Mus.* [Gr. φωνή voice, sound], composed in eight parts. **octapodic** (-ˈpɒdɪk) *a. Pros.* [Gr. ὀκταπόδ-ης, ὀκτάπους, -ποδ- eight-footed], containing eight metrical feet; **octapody** (-ˈæpədɪ), a verse of eight feet. **octasemic** (-ˈsiːmɪk) *a. Pros.* [L. *octasēmus*, Gr. ὀκτάσημος], containing eight moræ or units of time. **octastrophic** (-ˈstrɒfɪk) *a. Pros.*, consisting of eight strophes or stanzas.

1900 H. W. SMYTH *Greek Metric Poets* 195 We might arrange (the passage) in Octapodies.

b. In *Chem. octa-, oct-* (sometimes *octo-*) indicates the presence of eight atoms or units of an element or radical, as in ***octacarbon, octachloride, octammonio-***; **octadecanol**, any of the alcohols with the formula $C_{18}H_{37}OH$; spec. ***normal*** (or ***n-***) ***octadecanol***, a crystalline primary alcohol which is present in whale and dolphin oils, also called stearyl alcohol; **octaˈpeptide**, any peptide composed of eight amino-acid residues.

1877 Octachloride [see OCTAD 3]. **1914** *Jrnl. Chem. Soc.* CV. 2233 The acetates of the dextrorotatory carbinols from ethylbutylcarbinol (γ-heptanol) on to ethylpentadecylcarbinol (γ-octadecanol) are all of negative rotation. **1949** E. CHAIN in H. W. Florey et al. *Antibiotics* II. xvii. 709 Antifoam reagent (3 per cent. octadecanol in lard oil). **1970** *Chem. & Physics Lipids* IV. 246 The major long-chain alcohols found in heart and brain tissues are hexadecanol, octadecanol and octadecenol. **1873** WATTS *Fownes' Chem.* (ed. 11) 425 The octammonio-diplatinic compounds consist of double molecules of tetrammonio-platinic compounds having two or more molecules. **1931** *Chem. Rev.* VIII. 390 Curtius..found that when his triglycylglycine ester was heated to 100°C. *in vacuo* it was converted into an insoluble infusible material having the composition—$NHCH_2CO$—. He assigned to this material the structure of a cyclic octapeptide, but a much more highly polymeric open chain structure seems more probable. **1957** *Science* 3 May 886/1 (*heading*) Synthesis and pharmacology of the octapeptide angiotonin. **1972** *Lancet* 17 June 1320/1 The superb work of Wieland and his school established that the toxins are either cyclic heptapeptides or octapeptides.

octachord (ˈɒktəkɔːd), *a.* and *sb. Mus.* Also octo-. [ad. late L. *octachord-os*, a. Gr. ὀκτάχορδ-ος eight-stringed, f. ὀκτα- OCTA- + χορδή string, CHORD. In mod.F. *octacorde* (Littré).]

A. *adj.* **a.** Having eight strings. **b.** Relating to a scale of eight notes.

1760 STILES in *Phil. Trans.* LI. 737 In the time of the octachord lyre. *Ibid.* 771 Denying that the octachord system could have anything to do with his invention.

B. *sb.* **a.** A series of eight notes, as the ordinary diatonic scale. (Cf. *tetrachord, hexachord.*) **b.** A musical instrument having eight strings.

1776 BURNEY *Hist. Mus.* I. 35 Forming then the whole system of the octachord, or heptachord, as I understand it. **1811** BUSBY *Dict. Mus.* (ed. 3), *Octachord*, an instrument, or system, comprising eight sounds, or seven degrees. The Octachord, or lyre, of Pythagoras, comprehended the two disjunct tetrachords expressed by the letters E, F, G, A, B, C, D, E. **1882** *Academy* 15 Apr. 276 His mode of reasoning is..like the octochord itself, somewhat artificial.

Hence **octaˈchordal** (octo-) *a.*, of the octachord.

1882 *Academy* 15 Apr. 276/3 The octochordal scale is of great antiquity.

octactinal (ɒktækˈtaɪnəl, -ˈæktɪnəl), *a. Zool.* [f. Gr. ὀκτώ or ὀκτα- eight + ἀκτίς, ἀκτῖν- ray + -AL[1]: cf. ACTINAL.] Having eight rays; *spec.* belonging to the *Octactiniæ* or *Octocoralla*, sub-class of *Anthozoa* (see OCTO-). So **octacˈtinian** *a.* and *sb.*

1888 ROLLESTON & JACKSON *Anim. Life* 769 Jickeli suggests..that the Graptolites are possibly Octactinians. **1891** *Cent. Dict.*, Octactinal.

octad (ˈɒktæd). [ad. L. *octas, octad-*, a. Gr. ὀκτάς, -άδα a group of eight: see -AD 1 a.]

1. A group or series of eight; *spec.* in ancient systems of arithmetical notation: A group or series of eight characters corresponding to successive powers of ten (analogous to the groups of six figures marking millions, billions, etc. now used).

1883 SIR E. C. BAYLEY *Geneal. Mod. Numerals* II. in *Jrnl. R. Asiat. Soc.* XV. 48 [The Greeks] had, however, a system of 'octads' and 'tetrads' for expressing numbers of very high value. *Ibid.* 49 By collecting the alphabetical signs in groups of eight or 'octads', decimally arranged.

2. *Math.* **a.** *Mod. Geom.* The set of eight intersections of three quadric surfaces.

1889 CAYLEY in *Messenger* XVIII. 149 The eight points of intersection of any three quadric surfaces are an octad.

†**b.** *pl.* A system of eight imaginaries analogous to quaternions, also called *octaves*. *Obs.*

1845 J. T. GRAVES in *Phil. Mag.* XXVI. 315-20. **18..** CAYLEY *Collected Papers* I. 586.

3. *Chem.* An element or radical that has the combining power of eight units, i.e. of eight atoms of hydrogen.

1877 WATTS *Fownes' Chem.* I. 268 Ru[bidium] and Os[mium] form tetroxides (analogous to octochlorides), and may therefore be regarded as octads.

Hence **octadic** (ɒkˈtædɪk) *a.*, of or pertaining to an octad. ***octadic surface*** (*Mod. Geom.*), a quartic surface, eight of whose nodes form an octad.

1870 CAYLEY in *Proc. Lond. Math. Soc.* III. 20.

octadrachm (ˈɒktədræm), **octo-**. [ad. Gr. ὀκτάδραχμ-ος adj., weighing or worth eight drachmæ, f. ὀκτα- + δραχμή DRACHMA.] An ancient Greek coin of the value of eight drachmæ.

1876 HUMPHREYS *Coin-Coll. Man.* v. 41 The Edonians coined octodrachms, pieces of eight drachms. **1885** *Athenæum* 28 Feb. 284/1 A silver octadrachm of the town of Ichnæ, in Macedon, and a very fine tetradrachm of Camarina.

octaedral, etc.: see OCTAHEDRAL, etc.

octaeterid (ˌɒktəɪˈtɪərɪd). Also in Gr. form **octaeˈteris**. [ad. Gr. ὀκταετηρίς, -ιδ-, f. ὀκτα- OCTA- + ἔτος year. In F. *octaétéride* (1732 in *Dict. Trévoux*).] In the ancient Greek calendar, a period of eight years, in the course of which three months of 30 days each were intercalated so as to bring the year of 12 lunar months into accord with the solar year. So **octaeteric** (-ɪˈtɛrɪk) *a.*, of or belonging to this period.

a **1727** NEWTON *Chronol. Amended* (1728) i. 75. **1727-41** CHAMBERS *Cycl.*, *Octaeterides*, in chronology, etc. the space, or duration of eight years. **1753** —— *Cycl. Supp.*, *Octaeteris*, ..in antiquity, a cycle, or term, of eight years, at the end of which three entire lunar months were added. **1846** GROTE *Greece* II. II. ii. 353 *note*, The properties of the octaeteric or enneaeteric period. **1862** SIR G. C. LEWIS *Astron. Ancients* 38 The octaëteric cycle, attributed to Cleostratus. *Ibid.* 9 Three months of thirty days apiece were intercalated in each of the two first octaeterids. **1899** WARDE FOWLER *Roman Festivals* 2 In the *octaeteris* or 8-year cycle there were 99 lunar months.

octagon (ˈɒktəgən), *sb.* and *a.* Also 7 **octagone, octogone**, 7–8 **octogon**. [ad. L. *octă-, octōgōn-os* adj., a. Gr. ὀκτάγων-ος eight-cornered, f. ὀκτα- OCTA- + stem of γωνία corner, angle. In F. *octogone* (1520 in Hatz.-Darm.).]

A. *sb.* **1.** *Geom.* A plane figure having eight angles and eight sides. Hence applied to material objects of octagonal form or section.

1656 BLOUNT *Glossogr.*, *Octogon.* **1660** BARROW *Euclid* IV. xi. *Schol.*, Then will AB be the side of Octagone. **1674** tr. *Scheffer's Lapland* xvi. 84 They [the tents] were octogons somewhat broader towards the bottom. **1757** POCOCKE *Trav.* (1889) II. 284 A tower at each corner, which..are octagons. **1868** *Morn. Star* 26 Mar., The ceiling of the room is coffered in octagons geometrically arranged.

2. *Fortif.* A fort having eight bastions.

1706 in PHILLIPS. **1727-41** in CHAMBERS *Cycl.*

B. *adj.* = OCTAGONAL.

1679 M. RUSDEN *Further Discov. Bees* 81 The form is octagon or eight square. **1762-71** H. WALPOLE *Vertue's Anecd. Paint.* (1786) IV. 134 The octagon buildings at each end. **1774** *Westm. Mag.* II. 316 A..magnificent octogon hall. **1808** SCOTT *Marm.* v. xxv, Dun-Edin's cross, a pillared stone, Rose on a turret octagon. **1862** MISS BRADDON *Lady Audley* vii. 50 An octagon ante-chamber.

C. *Comb.*, as **octagon-faced** *a.* (after *double-faced*); **octagon-stitch**, a stitch in crochet-work.

1885 MRS. BURNETT *Theo* iv. (1888) 81, I will show you how to do the octagon-stitch. **1892** B. HINTON *Lord's Return* 203 This personage must be octagon-faced, at the least.

octagonal (ɒkˈtægənəl), *a.* Also 6–8 octo-. [In 16th c. *octogonal*, ad. mod.L. *octōgonāl-is*, in F. *octogonal* (1520 in Hatz.-Darm.): see prec. and -AL[1].] Of the form of an octagon; eight-sided.

1571 DIGGES *Pantom.* IV. xxv. Gg ij, A figure..enuironed with 6 equiangle Octogonall and 8 equilater triangular playnes or bases. **1782** WARTON *Hist. Kiddington* 4 The Gothic mouldings on the faces of its [a font's] octogonal panes. **1812-16** J. SMITH *Panorama Sc. & Art* I. 17 A.. triangular, square, or octagonal bar. **1860** TYNDALL *Glac.* I. v. 40 A little octagonal building.

Hence **ocˈtagonally** *adv.*, in an octagonal form.

1753 JOHNSON in *Bibl. Topogr. Brit.* III. 433 Our cockpit built octagonally.

†**octaˈgonian**, *a. Obs.* Of or belonging to an octagon.

Applied to a Dissenting congregation in Liverpool, worshipping in a building known from its shape as the Octagon.

1598 [see HEXAGONIAN]. **1813** JEFFERSON *Writ.* (1830) IV. 225 The best collection of these psalms is that of the Octagonian dissenters of Liverpool.

octagynia, etc.: see OCTOGYNIA, etc.

octahedral (ɒktəˈhiːdrəl, -ˈhɛdrəl), **octo-**, *a.* Also **octaedral, octoedral**. [f. late L. *octa(h)edros*, a. Gr. ὀκτάεδρ-ος eight-sided: see OCTAHEDRON and -AL[1].] Having the form of an octahedron; contained by eight plane (esp. triangular) faces.

1758 REID tr. *Macquer's Chym.* I. 222 The crystals of Alum are octaedral... These octaedral solids are triangular pyramids, having their angles cut away, so that four of their surfaces are hexagons, and the other four triangles. **1796** HATCHETT in *Phil. Trans.* LXXXVI. 292 Various modifications between the octoedral figure and the cube. **1811** PINKERTON *Petral.* I. 312 Some detached crystals of octahedral iron. **1869** PHILLIPS *Vesuv.* iii. 94 Crystallized in cubes and octahedral forms.

b. Of or belonging to an octahedron.

1878 GURNEY *Crystallogr.* 88 At each angle of the octahedral face.

octahedrally (ɒktəˈhiːdrəlɪ), *adv.* [f. OCTAHEDRAL, OCTO- *a.* + -LY[2].] In an octahedral shape or arrangement.

1872 *Geol. Mag.* IX. 356 The octahedrally crystallized magnetic particles do not contain any traces of nickel. **1947** *Q. Rev. Chem. Soc.* I. 253 Half of the metal ions are surrounded, approximately octahedrally, by four oxygen atoms of AsO_4 (or PO_4) ions and by two OH ions. **1970** *Nature* 11 Apr. 141/2 It is a reasonable guess that the molecules around the ion are disposed octahedrally.

octahedric (-ˈhɛdrɪk), *a. rare.* Also octo-. [f. Gr. ὀκτάεδρος (see OCTAHEDRON) + -IC: in mod.F. *octaédrique* (Littré).] = OCTAHEDRAL. Also †**octaˈhedrical, octo-** *a.*

1657 W. RAND tr. *Gassendi's Life Peiresc* I. 44 The forming of Alum into an octahedricall figure. *a* **1691** BOYLE *Hist. Air* (1692) 249 The alum appeared to be..coagulated in many Octaedrical grains. **1730-6** BAILEY (folio), *Octoedrical*. **1847** *National Cycl.* II. 868 Nitrate of barytes appears as octahedric crystals.

octahedrid (ɒktəˈhiːdrɪd, -ˈhɛdrɪd), *a. Cryst.* [f. as prec. + -ID[2].] Applied to any plane, in a crystallographic system, which intersects all the three axes of coordinates; so called because a group of eight such planes would form an octahedron. Opposed to *prismatoid* and *pinakoid*.

1895 STORY-MASKELYNE *Crystallogr.* ii. §18.

octahedrite (ɒktəˈhiːdraɪt, -ˈhɛdraɪt). *Min.* Also octo-. [f. as prec. + -ITE[1] 2 b.] **1.** Native dioxide of titanium, occurring in crystals of octahedral and other related forms; also called ANATASE.

1805 R. JAMESON *Syst. Min.* II. 493. **1831** BREWSTER *Optics* xvii. 149. **1868** DANA *Min.* (ed. 5) 241.

2. An iron meteorite which shows a Widmanstätten structure on etching due to intimate intergrowths of plates of kamacite with narrow borders of tænite oriented parallel to the faces of a regular octahedron.

1916 *Mineral. Mag.* XVIII. 42 (*table*) Nickel-poor octahedrites. **1944** C. PALACHE et al. *Dana's Syst. Min.* (ed. 7) I. 120 A similar structureless aspect can be obtained in an octahedrite by prolonged heating at about 900°. **1974** *Encycl. Brit. Micropædia* VII. 477/2 Besides nickel-iron, major minerals in octahedrites are troilite and schreibersite.

octahedron (ɒktəˈhiːdrən, -ˈhɛdrən), **octo-**. Pl. **-ons** or **-a**. Also 6–8 **octa(h)edrum**, 6–9 **octaedron**, 7–9 **octoedron**. [a. Gr. ὀκτάεδρον an octahedron, neuter of ὀκτάεδρος adj., eight-sided, f. ὀκτα- OCTA- + ἕδρα seat. In L. *octaëdron*, med.L. *octa(h)edrum* (Du Cange), F. *octaèdre*, also *octohèdre* (1587 in Hatz.-Darm.).]

Geom. A solid figure contained by eight plane faces; usually, one contained by eight triangles (such as is formed by two pyramids on opposite sides of a quadrilateral base); *spec.* the ***regular octahedron***, one of the five regular solids, contained by eight equal equilateral triangles (formed by two equal pyramids with equilateral faces on a square base). Hence *gen.* Any material body, esp. a crystal, of this form.

truncated octahedron, a fourteen-sided solid formed from the regular octahedron by truncating its six corners, and thus forming six new square faces, while cutting down the eight original triangular faces into regular hexagons.

1570 BILLINGSLEY *Euclid* XIII. xiv. 406 An octohedron is deuided into two equall and like Pyramids. **1655** H. MORE *Antid. Ath.* App. (1712) 183 There are Fiue regular Bodies ..the Cube, the Tetraedrum, the Octaedrum, the Dodecaedrum, and the Eicosaedrum. **1656** STANLEY *Hist. Philos.* v. (1701) 186/2 The Octaedrons consist of eight like sides. **1823** H. J. BROOKE *Introd. Crystallogr.* 141 Octahedrons with rhombic bases. **1851** RICHARDSON *Geol.* v. 76 If we take a cube and cut off all the eight corners till the original faces disappear, we shall make it an octohedron. **1880** CLEMINSHAW tr. *Wurtz' Atom. Th.* 142 The nitrates of barium, strontium, and lead,..crystallise in octohedra.

†**octaˈhedrous**, *a. Obs.* In 8 octoedrous. [f. stem of prec. + -OUS.] = OCTAHEDRAL.

1702 R. THORESBY in *Phil. Trans.* XXIII. 1072 Copper Ore..shot into an Octoedrous form.

octakis-, Gr. ὀκτάκις eight times, as in ˌ**octakishexaˈhedron** *Cryst.*, a solid figure contained by forty-eight scalene triangles.

1878 [see HEXAKIS-].

octal (ˈɒktəl), *a.* and *sb.* [f. OCT- + -AL.]

A. *adj.* **1.** *Electronics.* Applied to valve bases and plugs (and the corresponding sockets) having a standard circular arrangement of eight pins with a central moulded key for determining the orientation.

1936 *Wireless World* 20 Nov. 557 (*heading*) 8-pin base (octal) connections. **1943** C. L. BOLTZ *Basic Radio* x. 165 Then from America came the international octal base, with eight pins symmetrically arranged in a circle. **1961** *Engineering* 14 July 42/4 The unit is constructed as a plug-in module..connecting with associated circuits through a standard octal plug. **1976** *Gramophone* Feb. 1403/1 At the left is an octal valve socket designed for use with a matching transformer when a moving coil cartridge is used.

2. *Math.* and *Computers.* Pertaining to or being a system of numerical notation that employs 8 rather than 10 as the base.

1948 *Math. Tables & Other Aids to Computation* III. 295 Binary numbers are set into the keyboard in the octal (radix 8) notation. **1962** T. C. BARTEE et al. *Theory & Design Digital Machines* 307 In the octal system the sequence 624 represents the sum $6 \times 8^2 + 2 \times 8^1 + 4 \times 8^0$ which is equal to the sequence 404 in the decimal system. **1963** *Rep. Comm. Inquiry Decimal Currency* 4 in *Parl. Papers 1962–3* (Cmnd. 2145) XI. 195 If.. we have in mind electronic rather than human computers, a case can be made for counting in eights—an octal system—because this can be related more easily to the binary system used by such computers. **1973** *Nature* 27 Apr. 620/1 The octal system is widely used in listing machine instruction programs for small computers, where groups of six octal digits are written in place of sixteen to eighteen binary digits.

B. *sb.* The octal system; rarely *pl.*

1948 *Math. Tables & Other Aids to Computation* III. 295 The conversions octal-binary and binary-octal are very elementary. **1961** EVANS & PERRY *Programming & Coding* iii. 89 The two representations ·101010101 in binary, and ·525 in octal, are different representations of the same magnitude. **1961** *Times* 28 Dec. 9/5 (*heading*) Thinking in octals. Advantages over decimals. **1967** KLERER & KORN *Digital Computer User's Handbk.* I. ii. 39 Since $2^3 = 8^1$, a binary series of digits may be converted to octal by grouping the binary digits into three to left or right of the decimal point. Thus the binary integer $(1001011011)_2 = (1\ 001\ 011\ 011)_2 = (1133)_8$. **1977** D. BAGLEY *Enemy* xxxi. 253 This gadget is working in octal instead of decimal... Many computers work in octal internally.

octamerous (ɒk'tæmərəs), *a.* *Nat. Hist.* Also **octomerous** (-'ɒm-). [f. Gr. ὀκταμερ-ής in eight parts (μέρος part) + -OUS.] **a.** *Bot.* Having the parts of the flower in series of eight. (Often written 8-*merous*.) **b.** *Zool.* Having the radiating parts or organs eight in number, as an actinoid zoophyte.

1864 WEBSTER, *Octamerous* (*Bot.*), having the parts in eights. *Gray.* **1875** BENNETT & DYER tr. *Sachs' Bot.* 565 Pentamerous flowers and.. those which are truly tetramerous (or octamerous). **1877** HUXLEY *Anat. Inv. Anim.* iii. 159 The finally hexamerous Anthozoon passes through a tetramerous and an octomerous stage.

So **oc'tamerism**, the state of being octamerous (*humorously*, the state of being in eight parts).

1873 WHITNEY *Orient. Stud.* 133 Announced.. to form eight volumes.. perhaps the estimated octamerism of the work was meant to be understood in some peculiar sense.

octameter (ɒk'tæmɪtə(r)), *a.* and *sb.* *Pros.* Also **octometer** (-'ɒm-). [ad. L. *octameter*, *-trum* adj., a. Gr. ὀκτάμετρ-ος (μέτρον measure).]

a. *adj.* Consisting of eight measures or feet. **b.** *sb.* A verse containing eight measures or feet.

a **1849** POE *Philos. Composition*, The rhythm.. of the 'Raven'.. is trochaic, is octameter acatalectic, alternating with heptameter catalectic.. and terminating with tetrameter catalectic. **1889** *Athenæum* 25 May 657/1 'March: an Ode' [by Swinburne], is the only instance in the language of a poem written in octometers. **1900** H. W. SMYTH *Greek Metric Poets* 259 The long, swelling octameter.

ˌocta'methylˌcycloˌtetrasi'loxane. *Chem.* [f. OCTA- + METHYL + CYCLO- + TETRA- + SILOXANE.] A colourless oily liquid that is a cyclic tetramer, $[(CH_3)_2SiO]_4$, and an intermediate in the manufacture of many silicones.

1946 M. J. HUNTER et al. in *Jrnl. Amer. Chem. Soc.* LXVIII. 361/1 When a few drops of concentrated sulfuric acid are added to a quantity, say 10 c.c., of octamethyl*cyclo*tetrasiloxane, $[(CH_3)_2SiO]_4$, there is no marked change in appearance or temperature. **1962** BARRY & BECK in Stone & Graham *Inorg. Polymers* v. 216 The slow addition of dimethyldichlorosilane to excess water at 15 to 20°C yields a mixture consisting of 0·5% hexamethyl-cyclotrisiloxane (D_3), 42·0% octamethylcyclotetrasiloxane (D_4), 6·7% decamethylcyclopentasiloxane (D_5), [etc.]. **1970** *Encycl. Polymer Sci. & Technol.* XII. 503 Almost all strong inorganic alkalis and most quaternary ammonium hydroxides and phosphonium hydroxides will polymerize octamethylcyclotetrasiloxane to a high-molecular-weight polymer.

octan ('ɒktən), *a.* [a. F. *octane*, in Paré, 16th c., *octaine*, ad. L. *octānus*, found only in sense 'of the 8th legion', but cf. *quartan*, *quintan*.] ***octan fever***: a fever in which the paroxysms occur every eighth day (both paroxysmal days being counted).

1897 *Allbutt's Syst. Med.* II. 318 Further modifications have been recognised by nosologists as quintan, sextan, octan.

‖**Octandria** (ɒk'tændrɪə). *Bot.* [mod.L. f. Gr. ὀκτώ eight + ἀνδρ- (ἀνήρ) man, male: see -IA[1].] A class in the Linnæan Sexual System, comprising plants with eight stamens. Hence **oc'tander**, a plant of this class; **oc'tandrian** *a.*, **oc'tandrious** *a.*, belonging to this class; **oc'tandrous** *a.*, having eight stamens.

1753 CHAMBERS *Cycl. Supp.*, *Octandria*,.. a class of plants with hermaphrodite flowers, and eight stamina, or male parts in each. **1828** WEBSTER, *Octander*.. *Octandrian.* **1830** LINDLEY *Nat. Syst. Bot.* 69 Octandrous genera belonging to this family. **1880** SIR E. REED *Japan* II. 43 The flowers are octandrous.

octane ('ɒkteɪn). *Chem.* [f. OCT(A-, OCT(O- + -ANE 2 b.] **1. a.** The paraffin of the octacarbon series (C_8H_{18}). So **'octene** (-iːn) [-ENE], the olefine of the same series (C_8H_{16}), also called *octylene*; **'octine** (-aɪn) [-INE[5]], the hydrocarbon of the same series (C_8H_{14}) homologous with acetylene or ethine; **oc'toic** *a.*, applied to fatty acids, etc. of the same series, as ***octoic acid*** ($C_8H_{16}O_2$), one isomeric form of which is *caprylic acid*.

1872 WATTS *Dict. Chem.* VI. 877 *Octane.* C_8H_{18}. This hydrocarbon is one of the constituents of American petroleum. *Ibid.* 710 Hydrocarbons.. Second Series... Olefines.. Octene or Octylene, C_8H_{16}. **1877** —— *Fownes' Chem.* II. 59 Third Series... Ethine or Acetylene Series... Octine, C_8H_{14}. **1881** —— *Dict. Chem.* VIII. 1424 Octoic acids, $C_8H_{16}O_2$.

b. *ellipt.* for *octane number*, esp. with prefixed numeral, e.g. ***105 octane***, or adj., e.g. ***high octane***.

1932, etc. [see *high-octane* s.v. HIGH *a.* 22 a]. **1935** *Oil & Gas Jrnl.* 4 July 16/1 Until this spring, 87 octane gasoline was the highest quality used for commercial take-offs. **1954** [see ISOOCTANE b]. **1960** J. B. HILL in V. B. Guthrie *Petroleum Products Handbk.* iv. 20 A particular gasoline may have a Research octane of 88 and a Motor octane of 78. **1966** *McGraw-Hill Encycl. Sci. & Technol.* III. 309/2 High octane gasoline burns in the same manner and with the same flame velocity as low octane gasoline. **1973** J. LEASOR *Host of Extras* vii. 136 Adrenalin surged round my body like 105 octane petrol.

2. *attrib.* and *Comb.*, as (sense 1 b) ***octane-booster***, ***-quality***; ***octane-scented*** adj.; **octane number, rating**, a number indicating the anti-knock properties of a motor or aviation fuel, equal (for numbers below 100) to the percentage by volume of isooctane in an isooctane/normal heptane mixture of equivalent peformance (see also quot. 1966).

1971 *New Scientist* 5 Aug. 323/1 Those spokesmen of the oil industry who have been arguing that alkyl lead (added to petrol as an octane-booster..) is not a health hazard. **1931** *Automobile Engineer* Aug. 308/3 Lead tetra-ethyl is the only other practical alternative to cracked spirits as a means of raising the anti-knock value of motor spirit to an octane number of 70 or more (this now being the prime consideration of a premium gasoline or petrol). **1933** *Flight* 4 May 408/1 The British Air Ministry is, rightly or wrongly, taking its time over considering the matter of octane number. **1966** *McGraw-Hill Encycl. Sci. & Technol.* IX. 273/1 Fuels with octane numbers above 100 are usually rated by finding the number of milliliters of tetraethyllead required per gallon of isooctane to give the same resistance to detonation as the fuel sample. **1972** PATTERSON & HENEIN *Emissions from Combustion Engines* ii. 63 The octane number of the fuels on the market is about 94 for regular gasoline and 100 for premium gasoline. **1959** R. J. HENGSTEBECK *Petroleum Processing* i. 3 The octane quality of a gasoline may be rated differently by different engines. **1940** A. W. JUDGE *Aircraft Engines* I. v. 114 If it was found that a mixture of 78 per cent. of iso-octane and 22 per cent. of heptane matched the particular fuel under test in 'knocking' qualities the fuel in question would be said to have an octane rating of 78. **1959** R. J. HENGSTEBECK *Petroleum Processing* i. 3 Octane ratings above 100 are proportional to their performance potentials. **1972** *Daily Tel.* 15 Mar. 11/7 Lead has been used in growing quantities to raise the octane rating of petrol, allowing modern engines to make more efficient use of the fuel. **1946** *R.A.F. Jrnl.* May 151 Newly-arrived from the octane-scented atmosphere of Station life and full of inspiration.

'octangle, *a.* and *sb.* ? *Obs.* [ad. post-cl. L. *octangul-us* adj. eight-angled, f. *octo* eight + *angulus* ANGLE.] **a.** *adj.* Having eight angles, octagonal. **b.** *sb.* A figure with eight angles, an octagon.

1613–14 CHAPMAN *Masque Mid. Temple* a j, A siluer Temple of an octangle figure. **1651** J. F[REAKE] *Agrippa's Occ. Philos.* 253 The other figures, viz. triangle, quadrangle, sexangle, septangle, octangle. **1686** AGLIONBY *Painting Illustr.* 322 The Octangles which inviron the Ceiling. **1726** LEONI tr. *Alberti's Archit.* III. 4/1 The middle Rays of this Octangle may be a Pyramid of eight Faces.

octangular (ɒk'tæŋgjʊlə(r)), *a.* [f. L. *octangul-us* (see prec.) + -AR: cf. *angulāris* ANGULAR.] Having eight angles; octagonal.

1644 EVELYN *Diary* 22 Oct., A Cabinet of an octangular forme. **1712** J. JAMES tr. *Le Blond's Gardening* 27 An octangular Bowling-green. **1807** G. CHALMERS *Caledonia* I. I. iv. 159 An octangular vase of brass. **1877** W. JONES *Finger-ring* 147 An octangular ring of iron.

Hence **oc'tangularness** (Bailey vol. II, 1727).

octanoic (ɒktə'nəʊɪk), *a.* *Chem.* [f. OCTAN(E + -OIC.] = CAPRYLIC *a.*

1909 *Jrnl. Chem. Soc.* XCVI. II. 1378/1 (Index), Octanoic acid, ε-hydroxy-, and its lactone. **1940** T. P. HILDITCH *Chem. Constitution Nat. Fats* iii. 99 In the milk fats of sheep and goats.., the proportions of octanoic and decanoic (caprylic and capric) acids are much greater and approach, or even exceed, that of butyric acid in cow milk fats. **1972** *Materials & Technol.* V. ix. 244 $CH_3(CH_2)_6COOH$, octanoic acid, was first described in 1844 by Lerch who isolated it from butter.

Hence **octa'noate**, the anion, or an ester or salt, of octanoic acid; **'octanoyl**, the radical $CH_3(CH_2)_6CO$— present in octanoic acid; also called *caprylyl*.

1945 *Jrnl. Biol. Chem.* CLXI. 416 Of the tested fatty acids octanoate was the most reactive under these conditions. **1949** *Union Internat. Chim. Pure et Appl., Compt. Rend.* XV. 145 Rule 58.3... Octanoyl. Replacing 'capryloyl' and 'caprylyl'. **1954** A. WHITE et al. *Princ. Biochem.* xviii. 482 The reaction sequence.. by which octanoate might give rise to acetoacetate. **1973** *Agric. & Biol. Chem.* (Tokyo) XXXVII. 2713/2 During this acylation process with *n*-octanoyl chloride, esterification of two OH groups of 2 moles of Thr contained in a colistin nonapeptide molecule was possible. **1974** *Acta Crystallogr.* XXX. B. 2913/2 Copper(II) octanoate was prepared by adding copper carbonate to an excess of solution of octanoic acid in ethanol.

octanol ('ɒktənɒl). *Chem.* [f. as prec. + -OL.] Any saturated aliphatic monohydric alcohol containing eight carbon atoms, $C_8H_{17}OH$, of which many isomeric forms exist; *esp.* the primary straight-chain alcohol (*n*- or 1-octanol), or the secondary alcohol, $CH_3(CH_2)_5CH(OH)CH_3$ (2-octanol), both of which are colourless odoriferous liquids used chiefly in the perfume and plastic industries; octyl alcohol.

1905 *Jrnl. Chem. Soc.* LXXXVIII. I. 573 δ-Octanol is a mobile liquid with a pleasant odour which boils at 71° under 10 mm. pressure. **1932** *Physical Rev.* XL. 830 The series consists of twenty-one octanols which differ from one another only in the relative positions of a methyl and hydroxyl group along the chain. **1947** KIRK & OTHMER *Encycl. Chem. Technol.* I. 317, 1-Octanol.. is a colorless liquid with a penetrating odor. *Ibid.*, The technical grades of 2-octanol are used as solvents for many resins and in some protective formulations to improve flow and leveling. **1950** I. MELLAN *Industr. Solvents* (ed. 2) xi. 511 Commercial *n*-octanol is derived synthetically from coconut oil. **1975** J. M. TEDDER et al. *Basic Org. Chem.* V. xii. 450 Long chain fatty alcohols (mainly octanol and decanol) are used to inhibit terminal bud growth and hence stimulate branching in many plant species.

octant ('ɒktənt). [ad. late L. *octans*, *-tant-em* a half quadrant (Vitruv.), f. *octo* eight: cf. *quadrans* QUADRANT. So F. *octant*, in sense 3 (1683 in Hatz.-Darm.).]

1. The eighth part of a circle; *i.e.* either (*a*) an arc of a circle, forming one eighth of the circumference, or (*b*) one eighth of the area of a circle, contained within two radii at an angle of 45°.

1750 *Phil. Trans.* XLVII. 69 Thro' the whole octant OA, it is continually decreasing. **1875** T. R. ROBINSON *ibid.* CLXV. 411 The irregularity of the wind.. varies in each octant.

b. Each of the eight parts into which a solid figure or body (*e.g.* a sphere), or the space around a central point, is divided by three planes (usually mutually at right angles) intersecting at the central point.

1790 WILDBORE in *Phil. Trans.* LXXX. 497 Disposed in the eight octants of a regular parallelopipedon. **1875** BENNETT & DYER tr. *Sachs' Bot.* 288 The globule [= antheridium of *Nitella*] now consists of four lower and four upper octants of a sphere... Each octant now breaks up.. into an outer and an inner cell. **1895** STORY-MASKELYNE *Crystallogr.* ii. §15 These planes, *YZ*, *ZX*, *XY*, divide the space round the origin into eight hollow quoins or octants.

2. *Astron.* That point in the apparent course of a planet at which it is 45° distant from another planet, from the sun, or from some particular point; *spec.* each of the four points at which the moon is 45° from conjunction with or opposition to the sun, or midway between the syzygies and quadratures.

1690 LEYBOURN *Curs. Math.* 773 About the Octants from the Aphelion and Perihelion. **1706** PHILLIPS, *Octant* or *Octile* (in Astrol.), when a Planet is in such an Aspect or Position with respect to another, that their Places are only distant an eighth part of a Circle, or 45 Degrees. *c* **1716** MACHIN in Rigaud *Corr. Sci. Men* (1841) I. 275 It will be of great use, if I could have a few places of the moon when in the octants or near. **1787** BONNYCASTLE *Astron.* xxi. 363 In her third octant.. she again appears gibbous. **1834** *Hist. Astron.* ix. 45/1 (U.K.S.) A third [inequality of the moon], called the variation,.. is greatest in the octants.

3. An instrument in the form of a graduated eighth of a circle, used for making angular measurements, esp. in astronomy and navigation. (In Fr., mentioned 1683 in Le Cordier, *Instruments des Pilotes*.)

1731 HADLEY in *Phil. Trans.* XXXVII. 150 The Instrument consists of an Octant *ABC*, having on its Limb *BC* an Arch of 45 Degrees, divided into 90 Parts or half Degrees. **1774** M. MACKENZIE *Maritime Surv.* 2 The principal Instruments used in surveying; such as the Theodolite, the astronomical Quadrant, and Hadley's Octant, or Sextant. **1825** J. NICHOLSON *Operat. Mechanic* 316 Binding himself to divide all sextants and octants by the same engine.

Hence **oc'tantal** *a.*, of or pertaining to an octant; vanishing once in each octant of the compass.

1776 HORSLEY in *Phil. Trans.* LXVI. 363 If from these.. we reject the octantal days. **1928** L. S. PALMER *Wireless Princ. & Pract.* xii. 472 Any error of this nature occurring twice in each quadrant is termed an octantal error. **1954** *Electronic Engin.* XXVI. 39/1 Marconi's have developed a unique fixed (non-rotating) aerial with low octantal error.

‖**octapla** ('ɒktəplə). Also anglicized **octaples**. [ad. Gr. ὀκταπλᾶ, neuter pl. of ὀκταπλοῦς eight-fold, after HEXAPLA. Cf. mod.F. *octaples*

(Littré).] A text consisting of eight versions, esp. of the Scriptures, in parallel arrangement.

1684 N. S. *Crit. Enq. Edit. Bible* xviii. 178 Origen never wrote any Octaples. **1705** HICKERINGILL *Priest-cr.* IV. (1721) 216 St. Hierome had not only the Aid of the Learned Origen (his Hexaples and Octaples) but he himself also was a great Hebraition. **1727–41** CHAMBERS *Cycl.*, *Octapla*, a term in the sacred learning, used for a kind of ancient polyglot bible, consisting of eight columns. **1831–3** E. BURTON *Eccl. Hist.* xxiv. (1845) 516 Having succeeded in finding 2 other Greek translations, he [Origen] added them to the rest (the Hexapla); and thus the whole was arranged in eight columns, and was published with the name of Octapla.

octaploid, var. OCTOPLOID *a.* (*sb.*)

octapodic, -pody: see OCTA-.

octapole, var. OCTUPOLE.

octarch ('ɒktɑːk), *a. Bot.* [f. Gr. ὀκτ-ώ eight + ἀρχή beginning, origin: cf. DIARCH.] Arising from eight distinct points of origin, as the woody tissue of a root.

1884 BOWER & SCOTT *De Bary's Phaner.* 350 In the heptarch or octarch examples of L. clavatum investigated, I almost always found one of the concave plates larger, and of narrow horseshoe-like cross-section, the other smaller and much flatter. *Ibid.* 363 In the species of Trichomanes investigated, triach to octarch bundles usually occur.

octarchy ('ɒktɑːkɪ). [f. Gr. ὀκτώ eight + -αρχία rule, f. -αρχος ruling, ruler.] A government by eight rulers; an aggregate of eight tribal or petty kingdoms each under its own ruler: applied by some historians (instead of HEPTARCHY) to the eight kingdoms reckoned by them to have been established by the Angles and Saxons in Britain.

1799–1805 S. TURNER *Anglo-Sax.* (1836) I. III. v. 190 Eight Anglo-Saxon governments were established... This state of Britain has been improperly denominated the Saxon heptarchy. When all the kingdoms were settled, they formed an octarchy. **1854** MILMAN *Lat. Chr.* II. 91 One of the northern kingdoms of the Octarchy. **1889** *Sat. Rev.* 16 Nov. 566/2 His plan for the division of England..into an octarchy of provinces.

octaroon: see OCTOROON.

octar'ticulate, *a. Nat. Hist.* [f. L. *octo* eight + *articul-us* joint: cf. *articulate*.] Having eight joints; eight-jointed.

1856–8 W. CLARK *Van der Hoeven's Zool.* I. 340 Antennæ octarticulate.

octastich ('ɒktəstɪk). Also 6–9 in Gr. form **octastichon**, 7 **octo-**, **octastick**. [ad. Gr. ὀκτάστιχ-ος of eight verses (στίχος row, line).] A group of eight lines of verse.

1577–87 HOLINSHED *Chron.* III. 922/2 When I. Leland the famous antiquarie wrote this welwishing octastichon vnto the said Wolseie. **1656** BLOUNT *Glossogr.*, *Octostick*. *a* **1693** URQUHART *Rabelais* III. xvii. 143 It is metrified in this Octastick. **1891** DRIVER *Introd. Lit. O.T.* (ed. 3) 375 Several pentastichs and hexastichs, a heptastich and an octastich also occur.

octastichous (ɒk'tæstɪkəs), *a. Bot.* Also **oc'tostichous**. [f. as prec. + -OUS.] Having eight leaves in the spiral row, and thus eight vertical rows in the phyllotaxis.

1870 BENTLEY *Man. Bot.* (ed. 2) 138 A fourth variety of Phyllotaxis..is the octastichous or 8-ranked. **1880** GRAY *Struct. Bot.* 124 Octostichous, or Eight-ranked..occurs in the Holly, Aconite.

octastyle ('ɒktəstaɪl), *a.* and *sb. Arch.* Also **octo-**. [ad. late L. *octastȳl-us* (Vitruv.), a. Gr. ὀκτάστυλ-ος (στῦλος pillar). Cf. mod.F. *octostyle* (1580), earlier *octastyle* (1547 in Hatz.-Darm.).]

a. *adj.* Having eight columns in front or at the end, as a building. **b.** *sb.* A building or portico having eight columns.

1706 PHILLIPS, *Octastylos* or *Octastyle*, a Building that has eight Pillars in Front. **1727–41** CHAMBERS *Cycl.* s.v., The eight columns of the octostyle may either be disposed in a right line..or in a circle. **1846** ELLIS *Elgin Marb.* I. 235 The Parthenon, which was octastyle. **1866** FELTON *Anc. & Mod. Gr.* II. I. viii. 142 The temple is Doric, octostyle, or with eight columns at each end.

Octateuch ('ɒktətjuːk). Also **octo-**. [ad. late L. *octateuch-us* (Cassiod.), a. Gr. ὀκτάτευχ-ος containing eight books (τεῦχος book); (sc. βίβλος) the volume containing the first eight books of the O.T. (Euseb.). In mod.F. *octateuque* (Littré).] The first eight books of the Old Testament collectively; the Pentateuch together with the books of Joshua, Judges, and Ruth. Also, a manuscript or edition of the Octateuch.

1677 HANMER *View Antiq.* 37 Not unlike unto that [style] of Theodoret in his questions upon the Octoteuch. **1706** HEARNE *Collect.* 14 Mar. (O.H.S.) I. 204 The first Volume is to be confin'd to ye Octateuch. **1849** CURZON *Visits Monast.* 204 One MS. of the Octoteuch, or first eight books of the Old Testament. **1967** R. L. S. BRUCE-MITFORD *Art of Codex Amiatinus* 9 They may be read as follows: OCT·LIB LEG..(i.e. eight books of the Octateuch and the Law..). **1976** *Amer. N. & Q.* XV. 61/2 The Octateuch of Vatopédi, going back to the thirteenth century and considered one of the most valuable of the five known octateuchs. **1977** D. CUPITT in J. Hick *Myth of God Incarnate* vii. 143 A miniature in the Smyrna Octateuch.

octaval (ɒk'teɪvəl), *a.* [f. as OCTAVE *sb.* (*a.*) + -AL[1].] Pertaining to an octave; proceeding by octaves, or by eights; octonal. (In quot. opposed to *decimal*.)

1884 *Science* IV. 415/2 An octaval system of numeration, with its possible subdivision 8, 4, 2, 1, would have been originally better.

octavalent (ɒktə'veɪlənt), *a. Chem.* Also (now *rare*) **octo-**. [f. OCTA-, OCTO- + L. *valent-em*, pres. pple. of *valēre* to be worth.] Characterized by a valency of eight.

1880 Octovalent [see PER-[1] 5 b]. **1909** J. N. FRIEND *Theory of Valency* xvii. 117 Osmium apparently functions as an octavalent atom in the tetroxide OsO_4, as does ruthenium in RuO_4. **1950** N. V. SIDGWICK *Chem. Elements* II. 1458 There are a fair number of octovalent osmium compounds. **1973** S. E. LIVINGSTONE in J. C. Bailar et al. *Comprehensive Inorg. Chem.* III. xliii. 1209 The octavalent state [of osmium] is more stable than that of ruthenium.

Hence **octa'valency**, the property of being octavalent.

1925 *Ann. Rep. Progr. Chem.* XXI. 54 These facts are held to confirm the octavalency of osmium.

octave ('ɒktəv), *sb.* (*a.*) Also in sense 1 (*pl.*) 4 **utaves**, 4–6 **utas**, 5 **oeptaves**, **optas**, **oeptas**, 7 **outas**. [a. F. *octave* (12th c. in Hatz.-Darm.), ad. L. *octāva* fem. of *octāv-us* eighth (sc. *dies* day), which superseded the pop. OF. *oitieve* (*witieve*, *huitieve*), sing. f., also *huiteus*, *uyteaus*, pl. masc. (perh.:—L. *octālēs*); semi-popular forms in OF. in sense 1 (pl.) were *otaves*, *outaves*, *oectaves*, *octawes*, AF. *oeptaves*, whence the early ME. forms in α.]

1. *Eccl.* (Formerly always in *pl.*: so med.L. *octavæ*, OF. *huitieves*.) **a.** The eighth day after a festival (both days being counted, and so always falling on the same day of the week as the festival itself). **b.** (In later use.) The period of eight days beginning with the day of a festival.

in the octaves answered to med.L. *in octavis* 'on the eighth day' of a festival.

α. [**1352** *Act 25 Edw. III* (Stat. of Provisors), A les oeptaves (*16th c. tr.* utas) de la purificacion Nostre Dame.] **13..** *Trental of Gregory* (Vernon MS.) 126 Let sei þeos Masses bi ȝoure hestes Wiþ-inne þe vtaues of þe ffestes. **1387** TREVISA *Higden* (Rolls) VII. 259 In þe utas [*v.rr.* eotas, eoytaues] of Esterne. *c* **1420** *Chron. Vilod.* st. 766 Wᵗinne þe utaus of hurr' douȝter Seynt Ede. **1429** *Rolls of Parlt.* IV. 342/2 Atte the oeptaves of Seynt Martyn in Wynter. **1463** *Bury Wills* (Camden) 28 To contynwe sevene nyght aftir tyl the Vtas of my yeerday be passyd. **1472–3** *Rolls of Parlt.* VI. 28/2 He appiered not..in the optas of saint John the Baptiste. **1493** *Festivall* (W. de W. 1515) 49 b, For eche houre of the day..and euery daye of the utas. **1599** *Life Sir T. More* in Wordsw. *Eccl. Biog.* (1853) II. 174 It is Saint Thomas's Eve, and the Utas of Saint Peter. **1610** HOLLAND *Camden's Brit.* II. Ireland 166 A Parliament was held at Kilkenny in the Outas of the Purification of the Blessed Virgin Mary. *Ibid.* 181 On the Monday after the Outas of Easter.

β. **1387** TREVISA *Higden* (Rolls) VIII. 323 Þat ȝere in þe occabis [*v.rr.* octavas, eotaves, octaves, HIGDEN in octavis Epiphaniæ] of þe twelfþe day was made a parlement at Londoun. **1432–50** *Ibid.*, In whiche yere a parliamente was kepede at London in the octaves of the Epiphany. **1483** CAXTON *Gold. Leg.* 436/2 Betwyxe the octaues of ester and penthecoste. **1563–87** FOXE *A. & M.* (1596) 201/2 Driving off the time from the daie of Saint Martine to the octaues following. **1580** FULKE *Against Allen* 356 (T.) Celestine granted from the feast,—and in the octaves, every day, thirty thousand years of pardon! **1688** DRYDEN *Brit. Rediv.* 21 When his wondrous octaue roll'd again, He brought a royal infant in his train. **1739** WHITEFIELD in *Life & Jrnls.* (1756) 169 The Vicar takes care to observe the Octaves of Easter. **1818** CRUISE *Digest* (ed. 2) V. 394 A writ of entry was returnable on the octave of St. Michael, which was the 9th of October. **1883** W. H. RICH-JONES *Reg. S. Osmund* (Rolls) I. 80 *note*, The festival of S. Silvester is on December 31, so that it is always within the octave of Christmas.

c. *transf.* A period of festivity.

1597 SHAKS. *2 Hen. IV*, II. iv. 22 Here will be old Vtis: it will be an excellent stratagem. **1602** *Cont. Liberal. & Prod.* III. iii. in Hazl. *Dodsley* VIII. 355 Let us begin the utas of our jollity.

2. A group of eight lines of verse; a stanza of eight lines (*spec.* = OTTAVA RIMA); = OCTET 2.

a **1586** SIDNEY *Arcadia* (1622) 357 With monefull melodie it continued this octaue. **1604** E. G[RIMSTONE] *D'Acosta's Hist. Indies* VI. xxviii. 492 They have likewise put our compositions of musicke into their language, as Octaves, Songs, and Rondells. **1818** BYRON *Let. to Murray* 19 Sept., I have finished the First Canto (a long one, of about 180 octaves). **1881** *Athenæum* No. 2811. 328/2 A group of sonnets..written in the regular form of octave and sestet.

3. *Mus.* (Formerly EIGHTH, q.v. Sometimes abbrev. 8ve.) **a.** The note eight diatonic degrees above (or below) a given note (both notes being counted), which is produced by vibrations of twice (or half) the rate; it forms the starting-point of a new scale of identical intervals but different pitch, and thus has the same name as the given note, and is treated in harmony as a replicate of it. Hence, by extension, any of the notes at successive intervals of eight degrees above or below a given note (*second octave*, *third octave*, etc.). **b.** The interval between any note and its octave; an interval of eight (or strictly seven) degrees of the diatonic scale, comprising five tones and two diatonic semitones. **c.** A series of notes, or keys of an instrument, extending through this interval. **d.** The concord of a note and its octave; two notes an octave apart played or sung together.

CONSECUTIVE *octaves*, HIDDEN *octaves*: see these words. ***rule of the octave***, a scheme, formerly in vogue, of harmonies for the successive notes of the scale. ***short octave***, the lowest octave in some early organs, in which certain notes were omitted.

1656 BLOUNT *Glossogr.*, *Octave*, an eighth in Musick. **1677** PLOT *Oxfordsh.* 299 One Hooper..could so close his lips, as to sing an octave at the same time. **1694** HOLDER *Harmony* iv. (1731) 40 A Tenth ascending is an Octave above the Third... The Octave being but a Replication of the Unison, or given Note below it..it closeth and terminates the first perfect System, and the next Octave above it ascends by the same Intervals..and so on. **1749** *Power Pros. Numbers* 21 The Octave..is the most perfect Concord. **1776** BURNEY *Hist. Mus.* (1789) I. i. 3 The Greek scale in the time of Aristoxenus..extended to two octaves. **1840** *Penny Cycl.* XVI. 396/2 *Octave, the Rule of*. *Ibid.* 491/2 A complete..organ should have three sets of keys, and at least two octaves of pedals. **1853** HERSCHEL *Pop. Lect. Sci.* vii. §97 (1873) 312 The ear..can discriminate tones only between certain limits, comprising about nine octaves. **1876** HILES *Catech. Organ* i. (1878) 5 Short Octaves only occur in very old Organs. **1887** BROWNING *Parleyings, Chas. Avison* ii, Ere my hand could stretch an octave. **1889** E. PROUT *Harmony* ii. §33 The division of any string into halves, quarters, eighths, or sixteenths, gives the various upper octaves of the 'generator'. *Mod.* Playing octaves with both hands.

e. An organ-stop sounding an octave higher than the ordinary pitch; more usually called *principal* (but sometimes distinguished as of a different quality of tone).

1716 *Specif. Organ St. Chad's, Shrewsbury* in Grove *Dict. Mus.* II. 596 Great Organ..1. Open Diapason. 2. Stopped Diapason. 3. Principal. 4. Octave to middle C. **1880** E. J. HOPKINS *ibid.* II. 492 *Octave*, or *Principal*, an open metal cylindrical organ-stop, of four feet on the manual and eight feet on the pedal... In the Temple organ the two stops, of metal, are called 'Octave' and 'Principal' respectively; the former being scaled and voiced to go with the new open diapason, and the latter to produce the first over-tone to the old diapason.

f. *transf.* An interval analogous to the musical octave; *e.g.* the difference of vibration-period of rays of light or heat whose rates of vibration are as 1 : 2.

1870 TYNDALL *Notes on Light* §254 While..the musical scale, or the range of the ear, is known to embrace nearly eleven octaves, the optical scale, or range of the eye, is comprised within a single octave. **1923** GLAZEBROOK *Dict. Appl. Physics* IV. 891/2 The continuous spectrum was thus extended to thirty-nine times the wave-length of sodium yellow, or five octaves into the infra-red. **1960** [see INFRA-RED *a.* and *sb.* B]. **1961** BERKNER & ODISHAW *Sci. in Space* i. 3 Even if we add the radio-frequency window to the narrow light-wave window, the sum gives astronomy about twenty octaves..of the electromagnetic spectrum with which to investigate the universe from the Earth.

4. a. A group or series of eight.

a **1806** K. WHITE *Rem.* (1837) 406 Plato's syrens sing not only from the planetary octave. *c* **1817** HOGG *Tales & Sk.* II. 15 James and Elizabeth led the ring and the double octave that evening. **1868** MISS YONGE *Pupils St. John* xv. 240 That Creation was due to an Ogdoad, or Octave of Principles. **1898** *Tit-Bits* 9 Apr. 30/3 The..tallest brother of this remarkable octave stands 6 ft. 11½ in.

b. ***law of octaves*** (*Chem.*), the 'periodic law' as originally stated by its discoverer Newlands, according to which, the elements (excluding hydrogen) being arranged in order of their atomic weights, a recurrence of similar properties occurs (generally) at every eighth (or strictly seventh) term of the series.

1865 J. A. R. NEWLANDS in *Chem. News* 18 Aug. 83/2 This peculiar relationship I propose to provisionally term the 'Law of Octaves'. **1887** *Athenæum* 3 Sept. 299/3 Mr. Newlands..provisionally called his generalization the 'Law of Octaves'... At length the Law of Octaves, modified and much amplified, emerged as the 'Periodic Law'. **1932** J. N. FRIEND *Text-bk. Physical Chem.* I. xvi. 330 According to Newlands' Law of Octaves, when the elements are arranged in the order of increasing atomic weights, the first and last of any eight consecutive elements possess similar properties. **1965** D. ABBOTT *Inorg. Chem.* i. 31 In 1864 Newlands put forward his Law of Octaves, in which he likened the classification of elements to the musical scale.

†**c.** = OCTAD 2 b. *Obs.*

†**5.** A Portuguese gold coin: the Dobre of 12,800 reis. *Obs.*

1747 *Gentl. Mag.* 499/1 The Pernambuco fleet..arrived at Lisbon, Sept. 22, and brought..13,740 octaves of gold, and 439,980 crusades of silver. **1775** *Ann. Reg.* 144 Arrived, at Lisbon, from the Brazils, a fleet with 1500 octaves of gold, 200,000 crusades of silver.

6. *Fencing.* (In full ***octave parade***.) The position of parrying or attacking in the low outside line with the sword-hand in supination (if in pronation, it is *seconde*, q.v.).

1771 OLIVIER *Fencing Familiarized* 25 The octave parade ..is the opposition contrary to the half-circle [now called *septime*], and one of the most useful parades in fencing. **1784** MCARTHUR *Fencing* 12 Octave parade..is a lower outward parade. **1809** ROLAND *Fencing* 45 By this method your foil must, for certain, arrive at his body, if he does not change to an octave, or any other parade. **1889** W. H. POLLOCK, etc. *Fencing* 44 *Octave*, the same as *seconde*, but the hand in supination. *Ibid.* p. xi, Time Thrust in Octave.

7. A small wine-cask containing the eighth part of a pipe, or 13½ gallons.

1880 in WEBSTER *Suppl.* 1881 *Price List*, Importing and delivering Sherries in Octaves.

8. *attrib.* (or as *adj.*) and *Comb.*, as **octave coupler**, a device on an organ for connecting keys an octave apart (see COUPLER 2 a); **octave flute**, (*a*) a small flute sounding an octave higher than the ordinary flute, a piccolo; (*b*) a flute-stop on an organ sounding an octave higher than the ordinary pitch; **octave key**, a key on a wind-instrument used to produce a note an octave higher than the note that is being fingered; † **octave rime** = OTTAVA RIMA; **octave stanza**, a stanza of eight lines, *spec.* = *octave rime*; **octave stop** = 3 e; **octave-stretch**, the stretch of the hand over an octave on a keyboard (in quot. *fig.*).

1880 E. J. HOPKINS in Grove *Dict. Mus.* II. 596 In 1726 John Harris and John Byfield, sen. erected a fine.. organ for the church of St. Mary Redcliff, Bristol... The Redcliff organ.. contained the first '*octave coupler' that was ever made in England. 1798 ARNOT *Let.* in Kegan Paul *Life Godwin* I. 314 Pulled out my little *octave flute. 1852 SEIDEL *Organ* 20 In 1590, the octave-flute was invented by Compenio. 1880 GROVE *Dict. Mus.* II. 487/1 In more modern instruments [*sc.* oboes] a second *octave-key has been introduced.. which is usually lifted on reaching A above the stave. 1911 *Encycl. Brit.* XXIV. 274/1 The first 15 semitones are obtained by opening successive keys, the rest of the compass by means of octave keys enabling the performer to sound the harmonic octave of the fundamental scale. 1957 A. C. BAINES *Woodwind Instrum.* iv. 106 With full automatic octave keys, the G♯ key, when pressed, holds down ring III. 1700 DRYDEN *Pref. Fables* Wks. (Globe) 494 Boccace.. is said to have invented the *octave rhyme, or stanza of eight lines. 1821 BYRON *Lett. to Moore* 1 Oct., A poem, in *octave stanzas. 1887 COLVIN *Keats* vii. 149 The octave stanza introduced in English by Wyatt and Sidney. 1880 E. J. HOPKINS in Grove *Dict. Mus.* II. 492 In foreign organs the *Octave stop sounds the first octave above the largest metal Register of Principal (Diapason) measure on the clavier. *a* 1861 MRS. BROWNING *Little Mattie* vi, The *octave-stretch.. Of your larger wisdom!

Hence **'octave** *v.*, (*a*) to add strings, as in a harpsichord, giving notes severally an octave higher than the ordinary ones, so as to reinforce the tone; (*b*) to play in octaves (*Cent. Dict.* 1891).

1885 A. J. HIPKINS in *Encycl. Brit.* XIX. 74/1 Imitation of the harpsichord by 'octaving' was at this time [about 1772] an object with piano makers.

octavian (ɒk'teɪvɪən). *Sc. Hist.* [f. L. *octāv-us* eighth + -IAN.] One of the eight members of a finance committee appointed by James VI in 1595 to have control of the royal exchequer.

1596 J. CAREY *Let. to Burghley* 9 June (Bain's Calend. II. 135) Some of the Octaveyans of the Secret Council. — *Ibid.* 26 Aug. (ibid.), I will henceforth send only such as I get from verie good men, as from some of the Kinges Octaveyans. 1596 in Spotiswood *Hist. Ch. Scotl.* (1655) 422. *c* 1602 J. MELVILL *Diary* (Wodrow Soc.) 330 The Kings haill effeares.. was put in the hands of aught.. thairfor named *Octavians*. *c* 1634 ROW *Hist. Kirk* (Wodrow) 165. 1649 BP. GUTHRIE *Mem.* (1702) 5 The Multitude.. would in all probability have.. done Mischief, at last to those call'd Octavians, whom they blam'd for all. 1759 ROBERTSON *Hist. Scot.* II. 224. 1870 BURTON *Hist. Scot.* (1876) V. lx. 299 The battle of the octavians, with the zealots of the Church on one side and the 'cubiculars' of the Court on the other, lasted for eighteen months.

octavic (ɒk'teɪvɪk), *a.* and *sb. Math.* [f. L. *octāv-us* eighth + -IC.] **A.** *adj.* Of the eighth order or degree. **B.** *sb.* An octavic polynomial or curve.

1854 *Cambr. & Dublin Math. Jrnl.* IX. 94 The biquadratic and octavic function of $x, y, (x, y)^4, (x, y)^8$. 1879 *Amer. Jrnl. Math.* II. 251 For the first four orders there is but one such block, for the quintic and the sextic two, for the seventhic five, for the octavic three, and for the 9ic and 10ic four. 1897 *Nature* 11 Nov. 47/1 More general forms of octavic curves with six double points.

octavo (ɒk'teɪvəʊ). Abbrev. 8vo. or oct. [L., abl. of *octavus* eighth, in the phrase *in octavo* in an eighth (*sc.* a sheet); F. *in-octavo* sb.; Sp. *en octavo*.]

1. The size of a book, or of the page of a book, in which the sheets are so folded that each leaf is one-eighth of a whole sheet. Orig. in L. phr. *in octavo*, afterwards apprehended and treated as Eng. prep. and sb.

1582 PARSONS *Def. Cens.* 148, I haue two editions in greeke: the one of learned Pagnine *in folio*, the other of Plantyne *in octavo*. 1607 MIDDLETON *Five Gallants* I. i, Neither in folio nor in decimo sexto, but in octavo, between both. 1619 H. HUTTON *Follie's Anat.* Postscr. 59 My head, my muse, I bring to thee to presse.. In quarto's forme 't shall not be formed; tut! Pray, trim my head in spruce octavo's cut. 1700 MAIDWELL in *Collect.* (O.H.S.) I. 313 In octavo.. makes 16 pages to one sheet. 1798 CREECH *Let. to Davis* 15 Jan. (Sotheby's Catal.), Pray enquire of Mr. Cadell his determination respecting the mode of printing Burns. I am rather inclined to the Octavo. 1837–9 HALLAM *Hist. Lit.* I. I. iii. §148. 250 Mattaire.. mentions a book printed in octavo at Milan in 1470.

2. A book or volume *in octavo*.

1712 ADDISON *Spect.* No. 529 ¶ 1 The Author of a Folio.. sets himself above the Author of a Quarto; the Author of a Quarto above the Author of an Octavo; and so on. 1728 POPE *Dunc.* I. 141 Quarto's, Octavo's, shape the less'ning pyre. 1834 MEDWIN *Angler in Wales* I. Pref. 9 Imparting his lucubrations to the world in the shape of one or two octavos. 1850 LD. HOUGHTON in *Life* (1891) I. x. 445 Wordsworth's new poem.. a goodly octavo of blank verse.

3. *attrib.* passing into *adj.*, as in 'octavo edition' = 'edition *in octavo*'.

1704 SWIFT *Bat. Bks.* Misc. (1711) 248 She.. gather'd up her Person into an Octavo Compass. 1712 ADDISON *Spect.* No. 529 ¶ 3 Every Octavo Writer in Great Britain, that had written but one Book. 1799 *Med. Jrnl.* II. 193 The mosses are.. pasted to coloured octavo pages. *a* 1852 MOORE *Lit. Advert.* v, Enough to fill handsomely Two Volumes, *oct.* 1862 LD. BROUGHAM *Brit. Const.* App. ii. 420 In three large octavo volumes. 1875 JOWETT *Plato* (ed. 2) I. p. vii, The latest 8vo. edition of Stallbaum.

octennial (ɒk'tɛnɪəl), *a.* (*sb.*) [f. L. *octennium* a period of eight years (f. *octo* eight + *ann-us* year) + -AL[1]: cf. *biennial*, etc.] Of or pertaining to a period of eight years; occurring, or lasting, during eight years; recurring every eighth year.

Octennial Act, an act passed in 1768 limiting the duration of the Irish Parliament to eight years.

1656 in BLOUNT *Glossogr.* 1762 tr. *Busching's Syst. Geog.* III. 679 [His] office is octennial. 1769 LD. TOWNSHEND in Lecky *Eng. in 18th C.* (1882) IV. 386 The Octennial Bill.. gave the first blow to the dominion of aristocracy in this kingdom. 1847 GROTE *Greece* (1862) III. xxviii. 52 The octennial solemnity in honour of the God. 1865 —— *Plato* I. iii. 123 An octennial period of octaetêris.

† **B.** as *sb.* A period of eight years. *Obs. rare.*

1679 J. LEANERD in E. Ecclestone *Noah's Flood* A, I'de an Octenial spend to reach the height.

Hence **oc'tennially** *adv.*, once in eight years.

1864 in WEBSTER.

octet, octette (ɒk'tɛt). Also ottett, octett. [mod. f. L. *octo*, after *duet, quartet*: in It. *ottetto*, Ger. *oktett*.]

1. *Mus.* **a.** A musical composition for eight instruments or voices. **b.** A company of eight singers or players who perform together.

1864 H. F. CHORLEY in Lady Wallace tr. *Mendelssohn's Lett.* (ed. 3) p. xvii, Among Mendelssohn's published chamber-music may be specified an Ottett, two Quintetts, eight Quartetts for stringed instruments. 1880 GROVE *Dict. Mus.* II. 492 *Octet*, or *Ottett* (*Ottetto*), a composition for eight solo instruments... Mendelssohn's Octet for strings is a splendid example. 1886 *Pall Mall G.* 7 Dec. 5/1 Schubert's Octet in F was to be repeated.

2. A group of eight lines of verse; *spec.* the first eight lines of a sonnet.

1879 *N. & Q.* 5th Ser. XI. 459/1 Where is the octet called 'Prospective Faith'? 1896 E. GOSSE *Crit. Kit-Kats* 7 No fault can be found with the structure of her [Mrs. Browning's] octetts and sextetts.

3. **a.** *gen.* A group of eight persons or things.

1894 *Scot. Leader* 16 Mar. 3 The octette which rowed against Oxford yesterday.

b. A stable group of eight electrons in an electron shell of an atom.

1919 I. LANGMUIR in *Jrnl. Amer. Chem. Soc.* XLI. 888 After the very stable pairs.. the next most stable arrangement of electrons is the group of 8 such as forms the outside layer in atoms of neon and argon. We shall call this stable group of 8 electrons the 'octet'. 1927 N. V. SIDGWICK *Electronic Theory of Valency* x. 175 The trivalent elements, having incomplete octets, strive to complete them by co-ordination. 1965 D. ABBOTT *Inorg. Chem.* ii. 70 Some atoms can remain stable when surrounded by more than an octet of electrons (they expand their octets).

c. *Nuclear Physics.* A multiplet (sense b) of eight sub-atomic particles.

1961 in GELL-MANN & NE'EMAN *Eightfold Way* (1964) i. 13 The most important prediction is.. that the eight baryons should all have the same spin and parity and that the pseudoscalar and vector mesons should form 'octets', with possible additional 'singlets'. 1962 *Physical Rev.* CXXV. 1068/2 The baryons, as well as the mesons, can form octets and singlets. 1963 [see NONET 2]. 1968 M. S. LIVINGSTON *Particle Physics* xii. 213 Here [*sc.* in SU(3) theory] the basic octet of states is identified with the nucleon, the Σ-particle triplet, the Λ^0 particle, and the Ξ-particle doublet.

octic ('ɒktɪk), *a.* and *sb. Math.* [f. L. *octo* eight + -IC.] = OCTAVIC *a.* and *sb.*

1877 *Encycl. Brit.* VI. 726/1 ϕ is not expressible as the square root of an octic function of θ. 1916 G. A. MILLER et al. *Theory & Applic. Finite Groups* i. 4 The Octic Group. There are eight movements of a plane which transform into itself a square situated in this plane. 1938 *Duke Math. Jrnl.* IV. 285 Normal octics with the group $G(2, 2, 2)$. 1978 *Amer. Math. Monthly* LXXXV. 470 (*heading*) Rational octic and higher reciprocity laws.

octile ('ɒktaɪl), *a.* and *sb. Astron.* [ad. mod.L. *octīlis*, f. *octo* eight, after *quintīlis, sextīlis*, etc.: cf. F. *octil* (1732 in *Dict. Trévoux*).]

A. *adj.* Said of the 'aspect' of two planets distant 45° (= ⅛ of a circle) from each other.

1690 LEYBOURN *Curs. Math.* 759 In an Octile Aspect, before the Syzygies.

B. *sb.* = Octile aspect, OCTANT 2.

1690 LEYBOURN *Curs. Math.* 759 When the Octile is before the Quadrature. 1706 PHILLIPS, *Octile*, one of the new Aspects.

octillion (ɒk'tɪljən). [a. F. *octillion* (La Roche 16th c.), f. L. *octo* eight, after *million*: see BILLION.] The eighth power of a million, denoted by 1 followed by 48 ciphers. (In U.S., following later French usage, The ninth power of a thousand, denoted by 1 with 27 ciphers.) Hence **oc'tillionth**.

1690 [see BILLION]. 1848 *Fraser's Mag.* XXXVII. 647 The millionth of a grain is a very common dose; and a trillionth, octillionth, even a decillionth, very usual ones. 1870 *Eng. Mech.* 28 Jan. 491/1 A quadrillion is the next highest number to a trillion; then quintillions, sextillions, septillions, octillions. 1882 *Knowledge* No. 12. 241 Professor Young uses what we take to be the erroneous American system of notation, saying that the earth's mass amounts to about two octillions of tons.

octine (*Chem.*): see under OCTANE.

octingentenary (ɒktɪn'dʒɛntɪnərɪ, -dʒɛn'tiːnərɪ). *rare.* [f. L. *octingentī* eight hundred, after *centenary*.] The eight-hundredth anniversary of an event.

1893 *Cath. News* 17 June 5/2 The late octingentenary at Winchester.

octipartition, -reme: see OCTOPARTITION, -REME.

‖ **octli** ('əʊktlɪ). [Mex. Sp.] = PULQUE.

1845 *Encycl. Metrop.* XVI. 528/1 The most favourite spirit of the Mexicans is *pulque* or *octli*, a thick ropy juice which flows from a wounded agave or maguey. 1883 *Encycl. Brit.* XVI. 213/1 The juice extracted by tapping the great aloe before flowering was fermented into an intoxicating drink about the strength of beer, *octli*, by the Spaniards called *pulque*. 1914 T. A. JOYCE *Mexican Archaeol.* ii. 43 This awakening after heavy sleep.. connected the octli gods with the waxing and waning of vegetation and the moon. 1938 *Times Lit. Suppl.* 5 Mar. 157/1 Other mistakes relate to the preparation of the fermented drink 'octli'.

octo- (before a vowel **oct-**), combining form of L. *octo*, and sometimes of Gr. ὀκτώ eight. (The Greek form is more frequently ὀκτα-, OCTA-.) The more important combinations of *octo-* will be found in their alphabetical places; the following are technical terms of less frequent use:

'octoblast (-blæst) *Biol.* [Gr. βλαστός bud], an ovum at that stage of segmentation when it consists of eight cells. **octobrachiate** (-'brækɪət) *a. Zool.* [L. *brachium* arm], having eight 'arms', as a cephalopod; octopodous. **octocarbon, -chloride**: see OCTA-. **octocerous** (-'ɒsərəs), **octoceratous** (-'sɛrətəs) *adjs. Zool.* [Gr. κέρας horn], eight-horned; belonging to the *Octocera*, a name proposed by some naturalists for the *Octopoda* (cf. *decacerous* s.v. DECA-). **octocorallan** (-kə'rælən), **-coralline** (-'kɒrəlaɪn) *adjs. Zool.* [CORAL], belonging to the *Octocoralla*, one of the main divisions of *Anthozoa* or corals, characterized by eight chambers of the body-cavity and eight tentacles (cf. *hexacorallan* s.v. HEXA-); as *sb.* one of these corals. **octo'cotyloid** *a. Zool.*, having eight cotyloid fossettes, as a worm. **octo'dactyl, -'dactylous** *adjs. Zool.* [Gr. δάκτυλος digit], having eight digits. **'octode** *Radio* [-ODE[2]], any thermionic valve with eight electrodes, some of which have been used as frequency changers in superheterodyne receivers. **octo'decimal** *a. Cryst.* [L. *decem* ten], having eight faces on the prism or middle part, and five on each of the two summits; so *octoduodecimal* (eight and twelve), *octosexdecimal* (eight and sixteen). **octo'dentate** *a.* [L. *dens* tooth], having eight teeth (Webster, 1828). **ˌoctodesex'centenary** *a.* [L. *octo dē sexcentīs* eight from six hundred; cf. *centenary*], applied to a period of 592 years. **octoduo'decimal** *a.*: see *octodecimal*. **'octofid** *a.* [L. *-fidus* = cleft], divided into eight segments, as a calyx or corolla. **'octofoil** *a.* [after *trefoil*, etc.: see FOIL *sb.*[1]], *sb.* an ornamental figure consisting of eight leaves or lobes; *adj.*, eight-lobed (also **'octofoiled**). **oc'togamy** *nonce-wd.* [after *bigamy*], the marrying of eight spouses. **'octoglot** *a.* [Gr. γλῶττα, γλῶσσα tongue: cf. *polyglot*], written in eight languages. **octo'lateral** *a.* [L. *latus* side: LATERAL], eight-sided, formed of eight straight lines, as in *octolateral dodecagon*, a figure formed of eight straight lines connecting twelve points on a cubic curve. **octo'locular** *a. Bot.* [L. *loculus*, dim. of *locus* place], having eight cells, as a seed-vessel (Webster, 1828). **octonematous** (-'niːmətəs), **-'nemous** *adjs.* [Gr. νῆμα thread], having eight filaments or filamentous organs. **octo'petalous** *a. Bot.* [PETAL], having eight petals (Bailey (folio) 1730–6). **octoph'thalmous** *a. Zool.* [Gr. ὀφθαλμός eye], having eight eyes. **octophyllous** (-'fɪləs) *a. Bot.* [Gr. φύλλον leaf], consisting of eight leaflets. **octo'radial, -'radiate, -'radiated** *adjs.* [L. *radius* ray], having eight rays. **octo'radiant** *a.* = *octoradial* adj. **'octose** [a. G. *octose* (E. Fischer 1890, in *Ber. d. Deut. Chem. Ges.* XXIII. 934): see -OSE[2]], any monosaccharide having eight carbon atoms in the molecule. **octo'sepalous** *a. Bot.*, having eight sepals (Gray *Struct. Bot.* 1880). **octosex'decimal** *a.*: see *octodecimal* above.

octo'spermous *a. Bot.* [Gr. σπέρμα seed], producing or containing eight seeds (Webster, 1828). **'octospore** *Bot.* [SPORE], name given to each of the eight carpospores produced by certain algæ; so **oc'tosporous** *a.*, producing eight spores. **oc'tovalent** *a. Chem.* [L. *valēnt-em* having power or value], having the combining power of eight atoms of hydrogen; octadic. †**oc'tovirate** [L. *octovir* member of a council of eight; cf. DECEMVIR], a body of eight men, a council of eight.

1857 MAYNE *Expos. Lex.* 791/1 *Octoceratous. **1888** *Proc. Zool. Soc. London* 152 Pleading the cause of an *octodactyle 'Urform'. **1857** MAYNE *Expos. Lex.*, *Octodactylus, Zoöl.* Having eight fingers.. *octodactylous. **1934** A. W. HASLETT *Radio round World* 191 There are many more complicated types of valve, ranging up to the *octode which has eight different components instead of only three. **1943** *Electronic Engin.* XV. 339 Table A shows the more important frequency changers..and it may be noted that three of these, the pentode, the octode and the heptode mixer, owe some of their success to their high anode impedance. **1961** *Amat. Radio Handbk.* (ed. 3) ii. 58/2 When provided with an additional grid used as a suppressor it [*sc.* the heptode] was referred to as an octode. **1805–17** R. JAMESON *Char. Min.* (ed. 3) 206 *Octo-decimal artificial blue vitriol. **1677** PLOT *Oxfordsh.* 222 [Thomas Lydiat] first contrived the *Octodesexcentenary Period. [Cf. 223 So that the whole period, or 592 Lydiatean years, do anticipate so many Julian ones by five days.] **1805–17** R. JAMESON *Char. Min.* (ed. 3) 206 *Octo-duodecimal artificial blue vitriol. **1760** J. LEE *Introd. Bot.* II. xxxii. (1765) 157 *Laurus*, with an *octofid Corolla. **1785** MARTYN *Rousseau's Bot.* xxiv. (1794) 341 The exterior calyx..in Hibiscus is octofid. **1875** DARWIN *Insectiv. Pl.* xiii. 300 The minute octofid processes with which the leaves are studded. **1886** *Athenæum* 6 Mar. 331/1 An engraved figure of the Agnus Dei..within an *octofoil depression. **1890** MACKLIN *Monum. Brasses* iv. 88 Floriated octofoil cross. **1958** *Times* 11 Dec. 12/4 An octofoil plain salver. **1846** *Ecclesiologist* N.S. III. 70 A piscina with two orifices—one circular, one *octofoiled. **1848** B. WEBB *Contin. Ecclesiol.* 45 The aisle windows are large octofoiled circles. *c* **1386** CHAUCER *Wife's Prol.* 33 Of no nombre mencion made he, Of bigamye or of *Octogamye. **1888** *New Eng. Dict.* s.v. *Calepin*, There was an *octoglot edition by Passerat in 1609. **1857** MAYNE *Expos. Lex.* 791/2 Having eight arms or tentacula, as the umbrellæ of the *Favonia octonema*: *octonemous. *Ibid.*, Composed of eight folioles ..*octophyllous. **1890** *Athenæum* 12 July 66/3 A simple *octoradial medusa. **1911** BEERBOHM *Zuleika D.* xviii. 271 He affixed to his breast the *octoradiant star, so much larger and more lustrous than any actual star in heaven. **1857** MAYNE *Expos. Lex.* 792/1 *Octoradiate. **1828** WEBSTER, **Octoradiated*. **1890** *Octose [see *heptose* s.v. HEPTA-]. **1931** R. J. WILLIAMS *Introd. Biochem.* iii. 26 Aldoheptoses, octoses, nonoses and a decose have been made synthetically. **1962** D. J. BELL in Florkin & Mason *Comparative Biochem.* III. vii. 297 The first natural octose, D-glycero-D-mannoctulose..has recently been isolated from an aqueous extract of the Californian avocado. **1805–17** R. JAMESON *Char. Min.* (ed. 3) 312 Observed in the *octosexdecimal topaz. **1870** BENTLEY *Man. Bot.* (ed. 2) 384 The *octospores ultimately decay unless fecundated by antherozoids. **1857** BERKELEY *Cryptog. Bot.* 247 In *Nectria inaurata* the same hymenium produces ordinary *octosporous asci, and others filled with a multitude of far more minute bodies. **1874** COOKE *Fungi* 182. **1880** CLEMINSHAW *Wurtz' Atom. Th.* 233 In perruthenic acid and in osmic acid..ruthenium and osmium act as *octovalent elements. **1610** J. FORBES *Rec. Kirk* (1846) 355 The cheiffest of that *Octovirat were ever Papists in their hearts.

octoad ('ɒktəʊæd). [Arbitrarily f. Gr. ὀκτώ eight.] = OGDOAD.

1827 G. HIGGINS *Celtic Druids* 180 The ever-happy Octoad of the Christian heretics.

'octobass. [a. F. *octobasse* (Littré Suppl., *octabasse*), f. L. *octo* eight + *basse* BASS.] A very large instrument of the viol family, invented by J. B. Vuillaume about 1849; it had three strings, which were stopped by keys worked by the fingers and feet.

1875 KNIGHT *Dict. Mech.*, *Octo-bass*, an instrument of the viol family, the low octave of the violoncello. **1889** GROVE *Dict. Mus.* IV. 341 He [J. B. Vuillaume] sent his 'Octobasse' ..to the Paris Exhibition of 1849... At the London Exhibition of 1851 he had..his perfected 'Octobasse', for which he was awarded the Grand Council medal.

October (ɒk'təʊbə(r)). Also 3–7 **-bre**; in 7 sometimes abbrev. 8bre, 8^{ber}. [In OE. and mod.Eng. a. L. *Octōber*, *-ōbrem*, f. *octo* eight (orig. the eighth month of the year); in ME. a. F. *Octobre* (1303 in Hatz.-Darm.), ad. L. *Octōbrem*, which supplanted the popular OF. *oitovre*. Med.L. had also the analogical form *Octember*, *-imber*, 13th c. F. *Octembre*, Pr. *Octembre*.]

1. The tenth month of the year (according to the modern reckoning).

c **1050** *Byrhtferth's Handboc* in *Anglia* VIII. 316 Forðon september & october habbað lunam. **1297** R. GLOUC. (Rolls) 10382 þe verste day of octobre þis conseil bigan. **1398** TREVISA *Barth. De P.R.* IX. xviii. (MS. Bodl.) lf. 95/1 Octobre..is kindelich colde and druye. *a* **1548** HALL *Chron., Hen. VI*, 166 b, In the moneth of October this present yere. **1679** *Hatton Corr.* (Camden) 190 The Privy Counsell wch wase adjourn'd till ye 2^{d} of 8bre. **1684** WILDING in *Collect.* (O.H.S.) I. 254, 8^{ber} ye 6th. **1713** SWIFT *Hor. Sat.* II. vi, 'Tis (let me see) three years and more (October next it will be four). **1848** CLOUGH *Bothie* vi, Bright October was come, the misty-bright October.

2. Ale brewed in October. (Common in 18th c.)

1709 STEELE *Tatler* No. 118 ¶6 Hours he spent..in swelling himself with October. **1741** RICHARDSON *Pamela* (1824) I. 215 He ordered Jonathan to let the evening be passed merrily..with what everyone liked, whether wine or October. **1796** MRS. GLASSE *Cookery* xxii. 348 For strong October, five quarters of malt to three hogsheads, and twenty-four pounds of hops. **1855** MACAULAY *Hist. Eng.* xv. III. 533 A great crowd of squires after a revel, at which doubtless neither October nor claret had been spared.

3. *attrib.*, as ***October beer***; **October-bird**, name in the West Indies for the rice-bird or bobolink; from the time of its appearance there; **October Revolution**, name given to the revolution in which the Provisional Government in Russia was overthrown by the Bolsheviks in 1917 on 25 October Old Style (7 November New Style); also *transf.*

1742 *Lond. & Country Brew.* I. (ed. 4) 28 When Stout or October Beer is to be made. **1793** B. EDWARDS *Brit. W. Ind.* (1801) I. iv. 124 *note*, The most delicious bird in the West Indies is the Ortalan, or October-bird. **1917** *Times* 13 Dec. 8/4 The October revolution, having broken the power of the capitalists and landlords,..set up a 'Government' of People's Commissioners. **1925** P. A. SOROKIN *Sociol. of Revolution* xvii. 390 Since the latter party included the workmen, the enormous mass of soldiers.., and the peasants..the October revolution was becoming inevitable. **1932** M. EASTMAN tr. *Trotsky's Hist. Russ. Revolution* I. 17 In the historic conditions which formed Russia..we ought to be able to find the premises both of the February revolution and of the October revolution which replaced it. **1952** E. H. CARR *Bolshevik Rev.* II. xvi. 71 Even before the October revolution conditions in Petrograd..were particularly acute. **1965** *Guardian* 14 Oct. 10/2 Russian visitors..might..conclude that our October Revolution is still to come. **1965** B. PEARCE tr. *Preobrazhensky's New Economics* 77 It would be no exaggeration to say that the most interesting and exciting question since the October revolution of 1917..is the question of what the Soviet system is. **1974** tr. *Sniečkus's Soviet Lithuania* 56 The October Revolution opened up a new era in mankind's social progress.

Octoberist, -brist (ɒk'təʊb(ə)rɪst). [f. OCTOBER + -IST] **1.** [After SEPTEMBRIST.] (See quot.) *nonce-wd.*

1796 BURKE *Regic. Peace* iv. Wks. IX. 19 But in comes a gentleman in the fag end of October, dripping with the fogs of that humid and uncertain season... This is what the Octoberist says of the political interests of England.

2. (Chiefly in form *Octobrist.*) **a.** [Russ. *oktyabríst.*] In Russian politics, a member of the League of the 17 October 1905 Old Style (30 October New Style), formed in response to the Imperial Constitutional Manifesto of the same date. Also *attrib.* or as *adj.*

1906 *Daily Chron.* 10 Apr. 3/6 Count Peter Heyden, of the Octoberist party. **1906** *Westm. Gaz.* 29 Aug. 2/2 One of the chief questions in Russia has been whether the Octobrists would join the Reactionaries or make terms with the Constitutional Democrats. **1912** D. M. WALLACE *Russia* (rev. ed.) xxxix. 738 The weak point in the present Assembly is that the Octobrists—the moderate party which accepts the famous October manifesto in its natural sense, and wishes to co-operate with the Government in legislative work—do not possess an absolute majority. **1958** *Times Lit. Suppl.* 10 Jan. 14/3 The majority of the *zemstva* liberals found themselves on the side of the more left-wing Kadets, and only the minority among the Octobrists. *a* **1967** A. RANSOME *Autobiogr.* (1976) xxii. 195 Pares was intimate with Gutchkov of the Octobrists.

b. [Russ. *oktyabryónok.*] A member of a Russian communist organization founded in 1925 for young people below the normal age of the 'Pioneers' (see PIONEER *sb.* 3 c).

1929 S. N. HARPER *Civic Training in Soviet Russia* iv. 66 A widening of the scope of the movement also came in 1925. .. The Pioneers were given the task of working among their younger brothers and sisters and of organizing them into groups of 'Little Octobrists', in honour of the Bolshevik revolution of October 1917. **1935** S. & B. WEBB *Soviet Communism* I. v. 401 The Pioneers were given the task of bringing their younger brothers and sisters, as young as eight years old, into groups of Little Octobrists. By 1926 the two junior organisations had over two million members (1,800,000 Pioneers and 250,000 Octobrists). **1959** D. W. TREADGOLD *20th Cent. Russia* III. xviii. 288 The Little Octobrists for children eight to eleven years of age, the Pioneers..and the Komsomol..were together designed to produce adults who accepted the fundamental ideological commitments and values of the Party proper. **1960** A. KASSOF in C. E. Black *Transformation Russ. Society* v. 485 The Octobrists..includes members from seven through nine years of age. *Ibid.* 496 Of particular significance was the recent decision to re-establish the Octobrists for children younger than Pioneer age. **1974** T. P. WHITNEY tr. *Solzhenitsyn's Gulag Archipel.* I. I. viii. 333 It was just such a well-nourished little imp that our Octobrist child—Law —began to grow.

octocentenary (ɒktəʊ'sɛntɪnərɪ). [Arbitrary f. L. *octo* eight + CENTENARY. The etymological form from L. is *octingentenary*.] The eight-hundredth anniversary of an event. Also *attrib.* or as *adj.* So **octocen'tennial** *a.*

1889 *Times* 20 June, The programme of festivities in celebration of the octocentenary of the House of Wettin. **1893** *Athenæum* 30 Dec. 911/1 In prospect of the 'octocentenary' of the consecration of Harrow Church, Mr. Bushell has reprinted..three documents. **1889** *Times* 19 June 7/2 The celebration of its octocentennial day of honour.

octochord: see OCTACHORD.

octodecimo (ɒktəʊ'dɛsɪməʊ). [For *in octodecimo*, from L. *octodecimus* eighteenth, as in *octavo*, *duodecimo*, etc.] The size of a book, or of the page of a book, in which each leaf is one-eighteenth of a whole sheet; a book of this size. Abbrev. 18mo.

1858 O. W. HOLMES *Aut. Breakf.-T.* (1883) 19 A little dark platoon of octo-decimos.

‖**Octodon** ('ɒktədɒn). *Zool.* [mod.L., f. Gr. ὀκτώ eight + -όδων = -όδους -tooth.] **a.** A genus of South American rodents, resembling rats. **b.** A genus of coleopterous insects.

1841 *Penny Cycl.* XX. 62. **1849** *Sk. Nat. Hist.*, *Mammalia* IV. 100 Cuming's Octodon in size and shape resembles a water-rat.

So **octodont** (-dɒnt) *a.*, having eight teeth; *sb.* = sense a above.

octodrachm: see OCTADRACHM.

octodrant, erron. for OCTANT (after *quadrant*).

1688 R. HOLME *Armoury* III. 372/1 Another sort of semi-Quadrant, or Octodrant.

octoedral, etc.: see OCTAHEDRAL, etc.

octogenarian (ˌɒktəʊdʒɪ'nɛərɪən), *a.* and *sb.* [f. L. *octogēnāri-us* (see next) + -AN.]

A. *adj.* Of the age of eighty years; also *transf.* of or belonging to a person eighty years old.

1818 BYRON *Ch. Har.* IV. xii, Blind old Dandolo! Th' octogenarian chief, Byzantium's conquering foe. **1843** PRESCOTT *Mexico* (1850) I. 73 His papers were recovered.. and the octogenarian author began the work of translation from the Mexican. **1868** STANLEY *Westm. Abb.* iv. 280 The closing scene of Lord Palmerston's octogenarian career.

B. *sb.* A person eighty years old.

1815 *Paris Chit-chat* xvii. (1816) II. 35 Pity at least is due to a feeble octogenarian. **1841** MISS SEDGWICK *Lett. Abr.* I. 38 Three or four women, octogenarians. **1869** J. MARTINEAU *Ess.* II. 229 [They] astonish us..as the production of an octogenarian.

Hence **octoge'narianism**, the state of being eighty years old.

1883 *Congregationalist* Nov. 902 My brother John and I have lived in the greatest amity for a period approaching octogenarianism. **1895** *Forum* (N.Y.) May 272 The ripening quiet of octogenarianism.

octogenary (ɒk'tɒdʒɪnərɪ), *a.* (*sb.*) Now *rare.* [ad. L. *octogēnāri-us* containing eighty, aged eighty, f. *octogēnī* eighty each: see -ARY. Cf. F. *octogénaire* (1603 in Hatz.-Darm.).] = prec. A.

a **1696** AUBREY *Lives, de Laune* (1898) I. 216 Being then octogenary, and very decrepit with the gowt. **1823** JEFFERSON *Writ.* (1830) IV. 380 A hobby..whose easy amble is still sufficient to give exercise and amusement to an octogenary rider. **1873** BROWNING *Red Cott. Nt.-cap* 1259 After how long a slumber..Was it, he stretched octogenary joints?

b. *sb.* = prec. B.

1828 in WEBSTER, citing J. ADAMS.

octogon, etc., obs. forms of OCTAGON, etc.

‖**Octogynia** (ɒktəʊ'dʒɪnɪə). *Bot.* Also **octa-**. [mod.L., f. Gr. ὀκτώ eight + γυνή woman, female + -IA.] An order in several classes of plants in the Linnæan System, comprising those with eight pistils. Hence **octo'gynious, oc'togynous** *adjs.*, belonging to this order; having eight pistils.

1760 J. LEE *Introd. Bot.* II. xiv. (1765) 100 Octogynia. **1846** WORCESTER, *Octogynous*, having eight styles. *Loudon.* **1857** MAYNE *Expos. Lex.*, Octagynious. **1880** GRAY *Struct. Bot.* 422/1 With Octagynous (eight-styled) flowers.

octohedral, etc.: see OCTAHEDRAL, etc.

octoic *a.* (*Chem.*): see under OCTANE.

octomeral (ɒk'tɒmərəl), *a. Nat. Hist.* [f. Gr. ὀκτώ eight + μέρ-ος part + -AL[1]: cf. the more etymological OCTAMEROUS.] Having parts in sets of eight, octamerous; *spec.* in *Zool.* belonging to the division *Octomeralia* of *Scyphomedusæ*.

octomerous, octometer: see OCTA-.

octonal ('ɒktəʊnəl), *a.* [f. L. *octōn-ī* eight at a time, by eights, f. *octo* eight + -AL[1].] Proceeding by eights: = OCTONARY A.

1883 L. F. WARD *Dynamic Sociol.* II. 65 The advantages of the octonal system. **1887** *Longm. Mag.* Sept. 517 The advantages possessed by a decimal over a duodecimal or octonal system [of coinage].

octonare ('ɒktəʊnɛə(r)). *Pros.* [ad. L. *octōnārius versus*, an Iambic verse of eight feet.] A verse of eight feet, an octapody.

1886 *Amer. Jrnl. Philol.* VII. 399 All stichic divisions of the iambic octonares.

octonarian (ɒktəʊ'nɛərɪən), *a.* and *sb. Pros.* [f. L. *octōnāri-us* (see prec.) + -AN.] **a.** *adj.*

Consisting of eight feet. **b.** *sb.* A verse of eight feet.

1891 *Athenæum* 28 Feb. 275/1 Octonarian and septenarian iambic lines. **1892** A. S. WILKINS in *Classical Rev.* May 221/2 In Varro ὄνος λύρας vii. it is a pity not to recognize the unmistakable octonarians.

octonary (ˈɒktəʊnərı), *a.* and *sb.* [ad. L. *octōnāri-us* containing eight, f. *octōnī* (see OCTONAL).]

A. *adj.* Pertaining to the number eight: consisting of eight; proceeding by eights; *spec.* = OCTAL *a.* 1.

1615 JACKSON *Creed* IV. iv. §4 Eight..compared with seven is a greater number,..and yet the octonary number applied to nine, is less than the septenary applied to seven material numerables. **1633** T. ADAMS *Exp. 2 Peter* iii. 17 In Noah's octonary family, one was a son of Belial. **1845** B. THORPE *Lappenberg's Eng. under Anglo-Sax. Kings* I. 82 Of greater importance..would be the knowledge of the numeral system in use among the Saxons. I am inclined to the belief that the octonary..was the one followed. **1891** *Bull. N.Y. Math. Soc.* I. 5 The distinction between numbers of the form $4n + 1$ and those of the form $4n + 3$ is of great importance in the theory of numbers, and in the octonary system it would be obvious at a glance to which of these classes a given uneven number belongs. **1957** D. D. MCCRACKEN *Digital Computer Programming* iii. 33 The simple reason for the use of octal (also sometimes called octonary) numbers is that the conversion from binary to octal can be carried out mentally. **1963** L. SCHULTZ *Digital Processing* i. 22 Requiring eight symbols, the octal (sometimes, 'octonary') system proves to be a convenient means of expressing a binary value in a number approximately one-third the length of the binary number.

B. *sb.* A group of eight, an ogdoad; a group or stanza of eight lines of verse (esp. used of the divisions of the 119th Psalm).

1535 *Goodly primer*, Commendations Ps. cxix, The first Octonary. *Aleph*... The second Octonary. *Beth.* [etc.]. **1657** TRAPP *Comm. Ps.* cxix. 1 Pindarus and other Poets had their Ogdoades or Octonaries. *a* **1677** MANTON *Serm. Ps.* 119. lxiii. verse 56. **1882** SPURGEON *Treas. Dav.* Ps. cxix. *title*, The whole Psalm proceeds by octonaries.

octonocular, *a.* ? *Obs.* [f. L. *octōn-ī* eight at a time, eight + *ocul-us* eye + -AR: cf. *ocular*.] Having eight eyes.

1703 S. MORLAND in *Phil. Trans.* XXIII. 1322 The Tarantula is an Apulian Spider of the Octonocular kind. **1713** DERHAM *Phys.-Theol.* VIII. iii. 401 Most Animals are Binocular, spiders for the most part Octonocular, and some Senocular.

octoon (ɒkˈtuːn). [f. L. *octo* eight + *-oon* in *quadr-oon*.] Variant of OCTOROON.

1840 R. H. DANA *Bef. Mast* xiii. 29 The least drop of Spanish blood, if it be only of quatroon or octoon, is sufficient to raise them from the rank of slaves.

octopamine (ɒkˈtəʊpəmiːn). *Biochem.* [f. OCTOP(US + AMINE, the compound having been first identified in salivary extracts from an octopus.] A weakly sympathomimetic amine, $HO{\cdot}C_6H_4{\cdot}CHOH{\cdot}CH_2NH_2$, which under the action of monoamine oxidase inhibitors may accumulate in nerves in place of the closely related noradrenaline, thereby inhibiting the transmission of nerve impulses and causing vasoconstriction; 1-(3-hydroxyphenyl)-2-aminoethanol

1948 V. ERSPAMER in *Acta Pharmacol.* IV. 245 It is suggested that the parent substance of the adrenaline-like principle in the salivary extracts should be called 'Octopamine'. **1952** *Nature* 1 Mar. 376/1 Having identified octopamine as norsynephrine, it was obvious to expect that hydroxyoctopamine could be identified as..noradrenaline. This assumption was confirmed experimentally. **1970** PASSMORE & ROBSON *Compan. Med. Stud.* II. xv. 32/2 Octopamine is a much weaker adrenergic receptor activator than noradrenaline and replacement by it of a portion of the noradrenaline released by nerve stimulation could result in a diminished response of the effector tissue. **1972** FLORKIN & BRICTEUX-GRÉGOIRE in Florkin & Scheer *Chem. Zool.* VII. x. 323 Octopamine may result from the decarboxylation of *p*-hydroxyphenylserine.., but it is known that octopamine may also result from the oxidation of tyramine... Octopamine itself can be oxidized into.. noradrenaline.

octopartite (ɒktəʊˈpɑːtaɪt), *a.* [ad. med. or mod.L. *octopartītus*, f. *octo* eight + *partītus* divided.] Divided into or consisting of eight parts; *spec.* in *Law*, of a contract, indenture, etc.: Drawn up in eight corresponding parts, one for every party: now disused. (In quot. 1854, Of an eighth part.)

1752 CARTE *Hist. Eng.* III. 561 Sir James Balfour.. brought with him the octopartite indenture signed by Morton among others. **1854** *Tait's Mag.* XXI. 451 The Lichtenstein, sovereign and subject at once; octopartite possessor of a vote dietical. **1879** SIR G. SCOTT *Lect. Archit.* II. 196 This may be carried out on all four sides, and thus become an octopartite vault.

†**octoparˈtition.** *Obs. rare.* In 7 octi-. [f. L. *octo* eight + PARTITION.] Division into eight (equal) parts.

1674 JEAKE *Arith.* (1696) 34 Octipartition, or to divide by 8, is but to take half the quarter part.

octopean (ɒkˈtəʊpiːən), *a.* [irreg. f. OCTOPUS; cf. *Briarean*.] Pertaining to, or like that of, an octopus.

1896 *Law Times* CI. 558/1 Attempts..to escape the octopean grasp of a stringent Arbitration Clause.

octoped (ˈɒktəpɛd). Also -pede. [f. L. *octo* eight + *pes, ped-em* foot.] An eight-footed animal or thing.

1822 *Blackw. Mag.* XI. 591 The table is standing a most steady octoped on a most trustworthy floor. **1841** LYTTON *Night & Morn.* I. vi. I. 145 One class of spiders, industrious, hardworking octopedes.

ocˈtopian, *a.* [f. OCTOP(US + -IAN.] Suggestive of an octopus; = OCTOPEAN *a.* Also **ocˈtopic** [-IC], **ˈoctopine** [-INE[1]], *adjs.*

1914 CHESTERTON *Flying Inn* 248 The Captain prepared to swing himself on to one of the octopine branches [of a tree]. **1922** C. E. MONTAGUE *Disenchantment* i. 11 He had.. struck..a crate, from which some octopian beast..had reached out at him. **1968** *Punch* 6 Nov. 667/3 The sight of a Breton fisherman pulling the suckers off a live octopic leg.

octoploid (ˈɒktəplɔɪd), *a.* (*sb.*) *Biol.* Also octa-. [f. OCTO- + -PLOID.] (Made up of somatic cells) containing eight sets of chromosomes. Also as *sb.*, an octoploid organism.

1925 C. C. HURST *Experiments in Genetics* xxxviii. 542 By successive losses of septets the decaploid species would give rise to an octoploid species, the octoploid to a hexaploid species, the hexaploid to a tetraploid species. **1931** *Genetics* XVI. 462 The octoploid may be considered as having a replication of eight basically similar genoms. **1943** *Hereditas* XXIX. 193 (*heading*) Notes on octaploid *Solanum punæ* plant. **1961** *Lancet* 26 Aug. 488/1 The finding of 8 sex-chromatin bodies in an octaploid XXXY cell can be predicted from the above formula. **1973** *Nature* 11 May 87/2 Triploids.., artificial tetraploids and octoploids were all found to synthesize orientin isomers. **1974** *Sci. Amer.* Aug. 73/2 If a hexaploid wheat (*T. aestivum*) is crossed with rye, the result is an octoploid triticale.

Hence **ˈoctoploidy**, the state or condition of being octoploid.

1934 *Gen. Program 3rd Pittsburgh Meeting Amer. Assoc. Adv. Sci.* 34 Octoploidy and diploidy in *Miastor americana*. **1948** *Jrnl. Heredity* XXXIX. 42/1 Instead of abrupt doublings of the chromosome number as in mitosis, there is therefore a gradual change from diploidy to tetraploidy, from tetraploidy to octoploidy and so on. **1970** AMBROSE & EASTY *Cell Biol.* 496 (Index), Octoploidy.

octopod (ˈɒktəpɒd), *sb.* and *a.* [ad. Gr. ὀκτώποδ- (also ὀκτάποδ-), stem of ὀκτώπους OCTOPUS, in neuter pl. ὀκτώποδα *Octopoda*.]

A. *sb.* An animal having eight feet; *spec.* an octopus, or other member of the suborder *Octopoda* of cephalopods.

1835-6 TODD *Cycl. Anat.* I. 522 The Dibranchiate Octopods. **1839** JOHNSTON in *Proc. Berw. Nat. Club* I. No. 7. 198 When at rest this octopod lies prone on the belly. **1851-6** WOODWARD *Mollusca* 64 In the argonaut, and some octopods, there are blue cells besides.

B. *adj.* Eight-footed.

1826 KIRBY & SP. *Entomol.* III. 26 In the Octopod branch [of the *Aptera*] a further dichotomy takes place. **1835-6** TODD *Cycl. Anat.* I. 246/1 The Arachnidans are octopod.

So **ocˈtopodan** *a.* and *sb.*; **ocˈtopodous** *a.*

1835-6 TODD *Cycl. Anat.* I. 557/1 In the..Octopodous tribes. **1891** *Cent. Dict.*, *Octopodan*.

octopole, var. OCTUPOLE.

‖**octopus** (ˈɒktəpəs, ɒkˈtəʊpəs). Pl. **octopodes** (ɒkˈtəʊpədiːz), anglicized **octopuses**. [mod.L. *octōpus*, a. Gr. ὀκτώπους, acc. ὀκτώποδ-α eight-footed, f. ὀκτώ eight + πούς, πόδ- foot.] A genus of cephalopod molluscs, characterized by eight 'arms' surrounding the mouth and provided with suckers; an individual of this genus (*esp.* one of the larger and more formidable species).

1758 BAKER in *Phil. Trans.* L. 778 The Polypus, particularly so called, the Octopus, Preke, or Pour-contrel. **1835** KIRBY *Hab. & Inst. Anim.* I. x. 308 The body of the octopus is small, it has legs sometimes a foot and a half in length, with about two hundred and forty suckers on each leg. **1880** BROWNING *Pietro of Abano* 401 Help! The old magician clings like an octopus! **1884** H. M. LEATHES *Rough Notes Nat. Hist.* 46 Saying that enormous octopuses existed on the western side of Panama, in the Pacific Ocean.

b. *fig.*; usually applied to an organized power having extended ramifications and far-reaching influence, esp. harmful or destructive.

1882 GREG *Misc. Ess.* ii. 37 We are the very octopus of nations. **1893** *Boston* (Mass.) *Jrnl.* 25 Mar. 2/1 The electric octopus. Formal organization of the New England Street Railway Company. **1894** *Westm. Gaz.* 12 Mar. 2/1 He was an administrative octopus, a cormorant of toil.

c. *attrib.* and *Comb.*

1880 G. MEREDITH *Tragic Com.* (1881) 206 Then they laid octopus-limbs on her. **1894** *Outing* (U.S.) XXIV. 460/1 An octopus power sought to tear the human limpet from its clinging place. **1898** P. MANSON *Trop. Diseases* i. 9 A strange-looking octopus-like creature.

octopush (ˈɒktəpʊʃ). [f. OCTO(PUS + PUSH *sb.*[1]] A game of underwater hockey (see quots.). Hence **ˈoctopusher**, one who plays octopush.

1970 *Times* 18 Feb. 11 Octopush..is a new form of underwater hockey... The game is played by teams of six. .. The object of the game is to propel or shovel the puck.. along the bottom of the pool and into the opponents' gull [*sc.* goal]. **1971** *Observer* 23 May 19/2 (*caption*) Octopush..the name of the game for skindivers. Players try to push a lead puck (called a squid) through the other team's goal (gulley). **1973** *Sunday Mail* (Brisbane) 7 Jan. 2/3 Octopush..is played like underwater hockey. The teams, in flippers and face masks, but no oxygen tanks, play in a pool six feet deep. Instead of hockey sticks they use pushers,—shaped something like a rake with a blade where the prongs should be. **1973** *Telegraph* (Brisbane) 7 Mar. 3/2 Not mermaids but octopushers..are members of the Safari Women's team which plays the new game of octopush—diving to push a lead weight along the bottom of a swimming pool into the opposing team's goal.

octoreme (ˈɒktəriːm). Also **octireme**. [f. L. *octo* eight + *rēm-us* oar.] An (ancient) ship with eight ranks of oars. (In quot. 1890 humorously for 'eight-oared boat'.)

1799 CHARNOCK in *Naval Chron.* I. 132 Ancient galleys, called Triremes, Quadriremes, Quinquiremes and Octoremes. **1890** *Daily News* 25 Jan. 5/2 There is a bad race between the Trial Eights, and this is how Thucydides would infallibly have described it: 'And when the antagonistic octoremes appeared' [etc.]. **1891** *Cent. Dict.*, *Octireme*.

octoroon (ɒktəˈruːn). [A non-etymological formation from L. *octo* eight, after *quadroon* (in which the suffix is *-oon*).] A person having one-eighth negro blood; the offspring of a quadroon and a white; sometimes used of other mixed races.

1861 D. BOUCICAULT (*title*) The Octoroon. **1862** J. E. CAIRNES *Revol. Amer.* 17 The mulattoes, quadroons and octoroons..who now form so large a proportion of the whole enslaved population of the South. **1864** WEBSTER, *Octaroon*, see *Octoroon*. **1891** *Times* 8 Jan. 9/3 The mulatto, the quadroon, and the octoroon are chiefly products of the slavery period.

octostichous, octostyle: see OCTA-.

octosyllabic (ˌɒktəʊsɪˈlæbɪk), *a.* and *sb.* [f. late L. *octosyllab-us* (Mar. Vict.), in late Gr. ὀκτασύλλαβ-ος (Draco *De Metris*), f. Gr. ὀκτώ, ὀκτα- eight + συλλαβή, L. *syllaba* syllable: cf. SYLLABIC.]

A. *adj.* Consisting of eight syllables (chiefly in *Pros.*, of a 'verse' or line of poetry); composed of lines of eight syllables each.

a **1771** GRAY *Corr.* (1843) 256 Octosyllabic, Mixed. **1814** BYRON *Let. to Moore* 2 Jan., Scott alone, of the present generation, has hitherto completely triumphed over the fatal facility of the octo-syllabic verse. **1837** LOCKHART *Scott* May, an. 1810 The octosyllabic measure of the Lady of the Lake. **1884** *Pall Mall G.* 15 Aug. 4/2 [He] succeeded in managing the octosyllabic stanza.

B. *sb.* A 'verse' or line of eight syllables.

1842 MRS. BROWNING *Grk. Chr. Poets* 116 As flowing a rhythm as may bear comparison with many octosyllabics of our day. **1882** *Athenæum* 27 May 660/3 Scott..produced 'The Lay of the Last Minstrel', which soon set..every versifier from Byron downwards writing romantic stories in octosyllabics with anapæstic variations.

So **octosyˈllabical** *a. rare*—[0].

1846 in WORCESTER.

octosyllable (ɒktəʊˈsɪləb(ə)l), *sb.* and *a.* [f. L. *octosyllab-us*, after *syllable*: cf. F. *octosyllabe* (1611 in Cotgr.).] **a.** *sb.* = prec. B.; also, a word of eight syllables. **b.** *adj.* = prec. A.

1775-8 TYRWHITT *Lang. Chaucer* Note 60, I call this the octosyllable metre, from what I apprehended to have been its original form. **1827** HARE *Guesses* Ser. II. (1873) 364 The octosyllable metre, of which modern writers are so fond. **1846** WORCESTER, *Octosyllable, n.* A word of eight syllables. *Clarke.* **1882** SAINTSBURY in *Spenser's Wks.* (Grosart) III. p. lxvi, A poem in octosyllables.

octoteuch: see OCTATEUCH.

octrain (ˈɒktreɪn). *rare.* [irreg. f. L. *octo* eight, after *quatrain* (in which the suffix is *-ain*).] A group of eight lines of verse.

a **1827** J. M. GOOD in Spurgeon *Treas. Dav.* Ps. cxix. 1 Twenty-two octrains or discourses of eight lines each.

‖**octroi** (ɔktrwa, ˈɒktrɔɪ). Also 7–8 octroy, 8 octroit. [F. *octroi*, from *octroyer*: see next.]

†**1.** A concession, a grant; a privilege granted by a government, *esp.* a commercial privilege, as an exclusive right of trade. *Obs.*

1614 W. COLWALL in *Buccleuch MSS.* (Hist. MSS. Comm.) I. 151 Those merchants..much importune the Lords for octroy to make a company. He answered me, that they purposed..not as yet to grant any octroy. **1721** *Lond. Gaz.* No. 5920/1 They may obtain an Octroy or Grant for 15 Years.

2. A duty or tax levied on certain articles on their admission into a town (esp. in France and other European countries).

1714 *French Bk. of Rates* 25 Duties called the Octroits, in the City of Roan, upon Sugar, Wax, and Tobacco. **1848** MILL *Pol. Econ.* V. v. §4 (1876) 520 An octroi cannot produce a large revenue, without pressing severely upon the labouring classes of the towns. **1877** C. GEIKIE *Christ* (1879) 196 The octroi at the gates of towns.

b. The barrier or limit at which the tax is paid; also, the service by which, or body of officers by whom, it is collected.

1861 NEALE *Notes Dalmatia* iii. 41 At the octroi our driver gave out his destination. **1873** BROWNING *Red Cott. Nt.-cap* I. 364 This is the criminal Saint-Rambertese Who smuggled in tobacco, half-a-pound! The Octroi found it out and fined the wretch.

c. *attrib.*
1862 Thackeray *Philip* (1869) II. viii. 119 The *octroi* officers never stop gentlemen going out..upon duelling business. **1865** *Day of Rest* Oct. 582 Articles liable to the town or octroi tax. **1884** V. Stuart *Egypt* 142 The octroi duties are very mischievous and vexing.

octroy ('ɒktrɔɪ), *v.* [ad. F. *octroy-er* (15th c. in Littré), for earlier *ot(t)royer, otreier* = Pr. and OCat. *autreiar*:—L. **auctōricāre* or *auctōrizāre* (through a pronunciation **octoridiāre*: see Hatz.-Darm. s.v.) to authorize.] See also OTTROYE *v.*

1. *trans.* To concede, grant, accord: said of a government or appointed authority.
[**1292** Britton ii. xiv. §3 Si, pur sa poverte, luy eoms ottreyé par sa surté de sa fei a sure sa pleynte. **1477–1546** see OTTROYE.] **1480** Caxton *Ovid's Met.* xi. ii, Bacchus octroyed and graunted hym this yfte. **1845** Ld. Campbell *Chancellors* (1857) IV. lxxxiv. 144 The Chief Justice..thought that all our liberties were octroyed or granted by the Crown.

2. To impose by authority, to dictate. [= Ger. *octroyiren.*] *rare.*
1865 *Fortn. Rev.* I. 505 The doctrine of State rights, though severely stricken, has sufficient vitality to prevent the President from octroying State constitutions.

octuor ('ɒktjuːɔː(r)). *Mus.* [F., irreg. f. L. *octo* eight, after *quatuor* four (in *Mus.* used as = *quartet*).] = OCTET 1.
1864 in Webster. **1880** Grove *Dict. Mus.* s.v. *Octet*, Beethoven's 'Grand Octuor' (op. 103)..is an arrangement of his early String Quintet (op. 4), for 2 oboes, 2 clarinets, 2 horns, and 2 bassoons.

octuple ('ɒktjuːp(ə)l), *a.* (*sb.*) [ad. L. *octupl-us* eightfold, f. *octo* eight + *-plus*, as in *duplus* DOUBLE. Cf. F. *octuple* (1552 in Hatz.-Darm.).]

A. *adj.* Eightfold; eight times as much as...; composed of eight.
1603 Holland *Plutarch's Mor.* 1046 The Diameters of Venus and the earth, are in double proportion, but their globes or sphæres beare octuple proportion, to wit, eight for one. **1656** Stanley *Hist. Philos.* v. (1701) 162/2 The Overseers of the Altar, made all the four sides double to what they were before, so instead of doubling the Altar they made it Octuple to what it was. **1677** Plot *Oxfordsh.* 293 To quadruple the distance..in octuple the time. **1816** Kirby & Sp. *Entomol.* (1843) I. 56 Its..triple or sometimes octuple teguments. **1879** H. W. Warren *Recr. Astron.* x. 214 The octuple star *σ* in Orion.

B. *sb.* That which is eight times something else, or consists of eight parts.
1692 *Capt. Smith's Seaman's Gram.* ii. xv. 123 The Octuple thereof is 2.0. **1856** *Illustr. Lond. News* 2 Feb. 110/3 A monster negotiation..called the 'Octuple', because eight separate Companies were parties to it.

'**octuple,** *v.* [f. prec. sb.: cf. F. *octupler* (1798 in *Dict. Acad.*).] *trans.* To make eight times as much, increase eightfold.
1837 T. Doubleday in *Blackw. Mag.* XLI. 367 This prolific community had at least octupled itself in forty years. **1893** G. B. Longstaff *Rural Depopul.* 31 In New Hampshire..the new town populations have trebled the additions to the rural community, and in the case of Massachusetts have octupled them.

'**octuplet.** [f. as prec., after *triplet*, etc.] A set or combination of eight; in *Mus.* 'A group of eight notes which are to be played in the time of six' (Stainer & Barrett *Dict. Mus. Terms* 1898).
1852 De Morgan in R. P. Graves *Life Sir W. R. Hamilton* (1889) III. 338 Then if AB to BC, CD to DE, EF to FA, compounded, also give a ratio of equality, why not say ABCDEF are harmonics? We have then an harmonic quadruplet and sextuplet, and we might have octuplets, &c.

'**octuplex,** *a.* [a. L. type **octuplex, -plic-em* (whence *octuplicātus*), f. *octo* eight + *-plex*, -fold, as in *duplex, triplex*, etc.] Applied to a system of electric telegraphy by which eight simultaneous messages can be sent along the same wire. Hence '**octuplex** *v. trans.*, to render octuplex.
1889 *Times* (weekly ed.) 29 Mar. 5/2 If the line..is quadruplexed, the phonophoric instruments will 'sextuplex' or 'octuplex' it. **1893** *Rev. of Rev.* Dec. 606 Mr. Edison is confident of attaining sextuplex and octuplex systems.

†**octupli'cation.** *Arith. Obs.* [ad. late L. *octuplicātiōn-em* (Mart. Cap.), n. of action from **octuplicāre*, f. *octuplex.*] Multiplication by eight.
1674 S. Jeake *Arith.* (1696) 25 Octuplication, or to multiply by 8.

octupole ('ɒktuːpəʊl). *Physics.* Also **octa-, octo-**. [f. *octu-* (in OCTUPLE *a.* (*sb.*), OCTUPLET: cf. QUADRUPOLE), OCTA-, OCTO- + POLE *sb.*[2]] A multipole of order $l = 3$. Freq. *attrib.* or as *adj.* Cf. MULTIPOLE *sb.*
1929 P. Debye *Polar Molecules* ii. 26 The next configuration, constructed by a displacement of the quadrupole in an arbitrary direction, will give the octupole. **1950** D. Halliday *Introd. Nucl. Physics* ii. 57 Gamma-emission processes can be classified as to multipole order; we speak, for example, of dipole, quadrupole, octopole, and still higher-order transitions. **1954** *Physical Rev.* XCIV. 1799 (*heading*) Hyperfine structure of In^{115}. Evidence of a nuclear octupole moment. **1961** A. Abragam *Princ. Nucl. Magnetism* vi. 170 The existence of magnetic octopoles has been established by atomic beam methods. **1970** G. K. Woodgate *Elem. Atomic Struct.* ix. 166 The only multipole (2^k-pole) moments which do not vanish are: magnetic dipole ($k = 1$), electric quadrupole ($k = 2$), magnetic octupole ($k = 3$), electric hexadecapole ($k = 4$), etc. **1971** *Nature* 27 Aug. 609/1 The magnetic dipole and octapole and electric quadrupole moments all appear to vanish as $(Z_c + 1)^{-2}$ as Z_c, the redshift of light coming from the centre of the disk, goes to infinity.

octyl ('ɒktɪl). *Chem.* [f. OCT(A-, OCT(O- + -YL.] The hydrocarbon radical of the octacarbon series (C_8H_{17}); sometimes called *capryl.* Also *attrib.* as ***octyl alcohol***, etc. Hence **oc'tylamine**, the amine of the same series ($C_8H_{19}N$); '**octylene** = *octene* (see under OCTANE); **oc'tylic** *a.*, of or pertaining to octyl, as ***octylic acid, alcohol***, etc.
1866–77 Watts *Dict. Chem.* IV. 170 Octyl. Capryl. C_8H_{17}. *Ibid.*, Hydrate of Octyl. Octylic Alcohol. Caprylic Alcohol. C_8H_{17}.H.O. *Ibid.* 172 Octylamine is a colourless, bitter, very caustic, inflammable liquid, having an ammoniacal fishy odour. *Ibid.*, Octylene is a very mobile oil, lighter than water and insoluble therein, very soluble in alcohol and ether. **1871** Roscoe *Elem. Chem.* 333 Octyl alcohol is obtained by distilling castor oil with potash. *Ibid.* 345 Dibutyl or octyl hydride.

ocular ('ɒkjʊlə(r)), *a.* and *sb.* Also 6 **ocul-, occul-, ocullare**, 6–7 **occular**. [ad. L. *oculār-is*, f. *ocul-us* eye. Cf. F. *oculaire* (R. Estienne 1549).]

1. Of, belonging to, or connected with the eye as a bodily organ; seated in, or in the region of, the eye. *spec.* in *Entom.*, pertaining to the compound eye of an insect (distinguished from *ocellar*).
1597 A. M. tr. *Guillemeau's Fr. Chirurg.* 12 b/2 The Eye, or ocullare vayne. **1677** Plot *Oxfordsh.* 95 Ocular distempers in Horses. **1786** R. W. Darwin in *Phil. Trans.* LXXVI. 313 When any one has long and attentively looked at a bright object..an image..continues some time to be visible: this appearance in the eye we shall call the ocular spectrum of that object. **1828** Stark *Elem. Nat. Hist.* II. 150 Exterior antennæ..inserted near the ocular peduncles. **1831** Brewster *Optics* xxxvi. 304 The bluish green image of the wafer is called an *ocular spectrum*, because it is impressed on the eye. **1851–6** Woodward *Mollusca* 49 Snails, whose ocular tentacles have been destroyed, reproduce them completely in a few weeks. **1885** Thomas *Med. Dict.*, *Ocular Cone*,..a cone formed in the eye by the rays of light, the base being on the cornea, the apex on the retina. **1898** E. E. Maddox *Ocular Muscles* iii. 65 Our studies of the ocular motions up to this point have been quite independent of the ocular muscles.

b. Used for, applied to, or relating to the eye.
1599 A. M. tr. *Gabelhouer's Bk. Physicke* 53/1 A tryede Oculare vnguent. **1661** Lovell *Hist. Anim. & Min.* 83 It's used in ocular remedies. **1665–6** *Phil. Trans.* I. 120 He hath already begun his Object-Glasses for the mentioned two Ocular ones. **1889** *Anthony's Photogr. Bull.* II. 157 Abraded by the constant..insertion and withdrawal of the different eye pieces, leaving a..shining and reflecting surface at the ocular end.

c. Of the nature, form, or function of an eye.
1640 Somner *Antiq. Canterb.* 171 The ocular and peeked or pointed form of the arch. **1659** D. Pell *Impr. Sea* 195 The excellency of that ocular Organ that God hath bestowed upon man. **1841–71** T. R. Jones *Anim. Kingd.* (ed. 4) 491 An ocular apparatus..composed of two eyes united together.

d. Expressed by the eye; conveyed by the look of the eye.
1627 Donne *Serm.* V. 48 They did countenance that which was said with..ocular applause with fixing their eyes upon the Preacher. **1860** Emerson *Cond. Life, Behaviour* Wks. (Bohn) II. 384 The eyes of men converse as much as their tongues..the ocular dialect needs no dictionary.

2. Belonging to the action of the eye, and hence to the sense of sight; visual.

a. Made or performed by the eye or sight; done by means of the eye: chiefly in ***ocular inspection***.
c **1575** *Balfour's Practicks* (1754) 382 The Lordis of counsal, be ocular inspectioun, may decern..ony letter, contract..or uther writ, to be false and feinzeit. **1642** Howell *For. Trav.* (Arb.) 13 One's owne Ocular view..will still find out something new. **1830** Herschel *Stud. Nat. Phil.* §194 To make the induction of their law a matter of ocular inspection. **1853** Kane *Grinnell Exp.* xli. (1856) 372 In these regions we have learned to distrust ocular measurements of distance.

b. Obtained by the use of the eye; derived from what one has actually seen: as ***ocular testimony***. ***ocular witness***, an eye-witness. Now *rare* or *Obs.*
1608 Dekker *Dead Tearme* D iv, To bee an Occuler witnesse-bearer of what I speake. **1650** Bulwer *Anthropomet.* 93 Which will appeare more credible by the modern relations of some ocular witnesses. **1670** Walton *Lives* i. 44 He gave an ocular testimony of the strictness and regularity of [his life]. **1767** Blackstone *Comm.* II. xx. 313 Depending on the ocular testimony and remembrance of the witnesses.

c. Addressed to the eye; perceived by or manifest to sight; visible; conveyed to the mind through the actual sight of a thing. (Chiefly, now almost exclusively, in ***ocular demonstration*** and the like; formerly said also of material things.)
1589 Puttenham *Eng. Poesie* ii. x[i]. (Arb.) 98 Your occular proportion doeth declare the nature of the audible: for if it please the eare well, the same represented by delineation to the view pleaseth the eye well. **1604** Shaks. *Oth.* iii. iii. 360 Giue me the Occular proofe. **1615** Chapman *Odyss.* xxiii. 349 The scar That still remaines a marke too ocular To leaue your heart yet blinded. **1638** Rouse *Heav. Univ.* Advt. (1702) 3 Giving his Testimony, by Ocular Demonstration. **1726** Butler *Serm. Rolls* ii. 27 The Science of Opticks, deduced from ocular Experiments. **1875** Jowett *Plato* (ed. 2) III. 383 Of my zeal you shall have ocular demonstration.

d. Of or pertaining to the sense of sight.
1831 Faraday *Exp. Res.* xliv. 291 A peculiar ocular deception. **1849** Ruskin *Seven Lamps* vi. §4. 166 It is not a question of mere ocular delight.

B. *sb.* †**1.** Ocular quality or property; that which is manifest to sight: cf. A. 2 c. *Obs.*
1656 S. H. *Gold. Law* 70 Its Natures, and not Names; its occults, and not occulars, entitle to the title King.

2. The eye-piece of a telescope, microscope, or other optical instrument.
1835 Lindley *Introd. Bot.* (1848) I. 17 An Amici's achromatic ocular. **1876** Webb in G. F. Chambers *Astron.* 745 The Ramsden ocular is never achromatic. **1890** *Anthony's Photogr. Bull.* III. 84 The objectives and compensating oculars now available for microscopical research.

3. Humorously for 'ocular organ', 'eye'.
1825 C. M. Westmacott *Eng. Spy* I. 164 The queerest looking oculars I had ever seen. **1881** W. S. Gilbert *Patience*, To cut his curly hair, and stick an eye-glass in his ocular.

†'**ocularily,** *adv. Obs.* [f. OCULARY + -LY[2].] = OCULARLY 2.
1629 Chapman *Juvenal* Pref., Ocularily to present you with example of what I esteem fit [etc.].

ocularist ('ɒkjʊlərɪst). [a. mod.F. *ocularistе* (Littré), f. *oculaire* OCULAR: see -IST.] A maker of artificial eyes.
1866 *Morn. Star* 18 Feb., French artists..these, not oculists, but ocularists. **1893** Vizetelly *Glances back* II. xxxiii. 249 In several ocularists' waiting rooms collections of artificial eyes were displayed.

ocularly ('ɒkjʊləlɪ), *adv.* [f. OCULAR + -LY[2].]

1. With or by means of one's eyes or sight; by ocular testimony (quot. 1646).
1646 Sir T. Browne *Pseud. Ep.* vii. xv. 369 Andrew Thevet in his Cosmography doth ocularly overthrow it; for hee affirmeth, he saw an Asse with his saddle cast therein, and drowned. **1660** tr. *Paracelsus' Archidoxis* i. i. 5 Wee are made certain, and do ocularly behold that the thing is truly so. **1891** *Blackw. Mag.* CL. 22/1 Tender invitation, expressed verbally or ocularly.

2. To the eyes or sight; by ocular demonstration; visibly.
1628 Jackson *Creed* ix. iii. §1 The other passages in the same psalm were ocularly exemplified and fulfilled in Him. **1664** Power *Exp. Philos.* i. 58 It is ocularly manifest. **1831** Brewster *Optics* xxix. 247 That the multiplication and colour of the images is owing to the causes now explained may be proved ocularly.

†'**oculary,** *a. Obs. rare.* [ad. L. *oculāri-us*, f. *ocul-us* eye: see -ARY.] = OCULAR *a.*, 1 b, 2 c.
1600 W. Vaughan *Golden Groue* (1608) I v, Heynous, literall, oculary vntrueths. **1601** Holland *Pliny* II. 272 Eie-salues, and other ocularie medicines.

oculate ('ɒkjʊlət), *a.* Also 7 **occ-**. [ad. L. *oculāt-us* possessed of eyes, f. *ocul-us*: see -ATE[2].]

†**1.** Furnished with or possessed of eyes or sight; sharp-sighted; observant. *Obs.*
1549 E. Becke *Matthew's Bible* Ded., He that walketh without this lanterne..be he neuer so oculate..yet he is but blynd. **1615** Crooke *Body of Man* 221 It cannot be perceiued vnlesse the Anatomist be very diligent and occulate. **1657** Tomlinson *Renou's Disp.* 277 An oculate faithfull Narrator. **1660** Burney Κέρδ. δῶρον (1661) 115 Kings are as Intuitive Angells to..set a living pattern.. before the Oculate Judges, that they may judge righteous judgement, by sight more than by quidditie.

2. *Nat. Hist.* Having eye-like spots or holes resembling eyes.
1656 Blount *Glossogr.*, *Oculate*, full of eyes or holes. **1661** Lovell *Hist. Anim. & Min.* Isagoge, Raie undulate and oculate..stellarie oculate and clavate. **1706** Phillips, *Oculate*, full of holes like eyes. **1857** in Mayne *Expos. Lex.*

†'**oculate,** *v. Obs. rare*[−1]. In 7 **occ-**. [f. L. *ocul-us* eye: cf. It. *occhiare* 'to eye, or looke neerely vnto' (Florio). (L. *oculāre* had not this sense.)] *trans.* To set eyes upon; to eye, see, behold.
1609 *Ev. Wom. in Hum.* v. i. in Bullen *O. Pl.* IV, Diana bathing herself, being discovered or occulated by Acteon.

'**oculated,** *a.* Also 8 **occ-**. [f. L. *oculāt-us* (OCULATE) + -ED.] = OCULATE *a.* 2.
1711 *Phil. Trans.* XXVII. 344 Occulated Butterflies. **1752** Sir J. Hill *Hist. Anim.* 152 The oblong, oculated Porcellana..The Argus-shell.

†**ocu'lation.** *Obs. rare*[−0]. [n. of action f. L. *oculāre* to furnish with eyes, after *oculus* in sense 'eye or bud' of a plant.] = INOCULATION 1.
1611 Florio, *Innestare ad occhio*, to inoculate, to graffe by way of oculation. **1623** in Cockeram. **1857** Mayne *Expos. Lex.*, *Oculatio, Bot.* a term for grafting: oculation.

ocu'liferous, *a.* [f. L. *oculus, oculi-* eye + *-fer*: see -FEROUS.] Bearing an eye or eyes, as the tentacles or horns of snails, and the pedicels of certain Crustacea.
1856–8 W. Clark *Van der Hoeven's Zool.* I. 319 A transverse petiole, oculiferous at its apex.

So **ocu'ligerous** [-GEROUS] *a.*, in same sense.

'oculiform, *a.* [f. as prec. + L. *-formis* -FORM.] Having the form of an eye; eye-like.

1828 WEBSTER s.v., An oculiform pebble. **1841–71** T. R. JONES *Anim. Kingd.* (ed. 4) 107 The central ganglion situated beneath the oculiform spot. **1892** *Syd. Soc. Lex., Oculiform points*, the marginal corpuscles of the Medusæ.. supposed to be visual organs.

oculi'motor, oculi'motory *a.* = OCULOMOTOR.

oculism ('ɒkjʊlɪz(ə)m). *rare.* [f. L. *ocul-us* eye + -ISM; after OCULIST.] The business of an oculist; knowledge of defects of vision, diseases of the eye, etc., and the remedies.

1909 W. BOOTH in H. Begbie *Life W. Booth* (1920) II. 433 The gentleman.. was a doctor and.. he knew something of oculism.

oculist ('ɒkjʊlɪst). [a. F. *oculiste* (in Paré 16th c.), f. L. *ocul-us* eye: see -IST.]

1. One versed in the knowledge or treatment of the eyes; a physician or surgeon who treats diseases and affections of the eye.

1615 CROOKE *Body of Man* 538 Those whom we call Oculists, that is, such as professe and intend the cure of the eies. **1630** BRATHWAIT *Eng. Gentlem.* (1641) 197 It is observed by profest Oculists, that whereas all creatures have but foure muscles to turne their eyes round about, man hath a fift to pull his eyes up to heaven. **1711** ADDISON *Spect.* No. 124 ¶6 Having consulted many Oculists for the bettering of his Sight. **1866** MISS BRADDON *Lady's Mile* xxviii. 313, I must go at once to an oculist.

†**2.** One who has good eyes, or uses them well; a sharp-sighted or observant person. *Obs. rare.*

1660 BURNEY *Κέρδ. δῶρον* Ep. Ded. (1661) 6 As a sacred Oculist that could see to the end of a storm. **1833** *Men & Mann. Amer.* I. viii. 258 The fair oculist continued our fellow traveller.

3. *Comb.* **oculist-stamp** (also *oculist's stamp*), the more usual name among antiquaries for *medicine seal, stamp* (MEDICINE *sb.*[1] 6 a).

1778 *Gentl. Mag.* XLVIII. 509 An inscription on an oculist's stamp. **1851** *Monthly Jrnl. Med. Sci.* XII. 42 Above sixty Roman oculist-stamps have been now discovered in different parts of western Europe. **1886** *Guide Exhib. Galleries Brit. Mus.* 200 Roman Implements, such as steelyards and their weights, oculists' stamps, locks and keys. **1954** R. SUTCLIFF *Eagle of Ninth* viii. 87 An oculist's stamp is a talisman to carry a man safely where a Legion could not go.

Hence **ocu'listic** *a.*, of or belonging to an oculist; practising as an oculist.

1866 *Lond. Rev.* 24 Nov. 569 Manly eyes.. beamed upon her without arousing in her mind any but an oculistic curiosity. **1883** *Pall Mall G.* 22 Sept. 16 *Advt.* Mr. —— Oculistic Optician. **1893** *Brit. Med. Jrnl.* 9 Sept. 607 Men whose oculistic work seemed to have extended.. over a great part of the country.

oculo- (ˌɒkjʊləʊ), before a vowel ocul-, used as combining form of L. *oculus* eye (see -o) in several terms of Anatomy, etc., as **ocu'lauditory**, *a.* [AUDITORY], having the functions of an eye and an ear together, as certain sense-organs in some Hydrozoa; **oculo-a'gravic** *a.* [f. *oculogravic* with insertion of A- 14], applied to an illusion of an apparent upward movement of objects in the visual field that is experienced when the effective force acting on a person is reduced; **oculofrontal** (-'frʌntəl) *a.*, belonging or relating to the eye and the forehead; **oculo'gravic** *a.* [L. *grav-is* heavy], applied to an illusion of apparent tilting that is experienced when a person undergoes an acceleration that causes the effective force acting on him to change direction; **oculo'gyral** *a.* [Gr. γῦρ-ος ring, circle], applied to an illusion of apparent rotation that is experienced during or just after rotational accelerations of the body; **oculo'gyric** *a.* [Gr. γῦρ-ος ring, circle], relating to or involving the turning of the eyeball in its socket; *oculogyric crisis*, an attack involving the involuntary movement of the eyeball to an exaggerated position, usu. with the gaze directed upwards, and the maintenance of this position for a period; **oculomotor** (-'məʊtə(r)) *a.*, serving to move the eye; epithet of the third pair of cranial nerves, which supply most of the muscles of the eyeballs; *sb.* the oculomotor nerve; **oculonasal** (-'neɪzəl) *a.*, belonging or relating to the eye and the nose; **oculopalpebral** (-'pælpɪbrəl) *a.* [PALPEBRAL], to the eye and the eyelid; **oculozygomatic** (-zɪgəʊ'mætɪk) *a.*, to the eye and the zygoma.

1958 GERATHEWOHL & STALLINGS in *Jrnl. Aviation Med.* XXIX. 504 We predicted an apparent motion under conditions of reduced gravity which would be opposite in direction to the one observed at increased accelerative force. This hypothetical phenomenon, which may be observed best in the zero-gravity state, is called the *oculo-agravic illusion. **1961** H. G. ARMSTRONG *Aerospace Med.* xv. 232/1 The authors attribute the oculoagravic illusion to an otolith response and noted that the direction of apparent movement of the image was the opposite of that expected from the previous work.. on the oculogravic illusion. **1968** R. A. WEALE *From Sight to Light* vi. 117 The oculo-agravic illusion has been studied by means of the apparent movement of an after-image. **1892** *Syd. Soc. Lex.*, **Oculo-frontal.. O. rugæ*, the vertical furrows in the skin which extend upwards from the root of the nose. **1947** A. GRAYBIEL et al. in *Jrnl. Exper. Psychol.* XXXVII. 170 The *oculo-gravic illusion refers to the apparent displacement of an object in space which may be observed when the sensory receptors in the otolith organs are stimulated by an accelerative force which forms a resultant vector with the force of gravity. **1968** R. A. WEALE *From Sight to Light* vi. 116 The oculogravic phenomenon was accompanied by a downward turn of the eyes as acceleration increased and if no fixation light was provided. **1946** GRAYBIEL & HUPP in *Jrnl. Aviation Med.* XVII. 3/1 If.. visual cues are reduced by darkness, relatively weak stimulation of the labyrinth may cause strong illusions of apparent motion which may persist after all other sensations of rotation have disappeared. To this visual phenomenon, produced in this manner, we have applied the term '*oculo-gyral illusion'. **1953** R. A. MCFARLAND *Human Factors Air Transportation* iv. 192/1 The oculogyral illusion has its origin in the stimulation of the vestibular mechanism rather than in the eye alone. **1968** R. A. WEALE *From Sight to Light* vi. 115 The astronaut Glenn reported on the oculogyral effect that he experienced in orbit. **1922** STEDMAN *Med. Dict.* (ed. 7) 690 **Oculogyric*, ophthalmogyric, oculomotor. **1927** *Jrnl. Neurol. & Psychopath.* VIII. 27 Other features may.. be present, such as oculogyric crises or respiratory disorders. **1954** S. DUKE-ELDER *Parsons' Dis. Eye* (ed. 12) xxvii. 461 (*caption*) The cerebral ocular motor connections.... OGA, oculo-gyric area; OGT, oculo-gyric tract. **1973** DUKE-ELDER & WYBAR in S. Duke-Elder *Syst. Ophthalm.* VI. xii. 846 The most typical spasm of vertical movements is seen in oculogyric crises, a striking phenomenon wherein spasmodic deviations of the eyes occur in any direction but usually upwards and less frequently downwards, lasting from a few seconds to some hours. **1881** A. M. MARSHALL in *Jrnl. Microsc. Sc.* Jan. 78 The third or *oculomotor nerve. **1892** *Syd. Soc. Lex.*, **Oculo-nasal.* **1874** LAWSON *Dis. Eye* 69 The *oculopalpebral fold of mucous membrane which extends from the posterior edge of the cartilage on to the eye. **1875** WALTON *Dis. Eye* 847 The oculopalpebral and ocular portions. **1892** *Syd. Soc. Lex.*, **Oculozygomatic.*

‖**oculus** ('ɒkjʊləs). Pl. oculi (-aɪ). [L. *oculus* eye, used in technical and transf. senses.]

1. *Nat. Hist.* **a.** An eye; *spec.* a compound eye, as in insects (distinguished from *ocellus*). **b.** A spot resembling an eye; an ocellus.

1857 MAYNE *Expos. Lex.*, *Oculus, Anat., Med., Physiol.*, the eye or organ of vision.

2. *Bot.* A leaf-bud: = EYE *sb.* 10 a.

1727–41 CHAMBERS *Cycl.*, *Oculi, Eyes*, in botany, the gemmæ, or buds of a plant just putting forth. **1866** *Treas. Bot.* 802/1 *Oculus*, an eye, i.e. a leaf-bud.

3. *Arch.* **a.** 'Applied to the large circular window at the west end of a church, common in foreign churches, but not usual in England' (Parker *Goth. Arch.*). **b.** A round hollowed stone.

1848 RICKMAN *Architecture* p. xvii, The circular window .. in the centre of the west front.. was a common feature in the Norman style, and was called the 'Oculus', or eye of the building. **1892** T. F. T. DYER *Church Lore Glean.* 133 At Waverley Abbey, Surrey, in 1731, there were found in a stone oculus, two leaden dishes soldered together, containing a human heart, well preserved in pickle.

4. oculus Christi (= *Christ's eye*), mediæval Latin name of two plants: (*a*) Wild Clary or Sage, *Salvia Verbenaca*; (*b*) a Composite plant, *Inula Oculus-Christi*.

c **1440** *Promp. Parv.* 361/2 Oculus Christi, herbe, *hispia*. **1538** TURNER *Libellus, Verbena*,.. uerbena supina que uulgo uocatur Oculus christi. **1597** GERARDE *Herbal* II. cclv. 628 Wilde Clarie is called after the Latine name Oculus Christi, of his effect in helping the diseases of the eies. **1658** PHILLIPS, *Oculus Christi*, a certain herb very good for the eyes, otherwise called wild clary.

5. oculus mundi (= *eye of the world*), mediæval name of the variety of opal called HYDROPHANE.

1672 BOYLE *Virtues of Gems* Postscr. ii. Wks. 1772 III. 543 Though the *Oculus mundi* be reckon'd by Classic Authors among the rare Gems. **1794** SULLIVAN *View Nat.* I. 446 The *oculus mundi*, which has the property of becoming transparent in water, is nothing but an opaque, decomposed opale. **1796** KIRWAN *Elem. Min.* (ed. 2) I. 299 (Calcedony). This is the stone called *Oculus Mundi*.

6. Oculi Sunday, a name for the third Sunday in Lent, from the beginning of the introit (Ps. xxiv. [xxv.] 15), *Oculi mei semper ad Dominum*.

ocum, ocupie, ocupy(e, obs. forms of OAKUM, OCCUPY.

ocur, var. OCKER *Obs.*; obs. f. OCHRE.

ocydrome ('ɒsɪdrəʊm). *Ornith.* [ad. mod.L. *Ocydromus* (Wagler, 1830), ad. Gr. ὠκύδρομος swift-running.] A bird of the genus *Ocydromus* (family *Rallidæ*), natives of New Zealand, incapable of flight, but swift runners. So **ocydromine** (ɒ'sɪdrəmaɪn) *a.*, belonging to the subfamily *Ocydrominæ*, typified by the genus *Ocydromus*.

1895 *Pop. Sci. Monthly* Apr. 765 The 'ocydromes', curious birds with perfect wings yet incapable of flight. **1896** NEWTON *Dict. Birds* s.v. *Weka*, The chief interest attaching to the Ocydromes is their inability to use in flight the wings with which they are furnished, and hence an extreme probability of the form becoming wholly extinct in a short time.

†**'ocyme.** *Obs.* [ad. L. *ocimum*, a. Gr. ὤκιμον basil.] The plant Basil, *Ocymum basilicum*.

1621 BURTON *Anat. Mel.* II. iv. I. iii, To these [remedies for melancholy] I may add.. Ocyme, sweet Apples, Wine.

ocypode ('ɒsɪpəʊd), *a.* and *sb.* *Zool.* [ad. mod.L. *Ocypoda*, f. Gr. ὠκύπους, ὠκύποδ- swift-footed.]

a. *adj.* Belonging to the genus *Ocypoda* or family *Ocypodidæ* of crabs, characterized by long legs with which they run swiftly. **b.** *sb.* A crab of this genus or family; a sand-crab or racing crab. Also **ocypodan** (ɒ'sɪpədən) *a.* and *sb.*

1897 *19th Cent.* Aug. 301 The red Ocypode Crab.

od[1], **'od** (ɒd). Also odd. A minced form of *God* (GOD *sb.* 13, 14, GAD *sb.*[5]), which came into vogue about 1600, when, to avoid the overt profanation of sacred names, many minced and disguised equivalents became prevalent. Very frequent in 17th and early 18th c.; now *arch.* and *dial.*

1. Used interjectionally, by way of asseveration: cf. GAD *sb.*[5] 2, GOD *sb.* 13. Still *dial.* (with little or no consciousness of its origin).

1695 CONGREVE *Love for L.* III. iv, Odso, my son Ben come? Odd, I'm glad on't: Where is he? *Ibid.* v. ii, Odd! I have warm blood about me yet. **1775** SHERIDAN *Rivals* I. i, Odd! Sir Anthony will stare! *c* **1817** HOGG *Tales & Sk.* VI. 65 But od, you see, I couldna hae injured a hair of the lovely creature's head. **1824** SCOTT *Redgauntlet* Let. x, Od, ye are a clever birkie! *Mod. Sc.* (Roxb.), Od, man, but it's a queer story.

b. In imprecations and exclamatory phrases, as *od rabbit it, od rat it* (*'drat it*, cf. DRAT), *od save's*, etc. Still common dialectally from Cumbria to I. of Wight, Kent, and Devon.

1749 FIELDING *Tom Jones* XVI. ii, Odrabbit it. *Ibid.* XVII. iii, When we imagined we had a fox to deal with, od-rat it, it turns out to be a badger. **1775** SHERIDAN *Rivals* I. i, Odd rabbit it! when the fashion had got foot on the Bar, I guess'd 'twould mount to the Box! **1803** TANNAHILL *Soldier's Ret.* 27 Oddsaffs! my heart neer did wallop cadgier. **1812** H. & J. SMITH *Rej. Addr.* ix. *The Burning*, What are they fear'd on? fools! 'od rot 'em! **1869** *Lonsdale Gloss.*, *Od swinge*, a rustic oath. *'Od drat it, 'Od rabbet it, 'Od rot it, 'Od wite it*, a species of mild imprecation. **1881** *I. of W. Gloss.*, *Odd rot it*, an exclamation. **1887** *Kent Gloss.*, *'Od rabbit it.* **1888** *Berksh. Gloss.*, *Odd drat-ut*, an angry expression.

2. The possessive of *'od's* (*od's*, *odds*, also ADS, UDS) occurs like *God's*, *Gad's*, in many asseverative or exclamatory formulæ. See GOD 14 a, b, c, GAD[5] 3.

The origin of *'od's* being forgotten, it was written *ods*, *odds*, or run together with the following word, as *ods-*, *odz-*. Among the phrases (now mostly *obs.*, *arch.*, or *dial.*) are ***'od's blood, body, bones, death, feet, flesh, foot, life, mercy, truth, vengeance, blessed will, wounds***, etc.; also with diminutives and perversions of words, as ***od's bob, bobs, bodikins, bud*** (= *blood*), ***fish***, ***'odslid, odd's lifelings, odsnigs, odsnouns, odsoons*** (= *wounds*), ***od's-pittikins, pittkins, pitlikins*** (*pity*), ***od's wucks, odzooks*** (= *hooks*), ***-zookers*** (*-swookers*), ***od zounds*** (= *wounds*), etc.; also ludicrously, ***'od's haricots, kilderkins***, etc. (Cf. Bob Acres' fancy oaths in Sheridan *Rivals* II. i.)

1856 BOKER *Poems* (1857) II. 66 *'Ods blood! I hate them! **1748** SMOLLETT *Rod. Rand.* (Tauchn. 1845) 14 *Odds bob! I'd desire no better news. **1621** FLETCHER *Wild-goose Ch.* I. iii, Hark ye, hark ye! *Ods-bobs, you are angry, lady. **1800** MRS. HERVEY *Mourtray Fam.* I. 288 Odds bobs! how you talk! **1709** STEELE *Tatler* No. 137 ¶2 *Odsbodikins, you do not say right. **1733** FIELDING *Don Quix. in Eng.* II. viii, As sure as a gun—this is he—Odsbodlikins! **18..** H. AINSWORTH *Rookwood* I. ix, 'Odsbodikins!' exclaimed Titus, 'a noble reward!' *a* **1895** LD. C. E. PAGET *Autobiog.* iv. (1896) 99 '*Odds bones!' said I, 'don't they mean to give any quarter, then?' **1695** CONGREVE *Love for L.* II. v, *Odsbud, I would my Son were an Egyptian Mummy for thy sake. **1889** DOYLE *Micah Clarke* 205 Od's bud, man, you have lived two centuries too late. **1724** SWIFT *Quiet Life*, Thy wife has dev'lish whims; *Ods-buds, why don't you break her limbs? **1681** OTWAY *Soldier's Fort.* I. i, *Odds fish I have a peep-Hole for thee. **1823** SCOTT *Peveril* xlix, 'Oddsfish', said the King, 'the light begins to break in on me'. **1715** VANBRUGH *Country Ho.* II. Wks. (Rtldg.) 465/2 *Odsflesh! we shall break all the inns in the country. **1667** DK. NEWCASTLE & DRYDEN *Sir Martin Mar-all* v. i, *Ods foot, sir, there are some bastards.. that are as well worthy to marry her, as any man. **1809** MALKIN *Gil Blas* x. x. ¶33 *Ods haricots and cutlets! thought I. **1694** MOTTEUX *Rabelais* IV. xxiii. (1737) 99 *Odskilderkins, it seems.. we are within two Fingers breadth of Damnation. **1742** YARROW *Love at First Sight* 81 *'Odslid that was ill Luck indeed. *c* **1718** PRIOR *Better Answer* 12 *Odds life! must one swear to the truth of a song? **1601** SHAKS. *Twel. N.* v. i. 187 *Odd's lifelings, heere he is. *a* **1643** CARTWRIGHT *Ordinary* II. iv. in Hazl. *Dodsley* XII. 249 *'Odsnigs, I guess'd so. **1794** WOLCOTT (P. Pindar) *Duck of Richmond's Dog* Wks. 1812 III. 238 And lifted hands.. and cried Odsnigs! **1598** SHAKS. *Merry W.* IV. i. 25 *E.* How many Numbers is in Nownes? *W.* Two. *Q.*.. I thought there had bin one Number more, because they say *od's-Nownes. **1694** MOTTEUX *Rabelais* v. viii. (1737) 30 *Odsoons, said Æditius. **1889** DOYLE *Micah Clarke* 114 Od's 'oons, I drank deep last Night. **1611** SHAKS. *Cymb.* IV. ii. 293 *'Ods pittikins: can it be sixe mile yet? **1826** HOR. SMITH *Tor Hill* (1838) I. 173 'Ods pittikins! my master', cried Sib. **1831** PEACOCK *Crotchet Castle* vii. (1887) 93 *Od's vengeance, sir, some Aspasia and any other Athenian name of the same sort of person you like. **1598** SHAKS. *Merry W.* I. i. 273 *Od's plessed-wil: I will not be absence at the grace. **1728** VANBR. & CIB. *Prov. Husb.* I. i, Were Measter but hawf the Mon that I am—*Ods wookers! **1889** DOYLE *Micah Clarke* 394 *Od's wounds! How many are yours? **1785** *Span. Rivals* 9 *Odd's wucks and tar! no, no, bar snaps there. **1695** CONGREVE *Love for L.* v. ii, *Odzooks I'm a young Man. **1749** FIELDING *Tom*

Jones xviii. xii, *Odzookers!..I will go with thee. **1835** Hood *Dead Robbery* iv, *Odd zounds! Ten pounds, How sweet it sounds.

b. In ***od's me, od's my life, od's my will***, and the simple ***'od's, odds***, originating from the foregoing through some confusion; or perhaps (as has been suggested) *'s* is for *save*, but no fuller form appears. Cf. GOD 14 c.

1598 Shaks. *Merry W.* I. iv. 64 Od's-me: *que ay ie oublie.* **1600** —— *A.Y.L.* III. v. 43 'Ods my little life, I thinke she meanes to tangle my eies too. *Ibid.* IV. iii. 17 'Od's my will, Her loue is not the Hare that I doe hunt. **1632** Brome *North. Lasse* II. vi. Wks. 1873 III. 42 Ods me I must go see her. **1700** Congreve *Way of World* III. v, Odds my life, I'll have him murdered! **1710** *Mischief of Prej.* 3 Odds He's a brave Man indeed. **1763** Foote *Mayor of G.* II. Wks. 1799 I. 179 Odds me, brother Bruin, can you tell what is become of my wife? **1823** Scott *Peveril* iii, Odds-my-life, madam..mine errand can speak for itself.

od[2] (ɒd, əʊd). [Arbitrary term: see quot. 1850.] A hypothetical force held by Baron von Reichenbach (1788–1869) to pervade all nature, manifesting itself in certain persons of sensitive temperament (streaming from their finger-tips), and exhibited especially by magnets, crystals, heat, light, and chemical action; it has been held to explain the phenomena of mesmerism and animal magnetism. Also *attrib.* as *od force*, etc. (Cf. ODYLE.)

1850 Ashburner tr. *Reichenbach's Dynamics* 224, I will take the liberty to propose the short word *Od* for the force which we are engaged in examining. Every one will admit it to be desirable that a unisyllabic word beginning with a vowel should be selected..for the sake of convenient conjunction in the manifold compound words. **1851** H. Mayo *Pop. Superst.* (ed. 2) 13 To his new force..Von Reichenbach..gave the arbitrary but convenient name of Od, or the Od force. **1856** Mrs. Browning *Aur. Leigh* VII. 295 That od-force of German Reichenbach Which still from female finger-tips burns blue. **1885** H. S. Olcott *Theosophy* 212 So much of light is let into the old domain of Church 'miracles' by mesmerism and the Od discovery.

b. Forming the second element in various derivatives, as *biod* the 'od' of animal life, *chymod* chemical 'od', *crystallod* the 'od' of crystallization, *elod* electric 'od', *heliod* the 'od' of the sun, *magnetod* magnetic 'od', *pantod* 'od' in general, *selenod* or *artemod* lunar 'od', *thermod* heat 'od'.

1850 Ashburner tr. *Reichenbach's Dynamics* 224 Instead of saying, 'the Od derived from crystallization', we may name this product crystallod.

od, ME. form of AD *Obs.*, funeral pyre.

od, obs. form of ODD, WOOD.

‖**oda** ('əʊdə). [a. Turk *ōṭah, ōdah* chamber, hall.] A chamber or room in a harem; *transf.* the inmates of such a room.

1625 Purchas *Pilgrims* II. IX. 1592 They haue Roomes, which the Turkes call Oda's, but we may more properly (in regard of the vse they are put vnto) call them Schooles. **1684** J. Phillips tr. *Tavernier's Grd. Seignor's Serag.* 2 Four several Chambers, called Oda's, which are as it were four Forms, where they learn..whatever is convenient for young persons. **1822** Byron *Juan* VI. lxxi, Upstarted all The Oda, in a general commotion. **1886** Burton *Arab. Nts.* (abr. ed.) I. 252 The women made ready sweetmeats..and distributed them among all the Odahs of the Harem.

odacine ('ɒdəsaɪn). *Zool.* [f. mod.L. *Odacinæ* pl., f. *Odax* a genus of fishes, ad. Gr. ὀδάξ adv. 'by biting with the teeth'.] Of or related to the genus *Odax* of labroid fishes.

odæum, obs. variant of ODEUM.

odal ('əʊdəl), *sb.* (*a.*) See also UDAL. [a. ON. *óðal* property held by inheritance (Norw. *odal* sb., Sw. *odal*, Da. *odel* now adj. and in comb.) = OHG. *uodal*, also *uodil*, OS. *ôðil*, OE. *œ̄ðel*, *ēðel*, f. root *að*, *ôð*, whence also OHG. *adal*, Ger. *adel* noble descent, OHG. *ędili*, Ger. *edel*, OE. *æðele*, *eðele* noble.] Land held in absolute ownership without service or acknowledgement of any superior, as among the early Teutonic peoples; *esp.* such an estate among the Scandinavian peoples, or in Orkney and Shetland (where the usual form of the word is UDAL, q.v.). Chiefly *attrib.* and in *Comb.*, as *odal-born* adj., *odal-land*, *odal-right*.

In reference to Norway, the Da. form *odel* is often retained.

[**1755** tr. *Pontoppidan's Nat. Hist. Norway* 289 Every freeholder in Norway has vanity enough to think himself as good as noble by Odel, or right of inheritance.] **1839** Keightley *Hist. Eng.* I. 77 The most probable opinion respecting the Folcland, seems to be that which regards it as the same with the Odal-land of Scandinavia. **1847** I. A. Blackwell *Mallet's North. Antiq.* 289 Not retainers, but Odal-born freemen. **1860** D. Balfour (*title*) Odal Rights and Feudal Wrongs, a Memorial for Orkney. **1874** Stubbs *Const. Hist.* I. iii. §24. 52 The homestead of the original settler..with the share of arable and appurtenant common rights, bore among the northern nations the name of Odal, or Edhel. [**1886** J. Corbett *Fall of Asgard* I. 93 'A fair odel you have here, Heidrek', said Gudrun. *Ibid.* 136 Olaf Haroldsson..deems himself, in pure odel-right, heir to Tryggvason's kingdom.]

‖**odalisque** ('əʊdəlɪsk). Also 7 -ische, 8–9 -isc, 9 -isk. [a. F. *odalisque* (1664 in Hatz.-Darm.), corrupt. Turk. *ōdaliq*, f. *ōdah* ODA + *-liq*, *-lik* expressing function.] *Hist.* A female slave or concubine in an Eastern harem, esp. in the seraglio of the Sultan of Turkey. Also *transf.* and *fig.*

1681 Blount *Glossogr.*, *Odalisque*, a Slave. **1696** tr. *Du Mont's Voy. Levant* xxi. 270 He had seen and spoken with one of Mahomet the Fourth's Odalisches. **1798** Sotheby tr. *Wieland's Oberon* (1826) II. 170 A feast..In honour of fair Zoradone prepar'd, Where every odalisc the labour shar'd. **1798** [see *domestic slave* s.v. DOMESTIC *a.* 7]. **1823** Byron *Don Juan* VI. xxix, He went forth with the lovely Odalisques. **1834** R. H. Barham *Let.* 26 June (1870) I. v. 239 My seraglio of twelve elderly odalisques certainly does, now and then, furnish me with a job in the way of composing differences which will occasionally arise even in their well-regulated minds. **1874** O'Shaughnessy *Music & Moonlight* 28 An Odalisc, unseen, Splendidly couched on piled-up cushions green. **1903** G. B. Shaw *Let.* 8 May (1972) II. 322 What you want is a repertory of plays which you can carry on your own shoulders, and in which you cannot come into competition with the young odalisques of the west end. *a* **1915** Joyce *Giacomo Joyce* (1968) 14 She leans back against the pillowed wall: odalisque-featured in the luxurious obscurity. **1926** A. Bennett *Lord Raingo* I. v. 21 Withal she was no odalisque. She tried to improve herself, to make herself interesting to him. **1938** *Times* 18 Feb. 19/1 Evening gowns include such opposite styles as the odalisque type, with a transparent dancing skirt in black over a gown in gold lamé. **1967** *Listener* 16 Mar. 366/1 Is the creation of a cubist odalisque 'of consequence', and the devoutly humble production of an ikon not?

odaller ('əʊdələ(r)). [f. ODAL + -ER[1].] A free possessor by odal tenure: = UDALLER.

1860 D. Balfour *Odal Rights* 13 The coming shadow of the first feudal grant which menaced the freedom of their Odal soil, roused the long-suffering Odallers into rebellion. **1872** E. W. Robertson *Hist. Ess.* Introd. 31 Every member of the free community was an Ætheling, Adaling or Odaller. **1874** Stubbs *Const. Hist.* I. v. 100 *note*, In the trithing he sees the threefold division of the land allotted to the Norse odallers.

†**'odam.** *Obs.* Forms: 1–3 **áðum**, 3 **oðem, oðom**, 4 **odame**. [OE. *áðum* = OFris. *âthom*, OHG. *eidum*, *eidam* (MHG. *eidem*, obs. G. *eidam*, now dial. *êdm*, *êtn*, *êdn*):—OTeut. **aiþmo-z*: possibly related to **aiþo-z*, OHG. *eid*, OE. *áð*, OATH.] A son-in-law.

c **1000** Ælfric *Gen.* xix. 12 Hæfst þu suna oþþe dohtra on þisre byriȝ oþþe aþum? *c* **1200** *Trin. Coll. Hom.* 165 Nis þe gist siker of þe husebonde..Ne þe aldefader of hi[s] oðem. *c* **1205** Lay. 3619 Leir..gret Aganippum: þat was his leue aðum [*c* **1275** oþom]. *Ibid.* 23106 Ich wulle mid me leden: Lot mine oðem. **1297** R. Glouc. (Rolls) 3768 Lot þat was is oþom þulke kinges neueu was. **13..** *K. Alis.* 2081 Octiatus, Daries' odame, After theose ostes he cam.

odd (ɒd), *a.* (*sb.*) and *adv.* Forms: 4–6 **ode**, 4–7 **odde**, **od**, (4 **hod**, 5 *Sc.* **oyd**), 5– **odd**. [ME. *odde*, a. ON. *odda-* in comb. in *odda-maðr* (acc. *odda-mann*) third man, odd man, who gives the casting vote, *odda-tala* odd number, in which *odda-* is genitive or comb. form of *oddi* 'point, angle, triangle', whence 'third or odd number'. The root of *oddi*:—**ozdon-* is also that of *oddr* point, spot, place, OHG. *ort* angle, point, place, OS., OFris. *ord*, OE. *ord* point, tip, beginning, origin:—OTeut. **ozdoz*; but none of the other languages have developed from 'point' the notion of 'third or odd number'.

The sense seems to have been extended from the third or unpaired member of a group of three, to any single or unpaired member of a group, and from 3 as the primary 'odd number', to all numbers containing an unpaired unit. But this development was anterior to English use as recorded in documents.]

A. *adj.* **I.** With reference to number.

1. Of an individual: That is one in addition to a pair, or remaining over after distribution or division into pairs; constituting a unit in excess of an even number.

odd man [ON. *oddamaðr*], the third (fifth, etc.) man in a body of arbitrators, a committee, etc., who, in case of a division of opinion, may give the casting vote; a thirds-man, an umpire. ***odd trick***, in whist, the thirteenth trick, won by one side after each side has won six.

13.. *E.E. Allit. P.* B. 505 Noe of vche honest kynde nem out an odde & heuened vp an auter & halȝed hit fayre. **1398** Trevisa *Barth. De P.R.* v. lx. (Add. MS. 27944), And synowes beþ acounted in alle too & þritty peyre & one odde synowe. **1487–8** *Burgh Rec. Prestwick* 21 Jan. (1834) 32 Thai batht tuk Michel Masoun of Aire the oyd man for thaim batht. **1530** Tindale *Pract. Prelates* Wks. (Parker Soc.) II. 270 That six lords of Almany..with the King of Bohemia the seventh, to be the the odd man and umpire, should choose him for ever. **1567** Maplet *Gr. Forest* 68 b, They flie two a breast, and the fift or odde Crane..flieth all alone before. **1581** *Sc. Acts Jas. VI* (1814) III. 231/1 Quharethrow his hines as odman and owrisman commonlie chosin be bath the saidis partijs..may gif finall decisioun. *a* **1654** Selden *Table-t.* (Arb.) 41 They talk (but blasphemously enough) that the Holy Ghost is President of their General-Councils, when the truth is, the odd man is still the Holy-Ghost. **1710** *Brit. Apollo* II. No. 101. 2/1 The Party..got..the Odd Trick. **1837** Lytton *E. Maltrav.* 239 Three to one now on the odd trick. **1888** Bryce *Amer. Commw.* I. v. 62 This fifth was the odd man whose casting vote would turn the scale. **1900** Foster *Bridge* 55 A player should always go over when he has any chance for the odd trick.

2. a. Of a number: Having one left over as remainder when divided by two; opposed to *even*.

c **1375** *Sc. Leg. Saints* xii. (*Mathias*) 308 Sa to be in nowmyre ode, It wes nocht til þai dwelte with god; for-thy he wald þai ware twelfe ewyn. *c* **1430** *Art of Nombrynge* (E.E.T.S.) 15 Compt the nombre of the figures, and wete yf it be ode or even. **1542** Recorde *Gr. Artes* (1575) 170 There is no iuste halfe of any odde number. **1598** Shaks. *Merry W.* v. i. 3 This is the third time: I hope good lucke lies in odde numbers. **1698** Fryer *Acc. E. India & P.* 303 Three, Seven, or Nine Times; as if God delighted in an Odd Number. **1743** Emerson *Fluxions* 80, *m* is the half of any positive odd Number. **1825** J. Nicholson *Operat. Mechanic* 516 It [a wheel] in general contains an odd number of teeth.

b. Numbered with or known by such a number. (The form of expression in quot. 1575 is obs.; we should now say 'an odd number of dog's hairs'.)

1398 Trevisa *Barth. De P.R.* IX. iv. (MS. Bodl.) lf. 91 b/1 An euen monþe ansuereþ to an odde moneþ and an odde moneþ to an euen monþe. **1575** Turberv. *Venerie* 230 Some haue vsed in times past, to put a dogges haires odde into an Ash or Ceruisetree. **1674** N. Fairfax *Bulk & Selv.* 145 If you make two such bodies..to run a tilt upon such a line of odd leastings. **1882** Minchin *Unipl. Kinemat.* 25 If the direction-angle of one equals that of the other increased by any odd multiple of π. **1955** J. A. Wheeler in W. Pauli *Niels Bohr* 166 The spontaneous fission rates of nuclei of odd mass number are observed to be slower than the rates for the corresponding even nuclei. **1966** *Mathematical Rev.* XXXI. 36/1 Matrices *M* of even order behave somewhat differently from those of odd order. **1970** O. Dopping *Computers & Data Processing* ii. 50 The most common form of redundancy check is the parity check, in which the value of a check bit is determined by the parity (odd or even) of the number of ones in the unit to be checked.

c. †***even and odd***, all included, without exception, one and all; † ***even nor odd***, none at all. †***for odd or even***, on any account; ***for odd nor for even***, on no account. †***for even or odd***: see EVEN *a.* 15 c. ***evenly odd, oddly odd***: see quots.

c **1375** *Sc. Leg. Saints* x. (*Mathou*) 382 How dar þu þane for hod or ewyn fra þi lorde tak hyre to þe? *c* **1440** *Syr Gowther* 285 Speke no word, even ne odde. *c* **1440**, **1460**, **1485** [see EVEN *a.* 15 c]. **1570** Billingsley *Euclid* VII. def. 9. 185 A number euenly odde..is that which an euen number measureth by an odde number. *Ibid.* def. 10. 185 b, A number odly odde is that, which an odde number doth measure by an odde number. **1796** Hutton *Math. Dict.* I. 450/2 *Evenly Odd Number.*

d. ***odd and*** (***or***) ***even*** (dial. ***odds or evens***): a game of chance = *even or odd* (see EVEN *a.* 15 d).

[**1552** Huloet, Euen or odde, *par*, *impar*, a game much vsed now a dayes amonge chyldren.] **1836** E. Howard *R. Reefer* xii, Playing at odd-and-even for nuts. **1840** Dickens *Barn. Rudge* xxxvii, They presently fell to pitch and toss, chuckfarthing, odd or even. **1882** *Lanc. Gloss.*, *Odd-or-even*, a child's game, played by holding in the closed hand one or two small articles, the opposing player having to guess the number.

e. *absol.* as *sb.* ***the odd***, uneven number.

1589 Puttenham *Eng. Poesie* II. iii[i.] (Arb.) 85 Your ordinarie rimers vse very much their measures in the odde as nine and eleuen. *Ibid.* 86 This sort of composition in the odde I like not. **1875** Jowett *Plato* (ed. 2) I. 328 Just as the odd is a part of number, and number is a more extended notion than the odd.

f. *Physics.* Having odd parity.

1930 *Physical Rev.* XXXVI. 617 In the case of homonuclear molecules..any electron state may be either 'odd' or even. An electron state of a homonuclear molecule is said to be odd if the electronic factor of 4 changes sign on reflection in the midpoint of the line joining the nuclei, even, if it does not change sign. [*Note*] The use of 'odd' and 'even' in this sense was introduced by Hund... The words..are applied by Kronig, in a sense different from that used by Hund, to the *complete* 4 function of any molecule, homonuclear or heteronuclear. **1940** *Ibid.* LVIII. 104/1 The nearest one could come..would be to assume for the correct wave function a linear combination of two wave functions... These would correspond, respectively, to an even and odd state of the core. **1961** *Encycl. Dict. Physics* II. 786/2 Homonuclear molecules..can have even (*g*) orbitals (*g* for 'gerade') and odd (*u*) orbitals (*u* for 'ungerade') which are, respectively, symmetric and antisymmetric with respect to interchange of the nuclei.

3. Used in numeration to denote a remainder or numerical surplus over and above a 'round number' (as of units over tens, dozens, or scores); and thus becoming virtually an indefinite cardinal number of lower denomination than the round number named.

a. in phr. ***and odd*** preceding the sb. qualified.

13.. *E.E. Allit. P.* B. 426 Of þe lenþe of Noe lyf to lay a lel date, Þe sex hundreth of his age & none odde ȝerez. *a* **1548** Hall *Chron., Hen. VI*, 166 b, Had contynued in the English possession, from the yere of our Lord .M. lv. which is .iii. C. and od yeres. **1584** R. Scot *Discov. Witchcr.* III. v. (1886) 36 Bodin confirmeth them with an hundred and odd lies. **1688** *Lond. Gaz.* No. 2356/4 With 200 and odd Pounds. **1748** *Anson's Voy.* II. i. 109 Two hundred and odd men. **1865** M. Arnold *Ess. Crit.* i. 29 Go into ecstasies over the eighty and odd pigeons.

b. ***and odd***, following the sb. *arch.* or *Obs.*

1399 Langl. *Rich. Redeles* Prol. 68 They shall [fynde] ffele ffawtis, ffoure score and odde. *c* **1460** *Towneley Myst.* iii. 57 Sex hundreth yeris & od haue I,..In erth,..liffyd. *a* **1548** Hall *Chron., Hen. VIII*, 120 The nomber whiche departed..were..five hundreth horsemen and odde wel and warlike. **1634** Sir T. Herbert *Trav.* 134 Distant sixtie miles and odde. **1642** Rogers *Naaman* 10 Full one thousand six hundred years and odde.

c. without *and* (chiefly after tens).

1593 SHAKS. *Rich. III*, IV. i. 96 Eightie odde yeeres of sorrow haue I seene. **1660** BOYLE *New Exp. Phys. Mech.* xxv. 202 Forty odde, if not fifty great bubbles of Air. **1703** MARLBOROUGH *Lett. & Disp.* (1845) I. 170 We have fifty odd of our troops taken. **1793** JEFFERSON *Writ.* (1859) IV. 75 Fleeced of seventy odd dollars. **1885** *Law Times* LXXIX. 159/1 The 1300 odd pages..contain much of extreme value.

d. *ellipt.* denoting age, the word 'years' being understood. *colloq.*

1845 HOOD *Faithless Sally Brown* xvii, His death, which happen'd in his berth, At forty-odd befell. **1862** THACKERAY *Wks.* (1872) X. 223 At sixty odd, love, most of the ladies of thy orient race have lost the bloom of youth.

4. a. Used to denote a surplus over a definite sum, or a remainder of lower denomination of money, weight, or measure.

1382 *Pol. Poems* (Rolls) I. 268 Of twelve monethes me wanted one, And odde days nyen or ten. **1613** PURCHAS *Pilgrimage* (1614) 806 The Mexicans divided the yeare into eighteene moneths, ascribing to each twentie dayes, so that the five odde dayes were excluded. **1722** DE FOE *Col. Jack* (1840) 90 It was 22*s.* 6½*d.*; 21*s.* I had been to fetch, and the odd money was my own before. **1873** HALE *In His Name* i. 1 He would relax his hold on the odd sols and deniers.

†b. *and odd* or *odd* (denoting an indefinite number) qualifying a sb. of lower denomination. *Obs.* or *arch.*

a **1548** HALL *Chron., Hen. IV*, 32 b, When he had reigned .xiii. yeres, v. monthes and odde daies. **1603** PETOWE *Stanzas* in Farr *S.P. Jas. I* (1848), Three thousand and od hundred clowds appere. **1634** SIR T. HERBERT *Trav.* 43 It is in the latitude of twenty two degrees, odde minutes north. **1714** *Lond. Gaz.* No. 5213/4, 11 Foot odd Inches in the Hold. **1813** SIR R. WILSON *Priv. Diary* I. 434 Thirty-eight thousand odd hundred infantry, two thousand odd hundred cavalry.

†c. *(and) odd money*, denoting a surplus sum of lower denomination. *Obs.*

1472 JOHN PASTON in *P. Lett.* III. 48 Your byll a lone drawyth iiij mark and ode monye. **1550** EDW. VI *Jrnl.* Rem. (Roxb.) 267 The det of thirty thousand pound and ode money was put over an yere. **1689** WOOD *Life* 8 June (O.H.S.) III. 304 [They] broke as many windows as came to 7*li.* and od money. **1742** RICHARDSON *Pamela* III. 93 Pay the Thirty-five Pounds odd Money..; and the remaining Four Pounds odd will be a little Fund..towards the Childrens Schooling.

d. A surplus of lower denomination of money, weight, or measure (as in b and c) is now expressed simply by adding *odd* or *odds*.

1742 [see c]. **1835** MARRYAT *Jac. Faithf.* ii, The proceeds of the exhibition and sale amounted to 47*l.* odd. **1892** *Law Times Rep.* LXVII. 52/2 It was orally agreed..that the amount of such costs should be taken at 63*l.* odd. **1930** *Times* 25 Mar. 24/1 The balance-sheet shows a loan from the bankers of the company as at December 31 of £118,413 odds.

5. *Math.* Of a function of one variable: having the property that changing the sign of the argument changes the sign, but not the magnitude, of the function (i.e. $f(-x) = -f(x)$).

1886 A. G. GREENHILL *Differential & Integral Calculus* ii. 80 fx is an odd function, so that f(−x) = −fx. **1899** F. G. TAYLOR *Introd. Differential & Integral Calculus* xi. 106 A function of *x* is said to be even when it is not altered..on changing *x* into −*x*; it is said to be odd when it is altered in sign, but not in magnitude. **1946** *Ann. Computation Lab. Harvard Univ.* I. 17 This feature is especially valuable when dealing with the interpolation of odd functions. **1969** A. M. HOWATSON *Princ. Appl. Electricity* iv. 74 Some waveforms ..can be represented either by an even or by an odd function according to the choice of origin of θ. Others can be even but not odd..or odd but not even.

II. Transferred senses.

6. That exists or stands alone; single, sole, solitary, singular. Now only *dial.* **†** *by odd*, separately, by itself, alone (*obs.*). **†** *all and odd*, all and each, one and all (*obs.*). *an odd one* (*north. dial.*) a single one, one only.

c **1330** R. BRUNNE *Chron. Wace* (Rolls) 4614 Long pyles.. dide þey make; ffaste yn Temese dide þey hem stake,.. Ageyn þe schipes stod ilkon od. *c* **1375** *Sc. Leg. Saints* xx. (*Blasius*) 140 Say nocht of godis, bot of god, Fore þat word afferis ay be ode. *c* **1510** MORE *Picus* Wks. 28 As he [God] in soueraine dignitie is odde, So will he in loue no parting felowes haue. **1556** LAUDER *Tractate* 165 Cause ȝour prechours, all and od, Trewlie sett furth the wourd of God. **1869** *Lonsdale Gloss.*, *Odd*, adj. single. **1876** *Mid. Yorks. Gloss.*, *Odd-house*, a single dwelling, amid-land, always gets this name. **1877** *N.W. Linc. Gloss.*, *Odd*,..single, lonely... 'Odd kitlin, puppy, pig, chicken, stocking' &c. **1888** *Sheffield Gl.*, *Odd*, lonely. 'An *odd* house', 'an *odd* place'.

†7. Singular in valour, worth, merit, or eminence; unique, remarkable; distinguished, famous, renowned; rare, choice. *Obs.* (Compared *odder*, *oddest*.)

c **1400** *Destr. Troy* 4097 With Eleuon od shippes abill to werre. *Ibid.* 4165 So od men in armys, & egur to fight. *a* **1400–50** *Alexander* 189 Ane of þe oddist Emperours of þe werde. *Ibid.* 2121 Þe honouris of þat odd clerke Homore þe grete. *Ibid.* 3783 Kyng porrus..eft had assemblid Anoþire ost of odmen him eft on to ride. *a* **1568** ASCHAM *Scholem.* II. (Arb.) 101 For our tyme, the odde man to performe all three perfitlie..is, in my poore opinion, *Iohannes Sturmius.* **1570** DEE *Math. Pref.* 20 A Gentleman (which..for skill in the Mathematicall Sciences and Languages is the Od man of this land). **1577–87** HOLINSHED *Chron.* II. 38/2 He would.. haue beene..knowne for as od a gentleman..as anie in the English pale of Ireland. **1592** MONTGOMERIE *Misc. Poems* lv. 3 Good Robert Scot..Vho, vhill thou livd, for honestie wes od. **1611** COTGR., *Rebras, Vn entendement à double rebras*, an odde head, a notable wit, a terrible pate. *a* **1661** FULLER *Worthies, Wales* (1662) 34 He was an Odde man indeed, for all the Popish party could not match him with his equal in Learning and Religion. **1698** FRYER *Acc. E. India & P.* 249 Where were many Neat Tombs; but the Oddest, because New, was one beset with Young Cypress Trees.

†8. a. Not even, accordant, or conformable; uneven, unequal, discrepant, diverse, different. *Obs.*

1390 GOWER *Conf.* III. 138 The word under the coupe of hevene Set every thing or odde or evene. **1542** UDALL *Erasm. Apoph.* 162 b, How ferre odde those persones are from the nature of this prince. **1551** HADDON *Exh. Repent.* in Furnivall *Ballads* I. 330 Lorde! that their lyves were nothing od Vnto their sayenge that they tell! **1556** ROBINSON tr. *More's Utopia* (ed. 2) Transl. to Rdr., The successe and our intente proue thinges farre odde. **1596** ROYDON *Elegy on Sidney's Astrophel* v, Upon the branches of those trees, The airie-winged people sat, Distinguished in od degrees, One sort is this, another that.

b. Not even or 'square', having a balance on the wrong side. *to be odd with*, to fail of being 'even' or 'quits' with. Cf. EVEN *a.* 10, 10 c. *Obs.*

1450–70 *Golagros & Gaw.* 734 Than said bernys bald,.. We sal evin that is od, or end in the pane. *a* **1529** SKELTON *Agst. Garnesche* Wks. 1843 I. 120, I caste me nat to be od With neythyr of yow tewyne.

c. At variance or strife; at odds (*with*). *rare. Obs.*

1562 HEYWOOD *Prov. & Epigr.* 191 Thrift and thou art od. **1606** SHAKS. *Tr. & Cr.* IV. v. 265 The generall state I feare, Can scarce intreat you to be odde with him.

9. a. Extraneous or additional to what is reckoned or taken into account; hence, That is not, or cannot be, reckoned, included, or co-ordinated with other things; not belonging to any particular total, set, or group; not forming part of a regular series; unconnected; irregular; casual. Also, in weakened sense, merely conveying a notion of indefiniteness or fortuity, esp. with indef. adjs., as *some odd* (= 'some or other'), *any odd* (= 'any chance', 'any stray'). *odd ends, odd things*, odds and ends (see ODDS *sb.* 7).

a **1450** MYRC 198 Loke also they make non odde weddynge. *a* **1500** *MS. Ashmole* 344 (Bodl.) lf. 22 Thus shalt thou bryng in þi odde drawghtes in cas þu be a drawght behynde. **1567** HARMAN *Caveat* 62 There sekinge aboute for odde endes, [he] at length founde a lytle whystell of syluer. **1577** HARRISON *England* II. vi. (1877) I. 150 Bridales, purifications of women, and such od meetings. **1577** tr. *Bullinger's Decades* (1592) 286 Vnhoneste sparing of euerie odd halfe-penie. **1594** SHAKS. *Rich. III*, I. iii. 337 Odde old [*Qo.* (1597) old odde] ends, stolne forth of holy writ. **1656** COWLEY *Pindar. Odes, Brutus* v, When we see perish thus by odd Events, Ill men, and wretched Accidents, The best Cause. *a* **1700** PLUME *Life Bp. Hacket* (1865) 137 He often said..many years before his death, that some odd October would part us. **1707** W. FUNNELL *Voy. round World* 33 This second Prize, after we had taken out a few odd Things, was ..dismist. **1749** FIELDING *Tom Jones* XII. ix. *heading*, Containing little more than a few odd observations. **1821** CLARE *Vill. Minstr.* I. 131 Odd rain-drops damp'd his face. **1871** C. GIBBON *Lack of Gold* i, They had come to see what odd pence they could pick up. **1883** *Almondbury Gloss.* s.v., An *odd child* is an illegitimate child. **1930** *Daily Tel.* 1 Dec. 9/3 The 'odd' heavy tweed skirt that is worn in the English country can be left behind. **1949** D. M. DAVIN *Roads from Home* III. i. 210 He'd still be able to save the odd quid. **1959** *Times Lit. Suppl.* 7 Aug. p. ix/4 An endearing wizard liable to irritability and the odd fit of despair. **1973** G. MOFFAT *Deviant Death* i. 18 [He] could have made scarcely enough money from book reviews and the odd feature on country life to pay his petrol bill.

b. Of a place: Situated apart from the general body of places; out of the way; in phr. *odd corner (angle)* (see CORNER *sb.*[1] 6), and *dial.*

1576 FLEMING *Panopl. Epist.* 402 Being but a private man, and shutt up close in an odde corner. **1582** STANYHURST *Æneis* I. (Arb.) 28 Vs to this od corner thee wynd tempestuus hurled. **1610** SHAKS. *Temp.* I. ii. 223 In an odde Angle of the Isle. **1631** WEEVER *Anc. Fun. Mon.* 645 He was constrained to..seeke odde corners for his safety. **1832** TENNYSON *Miller's D.* 68 From some odd corner of the brain.

c. Of an interval of time: Occurring casually between times of fixed occupation.

1644 MILTON *Educ.* Wks. (1847) 100/2 They may have easily learned at any odd hour the Italian tongue. **1819** ARNOLD *Let.* in Stanley *Life* (1844) I. ii. 61, I fear I..do not make the most of all the odd five and ten minutes' spaces which I get in the course of the day. **1853** LYTTON *My Novel* v. vii, He..bought a 'Peerage', and it became his favourite study at odd quarters of an hour. **1893** JESSOPP *Stud. by Recluse* Pref. 9 The great teachers are not they who pick up their knowledge at odd moments.

d. Not forming part of a regular course of work, as *odd job*, a casual disconnected piece of work. Hence *odd-jobber*, *odd-job(s) man* one who does odd jobs (also *fig.*) and similarly *odd man, lad, hand*, etc.; *odd-job* v. intr., to do odd jobs; *odd-jobbing* vbl. sb.; *odd-timer*, *odd work*.

1743 W. ELLIS *Mod. Husbandman* Oct. xxii. 149 The Odd-man's Wages is from fifty Shillings, to four Pounds a Year. *c* **1770** in de Vries & Fryer *Venus Unmasked* (1967) 33 Miss E. P.... R.. has not received her stated allowance; is therefore obliged, in order to keep up appearances, to do *odd jobs.* **1798** J. WOODFORDE *Diary* 24 Nov. (1931) V. 148 Paid John Buck, Blacksmith, for divers odd Jobbs for the Year 1798 the Sum of 2.14.10. **18..** MRS. SPOFFORD *Pilot's Wife*, Pottering..about the house, and finding little odd jobs to attend to. **1853** MRS. GASKELL *Ruth* II. iii. 64 Just try for a day to think of all the odd jobs as to be done well. **1859** DICKENS *T. Two Cities* II. i, Outside Tellson's..was an odd-job man. *Ibid.* III. ix. 206 A gentleman like yourself wot I've had the honour of odd jobbing till I'm grey at it. **1860** —— *Gt. Expect.* (1861) I. vii. 90, I was.. odd-boy about the forge. **1861** MRS. BEETON *Bk. Househ. Managem.* 964 Where a single footman, or odd man, is the only male servant then ..he is required to make himself generally useful. **1863** *All Year Round* 11 July 472/2 Either can rest occasionally by employing an 'odd man', of whom there are several..ready to do 'odd' work. **1877** *N.W. Linc. Gloss.*, *Odd jobs*, various small things on a farm, or in a large household, which require doing, but belong to no person's regular work. **1886** H. F. LESTER *Under two Fig Trees* 99 All that the odd-jobber did was to stack the soil. **1892** W. S. GILBERT *Foggerty's Fairy* 161 A chambermaid and a nondescript odd-man constituted her staff of assistants. **1894** *Northumbld. Gloss.*, *Odd-laddy*, a boy kept on farms to do odd..jobs, such as carting turnips, manure, etc. The horse he drives is called the odd-horse; his cart the odd-cart, etc. **1897** E. L. VOYNICH *Gadfly* 190, I lived by odd-jobbing for the blacks on the sugar plantations. **1905** Odd-man [see DOORMAN 2]. **1909** J. R. WARE *Passing Eng.* 186/1 *Odd job man*, modified description of the Shyster, who professes to do anything and only does his employer. **1915** R. BROOKE *Let.* 20 Apr. (1968) 681 Ian Hamilton..asked me if I'd like to be attached to his staff as a sort of 'galloper' and odd-jobber—'A.D.C.'. **1916** H. G. WELLS *Mr. Britling* I. i. 28 They become villa parasites and odd-job men. **1925** A. S. M. HUTCHINSON *One Increasing Purpose* I. xviii. 113 She's an odd-timer on Miss Marr's typist staff. **1933–4** WITTGENSTEIN *Blue & Brown Bks.* (1958) 44 We are tempted to describe the use of important 'odd-job' words as though they were words with regular functions. **1938** D. SMITH *Dear Octopus* I. 22 Just a sort of receptionist and general odd-jobber. **1940** L. MACNEICE *Last Ditch* 25 He was not able to read or write, He did odd jobs on gentlemen's places, Cutting the hedge or hoeing the drive. **1944** F. CLUNE *Red Heart* 32 He taught, biked, and odd-jobbed his way around Great Britain for a year. **1948** in D. M. Davin *N.Z. Short Stories* (1953) 195 The odd-jobs man who was also the cowman and gardener at the homestead. **1973** A. CHRISTIE *Postern of Fate* II. ii. 69 I've done odd jobbing, you know. **1977** *Private Eye* 4 Mar. 20/2 (Advt.), Carpentry, cleaning, electrics, decorating, gardening, handy persons, odd jobbers.

e. Forming part of an incomplete pair or set.

1746 H. WALPOLE *Lett.* (1846) II. 105 Calling odd man! as the hackney chairmen do when they want a partner. **1757** MILLS in *Phil. Trans.* L. 108 It melted..a pair of sheepshears, and some odd brass buckles and candlesticks that lay on the wall. **1764** FOOTE *Patron* I. (1781) 25 With what stock did you trade? I can give you the catalogue... Two odd volumes of Swift; the Life of Moll Flanders [etc.]. **1851** MAYHEW *Lond. Labour* I. 229 Sellers of odd numbers of periodicals and broadsheets. **1870** DICKENS *E. Drood* iii, Odd volumes of dismal books.

†f. Extra; given over and above. *Obs.*

1602 SHAKS. *Ham.* V. ii. 185, I will win for him if I can: if not, Ile gaine nothing but my shame, and the odde hits. **1602** *2nd Pt. Return fr. Parnass.* I. iii. 349 You shall haue 40 shillings and an odde pottle of wine.

10. a. Differing in character from what is ordinary, usual, or normal; out of the ordinary course; extraordinary, strange. (Compared *odder*, *oddest*.)

a **1592** H. SMITH *Serm.* Wks. 1866 II. 84 Amongst the heathen they had many odd conceits. **1603** SHAKS. *Meas. for M.* V. i. 61 If she be mad..Her madnesse hath the oddest frame of sense. **1679** L. ADDISON *1st St. Mahumedism* A ij b, Though many odde things are here set down of this Imposter, yet they are all own'd by his Sectaries. **1711** ADDISON *Spect.* No. 72 ¶2 He was a Member of the Everlasting Club. So very odd a Title raised my curiosity. **1772** T. SIMPSON *Vermin-Killer* i, Some may think it odd for a man to sit down and write on so trifling a subject as vermin. **1852** MISS MITFORD in L'Estrange *Life* III. xiii. 243 An odd circumstance is that the oak-leaves this year are falling as soon as those of the elm. **1868** FREEMAN *Norm. Conq.* II. ix. 333 *note*, It is odd that they are not spoken of. *a* **1902** *Mod.* I know something still odder than that.

b. Of persons, their actions, etc.: Strange in behaviour or appearance; peculiar; eccentric; *odd bod* (freq. in *pl.*) [BOD].

1588 SHAKS. *L.L.L.* V. i. 15 He is too picked, too spruce, too affected, too odde, as it were. **1599** —— *Much Ado* III. i. 72 So odde, and from all fashions, As Beatrice is. **1679** L. ADDISON *1st St. Mahumedism* 33 Going up and down after an odd distracted manner. **1711** STEELE *Spect.* No. 14 ¶1 An odd Fellow, whose Face I have often seen at the Playhouse, gave me the following Letter. **1741** FIELDING *Conversation* Wks. 1784 IX. 369 One of these [philosophers], when he appears..among us, is distinguished..by the name of an odd fellow. **1796** NELSON 18 Aug. in Nicolas *Disp.* (1845) II. 243 Maurice Suckling..may be odd, but I believe none will do more real good with the estate. **1882** OUIDA *Maremma* I. 38 The village people thought her odd, and were a little afraid of her. **1955** [see BOD]. **1966** *Courier-Mail* (Brisbane) 15 Sept. 1/7 A family of 12 self-styled 'odd bods' is immigrating to Spain because Australia is 'too conventional'. **1976** 'J. ROFFMAN' *Why Someone had to Die* 78 Anyone would, except you who have an inborn bias toward the odd bods in society.

c. Of material things: Strange in appearance, fantastic, grotesque.

1613–39 I. JONES in Leoni *Palladio's Archit.* (1742) II. 50 This Basement..does well enough; not but that it is something odd. **1697** DAMPIER *Voy.* I. 517 He busied himself in making a Chest with 4 boards... It was but an ill shaped odd thing. **1838** *Murray's Hand-bk. N. Germ.* 484 In the garden of the château is an odd, many-sided building, resembling a Chinese temple. **1858** DICKENS *Lett.* (1880) II. 66 It is the oddest carriage in the world.

B. *sb.* (elliptical use of the *adj.*)

a. An odd thing; that which is odd. **b.** *Golf.* (See quot. 1881.) **c.** *dial.* A small point of land (= ON. *oddi, oddr*).

1830 GALT *Lawrie T.* II. vii. (1849) 63, I have now and then meddled with an odd or an end. **1833** MACAULAY *Ess., H. Walpole* (1887) 288 With the Sublime and the Beautiful Walpole had nothing to do..the Odd was his peculiar domain. **1869** *Lonsdale Gloss.*, *Odd*, n. a small point of land or promontory; as 'Green Odd'. **1881** *Golfer's Handbook* 35 (Jam. Suppl.) (1) 'An odd', 'two odds', etc. per hole, means the handicap given to a weak opponent by deducting one, two, etc. strokes from his total every hole. (2) To have played 'the odd' is to have played one stroke more than your adversary. **1900** *Westm. Gaz.* 8 Nov. 10/2 Mr. Douglas English contributes an interesting preface on 'The Photography of the Odd', with some excellent pictures—tree frog, caterpillar, dormouse, and so on.

C. *adv.* and quasi-*adv.*

†**1.** In a singular or unusual degree, extraordinarily, eminently; absolutely, completely. *Obs.*

c **1400** *Destr. Troy* 7466 His armour was od good. *Ibid.* 10839 Pantasilia.. That honerable Ector od myche louyt. *Ibid.* 9597 Deffibus.. Pletid vnto Paris.. Whether the Duke were od dede. *c* **1450** *Merlin* 159 These kynges were odde noble knyghtes.

2. quasi-*adv.* in various senses: see the adj.

1567 P. Beverley *Verses* in *Fenton's Trag. Disc.*, Wherin he lives so odde from right and lawe. **1579** E. Hake *Newes out of Powles Churchyarde* vi, I meane professors of the trueth, How far yet live they od! **1602** Shaks. *Ham.* I. v. 170 How strange or odde so ere I beare my selfe. **1876** 'P. Pyper' *Mr. Gray and Neighbours*, 'We lives odd, yer honour, in a tent'. 'Living odd'.. means in Marshland phraseology living in a house standing by itself.

D. *Comb.*

1. General comb. of the adj.: **a.** parasynthetic, as (sense 2) ***odd numbered, -toed*** adjs; (sense 10) ***odd-conceited*** (†***-ceited***), ***-humoured, -mannered, -peaked, -shaped, -sighted*** adjs.

1591 Shaks. *Two Gent.* II. vii. 46 Ile knit it vp in silken strings, With twentie *od-conceited true-loue knots. **1641** Brome *Joviall Crew* IV. i. Wks. 1873 III. 423, I have heard much of this old od-ceited Justice Clack. **1665** Needham *Med. Medicinæ* 41 If an *odd-humor'd disease happen. **1882** *Contemp. Rev.* Aug. 235 Placing two settlers on homesteads on each even-numbered section and also two settlers on each *odd-numbered section. **1774** Goldsm. *Nat. Hist.* VI. 293 A number of *odd shaped animals. **1921** W. de la Mare *Crossings* 54 He.. carries an odd-shaped fiddle. **1967** Karch & Buber *Offset Processes* ii. 34 Products include paper and board too large for conventional presses (over 80 inches), odd-shaped objects, posters, [etc.]. **1977** P. D. James *Death of Expert Witness* III. 169 The gathering of those odd-shaped pieces of information.. which, in the end, would click together to form a picture. **1690** Bentley *Phal.* 505 What an *odd sighted Examiner I have to deal with; that.. can see in Books what never was there. **1872** Nicholson *Palæont.* 424 The hind feet are *odd-toed.

b. the adj. or adv. with a pple., as ***odd-contrived, -looking, -sounding, -thinking, -turned*** adjs.

a **1682** Sir T. Browne *Tracts* 127 If he delighteth in *odd contrived phancies. **1774** Goldsm. *Nat. Hist.* VI. 99 This *odd-looking animal. **1876** 'Geo. Eliot' *Dan. Der.* III. v. xxxviii. 135 Spectators would be likely to think of him as an odd-looking Jew. **1976** J. B. Hilton *Gamekeeper's Gallows* ii. 23 Beresford was curious to know what this odd-looking character was carrying. **1670** Eachard *Cont. Clergy* 45 Such far-fetch'd and *odd-sounding expressions. **1853** Mrs. Gaskell *Cranford* vii. 131 There she sat, as stately and composed as though we had never heard that odd-sounding cough. **1942** Partridge *Usage & Abusage* (1947) 15/1 *Admittable* is rare and odd-sounding for *admissible*. **1717** Prior *Alma* III. 47 Some *odd-thinking youth, Less friend to doctrine than to truth. **1772** *Ann. Reg.* 47 He had an *odd-turned mind, and a bad heart.

c. the adj. with a sb., forming an attrib. phr., as ***odd-number, -order, -parity.***

1922 F. F. Potter *Teaching of Arithmetic* xvii. 325 The simple *odd-number series. **1957** L. Fox *Numerical Solution Two-Point Bound. Probl.* vi. 141 This too is connected with the use of central differences for even-order equations, but of mean central differences for *odd-order equations. **1962** *Gloss. Terms Automatic Data Processing* (*B.S.I.*) 33 When the numbers of ones (or zeros) is required to be odd the check is called an *odd parity check, and when even an even parity check. **1967** *Bodl. Libr. Rec.* VIII. 3 The second drawback is the use of an odd-parity code, with seven-hole punching necessary for a plain tape-feed.

2. Special comb.: **odd-and-end** *a.*, promiscuous, miscellaneous, consisting of odds and ends: see ODDS 7; **odd-come-short**, a short length of cloth forming the end of a piece; an odd remainder or fragment; *pl.* odds and ends; **odd-come-shortly**, some day or other in the near future; **odd-even** *a. Nuclear Physics*, (*a*) of or pertaining to nuclei of odd mass number and those of even mass number; (*b*) applied to nuclei containing an odd number of protons and an even number of neutrons; **odd-gaits, -gates** *local* [GATE *sb.*[2] 9 b], odd, strange, out of the way; **odd-horse** = *odd-man-out* (a); **odd man out**, (*a*) a mode of singling out, by tossing or the like, one person from among three or more, to perform some part, pay the reckoning (hence ***to go the odd man***), etc.; (*b*) a person or thing differing from all others of a group in some respect; **odd-man-wins**, a gambling game in which three toss coins, and the one who tosses with a different result from the two others, wins; **odd-mark**, 'that portion of the arable land of a farm set apart for a particular crop, as it comes in order of rotation under the customary cultivation of the farm' (Miss Jackson *Shropsh. Word-bk.*); **odd-odd** *a. Nuclear Physics*, (*a*) of or pertaining to nuclei of odd mass number only; (*b*) applied to nuclei containing an odd number of protons and an odd number of neutrons; **odd-pinnate** *a.*, pinnate (as a leaf) with an odd terminal leaflet, imparipinnate. See also ODDFELLOW, ODDWOMAN.

1846 J. Brown *Lett.* (1912) 90, I have no continuity and thoroughness of thought,.. and my style, if style it can be called, is the piebaldest, *oddandendest. **1863** N. Macleod *Remin. Highland Parish* ii, A little world of its own, to which wandering pipers, parish fools.. with all sorts of odd-and-end characters came. **1836** T. Hook *G. Gurney* III. 316 Some supplementary parcels, and what elderly ladies in country towns call '*odd-come-shorts'. **1873** Rhoda Broughton *Nancy* I. 79 A dinner-party.. a squire or two, a squiress or two, a curate or two—such odd-come-shorts as can be got together.. at briefest notice. **1876** —— *Joan* (1877) 46 An old laurel tree, into which every odd-come-short that the family has not known where else to deposit.. has been put. **1738** Swift *Polite Convers.* i, *Col.* Miss, when will you be married? *Miss.* One of these *odd-come-shortly's, colonel. **1821** Scott *Lett.* II. 110, I will write her a long letter one of these odd-come-shortlys. **1936** *Physical Rev.* XLIX. 897/1 The transitions are of the *odd-even type. **1949** Gamow & Critchfield *Theory of Atomic Nucleus* iv. 88 $\delta A = 0$ for even-even nuclei, $= 1$ for odd-even nuclei, $= 2$ for odd-odd nuclei. **1955** J. A. Wheeler in W. Pauli *Niels Bohr* 166 Odd-even differences in spontaneous fission. The spontaneous fission rates of nuclei of odd mass number are observed to be slower than the rates for the corresponding even nuclei. **1970** G. K. Woodgate *Elem. Atomic Struct.* ix. 195 The tentative explanation of this phenomenon, called odd-even staggering, is beyond the scope of this discussion. **1906** Kipling *Puck of Pook's Hill* 263 Won'erful *odd-gates place—Romney Marsh. **1957** H. Hall *Parish's Dict. Sussex Dial.* 88/2 *Oddgaits*, extraordinary. 'It's an odd-gaits sort of place.' **1801** *Sporting Mag.* XIX. 115 No cards, dice, *odd-horse, or tossing-up to be permitted. **1840** Dickens *Old C. Shop* xxxvi, Going the *odd man or plain Newmarket for fruit, ginger beer. **1889** *Sat. Rev.* 2 Feb. 128/2 The good luck which attends us in the political '*odd-man-out' game. **1928** F. W. Crofts *Sea Mystery* xvi. 263 Mrs. Berlyn as hostess would reasonably be the odd man out when the change was made from snooker to billiards. **1935** Mrs. Belloc Lowndes *Let.* 10 Aug. (1971) 129 Rex Whistler.. is rather 'odd man out', though he is so quiet and unassuming that everyone likes him. **1945** F. L. Green (*title*) Odd man out. **1958** *Times* 29 Nov. 9/1 Here.. is the fallen foe [*sc.* the pike]; not merely our foe, but.. the odd man out in Nature and in the sporting Canon. **1969** in Halpert & Story *Christmas Mumming in Newfoundland* 33 These settlements are 'odd men out'; at odds with outside economic forces. **1970** *Guardian* 19 Nov. 11/4 The products.. would look odd men out in a formal setting. **1973** *Listener* 15 Nov. 658/1 Eight of the present nine members of the EEC voted in favour, the odd man out being.. Denmark. **1884** *St. James's Gaz.* 5 Dec. 6/1 At coin-spinning the game generally played is '*odd man wins'. **1805** Duncombe in *Jrnl. R. Agric. Soc.* (1853) XIV. II. 455 Nearly one third of the arable land is constantly under the culture of wheat, and that third, during its preparation for the seed, is termed the *odd mark. **1855** *Ibid.* XVI. II. 557 Supposing his oddmark of wheat about 20 acres.. he sacrificed the full amount of the half year's rent. **1936** *Physical Rev.* XLIX. 897/1 The transition is of an *odd-odd or even-even type. **1937** *Ibid.* LI. 951/2 The condition.. for the instability of odd-odd nuclei should read $g + 2g\sigma < gm$. **1956** *Proc. Physical Soc.* A. LXIX. 635 (*heading*) The magnetic moments of odd-odd nuclei.

†**odd**, *v. Obs. rare*[−1]. [f. ODD *a.*] *trans.* To make odd or irregular (in quot. in reference to syncopation).

1597 Morley *Introd. Mus.* 89 The third is a driuing waie in two crotchets and a minime, but odded by a rest, so that it neuer commeth euen till the close.

oddball ('ɒdbɔːl). *colloq.* (orig. *U.S.*). Also **odd-ball, odd ball.** [f. ODD *a.* + BALL *sb.*[1]] An eccentric person; a person of unconventional views or habits. Also *attrib.* or as *adj.*, eccentric, exceptional, peculiar.

1948 *Amer. Speech* XXIII. 221 *Odd Ball*.. connoted that the individual's strangeness was not the result of prison camp experiences. **1953** Berry & Van den Bark *Amer. Thes. Slang* (1954) §411/2 Peculiar or eccentric person.. oddball, odd-fellow, odd stick. *Ibid.* §454/3 Social dud or bore; 'drip'.. oddball, ooly-drooly, pain. **1956** W. H. Whyte *Organization Man* (1957) ix. 123 There are exceptions, but one must be a very odd ball to be one. **1956** Wallis & Blair *Thunder Above* (1959) xvi. 158 A phlegmatic odd-ball in a world of make-believe. **1957** *Time* 2 Sept. 23/2 Officialdom in Saigon thought that the threat of rebellions by the country's fanatic, odd-ball religious groups was ended at last. **1959** *Washington Post* 19 Oct. B. 10/6 Life aboard a submarine has its oddball moments. **1968** *Canad. Antiques Collector* Dec. 10/1 The classic tradition was too strong at the end of the 18th c. for any but obvious odd balls to find a 'better way' of building their houses. **1969** *Daily Mail* 15 Jan. 5/4 If that burn-time was not correct we could have gone into all sort of odd-ball orbits. **1971** C. Fick *Danziger Transcript* (1973) 41 They had been oddball friends since Harvard. **1973** M. Truman *Harry S. Truman* xvi. 331 Earlier in 1946 an oddball broke into the National Gallery and cut a hole in Dad's portrait. **1974** *Peace News* 15 Mar. 10 It's always been very much an odd ball way of doing it. **1974** D. Sears *Lark in Clear Air* ii. 27 The oddest of a family where odd-balls were not the exception.

odder, compar. of ODD *a.*; obs. form of OTHER.

'Odd,fellow, Odd-fellow. [A fanciful appellation: cf. ODD *a.* 9 b.] A member of a society, fraternity, or 'order', organized under this name, with initiatory rites, mystic signs of recognition, and various 'degrees' of dignity and honour, for social and benevolent purposes, especially that of rendering assistance to members in sickness, distress, or other need.

The name 'Odd Fellows' appears to have been originally assumed by local clubs formed in various parts of England during the 18th c. for convivial and social purposes, usually with rites of initiation, passwords, and secret ceremonies, supposed to imitate those of Freemasonry. Associations of these clubs were formed from time to time for purposes of mutual recognition; of which that styled the 'Independent Order of Oddfellows, Manchester Unity', formed about 1813, has grown into a vast organization, having local branches or 'lodges' throughout Great Britain and the Colonies, as well as in the United States and some foreign countries. Besides this, there are numerous smaller societies of the same 'order' in Great Britain and the Colonies; a distinct federation also exists in the United States, which, beginning in 1819 in connexion with the Manchester Union, separated from it in 1842, and is now a great and important organization.

1795 in R. Humphreys *Mem. J. Decastro* (1824) 247 As many Grands and Brothers of the Odd Fellows, Bucks, Masonic and other Lodges. **1800** *Sporting Mag.* XVI. 59/1 A Member of the Odd Fellows. **1811** *Lex-Bal.*, *Odd Fellows*, a convivial society; the introduction to the most noble grand, arrayed in royal robes, is well worth seeing at the price of becoming a member. **1951** McWhiney & Simkins in A. Dundes *Mother Wit* (1973) 594/2 This mummery manifests itself in numerous other secret organizations such as the Odd Fellows, the Masons, and the Knights of Columbus. **1854** Thoreau *Walden* viii. (1886) 170 Men will.. if they can, constrain him to belong to their desperate odd-fellow society. **1887** *Pall Mall G.* 2 Sept. 8/2 A great gathering of Oddfellows was held last evening at the Masons' Hall tavern .. to welcome the grand master of the Manchester Unity. **1887** *Scotsman* 16 May 6/5 A General Council Meeting of the Scottish Order of Oddfellows' Friendly Society was held on Saturday at the Oddfellows' Hall, Edinburgh. **1970** *New Yorker* 14 Nov. 175/1 Members of the Independent Order of Odd Fellows stuck to their symbol of an axe left cleaving into a realistic log. **1977** P. D. James *Death of Expert Witness* I. 16 A ticket for the local Oddfellows' hop.

Hence **'Odd,fellowship**, the status of an Oddfellow; the principles and organization of the 'Oddfellows'.

1871 *Daily News* 30 June, I am forgetting that some of my readers are, perhaps, unacquainted with the rudiments of Odd-Fellowship. **1883** *Chambers' Encycl.* VII. 36/1 On its institution in Manchester, the main purpose of Odd-fellowship was declared by its laws to be, 'to render assistance to every brother who may apply through sickness, distress, or otherwise, if he be well attached to the King and government, and faithful to the Order'. **1907** C. E. Jackson *Poet Wildey* 11 It is the Independent Order of Odd Fellows, or if you like the term better, American Odd Fellowship. **1972** *Fairbanks* (Alaska) *Daily News-Miner* 3 Nov. 7/7 Odd Fellowship.. is a benevolent, fraternal order banded together for mutual benefit.

oddish ('ɒdɪʃ), *a.* [f. ODD *a.* + -ISH[1].] Somewhat odd or peculiar.

1705 Rowe *Biter* II. i, Such a scurvy, abominable.. oddish .. kind of a Husband. **1819** *Metropolis* I. 212 Some oddish coincidences occurred in the theatre. **1854** *Fraser's Mag.* XLIX. 292 He's odd-ish, and quite unlike other people.

odditorium (ɒdɪ'tɔərɪəm). [f. ODDIT(Y + -ORIUM.] A shop or venue for the display or retailing of oddities. Also *transf.*

1914 R. & E. Shackleton *Four on Tour* 182 We happened upon an 'odditorium', a delightful name adopted by a very shabby shop in a very narrow lane [in Kingston-upon-Thames] where we found some very attractive bits of old silver and china. **1933** *Sun* (Baltimore) 16 Dec. 10/6 Mr. Miller.. manages the Ripley Believe It or Not 'odditorium' at Horticulture Hall, which contains thirty-nine oddities. **1940** *Time* 26 Feb. 42/2 Sanka Coffee's Tuesday-night odditorium of the air.

oddity ('ɒdɪtɪ). [f. ODD *a.* + -ITY.]

1. The quality or character of being odd or peculiar; peculiarity, strangeness, singularity.

1750 tr. *Leonardus' Mirr. Stones* Pref., All Manner of precious Stones that have been ever valued for their Beauty, Colour, Oddity, Curiosity. **1824** Scott *St. Ronan's* xxiii, Pray do not set up for wit and oddity; there is nothing in life so intolerable as pretending to think differently from other people. **1888** Frith *Autobiog.* III. vi. 144 The oddity of the situation seemed to strike both at the same time.

2. An odd characteristic or trait, a peculiarity.

1713 Steele *Guardian* No. 144 ¶1 Our very street-beggars are not without their peculiar oddities. **1826** Disraeli *Viv. Grey* II. xv, All people have their oddities. **1877** Dowden *Shaks. Prim.* v. 48 Love's Labour Lost is.. a comedy of oddities of dialogue.

3. a. An odd or peculiar person.

1748 Smollett *Rod. Rand.* xlv. (1804) 309 This ridiculous oddity danced up to the table at which we sat. **1873** Black *Pr. Thule* xii. 180 He did not wish to gain the reputation of having married an oddity.

b. Something odd or peculiar; a fantastic, grotesque, or strange-looking object; a strange event.

1834 L. Ritchie *Wand. by Seine* 49 When any oddity took place in the town, such as an ill-assorted marriage, or a ridiculous love-suit. **1840** Miss Mulock *Ogilvies* iv, Hugh ..had often glanced half-contemptuously at the various oddities which decorated the chamber of the old politician.

'oddlegs. [ODD A. 8.] = JENNY 6.

Yorkshire Correspondent, The tools called *Jennies* are sometimes called *oddlegs* or *moffs*. They are compasses with one bent leg.

'oddlike, *a. Sc.* and *north. dial.* [f. ODD *a.* + -LIKE.] Odd-looking.

1718 Ramsay *Christ's Kirk Gr.* III. v, An odd-like wife, they said, that saw A moupin runkled granny. **1815** Scott *Guy M.* xxxix, Is not it an odd-like thing that ilka wauf carle in the country has a son and heir, and that the house of Ellangowan is without male succession? **1894** *Northumbld. Gloss.*, *Oddlike*, *oddishlike*, odd-looking.

oddlings ('ɒdlɪŋz), *sb. pl.* [f. ODD *a.* + -LING[1].] = ODDMENTS *sb. pl.*

1854- in *Eng. Dial. Dict.* **1900** *Windsor Mag.* XI. 354 A hundred odd bits, that's all—but they are a manufacturer's oddlings.

odd lot ('ɒd lɒt). [f. ODD *a.* + LOT *sb.*] **1.** An incomplete set or random mixture (of articles of commerce).

1897 *Sears, Roebuck Catal.* 173/1 The pants are not the size to fit the coats and vests. We then throw them into what we call our 'Odd Lots', or mixed suits. **1931** C. MAUGHAN *Markets of London* 105 Parcels of five bags or less are known as 'odd lots' and are sold separately at the end of the auctions, with the exception of pea-berries, which are sold irrespective of the size of the lots.

2. *U.S. Stock Exchange.* Used *attrib.* of transactions involving numbers of shares smaller than is normally dealt in. Hence **odd-lotter**.

1929 *Times* 1 Nov. 22/5 The list generally moved up under heavy accumulation of standard issues, together with reports of a tremendous volume of odd-lot bargain buying. **1939** C. O. HARDY *(title)* Odd-lot trading on the New York Stock Exchange. **1968** *Economist* 28 May 94/1 The unit trust investor is not quite an odd-lotter—the American term for a small investor. **1970** *Washington Post* 30 Sept. D. 10/3 Odd lot transactions by principal dealers. **1976** *National Observer* (U.S.) 28 Feb. 8/4 But odd-lot figures.. suggest that small investors were, on balance, selling in November and December of 1972 and in January of 1973. *Ibid.*, There is some statistical evidence that odd-lotters have been wrong far too often in the past.

oddly ('ɒdlɪ), *adv.* [f. ODD *a.* + -LY[2].] In an odd manner.

1. In reference to number: Not evenly; in ***oddly even, oddly odd***: see EVEN *a.* 15 c, ODD A. 2 c.

1674 JEAKE *Arith.* (1696) 5 Even Numbers Oddly, these may be parted into equal halves, but the halves will be odd.

†**2.** Singly, solely, alone. *Obs.*

13.. *E.E. Allit. P.* B. 923 þou art oddely þyn one out of þis fylþe.

†**3.** Singularly; remarkably; nobly, rarely, choicely. *Obs.*

13.. *E.E. Allit. P.* B. 698, I compast hem a kynde crafte .. & amed hit in myn ordenaunce oddely dere. *c* **1400** *Destr. Troy* 6859 So odly þai foght, That the grekes gaf bake. *c* **1425** *St. Christina* iii. in *Anglia* VIII. 120/40 þen was I odly mery. **1526** SKELTON *Magnyf.* 1624 Thy wordes & my mynde odly well agree. **1541** ELYOT *Gov.* III. vi, Cutting an odly great pomegranate.

4. In an uneven, irregular, or incongruous manner; †so as not to be even or equally balanced (*obs.*); irregularly; in a haphazard way.

1592 SHAKS. *Rom. & Jul.* II. v. 61 How odly thou repli'st: Your Loue saies like an honest Gentleman: Where is your Mother? **1596** —— *Merch. V.* I. ii. 79 How odly he is suited. **1638** SIR T. HERBERT *Trav.* (ed. 2) 166 In Persia.. Justice is so odly ballanced. **1649** G. DANIEL *Trinarch., Rich. II*, ccxcv, Nothing comes odly in; but from a fixt Determination, all things Rise or Fall. **1722** DE FOE *Plague* (1884) 192 People.. who having no Subsistence or Habitation.. liv'd oddly. **1821** CLARE *Vill. Minstr.* I. 89 Pattering acorns oddly drop.

5. In an extraordinary, unusual, or peculiar manner; strangely; fantastically, grotesquely.

1610 SHAKS. *Temp.* v. i. 197 How odly will it sound, that I Must aske my childe forgiuenesse? **1673** RAY *Journ. Low C.* 28 A Japan Letter, odly painted. **1713** BERKELEY *Hylas & Phil.* i. Wks. 1871 I. 271, I profess it sounds oddly, to say that sugar is not sweet. *a* **1839** PRAED *Poems* (1864) II. 44 How oddly beauties will behave! **1877** BLACK *Green Past.* xxiv. (1878) 190 Oddly enough he seemed to take a greater interest than ever in the Von Rosens.

b. Often hyphened to pples. used *attrib.*

a **1704** LOCKE (J.), Some oddly-shaped fetus. **1863** KINGLAKE *Crimea* (1876) I. xiv. 302 The most strenuous adversaries of this oddly-fated Prince. **1879** DOWDEN *Southey* v. 136 The oddly-assorted pair met in Taylor's house. **1886** E. S. MORSE *Jap. Homes* vi. 275 Oddly-shaped stones.

odd-man: see ODD A. 1, 6, 8 d, D. 2.

odd-me-dod, dial. corr. of HODMANDOD.

1880 JEFFERIES *Greene Ferne F.* 257 There, you great odd-me-dods—you don't know what it is!

oddments ('ɒdmənts), *sb. pl.* [f. ODD *a.* + -MENT.] Odd articles, items, fragments, or remnants; odds and ends; esp. articles belonging to broken or incomplete sets, as offered for sale.

In *Printing* applied to the parts of a book other than the text, i.e. the title-page, preface, contents, etc.; sometimes to the pages, whether of text or other matter, remaining over after making up complete sections or 'sheets'.

1796 MAD. D'ARBLAY *Lett.* 10 July, I have still so many book oddments of accounts.. to arrange. **1821** CLARE *Vill. Minstr.* II. 85 I'm your age treble, with some oddments to 't. **1836** *Lett. fr. Madras* (1843) 22 Everybody made up a parcel of clothes or some little oddments. **1873** MISS BRADDON *Str. & Pilgr.* I. vi. 64 Massed into one lot of oddments at an auction. **1883** *Sat. Rev.* 13 Oct. 467/1 Made up of plasters and match-boxes and medicine-bottles and heaven knows what other oddments. *Mod. Advt.*, To clear off: special offer of Remnants, Oddments, &c.

oddness ('ɒdnɪs). [f. ODD *a.* + -NESS.]

1. Unevenness of number.

1398 TREVISA *Barth. De P.R.* XIX. cxxvi. (Add. MS. 27944), And so in euene diuision is nouȝt euenenesse medled wiþ oddenesse, nouþer oddenesse wiþ euenenesse. **1589** PUTTENHAM *Eng. Poesie* II. iii[i.]. (Arb.) 85 The first seemes shorter then the later, who shewes a more odnesse.. by reason of his sharpe accent which is vpon the last sillable. *a* **1619** FOTHERBY *Atheom.* II. x. §4 (1622) 307 Take but One, from Three; and you.. destroy the odnesse. **1875** JOWETT *Plato* (ed. 2) I. 407 The number three, which participates in oddness, excludes the even.

†**2.** Unique or rare character, singularity. *Obs.*

1581 MULCASTER *Positions* xxxix. (1887) 188 Oftimes the report of that odnesse which we see not in effect, but heare of in speeche, falles out very lame. **1625** BP. J. WILLIAMS *Gt. Brit. Salomon* 36 So will I compare these two Kings.. that you may see, by the odnesse of their proportion, how they differ from all Kings beside. **1666** J. DAVIES *Hist. Caribby Isls.* 127 So neatly made, that the eye cannot be cloy'd with considering the odness of their shapes.

3. Divergence from what is ordinary or usual; strangeness, peculiarity; eccentricity.

1611 COTGR., *Bigearrure*,.. odnesse of humor, fantasticalnesse. **1711** ADDISON *Spect.* No. 7 ¶1, I was reflecting with my self on the Oddness of her Fancy. **1785** SARAH FIELDING *Ophelia* I. xiii, The oddness of the event would make people curious. **1836** MACGILLIVRAY tr. *Humboldt's Trav.* xxii. 315 The oddness of the dresses of the principal personages.

†**4.** Want of congruity or harmony, irregularity. *Obs. rare.*

1680 OTWAY *Orphan* IV. ii, In my house I only meet with oddness and disorder.

5. With *an* and *pl.* Something odd; †an irregularity, a discrepancy (*obs.*); a peculiarity.

1713 STEELE *Guardian* No. 10 ¶7, I shall be enabled.. to introduce several pretty oddnesses in the taking and tucking up of gowns. **1714** *Hue & Cry after Dr. S——ft* in Somers *Tracts* I. 390 Take Pen in Hand: Write some Odnesses. **1738** WHELER in *Phil. Trans.* XLI. 123 Neither of these Solutions would account for the Variety of Oddnesses I have met with. **1866** GEO. ELIOT *F. Holt* xxxvi, It seemed an oddness requiring explanation.

odds (ɒdz), *sb.* Also 6-7 oddes, ods, (6 *Sc.* oddis, odis, 7 odd's, *pl.* oddses). [app. pl. of ODD *a.* taken subst.: cf. *news*. In 16th c. regularly, and in 17th and 18th c. usually, construed as a singular, 'the odds *is* or *was*'; an isolated instance of 'the odds *were*' appears in 1614, but this construction is unusual before the 19th c.

It is somewhat difficult to comprehend how the plural of *odd* came to be taken to express the sense 'difference', and also how a word originally plural should, while still retaining the plural form, have been so constantly viewed and construed as singular. The most likely explanation is that *oddes, oddis* first meant 'odd' or 'unequal things' (cf. *news* = 'new things or matters'), a relic of which appears to exist in the phrase 'to make odds even' found in the earliest quotation. But the notion of two odd or unequal things so essentially involves that of the relation between them as easily to pass into that of 'inequality' or 'difference', as it perhaps already did in the phrase in question, and as is fully developed in sense 2. After the sense 'difference' was once established, the plural character of the word might be lost sight of, the more easily that in this sense no singular was in use, nor, from the suggested origin, possible. We may compare the history of *news, means, truce*.]

1. (?) Odd or unequal things, matters, or conditions; inequalities; hence ***to make odds even***, to equalize or level inequalities, to adjust or do away with differences; †to do away with, atone for, remit, or forgive shortcomings and transgressions; not to reckon his sins or crimes against a person.

[Cf. ODD *a.* 8 b, quot. 1450-70, 'We sal evin that is od'.] **1500-20** DUNBAR *Poems* lxxxv. 56 Implore, adore, thow indeflore, To mak our oddis evyne. **1570** *Satir. Poems Reform.* xvi. 70 Quhen ȝe forgaif him all his cryme, And maid his oddis euin. **1603** SHAKS. *Meas. for M.* III. i. 41 Yet death we feare That makes these oddes all euen. *a* **1839** PRAED *Poems* (1864) II. 171 Death looks down with nods and smiles, And makes the odds all even.

2. a. The condition or fact of being unequal; inequality; disparity in number, amount, or quality; dissimilarity: = DIFFERENCE *sb.* 1. Now *rare.* † ***at odds***, unequal, different (*obs.*).

1542 UDALL *Erasm. Apoph.* II. (1877) 282 Augustus.. admonished his doughter Iulia, to marke what great difference and oddes there was, betwene twoo women of high estate. **1548** W. PATTEN *Exp. Scot.* in Arb. *Garner* III. 60, I am so certain the excellency of his acts, and the baseness of my brain to be so far at odds. **1565** HARDING in Jewel *Def. Apol.* (1611) 98 Euen among the most blessed Apostles.. in likenesse of honour there was ods of power. **1565** JEWEL *ibid.* 612 Priesthood and Princehood haue one Originall and little oddes and small difference. **1587** HARRISON *England* II. i. (1877) I. 36 There is an irreconciliable ods betweene them and those of the papists. **1613** M. RIDLEY *Magn. Bodies* Pref. 2 Their proportion.. being at too great oddes. **1614** RALEIGH *Hist. World* II. v. iii. §15. 522 But whatsoeuer disproportion was betweene the two Armies; farre greater were the oddes betweene the Captaines. **1631** MAY *Lucan* Contin. VII. 329 Twixt whom and Cæsar was as great an ods Almost, as twixt the Furies and the Gods. **1690** LOCKE *Hum. Und.* IV. xvi. §12 Tho' there be a manifest odds betwixt the Bigness of the Diameter. **1756** MRS. CALDERWOOD in *Scotsman* (1884) 13 Dec. 9/6 To see the odds of clergymen in one country from another.. entirely puts out bigotry. **1823** GALT *Entail* I. viii. 58, I ken nae odds o' her this many a year. **1838-9** HALLAM *Hist. Lit.* III. III. iv. §58. 167 Nature has made little odds among men of mature age as to strength or knowledge. **1854** LOWELL *Cambridge Thirty Yrs. Ago* Pr. Wks. 1890 I. 80 The New England proverb says, 'All deacons are good, but—there's odds in deacons'.

b. The amount by which one number or quantity differs from another, or by which one thing exceeds or excels, or falls short of or below another; amount in excess or defect; difference.

1548 UDALL *Erasm. Par. Luke* vi. 75 Whiche is by a great oddes higher. **1605** VERSTEGAN *Dec. Intell.* ii. (1628) 27 More words by oddes then these may be found. **1640** W. BRIDGE *True Souldiers Convoy* 86 What shall weigh downe this odds but prayer? **1667** MILTON *P.L.* IV. 447, I chiefly who enjoy So farr the happier Lot, enjoying thee Preëminent by so much odds. **1671** MARVELL *Corr.* Wks. 1872-5 II. 384 It [a bill] was retained by the odds of two voices. **1799** WASHINGTON *Writ.* (1893) XIV. 234 The cheapest and by odds the most convenient mode. *a* **1845** HOOD *Agric. Distr.* vi, At long and last the odds we split. **1866** HOWELLS *Venet. Life* 50 By all odds, the loungers at Florian's were the most interesting.

c. Difference in the way of benefit or detriment. Now *colloq.* in ***what's the odds? it is*** or ***makes no odds***.

1642 ROGERS *Naaman* To Rdr., So great the oddes is, in what way a truth be uttered. **1657** W. MORICE *Coena quasi κοινὴ* Def. xv. 212 Aristippus would have found no odds in dying by the bite of a Lion. **1691** LOCKE *Money* Wks. 1727 II. 95 Whether it be any Odds to England. **1776** G. CAMPBELL *Philos. Rhet.* (1801) I. I. v. 118 Their being compounded would make no odds. **1826** *Sessions Papers* 11 Dec. 86/1, I asked Jackson whose they were—he said, 'What odds; they are mine.' **1840** THACKERAY *Shabby Genteel Story* ix, in *Fraser's Mag.* Oct. 410/1 Suppose I do die,.. what's the odds? Caroline doesn't care for me. **1844** DICKENS *Mart. Chuz.* xiii, It makes no odds whether a man has a thousand pounds or nothing there. **1855** GEO. ELIOT in *Fraser's Mag.* June 699/1 'What's the odds, so long as one can sleep?' is your *formule de la vie*. **1885** T. A. GUTHRIE *Tinted Venus* viii. 94 But there, it's no odds. **1886** BESANT *Childr. Gibeon* I. ix, What's the odds to a working-man whether he spells right or wrong? **1890** KIPLING *Soldiers Three* 79 'Wot's the odds as long as you're 'appy?' said Ortheris. **1923** D. H. LAWRENCE *Kangaroo* xvi. 345 That sense of sardonic tolerance, endurance. 'What's the odds, boys?' **1967** N. FREELING *Strike Out* 84 You do neo-expressionism, or.. neo-whatever-you-like, it makes no odds,.. you'd still be up against the machine. **1973** 'M. UNDERWOOD' *Reward for Defector* xxii. 158 What's the difficulty?.. Not that it makes any odds.

3. Disagreement, dissension, variance, strife; = DIFFERENCE 3. Chiefly in ***at odds***, † ***bring to odds*** (cf. DIFFERENCE 3 b).

1587 HARRISON *England* II. ix. (1877) I. 208 Those.. who otherwise would liue at strife, and quickelie be at ods. **1588** GREENE *Pandosto* (1843) 12 A compacted knavery.. to bring the king and him to oddes. **1604** SHAKS. *Oth.* II. iii. 185, I cannot speake Any beginning to this peeuish odds. **1611** BIBLE *Transl. Pref.* 9 The father.. findeth so great fault with them for their oddes and iarring. **1659** B. HARRIS *Parival's Iron Age* 27 In Germany, they.. fell to oddes principally about the Sacrament of the last Supper. **1694** MOTTEUX *Rabelais* IV. xxix. (1737) 121 Enemies; against whom he is eternally at odds. **1765** STERNE *Tr. Shandy* VIII. x, About which your reverences have so often been at odds with one another. **1873** BROWNING *Red Cott. Nt.-cap* 155 Old folk and young folk, still at odds, of course!

4. a. Difference in favour of one of two contending parties; balance of advantage; superiority in numbers or resources. ***at*** (†***with***) ***odds***, with the balance of advantage for or against one.

1574 HELLOWES *Gueuara's Fam. Ep.* Ep. Ded. (1577) 1, I was constreined with too much oddes, to endure combate with both these furious spirites. **1587** *Mirr. Mag., Albanact.* xxxviii, At home, with oddes, they durst not byde the stroke. **1600** SHAKS. *A.Y.L.* I. ii. 169 You wil take little delight in it, .. there is such oddes in the man. **1628** WITHER *Brit. Rememb.* Pref. 235 The ods is more then ten to three. **1676** HOBBES *Iliad* xx. 136 Nor does it need; so much we have the ods. **1708** SWIFT *Sacram. Test* Wks. 1755 II. I. 129 There appeared at least four to one odds against them. **1834** MEDWIN *Angler in Wales* I. 259 The odds were now greatly in their favour. **1856** FROUDE *Hist. Eng.* (1858) I. ii. 112 England had many times fought successfully against the same odds.

†**b.** Superior position, advantage. ***to take odds of***, to take advantage of. *Obs.*

1596 SPENSER *F.Q.* VI. ii. 18 Unarm'd all was the knight.. Whereof he taking oddes, streight bids him dight Himselfe to yeeld his Love. **1628** HOBBES *Thucyd.* (1822) 94 When.. we come to undertake any danger we have this odds by it. **1727** A. HAMILTON *New Acc. E. Ind.* I. p. xvi, I am not ignorant of the great Odds that the Bishop had of me, both in Education and Capacity. **1750** J. NELSON *Jrnl.* (1836) 23, I have the odds of you, for I have a much worse opinion of myself than you can have.

c. Equalizing allowance given to a weaker player or side in a game of skill or an inferior competitor in a handicap. Also *fig.*

1591 FLORIO *2nd Fruites* 73 *A.* What aduantage or oddes will you giue me? *S.* None at all: why should I giue you oddes? *A.* Because you play better than I. **1593** SHAKS. *Rich. II*, I. i. 62 Which to maintaine, I would allow him oddes, And meete him, were I tide to runne afoote, Euen to the frozen ridges of the Alpes. **1642** FULLER *Holy & Prof. St.* IV. xx. 346 Warre is a game wherein very often that side loseth which layeth the oddes. **1725** BAILEY *Erasm. Colloq.* I. 82 There's no great Honour in getting a Victory when Odds is taken. **1888** BRYCE *Amer. Commw.* II. li. 284 Each side feels that it cannot allow any odds to the other.

d. Phr. ***to ask*** (or †***beg***) ***no odds***: to desire no advantage; to seek no favour. *U.S.*

1806 *Baltimore Even. Post* 5 Mar. 2/2 (Th.), No odds he begs Of any beast that walks upon four legs. **1834** *Vermont Free Press* 7 June (Th.), A Varmounter never uses a dog... Give him a gun, and he asks no odds. **1894** *Congress. Rec.* 29 May 5447/1 South Dakota asks no odds of any State of the Union.

e. ***over the odds***, past the limit, above a generally agreed rate.

1922 'SAPPER' *Black Gang* xviii. 306, I admit it seems a bit over the odds, but every word I've told you is gospel. **1930** —— *Finger of Fate* 103, I admit..that to be called a damned Englishman by Pedro Gonsalvez is a bit over the odds. **1972** *Which?* Feb. 50/1 You could even pay more than the list prices. We found some of the tools being sold for perhaps a pound or so over the odds. **1972** *Listener* 28 Dec. 897/2 Sir Michael Swann, the new Chairman of the BBC's Board of Governors..felt that Alf Garnett went 'over the odds' occasionally. **1974** 'D. CRAIG' *Dead Liberty* xxxi. 187 His.. means of pushing his conscience underground was by paying a little over the odds.

5. a. In *Betting*, Advantage conceded by one of the parties in proportion to the assumed chances in his favour; the inequality of a wager, consisting in the ratio in which the sum to be given stands to that to be received. ***to lay*** (***give***, etc.) ***odds***, to offer a wager on terms favourable to the other party; ***to take odds***, to accept a wager thus proposed.

1597 SHAKS. *2 Hen. IV*, v. v. 111, I will lay oddes, that ere this yeere expire, We beare our Ciuill Swords..As farre as France. **1602** —— *Ham.* v. ii. 272 Your Grace hath laide the oddes a' th' weaker side. **1670** COTTON *Espernon* I. IV. 156 He was so confident of his skill, as to offer odds, that..he would either kill the Duke of Espernon, or very much endanger his life. **1748** *Whitehall Evening-Post* No. 405 The Odds, at starting, were on Babram. **1845** DISRAELI *Sybil* I. i, 'I'll take the odds against Caravan'. 'In ponies?' 'Done'. **1855** MACAULAY *Hist. Eng.* xxi. IV. 593 The Jacobites.. would not give the odds, and could hardly be induced to take any moderate odds. **1875** W. S. HAYWARD *Love agst. World* 100 What odds will you lay against him?

b. Phr. ***to shout the odds*** (see quot. 1925).

1925 FRASER & GIBBONS *Soldier & Sailor Words* 257 *To shout the odds*, to talk too much: to brag: to grumble. **1958** F. NORMAN *Bang to Rights* I. 10 He was still shouting the odds about this blag which was..nothing but a dirty great romance. **1960** L. COOPER *Accomplices* II. i. 76 There are always a few bloody fools who shout the odds about British justice and fair trials. **1967** *Sunday Times* 15 Oct. 9 For years he's shouted the odds about the Scouse way of life. **1973** 'J. PATRICK' *Glasgow Gang Observed* xv. 131 He still shouts the odds fae the windae when there's a ba'le [*sc.* battle] oan. 'Get *right* intae it, Tim,' he says.

6. a. 'Chances' or balance of probability in favour of something happening or being the case; esp. in ***it is odds*** (***that, but***), now usually ***the odds are***.

1589 *Pappe w. Hatchet* (1844) 44 Tis ods but I shall thrust thee through the buckler into the brain. **1625** BACON *Ess., Delays* (Arb.) 525 If a Man watch too long, it is odds he will fall asleepe. **1650** JER. TAYLOR *Holy Living* (1727) 245 It is infinite odds but he will quench the Spirit. *a* **1680** BUTLER *Rem.* (1759) I. 84 Those that..Can tell the Oddses of all Games. **1697** DRYDEN *Virg. Georg.* Ded., The Odds are against him that he loses. **1720** DE FOE *Capt. Singleton* viii. (1840) 148 It was a million to one odds that ever he could have been relieved. **1748** CHESTERF. *Lett.* (1792) II. clxvii. 116 It is odds but you touch some body or other's sore place. **1847** DE QUINCEY *Sp. Mil. Nun* viii. 17 It was odds but she had first embarked upon this billowy life from the literal Bay of Biscay. **1871** R. H. HUTTON *Ess.* (1877) I. 48 A game of chance where the odds are a hundred to one against you.

b. ***by all odds***, by far. *U.S.*

1866 W. D. HOWELLS *Venetian Life* 50 By all odds, the loungers at Florian's were the most interesting. **1951** J. P. MARQUAND *Melville Goodwin* x. 163 Lee said that McClellan was the best Union general he fought against by all odds.

7. a. Odds and ends, odd fragments or remnants, miscellaneous articles or things. Cf. END *sb.* 5.

Perhaps, in origin, an alteration of *odd ends*, found in same sense much earlier (see ODD *a.* 9); the later form having a better jingle, and more comprehensive appearance.

c **1746** J. COLLIER (Tim Bobbin) *View Lanc. Dial.* Gloss., *Odds-on-eends*, odd trifling things. **17..** —— *Lett. in Rhyme, To R. Townely*, 'Twas Thursday last, when I, John Goosequill, Went for some odds-and-ends to Rochdale. **1779** G. KEATE *Sketches fr. Nat.* (ed. 2) I. 51 'Tis but unstrapping my chaise trunk, laying out my odds and ends, and the affair is over. **1821** BYRON *Juan* III. lxxxiii, Having pick'd up several odds and ends Of free thoughts. **1844** DICKENS *Mart. Chuz.* xi, Fragments of old patterns, and odds and ends of spoiled goods. **1852** MRS. CARLYLE *Lett.* II. 193 There are still some odds and ends for the carpenter to do. **1860** SMILES *Self-Help* iv. 82 The very odds and ends of time may be worked up into results of the greatest value.

b. ***odds and sods*** (orig. Services' slang): see quots. 1930 and 1948; now in gen. use as a variant of *odds and ends*.

1930 BROPHY & PARTRIDGE *Songs & Slang 1914–1918* 143 *Odds and Sods*, 'details' attached to Battalion Headquarters for miscellaneous offices: batmen, sanitary men, professional footballers and boxers on nominal duties, etc. *a* **1935** T. E. LAWRENCE *Mint* (1955) II. ix. 125 Ten minutes late for dinner. Odds and sods to eat. **1941** *Argus* (Melbourne) *Week-End Mag.* 15 Nov. 1/4 *Odds-and-sods*, men not attached to a particular unit. **1944** *Penguin New Writing* XX. 44 The section was mixed up with the Police and one or two odds and sods as usual. **1948** PARTRIDGE *Dict. Forces Slang* 130 *Odds and sods*, men on miscellaneous duties. Men not classified. Members of other denominations than Roman Catholic, Church of England and Presbyterian. (Army). (2) In the Navy, the rank and file—the *hoi polloi*—of the lower-deck. **1950** G. WILSON *Brave Company* xiii. 193 Add three-inch mortar, four-point-two inch mortar, Vickers and all the odds and sods. **1955** E. WAUGH *Officers & Gentlemen* I. vi. 64 They left me behind with the other odds and sods. **1971** B. W. ALDISS *Soldier Erect* 205 We've got precious little strike-power..—the Assam Regiment,..a few odds and sods of the Burma Regiment, and our friends and allies of the Nepalese army! **1975** *Time Out* 26 Sept. 57/4 Although Tolkien's planned preface to the poems was never realised, his son Christopher has created one mostly out of his father's odds and sods—a radio talk plus notes. **1976** A. HILL *Summer's End* iv. 61 Beyond these were oblong-shaped archway bricks, chimney-cowlings, roof-tiles and other odds and sods I couldn't put names to.

8. *Comb.*, as (sense 5) ***odds-giver***, ***-receiver***; **odds-on** *a.*, on which odds are laid; also *fig.*; also (occas. without hyphen) as *adv.* and as *sb.*, the state of betting when odds are less than 1:1; an odds-on favourite.

1890 *Daily News* 10 Dec. 3/8 The proceedings were brought to a conclusion by the defeat of an odds-on fancy, Peerage. **1892** *Ibid.* 12 Sept. 3/4 Singularly enough the odds-giver was never in the race. **1898** *Ibid.* 30 May 11/3 Every even-money or odds-on favourite was bowled over. **1900** *Westm. Gaz.* 21 Apr. 3/3 We have played games by the hundred giving the odds of the QR, and have invariably made use of the right of castling QR without the least objection from the odds receiver. **1917** [see AUSSIE *sb.* and *a.* 2]. **1923** WODEHOUSE *Inimitable Jeeves* xiii. 153 'Something's gone wrong with the favourite.' 'Which is the favourite, sir?' 'Mr. Heppenstall. He's gone to odds on.' **1926** E. WALLACE *More Educated Evans* x. 222 Six successive odds-on chances. **1928** *Daily Mail* 31 July 11/4 The favourite..started at heavy odds-on. **1941** BAKER *Dict. Austral. Slang* 50 *An odds-on*, an odds-on favourite. **1945** J. B. BLAIR in *Coast to Coast 1944* 136 It seemed odds on that Wang would stop a bullet. **1955** *Times* 11 May 5/1 Lions Love..was made odds-on for the race for two-year-old fillies. **1962** D. FRANCIS *Dead Cert* i. 7 Admiral, the odds-on certainty who had lost his first race for two years. **1972** *Guardian* 5 Dec. 13/4 In one area near Poona there have been 22 drought years in the past 30... There, as in other places, it is a two to one odds-on probability. **1973** [see NAP *v.*[4]]. **1976** H. TRACY *Death in Reserve* xix. 147 'Odds on they've gone to France.' said Phoenix. 'He'd have enough fuel.'

odds (ɒdz), *v. dial.* [f. prec. sb.] **1.** *trans.* To make different, alter; to balance.

1863 KINGSLEY *Water Bab.* vi. 263 So they odds it till it comes even, as folks say down in Berkshire. **1876** *S. Warwick. Gloss., Odds*, to alter, make different. 'It'll all be odds'd in a bit.' **1883** *Hampsh. Gloss., Odds*, to alter. 'I can't odds 'un.' **1884** *Upton-on-Severn Gloss., Odds*, to balance, as an account, or to alter.

2. *slang.* To elude, to evade.

1958 F. NORMAN *Bang to Rights* II. 52, I used to go to church every Sunday only because I couldn't odds it. **1970** G. F. NEWMAN *Sir, You Bastard* iv. 124, I can't odds being mixed up in crime.

oddsbob, oddsbud, etc.: see OD[1].

oddside ('ɒdsaɪd). *Founding.* [f. ODD *a.* + SIDE *sb.*[1]]. A temporary cope, usu. made of sand or plaster of Paris, in which part of a pattern is bedded while the final mould is made of the upper, exposed portion.

1836 W. H. SMITH *Birmingham* III. 33 The patterns still lie on the sand of the 'odd side', as it is termed. **1903** *Work* 11 July 364/1 It is necessary, when the mould is commenced, either to block up the half of the flask to a level with the parting line on the pattern, or to sink the same into a bed of sand as far as its greatest diameter. This bed of sand is known as a match or 'oddside', and it has importance as a time-saver. **1928** W. RAWLINSON *Mod. Foundry Operations* xiii. 177 The use of oddsides eliminates the necessity of making a joint in the moulding operation, as is the case when moulding with a loose pattern. **1960** R. LISTER *Decorative Cast Ironwork* ii. 45 When the plaster has set, the sections are removed and placed aside, and the bottom section placed in another oddside. **1972** P. R. BEELEY *Foundry Technol.* viii. 351 Where a flat parting plane intersects the pattern, moulding is simplified by providing a split pattern and dispensing with the oddside.

†'**oddsman**. *Sc. Obs.* In 6 **odisman, odsman**. [Alteration of *odd man* (ODD *a.* 1): cf. *thirdsman*, *daysman*, etc.] An umpire, an arbiter.

1581 *Sc. Acts Jas. VI* (1814) III. 230/1 Referrit be the saidis parteis..to our souerane lord as ouris man and odisman. **1583** *Decreet Arbitral of Jas. VI Gov. Edinb.* (1742) 8 Ods-man and Overs-man, commonly chosen be Advice and Consent of baith the saids Parties.

†'**oddwoman**. *Sc. Obs.* [f. ODD *a.* + WOMAN, after *odd man.*] A female umpire, an arbitress.

1587 *Sc. Acts Jas. VI* (Jam.), And vmquhile the quene our souerane lordis derrest moder as odwoman and ourwoman.

oddzooks, oddzounds: see OD[1].

ode (əʊd). Also 7 **oade**. [a. F. *ode* (*c* 1500 in Hatz.-Darm.), = It., Sp., Pg. *oda*, ad. late and med.L. *ōda*, earlier also *ōdē*, a. Gr. ᾠδή (contracted from ἀοιδή) song, f. ἀείδειν to sing.]

1. a. In reference to ancient literature (and in some early uses of the word in English): A poem intended or adapted to be sung; e.g. the Odes of Pindar, of Anacreon, of Horace. ***Choral Odes***, the songs of the Chorus in a Greek play, etc.; *spec.* a short Old English poem, esp. *The Battle of Brunanburh*. **b.** In modern use: A rimed (rarely unrimed) lyric, often in the form of an address; generally dignified or exalted in subject, feeling, and style, but sometimes (in earlier use) simple and familiar (though less so than a *song*).

It rarely extends to 150 lines, and some poems so named are quite short, though prob. the name would not now be given to such. The metre in longer odes is usually irregular (e.g. Dryden *Alexander's Feast*, Wordsworth *Intimations of Immortality*), or consists of stanzas regularly varied (Gray's *Pindaric Odes*); but, in shorter 'odes', sometimes of uniform stanzas (Gray's shorter odes).

1588 SHAKS. *L.L.L.* IV. iii. 99 Once more Ile read the Ode that I haue writ. **1589** PUTTENHAM *Eng. Poesie* I. xxx. (Arb.) 72 Out of the primitiue Greeke and Latine, as Comedie, Tragedie, Ode, Epitaphe, Elegie, Epigramme, and other moe. **1609** HEYWOOD *Brit. Troy* XII. xviii, They Oades and Cantons sing. **1629** MILTON *Ode Nativity* 24 O run, prevent them with thy humble ode, And lay it lowly at his blessed feet. **1755** GRAY (*title*) The Progress of Poesy, a Pindaric Ode. **1770** T. PERCY tr. *Mallet's Northern Antiquities* II. 196 Compare the Anglo-Saxon Ode on Athelstan's Victory, preserved in the Saxon Chronicle. **1783** COWPER *Lett.* 4 Aug., We have few good English odes. **1798** S. HENSHALL *Saxon & Eng. Lang.* 39 The first specimen we shall exhibit is the conclusion of a Saxon Ode on a Victory of King Athelstan's. **1803–6** WORDSWORTH (*title*) Ode. Intimations of Immortality. **1805** —— *Ode to Duty*, This ode is on the model of Gray's Ode to Adversity, which is copied from Horace's Ode to Fortune. **1807** S. TURNER *Hist. Anglo-Saxons* (ed. 2) II. 323 It will be sufficient to add to the already copious specimens of the Anglo-Saxon poetry, the following Ode, which is appended to the menology. **1825** MACAULAY *Ess., Milton* (1887) 7 The Greek drama..sprung from the ode. **1847** F. MADDEN *Lazamon's Brut* I. p. xxiii, No one can read his descriptions of battles and scenes of strife without being reminded of the Ode on Æthelstan's victory at Brunanburh. **1852** TENNYSON (*title*) Ode on the Death of the Duke of Wellington. **1871** H. SWEET in W. C. Hazlitt *Warton's Hist. Eng. Poetry* II. 7 There are only two poems of any merit to which we can assign with any certainty a southern origin. These are the ode on the battle of Brunanburh, and the narrative of the battle of Maldon, which were, no doubt, composed immediately after the events they record. **1885** THEOD. WATTS in *Encycl. Brit.* XIX. 270/2 Enthusiasm is, in the nature of things, the very basis of the ode; for the ode is a monodrama, the actor in which is the poet himself. *Ibid.* 272/1 Coleridge's Ode to France, the finest ode in the English language, according to Shelley. **1890** R. G. MOULTON *Anc. Class. Drama* ix. 296 From the entry of the Chorus a comedy consists in the alternation of Episodes and Choral Odes to any number of each.

fig. **1841–4** EMERSON *Ess., Poet* Wks. (Bohn) I. 164 A tempest is a rough ode, without falsehood or rant.

2. *Gr. Church.* Each of the nine Scripture canticles; also, each song or hymn of a series called the ***canon of the odes***.

1881 LD. SELBORNE in *Encycl. Brit.* XII. 580/1 The system [of Greek hymnody] has a peculiar technical terminology, in which the words 'troparion', 'ode', 'canon' ..chiefly require explanation. The *troparion* is the unit of the system, being a strophe or stanza..divisible into verses or clauses, with regulated cæsuras... An *ode* is a song or hymn compounded of several similar *troparia*—usually three, four, or five... A system of three or four odes is 'triodion' or 'tetraodion'. A canon is a system of eight (theoretically nine) connected odes, the second being always suppressed.

3. *Comb.*, as ***ode-factor***, ***-maker***, ***-metre***, ***-writing***; ***ode-composing*** adj.; **odeman**, a writer of odes.

a **1737** POPE *Lett., to Ladies* iv. Wks. 1737 V. 122 My supper was..with a great Poet and Ode-maker. **1748** ARMSTRONG *Univ. Almanac* Nov., They'll lie somewhat heavy upon the hands of the ode-factors. *c* **1785–90** WOLCOTT (P. Pindar) *Progr. Curiosity* Argt. ii, Laurelled Odeman. **1795** —— *Coronation Bill* Wks. 1812 III. 377 Ode-composing Peter. **1791** LANGTON in Boswell *Johnson* an. 1780, A gentleman present..had been running down ode-writing in general, as a bad species of poetry. **1901** *Academy* 14 Dec. 585/2 That so-called 'irregular' ode-metre which they [*sc.* Patmore and Henley] use in common.

ode, obs. form of ODD, WOAD.

-ode, *formative suffix*[1], repr. Gr. -ώδης, -ώδες, adj.-ending = 'like, of the nature of', contracted from -οειδής = -o- final of root or comb. vowel + -ειδής like; e.g. λιθώδης stony, σαρκώδης fleshy, ὑλώδης woody, φυλλώδης leaflike. Thence have been formed mod.L. sbs. in *-ōdium*, Eng. *-ode*, in the sense of 'something of the nature of' that expressed by the first element. Examples: *cladode*, *geode*, *phyllode*, *sarcode*, *staminode*. (Not the same as *-ode* = Gr. ὁδός way, path, in *anode*, *cathode*, *electrode*, etc.)

-ode, *suffix*[2], formative element repr. Gr. ὁδός way, path, first used in *anode*, *cathode*, *electrode*, and later in the names of thermionic valves with a specified number of electrodes, as *diode*, *triode*, *tetrode*, etc. (with two, three, four electrodes); (certain of these latter—e.g. *diode*, *hexode*—were orig. coined directly from the Gr. to describe forms of multiplex telegraphy).

odel: see under ODAL.

odelet ('əʊdlɪt). [f. ODE + -LET: cf. F. *odelette* (16th c. in Hatz.-Darm.).] A short or little ode.

1589 PUTTENHAM *Eng. Poesie* II. xi[i]. (Arb.) 110 Philo to the Lady Calia, sendeth this Odelet [*pr.* Odolet] of her prayse in forme of a Piller. **1656** in BLOUNT *Glossogr.* **1819** W. TAYLOR in *Monthly Mag.* XLVII. 120 He has trifled, and written many an odelet to entertain his friend. **1883** *Athenæum* 22 Dec. 811/1 The gay and charming odelet 'To Minerva'.

'**odeling**. *nonce-wd.* [f. as prec. + -LING.] A diminutive or 'bantling' ode.

a **1845** HOOD *To Hahnemann* xii, An Ode-ling more will set you all to rights.

odeon ('əʊdiːən). [ad. Gr. ᾠδεῖον a building for musical performances.] **1.** Also **odeion** (əʊ'daɪən). = ODEUM.

1902 ANDERSON & SPIERS *Archit. Greece & Rome* vii. 117 No Greek example exists of the Odeon. *Ibid.* 280 *Odeon*, a circular building in which rehearsals and musical contests took place in Greece. **1908** W. R. LETHABY *Greek Buildings* IV. 196 The rotundas at Olympia..must have been covered by low cones. So must the Odeon and the Skias at Athens. **1909** A. MARQUAND *Greek Archit.* vi. 355 The Odeion (ᾠδεῖον), or music hall, was designed for musical contests and rehearsals of plays. **1961** L. MUMFORD *City in Hist.* Note to plate 12, What modern town..can point to..as many handsome examples of bath, theater, odeon? **1977** *Jrnl. R. Soc. Arts* CXXXV. 485/2 The Department of Antiquities.. is now excavating an Odeon.

2. (With capital initial.) The name of any of numerous cinemas in a chain built by Oscar Deutsch or his company in the 1930s. Hence in wider use, any cinema, esp. of similar lavish architectural style. Also *attrib.* and as *adj.*, designating this style.

1937 KLINGENDER & LEGG *Money behind Screen* 46 *Odeon Theatres, Ltd.*—Is a private company registered in October, 1933 with £100 capital... In November, 1936, the Odeon group of companies was increased by Cinema Ground Rents & Properties, Ltd... The object of the concern is stated to be primarily that of acquiring new sites for Odeon cinemas. **1946** J. P. MAYER *Sociol. of Film* iv. 51 Between August 1944 and June 1945 I spent approximately twenty Saturday mornings in the Odeon and Gaumont British Children's Cinema Clubs. **1952** A. WOOD *Mr. Rank* v. 87 People on holiday..would go into an Odeon because it would remind them of the Odeon at home. *Ibid.* 88 Beginning modestly.., Deutsch by 1937 had raised the total number of Odeons to over 200... His cinemas were all built to sumptuous standards, with the aim of providing something more luxurious than the rest... The Odeon cinemas became almost a symbol of the British way of life in the 1930s. **1954** J. BETJEMAN *Few Late Chrysanthemums* 40 An Odeon flashes fire Where stood their villa. **1960** C. MACINNES *Mr. Love & Justice* 224 The two girls carried on..joint excursions to their respective Odeons. **1964** *New Statesman* 10 Apr. 576/3 The whole occasion, with its foamy seats, Odeon hues and ice-cream girls, is organised to resemble film-going as closely as possible. **1970** COLLINS & DODD *Perishers Bk.* 8 4 Maisie..still finds Marlon attractive in a repulsive sort of way, especially when he wears his Odeon Admiral's uniform. **1972** H. C. RAE *Shooting Gallery* II. 243 It was the cinema, an Odeon in the heart of Glasgow, big and modern and comfortable. **1977** *Times* 12 Feb. 7/3 M. Barrier designed his own restaurant under the influence of *fin-de-siècle*, early Odeon, and fifties tubular.

oder, obs. form of OTHER.

‖**odeum** (əʊ'diːəm). Pl. odea (əʊ'diːə). [Late L. *ōdēum* (*odæum*), a. Gr. ᾠδεῖον a building for musical performances. Cf. F. *odéum* (1547 in Hatz.-Darm.), also *odéon*.] Among the ancient Greeks, and afterwards the Romans, a roofed building, akin to a theatre, for vocal and instrumental music; also, sometimes applied to a modern theatre, hall, etc., or gallery in such a building, used for musical performances.

[**1603** HOLLAND *Plutarch's Mor.* 277 Go to the gallerie *Stoa*, the learned schoole *Palladium*, or the Musicke-schoole *Odæum*.] **1682** *Lond. Gaz.* No. 1726/4 To this succeeded a Suit of Vocal and Instrumental Musick from the Odeum or Musick Gallery. **1775** R. CHANDLER *Trav. Asia Minor* 53 We saw here no stadium, theatre, or odéum. **1841** W. SPALDING *Italy & It. Isl.* I. iv. 156 In the free days of the nation, she and her colonies erected fortifications, theatres, odea, stadia, and temples. **1866** FELTON *Anc. & Mod. Gr.* I. II. iv. 336 The market, the court, the gymnasium, the odeum, the theatre..filled up the days of the citizen.

odeur, obs. form of ODOUR.

†'**odible**, *a. Obs.* [ad. L. *odibil-is* hateful, f. verbal stem *od-* hate: see ODIUM and -IBLE.] Worthy to be hated, hateful, odious.

1412-20 LYDG. *Chron. Troy* III. xxiv, His face was so hatefull and so odyble. *a* **1450** *Mankind* (Brandl) 724 All naturall nutriment to me as carene ys odybull. **1521** BP. CLERK in Ellis *Orig. Lett.* Ser. II. I. 307 The Spanyards.. being..as odybyll peopyll unto this nation as any cane be. **1614** RICH *Honest. Age* (1844) 58 There is not a vice so odible, but they haue skill to maske it with the visard of vertue. **1675** BAXTER *Cath. Theol.* II. v. 74 And is it possible ..to live continually with intelligible, amiable or odible Objects?

odic ('əʊdɪk), *a.*[1] *rare.* [f. ODE + -IC.] Of the nature of or pertaining to an ode.

1863 W. BARNES in *Macm. Mag.* May 36 That the dramatic and odic poetry of the Greeks..was a natural growth from the song-dances of savage life.

odic ('ɒdɪk), *a.*[2] [f. OD[2] + -IC.] Of or pertaining to the hypothetical force called OD.

1850 ASHBURNER tr. *Reichenbach's Dynamics* Pref. 11 The establishment of the existence of the odic force is that which was wanting to reply to most of the questions respecting life. **1869** *Punch* 21 Aug. 68/1 The magnetic or odic lights which Reichenbach photographed. **1895** ELIZ. S. PHELPS *Chapt. fr. Life* vii. 131 That odic force whose mysterious existence science cannot deny, and speculation would not.

†**odiferant, odiferous,** shortened forms of ODORIFERANT, -FEROUS.

14.. in Ashm. *Theat. Chem.* (1652) 220 Hys smel; That ben so swete and so odeferus. *a* **1529** SKELTON *Bk. 3 Foles* Envye, I thought for to have taken abyaunce with an odyfferaunt flowre. **1542** BOORDE *Dyetary* iv. (1870) 237 That there be no fylth in them, but good & odyferous sauours. **1552** HULOET, *Odiferous*, loke in odoriferous, for the laste is the better phrase. **1646** SIR T. BROWNE *Pseud. Ep.* 69 Working upon humane ordure and by long preparation rendring it odiferous. **1851** V. LUSH *Jrnl.* 8 Aug. (1971) 83 It looked marvellously strange to see so rough a looking man taking up bottle after bottle with all the air of a connoisseur, and at last after much deliberation selecting those which seemed to his olfactory nerves the most odiferous. **1977** *Fanfare* (Toronto) 6 July 3/1 German barbers worked busily for years on odiferous brews to suppress the dangerous shade.

Odinism ('əʊdɪnɪz(ə)m). [f. *Odin* + -ISM.] The worship of Odin, called the *All-father*, the chief deity of Norse mythology, corresponding to the OE. Woden, from whom most of the kingly lines of the Angles and Saxons reckoned their descent; the mythology and religious doctrine of the ancient Scandinavian people before the introduction of Christianity.

1848 O. BROWNSON *Wks.* V. 257 A revival of Odinism, or the old Scandinavian heathenism. **1867** PEARSON *Hist. Eng.* I. 115 Odinism, in the 5th and 6th centuries, was probably very different from what it became at a later date.

So **O'dinian, O'dinic, Odi'nitic** *adjs.*, of or pertaining to Odin or Odinism; **'Odinist**, a votary of Odin; a student of Odinism; also *attrib.* or *adj.*

1864 WEBSTER, *Odinic.* **1864** MISS COBBE in *Fraser's Mag.* Mar. 310 The worst penalty of wickedness threatened by the Odinist religion. **1869** STUART GLENNIE *Arthurian Local.* iv. 111 So in what I may call Odinian Scotland, have we memorials of the Norsemen. **1879** KARL BLIND in *19th Cent.* June 1105 The apparently Arthurian, in reality Odinic, character of various North-British legends. **1883** in *Homilet. Monthly* (N.Y.) Jan. (1884) 198 The Odinitic raven, the bird of memory of the old Norse Mythology. **1891** *Edin. Rev.* Apr. 351 The Odinic code countenanced the exposure of sickly or superfluous infants.

†**odi'ose**, *a. Obs. rare.* [ad. L. *odiōs-us*.] = next.

1560 DAUS tr. *Sleidane's Comm.* 36 That their name was in times past odiose, and hated of him.

odious ('əʊdɪəs), *a.* [a. AF. *odious* = OF. *odieus* (1376 in Godef.), F. *odieux*, ad. L. *odiōs-us*, f. *odium* hatred, ODIUM: see -OUS.]

1. Deserving of hatred, hateful; causing or exciting hatred or repugnance, disagreeable, offensive, repulsive; exciting odium.

c **1380** WYCLIF *Sel. Wks.* III. 139 þo passioun of Crist is myche for to preyse, bot sleeyng of his tormentoures is odiouse to God. *c* **1386** CHAUCER *Sompn. T.* 484 Sire quod he an odious meschief This day bityd is to myn ordre and me. *a* **1400** *Octavian* 1071 He bote hys lyppys and schoke hys berde, That hodyus hyt was to see. **1502** ATKYNSON tr. *De Imitatione* III. v. 199 So that nothyng be to the so odyous as synne & wyckydnes. **1577** HARRISON *England* II. v. (1877) I. 111 A number of their odious comparisons and ambitious titles are now decaied. **1604** SHAKS. *Oth.* v. ii. 180 You told a Lye, an odious damned Lye. **1759** JOHNSON *Idler* No. 86 ¶11, I am asked twenty times a day when I am to leave those odious lodgings. **1861** GEO. ELIOT *Silas M.* iii, The unhappy woman..whose image became more odious to him every day. **1866** DK. ARGYLL *Reign Law* vii. (1871) 327 The most odious conceptions of human society which the world has even seen.

†**2.** Regarded with hatred; hated. *Obs.*

1382 WYCLIF *Deut.* xxi. 15 If a man haue two wyues, oon loued and another odyows. *c* **1440** *Promp. Parv.* 362/1 Odyows, or be-hatyd, *odiosus*.

odiously ('əʊdɪəslɪ), *adv.* [f. prec. + -LY[2].] In an odious manner; so as to cause or incur hatred or odium; hatefully, abominably.

c **1460** G. ASHBY *Dicta Philos.* 1117 The malice of evil men Rebellith And makithe theime to lyve odiously. **1561** T. NORTON *Calvin's Inst.* I. xiii. (1634) 44 So charity is broken by odiously brawling together. **1642** R. CARPENTER *Experience* II. vii. 160 The Spaniards are odiously proud. **1675** MARVELL *Corr.* Wks. 1872-5 II. 467 No men were ever grown so odiously ridiculous [as the bishops were]. *a* **1715** BURNET *Own Time* (1823) I. 390 This was represented very odiously at Oxford. **1885** J. H. MCCARTHY *Camiola* xxxii, He was becoming dangerously, odiously complimentary.

odiousness ('əʊdɪəsnɪs). [f. as prec. + -NESS.] The quality of being odious or hateful; repulsiveness; the quality of causing odium; hatefulness.

1494 FABYAN *Chron.* VII. 644 Olyuer Deuyll, whom, for the odiousnesse of the name, ye Kynge causyd it to be chaungyd, & to be named Daman. **1561** T. NORTON *Calvin's Inst.* I. xvi. (1634) 86 Some men doe goe about with the odiousnesse thereof to bring God's truth in hatred. **1613** SHERLEY *Trav. Persia* 71 A thing..of infinite odiousnesse. *a* **1715** BURNET *Own Time* (1766) I. 226 The odiousness of the crime. **1884** *Manch. Exam.* 14 May 5/2 We say nothing of the impossibility of the task. It is enough to speak of its odiousness.

odir(e, obs. forms of ODOUR, OTHER.

Odissi (ɒ'dɪsɪ). *India.* [f. the place-name *Orissa*, Skr. *odra*.] A style of Indian dance, believed to be one of the oldest in India, originating in the eastern state of Orissa. Also called ORISSI.

1965 E. BHAVNANI *Dance in India* vi. 49 The classical dance as practised in Orissa, a State on the mid-north-eastern coast of India, is known as Orissi or Odissi. **1967** SINGHA & MASSEY *Indian Dancer* xxv. 203 Odissi did not escape a decline any more than the other dances of India... Odissi draws upon several ancient texts in Sanskrit and Oriya. *Ibid.* 205 Although Odissi recitals are nowadays given on the stage, they are nevertheless essentially a form of worship in which the dancer performs an act of adoration. **1971** *Femina* (Bombay) 30 Apr. 29/1 A student of Hindustani classical music, she knows many Oriya songs and is in demand in Bombay to accompany young Odissi dancers. **1972** *Daily Tel.* 26 Apr. 14/4 Her Odissi section could hardly have been more different. In this quintessentially feminine style, she showed the ancient thrice-bent sculptural positions as well as a wide variety of spins.

odist ('əʊdɪst). *rare.* [f. ODE + -IST.] A writer or composer of an ode; an ode-maker.

1797 CANNING & GIFFORD in *Anti-Jacobin* 18 Dec., The original Odist thus parodied by his friend. **1890** *Harper's Mag.* July 272/1 This sudden transformation of the hymn writer into the odist of Phœbus Apollo.

odium ('əʊdɪəm). [a. L. *odium*, f. vb. stem *od-*, *odi-* to hate.] Hatred, dislike, aversion, detestation. **a.** as a feeling or quality of the subject.

1654 tr. *Scudery's Curia Pol.* 139 Before his death he discern'd himself the object of the Peoples scorne, and odium. **1654** H. L'ESTRANGE *Chas. I* (1655) 65 Ambitious by some meritorious service to earn a better gust, or correct the universal odium against him. **1776** O. SCHUYLER in Sparks *Corr. Amer. Rev.* (1853) I. 287, I will no longer suffer the public odium, since I have it most amply in my power to justify myself. **1826** E. IRVING *Babylon* II. 389 Though it expose me to odium in every form, I have no hesitation in asserting it.

b. as a condition affecting the object: The fact or state of being hated or exposed to hatred.

1602 WARNER *Alb. Eng.* Epit. (1612) 387 Obseruing the King..to be in Odium with his Subiects. **1691** BP. KEN *Let. to Mrs. Griggs* 7 June (Add. MS.), To avoid yt odium vnder wch I lye. **1726** G. ROBERTS *Four Years Voy.* 64, I should have fallen under an Odium with them. **1875** JOWETT *Plato* (ed. 2) IV. 36 The odium which attached to him when alive has not been removed by his death.

c. The reproach attaching to some hated act or fact; odiousness; opprobrium.

1678 CUDWORTH *Intell. Syst.* I. iv. §20. 369 That he might decline the Odium of being accompted an Atheist. *a* **1680** BUTLER *Rem.* (1759) I. 348 Nero..having set Rome on fire himself..laid the Odium of it on the Christians. **1734** WATTS *Reliq. Juv.* lvii. (1789) 187 Men..who shall seek truth with an unbiassed soul; and shall speak it freely to mankind, without the fear of parties or the odium of singularity. **1826** SCOTT *Nigel* iv, When the odium of the transaction shall be forgotten. **1879** FROUDE *Cæsar* viii. 85 On him had fallen the odium of the proscription and the stain of the massacres.

†**d.** The object of hatred or dislike. *Obs.*

1681 HICKERINGILL *Sin Man-Catching* Wks. 1716 I. 189 Is not this better than to..become the common odium and object of the Peoples Hatred and just Indignation?

‖**e.** ***odium theologicum*** (mod.L.), the hatred which proverbially characterizes theological dissensions. Hence, by imitation, ***odium æstheticum*** (æsthetic), ***medicum*** (medical), ***musicum*** (musical), etc. Also, by imitation, ***odium academicum*** (academic), ***archæologicum*** (archæological), ***biologicum*** (biological), ***ethicum*** (ethical), ***philologicum*** (philological), ***philosophicum*** (philosophical), ***scholasticum*** (scholarly).

[**1673** J. FLAVEL *Fountain of Life* xxx. 414 Strigelius desired to die, that he might be freed *ab implacabilibus odiis theologorum*, from the implacable strifes of contending Divines.] **1734** 'PHILALETHES CANTABRIGIENSIS' *Geometry No Friend to Infidelity* 13 This is the very method which the *Odium Theologicum*, the intemperate zeal of Divines has always pursued. **1758** HUME *Ess. & Treat.* xxiv. 121 *note*, The *Odium Theologicum*, or Theological Hatred, is noted even to a proverb, and means that degree of rancour, which is the most furious and implacable. **1856** FROUDE *Hist. Eng.* II. vii. 137 The *odium theologicum* is ever hotter between sections of the same party which are divided by trifling differences, than between the open representatives of antagonist principles. *a* **1866** J. GROTE *Exam. Utilitarian Philos.* (1870) 9 The 'odium ethicum' is even more unreasonable than the 'odium theologicum'. **1875** LOWELL *Wordsworth* Pr. Wks. 1890 IV. 354 Something of the intensity of the *odium theologicum* (if indeed the *aestheticum* be not in these days the more bitter of the two). **1879** *19th Cent.* 1069 On such ground it is little wonder if the *odium musicum* sometimes approximates in character to the *odium theologicum*. **1893** *Westm. Gaz.* 23 Feb. 4/1 But the *odium medicum* of the main body of the profession has generally proved too strong for the heads of it. **1946** *Mind* LV. 98, I am accused of indulging in 'quixotic denunciations' of Spinoza, and of being actuated by a spirit of *odium philosophicum* against his memory. **1959** *Listener* 10 Sept. 405/2 The *odium biologicum* which it now seems scarcely possible for the acknowledged biologist wholly to avoid. *Ibid.* 29 Oct. 743/3 A kind of *odium archaeologicum* has been added to an *odium theologicum*. **1962** *Ibid.* 10 May 821/1 The lay public is now familiar with the wars of the learned... With Professor Dumond we are involved in something more than *odium academicum*. **1963** *Times* 14 Feb. 15/1 The question, then, arises whether the college to which he belongs and the cause of education in Oxford are to be sacrificed to the *odium theologicum* of a few infatuated dignitaries. **1970** *Language* XLVI. 246 The public will not change, and we will continue to suffer from the odium philologicum unless we can find a way of establishing more friendly communication. **1973** *Times Lit. Suppl.* 30 Mar. 347/4 Does not conceal her *odium scholasticum* at being anticipated by Firbank's bibliographer and first biographer. **1974** *Times* 21 Mar. (Art & Antiques Suppl.) p. iii/2 No punches are pulled in the book reviews, which are often filled with *odium scholasticum*, as one expert dissects the researches of another. *Ibid.* 9 Nov. 13/6 The *odium theologicum* that often characterises academic debate.

odize ('ɒdaɪz, 'əʊdaɪz), *v. rare.* [f. OD² + -IZE.] *trans.* To charge or impregnate with odic force.

1850 ASHBURNER tr. *Reichenbach's Dynamics* §488. 513 There is some probability that odic smoke is odized air, in the same way that the so-called magnetized water is odized water, that is, air and water charged with Od. *Ibid.*, Water ..when odized..becomes visible in the dark..exactly as odized metals acquire or increase in odic incandescence.

†**odling**, *vbl. sb.* (?) *Obs. rare*⁻¹. Meaning uncertain: 'must have some relation to tricking and cheating' (Nares). Perh. an error of some kind.

1599 B. JONSON *Ev. Man out of Hum.* Characters, *Shift*, A thread-bare shark; one that never was a soldier, yet lives upon lendings. His profession is skeldring and odling.

odly, -ment, -ness, obs. ff. ODDLY, etc.

odmyl ('ɒdmɪl). *Chem.* [f. Gr. ὀδμή (Ionian form of ὀσμή) smell + -YL.] A mobile sulphur-containing liquid found in the volatile substance given off in the preparation of balsam of sulphur; it has a garlicky smell, and boils at 71°C.

1866-72 WATTS *Dict. Chem.* IV. 173. **1892** *Syd. Soc. Lex.* s.v.

odograph: see HODOGRAPH 2.

o'dology. [f. OD² + -LOGY.] The science or doctrine of the hypothetical force called *od.*

1851 ROBERTSON in *Life & Lett.* ix. II. 26 Mesmerism, electro-biology, odology.

odometer (əʊ'dɒmɪtə(r)). Also 9 **hodometer.** [ad. F. *odomètre* (1724 in Hatz.-Darm.), f. Gr. ὁδός way + μέτρον measure; the spelling with *h*, following the Greek etymology, is rare.]

An instrument for measuring the distance traversed by a wheeled vehicle, consisting of a clockwork arrangement attached to the wheel or bearing, which records the number of revolutions of the wheel; now *esp.* one in a motor vehicle; also, an instrument for measuring distances in surveying, consisting of a large light wheel, having such a recording apparatus in the centre, and trundled along by a handle. Also applied to an instrument for measuring distances otherwise traversed, e.g. a pedometer.

1791 JEFFERSON in *Harper's Mag.* (1885) Mar. 536/1 Pd. Leslie for an odometer 10 D[ollars]. **1824** *Mechanic's Mag.* No. 34. 92 An odometer is a machine by which the steps of a person who walks..may be counted. **1848** SIR J. HERSCHEL *Ess.* (1857) 318 To each of these cars..a hodometer, marking the distances travelled..was attached. **1885** J. BIGELOW in *Harper's Mag.* Mar. 536/1 The number of revolutions of the wheels of his phaeton..were registered by the odometer. **1885** *Tradesman's Price List*, Patent Odometer accurately registers the distance travelled by Bicycle or Tricycle. **1913** *Collier's* 11 Jan. II. 57/1 The Corbin-Brown Speedometer records speed accurately... Its hand is steady; its odometer absolutely dependable. **1962** *Which? Car Suppl.* Jan. 28/2 We measured the accuracy of speedometer, mileage recorder (odometer) and fuel level gauge. **1968** *Chicago Tribune* 9 July I. 12/1 He went out the next week-end in his sportscar and, using the auto's odometer, plotted running courses from his home. **1969** B. WEIL *Dossier IX* v. 34 He checked the odometer which he had zeroed at the Porte de Versailles. Three more kilometres, then a right turn. **1972** *Drive* Spring 84 Cruising speed was restricted to 55 mph in deference to the 90,000 miles already clocked up on the broken odometer.

ödometer: see ŒDOMETER.

odometrical, -metry: see HODOMETRICAL, -METRY.

‖**odontalgia** (ɒdɒn'tældʒɪə). Also 7-8 in anglicized form **odontalgy.** [a. Gr. ὀδονταλγία toothache, f. ὀδοντ- tooth + -αλγια, from ἄλγος pain, suffering. Cf. F. *odontalgie* (1694 in Hatz.-Darm.).] Toothache.

1651 BIGGS *New Disp.* ¶248 The odontalgie or pain of the tooth. **1706** PHILLIPS, *Odontalgia.* **1727-41** CHAMBERS *Cycl.* s.v. *Alveoli*, From whence, and the nerve, proceeds that pain called odontalgy, or tooth-ach. **1800** *Med. Jrnl.* III. 403 Odontalgia, or the Tooth-Ach, the most frequent and painful disease incident to the human body. **1876** HARLEY *Mat. Med.* (ed. 6) 342 It is employed externally as an anodyne, as in neuralgia and especially odontalgia.

odontalgic (ɒdɒn'tældʒɪk), *a.* and *sb.* [f. as prec. + -IC; in F. *odontalgique.*]

A. *adj.* Of or pertaining to toothache.

1727 BAILEY vol. II, *Odontalgick*, pertaining to the Tooth-Ache. **1737** BRACKEN *Farriery Impr.* (1757) II. 102 Some Odontalgic Drop, or other Nostrum. **1888** H. F. WOOD *Passenger fr. Scotl. Yd.* xv. 181 That odontalgic expert—thought the detective—'looked extractions at him'.

B. *sb.* A medicine for toothache.

1737 BRACKEN *Farriery Impr.* (1757) II. 263 Opiates are Ophthalmics, as well as Odontalgics. **1861** HULME tr. *Moquin-Tandon* II. III. 159 The Larinus Odontalgicus of Dejean..has obtained a reputation as an odontalgic.

‖**odontiasis** (ɒdɒn'taɪəsɪs). [mod.L., f. Gr. ὀδοντιά- ειν to cut teeth: see -ASIS. In F. *odontiase.*] The cutting of the teeth; dentition, teething.

1706 in PHILLIPS. **1811** in HOOPER. In mod. Dicts.

odontic (əʊ'dɒntɪk), *a.* and *sb.* [ad. Gr. ὀδοντικός fit for the teeth, f. ὀδούς, ὀδοντ- tooth: see -IC.]

a. *adj.* Of or belonging to the teeth. **b.** *sb.* in *pl.* (*a*) Medicaments or remedies for the teeth (*Syd. Soc. Lex.* 1892); (*b*) Matters relating to the teeth.

1657 *Physical Dict.*, *Odentick*, belonging to the teeth. **1854** BADHAM *Halieut.* 303 Aristotle..says of his belone, that it is 'smooth' and 'toothless', which statement, as regards the odontics of the gar-fish, is the reverse of fact.

odontist (əʊ'dɒntɪst). [f. Gr. ὀδούς, ὀδοντ- tooth + -IST.] A dentist.

1819 *Blackw. Mag.* V. 607 It was Dr. Scott, the celebrated Odontist of Glasgow. **1821** *Ibid.* X. 214 His Majesty's Odontist had disappeared.

‖**odon'titis.** [f. Gr. ὀδοντ- tooth: see -ITIS. Cf. mod.F. *odontite* (Littré *Supplt.*).] Inflammation or pain of a tooth (Mayne *Exp. Lex.* 1857).

odonto-, before a vowel **odont-,** combining form of Gr. ὀδούς, ὀδοντ- a tooth, in terms of Zoology, Dentistry, etc., as in **o'dontocete** (-siːt) [Gr. κῆτος whale] *a.*, of a cetacean: having teeth instead of whalebone, opposed to *mysticete*; *sb.* a toothed cetacean; hence **odonto'cetous** *a.* **odonto'genic** *a.*, pertaining to the origin and development of teeth. **odon'togeny** [see -GENY], the generation or origin and development of the teeth; embryology of dentition (Dunglison *Med. Lex.* 1853). **odon'tognathous** *a. Zool.* [Gr. γνάθος jaw], having teeth or transverse ridges in the jaw, as helicoid Gasteropods. **o'dontolite** [Gr. λίθος stone], a fossil tooth; with lapidaries, a fossil tooth or other bone coloured blue by mineral impregnation, occurring in tertiary strata. **o'dontolith** [as prec.], tartar of the teeth. ‖**o,dontone'crosis,** necrosis or death of a tooth or part of a tooth (C.A. Harris *Dict. Med. Terminol.* 1867). **o,dontono'sology** [NOSOLOGY] (see quot. 1867). **o,dontor'nithic** *a.* [ORNITHIC], belonging to an extinct section of birds with teeth (*Odontornithes*). **odonto'rhynchous** *a. Ornith.* [Gr. ῥύγχος snout], having toothlike serrations in the bill, serrirostrate (as geese and ducks). **odonto'stomatous, odon'tostomous** *a.* [Gr. στομα(τ-) mouth], having jaws which bite like teeth; mandibulate (as an insect); see also quot. 1892. **odon'totrypy,** *Dentistry* [Gr. τρῦπα hole, τρυπά-ειν to bore], the operation of perforating a tooth to draw off pus from an internal abscess (C. A. Harris 1867).

1883 *Encycl. Brit.* XV. 393 The Mystacocetes have passed beyond the *Odontocetes in specialization. **1819** THOMSON in *Ann. Philos.* XIV. 416 *Odontolite Turquoise deserves to be treated as an object of zoognosy. **1868** DANA *Min.* (ed. 5) 581 Most of the turquois (not artificial) used in jewelry.. was bone-turquois (called also odontolite). **1847-9** TODD *Cycl. Anat.* IV. 83/1 The calculous matter which gathers round the teeth..called tartar or *odontoliths. **1857** MAYNE *Expos. Lex.*, *Odontonosologia*,..*odontonosology. **1867** C. A. HARRIS *Dict. Med. Terminol.*, *Odontonosology*, a treatise on the diseases of the teeth; also that branch of medicine which treats of the diseases of the teeth. **1874** W. C. WILLIAMSON in *Owen's Coll. Ess.* vii. 202 Professor Marsh's new *odontornithic bird. **1892** *Syd. Soc. Lex.*, **Odontorrhynchous*, having the mandibles dentated. *Ibid.*, **Odontostomatous*, having a dentated mouth or opening, as the *Bulimus odontostoma.*

odontoblast (əʊ'dɒntəblæst). [f. ODONTO- + -BLAST, germ, embryo.] A tooth-cell that produces dentine; any tooth-secreting cell. Hence **odonto'blastic** *a.*, of or pertaining to such a cell.

1878 T. BRYANT *Pract. Surg.* I. 558 The dentine is developed from the 'dentinal pulp' of vascular connective tissue by the immediate agency of a superficial layer of cells called odontoblasts. **1881** CARPENTER *Hum. Physiol.* (ed. 9) 56.

‖**odontoglossum** (əʊ,dɒntəʊ'glɒsəm). *Bot.* [mod.L., f. Gr. ὀδούς (see ODONTO-) + γλῶσσα, γλῶττα tongue.] A genus of orchids having flowers remarkable for their size and the beauty of their colours; also, a plant or flower of this genus.

1880 OUIDA *Moths* I. 178 Vere looked up from the golden blossoms of an Odontoglossum. **1891** *Athenæum* 4 July 40/2 Mr. R. A. Rolfe showed two hybrid odontoglossums.

So **o'dontoglot,** rare anglicized form of prec.

1879 BODDAM-WHETHAM *Roracina* xxi. 240 The heavier odour of a chocolate-tinted odontoglot.

odontograph (əʊ'dɒntəgrɑːf, -æ-). [f. ODONTO- + -GRAPH.] An instrument, invented by Professor R. Willis, for marking or setting out the teeth of gear-wheels.

1857 RANKINE in *Encycl. Brit.* (ed. 8) XIV. 396/1 To facilitate the drawing of epicycloidal teeth in practice..Mr. Willis has published tables of ρ-c and ρ'-c, and invented an instrument called the 'Odontograph'. **1866** BRANDE & COX *Dict. Sci.*, etc. s.v., Tables are given on the odontograph for finding the graduation on the scale corresponding to any given pitch and number of teeth.

odontography (ɒdɒn'tɒgrəfɪ). [f. ODONTO- + -GRAPHY.] A description, or history, of the teeth.

1840-5 OWEN (*title*) Odontography; or, a Treatise on the Comparative Anatomy of the Teeth. **1842** *Penny Cycl.* XXIV. 142/1. **1892** *Pall Mall G.* 19 Dec. 3/2 Minute anatomy, odontography, and many cognate branches, all fell under his [Owen's] observation in turn.

Hence **odonto'graphic** *a.*, of or pertaining to odontography.

1880 WEBSTER *Suppl.*

odontoid (əʊ'dɒntɔɪd), *a.* and *sb.* [ad. Gr. ὀδοντοειδής tooth-like: see ODONTO- and -OID. Cf. F. *odontoïde* (1690 in Hatz.-Darm.).]

A. *adj.* **1.** Resembling or having the form of a tooth; tooth-like; *spec.* in ***odontoid process*** (***odontoid peg***), a tooth-like projection from the body of the axis or second cervical vertebra of certain mammals and birds; when this process does not coalesce with the body of the axis, as in *Ornithorhynchus* and many reptiles, it is sometimes called the ***odontoid bone.***

1819 *Pantologia*, *Odontoid Process*, a process of the second vertebra of the neck. **1831** R. KNOX *Cloquet's Anat.* 179 The posterior surface of this ligament rests upon the odontoid process. **1872** MIVART *Elem. Anat.* 217 In many animals we have a distinct 'odontoid' bone, instead of an odontoid process. **1872** HUXLEY *Phys.* vii. 171 The skull does not move upon the atlas, but the atlas slides round the odontoid peg of the axis vertebra.

2. (*attrib.* use of B.) Of or belonging to the odontoid process, as ***odontoid ligament, tubercle.***

1840 G. V. ELLIS *Anat.* 277 The odontoid or check ligaments are two strong, round, fibrous processes, about half an inch long, attached, below, to the apex and sides of the odontoid process. **1892** *Syd. Soc. Lex.*, *Odontoid tubercle*, a rough elevation on the inner border of each condyle of the occipital bone for the attachment of the alar odontoid ligament.

B. *sb.* The odontoid process.

[**1706** PHILLIPS, *Odontoides* (in Anat.), a Part shap'd like a tooth; as The Tooth of the second Vertebra..and of some other Bones.] **1854** OWEN *Skel. & Teeth* in *Circ. Sc.*, *Organ. Nat.* I. 217 The rest of the body of the atlas, or 'odontoid', has coalesced with its proper neural arch. **1896** NEWTON *Dict. Birds* 852 The intervertebral pad connecting the Odontoid with the body of the Axis.

odontology (ɒdɒn'tɒlədʒɪ). [f. ODONTO- + Gr. -λογία discourse: see -(O)LOGY. Cf. F. *odontologie* (1771 in *Dict. Trévoux*).] That branch of the science of anatomy which treats of the structure or development of the teeth.

1819 *Pantologia* (title of Article), *Odontology.* **1842** BRANDE *Dict. Sci.*, etc., *Odontology*, the branch of anatomical science which treats of the teeth. **1911** *Chambers's Jrnl.* June 375/1 The British Medical Association has recently founded a Section of Odontology. **1966** G. GUSTAFSON (*title*) Forensic odontology. **1974** *Encycl. Brit. Macropædia* XI. 814/1 Other specialties on which the courts frequently require expert opinion include forensic odontology.

So **odonto'logic, odontological** (əʊ,dɒntəʊ'lɒdʒɪkəl) *adjs.*, of, pertaining to, or treating of the teeth, or of odontology; **odonto'logically** *adv.*; **odon'tologist,** one versed in the subject of the teeth or in odontology.

1788 V. KNOX *Winter Even.* I. ii. 24 It would not be surprising to see a barber style himself..Odontologist. **1856** S. CARTWRIGHT in *Trans. Odontological Soc. Gt. Brit.* I, The necessity of a union [amongst Dentists] has given rise to the formation of the Odontological Society.

odontome (əʊ'dɒntəʊm). *Path.* Also in mod.L. **odon'toma.** [f. Gr. type *ὀδόντωμα tooth-formation, f. ὀδοντ- tooth; in mod.F. *odontome* (Littré).] A small tumour or growth composed of dentine; more generally, any hard outgrowth from a tooth.

1870 tr. *Stricker's Hum. Histol.* xv. 470 We find in the dentine of the teeth, especially in pathological conditions, masses with bone lacunæ, termed Odontomes by Virchow. **1878** T. BRYANT *Pract. Surg.* I. 559 Tumours which result from the abnormal and excessive development of the dental structures at any time during the tooth's formation have been grouped together by M. Broca under the name of Odontomes. **1892** *Syd. Soc. Lex.*, *Coronary odontoma*, Broca's term for an odontoma which arises during the formation of the crown of a tooth.

odontophoral (ɒdɒn'tɒfərəl), *a. Zool.* [f. as ODONTOPHORE + -AL¹.] **a.** Of or pertaining to an odontophore. **b.** = ODONTOPHORAN *a.*

1877 HUXLEY *Anat. Inv. Anim.* viii. 490 Certain of the muscular bundles are also attached to the fore part of the odontophoral cartilages themselves.

odontophoran (ɒdɒn'tɒfərən), *a.* and *sb. Zool.* [f. mod.L. *Odontophora* (neut. pl. of Gr. ὀδοντοφόρος: see next), a proposed primary division of the Mollusca, including all those which have an odontophore, i.e. the Cephalopoda, Gasteropoda, and Pteropoda, with the tooth-shells, and chitons: see -AN.]

a. *adj.* Of or belonging to the *Odontophora.* **b.** *sb.* A mollusc of this group.

1877 HUXLEY *Anat. Inv. Anim.* viii. 506 In such a slightly modified Odontophoran as Chiton, the heart presents its normal position in the posterior region of the haemal face of the body.

odontophore (əʊˈdɒntəfɔə(r)). *Zool.* [ad. Gr. ὀδοντοφόρ-ος bearing teeth, f. ὀδούς, ὀδοντ- tooth + -φόρος bearing.] A ribbon-like or strap-like structure covered with teeth, forming the masticatory organ of certain molluscs; the lingual ribbon or 'tongue'. Also *attrib.*

1870 NICHOLSON *Man. Zool.* 251 The intestine has a neural flexure, and there is no odontophore. **1877** HUXLEY *Anat. Inv. Anim.* viii. 514 The mouth is..provided..with a well-developed odontophore. **1888** ROLLESTON & JACKSON *Anim. Life* 452 The stomodaeum in the *Glossophora*.. contains an organ known as radula, composed of a chitinous membrane bearing chitinoid teeth, developed within a sac (radular or odontophore sac), and growing throughout life.

odontophorous (ɒdɒnˈtəʊfərəs), *a. Zool.* [f. as prec. + -OUS.] Possessing an odontophore.

1870 ROLLESTON *Anim. Life* Introd. 87 The three classes Cephalopoda, Gasteropoda, Pteropoda, are placed together in one division as odontophorous Mollusca. **1877** HUXLEY *Anat. Inv. Anim.* viii. 513 These are odontophorous Mollusks which breathe air directly.

‖**odoom** (əʊˈduːm). [Ashanti *odúm*.] A West African timber tree (*Chlorophora excelsa*).

1887 MOLONEY *Forestry W. Afr.* 213 The 'Odoom' tree of the Gold Coast..To those Colonies this wood is invaluable, as it can withstand for years not only the weather, but also the attacks of the 'white ant'. *Ibid.* 247 Where such wood as 'odoom' ('oroko') is available. **1900** *Daily News* 6 Mar. 2/1 Two trees, the mahogany and a tree known locally as Odoom, which are found of large size and in considerable abundance, are admirably adapted for mine timbers.

odophone (ˈəʊdəfəʊn). [irreg. f. Gr. root ὀδ- smell + φωνή sound, tone.] A scale of scents or odours.

1885 C. H. PIESSE in *Encycl. Brit.* XVIII. 525 Tinctures.. made upon a quasi-scientific basis, namely, that of the odophone or gamut of odours of the late Dr. Septimus Piesse.

odor, another spelling of ODOUR.

†ˈ**odorable**, *a. Obs.* [ad. late L. *odōrābilis* perceptible by smell, f. *odōrā-rī* to smell, scent; cf. OF. *odorable* (14th c. in Godef.).] That can be smelt; perceptible to the sense of smell.

1589 PUTTENHAM *Eng. Poesie* II. i. (Arb.) 78 The audible [is measured] by stirres, times and accents: the odorable by smelles of sundry temperaments. **1684** BOYLE *Porousn. Anim. & Solid Bod.* viii. 125 The directly visible or odorable Expirations of Bodies.

†ˈ**odorament**. *Obs.* [ad. L. *odōrāment-um* perfume, f. *odōrāre* to scent, perfume. Cf. OF. *odorement*.] Anything used for its scent or perfume; an odoriferous or odorous substance; a perfume.

1382 WYCLIF *Rev.* xviii. 13 Alle vessels of precious stoon ..and of odoramentis, and oynementis, and encense. **1590** BARROUGH *Meth. Physick* I. xxiv. (1639) 41 [In Epilepsy] it is good to quicken the senses with odoraments. **1657** TOMLINSON *Renou's Disp.* 212 Pleasant odoraments must needs be grateful to the brain.

†**odoˈraminous**, *a. Obs. rare*$^{-0}$. [f. L. *odōrāmen, -min-* perfume + -OUS.] (See quot.)

1656 BLOUNT *Glossogr.*, *Odoraminous*, smelling sweet, fragrant, odoriferous, pertaining to odour.

odorant (ˈəʊdərənt), *a.* and *sb.* [a. F. *odorant* (15–16th c. in Godef.), ad. L. *odōrānt-em*, pr. pple. of *odōrāre* to perfume.] **A.** *adj.* That emits a scent: = ODOROUS, ODORIFEROUS. Now *rare*.

a **1465** *MS. Bodl.* 423 lf. 204 Disposed plentuously..With odoraunt odoure ful copiously. **1494** FABYAN *Chron.* VII. 239 The welle of bountie, that Flowre most odorande, By whose humylytie, man firste comforte fande. **1601** HOLLAND *Pliny* II. 33 The tast..of Parsly, Dill, and Fennell, sharpe, and yet odorant withall. **1791** tr. *Chaptal's Elem. Chem.* (1800) III. 42 The aroma..may be again restored by re-distilling it with the odorant plant which originally afforded it. **1872** J. H. INGRAHAM *Pillar of Fire* 169 At night, the odorant forests echo with the dread roar of fierce monsters.

B. *sb.* Also **odourant**. An odoriferous substance; *spec.* one used to impart a desired odour to a product. Also *attrib.*

1944 R. W. MONCRIEFF *Chemical Senses* viii. 166 Reactions to odorants are usually mild and undefined, a sniff, a drawing away, or..disgust. **1952** KIRK & OTHMER *Encycl. Chem. Technol.* VIII. 142 Biacetyl has been used as an odorant for butter, cream, milk, margarine.., cheese, coffee, confectionery.., ice cream mixes, and tobacco. **1971** *Nature* 24 Sept. 231/1 Theories of olfaction are thus legion; all attempt to answer the central question as to what properties of the odourant molecules are responsible for the wide variety of odour quality. **1972** *Materials & Technol.* V. xiv. 526 In microcellular soling mixes,..odorants which confer the odour of leather to the soles are frequently incorporated.

odorate (ˈəʊdərət), *a.* (*sb.*) Now *rare*. [ad. L. *odōrāt-us*, pa. pple. of *odōrāre* to perfume, scent. Cf. F. *odorat*.] Scented, fragrant.

1626 BACON *Sylva* §389 Where there is Heat and Strength enough in the Plant, to make the Leaves Odorate, there the smell of the Flower is rather Evanide and Weaker, than that of the Leaves. **1629** MAXWELL tr. *Herodian* (1635) 228 All kinde of fragrant and odorate Fruits, Herbes, and Gums. *a* **1715** R. LUCAS *Divine Breathings* (1772) §84 A rose set by garlick is sweeter, because the more foetid juice of the earth goes into the garlick, and the more odorate into the rose. **1800** *Med. Jrnl.* IV. 366 He found them to contain..of albuminous and farinaceous matter, but a small quantity, besides some odorate.

B. *sb.* A scented or fragrant substance.

a **1682** SIR T. BROWNE *Tracts* (1684) 213 A transcendent Perfume made of the richest Odorates of both the Indies.

So ˈ**odorating** *a.*, diffusing odour or scent.

1828 in WEBSTER. Hence in mod. Dicts.

odoˈration. *rare*$^{-0}$. [ad. L. *odōrātiōn-em* (rare), n. of action f. *odōrāre* to perfume. Cf. F. *odoration* (16th c. in Godef.).]

1623 COCKERAM, *Odoration*, a sauoring or smelling.

odorator (ˈəʊdəreɪtə(r)). [agent-n. in L. form from *odōrāre* to scent.] An atomizer for diffusing perfumes, etc.

odoriferant (əʊdəˈrɪfərənt), *a.* Now *rare*. [a. F. *odoriférant* (*c* 1420 in Hatz.-Darm.), pr. pple. of *odoriférer* to smell, shed perfume; cf. med.L. *odōriferens* for cl. L. *odōrifer*.] = ODORIFEROUS, ODOROUS.

1549 *Compl. Scot.* vi. 37 The sueit fragrant smel..of hoilsum balmy flouris maist odoreferant. **1578** LYTE *Dodoens* VI. lxxxiii. 764 White Rosen..which is moyst and odoriferant. **1604** E. G[RIMSTONE] *D'Acosta's Hist. Indies* IV. xxx. 292 Cedars..some white, and some redde, very odoriferant. **1727** BRADLEY *Fam. Dict.* s.v. *Florist*, Odoriferant or medicinal Drugs. **1892** in *Syd. Soc. Lex.*

†**odorifere**, *a. Obs. rare*$^{-1}$. [a. F. *odorifère* (15th c.), or ad. L. *odōrifer*.] = ODORIFEROUS.

1527 ANDREW *Brunswyke's Distyll. Waters* Q iv, The same [rose] water bryngeth them [weak limbs] agayne in theyr myght, with his smellyng and odoryfere vertue and styptysyte.

†**odoriferent** (əʊdəˈrɪfərənt). *Obs. rare*$^{-1}$. [f. med.L. *odōriferens* (see ODORIFERANT *a.*).] = ODORANT *sb.*

1858 G. A. SALA *Journey Due North* viii. 130 These boots have a peculiar..odour..of myrrh, frankincense, sandalwood, benzoin, and other odoriferents.

odoˈriferize, *v. rare*$^{-1}$. [f. L. *odōrifer* (see next) + -IZE.] *trans.* To render odoriferous; to scent or perfume.

1824 *Blackw. Mag.* XVI. 659 Perfumers, able to odoriferise and adorn the universe.

odoriferous (əʊdəˈrɪfərəs), *a.* Also 5–6 odory-, 6–8 oderi-. [f. L. *odōrifer* (f. *odor, odōri-* ODOUR + *-fer* bearing) + -OUS.]

1. That bears or diffuses scent or smell; odorous; fragrant; *rarely*, of an unpleasant odour.

c **1425** LYDG. *Assembly of Gods* 336 Of sauerys odoryferous was her sustynaunce. **1497** BP. ALCOCK *Mons Perfect.* A ij b/2 The odoriferous & swete vyolettes of all obedyence. *a* **1548** HALL *Chron., Hen. VII*, 54 What should I speke of the oderiferous skarlettes, the fyne veluet [etc.]. **1602** WARNER *Alb. Eng.* XI. lxi. (1612) 268 If odorifrous sents he smelt, he fathers them on her. **1749** LAVINGTON *Enthus. Meth. & Papists* II (1754) 67 Her dead Body was surprizingly beautiful and odoriferous..and it remains odorous and uncorrupt to this Day. **1822** SCOTT *Nigel* iii, Free air, impregnated, however, with the odoriferous fumes of the articles in which the ship-chandler dealt. **1843** PRESCOTT *Mexico* (1850) I. 129 The courts [were] strewed with odoriferous herbs and flowers. **1887** *Pall Mall G.* 2 Nov. 3/1 When..busy wharves take the place of the present muddy and odoriferous foreshore.

2. *fig.* Pleasing, sweet; 'fragrant'.

1577 HELLOWES *Gueuara's Fam. Ep.* 375 That which was in your lawe, cleare, neate, precious, and odoriferous. **1597** J. PAYNE *Royal Exch.* 11 Whose prayers and prayses is.. oderiferouse..before the lorde.

Hence **odoˈriferously** *adv.*, in an odoriferous manner; with scent or fragrance; fragrantly. **odoˈriferousness**, fragrance.

1599 A. M. tr. *Gabelhouer's Bk. Physicke* 42/1 Yet ther may heervnto be addede, a little Muscke, for odoriferousnes. **1601** CHESTER *Love's Mart.* lix, It makes them smell so odoriferously. *a* **1674** MILTON *Hist. Mosc.* iii. Wks. (1851) 487 Thir Markets smell odoriferously with Spices. **1855** H. SPENCER *Princ. Psychol.* (1872) II. VI. xi. 144 The atomic expulsion from which odoriferousness results, is one of the reactions consequent on the reception of heat. **1886** RUSKIN *Præterita* I. ix. 283 The coffee generally roasting odoriferously in the street.

†**odoˈrific**, *a. Obs. rare*$^{-1}$. [f. L. *odor, odōri-* ODOUR + -FIC.] = ODORIFEROUS.

1796 MORSE *Amer. Geog.* II. 568 They extract waters of a salubrious and odorific kind.

odorimeter (əʊdəˈrɪmɪtə(r)). [f. L. *odor, odōri-* ODOUR + -METER.] An instrument for measuring the intensity of odours.

1898 *Amer. Jrnl. Psychol.* X. 85 We are indebted to Dr. Zwaardemaker for the words 'olfactometry' and 'olfactometer'.., 'odorimetry' and 'odorimeter'. **1966** *New Scientist* 29 Dec. 726/3 The odorimeter is well adapted for plant control, for the regular injections of plasticizer can be made to coincide with the repeated inspection of batches being deodorized.

Hence **odoriˈmetric** *a.*, of or pertaining to odorimetry; **odoˈrimetry**, the measurement of the intensity of odours.

1898 *Amer. Jrnl. Psychol.* X. 85 Odorimetry is a 'side issue' of olfactometry. **1917** *Jrnl. Exper. Psychol.* II. 437 The preceding odorimetric method..enables one to stimulate the nose continuously for any desired time by means of an air current containing a known proportion of odorous molecules. **1922** *Perfumery & Essent. Oil Rec.* XIII. 5/2 Odorimetry..enables us to compare this value with fortuitous smells. **1935** *Bull. Neurol. Inst. N.Y.* IV. 15 (*heading*) Theoretical considerations, significance for quantitative and qualitative odorimetry and olfactometry. **1972** *Biol. Abstr.* LIV. 349/2 (*heading*) Odorimetric appraisal of polymers used in the construction of sealed chambers.

†ˈ**odorine**. *Chem. Obs.* [f. L. *odor* ODOUR + -INE[5].] (See quots.)

1842 BRANDE *Dict. Sci.*, etc., *Odorin*, one of the products of the redistillation of the volatile oil obtained by distilling bone; it has a very concentrated and diffusible empyreumatic odour, and is regarded by Unverdorben as a peculiar salifiable base. **1846** WORCESTER, *Odorine*. **1866–72** WATTS *Dict. Chem.* IV. 174 *Odorine*, a volatile base obtained by Unverdorben from bone-oil. It appears to have been impure picoline.

odoriphore (ˈəʊdərɪfɔə(r)). Also **odorophore**. [ad. G. *odoriphor* (H. Zwaardemaker *Die Physiol. des Geruchs* (1895) xiv. 240), f. as ODORIMETER: see -PHORE.] = OSMOPHORE 1.

1919 *Physiol. Abstr.* IV. 13 Adsorption is..but the first step [in olfaction], on which follows the solution of the odorous substance and its odorophore in the lipoids of the epithelial cell. **1922** *Ibid.* VII. 174 The natural groups of odours..are characterised by the presence, number, size, and arrangement of odoriphore groups. **1944** R. W. MONCRIEFF *Chemical Senses* xii. 306 Zwaardemaker considered that odour was dependent on the presence of odoriphores, special chemical groups, each of which was responsible for a special odour.

Hence **odoriˈphoric** *a.*

1944 R. W. MONCRIEFF *Chemical Senses* xii. 307 Odoriphoric groups. **1968** W. MCCARTNEY *Olfaction & Odours* 169 That odorous energy is molecular-vibratory.. seemed to him [*sc.* A. Heyninx] the sole admissible view and on it he reached the following conclusions:..4. The specific vibrations of the 'odoriphoric' groups of the odorous molecules cause the olfactory mucous membrane..to vibrate.

odorivector (ˈəʊdərɪvɛktə(r)). [ad. F. *odorivecteur* (A. Heyninx *Essai d'Olfactique physiol.* (1919) i. 2), f. as prec. + F. *vecteur* VECTOR.] Any substance the molecules of which stimulate the olfactory system.

1926 *Nature* 24 Apr. 591/2 The quality of the sensation depends on the molecular structure of the odorivector. **1964** *Ann. N.Y. Acad. Sci.* CXVI. 431 The final result of interaction of the odorivector molecules with the olfactory area is a modification in the electrical activity of the nerve cells which communicate with the sensors. **1967** J. W. JOHNSTON in T. Hayashi *Olfaction & Taste II.* 46 It is problematical whether there are pure odorivectors that stimulate one type of sensor unit.

odorize (ˈəʊdəraɪz), *v. rare.* [f. L. *odor* ODOUR + -IZE.] *trans.* To fill with an odour; to scent.

1884 *American* VIII. 301 The gas pours out in a cloud, odorizing the country for a long distance. **1897** *Chr. Herald* (N.Y.) 30 June 518/3 Put the mixture [rose leaves and spices] in a fancy jar with a lid. Keep closed, but open once a day to odorize the room.

odoˈrosity. *rare*$^{-1}$. [f. as next + -ITY.] The quality of being odorous; odorousness.

1847 LEWES *Hist. Philos.* (1867) II. 363 In like manner it possesses Saporosity, Odorosity.

odorous (ˈəʊdərəs), *a.* [f. L. *odor, odōr-em* ODOUR (or *odōr-us* fragrant) + -OUS; perh. after obs. F. *odoreux* (16–17th c. in Godef.) or It. *odoroso* (Florio). Formerly somet. pronounced (əʊˈdɔərəs).] Emitting a smell or scent; scented, odoriferous; more usually, sweet-smelling; fragrant.

1550 BALE *Image Both Ch.* I. viii. 107 The sweete smoke of the odorous incense. **1590** SHAKS. *Mids. N.* II. i. 110 An odorous Chaplet of sweet Sommer buds. **1675** T. R. tr. *Marini's Slaughter Innocents* 60 The hills, and dales, that plants odorous bare. **1697** DRYDEN *Virg. Georg.* I. 273 If od'rous Blooms the bearing Branches load. **1749** LAVINGTON *Enthus. Meth. & Papists* II. (1754) 8 Most of the Popish Saints dead bodies always remain odorous and uncorrupted. **1791** COWPER *Iliad* III. 454 Venus..in his chamber placed him, With scents odorous, spirit-soothing sweets. **1807** T. THOMSON *Chem.* (ed. 3) II. 237 At the same time the prussic acid becomes more odorous and more volatile. **1860** PUSEY *Min. Proph.* 205 A rich ointment..to which odorous substances, myrrh, cinnamon,..and cassia gave scent.

Comb. **1834** *Tait's Mag.* I. 221/1 Sweetest of younger sisters, odorous-tressed, Whose lips are worshipped by the breezes, Spring!

Hence ˈ**odorously** *adv.*, in an odorous manner, with smell or scent; ˈ**odorousness**, the quality of being odorous.

1727 BAILEY vol. II, *Odorousness*, sweet-scentedness. **1843** R. H. HORNE *Orion* II. i. 199 Odorously Glistened the tear-drops of a new-fall'n shower.

ˈ**odorscope**, ˈ**odoroscope**. [f. L. *odōr-em* ODOUR + -(O)SCOPE.] An instrument devised by Edison for determining or testing an odour.

1893 *Rev. of Rev.* Dec. 606 Odoroscope.

odour, odor (ˈəʊdə(r)). Forms: 3–4 odur, 4– odour, 4, 6– odor, (4 odere, -yre, 4– 5 odir, -e, 5 odure, hodure, 5–6 odoure, -owr(e, -eur). [a. AF. *odour*, OF. *odor, odur*, ad. L. *odōr-em* smell, scent. The spelling *odor*, occasional in ME., become obs. in 14th c., but arose again in 16th c. after L., was frequent in 17th c., and is now usual in U.S.]

1. That property of a substance that is perceptible by the sense of smell; scent, smell; sometimes *spec.* sweet or pleasing scent; fragrance.

a **1300** *Land of Cokaygne* 76 in *E.E.P.* (1862) 158 Trie maces beþ þe flure, þe rind, canel of swet odur. *a* **1300** *Cursor M.* 3701 þe odor [*v.r.* odour] o þi uestement It smelles als o piement. *c* **1375** *Sc. Leg. Saints* xvi. (*Magdalena*) 114 Al þe place Fulfillyt of þat odyre was. **1422** tr. *Secreta Secret., Priv. Priv.* 208 By the noos-thurles we haue knowlech of odeurs and stynches. *Ibid.* 247 In wyntyr the hodure of hote thynges;.. In somer odure of colde thynges. **1514** BARCLAY *Cyt. & Uplondyshm.* (Percy Soc.) p. xlii, To see suche dishes & smell the swete odour And nothing to taste is utter displeasour. **1646** SIR T. BROWNE *Pseud. Ep.* II. ii. (1686) 50 The effluvium or odor of Steel. **1664** BUTLER *Hud.* II. i. 574 All Spices, Perfumes, and Sweet Powders Shall borrow from your breath their Odours. **1697** DRYDEN *Virg. Georg.* III. 628 Fume with stinking Galbanum thy Stalls: With that rank Odour from thy Dwelling-place To drive the Viper's Brood. **1784** COWPER *Task* I. 317 The lime at dewy eve Diffusing odours. **1835** WILLIS *Pencillings* I. ii. 18 A more nauseating odour I never inhaled. **1873** BLACK *Pr. Thule* (1874) 45 There is an odour of sweet brier about, hovering in the warm, still air.

2. *transf.* A substance that emits a sweet smell or scent; a perfume; *esp.* incense, spice, ointment, etc.; also, an odoriferous flower. *arch.* or *Obs.*

1388 WYCLIF *Rev.* v. 8 The foure and twenti eldre men.. hadden ech of hem harpis, and goldun violis ful of odours. **1503** DUNBAR *Thistle & Rose* 6 Quhen.. lusty May.. Had maid the birdis to begyn thair houris Amang the tendir odouris reid and quhyt. **1526** TINDALE *Luke* i. 9 His lott was to bren odoures [*R.V.* incense]. **1534** —— *John* xix. 40 Then toke they the body of Iesu and wounde it in lynnen clothes with the odoures [1611 spices]. **1629** MAXWELL tr. *Herodian* (1635) 227 They throw in (by heapes) all Sorts of Spices, and Sweet Odours. **1697** DRYDEN *Virg. Georg.* IV. 601 With Nectar she her Son anoints.. Down from his Head the liquid Odours ran. **1709** PRIOR *Song, 'If wine and music'*, Thy Myrtles strow, thy Odours burn. **1871** R. ELLIS *Catullus* lxiv. 87 A royal virgin, in odours silkily nestled.

†**3.** The sense of smell. *Obs. rare.*

1398 TREVISA *Barth. De P.R.* xv. lxxiii. (MS. Bodl.) lf. 156b/1 Men wiþoute mouþe, and þei.. lyueþ onliche bi odoure and smell of noseþrelles. **1432–50** tr. *Higden* (Rolls) I. 291 Turfes.. whiche be more vile than woode.. and more tedious to the odoure.

4. *fig.* **a.** 'Fragrance'; 'savour'.

a **1340** HAMPOLE *Psalter* cxxxiv. 18 þei can not see the riȝt way, and þei fele not þe gode odor of crist. **1382** WYCLIF *2 Cor.* ii. 14 Therfor thankingis to God, that.. schewith by vs the odour of his knowynge [1582 (Rhem.) the odour of his knowledge]. —— *Eph.* v. 2 Crist.. ȝaf him silf for vs an offryng and sacrifice to God, in to the odour of swetnesse. **1526** *Pilgr. Perf.* (W. de W. 1531) 59 b, Let the swete odour of deuocyon and prayer spyre out and ascende vp to thy lorde. **1605** B. JONSON *Volpone* IV. i, I had thought the odour, sir, of your good name Had been more precious to you. **1791** BOSWELL *Johnson* i, The political principles in which he was educated, and of which he ever retained some odour. **1873** BURTON *Hist. Scot.* VI. lxv. 12 No odour of religious intolerance attaches to it.

b. (*good* or *bad*) Repute, favour, estimation. Also without qualifying adj.

1835 DICKENS *Let.* 16 Dec. (1965) I. 106 As the Tories are the principal party here, *I* am in no very good odour in the town. **1847** *Illustr. Lond. News* 24 July 62/1 To day he was in better odour. **1864** D. G. MITCHELL *Wet Days at Edgewood* 166 Hartlib was in good odor during the days of the commonwealth. **1886** SPURGEON *Treas. Dav.* Ps. cxlii. 4 When a person is in ill odour it is quite wonderful how weak the memories of his former friends become. **1954** N. MITFORD *Mme de Pompadour* xviii. 230 In 1760 St. Germain fell into bad odour with the police and Choiseul sent him packing. **1977** *Bulletin* (Sydney) 22 Jan. 33/1 There is no doubt that the Daoud affair, which has brought France into such odour abroad including a call for the boycott of French goods in the United States, was the result of conflicting interests between French diplomats and French security services.

5. odour of sanctity (F. *odeur de sainteté*, 17th c. in Littré): a sweet or balsamic odour stated to have been exhaled by the bodies of eminent saints at their death, or on subsequent disinterment, and held to attest their saintship; hence, *fig.*, gracious manifestation of saintliness; good repute as a saint, reputation for holiness: sometimes used ironically or sarcastically.

(For statements of the reputed fact, or references to it, see ENGELGRAVE *Cæleste Pantheon* (1727) I. 110; *Selecta Martyrum Acta* (Gaume, Paris) IV. 111, 198–9; *Fioretti di S. Francesco* (1546) xlviii. 66 b; PELLISSON *Lett. Hist.* I. 131; J. DE LA BARRE *Contin.* Bossuet's *Hist. Univers.* (1771) II. 270; VOLTAIRE *La Pucelle* (1780) I. 22; BÆDA *Hist. Eccles.* III. viii; *St. Guthlac* (Cod. Exon.) 1272, 1318; WILLIAM OF MALMESB. *Gesta Reg.* I. II. §216 (tr. Bohn II. xiii. 244); MALORY *Arthur* XXI. xii; FREEMAN *Norm. Conq.* III. xi. 32; also quots. 1749 in ODORIFEROUS, ODOROUS.)

1756 ALBAN BUTLER *Lives Saints* 24 Apl. II. 169 She [St. Bona] died in 673, leaving behind her a sweet odour of her sanctity and virtues to all France. **1778–84** COOKWORTHY tr. *Swedenborg's Heaven & Hell* §449 There was also a sensation of aromatic odour, as of a dead body embalmed, for when the celestial angels are present, what is cadaverous then excites a sensation as of what is aromatic. (*Note by* T. HARTLEY 1778. This may serve to explain what.. [is] related by authors of good credit, concerning certain persons of eminent piety, who are said to have died in the *odour of sanctity* from the fragrancy that issued from their bodies after death.) **1819** SCOTT *Ivanhoe* iv, My respected grandmother, Hilda of Middleham, who died in odour of sanctity, little short.. of her glorious namesake, the blessed Saint Hilda of Whitby. **1829** SOUTHEY *Pilgr. Compostella* Poet. Wks. VII. 264 These blessed Fowls, at seven years end, In the odour of sanctity died. **1833** RAINE *Brief. Acct. Durham Cath.* 64 Saints sleeping in all the odour of incorruptibility. **1856** R. A. VAUGHAN *Mystics* (1860) I. 90 There is an odour of iniquity, you must know, as well as an odour of sanctity.

6. *Comb.*, as ***odour-current, -reek, -wind; odour-breathing, -faded, -free, -laden, -like, -proof*** adjs.; **odour-blindness**, an inability to perceive a particular smell or range of smells.

1931 *Eugenical News* July 106/1 Some were thus 'blind' to fragrance in the red flowers though perceiving fragrance in the pink while others were just reversed in their odor 'blindness'. **1973** *Nature* 23 Mar. 271/2 Three types of odour-blindness or specific anosmia have been studied. **1821** SHELLEY *Prometh. Unb.* II. i, The odour-breathing sleep Of faint night flowers. **1876** LANIER *Poems, Psalm of the West* 182 What wavering way the odor-current sets. **1821** SHELLEY *Prometh. Unb.* III. iii, It feeds the quick growth of.. odour-faded blooms. **1955** *Jrnl. Appl. Physiol.* VIII. 341/2 The odorant.. introduced through an ultramicroburette was vaporized into the odor-free test room by an atomizing jet of odor-free air. **1962** W. D. HISLOP in H. W. Chatfield *Sci. Surface Coatings* xviii. 531 Use can be made of catalytic oxidation to treat the exhaust and render it odour-free. **1885** W. B. YEATS in *Dublin Univ. Rev.* Apr. 58/1 Dreaming in their soft odour-laden sleep. **1900** —— *Shadowy Waters* 44 Where time is drowned in odour-laden winds. **1626** BACON *Sylva* §904 Under this head, you may place all Imbibitions of Aire, where the substance is materiall, Odour-like. **1934** WEBSTER, Odorproof. **1950** *Amer. Jrnl. Psychol.* LXIII. 433 The need for rigorous experimental controls for smell soon became apparent. A large odor-proof globe.. was first thought of. **1951** M. MCLUHAN *Mech. Bride* (1967) 62/1 A special caste of robots, who would care for the victims of such necessities in germ- and odor-proof laboratories. **1960** *Farmer & Stockbreeder* 1 Mar. 55/3 The odour-proof film minimizes the risk of contamination. **1932** W. FAULKNER *Light in August* viii. 187 The odorreek of all anonymous men.

Hence (*nonce-wds.*) **'odouret**, a faint smell; **'odourful** *a.* = ODOROUS.

1825 L. HUNT *Redi Bacchus in Tuscany* 573 He makes odourets. **1889** *Chicago Advance* 30 May, More lasting, precious, odorful, than all The flowers of polar or of tropic seas.

odourant, var. ODORANT *sb.*

odoured ('əʊdəd), *a.* [f. ODOUR + -ED^2.] Having an odour; scented; chiefly in comb.

1422 tr. *Secreta Secret., Priv. Priv.* 242 Hit is good to reste .. in a softe bedde, in clothis fresshe wel oduret. **1595** SPENSER *Epithal.* 304 And odourd sheets, and Arras couerlets. **1817** GODWIN *Mandeville* I. 250 A gilded, nauseous, ill-odoured idol. **1878** LANIER *Poems, To our Mocking-bird* 4 Drift down through sandal-odored flames.

odourless ('əʊdəlɪs), *a.* [f. ODOUR + -LESS.] Without odour or scent; inodorous. Hence **'odourlessness**, the condition of being without odour.

18.. POE *Hans Pfaal* Wks. 1896 II. 12 It is tasteless, but not odorless. **1859** WILSON & GEIKIE *Mem. E. Forbes* IV. 127 Colourless, odourless crystals. **1879** HARTWIG *Aerial W.* ii. 19 The oxygen of the air.. odourless and tasteless. **1890** *Retrospect Med.* CII. 149 The odourlessness of Aristol.. renders the drug most useful in the treatment of soft chancre. **1901** *Westm. Gaz.* 24 Dec. 9/1 We would again lay stress on the odourlessness; it is a whale, not a smelt. **1963** W. SUMMER *Methods Air Deodorization* iii. 101 The simultaneous olfaction of two selected and matched odours will cause the psychological effect of odourlessness. **1968** [see OSMOCEPTOR].

o-dreghe, variant of A-DRIGH *Obs.*, away.

ods, obs. form of ODDS.

odsbob, -bodikins, -body, -bud, -fish, -heart, -life, -nigs, etc.: see OD^1.

†**'odso**, *int. Obs.* [Minced form of GODSO, as OD^1 for *God*; cf. GADSO.] An exclamation of surprise or asseveration.

1695 CONGREVE *Love for L.* II. v, Odso, let me see; Let me see the Paper. **1713** SWIFT *Jrnl. to Stella* 6 June, Wks. 1883 III. 158, I will speak to lord-treasurer.. to-morrow.—Odso! I forgot; I thought I had been in London. **1799** *Piece Family Biog.* I. 133 'Odso!.. you've begun, I see'.

odsoons, odspittikins, etc.: see OD^1.

odum (əʊ'du:m). [Native name in Ghana.] = IROKO.

1920 *Nature* 29 July 692/1 Another valuable wood is that labelled Odum.. which has also been exported as Iroko, sometimes falsely termed African teak... It possesses none of the qualities of teak with the exception of a superficial resemblance in colour. **1959** A. ABBS *Ashanti Boy* i. 34 The thick, odum stick he kept beside his bed. *Ibid.* 38 Low easy-chairs made of local mahogany or odum wood. **1962** *Listener* 6 Sept. 359/2 The big odum tree near the school park [in Ghana].

odur(e, obs. ff. ODOUR, ORDURE, OTHER.

odyfferaunt, -ferous: see ODIFERANT, -OUS.

odyl ('əʊdɪl, 'ɒdɪl). Also **-yle**. [f. OD^2 + Gr. ὕλη material: see -YL.] = OD^2.

1850 W. GREGORY *Lett. Anim. Magn.* p. xv, Of all the known influences, that of odyle appears to offer the best prospect of success to the investigator. **1885** H. S. OLCOTT *Theosophy* 156 The whole starry heavens is pervaded with a subtle aura, or.. imponderable fluid... He called it Od or Odyle. *Ibid.* 158 Heat he found to enormously increase quantitatively the flow of Odyle through a metal conductor.

Hence **o'dylic** *a.*, of or pertaining to odyl or od; **o'dylically** *adv.*, by means of odyl; **'odylism**, the doctrine of odyl or od; **odyli'zation**, the action or process of odylizing, the communication of animal magnetism from one person to another; **'odylize** *v. trans.*, to subject to or affect with odyl.

1853 CARPENTER *Hum. Phys.* (ed. 4) §924 No hypothetical '*odylic' or other concealed agency. **1871** M. COLLINS *Mrq. & Merch.* II. iv. 113 When a man and woman meet there is always a certain magnetic or odylic communication between them. **1880** MRS. WHITNEY *Odd or Even* iv. 41 An odylic thrill in the fingers that held her side of the cover. **1885** H. S. OLCOTT *Theosophy* 158 The Brahmin.. submitting his *odylically-tainted metallic vessel to the fire. **1862** *Fraser's Mag.* Oct. 517 Mesmerism.. with its kindred subjects, variously known as animal magnetism, electro-biology, clairvoyance, *odylism, hypnotism. **1876** CARPENTER in *Contemp. Rev.* Jan. 282 The curious phenomena which, under the names of mesmerism, odylism, electro-biology, psychic force, and spiritual agency, have been supposed to indicate the existence of some new and mysterious force in nature. **1883** SINNETT *Esoteric Buddhism* v. (1884) 86 The spirit of the sensitive getting *odylized.. by the aura of the spirit in the Devachan.

odynometer (ɒdɪ'nɒmɪtə(r)). [f. Gr. ὀδύνη pain + -(O)METER.] A register or measurer of pain. Hence **odyno'metrical** *a.*, of or pertaining to the measurement of pain.

1889 J. M. DUNCAN *Lect. Dis. Wom.* iii. (ed. 4) 9 As yet, we have no odynometer, or even good odynometrical resources, to test and measure pain. **1893** *Daily News* 23 Dec. 4/8 But we have no odynometer, and cannot tell whether, when one person bears pain better than another, he is bearing.. the same amount and quality of pain.

odynphagia (ɒdɪn'feɪdʒɪə). *Pathol.* [mod.L., badly f. Gr. ὀδύνη pain + -φαγια eating.] Painful swallowing (as a symptom of disease).

1880 M. MACKENZIE *Dis. Throat & Nose* I. 26 There is.. sometimes odynphagia of the most severe character. **1897** *Allbutt's Syst. Med.* IV. 835 In consequence of the odynphagia, the saliva collects.

odyous(e, odyr(e, obs. ff. ODIOUS, ODOUR, OTHER.

Odyssey ('ɒdɪsɪ). Also 7 **Odyssæa, -ysee, -isse**, 8 **-ysse**. [ad. L. *Odyssēa*, a. Gr. Ὀδύσσεια, f. Ὀδυσσεύς Ulysses, a king of Ithaca. Cf. F. *Odyssée*.]

1. One of the two great epic poems of ancient Greece, attributed to Homer, which describes the ten years' wanderings of Odysseus (Ulysses) on his way home to Ithaca after the fall of Troy.

1601 HOLLAND *Pliny* II. 372 In his Odyssæa, where he discourseth of the aduentures, trauels, & fortunes of prince Vlysses. **1603** —— *Plutarch's Mor.* 203 The Odysee or Ilias of Homer. **1701** SWIFT *Contests Nobles & Comm.* Wks. 1755 II. I. 25 Several passages in the Odysses. **1818** BYRON *Juan* I. xli, Their Æneids, Iliads, and Odysseys. **1876** GLADSTONE *Homeric Synchr.* 169 In the fourth Odyssey he is described as the slayer of Antilochos... In the eleventh Odyssey, he is named for his personal beauty.

2. *fig.* A long series of wanderings to and fro; a long adventurous journey.

1889 *Daily News* 10 Oct. 4/7 He is on this odyssey of rebellion now, though we do not know precisely among what people, or at what Court. **1894** *Westm. Gaz.* 10 Aug. 8/1 The odysseys of historical [music] scores might form the subject of an interesting volume. **1899** *Edin. Rev.* Oct. 326 Scraps of adventitious mineral that, after whole Odysseys of adventure, have come to rest within the shelter of a glass case.

Hence **Odyssean** (ɒdɪ'si:ən) *a.*, of, pertaining to, or having the characteristics of the Odyssey.

a **1711** KEN *Hymnotheo* Poet. Wks. 1721 III. 289 Odyssean risks upon the Main. **1870** LOWELL *Among my Bks.* Ser. I. (1873) 155 Even common sailors could not tell the story of their wanderings without rising to an almost Odyssean strain. **1892** AGNES M. CLERKE *Fam. Stud. Homer* ii. 49 The poet does not appear to feel any need of bringing it into harmony with the Odyssean vision.

odzookers, odzooks, odzounds: see OD^1, and ZOOKS, ZOUNDS.

‖**oe** (əʊ). *rare*$^{-1}$. [For Da. *öe*, *ö* = Norw. *öy*, Icel. *ey*, OE. *ieȝ*, isle, islet.] A small island.

1817 SCOTT *Harold* III. x, The bold Baltic's echoing strand Looks o'er each grassy oe [*rime* grow].

oe, another form of OY *sb. Sc.*, grandson.

oe, obs. variant of O *sb.*^{1}, O *adj.* one, O *vb.*

œ (in the earliest times, and now often, written separately *oe*) was in Early Old English the symbol of the *i*-umlaut of *ó*, *o*, as in *fœt*, *foet*, *soecan*, *œhtan*, *oehtan*, doubtless originally sounded like Ger. *ö*, *œ*, but afterwards written (and sounded) simply *é*, *e*, in which form it came down into Middle English.

In modern Eng. *œ*, *oe* reproduces the usual L. spelling of Gr. οι, which often in med.L., and in Romanic, was treated like simple *ē*. In words that have come into Eng. through med.L. or Fr., or other Romanic langs., Eng. has usually a simple *e*, as in *economy*, F. *économie*, L. *œconomia*, Gr. οἰκονομία; *penal*, F. *pénal*, L. *pœnālis*, f. *pœna*, Gr. ποινή; *cemetery*, L. *cœmeterium*, Gr. κοιμητήριον; but in recent words derived immediately from L. or Gr., *œ*, *oe* is usually retained, esp. (1) in proper names, as *Œdipus*, *Eubœa*, *Phœbe*; (2) in words referring to classical antiquities, as *œcist*, *Pœcile* (in which, however, some represent Gr. οι by *oi*, as *oikist*); (3) in scientific and technical terms, as *amœba*, *œnothera*, *œstrus*, *diœcious*, *diarrhœa*, *homœopathy*, *pharmacopœia*, *onomatopœic*; but there is a tendency, stronger in America than in Great Britain, to substitute *e* for *œ* in these words when they pass into popular use or become familiar, e.g. *diarrhea*, *esophagus*, *homeoid*. This *œ*, being orig. a diphthong and subsequently a long vowel, is usually pronounced as 'long *e*' (iː), rarely as 'short *e*' (ɛ); when changed to *e*, it submits to the same usages as ordinary *e* from Gr. and L.

In French, *œ* is an occasional etymological or orthographical substitute for *e* in the diphthongs *œi*, *œu*, as in *œil*, *œuf*, *cœur*; when these words are borrowed in Eng. they retain the Fr. spelling. *œ*, *oe* also occasionally represents Ger. *ö*, *œ*, *oe* (*Goethe*), and the *ö*, *ø* of Scandinavian tongues (*Faroe*).

œcist (ˈiːsɪst), **œkist** (ˈiːkɪst). Also oikist. [ad. Gr. οἰκιστής, agent-n. from οἰκίζ-ειν to settle (a colony), f. οἶκος house, dwelling.] The founder of an ancient Greek (rarely *transf.* a modern) colony.

1846 GROTE *Greece* I. xviii. II. 41 The legend of the Rhodian archæologists respecting their œkist Althæmenês. **1878** *Blackw. Mag.* Sept. 340 The œkist of Cape Colony, Van Riebeck. **1880** *Daily News* 17 Dec. 5/3 The Oecist of Gilead, to give Mr. Oliphant his proper designation. **1885** JANE E. HARRISON *Stud. Grk. Art* iv. 152 Megara Hyblæa in Sicily..sent for an oikist, or colony leader, from her old home, Megara in Hellas proper.

† **œco'domical**, *a. Obs. rare.* [f. Gr. οἰκοδομικ-ός (f. οἰκοδόμος builder, architect) + -AL[1].] Relating to the building of houses; architectural.

1678 CUDWORTH *Intell. Syst.* I. iii. §37. 155 If the Oecodomical Art, which is in the Mind of the Architect, were supposed to be transfused into the Stones, Bricks and Mortar.

œcoid (ˈiːkɔɪd). *Biol.* Also oikoid. [f. Gr. οἶκος house, dwelling: see -OID.] (See quot.)

1892 *Syd. Soc. Lex.*, *Œcoid*, Brücke's term for the substance, or stroma, of a red blood-corpuscle which is charged with or contains the coloured matter and the nucleus, where there is one, together called the zooid. Also, the same as the spongioplasm of an amœboid cell.

œcology, œcological, etc.: see ECOLOGY, ECOLOGICAL.

œconomic, -nomy, etc.: see ECONOMIC, etc.

‖ **œconomus** (iːˈkɒnəməs). *Hist.* Also 6 *Sc.* economus, iconymus, yconomus, -nimus. [L., a. Gr. οἰκονόμος house-steward.] The steward or manager of the temporalities of a religious foundation or society; the steward of a college.

1584 in *Life A. Melville* (1819) I. 481 Discharging..all vders economus, intrometters, factors or vder personis whatsoever. **1592** *Sc. Acts Jas. VI* (1814) III. 589/1 Ludouick, duke of lennox commendater of þe priorie of sanctandrois and his yconomus. **1599** *Ibid.* IV. 189/1 That thair salbe..ane counsall of that vniuersitie [St. Andrews].. quhilkis salhaif poware to haif the yconimus in euerie colledge. **1659** BAXTER *Key Cath.* II. iii. 404 Christ Jesus, dispensing them all by himself and administering them severally, not by any one oeconomus, but by the several Bishops as inferiour Heads. **1725** tr. *Dupin's Eccl. Hist. 17th C.* I. II. iii. 41 All the Alms, and all the Revenues..were kept in common, under the Care of the Deacons, and Oeconomi. **1854** MILMAN *Lat. Chr.* I. 373 A steward or œconomus must be appointed in each church.

† **œ'cumenacy.** *Obs. rare*[−1]. [irreg. f. Gr. οἰκουμένη (Romanized *œcūmenē*) the inhabited earth, the whole world + -ACY as in *episcopacy*, *papacy*, *primacy*.] The ecclesiastical primacy or supremacy of the world.

1646 CHAS. I in *Cert. Relig.* (1649) 45 When the Romane Monarck stretch'd forth his arms from East to West, he might make the Bishops of Roms œcumenacy as large as was his Empire.

‖ **œcumene** (iːˈkjuːmɛniː). Also ecumene, oik(o)umene. [a. Gr. οἰκουμένη (see ECUMENIC *a.*).] The inhabited world as known to the ancient Greeks; the Greeks and their neighbours regarded in the context of development in human society. Also *transf.*, the inhabited world (or a part of it) as known to or embraced by a later civilization.

1911 E. C. SEMPLE *Influences Geogr. Environment* vi. 171 Humanity's area of distribution and historical movement we call the Oikoumene. **1926** M. T. BINGHAM tr. *P. Vidal de la Blache's Princ. Human Geogr.* 18 Ocean solitudes long divided inhabited countries (oikoumenes). *Ibid.* ii. 49 Recent conquests by the *oikoumene*. **1941** *Antiquity* XV. 6 By reinstating the archaeological evidence the continuum of the oikumene, made explicit in the medieval travellers' narratives, could be displayed as an enlargement of one already implied in the Bronze Age by the 24th century B.C. **1946** V. EHRENBERG *Aspects Anc. World* iii. 32 Greeks and Romans alike regarded the inhabited earth, the *oecumene*, as an area round the Mediterranean. **1953** *Ann. Assoc. Amer. Geogr.* XLIII. 92 Distribution of people in its..global scale, involves dividing the land portions of the earth into permanently inhabited as compared with uninhabited, or temporarily inhabited, parts. The terms ecumene and non-ecumene have been employed to represent these two major sub-divisions. **1956** A. TOYNBEE *Historian's Approach to Relig.* 214 The political partition of the *Oikoumenê* into sixty or seventy self-governing parochial states. **1962** B. LEWIS in Lewis & Holt *Historians of Middle East* xvi. 182 It [*sc.* the common stock of Muslim universal history] appears chiefly in the general introductory matter, leading up to the establishment of the Islamic oecumene. **1967** *Economist* 18 Nov. 742/2 Should the political scientist make change itself his theme? And if so, in an interdependent world, can the boundaries of his study be less than the *oikumene* itself? **1967** H. R. FRIIS *Pacific Basin* ii. 20 Eratosthenes..was like other philosophers before him concerned with the extent of the inhabited world—the *oikoumene*. **1972** D. M. NICOL *Last Centuries of Byzantium* v. 78 The paterfamilias, the head of the Christian family or *oikoumene*, was the emperor in Constantinople.

œcumenian (iːkjuːˈmiːnɪən), *a. rare.* [f. as ŒCUMENACY + -IAN.] = ECUMENICAL I.

1865 LIGHTFOOT *Galatians* (1874) 192 Two anonymous Commentators in the Oecumenian Catena.

œcumenic, *a.*, etc.: var. ECUMENIC *a.*, etc.

† **'œdem, œ'deme,** obs. anglicized forms of next. [Cf. F. *œdème* (1545 in Hatz.-Darm.).]

1591 JAS. I *Poet. Exerc.*, *Furies* 889 Together with the Hyves, and..The boudned Oedems cleare. **1598** SYLVESTER *Du Bartas* II. i. III. *Furies* 486 Tumours, Begot of vicious indigested humours: As Phlegmons, Oedems, Schyrrhes, Erisipiles. **1616** BULLOKAR *Eng. Expos.*, *Oedeme*, a waterish swelling in the body without paine.

‖ **œdema** (iːˈdiːmə). *Path.* Also 5 vdimia, 9 edema. [mod.L., a. Gr. οἴδημα (-ματ-) swelling, swollen condition, f. οἰδέ-ειν to swell.] 'A swelling produced by the presence of serous fluid in the areolar tissue or in the substance of a part; being a local dropsy' (*Syd. Soc. Lex.* 1892).

c **1400** *Lanfranc's Cirurg.* 206 An enpostym þat comeþ of fleume, is clepid vdimia or zima. **1541** R. COPLAND *Galyen's Terapeut.* 2 F ij, Tumour, yᵗ is called oedema. **1683** SALMON *Doron Med.* II. 428 It resolves Oedema and discusses all sorts of cold and Hard Tumors. **1758** J. S. tr. *Le Dran's Observ.* (1771) 92 An *Œdema*..is almost a certain Symptom of a Suppuration. **1874** BUCKNILL & TUKE *Psych. Med.* 587 Œdema of the brain, a state in which the tissue of the organ is permeated by water or serosity.

attrib. **1896** *Allbutt's Syst. Med.* I. 651 An area which.. contains a considerable quantity of œdema fluid.

Hence **œde'matic, œ'dematose** *adjs.* = next.

a **1658** HARVEY (J.), A phlegmonous or *oedematick tumour. **1819** H. BUSK *Vestriad* IV. 743 Rudely they press his œdematic toes. **1884** *Brachet's Aix-les-bains* I. 105 The œdematic state. **1710** T. FULLER *Pharm. Extemp.* 213 *Oedematose Tumours.

œdematous (iːˈdiːm-, iːˈdɛmətəs), *a.* Also 9 oid-, ed-. [f. Gr. οἰδηματ- (see prec.) + -OUS.] Pertaining to or of the nature of œdema; affected with œdema, swollen with serous fluid; dropsical.

1646 SIR T. BROWNE *Pseud. Ep.* IV. iii. 183 An Inflammation..Oedematous, Schirrous, Erisipelatous according to the predominancy of melancholy, flegme, or choler. **1718** QUINCY *Compl. Disp.* 122 To dissolve hard Tumours, dissipate Oedematous swellings. **1828** WEBSTER, *Edematous*. **1854** JONES & SIEV. *Pathol. Anat.* (1874) 234 A general œdematous condition of the brain.

Hence **œ'dematously** *adv.*

1782 HEBERDEN *Comm.* xxii. (1806) 108 Healthy young women will often have their legs swell œdematously. **1898** *Allbutt's Syst. Med.* V. 577 The joints..are œdematously swollen and tender on pressure.

Œdipal (ˈiːdɪpəl), *a. Psychol.* [f. ŒDIP(US + -AL.] Characterized by an Oedipus complex; of or pertaining to the desire felt for a parent of the opposite sex.

1939 H. V. DICKS *Clin. Stud. Psychopathol.* v. 79 The analysis was devoted to working out the Oedipal, strongly sexualized, love for him. **1950** E. FRENKEL-BRUNSWIK in T. Wiesengrund-Adorno et al. *Authoritarian Personality* ix. 316 The problem of homosexuality relates to the different ways of failure in resolving the Oedipal conflict. **1960** *New Left Rev.* Nov.-Dec. 69/1 They interpreted the assassination in Oedipal terms, Trotsky being..the hated father-substitute. **1967** T. STOPPARD *Rosencrantz & Guildenstern* II. 59 He at last confronts his mother and in a scene of provocative ambiguity (*a somewhat oedipal embrace*) begs her to repent. **1972** *Jrnl. Social Psychol.* LXXXVI. 157 The less dramatic resolution of the Oedipal complex experienced by females causes them to have a weaker superego than males. **1975** C. DENNIS *Somebody just grabbed Annie!* 132 There was nothing Oedipal in his sleeping habits. He was just able to relax more easily in his old room.

Œdipean (iːd-, ɛdɪˈpiːən), *a.* [irreg. f. ŒDIPUS: see -EAN.] Pertaining to, or like that of, Œdipus; clever at guessing a riddle.

(In quot. 1822 with allusion to the story of Œdipus putting out his own eyes on discovering that he had unwittingly married his mother.)

1621 QUARLES *Argalus & P.* Introd., Many have ventured (trusting to the Oedipean conceit of their ingenious Reader) to write non-sense. **1822** LAMB *Lett.* II. (1841) 22 Did the eyes come away kindly with no Œdipean avulsion. **1876** *Spectator* 9 Sept. 1131/2 The Œdipean trilogy of Sophocles. **1972** P. H. KOCHER *Master of Middle-Earth* (1973) iii. 43 In striving to avert a danger he thinks he sees lying ahead he may take the very measures which are necessary to bring it about. All finite knowledge about the future is cursed by this Oedipean paradox.

Œdipo'dean, *a.* [f. Gr. Οἰδιπόδειος of Oedipus + -AN.] **a.** Of or pertaining to Oedipus or his family. **b.** = ŒDIPAL *a.*

1947 E. F. WATLING *Sophocles' Theban Plays* 13 Each of the three plays deals with a situation in the Oedipodean family history. **1959** S. NEILL *Genuinely Human Existence* x. 239 The Laian situation precedes the Oedipodean situation. **1968** H. J. SCHONFIELD *Those Incredible Christians* xiii. 202 Athenagoras similarly speaks of the heathen charges of 'atheism, Thyestean feasts and Oedipodean intercourse'.

† **œdi'podic,** *a. Obs. nonce-wd.* [f. Gr. οἰδίπους, -ποδ- (see ŒDIPUS) + -IC.] Swollen-footed, gouty.

1694 MOTTEUX *Rabelais* IV. xliii, Oh! what good wou'd it not do my oedipodic Leg.

Œdipus (ˈiːd-, ˈɛdɪpəs). Also 6 Edipus. [a. Gr. Οἰδίπους, Οἰδιποδ-, lit. 'swollen-footed', a proper name.] Name of the Theban hero who, according to the ancient Greek legend, solved the riddle propounded by the Sphinx.

1. Allusively applied to one who is clever at guessing riddles.

1557 N. GRIMALD *Cleobulus' Riddle* in *Tottel's Misc.* (Arb.) 102 Incase you can so hard a knot vnknit: You shall I count an Edipus in wit. **1603** B. JONSON *Sejanus* II. iii. [III. i.], I am not Oedipus inough, To vnderstand this Sphynx. **1628** EARLE *Microcosm.*, *Too idly reseru'd Man* (Arb.) 35 Hee h'as beene long a riddle himselfe, but at last finds Oedipusses. **1777** H. WALPOLE *Lett.* (1857) VI. 449 No mortal man could be found to expound those letters: not an Œdipus in the whole society.

2. *Psychol.* Used *attrib.* in ***Œdipus legend, love object, phantasy, phase, situation, theory,*** with reference to the psychoanalytic interpretation given to Sophocles' play *Œdipus Tyrannus* (in which Oedipus unknowingly kills his father and marries his mother) by Freud, and seen by him to exemplify the desires felt for the parent of the opposite sex by a child at an early stage of sexual development.

1910 *Amer. Jrnl. Psychol.* XXI. 97 The illustration of the attitude of son to parent is..transpicuous in the Œdipus legend. **1913** E. JONES *Papers on Psycho-Anal.* xviii. 381 (*heading*) Note on the Œdipus Saving Phantasy. **1926** J. I. SUTTIE tr. *Ferenczi's Further Contrib. Theory & Technique Psycho-Anal.* ix. 112 The patient..was here realizing sexual intercourse displaced 'from below upwards' (from the 'Oedipus phantasy'). **1943** H. READ *Educ. through Art* vi. 179 It is the Oedipus situation which gives rise to those idealistic tendencies in humanity which we know as religion, morality, custom, etc. **1957** N. FRYE *Anat. Crit.* iii. 181 A kind of comic Oedipus situation in which the hero replaces his father as a lover. **1963** A. HERON *Towards Quaker View of Sex* 59 That acceptance which would permit the Oedipus phase to be 'worked through'. **1964** M. ARGYLE *Psychol. & Social Probl.* i. 19 The Oedipus theory has been found not to be universal. **1972** H. L. MUSLIN in S. C. Post *Moral Values & Superego Concept* v. 109 Guilt as a result of the introjection of the Oedipus love objects.

b. Œdipus complex, the name given by Freud to the complex of emotions which he found were aroused in a child by its subconscious sexual desire for the parent of the opposite sex, which, if not resolved naturally, may lead to repression, guilt feelings, and an inability to form normal emotional or sexual relationships. Cf. ELECTRA.

1910 E. JONES in *Amer. Jrnl. Psychol.* XXI. 72 (*heading*) The Œdipus-complex as an explanation of Hamlet's mystery. **1920** S. FREUD in *Internat. Jrnl. Psycho-Anal.* I. 133 The girl had quietly passed through the normal stage of the feminine Oedipus complex, and had..begun to replace her father by a brother slightly older than herself. **1925** G. B. SHAW *Let.* 22 Feb. in J. Barrymore *Confessions of Actor* (1926) 122 [In 'Hamlet'] You..offer..a demonstration of that very modern discovery called the Œdipus complex, thereby adding a really incestuous motive on Hamlet's part. **1927** [see ELECTRA]. **1942** KOESTLER *Yogi & Commissar* (1945) I. i. 9 He believes that all the pests of humanity, including constipation and the Oedipus complex, can and will be cured by Revolution. **1951** M. MCLUHAN *Mech. Bride* (1967) 76/2 Did I give my baby an Oedipus complex? **1965** T. S. SZASZ *Ethics of Psychoanal.* I. iii. 50 According to classical analysis, he [*sc.* the psychoanalyst] teaches the patient about his early family situation, the Oedipus complex..transference, and resistance. **1969** *Listener* 17 Apr. 543/3 'I have to tell you, madam,' the psychiatrist said, 'that your son is suffering from an Oedipus complex.' 'What does it matter,' she replied, 'so long as he loves his mum?' **1971** J. Z. YOUNG *Introd. Study Man* i. 4 Psychoanalysis.. has revealed some startling features of our lives, but 'man is more than his Oedipus complex'. **1973** *Jrnl. Genetic Psychol.* CXXII. 156 The basic dynamics of the feminine 'Oedipus' complex are already fairly well known.

c. Œdipus effect, a term derived from that part of the legend of Oedipus which evidences the self-fulfilling nature of a prophecy or prediction (see quot. 1957).

1957 K. R. POPPER *Poverty of Historicism* i. 13, I suggest the name '*Oedipus effect*' for the influence of the prediction upon the predicted event.. whether this influence tends to bring about the predicted event, or whether it tends to prevent it. **1961** A. FLEW *Hume's Philos. of Belief* vii. 152 Hume is here in his own way taking note of the particular sort of feedback which has recently been given the mnemonically useful label *Oedipus effect*. **1972** I. C. JARVIE *Concepts & Society* iv. 124 By our belief in them [*sc.* class beliefs] and an acute Oedipus effect, they verify themselves. **1974** *Brit. Jrnl. Pol. Sci.* IV. 255 It is precisely this research perspective which in a dialectical fashion lends strength to an objection based on the Oedipus effect.

œdometer (iː'dɒmɪtə(r)). Also (*rare*) ödometer. [f. Gr. οἴδ-ημα swelling, swollen condition + -OMETER.] A device for measuring the swelling of a gel when water is absorbed or the compressibility of soil.

1915 W. W. TAYLOR *Chem. Colloids* xi. 158 Reinke used the oedometer, by means of which he measured the pressure of imbibition, to determine the velocity of the process. **1926** C. TERZAGHI in *Colloid Symposium Monograph* IV. 73 My own tests performed with coarse grained sands, by using a method which in every respect corresponds to the Ödometer method for measuring the swelling pressure of gels. **1938** *Nature* 24 Sept. 584/2 From the results of tests made with the Terzaghi oedometer together with calculation of the distribution of pressure from the building, it is possible to estimate the amount of settlement to be expected. **1969** LAMBE & WHITMAN *Soil Mech.* ix. 116 In the oedometer test, stress is applied to the soil specimen along the vertical axis, while strain in the horizontal directions is prevented.

œgopsid (iː'gɒpsɪd), *a.* and *sb. Zool.* Also oigopsid. [f. Gr. οἴγ-ειν to open + ὄψις vision, pl. eyes + -ID.] **a.** *adj.* Belonging to the *Œgopsida* (-æ), a division of decapod dibranchiate Cephalopoda, having the cornea of the eye 'open', i.e. perforated by an aperture. **b.** *sb.* A cephalopod of this division. (Opp. to *myopsid*.)

[**1888** ROLLESTON & JACKSON *Anim. Life* 460 In certain *Decapoda*, the *Oegopsidae*.] **1891** *Cent. Dict.*, Oigopsid.

‖**œil-de-bœuf** (œjdəbœf). [F., lit. 'ox-eye', term for a round window, etc.]

1. A small round window: = BULL'S-EYE 6.

1849 THACKERAY *Pendennis* xxv, Take a peep at the ladies in the hall through an *œil-de-bœuf*.

2. The name of a small octagonal vestibule lighted by a small round window in the palace at Versailles; hence *transf.* and *fig.*

1826 SCOTT *Woodst.* xii, This movement conveyed him to a sort of *œil-de-bœuf*, an octagon vestibule, or small hall, from which various rooms opened. **1837** CARLYLE *Fr. Rev.* I. III. i, To govern France were such a problem; and now it has grown well-nigh too hard to govern even the *Œil-de-Bœuf*. **1862** WRAXALL tr. *Mem. Q. Hortense* II. iv. 57 The royalist gentry had preserved the manners and levity which had once distinguished them in the *œils de bœuf* and *petites maisons* of old France.

‖**œil-de-perdrix** (œjdəpɛrdri). [Fr., lit. 'partridge-eye'.] **1.** In French pottery and porcelain, a design of dotted circles, usu. on a coloured background, first used *circa* 1760 on Sèvres porcelain.

1865 F. B. PALLISER *Hist. Lace* iv. 70 The lovely diapered ground recalls the may-flower of the Dresden and the oeil-de-perdrix of the Sèvres china of that time. **1925** W. W. WORSTER tr. *E. Hannover's Pott. & Porc.* III. 276 Next to the monochrome grounds, a favourite method was.. that of dotting the porcelain over with some little simple design repeated without a break in the manner of textiles. One of these was the famous *œil-de-perdrix* pattern, consisting of tiny circles or double circles dotted in green or blue and reserved in white on a monochrome or dotted ground. **1953** F. TILLEY *Litchfield's Pott. & Porc.* (ed. 6) vi. 234 The names of some other decorations [on Sèvres work] occur in various catalogues and inventories: thus the *œil de perdrix*, the well-known partridge eye-pattern. **1971** *Canad. Antiques Collector* Feb. 16/2 The rim has a light blue ground upon which is the oeil-de-perdrix pattern leaving three oval reserves.

b. A similar design used as a ground in lace-making (see quots.).

1891 A. S. COLE *Suppl. Descr. Catal. Specimens Lace S. Kensington Mus.* 23 The pattern consists of tape-like stems ..with a coarse ground of 'oeil de perdrix' devices or irregular little hexagons. *Ibid.* 31 The scheme of pattern consists of a series of oval compartments.., on an oeil-de-perdrix ground. **1899** A. M. SHARP *Point & Pillow Lace* vi. 148 This Lace [*sc.* Flemish Mechlin] is sometimes grounded with an ornamental 'réseau', instead of one in the usual hexagonal shape, called 'Fond de neige' or 'Œil de perdrix'. **1953** M. POWYS *Lace & Lace-Making* xi. 207 (*heading*) Fond de Neige, so-called Oeil de Perdrix. An elaborate ground, often used as a filling. **1960** H. HAYWARD *Antique Coll.* 178/2 Other grounds were sometimes used such as the *œil de perdrix*.

2. Applied to wines which are pink or pale red in colour. Hence *ellipt.* as *sb.*

1872 E. BRADDON *Life in India* viii. 305 If he required.. anything from Holloway's pills to œil de perdrix champagne ..he was compelled to lay in such a stock as would carry him through. **1920** G. SAINTSBURY *Notes on Cellar-Bk.* v. 80 The true *œil-de-perdrix* tint is not..'synthetically' attainable. *Ibid.* xii. 188 A glass, filled with *œil-de-perdrix* wine. **1959** W. JAMES *Word-Bk. Wine* 135 *Œil de perdrix.* A partridge-eye wine is a pink wine; the term is applied to pink champagnes, light-coloured sparkling burgundies, and to some wines made from a mixture of red and white grapes. **1966** *Country Life* 6 Oct. 820/1 In 1784 'L' Oeil de Perdrix Celleroy', presumably what we would now call pink champagne, fetched 48s. as against 38s. for ordinary Celleroy. **1971** *Times* 29 Mar. (Switzerland Suppl.) p. iii/6 From Neuchâtel..comes the best-known rosé, Oeil de Perdrix.

‖**œillade.** Forms: 6 oeyliade, 7 aliad, eliad, illiad, iliad, 9 œillade. [a. F. *œillade* (1460 in Hatz.-Darm.), f. *œil* eye + -ADE 1 a, as in *cannonade, fusillade*. Formerly more or less naturalized ('eɪlɪad, 'ɪlɪəd); now consciously French (œjad).] A glance of the eye, *esp.* an amorous glance; an ogle.

1592 GREENE *Disput.* Addr. 2 What amorous glaunces, what smirking Oeyliades. **1598** SHAKS. *Merry W.* I. iii. 68 Pages wife..gaue mee good eyes too; examind my parts with most iudicious illiads. **1605** —— *Lear* IV. v. 25 She gaue strange Eliads, and most speaking lookes To Noble Edmund. [*Qos.* aliads, *later Folios* Iliads.] *a* **1803** C. L. LEWES *Mem.* (1805) I. 98 With a most impressive œillade from the white of his eyes only. **1855** SMEDLEY *H. Coverdale* iv. 22 Horace..favouring Alice with a languishing *oeillade*.

œillet, œlet: see OILLET.

œkology, var. spelling of ECOLOGY.

œllacherite (œ'lækəraɪt). *Min.* [f. the name of J. *Œllacher* (b. 1804), Hungarian chemist + -ITE[1].] A white or pink variety of muscovite containing a significant proportion of barium.

1867 J. D. DANA in *Amer. Jrnl. Sci.* XCIV. 256 (*table*) Œllacherite. [*Note*] Œllacher's margarite from Pfitschthal [Tyrol]. **1933** *Amer. Mineralogist* XVIII. 30 A massive pink mineral with obscure cleavage..appeared under the microscope to have a micaceous texture and had about the optical characters of muscovite... The varietal name oellacherite is given by Dana to this barium-muscovite. **1949** *Chem. Abstr.* XLIII. 6120 The discovery of a previously unknown mineral in the mountains of Kara-Tau in Kazakhstan is reported... The chem. compn. corresponds to œllacherite in which a part of the AL_2O_3 is isomorphically displaced by V_2O_3. **1962** W. A. DEER et al. *Rock-Forming Min.* III. 14 It is probable that roscoelite and oellacherite are distinct chemical and structural species and that there is not a complete series between each of them and muscovite.

oen, obs. form of OWE.

œnanthic (iː'nænθɪk), *a. Chem.* [f. L. *œnanthē*, a. Gr. οἰνάνθη (f. οἴνη vine + ἄνθη blossom, bloom), a vine-shoot or bud, vine-blossom, vine. (Also a plant like the vine, applied by Pliny to an umbelliferous plant, and taken by Linnæus as the name of a genus of *Umbelliferæ* including the poisonous Water Dropwort.)] Having the characteristic odour of wine. ***œnanthic acid***, an acid (or mixture of acids), $C_{14}H_{26}O_2$ + H_2O, obtained from œnanthic ether, forming a colourless oil solidifying at 13° C. into a buttery mass. ***œnanthic ether***, a mobile oily liquid, the source of the peculiar odour of wines, obtained by distillation of wine-lees.

1838 T. THOMSON *Chem. Org. Bodies* 138 Of œnanthic acid. This acid was discovered by Liebig and Pelouze, constituting one of the component parts of œnanthic ether to which wines owe their peculiar smell. **1880** BLOXAM *Chem.* (ed. 4) 522 Caproic, œnanthic, and caprylic alcohols, are all liquid at the ordinary temperature. **1897** *Allbutt's Syst. Med.* II. 843 The bouquet and aroma [of wine] are due to the compound ethers, especially to œnanthic ether.

So **œ'nanthol, œ'nanthyl, œ'nanthylene, œnan'thylic** *a. Chem.* (see quots.); **œ'nanthylate**, a salt of œnanthylic acid.

1857 W. A. MILLER *Elem. Chem.* III. 139 *Œnanthylic Aldehyd; Œnanthol*..is furnished by the destructive distillation of castor oil. *Ibid.* 397 Œnanthylate of potash. *Ibid.* 191 Heptylene or Œnanthylene. **1866–77** WATTS *Dict. Chem.* IV. 176 *Œnanthyl*, $C_7H_{13}O$, the hypothetical radicle of œnanthylic acid and its derivatives. The same name is sometimes, but inappropriately, given to heptyl, C_7H_{15}. *Ibid.* 177 *Œnanthylic acid*, $C_7H_{14}O_2$..is a transparent colourless oil, having an unpleasant odour like that of cod-fish.

œnanthin (iː'nænθɪn). *Chem.* [f. Bot. L. *Œnanthe*, name of a genus (see prec.) + -IN.] A poisonous resinous substance obtained from Water Dropwort (*Œnanthe fistulosa*).

1892 in *Syd. Soc. Lex.*

œno- (iːnəʊ), occasionally oino- (ɔɪnəʊ), combining form of Gr. οἶνος wine, used in a few scientific and quasi-scientific compounds. **'œnocyte** (also †-cyth) *Ent.* [ad. G. *oenocyth* (H. R. von Wielowiejski 1886, in *Zeitschr. f. wissensch. Zool.* XLIII. 515): see -CYTE], a large, probably secretory, wine-coloured cell of insects that is often grouped into glands and is produced in the epidermis, either remaining there or migrating elsewhere (esp. to the fat body). **œno'cytoid** *Ent.* [ad. F. *œnocytoïde* (E. Poyarkoff 1910, in *Arch. d'Anat. microsc.* XII. 344)], a large, round, non-phagocytic cell, similar in appearance to an œnocyte, that occurs in the hæmolymph of some insects. **œnogen** ('iːnədʒɪn) *nonce-wd.* [after *oxygen*] (see quot.). **œnolin** ('iːnəlɪn) *Chem.* [see -OL and -IN], a colouring-matter ($C_{10}H_{10}O_5$) obtained from red wine. **œnology** (iː'nɒlədʒɪ) [-LOGY], the knowledge or study of wines; so **œno'logical** *a.*, pertaining to œnology; **œ'nologist**, one versed in œnology, a connoisseur in wines. **œnomancy** ('iːnəmænsɪ) [-MANCY], divination by means of wine. **œnomania** (iːnəʊ'meɪnɪə), oino- [MANIA], (*a*) a mania or insane craving for wine or other intoxicating drink, dipsomania; (*b*) mania resulting from intoxication, delirium tremens; hence **œno'maniac**, a person affected with œnomania. **œnometer** (iː'nɒmɪtə(r)) [-METER], a hydrometer for measuring the alcoholic strength of wines; an alcoholometer (Webster, 1864). **œnophil** ('iːnəʊfɪl), **œnophile** ('iːnəʊfaɪl) = *œnophilist*; so **œno'philic** *a.*, wine-loving. **œnophilist** (iː'nɒfɪlɪst) [Gr. -φιλος loving], a lover of wine. **œnophobist** (iː'nɒfəbɪst), oino- [Gr. -φοβος fearing], one who has a dread of, or aversion to, wine. **œnopoetic** (iːnəʊpəʊ'ɛtɪk) *a.* [Gr. ποιητικός making], pertaining to wine-making. **œnothionic** (-θaɪ'ɒnɪk) *a. Chem.* [Gr. θεῖον sulphur], in ***œnothionic acid***, an acid ($C_2H_6SO_4$) obtained by treating alcohol with sulphuric acid; *ethylsulphuric* or *sulphovinic acid*.

1886 *Jrnl. R. Microsc. Soc.* 964 The second kind of cell is, in consequence of its colour, called the '*œnocyth'; these were found arranged in groups, or were very small, or formed rows, or plexiform plates or larger complexes or plates. **1891** *Ibid.* 587 Prof. V. Graber discusses the complex tissue found in the body-cavity of most insects. It includes ..the yellow 'œnocytes', which Wielowiejski finds to be usually arranged in segmental groups. **1970** *Nature* 7 Nov. 581/1 Oenocytes, sometimes called abdominal endocrine glands, are the cells most probably interacting with the prothoracic glands in the control of moulting. **1925** A. D. IMMS *Gen. Textbk. Entomol.* I. 125 The leucocytes exist in several forms and four types..are recognized by Hollande ..as being present in most insects... These are—(1) Proleucocytes... (2) Phagocytes... (3) Granular leucocytes. .. (4) *Œnocytoids. **1969** R. F. CHAPMAN *Insects* xxxiii. 676 Oenocytoids are found in Coleoptera, Lepidoptera and some Diptera and Heteroptera. **1974** *Nature* 29 Nov. 391/2 Five cell types were identified in the haemolymph of *G[alleria] mellonella*; prohaemocytes, plasmatocytes, granular cells, spherule cells and oenocytoids. **1817** T. L. PEACOCK *Melincourt* (1875) 275 Inflated with *oenogen gas, or, in other words, with the fumes of wine. **1866–77** WATTS *Dict. Chem.* IV. 178 *Œnolin. **1824** *Blackw. Mag.* XVI. 12 The different branches of *oinological science. **1887** *Pall Mall G.* 13 July 5/1 The Oinological and Pomological Academy for the scientific culture of the future cultivators. **1894** THUDICHUM *Wines* Pref. 7 French œnological literature..includes many works of interest and importance. **1865** *Sat. Rev.* 12 Aug. 215/1 Our medical *œnologist. **1894** *National Observer* 6 Jan. 194/2 The genuine œnologist, as Dr. Thudichum calls him. **1814** *Sch. gd. Living* 196 His *œnology of British wines. **1865** *Sat. Rev.* 12 Aug. 215/1 To give, not milk, but strong drink to the babes in œnology. **1652** GAULE *Magastrom.* 165 *Oinomancy, divining by wine. **1842** BRANDE *Dict. Sc.*, Œnomancy. **1880** WEBSTER *Suppl.*, *Œnomania. **1897** *Allbutt's Syst. Med.* II. 871 Dipsomania or oinomania is a form of recurrent mania attended with impulsive drunkenness. **1857** J. MILLER *Alcohol* (1858) 20 A lady who had become a frightful *oinomaniac. **1874** BUCKNILL & TUKE *Psych. Med.* (ed. 3) 293 The thirst for drink..blindly leads the oinomaniac to a course against which his reason and his conscience alike rebel. **1930** *New Statesman* 28 June 366/1 Professor Saintsbury, an *oenophile who is free from the snobbish contempt his kind affect for whisky. **1961** C. WILLOCK *Death in Covert* iii. 68 This man, who described himself as an oenophil, believed that wine was the only fit alcoholic drink. **1962** *Punch* 6 June 869/2 For not-too-adventurous oenophiles I commend Ice Peach Wine. **1969** *New Scientist* 13 Feb. 357/2 Scientific oenophiles would not need the sometimes drastic oversimplification of scientific matters. **1976** *Times* 5 May 16/8 British Transport Hotels invited distinguished oenophiles to sip and sniff their way through a representative selection of English wines. **1957** *Times Lit. Suppl.* 20 Dec. 778/2 Merely a salon volume designed for presentation to *oenophilic friends. **1859** THACKERAY *Virgin.* xxxi, Are the Vegetarians to bellow 'Cabbage for ever'? and may we modest *Œnophilists not sing the praises of our favourite plant? **1893** SYMONDS *In the Key of Blue* 37 Those surprises which reward the diligent œnophilist in Italy. **1867** *Blackw. Mag.* CII. 209 The English and American *oinophobists. **1894** THUDICHUM *Wines* Pref. 8 The work of B. A. Lenoir consists of a first viticultural and a second *œnopoetic part. **1857** MAYNE *Expos. Lex.*, *Œnothionic.

‖**œnochoe** (iː'nɒkəʊiː). *Gr. Antiq.* Also oino-. [a. Gr. οἰνοχόη, f. οἰνο- wine + -χοος, -χοη pouring.] A vessel used for dipping wine from the crater or bowl and filling the drinking-cups.

1871 *Guide to 1st Vase Room, Brit. Mus.* (ed. 4) 29 On the *oinochoê*, No. 162 (Case 60), the figures are drawn in outline, on a white ground. **1895** *Atlantic Monthly* Mar. 315 An œnochoe (a dipper-like utensil for filling the wine-cup). **1895** *Catal.*, Oenochoe of rare form, with strainer at top of neck.

œnomel ('iːnəʊmɛl). Also 7–9 oino-. [ad. L. *œnomeli* (late L. *-melum*), a. Gr. οἰνόμελι, f. οἶνος wine + μέλι honey. So mod.F. *œnomel* (Littré).]

1. A mixture of wine and honey, used as a beverage by the ancient Greeks.

1574 HYLL *Ord. Bees* 35 The best Oenomell is that which is made of olde and tart wine and the best purifyed hony. **1657** TOMLINSON *Renou's Disp.* 101 Amongst sweet potions is reckoned oinomel. **1860** LD. LYTTON *Lucile* II. v. §6. 24

Wherever new flowrets, by lawn or by dell, Held on tiptoe for him their divine œnomel.

2. *fig.*; *esp.* applied to language or thought in which strength and sweetness are combined.

1844 MRS. BROWNING *Wine of Cyprus* xxii, Those memories..Make a better œnomel. **1882** MYERS *Renew. Youth* 54 While night serenely fell, Imparadised in sunset's œnomel. **1891** *Guardian* 28 Oct. 1755 Book-depths from which thou knew'st so well To mix for mind or heart an œnomel.

‖**œnothera** (iːnəʊˈθɪərə, commonly iːˈnɒθərə). *Bot.* [L. *œnothēra*, a. Gr. οἰνοθήρας, name of some plant, f. οἶνος wine + -θήρας -catcher: commonly taken as = 'wine-trap' (see quots.); but some Gr. authors have the name as ὀνοθήρας ass-catcher (in Pliny *onothēra*); another name was ὀνάγρα = ass-trap.] The typical genus of *Onagraceæ*, comprising plants (chiefly natives of America) with large handsome flowers, yellow, white, or purple, in some species opening in the evening; commonly called *evening primrose*.

1601 HOLLAND *Pliny* II. 259 Likewise Oenothera, otherwise named Onuris,..an herb good also in wine to make the heart merry. **1788** REES *Cycl.*, *Primrose, night* or *tree*, œnothera. **1817** J. BRADBURY *Trav. Amer.* 82 A number of large white flowers..belonging to a species of oenothera. **18..** BAIRD in Worcester *Dict.* s.v., The roots of the species *Oenothera biennis* are eatable, and were formerly taken after dinner to flavor wine, as olives now are; hence the name *Œnothera*, or wine-trap. **1863** J. SURAT *Life in South* II. 304 Splendid phloxes, œnotheras, mimosas.

†**oeps.** *Obs.* [a. AF. *oeps* (earlier *oes*, Britton) = OF. *oes, ous, ues, wes, eus, ops, oups, oeps, oefs*, etc., work, need, use, benefit, profit:—L. *opus* work, use (for), need (of).] Use, benefit, profit.

[**1292** BRITTON I. xxii. §2 Et ausi soit enquis de toutes lour prises a noster oes, et a lour. **1383** *Act 7 Rich. II*, c. 12 Soit il a son propre oeps ou al oepz dautre.]

1428 *Surtees Misc.* (1888) 3 To be raysed..to þe oeps of our soverayne lorde þe kyng. *Ibid.* 5 To þe oeps and profet of þe cite. **1429** *Rolls of Parlt.* IV. 349/2 Which peynes shall be areisid to the Kyngis oeps. **1436** *Ibid.* 501/2 Thoo enhabitauntz..that..have estat to her owen oeps, or thoo to whos oeps othre persones have estat.

oeptas, oeptaues, obs. ff. *octaves*, OCTAVE I.

o'er (ɔə(r)), poetic and dialectal contraction of OVER; also in combination: see words in OVER-.

Oerlikon (ˈɜːlɪkən). Also **oerlikon**. [Name of the suburb of Zurich where the guns are manufactured.] The proprietary name used by Werkzeugmaschinenfabrik Oerlikon Buhrle & Co. for guns and fittings manufactured by them; usu. *ellipt.* for an Oerlikon light anti-aircraft cannon.

1944 *R.A.F. Jrnl.* Aug. 272 (*caption*) Battleship..; carries ..a varying number of Oerlikons..., sometimes sixty. **1949** S. P. LLEWELLYN *Troopships* 31 Their forward and after decks cluttered with..pom-poms, oerlikons, and improvised wash-houses, the troopships cleared Wellington heads. **1970** *Trade Marks Jrnl.* 7 Oct. 1667/2 Oerlikon... Guns and parts and fittings therefor..ammunition for cannon; apparatus..for launching rockets; and rockets (missiles). Dieter Buhrle and Charlotte Buhrle-Schalk, trading as Werkzeugmaschinenfabrik Oerlikon Buhrle & Co.,..Zurich,..Switzerland; manufacturers and merchants. **1973** D. LEES *Rape of Quiet Town* x. 165 The frigate..sprayed the sub with Oerlikon fire.

oersted (ˈɜːstɛd). *Physics.* [f. the name of H. C. *Oersted* (1777–1851), Danish physicist.]

†**a.** (Written **oerstedt**.) (See quots.) *Obs.*

1879 J. D. EVERETT *Units & Physical Constants* xi. 139 The practical unit of current is the current due to an electromotive force of 1 volt working through a resistance of 1 ohm. It is called a current of 1 weber per second. Its theoretical value is 1 weber per second = 1/10 of the C.G.S. unit of current. In the 'Testing Instructions of the Indian Telegraph Department' it is called the Oerstedt. **1885** W. WILLIAMS *Man. Telegr.* 206 The unit current..has already been described as the Ampère or Oerstedt.

†**b.** The electromagnetic unit of reluctance in the C.G.S. system, defined as one gilbert per maxwell. (In the International System of Units replaced by the reciprocal heury, equal to approximately $1{\cdot}26 \times 10^{-8}$ gilberts per maxwell.) *Obs.*

1893 [see GILBERT[2]]. **1896** M. MACLEAN *Physical Units* 92 The committee on Notation of the Chamber of Delegates of the International Electrical Congress of 1893 in Chicago recommended that—unit field intensity, unit magnetic induction, and unit magnetising force be each called a Gauss; unit flux of magnetic force a Weber; unit magnetomotive force a Gilbert; and unit reluctance or magnetic resistance an Oersted. **1903** *Electr. World & Engin.* XLI. 1010/2 For practical work..the magnetic reluctance of a cubic centimeter of all non-magnetic materials..is the same as that of an air-pump vacuum. This unit of reluctance is called the 'oersted'. **1931** S. R. WILLIAMS *Magn. Phenomena* i. 46 The oersted of reluctance corresponds to the ohm of resistance.

c. The electromagnetic unit of magnetic field strength in the C.G.S. system, equal to the field strength produced at a distance of one centimetre by a unit magnetic pole or a thin straight wire carrying half an e.m.u. (i.e. five amp.) of current; one maxwell per square centimetre. Cf. GAUSS. (In the International System of Units the oersted is replaced by the ampere per metre, equal to $4\pi \times 10^{-3}$ (approximately 0·0126) oersted.)

1930 *Engineering* 25 July 113/2 At the meeting of the International Electrotechnical Commission..it was.. recommended that the names of maxwell, gauss, oersted and gilbert should be applied to the C.G.S. units for magnetic flux, flux density, magnetic field intensity and magnetomotive force respectively. **1938** R. W. LAWSON tr. *Hevesy & Paneth's Man. Radioactivity* (ed. 2) ii. 26 By means of deflexion experiments in very strong magnetic fields (23,000 oersteds) a fine structure of the α-particles from thorium C ..has been detected. **1959** *Sci. News* LI. 17 For instance, at a temperature of 0·01° K a magnetic field of the order of 100,000 oersted is needed in order to achieve the necessary nuclear alignment for the subsequent cooling by demagnetization. **1962** [see GAUSS]. **1963** JERRARD & MCNEILL *Dict. Sci. Units* 97 The earth's magnetic field has a magnetizing force of the order of 0·2 to 0·3 oersted. **1974** *Nature* 16 Aug. 535/2 Few, if any [geomagneticians] have really cared whether their magnetometers have measured *B* or *H*; the gauss, the c.g.s. unit of *B*, has by usage become totally interchangeable with the oersted, the c.g.s. unit of *H*. **1976** *Ibid.* 26 Feb. 652/1 All 36 specimens were submitted to magnetic study, including alternating field treatment up to 850 oersted.

oes, pl. of O; obs. form of OOZE.

œ'sophagal, *a.* = ŒSOPHAGEAL.

1778 [W. MARSHALL] *Minutes Agric.* 16 Jan. 1776, Perhaps he surcharged his stomach; and..the repletion closed the œsophagal orifice.

†'**œsophage.** *Obs.* [prob. a. F. *œsophage*, in 14th c. *ysophague* (Hatz.-Darm.).] = ŒSOPHAGUS.

1541 R. COPLAND *Galyen's Terapeut.* 2 Hj, Thycke medycamentes do crud & make concrecyon in yᵉ partyes of the bulke or oesophage. **1594** T. B. *La Primaud. Fr. Acad.* II. 343 The whole passage and pype, called oesophage or the throate. **1657** TOMLINSON *Renou's Disp.* 499 That it may stick longer in the œsophage.

œsophageal (iːsəʊˈfædʒɪəl), *a.* Also 9 eso-. [f. mod.L. *œsophage-us* (f. *œsophag-us*) + -AL[1].] Of, belonging to, or connected with the œsophagus.

1807 HOME in *Phil. Trans.* XCVII. 157 The orifices of the œsophageal glands. **1851–6** WOODWARD *Mollusca* 22 The lower side of the œsophageal ring. **1879** *St. George's Hosp. Rep.* IX. 215 A case of œsophageal obstruction.

Also, in same sense, **œso'phagean** *a.* [cf. F. *œsophagien*]. **œso'phagiac** *a.* [irreg. after *cardiac*].

1856 WEBSTER, *Esophagean.* **1892** *Syd. Soc. Lex.*, *Œsophagean.* **1858** J. H. BENNET *Nutrition* i. 11 The œsophagiac orifice [of the stomach].

œsophagitis (iːsɒfəˈdʒaɪtɪs). *Path.* [f. ŒSOPHAG-US + -ITIS. In mod.F. *œsophagite* (Littré).] Inflammation of the œsophagus.

1857 in MAYNE *Expos. Lex.* **1859** SEMPLE *Diphtheria* 277 Sometimes œsophagitis and pseudo-membranous gastritis are found. **1897** *Allbutt's Syst. Med.* II. 859 Chronic œsophagitis has been attributed to alcoholic excess.

œsophago- (iːˈsɒfəgəʊ), also **esophago-**, before a vowel **œsophag-**, combining form of Gr. οἰσοφάγος, ŒSOPHAGUS, in various terms of Pathology and Surgery, as **œsophagalgia** (-ˈældʒɪə), **-algy** [Gr. ἄλγος pain], pain in the œsophagus (Mayne *Expos. Lex.* 1857). **œsophagectomy** (-ˈgɛktəmɪ) [Gr. ἐκτομή cutting out, excision], excision of a portion of the œsophagus. **œ'sophagocele** (-siːl) [Gr. κήλη tumour, hernia], 'hernia of the mucous membrane of the œsophagus through an opening in the muscular wall' (*Syd. Soc. Lex.* 1892). **œsophagodynia** (-əʊˈdɪnɪə) [Gr. ὀδύνη pain], pain in the œsophagus (Mayne). **œ,sophago'gastric** *a.*, pertaining to both the œsophagus and the stomach. **œsophagopathy** (-ˈgɒpəθɪ) [Gr. πάθος suffering], disease of the œsophagus (Mayne). **œsophagoplegia** (-ˈpliːdʒɪə), **-plegy** [Gr. πληγή stroke], sudden paralysis of the œsophagus (Mayne). **œsophagorrhagia** (-ˈreɪdʒɪə), **-'orrhagy** [Gr. -ραγια bursting], hæmorrhage from the œsophagus (Mayne). **œ'sophagoscope** (-skəʊp) [-SCOPE], an instrument for inspection of the œsophagus; so **œsophagoscopic** (-ˈskɒpɪk) *a.*; **œsopha'goscopy**, inspection of the œsophagus. **œ'sophagospasm**, spasm of the œsophagus (Mayne). **œsopha'gostomy** [Gr. στόμα mouth], 'an operation for opening the œsophagus and keeping the opening permanent, so that food may be supplied to the stomach by its means' (*Syd. Soc. Lex.*). **œ'sophagotome** (-təʊm) [Gr. -τομος cutting], an instrument for cutting into the œsophagus; so **œsopha'gotomy**, incision into the œsophagus.

1892 *Syd. Soc. Lex.*, *Œsophagectomy. **1897** *Allbutt's Syst. Med.* III. 371 In the rare condition of simple or membranous stricture Mr. Kendal Franks has performed œsophagectomy with success. **1857** MAYNE *Expos. Lex.*, *Œsophagocele. **1954** *Amer. Jrnl. Surg.* LXXXVIII. 330/2 The procedure could be considered for *esophagogastric resection for gastric and esophageal varices secondary to portal hypertension and cirrhosis. **1971** *Nature* 9 July 117/1 The stomach was isolated between ligatures at the oesophago-gastric and gastro-duodenal junctions. **1884** M. MACKENZIE *Dis. Throat & Nose* II. 14 Dr. Waldenburg invented an *oesophagoscope. **1897** *Allbutt's Syst. Med.* III. 361 Œsophagoscopes..are hardly ever used in practice. **1893** *Brit. Med. Jrnl.* 30 Sept. 738 On *œsophagoscopic examination. **1872** COHEN *Dis. Throat* 46 There are great anatomical obstacles to the performance of *œsophagoscopy. **1884** MACKENZIE *Dis. Throat & Nose* II. 135 The remaining operations, internal oesophagotomy, *oesophagostomy, and gastrostomy. *Ibid.* 21 The *oesophagotome..consists of a gum-elastic bougie about fifteen inches long [etc.]. **1839–47** TODD *Cycl. Anat.* III. 576/1 The operation of *œsophagotomy. **1868** D. W. CHEEVER (*title*) Two Cases of Œsophagotomy for the Removal of Foreign Bodies. **1878** T. BRYANT *Pract. Surg.* I. 596 Œsophagotomy has an established position in practical

œsophagus (iːˈsɒfəgəs). Also 5–6 **ysophagus**, 6 **isofagus, hysophagus, oisophagus**, 8–9 **esophagus.** [mod.L., a. Gr. οἰσοφάγος the gullet; of uncertain origin (see below). The med. and early mod.L. representatives of Gr. οἰ-, were *i-*, *-y*: cf. F. *ysophague* (14th c. in Littré).] The tube or canal (in man and the higher animals musculo-membranous) extending from the mouth to the stomach, and serving for the passage of food and drink; the gullet.

In *Zool.* extended to include a canal in any class of animals by which food enters the organism.

1398 TREVISA *Barth. De P.R.* v. xxiv. (MS. Bodl.) lf. 14/1 Ysophagus, þat is þe wey of mete and drinke. **1525** tr. *Jerome of Brunswick's Surg.* I iij b/2 The throwte goll callyd hysophagus and trachea. **1541** R. COPLAND *Guydon's Quest. Chirurg.* F ij b, The Meri otherwyse called Ysophagus is yᵉ way of the mete & this Meri commeth out of the throte and thyrleth the mydryfe vnto yᵉ bely or stomacke. **1543** TRAHERON tr. *Vigo's Chirurg.* I. iv. 6 Called Meri or Oisophagus. **1633** P. FLETCHER *Purple Isl.* IV. 45 *note*, The Œsophagus, or meat-pipe conveying meats and drinks to the stomach. **1772** NUGENT tr. *Hist. Friar Gerund* I. 159 The enterance to the Esophagus being discovered. **1888** ROLLESTON & JACKSON *Anim. Life* 840 *Protozoa*... Class *Mastigophora*... A mouth and oesophagus sometimes present.

[*Note.* Aristotle *Hist. An.* I. 16. 495ᵃ 18 says 'the so-called οἰσοφάγος, which gets its name from its length and its narrowness', but does not explain how. According to its elements, Gk. οἰσοφάγος ought to mean 'eater of osiers'; which seems inept. A late Greek or Byzantine Scholiast on Oppian, explains it as from οἴω (an imaginary pres. to οἴσω) = κομίζω I carry + φαγεῖν to eat, which, though plausible in sense, is really impossible, -φάγος in all compounds meaning 'eating (something)', 'eater'.]

oest, obs. form of HOST *sb.*[1], a company.

œstradiol (iːs-, ɛstrəˈdaɪɒl). *Biochem.* Also (*U.S.*) **estr-**. [f. ŒSTRA(NE + DI-[2] + -OL.] The most active known naturally occurring œstrogenic hormone in mammals, $C_{18}H_{22}(OH)_2$, which is formed in the ovarian follicles, controls the growth of the female sexual organs and some functions of the uterus, and is used, e.g., in treating the menopausal syndrome and conditions associated with hypoplasia of the genital tract.

1934 K. DAVID et al. in *Biochem. Jrnl.* XXVIII. 1366 The increased oestrogenic potency of these substances is associated with an increased effect on the seminal vesicles. Oestradiol is about twice as oestrogenic as oestrone. **1951** A. GROLLMAN *Pharmacol. & Therapeutics* xxvi. 579 Estradiol is also marketed in the form of its benzoic acid ester in which form its activity is greatly enhanced. **1955** *Sci. News Let.* 17 Sept. 179/3 Drs. Emil Witsch and C. Y. Chang..told..that they were able to change male Xenopus toads into egg-laying females..under the influence of a female hormone, estradiol. **1968** *Times* 4 Oct. 9/2 Injections of male or female sex hormones, testosterone or oestradiol, prevent the shedding of old antlers.

œstral (ˈiːs-, ˈɛstrəl), *a.* Also (*U.S.*) **estral.** [f. ŒSTR(US + -AL.] = ŒSTROUS *a.*

1883 *Brit. Med. Jrnl.* 10 Mar. 446/2 The 'œstral' products had never found vent from the uterus. *Ibid.*, The lower animals do certainly have an 'œstral' discharge. **1972** *Biol. Abstr.* LIV. 6236/1 (*heading*) Change in the estral cycle of white rats..exposed to the..effect of gasoline..vapors.

œstrane (ˈiːs-, ˈɛstreɪn). *Biochem.* Also (*U.S.*) **estr-**. [f. ŒSTR(IN + -ANE.] (See quot. 1933.)

1933 N. K. ADAM et al. in *Nature* 5 Aug. 205/2 The parent saturated hydrocarbon of the œstrin group, $C_{18}H_{30}$, containing the sterol skeleton with one methyl group but without the side chain, may be termed 'œstrane'. **1947** H. SELYE *Textbk. Endocrinol.* i. 71/2 A side-chain at C_{17} does not necessarily decrease folliculoid activity in the estrane series and..it may even increase it. **1973** *Biochemistry* (Easton, Pa.) XII. 2221/1 All neutral and charged derivatives of estrane and androstane inhibit hydrolysis of *bovine* albumin.

oestre, oestridge, obs. ff. OYSTER *sb.*, OSTRICH.

œstrin (ˈiːs-, ˈɛstrɪn). *Biochem.* Also (*U.S.*) **estr-**. [f. ŒSTR(US + -IN[1].] Any of various preparations of œstrogenic material; an œstrogen, *spec.* œstrone.

1926 PARKES & BELLERBY in *Jrnl. Physiol.* LXI. 573 We suggest that 'oestrin' or some such term..should be applied to the oestrus-producing principle of the ovary. **1933** [see prec.]. **1935** B. HARROW in Harrow & Sherwin *Textbk. Biochem.* xxx. 756 The true theelin or estrin, as well as several related compounds, has been isolated in the chemically pure form. **1938** *Ann. Reg.* 1937 348 Oestrin, styryl blue, the acenaphthene derivatives and squalene can act as efficient evocators in embryological induction. **1970** W. B. Yapp *Introd. Animal Physiol.* (ed. 3) viii. 293 Collectively all are called oestrins or oestrogens; they are steroids.

œstriol ('iːs-, 'ɛstrɪɒl). *Biochem.* Also (*U.S.*) **estr-.** [f. Œs(trane + tri- + -ol.] An œstrogenic hormone, $C_{18}H_{21}(OH)_3$, which is one of the metabolic products of œstradiol and is produced in the placenta during pregnancy.

1933 N. K. Adam et al. in *Nature* 5 Aug. 206/1 The full chemical names of two important derivatives..are 3,16,17-trihydroxy 1,3,5-œstratriene, and 3-hydroxy 17-keto 1,3,5-œstratriene. These names, though suitable for chemical literature, are cumbrous for general and biological use. We suggest as common names, for use where the chemical nature of the principle has been identified, 'œstriol' for the trihydroxy compound, and 'œstrone' for the keto-hydroxy compound. **1950** L. Levin in S. Soskin *Progr. Clin. Endocrinol.* xi. 410 The separation of estriol from estrone on the basis of the somewhat greater acid dissociation of estriol. **1958** *Sci. News* XLVII. 88 Oestrone has also been obtained from palm kernel extracts, and oestriol from female willow flower. **1968** *New Scientist* 22 Feb. 399/3 Measurement of the mother's oestriol excretion is a guide to the well-being of both the foetus and the placenta that nourishes it.

œstro, variant of estro *Obs.* = œstrus 2.

1848 Lytton *K. Arthur* ix. lxxxvii, The knight sublimely stung Caught the full œstro of the poet's fire.

œstrogen ('iːs-, 'ɛstrədʒən). *Med.* Also (*U.S.*) **estro-.** [f. Œstr(us + -o + -gen.] Any natural or synthetic substance which can produce or maintain the secondary female sex characteristics in a mammal and which initiates certain bodily changes associated with the menstrual or œstrous cycle.

1927 *Official Gaz.* (U.S. Patent Office) 22 Nov. 788/1 Parke, Davis & Company, Detroit, Michigan... *Estrogen*... Extract of gland tissue for use in the treatment of various types of ovarian disfunctions. Claims use since May 25, 1927. **1928** *Endocrinology* XII. 151 (*heading*) Estrogen, a new sex hormone. **1936** *Jrnl. Amer. Med. Assoc.* 10 Oct. 1223/2 'Estrogen' is a registered trade mark belonging to Parke, Davis and Company... This firm has commendably agreed to relinquish its proprietary rights in the name on its adoption by the Council as a generic term. **1943** *Endeavour* II. 29/2 This soon led..to the synthesis of artificial oestrogens of extraordinary potency. **1951** A. Grollman *Pharmacol. & Therapeutics* xxvi. 583 Diethylstilbestrol and other estrogens exert an ameliorative effect in carcinoma of the prostate and in certain cases of mammary carcinoma occuring in post-menopausal women. **1960** *Which?* Feb. 24/1 Oestrogens, originally, seem to have been incorporated into face creams without any direct *evidence* that they could affect the skin. **1968** Passmore & Robson *Compan. Med. Stud.* I. xxxvii. 11/1 The principal ovarian hormones..fall into three broad functional categories, oestrogens, progestagens and androgens. **1968** *Times* 28 Nov. 14/4 Most oral contraceptive pills contain both a progestogen and an oestrogen—another type of ovarian hormone which is thought to be responsible for most of the side effects, such as changes of weight. **1974** *Nature* 12 Apr. 616/2 The role of oestrogens in male reproduction remains an enigma.

b. *attrib.* and *Comb.*, as *œstrogen effect, excretion, ointment, pill, therapy*; *œstrogen-induced, -secreting, -treated* adjs.

1957 *Times* 2 Dec. (Agric. Suppl.) p. vi/4 A source of greater fear to those familiar with oestrogen effects is the inhalation of dust from a concentrated premix. **1972** *Endocrinology* XCI. 1273 (*heading*) Early estrogen effects on lipid metabolism in the rat uterus. **1946** *Nature* 24 Aug. 276/2 The significance of androgen and oestrogen excretion in the urine in relation to ageing. **1972** *Brit. Vet. Jrnl.* CXXVIII. 565 Urinary oestrogen excretion has been studied during the oestrus cycle in a variety of domestic animals. **1956** *Nature* 10 Mar. 478/2 Progesterone.. prevents oestrogen-induced abdominal fibroids. **1960** *Which?* Feb. 24/2 In aged women..it was claimed that treatment with oestrogen ointment had an effect. **1972** F. Warner *Maquettes* 44 Oestrogen-pills on prescription. **1948** L. Martin *Clin. Endocrinol.* ix. 191 Œstrogen-secreting ovarian tumours composed of cells resembling those of the membrane granulosa of the Graafian follicle. *Ibid.* 170 Prolonged œstrogen therapy causes hypertrophy of the uterus and endometrium and enlargement of the breasts. **1974** *Jrnl. Amer. Med. Assoc.* 4 Feb. 522/1 Patients with preexisting hyperlipemia should probably not receive estrogen therapy. **1957** *A.M.A. Arch. Path.* LXIV. 595/2 Stratified squamous epithelium may be produced in the uterus of estrogen-treated rats by two separate..methods.

œstrogenic (iːs-, ɛstrə'dʒɛnɪk), *a.* Also (*U.S.*) **estro-.** [f. prec. + -ic.] Of the nature of, or having the actions of, an œstrogen.

1930 *Endocrinology* XIV. 101 Estrogenic material has been obtained from follicular fluid. **1938** *Ann. Reg. 1937* 348 Knowledge [was] advanced of the relation between molecular structure and the oestrogenic activity of the sex hormones. **1951** A. Grollman *Pharmacol. & Therapeutics* xxvi. 579 The naturally occurring estrogenic substances have been displaced in therapeutics to a large extent by a number of cheaper synthetic compounds. **1957** *Times* 2 Dec. (Agric. Suppl.) p. ii/7 Recently, fresh developments have taken place in the use of oestrogenic hormones such as stilboestrol and hexoestrol for beef production both in the United States and in this country. **1965** Lee & Knowles *Animal Hormones* iii. 52 Whether oestrogenic substances are secreted by the testes [of reptiles] has yet to be clarified.

Hence **œstro'genically**, *adv.*, as regards œstrogenic properties; **œstroge'nicity**, œstrogenic property.

1930 *Endocrinology* XIV. 389 A relationship between estrogenicity and the portion of a plant used as a source of extract. **1935** *Jrnl. Biol. Chem.* CXII. 425 In the commercial extraction of theelin and theelol from human pregnancy urine, an acidic, nitrogenous, crystalline substance may be separated from the crude extract. Preliminary Allen-Doisy tests showed this compound to be estrogenically inert. **1966** *Internat. Jrnl. Fertility* XI. 399 Both norethynodrel and norethisterone are active as a result of their estrogenicity. **1968** A. White et al. *Princ. Biochem.* (ed. 4) xliv. 948 They are estrogenically active when given orally.

œstrogenized ('iːstrədʒənaɪzd), *a. Med.* Also (chiefly *U.S.*) **estr-.** [f. œstrogen + -ize + -ed[1].] Treated with œstrogen. Also **,œstrogeni'zation**, the action or result of treating with œstrogen.

1946 *Nature* 20 July 96/1 The mobilization of lipo-chrome ..in the serum of œstrogenized or actively laying fowl must ..be familiar to all who have prepared phospholipid extracts from the sera of such birds. **1961** *Proc. 4th Nat. Cancer Conf.* (U.S.) 42/1 The lymphoid neoplasms that follow chronic estrogenization in some strains of mice. **1974** *Brain Res.* LXXX. 152 (*heading*) Inhibitory effect of neonatal estrogenization on the incorporation of [³H]lysine in the Purkinje cells of the adult male and female rat. **1975** *Nature* 5 June 498/1 The oestrogenised pituitary glands, without bromocryptine, stored less and released more prolactin.

œstrone ('iːs-, 'ɛstrəʊn). *Biochem.* Also (*U.S.*) **estr-.** [f. œstr(ane + -one.] An œstrogenic hormone, $C_{18}H_{22}O_2$, obtained from the urine of pregnant women and mares with actions and uses similar to those of œstradiol.

1933 [see œstriol]. **1951** A. Grollman *Pharmacol. & Therapeutics* xxvi. 579 Several preparations of amorphous concentrates of pregnancy urine or placental tissue, which consist principally of estrone sulfate, are prepared commercially for oral use. **1958** *Sci. News* XLVII. 87 Oestrone was the first naturally occurring oestrogen to be isolated in pure crystalline form. **1968** R. O. C. Norman *Princ. Org. Synthesis* xix. 651 There are four asymmetric carbon atoms in oestrone, so that there are eight enantiomorphic pairs of stereoisomers, all of which have been synthesized.

œstrous ('iːstrəs, 'ɛs-), *a.* Also (*U.S.*) **estrous.** [f. L. *œstr-us* (see below) + -ous.] Pertaining to, or causing, an œstrus (sense 2b); in heat; ***œstrous cycle***, the cyclic series of changes preceding, including, and following œstrus that takes place in most female mammals and involves esp. the reproductive and endocrine systems.

1900 *Q. Jrnl. Microsc. Sci.* XLIV. 60 The sexual season of all mammals is evidenced by a series of phenomena which constitute, in the absence of the male, one œstrous cycle (monœstrous mammals) or a series of œstrous cycles (polyœstrous mammals). **1901** *Brit. Med. Jrnl.* No. 2097. 594 The recurrent presence in the blood of an œstrous toxin. **1904** *Phil. Trans. R. Soc.* B. CXCVI. 47 (*heading*) The œstrous cycle and the formation of the corpus luteum in the sheep. *Ibid.* 73 (*heading*) Number of follicles discharging at an œstrous period. **1920** *Lancet* 2 Oct. 727/1 Under well-regulated food conditions the œstrous cycle in the guinea-pig is almost uniformly 16–17 days in duration. **1963** A. Heron *Towards Quaker View of Sex* 54 In most mammals, the oestrous cycle of the female, hormone-controlled, is an important factor. **1972** *Science* 5 May 519/1 Estrous rhythms and ovulation pattern had been reversed by substituting darkness for daylight. **1975** *Sci. Amer.* May 57/1 He [*sc.* a young male lion]..will mate if he encounters an unattended estrous female.

'œstrual, *a.* [irreg. f. œstrus + -al[1]; app. by association with *menstrual, menstruate*, etc.] Pertaining to or affected by an œstrus; œstrous. So **'œstruate** *v.*, to be affected by an œstrus, to be in heat, to rut; **'œstruation**, rutting.

1857 Mayne *Expos. Lex.*, *Œstrual*, of or belonging to the *œstrum* or orgasm. *Œstruation*,..the state of being under influence of the *œstrum*. **1859** J. C. Dalton *Treat. Human Physiol.* ii. v. 471 The ripening and discharge of the egg are accompanied by a peculiar condition of the entire system, known as the 'rutting' condition, or 'œstruation'. **1883** *Brit. Med. Jrnl.* 3 Mar. 398/1 Observation of wild animals.. shows that, after a definite period of quiescence, œstruation, or the 'rut', invariably recurs at epochs which strictly conform to some multiple of weeks. **1891** *Cent. Dict.*, *Œstruate*. **1924** *Amer. Jrnl. Physiol.* LXVIII. 294 (*heading*) The effect of pubescence, oestruation and menopause on the voluntary activity in the albino rat. *Ibid.* 303 The oestrual cycles became more and more irregular..as the animals approached the end of their sexual life. **1936** *Ibid.* CXVI. 5 Oestrual behavior in cats represents a specific pattern of response. **1961** *Nature* 16 Dec. 1043 (*heading*) Variations in the nuclear deoxyribonucleic acid content in the adrenal cortex of the female white rat during the œstrual cycle.

‖**œstrum** ('iːstrəm, 'ɛs-). Also 8 œstron. [med.L., var. of œstrus (Isidore *Orig.* xii. viii. 15).]

1. = œstrus 1; in quot. 1656 applied to a flea; in 1854 a parasite infesting fish (a sense of Gr. οἶστρος).

1656 S. Holland *Zara* (1719) 17 Defying the eagerness of those sanguine-coated Æstrums. **1706** Phillips, *Œstrum*, or *Œstrus*, the Gad-Bee. **1778** *Sketches for Tabernacle Frames* 26 Madd'ning Mares, by Lust or Oestron stung. **1854** Badham *Halieut.* 186 The conduct of the poor thunny under the scourge of the sea œstrum.

2. a. *fig.* = œstrus 2a.

1663 Butler *Hud.* i. ii. 495 What Oestrum, what Phrenetick Mood Makes you thus lavish of your Blood? **1728** Jefferson *Notes Virginia* 234 Love is the peculiar œstrum of the poet. **1848** Clough *Bothie* iii, Other times stung by the œstrum of some swift-working conception. **1886** Symonds *Renaiss. It., Cath. React.* (1898) VII. ix. 83 When..the real divine oestrum descends upon him.

b. *Physiol.* = œstrus 2b.

1772 *Ann. Reg.* 173/1 The times, in which animals of different species feel the œstrum, by which they are stimulated to the propagation of their respective kinds. **1857** in Mayne *Expos. Lex.*, *Œstrum, Œstrus.* **1878** G. Fleming *Text-bk. Vet. Obstetr.* 55 The rutting, heat, œstrum, or venereal œstrum of animals is analogous to 'menstruation' in woman. **1900** [see oestrus 2b]. **1925** [see acceptance 1b]. **1939** *Brit. Birds* XXXII. 251 The 'false œstrum' which temporarily affects so many birds during this period. **1963** Jubb & Kennedy *Path. Domestic Animals* I. i. 11/1 Oestrum may not occur, or be irregular.

‖**œstrus** ('iːstrəs, 'ɛs-). Also (*U.S.*) **estrus.** [L. *œstrus*, a. Gr. οἶστρος gad-fly, breeze, also sting, hence frenzy, mad impulse.]

1. *Entom.* A genus of dipterous insects, of which the larvæ are parasitic in the bodies of various animals; an insect of this genus or of the family *Œstridæ*; a gad-fly or bot-fly.

1697 Dryden *Virg. Georg.* iii. 238 This flying Plague.. Oestros the Grecians call: Asylus, we: A fierce loud buzzing Breez. **1752** Sir J. Hill *Hist. Anim.* 30 The black and yellow-bodied Œstrus, with black variegations in the wings. **1846** Prowett *Prometheus Bound* 59 Virgil powerfully describes the terrors of the maddened cattle from the torment of the œstrus. **1876** Duhring *Dis. Skin* 585 Œstrus, or Bot Fly deposits the ova unknown to the individual.

2. a. *fig.* Something that stings or goads one on, a stimulus; vehement impulse; passion, frenzy.

1850 E. FitzGerald *Lett.* (1889) I. 208 The Impetus, the Lyrical oestrus, is gone. **1874** Morley *Compromise* iii. (1888) 114 They too were pricked by the œstrus of intellectual responsibility. **1880** M. Pattison *Milton* xii. 161 [Milton] would not write more verses when the œstrus was not on him.

b. *Physiol.* A vehement bodily appetite or passion; *spec.* sexual orgasm; the rut of animals. In mod. use: The rut or heat (heat *sb.* 13) of female mammals, or the period during which this lasts.

1890 Billings *Nat. Med. Dict.* II. 233 *Œstrus*... 1. Rut, orgasm, clitoris. **1900** *Q. Jrnl. Microsc. Sci.* XLIV. 6 Œstrus may be a brief period and exist for only a few hours. *Ibid.*, The period of œstrus is referred to by various writers as 'Brunst', 'rut', 'heat', 'season', 'brim', or 'œstrum'. *Ibid.* 17 The duration of the œstri. **1904** *Phil. Trans. R. Soc.* B. CXCVI. 67 Œstrus was noted in a Black-faced ewe. **1963** A. Heron *Towards Quaker View of Sex* 54 In the baboon.. females in oestrus will mate with other males if their overlord's attention is temporarily distracted. **1974** *Encycl. Brit. Macropædia* VIII. 1083/1 Estrogens are substances that evoke the cyclical onset of heat, or estrus, during which the animal is sexually active and receptive to the male. **1974** *Country Life* 12 Dec. 1853/1 There was mention of what is termed 'synchronised oestrus'. By the use of drugs cows are induced to come in season at a prearranged time.

‖**œuf en cocotte** (œf ɑ̃ kɔkɔt). Also **œuf cocotte.** Pl. **œufs (en) cocotte(s).** [Fr., lit. 'egg in cocotte': see cocotte 2.] An egg cooked in a cocotte, *spec.* in *pl.*, a French dish of eggs baked in butter in individual cocottes or ramekins and served thus.

1900 *French Cookery for Eng. Homes* 142 Eggs with Sweet Herbs (*Oeufs en cocottes aux fines hérbes* [sic]). Colour in 1½ oz. of butter, some chopped onions, mushrooms, and parsley... Pour over each egg a teaspoonful of good raw cream. **1909** C. H. Senn *New Cent. Cookery Bk.* (ed. 3) xxx. 690 *Oeufs en Cocottes.* 6 to 8 eggs, a little butter, 1 tablespoonful..parsley, 6 to 8 dessertspoonfuls cream... Dish up and serve in the pipkin pans. **1960** E. David *French Provincial Cooking* 190, I always thought *œufs en cocotte* were soft. **1962** G. Z. Stone *Althea* (1964) 70 Eggs should be either very soft or thoroughly cooked,..that was what was the matter with *oeufs en cocotte*. **1963** I. Fleming *On H.M. Secret Service* ii. 27 In England he lived on grilled soles, oeufs cocotte and cold roast beef. **1966** *Observer* (Colour Suppl.) 25 Sept. 45/3 Perhaps the perfect egg dish is *oeufs en cocotte*. **1974** *She* Jan. 83/2 Dined at home. *Oeufs en cocotte* and grouse.

‖**œuvre** (œvr). [Fr., = work.] A work of art, music, or literature; the corpus of work produced by an artist, composer, or writer, considered as a whole. Cf. chef d'œuvre. Hence ***œuvre-catalogue***, a catalogue of an artist's complete work; ***œuvre de vulgarisation***, a work conveying knowledge of an academic or esoteric subject for the popular taste.

1875 Geo. Eliot *Let.* 10 Oct. in J. W. Cross *George Eliot's Life* (1885) III. xvii. 264 Our unprinted matter, our *œuvres inédites*, were safe. **1889** E. Dowson *Let.* 31 July (1967) 97 If I can only shake off Cursitor St I will go to the oeuvre like one oclock. **1890** —— *Let.* 10 or 11 June (1967) 153 The bêtise of a public which boycotts his oeuvre & buys Chomondley's pretty little ineptiae. **1898** C. Phillips *Later Work of Titian* iii. 66 The technical execution of these canvases, the treatment of landscape in the former would lead the writer to place them some years farther on still in the *œuvre* of the master. **1917** R. Fry in *Burlington Mag.* Aug. 61/2 A better opportunity for a general study of Cézanne's *oeuvre* than any other book. **1934** T. S. Eliot *Eliz. Ess.* 136 Even without an *œuvre*, some dramatists can effect a satisfying unity and significance of pattern in single plays. **1938** W. S. Maugham *Summing Up* 184 A body of work, an *œuvre*, is the result of long-continued and resolute effort. **1958** *Listener* 2 Oct. 540/1 The spreading abroad of his [*sc.* Palestrina's] bulky *oeuvre* gained considerably from the attentions of the romantics. **1959** *Ibid.* 20 Aug. 289/1 Were they in fact *oeuvres de vulgarisation* or attempts to stimulate craftsmen to new formal conquests? **1962** *Economist* 14 Apr. 141/3 An *oeuvre de vulgarisation* to bring his fifteen volume history . . before a wider public. **1965** *New Statesman* 16 July 92/1 Only four oil-paintings before 1913 are listed in his oeuvre-catalogue. **1974** *Listener* 17 Jan. 66/2 A television serial which should incorporate the Palliser oeuvre entire. **1976** *Publishers Weekly* 15 Mar. 57/2 The author tells his engaging tale with disarming simplicity and the illustrator's pictures do justice to the *oeuvre*. **1976** *Times* 16 July 12/1 Raymond Lister at Cambridge . . is currently working on an oeuvre catalogue for [Samuel] Palmer. **1978** *Times Lit. Suppl.* 25 Aug. 950/2 His oeuvre is the perfect place of exercise for . . jocular pedantry.

oeyliade, obs. form of ŒILLADE.

of (ɒv, (ə)v), *prep.* Also (3 *Orm.*) 5–7 off (6 offe); 3–6 o, 6– o': see O *prep.*[2] [OE. *of*, weak or unaccented form of the word whose rare strong form was *æf*, originally *af*, corresp. to OFris. *af*, *of*, *ofe*, OS. *af*, MLG. *af* prep. and adv. (MDu. *ave*, *af*, *of*, Du. *af* adv. 'off'), OHG. *aba*, *ab*, MHG. *abe*, *ab-* prep. and adv., Ger. *ab* adv. 'off', 'away', ON. *af*, Goth. *af* prep. and adv.:—OTeut. *aba*, unaccented by-form *ab*; corresp. to Skr. *apa* away from, down from, Gr. ἀπό, L. *ab*.

The form whence the OE. was immediately derived was *af* (as in OS., ON., and Goth.). Like other prepositional advbs., this developed two forms, according as it was stressed or stressless; in primitive OE., *æf* and *of*. In historic times the stressed form appeared only in a few nominal compounds (e.g. *'æfþunca* displeasure, *'æfweard* absent), while the originally unstressed *of* survived, as inseparable verbal particle and preposition. In OE. this *of* began to be used also as a separable particle or adv. (as in inf. *of dón*, dat. inf. *of to dónne*, pa. pple. *of(ȝe)dón*, imperative *dó of*, pa. t. *he dyde of*, in subord. cl. *þe he of dyde*); and, as the adv. in this position always received the stress, this gave rise to a new stressed form. But to the end of the ME. period, and often to 1600 or later, both unstressed and stressed forms were written *of*. About 1400, the spelling *off* appears casually, and usually (but not always) for the stressed form, to which it gradually came in course of the 16th c. to be appropriated (though *of* was sometimes used even in the 17th c.). This emphatic form was restricted to the adv. and those emphatic senses of the prep. which are akin to or derived from the adv. (*be off! get off the table! hands off! hands off the money!*); while the original spelling *of* (pronounced ɒv, əv), further reduced dialectally, colloquially, and in certain connexions, to *o'* (see O *prep.*[2]), remains for the weak senses of the preposition. Thus *of* and *off* now rank as different words.]

General Signification. The primary sense was *away*, *away from*, a sense now obsolete, except in so far as it is retained under the spelling OFF. All the existing uses of *of* are derivative; many so remote as to retain no trace of the original sense, and so weakened down as to be in themselves the expression of the vaguest and most intangible of relations. The sense-history is exceedingly complicated by reason of the introduction of senses or uses derived from other sources, the mingling of these with the main stream, and the subsequent weakening down, which often renders it difficult to assign a particular modern use to its actual source or sources. From its original sense, *of* was naturally used in the expression of the notions of removal, separation, privation, derivation, origin or source, starting-point, spring of action, cause, agent, instrument, material, and other senses, which involve the notion of taking, coming, arising, or resulting *from*. But, even in OE., this native development was affected by the translational character of the literature, and the employment of *of* to render L. *ab*, *dē*, or *ex*, in constructions where the native idiom would not have used it. Of far greater moment was its employment from the 11th c. as the equivalent of F. *de*, itself of composite origin, since it not merely represented L. *dē* in its various prepositional uses, but had come to be the Common Romanic, and so the French, substitute for the Latin genitive case. Whether *of* might have come independently in Eng. to be a substitute for the genitive is doubtful. In the expression of racial or national origin, we find *of* and the genitive app. interchangeable already in the 9th c. (tr. Bæda's *Eccl. Hist.* III. xix, Wæs þes wer . . of þæm æþelestan cynne Scotta = *de nobilissimo genere Scottorum*; Ibid. III. xxi, Se nyhsta wæs Scyttisces cynnes = *natione Scottus*; se wæs eac Scotta cynnes = *de natione Scottorum*); and this might have extended in time to other uses; but the great intrusion of *of* upon the old domain of the genitive, which speedily extended to the supersession of the OE. genitive after adjectives, verbs, and even substantives, was mainly due to the influence of F. *de*. Beside this—the most far-reaching fact in the sense-history of *of*—the same influence is also manifest in numerous phraseological uses, and esp. in the use of *of* = F. *de*, in the construction of many verbs and adjs. Many of these can be clearly distinguished; but, in other cases, the uses derived from F. *de* have so blended with those derived from OE. *of*, giving rise again to later uses related to both, that it would be difficult, if not impossible, to separate the two streams, with their many ramifications. All that can be done here is to exhibit the main uses of the preposition, and to show generally how far back each of these is exemplified. It has not been attempted to classify or even mention all the vbs. and adjs. which are or have been construed with *of*; examples occur under the chief senses and uses, but the construction of any individual vb. or adj. must be looked for under that word itself, where also will be seen what other prepositions share or have shared the same function with *of*.

I. Of *motion, direction, distance.*

†**1. a.** Indicating the thing, place, or direction whence anything goes, comes, or is driven or moved: From, away from, out of. *Obs.* exc. in the restricted sense in which it is now written OFF, q.v.

a **855** *O.E. Chron.* an. 658 Þis wæs ȝefohten siþþan he of East Englum com. *Ibid.* an. 794 And Ceolwulf biscep and Eadbald biscep of þæm londe aforon. *Ibid.* an. 823 Þa sende he Æþlwulf his sunu of þære fierde . . to Cent. *c* **893** K. ÆLFRED *Oros.* III. xi. §9 Hie þa Demetrias of þæm rice adrifon. **971** *Blickl. Hom.* 5 Crist of heofona heanessum on ðinne innoþ astiȝeþ. *Ibid.* 19 Faran of stowe to oðerre. *a* **1175** *Cott. Hom.* 219 [He] hi alle adrefde of heofan rices mirhðe. **1297** R. GLOUC. (Rolls) 11508 A certein day hom was iset, of londe vor to fle. *a* **1300** *Seven Sins* 36 in *E.E.P.* (1862) 19 Þat he sal of þis world wend. *a* **1300** *Cursor M.* 11596 (Gött.) Wit naghtertale he went of [*Cott.* o] toune. *c* **1330** R. BRUNNE *Chron. Wace* (Rolls) 8544 Þe sparkles fleye as fir of flyntes. **1439** *Rolls of Parlt.* V. 30/1 The said Places of the whiche thei wer remeved. **1489** CAXTON *Sonnes of Aymon* xiv. 337 Whan Longys dyde shove the spere in to your dygne syde, the water ranne of it. **1542–3** *Act 34 & 35 Hen. VIII*, c. 4 If anie suche person . . do withdrawe him selfe of this realme. *a* **1572** KNOX *Hist. Ref.* Wks. (1846) I. 346 [They] did secreidlie convey thame selfis and thair cumpanyeis of the town. **1613** PURCHAS *Pilgrimage* (1614) 541 With the least drawing bloud of another.

b. Indicating the place or quarter whence action (e.g. shooting, calling, writing, looking) is directed: From. *Obs.* (In quot. 1569–70, prob. after L. *ex.*)

c **893** K. ÆLFRED *Oros.* III. vii. §7 On ðæm dæȝe pleȝedon hie of horsum. *c* **1000** *Ags. Ps.* (Th.) xiii. 3 [xiv. 2] Drihten locað of heofenum. *c* **1230** *Hali Meid.* 5 Of þat syon ha bihalt al þe world under hire. *a* **1340** HAMPOLE *Psalter* xiii. 3 Lord lokyd of heuen on þe sonnes of men. **1569–70** KNOX *Let. to Cecil* 2 Jan. (S.P.O.), In haste, of Edinburgh, the second of Janur. Yours . . John Knox.

c. Following an adv., with which it is sometimes closely connected: e.g. ***down of, up of, off of.*** *dial.* or *Obs.* exc. in FORTH *of*, OUT *of*, q.v.

c **1000** ÆLFRIC *Gram.* xlvii. (Z.) 272 Se wyll astah up of ðære eorðan. **1123–31** *O.E. Chron.* an. 1123 Se kyng alihte dune of his hors. *c* **1290** *Beket* 1799 in *S. Eng. Leg.* I. 158 Ase he come op of þe se. *a* **1300** *Cursor M.* 2842 (Cott.) Our lauerd raind . . Dun o lift [*Fairf.* doun of þe lift], fire and brinstan. *c* **1380** *Sir Ferumb.* 1121 Þay comen doun of þe tour. *a* **1548** HALL *Chron., Hen. VIII* 26 b, He a lighted downe of his horse. **1748** RICHARDSON *Clarissa* (1811) V. 211 Biting my lip, got off of that, as fast as possible.

2. Indicating a point of time (or stage of life, etc.) from which something begins or proceeds. *Obs.* (supplied by *from*) exc. in archaic expressions, and in such phrases as ***of late, of recent years, of old, of yore***, which have gradually come to have the sense of 'during', 'in the course of' the time indicated: see 54.

c **900** tr. *Bæda's Hist.* I. xii. [xv.] (1890) 52 Of þære tide þe hi ðanon ȝewiton oð to dæȝe. *c* **1000** *Ags. Gosp.* Mark x. 20 Eall ðis ic ȝeheold of minre ȝeoȝuðe. *a* **1225** *Leg. Kath.* 79 Ðis meiden was . . faderles & moderles of hire childhade. *c* **1425** LYDG. *Assembly of Gods* 457 Thus haue I dewly, with all my dilygence, Executyd the offyce of olde antiquyte. *c* **1470–** [see LATE *a.*[1] B. 2]. **1483** CAXTON *G. de la Tour* H v, One his chamberlayne whiche he had nourysshed and brought up of his yougthe. **1520** WHITINTON *Vulg.* (1527) 8 b, Brought vp togyder of lytell babes. **1526** TINDALE *Mark* ix. 21 How longe is it a goo . . ? And he sayde, of a chylde. **1551** ROBINSON tr. *More's Utop.* II. ix. (1895) 291 The newe yeare . . whyche they doo begynne of that same hollye daye. **1591** SHAKS. *Two Gent.* IV. iv. 3 One that I brought vp of a puppy. **1613** PURCHAS *Pilgrimage* (1614) 534 Of auncient time they were subject to the Chinois, untill [etc.]. *a* **1625** in Gutch *Coll. Cur.* I. 186, I bred him of a Child.

†**3.** Indicating a situation, condition, or state, the departure from or emergence out of which is figured as (and often accompanied by) actual movement. *Obs.* (supplied by *from* or *out of*).

c **1000** ÆLFRIC *Hom.* I. 66 Þæt þu of deaðe arise. *c* **1200** *Trin. Coll. Hom.* 23 On þe þridde dai he aros of deaðe. *c* **1205** LAY. 11737 Fiftene þusende þer weoren islaȝen And idon of lif-dæȝen. *c* **1300** *St. Brandan* 451 As hi awoke of slepe. *c* **1380** *Sir Ferumb.* 2143 Many was þe cristene mon þat he had broȝt of dawe. *a* **1450** *Le Morte Arth.* 2006 Off swounynge whan he myght A-wake. **1513** DOUGLAS *Æneis* VIII. Prol. 38 The thrall to be of thirllage Langis ful sayr. **1579–80** NORTH *Plutarch* (1676) 14 Being delivered of his captivity. *a* **1586** SIDNEY *Arcadia* (1622) 34 To be thus banished of thy counsels.

4. Expressing position which is (or is treated as) the result of departure, and is therefore defined with reference to the fixed point.

†**a.** Away from, out of. ***of live***, out of life, dead. *Obs.*

c **1000** *Sax. Leechd.* III. 272 Fixas cwelað gyf hi of wætere beoð. *c* **1205** LAY. 9057 Heo cudden Kinbeline þat his fader wes of liue. *a* **1300** *K. Horn* 652 Heo saȝ Rymenild sitte Also he were of witte. *c* **1350** *Will. Palerne* 420 Sone of his seiȝt þe bestes seþþen ware. *a* **1425** *Cursor M.* 12478 (Trin.) Ioseph . . wende þe maistir were of lyue.

b. Now used only in certain phrases, as ***north of, south of***, etc., ***within*** (a mile, an hour, an ace, etc.) ***of, wide of, back of*** (U.S.), ***backwards of*** (arch.), ***upwards of*** (a number or amount): see these words.

1494 *Act 11 Hen. VII*, c. 23 Every such Fish should be splatted down to an Handful of the Tail. **1537** *Lett. Suppress. Monast.* (Camden) 157 Within x. or xij. mylles of hit. **1588** SHAKS. *L.L.L.* I. i. 119 That no woman shall come within a mile of my Court. **1597** —— *2 Hen. IV*, IV. i. 19 West of this Forrest, scarcely off a mile, . . comes on the Enemie. **1762** *Chron.* in *Ann. Reg.* 104/2 Upwards of 15,000 lb. weight. **1778** ROBERTSON *Hist. Amer.* I. 431 Countries . . situate to the east of those [etc.]. **1843** *Blackw. Mag.* LIV. 160 Bill was generally pretty wide of his mark. **1885** *Act 48 & 49 Vict.* c. 54 §14 Churches . . within four miles of one another. **1885** FISCHER in *Law Rep.* 29 Chanc. Div. 453 Commenced within a few days of each other.

c. *N. Amer.* and *dial.* In expressing the time: from or before (a specified hour); = TO *prep.* 6 b. Also *ellipt.*

1817 T. DEAN *Jrnl.* 31 May in *Indiana Hist. Soc. Publ.* (1918) VI. 278 At 15 minutes of 10 A.M. Paul Dick arrived. **1857** M. J. HOLMES *Meadow Brook* v. 64 Five minutes of nine, and round the corner at the foot of the hill appeared a group of children. **1912** in *Sc. Nat. Dict.* (1965) VI. 466/3 It is a quarter of twelve. **1972** H. MACINNES *Message from Málaga* xix. 264, I have to leave by a quarter of four—at the latest. **1973** D. MACKENZIE *Postscript to Dead Let.* 22 It was a quarter-of-seven. **1976** I. LEVIN *Boys from Brazil* iv. 135 'Can I go with you?' 'Sure. . . I leave at five of.'

II. Of *liberation* and *privation*. Expressing separation from or of a property, possession, or appurtenance. (In OE. expressed by *of*, *from*, or genitive case.)

5. In the construction of transitive verbs, of various classes; as

a. *to cure, heal, recover; cleanse, clear, purge, wash; bring to bed, deliver, disburden, ease, empty, free, lighten, rid of*, etc. **b.** *to bereave, deprive, divest, drain, exhaust, oust, rob, spoil, strip of*, etc.

In these, by a kind of transposition, *of* introduces that which is removed, the person or thing whence it is removed being made the grammatical object: thus, a prisoner is said to be stripped *of his clothes*, when in reality the clothes are stripped *off* or *from the prisoner*.

a **900** K. ÆLFRED *Solil.* 167 Us ȝeclensast of æallum urum synnum. *c* **1000** *Ags. Gosp.* Matt. vi. 13 Alys us of yfele. —— Luke vii. 21 He ȝe-hælde manega of adlum ȝe of witum and of yfelum gastum. **1124–31** *O.E. Chron.* an. 1124 Six men [he] spilde of here æȝon and of here stanes. *c* **1200** *Trin. Coll. Hom.* 169 Ared me louerd of eche deaðe. *c* **1380** WYCLIF *Sel. Wks.* III. 453 Allagatis a man most first be purged of dedly [synne]. *a* **1400** *Relig. Pieces fr. Thornton MS.* (1867) 37 We pray þat we be delyuered of all ill thynge. *c* **1440** *Tundale* 10 Ʒyf he . . clense hym here of his mysdede. **1526** *Pilgr. Perf.* (W. de W. 1531) 5 As yͤ iewes spoyled Egypte of theyr rychesse. **1616** W. HAIG in J. Russell *Haigs* vii. (1881) 163, I humbly beseech your sacred Majesty . . to free me of this close prison. **1632** J. HAYWARD tr. *Biondi's Eromena* 22 Without stripping himselfe of his cloathes. **1670** R. MONTAGU in *Buccleuch MSS.* (Hist. MSS. Comm.) I. 473 The King . . would release his Christian Majesty of his word. **1697** DRYDEN *Virg. Georg.* III. 486 The Pastor . . eases of their Hair, the loaden Herds. **1711** ADDISON *Spect.* No. 1 ¶2 She dreamt that she was brought to Bed of a Judge. **1820** KEATS *Grecian Urn* iv, What little town . . Is emptied of its folk this pious morn? **1847** C. G. ADDISON *Law of Contracts* II. iii. §3 (1883) 635 A recovery by one party ousts the other of his right to recover.

6. In the construction of some classes of intrans. verbs; as

a. *To recover.* †**b.** *To blin, cease, stint.*

13.. *Guy Warw.* (A.) 849 Of rideing wil þai neuer stent. *c* **1450** *St. Cuthbert* (Surtees) 5130 þe se of flowyng in abade. *c* **1450** *Merlin* 39 Neuer to entermete of that arte. *c* **1460** *Towneley Myst.* xxvi. 92 Centurio, sese of sich saw. **1602** SHAKS. *Ham.* I. iv. 3, I thinke it lacks of twelue. **1844** J. T. HEWLETT *Parsons & W.* xiii, He recovered of his wounds.

7. In the construction of verbal sbs. and nouns of action, akin to the preceding verbs. (Now mostly *Obs.* and replaced by *from.*)

a **1000** *Ags. Ps.* (Th.) xxii. (*heading*), He þancað Gode his alysnesse of his earfoðum. **1426** in *Surtees Misc.* (1888) 7 To pray . . for ease of þe said John Lyllyng. **1463** G. ASHBY *Prisoner's Refl.* 349 Of fre liberte a sharp abstinence. *c* **1500** *Melusine* 151 The rescue of the daunger . . is worth & ynough for a conqueste. **1534** WHITINTON *Tullyes Offices* I. (1540) 75 The rest of cares. *c* **1645** HABINGTON *Surv. Worcs.* (Worcs. Hist. Soc. Proc.) I. 121 For hys salvation and redemption of hys synnes. **1761** MRS. F. SHERIDAN *Sidney Bidulph* I. 14 He . . had been ordered by the physicians to Spa for the recovery of a lingering disorder.

8. In the construction of adjs.: **a.** *whole* (*of a wound*); *clean, clear, free, pure, quit, rid*, etc.; **b.** *bare, barren, destitute, devoid, empty, naked, void*, etc. Some of these, e.g. *clean, empty, free, naked*, etc. were in OE. followed by the genitive (cf. IX.); in some *from* has now taken the place of *of*: see under the adjs.

c **1000** *Ags. Gosp.* Mark v. 34 Beo of ðisum [*a plaga tua*] hal. *c* **1175** *Lamb. Hom.* 63 Of ure sunne make us clene. *c* **1375** *Cursor M.* 24648 (Fairf.) Lauedi of sorou þou mai be liȝt. **1470–85** MALORY *Arthur* VIII. xiii, Sir Tristram was . . hole of his woundes. **1574** tr. *Marlorat's Apocalips* 6 Their disputing of vertue, is voyde of the holye Ghost. **1611** SHAKS. *Cymb.* II. iii. 94, I am poor of thanks. **1697** DRYDEN *Virg. Georg.* I. 427 The Farmer, now secure of Fear. **1785** BURNS *Earnest Cry & Prayer* viii, Picking her pouch as bare as winter Of a' kind coin. **1876** GLADSTONE *Glean.* (1879) II. 273 Macaulay was singularly free of vices.

III. Of *origin* or *source.* Indicating the thing or person whence anything originates, comes, is acquired or sought.

9. a. Expressing racial or local origin, descent, etc.: after the vbs. *arise, be, come, descend, spring, be born, bred, propagated,* and the like.

c **897** K. ÆLFRED *Gregory's Past.* xxxv. 240 Of hwæm hit ærest com. *c* **900** tr. *Bæda's Hist.* I. xii. [xv.] (1890) 52 Of Geata fruman syndon Cantware.. Of Seaxum..coman Eastseaxan and Suðseaxan and Westseaxan. *Ibid.* IV. xxv[i]. 350 Sum wer of Scotta þeode. *c* **1000** *Ags. Gosp.* John iii. 6 þæt þe of gaste is acenned þæt is gast. **1129–31** *O.E. Chron.* an. 1129 Boren of þa ricceste men of Rome. *c* **1175** *Lamb. Hom.* 17 He wes iboren of ure lefdi Zeinte Marie. *c* **1200** ORMIN 495 Alle..þatt off þa tweʒʒen prestess comenn. *c* **1205** LAY. 320 His kun þe he of icumen wes. *Ibid.* 11117 He wes of heore cunne. *a* **1300** *Cursor M.* 14340 (Cott.) Fader i wat i am o [*v.r.* of] þe. *c* **1425** *Prymer* 6 Sikirli, maide marie ..of þee is risun þe sunne of riȝtwisnesse, oure lord ihesu crist. *c* **1435** *Torr. Portugal* 1068 'Sir', quod the kyng, 'of whens are ye?' 'Of Portingale, Sir', said he. **1513** MORE in Hall *Chron., Edw. V,* 1 Ye muste first considre of whom he and his brother dessended. **1590** SPENSER *F.Q.* II. vii. 12 Infinite mischiefes of them do arize. **1610** SHAKS. *Temp.* II. i. 82 She was of Carthage, not of Tunis. **1626** BACON *Sylva* §696 Fleas breed principally Of Straw or Mats. **1669** WORLIDGE *Syst. Agric.* (1681) 97 It is propagated of the Keys, as the Ash. **1709** STEELE *Tatler* No. 112 ¶5 Young Gentlemen, descended of honest Parents. **1826** DISRAELI *Viv. Grey* v. vi, Are you of Dorsetshire? **1851** THACKERAY *Eng. Hum.* i. (1853) 2 Of English parents, and of a good English family of clergymen, Swift was born in Dublin. **1888** *Athenæum* 3 Nov. 588/3 The force born of strong womanly instinct.

†**b.** Expressing the origin or derivation of a name: with various vbs. *Obs.* (Now *from.*)

c **1000** ÆLFRIC *Gram.* xv. (Z.) 93 Ða oðre seofan syndon *dirivativa,* þat is, þæt hi cumað of þam oðrum. **1387** TREVISA *Higden* (Rolls) I. 93 Assyria haþ þe name of Asur Sem his sone. *c* **1450** *St. Cuthbert* (Surtees) 6675 It takes name of a watir strynde. **1559** W. CUNNINGHAM *Cosmogr. Glasse* 18 Horizont..is said of ὁριζω, whiche signifieth to decerne, or ende. **1568** GRAFTON *Chron.* II. 83 Named Portgreves..the which is derived of two Saxon wordes. **1570–6** LAMBARDE *Peramb. Kent* (1826) 155 He..called it (of the sandie place where it is pitched) Sandgate Castle. **1605** CAMDEN *Rem.* (1637) 127 Names also haue been taken of civill honours, dignities, and estate, as King, Duke, Prince, Lord, Baron, Knight,.. Squire, Castellan.

10. After trans. vbs., their pples., gerunds, etc.

a. After *borrow, buy, gain, hold, purchase, receive, win,* and the like, in which it varies with *from*; formerly also with *get, have, steal, take,* etc. where *from* is now used. See also OFF *prep.* 2.

Still used after *take advantage, take leave, take an oath, take vengeance.*

c **1000** ÆLFRIC *Job* ii. 10 ʒif we god underfengon of godes hande. **1127–31** *O.E. Chron.* an. 1127 For to hauene sibbe of se eorl of Angeow. **1140** *Ibid,,* Hi nan helpe ne hæfden of þe kinge. *c* **1175** *Lamb. Hom.* 7 Drihten þu dest þe lof of milc drinkende childre muðe. *c* **1205** LAY. 2093 Of Ignogen his quene he hefde þreo sunen scene. *Ibid.* 29746 We..habbeoð ure irihte of ure arche-biscpe. *c* **1290** *St. Michael* 450 in *S. Eng. Leg.* I. 312 Alle habbez liȝt of hire. *a* **1300** *Cursor M.* 460 (Cott.) O me [*Gött.* of me] seruis sal he non gette. **1377** LANGL. *P. Pl.* B. XIII. 234, I haue none gode gyftes of þise grete lordes. *c* **1440** *Jacob's Well* 208 Takyth exaumple of hym! **1640** YORKE *Union Hon.* 154 Joan, wife to Gilbert.. of whom hee begot one daughter. **1642** tr. *Perkins' Prof. Bk.* viii. § 533. 233 He shall hold off him of whom his feoffor held. **1697–8** EVELYN *Mem.* 8 Feb., The use which may be derived of such a collection. **1724** DE FOE *Mem. Cavalier* (1840) 187 The kings enemies made all the advantages of it that was possible. **1741** RICHARDSON *Pamela* I. 92, I would not take them of her. **1755** AMORY *Mem.* (1769) I. 240, I hope you will not take it ill of me, that I offer my advice. **1833** HT. MARTINEAU *Loom & Lugger* II. iii. 45 She would have had much more comfort of her son if he had lived. **1885** *Law Rep.* 14 Queen's Bench Div. 735 They agreed to hire another room of the defendants.

b. After *ask, beg, crave, demand, desire, entreat, expect, inquire, request, require, seek,* and the like; also after *learn, hear.* (Some of these, as *ask, inquire,* were formerly constr. with *at*; in some *of* varies with *from.*)

c **893** K. ÆLFRED *Oros.* II. v. §3 He hæfde of oþerum þeodum abeden IIII C M. **1297** R. GLOUC. (Rolls) 2477 Bidde of me what þou wolt. **1362** LANGL. *P. Pl.* A. I. 47 He asked of hem of whom spac þe lettre. **1382** WYCLIF *Matt.* ii. 4 He ..enquiride of hem, wher Crist shulde be borun. *c* **1386** CHAUCER *Doctor's T.* 197 This cursed Iuge wolde no thyng tarie, Ne heere a word moore of Virginius. *a* **1425** *Cursor M.* 6819 (Trin.) Lerne not of him þat is lyere. **1444** *Rolls of Parlt.* V. 75/1 Without any suyt of any licence of oure Lord Kyng. **1596** SHAKS. *1 Hen. IV,* v. iv. 23 Lustier maintenance then I did looke for Of such an vngrowne Warriour. **1610** HEALEY *St. Aug. Citie of God* 93 Sylla ..demanded helpe of his armie. **1791** COWPER *Retired Cat* 10, I know not where she caught the trick..Or else she learned it of her master. **1821** J. F. COOPER *Spy* viii, It is all that is required of me. **1854** DICKENS *Hard T.* II. vii, You expect too much of your sister. **1859** G. MEREDITH *R. Feverel* xxxiv, I do not beg of you to forgive him now.

c. After various other vbs. Mostly *Obs.*

a **1300** *Cursor M.* 10670 To godd þan was i giuen ar mi moder me of bodi bare. **1660** F. BROOKE tr. *Le Blanc's Trav.* 5 The houses are built of the Moresco modell, with galleries.

11. a. After a sb. Arising from the elision of a pple. of some vb. of the foregoing classes.

c **888** K. ÆLFRED *Boeth.* i. §1 On ðære tide ðe Gotan of Sciððiu mæʒðe wið Romana rice ʒewin up ahofon. *c* **900** tr. *Bæda's Hist.* III. xx. [xxviii.] (1890) 246 Tweʒen biscopas of Bretta ðeode. *c* **1000** ÆLFRIC *Gen.* vii. 8 þa nitenu of eallum cinne and of eallum fuʒelcynne. **1520** in *Vicary's Anat.* (1888) App. viii. 213 Camme Pereson & Bankes..& Showed forthe their Graunte of Kyng Edward iiij[th]. **1789** BURNS *Whistle* v, Three noble chieftains, and all of his blood. **1818** CRUISE *Digest* (ed. 2) IV. 380 Such person as should be heir male of the body of the wife at her death. **1885** SIR R. BAGGALLAY in *Law Rep.* 10 P.D. 192 There was one child of the marriage.

b. esp. in reference to local origin.

Here the notion of *from* passes into that of *belonging to* a place, and so becomes identified with sense 47, q.v.

IV. Of the source or *starting-point of action, emotion,* etc.; *motive, cause, ground, reason.*

12. a. Indicating the mental or non-material source or spring of action, emotion, etc.: Out of, from, as an outcome, expression, or consequence of.

Esp. in many phrases, treated, when necessary, under the sbs., as *of one's own accord, of choice, consequence, course, force, goodwill, one's own head, one's own knowledge, necessity, one's own good pleasure, purpose, right, one's own will*; also *of courtesy, custom, duty, favour, grace, instinct, kind, nature, office, reason,* etc.

This connects the notions of origin and cause.

c **888** K. ÆLFRED *Boeth.* xiii. §1 Hit is of his aʒenre ʒecynde, næs of þinre. *c* **897** —— *Gregory's Past.* xxi. 157 Ðonne hie of yflum willan ne ʒesyngað ac of unwisdome. *c* **900** tr. *Bæda's Hist.* I. xvi. [xxvii.] (1890) 68 þonne is hit of lufan to donne. *a* **1225** *Leg. Kath.* 1361 þe Keiser kaste his heaued as wod mon, of wraððe. **1340** HAMPOLE *Pr. Consc.* 5773 Other werkes noght done of mercy. *c* **1400** MAUNDEV. (Roxb.) xxix. 131 Godd of his speciall grace herd his praier. *c* **1425** LYDG. *Assembly of Gods* 81 Desyryng of fauour to haue audyence. *c* **1520** *Trevelyan Papers* (Camden) 135 Contryvyd and ymagyned of malyce and dyspleasure. **1541** R. COPLAND *Guydon's Quest. Chirurg.,* Galyen sayeth of the auctoryte of Ypocras, that [etc.]. **1577** *St. Aug. Manual* (Longman) 6 It is of thy goodnes that we be made, of thy justice that we be punished, and of thy mercy that we be delivered. **1578** LYTE *Dodoens* III. lxxxv. 439 Apples of loue grow not of their owne kinde in this Countrie. **1581** MULCASTER *Positions* xxxix. (1887) 218 If some of choice became both diuines, and physicianes. **1624** CAPT. SMITH *Virginia* II. (Arb.) 370 They..serue him more of feare then loue. **1721** *St. German's Doctor & Stud.* 120 It seemeth of Reason. *Ibid.* 313 The Justices of favour will most commonly help forth the party. **1776** *Trial of Nundocomar* 32/1 Did you know of any bond..of your own knowledge? **1849** MACAULAY *Hist. Eng.* ix. II. 433 Lewis..laboured, as if of set purpose, to estrange his Dutch friends. **1894** CROCKETT *Raiders* 15, I seized my oars of instinct and rowed shorewards.

b. *of oneself,* by one's own impetus or motion, spontaneously, without the instigation or aid of another.

c **1000** *Ags. Gosp.* John viii. 28 Ic ne do nan þing of me sylfum. *Ibid.* xviii. 34 Cwyst þu þis of ðe sylfum? **1382** WYCLIF *John* v. 19 The sone may not of him silf do ony thing, no but that thing that he schal se the fadir doynge. *c* **1400** MAUNDEV. (Roxb.) vii. 24 þe cuntree es strang ynogh of þe self. **1542** UDALL *Erasm. Apoph.* 152, Whatsoever thyng wer not of it self eivill. **1598** CHAPMAN *Blinde Begger of Alexandria* Wks. 1873 I. 11 A man that of himselfe Sits downe and bids you welcome to your feast. **1607** TOPSELL *Four-f. Beasts* (1658) 67 When an Oxe or Cow in ancient time did dye of themselves. **1621** BP. MOUNTAGU *Diatribæ* 503, I speake not of my selfe or without booke. **1707** W. FUNNELL *Voy. round World* 20 The Goats..would many of them come of themselves to be milked. *a* **1774** GOLDSM. *Surv. Exp. Philos.* (1776) I. 106 Matter is of itself entirely passive, incapable of moving itself. **1836** CARLYLE *Let. to sister Jenny* 16 May, I judged that Robert and you were happy enough of yourselves for the present. **1886** *Athenæum* 30 Oct. 561/1 [They] therefore can do nothing good of themselves.

13. Indicating the cause, reason, or ground of an action, occurrence, fact, feeling, etc.

a. After an intrans. vb. (e.g. *die, perish*; *savour, smack, smell, taste, ring*; etc.) In some of these *obs.* and supplied by *with, from, at.*

The sense of cause is sometimes weakened into that of the subject-matter of the action (VIII).

c **893** K. ÆLFRED *Oros.* I. iv. §1 þæt he of ðæm cræfte Pharaone þæm cyninge swa leof wurde. **1119–31** *O.E. Chron.* an. 1119 Forð-ferde se eorl Baldewine of Flandran of þam wundan þe he..ʒefeng. **1124–31** *Ibid.* an. 1124 Se man ..þe nan [god] ne heafde stærf of hungor. *c* **1205** LAY. 31482 Heo..menden heom to Pendan Of Oswy þan kinge. *c* **1305** *St. Edmund Conf.* 394 in *E.E.P.* (1862) 81 Of him wondrede euerech man. *c* **1315** SHOREHAM 48 Word that of God smaketh. **1470–85** MALORY *Arthur* VIII. xii, My moder dyed of me. *Ibid.* x. xii, All the forrest rang of the noise. **1548–9** (Mar.) *Bk. Com. Prayer, Litany,* All women labouryng of chylde. **1697** DRYDEN *Virg. Georg.* IV. 602 He breath'd of Heav'n, and look'd above a Man. **1843** *Fraser's Mag.* XXVIII. 277, I am dying of fatigue. **1886** *Manch. Exam.* 18 Jan. 5/5 It savours more of statecraft than of statesmanship.

†**b.** After a trans. vb. or its object (e.g. *to esteem, praise, thank, blame,* etc.). *Obs.* (Supplied by *for, on account of,* etc.)

c **1350** *Will. Palerne* 500 þat perles..is preised ouer alle, Of fairnesse of facion and frely þewes. **1377** LANGL. *P. Pl.* B. VI. 129 We preye..þat god..ȝelde ȝow of ȝowre almesse þat ȝe ȝiue vs here. **1483** CAXTON *G. de la Tour* G ij, Behynd her bak he mocked her of it. *a* **1533** LD. BERNERS *Huon* lxi. 212, I thanke you of your courtesye. **1611** BIBLE *Transl. Pref.* 3 How can wee excuse ourselues of negligence? **1613** [see ARREST *v.*]. **1657** TRAPP *Comm. Ps.* lxviii. 17 Angels, who are here called, Shinan, of their changeableness.

14. After an adj. or sb., indicating that which causes or gives rise to the quality, feeling, or action.

a. After an adj. (e.g. *dead, sick, weary*; *ashamed, afraid, fearful*; *glad, joyful, sorry*; *proud, vain*; etc.): Because of, on account of.

[In OE. with genitive: cf. 30. In Fr. with *de.*] In some of these now *obs.*: see the words themselves.

c **1200** ORMIN 794 Oþre menn unnfæwe Well glade & bliþe sholldenn ben Ec off þatt childess come. **1297** R. GLOUC. (Rolls) 11178 þo were þe porters agrise sore of þulke siȝte. **1426** LYDG. *De Guil. Pilgr.* 3645 As thoȝ ye were In party dronken of your wynes. *a* **1450** *Knt. de la Tour* (1868) 99 She held her..ashamed of that she had be warned of her demaunde and requeste. **1526** TINDALE *Matt.* viii. 14 Lyinge sicke of a fevre. **1535** COVERDALE *Jonah* iv. 6 And Ionas was exceadinge glad of the wylde vyne. **1568** TILNEY *Disc. Marriage* B ij b, They had nothing to be prowde off. **1610** SHAKS. *Temp.* v. i. 230 We were dead of sleepe. *a* **1653** BINNING *Serm.* (1743) 607 Would not dyvours and prisoners be content of a deliverance? **1715–20** POPE *Iliad* VI. 105 Press'd as we are, and sore of former fight. **1842** MACAULAY *Ess.* (1848) I. 321 Sick of inaction.

b. After a sb. (e.g. *anger, grief, joy, thanks*). Mostly *Obs.* (supplied by *on account of, for, at*).

13.. *Guy Warw.* (A.) 275 Sorwe he makeþ wiþ þe mest Of Felice þat feir may. *c* **1450** *Merlin* 227 Feire lady, with goode will, and gramercy of youre seruyse. **1497** BP. ALCOCK *Mons Perfect.* B iij b, Some in pryde of worde, of garment, & of blood. **1595** SHAKS. *John* IV. i. 114 You will but make it blush, And glow with shame of your proceedings. **1598** GRENEWEY *Tacitus, Ann.* XIII. xii. (1622) 198 For want of remedy, and anger of such a destruction. **1599** SHAKS. *Much Ado* II. i. 200, I wish him ioy of her. **1611** —— *Wint. T.* v. ii. 54 Ready to leape out of himselfe, for ioy of his found Daughter. **1749** FIELDING *Tom Jones* XVIII. x, She..wished him heartily Joy of his new-found Uncle. **1760–72** H. BROOKE *Fool of Qual.* (1809) II. 112 Pouring forth her tears ..for grief of having found him in that condition.

V. Indicating the *agent* or *doer.*

15. Introducing the agent after a passive verb. (The regular word for this is now BY (sense 33), which began to come in *c* 1400; but *of* prevailed till *c* 1600, and is still in literary use, as a biblical, poetic, or stylistic archaism, or by association with other constructions, e.g. 'on the part of'. In OE. less used than *from*: cf. Ger. *von* from, of.)

The use of *of* is most frequent after pa. pples. expressing a continued non-physical action (as in ***admired, loved, hated, ordained of***), or a condition resulting from a definite action (as in ***abandoned, deserted, forgotten, forsaken of,*** which approach branch II). It is also occasional with ppl. adjs. in *un-*, as ***unseen of, unowned of.*** *Of* often shows an approach to the subjective genitive: cf. 'he was chosen of God to this work' with 'he was the chosen of the electors'. In other senses the agent has passed into the cause, as in ***afeard, afraid, frightened, terrified of***; or the source or origin, as in ***born of.*** Eng. *of* and *by* correspond somewhat to F. *de* and *par.*

c **893** K. ÆLFRED *Oros.* Contents I. x, Hu II æþelingas wurdon afliemed of Sciþþium. *c* **1050** *O.E. Chron.* an. 924 (MS. C) Æþelstan wæs of Myrcum ʒecoren to cinge. *Ibid.* an. 1030 Her wæs Olaf cing ofslaʒen..of his aʒenum folce. **1154** *Ibid.* (Laud MS.), Wæl luued of þe kinge and of alle gode men. *a* **1225** *Ancr. R.* 48 Ich wolde þet heo weren of alle iholden. **13..** *K. Alis.* 7709 Adam was byswike of Eve. *c* **1380** WYCLIF *Wks.* (1880) 427 þe puple trowiþ betere þerto whanne it is seyd of a maistir. *c* **1400** MAUNDEV. (1839) xxi. 222 He was cursed of God. *c* **1440** *Jacob's Well* 230 My preyerys arn noȝt herd of god for þe. **1459** *Paston Lett.* I. 441 Sir Thomas shuld a ben there, but he is hurte of an hors. **1548–9** *Bk. Com. Prayer* 2nd Exhort. Communion, I am commaunded of God, especially to moue and exhorte you. *c* **1550** BECON (*title*) The Principles of Christen Religion, necessary to be knowen of the faythful. **1558** GOODMAN (*title*) How superior powers oght to be obeyd of their subiects. **1577** B. GOOGE *Heresbach's Husb.* (1586) 13 That the juice that the ground requires be not sucked out of the sunne. **1590** STOCKWOOD *Rules Construct.* 32 The relatiue is not alwaies gouerned of the verbe that he commeth before. **1600** SHAKS. *A.Y.L.* III. ii. 361, I have been told so of many. **1611** BIBLE *Matt.* ii. 12 Being warned of God in a dreame. —— *Acts* xii. 23 Herod..was eaten of wormes. **1711** STEELE *Spect.* No. 152 ¶3 He is beloved of all that behold him. **1725** POPE *Odyss.* VII. 34 A wretched stranger, and of all unknown! **1847** D. G. MITCHELL *Fresh Glean.* (1851) 232 Otho was not loved of his kinsfolk in his home. **1869** FREEMAN *Norm. Conq.* III. xii. 222 A wretch forsaken of God and man. **1898** *Daily News* 10 Oct. 6/3 Everything.. seems to be done of those who govern Spain to keep travellers out of that country.

16. Indicating the doer of something characterized by an adj., as *it was kind of you* (= a kind act or thing done by you, on your part) *to help him.* Used with an adj. and sb., as *a cruel act, a cunning trick, a foolish fancy, a good thought, a kind deed, an odd thing*; a qualified pa. pple., as *cleverly managed, ill done, well done, well thought*; or an adjective alone, as *good, bad, right, wrong, wise, foolish*; *clever, stupid, rude, silly, unkind,* or any adj. by which conduct can be characterized.

Followed by *to do* (something), less frequently *that* (*he*) *did* (something), which is the logical subject or object of the statement; e.g. I took it kind of him to tell me = I took his telling me as a thing kindly done by him.

1532 TINDALE *Expos.* 73 Is it not a blind thing of the world that either they will do no good works,..or will..have the glory themselves? *c* **1592** MARLOWE *Jew of Malta* IV. v, 'Tis a strange thing of that Iew, he lives upon pickled grasshoppers. **1602** SHAKS. *Ham.* III. ii. 110 It was a bruite part of him, to kill so Capitall a Calfe there. **1668** H. MORE *Div. Dial.* II. 383 That's a very odd thing of the men of Arcladam. **1733** TULL *Horse-hoeing Husb.* 266 Is it not very unfair of Equivocus to represent [etc.]? **1760–72** H. BROOKE *Fool of Qual.* (1809) I. 52 Indeed, it was very naughty of him. **1849** F. W. NEWMAN *The Soul* 104 It was not a proud thing of Paul to say, but a simple truth. **1887** L. CARROLL *Game of Logic* iv. 92 It was most absurd of you to offer it!

17. a. After a sb., expressing the relation of doer, or that of maker or author (= *subjective genitive*).

a **1175** *Cott. Hom.* 217 Þenche ȝie ælc word of him swete. *a* **1300** *Cursor M.* 24985, I tru in..vprising o [*v.r.* of] flexs, and lijf wiðuten end. *c* **1380** WYCLIF *Serm.* Sel. Wks. II. 197 In þe aȝenrysyng of just men. **1497** BP. ALCOCK *Mons Perfect.* B ij, Grete temptacions of yᵉ worlde, the flesshe, & the deuyl. *a* **1548** HALL *Chron., Hen. VIII* 253 As trew as the allegation of him that is burnt in the hande, to saye he was cut with a sikle. **1601** BP. W. BARLOW *Eagle & Body* (1609) C j, By the traditions of antiquitie and the Definitions of Councels. **1656** EARL MONM. tr. *Boccalini, Pol. Touchstone* (1674) 262 The general ransacking of the Vice Roys. **1659** B. HARRIS *Parival's Iron Age* 13 The conquest of the Romans over them was more sure. **1754** SHERLOCK *Disc.* (1755) I. viii. 247 The Evidence of the Spirit is not any secret Inspiration. **1856** FROUDE *Hist. Eng.* (1858) I. iii. 269 He had the secret approbation of his prince.

b. Indicating the maker or author of a work: Made, written, painted by. Often expressed by the possessive case, as 'The tragedies of Shakspere', 'Shakspere's tragedies', or by a combination of this with the partitive *of* (44), as 'a sonata of Beethoven's'.

1382 WYCLIF *Bible* (heading), Heere bigynnith the epystle of saynt Jerom preest of alle the bokes of Goddis storye. —— *Prov.* i. 1 The parablis of Salamon. *Ibid.* xxxi. 1 The wrdis of Lamuel, the king. **1576** FLEMING *Panopl. Epist.* 398 The Epistles of Seneca are full of Philosophie. **1812** JEFFERSON *Writ.* (1830) IV. 175 The letter of the applicant. **1830** D'ISRAELI *Chas. I*, III. vi. 92 There exist no autographs of Charles, except some letters. **1871** HAWEIS *Music & Mor.* (1874) 57 A movement of Beethoven. **1885** *Sat. Rev.* 29 Aug. 300 The Cornish Ballads of the Rev. R. S. Hawker. *Mod.* The Iliad of Homer, the Æneid of Virgil. The 'Holy Family' of Rubens, the landscapes of Claude Lorraine. The phonograph of Edison, the kaleidoscope of Brewster.

VI. Indicating *means* or *instrument*.

†**18. a.** Indicating that by means of or with which something is done. *Obs.* or *dial.* (Now usually *with*.)

c **897** K. ÆLFRED *Gregory's Past.* xxxvi. 248 Ðylæs fremde men weorðen ȝefylled of ðinum ȝeswince. *c* **900** tr. *Bæda's Hist.* I. xvi. [xxvii.] (1890) 76 Þætte þære menniscan ȝecynde of ælmehteȝes Godes ȝefe ȝehealden wæs. *c* **1000** *St. Andrew*, etc. (1851) 28 He of v. hlafon and of twam fixum fif þusend manna ȝefylde. *c* **1175** *Lamb. Hom.* 139 Sunnendei weren engles makede of godes muðe. **13..** *E.E. Allit. P.* B. 1277 Þe gredirne & þe goblotes garnyst of syluer. *c* **1386** CHAUCER *Knt.'s T.* 1033 The circuit a myle was aboute Walled of stoon. *c* **1400** MAUNDEV. (Roxb.) viii. 32 Whare Moyses strake on þe stone with his ȝerde, and it ran of water. *Ibid.* (1839) xii. 132 Rennynge of mylk and hony. *c* **1477** CAXTON *Jason* 17 In makyng reed hys swerd of the bloode of the Esclauon king. *c* **1489** —— *Sonnes of Aymon* xvi. 374 So I defended me of all my power. **1551** ROBINSON tr. *More's Utop.* II. v. (1895) 165 They begin euerye dynner and supper of reading sumthing that perteineth to good maners and vertue. **1652** EVELYN *Mem.* 6 Mar., A chariot canopied of black velvet. **1824** MISS FERRIER *Inherit.* xxvii, It was pouring of rain.

b. Indicating that on which any one lives, feeds, etc. *Obs.* or *arch.* (Now usually *on*.)

a **1420** HOCCLEVE *De Reg. Princ.* 1193, I lyue of almesse. **1533** GAU *Richt Vay* 93 Lat wsz noth liff of okir or be ony falsait. **1581** SAVILE *Tacitus, Hist.* IV. lx. (1591) 214 Feeding of branches and sprigges. **1588** J. UDALL *Diotrephes* (Arb.) 8 Euerie man muste liue of his trade. **1613** PURCHAS *Pilgrimage* (1614) 540 They live of bread made of pith of trees. *a* **1718** PENN *Maxims* Wks. 1726 I. 825 [The covetous man] lives of the Offal. **1896** MRS. CAFFYN *Quaker Grandmother* 43 He hobnobbed with soldiers, and was nourished of carnage.

†**19.** After an adj., indicating that with which anything is *filled*, *imbued*, *coloured*, etc. *Obs.* (exc. after *full*, which perh. does not belong here.)

1137-54 *O.E. Chron.* an. 1137 And fylden þe land ful of castles. *c* **1430** *Syr Gener.* (Roxb.) 4098 The ground of bloode was al wete. *c* **1450** *Merlin* 155 The water was all reade of blode. **1450-1530** *Myrr. our Ladye* 248 Hys face made redde of the blode.

VII. Indicating the *material* or *substance* of which anything is made or consists.

20. a. After verbs signifying to make, to be made, to consist, to be. Hence such fig. phrases as ***to make a fool of***, ***to make much of***, ***make the best of***, etc.: see MAKE, etc.

c **893** K. ÆLFRED *Oros.* IV. xiii. §1 Hie worhton sume of seolfre, sume of treowum. *a* **1000** *Cædmon's Gen.* 365 Adam ..þe wæs of eorþan ȝeworht. *c* **1200** ORMIN 11081 He wrohhte win Off waterr þurrh hiss mahhte. *c* **1205** LAY. 17180 Þat weorc is of stane. *a* **1300** *Cursor M.* 21315 Þe first his greff of irin was, Þe toiþer o þaim was wroght o [*v.r.* of] bras. *c* **1386** CHAUCER *Knt.'s T.* 2184 To meken vertu of necessitee. *c* **1400** *Sowdone Bab.* 129 The sailes were of rede Sendelle. **1565** [see CONSIST *v.* 7]. **1590** SPENSER *F.Q.* II. vii. 17 Of which the matter of his huge desire..he did compound. **1601** SHAKS. *Twel. N.* III. ii. 14 Will you make an Asse o' me? **1611** BIBLE *Job* vi. 12 Is my flesh of brasse? **1667** MILTON *P.L.* II. 258 When great things of small..We can create. **1769** *De Foe's Tour Gt. Brit.* II. vii. 412 The Pulpit is old, and of Stone. **1846** MᶜCULLOCH *Brit. Empire* (1854) I. 623 The houses..are built of brick. **1859** SALA *Gaslight & D.* xxviii. 325 They..make much of one another.

b. Expressing transformation from a former condition. *arch.* (This has also affinities with 3.)

c **900** tr. *Bæda's Hist.* I. vii. (1890) 38 Ða wæs þes man ðurh Godes ȝyfe of ehtore ȝeworden soðfæstnesse freond. **1526** TINDALE *Heb.* xi. 34 Off [Gr. ἀπὸ, L. *de*] weake were made stronge, wexed valiant in fyght. **1548** E. COURTENAY tr. *Paleario's Benefit Christ's Death* iv. (1855) 121 God..hath made us of enemies most dear children. **1590** SPENSER *F.Q.* II. xii. 86 Streight of beasts they comely men became. **1666** SOUTH *Serm., Titus* ii. 15 (1715) I. 207 When Sampson's Eyes were out, of a Publick Magistrate, he was made a Publick Sport. *a* **1680** CHARNOCK *Attrib. God* (1834) I. 430 Of angry he becomes appeased. **1814** CARY *Dante, Paradise* XXXI. 75 Of slave Thou hast to freedom brought me. **1846** MANNING *Serm.* (1848) II. i. 8 Our humanity needed to be strengthened and hallowed; of fleshly, to be again made spiritual.

21. After a sb., *of* connects the material immediately with the thing. (Also commonly expressed by a preceding adj. or the sb. used attrib. e.g. 'a floor of wood or tiles', 'a wooden or tile floor'.)

c **1000** *Cædmon's Daniel* 175 Þære burȝe weard Anne manlican..Gyld of golde gumum arærde. *c* **1000** *Ags. Gosp.* Matt. iii. 4 Se Iohannes..hæfde reaf of olfenda hærum. *c* **1205** LAY. 30805 Ænne ring of rede golde. **1377** LANGL. *P. Pl.* B. Prol. 168 To bugge a belle of brasse, or of briȝte syluer. *c* **1430** *Two Cookery-bks.* 7 Fride Creme of Almaundys. **1555** in Burgon *Life Gresham* (1839) I. 189 A case of black leather. **1632** MILTON *L'Allegro* 21 There on Beds of Violets blew. **1634** SIR T. HERBERT *Trav.* 92 A Carravans-raw of white free stone, and the first building of that materiall I saw in those parts. **1760** GOLDSM. *Cit. W.* xxxix. ¶8 He sent me a very fine present of duck-eggs. **1895** *Pall Mall G.* 10 Oct. 2/1 A kind of whip of three flaps of leather. *Mod.* A bridge of boats. A floor of wood or tiles. A house of cards.

22. a. After a collective term, a quantitative or numeral word, or the name of anything having component parts, *of* introduces the substance or elements of which this consists. [= OE. genitive.]

c **1200** ORMIN 170 He shall turrnenn mikell flocc Off þiss Iudissken þeode. *c* **1205** LAY. 306 Heo funden ane heorde Of heorten. *Ibid.* 23434 Ten hundred punde Of seoluer and of golde. *c* **1489** CAXTON *Blanchardyn* xl. 151 Sadoyne..lefte wythin his cyte..foure thousand of goode knyghtes. **1497** BP. ALCOCK *Mons Perfect.* C iij, By a longe tracte of tyme. **1535** STEWART *Cron. Scot.* II. 709 Within les space nor tua or thre of ȝeir. *a* **1548** HALL *Chron., Edw. IV* 227 b, A pece of Crymosen Velvet. *Ibid., Hen. VI* 135 With bagges of money, or chestes of plate. **1623** GOUGE *Serm. Ext. God's Provid.* §15 A masse of ancient heresies. **1657** R. LIGON *Barbadoes* (1673) 54 A family of a dozen persons. **1786** W. THOMSON *Watson's Philip III* (1839) 353 With a Spanish army..of thirty thousand men. **1849** MACAULAY *Hist. Eng.* v. I. 533 A reward of five hundred pistoles. **1896** *Law Times Rep.* LXXIII. 615/1 A distance of over 700 yards.

b. After *class*, *order*, *genus*, *species*, *kind*, *sort*, *manner*, etc. See these words.

1382- [see KIND *sb.* 14]. **1602** CAREW *Cornwall* (1811) 63 Of wheat there are two sorts. **1698** FRYER *Acc. E. India & P.* 344 All manner of Hairs. **1774** GOLDSM. *Nat. Hist.* (1776) V. 312 Of the..eagle, there are but few species. **1870** ANDERSON *Missions Amer. Bd.* II. xi. 80 It was a sort of travelling school.

23. *Of* connects two sbs. of which the former denotes the class of which the latter is a particular example; or, of which the former is a connotative and the latter a denotative term (= *genitive of definition*).

Often passing into grammatical apposition, e.g. the River Thames, formerly 'the River of Thames'; the city of Rome, OE. Rome-burh: cf. L. *urbs Roma*, *urbs Buthroti*.

1123-31 *O.E. Chron.* an. 1123 Forbearn eall meast se burh of Lincolne. *c* **1175** *Lamb. Hom.* 89 Wiðinne þere buruh of ierusalem. **1297** R. GLOUC. (Rolls) 2827 Þe lond of armore. **1340** *Ayenb.* 45 Þe gemenes of des and of tables. **1432-50** tr. *Higden* (Rolls) I. 93 The floode of Tigris. **1530** PALSGR. 319/2 Of the colowre of scarlet. *a* **1548** HALL *Chron., Hen. VII* 3 b, Within the cytie of London. **1556** ROBINSON tr. *More's Utop.* II. (Arb.) 77 *marg.*, In the riuer of Thamys. **1593** SHAKS. *Rich. II*, I. iii. 196 This fraile sepulchre of our flesh. *a* **1661** FULLER *Worthies* (1840) II. 518 He was brought into the barn of the grave. **1749** FIELDING *Tom Jones* I. viii, The month of November. **1854** DE QUINCEY *Autobiog. Sk.* II. *Coleridge* 176 In the novel of 'Edmund Oliver', written by Charles Lloyd. **1861** M. PATTISON *Ess.* (1889) I. 44 The free towns of Lübeck, Bremen, and Hamburg. *Mod.* The name of John. The Isle of Wight. The peninsula of Spain and Portugal. The hour of eleven. The action of running. The vice of drunkenness. The fact of your meeting him. The circumstance of there being no one near. A state of rest.

24. Between two sbs. in sense-apposition.

a. in the sense 'in the person of; in respect of being, to be, for'. *arch.*

The leading sb. is the former, of the qualification of which the phrase introduced by *of* constitutes a limitation; thus 'he was the greatest traveller of a prince', i.e. the greatest traveller in the person of a prince, or so far as princes are concerned. The sense often merges on that of the partitive genitive, 43.

1470-85 MALORY *Arthur* III. xv, He was a ryght good knyght of a yonge man. *Ibid.* XXI. xiii, The trewest louer of a synful man that euer loued woman. **1599** HAKLUYT *Voy.* II, The king [is] a very good man of a Moore king. **1697** DRYDEN *Virgil* (1721) I. Life 46 Cæsar..the greatest Traveller, of a Prince, that had ever been. **1748** CHESTERF. *Lett.* (1792) II. clxxii. 137 Allowed to be the best scholar of a gentleman in England. **1871** R. ELLIS *Catullus* xlix. 1 Greatest speaker of any born a Roman, Marcus Tullius.

b. in the sense 'in the form of'.

The leading sb. is the latter, to which the prec. sb. with *of* stands as a qualification, equivalent to an adj.; thus 'that fool of a man' = that foolish man, that man who deserves to be called 'fool'; 'that beast of a place' = that beastly place.

a **1450** *Knt. de la Tour* (1868) 38 Here is a faire body of a woman. **1599** NASHE *Lenten Stuffe* 57 Some euill spirit of an heretique it is. **1663** BUTLER *Hud.* I. iii. 337 'Twas a strange riddle of a lady. **1683** EVELYN *Mem.* 5 Dec., That monster of a man, Lord Howard of Escrick. **1769** BICKERSTAFFE *Dr. Last in his Chariot* III. ix, O! devil of a help-mate, have I found you out? **1849** THACKERAY *Pendennis* lxi, That scamp of a husband of hers. *Mod.* An angel of a woman. A gem of a poem. A duck of a hat (*colloq.*).

25. †**a.** Indicating a person in whom one has, finds, or loses something: = in the person of. *Obs.* (supplied by *in*).

1470-85 MALORY *Arthur* XV. vi, Thow hast not thy pyere [peer] of ony erthely synful man. **1496-7** *Plumpton Corr.* 122 Ye have a great treasour of Mr. Gascoyne. **1523** LD. BERNERS *Froiss.* I. 631 The towne of Gaunte hath lost of hym a right valyant man. **1601** SHAKS. *All's Well* I. i. 7 You shall find of the King a husband Madame, you sir a father. *Ibid.* IV. ii. 65 You haue wonne A wife of me. *Ibid.* V. iii. 1 We lost a Iewell of her. **1651** C. CARTWRIGHT *Cert. Relig.* I. 2 It may be your Lordship hopes to meet with a weaker Disputant of me. **1760-72** H. BROOKE *Fool of Qual.* (1809) II. 153 We shall have a heavy loss of our friend Ned. **1820** BYRON *Wks.* IV. 347 A precious representative I must have had of him.

b. Of things, as in 'to have a bad time of it'.

of it appears orig. to mean 'consisting of' or 'comprised in' the fact or circumstance referred to.

1643 TRAPP *Comm. Gen.* xxxii. 31 Our Captain had a bloody victory of it. **1670** R. MONTAGU in *Buccleuch MSS.* (Hist. MSS. Comm.) I. 485 Conte de Grammont has had a troublesome journey of it. **1741** RICHARDSON *Pamela* II. 32 What a fine Time a Person..would have of it. **1872** RUSKIN *Fors Clav.* xv. 3 Living quite as hard a life of it. *Mod.* You will have a bad quarter of an hour of it, I assure you.

VIII. Indicating the *subject-matter of thought*, *feeling*, *or action*, i.e. that about which it is exercised.

26. In sense: Concerning, about, with regard to, in reference to. After verbs, substantives, and adjectives.

a. After intransitive verbs; esp. those of learning, knowing, thinking, and expressing thought, as *hear*, *read*, *know*, *think*, *dream*, *judge*, *tell*, *relate*, *write*, and the like. In subject-headings, titles of chapters, etc., often without a vb. as 'Of Snakes in Iceland'; here, *of* is now often omitted. To these may be added such as *joy*, *complain*, *doubt*, *despair*, etc., which are closely akin to IX.

Rare in OE. (which commonly used *be*, or with some vbs. the genitive); but *of* occurs after *secgan* to tell, and in late OE. after *sprecan* to speak.

c **900** tr. *Bæda's Hist.* Pref. ii. (1890) 2 Swyðost he me sæde of Þeodores ȝemynde. **1129-31** *O.E. Chron.* an. 1129 And þær scolden sprecon of ealle Godes rihtes. *a* **1175** *Cott. Hom.* 217 Þat we hine lufie and of him smaȝe and spece. *c* **1200** ORMIN Ded. 162-71 All wrohht and writenn uppo boc Off Cristess firste come, Off hu soþ Godd wass wurrþenn mann ..And off þatt he shall cumenn efft To demenn alle þede. *a* **1300** *Cursor M.* 24738 (Cott.) Þat i mai of hir louuing rede. **13..** *Ibid.* 5495 *heading* (Gött.), Of moyses nou wil i tell. *c* **1325** [see DOUBT *v.*]. *c* **1435** *Torr. Portugal* 587 Leve we now of Torrent there, And speke we of thys squyer more. *Ibid.* 1104 Listonyth, lordis, of a chaunce. **1444** *Rolls of Parlt.* V. 110/2 To enquere, here, and determyne of Office. *c* **1540** tr. *Pol. Verg. Eng. Hist.* (Camden No. 29) 56 The Burgoignions & Frenchemen begonne to treate of trewce. **1542** UDALL *Erasm. Apoph.* 85 b, Of these games is afore mencioned. **1590** SPENSER *F.Q.* I. Introd. 1 [To] sing of Knights and Ladies gentle deeds. *a* **1592** GREENE *Jas. IV*, IV. ii, Understanding of your walking forth. **1607** TOPSELL *Four-f. Beasts* (1658) 2 Of the Ape. *Ibid.* 242 Of the disposition of Horses in general. **1658** ROWLAND tr. *Moufet's Theat. Ins.* I. ii, Of the Politick, Ethick, and Oeconomick virtues of Bees. **1667** MILTON *P.L.* I. 1 Of Mans First Disobedience..Sing Heav'nly Muse. **1697** DRYDEN *Virgil's Georg.* III. 819 The learned Leaches..shake their Heads, desponding of their Art. **1709** STRYPE *Ann. Ref.* I. xlix. 498 All these bills were then referred to committees to consider of them. **1816** J. WILSON *City of Plague* I. i. 200 Father, judge kindly of us. **1818** MOORE *Fudge Fam. Paris* iii. 1 You may talk of your writing and reading. **1855** BROWNING *Women & Roses* i, I dream of a red-rose tree. **1863** DE MORGAN in *Fr. Matter to Spirit* Pref. 8 Far more useful than he knows of, though not exactly in the way he thinks of. **1874** MICKLETHWAITE *Par. Churches* §XI, Of Lecterns. **1895** *Bookman* Oct. 12/2 He was disposed to thing very well of it.

b. After trans. vbs. and their objects; e.g. after the trans. construction of *hear*, *tell*, *read*, etc. (see a), and after such as *inform*, *admonish*, *advise*, etc.

(These blend with 29 b.)

c **893** K. ÆLFRED *Oros.* I. i. §15 Fela spella him sædon þa Beormas..of þæm landum þe ymb hie utan wæron. **1127-31** *O.E. Chron.* an. 1127 Of his utgang ne cunne we iett noht seggon. *a* **1225** *Ancr. R.* 54 Uor to warnie wummen of hore fol eien. *a* **1250** *Owl & Night.* 9 Either seide of otheres custe That alre-worste that hi wuste. *c* **1320** *Cast. Love* 373 Thow owest not to here Mercy Of noo bone that she besecheth the. **1340-70** *Alex. & Dind.* 66, I haue founde ȝou folk faiþful of speche Me to lere of ȝour lif. **1444** *Rolls of Parlt.* V. 112/2 Warn the maister..of the saide covenaunt. **1525** LD. BERNERS *Froiss.* II. cxxix. [cxxv.] 366 Men..well enstructed of your busynesse. **1526** TINDALE *John* xviii. 34 Did other tell ytt the of me? **1653** WALTON *Angler* viii. 164 The like I have known of one that has almost watched his Pond. **1654-66** EARL ORRERY *Parthen.* (1676) 650, I first acquainted her of the danger. **1861** M. PATTISON *Ess.* (1889) I. 36 To observe the young prince, and to inform himself of his character. *Mod.* Have you heard any news of the travellers? To inform his friends of the result.

c. With other vbs. or phrases.

1129-31 *O.E. Chron.* an. 1129 Þa weorð hit eall of earcedæcnes wifes and of preostes wifes. *c* **1330** R. BRUNNE *Chron. Wace* (Rolls) 4584 He dred hym of his tresour. *c* **1380** WYCLIF *Wks.* (1880) 75 Þus it stondiþ of mannus curs. *c* **1450** tr. *De Imitatione* II. v, Yf þou kepe silence of oþir men, & specialy beholde þiself. *c* **1470** HENRY *Wallace* I. 166 King Herodis part thai playit..Off ȝong childer that thai befor thaim fand. **1579** FULKE *Heskins' Parl.* 495 Maister Heskins..tryfleth off the nearnesse of the bloud of Christe, which hee layeth wee denye. *c* **1590** MARLOWE *Faust.* vi, Examine them of their several names. **1655**

STANLEY *Hist. Philos.* (1701) 2/1 Of this Colony see Herodotus, Strabo, and Ælian. **1680–90** TEMPLE *Ess. Health* Wks. 1731 I. 272 Of the first I find no Dispute. *a* **1770** JORTIN *Serm.* (1771) IV. i. 6 We need not suppose of him that he prayed against riches. **1849** RUSKIN *Sev. Lamps* i. §2. 9 To enter into dispute of all the various objections.

†**d.** After *do. Obs.* (Now *with*: cf. VI.)

1297 R. GLOUC. (Rolls) 7106 Of þe croune of engelond he nuste wat best do. *a* **1300** *Cursor M.* 19040 Þai sald þam and þe pris laght, Be-for þe apostels fete it broght, Þar-of to do quat þaim god thoght. *c* **1386** CHAUCER *Melib.* ¶67 (Harl. MS.) To knowen what schulde be doon of [*so Cambr. & Petw. MSS.*; *other 4 MSS.* with] hir persone. *c* **1489** CAXTON *Sonnes of Aymon* i. 26 We..shalle doo of hym that he troweth to doo of me. *c* **1500** *Melusine* 353 Here ben your enemyes as prysonners, doo of them your playsyr. **1566** in Peacock *Eng. Ch. Furniture* (1866) 32 What was done of them we knowe not.

e. After *become*; formerly also *befall*, *fortune*, etc.

c **1440** *Tundale* 18, I will ȝou telle how it befell þanne..of a ryche monne. **1523** LD. BERNERS *Froiss.* I. 774 Thus it fortuned of this adventure. **1535–** [see BECOME 4]. **1568** GRAFTON *Chron.* II. 213 Thus it befell of this..enterprise.

27. After sbs. *Obs.* or *arch.*

c **1375** *Cursor M.* 755 (Fairf.) How adam brake goddis comandement of the appil. *c* **1400** *Rom. Rose* 5661 That may these clerkis seyn and seye In Boice of Consolacioun. **1551** ROBINSON tr. *More's Utop.* title-p., A fruteful and pleasaunt worke of the beste state of a publyque weale. **1611** RICH *Honest. Age* (1844) 77, I remember a pretty iest of Tobacco. **1684** HACKE *Coll. Voy.* I. 7 We concluded the discoursing of Women at Sea was very unlucky. **1688** PENTON *Guard. Instr.* (1897) 15 Reade Barrow of Charity. **1711** ADDISON *Spect.* No. 47 ¶1 Mr. Hobbs, in his Discourse of Human Nature. *a* **1715** BURNET *Own Time* (1823) I. 41 The court judged the paper to be seditious, and to be a lie of the king and his government.

28. After adjs.

c **1489** CAXTON *Sonnes of Aymon* i. 30, I am moche wrothe and sory of my son Lohyer. **1548** UDALL, etc. *Erasm. Par. Acts* 24 They..were afraied of themselues, lest they..should be stoned. **1615** BEDWELL *Moham. Imp.* III. §113 When I do see man..without any crosse at all,..I am afraid of him [= concerning him]. **1886** SIR N. LINDLEY in *Law Rep.* 32 Chanc. Div. 28 The same observations are true of all other contracts similarly circumstanced.

IX. Representing an original *genitive dependent on a verb or adjective.*

Many vbs. and adjs. in OE. were followed by a genitive case as an object or complement. In Latin, also, many adjs. and some vbs. were construed with a genitive, represented in French by *de*. These are represented in Middle and Mod. English by construction with *of*. Such of these as now attach themselves closely in sense to one or other of the preceding branches, have been there mentioned; but there remain many verbs and adjs. after which *of* has hardly more than a constructional force, or in which it does not clearly fall under any of those branches. Many of these come close in sense to branch VIII, while others, esp. the adjs., often approach or coincide with the objective genitive in branch X. It is convenient therefore to consider them here.

29. In the construction of verbs.

a. After intrans. vbs. Many of these in OE. took the genitive, and are found with *of* in Middle and Early Modern English, but this is now rare, except where *of* falls in sense under one of the branches already treated; instances are *to reck*, *repent*, *rue*, *beware* (orig. *be ware*) *of*. Verbs of sense, e.g. *feel*, *smell*, *taste*, *touch* (still with *of* in dial. or vulgar use), verbs of asking, as *ask*, *beseech*, *demand*, *desire*, *entreat*, and others, e.g. *distinguish*, *esteem*, *forget*, *like*, *seize*, formerly construed with *of*, now take a simple object; some, as *accept*, *admit*, *allow*, *approve*, *conceive*, *recollect*, *remember*, still have both constructions; with others, as *hope*, *look*, *thirst*, *wait*, etc., *of* has been displaced by *for* or some other preposition.

1340–70 *Alex. & Dind.* 868 No [= ne] like no lud of his luþur fare. *c* **1380** WYCLIF *Sel. Wks.* III. 361 Þe assoilyng serveþ of nouȝt. *c* **1450** *St. Cuthbert* (Surtees) 5287 To pray to god and saynt cuthbert Of help. **1523** LD. BERNERS *Froiss.* I. 447 They feared of a siege to be layed to them. *a* **1555** RIDLEY *Pituous Lament.* (1568) D viij b, To fele the smarte, and to fele of the whyp. **1568** E. TILNEY *Disc. Marriage* A v, Some liked well of carding and dicing, some of dauncing, and other some of chestes. **1575** ABP. PARKER *Corr.* (Parker Soc.) 477 As for the earthquake, I heard not of it, nor it was not felt of here. **1576** WHETSTONE *Life Gascoigne* xli, Death waites of no man's will. **1624** CAPT. SMITH *Virginia* III. 62 We had ranged vp and downe..looking of stones, herbs, and springs. *a* **1628** PRESTON *Mt. Ebal* (1638) 42 It is not any..niggardly kinde..that hee will like of. **1660** F. BROOKE tr. *Le Blanc's Trav.* 83 Two Portuguais ships..seized of the Haven. **1719** DE FOE *Crusoe* I. iv, She went to it, smelled of it, and ate it. **1852** R. S. SURTEES *Sponge's Sp. Tour* xvi. 81 Don't wait of me, my dear Mr. Sponge..don't wait of me, pray. **1867** DICKENS & W. COLLINS *No Thoroughfare* v, When I felt of his heart, there was no beat. **1888** BRYCE *Amer. Commw.* I. xiv. 194 Resolutions which perhaps no single member in his heart approves of.

b. After transitive vbs., the secondary or thing-object is often introduced by *of* representing an original genitive. Such are *balk*, *cheat*, *defraud*, *disappoint*, *frustrate*; *accuse*, *arrest*, *blame*, *convict*, *suspect*; *possess*, *seize* (a person *of*); *avail*, *bethink* (oneself *of*); also with impersonal vbs. as *it repents me of*; and formerly with *ask*, *beg*, *beseech*, *thank* (a person *of*), etc.

c **1200–** [see BETHINK]. **1362** LANGL. *P. Pl.* A. v. 227 Bidde god of grace. *a* **1375** *Joseph Arim.* 561 He bi-souȝte him of grace. **1483** CAXTON *G. de la Tour* M iv, She made hym to be serued of grete plenty of good and delicate metes. *a* **1555** LATIMER *Serm. & Rem.* (1845) 174 He came..desiring him of help. **1581** SAVILE *Tacitus, Hist.* III. ii. (1591) 114 To furnish them of men, horses and money. **1590** SPENSER *F.Q.* II. ix. 42 Of pardon I you pray. **1635** LAUD *Wks.* (1860) VII. 182 That Ireland should serve itself first of its own land. **1737** WHISTON *Josephus, Hist.* III. v. §1 Providing themselves of such houshold servants. **1820** HAZLITT *Lect. Dram. Lit.* 28 Shakespear..availed himself of the old Chronicles. **1844** ALB. SMITH *Adv. Mr. Ledbury* iii. (1886) 11 Our two friends bethought themselves of trying to catch a little slumber.

c. In many verbal phrases, as ***to have the advantage of***; also formerly in ***to have compassion***, ***mercy***, ***pity of***, ***to keep watch***, ***demand*** or ***do justice of*** (= on), ***have the victory of*** (= over).

a **1240** *Lofsong* in *Cott. Hom.* 209 Haue merci of me. *c* **1400** MAUNDEV. (Roxb.) ii. 5 When any man had þe victory of his enmy. *c* **1420** *Chron. Vilod.* st. 489 Haue pyte of me. *c* **1489** CAXTON *Sonnes of Aymon* xiv. 341 We shall doo iustyce of kyng yon. **1523** LD. BERNERS *Froiss.* I. xvii. 18 That the archers shulde haue noo vauntage of hym. **1737** WHISTON *Josephus, Antiq.* II. vi. §8 Take pity of his old age. *a* **1774** GOLDSM. *Hist. Greece* I. 312 Those were intimidated who demanded justice of the murderers. **1891** *Scribner's Mag.* Sept. 279/2 The traveller must keep watch of his clothes.

30. In the construction of adjectives. Besides those mentioned under the preceding divisions, many adjs. are construed with *of* and an object; the following are representatives of some of the chief groups: *fruitful*, *prolific*, *ominous*, *redolent*; *liberal*, *lavish*, *prodigal*, *scant*, *short*, *sparing*; *capable*, *incapable*, *susceptible*; *worthy*, *unworthy*, *guilty*, *guiltless*, *innocent*; *certain*, *uncertain*, *confident*, *diffident*, *doubtful*, *sure*; *aware*, *conscious*, *unconscious*, *ignorant*, *sensible*, *insensible*; *careful*, *careless*, *forgetful*, *heedful*, *heedless*, *hopeful*, *hopeless*, *mindful*, *unmindful*, *reckless*, *regardless*, *thoughtless*, *neglectful*, *negligent*, *observant*, *watchful*; *ambitious*, *desirous*, *eager*, *emulous*, *enamoured*, *envious*, *fond*, *greedy*, *jealous*, *studious*, *suspicious*; *disdainful*, *indulgent*, *patient*, *impatient*; those in *-ive*, as *apprehensive*, *communicative*, *descriptive*, *destructive*, *expressive*, *indicative*, *productive*; and some in *-ic*, as *characteristic*, *symbolic*.

Many of these involve a substantive, which may be considered as the subject of the genitive relation; e.g. ***hopeful of***, having hope of, ***envious of***, having envy of, etc.; others are verbal derivatives, and are closely akin to the objective-genitive group X, e.g. ***expressive of*** = that expresses.

a **1225** [see GUILTY]. **1382** WYCLIF *Ps.* xxxix. 18 [xl. 17] The Lord is bisi of me. *c* **1450** *Merlin* 32 He that wende to be siker of me hath failed. *c* **1489** CAXTON *Blanchardyn* xlvii. 180 They sholde neuer be consentyng of that infydelyte and grete trayson. **1535** COVERDALE *Matt.* x. 10 The workman is worthy of his meate. *a* **1548** HALL *Chron., Edw. IV* 211 For suche thynges as wee se before our iyes, we be well ware of. **1567** MAPLET *Gr. Forest* 85 He is of good memorie and long mindfull of a good tourne. **1687** A. LOVELL tr. *Bergerac's Com. Hist. Sun* 2, I was impatient of seeing him. **1697** DRYDEN *Virg. Georg.* III. 83 The Generous Youth..studious of the Prize. *Ibid.* IV. 796 Four Heifars..all unknowing of the Yoke. *a* **1715** BURNET *Own Time* (1823) I. 572 They were very..oppressive..of those of the other side. **1755** DODDRIDGE *Hymn*, '*Ye servants of the Lord*' i, Observant of his heavenly word. **1820** LAMB *Elia* Ser. I. *Christ's Hospital*, I am constitutionally susceptible of noises. **1820** *Broderip & Bingham's Rep.* I. 433 It is conclusive of the facts stated in it. **1873** BROWNING *Red Cott. Nt.-cap* 143 Symbolic of the place and people too.

X. Expressing the relation of the *objective genitive.*

31. After a vbl. sb. in *-ing*.

When the vbl. sb. is preceded by *the* or other determinative word, *of* is still used (a.); otherwise the form in *-ing* is treated as a gerund taking a direct object without *of*; but the form with *of* is still in archaic and dial. use (b.). See -ING[1].

a. *a* **1240** (*title*) Þe Wohunge of ure Lauerd. **1382** WYCLIF *Gen.* xiv. 17 The Kyng of Sodom ȝede out into the aȝengoyng of him. **1551** ROBINSON tr. *More's Utop.* II. (Arb.) 150 For the auoydinge of strife. *a* **1631** DONNE *Serm.* IV. xcii. 171 Not the Clothing nor Feeding of Christ but the housing of him. **1642** ROGERS *Naaman* 128 The robbing of the church for the saving of some mony. **1712** ADDISON *Spect.* No. 291 ¶2 Any..Notions and Observations which he has made in his reading of the Poets. **1824** DIBDIN *Libr. Comp.* p. i, The imparting of a moral feeling. **1849** RUSKIN *Sev. Lamps* 3 To enter into any curious or special questioning of the hindrances.

b. *c* **1340** HAMPOLE *Prose Tr.* 11 Here is forboden vnryghtwyse hurtynge of any persone. **1523** LD. BERNERS *Froiss.* I. cxxvi. 152 The Englysshmen departed without wynning of any thynge. *c* **1555** HARPSFIELD *Divorce Hen. VIII* (Camden) 84 For avoiding of prolixity. **1642** ROGERS *Naaman* 451 Rebuked for greeving of God. *a* **1687** PETTY *Pol. Arith.* v. (1691) 88 The Burthen of protecting of them all, must lye upon the chief Kingdom England. *a* **1715** BURNET *Own Time* (1823) I. 340 His fear of the danger the king was in by the duke's having of guards. **1750** PALTOCK *P. Wilkins* (1884) I. 159, I can't help loving of you heartily for it. *a* **1800** T. BELLAMY *Beggar Boy* (1801) II. 187 By stealing of children. **1874** RUSKIN *Fors Clav.* xlviii. 278 We must cease throwing of stones either at saints or squirrels. **1875** DASENT *Vikings* I. 272 He that owned to burning of churches in the West.

32. After what was formerly a verbal sb. governed by *in* or *a*, but is now identified with a present participle. The use of *of* is now *dial.* or vulgar.

[**1523** LD. BERNERS *Froiss.* I. 116 He was thre dayes a landyng of all his prouisyon. **1534** TINDALE *Matt.* ix. 9 He sawe a man syt a receauynge of custome. **1580** LYLY *Euphues* (Arb.) 367 Camilla, whome he founde in gathering of flowers. **1684** BUNYAN *Pilgr.* II. 15 She is..a taking of her last farewel of her Country.]

1563–87 FOXE *A. & M.* (1631) III. xii. 897/1 Hee found the Bishop basting of himselfe against a great fire. **1593** *Tell-Troth's N.Y. Gift* 4 Who was making faste of the brand gates. **1607** SHAKS. *Timon* v. i. 188 Why, I was writing of my epitaph. **1666** PEPYS *Diary* 19 Mar., They being altering of the stage. **1694** ECHARD tr. *Plautus* 178 I'll go see what the merchant..is doing of. **1749** LADY M. W. MONTAGU *Let. to C'tess Bute* 20 Aug., If ever you catch her stealing of sweetmeats.

33. After a noun of action.

1135 *O.E. Chron.*, God man he wes, and micel æie wes of him. *c* **1200** ORMIN Ded. 19 Ʒiff Ennglissh follc, forr lufe off Crist, Itt wollde ȝerne lernenn. *a* **1300** *Cursor M.* 24984 (Gött.), I tru in..hali kirke,..forgiuenes of sinnes. *c* **1380** WYCLIF *Wks.* (1880) 147 Gret desir of heuenely þynges. *c* **1400** (*title*) The Sege off Melayne. *a* **1548** HALL *Chron., Edw. IV* 236 Testifying the receipte of the pencion. **1563** *Homilies* II. *Com. Prayer & Sacram.* (1859) 356 Confirmation of children, by examining them of their knowledge. **1676–7** MARVELL *Corr.* Wks. 1872–5 II. 512 Obstruction of the publick justice. *a* **1715** BURNET *Own Time* (1823) II. 348 He had the management of a secret press. **1791** MRS. INCHBALD *Simp. Story* I. v. 44 An inordinate desire of admiration. **1861** M. PATTISON *Ess.* (1889) I. 48 A domiciliary visit in search of heretical books. **1873** MORLEY *Rousseau* I. 344 The betrayal of a secret. **1888** *Athenæum* 3 Nov. 595/3 His explanation of various facts is not ours.

34. After an agent-noun.

Sometimes closely approaching the relation of the object possessed, in 48 b.

a **1240** *Lofsong* in *Cott. Hom.* 217 Ich bileue on god feder al-mihti schuppare of heouene and of eorðe. **1382** WYCLIF *Matt.* iv. 19, I shal make ȝou to be maad fisheris of men. **1444** *Rolls of Parlt.* V. 124/1 Sellers of ale, that breken th'assise. **1559** W. CUNNINGHAM *Cosmogr. Glasse* 173 They are great drinkers of *Aqua vitæ*. **1601** SHAKS. *Twel. N.* I. iii. 90, I am a great eater of beefe. **1684** I. P. tr. *Fambresarius' Art Physick* I. 48 Nature, the Architectress of the Body. *a* **1849** J. C. MANGAN *Poems* (1859) 397 The Arbitress of thrones. **1856** 'CRAWLEY' *Billiards* (1859) 6 Many foreigners are very excellent handlers of the cue.

XI. Indicating that *in respect of* which a quality is attributed, or a fact is predicated.

35. a. After an adj. (e.g. *swift of foot*): In respect of, in the matter of, in point of, in. Now literary and somewhat archaic, exc. in particular phrases, as *blind of one eye*. (In OE. *on*; F. *de*; L. abl., gen. (*acc.* of respect).)

The *of*-clause is grammatically an adverbial qualification of the adj., for which an adv. may often be substituted, e.g. *weak of mind*, 'mentally weak'. Taken together, the adj. + the *of*-clause = a compound (parasynthetic) adj., e.g. *light of foot*, 'light-footed', *strong of limb*, 'strong-limbed'. It is further equivalent to the *of*-clause of quality in XII, e.g. 'a man weak of mind' = 'a man of weak mind'; the latter being the ordinary prose form.

a **1225** *Ancr. R.* 158 Ʒung of ȝeres ase he was. *a* **1300** *Cursor M.* 3730 (Gött.) Mith i noght be sua liht of [*Cott.* o] fote. **1362** LANGL. *P. Pl.* A. x. 32 Mon is him Most lyk of Marke and of schap. **1393** *Ibid.* C. xv. 187 Þe larke..is loueloker of lydene, And swettur of sauour and swyfter of wynge. *c* **1400** MAUNDEV. (Roxb.) vii. 24 Þai er blakk of colour. *c* **1420** *Sir Amadace* (Camden) lviii, That ladi..bryȝte of ble. *a* **1533** LD. BERNERS *Huon* 314 The emperour was hole of his thygh that Huon had broken. **1605** SHAKS. *Macb.* II. ii. 52 Infirme of purpose. **1611** BIBLE *2 Sam.* iv. 4 A sonne that was lame of [COVERD. on] his feete. **1697** DRYDEN *Virg. Georg.* III. 120 Of able Body, sound of Limb and Wind. **1783** MORELL *Ainsworth's Lat. Dict.* II, *Luscus*, blind of one eye. **1891** *Cornh. Mag.* Oct. 416 Hard he was of hand and harder of heart.

b. After *long*, *late*, *quick*, *slow*, *hard*, etc., and followed by a vbl. sb. Still in use, esp. in *dial.* (Sc. *lang o'* or *i'*), but more frequently expressed by *in*, *at*: see the adjs.

1477 *Paston Lett.* III. 204, I beleve yt not, by cause they have ben so long of comyng. **1741** MONRO *Anat. Bones* (ed. 3) 36 The Bones..are so long of hardning. **1824** MISS FERRIER *Inher.* xxii, That day may be a while of coming. **1842** ALISON *Hist. Europe* (1850) XI. lxxiii. §122 The winter was unusually late of setting in. **1887** BESANT *The World went*, etc. xxviii. 209 [He] was slow of catching news. *Mod.* He is rather hard of hearing. I am so quick of catching cold.

c. ***of length***, ***breadth***, ***height***, ***depth***, or the like, define the reference of a statement of measure. *Obs.* exc. in ***of age***; in other cases supplied by ***in***.

c **1400** MAUNDEV. (Roxb.) ii. 6 Þe crosse..was of lenth viii. cubits. *c* **1450** *Merlin* 31 The werke of this tour is iii or iiij fadom of height. **1523** LD. BERNERS *Froiss.* I. cccxxv. 507 The blade was two els of length. **1526** TINDALE *Luke* iii. 23 Iesus him silfe was about thirty yere of age. **1843** *Fraser's Mag.* XXVIII. 652 He is..fifty-three years of age.

†**36.** Following a verb: In respect of. *Obs.* (supplied by *in*).

13.. *Cursor M.* 10613 (Gött.) As scho of body wex [*Cott* . wex on her licame]. *c* **1400** *Three Kings Cologne* 6 Þat hille of Vaws passeþ of heithe all oþer hilles in þat contrey of Ynde. *c* **1450** *Merlin* 92 The tother party..encresed moche of peple. **1563** HYLL *Art Garden.* (1593) 40 To make it spread of breadth in the growing. **1690** W. WALKER *Idiomat. Anglo-Lat.* 346 Land rose of price very much.

37. Following a sb.: In respect of, in, by. *arch.*

c **1350** *Will. Palerne* 442 Þat barne..þat flour is of alle frekes of fairnes and miȝt. **1483** CAXTON *G. de la Tour* F j, A man..whiche of his craft was a rope maker. **1535** COVERDALE *Prov.* xvi. 28 He yt is a blabbe of his tonge, maketh deuysion amonge prynces.

XII. Indicating a *quality* or other distinguishing mark by which a person or thing is characterized. (For OE. genitive; F. *de*; = *genitive of quality or description*.)

38. a. Indicating a quality possessed by the subject.

The quality is usually expressed by a sb. qualified by an adj., but may consist of a sb. alone, as in 'a man of tact', 'a text-book of authority'. It is often equivalent to an adj. as in 'a man of tact' = a tactful man, 'a work of authority' = an authoritative work; 'a flag of three colours' = a tricolor flag; 'a people of many languages' = a polyglot people.

c1200 Ormin 49 Alls iff þe33 karrte wærenn Off wheless fowwre. **c1290** *S. Eng. Leg.* I. 457/25 A tour of gret bolde. **13..** *Cursor M.* 27685 (Fairf.) Sum sais he is..of [*Cott.* o] grete almus of grete praier. **c1380** Wyclif *Paternoster* in *Eng. Wks.* (1880) 201 It is of most auctorite. **c1430** *Syr Tryam.* 868 Syr Barnard was of myght. **c1430-** [see age *sb.* 3]. **c1440** *Promp. Parv.* 363/1 Of o colowre. **1512** *Act 4 Hen. VIII*, c. 4 §1 To be utterly voyde and of noo force ne effect. **1526** Tindale *Matt.* ix. 2 Sonne be off good chere. **1559** W. Cunningham *Cosmogr. Glasse* 80 By the promontory of good hope. **1560** Daus tr. *Sleidane's Comm.* 19 He is still of the same minde. **1591** Spenser *Ruins of Time* 563 Two Beares..Of milde aspect, and haire as soft as silke. **1634** Sir T. Herbert *Trav.* 93 Stealing a trifle, of two shillings value. **1662** Stillingfl. *Orig. Sacr.* III. iii. §4 A God of Infinite Justice, Purity, and Holiness. **1711** Steele *Spect.* No. 6 ¶2 He was of opinion none but men of fine parts deserve to be hanged. **1741** Richardson *Pamela* II. 360 Four Misses all pretty much of a Size. **1794** *Hist.* in *Ann. Reg.* 38 Several..officers of note fell. **1817** Byron *Manfred* II. i. 36 That word was made For brutes of burthen, not for birds of prey. **1886** *Manch. Exam.* 16 Jan. 5/4 An Evangelical of moderate views. **1891** *Law Rep.* Weekly Notes 72/2 All the parties..were not of age.

b. qualified by *all*, indicating (temporary) condition.

1653 H. Cogan tr. *Pinto's Trav.* v. 12 The masts and sail yards were all of a flame. **1766** Goldsm. *Vic. W.* ix, She observed, that..she was all of a muck of sweat. **1826** Disraeli *Viv. Grey* vi. i, The poor man, sir, was all of an ague. **1849** Thackeray *Pendennis* xvi, 'Do you say so?' Smirke said, all of a tremble.

39. a. Indicating quantity, age, extent, price, etc.

c1205 Lay. 377 A 3ung mon Of þriti 3eren. **c1230** *Hali Meid.* 11 For an eðelich delit of an hond-hwile. **c1450** *St. Cuthbert* (Surtees) 6623 Before he was of 3eres fourtene. **1523** Ld. Berners *Froiss.* I. ccxv. 270 Theyr speares of syxe foote of lengthe. **1603** Shaks. *Meas. for M.* II. i. 204 Are you of fourescore pounds a yeere? **1621** Burton *Anat. Mel.* III. ii. IV. i. (1651) 520 Calf-skin gloves of four pence a pair. **1634** Sir T. Herbert *Trav.* 11 A Portugall Carrack of above fifteene hundred tunne. **1788** *Misc.* in *Ann. Reg.* 134 A woman turned of forty. **1865** Dickens *Mut. Fr.* I. 11, A boy of fourteen. **1878** Marg. Stokes *Early Chr. Archit. Irel.* 4 Simple churches of one chamber. **1891** *N. & Q.* 26 Dec. 511/2 Small farms of from twenty to one hundred acres.

b. To this construction with *of* an adj. is sometimes added: this is frequent in the case of *old*; less so with *long, broad, high, deep*, etc. See old *a.* 3b.

1528 Paynel *Salerne's Regim.* (1575) 26 Lammes of a yeare olde. **1611** Shaks. *Cymb.* II. v. 31 One Vice, but of a minute old. **1670** Narborough *Jrnl.* in *Acc. Sev. Late Voy.* I. (1711) 68 Large Smelts of 20 Inches long. **1750** G. Hughes *Barbadoes* 234 The stalk..of near one fifth part of an inch thick. **1863** Hawthorne *Our Old Home, Consular Experiences*, A shabby..edifice of four stories high.

40. Indicating an action, fact, or thing that distinguishes, characterizes, or specifies a time, place, etc.

This passes into XIV.

1340- Day of doom [see doom *sb.* 7, day *sb.* 8b]. **1382** Wyclif *2 Sam.* xxiii. 20 In the dais of snow3 [1611 in time of snow]. —— *Eccl.* iii. 4 Time of weping, and time of la3hing; time of weiling, and time of leping. **c1470** *Golagros & Gaw.* 1 In the tyme of Arthur. **1638-** Angle of incidence, etc. [see angle *sb.*² 1 ¶]. **1660** F. Brooke tr. *Le Blanc's Trav.* 5 Caves..formerly inhabited by the Christians in time of persecution. **1795** *Gentl. Mag.* 545/1 The places of our birth and education. **1816** J. Wilson *City of Plague* I. i. 22 Is it the hour of prayer? **1845** M. Pattison *Ess.* (1889) I. 10 You will find yourself in the country of the mulberries.

41. Followed by a noun of action with possessive, equivalent to a passive participial phrase, *e.g.* 'trees of our planting' = trees planted by us.

This has affinities with III and XIII.

1526 *Pilgr. Perf.* (W. de W. 1531) 2 Not of myne inuencion. **1553** T. Wilson *Rhet.* (1580) 5 To dispose and order matters of our owne invention. **1607** Shaks. *Cor.* I. i. 220 Fiue Tribunes..Of their owne choice. **1611** Bible *Ezek.* xxvii. 16 Syria was thy merchant by reason of the multitude of the wares of thy making. **1825** Montgomery *Hymn*, Stand up and bless the Lord, Ye people of His choice. **1844** Lingard *Anglo-Sax. Ch.* (1858) I. v. 195 Their immediate superior was of her appointment. **1885** Bible (R.V.) *Ps.* cvii. 30 *margin*, The haven of their desire. —— *Isa.* v. 7 *margin*, The plant of his delight. *Mod.* Vegetables of his own growing. A canoe of my son's construction. The new nobility of Henry VII's creation.

XIII. In *partitive* expressions; indicating things or a thing of which a part is expressed by the preceding words.

42. a. Preceded by a word of number or quantity.

Of may here render L. *ex* or *de*. OE. had more commonly the genitive case, e.g. **c900** tr. *Bæda's Hist.* III. vi[ii]. (1890) 174 Moni3e þara broðra. **c1000** *Laws of Æthelred* viii. §1 Ðis is an þara 3erædnessa. See const. of one, some, etc.

c900 tr. *Bæda's Hist.* III. xix. 240 Wæron þær in þa tiid moni3e of Ongelþeode [*multi de gente Anglorum*]. **c1000** *St. Andrew* (1851) 16 þu ne 3esihst æni3ne of Godes þam hal3um. **c1000** *Ags. Gosp.* Matt. x. 29 An of ðam [*unus ex illis*] ne befylð on eorðan. **c1000** *Ibid.* Luke vi. 2 Ða cwædon sume of þam sundor-hal3an [*quidam Pharisæorum*]. *Ibid.* vi. 13 He..3eceas twelf of him [*duodecim ex ipsis*]. **1137-54** *O.E. Chron.* an. 1137 In mani of þe castles wæron lof and grin. *Ibid.* an. 1138 [Hi] sloghen suithe micel of his genge. **c1175** *Lamb. Hom.* 35 Eni of þine cunne. **c1205** Lay. 613 Six hundred of his cnihten. *Ibid.* 30803 An of hire ringe. **1340** *Ayenb.* 219 Yef tuo of ou oneþ ham to-gidere, me uor to bidde. **1382** Wyclif *Luke* xxii. 24 And stryf was maad among hem, which of hem schulde be seyn to be more. **1523** Ld. Berners *Froiss.* I. cccxxii. 501 More than any of his predecessours. **1596** Danett tr. *Comines* (1614) 338 Whither euery of their confederates should send their ambassadors. **1625** Bp. Mountagu *App. Cæsar* 149 Either of the two States disjoynedly. **1660** F. Brooke tr. *Le Blanc's Trav.* 3 Of sixty five persons that we were in all, but five escaped. **1679** Oldham *Poems* (1686) 34 Not Knights o'th Port Show more of impudence. **1812** Jefferson *Writ.* (1830) IV. 176 The rest of the world. **1849** Macaulay *Hist. Eng.* viii. II. 328 Of sixty magistrates and deputy lieutenants..only seven had given favourable answers. **1865** Grote *Plato* (1875) Pref. 8 There..[was] little of negation or refutation in their procedure. **1895** *Bookman* Oct. 17/1 For which some of us would gladly give all the novels ever written.

b. Preceded by a sb. (or adj. used *absol.*).

c900 tr. *Bæda's Hist.* v. iii. 392 Sumu fæmne of ðara nunnena rime [*de numero virginum*]. **c1000** Ælfric *Gen.* ii. 11 An ea of þam hatte Fison. **1382** Wyclif *John* iii. 1 Ther was a man of Pharisees [L. *ex Pharisæis*], Nicodeme bi name, a prince of the Jewis. **1567** Maplet *Gr. Forest* 78b, In the high grasse, wherin nothing can be espied of him saving onelye his hornes. **1792** Maria Riddell *Voy. Madeira* 61 The only birds of this order. **a1800** Cowper *Wks.* IV. 195 The sagacious of mankind. **1805** *Oracle* in *Spir. Pub. Jrnls.* (1806) IX. 190 The drudger of the party. **1888** *Athenæum* 3 Nov. 597/1 Had three sons, of whom Thomas married twice.

c. Under the partitive form the whole may be included. (In sense these have affinity with 22.)

1479 W. Paston in *P. Lett.* III. 241 Ther be ii systers of them. **1481** Caxton *Reynard* (Arb.) 71 Thaugh ther of vs were fyue we coude not defende vs. **a1548** Hall *Chron., Hen. VIII* 261b, You of the Clergie preache one against another. *Ibid.*, You of the temporaltie, bee not cleane and unspotted of malice and envie. **1596** Shaks. *1 Hen. IV*, II. iv. 205 If I fought not with fiftie of them, I am a bunch of Radish. **1711** Addison *Spect.* No. 93 ¶1 We all of us complain of the Shortness of Time. *Mod.* There were only five of us; and more than twice as many of them. Take part of it, not the whole of it.

d. Followed by an adj. used absol. (after F. or L.).

1650 Earl Monm. tr. *Senault's Man. bec. Guilty* 307 Love undertaketh nothing of generous, without the assistance of desire. **1673** Ray *Journ. Low C.* 67 This Source hath that of peculiar to itself, that [etc.]. **1788** *Lond. Mag.* 429 If their souls carried nothing with them of terrestrial. **1800** Fox in *Corr. w. Wakefield* (1813) 134 In the last..there is something of comic. **1821** Byron *Wks.* VI. 402 All that it had of holy he has hallowed. **1866** Ruskin *Crown Wild Olive* (1873) 143 Whatever of best he can conceive.

43. a. Preceded by a superlative or comparative; or by a word equivalent to a superlative, e.g. *chief, flower, cream, dregs*.

c1205 Lay. 27601 He of alle monnen mæst hine lufede. **c1350** *Will. Palerne* 442 þat barne..þat flour is of alle frekes. **a1400-50** *Alexander* 307 Ane of þe grettist of oure godis. **1476** Sir J. Paston in *P. Lett.* III. 166 Ye sholde have that maner in joynture with yowr wyffe to the lenger lyver off yow bothe. **1559** W. Cunningham *Cosmogr. Glasse* 43 Th' Earth..is lowest of all Elementes. **1576** Fleming *Panopl. Epist.* 398, I count him the rather of the twaine to bee chosen. **1590** Spenser *F.Q.* I. i. Introd. 2 O holy virgin, chiefe of nyne. **1697** Dryden *Virg. Georg.* IV. 200 He gather'd first of all In Spring the Roses, Apples in the Fall. **1820** L. Hunt *Indicator* No. 49 (1822) I. 389 The absurdest as well as the most impious of all the dreams of fear. **1834** Medwin *Angler in Wales* II. 163 We made the best of our way back to Tregaron. **1892** *Bookman* Oct. 27/2 The most dogged of fighters, the most dangerous of enemies. *Mod.* Which is the elder of you two?

b. ellipt. *of all* (*of any*) = most of all; especially. Freq. in phrases expressing surprise at something or someone unexpected.

?1370 *Robt. Cicyle* 58 He trowyd of alle thynge, Hys bredur schulde have made hym kynge. **c1460** *Towneley Myst.* xi. 31 Blyssed be thou of alle women. **1594** Shaks. *Rich. III*, III. i. 68, I doe not like the Tower of any place. **1732** Berkeley *Alciphr.* I. §5 It is what I desire of all things. **1848** A. Jameson in G. Macpherson *Mem. Life A. Jameson* (1878) ix. 254, I ran to Ireland, of all places in the world. **1870** Trollope *Phineas Finn* 400 The Earl desired it of all things. **1885** *Manch. Exam.* 20 Oct. 5/1 He, of all men, should have some sympathy with doubters like himself. **1896** *Month* May 135 'I should like it of all things,' said his sister. **1906** W. Churchill *Coniston* I. xiv. 178 'Well, of all people, Cynthia Wetherell!' he cried. **c1921** D. H. Lawrence *Mr. Noon* i. in *Mod. Lover* (1934) 175 'Well, of all the idle scawd-rags!' he said as he entered with the tray. **1926** D. O. Stewart *Mr. & Mrs. Haddock in Paris* x. 266 'Maybe you would like to take a little rest—perhaps at a nice, comfortable movie.' 'Well, of all things, Will Haddock!' **1953** A. Huxley *Let.* 17 Aug. (1969) 683 It is to appear serially—of all places—in *Esquire*—which is at present engaged in serving God and Mammon. **1956** S. Beckett *Waiting for Godot* I. 40 (*He fumbles in his pockets.*)..What have I done with my spray? (*He fumbles.*) Well, of all the —— (*he looks up, consternation on his features. Faintly.*) I can't find my pulverizer! **1958** W. Plomer *At Home* ii. 38 He actually filled a glass with (of all things, on a black November afternoon) ginger beer.

c. *of* (*all*) *other*, and the like, in which *other* after a superlative is illogical (unless *of* orig. had the notion of 'singled out from', 'taken from').

c1380 Wyclif *Sel. Wks.* III. 342 Cristis viker shulde be porerste man of oþir, and mekerst of oþir men. **1470-85** Malory *Arthur* x. xiv, Thou art fayrest of alle other. **1559** W. Cunningham *Cosmogr. Glasse* 82 The place most excellent of other in the Earth for pleasure. **1605** Shaks. *Macb.* v. viii. 4 Of all men else I haue auoyded thee. **1635** A. Stafford *Fem. Glory* 43 It comes to them the last of all other. **1667** Milton *P.L.* iv. 324 The fairest of her Daughters Eve. **1884** *Times* (weekly ed.) 17 Oct. 4/4 It is the thing of all others that we want you to do.

d. (One) distinguished out of a number, or out of all, on account of excellence. Also with repetition of sb., sometimes intensive, as in the Hebraistic ***Song of songs, holy of holies***; so ***book of books, man of men, heart of hearts***; also used to denote a person who shows strong (*spec.* national) characteristics.

1382 Wyclif *Song Sol.*, Heer gynneth the booc that is clepid Songus of Songis. **1594** Marlowe & Nashe *Dido* III. iii, That man of men. **1684** Bunyan *Pilgr.* II. 169 Now the Glass was one of a thousand. **1831** Macaulay in *Life & Lett.* (1880) I. 243 He gave me a dinner of dinners. **1866** W. Collins *Armadale* IV. ii. II. 270 The new sailing-master is a man of ten thousand. **1895** G. A. Sala *Life* (ed. 2) I. vi. 64 Morris Barnett..was a remarkably clever man—a Hebrew of the Hebrews, with a pronounced musical faculty. **1976** *Times* 15 May 14/7 Tévic the Milkman is a Jew of the Jews in character and behaviour, yet his problems are not peculiarly Jewish. **1976** *Lancet* 13 Nov. 1094/2 A Scot of Scots, he was born in 1912 and was educated at St Andrews and Edinburgh Universities.

44. Followed by a possessive case or an absolute possessive pronoun.

Originally partitive, but subseq. used instead of the simple possessive (of the possessor or author) where this would be awkward or ambiguous, or as equivalent to an appositive phrase; e.g. *this son of mine* = this my son; *a dog of John's* = a dog which is John's, a dog belonging to John. (All the early examples, and many of the later, are capable of explanation as partitive.)

a1300 *Cursor M.* 6480 þi neghbur wijf 3erne noght at haue, Ne aght [*Gött.* nor best, *Trin.* beest] of his, ne mai, ne knaue. **c1374** Chaucer *Troylus* I. 492 (548) A frend of his þat called was Pandare. **c1386** —— *Monk's Prol.* 13 Any neighebore of myne. **c1400** *Gamelyn* 241-2 'Now I haue i-proued many tornes of thyne, Thow most', he seyde, 'prouen on or tuo of myne'. **1463** *Bury Wills* (Camden) 23, I 3eve here..the clothes of myn that longe to the bedde that she hath loyen in. **1502** *Privy Purse Exp. Eliz. of York* (1830) 79 A yong hors of the Quenes. **1527** R. Thorne in Hakluyt *Voy.* (1589) 252 Two Englishmen, friends of mine. **1535** Coverdale *Micah* vii. 8 O thou enemie of myne, reioyce not at my fall. **1600** Shaks. *A.Y.L.* v. ii. 82 Looke, here comes a Louer of mine, and a louer of hers. **1637** Milton *Lycidas* 102 That sacred head of thine. **1638** Ld. Digby, etc. *Lett. conc. Relig.* i. (1651) 1 Many personall defects of mine own. **1687** Congreve *Old Bach.* III. vi, Adsbud, who's in fault, mistress of mine? **1718** Watts *Ps.* cxix. III. vi, Thou hast inclin'd this heart of mine Thy statutes to fulfil. **1724** De Foe *Mem. Cavalier* (1840) 255 This was..a false step of the..general's. **1870** Lowell *Study Wind.* 2 It is positive rest to look into that garden of his.

45. a. Without prec. partitive word, as obj. of a verb, or pred. after *be*: = a portion of, one of, some of, some. Mostly *arch.*

c900 tr. *Bæda's Hist.* III. xx. 246 Wæs he of discipulum Aidanes [*erat de discipulis*]. **c1000** Ælfric *Saints' Lives* II. xxvi. 260 Ic hæbbe of ðam stocce ðe his heafod on stod. **c1000** —— *Gen.* iii. 6 Heo..3enam þa of þæs treowes wæstme. **c1000** *Ags. Gosp.* Matt. xxv. 8 Syllaþ us of eowrum ele. **c1205** Lay. 14473, I þan norð ende 3if heom of þine londe. *Ibid.* 31771 He æt of ane uisce. **1340-70** *Alex. & Dind.* 126 þan comaundede þe king cofli to feche Of þat freliche frut. **c1386** Chaucer *C.T.* Prol. 146 Of smale houndes hadde she þat she fedde With rosted flessh. **c1450** *Merlin* i. 23 Like as thei hadden ben of the slayn. **1597** Shaks. *2 Hen. IV*, II. iv. 354 Is shee of the Wicked? **1654-66** Earl Orrery *Parthen.* (1676) 535 To lose of his own Men, or to kill of the Kings, were equal advantages. **1710** Steele *Tatler* No. 166 ¶2 You see of them in every Way of Life, and in every Profession. **1820** Keats *Ode Nightingale* i, As though of hemlock I had drunk. **1890** Healy *Insula Sanctorum* 92 When the horses tasted of the grass, they both fell dead.

b. After *partake* (also formerly *part, participate*).

c1380 *Antecrist* in Todd *Three Treat. Wyclif* (1851) 138 Crist parted wiþ folke of goodis þat he had. **1611** Bible *Rom.* xi. 17 And thou..with them partakest of the roote and fatnesse of the Oliue tree. **1654-66** Earl Orrery *Parthen.* (1676) 687 My looks participated of my hopes. **1848** FitzGerald *Letters*, etc. (1889) I. 191 Whose turkey I accordingly partook of.

46. a. = One of, a member of; hence, belonging to, included in, taking part in.

1425- [see counsel *sb.* 6]. **c1440** *Tindale* 1671 He was sum tyme with hym of meyne. **1615** G. Sandys *Trav.* 103 Their Priests were..of his councell in all businesses of importance. **1657** Cromwell *Sp.* 21 Apr. in *Carlyle*, Who..were all of a piece upon that account. **1673** Ray *Journ. Low C.* 36 If any desire to be admitted of the University. **a1709** Atkins *Parl. & Pol. Tracts* (1734) 15 Keble, of Counsel for the Lord B. **1748** Richardson *Clarissa* (1811) IV. 348, I am ever of party against myself. **1806** Jefferson *Writ.* (1830) IV. 47 Tracy has been of almost every committee during the session. **1845** Browning *Lost Leader* i, Shakespeare was of us, Milton was for us, Burns, Shelley, were with us. **a1859** Macaulay *Hist. Eng.* xxiii. V. 83 He had not been sworn of the Council.

b. Followed by an adj. in the superlative: = one of, some of, something of; formerly also *advb.* = as a thing of.

1542 Udall *Erasm. Apoph.* 212b, The matter gooeth not all of the wurst. **1548** —— *Erasm. Par. John* 7 If any man do not vse all of the best that thing whiche of his nature is..the very best. **a1648** Ld. Herbert *Hen. VIII* (1683) 293 Those who thought the late Proceedings to have been of the severest. **1709** Mrs. Manley *Secr. Mem.* (1736) I. 109 That Satisfaction..he was now afraid came of the latest to him. **1877** J. D. Chambers *Div. Worship* 230 The bread should be of the whitest and finest. **1878** Fr. A. Kemble *Rec. of a Girlhood* II. i. 35 My person was indeed of the shortest.

XIV. In the sense *belonging* or *pertaining to*; expressing possession and its converse: 'the owner of the house', 'the house of the owner'.

Formerly expressed by the genitive, and still to some extent by the possessive case (with transposition of order). The use of *of* began in OE. with senses 47, 48, expressing origin. After the Norman Conquest the example of the French *de*, which had taken the place of the L. genitive, caused the gradual extension of *of* to all uses in which OE. had the genitive; the purely possessive sense was the last to be so affected, and it is that in which the genitive or 'possessive' case is still chiefly used. Thus, we say *the King's English*, in preference to *the English of the King*; but *the King of England* in preference to *England's King*, which is not natural or ordinary prose English.

47. a. Belonging to a place, as a native or resident.

This occurs in OE. with the sense of origin = 'springing or coming from, belonging by origin to' (properly 11 b); in the 11th c. this passed into the sense 'belonging to as inhabitants or occupants', 'living in', and so of things 'situated in or at'.

c **893** K. Ælfred *Oros.* Contents II. viii, Hu Gallie of Senno abræcan Romeburȝ. *Ibid.* II. iii. §3 Mutius..an monn of ðære byriȝ. *a* **900** *O.E. Chron.* an. 896 Ða men of Lunden byriȝ. **971** *Blickl. Hom.* 71 Hit is se Nadzarenisca witȝa of Galileum.

1137–54 *O.E. Chron.* an. 1137 ¶2 Hi suencten suyðe þe uurecce men of þe land mid castel weorces. *Ibid.* ¶7 þe Iudeus of Noruuic bohton an xristen cild. *c* **1175** *Lamb. Hom.* 129 Ðet weter..wes liðe and swete þan folce of israel. þe wes sur and bitere alle þon monnen of þan londe. *c* **1205** Lay. 632 þa cnihtes of þan castle. **1382** Wyclif *Matt.* xii. 41 Men of Nynyue shall ryse in dome with this generacioun. **1388** —— *Judges* ix. 15 Fier go out..and deuoure the cedris of the Liban. **1523** Ld. Berners *Froiss.* I. 102 They of the towne wyst nat wher the countesse was become. **1568** Grafton *Chron.* II. 331 They of London, namely the honest Citizens were greatly afrayed. **1708** *Lond. Gaz.* No. 4464/8 Nathaniel Ogborne of Chipping-sodbury.., Cheese-Factor. **1830** Lindley *Nat. Syst. Bot.* 98 The Black Birch of North America. **1847** Tennyson *Princess* II. 34 We of the court.

b. Belonging to a place, as situated, existing, or taking place there; belonging to a place or thing, as forming part of it or of its equipment, or as attached to or derived from it (in which sense it approaches the partitive).

c **1122** *O.E. Chron.* an. 1102 þeofas..breokan þa mynstre of Burh. *Ibid.* an. 1116 On þisum ylcan ȝeare bærnde eall þæt mynstre of Burh..and..eall þa mæste dæl of þa tuna. *c* **1250** *Gen. & Ex.* 469 Tubal..Wopen of wiȝte and tol of grið Wel cuðe eȝte [*read* feȝte]. **1375** Barbour *Bruce* xx. 324 He salit, and left the grund of Spanȝe On north half hym. **1411** *Rolls of Parlt.* III. 650/1 Robert Tirwhit Justice of the Kinges Bench. **1424** *Paston Lett.* I. 13 On the yates of the Priorie of the Trinite chirche of Norwiche. **1608** Willet *Hexapla Exod.* 165 The fables of his religion as he impiouslie calleth them. **1613** Purchas *Pilgrimage* (1614) 559 The Deserts of Lybia have in them many Hydra's. **1639** De Grey *Compl. Horsem.* 306 Take of the oyle of Aspick one ounce. **1756** Mrs. Lennox tr. *Sully's Mem.* II. (1778) 124 One side of the barricadoes. **1809** Malkin *Gil Blas* VII. xvi. ¶13 Innumerable articles of housekeeping. **1843** *Fraser's Mag.* XXVIII. 698 Napoleon reached the plains of Gera. **1844** Lingard *Anglo-Sax. Ch.* (1858) I. iii. 125 Companions of his exile. **1891** *Law Times* XCII. 107/1 The 8th section of the Act.

c. Belonging to a time, as existing or taking place in it.

1526 Tindale *Matt.* v. 21 It was sayd vnto them off the olde tyme [Wyclif to eld men; 1611 by them of old time]. **1540** *Prymer* title-p., With the Pystels and Gospels of Sondayes and holydayes in Englysshe. **1560** Daus tr. *Sleidane's Comm.* 378b, Your letters..of the xxi. of December. **1656** Earl Monm. tr. *Boccalini's Advts. fr. Parnass.* II. xc. (1674) 243 They..finished that which appeared so dreadful to men of former times. **1851** Thackeray *Eng. Hum.* i. (1853) 13 A man of that time. **1861** M. Pattison *Ess.* (1889) I. 44 The massive and imposing style of the fourteenth century. **1870** Bryant *Iliad* I. IV. 120 By rules like these The men of yore laid level towns and towers. **1885** *Manch. Exam.* 15 May 5/7 A thing of the near future. **1893** W. P. Courtney in *Academy* 13 May 413/1 The best landscape gardeners of the day.

d. Typical or characteristic of (a particular period).

1923 H. Simpson (*title of play*) A man of his time. **1940** M. K. Tippett (*title of oratorio*) A child of our time. **1965** *Listener* 11 Nov. 760/1 It is a highly original picture, but like any work of art it has roots. It is absolutely of its time: all the enthusiasms of those last pre-war years are contained in it at boiling point. **1968** *Ibid.* 4 July 9/2 The 'Four' were very much of the 1890s.

48. a. Belonging to a place as deriving a title from it, or as its lord or ruler, as ***king, earl, bishop, abbot of***.

Prob. also from the notion of origin. Rare in OE. till 11th c., when it became the regular equivalent of Fr. *de*, *of* and its object being found in apposition with a genitive case.

c **893** K. Ælfred *Oros.* I. xi. §1 Alexander, Priamises sunu þæs cyninges of Troiana þære byriȝ, ȝenom þæs cyninges wif Monelaus of Læcedemonia Creca byriȝ. **10..** Ælfric *Gen.* xiv. 10 Ða feollon ða ciningas..ofslaȝene of Sodoman and Gomorran þæra manfulra þeoda. *a* **1070** *O.E. Chron.* an. 1066 (MS. C) Harold cyningc of Norweȝan [*Laud MS.* Harold se Norrena cyng] and Tostiȝ eorl. *c* **1122** *Ibid.* an. 1102 (MS. E) Se cyng and se eorl Rotbert of Bælæsme. *Ibid.* an. 1104 Se eorl Rotbert of Normandiȝ and Rotbert de Bælesme. *Ibid.* an. 1120 Seo cyng of Engle lande and se of France..Se eorl of Flandrand and se of Puntiw. *c* **1205** Lay. 24459 þe ærchebiscop of Lundene eode an his riht honden and bi his luft side þe [ilke] of Eouerwike. *c* **1425** Lydg. *Assembly of Gods* 469 Godfrey of Boleyn. **1612** Shelton (*title*) The History of..Don Quixote of the Mancha. **1772** *Hartford Merc.* Suppl. 18 Sept. 2/2 [He] created Lord Herbert, Baron Herbert of Cherbury and of Ludlow. **1791** Boswell *Johnson* 28 Apr. an. 1778, Mr. John Spottiswoode the younger, of Spottiswoode. *Mod.* The King of Great Britain, Prince of Wales, Archbishop of Canterbury, Duke of Wellington, Earl of Derby, etc.

b. Related to a thing or person as its ruler, superior, possessor, or the like. (Akin to the objective genitive, sense 34; and sometimes interchangeable with a possessive case, esp. when the object is a person.)

1127–31 *O.E. Chron.* an. 1127 He wæs legat of ðone Romescott. *c* **1200** Ormin 298 Moysæs wass hæfedd mann Off Issraæle þeode. *Ibid.* 344 þatt streon þatt wass Allmahhtiȝ Godd, & King off alle kingess, & Preost off alle preostess ec. *c* **1250** *Gen. & Ex.* 29 Fader god of alle ðinge. *Ibid.* 122 Of euerilc ouȝt, of euerilc sed, Was erðe mad moder of sped. **1382** Wyclif *Luke* viii. 41 He was prince [1526 Tindale, etc., a ruler] of a synagogue. —— *2 Cor.* i. 3 Blessid be God and the fadir of oure Lord Jesu Crist, fadir of mercies and God of al comfort. *c* **1386** Chaucer *Knight's T.* 81 Creon..That lord is now of Thebes the Citee. **1424** *Paston Lett.* I. 16 The Styward of the seyd Duc of Norffolk, of al hese lordshippes in Norffolk and Suffolk. **1596** Shaks. *Merch. V.* III. ii. 170 But now I was the Lord Of this faire mansion, master of my seruants. **1618** J. Taylor (Water P.) *Penniless Pilgr.* Wks. (1883) 62 The Master of the house. **1662** Stillingfl. *Orig. Sacr.* I. iv. §3 Gideon the Judge of Israel. **1712** Steele *Spect.* No. 496 ¶2 The father of him was a coxcomb. **1846** McCulloch *Acc. Brit. Empire* (1854) II. 219 The dean of guild, or head of the Merchant Company.

49. a. Belonging to a person (etc.), as something that he (etc.) has or possesses. (= the *possessive genitive*, and akin to the subjective, sense 17.)

In OE. always, in ME. most frequently, and in Mod.Eng. preferably expressed by the genitive or possessive case, except when for some reason this is difficult or awkward, e.g. in quots. 1386 (second), 1596, 1895.

c **1200** Ormin 666 ȝiff þatt itt..seþ þe wlite off ennglekinde. *a* **1300** *Cursor M.* 20063 (Gött.) Ur aun Langage of þe norþren lede. **1382** Wyclif *1 Cor.* i. 12 Forsoth I am of Poul [Vulg. *Pauli*], forsoth I of Appollo, treuly I of Cephas, forsoth I of Crist. [OE. *Gregory's Past. C.* 210 Paules..Apollan..Petres..Cristes.] *c* **1386** Chaucer *Knight's T.* 70 In the temple of the goddesse clemence. *Ibid.* 134 The bones of his frendes that weren slayn. **1535** Coverdale *Ruth* Contents i, Ruth the wife of the one sonne. **1559** W. Cunningham *Cosmogr. Glasse* 177 The soules of men and women. **1590** Spenser *F.Q.* II. ii. 13 The children of one syre by mothers three. **1596** Shaks. *Tam. Shr.* v. i. 89 He is..heire to the Lands of me signior Vincentio. **1700** Tyrrell *Hist. Eng.* II. 820 The Ayries of Hawks. **1712** Pope *Spect.* No. 408 ¶5 The Milk of a Goat. **1808** Forster *Perenn. Calend.* 21 May, The leaves of plants. **1886** *Pall Mall G.* 17 July 5/7 The tomb of England's first martyr. **1895** *Law Times* C. 133/2 The widow of a man who had been killed at a level crossing.

b. Belonging to a person or thing as a quality or attribute. (Also interchanging with the possessive case, esp. when the object is a person, animal, or space of time, as 'a month's salary'.)

c **1220** *Bestiary* 119 Ðurȝ grace off ure driȝtin. *a* **1300** *Cursor M.* 27033 For grettnes of his gilt. *c* **1386** Chaucer *C.T.* Prol. 39 To telle yow al the condicion Of ech of hem. *c* **1450** *Pol. Rel. & L. Poems* 104 It is of þe for to forgyfe Alkyn trespas both more and mynn. **1502** Arnolde *Chron.* (1811) 280 In the tendir age off you. *a* **1548** Hall *Chron., Hen. VIII* 248b, The value of the grounde so lytle. **1559** Aylmer *Harborowe* D iv b, The welfare or ilfare of the whole realm. **1604** Shaks. *Oth.* IV. i. 206 But yet the pitty of it, Iago; oh Iago, the pitty of it, Iago. **1648** *Royalist's Defence* 109 Words cannot express the barbarousnesse of it. **1714** Addison *Spect.* No. 556 ¶14 The chief Tendency of my Papers. **1793** Smeaton *Edystone L.* §239 The little irregularities of boring. **1802** Mar. Edgeworth *Moral T.* (1816) I. Pref. 8 The scene of 'The Knapsack' is laid in Sweden. **1843** *P. Parley's Ann.* IV. 346 The breezeless stillness of the summer air. **1886** *Athenæum* 30 Oct. 560/3 His failure seems..to be due to a want of singleness of aim.

50. Belonging to a thing, as something related in a way defined or implied by its nature; e.g. the *cause, effect, origin, reason, result of*; the *correlative, counterpart, match, opposite, original of*; a *copy, derivative, image, likeness of*; the *square, cube, logarithm, tangent, differential*, or other mathematical function *of*. See under these words.

c **1200** Ormin 706 Hiss sune shollde ben Biginning off þatt blisse. *c* **1315**- [see cause *sb.*]. *c* **1386**- [see effect *sb.*]. **1389**- [see copy *sb.*]. **1483** Caxton *G. de la Tour* E iv, The peyntynge of her face..was cause and occasion of suche horryble countrefaiture. **1559** W. Cunningham *Cosmogr. Glasse* 71, I am glad you understand the reason of it. **1601**- [see correlative *sb.*]. **1617**- [see counterpart]. **1639** Laud *Wks.* (1849) II. 277 No good cause can be assigned of it. **1646**- [see cube *sb.*[1]]. **1709** Steele *Tatler* No. 130 ¶10 The Anniversary of the Birth-day of this Glorious Queen. **1776** *Maiden Aunt* II. 16, I informed them the cause and event of my ramble. **1804** Mitford *Inq. Princ. Harmony Lang.* (ed. 2) 405 The analogy of the language. **1807** Hutton *Course Math.* II. 281 We may also derive the fluxion of any fraction, or the quotient of one variable quantity divided by another. **1847** Lytton *Lucretia* 91 Wait..the effect of the cataplasms I have applied.

51. Belonging to an action or the like, as that to which it relates.

1534 Ende of felycitie [see end *sb.* 15]. **1593** Shaks. *Lucrece* 113 Far from the purpose of his coming hither, He makes excuses for his being there. **1677** Marvell *Corr.* Wks. 1872–5 II. 540 Those two days afforded litle matter of writing. **1812** Jefferson *Writ.* (1830) IV. 175 It would only change the topic of abuse. **1886** *World* 18 Aug. 18 The weather is the solitary topic of conversation.

XV. Indicating *a point or space of time*.

52. a. At some time during, in the course of, on.

App. taking the place of the Com. Teut. and OE. genitive of time. Now only in the colloquial ***of an evening, of a morning, of a Sunday afternoon***, and the like.

[**921** *O.E. Chron.* (MS. A.), þa æfter þam þæs ilcan sumeres ȝegadorode micel folc hit. *c* **1100** *Ibid.* an. 47 þis was þes feorðes ȝeares his rices. *c* **1205** Lay. 2861 Fure þe neuer ne aþeostrede, winteres ne sumeres. *Ibid.* 3255 Heo wolden ..feden..þane king..dæies and nihtes.] **1382** Wyclif *Gen.* xx. 8 Anoon of the nyȝt [1388 bi nyȝt] rysynge, Abimalech [etc.]. **1472** *Presentm. Juries* in *Surtees Misc.* (1888) 23 Maid asalt..& afrayd his neyghburs of Palmsondai. **1590** Shaks. *Mids. N.* II. i. 253 There sleepes Tytania, sometime of the night. **1612** *Acct.-bk. W. Wray* in *Antiquary* XXXII. 214 Great thunder..and also the like of new yeares day following. **1657** *Manchester Court Leet Rec.* (1887) IV. 212 For buying and selling pullen both of one day. **1741** Richardson *Pamela* II. 149 Of a Thursday my dear Father and Mother were marry'd. **1741** C'tess Pomfret *Corr.* (1805) III. 178 Here the company meet of a summer's evening. **1830** J. H. Newman *Lett.* (1891) I. 222 My practice to walk of a day to Nuneham. **1831** Carlyle *Sart. Res.* I. iii, All the Intellect of the place assembled of an evening. **1899** W. J. Knapp *Life Borrow* I. 79 The father made his last Will and Testament of a Monday.

b. Sometimes the genitival *-s* is retained; perh. often understood as plural. Cf. a-nights.

1740 Chesterf. *Lett.* (1792) I. lxviii. 190 [To] sleep sound of nights. **1753** A. Murphy *Gray's Inn Jrnl.* No. 50 [They] begin to drop in here of Evenings. **1820** Lamb *Elia* Ser. I. *Christ's Hosp. 35 Yrs. ago*, Shut up by himself of nights. **1849** Thackeray *Pendennis* xix, Dice can be played of mornings as well as after dinner. **1867** 'E. Kirke' *On Border* iii. 67, I don't forget..how you worked of nights. **1891** Barrie *Little Minister* III. xl. 156 So long as women sit up of nights listening for a footstep. **1897** J. L. Allen *Choir Invisible* xvii. 252 You have holiday of Saturdays. I have not, you see.

c. ***of this date***, dating from this day. (*Sc.* and *U.S.*)

1866 *Glasgow Trade Circular*, The Subscriber..has retired of this date from the Company. **1882** Schouler *Hist. U.S.* II. 284 All interdictions against Great Britain would cease of the same date [10th of the next June].

53. During, for (a space of time). (In later use only with a negative.) *Obs.* or *arch.*

c **1369** Chaucer *Dethe Blaunche* 1105, I was warished of all my sorwe Of al day after. *c* **1374** —— *Troylus* v. 282 This Pandare þat of al þe day by-forn Ne myght haue comen Troylus to se. *c* **1400** *Destr. Troy* 13456 The biggyng..was of long tyme beleft. *c* **1430** *Syr Gener.* (Roxb.) 1723 Nathanael of al that long night For verrey sorow noght slepe might. **1523** Ld. Berners *Froiss.* I. x. 10 They wist nat of two dayes wher they were. **1587** Mascall *Govt. Cattle, Hogges* (1627) 265 Giue him no meat of an houre or two after. **1631** Weever *Anc. Fun. Mon.* 220 That he should not weare a shirt of three yeares. **1674** P. Henry *Diaries & Lett.* (1882) 267 It had not rayn'd of many weekes before. **1760–72** H. Brooke *Fool of Qual.* (1809) III. 73 Not seeing or hearing from him of a long time. **1833** S. Austin *Charac. Goethe* II. 334 Persons whom we have not seen of a long time.

54. ***of old, of yore, of late, of late years***, and the like, prob. orig. were in sense 2; but have come to mean In or during the time specified.

c **1400** *Destr. Troy* 13454 Thedur kynges wold come by custom of olde, For to hunt at the hert by the holt sydes. **1423** *Rolls of Parlt.* IV. 406/1 Ye verray and trewe makyng of old used and continued. *c* **1470** [see late B. 2]. **1576** Fleming *Panopl. Epist.* 401 Wee sawe (of late yeares) the epistles..both bredd..and also buried. **1634** Sir T. Herbert *Trav.* 118 Cazbeen is that City which of past ages was cald Arsatia. **1766** Goldsm. *Vic. W.* xxii, Your poor father and I have suffered very much of late. **1812** Byron *Ch. Har.* I. xxix, Where dwelt of yore the Lusians' luckless queen. **1885** *Law Times* LXXIX. 181/1 The duties..have been very much lightened of late years.

XVI. In *Locative* and other obsolete uses.

Many former uses of *of* are difficult to class. Some of these arose from employing it as a literal rendering of French *de* (or of L. *ab, ex, de*), in phrases where English idiom would have required some other preposition; others arose from a confusion with *on*, or erroneous expansion of *a*, *o* = *on* (a *prep.*[1], o *prep.*[1]), or of Sc. *a'* for *i'* = in. Others were app. due to confusion of constructions. Without endeavouring to distinguish these, examples are here given in various senses.

†**55. a.** In sense *on*. *Obs.*, *colloq.*, or *vulgar*.

c **1380** Wyclif *Sel. Wks.* III. 357 þis is not groundid of Crist. **1389** in *Eng. Gilds* (1870) 4 Of peyne of a pond wax to þe bretherhede. **1440** J. Shirley *Dethe K. James* 23 Thare heddes set upe of the gates of Sent Johannes Towne. **1516** *Test. Ebor.* (Surtees) V. 80, I will that myn ex[rs] lay a stone of my grave and that an ymage of our Lady be sett of the same. **1535** Coverdale *Mark* vi. 33 Many..ranne thither together of fote. **1589** *Marprel. Epit.* (1843) 60 Ile bestow a whole booke of him. **1596** Shaks. *Merch. V.* II. ii. 104, I am sure he had more haire of his taile then I haue of my face. **1597** Lyly *Wom. in Moone* III. ii, Of that condition I am yours. **1604** *Meeting of Gallants at Ordinarie* (Percy Soc.) 23 Pulling downe a house of Fyre. **1607** Dekker *Knt.'s Conjur.* (1842) 63 Mercurie (that runs of all the errands betweene the gods). **1621** *Bury Wills* (Camden) 167 Desiringe..he would bestowe some of my howsholde of my brother Nicke. **1662** Gurnall *Chr. in Arm.* xxiv. §5 (1669) 318/2 They turn their back of that light. **1668** Dryden *Even. Love* IV. iii, A mischief of all foolish disguisements! **1736** Earl Waldegrave in *Buccleuch MSS.* (Hist. MSS. Comm.) I. 389, I could not light of the Duc..till yesterday. **1746** Wesley *Wks.* (1872) II. 15 She might send him of an errand. **1777** Sheridan *Sch. Scand.* v. i, Oh, plague of his nerves!

b. esp. with *side, hand, part*, or similar word. Cf. F. *du côté de*, L. *ab, ex parte*, etc. *Obs.*

1432–50 tr. *Higden* (Rolls) I. 93 Assyria hathe on the este parte of hit [*ab ortu*] Ynde, of the sowthe [*ab austro*] Media, of the weste parte the floode of Tigris. *c* **1489** Caxton *Sonnes of Aymon* iii. 73 Of the one side of it [a high rock] was betyng a grete river. **1526** Tindale *Rev.* xxii. 2 Off ether syde [*ex utraque parte*] off the ryuer was there wode off lyfe. **1535** COVERDALE *1 Macc.* v. 46 They coude not go by it, nether of the right honde ner of the left. **1548-9** (Mar.) *Bk. Com. Prayer* Offices 23 Of theyr parte a great token of charitie. **1579-80** NORTH *Plutarch* (1676) 66 Of his Fathers side, he was descended of King Codrus. **1583** STOCKER *Civ. Warres Lowe C.* I. 64b, They..of all handes bestirred them. **1662** J. DAVIES tr. *Olearius' Voy. Ambass.* 300 Enclos'd of all sides with a high Wall. **1708** BURNET *Lett.* (ed. 3) 136 They thought the Advantage was wholly of that Side. **1779** FORREST *Voy. N. Guinea* 83 Six banks of paddles, three banks of a side.

†**56.** In sense *in.* Mostly *Obs.*

c **1430** LYDGATE *Lyke thyn Audience, etc.* 90 in *Pol. Rel. & L. Poems* 28 Antonye and poule.. Lyuyd in desert of wilfulle pouert. **1525** LD. BERNERS *Froiss.* II. cxlvi. [cxlii.] 403 They ..made the greattest reuell of the worlde. **1546** *Nottingham Rec.* IV. 131 He dothe soffer the horses of the market. **1568** Of conscience [see CONSCIENCE *sb.* 10]. **1609** BIBLE (Douay) *Num.* xxxii. 17 Because of the lying of wayte of the inhabitantes. **1613** *Hibbaldstow, Lincolnshire MS. Court Roll,* Those that are resident of their house which they keep comons for. **1773** GOLDSM. *Stoops to Conq.* II. i, I have just been mortified enough of all conscience.

†**57.** In sense *at* (or *on*). *of all,* at all = F. *du tout* (see also AVA). *Obs.*

1419 *Searchers Verdicts* in *Surtees Misc.* (1888) 15 Twa postes..be set in of hys coste. ?*a* **1500** *Wycket* (ed. Pantin 1828) p. xvii, That her two sonnes..myght syt one of hys ryght syde & one at hys left syde. *a* **1548** HALL *Chron., Hen. VI* 137 All other graynes, wer sold of an excessive price, above the olde custome. *c* **1550** CHEKE *Matt.* xx. 21 Y^t yees mi ij sones mai sit th'oon of y^i right hand and th'other of y^i left hand. **1588** A. KING tr. *Canisius' Catech.* 220 Thay hauing in tham selues na merits of al. **1690** W. WALKER *Idiomat. Anglo-Lat.* 94 It is cheap of twenty pounds. **1696** J. F. *Merchant's Ware-ho.* 32 They look very fine of the Price.

†**58.** In sense *to. Obs.*

1523 LD. BERNERS *Froiss.* I. cccciv. 702 They..set fyer of dyuers vyllages in Flaunders. **1604** E. GRIMSTONE *Hist. Siege Ostend* 68 He..would set fire of one of the Magazins.

†**59.** In sense *by. of himself,* by himself, alone. *Obs.* (Cf. 12 b.)

1340-70 *Alex. & Dind.* 33 We ben sengle of us silf, & se men ful bare. **1605** BACON *Adv. Learn.* I. vii. §9 She was solitary, and of herselfe. **1626** —— *Sylva* §323 Another apple, of the same kind, that lay of it Self.

†**60.** In sense of A *prep.*[1] (= on, in, into): *of thre* = A-THREE, in three: *fall of* = fall a-.

13.. *Seuyn Sag.* (W.) 782 The grehound wolde nowt sessed be, Til that adder ware toren of thre. **1451** *Rolls of Parlt.* V. 216/1 For asmoche as the persones..named, hath been of mysbehavyng aboute youre Roiall persone. **1672** MARVELL *Reh. Transp.* I. 269 Others fell of oyling and furbishing their Armour.

†**61.** In sense *with.* Mostly *Obs.* (See also 26 d.)

1523 LD. BERNERS *Froiss.* I. ccxiii. 262 Then they fell in communycacion of the lord Charles of Bloys, and of the lord Iohn of Mountfort. **1826** COBBETT *Poor Man's Friend* ii, These severe critics found fault of this working. **1843** LONGF. *Span. Student* I. v, Padre Francisco! Padre Francisco! What do you want of Padre Francisco?

XVII. Phrases.

62. a. *Of* followed by a sb. forms attrib. or advb. phrases: as, *of age, of a certainty, of choice, of consequence, of course, of force, of kin,* †*of life, of necessity, of purpose, of right, of a truth, of use, of wrong,* etc.: see the sbs.; also *of old,* etc. in 54.

†**b.** *Of* followed by an adj. (or adv.) formerly formed advb. phrases [cf. F. *d'avant, de loin, de nouveau,* etc.]: as *of before, of certain, of enough, of ere, of far, of fore, of fresh,* (*of afresh*), *of hard, of high, of light, of more, of new,* (*of anew*), *of night, of ordinary, of the same. Obs.* exc. in *of a sudden,* or as repr. by worn-down forms in *a-* (*afar, afresh, alight, anew*).

1297 R. GLOUC. (Rolls) 592 Ac noȝt vor þan þat oþer maide he louede more of inou. *Ibid.* 8018 A worse peire of inou þe oþer suþþe him broȝte. *a* **1425** *Cursor M.* 10748 (Trin.) If he spoused were of ere. *c* **1470** HENRY *Wallace* XI. 293 In my mater, as I off for began, I sall conteyn. **1483** CAXTON *G. de la Tour* D vj b, The deth that of nyghe foloweth them. *c* **1489** —— *Sonnes of Aymon* ii. 62 He.. called of heyghe, 'Barons! kepe well that Reynawde scape not'. *Ibid.* iii. 110 Began the batayll of a freshe. **1600** W. WATSON *Decacordon* (1602) 62 They being of fresh tormented. **1668** H. MORE *Div. Dial.* I. 59 That the same thing..may..be produced of a-fresh.

63. *Of* forms the last element of many prepositional phrases: e.g. *because of; by means of, by reason of; for fear of, for the sake of, for want of; in behalf of, in case of, in comparison of, in consequence of, in face of, in lieu of, in regard* or *respect of, in spite of, instead of; on account of, on behalf of, on condition of, on the point of;* etc. See the sbs.

of (ɒv, əv), joc. (being erroneous in Received Standard) or dial. var. HAVE *v.* (representing the unstressed pronunc. of *have,* esp. in such phrases as ***could have, might have, must have,*** and ***would have***).

1837 W. TAYLER *Diary* 10 May in J. Burnett *Useful Toil* (1974) II. 181 Soposing seven hundred and sixty [servants] to of advertised and the same number not to of advertised. **1844** *Southern Lit. Messenger* X. 486/2, I never would of married in the world, ef I couldn't of got jist exactly suited. **1854** M. J. HOLMES *Tempest & Sunshine* viii. 115, I don't see why in the old Harry he couldn't of lived. **1913** C. MACKENZIE *Sinister St.* I. I. iv. 60 Mrs. Frith used to talk about 'people as gave theirselves airs which they had no business to of done.' **1916** [see FAIR *sb.*[2] 1 c]. **1924** A. S. NEILL *Dominie's Five* ii. 31 If Neill had been 'ere, 'e could of told us. **1931** E. LINKLATER *Juan in Amer.* II. iv. 79 There's no beer-racket in Paris or Rome, and even if there had been I wouldn't of tried to muscle in on it. *Ibid.* III. iii. 226 If I hadn't of worked nights on a correspondence course I'd of been firing a furnace still. **1945** A. KOBER *Parm Me* 26 I'm certainly glad to of made your acquaintance. **1946** K. TENNANT *Lost Haven* (1947) i. 19 There might have been a time when I thought Kelly was too hard on the kids, and.. I might of been glad when he went off with that bloody moll. *Ibid.* xiii. 202 She must of forgot. **1957** [see BLOWER[1] 3 e]. **1959** [see DOZER[2]]. **1977** *New Yorker* 6 June 56/3 Sometimes I get to thinking that I could of raised up four girls and worn out a couple of saddles.

of-, *prefix*[1], the prepositional adv. OF, OFF, in comb., corresp. to OS. *af-,* ON. *af-,* Goth. *af-,* OHG. *ab-;* L. *ab-,* Gr. ἀπο-, Skt. *apa-,* forming compounds of different ages.

1. In vbs. and their derivatives of Germanic or OE. age, retained in ME., but now obs. In these the original literal sense 'away, off' seldom survived even in OE.; the compound verb, formed by the close union of particle and verb, having usually undergone a modification, extension, or transference of meaning, in which the original sense of the elements, esp. of the particle, was obscured or lost. Examples: *ofhold* to hold from, withhold, *ofsake* to put away a charge, deny, *ofthink* to displease, grieve, *ofask* to ask for, get by asking, *ofclepe* to call for, *ofsend* to send for. *Of-* frequently added to the verbal notion that of 'to do away with, finish off, destroy, kill', as in *ofslay, ofsting, oftread;* of 'to injure, hurt', as in *oflie, ofset, ofsit;* of 'to outdo or overcome', as in *ofride, ofrun.* Closely allied to this is the sense, in participial adjectives, of 'overcome or exhausted with the action expressed by the vb.', as in *ofcalen, offought, ofhungered, ofthirst.* Words of this class which came down into ME. will be found in their alphabetical places.

In ME. *of-* before a cons. was frequently reduced to *o-, a-,* and thus identified in form with several other prefixes of different origin: see A- *prefix,* and OF- *prefix*[2]; and cf. ADOWN, OF-HUNGERED, A-HUNGERED, OFTHIRST, ATHIRST, etc.

2. In later combinations of OE. and ME. age, the sense of the two elements remains manifest, the particle being usually = 'off'; the union is much looser, the particle being in vbs. mostly separable, with its position depending on the syntax. It was only in pples., verbal adjs., and sbs., that the combination became more or less permanent. In the 16th c., *of-* in this connexion passed imperceptibly into *off-,* which is always the form in later combinations. Hence these naturally attach themselves to OFF- *pref.,* under which see the ME. examples.

of-, *prefix*[2], in ME. appears sometimes to represent an earlier *a-.* OE. *of-* being often phonetically reduced to *a-,* there arose a confusion between the prefixes, so that original *a-* was sometimes expanded to *of-.* See OFFEAR, OFFRIGHT, OFGRAME, OFGRISEN, OFKEN, OFSCAPE, OFWAKE (in some of which, however, *of-* may be original).

of-, *prefix*[3], in ME. sometimes varies with *ofer,* OVER, from which it may be shortened. Cf. OFGO, OFHEAR, OFTAKE. But this cannot always be distinguished from OF- *prep.*[1] in the sense 'outdo or overcome' as in *ofride, ofrun.*

of, erroneous form of *oð, oþ,* OTH *conj.* until.

of, apocopate form of *þof,* THOUGH *conj.*

ofald, variant of OFOLD *a. Obs.,* single.

ofall, obs. form of OFFAL.

†**of-'ask,** *v. Obs.* [OE. *ofácsian, -áxian,* f. OF-[1] + *ácsian* to ASK.] *trans.* To inquire, to ask for; to get or learn by inquiry.

c **1000** ÆLFRIC *Gen.* ix. 21 Ða he ofaxode hwæt his suna him dydon. *a* **1100** in *Leg. Rood* 7 þæt hio þær ofaxian scolde þa halȝan rode. *c* **1305** *St. Kenelm* 343 in *E.E.P.* (1862) 56 Heo of eschte what men hit were. **1340** *Ayenb.* 153 He ne deþ noþing bote hit by wel of acsed and y-trid. *c* **1400** *St. Alexius* (Laud 622) 362 Whan þai miȝtten nouȝth spede, Ne hym of axen in no þede.

ofay ('əʊfeɪ). *U.S. slang* (chiefly used by Blacks). [Orig. unknown: the balance of probability is that it is a word of African origin (but the precise attribution in quot. 1932 lacks foundation). The suggestion that it is Pig Latin for *foe* seems no more than an implausible guess.] In the use of American Blacks: an offensive term for 'a white person'. Also *attrib.* or as *adj.* Cf. FAY *sb.*[4]

1925 *Inter-State Tattler* 6 Mar. 8 We hear that 'Booker Red' has three ofays on his staff. **1926** [see DICTY *a.*]. **1927** *Amer. Mercury* Dec. 392 Ugly people there are, certainly, but the percentage of beautiful folk is unquestionably larger than among the ofay brethren. **1932** *Africa* V. 506 The last of the five words contributed indirectly by Ibibio to the English language is *Offay*... The root of the word appears to come from the Ibibio *Afia,* white or light-coloured. Hence in Harlem *Offay* means any light-coloured person and therefore a European. **1936** MENCKEN *Amer. Lang.* (ed. 4) v. 214 The word *ofay,* which may have come from the French *au fait* (signifying mastery), is in general use in the Negro press of the United States to designate a white person. **1940** *New Republic* 7 Oct. 472 When he goes downtown to this civil-service office, they take him for ofay. .. One of them young ofay chicks what clerk down there, she even tries to flirt with him. **1946** *Variety* 23 Oct. 114 Boys start out with a Negro spiritual, with their inflection and harmony making it racially authentic, although they're ofay. **1952** M. STEEN *Phoenix Rising* iii. 70 'Dey run him out.' 'What for?' Karl sounded bored. 'Got after Harry's ofay chick—' **1956** B. HOLIDAY *Lady sings Blues* (1973) v. 52 Most of the ofays, the white people, who came to Harlem those nights were looking for atmosphere. *Ibid.* ix. 89 'What will people think?' is a big deal in ofay circles. **1968** M. RICHLER *Cocksure* iv. 25 Was she amused by his dilemma? His ofay dilemma. **1971** *Black World* Apr. 62, I was attendant in the ofay ladies lounge. **1971** B. MALAMUD *Tenants* 48 Who are those cats, brothers or ofays? *Ibid.* 74 The black replies. 'No ofay mother-fucker can put himself in *my* place.' **1977** *Amer. Speech 1975* L. 89 That this word [*sc.* Yoruba *ofe*] could have been brought to the United States by slaves is altogether possible... Thus *ofay* may be taken as a word said for self-protection in times of threat, which was then transferred to the source of threat, and so came to mean 'whiteman'.

†**of'cale(n,** *ppl. a. Obs.* [OE., f. OF-[1] + *calen,* pa. pple. of *calan* to be cold. See also ACALE.] Affected with cold, chilled, frozen.

c **1000** ÆLFRIC *Hom.* II. 248 Petrus stod ofcalen on ðam cauertune. **1297** R. GLOUC. (Rolls) 6580 þat water..vpward it stey So þat is hupes smorte and of cale [*v.rr.* of cold, of cal, acolde, colde] were ney.

†**of'clepe,** *v. Obs.* [OE. *ofclipian, -clypian,* f. OF- + *clipian* to CLEPE, call.] *trans.* To call for, summon, get by calling.

c **1000** ÆLFRIC *Saints' Lives* ii. (*Eugenia*) 219 Butan heo mid hreame hyre hræddinge ofclypode. **13..** *K. Alis.* 1810 He..ofclepith his chaunselere. *c* **1330** *Arth. & Merl.* 1742 Vp him stirt sir Fortiger And ofcleped his chaunceler.

ofdaw, variant of ADAW *v.*[1] *Obs.,* to wake up, recover from a swoon.

of-down, ofdune: see ADOWN.

†**of'draw,** *v. Obs.* [f. OF- 2, OFF- 1 + DRAW *v.*] *trans.* To draw away, draw to oneself, attract.

a **1225** *Ancr. R.* 258 þeo þet of-drauhð ear þus luue of oðer. *Ibid.* 386 Muchel ȝeoue of-draweð luue. *Ibid.* 392 Uorte of-drawen of us ure luue touward him.

†**of'drede,** *v. Obs.* Chiefly in *pa. pple.* 1 ofdræ̆d(d), 2-3 ofdred, 2-4 ofdrad, afterwards reduced to *adred,* ADRAD, q.v. [f. OF- + OE. *drǽd-an* to DREAD; in OE. only in pa. pple.] *trans.* To terrify, frighten; *pa. pple.* frightened, afraid; *refl.* to fear, be afraid.

c **1000** *Ags. Gosp.* Matt. xxv. 25 Ic ferde ofdræd, and behydde þin pund on eorþan. **1135-54** *O.E. Chron.* an. 1135 Wurþen men suiðe of uundred & ofdred. *a* **1200** *Moral Ode* 43 (Lamb. MS.) Ne þerf he bon of-dred [*Trin., Egert.* of-drad, *Jesus* adred] of fure. *Ibid.* (Jesus MS.) 163 þer we muwen beon aferd and sore vs of-drede [*Trin.* ofdrade, *Egert.* adrede, *Lamb.* adreden]. *c* **1205** LAY. 7575 His men weoren of-dredde [*c* **1275** adradde]. *a* **1300** *Assump. Virg.* (Camb. MS.) 91 Ne beo noȝt ofdrad þeȝ ihc beo her. *a* **1300** *K. Horn* (MS. O) 302 Wel sore y me of drede [*MS. L.* adrede] þat hye wile horn mis rede. *Ibid.* 1205 Wel sore hyre of dradde þat horn child ded were. *c* **1380** *Sir Ferumb.* 3723 Alle þay waxen sore of-drad.

†**of'drunken,** *v. Obs.* In 2-3 *Orm.* offdrunncnen. [f. OF- + DRUNKEN *v.*[1]] *trans.* To drown, swallow up in water.

c **1200** ORMIN 14611 þær haliȝ waterr att te funnt Offdrunncneþþ alle sinness. *Ibid.* 14852 Faraoness genge, þatt wass offdrunncnedd i þe sæ.

ofeald, variant of OFOLD *a., Obs.,* single.

†**of-'earn,** *v. Obs.* Also 2 of-ern. [f. OF- 1 + EARN *v.*] *trans.* To earn, deserve.

c **1200** *Trin. Coll. Hom.* 189 He haueð þer þurh forloren heuene wele and of-erned helle pine. *a* **1225** *Ancr. R.* 188 ȝif ȝe þolieð wo ȝe habbeð wurse of-earned. *Ibid.* 194 Sum likunge is & sum mislikunge, þet of-earneð muche mede.

ofen, ofer, obs. forms of OVEN, OVER.

ofer, oferre, obs. forms of AFAR.

off (ɒf, ɔːf), *adv., prep., a.,* and *sb.*[1] Forms: 1-7 of, (5 ofe, 6 offe), 5- off (*Sc. dial* aff). [Originally the same word as OF, as explained under that word; *off* being at first a variant spelling, which was gradually appropriated to the emphatic form, i.e. to the adverb and the prepositional senses closely related to it, while *of* was retained in the transferred and weakened senses, in which the prep. is usually stressless and sinks to (ǝv). *Off* appears casually from *c* 1400, but *of* and *off* were not completely differentiated till after 1600: cf. A. 3, B. 1.]

In this article are included all examples of the adv., whether under (α) the earlier spelling *of*, or (β) the later *off*; but, of the prep., only those uses for which *off* is now the recognized form; for others see OF.

A. *adv.* I. Simple senses.

1. a. Expressing motion or direction from a place: To a distance, away, quite away; as in ***go, run, drive off.*** Also expressing resistance to motion towards: as in ***beat, hang, keep, ward off.***

α. **971** *Blickl. Hom.* 5 Man sceolde mid sare on ðas world cuman,..and mid sare of ʒewitan. *c* **1386** CHAUCER *Reeve's T.* Prol. 58 Leueful is with force force of showue. *c* **1485** *Digby Myst.* III. 379 Com of þan, let vs be-gynne. **1526** *Pilgr. Perf.* (1531) 80 Come of..thou that art disposed to leue all for the loue of Iesu. *a* **1548** HALL *Chron., Hen. VIII*, 262 b, Peces of ordinaunce whiche shot of.

β. **1567** MAPLET *Gr. Forest* 12 Neyther could we keepe off, ..our outward enimies. **1659** D. PELL *Impr. Sea* 557 To drive off his melancholy thoughts. **1726** G. ROBERTS *Four Years Voy.* 28 To send my Mate off with the Boat. **1766** GOLDSM. *Vic. W.* xvii, She is gone off with two gentlemen in a post chaise. **1840** DICKENS *Old C. Shop* vi, Mr. Quilp put his hat on and took himself off. **1896** *Law Times* C. 508/1 [He] succeeded in getting the animal under control, and rode off.

b. *fig.*

α. *c* **1000** *Laws of Ine* c. 74 §2 Buton he him wille fæhþe of aceapian. **1523** LD. BERNERS *Froiss.* I. cxxiv. 150 The kynge bought of sir Thomas Hallande,..and therle of Tankernyll, and payed for them twentie thousande nobles.

β. **1568** GRAFTON *Chron.* II. 170 With fayre wordes [he] put them off for that tyme. **1629**, etc. [see BUY *v.* 7 a]. **1666** J. DAVIES *Hist. Caribby Isls.* 268 They will fall off from what they have promised. **1707** W. FUNNELL *Voy. round World* 259 A small matter of Money will buy off a great Fault. **1902** G. H. LORIMER *Lett. Merchant* xiv. 203 By the time the real weather comes along everybody has guessed wrong and knocked the market off a cent or two. **1934** G. B. SHAW *On Rocks* I. 25 You have to buy him off with a scrap of dole. **1971** *Nature* 30 Apr. 604/1 Halfway through the book, the reasons why the rapid development of fluidics in the early 1960s has tended to fall off recently become clear.

c. In nautical lang.: Away from land, or from the ship; also, away from the wind.

1610 SHAKS. *Temp.* I. i. 53 Lay her a hold, a hold, set her two courses off to Sea againe, lay her off. **1611** BIBLE *Acts* xxvii. 32 Then the souldiers cut off the ropes of the boat and let her fall off [*all prec. vv.* away]. *a* **1621** BEAUM. & FL. *Thierry & Theod.* IV. ii, I would I had A convoy too, to bring me safe off. **1697** DAMPIER *Voy.* I. 132 He stood off to Sea, and we plied up under the shore. **1699** *Ibid.* II. II. 22 Then she would fall off 2 or 3 Points from the Wind. **1723** G. ROBERTS *Four Years Voy.* 27 To sail to the Isle of Sal, and bring off all the People. **1882** NARES *Seamanship* (ed. 6) 107 *Nothing off*... To bring the ship's head nearer to the Wind.

d. *ellipt.* Gone off, just going off. Also *fig.* fallen or falling asleep.

1791 'G. GAMBADO' *Ann. Horsem.* ix. (1809) 106 My horse ..was off with me in a jiffey. **1815** *Chron.* in *Ann. Reg.* 16 He raised himself up..and said almost inarticulately, 'I am off', and expired. **1822–56** DE QUINCEY *Confess.* (1862) 76 I'm off for the Red Sea. **1852** MRS. SMYTHIES *Bride Elect* xliv, Come, Geraldine, it is time to be off! **1861** H. KINGSLEY *Ravenshoe* xxxviii, He was as fast off as a top. **1865** DICKENS *Dr. Marigold's Prescript.* v. 32 'Why, you're talking in your sleep!'..'What was I talking about?'..'Greek, I think..but I was just off too'.

e. ***they're off*** (occas. ***they are off***): a colloq. phrase indicating that a race has started; ***to be off and running***: to be making good progress.

1833 *Mirror of Lit.* 27 July 59/2 *They are off!* 'No, no' — cries one jockey whose horse turned his tail to the others. **1846** 'SYLVANUS' *Pedestrian & Other Reminisc.* xxiv. 227 The horses are paraded, the flag is dropped—'they're off!' is repeated by twenty thousand tongues. **1872** B. JERROLD *London* viii. 74 *Clear the course!*... A flutter goes through the sea of heads on the Grand Stand... *They're off!* **1928** E. O'NEILL *Strange Interlude* VIII. 288 They're off!.. Navy and Washington are leading—Gordon's third. **1967** *Boston Herald* 1 Apr. 1/1 Although he has not announced it officially, Wallace appears to be off and running for the presidency. **1970** WILSON & MICHAELS tr. *Charrière's Papillon* vi. 211 We were off and running.

f. *ellipt.*, = off one's head (HEAD *sb.*[1] 34): (somewhat) crazy. *colloq.* or *dial.*

1866 W. GREGOR *Dial. Banffshire* in *Trans. Philol. Soc.* 215 *Aff, to be*, to be deranged; as, 'He wiz lang jummlet; bit he's *aff* athegeethir noo.' **1887** *Lantern* (New Orleans) 9 Apr. 3/2 Humor him as he was a little off. **1904** W. H. SMITH *Promoters* i. 8 I've sometimes thought you were a trifle visionary, but I never considered you seriously off. **1927** W. E. COLLINSON *Contemp. Eng.* 116 Mental debility finds adequate expression in a whole series: he's not all there, a bit off (the top), he's off his chump. **1975** B. WOOD *Killing Gift* II. i. 47 He was an old man, after all; perhaps he was just a little off... 'No, gentlemen, I'm not senile.'

g. In bad condition; wrong, abnormal, odd; *spec.* (*a*) of a horse or athlete: not in good condition or form; off-form; (*b*) of food: stale, sour, contaminated; (*c*) of social behaviour: unacceptable; ill-mannered; esp. in phr. (***it's***) ***a bit off.***

Not always clearly distinguishable from sense 2 c.

1846 *Spirit of Times* 18 Apr. 91/1 He had endurance and speed enough to make a good race in any crowd, when 'all right', but then, he [*sc.* a horse] was liable to be oftener 'off' than otherwise. **1868** H. WOODRUFF *Trotting Horse* xxxvi. 300 When a trotter wins with great ease,..it is assumed, not that the loser was 'off', but that the winner is greatly superior. **1902** G. H. LORIMER *Lett. Merchant* xvi. 231, I may be off in sizing this thing up, because it's a little out of my line. **1916** 'TAFFRAIL' *Pincher Martin* ix. 153 'S'pose I'd best be makin' a move, though,' he added ruefully. 'Bit orf, I calls it!' **1922** J. CANNAN *Misty Valley* 58 Audrey had taken them sailing, but she had upset the boat, and they had drifted down stream, clinging to the sail, saying that it was a bit off. Whereafter they would go down to the pier and knit jumpers. **1941** E. BOWEN *Look at Roses* 68 'Your caller sounded to me a bit off.' 'Oh, Mrs. Massey's had bad news. She..didn't feel well.' **1951** C. ARMSTRONG *Black-Eyed Stranger* (1952) xiv. 117 Ambielli's got principles. They are a little off, slightly out of whack, you know. **1952** R. FINLAYSON *Schooner came to Atia* 140 Meat that tasted 'off'. **1953** K. AMIS *Lucky Jim* v. 56 It was rather rude, all the same. I could see Mrs. Neddy thought it was a bit off. **1960** 'A. BURGESS' *Right to Answer* ii. 23 That tomato juice is a bit off. Been in the tin too long. **1966** 'W. COOPER' *Mem. New Man* II. v. 155 It *is* just a teentsy-weentsy bit off, isn't it, darling, not to let you know he was coming. **1974** *Listener* 24 Jan. 102/1 Something was a little off with the mechanism, so the feeder-belt chewed up the baggage in transit.

2. a. At a distance; distant. Often after a statement of the distance; also in AFAR *off*, FAR *off.*

α. *a* **1500** GREGORY *Chron.* in *Hist. Coll. Citizen Lond.* (Camden) 213 One come and sayd that she was ix myle of. **1526** TINDALE *Matt.* xxvi. 58 Peter folowed hym a farre of [*so 16th c. vv.*, **1611** off].

β. **1573** J. SANDFORD *Hours Recreat.* (1576) 213 Greete a redde man and a bearded woman three myles off. **1613** PURCHAS *Pilgrimage* (1614) 610 A little off runneth a River. **1638** SIR T. HERBERT *Trav.* (ed. 2) 14 We see the Cape or extreame point of Africk 12 leagues off. **1671** R. MONTAGUE in *Buccleuch MSS.* (Hist. MSS. Comm.) I. 501 These are projects a great way off. **1749** FIELDING *Tom Jones* xv. xii, A street or two off. **1874** DASENT *Half a Life* II. 173 We shall meet at Oxford in October, not much more than a month off. **1897** HALL CAINE *Christian* xi, Glory stood off from the looking-glass and looked.

b. *Naut.*

1697 DAMPIER *Voy.* I. 44 In the morning we descryed a Sail off at Sea. **1726** G. ROBERTS *Four Years Voy.* 26, I lay off at an Anchor.

c. *fig.* Distant or remote in fact, nature, character, feeling, thought, etc. *Obs.* or *arch.* (in Gr. Britain).

a **1555** RIDLEY *Wks.* 173 So far off is it that they do confirm this opinion of transubstantiation, that [etc.]. **1571** BUCHANAN *Detect. Mary* B iv, So far was it of that hys lodging and thynges..was prouidit for him..that he found nat any ane token toward him of a freindly minde. **1607** SHAKS. *Cor.* II. ii. 64 That's off, that's off. *a* **1641** BP. MOUNTAGU *Acts & Mon.* (1642) 280 Cæsar..was altogether off from thinking it probable. **1887** *Presbyt. Banner* (U.S.) Oct., The leader..is not merely off on the subject of future probation, but also with regard to the Lord's day.

3. a. Expressing separation from attachment, contact, or position *on*; as in *to break, cast, cut, put, shake, take off*, etc.

α. *c* **1000** *Ags. Gosp.* Matt. v. 30 ʒif þin swiðre hand þe aswice, aceorf hi of & awurp hi fram þe. *c* **1200** *Trin. Coll. Hom.* 139 He hit bad of acken. *c* **1290** *S. Eng. Leg.* I. 32/98 þo is heued was of i-smite. **1362** LANGL. *P. Pl.* A. v. 170 þenne Clement þe Cobelere caste of his cloke. *c* **1449** PECOCK *Repr.* I. x. 52 Y wole leie myn arme to be smyte of. **1535** STEWART *Cron. Scot.* III. 449 He..of his claithis suddantlie hes done. **1568** TURNER *Herbal* III. 54 Yelowe scales: whiche with a light occasion fall of. **1571** DIGGES *Pantom.* II. xix. O iij b, To cut of from any Trapezium..what part therof ye list. **1646** J. HALL *Horæ Vac.* 67 The taking of the Plumets of a clocke to make it goe in the better Order. **1703** MOXON *Mech. Exerc.* 59 Good Steel breaks short of all Gray.

β. **1382** WYCLIF *Matt.* xix. 7 To ʒeue a litil boke of forsakynge, and to leeue off [1388 leeue of]. *c* **1400** MAUNDEV. (Roxb.) viii. 31 Do off þi schone of þi fete. **1535** COVERDALE *Song Sol.* v. 3, I haue put off [**1611** off] my cote. **1568** TILNEY *Disc. Marriage* C iv b, [He] bit off his owne tongue. **1637** *Star Chamb. Decree* §30 In the putting off the knots. *a* **1756** MRS. HEYWOOD *New Present* (1771) 43 Let it stew..then strain it off. **1834** MEDWIN *Angler in Wales* II. 154 The ball..struck one of the metal buttons on the breast of my coat, and glanced off. **1886** *Manch. Exam.* 22 Feb. 6/1 The entire surface of a country..divided off into farmsteads.

b. *fig.* In quot. 1710 for 'off their hands'.

1576 FLEMING *Panopl. Epist.* 356 Let us shake off this slouthfulnesse. *a* **1600** MONTGOMERIE *Misc. Poems* xxiv. 75 Cast of thy comfort. **1710** STEELE *Tatler* No. 248 ⁋8 The common Design of Parents is to get their Girls off as well as they can. **1711** ADDISON *Spect.* No. 105 ⁋3 Will. laught this off at first as well as he could. **1777** WATSON *Philip II* (1839) 121 The people threw off the reserve which they had hitherto maintained.

c. with ellipsis of pa. pple. = *come, cut, fallen off*; esp. *put* or *taken off* as clothes; no longer *on.*

a **1425** *Cursor M.* 7211 (Trin.) [My strengþe] is he seide in my here: If hit were of, I were not þon No strenger þen anoþer mon. **1530** TINDALE *Pract. Popish Prelates* Wks. (1573) 350/1 When the ring was of, he commaunded to burye her. **1602** MARSTON *Antonio's Rev.* II. i. Wks. 1856 I. 90 Enter Balurdo with a beard, halfe of, halfe on. **1724** DE FOE *Mem. Cavalier* (1840) 211 With some of his clothes on, and some off. **1797** *Anecd. Ld. Chatham* (ed. 6) I. xiii. 253 The blossom was off, and the fruit was set. **1868** *Law Rep.* 3 C.P. 423 The horse had his bridle off and a nose-bag on.

d. *Theatr.* = OFF STAGE *adv.* Also *transf.* and *fig.*

1774 [see STAGE *sb.* 5]. **1775** T. CAMPBELL *Diary* 4 Mar. (1947) 44 The players..stood their ground for a long time —but were at length hissed off. *Ibid.*, Mr. Vernon attempted to speak, but he w[d] not be heared—still the cry was off, off. **1805** T. DIBDIN in G. Colman *John Bull* p. i, To whom, thus midway placed, I say, be kind, John Bull before, Oh, spare John Bull behind (*pointing off*.). **1836** DICKENS *Sk. Boz* 1st Ser. II. 255 'But you must take care you don't knock a wing down...' 'I shall fall with my head "off", and then I can't do any harm.' *c* **1863** T. TAYLOR *Ticket-of-Leave Man* I. 7 The Bellevue Tea Gardens,..ornamental orchestra and concert room... Music heard off. **1909** 'I. HAY' *Man's Man* vi. 83 Portentous trampings 'off' announced the return of the glee-party. **1923** *Referee* 12 Aug. 3/3 The leopardess..was heard to roar a good deal 'off',..making her only appearance [on the stage]—in a cage. **1924**, etc. [see NOISE *sb.* 3 c]. **1954** T. S. ELIOT *Confid. Clerk* I. 27 *Lady Elizabeth Mulhammer's voice off*: Just open that case, I want something out of it. **1965** *New Statesman* 7 May 739/1 The elaborate framework of posh voices off intoning fragments of letters.

e. Of an item of food: deleted from the menu; not available. *colloq.*

[**1870** D. J. KIRWAN *Palace & Hovel* x. 154 On 'off' days they have soup and thick gruel for breakfast.] **1902** FARMER & HENLEY *Slang* V. 89/2 'Chops is hoff' = 'there are no more chops to-day'. **1933** [see BAWL *v.* 3 c]. **1953** 'M. INNES' *Christmas at Candleshoe* ii. 24 The celerity with which the less unpalatable dishes are prone to be 'off' in English hotels. **1966** N. FREELING *Dresden Green* II. 123 Sorry sir, said the waitress in the teashop, the pudding's *off*. We can do you a nice ice-cream though. **1974** D. CHANTLER *Man who Followed* II. 60 Tell the waiters..the Tutti-Frutti is off.

4. a. So as to interrupt continuity or cause discontinuance; as in ***break off, leave off, declare off***, etc.

α. *c* **1340–** [see BREAK *v.* 54]. **1387** TREVISA *Higden* (Rolls) VII. 377 Leve of [L. *Desiste*], Alwyn, wiþ þy good wille. *c* **1475** *Rauf Coilȝear* 172 Is nane sa gude as leif of, and mak na mair stryfe. **1596** SPENSER *F.Q.* VI. v. 36 His deuotion..breaking of.

β. **1567** MAPLET *Gr. Forest* 31 b, It will soone wax barraine, and leave off fruit bearing. **1657** R. LIGON *Barbadoes* (1673) 43 Upon Saturday..they break off work sooner by an hour. **1818** *Sporting Mag.* III. 91 The match went off, and all bets were declared void. **1819** *Metropolis* II. 69 The Duke has declared off, and the wounded lover does not seem to be anxious to make his proposals of marriage. **1892** *Bookman* Oct. 27/2 Zola began by being an idealist. He has not left off being one. *Mod.* To cut off supplies; to turn the water or gas off.

b. Discontinued, stopped, given up; no longer in operation or going on.

1752 MRS. LENNOX *Fem. Quix.* I. v, His illness having been only a violent head-ache,..being now quite off. **1760** R. HEBER *Horse Matches* ix. p. xxv, Match off, by consent. **1785** MRS. FLETCHER in *Wesley's Serm.* lvii. III. 12, Wks. 1811 IX. 36 His fever seemed quite off. **1882** *Daily News* 15 Aug. 2/1 He understood that the whole negotiation was now off. **1901** *Scotsman* 12 Mar. 5/4 When football is 'off' and cricket not yet 'on'. *Mod.* The gas is off at the meter. The water has been off for some hours.

c. *transf.* Of a person: Disengaged, done ***with.***

1710 STEELE *Tatler* No. 223 ⁋5 A Youth married under Fourteen Years old may be off if he pleases when he comes to that Age. **1818** SCOTT '*Old Song*' in *Br. Lamm.* xxix, It is best to be off wi' the old love, Before you be on wi' the new.

d. Away or free from one's work, school, service, etc.

1861 J. O'NEIL *Diary* 1 Apr. in J. Burnett *Useful Toil* (1974) I. 78 At Low Moor there is a great many off. There is above a hundred looms standing. **1882** J. D. MCCABE *New York* 384 Then begins five hours' patrol..after which he is 'off'. **1883**, etc. [see *day off* s.v. DAY *sb.* 19]. **1885**, etc. [see NIGHT *sb.* 5 a]. **1916** B. RUCK *Girls at his Billet* xviii. 242, I am sure your auntie..would be quite agreeable to letting us have the afternoon off for the ceremony. **1940** F. SARGESON *Man & Wife* (1944) 21 Of course Sally wasn't off for long. And they gave her a rise. **1970** 'D. HALLIDAY' *Dolly & Cookie Bird* v. 74, I was..bedding the avocados in lettuce. Anne-Marie was off but Helmuth did the last stages. *Ibid.* viii. 128 It was Anne-Marie's afternoon off.

5. a. So as to exhaust or finish; so as to leave none; to the end; entirely, completely, to a finish; as ***to clear off, drink off, pay off, polish off, work off.***

c **1440** *St. John* 228 in Horstmann *Altengl. Leg.* (1881) 471 þou..saynede þe coppe swetely and suppede it off syne. **1567** MAPLET *Gr. Forest* 47 Socrates..compelled of malicious Iudges to take ye Cup,..and so to drink it off. **1660** MARVELL *Corr.* Wks. 1872–5 II. 18 Some seauenteen shipps to be payd of. **1818** CRUISE *Digest* (ed. 2) II. 167 Contented to pay off the mortgage. **1883** GILMOUR *Mongols* xvii. 201 No set form of liturgy to be got off by heart and repeated. **1890** G. A. SMITH *Isaiah* II. xii. 202 We do not..kill them off by gladiatorial combats. **1897** *Westm. Gaz.* 20 July 7/2 These two..will have to shoot off the tie for the Bronze Medal. **1900** *Ibid.* 13 Dec. 2/3 What is known amongst breeders as 'feeding off' for table poultry is a thriving industry.

b. Finished, worked off; done with work.

1683 MOXON *Mech. Exerc., Printing* 385 A Press-man usually says, I am off, meaning he has Wrought off his Token, his Heap, his Form. **1707** HEARNE *Collect.* 26 Aug. (O.H.S.) II. 36 When ye Text of Livy is off I will consider.

6. a. In the way of abatement, diminution, or decay; as in ***to fall off, cool off, go off***; also, ***to be off.***

1632 *Star Chamb. Cases* (Camden) 121 Judgment was stayed and the Costes taken off. **1797** *Monthly Mag.* III. 501 Out of every thousand men, 28 die off annually. **1826** *Examiner* 695/1 The novelty had gone off a little. **1862** LOWELL *Biglow P.* Poems 1890 II. 260 They'll cool off when they come to understand. **1893** *National Observer* 7 Oct. 536/1 The place seemed to have gone off a good deal.

b. Of stocks, shares, etc.: lower in value or price (by a specified amount or numbered points).

1929 *Times* 30 Oct. 14/1 Duke Power 'opened' at 130 off 39½ points, Newhaven Railway at 90 off 18. **1931** *Daily Express* 21 Sept. 14/4 Japanese bonds were only slightly off. **1964** *Financial Times* 12 Mar. 21/5 Belfast Ropework were 6d off to 35s 6d. **1977** *Times* 19 Nov. 17/5 By the close the *FT* Index was just 0·5 off at 480·5.

c. with ellipsis of *taken.* Of retail commodities: reduced in price by a specified amount.

1965 *New Statesman* 9 Apr. 562/1 Don't be put off by the fact that both packets also say '3d off'. **1966** 'J. ASHFORD' *Consider Evidence* i. 5 Tomato soup was being sold at threepence a tin off. **1968** 'J. LE CARRÉ' *Small Town in Germany* v. 71 Don't matter what you fancy: radios, dish-washers, cars; he'll get you a bit off, like.

7. In all senses, *off* may be followed by *from*; formerly, and still *colloq.* and *dial.* by *of*.

a. 1526 TINDALE *Matt.* viii. 30 A good waye off from them. **1542** BOORDE *Dyetary* viii. (1870) 246 Stand or syt a good wayе of from the fyre. **1697** DAMPIER *Voy.* I. 109 The wind is commonly off from the Land. **1871** CARLYLE in *Mrs. C.'s Lett.* III. 200 She wished to be off from the July bargain.
b. 1593 SHAKS. *2 Hen. VI*, II. i. 96 A fall off of a Tree. **1667** MARVELL *Corr.* Wks. 1872–5 II. 224 The Lords and we cannot yet get off of the difficultyes risen betwixt us. **1678** BUNYAN *Pilgr.* I. 49 About a furlong off of the Porters Lodge. **1712** STEELE *Spect.* No. 306 ¶6, I could not keep my Eyes off of her. **1775** P. OLIVER in *T. Hutchinson's Diary* 7 Dec. I. 581 A Rebell Pirate.. taken.. off of Cape Ann. **1824** J. WIGHT *Mornings at Bow St.* 21 Two young men.. were charged by a watchman with having 'bother'd him on his *bate*,' and refused to 'go along off of it when he *tould* 'em.' **1843** T. C. HALIBURTON *Attaché* 1st Ser. II. xii. 210 The groom has stole her oats, forgot to give her water, and let her make a supper sometimes off of her nasty, mouldy, filthy beddin'. **1875** P. BROOKS *New Starts in Life* viii. 129 If you could have filled his pockets with gold, and feasted his hunger off of silver dishes. **1884** 'MARK TWAIN' *Huck. Finn* vi. 32 I'd borrow two or three dollars off of the judge for him. *a* **1922** T. S. ELIOT *Waste Land Drafts* (1971) 5 The reputation the place gets, off of a few barflies. **1962** F. NORMAN *Guntz* i. 15, I got hold of this very very old typewriter off of a friend of mine. *Ibid.* iii. 24 After his secretary had picked him off of the floor he got on the blower to his accounts department. **1965** T. PARKER *Five Women* i. 45 They'll thieve off-of anyone and jump in bed with anyone. **1974** J. STUBBS *Painted Face* xxiii. 284 Get off of me, will you, sir?

II. In phrases and locutions.

8. *Off* is used idiomatically with many verbs, as BUY, COME, DASH, GET, GO, LOOK, MARK, PALM, PASS, RATTLE, SHOW, TAKE, etc. q.v.

9. a. Used with ellipsis of *come, go, take*, etc., so as itself to function as a vb. ***off with*** = take or put off.

c **1205** LAY. 5084 Awei he warp his gode breond: & of mid þere burne. **14..** W. PARIS *Cristine* 295 in Horstmann *Altengl. Leg.* (1878) 187 Hire hede shalle ofe fulle sekyrly To morne. **1611** SHAKS. *Wint. T.* II. iii. 63 Ile off, But first, Ile do my errand. **1617** RICH *Irish Hubbub* (1623) 24 He that pledgeth must likewise off with his cap. **1634** SIR T. HERBERT *Trav.* 111 If hee returned without victory, hee knew his head should off. **1646** N. LOCKYER *Serm.* 19, I cannot hand off nor heart off. **1753** FOOTE *Eng. in Paris* II. Wks. 1799 I. 52 We'll off in a post-chaise directly. *Mod. vulgar colloq.* He off and bought another.

b. esp. in imperative phrases. ***off!*** = stand off! be off! ***off with you!*** = be off!

1594 SHAKS. *Rich. III*, v. iii. 344 Off with his sonne George's head. **1601** —— *All's Well* I. i. 168 Off with 't while 'tis vendible. **1717** E. SMITH *Phædra* v. 54 Off, or I fly for ever from thy sight. **1809** MALKIN *Gil Blas* II. vii. ¶1 Off with you! and do not return. **1822** BYRON *Vis. Judgm.* xciii, Some cried 'Off, off!' As at a farce. **1877** SPURGEON *Serm.* XXIII. 402 Off with your caps and throw them up and cry 'Hurrah!'

10. ***right off, straight off***: straightway, forthwith, immediately. See RIGHT, STRAIGHT.

11. Subjoined to *well, ill, better, worse, badly, comfortably*, and similar advbs., and after *how* ('How are they off?'), *off* has the force of '-circumstanced', '-conditioned', esp. as regards command of the means of life; ***well off***, in good circumstances, etc. Rarely *attrib.* or as *adj.*

This prob. arose from the phrase *come off* (COME *v.* 61 f). One who has 'come well out' of a doubtful affair is said to be 'well out' of it; so one who has 'come well off' from (or in) a struggle may be said to be 'well off'; cf. esp. quots. 1733–62. The most common use may be explained as 'that has come off, or fared (well or ill)', in the battle of life.

1733 SWIFT *Apology*, Since I 'scap'd being made a scoff, I think I'm very fairly off. **1741** RICHARDSON *Pamela* II. 251 Let me sit down, Miss, anywhere.. for I have been sadly off. **1762** GOLDSM. *Cit. W.* lxxxviii, Marriage is at present so much out of fashion, that a lady is very well off, who can get any husband at all. **1776** C. LEE in Sparks *Corr. Amer. Rev.* (1853) II. 485 How are you off in the article of intrenching tools? **1845** MOZLEY *Laud* Ess. (1892) I. 179 The clergy.. had lost the advantages of obits [etc.], and were miserably off. **1851** H. MAYO *Pop. Superst.* (ed. 2) 186 The earth is the best off. **1865** DICKENS *Mut. Fr.* IV. xii, I am in another way of business. And I am rather better off. **1873** MRS. OLIPHANT *Innocent* III. xxi. 351 He was not well enough off to marry. **1884** H. SPENCER in *Contemp. Rev.* June 772 While to the well-off the exaction means loss of luxuries, to the ill-off it means loss of necessaries. **1884** G. ALLEN *Philistia* III. 161 They are very badly off, poor people. **1888** J. PAYN in *Illustr. Lond. News* 10 Mar. 236/1 A well-known and well-off man of letters.

12. ***either off or on***, either one way or another, in any way. ***neither off nor on***, without reference, irrelevant (*to*): cf. 'neither here nor there'; irresolute, fickle. See also OFF AND ON.

1549 LATIMER *6th Serm. bef. Edw. VI* (Arb.) 159 It was neyther of nor on, to that that Paule sayed.

13. Used with a preceding numeral to represent a quantity in production or manufacture, esp. ***one off*** (see ONE 30 b).

1934, etc. [see ONE 30 b]. **1947** CROWTHER & WHIDDINGTON *Science at War* 49 Manufacturers found it very difficult to give up mass production, in order to make the 200 or so sets 'off'. **1970** *Cabinet Maker & Retail Furnisher* 30 Oct. 205/2 Without barrier coats mould breakdown can start after 60 units off. **1973** *Physics Bull.* Apr. 238/2 (Advt.), Kienzle printers. 6 off, surplus to manufacturing requirements.

B. *prep.*

I. Of motion or direction.

1. a. Of removal from a position *on, attached to*, or *in contact with* (anything): Away from, down from, up from, so as no longer to lie, rest, or lean on.

α. *a* **855** *O.E. Chron.* an. 797 Her Romane.. hine of his setle afliemdon. *c* **1200** *Trin. Coll. Hom.* 201 We habbeð don of us þe ealde man. *c* **1205** LAY. 30802 þat maiden.. droh of hire uingre An of hire ringe. *a* **1300** *Cursor M.* 15024 (Cott.) Branches þai brak o [*Gött., etc.* of] bogh. **1398** TREVISA *Barth. De P.R.* XVII. i. (1495) 592 Leues fall of trees in wynter tyme. *c* **1440** *Generydes* 2798 Of his hors he felle vppon the playn. **1642** tr. *Perkins' Prof. Bk.* iii. §209. 93 To deliver seisin of land by force off a feoffment is to remove all persons of the land. **1665** MARVELL *Corr.* Wks. 1872–5 II. 184 Our navy is speeding to chase the Dutch again of our seas.

β. *c* **1400** MAUNDEV. (Roxb.) ii. 6 Foure graynes of þe same tree þat his fader ete þe appel off. *Ibid.* vi. 20 He.. takes þe ryng off his fynger. **1568** GRAFTON *Chron.* II. 89 His kerchefe was pulled off his head. **1596** SHAKS. *Tam. Shr.* IV. i. 80 How she waded through the durt to plucke him off me. **1600** —— *A.Y.L.* I. iii. 16, I could shake them off my coate. **1670** NARBOROUGH in *Acc. Sev. Late Voy.* I. (1711) 84 And gathered several green Apples off the Trees. **1711** ADDISON *Spect.* No. 159 ¶7 Take thine Eyes off the Bridge, said he. **1743** H. WALPOLE *Lett.* (1857) I. 226 A man falling off a ladder. **1873** KINGSLEY *Prose Idylls* 129 The sheep have been driven off the land below. **1881** KEENE *Six Months in Meccah* vi. 158, I came across an object that nearly brought me off my beast.

b. *fig.* From resting, depending, determining, etc. upon. *off one's* HANDS, *one's* HEAD: see the sbs.

α. *c* **1380** WYCLIF *Wks.* (1880) 291 Vnderstond, ȝe kingis; and schaak of ȝou rudenesse, ȝe þat jugen londis.
β. **1601** SHAKS. *All's Well* II. iii. 250 Thou hast a sonne shall take this disgrace off me. **1724** DE FOE *Mem. Cavalier* (1840) 264, I had persuaded him off that. **1737** BRACKEN *Farriery Impr.* (1757) II. 52 If we took such Foals off their Dams the first Week they were dropt. **1742** FIELDING *J. Andrews* IV. iii, He hath taken several poor off our hands. **1809** MALKIN *Gil Blas* I. ii. ¶3 An honest jockey who would take it [my mule] off my hands. **1889** J. S. WINTER *Mrs. Bob* (1891) 152 That woman must be going off her head. **1894** DOYLE *Mem. S. Holmes* 215, I have been off my head ever since the blow fell.

2. Of source: From the hands, charge, or possession of; esp. with *take, buy, borrow, hire*, and the like. Also expressed by FROM. Cf. OF.

1535 COVERDALE *2 Chron.* xxxv. 11 And they kylled the Passeouer, and the prestes toke it off their handes, and sprenkled it. **1669** STURMY *Mariner's Mag.* I. 33 These Lines are taken off a Scale, that is divided into 20 parts to an Inch. *Ibid.* 60 Take off your Scale of Equal Parts with your Compasses 169. **1753** HOGARTH *Anal. Beauty* x. 108 It was drawn from a plaster-of-Paris figure cast off nature. **1885** *Act 48 & 49 Vict.* c. 41 §9 (3) A grand jury may.. present any sum, to be raised off the county at large.. for the purpose. **1891** C. JAMES *Rom. Rigmarole* 36 A villager had come.. to know whether Blincoe 'would take a goose off him'. **1897** *Daily News* 1 June 3/5 She admitted borrowing the 1*l.* off the plaintiff.

3. Of material or substance: with *dine, eat*, etc.

1815 W. H. IRELAND *Scribbleomania* 305 He always.. eats a supper off pork steaks, nearly raw. **1828** P. CUNNINGHAM *N.S. Wales* (ed. 3) II. 213 Each day the convict sits down to dinner off either beef, pork, or plum-pudding. **1861** G. MEREDITH *Evan Harrington* viii, An old gentleman who had dined there.. four days in the week, off dishes dedicated to the particular days.

4. Of deduction, or abatement: From.

1833 ALISON *Europe* (1849) I. iii. §15. 259 The sums.. which she saved off her allowance. *Mod.* To get something taken off the price.

II. Of position.

5. a. Away from being on; not on; *esp.* no longer on.

†***off the stones***, off the city pavement, out of the town. [*c* **1330** R. BRUNNE *Chron.* (1810) 141 If I were of lond, þe werre suld sone bigynne.] **1688** R. HOLME *Armoury* III. 235/1 It is reported of the Spanish Dominions that the Sun is never off some part of it. **1759** BROWN *Compl. Farmer* 112 As soon as the dew is off the ground. **1797** MRS. RADCLIFFE *Italian* xii, They are all off the bridge now. *a* **1845** HOOD *Ode imitated fr. Horace*, Not thus the city streamlets flow; They make no music as they go, Tho' never 'off the stones'. **1870** *Gd. Words* 133/2 You can scarcely find footing when once off the beaten road.

b. *fig.* Of state, or condition: (*a*) Away from (something normal or usual). (*b*) Not occupied with, engaged in, or bent upon; disengaged from; also, having lost interest in; averse to; ***off form***: in bad form; ***off one's game***: see GAME *sb.* 6 f. See also OFF DUTY *phr.*

1681 LUTTRELL *Brief Rel.* (1857) I. 67 The grand jury for Middlesex were about finding a bill against the Kings guards as rioters, but they are now off it. **1682-** [see GUARD *sb.* 5 b]. **1699** DAMPIER *Voy.* II. I. 166 Finding it to be nought, he would have been off his Bargain. **1795** WOLCOTT (P. Pindar) *Pindariana* Wks. 1812 IV. 111, I am off my feeding. **1807** SCOTT *Let.* 14 Mar. (1932) I. 359 This principle that the pursuers are entitled to have their time compensated when they were *bona fide* off work. **1816-** [see FEED *sb.* 1 b]. **1827** *Examiner* 187/2 She was scolding him, because he was off work. **1853** MRS. GASKELL *Cranford* iv. 74, I had a note to say her mistress was 'very low and sadly off her food'. **1889** E. DOWSON *Let.* 16 Nov. (1967) 117 You are perhaps right in being 'off' Gortsachoff's though the cooking is less deleterious than Pinolis. **1909** W. B. YEATS *Let.* 10 Dec. (1954) 544 She seemed as eager as ever about the play. I had thought she was off it. **1910** *Ibid.* 8 Jan. 546, I have not touched the long play but will come to it fresh from being so long off it. **1912** C. MATHEWSON *Pitching in a Pinch* vii. 142 The Chicago pitchers were away off form in the series. **1913** C. MACKENZIE *Sinister St.* I. II. xviii. 452 He said he was 'off girls' at the moment. **1929** E. BOWEN *Last Sept.* xxiv. 308 'What about their bungalow?' 'Oh, that was just an idea; they are quite off it.' **1973** 'H. CARMICHAEL' *Too Late for Tears* xiii. 153 I'm off my food, that's all.

6. a. Distant from (*lit.* and *fig.*).

a **1627** MIDDLETON *Widow* III. ii, Two mile off this place. **1705** ADDISON *Italy* 375 About Two Miles off this Town. **1863** GEO. ELIOT *Romola* xiv, He caught sight of Tessa, only two yards off him. **1885** HOWELLS *Silas Lapham* (1891) I. 73 White, or a little off white.

b. *Naut.* To seaward of; opposite or abreast of to seaward; also, away from (the wind): see WIND. See also OFF-SHORE.

1669 STURMY *Mariner's Mag.* IV. 138 Ready to give his best Judgement of his Distance off the Shore. **1707** W. FUNNELL *Voy. round World* 126 Off it lie two Rocks or small Islands. **1726** G. ROBERTS *Four Years Voy.* 3 The Stagg Rocks off the Lizard. **1776** GIBBON *Decl. & F.* xiii. (1827) I. 426 The fleet.. had been stationed off the Isle of Wight. **1813** *Examiner* 4 Jan. 6/1 The enemy keeping two points off the wind. **1879** FROUDE *Cæsar* xvi. 256 A sea battle.. was fought off the eastern promontory of the Bay of Quiberon.

7. *ellipt.* Opening or turning out of.

1845 MRS. CARLYLE *Lett.* I. 312 In Mary's little room (off my uncle's). **1851** H. MAYHEW *Lond. Labour* II. 225 (Hoppe) Watling-street, Bow-lane, Old-change, and other thoroughfares off Cheapside and Cornhill. **1860** *All Year Round* No. 66. 372 In a small street off one of the west-central squares.

8. from off: = sense 1, *off from* (A. 7).

a **1425** *Cursor M.* 25596 (Fairf.) þen ihesus þou was tane fra of þe crosse in flesshe & bane. **1590** SPENSER *F.Q.* III. iii. 43 Shall.. quite from off the earth their memory be raste? **1595** SHAKS. *John* I. i. 145 Would I might neuer stirre from off this place. **1768** STERNE *Sent. Journ.* (1778) I. 135 (*Amiens*) Wiping them [tears] away from off the cheeks of the first and fairest of women. **1819** BYRON *Juan* II. lxxxviii, As if to win a part from off the weight He saw increasing on his father's heart. **1845** AYTOUN *Bon Gaultier Ball.* 90 He lighted down from off his steed.

9. In combs. with *the* and a sb., used *attrib.* or as *adj.*, as **off-the-course**, occurring away from a race-course; **off-the-face**, of a hat: not covering or shading any part of the face; **off-the-job**, (*a*) done or happening away from one's work; (*b*) unemployed; **off-the-rack** = *off-the-peg*; **off-the-road**, located, operated, or occurring away from roads; **off-the-shelf**, obtained from stock; ready-made; also *fig.* Also ***off-the-cuff, off-the-map, off-the-peg, off-the-shoulder***; see these sbs.

1961 *Times* 2 June 22/2 She makes a tremendous off-the-course bet. **1908** *Sears, Roebuck Catal.* 1036/2 Pretty 'off the face' hat for children. **1953** *News Chron.* 2 June 1/4 The Queen Mother, in a white feathered gown and off-the-face white hat. **1962** *Guardian* 3 Oct. 8/2 Off-the-job training of men over 25 for semi-skilled work. **1967** *Time* 21 July 51 Some sort of new company-financed plan enabling an off-the-job worker to maintain 'his normal living standard' for up to a year. **1970** *Times* 9 Feb. 19 The off-the-job study is essential because it removes the pressures and distractions of the shop-floor. **1970** *Capital Times* (Madison, Wisconsin) 21 Feb. (Green Sheet Sect.) 4/2 An off-the-rack mod suit. **1974** H. WAUGH *Parrish for Defence* (1975) xxxvii. 173 The dress wasn't made for it [*sc.* her figure]. That was the trouble with off-the-rack clothes. **1975** 'A. THACKERAY' *One Way Ticket* I. 24 He wore off-the-rack clothes. **1962** *Guardian* 4 Oct. 14/2 Off-the-road training grounds for learner drivers. **1973** *Country Life* 18 Oct. 1172/2 Another type of off-the-road transport is the all-terrain vehicle, or ATV. **1966** *Electronics* 17 Oct. 38 The fact that its roll in a normal ocean is only 1° means that off-the-shelf, land-rated equipment can be used. **1971** *Engineering* Apr. 88 (Advt.), No chance of errors and 'off-the-shelf' service.

C. *adj.* [The *adv.* used *attrib.*]

(Arising apparently from the dropping of the hyphen in an adverbial combination: thus *off-side, off side*. See OFF- 4.)

1. a. Situated farther off, more distant, farther, far.

1856 MRS. CARLYLE *Lett.* II. 286 To leap from the top of the wall, which was only high on the off-side. *Mod. Newspr.* It is on the 'off' side of the spectator.

b. *Naut.* Farther from the shore; seaward.

1666 *Lond. Gaz.* No. 66/4 The *Lilly* Fregat,.. then in the off-gage of her station, near this Coast. **1719** DE FOE *Crusoe* II. xii, Our men.. were at work.. on the off side. **1726** SHELVOCKE *Voy. round World* 207 It was happy for us that our masts fell all over the off side. **1745** *Lond. Mag.* 397 Whilst I had to do with this Ship, the largest of all got on my Off-Bow, put me between two Fires.

2. *spec.* **a.** Of horses and vehicles: opposed to the *near* side, on which the driver walks, the rider mounts, and the passenger enters a vehicle. Hence ***off horse*** (of a pair), ***off foot, lead, leader, leg, ox*** (also *fig.*, a clumsy or stubborn person), ***wheel, wheeler***, etc. (Often hyphened.)

1675 *Lond. Gaz.* No. 1002/4 A black stone Horse, four years old, roweld for a lameness behind on the off-side. **1708** *Ibid.* No. 4477/4 His off-Knee is broke. **1721** *Ibid.* No. 5929/3 His Off Foot behind white. **1764** *Museum Rusticum* II. xiv. 52 To drive the cart so as the off-wheel should go in the same tract that the near wheel went in before. **1789** *Trans. Soc. Arts* VII. 70 Enables the off-horse.. to walk in the furrow. **1800** *Gentl. Mag.* I. 167 The [Mamelûke] rider always mounts on the off side of the horse. **1807** *Balance* (Hudson, N.Y.) 25 Aug. 267 (Th.), We behold a clumsy, awkward off ox trying the tricks of a kitten. **1823** J. F. COOPER *Pioneers* I. iv. 51, I knew just the spot where to touch the off-leader. **1842** SYD. SMITH *Let. Locking in on Railways* Wks. 1859 II. 234/1, I know very well the danger of getting out on the off-side. **1848** J. R. LOWELL *Biglow Papers* 1st Ser. 90 Ez to the answerin' o' questions, I'm an off ox at bein' druv. **1849** DE QUINCEY *Eng. Mailcoach* Wks.

1862 IV. 339 With the haunch of our near leader we had struck the off-wheel. **1884** E. L. ANDERSON *Mod. Horsemanship* I. ii. 8 The rider should practise mounting and dismounting upon the right or off side of the horse, as well as upon the usual side. **1887** E. CUSTER *Tenting on Plains* xii. 354 The old reliability of a mule-team is the off-wheeler. **1890** KIPLING *Barrack-Room Ballads* (1892) 35 Two's off-lead 'e answered to the name o' *Snarleyow*. **1894** DOYLE *Mem. S. Holmes* 25 Silver Blaze with his white forehead and his mottled off fore leg. **1910** J. HART *Vigilante Girl* x. 140 An iron 'jockey-stick' ran from the near leader's hames to the off-leader's bit. **1915** *Dialect Notes* IV. 209 My grandfather was always an off-ox. **1933** *Daily Progress* (Charlottesville, Va.) 1 Apr. 4/3, I don't know him from Adam's (or God's) off-ox.

b. *Cricket.* Applied to that side of the wicket, or of the field, opposite to that on which the batsman stands (*i.e.* in the case of right-hand batting, the side on the right of the wicket-keeper); also of a ball or hit on this side, or a batsman who hits the ball in this direction; **off-cutter**, a cutter (see CUTTER *sb.*[1] 5 b (*b*)) that turns from the off side.

1773 in G. B. Buckley *Fresh Light on 18th Cent. Cricket* (1935) 61 Having run a considerable number of notches from off-strokes. **1816** W. LAMBERT *Instr. & Rules Cricket* 31 Wide Bowling..should be directed at the off side of the wicket. **1836** *New Sporting Mag.* July 195 Crossing the leg over at off-balls is another rule that I should like to see more men adopt. *Ibid.*, The mode of handling the bat, for 'On hitting' must be similar to what is requisite for 'Off hitting'. **1836** E. JESSE *Angler's Rambles* 298 His off-hits between point and slip, were the admiration of the club. **1850** 'BAT' *Crick. Man.* 43 The long-stop is frequently obliged to cover many slips from the bat, both to the leg and off side. **1851** J. PYCROFT *Cricket Field* vii. 151 A good off-hitter should send the ball according to its pitch, not to one point only, but to three or four. **1854** *Ibid.* (ed. 2) 117 A bat brought forward from the centre stump to a ball Off or to leg, must..form an angle sufficient to make Off or On hits. **1884** I. BLIGH in *Lillywhite's Cricket Ann.* 3 Some of his far-pitched balls on the off side. **1885** *J. Lillywhite's Cricketers' Compan.* 91 Mr. W. H. Woodhouse..a brilliant off-hitter. **1888** A. G. STEEL in Steel & Lyttelton *Cricket* iii. 183 Left-handed batsmen are notoriously strong and powerful in their off hitting. **1895** H. G. HUTCHINSON *P. Steele* i. 28 This off-ball Peter..drove..so hard..that [etc.]. **1900** P. F. WARNER *Cricket in Many Climes* 182 Blanckenberg..made some very good off-side strokes. **1904** F. C. HOLLAND *Cricket* 9 Nearly all off strokes can be classed under one of the four principal hits—the off drive, the cut drive, the square cut, and the late cut. **1955** *Times* 5 July 4/2 Singh..was making his off-cutters seem more sinister than one feels they really were. **1956** R. ALSTON *Test Commentary* xiii. 114 Benaud packed the off-side. **1966** [see CUTTER *sb.*[1] 5 b].

c. ***off-verse*** [tr. G. *Abvers*]: the second half-line of a line of Old English verse. Cf. *on-verse* (ON *a.* 1 b).

1935 K. MALONE in *ELH* II. 291 The chief function of alliteration in OE poetry is that of binding together the two halves (i.e. the on- and off-verses) of the so-called long line. **1953** [see ICTUS 1]. **1953** *Speculum* XXVIII. 451 In the on-verse position *Beówulf* 2795 has *Wuldorcyninge* and in the off-verse position *eorþ-*, *hēah- þeódcyninges*, also *Frís-cyninge*, and *sǣ-cyninga*. **1963** F. P. MAGOUN in Brown & Foote *Early Eng. & Norse Stud.* 134 These verses tend to be used as off-verses. **1970** *Rev. Eng. Stud.* XXI. 134 The Anglo-Saxon poets apparently preferred beginning new clauses with the off-verse.

3. a. Lying off from, situated aside from, leading out of the main part. Cf. OFF *prep.* 7. See OFF- 4, in precisely the same sense.

1851 MAYHEW *Lond. Labour* II. 201/1 The 'off' parts of St. Paul's Church-yard. *Ibid.* 423/2 Friar-street is one of the smaller off thoroughfares. **1897** W. H. THORNTON *Remin.* i. 10, I rode with him one day to his off farm..and bought my first horse.

b. ***off chance***, ***off-chance***, a contingency out of the probable course; a remote chance, a by-chance.

1861 WHYTE MELVILLE *Good for Nothing* I. 109 To be sure, there is the off-chance of a settlement by a violent death. **1875** *Times* 2 July, It is always a very off-chance whether an officer..may in quiet times have the slightest opportunity of finding his abilities roughly tested. **1893** STEVENSON *Beach of Falesá* 144, I thought there was an off-chance he might go back on the whole idea.

4. a. Said of a day, evening, season, etc., when one is 'off work', or when the ordinary work, business, or course of affairs is suspended, or does not take place or occur. Also said of a shorter period of time to denote an interval of leisure or relaxation, and of a day, night, etc., when one does not feel fit or when one's performance is not up to the usual standard. The precise meaning depends on the context. Also *transf.* (Sometimes hyphened.)

1826 F. REYNOLDS *Life & Times* I. iv. 151 On Mrs. Siddons's nights, Mr. Harris (being sure of an over-flow from Drury-lane,) only put up his weakest bills, reserving the strongest for his *off nights*. **1843** *Knickerbocker* XXII. 325 After an 'off night' when I was allowed to stay in town. **1848** THACKERAY *Van. Fair* ix, It was with a team of these very horses, on an off-day, that Miss Sharp was brought to the Hall. **1875** *All Year Round* 3 Apr. 23/1 That estimable lady..had arranged those meetings on the quiet off-evenings. **1876** 'MARK TWAIN' *Old Times Mississippi* 25 The 'off-watch' was just turning in, and I heard some brutal laughter from them. **1880** MISS BRADDON *Just as I am* xxxv, Driving..to Blatchmardean on the off days. **1880** *Inter-Ocean* (Chicago) 28 May 8/3 Peters had an 'off' day. **1882** *Garden* 18 Mar. 182/1 Last year..being what we here call the 'off year' for Apples. **1897** *Manch. Guard.* 16 Oct., That in future all such meetings be held on 'off days' in preference to 'market days'. **1899** J. PENNELL in *Fortn. Rev.* LXV. 123 This has been an off, a profitless, year in practical cycle construction. **1905** G. B. SHAW *Let.* 3 Jan. (1972) II. 487, I had quiet literary offnights at the New Shakespear Society under F. J. Furnival, and breezy literary offnights at the Browning Society. **1908** *Sketch* 11 Sept. 340/2 Rhodes had an 'off-day' and could do nothing. **1913** A. G. BRADLEY *Other Days* v. 161 On the rare off-days [we] raided such crows and magpies' nests as we could find. **1928** *Weekly Dispatch* 18 Mar. 2/4 He'd never have picked up that skill in the Lagos Lagoon in the few off-watches he'd get from a branch-boat. **1929** *Star* 21 Aug. 5/2 It was certainly Elder's off-night. He was not feeling in the best of form. **1930** F. E. BAILY *It won't do any Harm* xiii. 260 You happened to ask me when I was in what I call an off-moment. **1932** E. E. REYNOLDS *Nansen* i. 9. There was plenty of fun as well as hard work. One account of an off-hour is worth extracting as illustrating Nansen's geniality in whatever company he might find himself. **1946** R. LEHMANN *Gipsy's Baby* 28 She was having a bit of an off-day, unfortunately. **1959** *Manch. Guardian* 24 July 4/2 Tolstoy or Balzac in an off-moment might be almost anyone. **1959** T. GRIFFITH *Waist-High Culture* (1960) 169 Such doubts arise in us all, at least on our off days. **1969** *Guardian* 21 Aug. 3/6 On off-days he tends his private camellias and on off-nights listens to Mozart and The Three B's. **1974** *Melody Maker* 13 Apr. 48 Everyone has their off nights and so the one who's feeling better helps the other one. **1976** *National Observer* (U.S.) 17 Jan. 19/2 Dr. Moskowitz is passionate about reading, theater, music, and writing, which is her newest off-hours activity.

b. ***off year***, in the U.S., a year in which there is a Congressional election but no Presidential election. Also *attrib.*

1873 B. A. HINSDALE *Let.* 17 Oct. in *Garfield-Hinsdale Lett.* (1949) 247 About one half is lost because it is the 'off year' in politics. **1906** *N.Y. Even. Post* 5 Nov. 4 In this off-year election. **1950** *Manch. Guardian Weekly* 24 Aug. 15 A full-dress State election in an 'off-year', that is a year when there is no Presidential election. **1972** *Times* 27 Dec. 5/7 Soon after he succeeded to the Presidency the Republicans, in the off-year elections of 1946, won both Houses of Congress.

5. In reference to the sale of excisable liquors: Short for 'off the premises': see OFF LICENCE, OFF-SALE.

6. Corresponding to or producing the state (of an electrical device) of being off (OFF *adv.* 4 b).

1899 J. PIGG *Railway 'Block' Signalling* vii. 363 In the 'off' position of the signal arm the switch makes such contacts as passes a 'holding down' current from the battery at the local station. **1935** D. L. SAYERS *Gaudy Night* xvi. 327 The switch ..stood in the 'Off' position, and she struck it down. **1960** *Practical Wireless* XXXVI. 425/2 A two-pole toggle switch ..could be used in the S1 position thus isolating the mains completely from the equipment when the switch is in the 'off' position. **1975** L. DEIGHTON *Yesterday's Spy* vii. 52 Schlegel bashed the 'off' button and the music ended with a loud click.

7. *Physiol.* Of, pertaining to, or exhibiting the electrical activity that occurs briefly in some optic nerve fibres in vertebrates when illumination of the retina ceases.

1903 F. GOTCH in *Jrnl. Physiol.* XXIX. 393 The third or terminal portion is a second rise due to the sudden change from light to darkness; this I propose for brevity to term the OFF effect. *Ibid.* 401 The rate of development of the OFF change. *Ibid.* 403 In no instance is the OFF delay greater than the ON. **1934** *Ibid.* LXXXI. 26 The increase in P III and its rapid return at 'off' account for the increased off-effect of the light-adapted eye. **1941** S. H. BARTLEY *Vision* xii. 287 The off-response first appears when the light flash is very short. **1948** *Jrnl. Physiol.* CVII. 57 Of the 164 elements, 16% were pure on-elements, 5% pure off-elements, and 79% on-off-elements. *Ibid.*, The on-sensitivity to blue (*B*-on) was taken as the fundamental sensitivity... For those elements which showed no on-effect the off-sensitivity to blue (*B*-off) was used. **1972** H. TAMAR *Princ. Sensory Physiol.* iv. 153/2 Some 5 per cent of all color-responsive ganglion cells seem really to have receptive fields with centers which are either 'on' or 'off' to one color.

D. *sb.* [absolute or ellipt. uses of the adj.]

1. *Naut.* = OFFING.

1599 HAKLUYT *Voy.* I. 291 The shippe lay thwart to wende a flood, in the off, at the Southsoutheast moone.

2. The condition or fact of being off.

a **1669** TRAPP in Spurgeon *Treas. Dav.* Ps. cxvi. 10, I have had my offs and my ons,..I have passed through several frames of heart and tempers of soul. **1895** MISS DOWIE *Gallia* 119, I love to feel the on and off of the break and to watch the way the pole seems to feel its way through the traffic.

3. *Cricket.* = Off side: see C. 2 b. Hence *Comb.*: OFF-DRIVE *sb.* and *v.*; **off-theory**, a theory that favours concentrating the fielders on the off side and bowling the ball at or outside the off stump.

1836 *New Sporting Mag.* XI. 193 Thus if the bat be brought forward in a straight line to meet the ball moving in the same line, the ball will be struck directly to the bowler. It is on this principle, that more to the on or off, so will it be returned, and according as it is bowled, more to his left or right. **1847** [see BREAK *v.* 32 b]. **1857** HUGHES *Tom Brown* II. viii, Johnson the young bowler is getting wild, and bowls a ball almost wide to the off. **1881** *Standard* 28 June 3/1 Whiting drove Studd to the off for four. **1883** W. L. MURDOCH in *Longman's Mag.* Jan. 292 At the present time, when bowlers place their men on the off side and bowl on what I might term the 'off theory', batsmen should be very careful what ball they hit at. **1894** *Daily News* 23 Nov. 6/3 Steady cultivation of a break from the off is a better amusement than the premature affectation of being an Amphitryon. **1960** H. S. ALTHAM in A. Ross *Cricketer's Compan.* 292 The off-theory was being to some extent abandoned. **1975** *Cricketer* May 14/2 Max Walker showed his 'leg-cutter' that snapped back from the off.

4. (See quot.)

1829 [J. R. BEST] *Pers. & Lit. Mem.* 257 To buy Lincolnshire hogs or offs, lambs taken off from their mothers.

5. The start of a race (cf. sense A. 1 e above); also *transf.*, the start, the beginning; departure; a signal to start or depart. *colloq.*

1959 *Times* 14 Sept. 3/1 Matthews broke once and on the second 'off' knocked down the first hurdle. **1963** L. Meynell *Virgin Luck* vii. 174 The price shortened and just before the 'off' I noticed it was being offered at nine to two. **1966** J. PORTER *Sour Cream* xiv. 180 It was too late. The students nearest to him..thought this was the off. They began to move forward. **1968** 'H. CALVIN' *Miranda must Die* iii. 34 'Time for off,' he said... He was gone. **1973** T. ALLBEURY *Choice of Enemies* xiii. 62 Jock..waited for someone to give him the off, and James said, 'O.K. Jock, you just give us the general picture.' **1973** 'I. DRUMMOND' *Jaws of Watchdog* xviii. 240 How long before the off will they try to put the poison in? **1978** *Lancashire Life* Apr. 50 (*caption*) Tangle-wrangle: Stan Lyons waits on the slipway for the 'off', while helpers sort-out the lines from his harness.

off, *v.* [Elliptical (chiefly colloq. or illiterate) uses of OFF *adv.*, at length inflected as a vb.: cf. to IN, to BACK.]

†**1.** *trans.* To put off; to defer. *Obs.*

1642 SIR E. DERING *Sp. on Relig.* 96 The further debate of this was offed [*printed* ofted] to the next day.

2. *intr.* To go off, make off. (*illiterate.*) Also ***to off it***, to depart; also (*slang*), to die. Cf. OFF *adv.* 9.

1889 T. E. BROWN *Manx Witch* 18 'And will you go linkin with me?' says Jack... 'I'm thinkin I'd better,' says Nessy. .. And offs with him. **1890** *Punch* 28 June 310/2 He found out after they'd off'd it that they didn't own a white mouse among 'em! **1895** *Westm. Gaz.* 21 Sept. 2/1 He took down his hat, an' off'd. **1930** J. BUCHAN *Castle Gay* iv. 72 He has probably offed it abroad. **1930** BROPHY & PARTRIDGE *Songs & Slang 1914–18* 143 *Off it*, to die. **1965** *Listener* 27 May 797/2 He ups and offs from wife, job, kids.

3. *Naut.* Of a ship: To move off from shore. In pr. pple. *offing*.

1882 OGILVIE (Annandale), We were offing at the time the accident happened.

4. *trans.* To take off, eat off, swallow. *rare.*

1887 BROWNING *Fust & Friends* 76 Awaiting thy sign To out knife, off mouthful.

5. ***to off with***, to take off instantly. (Cf. OFF *adv.* 9.) *illiterate*, or *humorous colloq.*

1892 *Daily News* 23 Feb. 5/1 They offed with his head. **1895** K. GRAHAME *Golden Age* 56 When the Queen said 'Off with his head!' she'd have offed with your head. **1895** *Pall Mall Mag.* Sept. 111 'So then he offs with his diamond ring'.

6. To kill.

Recorded chiefly in Black English contexts in the U.S.

1968 N. GIOVANNI *Revolutionary Tale* in *Negro Digest* June 77/1 The only way we can ever justify offing a brother is if we have already offed twenty whiteys. **1970** *Time* 11 May 29 At the swamp, Alex was offed... Warren shot him first, Lonnie hit him a second time. **1970** *Time* 2 Nov. 25/1 The Panthers' rhetoric is inflammatory and irresponsible, and it is impossible to say how many people take their 'off the pig' injunctions seriously. **1971** *Black Scholar* Sept. 40/2 If they caught a bitch or dude fuckin' around with the honkies, they offed 'em. **1974** R. B. PARKER *Godwulf Manuscript* (U.S. ed.) iii. 18 There were various recommendations about pigs being offed scrawled on the sidewalk. **1977** *Time* 31 Jan. 52/1 There is a contract out on him and he will be offed as sure as next morning's sunrise.

off-, *prefix.* The adv. *off* occurs in combination with verbs, ppl. adjs., vbl. sbs., and other sbs. In earlier times, it was written *of-*, as explained under OF- *pref.* 2; but such of the ME. compounds as survived into modern Eng. were then written *off-*, which is the only form found in recent compounds. In verbs, generally, the combination is very loose (see 1 below); in participles used as adjs. the union is closer, and in vbl. and other sbs. it becomes permanent, though combinations of this kind can be formed at pleasure whenever the sense requires. In a few cases, the combination is so specialized in sense, or otherwise important, as to require treatment as a main word. In verbs, the stress is now usually upon the root; in the other classes (2–4) on *'off-*.

1. With verbs, *off-* (ME. *of-*) enters into quasi-combination, chiefly as a separable particle, like Ger. *ab-* in *ab-reisen*, *ab-schreiben*, etc., in which the particle stands before the vb. only in certain syntactical conditions. In ME. *of* was frequently put before the vb. in the infinitive, as in *of glide*, *of hew*, and in this position (though usually written as a separate word in the MSS.) is often hyphened by modern editors (*of-glide*, *of-hew*); modern prose usage prefers the order *glide off*, *hew off*; but in the pples. the adv. is still sometimes put first, and is then sometimes hyphened to the vb. (as is regularly done in 2). ME. examples are the obsolete *of-cwell*, *of-quell* (to kill off), *of-*, *off-drive*, *of-glide*, *of-hew*, *of-hurl*, *of-race* (to pluck or tear off), *of-rive*, *of-shear*, *of-shred*, *of-smite*, *of-swipe* (to cut off with a sweep of the sword), *of-tear*, *of-turn*, *of-twitch*, *of-weve* (to twist off), *of-wip* (to whip off). Later examples are *off-chop*, *of- off-shake*, *off-stand*, *off-trench*, etc., but these are exemplified chiefly in the pa. pple., where the hyphen may be regarded as simply syntactical as in 2. See also OFF-DRIVE, OFF-LOAD, etc.

a **1618** SYLVESTER *Mem. Mortalitie* xli, Her head shee felt with whiffing steel *off-chopt. *c* **1200** ORMIN 8104 Forr þatt teȝȝ shollden att hiss dæþ þa riche menn *offcwellenn. *c* **1275** *Luue Ron* 23 in *O.E. Misc.* 93 Pyne and deþ him wile *of-dryue. **1555-8** PHAER *Æneid.* I. Cij b, With the light of torches great the darke offdriue atones. *c* **1400** *Rowland & O.* 475 The Nasell of his helme *of-glade. *c* **1400** *Destr. Troy* 6474 Hondes [he] *ofhew heturly fast. *Ibid.* 6722 His helme *of hurlit, & his hed bare. **1340** HAMPOLE *Pr. Consc.* 6704 Þe strenthe of hungre sal þam swa chace þat þair awen flesshe þai sal *of-race. *Ibid.* 7379 And thair awen flessch *of-ryve and race. **1570-6** LAMBARDE *Peramb. Kent* (1826) 219 They not their sinnes.. *of shake. *a* **1618** SYLVESTER *Job Triumph.* ii. 76 His fruit, yer ripe, shall be off-shaken all. **1892** ZANGWILL *Childr. Ghetto* II. 20 We rest not, but stand, Off-shaken our sloth. *c* **1320** *Sir Beues* 816 (MS. A) A spanne of þe groin be-forn Wiþ is swerd he haþ *of schoren. **1533** GAU *Richt Vay* 58 Thay ar heretikis offchorne fra ye kirk of Christ. **1390** GOWER *Conf.* I. 138 The leves let defoule in haste.. And let *of schreden euery braunche. *c* **1205** LAY. 26071 Arður.. of-toc þene eotend.. And þat þih him *of-smat [1275 of-smot]. *Ibid.* 28721 Þe king mid his sweorde þat hefd him *of swipte. **1390** GOWER *Conf.* I. 346 That he hire Pappes sholde *of tere Out of hire brest. **1515** BARCLAY *Egloges* (1570) B v b, His nose and eares *off trenched were also. *c* **1350** *Will. Palerne* 2590 William hent hastili þe hert, and meliors þe hinde, And as smartli as þei couþe þe skinnes *of turned. *c* **1320** *Sir Beues* 3882 (MS. A) His sclauin ech palmer *of twiȝte. *c* **1330** *Arth. & Merl.* 6883 Ther was mani heued *of weued. *a* **1400** *Sir Beues* (MS. S) 868 Her heued *of wypt at a drauȝte.

2. with pres. and pa. participles, forming adjs. (stress on *off*), as *'off-bitten* (= bitten off), *off-shed, off-sloping, off-standing, off-thrown*, etc. (Such combinations are possible with any pple. of suitable sense.) See also OFF-LYING.

1568 TURNER *Herbal* III. 43 It maye be called also Ofbiten, because a pece of the roote is biten of. **1674** N. FAIRFAX *Bulk & Selv.* 47 The worlds whole throng of hard, wide, and off-standing bodies. **1813** COLERIDGE *Remorse* II. i. 171 A small green dell Built all around with high off-sloping hills. **1853** KANE *Grinnell Exp.* xlix. (1856) 466 It has surrounded us with the off-shed fragments of the floes. **1888** LELAND *Pract. Educ.* i. 27 An offshooting twig.

3. with vbl. sbs. and nouns of action, forming sbs., sometimes concrete (stress on *off*): *'off-cutting, off-setting, off-shaving, off-standing, off-taking, off-turning*; *off-fall, off flow, off-look*, etc. See also OFF-BREAK, OFF-FALLING, OFFSCOURING, OFF-CUT, OFF-GO, OFF-PRINT, OFFSET, etc.

1565 JEWEL *Repl. Harding* (1611) 182 The ofshauing of the World, and the vilest of all people. **1591** R. BRUCE *Serm.* (1843) 223, I have.. woven my web of life to the off-cutting. **1612** WOODALL *Surg. Mate* Wks. (1653) 185 As it were off-scouring, or off-shavings of the intestines. **1674** N. FAIRFAX *Bulk & Selv.* 87 Two such worlds would touch without any more ado; there being no off-standing betwixt them. **1796** PEGGE *Anonym.* (1809) 352 Not imagining he could want any assistance on the off-setting.

1724 R. SMITH in *Coll. Dying Testim.* (1806) 214 Not-withstanding of Mr. Kid's.. off-fall from us. **1881** *Atlantic Monthly* XLVIII. 520 The superb outlooks and offlooks from its windows and porch.

4. a. with other sbs., usually with the sense, 'lying or leading off from the main trunk, etc.': as in *'off-branch, off-drain, off-spur, off-stream.* By omission of the hyphen, *off* comes to function as an adj.: see OFF *a.* Other compounds of *off-* with sbs. appear in their alphabetical places.

1793 W. CHAPMAN (*title*) Report.. on the means of working Woodford River,.. as an off-branch from the Lough-Erne and Ballyshannon Navigation. **1851** MAYHEW *Lond. Labour* II. 27 (Hoppe) The many off-streets and alleys which may be called the tributaries to those great second-hand marts. **1854** *Jrnl. R. Agric. Soc.* XV. I. 67 Crooked off-spurs of flat land. **1876** GLADSTONE *Homeric Synchr.* 224 An off-stream from the river Styx. **1884** *Kendal Merc.* 8 Feb. 4/7 These smaller off-drains should be flushed into the main street drain. **1890** *Antiquary* XXII. 9 In an off-room is exhibited the Hermaphrodite statue. **1896** *Westm. Gaz.* 4 Mar. 7/2 A very significant announcement is hid away in an off-corner of the *Daily Telegraph.*

b. With sbs. used *attrib.* or as *adj.*, as **off-course**, situated or taking place away from a race-course; **off-design**, that is not allowed for or expected; of or pertaining to such circumstances; **off-farm**, produced or sold away from a farm; **off-gold**, of a nation: not using the gold standard; **off-highway**, of or pertaining to travel that is not on highways; **off-ice**, of or pertaining to ice-hockey players when they are not engaged in a game; **off-pitch** *Mus.*, of a note: not of the correct pitch; **off-road**, used or taking place away from roads; **off-site**, occurring away from a site; removed from a site; **off-track**, (*a*) that is off one's intended route; (*b*) done away from a race-track (*spec.* of betting). See also main entries: OFF-AIR, OFF-COLOUR, etc.

1963 *Times* 7 Mar. 3/2 Those who bet on racecourses and have off-course businesses as well must include the net profit of the racecourse business when determining their category. **1964** A. WYKES *Gambling* viii. 195 In France, bookmaking is illegal; and the law against off-course, non-totalizator gambling is strictly enforced. **1977** *Times* 2 Apr. 14/2 If it [*sc.* the Tote] had a monopoly of off-course betting.. it could provide.. £35m a year for racing. **1962** S. L. BRAGG *Rocket Engines* ii. 34 Its performance at off-design pressure ratios is better than that of a conventional nozzle. **1972** *Lebende Sprachen* XVII. 134/1 Motors designed for high altitude use are frequently tested under off-design conditions. **1962** *Economist* 24 Mar. 1098/2 Target prices for off-farm dairy products.. are pitched at a much lower level. **1963** *Times* 11 Jan. 9/3 In agriculture the slow progress of both total output and off-farm sales has meant that the income of the collective farm economy has not risen fast enough. **1935** *Economist* 20 Apr. 900/2 The bulk of their trade is done with off-gold countries, and in commodities whose prices are determined by conditions in those off-gold countries. **1961** *Engineering* 10 Nov. 626 The problem of off-highway mobility. **1968** *Globe Mag.* (Toronto) 17 Feb. 5 There are now lucrative possibilities in many parts of North America for Leafs who once sold their off-ice services, personal appearances and so on very cheap. **1945** Off-pitch [see BLUE *a.* 3 d]. **1961** *Engineering* 10 Nov. 628 Spheres of off-road and industrial haulage. **1968** *Economist* 21 Sept. 82/2 The new engine.. is more suited.. to off-road vehicles (dump trucks and earth movers of all sorts). **1973** *Observer* (Colour Suppl.) 2 Sept. 51/3 Off-road racing started in California about seven years ago with the development of beach buggies and other fun cars. **1975** *Courier-Mail* (Brisbane) 11 Apr. 16/2 Off-road and recreational vehicles are becoming more and more popular. **1969** *Ibid.* 22 Feb. 14/2 Anybody involved in a fight is automatically 'off site' on the next plane. In other words all parties involved lose not only their jobs but their accommodation and have to find a new town. **1970** *Guardian* 22 Aug. 2/4 Underground nuclear explosions in Nevada.. would have negligible off-site effects. **1956** WALLIS & BLAIR *Thunder Above* (1959) i. 7 He could have deviated up into Scotland for an off-track landing at Prestwick. **1964** A. WYKES *Gambling* 340 Whereas the on-track betting turnover was the equivalent of $64,680,000, off-track betting brought in $65,240,000. The only legal way to make an off-track bet is through the Totalization Agency Board. **1970** *Globe & Mail* (Toronto) 26 Sept. B1/1 Very little of the money bet through off-track messenger betting shops reaches the pari-mutuel machines. **1976** *Times* 20 Mar. 14/6 Many off-track activities including a *concours d'elegance* of classic road cars.

5. Prefixed to the names of colours to denote colours that are almost the same as the colour specified, as ***off-black, -green, -yellow***; also OFF-WHITE *sb.* and *a.*

1927, etc. [see OFF-WHITE *sb.* and *a.*]. **1930** *Daily Express* 8 Sept. 5 One of the new off-black shades.., a sort of unripe blackberry colour, is used for the third model. **1958** J. BETJEMAN *Coll. Poems* 250 The walls are alternately painted Off-yellow and festival mauve. **1960** *Guardian* 9 Dec. 8/5 A feeling for the gentler blues and off-greens. **1978** *Detroit Free Press* 2 Apr. 10D (Advt.), Colors included.. nocturne (off-black).

offa ('ɒfə, ɔː-). Repr. U.S. colloq. pronunc. of *off of* (see OFF *adv.* 7 b).

1935 Z. N. HURSTON *Mules & Men* II. i. 233 Ah keeps her offa me too. **1954** W. TUCKER *Wild Talent* (1955) iv. 43 Roll your tail offa there and come on! **1973** *Black World* Jan. 65/2 She just couldn't take her eyes offa me. **1976** G. V. HIGGINS *Judgement D. Hunter* xiii. 128 Get offa the pot, willya?

offage ('ɒfɪdʒ). [f. OFF *adv.* + -AGE, as in *luggage, garbage*.] Refuse.

1727 tr. *Switzer's Pract. Gard.* VI. l. 267 Into beds made of the mowings of grass, offage herbs, greens, or long light dung.

off-'air, *a.* and *adv.* [OFF- 4 b, OFF *prep.* + AIR *sb.*[1]] **A.** *adj.* **a.** Operating on a closed circuit; not involving the broadcasting of programmes.

1961 *Times* 2 June 14/6 (Advt.), The ship of the year.. relies on Marconi Marine.. for closed circuit television. A completely co-ordinated internal and 'off-air' television system—.. providing passengers with closed circuit telecine and live television programmes.

b. Involving the transmission of programmes by broadcasting.

1971 *Morning Star* 10 Dec. 4/1 An attempt to prevent the allocation to ITV of Britain's last off-air television channel. **1975** *ITV Evidence to Annan Committee* i. 30 The cable companies are eager.. to deliver programmes into homes by cable rather than from off-air transmission by the IBA and the BBC. **1977** *Rep. Comm. Future of Broadcasting* (Cmnd. 6753) xiv. 218 The Cable Television Association.. saw no reason why those who currently contribute to off-air television should not also participate in programme making for cable television.

c. Carried out or done from received broadcast transmissions.

1973 *B.B.C. Handbk. 1974* 45/2 The off-air recording of educational programmes by educational institutions is another problem. **1980** *Amat. Photographer* 15 Mar. 119 (*caption*) Transferring film to video tape... Tuner/timer (for 'off-air' recording).

B. *adv.* From broadcast transmissions.

1974 *Author* Winter 149 A video cassette player/recorder.. will.. record off-air (you can record BBC 1 while watching ITV or BBC 2). **1975** *ITV Evidence to Annan Committee* i. 31 The cable companies, if they are to offer anything more than is already available off-air, will be forced to provide a menu of feature films and big sporting occasions. **1977** *Gramophone* June 124/1 The BBC's Matrix H tapes (including one recorded 'off-air') were as good a compromise as I have heard.

offal ('ɒfəl). Also 4 ofall, 5 offale, -aile, 6 offalle, -awle, 6–7 offall, 7–8 off-fall, (7 offell, uffal(l), 9 *dial.* offald, offil. [f. OFF *adv.* + FALL *sb.*[1]: cf. Du. *afval* shavings, refuse, garbage, Ger. *abfall* waste, rubbish, *pl.* parings, shavings.]

1. That which falls off or is thrown off, as chips in dressing wood, dross in melting metals, etc.; the part which, in any process, is allowed to fall off or neglected as valueless or of no immediate use; refuse, waste; also *pl.*, Scraps of waste stuff or refuse. Now only *techn.* or *dial.* = *offal corn* or *wheat, offal leather, offal wood* (cf. 6 a).

1398 TREVISA *Barth. De P.R.* xv. iv. (Tollem. MS.), Þe pouder of þe offal of golde. *Ibid.* XVII. cxxxv. (1495) 691 Hulkes and ofall and out caste of corne. *c* **1440** *Promp. Parv.* 362/1 Offal, that ys bleuit of a thynge, as chyppys, or oþer lyke. **1552** HULOET, Offall of beanes, *fabalia.* **1581** MULCASTER *Positions* xv. (1887) 68 To digest the good nurriture, and to auoide the offall. **1641** BEST *Farm. Bks.* (Surtees) 67 Every hives offell will serve to sweeten three gallons of water, and to make sufficient and good meade of the same. **1663** GERBIER *Counsel* (1664) 49 To manage the uffal of the Timber. **1736** BAILEY *Househ. Dict.* 514 They.. distil their rum from the offal of sugar. **1776** ADAM SMITH *W.N.* I. xi. (1869) I. 235 The offals of the barn and stables will maintain a certain number of poultry. **1876** SCHULTZ *Leather Manuf.* 284 The term offal applies to all the parts outside the bends. **1877** *N.W. Linc. Gloss.*, *Offals*, refuse of any kind, but more particularly refuse corn. **1882** *W. Worc. Gloss.*, *Offal*, waste wood.

†**b.** In collective sing. and pl.: Fragments that fall off in breaking or using anything; crumbs; leavings; relics, remnants. *Obs.*

1563-87 FOXE *A. & M.* (1684) II. 328 There were left twelve baskets, twelve maunds full of brokelets and offalls at that meal. **1582** STANYHURST *Æneis* II. (Arb.) 64 If Gods eternal thee last disseuered offal Of Troy determyn too burne. **1621** BURTON *Anat. Mel.* III. i. III. iii. (1651) 430 Poor Lazarus.. only seeks chippings, offals. **1659** D. PELL *Impr. Sea* 295 Upon these Plancks, Yards, Masts, and offals of the Vessel, have all the Mariners got safe to the Shore. **1786** A. MACLEAN *Christ's Commiss.* iii. (1846) 156 To partake of the crumbs and offals in common with the dogs.

2. a. The parts which are cut off in dressing the carcase of an animal killed for food; in earlier use applied mainly to the entrails; now, as a trade term, including the head and tail, as well as the kidneys, heart, tongue, liver, and other parts. †Formerly also in *pl.*

c **1420** *Liber Cocorum* (1862) 29 Take tho offal and tho lyver of tho swan In gode brothe thou sethe hom than. **1464** *Mann. & Househ. Exp.* (Roxb.) 543 Receyved.. for the fete and the offaile of a boloke, iiij.*d.* **1555** W. WATREMAN *Fardle Facions* II. vii. 156 Some.. when thei haue slaine the beaste (in sacrifice), vse to laye parte of the offalle in the fire. **1595** *Enq. Tripe-wife* (1881) 149 The Butchers offals were thy sweetest ware. *a* **1735** ARBUTHNOT (J.), He let out the offals of his meat to interest, and kept a register of such debtors in his pocket-book. **1868** *Daily News* 19 June, What is technically termed the 'offal' of slaughtered animals.. forms a most important feature of the metropolitan dead-meat trade. **1877** *Holderness Gloss.*, *Offal*, the cuttings of pork when a pig is killed.

b. Contemptuously: The parts of a slaughtered or dead animal unfit for food; putrid flesh; carrion; also, opprobriously, the bodies or limbs of the slain.

1581 DERRICKE *Image Irel.* II. Fj, Though durtie tripes and offalls like please vnderknaues enoufe. **1598** SHAKS. *Merry W.* III. v. 5 Haue I liu'd to be carried in a Basket like a barrow of butchers Offall? and to be throwne in the Thames? **1602** —— *Ham.* II. ii. 608, I should haue fatted all the Region Kites With this Slaues Offall. **1667** MILTON *P.L.* x. 633 Till cramm'd and gorg'd, nigh burst With suckt and glutted offal. **1735** SOMERVILLE *Chase* III. 223 Dripping Offals, and the mangled Limbs Of Men and Beasts. **1828** SCOTT *F.M. Perth* xv, Where is the hand.. Is it nailed on the public pillory, or flung as offal to the houseless dogs? **1838** PRESCOTT *Ferd. & Is.* (1846) I. iv. 212 Supporting life by feeding on the most loathsome offal, on cats, dogs, etc. **1867** BAKER *Nile Tribut.* iv. (1872) 61 A flock of ravenous beaks were tearing at the offal.

3. In the fish trade: Low-priced and inferior fish as opposed to those called *prime*; *esp.* small fish of various kinds caught in the nets along with the larger or more valuable kinds.

1859 SALA *Tw. round Clock* (1861) 17 'Offal' means odd lots of different kinds of fish, mostly small and broken, but always fresh and wholesome. **1887** E. J. MATHER *Nor'ard of Dogger* ii. (1889) 19 Prime and offal were rigorously kept apart. The prime fish are soles, turbot, halibut and brill. Plaice, haddock, cod, ling, etc. come under the technical name of offal.

4. Refuse in general; rubbish, garbage. Now chiefly *sing.*

1598 BARRET *Theor. Warres* v. iv. 137 Great pits to bury and to cast therein, the garbedge, filthinese, and offalls of the campe. **1798** *Anti-Jacobin* No. 9 (1799) 280 Express orders were given to afford them no other subsistence than the offals that might be collected in the streets. **1877** S. COX *Salv. Mundi* iv. (1878) 69 It became the common cesspool of the city into which all the offal was cast.

5. *fig.* Refuse, offscourings, dregs, scum. Chiefly in *collect. sing.*

1581 MULCASTER *Positions* xxxvii. (1887) 159 That barbarous offall of all kinde of people. **1590** SPENSER *F.Q.* II. iii. 8 The Miser threw him selfe, as an Offall, Streight at his foot in base humilitee. **1601** SHAKS. *Jul. C.* I. iii. 109 What trash is Rome? What Rubbish, and what Offall? **1728** MORGAN *Algiers* I. Pref. 2 Those Varlets, generally.. the very Offal of the Ottomans. **1828** MACAULAY *Ess.*, *Hallam* (1851) I. 86 Wretches.. whom every body now believes to have been.. the offal of gaols and brothels.

6. *attrib.* or as *adj.* **a.** *lit.* (See preceding senses.)

1596 *Stanford Churchw. Acc.* in *Antiquary* (1888) May 211 Chippes and offall woodd of the tree felled. **1599** MARSTON *Sco. Villanie* III. xi. 227 Fed with offall scraps, that sometimes fall From liberall wits. **1645** QUARLES *Sol. Recant.* XI. 76 Fair Crops from offall Corn are rarely found. **1717** tr. *Frezier's Voy.* 238 Offal Meat, which consists in Heads, Tongues, Entrails, Feet,.. which they eat on Fish-Days. **1764** *Museum Rusticum* III. xii. 40, I supposed.. that they would go to the tailing, or off-fall corn. **1778** [W.

MARSHALL] *Minutes Agric.* 17 Nov. 1776, Any offal-stick.. eighteen inches long answers the purpose. **1825** ESTHER HEWLETT *Cottage Comf.* vi. 49 Any offal milk. **1880** *Times* 2 Dec. 8/2 For sale by auction, at Her Majesty's Dockyard,.. offal wood.. about 30 tons. **1886** *Chesh. Gloss.*, *Offal corn*, *offal wheat*, the lighter grains winnowed from the marketable samples, and used for feeding fowls. **1891** J. J. LALOR in *Cycl. Temp. & Prohib.* 253/2 Patent, sole, harness, band and offal leather.

b. *fig.* Outcast; worthless; vile. Now esp. *dial.* *c* **1605** ROWLEY *Birth Merl.* III. vi, The offal fugitives of barren Germany. **1839** *Times* 5 Feb., The last four years being the period of the M—— or offal ministry in this island. **1860** GEO. ELIOT *Mill on Fl.* I. iv, He's an offal creatur as iver come about the primises. **1877** *Holderness Gloss.*, *Offal*, worthless; vile.

7. *Comb.*, as *offal-eater*. **1889** J. JACOBS *Æsop's Fables* I. 66 The refuse-eater and the offal-eater Belauding each other.

Hence **'offalist** (*nonce-wd.*), a gatherer of offal. **1822** *Sporting Mag.* IX. 230 Athenæus, that offalist and great gatherer of all town and country talk.

† **of-'fall**, *v. Obs.* [OE. *offeallan*, f. OF- + *feallan* to FALL.] *trans.* To fall upon; to kill, destroy. *a* **1000** *O.E. Chron.* an. 962 (Parker MS.) Sigferð cyning hine offeoll. *c* **1000** ÆLFRIC *Hom.* II. 510 [þæt treow].. fornean offeoll ða ðe hit ær forcurfon. *c* **1275** LAY. 28043 Waweyn was of-falle. **1387** TREVISA *Higden* (Rolls) VII. 535 (MS. Harl. 1900) That hir sone was ded and al hir meyne alayde and afalle [*MS. Cott. Tib. D. vii* offalle].

off and on, *adv. phr.* (*a.*, *sb.*) (See also ON AND OFF.) [OFF *adv.* 4, 1 c, 12.]

1. With interruption and resumption of action; intermittently, at intervals, now and again. 'Of an on', *Torr. Portugal* 543, is app. a corrupt reading. **1535** COVERDALE *1 Chron.* xxviii. 1 Officers waytinge vpon the kynge, to go of & on after their course. **1681** NEVILE *Plato Rediv.* 107 A bloody War ensued, for almost forty years, off and on. **1779** GREENE in Sparks *Corr. Amer. Rev.* (1853) II. 272 They had been hammering upon the business for almost two months, off and on. **1860** MRS. CARLYLE *Lett.* III. 41, I.. slept off and on.. all the way to Crewe.

2. *Naut.* On alternate tacks, away from and towards the shore. *a* **1608** SIR F. VERE *Comm.* 29, I plied onely to windward, lying off and on from the mouth of the Bay to the sea. **1666** *Lond. Gaz.* No. 113/3 Their Convoyer in his return, standing off and on for high water. **1722** DE FOE *Col. Jack* (1840) 192 Some.. privateers lay off and on in the soundings. **1852** TH. ROSS *Humboldt's Trav.* I. iii. 146 The Captain preferred standing off and on till daybreak. **1894** CROCKETT *Raiders* (ed. 3) 66 She's been beating off and on a' day with her tops'ls reefed.

b. Used prepositionally. **1708** *Lond. Gaz.* No. 4420/6 We lay off and on Buccaness all Day Yesterday. **1769** FALCONER *Dict. Marine* (1789) s.v. *Off*, When a ship is beating to windward, so that by one board she approaches towards the shore, and by the other sails out to sea-ward, she is said to stand off and on shore, alternately.

3. In vacillation between connexion and the reverse; with a see-saw policy. *a* **1641** BP. MOUNTAGU *Acts & Mon.* (1642) 467 In this sort stood the Samaritans wavering off and on with the Jewes a long time.

4. *lit. to play off and on with*, to take off and put on alternately. **1845** *Tait's Mag.* XII. 4 Sarah.. in deep confusion, played off and on with one of the richly jewelled rings she wore.

B. *predicatively* or as *adj.* Sometimes off and sometimes on; intermittent, taking place at intervals; vacillating, inconstant; *dial.* (of a sick person) sometimes better and sometimes worse. **1583** GOLDING *Calvin on Deut.* xv. 88 Their hoping is but off and on at al-aduenture. **1640** SANDERSON *Serm.* (1681) II. 144 We are wavering and loose, off and on, and no hold to be taken of us. **1688** R. HOLME *Armoury* II. 305/2 The Proverb, Off and on, like a Cock Sparrow. **1805** WORDSW. *Prelude* IV. 187 The faithful dog, The off and on companion of my walk. **1866** MRS. CARLYLE *Lett.* III. 316 After about two hours of off-and-on sleep, I awoke.

C. as *sb.* (by ellipsis of a vbl. sb.) Intermittent or inconstant action, see-sawing, vacillation. **1875** W. CORY *Lett. & Jrnls.* (1897) 386 After many years of off and on, he has taken to calling me his 'dear old friend'.

off-'axis, *a.* and *adv.* [f. OFF- 4 b, OFF *prep.* + AXIS[1].] (Situated) away from an axis. **1939** *Sci. Amer.* Aug. 120/2 The 'off-axis' type.. is exceedingly useful in practice because, with this arrangement, the photographic plate or film may be placed outside the light beam. **1962** A. NISBETT *Techinque Sound Studio* ii. 36 Place the second person just the same amount off-axis in the other direction. **1971** J. H. RICHARDSON *Optical Microscopy for Materials Sci.* i. 47 Even though a lens may be spherically corrected for objects situated on the microscope axis, spherical aberration may exist for off-axis objects.

off base, off-base, *phr.* (*adv.*) and *a.* [OFF *prep.*, OFF- 4 b.] **1.** Unawares, off one's guard, by surprise; mistaken. Cf. BASE *sb.*[1] 15 d. *U.S.* **1936** J. STEINBECK *In Dubious Battle* vii. 109 If they can catch us off base, they'll bounce us. **1947** *Time* 20 Oct. 11/1 Your Latin American department was off base in its comparison of the Portillo Hotel in Chile with our famous Sun Valley. **1948** *Daily Ardmoreite* (Ardmore, Okla.) 26 May 6/4 There are more men caught off base at cocktail parties than ball games. **1955** W. C. GAULT *Ring around Rosa* vii. 88 You're way off base, Bobby, and I think this kind of talk is in poor taste. **1971** B. MALAMUD *Tenants* 141, I don't feel lovely. I feel off-base, off-key, dissatisfied. **1974** *Publishers Weekly* 18 Mar. 43/1 Off base with his moralizing, an innocent in economics, overshadowed by the Kennedys.

2. Situated elsewhere than on a military base (BASE *sb.*[1] 16 and 16 b). **1962** *Economist* 1 Dec. 921/2, 136 families live on the base, 220 in an off-base village. **1967** *Ibid.* 30 Sept. 1196/3 The defence establishment has often been a pioneer in ending the colour bar, both at its own installations and 'off-base'. *Ibid.*, To fight off-base discrimination against Negro Soldiers. **1977** R. GADNEY *Champagne Marxist* xiv. 92 'I'd like to speak with you.' 'Fine.' 'Off-base?' 'Of course, if that's what you want.'

off beam, off-beam, *phr.*, *a.*, and *adv. colloq.* Also **off the beam**. [f. OFF *prep.*, OFF- 4 b + BEAM *sb.*[1] 24 c.] On the wrong track; wrong, mistaken. **1951** 'J. TEY' *Daughter of Time* ix. 121 'He's away off the beam. Away off.' 'I suspected as much. Let us have the facts.' **1958** *Woman* 20 Sept. 4/4 Funny how we all get off-beam ideas of each other, isn't it? **1960** *Spectator* 20 May 729 My thinking, which was quite off-beam, convinced me at that time that the man was a charlatan. **1973** *Guardian* 15 Feb. 14/4 Mr. Patrick is far from off-beam in tracing connections between environment and the behaviour he describes. **1977** *Time Out* 17–23 June 10/3 'A Question of Ulster' was not only way off beam for explanation, it was also five years ago.

off-bear ('ɒfbɛə(r), ɔ:-), *v.* [f. OFF *adv.* + BEAR *v.*] *trans.* To bear or carry off; *spec.* in *Brick-making*, etc. (see quots.). So **'off-ˌbearer**. **1866** *5th Rep. Children's Employment Commission* 142/1 in *Parl. Papers* XXIV. 1 The walk flatter is often a young woman, and the off-bearer a young man. **1884** C. T. DAVIS *Bricks & Tiles* 18 Others still are off-bearing [*ed.* 1889 bearing off] the bricks. *Ibid.* (1889) 130 The off-bearer rakes the dried sand into a pile, and sieves it into a half-barrel, called 'the tub'. *Ibid.* 132 A moulding gang consists of one laborer called the 'moulder', and one able-bodied man called the 'wheeler', and one boy called the 'off-bearer'. **1887** A. A. BROWN *Lumbering on the Cumberland* 47 Caleb occupied the position of honor, and acted as 'sawyer'. Abe was 'setter', and Eph was 'off-bearer'. **1894** *Columbus (O.) Disp.* 8 Mar., An off-bearer at ——'s saw mill.. was horribly mangled to-day. **1939** D. HARTLEY *Made in England* v. 170 In one shed there seemed to be about six workers, and their names indicated their share of the job; 'moulder', 'temperer', 'off-bearer', [etc.].

'off-beat, *sb.* and *a.* [f. OFF *prep.*, OFF- 4 b + BEAT *sb.*[1]] **A.** *sb. Mus.* An unaccented beat; = UPBEAT *sb.* 1; *spec.* the second or fourth beat in common time; a heavy accent on these beats. **1928** *Grove's Dict. Mus.* (ed. 3) V. 424/2 It is therefore in the nature of things that much music should begin on the offbeat. *Ibid.*, It is convenient to confine 'upbeat' to the last of the bar, leaving 'offbeat' for any other note than the first. **1946** A. HUTCHINGS in A. L. Bacharach *Brit. Music* xvi. 205 A rhythmic figure.. beginning on an off-beat so that its entry in another part will be effective and beget movement. **1958** C. WILFORD in P. Gammond *Decca Bk. Jazz* ii. 31 The pianist's left hand marks the beat firmly and unvaryingly, usually also with sharply staccato off-beats. **1973** J. WAINWRIGHT *Pride of Pigs* 175 The washboard player tapped the off-beats with the tips of his thimbles.

B. *adj.* **1.** *Mus.* Of, pertaining to, or comprising off-beats; having a marked rhythm on the off-beats. Also *transf.* **1927** *Melody Maker* Sept. 926/2 In a thirty-two bar passage the rhythm might appear thus: Six bars 'off-beat', two bars 'charleston', six bars 'four in a bar', [etc.]. **1936** *Metronome* Feb. 61/2 *Off beat cymbal*, sock cymbal. **1952** J. STEINBECK *East of Eden* xvi. 151 Samuel Hamilton rode back home... Doxology's loud off-beat hoofsteps silenced the night people until after he had passed. **1959** D. COOKE *Lang. Mus.* v. 263 Another 'oom-pah' bass without the 'oom' (the cheapest of jazz-rhythms, emphasized by off-beat side-drum taps). **1970** P. OLIVER *Savannah Syncopators* 15 Off-beat phrasing of melodic accents.

2. Unusual, unconventional; strange, eccentric. *colloq.* (orig. *U.S.*). Occas. with even stress. **1938** D. BAKER *Young Man with Horn* I. iv. 35 He tried.. to teach him to sweep with a utilitarian slant, all the strokes going in the same direction in such a way that.. you inevitably have a pile of whatever it is, right there in front of your broom... But.. Smoke would go right back into his off-beat swishing. **1951** *N.Y. Herald-Tribune* 13 Dec. 34 The author.. has a highly individual wit, a fey and off-beat slant on the process of making people laugh. **1958** S. ELLIN *Eighth Circle* (1959) II. xiii. 140 One of those types who are a little offbeat when they talk to you. **1958** *Economist* 13 Dec. 993/1 The most important postwar development has been the enormous popularity of the 'off-beat' greeting card, which was first introduced seven or eight years ago. **1959** *Observer* 5 Apr. 11/4 It is the off-beat things, the eccentricities, that help give salerooms their perpetual appeal and surprise. **1960** P. CARSWELL (*title*) Offbeat spirituality. **1963** [see FAR-OUT *a.* b]. **1967** *Daily Tel.* 16 Feb. 15/5 Suzanne Hywel, 23, looks off-beat but in fact has a yearning for the country that she left behind in Kent. **1976** *Times* 9 Aug. 10/1 One of London's oldest adult education institutions ran an off-beat course for reviewing the arts.

Hence **off-beatness**, the quality of being 'off-beat'; unconventionality. **1960** *Guardian* 11 Oct. 7/2 There is no deliberate off-beatness about her. **1962** J. M. BERNSTEIN tr. *Levi's Two-Fold Night* i. 7 There is.. a hint of 'off-beatness' in their conformism, which is the city's tradition.

off-board, *a. U.S.* [f. OFF- 4 b + BOARD *sb.* 8 c.] Of stocks, bonds, etc.: dealt in or sold elsewhere than at the stock exchange; = OVER THE COUNTER *adv.* (*a.*) a. **1950** in WEBSTER Add. **1968** *Economist* 6 Jan. 56/2 It is suspected in Wall Street that the agency's wily staff goes out of its way to prop up those offboard markets mainly to keep 'sassy' Wall Streeters off balance. **1977** *N.Y. Times* 14 Nov. 53/4 Most brokerage and investment banking firms, however, agree that the eventual elimination of what are called 'off-board trading restrictions' is inevitable.

off-branch: see OFF- 4.

off-break, *sb.* [OFF- 3.] **1.** The act or result of breaking off; a schism. **1866** W. GREGOR *Dial. Banffshire* 7 in *Trans. Philol. Soc.* The Free-kirk's an aff-brack fae the Aul' Kirk. **1892** G. M. RAE *Syrian Ch. India* 195 Her ranks had been greatly thinned by the off-break of Protestantism. **1934** *Discovery* Mar. 60/1 The line offering the most advantageous terrain must be carefully observed, glacier off-breaks noted, where and how often breaks occur.

2. *Cricket.* A ball bowled in such a way that, on pitching, it changes direction towards the leg side; such a change of direction. Also *attrib.* **1888** A. G. STEEL in Steel & Lyttleton *Cricket* iii. 117 The next spin or twist on the ball.. is the rotary motion from left to right. This, in cricket phraseology, is termed the 'off' break. **1903** G. L. JESSOP in H. G. Hutchinson *Cricket* v. 134. On a bad wicket and with an off-break bowler the position of short leg is indispensable. **1927** G. A. TERRILL *Out in Glare* iv. 74 If the spin meant the usual off-break, the ball was straighter than Verlenden had intended. It would break right away to leg. **1955**, **1963** [see CHINAMAN 4].

'off-break, *v.* [OFF- 1.] **1.** *trans.* To break off, rescind. *Sc. rare*[−1]. **1872** M. MACLENNAN *Peasant Life* (Ser. 2) 47 She winna be ony speckilation tae the pairish by offbraikin' the banns.

2. *intr. Cricket.* Of a ball: to break towards the leg side. Usu. as **'off-ˌbreaking** *ppl. a.* **1904** *Westm. Gaz.* 10 Aug. 3/1 Mr. Bosanquet.. dismissed three batsmen lbw with his 'off-breaking leg-break'. **1907** *Ibid.* 18 July 4/2 The off-breaking leg-break of the Bosanquet school has exercised a great influence over South African cricket.

off-Broadway (ˌɒf'brɔ:dweɪ, ɔ:-), *a.* and *sb.* orig. *U.S.* [f. OFF *prep.* + BROADWAY.] **A.** *adj.* Of a theatre, play, or performer: located in, appearing in, or associated with an area of New York other than the Broadway theatrical area; esp. with reference to experimental productions. Also *transf.* **1953** *Plays & Players* Dec. 24/3 There are still two other plays to consider... The former began life at an off-Broadway theatre and after some revisions was brought to the Vanderbilt on October 14. **1954** *New Yorker* 9 Oct. 38/1 Making a new translation of 'The Wild Duck' for an off-Broadway production. **1959** CORDELL & MATSON (*title*) The off-Broadway theatre. **1965** *Listener* 20 May 738/2 The Theatre of Drama and Comedy—a sort of off-Broadway Muscovite theatre. **1970** [see FIT-UP]. **1971** B. MALAMUD *Tenants* 31 The black said his chick was an Off-Broadway actress.

B. *sb.* Off-Broadway theatres or productions collectively. **1958** *Observer* 14 Dec. 14/4 The small downtown play-houses generically known as 'off-Broadway'. **1960** L. KAUFFMANN *Waldo* (1962) vi. 69 What I say is, off-Broadway is going downhill. **1966** *Saturday Night* (Toronto) Oct. 25 Off-Broadway, basing itself in and around the [Greenwich] Village area, began to rock the American theatre with Albee's plays and the latest works from Europe. **1973** *Black World* Apr. 28/2 Many theater people went to Harlem and off-Broadway in hopes of improving their careers.

Hence **off-off-Broadway**, a collective term for theatres or theatrical productions away from 'off-Broadway', esp. those that are experimental or avant-garde; also *attrib.* and *ellipt.* as *off-off*. **1967** *National Observer* (U.S.) 10 Apr. 20/1 It had to happen and it did. The small, experimental theater circuit known as 'Off-Off Broadway'—more simply, just plain OOB—is changing. **1967** *Sat. Rev.* (U.S.) 10 June 20 These off-off Broadway playwrights are emerging in a period when no producer can expect to present their unconventional works except at a financial loss. **1967** *Listener* 31 Aug. 266/2 Off-Broadway and off-off Broadway are for those who genuinely love theatre. **1968** *Guardian* 8 Oct. 5/3 Off-off Broadway.. never takes place in a 'real' theatre; instead, Off-off Broadway uses cafés, rooms, lofts, churches. **1971** 'T. COE' *Jade in Aries* (1973) vi. 63 He's had a couple of things produced. In coffee houses, you know. Off-Off-Broadway. **1973** *Guardian* 1 Mar. 20/3 Pierre.. produces an off off-Broadway version of Peter Pan where all the characters are played by actors over sixty. **1975** *Times* 26 Apr. 7/6 The Off-Off-Broadway scene has changed... Off-Off has turned into either grant-oriented classical or imported productions, or showcases for Broadway.

off camera, off-camera, *phr.* and *adv.* Also as *adj.* [f. OFF *prep.* + CAMERA.] Outside the range of a film or television camera; when not being filmed or televised. **1960** *News Chron.* 15 July 4/5 He is certainly the most telegenic personality of our time—yet off camera he is shy. **1970** *Guardian* 14 Nov. 8/3 Off camera Garbo.. would display a charming naïveté very different from the sophistication of the rôles she played. **1973** L. SNELLING *Heresy* I. iii. 20 If Frank thinks I'm going to let that pretentious little prick.. keep me off-camera.. he's crazy. **1976** *Scotsman* 25 Nov. 15/4 Information on.. cuts is passed to Rippon by the director at a moment when she is off-camera. **1980** *N.Y. Times* 21 Sept. III. 21/1 In the new commercials, an offcamera voice asks a woman why she buys Crest for her family.

off-campus, *a.* and *adv.* orig. *U.S.* [f. OFF- 4 b, OFF *prep.* + CAMPUS.] Outside a campus;

existing or available away from a campus. Also *ellipt.* as *sb.*

1951 M. McCarthy in *Holiday* May 162/2 Today, 'off-campus' for the students is mainly represented by Alumnae House. *Ibid.*, There is no compulsion on the part of the college that off-campus social life should be conducted under these auspices. **1965** *Times Lit. Suppl.* 25 Nov. 1057/3 The available off-campus communities were relatively few. **1969** *Listener* 8 May 632/1 Amnesty is another favourite word, and it means that student rioters shall not be bound by the laws that apply off-campus. **1972** *Sat. Rev.* (U.S.) 4 Mar. 23/3 Off-campus housing is tight and expensive. **1975** *New Yorker* 21 Apr. 8/3 It's no wonder that this wood- and brick-walled beer-and-hamburger haunt serves as an extracurricular, off-campus student union. **1978** *N.Y. Times* 30 Mar. A1/6 Most of the off-campus programs operated in Westchester have been set up in the last decade.

† **'off-'cap**, *v. Obs. nonce-wd.* [f. the expression *Off caps!*] *intr.* To take off or doff the cap, in reverence or respect *to* (a person). So † **off-cap** *sb.*, doffing of the cap.

1604 Shaks. *Oth.* I. i. 10 Three Great-ones of the Cittie, (In personall suite to make me his Lieutenant) Off-capt to him. **1606** tr. *Rollock's Comm. 2 Thess.* 170 (Jam.) They are enemies,..all their doings, becking, and off-cap, and good dayes..are fained.

off-cast, offcast ('ɒfkɑːst, ɔː-, -æ-), *ppl. a.* and *sb.* Also 6 ofcast. [f. off *adv.* + *cast*, pa. pple. of cast *v.*]

A. *ppl. a.* Cast off, rejected. (*lit.* and *fig.*)

1571 Golding *Calvin on Ps.* xlvii. 10 The ofcast Jews whom their own misbeleif hath banished from the Church. **1637** *Songs Costume* (Percy Soc.) 143 Some borrow'd off-cast vaine attire. **1674** N. Fairfax *Bulk & Selv.* To Rdr., The slighted and off-cast words in the mouths of Handy-crafts-men. **1821** T. Erskine *Internal Evid. Relig.* iv. 102 Mercy towards this off-cast race.

B. *sb.* A thing or person that is cast off or rejected (*lit.* or *fig.*). Cf. *outcast*.

1587 Golding *De Mornay* xxxii. 515 How would those greate men haue yeelded to such an offcast? **1594** J. Davis *Seamans Secrets* Ded. Wks. (Hakl. Soc.) 236 The worde of God published to the blessed recouery of the forraine of-castes. **1852** Savage *R. Medlicott* iii. vi. (1864) 310 The off-casts of all the professions—doctors without patients, lawyers without briefs. **1853** Kane *Grinnell Exp.* iv. (1856) 30 This wood..is the offcast of the great Siberian and American rivers. *Ibid.* xlviii. 450 Their offcasts, the bergs.

So **'off,casting** *vbl. sb.*, (*a*) the action of casting off, rejection; (*b*) *concr.* that which is cast off.

1589 R. Bruce *Serm.* (1843) 129 Sic a loath, disdain and offcasting of this heavenlie food. **1893** *Graphic* 15 Apr. 415/1 Shabby tweed suits, the offcastings of generations of.. tourists.

off centre, off-centre, *phr.* (*adv.*) and *a.* Also (*U.S.*) -center. [f. off *prep.*, off- 4 b + centre *sb.* and *a.*] Not quite coinciding with a central position, awry; wrong, mistaken; eccentric.

1929 D. Hammett *Dain Curse* (1930) xii. 127 He had gone off center, was a dangerous maniac. **1932** *Kansas City* (Missouri) *Times* 30 May 12 This dear old country of ours can't be so terribly off center. **1934** Webster, *Off-center, Philately*, of a stamp, having margins of unequal width. **1947** J. Steinbeck *Wayward Bus* xviii. 291 The scar on his lip made the smile off-center. **1952** L. A. G. Strong *Darling Tom* 12 A round mahogany table with a doily a little off-centre. **1958** *Observer* 25 May 16/7 Miss Anna Kavan's weird, off-centre art. **1960** *Times* 23 June 15/2 The need to write..cannot be assuaged without tugging the character of its victim a little off-centre. **1971** *Listener* 25 Nov. 714/3 An out-of-date idea hung onto by slightly off-centre intellectuals. **1975** J. Wainwright *Square Dance* 196 The arrival of the Watfords had thrown little Thelma more than slightly off-centre.

off-centre, *v.* Also (*U.S.*) -center. [f. prec.] *trans.* To place or position off centre. So **off-centred** *ppl. a.*, not central; eccentric; **off-centring** *vbl. sb.*, displacement from a centre.

1947 R. H. Müller in J. S. Hall *Radar Aids to Navigation* vii. 273 A point 70 miles from the radar site has been designated by the intersection of two straight lines. This appears on the scope, with an off-centering of about 1·5 radii. **1947** Miller & McLaughlin in *Ibid.* ix. 351 The off-center PPI is, unfortunately, rather badly distorted as soon as it is off-centered by more than one tube diameter. **1958** *Proc. Inst. Electr. Engin.* CV. B. Suppl. No. 8. 355/1 Few radars are capable of off-centring the display by any appreciable amount. **1973** *Sci. Amer.* Dec. 87/2 When Copernicus introduced his heliocentric arrangement, the earth became one of the family of planets revolving in off-centered circles around the sun.

off-chance, off-chop: see off *a.* 3 b, off- 1.

'off 'colour, 'off-,colour, *phr.* and *a.* Also (*U.S.*) off color. [off *prep.* 5 b.]

1. *Phrase.* Not of natural or proper colour, paler or darker than usual; hence, not up to the mark, defective, deficient, out of order; also, not in good health, slightly unwell.

1876 B. Harte *Gabriel Conroy* II. iv. iv. 90 Mr Hamlin had not been well, or, as he more happily expressed it, had been 'off colour'. **1879** *Scribner's Mag.* XIX. 680/2 He looked rather 'off color'. **1885** T. A. Guthrie *Tinted Venus* v. 60, I know I'm a wee bit off colour. **1893** Stevenson *Beach of Falesá* 120 He had mighty little English, and my native was still off colour. **1898** G. Giffen *With Bat & Ball* xi. 195 The devil with which the ball..seemed to rise from the pitch..made him a nasty bowler when the wicket was off-colour. **1898** G. B. Shaw *Mrs. Warren's Profession* III. 200 *Frank*: Off colour? *Rev. S.*: (repudiating the expression) No sir: unwell this morning. **1899** *Strand Mag.* Mar. 313/1 Even the flute was off-colour. **1931** A. J. Cronin *Hatter's Castle* I. iv. 80, I haven't been myself at all these last few days—quite off colour. **1955** *Times* 10 Aug. 3/3 Hampshire if slightly off colour at the end, duly won at Portsmouth yesterday. **1966** 'J. Hackston' *Father clears Out* 86 He did not sit in the shed for just a while, as a man does when he suddenly feels off-colour. **1974** A. Fowles *Pastime* ii. 12 'Where's Christine?' he said. 'Over her mum's. Her mum's off colour. She's staying..till she picks up.'

2. *adj.* ('off-,colour). Not of the right colour or shade, and so of inferior value: of diamonds, etc.

1860 A. de Barrera *Gems & Jewels* 164 If the manufactured diamond is found to contain a flaw, or what is technically termed 'off-color', its value is proportionately diminished. **1878** *Scribner's Mag.* XVI. 663/2 Diamonds.. are referred to as white, Cape white, bye water, off color and yellow. *Ibid.* 667/1 Definite varieties, such as 'Cape white', 'bye water', 'off-color', and 'yellow'. **1894** *Daily News* 7 July 6/3 Purchasing 'off-colour diamonds' and substituting them for others of the first quality.

3. Of questionable taste, disreputable, improper, indecent; esp. of jokes; risqué; hinting at obscenity; = dirty *a.* 2.

1875 J. G. Holland *Sevenoaks* in *Scribner's Monthly* Mar. 582/1 Everybody invited her, and yet every body, without any definite reason, considered her a little 'off color'. **1883** *National Police Gaz.* (U.S.) 17 Mar. 3/1 A few choice specimens of the off color morals and hypocritical manners of the stage. **1915** *Sat. Even. Post* 23 Jan. 27/3 It is almost inevitable that sooner or later some one would be moved to tell an off-color story. **1932** *Kansas City* (Missouri) *Times* 25 Mar. 21 It seemed a bit strange for a minister to be so devoted a reader of such a (then) decidedly off-color publication. **1952** [see fest]. **1954** Koestler *Invis. Writing* 58 It was still possible among intimate friends to pass on a joke that was politically off colour. **1958** *Spectator* 20 June 803/2 Landladies with their slangy off-colour jokes. **1972** 'G. Black' *Bitter Tea* (1973) iv. 56 He had never played an off-colour commercial trick on me, possibly because I had never given him the chance.

So **'off-,coloured** *a.*

1896 *Cape Times* in *Daily News* 2 June 8/5 Coloured and off-coloured professional gaol-birds in convict suits. **1897** *Outing* (U.S.) XXIX. 487/1 The off-colored puppy may or may not be the best one of the litter. **1904** *Daily Chron.* 18 May 3/4 These were the 'off-coloured', the half-castes, the outcome of white supremacy in a black country. **1913** C. Pettman *Africanderisms* 317 *Mêlées*, the off-coloured diamonds from two carats down. **1936** *Times Lit. Suppl.* 12 Sept. 717/2 A rabble of races, white, black and off-coloured, thus inhabits the Southern Africa of to-day.

offcome ('ɒfkʌm, ɔː-). Also 6 ofcome. [f. off *adv.* + come *v.*]

† **1.** *Arith.* The product of multiplication. *Obs.*

1542 Recorde *Gr. Artes* (1575) 127 The ofcome or product. **1570** Billingsley *Euclid* xi. xxxiv. 349 The roote Cubik of that ofcome or product, shall be the second number sought. **1674** Jeake *Arith.* (1696) 21 Which is called the *Multiplee*..and..sometime the *Offcome*.

† **2.** A conclusion, finish of an argument: cf. come-off 2. *Obs.*

1653 R. Baillie *Dissuas. Vind.* (1655) 28 To have set down..some solution of these knots, and not to have left them with a meer general offcome. *Ibid.* 67 But your true offcome is, that these elect infants are not knowne to men.

3. The way in which one 'comes off' or succeeds in an affair; (good or ill) success. *Sc.*

1691 Z. Haig in J. Russell *Haigs* xi. (1881) 327 Lest I have a foolish offcome, and receive disgrace. **1901** *Blackw. Mag.* Aug. 197/2 There were others..who chuckled at Rab's successful offcome.

4. A way of 'getting off' (cf. come *v.* 61 g); an excuse. *Sc.*

a **1700** Shields *Faithful Contend.* (1780) 179 (Jam.) For giving us the fairer off-come in the eyes of the world. **1717** *Wodrow Corr.* (1843) II. 270 The offcome of the Presbytery was, that he wavered so in his answers, that they behoved to set them down in write. **1841** Trench *Parables* xxi. (1877) 364 The excuses or 'offcomes', as they would be called in one of our northern dialects.

5. An outsider, stranger; one who is not a native of the district. *north. dial.*

1859 J. S. Bigg *Alfred Staunton* i. 6 'Is this Morecambe Bay?'..'Eye! eye! Morkim Bay ye offcomes ca' t'; but we ca' 't t' Sands!' **1899** H. S. Cowper *Hawkshead* v. 298 The Burtons were 'offcomes', for the name does not occur in the older register. **1946** M. Lane *Tale of Beatrix Potter* v. 97 The north-country preference for distinguishing newcomers for at least a generation as 'off-comes', which can be..translated as 'rubbishing foreigners'. **1961** *Guardian* 18 Dec. 6/2 Farm workers cannot compete for cottages with.. weekending 'off-comes' out of Lancashire.

So **'offcomed** *ppl. a.*, coming or having come from outside; **'offcomer**, an outsider.

1882 A. B. Taylor *Westmoreland Sketches* 27 Ise nivver fergit them two off-cumt chaps singin. **1895** *Leeds Mercury* (Weekly Suppl.) 28 Sept. 3/8 Yond's a off-comed un. **1898** B. Kirkby *Lakeland Words* 109 *Off-comer*, a stranger in the sense of not having been born in the locality. Ther's nin seea mich good i' some o' ther off-comers. **1958** *Listener* 26 June 1054/2 The educated people..are almost entirely strangers, off-comers. **1971** *Country Life* 9 Sept. 630/2 'Ah'll wager 'twas yon.' 'Why?' 'He's an off-comer.' **1972** 'G. North' *Sgt. Cluff rings True* i. 10 Give them three years: they'll cotton on to you... In the old days you were still an off-comed-un after twenty.

off-corn ('ɒfkɔːn, ɔː-). [off *adv.* 1.] The corn which is thrown out or separated in winnowing, either as being light, or not separated from the chaff; waste or 'offal' corn.

1573 Tusser *Husb.* (1878) 176 Such ofcorne as commeth giue wife to hir fee. *a* **1641** Bp. Mountagu *Acts & Mon.* (1642) 6 Mixed here with chaffe, off-corne, tares. **1856** *Farmer's Mag.* Nov. 384 The expense of carting, which would be paid by the off-corn.

offcut ('ɒfkʌt, ɔː-). [f. off *adv.* 3 + cut *v.*]

1. Something that is cut off, *e.g.* one of the pieces cut off in shaping a block of stone, etc; *esp.* an odd or waste piece left after the sawing of timber. In *Printing*, a piece cut off from a sheet to reduce it to the proper size; also, a part cut off the main sheet and folded separately, as in a sheet of duodecimo.

1663-4 in Swayne *Church-w. Acc. St. Thomas', Sarum* (Wilts Rec. Soc.) 337 C. Horton work abt the leads 16s. with 18lb. of old offcuts. **1865-7** Brande & Cox *Dict. Sci.* etc., *Offcut*,..is that part of a printed sheet which is cut off, and which, when folded, is inserted in the middle of the other part. **1883** *Stonemason* Jan. 3 The off-cuts and rubble are closely packed in the disused workings. **1960** 'N. Shute' *Trustee from Toolroom* 284 The offcuts were turned into pulpwood for newsprint. **1967** *Times Rev. Industry* July 44/2 On the building site..a litter of broken and unbroken bricks, torn cement bags,..and timber offcuts is commonplace. **1973** *Listener* 30 Aug. 291/1 There was another piece of filming about canals which looked like the off-cuts from some more ambitious documentary.

2. The act of cutting off. *rare*$^{-1}$.

1674 N. Fairfax *Bulk & Selv.* 29 If my soul does not thus featly stick out of my body, then it withdrew at the off-cut.

off-cutting: see off- 3.

off-diagonal (ɒfdaɪ'ægənəl, ɔː-), *a.* (*sb.*) *Math.* [f. off- 4 b, off *prep.* + diagonal *sb.*] Applied to an element of a square matrix that is not on the principal diagonal (from top left to bottom right). Also as *sb.*, such an element.

1940 *Physical Rev.* LVIII. 108/2 The only approximation made..is the neglect of the off-diagonal elements. **1957** L. Fox *Numerical Solution Two-Point Boundary Probl.* iii. 59 In *U* the off-diagonal terms are identical with those in the corresponding positions of the original matrix *A*. **1972** *Jrnl. Social Psychol.* LXXXVI. 198 *All* possible comparisons are set out here—i.e., including the congruences in the off-diagonals. *Ibid.*, The off-diagonal entries are the congruences between one factor in the one study and every other factor in the other study.

off-drive ('ɒf,draɪv, ɔː-), *sb. Cricket.* [f. off *adv.* + drive *sb.*] A drive to the off (off D.3).

1867 *Australasian* 2 Feb. 140/2 He made a very good off drive for four. **1881** *Daily News* 9 July 2 Making an off drive for four. **1882** *Daily Tel.* 19 May, An off-drive for 3. **1963** *Times* 13 Feb. 4/3 A slightly mistimed off-drive let to a fine catch by Knight, running around in front of the screen.

off-drive ('ɒf,draɪv, ɔː-), *v. Cricket.* [f. prec. sb.] *trans.* To drive to the off (off D.3); also with the bowler as object. Hence ***off-driver***, ***off-driving*** vbl. sb.

1884 *J. Lillywhite's Cricketers' Ann.* 5 Leslie's 144 was an example of that player's very best style, his..off-driving being masterly. **1888** *Pall Mall G.* 22 Sept. 9/1 Then he off-drove his next ball to the ropes. **1893** R. Daft *Kings of Cricket* vi. 103 C. G. Lane..could, I think, 'off drive' Jackson better than any other player of the day. **1897** *Westm. Gaz.* 18 May 9/1 At 235 Ranjitsinjhi off-drove the new bowler for 4. **1904** F. C. Holland *Cricket* 10 Ernest Hayes of Surrey is as hard an off-driver as any. **1927** G. A. Terrill *Out in Glare* v. 95 Clement played his first ball defensively; ..off-drove the next for three. **1955** *Times* 13 July 8/5 Off the third ball of what might have been the penultimate over Waite off-drove Tyson over the top of Lock. **1977** *Guardian* 3 Jan. 11/6 Greig began by off driving Chandra for four.

off duty, off-duty, *phr.* (*adv.*) and *a.* [f. off *prep.*, off- 4 b + duty.] Of a person: not engaged or occupied with one's normal work; of things, actions, etc.: of, pertaining to, or suggestive of this state. Hence *ellipt.* as *sb.*, time spent off duty.

1851 H. Mayo *Pop. Superst.* (ed. 2) 79 The attention is off duty. **1852** [see duty 5 e]. **1903** 'G. Thorne' *When it was Dark* iii. v. 352 The ship..wore a somewhat neglected, 'off-duty' aspect. **1904** *Daily Chron.* 23 Dec. 4/4 The off-duty policeman. **1937** D. L. Sayers *Busman's Honeymoon* vii. 153, I like to do a bit o' reading in my off-duty. **1946** *Nature* 9 Nov. 646/2 To provide facilities for adults to educate themselves in their off-duty hours. **1962** R. P. Jhabvala *Get Ready for Battle* iv. 173 Joginder yawned, the luxurious off-duty yawn of a hardworking man. **1968** K. O'Hara *Bird-Cage* xxii. 180 Maureen took her off-duty in the morning. **1973** W. J. Burley *Death in Salubrious Place* i. 14 As on other off-duty Sundays, at twelve o'clock Matthew went into the Seymour Arms.

† **offe**, *sb. Obs. rare*$^{-1}$. [ad. L. *offa* bite, bit, morsel.] A small piece, morsel, crumb. Hence † **offe** *v. trans.* to break into bits, to crumble.

c **1420** *Pallad. on Husb.* i. 688 Half a stryke Of barly mele, enoyled offed lyte, In dayes thries x, let make hem slyke And faat ynough, so that theyr appetite Be seruyd wel, and that non offis [*v.r.* offes] white Englame vppon the rootes of theyr tonge.

† **offe**, *adv.* and *prep. Obs.* Also 3 oue. [An early ME. deriv. form from of, on the analogy of inne, *ute*, oute, uppe: used advb. and at end of a clause.]

A. *adv.* = off.

c **1175** *Lamb. Hom.* 29 ȝif þin hefet were offe. *c* **1200** Ormin 14032 To wasshenn offe þeȝȝre lic. *a* **1225** *Ancr. R.* 150 Hwonne þeos rinde is offe..hwiteð hit wiðuten.

B. *prep.* = of (following relative pron.: cf. inne *prep.* 1 β.).

c1200 Trin. Coll. Hom. 93 þat holie gestninge þe he offe specð. c1200 Ormin 462 þiss gode prest, þatt we nu mælenn offe. Ibid. 4097 Amang þatt Judewisshe follc þatt Crist wass borenn offe. c1275 Lay. 451 þat we beoþ oue [c 1205 of] icomen.

offe, obs. form of woof.

†**of-fear, o'ffear**, v. Obs. Forms: 2–3 offearen, 2–4 offeren, 3 of-færen, oferen. Chiefly in pa. pple. of-feared, of-fered, (of-ferd). [Late OE. f. of- + OE. fǽran to terrify: see fear v. OE. had in the same sense afǽran: see afear v.] trans. To frighten, terrify; in pa. pple. frightened, afraid.

1131 O.E. Chron., Ealle ðe hit sæȝon wæron swa offeared swa hi næfre ær ne wæron. a1200 Moral Ode 157 Þer we muȝen bon eþe offerd and herde us adreden. c1205 Lay. 15491 Swa wes al þa uerde Ladliche of-færed. Ibid. 23424 Þa wes þe king Frolle Laðliche of-fered [c 1275 afered]. a1225 Leg. Kath. 669 Ha wes sumdel offruht and offearet. a1250 Owl & Night. 976 Hi miȝte oferen here brost. c1315 Shoreham 129 Most here no fend offere.

offen ('ɒfən, ɔː-), prep. dial. (also U.S.). Also affn, offan, off'n. [var. of off of (see off adv. 7), by substitution of on for o': see o prep.[1] and prep.[2]] Off from; off.

1824 Blackw. Mag. Oct. 457/1 'Set down that bottle,' quoth I, wiping the saw-dust aff n't with my hand. 1871 E. Eggleston Hoosier Schoolmaster xxxi. 216 He told his wife that the master had jist knocked the hind-sights offen that air young lawyer from Lewisburg. 1871 S. Lanier Wks. (1945) I. 23 He picked all the rocks off'n the groun'. Ibid. 195, I got down off'n my load. 1903 'O. Henry' in Ainslee's Feb. 60/2 He'd jest light off'n his bronco and hunt a place to camp. 1922 E. O'Neill Hairy Ape (1923) v. 45 Clean, ain't it? Yuh could eat a fried egg offen it. 1930 Life & Work Feb. 63 Lottie says A maun stop letting ye borrow offan me. 1938 M. K. Rawlings Yearling i. 14 You knock them plates offen the table..and you'll see who's riled. 1940 W. Faulkner Hamlet I. ii. 43 She was taking Ab's breakfast offen the stove, onto two plates. 1944 C. Himes Black on Black (1973) 198 That made me mad, them sendin' that jalopy for me. But I was so high off'n them dreams I let it pass. 1977 J. Cleary Vortex v. 121 Who took the gun off'n her, then?

offen, obs. form of offing.

Offenbachian ('ɒfən,bɑːkɪən), a. [f. Offenbach + -ian.] Of, pertaining to, or characteristic of the French composer Jacques Offenbach (1819–80), or his music.

1869 Porcupine 24 July 152/3 The Offenbachian piece which is now drawing all London to the theatre of the Brahams. 1888 G. B. Shaw London Music 1888–89 (1937) 36 Its absurdly Offenbachian finale to the first act. 1937 Scrutiny Dec. 286 The peculiar poised vivacity of Offenbachian opéra bouffe is partly explained by Shaw. 1970 Daily Tel. 21 May 16/3 Poulenc's one-act opera..is an amusing piece in his most Offenbachian vein.

offence, offense (ə'fɛns), sb. Forms: 5–6 offens, (Sc. 6 offenns), 4– offence, offense, (5 afence). [Two forms: ME. offens, a. OF. offens injury, wrong, annoyance, misdeed, ad. L. offensu-s offence, annoyance, f. offens-, ppl. stem of offendĕre (see offend); and ME. offense, offence, a. F. offense (1295 in Hatz.-Darm.), ad. L. offensa a striking against, hurt, injury, wrong, disfavour, displeasure, f. offens-us, pa. pple. of offendĕre, analogous to sbs. in -āta, -ade, -ée; cf. the two forms of defence. The spelling offence would regularly represent the former of these: cf. hence, pence; it has been extended to both. In U.S. the spelling offense is now usual.]

†1. In Biblical use: Striking the foot against; stumbling. lit. and fig. Obs. rare.

1382 Wyclif Lev. xix. 14 Ne before the blynde thow shalt putte thing of offence. 1560 Daus tr. Sleidane's Comm. 31 The Scripture calleth Christ himselfe the stone of offence. 1611 Bible Isa. viii. 14.

2. A stumbling-block; a cause of spiritual or moral stumbling; an occasion of unbelief, doubt, or apostacy.

c1400 Apol. Loll. 35 Þei are mad in þe house of Israel in to offens of wickednesse. 1526 Tindale Gal. v. 11 Then had the offence which the cross geveth ceased. 1610 Carleton Jurisd. 288 That monstrous and horrible offence, which is giuen by many, concluding from texts grossely vnderstood. 1736 Butler Anal. II. iii, To me there seems no difficulty at all in these precepts but what arises from their being offences, i.e. from their being liable to be perverted..to mislead the weak and enthusiastic. 1865 Lightfoot Galatians (1874) 220/1 The offence of the Cross shall be my proudest boast.

3. a. The action of attacking or assailing; attack, assault. arms of offence, offensive weapons.

c1400 Destr. Troy 13911 In offens of the freike..He drof at hym with þe dart. c1440 Promp. Parv. 7/1 Afence, or offence, offensa. c1450 Holland Howlat 602 Richt so did the ferd..ȝaipe..to faynd his offens. 1598 Barret Theor. Warres 131 Against batteries, assaults, and other offences of the enemy. a1677 Barrow Serm. Ord. in Wks. Creator in Beauties Barrow (1846) 257 The woods..yield..shelter from offences of weather and sun. 1692 Bentley Boyle Lect. v. (1735) 176 Without Arms of Offense, without Houses or Fortifications. 1833 Ht. Martineau Fr. Wines & Pol. iv. 56 Here are no weapons of offence. 1879 Lubbock Addr. Pol. & Educ. vii. 145 If it would weaken our power of offence, it would..increase our strength for defence.

†b. Obstruction, opposition. Obs.

1600 Hakluyt Voy. (1810) III. 83 The Sunne..without any offence or hinderance of the night, giveth his influence.

†4. a. Hurt, harm, injury, damage. Obs.

c1374 Chaucer Troylus iv. 171 (199) Litel witen folk what is to ȝerne þat they ne fynde in hire desire offence. c1386 —— Sompn. T. 350 The reuers shaltou se..That wyn ne dooth to folk no swich offence. 1411 Rolls of Parlt. III. 650/2, I..dyd assemble thise persones..nought for to doo harme ne offence to yowe, My Lord the Roos. 1500–20 Dunbar Poems lxxxiv. 27 Thir folkis..Hes teichit ws quhat skaithis and offence That women dois with cullourit eloquence. 1582 Hester Secr. Phiorav. II. xxxii. 110 Woundes in the head where there is offence of the braine, are mortall. 1601 Shaks. Jul. C. iv. iii. 201 'Tis better that the Enemie seeke vs, So shall he waste his meanes..Doing himselfe offence. 1655 Sir T. Browne in Hartlib Ref. Commw. Bees 5 Which bare place..should be covered with a very thin hoop of iron..for there..it may receive offence. a1705 Ray Creation (1714) 139 Without offence to his eyes.

b. Feeling of being hurt, painful or unpleasant sensation, pain. Obs.

c1400 Rom. Rose 5677 Many a burthen..The whiche doth him lasse offense, For he suffrith in pacience. c1566 J. Alday tr. Boaystuau's Theat. World D viij b, Not without great violent dolors and offence of his tender and delicate bodie. 1626 Bacon Sylva §694 As the pains of the touch are greater than the offences of other senses; so likewise are the pleasures. 1674 Playford Skill Mus. III. 38 In few parts they leave an offence in the ear.

5. a. The act or fact of offending, wounding the feelings of, or displeasing another; usually viewed as it affects the person offended; hence, b. Offended or wounded feeling; displeasure, annoyance, or resentment caused (voluntarily or involuntarily) to a person. c. Phrases: to give offence to, to offend, displease; to take offence, to be offended, to feel resentment, to take umbrage; without offence, without giving, or taking offence. Colloq. phr. no offence: do not take offence; no offence is meant or taken.

c1386 Chaucer Man of Law's T. 1040 Hym ne moeued outher conscience Or Ire or talent or som kynnes affray Enuye or pride or passion or offence. c1425 Lydg. Assembly of Gods 653 Scysme, Rancour, Debate, and Offense. 1604 Shaks. Oth. II. iii. 52 As full of Quarrell, and offence As my yong Mistris dogge. 1606 —— Ant. & Cl. IV. xv. 45 Let me rayle so hye, That the false Huswife Fortune, breake her Wheele, Prouok'd by my offence.

b. c1374 Chaucer Boeth. III. pr. iv. 57 (Camb. MS.) For no peril þat myhte befallen the by offense of the kyng Theodoryke. 1560 Daus tr. Sleidane's Comm. 99 b, Whiche through their impudent marchandise, gave occasion of offence. 1580 J. Stubbs in Lett. Lit. Men (Camden) 42 To have incurred hir Majesties greate offence and judiciall sentence of transgressing the Lawe. 1666 Pepys Diary 7 Oct., I..did only answer, that I was sorry for his Highness' offence. 1692 Bentley Boyle Lect. 7 It was the opinion of many of the ancients, that Epicurus introduced a deity into his philosophy..purely that he might not incurr the offence of the magistrate. 1771 Wesley Wks. (1872) VI. 82 This is particularly observable in the case of offence; I mean, anger at any of our brethren.

c. 1390 Gower Conf. I. 111 The kinges brother in presence Was thilke time, and gret offence He tok therof. 1553 Eden Treat. Newe Ind. (Arb.) 9 Other poore byrdes may not without offence seke theyr praye. 1606 Shaks. Ant. & Cl. II. v. 99 Take no offence, that I would not offend you. 1663 Gerbier Counsel 108 Let them have somewhat that is called meum without offence. 1712 Addison Spect. No. 267 ¶8 Pleasing the most delicate Reader, without giving Offence to the most scrupulous. 1859 Tennyson Elaine 112 Many a bard, without offence, Has link'd our names together in his lay. 1866 G. Macdonald Ann. Q. Neighb. xii. (1878) 234 As I never took offence, the offence I gave was easily got rid of. 1882 A. W. Ward Dickens iii. 53 Unfortunately, offence is usually taken where offence is meant. 1829 G. Griffin Collegians II. xvii. 37 'Is poor Dalton really dead?' 'He is, sir. I have already said it.' 'No offence my boy. I only asked, because if he be..it is a sign that he never will die again.' 1833 Ht. Martineau Manchester Strike iii. 25 There was no offence in such a comparison. 1855 Mrs. Gaskell North & South II. iii. 32 I'd rather think yo' a fool than a knave. No offence, I hope, sir. 1973 R. Busby Pattern of Violence ii. 24 Be better when I'm out of this piss hole—no offence, gents.

†d. The condition of being regarded with displeasure; disfavour, disgrace. Obs.

1387 Trevisa Higden (Rolls) II. 221 Man..fel..out of homlynesse into offence [L. offensam] and wreþþe. 1601 Shaks. Twel. N. iv. ii. 75, I am now so farre in offence with my Niece, that I cannot pursue with any safety this sport.

†6. a. The fact of being annoying, unpleasant, or repulsive; offensiveness. b. Something that causes annoyance or disgust; an offensive object, quality, feature, or state of things; a nuisance. Obs.

c1430 Lydg. Min. Poems (Percy Soc.) 48 This litel schort dyte..lat it be noon offence To your womanly mercifulle pyte. 1596 Harington Metam. Ajax (1814) 51 They quickly found not only offence but infection to grow out of great concours of people. 1601 Shaks. All's Well II. iii. 270 Meethink'st thou art a generall offence, and euery man shold beate thee. 1660 F. Brooke tr. Le Blanc's Trav. 263 There was not the least offence of bruitishnesse to be observed in the..Ape.

7. a. A breach of law, duty, propriety, or etiquette; a transgression, sin, wrong, misdemeanour, or misdeed; a fault. Phr. to commit (†do, make) an offence. Const. against.

1382 Wyclif Phil. i. 10 That ȝe be clene and withoute offence in the day of Crist. 1423 Jas. I Kingis Q. xxxviii, Quhat haue I gilt to him or doon offense, That I am thrall? 1433 Rolls of Parlt. IV. 479/1 Any affray in offence of the Kynges pees. c1470 Henry Wallace viii. 1223 Wallace to sic did neuir gret owtrage, Bot gyff till him thai maid a gret offens. 1548–9 (Mar.) Bk. Com. Pr., Litany, Remember not lorde, our offences, nor the offences of our forefathers. 1603 Shaks. Meas. for M. III. ii. 15 What offence hath this man made you, Sir? 1604 —— Twel. N. III. iv. 345 If this yong Gentleman Haue done offence, I take the fault on me. 1651 Hobbes Leviath. II. xxvii. 156 Only Children, and Mad-men are Excused from offences against the Law Naturall. 1771 Junius Lett. lxiv. 327 The penalties imposed..bear no proportion to the nature of the offence. 1841 Lane Arab. Nts. I. 95 We have not seen him commit any offence against thee. 1845 Jebb Gen. Law in Encycl. Metrop. II. 711/1 Hitherto our attention has been exclusively devoted to offences against the rights of others. 1875 Whitney Life Lang. ix. 155 A host of inaccuracies, offenses against the correctness of speech.

b. spec. in Law: see quot. 1848.

1780 Bentham Princ. Legisl. xix. §1 An offence is an act prohibited, or, (what comes to the same thing) an act of which the contrary is commanded by the law. 1797 Tomlins Law Dict., Offences are capital or not: capital, those for which the offender shall lose his life: not capital, when an offender may forfeit his lands and goods, be fined, or suffer corporal punishment, or both. 1847 Act 10 & 11 Vict. c. 82 (Juvenile Offenders' Act) §1 Every Person..charged with having committed..any Offence which now is or hereafter shall or may be by Law deemed or declared to be Simple Larceny, or punishable as Simple Larceny, and whose Age..shall not..exceed the Age of Fourteen Years. Ibid. §4 For the more effectual Prosecution of Offences punishable upon summary Conviction by virtue of this Act. 1848 Wharton Law Lex., Offence, crime; act of wickedness. It is used as a genus, comprehending every crime and misdemeanor; or as a species signifying a crime not indictable, but punishable summarily, or by the forfeiture of a penalty. 1854 Act 17 & 18 Vict. c. 86 §2 Whenever..any Person under the Age of Sixteen Years shall be convicted of any Offence punishable by Law, either upon an Indictment or on Summary Conviction before a Police Magistrate.

†8. A fault, a blemish. Obs. rare.

1567 Maplet Gr. Forest 11 b, Rust therefore is nothing else but a defaulte and an offence in the..impurenesse of any substaunce.

9. (See quot. 1961.) N. Amer.

1928 G. H. Ruth Babe Ruth's Own Bk. Baseball ii. 19 A game of baseball is like a battle... It's a battle of defense against offense and the best organization wins. 1961 J. S. Salak Dict. Amer. Sports 303 Offense, the team, or a player of the team, on the attack, being at bat (as in baseball) or in possession of the ball (as in football). 1969 Internat. Herald Tribune 6 Nov. 13/4 The Leafs, with Dave Keon and Murray Oliver leading the offense.., whipped Oakland 5–2. 1970 Toronto Daily Star 24 Sept. 18/4 Knechtel can play offence if somebody gets hurt. 1974 State (Columbia, S. Carolina) 3 Mar. 3-D/4 The Bears had to look elsewhere for their offense, and it came in the person of Pat Edwards, who led the charge with 16. 1976 Washington Post 19 Apr. D1/6 The chief defect of the Washington Bullets has been made painfully obvious in their last two playoff games with the Cleveland Cavaliers—the team is suffering from a sick offense.

†**o'ffence, o'ffense**, v. Obs. [a. OF. offenser, offencer (15th c. in Hatz.-Darm.), ad. L. offensāre, frequentative of offendĕre.] = offend v.

1512 Helyas in Thoms Prose Rom. (1828) III. 48 By thee have we over grevously offenced God. 1549 Compl. Scot. xiv. 118 Ane seruand that offensit his maister. 1570 Buchanan Admonit. Wks. (1892) 35 Punissing sic ar gilty in offenceing. 1614 Sylvester Bethulia's Rescue vi. 345 Every Nation, whom Thine Arms offenc't.

o'ffenceful, a. rare. [f. offence sb. + -ful.] Full of offence, sinful.

1603 Shaks. Meas. for M. II. iii. 26 Your most offence full act Was mutually committed. 1970 V. Nabokov in New Yorker 23 May 44 With each year..That separation seems more offenseful. And the offense more absurd.

o'ffenceless, a. [f. as prec. + -less.] Without offence; unoffending, inoffensive; not causing offence or disgust; incapable of offence or attack.

1604 Shaks. Oth. II. iii. 275 Euen so as one would beate his offencelesse dogge, to affright an Imperious Lyon. 1611 Chapman May Day Plays 1873 II. 325 O most offenceless fault. 1642 Milton Apol. Smect. Introd., Wks. (1851) 274, I shall endeavour it may be offencelesse to other mens eares. a1763 Shenstone Love & Hon. 126 A soft-ey'd maid, a mild offenceless prey. 1889 Swinburne Poems and Ball., Armada, Tame and offenceless, and ranged as to die.

Hence o'ffencelessly adv., without offence.

a1631 Donne Ess. Div. (1651) 135 We may (offencelesly since there is nothing but [God] himself so large as the world) thus compare him to the World. 1866 Ruskin Cr. W. Olive Pref. 29 If I might offencelessly have spoken.

offencible, offencion, etc.: see offens-.

†**o'ffencious**, a. Obs. rare^{-1}. [f. offenci-on, offension + -ous.] = offensive 5.

c1592 Marlowe Massacre Paris I. B iij, Wherein hath Ramus been so offencious?

offend (ə'fɛnd), v. Also 4–6 offende, (afend(e); 4–7 pa. pple. offend, 5 pa. t. and pa. pple. offende. [a. OF. offend-re to strike against, attack, injure, wrong, sin against, excite to anger, do amiss, etc. = Sp. ofender, Pg. offender, It. offendere, ad. L. offendĕre to strike against, stumble, commit a fault, displease, vex, hurt, injure, etc., f. ob- (ob- 1 b) + -fendĕre (found only in compounds).]

I. †1. intr. To strike with the feet against something, to stumble. Obs. rare.

1382 Wyclif Zech. xii. 8 He that shal offende [Vulg. qui offendit, R.V. is feeble or that stumbleth] of hem in that day. —— Rom. xi. 11 Wher thei offendiden so that thei schulden falle doun? c **1450** *Cov. Myst.* (Shaks. Soc.) 230 If men walke whan it is nyght, Sone they offende in that dyrknes.

2. To make a false step or stumble morally; to commit a sin, crime, or fault; to fail in duty; to do amiss, transgress. Const. *against*, †*to*, †*unto*.

1382 Wyclif *James* iii. 2 Alle we offenden in many thingis. If ony man offendith not in word, this is a parfijt man. c **1440** *York Myst.* xviii. 66 What ayles þe kyng at me? For vn-to hym I neuere offende. **1490** Caxton *Eneydos* xxi. 76, I neuer dyde amys, nor neuer offended ayenst hym. **1552** *Bk. Com. Prayer* Gen. Conf., We haue offended agaynst thy holy lawes. **1560** Daus tr. *Sleidane's Comm.* 45 They that offende herein to be presented to the Magistrates and punished. **1709** Pope *Ess. Crit.* 159 Great wits sometimes may gloriously offend, And rise to faults true Critics dare not mend. **1854** Dobell *Balder* iii, Such forgiveness as we bring to those Who can offend no more.

†**3.** *trans.* To sin against; to wrong (a person); to violate or transgress (a law, etc.). *Obs.*

c **1320** *Cast. Love* 1015 But ȝef thei hem amende Of that that they dude God afende. **1340** Hampole *Prose Tr.* 21 Breke doune Couatise..þat þou..offende not thi conscience. **1390** Gower *Conf.* III. 201 Justice natheles Was kept and in nothing offended. **1484** Caxton *Fables of Æsop* i. xix, Thow hast so gretely offendyd and blasphemyd the goddes. **1540** *Act 32 Hen. VIII*, c. 14 Sundry persons.. haue not feared..to offende the said lawes. **1603** Shaks. *Meas. for M.* iii. ii. 16 Marry Sir, he hath offended the Law. **1651** Hobbes *Leviath.* iii. xxxviii. 248 The person offended, is Almighty God.

†**4.** In Biblical use: To be a stumbling-block, or cause spiritual or moral difficulty, to (a person); to shock; to cause to stumble or sin. *Obs.*

1526 Tindale *Matt.* xviii. 6 Whosoever offend one of these lytell wons which beleve in me. —— *Mark* ix. 43 Yf thy hande offende the cut hym of. **1577** Hanmer *Anc. Eccl. Hist.* (1619) 114 That, if it were possible, the very Elect themselves should be offended. **1658** *Whole Duty Man* ix. §7 If our very eyes or hands offend us (that is, prove snares to us) we must rather part with them.

†**b.** *intr.* To be caused to stumble, to be spiritually or morally shocked. *Obs.*

1382 Wyclif *Rom.* xiv. 21 It is good for to not ete fleisch, and for to not drynke wyn, nether in what thing thi brother offendith [Vulg. *offenditur*, *16th c. vv.* stumbleth, *Rheims* is offended], or is sclaundrid, or is maad syk. **1611** Bible *1 Cor.* viii. 13 If meate make my brother to offend.

II. †**5.** *trans.* To attack, assault, assail; also *absol.* to act on the offensive. *Obs.*

c **1374** Chaucer *Troylus* i. 549 (605) Loue..With desespeir so sorwfully me offendeth That streyght vn to þe deth myn herte ffayleth. c **1400** *Destr. Troy* 12350 Make hym kyng of þis kith..your fos to offend. **1540** *Act 32 Hen. VIII*, c. 14 The nauy..is..a great defence and surete of this realme in tyme of warre, as well to offende as defende. **1653** *Nissena* 25 The fiercest Tygers..shall not offend you, whilst [I am] by your side. **1726** Leoni tr. *Alberti's Archit.* I. 81/1 A Fort..well disposed for offending its enemies. **1744** Ozell tr. *Brantome's Sp. Rhodom.* 210 Some Swissers.. who cou'd neither Stop, nor Follow, nor Offend M. de Guise. [**1881** Duffield *Don Quix.* II. 305 Don Quixote,.. very proud to see how well his squire defended and offended.]

†**6.** To strike so as to hurt; to wound, to hurt; to give (physical) pain to; to harm, injure. *Obs.*

c **1385** Chaucer *L.G.W.* Prol. 392 Whan a flye offendith him or biteth He with his tayle awey the fle smyteth. **1483** Caxton *Gold. Leg.* 79/1 The blynde fader aroos and began offendyng hys feet to renne to mete hys sone. c **1566** J. Alday tr. *Boaystuau's Theat. World* S vij b, Some..coulde not by no meanes be offended or grieved with any kinde of poyson or venom. **1590** Spenser *F.Q.* iii. x. 1 His late fight With Britomart so sore did him offend, That ryde he could not till his hurts he did amend. **1685** Boyle *Effects of Mot.* v. 48 The heat..will offend one's hand at several times the distance. **1687** B. Randolph *Archip.* 81 A small fort..very strongly arch't over, so as no bomb can offend it. **1758** J. S. *Le Dran's Observ. Surg.* (1771) 284 The Passage of the Sword..penetrated into the Thorax, without offending the Lungs.

7. To hurt or wound the feelings or susceptibilities of; to be displeasing or disagreeable to; to vex, annoy, displease, anger; now *esp.* To excite a feeling of personal annoyance, resentment, or disgust in (any one). (Now the chief sense.)

13.. Chaucer *Compl. to Lady* 129 Wel lever is me lyken yow and deye Than for to any thing or thinke or seye That mighte yow offende in any tyme. **1387** Trevisa *Higden* (Rolls) III. 269 Furius Camillus offended þe peple in delynge of prayes. **1560** Daus tr. *Sleidane's Comm.* 353 b, Many thynges whiche myght offende mens myndes. **1598** Shaks. *Merry W.* iii. v. 94 The rankest compound of villanous smell, that euer offended nostrill. **1603** —— *Meas. for M.* iv. iii. 188 If baudy talke offend you, we'el haue very litle of it. **1667** Milton *P.L.* viii. 379 Let not my words offend thee, Heav'nly Power. **1732** Berkeley *Alciphr.* vii. §25 If I were not afraid to offend the delicacy of polite ears. **1842** Tennyson *Day-Dream* 214 You shake your head. A random string Your finer female sense offends. **1859–60** J. H. Newman *Hist. Sk.* (1873) III. ii. ii. 232 A zealous Christian preacher offends not individuals merely, but classes of men.

b. *to be offended*: to be displeased, vexed, or annoyed. Now, usually, To feel personal annoyance; to feel hurt, to take offence. Const. *with*, *at*, or with clause.

a **1548** Hall *Chron., Hen. VII* 17 [He] was sore offended and greatly greved with the Flemynges..for kepyng from him perforce hys sonne and heyre. **1576** Fleming *Panopl. Epist.* 112 Although I was offended at the enterprise, I was loath to forsake my frende. **1634** *Documents agst. Prynne* (Camden) 16 The truthe is, Mr. Pryn..would make the people altogether offended with all things att the present. **1700** Dryden *Fables* Pref., I find some people are offended that I have turned these tales into modern English, because they think them unworthy of my pains. **1833–6** J. Eagles *Sketcher* (1856) 340 You cannot think of them together without being offended at the labour and timidity of Claude. **1559** W. Cunningham *Cosmogr. Glasse* 137, I praye you be not offended althoughe at thys presente I interrupte you. **1646** J. Hall *Horæ Vac.* 28 Wander they in their pleasing darknesse, offended if you shew them light. **1774** Kelly *Sch. for Wives* iv. ii, Don't be offended because I decline to do you an additional wrong. *Mod.* He was highly offended at being passed over. You are offended with me. I assure you I am not in the least offended.

†**c.** *intr.* = prec. *Sc. Obs. rare.*

1561 Q. Mary in Spottiswood *Hist. Ch. Scot.* iv. (1677) 178 The Queen offendeth that I use the Title and Arms of England. a **1578** Lindesay (Pitscottie) *Chron. Scot.* I. 6. a **1639** Spottiswood *Hist. Ch. Scot.* iii. (1677) 174 A Noble man..answered, that it was a devout imagination, wherewith John Knox did greatly offend. *Ibid.* vi. 370 The King did highly offend at his escape.

Hence **o'ffended** *ppl. a.*; **o'ffendedly** *adv.*, in an offended manner.

c **1440** *Promp. Parv.* 7/1 Afendyd, or offendyd, *offensus*. **1607** Topsell *Four-f. Beasts* (1658) 200 These being all mingled together, let the offended place be rubbed therewith. **1611** Shaks. *Cymb.* i. i. 75 So soone as I can win th' offended King, I will be knowne your Aduocate. **1667** Milton *P.L.* x. 566 They..Chewd bitter Ashes, which th' offended taste With spattering noise rejected. **1746–7** Hervey *Medit.* (1818) 87 To obtain peace and reconciliation with their offended Jehovah. **1804** Eugenia de Acton *Tale without Title* I. 194 Our modern misses; who..look offendedly grave at those freedoms in conversation. **1847–9** Helps *Friends in C.* (1851) I. 116 Offended vanity is the great separator. **1876** G. Meredith *Beauch. Career* I. vii. 102 She disdained to notice them, and blinked offendedly to have her clear sight of the weakness.

o'ffendable, *a. rare*$^{-1}$. [f. prec. + -able.] Capable of being or liable to be offended.

1868 Helps *Realmah* xvii. (1876) 482, I am the least offendable of mortal men.

offendant (ə'fɛndənt), *a.* and *sb.* Also 7 -ent. [a. F. *offendant*, pr. pple. of *offendre* to offend. (The spelling *-ent* is after Latin: see -ent.)]

†**A.** *adj.* Causing injury or mischief. *Obs.*

1547 Boorde *Brev. Health* cccxxxii. 107 b, Reforme the matter the which is offendant.

B. *sb.* **1.** One who offends or does wrong; a transgressor, an offender. Now *rare*.

1597 Beard *Theatre God's Judgem.* (1612) 439 Neither was his anger appeased, vntill that the offendant..was stoned to death and burnt. **1648** Gage *West Ind.* xviii. (1655) 127 It was expected the offendants, some should be hanged, some banished, some imprisoned. **1831** *Fraser's Mag.* IV. 549 Ah! speak, offendant of the goddess!

†**2.** An assailant. *Obs.*

1644 Nye *Gunnery* (1670) 73 Granadoes..the effects whereof are of no less esteem; whether it be for the offendants or..defendants. **1646** *View Ld. Falkland's Infallibility* 155 If he make a thrust..he then turnes offendent or arguer.

offender (ə'fɛndə(r)). Also 5–6 -our, 6–7 -or. [f. offend *v.* + -er^{1}, or a. AF. **offendour*.] One who offends, who transgresses a law, or infringes a rule or regulation; one who gives offence, displeases, or excites resentment; †an assailant (*obs.*). In *Law.* One who commits an offence (sense 7 b). See also *first offender* s.v. first *a.* (*sb.*) and *adv.* C. 2; *old offender* s.v. old *a.* (*adv.*, *sb.*^{1}) D. 4.

juvenile offender, a person under a certain age (14 or 16) who commits an offence, and for whose case special statutes have been passed. *first offender*, one who has committed a first offence, and obtains the conditional remission of punishment provided by the 'First Offenders' Act' of 1888, etc.

1464 *Rolls of Parlt.* V. 568/2 An Action therof ayenst the seid offendour. **1526** *Pilgr. Perf.* (W. de W. 1531) 51 b, A synner and offender of god. **1532–3** *Act 24 Hen. VIII*, c. 4 They shall haue full power..to make proces agayne the offendours of this acte. **1552** *Bk. Com. Prayer* Gen. Conf., Haue mercy vpon vs miserable offendors. **1665** Manley *Grotius' Low C. Warres* 843 Spinola..proceeded against them as Offenders against the Law. **1794** *Hope's new Meth. Fencing* 219 As I have put Restrictions upon the Defender, so the Offender or Thruster must be likewise limited. **1847** *Act 10 & 11 Vict.* c. 82 An Act for the more speedy Trial and Punishment of Juvenile Offenders... In certain Cases, to ensure the more speedy Trial of Juvenile Offenders..it is expedient to allow of such Offenders being proceeded against in a more summary manner than is now by Law provided. **1854** *Act 17 & 18 Vict.* c. 86 An Act for the better Care and Reformation of Youthful Offenders in Great Britain... Whereas Reformatory Schools for the better training of Juvenile Offenders have been..established. **1861** M. Pattison *Ess.* (1889) I. 47 A blow or an abusive expression subjected the offender to a fine.

†**o'ffendicle.** *Obs.* [ad. L. *offendicul-um*, f. *offendĕre* to offend (see -cule), or a. OF. *offendicle* (16th c. in Godef.).] A stumbling-block; something that causes spiritual stumbling; a cause of offence; an occasion of sin or spiritual difficulty.

1545 Joye *Exp. Dan.* viii. Q vj, In the middes of these afflictions and offendicles. a **1564** Becon *Demands Holy Script., Of Prayers*, etc. (Parker Soc.) 610 What is a slander, to offend, or to be offendicle to any man? **1573** Abp. Parker *Corr.* (Parker Soc.) 454, I am a principal party, and an offendicle to him.

offending (ə'fɛndɪŋ), *vbl. sb.* [f. offend + -ing^{1}.] The action of the verb offend; offence, transgression; †hurting; a stumbling-block (*obs.*).

1388 Wyclif *Jer.* iv. 1 If thou takist awei thin offendyngis [1382 hurtende thingus] fro my face, thou schalt not be mouyd. **1500–20** Dunbar *Poems* ix. 39 To forgif my nychtbouris offending. **1604** Shaks. *Oth.* i. iii. 80 The verie head, and front of my offending, Hath this extent; no more. **1864** *Realm* 1 June 7 Signor Scalese's offendings in this respect..were very slight and few.

o'ffending, *ppl. a.* [f. as prec. + -ing^{2}.] That offends (in various senses of the verb).

1552 Huloet, Offendynge, *offensans*. c **1586** C'tess Pembroke *Ps.* lxxviii. iv, Offending bowes, and armor for defence. **1599** Shaks. *Hen. V*, iv. iii. 29 If it be a sinne to couet Honor, I am the most offending Soule aliue. **1694** Salmon *Bate's Dispens.* (1713) 201/2 It gives Ease and Help in most Diseases of the Breast and Lungs,..calling forth the offending Matter which causes Coughs, Hoarseness [etc.]. **1713** Swift *Cadenus & Vanessa* 240 Offending daughters oft wou'd hear Vanessa's praise rung in their ear. **1856** Froude *Hist. Eng.* (1858) I. iii. 249 They determined to compel the offending bishop to withdraw his words.

o'ffendress. *rare*$^{-1}$. [f. offender + -ess.] A female offender.

1601 Shaks. *All's Well* i. i. 153 Virginitie murthers it selfe, and should be buried in highwayes out of all sanctified limit, as a desperate Offendresse against Nature.

†**o'ffensable**, *a. Obs.* [a. OF. *offensable*, f. *offenser*: see offence *v.*] Offensive, aggressive.

1489 Caxton *Faytes of A.* iii. v. 176 Deffensable werre is preuyleged moche more than is werre offensable.

†**o'ffensant**, *a. Obs. rare.* [a. F. *offensant*, pr. pple. of *offenser*: see offence *v.*] Hurting, hurtful; injurious.

1578 Banister *Hist. Man* i. 24 That the..roughnes of the ribbes, might not be at any time, to the sensibilitie of the same [membrane] offensaunt.

offense, variant spelling of offence.

offensible (ə'fɛnsɪb(ə)l), *a.* Also 7 -cible. [a. obs. F. *offensible*, *-cible* (16th c. in Godef.), ad. L. *offensibilis* liable to stumble, f. *offens-*, ppl. stem of *offendĕre* to offend.]

†**1.** Of the nature of an offence, fault, or crime; hurtful, harmful, injurious; offensive. *Obs.*

1574 Hellowes *Gueuara's Fam. Ep.* 239 Those y^{t} wil take in hand any enterprise that naturaly is seditious or offensible. **1575** *Brieff Disc.* (1846) 52 Hurtefull and offensible ceremonies. **1601** Breton *Ravisht Soule*, That Glorie might not be offensible That in a Shadowe onely, should be showne. **1611** Cotgr., *Offensible*, offencible, hurtfull.

2. Liable to take offence, easily offended. *rare*$^{-1}$.

18.. Mrs. Browning *Lett. R. H. Horne* (1877) I. xxix. 192 From my own proper consciousness of offensible self-love.

†**o'ffension.** *Obs.* Also 4–6 -cioun, etc. [a. OF. *offension* (13th c., *offencioun* in Gower *Mirour*), ad. L. *offensiōn-em* injury, offence, stumbling-block, etc., n. of action from *offendĕre* to offend.]

1. Hurt, injury, damage; displeasure, annoyance; what is offensive or causes disgust; wrong-doing, misdeed, fault: = offence *sb.* 4–7.

c **1374** Chaucer *Boeth.* i. pr. iv. 13 (Camb. MS.) But yif þat thow of thy fre wille rather be blemished with myn offencion. c **1386** —— *Knt.'s T.* 1558 My beerd myn heer.. That neuere yet ne felte offensioun Of rasour nor of shere. **1412–20** Lydg. *Chron. Troy* iv. xxx, He was aferde agayne them of the towne In his person to do offenciowne. c **1470** Henry *Wallace* vii. 456 Fylth off carioune..rycht foull off offensioune. **1582** Bentley *Mon. Matrones* ii. 190 Thy mercie exceedeth all offension.

2. Stumbling; striking against some obstacle.

1543 Traheron *Vigo's Chirurg.* iii. *Wounds* ii. i. 114 Offension or stomblyng, is when one hurteth hymself by occasion of some thynge lyenge in hys way. **1559** Morwyng *Evonym.* 344 For woundes, prickinges and all kyndes of offensions and the swellinges that cum therupon. **1656** Stanley *Hist. Philos.* I. viii. 75 The offensions of bodies may happen without any fault, those of the soule cannot.

b. Spiritual stumbling, or the occasion of it.

1382 Wyclif *Ecclus.* xxxi. 7 The tree of offencioun is gold of men sacrefiende. —— *Rom.* ix. 32 Lo! I putte a stoon of offencioun [**1388** -sioun] in Syon, and a stoon of sclaundre. —— *2 Cor.* vi. 3 To no man ȝyuynge ony offencioun, that oure mynisterie be not reprouyd.

offensive (ə'fɛnsɪv), *a.* (*sb.*) Also 6 -syve, 7 -cive, -siff. [ad. med.L. *offensīv-us*, f. ppl. stem of *offendĕre* to offend (see -ive); in F. *offensif*, *-ive* (1538 in Godef. *Compl.*).]

A. *adj.* **1.** Pertaining or tending to offence or attack; attacking; aggressive; adapted or used for purposes of attack; characterized by attacking. Opposed to *defensive*.

1547–64 Bauldwin *Mor. Philos.* (Palfr.) 119 They beare armour defensiue to defend their owne euils, and armour offensiue to assayle the good manners of others. **1581** Savile *Tacitus, Hist.* iii. xi. (1591) 147 A power..sufficient..to make warre offensiue, not onely to stande vppon their defence. **1611** BIBLE *Transl. Pref.* 3 A whole armorie of weapons, both offensiue and defensiue. **1638** SIR T. HERBERT *Trav.* (ed. 2) 322 A long muzzle, her teeth sharp, and offensive. **1654** H. L'ESTRANGE *Chas. I* (1655) 16 Conjunction with them in a league Offensive and Defensive against their common enemies. **1781** GIBBON *Decl. & F.* xxx. III. 143 The four magazines and manufactures of offensive and defensive arms. **1838** THIRLWALL *Greece* III. 229 Ducetius now felt himself strong enough to attempt some offensive movements against the Greeks. **1847** T. N. SAVAGE in *Boston Jrnl. Nat. Hist.*, They [Gorillas] are exceedingly ferocious, and always offensive in their habits.

†**2.** Hurtful, harmful, injurious. *Obs.*

a **1548** in Ellis *Orig. Lett.* Ser. III. III. 237 All customys, usages, and maners..that hath byn offensyve to Godds pepyll. *a* **1592** GREENE *Jas. IV*, v. i, Beware in taking air Your walks grow not offensive to your wounds. **1681** CHETHAM *Angler's Vade-m.* viii. §10 Thunder and Lightening are very offensive and spoil the Angler's sport. **1732** ARBUTHNOT *Rules of Diet* 289 Water Fowl are offensive to the Stomach sometimes by reason of their Oiliness. **1813** SIR H. DAVY *Agric. Chem.* (1814) 219 A number of chemical substances which are very offensive and even deadly to insects.

3. Giving, or of a nature to give, offence; displeasing; annoying; insulting.

1576 FLEMING *Panopl. Epist.* 114 Neither will I commit any thing, which might seeme scrupulous and offensive [orig. *quod displiceat*]. **1597** SHAKS. *2 Hen. IV*, IV. i. 210 Like an offensiue wife, That hath enrag'd him on, to offer strokes. **1612** BRINSLEY *Lud. Lit.* xxx. 298 When by long custome the order is once made knowne, it will be no more offensive. **1703** DE FOE in *15th Rep. Hist. MSS. Comm.* App. IV. 76, I would do nothing..that should be offensive to my benefactors. **1815** J. W. CROKER in *C. Papers* (1884) I. iii. 62 The Prussians are very insolent, and hardly less offensive to the English than to the French. **1875** WHITNEY *Life Lang.* ix. 156 The nursery..has its dialect, offensive to the ears of old bachelors.

4. Causing painful or unpleasant sensations; now in reference to taste or smell, or to the moral feelings: disgusting, nauseous, repulsive.

1594 PLAT *New sorts Soyle* 6 Such springes as be offensive in smel. **1634** SIR T. HERBERT *Trav.* 213 They [bats] sqweake and call one the other, in most offensive cryes. **1784** COWPER *Task* II. 96 The rivers die into offensive pools. **1798** FERRIAR *Illustr. Sterne* i. 9 The offensive details..could persuade us of the extreme corruption of manners. **1819** J. W. CROKER in *C. Papers* (1884) I. v. 145, I am agreeably disappointed at finding 'Don Juan' very little offensive. **1886** *Law Times* LXXXI. 59/2 Permitting offensive smells to emanate from certain drains.

†**5.** Having the quality of transgressing or committing offence; of the nature of a transgression.

1607 NORDEN *Surv. Dial.* I. 31 The most offensiue will speake most of theyr wrong. **1609** TOURNEUR *Fun. Poeme Sir F. Vere* 242 Offensive minds were more discouraged By mercie than by justice. **1621** BRATHWAIT *Nat. Embassie* (1877) 133 When thy offensiue life mispent shall grieue thee. **1649** BP. HALL *Cases Consc.* (1650) 219 Some things are forbidden because they are justly offensive; and some other things are onely therefore offensive because they are forbidden.

†**6.** Causing offence (sense 1, *fig.*); that is an occasion of stumbling. *Obs.*

a **1640** J. BALL *Answ. Canne* (1642) I. 110 In a false church ..to continue a member..may be scandalous and offencive, an appearance of evill.

7. In sports, of or pertaining to the offence (OFFENCE *sb.* 9). *N. Amer.*

1912 C. MATHEWSON *Pitching in a Pinch* vi. 124 Offensive coaching means the handling of base runners, and requires quick and accurate judgment. **1928** G. H. RUTH *Babe Ruth's Own Bk. Baseball* ii. 23 The change from defensive to offensive play came gradually. **1969** *Eugene* (Oregon) *Register-Guard* 3 Dec. 1D/2 They picked Oregon's Bob Moore as the outstanding sophomore offensive back, and he more than lived up to expectations. **1970** *Toronto Daily Star* 24 Sept. 18/6 Argos had to keep an extra offensive lineman right from the start. **1974** *Anderson* (S. Carolina) *Independent* 18 Apr. 6C/1 In 1972, Heard was voted most valuable defensive player and in '73 he was picked most valuable offensive player. **1978** *Detroit Free Press* 2 Apr. 6E/2 He mentions the offensive linemen simply because they caught such hell for past Lions failures.

B. *sb.* **1.** [Absolute use of A. 1.] ***the offensive***: the position or attitude of attack; aggressive action. Phrase, ***to act on the offensive***.

1720 WATERLAND *Eight Serm.* Pref. 2 In my Vindication ..I was chiefly upon the Offensive, against the Adversaries of our common Faith. **1838** THIRLWALL *Greece* IV. 163 We do not know whether..the council now..felt itself strong enough to act on the offensive against him. **1851** GALLENGA *Italy* 319 He showed no disposition to shut himself up in Mantua, or even to give up the offensive. **1879** A. FORBES in *Daily News* 13 June 5/6 Haphazard offensive is one thing; judicious offensive quite another thing.

2. *fig.* Forceful action or movement directed towards a particular end; a sustained campaign or effort; esp. in ***peace offensive***.

1918 in S. Sassoon *Siegfried's Journey* (1945) vii. 72 There are indications that the enemies' peace offensive is creating the danger which is its object. **1919** G. B. SHAW *Peace Conf. Hints* ii. 18 Even when Germany capitulated they [*sc.* the Jingos] were still under such a terror of peace that they called her collapse 'a peace offensive'. *Ibid.* 29 There was only one really valid word in England about peace; and that was that those who preached it were the enemies of their country. Peace proposals were called peace offensives. **1939** *War Illustr.* 21 Oct. 192/1 Mr. Chamberlain stated in the House of Commons that nothing in the German 'peace offensive' could modify the attitude which Great Britain had felt it right to take. **1943** J. D. WILSON *Fortunes of Falstaff* i. 1 An excursus on Falstaff published in 1927 is, for instance, one of the more powerful offensives in the perennial campaign which Professor Stoll wages against the romantic school of Shakespearian criticism. **1952** *Ann. Reg. 1951* 321 China..publicly supported the various manifestations of the Soviet 'peace offensive'. **1970** R. LOWELL *Notebk.* 189 You mean our National Peace Offensive?

offensively (əˈfɛnsɪvlɪ), *adv.* [f. prec. + -LY².] In an offensive manner.

1. By way of attack or aggression; aggressively.

1556 J. HEYWOOD *Spider & F.* lxxxvii. 142 Flies (without your leaue) passing offensiuelie. **1560** DAUS tr. *Sleidane's Comm.* 97 They devise a league, not offensively but defensively. **1683** *Lond. Gaz.* No. 1824/2 That Crown will not be in a posture to act offensively against the Turks this Summer. **1792** BURKE *Pres. St. Aff.* Wks. VII. 93 They must make war..either offensively or defensively. **1807** G. CHALMERS *Caledonia* I. I. iii. 109 By thus daring to act offensively, they are said to have inspired terror.

2. So as to excite displeasure, resentment, or disgust; disagreeably, unpleasantly, insultingly; †injuriously, hurtfully (*obs.*).

1576 FLEMING *Panopl. Epist.* 110 Any thing..offensively spoken in the dispraise of your person. **1660** BOYLE *New Exp. Phys. Mech.* xi. 82 The surrounding sides of the Receiver were sensibly, and almost offensively heated by it. **1726** SWIFT *Gulliver* II. iii, Smelling very offensively. **1803** *Med. Jrnl.* X. 100 You will readily believe that what I have thought freely, I could not mean to express offensively. **1885** *Manch. Exam.* 16 June 4/7 Last night the same insubordination was displayed still more offensively.

†**3.** With displeasure, with resentment. *Obs. rare.*

1589 PUTTENHAM *Eng. Poesie* III. xxiii. (Arb.) 275 The king laughed hartily and tooke it nothing offensiuely. **1604** E. G[RIMSTONE] *D'Acosta's Hist. Indies* I. i. 4 Wee ought not to take it offencively.

†**4.** In violation of law or order. *Obs. rare.*

1607 *Nottingham Rec.* IV. 284 Tymber lyinge vpon the same Hill offensively.

offensiveness (əˈfɛnsɪvnɪs). [f. as prec. + -NESS.] The quality, character, or fact of being offensive; injuriousness, hurtfulness; *esp.* unpleasantness, disgustingness.

1618 LATHAM *2nd Bk. Falconry* (1633) 23 Otherwise.. there is no content to bee had..but altogether offensiuenesse and vexation. **1628** VENNER *Baths of Bathe* (1650) 357 In regard of their offensivenesse to the stomack. *a* **1688** W. CLAGETT *17 Serm.* (1699) 83 The offensiveness of these offences is..abated. **1755** HALES in *Phil. Trans.* XLIX. 344 The smell of the ascending vapour was very offensive, which offensiveness abated much in five minutes. **1856** FROUDE *Hist. Eng.* (1858) II. viii. 244 The offensiveness of the evil was disguised by the charm of the good.

offer (ˈɒfə(r)), *sb.* Also 5–6 offre, 6 *Sc.* offir(r. [a. F. *offre* (OF. *ofre*, 12th c. in Littré), vbl. sb. f. *offr-ir* to OFFER. (The cognate Teut. langs. have a parallel formation from the vb. in the sense 'offering, sacrifice' (ON. *offr*, Sw., Da., Du. *offer*); but no analogous sb. existed in OE.).]

1. a. An act of offering (see OFFER *v.* 3, 4); a holding forth or presenting for acceptance; an expression of intention or willingness to give or do something conditionally on the assent of the person addressed; a proposal.

1433 *Rolls of Parlt.* IV. 425/1 My said Lord of Bedford.. made hem þerinne diverse faire overtures and offris. *Ibid.*, Of the whiche his liberall offre þe said Lords þankid hym. *c* **1489** CAXTON *Sonnes of Aymon* xii. 298 Sire, leve that offre that reynawde gyveth to you. **1590** MARLOWE *2nd Pt. Tamburl.* v. iii, There should not one..Live to give offer of another fight. **1613** PURCHAS *Pilgrimage* (1614) 546 If any of his subjects hath any precious stone of value, and make not him the offer of it, it is death to him. **1647** HAMMOND *Power of Keys* iv. 60 This magisteriall affirmation having no tender or offer of proof annext to it. **1711** ADDISON *Spect.* No. 89 ¶7 A virtuous Woman should reject the first Offer of Marriage. **1868** E. EDWARDS *Ralegh* I. xvi. 319 [He] had long been profuse in his offers of service.

b. *ellipt.* A proposal of marriage.

a **1548** HALL *Chron., Hen. VII* 7b, [She] there receaved a corporall othe of him to mary her eldest daughter, which offre she abode not by. **1619** T. LORKIN 4 May in *Crt. & Times Jas. I* (1848) II. 156, I would not wish any good offer for your niece should be refused, in hope of this. **1712–14** POPE *Rape Lock* I. 82 When offers are disdained, and love denyed. **1807–8** W. IRVING *Salmag.* (1824) 144 It was owing to her never having had an offer. **1847** A. BRONTË *Agnes Grey* xiv. 219 The conceited wretch chose to interpret my amiability of temper his own way, and at length..he actually —made me an offer! **1971** G. MITCHELL *Lament for Leto* iv. 121 Ronald Dick..certainly would make me an offer if I were free. **1976** *Scottish Rev.* Spring 6 She had plenty of flames and several guid offers.

c. The act of offering a price or equivalent for something; a bid.

c **1550** *Plumpton Corr.* 257 For your hofer, it likes not; I shud a sold it, I truste, for 4*s.* or better. **1721** SWIFT *South-Sea Project* xx, When stock is high they come between, Making by secondhand their offers. **1890** *Times* 19 July 16/1 The proprietor does not bind himself to accept the highest or any offer.

d. The condition of being offered; in *Comm.* the fact of being offered for sale, esp. at a low price, as sales promotion. ***on offer***, on sale.

1794 GOUV. MORRIS in Sparks *Life & Writ.* (1832) III. 48 A chateau was in my offer on most eligible terms. **1881** *Daily News* 23 Aug. 3/6 (*Market Report*) Old wheat scarce and dear. Very little barley on offer. **1966** *Listener* 9 June 830/1 The cheaper and nastier Hollywood series, which are always on offer. **1967** *Ibid.* 1 June 704/1 Purchasing the most sophisticated weapons we have on offer. **1971** *Woman's Own* 27 Mar. 21 Next week..bargain vanity case offer.

2. *concr.* That which is offered. **a.** Something presented in worship or devotion; an offering. Now *rare* or *Obs.*

1548 GEST *Pr. Masse* in H. G. Dugdale *Life* (1840) App. i. 72 No man must attempt to appear before him withoute hys offre, more or less. *a* **1586** SIDNEY (J.), Fair streams,.. let the tribute offer of my tears procure your stay awhile. **1840** MISS MITFORD in L'Estrange *Life* III. vii. 105 A tuft of flax to a Grecian bride Was ancient Hymen's offer.

†**b.** Something presented for acceptance. *rare.*

1634 MILTON *Comus* 702 Were it a draft for Juno when she banquets, I would not taste thy treasonous offer.

c. An opportunity or 'opening'. *dial.* or *colloq.*

1831 S. LOVER *Legends & Stories of Ireland* 9 The first offer afther I make her as good as new. **1877** *Coursing Calendar Autumn 1876* 302 Napoleon went past Countess in the race to the hare, and..never gave his antagonist an offer. **1925** *Dialect Notes* V. 337 *Offer*, a chance (at seals).

3. a. An attempt, an essay at doing something, or a show of this; the act of aiming at something, an aim. Now *rare* or *Obs.*

1581 LAMBARDE *Eiren.* I. iv. (1602) 19 To represse all intention of vproare & force..before that it should growe vp to any offer of danger. **1597** BACON *Coulers Good & Evill* x. in *Ess.* (Arb.) 154 Many inceptions are..imperfect offers and essayes. **1683** MOXON *Mech. Exerc., Printing* xvii. ¶2 The right side..[is] too thick, and must by several offers be Filed away,..not all at once. **1705** ADDISON *Italy* 526 One sees in it a kind of Offer at Modern Architecture. **1711** STEELE *Spect.* No. 118 ¶2 He had no sooner spoke these Words, but he made an Offer of throwing himself into the Water. **1842** S. LOVER *Handy Andy* xv. 140 You'd make a fair offer at anything but an answer to your school-master.

b. A knob or bud showing on a stag's antler.

1884 JEFFERIES *Red Deer* iv. 69 Little knobs appear on the beam like points about to grow, which are said to be 'offers', as if a point had offered to grow there. **1893** *Athenæum* 1 Apr. 400/2 A splendid red deer from Morena—with fourteen good points and an 'offer' or two.

offer (ˈɒfə(r)), *v.* Forms: 1–2 offrian, 2–3 offrien, 3 offren, (offri, 4 offir, -yr, 4–5 -ire, 4–6 ofre, 5 offere), 4–7 offre, 4– offer. [OE. *offri-an* = OFris. *offria*, *offaria*, OS. *offrôn* (MLG., MDu. *offeren*, LG. *offern*, Du. *offeren*), Icel., Sw. *offra*, Da. *offre* to offer a sacrifice; ad. L. *offer-re* to bring before, present, offer, bestow, inflict, in Vulg. and Christian L. to offer to God, offer sacrifice. In these last senses the L. verb was adopted with Christianity in OE. and the cognate langs. Meanwhile the more primary senses continued in F. *offr-ir* (ONFr. *offr-er*, Pr. *offrir*, Cat. *oferir*, It. *offerire*), and, after the Norman Conquest, gradually passed into Eng., sense 2 being a natural transition. With the exception of Dutch (? from Fr.) the other Teut. langs. retain only the sense 'to offer in sacrifice'.]

1. a. *trans.* To present (something) to God (or to a deity, a saint, or the like) as an act of worship or devotion; to sacrifice; to give in worship. Also with *up*. Const. *to* or formerly with simple dative.

The object may be a material thing, as a slain animal, vegetable produce, incense, money, etc. (cf. OFFERING *vbl. sb.* 2); or, by extension, prayer, thanksgiving, etc.

c **825** *Vesp. Psalter* lxv. 15 Onsegdnisse merȝlice ic ofriu ðe [L. *holocausta medullata offeram tibi*]. *c* **1000** ÆLFRIC *Exod.* xii. 6 And offrian eall Israhela folc þæt [lamb] on æfen. *c* **1000** —— *Hom.* II. 456 Hit wæs ȝewunelic..þæt man Gode ðyllice lac offrode on cucan orfe. *c* **1175** *Lamb. Hom.* 87 Heo sculden offrien of elchan hiwscipe gode an lomb. *c* **1200** ORMIN 1003 And aȝȝ wass sallt wiþþ iwhillc lac Biforenn Drihhtin offredd. **1382** WYCLIF *1 Cor.* x. 20 Tho thingis that hethene men offren, thei offren to deuelis and not to God. *c* **1400** *Destr. Troy* 2881 He offert onestly in honour of Venus, A gobet of gold. **1463** *Bury Wills* (Camden) 27 The seid preests to haue jd. ob. to offre at the messe. **1550** CROWLEY *Last Trump.* 473 Christe was once offered for all, To satisfie for all our synne. **1602** MARSTON *Antonio's Rev.* III. ii, I have a prayer or two to offer up. **1613** PURCHAS *Pilgrimage* (1614) 792 Then did he offer Incense to Vitzliputzli. **1711** ADDISON *Spect.* No. 159 ¶2 After having washed myself, and offered up my Morning Devotions. **1868** TENNYSON *Lucretius* 69, I would not one of thine own doves, Not ev'n a rose, were offer'd to thee. **1875** JOWETT *Plato* (ed. 2) III. 311 Offer up a prayer with me and follow.

b. *absol.* To present a sacrifice or offering; to sacrifice; to make a donation as an act of worship.

c **893** K. ÆLFRED *Oros.* I. xiv. §1 Mesiane noldon ðæt Læcedemonia mægdenmin mid heora offrian. *c* **1000** ÆLFRIC *Exod.* v. 1 Forlæt min folc, þæt hit mæge offrian me on þam westene. **1297** R. GLOUC. (Rolls) 325 Brut..offrede to þis maumet & honoured it inow. **1377** LANGL. *P. Pl.* B. XIII. 197 And þe pore widwe for a peire of mytes, þan alle þo that offreden in-to gazafilacium. *c* **1400** *Three Kings Cologne* 133 All þe pepil..come & visitid hem and offrid to hem wiþ gret deuocioun. *a* **1533** LD. BERNERS *Huon* lvii. 191 We..are goyng to offre at yᵉ holy sepulcre. **1548–9** *Bk. Com. Prayer, H. Communion*, Rubric, So many as are disposed, shall offer unto the poore mennes boxe. **1638** SIR T. HERBERT *Trav.* (ed. 2) 92 Bannyans have repayred to offer here and to wash away their sinnes in Ganges. **1725** tr. *Dupin's Eccl. Hist. 17th C.* I. v. 139 When it is forbidden in the Canons to the Deacons to offer. **1893** G. L. KITTREDGE in *Atlantic Monthly* LXXII. 830/2 Those who offer to his relics and receive his absolution.

†**2. a.** *gen.* To give, present, make presentation of (*spec.* to a superior as an act of homage, etc.). Const. as in 1. *Obs.*

The first two quots. may be regarded as intermediate between 1 and 2, the purpose being religious.

c **1122** *O.E. Chron.* an. 963 He nam up Sc̃a Kyneburh and S. Kynesuiđ..and S. Tibba..and brohte heom to Burch, and offrede heom eall S. Peter on an dæi. *Ibid.* an. 1013 Ælfsige..bohte..sc̃e Florentines lichaman, eall buton þe heafod, to .v. hundred punda, &..offrede hit Crist & sc̃e Peter. *c* **1250** *Gen. & Ex.* 3619 Ðis folc..Offreden him siluer and golde..He it bi-taȝte besseleel. *c* **1330** R. Brunne *Chron. Wace* (Rolls) 4554 When þis grete lordynges Seyen Cesar ofre þem swylke þynges. **1411** *Rolls of Parlt.* III. 650/2 Offre yow v c. mark to ben paied at youre will. *a* **1548** Hall *Chron., Edw. IV* 239 That all his heyres..should offer a hart of lyke weight and value, as a releve and homage done. **1568** Grafton *Chron.* II. 193 To sweare unto him homage and fealtie, the which every one..did willyngly offer.

b. *absol.* To give something as a present.

1671 L. Addison *West Barbary* 186 The Negro's likewise call every one by name who Offer, saying Fulano (or such an one) lays on so much.

3. a. To present or tender for acceptance or refusal; to hold out (a thing) to a person to take if he will. (The prevailing sense.) Const. indirect (dat.) and direct obj., or direct obj. and *to*, †*unto*: either obj. may be the subject of the passive voice: 'the place was offered to him', or 'he was offered the place'.

c **1375** *Sc. Leg. Saints* xxxiii. (*George*) 322 þe king þane ane infinite Of gret tresore gert offerit be To george. *c* **1400** Maundev. (1839) viii. 83 Thei offren hem to do alle, that the berere askethe. *a* **1548** Hall *Chron., Hen. V* 49 b, To inquyre what raunsome he would offer. **1596** Shaks. *Tam. Shr.* II. i. 383 Nay, I haue offred all, I haue no more, And she can haue no more then all I haue. **1611** Bible *2 Sam.* xxiv. 12, I offer thee three things; chuse thee one of them. **1665** Manley *Grotius' Low C. Warres* 43 He offered himself as a Peacemaker between them. **1791** Mrs. Radcliffe *Rom. Forest* ix, I cannot accept the honour you offer me. **1849** Macaulay *Hist. Eng.* vi. II. 116 One of the ringleaders..was offered a pardon if he would own that Queensberry had set him on. **1875** J. W. Dawson *Dawn of Life* Pref. 7, I offer no apology.

b. with dat., and inf. as direct obj.

(The object being what the person is permitted to do or have.)

1634 Sir T. Herbert *Trav.* 34 He offered her faithfully to haue remission, and that the Infant Mogull out of his clemency should forget all former Quarrels. **1654** Dor. Osborne *Lett.* (1888) 263 If he offers me to stay here, this hole will be more agreeable to my humour than any place that is more in the world. **1939** C. Morley *Kitty Foyle* 328, I offered him to go in the bathroom to wash.

†**c.** with *obj. cl.* To make the proposal, suggest (*that* something be done). *Obs.*

1660 Marvell *Corr.* Wks. 1872–5 II. 21 Some offerd..that onely the lands 'in capite', which receive the benefit, should be taxed with the revenue. **1727** Pope, etc. *Art of Sinking* 114 It is therefore humbly offered, that all and every individual of the bathos do enter into a firm association.

d. *absol.* To make an offer or proposal; to make an offer of marriage, to 'propose'.

1596 Shaks. *1 Hen. IV*, v. i. 114 We offer faire, take it aduisedly. *Prin.* It will not be accepted. **1847** Tennyson *Princ.* III. 143, I offer boldly: we will seat you highest. **1852** R. S. Surtees *Sponge's Sp. Tour* i. 2 He never hesitated about offering to a lady, after a three days' acquaintance.

e. *Comm.* To present for sale.

1632 J. Hayward tr. *Biondi's Eromena* 25, I understand that your Steward hath offered to sale your goods. **1741** Middleton *Cicero* I. v. 370 A particular estate..which she was now offering to sale. **1899** *Daily News* 29 May 10/5 Short attendance and very little wheat offering.

f. In *to offer battle*, etc. there is perh. some connexion with sense 5.

1560 Daus tr. *Sleidane's Comm.* 64 So great a number of ennemies are assembled to offer battell. **1576** Fleming *Panopl. Epist.* 218 To keepe off Fortune furiously offering the combate. **1596** Shaks. *Tam. Shr.* v. ii. 162, I am asham'd that women are so simple, To offer warre, where they should kneele for peace. **1839** Thirlwall *Greece* li. VI. 239 Darius ..was about to meet him and to offer battle.

g. *refl.* To present (oneself) to a person for acceptance or refusal; to put (oneself) forward, *spec.* as a suitor.

1765 H. Walpole *Castle of Otranto* i. 18 In short, Isabella, since I cannot give you my son [in marriage], I offer you myself. **1893** M. E. Mann *In Summer Shade* II. xi. 28, I have this evening offered myself to Mary Burne, and she has accepted me. **1903** *Eng. Dial. Dict.* IV. 332/2 He did nothing but offer himself for her for so long as she lived. **1930** G. B. Shaw *Apple Cart* II. 75 It is my intention to offer myself to the Royal Borough of Windsor as a candidate at the forthcoming General Election. **1978** I. Murdoch *The Sea, The Sea* 436 Charles, darling, tell me... When you came here today were you going to offer yourself to me?

†**h.** *intr.* To stand as a candidate for office. *Obs.*

1766 J. Wedgwood *Let.* 4 June (1965) 40 Some of our friends suspected a Candidate would offer who lived at too great a distance from the centre of the business. **1803** W. R. Davie *Let.* 20 Aug. in J. Steele *Papers* (1924) I. 405 The Gentlemen who prevailed upon me 'to offer' as they call it, consisted principally of the moderate men of both parties. **1835** A. B. Longstreet *Georgia Scenes* 234 Then lowering his voice to a confidential but distinctly audible tone, 'what you offering for?' continued he.

i. *trans.* With spoken words as object: to say tentatively or helpfully.

1881 M. Crommelin *Miss Daisy Dimity* I. ii. 32 'There are two hens to be set with Brahma eggs this morning, and a brood of young Cochins coming out,' offered Polly hesitatingly. **1894** 'R. Andom' *We Three & Troddles* iv. 21 'A coffee-mill,' suggested Wilks. 'Or a sewing machine,' I offered. **1973** J. Rossiter *Manipulators* v. 51 'Perhaps,' Bradley offered helpfully, 'you've been name-calling somebody. And they didn't like it.' **1974** 'E. Lathen' *Sweet & Low* v. 52 'Just like civil war in Nigeria,' offered Charlie sagely.

j. *Telephony.* To direct (a call) *to* a piece of apparatus.

1950 J. Atkinson *Herbert & Procter's Telephony* (new ed.) II. ii. 33/2 It is readily possible to read off the traffic offered to any particular contact for any value of total traffic. **1960** R. Syski *Introd. Congestion Theory Teleph. Syst.* v. 194 The *N* sources originate calls which are offered to *R* channels. **1960** *Post Office Electr. Engineers' Jrnl.* LIII. 76/2 This form of control will facilitate the provision of automatic alternative routing, which will permit traffic to be offered to a direct route and then, if all circuits are engaged, to overflow to the transit network.

4. with *inf.* To propose, or express one's readiness (to do something), conditionally on the assent of the person addressed.

1433 *Rolls of Parlt.* IV. 425/1 My said Lord of Bedford..offerd and agreed hym to serve þe Kyng. *a* **1533** Ld. Berners *Huon* lix. 203 He offeryth to make amendes. **1588** Hunsdon in *Border Papers* (1894) I. 306, I..did offer to send Sir John Selby and towe others to confer with them. **1634** Sir T. Herbert *Trav.* 185 They have too great plenty, and offred to sell us some. **1724** De Foe *Mem. Cavalier* (1840) 270, I offered to go to the king. **1865** Trollope *Belton Est.* i. 15 He had offered to accompany her to Belton.

5. a. To make an attempt to inflict, deal, or bring to bear (violence, or injury of any kind); to put forth one's effort to make (attack, resistance).

1530 Palsgr. 646/1 Every man offerith hym wronge. *c* **1590** Marlowe *Faust.* x, For the injury he offered me here in your presence. **1597** Shaks. *2 Hen. IV*, IV. i. 211 That hath enrag'd him on, to offer strokes. **1613** Purchas *Pilgrimage* (1614) 708 [They] avenged themselves for such wrongs as by the Turkes..had beene formerly offered them. **1781** Gibbon *Decl. & F.* xxviii. III. 84 The insults which he offered to an ancient chapel of Bacchus. **1863** P. Barry *Dockyard Econ.* 202 Offering..serious resistance from the forts and batteries.

b. with *inf.* To make an attempt or show of intention (to do something); to essay, try, endeavour. (In early use sometimes nearly = to venture, dare, presume, have the hardihood.)

1540–1 Elyot *Image Gov.* 29 After that the emperour had concluded in this wise his reson, there was no man offred to reply thereto. *a* **1553** Udall *Royster D.* III. v. (Arb.) 58, I knocke your costarde if ye offer to strike me. **1613** Jackson *Creed* II. xxx. §17 Heauing and offering with might and maine to get out. **1656** Bp. Hall *Breath. Devout Soul* (1851) 201, I may not offer to look into the bosoms of men, which thou hast reserved for thyself. **1703** Moxon *Mech. Exerc.* 37 You should not offer to cut the Grooves to their full width at the first. **1865** Trollope *Belton Est.* xxiv. 284 He did not offer to kiss her.

c. *intr.* with *at*: To make an attempt at or upon; to aim at. Now *rare* or *Obs.*

1611 B. Jonson *Catiline* II. i. (Rtldg.) 278/1 Offering at wit too? why, Galla, Where hast thou been? **1649** Milton *Eikon.* Pref., This Man, who hath offer'd at more cunning fetches to undermine our Liberties..then any British King before him. **1683** Burnet tr. *More's Utopia* (1684) 36 The Jests at which he offered were so cold and dull. **1687** —— *Trav.* iii. (1750) 169, I will not offer at a Description of the glorious Chapel. **1701** W. Wotton *Hist. Rome, Alexander* iii. 521 Several offer'd at the Empire during his time, who came to nothing. **1847** Mrs. Carlyle *Lett.* II. 3 He did not offer at coming in.

†**6.** *intr.* To incline, tend in some direction; to have an inclination or disposition *to*. *Obs.*

1639 Fuller *Holy War* IV. xiv. (1840) 203 They suspected him to be unsound in his religion, and offering to Christianity. *Ibid.* v. xxv. (1840) 28 We find some straggling rays and beams of valour offering that way.

7. a. *trans.* To bring forward or put forth for consideration, to propound. (In quots. 1634, 1638, To 'give', let one have; to mention or cite by way of example.)

1583 Burleigh *Let. to Whitgift* in Fuller *Ch. Hist.* IX. v. §9 But now they coming to me, I offer how your Grace proceeded with them. **1634** Sir T. Herbert *Trav.* 43, I will offer you a little of the Arabian Tongue as is more spoken in that Countrey. **1638** *Ibid.* (ed. 2) 232 The rest I offer not, this in my conceit sufficing. **1710** Prideaux *Orig. Tithes* v. 316 When all that I have offered hath been duly considered. **1796** H. Hunter tr. *St.-Pierre's Stud. Nat.* (1799) I. 524 We shall offer a few thoughts hereafter on this part of Harmony. *Mod.* On this I wish to offer a few remarks.

b. To put (a part of a structure, etc.) in place to see how it looks or whether it fits properly; to hold up or display (something) to test its appearance or correctness. Usu. const. *up* (occas. *on*). orig. *dial.*

1854 A. E. Baker *Gloss. Northamptonshire Words* II. 73 One of his workmen said, 'Shall I offer up, or offer on, that frame, to see if it will fit the picture?' **1887** Parish & Shaw *Dict. Kentish Dial.* 110, I once heard a master paper-hanger say to his assistant, when a customer was inspecting some wall-papers, 'Just offer this paper up for the lady to see.' **1903** *Eng. Dial. Dict.* IV. 332/2, I will offer the shrubs before planting them. **1952** Granville *Dict. Theatr. Terms* 125 *Offer up*, to show the producer the position of a picture or an ornament for approval before fixing it permanently, particularly mirrors which reflect the stage lighting. (2) Carpenters *offer up* doorways to fit into the door-frames, in fact they offer up anything before it is approved. The term is used by carpenters outside the theatre and is peculiar to their trade.

8. a. Of a thing: To present (to sight, notice, etc.); to furnish, afford, give.

1576 Fleming *Panopl. Epist.* 44 Sundrie circumstances which offered them selves to my judgement. **1698** Fryer *Acc. E. India & P.* 56 A gravelly Forest with tall benty Grass, offers, besides its taking Look, diversity of Game. **1729** Butler *Pref. Serm.* Wks. 1874 II. 5 It is scarce possible to avoid judging..of almost every thing which offers itself to one's thoughts. **1834** Mrs. Somerville *Connex. Phys. Sc.* iv. (1835) 42 Their motions offer the singular phenomenon of being retrograde. **1892** Westcott *Gospel of Life* 41 Each age offers its characteristic riddles.

b. *intr.* for *refl.* To present itself; to occur.

1601 Holland *Pliny* I. 57 There offereth to our eie, first the towne Nicæa. **1696** *Lond. Gaz.* No. 3222/3 If the Wind and Weather offer for his Embarking. **1697** Dryden *Virg. Georg.* IV. 631 Th' Occasion offers, and the Youth complies. **1709** Steele *Tatler* No. 4 ⁋1, I..shall take any Thing that offers for the Subject of my Discourse. **1809** Malkin *Gil Blas* I. x. ⁋8 Taking the first path that offered, we soon galloped out of the forest. **1891** A. H. Craufurd *Gen. Craufurd & Light Division* 7 He..distinguished himself wherever an occasion offered.

offerable (ˈɒfərəb(ə)l), *a.* *rare.* [f. prec. + -able.] That can or may be offered.

1577 Fulke *Confut. Purg.* 290 The onely once offered and no more offerable sacrifice of Christ his death. **1648** W. Mountague *Devoute Ess.* I. x. §7. 124 Allowing all that hath Cesars Image onely on it, offerable to Cesar. **1917** E. Pound *Let.* 26 Aug. (1971) 120 The minimum offerable arrangement would be six articles a year at 10 dollars each.

offerand, variant of offrand *Obs.*, offering.

†**offerd, offered**, obs. ff. afeard, afraid.

c **1200** *Trin. Coll. Hom.* 195 He beđ of harme offered. *a* **1300** *Floriz & Bl.* 632 Sore hi beoþ offerd.

offered (ˈɒfəd), *ppl. a.* [f. offer + -ed.]

1. a. Brought as an offering; presented for acceptance, etc.: see the verb.

c **1175** *Lamb. Hom.* 87 þet ioffrede lomb þet þe engel het offrian bitacneđ cristes deđþe. **1566** Securis *Detection* C vij b, The common prouerbe saith, that offered seruice stynketh. **1667** Milton *P.L.* IX. 300 Thou thy self with scorne And anger wouldst resent the offer'd wrong. **1681** Flavel *Meth. Grace* xxxiii. 550 The refusal of offered salvation. **1697** Dryden *Virg. Georg.* II. 547 A..Goat..Whose offer'd Entrails shall..drip their Fatness from the Hazle Broach. **1885** *Athenæum* 25 July 104/2 Faust..discarded the offered aid.

b. In the sense of offer *v.* 3 j.

1960 R. Syski *Introd. Congestion Theory Teleph. Syst.* v. 194 If an offered call cannot be served immediately because at the instant of its arrival no free channel is available, the source which originated it nevertheless continues to demand service. **1974** Cox & Reudink in W. C. Jakes *Microwave Mobile Communic.* vii. 550 Sometimes estimates of offered traffic are made directly instead of estimating attempt rates and holding times separately.

2. [f. offer *sb.* 1 b.] That has received an offer (of marriage). *rare.*

1709 Steele *Tatler* No. 52 ⁋3 It..assigns to a long Despair the Woman who is well offer'd, and neglects that Proposal.

offeree (ɒfəˈriː). [f. offer *v.* + -ee[1].] A person to whom something is or has been offered. Also *attrib.*

1952 *All England Law Reports* I. 1092 Provided the offer is not one which for some reason the offeree is entitled to refuse. **1967** *Economist* 20 May 754/1 The now-familiar rise in the price of an offeree company's shares before the announcement of a bid. **1972** *Real Estate Rev.* Winter 56/2 The statutes define such offerings in terms of the number of buyers, or the number of offerees, or the total number of stockholders or security holders after completion of the offering, or combinations thereof.

offerer (ˈɒfərə(r)). [f. offer *v.* + -er[1].]

1. One who offers a sacrifice, or prayer, etc.; one who brings an offering.

1382 Wyclif *Exod.* xxix. 33 That it be a pesible sacrifice, and that the hondes of the offrers ben halowid. **1526** Tindale *Heb.* x. 2 The offerers once pourged shulde have hadde no moare consciences of sinnes. **1624** F. White *Repl. Fisher* 375 Prayers and Praises which the offerers vnderstand not. *a* **1716** South *Serm.* (1718) II. 99 A fire, that will be sure to destroy the offering, though mercy should spare the offerer. **1818** Lamb *Poems, In a leaf of 'Lives of Saints'*, The lone mite, the cup of water cold That in their way approved the offerer's zeal.

2. a. In other senses of offer *v.*, q.v.: One who presents something for acceptance; one who makes an offer or proposal; one who makes an attempt *at* something; a bidder, etc.

1581 Mulcaster *Positions* xxxvii. (1887) 161 One may more then halfe gesse, what they will receiue, when none seeth but the offerer. **1612** *Two Noble K.* v. vi, Nay, let's be offerers all. **1660** Fuller *Mixt Contempl.* (1841) 169 The sufferers of violence would have been offerers of it, if empowered with might equal to their malice. **1675** Wycherley *Country Wife* I. i. (1735) 14 He's one of those nauseous offerers at wit. **1826** Lamb *Elia* Ser. II. *Pop. Fallacies* xi, There are favours..which confer as much grace upon the acceptor as the offerer. **1868** *Perthsh. Jrnl.* 18 June, The present Tenant (who is not to be an Offerer) will give directions for showing the boundaries.

b. *spec.* (with spelling offeror). One who offers something for sale, esp. shares.

1930 A. Palmer *Company Secretarial Pract.* vi. 46 Any document by which the offer for sale is made shall..be deemed to be a prospectus issued by the company, but without prejudice to the liability of the offerors in respect of the offer. **1955** *Times* 18 May 3/8 There was no binding contract until notice of the acceptance was received by the offeror. **1972** *Mod. Law Rev.* XXXV. 74 The offer was to remain open until May 14, 1970, with the usual right being reserved to the offeror to extend the time during which the offeree shareholders could tender their acceptances.

offering ('ɒfərɪŋ), *vbl. sb.* Forms: 1 offrung, 2–3 ofrung, 2–5 offringe, (3 -inke, -ingue), 3–6 offring, -yng(e, 4–6 offeringe, -yng(e, 6– offering. [OE. *offrung* vbl. sb. from *offrian* to offer. (Senses 1 a and 2 a were also expressed in ME. by OFFRAND from Fr.)] The action of the verb OFFER; that which is offered.

1. a. The presenting of something to God (or to a deity or object of worship) as an act of worship or devotion; sacrifice; oblation.

c **1000** ÆLFRIC *Hom.* II. 456 Seo offrung is nu unalyfedlic æfter Cristes ðrowunge. *c* **1000** *Ags. Gosp.* Matt. xxiii. 19 Hwæþer ys mare þe offrung þe þæt weofud þe ȝe-halȝað þa offrunge? *c* **1160** *Hatton G.* ibid., þe offreng..þa offrenge. *c* **1200** *Trin. Coll. Hom.* 47 þat on is childbed, and þat oðer chirchgang, and þe pridde þe offring. *c* **1250** *Old Kent. Serm.* in *O.E. Misc.* 27 Me sal to dai mor makie offrinke þan an oþren dai. *c* **1330** R. BRUNNE *Chron.* (1810) 154 To þe fertre of Saynt Agate Richard made offeryng. *c* **1386** CHAUCER *C.T.* Prol. 450 In al the parisshe wif ne was ther noon, That to the offrynge bifore hire sholde goon. *c* **1400** MAUNDEV. (1839) v. 35 The kynges that made offryng to oure lord whan he was born. **1546** J. HEYWOOD *Prov.* (1867) 80 Men saie long standyng and small offring Maketh poore persons. **1847** TENNYSON *Princ.* IV. 112 And dress the victim to the offering up.

transf. *c* **1430** LYDG. *Minor Poems* (Percy Society) 53 And with his wynnyngis he makith his offryng At ale stakis, sittyng ageyn the moone.

b. The action of the verb OFFER, in other senses: tender or presentation for acceptance, for sale, etc.

1668 WILKINS *Real Char.* II. i. §5. 40 Offering,..profer, tender, bid,..overture. **1706** PHILLIPS, *Offering*, the Act of him that offers. **1884** tr. *Lotze's Logic* 404 Offering seems, speaking generally, in favour of the seller..bidding is in favour of the buyer. **1900** *Daily News* 18 Sept. 2/5 Only moderate offerings of breadstuffs were made..holders still adopting an attitude of reserve.

2. *concr.* **a.** Something presented to God (or to a deity, etc.) in worship or devotion; *e.g.* a slain animal, fruits, money, or other things, given as an expression of religious homage or as a feature of religious worship; a sacrifice; an oblation.

Often qualified by a prec. word expressive of its nature or purpose, esp. in Biblical terms relating to the Levitical Law; as *burnt-*, *drink-*, *free-will-*, *guilt-*, *heave-*, *meal-*, *meat-*, *peace-*, *sin-*, *thank-*, *trespass-*, *wave-offering*, etc.; see these under their first elements.

c **1000** ÆLFRIC *Gen.* xxii. 7 Ic axiȝe hwær seo offrung siȝ. her ys wudu and fyr. *c* **1160** *Hatton Gosp.* Matt. xxiii. 18 Swa hwilc swa swereð on þare ofrunge þe ofer þ weofed ys, se is geltiȝ. **1297** R. GLOUC. (Rolls) 11326 He wende to seinte freþeswiþe..& wel vaire is offringe to þe heye weued ber. *c* **1386** CHAUCER *C.T.* Prol. 489 Rather wolde he yeuen out of doute Vn to his poure parisshens aboute Of his offryng. **1451** *Rolls of Parlt.* V. 219/1 Tithes or offringes beyng in Spirituelx mens hondes. **1552** ABP. HAMILTON *Catech.* (1884) 24, I preferre the trew knawlege of God abone all brount offeringis. **1601** SHAKS. *Jul. C.* II. ii. 39 Plucking the intrailes of an Offering forth. **1667** MILTON *P.L.* XI. 441 His Offring soon propitious Fire from Heav'n Consum'd. **1756–7** tr. *Keysler's Trav.* (1760) II. 341 That jewels..to the amount of many millions, shine as useless offerings in the church of Loretto. **1887** BOWEN *Virg. Æneid* III. 406 At the hallowed fires, when the offerings blaze to the skies.

b. Something offered to a person for his acceptance, esp. as a tribute of honour or esteem; a present, a gift.

c **1440** *Promp. Parv.* 362/2 Offerynge, or presaunt to a lorde at Crystemasse, or oþer tymys. **1634** SIR T. HERBERT *Trav.* 156 All which rabble receive liberally from such as meet them, Offerings of good will and Charitie. **1776** GIBBON *Decl. & F.* xi. I. 315 Crowns of gold, the offerings of grateful cities. **1882** MISS BRADDON *Mt. Royal* II. v. 105, I was not obliged to fling his offerings back in his face.

c. Something offered to the public for entertainment, patronage, purchase, etc.; *spec.* a theatrical production.

Quot. 1820 has connotations of sense 2 a.

1820 *Offering of Sunday-School Teacher* p. iv, The Book is really what its title imports,—'The Offering of a Sunday-School Teacher' etc.; and it is equally adapted to the Sunday Schools of every denomination of Christians. **1834** *Offering* p. i, The increased demand for works of this description, has induced the Editor of '*The Offering*' to usher into the world another of the class of books which, of all others, has met with the largest share of public patronage; and it is with peculiar pleasure that he again presents himself before his friends in the capacity of a compiler or gatherer. **1848** *Sporting Life* 29 Apr. 103/2 The Easter offerings at this house [*sc.* the Strand Theatre] are *Woman's Faith* and a new burlesque extravaganza. **1901** *Munsey's Mag.* July 587/1 There were so many offerings which critics and first night audiences liked,..which the paying public regarded with indifference. **1903** *Boston Even. Transcript* 29 Aug. 8/2 On Saturday next the Transcript will print an unusually attractive line of real estate offerings. **1932** *New Yorker* 11 June 46/2 If Mme. Sylva can summon so many listeners for subsequent offerings, her company should thrive.

3. *attrib.* and *Comb.* as †*offringlac* (LAKE *sb.*[1]).

995 in Kemble *Cod. Dipl.* VI. 130 Hio becwið vnto Cyrcan ..hyre beteran ofring-sceat. *c* **1200** ORMIN 639 Offringlac rihht god inoh Affterr hiss Faderr wille. **1512** in *Southwell Visit.* (1891) I. 15 That..the grettist bell..be rongen..all the offeryng tyme. **1548–9** (Mar.) *Bk. Com. Prayer, Communion*, Rubric, At the offeryng daies appoynted, euery manne and woman shall paie to the Curate, the due and accustomed offerynges. **1591** PERCIVALL *Sp. Dict.*, *Obléa*, an offering, a rounde offering cake. **1613** PURCHAS *Pilgrimage* (1614) 490 They set it downe on their offering-stone, and worship it. **1784** SIR J. CULLUM *Hist. Hawsted* (1813) 13 In 1358, the customary tenants paid their lord at Christmas a small rent, called *offering-silver*. **1853** ROCK *Ch. of Fathers* III. ii. 33 Their offerings of bread and wine, which they brought..having their hands muffled up in a very clean fine linen cloth or offering-sheet. **1938** HERBERT & PROCTER *Telephony* (ed. 2) II. ix. 371 The trunk offering selector and the trunk offering final selector together cater for a 4-digit numbering scheme. **1950** J. ATKINSON *Herbert & Procter's Telephony* (new ed.) II. xxv. 778/1 The telephonist dials a special number over the trunk offering switching train to the exchange concerned. **1964** K. H. BRINKMANN tr. *Trautmann's Design Automatic Teleph. Exch.* II. 63 An offering subgroup comprises the offering trunks which carry the traffic to such a subgroup.

'**offering,** *ppl. a.* [f. OFFER *v.* + -ING[2].] That offers, in various senses: see the verb.

1596 SHAKS. *1 Hen. IV*, IV. i. 69 Wee of the offring side, Must keepe aloofe from strict arbitrement. **1656** HEYLIN *Surv. France* To Rdr., Men..must not expect to be alwaies on the offering hand, but be content to take such money as they use to give. *a* **1715** BURNET *Own Time* II. (1724) I. 159 No person..had the courage to move the offering propositions for any limitation of prerogative.

offeror: see OFFERER 2 b.

offertorial (ɒfə'tɔərɪəl), *a. rare.* [f. L. *offertōrium* OFFERTORY + -AL[1].] Pertaining to an offertory; used in sacrificial offerings.

1856 *Tracts on Increase of Episcopate in Eng. & Wales* II. 9 To meet the continual demands for Church extension by stated Offertorial collections. **1887** J. R. HUTCHINSON tr. *Viresalingam's Fortune's Wheel* vi. 65 [He] lighted some offertorial camphor.

offertory ('ɒfətərɪ). Also 4 offretory, 5 offry-, offra-, 6 offi-, offytorie. [ad. eccl. L. *offertōri-um* (Isidore, *a* 640), offering-place, offering, oblation, etc. (cf. late L. *offertor* offerer (Commodianus, *c* 245), med.L. *offerta* offering), f. late L. and Romanic *offert-* ppl. stem, substituted for *oblāt-*, of *offerre* to OFFER: see -ORY. Cf. F. *offertoire* offering (14th c. in Hatz.-Darm.), It. *offertorio* 'an offering, an offring place' (Florio).]

1. *R.C. Ch.* An anthem sung or said in the Mass immediately after the Creed, while the offerings of the people are being received, and the unconsecrated elements are being placed on the altar. In the *Ch. of Eng.*, applied to the Scriptural sentences read or sung in the corresponding part of the Communion Service (now usually called *offertory sentences*).

c **1386** CHAUCER *C.T.* Prol. 710 Wel koude he rede a lesson or a storie But alderbest he song an Offertorie [*Camb. MS.* offratory]. **1387** TREVISA *Higden* (Rolls) V. 231 þat þe grayel and þe offertorie [*v.r.* offretory] schulde be i-seide to fore þe sacrement [CAXTON, sacrynge]. **1483** CAXTON *Gold. Leg.* 437/2 After the preest sayth Oremus..thenne he sayth the offrytorye. *c* **1532** DU WES *Introd. Fr.* in Palsgr. 1063 Wherfore than sayth the preest after the offytorie..pray for me, etc.? **1548–9** (Mar.) *Bk. Com. Prayer, Communion* Rubric, Then shall folowe for the Offertory, one or mo, of these Sentences of holy scripture, to be song whiles the people doo offer. **1729** C. WHEATLEY *Bk. Com. Prayer* (ed. 6) vi. §10. 284 The Sentences..are in the place of the Antiphona or Anthem which we find in the old Liturgies after the Gospel, and which from their being sung whilst the People made their Oblations at the Altar were call'd the Offertory. **1885** *Cath. Dict.* (ed. 3), *Offertory*. (1) An antiphon which used to be sung by the choir while the faithful made their offerings of bread and wine for the Mass, of gifts for the support of the clergy, etc... The Offertory is said immediately after the Creed.

2. That part of the Mass or Communion Service at which offerings are made; the offering of these, or the gifts offered. Also in *R.C. Ch.* applied *spec.* to the anticipatory oblation (see OBLATION 2).

1539 *Bk. Ceremonies* in Strype *Eccl. Mem.* (1721) I. II. App. cix. 287 Then followeth the offertory, wherby we be learned to prepare our selves by Gods grace to be an acceptable oblation to him. **1555** EDEN *Decades* 224 When the preeste was at mid masse at the offitorie, the kings profered them selues to go to kysse the crosse with the capytayne, but offered nothynge. **1662** *Bk. Com. Prayer, Communion*, Then shall the Priest return to the Lords Table, and begin the Offertory, saying one or more of these sentences following, as he thinketh most convenient in his discretion. **1852** HOOK *Ch. Dict.* (1871) 542 The offertory is so called because it is that part of the Communion Service at which the offerings are made. **1885** *Cath. Dict.* (ed. 3) s.v., The great oblation of Christ's body and blood must be carefully distinguished from the Offertory or anticipatory oblation of bread and wine.

3. *transf.* †**a.** The offering *of* anything, esp. to God. *Obs.*

1607 MARKHAM *Caval.* VII. Ded., To offer to your vertues this poore offertory of my labours. **1622** BACON *Hen. VII*, 8 Hee made Offertorie of his Standards, and had Orizons, and Te Deum againe sung. **1649** JER. TAYLOR *Gt. Exemp.* Ad Sect. v, We shall..exhibit to God an offertory in which he cannot but delight. **1660** EVELYN *News fr. Brussels unmasked*, Many..would willingly sacrifice..their present fortunes, and some of them their lives too, as a graceful offertory for such a seasonable and all-healing mercy. **1684** T. HOCKIN *God's Decrees* 162 The Jews did make these offertories by the especial dictates of God.

b. In recent use, An offering or collection of money made at a religious service.

1862 BP. MEDLEY in *Coventry Standard* Aug., Our offertory ever since the cathedral has been opened for divine worship has been about £300 instead of £96. **1874** SYMONDS *Sk. Italy & Greece* (1898) I. xiv. 297 After the ceremony we ..contributed to three distinct offertories. **1879** FARRAR *St. Paul* II. 6 He ordered collections to be made for the poor at Jerusalem by a weekly offertory every Sunday. **1891** *Ch. Times* 22 May 496 It is within a few years only that the word 'offertory' has been freely used for any collection of money for religious purposes.

4. a. A cloth used in the celebration of the Eucharist. **b.** A piece of plate used in the same. (Cf. Du Cange, *offertorium*, for both senses.)

1672 in *Archæol. Cantiana* (1886) XVI. 354 *note*, Given.. towards buying some Plate, viz. a flagon, offertory, patten, and chalice with a cover, for yᵉ holy Communion. [**1706** PHILLIPS, *Offertorium* (in old Latin Records), a piece of Silk or fine Linnen, antiently us'd to wrap up the Occasional Oblations or Offerings, made in the Church.] **1725** tr. *Dupin's Eccl. Hist. 17th C.* I. v. 64 The Chalices were cover'd with a Piece of Linen which was call'd the Offertory.

5. *attrib.*

1641 J. JACKSON *True Evang. T.* II. 90 So was the Paschall Lambe [the type of Christ], and the other offertory Lambes too. **1724** *Lond. Gaz.* No. 6290/2 The Offertory Sentence being read. **1849** ROCK *Ch. of Fathers* I. v. 402 Beside the tunicle, there is worn by the subdeacon,..the offertory-veil. **1877** J. D. CHAMBERS *Div. Worship* 274 A principal Ornament to be used in Celebration is the 'Offertorium', or Offertory Veil. **1879** HESBA STRETTON *Through a Needle's Eye* I. 90 The offertory money passed through Mrs. Cunliffe's hands. **1886** *Chr. Herald* (N.Y.) IX. 285 An offertory-box placed at the door of a famous place of worship.

†'**offerture.** *Obs.* [a. F. *offerture* offer (16th c. in Godef.), or ad. med.L. *offertūra* offering, oblation, f. late L. and Romanic *offert-*: see prec. and -URE.]

1. Offering in worship.

1595 BARNES *Sonn.* xxvi, As those three ki[illegible]gs,..By presents rich made royal offerture, Our new-borne Saviour's blessing to procure. **1624** F. WHITE *Repl. Fisher* 288 Their excessiue worship by Vowes, Oathes, Offertures.

2. The offering of something for acceptance; an offer, proposal, overture.

1631 *Celestina* x. 117 How much more advantageous.. would an intreated promise have been, then a forced offerture? **1648** *Eikon Bas.* 29 Thow hast prevented us with offertures of Thy love. **1657** W. MORICE *Coena quasi Κοινὴ* Pref. 8, I..received with much complacency this amicable offerture. **1684** T. HOCKIN *God's Decrees* 355 More transported with the love of poor empty enjoyments, than with the offerture of an eternal possession.

off-fal(l, obs. form of OFFAL.

'**off-,falling.** *Sc.* [f. OFF *adv.* + FALLING *vbl. sb.*]

a. That which falls off; *pl.* crumbs or scraps that fall from the table; also *fig.* **b.** A falling off in health, excellence, or goodness.

1636 RUTHERFORD, *Lett., to Lady Kenmure* (1671) I. 24 O how many rich off-fallings are in my Kings house! **1637** *Ibid.* (1881) 349 O that I had but Christ's odd off-fallings! *a* **1649** DRUMM. OF HAWTH. *Hist. Scot., Jas. I* (1655) 20 Many who were accustomed to be Copartners of such off-fallings, began to storm and repine at his actions. **1825** JAMIESON, *Off-falling*, a declension. It is often used of one who declines in health or external appearance; also in a moral sense.

So '**off-,faller** (*Sc.*), one who falls off; a deserter.

a **1688** HAMILTON *Let. J. Renwick* in Shields *Faithful Contend.* (1780) 40 (Jam.) Shot at by all ranks of off-fallers from the cause of God.

off flavour, off-flavour. [Cf. OFF *adv.* 1 g.] A stale, rancid, or unnatural flavour in food.

1947 *Richmond* (Va.) *News-Leader* 3 Apr. 36/1 There are several good reasons for what they term 'off-flavors' in milk. **1950** *N.Z. Jrnl. Agric.* Mar. 265/3 White clover, subterranean clover, red clover, silage, lucerne, and chou moellier all produce an off flavour [in the cows' milk]. **1952** *Chambers's Jrnl.* June 340/2 They found that meat put under this apparatus loses its red colour, goes brown, and has a definite off-flavour. **1958** [see ANTI-OXIDANT]. **1971** *Guardian* 19 May 8/1 Yogurts..are made with a living culture... The process is strictly controlled throughout so that off-flavours cannot develop.

off form, off-form, *phr.* and *a.* [f. OFF *prep.* + FORM *sb.*] In poor condition; 'out of form' (see FORM *sb.* 16).

1912 C. MATHEWSON *Pitching in a Pinch* 142 The Chicago pitchers were away off form in the series. **1961** *Times* 20 Feb. 6/2 Mr. Ferber sounded a little off-form. **1965** *Listener* 24 June 930/1 There is scarcely a topic in the history of science that has attracted more great men to it—yet found them so sadly off-form—than the question of whether his intelligence is inherited or due to his upbringing. **1972** H. A. WILLIAMS *True Resurrection* ii. 35 They don't say, 'He's not as good as he was,' but just, 'He's off-form today.' **1976** *Listener* 26 Feb. 250/2 The musicians may be tired, off-form.

off-'gauge, *a.* [f. OFF *prep.* + GAUGE, GAGE *sb.*] Of steel strip: having a thickness outside the permitted tolerance. Freq. *absol.*

1940 *Sheet Metal Industries* XIV. 611/1 It is believed that the predominating cause for off gauge while at running speed is the variation in the incoming strip. **1947** *Jrnl. Iron & Steel Inst.* CLVI. 398/2 The phenomenon undoubtedly contributes to 'off-gauge' strip in wide-strip mills and other mills rolling thin-gauge material, during acceleration and deceleration. **1953** *Engineering* 9 Jan. 33/1 As the measuring head cannot be mounted close to the roll gap, there is a delay between the rolling of off-gauge strip and its indication. **1962** C. W. STARLING *Theory & Pract. Flat Rolling* ix. 149 Probably the most common cause of rejections in cold rolled sheet is 'off gauge', and as the tendency is to decrease gauge tolerances, accurate gauge control is of the utmost importance.

'off-glide. *Phonetics.* [f. OFF *a.* + GLIDE *sb.*] A glide that terminates the articulation of a speech-sound, when the vocal organs either return to a neutral position or adopt a position anticipating the formation of the next sound. Cf. ON-GLIDE. Hence **off-gliding** *ppl. a.*

1879 [see BREATH 10]. **1888** [see ON-GLIDE]. **1927** J. J. HOGAN *Eng. Lang. in Ireland* 71 An important difference between I. [*sc.* Irish] and E. [*sc.* English] is the greater value of the off-glides of the Irish consonants. **1934** [see ON-GLIDE]. **1954** F. G. CASSIDY *Robertson's Devel. Mod. Eng.* (ed. 2) v. 104 An on-glide is one preceding the vowel (or consonant) and therefore gliding on toward it; an off-glide follows the vowel. *Ibid.*, Diphthongs develop from the addition of either on-gliding or off-gliding elements. **1964** E. J. A. HENDERSON in D. Abercrombie et al. *Daniel Jones* 418 There is frequently still sufficient pressure of air behind it for a weak off-glide to be audible. **1972** *Language* XLVIII. 865 The backness and roundness values of the following off-gliding vowels.

'off-go. *Sc. colloq.* [f. OFF- 3 + GO *sb.*[1]] A start, beginning: = GO-OFF.

1886 STEVENSON *Kidnapped* i. 5 The first..will likely please ye best at the first off-go. **1896** IAN MACLAREN *Kate Carnegie* 96 He wes a wee fractious an' self-willed at the off-go.

So **'off-ˌgoing** *vbl. sb.*, departure, going away, removal (in quot. 1770 *attrib.*); **off-going** *ppl. a.*, that goes off or away, or is being removed.

1727 P. WALKER *Life Welwood* in *Biog. Presbyt.* (1827) I. 186 He'll get a sudden and sharp Off-going. **1770** *E. Heslerton Inclos. Act* 14 Leading and taking away the offgoing crop. **1861** W. BARNES in *Macm. Mag.* June 130 The paths of the oncoming and offgoing bird. **1892** *Salisbury Jrnl.* 6 Aug. 4/4 Annual Sale by Auction of about 3500 off-going Dorset Down Ewes, Lambs and Wethers.

off-grain, *adv.* and *a.* [f. OFF *prep.*, OFF- 4 b + GRAIN *sb.*[1]] Of a fabric: against the direction of the threads; having a grain that is not straight.

1964 *McCall's Sewing* iii. 38/2 Finishing or printing processes will often pull them [*sc.* fabrics] off-grain. In some cases a permanent finish may lock the threads in the off-grain position and the fabric can never be straightened. *Ibid.* vii. 97/1 There are several ways to straighten off-grain fabrics. **1968** J. IRONSIDE *Fashion Alphabet* 88 Cheap fabrics are often printed 'off-grain' and one is faced with the decision of either having the grain right (so that the garment hangs properly) or the pattern straight!

off-hand, offhand (see below), *adv.* and *adj. phr.* [f. OFF *prep.* + HAND *sb.*]

A. *adv.* (ˌɒfˈhænd, ˌɔː-).

1. At once, straightway, forthwith; without preliminary deliberation or preparation, extempore.

1694 WOOD *Life* 3 Mar. (O.H.S.) III. 446 The speech before mention'd..being off-hand upon the debates of the House of Commons, was burnt by command of the House. **1711** HEARNE *Collect.* (O.H.S.) III. 207 He was a learned Man..and would..speak very neatly offhand in Latin. **1764** *Mem. G. Psalmanazar* 189 He read the office all in a good Latin off-hand, as the saying is, and without any hesitation or solecism. **1849** FITZGERALD *Lett.* (1889) I. 195 Wonderful bits of Poems, written off hand at a sitting, most of them. **1872** LOWELL *Wks.* (1890) IV. 243 Habit is a growth and cannot be made off-hand.

2. *lit.* From the hand with no other support. *U.S.*

1833 *Sk. & Eccentr. D. Crockett* ix. 119 Forty yards off-hand, or sixty with a rest, is the distance generally chosen for a shooting match. **1840** A. B. LONGSTREET *Georgia Scenes* (1848) 203 That they [rifles] should be fired off-hand, while the shot-guns were allowed a rest, the distance being equal. **1970** *Amer. Speech 1968* XLIII. 217 The shot could be made with a single-shot muzzle-loading rifle or with a *two-shoot gun*, fired either *off-hand* or *with a rest*.

3. *to farm off-hand*, to own or hold a farm without residing on it. *dial.*

1879 *Norfolk Archaeol.* VIII. 171 A farmer having an occupation apart from his homestead is said to farm it off-hand. **1898** *Longman's Mag.* Sept. 408 The land had been farmed 'off-hand', that is to say, the tenant did not live on the farm, but put in a working bailiff.

B. *adj.* (ˈɒfˌhænd, ˈɔː-; *as predicate somet.* ˌɒfˈhænd, ˌɔː-).

1. Of action, speech, etc.: Done or made off-hand (see A. 1); unpremeditated, extemporaneous, impromptu; having the air or style of something so done, free and easy, unstudied, unceremonious.

1719 *Free-thinker* No. 107 ¶2 A very Familiar, Off-hand Epistle.. from a young Gentleman. **1785–90** R. CUMBERLAND *Observer* No. 109 (R.) This..supplies him with many an apt couplet for off-hand quotations. **1822** HAZLITT *Table-t.* Ser. II. xvii. (1869) 344 The dashing off-hand manner of the mere man of business. **1844** DICKENS *Mart. Chuz.* vi, Speaking in his rapid, off-hand way. **1879** G. MEREDITH *Egoist* xvi. (1889) 147, 'I do not ride', Laetitia replied to the off-hand inquiry.

2. *transf.* **a.** Of persons: Doing or saying things off-hand, free and ready in action or speech; acting in an off-hand manner, unceremonious, curt, brusque.

1708 *Brit. Apollo* No. 89. 3/2 Who come like Master of a Riddle Or Off-hand Man upon a Fiddle. **1744** OZELL tr. *Brantome's Span. Rhodomontades* 1 An off-hand ready Wit, and lofty Words. **1853** LYTTON *My Novel* II. vi, Egerton is off-hand enough where he runs glibly thro' paragraphs that relate to others. **1876** T. HARDY *Ethelberta* (1890) 117 They are painfully off-hand with me, absolutely refusing to be intimate.

b. *Mining.* (See quots.)

1888 W. E. NICHOLSON *Gloss. Terms Coal Trade, Offhandmen*, a term applied to all colliery workmen except hewers and putters. **1921** *Dict. Occup. Terms* (1927) §047 *Odd worker, off hand man, wage man*, general terms for men or boys employed above or below ground and paid by the day. **1926** [see *face-worker* s.v. FACE *sb.* 27].

3. Of a shot: fired from a gun held in the hand without other support. *U.S.*

1856 R. GLISAN *Jrnl. Army Life* (1874) xxiv. 328, I surprised everybody by killing the duck at an off-hand shot.

4. Of a farm: owned or held by a person who does not reside there. *dial.*

1873 F. T. CHEVALLIER *Let.* 6 May in Thirsk & Imray *Suffolk Farming in Nineteenth Cent.* (1958) 106 On the off-hand farm I shall have a good opportunity of seeing what will be required during the ensuing year. **1880** R. S. CHARNOCK *Gloss. Essex Dial.* 33 Some who hold farms in different parishes call those farms where they do not reside 'off-hand farms'. **1898** *Longman's Mag.* Sept. 408 The labourer in charge of an off-hand farm. **1960** G. E. EVANS *Horse in Furrow* vii. 99 The whole capital he had sunk in the farms (the *Bransons Land* referred to was an *off-hand* holding) was not giving him the return it would have done if invested elsewhere. *Ibid.* xvi. 209 We generally spent two days at a farm, and perhaps another day at an 'off-hand' farm belonging to it.

5. *Engin.* Carried out with the workpiece held in the hand. Of a machine: intended for off-hand operations.

1931 E. P. VAN LEUVEN *Cold Metal Working* iv. 65 We refer to grinding as off-hand, semiprecision or precision grinding, depending on the type of machine and the degree of accuracy required. **1961** L. E. DOYLE et al. *Manuf. Processes* xxviii. 643 Nonprecision grinding, common forms of which are snagging and off-hand grinding, is done primarily to remove stock that cannot be taken off as conveniently by other methods. **1966** G. H. THOMAS *Metalwork Technol.* xiii. 150 'Off-hand' grinders..are of two types—bench models and pedestal (or floor) models. **1969** C. R. SHOTBOLT *Workshop Technol.* I. vi. 120 The author does not believe in any expensive cutting tool being ground by hand on an off-hand grinding machine.

6. Designating glass-ware made by hand, without a mould; also denoting such a process.

1941 C. J. PHILLIPS *Glass* viii. 156 The glass employed in 'offhand' glass blowing is usually melted in pots. **1949** P. DAVIS *Devel. Amer. Glass Industry* iv. 49 The process of blowing in a mold was closely similar to the off-hand method. **1967** C. GASKIN *Edge of Glass* vi. 144 He..took up his empty wineglass. 'If you were making this by the "off-hand" method—that's entirely by hand—you'd start with heating your batch.' **1970** *Canad. Antiques Collector* July–Aug. 14/2 You can feel the intrinsic beauty of an off-hand glass chain.

off-handed (ˌɒfˈhændɪd, ɔː-), *a.* **a.** = OFF-HAND B.: esp. in reference to style or manner. (In quot. 1840 irreg. as *adv.* = OFF-HAND A. 1.)

1835 MOORE *Diary* 15 Aug. in *Mem.* (1856) VII. 103 Found Babbage very off-handed and agreeable. **1840** BARHAM *Ingol. Leg.*, *Hand of Glory* ii, Nor, I'll venture to say, without scrutiny could he Pronounce her, off-handed, a Punch or a Judy. **1890** 'ROLF BOLDREWOOD' *Col. Reformer* (1891) 182 He's an off-handed chap.

b. *Mining.* = OFF-HAND B. 2 b. *dial.*

1846 W. E. BROCKETT *J.T. Brockett's Gloss. North Country Words* (ed. 3) II. 59 All workmen about a coal-pit are said to be *off-handed* who are not engaged in the business of hewing and putting the coal. **1906** *Daily Chron.* 16 Oct. 5/2 The 'off-handed' men..dispersed into the four seams of the pit.

Hence **ˌoff-ˈhandedly** *adv.*, in an off-handed manner, in a free and easy style, without ceremony; **ˌoff-ˈhandedness**, the quality of being off-handed.

1823 *New Monthly Mag.* VIII. 364 There is in them..an open off-handedness (to use a significant Irishism). **1883** F. M. PEARD *Contrad.* xix, He was quite conscious of the off-handedness of Dorothy's manner. **1886** *19th Cent.* Oct. 541 The newspaper moralisers speak off-handedly of the skilled workman earning his two or three pounds a week. **1893** G. ALLEN *Scallywag* I. 40 Isabel Boyton answered a little offhandedly. **1905** G. B. SHAW *Let.* 3 Jan. (1972) II. 485 At my third meeting I was asked to take the chair. I consented as offhandedly as if I were the Speaker of the House of Commons. **1973** J. WAINWRIGHT *Pride of Pigs* 123 He could have felt sorry for Fuller..to be systematically, off-handedly squashed.

offhandish (ɒfˈhændɪʃ, ɔː-), *a.* [f. OFF-HAND, OFFHAND *adj. phr.* + -ISH[1].] Somewhat off-hand; off-handed. Hence **offˈhandishly** *adv.*, off-handedly.

1886 in H. Baumann *Londinismen* 124/2. **1926** E. M. ROBERTS *Time of Man* i. 28 The brown colt came from the other side of the enclosure, nibbling offhandishly at the wilted grass and edging always a little nearer. **1952** *Ethics* LXIII. 66/1 Commitments acknowledged only in an offhandish way by Moore.

office (ˈɒfɪs), *sb.* Also 3 offiz, 3–4 -is, 4 -iss, -ise, -ys, ofice, 4–6 offyce, (5 offyz, -ez, -esse, offic, ofic, 6 offes, *pl.* 6–7 officies). [a. AF. and OF. *office* (12th c. in Hatz.-Darm.) = Sp. *oficio*, It. *officio*, *uffizio*, ad. L. *officium* service, duty, function, ceremonial observance, business, place, appointment, in med.L. also service prescribed by the Church, introit, ecclesiastical court, building or place for work; f. *ob-* (OB- 1 a) + *-ficium* doing.]

1. Something done toward any one; a service, kindness, attention. Chiefly with qualification, as *good*, *kind office*; *office of kindness*, etc. Hence with adj. of the opposite kind, as *ill*, etc.: A disservice.

1382 WYCLIF *2 Cor.* ix. 12 For the mynysterie of this office ..aboundith by manye in doynge of thankingis to the Lord. **1575** Q. ELIZ. in Ellis *Orig. Lett.* Ser. I. II. 278 Which we have hitherto forborne to graunt..for the evell offices whiche her other Secretary did there. **1593** SHAKS. *Rich. II*, II. ii. 137 Little office Will the hatefull Commons performe for vs. **1598** —— *Merry W.* I. i. 102, I would I could doe a good office betweene you. **1655** SIR M. LANGDALE in *Nicholas Papers* (Camden) III. 128 He suspectes father Talbot hath donne him some ill office. **1674** *Essex Papers* (Camden) I. 222, I know..that..yᵉ design of getting themselves into yᵉ place will encourage divers to doe me spightfull Offices. **1761** HUME *Hist. Eng.* II. xliv. 505 Those ill offices which his enemies..could employ against him. **1877** SPARROW *Serm.* x. 128 Making men capable of mutual offices of kindness. **1887** JESSOPP *Arcady* ii. 33 In return she gets some little kindly office done for her.

2. That which one ought, or has, to do in the way of service; that which is required or expected: † **a.** *gen.* Duty towards others; a moral obligation (*obs.*). **b.** Duty attaching to one's station, position, or employment; a duty, service, or charge falling or assigned to one; a service or task to be performed; business; function, one's part.

a **1300** *Cursor M.* 28366, I..did min office na-þe-lese þat vn-despensed sang i messe. *c* **1330** R. BRUNNE *Chron.* (1810) 55 Forto reise þe treuage..Pader & Thurston to þat office were fette. *c* **1400** MAUNDEV. (Roxb.) xxv. 114 Ilkane wate what he schall do and bisily tentez till þaire officez. **1483** CAXTON *Cato* I v b, Thou oughtest to be swete gracious and humble in thyn offyce or seruyse. **1534** WHITINTON *Tullyes Offices* I. (1540) 27 Honesty, that is the offyce and dutie of man. *a* **1548** HALL *Chron.*, *Hen. VII* 61 To thentent yt he worthely might be called a king, whose office is to rule and not to be ruled of other. **1603** SHAKS. *Meas. for M.* II. ii. 13 Doe you your office, or giue vp your Place. **1656** STANLEY *Hist. Philos.* v. (1701) 183/1 To make a Helm is the Office of a Ship-wright, but to use it rightly of a Pilot. **1669** J. JACKSON in *Pepys' Diary* VI. 212 The Cardinal de Bouillon, appointed by the Pope to perform this office in his stead. *a* **1756** MRS. HAYWOOD *New Present* (1771) 252 Her next office..is to rub the stove and fire-irons. **1832** HT. MARTINEAU *Hill & Valley* v. 73 He..had..taken upon him the preacher's office. **1878** GLADSTONE *Prim. Homer* viii. 111 They exercise the offices of the judge, the priest, the counsellor.

† **c.** Performance of a duty or function, service, attendance. *Obs.*

c **1320** *Sir Beues* 3555 (MS. A.) þanne eueriche marchal His ȝerde an honde bere schal. While Beues was in þat office þe kinges sone..A ȝede to Beues stable. **1535** COVERDALE *1 Kings* x. 5 Whan the Quene of riche Arabia sawe all the wyszdome of Salomon..& the offyces of his ministers, and their garmentes..she wondred exceadingly. **1621** QUARLES *Div. Poems, Esther* (1638) 104 We gave command..That by the office of our Eunuchs band, Queen Vashti should in state attended be.

3. a. That which is done or is intended to be done by a particular thing; that which anything is fitted to perform, or performs customarily; = FUNCTION *sb.* 3.

1340 *Ayenb.* 50 þe mouþ heþ tuo offices, huer-of þe on belongeþ to þe zuelȝ..þe oþer zuo is in speche. **1390** GOWER *Conf.* III. 85 The laste science..is Practique, whos office The vertu tryeth fro the vice. **1546** BP. GARDINER *Declar. Joye* 80 Then do you..offende in deuising the wordes (office and correlatiue) to signifie what fayth doth. **1688** R. HOLME *Armoury* III. 320/2 It hath its name Cooler, from its Office, which is to cool the Hot Wort. **1774** GOLDSM. *Nat. Hist.* (1776) VII. 247 It sometimes happens, that when the animal is interrupted in performing the offices of exclusion, the young ones burst the shell within the parent's body. **1830** R. KNOX *Béclard's Anat.* 198 The office of the arteries is to lead the blood from the heart into all the parts of the body.

† **b.** A bodily or mental function as operating; the proper action of an organ or faculty. *Obs.*

c **1374** CHAUCER *Boeth.* I. pr. ii. 4 (Camb. MS.) Whan she say me..with-owten office of tunge and al dowmb. *c* **1425** *Found. St. Bartholomew's* 52 The same day was restorid to hym the office of his tonge. **1604** SHAKS. *Oth.* III. iv. 113 Whom I, with all the Office of my heart Intirely honour. *a* **1656** USSHER *Ann.* VI. (1658) 778 A certain young man, who wanted his armes..performed all things by the office of his feet.

† **c.** *spec.* The function or action of discharging excrement, etc.; excretion. *Obs.* (Cf. *house of office*, HOUSE *sb.* 14 b.)

c **1386** CHAUCER *Wife's Prol.* 127 They beth maked for bothe That is to seye for office and for ese Of engendrure. **1613** PURCHAS *Pilgrimage* (1614) 623 Washing themselves, as they doe also after the offices of Nature.

4. a. A position or place to which certain duties are attached, esp. one of a more or less public character; a position of trust, authority, or service under constituted authority; a place in the administration of government, the public service, the direction of a corporation, company, society, etc.

c **1250** *Gen. & Ex.* 2071 Ðu salt ben ut of prisun numen, And on ðin offiz set aȝen. *a* **1300** *Cursor M.* 25031 Pilate was o gret officis [*v.r.* office] for ouer Iuus he was iustis. *c* **1400** MAUNDEV. (Roxb.) xxx. 136 Ilkane of þam hase sum office in þe emperour courte. **1433** *Rolls of Parlt.* IV. 476/2 Chosen to the Office of Corouner. *a* **1548** HALL *Chron.*, *Hen. VI* 135 b, The duke of Yorke was discharged of the office of Regent. **1622** BACON *Hen. VII*, 38 He was taken into service in his court to a base office in his kitchen. **1771** *Junius Lett.* xlix. 255, I..do not esteem you the more for the high office you possess. **1855** PRESCOTT *Philip II*, II. ix. (1857) 305 He avowed his purpose of throwing up..all the offices he held under government. **1874** GREEN *Short Hist.* Epil. 819 The claims of the Nonconformists were met in 1868..by the abolition of all religious tests for admission to offices or degrees in the Universities.

b. In absolute sense: Official position or employment; *spec.* that of a minister of state. Hence ***to take office, leave office,*** etc. ***man of office,*** an officer or official. ***Jack in*** (***out of***) ***office:*** *see* JACK *sb.*[1] 37.

†***of office*** (L. *ex officio*), by virtue of office, officially. *Obs.*

1297 R. GLOUC. (Rolls) 9600 To abbe men in offis Mid him þat of conseil were god and wis. *a* **1300** *Cursor M.* 27170 Man of office or dignite..werlds man, or clerc. **1389** in *Eng. Gilds* (1870) 21 It is ordeynede..what brother of yis gilde be chosen in to office. *c* **1450** *St. Cuthbert* (Surtees) 6959 He kepyd þe kirk of office. **1526** *Pilgr. Perf.* (W. de W. 1531) 302 A straunger and alyant, put in offyce by the Romayns. **1607** SHAKS. *Timon* I. ii. 208 Would I were Gently put out of Office, before I were forc'd out. **1784** COWPER *Task* IV. 412 The rugged frowns and insolent rebuffs Of knaves in office. **1845** DISRAELI *Sybil* IV. xiv. II. 306 'Peel ought to have taken office', said Lord Marney. **1880** MCCARTHY *Own Times* IV. lviii. 259 He had come into office at the head of a powerful party.

c. Personified, or denoting an office-holder or office-holders as a body.

1602 SHAKS. *Ham.* III. i. 73 The insolence of Office. **1634** MASSINGER *Very Woman* III. ii, Now, master Office, What is the reason that your vigilant Greatness..locked up from me The way to see my mistress? **1765** BEATTIE *Judgm. Paris* cii, Coward Office..sneaks secure in insolence of state. **1781** COWPER *Charity* 484 Except that Office clips it as it goes.

5. A ceremonial duty or service; a religious or social observance; *esp.* the rite or rites due to the dead, obsequies; now chiefly in ***last office***(***s***).

1387 TREVISA *Higden* (Rolls) III. 459 No fader folweþ þe offys of his sones deeþ [L. *filii comitatur exsequias*]. **1535** COVERDALE *1 Chron.* xxix. 14 Golde (gaue he him)..for all maner of vessels of euery offyce. **1618** ROWLANDS *Sacred Mem.* 37 To show their loue in this last office done To a dead friend. **1662** STILLINGFL. *Orig. Sacr.* II. vii. §10 The other great offices wherein their Religion did so much consist, viz. Sacrifices, distinction of meats, observation of Festivals, circumcision, and such like. **1711** ADDISON *Spect.* No. 135 ¶1 An eminent Person..used in his private Offices of Devotion to give Thanks to Heaven that he was born a Frenchman. **1822** SCOTT *Nigel* xxxvi, I..will be first to render thee the decent offices due to the dead.

6. *Eccl.* An authorized form of divine service or worship: **a.** The daily service of the Roman breviary, comprising psalms, collects, and lections for the several canonical hours, which vary with the day (more fully ***Divine Office***); in the Church of England, Morning and Evening Prayer. ***to say office,*** to recite the Divine Office. **b.** The introit, sung at the begining of the Mass or Holy Communion; also, the whole service of the Mass or Holy Communion. **c.** Any occasional service, as the ***Office for the Dead, for Baptism, for the Visitation of the Sick,*** etc.; also, a special form of service appointed for some particular occasion.

c **1290** *Becket* 942 in *S. Eng. Leg.* I. 133 þis holi man..song ane Masse of seinte steuene..þe furste offiz is propre inov: to þe stat þat he was Inne. *a* **1340** HAMPOLE *Psalter* xxii. 7 þis psalme is songen in þe office of ded men. *c* **1375** *Lay Folks Mass Bk.* (MS. B) 86 Bi þis tyme..þo prest bigynnes office of messe. *Ibid.* 581 þo preste turnes til his seruyce And saies forthe more of his office. **1548–9** (Mar.) *Bk. Com. Prayer* 121 The office, or Introite (as they call it). **1556** *Chron. Gr. Friars* (Camden) 60 The byshoppe of Cauntorbery came sodenly to Powlles..and dyd the offes hym selfe in a cope and no vestment, nor mytter, nor crosse, but a crose staffe. **1663** CHAS. II in Julia Cartwright *Henrietta of Orleans* (1894) 150 She is not only content to say the greate office in the breviere, every day. **1683** EVELYN *Mem.* 9 Sept., It being the day of publiq thanksgiving for his Majesty's late preservation..there was an office us'd, compos'd for the occasion. *a* **1746** in Wesley *Princ. Methodist* 29 Whoever..does not worship God in the Manner she prescribes..must be supposed to slight and contemn her Offices and Rules. **1845** STEPHEN *Comm. Laws Eng.* (1874) II. 246 The celebration of marriage in this country according to the office of the Church. **1850** MRS. JAMESON *Leg. Monast. Ord.* (1863) 149 Every day she recited the Office of the Virgin. **1859** JEPHSON *Brittany* ix. 142 Proceeded to sing the office of the dead. **1896** *Ch. Times* 13 Nov. 520/4 There is an office for the reopening of a church in the Priest's Prayer-book.

7. An official inquest or inquiry concerning any matter that entitles the king to the possession of lands or chattels: = ***inquest of office,*** INQUEST 1 b. ***to find*** (†***take,*** †***return***) ***an office,*** to return a verdict showing that the king is thus entitled. ***office found,*** a verdict having this effect.

1432 *Rolls of Parlt.* IV. 396/2 Of the which Maner the saide Oratrice..be an office was put out. **1472–3** *Ibid.* VI. 25/2 That all Offices founden of the premisses or of any of theym..be..voide. **1509–10** *Act 1 Hen. VIII*, c. 8 Diverse ..have been..disherited by escheatours and commyssyoners causyng untrue offices to be founden. **1607** COWELL *Interpr., Office* doth signifie..also an Inquisition made to the Kings vse of any thing by vertue of his office who inquireth. And therefore wee oftentimes reade of an office found, which is nothing but such a thing found by Inquisition made *ex officio*. *a* **1645** HABINGTON *Surv. Worcs.* (Worcs. Hist. Soc.) III. 531 Bewdley..became..the joynter of hys widowe..as was found by an office after her descesse. **1768** BLACKSTONE *Comm.* III. xvii. 259 If they find the treason or felony..of the party accused..the king is thereupon, by virtue of this office found, intitled to have his forfeitures. **1877** BURROUGHS *Taxation* 277 There may be a forfeiture without such office found.

8. a. A place for the transaction of private or public business of some kind; often including the 'staff' by which the business is conducted, or denominating the department of which they are officers. Applied to the room or department in which the clerkly work of an industrial or other establishment is done, a counting-house; also to that in which the business of any particular department of the operations of a large concern is conducted, as the ***booking-office, goods office, inquiry office, lost property office, superintendent's office,*** etc. at a railway station. Formerly used of the court of an ecclesiastical official, as still of a police court (*police office*); now, often preceded by a possessive case, or combined with a sb. indicating the business or purpose, as *collector's, inspector's, surveyor's, town clerk's office; assay-, box-, coach-, Crown-, fire-, post-, telegraph-office,* etc. The more important of these are noticed as combinations under the first element or as main words.

c **1386** CHAUCER *Friar's T.* 279, I wol han .xij. pens..Or I wol sompne hire vn-to oure office. *c* **1440** *Promp. Parv.* 363/1 Offyce, or place of offyce, *officina*. **1521** in Foxe *A. & M.* (1583) 822/1 Whether she was euer detected to the office of Willi. Smith late Bishop of Lincolne. **1611** BIBLE *2 Chron.* xxiv. 11 At what time the chest was brought vnto the kings office. **1625** MASSINGER *New Way* IV. iii, A debt to which My vows, in that high office registered, Are faithful witnesses. **1631** [see CROWN OFFICE]. **1642** Assurance-office [see ASSURANCE 5]. **1735** POPE *Donne Sat.* II. 71 His Office keeps your Parchment fates entire. **1819** KEATS *Let. to Reynolds* 22 Sept. in Ld. Houghton *Life* (1848) II. 26 There will be some of the family waiting for you at the coach-office. **1849** THACKERAY *Pendennis* xxxv, The 'Pall Mall Gazette' had its offices..in Catherine street. **1855** MACAULAY *Hist. Eng.* xviii. IV. 131 The offices [of the East India Company] which stood on a very small part of the ground which the present offices cover. **1885** *Law Times Rep.* LIII. 459/1 Griffith, having taken offices a few doors off, also carried on the business of a solicitor.

fig. **1665** NEEDHAM *Med. Medicinæ* 382 The Liver is not the office of Sanguification.

b. Sometimes transferred from the place of business to the company or corporation there established, as in *assurance* or *insurance office* (cf. *the post office*).

1646 Insuring-Office [see INSURING *vbl. sb.*]. **1651–1841** Insurance Office [see INSURANCE 5]. **1693** Assurance Office [see INSURE *v.* 4 c]. **1782** (*title*) The Phœnix Fire Office. **1858** LD. ST. LEONARDS *Handy-Bk. Prop. Law* v. 29 The tenant's ..insuring in an office..not authorized by his lease. **1870** T. B. SPRAGUE in *Jrnl. Inst. Actuaries* XVI. 77 The Office assures to him..a sum of money payable in certain contingencies. **1883** *Chambers' Encycl.* V. 601 *Proprietary Companies* being those offices possessing a capital the property of the partners. *Mutual Offices*, where the members themselves constitute the company. *Mod.* In what office are you insured? That is an old-established office.

c. (With capital O.) With defining adj. or attrib. sb.: The building or set of rooms in which the business of a department of government administration is carried on, as the *Colonial, Foreign, Home, War Office,* etc.; the persons engaged in carrying on the business of the department; esp. the responsible head of the department and his immediate coadjutors. See FOREIGN, HOME, WAR, etc.; also POST OFFICE. Also followed by defining phrase, as ***Office of Works.***

1707 J. CHAMBERLAYNE *St. Gt. Brit.* 599 A List of the Officers of the Admiralty-Office. *Ibid.* 690 The Places where the several Offices are kept..The Treasury Office is in the Cockpit..Stamp-Office, is in Lincolns-Inn Square [etc.]. **1839** *Penny Cycl.* XIV. 116 (London—Public Buildings) Excise Office 1769. Plain in design, but of most commanding aspect. *Ibid.* State-Paper Offices, St. James's Park. **1863** H. COX *Instit.* III. viii. 712 Before [1854]..the civil administration of the army was divided..among the offices of the Secretary of State, the Secretary-at-War, the Ordnance Office, and the Commissariat. *Ibid.*, In 1855 the office of Secretary-at-War was consolidated with that of the Secretary of State for War..The department thus constituted is the existing War Office. *Ibid.* 713 Officers of the Commissariat..render directly to the Audit Office.. accounts of the whole of their cash and store transactions. **1880** E. W. HAMILTON *Diary* 11 Sept. (1972) I. 49 His [*sc.* W. P. Adam's] place will have to be filled up at the Office of Works. **1935** *Discovery* Aug. 217/1 Mr. J. H. Markham, F.R.I.B.A., of H.M. Office of Works, has made a notable addition to London's public monuments. **1936** *Ibid.* July 199/1 A change in the Office of Works which archaeologists cannot but view with regret.

d. Holy Office (*R.C. Ch.*), an ecclesiastical tribunal for the suppression of heresy and punishment of heretics: = INQUISITION 3.

1727–41 CHAMBERS *Cycl., Inquisition* or the *Holy Office*. **1797** MRS. RADCLIFFE *Italian* xvi, A true instrument of arrestation from the Holy Office. **1855** PRESCOTT *Philip II*, II. iii. (1857) 223 A platform was raised..on which were ranged the seats of the inquisitors, emblazoned with the arms of the Holy Office. **1862** LONGF. *Wayside Inn, Torquemada* 112 'The Holy Office, then, must intervene!'

e. *Aeronaut. slang.* The cockpit of an aircraft.

1917 'CONTACT' *Airman's Outings* 123, I strapped our baggage, some new gramophone records, and myself into the observer's office. *Ibid.* 161, I withdraw into 'the office', otherwise the observer's cockpit. **1918** *Blackw. Mag.* Oct. 526/2 'Wouf!'—a deafening crash, and the old bus shakes violently as I put my head into the office. **1934** V. M. YEATES *Winged Victory* iv. 34 He put his head in the office and flew by the instruments. **1941** [see GREENHOUSE 3]. **1942** 'B. J. ELLAN' *Spitfire!* p. x, The cockpit is called the office. **1966** *New Statesman* 13 May 687/2 'Up in the office they too knew it.' 'The office? You mean the flight deck?' 'Just that. No more. No less. The office.'

9. a. *pl.* The parts of a house, or buildings attached to a house, specially devoted to household work or service; the kitchen and rooms connected with it, as pantry, scullery, cellars, laundry, and the like; also, often including stables and other out-houses, the barns and cowhouses of a farm, etc.

[*c* **1386** CHAUCER *Clerk's T.* 208 Houses of office stuffed with plentee Ther maystow seen of deynteuous vitaille.] *a* **1548** HALL *Chron., Hen. VIII* 74 Pitcher house, Larder and Poultrie, and all other offices large and faire. **1662** GERBIER *Princ.* 36 The Kitchin or other Offices and Selleridge. **1798** *Times* 28 June 4/3 To be sold..a..freehold house, with..numerous attached and detached offices of every description. **1799** J. ROBERTSON *Agric. Perth* 52 The offices are also improved..forming generally a square behind the dwelling-house, with the dunghill or straw-yard in the center. **1846** MRS. GORE *Eng. Char.* (1852) 57 As he passed by the areas of the fashionable squares, and imbibed the aroma of stews and ragoûts issuing from the offices. **1881** RUSSELL *Haigs* Introd. 7 The usual outbuildings and Offices which such fortified places contained.

b. *sing.* A privy. Cf. EASE 8 b. Also in *pl.*; *spec.* in phr. ***usual office***(***s***).

1727 (*title*) The Grand Mystery..proposals for erecting 500 Publick Offices of Ease in London and Westminster. **1871** E. JENKINS *Ginx's Baby* i. (1879) 9 The forty-five big and little lodgers in the house were provided with a single office in the corner of the yard. **1938** N. MARSH *Artists in Crime* vi. 84, I imagine it was to pay a visit to the usual offices. **1948** J. CANNAN *Little I Understood* ix. 124 Mildred had been too shy when Adam, indicating a door, had said, '"The usual offices"..', to open the door and look in. **1951** N. MARSH *Opening Night* ix. 220, I went to the usual office at the end of the passage. **1955** N. FITZGERALD *House is Falling* xi. 188 He was having the usual offices in his house duplicated. **1957** J. BRAINE *Room at Top* i. 13 The bathroom's to the right and the usual offices next to it. **1959** W. GOLDING *Free Fall* ii. 36 There are the usual offices indoors now. **1963** *Gloss. Gen. Building Terms* (*B.S.I.*) 10 '*Offices*' (deprecated), service rooms and W.C.s.

†**10. a.** A keeper's beat. *Obs.*

1617 ASSHETON *Jrnl.* (Chetham Soc.) 60 All hunt in James Whitendales office.

b. *transf.* (See quot.) *slang. Obs.*

a **1700** B. E. *Dict. Cant. Crew* s.v., *His Office*, any Man's ordinary Haunt, or Plying-place, be it Tavern, Ale-house, Gaming-house.

11. *slang.* A hint, signal, or private intimation; esp. in phr. ***to give*** (or ***take***) ***the office.***

1803 *Sporting Mag.* XXI. 327 Giving the office—is when you suffer any person, who may stand behind your chair, to look over your hand. **1811** *Lex Bal.* s.v., To give the office; to give information, or make signs to the officers to take a thief. **1812** J. H. VAUX *Flash Dict., Office*, a hint, signal or private intimation..to *take the office*, is to understand and profit by the hint given. **1841** J. T. HEWLETT *Parish Clerk* II. 258 Playing us foul, and giving the office to the Philistines. **1890** 'ROLF BOLDREWOOD' *Robbery under Arms* xiv, Ride about the country till I give you the office. **1897** *Outing* (U.S.) XXX. 112/2 The dropping of the hands is called 'giving the office' to start [a four-horse coach].

12. *attrib.* and *Comb.* **a.** attrib., as (senses 2, 4) ***office badge, chair, duty,*** †***-fellow***; (sense 6) ***office-book***; (sense 8) ***office bell, boy*** (also in extended use), ***building, clerk, copy*** (*spec.* see quot. 1957), ***desk, drawing, door, equipment, expenses, furniture, girl, job, politics, routine, stool, work,*** etc.; **b.** objective and obj. genitive, as (sense 4) ***office giver, -holder, -holding, -hunter, -hunting, -jobbing, -mongering, -seeker, -seeking; office-holding, -seeking*** adj.; (sense 8) ***office-cleaner, -keeper, worker; office-bound*** adj. Also OFFICE-BEARER, -HOUSE, etc.

1594 *Contention* II. ii. 25 This my staffe, mine *Office badge in Court. **1841** J. T. HEWLETT *Parish Clerk* II. 71 A brass plate with '*office-bell' upon it. **1869** FREEMAN *Norm. Conq.* III. xi. 30 The two chief ministers of the funeral ceremony..bearing their *office-books in their hands. **1961** *Times* 12 Oct. 16/2 The bliss of an *office-bound youngster. **1972** *Daily Tel.* 24 Apr. 25/1 'I couldn't bear being office-bound from nine to five each day' is the cry of many a sixth-former. **1846** *Knickerbocker* XXVII. 457 No songs for you, my sad street-sweeper!.. Nor for you, melancholy *office-boy! **1865** A. J. MUNBY *Diary* 15 June in D. Hudson *Munby* (1972) 209 She kept on writing, in a hand like an office-boy's. **1899** *Westm. Gaz.* 17 Apr. 4/1 The officials [in New York] intend to dismiss the large force of office boys in the various departments and replace them by office girls. **1914** G. B. SHAW *Misalliance* p. lxv, An office boy of fifteen is often more of a man than a university student of twenty. *Ibid.* 7, I said, 'Make him the Office Boy.' **1944** J. S. HUXLEY *On Living in Revolution* 118 Quoting from a recent address of David Lilienthal... 'An overcentralized administration is always characterized by the fact that its field officers tend to become messengers and office boys.' **1973** A. BEHREND *Samarai Affair* i. 15 His first job had been that of office boy. **1975** *Times* 13 Oct. 13/1 Mr [Ian] Smith..has to demonstrate to his hard-liners that he is not Pretoria's office-boy. **1840** *Niles' Reg.* 23 May 182/1 The Free Trader *office building has been crushed in and much shattered. **1924** R. GRAVES *Mock Beggar Hall* 62, I was aware that during the war Mock-Beggar Hall had been used as a Government office-building. **1942** *London Replanned* (R. Academy) 25/1 The Surrey bank of the River is developed with Embankment gardens and office buildings. *a* **1715** WYCHERLEY *Posth. Wks.* (1728) 168 How many Sots have had the Luck to wear A Chain of Gold, and fill the

*Office-Chair! 1874 'H. Churton' Toinette xl. 404 The old surgeon laid down his pen..and turned his office-chair round toward his visitor. 1899 Daily News 21 Apr. 5/2 Charwomen, *office-cleaners, pensioners. 1944 Times 7 June 2/2 Mr. E. Granville..asked the Secretary to the Treasury if he would arrange that..the members of the Government Minor and Manipulative Grades Association of Office Cleaners were referred to as such, and not as charwomen or charladies, which term..was resented. 1971 J. Aitken Nightly Deadshade vii. 79 Here I am, on the spot after the office cleaners have cleared off. 1974 Times 4 Jan. 12/3 There are practically no Hutu left in government or the civil service—not even at chauffeur or office-cleaner level. 1880 G. Meredith Tragic Com. (1881) 126 'Am I not precise as an *office clerk?' she said. 1789 J. Morgan Essays Law of Evidence I. 87 Of *Office Copies. 1836 S. F. Austin Let. 22 Nov. in Ann. Rep. Amer. Hist. Assoc. 1907 (1908) II. 142 It contains your commission, a letter of credence to the secretary of the United States, and office copies of them. 1848 Wharton Law Lex., Office copy, a transcript of a proceeding filed in the proper office of a court under the seal of such office. 1928 F. M. Ford Let. 16 Apr. (1965) 178, I don't know if you have..an office copy that you would care to sell. 1946 J. Irving Royal Navalese 126 Office copy, the, the other half (of the drink in hand). 1957 Clark & Gottfried University Dict. Business & Finance 246/1 Office copy, in general, a copy or transcript of any document.. retained for office use. In law, a copy of a document made by an officer of the court or other public officer. 1881 Rep. Indian Affairs (U.S.) 151 The articles manufactured by the carpenters..were as follows..one *office-desk [etc.]. 1907 G. B. Shaw John Bull's Other Island I. 3 Against the right hand wall is a filing cabinet,..and, nearer, a tall office desk and stool for one person. 1954 T. S. Eliot Confid. Clerk II. 69 It's an office desk. Sir Claude got it for me... You see, I shall do a good deal of my work here. 1715 Boston News-Let. 11 Apr. 2/2 A fair Alphabetical List..hung up at the *Office Door, would soon resolve any Person. 1863 'E. Kirke' My Southern Friends xxiii. 235 A short rap came at the office door. 1855 Ecclesiologist XVI. 294 Mr. Slater sends an *office-drawing..of a projected cathedral for South Australia. 1672 Owen Disc. Evang. Love 221 If it be not part of their *Office-Duty, to walk over them. a1885 G. B. McClellan Own Story (1887) xxxii. 534 He said that he was so much occupied with office-duty that it was impossible for him to leave. 1942 D. Powell Time to be Born (1943) ii. 44 The profits..had been..put back into the business, new *office equipment, printing, one thing and another. 1962 D. Francis Dead Cert x. 115 It had once been an elegant room and even the office equipment could not entirely spoil its proportions. 1972 Guardian 7 June 9/6 There is really no reason why office equipment shouldn't be good looking enough to go into private houses too. 1869 Bradshaw's Railway Manual XXI. 161 Expended..*Office expenses, &c—£438. 1887 'Mark Twain' Lett. to Publishers (1967) 233 On first 10,000, we deduct $5,000 office expenses and $1750 for author. 1972 P. Griffin A-Z Office Guide 86 They [sc. IOUs] should not be allowed to build up to a point when cash becomes short for office expenses. 1553 Grimalde Cicero's Offices III. (1558) 138b As yet Aquilius, my *office felowe, and familiar, had not sette forth the cases, that shoulde be counted couine. 1903 G. B. Shaw Man & Superman II. 66 If you were to marry the son of an English manufacturer of *awffice furniture, your friends would consider it a misalliance. 1911 Daily Colonist (Victoria, B.C.) 4 Apr. 4/4 (Advt.). We are selling lots of office furniture these days. 1974 N. Freeling Dressing of Diamond 188 A dislike of metal office furniture. 1863 A. D. Whitney Faith Gartney's Girlhood xi. 97 Faith looked up, and remembered the poor *office girl of three years since. 1972 J. McClure Caterpillar Cop xii. 193 Ye Olde Englishe Tea Shoppe..was crowded with office girls, buying roast beef sandwiches with luncheon vouchers. 1817 W. Irving in Life & Lett. (1864) I. 392, I should not like to have my name hackneyed about among the office-seekers and *office-givers at Washington. 1818 H. B. Fearon Sk. Amer. 143 Those dangerous abuses in government, introduced by *office-holders, which..threaten..to become inveterate. 1854 J. L. Stephens Centr. Amer. (1854) 4 Office-holders, civil and military. 1860 Motley Netherl. (1868) I. i. 12 The office holders..were not greedy for the spoils of office. 1957 P. Worsley Trumpet shall Sound 269 The tendency of the office-holder to merge his personal interests with those of his office. 1970 R. Lowell Notebk. 56 The communist committed to his commune, Artist and office-holder to a claque of less Than fifty souls. 1835 D. Crockett Acct. Col. Crockett's Tour 106 The *office-holding gentry..will meet with their match in an indignant people. 1857 [see office-seeking]. 1890 Gross Gild Merch. I. 110 Their anxiety to be rid of the burden of office-holding. 1936 Discovery Feb. 63/1 The burden of compulsory office-holding ruined the well-to-do. 1957 V. W. Turner Schism & Continuity in Afr. Society iv. 93 Social Drama I illustrates the conflict that may arise..when only a few men remain in the senior, office holding generation in a village. 1806 Deb. Congress U.S. 24 Feb. (1852) 506/2 It would be a struggle between *office-hunters and the people. 1810 W. Irving in Life & Lett. (1864) I. 243 The crowd of office-hunters. 1845 W. L. Mackenzie Lives Butler & Hoyt 75 General Spicer was a keen office-hunter. 1824 Niles' Reg. 20 Mar. 37/2 (heading) *Office hunting. 1889 Farmer Americanisms 397 Office-hunting is quite a business with the thousand-and-one 'hangers-on' to the skirts of political parties. 1923 H. Crane Let. 26 Oct. (1965) 153 My mind is divided between them and an *office job. 1937 M. Hillis Orchids on your Budget (1938) iv. 68 We ourselves have run our one-woman ménage both with and without an office job. ?c1670 (title) An Humble Proposal to Parliament against *Office-Jobbing. 1707 J. Chamberlayne St. Gt. Brit. 509 The Lord Privy Seal and his Officers..Richard Fountain, *Office-keeper. 1766 Goldsm. Vic. W. xx, He assured me that I was on the very point of ruin, in listening to the office-keeper's promises. 1834 Chambers's Edin. Jrnl. III. 229/1 Has the office-keeper acquainted you with the particulars I require? 1938 Times 16 Feb. 8/7 A short time ago a telegram was delivered at my office..after I had left for the day. The office keeper..had it re-telegraphed to my home address. a1919 T. Roosevelt in Ld. Charnwood Theodore Roosevelt (1923) 250 These men have a gift at *office-mongering, just as other men have a peculiar knack in picking pockets. 1917 H. Grant Two Sides of Atlantic 45 This is known in the States as '*office-politics'. 1961 'J. Wyndham' Consider her Ways 216 Office politics, very likely... Many a young man's gifts are stunted by them. 1907 G. B. Shaw Major Barbara III. 258 He could learn the *office routine without understanding the business. 1911 W. Owen Let. 25 Apr. (1967) 70, I am not too young to..turn to Office Routine, Customs, Revenues. 1925 H. Crane Let. 7 May (1965) 204 A change from office routine for awhile. 1813 Deb. Congress U.S. 6 Jan. (1853) 582/2 It would augment the *office-seekers, who, with the friends of the Administration, were continually haunting the Executive. 1817 [see office-giver]. 1845 Knickerbocker XXV. 374 A Friend writing from Washington..give us this pleasant sketch of a 'Sucker' office-seeker. 1877 Talmage 50 Serm. 2 The office-seekers had all folded-up their recommendations and gone home. 1882–3 W. Whitman Specimen Days 259 The members.. were..the meanest kind of bawling and blowing office-holders, office-seekers. 1977 Listener 11 Aug. 163/1 In 1881 ..James A. Garfield..was assassinated by a disappointed office-seeker from his own party ranks. 1857 W. R. Alger Genius & Posture of Amer. 4 Office-holding partisans, *office-seeking demagogues. 1860 H. Greeley Overland Journey 68 If he will work right ahead,..keeping clear of speculation and office-seeking, he can hardly fail to do well. 1884 Manch. Exam. 16 Oct. 5/2 The office-seeking throng, who do so much to win elections. 1884 F. M. Crawford Amer. Politician I. iv. 76 We are sick with the foul disease of office seeking. 1837 Dickens Pickw. lv, Wilkins Flasher, Esquire, was balancing himself on two legs of an *office stool. 1907 G. B. Shaw John Bull's Other Island I. 13 He seats himself on the office stool, and tilts it back. 1953 J. Wain Hurry on Down v. 91 You couldn't rightly say whether a fella was a workman or an office stool percher or a manager. a1678 J. Westley in E. Calamy Continuation of Acct. of Ministers Ejected (1727) I. 441 They are not a People that are fit Subjects, for me to exercise *Office-work among them. 1849 Dickens Dav. Copp. (1850) xvi. 167, I am not doing office-work... I am improving my legal knowledge. 1886 C. M. Yonge Chantry House II. xiv. 136 He had spent an entire day on his hands and knees..—the office-work, as we declared. 1889 Jessopp Coming of Friars iii. 130 The greater portion of work done in the Scriptorium was mere office work. 1956 'C. Blackstock' Dewey Death iv. 83, I cannot see why all the office work should be held up. 1936 Discovery May 146/2 The lowest value of natural illumination which an *office worker requires. 1956 A. H. Compton Atomic Quest 333 Mechanics and office workers and laborers of many kinds. 1973 'E. McBain' Hail to Chief viii. 136 The homeward rush of office workers had already begun.

c. Special Combs., as **office block**, a block (sense 14f) containing offices; also *attrib.* and *fig.*; **office hours**, (*a*) the hours of work at an office; (*b*) a disciplinary session *U.S. Forces' slang*; **office hymn** (see quot. 1938); **office junior**, the youngest or newest member of the staff of an office; **office party**, a party held for members of the staff of an office; **office piano** *slang*, a typewriter; **office wife**, a business man's female secretary.

1942 London Replanned (R. Academy) 26/2 The large octagonal building prominent in the drawing..is a suggested office block with garden court or car park. 1951 Ann. Reg. 1950 406 The architectural standard of most of these buildings..was very poor; most of them..resembled pre-war commercial office blocks at their most tasteless. 1963 Listener 10 Jan. 71/1 Harry Bertoia's beautiful but boring silvery puffball of wire is the apotheosis of what I once heard called 'office-block art'—the triumph of taste and craftsmanship over feeling. 1967 B. Patten Little Johnny's Confession 47 Maud, is that you I see Alone among the office blocks? 1972 M. Gilbert Body of Girl xxv. 211 If there is a covering party, I guess it'll be in the office block opposite. 1802 D. Rawn Let. 29 Oct. in J. Steele Papers (1924) I. 326 He receives in addition thereto, 300 Dollars for services termed extra, but wholly performed during the usual Office hour. 1841 Thackeray Gt. Hoggarty Diamond (1849) ix. 100 Gus Hoskins and I, who hunted after office hours in couples. 1852 Beck's Florist 260 Early rising has compensated for long office-hours. 1898 J. H. Parker Hist. Gatling Gun Detachment 23, I don't want to hear anything about it... If you want to see me about this subject, come to me in office hours. 1903 G. B. Shaw Man & Superman III. 80 It is the custom..always to put off business until to-morrow. In fact, you have arrived out of office hours. 1922 Marine Corps Gaz. June 212 One morning after Office Hours the C.O. was sitting at his desk grumbling to himself and holding his head in his hands. 1933 Leatherneck Apr. 14 No 'office hours' were held during the month of January for any 'A' Company Marines. 1967 A. Dubus Lieutenant 41 He committed an offense, he was brought in to office hours. 1972 'H. Howard' Nice Day for Funeral iii. 41 We only meet outside office hours. I never impose on social relationships. 1907 New Office Hymn Bk. II. p. v, The Office Hymns are the Hymns in the Divine Office. 1931 N. & Q. 19 Sept. 216/2 We are told that the best place for the Office Hymn both at Matins and Evensong is immediately before the Psalms. 1938 Oxf. Compan. Mus. 629/1 Office hymn, a liturgical hymn appointed for the Office, or Service of the day... The Office Hymns of the Roman Breviary were not transferred to the English Prayer Book. 1959 J. C. Denyer Office Managem. xi. 83 For office juniors, the appropriate official to approach is the Juvenile Employment Officer. 1970 J. Cooper How to survive from Nine to Five 81 The office junior has used hair lacquer under her arms instead of deodorant and is walking round like a penguin. 1974 R. Gadney Something Worth Fighting For ix. 64 A young man, neatly dressed, the obvious clerk or what is sometimes known as an office junior. 1955 W. Gaddis Recognitions I. iii. 101 Who made the first one? Will somebody tell me that? said The Boss at an office party. 1967 E. McGirr Here lies my Wife iii. 105 Kellerman had been in New Orleans the previous Christmas and so had missed the..office party. 1972 G. Bromley In Absence of Body xii. 142 'You seem to have a lot of office parties.' 'Yes. People leaving or getting married, or entertaining clients.' 1942 Berrey & Van den Bark Amer. Thes. Slang §75/38 Typewriter, mill, office piano. 1945 L. Shelly Jive Talk Dict. 29/2 Office piano, typewriter. 1970 C. Major Dict. Afro-Amer. Slang 87 Office piano,..a typewriter. 1942 Berrey & Van den Bark Amer. Thes. Slang §542/19 Girl Friday, office wife, a female secretary. 1952 G. W. Brace Spire (1953) xxvii. 268 I've been a pretty faithful office wife to him, and though he has never invited me to share a bed..he does hate to part with me. 1955 H. Kurnitz Invasion of Privacy (1956) vii. 52, I know all about American business executives and their secretaries. Office wives, isn't that what you call them? 1972 C. Weston Poor, Poor Ophelia (1973) viii. 41 The secretary smiled sweetly.. 'I'll do that, Mr. Farr. Get a good night's sleep now. 'Bye.' My office wife, he thought sourly.

ˈoffice, *v.* [f. prec. sb. Cf. officy *v.*]

†**1.** *intr.* To perform divine service: = officiate *v.* 1. *Obs.*

c1449 Pecock Repr. II. vi. 173 The same preest schulde office to God. 1502 Ord. Crysten Men (W. de W. 1506) IV. xxi. 237 The clerke so ordeyned sholde not offyce.

†**2.** *trans.* To perform in the way of duty or service. *Obs. rare*⁻¹.

1601 Shaks. All's Well III. ii. 129 Although The ayre of Paradise did fan the house, And Angles offic'd all.

†**3.** To appoint to, or place in, office. *Obs. rare.*

1611 Shaks. Wint. T. I. ii. 172 So stands this Squire Offic'd with me. 1763 Churchill Duellist II. 223 Before her Magna Charta lay, Which some great Lawyer..was offic'd to explain.

†**4.** To drive by virtue of one's office. *Obs. nonce-use.*

1607 Shaks. Cor. v. ii. 68 You shall perceiue, that a Iacke gardant cannot office me from my Son Coriolanus.

5. *slang.* To 'give the office' to (a person); to give private notice of (something): see office *sb.* 11. Hence **ˈofficing** *vbl. sb.*

1812 Sporting Mag. XXXIX. 283 This letter was to office Trist about laying bets on thick. 1819 Moore Tom Cribb's Mem. 19 To office, with all due dispatch, through the air, To the Bulls of the Alley the fate of the Bear. 1841 Swell's Night Guide (Gloss.) Office, giving warning. 1846 Ibid. 58 She eased him of his fawney,..officed her cullies, they pasted his nibs, and scarpered rumbo. 1859 G. W. Matsell Vocabulum 60 Officing, signalizing; a preconcerted signal by a confederate. 1914 Jackson & Hellyer Vocab. Criminal Slang 63 Office, noun,..a signal;..a warning... Used also as a verb in the same sense. 1926 J. Black You can't Win xiii. 182 Sanc closed the door..and 'officed' me to follow him out. 1949 Partridge Dict. Underworld 479/1 Officing, a preconcerted signal. 1955 Publ. Amer. Dial. Soc. xxiv. 73 The tool offices that they will clip him as he enters the ramp. .. The tool offices for a left bridge and a left prat, and the frame closes.

6. *intr.* To have or work in an office (sense 8a); to share an office *with* someone. *U.S.*

1892 Nation (N.Y.) 21 Apr. 303/2 An attorney officing in the same building. 1917 Dialect Notes IV. 347 Office with,.. to share an office with. 1936 Atlantic Monthly July (Contributors' Col., 4) A local newspaper has just carried two want ads containing this wording:—'Chance for public accountant to office with lawyer.' 'Chance for high grade realtor to office with lawyer.' 1973 N.Y. Times 11 Aug. 10/1 Mr. Mardian spoke of a man who 'officed in that same agency'.

Hence †**ˈofficed** *ppl. a.*, (*a*) Having a particular function; (*b*) Of a church: see quots. 1598, 1611.

1598 Florio, Officiata chiesa, a church well officed, id est, well serued, or duly serued. 1604 Shaks. Oth. I. iii. 271 When light wing'd Toyes Of feather'd Cupid, seele..My speculatiue, and offic'd [Qos. active] Instrument. 1611 Florio, Officiata Chiesa, a Church officed or serued. Officiato, officed, serued with due office.

office-bearer (ˈɒfɪsˌbɛərə(r)). One who bears or holds office; an officer.

1645 Durye Israel's Call 12 Civill and Ecclesiasticall office-bearers. 1855 Macaulay Hist. Eng. xvi. III. 694 One [Act]..required every officebearer in every University of Scotland to sign the Confession of Faith. Ibid. xix. IV. 376 The right..of the office bearers of the Church to meet and deliberate touching her interests. 1865 M. Arnold Ess. Crit. (1875) 10 As a plain citizen of the republic of letters, and not as an office-bearer in a hierarchy.

officeful (ˈɒfɪsfʊl). Also office-full. [f. office *sb.* + -ful.] That amount or number of anything which would fill an office.

1963 'W. Haggard' High Wire vi. 63 He had an officeful of paper. 1966 'E. Peters' Piper on Mountain ii. 26 Put him among an office-full of civil servants, and you could lose him in a moment. 1976 J. Wainwright Who goes Next? 66 'You'll have witnesses, of course, sir?'.. 'A whole office-full, officer.'

ˈoffice-house. A 'house of office' (house *sb.*[1] 14); now only *pl.* apartments or outhouses for the work of domestics, offices (office *sb.* 9).

c1450 St. Cuthbert (Surtees) 8018 Þe bischope gart make all þe kirke, þe monkys þaire office hous gart wyrke. 1632 Lithgow Trav. x. 444 This Pallace..hath neither outward walles nor gates..saue onely some office houses without. 1637 Rutherford Lett. (1862) I. 211 A field and an office-house for the zeal of His servants to exercise themselves in. 1720 Lond. Gaz. No. 5866/3 A large fine House and convenient Office houses of all Kinds. 1827 Carlyle Germ. Rom. II. 120 A hut, and various ruined office-houses.

officeless (ˈɒfɪslɪs), *a. rare.* [See -less.] Having no office, out of office.

1483 Cath. Angl. 258/2 Officeles, immvnis..officiperdus. 1834 Fraser's Mag. X. 739, I now must wander through a world All officeless and cold.

ˈoffice-man. †**1.** An officer; an official. *Sc. Obs.*

a1578 Lindesay (Pitscottie) Chron. Scot. (1899) I. 305 [The king] thair tuike wpe house with all maner of office men that was necessar to be had ffor him. 1583 in Maitland Hist. Edin. (1753) 230 The Magistratts and Office Men, sic as the Provest, Baillies, Dean of Gild and Thesaurer. a1639 Spottiswood Hist. Ch. Scot. VI. (1677) 407 The Ambassador..had office-men standing by him to wait.

2. A man who works in an office; *spec.* a detective who remains at headquarters.

1904 'No. 1500' *Life in Sing Sing* xiii. 256/2 *Office Man*, headquarters detective. **1908** J. M. SULLIVAN *Criminal Slang* 17 *Office man*, headquarters detective. **1921** *Daily Colonist* (Victoria, B.C.) 12 Oct. 16/2 (Advt.), Wanted—position as office man, watchman, warehouse, or place of trust. **1949** PARTRIDGE *Dict. Underworld* 479/1 *Office man*, a headquarters detective.

officer ('ɒfɪsə(r)), *sb.* Also 4 officere, -iser, -yser, oficere, 4–6 offycer, 4–7 -icier, 5 -ycere, -ysere, (-ycyr, -iceer, 6 offecer, -eser, -esar), *Sc.* 5–7 officiar, (6 -iciare, -iecear). [a. AF. *officer* = OF. *officier* (1334 in Godef. *Compl.*), ad. med.L. *officiārius*, f. *officium* OFFICE: see -ER².]

†**1.** One to whom a charge is committed, or who performs a duty, service, or function; a minister; an agent. *Obs.* exc. when qualified as in 2.

c **1380** WYCLIF *Sel. Wks.* III. 346 So if apostlis..sawen þus prestis serve in þe Chirche, þei wolden not clepe hem Cristis officeris, but officeris of Anticrist. *c* **1425** LYDG. *Assembly of Gods* 446 Remembre howe ye made me your offycere, All tho with my dart fynally to chastyse That yow dysobeyed. **1601** SHAKS. *All's Well* III. v. 18, I know that knaue,..a filthy Officer he is in those suggestions for the young Earle. **1619** SIR J. SEMPILL *Sacrilege Handled* 28 So long as God hath Officiars of his worship on Earth; so long must Tithes be their Inheritance. **1634** MILTON *Comus* 218 He, the Supreme Good, to whom all things ill Are but as slavish officers of vengeance. **1669** PENN *No Cross* xiv. §2 The Luxurious Eater and Drinker..has an Officer to invent, and a Cook to dress..the Species.

2. One who holds an office, post, or place.

a. One who holds a public, civil, or ecclesiastical office; a servant or minister of the king, as one of the great functionaries of the royal household, etc.; a person authoritatively appointed or elected to exercise some function pertaining to public life, or to take part in the administration of municipal government, the management or direction of a public corporation, institution, etc. In early use, applied esp. to persons engaged in the administration of law or justice.

Often with qualification defining the nature of the office, as *officer of health* (see HEALTH 1 b), *of the Household, of Justice, of the Law, of State*, etc.; *government, municipal, public*, CUSTOM-HOUSE, MEDICAL, RETURNING, REVENUE *officer*, etc.

c **1325** *Song Deo Gratias* 73 in *E.E.P.* (1862) 126 ȝif þou be made an officer..What cause þou demest loke hit be cler. *c* **1330** R. BRUNNE *Chron.* (1810) 312 Þe Kynge's ansuere was smert, & said, 'I se [ȝe] wille..so lowe me to chace, myn officers to change, & mak þam at ȝour grace'. **1375** BARBOUR *Bruce* I. 191 Schyrreffys and bailȝheys..And alkyn othir officeris, That for to gowern land afferis. *c* **1400** MAUNDEV. (Roxb.) ii. 7 Afterward was oure Lord ledd before þe bischope and þe officers of þe lawe. **1413** *Pilgr. Sowle* IV. xxxviii. (1859) 65 In your assyses al your offycers in the countre, done wel theyr deuoyre. *c* **1430** LYDG. *Min. Poems* (Percy Soc.) 54 Off all thi warde thou art made officeer. *c* **1460** FORTESCUE *Abs. & Lim. Mon.* xv. (1885) 148 Þe grete officers off þe lande, as Chaunceler, tresourer, and prive seell. **1479** in *Eng. Gilds* 423 Paiementes..to the Maire, Shiref, Recorder, and othir officers. **1578** in Spottiswood *Hist. Ch. Scot.* VI. (1677) 291 According to this division arises a sort of threefold Officiars in the Church. **1607** SHAKS. *Cor.* V. ii. 3, I am an Officer of State, and come to speak with Coriolanus. *a* **1677** HALE *Prim. Orig. Man.* I. i. 4 What fashion Cloaths the Roman Officers, Military, Civil or Sacred used. **1802** HAMILTON *Wks.* (1886) VII. 233 The first officer of the government..speaking in his official capacity. **1834** *Act 4 & 5 Will. IV*, c. 76 §109 The Word 'Officer' shall be construed to extend to any..Person who shall be employed in any Parish or Union in carrying this Act or the Laws for the Relief of the Poor into execution. **1845** MCCULLOCH *Taxation* II. ix. (1852) 328 Governments have usually consulted the officers employed in the collection of the revenue respecting the best modes of rendering taxes effectual. **1849** MACAULAY *Hist. Eng.* ii. I. 175 Another act..required every officer of a corporation to swear that he held resistance to the king's authority to be in all cases unlawful. *a* **1860** *Order* in Archbold *Poor Law* (ed. 10) 71 The guardians shall..appoint fit persons to hold the under-mentioned offices,..1. Clerk to the Guardians... 4. Medical Officer for the Workhouse. 5. District Medical Officer. 6. Master of the Workhouse... 10. Porter. 11. Nurse. 12. Relieving Officer. **1874** STUBBS *Const. Hist.* xi. I. 343 The great officers of the household..furnish the king with the first elements of a ministry of state.

b. A person engaged in the management of the domestic affairs of a great household or collegiate body, of a private estate, etc.; †formerly, also, a subordinate of such an officer; a menial, domestic.

c **1386** CHAUCER *Clerk's T.* 134 Heer vp on he to hise officeres Comaundeth for the feste to purveye. —— *Shipman's T.* 65 [This Monk hath] eek an Officer out for to ryde To seen hir graunges and hire bernes wyde. ? *c* **1475** *Sqr. lowe Degre* 460 The officers sone can he call, Both ussher, panter, and butler. **1526** *Pilgr. Perf.* (W. de W. 1531) 151 For the officers in monasteryes of religyon vseth the workes of the actyue lyfe. **1601** SHAKS. *Twel. N.* II. v. 53 Calling my Officers about me, in my branch'd Veluet gowne. **1611** —— *Cymb.* III. i. 65 Cæsar, that hath moe Kings his Seruants, then Thy selfe Domesticke Officers.

c. A person holding office and taking part in the management or direction of a society or institution, *esp.* one holding the office of president, treasurer, or secretary; an office-bearer.

1711 STEELE *Spect.* No. 78 ¶5 At last the Society was formed, and proper Officers were appointed. **1862** *Rules* §10 in *Trans. Philol. Soc.* p. iv, A General Meeting shall be held annually..to elect the Officers for the ensuing year. **1897** T. HOLMES in *Charity Organis. Rev.* Apr. 201 A hospital in old times was a place for the gratuitous reception of cases grave enough, in the judgment of its officers, to need treatment in the wards.

d. *officer of (at) arms*, a herald, pursuivant. Cf. ARM *sb.*² 15, HERALD *sb.* 1 d, KING-OF-ARMS.

c **1500** *Three Kings Sons* 32 Som officers of armes & purceuantes that had be at this iourney wente in all haste to the kynge, & tolde hym all the maner..therof. *a* **1548** HALL *Chron., Edw. IV*, 229 This counterfeight Herault..there put on his cote of Armes. The Englishe out-skourers perceivyng by his cote, that he was an officer of armes, gently saluted hym. **1593** SHAKS. *Rich. II*, I. i. 204 Lord Marshall, command our Officers at Armes, Be readie to direct these home Alarmes.

3. *spec.* **a.** A petty officer of justice or of the peace; a sheriff's serjeant, bailiff, catchpole; a constable (now *rare* in England); †a jailer; an executioner (*obs.*). See also PEACE *officer*, POLICE *officer*, SHERIFF'S *officer*.

[*c* **1440** *Promp. Parv.* 363/1 Offycere of cruelte, as bayly, or iaylere, or other lyke.] **15..** *Adam Bel & Clym of Clough* 321 Wyllyam sterte to an officer of the towne, Hys axe out of hys hande he wronge. **1584** J. NEWBERY *Let.* in Arb. *Garner* III. 182 With officers, I went divers times out of the Castle in the morning, and sold things; and, at night, returned againe to prison. **1593** SHAKS. *3 Hen. VI*, V. vi. 12 The Theefe doth feare each bush an Officer. **1596** —— *Rich. III*, V. i. 28 Come leade me Officers to the blocke of shame. **1597** SKENE *De Verb. Sign.* s.v. *Schireffe*, The Schireffis serjand, or officiar, suld haue ane horne. **1609** —— *Reg. Maj.* 7 The summons sall be made be ane lawfull summoner (or officiar). **1819** SHELLEY *Cenci* V. i. 35, I doubt not officers are, whilst we speak, Sent to arrest us. **1884** *Boston* (Mass.) *Jrnl.* 23 Aug., Sergeant McBryan.. was set upon by a crowd of roughs, who threw him down and kicked him in a most brutal manner. In trying to use his revolver the officer shot himself through the left thumb. **1888** E. H. MARSHALL in *N. & Q.* 7th Ser. VI. 237/2 It is no solecism to call a police constable an 'officer'..A police-constable is a peace officer, with the rights and duties of such, and is therefore entitled to be styled an 'officer'.

b. Used as a mode of address to a police officer.

1899 J. S. CLOUSTON *Lunatic at Large* II. v. 140 Keep your eye on that man, officer,..and put your plain-clothes' men on his track. **1926** GALSWORTHY *Silver Spoon* I. vii. 50 'Pardon me, officer,' he said, 'but where is Wren Street?' **1934** D. L. SAYERS *Nine Tailors* 143 It is said..that the plain bobby considers 'officer' a more complimentary form of address than 'my man', or even 'constable'. **1946** E. O'NEILL *Iceman Cometh* (1947) IV. 211 She knows I was insane. You've got me all wrong, Officer. I want to go to the Chair... God, you're a dumb dick! **1965** M. ALLINGHAM *Mind Readers* iii. 44 'Officer!' said the voice.., 'I wish to give this lady in charge.' **1976** [see OFFICEFUL].

4. a. A person holding a military or naval command, or occupying a position of authority in the army, navy, air force, or mercantile marine; *spec.* one holding a commission in the army or navy.

Officers in the army and navy are sometimes divided into *combatant* and *non-combatant* (the latter comprising medical and commissariat officers, paymasters, etc.). In the army they are distinguished as *general, staff, commissioned* (*field* and *company*), *brevet*, and *non-commissioned* officers; in the navy as *commissioned, warrant*, and *petty* officers. (See these words.) † *commission-officer*: see COMMISSION *sb.* 13. *officer of the day*, 'an officer whose immediate duty is to attend to the interior economy of the corps to which he belongs, or of those with which he may be doing duty' (Stocqueler). *officer of the deck*, the officer temporarily in charge of the deck of a vessel, and responsible for the ship's management. FLAG-OFFICER: see the word. (The appellation was app. used on shipboard earlier than in the army.)

? **1565** *Sir J. Hawkins' 2nd Voy.* in Arb. *Garner* V. 88 In cutting of the foresail, a marvellous misfortune happened to one of the Officers in the ship. **1598** W. PHILLIPS *Linschoten* in Arb. *Garner* III. 422 All the Officers of the ship assembled. *Ibid.* 423 There grew a great noise and murmuring in the ship, that cursed the Captain and Officers, because the ship was badly provided. **1599** SHAKS. *Hen. V*, IV. i. 37 *Pist.*..Art thou Officer, or art thou base, common, and popular? *King.* I am a Gentleman of a Company. **1607** —— *Cor.* IV. vi. 30 Caius Martius was A worthy Officer i' th' Warre. **1665** MANLEY *Grotius' Low C. Warres* 297 Hereupon, the other Officers and Souldiers also earnestly perswaded Frederick to surrender. **1698** LUTTRELL *Brief Rel.* (1857) IV. 392 All the disbanded officers, that are to have half pay, to doe duty in the standing regiments. **1706** *Wooden World Dissected* (1708) 8 He allows no Distinction betwixt an Officer and a Swabber. **1766** *Char.* in *Ann. Reg.* 10 They become colonels, before they are officers, and then generals, without any other difference than time. **1788** NELSON 26 Dec. in Nicolas *Disp.* (1845) I. 277 The want of good Petty Officers, and consequently good Lieutenants,..[was] most severely felt during the late War. **1844** *Regul. & Ord. Army* 138 The Captain, or Officer of the Day, is..to inspect the meals, in order to see that they are wholesome, sufficient, and properly cooked. **1867** SMYTH *Sailor's Word-bk.*, *Officer of the Watch*, the lieutenant or other officer who has charge of, and commands, the watch. **1881** *Morn. Post* 29 Sept. 5/4 The staff is entirely composed of cavalry officers. **1884** PAE *Eustace* 5, I would rather be a naval officer. **1943** C. H. WARD-JACKSON *Piece of Cake* 4 The Service experiences of all sorts of people—pilots,..old R.N.A.S. and R.F.C. officers, padres,..and the rest. **1948** PARTRIDGE *Dict. Forces' Slang* 148 R.A.F. officer term. **1952** *Oxf. Jun. Encycl.* X. 493 Members of the three [women's] services..are administered by their own officers. **1959** *Chambers's Encycl.* I. 184/2 If aircraft were used in attack and defence,..it could be argued that they were manned..by officers and men who could claim to be members of a service which belonged neither to the navy nor to the army. **1973** K. GILES *File on Death* iii. 63 Miss Sloper..had worked as an officer in the Second World War.

b. Phr. *(an) officer and (a) gentleman*, applied to a person embodying the civilized qualities expected of both, freq. used ironically, also (occas. with hyphens) *attrib.* or as *adj. phr.* Hence ***officer-and-gentlemanly*** adj.

1845 MRS. GASKELL *North & South* (1855) I. xiv. 164, I will bear with all proper patience everything that one officer and gentleman can take from another. **1871** *Porcupine* 29 July 275/3 They want their purchase, their officer-and-gentleman hobby, their..agreeable club of an army left undisturbed. **1888** KIPLING *Plain Tales from Hills* 123 Golightly spent..that summer trying to get the Corporal..tried by Court-Martial for arresting an 'officer and a gentleman'. **1926** —— *Debits & Credits* 334 Ignatius is one of the subtlest intellects we have, and an officer and a gentleman to boot. **1946** E. O'NEILL *Iceman Cometh* (1947) I. 48, I give you my word of honour as an officer and a gentleman, you shall be paid tomorrow. **1962** I. MURDOCH *Unofficial Rose* xxxi. 304 He was paying the penalty..for being an officer and a gentleman. **1966** A. PRIOR *Operators* iii. 28 Oh, coming the officer and gentleman touch, was he? **1969** K. GILES *Death cracks Bottle* x. 110 We will just be very nice to the police in an officer-and-gentlemanly way. **1971** 'H. CALVIN' *Poison Chasers* ix. 135 ''Evening, Sergeant,' I said. Hard, officer-and-gentleman tone. **1974** 'J. GRAHAM' *Bloody Passage* i. 11 There wasn't much I could do except put my head on the block like an officer and a gentleman.

c. ***Officers Training Corps***, an organization set up in schools and universities for the preliminary training of boys and young men who may later become officers in the armed forces.

1907 *Interim Rep. War Office Comm. Provision of Officers* 10 (*heading*) in *Parl. Papers* (Cd. 3294) XLIX. 549 Proposals respecting the Officers Training Corps at Universities. **1908** *Oxford Univ. Officers Training Corps* (Misc. Paper) 1 The present Oxford University Volunteer Corps is about to be transformed into a unit of 'The Officers Training Corps'. **1925** *Officers Training Corps Gaz.* Nov. 1/1 Though our first number is devoted to the University of London Contingent, ..it is proposed to include all University units of the Officers Training Corps. **1957** *Encycl. Brit.* XXII. 392/2 The Officers' Training corps (O.T.C.) was set up in 1909 under the Haldane scheme... The junior division.. consisted of boys in public secondary schools..; the senior division of university contingents... After World War II the training corps was replaced by the Combined Cadet force.

5. A member of a grade in some honorary orders.

(In the Legion of Honour, a member of the grade next above that of chevalier.)

1846 *Penny Cycl.* Suppl. II. 193/2 *Legion of Honor*... This order consists of five divisions: *chevaliers*,..*officers*, *commanders*, *grand officers*, and *grand crosses*... To obtain the rank of officer it is necessary to have served four years as a chevalier; an officer must serve two years to become commander.

6. *attrib.* and *Comb.* (chiefly in sense 4), as ***officer cadet*** (also *fig.*), ***-caste***, ***-class*** (also *attrib.* or as *adj.*), ***-instructor***, ***-type***; ***officer-like*** adj.; **officer material**: see MATERIAL *sb.* 7; **officer-tree**, an officer's saddletree.

1925 *Officers Training Corps Gaz.* Nov. 1/1 Our object.. is to foster a spirit of Unity and Co-operation among *Officer Cadets. **1955** T. H. PEAR *Eng. Social Differences* iii. 101 When..the functions of Sandhurst were modified, 'officer'-cadets succeeded 'gentleman'-cadets. **1962** L. DEIGHTON *Ipcress File* xiii. 74 [He] reminded me of those N.C.O.'s who drilled officer cadets. **1973** 'S. HARVESTER' *Corner of Playground* I. iv. 38 Officer cadets due to receive their commissions at the passing-out parade. **1976** *Listener* 5 Feb. 139/1 We were a grateful generation... The fittest had survived to become the officer-cadets of the intellect. **1937** 'G. ORWELL' in *New English Weekly* 29 July 308/2 The Popular Army..modelled as far as possible on an ordinary bourgeois army, with a privileged *officer-caste, immense differences of pay, etc., etc. **1936** 'N. BLAKE' *Thou Shell of Death* v. 78 His army training had given him a possibly misplaced belief in the superior wisdom of what he would never have thought of calling 'the *officer class'. **1950** G. GREENE *Third Man* ii. 25 'Be quiet, can't you, sir,' my driver said. He had an exaggerated sense of officer-class. **1954** 'N. BLAKE' *Whisper in Gloom* II. xiii. 173 He treated his church wardens with a certain officer-class brusqueness. **1958** P. SHORE in N. Mackenzie *Conviction* 28 The managers are often described as an officer class and this is..an apt analogy. **1968** A. LASKI *Keeper* i. 10 Ralph's turning to Colin and saying, in the same frankly brutal officer-class manner [etc.]. **1859** *Musketry Instr.* 63 The diagrams of the performances of each squad or section are..to be handed over to the *officer-instructor, or battalion sergeant-instructor. **1898** *Westm. Gaz.* 21 Apr. 6/3 The Russians have..insisted on the dismissal of the British officer-instructors in the Chinese naval torpedo schools, who are to be replaced by Russian naval officers. **1778** HAMILTON *Wks.* (1886) VII. 537 Such carelessness and indifference to the service as is subversive to every *officer-like quality. **1862** MARG. GOODMAN *Exper. Eng. Sister of Mercy* 231 The medical officer of the 42nd, an exceedingly officer-like and handsome man. **1894** *Harper's Mag.* Feb. 350, I carefully adjusted my Whitman's *officer-tree over a wealth of saddle blanketing. **1942** E. WAUGH *Put out More Flags* i. 64 'What do you think is the right type of officer?' 'The *officer-type.' ..'Now three-quarters of your officer-type live in towns'.

Hence (*nonce-wds.*) **'officerage**, the action of an officer; **'officeress**, a female officer; **offi'cerial** *a.*, of or pertaining to an officer or officers; **'officerhood**, **'officerism**, the position or function of an officer; a body of officers.

1837 CARLYLE *Fr. Rev.* III. v. vi, Spanish Field-officerism struck mute at such cat-o'-mountain spirit. **1838** *Fraser's Mag.* XVII. 687 They were..of the class officerial. **1839** *Ibid.* XIX. 742 They..say, not only that such an officeress exists, but that she keeps a Clerk. **1841** *Blackw. Mag.* L. 333 How much have they not to pay for carriage, porterage, overweightage, custom-house officerage. **1884** A. Forbes *Chinese Gordon* xi. 55 The belief..that he had sufficient influence with the officerhood of Gordon's force to bring them over.

officer (ˈɒfɪsə(r)), *v.* [f. prec. sb.]

1. *trans.* **a.** To furnish with officers, esp. military or naval (cf. *to man*). **b.** To lead, command, or direct as an officer. Esp. in *pass.*

1670 Cotton *Espernon* I. v. 229 Perhaps no Militia in Europe were better Disciplin'd, nor better Officer'd than they. **1709** Steele *Tatler* No. 39 ¶29 They seem to be the proper Men to officer, animate, and keep up an Army. **1804** Wellington in Owen *Mrq. Wellesley's Desp.* (1877) 276 Both these corps were commanded, and in general officered by Frenchmen and other foreigners. **1852** Miss Yonge *Cameos* II. xxxiii. 342 The French must have been very badly officered. **1858** *Merc. Marine Mag.* V. 65 The apprentice system..has *officered* our ships. **1870** Baldw. Brown *Eccl. Truth* 276 Our system of officering the army.

2. *transf.* To command, direct; to lead, conduct, manage; to escort.

1838 Dickens *Nich. Nick.* xvii, Kate..accompanied by Miss Knag, and officered by Madame Mantalini. **1841–4** Emerson *Ess., Prudence* Wks. (Bohn) I. 97 Society is officered by men of parts, and not by divine men. **1864** *Daily Tel.* 26 Nov., The fire had only been partially got under,.. the steam fire-engines,..although well officered, being apparently powerless.

Hence **ˈofficered** *ppl. a.*; **ˈofficering** *vbl. sb.*

1687 T. Brown *Saints in Uproar* Wks. 1730 I. 78 Whether you were single or double officer'd. **1785** Paley *Mor. Philos.* (ed. 21) II. 435 The direction and officering of the army. **1855** Macaulay *Hist. Eng.* xx. IV. 460 An ill drilled and ill officered militia. **1889** *Pall Mall G.* 29 July 2/1 His troops are all either black or English-officered fellaheen. **1890** *Century Mag.* Dec. 207 The American system of officering ..was superior to that of the English. **1907** *Daily Chron.* 15 Feb. 7/4 The preponderance of the Japanese forces;..their energetic and capable officering. **1933** Belloc *Charles I* 231 The army was still quite unfitted to meet the better training, the larger numbers and the superior officering of the enemy. **1977** *Listener* 16 June 779/4 It was..to the manning of the Empire, or rather the officering of it, that the best products of the classical 'classical education' were destined.

ˈofficerless, *a.* [f. officer *sb.* + -less.] Without an officer or officers.

1893 R. Kipling *Many Invent.* 172 This officerless, rebel regiment. **1898** *Westm. Gaz.* 18 July 5/3 The officerless privates then went in and did nobly.

ˈofficership. [f. as prec. + -ship.] The position or rank of an officer; a staff of officers.

1856 Miss Yonge *Daisy Chain* I. xxiv. (1879) 249 He.. shook hands with him, as if able, in the plenitude of his officership, to afford plenty of good-humoured superiority. **1883** *New Eng. Jrnl. Educ.* XVIII. 72 To the whole officership, under the very popular and able presidency of Mr. W——. **1890** *Pall Mall G.* 13 Aug. 1/2 To the vacant officership, Mr. B——..has been appointed.

officery, *a.* [f. officer *sb.* + -y[1].] Resembling an officer; having the character or nature of an officer.

1905 H. G. Wells *Kipps* III. i. 289 Saw a lot of young officery fellers coming along.

officese (ɒfɪˈsiːz). [f. offic(e *sb.* + -ese.] = commercialese.

1935 A. P. Herbert in *Punch* 19 June 730/2 It is just the misplaced effort to 'write like a book', to be elegant and flowery, that yields the sickliest growths of 'officese' and Jungle English—all these 'inst.'s' and 'ult.'s' and 'in regard to's' and 'favours' and 'representatives'. **1942** Partridge *Usage & Abusage* 218/2 Commercialese or Business English (or, as A. P. Herbert calls it, *Officese*). **1960** —— *Charm of Words* i. 22 Commercialese..has also been called officese.

†officeship. *Obs. rare.* (See quot.)

1611 Florio, *Vfficiatúra,* an officeship, officiousnesse.

official (əˈfɪʃəl), *sb.* [In branch I, a. F. *official* (12–13th c. in Godef.), ad. L. *officiāl-is* sb., absol. use of *officiālis* adj.: see next. In branch II, sb. use of next.]

I. One who is invested with an office.

†1. One who holds office in a household. *Obs.*

1340 *Ayenb.* 37 Zuyche byeþ þe greate officials þet byeþ ine þe house of riche men.

2. *Eccl.* In the Ch. of Eng., the presiding officer or judge of an archbishop's, bishop's, or archdeacon's court; now usually styled *Official Principal.*

The Official Principal of the two Archbishops' courts is now the Dean of Arches or Judge of the Court of Arches; in the Bishops' courts, the office is united with that of Chancellor of the Diocese; the title is more ordinarily known as that of the presiding officer of an Archdeacon's court.

[**1314–15** *Rolls of Parlt.* I. 293/1 Le libel enseale du seal autentik le Official ou Evesqe.] *a* **1327** *Poem times Edw. II* (Percy) xxxvi, Official & denys That chapitres schuld holde. *c* **1400** *Rom. Rose* 6420 There shalle no jugge imperial, Ne bisshop, ne official, Done jugement on me. **1456** *Pol. Poems* (Rolls) II. 236 W[ith] offycyal nor den no favour ther ys, But if sir symony shewe them sylver rounde. **1535** Stewart *Cron. Scot.* III. 285 Of Glasgow officiall than wes he. *a* **1639** Spottiswood *Hist Ch. Scot.* II. (1677) 105 [He] was preferred first to be Official of Glasgow, afterwards made Official of St. Andrews. **1707** Hearne *Collect.* 12 Nov. (O.H.S.) II. 71 Mr. Proast..was made official of Berks. **1899** *Reg. J. de Grandisson* III. Pref. 30 John B., Official of the Court of Canterbury, and lately his [the Bp. of Exeter's] Official-Principal. **1900** *Whitaker's Alm.* 238 Province of York. Official Principal and Auditor of the Chancery Court, The Hon. Sir Arthur Charles.

3. One who is invested with an office of a public nature, or has duties in connexion with some public institution; as a *government, municipal,* or *railway official.*

1555 Eden *Decades* 194, I being then..thofficial of Iustice in that citie at yowre maiesties appoyntemente. **1598** Hakluyt *Voy.* I. 68 The sayde Emperour, hath..an Agent, and Secretary of estate, with Scribes and all other Officials, except aduocates. **1797** Mrs. Radcliffe *Italian* xvi, The official repeated the summons without deigning to reply. **1856** Froude *Hist. Eng.* (1858) I. v. 375 He regarded himself as an official of the state religion. **1874** W. P. Mackay *Grace & Truth* 73, I could travel thus, and the railway officials could find no fault. **1886** *Pall Mall G.* 26 Nov. 11/2 The Irish Under-Secretaries..are supposed to be impartial administrative officials.

II. 4. a. Short for *official letter.* **†b.** *pl.* Official performances, rites: cf. office *sb.* 5.

1768 Sterne *Sent. Journ.* (1775) IV. 224 One must be almost a stone, not to raise a risible muscle at many of their officials. **1884** C. G. Gordon *Jrnls.* 5 Nov., I then wrote him an official; he wanted me to write him an order. I said 'No.'

official (əˈfɪʃəl), *a.* [ad. L. *officiālis,* f. *officium* office: see -al[1]. Cf. OF. *official* (14th c. in Godef.); also mod.F. *officiel* (1791 in Hatz.-Darm.).]

†1. Relating to duty. *Obs.*

1588 A. King tr. *Canisius' Catech.* 177 Quhilk [cardinal] vertues ar also called official or dewetifull, for that of thame proceids..al kynd of offices, and dewties.

†2. Performing some office or service; subservient *to* something else or *to* some purpose. ***official member,*** a bodily organ which serves the needs or purposes of a higher organ. *Obs.*

1533 Elyot *Cast. Helthe* (1541) 12 Offycialle members [are] Synewes, whiche doo serve to the braine: Arteries, or pulses, whiche do serve to the harte. **1547** Boorde *Brev. Health* ccxxvi. 77 Princypal members be foure, the herte, the brayne, the lyver, and the stones... All other members be officiall members, and dothe offyce to the pryncypal members. **1614** W. B. *Philosopher's Banquet* (ed. 2) 3 The braine, and Strings thervnto offitiall. **1646** Sir T. Browne *Pseud. Ep.* 198 The Oesophagus or gullet,..a part officiall unto nutrition. **1667** —— *Misc.* II. Posth. Wks. (1712) 6 Inscriptions commonly signified the Name of the Person interr'd, the Names of Servants Official to such Provisions [etc.].

3. a. Of or pertaining to an office, post, or place; belonging to the discharge of duties; connected with the tenure of office.

official arms (*Her.*), arms representing those of an office or dignity, as those of a city, as used by the Mayor and officers of the corporation.

1607 Shaks. *Cor.* II. iii. 148 The Tribunes endue you with the Peoples Voyce, Remaines, that in th'Officiall Markes inuested, You anon doe meet the Senate. **1796** H. Hunter tr. *St.-Pierre's Stud. Nat.* (1799) II. 583 The enormous accumulation of landed and official property. **1828** Carlyle *Misc.* (1857) I. 154 Perorating in official garments from the rostrum. **1842** Bischoff *Woollen Manuf.* II. 26 The subjoining official documents will render this obvious. **1865** Livingstone *Zambesi* Pref. 7 A series of papers in the Portuguese Official Journal. **1897** Gladstone *E. Crisis* 1 A trustworthy appeal from the official to the personal conscience.

b. ***official secrets,*** information the disclosure of which outside official circles would constitute a breach of national security; so ***Official Secrets Act.***

1889 *Act 52 & 53 Vict.* c. 52 §10 This Act may be cited as the Official Secrets Act, 1889. **1911** *Encycl. Brit.* XXIV. 571/1 By the Official Secrets Act 1889 it was made a misdemeanour for an official to communicate any information or documents concerning the military or naval affairs of Her Majesty, to any person to whom it ought not to be communicated. **1931** 'G. Trevor' *Murder at School* vi. 127 'I think once again I must plead the Official Secrets' Acts,' he answered, jocularly. **1931** *Economist* 28 Nov. 1001/1 The editor of a German Radical newspaper has been sentenced to 18 months' imprisonment on the ground that, in the course of an article on civil aviation, he revealed official secrets, whose disclosure endangered national security. **1966** A. Firth *Tall, Balding, Thirty-Five* v. 61 He pushed forward the buff paper. It was a shortened version of the form of submission to the Official Secrets Act of 1929. **1973** *Guardian* 29 June 14/3 Today the House of Commons debates the Franks report on the Official Secrets Acts. **1976** *Howard Jrnl.* XV. I. 24 The workings of the Official Secrets Act and the requirement of 'submission for prior approval' before a prison official can make a public statement do not encourage the development of penological expertise.

4. Of persons: Holding office; employed in some public capacity; authorized to exercise some specific function.

1833 Ht. Martineau *Loom & Lugger* II. v. 96 It must be to some official person. **1838** Dickens *Nich. Nick.* xxii, The heavy footfall of the official watcher of the night. **1855** Macaulay *Hist. Eng.* xix. IV. 308 The Bill..was strongly opposed by the official men, both Whigs and Tories.

5. a. Derived from, or having the sanction of, persons in office; authorized or supported by the government, etc.; hence, Authorized, authoritative.

1854 H. Rogers *Ess.* II. i. 81 Adverting to the truer and far more important solution 'by the way', and omitting it in the 'official chapter on Cause'. **1871** Morley *Crit. Misc.* Ser. I. *Condorcet* (1878) 66 The official religion of the century.. was lifeless and mechanical. **1895** *United Service Mag.* July 414 The Official History of the War of 1882. **1898** T. Mackay *State & Charity* vi. 92 The above cited preamble ..still remains the official definition of a charity. **1957** J. Passmore *100 Yrs. Philos.* i. 28 The 'Scottish school'.. lingered on..in the United States, where it became a sort of 'official philosophy' in the less adventurous Colleges. **1959** *Chambers's Encycl.* XII. 745 English and Afrikaans are treated on a footing of equality as official languages... Every child shall learn the second official language. **1970** *Cape Times* 28 Oct. 22/6 (Advt.), A knowledge of both official languages is required. **1976** *Scotsman* 27 Dec. 5/1 At Celtic Park, the official attendance was 47,000. **1977** *Belfast Tel.* 24 Jan. 9/4 Sinn Fein..has failed to gain any significant support at the polls, mainly because it has been regarded as the 'front organisation' for the official IRA.

b. *Med.* Authorized by the pharmacopœia; officinal.

1884 *Pharmaceut. Soc. Prosp.* 9 The official preparations and active principles of each drug are enumerated. **1893** *Pharmacopœia of U.S.* Pref. 36 (Funk) The word 'official' has been used in this edition of the Pharmacopœia in place of the word 'officinal'. The change was made by a special vote of the Committee at one of its first meetings in 1890. **1898** *Rev. Brit. Pharm.* 12 An official quinine-pill had become almost a necessity.

6. Having the manner or air proper to one in office, or denoting relations which arise from one's office, as distinct from those which are personal; formal, ceremonious.

1882 Miss Braddon *Mt. Royal* III. i. 5 Handing it with official solemnity to Mrs. Tregonell. **1896** 'M. Field' *Attila* I. 27 Be distant and official.

officialdom (əˈfɪʃəldəm). [See -dom.] The position of an official; official routine; the domain or sphere of officials; officials collectively. (Often in hostile sense: cf. officialism.)

1863 *Temple Bar Mag.* July 487 The little man..made an elaborate speech to officialdom, and at me, and led me away. **1880** Miss Bird *Japan* I. 57 The stage, one half of which was reserved for foreigners, the other half for Japanese officialdom. **1884** *Liverpool Mercury* 22 Oct. 5/6 [He] has burst the bonds of officialdom. **1888** *Cornh. Mag.* Oct. 369 The language of officialdom is entirely French.

oˌfficiaˈlese. [f. as prec. + -ese.] The language characteristic of officials or official documents.

1884 Yates *Recoll.* iii. I. 126 What was called, in delightful officialese, 'the double Secretariat' was abolished. **1924** P. MacDonald *Rasp* vi. 84 My—what's the officialese for it? —'suppression of the truth' gave Boyd clue number one. **1932** *New Statesman* 2 Jan. 7/1 Drink to me only with thine i's, and I will cross the t's, But leave no kiss within this cup of crabb'd officialese. **1941** *Manch. Guardian Weekly* 14 Mar. 214/3 Let us be fair to the Civil Servant: the official is not the only dealer in officialese. **1953** E. Simon *Past Masters* IV. ii. 220 One was left to infer between the lines of officialese. **1960** S. Foot *Emergency Exit* xiii. 110 Constitutional English is such a splendid language..but this was constitutional officialese. **1973** *Listener* 15 Feb. 221/3 The vocabulary Don Haworth's characters use.. embodies chunks of jolting officialese. **1975** B. Garfield *Hopscotch* iii. 50 'You've read the backgrounding.' It was phrased in dry officialese.

officialism (əˈfɪʃəlɪz(ə)m). [f. official + -ism.] The mode of action characteristic of officials; perfunctory and literal discharge of the duties of office; official system or routine; officials collectively or in the abstract. (Often in derogatory sense = *red tape, red tapeism.*)

1857 Smiles *Stephenson* (1859) 233 Their greatest national enterprises have not been planned by officialism. **1873** H. Spencer *Stud. Sociol.* (1882) 170 The unwisdom of officialism is daily illustrated. **1886** J. Martineau *Ch. Eng.* in *Contemp. Rev.* L. 15 There is necessarily an indefinite amount of unreality and officialism in worship, i.e. of worship simulated by mechanical imitation. **1895** *Times* 7 Jan. 4/1 What was lacking..was a little common-sense to help officialism at headquarters to grasp the practical situation.

officiality (əfɪʃɪˈælɪtɪ). [a. F. *officialité* (1285 in sense 1, in Hatz.-Darm.), or ad. late L. *officiālitās,* f. *officiāl-is* official: see -ity.]

1. The office or dignity of an ecclesiastical official (official *sb.* 2); the court of such, or the building in which it assembles. *Obs.* exc. *Hist.*

a **1662** Heylin *Laud* (1668) 288 Bird, who had the Officiality of the place. **1692** Wood *Life* 3 Oct. (O.H.S.) III. 403 Mr. Jonas Proast..had the officiality of Berks confer'd on him by Mr. William Richards archdeacon of Berks. **1742** Hume *Ess., Miracles* (1817) II. 463 *note,* Many of the miracles of Abbé Paris were proved immediately before the officiality, or bishop's court, at Paris. **1858** Neale *Hist. Jansenist Ch.* Introd. 49 The officiality was, for some time, kept open both by night and by day.

2. = officialism. *rare.*

1841 Carlyle *Heroes* vi. 347 To us it is no dilettante work, no sleek officiality. **1858** —— *Fredk. Gt.* I. III. x. 277 'Philip is not permitted to go', said Imperial Officiality. **1881** *Daily Tel.* 4 Feb., It may be surmised that officiality will not offer any objections.

b. Something official; an official post, notice, duty, etc.

1843 Carlyle *Past & Pr.* II. i, [He] held some '*obedientia*', subaltern officiality there. **1862** —— *Fredk. Gt.* (1872) III. IX. iii. 92 An actual Prussian Commissary hangs out his announcements and officialities at Donauwörth. **1867** —— *Remin.* (1881) II. 155 A cheerful, lively element, in spite of Reform Bills and officialities..which, before long, supervened.

officialize (əˈfɪʃəlaɪz), *v.* [f. official + -ize.]

1. *intr.* To do official work. *rare.*

1850 Sir S. Northcote in *Life* (1890) I. iii. 90, I should be just as contented if I were set to grind coffee..as when I am farming or officialising.

2. *trans.* To render official, give an official character to; to bring under official control.

1887 *Sat. Rev.* 16 Apr. 554 The most officialized of officials, smooth, monotonous, colourless. **1895** *Q. Rev.* July 273 This officialising of voluntary effort would..give the working classes a larger influence. **1897** *Spectator* 4 Sept. 297/2 An Empire officialised and regulated to death!

Hence **officiali'zation**, the rendering official in form or character.

1907 *Daily Chron.* 9 Nov. 4/4 One fails to detect a craving for any such officialisation.

officially (əˈfɪʃəlɪ), *adv.* [f. as prec. + -LY².] In an official manner or capacity; by virtue, or in consequence, of one's office; with official authority, sanction, or formality; by or in presence of an official; for official purposes; in official or public statements, reports, etc. (but not in actuality).

1790 BURKE *Fr. Rev.* 241 No excess is good; and therefore too great a proportion of landed property may be held officially for life. **1816** J. SCOTT *Vis. Paris* (ed. 5) Pref. 58 Buonaparte is officially announced to have quitted Malmaison for Rochefort. **1861** GEO. ELIOT *Silas M.* vi, He winked..at two of the company, who were known officially as the 'bassoon' and the 'key-bugle'. **1868** DICKENS *Uncomm. Trav.* xviii, Some gentle-hearted functionary.. who I suppose was officially present at the Inquest. **1871** MORLEY *Voltaire* (1886) 8 The fiery darts of the officially orthodox. **1938** E. AMBLER *Cause for Alarm* x. 163 The price per machine will..be higher... Officially, this fact will be accounted for by the modifications. Actually, those modifications are purely nominal. **1964** L. DEIGHTON *Funeral in Berlin* vii. 51 'Does anyone have phones going across..Berlin?' 'Officially one. It connects the Russian Command..with the Allied Command.'.. 'Unofficially?' 'There *have* to be lines.' **1976** 'B. SHELBY' *Great Pebble Affair* I. 30 Officially, I had been renting my apartment for three months before I even saw it.

official principal: see OFFICIAL *sb.* 2.

†**o'fficialry.** *Obs.* [See -RY.] An official post.

1716 M. DAVIES *Athen. Brit.* III. 10 A Country-Justiciary, or Custom-House-Attendancy, or Excise-Officialry.

†**o'fficialship.** *Obs.* [f. OFFICIAL *sb.* + -SHIP.] The post of an ecclesiastical official; a body of such officials; = OFFICIALITY I.

?**1461** *Liber Niger Domus Edw. IV* in *Househ. Ord.* (1790) 27 These lordes rewarde theire..chapeleyns..with officyalshippes, deaneries, prebendes. **1533** CRANMER *Let.* in *Misc. Writ.* (Parker Soc.) II. 266 Which said Thomas Eton..exercised the room of the officialship in Exeter. **1691** WOOD *Ath. Oxon.* I. 345 A Canonry, and an Officialship of the said Church, he kept to his dying day. **1762** tr. *Busching's Syst. Geog.* IV. 331 The officialship has the direction of all persons and things relating to the service of religion.

officialty (əˈfɪʃəltɪ). *rare.* [f. OFFICIAL *sb.* + -TY.]

†**1.** = OFFICIALITY I. *Obs.*

1726 AYLIFFE *Parergon* 163 An Officialty to an Archdeacon.

2. = OFFICIALITY 2, OFFICIALISM.

1876 T. HARDY *Ethelberta* ii. (1877) 22 When pleasant malt liquor..had..neutralised some of the effects of officialty.

officiant (əˈfɪʃ(ɪ)ənt). [ad. med.L. *officiānt-em*, pr. pple. of *officiāre* to OFFICIATE: cf. F. *officiant* (1690 in Hatz.-Darm.).] One who officiates at a religious ceremony or conducts a (formal) religious service; an officiating priest or minister.

1844 LINGARD *Anglo-Sax. Ch.* (1858) I. vii. 273 A prayer, pronounced by the bishop or officiant. **1881** FAIRBAIRN *Stud. Life Christ* xvi. 286 The priests were essentially officiants. **1895** SIR W. HUNTER *Old Missionary* 136 The officiants at the mosque..lined the wayside and salaamed.

officiar, obs. Sc. form of OFFICER.

offici'arian. *rare*⁻¹. [f. as next + -AN.] One who makes duty the principle of ethics.

1865 J. GROTE *Moral Ideals* (1876) 126 There hence arises ..a continual contest between the moralists of duty and the moralists of feeling, the officiarians and emotionalists.

officiary (əˈfɪʃɪərɪ), *sb.* [In I, f. as next; in II, ad. med.L. type **officiāria*, f. *officiārius* OFFICER.]

I. 1. An officer or official. *rare.*

1611 SPEED *Hist. Gt. Brit.* IX. xxi. §98. 1025 Without any trouble, vexation or impeachment..by his heires, or by any his Officiaries, Ministers, or Subjects. **1814** COLERIDGE *Lett., to D. Stuart* 30 Oct. (1895) 635 Human jurisprudence ..knows nothing of persons, other than as properties, officiaries, subjects. **1845** J. MARTINEAU *Misc.* (1852) 144 The staff of government officiaries.

2. A body of officers; an official body. *U.S.*

1888 *Voice* (N.Y.) 5 Apr., It would be next to impossible ..to get a city officiary in sympathy with the law. **1889** *Chr. Union* (N.Y.) 10 Jan., The virtual contract between officiary and pew-holder.

II. 3. A division of a Highland estate, in charge of a ground officer. Still (1902) in use on the Breadalbane (and possibly on some other large) estates, where, however, several officiaries are now in charge of one ground officer.

1799 J. ROBERTSON *Agric. Perth* 39 The great estates are divided into officiaries, each consisting of an ancient barony, or a tract of land sufficient to entitle the possessor to the privileges of a baron of the realm, provided he held his land of the crown. In each of these districts resides a ground-officer, from which circumstance they have derived their modern appellation. *Ibid.* 418. **1902** A. SEATH (Breadalbane Estate Office) in *Let.* Apr. 17 There are 13 officiaries on the Perthshire Estate under the care of only 2 Ground Officers.

officiary (əˈfɪʃɪərɪ), *a.* [ad. med.L. *officiāri-us*, f. *officium* OFFICE: see -ARY¹.]

1. Of a title, etc.: Attached to or derived from an office held. Of a dignitary: Having a title or rank derived from office.

1612 SELDEN *Illustr. Drayton's Poly-olb.* xi. 193 The title being officiary, not hereditary. **1670** HEYLIN *Hist. Presbyt.* 3 The City and Signiory of Geneva..was governed by Officiary and Titular Earls. **1707** CHAMBERLAYNE *St. Gt. Brit.* III. iii. 274 The Earl Marshal of England, is not only Honorary, as all the rest, but also officiary. **1801** R. PATTON *Asiat. Mon.* 145 The zemindar's appointment was officiary.

2. Belonging to, or holding, office; official. *rare.*

1755 AMORY *Mem.* (1769) I. 296 The Romish mass and rites..successors of the pagan gods in officiary dignity. **1857** HEAVYSEGE *Saul* (1869) 62, I hold thee light, officiary angel.

officiate (əˈfɪʃɪeɪt), *v.* [f. ppl. stem of med.L. *officiāre* to perform divine service, f. *officium* OFFICE.] To discharge an office.

1. *intr.* To discharge the office of a priest or minister; to perform divine service, or any rite or ceremony, in an official capacity.

1641 HEYLIN *Hist. Episc.* II. (1657) 446 There were many Parish Churches..as doth appeare by Epiphanius, who.. tells us also who officiated in the same, as Presbyters. **1683** *Brit. Spec.* 34 The Druids officiated only in Groves of Oak. **1714-26** GIDEON GUTHRIE *Mem.* (1900) 43 An earnest invitation..to oversee his only son and officiate in his family. **1834** MEDWIN *Angler in Wales* I. 211 *note*, Bonaparte had some difficulty in persuading Pope Pius VI to officiate at his coronation. **1876** J. SAUNDERS *Lion in Path* i, The Earl kept a good old Protestant Chaplain to officiate.

†**b.** *trans.* To perform, celebrate (a religious service or rite); to execute, exercise (a spiritual charge or function). *Obs.*

1631 WEEVER *Anc. Fun. Mon.* 127 Deacons had the charge to..helpe the Priest in diuine Seruice (a place officiated now by our Parish Clerkes). **1648** E. BOUGHEN *Geree's Case Consc.* 108 Which house..did duely officiate the Cure, by one of their own fraternity. **1717** *Entertainer* No. 8. 52 A Priest officiating the Common-Prayer. **1718** CIBBER *Non-juror* v. 106 He..has..been seen..to officiate Publick Mass in the Church of Nostre Dame at Antwerp.

c. To serve (a church). *rare.*

1894 *Critic* (U.S.) 7 July 8/1 'The Church of the Holy Sepulchre', he continues, 'is officiated by the Latins'.

2. *intr.* To perform the duties attaching to an office or place, or any particular duty or service.

1683 *Col. Rec. Pennsylv.* I. 91 To put him in Master of yᵉ Rolls, who doth Solemnly promise to officiate therein with care and Diligence. **1686** J. S. *Hist. Monast. Convent.* 156 Under him are ten Officers, that officiate in Buying up Corn. **1746-7** *Act 20 Geo. II*, c. 43 §40 The clerks or other officers officiating in the circuit courts. **1841** MISS MITFORD in L'Estrange *Life* (1870) III. viii. 115 Lord Sidmouth retains his unmarried daughter, who officiated as his private secretary when he was Prime Minister.

†**b.** Of a bodily organ, etc.: To perform its function, to act, operate. *Obs.*

1655 CULPEPPER, etc. *Riverius* x. iii. 288 Nature will grow dull by too much use of Clysters, and at length will never officiate that way. **1737** BRACKEN *Farriery Impr.* (1756) I. 53 To the End that when one Lobe of the Lungs is hurt by a Wound, the other..may officiate.

†**3.** *trans.* To perform the duties of (an office or place); to execute, fulfil, do (a duty or charge, business). *Obs.*

1652 EARL MONM. tr. *Bentivoglio's Hist. Relat.* 58 Her place is in many things officiated by her Niece the Lady Katherine Livia. **1683** MOXON *Mech. Exerc., Printing* xviii. ¶2 A Man (nay, a Boy) might officiate all this Work. *a* **1704** T. BROWN *Praise Proverty* Wks. 1730 I. 93 Officiating only the place of my brother Lucius. **1727** *Philip Quarll* 249 This lovely Animal was officiating the Charge it had of its own accord taken.

†**4. a.** *trans.* To minister, supply. **b.** *intr.* To minister, be subservient. *Obs. rare.*

1659 H. L'ESTRANGE *Alliance Div. Off.* 217, I see not how the either precept or use thereof,..can at all officiat to the errour of Transubstantiation. **1667** MILTON *P.L.* VIII. 22 The Firmament..And all her numberd Starrs, that seem to rowle..meerly to officiate light Round this opacous Earth.

Hence **o'fficiating** *vbl. sb.* and *ppl. a.*

1651 BAXTER *Inf. Bapt.* 245 The Baptizers of Infants you scornfully call 'Officiating Priests'. **1657-61** HEYLIN *Hist. Ref.* II. i. §11. 55 Of a set and appointed place, for the officiating of God's publick Service. **1868** DICKENS *Lett.* 29 Jan. (1880) II. 348 The officiating minister..was brought in between two big stewards.

officiate, *sb. rare*⁻¹. [f. L. type **officiātus*, f. ppl. stem of *officiāre*: see prec. and -ATE¹.] A body of officials or officers.

1865 *Even. Standard* 10 Mar., There were present..about fifty members of the Senate, including most important acting members of the University officiate.

offici'ation. [f. OFFICIATE *v.*: see -ATION.] The action of the verb OFFICIATE; performance of a religious, ceremonial, or public duty.

1798 N. DRAKE *Lit. Hours* (1820) III. lvii. 252 He introduced the erection of temples, the officiation of Priests and Priestesses. **1873** B. GREGORY *Holy Catholic Ch.* xv. 163 The unity of the Church lies deeper than any organization, ordinance, or officiation whatsoever. **1890** E. T. EVANS *Hist. Hendon* 195 The magistrate, during whose officiation the entries are very carefully made.

†**o'fficiative,** *a. Obs. rare*⁻¹. [f. as OFFICIATE *v.* + -IVE.] Of or pertaining to officiation.

1653 GAUDEN *Hierasp.* 311 It is only meant of those peculiar gifts, or powers of the Holy Spirit, which are properly ministeriall and officiative; as from Christ and in his name.

officiator (əˈfɪʃɪeɪtə(r)). [a. med.L. *officiātor*, agent-n. f. *officiāre* to OFFICIATE.] One who officiates; *esp.* an officiating priest or minister.

1830 MOORE *Diary* 24 Oct. in *Mem.* (1854) VI. 155 After breakfast proceeded to the little church..Fisher, the officiator. **1857** *Old Commodore* II. 297 The officiator.. made a bow equally low. **1877** J. D. CHAMBERS *Div. Worship* 4 The office of the Choir representing the people, was to respond to the officiator or officiators.

officier, obs. form of OFFICER.

‖**officina** (ɒfɪˈsaɪnə). [L., = workshop, laboratory; contr. of *opificīna*, f. *opifex* workman; cf. F. *officine* pharmaceutical laboratory or shop; *fig.* manufactory (of calumnies, plots, etc.).] **a.** Workshop; place of production.

1835 J. W. CROKER *Ess. Fr. Rev.* vi. (1857) 332 The Legislative..showed..it was..the real *officina* of business, the chief mart of popularity, and the widest arena for political struggle.

b. Phr. ***officina gentium***, a country or area from the inhabitants of which several nations develop; also ***officina gentis***, the place of origin of a nation or people.

[*c* **550** JORDANES *Getica* (1882) iv. 25 Scandza..quasi officina gentium aut certe velut vagina nationum.] **1821** DE QUINCEY *Confess.* (1822) 169 Southern Asia is..the great *officina gentium.* **1832** *Edin. Rev.* LV. 499 The New Englanders have been the *officina gentis* to the American people. **1877** D. M. WALLACE *Russia* (ed. 2) II. xxiv. 106 As Scandinavia was formerly called *officina gentium*—a workshop in which new nations were made. **1904** W. P. KER *Dark Ages* iii. 131 [Jordanes] has a lofty conception of the destiny and fortunes of the Gothic race, and his account of the origin of the warlike nations in the Northern island, Scanzia, *officina gentium*, corresponds in prose to the epic genealogies of the poets. **1961** L. F. BROSNAHAN *Sounds of Language* ix. 195 The *officina gentium* which was Scandinavia at this period.

officinal (əˈfɪsɪnəl), *a.* and *sb.* [ad. med.L. *officinal-is*, f. *officina*: see prec.

Officīna, in ancient L. 'a workshop, manufactory, or laboratory', was applied in med.L. also to a store-room of a monastery in which provisions, medicines, or necessaries of any kind were kept for use; in later use it seems to have been extended, like 'shop', from a work-shop to a sale-shop. In monastic L. *officīnālis domus, officīnāle*, occurs also in the same sense as *officīna*. As used of herbs and drugs, it is not quite clear whether *officīnālis* meant 'of the sort used in the pharmaceutical laboratory', or 'of the sort kept in the shops of herbalists and druggists', the resultant sense, 'used or recognized in pharmacy or medicine', being the same in either case.]

A. *adj.* **1.** Of a herb, plant, drug, etc.: Used in medicine or the arts. Of a medical preparation: Kept in readiness in apothecaries' shops; made according to the recipe prescribed in the pharmacopœia. Of a scientific name: Adopted by the pharmacopœia.

As applied to plants, it answers to the Linnæan specific name *officinālis, -āle*, given to that species of a genus which has been used in medicine, and known 'in the shops' by the generic name; e.g. *Anchusa, Borago, Pulmonaria officinalis, Lithospermum, Symphytum officinale*, = *Anchusa* of the shops or herbalists, Common Alkanet, etc.

In the transferred sense, 'recognized by the pharmacopœia', *officinal* has been recently superseded by OFFICIAL (5 b).

c **1720** W. GIBSON *Farmer's Dispens.* xv. (1734) 278 Those officinal Oils and Ointments that are most used in the Farriers practise. **1754** HUXHAM in *Phil. Trans.* XLVIII. 844 This I have long ordered to be kept here as an officinal medicine. **1769** *Gentl. Mag.* Dec. 607/1 Was presented to the Society of Arts, a large root of the true officinal rhubarb. **1785** MARTYN *Rousseau's Bot.* xii. (1794) 124 It [*Veronica officinalis*] has the trivial name of officinal, because an infusion of it is sometimes used medicinally. **1834** W. MACGILLIVRAY *Lives Zoologists* 308 He gives the Swedish officinal name. **1853** G. JOHNSTON *Nat. Hist. E. Bord.* I. 128 The order is comparatively rich in officinal herbs. **1866** AITKEN *Pract. Med.* II. 66 It is not altogether immaterial which of the numerous officinal preparations of iron are to be prescribed. **1876** HARLEY *Mat. Med.* (ed. 6) 67 Boracic acid is not officinal.

2. Of or pertaining to a shop; 'shoppy'. *rare.*

1751 JOHNSON *Rambler* No. 123 ¶5, I had always in my officinal state been kept in awe by lace and embroidery. **1856** EMERSON *Eng. Traits, Times* Wks. (Bohn) II. 121 'The Times'..its tone is prone to be official, and even officinal.

B. *sb.* An officinal drug or medicine.

1693 *Phil. Trans.* XVII. 926 Since his time many Officinals have been fully illustrated in Print. **1790** BLANE *ibid.* LXXX. 292 The officinals which have kept their ground..under the names of Mithridate and Venice Treacle.

o'fficinally, *adv.* [f. OFFICINAL *a.* + -LY².] In official use; according to the pharmacopœia.

1822-34 *Good's Study Med.* (ed. 4) I. 630 The three species of cinchona used officinally. **1875** H. C. WOOD *Therap.* (1879) 147 The digitalin of the U.S. Pharmacopœia is officinally described as 'a white or yellowish-white powder, without odor, and having a very bitter taste'.

† **'officine.** *Obs.* [a. F. *officine* (12th c. in Hatz.-Darm.), ad. L. *officina*; see above.] A workshop, a laboratory; an office in a monastery.

c **1425** *Found. St. Bartholomew's* (E.E.T.S.) 14 Who shulde nat be astonyid ther to see..thonorable byldynge of pite..where sumtyme was a comyn officyne of dampnyd peple. **1546** BALE *Eng. Votaries* I. (1550) 12 As testifieth Johan Textor in his officines. **1655** FULLER *Ch. Hist.* VI. ii. (1845) III. 301 Of the prime officers and officines of Abbeys. **1657** TOMLINSON *Renou's Disp.* 166 Which should be inspissated by a longer coction in our Officine.

† **offici'osity.** *Obs. rare.* [ad. late L. *officiōsitās*, f. *officiōsus*: see -TY.] The quality of being officious; attentiveness, dutifulness.

1565 STAPLETON tr. *Bæda's Hist. Ch. Eng.* V. iv. 157 She ..ceasyd not to vse such courteous officiosytye, all the dynner time.

officious (ə'fɪʃəs), *a.* [ad. L. *officiōs-us* obliging, dutiful, f. *officium* OFFICE: cf. F. *officieux*.]

† **1.** Doing or ready to do kind offices; eager to serve or please; attentive, obliging, kind. *Obs.*

1565 STAPLETON tr. *Bæda's Hist. Ch. Eng.* V. iv. 157 She ..came to the table, shewed her selfe very officious in caruinge..to the bysshope and all the hole table. **1570** *Marr. Wit & Sc.* II. i. in Hazl. *Dodsley* II. 339 Shew thyself officious and servicable still. **1679** *Season. Adv. Protest.* 6 The Peoples aversion they took away by degrees by their officious kind behaviour. **1782** JOHNSON *Death of Levet* ii, Officious, innocent, sincere, Of every friendless name the friend. **1790** BURKE *Fr. Rev.* Wks. V. 251 They were tolerably well-bred; very officious, humane, and hospitable. **1827** KEBLE *Chr. Y., Burial Dead* v, Feeling more bitterly alone For friends that press officious round.

† **b.** *officious lie* (L. *mendacium officiosum*, F. *mensonge officieux*): a lie told as an act of kindness to further another's interests. So *officious falsity*. *Obs.*

1577 tr. *Bullinger's Decades* (1592) 321 An officious lye, that is, when I fitten or tell an vntruth for duties sake to the end that by my lye, I may keepe my neighbour harmlesse. **1608** WILLET *Hexapla Exod.* 416 An officious lie, when one telleth a lie to do another good. **1633** BP. HALL *Hard Texts, N.T.* 39 Make this merry and officious lie for my sake. **1676** G. TOWERSON *Decal.* 520 Concerning officious falsities. **1678** CUDWORTH *Intell. Syst.* I. iv. §16. 283 Ignorantly zealous Christians, who were for Officious Lyes and Pious Frauds. **1788** WESLEY *Wks.* (1872) VII. 42 Concerning *officious* lies, those that are spoken with a design to do good, there have been numerous controversies.

† **2.** Dutiful; active or zealous in doing one's duty. *Obs.*

1588 SHAKS. *Tit. A.* V. ii. 202 Come, come, be euery one officious, To make this Banket. **1598** BACON *Sacr. Medit., Hypocrites* Ess. (Arb.) 117 As to these others who are so officious towards God. **1642** R. CARPENTER *Experience* I. iv. 13 To stand like officious and dutifull servants. **1726–46** THOMSON *Winter* 311 In vain for him the officious wife prepares The fire fair-blazing and the vestment warm. a **1770** AKENSIDE *Odes* I. vi. *To Cheerfulness*, The officious daughters pleas'd attend.

b. Of a thing: Performing its office or function, serving its purpose, efficacious. *rare.*

1618 BP. HALL *Contempl., N.T.* I. i, If twise in the day we doe not present God with our solemn invocations, we make the Gospell lesse officious, than the Law. **1884** LD. SELBORNE in *Law Times Rep.* L. 314/1 That interpretation which makes [the words] more officious with respect to the ..purpose of the instrument is to be preferred.

3. Unduly forward in proffering services or taking business upon oneself; doing, or prone to do, more than is asked or required; interfering with what is not one's concern; pragmatical, meddlesome.

1602 WARNER *Alb. Eng.* IX. xlv. (1612) 213 Wolsey, that slye, officious, and too Lordly Cardnall. **1676** ETHEREDGE *Man of Mode* I. i. (1684) 13 He..knows not whom, without Some officious Sot has betray'd me. **1770** LANGHORNE *Plutarch* (1879) I. 163/2 He would not be so officious as to interpose. **1826** DISRAELI *Viv. Grey* V. vi, One of those officious, noisy little men who are always ready to give you unasked information. **1863** GEO. ELIOT *Romola* xxv, He glanced suspiciously at the officious stranger.

† **4.** Pertaining to an office or business, official; hence, formal. *Obs.*

1610 J. DOVE *An Advert.* 16 He sheweth, that, as there is one adoration which is religious, belonging to God, so there is an other, onely officious, belonging to all ecclesiasticall rites and ceremonies. a **1734** NORTH *Lives* (1826) II. 44 He put off officious talk of government or politicks with jests. **1796** BURNEY *Mem. Metastasio* II. 264 To waste his precious moments in answering letters purely officious. **1852** J. H. NEWMAN *Scope Univ. Educ.* 221 The Sermons..of Protestant Divines in the seventeenth century, how often are they mere repertories of miscellaneous and officious learning.

5. *Diplomacy.* As opposed to *official*: Having an extraneous relation to official matters or duties; having the character of a friendly communication, or informal action, on the part of a government or its official representatives. (= F. *officieux* (Littré), It. *uffizioso*.)

1852 LD. PALMERSTON in *Mem. Ld. Malmesbury* (1885) 238 When the *diplomates* call, do not be too reserved, but preface your observations by stating that what you say is *officious*. *Ibid.* 226 *note*, Old diplomatists must know the difference between an *officious* and an *official* conversation. The first is the free interchange of opinions between the two Ministers, and compromises neither; the latter would do so, and bind their Governments. **1866** *Pall Mall G.* No. 447. 165/1 Feelers put out in the officious press. **1887** *Ibid.* 9 Nov. 2/1 Every individual who receives [official] protection from a foreign Government becomes in his turn a centre of protection to his friends and dependants, and spreads this diluted form which is known as 'officious' protection at a rate of arithmetical progression. **1900** *Westm. Gaz.* 16 Aug. 2/1 We want the great European Powers to consent to be our guarantees with the Sultan. They would act in an officious, if not in an official capacity.

officiously (ə'fɪʃəslɪ), *adv.* [f. prec. + -LY².] In an officious manner.

1. With eagerness to serve; attentively; obligingly, courteously.

1603 B. JONSON *Entertainm. at Althorpe* 220 A morrise of the clowns there-about, who most officiously presented themselves. **1708** J. HUDSON *Let.* in Hearne *Collect.* (O.H.S.) II. 124 He made me dine wth him, and officiously conducted me to ye Ferry. **1766** GOLDSM. *Vic. W.* vi, Little Dick officiously reached him a chair. **1824** SCOTT *St. Ronan's* xxviii, Her two fugitive handmaidens.. endeavoured to suppress a smuggled laugh..by acting very officiously in Mr. Touchwood's service.

† **2.** Dutifully, duteously. *Obs.*

1603 H. CROSSE *Vertues Commw.* (1878) 155 They ought ..holding sacred places, to labour earnestly and officiously, to suppresse those horrible euils. a **1677** BARROW *Serm.* (1686) III. xlv. 535 Let us demean ourselves modestly, consistently, and officiously toward him. **1700** DRYDEN *Ceyx & Alc.* 106 As danger taught Each in his way officiously they wrought.

3. In an unduly forward or obtrusive manner; with importunate forwardness; †without being asked or required; gratuitously.

1600 W. WATSON *Decacordon* (1602) 31 Officiously intruding them selues for bribes. **1732** BERKELEY *Alciphr.* III. §16 Would you officiously set an enemy right that was making a wrong attack? a **1734** NORTH *Lives* (1826) II. 160 He would not be exposed to them, although he had not officiously hurt any of them. **1818** JAS. MILL *Brit. India* II. IV. ix. 288 The French East India Company, the affairs of which the ministers of the French King had so officiously controled. **1848** W. H. BARTLETT *Egypt to Pal.* x. (1879) 221 The Arabs officiously picked up specimens of poor turquoise and small pieces of iron-ore.

4. As opposed to *officially*: Informally on the part of authority or its agents.

1863 F. W. GIBBS *Recognition* 10 When Mr. Deane.. applied to the French Government for two hundred guns, he was refused officially, but officiously referred to Beaumarchais. **1888** *Times* 12 Apr. 9/4 They [the Municipalities] fix the price 'officiously'—that is, at a quotation which may serve to guide the public without acting as a legal restraint on the baker.

officiousness (ə'fɪʃəsnɪs). [f. as prec. + -NESS.] The quality of being officious; officious conduct.

† **1.** Readiness in doing good offices, performing one's duty, or discharging any function; eagerness to serve or please; dutifulness; diligence. *Obs.*

1598 FLORIO, *Officiosità*, officiousnes, seruiceablenes. **1602** WARNER *Alb. Eng.* XI. lxi. (1612) 268 His Vertues and officiousnes to her-wards so had wrought, That vnto little lesse than Loue she, by Degrees, was brought. **1676** G. TOWERSON *Decalogue* 520 The bare officiousness of a lye. **1783** JOHNSON *Lett. to Mrs. Thrale* 20 Nov., The interchange of that social officiousness by which we are habitually endeared to one another. **1824** MISS MITFORD *Village* Ser. I. (1863) 232 We had missed the pleasant bustling officiousness..which our good neighbour loved so well.

2. Overforwardness in proffering services or taking anything upon one as a duty; well-intentioned meddlesomeness.

1613 PURCHAS *Pilgrimage* (1614) 734 Of other their rootes and fruites I am loath to write, least I wearie the Reader with tedious officiousnesse. **1698** FRYER *Acc. E. India & P.* 139 The sneaking Officiousness of the Banyans, who pressed on my Heels, and..waited like Lacquies. **1781** GIBBON *Decl. & F.* xix. II. 152 Constantius had a right to disclaim the officiousness of his ministers, who had acted without any specific orders from the throne. **1849** MACAULAY *Hist. Eng.* vii. II. 179 Of all faults officiousness and indiscretion were the most offensive to him; and Burnet was allowed..to be the most officious and indiscreet of mankind.

† **o'fficiperd, -pard.** *Obs. rare*⁻¹. [cf. L. *officiperda*, *officiperdus* one who makes an ill use of favours; in late L., one who throws away his labour.] The throwing away of one's labour.

1600 W. WATSON *Decacordon* (1602) 157, I thought it meete..to will and commaund my said seruant..vnder paine of officipard to do nothing without my Prouinciall Garnets counsell.

† **'officy,** *v. Obs.* [a. F. *officier* (13th c. in Godef.), ad. med.L. *officiāre* to OFFICIATE.] *intr.* To perform divine service: = OFFICIATE *v.* 1.

c **1449** PECOCK *Repr.* II. vi. 174 It is not to be trowid that dekenes officieden where that preestes were not officiyng. *Ibid.* 522 What for dyuersite of outward habit..and of diet and of waking and of officiyng.

† **of-'fill,** *v. Obs. rare*⁻¹. In 3 of-fullen. [app. f. OF-² + FILL *v.*: cf. AFILL.] *trans.* To fill completely.

c **1205** LAY. 20438 þa wes Ænglene lond: mid ærmþe of-fulled [c 1275 i-fulled].

offing ('ɒfɪŋ, 'ɔː-). Also 7 offen, 7–9 offin. [f. OFF *adv.* + -ING¹.]

1. *Naut.* The part of the visible sea distant from the shore or beyond the anchoring ground.

1627 CAPT. SMITH *Seaman's Gram.* ix. 44 The Offing..is the open Sea from the shore, or the middest of any great streame is called the Offing. **1659** D. PELL *Impr. Sea* 328 Yonder's ships in the Offin of the Sea. **1666** *Lond. Gaz.* No. 75/2 At Two this day..the Generals discovered Trump..in the Offen. **1796** *Log of 'Captain'* 26 June in Nicolas *Disp. Nelson* (1846) VII. p. lxxxix, Found at anchor His Majesty's Ship the Inconstant, the Gorgon and Sincere, with a Convoy in the Offing. **1860** MAURY *Phys. Geog. Sea* §127 In the offings of the Balize, sometimes as far out as a hundred miles or more from the land, puddles or patches of Mississippi water may be observed on the surface of the sea.

2. *Naut.* Position at a distance off the shore. Esp. in phrases, as ***to gain, get, keep, make, take an offing***.

1688 R. HOLME *Armoury* II. 31/1 An Offen or Offing is to be out in the open Sea from the shore-ward. **1703** DAMPIER *Voy.* III. 119 By Nine a Clock at night we had got a pretty good Offin. **1748** *Anson's Voy.* I. viii. 83 By noon we had gained an offing of near twenty leagues. **1861** SMILES *Engineers* II. VII. viii. 218 A sailing vessel..could lie out upon either tack, and make an offing. **1883** CLARK RUSSELL *Sea Queen* II. ii. 21 My father had..kept so wide an offing that the English shores were but little more than a cloud upon the distant water.

3. ***in the offing***: nearby, at hand, in prospect, likely to happen in the near future; (in quot. 1779, exceptionally, in the distant future).

1779 J. WEDGWOOD *Let.* 30 May (1965) 234, I hope soon to say as far as 30 inches, perhaps ultimately up to 36 inches by 24, but that is at present in the offing. **1914** T. DREISER *Titan* xvii. 139 The possibility of another woman equally or possibly better suited to him was looming in the offing. **1942** D. POWELL *Time to be Born* (1943) x. 239 Somehow it didn't seem like real love without a husband in the offing. **1949** N. MITFORD *Love in Cold Climate* I. v. 57 That look of concentration which comes over French faces when a meal is in the offing. **1970** G. F. NEWMAN *Sir, You Bastard* viii. 241 Number six could be afforded if he got promoted, but promotion wasn't in the offing.

offir(e, obs. forms of OFFER.

offis(s, -ise, offiser(e, obs. ff. OFFICE, OFFICER.

offish ('ɒfɪʃ, ɔː-), *a. colloq.* [f. OFF *adv.* + -ISH¹: cf. *uppish*.] Inclined to keep aloof; distant in manner. Cf. STAND-OFFISH. Hence **'offishness**.

1834 C. A. DAVIS *Lett. J. Downing* 75 Others are a little offish. **1842** *Betsy Bobbet* 289 (Farmer), I am naturally pretty offish and retirin' in my ways with strange men folks. **1860** BARTLETT *Dict. Americanisms*, *Offish*, distant or unapproachable in manners. **1874** T. HARDY *Far fr. Madding Crowd* lii, She is..quite offish and careless, I know. **1882** *Standard* 29 Sept. 5/2 With..all our 'offishness' ..we and our cousins in the Far South get along amazingly well. **1899** F. GREENWOOD in *Blackw. Mag.* June 1039/2 The robust self-dependence, selfishness, offishness of wild life. a **1963** S. PLATH *Crossing Water* (1971) 31 She stopped fitting me so closely and seemed offish.

off-island, *adv.* (*phr.*), *sb.*, and *a.* [f. OFF *prep.*, OFF- 4 b + ISLAND *sb.*] **A.** *adv.* (*phr.*) Away from an island; spec. *U.S.*, away from the island of Nantucket.

1917 *Dialect Notes* IV. 335 *Off island*, elsewhere than on the island (Nantucket). 'What would I want to go *off island* for?' **1971** *N.Y. Times* 27 June 3 One islander was heard to remark recently that he never carried more than 30 cents in his pocket unless he planned to go off-island.

B. *sb.* An island off the shore of a larger or central island.

1969 *Sunday Times* 23 Feb. 63 The off-islands may seem to be just across the nautical street but the journey can still be an experience on a rough day. **1973** W. J. BURLEY *Death in Salubrious Place* i. 14 The pleasure boats were on their various ways to the off-islands. **1973** *Publishers Weekly* 19 Nov. 61/1 Letty Ward lives with her parents on Innish, an Irish off-island. **1976** *London Calling* Apr. 2/1 The Isles of Scilly... The four inhabited 'off-islands', as they are always called, are Tresco,..St. Martin's, St Agnes and Bryher.

C. *adj.* Visiting or temporarily residing on an island.

1965 *New Yorker* 13 Feb. 42 This upset afforded small comfort to off-island Republicans here..because while the Guamanians are American citizens, they cannot vote in our Presidential elections.

So **off-islander,** (*a*) a visitor or temporary resident on an island; spec. *U.S.*, in Nantucket; (*b*) an inhabitant of an off-shore island.

1882 J. G. AUSTIN (*title*) Nantucket scraps: being the experiences of an off-islander, in season and out of season, among a passing people. **1935** [see NANTUCKETER]. **1939** S. CHAMBERLAIN *Nantucket* 4 Artists and summer visitors have discovered its allure, and many fortunate 'off islanders' now live in old Nantucket houses. **1961** D. M. DOUGLASS *Saba's Treasure* (1963) vi. 98 Off-islanders like other harbors better. **1967** *Daily Tel.* 17 May 21/1 Mr. John Knott, Conservative MP for St. Ives, Cornwall, is to meet representatives of the Duchy of Cornwall, the Scillies Council, the Steamship Co. and 'off-islanders' on Saturday. **1968** *Time* 26 July 67 Many 'off-islanders', the regular summer residents, are concerned lest their historic hideaway lose its charm.

offitorie, obs. corrupt form of OFFERTORY.

† **o'ffivorous,** *a. nonce-wd.* [irreg. f. OFFAL + -VOROUS.] Offal-eating.

1713 DERHAM *Phys.-Theol.* IV. xi. (1727) 197 *note*, In a Dog, and other offivorous Quadrupeds, 'tis very large.

off key, off-key, *adv.* (*phr.*) and *a.* [f. OFF *prep.*, OFF- 4 b + KEY *sb.*¹] Without tonal organization; out of tune; also *fig.*, wrong(ly), inappropriate(ly).

1929 M. LIEF *Hangover* 235 Eulalia Duncan sang so off-key last night that she had great difficulty moving her vowels. **1943** R. CHANDLER *Lady in Lake* xxxi. 171 There's something a little off key about everything you do. **1952** *Sci.*

Amer. May 65 Friends..who sing everything in a monotone or in the same off-key pattern. **1953** *N.Y. Times* 29 Jan. 25/2 Miss Davis' performance in this scene is foolishly false—a travesty of sexy movie acting, illogical and wholly off-key. **1965** G. McInnes *Road to Gundagai* iii. 53 A faintly off-key piano. **1971** [see OFF BASE *phr.* (*adv.*) and *a.*]. **1973** J. Wainwright *Devil you Don't* 18 He had a peculiar, off-key voice.

offlap ('ɒflæp, ɔː-). *Geol.* Also **off-lap.** [f. OFF *adv.* + LAP *v.*[2], after OVERLAP *v.* 3.] A progressive diminution in the lateral extent of conformable strata in passing upwards from older to younger strata, so that each stratum leaves a portion of the underlying one exposed; a set of strata exhibiting this.

1913 A. W. Grabau *Princ. Stratigr.* xviii. 734 (*caption*) Diagram illustrating regressive overlap (off-lap) and the formation of a sandstone of emergence..into which the shore-ends of the successive members of the retreatal series ..grade. **1948** *Jrnl. Geol.* LVI. 147/1 Marine blanket sands represent the horizontal welding of many parallel prismatic shore lines during a long, continuous period of over-lap or off-lap. **1969** Bennison & Wright *Geol. Hist. Brit. Isles* i. 14 The offlaps of marine sedimentation are accompanied, in this case, by lateral and vertical gradation into beds of continental facies. **1975** *Nature* 10 Jan. 107/1 The stratigraphic relationship of the Devensian Tills of eastern England is therefore one of offlap..and not of overlap.

So **'offlapping** *ppl. a.*

1906 A. W. Grabau in *Bull. Geol. Soc. Amer.* XVII. 615 Examples of regressively overlapping or, better, offlapping formations are frequently met. **1921** —— *Textbk. Geol.* I. xvii. 559 If, after a retreatal movement of the sea and the formation of an offlapping series.., a transgressive movement with overlapping of formations should follow, the sandstone bed of emergence would be in part reworked. **1974** *Nature* 15 Nov. 200/1 The sealevel curve is based on the series of transgression-regression cycles identified from successions of offlapping coral reefs.

offlet ('ɒflɪt, ɔː-). [f. OFF- 3 + LET *v.*[1]: cf. *inlet, outlet.*] A channel or pipe for letting water off.

1838 F. W. Simms *Pub. Wks. Gt. Brit.* iii. 9 Offlets.. constructed to carry away the water. **1875** Alex. Smith *New Hist. Aberdeen* II. 936 The mouth or offlet of the loch. **1886** *Cassell's Encycl. Dict., Offlet*, a pipe laid at the level of the bottom of a canal, etc., to let off the water.

offlete, variant of OFLETE *Obs.*, wafer.

off licence, off-licence. [OFF *a.* 5.] A shop or other establishment where alcoholic liquors are sold for consumption off the premises; also, a licence permitting such sales. Also *attrib.* Hence **off-licensed** *ppl. a.*; **off-licensee**.

1891 *Leeds Merc.* 22 Sept. 7 Five beer houses 'on' and six 'off' licenses. **1892** W. B. Kingston *Intemperance* 61 A circumstance entirely due to the competition of the 'off' licensee. **1892** *Daily News* 31 Oct. 3/2 Three big gin palaces and a swarm of off-licensed houses. **1897** *Ibid.* 28 Aug. 6/4 Four new off-licences were granted by the magistrates. **1907** *Daily Chron.* 16 Apr. 3/6 The number of off-license [*sic*] premises at the beginning of 1906 was 25,281. **1959** J. Braine *Vodi* iv. 55 It was an off-licence, very cool and smelling both earthy and antiseptic, with overtones of stale beer and tobacco. **1961** E. A. Powdrill *Vocab. Land Planning* iii. 42 To double the population is to increase considerably the range of shops that are required, for instance, cafes, off-licences, ladies' shops, etc. **1971** *Oxford Times* 15 Oct. 9 (Advt.), From our off-licensed branches. Guinness—small cans. 9p. **1975** J. Aiken *Voices in Empty House* iii. 105 The old lady tottering..to the off-licence on the corner. **1978** *Morecambe Guardian* 14 Mar. 4/1 (Advt.), We cordially invite all Hoteliers Restaurateurs Off-Licensees, etc. to visit our new Wines & Spirits department.

off limits, off-limits, *adv.* (*phr.*) and *a.* orig. *U.S.* [f. OFF *prep.* + *pl.* of LIMIT *sb.*] Of an area, place, etc.: outside the limits within which a particular group or class of people must remain; not to be frequented or patronized, esp. by military personnel; out of bounds. Also *transf.* and *fig.*

1952 R. Cutforth *Korean Reporter* xv. 137 Over the door an official army notice barked in iron-mouthed print: Strictly Off Limits. **1959** *Amer. Speech* XXXIV. 155 As long as the infatuation lasts, the man is said to be *attached* and strictly *off limits* to other girls. **1960** *Encounter* Feb. 38/1 The Negroes do not blame the residents but know that..the white G.I.'s in effect declare a town off-limits. **1968** A. Diment *Bang Bang Birds* v. 58 We ain't going to take them out because they're brothels. If it was just that we'd mark them Off Limits to service personnel. **1968** *Economist* 5 Oct. 46/3 The federation's leaders have declared the UAW-Teamsters group to be off-limits, describing it as 'a dual labour organisation, rival to the AFL-CIO'. **1971** 'S. Ransome' *Trap 6* (1972) xiii. 139, I didn't intrude into the investigators' office. So far as I'm concerned that's off limits. **1973** A. Dundes *Mother Wit* 259 White females were off-limits to Negro males. **1975** *N.Y. Times* 15 Sept. 9/1 In this central highlands town, which houses the legion's Corsican command post, three bars are off limits.

off-line (stress variable), *a.* and *adv.* [f. OFF *prep.* + LINE *sb.*[2]] **A.** *adj.* **1.** Not situated or performed on a railway or by rail.

1926 Huebner & Johnson *Railroad Freight Service* xvii. 338 Many railroads maintain 'off-line' offices or agencies at important industrial and commercial centers which they reach via connecting lines. **1973** E. Rath *Container Systems* vii. 175 Bimodal containerization uses truck trailers or other highway vehicles or special containers... This service uses the rail network as the main artery and as prime source of railroad revenue. The off-line service is given as an accommodation to the freight market. **1973** *Sci. Amer.* Oct. 24/3 The achievement is made possible by off-line loading and automatic, positive control of all motions of the vehicle.

2. *Computers.* Not on-line; other than on-line.

1950 W. W. Stifler *High-Speed Computing Devices* ii. 7 For other applications, off-line operation, involving automatic transcription of data in a form suitable for later introduction to the machine, may be tolerated. **1957** D. D. McCracken *Digital Computer Programming* xii. 157 The reel of tape may then be removed from the auxiliary ('off-line') tape unit, placed on a tape unit which is connected to the computer ('on-line'), and read in at high speeds. **1959** [see IN-LINE *a.* 3c]. **1967** C. Berners-Lee in Wills & Yearsley *Handbk. Managem. Technol.* 16 Off-line equipment is, typically, a keyboard device preparing a paper tape to be read into a computer later. An on-line keyboard, on the other hand, is one wired directly into the computer. **1969** *Sunday Times* (Colour Suppl.) 16 Feb. 22/3 The clearance and updating must be done when the computer is ..'off-line', i.e. is uncoupled from any systems that the computer itself is controlling. **1972** *Accountant* 26 Oct. 530/2 Off-line operation at Hendon is through a Varian 6201 computer and dual tape unit, transferring data to tape for processing later on the 370/145.

B. *adv. Computers.* With a delay between the production of data and its processing; not under direct computer control.

1950 W. W. Stifler *High-Speed Computing Devices* ii. 7 Some teletype machines operate on line. Their operators are in instantaneous communication. Other teletype machines are operated off line, through the intervention of punched paper tape. **1959** J. K. Brigden in E. M. Grabbe et al. *Handbk. Automation, Computation, & Control* II. xx. 4 Obviously all the equipment used for on-line purposes can also be used off-line. **1964** T. W. McRae *Impact of Computers on Accounting* i. 17 The tape is then..transferred to a smaller computer and printed off-line on the output printer of that computer. **1967** D. Wilson in Wills & Yearsley *Handbk. Managem. Technol.* 43 Because removable media systems can store inactive data off-line, the total capacity of these systems..is virtually unlimited. **1970** *Computers & Humanities* V. 36 Although the plotter, when run 'off line', is relatively cheap, it is slow. **1971** *Sci. Amer.* Sept. 17/1 (Advt.), Until recently, the best solution was to use the complex mathematics of the Fourier transform and program a computer to do the complex signal analysis computations off-line.

off-load ('ɒf,ləʊd, 'ɔː-; ,ɒf'ləʊd ,ɔː-), *v.* orig. *S. Africa.* [f. OFF- 1 + LOAD *v.*, after Du. *afladen.*] *trans.* To unload. Also *transf.* and *fig.*, to discard, get rid of, relieve oneself of (a person or thing). Hence **off-'loading** *vbl. sb.* and *ppl. a.*

1850 R. G. Cumming *Hunter's Life S. Afr.* (ed. 2) I. 5 No, no, mynheer, you must not off-load. **1850** R. G. Cumming *Five Yrs. Hunter's Life S. Afr.* II. xx. 82 Having off-loaded my waggon, I handed it over to Mr. Arnott, the resident blacksmith, to undergo repairs. **1863** W. C. Baldwin *Afr. Hunting* 222 The wagon stuck fast and we had to off-load. **1889** F. Oates *Matabele-Land* 131 At last we off-loaded a large part of our cargo. **1896** *Westm. Gaz.* 21 Feb. 5/1 The rules are that dynamite must be off-loaded within twenty-four hours after arrival [at Johannesburg]. **1903** Kipling *Five Nations* 208 Ubique means 'Off-load your guns'—at midnight in the rain! **1916** *Chambers's Jrnl.* June 373/2 At railhead the train is off-loaded into the motor-lorries. **1942** W. S. Churchill *Second World War* (1951) IV. I. ix. 146 It will..be necessary for the *Indomitable* squadrons to be off-loaded in Ceylon. **1949** *Sun* (Baltimore) 21 Feb. 4/3 The machinery was off-loaded and shipped on to Nottingham by railway. **1950** *Daily Progress* (Charlottesville, Va.) 30 Jan. 1/5 Salvage team personnel have completed offloading the Big Mo's ammunition and all beach gear has been placed. **1952** C. Day Lewis tr. *Virgil's Aeneid* v. 113 They enrolled the women for the colony, off-loaded the men who wanted To stay there. **1957** *Economist* 2 Nov. 429/1 The vehicle industry finds that it has to offload more of its rising production of cars and lorries on to the home market. **1958** *Times* 19 Mar. 14/2 Bales were off-loaded. *Ibid.*, Cotton was stolen from the Liverpool Docks in the off-loading of 12 different ships. **1968** M. Woodhouse *Rock Baby* v. 43 A Director who has to offload one of his staff and is embarrassed. **1971** C. Bonington *Annapurna South Face* iii. 30 This period being taken up with off-loading, Customs clearance and the journey across India. **1972** *Daily Tel.* 1 Apr. 3/2 It arrived at Heathrow as mishandled luggage, having been wrongly off-loaded in Rome from a flight from Australia to London. **1977** J. McClure *Sunday Hangman* ii. 17[He] side-stepped into the shadow of an off-loading Coke truck.

† **of-'flyght**, for *aflight* frightened, pa. pple. of AFLEY *v. Obs.* [See OF-[3].]

c **1315** Shoreham (E.E.T.S.) 153/696 Lord, þo we herde þe, We were of flyȝte.

'off-,lying, *a.* [f. OFF- 2 + *lying*, pr. pple. of LIE *v.*[1]] Lying off, at a distance or out of the way; remote; lying off from the central or main part.

1864 *Pall Mall G.* 31 Aug. 1/1 The off-lying colonies of Nova Scotia, New Brunswick, and Newfoundland. **1886** Child *Ballads* IV. xcviii. 373/2 An off-lying apartment in which she sleeps with her maids.

off microphone, off-microphone, *adv.* (*phr.*) and *a.* [f. OFF *prep.* + MICROPHONE.] Away from a microphone; that is distant from, or not facing, a microphone. Also colloq. abbrev. **off-mike.**

1937 *Printers' Ink Monthly* May 39/3 *Off mike*, a position away from a performer or performer's position away from the microphone. **1940** A. Oboler *Fourteen Radio Plays* 201 *Pa* (*off mike*). Hangin' around with loafers in the gymnasiums! *Ibid.* 257 Dialogue or effect is off-microphone, in other words, not all full volume in relation to other speeches or effects. **1958** *Listener* 13 Nov. 799/1 Those who may have wondered what goes on in the studios before the red light comes on were given an amusing picture of off-mike life in Mr. Robert Kemp's comedy, 'Young Mother Hubbard'. **1959** *Ibid.* 30 Apr. 774/1 The story..forced Mr. Naughton to move his magnifying glass from the street and to take it, as it were, off-mike. **1962** *Times* 3 Apr. 15/2 Goonery is not the most evident attribute of his off-microphone personality. **1962** A. Nisbett *Technique Sound Studio* ii. 40 The pages should be turned well off-microphone. *Ibid.* 48 Off-microphone voices and spot effects could be blended with on-microphone voices. **1973** *Washington Post* 5 Apr. B. 2 Something electric goes on between the comedienne and her husband... There are off-mike private jokes. **1977** *Rolling Stone* 19 May 89/1 Coltrane is occasionally off-mike.

off'n, var. OFFEN *prep.*

off-off, off-off-Broadway: see OFF-BROADWAY *a.* and *sb.*

† **of-'fought,** *pa. pple. Obs.* Also 4 of-fouȝten. [f. OF-[1] + *fought*, pa. pple. of FIGHT *v.*] Exhausted with fighting.

c **1320** *Sir Beues* 799 (MS. A) Þat Beues was so weri of fouȝte, Þat of his lif he ne rouȝte. *Ibid.* 1187 Icham weri of-fouȝte sore. *a* **1375** *Joseph Arim.* 552 Þei were weri of-fouȝten.

off-peak, *a.* [f. OFF- 4b + PEAK *sb.*[2]] That is not at the maximum; of or pertaining to a period of less than busiest use, consumption, business, etc.

1920 A. C. Pigou *Econ. of Welfare* II. xv. 261 If it is impracticable to charge differential rates directly as between peak and off-peak service, this may sometimes be attempted indirectly by differentiation between continuous and intermittent services. **1924** *World Power* I. 4 (*heading*) Electric heating by off-peak load. *Ibid.*, The continental technical press..gives particulars of successful applications of off-peak power for night uses at low tariffs. **1930** *Engineering* 11 Apr. 493/2 Such systems are generally arranged for supply by off-peak current. **1933** *Discovery* Apr. 111/2 Power is sold in large quantities at a very cheap rate so long as it is used during 'off-peak' hours. **1958** *Oxf. Mag.* 6 Mar. 336/2 Televised religious discussions attract over a million viewers even at off-peak times. **1971** *Times* 2 Oct. 13/2 The new off-peak fares should actually increase carryings. **1973** *Times* 21 Nov. 19/5 To prohibit the use of off-peak electric storage heating will not help the overall fuel position. **1976** P. R. White *Planning for Public Transport* v. 113 Operating costs incurred for specified service levels are related to the ratio of peak to off-peak demand.

offprint, off-print ('ɒfprɪnt, ɔː-), *sb.* [f. OFF- 3 + PRINT, in imitation of Ger. *Separatabdruck*, Du. *afdruk.*] A separately printed copy of an article, etc., which originally appeared as a part of a larger publication.

1885 Skeat in *Academy* 22 Aug. 121 Various terms, such as 'deprint', 'exprint', etc., have been proposed to denote a separately-printed copy of a pamphlet... By comparison with 'offshoot' I think we might use 'offprint' with some hope of expressing what is meant. **1888** F. H. Woods in *Academy* 21 Apr. 276 Having now obtained, through Canon Taylor's courtesy, an off-print of his paper. **1893** E. W. B. Nicholson *Ibid.* 11 Nov. 415, I have..examined five photographs of it, two of them attached by Lord Southesk to an off-print of his paper.

offprint (,ɒf'prɪnt, ,ɔː-; 'ɒfprɪnt, 'ɔː-), *v.* [f. OFF- 1 + PRINT *v.*, after prec.] *trans.* To print off or reprint (as an excerpt).

1895 in *Funk's Stand. Dict.* **1951** *Catalogues MS. Collections Brit. Mus.* (verso rear cover) Offprinted from the Journal of Documentation Volume 7. **1952** M. McCarthy *Groves of Academe* (1953) i. 8 Maynard Hoar, author of a pamphlet, 'The Witch Hunt in Our Universities' (offprinted from the *American Scholar* and mailed out gratis by the bushel to a legion of 'prominent educators').

off-put ('ɒfpʊt, 'ɔː-). Chiefly *north.* [f. OFF- 3 + PUT *v.*] An act of putting off (in any sense: see PUT *v.*). Also, one who puts off, procrastinates, or wastes time.

1730 *Wodrow Corr.* (1843) III. 458 The delays and off-puts in the matter of Mr. Glass are what I do not understand. **1835** Mrs. Carlyle *Lett.* I. 36 He replied he was just setting off to town..I supposed this..a mere off-put. **1866** S. Gilpin *Songs & Ballads of Cumberland* 57 It was just for an off-put. **1893–4** R. O. Heslop *Northumb. Words* II. 509 *Off-put*, delay, one that puts off time. 'Ye'r jeest an off-put o' time, laddy.' **1923** G. Watson *Roxburghshire Word-Bk.* 223 It was duist an offpit! A ken 'im owre weel!

So **off-put** *v. trans.*, to put off; to disconcert; to repel; **'off-,putter**, one who puts off; *spec.* (on the Tyne), 'the loader of coals into a vessel at a staith or spout' (Heslop *Northumberland Wds.*); **off-putting** *vbl. sb.* the action of putting off; **off-putting** *ppl. a.*, that puts off; *spec.* creating an unfavourable impression, causing displeasure; **off-'puttingly** *adv.*, in an off-putting manner; so as to disconcert or repel.

1387 Trevisa *Higden* (Rolls) VI. 409 Þanne he [Sergius] hym self occupiede þe poperiche. And in wreche of his of puttynge he made hem take up Formosus þe pope out of his grave, and smyte of his heed, and þrewe þe body into Tyber. *a* **1578** Lindesay (Pitscottie) *Chron. Scot.* (S.T.S.) II. 19 Quhene the earle knew thair promisse of na effect bot ane offputting of tyme. **1788** *Act* in Brand *Newcastle* (1789) I. 660 Acting as an off-putter or off-putters at any coal staith upon the said river. **1828** Mrs. B. Hall *Let.* 25 June in *Aristocratic Journey* (1931) 295 Forgetting that we had exchanged dilatory off-putting habits of the South for the anticipation in appointments of the North. **1833** *Chambers's Edin. Jrnl.* II. 234/1 Weel, mistress,..this off-putting will do nae langer. **1866** W. Gregor *Dial. Banffshire* 6 *Aff-pittan*, the act of procrastination. **1893–4** R. O. Heslop *Northumb. Words* II. 509 *Offputtin*, putting off, procrastinating, dallying. 'He's varry offputtin.' **1894** *Westm. Gaz.* 20 Nov. 6/2 Sir John used to answer his affectionate suitors with an 'off-putting' type-written letter. **1935** 'A. BRIDGE' *Illyrian Spring* xvii. 221 Your face isn't in the least off-putting, except when you're cross. **1951** WALLACE & BAGNALL-OAKELEY *Norfolk* vi. 66 The approach from the station is very off-putting:..Victorian and later ribbon-development soon started along the station road. **1955** M. ALLINGHAM *Beckoning Lady* xii. 169 Very off-putting, homely finances. **1960** M. SPARK *Bachelors* viii. 120 'Shut up about Ronald,' Tim said. 'It's jolly off-putting.' **1961** *Times* 4 Nov. 9/4 There is something..off-puttingly impersonal about a typed letter. **1969** D. FRANCIS *Enquiry* ix. 122 Composed, cool, off-puttingly gracious, she looked ..flawless. **1970** *Guardian Weekly* 7 Nov. 15 The peculiarity of a faith that can..be so offput by the female of any species that not even a cow is allowed to pasteurise here. **1973** *Nature* 16 Mar. 212/3 The appearance of the book is a little off-putting. **1974** *Country Life* 18 July 174/1 All this may sound offputtingly sporty. **1977** *Verbatim* Dec. 10/1 In case the number of pages is off-putting, it should be mentioned that the page size is 8-1/2" × 11".

off-ramp. *U.S.* [OFF- 4.] A sloping one-way road leading off a main highway.

1954 HEWES & OGLESBY *Highway Engin.* viii. 160 Capacity of off-ramps is affected by the number of through vehicles using the right-hand expressway lane. **1966** M. & G. GORDON *Undercover Cat prowls Again* v. 40 He took the Hollywood Freeway... Turning right at the Balboa off-ramp, he passed a city golf-course. **1968** 'R. MACDONALD' *Instant Enemy* xxx. 192, I took the first off-ramp and drove to the Langstons' neighborhood. **1973** W. MCCARTHY *Detail* iii. 247 Stuart looked for an off ramp... The next turnoff was ten miles ahead.

† **offrand, offerand.** *Obs.* Forms: 2 ofrende, 3–5 offrend(e, 4 ofrande, 4–5 offrond(e, 4–6 offrand(e, offerand(e, 5 offerond, offorand. [Early ME., a. OF. *ofrende* (11th c. in Littré), ad. med.L. *offerenda* 'offering, oblation', lit. '(thing or things) to be offered', gerundive of *offerre* to OFFER. Used in ME. in same sense as OFFERING, and still (? under Fr. influence) by Gower and Caxton, but otherwise peculiar to north. dial. after 1350, and after 1500 only Sc. The northern texts of Cursor Mundi, Hampole, Maundeville, etc., have regularly *offrand*, where the southern texts have *offring, offering*. In later times often spelt *offerand*, and prob. associated with *offerand*, northern form of *offering*, pr. pple. of *offer* vb.] = OFFERING *vbl. sb.* 1, 2.

c **1200** *Vices & Virtues* 85 Al swa ðe gode hlauerd ðe sent his menn ofrende for his aȝene wurscipe. *c* **1250** *Old Kent. Serm.* in *O.E. Misc.* 26 Al swo hi hedden aparailed here offrendes swo kam si sterre þet yede to-for hem. *a* **1300** *Cursor M.* 1063 (Cott.) For his offrand [*Fairf.* offerande, *Trin.* offrynge] was rightwys. *Ibid.* 1940 (Cott.) Our lauerd drightin..Him liked wel in his offrand [*F.* offerande, *Tr.* offrynge]. *Ibid.* 5974 (Cott.) 'Gas' he said 'her in mi land And to your lauerd yee mak offrand' [*F.* offerande, *Tr.* offronde]. **1340** *Ayenb.* 41 þe rentes þo offrendes þe tendes and þe oþre riȝtes of holy cherche. **1390** GOWER *Conf.* III. 307 With great offrende and sacrifise. *c* **1400** MAUNDEV. (Roxb.) vi. 18 Ane of þe three kynges þat made offerand [*Cott. MS.* offryng] til oure Lord. *c* **1440** *York Myst.* x. 162 Bot wher-of sall oure offerand be? *c* **1477** CAXTON *Jason* 98 Whan the preest had understande Iason that he promysed so good an offrande. **1513** DOUGLAS *Æneis* XII. xiv. 147 Pallas ..Of the ane offerand to the Goddis makis. **1549** *Compl. Scot.* 8 He estimeit the grite offrandis that vas offrit be riche opulent men. *a* **1572** KNOX *Hist. Ref.* Wks. 1846 I. 39 That ..thair offerand may be augmented.

offre, offring, obs. ff. OFFER, OFFERING.

† **'off-'reckon,** *v. Obs.* [f. OFF- 1 + RECKON *v.*] *trans.* To reckon off, deduct from the reckoning.

1721 A. HILL in *Buccleuch MSS.* (Hist. MSS. Comm.) I. 370 Whatever he might make by..Balls, Concerts, or the like, ought to be off-reckoned.

'off-,reckoning. Usu. in *pl.* [f. OFF- 3 + RECKONING *vbl. sb.* Cf. Du. *afrekening*, Ger. *abrechnung* deduction, settlement of accounts.] A deduction; formerly, in the British army, the name of a special account between the government and the commanding officers of regiments in reference to the clothing, etc., of the men.

1687 *Royal Order* 27 Nov. in *Lond. Gaz.* No. 2299/1 Each Soldier to which the Off-Reckonings or Residue of their Pay hath not formerly been liable. *Ibid.*, The said Off-Reckonings to be employed by the Colonel of each respective Regiment, for the Cloathing and Poundage. **1713** *Off Notice* ibid. No. 5126/10 South-Sea Stock is issued to answer the Off-reckonings of the six Marine Regiments. **1752** CHESTERF. *Lett.* (1792) III. cclxxxviii. 320 What we call the off-reckonings, that is deductions from the men's pay. **1816** JAMES *Mil. Dict.*, *Off-Reckonings*, a specific account, so called, which exists between Government and the Colonels of British Regiments, for the Clothing of the men. This Account is divided into two parts, viz. gross off-reckonings and net off-reckonings. **1845** STOCQUELER *Handbk. Brit. India* (1854) 47 The Commander-in-Chief [receives] 10,000*l.*, and very often the off-reckonings of a regiment of which he may be the colonel. **1867** SMYTH *Sailor's Word-bk.*, *Off-reckoning*, a proportion of the full pay of troops retained from them, in special cases, until the period of final settlement, to cover various expected charges (for ship-rations and the like).

† **'offredge.** *Obs.* [app. for **offrage*, f. OFFER *v.* + -AGE.] The act of offering, or that which is offered; offering, sacrifice.

1548 GEST *Pr. Masse* in H. G. Dugdale *Life* (1840) App. 72 He estemeth..not the value and bygnes of thi offredge. *Ibid.* 108 Therfore he mencyonethe only yᵉ partaking and not theyr offredge also.

offretite ('ɒfrətaɪt). *Min.* Also † **offrétite.** [ad. F. *offrétite* (F. Gonnard 1890, in *Compt. Rend.* CXI. 1002), f. the name of Albert *Offret* (b. 1857), French mineralogist: see -ITE[1].] A hydrated aluminosilicate of potassium and calcium, which belongs to the zeolite group and is found as colourless hexagonal crystals at Mount Semiol, France.

1891 *Jrnl. Chem. Soc.* LX. 407 Offrétite is a zeolite which occurs in very small quantity, associated with christianite and chabasite, in the basalt of Mount Simionse [*sic*], near Montbrison. **1892** E. S. DANA *Dana's Syst. Min.* (ed. 6) 1043 Offrétite. **1894** *Amer. Jrnl. Sci.* CXLVIII. 188 Offretite. **1967** *Nature* 3 June 1005/2 Offretite and erionite are evidently two distinct but closely related minerals, which can intergrow. **1970** *Trans. Faraday Soc.* LXVI. 1616 Synthetic unfaulted offretite can provide a wide pore molecular sieve which can sorb molecules up to ~7·1 Å in critical dimension... This zeolite appears to have possibilities as a versatile molecular sieve. **1975** *Nature* 28 Aug. 718/2 Offretite is a rare natural zeolite whose synthetic equivalent, zeolite O, is commercially important as a molecular sieve.

offretory, offrytorye, obs. ff. OFFERTORY.

off-rhyme. [OFF- 4.] A partial or near rhyme.

1938 L. MACNEICE *Mod. Poetry* vii. 131 One can use internal rhymes, off-rhymes, bad rhymes, 'pararhymes'. **1944** —— *Christopher Columbus* 8 Your significant variations of rhythm, your internal rhymes, your off-rhymes and assonances and technical surprises, will get in the composer's way. **1956** E. WILSON *Piece of My Mind* (1957) vii. 124 Many kinds of liberties are countenanced—in the way of off-rhymes and irregular rhythms—in the writing of modern poetry. **1972** *Computers & Humanities* VII. 19 Taylor is not as unsystematic as might have been thought in his use of off-rhymes. **1972** J. WAIN in Cox & Dyson *20th-Cent. Mind* I. xi. 405 These half-rhymes of Owen's (para-rhymes, off-rhymes, even meta-rhymes, as they have been variously dubbed). **1977** *N.Y. Rev. Bks.* 9 June 29/4 Internal rhymes (trunks, sunk), off-rhymes (salt, silt), a lyrical vocabulary (sweetness, enchanted)—all these things are here, but none of them is obtrusive.

† **o'ffright,** *v. Obs.* Forms: *pa.t.* 3 offurhte(ü), offrihte; *pa. pple.* 2 offriht, 3 offuriht, offruht(ü), offruiht, offruyht, offriȝt, o-friȝt, ofright. [f. OF-[2] + OE. *fyrhtan* to FRIGHT, to be afraid. Orig. and chiefly in pa. pple., which may have been altered from OE. *afyrht* AFFRIGHT *ppl. a.*, into which it again finally passed, through *ofright.* See OF- *pref.*[2]]

1. *trans.* To frighten, terrify. *pa. pple.* Frightened, afraid.

c **1160** *Hatton Gosp.* Matt. viii. 26 To whi sænde ȝe offirhte [*Ags. Gosp.* forhte] ȝe litles ȝeleafan. *c* **1200** *Trin. Coll. Hom.* 31 Hie waren swiðe offurihte and ofdredde. *c* **1250** *Gen. & Ex.* 3652 Fele it brende and made o-friȝt. *c* **1275** *O.E. Misc.* 54 Hi weren aferd and offruyht. *c* **1330** R. BRUNNE *Chron.* 158 þe mayden Berenger scho was alle ofright.

2. *intr.* To be afraid.

c **1205** LAY. 32113 Strongliche he wes auæred; laðliche of-furhte. *c* **1275** *Ibid.* 30267 And þe king of-frihte and a-wok of sleape.

'off,saddle, off-saddle, *v.* Chiefly *S. Africa.* [f. OFF- 1 + SADDLE *v.*, after Du. *afzadelen.*] *trans.* To take the saddle off (a horse) for a rest, feeding, etc.; to unsaddle; also *absol.*; *transf.* to make a break in a journey.

1837 F. OWEN *Diary* (1926) 78 We off-saddled and sat on the ground on the outside of the fence. **1850** R. G. CUMMING *Five Yrs. Hunter's Life S. Afr.* I. 119 Accordingly we off-saddled, and in a few minutes I was once more asleep. *Ibid.* 129 Having off-saddled our horses, we knee-haltered them. **1863** W. C. BALDWIN *Afr. Hunting* 389, I offsaddled Kebon, kneehaltered him and then lay under the shade of a tree. **1879** A. FORBES in *Daily News* 21 Aug., I mean to trek for home, perhaps I shall outspan for a few days at Capetown; perhaps I shan't off-saddle at all. **1887** RIDER HAGGARD *Jess* 323 John was sharply ordered to dismount and offsaddle his horse. **1893** SELOUS *Trav. S.E. Africa* 21 Here..I had determined to off-saddle for the first time. **1915** KIPLING *New Army* 22 The batteries off-saddled in silence. **1939** [see KNEE-HALTER *v.*]. **1974** B. MATHER *White Dacoit* ii. 22 They halted and off-saddled and picqueted the horses half a mile downstream.

Hence **off-saddling** *vbl. sb.*

1906 RIDER HAGGARD *Benita* ix. 120 Directions as to their herding, and the off-saddling of the horses.

'off-saddle, *sb.* [f. the vb.] A break or rest in a journey during which horses are unsaddled.

1900 *Pall Mall Gaz.* 4 Jan. 1/3 The Cape horse..can canter along steadily all day under a burning sun, with an occasional off-saddle. **1908** *Daily Chron.* 10 Nov. 3/5, I had him by the hip at 'off-saddle' time.

off-sale. [OFF *a.* 5.] The sale of alcoholic liquors for consumption elsewhere than at the place of sale.

1899 *Daily News* 19 May 8/5 That licensed houses should be closed in England throughout Sunday, except for one hour of off-sale at mid-day, and two hours of off-sale in the evening. **1933** *Sun* (Baltimore) 17 Apr. 4/4 The local act also holds up issuance of an 'off sale' of beer in packages by Dressman Bros., grocers. **1963** *Times* 23 Apr. 20/3 Sales of bottles to take home ('Off-Sales') have increased very considerably, and there has been a reduction of sales by the glass. **1970** *Times* 18 Aug. 20 M. & B. wants to stop off-sales in favour of the 23 Wine Sellers off-licences it has opened in Birmingham. **1977** 'J. FRASER' *Hearts Ease* ix. 104, I see you're licensed for off-sales... Does that mean you have any wines?

offscape ('ɒfskeɪp, ɔː-), **offskip** ('ɒfskɪp, ɔː-). Now *rare* or *Obs.* [f. OFF- 3 + *-scape*, taken, in the sense of 'view, scene', from *landscape*: cf. *sea-scape.*] A distant view or prospect; the distant part of a view or prospect, the distance, background.

1711 *Brit. Apollo* III. No. 133. 4/2 A Perspective View of Portsmouth..with an Off-scape of the Sea. **1752** AVISON *Mus. Express.* 26 In Painting there are three various Degrees of Distances established, viz. the Fore-Ground, the intermediate Part, and the Off-skip. **1774** T. WEST *Antiq. Furness* (1822) 19 On a fine day the offscape at Hawcoat is circular and takes in the whole extent of the isle of Man, the isle of Anglesey, the Mountains of..North Wales, &c. **1820–2** PYNE *Wine & Walnuts* (1824) I. iv. 33 Her study.. commanding an off-skip, bird's-eye view all along St. George's Fields. **1838** JAMES *Robber* i, The first slopes of the offscape appeared.

'off'scour, *v. rare.* [f. OFF- 1 + SCOUR *v.*] *trans.* To scour off; in quot. to scour or cleanse from defilement. So **'off,scourer,** one who scours off.

1578 LYTE *Dodoens* III. vi. 322 They of scoure and clense al inwarde partes. **1856** RUSKIN *Mod. Paint.* V. IX. xi, England..becoming thus the offscourer of the earth, and taking the hyena instead of the lion upon her shield.

offscouring ('ɒf,skaʊərɪŋ, 'ɔː-). [OFF- 3.]

1. The action of scouring off. *rare.*

1896 MRS. CAFFYN *Quaker Grandmother* 21 My microscopical coating of dross needs no sweat of brow for its off-scouring.

2. That which is scoured off; filth or defilement cleaned off and cast aside; refuse, rubbish. **a.** *lit.* (Almost always in *pl.*; cf. *sweepings.*)

1674 N. FAIRFAX *Bulk & Selv.* 196 Light may otherwise arise than from suns (as may be seen by..stale Sprats,..the off-scourings of an Oyster-shell). **1859** JEPHSON *Brittany* ii. 16 Having carefully picked my way through the off-scourings of the lofty houses on either side of me. **1878** *N. Amer. Rev.* CXXVI. 344 [Fires] consumed the offscourings of a great city.

b. *fig.* of persons. (In *collective sing.* (after 1 Cor. iv. 13) or *pl.*)

1526 TINDALE *1 Cor.* iv. 13 The of scowrynge of all things. **1575–85** ABP. SANDYS *Serm.* (1841) 188 They are accounted as the offscourings, refuse, and baggage of the world. *a* **1631** DONNE *Lament. Jeremy* III. xvii, Thou hast made us fall As refuse, and off-scouring to them all. **1775** ADAIR *Amer. Ind.* 413 White people, who are generally the dregs and off-scourings of our colonies. **1834** L. RITCHIE *Wand. by Seine* 10 The army..included..the very offscourings of society. **1835** J. P. KENNEDY *Horse-Shoe Robinson* I. xiv. 180 Why, you off-scouring,..it is enough to make Old Scratch laugh, to hear you talk about conscience! **1871** *Scribner's Monthly* II. 546 Every Protestant is counted but the off-scouring of decent society. **1928** H. W. SHOEMAKER in *Publ. Pennsylvania Folk-Lore Soc.* I. IV. 10 That dressy offscouring will not come back for her... I've known him and his kind too well for more than fifty years. **1972** F. W. LINDSAY *Cariboo Dream* 13/2 Thugs, gamblers and the off-scourings of the world.

off screen, off-screen, *adv.* (*phr.*) and *a.* [f. OFF *prep.* + SCREEN *sb.*[1]] Not appearing on a film or television screen; = OFF CAMERA *phr.* and *adv.* Also *fig.*

1935 *Motion Picture* Nov. 15/1 In addition, of course, you are the perfect lady, off-screen. **1953** K. REISZ *Technique Film Editing* i. 62 A reaction shot is shown and held while the character off screen is speaking his lines. **1958** *New Statesman* 9 Aug. 168/1 There were, of course, a few minor, off-screen, political controversies. **1962** *Guardian* 14 Aug. 5/3 This disarmingly frank and articulate off-screen comedian. **1973** 'E. MCBAIN' *Let's hear It* xiv. 209 The actors made important plot points offscreen, their voices floating in over the picture. **1974** *Times* 10 Apr. 13/8 The off-screen audience, real or canned, goes into mad paroxysms.

offscum ('ɒfskʌm, ɔː-). Also 6 offscome, ofscombe, 7 off-scumme, of-scum(me. [f. OFF- 3 + SCUM.] That which is skimmed off; scum, dross, refuse; *fig.* that which is rejected as vile or worthless (usually of persons, in *collective sing.* or *pl.*; formerly also of one person).

1579 LODGE *Def. Plays* 3 A little pamphelet..I fynd it the offscome [*mispr.* oftscome] of imperfections. **1581** J. BELL *Haddon's Answ. Osor.* 40 b, The ofscombe of that unsavory schoolkitchen. **1605** SYLVESTER *Du Bartas* II. iii. III. *Lawe* 328 These off-scums all at once Too idlely pampred, plot Rebellions. *a* **1670** HACKET *Abp. Williams* II. (1692) 161 The roguy off-scum in the streets of Westminster talk'd so loud. **1763** J. BROWN *Poetry & Mus.* iii. 28 The Off-scum of civilized Nations. **1863** FR. A. KEMBLE *Resid. in Georgia* 11 The offscum and the offscouring of the very dregs of your society.

attrib. **1626** tr. *Boccalini's New-found Politicke* III. xiii. 207 A most vile Game deuised by the off-scum raskals of men.

off season, off-season. A period when ordinary business or course of affairs is suspended or does not occur; a time of year other than the busiest or most popular time for a particular activity. Also *attrib.* or as *adj.*

1848 THACKERAY *Van. Fair* xxxvi, She has to board two or three of her sisters in the off-season. **1868** YATES *Rock Ahead* III. iii, In the off-season [they] went round to the different watering-places..giving a little musical entertainment. **1897** [see HIGH *a.* 4 a]. **1902** *Chambers's Jrnl.* July 433/2 The collection was not one of those which bore an historic name ..and the sale took place in the off-season. **1905** A. BENNETT *Let.* 5 Apr. (1966) I. 61, I have a great notion of books being issued in off-seasons. **1908** *Daily Chron.* 21 Apr. 3/5 A great part of Miss Elwin's off-season work consists in meeting girls on their way to and from school. **1930** *B.B.C. Year-bk. 1931* 25 During the summer period, normally regarded as an 'off season', the average number of new licences taken out each month..was in excess of 20,000. **1957** L. F. R. WILLIAMS *State of Israel* 44 The coaches..are primarily intended for tourists, but..carry domestic traffic in the off-season. **1959** [see BUDGET *sb.* 4]. **1971** W. J. BURLEY *Guilt Edged* iii. 59 The newcomers..disturbed the off-season peace of the Treen Hotel. **1976** *Washington Post* 19 Apr. D 1/6 With the series clinched, the Caps looked as though they were running their motors down for the offseason that begins when they fly off for a week's vacation in Hawaii.

offset ('ɒfsɛt, 'ɔː-), *sb.* [f. OFF- 3 + SET. Cf. SET-OFF.]

1. The act of setting off (on a journey or course of action); outset, start.

a **1555** LATIMER *Serm. & Rem.* (1845) 311 When you thus get out of your way at the first off-set. **1803** SOUTHEY *Lett.* (1856) I. 235 He addressed a letter to me, announcing their off-set. **1899** *Eclectic Mag.* Feb. 201 At the offset I was out of it.

2. A short lateral offshoot from the stem or root of a plant (esp. from a bulb), serving for propagation.

1629 J. PARKINSON *Parad.* xi. 114 The root is..compassed with a number of small rootes, or of of-sets round about it. **1664** EVELYN *Kal. Hort.*, *July* (1729) 211 Take up your Gladiolus now yearly..or else their Off-sets will poison the ground. **1667** *Decay Chr. Piety* ix. §6 This root of bitterness ..sent forth some offsets to preserve its kind. **1796** C. MARSHALL *Garden.* vi. (1813) 81 The young offsets from strawberries slipped in autumn..will do for plants. **1856** E. S. DELAMER *Flower Garden* (1861) 21 The capability of propagation by offsets is another point of interest belonging to bulbs. **1880** GRAY *Struct. Bot.* iii. §1. 33 Houseleeks..and such-like fibrous-rooted succulent plants multiply freely by offsets. **1925** A. J. MACSELF *Bulb Gardening* xiv. 215 Almost all bulbs and corms throw what are termed offsets, which are first attached to the basal wing of the bulb, drawing nourishment from the parent bulb, but later developing an independent root system. **1970** *Sunday Tel.* 3 May 19/2 The striped pineapple plant..which I have known having to be guarded at Chelsea Show for fear of the offsets that slowly form the new plants getting missed.

3. *transf.* and *fig.* **a.** Something that springs or is derived from another; a lateral branch, an offshoot.

1756 AMORY *Buncle* (1770) II. 22 *note*, He has omitted.. many antiquities that are to be found in off-sets by the way. **1806** C. ANDERSON *Let.* in *Life* iv. (1854) 65 Mr. Macfarlane's Church (an offset from the Tabernacle). **1853** KANE *Grinnell Exp.* viii. (1856) 56 The glaciers which abut upon this sound are probably offsets from an interior mer de glace. **1863** M. J. BERKELEY *Brit. Mosses* iii. 19 The female organs..are disposed in little special offsets from the stem. **1870** ROCK *Text. Fabr.* Introd. 137 As an offset from symbolism, heraldry sprang up.

b. *spec.* A person, or tribe, springing collaterally from a specified family or race; a 'scion'.

1711 W. KING tr. *Naude's Ref. Politics* iii. 88 The kingdom at last..came to Pepin an off-set of the family of Clodion. **1834** MCMURTRIE *Cuvier's Anim. Kingd.* 42 Others assert that they are mere degenerate offsets from the Scythian and Tartar branch of the Caucasian stock. **1837** W. IRVING *Capt. Bonneville* II. 126 They speak the Shoshonie language, and probably are offsets from that tribe.

c. A minor branch of a mountain range; a spur.

1833 *Penny Cycl.* I. 139/2 A hill, called Mount St. Elias.. with its offsets, occupies the southern part of the island [Ægina]. **1879** L. G. SEGUIN *Blk. Forest* vi. 85 Hills, which are an offset of the Black Forest range.

d. *Naut.* A current flowing outwards from the shore. Also *attrib.*

1902 *Daily Chron.* 30 Aug. 5/6 There was..what maritime men call an offset at the time Holbein was swimming. *Ibid.* 2 Sept. 5/5 He had got the benefit of a good off-set current under him.

4. Something that 'sets off', embellishes, or throws something else into prominence; a set-off.

1675 G. R. tr. *Le Grand's Man without Passion* 53 The excellency of Vertue needs no off-sets. **1721** RAMSAY *Content* 371 Three waiting-maids..One mov'd beneath a load of silks and lace, Another bore the off-sets of the face. *a* **1864** FERRIER *Grk. Philos.* (1866) I. xii. 338 A foil or offset or complement.

5. Something 'set off' against something else so as to counterbalance it, as an item on one side of an account equivalent to one on the other side; anything that counterbalances, compensates, or makes up for something else: a set-off.

1769 *Conn. Col. Rec.* (1885) XIII. 207 A petition..setting forth that the petitioner and petitionee have executions against each other now in the hands of Ezekiel Williams,.. upon which the petitioner prays for an off-set of the same. **1792** N. CHIPMAN *Rep.* (1871) 83 Defendant may plead an offset of any sum due to him by the plaintiff. **1832** G. DOWNES *Lett. Cont. Countries* I. 305 As an offset to this, its luxury of flagging is very gratifying to British soles. **1870** LOWELL *Study Wind.* 219 The Spanish and English [tragedies] agree in the Teutonic peculiarity of admitting the humorous offset of the clown. **1932** *Daily Progress* (Charlottesville, Va.) 13 Aug. 1/3 Mr. Minor's action is what is known as an offset. He is asking the difference between $5,000 and the amount he alleges is due to him, or slightly more than $21,000. **1973** *Times* 11 June 14/1 Instead of being 50p better off, she gained only 15p a week. The High Court ruled that this automatic offset, which was standard commission procedure, was unlawful.

6. *Surveying.* A short distance measured perpendicularly from a main line of measurement, as from the straight line joining the two ends of an irregular boundary, to a point (*e.g.* an angle) in the boundary, in order to calculate the area of the irregularly bounded part.

1725 BRADLEY *Fam. Dict.* s.v. *Surveying*, Before you begin to measure the Line, take the Off-set to the Hedge, viz. the Distance ⊙ *e*. **1807** HUTTON *Course Math.* II. 62 Observe when you are directly opposite any bends or corners of the boundary..and from these measure the perpendicular offsets..with the offset-staff, if they are not very large, otherwise with the chain itself. **1879** *Cassell's Techn. Educ.* IV. 94/2 Before he proceeds to the determination of the distances or dimensions, technically called 'offsets'.

7. a. *Arch.* A horizontal or sloping break or ledge on the face of a wall, pier, etc., formed where the portion above is reduced in thickness.

1721 PERRY *Daggenh. Breach* 105 The Work being carry'd up with good Earth by proper Off-sets. **1772** HUTTON *Bridges* 97 Made with a broad bottom on the foundation, and gradually diminished in thickness by offsets. **1861** SMILES *Engineers* II. VII. vi. 183 Longitudinal bearers, firmly fixed to the offsets of the piers and abutments.

b. A horizontal terrace on the side of a slope or hill. (*local U.S.*)

1856 *Porter's Spirit of Times* 18 Oct. 106/3 The hearth-stone, garden, 'offsets',..and a thousand delicious memories..swarm before us now. **1864** in WEBSTER. **1873** J. H. BEADLE *Undevel. West* xxvi. 555 He then walked along a flat offset five or six feet below the house. **1878** —— *Western Wilds* x. 157 About half way up the cliff is a small offset, where grows a beautiful pine. **1889** in FARMER *Americanisms*.

8. See quot. (*U.S.*)

1884 KNIGHT *Dict. Mech.* Suppl., *Offset.* (*Carriage Hardware.*) The fork at the point in the back-stay where the branches separate to reach the hind axle at two points.

9. A more or less abrupt bend in a pipe, made to carry it past an obstruction in its course.

10. *Printing.* **a.** = SET-OFF: see quot.

1888 JACOBI *Printers' Voc.* 90 *Off-set*, the set-off of ink from one sheet to another of printed work whilst wet.

b. Used, freq. *attrib.*, of a printing process whereby an image is first impressed on a rubber-covered cylinder and thence transferred to the paper; also used *attrib.* of paper suitable for use in this process.

1906 *Brit. Printer* Oct. 283/2 The offset process—that is, working first on the blanket and offsetting from this on to the paper fed into the machine—is as the usual method. **1909** *Brit. Pat. 25,446* 4 Nov., For printing in lithographic machines by the so-called offset process, the lithographic design used as the basis of printing is generally the opposite or the reverse of that which would be used in ordinary direct lithographic printing... By our invention we provide a press ..for conveniently reversing designs or pulling proofs from reversed designs, such works being carried out by the offset method. **1918** *Pall Mall Gaz.* 29 June 8/5 A Litho Offset Press. **1921** *Dict. Occup. Terms* (1927) § 526 *Offset-litho operator*, a photographer..who obtains a negative, not reversed in position, with or without using a screen. **1926** *Encycl. Brit.* III. 220/2 By the offset method any paper, whether smooth- or rough-surfaced, may be used... Offset seems to be particularly adapted to colour-work. **1928** *Penrose Ann.* 111 The faulty soluble coating in so many classes of so-called offset papers, engenders printing troubles. **1929** *Horse* I. 61 The process employed in reproducing this notable painting is that known as offset. **1931** *Times Lit. Suppl.* 25 June p. viii/3 The rollicking offset-lithographs of Elsa Moeschlin. **1937** *Discovery* Oct. 297 An offset—a print made in a non-greasy powdered chalk. **1958** J. R. BIGGS *Woodcuts* 91 Offset cartridge, that is, the paper made for printing offset lithography, has a kindly surface, and a firm feel which is suitable for some subjects. **1958** *Times Lit. Suppl.* 4 Apr. 188/3 Dr. Willoughby's book, printed by offset from type-written script. **1967** KARCH & BUBER *Offset Processes* Pref., Although growth for the entire [printing] industry has been great, offset-lithography has grown at twice the rate of the industry as a whole. *Ibid.* ii. 12 Letterpress printed halftones..can often be..rescreened for printing by the offset-lithographic process. **1970** [see FLEXOGRAPHY]. **1976** *Sci. Amer.* Jan. 135/1 This work is unappealing typographically, dominated by crowded typewritten copy in grayish offset.

11. *Comb.* **offset-blanket**, a blanket or sheet of thick soft paper attached to a special cylinder on a printing-press for the purpose of receiving the offset, or excess of ink, on freshly printed sheets of paper; **offset-glass**, an oil-cup or journal-oiler with a glass globe flattened on one side so as to allow it to stand close to the side of an object (Knight *Dict. Mech.* Suppl. 1884); **offset-pipe**, a piece of pipe having a bend, used for effecting an offset: see 9 (ibid.); **offset purchase** *Econ.*, a purchase made abroad by agreement to counter-balance revenues spent in the buying country by the selling country; **offset-sheet** (*Printing*) = *set-off sheet*: see SET-OFF; **offset-staff** (*Surveying*), a rod used in measuring offsets; **offset well** (see quot. 1971); also *ellipt.* **offset**.

1966 *Economist* 20 Aug. 731/2 The Germans continue to be slow in making their military 'offset' purchases to counter the dollars which are drained away by the cost of keeping American troops in Germany. *a* **1974** R. CROSSMAN *Diaries* (1975) I. 550 There was an appalling incident in the House when he was caught out about our attempt to pay for the new American planes with offset purchases. **1807** HUTTON *Course Math.* II. 57 An offset-staff..for measuring the offsets and other short distances. It is 10 links in length, being divided and marked at each of the 10 links. **1922** *Petroleum Gloss.* (Pan Amer. Petroleum & Transport Co.) 32 *Offset well*, a well drilled opposite to a well on an adjoining property. **1924** *Amer. Review of Reviews* Mar. 231 Adjacent to one of the California reserves were oil lands that were under active development, with wells near enough to the boundary lines of the naval territory to cause a draining away of a certain amount of oil that lay beneath the navy's property. Under such circumstances, it is customary to sink what are known as 'offset wells'. **1932** *World Petroleum* III. 467/1 Production in the light oil zone at the discovery well in the center of the field..has since been considerably augmented by the completion of offset wells. **1971** WILLIAMS & MEYERS *Oil & Gas Terms* (ed. 3) 294 *Offset well*, a well drilled on one tract of land to prevent the drainage of oil or gas to an adjoining tract of land, on which a well is being drilled or is already in production. **1974** R. D. GRACE in P. L. Moore et al. *Drilling Practices Manual* 349 Deviation to 10 degrees was recorded in the north offset.

offset (ˌɒf'sɛt, ˌɔː-), *v.* [f. OFF- 1 + SET *v.*[1]]

1. *trans.* To set off as an equivalent *against* something else or part of something else; to balance by something on the other side or of contrary nature. Also said of the equivalent: To counterbalance, compensate.

1792 N. CHIPMAN *Rep.* (1871) 84 The demands of plaintiff and defendant must be mutual..or they will not be allowed to offset one against the other. **1860** EMERSON *Cond. Life*, *Power* Wks. (Bohn) II. 340 In human action, against the spasm of energy we offset the continuity of drill. **1877** *Scribner's Mag.* XV. 196/1 He had lost twenty-four Whig votes to offset the twenty-five Democratic votes which Lathers received. **1898** *Atlantic Monthly* Apr. 456/2 We traveled southward; but an ascent of a thousand feet offset, and more than offset, the change of latitude. **1930** G. B. SHAW *Androcles & Lion* Pref. 58 The triumphant solution of the first by our inventors and chemists has been offset by the disastrous failure of our rulers to solve the other. **1936** *Discovery* Sept. 278/1 To have a large family, it is essential for the parents to start at an early stage, and this is offset by the tendency to postpone marriage. **1968** *Lebende Sprachen* XIII. 51/2 The customer can offset claims on the bank only against liabilities in the same currency. **1975** E. F. L. BRECH *Princ. & Pract. Managem.* (ed. 3) v. x. 813 Companies were required to deduct tax at the standard rate from all dividends paid... The only exception to this rule was if the company had itself received a dividend under deduction of tax from some other UK company... The tax on the latter could then be offset and only the net balance was remittable.

2. a. *intr.* To spring, branch off, or project as an offset *from* something else (cf. prec. 3 a).

1853 KANE *Grinnell Exp.* xli. (1856) 371 Ridges, offsetting from the higher range, project in spurs laterally. **1877** R. F. BURTON in *Athenæum* 3 Nov. 568/3 To the north-west offsets the Ngombe..stream.

b. *trans.* To furnish with an offset (see prec. 9).

1889 *Sci. Amer.* 17 Aug. 107/1 Bending and offsetting of the pipe is a matter of economy or taste with the pipe fitters.

3. *Printing. intr.* To cause an off-set or set-off.

1888 JACOBI *Printers' Voc.* 122 When the ink off-sets from one sheet to another.

Hence **'off,setting** *vbl. sb.* and *ppl. a.*; *offsetting-blanket* = *offset blanket*: see OFFSET *sb.* 11.

1856 KANE *Arct. Expl.* I. iii. 33 Made the offsetting streams of the pack, and bore up to the northward and eastward. **1857** DICKENS *Perils Eng. Prisoners* iii, in *Househ. Words* Extra Christmas No., 7 Dec. 30/2 The off-settings and point-currents of the stream. **1889** [see 2 b]. **1908** *Daily Chron.* 24 Aug. 9/7, I was swimming against a strong offsetting tide. **1946** E. HODGINS *Mr. Blandings builds his Dream House* (1947) xvi. 208 The Blandings saw their house ..in all its gleaming whiteness, the delicate waving leaves.. the perfect offsetting foils. **1970** P. OLIVER *Savannah Syncopators* 28 The offsetting of the rhythms of the different drums against the gongs and against each other, sets up an exhilarating tension. **1975** *Times* 10 July 4/8 Mr Callaghan ..sees the release of Mr Hills as unconditional. No offsetting arrangement will be discussed.

off-set ('ɒfsɛt, ɔː-), *ppl. a.* [f. OFF *adv.* + SET *ppl. a.*] Set at an angle; placed off-centre or out of line.

1950 H. L. LORIMER *Homer & Monuments* v. 169 It lacks the off-set rim characteristic of the hoplite shield. **1950** *N.Z. Jrnl. Agric.* June 583/1 Equipment was further improved by acquiring sets of both tandem and off-set discs. **1960** *Farmer & Stockbreeder* 29 Mar. 76/3 This new 43in-cut offset harvester, known as the Taarup Tiger, weighs only 9½cwt.

off-set, *adv.* [f. OFF- 2 + SET *sb.*] Out of range of the cameras in a film or television set or studio.

1948 L. LEVY *Music for Movies* ii. 13 When we had decided on a piece of music to accompany any one scene, the band would play off set while the actor went through his actions or lines in time with the music. **1968** M. WOODHOUSE *Rock Baby* vii. 64 In the next shot he'd gone off-set, the camera had moved in.

'off-'ship, *a.* [f. OFF *prep.* + SHIP *sb.*; cf. *off-shore.*] That is off the ship.

1853 KANE *Grinnell Exp.* xxxiv. (1856) 310 When the ship's thermometer gave us −46°; my offship spirit −52°.

offshoot ('ɒfʃuːt, ɔː-). [f. OFF- 3 + SHOOT.]

1. A shoot springing from the stem or other part of a plant, a lateral shoot; a lateral branch projecting from the main part of anything material, as a nerve-trunk, mountain-range, street, etc.

1814 J. MURRAY in Smiles *Life* (1891) I. xi. 254 Stunted offshoots of felled trees. **1851** CARPENTER *Man. Phys.* (ed. 2) 230 The vesicular matter of the retina is an offshoot (so to speak) from that of the optic ganglion. **1872** RAYMOND *Statist. Mines & Mining* 275 A constant succession of mountain ranges, spurs, and offshoots from the great central chains. **1872** JENKINSON *Guide Eng. Lakes* (1879) 242 Lonscale Fell is the most eastern offshoot of Skiddaw.

b. *fig.* A collateral branch or descendant from a (specified) family or race.

1710 ADDISON *Tatler* No. 157 ¶10 [She] finds her self related, by some Off-shoot or other, to almost every great Family in England. **1874** SYMONDS *Sk. Italy & Greece* (1898) I. ix. 188 An offshoot of the great house which had already given Dukes to Florence.

c. Something which originated as a branch of something else; a derivative.

1801 STRUTT *Sports & Past.* III. vi. 222 Off-shoots from the Saturnalian disfigurement. **1867** LADY HERBERT *Cradle L.* ix. 139 A large school in the town, which has offshoots in the surrounding villages. **1878** BOSW. SMITH *Carthage* 9 The much older settlement of which it may have been an offshoot.

†**2.** Something that 'shoots off' or emanates; an emanation. *Obs. rare*$^{-1}$.

1674 N. FAIRFAX *Bulk & Selv.* 28 The body is..reeking out whole steams of little unseen off-shoots.

off shore, 'off-'shore, *adv. phr.* (*adj.*) [f. OFF *prep.* + SHORE *sb.* Opposed to IN SHORE.]

A. *adv.* **a.** In a direction away from the shore.

1720 DE FOE *Capt. Singleton* xvii. (1840) 285 The wind blowing off shore. **1854** G. B. RICHARDSON *Univ. Code* v. (ed. 12) 637 Lay her head off shore. **1895** *Chamb. Jrnl.* XII. 634/2 The dab travels in any direction, offshore or inshore, or along the coast.

b. At some distance from the shore. (In quot. 1745, inland from the shore.)

1745 P. THOMAS *Jrnl. Anson's Voy.* 50 Gusts of Wind from the Mountains Off Shore. **1887** *Fisheries U.S.* Sect. v. II. 16 The best months for whaling offshore are from September to May.

B. *adj.* (*attrib.* 'ɒfʃɔə(r), ɔː-). **a.** Moving or directed away from the shore.

1845 DARWIN *Voy. Nat.* viii. 159 An insect on the wing, with an off-shore breeze, would be very apt to be blown out to sea. **1860** *Merc. Marine Mag.* VII. 230, I might take the off-shore tack.

b. Situated, existing, or operating at a distance from the shore. Also, away from the mainland. Esp. in *off-shore island*, an island close to the mainland; *spec.* (*a*) any of a number of small islands off the coast of China, in the Formosa Strait; (*b*) Great Britain, jocularly regarded as an 'off-shore island' of Europe; hence *off-shore islander*.

1883 G. B. GOODE *Fish. Indust. U.S.A.* 20 (Fish. Exh. Publ.) The off-shore fisheries are prosecuted on the great oceanic banks extending from Nantucket to Labrador. **1884** *Science* 14 Nov. 463 The crews of the offshore fishermen. **1921** *Daily Colonist* (Victoria, B.C.) 5 Apr. 7/2 The seas were breaking so high over the bar here yesterday and today that some off-shore shipping was compelled to remain outside. **1946** *Sun* (Baltimore) 30 Jan. 11/3 Drastic measures should be taken to complete whatever trade negotiations and shipping are necessary to hasten receipt of raw sugars and off-shore refined sugars. **1958** *New Statesman* 30 Aug. 241/2 It is impossible to say whether it is intended merely to put a stop to the various patrol activities which Chiang's forces mount from the Quemoy and Matsu groups of islands; whether it is a prelude to the occupation of these off-shore islands; or whether, possibly, we are witnessing the first stage in the invasion of Formosa itself. **1959** M. LASKI (*title of play*) The offshore island. **1963** *Listener* 14 Feb. 310/2 Reflect (as often) on the advantages of being an off-shore islander living in an intellectual fog where there is no black and white. **1966** *Economist* 8 Jan. 119/3 British Petroleum is busily finding itself another offshore rig to replace the defunct 'Sea Gem'. **1968** *Listener* 29 Feb. 264/1 The Empire had gone: England was an offshore island in competition with the giants of the world. **1972** *Guardian* 16 Aug. 12 (*heading*) View from an offshore island. Linda Christmas on the Isle of Man. **1972** P. JOHNSON *Offshore Islanders* 79 William I's work in rebuilding the Old English monarchy was..continued by an Angevin who became a thorough offshore islander in his turn. **1973** *Guardian* 17 Jan. 10/1 The purpose of Mr Peter Walker's new Offshore Supplies Office is..to bring more work and wealth to Britain. *Ibid.* 11 Opportunities for British industry from offshore oil and gas developments. **1973** C. CALLOW *Power from Sea* iv. 89 All the big off-shore pipelines have been supplied by foreign groups. **1974** E. AMBLER *Dr. Frigo* I. 45 Off-shore oil? Is that what they were looking for? **1975** *Petroleum Rev.* XXIX. 397/3 With the North Sea rapidly becoming the area for the most intensive offshore diving activity in the world, the growing pains of this..profession are felt..in the UK. **1975** *Weekend Mag.* (Montreal) 15 Nov. 7/3 Jamaicans are luckier than most offshore workers. Because their government has a tax convention with Canada, they are exempt from paying income tax and Canada pension.

c. Of, pertaining to, or designating goods purchased with American dollars by and from countries other than the United States (see quots.). Also, designating the dollars used in this way.

1948 *Economist* 8 May 768/1 The 16 nations will be provided with 'off-shore' dollars for buying from Germany. **1949** *Times* 10 Sept. 5/7 *Off-shore purchases*, the name given to supplies to countries in receipt of Marshall aid, which are financed by Marshall aid but which do not come from the United States itself. **1952** *Economist* 13 Dec. 759 An off-shore purchase, as its name implies, is the buying of goods from countries other than the United States with dollars supplied by the United States. **1953** *Ann. Reg. 1952* 220 'Off-shore' orders for military equipment were placed with Italian industry. **1960** *New Left Rev.* July–Aug. 45/2 The buoyancy of the Japanese economy..has been..guaranteed by massive off-shore purchases of military equipment.

d. *offshore funds* (see quot. 1972).

1972 *Observer* 8 Oct. 18/1 Offshore funds, investment funds similar to unit trusts but registered abroad, usually in countries with advantageous tax situations. **1977** *Times* 29 Nov. 22/5 (*heading*) Authorized Units, Insurance & Offshore Funds.

off side, 'off-'side. *phr.* [f. OFF *prep.* + SIDE.] Away from one's own side; on the wrong side, *i.e.* in Football, Hockey, etc., between the ball and the opponent's goal. (The specific meaning varies in the different games.) **a.** As *advb. phrase.*

1867 *Sheffield Football Assoc. Rules*, Any player between an opponent's goal and goalkeeper (unless he has followed the ball there), is offside and out of play. **186.** *Rugby School Football Rules* vi. in *Footb. Ann.* (1868), A player is off side when the ball has been (kicked, touched) or is being run with by any of his own side behind him. **1882** *Standard* 20 Nov. 2/8 W. succeeded in kicking a goal, but he was declared to be off side at the time. **1897** *Outing* (U.S.) XXX. 284/2 We don't consider it fair to strike when off-side of an opponent.

b. *attrib.* or as *adj.* ('ɒfsaɪd, ɔː-). Also with stress on second syllable. Also quasi-*sb.*, an occasion on which a player is, or becomes, off side.

186. *Cheltenham Coll. Football Rules* vii. in *Footb. Ann.* (1868), No offside play is allowed. **1887** in B. James *England v Scotland* (1969) ii. 50 Dewhurst shot the ball in, and Cobbold helped it past Macauley, an appeal for offside by Dewhurst being disallowed. **1891** *Pall Mall G.* 16 Nov. 1/2 The majority of the critics averring that the Scottish half played a persistently offside game. **1895** *Outing* (U.S.) XXVII. 250/2 The off-side rule should be clearly understood. **1899** A. H. QUINN *Pennsylvania Stories* 24 Claims of 'off-side' were freely made and repudiated by the captains. **1925** *Kansas City* (Missouri) *Star* 22 Nov. 16/4 The ball was called back, and Kansas was penalized five yards for off-side. **1972** G. GREEN *Great Moments in Sport: Soccer* i. 24 Menti..twice put the ball in the England net, but each time the 'goal' was disallowed for offside. **1976** *Wymondham & Attleborough Express* 19 Nov. 24/4 Hempnall were not to be denied and hit back immediately, Borroughes beating the offside trap to convert a fine pass from Tweedale. **1976** *Norwich Mercury* 10 Dec. 8/5 However, their well-drilled off-side trap prevented Thurton from ever really getting to grips with the bone-hard ground and getting any rhythm into their game.

c. See also OFF *a.*

off-side, offside, *v. Austral. colloq.* [Back-formation from OFF-SIDER.] *intr.* To act as an off-sider or assistant. So **off-siding** *vbl. sb.*

1883 in M. Durack *Kings in Grass Castles* (1959) xxvi. 256, I have put up a yard on Galway since Uncle Jerry left—Pumpkin and Kangaroo offsiding. **1917** R. D. BARTON *Reminisc. Austral. Pioneer* vii. 93, I met a black-fellow..who was offsiding for the horsedriver, and was called Archie. **1930** V. PALMER *Passage* I. v. 41 A boy like Hughie might as well climb into his coffin right away as go off-siding for old Kunkel. **1936** I. L. IDRIESS *Cattle King* iii. 18 I'll get you a job offsidin' for me. **1953** A. UPFIELD *Murder must Wait* iv. 30 He's up at Mitford, and has asked me to send you up to off-side for him. **1960** —— *Bony & Kelly Gang* 167 Bony was asked to offside for Joe Flanagan, the settlement's electrician.

'off-sider, offsider. [f. OFF SIDE *phr.* + -ER[1].]

1. An animal on the off side (see OFF *a.* 2 a) of a team (see also quot. 1898); hence, an assistant, *spec.* a bullock-driver's assistant; a companion, deputy, partner. orig. and chiefly *Austral.* and *N.Z. colloq.*

1880 H. C. KENDALL *Songs from Mountains* 41 And, as to a team, over gully and hill He can travel with twelve on the breadth of a quill, And boss the unlucky 'offsides'. **1898** *Bulletin* (Sydney) 17 Dec. (Red page), In draught work the laziest or worst horse is on the off-side, under the whip; thus it is an inferior man or thing that is *a bit off*, *off color*, or *an offsider.* **1903** 'T. COLLINS' *Such is Life* 46 Jam him agen the off-sider, so's he can't shift. **1905** A. B. PATERSON *Old Bush Songs* 6 They say there's no delay To get an off-sider For the old bullock dray. *Ibid.* 8 An offsider is a bullock-driver's assistant. **1924** 'R. DALY' *Outpost* xx. 191 A high and mighty gentleman is Mr. Whelan nowadays! Seems to think I'm only an off-sider, and that miners are the only people who know anything about the country. **1929** W. SMYTH *Girl from Mason Creek* 206 The Maori boy who acted as the cook's offsider. **1931** V. PALMER *Separate Lives* 244 Shorty's advent as off-sider did nothing to help matters. He and the bullock-driver had long arguments on the way. **1934** T. WOOD *Cobbers* 19 Friends with everybody though, and an off-sider of the Governor, too. **1942** 'M. INNES' *Daffodil Affair* II. 46 Too right, Mr Wine. You couldn't have a better off-sider than Ron. **1952** A. GRIMBLE *Pattern of Islands* 243 There was nothing for it but to leave me hanging around at Ocean Island as offsider to anyone the High Commissioner might send up to take charge. **1962** *John o' London's* 19 July 64/2 Jill Dawson takes a job as an off-sider—'more than a secretary and different'. **1973** *Nation Rev.* (Melbourne) 31 Aug. 1451/1 'Would you wait outside,' 'Salisbury' now said to his offsider. 'I'd like a word with matron in private.' **1977** *National Times* (Austral.) 17 Jan. 5/5 He now works as a truckie's offsider.

2. In certain games: a player who is off side. *rare.*

1927 *Daily Tel.* 21 Feb. 14/1 Nor did the referee have an eagle eye for the offsider.

offskip, variant of OFFSCAPE.

off spin, 'off-'spin. *Cricket.* [OFF *a.* 2 b.] Spin that causes the ball to turn from the off side towards the leg side; bowling with this spin. Also *attrib.* Hence **off-spinner,** (*a*) a bowler who causes the ball to turn in this way; (*b*) a ball bowled with this spin; **off-spinning** *ppl. a.*

1904 P. F. WARNER *How we recovered Ashes* ii. 42 Arnold ..occasionally managed to get a little off-spin on the ball. **1924** N. CARDUS *Days in Sun* 52 It is not that bowling is deadlier nowadays than it was, say, in the days of conventional off-spinners like Hearne and Wainwright. **1955** MILLER & WHITINGTON *Cricket Typhoon* 189 The off-spinning Ian Johnson. **1955** *Times* 14 May 4/4 The latter.. was now bowling his normal off-spinners. **1956** R. ALSTON *Test Commentary* vi. 41 A superb piece of accurate off-spin bowling. *Ibid.* 42 This happy-looking cricketer..bowls a species of slow-medium off-spinner. *Ibid.* 43 He set about Johnson as no self-respecting off-spinner ought to behave to another of his kind. **1963** *Times* 14 May 4/5 Miller, of Cambridge, produced an excellent bowling performance, taking six wickets for 64 runs with his off-spin. **1975** *Cricketer* May 9/1 The 6 ft 3 ins off-spinner's recent games against England were in his winter Test rubber. **1977** *South China Morning Post* (Hong Kong) 13 Apr. 15/8 Richard Austin, better known as an opening bat and an off-spin bowler, was brought on.

offspring ('ɒfsprɪŋ, ɔː-). Forms: 1–7 **ofspring,** 1 **-springc,** 1–2 **-sprinc,** 2 **-sprinke,** 2–4 **-spreng(e,** 2–6 **-springe,** 3 **of sprench, ofsprung,** 3–6 **-spryng(e,** 3–7 **of-spring,** 5–6 **offsprynge,** 6–7 **-springe,** 3 (*Orm.*), 5– **offspring,** (7–8 **off-spring**). *β.* 3–5 **ospring(e,** (3–4 **osspringe,** 4 **ospreng, hospring, oxspring, oxpring**). [OE. *ofspring*, f. *of* prep. adv. OF, OFF + *spring-an* to SPRING.]

1. The progeny which springs or is descended from some one; children or young (or, more widely, descendants) collectively; progeny, issue. Applied without indef. art. to a number, or to one; with indef. art. always collective, and usually with an adj., as *a numerous offspring.* (Rarely of plants.)

c **949** in Kemble *Cod. Dipl.* II. 300 þis sy gedon for Siferð and for his ofspringc. *c* **1000** ÆLFRIC *On O. & N. Test.* (Grein 1872) 3 Eall heora ofspring ðe him of com. *c* **1175** *Lamb. Hom.* 75 On adam and on eue and on al heore ofsprinke. *c* **1200** ORMIN 16446 þatt all hiss offspring shollde ben Todrifenn and toskeȝȝredd Inn all þiss middellærd. *c* **1275** *Duty Christians* 21 in *O.E. Misc.* 142 We beoþ alle his of-sprung. **1297** R. GLOUC. (Rolls) 499 To him and to his of spring [*v.rr.* ospryng, osprynge]. *a* **1300** *Cursor M.* 135 (Cott.) Siþen i will of adam tell, Of hys oxspring [*Gött.* hospring; *Trin.* ospringe], and of noe. *c* **1400** MAUNDEV. (Roxb.) vii. 24 Whare Iacob þe patriarc and his offspring dwelt. *a* **1547** SURREY *Æneid* IV. (1557) D iij, Of Goddish race some ofspring shold he be. *a* **1577** SIR T. SMITH *Commw. Eng.* (1609) 14 Any of his sonnes or of spring. **1632** J. HAYWARD tr. *Biondi's Eromena* 187 Not onely a mother of a numerous off-spring, but also likely to be shortly a grand-mother. **1712** STEELE *Spect.* No. 263 ¶1 The Son endeavouring to appear the worthy Offspring of such a Father. **1770** GOLDSM. *Des. Vill.* 168 To tempt its new-fledg'd offspring to the skies. *a* **1814** *Forgery* III. ii. in *New Brit. Theatre* I. 474 The joyful promise of an off-spring from thee. **1875** BENNETT & DYER *Sachs' Bot.* 820 In the variety-hybrids [of plants]..some of the non-essential characters of the parents sometimes present themselves in the offspring uncombined side by side. **1881** J. OWEN *Even. w. Skeptics* I. 446 The modern hereditarian regards himself as the offspring mentally as well as physically of a long line of ancestors.

b. Rarely in *pl.*: †(*a*) in individual sense = children or descendants (*obs.*); (*b*) in collective sense = progenies, broods, families.

a **1548** HALL *Chron.*, *Edw. IV*, 237 The erle of Richemond, one of the ofsprynges, of the bloud of kyng Henry the sixte. **1675** TRAHERNE *Chr. Ethics* 300 As the woman was the glory of man, so were their off-springs the glory of both. **1686** PLOT *Staffordsh.* 277 The Naturalists took care to transmit to Posterity the birth-places..of all numerous Off-springs. **1756** TOLDERVY *Hist. 2 Orphans* IV. 209 The widows, and the offsprings of the poorer, the indigent clergy. **1808** *Mem. Female Philos.* I. 73 How much do these beloved offsprings add to our love and our happiness!

c. *fig.* Of persons in relation to place of birth, or origin.

1695 TRYON *Dreams* iii. 27 Man..is an Abridgment or Epitome thereof [the World], or if you please, its Son, or Off-Spring. **1697** DRYDEN *Virg. Georg.* I. 685 And there Euphrates her soft Off-spring arms. *a* **1839** PRAED *Poems* (1864) II. 300 Beautiful Athens, we will weep for thee; For thee and for thine offspring!

2. *fig.* That which springs from or is produced by something; produce, product; issue, outcome, result; 'fruit'. **a.** usually collective.

1609 BIBLE (Douay) *Lev.* xix. 25 The fifth yeare you shal eate the fruites, gathering the ofspring, that they bring forth. **1666** BOYLE *Orig. Formes & Qual.* Wks. 1772 III. 72 The prolific buds that are the genuine ofspring of the stock. **1669** STURMY *Mariner's Mag.* Ded., Accept..this Off-spring of some spare Hours. **1725** N. ROBINSON *Th. Physick* 209 Whey is the Offspring of Milk. **1826** KENT *Comm.* (1858) I. 4 The law of nations..is the offspring of modern times. **1856** FROUDE *Hist. Eng.* (1858) I. i. 69 The discoveries of Newton were the offspring of those of Copernicus.

†**b.** with *an* and *pl.* in individual sense. *Obs.*

1609 BIBLE (Douay) *Ezek.* xxxvi. 30, I wil multiplie the fruite of the tree, and the offsprings of the filde. 1748 HARTLEY *Observ. Man* II. iii. §1. 200 Almost all Kinds of Vice are the Excesses and monstrous Offsprings of Natural Appetites. 1760–72 H. BROOKE *Fool of Qual.* (1809) IV. 44 Our spirits are the offsprings of his divine spirit. *a* 1814 *Forgery* III. ii. in *New Brit. Theatre* I. 465 These dark engender'd looks,..offsprings of detestable despair.

†3. A GENERATION (sense 5). *Obs.*

a 1300 *Cursor M.* 11415 (Cott.) þar þai offerd, praid, and suank, Thre dais noþer ete ne dranc, þus thoru ilk oxspring [*Gött.*, *Trin.* ospring, *Laud* ofsprynɡ] þai did. 1587 GOLDING *De Mornay* vi. 63 Yᵉ begetting, ingendring and spreading foorth of al things from offspring to offspring.

†4. The fact of springing or descending from some ancestor or source; descent, origination, derivation, origin. *Obs.*

c 1420 *Sir Amadas* (Weber) 48 Y-comen of hye osprynɡ. *c* 1510 BARCLAY *Mirr. Gd. Manners* (1570) D ij b, Eacus..Of whom this saide Pyrrus had his birth and ofspring. 1551 T. WILSON *Logike* 10 b, These vertues, though their ofspryng bee from God, yet tyme maketh theim perfecte in the iyes of man. 1644 J. BERKENHEAD *Serm.* 4 All the armies upon earth were to deduce their offspring from that one Adam, by generation. 1698 J. CRULL *Muscovy* 3 The..Duina owes its name and off-spring to a Lake of the same Name. 1715 M. DAVIES *Athen. Brit.* I. 283 A great inlet into the offspring of those Deluding Antiquities.

†**b.** *transf.* Family, race, stock; ancestry. *Obs.*

a 1300 *Cursor M.* 13598 (Cott.) þe neist men of his oxspring Did þai þan be-for þam bring. *c* 1300 *Harrow. Hell* 20 And so wes seid to Davyd the kyng, That wes of Christes oune ofsprynɡ. *c* 1440 *Promp. Parv.* 372/1 Osprynge..*idem quod* kynrede. 1560 DAUS tr. *Sleidane's Comm.* 12 b, The Frenchmen come of the same ofspringe that we do. 1582 STANYHURST *Æneis* II. (Arb.) 46, I may not, I wyl not deny my Greecian ofspring. 1612 BREREWOOD *Lang. & Relig.* xiii. 117 What if the innumerable people of..the huge continent of America, be also of the same off-spring?

†5. That from which anything springs or originates: spring, fountain, source, original. *Obs.*

1538 LELAND *Itin.* V. 64 Wher as the very Hed of Isis ys in a great Somer Drought apperith very litle or no water, yet is the stream servid with many Ofspringes resorting to one Botom. 1597 A. M. tr. *Guillemeau's Fr. Chirurg.* 22 b/1 Having discovered and denudatede the Polipum vnto his roote or first offspringe and originalle. 1604 PARSONS *3rd Pt. Three Convers. Eng.* 85 The fountaines or offsprings, from whence this diuersity hath taken her beginninge.

¶ The alleged sense 'Propagation, generation', repeated in Dicts. from J., appears to be an error, J.'s quot. being app. in sense 1.

1594 HOOKER *Eccl. Pol.* I. v. §2 That which cannot hereunto [to eternal existence] attain personally, doth seek to continue itself another way, that is by offspring and propagation.

[**off-square**: see *half-square* in HALF-, II n.]

off stage, off-stage, *adv.* (*phr.*) and *a.* [f. OFF *prep.*, OFF- 4 b + STAGE *sb.*] Away from the stage; that is not appearing or occurring on a stage (see also quot. 1952). Also *transf.* and *fig.*

1922 *Times Lit. Suppl.* 12 Oct. 647/1 It is of no relevance to the story whether the apathy is produced by cocaine or Buddhism; the cause, whatever it is, is 'off stage', as it were. 1933 ST. JOHN ERVINE *Theatre in My Time* vii. 43 A player with a distinctive and adenoidal voice..made his first speech off-stage. 1942 BERREY & VAN DEN BARK *Amer. Thes. Slang* §585/1 *Offstage leading lady*, an actor's sweetheart. 1948 *Times* 17 Jan. 5/3 The off-stage noises of those who work to distract attention from what is really going on. 1952 GRANVILLE *Dict. Theatr. Terms* 125 *On-stage*. Like off-stage, this is a somatic adjective. The on-stage arm is the one nearest the centre of the stage when an artiste faces the audience. Thus, in position *stage left*, the right will be the on-stage arm, and the left the offstage one... The same applies to furniture and properties so positioned. 'Bring the settee a little more off-stage' (i.e. towards the side). 1959 J. WAIN *Travelling Woman* viii. 110 The philosopher emptied one final shovelful of ashes into the bucket, carried it off to some unknown destination offstage, came back. *Ibid.* ix. 128 You didn't know me. I was just a figure off-stage somewhere. 1961 J. MCCABE *Mr. Laurel & Mr. Hardy* (1962) i. 31 If any of America's millions had seen the offstage Charles Spencer Chaplin of 1910, they might well [etc.]. 1967 M. ARGYLE *Psychol. Interpersonal Behaviour* vii. 125 People do not work at their image-projection all the time; there is a difference between being 'on-stage' and 'off-stage'; in the former, people feel under observation and are very concerned about the image they are projecting. 1975 *New Yorker* 21 Apr. 103/3 The climax is the obligatory offstage pistol shot.

off-street, *a.* [f. OFF- 4 b + STREET *sb.*] That is not on a street; esp. of parking facilities: located away from main streets. Also, that does not take place on a street.

1929 *Amer. City* Sept. 133/1 Off-street loading facilities.. reducing traffic congestion. 1937 *Sun* (Baltimore) 4 Dec. 8/1 Provision for off-street parking..should help solve the parking problem in that vicinity. 1947 *Evening Sun* (Baltimore) 12 Sept. 2/5 Fringe parking on the perimeter of the business district would help relieve traffic congestion whereas providing more off-street space for automobiles in the heart of a city would actually aggravate the problem. 1958 *Times* 1 Aug. 5/5 The provision of authorized long-term street parking places in the vicinity of railway stations where there are insufficient off-street facilities. 1969 [see FEED *v.* 7 b]. 1977 *Stornoway Gaz.* 27 Aug. 1/5 The Council say the proposals contain inadequate provision for the off-street servicing of the premises.

offtake ('ɒfteɪk, 'ɔː-). [f. OFF- 3 + TAKE *sb.*]

1. The action of taking off; *spec.* the taking of commodities off the market; purchase of goods. Also, the removal of oil from a reservoir or supply. Also *attrib.*

1885 *Manch. Exam.* 10 June 4/4 In jacconets..supply and offtake seem to have been brought pretty well into conformity. 1896 *Westm. Gaz.* 9 Sept. 2/2 The proportion of the total off-take of the Shanghai market supplied by Great Britain or her Colonies was 79 per cent. 1955 *Times* 12 May 17/2 Producers have not been keen recently to tender metal for the stockpile because of the high rate of commercial off-take. *Ibid.* 25 June 9/1 A reduced offtake at home has ensued on top of a persistent decline in export sales. 1960 *Farmer & Stockbreeder* 19 Jan. 5/1 Only a moderate offtake is reported for English barley but offers remain generally small. 1969 *Hindu* (Madras) 3 Aug. 1/5 With the opening of free market shops, the off-take from the existing ration shops would go down. 1973 'D. JORDAN' *Nile Green* iv. 23 We might work out some sort of guarantee based on the projected offtake of their new oil discoveries in the Western Desert. 1974 *Information Handbk.* 1974–5 (Shell Internat. Petroleum Co.) 73 In Spain the Amposta field..started production in February 1973 and at the end of the year had averaged 16 800 b/d: owing to offtake difficulties, well below the scheduled 30 000 b/d. 1975 *Petroleum Rev.* XXIX. 317/1 Links with local supply systems are effected at small offtake stations, where the pipework and associated control valves appear above ground.

2. That which is taken off; a deduction.

1892 *Labour Commission Gloss.*, *Off-takes*, all deductions retained from the men's wages for house-rent, house-coal, doctor's fees, tool-sharpening, closed lights, etc.

3. A channel by which, or place where, something is taken off: *spec.* **a.** *Mining.* A subsidiary drainage-level: see quot.

1875 *Ure's Dict. Arts* III. 320 There are subsidiary levels, called off-takes or drifts, which discharge the water of a mine, not at the mouth of a pit, but..where, from the form of the country, it may be run off level free.

b. The taking off or flowing out of a branch-stream from the main channel of a river; the place of such outflow.

1888 *19th Cent.* Jan. 44 The third of the Hugli headwaters has its principal offtake from the Ganges again about forty miles further down.

off target, off-target, *adv.* (*phr.*) and *a.* [f. OFF *prep.*, OFF- 4 b + TARGET *sb.*[1]] So as to fail to reach a target; that misses a target (freq. *fig.*).

1959 J. L. AUSTIN *Sense & Sensibilia* (1962) ix. 89 The second example is ineffective, off-target, in a rather similar way. 1960 V. JENKINS *Lions Down Under* 112 His kicking, for once, was off-target. 1967 *N.Y. Herald Tribune Internat.* 11–12 Feb. 10/6 The 'Daily Mail' carried Philip's entire speech with the headline 'Never Before a Royal Speech as Outspoken as This' and said in an editorial it thought he was way off target. 1977 R. E. HARRINGTON *Quintain* vi. 54 Though it was off-target, and glancing, the blow rocked him back.

off-the-peg: see PEG *sb.*[1] 1 e.

off time, off-time, *sb.* [OFF *a.* 4.] A time when one is off duty or free from work; a holiday; a time when normal activity is reduced or suspended.

1866 DICKENS *Mugby Junction* in *All Year Round* Extra Christmas No. 10 Dec. 6/1 The answer to his inquiry, 'Where's Lamps?' was..that it was his off-time. 1894 MRS. H. WARD *Marcella* II. III. iv. 323 In hospital..every hour was full, and there were always orders to follow. And the 'off' times were no trouble—I never did anything else but walk up and down the Embankment..or go to the National Gallery. 1902 *Westm. Gaz.* 26 Aug. 8/1 The York Meeting ..marks the close of the 'off' time, which has been experienced since the Goodwood gathering. 1936 W. R. TITTERTON *G. K. Chesterton* II. iii. 139, I used the stage there at off times to advertise the plays that we ran. 1940 C. DAY LEWIS tr. *Georgics of Virgil* I. 24 Winter's an off-time for farmers. 1956 'J. WYNDHAM' *Seeds of Time* 216 In his off times he occupied himself..in teaching Lellie. 1975 *BP Shield Internat.* May 1/3 We are insisting on their having their homes within 70 miles of Aberdeen because, should there be an emergency, then they can be easily called in during their off-time to deal with it.

off-time, *a.* *U.S. slang.* [f. OFF 4 b + TIME *sb.*] Out of time; badly timed (see also quots.).

1942 BERREY & VAN DEN BARK *Amer. Thes. Slang* §582 *Off-time jive*, a sorry excuse. 1946 MEZZROW & WOLFE *Really Blues* xiii. 237 If somebody passed a remark that wasn't in line, he'd start singing and beating on the offtime cat. *Ibid.* 377 *Offtime*, out of harmony, old-fashioned, corny, offensive. 1973 C. HIMES *Black on Black* 188, I can stop in front of a joint where the jukebox's playing and cut a step of off-time boogie.

†'**offtract.** *rare.* [irreg., app. f. OFF *adv.* + *-tract* in *abstract*, *extract*. Cf. Ger. *abzug*.] That which is drawn or taken from something as its source.

1784 J. BARRY in *Lect. Paint.* i. (1848) 77 The energies of language were easier, more at command, and, as the more immediate offtract [*printed* offtrack] of thought, naturally antecedent to the energies of art. *Ibid.* ii. 117 It is the mind of the artist which is visible in what he does: the one must necessarily be an offtract of the other.

†**o'ffusc,** *a.* *Obs. rare*⁻¹. [a. F. *offusque* (15th c. in Godef.), or ad. It. *offusco* (Florio), L. type **offusc-us* (not found in ancient L.) f. *of-*, *ob-* (OB- 1) + *fuscus* dark.] Dark, dusky: = OBFUSCOUS.

1849 LYTTON *Caxtons* lii (*Blackw.* Mar. 287) Does it [silence] not wrap a man round with as offusc and impervious a fold?

†**o'ffuscant.** *Obs.* [ad. L. *offuscānt-em*, pr. pple. of *offuscāre* to darken (see next); or ad. corresp. F. *offusquant*.] One who obfuscates or obscures; one who opposes enlightenment, an obscurantist.

1799 W. TAYLOR in *Monthly Rev.* XXIX. 180 The offuscants (as they [the 'Illuminés'] affected to call the teachers of vulgar credulity). 1806 —— in *Ann. Rev.* IV. 722 They are systematic offuscants; not reasoners, but mystics.

o'ffuscate, *ppl. a.* Now *rare.* [ad. L. *offuscāt-us*, pa. pple.: see next.] = OBFUSCATE *ppl. a.*

1603 HOLLAND *Plutarch's Mor.* 658 Their eie sight..is offuscate and darkened by the great light. *a* 1615 DONNE *Ess.* (1651) 104 The certainty of the Person or History is therby offuscate. 1840 *New Monthly Mag.* LVIII. 458 His offuscate eyes.

o'ffuscate, *v.* Now *rare.* [f. L. *offuscāt-*, ppl. stem of *offuscāre* to darken, f. *of-*, *ob-* (OB- 1) + *fuscāre* to darken, *fusc-us* dark. See also OBFUSCATE.]

1. = OBFUSCATE *v.* 1.

1656 BLOUNT *Glossogr.*, *Offuscate*, to make black or dark. 1659 B. HARRIS *Parival's Iron Age* 236 The exhalations.. which offuscate, or darken the Sun. 1693 EVELYN *De la Quint. Compl. Gard.* I. II. xvi. 45, I should fear those Dwarfs might grow so large as to offuscate or shadow the Wall-Fruit or Espaliers. 1807 HERSCHEL in *Phil. Trans.* XCVII. 184 The brilliancy of the metalline ground on which these faint rings are seen, the contrast of which will offuscate their feeble appearance. 1816 F. H. NAYLOR *Hist. Germany* I. II. xiv. 677 A constellation, by whose transcendent radiance all inferior luminaries were offuscated.

2. = OBFUSCATE *v.* 2.

1623 HART *Arraignm. Ur.* Ded. A, Hee was forced to yeeld to such conditions as did much offuscate the splendor of his former victories. *a* 1734 NORTH *Exam.* II. v. §1 (1740) 315 To take all Occasions and Handles that may operate in that Design, and to drop or offuscate all the rest. 1834–43 SOUTHEY *Doctor* cxlix. (1862) 389 That knowledge is.. obliterated or offuscated by its [the soul's] union with the body. 1841 D'ISRAELI *Amen. Lit.* (1867) 358 His gaiety and his gravity offuscate one another.

3. = OBFUSCATE *v.* 3.

1632 J. HAYWARD tr. *Biondi's Eromena* 93 She had her spirits so offuscated as..not to know her selfe. 1727 *Philip Quarll* 241 The Tears..which offuscated his Sight. *a* 1734 NORTH *Lives* (1826) I. 336 Some men's timidity offuscates their understandings. 1871 M. COLLINS *Mrq. & Merch.* III. ix. 230 Mowbray's brain..was somewhat offuscated.

Hence **o'ffuscated, o'ffuscating** *ppl. adjs.*

a 1659 OSBORN *Misc.*, etc. (1673) 582 Such a perplexed knowledge, as renders their understanding..more offuscated and gloomy. 1708 *Brit. Apollo* No. 33. 2/1 To Inlighten their Offuscated Intellects. 1798 W. TAYLOR in Robberds *Mem.* I. 237 The future offuscating philosophy. 1828 D'ISRAELI *Chas. I*, I. iii. 35 These vain and offuscating disputations.

offu'scation. Now *rare.* [ad. L. *offuscātiōn-em*, n. of action from *offuscāre* (see prec.): cf. F. *offuscation*, also *obf-* (14th c.).] = OBFUSCATION.

1502 *Ord. Crysten Men* (W. de W. 1506) IV. xx. 220 To knowe offuscacyon of the very knowlege. 1629 BP. HALL *Reconciler* 16 The wofull and gloomie offuscations of the Church. 1755 *Phil. Trans.* XLIX. 410 The atmosphere.. had the appearance of clouds and notable offuscation. 1863 LYTTON *Caxtoniana* II. 191 This offuscation of intelligence in verse-writers.

†**o'ffusque,** *v.* *Obs. rare.* [a. F. *offusque-r* (14th c. in Hatz.-Darm.), ad. L. *obf-*, *offuscāre* to darken: see OFFUSCATE and the earlier *obfusque*, OBFUSK.] *trans.* To obfuscate, obscure: = OBFUSK.

Richardson cites BOLINGBROKE, but the orig. ed. has *obfusques*: see OBFUSK *v.* 9, quot. *a* 1751.

offward ('ɒfwəd, ɔː-), *adv.* (*sb.*) and *a.* [f. OFF *adv.* + -WARD.]

A. *adv.* In a direction or position off or away from something; *spec.* (*Naut.*) away from the shore. Also quasi-*sb.* in phr. *to the offward.*

1600 ABP. ABBOT *Exp. Jonah* 567 Then Ionas was so wise, to be as far of-ward as possibly he might. 1692 *Capt. Smith's Seaman's Gram.* I. xvi. 80 *Off-ward*, is contrary to the shore; as the stern of a Ship lies to the Off-ward, and her head to the shoreward. 1778 [W. MARSHALL] *Minutes Agric.* 13 May 1775, The cattle may be eased, by turning *offward* or *toward*, at pleasure. 1794 *Rigging & Seamanship* II. 254 **Offward*, from the shore. 1867 SMYTH *Sailor's Word-bk.* s.v., The ship heels offward.

B. *adj.*

†**1.** Turned or directed off or away; averse. *Obs.*

1563 MAN *Musculus' Common-pl.* 22 To haue any ofwarde will and turned from God. 1626 BP. ANDREWES *Serm.* (1641) 163 Righteousnesse was not so off-ward before, but she is now as forward.

†**2.** = OFF C. 2 a. *Obs. rare*⁻¹.

1710 *Lond. Gaz.* No. 4727/4 A little white on his offward Heel behind.

Hence †'**offwardness** *Obs.*, state of being turned away, averseness, aversion.

1600 ABP. ABBOT *Exp. Jonah* 1 His of-wardnesse from God and God's favourable inclination ever more to him. *Ibid.* 137 Their marvellous of-wardnesse and unwillingness ..to the shedding of bloud.

'**offwards,** *adv.* *rare*⁻¹. [f. as prec. + -WARDS.] = OFFWARD A.

1692 *Capt. Smith's Seaman's Gram.* II. xv. 123 For the Rack offwards 7 foot.

off-white, *sb.* and *a.* [OFF- 5.] **A.** *sb.* A colour very close to white, usu. with grey or yellow tinge. **B.** *adj.* Almost white. Also *fig.*, not standard; not socially acceptable; ***off-white collar***: of a worker or occupation: not manual but not quite 'white collar'.

1927 *Daily Mirror* 10 Dec. 16/1 Jumper suits in white, yellow, or what the Paris dressmakers call 'off whites' will see you through. **1931** *Daily Express* 18 Mar. 5/3 Fashionable colours are all off-white shades such as palest blues, greys, pinks, and greyish-greens. **1937** F. STARK *Baghdad Sketches* 187 A voluminous nightdress very much 'off white'. **1951** H. NICOLSON *Diary* 29 Aug. (1968) 208, I go to the B.B.C. to listen to recordings of King George's broadcasts. His voice is so like the present King's... it is what the B.B.C. would call 'off-white', meaning slightly cockney. **1954** M. PROCTER *Hell is City* III. ix. 120 The interrogation room..had white-tiled walls and an off-white ceiling. **1962** *Guardian* 13 Apr. 1/7 Off-white-collar workers ..are showing an unpatriotic reluctance to subsidise richer men's meals. **1962** A. G. FRANK in *Monthly Rev.* (N.Y.) Nov. 384 There is movement into white or off-white collar jobs. **1962** M. ALLINGHAM *China Governess* (1963) iii. 51, I can be as 'off-white' as I like. I've no code to live up to. **1965** —— *Mind Readers* ix. 94 'You're telling me!' The voice could produce an off-white accent. **1969** Y. CARTER *Mr. Campion's Farthing* ii. 9 A very slight off-white accent... A suggestion of the lower orders. **1971** *Nature* 15 Jan. 175/2 It yielded about 200 mg of pure wildfire toxin as a fluffy, off-white powder.

off-wring, *v. poet. rare*$^{-1}$. [OFF- 1.] *trans.* To wring or wrench off.

a **1889** G. M. HOPKINS *Poems* (1918) 90 His twiny books Fast he opens, last he offwrings Till walk the world he can with bare his feet.

offytorie, obs. corrupt form of OFFERTORY.

† **of-'gast** *ppl. a.*, obs. by-form of AGAST, AGHAST: see OF-^{2}.

c **1305** *St. Kenelm* 212 in *E.E.P.* (1862) 53 So sore hi were of gaste.

of'get, *v. Obs. rare.* In 3 of-ȝete(n, -ȝiten. [f. OF- + OE. *ȝietan, -ȝitan* to GET. Cf. ONGET, OE. *onȝietan* to perceive.] *trans.* To perceive, discern.

c **1205** LAY. 25777 ȝif þu hine miht of-ȝiten. *c* **1275** *Ibid.* 26623 ȝef hii of-ȝete mihte.

† **of'go**, *v. Obs.* [OE. *ofgán*, f. OF-^{1} + *gán* to GO. For sense-development, cf. Ger. *bekommen* to obtain. For senses 3, 4, see OF-^{3}.]

1. *trans.* To demand, require, exact.

c **1000** ÆLFRIC *Hom.* II. 340 Ic ofga his blodes gyte æt ðinum handum. *c* **1175** *Lamb. Hom.* 117 Ic of-ga et þe mid groman his blod.

2. To gain, win, obtain; to obtain by merit, to deserve, earn.

c **1000** ÆLFRIC *Hom.* I. 118 We sceolon..mid halȝum mæȝnum ðone eard ofgan þe we..forluron. *c* **1100** *O.E. Chron.* an. 1098 His broðer Rodbert wearð his yrfe numa, swa swa he hit æt þam cynge of-eode. *a* **1225** *Ancr. R.* 390 Ich hit wulle heorteliche uorto of-gon þine heorte. **1340** *Ayenb.* 13 He ssell come ate day of dome to..yelde to echen be þet he heþ of-guo ine þise wordle. **1377** LANGL. *P. Pl.* B. IX. 106 To go..and agon [*MS. W* ofgon] her lyflode.

3. To go through, permeate.

1297 R. GLOUC. (Rolls) 3173 Vor þe poyson in is slep þe veines so þoru soȝte þat it of eode [*v.r.* ouerwent] al þat body and to deþe him sone broȝte.

4. To come up with, overtake.

c **1300** *Beket* 52 Me ne miȝt hem noȝt ofgo.

Hence † **of'going** *vbl. sb.*, deserving, earning.

1340 *Ayenb.* 215 Hare Demere..ham ssel yelde be hare ofgoinge.

† **of'grame**, *v. Obs. rare.* [f. OF-^{2} + GRAME *v.*] *trans.* To vex, irritate. Known only in pa. pple. ***of-gramed*** vexed: cf. AGRAMED.

c **1200** *Trin. Coll. Hom.* 69 Þus here aȝene sinnes hem shendeð and hie ben of-gramede wið hem selfen.

† **of'grede**, *v. Obs. rare.* Pa. t. 4 ofgrad. [f. OF-^{1} + GREDE *v.* to cry.] *trans.* To call for, summon.

13.. *K. Alis.* 581 (Bodley MS.) The kyng it seiȝ and wonder had: Alle his maistres he of-grad.

† **of'greet**, *v. Obs. rare.* Pa. t. 4 ofgrett. [app. f. OF-^{2} + GREET *v.*^{1} 2.] *trans.* ? To strike off.

c **1330** *Arth. & Merl.* 5946 (Kölbing) Þe heþen hounde, Þat ich of hem who so mett Hastiliche þe heued ofgrett.

† **of'grisen**, *ppl. a. Obs. rare.* [By-form of *agrisen*, pa. pple. of AGRISE *v.*: see OF-^{2}.] Terrified.

c **1200** *Trin. Coll. Hom.* 135 Ne beo þu zacharie noht of-grisen. *Ibid.* 173 Hie..beð swiðe of-grisen.

† **of'hear**, *v. Obs. rare.* [f. OF-^{3} + HEAR *v.*] *trans.* To hear; or ? to overhear.

a **1300** *K. Horn* 41 A Payn hit of-herde And hym wel sone answarede.

† **of'heat**, *v. Obs. rare.* Pa. pple. in 3 ofhæt. [f. OF-^{1} + OE. *hǽtan* to HEAT.] *trans.* To overcome with heat.

c **1205** LAY. 9314 He wes swiðe of-hæt [*c* 1275 a-feat] þat al his burne wes bi-swat.

† **of'hold**, *v. Obs.* [OE. *ofhealdan*, f. OF-^{1} + *healdan* to HOLD.] *trans.* To withhold, keep back.

1035-50 *O.E. Chron.* an. 1035 (MS. C) He..let niman of hyre ealle ða betstan gærsuma ðe heo ofhealdan ne mihte. **1340** *Ayenb.* 9 Þis heste ous uorbyet to nimene and of-hyealde oþre manne þing. *Ibid.* 46 He ne may naȝt ine guode manere of-healde þet he wynþ. **1393** LANGL. *P. Pl.* C. III. 238 Mynstrales and messagers..with-helde [*MS. I* of-helden] hym halfe a ȝere.

† **of'hungered**, *a. Obs.* Forms: 1 ofhingrod, 3 of-hungret, (of-fingred), 3-4 of-hongred, of-hungred, 4 of-hongret. (Hence AFINGERED, q.v.) [OE. *ofhyngred, -od*, f. OF-^{1} + pa. pple. of *hyngran, -ian* to HUNGER.] Afflicted with hunger, very hungry, famished.

c **1000** ÆLFRIC *Hom.* I. 204 Eadiȝe beoð þa þe sind of hingrode and oflyste rihtwisnysse. *c* **1205** LAY. 31804 No nan uolc on londe: þat of-fingred nes sære. *a* **1225** *Ancr. R.* 376 ȝif þu ert of hungred efter þe swete. *Ibid.* 404 ȝif þi uo is offingred, ȝif him uode. *c* **1290** *S. Eng. Leg.* I. 420/15 Þulke þat weren a-cale and of-hongred. *c* **1330** *Amis & Amil.* 1908 Wel sore of-hungred and cold. **1393** LANGL. *P. Pl.* C. XII. 43 Boþe a-fyngred [*v.r.* of-hongret] and a-furst.

ofice, oficere, obs. ff. OFFICE, OFFICER.

‖ **oficina** (ɒfɪ'siːnə). [Sp., ad. L. *officīna*: see OFFICINA.] A factory or 'works' in a Spanish-speaking country, as in South America or Mexico.

1889 *Daily News* 10 Dec. 2/2 The extension of the Nitrate Railway Company to the Southern nitrate deposits must prove to be of great importance in the future.. It is probable that one or two other oficinas might use the line when made. **1897** *Westm. Gaz.* 4 Nov. 8/1 The directors had the oficina closed down entirely..and the works will remain closed until there is a reasonable advance in the price of nitrate. **1942** *Econ. Geol.* XXXVII. 198 Fig. 9 shows an oficina that has derived its nitrate from one of the small 'islands' or 'peninsulas' rising above the playa. **1966** POHL & ZEPP *Latin Amer.* vii. 120 Most of the *oficinas* are in the north, where groundwater is available.

† **of'ken**, *v.*^{1} *Obs. rare.* [f. OF-^{2} + KEN *v.*^{1}: cf. AKEN *v.*^{1}] *trans.* To recognize, descry, perceive.

c **1275** LAY. 1659 Þo Goffare þe king þane castel of-kende [*c* 1205 kennede].

† **of'ken**, *v.*^{2} *Obs. rare.* [f. OF-^{2} + KEN *v.*^{2}: cf. AKEN *v.*^{2}] *trans.* To bring forth, give birth to.

c **1250** *Doomsday* 42 in *O.E. Misc.* 164 Heo schulen iseon the lauedi þat ihesu crist of-kende.

Oflag ('ɔflag). [G., abbrev. of *offizier(s)lager* officers' camp.] In Nazi Germany: a prison-camp for captured enemy officers.

1941 [see ILAG]. **1945** *News Chron.* 20 Apr. 1/6 Unlike the guards of the stalags and oflags, they never wait to give themselves up. **1958** P. KEMP *No Colours or Crest* xii. 265 Her husband..had been a prisoner of the Germans since 1939 in an Oflag in Posen. **1969** *Listener* 10 Apr. 503/3 Wing-Commander Wassler (who for practical purposes is still in his wartime Oflag). **1974** *Times* 12 Oct. 12/7 He found himself in Oflag IHA/H, a prisoner-of-war camp in Spannenburg.

'oflete. *Obs.* Forms: 1 oflǽte, -láte, -léte, (ofeléte), 2 ouelete, (3 ouelete), 9 of(f)lete. [mod. ad. OE. *oflǽte, -láte* wk. fem., ad. eccl. L. *oblāta*, sb. use of fem. pa. pple. of *offerre* to offer; cf. O.Icel. *obláta, oblát*, OHG. *oblâta* (Ger. *oblate*), and see OBLEY. (If the old word had survived, its mod. form would have been *ov(e)let*, or *owlet*.)]

1. An offering, sacrifice, oblation.

c **825** *Vesp. Psalter* I. 21 Ðonne ðu onfoest onseȝdnisse rehtwisnisse oflatan. *c* **1000** *Ags. Ps.* xxxix. 6 Noldest þu na offrunga and oflata nane. *a* **1300** *E.E. Psalter* ibid., Offrand and ouelote wald þou noght se. [**1881** T. E. BRIDGETT *Hist. Holy Eucharist* I. 167 A pure oflete or oblation.]

2. A sacramental wafer; a wafer generally.

c **1000** ÆLFRIC *Hom.* II. 174 Benedictus..asende ane ofeletan, and het mid þære mæssian for ðam mynecenum. *c* **1000** *Sax. Leechd.* III. 42 Wið weorh man sceal niman .vii. lytle oflætan swylce man mid ofrað & writtan þas naman on ælcre oflætan. *c* **1200** *Trin. Coll. Hom.* 97 Erest it beð ouelete ..and efter..turneð þe bred to fleis. [**1844** LINGARD *Anglo-Sax. Ch.* (1858) I. vii. 268 The *offlete* or bread for the oblation. **1849** ROCK *Ch. of Fathers* I. ii. 156 Instead of ofletes these [altar] Breads came to be called by the name either of 'Obley', or of 'singing-bread'. **1884** A. J. BUTLER *Anc. Copt. Ch.* II. 50 The Greek rubric sanctions the use of a napkin or corporal to fan the oflete.]

† **of'lie**, *v. Obs.* [OE. *oflicgan*, f. OF-^{1} + *licgan* to LIE.] *trans.* **a.** To injure by lying; to overlie. **b.** To fatigue with lying. **c.** To lie with. Cf. FORLIE.

c **1000** *Modus Impon. Penit.* c. 41 in Thorpe *Laws* II. 276 ȝif hwa on slæpe his bearn oflicge ðæt hit dead wurðe. *c* **1205** LAY. 19300 Heom biuten twælf cnihtes dæies and nihtes þa weoren weri of-læien [*c* 1275 for-leie]. *a* **1250** *Owl & Night.* 1505 ȝif thu bi-thenchest hwo hire of-ligge, Thu miȝt mid wlate the este bugge.

of-lofte: see LOFT *sb.*

† **of'longed**, *ppl. a. Obs.* [OE. *oflangod*, f. OF-^{1} + *langod*, pa. pple. of *langian* to LONG, cause longing.] Seized or overcome with longing.

c **1000** ÆLFRIC *Hom.* II. 176 Swiðor for ðære sibbe þonne for Godes dæle wearð þa oflangod unȝemetlice. *c* **1200** *Trin. Coll. Hom.* 183 Hwu shal ich of-longed wið-ute þe libben. *c* **1205** LAY. 19034 Æfter þe ic wes of-longed [*c* 1275 of-langet]. *c* **1275** *Passion of our Lord* 14 in *O.E. Misc.* 37 He wes swiþe of-longed to his fader blysse.

† **of'lust, -list**, *ppl. a. Obs.* [OE. *oflysted, oflyst*, f. OF-^{1} + *lyst-ed*, pa. pple. of *lystan*, to delight, cause desire, LIST *v.*] Possessed with a strong desire, affected with longing.

c **888** K. ÆLFRED *Boeth.* xxxv. §6 Forþam he wæs oflyst ðæs seldcuþan sones. *c* **1000** ÆLFRIC *Hom.* I. 136 Ða wæs ðes man swiðe oflyst ðæs Hælendes to-cymes. *c* **1205** LAY. 30554 Þa wes he wræccheliche of-lust After deores flæsce.

† **'ofold**, *a. Obs.* Also 3 ofeald, 4 ofald. [Reduced f. *ônfold, OE. *ánfald*: see AFALD; also ONEFOLD.] **a.** Single. **b.** Simple.

c **1200** *Trin. Coll. Hom.* 187 Ofeald oðer twifeald is ilch man. *a* **1300** *Cursor M.* 25024 (Gött.) 'Anelepi' qui es he cald and knaun Bot for he es ofald [*Cott.* anfald] his fader aun? **13..** *Minor Poems fr. Vernon MS.* xlvi. 278 Now knowe I wel þat hit mai be þat O-fold god Is in þre. *c* **1440** *Jacob's Well* 197 Þou woldyst restore hym o-fold, þat is, euen in-as-myche as þou dedyst him harm!

ofor, obs. form of OVER.

oforn, variant of *aforn*, obs. form of AFORE.

13.. *Guy Warw.* (A.) 2756 Than seyd þemperour on þis maner To þe douke Segyn oforn hem þer.

† **of'pine**, *v. Obs. rare.* [f. OF-^{1} + PINE *v.*] *trans.* To torment.

13.. *Minor Poems fr. Vernon MS.* xxxvii. 117 Þauȝ he ofpyne me in seknesse sore, Hit is for my gode.

ofre, obs. form of OFFER.

† **of'reach**, *v. Obs.* [f. OF-^{1} + REACH *v.*] *trans.* To reach, get at.

a **1225** *Juliana* 57 Hwet se hit of rahte [*v.r.* hit rahte]. *a* **1300** *K. Horn* 1283 Þat lond ischal ofreche, And do mi fader wreche. *c* **1320** *Sir Beues* 867 (MS. A) And sum kniȝt Beues so ofrauȝte, Þe heued of at þe ferste drauȝte. *c* **1350** *Will. Palerne* 3874 No rink þei miȝt of-reche recuuered neuer after. **1377** LANGL. *P. Pl.* B. XVIII. 6 Of crystes passioun and penaunce þe peple þat of-rauȝte.

† **of'rede**, *v. Obs. rare.* [f. OF-^{1} + REDE *v.*, to counsel.] *trans.* To outdo in counsel, to outwit.

c **1275** [see OFRIDE].

† **of'ride**, *v. Obs.* [OE. *ofrídan*, f. OF-^{1} + *rídan* to RIDE.] *trans.* To ride down, overtake by riding, overtake.

901 *O.E. Chron.*, Se cyng het ridan æfter, and ne mehte hine mon ofridan. *c* **1000** ÆLFRIC *Gen.* xiv. 14 Abram efste wið ðæs heres oþ ðæt he hiȝ ofrad. *c* **1275** *Prov. Ælfred* 641 in *O.E. Misc.* 136 For þe helder mon me mai of-riden, Betere þenne of-reden.

† **of-'run**, *v. Obs.* In 1 of-irnan, 3 of-ærne, of-herne, of-urne. [OE. **ofrinnan, ofirnan*, f. OF-^{1} + **rinnan, irnan* to RUN.] *trans.* **a.** To overtake by running. **b.** To run away from, flee from.

c **888** K. ÆLFRED *Boeth.* xxxix. §13 Færþ he þonne æfter þære sunnan..oþ he ofirnþ þa sunnan hindan. *c* **1000** ÆLFRIC *Hom.* I. 400 Ðæs witeȝan cnapa, Gyezi..ofarn ðone ðeȝen Naaman. *c* **1205** LAY. 13149 þe abbed an horse leop.. And sone gon of-ærne þe eorl Uortigerne. *c* **1275** *Ibid.* 18267 Octa sende his sonde..After þaie Yresse þat Vther weren of-vrne [*c* **1205** þæ Vðer æt-urnen].

† **of'sake**, *v. Obs.* [OE. *ofsacan*, f. OF-^{1} + *sacan* to contend, charge, accuse.] *trans.* To deny.

c **1000** *Laws of Æthelstan* c. 4 §7 in *Thorpe*, ȝif hwa ofsacan wille, do ðæt mid eahta and feowertiȝ fulborenra þeȝena. *c* **1305** *Christopher* 60 in *E.E.P.* (1862) 61, I ne mai hit noȝt ofsake..& þat me rueþ sore. **13..** *Birth Jesus* 785 in Horstmann *Altengl. Leg.* (1875) 97 þat þe giwes ne of soke it nouȝt.

† **of'scape**, *v. Obs.* [f. OF-^{2} + SCAPE *v.*; altered from ASCAPE, ESCAPE.] *intr.* To escape.

1297 R. GLOUC. (Rolls) 459 Hii þat miȝte ofscapie [*v.rr.* of-scape, askape] bigonne to fle vaste. *Ibid.* 582 Þou ne ssalt, bi hem þat made me, ofskapie so liȝte. *Ibid.* 1196 He was sori & made gret ymone Of hom þat ofscapede.

† **of'seche**, *v. Obs.* [ME. f. OF-^{1} + *sechen* to SEEK. Cf. ON. *ofsœkia* to persecute.]

1. *trans.* To seek after, search for; *absol.* to make a search; *fig.* to attack (as a disease); to approach or come up to.

a **1225** *Ancr. R.* 232 Þe þet..ofsecheð wel ut his owune feblesce. **1297** R. GLOUC. (Rolls) 3048 He was sone of soȝt. *c* **1305** *St. Swithin* 13 in *E.E.P.* (1862) 43 He nom wiþ him folc ynouȝ: and to þe gywene gan wende And let ofseche oueral. **1340-70** *Alisaunder* 25 Case fell, þat this Kyng.. Was with siknes of-sought. *Ibid.* 1217 On euery syde þe sea of-souhte the walles. *c* **1350** *Will. Palerne* 1676 Þat noþer clerk nor kniȝt nor of cuntre cherle Schal passe vnperceyued and pertiliche of-souȝt.

2. To beseech, entreat.

1297 R. GLOUC. (Rolls) 8882 Þe king of soȝte hire suiþe ynou.

† **of'see**, *v. Obs.* [OE. *ofséon*, f. OF- + *séon* to SEE.] *trans.* To see, perceive by sight, catch sight of, observe.

c **1000** ÆLFRIC *Saints' Lives* xxiii. (*Seven Sleepers*) 545 Ða ofseah he ænne ȝeongne man. —— *Gen.* xvi. 7 Ða ofseah hiȝ Godes engel. *c* **1320** *Sir Beues* 1288 (MS. A) Vnder a faire medle tre, þat sire Beues gan of-see. *Ibid.* 1832 Beues hire sone of-say. *c* **1350** *Will. Palerne* 48 Þanne of-saw he ful sone þat semliche child. *c* **1380** *Sir Ferumb.* 3739 Wanne a cam þe pauylons neȝ, þe Amyrel wel sone him of-seȝ.

†**of'send**, *v. Obs.* [OE. *ofsendan*, f. OF-[1] + *sendan* to SEND.] *trans.* To send for.

c **1121** *O.E. Chron.* (Laud MS.) an. 1048 Ofsænd se cyng Godwine eorl. *c* **1205** LAY. 15748 Heo him radden..þat he of-sende Magan þat wes a selcuð mon. **1297** R. GLOUC. (Rolls) 6478 Seint edwardes moder þeruore he of sende, Emme quene of engelond, þat heo hider wende. **1362** LANGL. *P. Pl.* A. II. 37 Sir Simonye is of-sent to asseale þe Chartres. *c* **1380** *Sir Ferumb.* 1516 Moradas askede for wat nede þat þay wern of-sent.

†**of'serve**, *v. Obs.* [f. OF-[1] + SERVE *v.* (*c* 1225): perh. after OF. *deservir*; but the *of-* has the same force as in *ofswink*.] *trans.* To deserve, merit; to obtain by deserving; to earn.

a **1225** *Ancr. R.* 236 So mid rihte ofserueden kempene crune. *a* **1225** *Juliana* 34 þu hauest inoh min freontschipe of-seruet. **1297** R. GLOUC. (Rolls) 2699 As he it adde of serued, ynou he adde of wo. *c* **1315** SHOREHAM 32 Thou hest of-serued dygnelyche The pyne of helle vere.

Hence †**of'serving** *vbl. sb., Obs.*, deserving, desert, merit.

a **1240** *Lofsong* in *Cott. Hom.* 215 þu nowest none mon nowicht þurh his of-seruunge. **1340** *Ayenb.* 101 þise grace god ous made þe uader wyþoute oure ofseruinge.

†**of'set**, *v. Obs.* [OE. *ofsett-an*, f. OF-[1] + *sett-an* to SET.] *trans.* To beset, oppress.

c **1000** *Judges* iii. 8 in Thwaite *Heptat.*, He hiȝ ofsette and ȝeswencte for þearle. *c* **1000** *Sax. Leechd.* III. 202 On maneȝum leahtrum biþ ofsett. **1340–70** *Alex. & Dind.* 987 We ben of-set wiþ no sinne for vnsely godus. **1340–70** *Alisaunder* 308 Ðus was þe citie of-sett and siþþen so wonne.

†**of'shame**, *v. Obs.* [OE. *ofsceamian*, f. OF-[1] + *sceamian* to feel SHAME.] *trans.* To put to shame. Usually in pa. pple. **of-shamed**, put to shame, ASHAMED.

c **888** K. ÆLFRED *Boeth.* iii. §4 ȝif þu þe ofsceamian wilt ðines ȝedwolan. *c* **1000** ÆLFRIC *Hom.* II. 416 Se dry þær stod eadmod and ofsceamod. *c* **1200** *Trin. Coll. Hom.* 173 Hie.. bieð swiðe of-shamede of hem. *c* **1275** *Passion of our Lord* 137 in *O.E. Misc.* 41 þeyh alle of-schomed beo. **1297** R. GLOUC. (Rolls) 7020 þo was þis luþer godwine of ssamed suiþe sore. *c* **1315** SHOREHAM 160 Anon opened thei bothe hare eȝen..And woxe of-schamed.

†**of'sit**, *v. Obs.* [OE. *ofsitt-an*, f. OF-[1] + *sitt-an* to SIT.] *trans.* To sit upon, occupy, oppress, repress.

c **888** K. ÆLFRED *Boeth.* xviii. §1 Eall þæt seo sæ hes ofseten hæfþ. *c* **1000** *Judges* v. Annot. in Thwaite *Heptat.* 156 þe..mid unrihtwisnisse þa earman ofsittaþ. *c* **1175** *Lamb. Hom.* 115 Ðet is Kinge's rihtwisnesse þet he mid wohȝe ne of-sitte ne ermne ne eadine.

†**of'slay, of'sle**, *v. Obs.* Forms: see SLAY. [OE. *ofsléan*, f. OF-[1] + *sléan* (:—*slahan*) to strike, SLAY.] *trans.* To kill off, slay.

c **893** K. ÆLFRED *Oros.* IV. i. §5 He ofsloȝ micel ðæs folces. *c* **900** tr. *Bæda's Hist.* I. xviii. [xxiv.] (1890) 92 Ðeodbald.. wæs ofslæȝen mid ealle þy weorode þe he lædde. *c* **1000** *Sax. Leechd.* I. 168 ȝenim þas wyrte þe man *solago minor*.. nemneð..heo þa wyrmas ofslihþ. *c* **1205** LAY. 685 Bi þone toppe he hine nom Al swa he hine walde of-slean. *Ibid.* 2559 þer he his broðer of-sloh. *c* **1250** *Gen. & Ex.* 4077 Godes wreche ðor haueð of-slaȝen xxiii. ðusent of ðagen. *c* **1320** *Sir Beues* 2520 (MS. A) For to bringe þis quene aȝen And þe, Beues, her of-slen.

†**of'spring**, *v. Obs. rare.* [f. OF-[1] + SPRING *v.*] *intr.* To spring, descend.

c **1275** LAY. 26418 Belyn and Brenne Of wam we beoþ of-spronge.

†**of'stand**, *v. Obs. rare.* [OE. *ofstand-an*, f. OF-[1] + *standan* to STAND.]

1. *intr.* To remain standing, remain, stay. Cf. ATSTAND *v.* 1, 2. (Only in OE.)

c **1000** *Sax. Leechd.* II. 194 ȝif him ofstondeþ on Innan æniȝu ceald wæte.

2. *trans.* To withstand. Cf. ATSTAND *v.* 3.

c **1400** R. GLOUC. (Rolls) 1300 (MS. B) þe emperour of Rome þat no lond ne myȝte ofstonde [*v.r.* at stonde].

†**of'sting**, *v. Obs.* [OE. *ofsting-an*, f. OF-[1] + *sting-an* to STING, pierce.] *trans.* To kill by a thrust; to pierce, gore, stab to death.

c **893** K. ÆLFRED *Oros.* IV. i. §5 He hiene [þone ylp] on þone nafelan ofstang. *a* **1000** *O.E. Chron.* (Laud MS.) an. 626 He [Eomer] wolde of-stingan Eadwine cininge, ac he ofstang Lillan his ðeȝn. *c* **1205** LAY. 5034 þat ich for þine þinge Mid sæxe me of-stinge. *Ibid.* 10653 Carrais him on þrong and mid spere him of-stong.

†**of'strength**, *v. Obs. rare.* [f. OF-[1] + STRENGTH *v.*] *trans.* To fortify.

1297 R. GLOUC. (Rolls) 2968 Ac octa hengistes sone and is poer attelaste Of scapede to euerwik and of strengþede þen toun vaste.

†**of'swink**, *v. Obs.* [f. OF-[1] + SWINK *v.*] *trans.* To gain by labour, labour for.

c **1300** *Beket* 9 In strong swynche niȝt and dai: to of-swynche here Mete stronge. *c* **1350** *Leg. Rood* (1871) 26 He ..of-swonke is owe mete. *a* **1400** *Chron. R. Glouc.* 944 (MS. B) þat we myȝte of swynke [*MS. A* biswinke] oure mete, & libbe by oure swynke.

oft (ɒft, ɔ:-), *adv.*, *a.* Now *arch.*, *poet.*, and *dial.*; repr. in ordinary use by *often*. Forms: α. 1– oft, (4–5 offt, 8 *Sc.* aft). β. 2–6 ofte, (3 hofte, 3–5 offte, 5 owghte). [Comm. Teut.: OE. *oft* = OFris. *ofta*, *ofte*, OS. *oft*, *ofto* (MDu. *ofte* rare), OHG. *ofto* (MHG. *ofte*, *oft*, Ger. *oft*), ON. *oft*, *opt* (SW. *ofta*, Da. *ofte*); Goth. *ufta*. In early ME. *oft* was extended to *ofte* (app. in imitation of advbs. in *-e*), which became 1200–1500 the only form in south. and midl., *oft* being confined to north. dial. or writers under northern influence. In 16th c. with the mutescence of final *e*, *oft* gradually displaced *ofte*, which occurs however as a graphic var. till *c* 1580. See also OFTEN.]

A. *adv.* **a.** = OFTEN A.

α. *c* **950** *Lindisf. Gosp.* Matt. xvii. 15 Oft fallas in fyr and symle in wætre. *c* **1000** *Ags. Gosp.* Luke xiii. 34 Hu oft ic wolde þine bearn ȝegaderian. *c* **1175** *Lamb. Hom.* 109 Ac þas twa þing deriað oft þan alden. *a* **1300** *Cursor M.* 3747 (Cott.) He has me don oft vn-resun. **1388** WYCLIF *Eccl.* vi. 1 It is oft vsid anentis men. *c* **1400** *Destr. Troy* 13466 Oft went þat wegh to the water syde. **1526** TINDALE *1 Cor.* xi. 25 This do as oft as ye drinke it, in the remembraunce off me. **1535** COVERDALE *Judith* v. D, As oft as they were sory. **1551** BIBLE *2 Cor.* xi. 23 In pryson more plenteously: in death oft [WYCLIF ofte tymes, TIND., CRANM., *Geneva* ofte, *Rheims* often, 1611 oft]. **1576** FLEMING *Panopl. Epist.* 255 It commeth to passe, many times and oft. **1611** BIBLE *Transl. Pref.* 1 b, Not only as oft as we speake..but also as oft as we doe any thing. **1717** LADY M. W. MONTAGU *Let. to Mrs. Hewet* 1 Apr., Let me hear as oft as you can. **1752** HUME *Ess. & Treat.* (1777) I. 193 [It] is commonly a painful, oft a fruitless occupation. *a* **1774** GOLDSM. tr. *Scarron's Com. Romance* (1775) I. 29 Many's the time and oft. **1786** BURNS *Dream* xi, Yet aft a ragged cowte's been known To mak a noble aiver. **1806** H. K. WHITE *Hymn*, Much in sorrow, oft in woe, Onward, Christians, onward go! **1852** MRS. STOWE *Uncle Tom's C.* xxviii. 260 A strife..suspended oft, but yet renewed again. *Mod. Sc.* Hae ye been oft there?

β. *c* **1175** *Lamb. Hom.* 147 Ofte for his sunne [he] swingeð him mið smele twige. *c* **1200** ORMIN 9016 Forr ȝuw birrþ uppo kirrkeflor Beon fundenn offte & lannge. *c* **1205** LAY. 3363 For ofte [*c* **1275** hofte] hit ilimpð þat eft hit him of-þincheð. *c* **1250** *Gen. & Ex.* 4144 Ydolatrie..ofte vt-wrogte hem sorges dref. **1297** R. GLOUC. (Rolls) 53 Of þe folc of denemarch..þat ofte wonne engelond. **1340** *Ayenb.* 236 Hit be-houeþ..ofte wesse his herte of kueade lostes. **1362** LANGL. *P. Pl.* A. II. 16 þat is Meede þe Mayden..þat haþ me marred ofte. *c* **1386** CHAUCER *Clerk's T.* 170 She wolde brynge Wortes or othere herbes tymes ofte [*rime* softe, lofte; *so* 5 *MSS.*; *Petw. & Lansd.* oft, soft, loft]. *c* **1440** *Promp. Parv.* 231/1 Hawntyn, or ofte vsyn. **1442** *Rolls of Parlt.* V. 54/2 Upon the peyne of xl. li., to be forfait as ogwhte as they do the contrarie. **1470–85** MALORY *Arthur* XVI. xvi, Thenne ofte Colgreuaunce cryed vpon syre Bors. **1512** *Act 4 Hen. VIII*, c. 1 §4 As ofte and as many tymes as nede shall require. *c* **1582** E. SKORY in *Nature* (1883) XXVII. 316 The fyers doe ofte breake forth.

Comparative: 1 oftor, 2–7 (9 *arch.* and *dial.*) ofter, (3 -ere, 4 *Sc.* -yre, 5 -ir, *Sc.* -ar).

c **897** K. ÆLFRED *Gregory's Past* lvi. 435 Hi beoþ ðæs ðe lator ðe hi oftor ymbðeahtiað. *c* **1175** *Lamb. Hom.* 21 We sunegiet..welle ofter þene we scolde. **1297** [see OFTSITHE]. *c* **1386** CHAUCER *Nun's Pr. T.* 608 If thou bigyle me any ofter than ones. *c* **1449** PECOCK *Repr.* I. viii. 39 That the reders be the more and the oftir remembrid. **1551** TURNER *Herbal* (1568) Piij, I haue not sene it in Englande ofter than ones. **1615** LATHAM *Falconry* (1633) 16 The more ofter that you doe use her unto them, the quieter she will be. **1828** *Craven Gloss.* (ed. 2), *Ofter*, more frequently. **1856** MRS. BROWNING *Aur. Leigh* III. 907 She laughed sometimes..But ofter she was sorrowful. **1868** ATKINSON *Cleveland Gloss.*, *Ofter*, more frequently, oftener.

Superlative: 1 oftost, -ust, 3–7 -est. ? *Obs.*

c **950** *Lindisf. Gosp.* Mark v. 4 Forðon oftust mið feotrum & mið hracenteȝum ȝebunden wæs. *a* **1225** *Leg. Kath.* 114 Ah eauer ha hefde on hali writ ehnen oðer heorte, oftest ba togederes. **1393** LANGL. *P. Pl.* C. IV. 439 That he þat seith most sothest [*v.r.* oftest seiþ soþ]. **1480** CAXTON *Descr. Brit.* 23 Netheles oftest and longest they were vnder the kyngis of Mercia. **1599** JAS. I *Βασιλ. Δωρον* (1682) 35 Vertue followeth oftest noble blood. **1671** MILTON *P.R.* II. 228 Rocks whereon greatest men have oftest wreck'd.

b. At frequent intervals of space. *rare.*

1617 MORYSON *Itin.* I. 30 Of the villages oft intermixed, some are subject to the Margrave..and some to divers Bishops. **1634** SIR T. HERBERT *Trav.* 94 Shee is diuided and sub-diuided so oft and into so many streames.

c. Like other advbs., usually hyphened to a ppl. adj. used *attrib.*, as *oft-told*. (In this construction still frequent.) Cf. OFTEN A. 3.

a **1586** SIDNEY *Arcadia* (1622) 121 Partaker of this oft-blinding light. **1671** MILTON *Samson* 575 Oft-invocated death. **1715–20** POPE *Iliad* XIII. 495 The oft-heav'd axe. **1818** BYRON *Ch. Har.* IV. cxxiii, Reaping the whirlwind from the oft-sown winds. **1851** D. JERROLD *St. Giles* v. 39 To thwart an oft-told prophecy. **1858** in *Proc. Amer. Phil. Soc.* VI. 318 The attacks of an oft-recurring malady. **1864** BURTON *Scot Abr.* I. v. 270 An old and oft-repeated tale. **1906** P. E. MORE *Shelburne Ess.* (4th ser.) 198 There are single lines here and there, such as the oft-quoted 'White arms out in the breakers tirelessly tossing', which have a magical power of evoking an image or the memory of subtle sounds and odors. **1922** JOYCE *Ulysses* 269 Her first merciful lovesoft oftloved word. **1954** O. NASH *Face is Familiar* (rev. ed.) 115 The oft-quoted remark of the prominent and respectable dignitary. **1976** M. BUTTERWORTH *Remains to be Seen* i. 11 The wary air of an oft-disappointed augur reading entrails.

†**B.** *adj.* = OFTEN B. (Chiefly with *vbl. sbs.*)

With gerunds and verbal sbs., and so essentially adverbial.

1387 TREVISA *Higden* (Rolls) V. 311 þis hermyte..was blynde for ofte wepynge þat he usede in his beedes. *c* **1450** tr. *De Imitatione* I. i. 2 Many feliþ but litel desire of offte heringe of þe gospel. **1483** *Cath. Angl.* 258/2 Ofte, *creber, frequens, nu[m]erosus.* **1548** UDALL, etc. *Erasm. Par. Mark* 74 b, I ascribe my safety to myne oft fastynges. *a* **1568** ASCHAM *Scholem.* (Arb.) 85 To breede occasion of ofter meeting of him and her. **1624** QUARLES *Div. Poems, Sion's Sonn.* xx. 17 Brests, whose beautie reinvites My oft remembrance to her oft delights. **1671** MILTON *Samson* 382 Warn'd by oft experience.

C. *Comb.* With sbs. denoting time, as †*oft-seasons*; see also OFTSITHE, -S, OFT-TIME, -S.

1542 UDALL *Erasm. Apoph.* 7 b, Thou walkest too and fro, ofteseasons in maner all y[e] whole daye.

oft, obs. or dial. form of AUGHT, OUGHT *v.*

1575 *Gamm. Gurton* III. iii, Did I (olde witch) steal oft was thine? **1576** *Parad. Dainty Devices*, If I may of wisedome oft define. **1590–** [see OUGHT *v.*].

†**of'take**, *v. Obs.* For forms and inflexions see TAKE *v.*

1. [f. OF-[3] + TAKE *v.*] *trans.* To overtake, come up with.

c **1205** LAY. 26069 Arður wes swiftre And of-toc þene eotend. **1297** R. GLOUC. (Rolls) 1468 He of tok [*several MSS.* ouer tok] him at an hauene and slou him riȝt þere. **13..** *Guy Warw.* (A.) 6412 His gode stede he bi-strod And of-tok hem wiþ-outen abod. *a* **1400** *Octouian* 1625 All that they myghte with wepene of-take.

b. To overtake or detect (in a fault).

c **1350** *Usages of Winchester* in *Eng. Gilds* (1870) 355 þat he ne mowe wiþ-segge ȝif he is of take oþer þan weel.

2. To take off or away. (In pa. pple.) [Belongs to OFF- 1.]

c **1386** CHAUCER *Prioress' T.* 213 Til fro my tonge of taken is the greyn. **1432–50** tr. *Higden* (Rolls) VII. 201 Lest thei scholde have skornede hym or elles oftaken the rynge awey in his absence.

often ('ɒf(ə)n, 'ɔ:-; 'ɒftən, 'ɔ:-), *adv.* and *a.* Also 4 oftin, 5 oftyn(e, -on, 6 hoften, 8 *Sc.* aften. [An extended form of OFT, or of its ME. variant *ofte*. In Chaucer we find *ofte* before a consonant, *often* before a vowel or *h*, as if in imitation of inflexional endings in *-en* reduced before a consonant to *-e*; but the earliest examples appear to be northern, and in them *oftin* occurs before a cons. The word is not common in Standard English till the 16th c.]

A. *adv.* **1. a.** Many times; at many times, on numerous occasions; frequently. Opposed to *seldom*.

13.. *Cursor M.* 3520 (Gött.) Esau went for to hunt A day, as he was oftin wont [*Cott.* oft, *Trin.* ofte]. *Ibid.* 7699 (Gött.) þat oftin [*Cott.* oft, *Tr.* often] chancis sua it bi-fell. *c* **1386** CHAUCER *C.T. Prol.* 310 That often [*v.r.* oftyn] hadde ben at the Parys. *c* **1400** MAUNDEV. (1839) ix. 100 And the erthe and the lond chaungeth often his colour. *c* **1440** *Promp. Parv.* 363/1 Oftyne, *sepe, multocies, frequenter.* **1509** FISHER *Fun. Serm. C'tess Richmond* Wks. (1876) 292 Full often she complayned that [etc.]. **1526** TINDALE *Matt.* xxiii. 37 Howe often [WYCLIF oft, **1388** ofte] wolde I have gaddered thy children to gedder. **1697** DAMPIER *Voy.* I. 251, I have often wonder'd at his Expressions and Actions. **1701** DE FOE *True-born Englishm.* II. 128 Seldom contented, often in the wrong. **1709** STEELE *Tatler* No. 149 ¶7 Let me beg of you to write to me often. **1861** M. PATTISON *Ess.* (1889) I. 34 The crown of England, always at strife, and often at open war, with its own barons. **1883** MISS JEWSBURY in *Mrs. Carlyle's Lett.* II. 274 The mortifications and vexations she felt.. were often and often self-made.

Comparative and *Superlative*.

1467 *Ordin. Worc.* in *Eng. Gilds* 380 [They] shullen com and assemble togeder in euery quarter of the yere, ones or oftener and it nede. **1558** BP. WATSON *Sev. Sacram.* xi. 61 He..that the oftneste and with moste reuerence commeth. **1660** BOYLE *Seraph. Love* xvi. (1700) 99 He is rather welcom'st to God that comes to him oftenest, and stays with him longest. *a* **1715** BURNET *Own Time* (1766) I. 246 As has happened oftner than once before. **1784** COWPER *Task* I. 411 An idol at whose shrine Who oft'nest sacrifice are favour'd least. **1866** DARWIN *Orig. Spec.* (ed. 4) iv. 104 Those individual flowers..would be oftenest visited by insects, and would be oftenest crossed.

b. In colloq. phrases: *(as) often as not*, *more often than not*, at least half the time; frequently; *every so often*: see EVERY *a.* 1 f; *once too often*: see ONCE *adv.* 8 d.

1911 G. B. SHAW *Getting Married* Pref. 149 Such a transaction..is as often as not the inauguration of a lifelong squabble. **1919** E. O'NEILL *In Zone* in *Moon of Caribbees* (1923) 16 All them German spies they been catchin' in England has been livin' there for ten, often as not twenty years. **1960** *Observer* 25 Dec. 7/6 The driver often as not wore chauffeur's livery. **1962** M. DRABBLE *Summer Bird-Cage* xi. 185, I..use a small red plastic colander, and everything eels into the sink as often as not. **1977** F. ROSS *Dead Runner* I. 64 More often than not the only successful outcome of a dead-run operation was the runner's grave.

2. In many instances; in cases frequently occurring.

Here *often* lies properly outside the statement, referring to the frequency of cases in which it can be said; thus quot. 1807–26 really means 'it often happens that the disease will remain stationary during life'; quot. 1878 'it often happens that a good character is worth', etc.

c **1386** CHAUCER *Miller's T.* 44 Youthe and elde is often at debaat. **1509** FISHER *Fun. Serm. C'tess Richmond* Wks. (1876) 290 Full often suche as come of ryght pore and vnnoble fader and moder, haue grete abletees of nature. *a* **1548** HALL *Chron., Hen. VII* 8 Worldly chaunces..in adversitye often chaunge from evell to good and so to bettre. **1652** CULPEPPER *Eng. Physic.* 83 It groweth in moist grounds..ofner than in the dry and open fields. **1693** DRYDEN *Juvenal* x. 8 Whole Houses, of their whole Desires possest, Are often Ruin'd, at their own Request. **1707** FREIND *Peterborow's Cond. Sp.* 58 Such effects..are too often paid for by an after-reckoning. **1807–26** S. COOPER *First Lines Surg.* xv. (ed. 5) 354 The disease will often remain stationary during life. **1878** JEVONS *Prim. Pol. Econ.* vii. 59 A good character is often worth a great deal of money. **1886** PATER *Appreciations* (1890) 137–8 A museum is seldom a cheerful place—oftenest induces the feeling that nothing could ever have been young.

3. Like other advbs., commonly hyphened to a ppl. adj. when this is used *attrib.* (cf. HIGHLY).

1601 *Mary Magd. Lament.* II. xx, This often-heard report. **1627** DONNE *Serm.* xxii. 216 Second or oftener-iterated Marriages. **1766** BLACKSTONE *Comm.* II. v. 70 In the often-cited charter of Henry the first. **1859** I. TAYLOR *Logic in Theol.* 316 That often-recurrent affirmation concerning the purpose of the death of Christ. **1877** A. S. HEWITT in Raymond *Statist. Mines & Mining* 374 At often-recurring intervals.

B. *adj.* (The adv. used with gerundial and verbal sbs., and at length with other sbs.) Done, made, happening, or occurring many times; frequent. (Very common in 16th and 17th c.; but rare after 1688, and now *arch.*)

1450–1530 *Myrr. our Ladye* 244 Had not be hys often comfortes: she myghte not haue abyden the tyme of hys passyon wyth her lyfe. **1526** TINDALE *1 Tim.* v. 23 Vse a lytell wyne for thy stommakes sake, and thyne often diseases. **1530** PALSGR. 315/2 Hoften, *frequentatif.* **1558** in Strype *Ann. Ref.* (1824) I. II. iv. 397 There should be no often changes in religion. **1573** G. HARVEY *Letter-bk.* (Camden) 24 Esspecial thanks for your ernest and often letters in mi behalf. **1601** B. JONSON *Poetaster* IV. ii, Any favours, that may worthily make you an often courtier. **1640** BP. REYNOLDS *Passions* xiii, Liable to an oftner anger. *a* **1679** HOBBES *Rhet.* III. iii. (1681) 105 Long, impertinent, and often Epithets. **1685** EVELYN *Mrs. Godolphin* 8 To my often admiration. **1729** FENTON in *Waller's Wks.* Observ. 19 Her blood is kept pure, by often alliance with great and Princely families. **1831** CARLYLE *Sart. Res.* I. v, The greatest and oftenest laugher. **1896** HOWELLS *Impressions & Exp.* 210, I knew those lemons..from often study of them on their shelf.

C. *Comb.* With nouns denoting time, as † **often-sithe**, † **-tide**, **-while**, **-s** = OFTENTIME, -S.

c **1330** R. BRUNNE *Chron.* (1810) 289 Boste & deignouse pride & ille avisement Mishapnes oftentide. *c* **1386** CHAUCER *Knt.'s T.* 1019 And thonken hym..often sithe [*Hengwrt & Cambr.* ofte sythe; *Corp. & Harl.* ofte siþe; *Lansd.* oft siþe; *Petw.* mony sith]. *a* **1577** GASCOIGNE *Wks.* (1587) (N.), For whom I sighed have so often sithe. **1605** SYLVESTER *Du Bartas* II. iii. IV. *Captains* 457 Even a holy Guile Findes with thee grace and favour often-while. *a* **1850** ROSSETTI *Dante & Circ.* I. (1874) 42, I had oftenwhiles many troublesome hours.

† **of'tene**, *v. Obs.* [f. OF-[2] + TENE *v.*: cf. ATENE *v.*] *trans.* To irritate.

a **1250** *Owl & Night.* 254 Þeos ule luste swiþe longe And was ofteoned swiþe stronge. **1340** *Ayenb.* 66 Þanne hit is oftyened: he [þe þorn-hog] kest out his eles of his bodye ariȝthalf and alefthalf.

oftening ('ɒf(ə)nɪŋ, ɔː-), *vbl. sb. rare*[−1]. [f. OFTEN *adv.* and *a.* + -ING[1].] Frequent repetition.

a **1889** G. M. HOPKINS *Jrnls. & Papers* (1959) 289 Repetition, *oftening, over-and-overing, aftering* of the inscape must take place in order to detach it to the mind.

† **'oftenly**, *adv. Obs. rare.* [f. OFTEN *a.* + -LY[2].] = OFTEN *adv.*

1577 *St. Aug. Manual* (Longman) 86 So much the more happily as hee doth it more oftenly. **1578** T. PROCTOR *Gorg. Gall. gall. Invent.* O iij, Yet oftenly we wisely heare may meate. **1591** PERCIVALL *Sp. Dict.*, *Frequentadamente*, oftenly. **1751** LAVINGTON *Enthus. Meth. & Papists* III. (1754) 35 Most oftenly the whole Discourse is the Devil's.

'oftenness. Now *rare.* [f. as prec. + -NESS.] The fact or condition of occurring often; frequency.

1565 Oftennesse [see OFTNESS]. **1594** HOOKER *Eccl. Pol.* I. viii. §8 Degrees..there could be none, except perhaps in the seeldomnes and oftennes of doing well. **1639** SCLATER *Worthy Commun.* 49 St. Paul is at his (ὀσάκις) his (oftennesse) of which Thomas gives a reason. **1656** BLOUNT *Glossogr.*, *Crebrity*, a multitude, oftenness. **1730–6** BAILEY (folio), *Crebritude*, frequency, oftenness. **1977** 'E. CRISPIN' *Glimpses of Moon* ii. 27 The Pisser's [*sc.* a pylon's] noise.. had actually intensified both in volume and in oftenness.

'oftens, *adv. Obs.* exc. *dial.* [f. OFTEN *adv.* with advb. genitive *-s* (as in *whiles, whilst*, etc.), perh. sometimes felt as a plural.] = OFTEN *adv.*

1567 DRANT *Horace, Ep.* I. xix. F vij, How haue your tumultes vyle Full oftens rasde my collor vp, and oftens made me smyle. *Ibid.* II. ii. H v, This thinge I oftens talke vpon And oft I thinke of this. **1825** BROCKETT *N.C. Gloss.*, *Oftens, offens*, the plural of *often.* Quite common. **1868** ATKINSON *Clevel. Gl.*, *Oftens* (*pr.* off'ns), often, oftentimes. **1889** PEACOCK *N.W. Linc. Gl.* 381, I ofens heärd tell o' fairies.

'oftentime, *adv.* (*a.*) *rare.* [f. OFTEN *adv.* + TIME, as an extended form of OFT-TIME.] = next. (In quot. 1876 as *adj.* Frequent.)

c **1400** MAUNDEV. (1839) ii. 14, I haue often tyme seen it. *c* **1450** *Sir Beues* (MS. C) 155/3335 Ȝe wot alle..That often tyme Saber þe hore Hath me greuyd full sore. **1853** TRENCH *Proverbs* ii. 28 Oftentime the proverb in its more popular form is so greatly superior to the same in this its Latin.. dress. **1876** MRS. WHITNEY *Sights & Ins.* II. xviii. 475 Where Cosmo of the Medici had his oftentime habitation.

oftentimes ('ɒf(ə)ntaɪmz, ɔː-), *adv.* Now only *arch.* or *literary.* [f. OFTEN *adv.* + *times*; an extended form of OFTTIMES.] Many times; on many occasions, or in many cases; frequently, often.

c **1430** *Syr Tryam.* Notes 60 The kynge..oftentymes dyde wepe. **1444** *Rolls of Parlt.* V. 117/2 He to forfaite as often tymes as he offendith. **1540–1** ELYOT *Image Govt.* 15 b, He shalbe oftentymes warned. **1611** BIBLE *Heb.* x. 11 Offring oftentimes [WYCLIF, TINDALE, etc. ofte tymes] the same sacrifices. **1774** J. BRYANT *Mythol.* I. 495 These buildings were oftentimes light-houses. **1800** WORDSW. *Pet Lamb* 62 This song to myself did I oftentimes repeat. **1845–6** TRENCH *Huls. Lect.* Ser. II. ii. 168 An oftentimes fatal readiness. **1875** GLADSTONE *Glean.* (1879) VI. 154.

† **b.** Rarely in compar. and superl. *oftener times, oftenest times. Obs.*

1562 COOPER *Answ. Priv. Masse* (Parker Soc.) 107 Many ..take of this sacrifice once in the whole year, some twice, some oftener times. **1592** WYRLEY *Armorie* 143 Oftenest times when least we do mistrust. **1607** TOPSELL *Four-f. Beasts* (1658) 450 The female is oftener times taken then the male.

† **of'think**, *v. Obs.* Forms: 1 ofþyncan, 2–3 -þunche(n (*ü*), -þinche, 3–4 -þinke, -þenke, 4 -þynke, -thenche, 4 othynke, 5 othenkyn; *3rd sing.* 1 ofþyncþ, 2 ofþincþ, 3 -thencheþ, -thenkth, 3–4 -thinkeþ, -þynketh. *Pa. t.* 1–2 ofþuhte, 2 -þuchte, -þouhte, 3 -þoȝte, -þouȝte, -thoȝte, 5 othoȝte. See also ATHINK. [OE. *ofþyncan*, f. OF-[1] + *þyncan* to seem fit, to seem: see THINK *v.*[2]]

1. To seem not good; to displease, vex, grieve. Chiefly used *impersonally*, with dative of person, and genitive of thing, or *that.*

Beowulf 2035 Mæȝ þæs þonne ofþyncan ðeoden Heaðobeardna. *c* **888** K. ÆLFRED *Boeth.* xxxv. §4 Ða sceolde þam gigantum of þyncan þæt he hæfde hiera rice. *c* **893** —— *Oros.* II. v. §4 Him þa ofþyncendum ðæt his folc swa forslaȝen wæs. *c* **897** —— *Gregory's Past.* xxi. 161 Ðonne him hiera [scylda] na ne ofðyncð. *c* **1000** ÆLFRIC *Hom.* I. 86 Him ðæs slæpes ofþuhte. *c* **1175** *Lamb. Hom.* 55 Þenne ofþuncheð hit him sare. *Ibid.* 157 Hom ofþuchte þet þis orliche lif hom to longe leste. **1297** R. GLOUC. (Rolls) 759 Hit of þouȝte þe luþer quene þat hire fader adde to muche. *c* **1300** *Beket* 1001 Ous hit ofthinketh sore.

2. *impers.* To cause (one) grief or regret (to have done something); to 'repent'.

c **1000** *Ecgbert. Confess.* Proem in Thorpe *Laws* II. 130 Ofþinceð þe ealles þe ðu to yfele hæfst ȝeworht? *c* **1000** ÆLFRIC *Gen.* vi. 7 Me of-þincþ þæt ic hiȝ worhte. *c* **1000** ÆLFRIC *Gram.* xxxiii. (Z.) 207 *Poenitet*, me ofþincþ. *a* **1175** *Cott. Hom.* 225 Him of-þuhte þat he efre mancinn ȝesceop. *a* **1200** *Moral Ode* 164 Gif him her of-þincþ his gult. *Ibid.* 271 Þo þe ofþouhte sore her here misdeden. *c* **1205** LAY. 3364 Eft hit him of-þincheð [*c* 1275 aþincheþ]. **1297** R. GLOUC. (Rolls) 1249 Sore ofþinkþ it me þat ich abbe vor oure Kinges loue ihold aȝen þe. *Ibid.* 3409 Sone dawes hom of þoȝte hor prute. *c* **1374** CHAUCER *Troylus* I. 987 (1043) Yet me of-þynketh [*v.r.* mathynketh = m'oþynkeþ] þat þis auaunt me a-sterte. **1382** WYCLIF *Exod.* xiii. 17 Lest perauenture it shoulde othenkyn hym [1388 repente the puple]. —— *Jer.* iv. 28 It othoȝte not me [1388 repentide not me].

b. (with personal subj.) To grieve, be sorry; to repent.

a **1225** *Ancr. R.* 118 Do ase deð þe pellican: of þunche hit swuðe sone. *c* **1250** *Death* 2 in *O.E. Misc.* 168 I-hereð of one þinge that ȝe ohen of þenche. *c* **1325** *Spec. Gy Warw.* 539 He þer-after of-þinkeþ sore And þer-of crieþ merci and ore. **1382** WYCLIF *Ecclus.* xxxii. 24 Aftir thi deede thou shalt not othynke [1388 repente].

Hence † **of'thinking** (in 3 **ofþunchunge**) *vbl. sb.*, displeasure, vexation, disgust, grief, sorrow.

a **1225** *Ancr. R.* 200 Þe þridde kundel is Of-þunchunge of oðres god. *c* **1230** *Hali Meid.* 7 Aȝaines an likinge habben twa of þunchunges.

† **of'thirst**, *ppl. a. Obs.* [OE. *ofþyrsted, ofþyrst*, f. OF- + **þyrsted*, pa. pple. of *þyrstan* to THIRST.] Earlier form of ATHIRST, q.v.

c **1000** *Judges* xv. 18 in Thwaite *Heptat.*, He [Samson] wearþ þa swiþe ofþyrst. *c* **1200** *Trin. Coll. Hom.* 199 Þenne hie beð of-þurst cumeð to sum welle. *c* **1275** *XI Pains of Hell* 166 in *O.E. Misc.* 151 Sore of-þurst and ful hungri. **1393** LANGL. *P. Pl.* C. x. 85 Boþe a-fyngrede and a-furst [*MS. M* of-þerst].

'oftly, *adv. rare.* [f. OFT *adv.* + -LY[2], after other advbs. in *-ly*; cf. OFTENLY.] Often.

1592 WYRLEY *Armorie, Ld. Chandos* 62 Oftlie returning vnto freends, I told, That I had seene of noblenes the flower. **1844** MRS. BROWNING *Catarina to Camoens* xii, Will you oftly Murmur softly.

oftner, oftnest, obs. comp. and sup. of OFTEN.

'oftness. *Obs.* or *arch.* Also 6–7 oftenes, -ness(e. [f. OFT *a.* + -NESS. The spelling *ofteness* unites this with *oftenness.*] = OFTENNESS.

1545 ELYOT *Dict.*, *Crebritas*, oftnes [1548–52 oftenesse, 1565 oftennesse]. **1572** J. JONES *Bathes of Bath* III. 25 b, Greatnesse of pulse, swiftnes and oftenes of the same. **1597** HOOKER *Eccl. Pol.* v. lxxii. §4 Not the oftnes [1617 oftenesse] of theer fasting, but their hypocrisie therein was blamed. **1642** ROGERS *Naaman* 428 So..oftnesse comprehends seldomenesse.

† **of'tread**, *v. Obs. rare.* [OE. *oftredan*, f. OF- + *tredan* to TREAD.] *trans.* To tread or trample down; to injure or destroy by treading.

c **893** K. ÆLFRED *Oros.* VI. iv. §4 Ðær wæron xxxM. ofslaȝen and æt ðæm ȝeate oftreden. *c* **1000** ÆLFRIC *Saints' Lives* xviii. (*Serm. Bk. Kings*) 347 Ða hors hi [Gezabel] oftrædan huxlice under fotum. *c* **1200** ORMIN 11650 Forrþi birrþ uss allre firrst Offtredenn gluterrnesse.

oft-seasons: see OFT C.

† **'oft,sithe**, *adv. Obs.* Forms: 3 oftesiðen, 3–4 ofte siþe, etc.: see OFT and SITHE: also 4 **ofte-syde**, **of-sith**, **of-siþe**. [In early ME. *oftesiðen*:—OE. **oftsiðon*:—**oftsiðum* dat. pl., corresp. to ON. *optsinnum* many times, oft-times (cf. OE. *on oftsiðas* on many occasions, oft-times); f. OFT + *siðum* dat. pl. of *sið* time: see SITHE. By normal phonetic processes *ofte-siðen* became *oftesiþe, oftsiþe, oftsith*, in which the original pl. form was lost, but app. reinstated in the later *oft-sithes*: see next, and *oftensithe* in OFTEN C.] = next.

a **1225** *Ancr. R.* 418 Of swuche witunge is i-kumen muchel vuel oftesiðen. **1297** R. GLOUC. (Rolls) 5337 Ofte siþe [*MS. Trin. Coll.* ofte seþþe, *MS. Digby* (*c* 1425) ofte tymes] aboue he was, and bineþe ofter [*v.r.* oftere] mo. *a* **1300** *Cursor M.* 12534 (Cott.) And of-sith [*F.* oft-siþe, *Gött.* ofte-syde, *Trin.* ofte] walawai! he said. *c* **1305** *Oxford Student* 17 in *E.E.P.* (1862) 40 Þeȝ þis child were ȝung, of þis deol ofte siþe hit þoȝte. **1340** HAMPOLE *Pr. Consc.* 7460–1 Als oft-sythe als þai here newed þair syn, Als oft-syth þair payn salle new þare bigyn. *c* **1380** WYCLIF *Sel. Wks.* III. 37 Ese and welþe drawiþ men oftsiþ to synne. *c* **1448** HOCCLEVE *Balade Dk. York* 51 If þat I..my colours sette ofte sythe awry.

'oft,sithes, *adv. Obs.* Forms: 4 oft siþes, (-is, -s), 4–5 ofte siþes, etc., 4–5 oftsithes, etc. Also *β.* 4 oftsyis(s, oftsiss, -syse, -sise, 4–5 -syss. [app. orig. a northern form (but also Kentish in *Ayenb.*) corresp. to southern *oftesiþe*: see prec. The *-s* was prob. a plural ending, taking the place of the lost dat. pl. *-en* in *ofte siðen* (cf. OE. *on oftsiðas* on many occasions, oft-times); less prob. the adverbial genitive *-s*, or repr. the *-is* of ON. *optsinnis* oft-times.] Oftentimes, often.

a **1300** *Cursor M.* 7703 (Cott.) Oftsithes [*Fairf.* oft siþe, *Gött.* oft sith, *Trin.* ofte] moght he him ha tan. *Ibid.* 16813. **1340** *Ayenb.* 249–50 To ane riche manne hit were ofteziþes to lite. **1340** HAMPOLE *Pr. Consc.* 3496 Ofte sythes of þe day men falles In syns, þat clerkes veniel calles. *c* **1386** CHAUCER *C.T.* Prol. 485 Swich he was y-preued ofte sithes [*rime* tithes]. *c* **1410** LOVE *Bonavent. Mirr.* xxii. (Pynson) G j b, He ..came to mete as he was wonte to do oft sythes. *c* **1491** *Chast. Goddes Chyld.* 18 Some haue had oftsithes swete sauours two dayes or thre togider.

β. **13..** *Cursor M.* 27580 (Cott.) We may se bitide and of-sise [*Fairf.* of siþe] þe standand fall, the falland rise. *c* **1375** *Sc. Leg. Saints* xviii. (*Egipciane*) 1121 Of kneis thankand god oft-syse. *c* **1450** HOLLAND *Howlat* 274 Thus argewe thai ernistly wounder oftsyss. *c* **1500** *Lancelot* 2594 Ȝhit he was pure, he prewit wel oft-syss. *a* **1568** in *Bannatyne MS.* (1878) 780/6 Oft syiss he sicht, and said, Allace.

'oft-,time, *adv.* (*a.*) *Obs.* or *arch.* Forms: see OFT and TIME; also 5–6 **oftyme**. [f. OFT *adv.* + TIME, substituted for *oft-sithe*: as in other phrases.] = next. In quot. 1896 as *adj.*: Frequent, that has often been: cf. *sometime.*

1414 BRAMPTON *Penit. Ps.* (Percy Soc.) 23 Thowȝ I do ofte tyme amys. **1483** CAXTON *G. de la Tour* H j, Oftyme hit displeaseth god. **1514** BARCLAY *Cyt. & Uplondyshm.* (Percy Soc.) 2 To se the cyte oftyme whyle he was ladde. **1567** *Satir. Poems Reform.* v. 147 For men oftyme of meinest sort, ..Hes geuin gude counsall to the wyse. **1896** *Daily News* 12 Sept. 5/1 The oft-time Premier of the Colony.

oft-times, ofttimes ('ɒft,taɪmz, ɔː-), *adv.* Now *arch.* and *poet.* Also 4–5 **oft times**, 4–6 **ofte times**; (5–6 **oftymes**, **oftimes**, 6 *Sc.* **aftymes**). [f. as prec.: the *-s* is prob. the plural ending, *times* being substituted for *sithes*, as in *fele times* (Langland) for *feolesiþes*, many times.] = OFTENTIMES.

1382 WYCLIF *Matt.* xvii. 15 For why oft tymys [*v.r.* oft time, **1388** ofte tymes, TINDALE oft tymes, **1551** ofte times, *Rheims* often, **1611** oft times] he fallith in to the fijr, and oft tymys [*16th c. vv.* oft, **1551** ofte, *Rheims* often] in to water. **1413** *Pilgr. Sowle* II. lx. (1859) 57 Ful oftymes thou hast excyted me to synne. **1526** *Pilgr. Perf.* (W. de W. 1531) 6 Than is he ofttymes moost nye the state of misery. **1567** MAPLET *Gr. Forest* 30 b, That which is holsome and good for one kind, oftetimes is hurtfull for another. **1588** A. KING tr. *Canisius' Catech.* 15 b, Aftymes to cal on the sueit name of Iesus. **1662** STILLINGFL. *Orig. Sacr.* III. i. §19 Prodigies, which oft-times presage revolutions in states. **1701** J. LAW *Counc. Trade* (1751) 59 They are ofttimes directly opposite to one another. **1814** CARY *Dante, Paradise* XXII. 104, I oft-times wail my sins. **1869** FREEMAN *Norm. Conq.* III. xii. 258 Ofttimes he laced and ofttimes he unlaced his helmet.

† **of'wake**, *v. Obs. rare.* [f. OF-[2] + WAKE *v.*: app. erron. extension of *a-wake.*] *intr.* To awake.

c **1330** *Arth. & Merl.* (Kölbing) 3800 He ofwoke & had wonder; His sweuen he teld his feren hard.

† **of'walked**, *pa. pple. Obs. rare.* [f. OF-[1] + *walked*, pa. pple. of WALK *v.*] Exhausted with walking.

1377 LANGL. *P. Pl.* B. XIII. 204 Whan þow art wery for-walked [*MS. W* of-walked].

† **og, ogg** (ɒg). *Obs. Austral.* and *N.Z. slang.* [Cf. HOG *sb.*[1] 8.] A shilling.

1937 PARTRIDGE *Dict. Slang* 580/2 *Ogg* or *og*, a shilling... A corruption of *hog* (a shilling). **1945** BAKER *Austral. Lang.* v. 109, 1s....*og* and *rogue* (probably a clipping of the English rhyming slang *rogue and villain*, a shilling). **1946** *Penguin New Writing* XXVIII. 125 Three quid and seven og.

OG, O.G., contracted form of OGEE.

ogain(e, ogaines, etc., obs. ff. AGAIN, AGAINST.

ogam, ogamic, var. OGHAM, OGHAMIC.

† **'ogart.** *Sc. Obs.* [Another form of *ongart*, ANGARD *sb.*, q.v.] Arrogance, presumption.

[*c* **1325** *Metr. Hom.* 49 Her may ye alle ensampel tak, Ongart and rosing to forsak.] *c* **1375** *Sc. Leg. Saints* xxx.

(*Theodera*) 215 Na ogart na pryd is þe with-in. *Ibid.* xl. (*Ninian*) 1334 Alace! for myn ogart I haf tynt grace! *c* **1470** HENRY *Wallace* x. 155 For thi ogart othir thow sall de, Or in presoun byd.

‖**ogbanje** (əʊg'bænʒiː). [Ibo.] (See quots.) Also *attrib.*

1958 C. ACHEBE *Things fall Apart* ix. 68 The child was an *ogbanje*, one of those wicked children who, when they died, entered their mothers' wombs to be born again. *Ibid.* 68 Okonkwo had called in another medicine-man who was famous in the clan for his great knowledge about *ogbanje* children. **1976** *CRC Jrnl.* July 18/1 His daughter Aku-nna is so thin and delicate that it is even suggested that she might be an 'ogbanje', a 'living dead', a child only on loan to this world who will be called back to the other world while still young.

ogdoad ('ɒgdəʊæd). Also 7 **ogdoade**. [ad. late L. *ogdoas, ogdoad-em*, a. Gr. ὀγδοάς, ὀγδοάδα, f. stem of ὀκτώ eight, ὄγδοος eighth.] **a.** The number eight. **b.** A group, set, or series of eight; *spec.* in *Gnosticism*, a group of eight divine beings or æons; also, the heavenly region.

1621 BP. MOUNTAGU *Diatribæ* 258 Their Ogdoades, Duodecads, Triacontads, Pleromaes, Bythos, Siges, and all the Æones, blasphemous speculations. **1660** STANLEY *Hist. Philos.* IX. (1701) 383/2 The Ogdoad, they said was the first Cube, and the only number evenly even under ten. **1803** G. S. FABER *Cabiri* I. 195 *note*, The arkite ogdoad, or the eight Cabiric gods of Egypt. **1833** CRUSE *Eusebius* v. xix. 203 Irenaeus also wrote the treatise on the Ogdoad, or the number eight. **1882–3** SCHAFF *Encycl. Relig. Knowl.* II. 879 Mind, Word, Intelligence, Wisdom, Power, Justice, Peace, —which with the Father, constitute the great Ogdoad, the type of the lower spheres. **1889** FARRAR *Lives Fathers* I. iii. 112 *note*, All things sprang from 'depth' ('Bythos', the unutterable) and silence ('Sige'), the immediate parents of 'Mind' and 'Truth', the 'Word' and 'Life', 'Man', and the 'Church'. These formed the Ogdoad and represent the Supreme Being absolutely and relatively.

‖**ogdoas** ('ɒgdəʊæs). *rare.* [Gr.] = prec.

1647 H. MORE *Song of Soul* I. II. xv, Upon this universall Ogdoas Is founded every particularment.

†'**ogdoastich**. *Obs.* Also 7 **-ick, -ique**, and in quasi-Gr. form **-icon**. [A by-form of OCTASTICH, after Gr. ὀγδοάς: see OGDOAD.] A poem or stanza of eight lines: = OCTASTICH.

1612 SELDEN *Illustr. Drayton's Poly-olb.* i. 19 His request to Diana, in an hexastick, and her answer in an ogdoastick.. are in the British story. **1631** WEEVER *Anc. Fun. Mon.* 673, I haue read this Ogdoasticon following. **1642** HOWELL *For. Trav.* (Arb.) 54 It will not be much out of the byas, to insert (in this Ogdoastique) a few verses of the Latine which was spoken in that age.

ogee (əʊ'dʒiː, 'əʊdʒiː). Also 5 *pl.* oggez. Sometimes written **OG** or **O.G.** [app. worn down from F. *ogive*, OGIVE, with which it is identified by Cotgrave and others in 17th c.: see sense 1 and OGIVE. See Paley, *Gothic Mouldings* (ed. 1865), 33, 35, 48, 52, and C. Brunel in *Romania* (1960) LXXXI. 293.]

†**1.** = OGIVE 1. *Obs.*

1428–9 *King's Hall Acc.* in Willis & Clark *Cambridge* (1886) II. 445 *note*, Item pro ij peciis [of stone] pro armis Regis viij *s.* Item pro iiij ped' de Oggez viij *d.* [App. worked stones from Burwell and Hynton.] **1611** COTGR., *Ogive*, an Ogiue, or Ogee in Architecture.

2. *Arch.* and *Joinery.* **a.** A moulding consisting of a continuous double curve, convex above and concave below; a cyma reversa.

In cross-section, its outline is a sort of *S* shape when the moulding (with reference to the solid on which it is worked) is towards the observer's left hand, and like this reversed when towards his right. If the *S* outline is towards his right, or the reversed shape towards his left, the moulding is termed a back-ogee, a cyma, or a cyma recta. An inverted back-ogee (frequently used as a base-moulding to a wall or plinth), and an inverted ogee, are such mouldings respectively turned upside down. The double-curved fall of a piano is a familiar example of the inverted ogee. The term ogee is sometimes applied to all the above curves indiscriminately.

1677 MOXON *Mech. Exerc.* (1703) 267 Scima recta, or Ogee. **1703** T. N. *City & C. Purchaser* 1 An O.G. with a Fillet over it. *Ibid.* 95 An O.G. is a Moulding, somewhat resembling an S. **1797** *Encycl. Brit.* (ed. 3) II. 234/2 There are eight regular mouldings in ornamenting columns.. cyma, talon, or ogee. **1847** SMEATON *Builder's Man.* 251 *Ogee*, a moulding, consisting of a portion of two circles turned in contrary directions, so that it is partly concave and partly convex. **1858** *Skyring's Builders' Prices* (ed. 48) 59 Beaded capping.. with OG under. **1862** RICKMAN *Goth. Archit.* 15 The ogee, which has the round uppermost and over-hanging. **1879** SIR G. SCOTT *Lect. Archit.* I. 152 The upper torus was often converted into a kind of ogee.

b. Any curve or line having this form.

1851 RUSKIN *Stones Ven.* I. x. §17 This double curve is called the Ogee; it is the profile of many German leaden roofs, of many Turkish domes. **1875** FORTNUM *Majolica* viii. 69 The dishes of this variety usually have the outer edge shaped in alternating ogee.

c. Short for *ogee arch, canopy, plane*: see 3 a, b.

1677 MOXON *Mech. Exerc.* (1703) 73 Planes in use amongst Joyners, called Molding-planes; as.. the Ogee. **1855** STREET *Brick & Marb.* (1874) 211 The window-head is of that earliest form of ogee, a circle just turned up to a point in the centre. **1862** RICKMAN *Goth. Archit.* 263 The second canopy is the ogee, which runs about half up the dripstone, and then is turned the contrary way, and is finished in a straight line running up into a finial.

3. *attrib.* **a.** Consisting of an ogee or a series of ogees; having the outline of an ogee; as, ***ogee character, curvature, curve, shape***; **ogee front**, the fall of a pianoforte shaped in an ogee curve; **ogee head, -top**, a roof or covering, the upper part of an opening, when shaped like an ogee; **ogee member**, the outline of an ogee as an element of form; **ogee mould**, a templet for running an ogee moulding in plaster, etc.; **ogee moulding** = OGEE 2; **ogee plane**, a joiner's moulding-plane with an ogee sole; **ogee wing** *Aeronaut.*, a wing whose outline is an ogee (used on some supersonic aircraft).

1688 R. HOLME *Armoury* III. 396/2 An other sort of Mould by which a cornice is run about a Room or Mantle-trees of Chimneys.. is termed an O.G. Mould. **1753** HOGARTH *Anal. Beauty* ix. 48 The variety introduced by the ogee member, which is entirely composed of waving lines. **1815** R. WORNUM *Price-list*, Harmonic [piano-forte].. O.G. front do. in rose wood. **1823** P. NICHOLSON *Pract. Build.* 162 A moulding of the ogee kind, called a Cyma-reversa. **1836** LOUDON *Encycl. Cottage Archit.* 1129 Ogee moulding, called also cyma reversa. **1849** FREEMAN *Archit.* 226 A circular tower.. crowned with an ogee cupola. **1851** RUSKIN *Stones Ven.* I. x. §18 The varieties of the ogee curve are infinite. **1862** RICKMAN *Goth. Archit.* 291 Triangular canopies.. some with ogee heads. *Ibid.* 357 Canopies.. are generally of the ogee character. *Ibid.* 385 Octagonal towers,.. with buttresses, pinnacles, and an ogee top. **1864** BOUTELL *Her. Hist. & Pop.* 318 The arches having an ogee curvature. **1875** KNIGHT *Dict. Mech.* II. 1547/1 *Ogee-plane*, a joiner's plane for working ogee-mouldings. **1892** W. B. SCOTT *Autobiog.* I. i. 10 It was framed by immense ogee stone lintels and architrave. **1960** *Aeroplane* XCIX. 791/1 The ogee wing is one of the highly swept delta wings with very low aspect ratio which are being proposed for supersonic airliners. Slender wings of this type have subsonic leading-edges and supersonic trailing edges. **1970** *New Scientist* 23 Apr. 172/2 The HS 133 is an ogee wing (Concorde shape).

b. ogee arch, an arch formed by the union of two contrasted ogees meeting at its apex. Similarly **ogee doorway, ogee window**, etc., a doorway, etc. having the form of an ogee arch.

1816 RICKMAN in J. Smith *Panorama Sc. & Art* I. 132 The ogee or contrasted arch, has four centres; two in or near the span, and two above it, and reversed. **1834** *Gentl. Mag.* CIV. 95 The beautiful ogee doorway. **1851** RUSKIN *Stones Ven.* I. xi. §14 But if the arch be of any bizarre form, especially ogee, the joints must be in particular places, and the masonry simple, or it will not be thoroughly good and secure; and the fine schools of the ogee arch have only arisen in countries where it was the custom to build arches of few pieces.

4. *Comb.*, as **ogee-headed** adj.

1851 TURNER *Dom. Archit.* I. vi. 218 This [window] is ogee headed.

Hence **o'geed, ogee'd** *a.*, furnished with an ogee or ogees; having the form of an ogee.

1851 RUSKIN *Stones Ven.* I. xi. §2 The form of the arch.. may be rounded, or lozenged, or ogee'd, or anything else. **1880** *Archæol. Cant.* XIII. 460 A piscina, in the south wall of the aisle, has an ogeed, five-foiled arch. **1882** *Ibid.* XIV. 364 On the exterior the labels are ogeed.

ogel, oggel *a.*, ugly, horrible: see OUGLE *a.*

Ogen ('əʊgɛn). Also with lower-case initial. [Place-name (see below).] The name of a kibbutz in Israel, used attrib. in **Ogen melon** to designate a small melon with pale orange flesh and brownish-orange skin ribbed with green, belonging to a variety first developed there.

1967 *Guardian* 14 June 6/7 The tiny Ogen melon... Paler-fleshed than its French antecedent, the Charentais, it has the same voluptuous flavour. **1969** *Oxf. Bk. Food Plants* 118/2 'Ogen Melon'. The name is derived from a kibbutz in Israel where it was bred and whence it has been exported during the last decade. It is said to belong to the cantaloupe group of varieties. **1973** *Observer* (Colour Suppl.) 1 July 39/1 The small ogen melon, orange ribbed with green.. was first grown by Nathan Fuchs at the Ogen kibbutz, north of Tel Aviv. **1976** *Listener* 12 Feb. 171/3 This one place on the Dead Sea.. is now the source of such fruits as the ogen melons we enjoy in London in midwinter.

-ogen (ədʒɛn), a suffix f. -O + -GEN, q.v. In *Biochem.* appended to the names, usu. terminating in *-in*, of biologically active compounds, esp. proteins, to form the names of their inactive precursors: as CHYMOTRYPSINOGEN, FIBRINOGEN, PEPSINOGEN, RENNINOGEN.

1961 *Rep. Comm. Enzymes Internat. Union Biochem.* ix. 49 The names of enzyme precursors should no longer be formed by the use of the suffix '-ogen'; the prefix 'pre-' should be used instead.

ogg, var. OG.

†**ogga'nnition**. *Obs. rare*$^{-1}$. [n. of action f. L. *oggannīre*, f. *ob-* (OB- 1 b) + *gannīre* to snarl. Cf. OBGANIATE.] Snarling, growling, grumbling.

1625 BP. MOUNTAGU *App. Cæsar* 288 Nor will I abstaine, notwithstanding your oggannition, to follow the steps and practice of Antiquity.

oggif, obs. form of OGIVE.

oggin ('ɒgɪn). *Naut. slang.* [A corruption of *hogwash.*] The sea.

1946 J. IRVING *Royal Navalese* 126 *Oggin*, the sea; the Drink; the Ditch. The term descends to us aitch-less from an earlier abuse of the sea as the Hog-Wash. **1949** W. GRANVILLE *Sea Slang Twentieth Cent.* 100 *Floggin' the 'oggin*, sailing the high seas. (Naval lower-deck.) *'Oggin* is a form of *'ogwash. Ibid.* 168 *'oggin*, the sea or *ditch.* A perversion of *'ogwash* (*hogwash*). **1973** D. LEES *Rape of Quiet Town* x. 165 No one told the two gunners that the sub was about to crash-dive and they had to run like hell to avoid being left behind in the oggin.

†'**oggle**, *v. Obs. rare.* In 5 ogyl. [app. for ***uggle**, freq. or dim. of UG, UGGE *v.*, to shudder. Cf. *ogel, oggel*, OUGLE *a.*] *intr.* To shudder or quiver for fear.

c **1450** *Cov. Myst.* xli. (Shaks. Soc.) 395 Myn herte gynnyth ogyl and quake for fer.

ogglesome, variant of UGGLESOME, horrible.

ogh, variant of OCH *int.*

1582 STANYHURST *Æneis* IV. (Arb.) 116 God Iuppiter, ogh lord: Quod she, shal hee scape thus?

ogh, oȝ, obs. forms of OWE *v.*

ogh, for *hogh*, obs. form of HEUGH.

ogham, ogam ('ɒgəm). Also **ogum, oghum**. [a. OIr. *ogam, ogum* (gen. *oguim*), mod.Ir. *ogham*, pl. *-uim*, Gaelic *oghum*, a name traditionally connected with a mythical inventor called in Irish legends *Ogma*, said to have invented the Ogam 'to provide signs for secret speech only known to the learned'. Cf. Ὄγμιος, the name according to Lucian of a Gaulish deity, who seems to have presided over language or eloquence. Rhŷs takes the word as possibly connected with Gr. ὄγμος straight line, row, furrow, Skr. *ajma* course, road.]

1. An alphabet of twenty characters used by the ancient British and Irish; the system of writing, or an inscription written, in such characters; also one of the characters themselves.

The characters consist each of a thin line or stroke, or a group of from two to five such parallel strokes, arranged along either side of, or drawn across, a continuous medial or guiding line. Thus *b, l, w* (*v, f*), *s, n*, are represented by 1, 2, 3, 4, 5 strokes under the line; *χ* (*h*), *d, t, c, q* by the same above the line; *m, g, y, z, r*, by long strokes crossing obliquely, thus /; *a, o, u, e, i* by short strokes crossing at right angles. In inscriptions, the edge of a squared stone usually serves as the continuous base line.

1677 O'MOLLOY *Grammatica* 133 Obscurum loquendi modum, vulgo *ogham*, Antiquarijs Hiberniæ satis notum... Alia adhuc vtebantur methodo in scribendo preter abbreuiationes, quam insuper vocabant *ogham*, peritioribus tantum-modo familiare. **1729** T. INNES *Crit. Ess. Anc. Inhab. North. Parts Brit.* II. 445 That the first author.. was Fenius-Farsaidh, who composed.. the alphabets of the Hebrews, Greeks and Latins; the Bethluisnion, and the Ogum. *Ibid.* 451 Waræus.. tells us, that the Ogum did not contain the Irish vulgar character, but a hidden way of writing. **1794** SULLIVAN *View Nat.* V. 77 The Ogham was the sacred character of the Druids. **1845** O'DONOVAN *Gram. Irish Lang.* Introd. **1851** D. WILSON *Preh. Ann.* (1863) II. IV. ii. 212 The Newton Stone oghams have hitherto baffled all attempts at interpretation. **1877** RHŶS *Lect. Welsh Philol.* VI. 272 Monuments in Ogam are known only in the British Isles. *Ibid.* 273 The continuous line merely represents the edge or ridge of the stones on which the Ogams are written.

2. An obscure mode of speaking used by the ancient Irish.

1627 CONNELL MAGEOGHEGAN tr. *Annals of Clonmacnoise* (in O'Donovan), A.D. 1328. Morish O'Gibelan,.. an excellent poet in Irish, an eloquent and exact speaker of the speech, which in Irish is called Ogham. **1677** [see 1].

3. *attrib.*, as ***ogham alphabet, inscription, stone***.

1784 T. ASTLE *Orig. Writing* vi. 180 King Charles I corresponded with the Earl of Glamorgan when in Ireland, in the Ogham cipher. **1814** SCOTT *Wav.* xxviii, Detecting the Oggam character.. upon the key-stones of a vault. **1827** G. HIGGINS *Celtic Druids* 21 These were the Ogham-beith, the Ogham-coll, and the Ogham-craoth, which means Ogum-branches. **1861** O'CURRY *Lect. MS. Materials* 464 Monumental stones with *Oghuim* characters and words. **18..** WHITLEY STOKES in Rhŷs *Lect. Welsh Philol.* (1877) 272 Genuine Ogham Inscriptions exist both in Ireland and Wales which present grammatical forms agreeing with those of the Gaulish linguistic monuments.

oghamic, ogamic ('ɒgəmɪk, ɒ'gæmɪk), *a.* [f. prec. + -IC: cf. OGMIC.] Of or pertaining to ogham; consisting of oghams.

1876 SULLIVAN in *Encycl. Brit.* V. 306/1 In.. the Book of Ballymote, compiled near the close of the 14th century, the different styles of Ogamic writing and the value of the letters are explained. **1887** *Athenæum* 6 Aug. 187/2 Material for Oghamic study.

o'ȝe, variant of *aȝé, ayé*, obs. form of AGAIN.

13.. *Guy Warw.* (A.) 3207 'Bi-leue þou here,.. Al what ich come now son oȝe'. 'Anon', seyd Gij, 'it schal so be'.

oghen, oȝen: see OWE *v.*

oghne, obs. f. OWN.

oght, -e, oȝt, obs. forms of AUGHT, OUGHT.

Oghuz (əʊ'guːz). [ad. Turk. *oğuz* (which is also the name of a legendary Turkish hero).] **1.** Also **Ghuzz** (via Arabic), **Oghus, Oğuz**. One of various Turkic tribes, now more usually included among the Turkmen, who originally inhabited Siberia and, later, Transoxiana but who crossed the Oxus in the 11th century and invaded Persia, Syria, and Asia Minor; also, a member of one of these tribes. Also *attrib.* or as *adj.*

1843 *Penny Cycl.* XXV. 395/2 For many centuries the Oghuzes were perpetually at war with the Persians. **1845** *Encycl. Metrop.* XXV. 868/2 They [*sc.* the Uz-beks] are called Ghuzz by the Arabs. **1854** G. Larpent in J. Porter *Turkey* I. 155 The Turks divided themselves into the Uigurs or Eastern Turks..and into the Oghus or Western Turks. **1888** *Encycl. Brit.* XXIII. 660/2 The old name Ghuzz, originally, as it seems, the Turkish Oghuz (an eponymous hero of whom Turkish chronicles tell many fables) was wholly superseded by the new name Turkman. **1899** Skrine & Ross *Heart of Asia* I. xix. 142 The Ghuz laid waste the whole of Khorāsān. **1947** Auden *Age of Anxiety* (1948) v. 103 The Ghuzz, the Guptas, the gloomy Krimchaks. **1953** [see Kipchak]. **1965** H. M. Smyser in Bessinger & Creed *Medieval & Linguistic Stud.* 93 Ibn Faḍlān's descriptions of..Oghuz (Ghuzz Turks)..are fascinating. **1972** [see Kipchak]. **1974** G. Lewis tr. *Bk. of Dede Korkut* 10 It is known that the term 'Oghuz' was gradually supplanted among the Turks themselves by *Türkmen*, 'Turcoman', from the mid tenth century on... The Turcomans were those Turks, mostly but not exclusively Oghuz, who had embraced Islam and begun to lead a more sedentary life than their forefathers. *Ibid.*, The stock epithet of the Oghuz ladies is 'white-faced'.

2. The southern division of the Turkic languages. Usu. *attrib.* or as *adj.*

1959 J. Benzing in *Philologiae Turcicae Fundamenta* I. 2 In what follows a survey is given of the Turkic languages, in which the individual languages and dialects are set together as they seem to me, on grounds of linguistic history (phonetic and especially grammatic) to be especially closely connected... b) Southern Turkic (the Oghuz group). Here belong: 1. Osmanli... 2. Azarbaijani... 3. Turkmen. **1974** *Encycl. Brit. Micropædia* X. 198/1 Turkmen is a member of the southwestern, or Oghuz, division of the Turkic languages.

So **O'ghuzian** *a.* and *sb.*

1603 R. Knolles *Gen. Hist. Turkes* 128 For although he [*sc.* Othoman] were a Turke borne, yet was he not of the Selzuccian family, as were the rest, but of another house and tribe, and therefore not of them fauoured or thought to have so good right vnto any of the late Sultans prouinces or territories, as had they who being of his house and holpen with the prescription of time, enuied at the sudden rising of this Oguzian Turke, being vnto them as it were a meere stranger. **1621** Heylin *Microcosmus* 312 Solyman the chiefe of the Oguzian family and Prince of Machan, flying the fury of the Tartars, was drowned in Euphrates. **1880** A. H. Sayce *Introd. Sci. of Lang.* II. ix. 263 The one-eyed giant.. reappears among the Turkish Oghuzians. *Ibid.* 264 In the Oghuzian version the story is amplified.

ogival (əʊ'dʒaɪvəl, 'əʊdʒɪvəl), *a.* (*sb.*) [f. next + -al¹, or a. F. *ogival* (in J. Michelet 1835).]

A. *adj.* **1. a.** Having the form or outline of an ogive or pointed ('Gothic') arch.

1841 *Blackw. Mag.* XLIX. 150 (tr. Michelet *Hist. France* II. 666) In the ogival triangle, in the ogive, two lines are bent. **1868** *Athenæum* 25 July 112/3 They..show..how a flat-headed shot must penetrate an inclined plate better than a shot with an ogival head. **1871** Hartwig *Subterr. World* xxiii. 269 Its roof is supported by an ogival vault or an arch. **1875** *Wond. Phys. World* I. ii. 88 Black lines forming parabolic or ogival curves. **1888** *Times* (weekly ed.) 30 Mar. 8/3 [The ship has] ogival ends like the head of a Palliser projectile. **1900** *Brit. Med. Jrnl.* 12 May 1156 With regard to the head of the bullet, the..type which offers..least resistance is that known as ogival, which means that the curve is..part of the circle, the radius of which is equal to two diameters of the base of the bullet.

b. Characterized by ogives or pointed arches.

1855 tr. *Labarte's Handbk. Arts Mid. Ages* v. 235 The style of ogival architecture. **1882** E. O'Donovan *Merv Oasis* I. xxv. 420 The peculiar ogival forms of Persian and Saracenic architecture. **1891** *Pall Mall G.* 10 Dec. 6/1 The rise and growth of the Ogival—or Gothic—style.

c. *Comb.*, as **ogival-cylindrical, -headed** adjs.

1868 *Rep. Munit. War* 126 A solid steel shot..having either a cylindrical or ogival-cylindrical shape. *Ibid.* 263 The ogival-headed shot..does not rack like spherical shot.

2. Having the shape of an ogee.

1962 *Flight Internat.* LXXXI. 269/1 One of the two Fairey FD.2 research aircraft owned by the Ministry of Aviation is being converted..to flight-test an ogival wing. **1965** *Times* 11 Sept. 7/6 Instead of being an ordinary, straight-sided delta, the Concord wing is ogival. Each wing starts as a sharp point.., spreads outwards and then curves in again. **1976** *Jane's Pocket Bk. Res. & Exper. Aircraft* 19 Special design features: Slender ogival delta wings.

B. *sb.* An ogival head of a shot.

1894 *Times* 2 Aug. 3/6 Its ogival and point had been fused ..as had been the case with the first shot.

ogive ('əʊdʒaɪv, əʊ'dʒaɪv). *Arch.* Also 3 oggif. [a. F. *ogive* (1468 in Godef. *Compl.*), formerly also *œgive* (1325), *orgive* (1399), *augive* (1459), *osive*, *oisive* (1462–3), *ogive* (1503); of uncertain origin; it has been conjecturally referred to F. *auge* trough; to It., Sp., Pg. *auge* 'the highest point of any planet' (Florio), culmination, highest point, ad. Arab. *auj* (prop. a term of Astrology or Astronomy); and to L. *augēre* to increase, augment (Littré).]

1. The diagonal groin or rib of a vault, two of which cross each other at the centre.

1357–8 *Ely Sacr. Rolls* (1907) II. 180 In lvj pedibus de oggifs empt. per pede iijd. ob. 16ˢ. 4ᵈ. **1611** Cotgr., *Branches d'augives*, branches ogiued; or, limmes with ogiues. [See also ogee 1.] **1727–41** Chambers *Cycl.*, *Ogives*, arches or branches of a Gothic vault, which, in lieu of being circular, pass diagonally from one angle to another... The middle, where the ogives cut or cross each other, is called the key, which is sometimes carved in form of a rose, or a *cul de lampe*. **1842** Gwilt *Encycl. Arch.* (1876) 232 *Ogive*.. designated originally a diagonal band in groined vaulting formed by the intersection either of barrel vaults or of keel vaults, to both of which the terms *voûte en croisée d'ogives*, or *voûte d'ogives*, were applicable. **1896** Vizetelly tr. *Zola's Rome* 361 [Referring to the church of Santa Maria sopra Minerva] The clustering columns cased in stucco imitating marble, the ogives which dared not soar, the rounded vaults condemned to the heavy majesty of the dome style.

†**2.** (See quots.) *Obs.*

(This explanation seems due to Cotgrave (who app. misunderstood the Fr. word, as no such sense appears in French dictionaries or authors). Blount who copied Cotgrave, and Phillips who plagiarized Blount, also identify *Ogive* with *Ogee*.)

[**1611** Cotgr., *Augive*, an ogiue; a wreath, circlet, round band, in Architecture.] **1656** Blount *Glossogr.*, *Ogive* or *Ogee* (Fr. *Augive* or *Ogive*), a wreath, circlet or round band in Architecture. **1658** in Phillips.

†**3.** An ogee moulding. *Obs.*

1703 T. N. *City and C. Purchaser* 214 O.G., Ogee, or Ogive, a sort of Moulding in Architecture. **1706** Phillips, *Ogive*, or *Ogee*,..a Member of a Moulding which consists of a Round and a Hollow.

4. a. A pointed (= 'Gothic') arch.

(Apparently so called from the shape of the spaces between the ogives or ribs of a vault. 'As equivalent to a pointed arch, *ogive* is merely the popular confirmation of an error committed by the ignorance of some writers in the present [19th] century'. Gwilt *Encycl. Arch.* (1842–76) 233.)

1841 *Blackw. Mag.* XLIX. 150 [see ogival a.]. *Ibid.* (tr. Michelet), The common aspiration of lines..which is the mystery of the ogive, is frequent in India and Persia. **1851** Ruskin *Stones Ven.* I. i. §33 It will be..difficult to distinguish the Arabian ogives from those..built under.. Gothic influence. **1893** *Funk's Stand. Dict.*, *Ogive*,..a pointed arch; hence, a window in the pointed style. **1894** *Nation* (N.Y.) 7 June 425/3 The architects freely mixed the two styles, at Laon sandwiching two stories of round arches between the ogives on the ground floor and those in the clerestory.

b. (Something having) the profile of an ogive, esp. the head of a projectile.

1904 *Sci. Amer.* 16 Jan. 44/1 It [*sc.* an airship] is cylindrical in form, with an ogive nose and a nearly hemispherical stern. **1947** L. E. Simon *German Research in World War II* 115 They studied the way in which the ogive (the tapering head of the projectile) broke up. **1950** E. A. Bonney *Engin. Supersonic Aerodyn.* v. 183 For a given base diameter, therefore, the drag of an ogive will be less than that of a cone of the same length. **1966** D. Stinton *Anat. Aeroplane* vi. 89 The shapes of such aircraft are determined by the need to produce favourable interactions between the relatively high-pressure regions behind shock waves and the adjacent airframe surfaces. The simplest example is shown in Fig. 6.9, in which an ogive, shedding a complete ogival Mach-cone, is split longitudinally and fitted with wings.

5. *Statistics.* A graph in which each ordinate represents the frequency with which a variate has a value less than or equal to that indicated by the corresponding abscissa, which for many unimodal frequency distributions has the form of an ogee. (In earlier use the ordinates and abscissas were interchanged.)

1875 F. Galton in *Phil. Mag.* XLIX. 35 When the objects are marshalled in the order of their magnitude along a level base at equal distances apart, a line drawn freely through the tops of the ordinates which represent their several magnitudes will form a curve of double curvature... Such a curve is called, in the phraseology of architects, an 'ogive'. *Ibid.* 46 A law of frequency of error founded on a binominal ogive. **1930** R. Pearl *Introd. Med. Biometry & Statistics* vi. 119 The ogive and integral forms of plotting a frequency distribution are fundamentally the same. The only difference is that in the case of the ogive frequencies are plotted along the abscissal axis, and in the integral along the *y* axis as usual. **1937** Yule & Kendall *Introd. Theory of Statistics* (ed. 11) viii. 150 The values of the percentiles may be used to draw what is known as Galton's ogive curve. **1939** J. F. Kenney *Math. of Statistics* (1940) I. ii. 26 The graphs of cumulative frequencies are called ogives. **1962** A. Battersby *Guide to Stock Control* iii. 31 This curve has been derived from sales figures with a Normal distribution... It is called the 'ogive' of the Normal curve. *Ibid.*, For Normal probability paper, the scale is drawn so as to turn the Normal ogive into a straight line.

6. *Geol.* A stripe or band of dark material stretching from side to side across the surface of a glacier, usu. arched in the direction of flow and arranged in a parallel series of similar bands.

1947 *Jrnl. Glaciology* I. 16 Then there is the question of 'Ogives' or pressure arches. **1949** *Ibid.* I. 327 Vareschi's latest and most important researches were made upon various systems of banding which appear in the tongue of the Great Aletsch Glacier, in particular what are locally called *Ogiven*. These are curved bands visible on the glacier surface, often in regular longitudinal series... The ogive itself is generally darker block ice, whilst between one ogive and the next is paler and higher *Buckel* ice. **1951** *Ibid.* I. 498 The study of the formation of ogives which in English-speaking countries are referred to as Forbes's Bands. **1974** *Encycl. Brit. Macropædia* IX. 183/1 In plan view, the ogives are invariably distorted into arcs or curves convex downglacier; hence the name ogive.

7. *attrib.* and *Comb.*, as ***ogive window***; ***ogive windowed*** adj.

1842 Barham *Ingol. Leg.*, *Blasphemer's Warn.*, The large ogive window that lighted the hall. **1882** E. O'Donovan *Merv Oasis* I. ii. 28 The houses of the genuine ogive-windowed, flat-roofed Persian type. **1898** T. Hardy *Wessex Poems* 212 High halls with tracery And open ogive-work.

Hence **ogived** *a.*, consisting of an ogive or ogives; having the form of an ogive or ogee.

1611 [see ogive 1]. **1845** Petrie *Eccl. Arch. Ireland* 232 Of the triangular or rather ogived label.., an example is found over a..doorway of a temple on a coin of the Emperor Licinius.

Oglala (ɒ'glɑːlə). Also **Ogalalla, Ogallalla(h), Oglalla.** [Native word.] The chief tribe of the Teton Sioux Indians; a member of this tribe; also, their language. Also *attrib.*

1837 *Missionary Herald* (Boston, Mass.) XXXIII. 369/2 Came to the village of the Ogallallah Indians, consisting of more than two thousand persons. **1838** S. Parker *Jrnl. Exploring Tour beyond Rocky Mts.* 63 They were Ogallallahs, headed by eight of their chiefs. **1857** *Porter's Spirit of Times* 21 Mar. 34/1 They proved to be a hunting-party of Ogallallah Sioux. **1867** *Harper's Weekly* 5 Oct. 629/2 The Commission..on August 19 held a council on the steamer..with the head chiefs of the Ogallas. **1876** H. T. Williams *Pacific Tourist* 47/1 Red Cloud is chief of the Ogalalla Sioux. **1897** C. King *Warrior Gap* (1898) 31 With him rode Baptiste,..whose mother was an Ogallala squaw. **1921** F. Hebert *40 Years Prospecting* 6 It was there that I saw Pawnee Killer, a big Ogalala Chief. **1933** [see Dakota *sb.* 2]. **1947** B. A. De Voto *Across Wide Missouri* 123 When Sublette & Campbell brought the Oglalas to the Platte in 1834 [etc.]. *Ibid.* 191 Fort Laramie..would draw all the wandering trappers,..the Oglala Sioux, and finally the United States Army. **1973** *Freedomways* XIII. 81 There is much emphasis on the dance and its symbolic meaning to the Oglala. **1974** *Black Panther* 19 Jan. 3/3 Both Mr. Means, an Oglala Sioux, and Mr. Banks, a Chippewa, have wove the right to make opening statements to the jury once they are seated.

ogle ('əʊg(ə)l), *sb.*¹ [f. the vb. or cognate with it.]

1. An eye; usually *pl.* the eyes. Orig. *Vagabonds' cant*; in early 19th c. in *Pugilistic slang*, etc.

a **1700** B. E. *Dict. Cant. Crew* s.v. *Ogling*, The Gentry-mort has rum Ogles, that Lady has charming black Eyes. **1705** E. Ward *Hud. Rediv.* (1708) I. vi. ix, He rowl'd his Ogles with a Grace Becoming so a zealous Face. **1711** —— *Quix.* I. 348 Turning up his Ogles tow'rd The Shining Heavens, in a Passion. **1819** Moore *Tom Cribb's Mem.* App. ii. 51 Round *lugs* and *ogles* flew the frequent fist. **1820** *Sporting Mag.* VI. 80 The latter..got a small taste over his left ogle. **1853** 'Cuthbert Bede' *Verdant Green* II. iv, That'll raise a tidy mouse on your ogle, my lad.

2. An amorous, languishing, or coquettish glance; an ocular invitation to advances.

1711 Addison *Spect.* No. 46 ¶8, I have..brought over with me a new flying Ogle fit for the Ring. **1775** *Davenant's Man's the Master* v. 65 Her ogles dart this way. **1823** Byron *Juan* vi. lx, If fond of a chance ogle at her glass, 'Twas like the fawn, which, in the lake displayed, Beholds her own shy, shadowy image pass. **1851** Thackeray *Eng. Hum.* ii. (1876) 189 You see him..delivering a killing ogle along with his scented billet. **1882** Mrs. Edwardes *Ballroom Repentance* I. 20 Enduring alike her wrong notes and her ogles.

†**ogle**, *sb.*² *Her. Obs.* Pl. 5 oglys. [Origin unknown: the sense is the same as that of ogress².] A representation of a cannon-ball as a bearing.

1486 *Bk. St. Albans, Her.* B iv b, Oglys be calde in armys gonestonys.

ogle ('əʊg(ə)l), *v.* Also 8 **augle, oagle.** [Appeared late in 17th c., as a cant word, app. from Du. or LG.: cf. LG. *oegeln*, freq. of *oegen* to look at (Bremisches Wbch. 1767), Ger. *äugeln* to ogle, to leer, freq. or dim. of *augen* to look about, to eye, f. *auge* eye. Cf. also early mod.Du. or Flem. *oogheler, oegheler* flatterer (Kilian); and for the sense the Du. *oogen* to direct or cast the eyes, in Hexham (1660) 'to cast sheepes eyes upon one, or to aime or take a mark by the Eyes', f. *oog* eye.]

1. *intr.* To cast amorous, coquettish, or insinuatingly familiar glances.

1682–87 [see ogling *vbl. sb.*]. *c* **1685** *Roxb. Ball.* (1885) V. 567 Wilt thou still sparkle in the Box, And ogle in the Ring? **1713** Lady M. W. Montagu *Lett., to Miss Wortley* Nov. (1887) I. 83 He sighs and ogles so, that it would do your heart good to see him. **1719** D'Urfey *Pills* I. 256 Here is one can Oagle finely. **1779** Mad. D'Arblay *Diary* Jan., I was watched the whole evening, but..the company behaved extremely well, for they only ogled! **1886** Fenn *Master of Cerem.* iii, Her sister ogled and smiled, and smirked under her paint and diamonds.

b. *trans.* To turn or bring by ogling.

1712 Arbuthnot *John Bull* III. iii, He would ogle you the outside of his eye inward, and the white upward. *a* **1814** *Manœuvring*, in *New Brit. Theatre* II. 119, I might ogle myself blind..before I should get a kind look from her.

2. *trans.* To eye with amorous, admiring, or insinuating glances; to 'make eyes' at.

1711 Addison *Spect.* No. 8 ¶7 As soon as the Minuet was over, we ogled one another through our Masques. **1715** Lady M. W. Montagu *Town Eclogues* i, The prince is ogled; some the King pursue; But your Roxana only follows You. **1840** Dickens *Old C. Shop* xxxiii, 'Is that my Sally?', croaked the dwarf, ogling the fair Miss Brass. **1844** —— *Mart. Chuz.* iv, Mr. Tigg..ogled the three Miss Chuzzlewits with the least admixture of banter in his admiration.

3. To keep one's eyes upon; to eye, to look at.

1820 W. Irving *Sketch Bk.* I. 150 There was a portly parson, whom I observed ogling several mouldy writers through an eye glass. **1833** M. Scott *Tom Cringle* (Farmer), She first ogled the superscription, and then the seal, very ominously. **1891** Clark Russell *My Shipmate Louise* 67 He stood ogling the wreck through his binocular.

ogler ('əʊglə(r)). [-er¹.] One who ogles.

1692 Southerne *Wives Excuse* Prol., To the Ladies, who must sit it out, To hear us prate, and see the Oglers shoot.

1709 *Tatler* No. 145 ¶1 A certain Sect of professed Enemies to the Repose of the Fair Sex, called Oglers. **1787** Wolcott (P. Pindar) *Ode upon Ode* Wks. 1812 I. 418 The sweet and tender style of Oglers. **1847** Le Fanu *T. O'Brien* 216 The most conspicuous ogler at court.

ogli, oglie, obs. forms of ugly.

ogling (ˈəʊglɪŋ), *vbl. sb.* [f. ogle *v.* + -ing¹.]

a. The action of the verb ogle; the throwing of amorous, languishing, or insinuating glances.

1682 Shadwell *Tegue o Divelly* ii. Epil. (1691) 80 They say their Wives learn ogling in the Pit [*side note*, A foolish Word among the Canters for glancing]. *a* **1700** B. E. *Dict. Cant. Crew*, *Ogling*, casting a sheep's Eye at Handsom Women. **1709** Hickes *Let. to Charlett* 15 Jan. (Bodl. Ballard MS. XII. 109), As for Augling.. I only used it, as a word which signifies to eye or look with a fixed eye. **1796** Burke *Regic. Peace* i. Wks. VIII. 106 It was not enough, that the speech from the throne.. threw out oglings and glances of tenderness. **1878** E. Jenkins *Haverholme* 99 If dining, and ogling, and flattering.. could have saved a party, the Whigs would now have been in the ascendant.

b. *attrib.* and *Comb.* **ogling-glass** *U.S. humorous*, a monocle.

1687 Congreve *Old Bach.* iii. iv, A penal mourning for the ogling offences of his youth. **1711** Addison *Spect.* No. 46 ¶8 Being thus qualified, I intend, by the Advice of my Friends, to set up for an Ogling-Master. **1843** *Knickerbocker* XXII. 111 There he was promenading,.. an ogling-glass lifted to his eye.

ˈogling, *ppl. a.* [f. as prec. + -ing².] That ogles; casting amorous or admiring looks.

a **1715** Ld. Halifax *On Countess Dowager of ——* 6 Have at the heart of every ogling beau. **1883** Stevenson *Silverado Sq.* 180 The ogling, well-shod lady with her troop of girls.

oglio, obs. form of olio.

†**ogloˈgarchial,** *a. Obs. rare*⁻¹. Erron. for *oligarchial*, from oligarchy. So †**ogloˈgarchian** *a.*

1600 W. Watson *Decacordon* (1602) 329 Intende they [the Jesuits] a Democracy or an Aristocracy, or an Oglogarchial? or what kind of gouernment is intended by them? *Ibid.* 224 The ecclesiasticall state in Scotland,.. their grounds, rules and principles of their gouernment Oglogerchian.

ogmic (ˈɒgmɪk), *a.* [f. *ogam*, ogham + -ic.] = oghamic.

1874-7 Rhŷs *Lect. Welsh Philol.* vi. 286 The Ogmic monuments in our island are not confined to the West, for others are known in Scotland. **1882** R. C. Maclagan *Scot. Myths* 35 The inventors of the Ogmic called each letter by the name of a different plant. **1893** Prof. Kirkpatrick in *Scotsman* 14 Apr. 7/5 A province that he [Prof. Rhŷs] had made peculiarly his own was Ogmic Epigraphy.

o'goblin: see goblin².

Ogopogo (ˈəʊgəʊˈpəʊgəʊ). *Canad.* [Fanciful, said to be from a British music-hall song by C. Clark (see quot. 1974).] The name of a water monster alleged to live in Okanagan Lake, British Columbia. Also *transf.*

No contemporary (1924) copy of the song referred to in quot. 1974 has been traced.

1926 *Province* (Vancouver) 24 Aug. 7 (*heading*) 'Ogopogo' now official name of the famous Okanagan sea serpent. **1927** *Ibid.* 25 Sept. 24 Alberta claims to have an Ogopogo all its own. **1933** *Sun* (Baltimore) 24 June 14/1 He blamed the 'ogopogo', famed lake monster. **1936** A. F. Cross *Cross Roads* 71 Ogopogo's head is slightly reminiscent of Henry VIII, he has a torso like an accordion, and a tail like a shillelagh. Ogopogo is, of course, a celibate, because he lost his wife in the Carboniferous Age, and after the customary dinosaurian 1,000-year period of mourning, was once more seen about again. **1955** *Daily Progress* (Charlottesville, Va.) 8 Feb. 12/6 The dispute arose when Ogopogo's name appeared on a new bridge across the South Saskatchewan. **1962** G. MacEwan *Blazing Old Cattle Trail* vii. 46 The way was described as rough and mountainous but no Ogopogo lake serpents were reported. **1974** P. Costello *In Search of Lake Monsters* x. 222 The old Indian name for the animal was Naitaka, or Nha'a'itk; the settlers name for it is now Ogopogo, which is far more recent in origin. It is not, as some seem to have thought, an Indian word. Back in 1924 the following music hall hit from London was sung one night in Vernon: His mother was an earwig, His father was a whale. A little bit of head, and hardly any tail, And Ogopogo was his name.

‖**o-goshi, ogoshi** (əʊˈgɒʃɪ). [Jap., f. *o(u)* big, major + *koshi* the waist or hips.] A hip throw in Judo.

1954 E. Dominy *Teach yourself Judo* 190 *Ogoshi*,.. Floating Hip Throw. **1957** Takagaki & Sharp *Techniques Judo* ii. iv. 47 *O-goshi*: major hip throw.... Throw by a pulling and twisting motion over your right hip. **1966** *Daily Tel.* 15 Nov. 21/4 A ballet dancer.. broke an arm.. while trying an O Goshi throw.

Ogpu (ˈɒgpuː). Also O.G.P.U. [f. the initials of the Russ. *Ob"edinënnoe Gosudárstvennoe Politícheskoe Upravlénie* United State Political Directorate.] An organization for investigating and combating counter-revolutionary activities in Soviet Russia, which superseded the Cheka and the G.P.U. (G. III. f) in 1923 and was replaced by the N.K.V.D. (N II. 1) in 1934.

1923 *Times* 24 Nov. 13/5 By special decree the Soviet Government has created a new Supreme International Cheka (State Political Department), which is called 'Ogpu' (Unified State Political Department). **1927** *Daily Tel.* 7 June 10/2 A report from Leningrad states that the Ogpu (Cheka) has officially announced the execution without trial of 'all the active members of a band of incendiaries'. **1927** *Glasgow Herald* 13 June 12/3 The fertile imagination of the Ogpu, or 'State Political Department'. **1927** *Daily News* 17 Nov. 7/4 Trotzky is under arrest.. and is being watched by officials of the O.G.P.U. (Secret Police). **1928** *Sunday Times* 8 Jan. 11/1 The day has gone by when Ogpu sought to conceal itself. **1939** *Ann. Reg. 1938* 211 The new chief of the O.G.P.U., one Beria, appointed only in November, is stated to have dismissed 470 of the highest officers. **1940** [see Gestapo]. **1940** *War Illustr.* 12 Jan. 608/1 Reported that Russians have brought up picked Ogpu troops into Karelian Isthmus. **1949** [see Cheka]. **1958** C. Cockburn *Crossing Line* vi. 97 Dedicated men.. with pistols in their hands ready to blaze away in case this OGPU desperado should get up to any tricks. **1972** T. Wittlin *Commissar* (1973) xxxiv. 248 For almost ten years an intensive chase after Agabekov was conducted by the men of the OGPU in Paris.

†**o'grant,** *a. Obs. rare*⁻¹. [app. for *agrant*; cf. agraunte *v.* and AF. *agraunter*, ONF. *agraanter* = OF. *acreanter* to promise, assure, guarantee, grant, agree, consent (Godef.). The form of the Eng. word is not easy to understand, unless it be short for *ogranted* pa. pple., which again makes the sense difficult.] ? Agreed, consentient.

c **1330** R. Brunne *Chron.* (1810) 51 Harald.. To be þer kyng & hede þe lond was wele ogrant.

-ography: the suffixal element -graphy, preceded by the connective *-o-*, belonging to the prec. element (see -o *suffix*¹ 3); applied to a branch of knowledge the name of which ends in this, as *biography*, *geography*, *hydrography*.

1828 *First Book, King's Coll.* 15 Your 'ologies and 'ographies.. as studies in a College.

†**ograve.** *Obs. rare.* Epithet of a variety of wheat: see quot.

1616 Surfl. & Markh. *Country Farme* 543 The next [wheat] is small Pollard, which loves an indifferent earth... Then Ograue wheat, which loueth anie well-mixt soyle.

ogre (ˈəʊgə(r)). Also 8 **hogre.** [a. F. *ogre* (first used by Perrault in his *Contes*, 1697).

The alleged instance of 1527 in Hatz.-Darm. is an error. It has been suggested that Perrault may have formed *ogre* on an It. dial. **ogro* for **orgo* = It. *orco* demon, monster, from L. *Orcus*, Hades, the god of the infernal regions, Pluto. The OSp. reprs. of *Orcus* were *huerco* (Percivall), *huergo*, *uergo* (Diez); Mod.Sp. *ogro* 'ogre' is from Fr. (Conjecture has tried to see in *ogre* the ethnic name *Ugri*, *Ungri*, *Ongri*, applied by early writers to the Hungarians or Magyars: see Ugrian. But this is historically baseless.)]

In folk-lore and fairy tales: A man-eating monster, usually represented as a hideous giant; hence, A man likened to such a monster in appearance or character.

1713 tr. *Arabian Nights* I. 78 He perceiv'd that the Lady.. was a *Hogress*, Wife to one of those Savage Demons call'd *Hogres*, who stay in remote places, and make use of a thousand wiles to surprize and devour Passengers. [So ed. 1785.] **1786** tr. *Beckford's Vathek* (1868) 27 With the grin of an ogre. **1830** Scott *Demonol.* iii. 116 Some doting ogre of a fairy tale. **1844** Dickens *Mart. Chuz.* ix, 'He's the most hideous, goggle-eyed creature,.. quite an ogre'. **1854** *Old Story-Teller, Hop-o'-my-Thumb* 93 She warned them that they were in the house of an ogre, who especially delighted in eating young children.

fig. **1850** Kingsley *Alt. Locke* x, Irresponsibility of employers, slavery of the employed,.. that is the system they represent.. Why, it is the very ogre that is eating us all up.

b. *attrib.* and *Comb.*, as **ogre-king, -land,** etc.

1846 R. Bell *Life Canning* viii. 215 Headed by the giant West India Interest, and followed by all the other ogre-monopolies. **1855** J. R. Planché tr. *C'tess d'Aulnoy's Fairy T., Bee & Orange Tree* (1858) 183 It is the custom in Ogreland, that the Ogre, Ogress, and the young Ogres, always sleep in their fine gold crowns. **1859** Ld. Lytton *Wanderer* (ed. 2) 288, I was lately wed With a diamond ring to an Ogre-king.

Hence **ogreism** (ˈəʊgərɪz(ə)m), the character or practices of ogres.

ogreish, ogrish (ˈəʊgərɪʃ, ˈəʊgrɪʃ), *a.* [f. ogre + -ish¹.] Resembling, or characteristic of, an ogre.

1852 Dickens *Bleak Ho.* II. iii. 41 There is an Ogreish kind of jocularity in Grandfather Smallweed to-day. **1864** G. Dyce *Bella Donna* II. 105, I know that I am a rude ogrish fellow. **1867** O. W. Holmes *Guardian Angel* xxv. (1891) 306 He glared at it in a dreadfully ogreish way.

Hence **ˈogreishly** *adv.*, in an ogreish manner.

1891 *Harper's Mag.* June 71/1 A great distorted silhouette.. appeared upon the wall, leaning ogreishly over the pillow.

ogress¹ (ˈəʊgrɪs). Also 8 **hogress.** [a. F. *ogresse*, fem. of *ogre*: see -ess¹.] A female ogre.

1713 [see ogre]. **1789** Gibbon *Autobiog.* (1854) 6 Three Ogresses, or female cannibals. **1840** Dickens *Barn. Rudge* ix, Like some fair ogress who had set a trap and was watching for a nibble from a plump young traveller.

ogress². *Her.* Also 8 **aggress.** [Origin unknown: the sense is the same as in ogle *sb.*²; but it is difficult to find a formal relation between them.] A 'roundel sable', *i.e.* a black circular spot on a shield, supposed to represent a cannon-ball: called also a *pellet*.

1572 Bossewell *Armorie* ii. 37 b, Beareth Verte, fiue Fermaulxz in Crosse D'Or, a Border d'Argent, charged with eight Ogresses: or, after the French blazon, '*Ogressèe de huit pieces*'. **1678** Phillips (ed. 4), *Ogresses* [ed. 1706 or *Agresses*], certain round figures in Heraldry resembling Pellets, always of a black colour. **1690** *Lond. Gaz.* No. 2525/4 A Fesse Argent between Estoiles charged with 3 Ogresses. **1766** Porny *Heraldry* Dict. (1787), *Ogress*, term used by English Heralds only, to express the black Roundelets, which are also called *Pellets* and *Gunstones*. **1882** Cussans *Her.* (ed. 2) iv. 73 The Pellet, or Ogress.

‖**ogrillon** (ɔgrijɔ̃). *rare*⁻¹ [a. F. *ogrillon*, f. *ogre* ogre + suff. *-illon* in *moinillon*, *négrillon*, *oisillon*, etc.] A little ogre.

1860 Thackeray *Round. Papers* xv. (1863) 235 What.. brutal behaviour to his children, who, though ogrillons, are children!

ogrufe: see groof.

ogtiern, ogum, var. ochiern, ogham.

Ogygian (əʊˈdʒɪdʒɪən), *a.* [f. L. *Ogygius*, Gr. Ὠγύγιος (f. personal name Ὤγυγος, Ὠγύγης) + -an.] Of or pertaining to the mythical Attic or Bœotian king Ogyges; of obscure antiquity; of great age.

Ogygian deluge, a famous flood said to have taken place in the reign of Ogyges.

1843 Horne *Orion* i. iii. 148 He.. wished the Ogygian deluge were returned. **1858** Hogg *Life Shelley* I. iv. 139 Sir Bysshe being Ogygian, gouty, and bedridden.

ogyl, variant of oggle *v.*, to shake.

oh (əʊ), *int.* (*sb.*) [Another spelling of *O* int., prob. intended to express a longer or stronger sound.] An exclamation expressing emotion of various kinds; formerly often used in all positions in which *O* is now more usual; now chiefly used when the exclamation is detached from what follows, and esp. as a cry of pain or terror, or in expression of shame, derisive astonishment, or disapprobation, in which case it is often repeated as *oh! oh!*

a **1548** Hall *Chron., Edw. IV* 231 b, Oh Lorde, Oh sainct George,.. have you thus doen in deede? **1552** Huloet, Oh, a voyce of an exceadynge disdeynynge, reioycinge, or sorowynge. *a* **1553** Udall *Royster D.* iv. viii. (Arb.) 78 Oh bones, thou hittest me. **1555** *Tract* in Strype *Eccl. Mem.* (1721) III. App. xliv. 124 Oh! what a heinous work is this in the sight of God. *Ibid.*, Oh! what damnable beasts are these. **1637** Rutherford *Lett.* (1862) I. 249 Oh for that cloud of black wrath and fury of the indignation of the Lord. **1653** Walton *Angler* iv. 105 Oh me he has broke all, there's half a line and a good hook lost. **1707** Watts *Hymn 'There is a land of pure delight'* v, Oh! could we make our doubts remove. **1711** Steele *Spect* No. 146 ¶3 Oh how glorious is the old Age of that great Man. **1798** Coleridge *Anc. Mar.* iv. ix, But oh! more horrible than that Is the curse in a dead man's eye! *Ibid.* v. i, Oh sleep! it is a gentle thing. **1820** Byron *Mar. Fal.* ii. i. 454 But never more—oh! never, never more.. shall Sweet Quiet shed her sunset! **1843** Hood *Song of Shirt* iv, Oh, Men, with Sisters dear! Oh, Men, with Mothers and Wives! **1875** Jowett *Plato* (ed. 2) I. 52 And Oh! let me put another case, I said.

B. *sb.* The interjection or exclamation *oh!*, as a name for itself. So **oh dear, oh fie,** etc.

1534 More *Comf. agst. Trib.* iii. x. (1847) 223 He fet a long sigh with an oh! from the bottom of his breast. **1597** Middleton *Wisdom of Solomon* xi. 14 God sent sad Ohs for shadows of lament. **1711** Steele *Spect.* No. 154 ¶2 He was reproved, perhaps, with a Blow of the Fan, or an Oh Fy! **1712** *Ibid.* No. 400 ¶4 An Interjection, an Ah, or an Oh, at some little Hazard in moving or making a Step. **1820** W. Tooke tr. *Lucian* I. 386 Never-ending ohs and ahs. **1852** Darwin in *Life & Lett.* (1887) I. 384 Oh! the professions; oh! the gold; and oh! the French—these three oh's all rank as dreadful bugbears.

Hence **oh** *v. intr.*, to exclaim 'Oh!'; *trans.* to greet with 'Oh?' Also **oh-oh** *v.*

1833 R. H. Froude in *Rem.* (1838) I. 321 People would.. 'Oh! oh!' *Ibid.* 323 There is no chance of its being 'Oh, oh!'-ed. **1848** Newman *Loss & Gain* ii. xix. (1876) 320 It is very well for secular historians to give up a tradition.. and for a generation to oh-oh it; but the Church cannot do so. **1855** Dickens *L. Dorrit* i. xxxiv, All their hearing, and ohing, and cheering.

oh, ohen, obs. forms of owe *v.*

ohelo (əʊˈheɪləʊ). [Hawaiian.] The red or yellow fruit of a blueberry native to Hawaii, *Vaccinium reticulatum*. Also *attrib.*

1843 J. J. Jarves *Hist. Hawaiian Islands* i. 9 The banana, yam, sweet potato,.. *ohelo* (a berry),.. are indigenous and plentiful. **1888** W. Hillebrand *Flora Hawaiian Islands* 272 The shining fleshy berry, the 'Ohelo',.. is the principal food of the wild mountain goose. **1977** *Time* 17 Oct. 41/1 Native Hawaiians have long attempted to placate the fire goddess Pele by dropping offerings—ohelo berries, liquor and, once upon a time, an occasional human—into the crater of the 4,090ft. volcano Kilauea.

ohia (əʊˈhiːə). Also **ohia lehua.** [Hawaiian.] = lehua. Also *attrib.*

1824 C. S. Stewart *Jrnl.* 15 June in *Jrnl. Residence Sandwich Islands* (1828) xi. 305 The only trees and plants known to us, which we saw.. were the koa, *acacia*, a large and beautiful tree of dark, hard wood, the Ohia, *eugenia malaccensis*, bearing a beautiful tufted, crimson flower, and a fruit called by foreigners, the native apple. **1825** [see kukui]. **1866** 'Mark Twain' *Lett. from Hawaii* (1967) xi. 99 Shady groves of forest trees.. and, handsomest of all, the ohia, with its feathery tufts of splendid vermilion-tinted blossoms. **1888** [see lehua]. **1917** *Nature* 20 Sept. 57/2 The ohia.. also called ohia lehua and lehua, resembles.. our white oak, but bears beautiful clusters of scarlet flowers with long, protruding stamens. **1937** D. & H. Teilhet *Feather*

Cloak Murders x. 185 A few gnarled ohia trees..grew between the twisted rocks. **1970** S. CARLQUIST *Hawaii* xvi. 301 The ohia lehua lends a somber air to wet forests because of its dark green foliage, dark gray bark, and often gnarled branches. Roots are formed on the sides of trunks of ohia trees... Ohia forest can be very tall, exceeding fifty feet... The tallest ohias are on the island of Hawaii.

Ohian (əʊˈhaɪən), *sb.* and *a.* = OHIOAN *sb.* and *a.*

1819 in J. Flint *Lett. from Amer.* (1822) 128 The Ohian is in many cases growing up to manhood. **1836** C. R. GILMAN *Life on Lakes* I. 54 He..is the very man..who should be called Buck Eye and not Ohian. **1963** *Guardian* 1 May 10/7 The average Ohian. **1977** *Financial Times* 18 Oct. 17/1 Ohians can with some justification claim to be a boilerhouse of U.S. manufacturing industry. *Ibid.* 17/7 Even those Ohian politicians who rose to national prominence rarely put their stamp on the country's affairs.

Ohio (əʊˈhaɪəʊ), the name of a North American river, a tributary of the Mississippi, and one of the United States, used *attrib.* in ***Ohio bluebell, buck-eye, sandstone***; **Ohio fever, spread** (see quots.).

1842 C. M. KIRKLAND *Forest Life* II. xxxix. 142 A beautiful perennial, here called the Ohio bluebell, a far larger plant than the one we know by that name. **1810** F. A. MICHAUX *Hist. Arbres Forestiers de l'Amérique Septentrionale* I. 38 Ohio buck eye.., nom donné par moi. **1832** D. J. BROWNE *Sylva Amer.* 227 It is called Buckeye by the inhabitants,..but..we have denominated it Ohio Buckeye, because it is more abundant on the banks of this river. **1948** *Chicago Sun-Times* 20 Apr. 32/2 The Ohio buckeye..is the first of all the big trees to burst forth with leaves. **1816** in T. W. Robinson *Hist. Morrill* (1944) 155 The 'Ohio Fever' took away many of our best farmers. **1831** T. BUTTRICK *Voyages* 57 The 'Ohio fever' became a well known expression for this desire to move West. **1835** *Knickerbocker* V. 274 Such..as some fifteen years since happened to reside in any part of New-England where what was called the 'Ohio fever' prevailed. **1881** *Harper's Mag.* Apr. 711/1 Lime stone..and gray Ohio sandstone are much used in construction. **1971** M. TAK *Truck Talk* 111 *Ohio spread*, a trailer with a separation of eight feet between the axles.

Ohioan (əʊˈhaɪəʊən), *sb.* and *a.* [f. OHIO + -AN.] **A.** *sb.* A native or inhabitant of Ohio in the United States. **B.** *adj.* Of or pertaining to Ohio.

1818 E. P. FORDHAM *Pers. Narr. Trav.* (1906) viii. 165, I do not choose the risk of being insulted by any vulgar Ohioans. *c* **1848** W. WHITMAN in *Amer. Speech* (1961) XXXVI. 297 Ohioans [are called] *Buckeyes*. **1906** A. B. HULBERT in B. A. Botkin *Treas. S. Folklore* (1949) III. i. 421 When exactly one half had passed on a hog gallop the Ohioan leaped down. **1927** H. CRANE *Let.* 7 May (1965) 296 Under the benign influence of Ohioan pollens during the months of June, July, Sept. & October. **1929** G. L. ESKEW in B. A. Botkin *Treas. S. Folklore* (1949) I. i. 13 Daniel Decatur Emmett, an Ohioan by birth, a traveling minstrel and showman by persuasion, made a song about 'Dixie, the Land of Cotton'. **1948** [see NEBRASKAN *sb.*]. **1973** *Time* 25 June 11/1 A fellow Ohioan and Wooster alumnus. **1978** *Amer. Speech* LIII. 42 A wave of Ohioans in the middle nineteenth century inundated northern Indiana and a large area of Illinois.

‖**ohm**[1] (oːm). [Ger., = AAM.] An obsolete German liquid measure equivalent to from 30 to 36 gallons according to the locality.

1851 LONGF. *Gold. Leg.* IV. *Convent Hirschau*, It comes from Bacharach on the Rhine..And costs some hundred florins the ohm [*rime* Rome].

ohm[2] (əʊm). *Electr.* [From the name of the German physicist Georg Simon *Ohm* (1787–1854), who determined mathematically the law of the flow of electricity (*Ohm's law*).] **1.** The unit of electrical resistance: see quots. Now incorporated in the International System of Units, and defined as the resistance that exists between two points when a potential difference between them of one volt produces a current of one ampere.

The word *ohma* was orig. proposed for the practical unit of 'tension' (voltage), along with *volt* for the unit of resistance (see quot. 1861, which also appears in *Electrician* (1861) 9 Nov. 4 and is from the paper read at the Sept. 1861 meeting of the British Association). The origin of the change in application of the word has not been traced in print.

1861 CLARK & BRIGHT in L. Clark *Exper. Investigation Laws Propagation Electr. Current* 49 Let us derive terms from the names of some of our most eminent philosophers... We shall then have the following table: A.—Tension. 1 Daniell's Element = 1 Ohma, or unit of tension... B.—Quantity. 1 Ohma, by 1 metre square at 1 milliometre [*sic*] distance = 1 Farad, or unit of quantity... D.—Resistance. 1 Farad per second = 1 Volt, or unit of resistance. *Ibid.*, The ohma, or unit of tension, is practically a very convenient one for all battery purposes. **1865** *Proc. R. Soc.* XIV. 159 It is proposed that the new standard [of resistance] shall not be..described as so many metre/seconds, but that it shall receive a distinctive name, such as the B.A. unit, or, as Mr. Latimer Clark suggests, the 'Ohmad'. **1867** W. H. PREECE in *Phil. Mag.* XXXIII. 397, I beg to suggest..to those physicists and electricians who have adopted the British-Association unit for electrical measurements, that in place of expressing this unit, as is variously done at present, by B.A. unit, Ohmad, Ohm, 10^7 metre/second, &c., it would be very convenient to adopt some universal symbol analogous to that used for degrees (°). The Greek letter ω appears to me very convenient. *Ibid.*, The conductivity of the Atlantic cable would be given by 7524^{ω}, and its insulation by 2349^{Ω} per knot, which may still be read Ohm and Megohm. **1867** R. S. CULLEY *Handbk. Pract. Telegr.* (ed. 2) ii. 30 The unit [of resistance] adopted by the electricians of this country is that determined by a Committee of the British Association, and is called the 'ohm'.., and sometimes the 'B.A. unit'. **1870** F. L. POPE *Electr. Tel.* iii. (1872) 25 The Ohm..is equivalent to about $\frac{1}{13}$ of a mile of galvanized No. 9 iron wire. **1876** PREECE & SIVEWRIGHT *Telegraphy* 5 It is convenient..to use a symbol to represent the ohm as we use ° to represent degrees, and ′ minutes. The symbol used by us is ω, the Greek *omega*. Thus we say that the resistance of a wire between London and Birmingham is 1500^{ω}. **1889** *Nature* 14 Feb. 368/2 It was in this country that..the term 'ohmad' or 'ohm', suggested by Sir Charles Bright and Mr. Latimer Clark at the meeting of the British Association in Manchester in 1861, first came into use as the name of a decimal multiple of the absolute unit of resistance convenient for practical purposes. At the Congress of Electricians in Paris in 1881, the Ohm was unanimously adopted as an international standard. **1892** *Gloss. Electr. Terms* in *Lightning* 3 Mar. Suppl., The Ohm is the resistance of a column of mercury of a constant section of one square millimetre and of a length of 106·3 centimetres, at the temperature of melting ice. **1943** F. E. TERMAN *Radio Engineers' Handbk.* II. 40 Wire-wound variable resistors of these types are available up to about 100,000 ohms, and are capable of dissipating up to about 15 watts. **1973** D. ALDOUS in *Pye Bk. of Audio* vii. 75/2 Most transistor amplifiers offer a wide range of output impedances, usually from 4 to 16 ohms.

2. *attrib.* and *Comb.*, as **ohm-centimetre**, the unit of electrical resistivity in the C.G.S. system, being the resistivity of a substance of which a centimetre cube has a resistance of one ohm; **ohm-metre**, the corresponding unit in the International System of Units, equal to 100 ohm-centimetres.

1920 W. T. MACCALL *Continuous Current Electr. Engin.* (ed. 2) iii. 18 The resistance of a conductor 1 cm. long and 1 sq. cm. cross-section..is called the specific resistance per centimetre cube... A better name is ohm-centimetre (or microhm-cm.). **1957** H. COTTON *Electr. Technol.* (ed. 7) iii. 67 It is..logical to express ρ as so many ohms-centimetre..or ohm-metre [*sic*]... For example, for copper at normal room temperature $\rho = 1{\cdot}72 \times 10^{-6}\ \Omega$-cm $= 1{\cdot}72 \times 10^{-8}\ \Omega$-m. **1974** *Encycl. Brit. Micropædia* VIII. 524/1 If lengths are measured in centimetres, resistivity may be expressed in units of ohm-centimetre. *Ibid.*, The resistivity of an exceedingly good electrical conductor, such as hard-drawn copper, at 20° C (68° F) is $1{\cdot}77 \times 10^{-8}$ ohm-metre, $1{\cdot}77 \times 10^{-6}$ ohm-centimetre, or 10·7 ohm-circular mils per foot.

Hence **ˈohmad** = OHM; **ohm-ˈammeter**, an instrument for measuring electrical current and resistance, a combination of an ammeter and an ohmmeter; **ˈohmmeter**, an instrument for measuring electrical resistance in ohms.

1866 R. M. FERGUSON *Electr.* 151 This is called the B.A. Unit of resistance 1864, or an Ohmad. **1891** *'Electrician' Primer* No. 12. 8 *Ohmmeters* indicate the ratio of the pressure between the ends of a conductor to the current passing through that conductor.

ˈohmic, *a.* [f. OHM[2] + -IC.] That obeys Ohm's law, or exhibits behaviour consistent with it.

1889 *Electr. Rev.* 11 Oct. 411 At present Dr. Fleming and a few others talk of 'ohmic' resistance, to distinguish resistance from the relation between the back electromotive force and the current. **1904** *Electrician* Nov. 150/1 The energy dissipation due to ohmic resistance in the metal. **1926** R. W. LAWSON tr. *Hevesy & Paneth's Man. Radioactivity* i. 14 This proportionality between current and potential..only maintains for the initial part of the curve (the region of Ohmic current, cf. Fig. 3). **1949** *Bell Syst. Techn. Jrnl.* XXVIII. 471 (*heading*) Semi-conductor with two *p-n* junctions and ohmic metal contacts. **1967** *Electronics* 6 Mar. 136/2 Ohmic heating in the device induces diffusions that form p-n junctions.

Hence **ˈohmically** *adv.*, by, or as a result of, ohmic resistance.

1919 *Radio Rev.* Dec. 144 A set of triodes arranged in an ohmically-coupled cascade. **1968** C. G. KUPER *Introd. Theory Superconductivity* i. 10 Changes in the field produce eddy currents, but they will decay Ohmically.

Ohm's law. [see OHM[2].] **1.** *Electr.* The law that the strength of a constant electric current in a circuit is proportional to the electromotive force divided by the resistance of the circuit, and that the potential difference between any two points of it is proportional to the resistance between them. (The name was formerly used of some related principles also.)

Propounded by Ohm in *Die galvanische Kette, mathematisch bearbeitet* (1827).

1850 *Phil. Mag.* XXXVII. 463 (*heading*) On a deduction of Ohm's laws, in connexion with the theory of electro-statics. **1863** *Rep. Brit. Assoc. Adv. Sci. 1862* I. 127 The first relation is a direct consequence of Ohm's Law. **1867** *Phil. Mag.* XXXIII. 321 (*heading*) On one of Ohm's laws relating to an insulated circuit. **1910** *Encycl. Brit.* IX. 182/2 This result..obtained by Cavendish in January 1781, that the current varies in direct proportion to the electromotive force, was really an anticipation of the fundamental law of electric flow, discovered independently by G. S. Ohm in 1827, and since known as Ohm's Law. **1921** W. S. IBBETSON *Motor & Dynamo Control* iv. 131 Generally speaking, A.C. circuits do not obey Ohm's law. **1973** J. W. GARDNER *New Frontiers in Electricity* vii. 138 Superconductors constitute a very dramatic violation of Ohm's law.

2. *Acoustics.* The law that a complex musical sound is heard as the sum of a number of distinct pure tones into which the sound can be analysed by Fourier's theorem.

Propounded by Ohm in *Ann. d. Physik* (1843) LIX. 513, and called *Ohm's Regel* by Helmholtz in *Die Lehre von den Tonempfindungen* (1863) ii. 54.

1875 A. J. ELLIS tr. *Helmholtz' On Sensations of Tone* ii. 51 Every motion of the air..which corresponds to a composite mass of musical tones, is, according to Ohm's law, capable of being analysed into a sum of simple pendular vibrations, and to each such single simple vibration corresponds a simple tone, sensible to the ear. **1924** WILKINSON & GRAY *Mechanism of Cochlea* i. 14 Ohm's Law is a generalisation from the results of experiment. **1974** S. E. GERBER *Introductory Hearing Sci.* vi. 134 Ohm's law has generated over a century of research, largely aimed at demonstrating its limitations. *Ibid.*, When tones of relatively low intensity which differ considerably in frequency are presented together, they are perceived as two distinct tones, in accordance with Ohm's law.

ohn, Sc. dial. var. of ON- = *un-*, without.

oho (əʊˈhəʊ), *int.* Also as two words **o ho, oh ho,** etc.; also 4 **o how**. [See HO *int.*[1] 5.] An exclamation expressing surprise, taunting, exultation, etc.; in quot. 1369 as a shout to arouse a sleeper. (Cf. HO *int.*[1])

13.. *Cursor M.* 12129 (Gött.) 'O ho!' alle þan gan þai cri, 'Qua herd euer sua grett ferli!' *c* **1369** CHAUCER *Dethe Blaunche* 179 This messager..cried O how, a-wake anoon. *c* **1460** *Towneley Myst.* viii. 28 O, ho! this is a wonderfull thyng to witt. **1601** SHAKS. *Twel. N.* III. iv. 71 Oh ho, do you come neere me now. **1610**—— *Temp.* I. ii. 349 Oh ho, Oh ho, would't had bene done. **1778** MAD. D'ARBLAY *Diary* 26 Aug., O ho, this is a good hearing! **1838** DICKENS *O. Twist* ii, 'Oho!..we are the fellows to set this to rights'. *c* **1874** D. BOUCICAULT *Shaughraun* in M. R. Booth *Eng. Plays of 19th Cent.* (1969) II. 224 Oho! if that's Robert Ffolliott, I'd like to know who's this? **1898** G. B. SHAW *Arms & Man* III. 56 Four telegrams—a week old. (He opens one). Oho! Bad news!.. My father's dead. **1933** E. O'NEILL *Ah, Wilderness!* III. i. 93 'Oho,' they cried, 'the world is wide, But fettered limbs go lame!' **1976** P. DICKINSON *King & Joker* ii. 27 Oho. So something had happened.

oh, oh (ˈɒəʊ), *int.* Also **ohoh.** [See O *int.* (*sb.*, *v.*) and OH *int.* (*sb.*)] An exclamation of alarm or dismay in response to adverse circumstances.

1944 E. S. GARDNER *Case of Black-Eyed Blonde* xvi. 156 Two police cars were closing in on them..'Oh, oh!' Della said under her breath. **1947** M. LOWRY *Under Volcano* v. 141 'Oh... Oh.' The Consul groaned aloud... It came to him he was supposed to be getting ready to go to Tomalín. **1958** J. MORGAN *Expense Account* i. 11 They were on the parkway, and Pete was thinking about the children, when he snapped his fingers and said, 'Oh, oh!' He had forgotten to buy them anything in Chicago. **1960** A. WEST *Trend is Up* vi. 259 Oh, oh, he thought, Silky is going to pass out before this night is through, that's for sure. **1962** J. F. POWERS *Morte d'Urban* iii. 58 'Oh, oh, I was afraid of that,' Wilf said.

-oholic: see -AHOLIC.

ohone (əʊˈhəʊn), **ochone** (əʊˈxəʊn), *int.* (*sb.*, *v.*) Forms: 5 **ochane,** 7 **oh hone, O hoan,** 7– **O hone,** 8– **ohon,** 9– **ochone, och hone, ohone.** [a. Gael. and Ir. *ochòin*, oh! alas! Often erroneously analysed, as if it contained the Eng. *O!*] A Scottish and Irish exclamation of lamentation.

c **1480** HENRYSON *Test. Cres.* 541 Ochane! Now is my breist with stormy stoundis stad. *c* **1604** I. C. *Epigr.* in *Shaks. Cent. of Praise* (1879) 63 He that made the Ballads of oh hone. **1621** BURTON *Anat. Mel.* II. iii. v. (1651) 341 Houling O Hone, as those Irish women. **1685** *Whigs Lament.* in *Roxb. Ball.* (1885) V. 534 What have the Whigs to say? O hone! O hone! Tories have got the day; O hone! O hone! **1714** RAMSAY *Elegy J. Cowper* i, John Cowper's dead—Ohon! Ohon! **1801** SCOTT *Glenfinlas* i, 'O hone a rie'! O hone a rie'!' The pride of Albin's line is o'er. *Note, O hone a rie'* signifies—'Alas for the prince, or chief'. **1816** —— *Antiq.* xx, Ohon! it's an ill feight whar he that wins has the warst o't. *c* **1850** in R. Ward *Penguin Bk. Austral. Ballads* (1964) 52 The trees grew so thick I couldn't find it, ochone, ..So bothered and lost was poor Paddy Malone. **1861** TROLLOPE *Tales of All Countries* (ser. 1) 67, I could plainly hear poor Larry's head strike against the stone floor. 'Ochone, ochone!' he cried at the top of his voice. **1884** D. BOUCICAULT *Shaughraun* 20/1 Och hone!—my darlin' boy, it will be a grand day for you, but your poor ould mother will be left alone..och-o-o-hone! **1913** W. B. YEATS *Countess Cathleen* in *Poems* 68 Ochone! The treasure room is broken in. **1919** G. B. SHAW *O'Flaherty V.C.* in *Heartbreak House* 186 Ochone! ochone! my son's turned agen me. Oh whatll I do at all at all? **1920** F. SCOTT FITZGERALD *This Side of Paradise* (1921) *A Lament for a Foster Son...* Ochone He is gone from me the son of my mind. **1939** JOYCE *Finnegans Wake* 277 His sevencoloured's soot (Ochone! Ochonal!).

b. as *sb.*

a **1680** BUTLER *Rem.* (1759) I. 180 The Members..repeated the Oh-hones Of his Wild Irish and chromatic Tones. **1855** KINGSLEY *Westw. Ho!* xi, They could now hear plainly the 'Ochone, Ochonorie', of some wild woman. **1977** *Irish Democrat* Mar. 6/3 When Sarsfield sailed away I wept as I heard the wild ochone.

c. as *v. intr.*

1829 G. GRIFFIN *Collegians* III. xxxiii. 54 I'm ashamed o' myself, to be always..moaning and ochoning, among the neighbours.

o-hoy, variant of AHOY, call used in hailing.

1885 RIDER HAGGARD *K. Solomon's Mines* (1889) 228 As he struck he shouted 'O-hoy! O-hoy!' like his Berserkir forefathers.

oh-so (ˈəʊsəʊ), *adv.* Also **oh, so.** [f. OH *int.* + SO *adv.* III.] Prefixed as an intensive (usu. with hyphen) to adjectives or adverbs, with the sense 'ever so', 'extremely' (usu. with sarcastic or ironical overtones).

1922 *Sketch* 29 Mar. 513/3 A big grey felt hat, which looked, oh, so Spanish! **1952** M. LASKI *Village* ii. 33 Her sweet but, oh, so uninteresting face. **1960** J. BETJEMAN *Summoned by Bells* vii. 66 That mawkish and oh-so-melodious book Holds one great truth. **1965** *Listener* 27 May 797/2 The book is worth a shelf-load of those fashionable intellectualities that oh-so-knowingly chart out the spirallings of psychotic zombies, incapable of feelings, incapable of contacts, their spiritual telephone-wires all cut. **1966** J. PORTER *Sour Cream* xiii. 166 It just never entered Azatov's curly head that his oh-so-upright wife was cuckolding him every time his back was turned. **1972** J. GORES *Dead Skip* xiv. 97 The mailboxes were set against the oh-so-rustic redwood slat fence. **1973** *Radio Times* 20 Dec. 18/2 Very suave thriller with Laurence Harvey being oh-so-smooth. **1977** *Gay News* 7–20 Apr. 22/1 Most people do feel oh-so-slightly apprehensive about meeting him.

oht, ohte, obs. forms of AUGHT, OUGHT.

oh yeah (əʊ 'jɛə), *int. colloq.* (orig. *U.S.*). Also O yeah. [f. OH *int.* + YEAH.] An exclamation or interrogative suggesting incredulity, disbelief, or scepticism; 'really?', 'is that so?'. Also as quasi-*adj.*

1930 *Forum* Dec. 376/2 Only recently, that cultural masterpiece *O yeah!* sounded its death rattle. **1931** LOEB & SCHENKER *Please Stand By* xii. 138 'Oh, are you William Wishtell,' the girl from the Globe asked... 'I've been dying to meet you.' 'Oh, yeah? Well, here I am in the flesh.' **1933** F. SCOTT FITZGERALD *Let.* 19 Oct. (1964) 237 No exclamatory 'At last, the long awaited, etc.' This merely creates the 'Oh yeah' mood in people. **1933** P. GODFREY *Back-Stage* xv. 194 They smiled indulgently, and greeted me with such remarks as 'I should worry' and 'Oh, yeah!' **1934** *Daily Mirror* 28 June 13/1 (*heading*) 'Oh Yeah!'.. Observe that when you say, 'Oh, yes,' it doesn't mean at all the same thing as 'Oh, yeah,' when..you say *that*. 'Oh, yeah' means, really, 'Oh, *no*'; or 'you think you know about that do you, you guy, but I don't think you do, I don't.' **1936** *Variety* 24 June 47/3 Oh, Yeah? Agency men claim they can guess within $250 of any quoted price on a picture name. **1937** H. G. WELLS *Star Begotten* vii. 120 Confronted with an idea the American says 'Oh yeah!' or 'Sez you'. **1943** *Amer. Speech* XVIII. 256 A representative group of Americanisms which have wide currency in Australia:..oh yeah. **1966** D. FRANCIS *Flying Finish* vi. 74 'You look out, pal, you mustn't go around admitting that sort of thing...' 'Oh yeah?' I said, laughing.

oh yes: see OYEZ.

Oi, oi (ɔɪ), repr. dial. or vulgar pronunc. I *pers. pron.*

1901 M. FRANKLIN *My Brilliant Career* xvi. 132 Sure O'i can't plaze yez anyhows. **1930** J. B. PRIESTLEY *Angel Pavement* iv. 188 Now, where was Oi? Losing mi plice, wasn't Oi?.. Ow, Oi know... Whoi dew the Catholics eat Fish on Froiday? **1939** JOYCE *Finnegans Wake* III. 551 Oi polled ye many but my fews were chousen. **1962** M. GREEN *Art of Coarse Sailing* ii. 20 Oi couldn't 'elp overhearing... If your friend's wife's 'aving 'er confinement she oughter come ashore... A Broads boat ain't no place for a babby to be born in. Shall Oi phone for the doctor? **1975** J. DRUMMOND *Slowly the Poison* i. 36 Oi washed down the cobbles. **1976** *Guardian* 6 Aug. 9 (Advt.), An' we're much 'bliged ta Whitbread, thassall oi can say.

oi, *int.*[1]: see OY, OI *int.*

oi (ɔɪ), *int.*[2] Repr. colloq. or vulgar pronunc. of HOY *int.* as a call to attract attention.

1962 JACKSON & MARSDEN *Educ. & Working Class* I. iii. 57 Father said, 'Oi, you two—you're not doing anything. Get some paint and paint under there!'

-oic, ending of the names of organic acids containing a carboxyl group, esp. in place of a methyl group. [App. first used in CAPROIC *a.*]

1971 *Nomencl. Org. Chem.* (I.U.P.A.C.) (ed. 2) C. 182 Carboxyl groups COOH replacing CH_3 at the end of the main chain of an alicyclic hydrocarbon are denoted by adding '-oic acid' or '-dioic acid' to the name of this hydrocarbon.

oick, oik (ɔɪk). *slang.* [Etym. obscure.] Depreciatory schoolboy word for a member of another school; an unpopular or disliked fellow-pupil. Also *gen.*, an obnoxious or unpleasant person; in weakened senses, a 'nit-wit', a 'clot'. Hence '**oikish** *a.*, unpleasant, crude; '**oickman** (see quot. 1925).

1925 *Dict. Bootham Slang, Hoick*,..spit. *Oick*,..to spit; abbreviated form of 'oickman'. *Oickman*,..labourer, shopkeeper, etc.; also a disparaging term. **1933** A. G. MACDONELL *England, their England* vi. 95 Those privately educated oicks are a pretty grisly set of oicks. Grocers' sons and oicks and what not. **1935** 'N. BLAKE' *Question of Proof* x. 189 Smithers is such an oick. **1940** M. MARPLES *Public School Slang* 31 Oik, hoik: very widely used and of some age; at Cheltenham (1897) it meant simply a working man, but at Christ's Hospital (1885) it implied someone who spoke Cockney, and at Bootham (1925) someone who spoke with a Yorkshire accent. **1940** M. DICKENS *Mariana* iv. 109 The old Oik mentioned it over a couple of whiskeys. **1946** G. HACKFORTH-JONES *Sixteen Bells* 260 Come to think of it he must have been a bit of an oik when he worked at Bullingham & Messer. That crack about long hair was well merited. **1957** F. KING *Widow* I. v. 63 He and Cooper had fought a battle with three 'oiks'—this was apparently school slang for the boys of the town. **1958** B. GOOLDEN *Ships of Youth* vii. 162, I only need my cap on back to front to look the complete oick. **1959** W. CAMP *Ruling Passion* xvi. 126 Who's that incredibly uncouth and oikish man? **1966** 'K. NICHOLSON' *Hook, Line & Sinker* viii. 95 So glad you got here before the oicks. **1968** *Melody Maker* 30 Nov. 24/5 Old Stinks from the third stream said: 'I say you oik, the Beach Boys latest is fab gear.' **1975** *Listener* 16 Jan. 83/1 The rigmarole about the flat was patent set-dressing, just to impress us oiks. **1975** *Times* 7 Aug. 7/7 His [*sc.* Oswald Mosley's] angels, a gang of gullible and bloodthirsty oiks.. would come pretty far down the roster of hell's legions.

oiconomical, obs. form of ECONOMICAL.

-oid (ɔɪd, əʊɪd), *suffix*, ad. mod.L. *-oīdēs*, Gr. -οειδής, i.e. -ο- of prec. element or connective + -ειδής 'having the form or likeness of', 'like', f. εἶδος form; cf. L. *-i-formis*: see -FORM. (A parallel Gr. formative was -ώδης: see -ODE[1].) Examples: αἱματοειδής (αἱματώδης) 'like blood, of the appearance of blood, hæmatoid'; ἀνθρωποειδής 'of human form, manlike, anthropoid'. In other mod. langs., as in Gr. and L., the *o* and *i* make distinct syllables (L. *anthrōpoīdēs*, F. *anthropoïde*, Ger. *anthropoïd*); in Eng. also, some pronounce (ænθrəʊ'pəʊɪd), but the prevalent pronunciation of the suffix (and in many words, as *alkaloid, asteroid*, the only one) is with the diphthong (oi) as in *void*.

Extensively used in scientific terms, taken from Greek prototypes, or formed on Gr. (rarely L.) words. These are primarily adjs. with the sense 'having the form or nature of, resembling, allied to'; but also (as sometimes in Gr.) sbs., in the sense of 'something having the form or appearance of, something related or allied in structure, but not identical'. The sbs. are esp. numerous in Mathematics, where, in imitation of *rhomboid* (Gr. ῥομβοειδής approaching a lozenge (ῥόμβος) in shape, a rhomboid) and *trapezoid* (Gr. τραπεζοειδής having somewhat of the form of a table (τράπεζα)), the suffix has been used to form the names of many geometrical figures.

Examples:—(*adj.*) Anat. *adenoid, arachnoid, arytenoid, coracoid, hyoid, sigmoid, thyroid*; Zool. *amœboid, anthropoid, cancroid, crinoid, echinoid, hydroid, ichthyoid, medusoid, simioid*; Bot. *ovoid, scorpioid*.

(sbs.) Math. *cardioid, cycloid, ellipsoid, hyperboloid, rhomboid, spheroid, trapezoid*; Astron. *asteroid, planetoid*; Chem. *albuminoid, alkaloid, amyloid, colloid, crystalloid, metalloid, selenoid*; Bot. *aroid, fucoid, rhizoid*; Zool. *zooid*; Min. *amygdaloid*.

The mod.L. *-oïda, -oïdea, -oïdeæ, -oïdei, -oïdeus* (Eng. *-oideous*), are derivatives of *-oīdēs, -oid*.

-oidal. When the form in *-oid* is a sb., an adj. is formed in *-oidal* (see -AL[1]); as *conchoidal, cycloidal, rhomboidal, trapezoidal*; so *alkaloidal, asteroidal, fucoidal*, etc.

oidematous, variant of ŒDEMATOUS.

oidiomycosis (əʊˌɪdɪəʊmaɪ'kəʊsɪs). [f. OIDI(UM + -O + MYCOSIS.] Infection of an animal or person with a fungus formerly classified in the genus *Oidium*, esp. the thrush fungus *Oidium* (now *Candida*) *albicans*. Now usu. called *candidiasis*. Cf. MONILIASIS.

1901 [see *blastomycosis* s.v. BLASTO-]. **1917** *Boston Med. & Surg. Jrnl.* CLXXVI. 771 (*heading*) Systemic oidiomycosis: with manifestations in the central nervous system. **1933** *Jrnl. Agric. Res.* XLVI. 169 Van Heelsbergen calls the disease oidiomycosis, and describes it as an affection of the mucous membrane of the mouth, fauces, esophagus, crop, stomach, and small intestine of birds, mammals, and man. **1938** H. T. KARSNER *Human Path.* (ed. 5) x. 297 (*heading*) Blastomycosis or oïdiomycosis. **1951** T. G. HUNGERFORD *Diseases of Poultry* (ed. 2) viii. 259 Fungus infection of the digestive tract is also known as thrush, moniliasis, oidiomycosis,..and sour crop. **1975** ARNALL & KEYMER *Bird Diseases* viii. 139 Candidiasis, Moniliasis, Oidiomycosis, Sour Crop or Thrush (*Candida albicans* infection). Turkeys, parrots, gamebirds and pigeons are mainly affected.

‖**oidium** (əʊ'ɪdɪəm). *Bot.* [mod.L., f. Gr. ᾠόν egg + -ίδιον dim. suffix.] A form-genus of parasitic fungi, comprising species now regarded as the conidial stage of various fungi of the family *Erysipheæ*; they cause various diseases of plants, and of the human subject. *spec.* The species *Oidium Tuckeri* (*Erysiphe Tuckeri*), or the disease of the vine produced by this; grape-mildew.

1857 BERKELEY *Cryptog. Bot.* §318 (L.) It has already been shown that these supposed species of oidium are not true moulds, but merely states of different species of erysiphe. **1859** *Times* 20 Sept. 8/3 The late rain has favoured the growth of the grapes which escaped the oïdium and the hail. **1868** *Rep. U.S. Commissioner Agric.* (1869) 571 The sulphur-cure for the oïdium, the most formidable disease that attacks the vine. **1882** *Contemp. Rev.* Dec. 956 The wet and sunless summer had brought on the oidium.

oier, oies, -ez, obs. ff. OYER, OYEZ.

oignement, obs. form of OINTMENT.

oigopsid, variant of ŒGOPSID.

oik: see OICK.

oikist, oikoid, variant of ŒCIST, ŒCOID.

oik(o)umene, var. ŒCUMENE.

oil (ɔɪl), *sb.*[1] Forms: see below. See also ELE *sb.* [Early ME. *oli, olie, oyle, oile*, a. ONF. *olie*, OF. 12th c. *oile, oille*, 13th c. *oele, uille*, 15th c. *oyle, huille*, 16th c. *huile* (orig. masc.), in Fr. dial. *ole, eule*, Pr. *ol*, Sp. and It. *olio* (It. formerly *oglio*):—L. *oleum* oil, olive oil; cf. *olea* olive. The OE. word was ELE, earlier *æle*:—**oli* = OHG. *oli*, Ger. *öl*, ad. L. *olium, oleum*; this was superseded in 12–13th c. by the Fr. word in two types, α. *oli(e*, β. *oile*, and their later reprs. (some of these perh. influenced by later F. (*h*)*uile*). The α. forms after 13th c. were only northern and esp. Sc., where *ulyie, uillie* ('øl(j)ɪ) still survives. The 13th c. *eoli, eolie* (see ELE), *eoile*, connect the OE. and F. types.]

A. Illustration of Forms.

α. 2–4 **oli**, 3 **oliȝe**, 3 (6 *Sc.*) **olie**, 4 *Sc.* **olȝe**, 5 **oly, oyly, ole**; *Sc.* 6 **olye, oley, oulie, vly(e, vlly**, 6–9 **ulye**, 8 **ulȝie**, 8–9 **ulyie, oolie, uley**.

c **1175** *Lamb. Hom.* 79 An helendis Mon..wesch his wunden mid wine and smerede mid oli. *c* **1250** *Gen. & Ex.* 2458 He ben smered..Wið crisme and olie. *c* **1440** *Promp. Parv.* 363/2 Oly, or oyl, *oleum*. **1483** *Cath. Angl.* 259/1 Ole, *oleum*. **1500–20** DUNBAR *Poems* xxvii. 48 The vly birstit out. **1513** DOUGLAS *Æneis* VI. iv. 37 The fat olie [*ed.* **1553** olye] did he ȝet. **1536** BELLENDEN *Cron. Scot.* (1821) I. p. xxxviii, Ane fontane..quhair stremis of oulie springis ithandlie. **1549** *Compl. Scot.* xix. 161 The..vlye makkis the fyir mair bold. **1568** *Bannatyne MS.* (Hunterian Club) 394 Sum of vlly spewis ane quairt. **1722** RAMSAY *Three Bonnets* II. 57 Wi' language glibe as oolie. *a* **1774** FERGUSSON *Election* Poems (1845) 39 The barber..straikit it wi' ulzie [= ulȝie]. **1816** SCOTT *Antiq.* x, Would ye creesh his bonny brown hair wi' your nasty ulyie? **1858** M. PORTEOUS *Souter Johnny* 33 Outowre the ulye, midnicht late. **1858** RAMSAY *Remin.* Ser. I. (1860) 261 The uley-pot, or uley cruse.

β. 3 **eoile**, 3–7 **oyle**, 3–8 **oyl**, 4–7 **oile**, (4 **uile, oyel**, 4–5 **oylle, oille**, 5 **oel, hoyle**, 6 **huill**), 4, 7– **oil**, (9 *vulgar* and *dial.* **ile**).

a **1225** *Leg. Kath.* 2519 Ȝet of þe lutle banes..floweð oðer eoile ut. **1297** R. GLOUC. (Rolls) 293 He let fulle corn & oyl & win bi eche side. **1340** *Ayenb.* 93 In þe writyngge ha clepeþ uile oure lhord..'vile of blisse uor wepinge'..Of þise oyle byeþ ysmered þo þet god heþ ymad kynges. *c* **1375** *Cursor M.* 11870 (Gött.) Pic and oil [*Cott.* oile, *Fairf.* oyle] til his bi-houe. *c* **1386** CHAUCER *Knt.'s T.* 2103 Who wrastleth best naked with oille [*v.rr.* oyle, oile] enoynt. *c* **1400** MAUNDEV. (Roxb.) xiv. 61 Þat table euermare droppez oel, as it ware of oliue. **1477** EARL RIVERS (Caxton) *Dictes* 70, I haue putte more oille in my lampe to studie by. **1659** STANLEY *Hist. Philos.* III. II. 132 One sort is fluid, as Honey, Oyle. **1684** R. WALLER *Nat. Exper.* 27 If..the Vial be filled with Oile. **1767** T. HUTCHINSON *Hist. Mass.* II. iv. 445 The consumption of oyl by lamps. **1888** Ile [see 3 f].

γ. *dial.* 6 **yolle**, 7 **yolld(?)**, **youll**.

c **1568** in Swayne *Sarum Church-w. Acc.* (1896) 116 Pynt of yolle for the Belles vd. **1610** *MS. Acc. St. John's Hosp., Canterb.*, For yolld and canndelles. *Ibid.*, For youll.

B. Signification.

1. A substance having the following characters (or most of them): viz. those of being liquid at ordinary temperatures, of a viscid consistence and characteristic smooth and sticky (unctuous) feel, lighter than water and insoluble in it, soluble in alcohol and ether, inflammable, chemically neutral.

a. without *an* or *pl.* In early use almost always = OLIVE-OIL. Now freq. 'mineral oil, petroleum'; cf. PETROLEUM.

c **1175** [see A. α]. *a* **1300** *E.E. Psalter* xxii[i]. 5 Þou fatted in oli mi heved yhit. *c* **1305** *Land of Cokaygne* 46 in *E.E.P.* (1862) 157 Þer beþ riuers..Of oile, melk, honi and wine. *c* **1400** MAUNDEV. (Roxb.) ii. 6 He wald send him of þe oile of þe tree of mercy. **1548–9** (Mar.) *Bk. Com. Prayer, Visit. Sick*, As with this visible oyle thy body outwardly is annoynted. **1649** JER. TAYLOR *Gt. Exemp.* II. Disc. viii. 84 The five foolish virgins..begd oyle. **1752** HUME *Pol. Disc.* iii. 41 'Tis the oil which renders the motion of the wheel more smooth and easy. **1860** *Chem. News* 6 Oct. 204/2 The wells yield, by pumping, from ten to twenty-five barrels per day of the crude oil. **1862** *Ibid.* 20 Sept. 149/2 It is believed that the United States and Canada possess natural supplies of petroleum to furnish the rest of the world, for ages to come, with sufficient quantities of oil to yield all the artificial light required, and perhaps much of the fuel also. **1868** BROWNING *Ring & Bk.* IV. 73 [They] spend their own oil in feeding their own lamp. **1907** V. B. LEWES *Liquid & Gaseous Fuels* iv. 85 In these early wells the oil had to be pumped, but in 1861 a well drilled to a depth of 460 feet yielded oil at such pressure that it rose to the surface and overflowed. **1930** C. T. BRUNNER *Probl. of Oil* p. iii, To-day the industrial importance of oil is incalculable... Transport interests.. depend mainly on oil..as the source of their power, while even the roads..are surfaced with a derivative of oil, bitumen. **1964** J. P. GETTY *My Life & Fortunes* ii. 23 Today, oil is big business, probably the biggest of all businesses. Without oil, there would be—there could be—no civilization as we know it. **1976** *Daily Tel.* 17 June 6/5 Converting more power stations from oil to coal would push up electricity charges.

b. with *an* and *pl.*, indicating a particular kind or different kinds.

The oils constitute a very large group of natural substances, of animal, vegetable, or mineral origin. They are divided into three classes: (1) *fatty* or *fixed oils* (see FATTY 6, FIXED 4 c), of animal or vegetable origin, which (in common with *fats*) are chemically triglycerides of fatty acids, and produce a permanent greasy stain on paper, etc.; these are subdivided into *drying oils*, which by exposure to air absorb oxygen and thicken into varnishes, and *non-drying oils*, which by exposure ferment and become rancid; they are used as lubricants, as illuminants, in making soap, and for various other purposes. (2) *essential* or *volatile oils* (see ESSENTIAL *a.* 5 b), chiefly of vegetable (sometimes of animal) origin, which are acrid and limpid, and form the characteristic odoriferous principles of plants, etc.; chemically, they are hydrocarbons, or mixtures of hydrocarbons with resins, etc.; they are extensively used in medicine and perfumery, and in some cases in the arts. (3) ***mineral oils***, which are chemically mixtures of hydrocarbons, and are used chiefly as illuminants.

1398 TREVISA *Barth. De P.R.* XVII. cxii. (MS. Bodl.) lf. 217/2 Many diuers oile is pressedde oute of many diuers þinges and some oile is semple: as oile of olife, oile of nottes, oile of popie..and some oile is medled and compowned. **1652** CULPEPPER *Eng. Physic.* 3 Used outwardly as an Oyl or Oyntment. **1695** W. HALIFAX in *Phil. Trans.* 100 Perhaps he distributed among them Sweet Oyls, to be used in or after their Bathings. **1732** ARBUTHNOT *Rules of Diet* 261. **1742** in *Nature* (1882) XXVI. 620 An oyle extracted from a flinty rock for the cure of rheumatick..and other cases. **1875** *Ure's Dict. Arts* III. 456 Essential oils..are not greasy to the touch, like the fat oils. **1892** MORLEY & MUIR *Watts' Dict. Chem.* III. 637/1 Oils are said to be 'fixed' when they cannot be distilled either alone or with steam without undergoing decomposition; oils that can be so distilled being termed volatile or essential oils... Fatty oils that absorb oxygen from the air, and thus become slowly converted into varnishes are termed drying oils, e.g. linseed, hazel-nut, hemp, and poppy oils. Drying oils contain glycerides of linoleïc and similar unsaturated acids.

c. ***holy oil***: oil used in religious or sacred rites, as the anointing of priests or kings, chrism, extreme unction, etc.

c **1305** *St. Katherine* 301 in *E.E.P.* (1862) 98 Of hire tumbe þer vrneþ ȝut holi oylle. **1382** WYCLIF *Num.* xxxv. 25 The greet preest that with hooli oyle is anoynt. **1559** *Mirr. Mag., Hen. VI*, v, When a crown in cradel made me king with oyle of holy thoumbe. **1613** SHAKS. *Hen. VIII*, IV. i. 88 She had all the Royall makings of a Queene; As holy Oyle, Edward Confessors Crowne. **1885** *Cath. Dict.* (ed. 3) 404/2 Since the seventh century the holy oils, formerly consecrated at any time, have been blessed by the bishop in the Mass of this day [Maundy Thursday].

†**d.** *Old Chem.* One of the five supposed 'principles' of bodies. *Obs.*

1706 PHILLIPS s.v., Among Chymists, Oil or Sulphur is one of the five Principles of their Art, being a subtil, fat Substance, capable of taking fire, which usually arises after the Spirit. **1727–41** CHAMBERS *Cycl.* s.v *Elements*, The four principles, salt, oil, water, and earth, are always found in all plants. *Ibid.* s.v. *Principle*, The chymists make five principles; three whereof are called active principles..such as salt; sulphur or oil; and mercury or spirit... The two passive principles..are phlegm and *caput mortuum*.

e. ***midnight oil***: see MIDNIGHT *sb.* 5.

2. In the names of the various kinds, unlimited in number: **a.** denoted by *oil of* with the name of the source (plant, animal, etc.), or sometimes of a person, as ***oil of almonds, amber, ben, cade, dill, eucalyptus, fennel, geranium, juniper, lavender***, etc., etc.; ***oil of Matthiole*** (see quot. 1861), ***oil of scorpions, oil of philosophers*** (see PHILOSOPHER).

1398 TREVISA *Barth. De P.R.* XVII. cxii. (MS. Bodl.) lf. 217b/1 Oile of popie..is moste made of blacke popie sede. [See also 1 b.] *c* **1400** *Lanfranc's Cirurg.* 312 Oile of rosis, & þe ȝelke of an ey, ben good þerfore. **1552** HULOET, Oyle of almondes, *metopion.* **1641** FRENCH *Distill.* iii. (1651) 73 There will remain..the true Oil or Essence of Antimony. **1662** R. MATHEW *Unl. Alch.* §89. 130 Anointing it with Oyl of Amber and Oyl of Roses mixed together. **1741** *Compl. Fam.-Piece* I. i. 57 Take Oil of Scorpions, and Oil of Bees-wax. **1834** SOUTHEY *Doctor* xxiv. I. 236 Oil of swallows.. procured by pounding twenty live swallows in a mortar with about as many different herbs. **1838** T. THOMSON *Chem. Org. Bodies* 469 Oil of Bitter Almonds may be obtained by distilling bitter almonds with water. **1850** DAUBENY *Atomic The.* x. (ed. 2) 345 A neutral sulphate of oxide of ethyle, commonly called oil of wine. **1861** HULME tr. *Moquin-Tandon* II. III. 65 The entire Animal..infused in oil.. Scorpion (Oil of Matthiole). **1870** J. POWER *Handybk. ab. Bks.* iii. 46 Pieces of cotton impregnated with oil of cedar or of birch. **1876** HARLEY *Mat. Med.* (ed. 6) 413 Oil of Cade is a brown inflammable tarry liquid, with a strong acrid taste.

b. The name of the source, or other defining word, preceding *oil*, as *argan oil, brick oil, cod liver oil, cottonseed oil, fish oil, linseed oil, olive oil*, etc., etc., *hair oil, salad oil*, etc. (see these words); **animal oil**, any oil obtained from an animal body; spec. ***Dippel's animal oil***, an oil prepared by distillation from stag's horns, etc. and used in medicine; **dead oil** (see DEAD D. 2); **sweet oil** = OLIVE-OIL.

1565 in *Reg. Privy Counc. Scot.* I. 360 Twa barrell of fische huill. **1581** MULCASTER *Positions* xxxiv. (1887) 123 Then were they oynted with sweete oyle. **1766** *Gentl. Mag.* Apr. 171/1 The oil called Zacchæus's oil, is expressed from the fruit of a tree that..is said..to be of the kind which Zacchæus climbed. **1823** CRABB *Technol. Dict., Dippel's animal oil*,..so called from the chemist who first observed it. **1836–41** BRANDE *Man. Chem.* (ed. 5) 1133 Beech-nut oil, the decorticated nuts of the beech-tree..yield about 15 per cent. of oil resembling olive oil. **1861** HULME tr. *Moquin-Tandon* II. III. 188 Animal oil is produced in great abundance by the Whale and the Porpoise. **1883** *Fisheries Exhib. Catal.* (ed. 4) 160 Whale Oil, White and Black Porpoise Oil,..Seal Oil, Sturgeon Oil, &c.

c. rarely, with defining word following, as †**oil castor** = CASTOR OIL, †**oil olive** = OLIVE-OIL.

1779 M. CUTLER in *Life, Jrnls. & Corr.* (1888) I. 75 Making a screw to express *oil castor. [**1309** *Durham Acc. Rolls* 6, j barello *olei olive.] **1469** in *Househ. Ord.* (1790) 102 Oyle olif for Lent. **1535** COVERDALE *Lev.* xxiv. 2 That they brynge pure oyle olyue beaten for lightes. **1545** *Nottingham Rec.* III. 224 A pynt oyle Olyve. **1673** *Phil. Trans.* VIII. 6002 That Aqua vitæ swims upon Oyl-olive.

d. in partly-anglicized phrases from French; †**oil-de-bay** (*-baies*) = oil of bay (obtained from the bay laurel); †**oil d'olive** = OLIVE-OIL; †**oil-de-rose**, tr. L. *oleum roseum*.

1545 *Rates of Customs* cjb, *Oyle debay the barrell conteinynge c. pounde. **1601** HOLLAND *Pliny* (1634) I. 434 Some take the Bay berries only, and thereout presse oile-de-Baies. **1607** TOPSELL *Four-f. Beasts* (1658) 273 A Goose feather anointed with Oyl-de-bay. *c* **1400** *Lanfranc's Cirurg.* 41 *Oile de oliue þat is nouȝt ripe. **1419** *Liber Albus* (Rolls) I. 224 Karke de oille dolive. **1535** LYNDESAY *Satyre* 4057 To ..mix..saiffrone with oyl-dolie. *a* **1585** POLWART *Flyting w. Montgomerie* 234 For thy feuer..take old-oly Mixt with a mouthfull of melancholy. *c* **1420** *Pallad. on Husb.* VI. 213 *Oilderose Me may baptize and name hit.

3. In figurative and allusive uses.

a. In allusion to the use of oil for anointing (ceremonial or medicinal), or for maintaining light or heat; *esp.* in reference to 'smooth', *i.e.* soothing or flattering, words (see also b); also with stronger implications: nonsense, falsehood.

c **1290** *S. Eng. Leg.* I. 5/146 With Oyle of milce smeorien him. *a* **1300** *Cursor M.* 955 þe oil o merci. *a* **1340** HAMPOLE *Psalter* cxxvii. 4 Enoynt wiþ oyl of charite. *a* **1380** WYCLIF *Serm.* Sel. Wks. II. 38 þis devocioun is þe oyle. **1382** —— *Ps.* xliv. 8 [xlv. 7] Therfore enoyntide thee God, thi God, with oile of gladnesse befor thi felawis. **1526** *Pilgr. Perf.* (W. de W. 1531) 154 Swete vnccyon of oyle of the holy goost. **1531** ELYOT *Gov.* III. xxv, Two or three drops of the sweete oyle of remembraunce. **1638** SHIRLEY *Mart. Soldier* III. iii, A little oyle of favour will scoure thee agen, And make thee shine as bright. **1657** TRAPP *Comm. Job* xxix. 25 He had so fourbished the sword of Justice with the Oyle of Mercy. **1781** in Hone *Every-day Bk.* II. 835 His wants are supplied by the oil of his tongue. **1877** G. DAWSON *Prayers* (1878) 46 When the oil of life has run out. **1917** *Amer. Mag.* Nov. 39/2 'Why dearie!' I remarks, kissin' her; 'You know I—'. 'Easy with the oil!' she cuts me off. **1924** [see BUSHWA, -WAH]. **1926** MAINES & GRANT *Wise-Crack Dict.* 14/2 *Throwing the oil*, telling glib falsehoods. **1940** M. MARPLES *Public School Slang* 130 At Winchester..oil = an evasion. **1940** WODEHOUSE *Eggs, Beans & Crumpets* 168 Coo to him, and give him the old oil. **1954** —— *Jeeves & Feudal Spirit* i. 7 It was imperative that they be given the old oil, because she was in the middle of a very tricky business deal with the male half of the sketch and at such times every little helps.

†**b.** Phr. *to hold* or *bear up oil*: to use flattering speech, flatter. *Obs.*

1387 TREVISA *Higden* (Rolls) III. 447 A greet deel of hem ..hilde up þe kynges oyl [L. *magna convivantium parte assentiente*]. **1390** GOWER *Conf.* III. 172 Prophetes false manye mo To bere up oil, and alle tho Affermen that which he hath told. **1399** LANGL. *Rich. Redeles* III. 186 For braggynge and for bostynge and beringe vppon oilles.

c. ***to add*** (***put***) ***oil to the fire, flames***, etc.: to heighten or aggravate fury, passion, or the like; to 'add fuel to the flame'.

a **1548** HALL *Chron.* (1809) 820 There were also certaine other malicious and busye persones who added Oyle..to the Fornace. **1560** DAUS tr. *Sleidane's Comm.* 229 As the common saying is, powred oyle vpon the fyre. **1647** COWLEY *Mistress, Incurable* iv, But Wine, alas, was Oyl to th' fire. **1822** SCOTT *Pirate* iv, Serving only like oil to the flame.

d. In various phrases referring to the use of an oil-lamp for nightly study; e.g. † ***to lose one's oil***, to study or labour in vain (*obs.*); ***to smell of oil***, to bear marks of laborious study; ***to burn the midnight oil***, to study late into the night.

a **1548** HALL *Chron., Hen. V*, 35b, That thei were like to lese bothe worke and oyle. **1576** NEWTON *Lemnie's Complex.* Epistle, None of indifferent iudgemente, shall thinke his oyle & labour lost. **1650** SIR T. BROWNE *Pseud. Ep.* (ed. 2) To Rdr. 3 A work of this nature..should smell of oyle if duly and deservedly handled. **1650** G. DANIEL *Trinarch., Crastini Anim.* 16 As were that worth our Braines, and Midnight Oyle. *a* **1668** DENHAM *Poems* 47 What from Johnson's oil and sweat did flow. **1675** E. WILSON *Spadacrene Dunelm.* 72 That work needs not smell of Oyl. *a* **1763** SHENSTONE *Elegies* xi. 27, I trimm'd my lamp, consum'd the midnight oil. **1812** *Edin. Rev.* XX. 227 He may have..wasted the midnight oil in preparing.. instruction.

e. ***to pour oil upon the waters***, etc.: to appease strife or disturbance; in allusion to the effect of oil upon the agitated surface of water. (Cf. OLEIC, quot. 1894.)

[**1774** *Phil. Trans.* LXIV. II. 445 (*heading*) Of the stilling of Waves by means of Oil. Extracted from sundry Letters between Benjamin Franklin LL.D. etc. *Ibid.* 447 Pliny's account of a practice among the seamen of his time to still the waves in a storm by pouring oil into the sea.] **1847** W. B. BARING in *Croker Papers* (1884) III. xxv. 103 Lord G. [Bentinck]..spoke angrily. D'Israeli poured oil and calmed the waves. **1855** MOTLEY *Dutch Rep.* v. i. (1866) 663 The fiery words of Don John were not as oil to troubled water. **1867** TROLLOPE *Chron. Barset* II. xiii, Then Mrs. Grantly.. strove to change the subject, and threw oil upon the waters.

f. ***to strike oil*** (orig. *U.S.*): *lit.* to reach the oil (petroleum) in sinking a shaft for it through the overlying strata; hence *fig.* (*colloq.*), to hit upon a source of rapid profit and affluence.

1862 *Amer. Ann. Cycl. 1861* 580/1 The oil, when first struck, has..been known to burst forth with great violence. **1866** *Punch's Almanack* (last page), Barber has struck 'Ile', but it will not do for the hair. **1875** *Punch* 6 Mar. 99/2 He has certainly 'struck oil' in the Costa Rica and Honduras loans. **1888** LOWELL *Wks.* (1890) VI. 207 We are a nation which has struck ile. **1930** 'SAPPER' *Finger of Fate* 180 The general consensus of opinion was that if his cricket was up to the rest of his form, Bob had struck oil. **1936** W. S. MAUGHAM *Cosmopolitans* 266 He'd struck oil a year or two ago and now he's got all the money in the world. **1973** N. GRAHAM *Murder in Dark Room* xiii. 94 You stopped with Scherz. I went a little further back and struck oil. **1975** *Times* 7 Oct. 5/2 When oil is struck..the oilman needs samples for laboratory analysis.

g. In humorously allusive phrases, imitating the names of kinds of oil (see 2, and cf. ANOINT 3b, 5, GREASE *v.* 4b, OIL *v.* 2): † ***oil of angels*** (ANGEL *sb.* 6), gold employed in gifts or bribes (cf. INDIAN *oil*); ***oil of barley, oil of malt***, malt liquor; ***oil of baston, birch, hazel, holly, whip, hazel oil, hickory oil, stirrup oil, strap oil***, a beating or flogging (with a birch-rod, hazel-stick, etc.); † ***oil of fool***, flattery used to befool a person (*obs.*).

1592 GREENE *Upst. Courtier* Ejb, The palms of their hands so hot that they cannot be coold vnlesse they be rubd with the oile of *angels. **1623** MASSINGER *Dk. Milan* III. ii, I have seen..his stripes wash'd off With oil of angels. *a* **1700** B. E. *Dict. Cant. Crew, Oyl of *Barley*, strong Drink. **1608** WITHALS *Dict.* 308 They call it vulgarly the oyle of *Baston, or a sower cudgell. **1828** *Craven Gloss.* (ed. 2), *Oil of *birch*, a flogging with a birchrod. **1785** WOLCOTT (P. Pindar) *9th Ode to R. A.'s*, Reynolds..prithee, seek the Courtier's school And learn to manufacture oil of *fool. *c* **1678** Oil of *hazel [see HAZEL[1] 1e]. **1825**, **1894** *Hazel-oil [see HAZEL[1] 4c]. **1825** BROCKETT *N.C. Gloss., Oil-of-hazel*, a sound drubbing. **1894** H. GARDENER *Unoff. Patriot* 168 If I'd behaved that way with my father he would have prescribed a little *hickory oil. **1608** *Pennyless Parl.* in *Harl. Misc.* (ed. Park) I. 183 The oil of *holly shall prove a present remedy for a shrewd housewife. *c* **1648–50** BRATHWAIT *Barnabees Jrnl.* title-p., The oyle of *malt and juyce of spritely nectar Have made my Muse more valiant than Hector. **1693** *Poor Robin* (N.), Now for to cure such a disease as this, The oyl of *whip the surest medicine is.

h. ***oil and vinegar***: *lit.* used together as condiments; *fig.* said of two elements or factors which do not agree or blend together, or of any two incongruous constituents, with reference to the incompatible characters of oil and vinegar when mixed.

1629 J. PARKINSON *Parad.* II. xxxvi. 503 The first shootes or heads of Asparagus..being boyled tender, and eaten with ..oyle and vinegar. **1747** H. GLASSE *Art of Cookery* i. 11 The French eat Oil and Vinegar with it [*sc.* broccoli]. **1777** R. POTTER tr. *Æschylus' Agamemnon* in *Tragedies* 232 Pour thou oil In the same vase and vinegar, in vain Wou'dst thou persuade th' unsocial streams to mix. **1820** KEATS *Let.* June (1931) II. 537 Men get such different habits that they become as oil and vinegar to one another. **1845** THACKERAY *Legend of Rhine* ix, in *George Cruikshank's Table Bk.* Sept. 194 Oil and vinegar, which he took with cucumber to his salmon. **1910** *Blackw. Mag.* Oct. 562/2 We might as well try to blend vinegar and oil, as mix together these two elements in one chamber. **1930** A. P. HERBERT *Water Gipsies* x. 120 'Why shouldn't our class marry his class?' 'It's oil and vinegar. They don't mix.' **1977** D. CLARK *Gimmel Flask* iii. 58 Your double oil and vinegar bottle.

i. Money; *spec.* money given in order to bribe or corrupt; a bribe. *U.S. slang.*

1903 A. H. LEWIS *Boss* 121 The sooner we get th' oil, th' sooner we'll begin to light up. **1935** *Detective Fiction Weekly* 31 Aug. 118/1 She didn't take care of her protection directly, that is, she didn't slip the oil to the cops herself. **1970** C. MAJOR *Dict. Afro-Amer. Slang* 87 *Oil*, graft, pay-off to authorities.

j. *Austral.* and *N.Z. slang.* Information, news, the true facts, esp. in phr. ***dinkum oil*** (see DINKUM *a.*).

1916, etc. [see DINKUM *a.*]. **1919** W. H. DOWNING *Digger Dial.* 36 *Oil*—News; information. **1930** *Bulletin* (Sydney) 1 Jan. 50/1 On a prospect..Old bloke what died gave me the dinkum oil. **1930** L. W. LOWER *Here's Luck* x. 84 We get the dinkum oil off him. **1944** J. H. FULLARTON *Troop Target* ii. 18 'What's the oil, Noel?' 'Yes, spill it.' **1946** F. I. COOZE *Ten Bob Each Way* 22 I'll give you the oil according to Hoyle. **1946** J. D. WOODS in *Coast to Coast 1945* 33 You'd better play a hand or two..and get the oil about the place. **1948** V. PALMER *Golconda* xvi. 133 If anything were afoot, he told himself, Mahony would be sure to have the real oil about it, and he himself had a right to any inside information that was going. **1965** *Telegraph* (Brisbane) 5 July 8 The good oil, the drum, the griff.

4. a. = OIL-COLOUR. Often in pl. *oils.*

[**1574** in W. H. Turner *Select. Rec. Oxford* 351 The.. payntinge and coloringe..wth good colo[rs] and oyles. **1594** PLAT *Jewell-ho.* III. 51 To refresh the colours of olde peeces that bee wrought in oyle.] **1663** GERBIER *Counsel* 84 Painters work of ordinary lights of windowes in oyl. **1841** W. SPALDING *Italy & It. Isl.* II. III. iv. 403 Landscape-painting in oils may be considered to have been by him [Poussin] brought almost to perfection. **1867** *Nat. Encycl.* I. 857 Antonello de Messina..the first Italian who painted in oils.

b. An oil-painting, a picture painted in oils.

1852 W. H. OXBERRY in W. Davidge *Footlight Flashes* (1866) xii. 110 An original painting of my father, by Drummond, and a little oil, by W. Beverly. **1890** *Eng. Illustr. Mag.* 272 Some fair oils by German artists. **1892** *Pall Mall G.* 28 May 5/1 Visitors to the studio will also find some thirty or forty small oils of dogs. **1912** W. OWEN *Let.* 26 Jan. (1967) 111, I herewith send a representation of my outward man; I[t] does not please me; nothing will, unless it were an oil by Sargent. **1938** W. T. WALSH *Philip II* xxviii. 573 One of the artists he employed was..Domenico Theotocópuli, whom he engaged to do a large oil of the martyrdom of St. Maurice. **1967** N. FREELING *Strike Out* 27 Over the chimney-piece was a large oil of three splendid horses. **1977** D. MACKENZIE *Raven & Kamikaze* iii. 39 A blackframed oil of a Labrador.

5. *colloq.* abbrev. of OILSKIN. Chiefly in *pl.*

1891 J. DALE *Round the World* 330 A young man dressed us in a full suit of 'oils'.

6. *attrib.* and *Comb.* **a.** *attrib.* Of, consisting of, pertaining to, or dealing with oil, as ***oil-broker, -brush, change, company, -cooper, dilution, -dregs*** (hence ***oil-dreg*** vb., to treat with oil-dregs), ***-fuel, -globule, -merchant, -minister, -monger, -mongery, immersion, impregnation,***

magnate, -particle, -patch, priming, reserve, revenue, -room, sheikh, storage, supply, tannage, etc.; containing or conveying oil, as ***oil-bomb, bottle, bunker, -canakin, -car, -cell, -closet, -cock, -drum, -duct, †-fat, -feed, filter, -horn, -jar, -ladle, -pan, -pot, -pump, -safe, shell, -sink, -sump, -tank, -valve, -vase, -vat, -vessel***, etc.; producing, or used in the production or distribution of oil, as ***oil depot, district, -factory, industry, -land, platform, refinery, -region, -shale, sheikdom, -shop, show*** [SHOW *sb.*[1] 5 c], ***state, terminal, -well, -works***, etc.; obtained or made from oil, as ***oil gas, spirit***; in which oil is used as fuel, etc., as ***oil-cooker, -engine, -heater, -lamp, -launch, -motor, -stove***; belonging or relating to oil-painting, painted in oils, as ***oil group, head, picture, portrait, sketch, -work***. **b.** Objective and obj. gen., as ***oil-bearing, -carrying, -containing, -distributing, -producing, -refining, -retaining, -yielding*** adjs.; ***oil-burning*** ppl. a. and vbl. sb.; ***oil-cracking, -drilling, -raising, -sinking, -throwing*** vbl. sbs.; ***oil-atomizer, catcher, -cooler, -crusher, -distributor, -drawer, -dripper, -feeder, gusher, -refiner, separator, -spreader***. **c.** Instrumental, etc., as ***oil-bathed, -bound, -cooled, -filled, -foul, -hardening, -immersed, -impregnated, -mixed, operated, -primed, -proof, -quenched, -related, -rich, -sleeked, -stained, tanned; oil-bright, -buttered, -dried*** (dried of oil, having the oil dried up), ***-driven, -fed, -fired, -laden, -lit, -smelling, -soaked*** adjs.; ***oil cooling, -firing, quenching, tanning*** vbl. sbs.; ***oil-harden*** vb. Also parasynthetic, as ***oil-bunkered, -engined, -tanked*** adjs. **d.** Similative, etc., as ***oil-like, -green, -yellow*** adjs.

1886 A. WINCHELL *Walks Geol. Field* 136 The particular causes and conditions of *oil-accumulation. **1932** *World Today* LIX. 262/2 The camshaft and valve-gear as a whole are *oil-bathed. **1770–4** A. HUNTER *Georg. Ess.* I. 57 Rape and hemp are *oil-bearing plants. **1863** *Jrnl. Franklin Inst.* LXXV. 271 The out-croppings of the lowest members of the Oil-Bearing Strata. **1946** *Nature* 28 Dec. 932/1 In the search for similar oil-bearing structures, geophysical surveys have been extended over wide areas. **1977** *Times* 9 Sept. 7/3 Mao Tse-tung..wanted Peking's parks to grow fruit and oil-bearing plants. **1918** E. S. FARROW *Dict. Mil. Terms* 417 **Oil bomb*, in trench warfare, a large oil drum containing oil and a quantity of high explosive, which dissipates the burning oil in all directions. **1947** *Illustr. London News* 25 Jan. 117/1 The magnificent hammer-beam roof of Westminster Hall..was extensively damaged by an oil bomb in 1941. **1945** *Archit. Rev.* XCVII. 42 Apart from the roof the remainder of the external steel finish is *oil-bound paint. **1963** *House & Garden* Feb. 77/2 Oil-bound distempers, in which the binding material is an emulsion of oil or varnish, are more correctly called water paints. **1863** *National Almanac & Ann. Rec.* 687/2 A leading Liverpool *oil-broker. **1977** *Yellow Pages Classified Telephone Directory: London (North)* 250/2 Oil Brokers. **1958** *Engineering* 28 Mar. 395/3 The closing of the Canal resulted in a sharp increase in the prices of *oil bunkers. **1909** *Times Lit. Suppl.* 3 June 205/2 A plutocrat..who could quell the North Sea with *oil-bunkered Dreadnoughts. **1886** *Marine Engineer* VII. 283/2 The *oil-burning apparatus has been fitted. **1898** *Railway Mag.* Sept. 246/1 If the atmospheric conditions of the tunnels serve as an excuse..why not use oil-burning locomotives? **1920** E. C. BOWDEN-SMITH *Oil Firing for Kitchen Ranges* iv. 89 With regard to filtering the oil, this depends a great deal on the oil-burning system and the class of burner. **1924** *Domestic Engineering* XLIV. 191/2 The development of oil burning for land purposes has been retarded by the fluctuations in the price of oil. **1960** G. J. GOLLIN in W. F. B. Shaw *Domestic Heating* viii. 134 (*caption*) A complete oil-burning boiler installation. **1961** V. C. MILES *Domestic Vapouriser Burner Pract.* vii. 83 The vapourising type burner is being used in increasing quantities for the conversion of solid fuel boilers to oil burning. **1598** E. GILPIN *Skial.* (1878) 29 Hence with these fidlers whose *oyle-buttred lines, Are Panders vnto lusts. **1843** L. M. CHILD *Lett. from N.Y.* xl. 273 Children are driving hither and yon, one with a..band-box, or *oil-canakin. **1876** J. S. INGRAM *Centenn. Exposition* 336 The oil ..was loaded by gravity upon *oil cars. **1897** KIPLING *Day's Work* (1898) 222 There were oil-cars, and hay-cars and stock-cars full of lowing beasts. **1850** *Rep. Comm. Patents 1849* (U.S.) 331 The complete hanger or pillow-block, with or without the *oil-catcher. **1884** *Rep. Comm. Agric.* (U.S. Dept. Agric.) 363 When the cellular structure of the rind has completely developed, and the *oil-cells have begun to fill. **1959** *Motor Manual* (ed. 36) x. 239 A second *oil-change should be made before many hundreds of miles have been run. **1976** H. MACINNES *Death Reel* xii. 105, I am putting my car in for an oil change. **1827** J. S. MILL in *Westm. Rev.* VII. 177 A prohibition of gas-lights might be called.. protection to the *oil-companies. **1951** in M. McLuhan *Mech. Bride* (1967) 116/2 It's an oil company spending more money to make a better motor oil. **1974** E. AMBLER *Dr. Frigo* I. 53 One oil company would be bad enough. A consortium of five..must be quite oppressive. **1932** E. BOWEN *To North* xxiv. 231 She went into the scullery; here the *oil-cooker was potent; she opened the window. **1977** J. THOMSON *Case Closed* vi. 81 A leanto scullery..that contained the sink and an oil-cooker. **1904** A. F. BERRY in M. Maclean *Mod. Electr. Pract.* II. I. vii. 79 Those [manufacturers] who use a shell-type *oil-cooled construction of transformer..keep the temperature of part of the coils as nearly as possible at the temperature of the oil by spreading out the coils. **1962** *Science Survey* III. 89 (*caption*) The magnet weighs 750 tons and is energised by oil-cooled copper windings. **1973** R. W. SILLARS *Electr. Insulating Materials* x. 205 Oil-cooled power equipment.. requires a medium which is fluid at all climatic and operating temperatures. **1940** *Chambers's Techn. Dict.* 590/1 **Oil cooler*, a small air-cooled radiator, used in aircraft and racing cars, for cooling the lubricant after its return from the engine and before delivery to the oil tank. **1911** BOHLE & ROBERTSON *Transformers* iv. 61 Another disadvantage of *oil-cooling is the fact that if a fault occurs necessitating the withdrawal of the oil and the removal of the transformer it is frequently necessary to rewind the coils. **1970** J. SHEPHERD et al. *Higher Electr. Engin.* (ed. 2) ix. 278 For larger transformers oil cooling is needed, especially where high voltages are in use. **1705** *Lond. Gaz.* No. 4174/4 An Apprentice to an *Oyl-Cooper in London. **1929** *Times* 31 May 9/3 Notable advances are being made in the technology of *oil-cracking processes. **1954** *Encounter* Sept. 34/1 Workmen in an oil-cracking plant in Oklahoma..got angry, because, in a collective bargaining session, the management had referred to them as semi-skilled. **1856** *Farmer's Mag.* Jan. 35 The price of cake..gives a higher profit to the *oil-crushers. **1863** *Oil depot [see *oil derrick*, sense 6 e]. **1970** W. G. ROBERTS *Quest for Oil* xiv. 141 Even the small barge which plies up and down a big river to supply a local oil depot will have to have a crew. **1949** *Gloss. Aeronaut. Terms* (*B.S.I.*) II. 6 **Oil-dilution system*, a system by which the oil can be diluted to assist cold starting. **1889** *Century Mag.* Mar. 714/2 For pilot-boats *oil-distributers [*sic*] are valuable when boarding vessels in breaking seas. **1909** *Daily Chron.* 17 Sept. 1/3 M. Blériot..was really thinking of the oil-distrubutor and the gauge showing the consumption of petrol. **1862** *Sci. Amer.* 22 Feb. 122/1 This *oil district is peculiar in many respects. **1910** *Chambers's Jrnl.* Nov. 752/1 The apparatus has..demonstrated its value to the oil-district. **1751** T. SHAPP in *Lett. Lit. Men* (Camden) 374 Tillotson..was a wet and dry-salter, or *oil-drawer in London. *c* **1420** *Pallad. on Husb.* I. 479 *Oildreggis mixt with cley. *Ibid.* 482 Drie hit wel, and then *oyldregge hit efte. **1552** HULOET, Oyle dregges, *Muria, Amarica, Amurca.* **1593** SHAKS. *Rich. II*, I. iii. 221 My *oyle-dride Lampe. **1937** M. HUXLEY *Let.* 13 Oct. in A. Huxley *Lett.* (1969) 427 We have seen so much, including..*oil drilling. **1974** *Evening News* (Edinburgh) 10 Apr. 13/7 The next generation of British oil-drilling experts will be trained and produced in Scotland. **1893** *Times* 20 Mar., This *oil-driven locomotive is at once an innovation and a success. **1896** *Westm. Gaz.* 17 Nov. 2/3 One of the modern oil-driven motors. **1909** *Daily Chron.* 24 July 6/3 Two small *oildrums will be fixed beneath the plank. **1975** *Times* 22 July 14/2 The white Anglo-Saxon bass oil drum player. **1896** *Westm. Gaz.* 1 Dec. 6/3 The first exhibition of any *oil-engines in this country..in 1887 in the Agricultural Hall. **1913** *Chambers's Jrnl.* Jan. 31/1 *Oil-engined ships are..being built. **1924** *Times Trade & Engin. Suppl.* 29 Nov. 250/3 The large oil-engined liner. **13..** *S. Eng. Leg.* (MS. Bodl. 779) in Herrig *Archiv* LXXXII. 396/124 A whit coluere..brouȝt an *oyl-fat in here bele. **1870** A. S. EVANS *Our Sister Republic* ii. 50 The watchmen..with muskets in their hands, and great *oil-fed lanterns by their sides. **1886** *Chambers's Jrnl.* 16 Jan. 47/2 A vessel..propelled entirely by oil-fed furnaces. **1905** *Westm. Gaz.* 15 Feb. 8/2 It has a horizontal engine,.. forced oil-feed, automatic carburation, [etc.]. **1900** CONRAD *Ld. Jim* vi. 74 He set the log for me; he..put a drop of oil in it too. There was the *oil-feeder where he left it nearby. **1904** A. F. BERRY in M. Maclean *Mod. Electr. Pract.* II. I. vii. 78 If a fire breaks out in the *oil-filled tank itself, the latter may be run out into the air. **1930** *Engineering* 24 Jan. 100/3 Various special designs, including the 132-kv. single-core oil-filled cables, which..are shortly to make their appearance in this country. **1957** W. J. JOHN *Mod. Electr. Engin.* I. iv. 126/1 In order to overcome the fire risk in oil-filled equipment, some attention has been paid to the use of chlorinated diphenyls. **1907** *Yesterday's Shopping* (1969) 713/3 *Oil Filters... For filtering oil that has been used and become dirty, thus rendering it available for use again. **1925** *Morris Owner's Manual* ii. 28 Unscrew the large plug at the bottom of the sump, when the oil filter, which is attached to it, may be withdrawn. **1977** *Belfast Tel.* 22 Feb. 26/8 (Advt.), Oil filters for all cars. **1886** A. WINCHELL *Walks Geol. Field* 137, I will now give you the whole philosophy of *oil-finding and oil-production. **1900** *Engineer* 22 June 651/1 It is coke instead of *oil-fired. **1932** *Discovery* Aug. 248/2 In the oil-fired..liner high-class labour can be employed in the stokehold. **1961** I. MURDOCH *Severed Head* xxi. 168 The famous oil-fired central heating seemed to be making little impression on the temperature of the room. **1970** V. CANNING *Great Affair* v. 74 Aga oil-fired stoves in the kitchen. **1903** *Work* 11 July 364/1 The two firemen to be carried for coal burning would probably be reduced to one, there being little labour in *oil firing. **1963** *Times* 12 Feb. 1/7 (*heading*) Trouble-shooting in oil-firing. **1931** W. FAULKNER *Sanctuary* xvi. 112 The white men sitting in tilted chairs along the *oil-foul wall of the garage. **1888** *Pall Mall G.* 23 Apr. 11/1 *Oil-fuel boats, and life-saving apparatus. **1823** J. BADCOCK *Dom. Amusem.* 79 *Oil Gas,.. that obtained from oil. **1958** *Times Rev. Industry* June 70/2 To build a..catalytic oil-gas process plant. **1580** HOLLYBAND *Treas. Fr. Tong*, *Vne buire à mettre l'huile*, an *oyle glasse, a vyole. **1845** BUDD *Dis. Liver* 207 Some cells contain small *oil-globules, marked by the clear rings. **1673** *Lond. Gaz.* No. 845/4 One *Oyl green Carpet. **1843** PORTLOCK *Geol.* 214 Of a fine oil green, or greenish-white colour. **1921** *Daily Colonist* (Victoria, B.C.) 12 Oct. 9/7 One *oil gusher in the new Fort Norman field, Northern Canada, produces 1,500 barrels a day. **1973** C. CALLOW *Power from Sea* i. 13 The big oil gushers being found in the North Sea. **1904** *Electrochem. Industry* Feb. 51/1 The usual method [for producing sorbite in steel] has been to reheat and *oil-harden. **1890** *Nature* 18 Sept. 503/1 This process of *oil-hardening, introduced first by Lord Armstrong in the case of barrels, is now almost universally adopted for all gun forgings. **1895** *Montgomery Ward Catal.* 424/1 *Oil Heater ..will comfortably warm a large room in very cold weather. **1972** P. RUELL *Red Christmas* i. 10 The presence inside [the vehicle] of a small oil-heater and a lot of travelling rugs cheered him up. **1535** COVERDALE *1 Sam.* xvi. 13 Then toke Samuel his *oyle horne, & anoynted him. *a* **1661** HOLYDAY *Juvenal* 136 That makes with his great oil-horn much a do. **1930** *Engineering* 9 May 599/3 Both sets of transformers are of the *oil-immersed type. **1955** *Gloss. Terms Radiology* (*B.S.I.*) 34 *Oil-immersed tube*, an X-ray tube designed for operation in oil. **1883** *Encycl. Brit.* XVI. 268/1 A given angle in a water or *oil immersion objective represents a much larger aperture than does the same angle in an air-objective. **1964** M. HYNES *Med. Bacteriol.* (ed. 8) xiv. 232 Growth may be obvious under the oil-immersion lens within 24 hours. **1940** *Chambers's Techn. Dict.* 591/1 **Oil-impregnated paper*, used for low and high voltage cables; the oil has resin in it to increase viscosity at working temperatures. **1946** *Nature* 28 Dec. 931/2 Such indications include seepages, gas-escapes, *oil-impregnations, elaterite veins, and bituminous coatings in fractures and joints. **1880** *Harper's Mag.* Dec. 65 The *oil industry has lent a powerful hand to the iron industry of Pittsburgh. **1951** in M. McLUHAN *Mech. Bride* (1967) 114 Competition is just as much a part of the oil industry as wells or refineries. **1851** MELVILLE *Moby Dick* I. xx. 155 This excellent hearted Quakeress..with a long *oil-ladle in one hand. **1813** E. WEETON *Jrnl. of Governess* (1969) II. 92 A painted glass cylinder..intended to contain within it, either an *oil lamp or a candle. **1831** BREWSTER *Nat. Magic* xiii. (1833) 323 A small oil-lamp on the floor. **1962** L. DAVIDSON *Rose of Tibet* iii. 56 A dark and malodorous shack, lit by oil lamps. **1605** TIMME *Quersit.* I. xv. Kiij b, Sulphur.. the natural, moist, original, *oylelike. **1872** GEO. ELIOT *Middlem.* I. xv. 264 A dim, *oil-lit street. **1974** G. JENKINS *Bridge of Magpies* vii. 107, I went down..to the shabby oil-lit cabin. **1927** U. SINCLAIR *Oil!* 312 Mountains on every side, and the *oil magnate owned everything in sight. *c* **1420** *Pallad. on Husb.* Tab. 274 Olyuys, putacioun, and *oil makynge. **1837** WHITTOCK, etc. *Bk. Trades* (1842) 349 Another species of *oil-merchants deal mostly in sweet oils, and a few leading articles of foreign produce, termed dry saltery. **1974** *Atlantic Monthly* Sept. 20 At the June meeting of OPEC in Quito, Ecuador, the Shah's *oil minister, Jamshid Amuzegar, blocked a move by Saudi Arabia to lower the price of oil by $2 on the posted price of $11.65 per barrel. **1986** *Economist* 26 Apr. 76/1 After 17 days yakking in Geneva's Intercontinental Hotel, OPEC's 13 oil ministers conceded the obvious on April 21st: they have lost the power to reverse this year's collapse in the oil price. **1912** *Chambers's Jrnl.* Apr. 287/2 *Oil-mixed concrete is best made by mixing the cement, sand, and water to a mortar, adding the oil to the mixture, [etc.]. **1896** *Daily News* 16 Nov. 4/2 The Daimler *oil-motors..were strongly in evidence. **1946** *Happy Landings* (Air Ministry) July 3/3 *Oil operated propellers are liable to 'run away' if the oil congeals. **1908** *Westm. Gaz.* 16 Apr. 4/3 Special *oil-pans are fitted on each end of the throw for scooping up the oil from the base-chamber. **1955** W. GADDIS *Recognitions* II. vii. 642 The paving hardpacked with that snow, its whiteness.. spotted and streaked from leaking oil-pans. **1965** M. BRADBURY *Stepping Westward* viii. 399 A floor covered with *oil-patches. **1973** C. CALLOW *Power from Sea* ii. 75 There was a conspiracy of silence among the oil companies working in the 'oil patch' at this time. **1786** J. WOODFORDE *Diary* 4 Mar. (1926) II. 229 Rec'd an *oil Picture from my Nephew Saml. from London. **1862** THORNBURY *Life Turner* I. 258 His early oil-pictures were dark and heavy. **1973** *Glasgow Herald* 7 Aug. 11/7 The *oil-platform proposals. **1974** *Evening News* (Edinburgh) 12 Apr. 7/4 The public inquiry into the proposal to build giant concrete oil platforms at Drumbuie, Loch Carron, has ended after 43 days of speeches and evidence. **1939** WYNDHAM LEWIS *Let.* 15 Dec. (1963) 268, 1 *oil-portrait and half-a-dozen chalk or pencil portraits. *c* **1440** *Promp. Parv.* 364/1 *Oly potte, or oly vesselle. **1669** R. MONTAGU in *Buccleuch MSS.* (Hist. MSS. Comm.) I. 448 A vinegar pot, oil pot, and sugar box. **1934** H. HILER *Notes Technique Painting* iii. 157 The ordinary *oil-primed canvases. *Ibid.* i. 67 May be primed with an *oil priming. **1845** STOCQUELER *Hand-bk. Brit. India* (1854) 37 Corn, cotton, *oil-producing plants, and sugar. **1959** *Daily Tel.* 13 Mar. 1/6 The Arab oil-producing countries. **1974** *Times* 21 Sept. 2/6 Scottish oil..could easily be undercut if the oil-producing states chose to lower their posted price. **1880** *English Mechanic* 24 Sept. 75/2 (*heading*) *Oil-proof cement. **1906** *Daily Chron.* 29 May 5/4 The licensing authority should require motor bus proprietors to provide an oil-proof receptacle under the bonnet of each omnibus. **1914** *Oil-quenched [see *air-hardened* ppl. a. (AIR *sb.*[1] II)]. **1943** *Gloss. Terms Electr. Engin.* (*B.S.I.*) 53 *Oil-quenched fuse*, a liquid-quenched fuse in which the liquid is oil. **1937** *Discovery* May 155/2 *Oil quenching..offers a uniform rate of cooling, without requiring the exercise of unusual care. **1910** *Chambers's Jrnl.* Nov. 750/1 This engineer, who has made a deep study of *oil-raising methods. **1863** *Oil refinery [see *oil derrick*, sense 6 e]. **1977** *Times* 21 Nov. (Eastern Province Suppl.) p. ii/8 (*caption*) Ras Tannurah, the country's main oil refinery and port. **1862** *Prelim. Rep. 8th Census* (U.S. Census Office) 72 The Pennsylvania *oil region. **1884** *Boston* (Mass.) *Jrnl.* 22 Nov. 2/5 The Pennsylvania oil-region. **1974** *Evening News* (Edinburgh) 12 Apr. 11/4 Minister of State at the Scottish Office, Mr Bruce Millan, will tour *oil-related developments in the Northeast of Scotland and Shetland during a three-day visit next week. **1975** *Petroleum Economist* Aug. 288/1 The Department of Energy,..expects that oil-related employment will increase as more companies enter the offshore market. **1950** *Chambers's Encycl.* X. 619/2 Table III shows the distribution of ownership of *oil reserves. **1966** P. O'DONNELL *Sabre-Tooth* iii. 58 Kuwait..holds a quarter of the world's known oil reserves. **1977** *Listener* 17 Mar. 335/3 Overseas companies..own around 60 per cent of the North Sea oil reserve in the British sector. **1907** *Westm. Gaz.* 5 Dec. 4/2 The spring is..connected to the gear-box by an *oil-retaining universal coupling. **1962** *B.S.I. News* Feb. 37 Bronze oil-retaining brushes and thrust washers for aircraft. **1975** P. SOMERVILLE-LARGE *Couch of Earth* x. 184 We should be prepared to forego a week's *oil revenues. **1977** *Sunday Times* 20 Nov. 53/4 Part of the oil revenue will have to be used to tackle some of Britain's deep-seated industrial problems. **1959** *Daily Tel.* 13 Mar. 1/6 The *oil-rich sheikhdoms of the Persian Gulf are still under British protection. **1975** N. LUARD *Robespierre Serial* iv. 16 The profile might have fitted any oil-rich Arab. **1877** *Harper's Mag.* Dec. 34/2 The three boys in the *oil-room have used, of all grades of oil, twenty gallons less. **1886** *Boy's Own Paper* 2 Oct. 11/3 Disagreeable smells, as if of a steamboat's lower regions, proved this to be the oil-room. **1934** *Discovery* Apr. 88/2 The cost of *oil separators is less than it used to be, and some of the prominent shipping companies are willing to introduce them. **1969** *Gloss. Terms Vacuum Technol.* (*B.S.I.*) 20 *Oil separator*, a device which reduces the loss of pump oil as droplets at the out-let. **1877** A. H. GREEN *Phys. Geol.* ii. §6. 72 When Shales contain enough bituminous matter to be used for the manufacture of Paraffin they are called *Oil Shales. **1960** *Spectator* 30 Sept. 493 Spiritual *oil-sheikhs waiting for their oil to be discovered. **1974** *Times* 31 Jan. 18/5 The oil shaikhs put paid to that as club after club buckled before the fuel crisis. **1972** *Guardian* 23 Feb. 2/1 Qatar is one of the smaller *oil sheikdoms. **1904** *Sci. Amer. Suppl.* 9 Apr. 23641/3 *Oil shells, that is, shells containing oil, which should distribute their contents upon the waves wherever they might happen to fall, could, by means of a cannon, be projected some distance in advance of a moving ship. **1679** OATES *Narr. Popish Plot* 32 Where they found an *Oyl-shop, which the said Groves bragg'd he fir'd. **1752** SIR J. HILL *Hist. Anim.* 315 They generally purchase.. the bottoms of the casks at our oil-shops. **1953** WILSON & METRE in *Sci. Petroleum* VI. I. 122/1 Despite the wide distribution of *oil shows and much exploratory drilling, only two oilfields of commercial importance have been found. **1977** *Offshore Engineer* May 8/1 (Advt.), All exploratory wells drilled—designated as either dry well, gas show, oil show, oilwell, gaswell, oil and gas well. **1884** F. J. BRITTEN *Watch & Clockm.* 47 *Oil sinks are formed in watch and clock plates so that.. the oil is kept close to the pivot. **1961** *Aeroplane* C. 127/2 A Cessna 180D has been specially fitted with equipment to keep holiday beaches clear of oil contamination... This process is known as '*oil sinking' and has been developed in Germany. **1856** D. G. ROSSETTI *Let.* 15 May (1965) I. 301 That *oil-sketch of the Queen and Page. **1977** *Times* 14 May 16/5 Oil sketches by Landseer, as opposed to large finished paintings, were fetching £10,000 and more a year or two back. **1952** C. DAY LEWIS tr. *Virgil's Aeneid* IV. 78 His chin and *oil-sleeked hair set off by a Phrygian bonnet. **1894** H. GARDENER *Unoff. Patriot* 173 It was the smell of smoke and *oil-soaked cloth. **1907** *Westm. Gaz.* 11 Apr. 4/2 'Hygiene,' the *Lancet* says, 'would condemn the highly seasoned and *oil-stained meerschaum or briar pipe.' **1944** *R.A.F. Jrnl.* Aug. 291 His cap, battered flat and copiously oil-stained, stuck on the back of his head. **1976** E. WARD *Hanged Man* xiii. 72 Quentin.. took Wallace's oil-stained shoes. **1973** *Listener* 22 Nov. 698/3 The *oil states are rich. **1974** *Times* 18 Apr. 5/6 (*heading*) Few concessions from oil states at UN debate. **1906** CONRAD *Mirror of Sea* xxxi. 164 Petroleum ships discharge their dangerous cargoes and the *oil-storage tanks low and round with slightly-domed roofs, peep over the edge of the foreshore. **1973** *Times* 1 Dec. 2/3 He lives in a cottage beside it, and spends his days servicing and maintaining his donkey and its four cylindrical oil storage tanks and logging the amount of oil. [**1865** *U.S. Pat. 45,957* 17 Jan., Coal-oil stove.] **1880** *Harper's Mag.* Aug. 400 *Oil stoves are objectionable because of the unpleasant odor of the fuel. **1884** *Health Exhib. Catal.* 66/2 Pottery Oil Stoves. **1921** *Daily Colonist* (Victoria, B.C.) 21 Oct. 6/6 (Advt.), Optimus oil stoves—solid brass, regular $10. **1933** DYLAN THOMAS *Let.* 11 Nov. (1966) 58 The oil-stove shines like a parhelion. **1977** A. CLARKE *Let. from Dead* ii. 18 'Could we give him a bed, Angy?'.. 'Of course. It'll have to be the front attic... I'll take one of the oil stoves up.' **1923** W. DEEPING *Secret Sanct.* ix. 85 A man was bending over one of the wings, pouring oil into the *oil-sump. **1909** *Q. Rev.* Oct. 575 Depôt ships for destroyers, mother-ships for submarines, and *oil-supply vessels. **1974** *Evening News* (Edinburgh) 10 Apr. 1/5, 27-year-old Spanish seaman decided to entertain women aboard a North Sea oil supply ship berthed at Leith last night. **1862** *U.S. Pat. 34,426* 18 Feb., *Oil tank. **1923** H. S. BELL *Amer. Petroleum Refining* 293 Corrosion in oil tanks occurs at three points. **1951** DYLAN THOMAS *Selected Lett.* (1966) 352 O evergreen ..*oil-tanked..cradle of Persian culture. **1903** H. R. PROCTER *Princ. Leather Manuf.* xxiv. 384 We may apply some of the ideas which we have formed with regard to *oil-tannages to the action of fats upon tanned leather. **1948** M. P. BALFE in *Progress in Leather Sci. 1920–1945* III. xxiv. 496 The oil tannage gave a leather which absorbed water more rapidly and to a greater extent than the combination tannage, and showed a greater degree of separation of the fibres. **1950** L. K. MASON *Pipe Dreams about Leather & Saddles* 15 *Oil Tannage*, or 'shamoying', used mainly for wash-leather sheepskins ('chamois') and the like. **1903** L. A. FLEMMING *Pract. Tanning* 46 Sheep and lambskins *oil-tanned. **1953** D. WOODROFFE *Leather Dressing* vii. 80 Chamois or oil tanned leather is usually yellow, clothy and porous. **1972** *Materials & Technol.* V. 411 Chamois or wash leather is the term applied to oil tanned products obtained from the flesh splits of sheepskins. **1903** L. A. FLEMMING *Pract. Tanning* 410 *Oil tanning with Turkey-red oil. **1958** C. GOERTH tr. A. Kuntzel in F. O'Flaherty et al. *Chem. & Technol. Leather* II. xxviii. 426 Oil tanning produces a leather having characteristics quite different from all other types of tanning. **1975** *Petroleum Rev.* XXIX. 387/3 The location of the *oil terminal was proposed by Orkney County Council. **1977** *Observer* 24 Apr. 1/6 The blow-out occurred..just over 200 miles from the British oil terminal at Teesport. **1963** BIRD & HUTTON-STOTT *Veteran Motor Car* 101 Inadequate cooling and excessive *oil-throwing. **1901** *Sketch* 17 July 498/1 Sand dropped into the *oil-valves. **1885** J. S. STALLYBRASS tr. *Hehn's Wand. Plants & Anim.* 94 The numerous *oil-vases given as prizes at the games instituted by Pisistratus. **1472** in Swayne *Sarum Church-w. Acc.* (1896) 5, ij *oylevates of silver. **1611** BIBLE *Transl. Pref.* 3 A whole cellar full of *oyle vessels. **1881** RAYMOND *Mining Gloss.*, **Oil-well*, a dug or bored well, from which petroleum is obtained by pumping or by natural flow. **1611** CORYAT *Crudities* 25 Many goodly pictures of some of the Kings and Queenes of France.. drawen out very liuely in *oyle workes. *Ibid.* 26 Pictures made in oyleworke vpon wainscot, wherein..the nine Muses are excellently painted. **1869** *Bradshaw's Railway Manual* XXI. App. 117 Oil refiners... Works: British Oil Works, Saltney, near Chester. Victoria Oil Works, Collyhurst Road. **1843** PORTLOCK *Geol.* 214 Of a rich yellowish-green, or *oil yellow colour. **1887** MOLONEY *Forestry W. Afr.* 76 The principal *oil-yielding seeds.

e. Special Combs.: **oil age**, an age in which oil is used extensively, esp. as a source of power; **oil baron** = *oil king* below; **oil-beetle**, a beetle of the genus *Meloe*, which exudes an oily liquid when alarmed; **oil-belt**, a zone containing oil-fields; **oil-berg** [after ICEBERG], a large body of oil floating in the sea; **oil-berry**, †(*a*) an olive; (*b*) ? a name for the fruit of the Oil-Palm (*Elæis guineensis*); **oil-bird**, name for various birds yielding oil; (*a*) the GUACHARO of the West Indies and S. America, *Steatornis caripensis*; (*b*) a FROGMOUTH of Ceylon, *Batrachostomus moniliger*; (*c*) the FULMAR, *Fulmarus glacialis*; **oil-box**, (*a*) a box in which oil is stored; (*b*) in *Machinery*, 'a box containing a supply of oil for a journal, and feeding it by means of a wick or other device' (Knight *Dict. Mech.* 1875); **oil-break** *a.* (see quot. 1943); **oil-bush** [BUSH *sb.*[2]], a socket containing oil in which an upright spindle runs; **oil-butt**, a butt (BUTT *sb.*[2]) containing oil; also *fig.* (see quot. 1937); †**oil-can**, a can for holding oil; *spec.* = OILER 3; also (*slang*), a German trench-mortar shell (*obs.*); †**oil-case** = OILSKIN (*obs.*); **oil-cellar**, (*a*) a cellar for storage of oil; (*b*) a small reservoir for oil in a piece of machinery; **oil circuit-breaker**, an oil-break circuit breaker; †**oil-clock** [CLOCK *sb.*[3]] = *oil-beetle*; **oil coal**, coal from which oil is obtained; **oil-coat**, a coat of oiled cloth, an oilskin coat (cf. OILED 1 c, quot. 1672); **oil-cup**, a small vessel to hold oil for lubricating, either portable (= OILER 3), or attached to the machinery and acting automatically (cf. *oil-box* b, *oil-cellar* b); **oil-derrick**, a derrick or frame used in boring for mineral oil; also *fig.*; **oil-drop**, (*a*) name for the rudimentary umbilical vesicle in the eggs of some fishes; (*b*) a drop of oil; freq. *attrib.* with reference to an experimental method of measuring the electronic charge; **oil-filler**, (*a*) one who or that which fills a container with oil, (*b*) an aperture through which an engine is filled with oil; (*c*) a coat of oil-paint used to fill in areas of a painted surface; **oil floor-cloth** (see OILCLOTH); **oil-garden**, a garden of olives grown for oil; **oil-gauge (-gage)**, a hydrometer for measuring the specific gravity of oils, an oleometer; **oil-gilding**, gilding in which the gold-leaf is laid on a surface formed of linseed-oil mixed with a yellow pigment (*oil-gold size*); **oil-gland**, a gland which secretes oil; *spec.* the uropygial or coccygeal gland in birds, which secretes the oil with which they preen their feathers; **oil-gold** (see *oil-gilding*); **oil-hole**, a small hole drilled in a machine, into which oil can be dropped for lubricating; **oil-jack**, a vessel with a spout, in which oil can be heated; **oil-jacket**, a seaman's jacket made of oil-skin; **oil king**, a magnate in the oil-trade; **oil-meal**, ground linseed cake; **oil-paint**, paint made by mixing a pigment with oil (= OIL-COLOUR); **oil-painter**, a painter in oils; **oil-painting**, (*a*) the action, or art, of painting in oils; (*b*) a picture painted in oils; also used in negative phrases to indicate an unprepossessing appearance; **oil-palm**, a palm tree yielding fruit from which oil is pressed, esp. *Elæis guineensis*, which is native to West Africa but widely cultivated in tropical regions; **oil-paper**, paper made transparent or waterproof by soaking in oil; **oil-plant**, any plant yielding an oil (usually with defining word, as *castor-oil plant*, *croton-oil plant*, etc.); *spec.* the GINGILI, *Sesamum indicum*; **oil pollution**, contamination with oil discharged from a ship; **oil pool**, an extent of rock in which oil is present throughout without interruption, forming a single reservoir; **oil-press**, an apparatus for expressing oil from fruits, seeds, etc.; **oil-presser**, one whose trade is to press oil from seeds, etc.; the manager of an oil-press; **oil province**, an extensive area containing a number of oil fields that are geologically related; **oil-resin**, used *attrib.* to designate a cooked varnish used on paintings, and in painting mediums; **oil rig**, a rig (RIG *sb.*[6] 3 a) employed in drilling for oil; **oil-rubber**, in *Engraving*, a roll of woollen cloth moistened with oil, used for cleaning plates, etc.; **oil-sand**, a stratum of sandstone yielding oil; also extended to any oil-bearing rock; **oil shale**, shale which contains kerogen and on distillation yields oil; **oil-shark**, any species of shark yielding oil, esp. *Galeorhinus zyopterus* of California; **oil-sheet**, a sheet made of oilskin or oil-paper; **oil-ship**, a vessel carrying whale-oil or fuel oil as cargo; **oil-silk** = OILED *silk*; **oil slick**, a film or layer of oil, esp. one floating on an expanse of water; so **oil-slicked** *a.*; **oil-smeller** (*U.S.*), a person who professes to discover oil-bearing strata for well-boring by the sense of smell; **oil-soluble** *a.*, soluble in oil; **oil spill**, an escape of oil into the sea; **oil-spot**, (*a*) a marking on Chinese porcelain caused by deposition of iron in firing, used chiefly *attrib.* of Honan ware so marked; (*b*) on industrial glass (see quot. 1962); **oil spring**, a spring of mineral oil (with or without admixture of water); **oil-stock** *Eccl.*, a vessel for containing holy oil; **oil-strike** orig. *U.S.*, a discovery of an oil-field by drilling; **oil string**, the inner-most length of casing (tubing) in an oil well, extending down to the oil-producing rock; **oil switch**, an oil-break switch; **oil-tanker**, a vessel having special tanks for the conveyance of oil; a vehicle designed for carrying oil; **oil-tawing**, the process of tawing skins in oil, in the manufacture of oiled leather; **oil-tempered** *a.* (of steel), tempered by means of oil; **oil-test**, **oil-tester**, a contrivance for ascertaining some property of oils, as their flashing-point, burning-point, or lubricating quality; **oil thrower** (see quot. 1964); **oil-tight** *a.* [after *watertight*], of such a degree of tightness as to prevent oil from passing through; **oil-tongued** *a.*, having an 'oily' tongue, characterized by smooth or flattering speech; **oil trap** (see TRAP *sb.*); **oil-tube**, a tube conveying oil, as the vittæ in the fruits of *Umbelliferæ*; **oil-water** *a.*, situated between or involving oil and water; **oil-way**, a channel for the admission of oil to lubricate a hinge or the like; **oil whetstone** = OILSTONE *sb.*; †**oil wort**, ? a vegetable yielding oil, or eaten with oil (*obs.*). See also OIL-BAG, OIL BURNER, etc.

1911 *Chambers's Jrnl.* July 465/1 That was the beginning of the great *Oil Age. **1969** M. PEI *Words in Sheep's Clothing* (1970) xx. 206 This favors Texas *oil barons, but not people who wear out their bodies and brains working for a living. **1974** N. MARSH *Black as he's Painted* iii. 75 From the oil barons at the top to ex-business men at the bottom. **1976** *Time* 27 Sept. 65/2 Since it was launched in 1973 by Reporter-turned-Lawyer Michael R. Levy, 30, *Texas Monthly* has taken on just about every sacred steer in the Lone Star State: college football, the Miss Texas Pageant, oil barons, the Texas Rangers, Dallas banks. **1658** ROWLAND *Moufet's Theat. Ins.* 1016 In English it may fitly be called the *Oyl-beetle, or the Oyl-clock. **1879** LUBBOCK *Sci. Lect.* 43 A small parasite..on one of the wild bees was the larva of the oil-beetle. **1865** *Harper's Mag.* Apr. 563/2 The Canadian wells now flowing hundreds of barrels of oil are located on the borders of Lake Erie, far to the west of the so-called *oil belt. **1901** *Chambers's Jrnl.* Feb. 126/1 The exploitation of.. the most prolific oil-belt of the world. **1904** *Dialect Notes* II. 385 *Oil-belt*, the district including the supposed course of subterranean rivers of oil. **1966** *Economist* 24 Sept. 1275/1 There are considerable areas of doubt about the performance in rough weather of ships over 300,000 tons... The danger of underwater damage to floating *oil-bergs with nearly 100 feet of ship below the surface is considerable. **1977** *Time* 10 Jan. 53/3 No scientists are willing to forecast the effects of the oil now spreading seaward from the *Argo Merchant*. Most believe that if the globs of oil, called oilbergs because most of their mass is below the surface, continue to move east, the damage will be held to a minimum. **1382** WYCLIF *Isa.* xvii. 6 As the shaking out of the *oile berie [1388 the fruyt of olyue tre]. **1878** H. M. STANLEY *Dark Cont.* II. ix. 281 The oil-berry tree, the black ivory nut-tree, which might be made a valuable article of commerce. **1893** *Westm. Gaz.* 27 Nov. 7/1 The *oil-bird of Trinidad, so called on account of its excessively plump, fat, not to say oily condition. **1893** NEWTON *Dict. Birds*, *Guacharo*, the Spanish-American name of what English writers have lately taken to calling the Oil-Bird, the *Steatornis caripensis* of ornithologists. **1799** *Sporting Mag.* XIV. 28 *Oil-boxes and hoop-fellied wheels are great improvements. **1904** W. E. WARRILOW in M. Maclean *Mod. Electr. Pract.* II. II. i. 230 Figs. 482, 483 illustrate an *oil-break switch for large powers, this type being suitable for a working current of 500 amperes at a pressure of 2000 volts. **1943** *Gloss. Terms Electr. Engin.* (*B.S.I.*) 62 *Oil-break*, applied to a switch, circuit-breaker or similar apparatus to denote that the circuit is opened in oil. **1851** H. MELVILLE *Moby Dick* III. xxix. 184 The cabin mess dined off the broad head of an *oil-but, lashed down to the floor for a centre-piece. **1937** PARTRIDGE *Dict. Slang* 581/1 *Oil-butt*, a black whale. **1839** THACKERAY *Major Gahagan* ix, Their fall upsetting the.. *oil-can. *a* **1917** E. A. MACKINTOSH *War, the Liberator* (1918) 156 'Look out, sirr,.. oil can coming over.' Instantly self-preservation reasserted itself. **1917** A. G. EMPEY *Over Top* 302 '*Oil Cans*', Tommy's term for a German trench mortar shell. **1741** *Gentl. Mag.* XI. 15 Tea in *oil-case bags. **1764** WESLEY *Jrnl.* 16 Jan., I was.. persuaded to put on an oil-case hood. *c* **1420** *Pallad. on Husb.* I. 499 Me may also doon other diligence Aboute an *oilcelar, hit for to warme. **1875** KNIGHT *Dict. Mech.*, *Oil-cellar*, an oil-reservoir in the bottom of a journal-box. **1924** W. A. COATES *Choice of Switchgear* v. 89 Only small, unimportant *oil circuit-breakers are operated by a hand lever directly upon the breaker itself. **1964** E. A. REEVES *Installation & Maint. Industr. Switchgear* iii. 32 Medium-voltage oil circuit-breakers may be either incorporated in a cubicle or fitted on the outside of a metal-clad unit. **1873** C. ROBINSON *New South Wales* 52 Deposits of brown cannel *oil coals and oil shales. **1653** *Flemings in Oxford* (O.H.S.) I. 62 For an *oyle-coat and hatt-case.. 16–00. **1850** CLOUGH *Dipsychus* I. iv. 34 It falls from off me like the rain From the oil-coat. **1850** *Rep. Comm. Patents 1849* (U.S.) 233 The combination of the tight *oil cup with the axle. **1875** KNIGHT *Dict. Mech.*, *Oil-cup*. When portable, for oiling machinery, they are considered as Oilers. **1895** *Mod. Steam Eng.* 39 Oil-cups for screwing into these openings may be purchased. **1863** *Boston Herald* 16 Aug. 3/3 You see, in close proximity on every side, oil depots, oil refineries, *oil derricks. **1902** 'MARK TWAIN' *Speeches* (1910) 367 That long, lank cadaver, old oil-derrick out of a job. **1948** *Ada* (Okla.) *Even. News* 2 July 1/3 The work scheduled for Friday called for the shooting of scenes at the oil derrick. **1976** *Scotsman* 24 Dec. 6/3 Aberdeen District planning and building control committee yesterday granted planning permission for a 96-ft steel oil derrick which is to be built above a 1000-ft deep test well..near their manufacturing site on the Bridge of Don estate. **1885** *Science* 22 May 425/1

The egg of the cod..buoyant, but without an *oil-drop. **1911** *Physical Rev.* XXXII. 393 Instead of using oil drops he sucks into the observing chamber the metallic dust arising from the volatilization produced in a metallic arc. **1913** *Ibid.* 2nd Ser. I. 218 Improvements which the 'oil drop method' introduced into the study of the Brownian movements. **1939** X. HERBERT in B. James *Austral. Short Stories* (1963) 115 The first sight that caught his eye was a row of sparkling oil-drops hanging from the face of yet another outcrop. **1946** *Nature* 30 Nov. 786/1 Oil drops..entered the field and were illuminated by flashes of light. **1968** M. S. LIVINGSTON *Particle Physics* ii. 13 The first precise measurement of the electronic charge came with the results of Millikan's oil-drop experiment in 1909. **1860** *Harper's Mag.* June 8/1 New Bedford is the chief seat of the whaling interest... Here the gaugers, clerks, super-cargoes, *oil-fillers..ply their busy offices. **1927** [see *dip-stick, dipstick*]. **1937** [see *guide coat*]. **1972** D. BLOODWORTH *Any Number can Play* xvi. 152 He.. unscrewed the radiator cap..and then glanced at the oil filler. *a* **1756** MRS. HEYWOOD *New Present* (1771) 258 Directions concerning *Oil Floor-Cloths. **1535** COVERDALE *1 Sam.* viii. 14 Youre best londe and vynyardes and *oyle-gardens shall he take. **1847** J. C. MAITLAND *Historical Charades* xv. 193 A gilder living in the village..explained to him the nature of *oil-gilding. **1835–6** TODD *Cycl. Anat.* I. 271/2 The neck of the bird..can be made to apply the beak to the coccygeal *oil-gland. **1893** NEWTON *Dict. Birds* s.v., Analysis of the secretion of the Oil-gland shews that its composition closely resembles that of the sebaceous product of Mammals. **1710** *Brit. Apollo* III. No. 89. 2/1 Night Peices ought to be..in *Oyl-Gold, or Oyl-Lacker. **1875** KNIGHT *Dict. Mech.* s.v. *Oil-gilding*, Oil-gold size, made of boiled linseed-oil and ochre. **1875** *Ure's Dictionary of Arts* III. 1055 (s.v. *Varnish*) The assistant is then to lift up the *oil-jack..laying the spout over the edge of the pot. **1851** H. MELVILLE *Moby Dick* II. vii. 54 That worthy,..buttoned up in his *oil-jacket. **1898** *Contemp. Rev.* Aug. 236 The Bill.. might have suited the English oil dealers; it was too much for the American *oil kings. **1886** C. SCOTT *Sheep-Farming* 51 Linseed cake, or *oil-meal as it is sometimes termed, is always relished by a sheep. **1790** ROY in *Phil. Trans.* LXXX. 184 The French rods were covered with several coats of *oil-paint to prevent their imbibing the salt water. **1898** *Westm. Gaz.* 17 Nov. 3/1 His splendid success in the use of oil-paint as an artistic material. **1765** T. H. CROKER et al. *Compl. Dict. Arts & Sci.* II. s.v. *Enamel*, Blue is made of the azure or lapis lazuli used by *oil-painters. **1842** *Ainsworth's Mag.* I. 232 There are difficulties in the way of even our first oil-painters. **1891** R. FRY *Let.* 4 Mar. (1972) I. 129 Raphael..is a fresco painter and not an oil painter. **1782** H. WALPOLE *Vertue's Anecd. Paint.* (ed. 3) I. 11 *note*, Mr. Raspe..has proved that *oil-painting was known long before its pretended discovery by Van Eyck. **1859** GULLICK & TIMBS *Paint.* 76 Until the time of Correggio and Titian, the peculiar beauties of oil painting were unknown. **1862** THORNBURY *Life Turner* I. 351 In this first period Turner's oil paintings were bold and dark. **1930** J. B. PRIESTLEY *Angel Pavement* ii. 64 "Member him, Edna?—teeth sticking out a yard, and all cross-eyed.'.. 'Still, we can't all be oil paintings.' **1932** N. MITFORD *Christmas Pudding* iii. 39 The poor girl's certainly no oil painting. **1955** L. P. HARTLEY *Perfect Woman* viii. 76, I may not be an oil-painting, but I'm all right in my way. **1966** 'O. MILLS' *Enemies of Bride* i. 10 She's no oil-painting, so she wouldn't be besieged with offers. **1973** *Listener* 23 Aug. 246/1 Mr Tillett was no oil painting, but he was a gentlemanly sort of man. [**1725** H. SLOANE *Voy. Jamaica* II. 113 (*heading*) The Palm Oil-Tree. **1731** P. MILLER *Gardeners Dict.* s.v. *Palma*. The Oily Palm grows in great Plenty on the Coast of Guiney..: But these Trees have been transplanted to Jamaica and Barbadoes, in both which Places they thrive very well... The Inhabitants make an Oil from the Pulp of the Fruit.] **1866** *Treas. Bot.* 443/2 *Elæis guineensis*, the African *Oil Palm, which yields the celebrated palm oil, is a native of tropical Western Africa. **1907** FREEMAN & CHANDLER *World's Commercial Products* 374 The well-known Oil Palm of the West Coast of Africa.. furnishes two different oils. **1954** R. E. HOLTTUM *Plant Life Malaya* vi. 81 Oil palms are the next most important oil crop [after coconut] in Malaya. **1966** E. J. H. CORNER *Nat. Hist. Palms* xiii. 305 The fruit of the oil-palm is a drupe one and a half inches long, with pulpy, red or black wall or pericarp and a small, pointed stone. **1975** T. C. WHITMORE *Trop. Rain Forests Far East* xvii. 219/2 Western man introduced plantation agriculture, initially to grow spices, later to grow the other cash crops, with coffee, tea, rubber, and oil palm predominating. **1836–9** DICKENS *Sk. Boz, Streets* ii, The candle in the transparent lamp, manufactured of *oil-paper, ..has been blown out. **1848** tr. *Hoffmeister's Trav. Ceylon & India* 208 *Sesamum* (*oil plant), *Ricinus* (castor-oil tree). **1884** MILLER *Plant-n.*, *Arachis hypogæa*,..Ground-nut or Earth-nut Oil-plant; *Bassia longifolia*, Ilpa, Illipoo, or Illupie oil-plant; *Carapa guianensis*, Carap, Crab, or Andiroba Oil-plant; *Croton Tiglium*, Croton-oil-plant; *Ricinus communis*,..Castor-oil-plant; *Sesamum indicum*,.. Gingelly-, or Gingilie-, Oil-plant, Tit-, or Teet-, Oil-plant; *S. indicum* and *S. orientale*, Benne-oil-plant. **1922** *Times* 15 June 2 (*heading*) *Oil pollution of the sea. **1973** V. CANNING *Flight of Grey Goose* iv. 67 Two great black-headed gulls that were recovering from the effects of oil pollution. **1903** *Bull. U.S. Geol. Survey* No. 212. 68 The foregoing account of the Gulf Coastal Plain has been given in some detail in order that the geologic environment of the *oil pools might be readily understood. **1938** *Sun* (Baltimore) 18 Jan. 1/3 Kilgore is in the heart of the vast east Texas oil pool, the world's largest. **1971** I. G. GASS et al. *Understanding Earth* ix. 139/1 The oil-water interface in a sub-surface abiogenic oil-pool. **1715** LEONI *Palladio's Archit.* (1742) I. 65 On the right-hand you have the *Oil-presses, and other places for the Oil. *c* **1865** LETHEBY in *Circ. Sc.* I. 105/1 Mr. Brotherton ..is a large *oil-presser. **1926** E. R. LILLEY *Oil Industry* iii. 22 [The writer will use the term 'province' when referring to an area containing connected or related fields.] *Ibid.* 539/2 (Index), *Oil province. **1940** *Bull. Amer. Assoc. Petroleum Geologists* XXIV. 1024 The Pure Oil Company's discovery in Marshall County, in what is virtually a new oil province, may encourage other operators to venture farther into the unknown. **1975** *North Sea Background Notes* (Brit. Petroleum Co.) 3 The North Sea..has now become one of the world's major offshore oil provinces. **1934** H. HILER *Notes Technique of Painting* iii. 163, I have used an *oil-resin medium for fifteen years. **1951** R. MAYER *Artist's Handbk.* i. 31 Some of the earlier American uses of tempera and oil-resin glazes are mentioned on page 27. **1885** *Engineering* 26 June 708/2 As I have referred to the Pennsylvanian *oil rig, a brief mention of its principle may not be out of place here. This machine is specially arranged for deep sinking. **1965** M. BRADBURY *Stepping Westward* viii. 391 They reached the section where the oil-rigs stand up. **1973** *Scotsman* 12 Jan. (Tayside Suppl.) p. vii/2 (*caption*) Montrose from the air. A new quay and purpose-built base will service up to 12 oil rig supply ships. **1974** *BP Shield Internat.* Oct. 17/2 It's the morning rush-hour to the North Sea oil rigs. **1975** *Times* 16 Sept. 3 (*heading*) Puzzle of oil-rig divers' death from overheating. *c* **1790** IMISON *Sch. Art* II. 44 The tools necessary for engraving are, the *oil-rubber, burnisher, scraper, oil-stone, needles, and ruler. **1883** *Century Mag.* July 330/1 When the *oil-sand is struck, the oil, mingled with gas, spurs up with great force. **1915** C. SCHUCHERT *Text-bk. Geol.* II. xxvii. 713 The oil and gas are stored in coarse, open-textured sandstones and conglomerates, and because of this the term *oil-sand* has come to be applied by drillers to all horizons yielding these volatile hydrocarbons. **1921** G. H. COX et al. *Field Methods Petroleum Geol.* 217 Because of the higher average porosity of sandstone, most 'oil sands' are true sandstones, but many are porous limestones. **1925** A. B. THOMPSON *Oil-Field Explor.* I. ix. 426 Twenty or more workable oil sands have been encountered to 2,500 ft [in the Bibi-Eibat oil-field]. **1974** *Globe & Mail* (Toronto) 23 May 8/3 Research is also progressing on development of a micro-organism that could be used in the reclamation of the Alberta oil sands, Dr. Kaneda said. **1873** *Oil shale [see *oil coal* above]. **1919** [see BOGHEAD, BOGHEAD]. **1956** *Nature* 4 Feb. 216/1 In 1858 Geikie was able to indicate to James Young, founder of the Scottish oil industry, the general distribution of West Lothian oil-shales. **1974** 'E. LATHEN' *Sweet & Low* xiv. 138 Yet another optimistic study of oil shale. **1975** *Petroleum Economist* Sept. 349/2 Morocco is preparing to exploit its large oil shale deposits at Timahdit in the Middle Atlas Mountains. **1851** H. MELVILLE *Moby Dick* II. xxxix. 257 However curious it may seem for an *oil-ship to be borrowing oil on the whale-ground. **1911** J. J. ABRAHAM *Surgeon's Log* vi. 195 No one is allowed to smoke on board the oil-ships. **1783** CAVALLO in *Phil. Trans.* LXXIII. 438 This slip of *oil-silk answers better than a piece of bladder or leather. **1870** G. H. LEWES *Jrnl.* 14 Apr. in *Geo. Eliot Lett.* (1956) V. 90 Bought oil silk for compress. **1938** *Times* 20 May 21/4 Oilsilk, that daughter of oilskin, has been developed into many types of mackintosh. **1965** M. THOMAS *Grannies' Remedies* 91 An envelope of wetted linen or cotton, oil-silk, and thick flannel. **1889** *Century Mag.* Mar. 710/2 It had..formed an *oil-slick thirty feet to windward. **1918** *Sat. Even. Post* 12 Oct. 90 The submarine when running close beneath the surface leaves what is known as an 'oil slick'. That is, the oil that is discharged in the exhausts floats on the top of the water in tell-tale streaks... 'Oil Slick' is American terminology. The British Admiralty did not approve at first. **1950** G. HACKFORTH-JONES *Worst Enemy* ii. 171 Meanwhile, no doubt, an 'oil slick' would be rising from the crumpled ballast tanks which must have suffered damage. **1973** *Guardian* 19 May 12/3, 200,000-ton tankers..letting loose their oil slicks in some of the most profitable fishing grounds in the world. **1958** *Oxford Mail* 15 Aug. 1/5 Wreckage picked up from the *oil-slicked section of the Atlantic by the searching ships. **1967** L. DEIGHTON *Expensive Place* xxvii. 164 The oil-slicked highway dared children and divided neighbours. **1976** *Leicester Mercury* 14 Oct. 10/2 The grey waters of the Clyde closed slowly over the oil-slicked plates of the huge submarine. **1865** J. H. A. BONE *Petroleum & Petroleum Wells* 20 A new class of people has sprung into existence under the cognomen of *oil smellers, who profess to be able to ascertain the proper spot for boring by smelling the earth. **1925** *Jrnl. Physical Chem.* XXIX. 1206 A water-soluble emulsifying agent opposes the action of an *oil-soluble agent. **1935** A. J. NORTON in P. H. Groggins *Unit Processes in Org. Synthesis* xiii. 636 Strictly speaking, the oil-soluble resins are a subdivision of the thermoplastic resins. **1971** *Jrnl. Econ. Entomol.* LXIV. 1399 (*heading*) Oil-soluble black dye in larval diet marks adults and eggs of tobacco budworm and pink bollworm. **1970** *Internat. & Compar. Law Q.* XIX. 343 Compensating governments and tanker owners for the costs incurred in cleaning *oil spills. **1975** *Offshore* Aug. 112/1 The company has been blocked from drilling for six years, initially by the moratorium imposed by the state following the January, 1969 oil spill. **1976** *Globe & Mail* (Toronto) 16 Feb. 9/3 Adequate contingency plans to deal with oil spills, especially in the ecologically sensitive Mackenzie delta and Beaufort Sea areas, have not yet been developed. **1922** A. L. HETHERINGTON *Early Ceramic Wares of China* xviii. 124 The markings may assume quite a different appearance and silvery spots or "oil spots' may take the place of the golden-brown streaks. *Ibid.*, A specimen with a Northern grey body and 'oil spot' glaze is shown in colour on Plate 38. **1934** *Burlington Mag.* May 214/2 A black glaze diapered with silvery spots..the much-prized 'oil-spot temmoku'. **1960** H. HAYWARD *Antique Coll.* 203/1 'Oilspot' glaze: some of the Chinese wares bearing so-called Honan brown and black glazes of the Sung dynasty bear attractive silver spots, caused by precipitated iron crystals. **1962** *Gloss. Terms Glass Industry* (*B.S.I.*) 40 *Oil spot*, a mottled, circular mark caused by carbonization of oil on electric lamp bulb or valve forming equipment. **1971** L. A. BOGER *Dict. World Pott. & Porc.* 154/2 Some Honan wares have a body of buff or buff-white, or of white or grey white... The rare oil spot temmoku generally belongs to this group. Occasionally a rare tea bowl is found that is covered with small silver spots which are actually a silver-like reflection caused by the metallic luster of the brown. This is referred to by the Chinese as the oil spot glaze. **1762** in *Pennsylvania Mag. Hist. & Biogr.* (1913) XXXVII. 174 Mullen brot me a Bottle of Oyle from ye *Oyl Spring at Mooskingum. **1832** B. DAVENPORT *New Gazetteer* 272/1 s.v. *Franklin*, The celebrated Oil Springs..rise from the bed of Oil creek [Pa.] and afford an inexhaustible supply of oil. **1839** Z. LEONARD *Adventures* 73/2 An oil spring, rising out of the earth. **1868** DANA *Min.* (ed. 5) 725 The oil spring of Cuba, Alleghany Co., N.Y., called the Seneca Oil Spring,.. was described by Prof. Silliman in 1833..as a dirty pool. **1897** W. WALSH *Secr. Hist. Oxf. Movem.* viii. (1898) 248 The *oilstock of the Holy Chrism is kissed in place of the Pax. **1864** *Harper's Mag.* Dec. 59/2 It is certain that great *oil-strikes are no longer looked for. **1973** *Scotsman* 21 Feb. 1/5 Ultramar shares moved up 1p to 271½p on hopes of an oil strike. **1921** W. H. JEFFERY *Deep Well Drilling* xii. 346 When the drilling conditions, depth to the producing formation, etc., are known, the perforated casing is sometimes added to the *oil string before the well is drilled in. **1943** *Bull. Amer. Assoc. Petroleum Geologists* XXVII. 519 The usual range of oil-string lengths is from 4,500 feet to 5,000 feet where casing is set above the 'pay'. **1946** *Mod. Petroleum Technol.* (Inst. Petroleum) 85 In low-pressure wells the upper section of the smaller diameter casing, the 'oil string', is sometimes removed as a measure of economy, but in wells in which gas or oil under high pressure is expected, each string of casing extends to the surface. **1960** C. GATLIN *Petroleum Engin.* xiv. 269/1 The final appearance of a typical completed well is shown in Figure 14.1. Note that three separate casing sizes are indicated: the surface pipe, the intermediate string, and the oil string. **1904** *Trans. Amer. Inst. Electr. Engin.* XXIII. 215 The design of the *oil-switch lends itself readily to operation by control from a distance. **1964** E. A. REEVES *Installation & Maint. Industr. Switchgear* iii. 57 The type of oil switch described is essentially a fault-making and load-breaking device. **1920** *Isle of Man Weekly Times* 21 Sept. 3 Kermode's supplied..installations..for..British Admiralty *oil-tankers. **1926** *Brit. Gaz.* 12 May 4/3 Many vessels have been docked and undocked, including oil tankers. **1927** *Daily Express* 20 Sept. 2/4 The goods train consisted mainly of oil-tankers. **1965** W. SOYINKA *Road* 21 Have you known any other driver take an oil-tanker from Port Harcourt to Kaduna non-stop? **1967** N. FREELING *Strike Out* 73 Dickie looks as poor as a rat on an oil-tanker. **1884** *Science* 13 June 724/1 Bars of *oil-tempered and untempered steel. **1875** KNIGHT *Dict. Mech.*, **Oil-test*, for ascertaining the degree of heat at which the hydrocarbon vapors of petroleum are liable to explode. **1898** *Daily News* 1 Oct. 7/2 Cement tester, *oil tester; apparatus for the testing of pressure and vacuum gauges and indicators. **1903** *Oil thrower [see CREEPAGE]. **1964** DORIAN & OSENTON *Elsevier's Dict. Aeronautics* 428 *Oil thrower*, a disk fixed on a shaft, so as to prevent oil from creeping along it, the oil being thrown off centrifugally. **1859** RANKINE *Steam Engine* (Cent.) An *oil-tight stuffing-box. **1972** *Practical Motorist* Oct. 168/2 As the nut is tightened the neoprene ring is squeezed out to give an oil-tight seal. **1631** MASSINGER *Emperor East* v. ii, The proud attributes, By *oil-tongued flattery imposed upon us. **1946** *Nature* 26 Oct. 572/1 An interesting series of transparent 50 per cent *oil-water systems was described. **1964** G. H. HAGGIS et al. *Introd. Molecular Biol.* iii. 70 The unfolding of protein molecules at air-water or oil-water interfaces must be briefly described at this point. **1971** Oil-water [see *oil pool* above]. **1840** *Archæologia* XXIX. 62 An oblique perforation in the stone served as an *oilway to render its revolutions easier. **1601** HOLLAND *Pliny* II. 514 *Oyle whetstones that barbars vse. **1493** *Festivall* (W. de W. 1515) 108 He ete but brede and *oyle wortes.

†oil, *sb.*[2] *Obs.* [An alteration of OLIO: perh. confused with It. *olio* oil.] = OLIO 1.

1706 PHILLIPS, *Oil* or *Olio* (in Cookery), a rich sort of Potage after the Spanish way, made of Buttock-beef, part of a Fillet of Veal, of a Leg of Mutton, and of raw Gammon of Bacon, with Ducks, Partridges, Pigeons, Chickens, Quails, Sausages, and a Cervelas, all fry'd brown, and afterwards boil'd with all sorts of Roots and Herbs. *Oils* (for Fish-Days) are also prepar'd with Peas-soop, several sorts of Fish, Roots and Pulse. **1725** BRADLEY *Fam. Dict.* s.v., To have an Oil for Flesh-Days, take all Sorts of good Meats, viz. Part of a Buttock of Beef [etc.].

oil, *v.* [f. OIL *sb.*[1]]

1. *trans.* To apply oil to; to anoint.

†a. To pour oil upon ceremonially, esp. in consecrating to the office of king: = ANOINT *v.* 2. *Obs.*

c **1440** *R. Gloucester's Chron.* 7243 (MS. Camb. Ee 4. 31) Fram king alfred, þe kunde more, þat uerst was oyled [*MS. Cotton Caligula A. xi.* yeled] at rome. *Ibid.* 5329 (MS. Digby 205) þe pope lyoun him blessede..And þe kinges croune of þis lond..Sette him on and oyled [*earlier MSS.* elede] him. *c* **1580** SIDNEY *Ps.* XXIII. iv, Thou oil'st my head, thou fill'st my cupp. **1764** CHURCHILL *Gotham* I. 337 Jehu, oil'd for Ahab's sin. **1851** H. MELVILLE *Moby Dick* (U.S. ed.) xxv. 124 A king's head is solemnly oiled at his coronation, even as a head of salad.

b. To put oil on; to moisten, rub, smear, or lubricate with oil; to rub (a person) with oil as a protection against sunburn (also *refl.*). Phr. ***to oil the wheels*** (also *fig.*).

to oil out, in *Painting*, to moisten (those parts of a picture intended to be retouched) with a thin coating of oil.

c **1440** *Promp. Parv.* 363/1 Oyle wythe oyle. **1598** *Ludlow Churchw. Acc.* (Camden) 169 Item, to William Glover, for oylinge and coloringe yt [an hour glass]. **1643** CARYL *Sacr. Covt.* 13 Would he have the Chariot move swiftly, who.. will not Oyle the Wheeles? **1703** MOXON *Mech. Exerc.* 171 So oft as the Workman has occasion to oyl the Centers of the Work. **1859** GULLICK & TIMBS *Paint.* 201 This operation is termed 'oiling out'. **1876** GEO. ELIOT *Dan. Der.* II. IV. xxxiii. 332 There's a bad style of humbug, but there is also a good style—one that oils the wheels and makes progress possible. **1884** SPEEDY *Sport* v. 67 They should be wiped clean and free from damp, then..oiled. **1896** C. M. SHELDON *His Brother's Keeper* ii. 39 Have you been greasing your boots with it?.. Half a pint wouldn't oil more than one of 'em. **1909** *Daily Chron.* 6 Sept. 3/3 Her craze for the 'psychic'..oils the wheels of the plot. **1941** A. CHRISTIE *Evil under Sun* vi. 107, I oiled myself and sunbathed. **1945** E. WAUGH *Brideshead Revisited* I. ii. 43 Anthony had helped oil fading beauties on sub-tropical sands. **1972** *Mainichi Daily News* (Japan) 6 Nov. 13/1 Advertisement [*sic*] is a powerful factor in boosting the economy in free countries and it is the strongest means of oiling the wheel of manufacturer-consumer relations. **1972** 'G. BLACK' *Bitter Tea* (1973) ix. 137 A cousin came over and oiled Sally's back. **1973** A. HOLDEN *Girl on Beach* 51 She changed into her swimsuit, oiled herself all over. **1976** D. FRANCIS *In Frame* xvi. 232 Our passage had been oiled by telexes from above. When we arrived..we found ourselves whisked into a private room. **1977** 'A. STUART' *Snap Judgement* 178 He set the deal up... He was oiling the wheels for when Brigitte arrived with the secrets.

c. To cover the surface of (water) with a film of oil in order to kill mosquito larvæ.

1921 M. Watson *Prevention of Malaria* (ed. 2) xvii. 190 When a clear pool containing the ordinary floating alga is 'oiled', the alga dies. 1952 P. F. Russell *Malaria* 133 Water recently oiled is unfit for bathing. 1959 A. A. Sandosham *Malariology* vi. 252 When oiling a ravine the seepages in which the ravine stream begins should get most attention.

2. *fig.* **a.** *to oil the hand (fist)*: to bribe (cf. anoint *v.* 3 b); also with the person as obj. Also, *to oil the knocker*: to bribe or tip a doorman. *slang.*

1602 *2nd Pt. Return fr. Parnass.* II. ii. 601 Must his worships fists bee needs then oyled with Angells? 1652 J. Wright tr. *Camus' Nat. Paradox* ix. 210 Speaking in private to the same Officer (whose hand he had already oyled). 1870 *Brewer's Dict. Phr. & Fable* 632/1 *To oil the knocker*, to fee the porter. The expression is from Racine, *On n'entre point chez lui sans graisser le marteau* (No one enters *his* house without oiling the knocker)—'*Les Plaideurs*'. 1901 *Daily Chron.* 13 Aug. 6/7 Certain officials had to be 'oiled'. 1901 Farmer & Henley *Slang* V. 93/1 *To oil the knocker*, to fee the porter. 1968 *Gloss. Brit. Argot* (Paramount Pictures), *Oil the knocker*, tip the porter or caretaker.

b. (*a*) To make 'smooth' or bland; *to oil one's tongue*, to adopt or use flattering speech. (*b*) To besmear with flattery, to flatter (= anoint *v.* 3 a).

1607 Dekker & Webster *Hist. Sir T. Wyatt* D.'s Wks. 1873 III. 102 Hast thou betraide me? yet with such a tongue, so smoothly oilde. *a* 1716 South *Serm.* (1727) IV. ix. 387 No wonder if Error, oiled with Obsequiousness,.. has often the Advantage of Truth. 1750 Shenstone *Rural Elegance* 108 The reptile race, That oil the tongue, and bow the knee. 1887 R. Buchanan *Heir of Linne* i, Oil my voice, and I'm your man.

3. a. To supply or feed with oil.

1614 Sylvester *Bethulia's Rescue* v. 120 Bagos, too-apt,.. Thus oyles the Fire, which but too-fast did burn. 1923 *Man. Seamanship* (Admiralty) II. 80 The pumps in the oiler should be started gradually, attempts should not be made to oil individual tanks too rapidly.

b. *intr.* To take in a supply of oil.

1914 H. H. Fyfe *Real Mexico* 201 Some day vessels will call here.. to 'oil' just as they now 'coal'. 1922 *Glasgow Herald* 21 Oct. 11 After that the Renown only stopped to oil.

4. a. To convert (butter or grease) into oil by melting.

1759 *Ann. Reg.* 66 The butter is oiled by hot water. 1842 Barham *Ingol. Leg., St. Cuthbert*, And the fish is all spoil'd, And the butter's all oil'd, And the soup's got cold in the silver tureen.

b. *intr.* To become of the consistence of oil.

1741 *Compl. Fam.-Piece* I. ii. 114 Take Care the Butter do not oil. 1796 Mrs. Glasse *Cookery* xi. 175 Boil all together and send it up immediately, or else it will oil. *Mod.* Add warmed butter, being careful not to allow it to oil.

5. *colloq.* To move or go in a quiet or stealthy manner; (const. *in*) to enter, (*fig.*) to interfere; (const. *out*) to depart, (*fig.*) to extricate oneself. Also const. other advbs.

1925 Wodehouse *Carry on, Jeeves!* vi. 139 As man to man, do you want to oil out of this thing? 1929 —— *Mr. Mulliner Speaking* i. 28 It would be a simple task to oil in, insert the soap, and buzz back undetected. 1930 —— *Very Good, Jeeves!* iv. 110, I.. oiled round to where Jeeves awaited me. 1945 'A. Gilbert' *Don't open Door* xix. 172 As soon as he was alone he'd oil out and they could think what they pleased. 1958 —— *Death against Clock* 119 She might oil in, and.. clinch a bargain on the spot. 1963 —— *Ring for Noose* x. 119 He deserves to lose his licence, oiling off and leaving you on your tod. 1968 G. Mitchell *Three Quick & Five Dead* i. 35 Do you think the girl was pestering for marriage, but that James wanted to oil out? 1977 'J. Le Carré' *Hon. Schoolboy* xxii. 527 That twerp Enderby is oiling through the back door.

6. *intr. to oil up*: to clog up with oil.

[1925: see *oiled-up* s.v. oiled *ppl. a.* 5.] 1960 [see foul *v.*[1] 1 b]. 1975 *Country Life* 5 June 1470/1 In traffic.. plugs oil up. And pedals are hard pressed to keep the engine alive.

'oil-bag. **a.** A sac or gland in an animal body which secretes or contains oil. **b.** A bag to contain material from which oil is to be expressed. **c.** A bag to contain oil for any purpose.

1713 Derham *Phys.-Theol.* vii. i. (1727) 334 *note*, In most .. Birds there is only one Gland; in which are divers.. Cells, ending in two or three larger Cells, lying under the Nipple of the Oil-bag. 1792 Belknap *Hist. New Hampsh.* III. 161 The oil-bag of the musquash, wrapped in cotton, affords a perfume, grateful to those who are fond of musk. 1875 Knight *Dict. Mech., Oil-bag*, a sack of horsehair or cocoa-nut fiber, used in pressing oleine from the stearine in a press. *a* 1889 in *Century Mag.* Mar. 710/1 [I] placed two oil-bags, filled with linseed oil, over the bows. 1961 F. H. Burgess *Dict. Sailing* 152 *Oil bag*, any container that permits oil to drip out slowly to help quell the sea.

'oil bath. Also oil-bath. [f. oil *sb.*[1] + bath *sb.*[1]]. **1.** A receptacle containing oil for cooling, heating, lubricating, or insulating apparatus immersed in it, or for other purposes.

1838 T. Thomson *Chem. Org. Bodies* 663 Exposed.. by means of an oil-bath, to a temperature between 300° and 350°. 1885 *Marine Engineer* 1 Sept. 151/2 The crank shaft at the lowest point of its revolution constantly touches the surface of an oil bath in the closed motion chamber. 1927 Mellanby & Cooper tr. *Kieser's Materials & Design Turbo-Gen. Plant* 52 The sudden drop in temperature is obtained by quenching the wheels in an oil bath. 1968 K. Ball *B.M.C. Autobk.* 4 198/2 *Oil-bath*... In air filters, a separate oil supply for wetting the wire-mesh element. 1970 —— *Fiat 600* 164/2 Oil bath Reservoir which lubricates parts by immersion. 1971 *Power Farming* Mar. 57/3 It forms an oil-bath for the drive, the oil being circulated by the gears to the outboard end and returned through piping.

2. *India.* (See quots.)

1909 *Westm. Gaz.* 28 Apr. 5/2 The term oil-bath is only a misnomer, inasmuch as the bath is not taken in oil. It is applied to a process involved in besmearing the body with oil and then bathing in a river or tank to remove the oil from the body. 1967 Singha & Massey *Indian Dancer* ix. 96 First, the entire body is given an 'oil-bath', that is, oil is rubbed into it.

'oil burner. **1.** A device in which oil is atomized and burned to produce heat.

1900 *Engineer* 22 June 651/3 A new muffle furnace with two oil burners of the luminous lamp type, but arranged to give a blue flame. 1946 K. Steiner *Fuels & Fuel Burners* xiv. 279 Domestic oil burners usually operate intermittently .., starting when heat is required and stopping when the heat demand is satisfied. 1946 E. Hodgins *Mr. Blandings builds his Dream House* (1947) ii. xv. 204 The oil burner, starting up in answer to the call of its thermostat. 1970 D. Kut *Warm Air Heating* xx. 338 The grade of oil fuel best suited for a particular installation depends on the type of oil burner and on the hourly through-put of oil.

2. a. A vehicle or ship burning oil as fuel.

1902 *Westm. Gaz.* 29 Sept. 5/2 Tank engines were the first to be fitted as oil-burners, and now some of the newest main line locomotives are to be fitted. 1911 *Daily Colonist* (Victoria, B.C.) 20 Apr. 14/3 The steamer will be practically a duplicate of the Princess Adelaide but will be constructed as an oil-burner. 1923 R. D. Paine *Comrades of Rolling Ocean* ix. 160 That ship of his.. is an oil-burner. 1942 Berrey & Van den Bark *Amer. Thes. Slang* §766/6 *Oil burner*, a diesel-powered truck. 1971 M. Tak *Truck Talk* 111 *Oil burner*, (1) a diesel truck, as opposed to a truck that runs on gasoline.

b. *slang.* A vehicle which, because of its poor condition, uses up great quantities of lubricating oil.

1938 *Amer. Speech* XIII. 307/2 *Oil burner*, a bus which uses excessive amounts of oil. 1975 B. Garfield *Hopscotch* xvii. 166 Even in an old oil-burner he could have gone three times as far in a day's drive if he'd wanted to.

oilcake ('ɔɪlkeɪk). The cake or mass of compressed seeds (rapeseed, linseed, cottonseed, or other kind) which is left after pressing out so much of the oil as can be thus extracted; used as a fattening food for cattle or sheep, or as manure. (Usually as a substance; less commonly with *pl.*)

1743 W. Ellis *Mod. Husbandman* June iv. 36 Dressing Ground with Lime, Chalk,.. Oil Cake Powder, Malt Dust [etc]. 1757 W. Thompson *R.N. Advoc.* 41 They shall not be fed with Graves, Oil Cakes, Horse-Flesh. 1805 *Trans. Soc. Arts* XXIII. 41 Feeding the cows with green food and oil-cake. 1859 *All Year Round* No. 29. 57 Our greatest agricultural revolution was produced by feeding mutton on oil-cake and sliced turnips. 1942 *Sun* (Baltimore) 26 Nov. 8/2 The ships, operating under a safe conduct agreement between Sweden and belligerent nations, were laden with grain, oilcake and piece goods. 1971 *Post* (S. Afr., Cape ed.) (Suppl.) 9 May 10/1 (*caption*) Easy oil cake.. easy and cheap to make. 1975 *Nature* 13 Feb. 488/3 The importance of the poppy crop lies primarily in the seed, as the principle [*sic*] source.., after extraction, of oil-cake for cattle feed.

Comb. 1865 Dickens *Mut. Fr.* i. x, An oilcake-fed style of business-gentleman.

oilcloth ('ɔɪlklɒθ, -ɔːθ).

1. A general name for any fabric of cotton, linen, hemp, etc. prepared with oil, so as to be rendered waterproof. **a.** = oilskin.

1697 tr. *C'tess D'Aunoy's Trav.* (1706) 135 Which Coaches.. are distinguished by this, that they are covered with green Oyl-cloth round. 1753 Hanway *Trav.* (1762) I. iii. xxxvi. 165 It was with difficulty that we could, by the help of oil-cloths and other conveniencies, keep ourselves dry. 1844 J. Tomlin *Missionary Jrnls.* 319 He brought his bible, carefully wrapped up in an oil-cloth. 1871 Tyndall *Fragm. Sc.* (1879) I. vii. 232 A suit and hood of yellow oilcloth covered all. 1885 C. G. W. Lock *Workshop Receipts* IV. 21/1 The manner of making oil-cloth or 'oil-skin' was at one period a mystery.

b. A canvas of various degrees of thickness, painted or coated with a preparation containing a drying oil, used for table-cloths, floor-cloths, etc.

1796 H. Walpole *Let.* 20 Nov. (1905) XV. 430, I mentioned *carpets* made from Mr. Lysons's mosaic pavements; I ought to have said *oil-cloths*, which cost a great deal less. 1803 [see 2]. 1819 *Pantologia, Oil-cloth*, linen cloth or canvas painted either plainly or ornamentally in oil-colours. 1828 Webster, *Oil-cloth*, cloth oiled or painted for covering floors. 1832 Babbage *Econ. Manuf.* 76 Those oil-cloths with the greatest variety of colours are most expensive. 1903 Kipling *Five Nations* 114 Then the oil-cloth with its numbers, as a banner fluttered free. 1904 G. Stratton-Porter *Freckles* 72 Freckles.. covered the [book-]case with oil-cloth. 1974 *Country Life* 3 Jan. 33/3 Fortunately preserved under later oilcloth is decoration in the upper hall and several of the bedrooms.

2. *attrib.* and *Comb.* Made of or covered with oilcloth.

1749 H. Walpole *Lett.* (1846) II. 265, I am not commonly fond of sights, but content myself with the oil-cloth-picture of them that is hung out. 1803 Jane Porter *Thaddeus* xxix. (1831) 259 Oilcloth floor and uncurtained windows. 1840 R. H. Dana *Bef. Mast* x. 23 We had on oil-cloth suits and south-wester caps. 1897 *Outing* (U.S.) XXX. 442/1 The meal spread on the oilcloth-covered table. 1917 W. Owen *Let.* 8 Aug. (1967) 481 Thus I need at once... The Oil-cloth raincoat. 1954 M. Sharp *Gipsy in Parlour* xiii. 133 Oilcloth-covered tables and bentwood chairs. 1974 R. B. Parker *Godwulf Manuscript* xii. 96 The kitchen with its oilcloth-covered table.

'oil-clothed, *a.* [f. oilcloth + -ed[2].] Laid or covered with oilcloth. So **'oilclothy** *a.*, suggestive of or resembling oilcloth.

1894 M. Dyan *All in Man's Keeping* II. x. 185 There came .. the tap of light heels on the oil-clothed landing. 1915 Galsworthy *First & Last* in *Cosmopolitan* June 12/2 He was in a gas-lighted passage, with an oil-clothed floor. 1923 U. L. Silberrad *Lett. J. Armiter* ix. 202 Everything was slippery and oilclothy. 1974 L. Thomas *Tropic of Ruislip* ii. 41 She.. followed Andrew into The Bombardier Café where he was sitting at one of the tables covered with decorated oilcloth depicting badges of Britain's fighting forces... She and her grandfather sat at the next oilclothed table staring directly at him.

'oil-,colour. 'Colour' or paint made by grinding a pigment in oil. (Chiefly in *pl.*)

1539 *Ld. Treas. Acc. Scotl.* in Pitcairn *Crim. Trials* I. 298* Painting of hir mastis, salis, and airis, with oley colouris. 1659 Wood *Life* (O.H.S.) I. 309 They were all painted over in oyl-colours this yeare (1659). 1703 Moxon *Mech. Exerc.* 349 Draw upon these marked Lines with Oyl Colours. 1821 Craig *Lect. Drawing* i. 33 In the time of those three great men, the practice of painting in oil colours became general.

'oildom. [f. oil *sb.*[1] + -dom.] The petroleum-producing districts of a country; petroleum producers and marketers regarded as a group.

1865 J. H. A. Bone *Petroleum & Petroleum Wells* 42 If he would see anything at all of oildom he must make the passage, unpleasant as it may be. 1880 *Harper's Mag.* Dec. 63 Huge shops.. send.. iron tanks into the oil regions—to hold the surplus of Oildom. 1904 I. M. Tarbell *Hist. Standard Oil Co.* I. 71 The rise [in freight rates] which had been threatening had come... At the news all oildom rushed into the streets. 1926 J. Ise *U.S. Oil Policy* xiii. 135 The new order immediately precipitated a fresh quarrel in oildom.

oiled (ɔɪld), *ppl. a.* [f. oil *v.* + -ed[1].]

1. a. Smeared, moistened, or lubricated with oil. †In early use, of a person, Anointed. Also *fig.* Cf. *to oil the wheels* (oil *v.* 1 b).

1550 Bale *Eng. Votaries* ii. Pref., This chaplayne of the deuyll was a general prouyder for the oyled fathers there. 1606 Sylvester *Du Bartas* ii. iv. iii. *Schisme* 345 Th' Oyled Priests that in Gods presence stand. 1624 Massinger *Parl. Love* v. i. Wks. (Rtldg.) 142/1, I have no oiled tongue; and I hope my bluntness will not offend. 1630 Fanshawe *Ode*, Free from the bait of oiled hands, And painted looks. 1894 Ld. Rosebery *Sp.* 18 Mar., If the Employers' Liability Bill had been presented to the House of Lords by a Conservative Government it would have been passed on oiled castors. 1932 D. L. Sayers *Have his Carcase* xx. 263 It was.. surprising to find the identification.. going like oiled clockwork. 1933 *Brit. Birds* XXVII. 45 Very little has been heard of 'oiled' birds during the two years. 1971 'D. Halliday' *Dolly & Doctor Bird.* i. 2 Lying oiled in the sun. 1972 *Daily Tel.* 9 Mar. 9/2 Oiled birds, mostly razorbills and guillemots, are coming ashore in north Cornwall. 1973 J. Burrows *Like an Evening Gone* i. 8 Greta was capable... Her unlikely scheme proceeded as on oiled wheels. 1976 M. Millar *Ask for me Tomorrow* (1977) xvii. 135 It was the only house on Camino de la Cima, an oiled dirt road.

b. Soaked, ground, preserved, etc. in oil.

1535 Coverdale *Lev.* viii. 26 An vnleuended cake, and a cake of oyled bred, and a wafer. 1658 Phillips s.v. *Distemper*, Painting in Distemper, or size,.. hath been ancientlier in use than that which is in oiled colours. 1883 *Fisheries Japan* 22 (Fish. Exh. Publ.) Oiled sardines, preserved oysters and tunny-fish, are exhibited in our Court.

c. Of a fabric, etc.: Impregnated with oil, esp. so as to be waterproof, as *oiled cloth* = oilcloth, *oiled silk*, etc. † *oiled boots*: cf. boot *sb.*[3] 3.

1624 Massinger *Parl. Love* v. i. Wks. (Rtldg.) 141/2 Perillus' brazen bull, the English rack, The German pincers, or the Scotch oiled boots. 1672 Dryden *Assignation* Prol., Your own oiled coats keep out all common rain. 1718 Motteux *Quix.* (1733) II. 209 Our Windows in the Winter were cover'd with Oil'd-cloth, and in the Summer shaded with Lattice. 1795 Ware *Rem. Ophthalmy* (ed. 3) p. vii, On the application of an oiled silk cap over the head. 1808 M. Wilmot *Russ. Jrnls.* (1934) 316 He *has* a suite of apartments in the Tartar taste with oil'd paper instead of Glass windows. 1816 J. Smith *Panorama Sc. & Art* II. 152 An inflammable air-balloon 33 feet in diameter, made of oiled silk. 1853 Morfit *Tanning & Currying* 433 Oiled leather is commonly known as chamois, or wash-leather. 1957 *Textile Terms & Definitions* (Textile Inst.) (ed. 3) 70 *Oiled wool*, unscoured or undyed knitting wool or wool dyed before spinning and containing added oil not subsequently removed. 1962 L. Deighton *Ipcress File* i. 15 His oiled teak desk. 1974 D. Ramsay *No Cause to Kill* i. 28 The carpeting was a basket weave.. effective against oiled walnut, the only wood present. 1977 J. R. L. Anderson *Death in City* viii. 119 A heavyweight oiled-wool pullover.

2. Converted or melted into oil.

1769 Mrs. Raffald *Eng. Housekpr.* (1778) 297 Beat it very fine in a mortar, with a little oiled butter. 1840 Hood *Up the Rhine* 111 A sauce made of oiled butter and hard-boiled eggs.

3. *slang.* Drunk; if unmodified (by *well*, etc.) only mildly drunk, tipsy.

1737 *Pennsylvania Gaz.* 6–13 Jan. 2 He's Oil'd. 1899 A. M. Binstead *Gal's Gossip* 169 He was certainly well 'oiled'. 1916 E. V. Lucas *Vermilion Box* 141 He was, as the slang phrase has it, 'oiled'; which is a condition of alcoholic comfort well on this side of inebriety. 1926 E. Wallace *More Educated Evans* ix. 218 He'll come out in a minute, oiled to the world. 1948 Wodehouse *Spring Fever* xvi. 162 Augustus Robb, if not actually plastered, was beyond a question oiled. 1976 J. Wainwright *Who goes Next?* 76 When they're nicely oiled, one of 'em sometimes trots around here, and buys something.

4. Executed in oil-colours.

1903 Ld. R. Gower *Rec. & Reminisc.* 246 To make an oiled copy of the framed 'Three Maries', by Carracci.

5. *Comb.*, as **oiled-down**, smoothed or plastered down with (hair) oil; **oiled-up**, fouled or choked with oil.

1907 M. A. von Arnim *Fräulein Schmidt & Mr. Anstruther* xiii. 49 Her long respectable face and oiled-down hair. **1956** H. Gold *Man who was not with It* (1965) xxviii. 264 A yellow-fleshed, oiled-down, slicked-up head. **1925** *Morris Owner's Manual* 81 Sooty or oiled-up plugs will cause erratic running, loss of power and..increased petrol consumption.

† **'oileous**, *a. Obs. rare.* [irreg. f. oil + -eous: cf. oleous, the regular formation.] Full of or containing oil; oily, oleous.

1597 Gerarde *Herbal* ii. xl. §4. 255 Thicke, fat, and oileous stalkes. **1603** Holland *Plutarch's Mor.* 659 Now is the sea fattie and oileous.

oiler ('ɔɪlə(r)). [f. oil *sb.* or *v.* + -er¹: cf. F. *huilier* oil-manufacturer, oil-merchant.]

† **1.** A manufacturer of, or dealer in, oil; an oil-man. *Obs. rare*—⁰.

1552 Huloet, Oyler or oyle maker, *Olearius.* **1818** Todd, *Oiler*, one who deals in oils and pickles. This word is in Huloet. We now say *oilman.*

2. One who oils or lubricates with oil. Also *fig.*

1846 Worcester, *Oiler*, one who oils. **1883** Ld. Granville in *Standard* 3 May 3/3 In the House of Commons you have some good oilers. **1899** *Daily News* 22 Mar. 9/2 An axle oiler at Charing Cross Station.

3. Any contrivance for oiling machinery, etc.; usually a small can with a long narrow nozzle through which to apply the oil.

1861 Olmsted *Journ. Cott. Kingd.* I. 57 He did not give himself the trouble to elevate the outlet of his oiler, so that a stream of oil..was poured out upon the ground. **1886** *Cycl. Tour. Club Gaz.* May 192/1 The old oilers, with screw caps..have seen their day.

4. An oilskin or oilcloth coat and/or trousers. *colloq.* (orig. *U.S.*).

1889 A. F. Higgins in *Scribner's Mag.* June 681 Some.. with oilers and rubber boots defy the waves. **1899** 'Q' *Ship of Stars* ix. 69 Taffy wore a suit of oilers, of which he was mighty proud. **1924** R. J. Flaherty *My Eskimo Friends* i. i. 6 Old Puggie, donning oilers and sou'wester,..settled down to the helm. **1969** *Islander* (Victoria, B.C.) 22 June 2/2 You can always spot Dolfie in his favorite open boat, because he almost invariably wears yellow oilers.

5. An oil-well. *U.S. colloq.*

1890 *Columbus* (O.) *Disp.* 24 May, The Ohio Oil Co... drilled in an oiler..that will be the largest one in this field.

6. a. 'A vessel engaged in the oil-trade. (Little used.)' (*Cent. Dict.*)

b. A naval vessel carrying oil for the use of other ships.

1916 'Taffrail' *Pincher Martin* xiv. 255 Perhaps they would be going alongside an oiler at dead of night to replenish their fuel, and the wind would get on the wrong bow. **1923** [see oiling *vbl. sb.* 3]. **1943** *Times* 8 Dec. 3/3 A flash was followed by a sheet of flame and the oiler was burning fiercely when our aircraft left. **1960** 'N. Shute' *Trustee from Toolroom* viii. 215 She was a Fleet oiler that had discharged her cargo at Christmas Island. **1973** *Times* 15 Mar. 5/4 Sightings included a Soviet F class diesel electric submarine together with..an oiler. **1974** *Union* (S. Carolina) *Daily Times* 22 Apr. 8/1 The carrier Kitty Hawk, several escorting destroyers and an oiler were expected to sail through the Strait of Malacca today.

c. A vehicle transporting oil.

1948 Mencken *Amer. Lang.* Suppl. II. 714 A tank-car is a car or oiler. **1975** I. K. Martin *Regan & Manhattan File* 54 That truck..was a General Mills sixteen-wheel oiler.

7. a. A vessel using fuel-oil.

1911 J. Barten *Compl. Nautical Pocket Dict.* 138/2 *Oiler*, Dampfschiff mit Oelfeuerung. **1915** *Chambers's Jrnl.* Oct. 664/1 The word 'oiler', like 'steamer', for oil-driven ships.. is coming into use.

b. An oil-engine.

1926 *Chambers's Jrnl.* Dec. 843/1 She is a cold-starter, two stroke 'oiler'.

c. A vehicle using oil as its fuel.

1935 *Economist* 7 Dec. 1136/2 As far as goods traffic is concerned, the growth of the Diesel lorry or 'oiler' has been at the expense of the 'steamer' as much as of the petrol vehicle.

8. *U.S. slang.* A Mexican. (*derogatory.*)

1907 S. E. White *Arizona Nights* i. iv. 82 A few oilers livin' near had water holes in the foothills. *Ibid.* iii. ii. 282 We're livin' like a lot of Oilers.

oilery ('ɔɪlərɪ). [f. oil *sb.* + -ery: cf. F. *huilerie* in same sense.] The business, business establishment, or stock of an oilman.

1864 Webster, *Oilery*, the business or the goods of a dealer in oils. **1886** *Lond. Gaz.* 65/2 Tradesmen who hold Warrants of Appointment from the Lord Steward.. Chocolate..Oilery.

oilet, obs. form of oillet.

'oil field. Also oilfield, oil-field. [f. oil *sb.*¹ + field *sb.*] An area or a tract of country underlain by oil-bearing strata, the oil usu. being present in amounts that justify commercial exploitation and occupying a number of distinct pools. Also *attrib.* Cf. *oil province* s.v. oil *sb.*¹ 6 e.

1894 *Dublin Rev.* Oct. 434 The principal sources of liquid fuel are the American and Russian oil-fields. **1912** Tower & Roberts *Petroleum* i. 11 In most cases there is a comparatively large area which can be called an 'oil field'... Within the main field there are usually several distinct areas, or 'pools', from which the chief production comes. **1926** E. R. Lilley *Oil Industry* iii. 21 The expression 'oil field' may be used to indicate an individual area of small extent such as the Salt Creek field of Wyoming.., or a group of such areas as the Lima-Indiana field.., or even an area of as wide extent as the Mid-Continent field which includes parts of Kansas, Oklahoma, Texas, Arkansas, and Louisiana. **1930** C. T. Brunner *Probl. of Oil* i. 11 The bulk of the American output still comes from the mid-Continental and Californian oilfields. **1964** *Oceanogr. & Marine Biol.* II. 136 There is a decline of sulphate with depth in the interstitial water of cores, due to the activity of sulphate-reducing bacteria and the interstitial water eventually comes to resemble oil field brine. **1973** *Scotsman* 21 Feb. 1/4 Another oilfield has been discovered in the North Sea, just inside the British sector and about 170 miles east-north-east of Aberdeen. **1975** *Offshore Engineer* Oct. 61 (Advt.), We will be fully equipped for on the spot repair and maintenance work of all oil field tools.

oilily ('ɔɪlɪlɪ), *adv.* [f. oily + -ly².]

1. *lit.* Like oil; with the consistence or appearance of oil.

1872 Tennyson *Gareth & Lynette* 795 Oilily bubbled up the mere. **1899** *Pall Mall Mag.* Sept. 211 The river.. slipped oilily past the wall below.

2. *fig.* Smoothly, blandly, flatteringly.

1862 Thornbury *Life Turner* II. 251 Parrying the thrust with the ordinary tradesman's skill of fence..quietly and oilily suggested. **1889** *Chr. World Pulpit* XXXV. 170 The love which smiles tolerantly and oilily upon all kinds of wrongs and insults.

oiliness ('ɔɪlɪnɪs). [f. as prec. + -ness.]

1. *lit.* Oily quality; the quality of being full of, covered with, or of the nature or consistence of, oil.

1598 Florio, *Oliosita*, oylienes, fatnes. **1611** Cotgr., *Oleaginité*, oylinesse, or an oylie substance. **1646** Sir T. Browne *Pseud. Ep.* 334 Unctuous bodies, and such whose oylinesse is evident. **1780** A. Young *Tour Irel.* II. 199 The oiliness and richness of the ground. **1884** *Public Opinion* 5 Sept. 302/1 The flax..wants that elasticity, pliancy, and oiliness, found in the produce of more temperate countries.

b. *concr.* The oily matter of anything.

1626 Bacon *Sylva* §521 Fat and succulent leaves, which oylinesse if it be drawn forth by the sunne..will make a very great change. **1641** French *Distill.* iii. (1651) 81 The oilinesse will separate from its body. **1799** G. Smith *Laboratory* II. 36 Get some bran, and with it rub off all the oiliness.

2. *fig.* Smoothness of behaviour or speech; bland or flattering manner; 'slipperiness'.

1851 Helps *Comp. Solit.* ii. (1874) 16 The hardness, oiliness, and imperturbability of the world. **1900** A. Hope *Quisante* iii. 32 In attempting smoothness, he fell into oiliness.

oiling ('ɔɪlɪŋ), *vbl. sb.* [f. oil *v.* + -ing¹.] The action of the verb oil.

1. a. The application of oil; anointing, lubrication, etc. with oil. Also, oil pollution; the discharge of oil from a ship.

c **1440** *Promp. Parv.* 364/1 Oylyynge wythe oyle, *oleacio.* **1562** *Burn. Paules Ch.*, Theyr Sacramente of an oylinge. **1683** Moxon *Mech. Exerc.*, *Printing* x. ¶5 So oft as the Nut and Spindle shall want Oyling. **1949** *Brit. Birds* XLII. 378 No signs of oiling were visible. **1970** *Nature* 9 May 573/2 A recent 'routine' winter oiling along the east coast of Scotland exacted a known toll of about 8,000 seabirds.

b. *spec.* The covering of the surface of water with oil. Cf. oil *v.* 1 c.

1887 *Pall Mall G.* 23 Aug., The sea had lost its power by reason of the oiling... The oiling was continued seven hours, and the small quantity of 5 lbs. was used. **1910** R. Ross et al. *Prevention of Malaria* vi. 270 (*heading*) Oiling. **1927** P. Hehir *Malaria in India* 313 Anopheles larvæ succumb to oiling more readily than Culex larvæ. **1949** F. C. Bishopp in M. F. Boyd *Malariology* II. lxi. 1340/1 Malaria cases have also been markedly reduced on estates where oiling has been practiced regularly. **1966** P. H. Manson-Bahr *Manson's Trop. Dis.* (ed. 16) iv. 70 Oiling kills mosquito larvæ probably in several ways.

2. Turning into oil, or into the consistence of oil.

1727 Bradley *Fam. Dict.* s.v. *Flummery*, Beat with some Spoonfuls of Milk for Fear of Oiling. **1769** Mrs. Raffald *Eng. Housekpr.* (1778) 7 Putting in now and then a little cream to prevent them [almonds] from oiling.

3. The taking of oil on board, esp. for fuel.

1906 *Westm. Gaz.* 27 Feb. 2/1 The difficulties in the way of 'oiling', to coin a word to correspond to 'coaling', at foreign ports. **1923** *Man. Seamanship* (Admiralty) II. 79 (*heading*) Oiling from an oiler.

4. The action of *to oil out* (cf. oil *v.* 1 b).

1859 [see oil *v.* 1 b]. **1962** R. G. Haggar *Dict. Art Terms* 231/2 *Oiling out*, in oil painting, the process of bringing out passages which have sunk in; a drying oil is applied.., the excess is removed and the surface gently polished.

† **'oilish**, *a. Obs.* [f. oil *sb.*¹ + -ish¹.] Resembling oil; having the consistence or appearance of oil; somewhat oily.

1471 Ripley *Comp. Alch.* Rec. xi. in Ashm. (1652) 189 That Oylysh substance. **1547** Boorde *Brev. Health* lxxiii. 22 b, Yf it [urine] be oylyshe it doth signifie a fever hectyke. *c* **1682** J. Collins *Making of Salt in Eng.* 67 Red, fat, oylish, soft and plyable.

oilless ('ɔɪllɪs), *a.* [f. as prec. + -less.] Devoid of oil; containing no oil; not lubricated, or not requiring to be lubricated, with oil.

a **1787** J. Brown *Sel. Rem.* (1807) 299 You content yourselves with an oilless lamp of a bare profession. **1850** Scoresby *Cheever's Whalem. Adv.* x. (1859) 140 Those beautiful oilless candles which are sold under the name of spermaceti. **1862** *Sat. Rev.* 8 Feb. 153 The dissonant wail of an oilless door. *a* **1902** *Mod.* A patent carboid oilless bearing. **1922** [see graphited *a.*]. **1940** *Chambers's Techn. Dict.* 591/1 *Oil-less circuit-breaker*, a circuit-breaker which does not use oil either as the quenching medium or for insulation purposes. **1972** H. Osborne *Pay-Day* i. 19 Panjeh had always been a poor relation on the Coast, an oil-less sheikhdom. **1974** *Economist* 21 Dec. 11/2 France..has come back in from its oilless cold to work with its allies.

Hence **'oillessness.**

1866 J. E. H. Skinner *After the Storm* II. 226 Those who burnt their fingers at the game [in oil shares] quickly vanished into outer oillessness.

oillet ('ɔɪlɪt). Forms: 4 **oylete**, 4–5 **-ett(e**, 4–9 **oylet**, 4–8 **oilet**, 5 **olyet**, 6 **oyliet**, 7 **œlet**, 8 **oeillet**, 9 **oeilette**, **oillet**. [a. OF. *oillet*, mod.F. *œillet*, dim. of *oil*, *oeïl* eye. The spellings *olyet*, *oyliet*, represented the F. *l mouillé.* In later use changed, under the influence of eye *sb.*, to eyelet.]

† **1.** A small round hole worked in cloth for purposes of fastening, etc.; = eyelet *sb.* 1 a. *Obs.*

1382 Wyclif *Exod.* xxvi. 5 The curtyn shal haue fifti oiletis in either parti, so set in, that o oylete [1388 *v.r.* oon oilet] may come aȝen another [1388 *v.r.* an other oylett]. *c* **1440** *Promp. Parv.* 363/2 Olyet, made yn a clothe, for sperynge. **1627** Capt. Smith *Seaman's Gram.* v. 23 Drawing a rope thorow a blocke or oylet to runne vp and down.

2. An aperture or loophole for observation, etc.; = eyelet *sb.* 2. Now only *Hist.*

1383-4 *Abingdon Rolls* (Camden) 46 Solut' Symoni vitreario pro oyletiis trium fenestrarum claustri xxxvs. iij*d.* *c* **1440** *Promp. Parv.* 363/2 Olyet, hole yn a walle (*H.*, *P.* lyteli hole). *c* **1450** Lonelich *Grail* xiv. 630 Thorwh the oylettes of his helm. **1786** tr. *Beckford's Vathek* (1868) 37 Diverting themselves..at the anxious faces they saw.. through the oilets of the tower. **1796** *Archæologia* XII. 147 The parapet often had the merlons pierced with long chinks ending in round holes, called oeillets. **1851** Turner *Dom. Archit.* I. vi. 234 A good battlement, with oillets. **1887** MacGibbon & Ross *Castell. & Dom. Archit.* II. 378 Lighted with narrow loops..with top and bottom oylets.

† **3.** A small eye of a plant; = eyelet *sb.* 3 b.

1574 Hyll *Planting* 86 Often..a man shall finde of oylets or eyes hard by the olde slender wood. **1601** Holland *Pliny* I. 434 Prouided alwaies that the œlets stand 3 foot asunder. *Ibid.* II. 84 The little oilets and shoots from the root.

4. *attrib.* and *Comb.*, as **oillet-hole** = eyelet-hole 1; **oillet-shell**, a shell of the genus *Terebratula* (or family *Terebratulidæ*), characterized by a circular perforation.

1530 Palsgr. 249/1 *Oyliet hole, *oillet.* **1634** Ford *P. Warbeck* ii. iii, Let my skin be punch'd full of oylet-holes with the bodkin of derision. **1687** A. Lovell tr. *Thevenot's Trav.* II. 91 A Waste-coat quilted with Cotton and set thick with Oilet-holes. **1852** Miss Yonge *Cameos* (1877) II. xxiii. 253 The collar worked with oylet-holes. **1873** W. S. Mayo *Never Again* xii. 164 Now studying stars, anon the ground, From narrow *oillet pane. **1708** *Phil. Trans.* XXVI. 79 *Terebratula*, the Hole-neb, or *Oilet-shell.

Hence **oilleted** *a.* [-ed²], furnished with eyelets.

1563-87 Foxe *A. & M.* (1684) III. 925 He prayed them to forbear a little, till he had put off his doublet, being oiletted.

oilman ('ɔɪlmən). **a.** A manufacturer or seller of oil. **b.** A dealer in sweet oils and eatables preserved in them, etc. **c.** A worker in an oil-mill. **d.** A man who oils machinery: = oiler 2.

c **1440** *Promp. Parv.* 363/2 Oly mann,..he that makythe, or syllythe oyle, *olearius.* **1607** Topsell *Four-f. Beasts* (1658) 517 A Hog at Basil, nourished by a certain Oyl-man. **1755** Johnson, *Oilman*, one who trades in oils and pickles. **1760** Foote *Minor* ii. Wks. 1799 I. 257 His uncle was an oil-man. **1865** *Sat. Rev.* 5 Aug. 173 Sold, not only by all druggists, but also by grocers, oilmen, and chandlers.

e. A person in the oil industry; an employee of an oil company.

1865 *Atlantic Monthly* XV. 388 She was still considering her probable success in finding an oil-man to take her down the Creek. **1880** *Harper's Mag.* Dec. 65 There are engines and boilers and pumps to be built for the oil men. **1912** Tower & Roberts *Petroleum* v. 83 The flowing or gushing wells are always regarded as lucky strikes among oilmen. **1951** T. Sterling *House without Door* i. 6 She knew what Texas oil men looked like. **1972** *Times* 27 Sept. 21/7 The oilmen look longingly at the areas north of the 62nd Parallel. **1973** A. Price *October Men* viii. 113 The oilman Ian Howard, just back from a year..in Saudi Arabia. **1975** *Lamp* (Exxon Corporation) Winter 11/1 When they began to commit sizable sums to North Sea oil development three and four years ago, oilmen expected the investment to be a costly one.

oil-mill. A machine in which seeds, fruits, etc. are crushed or pressed to extract oil; a factory where oil is expressed by such machines.

c **1420** *Pallad. on Husb.* i. 495 Oilmilles, whelis, wrongis, ..y nil not speke of now. **1525** *Test. Ebor.* (Surtees) V. 212 Also my oile mylne. **1747** Franklin *Let.* Wks. 1887 II. 75 We have many oil-mills in this province, it being a great country for flax. **1860** Geo. Eliot *Mill on Fl.* ii. vii, Because their fathers were professional men, or had large oil-mills.

'oil-nut. A name for various nuts and large seeds which yield oil; also for the plants producing them; *spec.* **a.** the Castor-oil Plant, *Ricinus communis*; **b.** the North American Butternut, *Juglans cinerea*; **c.** the North

American Buffalo-nut or Elk-nut; **d.** the Oil Palm, *Elæis guineensis*.

1694 *Town Rec. Topsfield, Mass.* (1917) I. 86/2 From thence on a straight line to an oylenut tree which is Isaac Burtons tree marked. **1707** SLOANE *Jamaica* I. 126 The Oil-Nut-Tree..seems not to be different from the European Ricinus. **1778** J. CARVER *Trav. N.-Amer.* 500 The Butter or Oilnut... The tree grows in meadows, where the soil is rich and warm. **1796** MORSE *Amer. Geog.* I. 189 White Walnut, Butternut, or Oilnut. **1813** H. MUHLENBERG *Catal. Plantarum Americæ Septentrionalis* 96 Oil nut, (*Pyrularia* or *Hamiltonia oleifera*). **1832** D. J. BROWNE *Sylva Amer.* 173 In Massachusetts, New Hampshire and Vermont it [*sc.* the butternut] bears the name of Oil Nut. **1866** WHITTIER *Marg. Smith's Jrnl.* Pr. Wks. 1889 I. 82 We passed many trees, well loaded with walnuts and oilnuts. **1877** J. A. B. HORTON in Moloney *Forestry W. Afr.* (1887) 40 The longer the oil-nuts remain underground the thicker the oil will be when made. **1884** MILLER *Plant-n.*, *Pyrularia oleifera*, Buffalo-nut, Elk-nut, or Oil-nut, of N. America. **1912** E. SETON *Forester's Manual* 41 White Walnut, Oil Nut, or Butternut (*Juglans cinerea*). **1933** J. K. SMALL *Man. S.E. Flora* 1250 P[yrularia] pubera... Buffalo-nut. Oil-nut. Mountain-coconut.

oilometer (ɔɪˈlɒmɪtə(r)). Also *erron.* oiliometer. [irreg. f. OIL *sb.*[1] + -(O)METER: cf. *gasometer*.] **a.** = OLEOMETER, ELÆOMETER. **b.** A reservoir for the storage of oil; cf. *gasometer*.

1876 *Catal. Sci. App. S. Kens.* 97 Oiliometer. An instrument for ascertaining the density of oils. **1897** *Westm. Gaz.* 12 Jan. 7/2 The Russian Oil Company, whose works.. include scores of 'oilometers', besides quantities of oil in every stage of preparation.

[**oilous**, error for OILEOUS in mod. Dicts.; Gerarde, who is cited for *oilous*, used *oileous*.]

oil-ring. **a.** In *Seal-engraving*, a ring with a small dish on top to hold a mixture of oil and diamond-dust; it is worn on the forefinger of the workman, and the wheel is allowed to rotate in the dish to replenish the engraving-tool. **b.** In *Machinery*, a ring surrounding and riding upon a journal, etc., which, whilst revolving, it continuously lubricates by raising oil from a reservoir in which it dips.

1900 *Mod. Cat. Electr. Co.*, Dissected Dynamo..Oil cock, Oil hole cover, Journal box, Oil ring.

ˈoil-seed. Any seed yielding oil, e.g. linseed, rapeseed, mustard-seed. *spec.* **a.** that of the Castor-oil plant, *Ricinus communis*; **b.** that of *Guizotia oleifera*, an East Indian Composite plant, the oil of which is used for lamps and as a condiment; **c.** that of the Gold-of-Pleasure or False Flax, *Camelina sativa* (*Siberian oil-seed*); **d.** cottonseed (also attrib. *oil-seed cake*).

1562 TURNER *Herbal* II. 134 Sesama whyche maye be called in English oyle sede is euell for the stomack. **1760** J. LEE *Introd. Bot.* App. 320 Oil Seed, *Ricinus*. **1887** MOLONEY *Forestry W. Afr.* 349 Imported into this country from the West Coast of Africa as an oil-seed. **1892** *Daily News* 3 Sept. 7/3 In the Punjab the season..was fairly good for oilseeds, the area under which was the largest on record. **1899** *Whitaker's Almanac* 584 Exports [from U.S.] to the United Kingdom in 1897..Oil seed cake, £767,702.

ˈoilskin. Cloth made waterproof by being treated with oil; a piece, or garment, of such cloth; = OILCLOTH 1 a.

1816 J. SCOTT *Paris Revis.* (ed. 3) 327 They proceeded to untie the oil-skins from the locks of their rifles. **1828** MISS MITFORD *Village* Ser. III. (1863) 97 A large package.. covered with oilskin. **1884** CLARK RUSSELL *Jack's Courtship* xxviii. II. 225 There were two men at the wheel in yellow oilskins.

b. Often *attrib.* (made of oilskin); also in *Comb.*

1812 H. & J. SMITH *Rej. Addr.*, *Tale Drury Lane* 97 The belt and oil-skin hat he wore. **1842** DICKENS *Amer. Notes* ii. (1850) 10/1 Clad in a suit of shaggy blue, with an oilskin hat. **1891** A. WELCKER *Woolly West* 71 Listeners, in yellow oil skin suits and damp and steaming overcoats..crowded about the red-hot stove.

Hence **ˈoilskinned** (-skɪnd) *a.*, dressed in oilskin.

1857 C. KINGSLEY *Two Yrs. Ago* I. iii. 80 Oil-skinned coast-guardsmen. **1897** *Century Mag.* Sept. 777/1 They lay ..oilskinned and sea-booted.

oilstone (ˈɔɪlstəʊn), *sb.* A smooth and fine-grained whetstone, the rubbing-surface of which is lubricated with oil; the stone of which such whetstones are made (Simmonds *Dict. Trade* 1858).

1585 HIGINS *Junius' Nomenclator* 412/1 *Cos cretica*,..an oylestone, or a Barbars whetstone smeared with oyle, or spitle. **1598** in FLORIO s.v. *Saliuaria*. **1709** *Phil. Trans.* XXVI. 493, I set it sometimes upon an Oyl-stone or Hone. **1812–16** J. SMITH *Panorama Sc. & Art* I. 24 They will leave the surface of metal..almost as smooth as an oil-stone. **1853** [see ABRASIVE B. *sb.*]. **1885** [see ARKANSAS 1]. **1947** J. C. RICH *Materials & Methods Sculpture* x. 300 Fine oilstones are generally used for sharpening flat chisels. **1966** A. W. LEWIS *Gloss. Woodworking Terms* 63 *Oilstone slips* or *slipstones*, oilstones of a variety of shapes used to sharpen gouges, [etc.].

Hence **ˈoilstone** *v. trans.*, to sharpen on an oilstone.

1876 J. ROSE *Pract. Machinist* iii. 51 If, therefore, a hole requires to be made unusually smooth, the [boring] tool must be given less top rake, and may then be oilstoned. **1888** C. M. WOODWARD *Manual Training* xv. (1890) 247 To grind his plane and oil-stone it.

oil-tree. Name for various trees and large shrubs which yield oil; as the Castor-oil plant (*Ricinus communis*), the Physic-nut tree (*Curcas purgans* or *Jatropha Curcas*), the Illupi (*Bassia longifolia*), and the Oil-palm (*Elæis guineensis*).

In Isa. xli. 19 a literal rendering of Heb. *ˁētz-shemen*, prob. oleaster or wild olive (cf. 1 Kings vi. 23, Neh. viii. 15 R.V.).

1611 BIBLE *Isa.* xli. 19, I will plant in the wildernes the Cedar, the Shittah tree, and the Myrtle, and the Oyle tree [COVERD. olyues]. **1760** J. LEE *Introd. Bot.* App. 321 Oil-tree, *Ricinus*. **1864** WEBSTER, *Oil-tree*,..an Indian tree of the genus *Bassia*. **1879** H. N. MOSELEY *Notes on 'Challenger'* ii. 57 A very thick growth of oil-trees (*Jatropha curcas*).

ˈoil well. Also oil-well, oilwell. [f. OIL *sb.*[1] + WELL *sb.*[1]] A shaft sunk to obtain oil or from which oil is obtained. Freq. *attrib.*

1847 L. COLLINS *Hist. Sk. Kentucky* 249 The American Oil well is situated three miles above Burksville. **1861** *Chem. News* 28 Sept. 164/2 He states that the yield from the wells has greatly decreased, and that the oil well region, for practical working, is of very limited extent. **1903** G. H. MONTAGUE *Rise & Progress Standard Oil Co.* i. 4 With the success of Drake's oil-well at Titusville, Pennsylvania, in 1859, refiners had been released from the necessity of distilling coal into petroleum before refining petroleum into kerosene. **1946** *Mod. Petroleum Technol.* (Inst. Petroleum) 86 There are two main systems employed in drilling oil-wells: (1) the rotary or mud-flush system, and (2) the cable-tool or percussion system. **1946** *Nature* 20 July 84/1 The oil industry uses large quantities of nitroglycerine explosives.. in the so-called oil-well 'shooting', where the explosives are employed to shatter the underground formation and thus open up fissures through which the oil may flow freely to the well. **1976** *Globe & Mail* (Toronto) 4 Feb. 7/4 The study made conclusions similar to those of Dr. Pimlott, saying existing technology could not cope with an oilwell blowout in the Beaufort Sea.

oily (ˈɔɪlɪ), *a.* (*adv.* and *sb.*) [f. OIL *sb.*[1] + -Y.]

A. *adj.* **1.** Of or pertaining to oil (in quot. *a* 1732, produced by the burning of oil); of the nature of or consisting of oil; having the consistence or appearance of oil. *oily acid* = FATTY acid.

1528 PAYNEL *Salerne's Regim.* E ij, Chese..made conueniently of good mylke sufficiently oyly. **1552** HULOET, Oylye, or of oyle, *oleaceus, olearis*. **1615** tr. *De Monfart's Surv. E. Indies* 28 Being cut it expelleth a kind of fat oylie liquor. **1697** DRYDEN *Virg. Georg.* I. 538 Sparkling Lamps their sputt'ring Light advance, And in the Sockets Oily Bubbles dance. **1725** DE FOE *Voy. round World* (1840) 84 Our men made some butter also..but it grew rank and oily. *a* **1732** GAY *Poems* (1745) I. 183 Oily rays Shot from the crystal lamp. **1807** T. THOMSON *Chem.* (ed. 3) II. 441 Whether the oily principle in all the fixed oils is the same. **1898** *Daily News* 21 Aug. 5/3 The Atbara..was flowing swift and oily, but quietly, between its banks.

2. a. Containing, full of, or impregnated with oil; smeared or covered with oil; greasy, fat.

1597 SHAKS. *1 Hen. IV*, II. iv. 575 This oyly Rascall is knowne as well as Poules. **1611** —— *Wint. T.* v. iii. 83 The ruddinesse vpon her Lippe is wet; You'le marre it, if you kisse it; stayne your owne With Oyly Painting. *a* **1756** MRS. HEYWOOD *New Present* (1771) 256 A piece of oily flannel. **1871** R. ELLIS *Catullus* xxv. 2 Or glossy goose's oily plumes, or velvet ear-lap yielding. **1879** BROWNING *Ned Bratts* 44 He mopped his oily pate.

b. oily grain, †**corn,** a name for the seed of *Sesamum orientale*.

1671 SALMON *Syn. Med.* III. xxii. 431 *Sesamum*..Oyley corn..is Emollient and helps bruises [etc.]. **1753** CHAMBERS *Cycl. Suppl.* App., *Oily-grain*, the name by which some call the Sessamum of botanical authors. **1857** MAYNE *Expos. Lex.*

c. oily wad, (*a*) a torpedo boat burning fuel-oil (*disused*); (*b*) a seaman without a special skill (see also quot. 1961).

1925 FRASER & GIBBONS *Soldier & Sailor Words* 213 *Oily wads*, a Navy nickname for a class of oil burning torpedo boat destroyers. **1929** F. C. BOWEN *Sea Slang* 97 *Oily Wads*. The name occasionally applied to seamen in the Navy who do not specialise in anything, from the amount of time they have to spend cleaning brass-work with oily wads. **1931** 'TAFFRAIL' *Endless Story* xxii. 344 Numbered from 1 to 36, they were generally known in the Service as the 'oily wads'. **1932** KIPLING *Limits & Renewals* 199 Some oily-wad of a *Bulleana* struck up about not having got his proper bird. **1961** F. H. BURGESS *Dict. Sailing* 152 *Oily wad*, a seaman with no ambition. **1963** *Times* 13 June 17/1 His first command, which he held from May 1908, to January 1910, was torpedo boat no. 14 in the Home Fleet, one of the first oil-burning ships in the Navy, known to those serving in them as 'oily wads'.

3. *fig.* 'Smooth' in behaviour or (esp.) in speech; subservient, compliant, 'supple'; bland, soothing, insinuating, fawning, 'unctuous'; 'slippery'.

1598 E. GILPIN *Skial.* (1878) 37 An oylie slaue: he angling for repute, Will gently entertaine thee. *c* **1605** ROWLEY *Birth Merl.* I. ii, By smoothing flattery or oily words. **1641** LD. BROOKE *Eng. Episc.* I. vii. 36 Courtesies and Hopes are the most oylie Bribes. **1765** DUNCOMBE in *Lett.* (1773) III. 149 He had a smooth oily tongue. **1784** COWPER *Task* IV. 64 Rills of oily eloquence. **1885** R. L. & F. STEVENSON *Dynamiter* 171 Only oily and common-place evasion. **1894** H. NISBET *Bush Girl's Rom.* 32 What had this oily scoundrel of a servant to do with her?

B. *adv.* = OILILY.

c **1842** TENNYSON in *Mem.* (1897) I. 196 The bay was oily calm.

C. *Comb.*, as *oily-bathed*, *-brown*, *-like*, *-looking*, *-smooth*, *-tongued*.

1807 T. THOMSON *Chem.* (ed. 3) II. 180 Thick oily-like liquid. **1838** —— *Chem. Org. Bodies* 334 An oily-looking body will be observed in the retort. **1854** MISS YONGE *Little Duke* v, An oily-tongued Count, who sat next the King. **1861** WHYTE MELVILLE *Mkt. Harb.* 22 A decanter of oily-brown sherry. **1875** BROWNING *Aristoph. Apol.* 131 The verse slips oily-bathed In unctuous music. **1884** [HAMILTON] *Jaunt in Junk* iv. 37 The oily-smooth rollers.

D. *sb.* An oilskin garment. Chiefly in *pl.*

1893–4 R. O. HESLOP *Northumb. Words* II. 510 *Oily*, an oilskin coat. **1898** G. A. RUSHTON in W. A. Morgan *'House' on Sport* I. 73 Still wind and rain the next day—but we.. putting on our oilies went ashore and tramped for miles. **1933** E. A. ROBERTSON *Ordinary Families* iv. 69 Soaked to the skin in spite of their oilies, Sootie and Ronald came down into the cabin. **1959** 'A. FRASER' *High Tension* x. 106, I..ran upstairs to put on a thick jersey... That and an oily would do. **1973** J. R. L. ANDERSON *Death on Rocks* vii. 127 His own oilies were in the club.

Hence **ˈoilyish**, *a. rare*, somewhat oily.

a **1722** LISLE *Husb.* (1752) 344 Give her a quart of cream ..before it is turning to butter, viz. when it is oilyish.

‖**oime, oimee** (oiˈmɛ), *int. rare.* [It. *oimè*, *ohimè*, f. *ohi!* alas! + *me* me.] Alas! Ah me!

1660 HOWELL *Parly of Beasts* 5 Oimee! I am afraid that Morphandra hath a purpose to re-transform me. **1820** BYRON *Mar. Fal.* III. ii. 341 Oime! Oime!—and must I do this deed?

oink (ɔɪŋk), *v.* [Echoic.] **a.** *intr.* Of a pig: to utter its characteristic sound. **b.** *transf.* To make a similar sound; to imitate this sound; to grunt like a pig. Also as *sb.*

1969 *New Yorker* 11 Oct. 55/2 (*caption*) I'm warning you —don't start oinking. **1971** *It* 2–16 June 11/4 Seale called the fab philosopher 'a moral coward who oinks like a pig'. **1971** E. BULLINS *Hungered One* 143 The pitter-patter of the returning dog's feet came from the road, and the cricket music and an occasional pig's oink and a drowsy duck quacked at the dark. **1972** J. WAMBAUGH *Blue Knight* (1973) iv. 55 One young guy..leaned back in his chair and made a couple of oinks and said, 'I smell pig.' **1973** *Times* 11 Apr. 13/5 The spasmodic oink-oink of chalk on cue. **1977** C. MCFADDEN *Serial* (1978) v. 16/2 They oinked at him, in concert, just about every time he opened his mouth.

oino-: see ŒNO-.

oint, *v. Obs.* or *arch.* Forms: 4–8 oynt, 6 oynct, 6–9 oint. [f. F. *oint*, 3 sing. pres. ind., or pa. pple. of *oindre*:—L. *ung(u)ĕre* to anoint.] *trans.* = ANOINT *v.*

1375 *Creation* 632 in Horstmann *Altengl. Leg.* (1878) 132 Of oyle taken ȝow som del, Wherwiþ ȝe mowen oynten me wel. ? *a* **1400** *Cursor M.* 7377 (Cott.) Vn-to king oynt þou him þer [*altered from* Vn-to king þou sal him smer]. *a* **1450** *Knt. de la Tour* (1868) 123 Beter is the frende that prikithe thanne the flatour that oyntethe. **1582** STANYHURST *Æneis* II. (Arb.) 51 His temples with black swart poyson ar oyncted. **1697** DRYDEN *Virg. Georg.* III. 683 They oint their naked Limbs with mother'd Oyl. *a* **1711** KEN *Christophil* Poet. Wks. 1721 I. 500 To me be Water, Oyl, Fire, Wind, To cleanse, oynt, warm, and wing my Mind. **1855** SINGLETON *Virgil* II. 338 Than whom none other was more fortunate In ointing jav'lins.

Hence **ˈointed** *ppl. a.*, anointed; **ˈointing** *vbl. sb.*, anointing, unction (also *attrib.*, as *ointing-box*, *-cloth*, *-oil*).

a **1340** HAMPOLE *Psalter, Canticles* 515 þe oyntynge of þe halygast. **1382** WYCLIF *2 Macc.* i. 10 Of the kyn of oyntyd prestis. *a* **1547** SURREY *Æneid* IV. 287 With ointed bush & beard. *a* **1623** AINSWORTH *Ps.* in Farr *S. P. Jas. I* (1848) 76 Thou makest fat mine head with ointing oil. **1652–62** HEYLIN *Cosmogr.* II. (1682) 192 Ointings, Washings, and the like Superstitious practices. **1697** DRYDEN *Æneid* x. 208 Directing ointed arrows from afar; And death with poyson arm'd. **1855** SINGLETON *Virgil* II. 237 Along the waters slips the ointed fir.

†**ˈointling.** *Obs. nonce-wd.* [f. OINT + -LING: cf. *shaveling*.] An anointed priest. (*contemptuous.*)

a **1603** T. CARTWRIGHT *Confut. Rhem. N.T.* (1618) 610 You..are blasphemous, by comparing your Ointlings with Melchisedec.

ointment (ˈɔɪntmənt). Forms: α. 3–5 **oygnement,** (3–4 *pl.* **-menz, -mens**), 4 **oigne-, oyni-, ungne-, une-, uine-,** 4–5 **oyne-,** 4–6 **oyn-,** 5 **ony-, hone-, unȝement.** β. 4–5 **untement,** 6 **ungt-,** *Sc.* **unt-;** 4–7 **oynt-,** 5–6 **oynte-,** 6 **oynt-, -oynct-,** 4– **ointment.** [ME. *oignement*, a. OF. *oignement*:—L. type **ungu(i)mentum* for *unguentum* UNGUENT, f. *unguĕre* to anoint. In 14th c. conformed to the vb. OINT as *ointment*; first in northern texts.]

1. An unctuous preparation, of a soft consistence like that of butter, often mixed with some medicament, used chiefly for application to the skin, for medicinal purposes, or as a cosmetic; an unguent. ***a fly in the ointment***: see FLY *sb.*[1] 1 e.

α. *c* **1290** *S. Eng. Leg.* I. 245/171 Nimeth here þis guode oygnement. *a* **1300** *Cursor M.* 17288 + 92 Mary maudlayn.. And marie salome, hade boght þam oynemenz. **13..** *Guy Warw.* (A.) 6105 An vnement purchast he þat made his visage out of ble. *c* **1350** *Will. Palerne* 136 A noynement anon sche made. *c* **1386** CHAUCER *C.T. Prol.* 631 Ne oynement that wolde clense and byte. *c* **1400** *Rule St. Benet* (E.E.T.S.) 23 Wen sho hauis laid hir plaisters and hir vinemens. **1422** tr. *Secreta Secret., Priv. Priv.* 247 Vsynge of honementys aftyr the tyme and complexcione. **1530** PALSGR.

249/1 Oynment, *oignement, oyncture*. **1536** Bellenden *Cron. Scot.* ii. xii. 17b, The unȝementis & drogareis y[t] our forbearis vsit.

β. *c* **1325** *Metr. Hom.* 17 Scho hauid boht this ointment. *c* **1375** *Cursor M.* 14005, 14062 (Cott. MS.). *c* **1400** *Destr. Troy* 7526 With oile and with ointment abill þerfore. **1435** Misyn *Fire of Love* 59 þe vntementis precius. *c* **1489** Caxton *Sonnes of Aymon* vii. 169 He enoynted Reynawde with an noyntement. **1526** Tindale *John* xii. 3 All the housse smelled off the savre off the oyntment. **1590** Spenser *F.Q.* i. ii. 42 The divelish hag..With wicked herbes and oyntments did besmeare My body. **1696** Whiston *The. Earth* Introd. 11 Our Lord says of the Woman who poured the Oyntment on him. **1750** tr. *Leonardus' Mirr. Stones* 137 Physicians dissolve it in the juice of certain herbs, and make an ointment of it. **1820** Scott *Ivanhoe* xxxvii, She had given him a pot of that precious ointment.

fig. *a* **1420** Hoccleve *De Reg. Princ.* 1429 The oynement of holy sermonynge Hym loþ is vp-on hem for to despende.

†**2.** Anointing, unction. *Obs.*

1510–20 *Everyman* in Hazl. *Dodsley* I. 132 Receive of him..The holy sacrament and ointment together. **1526** Tindale *1 John* ii. 20 Ye have an oyntment of the holy gost. **1621** Brathwait *Nat. Embassie* (1877) 85 But he expected ointment..there He stands.

3. *Comb.*, as ***ointment-maker***; ***ointment-like*** adj.; **ointment-carrier**, an instrument for introducing ointment into the body.

1382 Wyclif *Ecclus.* xxxviii. 7 The oynement makere shal make pymentis of swotenesse. **1398** Trevisa *Barth. De P.R.* xvi. iii. (1495) 553 The oynement boxe that the gospel spekith of. *c* **1540** *Recipe* in *Vicary's Anat.* (1888) App. ix. 226 A Cataplasme made vngtment-lyke. **1552** Huloet, Oyntment maker, *vnguentareus*. **1897** *Allbutt's Syst. Med.* III. 744 In place of the injection, ointment may be introduced by means of one of Allingham's ointment-carriers. **1899** *Daily News* 29 May 4/7 Coroner: What do you call yourself? Witness: Well, an ointment maker.

†**'oint-plaster.** *Obs.* In 6 oynt-playster. [Cf. oint *v.*, also OF. *oint* sb.] A plaster of ointment.

1578 Lyte *Dodoens* iii. cxiii. 306 To be applyed, outwardly in oynt-playsters.

†**ointu'ose,** *a.* *Obs. rare.* [Cf. OF. *ointeux, ointeuse*, It. *untoso* (Florio), L. *unctuōs-us* unctuous.] = unctuous.

c **1400** *Lanfranc's Cirurg.* 137 þat neiþer oile ne noon oyntuose þing fallip not wiþinne þe brayn panne.

†**'ointure.** *Obs.* *rare*$^{-1}$. In 5 oyn-. [a. OF. *ointure* (12th c. in Godef.):—L. *unctūra* uncture, f. *unguĕre* to anoint.] Ointment.

c **1430** *Pilgr. Lyf Manhode* ii. cxxvi. (1869) 123, I can with good oynture enoynte a shrewede wheel þat cryeth.

‖**oiran** ('ɔɪrən). [Jap.] A Japanese courtesan of high standing. Also *collect.*

1871 A. B. Mitford *Tales Old Japan* I. 67 They are employed to wait upon the *Oiran*, or fashionable courtesans. **1904** R. J. Farrer *Garden of Asia* xix. 181 Of all glories in Japan, the richest is that of the Oiran, or established beauty of the Yoshiwara. **1970** J. Kirkup *Japan behind Fan* 90 The boys..who are indistinguishable from the *oiran*, the geisha and other women. **1972** *Mainichi Daily News* (Japan) 6 Nov. 20/2 (Advt.), 'Oiran'—the glittering Yoshiwara courtesans—recreate the ceremonies attendant on greeting an honored patron.

oire, ois, obs. forms of eyre, oyez.

‖**Oireachtas** ('ɛrəxtəs). [Ir., = assembly, gathering, convocation.] **1.** The assembly and festival held annually by the Gaelic League of Ireland, a gathering similar in concept to the Welsh eisteddfod and Scottish mod. Also *attrib.*

1902 W. B. Yeats *Let.* 20 Jan. (1954) 364 Royalties..I shall ask A. P. Watt to send..to the Sec. of Gaelic League, Dublin. Do you think I should specify the purpose? Say an Oireachtas prize. **1910** *Encycl. Brit.* V. 616/1 In 1898 it was decided to hold a festival called the *Oireachtas* ('hosting, gathering') on the lines of the Welsh *Eisteddfod*. **1911** W. H. G. Flood *Story of Bagpipe* xx. 164 The *Mod* is somewhat analogous to the *Oireachtas* in Ireland. **1913** *Irishman* Feb. 4/1 The keynote of this Oireachtas must be that Irish shall be plainly and unmistakeably the dominant language. **1971** *Daily Tel.* 5 Aug. 10/3 Prominent among the tents on the field for the first time this year is one representing Eire's equivalent of the Eisteddfod—the Oireachtas, to be held in October.

2. The legislature or parliament of the Republic of Ireland, consisting of the president and two houses, a house of representatives (Dáil Éireann) the members of which are elected by proportional representation, and a partially nominated senate (Seanad Éireann).

In quot. 1947 *An t-Oireachtas* is the regular Irish form that includes the definite article.

1922 *Daily Mail* 4 Dec. 9 The Provisional Government will be out of office by Wednesday, and the Oireachtas, as the Free State Parliament will be known, will come into being, consisting of Seanad Eireann (Upper House), comprised of 60 senators, 30 of whom will be nominated by the Government, and the remainder by the elected deputies of the people, who will sit as a Lower House, under the name of Dail Eireann. **1923** W. B. Yeats *Senate Speeches* (1961) 53 A joint committee of both houses to consider how suitable accommodations for Oireachtas may be obtained. **1930** G. B. Shaw *John Bull's Other Island* Pref., in *Works* XI. 72 The Northern Parliament will not merge into the Oireachtas. **1938** *Ireland: Citizen's Manual* 27 The Oireachtas may not enact a law repugnant to the Constitution nor declare acts to be unlawful after their commission. **1947** S. Malone *Notes Procedure Oireachtas* p. vii, The National Parliament (An tOireachtas) consisting of the President and two Houses. **1969** Henig & Pinder *European Pol. Parties* xi. 447 To win an election was, and is, to win the right to a virtual monopoly of legislative and policy initiative and the power to manage and control the *Oireachtas* (Parliament). **1975** *Irish Times* 9 May 8/1 Mr. Lynch said that there had been a tradition among the staff of the Oireachtas that if there was to be any easement of Standing Orders, that easement would be given in favour of the Opposition. **1977** *Cork Examiner* 6 June 2/8 Ever since it has been bandied about both in accusation and refutation on the subsequent occasions of the passage of an electoral Bill through the Oireachtas.

ois(e, obs. form of use.

oi'sivity. *nonce-wd.* [ad. F. *oisiveté*: cf. ocivity.] Idleness, indolence.

1830 *Fraser's Mag.* I. 748 The indolent and hallucinatory oisivity of Campbell.

oisophagus, obs. variant of œsophagus.

oist, 16th c. Sc. form of hoast, host.

oister, oistrich, obs. ff. oyster *sb.*, ostrich.

oistie, oistillary, oistlair, -ler, obs. Sc. ff. hostie, hostelry, hosteler, hostelar.

oitemealle, oither, obs. ff. oatmeal, other.

oiticica (ɔɪtɪ'siːkə). [Pg., f. Tupi *oitisica*.] A name used for several tropical South American trees, esp. *Licania rigida*, of the family Chrysobalanaceæ, whose crushed seeds yield an oil used in paints and varnishes. Also *attrib.*

1918 E. R. Bolton in *Analyst* XLIII. 251 (*title*) Oiticica oil—a new drying oil. *Ibid.*, During the early part of 1917 we examined a new oilseed sent apparently for the first time from Brazil, bearing the native name of Oiticica or Oilizika. **1925** Morrell & Wood *Chem. Drying Oils* ii. 67 The oil is extracted from the kernels of oiticica (a name applied to several species of *Moquilea* and *Conepia*, belonging to the *Rosaceæ*). **1931** B. Miall tr. *Guenther's Naturalist in Brazil* vii. 124 The handsomest tree of the Sertão is the Oiticica. A sturdy trunk, divided into many branches, lifts itself from roots which run high over the ground. From the dense green roof of foliage the older leaves hang like silver tassels. **1944** H. G. Kirschen Bauer *Fats & Oils* vi. 88 Oiticica seed oil owes its outstanding drying properties to the presence of licanic acid. **1944** S. Putnam tr. *E. da Cunha's Rebellion in Backlands* ii. 123 An old abandoned shack overgrown with oiticica boughs. **1951** R. Mayer *Artist's Handbk.* iii. 112 Oiticica Oil is a Brazilian product. **1967** *Times* 27 Apr. 27/3 The rather bewildering news yesterday that the Oiticica crop in the State of Ceara in South America has been almost a complete failure may well have sent some commodity men hurrying for their dictionaries.

Ojibwa(y (əʊ'dʒɪbweɪ). Numerous varr. [Ojibwa, based on a root meaning 'puckered' (see quot. 1824); Chippewa is a corrupted form of *Ojibwa(y*.] **a.** A member of an Algonquian people of North American Indians, inhabiting the lands around Lake Superior and, in more recent times, certain adjacent areas from Saskatchewan to Lake Ontario. **b.** An Algonquian language spoken by this people. Also *attrib.* or as *adj.*

'*Chippewa* and *Ojibwa(y* are the same word. Of these the former was the common English form until well into the nineteenth century... *Chippewa* is now the common spelling in the U.S. and *Ojibwa(y* in Canada. Hence these forms tend to be used for somewhat different local groups, but the usage is not consistent. Ethnologists, and especially linguists, tend to use *Ojibwa(y* for all the groups in question.' (Dr. I. Goddard)

1700 in *Documents Colonial Hist. New-York* (1854) IV. 749 Upon the sides of [Lake Huron]..live several Nations, vizt. the Christinos, the Ochipoy [etc.]. **1783** in *Mass. Hist. Soc. Coll.* (1809) X. 123 Chactaws 600... Upichweys 3000. **1824** W. H. Keating *Narr. Expedition St. Peter's River* II. 151 The term Chippewa, which is generally applied to this nation, is derived from that of O'chepe'wag, which..signifies plaited shoes, from the fashion among those Indians of puckering their moccassins. **1835** C. F. Hoffman *Winter in West* II. 15 The Chippewa, or Ojibboai..is generally considered the *court language* of our North-western tribes. **1853** Dickens *Noble Savage* in *Househ. Words* 11 June 337/1 Mr. Catlin..with his Ojibbeway Indians. **1855** Longfellow *Hiawatha* i. 13 From the great lakes of the Northland, From the land of the Ojibways. **1872** W. F. Butler *Great Lone Land* viii. 110 Little ones..jabbered the smallest amount of English or French, and a great deal of Ojibbeway, or Cree, or Assineboine. **1903** Chesterton *R. Browning* i. 7 If his great-aunt had been a Red Indian, should we not have said that only in the Ojibways and the Blackfeet do we find the Browning fantasticality combined with the Browning stoicism? **1916** [see Montagnais *sb.* and *a.*]. **1921** E. Sapir *Language* 53 In many, as in Italian or Swedish or Ojibwa, long consonants are recognized as distinct from short ones. **1937** R. H. Lowie *Hist. Ethnol. Theory* ix. 133 Foremost among his earlier students was the part-Fox William Jones, who transcribed a superb series of Fox and Ojibwa texts. **1968** *Globe & Mail* (Toronto) 5 Feb. 6/3 A. E. Bigwin, an Ojibway who is a Toronto school principal, states [etc.]. **1972** W. B. Lockwood *Panorama Indo-Europ. Lang.* vii. 117 The biggest languages in this [*sc.* the Algonquian] family are Chippewa (USA) or Ojibwa (Canada) with 35,000 speakers, [etc.]. **1974** *Sat. Rev. World* (U.S.) 2 Nov. 23/2 Armed Ojibwa militants had occupied a 14-acre park..in the resort town of Kenora, Ontario.

‖**ojime** ('oːdʒime). [Jap., f. *o* string + *shime* fastening, fastener.] A bead or bead-like object, often very elaborate, used in Japan as a sliding fastening device on the strings of a bag or pouch, or of an inro.

1889 M. B. Huish *Japan & its Art* xii. 167 Japanese Art metal-work..consists of the following branches:-..4. Articles for personal use, notably pipes.., beads (*ojime*), [etc.]. **1902** F. Brinkley *Oriental Series: Japan* VII. v. 173 There is reason to think that the *ōjime* was the first highly ornate appendage of both the *inro* and the *kinchaku*. **1960** *Times* 2 Jan. 9/4 The inro consisted of interlocking compartments that..were opened and closed by means of sliding beads termed ojimes. **1972** *Times* 15 June 21/2 Each [inro] was complete with a coral ojime and ivory netsuke.

ok, var. ac *Obs.*; obs. f. eke, oak; obs. pa. t. of ache.

O.K. (əʊ'keɪ), *a.*, *sb.*, and *v.* *colloq.* (orig. *U.S.*). Also OK, o.k., ok. [App. f. the initial letters of *oll* (or *orl*) *korrect*, jocular alteration or colloq. pronunc. of 'all correct': see A. W. Read in *Amer. Speech* XXXVIII (1963), XXXIX (1964), etc.

From the detailed evidence provided by A. W. Read it seems clear that *O.K.* first appeared as a jocular alteration of the initial letters of *all correct* (i.e. orl korrect) in 1839, and that in 1840 it was used as an election slogan for 'Old Kinderhook' (see sense A b). Thence by stages it made its way into general use. Other suggestions, e.g. that *O.K.* represents the Choctaw *oke* 'it is', or French *au quai*, or that it derives from a word in the West African language Wolof via slaves in the southern States of America, all lack any form of acceptable documentation.]

A. *adj.* **a.** Chiefly in predicative use or as *int.*: all correct, all right; satisfactory, good; well, in good health; also in phr. ***O.K. by*** (*someone*): acceptable to (that person); freq. used as an exclamation expressing agreement: 'yes', 'certainly', 'all right'; also appended to a statement or declaration as a strong form of challenge or appeal in which affirmation or agreement is expected. Also as *adv.*

1839 C. G. Greene in *Boston Morning Post* 23 Mar. 2/2 He..would have the 'contribution box', et ceteras, *o.k.*—all correct—and cause the corks to fly, like *sparks*, upward. **1839** *Salem Gaz.* 12 Apr. 2/3 The house was O.K. at the last concert, and did credit to the musical taste of the young ladies and gents. **1839** *Evening Tattler* (N.Y.) 2 Sept. 2/2 These 'wise men from the East'..are right..to play at bowls with us as long as we are willing to set ourselves up, like skittles, to be knocked down for their amusement and emolument. OK! all correct! **1839** *Boston Even. Transcript* 11 Oct. 2/3 Our Bank Directors have not thought it worth their while to call a meeting, even for consultation, on the subject. It is O.K. (*all correct*) in this quarter. **1839** *Philadelphia Gaz.* 12 Nov. 2/1 Yes—that's good—O.K.—I.S.B.D. [*sc.* it shall be done]. **1840** *Morning Herald* (N.Y.) 30 Mar. 2/1 A few years ago, some person accused Amos Kendall to General Jackson of being no better than he should be. 'Let me examine the papers,' said the old hero. .. The General did so and found every thing right. 'Tie up them papers,' said the General... 'Mark on them, "O.K.",' continued the General. O.K. was marked upon them. 'By the eternal', said the good old General.., 'Amos is *Ole Kurrek* (all correct) and no mistake.' *Ibid.* 21 Apr. 2/4 The Brigadier..reviewed his Brigade..and pronounced every thing O.K. **1840** *Boston* (Mass.) *Daily Times* 15 Dec. 2/3 What is't that ails the people, Joe? They're in a kurious way, For every where I chance to go, There's nothing but O.K. **1847** Robb *Squatter Life* 72 (Farmer) His express reported himself,..assured Allen that all was O.K., and received his dollar. **1852** Judson *Mysteries of N. York* iv. (ibid.), 'Tis one of us; it's O.K. **1853** F. Townsend *Fun & Earnest* 14 To the earnest inquiries of another, he simply respondeth, O.K. **1864** *Boy's Own Mag.* Nov. 450/1 No thought of taking the trouble to find out whether the order was O.K., or 'orl korrect', as Sir William Curtis phrased it. **1865** W. H. Russell *Atlantic Telegraph* 61 The communication with shore continued to improve, and was, in the language of telegraphers, O.K. **1866** *N. & Q.* 18 Aug. 128/2 The following telegram has been received from Mr. R. A. Glass ..'O.K.', (all correct). **1874** E. S. Ward *Trotty's Wedding Tour* xiii. 133 We had an O.K. time till we went to bed. **1886** *Lantern* (New Orleans) 29 Sept. 3/2 Favetto umpired the game all O.K. **1888** *Troy Daily Times* 20 Feb. (ibid.), The Canadian customs-house is required to stamp an American vessel's paper O.K. **1894** C. H. Donovan *With Wilson in Matabeleland* xi. 253 As our American friends would say, we were still 'O.K.' **1898** *Daily News* 21 Jan. 7/1 In one of his letters from America defendant said..he was 'All O.K.'... Mr. Justice Ridley—It means 'all correct', I understand. **1900** *Law Times* 10 Nov. 35/2 The State Court [U.S.] seems to have decided that when a lawyer marks such a decree O.K., he is, by so doing, estopped from questioning that decree by appeal. **1918** [see wet *a.* 4b]. **1922** D. H. Lawrence *England, my England* 101 At first Joe thought the job O.K. **1922** J. Reith *Diary* 14 Dec. (1975) ii. 128 He said ..that if things went OK I should get a rise soon. **1932** H. Nicolson *Public Faces* i. 8 'O.K.,' he had said, 'I'll remind old Peabottle.'.. The expression 'O.K.' was not one which should be used in the Foreign Office, and least of all by an Assistant Private Secretary. **1937** D. L. Sayers *Busman's Honeymoon* viii. 148 'I say, Mr. Superintendent, are you going to want me any more? I've got to get back to Town.' 'That's O.K. We've got your address.' **1939** *Times* 24 Oct. 4/5 'O.K.' is an abbreviation of the expression 'Orl korrec' —all correct. It is English, I think Cockney—not an Americanism. I was born in the sixties and remember it when I was a boy. **1940** 'N. Blake' *Malice in Wonderland* i. ii. 20 Anything that was efficiently organised was O.K. by Paul Perry. **1941** *Coast to Coast 1941* 224 He'd have reckoned it was O.K. to have gone or to have done what I did. **1957** J. Montgomery *Twenties* xviii. 262 By mid-1929, when sound films had spread across Britain, there was hardly a town or village without some child who was saying 'O.K.' when previously he would have said 'Yes'. **1968** *Encounter* Sept. 22/1 Direct transliterations from Yiddish or 'Yinglish' versions thereof... O.K. by me. **1973** *Railway World* Apr. 172/2 It seems OK now to refer to that bit of the

Mae Khlaung as the 'River Kwai'. **1973** [see the verb, below]. **1976** *Publishers Weekly* 12 Jan. 52/2 The older dog asks if Pepper will allow him to go along for awhile and Pepper says ok. **1976** *Punch* 11 Feb. (recto front cover), Harold rules—OK? **1976** *Spectator* 15 May 3/1 George Davis was released by the Home Secretary, to the delight of headline writers, and the groans of others. The *Spectator* is bored by that line OK? **1976** *Sunday Times* 16 May 42 When George Davis stepped out of Parkhurst prison last week few headline writers could resist the temptation. *George Davis is free OK?* (the Sun), *George Davis is free—but is it OK?* (the Guardian). **1976** *Observer* 13 June 1/5 He added belligerently: 'I don't want to answer no more questions, OK? No disrespect to the court.' **1976** *Sunday Express* 4 July 6/3 He kept going on and on: '..there are certain standards to be maintained in first-class compartments.'.. And when he left the train..he gave..a look which said: 'First Class Rules—O.K.?' **1977** *Times* 26 Apr. 8/4 The popular graffiti— *Rules-OK*, which originated amongst the Glasgow razor gangs of the thirties. **1977** *Zigzag* June 31/1 We could have had a great album, rather than an OK album.

b. Used as a slogan by the Democrats in the American election campaign of 1840, influenced by the initials of *Old Kinderhook*, a nickname for Martin Van Buren (1782–1862), the Democratic candidate for the presidency, who was born at Kinderhook in New York State. ***O.K. Club***, a Democratic club of New York City in 1840. *Obs.* exc. *Hist.*

1840 *Democratic Republ. New Era* 23 Mar. 3/2 (Advt.), The Democratic O.K. Club are hereby ordered to meet at the House of Jacob Colvin. **1840** *Newark Daily Advertiser* 28 Mar. 2/4 The *war cry* of the locofocos was O.K., the two letters paraded at the head of an inflammatory article in the New Era of the morning. 'Down with the whigs, boys, O.K.' was the shout of these poor, deluded men. **1840** *National Intelligencer* (Washington) 7 Apr. 1/2 Already the Locofocos have got out their banners and procession, and 'the Butt-enders' and 'Point-enders' are marching at night through our streets, led by the so-called 'O.K.' club, which is just now a cant phrase in Tammany. **1840** *Democratic Republ. New Era* 27 May 2/6 We acknowledge the receipt of a very pretty gold Pin,.. having upon it the (to the 'Whigs') very frightful letters O.K., significant of the birth-place of Martin Van Buren, old Kinderhook, as also the rallying word of the Democracy of the late election, 'all correct'... Those who wear them should bear in mind that it will require their most strenuous exertions..to make all things O.K. **1948** Partridge *World of Words* (ed. 3) 175 O.K. was in 1840 the watchword of the O.K. Club, that Democratic Club of New York City which took its name from *Old Kinderhook*, nickname of Martin van Buren (1782–1862), born at Kinderhook in New York State and in 1836–40 the President of the United States.

c. Socially or culturally acceptable; correct; fashionable, modish; having or showing prestige, high-class.

1869 *Henry De Marson's New Singer's Jrnl.* xxxv. 246 The Stilton, sir, the cheese, the O.K. thing to do, On Sunday afternoon, is to toddle in the Zoo. **1899** R. Whiteing *No. 5 John St.* xxiii. 233 She objected to the parting of the ass's mane as 'too O.K. for a moke'. **1950** S. Potter *Some Notes Lifemanship* i. 30 The word 'diathesis'..is now on the O.K. list for conversationmen. *Ibid.* v. 78 Just as there are O.K.-words in conversationship, so there are O.K.-*people to mention* in Newstatesmanship. **1957** *Observer* 22 Sept. 5/4 She left her campaign to save the theatre in the elegant hands of the Piccadilly and St. James's Association Ltd.—a very O.K. organisation of local shopkeepers and business, who like to keep the district nice. **1958** *Spectator* 19 Sept. 360/3 Mr. Macmillan ended his letter by saying we must treat this crisis 'calmly and constructively'. Both these are very OK words just now. **1960** *New Left Rev.* May–June 55/1 To give up his clerk's post in favour of a much better paid (but socially less OK) job in a factory. **1963** *Listener* 17 Jan. 140/3 In an eminently 'Third Programme' talk..he drew a comparison between this opera and his recent *King Priam* which was bedevilled by O.K. names and words. **1973** *Times Lit. Suppl.* 8 June 650/5 Handy quotations from such OK literary luminaries as Macaulay, Nietzsche, Strindberg, [etc.].

B. *sb.* **a.** A member of the O.K. Club (see A. b, above). *Obs.*

1840 *Morning Herald* (N.Y.) 30 Mar. 2/1 The O.K.'s are now the most original and learned locofoco club of the day. *Ibid.* 4 Apr. 2/1 All the clubs of Buttenders, O.K.'s, N.C.'s, [etc.]. **1840** *Boston Even. Transcript* 15 Apr. 2/1 The tail of the Democratic party, the roarers, buttenders, ringtails, O.K.'s (flat burglary this latter) and indomitables.

b. The letters 'O.K.', esp. as written on a document or the like, to express approval of its contents; an endorsement, approval, or authorization.

1841 'Dow, Jr.' *Short Patent Sermons* 106 Fortitude.. infuses new life into his soul, while Hope adds an O.K. to his condition. **1896** *Congress. Rec.* 5 Mar. 2507/1 The deputy marshall..would send word to the prosecuting attorney asking for an 'O.K.' **1901** Merwin & Webster *Calumet 'K'* xiv. 273 A formal permit..signed by Porter himself, and bearing the O.K. of the general manager. **1910** S. E. White in *Sunset* Sept. 311/1 The high official added his OK to the others. **1925** H. Crane *Let.* 21 Oct. (1965) 218 My questionnaire..had won an OK sign in the upper right corner. **1930** *Liberty* 11 Oct. 30/3 Rube copped a sneak on the joint to find out if it was ready. In twenty minutes he gives us the O.K. **1956** *Rev. Eng. Stud.* VII. 440 It is Pound who is to give the O.K. to the gods (not to God). **1961** L. Mumford *City in Hist.* xvii. 535 The fifth vice-president whose name or O.K. sets the final seal of responsibility upon an action.

C. *v. trans.* To endorse by marking with the letters 'O.K.'; to approve, agree to, sanction, pass.

1888 *Missouri Republican* 25 Jan. 10/4 The expression, 'Please O.K. and hurry return of my account,' is grammatically correct. The noun account is governed by the preposition of, and is also the object of the active transitive verb O.K. **1891** *Congress. Rec.* 13 Feb. 2635/2 If those who were to go into the clerical service of the Government were to be 'O.K.'d' by any one except the Civil Service Commission. **1898** H. E. Hamblen *Gen. Manager's Story* 82 He hunted the hook over until he found the 227's report signed, Grinnell, O.K'd., and signed by the man who had done the work. **1921** R. S. Woodworth *Psychol.* xix. 505 Not that Freud would OK our account of dreams up to this point. Far from it. **1923** Galsworthy *Captures* 192 He finished pencilling, O.K.'d the sheets,..and went back to his room. **1932** E. Wilson *Devil take Hindmost* xxi. 224 The company submits plans to us and we O.K. them... We've O.K.'d Boulder City. **1942** E. Paul *Narrow St.* xxvii. 238 Of course, he [*sc.* Petain] had not counted on having the decrees he signed dictated by a German Führer, or at least O.K.'d when their hearts beat exactly as one. **1973** P. Dickinson *Gift* v. 76 'OK, OK,' said Mr Venn soothingly. .. But you know quite well head office wouldn't OK it... I'm not going to risk it.' 'OK,' said Mr Palozzi. **1976** *Columbus* (Montana) *News* 27 May 3/4 Smith's report..was not officially OKed by the War Department for release until July 9.

‖**oka, oke** (ˈəʊkə, əʊk). Forms: *α.* 7– **oka**, (7 **oquea, oqui**, 7–9 **okka**, 9 **ocha**). *β.* 7– **oke**, (7–8 **oque**, 9 **okk**). [a. It. *oca, occa* (1709 in Somavera), F. *oque, ocque*, ad. Turk. *ōqah*, Arab. *ūqiyah*; app. ad. (through Syriac) Gr. οὐγκία, L. *uncia*, although the actual weight is now very different. (Devic in Littré *Suppl.*)]

A Turkish and Egyptian measure of weight, in general equal to about $2\frac{3}{4}$ lb. English; also, a measure of capacity, equal to about $\frac{2}{3}$ of a quart.

α. **1625** Purchas *Pilgrims* II. vii. 1154 He sent him one hundred thousand *Oquies* of gold. **1653** H. Cogan tr. *Pinto's Trav.* iii. 5 Three hundred Oqueas of gold. **1682** Wheler *Journ. Greece* i. 77 We bought Wine..at four Aspers the Oka. **1684** tr. *Tavernier's Grd. Seignior's Serag.* 39 (Stanf.) Weighs a hundred Okkas. **1820** T. S. Hughes *Trav. Sicily* II. ix. 240 (Stanf.), 1400 ochas of flour. **1899** *Whitaker's Alm.* 703 Egypt..1 oka = 2·723 lbs. *Ibid.* 705 Turkey..1 Almud (8 Oka) = 1·1519 gallons.

β. c **1645** Howell *Lett.* (1655) II. lv. 65 He had at one time swallow'd three and thirty okes, which is a measure near upon the bignes of our quart. **1687** tr. *Thevenot's Trav. Levant* in Sir T. P. Blount *Nat. Hist.* (1693) 68 Seven and twenty thousand Oques, at fourscore and ten Oques the Chest. **1706** Phillips s.v., The greater Oke of Smyrna, is 2 Pounds, 11 Ounces and 13 Drams English; the middle Oke is 1 Pound, 11 Ounces 6 Drams; and the least Oke is 13 Ounces, 2 Drams. **1847** Disraeli *Tancred* iv. iv, We might ..buy it all up at sixty piastres per oke. **1850** W. Irving *Mahomet* xxxi. (1853) 162 To Abu Sofian he gave one hundred Camels and forty okks of silver.

oka, var. oca.

okam, okcome, okeham, obs. ff. oakum.

okapi (əʊˈkɑːpɪ). [Native name.] A rare ungulate mammal, *Okapia johnstoni*, of the family Giraffidæ, about the size of a horse and reddish-brown in colour, with horizontal white stripes on the legs; native to forested regions of the Congo, where it was discovered in 1900 by Sir Harry Johnston (1858–1927), the English explorer.

1900 H. Johnston in *Proc. Zool. Soc.* 775, I found the Bambuba natives dwelling alongside the dwarfs called it 'Okapi'. **1901** *Chambers's Jrnl.* July 493/1 The native name for this strange beast, which is quite inoffensive, is the *okapi.* **1930** *Punch* 24 Sept. 337/2 A photographer has succeeded in getting a 'close-up' of the shy okapi. **1958** *Listener* 23 Jan. 154/1 The Pygmies are excellent trappers and they are paid to catch various kinds of beasts including the rare okapi, the short-necked forest giraffe, which are sold to zoos. **1960** M. Spark *Ballad of Peckham Rye* iii. 35 'You look to me like an Okapi,' he said. 'A what?' 'An Okapi is a rare beast from the Congo. It looks a little like a deer, but it tries to be a giraffe.' **1974** Mochi & Carter *Hoofed Mammals of World* i. 7 The only living relative of the giraffe is the okapi, a forest animal living in the great rain forest of the Congo.

okay (əʊˈkeɪ), *a.*, *sb.*, and *v. colloq.* (orig. *U.S.*). Also **okeh, okey.** [Repr. pronunc. of O.K. *a.*, *sb.*, and *v.*] **A.** *adj.*

a. = O.K. *adj.* a. Also as *adv.*

1919 Mencken *Amer. Lang.* 161 Dr. Woodrow Wilson is said..to use *okeh* in endorsing government papers. **1929** J. P. McEvoy *Hollywood Girl* ix. 147 *Jimmy* (*dashing out door*): I'll kill the son of a—— *Girl* (*going back to kitchenette*): Okay, big boy. **1932** *Sunday Express* 3 July 9/6, I had given my hand to the comedian and heard him say: 'Hold on, baby... Hold on. It's okay. You're going to be fine.' **1934** N. Sainsbury *Gridiron Grit* xii. 142 Okay by me. **1936** J. B. Priestley *They walk in City* viii. 237 The short one took the letter... He nodded. 'Righty-o. Seems okay.' **1939** E. B. Wilson *My Memoir* 174 Approval was designated by 'Okeh, W.W.' on the margin of a paper. Someone asked why he [*sc.* Woodrow Wilson] did not use the 'O.K.' 'Because it is wrong,' Mr. Wilson said. He suggested that the inquirer look up 'okeh' in a dictionary. This he did, discovering that it is a Choctaw word meaning 'It is so'. **1944** 'N. Shute' *Pastoral* i. 7 Okay. I'll tell the boys. **1945** E. Waugh *Brideshead Revisited* 304 'Don't let on to anyone that we've made a nonsense of the morning.' 'Okey, Ryder.' **1953** J. Y. Cousteau *Silent World* 91 Tailliez came up and reported, 'Everything okay. They're playing chess.' **1966** D. M. Thomas in *Listener* 17 Feb. 247/1 Okay, my starsick beauty! .. Where would you like to go? **1972** *Publishers Weekly* 6 Mar. 31/2 He says most of that magazine's ex-staffers have done 'okay' in re-adjusting. **1974** 'E. Lathen' *Sweet & Low* xix. 185 He got through a third degree okay.

b. = O.K. *adj.* c.

1958 *Observer* 7 Sept. 13/4 Being in fusion is the really okay thing now. **1966** *New Statesman* 11 Mar. 348/1 The writer's ideas are rooted deep in the soil of experience and have not been processed into pet ideas and okay-words before they have ripened. **1970** G. Greer *Female Eunuch* 159 His secretary had..moved out of Haight Ashbury when it ceased to be okay to live there. **1974** *Listener* 16 May 642/1 The current psychiatric okay-word is the cautious and benign 'disturbed'. **1976** *New Society* 1 Jan. 5/1 In spite of the levelling effect of package holidays, skiing is still an okay sport. A survey..showed that British skiers were more likely to be upper middle class ABs living in the prosperous southern counties.

B. *sb.* = O.K. *sb.* b.

1925 Ade *Let.* 28 Mar. (1973) 104 If, while he was putting his okeh on this material, he privately disapproved of it and was sending word back east that the material was not what you wanted, of course he was putting me in a tough position. **1925** *Dollar Mag.* Dec. 207 To find new and more vivid forms of expression..in the hope that they will, in time, receive the okeh of the reading public. **1931** *North Amer. Rev.* Jan. 15/2 During the last two years Raskob has either put his okay on every major move that Jouett Shouse has made, or else suggested it himself in the first place. **1973** *Freedomways* XIII. 18 Nothing goes down without his okay. **1974** *Columbia* (S. Carolina) *Record* 25 Apr. 6-D/1 In the more than 14 years since the dam was first proposed, the estimated $75 million cost has more than doubled. Whether it will get an *okay* on environmental grounds has not been determined.

C. *v. trans.* = O.K. *v.*

1930 *Amer. Speech* VI. 119 Parachute company stock sale okehed. **1938** *Times* 18 Jan. 13/4 The proposal to call this haunt of pleasure the 'Non-stop Journal Kino' was taken to the Supreme Court before being—as the delighted proprietor probably put it—okayed. **1945** H. I. Phillips *Private Purkey's Private Peace* vii. 40 When they okayed me at that abduction center 'for the duration' I thought it meant just for the duration of the war. **1947** *People* 22 June 5/3 Micky and ex-light-weight champion Dave Crowley did the same fight 25 times before the final take was okayed. **1958** S. Ellin *Eighth Circle* (1959) i. i. 18 Every place where you can okay it, you put down O.K. and your initials. **1968** *Listener* 5 Dec. 771/1 Okayed by Western governments, the Prague festival enjoyed a substantial dollar bonus in the form of the Illinois State University Jazz Band. **1974** *Times* 22 Feb. 19/4 Scripts Limited comes in after the screenwriter has been commissioned by a film company, has written his first draft and had it okayed.

Okazaki (əʊkəˈzɑːkɪ). *Biology.* The name of Reiji *Okazaki* (1930–75), Japanese molecular biologist, used *attrib.* to designate fragments formed during the replication of chromosomal DNA, first described by Okazaki et al. in 1968 (*Proc. Nat. Acad. Sci.* LIX. 598).

1969 *Proc. Nat. Acad. Sci.* LXIV. 1065 Some of the Okazaki fragments are present in a single-stranded state in cell lysates prepared under nondenaturing conditions. **1971** *Jrnl. Molecular Biol.* LVII. 351 The assembly of small fragments of newly synthesized DNA—the so-called Okazaki fragments..—to form a larger structure. **1975** *Nature* 4 Sept. 76/3 The synthesis of new DNA strands during the process of DNA duplication seems to occur in rather short sections (now known to everyone as 'Okazaki pieces').

oke (əʊk), *a. colloq.* (orig. *U.S.*). [Abbrev. of pronunc. of O.K. *a.*, *sb.*, and *v.*] = O.K. *adj.* a.

1929 D. Hammett *Dain Curse* (1930) v. 45 Try not breathing so hard. Everything will probably be oke. **1932** A. Woollcott *Let.* 31 Dec. (1946) 95 Dear Lady Cavendish.. gets along famously with her mother-in-law, the Duchess of Devonshire. Has the Duchess saying 'Oke' already. **1933** Dylan Thomas *Let.* Oct. (1966) 38 Laleham arrangement, though in the air, is oke by me, and if there is any one expression worse than 'sez you' this is it. **1935** *Spectator* 15 Feb. 257/1 A child replied 'oke', to something I said. **1944** L. A. G. Strong *Director* 93 'How was it, Votty?' 'Oke.' **1951** Green & Laurie *Show Biz* 570/1 *Oke*, OK. **1960** S. H. Courtier *Gently dust Corpse* xiv. 196 He's oke now. Get some brandy.

oke: see oka; obs. f. oak; obs. pa. t. ache.

okecorne, okehorne, obs. forms of acorn.

okeh, okey, varr. okay *a.*, *sb.*, and *v.*

okenite (ˈəʊkənaɪt). *Min.* [Named 1828 (*okenit*), after Lorenz Oken, a German naturalist: see -ite[1].] A hydrous silicate of calcium, occurring in minute needle-shaped crystals, usually forming a tough fibrous mass, of a whitish colour, and subtransparent. Also called *dysclasite.*

1828 *Edin. Philos. Jrnl.* VI. 186 Okenite, a new species of zeolite. **1850** Dana *Min.* (ed. 3) 248 Okenite occurs in amygdaloid in Greenland.

okepy, okewpy, obs. forms of occupy.

†**oker.** *Obs. rare.* [app. ad. L. *ocrea*: see ocrea. (But cf. hogger, cocker.)] (See quot.)

1538 Elyot, *Carpatinæ*, ploughemens bootes, made of vntanned lether, they may be called okers [*so edd.* 1545–52; *ed.* 1565 (Cooper) cokers]. **1552** Huloet, Bootes for ploughmen called Okers.

okey-doke (ˌəʊkɪˈdəʊk), *a. colloq.* (orig. *U.S.*). Also **oakie-doke, okay-doke, okee-doke, okey-dokey, okie-dokie, okle-dokle.** [Redupl. O.K. *adj.*]

= O.K. *adj.* a.

1932 *Amer. Speech* VII. 334 *Okey-dokey*, O.K. **1934** M. H. Weseen *Dict. Amer. Slang* xiii. 190 *Okey dokey*, O.K. *Ibid.* xxi. 373 *Okay doke*, satisfactory; agreeable; all right. **1935** *Evening Sun* (Baltimore) 7 Feb. 7/1 An attorney asked Carl Bush, witness, to answer a 'yes or no' question. 'Oakie-Doke,' replied Bush. **1936** M. Harrison *All Trees were*

Green 305 Captain Sarsfield said: 'Everything okey-doke up at the mansion?' **1936** D. POWELL *Turn, Magic Wheel* I. 36 He saw that tiresome red-faced fellow.., the man who knew everybody and said 'okie-dokie' to everything. **1944** M. LASKI *Love on Supertax* iv. 53 Things are okey-doke for a lot of people now. **1947** B. SCHULBERG *Harder they Fall* vii. 121 'Hey, Killer, tell Jack to pick me up in front of the door right away.' 'Okle-dokle,' the Killer said. 'Where we goin'?' **1957** C. MACINNES *City of Spades* II. iii. 95 One Guinness stout, right, I thank you, okey-doke, here it is. **1968** C. BROWN in A. Dundes *Mother Wit* (1973) 236/1 There are certain classic soul terms... Among the classical expressions are: 'solid', 'cool',..'okee doke', [etc.]. **1977** J. FLEMING *Every Inch a Lady* I. i. 7 Light out, silence, everything okey dokey, she goes off to bed. **1977** *New Yorker* 16 May 33/1 Now, if for any reason you lose your paper clips, you're in big trouble. Okeydoke.

Okhrana (ɒx'rɑːnə). Also **Ochrana**. [a. Russ. *okhrána*, lit. 'guarding, protection'.] An organization of political police set up in 1881 in tsarist Russia after the assassination of Alexander II to maintain the security of the state and suppress revolutionary activities, and disbanded in 1917. Cf. CHEKA.

1899 P. KROPOTKIN *Mem. of Revolutionist* II. vi. 246 A secret league for the protection of the Tsar [Alexander III] was started... This league still exists in a more official shape, under the name of Okhrána (Protection). **1906** *Cosmopolitan* Dec. 237/2 The exact number, local distribution, and cost of the 'okhrana'..are known to no single official. **1920** *Contemp. Rev.* June 861 The Soviet authorities were confronted with the task..of abrogating individual laws permeated by the spirit of the Tsarist Okhrana. **1928** *Illustr. Hist. Russ. Rev.* I. 65 The confidential reports of the police and the 'Okhrana' furnish convincing evidence of the political nature of the unrest in the capital. **1930** A. T. VASSILYEV (*title*) The Ochrana: the Russian secret police. **1949** I. DEUTSCHER *Stalin* ii. 36 *Okhrana*, or the Third Department, was the political police set up in 1881, after the assassination of Alexander II. **1974** T. P. WHITNEY tr. *Solzhenitsyn's Gulag Archipel.* I. I. ii. 67 Section 13, presumably long since out of date, had to do with service in the Tsarist secret police—the Okhrana.

Okie ('əʊkɪ). *colloq.* [f. *Ok*lahoma, one of the United States + -IE (see -Y[6]).] A migrant agricultural worker, *spec.* one from Oklahoma forced to leave his farm during the depression of the 1930s. Also, a native or inhabitant of Oklahoma. Also *attrib.* Cf. OKLAHOMAN.

1938 *Forum & Century* Jan. 12 About a fifth of [the migratory workers in California] are Okies. **1939** J. STEINBECK *Grapes of Wrath* xviii. 280 Okie use' ta mean you was from Oklahoma. Now it means you're a dirty son-of-a-bitch. **1941** S. LONGSTREET *Last Man around World* 356 The hillbilly, the Okie..and people who once shook hands with Warren G. Harding..fill the land. **1948** *Daily Ardmoreite* (Ardmore, Okla.) 11 July 21/5 Sooners have less reason to be offended at being called 'Okies' than residents of other states have for their nicknames. **1957** J. KEROUAC *On Road* (1958) 167 This was an Okie from Bakersfield, California. **1964** *Amer. Folk Music Occasional* I. 87 The songs of the 'Okies', those modern Forty-niners from the depleted farm lands of the Southwest. **1964** E. A. NIDA *Toward Sci. Transl.* viii. 180 Procházka..describes the problem of reproducing in Czech the Okie speech used by some of Steinbeck's characters. **1970** J. HANSEN *Fadeout* (1972) viii. 67 I'm a dirty, ignorant Okie to him. **1975** *New Society* 19 June 705/1 Oklahoma got most attention, but migrants drifted from other places across the Great Plains and rural south... As time passed, nearly all migrants came to be called Okies once they had reached California. **1978** *Chicago* June 40/2 Glenn Allen Smith's new play about the zany misadventures of an Okie hero-type is not quite zany enough to carry its weight.

‖**okimono** (oːki'moːno). [Jap., = 'put thing', f. *oku* to put + *mono* thing.] A standing ornament or figure, esp. one put in a guest room of a house.

1886 W. ANDERSON *Pict. Arts Japan* III. xi. 112 The ornament pure and simple, the *Okimono* of the Japanese, was..made by artists in metal from a very early period... The first of the modern *Okimono* school appeared to have been a woman named Kamé or Kamé-jo. **1890** *Artistic Japan* V. 348 It is important to distinguish between netsukés, articles made for a special purpose..and okimonos..ornaments never intended either for use or wear. **1911** J. F. BLACKER *ABC of Jap. Art* vi. 116 Elephant's tusks..were used chiefly for *okimonos*—alcove ornaments. **1916** JOLY & TOMITA *Jap. Art & Handicraft* 198 (*caption*) 22 *Okimono*, figure of Fukurokujiu with staff and *tama*. **1961** *Times* 7 Nov. 24/5 (Advt.), A collection of Japanese colour prints, netsuke, and works of art.. including netsuke carved in wood and ivory, okimono and ivory carvings. **1962** F. A. TURK *Jap. Objets d' Art* II. 81 From the late figure-group Netsuke,..arose the *okimono* (i.e. a carving to stand in an alcove). **1975** *Times* 8 May 16/3 A mid-nineteenth century wood figure of a demon..is an okimono rather than a true netsuke, too elaborate and delicate to use as a button.

Okinawan (əʊkɪ'nɑːwən, ɒk-), *sb.* and *a.* [f. the place-name *Okinawa*, f. Jap. *okinawa*, lit. 'rope on the sea': see -AN.] **A.** *sb.* A native or inhabitant of the Okinawa Islands, esp. of Okinawa, the largest of the Ryukyu (Nansei) group south-west of Japan; also, the dialect of Japanese spoken there. **B.** *adj.* Of or pertaining to Okinawa or the Okinawa Islands, to its people or its language.

1944 *Civil Affairs Handbk.: Ryukyu Islands* (U.S. Navy Dept.) xiv. 44 These phonetic differences impart a characteristic accent to Japanese as spoken by Okinawans. **1945** *N.Y. Times* 3 Apr. 3/1 Hundreds of kimono-clad Okinawans who fled to the hills with the first shells of the American pre-invasion bombardment are now streaming into our lines. **1945** *Ibid.* 5 Apr. 3/1 Dozens of enterprising GI's..saddled small, shaggy-maned Okinawan ponies with their gear. **1947** *Sci. Monthly* Mar. 235/2 Since the dawn of recorded history the Okinawans, although nominally independent, were influenced by both China and Japan and at times paid allegiance and tribute to both. At one time Okinawan sailing vessels carried on widespread commerce with the Asiatic mainland and the islands of the Western and Southwestern Pacific. **1955** C. J. GLACKEN *Great Loochoo* 3 The most significant characteristic of Okinawan culture is the family system. *Ibid.* viii. 166 This fish is caught with the aid of a homemade triangular wire device (*yamaguchi* in Okinawan). **1960** B. LEACH *Potter in Japan* iii. 72 About seventy relatives, Okinawans and members of the Japanese Craft Society assembled. *Ibid.* 73 Two Okinawan scholars spoke next. **1964** *Listener* 24 Sept. 473/1 Brando..has appeared in comedy before—as the Okinawan Sakini in *The Teahouse of the August Moon.* **1966** P. S. BUCK *People of Japan* (1968) xiv. 176 Okinawans wish once again to become part of Japan. **1973** C. L. HOGG *Okinawa* 13 Take the very name of the island... Okinawans have always called it Uchina, but no one else has ever paid the slightest attention to what Okinawans call their island... Okinawa, the name bestowed on Uchina by the Japanese, may be translated 'rope in the offing'. **1973** *Guardian* 24 May 4/4 More than half of Okinawans dislike Americans, because of their offensive behaviour. *Ibid.* 4/6 Two Okinawan women waiting at a bus stop were killed by a drunken American driver.

okk, okka: see OKA.

ok(k)er, var. OCKER *Obs.*; obs. f. OCHRE.

Oklahoma (əʊkla'həʊmə). The name of a State in the south-west of the United States (see next), used *attrib.* and *absol.* to designate a kind of rummy orig. played in Oklahoma.

1945 A. A. OSTROW *Compl. Card Player* 578 *Oklahoma Rummy*... The cards rank in sequence as in standard rummy, but ace is high only and never low. Deuces are wild. **1948** [see CANASTA]. **1949** J. SCARNE *On Cards* (1955) ix. 63 *Oklahoma Gin.* In this variation the twenty-first card.. determines the maximum number of points in unmatched cards with which a player may knock. *Ibid.* 64 Oklahoma usually incorporates the Spades Double feature. *Ibid.* xiii. 163 *Oklahoma Rummy.* A variation of Fortune Rummy. Played for years throughout the Middle West. **1973** G. F. HERVEY *Hamlyn Illustr. Bk. Card Games* 110 Oklahoma may be played by any number of players from two to five, but is generally considered best when played by three.

Oklahoman (əʊkla'həʊmən). [f. *Oklahoma*, one of the United States, f. Choctaw *okla* nation, people + *homma* red: see -AN.] A native or inhabitant of the State of Oklahoma.

In quot. 1894 as the name of a newspaper.

1894 (*title*) Evening Oklahoman (Oklahoma City, Okla.). **1901** *Outlook* (N.Y.) 2 Feb. 280/1 Many of the old Oklahomans who are selling out expect to secure new homes at the opening. **1934** L. GANNETT *Sweet Land* iv. 40 The Texans held that 'Pretty Boy' was no Oklahoman at all. Some held that he was a genuine West Texan. **1948** *Durant* (Okla.) *Daily Democrat* 4 July 2/5 Every Oklahoman appreciates an agency which seeks to protect our lives and property. **1959** C. OGBURN *Marauders* (1960) ii. 53 John P. McElmurray, a very tall, very spare, taciturn, profane Oklahoman. **1973** *Black Panther* 1 Sept. 16/1 'Those animals,' declared Mrs. Johnson, a typical racist Oklahoman.

†**o-knes, o-knon**, *phr. Obs.* = On knees: see AKNEE and O *prep.*[1] b.

a **1225** *Ancr. R.* 16 Buinde oknon vorðward vpo ðe bed. *c* **1300** *Havelok* 2252 O-knes ful fayre he him sette.

O.K.-ness (əʊ'keɪnɪs). [f. O.K. *a.*, *sb.*, and *v.* + -NESS.] The fact or quality of being O.K.; acceptability.

1935 E. GILL *Let.* 31 Jan. (1947) 321, I rejoice..to have your assurance as to orthodoxy, decency & general o.k.ness of the..'article'. **1950** S. POTTER *Some Notes Lifemanship* 76 The absolute O.K.-ness of French literature..cannot be too much emphasised. **1962** M. DRABBLE *Summer Bird-Cage* iv. 55, I carried an aura of vicarious theatrical OK-ness. **1969** *Punch* 19 Feb. 256/2 The rest of us..should be able to talk quite fluently about the varying OK-ness of split, one-piece, or cracked-edge construction.

okom(e, okre, obs. forms of OAKUM, OCHRE.

okoume (əʊ'kuːmeɪ). Also **okoumé**. [Native name.] = GABOON, GABOON.

1922 C. T. CAMPION tr. *Schweitzer's On Edge of Primeval Forest* vi. 108 The chief sorts [of wood] dealt in are mahogany,..and okoume (*Aucoumea klaineana*), the so-called false mahogany. **1933** —— tr. *Schweitzer's My Life & Thought* xiii. 163 The trade in okoume wood..was just beginning to flourish in the Ogowe district. **1947** J. C. RICH *Materials & Methods Sculpture* x. 293 *Okoume* is another name for Gaboon Mahogany. The wood is soft and light-weight and is a light reddish-brown color. **1956** *Handbk. Hardwoods* (Forest Prod. Res. Lab.) 97 Gaboon is known as okoumé in France. The tree grows mainly in French Equatorial Africa.

okoure, variant of OCKER *Obs.*, usury.

okra ('ɒkrə). Also 8 ocra, 8–9 ocro, ockro, ochre, okro, 9 ochro, ochra, (occro, occra, okero, ookroo, ? okree). [app. West African: Christaller, *Dict. Asante & Fanti* (1881), has *nkru-ma* 'an annual plant, and its green seed-pods, used for soup, salad, pickles; okra, ochra, okro, *Hibiscus esculentus*'; where *-ma* is a formative suffix of nouns, the root-word being *nkru*: cf. *nkran*, the name of the town Europeanized as *Accra*. (J. Platt in *Athenæum* 1 Sept. 1900.)]

A tall malvaceous plant, *Hibiscus* or *Abelmoschus esculentus*, indigenous to Africa, now cultivated in the East and West Indies and the southern United States; the young mucilaginous capsules or 'pods' are used as an esculent vegetable and for thickening soup; the stem furnishes a fibre suitable for ropes. Also a name for the pods. (Also called *gumbo*.)

1707 SLOANE *Jamaica* I. 222 Ocra, this has a round green stem, which rises straight up to ten or twelve foot high. **1713** J. PETIVER in *Phil. Trans.* XXVIII. 211 Winged Birds Pease or Ochre. **1750** G. HUGHES *Barbadoes* 207 The flower is succeeded by a multangular fleshy pod, every way resembling that of an Ockro. **1777** G. FORSTER *Voy. round World* II. 321 The contents were the leaves of the okra (*hibiscus esculentus*). **1834** M. G. LEWIS *Jrnl. W. Ind.* 152 The only native vegetable, which I like much, is the ochra, which tastes like asparagus. **1858** CLARKE in Moloney *W. Afr. Fisheries* (1883) 37 (Fish. Exh. Publ.) This stew is made piquant and wholesome by the addition of salt, bitter tomatoes or ocroes, shallots,..and abundance of red peppers. **1873** GARDNER *Hist. Jamaica* 391 A quart of ockroes. **1894** A. SPINNER *Study Colour* 45 To help her mother gather the green okras for the soup. **1923** H. C. THOMPSON *Vegetable Crops* xxvii. 454 Okra is a tender plant and grows best in hot weather. **1953** G. LAMMING *In Castle of my Skin* xiv. 274 Slicing the ochroes was..painstaking. The prickly surface irritated the skin, and the slices fell off on the hand in a slimy mess. **1963** J. KIRKUP *Tropic Temper* 49 The chicken curry..is particularly good, with its rich, really hot sauce containing a curious, ribbed, tasteless vegetable called okras. **1964** E. HUXLEY *Back Street New Worlds* xiv. 141 The Shepherd's Bush market has a shop devoted wholly to West African foods..like gbure and okra, tete and apan. **1967** *Guardian* 8 Dec. 6/4 Fresh bhindi (which some people know as ladies' fingers, others as okra). **1971** *Advocate-News* (Barbados) 17 Sept. (Guyana Suppl.) p. ii/2 Now the Liliputians have completed planting of ground provisions, pumpkins, ochroes, blackeye peas, celery, bora and such permanent crops as breadfruit, citrus and breadnut. **1972** Y. LOVELOCK *Vegetable Bk.* 147 Perhaps the best known member [of the hibiscus family] is okra.., of African origin and said to have been cultivated in ancient Egypt. It is now grown widely in Africa, the Mediterranean region and the Americas.

b. Applied, with defining words, to other species of *Hibiscus* or *Abelmoschus*.

1840 *Penny Cycl.* XVI. 395/2 The okro..is very closely allied to *H. Abelmoschus*, now *Abelmoschus moschatus*,..by Browne, in his 'Nat. Hist. of Jamaica', called Musk-okro.

c. *attrib.* and *Comb.*

1756 P. BROWNE *Jamaica* 285 The Okro Plant. The pods of this plant are full of a nutritive mucilage, and the principal ingredient in most of the soops and pepper-pots, made in America. **1833** MARRYAT *P. Simple* (1863) 263 The negroes here get so tired of salt fish and occra broth, that they eat dirt by way of a relish. **1878** N. A. DONNELLEY *Lakeside Cook Bk.* 4/2 (*recipe*) Okra Gumbo. **1949** *Caribbean Q.* I. i. 33 The little yellow cups of witchery known as Okra flowers. **1952** S. SELVON *Brighter Sun* v. 82 Neighbour ask me bringam dry ochro seed for she to plant. **1973** *News & Courier* (Charleston, S. Carolina) 4 Nov. 3-E/1 A lunch of sandwiches and okra soup will be served from noon to 1 p.m.

‖**okrug** ('ɒkrʊg). [a. Russ. and Bulg. *ókrug*.] In Russia and Bulgaria, a territorial division for administrative and other purposes. Also *attrib.* Cf. OBLAST.

1886 *Encycl. Brit.* XXI. 69/2 Area and population of the Russian Empire... *Okrugs*, or *otdyels* (territories) under military government. **1902** *Ibid.* XXVI. 448/2 The country [*sc.* Bulgaria] is divided into twenty-two departments (*okrŭg*, pl. *okrŭzi*), each administered by a prefect. **1935** B. W. MAXWELL *Soviet State* I. i. 30 Russia, before the Revolution, was divided for purposes of administration into seventy-eight governments (*guberniya*), twenty-one regions (*oblast*), and one circuit (*okrug*). **1958** D. J. R. SCOTT *Russ. Polit. Institutions* ii. 74 The new administrative *okrugs*.. completed in 1952, were the product of a new acute phase of the persistent concern over effective supervision of districts by higher authorities... Shortly after the death of Stalin.. the *okrugs* began to be abolished again, and none of them is now in existence. **1971** J. S. RESHETAR *Soviet Polity* vii. 257 The least of the ethnic autonomous administrative units is the 'national area' (*okrug*). They have been established for the numerically small peoples of the Soviet Far North and Far East who inhabit large and sparsely populated areas. **1976** *Survey* Spring 65 There are [in the USSR] 14 union republic central committees, 10 *okrug* committees..and 4,243 city and *raion* committees.

†**okselle.** *Obs. rare*[−1]. [app. a. MDu. *oeksele* (Du. *oksel*, Flem. *oksele*):—OLG. **ōksla*, **ôhsla* arm-pit; from a root *óks-*, *óhs-*, seen in OE. *óx-n*, OHG. *uohs-ana*, *uoch-isa*, *och-asa*, MHG. *uohs-e*, *üehs-e*, also OE. *óhs-ta*, *ox-ta*, in Epinal G. *ócusta*, Sc. *ox-ter*; also, with weak grade, in OHG. *ahs-ala*, MHG. *ahs-el*, Ger. *achs-el*; further, in L. *axilla*, and OIr. *oxal*; all in the same or an allied sense.] The arm-pit; cf. OXTER.

1489 CAXTON *Faytes of A.* II. xxxv. 150 He dide putte two grete boteylles undre his okselles and swymed..in the see.

oksi, obs. form of ASK *v.*

okta ('ɒktə). *Meteorol.* [f. OCTA- by alteration.] (See quot. 1950.)

1950 *Meteorol. Gloss.* (Meteorol. Office) (ed. 3) Amendment List No. 4. 7 *Okta*, unit, equal to area of one eighth of the sky, used in specifying cloud amount. **1957** *Weather Map* (Meteorol. Office) (ed. 4) iv. 35 From January 1, 1949, cloud amount has been observed and reported in oktas or eighths of sky covered, code figure 0 representing a clear sky, 1 representing 1 okta (eighth) of sky covered or less, but not zero, 2 representing 2 oktas (eighths), and so on ..8 representing 8 oktas (eighths) (sky completely covered), and 9 representing sky obscured or cloud amount cannot be estimated. **1960** *Handbk. Aviation Meteorol.* (Meteorol. Office) xii. 178 The number of oktas of sky covered by any particular cloud layer is estimated as if no other clouds were present. **1961** C. E. WALLINGTON *Meteorol. for Glider Pilots* iii. 38 Cloud amount is usually reported in eighths of the sky covered... Sometimes the internationally convened word 'oktas' is substituted for 'eighths'. **1977** 'J. LE CARRÉ' *Hon. Schoolboy* xviii. 455 Cloud is anticipated at six to seven okta. .. One okta is one eighth of sky area covered.

okupie, okypy, obs. forms of OCCUPY.

okur, -yr(e, var. OCKER *Obs.*; obs. ff. OCHRE.

okym, ol, obs. forms of OAKUM, WHOLE.

ol (ɒl). *Chem.* [a. G. *ol* (A. Werner 1907, in *Ber. d. Deut. Chem. Ges.* XL. 2113), f. the suffix *-ol* -OL.] Used *attrib.* and in *Comb.* to designate a complex containing a hydroxyl group of which the oxygen atom is bonded to two metal atoms; also applied to the group itself.

1907 *Chem. Abstr.* I. 2537 There is no simple or normal hydroxyl group in these compounds because they will not add HX to form an aquo salt. Hence they should not be designated 'hydroxy' compounds, but may be designated 'ol' compounds, to signify that the hydroxyl group is in the complex radical. **1929** J. A. WILSON *Chem. & Leather* 29 Bjerrum succeeded in preparing an ol-compound with a nucleus containing 12 chromium atoms. **1931** *Jrnl. Physical Chem.* XXXV. 46 With the conversion of hydroxo groups to ol groups to oxo groups there results increasing resistance to the action of acids. *Ibid.* 47 The authors hazard the guess that the oxolation of ol complexes would result in a loss of the reaction with neutral salts. **1962** J. R. LEACH tr. *Grinberg's Introd. Chem. Complex Compounds* ix. 266 The acid-base equilibria can..be complicated by the formation of polynuclear complexes with 'ol' bridges, or with 'oxo' bridges. **1974** D. NICHOLLS *Inorganic Complexes* iii. 26 This species with the hydroxo or *ol* bridges can react in the presence of added base.

ol': see OLE, OL' *a.*

-ol, *suffix*, used to form chemical terms.

1. The termination of *alcoh-ol*, used to form the names of substances which are alcohols in the wider sense (ALCOHOL 5), or compounds analogous to alcohol; e.g. *carbinol* (methyl alcohol), *methol*, *pseudol*, *glycol* (2-atomic alc.), *glycerol* (3-atomic alc.), *phenol* (phenyl or benzene alc.), *naphthol* (naphthyl alcohol), etc. In some cases this systematic nomenclature has not displaced the name which the substance had previously received, e.g. *glycerol* is more commonly known as *glycerin* (or, commercially, *glycerine*).

2. From *phenol*, the ending has been transferred to bodies belonging to the group of *phenols* (which are alcohols), as *anthranol*, *anthrol*, *cresol*, *cymenol*, *eugenol*, *thymol*, and to some other phenol derivatives, as *anethol*, *creosol*, *guaiacol*, *phenetol*, *phlorol*, *pyrogallol*, *veratrol*, *xylenol*.

3. In some words *-ol* is a deriv. of L. *oleum* oil; in which case it is more systematically written -OLE (now the usual form); e.g. *furfurol*, *indol*, *oxindol*, *pyrrol*, *terpinol*.

ola, variant of OLLA², palm-leaf.

-ola, *suffix*. Chiefly *U.S.* Prob. derived from the second element of PIANOLA and now found esp. in commercial use as a suffix to form nouns, as MOVIOLA, PAYOLA, VICTROLA, etc.

See *Amer. Speech* (1961) XXXVI. 104-116.

‖**olam** (əʊˈlɑːm). [Heb. *ʿōlām* a long period of undefined limits, an age (Gr. αἰών), perh. properly 'that which is hidden', f. *ʿālam* to hide.] Used by some for: A vast period of time, an age, through a succession of which the universe or the earth is supposed to have passed. (Cf. ÆON.) Hence **o'lamic** *a.*, of or belonging to a vast period or age. (Cf. ÆONIAN.)

1872 T. LEWIS in *Lange's Comm. Eccles.* iii. 15 (ed. Clark) 73 Closely allied to the cyclical idea so prominent elsewhere in the book and the idea of the olam as the unity of the cosmos in time. *Ibid.* 44 Excursus on 'Olamic or aeonian words in Scripture'. **1877** DAWSON *Orig. World* vi. 132 The reference to God's olamic Sabbath. **1886** —— in *Expositor* Apr. 287 But man fell, and lost the perpetual or olamic sabbatism.

†**o'last**, var. ALAST *Obs.*, lastly: cf. O *prep.*¹ b.

a **1240** *Lofsong* in *Cott. Hom.* 207 Erest in his one hond and seoððen in his oðer, olast in his side þurlunge.

-olater, -olatry (see -O¹), the forms in which the suffixes -LATER, -LATRY usually occur.

olation (ɒˈleɪʃən). *Chem.* and *Tanning*. [f. OL + -ATION.

Though often attributed to Bjerrum and to Stiasny the word has not been found in their publications.]

Conversion of a complex into an ol form; linking of metal atoms by hydroxyl ligands. Used esp. with reference to chromium compounds used in tanning.

1931 *Jrnl. Physical Chem.* XXXV. 27 Bjerrum.. postulated that perhaps the hydroxo groups in the complex ions were becoming more firmly bound to form larger complexes... Bjerrum called this process 'olation'. **1931** *Chem. Abstr.* XXV. 2325 The basicity of the Cr salt in a one-bath Cr liquor is greater than that of the liquor as a whole because of 'olation'; the complex ol compds. react with the free acid only very slowly. **1941** D. WOODROFFE *Fund. Leather Sci.* viii. 107 This condensation is termed 'olation' and the larger complex compound obtained is described as an olated chromium salt. **1948** *Progress in Leather Sci. 1920-45* II. xxvi. 524 Stiasny..termed this process 'olation' and postulated that hydroxy groups react immediately with acid whereas 'ol-groups' only react after deolation. **1969** T. C. THORSTENSEN *Pract. Leather Technol.* viii. 120 At higher temperatures there is greater fixation of the chrome tanning compound by the hide protein and greater olation of the chrome complexes. **1974** D. NICHOLLS *Inorganic Complexes* iii. 26 The hydroxo-aquo complexes may combine together in a process known as *olation*.

Hence (as back-formations) **o'late** *v. intr.*, to form an ol group or compound; **o'lated** *ppl. a.*

1931 *Jrnl. Physical Chem.* XXXV. 45 The hydroxo groups then 'olated', resulting in the formation of large aggregates, eventually reaching colloidal size. *Ibid.*, It would be expected..that the greater the degree of olation, the more sluggish would be the reaction of the complex olated ion. **1936** E. W. MERRY *Chrome Tanning Process* i. 9 Chrome alum solutions prepared hot are green and contain strongly olated chromium compounds. *Ibid.*, It is not possible to forecast what will be the actual basicity of the chrome salts ..or the extent to which they will olate. **1941** [see above]. **1945** MCLAUGHLIN & THEIS *Chem. Leather Manuf.* xiv. 416 A chrome compound is said to be 'olated' when one or more of its hydroxyl groups is held between two chromium atoms.

Olbers' paradox (ˈɒlbəz). *Astr.* [named after H. W. M. *Olbers* (1758-1840), German astronomer, who propounded it in *Astron. Jahrb.* (1826) 110.] The paradox that if stars were distributed evenly (in sufficient numbers) throughout an infinite static universe, the sky should be as bright at night as in the daytime, owing to the fact that whilst the apparent brightness of individual stars decreases with distance the number of stars increases in the same proportion.

1952 H. BONDI *Cosmol.* iii. 23 Olbers' paradox does not arise in a static universe in which, roughly speaking, the stars did not start to radiate until some moment which can be determined..to have been between 10^8 and 10^{10} years ago. **1969** ROSSER & MCCULLOCH *Relativity & High Energy Physics* vi. 131 Olbers' paradox can be resolved by the fact that the distant stars..are going away from the earth at high speeds (the expanding universe).

old (əʊld), *a.* (*adv.*, *sb.*¹) Forms: see below. [Com. Teut.: Early ME. *old*:—OE. *ald* (WSax. *eald*) = OFris. and OS. *ald* (MDu. *out*, *oud-*, Du. *oud*, MLG. *old*, LG. *oll*), OHG. (MHG., Ger.) *alt*:—OTeut. **alđo-z*, orig. a ppl. formation (corresp. to Gr. forms in -τός, L. *-tus*) from OTeut. vb. stem *al-*, Goth. *al-an* to grow up, ON. *al-a* to nourish, bring up, cognate with L. *al-ĕre* to nourish: cf. COLD *a.* OTeut. **alđoz* was thus app. = 'grown up, adult', corresp. in form to L. *altus* grown or become great, tall. ON. wanted the positive (supplied by *gamall*; comp. *ellri*, superl. *ellztr*); Goth. had the related derivative form *alþeis* (:—**alþijoz*). The original OE. form *ald* (also in Early WSax. and Early Kent.), remained in Anglian, and has come down in Northern dial., in later Sc. written *awld*, *auld*, in north. Eng. dial. *aud*, *aad*, *ahd*. In midl. Eng., OE. *ald*, lengthened to *āld*, became regularly *ōld* (cf. *bold*, *cold*, *hold*, *sold*, *told*), which remains the standard Eng. form (in ME. also written *oold*, in dial. *wold*, *ould*, *owld*, *ole*, *owd*). The WSax. and Kentish *eald* came down into ME. as *eald*, *yeald*, *yald*, *eeld*, *eld*; it is now extinct (but cf. ELD *a.*). The original comparative and superlative, still retained in particular uses, are ELDER (:—**aldira*), ELDEST, q.v.; in the general sense these have been superseded by *older*, *oldest* (see also ALDER, ALDEST). Derivatives are †ALD, †ALDER *sb.*², ALDERMAN, ELD *sb.*², *v.*, ELDER *sb.*³]

A. Illustration of Forms.

α. 1-5 (*Sc.* -6) **ald**, (4-5 **alde**, 3-4 **hald**, 4 **alld**, **halde**), 4-5, *Sc.* 4-, **auld**, (4 **aulde**, **hauld**, 5-6 **awld**, **-e**, 7- *north. Eng. dial.* **awd**, **aud**, **aad**).

c **725** *Corpus Gloss.* 173 *Anus*, ald uuif. *Ibid.* 1854 *Senex*, ald. *a* **800** *Leiden Gloss.* 132 *Quotus*, hu ald; *totus*, suæ ald. *c* **825** *Vesp. Psalter* cxlviii. 12 Alde mid ȝingrum. *c* **875** *O.E. Chron.* an. 871 Sidroc eorl..se alda. *c* **950** *Lindisf. Gosp.* Luke i. 18 Ic forðon am ald. *c* **1200** ORMIN 126 Till þatt teȝȝ wærenn alde. *c* **1205** LAY. 2959 þe alde king. *a* **1250** *Owl & Night.* 1183 For þine alde niþe. *a* **1300** *Cursor M.* 9224 (Cott.) Four hundret winter ald [*Fairf.* halde, *Trin.* old]. *Ibid.* 12578 (Cott.) Ar he was tuelue yeir alld [*Gött.* ald, *Fairf.* alde]. **1340** *Ayenb.* 104 He ijs ald. *Ibid.* 219 A guod ald wyf. *c* **1375** *Sc. Leg. Saints, Egipciane* 413, I ame auld & febil bathe. *c* **1400** MAUNDEV. (Roxb.) iv. 12 In ane alde castell. *a* **1430** *Morte Arth.* 279 As awlde mene telles. **1549** *Compl. Scot.* i Oure ald enemies. **1588** A. KING tr. *Canisius' Catech.* H ij, Ye awld kallendar. **1611** MURE *Misc. Poems* i. 6 In auld Neptunus' source. **1790** BURNS *Tam o' Shanter* 15 Auld Ayr, wham ne'er a town surpasses.

β. 1-4 **eald**, 3 **æld**, 2-4 **eld**, 3 **eold**, 4-5 **eeld**, **yeald**, **yald**, 4-5 **elde** (**helde**).

c **831** *Kentish Charter* in Sweet *O.E. Texts* 446, [An] eald hriðer. *c* **888** K. ÆLFRED *Boeth.* xxxix. §3 Sie eald ȝesceaft. *c* **1000** *Ags. Gosp.* Luke i. 18 Ic eom nu eald. *c* **1175** *Lamb. Hom.* 9 On þa ealde laȝe [*Ibid.*, on þan alde laȝe]. *c* **1200** *Moral Ode* 4 (Egerton MS.) þech ich beo a wintre eald, to ȝung ich eom at rede. *c* **1205** LAY. 7031 þe ȝunge wifmen & þe ælde [*c* 1275 holde]. *c* **1275** *Ibid.* 2916 In þan eolde [*c* **1205** holde] daiȝe hit was a borh riche. *c* **1290** *Becket* 195 in *S. Eng. Leg.* I. 112 Are it were seue ȝer eld. **1340** *Ayenb.* 7 Ine þe yalde laȝe. *Ibid.* 46 Ine þe ealde laȝe. **1388** WYCLIF *2 Kings* iv. 14 Hir hosebonde is eeld. *c* **1440** *Promp. Parv.* 137/2 Elde or olde [**1499** *ed. Pynson* eeld or worne].

γ. 3- **old**, (3-5 **hold**, 4-5 **-e**, **oold**, **-e**, 4 **owd**, 5 **ole**, **wold**, **-e**, 5-6 **olde**, 6 **owld**, **-e**, 6-7 **ould**, **-e**, 8-9 *dial.* **owd**, **wold**).

c **1200** *Trin. Coll. Hom.* 199 þenne hie beð old. *c* **1205** LAY. 3002 þe olde [*c* **1275** holde] kinge. **1340-70** *Alex. & Dind.* 327 Whan we holde waxen. **1382** WYCLIF *Gen.* xliii. 27 Ȝoure oold fader. *c* **1400** *Apol. Loll.* 23 þe Wold Testament. **1426** AUDELAY *Poems* 73 Weder that he were hold or ȝong. *c* **1440** *Promp. Parv.* 363/2 Ole, for-weryd, as clothys. **1447** BOKENHAM *Seyntys* (Roxb.) 45 The wolde law. *c* **1489** CAXTON *Sonnes of Aymon* 452 There nys noo man so oolde. **1530** PALSGR. 250/1 Oulde house that is in ruyne. **1537** WRIOTHESLEY *Chron.* (1875) I. 62 The owld judgment of this realme. *c* **1746** COLLIER (Tim Bobbin) *Lanc. Dial.* Wks. (1862) 56 There's on owd Cratchenly Gentlemon. **1864** TENNYSON *Northern Farmer* 49 A mowt 'a taäen owd Joänes. **1891** T. HARDY *Tess* (1900) 8/1 I've got a wold silver spoon and a wold graven seal at home.

B. Signification. I. Having lived or existed a relatively long time.

1. That has lived long; far advanced in years or life. Said of men, animals, and plants, also of their limbs, organs, faculties, etc. (Opposed to *young*; less emphatic than *aged*.) ***old one***, ***old un***, an elderly person, *esp.* one's father or mother; ***any old***: see ANY *a.* and *pron.* 1 e.

Often absolutely: ***the old*** (pl.), old people; so ***old and young***, ***young and old*** (sc. *people*).

Beowulf 357 þær Hroðgar sæt eald ond unhar. *c* **950** [see A. *α*]. *c* **1050** *Byrhtferth's Handboc* in *Anglia* (1885) VIII. 299 Swa byð se ealda man ceald & snofliȝ. *c* **1200** [see A. *γ*]. *c* **1205** [see A. *α*]. *a* **1250** *Owl & Night.* 25 On old stoc. *a* **1300** *Cursor M.* 2779 (Cott.) Yong and ald, bath barn and man. **1377** LANGL. *P. Pl.* B. xviii. 9 How osanna by orgonye olde folke songen. **1398** TREVISA *Barth De P.R.* vi. xiv. (1495) 198 Of suche foules..the yonge fede the olde whan thei maye not for aege gete theyr owne mete. *c* **1420** *Pallad. on Husb.* iv. 723 Of myddil age, and rather yonge then olde. **1484** CAXTON *Fables of Æsop* ii. vii, Now when I am bycome old and feble. **1508** DUNBAR *Tua Mariit Wemen* 277 Weil couth I..bler his ald E. **1568** E. TILNEY *Disc. Mariage* A iv b, An olde Gentleman called M. Erasmus. **1593** SHAKS. *Rich. II*, i. ii. 67 What shall good old Yorke there see But empty lodgings? **1597** MIDDLETON *Wisdom of Solomon* xii. 3 Bald, because old, old, because living long. **1610** SHAKS. *Temp.* iii. iii. 2 My old bones akes. **1632** MILTON *L'Allegro* 97 When..young and old com forth to play On a Sunshine Holyday. **1770** GOLDSMITH *Deserted Vill.* 20 The young contending as the old survey'd. **1784** COWPER *Task* iv. 172 Under an old oak's domestic shade. **1836** DICKENS *Pickw.* (1837) xx. 204 'It's the old 'un.' 'Old one,' said Mr. Pickwick. 'What old one?' 'My father, Sir,' replied Mr. Weller. **1838** T. THOMSON *Chem. Org. Bodies* 947 Old trees are frequently affected with a kind of ulcer. **1841-4** EMERSON *Ess., Love* Wks. (Bohn) I. 71 This passion.. though it begin with the young, yet forsakes not the old. **1854** C. M. YONGE *Heartsease* I. ii. xiv. 341 He is the great pride of the old folks at Worthbourne. **1864** TENNYSON *Grandmother* 18 All my children have gone before me, I am so old. **1868** *Haileyburian* I. 4/2 The Present won the toss, and completely 'penned' the 'old 'uns'. **1915** N. L. MCCLUNG *In Times like These* xix. 130 Did you ever visit an old folks' home and notice the different spirit shown by the men and women there? **1921** G. B. SHAW *Back to Methuselah* v. 253 There! What have you to say to that, old one? **1968** M. BRAGG *Without City Wall* xxvi. 237 In the Women's Institute the streamers, well hung..were still taut, after the Old Folks' Tea. **1976** *National Observer* (U.S.) 21 Feb. 2/4 Many more old folks would pay an additional charge for the protection in any one year than would enjoy its benefits against large doctor and hospital bills. And that's not the best way to harvest votes among the elderly.

fig. **1500-20** DUNBAR *Poems* xlvii. 9 As the ta lufe vaxis auld, The tothir dois incress moir kene. **1638** FORD *Fancies* v. iii, Night draws on, And quickly will grow old. **1822** SHELLEY *Triumph of Life* 538 Long before the day Was old.

b. Having the characteristics (physical or mental) of age.

1832 LYTTON *Eugene A.* i. vi, We grow old before our time. **1837** MARRYAT *Percival Keene* xix, You appear to have an old head upon very young shoulders. **1842** TENNYSON *Gardener's D.* 52 So old at heart, At such a distance from his youth in grief. **1866** G. MACDONALD *Ann. Q. Neighb.* i. (1878) 3 It is not a pleasant thing for a young man..to have an old voice. **1895** *Daily News* 30 Nov. 3/1 'Nowadays', she says, 'it is only old people who do not grow old'.

c. Used disparagingly; esp. *colloq.* and *slang* in such collocations as *old bloke*, *buffer*, *cat*, *codger*, *fogy*, *trot* (see these words). ***old bag*** (see BAG *sb.* 17); ***old boy***, used of an old man (see also as main entry); ***old geezer*** (see GEEZER); ***old girl***: see GIRL *sb.* 2 a; ***old pot***, one's father (chiefly *Austral.*); ***old trot*** (see TROT *sb.*²); ***old trout*** [perh. var. of TROT *sb.*² infl. by TROUT *sb.*¹ 4], *colloq.* applied to an old woman.

1508 DUNBAR *Tua Mariit Wemen* 126, I dar nought keik to the knaip that the cop fillis, For eldnyng of that ald schrew. **1596** SHAKS. *Tam. Shr.* I. ii. 80 An old trot with ne're a tooth in her head. *a* **1625** FLETCHER *Hum. Lieut.* III. iv, Peace, you old fool. **1820** SHELLEY *Hymn to Mercury* xv, Halloo! old fellow with the crooked shoulder! You grub those stumps? **1866** CARLYLE *Remin.* I. (1881) 186 An 'agricultural dandy' or old fogie, of Hibernian type. **1888** R. BOLDREWOOD *Robbery Under Arms* (Farmer), I used to laugh at him, and call him a regular old crawler. **1893** G. B. SHAW *Widowers' Houses* II. iv. 43 He wont have any news to break, poor old boy: she's read all the letters already. **1916** C. J. DENNIS *Songs Sentimental Bloke* 124 *The old pot*, the male parent (from 'Rhyming Slang', the 'old pot and pan'—the 'old man'). **1930** G. B. SHAW *Apple Cart* I. 3 When they found him he was melancholy mad, poor old boy; and he never got over it. *a* **1938** C. J. DENNIS in *Penguin Bk. Austral. Ballads* (1964) 234 Oh, w'erefore art you Romeo, young sir? Chuck yer ole pot, an' change yer moniker! **1938** N. MARSH *Artists in Crime* ix. 128 Miss Troy thought I was good enough to come here, even if my old pot did keep a bottle store. *Ibid.* 129 'What about Mr. Pilgrim?' 'Aw, he's different... I get on with him good-oh, even if his old pot is one of these lords. Him and me's cobbers.' **1956** B. GOOLDEN *Singing & Gold* viii. 172 Drives old ladies about the town and that... Wouldn't suit me though. Don't see yours truly rushing to carry the old trouts' shopping baskets. **1958** J. CANNAN *And be a Villain* vi. 140 The old trout wasn't exactly throwing her money about, he'd say. **1964** R. BRADDON *Year Angry Rabbit* x. 90 Too high and mighty for his old trout of a mum nowadays is young Gary. **1972** N. MARSH *Tied up in Tinsel* xviii. 197 'Er old pot was killed saving the colonel's life. **1974** L. THOMAS *Tropic of Ruislip* ii. 42 You could scare the old boy and he'll spill his tea. He spills things all the time.

d. Proverbs.

c **1470** ASHBY *Active Policy* 615 Aftur the oolde dogge the yonge whelpe barkes. **1631** BRATHWAIT *Whimzies, Hospitall-man* 45 There is none so desperately old but he hopes to live one yeere longer. **1668** DAVENANT *Man's the Master* I. i, As the proverb says, put an old cat to an old rat. **1691** R. CROMWELL *Let.* in *Eng. Hist. Rev.* (1898) XIII. 109 There is an old proverb 'old yong, yong old'. **1883** READE *Many a Slip* in *Harper's Mag.* Dec. 141/1 A man is as old as he feels, and a woman's as old as she looks.

2. *transf.* Belonging to, or characteristic of, old persons; of or pertaining to advanced life; esp. in ***old age***, the period of life of the old or advanced in years, the latter period of life, = AGE 6; also *absol.* and *attrib.*, as in ***old age pension***, etc.

13.. *Seuyn Sag.* (W.) 22 He that schal, in thin eld age, Benime the thin heritage. *c* **1380** WYCLIF *Serm.* Sel. Wks. I. 365 It was miracle þat so oold folk brouȝten forþ þis child in her olde daies. *c* **1430** *Hymns Virg.* 79 Lete us praie þat god send us paciens in oure olde age. **1500–20** DUNBAR *Poems* xxxvi. 27 Thair cumis ȝung airis, That his auld thrift settis on ane ess. **1605** SHAKS. *Lear* I. i. 190 Hee'l shape his old course, in a Country new. **1610** —— *Temp.* I. ii. 369 Ile racke thee with old Crampes. **1611** BIBLE *Gen.* xxv. 8 Abraham.. died in a good old age [WYCLIF in a good elde]. **1707** *Lond. Gaz.* No. 4354/4, 176*l.* per Ann. in Lease (most of which are very old Lives). **1813** SHELLEY *Q. Mab* II. 152 Old age and infancy Promiscuous perished. **1868** FREEMAN *Norm. Conq.* (1876) II. ix. 414 The great Earl.. died in a good old age. **1891** *Pall Mall G.* 18 Dec. 2/1 There is extreme reluctance to devote any of their earnings.. to ensuring an old-age annuity.

3. Of material things: Having existed long, long-made, that has been long in use. (Opposed to *new*.) Hence, Worn with age or long use, or deteriorated through the effects of time; worn out, decayed, dilapidated, shabby, stale, etc.; also, Discarded after long use, disused, gone out of use.

Absolutely: ***the old***, that which is old.

Beowulf 2763 Þær wæs helm moniȝ eald ond omiȝ. *c* **1000** *Ags. Gosp.* Matt. ix. 16 Ne deþ.. nan man niwes claðes scyp on eald reaf. *Ibid.* xiii. 52 Niwe þing and ealde. *c* **1200** *Trin. Coll. Hom.* 163 Ðe chireche cloðes ben to brokene and ealde. *c* **1300** *Havelok* 545 In an eld cloth wnden. **1382** WYCLIF *Matt.* ix. 17 Nether men senden newe wijne in to olde botelis. —— *Luke* v. 39 No man drynkinge old [TINDALE olde wine], wole anon newe; sothli he seith, The olde is the betere. **1454** *Test. Ebor.* (Surtees No. 30) 175 On of my ald gownes furred. **1542** *MS. Acc. St. John's Hosp., Canterb.*, Rec. for ij olde bee fattis iiij*d.* **1598** B. JONSON *Ev. Man in Hum.* I. ii, Drake's old ship at Deptford may sooner circle the world again. **1601** WEEVER *Mirr. Mart., Sir John Oldcastle* iv, Mans memorie, with new, forgets the old. **1670** DRYDEN *Almanzor* Prol. 27 They bring old iron and glass upon the stage. *a* **1800** COWPER *Needless Alarm* 53 They [sheep] gathered close around the old pit's brink. **1841** THACKERAY *Gt. Hoggarty Diamond* iv, Pale sherry, old port, and cut and come again. *a* **1902** *Mod.* A dealer in old books, old china, and old pictures. A very old book with iron clasps.

†**b.** In old clothes, shabby. *Obs. rare*⁻¹.

1596 SHAKS. *Tam. Shr.* IV. i. 140 There were none fine, but Adam, Rafe, and Gregory, The rest were ragged, old, and beggerly.

c. ***any old***: see ANY *a.* and *pron.* 1 e.

4. Of (any specified) age or length of existence: e.g. *How old? ten days old.* When used *attrib.* with a prec. numeral and sb. these are usually hyphened to *old* (*year* being used instead of *years*), as in *a six-months-old child, a two-year-old sheep*, etc. These attrib. forms are also used *absol.* as sbs.: e.g. *a flock of two-year-olds*.

The numeral and sb. were in OE. in genitive as an advb. determination of *eald*, e.g. *þritiȝes ȝeara eald* (cf. Ger. *drei tage alt, eins tags alt*, F. *âgé de trente ans*); but by the 12th c. the genitive inflexion was dropped; cf. quots. 1110–1200. See also b.

c **897** K. ÆLFRED *Gregory's Past. Care* xlix. 385 Ær he wæs ðritiȝes ȝeara eald. *c* **1000** ÆLFRIC *Gen.* xlvii. 8 And [Pharao] axode hyne hu eald he wære. **1110–1123** *O.E. Chron.* an. 1110 He [se mona] wæs.. feowertyne nihta eald. **1135–54** *Ibid.* an. 1135 Suilc als it uuore thre niht ald mone. *c* **1200** ORMIN 7675 Ȝho wass sextiȝ winnterr ald. *c* **1205** LAY. 301 He was fiftene ȝer ald. *c* **1330** R. BRUNNE *Chron. Wace* (Rolls) 3720 Er he were seuen ȝer old. *c* **1420** *Pallad. on Husb.* IV. 919 A she asse oon yer olde. **1535** COVERDALE *Gen.* xvii. 12 Euery manchilde when it is eight dayes olde, shalbe circumcyded. **1590** SHAKS. *Com. Err.* I. i. 45 My absence was not sixe moneths olde. *Ibid.* II. ii. 150 In Ephesus I am but two houres old. **1598** B. JONSON *Ev. Man in Hum.* III. iii, Your son is old enough to govern himself. **1672** LADY M. BERTIE in *12th Rep. Hist. MSS. Comm.* App. v. 26 Wee expect the new Dutches.. she is not fifteen yeare old. **1711** STEELE *Spect.* No. 11 ¶4 The Story you have given us is not quite two thousand Years Old. **1780** A. YOUNG *Tour Irel.* I. 182 A child 7 years old earns 1*d.* a day spinning. **1857** HUGHES *Tom Brown* II. i, I say, young fellow.. How old are you? **1872** RUSKIN *Fors Clav.* xxi. 7 A wall which was just eighteen hundred years old. **1892** *Daily News* 26 Feb. 5/7 A five-year-old girl. **1899** *Westm. Gaz.* 25 Nov. 6/2 Under the century-old trees.

absol. **1769** *St. James's Chron.* 10–11 Aug. 3/4 (Horse-race) Five-year-olds, 9 st. **1849** ALB. SMITH *Pottleton Leg.* (repr.) 27 Rising two-score-olds. **1855** TENNYSON *The Brook* 137 That was the four-year-old I sold the Squire.

b. The expression '*x* years old' may be preceded by a prep., as if it were a sb. phrase = 'the age of *x* years': e.g. 'a child of ten years old', 'from two years old and under', 'at, under, or over six months old'.

This construction appears first with *of*, which may possibly represent the OE. (and Com. Teut.) genitive phr., or the corresponding Fr. phr. with *de* (see note to 4), so that 'a child of *x* years old' might be orig. = 'a child old (in respect) of *x* years'. But there is a chronological gap between the two constructions, the earliest examples of the later being in *Cursor M.* In one instance, the oldest text has 'o tua yeir eild', i.e. 'of two years' *age*', in which the later MSS. substitute *old* or *eild*. But in another instance, the reading 'of thre ȝer alde' is evidently original. Whether this implies a confusion between *old, eld* adj. and *eld* sb., as app. in the Chaucer quot. which follows, or the existence of two forms derived from OE. *preora ȝeara eald*, viz. 'three year old', and 'of three year old', is not clear; but what is evident is that '*x* year(s) old' soon came to be taken in the lump as a sb. phr. which might be preceded by any prep., since we find *c* 1420 'from iij yere olde til x', and in the next cent. 'at nine months old' = 'at the age of nine months'.

A similar usage is found with *high, long, broad, deep*, etc. (which also in OE. were preceded by a genitive or accus. phr. of dimension); but there the const. with *of* appears to be later, and that with other preps less usual: see OF 39 b.

13.. *Cursor M.* 11566 (Cott.) Wit-in þe land left he noght an O tua yeir eild [*G.* eilde, *F.* old, *Tr.* olde] þat he ne was slan. *Ibid.* 10587 (Gött.) Þis may [*v.r.* maiden], bot of thre ȝere alde [*C.* old, *F.*, *Tr.* olde] was on þe grece [= stair] i ar of tald. *c* **1374** CHAUCER *Anel. & Arc.* 78 (Harl. 372) Yong was this Quene, of xx^ti yere of eeld [So 2 other MSS.; *Harl.* 7333, of xx^ti yere eld; *Digby*, of xx^ti yeer olde; so *Caxton*]. *c* **1420** *Pallad. on Husb.* IV. 734 Caluyng from iij yeer olde Til x is best. *c* **1470** HENRY *Wallace* II. 273 Hyr dochtir had of xij wokkis ald a knayff. **1582** N. T. (Rhem.) *Matt.* ii. 16 From tvvo yere old & vnder [1611 two yeares; WYCLIF, fro two ȝeer age and with ynne; TIND., *Geneva*, as many as were two yere old and vnder]. **1593** SHAKS. *2 Hen. VI*, IV. ix. 4, I was made a King, at nine months olde. **1594** —— *Rich. III*, II. iv. 28 He could gnaw a crust at two houres old. **1625** J. MEAD in Ellis *Orig. Lett.* Ser. I. III. 201 A young man under thirty years old. **1697** DRYDEN *Virg. Georg.* IV. 421 A Steer of two Years old. **1727** SWIFT *Gulliver* I. vi, Those intended for apprentices are dismissed at seven years old. **1818** SHELLEY *Rev. Islam* II. xxv, This child of twelve years old.

5. *fig.* Of long practice and experience *in* some specified matter or respect, or as an agent or qualified person of some kind; practised, experienced, skilled; also, in slang use, Clever, knowing.

c **1000** *Ælfric's Canons* §17 in Thorpe *Laws* II. 348 Na þæt ælc eald sy, ac þæt he eald sy on wisdome. *c* **1220** *Bestiary* 90 Old in hise sinnes dern. *c* **1315** SHOREHAM 52 The sevende ordre hys of the prest, And hys icleped the ealde, Bote nauȝt of ȝeres, ac of wyt. **1552** HULOET, Olde souldier, *veteranus*. **1588** SHAKS. *L.L.L.* II. i. 254 Thou art an old Louemonger, and speakest skilfully. **1638** FORD *Fancies* II. ii, My stars, I thank ye, for being ignorant, Of what this old-in-mischief can intend! *c* **1652** MILTON *Sonn. to Sir H. Vane*, Vane, young in yeares, but in sage counsell old. **1716** *Lond. Gaz.* No. 5412/3 Frances Green,.. an old Offender. **1722** DE FOE *Col. Jack* (1840) 232 The Germans were too old for us there. **1820** SHELLEY *Lett. to M. Gisborne* 140, I, an old diviner, who know well Every false verse of that sweet oracle. **1853** LYTTON *My Novel* VIII. ii, Old in vices, and mean of soul! **1881** JOWETT *Thucyd.* I. 152 The Athenians were old sailors and they were only beginners.

b. In various colloq. and slang phrases: as ***old bird***, a person who has become knowing through experience, *spec.* an experienced thief; ***old coon*** (see quot. 1877); ***old hand*** (see D. 4); ***old*** FILE, SOLDIER, STAGER; ***to be old*** DOG ***at*** (a thing).

1589 [see DOG *sb.*¹ 15 i]. **1711** SHAFTESB. *Charac.* (1737) I. 35 With the old Stagers no matter whom they meet in a Coach, 'tis always Good your Honour! or Good your Lordship! **1722** DE FOE *Col. Jack* (1840) 99 The Captain [was] an old soldier at such work. **1784** J. POTTER *Virtuous Villagers* II. 9 Philip, who is an old Robin, as the saying is, demurred to the business. **1785** CUMBERLAND *Observer* No. 107 ¶6 Uncle Antony was an old dog at a dispute. **1835** A. B. LONGSTREET *Georgia Scenes* 216 To be sure I will, my old coon—take it—take it, and welcome. **1852** C. W. H[OSKINS] *Talpa* 62 One word of advice from an 'old file'. **1862** *Punch* 1 Feb. 42/2, I guess them saucy Britishers Won't easy get to leeward Of such an all-fired smart old 'coon As William H. Seward. **1877** *Five Years' Penal Servitude* i. 32 In nine cases out of ten an 'old bird' would betray himself. **1877** BARTLETT *Dict. Amer.* (ed. 4) 436 'He's an old coon,' is said of one who is very shrewd; often applied to a political manager. **1890** W. A. WALLACE *Only a Sister?* 263 Evidently the master was an old bird, he carefully retraced his steps and bolted the door at the foot of the stairs.

6. In colloq. use: = Great, plentiful, abundant, excessive; 'grand'. Now chiefly after other appreciative adjs., as *good, grand, high*.

c **1440** *Bone Flor.* 681 Gode olde fyghtyng was there. **1590** TARLTON *News Purgat.*, Sunday, at masse, there was old ringing of bells. **1599** SHAKS. *Much Ado* v. ii. 98 Yonders old coile at home. *a* **1604** HANMER *Chron. Irel.* 123 *note*, If they [certain monks] were as fat in those daies as most of them proved after, there would have beene old frying. **1654** GAYTON *Pleas. Notes* II. iv. 50 When fifteen joines to Seventy, there's old doings (as they say), the Man and Wife fitting together like January and May day. **1664** COTTON *Scarron.* 104 There was old drinking and old singing And all the while the Bells were ringing. **1705** HICKERINGILL *Priest-cr.* II. Wks. 1716 III. 77 There was old Bandying, and Cursing, and Fighting, and Railing in abundance. **1814** SCOTT *Wav.* xviii, So there was old to do about ransoming the bridegroom. **1818** —— *Rob Roy* xxxii, 'Here's auld ordering and counter-ordering' muttered Garschattachin. **1825** BROCKETT *N.C. Gloss.* s.v., *Old-doings*, great sport, great feasting—an uncommon display of hospitality.

II. Belonging to former times or an earlier period as well as to the present; long established.

7. a. Dating far back into the past; of ancient origin; made or formed long ago; also *poet.* of things which have always existed, as elemental forces, etc.: Primeval. (In OE. and early ME. applied to the Creator.)

Beowulf 945 þæt hyre eald metod este wære bearn-ȝebyrdo. *c* **888** K. ÆLFRED *Boeth.* xiv. §2 Se ealda cwide is swiðe soð þe mon ȝefyrn cwæð. *c* **1205** LAY. 24885 Ane huse þe wes biclused faste an ald stanene weorc. **1340** *Ayenb.* 104 Me zayth he is ine heuene.. he ys ald and yknawe and ydred and yworþssiped and yloued. *c* **1350** *Alex. & Dind.* 798 Ȝoure docturus sain in sawus ful olde. *c* **1400** MAUNDEV. (Roxb.) iv. 12 Scho lies in ane alde castell. **1596** SHAKS. *Tam. Shr.* III. i. 80 Old fashions please me best. **1634** MILTON *Comus* 33 An old, and haughty Nation proud in Arms. **1667** —— *P.L.* I. 543 A shout that tore Hells Concave, and beyond Frighted the Reign of Chaos and old Night. **1732** POPE *Ess. Man* I. 158 Who knows but he, whose hand the lightning forms, Who heaves old Ocean, and who wings the storms? **1863** H. COX *Instit.* III. iv. 643 His office was as old as the time of the Conquest.

b. In personal or other particular reference (as with agent-noun, etc.): That has long stood in some relation to one; that has been such from of old; not new or recent. ***old pal***: an old friend, freq. with reference to association or collusion in business, *spec.* in phr. ***old pal's act*** (and variants), favour or cooperation based on prior acquaintance.

a **1000** *Juliana* 623 (Gr.) Wrecað ealdne nið. *a* **1225** *Leg. Kath.* 1380 Þe deore Drihtin..toc read to ure alde dusischipes. *c* **1440** *York Myst.* xxii. 63, I wolde now som mete wer sene For olde acqueyntaunce vs by-twene. *c* **1470** HENRY *Wallace* I. 7 Our ald ennemys cummyn of Saxonys blud. **1500–20** DUNBAR *Poems* lx. 68 To thy auld schervandis have an E, That lang hes lippinit into the. **1549** *Compl. Scot.* vi. 67 Corriandir, that is gude for ane ald hoste. **1706** *Wooden World Dissected* (1708) 19 Not purely for their presumptuous Assumption of his proper Title, but out of an old Grutch. *a* **1727** RAMSAY *Auld Langsyne* 1 Should auld acquaintance be forgot Tho' they return with scars? **1840** R. H. DANA *Bef. Mast* xxvi. 86 Many a good ducking in the surf, did he get to pay up old scores. **1849** MACAULAY *Hist. Eng.* iv. I. 505 In satisfaction of an old debt due to him from the crown. **1875** JOWETT *Plato* (ed. 2) I. 81, I have a claim upon you as an old friend of your father. *a* **1966** M. ALLINGHAM *Cargo of Eagles* (1968) ii. 26 The Old Pal's Act isn't confined to you public school types above stairs now. **1972** E. GRIERSON *Confessions of Country Magistrate* i. 7 What is this mysterious process by which the man in the street is suddenly transformed into the magistrate on the bench? How, if not by the Old Pals' Act or the Signs of the Zodiac, is the miracle accomplished? **1973** *Times* 23 May 2/3 All these favours given by the Post Office on the old pals network. **1975** T. HEALD *Deadline* ii. 18 The old pals act will operate as far as the press is concerned.

c. Known or familiar from of old, or because of former association.

c **888** K. ÆLFRED *Boeth.* xxxix. §13 Healdað þa tunglu þa ealdan sibbe þe hi on ȝesceapne wæron. **1121** *O.E. Chron.* an. 1003 He teah forð þa his ealdan wrenceas. *c* **1386** CHAUCER *Man of Law's T.* 269 O Sathan enuious..Wel knowestow to wommen the olde way. **1588** SHAKS. *L.L.L.* v. ii. 417 Yet I haue a tricke Of the old rage. **1598** —— *Merry W.* IV. ii. 22 Your husband is in his olde lunes [*1st fol.* lines] againe. **1601** —— *Jul. C.* v. i. 63 *Ant.* Old Cassius still. **1784** COWPER *Tirocin.* 737 Following her old plan. **1820** SHELLEY *Hymn to Mercury* lxxxvii, While he conceived another piece of fun, One of his old tricks. **1855** MACAULAY *Hist. Eng.* xix. IV. 377 The old men had again met in the old hall. **1865** LIGHTFOOT *Galatians* (1874) 22 The Apostle had been travelling over old ground.

d. Phr. (*as*) ***old as the hills***, exceedingly old; perh. in allusion to Job xv. 7 'Art thou the first man that was born? or wast thou made before the hills?'

1819 *Metropolis* I. iii. 58, I thought he was going to make a die of it! Why he's as old as the Hills. **1820** SCOTT *Monastery* ix. 251 If you were as good a priest as the Pope, and as old as the hills to boot, you shall not carry away Mary's book without her leave. **1821** BYRON *Let.* 1 Oct. in *Works* (1901) V. 385 The Pulci Style, which the fools in England think was invented by Whistlecraft—it is as old as the hills in Italy. **1849** DICKENS *Dav. Copp.* (1850) xv. 156 All the angles and corners, and carvings and mouldings, and quaint little panes of glass, and quainter little windows, though as old as the hills, were as pure as any snow that ever fell upon the hills. **1898** *Tit-Bits* 23 Apr. 73/3 The superstition.. is almost as old as the hills. **1914** 'BARTIMEUS' *Naval Occasions* ix. 66 'Sides, she's as old as the hills. **1937** A. HUXLEY *Ends & Means* iv. 25 A violent revolution cannot achieve anything except the inevitable results of violence, which are as old as the hills. **1954** B. & R. NORTH tr.

Duverger's Pol. Parties II. i. 255 Dictatorship is as old as the hills. **1956** A. WILSON *Anglo-Saxon Att.* I. i. 14 Fifty-five must seem as old as the hills to a girl like you.

e. ***the old story*** (and variants), a familiar tale or excuse (usu. with a connotation of implausibility).

1700 [see STORY *sb.*[1] 6 a]. **1859** GEO. ELIOT *Adam Bede* I. iv. 75 'What! father's forgot the coffin?' 'Ay, lad, th' old tale; but I shall get it done.' **1898** J. D. BRAYSHAW *Slum Silhouettes* 28 'What brought 'em to that?' Oh, the old story—liftin' their little finger. **1919** R. FROST *Let.* 4 Jan. (1964) 80 Pelle was good reading. But none of it was any news. Not a phrase but was old story. **1938** E. AMBLER *Cause for Alarm* xi. 184 Too much or too little—empty stomachs or overfed ones—the old, old story.

8. Used as an expression of familiarity, **a.** in addressing or speaking of persons with whom one has an acquaintance of some standing, or whom one treats as such, as in the colloq. ***old boy, chap, fellow, man***; ***old bean***: see BEAN *sb.* 6 e; ***old boy***: see also BOY *sb.*[1] 5; ***old dear***: usu. of a woman (cf. DEAR *a.*[1] and *sb.*[2] B); ***old fellow*** (U.S.): an overseer or 'boss'; ***old fruit***: see FRUIT *sb.* 2 e; ***old girl***: see GIRL *sb.* 2 a; ***old hen*** (see HEN *sb.* 5 a); ***old horse*** (cf. HORSE *sb.* 4); ***old hoss***: see HORSE *sb.* 4, HOSS 2; ***old lady***: a girl or woman, esp. one's wife or mother; also *transf.* of a man whose behaviour resembles that of an old lady; ***old son*** (cf. SON *sb.*[1] 3 b); ***old sport***: see SPORT *sb.*[1]; ***old thing***: see THING *sb.*[1]; ***old top*** (cf. TOP *sb.*[2]). **b.** with names of places which one has long known, esp. of one's native country: see also 12 b. Often in the collocation ***good old***, a colloq. or cant expression of commendation or appreciation. (Cf. 6.)

a. 1588 SHAKS. *Tit. A.* IV. ii. 121 Looke how the blacke slaue smiles vpon the father; As who should say, old Lad I am thine owne. **1711** STEELE *Spect.* No. 17 ¶3, I never hear him so lavish of his fine things, as upon old Nell Trott. **1808** SCOTT *Marm.* VI. Introd. 81 England was merry England, when Old Christmas brought his sports again. **1898** DOYLE *Trag. Korosko* ix. 280 There they go giving the alarm! Good old Camel Corps!

1601 SHAKS. *Twel. N.* III. ii. 9 Did she see thee the while, old boy, tell me that. **1872** *Punch* 24 Aug. 81/2 A fellow who can take a joke good-naturedly like you can, old boy. **1892** ANSTEY *Voces Populi* Ser. II. 37 Never mind, old chap. **1880** [see DEAR *a.*[1] and *sb.*[2] B]. **1955** J. THOMAS *No Banners* ii. 23 Remember the old dear at La Souterraine who fed us on bread and ham and cheese and a bottle of wine? **1825** C. M. WESTMACOTT *Eng. Spy* I. 136, I say, old fellow. **1901** S. E. WHITE *Blazed Trail* xxvii. 187 He was intensely loyal to his 'Old Fellows' [= 'bosses' of lumber camps]. **1906** WODEHOUSE *Love among Chickens* v. 63 Garney, old horse, you're a marvel. You think of everything. We'll buckle to right away. **1924** —— *Ukridge* i. 12 It's a wearing life, laddie. A wearing life, old horse. **1942** *R.A.F. Jrnl.* 3 Oct. 11 'Well, old horse,' I thought, 'You're going to be disappointed.' **1960** A. CHRISTIE *Adventure of Christmas Pudding* 209 He said with a remarkable lack of medical decorum: 'That you, Poirot, old horse?' **1976** 'A. HALL' *Kobra Manifesto* ii. 24, I wish someone had told me, old horse. **1836** DICKENS *Let.* 21 Mar. (1965) I. 141 Let me have particular word how your rheumatism is, old lady. **1859** MRS. GASKELL *Lett.* (1966) 545 You must not send us any more work to do, old lady, for Caroline is slow, & there is a great deal to do. **1871** E. EGGLESTON *Hoosier Schoolmaster* (1872) xvii. 134 Here's the old lady and Shocky. **1914** CONRAD *Chance* II. i. 244 The old lady's first-rate, sir, thank you. **1932** D. L. SAYERS *Have his Carcase* xii. 152 'There, there, Mother,' muttered Henry... 'Bit of a staggerer for the old lady, this.' **1938** H. NICOLSON *Diary* 10 Nov. (1966) 378 This memorandum was not at all liked by the old ladies of the Executive. **1967** C. HIMES *Black on Black* (1973) 133 A man called T-bone Smith sat.. looking at television with his old lady, Tang. **1976** *New Yorker* 17 May 34/2 It is a sign that you wish to shave your old lady. **1870** 'MARK TWAIN' *Let.* 22 Mar. (1917) I. 172, I can make the money without lecturing. Therefore, old man, count me out. **1885** *Punch* 3 Jan. 4/1 You'll be thinking I've got the blue-mouldies, old man. **1890** R. BOLDREWOOD *Col. Reformer* (1891) 204 Take another tumbler, old man. **1916** 'TAFFRAIL' *Pincher Martin* viii. 142 'Ow are we, ole son? Feelin' a bit squeamish?' **1951** S. SPENDER *World within World* ii. 66 Do you know, old son, this is the first time you've ever talked with me that I haven't been completely bored? **1974** L. DEIGHTON *Spy Story* xx. 218 You're doing well, old son. **1974** N. FREELING *Dressing of Diamond* 41 Right then, old son. **1912** *Collier's* 28 Sept. 19/1 'Tough luck, old top,' he muttered. **1915** WODEHOUSE *Something Fresh* ii. 24, I say, Dickie, old top, I want to see you about something devilish important. **1932** A. J. WORRALL *Eng. Idioms* 56, I say, old top! Do you like these?

b. 1596 SHAKS. *Tam. Shr.* I. ii. 49 What happie gale Blowes you to Padua heere, from old Verona? **1659** D. PELL *Impr. Sea* 140, I may take upon mee to tell old England. **1732** BERKELEY *Alciphr.* II. §7 Hath not old England subsisted for many ages without the help of your notions? **1785** BURNS *Cotter's Sat. Nt.* xix, From scenes like these old Scotia's grandeur springs. **1808** SCOTT *Marm.* VI. Introd. 68 Nor failed old Scotland to produce, At such high-tide, her savoury goose. **1844** ALB. SMITH *Adv. Mr. Ledbury* (1856) I. xii. 90 There's old Gravesend!

c. In trivial use with connotations of familiarity and in jocular and mildly disparaging senses of persons and things.

1898 *Westm. Gaz.* 1 July 2/2 The lawyers in the House have had what.. we may be allowed to call a high old time. **1905** *Smart Set* Sept. 117/2 No one else is going to run off with your old car. **1913** F. H. BURNETT *T. Tembarom* xxxiv. 438 Whatever happens, you are both fixed all right... Whatever old thing happens. *a* **1917** E. A. MACKINTOSH *War, the Liberator* (1918) 91, I always wondered If our old barrage could Be half as bloody good As the Staff said it would. **1938** M. K. RAWLINGS *Yearling* i. 3 'There'll come a little old drizzly rain before night-fall,' he thought. **1942** Z. N. HURSTON in A. Dundes *Mother Wit* (1973) 28/2, I had done.. cooked you a great big old cake. **1945** *Tee Emm* (Air Ministry) V. 38 Getting the 'general impression'.. to register in the old brain-box. **1949** B. A. BOTKIN *Treas. S. Folklore* p. xx, It is a land where the word 'old'—the Old South,.. Old Man So-and-So, little old this-and-that—are terms of affection and pride. **1965** J. BINGHAM *Fragment of Fear* iv. 49 'I have been successful.'.. 'Good old you!' **1971** P. O'DONNELL *Impossible Virgin* i. 12 When you look in poor old Tina's tum there's just a grotty old mish-mash of bits and pieces. **1971** D. FRANCIS *Bonecrack* viii. 101 'They didn't take my advice.' 'Silly old them.'

9. Applied to the devil, **a.** orig. in reference to his primeval character; in OE. *se ealda* (= 'the old one'); also in particular appellations, as ***old serpent, dragon, enemy, adversary***, etc.

a **1000** *Leás.* 32 (Grein) Se ealda. *a* **1200** *Moral Ode* 285 Belsebub þe ealde. *c* **1200** *Trin. Coll. Hom.* 191 þe alde neddre þe bipehte eue and adam. *c* **1230** *Hali Meid.* 15 Nu bihalt te alde feond. **1382** WYCLIF *Rev.* xx. 2 The olde serpent, that is the deuel. **1629** MILTON *Nativity* 168 Th' old Dragon under ground. **1638** SIR T. HERBERT *Trav.* (ed. 2) 10 Soyling their hellish carkasses with juyce.. or what the old imposter infatuates them with. **1822** HOGG *Perils of Man* III. 38 Cuffed about by the 'auld thief', as they styled him.

b. So in various jocose appellations, as ***the old one, the old*** GENTLEMAN (*in black*); ***old*** HARRY, NICK, SCRATCH, etc. Also ***the old boy*** (see BOY *sb.*[1] 6).

1668 R. L'ESTRANGE *Vis. Quev.* (1708) 84 They were all sent to Old Nick. **1700** T. BROWN *Wks.* (1760) III. 102, I know not who'll take em for saints, but the old gentleman in black. *c* **1746** COLLIER (Tim Bobbin) *Gloss.*, *Owd Harry, Owd Nick*, names for the devil. **1762** SMOLLETT *L. Greaves* II. x, He must have sold himself to Old Scratch. **1785** BURNS *Addr. to Deil* i, O thou! whatever title suit thee, Auld Hornie, Satan, Nick, or Clootie. **1824** *Hist. Gaming Houses* 51 He would not stick at playing up Old Harry in every possible shape and manner. **1825** J. NEAL *Bro. Jonathan* I. 253 His Master.. the Old One. **1894** ASTLEY *50 Years Life* I. 213 The balls did whistle round like 'old Billy'.

III. Belonging to an age or period now past away; ancient; former.

10. Of or pertaining to the distant past; belonging to antiquity or to a bygone age; ancient, bygone, olden. (Opposed to *modern*.)

c **1000** *Ags. Gosp.* Luke ix. 8 Sume sædon eald witeȝa aras. *c* **1000** *Ags. Ps.* lxxvi. 5 (Gr.) þa ic ealde daȝas eft ȝeþohte. *a* **1067** in Kemble *Cod. Dipl.* IV. 202 Swa he on ældum timum ȝelæȝd wæs. *c* **1200** ORMIN 13724 þatt alde follc Off Godess hallȝhe lede. *c* **1205** LAY. 2916 A þan holde dawen [*c* **1275** eolde daiȝe]. **1340** *Ayenb.* 124 An ald filosofe þet hette platoun. **1382** WYCLIF *Matt.* v. 21 ȝee han herde that it is said to olde men [1388 elde men, 1526 TIND. vnto them off the old tyme, 1611 by them of old tyme]. ? *a* **1400** *Morte Arth.* 13 Elders of alde tyme. *c* **1425** LYDG. *Assembly of Gods* 294 Olde poetys sey she bereth the heruest horne. **1590** L. LLOYD *Diall Daies* 8 The old antient Romanes had.. certaine ceremonies. **1591** SHAKS. *1 Hen. VI*, I. ii. 56 The nine Sibyls of old Rome. **1635** SWAN *Spec. M.* ii. §3 (1643) 32 The old ancient order of the yeare. **1671** MILTON *P.R.* III. 178 The Prophets old, who sung thy endless raign. **1728** POPE *Dunc.* II. 144 A shaggy Tap'stry, worthy to be spread On Codrus' old, or Dunton's modern bed. **1784** COWPER *Task* v. 217 Tubal.. the Vulcan of old times. **1809** W. IRVING *Knickerb.* VII. ix. (1820) 513 The customs and manners that prevailed in the 'good old times'. **1842** TENNYSON *Golden Year* 65 Old writers push'd the happy season back.

b. Relating to past times: dealing with antiquity.

a **900** CYNEWULF *Crist* 1396 Nu ic ða ealdan race anforlæte hu þu æt ærestan yfle ȝehoȝdes. *c* **1330** R. BRUNNE *Chron.* (1810) 1, In Saynt Bede bokes writen er stories olde. **1375** BARBOUR *Bruce* I. 17 Aulde storys that men redys. **1667** MILTON *P.L.* XI. 386 Wherever stood City of old or modern Fame. **1820** SHELLEY *Œdipus* I. 42 Grasshoppers that live on noonday dew, And sung, old annals tell, as sweetly too.

c. Proper to antiquity or a bygone age; of ancient character, form, or appearance; antique.

c **1381** CHAUCER *Parl. Foules* 19 It happede me for to beholde Vp on a bok was wrete with letteris olde. **1573–80** BARET *Alv.* O 69 Men curious in vsing old and ancient wordes.. *Antiquarii homines.* **1601** SHAKS. *Twel. N.* II. iv. 44 O fellow come, the song we had last night: Marke it Cesario, it is old and plaine. **1709** POPE *Ess. Crit.* 324 Some by old words to fame have made pretence, Ancients in phrase. **1899** *Westm. Gaz.* 11 May 4/2 What they call the old blue, the shade seen in old enamelling.

d. Associated with ancient times (esp. with classical antiquity); renowned in history; esp. in poetry, as an epithet with proper names.

c **1631** MILTON *Arcades* 98 On old Lycæus or Cyllene hoar. **1710** POPE *Windsor For.* 316 From old Belerium to the northern main. **1820** SHELLEY *Witch of Atlas* lvii, To glide adown old Nilus, when he threads Egypt and Æthiopia. **1845** M. PATTISON *Ess.* (1889) I. 10 It is the old historical lands of Europe that the lover of history longs to explore.

11. Belonging to an earlier period (of time, one's life, etc.) or to the earlier or earliest of two or more periods, times, or stages; pertaining to an earlier condition of things; possessed, occupied, practised, etc. at a former time. (Opposed to *new*.) See also *old light(s* LIGHT *sb.* 6 d), *old school* (SCHOOL *sb.* 5 b), *old tenor* (TENOR *sb.*[1] 1 c).

a **1000** *Phenix* 321 þonne he ȝewiteð wongas secan his ealdne eard of þisse eþel-tyrf. *a* **1000** *Elene* 1266 (Gr.) ȝeoȝuð is ȝecyrred, ald onmedla. *c* **1375** *Sc. Leg. Saints* ix. (*Bertholomeus*) 140 Mychtyly he put hym owte of his ald seinȝnery. **1508** DUNBAR *Flyting* 320 Thow.. geris me.. thair ald sin with new schame certify. **1638** SIR T. HERBERT *Trav.* (ed. 2) 93 He projects the recovery of his old Eparchy of Brampore. *c* **1647** MILTON *Forcers of Conscience* 20 New Presbyter is but Old Priest writ Large. **1802** WORDSWORTH *Resol. & Indep.* iii, The pleasant season did my heart employ: My old remembrances went from me wholly. **1842** TENNYSON *Morte d'Arthur* 240 The old order changeth, yielding place to new. **1893** MAX MÜLLER *Theosophy* xii. (1899) 401 In order to bring his old Jewish belief into harmony with his new philosophical convictions.

b. That was or has been (the thing spoken of) at a former time.

1571 *Satir. Poems Ref.* xxvii. 54 Ald feyis ar sindle faythfull freindis fund. **1647** *Galway Arch.* in *10th Rep. Hist. MSS. Comm.* App. v. 496 Sherriffes and ould Sheriffes to goe in their blacke gownes. **1847–9** HELPS *Friends in C.* (1851) I. 2 Ellesmere the great lawyer, also an old pupil of mine. **1894** HALL CAINE *Manxman* III. xix. 189 His old master, the college friend of his father.

c. Prefixed to the name of a language, to denote an early period in its history, or the earliest of several periods, preceding that usu. called *middle* (see MIDDLE *a.* 4 b), as in *Old English* (see ENGLISH *sb.* 1 b), *Old Norse* (see NORSE *sb.* 3), *Old Prussian* (see OLD PRUSSIAN *sb.* b). Abbrev. O (see O 5 b).

d. Prefixed to a sb. or adj. to denote a former member of a particular institution or society, esp. a public school.

1824 M. R. MITFORD *Our Village* I. 147 One meets with an old Etonian, who retains his boyish love for that game [*sc.* cricket]. **1848** C. H. NEWMARCH *Recollections of Rugby* i. 1 'Oh! mihi præteritos referat si Jupiter annos,' is an exclamation, in which, remembering.. a duck hunt at Swift's, every old Rugbæan will, I hope, most heartily concur. **1857** *Manx Sun* 4 July in *Geo. Eliot Lett.* (1954) II. 337 The writer is a gentleman of our own acquaintance, an old Cantab. **1870** *Wellingtonian* May 152 The above Match proved a very exciting one.. inasmuch as it was only won by two wickets by the old Wellingtonians. **1892** (*title*) Eton of old.. by an Old Colleger. **1902** S. A. BARNETT in H. Barnett *Canon Barnett* (1918) II. xxxiv. 70 The 'Old Northeyites' has kept the educational side well in front. *Ibid.* 71 The 'Old Dalgleishers'—whose special feature is the Easter expedition—enjoyed it for the eighth year in succession. **1914** 'I. HAY' *Knight on Wheels* (ed. 2) xviii. 172 Each happened to be wearing an Old Studleian tie, so common ground was established at once. **1920** GALSWORTHY *In Chancery* I. iv. 42 He went out to dinner alone—an old Malburian [*sic*] dinner. **1936** G. M. YOUNG *Victorian England* xiv. 96 The Old Giggleswickian was not yet a named variety. **1964** C. MACKENZIE *My Life & Times* III. 52 Henry Cruft had been at Eton and then.. sent to Shrewsbury. He still considered himself an Old Etonian. *Ibid.* 126 Cyril Bailey.. was an Old Pauline who had left before I went to St Paul's in 1894. **1967** V. CANNING *Python Project* iii. 46 He.. straightened his Old Etonian tie. **1970** P. DICKINSON *Seals* i. 11 His Old Etonian tie was knotted round a starched white collar. **1975** *Listener* 6 Feb. 164/1 The son of an Army officer and an Old Harrovian.

12. Distinguishing the thing spoken of from something of the same kind newer or more recent: Of earlier date, prior in time or occurrence, former, previous. ***Old Year's Day***, the last day of the old year.

c **890** *O.E. Chron.* an. 885 Se Hloþwiȝ was Carles broþur ..se Hloþwiȝ was þæs aldan Carles sunu. *c* **1175** *Lamb. Hom.* 87 þes dei.. on þere alde laȝe. *c* **1200** *Vices & Virtues* 27 Oðer newe mone betere ðan æld-mone. **1387** TREVISA *Higden* (Rolls) VII. 407 Al holy writt, þe elde [*v.r.* olde] testament and þe newe. *c* **1460** FORTESCUE *Abs. & Lim. Mon.* ix. (1885) 128 Thai shulde than be vndir a Prince double so myghty as was thair old prince. **1548–9** (Mar.) *Bk. Com. Prayer, Baptism*, Graunte that the olde Adam.. maye so be buried, that the newe man may be raised vp agayne. **1590** SHAKS. *Mids. N.* I. i. 4 Foure happy daies bring in Another Moon! but oh, me thinkes, how slow This old Moon wanes. **1611** BIBLE Transl. Pref. 1 The making of a new Law for the abrogating of an old. **1671** MILTON *P.R.* IV. 278 All the schools Of Academics old and new. **1849** GROTE *Greece* II. lxvii. (1862) VI. 34 The gradual transition of what is called the Old Comedy into the Middle and New Comedy. **1888** KIPLING *Wee Willie Winkie* (1889) 6 The idea that he shared a great secret.. kept Wee Willie Winkie.. virtuous for three weeks. Then the Old Adam broke out, and he made.. a 'camp-fire' at the bottom of the garden. **1976** *Listener* 26 Feb. 232/1 The best way to keep evil and the old Adam down was to flog the child.

b. With names of countries: Known or inhabited at an earlier period, as ***Old England*** (hence ***Old Englander***), ***Old France, Old Spain*** (opposed to the American colonies of *New England, France, Spain*; now only *hist.*), and similarly in modern colonial use, ***the old country, old home*** = Great Britain; also applied to a (person's) country of origin other than Great Britain, *spec.* (occas. in *pl.*) to the countries of Europe, the 'old world'; hence ***old-countryman***; ***Old Commonwealth***: Canada, Australia, and New Zealand (cf. NEW COMMONWEALTH); ***the Old Dominion***: see DOMINION 2 b; ***Old South***, the southern states of the U.S. before the civil war of 1861–5; ***Old World***, the Eastern Hemisphere, as opposed to the New World of America. (In *Old England* and the like, there is often a blending with this of sense 8.)

c **1596** DONNE *Poems* (1912) I. 76 If you from spoyle of th'old worlds farthest end. **1647** WARD *Simp. Cobler* 43 Hee that prizes not Old England Graces, as much as New England Ordinances. **1755** MAGENS *Insurances* I. 393 W. H. Master of the Ship called St. George, belonging to London in old England. **1763** *Ann. Reg.* 121 Bills of exchange drawn by the government of Canada on that of Old France. **1780** *Ibid.* 213 Newly arrived from Old Spain. **1782** 'J. H. ST.

JOHN DE CRÈVECŒUR' *Lett. from Amer. Farmer* i. 3 A person who hath been to Paris,..and who hath seen so many fine things up and down the old countries. **1796** F. BAILY *Jrnl. Tour N. Amer.* 25 Dec. (1856) 172 The scenery..so very different from what we had been used to in the *old* country. **1812** *Examiner* 28 Dec. 826/1 General Miranda had sailed.. for Old Spain. **1817** J. BRADBURY *Trav. Amer.* 321 It gives them an opportunity of making enquiries respecting the 'old country'. **1828** *Amer. Q. Rev.* IV. 211 Even the illiterate in our country will distinguish an Englishman by his pronunciation, and will designate him as an 'old countryman'. **1837** HT. MARTINEAU *Soc. Amer.* III. 95 They are readers: their imaginations live in the Old World. **1840** *Southern Lit. Messenger* VI. 241/1 More of Old England is left in the hearts of the Old Dominion than in all the states beside, save [etc.]. **1844** MRS. HOUSTON *Yacht Voy. Texas* II. 127 Farming details which apply..to practice in the 'Old Country'. **1848** BARTLETT *Dict. Amer.* 239 *Old Countryman*, a native of England, Scotland, Ireland, or Wales. **1873** *Harper's Mag.* July 271/1 Never in her most boastful days did the old South, under her cherished system of slave labor, produce better crops. **1884** *Boston Jrnl.* 30 Dec. 2/4 Our goods are crossing the water to keep alive old England. **1886** LOWELL *Wks.* (1890) VI. 143 It [the founding of Harvard] insured our intellectual independence of the Old World. *Ibid.* 156 The more conservative universities of the Old Home. **1898** J. D. BRAYSHAW *Slum Silhouettes* 8 Loudly declaiming..about the injustice done to 'the ould counthry', and forcibly giving vent to his views upon 'Home Rule'. **1927** M. M. BENNETT *Christison* xiv. 133 In 1877, twenty-five years after he had sailed from Liverpool for Victoria, Christison left Australia to visit the Old Country. **1947** E. A. MCCOURT *Flaming Hour* vi. 32 In the old country..there would be spinach, brussels sprouts, artichokes. **1950** W. L. JAMES in A. Dundes *Mother Wit* (1973) 431/2 It was those cries which Negroes made famous in the Old South. **1965** *New Society* 26 Aug. 18/1 The 'old' Commonwealth consists of Canada, Australia and New Zealand; the 'new' Commonwealth includes all remaining Commonwealth countries. **1966** B. H. DEAL *Fancy's Knell* (1967) ii. 26 Bill was Old South and Mildred wasn't. **1973** *Guardian* 26 Jan. 1/2 The rules as drafted would lead to unacceptable treatment of people from the Old Commonwealth. **1973** *Sunday Bulletin* (Philadelphia) (Discovery Suppl.) 14 Oct. 17/2 People referred to Europe (or any nation therein) as 'the old country'. **1975** *Listener* 29 May 692/2 We now see not just the African Commonwealth, but also the Old Commonwealth and the Asian Commonwealth, beginning to make their own direct links with the Community. **1975** A. PRICE *Our Man in Camelot* i. 25 There was much more of the Old South in Shirley's voice.

c. *old style*: see STYLE. ***Old Christmas Day, Old Christmas Eve, Old Lady Day, Old May-day, Old Michaelmas-day, Old Midsummer***, etc., these days or times according to the computation of old style.

1783 W. OWEN *New Bk. of Fairs* 14 Friday before Old Michaelmas, meeting by custom for horned cattle. *Ibid.* 65 Monday before Old Midsummer July 5, for sheep and horned cattle. *Ibid.* 70 Monday before Old Lady Day, for broad and narrow cloths, and leather. **1825** HONE *Every-day Bk.* 1324 September 26..Old Holyrood. **1826** *Ibid.* II. 659 A festival called Beltane..annually held in Scotland on old May-day. *Ibid.* 1315 October 11. This is 'Old Michaelmas Day'. **1861** *Times* 16 Feb., The old style is still retained in the accounts of Her Majesty's Treasury... The first day of the financial year is the 5th of April, being old Lady Day. **1863** *Book of Days* I. 58 January 6 Epiphany or Twelfth Day (*Old Christmas Day*). *Ibid.* 52/2 *Auld Hansel Monday*, i.e. Handsel Monday old style, or the first Monday after the 12th of the month [January]. **1931** *Sun* (Baltimore) 7 Jan. 7/2 In the church calendar the day is known as Epiphany and in England as Twelfth Night, but among the Colonists it was known as 'Little Christmas' or 'Old Christmas', deriving the name from the fact that when the calendar was changed centuries ago an error was made. **1935** *Evening Sun* (Baltimore) 5 Jan. 18/3 On Old Christmas Eve, tomorrow night, daffodils, hops and elders are supposed to shoot mysterious sprouts through snow and frozen ground. **1948** *Richmond* (Virginia) *Times-Dispatch* 8 Jan. 26/1 In Rodanthe, N.C., and probably in some other remote places, 'Old Christmas' is observed on January 5. **1956** *Sun* (Baltimore) 5 Jan. 3/2 Why residents of the Outer Banks celebrate Epiphany or Old Christmas, as well as December 25..is something lost in antiquity. **1969** in Halpert & Story *Christmas Mumming in Newfoundland* 176 From before Christmas till Old Christmas Day called Twelfth Day, they held high carnival.

d. *old days* (or *times*): past times; freq. in phr. ***good*** (or ***bad***) ***old days*** (or ***times***).

1828 *Oscotian* (ed. 2) I. 1 However glorious those '*good old times*' may have been, they still were destitute of one very important advantage. **1856** GEO. ELIOT in *Westm. Rev.* X. 55 The aristocratic dilettantism which attempts to restore the 'good old times' by a sort of idyllic masquerading. **1898** G. B. SHAW *Mrs. Warren's Profession* II. 197 Suppose we were both as poor as you were in those wretched old days. **1906** *Nature* 3 May (Suppl.) p. vii/2 In writing of times that are past and gone, while still within our recollection, we have all to be on our guard against a popular illusion as to the 'good old days'. **1911** G. B. SHAW *Getting Married* 261, I felt that I had left the follies and puerilities of the old days behind me for ever. **1932** H. E. WILLIAMS in N. Hodgins *Some Canadian Essays* 225 While museums exemplify the distances that we have travelled since 'the good old days', they are not the best place in which to extract the old-time flavour. **1935** *Discovery* Jan. 29/2 Even in the bad old days, however, there are some things on which Canada may well pride herself. **1950** E. H. GOMBRICH *Story of Art* xxv. 379 There was one thing to be said for the 'good old days'—no artist need ask himself why he had come into the world at all. **1958** A. HUXLEY *Brave New World Revisited* (1959) 27 In the bad old days children with considerable, or even with slight, hereditary defects rarely survived. **1973** *Archivum Linguisticum* IV. 90 Associated with 'the old days', that is with the Rana regime.

e. *old ice*: in polar regions, ice formed before the most recent winter; similarly *old snow* (see quots. 1952, 1966).

1856 E. K. KANE *Arctic Explorations* I. xii. 128 Fissures.. were beginning to break in every direction through the young ice... I therefore made for the old ice to seaward. **1885** *Encycl. Brit.* XIX. 328/1 Old ice is believed to become thicker in a second winter, and even to attain a thickness of 10 feet. **1935** *Handbk. Weather, Currents & Ice* (Meteorol. Office) vii. 102 The Arctic peak consists of old ice, which due to rafting and hummocking forms massive fields. **1952** *Jrnl. Glaciology* II. 150 The definition of *firn*, adopted by the Eidg. Institut für Schnee- und Lawinenforschung, and included in the latest 'Draft on an International Snow Classification' suggested by the Committee on Snow Classification of International Association of Scientific Hydrology, is as follows: 'old snow which has outlasted one summer at least (transformed into a dense heavy material as a result of frequent melting and freezing)'. **1966** T. ARMSTRONG et al. *Illustr. Gloss. Snow & Ice* 30 *Old snow*, deposited snow whose transformation into *firn* is so far advanced that the original form of the ice crystals can no longer be recognized.

f. ***old quantum theory***: see QUANTUM THEORY; ***old red sandstone***: see SANDSTONE.

g. Of a coinage: designating a former monetary unit that has been replaced by a new one with the same name (see NEW *a.* 4).

The French *old franc* was replaced in 1960; in Britain 'new' decimal currency was introduced in 1971.

1959 *Times* 10 Nov. 10/6 The new 'heavy franc', which is worth 100 old francs, is to become legal currency on January 1 next year. **1965** R. FERGUSON *Woman with Secret* x. 76 She left me 40,000 francs. Old francs. **1969** *Times* 21 July (Decimal Currency Suppl.) p. 1/5 Below 5p the only old coin which will be an exact equivalent of the new will be sixpence ($2\frac{1}{2}$p). *Ibid.* 6 The $\frac{1}{2}$p coin being smaller than the old farthing..will be universally unpopular. **1972** D. LEES *Zodiac* 46 That's over four thousand dollars..more than two million old francs. **1974** L. THOMAS *Tropic of Ruislip* ix. 178 'Blimey,' she said. 'There's one of the old pennies in here. That's not yours, is it?' 'No,' he answered. 'I cashed all my old ones in.' **1976** *Listener* 8 Apr. 430/2 Gary was born on 5 April 1966... In those pre-decimal days, you could buy a loaf of bread for 15 old pennies.

†**C.** *adv.* In ancient times, long ago. *rare*[−1].

1608 SHAKS. *Per.* I. Prol. 1 To sing a Song that old was sung, From ashes, auntient Gower is come.

D. *sb.*[1] (elliptical uses of the adj.)

†**1.** = Old man, old woman. *Obs.*

c **1375** *Sc. Leg. Saints* iii. (*Andreas*) 155 Sa suld þat ald his penance mak. *Ibid.* xviii. (*Egipciane*) 326, & to þat auld þane sad scho rathe. **1426** LYDG. *De Guil. Pilgr.* 13113 O, thow Olde! what hastow do, Vnwarly me to smyte so? **1513** DOUGLAS *Æneis* II. ix. [x.] 34 Scho..Him towart hir hes brocht..And sete the auld doun in the haly sete. *c* **1532** *Crt. of Loue* 280 What doth this olde Thus far ystope in yeres?

2. *pl.* (*olds*). Old ones (of a set or class); old persons, etc. *mod. colloq.*

1883 BESANT *All in a Garden fair* II. vii. (1885) 167 Young clever people..are more difficult to catch than the olds. **1890** *Pall Mall G.* 30 Aug. 2/2 Although the 'Olds' have been the pioneers..of the movement, the 'Youngs' show an impatience with them at every meeting.

3. *pl.* (*olds*). Hops more than two and less than four years old. *old olds*, hops more than four years old.

1892 *Daily News* 22 Mar. 7/4 Old olds are still selling. **1898** *Ibid.* 25 June 7/7 Some few transactions are taking place in yearlings and olds.

b. *sing.* A type of ale noted for its strength. Hence *old and mild*, a combination of old and mild ale in equal parts.

1904 A. MAKINS *Licensed Victuallers' Handbk.* xiv. 224 The number of different kinds of malt liquors now produced are not numerous... 'Bitter', 'Stout', 'Mild', and 'Old' (usually called by the public 'Burton'). **1923** *Month* July 37 A glass of 'owd' (old ale) is his only inspiration. **1930** A. P. HERBERT *Water Gipsies* xxiii. 341 The total price of two mild and bitters, one old and mild, two small ports. **1932** L. GOLDING *Magnolia St.* I. iii. 56 Two quarts of old, please! **1933** A. G. MACDONELL *England, Their England* vii. 105 The row of gaffers on the rustic bench..called for more pints of old-and-mild. **1957** J. BRAINE *Room at Top* xx. 177 I'd had two pints of old at the St. Clair. **1967** A. BAILEY in L. Deighton *London Dossier* 66 Try Burton, sometimes called 'Old'...a strong, dark and sweet draught beer..often mixed in the glass with mild ale when it becomes..known as 'Old and Mild'. **1974** *Guardian* 19 Jan. 11/1 In the tap-room ..I encountered..a most impressive Old which is in effect a draught barley wine.

4. = Old time, the olden time; an earlier time or period: = ELD 5. Chiefly in ***men, times, days***, etc. ***of old***.

c **1400** *Destr. Troy* 10503 He has..desyred my doghter to wed, Pollexena the pert, by purpos of olde. **1535** COVERDALE *Ps.* lxxvi[i]. 5 Then remembred I the tymes of olde, & the yeares that were past. *c* **1586** C'TESS PEMBROKE *Ps.* LXXVII. iv, I fell to thinck..Upon the yeares of old. **1635** N. R. *Camden's Hist. Eliz.* I. an. ii. 7 Apparrelled in blacke after the manner of old. **1784** COWPER *Ep. Joseph Hill* 58 Some few that I have known in days of old. **1845** M. PATTISON *Ess.* (1889) I. 10 France..is..rich beyond all others in the traces of the men of old.

b. Advb. phrase. *of old*: of old time, in the olden time, long since, formerly; also, From old days, for a long time (preceding the present).

c **1386** CHAUCER *Friar's T.* 317 Pay me quod he..ffor dette which that thou owest me of old. **1423** *Rolls of Parlt.* IV. 406/1 Ye verray and trewe makyng of old used and continued. **1478** J. PASTON in *P. Lett.* III. 219, I am aqueyntyd with your condycyons of old. **1535** STEWART *Cron. Scot.* I. 4 Intill ane place callit Ecolumkill,..Lang of the ald thair wes thair sepultuir. **1599** SHAKS. *Much Ado* I. i. 146 You alwaies end with a Iades tricke, I know you of old. **1655** MILTON *Sonn. Massacre Piedmont*, Who kept thy truth so pure of old. **1774** J. BRYANT *Mythol.* I. 97 It was the.. sacred place, where of old the everlasting fire was preserved. **1871** R. ELLIS *Catullus* i. 4 You of old did hold them Something worthy.

E. Old- in Comb.

1. a. With another adj., in antithetic or consequential relation, as †*old cool*, †***old-excellent***; ***old-new***, ***old-young***. **b.** With a pr. pple., forming an adj., as ***old-growing*** (growing old), ***old-looking***. **c.** With a pa. pple., in advb. sense 'of old, long, anciently', as ***old-acquainted, -branded, -built, -cut, -established, -gathered, -landed, -licensed, -said*** adjs.

1592 SHAKS. *Rom. & Jul.* I. ii. 20 This night I hold an *old accustom'd Feast. **1535** CRANMER *Let. to Dean of Chapel Royal* in *Misc. Writ.* (Parker Soc.) II. 309 My *old acquainted friend, Master Shaxton. **1716** LADY M. W. MONTAGU *Let. to Lady* —— 16 Aug., This is a very large town, but most part of it *old built. **1607** TOURNEUR *Rev. Trag.* I. ii. Wks. 1878 II. 16 O what it is to haue a *old-coole Duke. **1601** CHESTER *Love's Mart.* cxvii, Those carued *old-cut stonie Images. **1785** *Daily Universal Reg.* 1 Jan. 3/2 The following articles, in Silver, at the *Old established Wholesale Prices. **1787** BENTHAM *Def. Usury* xiii. 141 Old-established trades. **1898** *Westm. Gaz.* 2 Apr. 6/1 Some of the older-established jobbers refuse to deal for cash at all. **1961** NEW ENG. BIBLE *Matt.* xv. 2 Why do your disciples break the old-established tradition? **1602** F. HERING *Anatomyes* 5 In the knowledge of Plants they are *old excellent. **1643** TRAPP *Comm. Gen.* xii. 1 Abraham was old-excellent at it [self-denial]. *a* **1586** SIDNEY *Arcadia* I. Wks. 1725 I. 61 According to the nature of the *old-growing world. **1824** MISS MITFORD *Village* Ser. I. (1863) 124 Apart from his *old-looking younger brother. **1837** *Blackw. Mag.* XLII. 235 All the oldest looking, shrivelled oak-apples. **1530** PALSGR. 250/1 *Ould sayd sawe, *prouerbe*. *c* **1570** *Marr. Wit & Science* v. i. in Hazl. *Dodsley* II. 379 An old-said saw it is ..Soon hot, soon cold. **1828** *Craven Gloss.* (ed. 2) s.v., It's an oud said say, and a true yan. **1834** 'NIMROD' in *New Sporting Mag.* VIII. 82 There stood before me, a round-shouldered, decrepid, tottering **old-young* man. **1907** *Daily Chron.* 8 July 3/3 Liverpool..the old-young city. **1932** V. WOOLF *Common Reader* 2nd Ser. 130 A 'round-shouldered, tottering old-young man bloated by drink'. **1951** DYLAN THOMAS *Lett.* (1966) 352 These old-young men are shipped back also, packed full with shame and penicillin. **1959** N. MAILER *Advts. for Myself* (1961) 21 The colourful old-young men of American letters. **1974** J. MANN *Sticking Place* v. 83 She was not a girl at all, on close inspection..but an old-young woman.

2. Parasynthetic combinations: **a.** general, as ***old-aged*** (of old age, aged), ***old-blooded*** (having old blood), ***old-branched, -faced, -hearted, -phrased, -sighted***, etc., adjs.; hence ***old-sightedness*** (= presbyopia). **b.** based on some recognized phrase, as ***old-bachelorish*** (having the character associated with an 'old bachelor'), ***old-boyish*** (of the nature of an 'old boy'); so ***old-boyishness, old-boy-like, old-cattish, old-fogydom, old-fogyish, old-gentlemanly, old-masterish, old-masterly***, etc., adjs.; ***old-bachelorship, old-fellowhood*** (the status of an 'old fellow', e.g. of a college), ***old-fogyism, old-ladyhood, old-liner*** (one of the 'old line'), ***old-lorist, -masterishness, old soldierism*** (the conduct of an 'old soldier'), etc., sbs. See also derivatives of OLD MAID, OLD WOMAN, etc.

1581 SIDNEY *Apol. Poetrie* (Arb.) 31 *Olde-aged experience goeth beyond the fine-witted Phylosopher. **1824** MISS MITFORD *Village* Ser. I. (1863) 198 Every thing was.. so provokingly in order, so full of naked nicety, so thoroughly *old-bachelorish. **1832** *Ibid.* Ser. v. 346 Every female present..prophesied old-bachelorship and all its evils, to the contrivers and performers. **1894** H. NISBET *Bush Girl's Rom.* 218 The hauteur..that woke in his proud, *old-blooded breast. **1846** MRS. GORE *Sk. Eng. Char.* (1852) 143 The curious weazened *old-boyish air of this..race of men. **1850** *Punch* 3 Aug. 52/1 There is a jolly-buckism or an *old-boyishness about the concern. **1597** DRAYTON *Mortimeriados* 25 A Forrest of *old-branched Oakes. **1780** MAD. D'ARBLAY *Diary* (1842) I. 303 Don't I begin to talk in an *old-cattish manner of cards? **1595** SHAKS. *John* II. i. 259 'Tis not the rounder of your *old-fac'd walles, Can hide you from our messengers of Warre. **1848** THACKERAY *Van. Fair* lviii, He had now passed into the stage of *old fellowhood. His hair was grizzled. *c* **1905** F. ROLFE *Nicholas Crabbe* (1958) xxvii. 188 Exasperate and purulent *oldfogeydom. **1920** T. P. NUNN *Education* xii. 147 At that age..old fogeydom already lays his hand on most of us, little as we may expect it. *a* **1877** in Bartlett *Dict. Amer.* (1877) (ed. 4) 437 He's slow and rather **old-fogyish*. **1883** A. FORBES in *19th Cent.* Oct. 722 The full side-face whiskers, which of late are becoming old-fogeyish. **1869** *Daily News* 30 Jan., [The *Quarterly Review*] never falls..into tradition, routine, or *old-fogyism. **1819** BYRON *Juan* I. ccxvi, A good *old-gentlemanly vice. **1888** *Lady* 25 Oct. 374/3 Caps,.. charmingly suggestive of pretty *old-ladyhood. **1855** *Richmond* (Virginia) *Whig* 15 Mar. 1/1 Endorsed thus by two '*old liners', he was most cordially received. **1884** *Boston* (Mass.) *Jrnl.* 25 Sept. 2/2 The old-liners appear to be out of the fight. **1903** *N.Y. Even. Post* 31 Oct. 5 The old-liners quietly backbite him for taking up a 'fanatic' like Johnson. **1908** R. W. CHAMBERS *Firing Line* xxix. 493, I didn't expect any cordiality..but..they classed us with the old-liners. **1880** *Academy* 14 Aug. 123 So solid and careful an *old-lorist. **1925** A. HUXLEY *Those Barren Leaves* I. ii. 14 One of those large, handsome, *old-masterish women. **1961** *Listener* 16 Nov. 822/3 There are no 'properties', no old-masterish bits and pieces, to keep the thing going. **1937** *Burlington Mag.* Mar. 137/1 The same contempt for '*old masterishness' and its devotees. **1882** *Athenæum* No. 2866. 439 This dignified and, if the term be allowed, *old-masterly work. **1968** S. HYNES *Edwardian Turn of Mind* ix. 317 A taste in painting that was neither Old Masterly..nor academic. **1911** H. S. HARRISON *Queed* xxii. 276, I think *old-soldierism is the meanest profession the Lord ever suffered to thrive. **1886** J. Corbett *Fall of Asgard* II. 178 He listened to him telling of..his *old-phrased oaths.

3. With a sb. (or adj. used absol.), forming an attrib. phrase, as ***old-book, old-country, old-home, old-issue, old-ivory, old-life, old-line*** (following the old lines), ***Old Line State*** (Maryland), ***old-master, old-Roman, old-school, old-service, old-standard, old-town, old-wave, old-year***, etc. See also old-time, old-world.

1862 Burton *Bk. Hunter* i. 25 In the *old-book trade there are opportunities for the exercise of ingenuity. *a* **1902** *Mod.* A well-known frequenter of the old-book shops. **1890** *Tablet* 21 June 981 Grooms in *old-day livery. **1928** Blunden *Undertones of War* xvii. 177 Flinging *old-home repartee at your pal passing by. **1959** *Word* XV. 147 Langer gives a considerable number of examples of old-home expressions which were lost and replaced. **1879** A. W. Tourgée *Fool's Errand* xvii. 87 Robert..was..an '*old-issue free nigger' (freed before the war). **1899** C. W. Chesnutt *Wife of his Youth* 214 Wright came of an 'old issue' free colored family, in which though negro blood was present in an attenuated strain, a line of free ancestry could be traced beyond the Revolutionary War. **1898** *Daily News* 2 Dec. 5/1 There is one book exhibited, which..has put on a true *old-ivory tone. **1863** A. C. Ramsay *Phys. Geog.* 51 That Palaeozoic or *old-life period. **1897** *Outing* (U.S.) XXX. 354/2 The return to the old-life routine. **1856** *Congress. Globe* 9 Jan. 180/3 Have they offered us one of my colleagues, an *old-line Whig? **1908** R. W. Chambers *Firing Line* xxi. 353 I'm in an old-line institution. **1928** F. Scott Fitzgerald *Let.* 1 Feb. (1964) 383, I rode..with the president of a very prominent club, not my own, a Princetonian of the rather old-line, conservative, very gentlemanly type. **1949** *Sun* (Baltimore) 7 Sept. 12/4 Mr. Taft's mental and moral force has been a reservoir of strength to the old-line men. **1958** *Spectator* 20 June 791/3 In spite of his reputation as an old-line Stalinist, Suslov supported Krushchev. **1962** R. Tyre *Douglas in Saskatchewan* v. 78 The Socialists had high hopes of winning the 1934 election but the farmers were not quite ready yet to abandon their traditional support of the old line parties. **1973** *Deb. Senate Canada* 28 Mar. 2710/1 The two old-line parties are afraid of treading on the toes of the financial institutions. **1872** Schele de Vere *Americanisms* xii. 660 Maryland bears the proud title of **Old-line State* from the *Old-Line* regiments which she contributed to the Continental Army in the War of the Revolution—the only State that had regular troops of 'the line'. **1948** Mencken *Amer. Lang.* Suppl. II. 604 *Maryland Free State*...has overshadowed all the old nicknames..including *Old Line State* and *Terrapin State*. **1950** D. Gascoyne *Vagrant* 56 Though that's what this *old-master lute-master opines. **1959** *Times* 19 Mar. 4/3 Still-life studies combining an old-master flavour with a slightly surrealist inclination. **1831** Carlyle *Sart. Res.* i. vii, *Old-Roman contempt of the superfluous. **1886** *N. Amer. Rev.* July 19 Adam, according to this *old-school Calvinism, was the Federal Head, the representative of his race. **1894** *Westm. Gaz.* 19 Apr. 6/2 One of the few remaining *old-service gaolers. **1838** J. F. Cooper *Home as Found* I. x. 163 That is the First Presbyterian, or the *old standard [church]; a very good house. **1962** *Listener* 30 Aug. 315/1 This reaction has not come from *Old Wave film makers. **1967** *Observer* 26 Feb. 21/3 All the addicts were middle-aged...typical old-wave addicts. But what of the new ones? **1897** R. M. Stuart *In Simpkinsville* i. 14 They got him to come to the old year party one year, jest for the fun of it.

4. Special combs. and phrases: **old bach** (see bach *sb.* 1); **Old Baptist, Old Christian (church)** *U.S.*, names of religious denominations; **old-bone** *v.*, to manure with old bones; †**old boy**, a kind of strong ale; **old-'clothes-man**, a dealer in old or second-hand clothes; **old-'clothes-shop**, a shop for the sale of old clothes; **old contemptible**: see contemptible *a.* 4; **old crock** (see crock *sb.*[3] 4); **old firm**, a group of friends or associates (cf. firm *sb.*[1] 2 c); **old gang** *colloq.*, a group or clique of friends or colleagues, esp. politicians, accustomed to supporting each other in matters of business or policy; **old gentleman**: see 9 b, also quot.; **Old Glory** *U.S.*, the 'Stars and Stripes'; †**old-grey** [grey *sb.* 5], old man, greybeard; **old guard** (see guard *sb.* 9 b); **old hand**, (*a*) one who has been long employed or has experience in any business, one who is skilful in doing something (see hand *sb.* 9); (*b*) one who has been a convict; also *attrib.*; **old holder** (see quot.); **old home week** *U.S.* (see quot. 1904); **Old Kingdom**, a name given collectively (*a*) to the Third, Fourth, Fifth, and Sixth Dynasties, which ruled Egypt from the 27th to the 22nd century B.C.; (*b*) to a period of Hittite history extending from the 18th to the 16th century B.C.; **old lady**, collectors' name for a species of moth, *Mania maura*; **old-like** *a.*, old in appearance (*obs.* exc. *Sc.* and *dial.*); **old master** *U.S.*, the former master of a (Negro) slave; also **old mistress** (see also ole, ol' *a.*); **old money**, old-established wealth; **old offender**, an habitual criminal; **old religion**, a religion or belief which is replaced or ousted by another, *spec.* (*a*) a pre-Christian religion; paganism; (*b*) witchcraft; (*c*) Roman Catholicism; **old-rich**, those whose wealth is old-established, opp. *new rich* (new *a.* 8 d); also *attrib.* or as *adj.*; **Old Ritualist** [tr. Russ. *staroobryádets*] = Old Believer; **old rope** *slang* (orig. *Naval*), rank tobacco; **old settler** [settler 2], one of the earliest settlers in a community; **old ship** *Naval slang*, an old shipmate; †**old-sir, old-sire**, an old man, an aged sire; **old sledge**, a game at cards = all fours[1]; **old soldier** *v.*, to 'come the old soldier over': see soldier *sb.* (*colloq.*); *sb. U.S. slang*, the remaining part of a smoked cigar or chewed quid; also, an empty liquor bottle (Webster 1909); **old sow**, the plant *Melilotus cærulea* (sweet trefoil), also a local name of *Antennaria margaritacea* (pearl cudweed) (Britten & H.); **old-spelling**, the unstandardized early spelling of English; **old squaw** the long-tailed duck, *Clangula hyemalis*; = long-tail 1 b, old wife 2; also *attrib.*; **old-standing** *a.*, that has stood or existed long, long-standing; **old style** *a.*, belonging to the old style, old-fashioned; *Typog.*, one of a group of typefaces first produced in the 19th century and modelled on the 18th-century old-face fount cast at the Caslon foundry; also *attrib.*; cf. Caslon, old-face; **old sweat** *slang*, an old soldier; **old thing** *Austral.* (see quots.); **old Thirteen** *U.S.*, the original thirteen American colonies, which declared their independence in 1776; also, the original 'Stars and Stripes', a flag with thirteen stars and thirteen stripes; **Old Tom**, a kind of strong gin; **old witch**, a children's game; **old witch-grass**, a North American panic grass, *Panicum capillare*.

1845 A. Wiley in *Indiana Mag. Hist.* (1927) XXIII. 18, I see nothing awaiting the '*old Baptist' churches but utter annihilation. **1889** P. Butler *Personal Recoll.* 252 'Hardshell' Baptists..wish to be known as Old Baptists, or United Baptists. **1849** Johnston *Exper. Agric.* 57 On the *old-boned field, the crop was four times as bulky as on the unboned field. *Ibid.*, This old-boning caused a large increase both in the turnip and in the corn crops. **1743** *Lond. & Country Brew.* iv. (ed. 2) 289 Then add to the same new Drinks, with their Sediments, and call it *Old-boy, Stout, or Nog. **1849** E. Chamberlain *Indiana Gazetteer* (ed. 3) 175 Presbyterians, Methodists, United Brethren, Christian,..*Old Christian, (or new Light) and Baptists. **1782** Wolcott (P. Pindar) *2nd Ode to R.A.'s*, Like an *Old-clothes-Man about London Street! **1834** *Chambers's Edin. Jrnl.* III. 141/1, I feel convinced that these old-clothes-men only address persons of gentlemanly appearance. **1968** *N.Y. City* (Michelin Tire Corp.) 82 The dark smoke-filled bars which alternate with old-clothes dealers along the street.. shopkeepers..tailors and old-clothes men. **1781** C. Johnston *Hist. J. Juniper* II. 252 The actor went to dress at his usual wardrobe, an *old-clothes shop. **1851** A. O. Hall *Manhattaner* 6 Groups of old clo' shops, gaudily set forth with parti-colored handkerchiefs. **1930** A. P. Herbert *Water Gipsies* vii. 72 Five shillings each way... Don't desert the *Old Firm! **1935** D. L. Sayers *Gaudy Night* iv. 64 If you ever want me, you will find the Old Firm at the usual stand. **1975** 'D. Jordan' *Black Account* xiii. 66 'Always happy to help the Old Firm,' he declared. **1885** J. Chamberlain in J. R. Ware *Passing Eng.* (1909) 187/1 In deference to his [*sc.* Lord Randolph Churchill's] opinion, there will no doubt be a clearance out of some of those whom the Fourth Party is in the habit of politely designating as the '*Old Gang'. **1889** *Judge* (N.Y.) XV. 368/1 Yankee Doodle came to town Astride his thorough-bred. He met the old gang going out With Grover at their head. **1891** G. B. Shaw *How to become Mus. Critic* (1960) 195 Mr Chappell has at last awakened to the fact that his stock players were becoming what vestry politicians call an old gang. **1900** —— *Let.* 4 Mar. (1972) II. 150 In excited times nominations are apt to be made freely; and what happens then is that though the old gang is pretty safe, the other seats go anyhow. **1901** *Punch* 3 Apr. 250/2 There is so much favoritism that only the Old Gang and Rank Outsiders get chosen. **1916** Mrs. Belloc Lowndes *Let.* 8 Dec. (1971) 78 Violet Markham thinks L.G. will last out a good while but that all 'the Old Gang' as people are beginning to call them, will gradually crystallise into a Peace Party. **1933** Wyndham Lewis *Old Gang & New Gang* 9 Every morning when Mr. Everyman opens his newspaper he reads about the doings of the 'Old Gang'—or rather about their non-doing and non-caring. **1934** G. G. Coulton in *S.P.E. Tract* XLIII. 103 Within six years he [*sc.* Hart] had gathered eleven colleagues whom, at a much later prize-giving, he affectionately described as 'the Old Gang', and of whom Fowler was one. **1940** H. Nicolson *Let.* 6 June (1967) 94 There is a growing feeling against what is called 'the old gang'... The men who have come back from the front feel that Kingsley Wood and Inskip let them down and must go. **1961** R. Hoggart *W. H. Auden: a Selection* 24 A feeling that 'the old gang' were always hopelessly out of touch and wrong. **1964** C. Barber *Ling. Change Present-Day Eng.* ii. 26 A rejection of Old Gang politics,..general resentment at the Establishment. **1828** G. Smeeton *Doings in London* 77 An '**old gentleman*' (a card somewhat larger and thicker than the rest of the pack, and now in considerable use amongst the 'legs'). **1862** W. Driver in *Salem* (Mass.) *Reg.* 10 Mar. 2, I carried my flag, '*Old Glory', as we have been used to call it, to the Capitol, presented it to the Ohio 6th. **1930** J. Dos Passos *42nd Parallel* ii. 153 They wrapped me in the Stars and Stripes and brought me home on a frigate to be buried..I was wrapped in Old Glory. **1973** *Sat. Rev. World* (U.S.) 4 Dec. 16/2 The right to substitute the peace symbol for the stars in Old Glory. **1975** *Times* 15 Apr. 6/7 Come what may, the American Ambassador to Saigon..will be rescued by the Marines, with the 'Old Glory' flag rolled in his arms. **1582** Stanyhurst *Æneis* ii. (Arb.) 64 Hee rested wylful lyk a wayward obstinat *oldgrey. **1785** Grose *Dict. Vulg. T.*, **Old hand*, knowing or expert in any business. **1845** C. Griffith *Present State of Port Philip* 76 The old hands are men, who, having been formerly convicts..have become free by the expiration of their sentences. **1848** Dickens *Dombey* xii, Toots, as an old hand, had a desk to himself. **1857** R. B. Paul *Lett. from Canterbury, N.Z.* ii. 26 Only enter the dwelling of the roughest 'old hand' among us, and you will meet with..much kindness. **1865** Tucker *Austral. Story* i. 85 Reformed convicts, or, in the language of their proverbial cant, 'old hands'. **1865** Nixon *Peter Perfume* 102 'Bosh-man', in the old-hand vernacular, signifies a fiddler. **1911** C. E. W. Bean *'Dreadnought' of Darling* xxxii. 283 Lots of these fellows near Bourke were 'old hands'. Some of them were decent, good fellows, and the rest—well, they were horrible—the blackest, unmitigated rascals, fearing neither God nor the devil, men who would stick at nothing. **1946** K. Tennant *Lost Heaven* (1947) i On one side is Limeburners', where the 'old hands' used to pound oyster shells for lime. **1810** *Sporting Mag.* XXXVI. 21 The defendants who have designated themselves as *old-holders—copyholders..who pay one heriot only, though they hold several messuages. **1904** *Boston Herald* 2 Aug. 6 In.. Massachusetts this first week in August is being observed as *Old Home Week, and preparations have been made for welcoming back..visitors who return to their native, or earlier, home to renew acquaintance with former scenes and companions. **1949** T. Rattigan *Harlequinade* 63 What with Mums in front and babies in the wings it's not so much a dress rehearsal as old home week. **1973** 'I. Drummond' *Jaws of Watchdog* i. 11 He and Jenny embraced warmly. 'Old home week,' said the Princess sourly. **1905** J. H. Breasted *Egypt through Stereoscope* 22 With the accession of the 3rd Dynasty..we see Egypt rising into her first great period of power and prosperity, which we call the *Old Kingdom. *Ibid.* 143 The king who made the sphinx must have dismantled some Old Kingdom mastabas to clear the rock. **1910** *Encycl. Brit.* IX. 39/1 A valuable stele from Sakkara of the beginning of the Old Kingdom was presented to the Ashmolean Museum at Oxford in 1683. **1928** C. Dawson *Age of Gods* vii. 151 We must be prepared to allow for a margin of error of more than 800 years in dealing with..the Old Kingdom of Egypt. **1938** E. M. Sanford *Mediterranean World in Anc. Times* i. 55 The foundation of the united Old Kingdom of the Hittites was delayed by the rivalry of individual states. **1952** O. Gurney *Hittites* i. 25 Telipinus is usually regarded as the last king of the Old Kingdom. **1961** A. Gardiner *Egypt of Pharaohs* i. iv. 60 Our evidence for the Old Kingdom is purely archaeological. **1973** R. J. Williams in D. J. Wiseman *Peoples Old Testament Times* iv. 83 Great advances were made in medicine, which reached heights in the Old Kingdom never surpassed in ancient Egypt. **1974** *Encycl. Brit. Macropædia* VI. 465/1 There is good reason to regard this king [*sc.* Khasekhemui] as the founder of the Old Kingdom. **1832** Rennie *Butterflies & Moths* 99 The *Old Lady appears the end of July or beginning of August. **1634** W. Tirwhyt tr. *Balzac's Lett.* (vol. I.) 34 It is one more *old-like than his Father, and as over-worne as a ship. **1855** Robinson *Whitby Gloss.*, *And like*, looking old. 'He is beginning to grow varry aud like'. **1872** S. Powers *Afoot & Alone* 61 Negroes everywhere..seemed to think they were not free unless they left the *old master. **1892** 'Mark Twain' *Amer. Claimant* viii. 81 When a bell ring..en old marster tell me to——. **1949** B. A. Botkin *Treas. S. Folklore* i. iii. 58 The chief protagonist and antagonist of master-slave folklore are Old Massa and Old John. **1859** D. D. Emmett *Dixie's Land* (song) (1960), *Old missus marry Will de Weaber... Here's a health to de next old missus. **1874** 'Mark Twain' in *Atlantic Monthly* Nov. 592/1 Well, bymeby my ole mistis say she's broke. **1963** *Times* 25 Feb. (Canada Suppl.) p. xv/3 Having noted that the Canadian rich, particularly the *old-money rich, tend to dwell among exquisite eighteenth-century chattels, the poorer folk aspire to antiques themselves. **1966** 'D. Shannon' *With a Vengeance* i. 22 There's a lot o' money—kind of substantial *old* money, you know—her husband was a banker. **1967** L. J. Braun *Cat who ate Danish Modern* ii. 18 People with Old Money always avoid publicity on their real estate. **1817** *2nd Rep. Comm. State of Police of Metrop.* 329 in *Parl. Papers* VII. 321 The greater part of these Juvenile Offenders,..are mixed indiscriminately with *old offenders of all ages. **1890** W. Booth *In Darkest Eng.* ii. v. 177 C.M. Old offender, and penal servitude case. **1970** P. Laurie *Scotland Yard* x. 263 If he is an old offender, the threat failed to deter him. **1848** W. D. Cooley tr. *Erman's Trav. in Siberia* II. xii. 306 The Bugoi of the Buraets of the *old religion, maintain that they know..how to deal with certain mischievous spirits. **1934** A. Huxley *Beyond Mexique Bay* 159 The old religion came ..boldly out into the open in 1745. **1964** *Listener* 12 Mar. 445/3, I am glad to see that the witch-religion is becoming so respectable... Jean Morris..now proposes..that the Templars were of the 'old religion'. **1967** D. Pinner *Ritual* x. 106 If the Old Religion possessed this village, I probably would be too frightened to be anything but a warlock voyeur. **1972** P. Dennison in N. Tiptaft *Religion in Birmingham* 140 Wherever a local squire remained Catholic there was a good chance for the survival of a small pocket of the old religion in his territory. **1973** J. Wainwright *High-Class Kill* 77 Some of 'em stumble against witchcraft. Sorcery. Demonology. The so-called 'old religion'. **1975** *Country Life* 6 Feb. 318/2 In Queen Mary's reign he was, as a reliable adherent of the old religion, put on the Council of the Welsh Marches. **1927** *Public Opinion* 18 Feb. 149/1 These mistakes..seem folly to an *old-rich man. *Ibid.* 149/2 The old-rich know these things well enough, but the new-rich never discover them. **1976** T. Allbeury *Only Good German* xiv. 101 The kind of places that the old rich go to rather than the new rich. **1885** A. J. C. Hare *Studies in Russia* vi. 301 In later times the schismatics have divided into the Stároobriádtsi, or *Old Ritualists..and the Bezpopoftsi, or priestless people. **1911** Old Ritualist [see Old Believer]. **1954** G. Vernadsky *Hist. Russia* (ed. 4) v. 132 Outstanding among the leaders of the Old Ritualists, as the anti-Nikonians eventually became known, was the archpriest Avvakum. *Ibid.* viii. 180 The movement of the Old Ritualists by 1800 ceased to be a unit and broke into several separate sects. **1974** R. Pipes *Russia under Old Regime* ix. 236 Russian dissenters are customarily divided in two basic groups: the Old Believers, known to themselves as 'Old Ritualists' (*Staroobriadtsy*) and to the official church as 'Splitters' (*Raskol'niki*), and the Sectarians. **1943** Hunt & Pringle *Service Slang* 48 **Old rope*, any tobacco which offends the nostrils of those present, and especially the finer varieties such as Egyptian. **1946** J. Irving *Royal Navalese* 127 *Old Rope*, any offensive smelling tobacco. **1744** *Colonial Rec. Georgia* (1906) VI. 117 Thomas Ellis has been an *old Settler in the Colony. **1815** Old settler [see settler 2 b]. **1854** R. B. Paul *Some Acct. Canterbury Settlemt.* 5 Having now resided more than two years in the Canterbury

Settlement..[I] may almost call [myself] an 'old settler'. **1964** S. M. MILLER in I. L. Horowitz *New Sociol.* 293 'Old-settler' Protestant recruits largely from farm and rural areas. **1927** *Daily Express* 11 Oct. 3/4 He gave a vivid description of waiting for the train at Charing Cross, then he met an '*old ship', and they went to have a drink. **1948** PARTRIDGE *Dict. Forces' Slang* 131 *Old Ship*, a former messmate (Navy). **1586** T. B. *La Primaud. Fr. Acad.* I. (1594) 79 Of a crooked *old-sire, we say that his spirit waxeth old with him. **1837** W. IRVING *Capt. Bonneville* I. 181 [This] threw a temporary stigma upon the game of '*old-sledge'. **1884** 'C. E. CRADDOCK' *In Tennessee Mts.* II. 82 The mingled charms of Old Sledge and apple-jack had occasioned comment. **1950** R. P. WARREN *World Enough & Time* iii. 101 The groups of men who played 'Old Sledge' and 'Brag' on the sidewalk. **1834** W. A. CARUTHERS *Kentuckian in N.Y.* I. 12, I smokes the *old sodgers what the gentlemen throws on the bar-room floor. **1869** 'MARK TWAIN' in *Buffalo Express* 4 Sept. 1/1 A wooden box of sand, sprinkled with cigar stubs and 'old soldiers'. *a* **1877** in Bartlett *Dict. Amer.* (1877) (ed. 4) 438 Ladies who swab our sidewalks,.. And..Haul off old soldiers lying there at rest. **1892** *Pall Mall G.* 3 Aug. 5/2 Mr. W. R. tried to 'old soldier' him, but, as Harry said in sententious vernacular, 'I wasn't having any'. **1936** *Amer. Speech* XI. 304/1 *Old soldier*, 'a partly-smoked cigar'... I have heard this more frequently as *dead soldier*, applied to empty beer or whiskey bottles but not to cigar butts. **1855** MORTON *Cycl. Agric.* II. 421 *Melilotus azureus*, a Swiss plant..with blue blossoms, has a singular porcine odour, whence it is vulgarly called '*Old Sow'; and is the plant which gives the peculiar flavour to Schapziger cheese. **1927** R. B. MCKERROW *Introd. Bibliogr.* III. i. 246 The composition rates for *old spelling texts are some 10 per cent above the normal rate. **1960** *Studies in Bibliogr.* XIII. 49 (*heading*) The rationale of old-spelling editions of the plays of Shakespeare and his contemporaries. **1969** *N.Y. Rev. Bks.* 30 Jan. 32/2 In the first place the words aren't old-spelling [in an edition of Shakespeare]. **1838** J. J. AUDUBON *Ornith. Biogr.* IV. 105 They have various appellations, among others those of 'old wives' and '*old squaws'. **1884** etc. [see SQUAW *sb.* (and *a.*) 4]. **1892** B. TORREY *Foot-Path Way* 41 The cliffs..offer an excellent position from which to sweep the bay in search of loons, old-squaws, and other sea-fowl. **1963** *Kingston* (Ontario) *Whig-Standard* 8 Feb. 11/2 Large numbers of Old Squaw ducks were sighted during the survey. **1971** *Islander* (Victoria, B.C.) 10 Oct. 13/1 Oldsquaw is one of the few ducks with two complete annual plumage changes. **1975** *Globe & Mail* (Toronto) 9 Dec. 11/5 Almost all the affected ducks are oldsquaws, long-tailed Arctic ducks that winter by the thousand on the Great Lakes. **1608–9** MIDDLETON *Widow* I. ii, Your college for your *old-standing scholar. **1897** *Allbutt's Syst. Med.* III. 47 Old-standing cases of chronic pericarditis. **1927** A. BENNETT *Let.* 14 Apr. (1966) I. 365 The Beaverbrook papers, which have my stuff at 1/6d a word under an oldstanding arrangement. **1962** A. SORSBY in A. Pirie *Lens Metabolism Rel. Cataract* 298 The characteristic subepithelial opacities seen in this affection are an oldstanding observation. *c* **1869** (*title*) Specimens of *old style types (Miller & Richard). **1873** BROWNING *Red Cott. Nt.-cap* 132 Dignified And gentry-fashioned old-style haunts of sleep. **1884** BIGMORE & WYMAN *Bibliogr. Printing* II. 42 Perceiving the tendency to go back to a former taste in printing, this foundry [*sc.* Miller & Richard], about 1850, commenced to cut a series of what they termed 'old-style founts', the success of which has been unexampled in the annals of type-founding. **1895** *Educat. Rev.* Sept. 123 The old-style naturalist had been working from time immemorial. **1913** J. H. QUINN *Library Cataloguing* xv. 222 'Old-style' in type does not mean old-fashioned, but the more artistic and readable type modelled on the lettering of the early printers, principally those of the Italian presses. **1966** H. WILLIAMSON *Methods Bk. Design* (ed. 2) viii. 101 In 1852 Miller and Richard..led the way to a new development by issuing specimens of a regularized old face which they named Old Style. The new class of old style types, of which this was the first, reverted to gradual shading and to oblique top-serifs, but retained vertical stress. **1919** *Athenæum* 8 Aug. 727/2 A 'gasper' is a cheap cigarette, an '*old sweat' an old soldier. **1924** A. J. SMALL *Frozen Gold* i. 38 You're a levelheaded old sweat, I know, or you wouldn't be carrying the button. *a* **1935** [see EASY *a.* 13 b]. **1955** J. THOMAS *No Banners* ix. 80 These were followed by two lank British privates, old sweats of the Regular Army. **1973** *Guardian* 16 Mar. 12/5, I speak feelingly as an 'old sweat' who served in Ireland in an earlier time of 'troubles'. **1848** H. W. HAYGARTH *Recoll. Bush Life Austral.* i. 6 The Traveller's entertainment is confined to the '*old thing', as it is contemptuously called, that is to say, beef and 'damper'. **1945** BAKER *Austral. Lang.* iv. 80 It was what W. W. Dobie called the *muttonous* diet of the outback that produced the expression *the Old Thing* for a meal of mutton and damper. **1845** *Southern Lit. Messenger* XI. 584/2 Charleston..[was] the chief commercial city of the '*Old Thirteen'. **1854** B. F. TAYLOR *Jan. & June* 68 The 'Old Thirteen' were blazing bright—There were *only* thirteen then! **1904** *Hartford* (Connecticut) *Courant* 30 Aug. 10 We want to see the Old Thirteen draw closer and closer together. **1821** P. EGAN *Real Life in London* I. ix. 187 **Old Tom*—It is customary in public-houses and gin-shops in London and its vicinity to exhibit a cask inscribed with large letters—OLD TOM, intended to indicate the best gin in the house. **1836–9** DICKENS *Sk. Boz, Gin-shops* (1892) 171 Great casks.. bearing such inscriptions as 'Old Tom, 549'. **1897** *Allbutt's Syst. Med.* II. 846 When sweetened and diluted by the retailers gin is known as gin cordial or 'Old Tom'. **1971** R. DENTRY *Encounter at Kharmel* iv. 75 A bottle of Old Tom and two hot-glasses. **1881** *Harper's Mag.* Jan. 184/2 The young solks..played at 'prisoner's base' or '*old witch by the wayside'. **1906** *Dialect Notes* III. 148 *Old witch*,..an outdoor game. The players circle around one of their number, the old witch, to whom the following is addressed: 'Chickamy, chickamy, crany-crow... What time is it, old witch?' **1859** W. DARLINGTON *Amer. Weeds* 403 *Old-witch grass... Sandy pastures, cultivated grounds; throughout the United States. **1894** J. M. COULTER *Bot. W. Texas* III. 508 Old witch grass... Annual... In cultivated land everywhere.

†**old**, *sb.*[2] *Obs.* Forms: α. 2–3 (*Sc.* 5–6) ald, (4 alde), 4–6 auld; β. 4–6 olde, (5 oolde), 5– old. [Early ME. *ald*, app. a. ON. *öld* (:—*aldâ* or *aldi*), gen. sing. *aldar*, etc., age, an age:—OTeut. **alđoz* OLD *a.* But the Eng. word may be in some, esp. later uses, directly from the adj. *old* in Eng., or may be an alteration of ELD *sb.* after *eld*, *old* adj.]

1. Age, duration of life or existence.

c **1200** [see ALD *sb.* 1].

2. An age, or secular period of the world.

c **1200** [see ALD *sb.* 2].

3. Old age, the advanced stage or period of life; also, The wane of the moon.

α. *c* **1205** LAY. 19411 Bruttes hafden muchel mode..for þas kinges alde. *a* **1300** *Cursor M.* 10969, I and mi wijf on ald tas. **1535** STEWART *Chron. Scot.* I. 444 Vnsaturabill bayth in ald and ȝouth.

β. [*c* **1315** SHOREHAM 2 Wanne man drawith into olde-ward, Wel ofte his bones aketh.] *c* **1386** CHAUCER *Knt.'s T.* 1284 He hadde a Beres skyn colblak for old. *c* **1420** *Pallad. on Husb.* II. 439 In old ek of this mone is this moost good. *c* **1425** *Seven Sag.* (P.) 641 He wille brynge the adown in olde. **1523** FITZHERB. *Husb.* §12 Let them be sowen in the olde of the mone. **1606** SHAKS. *Tr. & Cr.* II. ii. 104 Virgins, and Boyes; mid-age and wrinkled old [*Qo.* elders]. **1616** SURFL. & MARKH. *Country Farme* I. xiii. 63 They must not be gelded..in the old of the Moone.

†**old**, *v. Obs.* Forms: 1 aldian, 2 aldien, 3 alden, holden, 4–5 olden, 5–8 old, (6 *Sc.* auld). [ME. *olden* = early ME. *alden*:—OE. (Anglian) *aldian* = WSax. *ealdian*, f. *ald*, *eald*, OLD *a.*: see ELD *v.*[1]] *intr.* To grow old.

c **825** *Vesp. Psalter* vi. 8 Ic aldade betwih alle feond mine. *c* **1175** *Lamb. Hom.* 35 Vfel is þet mon aldeþ. *Ibid.* 109 þeo hearte ne aldeð naut. *c* **1275** LAY. 2937 þo holdede [*c* **1205** ældede] þe king and failede his mihte. **1382** WYCLIF *1 Macc.* xvi. 3 Nowe I haue oldid [**1388** eldid]. **1496** *Dives & Paup.* (W. de W.) IV. xxvii. 195/1 As they olde so they fade. *c* **1560** A. SCOTT *Poems* (S.T.S.) xxxiv. 83 Auldit rubiatouris. **1741** J. SPENCE *Let.* 13 Jan. in *Academy* (1875) 20 Feb. 192/1 The Pretender looks sensibly olded since I was here last.

old, obs. f. WOLD; var. HOLD *a.*, *Obs.*

Old A'cademy. Also old Academy. [ACADEMY 2.] The school of philosophy founded by Plato in the fourth century B.C., as distinguished from schools founded by later Heads of the Academy, the *Middle Academy* of Arcesilaus, and the NEW ACADEMY of Carneades. So **Old Aca'demic** *sb.* and *a.*

1702 S. PARKER tr. *Tully's Five Bks. of De Finibus* v. 281, I am..well pleas'd that you've fallen upon so seasonable a Subject of Discourse, my Cousin being ambitious of a right Notion of that Hypothesis which the Old Academicks and Peripateticks you speak of, propagated about Moral Ends. **1744** W. GUTHRIE tr. *Cicero's Academical Treatises* in *Morals of Cicero* 304 If it were not too much Trouble, I should desire to hear anew, from your Mouth, both that and the whole System of the old Academy. *Ibid.* 316 The old Academics did not hold that all Virtue consisted in Reason. **1811** W. WARD *Acct. Writings, Relig. & Manners Hindoos* I. 357 This was the doctrine taught by Anaxagoras, and after him by Plato, and the whole Old Academy. **1874** J. S. REID *Cicero's Academica* p. xviii, It is a positive duty to discuss all aspects of every question, after the example of the Old Academy and Aristotle. **1876** ALLEYNE & GOODWIN tr. *Zeller's Plato & Older Acad.* xvi. 617 The Old Academy had even then, in many of its members, departed very far from genuine Platonism. **1885** J. S. REID *Cicero's Academica* (new ed.) 15 Varro evidently means that Cicero, having in earlier works copied the *writings* of 'Old Academic' philosophers, is about to draw on the literary stores of the New Academy. **1908** *Encycl. Relig. & Ethics* I. 59/2 The 'Old Academy' carried on the discussion of the problems which Plato had raised in his oral teaching. **1937** *Oxf. Compan. Classical Lit.* 2/1 The Academy under these leaders was known as the Old Academy. **1950** F. MAYER *Hist. Ancient & Medieval Philos.* xiv. 198 Conventionally, the Platonic school is divided into three periods. The first is the period of the Old Academy, which lasted from 347 B.C. to 250 B.C. **1974** A. A. LONG *Hellenistic Philos.* v. 224 Antiochus saw a very sharp distinction between the Old and the New Academy.

old age pension. [OLD *a.* 2.] A pension paid in certain countries by the state or, less frequently, by a private institution, to persons who have reached a specified age and are eligible for such assistance; also *ellipt.*, as *old age*. Used *attrib.* with *act*, *scheme*, etc. So **old age pensioner**, one who receives an old age pension.

1879 *19th Cent.* VI. 903 When the great clubs are able to mature the scheme which they are already entertaining for the payment of old age pensions. **1890** *Chambers's Jrnl.* 8 Feb. 88/1 To qualify..the worker must contribute..for an old-age pension for fourteen hundred and ten weeks. **1892** *Q. Rev.* Apr. 507 Old age pensions commence at seventy years of age. **1895** W. S. COTTEW *Scheme for Old Age Pension Fund* 1/2 After all working and other expenses paid, interest, etc., to form an Old Age Pension Fund, and as a further addition to the fund, there shall be an Old Age Pension Rate, not to exceed one penny in the £. **1906** *Chambers's Jrnl.* 10 Mar. 239/1 There are two possible systems for an old-age pension scheme for this country. **1908** *Act 8 Edw. VII* c. 40 §1 The sums required for the payment of old age pensions under this Act shall be paid out of moneys provided by Parliament. **1909** *Westm. Gaz.* 4 Jan. 3/3 We..believe that the Old-Age Pensions Act was almost universally intended to create a new social stratum. **1910** G. B. SHAW *Let.* 24 July (1972) II. 936 A list..which includes a choice collection of old-age-pensioners. **1931** *Times Lit. Suppl.* 4 June 441/2 The inspiration served its avowed purpose in providing him with 'an old-age pension'. **1936** *Act 26 Geo. V. & 1 Edw. VIII* c. 31 §4 Not more than one old age pension..shall be payable to any one person. **1945** A. HUXLEY *Let.* 30 Jan. (1969) 514 A nation like England..by 1975, will probably have declined to under forty millions, one quarter of whom will be drawing old age pensions. **1951** *Bull. Nat. Old People's Welfare Comm.* Feb. 10 In one London Borough on a given day each week old-age pensioners may attend the Municipal Baths at a cost of 1d. per bath. **1959** *Daily Tel.* 9 Apr. 1/7 Old age pensioners had much to gain from stability of prices. **1967** K. GILES *Death & Mr. Prettyman* viii. 160 'Not the old-age?'... 'The old-age for tax evaders? You're joking!' **1973** A. CHRISTIE *Postern of Fate* III. 127, I must go and talk to some old age pensioners at their club. **1976** *Sunday Tel.* 30 May 1/6 Sixteen old-age pensioners were injured..when a coach from Dundee crashed over an embankment.

Old Be'liever. [tr. Russ. *starovér.*] A member of that section of the Russian Orthodox Church which refused to accept the liturgical reforms of the patriarch Nikon (1605–1681). Also called RASKOLNIK.

1814 R. PINKERTON tr. *Platon's Present State Greek Ch. in Russia* 293 On the death of the first leaders of the modern Raskolniks, some of the sects resolved to admit runaway priests into their communion, and to acknowledge their ordination on condition of their becoming Old Believers. **1879** L. B. LANG tr. *Rambaud's Hist. Russia* I. xxii. 433 She had arrested certain 'old believers'. **1911** *Encycl. Brit.* XIX. 692/1 This ruthlessness goes far to explain the unappeasable hatred with which the 'Old Ritualists' and the 'Old Believers', as they now began to be called, ever afterwards regarded Nikon and all his works. **1921** F. C. CONYBEARE *Russ. Dissenters* I. iii. 140 Court Kolovrat, the protector of the Old believers in Austria. **1931** *Times Lit. Suppl.* 12 Feb. 105/3 In Kiev, where he made the acquaintance of the community of Old Believers, who upheld the schism in the Orthodox Church. **1932** M. EASTMAN tr. *Trotsky's Hist. Russ. Revolution* I. i. 27 The struggle against the state church did not go farther than the creation of peasant sects, the faction of the Old Believers being the most powerful among them. **1957** *Oxf. Dict. Chr. Ch.* 960/2 His [*sc.* Nikon's] liturgical reforms were sanctioned..and the formation of the schismatical sect of the Old Believers followed. **1959** *Listener* 19 Feb. 338/3, I would put the number of practising Orthodox Christians (including Old Believers) [in the U.S.S.R.] somewhat lower than the figure ..suggested by Mr. Kolarz. **1962** K. S. LATOURETTE *Christianity in Revolutionary Age* IV. xix. 508 In 1957 the Old Believers were known to have a church in Moscow. **1963** V. NABOKOV *Gift* ii. 122 In 1862, sixty Russian Old-Believers with their wives and children lived for half a year in these parts. **1963** N. V. RIASANOVSKY *Hist. Russia* xix. 221 Shchapov and numerous others have stressed the social composition of the Old Believers and the social and economic reasons for their rebellion. **1973** *Guardian* 5 Mar. 2/7 The Soviet magazine Science and Religion..was criticising small groups of Old Believers..in Tuvinskaya province.

Old Bill.

1. The name of a cartoon character created during the war of 1914–18 by the British cartoonist Bruce Bairnsfather (1888–1959) and portrayed as a grumbling veteran soldier with a large moustache. Freq. in allusive and *transf.* use.

1915 *Bystander* III. 4 Again, 'Old Bill' and 'Our Bert' and 'Alf', seriously comical and comically serious, fill the pages with their humour. **1925** FRASER & GIBBONS *Soldier & Sailor Words* 213 *Old Bill*, a veteran. Any old Soldier; in particular one with a heavy, drooping moustache. (From Captain Bairnsfather's celebrated creation 'Old Bill'). **1930** *Daily Express* 6 Oct. 4/4 An enormous mouth fringed all around with stiff hairy bristles, just like an 'Old Bill' moustache. **1933** B. BAIRNSFATHER *Laughing through Orient* i. 15 Old Bill who, for many years, has been so closely entwined with my existence. **1939** H. HODGE *Cab, Sir?* 54 Here comes Old Bill himself. **1942** P. V. BRADSHAW *They make us Smile* 9 The creation of Old Bill was never deliberate. Bill somehow created himself. **1946** *R.A.F. Jrnl.* May 163 During the last war, Bruce Bairnsfather created 'Old Bill', a lovable grumbler, typifying the foot-slogger of the British Army in Flanders. **1973** *Times* 2 Nov. 13/7 The Old Bill moustache starts twitching.

2. *slang.* The police force; a policeman.

[**1939**: see BILL *sb.*[5]] **1958** F. NORMAN *Bang to Rights* 138 Two Old Bill's came up to me and told me they had a warrant for my arrest. **1967** *Guardian* 14 Mar. 8/6 He observed a couple of men supping nearby who looked suspiciously like plainclothes men. Coulson asked the landlord. 'Oh no,' he said, 'they're drinking pints. Old Bills only drink halves.' **1970** G. F. NEWMAN *Sir, You Bastard* viii. 272 Giving Old Bill a bung was still an offence, and there would have been no consideration for the information. **1973** K. ROYCE *Spider Underground* i. 19 It's me he's out to fix by bringing Old Bill about my ears. **1976** *New Statesman* 12 Mar. 322/3 If they were caught at it when the Old Bill (police) staged one of their frequent raids then we would all be up on a charge of 'maintaining a disorderly house'.

old boy. [f. OLD *a.* + BOY *sb.*[1]] A former pupil of a (particular) boys' school, esp. an English public school. Also as quasi-*adj.* Hence **old-boyish** *a.*, characteristic or suggestive of an old boy; **old-boyishness**. Also used *attrib.* (influenced by OLD *a.* 8 a), *spec.* in **old boy(s') net(work)**, to designate comradeship or favouritism shown among old boys; also *transf.*; **old boys' tie**, phr. suggesting attitudes or activities typical of old boys. See also *old girl* s.v. GIRL *sb.* 2 a.

1868 *Haileyburian* I. 4/2 On Nov. 30th, was played our first *Old Boys* football match. **1894** A. BEARDSLEY *Let.* 2–3 Oct. (1971) 76, I had hoped to be at the Old Boys' dinner next month but I fear it is out of the question. **1910** H. G. WELLS *New Machiavelli* (1911) I. iii. 92 (*heading*) The school chapel; and how it seems to an old boy. **1920** BEERBOHM *And Even Now* 297 The accounts given to me by 'old boys' of other schools. **1931** 'G. TREVOR' *Murder at School* i. 16 'It is always a pleasure for Oakington to receive her old boys.' .. A little old-boyishness in response seemed clearly indicated.. Within five minutes Revell had ceased to be old-boyish. **1936** 'G. ORWELL' *Keep Aspidistra Flying* iii. 57 He..developed unorthodox opinions about the C. of E., patriotism and the Old Boys' tie. **1959** 'J. BYROM' *Take only as Directed* viii. 88 'Well, blow me down!' I chose a phrase that seemed suitably Old Boy. **1959** *Guardian* 10 Nov. 8/4 The party must show that the Old Boy network of the Left does not prevent its speaking out when necessary. **1960** *Observer* 26 June 27/2 They write, therefore they are—that is, are part of literary history or, if the anthology is contemporary, part of the Old Boy circuit. **1960** *Punch* 10 Aug. 208/1 His [*sc.* Shakespeare's] marvellous understanding of the old-boy net as it was operated in the upper echelons of the Greek and Trojan armies. **1961** *Guardian* 19 Jan. 20/7 The atmosphere of old-boyishness and good-chappery which is a deadly threat to our society. **1964** *New Scientist* 24 Sept. 793/1 Dr. Bertrand Goldschmidt..managed to obtain, on an 'old boy basis', about 3 micrograms of plutonium. **1970** *Wall St. Jrnl.* 30 Mar. 1/1 Management experts here see a decline [in Britain] in the 'Old Boy Network'. *Ibid.*, The Old Boy Net is being replaced by professional managers who take perks for granted. **1971** J. R. L. ANDERSON *Reckoning in Ice* vii. 143 To hanker after reunions, Old Boys' gatherings and the like suggests that nothing in one's later life has ever quite matched school. **1972** *Daily Tel.* (Colour Suppl.) 1 Dec. 40/4 There is a clubbish sort of old boys' net in The Room [at Lloyd's]. **1973** A. PRICE *October Men* xii. 178 The Russians don't go much on the old boys' network. **1975** *Times* 27 Feb. 14/8 The [Central Intelligence] Agency..is a cosy gentleman's club whose members have a strict code of their own... They operate on an old boy net, extensive if exclusive.

Old Catholic: see CATHOLIC B. 3 b.

old chum: see CHUM *sb.*^{1} 1 b.

Old Dart. *Austral.* and *N.Z. colloq.* [Origin uncertain: cf. DART *sb.* 7.] The 'old country'; Great Britain, *esp.* England.

1908 E. S. SORENSON *Quinton's Rouseabout* 206 Murty unexpectedly came in for something like £800 by the death of a distant and almost forgotten relative in the old dart. **1933** *Bulletin* (Sydney) 13 Dec. 58/4 He was a forward in the British team of 1904, led by Bedell Sievwright, about the best side from the Old Dart to visit these shores. **1935** 'J. GUTHRIE' *Little Country* i. 6 The present generation..still finds under its skin a queer, rooted, and sometimes flowering love for the Old Dart. **1945** BAKER *Austral. Lang.* x. 184 He would be less maudlinly sentimental over *Home*, *the old country*, *the old dart*, or *the old land* as Britain was known. **1950** K. S. PRITCHARD *Winged Seeds* 357 'It means,' Dinny said slowly, 'that Australia's backin' the Old Dart with $31,500,000 worth of gold a year.' **1952** J. CLEARY *Sundowners* 157, I married her when I was over in the Old Dart during the war. **1966** 'J. HACKSTON' *Father clears Out* 143 If you'd come from the Old Dart yourself you'd have been the first to start chucking snow. **1973** *Austral. Women's Weekly* 25 July 79/3 Fresh from the Old Dart, I was as willing as they came. I wanted to write that success letter home to England.

olde (əʊld, 'əʊldiː), *a.* An affected form of OLD *a.*, supposed to be archaic and usu. employed to suggest (spurious) antiquity, *esp.* in collocations often also archaistically spelt, as *olde English(e)*, *Englyshe*, *worlde*, *worldly*. Also as *sb.*

Also *oldie*, *oldy*.

1927 C. CONNOLLY *Let.* 7 Mar. in *Romantic Friendship* (1975) 281 There remain consolations, such as finding places that aren't spoilt and not being surprised by their destruction into the..oldie worldie type. **1929** —— *Let.* [undated] in *Romantic Friendship* (1975) 325 Oldy-worldy England is such a dreary opposite [to America]. **1930** E. POUND *XXX Cantos* viii. 31 Ye spirits who of olde were in this land. **1931** M. ALLINGHAM *Look to Lady* v. 61 There's something so Olde English about you, Val, that I expect a chorus of rustic maidens. **1932** N. MITFORD *Christmas Pudding* v. 74 You just made the mistake..of confusing old world with olde worlde. You should have been more careful to find out whether or not there was an 'e'; so much hangs on that one little letter. **1933** A. G. MACDONELL *England, their England* vii. 101 It was as if Mr. Cochran had..brought Ye Olde Englyshe Village straight down by special train from the London Pavilion. **1934** C. LAMBERT *Music Ho!* V. 280 We..pour our bootleg gin into cracked leather bottles with olde-worlde labels. **1939** JOYCE *Finnegans Wake* I. 7 A glass of Danu U'Dunnell's foamous olde Dobbelin ayle. **1939** O. LANCASTER *Homes Sweet Homes* 10 All over Europe the lights are going out, oil-lamps, gas-mantles, electroliers, olde Tudor lanthorns, standards and wall-brackets. **1950** M. J. C. HODGART *Ballads* v. 106 We don't know what Percy's corrections were, but the Olde Englishe of this stanza may be suspected: Lord Thomas he saw Fair Annet wex pale. **1956** E. POUND tr. *Sophocles' Women of Trachis* 25 E'en from fond eyes, olde flowers are cast away. **1958** B. NICHOLS *Sweet & Twenties* viii. 105 The oldy-worldy cafés. **1959** *Good Food Guide* 38 A lot of olde realle beames in Amersham and a lot of olde phonie cookynge too. **1967** 'D. SHANNON' *Rain with Violence* (1969) i. 9 A little coffee shop ..Decorated in very pseudo Olde Englishe. **1970** P. GEDDES *November Wind* viii. 95 Bear... An olde Englishe, where-did-you-put-my-cricket-bat teddy bear. **1972** *Guardian* 4 Dec. 11/3 The interior is old but not olde worlde, the medieval oak beams have been left..without..horse brasses and warming pans. **1974** 'P. B. YUILL' *Bornless Keeper* vii. 65 Why did we have to come..to this quaint olde aleshoppe? **1976** *Rhyl Jrnl. & Advertiser* 9 Dec. 18/6 (Advt.), Gwaenysgor. Charming stone built olde worlde Cottage of immense character.

olde, obs. f. WELD, a plant used in dyeing.

olden ('əʊld(ə)n), *a.* [f. OLD *sb.*^{2} + -EN^4. (It has been suggested that the suffix may represent an earlier inflexion of *old*. Cf. Ger. *in der alten Zeit*.)]

1. Belonging to a bygone age or time; ancient, old: esp. in the phr. 'the olden time' (Shaks.). *literary* and *arch.*

a **1425** *Cursor M.* 18100 (Trin.) To ende he seide now com my sawes þat I seide bi olden dawes. **1426** AUDELAY *Poems* 22 The goodys of hole cherche..That other han ȝeven in holdoun dais. **1605** SHAKS. *Macb.* III. iv. 75 Blood hath bene shed ere now, i' th' olden time. **1806** KNOX & JEBB *Corr.* I. 305 To talk and write..like those of 'olden time'. **1816** SCOTT *Tales my Landlord* Ser. I. Introd., A young person.. who delighted in the collection of olden tales and legends. **1837** LONGF. *Flowers* i, In language quaint and olden. **1848** CLOUGH *Amours de Voy.* III. 79 The words of the olden-time inspiration. **1849** MISS MULOCK *Ogilvies* xlvi. (1875) 356 Some new bond had made the very memory of that olden pledge a sin.

2. *poetic* for OLD *a.* 1, 2. *rare.*

1823 BYRON *Juan* XII. xliii, Olden she was—but had been very young. **1871** R. ELLIS *Catullus* xxvii. 1 Boy, young caterer of Falernian olden.

Hence † **'oldenness**, olden quality, antiquity.

1422 tr. *Secreta Secret., Priv. Priv.* 193 The ij^e caus is that matremony ys to be comend is the oldennysse of hit, ffor this ordir ys not nyowely maket, but of oldennys hit passith all manner of orderis in erth.

olden ('əʊld(ə)n), *v. rare.* [f. OLD *a.* + -EN^5.]

1. *intr.* To grow old, to become older in appearance or character, to age.

1827 MARY FRAMPTON *Jrnl.* (1885) 329 Her face is oldened and more sallow. **1848** THACKERAY *Van. Fair* xviii, In six weeks he oldened more than he had done for fifteen years before. **1852** —— *Esmond* I. ix, She had oldened..as people do who suffer silently great mental pain.

2. *trans.* To cause to grow old, to make older in appearance or character, to age.

1850 THACKERAY *Pendennis* liii, It was curious how emotion seemed to olden him. **1863** *Denise* II. 188 When oldened by sorrow he might feel the deep spell that Denise possessed.

Hence **'oldened**, **'oldening** *ppl. adjs.*

1876 MRS. WHITNEY *Sights & Ins.* II. xxiv. 525 It was the joy of oldening years. **1892** *Temple Bar Mag.* Dec. 580 Her friend's oldened and altered looks.

olden, obs. f. *holden*, pa. pple. of HOLD *v.*

Old English.

1. The English language of an earlier period: see ENGLISH *sb.* 1 b.

2. *Typog.* A form of 'Black Letter' resembling that used by early English printers; now occasionally employed for ornamental purposes.

1849 MRS. GASKELL *Let.* 7 Dec. (1966) 94 Two birch-wood rocking chairs, with 'Mina' & 'Sam' carved in old English on the back of each. **1883** in A. Adburgham *Shops & Shopping* (1964) xix. 226 Woven ingrain red initial letters, old English style; whole names in old English or script. **1966** S. MARCUS *Other Victorians* ii. 34 In the index [of *Index Librorum Prohibitorum*], authors' names are in Small Capitals, titles are in Old English. **1967** E. CHAMBERS *Photolitho-Offset* ii. 13 Text type faces are of the style worked almost exclusively by Gutenberg and are sometimes known as 'Old English'.

3. *absol.* for B. 3.

1971 F. HAMILTON *World Encycl. Dogs* 77 The Old English is quite unlike the Collie varieties of sheepdog.

B. *adj. phr.* **1.** Designating or belonging to the English language of an earlier period: see ENGLISH *a.* 4 b.

2. *Typog.* Of a style resembling that used by early English printers.

1701 M. BULL *Let.* 12 June in *Private Corr. Samuel Pepys* (1926) II. 230 There is no picture in it, nor any thing writt in capital or Roman letters, but all printed in the old english letter. **1950** M. ALLINGHAM *Mr. Campion & Others* 191 The embossed address..in semi-Old English script. **1967** B. COPPER *No Flowers for General* vii. 85 [There] was a large white-painted board. In black Old English lettering it said: Fitzgoerge [*sic*] Country Club. **1974** *Listener* 24 Jan. 98 In those days..mortgage deeds were written out ('engrossed') and the word 'mortgage' appeared in Old English lettering on the back sheet.

3. Old English sheep-dog, a large, thick-set dog of the breed so called, with a long, blue-grey and white coat; also known as the bobtail. Also *absol.*

1890 R. B. LEE *Hist. & Descr. Collie* v. 81 The old English sheep dog was at one time pretty equally distributed through various parts of the kingdom. **1928** F. T. BARTON *Kennel Encycl.* 313 The type of old English sheep-dog varies considerably in different counties. **1971** F. HAMILTON *World Encycl. Dogs* 77 The Old English Sheepdog has been known as a distinct variety in Britain for at least two hundred years.

4. Made by English craftsmen of an earlier period, esp., of table silver, made to a pattern used from the mid-18th century, with plain shapes and flat stems spreading to the rounded ends.

1907 *Yesterday's Shopping* (1969) 215/1 Nickel Silver, Old English Pattern, Spoons and Forks. *a* **1910** 'MARK TWAIN' *Autobiogr.* (1924) II. 93 Her prized and precious old-English sugar bowl..was an heirloom in the family. **1973** *Country Life* 15 Feb. 389/3 William Bateman..was making Old English teaspoons as late as the 1820s, a decade after the fiddle pattern became fashionable.

older ('əʊldə(r)), *a.* and *sb.* [f. OLD *a.* + -ER^3.]

A. *adj.* The later 'levelled' comparative of OLD, which has superseded the earlier ELDER q.v., except in special uses. (The levelling down of the comparative appears to have begun with the form *alder*, found already *c* 1200.)

1. In the ordinary senses of OLD: Of greater age; that has lived or existed longer, of longer existence or standing; more ancient.

1205–1610 [see ALDER *a. compar.*]. **1592** SHAKS. *Rom. & Jul.* II. iv. 127 Young Romeo will be older [*Qos.* elder] when you haue found him. **1601** —— *Jul. C.* IV. iii. 31, I am a Souldier, I, Older in practice. Abler then your selfe To make Conditions. **1671** MILTON *Samson* 1489 Thy Son, Made older then thy age through eye-sight lost. **1713** J. WARDER *True Amazons* (ed. 2) 54 In June and July, they [wasps] are both older and bolder. **1863** LYELL *Antiq. Man* 8 Deposits of older date. *a* **1864** HAWTHORNE *Septimius Felton* (1879) 149 A house in the older part of the town. *Mod.* She is ten years older than her sister.

2. In the sense of ELDER *a. compar.* 1 b: the older of two of a family, etc.; senior. Only *dial.*

c **1205** LAY. 3750 Of þan aldre sustren. **1465** MARG. PASTON in *P. Lett.* II. 212, I have delyveryd your older sonne xx mark. *Mod. Sc.* He is my aulder brother.

B. *sb.* † **1.** *pl.* Predecessors: = ELDER B. 1. *Obs.*

a **1470** TIPTOFT *Orat. G. Flamineus* (Caxton 1481) F iv, To preche of the noble dedes of thyn olders, I wil..confesse that thyn auncestres have be of soverayne auctorite.

† **2.** (A person's) superior in age, senior (chiefly in *pl.*): = ELDER B. 2. *Obs.*

1483 CAXTON *G. de la Tour* K vj, Trewly this yonge man ..byleueth the counceylle of his older. *c* **1500** *How the Plowman lerned his Pater-Noster* 40 in Hazl. *E.P.P.* I. 211 As I haue herde myne olders tell. **1562** J. HEYWOOD *Prov.* (1867) 26, I haue herd of myne olders.

† **b.** A person advanced in life: = ELDER B. 2 b.

c **1440** CAPGRAVE *St. Kath.* v. 868 Oon of the olderes ageyn on-to hir seyth: 'O precyous spouse of god!'

older, erron. Sc. form of *owther*, EITHER *conj.*

oldest ('əʊldɪst), *a. superl.* [f. OLD *a.* + -EST.] The later 'levelled' superlative of OLD, which has superseded the earlier form ELDEST in all except special uses: see ELDEST *a. superl.* 2, 3, 5.

1. In ordinary senses derived from OLD: Farthest advanced in age; first made or produced; most ancient: = ELDEST 1, 3.

c **1400** MAUNDEV. (1839) iv. 30 It is on of the oldest townes of the world. **1597** SHAKS. *2 Hen. IV*, IV. v. 127 Haue you a Ruffian that will..commit The oldest sinnes, the newest kinde of wayes. **1605** —— *Lear* v. iii. 325 The oldest hath borne most, we that are yong, Shall neuer see so much. **1676** HOBBES *Iliad* Pref. (1686) 7 They that..look upon it with the oldest spectacles of a Critick, may approve it. **1743** BULKELEY & CUMMINS *Voy. S. Seas* 120 The oldest Seaman on board never saw a more dismal Prospect. **1790** BURKE *Fr. Rev.* 45 Our oldest reformation is that of Magna Charta. **1838** DE MORGAN *Ess. Probab.* 210 A's interest in the latter annuity..when A is the oldest of the three.

2. Occasionally found in uses properly belonging to ELDEST. Now *dial.* or *vulgar.*

13.. *E.E. Allit. P.* B. 1333 Bolde Baltazar þat watz his barn aldest. *c* **1400** *Destr. Troy* 11055 Pirrus, Polidamas brother..aldist but he. **1785** PALEY *Mor. Philos.* (1818) I. xxii. 225 The not making a will, is a very culpable omission ..where it leaves daughters, or younger children, at the mercy of the oldest son. **1899** *Tit-Bits* 12 Aug. 396/3 The oldest sister.

3. Phr. *oldest inhabitant*; freq. in joc. use.

1850 HAWTHORNE *Scarlet Letter* 13 The whereabouts of the Oldest Inhabitant was at once settled, when I looked at them. **1859** 'L.N.R.' *Missing Link* x. 130 No bedstead has been seen there in the 'memory of the oldest inhabitant'. **1914** 'I. HAY' *Lighter Side School Life* iv. 105 The Wag and the Oldest Inhabitant are usually permitted to offer observations. **1926** CHESTERTON *Incredulity of Father Brown* v. 160 A curse on the place, according to the guide-book or the parson or the oldest inhabitant or whoever is the authority. **1950** 'J. TEY' *To Love & be Wise* xv. 196 The Oldest Inhabitant..was a vain old party but he was the representative..of..Race Memory. *a* **1966** M. ALLINGHAM *Cargo of Eagles* (1968) xii. 141 'The ancient mariner in the corner of The Demon?' enquired Campion. 'The professional oldest inhabitant?' **1974** E. LEMARCHAND *Buried in Past* xi. 187 Good Lord, look at the Oldest Inhabitant stepping in front of a moving car...the chap's managed to pull up.

old-face. *Typog.* [See FACE *sb.* 22.] A typeface characterized by a pleasingly irregular appearance with little contrast between thick and thin strokes and with bracketed serifs, modelled on the roman and italic letters that were derived from classical inscriptions and early humanist hands and used by printers of the 15th to 18th centuries. Also *attrib.* Also **old-faced** *a.*

[**1824** J. JOHNSON *Typographia* II. xix. 647 Such letter.. could not possibly last so long as that of the old cut.] **1863** G. UNWIN (*title*) Specimens of the old-faced series of type in use at the Gresham Steam-press. **1875** *Caslon's Circular* July 1/1 He [*sc.* Charles Whittingham] was supplied by Mr. Caslon with the complete series of original old-face founts. *Ibid.*, There appeared in the market a modern imitation of the old-face character called Old Style. *Ibid.* 1/2 There followed a demand for the old-face founts. **1888** C. T. JACOBI *Printers' Vocab.* 90 Old-cut type, founts similar to the Caslon old-faced type. **1922** D. B. UPDIKE *Printing Types* II. xxi. 201 In England Caslon types are called 'old face'. **1923** MORISON & JACKSON *Brief Survey Printing* ii. 16 The raw material of the revival was ready as far back as the year 1720, when Caslon set up his type foundry and began the casting of the now famous old face founts which have become classical. **1931** *Times Lit. Suppl.* 25 June (Suppl.) p. i/2 Bold woodcuts stencilled with bright colours on a large page need stronger support than can be furnished by a quiet old-face in readable eleven-point. **1951** S. JENNETT *Making of Bks.* xii. 198 Text faces can be divided into two clear categories, known to the printer as 'old faces' and 'modern faces'; such types as had appeared up to and including Caslon..are grouped under the term 'old face'... The chief characteristic of old-face types is the fundamental relation of the line to that made by the pen. The stress is tilted..and the accent diminishes gradually into the thin stroke without obvious junction; exaggeration and artificial emphasis are generally avoided. **1972** P. GASKELL *New Introd. Bibliogr.* 210 The demand for the old faces came to an abrupt end. *Ibid.* 212 From the 1840s there was a gradually quickening revival of interest in old-face romans.

'old-ˌfangled, *a.* [f. after *new-fangled*: cf. FANGLE.] Characterized by adherence to what is old, old-fashioned. Hence **old-'fangledness.**

1842 BROWNING *Pied Piper* vi, Low it dangled Over his vesture so old-fangled. **1871** M. COLLINS *Mrq. & Merch.* I. vi. 208 Old-fangled cut glasses. **1894** *Harper's Weekly Mag.* 7 Apr. 315 Repelling the new-fangled remedy, [he] resorts to the oldest-fangled known. **1895** *Spectator* 23 Nov. 731/2 We like better, out of a certain old-fangledness, to turn back again to the oft-told stories of *Punch's* beginnings.

old-farrand: see AULD and FARRAND 3.

†**'old-ˌfashion,** *a. Obs.* [f. OLD *a.* + FASHION *sb.*] = OLD-FASHIONED.

1665 PEPYS *Diary* 22 July, I..viewed the new hall, a new old-fashion hall. **1683** MOXON *Mech. Exerc., Printing* ii. ¶2 They are now accounted old-fashion. **1796** CHARLOTTE SMITH *Marchmont* III. 67 A high, long, old-fashion room.

†**ˌold-'fashionable,** *a. Obs.* [f. as prec. + -ABLE.] = next. Hence **ˌold-'fashionably** *adv.*

1764 H. WALPOLE *Lett., to G. Montagu* 10 May (1846) IV. 420 No. 14..looked so old-fashionably, that I ventured to give eighteen shillings for it. **1807** E. S. BARRETT *Rising Sun* III. 18 Hypocrisy is decried as old-fashionable and useless in this liberal age.

ˌold-'fashioned, *a.* [See FASHIONED *ppl. a.*[2]]

1. a. Formed or conducted according to the fashion of former times; antiquated in form or character. Also *absol.*

1653 WALTON *Angler* ii. 64 They were old fashioned Poetry, but choicely good. **1683** MOXON *Mech. Exerc., Printing* 38 The Old-fashion'd Presses..used here in England. **1712** STEELE *Spect.* No. 308 ¶2 An old-fashioned Grate consumes Coals, but gives no Heat. **1897** MARY KINGSLEY *W. Africa* 145 Good, old-fashioned, long skirts. **1904** *Daily Chron.* 7 Jan. 3/3 She..does not hesitate to lean to the old-fashioned if occasion require.

b. Of a plant, belonging to an old-established variety no longer common in cultivation.

1920 'O. DOUGLAS' *Penny Plain* i. 8 A herbaceous border ..blazed in a sweet disorder of old-fashioned blossoms. **1939** S. SITWELL *Old Fashioned Flowers* i. 21 There can be more than a mere sentimental fondness for these old flowers. It is not enough that they are old-fashioned and in danger of being classed as quaint. **1960** F. C. STERN *Chalk Garden* v. 53 There are a number of 'old-fashioned' primroses which are great fun in the garden. **1975** R. GENDERS *Growing Old-fashioned Flowers* 7 In most cottage gardens there may still grow at least a few of the old-fashioned plants.

2. Attached to old fashions or ways; having the tastes of former times.

1687 T. BROWN *Saints in Uproar* Wks. 1730 I. 81 Those old-fashion'd sparks yonder. **1712** ADDISON *Spect.* No. 499 ¶7 Will is one of those old-fashioned men of wit and pleasure of the town. **1796** BURKE *Regic. Peace* iv. Wks. IX. 20 People, like me, old fashioned enough to consider, that [etc.]. **1866** GEO. ELIOT *F. Holt* i. (1868) 15 You have come back to a family who have old-fashioned notions.

3. Having the ways of a grown-up person; hence, precocious, intelligent, knowing. Chiefly *dial.*

1844 *Yorks. Comet* 18 (E.D.D.) A sleep-walker..began o'tunin' on't, as owd-feshioned as if his een had been wide oppen. **1848** DICKENS *Dombey* xiv. (1858) 96 The little fellow had a fine mind, but was an old-fashioned boy. **1858** R. M. BALLANTYNE *Coral Island* i. 11, I overheard them [*sc.* shipmates] sometimes saying that Ralph Rover was a 'queer, old-fashioned fellow'. **1874** BURNAND *My time* ii. 18, I suppose at this age I must have been very old-fashioned. **1886** *S.W. Linc. Gloss.* s.v., The pony was a bit old-fashioned, and could open the gate with his mouth. **1972** J. WILSON *Hide & Seek* iv. 76 She's not very happy at school. .. She can seem irritating and annoying at times—she has this quaint old-fashioned sort of knowing air, and she asks the teachers lots of questions.

4. Disapproving, tart, reproachful: used *spec.* of facial expression. Also as *adv.*, in a disapproving, reproachful or quizzical manner. Freq. in phr. ***to give*** (someone) ***an old-fashioned look***, ***to look old-fashioned at*** (someone).

Quot. 1911 may belong in sense 3.

1911 F. H. BURNETT *Secret Garden* xvii. 181 She.. examined them with a solemn savage little face. She looked so sour and old-fashioned that the nurse turned her head aside to hide the twitching of her mouth. *a* **1922** T. S. ELIOT *Waste Land Drafts* (1971) 13 No, ma'am, you needn't look old-fashioned at me. **1926** S. JAMESON *Three Kingdoms* vi. 154 Laurence listened, said: 'Oh. Bring her up in two minutes,' and gave Macdougal what he mentally classified as an old-fashioned look. **1933** E. WILLIAMS *Late Christopher Bean* II. 51, I was wrong thinking wrong things, and acting so old fashioned with you. **1935** *Archit. Rev.* LXXVII. 270/3 He straightened his back and gave me an old-fashioned look as who should say 'And I dare you to laugh at me in your damn superior way, blast you.' **1935** N. MARSH *Enter Murderer* vii. 83 'Don't you act old-fashioned at me,' snarled the man. **1943** P. CHEYNEY *You can always Duck* i. 15 She looks at me sorta old-fashioned. **1948** 'N. SHUTE' *No Highway* vi. 149 They'll probably look a bit old-fashioned at me. **1951** M. KENNEDY *Lucy Carmichael* VII. iv. 379 I've tried to tell her twice..and all I get is an old-fashioned look. **1959** 'R. SIMONS' *Houseboat Killings* xiii. 133 The commissionaire gave them an old-fashioned look as they spun the revolving doors, but it was lost on Wace. **1974** *Blackw. Mag.* Sept. 197/2 Comrade Supervisor gave her an old-fashioned look and answered: 'Lidia died the moment she fell, the moment she touched the ground.'

5. Special collocations: **old-fashioned cocktail** *U.S.*, a cocktail consisting principally of whisky, bitters, and sugar, served with ice; also *ellipt.*, as *old-fashioned*; **old-fashioned rose** = OLD ROSE a; **old-fashioned waltz**, a waltz played in quick time; **old-fashioned winter**, a winter marked by snow and hard frost.

1901 *Cocktail Bk.* 27 (*heading*) Whiskey Cocktail—Old-fashioned. **1930** H. CRADDOCK *Savoy Cocktail Bk.* I. 114 Old Fashioned Cocktail. 1 Lump Sugar. 2 Dashes Angostura Bitters. 1 Glass Rye or Canadian Club Whisky. **1942** D. POWELL *Time to be Born* (1943) x. 237 He charged ten cents more for old-fashioneds than Bill's did. **1958** G. GREENE *Our Man in Havana* v. iii. 212 A Scotch, sir? A sherry? An Old-Fashioned? **1963** E. CLARKE *Shaking in 60's* 95 Old fashioned cocktail. Use a small heavy tumbler glass... Place in 1 lump of sugar..add a lump of ice..pour into the prepared glass 2 measures of Bourbon. **1975** 'M. DUKE' *Death of Holy Murderer* ix. 111 We're drinking old-fashioneds beside the swimming pool. **1888** J. W. RILEY (*title*) Old-fashioned roses. **1889** *Garden* 6 July 14/3 If this conference does no more than further the cultivation of the many climbing and other old-fashioned Roses, it will have achieved a great object. **1937** C. SPRY *Flowers in House & Garden* 75 Grass paths divide large irregularly-shaped beds filled with..old-fashioned roses. **1962** A. CHRISTIE *Mirror Crack'd* i. 17 Laycock had cut down the old-fashioned roses in a way more suitable to hybrid teas. **1971** J. RAVEN *Botanist's Garden* vi. 120 We grow..four others of the showiest of the old-fashioned roses. **1927** *Melody Maker* Aug. 787/2 The old-fashioned tango is not so dissimilar to the modern, and there are still many sincere lovers of the old-fashioned waltz left. **1952** M. LASKI *Village* ii. 41 The Rhythm Ragamuffins were starting off with an old-fashioned waltz. **1865** M. EYRE *Lady's Walks S. of France* xvi. 189, I like an old-fashioned English winter—hard frosts and deep snows in their season. **1939** L. M. MONTGOMERY *Anne of Ingleside* xiii. 86 We never seem to have old-fashioned winters nowadays.

Hence **ˌold-'fashionedly** *adv.*, in an old-fashioned manner; **ˌold-'fashionedness**, the quality or condition of being old-fashioned.

1813 M. EDGEWORTH *Let.* 16 May (1971) 60 She is now huge and very plainly dressed old fashionedly but she must have been beautiful and graceful formerly. **1817** *Blackw. Mag.* I. 590 Old age was the ton—old fashionedness the rage. **1853** MRS. CARLYLE *Lett.* II. 218 It is comfortably but plainly and old-fashionedly furnished. **1886** *Athenæum* 27 Mar. 421/3 She has given a pleasing air of old-fashionedness to her language. **1967** V. GIELGUD *Conduct of Member* iii. 27, I don't see that we can ask for Lestrange's resignation because he's old-fashionedly moral. **1968** *Economist* 9 Nov. p. iii/3 He could be, obsessively and old-fashionedly, wrong. **1976** 'M. ALBRAND' *Taste of Terror* vii. 46 Kent had reacted old-fashionedly. If he lived with a woman..he would feel compelled to marry her.

old field. a. Land cultivated of old; esp., in U.S., cultivated by the Indians, before the coming of the white men.

1635 in *Amer. Legal Rec.* (Amer. Hist. Soc.) (1954) VII. 31 Mr. John wilkins made suit..for a neck of land.. boundeth..northerly on Cugleyes ould field. **1656** *Rec. of Braintree, Mass.* (1886) 7 A highway layed out in the old feild for goodman Hoydin to bring his corne out. **1765** J. BARTRAM *Jrnl.* 28 Dec. in Stork *Acc. E. Florida* (1766) 12 Landed at Mount-Royal, where there are 50 acres of cleared old fields. **1791** W. BARTRAM *Travels* 54 Their old field and planting land extend up and down the river. **1839** *Southern Lit. Messenger* V. 113/1 First..no such foreigner has the faintest idea of what an old-field is. **1859** *Trans. Illinois Agric. Soc.* III. 452 In 1840 I became possessed of the tract of land containing what was called the 'old field'. **1896** P. A. BRUCE *Econ. Hist. Virginia* I. 427. **1905** *Forestry Bureau Bull.* (U.S.) No. 63, 5 The life history of second-growth white pine on old fields and pastures in New England. **1938** G. H. COLLINGWOOD in *Amer. Forests* Sept. 417 Pure stands of young Virginia pine frequently follow on old fields when agriculture is abandoned.

b. *attrib.* in **old-field birch**, one of several North American birches, esp. the white birch, *Betula populifolia*; **old-field lark**, the field-lark; **old-field mouse**, a white-footed, pale brown mouse, *Peromyscus polionotus*, found in sandy regions of the south-eastern U.S.A.; **old-field pine**, one of several North American pines, esp. the loblolly pine, *Pinus tæda*.

1810 F. A. MICHAUX *Hist. Arbres Forestiers de l'Amérique Septentrionale* I. 26 White birch [ou] *Old field birch (Bouleau des terreins secs.). **1832** D. J. BROWNE *Sylva Amer.* 123 In the state of Maine,..[the name] Old Field Birch is..employed to distinguish the white birch from the canoe birch. **1946** W. D. BRUSH in *Amer. Forests* Sept. 431 This accounts for the tree quickly taking possession of burned-over, cutover and abandoned land, which has given it the name 'oldfield birch'. **1921** A. H. HOWELL in *N. Amer. Fauna* XLV. 44 The little *old-field mouse occurs rather commonly in suitable situations throughout the eastern, central, and northeastern parts of the State [of Alabama]. **1936** *Jrnl. Mammalogy* XVII. 420 A number of breeding stocks of old-field mice..were collected in parts of Alabama and Florida. **1971** *Nature* 12 Nov. 102/2 Crosses of *Peromyscus maniculatus*, the deermouse, and *P. polionotus*, the oldfield mouse,..showed that placental weights of foetuses..differed significantly from each other. **1797** B. HAWKINS *Let.* 23 Feb. (1916) 89 The whole grown up with *old field pine, some of them a foot and a half diameter. **1841** *Southern Lit. Messenger* VII. 452/1 The old-field pine had not intruded so largely on the domain of the plough-man and reaper. **1856** OLMSTED *Slave States* 89 Cannot some Yankee contrive a method of concentrating some of the valuable properties of this old-field pine, so that they may be profitably brought into use in more cultivated regions? **1894** J. M. COULTER *Bot. W. Texas* III. 554 *Pinus Taeda*... Extending from the Gulf States to the valley of the Colorado. 'Loblolly pine.' 'Old-field pine.' **1967** N. T. MIROV *Genus Pinus* ii. 118 This tendency of pines to occupy newly exposed ground can be observed even now in abandoned fields ('old field pine' is the common name for *P. tæda*).

c. ***old-field colt, ground, plum, preacher, school, school-master, scrub.***

1835 *Southern Lit. Messenger* I. 582, I could..only remember that every untrimmed *old field colt was a regular descendant of Eclipse. **1772** in *Maryland Hist. Mag.* (1919) XIV. 278 Our corn..is very good at all the quarters, some of this *old field ground..excepted. **1887** *Harper's Mag.* Sept. 588/2 She been goin' out..betewen times, and getherin' *old-field plums. **1904** T. WATSON *Bethany* II. iii. 168 The tremendous emphasis with which the *old field preacher uttered the words. **1834** W. A. CARUTHERS *Kentuckian in N.Y.* I. 26 He sold his horse and cart too, and then turned into keepin an *old-field school. **1853** J. G. BALDWIN *Flush Times Alabama* 125 The master of the old field school was one of the regular faculty. **1948** E. N. DICK *Dixie Frontier* 172 Schools...located on worn-out cultivated areas, were called 'old field' schools. **1853** J. G. BALDWIN *Flush Times Alabama* 106 He had been an *old-field schoolmaster. **1834** W. A. CARUTHERS *Kentuckian in N.Y.* I. 12, I bet you my horse Talleyrand..against an *old field scrub.

old girl: see GIRL *sb.* 2 a.

old gold: see GOLD[1] 8 b.

oldhamite ('əʊldəmaɪt). *Min.* [f. the name of Thomas *Oldham* (1816–1878), director of the Indian Geological Survey + -ITE[1].] Meteoric calcium sulphide of a pale-brown colour, found in small spherules.

1863 *Rep. Brit. Assoc. Adv. Sci. 1862* App. 11 In it [*sc.* an aërolite] Mr. Maskelyne has detected a mineral to which he gives the name of Oldhamite—a yellow transparent body of cubic crystallization. **1870** *Phil. Trans.* 195. **1892** DANA *Min.* (ed. 6) 65.

old hat. *slang.* [OLD *a.* + HAT *sb.*] Something considered to be old-fashioned, out of date, or unoriginal. Also *attrib.* or as *adj.*

1911 A. QUILLER-COUCH *Brother Copas* iv. 78 Men have ..put it, with like doctrines, silently aside in disgust. So it has happened with Satan and his fork: they have become 'old hat'. **1916** D. H. LAWRENCE *Let.* 19 Feb. (1962) I. 433 The whole of the consciousness and the conscious content is old hat—the millstone round your neck. **1920** —— *Touch & Go* I. i. 21 *Oliver.* What was the address about, to begin with? *Willie.* Oh, the same old hat—Freedom. **1932** G. B. SHAW *Platform & Pulpit* (1962) 250 If I mention that sort of thing I am told that is old hat, that I am a back number. **1940** R. CHANDLER *Farewell, my Lovely* xxi. 98 We curved..past the Georgian-Colonial vogue, now old hat, past the handsome modernistic buildings. **1944** W. STEVENS *Let.* 12 Sept. (1967) 474 This is all growing to be old hat now, and I am eager..to go on to something else. **1959** N. KNEALE *Quatermass Experiment* III. 82 All pious generalizations, plus old-hat background waffle. **1959** *Observer* 5 Apr. 18/3, I suppose we couldn't possibly revive 'The Nymph'? Too old hat. **1960** J. MACLAREN-ROSS *Until Day she Dies* ii. 30 This drammer..that's sure going to make *A Hatful of Rain* look just like a handful of old hat. **1961** *Listener* 16 Nov. 826/1 Today's contemp'ry is tomorrow's old-hat. **1963** *Ibid.* 3 Jan. 45/2 The late-romantic style of performance is now regarded as 'ham' and 'old hat'. **1970** *New Scientist* 5 Mar. 476/2 Those who have been told that they belong to an 'old-hat' arts culture are now looking to climb on a 'new-hat' science-culture bandwagon. **1974** V. GIELGUD *In Such a Night* xii. 110 She..had made all jokes on the subject of mothers-in-law not only 'old hat' but..meaningless.

old identity. *Austral.* and *N.Z.*: see IDENTITY 7.

oldie ('əʊldi:). *colloq.* Also **oldy.** [f. OLD *a.* + -IE (see -Y[6]).] **1.** An old or elderly person; an adult; an 'old hand'. Freq. in ironical contexts.

1874 L. TROUBRIDGE *Life amongst Troubridges* (1966) 89 We scurried off pretty quick, leaving all the oldies buried in spiders' nests (not their bodies but their minds). *Ibid.* 97, I am now in my seventeenth year, isn't it sad? I shall soon be an 'oldy'. I shan't wear a cap. **1936** *Silver Screen* Feb. 64 Ruthie is..upset at the thought of her sister marrying such an oldie as Mr. Kruger. **1957** W. CAMP *Prospects of Love* ix. 183 Of course Mrs. Lawrence must come too. She would keep the 'oldies' company. **1959** C. MACINNES *Absolute Beginners* 10 As for me, eighteen summers, rising nineteen, I'll very soon be out there among the oldies. **1959** *Encounter* Oct. 73/2 As for me, as an oldie and a taxpayer I dig this book. **1968** *Blues Unlimited* Dec. 26 The artists here are 'oldies, but goodies'. **1971** *Daily Tel.* 12 May 14/6 To oldies over 30, the mere phrase 'alternative society' is liable to be a cause for instant apoplexy. **1972** J. BROWN *Chancer* xv. 199 We've got our rights, haven't we, same as the oldies.

2. Something old or familiar; an old song, tune, film, etc. Also, an old or well known idea or suggestion.

1940 *Amer. Speech* XV. 205/1 *Oldies*, old tunes or films. **1951** *Daily Progress* (Charlottesville, Va.) 17 Dec. 3/5 If your old jalopy is cranky and has been acting up under the stresses of urban life, maybe you ought to retire it to Prudence Island... Real oldies are just the thing on Prudence Island. **1955** W. GADDIS *Recognitions* II. iv. 475

Here's an oldie, friends, Rudy Vallee singing, *Love Made a Gypsy Out of Me.* **1959** 'O. Mills' *Stairway to Murder* xv. 157 'But fiddling with the clock-face—what an oldie!'.. 'It's so well-worn, I don't think anyone'd still have the nerve to pull it.' **1962** *John o' London's* 4 Jan. 18/1 Then there is the slightly more dubious pleasure of watching goodish oldie films like *Rebecca*. **1970** E. Lee *Music of People* xiv. 236 These tunes..are frequently rehashed as new versions of 'good old oldies'. **1972** *Guardian* 22 May 11/1 The arguments against? To begin with, an oldie: do you punish an effect or cure the cause? **1972** *Practical Motorist* Oct. 162/1 On recirculatory heaters—used on the 'oldies'—a rheostat switch controls the speed of the fan. **1973** *Times* 29 Nov. (Christmas Bk. Suppl.) p. ii/5 Those two golden oldies, *Frenchman's Creek* and *Jamaica Inn.* **1975** *Listener* 9 Jan. 57/1 Dragging up old revue skits..patter songs.. golden oldies ('These Foolish Things'), one-liners and sketches. **1975** *Ibid.* 10 Apr. 486/1 There you are, sitting in your lovely home..watching a late-night oldie.

oldish ('əʊldɪʃ), *a.* [f. old *a.* + -ish[1].] Somewhat old.

1668–9 Pepys *Diary* 20 Feb., She is an oldish French woman. **1775** Mad. D'Arblay *Early Diary* (1889) II. 56 Miss Lake..is a very obliging and sweet-tempered, oldish maid. **1798** Charlotte Smith *Yng. Philos.* III. 120 A common cotton gown, an oldish black bonnet. **1855** Darwin in *Life & Lett.* (1887) II. 47 Time is slipping away, and we are getting oldish. **1884** Q. Victoria *More Leaves* 189 An oldish woman, a character, who worked me a book-marker.

old land. a. *dial.* Also olland, ollunt. Land newly ploughed after having been uncultivated for some time; also, arable land sown with grass for a period of more than two years.

1674 J. Ray *Coll. Eng. Words* 73 Old land: ground that hath layn untilled long time and is new plowed up. Suff[olk]. **1788** *Ann. Agric.* IX. 429 The following is the former [crop rotation]: 1 and 2. Ollond, or lay of two years, 3. Wheat or oats on one earth, 4. Turnips, 5. Barley. **1882** in *N. & Q.* 18 Nov. 406/2 It was the land ploughed out of grass (out-land), which was known as olland. **1895** P. H. Emerson *Birds, Beasts, & Fishes Norf. Broadland* 8 Newlays and ollunts close by the marsh farmhouse. **1909** *Eastern Daily Press* (Norwich) 23 Jan. 8/1 Oats also do much better on an olland than on loose land.

b. *U.S.* Land that has been in cultivation for a long time, or land exhausted by a long period of cultivation.

1715 in *Amer. Speech* (1940) XV. 290/2 At the Corner of the said Jones's old land. **1748** J. Eliot *Essay Field-Husbandry New Eng.* 16 The third sort of Land I would speak of is our old Land which we have worn out. **1833** B. Silliman *Man. Sugar Cane* 10 Violet cane..prefers old land, and that which is rather dry. **1872** *Rep. Indian Affairs 1871* (U.S.) 230 It is my intention, during the coming season, to..summer-fallow as much of the old land as can be spared from cultivation. **1919** D. L. Cady *Rhymes Vermont Rural Life* 67, I learnt soon after I was born To never use 'old land' for corn.

c. *Geol.* Usu. as one word. Land which lies behind a coastal plain of more recent origin, esp. where the coastal plain has been built up from sedimentary material derived from that same land; also, an area of very ancient crystalline rocks, esp. when reduced to low relief. Also *attrib.*

1895 *Geogr. Jrnl.* V. 133 The old-land streams..are extended across the new coastal plain by the addition of consequent lower courses. **1897** *Ibid.* IX. 538 For convenience all the land back of this initial shoreline will be called the 'oldland', and all alluvial accumulation built in front of the oldland..will be called 'foreland'. **1903** *Jrnl. Geol.* XI. 617 The Canadian shield of Suess..marks the site of the oldland area from which the materials of the later sedimentary deposits were derived. **1937** [see *fall zone* s.v. fall *sb.*[1] 29]. **1939** A. K. Lobeck *Geomorphol.* xiv. 447 It [*sc.* a coastal plain] may rest upon an oldland of simple structure or of complex structure. **1957** *Geogr. Jrnl.* CXXIII. 503 Observations carried out on the Dartmoor tract of the oldland of south-west England.

Old Left. [old *a.* 12.] The name given to older liberal elements in the socialist movement, as distinct from the more radical New Left. So **Old Leftist**, a member or supporter of the Old Left.

1960 *New Left Rev.* Sept.–Oct. 11/2 Side by side with the Old Left—and, at the present moment, 'objectively' reinforcing it—is a New Left, growing in strength. **1967** *Time* 21 Apr. 15 New York police on horseback—in contrast with the 'Cossack' image so many Old Leftists apply to them—kept the countermarchers from breaking up the parade. *Ibid.* 28 Apr. 14 The Old Left organized and proselyted, playing its part in bringing about the American welfare state. **1968** *Harper's Mag.* May 65 The New Left is, of course, an enormously diverse group, ranging from slightly disguised representatives of the Old Left to political fauna so bizarre as to defy classification. **1971** *N.Y. Times* 7 June 31 Daniel instead produces notes toward an autobiographical novel about his Old-Left parents.

†'**oldly**, *a. Obs. rare*⁻¹. [f. old *a.* + -ly[1].] Verging on old age, elderly.

1382 Wyclif *Job* xli. 23 [32] He shal eymen the se as an oldli man [Vulg. *quasi senescentem*].

'**oldly**, *adv. rare.* [f. old *a.* + -ly[2].]

a. In the manner of one that is old. b. In an old or bygone manner. c. In old time, long ago.

c **1200** Ormin 1229 Oxe ganngeþþ haȝheliȝ & aldelike lateþþ. *Ibid.* 2553 Ȝho toc onn full aldeliȝ To fraȝȝnenn Godess enngell. *c* **1440** *Bone Flor.* 248 He coghyth and oldely grones. **1494** Fabyan *Chron.* vii. 294 This so oldly foundyd Is so surely groundyd That no man maye confounde it. **1529** Wolsey in Ellis *Orig. Lett.* Ser. i. II. 13 With the ampliacion of the fee, above that wych ys oldely accustomyd, to the summe of xl[li]. **1562** J. Heywood *Prov. & Epigr.* (1867) 216 Talke or walke oldly or newly: Talke and walke plainly and trewly. **1582** Stanyhurst *Æneis* iv. (Arb.) 103 Fluds mightye be rowling From the chyn oldlye riueld. **1910** W. de la Mare *Three Mulla-Mulgars* xviii. 241 'On his woman-hand stood no fourth finger.' 'Was the little woman-finger newly gone, or oldly gone?' **1922** Joyce *Ulysses* 34 He raised his forefinger and beat the air oldly before his voice spoke. **1960** 'A. Burgess' *Doctor is Sick* 244 He chuckled oldly.

old maid.

1. A woman who remains single considerably beyond the ordinary marrying age; an elderly spinster: usually connoting habits characteristic of such a condition.

1530 Palsgr. 250/1 Oulde mayde, *luberdine.* **1673** *Lady's Calling* ii. i. §5 An old Maid is now..look'd on as the most calamitous Creature in nature. **1711** Addison *Spect.* No. 7 ¶4 An old Maid, that is troubled with the Vapours. **1819** *Metropolis* III. 232 The Miss Thing-em-tights, in Golden-square—fusty old maid frumps! **1887** Ruskin *Præterita* II. xi. 391 She..spent most of her summers in travel, with another wise old maid for companion.

2. A name of a bivalve mollusc of the family *Myidæ*, also called Gaper or Gaping Clam.

1865 J. G. Wood *Com. Shells of Sea-shore* (1869) 23 The Common Gaper-shell or Old Maid (*Mya arenaria*)... In some places the animal is sold for food, and is sold under the name of 'Old Maid'.

3. a. West Indian name of a plant, *Vinca rosea.*

1884 Miller *Plant-n.*, *Vinca rosea*, Madagascar Periwinkle, 'Old Maid' of the W. Indies.

b. *U.S.* The velvet-leaf or Indian mallow, *Abutilon theophrasti*, or a zinnia, *Z. elegans.*

1839 *Southern Lit. Messenger* V. 751/2 A particular spot in his garden was appropriated to the culture of old maids. **1880** *Scribner's Monthly* May 101/2 In my section an annoying weed is *Abutilon*, or velvet-leaf, also called 'old maid'. **1888** *Century Mag.* XXXVI. 896/1 The flower-garden overrun with..four-o'clocks, old-maids, and sun-flowers.

4. A simple round game at cards in which one card (usually a queen) is removed from the pack and the rest distributed among the players, who draw cards from one another till all are paired except the odd one, the holder of which receives this title.

1831 E. Leslie *Amer. Girl's Bk.* 144 *Old Maid*... When played by girls, three of the queens must be put away as useless. **1874** L. Troubridge *Life amongst Troubridges* (1966) ix. 89 After dinner..we had to begin a stodgy game of Old Maid, just us two. **1891** in *Cassell's Bk. Sports & Past.* 865. **1959** [see heart *sb.* 24 b].

Hence **old-'maiddom** = *old maidhood*; **old-'maidhood, -'maidenhood, -'maidship, -'maidenship**, the state or condition of an old maid; **old-'maidish, -'maidenish, -'maidenly** *adjs.*, like or characteristic of an old maid (hence *old-'maidishness*); **old-'maidery**, the habits or characteristics of an old maid; **old-'maidishly** *adv.*, in the manner of an old maid; **old-'maidism, -'maidenism** = *old-maidhood, old-maidery*; **old-'maidy** *a.* = *old-maidish* adj.

1920 D. H. Lawrence *Lost Girl* vi. 93 She was withering towards *old-maiddom. **1847** A. Brontë *Agnes Grey* ix. 144 Never marry at all, not even to escape the infamy of *old-maidenhood. **1889** C. M. Yonge *Reputed Changeling* II. xxvii. 184 Old maidenhood came earlier then than in these days. **1898** *Westm. Gaz.* 3 Oct. 2/1 The woman [was] one of the sort in which old-maidenhood is writ large on every fold of the gown. **1867** J. H. Stirling in *Fortn. Rev.* Oct. 381 The plain, simple,..but somewhat *old-maidenish and loquacious, Herr Professor Kant. **1782** Mrs. Cowley *Bold Stroke for Husband* 14 Till the horrors of *old maidenism frighten her into civility. **1835** *Mrs. Carlyle's Lett.* I. 26 The lady, verging on old-maidenism. **1784** R. Bage *Barham Downs* II. 285 She has only a few innocent *old-maidenly foibles about her. **1896** Mrs. Caffyn *Quaker Grandmother* 34 You know the cross-grained old-maidenly sort of a person that fate is. **1784** R. Bage *Barham Downs* II. 324 Betake ourselves to chastity, cards, and scandal, the solid comforts of *old-maidenship. **1804** *Something Odd* I. 199 Notwithstanding the *old-maidery and malevolence of dear Miss Freddy. **1821** T. D. Fosbroke *Berkeley MSS.*, Inclined to parsimonious old maidery. **1883** N. Sheppard *Geo. Eliot's Ess.* Introd. 14 Marriage for deliverance from poverty or *old-maidhood. **1757** Mrs. Griffith *Lett. Henry & Frances* (1767) III. 9 Sensible and agreeable, but formal and *old-maidish. **1862** *Gifts & Graces* x. 114 She was a very methodical and old-maidish little lady. **1975** 'P. Loraine' *Ask the Rattlesnake* ii. viii. 239 Clifford tut-tutted *old maidishly. **1824** Miss Mitford *Village* Ser. i. (1863) 213 If ever she betrayed an atom of *old-maidishness, it was on the score of her caps. **1875** H. James *R. Hudson* iii. 103 There is nothing like matrimony for curing old-maidishness. **1907** G. B. Shaw *Major Barbara* Pref. 185 Here am I,..economically disposed to the limit of old-maidishness. **1950** M. Peake *Gormenghast* xviii. 112 In spite of his old-maidishness, his clipped and irritatingly academic delivery.., he had a strongly developed sense of the ridiculous. **1975** J. Symons *Three Pipe Problem* xvi. 152 With precise old-maidishness he took a small key from his watchchain. **1776** Mrs. Delany *Lett.* Ser. ii. II. 193 To come to the letter so strongly tinctured with *old maidism. **1893** *Temple Bar Mag.* XCVIII. 539 He is faddy, almost to the point of old-maidism. **1861** *Sat. Rev.* 20 July 63 Till.. the chilling threshold of *old maidship has been reached. **1884** 'Mark Twain' *Huck. Finn* xxxv. 357 Whoever heard of getting a prisoner loose in such an *old-maidy way as that? **1905** J. C. Lincoln *Partners of Tide* i. 8 The old maids are pretty conscientious, spite of their bein' so everlastin' 'old maidy'. **1923** U. L. Silberrad *Lett. J. Armiter* xiii. 253 She is much nicer and better really than I, in my old-maidy prejudice, used to think.

old man.

1. a. *lit.* A man advanced in life. (Formerly sometimes as one word.)

the old man, familiar term for a husband or father. Also *U.S.* in ***old man eloquent***, applied after Milton's phrase (see quot. *c* 1645) to John Quincy Adams (1767–1848), sixth President of the United States.

c **1200** Ormin 13212 To gan biforenn alde menn Inn alle gode þæwess. *c* **1375** *Sc. Leg. Saints* iii. (*Andreas*) 207 Myn barne,..to þis aldman enerthand is. *c* **1400** *Destr. Troy* 126 Þat elde man..Hade a son. **1535** Coverdale *1 Sam.* ii. 31 There shal no oldeman be in thy house. *c* **1645** Milton *Sonn. to Lady M. Ley*, As that dishonest victory At Chæronea,.. Kil'd with report that Old man eloquent. **1768** Sterne *Sent. Journ.* (1778) II. 191 (*Grace*) His wife..join'd her old man again, as their children and grand-children danced before them. **1839** C. M. Kirkland *New Home* xii. 75 'I reckon you'd ha' done better to have waited till the old man got back.' 'What old man?' asked I... 'Why, *your* old man to be sure,' said he laughing. I had yet to learn that in Michigan, as soon as a man marries he becomes 'th' old man'. **1846** *Brackenridge's Mod. Chivalry* (rev. ed.) I. xxiii. 114 You are welcome, Sir, if you wish to stop..though since my old man's time, we don't take in strangers for common. **1846** *Quincy* (Illinois) *Whig* 3 Mar. 2/3 We should suppose that the 'old man eloquent', would pause in his career, and look about him. **1848** Thackeray *Van. Fair* xviii, His wife ..called him..her dear John—her old man—her kind old man. **1848** *Congress. Globe* 24 Feb. 388 Let not the grave of the old man eloquent be desecrated by unfriendly remembrances. **1871** E. Eggleston *Hoosier Schoolmaster* (1872) iii. 28 My ole man's purty well along in the world. **1892** M. C. F. Morris *Yorksh. Folk-Talk* 81 'T' au'd man —t' au'd woman' are synonymous with father or mother. **1900** *Congress. Rec.* 25 Jan. 1208/1 John Quincy Adams, the 'Old Man Eloquent', expressed very happily what we now.. believe. **1901** S. E. White *Claim Jumpers* i. 4 He's been pestering the old man to send him West. Old man doesn't approve. **1914** 'Bartimeus' *Naval Occasions* xix. 171 Not bad work,..bagging your Old Man's ship. **1932** [see kid *v.*[4]]. **1946** R. Allen *Home Made Banners* xiii. 163 My old man says Quebec or no Quebec they'll have to send the Zombies over. **1974** 'J. Le Carré' *Tinker, Tailor* vi. 47 She was a sight better qualified than her old man.

b. A familiar term for a ship's captain.

1835 N. Ames *Old Sailor's Yarns* 53 The commander of a merchantman, although perhaps under twenty years of age, is invariably called the 'old man', by all hands on board. **1840** R. H. Dana *Two Yrs. before Mast* xxxi. 374 The 'old man'..was determined to carry sail till the last minute. **1845** *Knickerbocker* XXVI. 206 I've known the Old Man come on deck at midnight. **1865** *Routledge's Ev. Boy's Ann.* 445 The term 'old man', so much applied by sailors to their commander,..was hardly aptly applied, seeing the captain was only twenty-five. **1873** 'Mark Twain' & Warner *Gilded Age* iv. 44 The 'old man' was the captain—he is always so, on steamboats and ships. **1897** Kipling *Capt. Cour.* vii. 143 The *Jennie Cushman*..cut clean in half—graound up an' trompled on at that! Not a quarter of a mile away. Dad's got the old man. **1916** 'Taffrail' *Pincher Martin* v. 68 Having a sherry-and-bitters with 'the old man'. **1924** 'P. Blundell' *Confessions of Seaman* ii. 22 You'd better come along and see the 'old man' now. He's just off ashore. **1958** N. Marsh *Singing in Shrouds* (1959) ix. 184 Did you ever know such a *bloody* Old Man! **1968** *Daily Tel.* 14 Aug. 15/4 'It was just like a furnace,' said Mr. Martin Jones, deckhand, of Slough, Bucks. 'The old man was grand.'

c. Hence applied in the other Services to a commanding officer.

1830 J. P. Martin *Narr. Adventures Rev. Soldier* viii. 190 They and some others of the men..were about to have some fun with 'the old man', as they generally called the Captain. **1890** Kipling *Life's Handicap* (1891) 41 An' whin I'm let off in ord'ly-room through some thrick of the tongue an' a ready answer an' the ould man's mercy, is ut smilin' I feel? **1917** A. G. Empey *Over Top* 311 '*The Old Man*', captain of a company. He is called 'the old man', because generally his age is about twenty-eight. **1942** *R.A.F. Jrnl.* 3 Oct. 24 It was preposterous to think of the Old Man on a bicycle... The idea of the Old Man riding a bicycle set us back a long way. **1948** Partridge *Dict. Forces' Slang* 131 *Old Man*, the Commanding Officer. The Air Force gets it from the Army, which gets it from the Navy, which gets it from the Merchant Service. **1967** *Everybody's Mag.* (Austral.) 18 Jan. 36/2 Today, in Vietnam, Australians are again catching up on American Army Slang... The Company Commanding Officer is a CCO or the Old Man—even if he's all of 23. **1977** 'D. MacNeil' *Wolf in Fold* xiii. 137 The Old Man had commanded longer than most lieutenant-colonels.

d. As a term of affectionate familiarity: see old *a.* 8.

e. *old man of the mountain(s)* [tr. Arab. *šaiḵ-al-jibal*], (*a*) named applied to Hasan ibu-al-Sabbah, founder of the Assassins (see assassin 1) and his successors; (*b*) applied allusively to other political murderers, and *fig.* to persons of ruthless ambition; (*c*) a rock formation resembling the face of an old man.

1579 J. Frampton tr. *Marco Polo's Travels* xvii. 27 That way,..could not be travelled to Crerima for the crueltie of the king of that countrie,..from whome fewe coulde scape, but eyther were robbed or slayne. And for this cause manye kings did paye him tribute, and hys name is as muche to saye, as the olde man of the mountayne. **1625** Purchas *Pilgrimes* III. i. iv. 72 Hauing spoken of the Countrey, the old man of the Mountayne shall bee spoken of, of whome Marco heard much from many. His name was Aloadine, and was a Mahumetan... Aloadine had certaine Youthes from twelve to twentie yeares of age,..other Lords and his Enemies were slaine by these his Assasines. **1773** W. Jones *Hist. Life Nader Shah* p. xiii, It may be worth while to remark in this place, that the Old man of the mountain, who is mentioned in our accounts of the Crusades, was no other than a Prince of the Ismaëlian family. **1777** J. Richardson

Dict. Persian, Arabic & Eng. p. xvi/1 He was stabbed by a Batanist, one of the subjects of the Old Man of the Mountain; whilst he was reading a petition which the assassin had presented. 1792 H. WALPOLE *Let.* 4 Sept. (1905) XV. 138 A whole senate has assumed the accursed dignity of the 'Old Man of the Mountain', and spawned a legion of assassins. 1818 W. MARSDEN tr. *Trav. Marco Polo* I. xxi. 112 (*heading*) Of the old man of the mountain; of his palace and gardens; of his capture and his death. *Ibid.* 114 There was no person however powerful, who having become exposed to the enmity of the Old man of the mountain, could escape assassination. 1837 H. MARTINEAU *Society in Amer.* I. II. 220 Our party.. was.. struck with the romance of the domestic history of the old man of the mountain, as the guide is called. 1871 *N.Y. Herald* 6 Sept. 6/6 It seems as if 'the Old Man of the Mountains' [*sc.* Brigham Young] meant to fight every step of the federal government for the supremacy of Utah. 1888 KIPLING *In Black & White* (1889) 67 He might have been the original Old Man of the Mountains. 1905 H. W. C. DAVIS *Eng. under Normans & Angevins* xi. 308 An Arab writer lays the blame on Saladin, affirming that he had offered the chief of the Assassins, the Old Man of the Mountain, a heavy bribe. 1934 A. HUXLEY *Beyond Mexique Bay* 80 The lessons of Loyola and the Old Man of the Mountain. 1936 J. BUCHAN *Island of Sheep* vi. 118 Desperadoes who had crushed their lives were in-spanned in Castor's sense... like the servants of the Old Man of the Mountain in the Crusades. 1939 G. B. PICKWELL *Deserts* 48/2 The devil's garden is well named: with boulders and 'barrels' and 'Old Men of the Mountain' it is a grotesque feature of the land of sun and wind and freakish rain. 1957 *Encycl. Brit.* II. 554/1 Before long perfervid imaginations detected the hand of the Old Man of the Mountain in political murders and attempts even in Europe. 1965 J. FLEMING *Nothing is Number* I. ii. 21 You are great *assassins*,.. the word itself is your very own, it comes from the Arabic *hashshash*, dating from the Crusades when your old sheik, Old Man of the Mountains, sent out his Moslem fanatics to kill the Christian leaders. They filled themselves with *hashish* to get themselves in the right mood.

f. ***old man of the sea***: in the story of Sinbad the Sailor in the *Arabian Nights*, the sea-god who forced Sinbad to carry him on his shoulders for many days and nights until he was thwarted by being made so drunk that he toppled off. Hence, allusively, a person of whose company one may not easily be rid; a heavy and encumbering burden, esp. in *fig.* use. Also *attrib.*

1712 tr. *Arabian Nights' Entertainments* (ed. 2) III. lxxxiv. 57 You fell say they into the Hands of the old Man of the Sea, and are the first that ever escap'd strangling by him. 1809 W. SCOTT *Let.* 7 Aug. in J. G. Lockhart *Scott* (1837) II. vii. 252 About three years ago I accepted the office I hold in the Court of Session, the revenue to accrue to me only on the death of the old incumbent. But my friend has since taken out a new lease of life... Such odious deceivers are these invalids. Mine reminds me of Sinbad's Old Man of the Sea, and will certainly throttle me if I can't somehow dismount him. 1850 C. M. YONGE *Henrietta's Wish* viii. 112 Uncle Roger has got hold of him, and he is as bad as the old man of the sea. 1856 G. MEREDITH *Let.* 15 Dec. (1970) I. 28 The *Dulness* is something frightful, and hangs on my shoulders like Sinbad's old Man of the Sea. 1874 M. CLARKE *His Natural Life* (1875) I. 9 The old-man-of-the-sea burden of parsimony and avarice which he had voluntarily taken upon him was not to be shaken off. 1899 *Strand Mag.* Mar. 308/1 When a man once gets a Cavalanci and plays to it, it sticks to him like the Old Man of the Sea. 1904 G. STRATTON-PORTER *Freckles* iii. 54 Again Freckles' 'old man of the sea' sat sullen and heavy on his shoulders and weighed him down until his step lagged and his heart ached. 1927 *Times* 22 July 15/4 The bad habit into which we slip almost unconsciously fixes itself about our necks as firmly as any Old Man of the Sea. 1947 M. LOWRY *Under Volcano* ix. 281 What could she do under the weight of such a heritage? How could she rid herself of this old man of the sea? 1957 C. F. MACINTYRE *Stephane Mallarmé: Selected Poems* p. viii, Mallarmé has been like the Old Man of the Sea, like the Biblical poor. There's no getting rid of him! 1965 N. FREELING *Criminal Conversation* II. xx. 186, I am tired. I find you like the Old Man of the Sea. 1971 A. PRICE *Alamut Ambush* xiv. 169 'He's a man who likes to use others to do his own work. He likes to ride on other people's backs.' The Old Man of the Sea, thought Roskill.

g. *Theatr.* An actor playing the role of an old man, *esp.* one who specializes in such roles. Also, the role itself. Cf. OLD WOMAN 1 c.

1747 T. WHINCOP *Scanderbeg* 243/1 An Actor of great Humour in low Comedy, especially in the Parts of Old Men. 1762 J. LOVE *Let.* 5 July in D. Garrick *Private Corr.* (1831) I. 144 His feeble old men, which he has only tried one season, will increase your hopes. 1775 T. HOLCROFT *Let.* 1 June in *Mem.* (1816) I. II. iv. 236, I have succeeded best in low comedy and old men. 1794 C. MATHEWS *Let.* 3 Aug. in A. Mathews *Mem. Charles Mathews* (1838) I. 101 He is a very respectable performer in a general line, but mostly 'old men'. 1849 *Theatrical Mirror* 24 Sept. 31 Mr. Basil Baker.. is engaged for the first old men at Drury Lane. 1901 C. MORRIS *Life on Stage* vii. 39 A company was generally made up of a leading man.., first old man, second old man, heavy man, first comedian, [etc.]. 1957 *Oxf. Compan. Theatre* (ed. 2) 772/1 The old stock company was formed of a group of actors each of whom undertook some special line of business... The Old Man played Sir Anthony Absolute and Sir Peter Teazle, and was a person of consequence.

h. A person set in authority over others: a master, overseer, or foreman; a superintendent or senior official; a 'boss'.

1837 *Southern Lit. Messenger* III. 86, I say, darkie, the old man keeps good liquor, and plenty of belly timber, don't he? 1844 *Knickerbocker* XXIII. 83 The 'old man' himself came to the door, and looking down at his apprentice, shook his head sorrowfully. 1845 E. J. WAKEFIELD *Adventure N.Z.* I. xi. 331 Tommy Evans, the 'old man' who headed the principal station, started.. to get on board. 1887 C. B. GEORGE *40 Yrs. on Rail* ix. 167 They feel that if they can only lay it before the 'old man' it will be properly dealt with. 1913 C. E. MULFORD *Coming of Cassidy* xii. 197 'Is there any chance to get a job here?' he asked anxiously. 'You'll have to quiz th' Old Man.' 1921 H. G. WELLS *Grisly Folk* in *Story-Teller* Apr. 14/1 There was no Old Man who was lord and master and father of this particular crowd. 1935 A. J. POLLOCK *Underworld Speaks* 82/2 *Old man*, the big underworld boss; boss politician. 1949 W. HERTRICH *Huntington Bot. Gardens* 32, I declined to accept it, but suggested that he deduct this amount 'from the Old Man's bill'. 1958 'CASTLE' & 'HAILEY' *Flight into Danger* x. 137 Is that you, Dave? Harry. Surprise for you—the Old Man is on the line. 1967 E. & M. A. RADFORD *No Reason for Murder* xii. 80 The Old Man is the traditional police name for a Chief Constable. 1974 'P. B. YUILL' *Bornless Keeper* xiii. 119 Has the old man been on? He'll be wanting to ask your old mates at the Yard for help. *Ibid.*, The old man wants to hear a progress report.

i. Substituted familiarly for 'old Mr.——'. orig. and chiefly *U.S.*

1843 'R. CARLTON' *New Purchase* I. 92 It ain't more nor a mile to ole-man Sturgisses. 1859 BARTLETT *Dict. Amer.* (ed. 2) 301 In the South and West, instead of saying.. 'Old Mr. Smith', it is customary to say, 'Old man Smith'. 1862 R. R. BUTLER *Let.* 8 Jan. in *Congress. Globe* (4 Mar. 1868) 1664/1, I send a few lines to you by old man Jesse Price. 1902 A. D. MCFAUL *Ike Glidden* xvii. 126 There is old man Spencer who had always been poor. 1930 *Chicago Daily Maroon* 28 Oct. 1/3 Old Man Stagg spoke a few words in commending .. the students for their show of enthusiasm. 1949 [see OLD *a.* 8 c]. 1961 'E. LATHEN' *Banking on Death* (1962) xv. 123 Old man Michaels didn't like him.

j. *slang.* The penis.

1902 FARMER & HENLEY *Slang* V. 99/1 *Old man*,.. the penis. 1968 R. LAIT *Chance to Kill* xxii. 139 There was David getting out of bed in his shirt, his old man hanging out. 1971 B. W. ALDISS *Soldier Erect* 23 She had been opening up her legs before the reprise. Those glorious mobile buttocks... I felt my old man perking up again at the memory.

k. *fig.* Applied to things; spec. ***Old Man River***, the Mississippi (see also quot. 1932).

1910 W. M. RAINE *Bucky O'Connor* iii. 37 When Old Man Trouble comes knocking at the door. 1919 C. P. THOMPSON *Cocktails* 252 Why, being officially booked to meet Old Man Death on ground, I had kept the appointment in the air. 1927 KERN & HAMMERSTEIN (*song-title*) Old man river. 1932 *Sun* (Baltimore) 24 Sept. 16/3 Old Man River Sinking. .. The north branch of the Susquehanna river is lower than it was 112 years ago. 1933 *Lit. Digest* 12 Aug. 28/2 (*heading*) Who Owns Old Man River? 1949 *Natural Hist.* Nov. 427/3 At last they have succeeded in vaulting the natural barriers between the Great Lakes and Old Man River. 1976 B. BOVA *Multiple Man* v. 55 St. Louis is a dull town... Old Man River is wide and sluggish.

2. *Theol.* Unregenerate human nature (OLD *a.* 12: cf. *Old Adam*).

1382 WYCLIF *Eph.* iv. 22 Do ȝe away vp the firste lyuyng the olde man. *c* 1450 tr. *De Imitatione* III. xxxix. 110 Allas! yit liueþ in me þe olde man; he is not all crucified. 1567 *Gude & Godly B.* (S.T.S.) 146 The haly Spreit vs geue, Quhilk may our auld man mortifie. 1733 *Revolution Politicks* II. 40 You provoke me to Wrath, and if you should raise the old Man, you can't tell what mischief may ensue.

3. A local name for the Rainbird of Jamaica (*Hyetornis pluvialis*).

1694 RAY in *Lett. Lit. Men* (Camden) 200 The referring of the *Old-men*, or Rain-fowls, to the Cuckow. 1725 SLOANE *Jamaica* II. 313 They are called Old-Men from the light brown, or grey colour their downy feathers are of. 1894 NEWTON *Dict. Birds* 654.

4. a. In *Australia*: A full-grown male kangaroo.

1828 P. CUNNINGHAM *N.S. Wales* (ed. 3) II. 151 He.. relates.. that he has been fortunate enough to kill *an old man* as he came along. 1873 J. B. STEPHENS *Black Gin* 39 The 'old man' fleetest of the fleet. 1884 R. BOLDREWOOD *Melbourne Mem.* iii. 24 The fiercest 'old man' forester did not seem to be too heavy weight for her.

b. *Austral.* and *N.Z. slang.* Used *attrib.* to denote the largeness or significance of the thing specified; freq. of animals (see also sense 4 a).

1834 G. BENNETT *Wanderings New South Wales* I. xv. 286 Many persons when alone are afraid to face a large 'old man' Kangaroo. 1845 R. HOWITT *Impressions Australia Felix* 233, I stared at a man one day for saying that a certain allotment of land was 'an old man allotment': he meant a large allotment, the old-man kangaroo being the largest kangaroo. 1866 R. HENNING *Let.* 18 July (1966) 226 Spring, a very fine kangaroo dog we have here, killed.. an old-man kangaroo about five feet high. 1888 D. MACDONALD *Gum Boughs* 7 Who that has ridden across the Old Man Plain. 1902 KIPLING *Just So Stories* 87 Still ran Kangaroo—Old Man Kangaroo... He ran till his hind legs ached. 1906 E. DYSON *Fact'ry 'Ands* xv. 199 Two 'underd ole-man rats that 'ad bin glued on t'Bunyip in mortil combat. 1930 J. DEVANNY *Bushman Burke* I. ii. 17 [He] had once taken an Old Man pig with a slasher. 1934 A. RUSSELL *Tramp-Royal in Wild Austral.* xxix. 190 An 'Old Man' sand storm. Lashed up and hurried along by a forty-mile-an-hour gale.. an inferno of swishing sand and gravel.. in Central Australia. 1936 I. L. IDRIESS *Cattle King* xii. 107 The river-bed is indicated by wide flats, mostly lignum bush, by big old-man coolabahs, and big old gums in places. 1941 —— *Great Boomerang* xi. 82 Fifteen years may pass before an old man flood brings a miracle to the land. 1945 BAKER *Austral. Lang.* xiv. 244 Especially heavy gales of this type are often called *old man southerlies* or *old man busters*. 1947 J. STEVENSON-HAMILTON *Wild Life S. Afr.* xxxi. 259, I was the owner of a large boarhound which killed a great many 'old men' baboons. 1953 A. UPFIELD *Murder must Wait* xviii. 157 An old-man red-gum growing close to the track. 1965 [see DOGGER[4]]. 1972 P. NEWTON *Sheep Thief* ii. 17 The homestead.. was fringed with a towering belt of real oldman pines. 1973 'D. SHANNON' *No Holiday for Crime* (1974) 78 You're going to be like Old Man Kangaroo, my girl. As per Mr. Kipling. Very truly sought after.

5. A name of the Southernwood (*Artemisia Abrotanum*); perh. from its hoary foliage.

1824 MRS. CAMERON *Marten & Scholars* ii. 13 She tied up two or three pinks and a rose with a bit of old-man and some sweetbriar. 1863 MRS. GASKELL *Sylvia's L.* i, A few 'berry' bushes, a black-currant tree or two.. with possibly a rose tree and 'old man' growing in the midst. 1884 *Harper's Mag.* July 234/2 Roses, and 'lad's-love', or 'old-man'. 1920 E. THOMAS *Collected Poems* 97 Old Man, or Lad's-love—in the name there's nothing To one that knows not Lad's-love, or Old Man, The hoar-green feathery herb. 1973 F. A. BODDY *Foliage Plants* iv. 62 Old world charm and sentimentality can be further satisfied with the grey, feathery, aromatic leaves of *Artemisia abrotanum*, commonly called southernwood, lad's love or old man.

6. *Mining.* An old vein or working which has become exhausted or has been abandoned for a long time; also, oreless stuff, waste or rubbish left from the working of a mine; see also quot. 1829.

1653 MANLOVE *Lead Mines* 225 No miner ought of an Old man to set To seek a Lead-mine, or Lead oar to get, Untill the Burghmaster a view hath taken And find such work an Old work quite forsaken. 1710 BP. NICOLSON in Hutchinson *Hist. Cumberld.* (1794) II. 214 A new belly was happily discovered before the forehead of the Old Man, which proved so rich, that in less than twenty-four hours they had filled several sacks with fine and clean-washed mineral. 1747 HOOSON *Miner's Dict.* N iv b, Crusht Wholes sometimes may be mistaken for Oldman. 1829 *Glover's Hist. Derby* I. 61 Ironstone, in cheeseshaped nodules, containing septariæ of carbonate of iron (*Old man*). 1866 JEVONS *Coal Quest.* (ed. 2) 300 The thousands of tons of cinder and slag—'old man' as it is locally called.. left by the Romans.

7. *Comb.* **old man cactus**, a Mexican plant (*Pilocereus* or *Cereus senilis*) with long grey hairs covering the top of the stem; † **old-man-house**, a hospital for old men; **old man salt-bush**, an Australian shrub, *Atriplex nummularia*, of the family Chenopodiaceæ, used as food for sheep in dry areas.

1634 BRERETON *Trav.* (Chetham Soc.) 49 Here [Haerlem] is a most dainty curious old-man-house. 1880 W. A. DIXON in *Jrnl. & Proc. R. Soc. New South Wales* XIV. 140 The order in which the salt-bushes proper are considered to stand from a grazier's point of view are 1st, *A. numularia* [*sic*], or old man salt-bush. 1900 *Daily News* 6 Sept. 3/1 Another singular product is Pilocereus Senilis, or 'old man cactus', from Mexico, the body of the plant being hidden by long grey hair. 1903 'T. COLLINS' *Such is Life* 16 He disappeared in the timber and old-man salt-bush. 1933 *Bulletin* (Sydney) 14 June 25/1 Old-man saltbush is a rapid grower and gives more fodder in drought-time than any other tree. 1954 B. MILES *Stars my Blanket* x. 58 A great valley, the floor.. thickly covered with Old Man Saltbush. 1965 *Austral. Encycl.* VII. 541/2 The round-leaved *Atriplex nummularia* (old-man or cabbage saltbush) is one of the tallest species and may reach 10 feet in height.

8. Combinations of *old man's* in plant names: **old man's beard**, (*a*) a name of the epiphytic plant *Tillandsia usneoides*, also called black-moss, long-moss, and Spanish moss; (*b*) the Traveller's Joy, *Clematis Vitalba*; (*c*) the Strawberry Saxifrage, *Saxifraga sarmentosa*; (*d*) the South European composite *Geropogon*; **old man's eyebrow**, *Drosera binata* (*Treas. Bot.* 1866); **old man's head**, (*a*) a name of the pink or carnation (*Dianthus*); (*b*) the old man cactus: see 7.

1742 W. ELLIS *Mod. Husbandman* June vi. 67 In this Month [*sc.* June], be sure to cut.. what we in Hertfordshire call the *Old-Man's Beard. 1756 P. BROWNE *Jamaica* 193 *Old-Man's-Beard*, this slender parasitical plant is found upon the trees in many parts of Jamaica... It is frequently imported from North America for the use of sadlers and coachmakers. 1760 J. LEE *Introd. Bot.* App. 321 Old Man's Beard, *Clematis*. 1821 CLARE *Vill. Minstr.* I. 84 Dig old man's beard from woodland hedge, To twine a summer shade. 1857 MAYNE *Expos. Lex.*, *Old Man's Beard*, common name for the Gerontopogon. 1952 *Cape Argus Mag.* 30 Aug. 2/4 That soft yellowy-green parasite that festoons itself so theatrically over the tops of the trees, giving the forests that appearance of hoary old age, is known as 'old-man's-beard'. 1965 E. RICHARDSON *Living Island* 10 Many standing trees are dead hosts to tattered Old Man's Beard and other lichens. 1972 R. & R. WRIGHT *Cariboo Mileposts* 86 Old man's beard lichen, the small green plant often seen in trees. 1974 *Islander* (Victoria, B.C.) 3 Nov. 7/3 Across the path and up into the old man's beard hanging from the pines. 1760 J. LEE *Introd. Bot.* App. 321 *Old Man's Head, *Dianthus*. 1858 HOGG *Veg. Kingd.* 341 Another curious species of this genus is what is popularly termed *The Old Man's Head* (*Cereus senilis*).

old-'mannish, *a.* [f. OLD MAN + -ISH[1].] Characteristic or suggestive of an old man.

1865 J. A. SYMONDS *Let.* 15 Apr. (1967) I. 535 Ughtred grows even more noisy, patronizing, old mannish, & goodnatured than he used to be. 1898 *Tit-Bits* 30 Apr. 85/1 We are all more or less acquainted with the precocious child—the 'old-mannish' boy or the 'old-womanish' girl. 1927 W. DEEPING *Kitty* vii. 91 His affection for that corner of the City of Westminster grew more deep and old-mannish.

old master. *Art.* See MASTER *sb.*[1] 16.

oldness ('əʊldnɪs). [-NESS.] The quality, fact, or condition of being old: in any sense of the adj.

c 1000 ÆLFRIC *Hom.* I. 194 We awurpon þa derigendlican ealdnysse. 1382 WYCLIF *Josh.* ix. 5 Olde shoon, the whiche to the doom of oldnes ben sowid with patchis. —— *Ezek.* xvi. 55 Thi sister Sodom and hir douȝtris shulen turne aȝen to her oldenes. —— *Rom.* vii. 6 That we serue in newenesse of spirit and not in oldnesse of lettre. 1470–85 MALORY *Arthur* XVII. xviii, My flesshe which was al dede of oldenes is become yonge ageyne. 1540 COVERDALE *Old Faith* i. Wks. (Parker Soc.) I. 13 Concerning the antiquity or oldness of our christian faith. **1616** SURFL. & MARKH. *Countrie Farme* 690 After foure yeares the wild Bore groweth leane through oldnesse of age. **1809–10** COLERIDGE *Friend* (1865) 65 How shall I avert the scorn of those critics who laugh at the oldness of my topics? **1893** J. PULSFORD *Loyalty to Christ* II. 267 Where the Spirit of the Lord is there is liberty. Oldness and deadness are shaken off.

Oldowan ('ɒldəuwən), *a.* Also **Olduwan**. [f. the name of the *Oldoway* (or Olduvai) Gorge, Tanzania + -AN.] Belonging to an African culture of the early Pleistocene period, characterized by primitive stone tools.

1934 L. S. B. LEAKEY *Adam's Ancestors* v. 104 In the Kanam deposits we find examples of a culture which has been given the name of Oldowan. This name is derived from Oldoway, the site where this culture was first recognized. **1964** K. P. OAKLEY *Frameworks for dating Fossil Man* iv. 172 The oldest known artifacts in the world are the Oldowan pebble-tools which occur in.. South Africa, East Africa and North Africa. **1972** [see NUT-CRACKER 5]. **1973** B. J. WILLIAMS *Evolution & Human Origins* xi. 189/2 Even among Olduwan materials (pre-handaxe) there are stone balls that have been rounded and smoothed to a far greater degree than can be explained by any possible functional requirement.

Old Prussian, *sb.* and *a.* [f. OLD *a.* + PRUSSIAN *a.* and *sb.*] **A.** *sb.* **a.** A member of a medieval people, related to the Lithuanians, who inhabited the shores of the Baltic sea east of the Vistula. **b.** The West Baltic language of this people, which ceased to be spoken in the 17th century. See also BALTIC A. *adj.* 2. **B.** *adj.* Of or pertaining to this people or their language.

1872 [see LETTIC *a.* (*sb.*)]. **1891** [see BALTIC *a.* 2]. **1917** *Encycl. Relig. & Ethics* IX. 487/1 Both the Este and the Old Prussians drank mare's milk and mead. *Ibid.* 488/1 References to Old Prussian religion occur in Lives of St. Adalbert. **1922** [see BALTO-]. **1933** L. BLOOMFIELD *Language* i. 13 A similar relation, though less close, was found to exist between the Baltic languages (Lithuanian, Lettish, and Old Prussian) and the Slavic. **1946** T. G. CHASE *Story of Lithuania* i. 3 The Old Prussians.. were annihilated by the Teutonic Knights. **1951** A. SPEKKE *Hist. Latvia* vi. 133 Christianus seems to have booked some success among the Old Prussian aristocracy. **1974** *Encycl. Brit. Micropædia* VII. 514/3 Old Prussian preserves many archaic Baltic features that do not occur in the related East Baltic languages.

old régime: see RÉGIME 2 b.

old rose. [f. OLD *a.* + ROSE *sb.* and *a.*] **a.** A shrub rose belonging to a species long in cultivation or a variety grown before the development of the hybrid tea rose about 1890, generally bearing fragrant, less formal flowers during a single mid-summer period.

1885 'E. V. B.' *Ros Rosarum* p. xx, In my own garden I gather together and fondly nurture every Old Rose that can be found. **1899** G. JEKYLL *Wood & Garden* vii. 78, I have also learnt from cottage gardens how pretty are some of the old Roses grown as standards. **1936** E. A. BUNYARD *Old Garden Roses* p. xi, The Old Roses are restrained and never garish. **1955** G. S. THOMAS *Old Shrub Roses* ii. 31 Many of the most shapely and sumptuous of our old roses were raised during the nineteenth century.

b. A shade of deep pink. Also *attrib.* or as *adj.*

1893 *Ladies' Home Jrnl.* Jan. 29/2 Old-rose and black.. is a specially fashionable combination. **1897** *Sears, Roebuck Catal.* 255/1, 36-inch all wood albatross, colors cream, pink, old rose, nile green. **1922** W. J. LOCKE *Tale of Triona* xxi. 241 Her mother's room, with the old rose curtains and Chippendale. **1923** W. DE LA MARE *Riddle* 290 The chest was empty, except that it was lined with silk of old-rose. **1932** G. ATHERTON *Adventures of Novelist* 349, I had brought with me an old-rose rug; I had the walls papered to match, and found an old-rose silken cover for the bed. **1948** 'J. TEY' *Franchise Affair* xi. 115 At the Alençon—cream paint and old-rose couches against the walls. **1973** *Harrods Christmas Catal.* 50 Cocktail bar with mahogany finish, and leather panels in old rose.. £130.

old school. [f. OLD *a.* + SCHOOL *sb.*[1] 5.] **a.** A group of people or a section of society noted for its conservative views or principles; members of a profession or a political party who adhere to its traditional views or methods. Freq. *attrib.* or as *adj.* Also, ***in the old school***: according to traditional or old-fashioned methods; ***of the old school***: traditional, old-fashioned.

1749 SMOLLETT tr. *Le Sage's Gil Blas* IV. i. 6 Mr. Doctor .. as I am a grand nephew to a physician of the old school give me leave to revolt with you against chymical medicines. **1798** *Monthly Mag.* Feb. 127/2 He was a whig of the old school. **1806** T. G. FESSENDEN *Democracy Unveiled* (ed. 3) II. 61 These bring grave old-school reflections. **1808** H. MORE *Lett.* (1925) 188 It was said more than twenty years ago, that I was the only one of the old school who strongly relished Cowper. **1815** *Niles' Reg.* IX. 120/2 The federal and 'old school' democratic candidate for congress. **1817** BYRON *Beppo* xxxiv, He was a lover of the good old school. **1818** M. EDGEWORTH *Let.* 19 Sept. (1971) 101 Lord Bathurst is.. an *agreeable* diplomatist.. dry faced—of the old school. *c* **1830** MRS. CAMERON *Houlston Tracts* III. No. 63. 2 Their family consisted of a son and three daughters, who were brought up more in the old school than is now customary. **1838** J. F. COOPER *Eve Effingham* II. iii. 81, I could just get a look of our clergyman's wig; for he was an old school man. **1842** F. A. KEMBLE *Let.* 2 Oct. in *Rec. Later Life* (1882) II. 268 Some old-school Whigs, sound politicians, and great friends of mine. **1911** G. B. SHAW *Doctor's Dilemma* I. 23 Did I hear from the fireside armchair the bow-wow of the old school defending its drugs? *a* **1963** S. PLATH *Crossing Water* (1971) 60 Bowing and truckling like an old-school oriental. **1972** 'E. PETERS' *Death to Landlords!* i. 20, I was trained in the old school.. and by hard work I built up the business. **1973** E. MCGIRR *Bardel's Murder* ii. 45 He saw Captain Joyningstowe doing the old-school act with a couple of stern dowagers. **1974** *Times* 18 Apr. 19/5 The Old School certainly accept the view that the rise in the price of oil is deflationary.

b. Used *attrib.* to designate conservative or traditional religious views, as ***old school Baptist, old school Church, old school Presbyterian.***

1816, etc. [see NEW SCHOOL a]. **1873** 'MARK TWAIN' & WARNER *Gilded Age* vii. 80 Grandmother.. was an Old-School Baptist. **1875** *Richmond* (Virginia) *Daily Whig* 3 Sept. 2/3 He should never have terminated his affiliation with the Old School Church. **1878** J. H. BEADLE *Western Wilds* xii. 183 The Old School Baptisses never went nigh the Methodis' meetin' house. **1898** I. H. HARPER *Life S. B. Anthony* I. 218, I recommend that you form an acquaintance .. with some well-settled Old-School-Presbyterian clergyman. **1933** *Sun* (Baltimore) 21 Oct. 6/8 More than one thousand members of the Old School Baptist Churches are meeting in a three-day session at Little Creek Church. **1949** *Pacific Northwest Q.* Apr. 124 In the period before the Civil War [they] generally preferred to be called Old School Baptists. **1961** K. S. LATOURETTE *Christianity in Revolutionary Age* III. vii. 166 We have seen the separation of the New School from the Old School Presbyterians.

old school tie. [f. OLD *a.* + SCHOOL *sb.*[1] 1 + TIE *sb.* 4.] A tie of characteristic pattern worn by former members of a particular school, esp. an English public school; used *transf.* and *fig.* to denote the wearer of such a tie and the behaviour and attitudes usually associated with it, esp. conservatism and group loyalty. Also *attrib.* or as *adj.* Hence **old school 'tieism**.

1932 KIPLING *Limits & Renewals* 86, I was thinking over the moral significance of Old School ties and the British social fabric. **1936** S. SMITH *Novel on Yellow Paper* 140 Cynthia was.. an old-school-tie acquaintance of mine. **1939** G. HOUSEHOLD *Rogue Male* 40 The only class-conscious people are.. the suburban old-school-tie brigade and their wives. **1942** A. CHRISTIE *Body in Library* iii. 35 The Inspector was tacitly accusing him of favouring his own class—of shielding an 'old school tie'. **1943** J. B. PRIESTLEY *Daylight on Saturday* ix. 58 Now this Old School Tie stuff .. is only a protest against inefficiency and nothing else. **1944** G. B. SHAW *Everybody's Pol. What's What?* i. 4 To the Old School Ties the dictators seem ignorant uneducated rebels. **1949** R. CHANDLER *Let.* 13 May in *R. Chandler Speaking* (1966) 139, I don't want to be revoltingly old-school-tie, but it does seem to me that a line has to be drawn. **1957** *Numbers* Mar. 17, I just met an old school-tie in the cloakroom. **1958** S. HYLAND *Who goes Hang?* xi. 54 He was an Etonian.. and he made his jokes unsmilingly as a concession to the old school tie convention. **1960** T. HUGHES *Lupercal* 45 As soon Let the old school tie be rent Off their necks. **1965** *Listener* 22 July 125/1 One thing I have learned is to distrust a lot of the familiar chat about old school ties. **1969** *Ibid.* 9 Jan. 41/1 He wore an old-school tie and an air of off-hand insolence which he thought of as easy and confident. **1973** 'S. HARVESTER' *Corner of Playground* I. v. 55 Their being boys from adjoining villages, the African version of old school tieism.

Oldspeak ('əuldspiːk). [f. OLD *a.* + SPEAK *v.*] The name used for Standard English, as opposed to the artificial language NEWSPEAK, in G. Orwell's novel *Nineteen Eighty-Four*, applied to normal English usage, *spec.* as distinct from technical or propagandist language. Hence **Oldspeaker**, one who uses Oldspeak.

1949 'G. ORWELL' *Nineteen Eighty-Four* I. 54 You haven't a real appreciation of Newspeak... Even when you write it you're still thinking in Oldspeak. *Ibid.* 299 It was expected that Newspeak would have finally superseded Oldspeak (or Standard English, as we should call it) by about the year 2050. **1960** *Encounter* Nov. 10/1 The substitution of 'Newspeak' for 'Oldspeak' (or present-day English) is designed to effect nothing less than the destruction of human reason by linguistic means. **1974** *Daily Tel.* (Colour Suppl.) 20 Sept. 10/3 Sometimes they say that 'real' freedom, being quite different from the crude concept mistakenly used by Oldspeakers, can exist only in a socialist state.

oldster ('əuldstə(r)). [f. OLD *a.* + -STER, after *youngster*.]

1. *Naut.* A midshipman who is no longer a 'youngster'; one of four years' standing.

1818 'A. BURTON' *Adventures J. Newcome* II. 77 An Oldster with a Gunter's scale Bestow'd his blows as fast as hail. **1829** MARRYAT *F. Mildmay* ii. 34, I became the William Tell of the party as having been the first to resist the tyranny of the oldsters. **1866** *Cornh. Mag.* Oct. 477 It is their duty as 'oldsters' to keep the 'youngsters' in order. **1886** *All Year Round* 4 Sept. 105 They, having been youngsters and felt the misery of it in their last ship, were determined to be oldsters, and let us know it in this.

2. *gen.* One who is no longer a 'youngster', youth, or novice; an elderly person; an old stager. Also *attrib.* *colloq.*

1848 DICKENS *Dombey* x, Her eyes would play the Devil with the youngsters before long,—'and the oldsters too, Sir, if you come to that', added the Major. **1883** E. E. HALE in *Harper's Mag.* Jan. 277/2 The carriages appeared for the oldsters, and the youngsters went on foot. **1938** [see MARRIED *sb.*]. **1942** *Sun* (Baltimore) 10 Oct. 10/3 The oldsters, travelling salesmen and the like, have learned to tote their own satchel. **1957** *New Yorker* 21 Sept. 33/3 Last week, our interest in nimble oldsters led us to the twenty-fifth floor of the Whitehall Building. **1964** *Wall St. Jrnl.* 5 Feb. 16 'The youngsters are chafing at the bit and aren't willing to wait and see how the civil rights bill shapes up,' he adds, 'and we oldsters can't hold back any longer.' **1973** M. AMIS *Rachel Papers* 112 What was more, the producers could afford only middle-aged actors and actresses. I shifted in my seat as the camera inexpertly focused on a parade of oldster genitals. **1974** *Anderson* (S. Carolina) *Independent* 18 Apr. 4A/2 By getting married, two oldsters in a Portland, Ore., nursing home had their Social Security cut from $412 a month to $309.40 a month because the regulations assume two can live as cheaply as one.

'old-time, *a.* Also **-times**. **1.** Of, belonging to, or characteristic of the ancient or olden time.

1824 in *Spirit Pub. Jrnls.* (1825) 495 An old-times chamber it was, sure enough. **1856** KANE *Arct. Expl.* II. xxii. 216, I took a Bible.. and we went through the old-times service. **1888** H. C. LEA *Hist. Inquis.* I. 422 Respect for the old-time prejudices of the Church. **1894** *Archæol. Jrnl.* Mar. 51 A piece of old-time folk-lore.

2. a. Pertaining to or characteristic of an earlier or former time.

1870 'MARK TWAIN' in *Buffalo Express* 1 Jan. 2/6 Conrad's color came back to his cheeks and his old-time vivacity to his eyes. **1936** F. CLUNE *Roaming round Darling* xiv. 120 Whitney, old-time driver for Cobb and Co.'s coaches (later a grazier), planted here a score of fig-trees. **1975** *Nature* 29 May 360/2 What they have is a lot of old-time researchers who are accustomed to pursuing their own interests.

b. In ballroom dancing, applied to styles of dance and music fashionable in the nineteenth and early twentieth centuries. Also in form ***old(e) tyme***. Also *absol.* as *sb.*

1887 E. SCOTT *Grace & Folly* iv. 64 It may not be uninteresting to enquire a little into the nature of some of the old-time dances. **1929** *Radio Times* 8 Nov. 389/2 Other records were... *Old Time Favourites*, the London Orchestra. **1933** AUDEN *Dance of Death* 11 Select partners for an old-time waltz. **1947** J. R. GILLESPIE (*title*) Old tyme dancing. **1950** A. WILSON *Such Darling Dodos* 116 Derek's crazy to take up dancing in a big way again. He adores all this old-time dancing. **1952** [see DRAG *v.* 1 e]. **1960** D. POTTER *Glittering Coffin* iii. 43 The primary school.. is opened only for occasional old-time dances. **1967** O. NORTON *Now lying Dead* iii. 54 Tuesdays he stays at home because that's Her night for her Old Time. **1974** *Radio Times* 11 Apr. 52/3 9.2 Time for Old Time in Radio 2 Ballroom. **1975** R. BUTLER *Where all Girls are Sweeter* vi. 75 'It's kind of romantic, really.'.. 'Like Old Tyme dancing on BBC radio, you mean?'

So **old-'time-like** *a.*, old-fashioned (*U.S.*); **old-'timer**, one whose experience goes back to old times; one of long standing in a place or position; an old-fashioned person or thing (orig. *U.S.*); **old-'timiness**, old-fashioned character.

1888 *New Princeton Rev.* Jan. 122 Most of us 'old-timers' .. are poor now. **1889** *Chicago Advance* 24 Jan., A small hotel, recommended to us as being more old-time-like than the others. **1882** W. H. BISHOP in *Harper's Mag.* Dec. 47/1 A few swarthy, lantern-jawed old-timers hang about the corners. **1887** *Blackw. Mag.* Feb. 224/1 A picture whose old-timiness would have thrown a Boston novelist into ecstasy. **1894** *Outing* (U.S.) XXIV. 34/1 A cutter of some six to eight tons.. a regular old-timer. **1910** [see FEST]. **1922** [see ANIMAL A. 6]. **1928** *Daily Mail* 25 July 2/3 Many types are represented. There is.. the old-timer, who knows more about Oxford than the inhabitants of the city themselves. **1928** D. H. LAWRENCE *Woman who rode Away* 60 But he was an old-timer miner. **1929** A. WOOLLCOTT in *New Yorker* 4 May 44/2 The big walnut tree that was an old-timer even in her day. **1939** *Sun* (Baltimore) 4 Apr. 12/7 Remarks about this type of vessel seem to have struck a responsive chord in the breasts of several old-timers. **1942** 'M. INNES' *Daffodil Affairs* II. ii. 46 You ought to meet some of the old-timers there, Mr Wine. **1962** *Coast to Coast 1961–62* 46 'Well thanks for the welcome, old-timer,'.. Marlett said. **1966** *Listener* 10 Mar. 344/2, I am not sure.. that some old-timers might not welcome a return to the traditional style of the Promenade Concerts. **1973** R. L. SIMON *Big Fix* (1974) xviii. 146, I raised the hoe... 'Sorry old timer,' I said and brought it down on the back of his neck. **1978** *Jrnl. R. Soc. Arts* CXXVI. 194/1 This may seem familiar stuff to some of you old-timers.

'old-timey, *a.* Also **old-timy**. [f. OLD-TIME *a.* + -Y[1].] Old-fashioned in character; (nostalgically or sentimentally) recalling the past.

1850 A. J. DOWNING in *Horticulturist* V. 265 The terraced garden, too, is quaint and 'old-timey'. **1879** F. R. STOCKTON *Rudder Grange* xvii. 206 Things that were apparently so 'old-timey'.. that David Dutton did not care to take them with him. **1892** KIPLING & BALESTIER *Naulahka* ix. 94 The venerable.. institution of matrimony is still in use here... The 'Doll's House' glanced right off this blessed old-timey country. **1921** O. W. HOLMES in *Holmes-Laski Lett.* (1953) I. 372, I must have mentioned Bryce's two nights with us I think—very pleasant and old timey. **1935** 'L. FORD' *Burn Forever* 28 They're real old-timey over at the Curriers. **1936** J. DOS PASSOS *Big Money* 221 Look how oldtimy the street looks. **1971** E. BULLINS in W. King *Black Short Story Anthol.* (1972) 62 Every year in August the Mary's Shore colored community gave an ole timey camp meetin'. **1973** —— *Theme is Blackness* 103 Well, man, I don't want to hear nothin' 'bout some fat ole-timey black bitch that I'm supposed to be like. **1974** *Columbia* (S. Carolina) *Record* 24 Apr. 14-B/4 Beds have old timey coverlets and primitive barn markings form popular wall plaques. **1975** *Publishers Weekly* 17 Nov. 98/3 Large format and illustration with old-timey black-and-white drawings.

old town. [f. OLD *a.* + TOWN *sb.* 4.] The older part of a city or town contained within its modern limits. Also *attrib.* Hence **old-towner**, an inhabitant of an old town.

1752 G. ELLIOT *Proposals Publ. Works Edin.* 32 In these cities, what is called the *new town*, consists of spacious streets and large buildings.. while the *old town*.. is more crouded than before these late additions were made. **1797** LADY NEWDIGATE *Let.* 16 July in A. E. Newdigate-Newdegate *Cheverels* (1898) xiii. 154, I am told that y[e] Steyne & everything beyond the Old Town has been built within y[e] last 30 years. **1842** QUEEN VICTORIA *Jrnl.* 3 Sept. in D. Duff *Victoria in Highlands* (1968) 32 We set off.. for Edinburgh. .. The procession moved through the Old Town up the High Street. **1924** 'P. BLUNDELL' *Confessions of Seaman* xi. 147 There is not, of course, any real 'old town' in Hamburg. Most of the city was burnt down in 1842. **1966** G. LYALL *Shooting Script* xxvi. 208 They are staying at the Colombo, on the beach front near the old town. Jiminez will control the old town, whatever happens. **1968** M. TRIPP *One is One* ii. 15 The beautiful Old Town in Annecy where ancient houses were backed by wooden galleries. **1973** *Guardian* 30 May 7/1 The fears of the old-towners are certainly understandable. The population has declined. Runcorn new town.. has been growing. **1973** R. PARKES *Guardians* viii. 137 The granite masses of old-town Helsinki.

†**'oldward**, *a. Obs. rare.* [f. OLD + -WARD.] Having the old tendency. ***at oldward***: at the old way of action.

1624 T. SCOTT *2nd Pt. Vox Populi* 19 Of their old-ward, and wonted policy. **1657** TRAPP *Comm. Ps.* cvi. 12 Ere they were three days older they murmured again;.. they were soon at oldward.

old wife, old-wife.

1. An old woman. Now usually disparaging (cf. OLD *a.* 1 c). (Formerly sometimes as one word.)

old wives' fable, story, tale, a foolish story such as is told by garrulous old women.

1340 *Ayenb.* 219 A guod ald wyf porchaceþ more of heuene ine one-lepi oure biddinde: þanne ssolde do a þouzond knyȝtes.. in lang time be hare armes. ? *a* **1400** *Morte Arth.* 986 Thane answers sir Arthere to that alde wyf. **1526** TINDALE *1 Tim.* iv. 7 Cast awaye vngostly and olde wyves fables [**1388** WYCLIF, elde wymmenus fablis; **1535** COVERDALE, olde wyuesh fables]. *a* **1619** FOTHERBY *Atheom.* II. xii. §2 (1622) 338 Countrymen doe vse to lighten their toyling; oldwiues, their spinning;.. by.. musicall harmonies. *a* **1680** BUTLER *Rem.* (1759) IV. 78 So simple were those Times, when a grave Sage Could with an Old-wive's-Tale instruct the Age. **1711** SHAFTESB. *Charac.* (1737) I. 6 A solid system of old-wives storys. **1875** JOWETT *Plato* (ed. 2) I. 47 These are the sort of old wives' tales which he sings and recites to us.

2. A name of the Long-tailed Duck (*Harelda glacialis*), also called Old Squaw.

1634 W. WOOD *New Eng. Prosp.* (1865) 34 The Oldwives be a foule that never leave tatling day or night, something bigger than a Ducke. **1894** NEWTON *Dict. Birds* 654 Old squaw and old wife are two.. names of the Long-tailed Duck.

3. A name of various fishes, esp. of the families *Labridæ* (wrasse), *Sparidæ* (sea-bream), *Balistidæ* (file-fish), and *Clupeidæ* (alewife and menhaden).

1588 HARIOT *Virginia* D iij, There are also.. Oldwiues; Mullets; Plaice. **1602** CAREW *Cornwall* 32 Of flat [fish there are] Brets, Turbets, Dories,.. Oldwife, Hake. **1655** MOUFET *Health's Improv.* xix. 184 Of Fresh-water Fish.. Old wives (because of their mumping and soure countenance) are as dainty and wholesome of substance, as they are large in body. **1756** P. BROWNE *Jamaica* 456 A saying.. That an Old Wife is the best of fish, and worst of flesh. **1847** CARPENTER *Zool.* II. 41 Several species [of *Labridæ*] are found upon our own coasts.. known among the fishermen by the name of 'Old Wives of the Sea'.

4. A cap or cowl to prevent a chimney from smoking. *Sc.*

1887 JAMIESON Suppl., *Auld wife*.. 3. The cowl or cover of a chimney-can, used as an aid-vent.

Hence **old-'wifely, old-'wifish** *adjs.*, resembling or characteristic of an old wife; **old-'wifery**, the habits or notions characteristic of an old wife.

1535 [see quot. 1526 in 1]. *c* **1542** A. ALANE *Auctor. Word of God*, Hethenyssh, old wiuyssh and capcyos fables. **1802** D. SIMPSON *Plea Relig.* (1834) 210 *note*, Opposed by a large number of old-wifely bishops. **1827** CARLYLE *Germ. Rom.* III. 177 This notion he named stuff and old-wifery. **1857** J. W. DONALDSON *Christian Orthod.* i. 7 *note*, 1 Tim. iv. 7:.. Deprecate the irreligious and oldwifish mythologies.

old woman.

1. a. *lit.* A woman advanced in years; hence, A person compared disparagingly to an old woman; a man of timid and fussy character. ***old woman's fable, tale, story***: see OLD WIFE 1.

1388 WYCLIF *1 Tim.* iv. 7 Eschewe thou uncouenable fablis, and elde wymmenus fablis. **14..** *Voc.* in Wr.-Wülcker 619/14 *Vetulana*, an old quene or an old wymman. *c* **1449** PECOCK *Repr.* v. i. 479 Eeld wommenys fablis. **1566** PAINTER *Pal. Pleas.* II. 379 The good olde woman, willing to follow hir minde, suffred hir alone. **1709** *Brit. Apollo* II. No. 22. 2/2 People are apt to call it an Old Woman's Story. **1722** DE FOE *Plague* (1754) 24 The old Women, and the Phlegmatic Hypochondriac Part of the other Sex, whom I could almost call old Women too. **1782** COWPER *A Fable* 21 For ravens, though, as birds of omen, They teach both conjurers and old women To tell us what is to befall. **1852** C. M. YONGE *Two Guardians* xv. 294 What does she do but let me go muddling on with that old woman Wells! **1867** TROLLOPE *Claverings* I. xi. 141 Who is it says so? A parcel of old women. **1876** G. M. HOPKINS *Let.* 23 Sept. (1956) 142 The Pope, it is well known, is a very fine looking man but there are some smutty smirking old-woman presentments of him. **1880** *Academy* 8 May 337 By old women of both sexes. **1911** *Chambers's Jrnl.* 46/1 The new commanding officer was, however, of the genus known in the service as 'old woman', and the regiment suffered accordingly. **1918** E. POUND *Pavannes & Divisions* 39 But surely the worst of your old-women are the male ones. **1953** E. SIMON *Past Masters* II. 74 Macphail is an old wooman [*sic*]... He thought it his duty to let me know. **1975** B. WOOD *Killing Gift* 177 He didn't want Marvin on guard against him... 'Give it some time, Marvin... Maybe I'm being a bit of an old woman.'

b. In *slang* use = wife ('my old woman'); mother.

a **1775** J. BOUCHER *Gloss. Archaic & Provinc. Words* (1832–3) p. l/1, Could my *old woman*, whilst I labour'd thus, At night reward me with a *smouch*, or buss. **1834** W. G. SIMMS *Guy Rivers* II. 97 The old woman, by whom we mean .. to indicate the spouse of the wayfarer, and mother of the two youths, was busied about the fire. **1839** C. M. KIRKLAND *New Home* xv. 96 If my old woman was to stick up that fashion, I'd keep the house so blue she couldn't see to snuff the candle. **1869** MRS. STOWE *Old-town Folks* xxxvii. 481 The old woman is just as choice of her boys as if [etc.]. **1916** 'TAFFRAIL' *Pincher Martin* xviii. 337 'Ow's Hemmeline an' Mrs Fig—yer ole woman? **1926** I. M. PEACOCKE *His Kid Brother* xiv. 216 His wife.. a small round dumpling of a woman with rosy cheeks, whom the policeman addressed as 'Old woman'. **1976** J. O'CONNOR *Eleventh Commandment* xi. 143 If you went home and found someone indoors with your old woman, what would you do?

c. *Theatr.* An actress playing the role of an old woman, esp. one who specializes in such roles. Cf. OLD MAN 1 g.

1838 A. MATHEWS *Mem. Charles Mathews* I. 101 Mrs. Davenport,.. the inimitable 'Old Woman' of Covent Garden Theatre, having succeeded Mrs. Webb in that line soon after this period. **1901** C. MORRIS *Life on Stage* vii. 40 Then came the leading lady, the first old woman (who was sometimes the heavy woman).. and the ladies of the ballet. **1957** *Oxf. Compan. Theatre* (ed. 2) 772/1 The Old Woman took Juliet's Nurse.

d. old woman's tooth, a simple kind of wooden router plane used by cabinet makers.

1846 C. HOLTZAPFFEL *Turning & Mech. Manipulation* II. xxiii. 487 This plane.. is generally called 'the old woman's tooth'. **1907** E. ROWE *Pract. Wood-Carving* 7 The router, very similar to the tool called by the joiner an 'old woman's tooth', may occasionally be used. **1969** E. H. PINTO *Treen* 389 Plate 417, *F*, is an 'old woman's tooth', a router plane of French walnut, probably 16th- or 17th-century.

2. = OLD WIFE 4.

1861 WHYTE MELVILLE *Mkt. Harb.* vi. 46 A chimney adorned with what is called an 'old woman'—an ingenious contrivance to prevent it from smoking.

3. *Comb.*: †**old-woman-house**, a hospital for old women: cf. OLD MAN 7. Also names of plants, as **old woman's bitter**, *Picramnia Antidesma*, and *Citharexylum cinereum*; **old-woman's tree** (Jamaica), *Quiina jamaicensis* (*Treas. Bot.* 1866).

1634 BRERETON *Trav.* (Chetham Soc.) 50 Here [Haerlem] are also five or six old-women-houses.

Hence **old-'womanish, old-'womanly, -like** *adjs.*, resembling or characteristic of an old woman; **old-'womanishness**, behaviour characteristic of an old woman; **old-'womanism**, the characteristics of old women; **old-'womanliness**, old-womanly quality; **old-'womanry**, an old-womanish trait or practice.

1775 S. J. PRATT *Liberal Opin.* cxxxiv. (1783) IV. 227 You are chained down by an *old womanish veneration, to a set of ideas. **1834** *Tait's Mag.* I. 661/2 The Cardinal appears to be surrounded by a tribe of fools, more idiotic, if possible, and old-womanish than himself. **1941** B. SCHULBERG *What makes Sammy Run?* xi. 266 An *old-womanishness that's won him the reputation of best-loved producer. **1977** *Listener* 28 Apr. 535/2 His mother's.. puritanism and old-womanishness.. seemed to hover over Owen's editorial shoulder. **1828** *Examiner* 359/2 The leaven of *old-womanism.. is made up of a Highland prophecy. **1859** *Autobiog. of a Beggar-Boy* 168 There is a species of old womanism about many of the provincial magistrates. **1721** AMHERST *Terræ Fil.* No. 4 (1754) 19 A great deal more of such *old-woman-like stuff. **1877** *Sunday Mag.* 53 [Girls] go about their business with an air of *old-womanliness and selfpossession. **1834** L. RITCHIE *Wand. by Seine* 114 *note*, Why should the bookselling trade continue to be fettered by these *old-womanly rules? **1882** *Macm. Mag.* XLVI. 195/2 The evils caused by this old-womanly kind of legislation. **1828** SCOTT *Diary* 9 Mar. in *Lockhart*, Trifling discussions about antiquarian *old womanries. **1892** A. LANG in *Longm. Mag.* XIX. 687 In the same receptacle of antiquarian old-womanries.

old-world ('əʊldwɜːld), *a.* [The phrase *old world* used attrib.: see WORLD.]

1. Of or pertaining to the old world or ancient order of things; belonging to, or characteristic of, early or bygone times.

1712 ARBUTHNOT *John Bull* III. iv, Silly auld warld Ceremonies. **1822** SCOTT *Nigel* xiii. **1850** MERIVALE *Rom. Emp.* (1865) II. xi. 9 The great old-world cities of Seleucia and Babylon. **1858** GEN. P. THOMPSON *Audi Alt.* I. xlvii. 185 The genus Statesman; which.. seems on the way to join the Megatheria of old world history. **1876** OUIDA *Winter City* ix. 257 She watched the simple pastoral old-world life around her.

2. a. Of or pertaining to the Old World or continents of Europe, Asia, and Africa, as opposed to the New World or America.

1877 *Harper's Mag.* Dec. 91/2 This was.. a beautiful garden kept in old-world order by a Scotch gardener. **1931** E. F. BENSON *Mapp & Lucia* i. 19 Seven bedrooms, four sitting-rooms h. & c., and an old-world garden. **1965** *Canad. Jrnl. Linguistics* X. 97 Consolidation with various Old-World stocks (Uralic, Indo-European) has been sought. **1967** *Boston Sunday Globe* 23 Apr. 23 (Advt.), Old world wood finish and antique polished bronze [lamp].. antique empire gold and black candelabra. **1977** *N.Y. Rev. Bks.* 13 Oct. 14/1 For most Americans political assassination was an Old World phenomenon of bomb-throwing Bolsheviks and Balkan fanatics.

b. Old World monkey, a catarrhine monkey belonging to the superfamily Cercopithecoidea or the family Cercopithecidæ, which includes the monkeys of Africa and Asia.

1863 H. W. BATES *Naturalist on River Amazons* II. v. 326 The Marmosets, have thirty-two teeth, like the Old World monkeys and man. **1894** H. O. FORBES *Hand-bk. Primates* I. 252 The family *Cercopithecidæ* includes all the Old World Monkeys except the Anthropoid or true Apes, and Man. **1936** E. G. BOULENGER *Apes & Monkeys* vi. 120 The old-world monkeys are very widely distributed. **1968** *Times* 15 Nov. 8/6 Two fossil monkeys of the primate group known as the Old World monkeys, or Cercopithecoidea. Living representatives of the group include baboons, mandrills and macaques. **1974** S. I. ROSEN *Introd. Primates* vi. 86 The Old World monkeys are biologically closer to man than the New World primates.

Hence **old-'worldish** *a.*, characteristic of the old world; **old-'worldism, old-'worldliness, old-'worldness**, old-world character or quality.

1886 W. J. TUCKER *E. Europe* 417 His notions are old-worldish. **1887** STUART CUMBERLAND *Queen's Highway fr. Ocean to Ocean* 8 Victoria is not a bustling place, neither is it sleepy; but there is an air of old-worldism, of quiet content about it. **1888** MRS. HUNGERFORD *Hon. Mrs. Vereker* I. i. 2 There was a touch of old-worldism, of a comfortable drowsiness, about everything. **1895** *Atlantic Monthly* Mar. 410 There is a sort of modern oldworldness. **1934** *Archit. Rev.* LXXV. 178 The patron public was becoming patina-conscious, aware of texture, age-effects, old-worldliness, the charm of mellowness.

‖**ole** ('ole), *sb.* [Sp. *ole* Andalusian dance.] The name of a Spanish folk-dance, which is accompanied by castanets and singing.

1846 R. FORD *Gatherings from Spain* xxiii. 328 The dance .. is called the *Ole* by Spaniards, the *Romalis* by their gipsies... The whole person.. trembles like an aspen leaf. **1950** L. ARMSTRONG *Dances of Spain* I. 9 *Olé*, Gaditanian (Cadiz) folk dance of apparently great antiquity. A solo with castanets. **1964** W. G. RAFFÉ *Dict. Dance* 360 *Ole* (Spain), a woman's solo dance with castanets... The dance is accompanied by rapid vocal acrobatics.. to the syllables 'ay' or 'olé' (from which the dance may take its name).

ole, ol' (əʊl), *a.* Also ol. A representation of a *colloq.*, *dial.*, and Black English pronunc. of OLD *a.*

1844 (*song-title*) Ole Bull and Ole Dan Tucker. **1874** [see *old mistress* s.v. OLD *a.* (*adv.*, *sb.*[1]) D.4]. **1880** J. C. HARRIS *Uncle Remus* i. 18, I speck de ole 'oman en de chilluns kin sorter scramble roun' en git up sump'n fer ter stay yo' stummuck. **1894** A. MORRISON *Tales of Mean Streets* 224 'That's all right, ol' cock,' roared Bill Napper. **1901** W. N. HARBEN *Westerfelt* iv. 44 How are you, ol' hoss... Glad to see you. **1907** G. B. SHAW *Major Barbara* II. 217 Youre ony a jumped-up, jerked-off, orspittle-turned-out incurable of an ole workin man. **1915** C. JOHNSON *Battleground Adventures* liv. 418 Holt met the ol' man comin' from the barn as hard as he could run. *Ibid.* 420, I got a little ol' box to sit on. **1935** Z. N. HURSTON *Mules & Men* I. iv. 101 It laid dere for thousands of years, then Ole Missus said to Ole Massa: 'Go pick up dat box.' **1936** M. MITCHELL *Gone with Wind* iv. 63 'Mammy gettin' ole,' said Dilcey, with a calmness that would have enraged Mammy. **1938** M. K. RAWLINGS *Yearling* iv. 34 He'll rip them leaves offen the stems and cram 'em in his ugly ol' mouth like a person. **1944** C. HIMES *Black on Black* (1973) 202 Just a li'l ol' knot at the bottom. **1950** R. AMES in A. Dundes *Mother Wit* (1973) 488/1 The old time darky's.. love for 'ole marse' and 'ole mist'ess'. **1962** J. D. SALINGER *Franny & Zooey* 85 That's the spirit... That's putting the ole foot down. **1971** *Jamaican Weekly Gleaner* 3 Nov. 18/2 Long debt better dan ole grudge. *Ibid.* 32/2 'Sure hate to be back at that same old school.' 'Same ol' tests.' **1972** G. BEARE *Bee Sting Deal* i. 12 'I work here,'.. 'But surely not at 5.30 a.m., ole gel.' **1973** S. HENDERSON *Understanding New Black Poetry* 21 Thus in the spirituals we have.. Tell ol Pharaoh to let my people go. **1973** [see LIMER[2]]. **1973** *Black World* May 13/1 They succinctly and repeatedly lay the flaming blame at Ole Massa's front door. **1974** *Sunday Guardian* (Port-of-Spain) 28 July 12/2, I took a bus to Martin's Bay, and there was laughter and ole talking all the way. Down on the wharf I find gangs of limers giving jokes and ole talkin. **1977** *Washington Post* 7 Dec. B1/1 Some people will be carried away by NBC's Bette Midler special, 'Ol' Red Hair is Back', at 10 o'clock tonight on Channel 4. **1977** *Time* 29 Aug. 31/1 'My God,' sighed Bell, 'I still wish we could get ole Frank Johnson to take it.'

‖**olé** (o'le), *int.* [Sp. *olé* bravo.] Bravo. Also as *sb.*, a cry of olé. Usu. assoc. with Spanish music and dance and with bullfighting.

1922 J. HERGESHEIMER *Bright Shawl* 55 An uproar of applause rose from the theatre, a confusion of cries, of Olé! Olé! Anda! Anda! Chiquella! **1940** E. HEMINGWAY *For whom Bell Tolls* v. 60 'Olé!' someone said. 'Go on, gipsy!' **1962** J. STEWART tr. *Cousseau's Death of Miss Cunningham* 44 The unheard *Olés* of the crowd.. in Caracas. **1966** R. E. PICKERING *Himself Again* vi. 42, I.. picked up the little glass, and drained it. 'Olé,' said Charley. **1967** J. POTTER *Foul Play* i. 17 Freda and Basil had launched themselves into a perilous exhibition tango, to encouraging olés from the surrounding circle of boozers. **1973** *Sat. Rev.* (U.S.) 25 Sept. 29/1 The *plaza de toros* was packed; and.. before I could even see the ring, I heard the *olés*.

ole, variant of OLLA[2], palm-leaf.

-ole, *suffix* [partly f. L. *oleum* oil, partly a var. -OL], used to form chemical names. **1.** In the names of compounds containing five-membered, unsaturated rings with at least one hetero-atom, e.g. *carbazole*, *indazole*, *indole*, *pyrrole*, *thiazole*, *triazole*.

Although applicable to older words like *pyrrole* (1835), this systematic use of *-ole* is of more recent date.

1928 *Jrnl. Amer. Chem. Soc.* I. 3078 For five-membered rings proposals made by Widman, Bouveault and others have found their way into use. The ending *-ol* or *-ole* appears in such names as pyrrole, imidazole and even dioxole (which is non-nitrogenous). It conflicts with the ending *-ol* for alcohols and phenols (hence the modified spelling *-ole*), but its use to denote a five-membered ring is well known. **1971** *Nomencl. Org. Chem.* (I.U.P.A.C.) (ed. 3) B. 53 (*table*) No. of members in the ring..5. Rings containing nitrogen: unsaturation..-ole... Rings containing no nitrogen: unsaturation..-ole.

2. Unsystematically, in the names of aromatic ethers, e.g. *anisole*, *phenetole*, *safrole*, which were regarded as being derived from carboxylic acids in the same way as 'benzole' (benzene) is from benzoic acid.

1852 *Rep. Brit. Assoc. Adv. Sci. 1851* I. 136 The use of the analogous termination *ole* for those [bodies] formed by the abstraction of 2 atoms of carbonic acid from the same [*sc.* vegetable acids] may be apt to cause some ambiguity. Thus we use the terms benzo*le*, pheno*le*, and aniso*le*, as being derived respectively from the benzoic, salicylic, and anisic acids.

olea, obs. f. OLIO; var. OLLA[1], pot, stew.

oleaceous (əʊlɪ'eɪʃəs), *a. Bot.* [f. mod.L. *Oleācе-æ*, f. *olea* olive-tree: see -ACEOUS.] Belonging to the Natural Order *Oleaceæ*, comprising trees and shrubs chiefly of temperate regions; the typical genus is *Olea*, the Olive.

1857 in MAYNE *Expos. Lex.*

oleaginous (əʊlɪ'ædʒɪnəs), *a.* [ad. F. *oléagin-eux, -euse*, f. L. *oleāgin-us, -āgineus, -āginius*, of or pertaining to *olea* the olive-tree; cf. (late) L. *oleāgina* the olive (Venant. Fort. *c* 600); also med.L. *oleāgo, -āgin-em* oily matter, such as in the bath was scraped from the oiled bodies of wrestlers.]

1. a. Having the nature or properties of oil; containing oil or an oily substance; oily, fatty, greasy.

1634 T. JOHNSON *Parey's Chirurg.* XXVI. xxiv. (1678) 645 There are three differences of these oleaginous juices. **1718** CHAMBERLAYNE *Relig. Philos.* (1730) I. xi. §14 Receptacles of a fat, or oleaginous Matter. **1799** KIRWAN *Geol. Ess.* 332 The soft oleaginous state of the shales on which they are found. **1875** MISS BRADDON *Str. World* I. i. 2 Like the oleaginous scum that pollutes the surface of a city river.

b. Producing oil.

1696 PHILLIPS (ed. 5), *Oleaginous*,..out of which Oyl may be press'd. **1712** tr. *Pomet's Hist. Drugs* I. 154 Having in it a little oleaginous Kernel. **1848** MILL *Pol. Econ.* I. I. ii. §3. 43 Growing flax, hemp..oleaginous plants. **1881** MIVART *Cat* 296 Sebaceous and oleaginous glands.

2. *fig.* = OILY 3.

1859 FARRAR *Julian Home* xx. 255 The lank party who snuffles the responses with such oleaginous sanctimony. **1922** JOYCE *Ulysses* 406 The scent, the smile.., the dark eyes and oleaginous address. **1945** R. HARGREAVES *Enemy at Gate* 31 The shifty, oleaginous, power-greedy place-man Olympius. **1966** *Listener* 18 Aug. 244/3 Many of the other works have a rather nasty oleaginous inconsistency of texture. **1973** *Daily Tel.* 13 Oct. 11/2 A piped programme that included an oleaginous instrumental version of part of a Chopin nocturne. **1976** *National Observer* (U.S.) 17 July 5/1 For years, the conferences have been sponsored and paid for by big companies and their oleaginous lobbyists.

Hence †**olea'ginity, oleagi'nosity, ole'aginousness**, †**ole'aginy**, the quality of being oleaginous, oily nature; **ole'aginously** *adv.*

1657 G. STARKEY *Helmont's Vind.* 314 One part of Alcali will turn two or three parts of Oyl into meer Salt, without any the least oleaginity. **1678** R. R[USSELL] *Geber* IV. ii. 241 The first Property of Differencies of the Medicine is Oleaginy. **1680** BOYLE *Produc. Chem. Princ.* II. 66 In speaking of the Oleaginousness of Urinous Spirits. **1694** SALMON *Bate's Dispens.* (1713) 126/1 Filtering and exhaling it to an Oleaginosity. **1861** J. LAMONT *Seasons w. Sea-horses* v. 69 From its oleaginousness it soon finds its own level in the casks. **1912** L. J. VANCE *Destroying Angel* x. 119 Three doors, in one of which a rotund Chinaman beamed oleaginously. **1912** W. DEEPING *Sincerity* xxxii. 247 His hands were fat, his neck full of red creases, his manner towards women oleaginously gallant. **1939** JOYCE *Finnegans Wake* 54 Whileas oleaginosity of ancestralolosis sgocciolated down the both pendencies of his mutsohito liptails.

oleander (əʊlɪ'ændə(r)). [a. med.L. *oleander*, in F. *oléandre* (15th c. in Hatz.-Darm.), It. *oleandro*, Sp. *eloendro*, Pg. *loendro*; origin obscure.

Conjectured by Diez to be a further corruption of *lorandrum*, recorded as a vulgar corruption of *rhododendron*, *-drum*, by Isidore *Origines* XVII. vii. 54 'Rhododendron [v.r. *rodandrum*] quod corrupte *lorandrum* [v.r. *laurandrum*] vocatur, quod est foliis *lauri* similibus, flore ut rosa, arbor venenata'. (Cf. the Fr. name *laurier-rose*.) Du Cange cites also the form *lauridendrum*, or *lauriendrum*; the latter may have given a further Romanic series *laure-* or *loreandro*, *l'oreandro*, *l'oleandro* (*l'* being taken as the article, and the final form perh. influenced by *olea* olive, *oleastrum*: cf. Alphita '*Oliandrum* i.e. siluestris olea.')]

a. An evergreen poisonous shrub, *Nerium Oleander* (N.O. *Apocynaceæ*), a native of the Levant, with leathery lanceolate leaves, cultivated for its handsome red or white flowers; also called *rose-bay*. Hence, by extension, any shrub of the genus *Nerium*, as the sweet oleander, *N. odorum*, a native of India, with fragrant flowers.

[*c* **1400** *Lanfranc's Cirurg.* (MS. A.) 192 Do þerto white litarge, elleborum nigrum, alumen vetus, oleandrum ana.] **1548** TURNER *Names of Herbes* 56 Nerion otherwyse called Rhododendron, and Rhododaphne..It maye be called in englishe Rose bay tree or rose Laurel. This tree is named of some oleander. **1562** —— *Herbal* II. 65 The floures and the leues of oleander ar poyson. **1671** SKINNER, *Holyander*, sic scribit Blake, credo idem quod Oleander. **1785** MARTYN *Rousseau's Bot.* xvi. (1795) 214 The Oleander is one of the most beautiful plants of this tribe—*Contortæ*. **1816** KIRBY & SP. *Entomol.* (1818) II. xx. 180 The oleander..yields a honey that proves fatal to thousands of imprudent flies. **1852** CONYBEARE & H. *St. Paul* (1862) I. vi. 158 The oleander, 'the favourite flower of the Levantine Midsummer', abounds in the lower water courses. **1880** G. W. CABLE *Grandissimes* xxvi. 193 Their long, over-arched avenues of oleander. **1915** H. H. THOMAS *Greenhouse* vi. 57 Oleanders require the protection of a cool greenhouse in winter. **1956** *Railway Mag.* Mar. 165/1 A fertile valley, with magnificent oleanders. **1962** *Coast to Coast 1961–62* 13 In the shade of the giant oleander bush sat Brett's half-Persian she-cat, licking and preening herself with a too obvious absorption.

b. *attrib.* and *Comb.*, as ***oleander-bud, -tree***; **oleander-fern**, a fern of the genus *Oleandra*, having fronds resembling the leaves of the oleander; **oleander hawk(-moth)**, a large moth, *Daphnis nerii*, of the family Sphingidæ whose caterpillars feed on oleander or periwinkle leaves.

1682 WHELER *Journ. Greece* I. 72 Wild-Vines..and Oleander-trees. **1843** HUMPHREYS & WESTWOOD *Brit. Moths* I. 21 The Oleander Hawk-moth..measures about $4\frac{1}{4}$ inches in the expansion of its fore wings, of which the ground colour is an olive-green. **1859** W. H. GREGORY *Egypt* II. 217 Water-courses, with oleander coverts. **1884** MILLER *Plant-n.*, *Oleandra neriiformis*, Oleander-Fern. **1884** RITA *Vivienne* VI. i, The crimson glory of the oleander-buds. **1907** R. SOUTH *Moths Brit. Isles* 1st Ser. 45 (*heading*) The Oleander Hawk-moth. **1955** E. B. FORD *Moths* i. 6 The other form [of green colouring]..is found..in some Sphingidae such as the Oleander Hawk. **1972** *Shooting Times & Country Mag.* 24 June 20/3 When they flew they reminded me of one of the hawk moths, the Oleander perhaps, or the Elephant Hawk moth.

oleandomycin (ˌəʊlɪːændəʊ'maɪsɪn). *Pharm.* [f. *oleand-rose*, a sugar of which a residue is present in the oleandomycin molecule (f. OLEANDR(INE + -OSE[2]) + -O + -MYCIN.] (The phosphate of) a macrolide, $C_{35}H_{61}NO_{12}$, produced by a strain of the bacterium *Streptomyces antibioticus*, which is active against a wide range of Gram-positive bacteria and has been used in treating staphylococcal enteritis and skin infections.

1956 B. A. SOBIN et al. *U.S. Pat. 2,757,123* 31 July, This invention relates to a new and useful antibiotic called oleandomycin. **1967** [see ERYTHROMYCIN]. **1968** [see MACROLIDE]. **1974** D. PERLMAN in W. O. Foye *Princ. Med. Chem.* xxxi. 742/1 Oleandomycin, a macrolide bacterial antibiotic closely related to erythromycin, has been losing value as a therapeutic agent for infections caused by gram-positive bacteria because of high incidence of side effects.

oleandrine (əʊlɪ'ændraɪn). *Chem.* [f. OLEANDER + -INE[5].] A yellow, bitter, poisonous alkaloid, the active principle of the leaves, etc. of the oleander.

1885 in J. THOMAS *Med. Dict.* **1892** in MORLEY & MUIR *Watts' Dict. Chem.*

olearia (əʊlɪ'ɛərɪə). [mod.L. (C. Moench *Suppl. Methodus Plantas Horti Botanici et Agri Marburgensis* (1802) 254), f. the name of Johann Gottfried *Olearius* (1635–1711), German theologian and horticulturist.] An evergreen shrub or tree of the Australasian genus so called, belonging to the family Compositæ and bearing clusters of white, yellow, or mauve flowers; = *daisy-tree* (DAISY *sb.* 7).

1839 G. DON *Sweet's Hortus Britannicus* (ed. 3) 344 (*heading*) *Olearia* DC. [English name] Olearia. **1852** *Curtis's Bot. Mag.* LXXVIII. 4638 Mr. Gunn's Olearia..ia another interesting plant of Van Diemen's Land, which braves the cold of England. **1868** *Trans. N.Z. Inst.* I. III. 4 Along the shore there is a profusion of shrub Veronicas and Olearias. **1882** T. H. POTTS *Out in Open* 64 Soon to be lost beneath a covering screen of *veronicas*, *olearias*, gnarled and knotted *griselinias*. **1918** *Chambers's Jrnl.* Apr. 221/1 The trees, especially the rata and the olearia, grow for nearly half their length along the ground. **1959** *Listener* 22 Jan. 174/1 He sometimes tears at the bark of the ceanolthus and olearias. **1971** *Homes & Gardens* Sept. 127/2 Many olearias have grey under-sides to the foliage.

oleaster (əʊlɪ'æstə(r)). Also 5 oli-. [a. L. *oleaster*, f. *olea* olive-tree: see -ASTER.] **a.** The true Wild Olive (*Olea Oleaster*), the wild variety (or sub-species) of the cultivated Olive, with more or less thorny branches and small worthless fruit. **b.** A small tree of the genus *Elæagnus*, a native of southern Europe and some parts of Asia, somewhat resembling the preceding, with abundance of fragrant yellow flowers, and reddish-brown inedible fruit; also called *wild olive*.

[*c* **1000** *Sax. Leechd.* II. 90 Gecnuwa lufestice & ellenrinde & oleastrum, þæt is, wilde elebeam.] **1398** TREVISA *Barth. De P.R.* XVII. cxiii. (1495) 676 Oliaster is a wilde oliue tree and hath that name for he is lyke to the oliue tree: but the leues thereof ben broder and this tree is bareyne and bytter and not tilthed. *c* **1420** *Pallad. on Husb.* IV. 115 Bareyn yf thin oliaster be. **1671** SALMON *Syn. Med.* III. xxii. 414. **1731–3** MILLER *Gard. Dict.* s.v. *Olea*, The Oleaster is very hardy, and will endure the severest Cold of our Climate.. This will grow to the Height of sixteen or eighteen Feet.. During the Season of its Flowering, (which is in June) it perfumes the circumambient Air to a great Distance. **1855** SINGLETON *Virgil* I. 185 Let the palm Or a huge oleaster th' outer court O'ershadow. **1874** FARRAR *Christ* (1881) 212 He had found in the oleaster what He had not found in the olive.

Hence †**ole'astral, -ial** *a. Obs.*, pertaining to a wild olive (with allusion to Rom. xi. 17).

1600 W. WATSON *Decacordon* (1602) 81 Seditious factions, and vnnaturall dispositions, sprong out of oleastriall graffes amongst us.

oleate ('əʊlɪːət). *Chem.* and *Pharm.* [f. OLE-IC + -ATE[4].] A salt of oleic acid; also applied to pharmaceutical preparations composed of alkaloids, or metallic oxides or salts, dissolved in this.

1831 T. P. JONES *Convers. Chem.* xxx. 303 Soap made with potash may be considered as an oleate and margarate of that alkali. **1841** BRANDE *Man. Chem.* (ed. 5) 1141 The solution now contains pure oleate of potassa. **1869** E. A. PARKES *Pract. Hygiene* (ed. 3) 46 When an alkaline oleate is mixed with pure water. **1899** G. M'GOWAN tr. *Bernthsen's Organ. Chem.* 177 Soaps consist of the alkaline salts of palmitic, stearic, and oleic acids, hard soaps containing soda salts, chiefly of the solid acids, while soft soaps contain potash salts, principally oleate.

†'**oleated**, *ppl. a. Obs. rare*[−1]. [f. L. *oleāt-us* oiled, preserved in oil + -ED.] Oiled.

1661 LOVELL *Hist. Anim. & Min.* 418–9 It's cured..by vomit with an oleated feather.

olebanum, obs. form of OLIBANUM.

‖**olecranon** (əʊlɪ'kreɪnən). *Anat.* Also 8 -**num**. [a. Gr. ὠλεκρᾶνον, shortened from ὠλενόκρᾶνον head or point of the elbow, f. ὠλένη elbow + κρᾶνίον head, skull, cranium.] The process or apophysis at the upper end of the ulna, forming the bony prominence at the elbow.

1727–41 CHAMBERS *Cycl.* s.v., The olecranum is received into the hind sinus of the lower end of the humerus. **1741** MONRO *Anat. Bones* (ed. 3) 248 The..Cavity lodges the Olecranon in the Extensions of that Member. **1804** ABERNETHY *Surg. Obs.* 99 A girl..had a collection of fluid under the triceps extensor cubiti, near the olecranon. **1836–9** TODD *Cycl. Anat.* II. 63/1 Posteriorly, the olecranon forms a remarkable prominence.

b. *attrib.*, as **olecranon fossa**, the depression in the humerus into which the olecranon fits when the arm is extended; **o. process** = *olecranon*.

1842 E. WILSON *Anat. Vade M.* (ed. 2) 66 Bounding the greater sigmoid notch posteriorly is the olecranon process. **1879** tr. *De Quatrefages' Hum. Spec.* 57 Desmoulins regarded the perforation of the olecranon process as one of the most decided characters of his Austro-African species of man.

Hence **ole'cranal, ole'cranial, ole'cranian** *adjs.*, pertaining to the olecranon; **ole'cranoid** *a.*, 'resembling the olecranon' (*Syd. Soc. Lex.*), but erron. used for *olecranal*.

1831 R. KNOX *Cloquet's Anat.* 689 The other passes backwards into the olecranal cavity. **1857** DUNGLISON *Med. Lex.* 940 These two eminences are separated..by the greater sigmoid, or semilunar fossa, or olecranoid cavity. **1881** MIVART *Cat* 93 The olecranal or anconeal fossa. **1883** N. JOLY *Man before Metals* II. viii. 353 The olecranian cavity is often perforated. **1892** *Syd. Soc. Lex.*, *Olecranial*.

olefactible, obs. variant of OLFACTIBLE *a.*

olefiant ('əʊlɪfaɪənt, əʊ'liːfɪənt), *a. Chem.* [a. F. *oléfiant*, in *gaz oléfiant*, the name given in 1795 by the Dutch chemists, Deiman, Paets van Troostwyk, Bondt, and Lauwerenburgh (*Crell. Ann.* 1795 II. 195, 310, 430); in form a pr. pple. of a vb. '*oléfier*' to make oil, to 'olefy'.] *lit.* Making or forming oil: only in ***olefiant gas***: the name originally given to heavy carburetted hydrogen or ETHYLENE (C_2H_4), from its forming with chlorine an oily liquid ('Dutch oil', 'D. liquid').

1807 T. THOMSON *Chem.* (ed. 3) II. 413 This gas, which was first examined by the Dutch chemists, received from them the name of olefiant gas. **1813** SIR H. DAVY *Agric. Chem.* iii. (1814) 124 Olefiant gas burns with a bright white light. **1873** WATTS *Fownes' Chem.* (ed. 11) 166 Olefiant gas is colourless, neutral, and but slightly soluble in water. **1877** —— *Fownes' Org. Chem.* II. 56 Ethene, or Ethylene, C_2H_4, also called Olefiant gas,..unites readily with chlorine, bromine, and iodine, forming oily liquids.

olefin ('əʊlɪfɪn). *Chem.* Also formerly olefine. [f. OLEFIANT with ending -IN[1], -INE[5].

The spelling *olefin* is now generally used in accordance with the practice of reserving -INE[5] for the naming of basic substances and heterocyclic compounds containing nitrogen.]

The general name for the series of hydrocarbons homologous with olefiant gas or ethylene, having the general formula C_nH_{2n}; forming with chlorine and bromine oily dichlorides and dibromides analogous to Dutch liquid (see prec.). Also *attrib.*, as ***olefin series***.

1860 F. GUTHRIE in *Jrnl. Chem. Soc.* [I] XII. 109 The isolation of the so-called organic radicals, the hydrides of the olefines. **1866** ROSCOE *Elem. Chem.* 297 The higher carbon series yield olefines corresponding to ethylene. **1873** WATTS *Fownes' Chem.* (ed. 11) 552 Olefines are polymeric. **1879** SCHORLEMMER *Rise & Devel. Organ. Chem.* (1894), The second series we call, with Guthrie, the Olefines, after the initial member which was first known as olefiant gas. **1899** E. F. SMITH *Richter's Organ. Chem.* I. 89 C_nH_{2n}: Olefines, Alkylens, Alkenes. **1923** T. G. PHILLIPS *Fundamentals Org. & Biol. Chem.* ix. 131 Similar series [of compounds] may be derived from the olefin hydrocarbons. **1949** R. F. GOLDSTEIN *Petroleum Chemicals Industry* vi. 124 The higher olefins are present in all fractions of the petrol range of thermally and catalytically cracked oils. **1968** R. O. C. NORMAN *Princ. Org. Synthesis* viii. 262 This discussion indicates the difficulties necessarily present in effecting the dimerization of an olefin.

Hence **ole'finic** *a.*, of, having the nature of, or characteristic of an olefin; applied *spec.* to a double bond between two carbon atoms such as is characteristic of olefins (cf. ETHYLENIC *a.*).

1898 J. WADE *Introd. Study Org. Chem.* lvi. 344 On gentle oxidation it [*sc.* linaloöl] yields an olefinic ketone. **1923** *Daily Mail* 15 Feb. 3 Those olefinic and empyreumatic substances which result from the distillation of coal or oil. **1968** R. O. C. NORMAN *Princ. Org. Synthesis* vii. 248 Although carbanions . . do not react with simple olefins, they do so if the olefinic double bond is conjugated to a group of $-M$ type. **1974** *Jrnl. Amer. Chem. Soc.* XCVI. 7934 (*heading*) Stereochemistry of olefinic cyclization.

oleic (əʊ'liːɪk, 'əʊliːɪk), *a. Chem.* [f. L. *ole-um* oil + -IC.] *lit.* Pertaining to or derived from oil; spec. in ***oleic acid***: one of the fatty acids ($C_{18}H_{34}O_2$), occurring in most fats, and a constituent of most soaps; obtained as an oily liquid, colourless, tasteless, and inodorous (when pure); also called *elaic acid*; in *pl.* extended to the series of acids to which this belongs: see quot. 1899. ***oleic ether***: a general name for the oleates of hydrocarbon radicals, *esp.* oleate of ethyl, $C_{18}H_{33}(C_2H_5)O_2$.

1819 J. G. CHILDREN *Chem. Anal.* 315 Oleic acid was obtained by Chevreul from the soluble portion of the soap formed with hog's lard and potassa. **1836** *Blackw. Mag.* XXXIX. 309 One of three acids, either the oleïc, margaritic, or cetic. **1866–77** WATTS *Dict. Chem.* IV. 192 Oleic acid crystallises from alcoholic solution in dazzling white needles. *Ibid.* 195 Oleate of Ethyl or Oleic Ether . . is a colourless liquid of specific gravity 0·87 at 18°. **1871** ROSCOE *Elem. Chem.* 387 The natural oils and fats are all compounds of glycerin, chiefly with palmitic, oleic, or stearic acids. **1894** *Daily Graphic* 20 Apr. 13/2 The smoothing of troubled waters by means of oil has been recently scientifically investigated, . . the quieting effect of all oils or soaps used is in direct proportion to the amount of free oleic acid they contain. **1899** E. F. SMITH *Richter's Organ. Chem.* 276 *Oleic Acids*, Olefine Monocarbonylic Acids, $C_nH_{2n-1}CO_2H$. The acids of this series, bearing the name *Oleic Acids*, because oleic acid belongs to them, differ from the fatty acids by containing two atoms of hydrogen less than the latter.

oleiferous (əʊliː'ɪfərəs), *a.* Also erron. **oliferous**. [f. L. type **oleifer*, f. *ole-um* oil: see -I-FEROUS.] Producing oil.

1804 *Med. Jrnl.* XII. 93 The oliferous Chinese radish . . is much cultivated in Piedmont and the Milanese. **1849** MURCHISON *Siluria* xviii. (1854) 443 The . . limestones of Trenton, which are more or less oleiferous from Quebec to the Manitoulin Islands. **1857** LIVINGSTONE *Trav.* xv. 272 Castor-oil-plant or various other oliferous seeds.

olein ('əʊliːɪn). *Chem.* [Named *oléine* by Chevreul, f. L. *ole-um* oil + -IN[1], after *glycerin.*]

1. *Chem.* The trioleate of glyceryl, $C_3H_5(C_{18}H_{33}O_2)_3$, one of the most widely diffused of the natural fats, obtained as a colourless oily liquid, solidifying at −6°C.; also called *elain*. In *pl.* applied to the oleates of glyceryl or glycerides of oleic acid in general; the above being distinctively called *triolein*.

1838 T. THOMSON *Chem. Org. Bodies* 126 Olein is white, very liquid, and lighter than water. *c* **1865** LETHEBY in *Circ. Sc.* I. 94/1 Tallow consists of several fats; one of which (oleine) is liquid at ordinary temperatures. **1866–77** WATTS *Dict. Chem.* IV. 179 [Drying oils] contain an olein different from that of the non-drying oils, and yielding by saponification, not oleic, but linoleic acid or an acid similar thereto.

2. (See quots.)

1893 THORPE *Dict. Appl. Chem.* III. 59/1 *Olein* . . is applied commercially to any liquid oil obtained from partly solid oils by pressure. . . The product of the cold pressing of cocoanut and palm oil is known as 'cocoanut olein' and 'palm olein' respectively. *Ibid.* 56 An impure oleic acid, known as *olein* or *wool oil*, and employed for oiling wool, and for making lubricants and soaps, is prepared from the 'Yorkshire grease' obtained from the soap used in cleaning . . fibres, yarns, and cloth.

† **o'leity.** *Obs. rare*$^{-0}$. [ad. L. *oleitās*, f. *olea* olive.]

1656 BLOUNT *Glossogr.*, *Oleity* (*oleitas*), the time of gathering Olives, or the Olives when they are gather'd to make oyl of; also oyliness.

† **olen, ollen.** *Obs.* [Russ. *o'len'* deer, stag = OSlav. *jelenĭ*, Pol. *jeleń*, Lith. *élnís*, OLith. *ellenís* stag; whence Ger. *elen*, *elend*, *elendthier*, transf. to the elk (Russ. *los'*, Pol. *loś*): see also ELAND, ELLAN, ELLEND.] A red deer, a stag.

1591 G. FLETCHER *Russe Commw.* (Hakluyt Soc.) 14 Their beasts of strange kinds are the losh [= elk], the ollen [= stag], the wild horse. **1598** HAKLUYT *Voy.* I. 284 He commanded them to kille fiue Olens or great Deere. *Ibid.* 337 Samoeds . . whose meate is flesh of Olens or Harts, and fish. **1613** PURCHAS *Pilgrimage* IV. xvii. 431 They worship the Sunne, the Ollen and the Losey [elk], and such like.

olenellid (ɒlə'nɛlɪd), *sb.* and *a.* [a. mod.L. family name *Olenellidæ*, f. generic name *Olenell(us* (E. Billings *Palæozoic Fossils* (1861) I. 11) + -ID[3].] A trilobite belonging to the family Olenellidæ; of or pertaining to this family.

1892 PEACH & HORNE in *Q. Jrnl. Geol. Soc.* XLVIII. 239 Among the *disjecta membra* of Olenellid trilobites from the dark shales . . are certain portions of the carapaces of a much larger species. *Ibid.* 240 One word of speculation as to the systematic position of the Olenellids may be admissible here. **1937** *Jrnl. Paleont.* XI. 577/1 Olenellids present a most interesting association of primitive and specialized characters. *Ibid.* 578/2 The olenellid shell is for its size excessively thin. **1969** BENNISON & WRIGHT *Geol. Hist. Brit. Isles* iv. 87 The fauna of the Lower Cambrian chiefly comprises Olenellid trilobites. **1973** P. TASCH *Paleobiol. Invertebr.* xi. 518/1 The so-called abortive segments in . . other olenellids might be evidence of the type of asexual budding that occurs in certain primitive polychaete worms.

† **o'lenght.** [O *prep.*[1] b and LENGTH 16.] Afar.

a **1340** HAMPOLE *Psalter* xxxvii. 12 þai þat ware biside me stode olenght.

olent ('əʊlənt), *a. rare.* [ad. L. *olēnt-em*, pr. pple. of *olēre* to smell.] Smelling, giving out a smell or scent.

1607 TOPSELL *Four-f. Beasts* (1658) 176 Martial calleth it [the fox] *olidam vulpem*—an olent or smelling beast. **1831** *Fraser's Mag.* IV. 523 The whole number is disgustingly olent of parliamentary affairs. **1868** BROWNING *Ring & Bk.* IX. 313 The cup, he [a butterfly] quaffs at, lay with olent breast Open to gnat, midge, bee and moth as well.

-olent, suffix of words from L., as *sanguinolent*, *vinolent*, *violent*: see -ULENT.

oleo ('əʊliːəʊ), *sb.*[1] and *a.*

A. *sb.* **1.** Commercial contraction for OLEOMARGARINE, esp. in the U.S. sense of artificial butter or MARGARINE.

1884 *Daily News* 11 Dec. 3/6 There is one firm in London which is able to turn out from ten to twenty tons of this valuable oleo per week. **1888** *Pall Mall G.* 26 Jan. 12/1 When the law [of Iowa] compelled the sale of 'oleo' for what it was. . . From 2c. to 3c. per pound more has been realized for the summer make of butter than would have been were it not for the 'oleo' law.

2. *Aeronaut.* An oleo strut or leg. (See B 2 below.)

1929 F. H. & H. F. COLVIN *Aircraft Handbk.* (ed. 4) iii. 64 To prepare oleo for use. 1. Pull piston out of cylinder and remove auxiliary piston. 2. Fill tube up to 6 inches from top with G.E. transformer oil No. 6. 3. Insert auxiliary piston with bolt head down. 4. Insert main piston. **1931** *Handbk. Aeronautics* (R. Aeronaut. Soc.) iii. 190 (*table*) 2 Large oleos. . . 2 Small oleos. . . 2 Front struts. . . 2 Rear struts. **1958** H. G. CONWAY *Landing Gear Design* ix. 184 The combination of tyre and oleo will thus have an efficiency well below 100 per cent. **1977** D. BEATY *Excellency* xx. 223 He felt the main wheels shake on their oleos.

B. *adj.* **1.** ***oleo oil***: a name given (esp. in U.S.) to OLEOMARGARINE (in the Eng. and Fr. sense).

1893 THORPE *Dict. Appl. Chem.* III. 59 Pressure is gradually applied, and the expressed oil constitutes the 'oleo oil', . . a soft, granular, tasteless, and nearly colourless fat. The hard fat remaining in the filter bags forms the 'beef' or oleo-stearin . . sold to the soap and candle makers. *a* **1895** *Westm. Gaz.* 11 Sept. 3/2 In this country . . they use oleo oil, or any other foreign fat, in order to make as close and good an imitation [of cheese] as they can.

2. [f. OLEO-.] Applied to (a system containing) a telescopic strut, used esp. in aircraft undercarriages, which absorbs shocks by means of a hollow piston into which oil is forced through a small orifice on compression of the strut (see also quot. 1965).

1916 N. J. GILL *Flyer's Guide* iii. 39 The commonest form of shock absorber is the rubber type, but Oleo gear are [*sic*] now also used to a considerable extent. **1920** *Flight* XII. 14/1 The undercarriage is at present of the usual Vee type with stream-line steel tube struts and rubber shock absorbers, but later an oleo undercarriage will be fitted. **1935** C. G. BURGE *Compl. Bk. Aviation* 596/1 The piston must return to the original position as quickly as possible after each impact, and to secure this the oleo leg frequently incorporates a compressed-air chamber. **1965** C. N. VAN DEVENTER *Introd. Gen. Aeronaut.* vii. 149/2 The more usual method of absorbing the impact of landing is through the use of oleo struts. Of the two general types, one has a moving piston . . and the other has a fixed piston and uses a spring instead of air. **1977** D. BEATY *Excellency* i. 17 The searchlight began fingering the fuselage. The port oleo leg blossomed a brilliant silver.

oleo ('əʊliːəʊ), *sb.*[2] *rare.* Abbreviation of OLEOGRAPH.

1921 GALSWORTHY *Captures* (1923) 57 Taking up the oleos, he turned his back on the photographs. **1932** *Daily Express* 25 June 9/3 A little room hung with lace and oleos.

oleo, obs. form of OLIO.

oleo- (əʊliːəʊ), used **a.** as combining form of L. *oleum* oil, in various technical and scientific derivatives and compounds. [Cf. late L. *oleomella*, *oleoselinon*, in Isidore *Orig.*, *a* 450.] The chief of these appear in their places as main words; the following are other examples.

'oleo,duct [after *aqueduct*], a duct or channel for the conveyance of oil from an oil-well or oil-field. **,oleo'jector**, an automatic apparatus for injecting oil for lubrication. **ole'ometer** [-METER], an instrument for determining the density, and so the purity, of oils; = ELÆOMETER. **oleo'philic** *a.* [-PHILIC], having an affinity for oils or oily materials; readily absorbing oil. **oleo'phobic** *a.* [-PHOBIC], tending to repel, or not to absorb, oils or oily materials. **oleo-pneu'matic** *a.*, applied to a device or system which absorbs shocks by a combination of forcing oil through an orifice and compression of air or another gas. **'oleop,tene**, *Chem.* [Gr. πτηνός winged, volatile], the liquid part of a volatile oil; = ELÆOPTENE (Webster, 1864). **,oleorefrac'tometer**, an instrument for measuring the refractive power of oils. ‖**,oleo'saccharum** [mod.L., f. L. *saccharum* sugar], a pharmaceutical preparation made by triturating an essential oil with sugar. **oleo'thorax** *Med.* [ad. F. *oléothorax* (A. Bernou 1922, in *Bull. de l'Acad. de Méd.* LXXXVII. 457)], a method of treatment, now disused, in which oil is introduced into the pleural cavity; introduction of oil in this manner.

b. as comb. form of *oleic*, *olein*, as in OLEOMARGARINE: so ***oleo-palmitin***, ***oleo-stearin*** (see OLEO *sb.*[1] *oil*, quot. 1893). **,oleopho'sphoric** *a. Chem.* in ***oleophosphoric acid***, 'a phosphoretted fatty acid contained in the brain' (Watts *Dict. Chem.*).

1886 *Pall Mall G.* 8 Oct. 11/1 The Government decided upon the construction of an *oleoduct. . . The line must start from Baku, but the terminal point on the Black Sea is left open for the present. **1884** *Health Exhib. Catal.* 110/1 Patent *Oleojector for lubricating steam engine cylinders. **1861** HULME tr. *Moquin-Tandon* II. III. i. 105 Cod-liver oil . . should stand at 392° of Lefebvre's *oleometer. **1866–77** WATTS *Dict. Chem.* IV. 181 Lefebvre . . has constructed . . a hydrometer of peculiar construction, called an oleometer, having a very large cylindrical bulb and a very long stem, on which are inscribed densities from 0·8 to 0·94 for the temperature 15°, each density corresponding to that of a commercial oil. **1957** *Brit. Jrnl. Appl. Physics* VIII. Suppl. 6. S23/2 For oils containing oleic acid, the behaviour is different. Zinc and copper behave initially as the other metals in becoming more oleophobic on continued contact with oil and water but this eventually gives place to a reverse trend to increasingly *oleophilic behaviour. **1967** [see HYDROPHOBIC *a.* (*sb.*) 2 a]. **1970** *Sci. Jrnl.* Feb. 21/3 Sawdust treated with appropriate silicones is water repellent but strongly oleophilic and will soak up many times its weight of oil. **1946** *Jrnl. Colloid Sci.* I. 513 The . . conclusion was that the observed phenomenon was due to the adsorption of eicosyl alcohol from solution upon the interior walls of the flask, to form a film possessing the property of being *oleophobic to (unwetted by) the oil solution. **1967** E. CHAMBERS *Photolitho-Offset* xiv. 210 Others were unsuitable because of extreme low sensitivity to light, or the inherent oleophobic (ink rejecting) character of the tanned coatings. **1839–47** TODD *Cycl. Anat.* III. 587/2 A peculiar fatty acid called *oleophosphoric. **1873** RALFE *Phys. Chem.* 18 Oleophosphoric Acid is a yellowish gummy substance, composed of oleic acid, glycerin, and phosphoric acid. **1909** *Aëronaut. Jrnl.* Apr. 64/1 The front wheel is fitted with an *oleo-pneumatic brake for safety purposes. **1930** *Engineering* 16 May 647/1 (*heading*) Oleo-pneumatic shock absorber for aeroplanes. **1960** *Times* 30 Aug. 4/5 All four wheels . . are independently sprung by means of wishbones and Girling oleo-pneumatic spring and damper units. **1897** *Daily News* 2 Oct. 2/5 This . . is an *oleorefractometer . . whose business it is to tell . . the truth about our butter, our oil, our fat. **1757** A. COOPER *Distiller* II. vi. (1760) 131 Take some fine Loaf Sugar and . . Oil, . . rub them well together in a Glass Mortar, which is what the Chemists call making an **Oleosaccharum*. **1922** *Jrnl. Amer. Med. Assoc.* 24 June 1996/2 The normal pleura would not bear this direct treatment, but in such pathologic conditions the *oleothorax answered the desired purpose. **1938** *Brit. Encycl. Med. Pract.* IX. 309 Oleothorax is a therapeutic method consisting in the introduction of a sterile oil or an oil containing an antiseptic into the pleural cavity. **1962** H. SPENCER *Path. Lung* xii. 384 They [*sc.* liquid paraffin granulomas in the lung] have also been reported following oleothorax. . . This form of pulmonary oil granuloma has now largely disappeared following the cessation of this form of therapy.

oleograph ('əʊliːəgrɑːf, -æ-). [f. OLEO- + -GRAPH.] A picture printed in oil-colours in imitation of an oil-painting. Hence **,oleo'graphic** *a.*, pertaining to oleographs or oleography; of the nature of or resembling an oleograph; **oleo'graphically** *adv.*; **ole'ographist**. Also **oleo'lithograph**.

1873 *Young Englishwoman* Sept. 466/1 Oleographs are now very cheap, and, if well chosen, are most pleasing. **1880** WEBSTER Suppl., *Oleograph.* **1885** *Pall Mall G.* 1 June 6/1 Conventional oleographic enlargements of individual figures. **1892** *Athenæum* 2 July 33/1 It is oleographic in its delineations of the gushing aspirations of the school-room miss. **1897** MARY KINGSLEY *W. Africa* 412 Framed oleographs of English farmyard scenes. **1897** W. ARCHER *Theatr. 'World' 1896* 173 Seems . . incredible even in Germany, with the sacred *eikon* of the Kaiser oleographically lowering over the scene. **1907** R. BROOKE *Let.* 23 Aug. (1968) 100 The book plate of one Frederick Leighton—the notable oleographist, I take it? **1922** JOYCE *Ulysses* 698 Artistic oleograph on inner face of door. **1928** D. L. SAYERS *Lord Peter views Body* 176 Lord Peter sat down on a red velvet arm-chair, fixed his eyes on a gilt-framed oleograph, and became wrapped in contemplation. **1939** J. CARY *Mr. Johnson* 45 He is the happy husband adoring and adored in a perpetual and rather solemn dignity like an oleolithograph of the Royal Family. **1974** N. FREELING *Dressing of Diamond* 57 It was only in books that kidnappers had a handy stammer or a gold tooth, and a flat with a large coloured oleograph on the wall of President Kennedy, or the Pope, or Marilyn Monroe.

oleography (əʊlɪ'ɒgrəfɪ). [f. OLEO- + -GRAPHY.] The art or process of printing pictures in oil-colours, by a method of chromolithography.

1873 *Contemp. Rev.* XXII. 270 They would employ the detestable art of Oleography. **1875** tr. *Vogel's Chem. Light* xv. 250 We must express an adverse opinion against oleography.

oleomargarine (ˌəʊliːəʊ'mɑːgəriːn, -ɪn, -'mɑːdʒəriːn). [f. OLEO- b + MARGARINE. 'Often mispronounced..as if spelt *-margerine*' (*N.E.D.*, 1902).] A fatty substance obtained by extracting the liquid portion from clarified beef fat by pressure, and allowing it to solidify; with the addition of butyrin, or more or less admixture of butter, milk, etc. and sometimes of refined lard, it forms a substitute for natural butter, formerly sold as *butterine*, but now legally called in Great Britain (also in France, Germany, Denmark, etc.) *margarine*.

In U.S., *oleomargarine*, popularly *oleo*, is a recognized name of the commercial product, the expressed fat being distinguished as *oleo-oil*.

The name *oléo-margarine* was applied as early as 1854 by the French chemist Berthelot (*Ann. Chim. Phys.* XLI. 242 footnote) to a solid substance obtained *c* 1838 by Pelouze and Boudet (*Comptes Rendus* VII. 665) from olive oil, which was regarded as a combination of the *oléine* and *'margarine'* of Chevreul and Berthelot. (See MARGARINE.) According to the view then held, *oléine*, *'margarine'*, and *stéarine*, were regarded as the essential constituents of animal fat. As butter, or the fat of milk, consists according to Chevreul mainly of *oléine* and *'margarine'*, with a small amount of butyrin and allied principles, M. Mège-Mouriès in 1869–71 experimented on its artificial production by the extraction of the oléine and 'margarine' from animal fat, with subsequent processes for the addition of butyrin, etc. Hence the name *oléo-margarine* for the supposed combination of oléine and 'margarine' thus extracted. As further research has shown that neither the *'margarine'* of Chevreul, nor the *oléo-margarine* of Berthelot are definite chemical substances, these names are no longer in chemical use, and 'oleo-margarine' has only a manufacturing or commercial use for the fatty substance described above, or (as in U.S.) for the artificial butter (MARGARINE) made from it.

[**1871** *Sci. Amer.* 26 Aug. 129 Since 1869 M. Mège has endeavoured to utilize the oleine and margarine obtained on pressing animal fatty matters in the manufacture of stearine. **1872** *Moniteur Scient.* 742 C'est avec l'oléo-margarine que M. Mège fabrique son beurre économique. **1873** BRIN *Patent Specif.* No. 3477. 6 A perfect combination of the 'oleine margarine' and milk is effected.] **1873** *U.S. Patent Specif.* No. 146,012 In order to separate the oleomargarine from the stearine, separated crystallizers or crystallizations, at unequal temperatures have been already employed. **1873** *Sci. Amer.* 18 Oct. 246 The manufacture of artificial butter by the 'Oleomargarine Manufacturing Company'. **1881** *Law of Illinois State* in *Chicago Times* 4 June, No person shall mix oleomargarine..with any butter or cheese.. without distinctly marking..the article or package. **1881–82** [see BUTTERINE]. **1888** BRYCE *Amer. Commw.* II. 201 Bills.. prohibiting the sale of oleomargarine as butter. **1891** THORPE *Dict. Appl. Chem.* II. 517/2 The greater proportion of the oleomargarine extracted in America and elsewhere is, however, exported direct to Holland, to be there converted into margarine. *Ibid.* 518/1 The term 'oleomargarine' should be confined to the animal oil used in making margarine. **1900** PERKIN & KIPPING *Organic Chem.* ix. 170 Artificial butter, or *margarine*, is prepared from oleomargarine..manufactured from the best ox-suet... When carefully prepared, it is a wholesome substitute for butter, and probably just as nutritious.

Hence **oleomar'garic** *a.*, consisting of olein and 'margarine'; pertaining to oleomargarine.

1873 *U.S. Patent Specif.* No. 146,012 The stearine is deposited in the form of teats at the middle of the oleomargaric liquid.

oleone, -on ('əʊliːəʊn). *Chem.* [f. L. *oleum* oil + -ONE.] An oily liquid, obtained by the distillation of oleic acid with lime; supposed to be the ketone of oleic acid.

1840 *Penny Cycl.* XVI. 425. **1866–77** WATTS *Dict. Chem.* IV. 196.

oleoresin (ˌəʊliːəʊ'rezɪn). [f. OLEO- + RESIN.] **a.** A natural mixture of a volatile oil and a resin; a balsam. **b.** A mixture of an oil (fixed or volatile) and a resin or other active substance, artificially obtained by evaporation from an ether tincture.

1853 G. JOHNSTON *Nat. Hist. E. Bord.* I. 248 The oleoresin of the Male-Fern is an excellent remedy for tapeworm. *c* **1865** LETHEBY in *Circ. Sc.* I. 106/2 Turpentine freely absorbs oxygen from the air, and is converted into an oleo-resin. **1876** HARLEY *Mat. Med.* (ed. 6) 405 These trees ..secrete a large quantity of oleo-resin which exudes as a varnish or in granular masses from cracks in the bark. **1898** *Allbutt's Syst. Med.* V. 82 The internal administration of.. the essential oils, the oleo-resins, and the balsams.

Hence ˌ**oleo'resinous** *a.*, of the nature of an oleoresin.

1861 BENTLEY *Man. Bot.* 474 Trees, which abound in an oleo-resinous juice. **1883** HALDANE *Workshop Receipts* II. 289/1 Dissolving any oleo-resinous deposit in..rectified spirit.

oleose ('əʊliːəʊs, əʊlɪ'əʊs), *a.* Now *rare.* [ad. L. *oleōs-us* oily, f. *ole-um* oil: see -OSE.] = OLEOUS.

1675 *Phil. Trans.* X. 484 Slime, out of which they suck something oleose. **1754** HUXHAM *ibid.* XLVIII. 837 The oleose part of the spirit of wine. **1869** *Eng. Mech.* 24 Dec. 357/2 It is of an oleose consistence.

ole'osity. Now *rare* or *Obs.* [f. as prec. + -ITY. Cf. It. *oliosità* 'oylienes, fatnes' (Florio 1598).] Oily quality or consistence; oiliness.

1610 B. JONSON *Alch.* II. v, By his viscositie, His oleositie, and his suscitabilitie. **1627** tr. *Bacon's Life & Death* (1651) 37 Saffron..is both notably Astringent, and hath besides an Oleosity.

oleous ('əʊliːəs), *a.* Now *rare* or *Obs.* [ad. L. *oleōs-us*, f. *ole-um* oil: see -OUS.] Of the nature or consistence of oil; containing oil; oily.

1601 HOLLAND *Pliny* II. 125 The root yeeldeth no oleous substance, but a reddish juice. **1682** T. GIBSON *Anat.* (1697) 9 It is bred of a viscous and oleous vapour of the blood. **1747** tr. *Astruc's Fevers* 148 They..may be combined with oleous remedies.

olephant, -aunte, obs. forms of ELEPHANT.

olepi, -y, var. ONLEPY *Obs.*, only, sole.

olepotride, obs. variant of OLLA PODRIDA.

oler, variant (now *dial.*) of ALDER.

1665–76 REA *Flora* (ed. 2) 18 A good quantity of short sticks of Oler, Withy, or any soft wood. **1879** BRITTEN & HOLLAND *Plant-n.*, Oler. See Owler... Owler, *Alnus glutinosa*, L.—*Ches.* (or Oler).

oleraceous (ɒlə'reɪʃəs), *a.* [f. L. (*h*)*olerāce-us* (f. (*h*)*olus*, (*h*)*oler-* pot-herb) + -OUS.] Of the nature of a pot-herb, or vegetable used in cookery; obtained from a pot-herb.

a **1682** SIR T. BROWNE *Tracts* 28 An herby and oleraceous vegetable. **1822–34** *Good's Study Med.* (ed. 4) I. 487 The oleraceous and especially the mucilaginous demulcents. **1848** HARDY in *Proc. Berw. Nat. Club* II. No. 6. 329 Caterpillars of various..moths that infest oleraceous plants.

†**b.** Belonging to the division *Oleraceæ* or *Holeraceæ* in Linnæus's proposed Natural System, corresponding to the *Chenopodiaceæ* and other apetalous Orders, and including various esculent herbs, as spinach, beet, etc. *Obs.*

1785 MARTYN *Rousseau's Bot.* xvii. (1794) 221 Among the *Oleraceous* plants in the natural orders of Linnæus, by other authors called *Apetalous*. Such are all the Goosefoots... Beet is very nearly allied to these... The Glassworts are also of this Oleraceous tribe.

olericulture ('ɒlərɪˌkʌltjʊə(r)). *rare.* [f. L. *olus*, *oler-* (see prec.), after *agriculture*, *horticulture*, etc.] The cultivation of pot-herbs or other esculent vegetables. So ˌ**oleri'culturally** *adv.*, in relation to olericulture.

1888 *Amer. Nat.* XXII. 807 *The Dwarf Kales*.. olericulturally considered they are quite distinct. **1966** *McGraw-Hill Encycl. Sci. & Technol.* XIV. 286/1 The term olericulture, referring to vegetable production, is used occasionally.

†**olerie.** *Obs. rare.* [a. OF. *olerie* ('les oleries de devant Noel'), 1478 in Godef.] See quot. and cf. O *int.* B. 2.

1892 KIRK *Abingdon Acc.* p. xxvi. *note*, The Oleries, or Anthems in Advent beginning with O.

†'**oleron.** *Obs.* Also 6 oldryn(n)e, olron, old(e)ron, oulderon. See also ALLRON. A kind of coarse fabric (app. for sail-cloth); ? originally made at Oléron in France.

1512 *Lett. & Papers Hen. VIII*, II. 1456, 148 bolts of 'oldrynnes', 12*s.* the bolt. **1545** *Rates of Customs* c j, Olrons the bolte vjs. viijd. **1583** *Ibid.* D v b, Oulderons the bolt containing xxx. Yardes xiijs. iiijd. **1561** in Rogers *Agric. & Prices* III. 490/4 Oldrons canvas 24 bolts @ 17/6. **1562** *Ibid.* 491/1 Olderon canvas.

oless, obs. form of UNLESS *conj.*

oleum ('əʊliːəm). Pl. oleums. [L., = 'oil'.] An oily liquid which is produced by dissolving sulphur trioxide in concentrated sulphuric acid in the contact process and is used in sulphonation and nitration processes; fuming sulphuric acid.

1905 BLOUNT & BLOXAM *Chem. for Engineers & Manuf.* (ed. 2) II. i. 23 Ordinary vitriol is still called in Germany English sulphuric acid, in contradistinction to the fuming acid or 'oleum'. **1949** P. W. VITTUM tr. *Fierz-David & Blangey's Fund. Proc. Dye Chem.* 83 When sulfonation is done with oleum, usually only the SO_3 is used up. **1954** *Thorpe's Dict. Appl. Chem.* (ed. 4) XI. 296/1 (*heading*) Boiling-points of oleums. **1973** *Times* 20 Jan. 3/1 It [*sc.* a tanker] was carrying a maximum load of 20 tons of oleum, a corrosive acid said to react violently when in contact with a small quantity of water.

O-level: see O 5 d.

oleyl ('əʊlɪɪl, -aɪl). *Chem.* [f. OLE(IC *a.* + -YL.] The radical $CH_3(CH_2)_7CH=CH(CH_2)_7CH_2-$, which has the same carbon atom skeleton as oleic acid; **oleyl alcohol,** an oily liquid, $C_{18}H_{35}OH$, which occurs in fish oils and is used in the manufacture of surface-active agents; *cis*-9-octadecen-1-ol.

1903 *Jrnl. Chem. Soc.* LXXXIV. i. 730 Ethyl oleate gave oleyl alcohol, $C_{18}H_{36}O$, as a colourless liquid. **1951** KIRK & OTHMER *Encycl. Chem. Technol.* VI. 271 The reaction of acetylene with oleyl alcohol gives vinyl oleyl ether, which is polymerizable and copolymerizable with other vinyl monomers. **1972** *Materials & Technol.* V. ix. 262 Oleyl alcohol can be epoxidised with peracids to yield polyhydroxy compounds. **1972** *Arch. Biochem. & Biophysics* CL. 199/2 Oleyl CoA inhibits the adenine nucleotide transport system..of rat liver mitochondria.

olfacient (ɒl'feɪʃ(ɪ)ənt). *rare.* [ad. L. *olfacientem*, pr. pple. of *olfacĕre* to smell (trans.), contr. from *olefacĕre*, f. *olē-re* to smell + *facĕre* to make.] Something that affects the sense of smell.

1822–34 *Good's Study Med.* (ed. 4) III. 200 An atmosphere, in which only a few particles of sternutatories or other acrid olfacients are floating.

†'**olfact,** *sb.* *Obs. rare*[−1]. [ad. L. *olfactu-s* smelling, smell, f. *olfacĕre*: see prec.] The organ or sense of smell.

1657 TOMLINSON *Renou's Disp.* 274 To the gust acrimonious, to the olfact fragrant.

'**olfact** (ɒl'fækt), *v.* *rare. affected.* [f. L. *olfact-*, ppl. stem of *olfacĕre*: see prec.] *trans.* To smell.

1663 BUTLER *Hud.* I. i. 742 There is a Machiavilian Plot (Though ev'ry Nare olfact it not). **1805** T. HARRAL *Scenes of Life* II. 105 Sweet olfacted scents in dear Bond Street. **1826** HOR. SMITH *Tor Hill* (1838) II. 335 Can you olfact this redolent ragout, and yet tear me from it?

olfactible (ɒl'fæktɪb(ə)l), *a.* Also 8 olefact-, 9 -able. [f. L. *olfact-*, ppl. stem (see prec.) + -IBLE.] That may be smelled.

c **1705** BERKELEY *Comm.-pl. Bk.* in Fraser *Life* (1871) 476 Gustable and olefactible perceptions. **1825** JAS. MILL in *Westm. Rev.* Jan. 188 Palpable virulence! he might as well have called it olfactable virulence. **1881** G. ALLEN *Evolutionist at Large, Microscopic Brains*, As our world is mainly a world of visible objects, theirs [ants'], I believe, is mainly a world of olfactible things.

olfaction (ɒl'fækʃən). [n. of action f. L. *olfacĕre*: see above.] The action of smelling or the sense of smell.

a **1846** DUNGLISON cited in Worcester. **1873** A. FLINT *Phys. Man, Nerv. Syst.* i. 16 The special senses, such as sight, audition, olfaction, and gustation. **1897** *Allbutt's Syst. Med.* IV. 695 If the neurosis of olfaction be due to local disease.

olfactive (ɒl'fæktɪv), *a.* [f. L. *olfact-*, ppl. stem (see above) + -IVE.] Of or pertaining to the sense of smell, olfactory.

1654 GAYTON *Pleas. Notes* IV. xxii. 274 He summons their olfactive forces before he will storme. **1686** W. HARRIS tr. *Lemery's Course Chem.* I. xxi. (ed. 3) 458 The tickling pleasure which this smell produces in the brain by means of the olfactive nerve. **1847–9** TODD *Cycl. Anat.* IV. 701/1 The contact of the odoriferous medium with the olfactive surface. **1874** CARPENTER *Ment. Phys.* I. ii. §38 Either the Optic, the Olfactive, or the Auditory nerve.

olfactometer (ɒlfæk'tɒmɪtə(r)). [f. as next + -OMETER.] **a.** An instrument for measuring the sensitivity of a subject to odours or the intensity of odours.

1889 H. ZWAARDEMAKER in *Lancet* 29 June 1301/1, I have lately constructed a small instrument which, I think, deserves the name of 'olfactometer'. Its component parts consist of two tubes fitting into each other. The outer one is lined with scented material, and made to glide up and down over the inner one, of which one end remains free and is bent to fit the nostril. **1922** G. H. PARKER *Smell, Taste & Allied Senses* iii. 51 Two single olfactometers may be combined so that one current carrying an odorous material..may be introduced into one nostril and another carrying a second odorous substance..into the other nostril. **1969** J. R. HUGHES et al. in C. Pfaffmann *Olfaction & Taste* 173 Stimuli have been presented by a portable two-channel olfactometer. **1969** *Daily Tel.* 9 Sept. 20/8 He has developed devices, known as olfactometers, which at present measure only the intensity of odours but do not differentiate between them.

b. A device for investigating the responses of animals to odours.

1926 *Jrnl. Econ. Entomol.* XIX. 552 Adult potato beetles were collected in potato patches and were tried in the insect olfactometer. **1969** *New Scientist* 17 Apr. 134/2 Some initial experiments using an olfactometer suggested that the sense of smell did not play any part in bringing the male and female spiders together.

olfactometry (ɒlfæk'tɒmɪtrɪ). [f. L. *olfact-*, ppl. stem of *olfacere* to smell (see OLFACIENT) + -O + -METRY.] The measurement of the sensitivity of the sense of smell, the use of an olfactometer; also, = ODORIMETRY.

1898 *Amer. Jrnl. Psychol.* X. 85 Olfactometry is that branch of psychophysics which is concerned with the measurement of the keenness of smell. **1898** [see ODORIMETER]. **1935** [see ODORIMETRY]. **1967** J. W. JOHNSTON in T. Hayashi *Olfaction & Taste II* 48 The characterization of a simple blend as a nonresinous woody odor by means of olfactometry and G-L chromatography has shown the way to the elusive correlation of the physical parameter, odorant intensity, and the psychological dimension, subjective (odorant) strength. **1968** W. MCCARTNEY *Olfaction & Odours* 151 When olfactometry is being practised, great care must be taken to avoid fatigue (adaptation) of the perceiving organ.

Hence **olfacto'metric** *a.*, of olfactometry.

1898 *Amer. Jrnl. Psychol.* X. 101 (*heading*) Control in Zwaardemaker's olfactometric method of the factors which determine the intensity of the stimulus. **1963** *Nature* 20 Apr. 272/2 As the syntheses were completed, the compounds were tested.., using advanced olfactometric techniques, for intensity and quality of odour. **1973** *Biol. Abstr.* LV. 2568/1 An olfactometric method is proposed for estimating the attractant properties of chemical compounds for insects.

olfactor (ɒlˈfæktə(r)). *rare*⁻¹. [agent-n. in L. form from *olfacĕre*: see above.] He who or that which smells; a smelling agent.

1829 SOUTHEY *Sir T. More* (1831) II. 276 And if thy nose ..were anything more than the ghost of an olfactor, I would offer thee a pinch [of snuff].

olfactorium (ɒlfækˈtɔərɪəm). Pl. **-ia**. [f. as OLFACTRONICS *sb. pl.* (const. as *sing.*) + -ORIUM.] A large odour-proof enclosure in which olfactory experiments are conducted.

1950 D. FOSTER et al. in *Amer. Jrnl. Psychol.* LXIII. 433 The design was..made cubical and the apparatus finally devised and described here was called the olfactorium. **1968** W. MCCARTNEY *Olfaction & Odours* 148 The 'olfactoria' (capacity 500 cubic feet, for example) that have recently been constructed in the U.S.A... are essentially the same as was Fischer and Penzoldt's test room.

olfactory (ɒlˈfæktərɪ), *a.* and *sb.* [ad. L. **olfactōri-us* adj. (found only in the absol. *olfactōria* bouquet), f. *olfactor*; see above and -ORY.]

A. *adj.* Of or pertaining to the sense of smell, connected or concerned with smelling.

1658 PHILLIPS, *Olfactory*, belonging to the sense of smelling. **1670** *Phil. Trans.* V. 2060 Vesalius was the first, that rightly observed the Olfactory Nerves. **1799** *Med. Jrnl.* I. 243 Daily experience proves the importance of the olfactory sensations. **1880** GÜNTHER *Fishes* 109 The olfactory organ is single in Branchiostoma and the Cyclostomes.

B. *sb.* An organ of smelling.

1823 J. BADCOCK *Dom. Amusem.* 166 Persons..who keep their olfactory out of the effluvia of other's ills. **1884** J. TAIT *Mind in Matter* (1892) 64 Something..that affects the mind through the olfactories.

†**b.** (See quots.) *Obs. rare*⁻⁰.

1656 BLOUNT *Glossogr.*, *Olfactory*, a Posie or Nose-gay, any thing to smell to. **1775** ASH, *Olfactory*, the power of smelling.

Hence **olˈfactorily** *adv.*, in the sense of smell.

1888 *Century Mag.* XXXV. 363 He was olfactorily impressed. **1944** R. W. MONCRIEFF *Chemical Senses* ix. 187 Structurally, the esters bear the same relation to the acids as the ethers do to the alcohols... Olfactorily, however, there is a difference. **1969** *Psychol. Bull.* LXXI. 60/1 Olfactorily acting and oral pheromones.

olfactronics (ɒlfækˈtrɒnɪks), *sb. pl.* (const. as *sing.*). [f. L. *olfact-*, ppl. stem of *olfacere* to smell (see OLFACIENT) + ELEC)TRONICS.] The detection, analysis, and measurement of vapours by means of instruments.

1964 *Aviation Week & Space Technol.* 16 Nov. 46/1 'Olfactronics.' Chicago—Combination of chemical analysis and electronic techniques appears to offer many interesting possibilities..beyond the detection of hidden explosives on aircraft, according to Dr. Andrew Dravnieks of the Illinois Institute of Technology. **1967** *N.Y. Times* 16 July IV. 8 Eventually olfactronics may be used to guard bank vaults against burglars. **1970** *Jrnl. Reproductive Med.* Apr. 69 (*heading*) Changes in vaginal odors... A study in applied olfactronics.

Hence **olfacˈtronic** *a.*, of or pertaining to olfactronics; **olfacˈtronically** *adv.*, by olfactronic means.

1966 *New Scientist* 15 Sept. 623/2 A human carries an olfactronic 'image' of his recent environment, provided that this environment contained some olfactronically distinguishable features. **1969** *Product Engineering* 10 Mar. 11 Acoustic or vibration sensors, heat-detection devices, and even olfactronic detectors might prove more effective. **1970** *Jrnl. Reproductive Med.* Apr. 70/1 The atmosphere around the study object..must be known and examined olfactronically.

†**ˈolfend.** *Obs.* Also 3 oluente, -onte, *Orm.* ollfennt. [Com. Teut.: OE. *olfend* and *olfenda* = MHG. *olbent*; also with change of formative OS. *olbundeo*, ON. *úlfaldi*, Goth. *ulbandus* masc., OHG. *olbanta*, *olbenta*, MHG. *olbande*, *olbende*, *olbente* fem. See note below.] A camel.

971 *Blickl. Hom.* 169 Se þe mid þon anum hrægle wæs ȝeȝyrwed þe of olfenda hærum awunden wæs. *c* **1000** *Ags. Gosp.* Matt. iii. 4 Johannes..hæfde reaf of olfenda hærum. *c* **1160** *Hatton Gosp.* ibid., Of oluende hære. *c* **1200** ORMIN 3208 Hiss claþ wass off ollfenntess hær. *c* **1200** *Trin. Coll. Hom.* 127 Stark haire of oluente [was] his wede. *Ibid.* 195 Seuen þusend shep and þrie þusend oluontes.

[*Note.* The similarity between this ancient Teutonic name for the camel, and the Gr. ἐλέφαντ- ELEPHANT, has excited much attention, without receiving any satisfactory explanation. Some have thought the Teut. word adopted from Gr., with mistaken identification of the animals; others think of an original relationship between pre-Hellenic **lebhant-* and pre-Teut. **lbhant*, as the name of some real or imaginary gigantic beast. But the resemblance may also be merely accidental; it is strongest in the case of OE. *olfend*, Ormin's *ollfennt* 'camel', and ME. *olifant*, *oliphant*, 'elephant'. The only app. certain cognates of Goth. *ulbandus* are Slavonic: OS. *velĭbadŭ*, *velĭblądŭ*, Russ. *vel-*, *verblʲud*, Czech *velbloud*, Lith. *verbludas*, which Miklosich considers to be adopted from OTeut. with modification by popular etymology.]

olhnen, olhtnen, var. OLUHNEN *v. Obs.*

oli, oliaster, obs. ff. OIL, HOLY, OLEASTER.

oliban (ˈɒlɪbən). [a. F. *oliban* (13–14th c. in Hatz.-Darm.), ad. L. *olibanum*.] = next.

c **1530** *Remedy Love* 214 Breathyng an Aromatike redolence Surmountyng Olibane. **1857** *Old Commodore* II. 54 Gum oliban and myrrh two ounces each.

‖**olibanum** (əʊˈlɪbənəm). Also 6 oly-, 7 ole-, olli-. [a. med.L. *olibanum*, 11th c. (in Sp., It. *olibano*, F. *oliban*), immed. or indirectly from Gr. λίβανος, late L. *libanus* (Vulgate) frankincense.]

An aromatic gum resin obtained from trees of the genus Boswellia, appearing in commerce in the form of irregular yellowish lumps; formerly used as a medicine but now chiefly as incense.

1398 TREVISA *Barth. De P.R.* XVII. clxxiii. (1495) 714 The tree..hyght Libanus and the gumme therof hyghte Olibanum, and hath that name of a mount in Arabia. *c* **1475** *Sqr. lowe Degre* 849 Cloves that be swete smellyng, Frankensence and olibanum. **1583** *Rates of Customs* D iv b, Olibanum the pound xiid. **1605** TIMME *Quersit.* III. 172 Take..aloes hepat., myrrhe, olebanum, mastic. **1625** PURCHAS *Pilgrims* I. III. xi. 273 A small Frigat of Shaher, laden with course Ollibanum. **1712** tr. *Pomet's Hist. Drugs* I. 200 Olibanum drops from the Tree plentifully, in roundish Drops. **1899** *Westm. Gaz.* 23 Sept. 8/3 It is popularly supposed that there is a trade secret in the making of incense, but..it is composed simply of gum olibanum, Siam benjamin, cascarilla bark, myrrh, and copal varnish.

[*Note.* Various suggestions have been offered to account for the med.L. form: e.g. that the word has been influenced by *oleum* oil, or was perh. contracted from *oleum libani*; that it contains the Gr. article ὁ λίβανος; that it is derived from or influenced by the Arabic *al-lubān*.]

olibene (ˈɒlɪbiːn). *Chem.* [f. prec. + -ENE.] A volatile oil, $C_{10}H_{16}$, obtained from olibanum.

1881 WATTS *Dict. Chem.* 3rd Suppl. 1433 Olibene, treated with dry hydrochloric acid gas, forms a crystalline hydrochloride, smelling like camphor..melting at 127°.

†**oˈlibian.** *Obs.* [irreg. f. L. *olib(anum* + -IAN.] = OLIBANUM. Chiefly *attrib.*, as ***olibian-tree***.

1605 TIMME *Quersit.* III. 177 Take..of the barke of the olibian tree. **1646** J. GREGORY *Notes & Obs.* Ep. Ded. (1650) 4 Like those Subterraneous Olibian Lampes.

†**oˈliche**, obs. form of ALIKE.

c **1330** R. BRUNNE *Chron. Wace* (Rolls) 41 Saxons Inglis hight alle oliche.

olid (ˈɒlɪd), *a.* [ad. L. *olid-us* smelling, f. *olēre* to smell: see -ID¹.] Having a strong disagreeable smell; fetid, rank.

1680 BOYLE *Produc. Chem. Princ.* I. iv. Wks. I. 608 Urine, of which..olid and despicable liquor I choose to make an instance. **1684** tr. *Bonet's Merc. Compit.* XIX. 771 The olid or rank smell of Belchings. **1822–34** *Good's Study Med.* (ed. 4) II. 341 The sweat is copious, but proves by its sour and olid smell, that it is a morbid secretion.

†**ˈolidous**, *a. Obs. rare*⁻¹. [-OUS.] = prec.

1646 SIR T. BROWNE *Pseud. Ep.* III. iv. 114 This humor may be a garous excretion, or a rancide and olidous separation.

olie, obs. form of OIL.

olifant: see OLIPHANT.

olife, obs. var. of *olive*, ALIVE.

oliff, olifiant, olifene: see OLIVE, OLEFIANT, OLEFINE.

oligacanthous: see OLIGO-.

oligæmia (ɒlɪˈgiːmɪə). *Med.* Also 9 oligemy, (*U.S.*) oligemia. [mod.L., ad. F. *oligaimie* (A. N. Gendrin *Traité philos. de Méd. pract.* (1838) I. i. 37), ad. Gr. ὀλιγαιμία (Arist.), f. ὀλίγος (see OLIGO-) + αἷμα blood.] = *hypovolæmia* s.v. HYPO-; now distinguished from *anæmia*, which is applied to a diminished concentration of blood cells.

1843 T. WATSON *Lect. Princ. & Pract. Physic* I. iv. 49 The blood is scanty and poor—what Andral calls (though with questionable propriety) anæmia. Oligæmia is the cacophonous but more exact name assigned to it by Gendrin; but poverty of blood is the ordinary English phrase for it, and the best of the three. **1857** MAYNE *Expos. Lex.*, *Oligæmia*..oligemy. **1861** T. H. TANNER *Man. Practice Med.* (ed. 4) I. i. 7 Anæmia.—Deficiency of blood (poverty of blood, spanæmia, hydræmia, or oligæmia) arises generally..where there has been deprivation. **1866** A. FLINT *Princ. Med.* (1880) 62 Under the name general anaemia are included diminution in the mass of blood or oligaemia [etc.]. **1942** M. M. WINTROBE *Clin. Hematol.* vii. 243 Anemia, which..refers to the concentration of oxygen-carrying substance in a certain volume of blood, is to be distinguished from oligemia, which signifies a reduction of the total amount of blood in the body. **1974** PASSMORE & ROBSON *Compan. Med. Stud.* III. iii. 2/1 Rarely, oligaemia with shock arises from loss of plasma proteins in the urine in the course of the nephrotic syndrome.

Hence **oliˈgæmic** *a.*

1848 C. D. MEIGS *Females & their Diseases* xxxii. 421 Your thin, pale oligæmic patient cannot take up enough oxygen out of the air she breathes, to make her *strong*. **1947** *Amer. Heart Jrnl.* XXXIII. 645 The cardiodynamic alterations are characteristic of progressive and terminal stages of shock associated with low blood volumes; that is, oligemic shock. **1965** *Proc. Soc. Exper. Biol. & Med.* CXIX. 884/1 Experimental animals were maintained until death or sacrifice at an oligemic hypotension of about 30 mm Hg.

oligandrous, oliganthous: see OLIGO-.

oligarch (ˈɒlɪgɑːk), *sb.* [ad. Gr. ὀλιγάρχ-ης, f. ὀλίγ-ος few + ἄρχ-ειν to rule. Cf. mod.L. *oligarcha*, mod.F. *oligarque* (19th c. in Littré).] A member of an oligarchy; one of a few holding power in a state.

a **1610** HEALEY *Theophrastus* (1636) 89 Olygarches, or principal men in a state, have these conditions. **1821** BYRON *Two Foscari* II. i, Groan'd under the stern oligarchs. **1849** GROTE *Greece* II. xliii. V. 287 He established the oligarchs in that town as citizens and sold the Demos as slaves. **1868** *Spectator* 14 Nov. 1333 In mediæval Hungary, the central power of the Crown had to contend with that of the great territorial oligarchs.

oligarch (ˈɒlɪgɑːk), *a. Bot.* [mod. f. Gr. ὀλίγ-ος few + ἀρχή origin.] Proceeding from few points of origin, said of the primary xylem (or wood) of the root.

1884 BOWER & SCOTT *De Bary's Phaner.* 353 In almost all Dicotyledons where the point has been investigated, the original bundle of the root is oligarch, usually with 2, 3, or 4 rays, more rarely with 6 or 8. *Ibid.* 387 Nearly related plants..show the usual behaviour of oligarch roots.

oligarchal (ˈɒlɪgɑːkəl), *a.* [f. OLIGARCH *sb.* (or mod.L. *oligarcha*) + -AL¹.] = next.

1787 GLOVER *Atheniad* XIII. Poems (1810) 123/1 The whole defence, Our oligarchal tyrants have to boast, Are poor barbarians, scarce three hundred strong. **1826** in Hare *Guesses* Ser. I. (1873) 79 Close boroughs are said to be an oligarchal innovation on the ancient Constitution of England.

oligarchic (ɒlɪˈgɑːkɪk), *a.* [ad. Gr. ὀλιγαρχικός, f. ὀλιγάρχ-ης OLIGARCH: see -IC; perh. through a mod.L. *oligarchic-us* or F. *oligarchique* (Oresme 14th c.).] Of, pertaining to, or of the nature of an oligarchy; carried on, administered or governed by an oligarchy; supporting or advocating oligarchy.

a **1649** DRUMM. OF HAWTH. *Skiamachia* Wks. (1711) 191 He sent a letter to the lords of his privy-council of Scotland, declaring the unjust proceedings of this oligarchick power against his royal person and kingly office. **1768–74** TUCKER *Lt. Nat.* (1834) II. 486 Grievous and crying abuses have been committed..in secular government under all its forms, whether democratical, oligarchic, or monarchical. **1871** BLACKIE *Four Phases* i. 129 The strong bulwark against autocratic or oligarchic oppression.

oligarchical (ɒlɪˈgɑːkɪkəl), *a.* [f. as prec. + -AL¹.] = prec.

1586 BRIGHT *Melanch.* xii. 59 Which popularitie of administration nature will none of, nor yet with any holygarcicall or mixt. **1586** T. B. *La Primaud. Fr. Acad.* I. (1594) 584 Megabyses..perswaded the oligarchicall government. **1621** BURTON *Anat. Mel.* III. ii. VI. iii. (1651) 569 She will..wear the breeches in her oligarchicall government. **1839** THIRLWALL *Greece* xliii. V. 261 A large share of power was thrown into the hands of an oligarchical faction.

Hence **oliˈgarchically** *adv.*, in an oligarchical manner, by an oligarchical government.

1850 GROTE *Greece* II. lv. VII. 19 Tegea, situated on the frontiers of Laconia and oligarchically governed, was tenaciously attached to Sparta.

oligarchism (ˈɒlɪgɑːkɪz(ə)m). [f. OLIGARCH *sb.* + -ISM.] Oligarchy as a principle or system.

1866 *Daily Tel.* 18 Jan. 5/2 The opposition to the.. feudalism of the King and the more dogmatic and intolerant oligarchism of M. de Bismarck.

ˈoligarchist. *rare.* [f. as prec. + -IST.] An advocate or supporter of oligarchy.

1659 HARRINGTON *Valerius & Publicola* Wks. (1700) 488 Such as are plainly Oligarchists, or shall exercise by a force, and without election by the People, such a Power as is both naturally and declaredly in the People, and in them only.

oligarchization (ɒlɪgɑːkaɪˈzeɪʃən). [f. OLIGARCH(Y + -IZATION.] Movement towards oligarchy.

1966 *Social Forces* XLIV. 328/1 Oligarchization may be defined as the concentration of power, in the Weberian sense, in the hands of a minority of the organization's members. **1974** tr. *Wertheim's Evolution & Revolution* 405 The Continued Revolution; China and the Iron Law of 'Oligarchization'.

oligarchize (ˈɒlɪgɑːkaɪz), *v.* [f. as OLIGARCHIST + -IZE.] *trans.* To convert into an oligarchy; to subject to an oligarchy.

1850 GROTE *Greece* II. lxii. VIII. 36 The remaining five to oligarchise the dependent allies. *a* **1873** LYTTON *Pausanias* III. iv. (1878) 471 Sparta..will no more have the power to oligarchise democracy.

oligarchy (ˈɒlɪgɑːkɪ). [ad. Gr. ὀλιγαρχία government in the hands of a few, f. as ὀλιγάρχης OLIGARCH + abstract ending -ία; probably through med.L. *oligarchia* (Du Cange); cf. F. *oligarchie* (Oresme, 14th c.).] Government by the few; a form of government in which the power is confined to a few persons or families;

also, the body of persons composing such a government.

1577 tr. *Bullinger's Decades* (1592) 169 But if these chief or head men vse euill meanes to come to authority..then is their gouernment not to be called an Aristocracie, but an Oligarchie. *a* **1618** RALEIGH *Rem.* (1644) 7 An Oligarchy is the swerving, or the corruption of an Aristocracy. **1651** HOBBES *Leviathan* II. xix. 95 They that are displeased with Aristocracy, called it Oligarchy. **1790** BURKE *Fr. Rev.* 283 An ignoble oligarchy founded on the destruction of the crown, the church, the nobility, and the people. **1835** THIRLWALL *Greece* I. 397 It ceased to be, in the Greek sense, an aristocracy; it became a faction, an oligarchy. **1861** BRIGHT *Sp. Amer.* 4 Dec. (1876) 99 Those whose sympathies warm towards the slave oligarchy of the South.

oligist ('ɒlɪdʒɪst). *Min.* [Named 1801 (*oligiste*) by Haüy, ad. Gr. ὀλίγιστος least, superl. of ὀλίγος few, little.] More fully ***oligist iron***: A variety of native iron sesquioxid or hæmatite: so called as containing less iron than the magnetic oxide.

1828 WEBSTER s.v., Oligist iron, so called, is a crystalized tritoxyd of iron. **1853** TH. ROSS *Humboldt's Trav.* III. xxxii. 397 The origin.. appears similar to that of oligist iron. **1865** *Reader* No. 148. 491/2 On the sublimed Oligist of Vesuvius. **1891** G. D'ALVIELLA *Hibbert Lect.* 17 The bones of the dead are painted red with oligist or cinnabar.

Hence **oligistic** (ɒlɪ'dʒɪstɪk), **oli'gistical** *adjs.*, containing or resembling oligist.

1828 WEBSTER, *Oligistic*. **1849** D. CAMPBELL *Inorg. Chem.* 185 Sesquioxide of iron..is found native occasionally in beautiful black metallic-like crystals, known as oligistic, or specular iron. **1869** PHILLIPS *Vesuv.* iv. 135 In crevices [of the lava] we found plenty of oligistic iron.

oligo- ('ɒlɪgəʊ), before a vowel **olig-**, combining form of Greek ὀλίγος small, little, pl. few, in forming nouns and adjectives, as: ὀλιγόκαρπος with little fruit, oligocarpous, ὀλιγόφυλλος having few leaves, oligophyllous. Hence many modern technical terms, on Greek models, or Greek analogies: **oliga'canthous** *a. Bot.* [Gr. ἄκανθα thorn], having few spines, as *Mimosa oligacantha* (Mayne *Expos. Lex.* 1857); **oli'gandrous** *a. Bot.* [see -ANDROUS], having fewer than twenty stamens; **oli'ganthous** *a. Bot.* [Gr. ἄνθος flower]: see quot.; **oligar'ticular** *a.* [L. *articulus* joint], 'confined to a few joints, as an arthritis' (*Cent. Dict.* 1890); **oligo'blennia** [Gr. βλέννος slime, βλεννός drivelling], deficiency of mucus (Dunglison *Med. Lex.* 1853); **oligo'carpous** *a. Bot.* [see above], having few fruits; **oligochro'mæmia** [Gr. χρῶμα colour, αἷμα blood], deficiency of hæmoglobin in the red blood-corpuscles; **oligochro'nometer**: see quots.; **oligo'cystic** *a.*, having few cysts or cavities; **oligocy'thæmia** [Gr. κύτος a hollow, αἷμα blood], deficiency of the red corpuscles of the blood; so **oligocy'thæmic** *a.*; **oligo'dontous** *a.* [Gr. ὀδοντ- tooth], having few teeth (Mayne); **oligody'namic** *a.* [ad. G. *oligodynamisch* (C. von Nägeli 1893, in *Neue Denkschriften d. allgem. schweiz. Ges. f. d. ges. Naturwiss.* XXXIII. I. II. 8)], effected or exerted by minute quantities of metallic ions in solution; acting or being active at very low concentrations; **oligo'ester** *Chem.*, an oligomer in which adjacent monomeric units are linked together by an ester grouping, –CO·O–; **oligoga'lactia** [Gr. γάλα, γάλακτ-, milk], scantiness of milk-secretion (Dunglison 1853); **oligo'glottism** [Gr. γλῶττα a tongue], slight knowledge of languages (*ibid.*); **oligo'haline** *Oceanogr.* [ad. G. *oligohalin* (H. C. Redeke 1922, in *Bijdragen tot de Dierkunde* (Amsterdam) XXII. 330), f. Gr. ἅλιν-ος of salt], characterized by salinity in the range immediately above that of 'fresh' water (a division of the MIXOHALINE category); **oligo'lectic** *a.* [Gr. λεκτ-ός chosen], of bees, gathering pollen from only a few closely related plants; **oligo'mania**, madness manifesting itself in a few directions only; **oligomeno'rrhœa, -rrhæa** or (*U.S.*) **-rrhea** [MENORRHŒA], defective menstruation; hence **ˌoligomeno'rrhœal, -'rrhœic** *adjs.*; **oli'gomerous** *a. Bot.* [Gr. μέρος part], having fewer divisions than is normal; so **oli'gomery**; **oligome'tochia**, *Philol.* [Gr. μετοχή a participle], avoidance of participles or participial constructions; so **oligome'tochic** *a.*, containing or using few participles; **oligo'mycin** *Pharm.* [-MYCIN], (any of) a group of antifungal antibiotics produced by the bacterium *Streptomyces diastatochromogenes*, which inhibit certain mitochondrial phosphorylation reactions; **oligo'nucleotide** *Biochem.* [ad. G. *oligo-nucleotid* (F. G. Fischer et al. 1941, in *Jrnl. f. prakt. Chem.* CLVIII. 81)], any polynucleotide whose molecules are made up of a relatively small number of nucleotides; **oligo'peptide** *Biochem.* [ad. G. *oligopeptid* (Helferich & Grünert 1940, in *Naturwissenschaften* 28 June 411/2)], any peptide whose molecules are composed of a relatively small number of amino-acid residues; **oligo'petalous** *a. Bot.*, having few petals (*Funk* 1893); **oli'gophagous** *a. Zool.* [-PHAGOUS], of insects, feeding on a limited number of plants; so **oli'gophagy** (-'ɒfədʒɪ); † **oli'gophorous** *a.* [Gr. -φορος bearing], of wine: that will bear but little water, weak; **oligo'phrenia** [Gr. φρήν mind], feeble-mindedness; **oligo'phyllous** *a. Bot.* [see above], having few leaves (Mayne 1857); **'oligopod** *a. Ent.* [ad. It. *oligopodo* (A. Berlese 1913, in *Redia* IX. 128) f. Gr. πούς, ποδ- foot], of an insect larva, having well-developed thoracic limbs; **oligo'prothesy** *Philol.* [Gr. πρόθεσις a preposition], sparing use of prepositions; so **oligopro'thetic** *a.*; **oligo'saccharide** *Biochem.* [ad. G. *oligosaccharid* (B. Helferich et al. 1930, in *Ber. d. Deut. Chem. Ges.* LXIII. 991)], any carbohydrate whose molecules are composed of a relatively small number of monosaccharide residues; **ˌoligosa'probic** *a. Ecology* [ad. G. *oligosaprob* (Kolkwitz & Marsson 1902, in *Mittheilungen aus der K. Prüfungsanstalt f. Wasserversorgung und Abwässerbeseitigung* I. 46): see SAPROBE], of, being, or inhabiting an aquatic environment that is rich in dissolved oxygen and (relatively) free from decayed organic matter; so **oligo'saprobe**, an oligosaprobic organism; **oligosi'deric** *a.* [Gr. σίδηρ-ος iron], containing only a small proportion of iron; **oligo'siderite**, a stony meteorite containing a small percentage of iron (*Funk* 1893); **oligo'spermia** *Med.* [Gr. σπέρμα seed], orig. the condition in which the amount of semen secreted is reduced; now usu. = *oligozoospermia* below; hence **oligo'spermic** *a.*; **oligo'spermous** *a.*, containing few seeds (Mayne); **oligo'sporean, -'osporous** *a.* [Gr. σπόρος sowing, seed], of or belonging to the *Oligosporea*, Schneider's name for the minute parasitic sporozoans of the genus *Coccidium*, the cysts of which produce a small definite number of spores (*Syd. Soc. Lex.*, *Cent. Dict.*); **oligo'stemonous** *a.* [Gr. στήμων] = *oligandrous* (*Syd. Soc. Lex.*); **oligosy'llabic** *a.* [Gr. ὀλιγοσύλλαβος], having less than four syllables; **oligo'syllable**, a word of less than four syllables; **oli'gotokous** *a. Ornith.* [Gr. ὀλιγοτόκος], laying less than four eggs (*Cent. Dict.*); **oli'gotrophy** [Gr. ὀλιγοτροφία], deficiency of nourishment; **oligo'tropic** *a. Zool.* [ad. G. *oligotrope* (E. Loew 1884, in *Jahrb. Bot. Gartens Berlin* III. 256): see -TROPIC], of bees, collecting nectar from only a few kinds of flower; **ˌoligozoo'spermia** *Med.* [*zoosperm* s.v. ZOO-], the condition of having the number of spermatozoa in the semen sufficiently reduced to affect fertility; **oligu'resia** [Gr. οὔρησις making water], **oli'guria** [Gr. οὔριος of urine], deficient secretion of urine; so **oli'guric** *a.*, of, pertaining to, or involving oliguria; also as *sb.*, one who suffers from oliguria.

1870 HOOKER *Stud. Flora* 36 *Lepidium*, Cress.. Flowers.. often apetalous and *oligandrous. **1857** MAYNE *Expos. Lex.*, *Oliganthus*, having but a small number of flowers, as the *Psychotrea oligantha*, *Opilobium oliganthum*: *oliganthous. *Ibid.*, *Oligocarpous. **1866** *Treas. Bot.* 811/1 Thus oligocarpous is applied to sori in which the spore-cases are few in number. **1866** A. FLINT *Princ. Med.* (1880) 62 When the blood contains many of these pale corpuscles..the condition is called achroiocythaemia or *oligochromaemia. **1899** CAGNEY tr. *Jaksch's Clin. Diagn.* i. (ed. 4) 9 So with oligochromæmia,—diminution of hæmoglobin. **1857** MAYNE *Expos. Lex.*, *Oligochronometrum*, term for an instrument invented by Del Negro for measuring the minute fractions of time: an *oligochronometer. **1876** *Catal. Sci. App. S. Kens.* 604 *Oligochronometer*, an instrument for measuring the smallest fractions of time.—Applied to the measurement of the velocity of projectiles. **1872** PEASLEE *Ovar. Tumours* 31, I have..adopted the term *oligocystic cystoma as more distinctive than monocystic. **1876** tr. *Wagner's Gen. Pathol.* (ed. 6) 524 *Oligocythæmia, diminished amount of red corpuscles, is the last to remain. **1858** THUDICHUM *Urine* 138 The amount of blood-corpuscles..so considerably diminished as to cause an anæmic, or better *oligocythæmic, condition. **1898** *Allbutt's Syst. Med.* V. 534 There are two classes—the hæmolytic and the oligocythæmic. **1893** *Nature* 3 Aug. 331/2 By *oligodynamic phenomena Nägeli means those produced by excessively small quantities of metallic substances in solution. **1941** *Jrnl. Marine Res.* IV. 186 Containers made of copper, zinc, tin or nickel alloys are not suitable for the collection of samples of sea water for bacteriological analysis due to the inimical oligodynamic action of the metals. **1965** B. E. FREEMAN tr. *Vandel's Biospeleol.* xix. 337 The Thiobacteria can synthesise oligodynamic substances (nicotinic acid..pyridoxine, vitamin B_{12}). **1973** *Times* 25 Apr. 19/5 The ability of minute amounts of these metals to exert a lethal effect upon micro-organisms is referred to as oligodynamic action. **1957** *Makromolekulare Chemie* XXIII. 31 Linear *oligoesters of terephthalic acid and glycol form three polymer-homologous series: ester-diols, ester-dicarboxylic acids, and ester-hydroxyacids. **1968** *Encycl. Polymer Sci. & Technol.* IX. 491 For the synthesis of oligoesters and amides, the carboxyl group is usually activated by transformation into acid chloride or azide, as well as to a mixed anhydride or active ester. **1951** *Rep. Comm. Treatise Marine Ecol.* (National Research Council, U.S.) XI. 50 As originally proposed by Redeke, this classification was related to chlorinity rather than to the total salinity... This scheme, as set up by Redeke..is best presented in tabular form:..Cl, o/oo... Brackish water. 0·1–1·0. *Oligohaline. **1971** *Nature* 24 Sept. 281/1 Next, there is a conglomerate which contains brackish oligohaline facies fauna. **1925** C. ROBERTSON in *Ecology* VI. 413, I have used the term *oligolectic for a bee collecting pollen from a species, genus or family, where the relationship of the flowers seems to determine the preference, and polylectic for one collecting pollen from unrelated plants. **1972** *Science* 12 May 601/2 There are very few oligolectic bees. **1973** PROCTOR & YEO *Pollination of Flowers* v. 151 Bees that visit only one or a few species of flowers for food are described as oligotropic, while those showing a similar restriction for pollen supplies are called oligolectic. **1842** *Med. News* I. 472 Reasons..to justify the substitution of the term *oligomania for monomania. **1885** W. ROBERTS *Treat. Urin. Dis.* xiv. (ed. 4) 672 She had suffered from anæmia and *oligomenorrhæa, but got quite well of these. **1974** PASSMORE & ROBSON *Compan. Med. Stud.* III. xxviii. 6/1 Although there are important exceptions, in general those conditions which cause primary amenorrhoea are congenital, while those causing secondary amenorrhoea or oligomenorrhoea are acquired. **1963** *Oligomenorrheal [see POLYMENORRHŒAL *a.*]. **1955** *Obstetr. & Gynecol.* V. 661 Five of the 7 patients were amenorrheic at the time of the first visit, while 2 were *oligomenorrheic with menses occurring once to three times a year. **1977** *Lancet* 15 Oct. 805/1 Bromocriptine restores normal gonadal function in some amenorrhœic or oligomenorrhœic patients who have normal serum-prolactin levels. **1897** WILLIS *Man. Fl. Plants & Ferns* I. 74 The gynoeceum,..in most cases has fewer members than the outer whorls or is *oligomerous. *Ibid.*, *Oligomery of the gynoeceum. **1888** GILDERSLEEVE in *Amer. Jrnl. Philol.* IX. 144 If then..the rhetoricians do consider the participle as an element of style, and if they are right in so considering it, **oligometochia* and *polymetochia* cannot be neglected by us. **1954** R. M. SMITH et al. in *Antibiotics & Chemotherapy* IV. 962 The purpose of this paper is to report a presumably new antifungal antibiotic, *oligomycin. **1958** *Jrnl. Amer. Chem. Soc.* LXXX. 6093/1 The oligomycins are active against the fungi producing oak-wilt and Dutch elm diseases. **1964** *Ann. Rev. Biochem.* XXXIII. 737 In loosely coupled mitochondria, oligomycin abolishes phosphorylation, and the available evidence is consistent with the conclusion that oligomycin inhibits ATP formation from all three coupling sites of the respiratory chain. **1969** J. DEKKER in D. C. Torgeson *Fungicides* II. xiii. 621 Oligomycin..is an antifungal antibiotic active against various fungal plant pathogens. The results, however, have not been good enough to warrant practical applications. **1942** *Chem. Abstr.* XXXVI. 785 From a study of dialysis coeffs., the *oligonucleotide has a mol. wt. 3·5–5·3 times that of a mononucleotide. **1961** *Lancet* 12 Aug. 377/2 Many oligonucleotides and polynucleotides stimulate the growth of protozoans. **1971** *Nature* 28 May 217/2 There were several oligonucleotides missing from the former RNA. **1941** *Chem. Abstr.* XXXV. 78 (*heading*) *N*-methanesulfonyl derivatives of amino acids and *oligopeptides. **1955** *Nature* 9 July 72/2 The importance of the amino-acids and oligopeptides and the complexity of their mixtures often encountered stimulate a demand for more powerful analytical tools. **1968** *New Scientist* 22 Aug. 402/2 The first section, that on the posterior pituitary hormones, is mainly concerned with the fact that these oligopeptides do not occur free in the nerve cells. **1920** C. T. BRUES in *Amer. Naturalist* LIV. 317 A distinction is made between vegetarian species with a single food-plant (Monophagous), those with several definitely fixed ones (*Oligophagous) and those with quite indiscriminate food habits (Polyphagous). **1946** —— *Insect Dietary* iii. 145 (*heading*) Polyphagy, oligophagy and monophagy. **1969** R. F. CHAPMAN *Insects* ii. 27 Other insects..feed on only a limited range of plants. They are called oligophagous. *Ibid.* 28 Oligophagy may also arise in this way [*sc.* the presence of particular chemical stimulants in certain plants]. **1600** SURFLET *Countrie Farme* VI. xxii. 802 The wines of high Normandie..be not strong or mightie, but *oligophorous. **1657** TOMLINSON *Renou's Disp.* 220. **1899** *Allbutt's Syst. Med.* VIII. 196 **Oligophrenia*, enfeeblements of cerebral (psychical) development, with a parallel enfeeblement in the evolution of personality. **1932** *Brit. Jrnl. Psychol.* XXIII. 21 The oligophrenia, or 'small wittedness' as Continental writers call the condition, is due to an insufficiently developed brain. **1972** *Encycl. Psychol.* II. 345/2 *Oligophrenia*, synonymous with the term *amentia* ..mental subnormality. [**1925** A. D. IMMS *Gen. Textbk. Entomol.* II. 179 In the *oligopod phase the embryo has reached an advanced condition.] **1934** R. A. WARDLE *Folsom's Entomol.* (ed. 4) iii. 173 A less active type of oligopod larva..has a cylindrical fleshy body. **1957** T. W. KIRKPATRICK *Insect Life in Tropics* iv. 64 Oligopod larvae usually have well-developed thoracic legs but no abdominal feet and are typical of most beetles and Neuroptera. **1969** R. F. CHAPMAN *Insects* xx. 399 The least modified [larval form] with respect to the adult is the oligopod larva. **1896** J. DONOVAN in *Classical Rev.* Feb. 63/1 The inquiry leads to the general law that prose is polyprothetic and poetry *oligoprothetic. The gradual development from extreme *oligoprothesy to considerable polyprothesy, in the Tragic writers, is especially dwelt on and fully demonstrated. **1930** *Chem. Abstr.* XXIV. 3762 The name **oligosaccharides* is suggested for the simpler cryst. sugars (intermediate between the monoses and the polysaccharides) which form 2 or more monoses on hydrolysis. **1957** *Sci. News* XLV. 87 Human breast milk..contains a number of oligosaccharides. **1968** Oligosaccharide [see MONOSACCHARIDE]. **1925** *Bull. Illinois Nat. Hist. Survey* XV. 441 The part of a stream lying between the mesosaprobic lower limit and that of the cleanest zone normal to rivers has been called by Kolkwitz and Marsson *oligosaprobic. **1933** *Water Pollution Res. Technical Paper* (D.S.I.R.) No. 3. 134 The classification of the organisms into poly-, meso-, and oligo-saprobic..is now generally in use in defining the ecological status of aquatic organisms. It is based on the conditions which result when sewage or similar polluting liquids flow into small streams or into series of lagoons; in such cases a characteristic succession of biological associations is found, beginning with the poly-saprobes living in the crude liquid and ending with the oligo-saprobes in the region where self-purification is complete. **1950** *Folia Limnologica Scand.* V. 77 The oligosaprobic zone is regarded chemically as the zone in which oxidation (mineralisation) is nearly completed. **1970** Oligo-saprobic [see *mesosaprobic* adj. s.v. MESO-]. **1881** *Nature* 17 Nov. 72 Bodies closely resembling some *oligosideric meteorites. **1848** DUNGLISON *Dict. Med. Sci.* (ed. 7) 599/2 **Oligospermia*, paucity of spermatic secretion. **1897** WHITE & MARTIN *Genito-Urinary Surg.* xxviii. 1027 Oligospermia, or a diminution in the quantity of semen ejaculated, may be due to deficiency in quantity or absence of any of the constituent parts of this fluid. **1936** H. BAILEY *Dis. Testicle* xviii. 148 The causes of male sterility are:...2. Oligospermia; spermatozoa are few and inactive. **1944** R. S. HOTCHKISS *Fertility in Men* ix. 185 Defective spermatogenesis results in the failure to supply the full complement of spermatozoa to the ejaculate. This varies in degree from complete atrophy of the seminiferous tubule to a reduced number of spermatozoa in the seminal discharge. The former condition produces azoospermia, while the latter causes oligospermia. **1974** PASSMORE & ROBSON *Compan. Med. Stud.* III. xxviii. 21/1 A diminution of fertility can be demonstrated when sperm density falls below 20 M/ml, and values below this level on repeated counts constitute oligospermia. **1892** *Syd. Soc. Lex.*, *Oligospermic. **1971** *Nature* 19 Feb. 534/2 In veterinary and medical practice artificial insemination facilitates the use of incapacitated or oligospermic males. **1830** COLERIDGE *Table-t.* 30 Apr., As long a sentence made up of as few words, and those as *oligosyllabic, as any I remember. **1706** PHILLIPS, **Oligotrophy*, a Decrease of Nourishment, or a very small one. **1730** in BAILEY. **1899** C. ROBERTSON in *Bot. Gaz.* XXVIII. 29 The difference between a monotropic and an *oligotropic bee may depend merely upon the accident that only one species occurs in the neighbourhood. **1919** J. H. LOVELL *Flower & Bee* 106 When a species of bee restricts its visits..to a few allied kinds of flowers [it is termed] an oligotropic bee. **1946** C. T. BRUES *Insect Dietary* iii. 107 Some more specialized bees and other insects restrict their visits to a much more circumscribed assortment of plant species. With these oligotropic kinds the advantages to the plant are obviously greater. **1892** F. P. FOSTER *Med. Dict.* IV. 2447/1 **Oligozoospermia*, of De Sinety, a variety of sterility in the male in which the spermatozooids are diminished in number and activity. **1897** WHITE & MARTIN *Genito-Urinary Surg.* xxviii. 1027 Oligozoöspermia indicates a condition in which the semen ejaculated contains few spermatozoa. **1962** *Lancet* 27 Jan. 218/1 There was nothing to suggest oligozoospermia due to external causes. **1876** DUNGLISON *Dict. Med. Sci.* (rev. ed.) 721/2 *Oliguria. **1899** CAGNEY tr. *Jaksch's Clin. Diagn.* vii. (ed. 4) 252 The oliguria and suppression which herald an attack of uræmia. **1961** *Lancet* 22 July 187/2 The œdema, oliguria, albuminuria, and absence of an impressive cardiac murmur may result in the condition being mistaken for acute nephritis. **1907** *Amer. Jrnl. Med. Sci.* CXXXIV. 77 The *oliguric urine..is of higher specific gravity and contains less indican. **1918** *Endocrinology* II. 95 In man it is common to observe diuresis, especially in oligurics. **1961** *Lancet* 16 Sept. 632/1 In mushroom poisoning hæmodialysis is obviously essential where..severe oliguric renal failure occurs.

Oligocene (ˈɒlɪgəʊsiːn), *a. Geol.* [mod. f. OLIGO- + Gr. καινός new, recent.] Of certain Tertiary strata: Of an intermediate age between the Eocene and Miocene formations.

1859 PAGE *Hand-bk. Geol. Terms, Oligocene*,..employed by M. Beyrich [1854] to designate certain Tertiary beds of Germany..which appear to be neither exactly of Eocene nor of Miocene age, but to occupy an intermediate position. **1872** R. B. SMYTH *Mining Statist.* 18 The Pliocene rocks of the Murray basin and those in Gipps Land, which..overlie Miocene and Oligocene and Eocene rocks. **1882** GEIKIE *Geol. Sk.* 281 As far back as Miocene or Oligocene times.

oligochæte, -chete (ˈɒlɪgəʊkiːt), *a.*, *sb.* [f. mod.L. *Oligochæta*, f. OLIGO- + Gr. χαίτη mane, taken in sense 'bristle'.] **a.** *adj.* Belonging to the *Oligochæta*, one of the divisions of the *Chætopoda* (see CHÆTOPOD), including the earthworms and lugworms; so called from the small number of their bristly foot-stumps or parapodia. **b.** *sb.* A worm of this order or division.

1876 tr. *Beneden's Anim. Parasites* 47 An oligochete worm, *Hemidasys agaso*, from the Gulf of Naples. **1896** *Naturalist* 77 Omission of..the embryology of oligochæts.

Hence **oligochætous** (-ˈkiːtəs) *a.*

1877 HUXLEY *Anat. Inv. Anim.* iv. 192 Albertia is an entoparasite, and Balatro an ectoparasite, upon oligochaetous Annelids. **1889** *Athenæum* 16 Nov. 678/3 On the anatomy of an oligochætous worm of the genus Dero.

oligoclase (ˈɒlɪgəʊkleɪs). *Min.* [Named 1826, f. OLIGO- + Gr. κλάσις breaking, fracture; because thought to have a less perfect cleavage than albite.] A lime- and soda-felspar, resembling albite, of light grey, yellow or greenish colour, occurring either in crystals or massive.

1832 SHEPARD *Min.* 246 Oligoklase. **1849** NICOL *Min.* 129 Oligoclase occurs in granite and gneiss. **1863** S. R. GRAVES *Yacht. Cruise to Baltic* 142 The felspar of this quarry is of two kinds, orthoclase and oligoclase, in large masses, the former pink, the latter quite white; both..equally in demand for the manufacture of porcelain.

oligodendrocyte (ɒlɪgəʊˈdɛndrəʊsaɪt). *Histology.* [f. OLIGODENDRO(GLIA + -CYTE.] A kind of neuroglial cell similar to an astrocyte (but with fewer processes), found characteristically round nerve cells in the central nervous system and concerned with the maintenance of myelin.

1932 [see OLIGODENDROGLIA]. **1966** WRIGHT & SYMMERS *Systemic Path.* II. xxxiv. 1243/2 The oligodendrocyte greatly outnumbers all other cells in the brain. **1974** J. A. G. RHODIN *Histol.* xv. 316/1 The primary function of the oligodendrocytes is the formation of the myelin sheath.

oligodendroglia (ˌɒlɪgəʊdɛndrəʊˈglaɪə). *Histology.* [ad. Sp. *oligodendroglía* (P. del Rio-Hortega 1921, in *Bol. de la Real Soc. Española de Hist. Nat.* XXI. 63): see OLIGO-, DENDRO-, and NEURO)GLIA.] Oligodendrocytes. Usu. const. as *pl.*

1924 *Brain* XLVII. 430 (*heading*) Oligodendroglia and its relation to classical neuroglia. **1932** W. PENFIELD *Cytol. & Cellular Path. Nervous Syst.* II. ix. 437 Oligodendrocytes or oligodendroglia were first demonstrated by Robertson (1899, 1900 *a*) under the name of mesoglia by means of his platinum method. Del Rio-Hortega (1921 *b*) independently re-discovered the cells by means of a more reliable and complete staining method. He called them oligodendroglia ..because, as compared with astrocytes or the astroglia, the branches of these cells were small and apparently few and he recognized them as one type of neuroglia. **1951** O. LARSELL *Anat. Nervous Syst.* (ed. 2) iv. 127 The elements of oligodendroglia are related to the astrocytes but are smaller and have smaller nuclei. **1962** [see MICROGLIA]. **1974** BERGMAN & AFIFI *Atlas Microsc. Anat.* vi. 111 Oligodendroglia are smaller than astrocytes and have a denser nucleus and cytoplasm. **1974** J. A. G. RHODIN *Histol.* xv. 314/2 Oligodendroglia or oligodendrocytes are small, angular cells of neural ectodermal origin.

Hence ˌ**oligodendroˈglial** *a.*

1929 *Jrnl. Path. & Bacteriol.* XXXII. 736 An oligodendroglial cell contains a spherical nucleus which is smaller than the nucleus of a neuroglial cell. **1972** *Science* 19 May 801/3 These vacuoles..were found..in axons, astrocytes, and oligodendroglial cells.

oligodendroglioma (ˌɒlɪgəʊdɛndrəʊglaɪˈəʊmə). *Path.* [f. OLIGODENDROGLI(A + -OMA.] A tumour derived from oligodendroglia.

1926 BAILEY & CUSHING *Classification Tumors of Glioma Group* 54 With few exceptions the true brain tumors may be classified under fourteen major categories as follows:.. Medullo-epithelioma... Oligodendroglioma... Neuroblastoma. **1929** *Jrnl. Path. & Bacteriol.* XXXII. 735 (*heading*) Oligodendrogliomas of the brain. **1967** *Nursing Times* 27 Jan. 108/1 Some of these, such as the oligodendroglioma, grow very slowly and are compatible with normal life in many cases for 10 years or more. **1978** *Jrnl. R. Soc. Med.* LXXI. 419 Oligodendroglioma, a tumour which, in *in vitro* studies..has been shown to have a high oxygen consumption.

oligohydramnios (ˌɒlɪgəʊhaɪˈdræmnɪəs). *Obstetrics.* [f. OLIGO- + HYDR(O- + AMNIOS.] A deficiency in the amount of amniotic fluid.

1889 [see POLYHYDRAMNIOS]. **1928** W. G. LEE *Childbirth* xv. 227 A 'dry uterus' and an oligohydramnios..often result in either a constriction ring or a uterus closely molded to the fetal mass. **1962** D. E. REID *Texbk. Obstetr.* xxiv. 630/2 In oligohydramnios, rather than the normal 1,000–2,000 ml., only 100–200 ml. is found. **1972** E. D. MORRIS in C. J. Dewhurst *Integrated Obstetr. & Gynaecol.* xxii. 381 Oligohydramnios is evident clinically in two particular circumstances: in association with a small-for-dates baby, and with severe renal anomalies of the foetus.

oligomer (əˈlɪgəmə(r)). *Chem.* [f. OLIGO- + -MER.] Any polymer whose molecules consist of relatively few repeating units.

1952 VAN DER WANT & STAVERMAN in *Rec. Trav. Chim. Pays-Bas* LXXI. 379 In the course of an investigation into the chemical and physical properties of polymers of different molecular weight it appeared desirable to us to have available condensation products of ε- amino-caproïc acid: $H[NH(CH_2)_5CO]_nOH$ with low and exactly specified values of n ('linear oligomers') e.g. $n = 2, 3, 4$ and 5. **1967** [see *leucoanthocyanidin* s.v. LEUCO-]. **1969** *Nature* 13 Sept. 1125/2 Table 1 shows the frequencies of monomers, dimers and higher oligomers of mitochondrial DNA. **1975** *Ibid.* 6 Mar. 83/2 The extent to which each of the characteristic oligomers (pentanucleotides and larger) of *Escherichia coli* 16S rRNA is conserved across phylogenetic lines.

Hence **oligoˈmeric** *a.*

1957 *Makromolekulare Chemie* XXIII. 32 The van der Wyk-rule, which permits calculation of the melting points of straight-chain paraffins, can be applied to the oligomeric esters of terephthalic acid and glycol after introduction of suitable constants. **1970** *Nature* 13 June 1004/2 A series of oligomeric substrates, up to twelve glucose units in length and labelled at the end-group, was prepared. **1974** *Sci. Amer.* Nov. 64/1 The *J* chain is present in oligomeric forms, and the dimer, when found in secretions such as saliva and tears, is bonded to yet another polypeptide.

oligomerization (əˌlɪgəməraɪˈzeɪʃən). *Chem.* [f. prec. + -IZATION.] The formation or production of an oligomer from a monomer.

1958 *Jrnl. Chem. Soc.* 3563 (*heading*) The cationic oligomerisation of the stilbenes. **1972** *Jrnl. Amer. Chem. Soc.* XCIV. 6968 (*heading*) The mechanism of the oligomerization of hydrogen cyanide and its possible role in the origins of life. **1974** *Encycl. Brit. Macropædia* XIII. 716/2 Aluminum alkyls also cause dimerization, oligomerization, or polymerization of olefins.

So **oˈligomerize** *v. trans.*, to form an oligomer of.

1967 *Nature* 29 Apr. 480/1 Hydrogen cyanide could be oligomerized to the dimer, trimer, tetramer, etc., to form the parent skeletons of glycine, alanine and aspartic acid, and other organic compounds. **1972** *Proc. Nat. Acad. Sci.* LXIX. 3389/1 Linear double-stranded molecules of simian virus (SV)40 DNA..are oligomerized by either ligase.

oligomictic (ɒlɪgəʊˈmɪktɪk), *a.* [f. OLIGO- + Gr. μικτ-ός mixed + -IC.] **1.** *Petrol.* [ad. Russ. *oligomiktovyĭ* (M. S. Shvetsov *Petrografiya Osadochnykh Porod* (1934) viii. 155).] (See quot. 1935.)

1935 *Jrnl. Sedimentary Petrology* V. 106/2 Rocks consisting of one to two dominant minerals are termed oligomictic and those composed of several minerals polymictic... The book is written in Russian... The review is based on a typewritten summary in English. **1949** F. J. PETTIJOHN *Sedimentary Rocks* xiv. 438 Schwetzoff..noted that oligomictic rocks are the characteristic deposits of epicontinental seas and are found rarely in geosynclinal depressions, whereas polymictic rocks are characteristic of geosynclinal regions. **1959** W. W. MOORHOUSE *Study of Rocks in Thin Section* xix. 337 The typical oligomictic conglomerate is composed predominantly of quartz. **1971** *Nature* 28 May 247/1 Structureless to planar cross-stratified, sheet-like bodies of oligomictic conglomerates and subarkoses are interbedded.

2. *Limnology.* Applied to a lake that exhibits a stable thermal stratification and only rarely undergoes an overturn.

1956 HUTCHINSON & LÖFFLER in *Proc. Nat. Acad. Sci.* XLII. 84 Although at low altitudes in the humid tropics small temperature gradients can maintain stable stratifications, no stable stratification develops at the low temperatures of high altitudes, where the density difference per degree centigrade is very small. The lack of seasonal variation, that permits almost perennial stratification at low altitudes in equatorial latitudes, thus permits perennial circulation at high altitudes in the same latitudes. We propose for these two types of equatorial lake the terms oligomictic and polymictic, respectively. **1968** R. W. FAIRBRIDGE *Encycl. Geomorphol.* 617/1 The lake water body is stratified, thus oligomictic.

oligopoly (ɒlɪˈgɒpəlɪ). [f. OLIGO- + Gr. πωλ-εῖν to sell, after MONOPOLY.] A state of limited competition when a market is shared by a small number of producers or sellers.

1895 J. H. LUPTON *Utopia of Sir Thomas More* I. 55/2 More makes an antithesis between *monopolium* and *oligopolium*. We have 'monopoly' but not 'oligopoly' (the sale by a few), and so cannot preserve the point of the sentence. **1933** E. H. CHAMBERLIN *Theory Monopol. Competition* i. 8 The theory of value..has been treated.. with particular reference to the problem of two sellers, or 'duopoly', and we may extend this terminology, adding 'oligopoly' for a few sellers. **1954** *Wall St. Jrnl.* 13 Dec. 3/3 'Oligopoly'—monopoly power in the hands of two or more companies. **1957** *Economist* 7 Sept. 769/2 The small but bustling textile industry is now giving a miniature demonstration of the oligopoly stage of capitalism as the big firms begin to mop up the smaller ones. **1959** [see DUOPOLY b]. **1967** J. K. GALBRAITH *New Industrial State* xvi. 180 Under the cognomen of oligopoly it is assumed in its price-making to have some of the powers of a monopoly and some of the restraints of competition. **1970** *Daily Tel.* 23 Jan. 18 Deciding when monopoly or oligopoly is or is not..'against the public interest'. **1974** M. B. BROWN *Econ. of Imperialism* iii. 52 The driving force behind the extension of commodity production under capitalism is the competition of capitalists, even under conditions of oligopoly. **1977** *Dædalus* Fall 92 Oligopolies will tend to have excess physical capacity.

Hence **oliˈgopolist**; **oliˌgopoˈlistic** *a.*

1939 J. A. SCHUMPETER *Business Cycles* I. ii. 60 The general statement that oligopolistic prices are indeterminate would be misleading. **1947** *Jrnl. Pol. Econ.* LV. 432/1 Observed price rigidities in oligopolistic industries. **1958** *Jrnl. of Business* (Chicago Univ.) XXXI. 198/1 Frequently, in the case of older products, some measure of oligopolistic uncertainty exists. **1959** *Economist* 28 Mar. 1175/1 Increases between 1953 and 1957 came about entirely from prices in the oligopolistic industries. **1959** DE CHAZEAU & KAHN *Integration & Competition in Petroleum Industry* xvii. 443 Having achieved the touchstone of crude oil production control, the leading firms and practically the industry as a whole behave like self-conscious oligopolists. **1967** *Spectator* 28 July 113/2 The big cleaning material manufacturers (I mean, of course, the soap and washing powder oligopolists) have all been making efforts to grab a slice of this easy market. **1971** K. HOPKINS *Hong Kong* 212 Oligopolistic industries dominated by large corporations do not exist in Hong Kong. **1975** *New Law Jrnl.* 11 Sept. 892/1 The provisions of article 86 of the EEC treaty are designed to proscribe monopolistic, oligopolistic or, in certain respects, a monopsonic position being exploited at the expense of other producers or of consumers in the European Common Market. **1977** *Dædalus* Fall 92 The world is not a two-person zero-sum game, and no oligopolist expects competitors to hold their prices or quantities fixed in response to his moves.

oligopsony (ɒlɪˈgɒpsənɪ). *Econ.* [f. OLIGO- + Gr. ὀψων-εῖν to buy provisions; after MONOPSONY; cf. OPSONY.] A marketing state in which only a small number of buyers exists for a product; also *attrib.* Hence **oliˈgopsonist**, **oliˌgopsoˈnistic** *a.*

1943 E. R. WALKER *From Econ. Theory to Policy* iv. 61 It is surely only a matter of time before [market situation] No. 23 is christened 'oligopsony'. **1949** W. FELLNER *Competition among Few* i. 11 The problem is that of oligopoly, oligopsony, and bilateral monopoly, and, of course, also of markets which are oligopsonistic on the demand side and oligopolistic on the supply side... The oligopsonist.. attempts to select a definite price to be paid for the materials and services he buys. **1961** N. F. KEISER *Introductory Econ.* v. 77 At one time the major cigarette manufacturers were oligopsonists in their purchases of tobacco. **1965** D. GREENWALD et al. *McGraw-Hill Dict. Mod. Econ.* 358 *Oligopsony*, a market structure with relatively few buyers... An oligopsonistic situation may lead to express or tacit collusion among the sellers. **1965** HAILSTONES & DODD *Econ.* (ed. 5) xi. 229 *Oligopsony* exists when a few buyers dominate the market... The author of a college textbook faces an oligopsonistic market in the publication of his manuscript. **1972** HUNT & SHERMAN *Econ.* xviii. 275 Some large firms have extra market power as large buyers of commodities (technically, oligopsony power). **1972** J. WINKLER *On Marketing Planning* xiii. 205 Companies operating in oligopsonistic markets find that great power flows to their salesmen.

oligotrophic (ɒlɪgəʊˈtrəʊfɪk), *a. Ecol.* [ad. G. *oligotroph* (A. Thienemann *Die Binnengewässer Mitteleuropas* (1925) iv. 198 (*-trophie* sb.), 200 (*-troph*)), f. Gr. ὀλίγος small, little + τροφή nourishment: see -IC.] Relatively poor in plant nutrients and (in the case of a lake) containing abundant oxygen in the deeper parts.

[**1928** *Proc. Linn. Soc.* CXL. 100 The typical oligotroph lakes are deep, with submerged beaches narrow or absent, inconsiderable or no littoral vegetation, and an indistinct littoral zonation.] **1931** R. N. CHAPMAN *Animal Ecol.* xvi. 304 The oligotrophic type of lake is rich in oxygen even to the bottom. It owes its characteristic partly to a geologic formation which permits relatively little inwash of organic material..; and partly to biotic conditions which do not favour rapid decomposition with the consequent oxygen consumption. **1943** G. K. FRASER *Peat Deposits of Scotland* I. 3 The remains of plants nourished on rich soils (technically termed eutrophic soils)..will be able to support a greater bacterial population than those of plants grown on poor or impoverished soils (oligotrophic soils). *Ibid.* 9 Acid ground waters are usually oligotrophic and can support only short herbage such as smaller sedges. **1955** *New Biol.* XVIII. 115 *N. alba* occupies a wide range of waters in the British Isles, from the oligotrophic, or nutrient-poor, peat-bottomed moorland lakes in Scotland and Ireland, to the eutrophic, or nutrient-rich, fen-lodes and broads of East Anglia. **1972** J. G. CRUICKSHANK *Soil Geogr.* vi. 186 Also acid and infertile is oligotrophic peat.

So **ˈoligotrophy**, an oligotrophic condition.

1928 *Proc. Linn. Soc.* CXL. 109 Even if the natural course is from oligotrophy to eutrophy, the opposite process may also be found. **1957** G. E. HUTCHINSON *Treat. Limnol.* I. ix. 644 Hutchinson set limits [on oxygen loss] of 0.017 mg. cm.$^{-2}$ day^{-1} for oligotrophy. **1967** [see EUTROPHY]. **1973** P. A. COLINVAUX *Introd. Ecol.* xviii. 258 It is the change from oligotrophy to eutrophy, simulating as it does the natural aging of a lake, which gives rise to the idea that polluted lakes are dying or actually dead.

olingo (ɒˈlɪŋgəʊ). [Amer. Sp., f. native name.] A small, nocturnal mammal of the genus *Bassaricyon*, belonging to the family Procyonidæ, native to forest regions of Central and South America, and distinguished from the kinkajou by a straight tail which is not prehensile.

1920 E. A. GOLDMAN in *Smithsonian Misc. Coll.* LXIX. No. 5. 155 (*heading*) *Bassaricyon gabbii gabbii* Allen. Bushy-tailed Olingo. **1964** L. S. CRANDALL *Managem. Wild Mammals in Captivity* 314 Closely allied to the kinkajou and apparently often confused with it is the olingo (*Bassaricyon gabbii*). *Ibid.* 315 The olingo is a grayer brown, over-all, than most kinkajous, with pale gray face and noticeably longer and more pointed muzzle. Its most obvious character is the long tail, which is very faintly ringed, somewhat bushy, and non-prehensile. **1965** D. MORRIS *Mammals* 278 Allen's Olingo bears a strong resemblance to the Kinkajou... Where the two species do differ, the Olingo is always the more primitive. **1975** *City Press* 4 Sept. 16/3 Who would suspect that the City has anything to do with 18,985 rats, 1,110 baboons, 10 anteaters and an olingo?

olio (ˈəʊlɪəʊ). Forms: 7 olleo, 7–8 ollio, oleo, 7–9 oglio, 7– olio. [a. Sp. *olla*, Pg. *olha* (both pronounced (ˈoʎa) pot, stew, hotchpotch = It. *olla* pot:—L. *olla* pot, jar; the final *a* being represented by the more sonorous *o*, as in *armado*, *bastinado*, and other words from Sp.: cf. OLLA[1].]

1. A dish of Spanish and Portuguese origin, composed of pieces of meat and fowl, bacon, pumpkins, cabbage, turnips, and other ingredients stewed or boiled together and highly spiced; by extension, Any dish containing a great variety of ingredients, a hotchpotch.

a **1643** SUCKLING *Lett.* (1646) 88 Like great Oleoes; they rather make a shew than provoke Appetite. **1668** DAVENANT *Man's the Master* v. i, A sea of olio, and in it hams of Baijon lying at Hull with sails furl'd up of cabbage-leaves. **1670** NARBOROUGH *Jrnl.* in *Acc. Sev. Late Voy.* I. 89 The first Course was Soppas, then Olleos, then Pullets. *a* **1763** SHENSTONE *Wks.* (1768) II. 8 Such a soup, or ollio..is much in vogue. **1773** BRYDONE *Sicily* xxiii. (1809) 227 The Olio still preserves its rank and dignity in the centre of the table. **1885** A. B. ELLIS *W. Afric. Isl.* xi. 276 The olio, that is, the ingredients of which the soup is made, served up as a second course.

Comb. **1750** E. SMITH *Compl. Housew.* (ed. 14) 159 To make an Olio-Pye.

2. *fig.* **a.** Any mixture of heterogeneous things or elements; a hotchpotch, farrago, medley.

1648 *Eikon Bas.* xv, Such an Oglio or Medley of various Religions. **1700** CONGREVE *Way of World* III. viii, I have such an Olio of affairs really I know not what to do. **1772** *Ann. Reg.* 69 The company were an olio of all sorts. **1819** MRS. GRANT in *Mem.* (1844) II. 246 This oglio of a letter. **1847** DISRAELI *Tancred* II. xiv, An olio of all ages and all countries. **1880** *St. James's Gaz.* 16 Oct. 11 Those olios of partisan opinion with the facts left out.

b. A collection of various artistic or literary pieces, as engravings, verses, etc.; a miscellany; a musical medley, a *potpourri*; *spec.* a variety act or show; also *attrib.*

1655 DUCHESS OF NEWCASTLE (*title*) The Worlds Olio. Nature's Pictures drawn by Fancie's Pencil to the Life. **1691** *Reas. Mr. Bays changing Relig.* (ed. 2) 17 Entertain them with..a fashionable Oglio at Lockets, or the Blue Posts. **1702** MOTTEUX *Prol. Farquhar's Inconstant*, An opera, like an oglio, nicks the age. **1809** S. BRECK *Recoll.* (1877) App. 271 We..rode round to Mr. Brent's,..with whose family we took tea, and afterward accompanied them to an olio concert. **1884** *Sat. Rev.* 7 June 740/1 The second part of a minstrel show is the 'olio'—and this is only a variety entertainment, of banjo-playing, clog-dancing, and the like. **1928** *Amer. Speech* IV. 68 Behind these *drops*,..are the *oleos*, or *act-curtains*. These..are used for small vaudeville acts... Such acts..are termed *oleo acts*, or *acts in one*. **1951** GREEN & LAURIE *Show Biz* 570/1 *Olio*, scenery, in front of which an act, generally a 'sidewalk comedy' team performs; also specialties performed between acts in burlesque. **1956** M. STEARNS *Story of Jazz* (1957) xi. 116 The second part, or olio (a word derived from the Spanish *olla*, meaning mixture), consisted of a series of solo acts that later evolved into variety or vaudeville. **1961** BOWMAN & BALL *Theatre Lang.* 237 *Olio*; *oleo*... A scene consisting of a specialty act ..played..while another scene is being set. Also as *olio act* (or *scene*)... A backing, drop, or tableau curtain for a front scene... Also as *olio drop*... A medley of songs, dances, comic sketches and the like. **1961** A. BERKMAN *Singers' Gloss. Show Business* 64 *Oleo*, miscellaneous Vaudeville or Variety Acts presented between the acts or during the intermissions of a play. **1964** *Punch* 2 Dec. 852/1 The audience is invited to stay..for the Olio,..which here means an Aftershow. **1976** *Publishers Weekly* 9 Feb. 96/3 It is a mixture of self-indulgent prose, sickening violence and unbelievable happenings. The whole olio is, clearly, a bid for Bicentennial attention.

olio, obs. variant of OLLA, palm-leaf.

ˈoliphant. *arch.* Also 3–5 olifa(u)nt. [a. OF. *olifant*: see ELEPHANT.] Obsolete form of ELEPHANT, occasionally retained by modern writers as a historical spelling in sense 'horn or trumpet of ivory': see ELEPHANT 4 b.

[*c* **1205** LAY. 23778 He [a shield] wes al clane of olifantes bane.] **13..** *K. Alis.* 1182 To mouth he set his olifaunt. *c* **1489** CAXTON *Blanchardyn* xlv, Many an horne, many an olyphaunt, & many a claryon & trompettes were blowen. **1851** E. J. MILLINGTON tr. *Didron's Chr. Iconogr.* I. 56 *note*, Roland..in his distress sounds the oliphant. **1855** tr. *Labarte's Arts Mid. Ages* 10 As a specimen of the sculptured ivory of the xiv[th] century, we give..a large oliphant or warder's horn. **1888** *Sat. Rev.* 24 Mar. 351/1 There were two ivory horns (or Oliphants, as they used to be called).

†**ˈoliprance.** *Obs.* exc. *dial.* Also 4–6 oly-, 4 -praunce. [Origin unknown. No similar word is known in continental Fr.] ? Pride, vanity, ostentation; in later use ? splendour, merry-making, jollity. **b.** 'Rude, boisterous merriment'; a romp. *dial.*

1303 R. BRUNNE *Handl. Synne* 4581 Pryde..Of ryche atyre ys here auaunce, Prykyng here hors wyþ olypraunce [Fr. *Lur orprance mustre al oyl*]. *Ibid.* 4695 Hem were leuer here of a daunce, Of bost, ande of olypraunce, þan any gode of God of heuene [Fr. *De pechier dunent enchesun, Seur seiez, li fol bricun*]. **13..** *E.E. Allit. P.* B. 1349 In pryde & olipraunce his empyre he haldes. ? *a* **1500** *Peebles to Play* x, Then thai to the taverne hous, With meikle olyprance. **1535** STEWART *Cron. Scot.* III. 552 Sone efter this with mekle oliprance Ane greit ambaxat send wes out of France. **17..** PERCY in Pinkerton *Sel. Sc. Ball.* (1783) II. 168 *Oly-prance*, is a word still used by the vulgar in Northamptonshire, for rude rustic jollity. *Olyprancing doings* are strange, disorderly, inordinate sportings formerly used in Pilgrimages. **1790** GROSE *Prov. Gloss.* (ed. 2), *Oly-prance*, oly-prancing doings, rude, boisterous merriment, a romping-match, *Northamptonsh.* **1850** MISS BAKER *Northamptonsh. Gloss.* s.v., When a party of young people go out gipsying or gathering violets, and..have had a day of great enjoyment, they will return home and say 'We've had a nice oly prance'.

olisbos (ˈɒlɪzbəs). [ad. Gr. ὄλισβος.] = DILDO[1].

1887 [see GODEMICHE]. **1941** G. R. SCOTT *Phallic Worship* x. 178 Aristophanes speaks of the use, by Milesian females, of an *olisbos* made of leather. **1955** V. NABOKOV *Lolita* I. xxii. 126, I had blazed in her face an olisbos-like flashlight. **1967** CROSLAND & DAVENTRY tr. *de Becker's Other Face Love* plate 13 (*caption*) Two women together using a double olisbos.

olistolith (ɒˈlɪstəʊlɪθ). *Geol.* [f. Gr. ὀλίσθ- stem of ὀλίσθημα slip, slide + -LITH.] One of the discrete bodies contained within the matrix of an olistostrome.

1956 [see next]. **1974** *Nature* 26 Apr. 745/1 It is possible that these domes represent olistoliths transported over a long distance from the Turkish shelf.

olistostrome (ɒˈlɪstəʊstrəʊm). *Geol.* [f. as prec. + Gr. στρῶμα bed.] A sedimentary deposit composed of a heterogeneous mixture of materials and formed by the sliding or slumping of semi-fluid sediment.

1956 G. FLORES in *Proc. 4th World Petroleum Congr. 1955* I. 122/2 By Olistostromes we define those sedimentary deposits occurring within normal geologic sequences that are sufficiently continuous to be mappable, and that are characterized by lithologically and/or petrographically heterogeneous materials, more or less intimately admixed, that were accumulated as a semi-fluid body. In any Olistostrome we distinguish a 'binder' or 'matrix' represented by prevalently pelitic, heterogeneous material. .. The name '*Olistolith*'..is applied to the masses included as individual elements within the binder. **1972** *Nature* 8 Dec. 328/2 The mixture is now floating in a matrix of middle Miocene olistostrome.

olitory (ˈɒlɪtərɪ), *a.* and *sb.* Now *rare.* [ad. L. *(h)olitōrius* of or belonging to a kitchen gardener or vegetables, f. *(h)olitor* kitchen gardener, f. *holus, holer-*, pot-herbs, vegetables: see -ORY.]

A. *adj.* Of or pertaining to pot-herbs or kitchen vegetables, or to the kitchen garden.

1658 EVELYN *Diary* 6 Dec., Now was publish'd my 'French Gardener', the first..that introduc'd ye use of the Olitorie garden. **1664** —— *Kal. Hort., July* (1729) 209 Let such Olitory-Herbs run to Seed as you would save. **1670** *Phil. Trans.* V. 1150 The Sylvan, Hortulan and Olitory affairs. **1785** [R. GRAVES] *Eugenius* II. i. 3 The proper supplies of herbs, and other olitory productions, for the kitchen. **1895** *Econ. Rev.* Oct. 447 Any vegetable cultivated in the olitory garden.

†**B.** *sb.* **1.** A pot-herb, a culinary vegetable. *Obs.*

1696 EVELYN *Mem.* (1857) III. 364 A world of vulgar plants and olitories. **1699** —— *Kal. Hort.* (ed. 9) 130 Trust not to the accidental Mildness of the Weather, so as to neglect timely Cover to your tender Olitories.

†**2.** A kitchen-garden. *Obs.*

1706 PHILLIPS, *Olitory*, or *Olitory Garden*, a Kitchen-Garden. **1745** ELIZA HEYWOOD *Female Spect.* No. 15 (1748) III. 125 The refreshing sallad, and all those early products of the useful olitory. **1793** W. ROBERTS *Looker-On* No. 65 (1794) III. 5 Why should I injure the olitory, by seeming thus to doubt of its attractions? **1900** *Echo* 12 June 1/5 No old-world garden was without its 'olitory' or garden of herbs, savoury, aromatic, and quaint.

oliue, obs. form of ALIVE: see also LIFE 14.

‖**oliva** (əʊˈlaɪvə). [L. *olīva* olive.]

1. *Zool.* A genus of gasteropod molluscs; a member of this genus; an olive-shell (see OLIVE *sb.* 5).

1839 DARWIN *Voy. Beagle* i. (1889) 9 Its polish, equal to that of the finest oliva shell. **1973** A. H. WHITEFORD *N. Amer. Indian Arts* 133 Trade routes from the Gulf of California and Mexico brought..oliva shells into the Southwest.

2. *Anat.* The olivary body (*Syd. Soc. Lex.* 1892).

3. 'Olive-tree gum' (Ogilvie).

olivaceo- (ɒlɪˈveɪʃ(ɪ)əʊ), used in *Nat. Hist.* as combining form of next, prefixed to other adjs., to denote a colour mixed or tinged with olivaceous, as **olivaceo-aeneous**, **olivaceo-cinereous**.

1847 HARDY in *Proc. Berw. Nat. Club* II. No. 5. 237 Head ..with the thorax nigro- or olivaceo-æneous. **1887** W. PHILLIPS *Brit. Discomycetes* 17 Stem 1 to 2 inches long.. black, olivaceo-cinereous at the base.

olivaceous (ɒlɪˈveɪʃəs), *a.* [f. mod.L. *olīvāceus*, F. *olivacé* olive-green, f. *olīva* OLIVE: see -ACEOUS.] Of a dusky green colour with a tinge of yellow (like the unripe fruit of the olive); olive-green; olive. (Chiefly in *Nat. Hist.*)

1776 PENNANT *Zool.* I. 376 The head, neck, back and wings are of an olivaceous ash-colour. **1836** *Family Tour through Holland* 96 The colour..being that of a rich olivaceous green. **1854** H. MILLER *Sch. & Schm.* xxi. (1857) 472 Both shale and nodules bore..an olivaceous tint. **1887** W. PHILLIPS *Brit. Discomycetes* 20 Pileus at first nearly even, olivaceous-umber, dark at the apex.

†**olivader**, *a. Obs. rare*$^{-1}$. = OLIVASTER, for which it is prob. a misreading or misprint.

1662 EVELYN *Diary* 30 May, A train of Portuguese ladies ..their complexions olivader and sufficiently unagreeable.

oliˈvander, *a. rare.* Error for OLIVASTER.

1855 ANNE MANNING *Old Chelsea Bun-ho.* i. 5 A lank.. Personage, of olivander Complexion. **1861** *Cornh. Mag.* Sept. 296 Her olivander cheek and chin.

olivart, *a. rare*$^{-1}$. [? erroneous ad. F. *olivâtre*.] Of olive complexion.

1885 MRS. EWING *Story of Short Life* vii, He had a smooth, oval, olivart face, and dreamy eyes.

olivary (ˈɒlɪvərɪ), *a.* Also 6 olivare. [ad. L. *olīvāri-us* of or pertaining to olives, f. *olīva* olive: see -ARY. Cf. F. *olivaire* (14th c. in Godef. *Compl.*).] Shaped like an olive. In specific applications:

a. *Surg.* Applied to a cautery or catheter with an oval head. **b.** *Anat.* ***olivary body***, each of two oval prominences of nerve-matter, one on each side of the medulla oblongata. ***olivary eminence***, (*a*) = prec.; (*b*) = next. ***olivary process***, a prominence on the sphenoid bone, supporting the commissure of the optic nerves. Also applied to parts of or connected with the olivary body, as ***olivary nucleus***, ***olivary peduncle***.

1541 R. COPLAND *Guydon's Quest. Chirurg.* P iij b, The seconde cautere is named Oliuare bicause it resembleth a kyrnell of Olyue. [**1706** PHILLIPS, *Olivaria Corpora*..two Protuberances or Knobs of the under part of the Brain.] **1831** R. KNOX *Cloquet's Anat.* 420 The olivary eminences.. are enveloped, like the rest of the spinal marrow, with a white external layer. **1837** QUAIN *Elem. Anat.* (ed. 4) 721 The olivary bodies are so called from their oval round form, like an olive. **1847** TODD & BOWMAN *Phys. Anat.* II. 104 It is not improbable that the true origin of each nerve is from the central part of the medulla oblongata, the olivary columns. **1892** *Syd. Soc. Lex.* O[livary] cautery.

†**oliˈvaster**, *a. Obs.* [a. F. *olivastre* (1575 in Hatz.-Darm.), now *olivâtre* somewhat olive-coloured: cf. OF. *olivastre* wild olive: see -ASTER,

and cf. OLEASTER.] Olive-coloured; having an olive complexion (see OLIVE 9).

1626 BACON *Sylva* §399 But the Countries..where they [men] are Tawney, and Olivaster, and Pale, are generally more Sandy, and Dry. **1658** PHILLIPS, *Olivaster*, of an olive colour; also a wild olive-tree. *a* **1697** AUBREY *Lives, Harvey* (1898) I. 300 Round faced, olivaster complexion, little eie, round, very black, full of spirit.

olive ('ɒlɪv), *sb.*[1] and *a.* Also 4 olife, 4–5 olyf, 4–6 olyue, 5–7 olyff(e, 7 oliff. [a. F. *olive*:—L. *olīva* olive and olive-tree.]

A. *sb.* **1. a.** An evergreen tree, *Olea europæa*, esp. the cultivated variety *O. sativa*, with narrow entire leaves, green above and hoary beneath, and axillary clusters of small whitish four-cleft flowers; cultivated in the Mediterranean countries and other warm regions, chiefly for its fruit and the oil thence obtained (see sense 2 b).

c **1200** *Trin. Coll. Hom.* 89 þat burh folc..beren on here honde blostme sum palm twig, and sum boh of oliue. **1297** R. GLOUC. (Rolls) 3986 Branches hii bere Of oliue as in signe þat hii aȝen pays nere. **1398** TREVISA *Barth. De P.R.* XVII. iii. (Tollem. MS.), With oute spray of olyue no messangeres were sente to Rome to ȝete pese, noþer to profre pees to oþer men. *c* **1430** LYDG. *Min. Poems* (Percy Soc.) 180 The olive..myght not forsake his fatnesse. **1549** *Compl. Scot.* vi. 57 Throucht the operatione of the sternis, the oliue, the popil, & the osȝer tree changis the cullour and ther leyuis. **1791** COWPER *Iliad* XVII. 64 As the luxuriant olive by a swain Rear'd in some solitude. **1813** BYRON *Br. Abydos* I. i, Where the citron and olive are fairest of fruit. **1839** tr. *Lamartine's Trav. East* 79/1 It was those very olives themselves, the venerable witnesses of so many days, written on earth and in heaven. **1870** YEATS *Nat. Hist. Comm.* 205 The olive is indigenous to Palestine, Greece, and the slopes of the Atlas mountains.

b. Extended to the whole genus *Olea*; also applied, with qualifying words, to various trees and shrubs allied to the common olive, or resembling it in appearance or in furnishing oil.

American olive, the Devil-wood, *Osmanthus americanus* (*Olea americana*); **bastard** or **mock olive**, *Notelæa ligustrina* (N.O. *Oleaceæ*) of Australia and Tasmania; **black olive**, *Bucida* (*Terminalia*) *Buceras* (N.O. *Combretaceæ*), and *Ximenia americana* (N.O. *Olacaceæ*), of the West Indies; **Californian olive**, *Oreodaphne* (*Umbellularia*) *californica* (N.O. *Lauraceæ*); **Chinese olive**, *Canarium commune* (N.O. *Amyridaceæ*), a tree bearing triangular drupes which yield an oil used as a condiment and for burning; **holly-leaved olive**, *Osmanthus ilicifolius* (*Olea ilicifolia*) of Japan; **negro's olive**, *Terminalia Chebula* (N.O. *Combretaceæ*); **spurge olive**, *Daphne Mezereum* (N.O. *Thymeliaceæ*); **sweet-scented olive**, *Osmanthus* (*Olea*) *fragrans* of China; **white olive**, the Fly-honeysuckle, *Halleria lucida* (N.O. *Scrophulariaceæ*) of South Africa. **wild olive**, the wild variety of the common olive (= OLEASTER a), or any wild species of *Olea*; also applied to various trees and shrubs resembling this, as *Elæagnus angustifolia* (= OLEASTER b); *Daphne Thymelæa*; *Rhus Cotinus* (N.O. *Ancardiaceæ*); *Putranjiva Roxburghii* (N.O. *Euphorbiaceæ*) of India; *Bontia daphnoides* (N.O. *Myoporaceæ*), *Bucida Buceras*, *B. capitata*, and *Ximenia americana*, of the West Indies. (See *Treas. Bot.* 1866, and Miller *Plant-n.* 1884.)

1577 B. GOOGE *Heresbach's Husb.* (1586) 107 b, The wilde Olive, in Greeke ἀγριέλαίας, in Latine Oleaster. **1753** CHAMBERS *Cycl. Supp.* App. s.v. *Olive*, Wild Olive of Barbadoes, a name by which some call the Bontia, a distinct genus of plants. **1756** P. BROWNE *Jamaica* 221 This tree is called the Black Olive in Jamaica. **1785** H. MARSHALL *Arbustrum Amer.* 98 American Olive tree..grows naturally in Carolina and Florida, and is a beautiful ever-green tree. **1866** RUSKIN (*title*) The Crown of Wild Olive. **1866** *Land We Love* (Charlotte, N. Carolina) May 78 American Olive..is a very fine evergreen, producing clusters of small white flowers. **1880** *S. Africa* (ed. 3) 136 Wild Olive..wood of small size and generally decayed at heart. Used for fancy turning. **1901** C. T. MOHR *Plant Life Alabama* 14 Their banks adorned with evergreen andromedas, American olive, ..sweet bay, and azaleas.

2. a. The fruit or 'berry' of *Olea sativa*, a small oval drupe, bluish-black when ripe, with bitter pulp abounding in oil, and hard stone; valuable as a source of oil, and also eaten pickled in an unripe state.

1398 TREVISA *Barth. De P.R.* XVII. cxi. (1495) 674 The more blacke oliues ben wythout: the more rype they be wythin. **1555** EDEN *Decades* 209 They are for the most part of the colour of an olyue. **1579** LANGHAM *Gard. Health* (1633) 438 The ripe Oliues overturne the stomach, and cause wambling therein. **1732** ARBUTHNOT *Rules of Diet* 258 Olives are anti-acid by their Oil. **1856** EMERSON *Eng. Traits, Voy. to Eng.* Wks. (Bohn) II. 12, I find the sea-life an acquired taste, like that for tomatoes and olives.

† **b.** *oil of olive*(*s* = OLIVE-OIL. *Obs.*

1382 WYCLIF *Lev.* xxiv. 2 Comaund to the sones of Ysrael, that thei bryngen to thee oyle of olyues. **1486** *Bk. St. Albans* C vj b, Anoynt it with oyle of Olyff. **1727–41** CHAMBERS *Cycl.* s.v. *Oil*, Oil of olives is the most popular, and most universal of all others.

3. a. A leaf, branch, or wreath of the common olive, an ancient emblem of peace; hence allusively.

c **1400** MAUNDEV. (1839) ii. 11 Olyve betokeneth Pes. **1567** MAPLET *Gr. Forest* 54 The valiant and noblest vanquishers ..were honoured and crowned with the Olive. **1591** SPENSER *Vis. Bellay* ix, His right hand did the peacefull olive wield. **1606** SHAKS. *Ant. & Cl.* IV. vi. 7 The three nook'd world Shall beare the Oliue freely. **1710** POPE *Windsor For.* 429 Where Peace descending bids her olives spring. **1741** SHENSTONE *Judgm. Hercules* 402 Peace rears her olive for industrious brows. **1849** C. BRONTË *Shirley* xvi. 238 But six months of the reign of the olive, and I am safe.

b. A child (= OLIVE-BRANCH 2); also *attrib.*

1803 ANNA SEWARD *Lett.* (1811) VI. 114, I hope..that the fair convalescent and her young olives are well. **1838** DICKENS *Nich. Nick.* xiv, Four olive Kenwigses who sat up to supper. **1891** MERIVALE & MARZIALS *Thackeray* 37 There is a ring of despair about the name of the tenth olive, Decima.

4. The wood of the common olive; olive-wood.

c **1400** MAUNDEV. (1839) ii. 10 The Table aboven his heved [on the Cros]..was of Olyue.

5. A gasteropod mollusc of the genus *Oliva* or family *Olividæ*; or its shell, of an elongated oval form and fine polish; an olive-shell.

1843 *Zoologist* I. 54 That beautiful, elegant and brilliantly polished genus of shells called Olives. **1856** WOODWARD *Mollusca* III. 353 Since the period of the English chalk-formation, there have been..Cones and Olives in the London Basin. **1865** GOSSE *Land & Sea* 132 Cowries and olives.

6. *Cookery.* (*pl.*) A dish composed of thickish slices of beef or veal, rolled up with onions and herbs, and stewed in brown sauce: cf. *olive pie* in C.

1598 *Epulario* C ij b, To make Oliues of Veale or any other flesh that is lean. **1598** FLORIO, *Tomacélla*,..that meate which we call oliues of veale. **1615** MARKHAM *Eng. Housew.* II. ii. (1664) 72 To roast Olives of Veal. **1769** MRS. RAFFALD *Eng. Housekpr.* (1778) 117 Beef Olives. **1861–80** MRS. BEETON *Bk. Household* §668 Beef Olives.

7. † **a.** A kind of oval bit for a horse (*obs.*). **b.** An oval button, or a piece of wood of the shape of an olive covered with silk or worsted, for fastening a cloak or other garment by means of a loop of braid. **c.** An oval perforated plate attached to the strap of a bag, through which a stud or button passes in fastening it.

1607 MARKHAM *Caval.* II. (1617) 56 Those Mellons or Oliues, must bee very smooth and full of holes, which the Horse will take great pleasure to sucke, and champe vpon. **1611** COTGR., *Olivette*..a little Oliue-bitt for a horse. **1875** KNIGHT *Dict. Mech.*, *Olive*, an escutcheon attached to the strap of a traveling bag or satchel and perforated for the passage of the swiveled stud or button.

8. *Anat.* The olivary body.

1899 *Allbutt's Syst. Med.* VI. 807 This connection with the nucleus of the sixth nerve, through the so-called peduncle of the superior olive being very intimate.

9. a. = Olive colour: see B.

1662 J. DAVIES tr. *Olearius' Voy. Ambass.* 287 A full face; but yellowish or inclining to an Olive. **1837** LOCKHART *Scott* viii, Charlotte Margaret Carpenter..was rich in personal attractions..a complexion of the clearest and lightest olive. **1884** *Christian World* 17 Jan. 52/1 All wool Rich Ottoman Dress Material..in..Olive. **1884** W. C. SMITH *Kildrostan* 92 The sun has dyed Her cheek with olive.

b. A woman or girl of olive complexion.

1713 ADDISON *Guard.* No. 109 ⁋5 Your fair women therefore thought of this fashion to insult the Olives and the Brunetts. **1828** *Lights & Shades* II. 216 One sees Olives and Brunettes trundling mops and crying mackerel.

10. A greenish-brown moth, *Zenobia* (or *Ipomorpha*) *obtusa*, of the family Noctuidæ, found in Europe and northern Asia.

1832 J. RENNIE *Conspectus Butterflies & Moths Brit.* 83 The Olive..feeds on the poplar. **1908** R. SOUTH *Moths Brit. Isles* 2nd Ser. 9 The Olive..is somewhat similar in general appearance to the last mentioned [*sc.* the Double Kidney]. **1974** B. GOATER *Butterflies & Moths of Hampshire* 376 The Olive..widespread but associated with *Populus* species.

11. a. A mayfly with an olive-coloured body belonging to the genus *Baetis*, which includes species with transparent wings, or the genus *Ephemerella*, esp. *E. ignita*, which has blue wings.

1889 F. M. HALFORD *Dry-Fly Fishing* ix. 206 The blue-winged olive..is known to modern entomologists as *Ephemerella ignita*. **1911** —— *Mod. Devel. Dry Fly* iii. 18, I think the dark olive is, as a rule, not so well taken by the fish as the common olive. **1949** A. C. WILLIAMS *Dict. Trout Flies* II. 267 Whereas other insects are seasonal, the olive is more or less always with us. **1971** *Country Life* 21 Oct. 1084/1 Often there is a good hatch of olives in the morning or afternoon—sometimes both—which usually brings a response not only from the grayling but from the trout.

b. An artificial fly made in imitation of an insect of this type.

1895 *Montgomery Ward Catal.* Spring & Summer 495/2 Bass Flies, consisting of the following styles:..Oak, Olive, Montreal, Professor, [etc.]. **1907** *Yesterday's Shopping* 674/2 Special Irish Salmon Flies... Golden Olive with Blue and Jay Shoulder. **1911** F. M. HALFORD *Mod. Devel. Dry Fly* iii. 18 No. 7 of the series of patterns is the olive dun male. **1921** G. E. M. SKUES *Way of Trout with Fly* II. ii. 109 The floating subimago I tried to imitate with a darkish variety of a stock pattern of olive. **1938** W. C. PLATTS *Mod. Trout Fishing* vii. 68 Among the wet flies in use may be mentioned ..various Olives. **1968** C. F. WALKER *Art of Chalk Stream Fishing* xvii. 147 My own choice would be the Rough Olive, a most successful fly.

B. *adj.* **a.** Of the colour of the unripe fruit of the olive, a dull somewhat yellowish green. **b.** Also, applied to a yellowish brown or brownish yellow, in the complexion of persons or races. **c.** Also, of the colour of the foliage of the olive, a dull ashy green with silvery sheen.

In 'olive colour' = 'colour of an olive', *olive* is strictly the sb. used attrib., as in 'mouse colour'; but in 'a greenish or olive colour', we see it treated as an adj., and in 'an olive complexion', 'an olive beauty', it has become a full adj.

a. **1657** R. LIGON *Barbadoes* (1673) 70 The Pomegranate ..the leaves small, with a green mixt with Olive colour. **1830** J. C. STRUTT *Sylva Brit.* 59 Its light and cheerful green ..contrasts agreeably with the Oak, whose early leaf has generally more of the olive cast. **1845** BUDD *Dis. Liver* 229 It has generally the greenish or olive colour proper to bile. **1853** W. GREGORY *Inorg. Chem.* (ed. 3) 250 Protoxide of Mercury..is a black or dark olive powder.

b. 1634 SIR T. HERBERT *Trav.* 48 The Inhabitants are of an Olive colour. **1713** ADDISON *Guard.* No. 109 ⁋5 You must know I am a famous olive beauty. **1774** GOLDSM. *Nat. Hist.* (1776) II. 224 Indians are of an olive colour, and, in the more southern parts, quite black. **1805** SOUTHEY *Madoc in Aztl.* II Her cotton vest..leaves her olive arms Bare in their beauty. **1894** DOYLE *Mem. S. Holmes* 218 A beautiful olive complexion.

fig. **1814** SIR R. WILSON *Priv. Diary* II. 388 We have just received the 'Moniteur' of the 2nd, with the conditions of peace. To my sight the treaty is not of an olive colour.

C. *attrib.* and *Comb.* **a.** Simple attrib., as ***olive crop***, ***culture***, ***-garden*** (= OLIVE-YARD), ***garland***, ***-ground***, ***grove***, ***industry***, ***leaf***, ***-lees***, ***-marc***, ***shade***, ***shoot***, ***spray***, ***-wreath***, etc. **b.** Instrumental, as ***olive-bordered***, ***-clad***, ***-hoary***, ***-shaded*** adjs. **c.** Similative, with words denoting colour, etc., expressing a colour resembling or suggesting that of an unripe olive, as ***olive-brown***, ***-green*** (= B.), ***-grey***, ***-yellow*** adjs. and sbs., ***olive-pale*** adj. **d.** Parasynthetic (from B.), as ***olive-backed***, ***-cheeked***, ***-sided***, ***-skinned*** adjs.; also with reference to the shape of an olive, as ***olive-shaped*** adj. **e.** Special Combs.: **olive-acanthus**, in decorative art, an ornamental form of acanthus leaf with lobes each resembling an olive leaf; **olive-back**, a North American forest thrush, *Hylocichla ustulata*, also known as Swainson's thrush; **olive-backed thrush** = *olive-back*, *olive thrush*; **olive-bark**, (*a*) the bark of the olive; (*b*) the West Indian tree *Bucida* (*Terminalia*) *Buceras*, of which the bark is used for tanning; **olive-berry** = sense 2; † **olive-bit** = sense 7 a; **olive cautery**, an olivary cautery (see OLIVARY); **olive crescent**, a pale greenish-brown European moth, *Trisateles emortualis*, of the family Noctuidæ; **olive-crown**, a wreath of olive (as a token of victory); **olive drab**, of a brownish green colour, used *spec.* of the colour of U.S. Army uniform; also *ellipt.*; **olive-fly**, an insect injurious to olive-trees; also ***olive fruit fly***; † **olive grape** (see quot.); **olive-nut**, the stone of the fruit of species of *Elæocarpus* (N.O. *Tiliaceæ*); **olive-ore** = OLIVENITE: see quot. 1805 s.v.; **olive pie**, a pie made with olives of veal (see 6); **olive-plum**, the drupaceous fruit of any tree of the genus *Elæodendron* (N.O. *Celastraceæ*), or the tree itself; **olive-shell** = sense 5; **olive thrush** = *olive-back*; **olive-tyrant**, any bird of the subfamily *Elæniinæ* of tyrant flycatchers, having generally olivaceous coloration; **olive whistler**, an Australian bird, *Pachycephala olivacea*; **olivewort**, Lindley's name for plants of the N.O. *Oleaceæ*.

1888 F. G. JACKSON *Decor. Design* vii. 152 Curved like the *olive acanthus, it is moulded with concave markings. **1845** S. JUDD *Margaret* I. xvi. 143 The *olive-backs trolled and chanted among the trees. **1892** B. TORREY *Foot-Path Way* 19 The olive backs began to make themselves heard. **1945** *Mass. Audubon Soc. Bull.* Mar. 43 Two thrushes of annual interest to students are the migrant Olive-back and the Gray-cheek. **1897** *Outing* (U.S.) XXX. 437/1 The red-finned, *olive-backed, foolish-looking fish. **1844** J. E. DEKAY *Zool. N.Y.* II. 74 The *Olive-backed Thrush is closely allied to the [hermit thrush]. **1892** B. TORREY *Foot-Path Way* 99 Two birds dashed by me—a blackpoll warbler in hot pursuit of an olive-backed thrush. **1946** T. M. STANWELL-FLETCHER *Driftwood Valley* 187 We spend the long bright evenings out on the lake, listening to the chorus of olive-backed thrushes. **1958** E. T. GILLIARD *Living Birds of World* 336/2 The Olive-backed Thrush.. winters south to Argentina. **1866** *Treas. Bot.* 177/2 The *Olive-bark, or Black Olive of Jamaica, produces wood which is valuable on account of its not being liable to the attacks of insects. **1526** TINDALE *Jas.* iii. 12 Can the fygge tree..beare *olive berries? **1869** MRS. STOWE *Oldtown Folks* xvi. 176, I guess our olive-berries are pretty well beaten off now. **1611** *Olive-bit [see 7]. **1706** PHILLIPS, *Olive-bit*, a kind of Bit for Horses. **1827** KEBLE *Chr. Y.* 1st Sund. Advent vii, Beside the *olive-bordered way. **1885–94** R. BRIDGES *Eros & Psyche* March xxv, Olive-border'd clouds o'er lilac led. **1796** WITHERING *Brit. Plants* (ed. 3) IV. 318 Pileus *olive brown..edge turned down. **1837** PRICHARD *Phys. Hist. Man.* (ed. 3) II. 345 The olive-brown or copper colour of the Bechuana. **1894** R. B. SHARPE *Handbk. Birds Gt. Brit.* I. 101 Eggs [Yellow Wagtail]..Some are uniform pale olive-brown, some darker olive, while others are nearly uniform pinkish-brown. **1597** A. M. tr. *Guillemeau's Fr. Chirurg.* C j b/1 This Cauterye may allmost be callede the *Olive Cauterye, because it is allmost like vnto an olive. **1866** HOWELLS *Venet. Life* xii. 193 A black-eyed, *olive-cheeked lady. **1832** J. RENNIE *Conspectus Butterflies & Moths Brit.* 146 The *Olive Crescent..resembles the Clay-Fan-Foot. **1908** R. SOUTH *Moths Brit. Isles* 2nd Ser. 88 The Olive Crescent..is exceedingly rare in England. **1974** B. GOATER *Butterflies & Moths of Hampshire* 411 Olive Crescent... One taken in bright sunlight..in late July, 1939. **1884** *Encycl. Brit.* XVII. 762/1 Apart from occasional damage by weather or organic foes, the *olive crop is somewhat precarious even with the most careful cultivation. **1977** J. AIKEN *Last Movement* ii. 42 Local staff, who came and went when the orange or olive crop demanded their attention. **1749** WEST *Odes Pindar* xi. (1753) I. 69 She.. decks thy *Olive-Crown with sweetly-sounding Lays. **1893** K. A. SANBORN *Truthful Woman in S. California* xii. 155 *Olive culture is just now the fad. **1957** *Encycl. Brit.* XVI. 774/1 Specialized olive culture is an important industry on hillsides throughout Greece. 1897 Sears, Roebuck Catal. 21/3 One gallon of this paint will cover (two coats) over 300 square feet of surface. Always order by color number as well as catalogue number... 214 *Olive Drab. 1908 Sears, Roebuck Catal. 71/2 Colors of.. house paint... Nile Green.. Olive Drab.. Cream. 1917 A. Woollcott Let. Oct. (1946) 28, I was afflicted because I had signed, have been in olive drab for three months—been away from America for almost three months. 1942 —— in Reader's Digest Nov. 23/2 Wherefore, as he [sc. Irving Berlin] toils away at something for the boys in olive-drab to sing out with real emotion, he has only to listen to the bugle notes for a motif. 1948 W. J. Stokoe Caterpillars Brit. Moths I. 274 The caterpillar.. is slaty-brown, inclining to olive-drab above. 1970 N. Armstrong et al. First on Moon iii. 66 Check the olive-drab lap and shoulder strapping for each man. 1886 R. C. Haldane Subtropical Cultivations 183 Musca oleæ (the *olive-fly) lays its eggs in the young fruit, and is a most destructive insect. 1972 Swan & Papp Common Insects N. Amer. 627 The *Olive Fruit Fly, Docus oleae, is a serious pest of olives in the Mediterranean area. 1809–10 Coleridge Friend (1865) 72 Its corn fields and *olive gardens. 1601 Holland Pliny I. 409 Another sort, which of the resemblance of oliues, is called the *Oliue grape,.. this is the last grape of any account.. known to haue bin found out. 1756–7 tr. Keysler's Trav. (1760) III. 17 The natural colour of these filaments is a kind of an *olive-green. 1801 Hatchett in Phil. Trans. XCII. 57 Prussiate of potash changed the colour of the.. solution to an olive-green. 1894 R. B. Sharpe Handbk. Birds Gt. Brit. I. 70 Lower back and rump *olive-greenish, streaked with dusky. 1862 R. H. Patterson Ess. Hist. & Art 29 Oil-paintings, in gilt frames, are effective on walls of *olive-grey. 1849 Grote Greece II. lx. (1862) V. 298 They found themselves enclosed in a walled *olive-ground. 1591 Percivall Sp. Dict., Azebuchal, an *oliue groue, Oleastrum. 1878 O. Wilde Ravenna 6 Dark olive-groves and noble forest-pines. 1959 Times 29 Sept. 12/6 Vineyards and olive groves. 1855 Tennyson Daisy 31 Or *olive-hoary cape in ocean. 1893 K. A. Sanborn Truthful Woman in S. California xii. 155 Pomona is head-quarters for the *olive industry. 1968 Encycl. Brit. XVI. 937/1 In South America and Australia, development of a commercial olive industry is.. recent. 1541 R. Copland Guydon's Quest. Chirurg. P iij b, Lyke to *Olyue Leafe. 1611 Bible Gen. viii. 11 Lo, in her mouth was an oliveleaf pluckt off. 1667 Milton P.L. xi. 860 An Olive leafe he brings, pacific signe. 1886 Sheldon tr. Flaubert's Salammbo i, Little dogs fattened on *olive-marc. 1864 Browning Jas. Lee's Wife iii. i, The water's.. *olive-pale To the leeward. 1617 Murrell Cookery II. (1638) 122 To make an *Olive Pie to be eaten hot. 1861–80 Mrs. Beeton Bk. Household §924 Veal Olive Pie. 1685 Dryden Theocritus xxvii. 15 The Sun's too hot; those *Olive-shades are near. 1800 Campbell Ode to Winter, On Calpe's *olive-shaded steep. 1908 Practitioner Sept. 360 The sounds which will best aid are those.. having interchangeable *olive-shaped metallic heads. 1930 T. S. Eliot tr. St.-J. Perse's Anabasis 65 He who fashions a leather tunic, wooden shoes and olive-shaped buttons. 1882 Ogilvie, Oliva, the *olive-shell, so named from the olive-like shape of the shell. 1884 Coues Key N. Amer. Birds 438 Contopus borealis, *Olive-sided Flycatcher. 1904 W. H. Hudson Green Mansions 4 The nervous *olive-skinned Hispano-American of the tropics. 1970 H. M. Davy Caring for your Appearance iii. 35 Some of your friends may have a very pale skin throughout all seasons... Some others, with the very darkest colouring, we may describe as olive skinned. 1864 J. R. Lowell Fireside Trav. 222 Climbing the sides of the nearer Monticelli in a gray belt of *olive-spray. 1957 Encycl. Brit. XVI. 773/2 The wild olive spray of the Olympic victor. 1552 Huloet, *Olyue stone, samsa, sansa. 1904 S. E. White Silent Places i. 4 The white-throats and *olive thrushes called in a language hardly less intelligible. 1911 J. A. Leach Austral. Bird Bk. 152 *Olive Whistler, Olivaceous Thick-head... Olive brown; head dark-gray... Liquid, whistling note. 1933 Bulletin (Sydney) 20 Sept. 21/1 A curious example of vocal variation among birds.. is found in the 'olive whistler'. 1944 A. Russell Bush Ways xxii. 105 A recluse of the open scrubs of the dry south-eastern interior, as the olive whistler is to the mountain mists of the coast ranges. 1965 Austral. Encycl. IX. 292/1 The olive whistler, of eastern Australia and Tasmania, is probably one of the sweetest singers among the birds of Australia. 1845 Lindley Veg. Kingd. (1853) 616 However heterogeneous the *Oliveworts may appear.. it is remarkable that the species will all graft upon each other. 1853 Hickie tr. Aristoph. (1872) II. 656 Place the *olive-wreaths near. 1894 R. B. Sharpe Handbk. Birds Gt. Brit. 100 General colour *olive-yellow above, and bright yellow below.

olive (ˈɒlɪv), *sb.*[2] Also 6 oliff. [Origin obscure: see quot. 1894.] Local name of a bird, the Oyster-catcher (*Hæmatopus ostrilegus*).

1541–2 in Househ. Ord. (1790) 223 [Prices of Foule] Crocards and Oliffs. 1607 J. Norden Surv. Dial. III. 111 Any Pibble, Peach, or Sea-bank, wherein breed sea-Pyes, Oliues, Pewets, or such. 1634 Althorp MS. in Simpkinson The Washingtons App. (1860) p. xii, Knotts, Olives, Redshankes. 1802 G. Montagu Ornith. Dict. (Rennie 1833) 351 Oyster-catcher.. 'Provincial. Pienet, Olive'. 1848 Col. Hawker Diary (1893) II. 286, 2 golden plovers, 2 olives, 5 curlews. 1894 Newton Dict. Birds, Olive,.. apparently a corruption of Olaf, which is said also to be used (Christy, B. Essex, 238);.. if so the word should be more properly spelt Olave.

ˈolive-ˈbranch.

1. a. *lit.* A branch of an olive-tree.

a 1300 Cursor M. 1904 An oliue branche in moth sco broght. 1535 Coverdale Ps. cxxvii[i]. 3 Thy children like the olyue braunches rounde aboute thy table. [So in 'Great Bible' 1539, and Bk. of Com. Prayer.] 1611 Bible Neh. viii. 15 Go forth unto the mount, and fetch olive-branches. 1838 Thirlwall Greece II. 294 They returned and spread their olive branches before the shrine.

b. As an emblem of peace; hence *fig.* anything offered in token of peace or goodwill. Also variously, in allusion to Gen. viii. 11.

c 1330 R. Brunne Chron. Wace (Rolls) 11446 Twelue messegers til hym were sent.. Wyþ olyue braunches in handes born. 1593 Shaks. 3 Hen. VI, iv. vi. 34 To whom the Heau'ns in thy Natiuitie, Adiudg'd an Oliue Branch, and Lawrell Crowne. 1622 Bacon Hen. VII 85 Yet did he make that Warre rather with an Olive-branch, then a Laurel-branch in his Hand more desiring Peace then Victorie. 1796 Burke Regic. Peace iii. Wks. VIII. 307 Our dove-like ambassador with the olive-branch in his beak. 1837 Marryat Perc. Keene iii, My mother.. had first tendered the olive branch, which had been accepted. 1856 R. Glisan Jrnl. Army Life (1874) xxiv. 324 The troops.. moved up Rogue River.. with the olive branch in one hand, and the sword in the other. 1936 Wodehouse Laughing Gas v. 60 He read his National Geographic Magazine. I read mine. And for some minutes matters proceeded along these lines. Then I thought to myself: 'Oh, well, dash it,' and decided to extend the olive branch. 1975 B. Garfield Hopscotch xxvii. 283 Abandoning the manuscript.. could be an olive branch: Kendig's.. assurance he was quitting.

2. usually *pl.* (in allusion to Ps. cxxviii. 3 (4): see sense 1, quot. 1535). Children. (Now humorous.)

1677 Baker in Rigaud Corr. Sci. Men (1841) II. 27 Having a just equal number of chargeable olive-branches. 1733 C'tess Granville Let. to Swift in Mrs. Delany's Lett. I. 422 My son, my daughter, and all our olive-branches salute you most tenderly. 1796 Jane Austen Pride & Prej. (1870) II. xxiv. 310 The rest of his letter is only about.. his expectation of a young olive-branch. 1838 Dickens Nich. Nick. xiv, The wife and olive branches of one Mr. Kenwigs.

ˈolive-ˌcoloured, *a.* = olive B: **a.** Olive-green, olivaceous; **b.** Dusky or brownish yellow.

1613 Purchas Pilgrimage vi. xv. (1614) 656 The tawney Moore, blacke Negro,.. oliue-coloured American, should with the whiter European become one sheepe-folde, under one greate Sheepheard. 1653 R. Sanders Physiogn. 173 If that woman be olive-coloured or yellowish, with her black eyes. 1752 Sir J. Hill Hist. Anim. 162 The large, smooth, olive-coloured Pinna. 1774 Goldsm. Nat. Hist. II. 220 The complexion olive coloured, and the hair black. 1859 Lang Wand. India 302 They were remarkably handsome birds, with.. olive-coloured feathers on their backs. 1863 Trevelyan Compet. Wallah (1866) 203 Hampered by liaisons with Hindoo women and by crowds of olive-coloured children.

olived (ˈɒlɪvd), *a. rare.* [f. olive + -ed[2].]

†**1.** Cut up into 'olives' (see olive 6). *Obs.*

a 1643 Cartwright Ordinary ii. i, Hav. No mild words shall bury My splitted, spitch cock'd—Sl. Oliv'd, hash'd.. Hav. Rost'd fury.

2. Furnished or adorned with olive-trees or olive-branches.

c 1749 W. G. Hamilton Parl. Logick, etc. (1808) 227 Jove's fair daughter, oliv'd Peace. 1749 Warton Triumph Isis 77 Green as of old each oliv'd portal smiles. a 1790 —— Poet. Wks. (1802) II. 176 Hoar Plato walks his oliv'd Academe.

oliveness (ˈɒlɪvnɪs). *rare.* [f. olive B. + -ness.] The quality of being of an olive colour.

18.. Cent. Dict. cites Coues.

olivenite (əʊˈlɪvənaɪt, ˈɒlɪvənaɪt). *Min.* [f. (1820) Ger. *o'liven-* (inflected case of *olive*) in *o'livenerz* (Werner, 1789) olive-ore + -ite[1].] A native arsenate of copper, occurring in crystals or masses, usually of olive-green colour.

[1805 R. Jameson Min. II. 249, I use the name Oliven-Ore in place of Olive Copper-ore.] 1820 Ibid. (ed. 3) II. 340 Earthy, Acicular Olivenite. 1858 Greg & Lettsom Min. 319 The finest specimens of Olivenite known have been found in Cornwall.

ˈolive-ˈoil. 1. The oil obtained from the pulp of olives. Formerly *oil of olive(s* (olive 2 b), *oil olive* (oil *sb.*[1] 2 c). Also *attrib.*

A fixed non-drying oil, of a pale yellow or greenish-yellow colour, insipid and inodorous, viscid and greasy to the touch, and very light; much used in cookery and medicine, and (the inferior kinds) also for illumination, lubrication, etc.

1774 Goldsm. Nat. Hist. (1776) VII. 207 His remedy which was nothing more than olive-oil. 1841 W. Spalding Italy & It. Isl. III. 386 The most important articles which our country receives from Italy are, Unmanufactured Silk, and Olive-Oil. 1870 Yeats Nat. Hist. Comm. 206 Olive oil is largely used.. in dressing woollen goods, and for machinery. 1895 Montgomery Ward Catal. Spring & Summer 109/2 A pure, natural color olive oil soap made of the finest selected oil imported for this purpose. 1957 Encycl. Brit. XVI. 774/2 California olive oil output is normally less than 1% that of Spain. 1970 'D. Halliday' Dolly & Cookie Bird ii. 10 They have.. vineyards and.. three olive-oil factories. 1977 P. Way Super-Celeste 52 The Mafia godfathers could.. declare they were olive oil merchants.

2. A jocular mispronunciation of *au revoir*.

1906 Dialect Notes III. 148 Olive oil, n. phr., au revoir. Facetious. 1909 J. R. Ware Passing Eng. 187/2 Olive oil (Music Hall, 1884). English pronunciation of au revoir. 1933 Partridge Slang To-day & Yesterday iii. iii. 206 For 'good-bye', the boys at Dulwich already in 1906 used.. olive oil (au revoir). 1960 Wentworth & Flexner Dict. Amer. Slang 364/2 Olive oil, good-bye.

ˈolive-ˌplant. 1. = olive 1.

c 1420 Pallad. on Husb. Tab. 268 Oliuis, to rere withouten oliue plauntis. 1611 Bible Ps. cxxviii. 3 Thy children like olive-plants round about thy table.

2. *pl.* (in allusion to Ps. cxxviii. 3.) Children. (= olive-branch 2.)

1616 Sir E. Sandys Ps. in Farr S.P. Jas. I (1848) 80 Thy children sweet, in virtue bred, Fair olive-plants, thy boord beset. 1842 J. Aiton Domest. Econ. (1857) 315 The training of the olive-plants that soon arise about a minister's table should be a matter of much anxiety and many prayers.

†**oliver**[1]. *Obs.* [a. AF. *oliver* = OF. *olivier* olive-tree, doublet of *olivaire*:—L. *olīvāri-us* of or pertaining to an olive: cf. med.L. *olivārium* olive garden or grove.] An olive-tree.

13.. K. Alis. 5785 (MS. Bodl.) And founden appel trewes, and fygeres, Peryes, cypres, and Olyuers. c 1386 Chaucer Monk's T. 46 And they brende.. alle hire Olyueres and vynes eke.

oliver[2] (ˈɒlɪvə(r)). [Origin uncertain.]

A tilt-hammer having the arm or handle attached to an axle, worked with the foot by a treadle which brings the hammer down, and with a spring which raises it; used esp. in the shaping of nails, bolts, and the like.

Such a contrivance is described in 1686 by Plot Oxfordsh. 390 'A large sledg.. set in an axis of wood, from whence goes a rodd of iron fastned to a pallet that reaches out a little beyond the anvil, which being drawn by the foot of the smith.. is returned again by three springs of holly that clasp the axis the contrary way.' This mention of 'springs of holly', together with the variant *holliper* in quot. 1883, has suggested that the origin may be found in *holly*, although the established spelling (which evidently goes back to times anterior to living memory) points to the proper name *Oliver*.

1846 Holtzapffel Turning & Mech. Manip. 962 The Oliver, or small lift hammer.. was used when the author first saw it, in making long stout nails, intended for fixing the tires of wheels. 1869 Eng. Mech. 31 Dec. 387/1. 1881 Greener Gun 257 The iron pins are.. stamped upon olivers, in much the same manner as described for stamping with dies. 1882 Standard 26 Dec. 2/3 The 'Oliver'.. on the top of which is fixed the stamp of the particular pattern and size of the nail required to be made. 1883 Crane Smithy & F. (1885) 30 The 'Oliver' or 'Holliper' consists of a top and bottom swage united by a spring. 1896 Cyclist 8 Jan. 26/2 The brazers' and smiths' hearths.. By them are the steam olivers and stamping presses.

Hence **ˈoliverman,** a man who works an oliver.

1883 B'ham Daily Post 11 Oct., Oliverman wanted, at once, used to small Coach Bolts.

Oliver[3] (ˈɒlɪvə(r)). *slang.* Also oliver. [A male Christian name, perh. alluding to *Oliver* Cromwell (1599–1658), leader of the Parliamentary troops in the Civil War.] The moon.

1781 [see whiddle v.]. 1834 W. H. Ainsworth Rookwood II. v. 360 Now Oliver puts his black nightcap on, And every star its glim is hiding. Ibid. III. v. 284 Oliver whiddles!—who cares—who cares If down upon us he peers and stares? Mind him who will? with his great white face, Boldly I'll ride by his glim to the chase. 1870 R. F. Burton Vikram & Vampire v. 171 But, look sharp, mind old Oliver, or the lamb-skin man will have the pull of us. 1882 Sydney Slang Dict. 6/2 Oliver, the moon. 'When Oliver looks pale,' when the moon is waning. 1895 New Rev. July 7 'There's a moon out.' 'The better for us to pick 'em off, Dan,' I returned, laughing at him. 'What—Oliver? damn Oliver!' said Zacchary. 'Let's push forward and come to quarters.' 1935 E. Weekley Something about Words vi. 107 Oliver, thieves' cant for the moon, is not in the Oxford Dictionary.

Oliver[4] (ˈɒlɪvə(r)). [The name of William *Oliver* (1695–1764), a physician of Bath, who invented the recipe.] = *Bath Oliver* (s.v. Bath *sb.*[2] 2 a). Also *attrib.*

1853 E. M. Sewell Experience of Life ii. 18 The Oliver biscuits, in the small, deep, old china dessert plates, were to my belief then never bought at any shop in Carsdale. Ibid. vii. 64 She was sitting.. at a table.. on which stood.. a china basket with Oliver biscuits.

Oliver, in *a Roland for an Oliver*: see Roland.

Oliverian (ɒlɪˈvɪərɪən), *sb.* and *a.* Also 7 -arian. [f. proper name *Oliver* + -ian.]

A. *sb.* A partisan or adherent of Oliver Cromwell; a Cromwellian.

1658 Wood Life 30 Aug. (O.H.S.) I. 258 Dennis Bond, a great Olivarian.. died on that day. 1707 E. Ward Hud. Rediv. II. xii. 28 A Scotch Brood of Presbyterians, Or pious English Oliverians. 1885 J. Brown Bunyan 132 The very Oliverians were becoming Royalist in their sympathies.

B. *adj.* Cromwellian.

1721 Amherst Terræ Fil. No. 15 (1754) 74 The principles of the revolution, and not of the Oliverian usurpation.

olivescent (ɒlɪˈvɛsənt), *a.* [f. olive + -escent.] Of colour: bordering on or slightly olive.

1900 Proc. Zool. Soc. 506 Kirontisa whiteheadi... Upper-side deep olivescent brown. Fore wing with two paler olivescent marks within.

olivet[1] (ˈɒlɪvɪt). *Obs.* exc. as in b. [ad. L. *olīvēt-um* olive-grove.] A place in which olive-trees are grown; an olive-grove.

1382 Wyclif Amos iv. 9 3our vijn 3erdis; and olyuetis [gloss or placis wher olyues wexen]. 1609 Bible (Douay) Exod. xxiii. 11 So shalt thou doe in thy vineyard and thy olivete. 1610 W. Folkingham Art Of Survey i. viii. 18 Good for graine, Elmes, Vine-yards, and Oliuets.

b. Now only as proper name of the Mount of Olives, the scene of the Ascension, on the east side of Jerusalem; hence allusively.

c 1275 Passion of our Lord 127 in O.E. Misc. 41 Vre louerd nom his apostles.. And forþ myd him ledde to þe Munt of olyuete. c 1440 Jacob's Well 252 3if þou be in þe ground of mercy þou art in olyuete. 1611 Bible Acts i. 12 The mount called Oliuet. 1866 Whittier Our Master 51 And faith has still its Olivet, And love its Galilee.

ˈolivet[2]. Also oliˈvette. [a. F. *olivette*, dim. of OLIVE: see -ET[1].]

1. = OLIVE *sb.*[1] 7 b.

1819 *Army List* in *Pall Mall Gaz.* (1891) 14 Nov. 3/2, 10th Hussars..Jacket blue, and cross loops and olivets in gold; blue facings. **1900** *Westm. Gaz.* 30 Aug. 2/2 The little cord olivettes and buttons..corresponded in colour to the cloth.

2. (See quot.)

1858 SIMMONDS *Dict. Trade, Olivet*, a kind of mock pearl or white bugle made for the African trade and prized by the negroes of Senegal.

Olivetan (ɒlɪˈviːtən). [From Monte Oliveto (or Uliveto) near Siena, the site of the mother convent: see -AN; in F. *olivétain*.] One of an order of monks founded in 1313 by John Tolomei of Siena, and subjected to the Benedictine rule.

1691 tr. *Emilianne's Observ. Journ. Naples* 35 Proper to associate with the Canon Regulars, or Olivetans. **1717** BERKELEY *Jrnl. Tour Italy* 19 Jan., Wks. 1871 IV. 526 In the vineyard of the Olivetans. **1850** MRS. JAMESON *Leg. Monast. Ord.* Introd. 42 The Olivetans, a congregation of Reformed Benedictines, produced some celebrated artists.

ˈolive-ˌtree. = OLIVE *sb.*[1] 1.

(Also with qualifying words: see OLIVE 1 b.)

c **1315** SHOREHAM 131 Þou ert þe coluere of noe, þat broute þe braunche of olyue tre. *c* **1489** CAXTON *Sonnes of Aymon* i. 47 Berynge braunches of olyue tree in their handes In token of peas. **1535** COVERDALE *Ps.* lii. 8, I am like a grene olyue tre in ye house of God. **1756–7** tr. *Keysler's Trav.* (1760) I. 475 The olive-tree is an ever-green, but the colour of it is not vivid, but faint, and resembles a willow. **1883** BROWNING *Jochanan Hakkadosh* 480 The wind makes olive-trees up yonder hill Whiten and shudder.

Olivetti (ɒlɪˈvɛtɪ). [Name of the manufacturers.] The proprietary name of a range of typewriters.

1949 *Trade Marks Jrnl.* 23 Mar. 255/1 Olivetti... Typewriters. Ing. C. Olivetti & C., Società per Azioni.., Ivrea, Province of Turin, Italy; machine manufacturers. **1966** AUDEN *About House* 18 The Olivetti portable, The dictionaries (the very Best money can buy). **1968** *Listener* 28 Nov. 736/1 You can still go for a walk down Gloucester Crescent and below the chatter of a dozen Olivettis catch the soft murmur of extra-marital associations. **1977** G. FISHER *Villain of Piece* i. 3, I..glared at my Olivetti. There was a sheet of copy paper in it.

ˈolive-ˌwood.

1. The wood of the common olive, *Olea europæa*; used in ornamental work.

1718 LADY M. W. MONTAGU *Let. to Abbé Conti* 19 May, There are others of mother of pearl and olive wood inlaid. **1812** J. SMYTH *Pract. of Customs* (1821) 294 Olive wood is beautifully veined, and has an agreeable smell. **1888** *Pall Mall G.* 6 Sept. 10/1 The manufacture..of objects of devotion in mother-of-pearl and olive-wood.

2. Any tree of the genus *Elæodendron* (N.O. *Celastraceæ*), furnishing an ornamental wood.

1866 in *Treas. Bot.*

olive-yard (ˈɒlɪvˌjɑːd). An inclosure or piece of ground in which olive-trees are cultivated.

1382 WYCLIF *Exod.* xxiii. 11 So thow shalt doon in thi vyne ȝeerd, and in thin oliue ȝeerd. **1611** BIBLE *Josh.* xxiv. 13 Of the vineyards and oliveyards which ye planted not do ye eat. **1703** MAUNDRELL *Journ. Jerus.* (1721) 64 We pass'd thro' large Olive-yards. **1760–72** tr. *Juan & Ulloa's Voy.* (ed. 3) II. 241. **1880** J. H. SHORTHOUSE *John Inglesant* xxxvii. 523 He had come into the cool pastures and olive yards. **1911** *Encycl. Brit.* XX. 87/1 Many olive-yards now exist in Upper Egypt.

oliˈviferous, *a.* *rare*⁻⁰. [f. L. *olīvifer* + -OUS.] Olive-bearing.

1656 BLOUNT *Glossogr., Oliviferous*, which bears or brings forth Olives. **1658** in PHILLIPS.

oliviform (əʊˈlɪvɪfɔːm), *a.* [See -FORM and cf. F. *oliviforme*.] Having the shape of an olive. In *Conchol.* Resembling an olive shell.

1857 MAYNE *Expos. Lex., Oliviform*, shaped like the olive.

olivil (ˈɒlɪvɪl). *Chem.* [a. F. *olivile*, f. *olive*.] A crystalline substance obtained from the gum of the olive-tree.

1810–26 HENRY *Elem. Chem.* II. 332 Olivile is a name given by M. Pelletier to the substance which remains after gently evaporating the alcoholic solution of the gum which exudes from the olive tree. **1866–77** WATTS *Dict. Chem.* IV. 200 *Olivil.* $C_{14}H_{18}O_5$..A neutral substance occurring..in the gum of the olive-tree.

Hence † **oˈlivilin**. *Chem. Obs.* = prec.

1838 T. THOMSON *Chem. Org. Bodies* 668 From the undissolved portion absolute alcohol dissolves the olivilin, which is deposited in crystals on evaporating the solution.

olivine (ˈɒlɪvaɪn, -ɪn). *Min.* Also -in. [Named 1790; f. L. *olīva* OLIVE: see -INE[5].] **a.** A variety of CHRYSOLITE, chiefly of olive-green colour, occurring in eruptive rocks and in meteorites.

1794 KIRWAN *Min.* 263 Olivin..is found generally in roundish grains. **1816** R. JAMESON *Min.* II. 74 Olivine is nearly allied to Augite. **1879** RUTLEY *Stud. Rocks* x. 116 Olivine is a common constituent of many eruptive rocks.

b. *attrib.* Containing or resembling olivine.

1872 W. S. SYMONDS *Rec. Rocks* i. 12 Micaceous and olivine rocks. **1884** *Bookseller* 6 Nov. 1190 These two books ..are bound in bevel boards, with olivine edges.

c. In *comb.* naming mixed minerals, as *olivine-diabase, -gabbro*.

1895 A. HARKER *Petrol.* 115 Numerous olivine-diabases are associated with the Carboniferous strata of the Midlands. *Ibid.* 68 The Tertiary gabbros of the western islands of Scotland..are in general olivine-gabbros. **1900** [see KENTALLENITE]. **1936** J. S. FLETT in Wilson & Knox *Geol. Orkney* xvii. 180 They are the only olivine-basalt dykes that have been discovered in the Orkneys. **1956** W. EDWARDS in D. L. Linton *Sheffield* 15 Boreholes in the southeastern part of the coalfield have revealed thick, sill-like beds of olivine-dolerite and analcime-dolerite. **1965** E. L. P. MERCY in G. Y. Craig *Geol. of Scotland* vii. 243/2 Rhythmic banding in the olivine-gabbros and troctolites has been described.

Hence **oliˈvinic, oliviˈnitic** *adjs.*, pertaining to, resembling, or containing olivine; **oliviˈniferous** *a.*, containing or yielding olivine.

1845 *Jrnl. Asiatic Soc. Bengal* XIV. 294 The narrow zone of oliviniferous trap. **1894** L. FLETCHER in *Mineralog. Mag.* X. 312 A silicate of the olivinic type.

olivite (ˈɒlɪvaɪt). *Chem.* [f. OLIVE + -ITE[1] 4.] A bitter substance obtained from unripe olives, and from olive-leaves.

1866–77 WATTS *Dict. Chem.* IV. 202.

† **oˈlivity.** *Obs. rare*⁻⁰. [ad. L. *olīvitās*, f. *olīv-a* OLIVE: see -ITY.]

1656 BLOUNT *Glossogr., Olivity* (*olivitas*), the time of gathering Olives, or making Oyl; see *Oleity*.

olk, obs. Sc. form of *ouk*, WEEK.

olla[1] (ˈɒlə). Also 7 ollia. [a. Sp. *olla* (pronounced ˈoʎa, whence spelling *ollia*. and OLIO), in Pg. *olha* pot, stew, hotchpot:—L. *olla* pot, jar.]

1. In Spain and Spanish-speaking lands, an earthen jar or pot used for cooking, etc.; also, a dish of meat and vegetables cooked in such a pot; hence = OLIO 1, OLLA PODRIDA.

1622 MABBE tr. *Aleman's Guzman d'Alf.* I. II. i. 110 We did alwaies finde a tricke to adde some-thing, though it were but for the boyling of their *Olla. Margin, Olla*, is a pot or Pipkin, wherein flesh, and other things are sod; by the Figure Metonym the Olla is taken for that which is boyled in it. *c* **1645** HOWELL *Lett.* v. xxxviii. (1650) 174 He can marinat fish, make gellies..; he is passing good for an *ollia*. **1771** SMOLLETT *Humph. Cl.* 11 Oct., He taught me..to cook several outlandish delicacies, such as ollas, pepper-*pots*, pillaws [etc.]. **1832** *Veg. Subst. Food of Man* 224 The olla.. with which a Spanish dinner commences. **1843** LONGF. *Span. Stud.* I. v, Give a Spaniard His mass, his olla, and his Doña Luisa. **1877** DORA GREENWELL *Basket of Summer Fruit* 69 Everything that is good in itself is good for an olla.

2. In parts of the United States formerly Spanish: A large porous earthen jar for keeping drinking-water cool by evaporation from its outer surface.

1851 MAYNE REID *Scalp Hunt* li. 390 The olla was filled with water from the adjacent stream. **1854** BARTLETT *Mex. Boundary* I. xi. 272 The olla or earthen pot almost their only domestic utensil. **1884** J. G. BOURKE *Snake Dance Moquis* x. 109, I found three large four or five gallon ollas.

‖**3.** An ancient cinerary urn. [Latin.]

1857 BIRCH *Anc. Pottery* (1858) II. 327 Of this pale red ware were also made the jars or *ollae* which held the ashes of the dead.

‖**olla**[2]. Also 7 olea, 8 olio, 8–9 ole, 9 ollah, ola. [a. Pg. *olla*, var. of *ola*, a. Malayālim *ōla* (Tamil *ōlai*).] A palm-leaf, esp. a leaf or strip of a leaf of the palmyra, used in Southern India, etc., for writing on; hence, a native letter or document written on such a leaf: = CADJAN 2.

1625 PURCHAS *Pilgrims* II. x. 1728 He sent another mandate, that he should doe nothing till he had an *Olla* or Letter written with his hand in letters of gold. **1698** FRYER *Acc. E. India* 66 The Houses are low, and Thatched with Oleas of the Cocoe-Trees. *Ibid.* Index, *Oleas*, leafs. **1718** *Propag. Gospel in East* III. 37 (Y.) Damulian Leaves, commonly called Oles. **1760** ALVES in Dalrymple *Oriental Repert.* (1808) I. 377 (Y.) Orders for Olios to be made out for delivering of what Englishmen were in his Kingdom to me. **1806** C. BUCHANAN *Chr. Researches* (ed. 2) 70 Many persons had their Ollahs in their hands, writing the sermon in Tamil shorthand. **1859** TENNENT *Ceylon* (1860) I. x. 512 The books of the Singhalese are formed to-day, as they have been for ages past, of *olas* or strips taken from the young leaves of the Talipat or the Palmyra palm.

‖**ollamh, ollav** (ˈɒləv). *Irish Antiq.* Also ollave, ollam. [a. Ir. *ollamh* (ˈɔlav, *nasal v*), OIr. *ollam*, learned man, doctor.] Among the ancient Irish, A master in some art or branch of learning; a learned man: a rank answering to that of a doctor or professor in a university.

1723 O'CONNOR tr. *Keating's Hist. Irel.* 132 Ollamh Fodhla was his Successor in the Throne. *Ibid.*, Ollamh signifies a Person that excells in Wisdom and Learning. **1845** PETRIE *Eccl. Archit. Irel.* 347 The author of this law refused to allow him more than the *ollave* in poetry, or the *ollave* in language, or the teacher. **1888** *Blackw. Mag.* Dec. 807 The Ollams being specially devoted to genealogy before the advent of the Normans. **1893** *Dict. Nat. Biog.* XXXIV. 430 A family of hereditary historians who were..ollavs (i.e. chief chroniclers or professional authors) of the O'Briens.

olland, var. OLD LAND.

ollapod (ˈɒləpɒd), abbrev. of OLLA PODRIDA.

1804 COLLINS *Scripscrap* A iij, This little Ollapod, made up of 'Trifles light as air'. *a* **1845** HOOD *To Hahnemann* i, Framed the whole race of Ollapods to fret.

Hence **ˈollapodism** (*nonce-wd.*), a sentence made up of various languages.

1837 *Tait's Mag.* IV. 157 His natural volubility, aided by ..a plentiful sprinkling of Ollapodisms..pleased the men.

olla podrida (ˌɒlə pəʊˈdriːdə). Also 7 olio (ollio) podrido, oleopodrido, olepotride, ollapod-, 9 olla-podrida. [a. Sp. *olla podrida* = 'rotten pot', f. *olla* (see OLLA[1], OLIO) and *podrida* = L. *putrida* putrid, rotten. The spelling *olepotride* simulates Fr.]

1. A dish of Spanish origin composed of pieces of many kinds of meat, vegetables, etc. stewed or boiled together: = OLIO 1.

1599 MINSHEU *Span. Dial.* 22, I desire to know, from whence or why they called it olla podrida [*marg.*, A rotten or putrified pot. Also a hotchpotch of many meats together]. **1615** MARKHAM *Eng. Housew.* II. ii (1668) 63 An excellent Olepotride..the only principle dish of boyled meat which is esteemed in all Spain. **1622** MABBE tr. *Aleman's Guzman d' Alf.* I. II. i. 110 *margin, Olla podrida*, is a very great one, contayning in it diuers things, as Mutton, Beefe, Hens, Capons, Sawsages, Piggs feete, Garlick, Onions, &c. It is called *Podrida*, because it is sod leisurely, til it be rotten (as we say) and ready to fall in peeces... In English it may well beare the name of Hodge-podge. **1647** R. STAPYLTON *Juvenal* (1682) 208 For foure hundred pieces to bespeake An ollio podrido. *a* **1648** LD. HERBERT *Autobiog.* (1886) 159 Nine dishes,..the first whereof was, three ollas podridas. **1846** *Edin. Rev.* LXXXIV. 175 Mr. Hughes evidently prefers a beefsteak to an *olla podrida*.

2. A hotchpoch, medley; a mixture of languages; = OLIO 2.

a **1634** RANDOLPH *Muse's Looking-glass* I. iv, A mere *Olla Podrida*, A medley, of ill-placed, and worse penn'd humours. **1663** COWLEY *Cutter Coleman St.* II. v, My little Gallimaufry, my little Oleopodrido of Arts and Arms. **1829** SCOTT *Napoleon* Introd., Wks. 1870 IX. 236 Their accusation was..an olla podrida. **1850** H. ROGERS *Ess.* II. iv. 169 An olla podrida, made up half of words supplied by the one language, and half of words supplied from the other. **1859** GREEN *Lett.* I. (1901) 30 That olla-podrida of a brain of mine.

Hence **ˌollapoˈdrida-ish, ˌollapoˈdridical** *adjs.* (*nonce-wds.*), heterogeneous.

1827 SCOTT *Jrnl.* 13 Mar., My ideas were olla-podrida-ish. **1830** *Fraser's Mag.* I. 748 Its omnigenous and ollapodridical character.

† **olle**, *v. Obs. rare*⁻¹. [ME., ? f. OE. *oll*, in phr. *mid olle* with scorn or contumely.] *intr.* ? To pour scorn or contempt (*on*).

a **1400–50** *Alexander* 1861 He set neuire his hope..To olle ay on his vndireling for ouer-laike a quyle.

ollen: see OLEN.

Ollendorffian (ɒlɪnˈdɔːfɪən), *a.* Also **Ollendorfian.** [f. the name of Heinrich Gottfried *Ollendorff*, German educator and grammarian (1803–65) + -IAN.] In the stilted language of foreign phrase-books.

[**1876** C. M. YONGE *Womankind* vi. 40 German [learnt] by the Ollendorf method.] [**1886** F. M. CRAWFORD in H. Norman *Broken Shaft* 18 The simple but instructive dialogues of Herr Ollendorff.] **1892** *New Rev.* Feb. 252 But the characters have as much individuality as the Ollendorffian prattlers about the gardener. **1900** *Sketch* 21 Feb. 191/2 She persisted in firing off Ollendorfian French at the waiters. **1905** *Westm. Gaz.* 8 July 2/3 'Views' which we snapshot, be they views of mountains or of men, and whether we use Kodak or Ollendorffian chit-chat to produce them. **1918** L. HUXLEY *Life J. D. Hooker* II. xliii. 327 He started them also, and very successfully, with colloquial Latin from an Ollendorffian French handbook. **1934** H. G. WELLS *Exper. Autobiogr.* II. ix. 766 A sort of Ollendorfian French.

olleo, ollio, obs. forms of OLIO.

† **ollite** (ˈɒlaɪt). *Min.* [f. L. *olla* pot + -ITE: in L. *lapis ollāris*, F. *pierre ollaire*.] An obsolete synonym of potstone, or steatite.

1811 PINKERTON *Petral.* I. 81 A dark ollite interspersed with golden mica. *Ibid.* 319 Saussure..calls steatite the substance which forms the base or the paste of ollite.

ollunt, var. OLD LAND.

olm (əʊlm). [G.] = PROTEUS 3 b.

1905 A. SEDGWICK *Student's Text-bk. Zool.* II. x. 307 *Proteus* Laur., the olm, 3 fingers, 2 toes, eyes hidden, Carniola subterranean waters. **1926** J. S. HUXLEY *Ess. Pop. Sci.* viii. 93 Three or four other species of animals, such as Proteus, the blind 'Olm' of Carniola, and Necturus, which ..are not known in a land-form at all. **1955** W. LEY *Salamanders* i. 3 The olm's rather restricted habitat..is a mountainous area in southern Europe, at the northern end of the Balkan peninsula. *Ibid.* 4 The olm is blind, having no use for eyes in the cold dark caves where it normally lives. **1965** B. E. FREEMAN tr. *Vandel's Biospeleol.* iii. 22 It was *Proteus* which firstly, because of its size, attracted the attention of man, and [was] also the first to receive a vernacular name, the olm.

Olmec (ˈɒlmɛk). [ad. Nahuatl *Olmecatl*, pl. *Olmeca* lit. 'inhabitants of the rubber country'.]

1. Also **Olmeca**. A native American people or peoples inhabiting the coast of southern Veracruz and western Tabasco during the 15th and 16th centuries, to where they probably migrated during the 12th century from the Mexican altiplano.

1787 C. CULLEN tr. *Clavigero's Hist. Mexico* I. II. 103 The Olmecas and the Xicallancas, whether one nation, or two distinct nations, but constantly allied and connected together, were so ancient in the country of Anahuac, that many authors account them prior to the Toltecas. **1883** P. J. J. VALENTINI in *Proc. Amer. Antiquarian Soc.* II. 193 (*heading*) The Olmecas and the Tultecas: a study in early Mexican ethnology and history. **1914** T. A. JOYCE *Mexican Archaeol.* v. 125 Though bows were found among the Olmec and Huaxtec, they must have been of quite late introduction. **1931** G. MASON *Columbus came Late* xi. 238 The Olmeca people that inhabited the damp country of southern Vera Cruz and western Tabasco. **1947** M. COVARRUBIAS *Mexico South* iv. 129 The builders of the cities of El Tajín and Teotihuacán..were the Olmecs proper. **1964** C. GIBSON *Aztecs under Spanish Rule* 9 The most important migrant peoples pertinent to Valley [of Mexico] history in the Post-Classic or late pre-colonial period were the Olmeca, Xicalanca, Tolteca, Chichimeca, Teochichimeca, Otomi... The first five of these were historically extinct, absorbed, or expelled by the time of the arrival of Europeans.

2. A prehistoric people inhabiting the same area *c* 1200–100 B.C. Also *attrib.* or as *adj.*; *spec.* designating the culture of this people or its characteristic artistic style, also found elsewhere in southern Mexico. So **'Olmecan, 'Olmecoid** *adjs.*

[**1927** H. BEYER in *El Mexico Antiguo* II. 306 (*caption*) Idolo Olmego di Piedra Verdosa.] **1929** *Indian Notes* (Mus. Amer. Indian, Heye Foundation) VI. 280 Beyer published a picture of what he calls 'an Olmecan idol' formerly in his possession and now in a private collection. *Ibid.* 285 This peculiar type of mask may be safely assigned to the ancient Olmecan culture, which apparently had its center in the San Andrés Tuxtla area around Lake Catemaco. **1932** *Natural Hist.* XXXII. 519/2 There is often described in the traditions a highly civilized people called the Olmec, who lived anciently as far north as Tlaxcala, but were later dispersed to southern Vera Cruz, Chiapas, southern Puebla, and eastern Oaxaca. They were famed for their work in jade and turquoise, and were credited with being the chief users of rubber in Central America. *Ibid.* 520/2 Perhaps investigations in the Olmec area would clarify the much discussed relationship between the Mexicans and the Mayas. **1943** M. W. STIRLING *Stone Monuments S. Mexico* 7 Two years later he released a study..of the giant head in which he emphasized its 'Ethiopian' features, features which have since been identified with the style of art called Olmec. *Ibid.* 54 The niche..represents the 'Olmec' open-jaguar-mouth motive. **1960** *Times* 6 Oct. 4/6 The Veracruz region, which is rich in..treasures of the Olmec..coastal cultures of ancient Mexico. **1962** G. ASHE *Land to West* viii. 222 A clay Fire-god of the prehistoric Olmecs on the Gulf coast. **1965** M. D. COE in R. Wauchope *Handbk. Middle Amer. Indians* III. II. 738 (*heading*) The Olmec style and its distributions. *Ibid.* 765 As one moves away from the core region and also into later time periods, many objects are encountered which are more or less Olmecoid, but these are not Olmec in our meaning. **1966** *Listener* 29 Dec. 957/1 The most ancient civilization of Mesoamerica is that of the Olmecs. **1967** L. DEUEL *Conquistadors without Swords* xxi. 287 (*caption*) Substructure of Pyramid E-VII with its Olmecoid stucco masks. **1973** *New Yorker* 24 Mar. 108/2 The Olmec civilization was not identified as such until the nineteen-forties. **1973** *Black World* July 13/1 The huge stone heads of Olmec deities, exhibited an unmistakably African physiognomy. **1973** *Times* 15 Oct. 11/8 The Olmec Forerunners, the archaic predecessors of the Maya though probably not themselves Maya. **1977** *Sci. Amer.* Mar. 116/1 The Olmec, one of the earliest of the complex societies in the region, built major ceremonial centres on the low-lying coastal plain of the Gulf of Mexico; examples are San Lorenzo and La Venta. *Ibid.*, At the same time the Olmec zone of cultural influence and Olmec trade extended into much of the high plateau.

o loft(e, olon, oloude, obs. forms of ALOFT, ALONE, ALOUD.

-ology, ology ('ɒlədʒɪ), *suffix* and quasi-*sb.*

1. *suffix.* The form in which the suffix -LOGY (Gr. -λογία) usually occurs in words derived from Gr., the *o* belonging etymologically to the prec. element (see -O); hence the form of the suffix in modern formations, often sportive nonce-words.

1803 FESSENDEN *Terrible Tractoration* I. (ed. 2) 18 *note*, Sublime discoveries in the abstruse sciences of insect-ology, mite-ology and nothing-ology. **1805** J. LAWRENCE *Treat. Cattle* (1809) 495 The contemplation, either of physiology, or commonsensology.

2. quasi-*sb.* Any one of the various sciences or departments of science. Also 'ology.

1811 E. NARES *Thinks-I-to-myself* (ed. 5) I. 68 She..was therefore supposed to understand Chemistry, Geology, Philology, and a hundred other ologies. **1823** *Edin. Rev.* XXXVIII. 420 This is the Ology of the day. **1854** DICKENS *Hard T.* II. ix. 236 Ologies of all kinds, from morning to night. If there is any Ology left..that has not been worn to rags in this house..I hope I shall never hear its name. **1866** CARLYLE *Inaug. Addr.* 189 Maid-servants, I hear people complaining, are getting instructed in the 'ologies'. **1884** J. ROBERTSON *Univ. Serm.* in *Cambr. Rev.* 5 Nov. Suppl. p. xxvi/1 The full shock of each new 'ology'. **1886** KIPLING *Departmental Ditties* (ed. 2) 57 And after—ask the Yusufzaies What comes of all our 'ologies. **1927** G. D. H. & M. COLE *Murder at Crome House* iv. 42 'I don't think she's interested in anything except some 'ology—' 'Psychology, I think, sir,' said Johnson. **1972** C. L. COOPER in W. King *Black Short Story Anthol.* 237 With Famat's help,..I came to grasp an ology that was an intermixture of Ax, orthodox Islam, and theory. **1976** A. PRICE *War Game* I. ix. 172 One's doing a thesis on geology now, and the other's writing a book on meteorology. Ology is about the only thing they have in common.

So **o'logical, olo'gistic,** *a. nonce-wds.*, of, pertaining to, or versed in the 'ologies'; **-'ologist, 'ologist,** a student or professor of an 'ology'.

1834–43 SOUTHEY *Doctor* cxxxix. (1848) 348/2 Not so for the scientific in gooseberries, the gooseberryologists. **1839** *New Monthly Mag.* LV. 444 We have eight or nine ologists of different sorts staying with us. **1854** DICKENS *Hard T.* I. xv. 120, I hope you may now turn all your ological studies to good account. *a* **1861** CLOUGH *Uranus* 25 Chaldean mumblings vast, with gossip light From modern ologistic fancyings mixed. **1890** *Pall Mall G.* 14 Mar. 6/1 Mr. C. is rising forty, amiable, and 'ological'. That is, he goes in hot for the 'ologies'. **1896** *Westm. Gaz.* 1 July 2/2 Every feature of the face..has long before now been made an 'index to character' by 'ologists' of various persuasions.

ololiuqui (əʊləʊ'l(j)uːkɪ). Also ololiuhqui. [ad. Amer. Sp. *ololiuque*, f. Nahuatl *ololiuhqui* 'one that covers'.] A Mexican climbing plant, *Rivea corymbosa* (*Ipomœa sidifolia*), of the family Convolvulaceæ; also, the narcotic drug prepared from its seeds. Also *attrib.*

1915 W. E. SAFFORD in *Jrnl. Heredity* VI. 311 It is very strange that Mexican botanists living in the country of the Ololiuhqui have not solved the mystery of its identity. **1926** *Chambers's Jrnl.* Aug. 513/2 [He] bemused himself with the seeds of the ololiuhqui. **1941** R. E. SCHULTES (*title*) A contribution to our knowledge of *Rivea corymbosa*, the narcotic ololiuqui of the Aztecs. **1954** A. HUXLEY *Let.* 2 Mar. (1969) 699 Ololiuqu(i) is used by the Mexican and Cuban witch doctors to increase ESP faculties and relieve disease. **1962** —— *Island* xi. 171 He began to talk about the indoles recently isolated from the ololiuqui seeds that had been brought in from Mexico last year. **1966** *New Scientist* 21 Apr. 156/1 In Mexico, the seeds of climbing convulvulus plants known as 'morning glory' are made into a drug called 'ololiuqui'. **1973** *Sci. Amer.* Oct. 130/2 The seeds of certain Mexican morning glories,..the source of a magic Aztec potion, ololiuqui, used to 'communicate with the gods and receive the secret things'.

Olonetsian (ɒləʊ'nɛtsɪən). Also Olonecian, Olonetzian. [f. *Olonets*, the name of a town and former government in N.W. Russia.] A dialect of Karelian spoken to the north east of Lake Ladoga. Also **O'lonets.**

1932 W. L. GRAFF *Lang.* xi. 405 Finno-Ugric..dialects. These are..: Carelian, Olonetsian, [etc.]. **1933, 1939** [see LUDIAN]. **1946–47** *Slavonic & E. European Rev.* XXV. 436 Olonecian (Aunus), heard on the eastern shores of Lake Ladoga.., and the Ingrian..of Ingria.., are dialectical varieties of Carelian. **1954** PEI & GAYNOR *Dict. Linguistics* 154 *Olonetzian*, a member of the Finnish group of the Finno-Ugric (or Uralic) sub-family of the Ural-Altaic family of languages. **1957** B. COLLINDER *Survey Uralic Lang.* p. v, The dialects spoken in the Karelian-Finnish Soviet Republic are called Karelian (kr, in the north) and Olonets (ol, in the south). **1965** —— *Introd. Uralic Lang.* i. 11 Olonets (Olonetsian) is a variant of Karelian, spoken in the former province of Olonets..and strongly influenced by Russian. **1975** G. F. CUSHING tr. *Hajdu's Finno-Ugrian Lang. & Peoples* 199 Tver Carelian is spoken in the Upper Volga region, Aunus or Olonets to the north-east of Lake Ladoga.

† **'olorine.** *Obs. rare.* [ad. L. *olōrīna* 'of swans', in *herba olorina* swans' grass.] A grass or 'herb' eaten with avidity by swans; swans'-grass.

The grass of Loch Spiney, referred to by Boece (see OLOUR) and Leslie, is app. *Glyceria fluitans*, called locally 'Swan girss' (Rampini *County Hist. Elgin* 58) and 'Pike girss'.

1596 DALRYMPLE tr. *Leslie's Hist. Scot.* I. 45 Moray hes a freshe water loch called Spynie, that mekle abundes in Swanis, in quhilke loch is a certaine herb verie rare and sindle to be found, in quhilke because the Swan hes sa gret delyte, we cal the herbe olorine (because the swan in latin is olor) [tr. LESLIE *De Orig.* (etc.) *Scot.* (1578) 28 Herba quædam rara..qua quòd olores impensè delectantur, Olorinam eam dicimus]. **1796** MORSE *Amer. Geog.* II. 150 The plant *olorina* which grows in its waters.

oloroso (ɒlə'rəʊsəʊ). [Sp. *oloroso* fragrant.] A type of dry or medium sherry; a glass of such sherry.

1876 H. VIZETELLY *Facts about Sherry* v. 46 The olorosos ..are deeper in colour than the amontillados. **1888** [see FINO]. **1908** C. E. HAWKER *Chats about Wine* vii. 105 There are several varieties of Sherry..the 'fino'..and the 'Oloroso'. **1920** G. SAINTSBURY *Notes on Cellar-Bk.* ii. 20 One might jangle a long time on Montillas and Olorosos. **1935** 'R. HULL' *Keep it Quiet* iv. 34 It seemed best..to let them try the proposed new Oloroso... Both..pronounced the new sherry to be disgusting. **1955** W. GADDIS *Recognitions* I. i. 59 He seemed prepared to sit over that dark oloroso sherry all evening. **1961** [see AMONTILLADO a]. **1966** *Harper's Bazaar* Mar. 105 Oloroso, the darker, fuller style of sherry which, although dry in the natural state, is almost invariably sweetened for export. **1972** *Times* 20 Oct. 4/6 (Advt.), A very old, rich oloroso cream sherry. **1974** *Times* 23 Feb. 13/5 In Jerez, the producers like to start the day with a glass of natural dry oloroso. **1976** *Daily Tel.* 26 Oct. 17 [Yesterday] it [*sc.* the High Court] gave the sherry producers of the Jerez district of Spain what they had sued to obtain in 1970—exclusive right in Britain to use the descriptions *amontillado, oloroso* and *fino.*

† **olour.** *Obs. rare.* [erron. f. L. *olōrum* gen. pl., 'of swans'.] = OLORINE.

1536 BELLENDEN *Cron. Scot.* (1821) I. xxxiv, The cause quhy the swannis multiplyis sa fast in this loch [Spynee], is throw ane herbe namit Olour [tr. BOECE *Scot. Hist.* (1526) Descriptio lf. ix, Herba quædam cuius semine [Holores] auidissime vescuntur, atque ob id Holorum cognominata].

olp, olph, olf (ɒlp, ɒlf), local variants of ALP².

a **1825** FORBY *Voc. E. Anglia, Green-olf*, the green finch, or, more properly, green grosbeak. *Parus viridus.* **1840** SPURDENS *Suppl. Forby, Olp.* This is nearer to the pronunciation in Suffolk, than Olf in Forby.

olpe ('ɒlpeɪ). *Greek Antiq.* [ad. Gr. ὄλπη leather oil-flask, ewer, wine-jug.] **a.** A leather flask for oil or some other liquid. **b.** A kind of jug with a pear-shaped body and a handle.

1883 J. W. MOLLETT *Illustr. Dict. Art & Archæol.* 233/2 *Olpê*..a kind of *aryballos* with a curved handle, but no spout (originally a leather oil-flask). **1937** *Times Lit. Suppl.* 6 Feb. 93/1 An interesting eye olpe. **1961** *Oxf. Univ. Gaz.* 10 Mar. 832/1 A small late (?) Corinthian olpe with waves, dots and wavy lines. **1969** R. MAYER *Dict. Art Terms & Techniques* 269/1 *Olpe*, in ancient Greek pottery, a short-necked jug tapering to a foot... The word also denoted a leather flask used for carrying liquids. **1974** SAVAGE & NEWMAN *Illustr. Dict. Ceramics* 207 *Olpe* (Greek), a type of wine-jug resembling an *oenochoë*.

oltra-, obs. form of ULTRA-.

oluente, variant of OLFEND *Obs.*, camel.

† **oluhnen,** *v. Obs.* Also 3 **olhnen.** [Early ME. *oluhnen* (*ü*) app. for **olühtnen*, f. OE. *ólyht* flattery (Blickl. Hom. 99), connected with *olehtan, oleccan* to flatter.] *trans.* and *intr.* To flatter.

a **1225** *Ancr. R.* 180 ȝif me is iluued more þen anoðer, & more ioluhned. *Ibid.* 248 Ne mei he buten scheawe þe uorð sumhwat of his apeware; & oluhnen, oðer þreaten þet me bugge þerof. *a* **1225** *Juliana* 53 þen laddliche of helle þat olhnede swiðe & bed tus & bisohte.

Hence † **oluhninge** (olhtninge, olhtnunge, olhnung(e), *vbl. sb.*, flattering, flattery.

a **1225** *Ancr. R.* 192 (MS. T.) Olhtninge oðer hereward mihte sone make sum of ou fulitohen. *a* **1225** *St. Marher.* 5 For al me is thin olhnung ant thin eie. *a* **1225** *Leg. Kath.* 1502 Ah al þe helpeð an þin olhnunge.

olupy, obs. form of ONLEPY *a.*, only.

oly, olybanum, obs. ff. OIL, OLIBANUM.

oly-cook, oly-koek ('əʊlɪkʊk). *U.S. local.* Also oliekoek, olycoek, -coke. [a. Du. *oliekoek*, lit. 'oil-cake'.] A cake of dough sweetened and fried in lard: originally a Dutch delicacy.

1809 W. IRVING *Knickerb.* (1861) 90 Balls of sweetened dough..called doughnuts, or olykoeks. **1818** —— *Sketch Bk., Leg. Sleepy Hollow* (1865) 440 There was the doughty dough-nut, the tenderer oly koek, and the crisp and crumbling cruller. **1851** H. MELVILLE *Whale* lxv. 334 Like old Amsterdam housewives' dough-nuts or oly-cooks. **1881** *Harper's Mag.* Mar. 533/1 His favorite city has surpassed all others in..olie koeks, and New Year cookies. **1889** R. T. COOKE *Steadfast* vi. 78 Refreshing him with hot flip, oly koek, or Indian preserves. **1895** *Dialect Notes* I. 387 In the Dutch-settled districts the word *olykoeks*, which Washington Irving has made classic, is used for some of the varieties [of doughnut]. **1947** R. BEROLZHEIMER et al. *U.S. Regional Cook Bk.* 138 The doughnut originated in Holland where it was called 'olie koeken'.

olyet, olyf, -yff(e, obs. ff. OILLET, OLIVE.

olyfant, -aunt, etc., obs. ff. ELEPHANT.

Olympia (əʊ'lɪmpɪə). The name of a town at the southern end of Puget Sound, the capital of the state of Washington, used *absol.* or *attrib.* in **Olympia oyster** to designate a small oyster, *Ostrea lurida*, native to the region.

[**1887** G. B. GOODE *Fisheries U.S.: Geogr. Rev.* 626 No fishing is done at Olympia, the harbor being nearly bare at low water and lined with oysters. The shipment of these oysters to San Francisco is the only fishing industry of the town. The first shipment of these oysters was made two or three years ago.] **1908** *Nat. Geogr. Mag.* Mar. 225/1 New beds will have to be planted, and it will be five years before the so-called 'Olympia oyster' will again be on the market. **1911** *Encycl. Brit.* XX. 97/1 Olympia oysters are widely known in the Pacific coast region; they are obtained chiefly from Oyster Bay, Skookum Bay, North Bay and South Bay, all near Olympia. **1953** R. FROMAN *One Million Islands* 180 The tiny Olympia oysters also have their own unique flavor. **1957** M. MCCARTHY *Memories Catholic. Girlhood* viii. 203 Tiny Olympia oysters... Olympia oyster cocktail. **1961** *Spectator* 8 Dec. 879/1 American ingredients and American cooking..have always to me seemed most mysterious... Olympia pan roast (olympia is an oyster) and Green Goddess dressing..turn out to be entirely local [i.e. West Coast] inventions. **1965** M. TRACY *Shellfish Cookery* v. 99 Olympia oysters are tiny West Coast oysters... They are ambrosial, and fabulously expensive even near their home waters.

Olympiad (əʊ'lɪmpɪæd). Also 5–7 **Olympias.** [a. F. *Olympiade* (1553 in Hatz.-Darm., but prob. earlier), ad. L. *Olympias*, acc. *Olympiadem*, a. Gr. Ὀλυμπιάς, -άδ-, f. Ὀλύμπιος OLYMPIAN: see -AD.] **1. a.** A period of four years reckoned from one celebration of the Olympic games to the next, by which the ancient Greeks computed time, the year 776 B.C. being taken as the first year of the first Olympiad. Also *attrib.*, as ***Olympiad era.***

1398 TREVISA *Barth. De P.R.* IX. iv. (MS. Bodl.) lf. 92/1 Þe grees..cleped þe firste fyue ȝeres þe furst Olimpias. *c* **1532** DU WES *Introd. Fr.* in Palsgr. 1079 The Greeks were wont to reken by Olympiades whiche ben four yere. **1601** HOLLAND *Pliny* I. 6 This nature of hers, Pythagoras of Samos first found out, about the 42 olympias. *Ibid.* II. 564 The originall and beginning of the Olympiades. **1682** SIR T. BROWNE *Chr. Mor.* I. §21 Let Ephemerides not Olympiads give thee account of His mercies. **1819** BYRON *Proph. Dante* III. 158 Not Hellas can unroll Through her olympiads two such names. **1876** SMITH *Dict. Gr. & Rom. Antiq.* 835/1 A new Olympiad aera..came into use under the Roman emperors. **1882** LIDDELL & SCOTT *Greek Lex.* (ed. 7) s.v. Ὀλυμπιάς, The 1st Olympiad began 776 B.C.; the 293rd and last in 393 A.D.

b. A quadrennial celebration of the ancient Olympic Games.

a **1490** J. SKELTON tr. *Diodorus Siculus' Bibliotheca Historica* (1956) I. 382 Whiche maner of fayttis, thus ordeyned by his former instytucion, were callyd Olympiades. **1614** RALEGH *Hist. World* I. II. xxiii. 576 These Olympiads... To tell the great solemnitie of them, and with what exceeding great concourse of all Greece they were celebrated, I hold it a superfluous labour. **1728** I. NEWTON *Chronol. Anc. Kingdoms Amended* i. 47 This Breviary seems to have contained nothing more than a short account of the Victors in every Olympiad. **1852** G. GROTE *Hist. Greece* X. 439 They revenged themselves by pronouncing the 104th Olympiad to be no Olympiad at all. **1913** F. A. M. WEBSTER *Olympian Field Events* I. i. 7 We have certain proof that it [*sc.* javelin throwing] was a part of the Pentathlon in the Ancient Olympiads. **1960** A. R. BURN *Lyric Age Greece* ix. 177 He [*sc.* Pheidon of Argos] was said to have marched west to Olympia and presided over the Games of the eighth Olympiad (748). **1977** *Jrnl. Hellenic Stud.* XCVII. 16 This no doubt partly accounts for the well-known string of Spartan victories in running events at the early Olympiads.

2. A (quadrennial) celebration of the modern Olympic Games revived in 1896. Hence, an occurrence of other competitions held on a regular basis. Also *fig.*

1907 *Westm. Gaz.* 1 Aug. 10/3 When the last Olympiad was held at St. Louis, U.S.A., in 1904, it was decided to hold the next in Rome. **1923** *Glasgow Herald* 26 Mar. 11/4 But the Oxford supporters were clamant in their championing, and by the time the final preparations were made the element of discord, like the seed of the apple of the Olympiads, had entered into the multitudes. **1935** *Encycl. Sports* 440/2 The next Olympiad, as the games came to be called, was held at Stockholm [in 1912]. **1957** W. PERELMAN tr. *Flohr's Twelfth Chess Tournament of Nations* 5 The first Olympiad was held in London in 1927,..when 16 countries took part. **1959** *Listener* 22 Oct. 706/3 There was no reason why a British team [of Bridge players] should not be successful in the first World Olympiad next spring. **1964** —— 29 Oct. 695/1 Next week the chess olympiad begins in Tel Aviv, Israel... Unlike the Olympic Games, this is a team event, held every two years. **1967** —— 17 Aug. 213/2 Sixth-form specialisation is indeed producing diminishing returns: is the flight from maths and science compensated for by the winning of a mathematical Olympiad? **1972** *Daily Tel.* 21 June 14/5 Britain scored 42 victory points out of 60 during Monday's play in the World Bridge Olympiad. *Ibid.* 30 Aug. 9/3 Miss Pauline Dukelow, 16, paralysed from the age of three, is to receive the Andrew and Booth Courage award for the 21st Olympiad of the Paralysed at Heidelberg this month. **1976** *Radio Times* 15 May 37/1 In the following six Olympiads the Soviet Union have won over 500 medals. **1977** *Daily Times* (Lagos) 25 Feb. 17/4 This great cultural Olympiad was a gigantic step towards pan-Africanism and the unity of the black man.

Hence **Olympi'adic**, †**Olympi'adical** *adjs.*, of or pertaining to an Olympiad or Olympiads.

1638 MEDE *Wks.* (1672) 698 In this third year of the King, and at the end of this Olympiadical year,..came forth the Edict of Darius. **1890** *Cent. Dict.*, Olympiadic era.

Olympian (əʊ'lɪmpɪən), *a.* and *sb.* [ad. late L. *Olympiān-us*, f. earlier *Olympi-us*, a. Gr. Ὀλύμπιος of Olympus. The fem. Ὀλυμπία (sc. χώρα) i.e. Olympian region, Olympia, was spec. applied to a district of Elis in Greece, by the city of Pisa, where the Ὀλύμπια (sc. ἱερά), Olympia, or Olympic games, were held.] **A.** *adj.*

1. a. Of or belonging to Olympus; heavenly, celestial.

1603 HOLLAND *Plutarch's Mor.* 1329 Our Olympian or celestiall earth. **1667** MILTON *P.L.* VII. 3 Above th' Olympian Hill I soare, Above the flight of Pegasean wing. **1749** G. WEST *Odes Pindar* ii. (1753) I. 22 O Son of Rhea, God supreme! Whose kingly Hands th' Olympian Sceptre wield! **1818** KEATS *Endymion* II. 911 Light..quick and sharp enough to blight The Olympian eagle's vision. **1900** G. C. BRODRICK *Mem.* 262 What Professor Max Müller well calls his 'Olympian manners' never repelled me.

b. A competitor in the modern Olympic Games.

1976 *Billings* (Montana) *Gaz.* 27 June 7-F/6 The games are part of a 12-game tour for the *Olympians*, coached by North Carolina's Dean Smith, in preparation for the Montreal Games in July. **1977** *Time* 13 June 21/1 To support themselves during the rigors of year-round training, many Olympians have accepted deals from manufacturers and fees for appearing in track and field meets, hiding their earnings from Olympic, Amateur Athletic Union and international sports federations officials.

2. Of or belonging to Olympia: = OLYMPIC A. 2.

1593 SHAKS. *3 Hen. VI*, II. iii. 53 Such rewards As Victors weare at the Olympian Games. **1667** MILTON *P.L.* II. 530 As at th' Olympian Games or Pythian fields. **1873** SYMONDS *Grk. Poets* vi. 163 The Olympian games were held in Elis once in five years, during the summer.

B. *sb.* **1.** A native or inhabitant of Olympia; an athlete who took part in the Olympic games.

1606 SHAKS. *Tr. & Cr.* IV. v. 194 When that a ring of Greekes haue hem'd thee in, Like an Olympian wrestling.

2. An inhabitant of Olympus; one of the greater gods of ancient Greek mythology; *spec.* (*the Olympian*) Zeus or Jupiter.

1843 CARLYLE *Past & Pr.* I. i, Midas longed for gold, and insulted the Olympians. **1894** SIR E. SULLIVAN *Woman* 85 If you entered a grove or bathed in a river, you might tumble over a nymph or a satyr, or perhaps an Olympian.

Hence **O'lympianism**, the polytheistic system of the ancient Greeks, in which the gods of Olympus were the chief deities; **O'lympianize** *v.*, (*a*) *trans.*, to turn into an Olympian; (*b*) *intr.*, to play the Olympian; **O'lympianly**, **O'lympianwise** *advs.*, in the style of an Olympian.

1871 *Echo* 21 June, The *Times*..A little too Olympianly, ..intimates that Mr. Gladstone's argument for the Bill 'perishes on analysis'. **1893** W. C. WILKINSON in Barrows *Parlt. Relig.* II. 1247 Olympianism—if I may use such a word to describe a certain otherwise nondescript polytheistic idolatry. **1897** *Edin. Rev.* Apr. 460 Orpheus became in a sense Olympianised. **1898** G. MEREDITH *Odes Fr. Hist.* 8 A..gemmed, elected few..its..game Olympianwise perform.

Olympic (əʊ'lɪmpɪk), *a.* and *sb.* [ad. L. *Olympic-us*, a. Gr. Ὀλυμπικός, orig. 'of Olympus', later 'of Olympia'.] **A.** *adj.*

1. Of or belonging to Olympus; Olympian; celestial. *rare.* ? *Obs.*

1600 TOURNEUR *Transf. Metamorph.* vii, Th' olimpique Globe is now a hollow ball.

2. a. Of or belonging to Olympia in Elis (see OLYMPIAN), in which the most famous games of ancient Greece (the ***Olympic Games***) were celebrated in honour of the Olympian Zeus. Also *transf.*

a **1610** HEALEY *Epictetus* (1636) 48 Wouldest thou be victor in the Olympicke games? **1711** ADDISON *Spect.* No. 173 ¶3. I have looked over all the Olympic Games, and do not find anything in them like an Ass-Race. **1839** THIRLWALL *Greece* l. VI. 193 Dionysodorus, who had gained an Olympic prize. **1875** JOWETT *Plato* (ed. 2) III. 348 Their life will be blessed as the life of Olympic victors.

b. Of or pertaining to the modern ***Olympic Games***, which were revived as a quadrennial international athletic meeting at Athens in 1896 and have been held in various places since then. Also *transf.*

1896 *Scribner's Mag.* Apr. 453/1 The revival of the Olympic Games. Restoring the Stadion at Athens. **1908** *Westm. Gaz.* 31 Mar. 8/3 There is now some confusion with regard to the International Olympic games. **1914** R. BROOKE *Let.* 5 Dec. (1968) 638 A New Zealand youth who was fighting in Mexico, heard the news in August, walked 300 miles to the coast, got a boat, and turned up here. He is also an Olympic Swimmer: and *knows* the *South Seas*. **1936** J. BUCHAN *Island of Sheep* iv. 60 It was not the Peter that you knew in the War, but Peter ten years younger, with no grey in his beard, and as trim and light and hard as an Olympic athlete. **1960** *Times* 5 Sept. 4/6 Hill..was representing a Germany united for Olympic purposes. **1962** *Listener* 1 Feb. 234/1 A match [at Bridge] between Italy and the U.S.A. in the Olympic event two years ago. **1964** D. M. KUNZLE in G. C. Kunzle *Parallel Bars* 14 It was the whole conception of modern Olympic Gymnastics which was under fire. **1965** V. CANNING *Whip Hand* xii. 134 He's also first class with foils and sabre, Wimbledon standard tennis, Olympic standard swimming, and a double-first Oxford. **1968** MRS. L. B. JOHNSON *White House Diary* 10 Mar. (1970) 637 Lyndon..can break an Olympic record for getting dressed... We were out the door in about eight minutes. **1972** G. LYALL *Blame the Dead* i. 7 He scuttled away, carrying the pencil and cartridge case in front like a little Olympic torch. **1972** *Guardian* 19 Aug. 1/4 It is very important that he doesn't bring any infection that could affect other athletes in the Olympic Village. **1974** *Times* 21 Jan. 4/3 The boys are encouraged to join in games with them, swim in the pool of Olympic dimensions and just talk to them during breaks between intelligence tests and interviews. **1976** *Scotsman* 20 Nov. (Weekend Suppl.) 2/6 She used 30 cameramen and shot more than a million feet of film glorifying the Olympic ideal.

c. *Comb.*, with reference to the modern Olympic Games, as ***Olympic-size***, ***-sized***, ***-style*** adjs.

1966 J. BALL *Cool Cottontail* (1967) 17 A beautifully decked Olympic-size swimming pool. **1970** 'E. LATHEN' *Pick up Sticks* (1971) iv. 36 The heart of Fiord Haven, where Havenites will enjoy an Olympic-size indoor swimming pool. **1969** *Guardian* 16 June 2/6 The 600-acre military 'city', 40 miles from Saigon..contains..an Olympic-sized swimming pool. **1966** *Times* 28 Feb. (Canada Suppl.) p. xiv/5 Canada's 1967 Pan-American Games, which includes Olympic-style amateur wrestling.

B. *sb.* An Olympic game: usually in *pl.* Used esp. of the revived Olympic Games. Also *transf.* and *fig.*

c **1640** [SHIRLEY] *Capt. Underwit* I. in Bullen *O. Pl.*, To see the Clownes sell fish in the hall and ride the wild mare, and such Olimpicks. **1678** W. DILLINGHAM *Serm. Fun. Lady Alston* 8 In the Greek Olympicks, or in the Roman Cirque. **1711** SHAFTESB. *Charac.* (1737) I. 269 At their fairs ..they perform their rude olympicks. **1928** in *Funk's Stand. Dict.* **1948** KIERAN & DALEY *Story of Olympic Games* (rev. ed.) xiii. 327 The 'surest thing' in the Olympics never looked surer. **1948** *Official Rep. Olympic Games* (Brit. Olympic Assoc.) 41/1 No boxing competition of comparable size had been attempted anywhere in the world since the Berlin Olympics of 1936. **1949** W. M. HUGILL in *Phoenix* (Toronto) III. 31 One school of thought has repudiated any connection between culture and the modern Olympics. **1951** *European Bridge Rev.* June 5/1 The 1951 Australian Jubilee Year World Olympic for contract bridge pairs. **1974** *Encycl. Brit. Macropædia* II. 274/1 The development of the modern Olympics into the pre-eminent athletic events in the world. **1976** *New Scientist* 28 Oct. 203/2 Any competitor in the gravitational Olympics must be able to pass the three classical tests of relativity that Einstein proposed in 1916.

Hence †**Olympicly** *adv.*, in Olympic fashion.

1599 NASHE *Lenten Stuffe* 33.

†**O'lympical**, *a. Obs.* [See -ICAL.] = prec. A.

1432-50 tr. *Higden* (Rolls) II. 423 Victorye..at the actes Olimpicalle. **1592** R. D. *Hypnerotomachia* 83 Removing from my heart, all fearefull thoughts, with her Olymphicall aspects. **1608** TOPSELL *Serpents* (1658) 653 Clemens Alexandrinus..hath these words:..'These fat, dull, grosse, and Olympicall enemies of ours are worser then wasps'.

Olympionic (əʊlɪmpɪ'ɒnɪk). [ad. Gr. Ὀλυμπιόνῑκος conquering in the Olympic games (νίκη victory).] An ode in honour of a victor in the Olympic games.

1799-81 JOHNSON *L.P.*, *Cowley* Wks. II. 49 In the Olympionick an oath is mentioned in a single word.

†**Olympionicest.** *Obs.* [irreg. f. L. *Olympionīcēs*, a. Gr. Ὀλυμπιονίκης a victor in the Olympic games.] A victor in the Olympic games.

a **1656** USSHER *Ann.* (1658) 89 Sirnamed..the *Olympionicest*, i.e. one that had won the bell in the games at Olympus.

Olympus (əʊ'lɪmpəs). (Also 6 **Olimp.**) [L. *Olympus*, a. Gr. Ὄλυμπος name of several lofty mountains, each app. the highest in its own district; esp. that mentioned below.] A mountain in the north of Thessaly, the fabled abode of the greater gods of ancient Greek mythology; hence applied to heaven as the divine abode; rarely, to the sky.

[**1549** *Compl. Scot.* Epistle 3 Vndir the machine of the supreme olimp. *Ibid.* v. 32.]

1580 STANYHURST *Upon the Death of Ld. G. Fitzgirald* in *Æneid*, etc. (Arb.) 152 Thy soul God gladdeth with saincts in blessed Olympus. **1607** SHAKS. *Cor.* v. iii. 30 As if Olympus to a Mole-hill should In supplication Nod. **1715-20** POPE *Iliad.* I. 551 To move thy suit I'll go To great Olympus crown'd with fleecy snow. **1878** J. PAYN *By Proxy* I. iii. 25 The gods of the Buddhist Olympus. **1879** FROUDE *Cæsar* ii. 16 The Greeks introduced them to an Olympus of divinities.

olypha(u)nt, -vaunt, obs. ff. ELEPHANT.

olyue, obs. form of ALIVE, OLIVE.

†**olyver currant**, *adv. phr. Obs.* [ad. OF. phr. *avoir l'olivier* or *son olivier courant* (in Cotgrave, *Il a tous ses oliviers courans*, hee hath his full swindge or libertie, he doth what he list); so med. L. *olivero currente* (Giraldus Cambrensis): origin unascertained. See Gaston Paris, *Romania* XVIII. 132 ff., Paul Meyer, *Ibid.* XXXII. 450-1, *Times Lit. Suppl.* 10 Aug. 1933, p. 537.] In accordance with one's plans or desires.

1470 SIR J. PASTON in *Paston Lett.* II. 415 If ye cowde fynde the meanes..to cawse [the] Meyr in my Lordes ere to telle hym..that the love of the contre and syte restyth on owr syde..thys wolde do nonn harme, if it be soo that that [*sic*] all thynge go olyver currant.

‖**om** (ɔːm), *int.* Also o'm. [Skr.] In Hinduism and Buddhism, an utterance of assent used in prayer and meditation. Also as *sb.*, an instance or example of this assent, and as *v. intr.*, to utter the assent. (See also quot. 1917.)

1788 W. JONES in *Asiatick Researches* I. 262, I am inclined, indeed, to believe, that not only *Crishna* or *Vishnu*, but even *Brahmà* and *Siva*, when united, and expressed by the mystical word *o'm*, were designed by the first idolaters to represent the Solar fire. **1810** E. MOOR *Hindu Pantheon* 410 The character, that, if uttered, would yield the sound of *o'm*; or, being triliteral, better, perhaps, written *aum*. *Ibid.* 412 A suppression of breath is thus explained by an ancient legislator to imply the following meditation: '*Om*! earth! sky! heaven!' **1899** R. WHITEING *No. 5 John St.* xv. 153 The Brahmin leads us gently to the outermost courts of Nirvana. In spite of the outward symbol, we look within, and there we may hope to find *om*. **1917** A. B. KEITH in *Encycl. Relig. & Ethics* IX. 490/2 The first evidence of this important position of the word is to be found in the *Aitareya Brāhmana* (v. 32) in which it is declared that *om* is the world of heaven and the sun, and where it is resolved into the three letters *a*, *u*, and *m*. **1937** M. COVARRUBIAS *Island of Bali* (1972) ix. 318 Typical Brahmana are the speculations about the sacred syllable *ong*, the Om of India. **1956** E. WOOD *Yoga Dict.* 113/1 *Om*, the greatest *mantra*..or word of power. *Ibid.* 114/1 *Om* is recited by devout Hindus at the beginning of all prayers, hymns and words of worship or aspiration. **1971** *Illustr. Weekly India* 4 Apr. 31/2 The note greets me, '*Hare Krishna*. Please accept my *Om* prayers for your eternal well being. I would like to see you for a few minutes.' **1972** P. HOLROYDE *Indian Music* ii. 58 The sound '*om*'.., pronounced 'a-u-m', rings out like the tolling of a cathedral bell. **1976** B. JACKSON *Flameout* i. 17 He..took deep yogic breaths, loudly hummed a long, resonant '*om—om—om—*'. ..'It's sure good to hear you *om*-ing.'

om, var. of *hom*, form of HEM *pron.*, them.

-oma, terminal element repr. Gr. -ωμα, in which ω repr. ω (or ο) in the parent word (usu. a vb.) and -μα is a Gr. suffix forming neut. sbs., exemplified in Eng. words adopted from the Gr. such as CARCINOMA, COLOBOMA, DERMA, DIPLOMA, ECZEMA, GLAUCOMA, PHYMA, PLASMA, SARCOMA, TRACHOMA, and in words on Gr. analogy such as LIPOMA. In *Bot.* -*oma* has usu. been anglicized to -OME. In *Med.* the examples of *sarcoma* (17th c. in English) and *carcinoma* (18th c.) have been taken as types on which to base new names of neoplasms and other localized swellings, *-oma* (†*-ome*) being used as a suffix denoting 'tumour, growth' (cf. also Gr. ὄγκωμα swelling): e.g. FIBROMA († FIBROME), CEMENTOMA, OLIGODENDROGLIOMA, TUBERCULOMA († TUBERCULOME).

omacle, erron. form of ONYCLE *Obs.*, onyx.

‖**omadhaun** ('ɒmədɔːn). Also 9 **omadaun, -dawn, -dhawn, -dhoun, -thaun**. [a. Ir. *amadan* fool.] A fool: as an Irish term of abuse.
1818 LADY MORGAN *Autobiog.* (1859) 32 Be aisy, you omadaun! **1841** S. C. HALL *Ireland* I. 263 The Omadawn!—to think of his taking in a poor soft boy like that, who was away from his mother. **1894** HALL CAINE *Manxman* 27 You gobmouthed omathaun. **1895** JANE BARLOW *Strangers at Lisconnel* 84 Big Hugh McInerney, whom people were apt to call an omadhawn.

omage, omager(e, obs. ff. HOMAGE, -ER.

Omaha ('əʊməhɑː). Also †**Maha**, †**Omawhaw**. Pl. **Omaha, Omahas**. [ad. Omaha *umonhon* upstream people.] A Siouan people in northeastern Nebraska, or their language; a member of this people. Also *attrib.* or as *adj.*
1804 W. CLARK in Lewis & Clark *Orig. Jrnls. Lewis & Clark Expedition* (1904) I. 34 As we were pushing off this morning two Canoos Loaded with fur &c came to from the Mahas nation. *Ibid.* 124 This Village was built by a Indian Chief of the Maha nation. **1814** H. M. BRACKENRIDGE *Views Louisiana* I. vi. 76 Mahas, (or Oo-ma-ha) Reside on the Maha creek. **1823** E. JAMES *Acct. Expedition Rocky Mts.* I. 190 Several of the Pawnee *caches*..had been broken open and robbed of their corn by the Omawhaws. **1839** *Boston Weekly Mag.* 12 Jan. 145/2 The Omaha village was one of the most beautiful that can be imagined. **1854** W. G. SIMMS *Southward Ho!* 406 The Pawnees and the Omahas were neighboring but hostile nations. **1900** G. B. GRINNELL *Indians of To-day* 12 He killed one more Omaha. **1920** [see AVUNCULATE]. **1936** F. B. STREETER *Prairie Trails* iv. 190 He went with the Omaha Indians on a buffalo hunt. **1957** [see KANSA]. **1964, 1968** [see CROW *a.* 2]. **1972** W. B. LOCKWOOD *Panorama Indo-Europ. Lang.* vii. 117 The plains between the Mississippi and the Missouri were occupied by the Siouan family [of languages], of which the most significant today are Dakota (45,000) and Omaha (10,000). **1974** *Encycl. Brit. Micropædia* VII. 528/3 *Omaha*, North American Indian people of the Dhegiha branch of the Siouan language stock. *Ibid.*, Omaha social organization was elaborate, with a class system of chiefs, priests, physicians and commoners.

‖**omalgia** (əʊ'mældʒɪə). *Path.* [f. Gr. ὦμ-ος shoulder + -αλγία from ἄλγος pain.] Rheumatism in the shoulder.
1892 *Syd. Soc. Lex.*, *Omalgia*,..pain in the shoulder. **1897** *Allbutt's Syst. Med.* III. 63 Varieties of muscular rheumatism..as omalgia when the shoulder muscles are affected.

omalo-, incorrect form of HOMALO-.

omander (əʊ'mændə(r)). A name of an East Indian ebony obtained from the tree *Diospyros Ebenaster*: akin to calamander.
1843 HOLTZAPFFEL *Turning*, &c. 82 Mr. Laird says there are three varieties of Coromandel; the *Calamander*,..the *Calemberri*,..and the *Omander*, the ground of which is as light as English yew, but of a redder cast, with a few slight veins and marks of darker tints. **1858** SIMMONDS *Dict. Trade*, *Omander-wood*.

omang, -e, obs. forms of AMONG.

omanhene ('əʊmænheɪneɪ). [Ashanti, f. *oman* council + *-hene* combining form of *ohene* chief.] Among the Ashanti people of West Africa, a paramount chief of a state or district, under whom are the lesser chiefs of villages.
1909 MOORE & GUGGISBERG *We Two in W. Africa* xi. 146, I met my first *omanhin* at Tarkwa—'king' he would have been called some years ago but his title is not officially recognised now, the head chief of a tribe being known by the native equivalent of *omanhin*. **1923** R. S. RATTRAY *Ashanti* xxii. 264, I am greatly indebted to an Ashanti chief, Osai Bonsu, *Omanhene* of Mampon, for permitting his drummer to drum this complete history into a phonograph. **1955** D. E. APTER *Gold Coast in Transition* iv. 94 The chief became known as the *omanhene* or head of council, among the Ashanti. **1959** A. ABBS *Ashanti Boy* i. 17 That was nothing strange to a conscientious Omanhene to whom the family in its widest sense meant 'the tribe'. **1961** *Guardian* 10 Nov. 1/1 Chiefs and their retinues from all over the country.. Nenes, Omanhenes, Nanas, Niis, Togbes, and..[the] Fiaga of Peki. **1962** C. G. BAËTA *Prophetism in Ghana* iii. 61 The head of the Church is referred to as *Omanhene* or 'Paramount Chief'.

Omani (əʊ'mɑːnɪ), *sb.* and *a.* Also 9 **Omanee, Omany**. [Arab., f. *Oman* name of a coastal region in the south-east of the Arabian peninsula + *-i* adj. suffix.] **A.** *sb.* A native or inhabitant of Oman. **B.** *adj.* Also in form *Oman* (the place-name used *attrib.*). Of or pertaining to Oman or its inhabitants.
c **1819** F. WARDEN in *Sel. Rec. Bombay Govt.* (1856) No. 24. 433 It would give the Omanees sufficient time to unite and assemble for their general defence. **1819** —— in *Ibid.* 44 It is probable that the Oman Chiefs of the Hinavi tribe will ..return to their former relations with the Imaum. **1838** J. R. WELLSTED *Trav. Arabia* I. ii. 16 In consequence of the difference in their faith, the Omán Arabs and Persians seldom intermarry. *Ibid.* xix. 292 The Omány in all ages is celebrated in the songs of the Arabs as the fleetest. **1865** W. G. PALGRAVE *Narr. Journey through Arabia* II. xv. 256 The principal family whose chiefs headed the original settlement was, according to 'Omânee tradition, that of the Ya'aribah. *Ibid.* 262 These new hostilities on the part of Islam suggested to the sectarian 'Omânees the expediency of new measures. **1871** G. P. BADGER *Hist. of Imâms & Seyyids of Omân* p. xvii, A battle was fought in which the 'Omânis were defeated with great loss. *Ibid.* p. xxxvii, In order to test the pluck of the 'Omâny sovereign..he sent him a viciously restive horse. **1928** A. T. WILSON *Persian Gulf* xii. 174 The inhabitants virtually deserted the island, by this means bringing the Omani occupation to an end. A year or two later..the Omanis seized certain islands off the Persian coast. **1931** E. WAUGH *Remote People* 165 Instead of the cultured, rather decadent aristocracy of the Oman Arabs, we have given them [*sc.* the Zanzibar Islanders] a caste of just, soap-loving young men with public school blazers. **1973** *Nat. Geographic* Feb. 209/1 Omanis danced in the streets for days. **1973** *Times* 15 Feb. 7/1 He saw in Muscat an Omani whom he recognized as having served as a political commissar in..Dhufar in 1971. **1973** *Black Panther* 4 Aug. 11/2 The struggle of the Oman people has..had wide success in the building of institutions to insure the people's survival. **1974** *Times* 18 Jan. 15/4 The 'Red Line' is the name given by the Omani guerrillas to the road linking the town of Salalah..to the Omani capital Muscat.

Omaresque (əʊmə'rɛsk), *a. rare.* [f. as next + -ESQUE.] Suggestive of Omar Khayyam or his poetry.
1892 *Academy* 5 Nov. 404/1 In shorter measures there is often an Omaresque effect of thought.

Omarian (əʊ'mɑːrɪən), *a.* and *sb.* [f. the name of the Persian mathematician and epigrammatist, Ghiyāthuddīn Abulfath *'Omar* bin Ibrāhīm al-Khayyāmī (*c* 1100) + -IAN.] **A.** *adj.* Of or pertaining to Omar Khayyam or his poetry; having the style or character of his poetry. **B.** *sb.* A student or admirer of Omar Khayyam; a member of the Omar Khayyam Club.
1898 *Daily News* 31 Jan. 6/3 To the devout Omarian a reproduction in black-and-white of this early MS. will carry something of the fragrance [etc.]. **1898** *Westm. Gaz.* 22 Feb. 3/4 The next service demanded of Omarian scholarship is an edition in the original Persian. **1901** *Ibid.* 8 Jan. 2/3 Marie's needs are almost Omarian in their simplicity. **1907** *Daily Chron.* 13 Feb. 3/3 Serious Omarians..are willing to do more for their master than merely turn down an empty glass. **1934** A. J. A. SYMONS *Quest for Corvo* xi. 154 An American Omarian..contributed an Introduction.

Hence **O'marianism, 'Omarism**, admiration or imitation of Omar Khayyam; the doctrines or cult of Omar Khayyam. So **'Omarite** = OMARIAN *a.*
1897 *Daily Chron.* 9 Dec. 7/2 All more or less imbued with the spirit of what is called 'Omarianism', and all.. decorously convivial. **1898** J. H. MCCARTHY in *Westm. Gaz.* 22 Feb. 3/3 The protest against what may be called Omarism. **1900** *Academy* 21 July 55/2 Mr. Fawcett called Omarism a fad. *Ibid.*, The Omarite message was interpreted: 'Get drunk as often as you can, and stay so long as you can, for there's nothing in life half so profitable.' **1918** *Naval Intelligence* xxxix. 180 Stanza after stanza, which he reeled off in an ecstatic and maudlin manner with his eyes half closed and his head wagging—all Omarites do this, you may have noticed.

omast, variant of OVEMEST.

‖**omasum** (əʊ'meɪsəm). [L., bullock's tripe.] The third stomach of a ruminant; the *psalterium* or manyplies.
1706 PHILLIPS, *Omasum*, the thick and fatty part of the Belly of an Ox, etc., fat Tripe: See *Abomasum*. **1892** in *Syd. Soc. Lex.*

Omayyad, var. UMAYYAD *a.* and *sb.*

ombe-: see UMBE-.

omber, obs. form of UMBER, a grayling.

omberty, variant of UMBERTY *Obs.*

ombra(h, obs. f. OMRAH, Muslim grandee.

ombrage, -eous, obs. ff. UMBRAGE, -EOUS.

ombre ('ɒmbə(r), 'ɒmbreɪ), *sb.*[1] Also 7 **l'ombre, l'hombre, umbre, 7–9 hombre, 8–9 omber**. [a. Sp. *hombre* (:—L. *hominem*) man (see quot. 1662), perh. through F. *hombre, ombre* (17th c. in Hatz.-Darm.).]

1. A card-game played by three persons, with forty cards, the eights, nines, and tens of the ordinary pack being thrown out.
Ombre was very popular in the 17th–18th centuries, but about 1726 it was superseded as the fashionable card-game by Quadrille.
1660–61 E. GOWER 26 Jan. in *5th Rep. Hist. MSS. Comm.* 202/1 To play at Hombre, the new game at cards now in fashion at court. **1662** COTGRAVE *Wits Interpr.* (ed. 2) 353 L'Ombre is a Spanish Game at Cards, wherein he who undertakes to play it saith *Jo soy L'Ombre*, i.e. I am the man; for so the word *L'Ombre* signifieth. **1668** ETHEREDGE *She would if she could* III. iii, Were [I] every afternoon at my Lady Briefes..at Umbre and Quebas. **1678** WYCHERLEY *Plain-Dealer* II. i, Captain, I beg your pardon: You will not make one at Hombre? **1691** ETHEREDGE *Poems* Wks. (1888) 378 Such ropes of pearl her arms encumber, She scarce can deal the cards at ombre. **1706** PHILLIPS, *Omber*, or *Ombre*. **1712–14** POPE *Rape Lock* III. 27 At Ombre singly to decide their doom. *a* **1761** J. CAWTHORN *Birth Genius* Poems (1771) 54 They taught him with address and skill To shine at ombre and quadrille. **1848** THACKERAY *Vanity Fair* xlvii, The night when he and the Marquis of Steyne won a hundred thousand from a great personage at Hombre. **1887** *All Year Round* 5 Feb. 68 Ombre and Quadrille are terribly complicated for a beginner.

2. The player at this game who undertakes to win the pool.
1727–41 CHAMBERS *Cycl.* s.v., If any will attempt for it [the stake or game], he henceforth is called the ombre. **1878** H. GIBBS *Ombre* 20 He is then the *Ombre* (El Hombre) the man of the moment—the champion who stands the game.

3. *Comb.*, as *ombre-box, -player, -table*.
1711 STEELE *Spect.* No. 140 ¶10 Ladies..who as soon as the Ombre-Table is called for..are immediately Transmigrated into the veriest Wasps in Nature. **1735** *Pope's Lett.* I. 319 Things..below the Consideration of a Wit, and an Ombre-player. **1878** H. GIBBS *Ombre* 9 A regular Ombre-box has four trays within it each with its several coloured counters, and in the middle a pool-dish.

‖**ombré** (ɔ̃bre), *sb.*[2] and *a.* Also **ombre**. [Fr., pa. pple. of *ombrer* to shade.] **A.** *sb.* A fabric woven or dyed in a series of colour tones graduating from light to dark and usu. producing a striped effect. Also, such an effect or design.
1895 *Funk's Stand. Dict.* II. 1227/2 *Ombré*.., a cheap grade of silk prints. **1921** A. GANSWINDT *Dyeing Silk* 147 *Ombres*. Shaded effects on hank silk can be obtained by binding the hanks firmly on rods, using only a small amount of dyestuff in the bath [etc.]. **1930** R. CUTHILL tr. *Schober's Silk* iv. 271 *Ombré*, a fabric in a number of colours, one fading off into the other, this effect being obtained by the use of yarns printed before weaving. **1966** A. J. BLISS *Dict. Foreign Words & Phrases Current Eng.* 264 *Ombré*.., (a fabric) woven with variably dyed yarns so as to produce a shaded effect. **1975** *Country Life* 30 Oct. 1192/2 Degradé, a fabric that is shaded from light to dark and sometimes called ombré in the dress side of the trade.

B. *adj.* Shaded from light to dark in tints of one or more colours.
1918 S. KLINE *Man. Processes Winding* iii. 61 Ombré warps. **1928** *Daily Express* 27 Feb. 5/5 Rainbow effects have been produced by the use of what are known as ombre yarns, in which cotton and artificial silk of different colours are admixed. **1963** *Times* 24 Jan. 12/4 He varies the plain colours with *ombré* effect and brilliant spots. **1969** *Daily Tel.* 21 Apr. 12/6 Other leather is speckly and *ombre* with tiny splatters of black on grey highlighted with *art nouveau* silver buckles. **1974** D. RAMSAY *No Cause to Kill* I. 9 She was tempted by a blue silk *ombré* plaid.

‖**ombre chevalier** (ɔ̃br ʃəvalje). Also **omble chevalier**. [Fr.] A freshwater race of the char, *Salvelinus alpinus*, of the family Salmonidæ, found in certain French and Swiss lakes, esp. the Lake of Geneva.
1884 G. B. GOODE *Fisheries U.S.: Nat. Hist. Aquatic Animals* 501 The Saibling of Bavaria and Austria is one and the same thing with the 'Ombre Chevalier' of France and Switzerland,..the 'Char' of England and Scotland. **1905** D. S. JORDAN *Guide to Study of Fishes* II. iv. 108 The only really well-authenticated species of charr in European waters is the red charr, sälbling, or ombre chevalier. **1940** A. SIMON *Conc. Encycl. Gastron.* II. 67/1 *Omble Chevalier*... The best fish of the Swiss and Savoy lakes; it never leaves the lakes for the running waters of rivers. **1960** E. DAVID *French Provincial Cooking* 38 Some *ombres-chevaliers* from the lac du Bourget, cooked and left to get cold in white wine. **1968** V. CANNING *Melting Man* iii. 58 Tonight I shall be in France, eating *omble chevalier*, straight from the lake. **1971** *Times* 29 Mar. (Switzerland Suppl.) p. iii/5 The *ombre chevalier*, a type of salmon trout, especially from the Lake of Geneva.

‖**ombrelle** (ɔ̃brɛl). *poet.* [Fr.] A parasol or sunshade.
1925 E. SITWELL *Troy Park* 75 What hotels Hide their bustles and their gay ombrelles. **1942** —— *Street Songs* 13 All that I knew of shade Was the cloud, my ombrelle of rustling grey Sharp silk.

‖**ombrellino** (ombrel'lino). [It.] (See quot. 1957.) Also, a parasol or sunshade.
1847 F. W. FABER *Let.* in R. Chapman *Father Faber* (1961) viii. 163 It was a dark still night, and the bell and lights and singing and the flashing *ombrellino* had a most touching effect among the trees. We deposited our Lord in His own tabernacle after receiving His Benediction. **1949** D. ATTWATER *Catholic Encycl. Dict.* (ed. 2) 354/1 *Ombrellino* (It., a little umbrella). A small flat canopy with one staff borne over the Blessed Sacrament when it is carried from its own altar to another for exposition, etc., and, in some countries, when it is taken to the sick. **1957** *Oxf. Dict. Chr. Ch.* 983/2 *Ombrellino*, in the W. Church the small umbrella-like canopy of white silk carried over the Blessed Sacrament when it is moved informally from one place to another. **1964** *Punch* 26 Feb. 326/3, I came round lying on the sand under an *ombrellino*.

‖**ombres chinoises** (ɔ̃br ʃinwaz). [Fr., Chinese shadows.] = GALANTY SHOW.
1785 LADY NEWDIGATE *Let.* 25 May in A. E. Newdigate-Newdegate *Cheverels* (1898) iv. 61 We talk of having another representation of our *Ombres Chinoises* on Friday. **1802** *Monthly Mag.* Sept. 132/1 Besides the great theatre, there are..several smaller ones for..different exhibitions, such as ombres Chinoises. **1968** G. SPEAIGHT in M. Batchelder *Puppet Theatre Handbk.* p. xx, 'Ombres chinoises' were extremely popular in France and England during the eighteenth century, but later fell from favour. **1950** H. W. WHANSLAW *Shadow Play* vi. 48 Tronchet describes the theatre of Francois-Dominique Seraphin, in the Palais Royale,..where he exhibited his famous *Ombres Chinoises-Le Spectacle des Enfants de France*. **1960** O. BLACKHAM *Shadow Puppets* 98 In March 1779 Astley re-opened his Amphitheatre near Westminster Bridge, and here the *ombres chinoises* continued to be advertised right up to the summer of 1790. **1974** *Encycl. Brit. Micropædia* VII. 530/2 *Ombres chinoises*.., European version of the Chinese

shadow puppet show, introduced in Europe in the mid-18th century by returning travellers.

ombrifuge (ˈɒmbrɪfjuːdʒ). *rare*$^{-1}$. [? irreg. f. Gr. ὄμβρος shower of rain + -FUGE.] A refuge or shelter against rain.

1868 BROWNING *Ring & Bk.* x. 465 The belfry proves a fortress of a sort,..Turns sunscreen, paravent, and ombrifuge.

ombro-, comb. f. Gr. ὄμβρος shower of rain: **omˈbrogenous** *a.*, of moorland or marsh, needing a high rainfall for its development; **ˈombrograph** [see -GRAPH], 'an automatic instrument for recording the time of occurrence, quantity, and rapidity of rainfall' (Funk, 1893); **omˈbrology** [see -LOGY], the branch of meteorology that deals with rain; hence **ombroˈlogical** *a.*; **omˈbrometer** [see -METER], a rain-gauge; **ˈombrophil** [see -PHIL], see quot.; **omˈbrophilous** *a.* [a. G. *ombrophile* (J. Wiesner 1893, in *Sitzungsber. Akad. Wiss. Wien* Abth. I. CII. 503)], of a plant, able to flourish in conditions of excessive moisture; so **omˈbrophily**; **ˈombrophobe** [see -PHOBE], see quot.; **omˈbrophobous** *a.* [a. G. *ombrophobe* (J. Wiesner 1893, *loc. cit.*)], of a plant, not well adapted to very wet conditions; so **omˈbrophoby**.

1939 A. G. TANSLEY *Brit. Islands & their Vegetation* xxxv. 718 Blanket moss or bog—*ombrogenous. **1946** *Proc. Prehist. Soc.* XII. 3 The blanket-bog is termed an 'ombrogenous' mire, to indicate the fact that its existence is directly determined by the rainfall and evaporation to which it is subject. **1952** P. W. RICHARDS *Trop. Rain Forest* ix. 215 The vegetation of the ombrogenous moors is tall evergreen forest. **1975** J. R. ETHERINGTON *Environment & Plant Ecol.* iii. 91 Some other peat soils are topogenous rather than ombrogenous. **1865** *Athenæum* No. 1942. 54/2 The *Ombrological Almanack. **1845** P. LEGH (*title*) Hints for Anemology and *Ombrology, with a Weather Almanac for 1840 and 1845. **1744** R. PICKERING in *Phil. Trans.* XLIII. 12 (2) Of the *Ombrometer. This Machine consists of a tin Funnel, whose Surface is an Inch square, a flat Board, and a glass Tube let into the Middle of it in a Groove,..and an Index. **1763** BORLASE *ibid.* LIII. 29 If you..keep an ombrometer, and register of the rain. **1794** *Gentl. Mag.* LXIV. I. 295, I found a very brief description of an instrument of this kind, but under the word *ombrometer*. **1897** WILLIS *Flower. Pl.* I. 153 Wiesner..divides plants into **ombrophiles*, which can undergo without injury long-continued rain, and **ombrophobes*, whose leaves soon decay or fall off under such circumstances. **1895** *Jrnl. R. Microsc. Soc.* 194 Plants which, on the one hand are uninjured (*ombrophilous) and on the other hand are injured (*ombrophobous) by excessive rainfall. *Ibid.*, Some species ..growing in moist shady situations, are nevertheless ombrophobous. *Ibid.*, Xerophilous plants..are hardly ever ombrophilous. **1903** W. R. FISHER tr. *Schimper's Plant-Geogr.* I. i. 2 Xerophytes perish after two or three days of continuous rain; they are rain-avoiding, ombrophobous, whereas hygrophytes are, as a rule, ombrophilous... Ombrophilous foliage is capable of being wetted, ombrophobous foliage is unwettable. *Ibid.* III. i. 225 Reference may here be made to Wiesner's investigations regarding the *ombrophily and *ombrophoby of tropical vegetation. **1897** *Jrnl. R. Microsc. Soc.* 412 Ombrophoby of flowers. By this term Prof. A. Hansgirg designates the phenomena of curvature by which many flowers protect themselves against injury from long-continued rain or other exposure to moisture.

ombú (ɒmˈbuː). Also ombu. [Amer. Sp., f. Guarani *umbú*.] An evergreen tree, *Phytolacca dioica*, of the family Phytolaccaceæ, native to temperate regions of South America. Also *attrib.*

1871 R. O. CUNNINGHAM *Notes Nat. Hist. Strait of Magellan* xiv. 466 A variety of cottages, each shaded by the umbrageous foliage of the large Ombu. **1878** E. CLARK *Visit S. Amer.* ix. 123 The gnarled ombus and willows, and poplars and peach trees, affording the welcome shade. **1902** W. H. HUDSON *El Ombú* i. 1 In all this district..you will not find a tree as big as this ombú, standing solitary, where there is no house. *Ibid.* 2 They say..that those who sit much in the ombú shade become crazed. **1923** *Chambers's Jrnl.* Dec. 828/2 A huge, gnarled tree, tremendously thick and spreading like an *ombú*. **1931** B. MIALL tr. *Guenther's Naturalist in Brazil* iv. 79 In the Argentine I have often admired the monumental character of one of the native trees, the Ombú. The roots rise from the ground like great brown bladders, lifting the trunk into the air, and from the trunk the branches spring like a tracery. **1941** E. NASH *I Liked Life I Lived* vi. 70 The humble dwelling was called the house of the twenty-five ombú trees. **1961** G. DURRELL *Whispering Land* i. 30 Small, neat *estancias*, gleaming white in the shade of huge, caruncculated *ombú* trees, that stood massively and grimly on their enormous squat trunks. **1969** T. H. EVERETT *Living Trees of World* 144/1 The ombú becomes 60 feet tall with a branch spread of more than 100 feet. From the bottom of its very thick trunk it develops extraordinary irregular outgrowths that look like fantastic and bulky roots. *Ibid.*, The elliptic or ovate leaves of the ombú are evergreen and male and female flowers are on separate trees; the fruits are small and berry-like. **1975** *New Yorker* 14 Apr. 36/1 They give shade from the bare sun to man and beast, and men mark their way on the endless plains by remembering this or that ombu tree.

Ombudsman (ˈɒmbʊdzmən). Also with lower-case initial. [Sw. (see below), f. *ombud* commissioner, agent, repr. ON. *umboð* charge, commission, *umboðsmaðr* commissary, manager.] An official appointed to investigate complaints by individuals against maladministration by public authorities; *spec.* in U.K., the Parliamentary Commissioner for Administration. (Corresp. to Sw. *justitieombudsmannen.*) Also *attrib.* and in extended and *fig.* uses.

In Sweden, an *ombudsman* is a deputy of a group, particularly a trade union or a business concern, appointed to handle the legal affairs of the group and protect its interests generally. With the definite suffix *-en* it normally denotes a particular office. The office of *justitieombudsmannen* (abbrev. *JO*), which was instituted in Sweden in 1809, is the one which is referred to in the following quotations, and it is this office which was established in New Zealand in 1962. In Sweden the office of *militieombudsmannen* (abbrev. *MO*) was also introduced in 1809 as a parliamentary commissioner appointed to supervise and enforce the observance of laws and statutes concerned with national defence. In 1968 the offices of *justitieombudsmannen* and *militieombudsmannen* were replaced by four independent officers under the joint name of *justitieombudsmännen*. The word *pressombudsman* connotes a public relations officer, and in its definite form *pressombudsmannen* an office instituted in 1969 to supervise and enforce ethical standards of the press.

The office of *ombudsman* was introduced in Finland in 1919, in Denmark in 1954, and in Norway in 1962.

[**1911** *Encycl. Brit.* XXVI. 195/2 By revisers elected annually the Riksdag controls the finances of the kingdom, and by an official (*justitieombudsman*) elected in the same way the administration of justice is controlled; he can indict any functionary of the state who has abused his power. **1914** J. GUINCHARD *Sweden* iii. 200 The Riksdag has yet another form of control over the High Court of Justice and the Supreme Administrative Court in that the 'Justitieombudsman' may in certain cases arraign a member of the Court before the Court of Impeachment. **1958** S. HURWITZ in *Public Law* Autumn 236 A precedent existed in Sweden, where a 'Justitieombudsman' and a 'Militieombudsman', appointed by Parliament, were introduced in 1809 and in 1915 respectively.] **1959** *Listener* 16 July 89/1 Sweden has been running the Ombudsman system for 150 years, and Denmark has a very active Ombudsman. **1963** *Times* 23 Apr. 13/6 The perfunctoriness with which the Government recently rejected the conclusions of the unofficial inquiry conducted by Justice into the Scandinavian *ombudsman* procedure was disappointing. **1966** *N.Z. News* 28 Sept. 3/2 Britain's Ombudsman, Sir Edmund Compton, is now in New Zealand consulting New Zealand's Ombudsman, Sir Guy Powles, about the workings of his office and the way in which he deals with complaints. **1966** S. OAKLEY *Story of Sweden* xiv. 164 The private citizen was protected from the bureaucracy by a so-called *ombudsman*, elected by the Estates to hear and investigate complaints against abuses of power by public servants. **1969** *Daily Tel.* 13 Dec. 1/5 Complaints from hospital patients and staff may shortly be dealt with by a special type of Ombudsman. **1970** MORRIS & HAWKINS *Honest Politician's Guide to Crime Control* 100 We do not doubt that the ombudsman system would work well here. **1970** *Harper's Mag.* Dec. 59/1 He had come to protest to the newspaper, his only ombudsman that day. **1971** *N.Y. Post* 15 Nov. 46 She was everywhere, doing everything—columnist, lecturer,..ombudsman for every injustice. **1972** *Daily Tel.* 23 Feb. 2 The Health Service is to have its own Ombudsman or Health Service Commissioner, who will be responsible for carrying out independent investigations into patients' complaints. **1973** *Daily Californian* 1 Feb. 2/1 A state ombudsman's office, sort of an official wailing wall. **1974** M. GILBERT *Flash Point* i. 12 He had approached..his own member of parliament..the Ombudsman and..the press. **1975** *Local Council Rev.* Autumn 95 A layman's guide to the complaints machinery set up under the 1974 Local Government Act. Explains what the ombudsmen can and cannot do, how complaints should be put to them. **1976** *Daily Tel.* 2 Dec. 2/5 He complained to the Department of Education and eventually to Baroness Serota, the Ombudsman for the area, who found Surrey education committee guilty of maladministration. **1978** *Times* 7 Mar. 4/8 The appointment of local ombudsmen has had a considerable impact on local authority procedures, in the view of the authors of the first critical appraisal of their work.

Hence *ombuds-committee*; **ˈombudsmanry**, the profession or practice of being an ombudsman; **ˈombudsmanship**, the office or function of an ombudsman; **ˈombudswoman**, a female ombudsman.

1961 *Observer* 12 Nov. 40/8, I suppose I have become a sort of ombudswoman on turnstiles. **1964** *Economist* 7 Mar. 875/2 A sort of Ombudscommittee for people who feel cheated. **1970** *Daily Tel.* 6 Aug. 2/4 A resolution calling for an inquiry into promotion procedures and for the setting up of an arbitration 'ombuds-committee' has been tabled. **1971** *New Society* 25 Mar. 489/3 It is obvious that local ombudsmanry on a national scale would mean setting up a new light industry. **1966** *Times* 5 July 13 The whole field of ombudsmanship and the scrutiny of administrative practice and legislative principle..at present goes largely unmarked. **1971** *New Scientist* 3 June 597/2 The loquacious ombudsmanship of Bernard Braden. **1965** *Manch. Guardian Weekly* 21 Oct. 6 The only answer is for more councillors to see themselves as Ombudsmen and Ombudswomen. **1972** *New Yorker* 30 Sept. 6/3 Mabel Mercer, ombudswoman to all who have ever played at love. **1973** *Maclean's Mag.* June 45/1 She had previously been ombudswoman for the Status of Women Council [etc.].

omdah, omdeh. Also omda. [ad. Arabic *ʿumdah* column, support, trustworthy authority, village-chief, f. root *ʿmd* to support.] The headman of a village in Arab countries.

1907 *Daily Chron.* 20 Aug. 3/7 Village omdehs to be elected by the whole mass of the villagers. **1922** *Q. Rev.* Apr. 428 Omdehs and others who may be tempted to revert to the old ways would do well to reflect. **1924** *Glasgow Herald* 23 Dec. 7 The numerous 'omdas', or village headmen, who were dismissed during the Zaghlulist regime. **1926** *Blackw. Mag.* Apr. 409/1, I was reluctantly compelled to accept the hospitality of the Omdah..for lunch. **1928** *Observer* 11 Mar. 19/3 The Omdas—representatives of the central authority in the villages. **1976** *Times* 31 July 10/2, I used to go from village to village, discussing their affairs with the omdas and shaikhs.

-ome, anglicized form of -OMA (partly through influence of G. *-om*, F. *-ome*), occurring chiefly in *Bot.* in terms such as CAULOME, HADROME, PHYLLOME, RHIZOME, and usu. signifying a structure or group of cells forming a normal part of the anatomy, in contrast with the abnormality implied by *-oma* (cf. MYCETOME, an organ in insects, MYCETOMA, a fungal skin disease). It also occurs in a few obs. forms of words now written *-oma*, e.g. FIBROME, TUBERCULOME.

omee (ˈəʊmɪ). *slang*. Also **omer, omie.** [Corruption of It. *uomo*, man.] A man, esp. a landlord or itinerant actor.

1859 HOTTEN *Dict. Slang* 70 *Omee*, a master or landlord. **1893** P. H. EMERSON *Signor Lippo* xiii. 42 When I got back the cullies said, 'Well, cully, how did you get on with the omer?' **1928** *Sunday Express* 14 Oct. 5 Man [in slang of busking] is 'omey'. **1937** N. MARSH *Vintage Murder* vii. 82 'A lot of omies the others were then.'..'Ted means they were bad actors doing worse shows in one-eyed towns up and down the provinces.' **1962** L. KNIGHT (*title*) A proper circus omie.

omega (ˈəʊmɪgə, əʊˈmɛgə). [Gr. ὦ μέγα i.e. 'great O', in contradistinction to ὂ μικρόν 'little O'.]

1. The last letter (Ω, ω) of the Greek alphabet, having originally the value of long open *ō*.

c **1400** MANDEVILLE *Trav.* (1725) iii. 25 What Lettres thei ben..with the Names..α Alpha, β Betha..ω Omega. [**1573–80** BARET *Alv.* O, The Greekes therefore haue ωμικρον standing for a short *o*: and ωμεγα for this double or long *o*, *oo*.] **1640** S. DAINES *Orthoepia Anglicana* (1908) 11 *Oa*, sounds generally after the Greeke *Omega*. *Ibid.* 12 *Oo* in *Poore* imitates in sound the Greek *Omega*. **1656** in BLOUNT *Glossogr.*, *Omega*. **1727–41** CHAMBERS *Cycl.* s.v. *O*, The Greeks had two O's, viz. omicron, ο, and omega ω. **1897** *Allbutt's Syst. Med.* III. 815 The outline of such a loop is that of a capital omega.

2. *transf.* **a.** The last of a series; the last word; the end or final development. ***alpha and omega***: see ALPHA 2. Also ***from alpha to omega***: from beginning to end; from top to toe.

1526 TINDALE *Rev.* i. 8, I am Alpha and Omega the fyrst and the laste. **1651** N. BACON *Disc. Govt. Eng.* II. xxviii. (1739) 132 Formerly the Pope usurped the power to be the Omega to the resolves of all Councils. **1746** WESLEY *Hymn, 'Love Divine'* ii, Alpha and Omega be. **1800** *Asiat. Ann. Reg., Proc. E. Ind. Ho.* 85/1 A letter..contained the alpha and the omega of the business. **1832** TENNYSON *Two Voices* 278 'Omega! thou art Lord', they said, 'We find no motion in the dead'. **1851** NEALE *Hymn, 'Draw nigh, and take'*, Alpha and Omega, to whom shall bow All nations at the Doom, is with us now. **1886** *Athenæum* 25 Dec. 863/3 These two volumes may be considered as the omega of Hebrew bibliography. **1929** D. G. MACKAIL *How Amusing!* 307, I was a gentleman..from alpha to omega. **1978** D. QUINN *Fear of God* II. 161 Vast explosions of silence..marching..from Alpha to Omega and..beyond the infinite.

b. Omega point, in the work of P. Teilhard de Chardin (1881–1955) a hypothesized point of convergence, absorption, or transformation which is the divine end, or God, towards which the forces of evolution are moving (see quot. 1964).

1959 B. WALL tr. *Teilhard de Chardin's Phenomenon of Man* ii. 57 He goes on to add these words which my readers would do well to recall when I come to unveil (with all due reservations and corrections) the perspective of the 'Omega point'. *Ibid.* IV. ii. 259 Accordingly its enormous layers, followed in the right direction, must somewhere ahead become involuted to a point which we might call *Omega*, which fuses and consumes them integrally in itself. **1964** N. DENNY tr. *Teilhard de Chardin's Future of Man* vi. 122 Ahead of, or rather in the heart of, a universe prolonged along its axis of complexity, there exists a divine centre of convergence... In order to stress its synthesising and personalising function, let us call it the *point Omega*. **1965** *Listener* 3 June 817/2 The idea has something in common with Teilhard de Chardin's concept of the 'Omega Point'. **1977** *Time* 28 Feb. 45/1 Teilhard believed man would eventually transcend his individualism and converge at the 'Omega Point' with the Omega—God.

3. *Nuclear Physics.* †**a.** (Written Ω.) A former designation of certain hyperons. *Obs.*

The decay schemes in quot. 1953 are those of the sigma (Σ) particles, whilst the mass specified in quot. 1954[2] (and elsewhere) is that of the xi minus. In quot. 1954[1] a lambda particle is referred to.

1953 *Nuovo Cimento* X. 1741 Two decay schemes have been proposed by analogy with the decay of V_1^0-particles. Adopting the nomenclature proposed at the Bagnères Conference these are: (*a*) $\Omega_\pi^\pm \rightarrow n + \pi^\pm + Q$, (*b*) $\Omega_p^+ \rightarrow p + \pi^0 + Q$. **1954** *Sci. News* XXXI. 62 Ω^0-particle. Mass, $2{,}184 \pm 7$ [$\equiv$ 1116 MeV]. Lifetime, $(3{\cdot}3 \pm 1) \times 10^{-10}$ seconds... Decay scheme: $\Omega^0 \rightarrow p^+ + \pi^-$. **1954** *Physical Rev.* XCVI. 543/1 The known hyperons, Λ^-, Ω^-, have masses equivalent to 1200 and 1320 Mev, respectively.

b. In full ***omega meson***. A neutral meson with zero hypercharge, zero isospin, unit spin, and negative parity that is observed as a resonance (as when protons and antiprotons of sufficient energy collide), has a mass of 784 MeV (1534 times that of the electron), and on decaying usu.

produces a positive, a negative, and a neutral pion. Freq. written as ω.

1961 B. C. MAGLIĆ et al. in *Physical Rev. Lett.* VII. 178/1 The existence of a heavy neutral meson with $T = 0$ and $J = 1^-$ was predicted by Nambu... Such a particle is also expected in the vector meson theory of Sakurai and.. according to the unitary symmetry theory; and for other reasons. We will refer to it as ω. *Ibid.* 181/1 We conclude that the data fit the qualitative criteria for an axial vector matrix element (ω meson). **1961** *New Scientist* 5 Oct. 48/1 Four physicists at the Lawrence Radiation Laboratory, Berkeley, have made observations.. that appear to indicate unequivocally the presence, in a proton-antiproton reaction, of the omega-meson. **1971** *Sci. News* 10 Apr. 250 It appears that electromagnetic forces are mediated to leptons directly by photons and to hadrons by phi, rho or omega. **1971** *Sci. Amer.* July 100/2 Three vector mesons with zero strangeness are currently known: the rho, the omega and the phi. **1974** *Nature* 6 Dec. 438/2 The omega meson, which has all the same normal quantum numbers as the phi,.. decays very rapidly to three pions.

c. ***omega minus*** (or ***particle***): a negatively charged hyperon having hypercharge of -2, zero isospin, a spin of 3/2, positive parity, and a mass of 1672 MeV (3272 times that of the electron), and decaying via the weak interaction into either a xi particle and a pion or a lambda particle and a kaon. Freq. written as Ω^-.

1962 M. GELL-MANN in *Proc. Internat. Conf. High-Energy Physics* 805/2 Starting with the resonance at 1238 MeV, we may conjecture that the Y_1^*, at 1385 MeV and the Ξ^* at 1535 MeV might belong to this supermultiplet... If $J = 3/2^+$ is really right for these two cases, then our speculation might have some value and we should look for the last particle, called, say, Ω^- with $S = -3$, $I = 0$. At 1685 MeV, it would be metastable and should decay by the weak interactions into $K^- + \Lambda$, $\pi^- + \Xi^0$, or $\pi^0 + \Xi^-$. **1964** *Physical Rev. Lett.* XII. 204/1 The multitude of resonances which have been discovered recently.. can be arranged as a decuplet with one member still missing... This particle (which we shall call Ω^-, following Gell-Mann) is predicted to be a negatively charged isotopic singlet with strangeness minus three. *Ibid.* 206/1 In view of the properties.. established for particle 3, we feel justified in identifying it with the sought-for Ω^-. **1964** *Daily Tel.* 21 Feb. 25/2 Dr. Maurice Goldhaber, director of Brookhaven, said yesterday: 'The discovery of Omega Minus forms the capstone in a building which was so far held together only by the bold imagination of Dr. Gell-Mann and Dr. Ne'eman.' **1964** *Listener* 30 Apr. 711/1 The new theory [*sc.* that of unitary symmetry] has made one striking prediction which was subsequently found to be correct: the observation of the negatively charged Omega particle. **1972** *Daily Colonist* (Victoria, B.C.) 24 Feb. 5/2 The physicists hope to make the first observation of 'quarks'.. by studying the activity of a rare and elusive sub-atomic particle called the omega-minus. **1974** FRAUENFELDER & HENLEY *Subatomic Physics* i. 6 The negative kaon.. collides with a proton and produces a positive kaon, a neutral kaon, and an omega minus. The Ω^- decays into a Ξ^0 and a π^-.

4. a. *attrib.* and *Comb.*, as ***omega-shaped*** adj.

1880 MRS. GRAY *14 Months in Canton* xxviii. 301 They are always in the Omega or horse-shoe form. **1885** *Where Chineses Drive* 19 The omega-shaped tombs so common in the south [of China].

b. Used *attrib.* (with capital initial) to designate a style of interior decoration and design associated with the Omega Workshops, a short-lived undertaking begun in London by the art critic Roger Fry in 1913 and influenced by the work of William Morris.

1922 D. H. LAWRENCE *Aaron's Rod* iii. 30 Into this reticence pieces of futurism, Omega cushions and Van-Gogh-like pictures exploded their colours. **1970** *Oxf. Compan. Art* 790/2 The Omega artists believed that the creative joy of the artist and craftsman should go into the making of articles for everyday use. **1973** *Guardian* 22 Jan. 8/1 Drawings and paintings of the Bloomsbury artists still crowd the walls... The dining-room's Omega chairs attend its round painted table.

omegatron (ˈəʊmɪgətrɒn). *Physics.* [f. OMEGA (ω being the symbol of angular frequency) + -TRON.] A mass spectrometer that employs the principle of the cyclotron to identify and measure gases at very low pressures, a radio-frequency electric field being applied at right angles to a magnetic field so that charged particles having a certain charge-to-mass ratio impinge on a collecting electrode.

1949 J. A. HIPPLE et al. in *Physical Rev.* LXXVI. 1878/1 Since this device measures ω, it is suggested that it be called the omegatron. **1966** W. SUMMER tr. *E. von Angerer & H. Ebert's Physical Lab. Handbk.* x. 208 The omegatron.. is useful as a gauge down to 10^{-12} torr. *Ibid.*, The ion-collecting efficiency of an omegatron is high and operation is satisfactory in the range 10^{-5} to 10^{-9} torr. Below 10^{-7} torr resolution up to $m = 30$ is very good... Resolution is less complete for $30 < m < 100$, but ions present can be identified. **1975** *Nature* 6 Feb. 408/2 Partial pressures were measured with an omegatron radio-frequency mass spectrometer which formed part of the UHV section.

omelet, omelette (ˈɒmlɪt, ˈɒməlɪt), *sb.* Also 7 **aumelet, -ette, ammulet, omlet, emlett,** 7–8 **amulet, aumulet,** 8 **amlet, aumlet.** [a. F. *omelette*, in 16th c. *homelaicte* (Rabel.), *aumelete* (O. De Serres), for earlier *amelette* (15th c. in Littré, also still in Fr. dial.), app. by metathesis from *alemette*, a synonym, by substitution of suffix, of *alemelle, alumelle*, lit. thin plate, 'the blade of a sword or knife' (Cotgr.); 'that is, the *omelet* was named from its thin flat shape' (Skeat). Menagier, 14th c., has 'alumelle (*v.r.* alumette) frite au sucre'. Godefroy exemplifies the successive forms *alumette, amelette, omelette, œufmolette, aumelette*. The forms in *am-* and *aum-* were also Eng. in 17–18th c. OF. *alemelle* appears to have itself arisen from *lamelle, lemelle*, ad. L. *lamella* dim. of *lamina*, by an erroneous analysis of *lalemelle*, i.e. *la lemelle*, as *l'alemelle*: cf. JADE *sb.*[2]]

a. A dish mainly consisting of eggs whipped up, seasoned, and fried; often varied by the addition of other ingredients, as cheese, apples, parsley, chopped ham, fish, mushrooms, etc.

1611 COTGR., *Haumelette*, an Omelet, or Pancake of egges. **1655** tr. *Com. Hist. Francion* I–III. 26, I was commanded to make an aumelet, it being Friday. **1657** R. LIGON *Barbadoes* (1673) 36 An Amulet of eggs. **1681** W. ROBERTSON *Phraseol. Gen.* (1693) 185 An Aumulet of Eggs. **1698** SIR H. SLOANE in *Phil. Trans.* XX. 70 A Fresh Egg in Fashion of an Ammulet. **1699** EVELYN *Acetaria* (1729) 125 In Omlets, made up with Cream, fried in Sweet Butter. **1748** MRS. S. HARRISON *House-kpr.'s Pocket-Book* ii. (ed. 4) 6 Eggs dress'd, in several sorts of Amlets. **1750** E. SMITH *Compl. Housew.* (ed. 14) 50 An Amulet of Eggs the savoury way. **1796** MRS. GLASSE *Cookery* v. 83 Make an Aumlet of yolks of eggs. **1806** A. HUNTER *Culina* (ed. 3) 203 The omelette is an extemporaneous dish that admits of great variation in its composition. **1860** HAWTHORNE *Marb. Faun* xxv. (1883) 257 Old Stella.. quickly followed it with a savory omelet. **1873** E. SMITH *Foods* 96 In preparing omelettes, the albumen is more consolidated.

b. *Proverb.* 'Omelets cannot be made without breaking eggs', transl. the French, *On ne saurait faire une omelette sans casser des œufs*, said in reference to operations which cannot be accomplished without the sacrifice of something in itself valuable.

1859 GEN. P. THOMPSON *Audi Alt.* II. xc. 65 We are walking upon eggs, and whether we tread East or tread West, the omelet will not be made without the breaking of some. **1898** *Times* 10 Jan. 13/3 Omelettes cannot be made without breaking eggs, and war cannot be waged without losses of this kind occurring.

c. *attrib.*, as ***omelette (frying)-pan***.

1846 *Jewish Manual, or Pract. Information Jewish & Mod. Cookery* v. 99 A small omelette frying-pan is necessary for cooking it [*sc.* the omelette] well. **1879** A. D. WHITNEY *Just How* 292 Finish beating and mixing the omelette, setting on the omelette-pan when almost ready. **1948** *Good Housek. Cookery Bk.* II. 369 To season a new omelet pan. Heat the pan slowly, then melt a knob of butter in it and rub it well in with a piece of soft paper. **1977** T. HEALD *Just Desserts* vii. 174 Gabrielle won't go anywhere without her favourite omelette pan.

d. omelette (aux) fines herbes, a savoury omelette flavoured with herbs; **omelette soufflée**, an omelette made by folding the separately beaten egg whites into the mixture.

1845 E. ACTON *Mod. Cookery* xix. 489 Seasoned with minced herbs,..[it] is then called an '*Omlette aux fines herbes*'. **1846** [see FINES HERBES]. **1928** A. CHRISTIE *Mystery of Blue Train* xix. 150 The Comte de la Roche had just finished *déjeuner*, consisting of an *omelette fines herbes*. **1977** D. RAMSAY *You can't call it Murder* ii. 108 During lunch.. they disposed of.. the most subtle of *omelettes fines herbes*. **1845** E. ACTON *Mod. Cookery* xix. 491 (*heading*) An omlette soufflée. **1930** W. S. MAUGHAM *Cakes & Ale* xii. 145 No one could make a better *omelette soufflée* than she. **1968** *Radio Times* 28 Nov. 25/1 Colourful Cookery.. Puffed Onion Tart .. Omelette Soufflée. **1975** HUME & DOWNES *Cordon Bleu Desserts* ii. 64 Omelet Soufflé with Strawberries... Omelet Soufflé 'en Surprise'.

'omelet, 'omelette, *v.* [f. the sb.] *trans.* To make into an omelet. Also *transf.*

1872 E. EGGLESTON *End of World* xxiii. 155 The eggs.. were not poached, they were not scrambled, they were not omeletted. **1908** *Westm. Gaz.* 6 Oct. 3/1 (*caption*), I don't want to be omeletted!

omelie, omely(e, obs. forms of HOMILY.

omell, var. AMELL *Obs.*, among, amid.

omen (ˈəʊmən), *sb.* [a. L. *ōmen*, OL. (according to Varro) *osmen*, perh. for *ausmen*, f. root of *audīre* to hear + *-men* (as in *carmen*, etc.).]

a. Any phenomenon or circumstance supposed to portend good or evil; a token significant of the nature of a future event; a prophetic sign, prognostic, augury.

1582 STANYHURST *Æneis* II. (Arb.) 66 You Gods of countrye this is eke your prosperus omen. **1600** B. JONSON *Cynthia's Rev.* IV. ii, I take it for no good omen, to find mine Honor so deiected. **1637** HEYWOOD *Dialogues* ii. Wks. 1874 VI. 113 Far be that Omen from vs [= L. *absit omen*!]. **1719** YOUNG *Busiris* III. 1, May all the gods watch o'er your life and empire, And render omens vain! **1836** W. IRVING *Astoria* I. 198 They retained much of the Indian belief in charms and omens. **1874** GREEN *Short Hist.* viii. §4. 497 Men noted as a fatal omen the accident which marked his first entry into Lambeth.

b. Without *an* and *pl.*: Indication of good or evil to come; foreboding; prognostication. In quot. 1742 personified.

1742 YOUNG *Nt. Th.* III. 114 And on her Cheek, the Residence of Spring, Pale Omen sat. **1825** LYTTON *Zicci* 78, I trust your business to our illustrious guest is of good omen and pleasant import. **1868** FREEMAN *Norm. Conq.* II. ix. 326 A day of the brightest omen. **1876** MOZLEY *Univ. Serm.* iv. (1877) 73 Birds of evil omen fly to and fro.

c. *attrib.* and *Comb.*, as ***omen-animal, -bearing, -bird, -hunter, -hunting, -monger,*** etc.

1695 CONGREVE *Love for L.* IV. xi, Directed by a dreamer, an omen-hunter. **1777** H. WALPOLE *Lett., to M. Cole* 16 Sept. (1846) V. 472, I hope fatalists and omen-mongers will be confuted. **1899** A. B. BRUCE *Moral Ord. World* 150 The eagle and other omen-bearing birds. **1902** *Man* II. 61 The chapters on the omen-animals and the cult of skulls are of special value.

omen (ˈəʊmən), *v.* [f. prec. sb. Cf. L. *ōmināre, -ārī.*] *trans.* To presage, prognosticate, forebode.

1805 SOUTHEY *Madoc* II. xi, An offering which shall more propitiate them, And omen sure success. **1818** SCOTT *Hrt. Midl.* xxiv, The yet unknown verdict, of which, however, all omened the tragical contents. **1871** CARLYLE in *Mrs. C.'s Lett.* III. 91 Good or ill luck for the whole year being omened by your liking or otherwise of the first person that accosts you on New Year's morning.

omened (ˈəʊmənd), *a.* [f. prec. sb. or vb. + -ED.] Having an omen. Chiefly in combs., as ***ill-, well-, happy-omened.***

1700 DRYDEN *Pal. and Arc.* I. 50 To meet my triumph in ill-omened weeds. **1725** POPE *Odyss.* xx. 131 Soon, with consummate joy to crown his prayer, An omen'd Voice invades his ravish'd ear. **1848** BUCKLEY *Iliad* 155 Command to observe well-omened words.

'omening, *vbl. sb.* [f. OMEN *v.* + -ING[1].] A foreboding, prognostication.

1796 COLERIDGE *Let. to Poole* 4 July in *Biog. Lit.* (1847) II. 369, I was afraid to give way to the omenings of my heart. **1823** SCOTT *Peveril* ii, These evil omenings do but point out conclusions.. most unlikely to come to pass.

ome'nology. [f. OMEN *sb.* + -OLOGY.] The study or science of omens.

1904 J. HASTINGS *Dict. Bible* V. 559/2 Such.. occurrences as the lunar eclipse, would serve as a basis for lunar omenology.

oment: see OMENTUM.

omental (əʊˈmɛntəl), *a.* [f. OMENTUM + -AL[1].] Of, pertaining to, or situated in the omentum.

1758 J. S. tr. *Le Dran's Observ. Surg.* (1771) Dict. C c viii, *Sarcoepiplocele*, a fleshy Omental Rupture. **1799** *Med. Jrnl.* I. 158 Singular Case of an Omental Hernia. **1898** *Allbutt's Syst. Med.* V. 218 To decide whether a tumour be glandular or omental.

omentocele (əʊˈmɛntəʊsiːl). *Path.* [f. OMENTUM + Gr. κήλη tumour.] Hernia of the omentum; = EPIPLOCELE. (*Syd. Soc. Lex.* 1892.)

omentopexy (əʊˈmɛntəʊpɛksɪ). *Surg.* [f. OMENT(UM + -O + -PEXY.] Any operation in which the omentum is sutured to another structure, e.g. the abdominal wall.

1905 *Jrnl. Amer. Med. Assoc.* 25 Nov. 1700/2 Omentopexy was undertaken to provide collateral circulation for the portal vein. **1957** J. G. ALLEN et al. *Surgery* xxxiii. 795/2 Omentopexy was introduced by Morison, Talma and others about 1900. **1962** *Lancet* 13 Jan. 66/2 Subsequently 1 (case 12) had an omentopexy, which controlled hæmorrhage for two years.

‖**omentum** (əʊˈmɛntəm). *Anat.* Pl. **-a.** Also 6 in anglicized form **oment.** [L. *ōmentum.*] A fold or duplication of the peritoneum connecting the stomach with certain of the other viscera, as the liver, spleen, and colon; the caul.

Three divisions of the omentum are commonly recognized: the ***gastro-colic*** or ***greater omentum*** descending over a part of the intestines from the lower border of the stomach to the transverse colon; the ***gastro-hepatic, hepato-gastric,*** or ***lesser omentum*** extending from the liver to the smaller curvature of the stomach; the ***gastro-splenic omentum*** connecting the cardiac end of the stomach with the spleen.

[**1545** RAYNOLD *Byrth Mankynde* H hh j, The kell called Omentum in laten.] **1547** BOORDE *Brev. Health* ccciv. 99 b, The oment or Siphac which is a pellicle the whiche doth compasse and doth bere up the guttes. **1682** T. GIBSON *Anat.* 25 The Omentum aboundeth with vessels of several sorts. **1767** GOOCH *Treat. Wounds* I. 105 Wounds of the omentum are of the mortal kind.. the effused blood, falling into the cavity of the abdomen, will kill the patient. **1845** BUDD *Dis. Liver* 16 The glands in the right border of the lesser omentum. **1873** MIVART *Elem. Anat.* xi. 458 A great, free, apron-like flap of the peritoneum called the great omentum, hangs down loosely in front of the bowels.

‖**omer** (ˈəʊmə(r)). [a. Heb. *ōmer.* (Identity of the word in the two senses uncertain.)]

1. A Hebrew measure of capacity equal to the tenth part of an ephah, or $5\frac{1}{10}$ pints Imperial measure. (Formerly rendered GOMER q.v.; also erroneously *homer*, in which form it is confounded with a much larger measure of capacity, HOMER[2].)

[**1000–1631**: see GOMER.] **1611** BIBLE *Exod.* xvi. 33 Take a pot, and put an Omer full of Manna therein. *Ibid.* 36 Now an Omer is the tenth part of an Ephah. **1623** COCKERAM, *Omer*, a pottle. *a* **1658** CLEVELAND *Model New Rel.* 21 For Sprats are rose an *Omer* for a Souse. **1706** PHILLIPS, *Homer*, a twofold Measure among the Hebrews; one liquid, and the other dry, the former containing three Pints and a half. **1876** *Helps Study Bible* 241, 1·8 cab = 1 omer.. 5·1 pts.

2. A sheaf; *spec.* the sheaf of the wave-offering: in ***Counting of the Omer***, the formal enumeration of the days (day by day) from the eve of the 2nd day of the Passover (when the *omer* was brought) till Pentecost is reached; a custom observed by the Jews in synagogue and in homes, after Leviticus xxiii. 15, 16.

1860 J. GARDNER *Faiths World* II. 560/2 The..'days of the omer'. **1871** *Daily Sabbath...Prayers*, etc., Introd. 19 The Counting of the Omer. **1892** ZANGWILL *Childr. Ghetto* II. 259 They counted the days of the Omer till Pentecost saw the synagogue dressed with flowers.

omer, obs. form of UMBER, grayling.

omer, var. OMEE.

‖**omertà** (omer'ta). [dial. form of It. *umiltà* humility, with reference to the Mafia code which enjoins submission of the group to the leader as well as silence on all Mafia concerns.] Refusal to give evidence by those concerned in the activities of the Mafia.

1909 *Evening Sun* (N.Y.) 13 May 8/1 There is..the belief that it is unmanly to tell anything about a fellow countryman which could get him into trouble. It is called 'Omerta' in the Sicilian tongue, which means manliness. **1963** R. I. McDAVID *Mencken's Amer. Lang.* 720 *Omertà*, the very strict code of the Mafia. **1965** *Times Lit. Suppl.* 25 Nov. 1058/4 He could call on a good many witnesses more bound to *omertà* than to the truth. **1965** J. WAINWRIGHT *Death in Sleeping City* II. vii. 129 They [*sc.* the Mafia] have a law... It's called the Omerta. It's an unwritten law—a code of conduct, really. **1968** *Listener* 29 Feb. 268/3 An island [Sardinia] where omerta is stronger than democracy. **1969** *Sunday Truth* (Brisbane) 30 Nov. 25/2 He had broken the highest law of the Mafia—omerta, or silence. **1970** G. GREER *Female Eunuch* 222 *Vendetta* and *omertà*..are not significant until the familial, regional community is threatened by political authority. **1977** *Time* 12 Sept. 43/1 The protection program was formally established after passage of the Organized Crime Control Act of 1970 to hasten the breakdown of *omertà*, the underworld code of silence.

omest, var. OVEMEST *Obs.*, highest, topmost.

-ometer ('ɒmɪtə(r)), the element -METER, Gr. μέτρον measure, preceded by *-o*, belonging to the prec. element, or merely connective (see -O[1]), in which form it usually appears in words from Greek, and hence in modern formations, as *dampometer*, *gasometer*, *olfactometer*, etc. Also as a quasi-*sb.*

1856 *Farmer's Mag.* Jan. 63 The barometers, thermometers, saccharometers, and other ometers.

Omeyyad, var. UMAYYAD *a.* and *sb.*

‖**omi** ('əʊmɪ). Also, with prefixed *ō-* 'great'. [Jap.] In early imperial Japan, a high-ranking administrative official claiming imperial ancestry (cf. MURAJI); a title of members of a family upon which such an office was bestowed.

1901 [see MURAJI]. **1931** G. B. SANSOM *Japan* I. ii. 37 We have the *ō-omi*, or great ministers, who were appointed from among the heads of clans closely related to the imperial family. *Ibid.*, The *omi* and *muraji* of lesser standing. **1964**, **1970** [see MURAJI].

omicron ('ɒmɪkrɒn, əʊ'maɪkrɒn). [Gr. ὁ μικρόν, lit. 'little O': cf. OMEGA.] The fifteenth letter (Ο, ο) of the Greek alphabet, originally having the value of the short *o*.

c **1400** MANDEVILLE *Trav.* (1725) iii. 25 What Lettres thei ben..with the Names..α Alpha, β Betha,..ο Omicron..χ Chi, [etc.]. **1631** R. HARRIS *Arraignement Whole Creature* xiii. 208 The whole Globe..cannot fill this little triangulary heart: so many Omicrons, cannot fill one little Delta. **1727-41** [see OMEGA 1]. **1893** E. M. THOMPSON *Handbk. Gr. & Lat. Palæogr.* x. 135 The very small size of *theta* and *omikron*, may also be noticed. **1947** *Jrnl. Investigative Dermatol.* IX. 215 Where *-oma* occurs as the ending in words *properly* formed from the Greek, the stem always ends in omicron or omega (as a lengthening of omicron). *Ibid.* 213 Many such Greek verb stems, but by no means all, end in *o* represented by omicron when the pronunciation is short (ŏ) or by omega (ω) when it is long (ō). **1959** A. G. WOODHEAD *Study of Greek Inscriptions* ii. 18 This differentiation, like that between *omicron* and *omega*, gradually spread to the rest of the Greek world.

omie, var. OMEE.

†'**ominal**, *a. Obs.* [ad. L. type **ōmināl-is*, f. OMEN: see -AL[1].] Of or pertaining to omens; from which an omen is drawn.

1651 J. F[REAKE] *Agrippa's Occ. Philos.* 110 But those are the chiefest which Ominall birds shall foretell. **1661** K. W. *Conf. Charac.* To Rdr. (1860) 8 The confounding rayes and sulphurus beams of his ominall countenance, which affrighted all loyall and natural eyes.

†'**ominate**, *v. Obs.* [f. ppl. stem of L. *ōminārī*, *-āre* to prognosticate, f. *ōmen*, *ōmin-* OMEN.]

1. *trans.* To prognosticate from omens, to augur, forebode.

1582 STANYHURST *Æneis* III. (Arb.) 82 By the God enstructed..to ominat eeche thing. **1652** GAULE *Magastrom.* 327 The augurs, ominating disastrous and unfortunate things to the Romane army. **1742** MIDDLETON in *Mrs. Montagu's Lett.* II. 173 To whom I have ever been wishing and ominating every thing that is good.

b. *intr.* To augur, to have or utter forebodings.

1637 HEYWOOD *Dial.* ii. Wks. 1874 VI. 127 Of doubtfull things thus ill you ominate. **1667** H. MORE *Div. Dial.* II. i. (1713) 88, I cannot ominate so well touching this Congress.

2. *trans.* To be a prognostic of, to portend.

1598 BARCKLEY *Felic. Man* III. (1603) 175 This unfortunate bird [i.e. an owl]..ominating some evill to followe. **1644** *Fifth of November* 12 If the staggering of the Arke of Gods worship should ominate the fall of it. **1706** PHILLIPS, *To Ominate*, to give an Omen of, to fore-bode or fore-shew. **1827** GALT *Let.* in *Ann. Parish* Mem. (1850) 47, I had no vultures to *omenate* wars and conquests.

b. *intr.* To be or serve as an omen, to portend.

1667 *Decay Chr. Piety* xv. §6 And this is it which ominates sadly as to our divisions with the Romanists. **1691** NORTH *Let.* 31 Dec. in *Lives* (1890) III. 228 May the new year be better than the beginning ominates. My brother Dudley died last night about seven.

Hence †'**ominating** *ppl. a.*

1663 SIR G. MACKENZIE *Religious Stoic* xiii. (1685) 116 These ominating presages. **1702** H. DODWELL *Apol.* §16 in S. Parker *Cicero's De Finibus*, This..filled them with confidence and well ominating Hopes.

†**omi'nation.** *Obs.* [ad. L. *ōminātiōn-em*, n. of action from *ōmināre*: see prec.] The action of omening or presaging; prognostication, foreboding.

1589 PUTTENHAM *Eng. Poesie* II. xi[i]. (Arb.) 124 If any other man by triall happen vpon a better omination. **1646** SIR T. BROWNE *Pseud. Ep.* v. xxi. 265 Nor was the same [falling of Salt] a generall prognosticke of future evill among the ancients, but a particular omination concerning the breach of friendship. **1650** TRAPP *Comm. Num.* xviii. 12 Adding happy ominations and gratulations. **1663** J. SPENCER *Prodigies* (1665) 102 Ominations by Words, Names, Places, Times, in so many several Chapters full of elaborate vanity.

ominous ('ɒmɪnəs), *a.* [ad. L. *ōminōs-us* portentous, f. *ōmen*, *ōmin-* OMEN: see -OUS. Cf. mod.F. *omineux* (Littré).]

1. Of the nature of an omen, serving to foretell the future, presaging events to come, portentous.

1592 WARNER *Alb. Eng.* VIII. xliii. (1612) 207 *H* the letter still Might be obserued ominous to Englands good or ill. **1646** J. GREGORY *Notes & Obs.* (1650) 29 'Twas a Rule..to undertake nothing..in-auspicato, without some ominous performance. **1766** GOLDSM. *Vic. W.* ii, Nor can I here pass over an ominous circumstance that happened, the last time we played together. **1821** BYRON *Heav. & Earth* i. 15, I feel a thousand fears Which are not ominous of right.

b. Founded upon omens.

1672 MARVELL *Reh. Transp.* I. 137, I do not reckon much upon those ominous criticismes.

†**2.** Of good omen, auspicious; fortunate. *Obs.*

1597 M. BOWMAN in A. M. tr. *Guillemeau's Fr. Chirurg.* xij b, Whom I pray to give ominouse and fortunate event to your divine attemptes. **1662** R. MATHEW *Unl. Alch.* 175 This Medicine is..most ominous in all kind of Fluxes.

3. Of ill omen, foreboding evil, inauspicious.

1589 WARNER *Alb. Eng.* VI. xxx. (1612) 151 If ought foresayd be ominous, should any feare, tis I. **1593** SHAKS. *3 Hen. VI*, II. vi. 107 Let me be Duke of Clarence, George of Gloster, For Glosters Dukedome is too ominous. **1666** J. DAVIES *Hist. Caribby Isls.* 321 If..a dog, as one would say, did bark at them, thinking it ominous, they immediately return. **1769** *Junius Lett.* xiv. 58 There is an ominous fatality in it, which even the spurious descendants of the family cannot escape. **1835** I. TAYLOR *Spir. Despot.* i. 6 The brightest and the fondest hopes we entertain..hang upon the auspicious or ominous aspect of English Christianity. **1871** L. STEPHEN *Playgr. Eur.* (1894) iv. 100 An ominous shake of the head supplied the remainder of the sentence.

b. Marked or attended by evil omens, disastrous.

1634 HEYWOOD *Maidenhead lost* III. Wks. 1874 IV. 140 O my ominous fate. **1669** MARVELL *Corr.* Wks. 1872-5 II. 289 It is the second fatall and ominous accident that hath faln out. **1671** R. BOHUN *Wind* 140 The E. Winds..being ominous to our Gardens and Fields, by blasting the corn and fruits.

c. Of doubtful or menacing aspect or appearance.

1877 A. B. EDWARDS *Up Nile* xxi. 647 Columns of hieroglyphic text, interspersed with ominous shapes, half-deity, half-demon. **1884** RUSKIN *Art. of Eng.* ii. 66 In the dimness or coruscation of ominous light.

ominously ('ɒmɪnəslɪ), *adv.* [f. prec. + -LY[2].] In an ominous manner, by way of omen or presage, portentously.

†**a.** In general sense; or *spec.* With presage of good, auspiciously, happily. *Obs.*

1597 A. M. tr. *Guillemeau's Fr. Chirurg.* 21/1, I have my selfe very luckylye and ominouslye done the same. *a* **1619** FOTHERBY *Atheom.* II. xi. §5 (1622) 319 His sublime and cœlestiall disposition, was ominously foretold him, in his very name. **1656** *Petition fr. Colchester* in *Eng. Hist. Rev.* XV. 657 That Interest which God hath been pleased soe ominously to owne in our dayes.

b. With presage of evil or disaster; inauspiciously, menacingly.

1649 MILTON *Eikon Bas.* i. Wks. (1847) 278/2 Which of all those oppressive acts..did he ever disclaim..till the fatal awe of this parliament hung ominously over him? *a* **1765** YOUNG *Statesman's Creed* (R.), Their execrable names, who high in power, And deep in guilt, most ominously shine. **1848** C. BRONTË *J. Eyre* vii, The same black column which had frowned on me so ominously from the hearth-rug of Gateshead. **1881** J. RUSSELL *Haigs* v. 106 The fact..speaks ominously as to the general state of misrule.

ominousness ('ɒmɪnəsnɪs). [f. as prec. + -NESS.] The quality of being ominous, or of presaging good or (more usually) evil to come.

1606 HOLLAND *Sueton.* 79 Avoyding and eschewing..but the unluckie ominousnesse of the name. *a* **1715** BURNET *Own Time* (ed. 3) II. 410 Such deluges of rain, as disgraced the shew, and heightned the opinion of the ominousness of this embassy. **1878** T. HARDY *Ret. Native* II. III. iii. 128 His mother's taciturnity was not without ominousness.

omis, obs. form of AMISS *adv.*

†**o'mise**, *v. Obs. rare*[−1]. In 5 omyse. [f. F. *omis*, pa. pple. of *omettre*, ad. L. *omittĕre* to OMIT. Cf. *demise*, *premise*.] *trans.* To omit: = OBMISS.

a **1425** *Foundat. St. Bartholomew's* 33 No thynge hath he omysid.

omissible (əʊ'mɪsɪb(ə)l), *a.* [f. L. *omiss-*, ppl. stem of *omittĕre* to OMIT + -IBLE.] Capable of being omitted.

1816 BENTHAM *Chrestomathia* I. Wks. 1843 VIII. 14 Least generally useful branches..in case of necessity, omissible. **1858** CARLYLE *Fredk. Gt.* VII. ii. (1872) II. 246 All mere puddle, omissible in this place. **1893** *Nation* (N.Y.) 27 Apr. 315/3 There is nothing omitted nor anything omissible.

Hence **omissi'bility**.

1961 in WEBSTER. **1966** *Amer. Speech* XLI. 182 Certain self-explanatory terms have been examined with a view to their omissibility from *NID 3* (Webster's Third New International Dictionary). **1971** D. CRYSTAL *Linguistics* 202 The omissibility of *here tomorrow*. **1971** T. F. MITCHELL in *Archivum Linguisticum* II. 43 The omissibility of a following noun.

omission (əʊ'mɪʃən). [ad. L. *omissiōn-em*, n. of action from *omittĕre* to OMIT. Cf. F. *omission* (1315 in *Rolls of Parlt.* I. 338/2).]

1. The action of omitting or leaving out, or fact of being omitted; failure or forbearance to insert or include; also, an instance of this.

1555 J. BRADFORD *Let.* in Coverdale *Lett. Mart.* (1564) 318 Ioseph myghte haue objected the omission of his vocation. **1628** T. SPENCER *Logick* 81 A cessation or omision of action. **1790** PALEY *Horæ Paul.* Rom. i. 10 To supply the omission in the preceding narrative. **1849** MURCHISON *Siluria* iii. 60 The omissions of certain deposits in some parts. **1887** BROWNING *Parleyings, F. Furini* ix, What does man see..but faults to mend, Omissions to supply?

2. The non-performance or neglect of action or duty; an instance of this.

c **1380** WYCLIF *Wks.* (1880) 410 Many men in omissioun synne aȝenus crist. **1526** *Pilgr. Perf.* (W. de W. 1531) 172 Y[t] synne..by the reason of wordes, dedes or thoughtes, omyssyons or other neglygences. **1597** HOWSON *Serm. 24 Dec.* 40 We haue auoided all sinnes of omission and commission. **1667** PEPYS *Diary* 19 June, His faults to me seem only great omissions. **1841** MISS MITFORD in L'Estrange *Life* (1870) III. viii. 121 If..he be sent to jail for my omissions, I should certainly not long remain to grieve over my sin, for such it is.

omissive (əʊ'mɪsɪv), *a.* [f. L. *omiss-*, ppl. stem of *omitt-ĕre* to OMIT + -IVE.] Characterized by omitting, neglecting to perform, or leaving out.

1629 BP. HALL *Serm. to Lords* 19 Feb. (R.), The first is an untowardnesse of omission, the second of commission. The omissive untowardnesse shall lead the way. **1681** BAXTER *Answ. Dodwell* iv. 62 This man hath the Gramatical skill to call *Omissive obedience* by the name of *Passive*. **1758** *Descr. Thames* 19 Should I be silent on the Occasion, I might well be deemed truly omissive to my Duty. **1805** W. TAYLOR in *Ann. Rev.* III. 207. **1816** COLERIDGE in *Lit. Rem.* (1836) I. 389 Actions, omissive as well as commissive. **1832** *Examiner* 193/2 We compared their careless and omissive part with the part of the people, performed with prodigious energy.

omit (əʊ'mɪt), *v.* See also OBMIT. [ad. L. *omittĕre* to let go, let loose, lay aside, disregard, f. *o-* = *ob-* (OB- 1) + *mittĕre* to send, let go.]

1. *trans.* To leave out, not to insert or include.

1432-50 tr. *Higden* (Rolls) IV. 33 [They were] lxxij. in nowmbre, but the consuetude of scripture is to omitte the litelle nowmbre if þat hit remayne, after the grete nowmbre. **1526** *Pilgr. Perf.* (1531) 162 So moche as they omitted or lefte vnsayd. **1547** BOORDE *Astronomye* Pref., Wher I have ometted & lefft out mani matters apertaynyng to this boke. **1605** CAMDEN *Rem.* 200 That I may omitte other of his speeches. **1736** BUTLER *Anal.* II. vii. 330 Parts of them..are omitted to be quoted. **1875** JOWETT *Plato* (ed. 2) III. 268 The intermediate passages are omitted, leaving only the dialogue.

†**b.** *intr.* with *of*. *Obs.*

1550 J. COKE *Eng. & Fr. Heralds* §44 (1877) 70 Other noble actes which, to breviate this matter, I omyt of.

2. *trans.* To fail or forbear to use or perform; to let alone, pass over, neglect, leave undone.

1533 MORE *Apol.* xxiv. Wks. 887/2 They had..omitted no charitable meane vnto him that came to theire mindes. **1560** DAUS tr. *Sleidane's Comm.* 180 b, He will omit nothynge, that conserueth hys dewtie. **1601** SHAKS. *Jul. C.* IV. iii. 220 There is a Tide in the affayres of men, which..Omitted, all the voyage of their life, Is bound in Shallowes, and in Miseries. **1606** G. W[OODCOCKE] *Lives Emperors* in *Hist. Ivstine* I j 6, And for his delight in hunting, horses, dogs.. omitting the affaires of the Empire. **1651** HOBBES *Leviath.* II. xxvii. 156 Which..to do, or omit, is contrary to the Lawes. **1751** JOHNSON *Rambler* No. 155 ¶12 To do nothing is in every man's power; we can never want an opportunity of omitting duties. **1854** FORD *Handbk. Spain* I. 53 No traveller ..should omit visiting the two latter.

b. Const. with *infin.*

1529 WOLSEY in Ellis *Orig. Lett.* Ser. I. II. 2 Withowt omyttyng so to do. **1632** J. HAYWARD tr. *Biondi's Eromena* 14 The Princesse..not omitting to visite her dayly. **1722** DE

FOE *Plague* 102 Some people, notwithstanding the danger, did not omit publicly to attend the worship of God. **1851** HUSSEY *Papal Power* i. 38 Innocentius did not omit to approve of this compliment.

†**c.** To leave disregarded, take no notice of.

1593 SHAKS. *2 Hen. VI*, III. ii. 382 But wherefore greeue I at an houres poore losse, Omitting Suffolkes exile, my soules Treasure? **1597** —— *2 Hen. IV*, IV. iv. 27 Therefore omit him not: blunt not his Loue.. By seeming cold, or carelesse of his will. **1603** —— *Meas. for M.* IV. iii. 77 What if we do omit This Reprobate?

†**3.** To forbear or cease to retain; to let go. *Obs.*

1604 SHAKS. *Oth.* II. i. 71 The gutter'd-Rockes, and Congregated Sands,..do omit Their mortall Natures, letting go safely by The Diuine Desdemona. **1646** SIR T. BROWNE *Pseud. Ep.* II. ii. (1686) 45 By the fire irons omit many drossie and scorious parts.

Hence **o'mitted** *ppl. a.*, **o'mitting** *vbl. sb.*

a **1548** HALL *Chron.*, *Hen. VIII* 250 b, In omittyng of their duitie. **1557** RECORDE *Whetst.* B iij b, I will set furthe here those omitted nombers. **1619** J. TAYLOR (Water P.) *Kicksey Winsey* Wks. (1630) II. 34 It is too late to put old omittings to new committings.

†**o'mittance.** *Obs. rare*$^{-1}$. [f. OMIT *v.* + -ANCE; cf. *admittance.*] = OMISSION.

1600 SHAKS. *A.Y.L.* III. v. 133, I maruell why I answer'd not againe, But that's all one: omittance is no quittance.

omitter (əʊ'mɪtə(r)). [f. OMIT *v.* + -ER[1].] One who omits or leaves unperformed.

1611 W. SCLATER *Key* (1629) 216 The omitting of a thing forbidden of God, erroneously iudged lawfull to be done, is a sin in the omitter interpretatiue, as the schooles speake. *a* **1661** FULLER (Webster 1864), The omitters thereof should not mutually censure each other.

‖**omlah** ('ɒmlɑː). *East Indian.* Also 9 **amlah**, **amla.** [ad. Arab. *umalā*, pl. of *āmil* AUMIL, 'operator, agent'; properly used as a collective pl.; but sometimes erron. with Eng. pl. *-s* added.] In northern India, A body or staff of native officials in a civil court.

c **1778** R. LINDSAY in *Lives Lindsays* (1849) III. 166, I was at this place met by the Omlah, or officers belonging to the establishment. **1834** *Baboo* I. xvii. 303 The table surrounded by the Amlah and the Mookhtars. **1845** STOCQUELER *Handbk. Brit. India* (1854) 57 The corruption of the omlah, or native officers of the courts. **1866** TREVELYAN *Dawk Bungalow* II. in *Fraser's Mag.* LXXIII. 390 We will hint to the omlahs to discover a fast which it is necessary that they shall keep with great solemnity. **1872** E. BRADDON *Life in India* vi. 253 The venality and turpitude of the native *amla* of our courts.

‖**om mani padme hum** (ɔːm mani padme hum), *int.* [Skr., lit. 'Hail! Jewel in the Lotus!' See OM *int.* and quot. 1848 below.] In Tibetan Buddhism, a mantra or mystic formula intoned in prayer and meditation. Also as *sb. phr.*

1774 G. BOGLE *Narr. Mission Tibet* (1876) iii. 29 Some old women.. were counting their beads and repeating their *Om mani padmi hums!* **1836** B. H. HODGSON in *Jrnl. Asiatic Soc. of Bengal* V. 88 The celebrated *Shadakshari Mantra*, or six-lettered invocation of him, viz. *Om! Mane padme hom!* of which so many corrupt versions and more corrupt interpretations have appeared. **1848** J. D. HOOKER *Himalayan Jrnls.* (1854) I. x. 229, I.. returned down the 'via sacra', a steep paved path flanked by.. low stone dykes, into which were let rows of stone slabs, inscribed with the sacred 'Om Mani Padmi om'.—'Hail to him of the lotus and jewel'; an invocation of Sakkya, who is usually represented holding a lotus flower with a jewel in it. **1863** E. SCHLAGINTWEIT *Buddhism in Tibet* viii. 84 Amitābha then blessed Padmapāni Bōdhisattva by laying his hands upon him, when, by virtue of this benediction, he brought forth the prayer 'Om mani padme hum'. **1895** L. A. WADDELL *Buddhism of Tibet* vi. 148 The commonest mystic formula in Lāmaism, the 'Om-ma-ni pad-me Hū-m,'—which literally means '*Om*! The Jewel in the Lotus! *Hūm*!'—is addressed to the Bodhisat Padmapāni who is represented like Buddha seated or standing within a lotus-flower. He is the patron-god of Tibet. **1901** KIPLING *Kim* ii. 47 In the pauses of their talk they could hear the low droning—'*Om mane pudme hum! Om mane pudme hum!*'—and the thick click of the wooden rosary beads. *Ibid.* v. 111 He clicked the beads, and began the '*Om mane pudme hum*' of his devotion. **1924** A. HUXLEY *Little Mexican* 16 A mystic formula, a kind of *Om mani padme hum.* **1970** J. BLOFELD *Way of Power* I. i. 38 Old women twirling their prayer-wheels and intoning *Om Mani Padme Hum* while riding in buses.

†**ommateum** (ɒmə'tiːəm). *Zool. Obs.* [mod.L., f. Gr. ὄμμα, ὀμματ- eye.] (See quots.) Hence **omma'teal** *a.*

1883 LANKESTER & BOURNE in *Q. Jrnl. Microsc. Sci.* XXIII. 182 This enlarged portion of the hypodermis is, in fact, the soft or living tissue of the eye [of the Scorpion], and may be distinguished from the lens in front of it by a special name. We propose to call it the ommatēum'. The ommateum and the lens together form the eye. *Ibid.*, A well-marked 'basement membrane', which in the region of the ommateum may be called the eye-capsule, or, better, the 'ommateal capsule'. **1884** [see next]. **1898** A. S. PACKARD *Text-bk. Entomol.* 250 (*heading*) The compound or facetted eye (ommateum).

‖**ommatidium** (ɒmə'tɪdɪəm). *Zool.* Pl. **-ia.** [mod.L., f. Gr. type *ὀμματίδιον, dim. of ὄμμα, ὀμματ- eye.] A structural element of the eyes of Invertebrates; *e.g.* one of the simple eyes which make up the compound eye of an insect.

1884 J. CARRIÈRE in *Q. Jrnl. Microsc. Sci.* XXIV. 674 The whole set of eye-units (ommatidia) of Musca vomitoria are enclosed in a chitinous capsule. [*Note*] The term 'ommateum' was introduced by Lankester in his memoir on the eyes of Scorpions to signify the entire soft parts of the non-segregate (unicorneal) eye of Arachnida and Hexapoda. .. The similar term 'ommatidium' is introduced in this paper to signify the units consisting each of a retinula and a vitrella, together with their sheath of pigment cells, into which the ommateum of the multi-corneal (polymeniscous) eye of Arthropods, is segregated. **1888** ROLLESTON & JACKSON *Anim. Life* 452 *note*, Patten.. points out.. the following general features... Every eye consists as a rule of a number of eye-elements or *ommatidia*, which may and do occur isolated as well as aggregated. Every ommatidium is composed of 2–4 central cells or *retinophoræ* fused together, and inclosing an axial nerve, and of one or more surrounding circles of pigmented cells or *retinulæ*. *Ibid.* 492 [Arthropoda] In a polymeniscous eye a single lens-facet, a vitrella, and retinula constitute an 'element', or the two latter.. an *ommatidium.* **1925** A. D. IMMS *Gen. Textbk. Entomol.* I. 79 The distinctness of vision depends partly upon the number and size of the ommatidia. **1932** METCALF & FLINT *Fund. Insect Life* iv. 110 It is believed that each ommatidium does not form an image of the whole object, but only preserves the intensity, pattern, and color of the light coming from the particular small part of the object that is in line with its long axis. Indeed, the several ommatidia, or 'tubes', are usually so isolated from each other by pigment, that no light can pass from one to the other. **1973** *Sci. Amer.* Dec. 35/3 The compound eye of *Drosophila* is a remarkable structure consisting of about 800 ommatidia: unit eyes containing eight receptor cells each.

Hence **omma'tidial** *a.*, pertaining to an ommatidium.

1890 *Anatomischer Anzeiger* V. 356 This spine-bearing cornea is soon shed and a faceted one formed, each facet.. often containing in the centre the remnants of an ommatidial spine. **1925** A. D. IMMS *Gen. Textbk. Entomol.* I. 76 The hypodermis between the ommatidial pillars becomes transformed into the secondary pigment cells. **1975** *Nature* 10 Apr. 522/2 The axons from seven retinula cells of one ommatidium interweave with those of their four neighbouring facets in such a way that four bundles of three fibres, heterogeneous with regard to their ommatidial origin, plus one single axon are produced.

ommatin ('ɒmətɪn). *Biochem.* Also **-ine.** [a. G. *ommatin* (E. Becker 1939, in *Biol. Zentralbl.* LIX. 622), f. Gr. ὄμμα, ὀμματ- eye: see -IN[1].] Any of the group of ommochromes characterized by weaker colours, less stability to alkalis, and lower molecular weights as compared with the ommins.

1940 *Biol. Abstr.* XIV. 1238/1 The 2 eye pigments [of *Ephestia*] are typical of those found among insects. The dark red or brown ommines occur in Lepidoptera, Hymenoptera, Coleoptera, Hemiptera Heteroptera, and in the nematocerous Diptera. The more weakly colored ommatines are found in the cyclorrhaphous Diptera, Odonata, and Orthoptera. **1965** [see OMMOCHROME]. **1969** R. F. CHAPMAN *Insects* vii. 109 Tyndall blues are rare in insects, but the blue of dragonflies is produced in this way, the dark background being provided by a brown-violet ommatin. **1975** D. G. COCHRAN in Candy & Kilby *Insect Biochem.* iii. 237 Storage of large quantities of 3-hydroxykynurenine occurs in vesicles or dilations of the endoplasmic reticulum of tubule cells [of *Drosophila*], and, at least in certain mutants, it is converted into ommatins and ommins.

ommatophore ('ɒmətəʊfɔə(r)). *Zool.* [a. mod.L. *ommatophorus*, f. Gr. ὀμματο- eye + -φόρος bearing.] In the Mollusca and other Invertebrates: Any part, as a tentacle, bearing an eye; an eye-stalk; *e.g.* the 'horn' of a snail. So **ommatophorous** (-'ɒfərəs) *a.*, bearing an eye, as an eye-stalk.

[**1878** BELL tr. *Gegenbaur's Comp. Anat.* 354 The tentacle ..which may be converted into a special eye-stalk (ommatophor).] **1892** *Syd. Soc. Lex.*, *Ommatophore.*

Ommiad(e, var. UMAYYAD *a.* and *sb.*

ommin ('ɒmɪn). *Biochem.* Also **-ine.** [a. G. *ommin* (E. Becker 1939, in *Biol. Zentralbl.* LIX. 611), f. Gr. ὀμμ-α eye: see :IN[1].] Any of the group of ommochromes characterized by stronger colours, greater stability to alkalis, and higher molecular weights as compared with the ommatins.

1940, etc. [see OMMATIN]. **1964** T. H. GOLDSMITH in M. Rockstein *Physiol. Insecta* I. x. 425 The principal ommin is widely distributed in arthropods and cephalopods. **1965** [see OMMOCHROME].

ommochrome ('ɒməkrəʊm). *Biochem.* [ad. G. *ommochrom* (E. Becker 1942, in *Zeitschr. f. indukt. Abstammungs- und Vererbungslehre* LXXX. 179), f. Gr. ὀμμ-α eye + χρῶμ-α colour: see -O.] Any of a group of insect pigments derived by condensation reactions from kynurenine and giving yellow, red, and brown body colours and commonly also found in the accessory cells of the eyes of insects.

1945 *Biol. Abstr.* XIX. 450/1 The distribution of this new group of pigments, the ommochromes, among arthropods has been examined. **1965** B. E. FREEMAN tr. *Vandel's Biospeleol.* xxv. 405 In the arthropods, melanines are replaced by ommochromes (ommines and ommatines). **1965** V. B. WIGGLESWORTH *Princ. Insect Physiol.* (ed. 6) xiii. 556 The ommochromes fall into two groups: the non-dialysable 'ommines', with large molecules, and the dialysable 'ommatines' with small molecules. **1970** *Nature* 26 Dec. 1336/2 The integumental pigments of the isopod Crustacea are ommochromes. **1974** *Ibid.* 30 Aug. 799/2 An early effect of ecdysoids at metamorphosis in some caterpillars is conversion of tryptophane into red ommochrome pigments.

omneity (ɒm'niːɪtɪ). *rare.* Also 7–9 **omniety.** [f. L. *omni-s*, *omne* all + -ITY: perh. immed. from a scholastic L. **omneitās*.

A more regularly-formed L. *omnitās* (of which the Eng. repr. would be *omnity*: cf. *quality* etc.) is used by Patricius *Nova de Universis Philosophia* (ed. Venice 1593) 13, app. transl. late philosophical Gr. παντότης (Prof. Bywater).]

The condition of being all; 'allness'.

1638 W. GILBERTE in *Ussher's Lett.* (1686) 494 In the apprehension of God's Omneity, and his own Nothing. **1643** SIR T. BROWNE *Relig. Med.* I. §35 So nothing became something and Omneity [*ed.* 1682 Omniety] informed Nullity into an Essence. **1816** COLERIDGE *Lay Serm.* 339 In the language of the old schools, Unity + Omneity = Totality. **1860** A. HAYWARD tr. *Goethe's Faust* Notes 167 The *Ganzen*.. is the *Omniety* of the metaphysicians.

omni ('ɒmnɪ). Abbrev. *omnirange.*

1949 *Proc. IRE* XXXVII. 832/1 The flag alarm of the course-deviation indicator is actuated by the omni receiver. **1950** *Time* 31 July 28/2 Each omni sends out a radio signal that is different for each direction from the station.

omni- (ɒmnɪ), combining form of L. *omnis* all, used already in ancient L. in forming compound adjs. as *omnifer* all-bearing, *omnigenus* of all kinds, *omniparens* all-producing, *omnipotens* all-powerful, *omnivorus* all-devouring. The number of these was increased in Christian and late L., by such additions as *omniscius* all-knowing, *omnifarius* omnifarious, *omnivalens* all-powerful, and in med. Schol. L. by such as *omnipræsens*, *omniscientia*; finally in mod.L. and esp. in Eng. itself by a multitude of words formed more or less on the model of these, or to supply a latinized equivalent to an Eng. compound in ALL-, as in ***omni-patient*** all-suffering, ***omni-percipient*** all-perceiving, etc. The longer-established and more used words in *omni-* will be found in their places as Main words; the following are of more occasional occurrence:

omni'active *a.*, active in all things or everywhere (also *absol.* as *sb.*); **'omni-antenna**, an omnidirectional antenna; **'omniarch** (-ɑːk), ruler of all things; **omnibe'nevolent** *a.* [after *omnipotent*, etc.], benevolent towards all; so **omnibe'nevolence**, universal benevolence; **omnicau'sality**, the fact of being the cause of all things; universal causality; **omni'cipient** *a.* = *omnipercipient*; **omnicor'poreal** *a.*, comprising all material bodies; **omnicre'dulity**, universal credulity, capacity of believing anything whatever; **omni-'erudite**, *a.*, learned in all (or very many) subjects, having universal erudition; **omni-'essence**, universal essence or being; **om'niferous** *a.* [L. *omnifer*: see -FEROUS] (see quot.); **om'nifidel** *a.* [after *infidel*], believing everything, holding all creeds; **omni'focal** *a.* *Ophthalm.*, designating a lens whose power changes continuously from top to bottom; also as *sb.*, such a lens; **omni'futuant**, **-'futuent** *adjs.* [L. *futuere* to have sexual relations with], practising or tolerant of both homosexual and heterosexual activity; **om'nigerent** (-dʒərənt) *a.* [L. *gerent-em*, pr. pple. of *gerĕre* to perform, carry on, do], universally working, performing all kinds of work; **'omnigraph** [see -GRAPH], 'a pantograph (*rare*)' (Webster 1864); **omni'lateral** *a.*, facing all directions; representing all points of view; so **omni'laterally** *adv.*; **om'nilegent** *a.* [L. *legent-em*, pr. pple. of *legĕre* to read], reading everything, acquainted with all (or a very great amount of) literature; **omnilingual** (-'lɪŋgwəl) *a.* [L. *lingua* tongue, language], speaking or understanding all languages; **om'niloquent** *a.* [L. *loquent-em*, pr. pple of *loquī* to speak], speaking of all things or on all subjects; **omni'lucent** *a.* [L. *lucēnt-em*, pr. pple. of *lucēre* to shine], shining upon all or everywhere; †**'omnimode**, **om'nimodous** *adjs.* [L. *omnimodus*, f. *modus* MODE], existing in all modes or ways, of all sorts; **omninescience** (-'nɛʃ(ɪ)əns) [after *omniscience*: see NESCIENCE], ignorance of everything, universal ignorance; so **omni'nescient** *a.*, ignorant of everything; **om'niparent** *a.* [L. *omniparens*: see PARENT], producing or bringing forth all things; in quot. 1609 as *sb.* = parent of all; **omni'parient** *a.* = prec. (in quot. *absol.*); **omni'parity** [see PARITY], the state of being all equal, universal equality; **om'niparous** *a.* [late L. *omnipar-us* (*c* 500), L. *-parus* bringing forth, producing] = *omniparent*; **omnipatient** (-'peɪʃənt) *a.*, patient of everything, having unlimited endurance; **omniper'cipient** *a.*, perceiving all things; so **omniper'cipience**, †**omniper'cipiency**; †**omni-'perfect** *a.*, all-perfect; **omni'pollent** *a.*, all-powerful; **omni'pregnant** *a.*, ready to produce anything; †**omni'prudent** *a.* [see PRUDENT], having universal foresight, or exercising universal providence; **omnipurpose** *a.*, serving all purposes; **'omnirange** *Aeronaut.*, (part of) a navigation system in which short-range omnidirectional VHF transmitters serve as radio beacons; **omnirepre'sentativeness**, the quality of being representative of all forms or kinds; †**omnisci'turient** *a.* [L. **scītūrīre* to desire to know], desiring to know everything; **omni'scribent, omni'scriptive** *adjs.* [L. *scrībere* to write], writing on all subjects; **omnisentience** (-'sɛnʃ(ɪ)əns), universal feeling or sensation; **omni'sentient** *a.*, having universal feeling or sensation; **omnisig'nificance**, universal significance or meaning; **omni'spective** *a.* [L. *spect-*, ppl. stem of **specĕre* (*-spicĕre*) to look], looking into or beholding all things; **omni'subjugant** *a.* [cf. SUBJUGE *v.*], subjugating everything or everyone; **omni'temporal** *a.* [L. *tempus* time], relating to all times; including in its meaning all the various tenses; so **omni'temporally** *adv.*; †**om'nitenent** *a.* [L. *omnitenens*, f. *tenēre* to hold], holding or containing all things; **omni'tolerant** *a.*, tolerant of everything; **omnitonic** (-'tɒnɪk) *a. Mus.* [F. *omnitone*], relating to all tones or tonalities (see quot.); **omni-tooled** *a.*, possessing many tools; **om'nivagant** *a.* [L. *vagānt-em*, pr. pple. of *vagāre* to wander, cf. L. *omnivagus*], wandering everywhere; †**om'nivalent** [late L. *omnivalens*], †**om'nivalous** *adjs.* [L. *valēre* to be strong], all-prevailing, all-powerful, omnipotent; so †**om'nivalence**, omnipotence. †**omni'various** *a.*, of all varieties or different kinds; **omniver'bivorous** *a.* [L. *verbum* word, *vorāre* to devour], capable of 'swallowing' all words (*humorous*); **omnivi'carious** *a.*, taking the place of (anything); **om'nividence** [L. *vidēre* to see: after *omnipotence*, etc.], the capacity of seeing all things; †**om'nividency**, a seeing of all things; 'universal inspection' (Davies); **omnivision** (-'vɪʒən), the action or faculty of seeing all things, omnividence; †**om'nivolent** *a.* [L. *omnivolus*], willing everything.

Among other self-explanatory compounds, chiefly nonce-words, which have been used, are ***omni-centralizing, omni-conclusive, omni-dexterity, omni-directive, omni-loving, omni-motive, omni-penetrative, omni-productive, omni-sciolism, omni-swallowing, omn-itinerant, omni-versifier, omnivivent*** (all-living). As derivatives from adjs., Bailey (vol. II, 1727) has ***omniferousness, omniparentness***.

1846 J. MARTINEAU *Misc.* (1852) 196 The simplicity of Monotheism cancels the pretended host, and takes the collective universe as the symbol of the Omnipresent and the *Omniactive Mind. **1873** *Contemp. Rev.* XIX. 29 He is everlastingly within creation as its inmost life, omnipresent and omni-active. **1974** *New Scientist* 24 Jan. 191 (*caption*) *Omni-antenna. **1976** *CB Mag.* June 110 (Advt.), Beam antennas vs. omni-antenna range. **1848** *Tait's Mag.* XV. 706 The hierarchy will extend from the unarch, or head of a phalange, to the *omniarch, or head of the universe. **1850** DOBELL *The Roman* vii, So the ordnance of the world, drawn up, might hail the Omniarch. **1834** L. HUNT *Jrnl.* No. 9. 65 The old dilemma between omnipotence and *omnibenevolence perplexed the understanding then as it does now. **1868** BROWNING *Ring & Bk.* XI. 2002 Omniscience sees, Omnipotence could stop, Omnibenevolence pardons. **1679** PENN *Addr. Prot.* II. 182 What an Omniscient and Omnipotent God did know and could do for Man's Salvation, an *Omnibenevolent God.. would certainly have done. **1678** CUDWORTH *Intell. Syst.* I. iv. §8. 200 Absolute perfection..does..not only comprehend..perfect knowledge or understanding, but also *omni-causality and omnipotence. **1899** BEERBOHM *More* 162 *Omnicipient in material, the master of many styles. **1678** CUDWORTH *Intell. Syst.* I. iv. §18. 347 [In ancient Egyptian theology] He [God] is both Incorporeal and *Omnicorporeal, for there is nothing of any Body, which he is not. **1845** *Q. Rev.* LXXV. 103 He loses no opportunity of showing his *omnicredulity. **1592** G. HARVEY *Pierce's Super.* in *Archaica* (1815) II. 194 What an ambidexterity, or rather *omnidexterity, had the man. **1835** SOUTHEY *Doctor* xcv. III. 211 That *omni-erudite man himself is likely to have seen the books from whence Gaffarel derived his knowledge. **1624** DONNE *Serm.* xliii. 431 In mine omnipotence, in mine omnipresence, in mine *omni-essence, he is equall partner with me. **1656** BLOUNT *Glossogr.*, **Omniferous* (*omnifer*), that beareth or bringeth forth all things, or of all kinds. **1848** *Athenæum* 8 Jan. 35 He is, then, rather *omnifidel than infidel. **1962** *Jrnl. Amer. Med. Assoc.* 19 May 595 (*heading*) The *omnifocal lens for presbyopia. **1962** *Arch. Ophthalm.* LXVIII. 777/1 (*heading*) Use of the omnifocal. *Ibid.*, Omnifocals are used binocularly but are effective monocularly in cases where only one eye can be used. **1965** *Maclean's Mag.* 20 Feb. 1 An optical company in Ohio offers to solve this problem with an 'omnifocal' lens which has power that's gradually increased from top to bottom with no blurred area or transition zone. **1974** *Year Bk. Ophthalm.* 38 Three types of lens included.. Varilux, Zoom and Omnifocal. **1929** A. HUXLEY *Do What you Will* 132 The ancient Greeks were evidently, in Sir Richard Burton's expressive phrase, '*omnifutuent'. **1966** *Listener* 24 Mar. 445/1 Stephen learns to accept himself as a homosexual only by entering a society which is innocently omnifutuant. **1967** *Ibid.* 30 Mar. 433/1 Anthony Burgess.. to whom, among others, I owe such words as *omnifutuant* and *futuancy*. **1865** E. BURRITT *Walk Land's End* 383 Here that old *omnigerent worker [the ocean] has turned lapidary. **1936** *Times Lit. Suppl.* 2 May 378/2 The present eight hundred pages set forth the science of *omnilateral aristology. **1953** *Essays in Crit.* III. II. 374 He [*sc.* Chaucer] sees life steadily, and if he is not omnilateral, he *is* manysided. **1936** *Times Lit. Suppl.* 2 May 378/2 Of old, man was *omnilaterally oriented. **1828** *Blackw. Mag.* XXIV. 872 In all the ranks of the *omnilegent philosophers. **1890** SAINTSBURY *Ess. Eng. Lit.* (1891) 331 De Quincey..was not exactly, as Southey was, 'omnilegent'. **1893** T. B. FOREMAN *Trip to Spain*, etc. 59 Antonio is apparently *omni-lingual. **1824** *New Monthly Mag.* X. 226 These *omniloquent professors of Facetiæ. **1840** MILL *Diss. & Disc.* (1859) II. 294 The bearer of encouragement and intelligence from omniloquent Zeus. **1651** BIGGS *New Disp.* 2 The serene and *omni-lucent fountain, the Intellect. **1891** M. MAARTENS *Old Maid's Love* II. ix. 213 The wide radiance of heaven.. omnipresent, omnilucent. **1656** BLOUNT *Glossogr.*, **Omnimode*,..of all manners or fashions, infinite in means, of every way. **1627** W. SCLATER *Exp. 2 Thess.* (1629) 132 You will be forced to confesse an *omnimodous desolation of the Roman Empire. **1694** HOWE *Wks.* (1834) 139 Absolute omnimodous simplicity. **1856** R. A. VAUGHAN *Mystics* (1860) I. 95 In *omni-nescience we approach Omniscience. **1886** *Athenæum* 18 Sept. 362/1 The astounding pretensions to universal knowledge and real omninescience displayed in all his novels and dramas. **1890** *Sat. Rev.* 22 Nov. 574/2 One of the omniscient, or *omni-nescient, persons who do 'London Correspondence'. **1609** J. DAVIES *Holy Roode* (1878) 12 O Thou all-powreful-kind *Omniparent, What holds thy hands that should defend thy head? **1647** H. MORE *Poems* 197 Omniparent Sol with golden Visage clear. **1886** SHELDON tr. *Flaubert's Salammbo* v. 99 The supreme Rabbet, the *Omniparient, the last-imagined. **1635** F. WHITE *Sabbath* Ep. Ded. 9 They command whatsoever their working-heads affect..to wit, *Omniparity of Churchmen. **1822** *New Monthly Mag.* V. 245 Worse than this..is the levelling and jumbling of ages by this preposterous omniparity of appearance. **1755** JOHNSON, *All-bearing*, that which bears everything; *omniparous. **1831** CARLYLE *Sart. Res.* II. iii, With this his so omnipotent or rather *omnipatient Talent of being Gulled. **1880** A. SOMERVILLE *Autobiog.* 167 That plain solid omnipatient man had within him some immense resource of high principle and pure passion. **1664** H. MORE *Antid. Idolatry* ii. 21 This Omnipresence or *Omnipercipience terrestrial. **1894** H. NISBET *Bush Girl's Rom.* 235 He saw many different phases of this omnipercipience, which may be bestowed at any moment upon the industrious devotee of this ancient lore, or black magic. **1664** H. MORE *Antid. Idolatry* ii. 23 The Communication of this *Omnipercipiency. *Ibid.* 20 An *omnipercipient Omnipresence, which does hear and see what-ever is said or transacted in the World. **1932** H. H. PRICE *Perception* vii. 202 This could only be avoided if we had been *omni*percipient. **1678** CUDWORTH *Intell. Syst.* I. iv. §18. 331 This is the Perfect and genuine Son of the first *Omniperfect [Gr. παντελείου] Being. **1922** JOYCE *Ulysses* 377 The certain sign of *omnipollent nature's incorrupted benefaction. **1611** DONNE *Panegyrical Verse Coryat's Crud.*, *Omniprægnant.. They hatch all wares for which the buyer cals. **1812** COLERIDGE in *Lit. Rem.* (1836) I. 316 A certain omnipregnant, nihili-parturient genius of my acquaintance. **1642** VICARS *God in Mount* (1644) 1 The omnipotent and *omniprudent great God of heaven and earth. **1961** *Omnipurpose [see OMNICOMPETENT *a.*]. **1947** *Electronics* Oct. 95/2 There are also voice channels on both the runway localizer and the *omnirange, which are used generally for traffic control and weather information. **1951** *Gloss. Aeronaut. Terms* (*B.S.I.*) III. 27 *V.H.F. Omni-range*, a short-range, very-high-frequency, omni-directional beacon which provides an indication in the aircraft of the bearing of the beacon, or left-right track indication. **1959** K. HENNEY *Radio Engin. Handbk.* (ed. 5) xxv. 27 As of June 30, 1955, there were 410 omniranges in operation. **1966** D. FRANCIS *Flying Finish* xvii. 199 The V.O.R.—Very high frequency Omni-range—by which one navigated from one radio beacon to the next. **1842** MRS. BROWNING *Grk. Chr. Poets* 25 The secret of his wonderful fertility and *omnirepresentativeness. **1837** C. LOFFT *Self-formation* I. 106 These *omnisciturient gentry resemble..one of the monster words of Aristophanes. **1891** *Sat. Rev.* 13 June 700/2 The subject has since been dealt with by the *omniscribent Sir Thomas Farrer. **1821** *Blackw. Mag.* VIII. 356 In short, he may be reckoned *omni-scriptive or pangraphic. **1851** J. B. HUME *Undine & Viking* II. ii. in *Poems of early years* 19 Mid-centre of the Universe, all feeling, eye and ear In *Omnisentience poised, he lives throughout the total sphere. **1932** H. H. PRICE *Perception* iv. 72 If we were **omnisentient* beings,..able to sense all at once all the sense-data which can ever be sensed by every sentient human or non-human. **1835** SOUTHEY *Doctor* xciii. III. 193 Which in its *omnisignificance may promise anything, and yet pledges the writer to nothing. **1743** S. BOYSE *Poems* III, Thee, great omniscient *omnispective Power! Thee first and last,—thee only, I adore! **1911** BEERBOHM *Zuleika D.* ii. 23 But would she ever meet whom, looking up to him, she could love—she, the *omnisubjugant? **1956** P. FLEMING *My Aunt's Rhinoceros* 141 After the war the bureaucrats no longer held their omnisubjugant trump. **1883** B. F. WESTCOTT *Historic Faith* xi. 144 The 'eternal' does not in essence express the infinite extension of time but the absence of time, not the *omni-temporal but the supra-temporal. **1890** *Classical Rev.* Oct. 381/1 In this sense it [the Infinitive] may be called timeless = omnitemporal. **1970** P. A. BERTOCCI *Person God Is* xii. 223 It is..my concern to press the question on both Advaitin and Visishtadvaitin: Why not reconceive the perfection of God so that good and evil, truth and error, progress and decay, can affect the qualitative manner in which God experiences himself and the world, and in a way consistent with his omni-temporal unity and continuity? **1961** E. NAGEL *Struct. of Sci.* iv. 70 Suppose there are (*omnitemporally) no physical objects that do not attract each other. **1964** *Philos. Rev.* LXXIII. 486 For something to qualify as being true omnitemporally. **1656** BLOUNT *Glossogr.*, **Omnitenent*,..that contains all things. **1855** BAGEHOT *Lit. Stud.*, *Cowper* (1879) I. 264 A vague, literary, *omnitolerant idleness. **1879** GROVE *Dict. Music* I. 517 The '*omnitonic' system [of Fétis], whose main principle is that harmonic combinations exist by which any given sound may be resolved into any key and any mode. **1851** H. MELVILLE *Moby Dick* III. xxi. 146 This *omni-tooled, open-and-shut carpenter, was,..no mere machine of an automaton. **1656** BLOUNT *Glossogr.*, **Omnivagant*, wandring every where, that runs up and down in all places. **1891** L. MERRICK *Violet Moses* III. xxiii. 200 Vice was omnivagant and reigned supreme. **1607** J. DAVIES *Summa Totalis* (1878) 17 Which Sonne is but the Sires Intelligence, Making another one *Omnivalence. **1609** —— *Holy Roode* 12 Is Sinne so strong, or so *Omniualent, That by Her pow'r, thy pow'r is vanquished? **1773** J. ROSS *Fratricide* I. 236 (MS.) By ocular proof of that omnivalent power. *Ibid.* II. 50 The dreadful dungeon of *omnivalous pains. **1624** HEYWOOD *Gunaik.* VIII. 395 Tiberius Cæsar builded that chamber, wherein were discovered the *omnivarious shapes of beastly and preposterous luxuries. **1858** O. W. HOLMES *Aut. Breakf.-t.* xi. 102, I am *omniverbivorous by nature and training. **1967** V. NABOKOV *Speak, Memory* (ed. 2) ii. 42 The game in use was the regular 'draw poker', with, occasionally, the additional tingle of jackpots and an *omnivicarious joker. **1884** E. A. ABBOTT *Flatland* II. xviii, *Omnividence is the attribute of God alone. *a* **1661** FULLER *Worthies* I. (1662) 26 Not to pretend inspection into the Book of life, seeing all other books have come under their *Omnividencie. **1861** MISS BEAUFORT *Egypt. Sep. & Syr. Shrines* I. v. 99 The hawk signifying *omnivision, and the scarabæus, chiefly typical of creation and of the world. **1656** BLOUNT *Glossogr.*, **Omnivolent*, that willeth or desireth all things.

omniana (ɒmnɪ'eɪnə). [f. L. *omnis* all, *omnia* all things + -ANA.] Notes or scraps of information about everything, or about all (or very many) kinds of things; '*ana*' of all kinds. Also *attrib.*

1807 W. TAYLOR in Robberds *Mem.* II. 185 Now it is only in the Athenæum that I get at the *omniana* passing in your brain. **1824** SOUTHEY *Lett.* (1856) III. 426, I should very well like to edit Sir T. Browne's works..and add such Omniana notes as my stores may enable me to furnish.

omnibenevolent, etc.: see OMNI-.

omnibus ('ɒmnɪbəs), *sb.* and *a.* [a. F. *omnibus* (*c* 1828, in Dict. Acad. 1835), a. L. *omnibus* 'for all', dative pl. of *omnis* all, in Fr. phrase *voiture omnibus* = *voiture pour tous*, 'vehicle for all'.]

A. *sb.*

1. a. A four-wheeled public vehicle for carrying passengers, with the inside seats extending along the sides, and the entrance at the rear, and with or without seats on the roof; usually plying along a fixed route. (Colloq. shortened to BUS.) ¶ ***omnibi***, representing a spurious 'plural' (in quot. 1889 genitive singular) form, occurs occasionally.

1829 SHILLIBEER *Mem. to Chairman of Board of Stamps* 3 Apr. 5, I am..engaged in building 2 Vehicles after the manner of the recently established French *Omnibus*, which when completed I purpose starting on the Paddington road. **1829** *Saunders' Newsletter*, The new vehicle, called the omnibus, commenced running this morning [4 July] from Paddington to the City. **1830** *Hist.* in *Ann. Reg.* 188/1 A barricade was formed across the street by one of those long coaches to which the Parisians have given the name of *Omnibus*. **1834** L. RITCHIE *Wand. by Seine* 179 *note*, A steam omnibus has also begun to ply regularly on the crowded thoroughfare of the City Road. **1835** MARRYAT *Olla Podr.* vi. (Rtldg.) 20 Omnibuses, diligences, or cars, which are attached to the..steam-tugs. **1840** W. HOWITT *Visits to Remarkable Places* (ser. I.) 200 Trains of omnibuses, or omnibi, are flying down to the Broomielaw every hour. **1862** B. TAYLOR *Home & Abr.* Ser. II. viii. 397, I was put down at the station, where omnibuses were in waiting. **1881** GRANT WHITE *Eng. Within & Without* iv. 79 The London omnibus, or 'bus as it is universally called..is in form a mere ugly square box on wheels. **1889** E. DOWSON *Let.* 23 June (1967) 85, I trust you arrived chez toi—in all sobriety last night & accomplished the de[s]census Av—I should say omnibi with discretion. **1969** *Times* 18 Jan. 20/3 The portmanteau term 'reprint' evades definition. It covers series, 'evergreens', omnibi, disinterments, defrostings, definitive editions, [etc.].

b. *fig.*

1831 W. IRVING in *Life & Lett.* (1864) II. 455 The great reform omnibus [the Reform Bill] moves but slowly. **1894** J. H. OVERTON *Eng. Ch. 19th Cent.* 121 His [Arnold's] scheme of making the Church a sort of theological omnibus never took any definite shape.

2. a. = *omnibus-box*: see B. 2.

1844 C. G. F. GORE *Quid pro Quo* (ed. 3) 81 What if I.. swell the 'Bravos' of the Omnibus? **1848** THACKERAY *Van. Fair* vi, Having just arrived from the omnibus at the opera.

b. Short for *omnibus book* (see sense B. 3).

The word 'omnibus' was also used in the sense 'omnibus journal', i.e. a newspaper comprising a variety of items, in two early 19th-century publications, *The National Omnibus; and General Advertiser* (1831), and *The Lancashire Omnibus, a Journal of Literature and Amusement* (1832).

1930 *Writer* Jan. 74/2 One of the recent omnibuses contained selected short stories. **1931** 'J. GROVE' (*title*) The omnibus of romance. **1937** 'A. ARMSTRONG' (*title*) The laughter omnibus. **1976** R. USBORNE *Wodehouse at Work* (rev. ed.) iii. 92 The Preface that Wodehouse wrote for the 1974 omnibus *World of Psmith*. **1978** *Bookseller* 8 Apr. 2196/3 When..Charles Pick..dreamed up those jumbo Heinemann Octopus omnibuses, it seemed..only a matter of time before Collins put some..authors into similar vehicles.

3. *Glass-making.* (See quot.)

1875 KNIGHT *Dict. Mech.*, *Omnibus*. 1. (*Glass-making.*) A sheet-iron cover for articles in a leer or annealing-arch, in order to protect them from drafts of air.

4. A man or boy who assists a waiter at an hotel, restaurant, etc.

1888 *Star* 11 Aug. 4/5 To pay to what is known in a restaurant as an 'omnibus', i.e. a lad that clears the tables. **1897** *Daily News* 19 June 2/6 Omnibuses..apprentices—who wait on the waiters.

5. *attrib.* and *Comb.*, as ***omnibus-cad*** (CAD[2] 3), ***-driver***, ***-driving*** adj., ***-fashion*** adv., ***-office***,

-riding adj., *sleigh*, *-ticket*, *trade*, *traffic*, *wheel*; **omnibus man**, the driver or conductor of an omnibus.

1848 THACKERAY *Bk. Snobs* xlix, A sceptical audience of *omnibus-cads and nursemaids. **1843** POE *Mystery of Marie Roget* in *Ladies' Compan.* (N.Y.) Feb. 166/1 The *omnibus-driver, Valence. **1870** 'F. FERN' *Ginger-Snaps* 304 This honored name, shouted from lungs that would not have disgraced an omnibus-driver. **1865** DICKENS *Mut. Fr.* IV. xvi, *Omnibus-driving expressions. **1857** *Christian Misc.* July 219/2 We know no class of men in this country who undergo a more severe life of toil..than the *omnibus-men and cabmen of London. **1900** *Daily News* 12 Nov. 6/6 For the benefit of the Omnibusmen's Superannuation Fund. **1854** M. CUMMINS *Lamplighter* xviii. 112 You know the way from the *omnibus-office. **1844** *Knickerbocker* XXIV. 91 His opinions against the *omnibus-riding of so many of our idle citizens. **1860** *Boston Auditor's Ann. Rep. 1859–60* 323 One covered *omnibus sleigh. **1852** E. E. HALE *If, Yes, & Perhaps* (1868) 3 This [sum]..would buy the *omnibus tickets. **1834** *Tait's Mag.* Feb. 41/1 The *omnibus trade became too flourishing to be limited to what are called the 'metropolis roads'. **1869** *Engineering* 26 Nov. 348/1 With some slight modifications of detail, Mr. Wright's doors might..be advantageously applied to many railway carriages employed in working metropolitan, or as it is often called, '*omnibus' traffic. **1883** E. W. HAMILTON *Diary* 15 Dec. (1972) II. 525 Trains worked by electricity admit of any amount of sub-division, which is no small consideration as it facilitates *omnibus* traffic and dispenses with the necessity of constructing the permanent way as strong as it now is. **1884** *Daily News* 19 Sept. 5/2 The railways must unite the facilities of omnibus traffic with their greater speed. **1868** *Less. Mid. Age* 2 The rattle of *omnibus wheels running down to the railway station.

B. *adj.*

1. Relating to or serving for numerous distinct objects at once; comprising a large number of items or particulars: e.g. an ***omnibus bill***, ***clause***, ***order***, ***faculty***.

1842 *Congress. Globe* 27th Congress 2 Sess. App. 661/1 These two articles..were caught in the omnibus, or dragnet section, which is placed in the rear of the bill. **1850** *Ibid.* 31st Congress 1 Sess. App. 524/1, I am opposed to all omnibus bills, and all amalgamation projects. **1857** in Herrig *Beiträge* XXII. 163 *Omnibus-bills*, bills which contain laws dissimilar in their character and purposes. **1884** *Western Daily Press* 22 Feb. 5/5 The Corporation Omnibus Bill has been rejected. **1887** *Pall Mall G.* 15 Aug. 2/1 The Revenue Bill which Mr. Goschen introduced..is an omnibus bill of four parts, dealing with Customs, Taxes, Stamps, Excise, and Miscellaneous, in twenty-six clauses. **1889** *Boston* (Mass.) *Jrnl.* 16 Feb. 6/4 The instructions moved..to the Conference Committee upon the omnibus Territorial bill. **1889** *Echo* 16 Nov. 2/3 Each man pays an 'omnibus' contribution of a shilling a week for benefits. **1891** *Daily News* 1 Oct. 5/6 There is what is called an 'omnibus resolution' embracing a whole programme of reforms. **1900** *Durham Dioces. Gaz.* Feb. 10 Omnibus Faculty for 1899 for the following works. **1968** *Globe & Mail* (Toronto) 3 Feb. 40/2 All organizations said, however, that changes in existing regulations are necessary and many of the Criminal Code amendments contained in an omnibus bill presented by Justice Minister Pierre Trudeau are good ones. **1972** *N.Y. Law Jrnl.* 10 Oct. 18/9 Defendant's omnibus motion is disposed of as hereinafter indicated. **1974** *Times* 30 Aug. 15/2 The plan..is to work up some omnibus convention which most will sign.

2. *spec.* **a.** ***omnibus box***, a name given to large boxes on the pit tier in some theatres and opera-houses, appropriated to a number of subscribers. **b.** ***omnibus train*** [after F. *train omnibus* (Hatz.)], a railway train stopping at all the stations on the route. **c.** In electrical works, applied to a bar, wire, etc. through which passes the whole of the current proceeding from the source.

1853 H. D. WOLFF *Pict. Span. Life* 50 Some..are hired for the season by families, while others are omnibus boxes, or let off in ephemeral places. **1864** B. LUMLEY *Reminisc. Opera* 15 [The great 'Tamburini Row' at opening of Opera season 1841]. The famous *omnibus* boxes were filled, towards the conclusion of the opera, with the fashionable allies of the coalition. *Ibid.* 16 The whole party of the noble and fashionable occupants of the omnibus boxes leaped on the stage...The gallant chevaliers of the 'omnibus' waved their hats triumphantly and shouted 'Victory!' **1882** SERJT. BALLANTINE *Exper.* I. 295 He was in the omnibus box at the opera. **1893** MARG. SYMONDS *Doge's Farm* 164 We..were advised..to travel to Padua by the ordinary omnibus train, and let the specials go by. **1894** *Times* 17 Jan. 7/5 A duster was found lying on the terminal..which was connected with the omnibus bar, and the deceased had, it was stated, left the omnibus plug on when it ought to have been off. **1902** *Chambers's Jrnl.* Dec. 823/2 On this level, where it touched the stage, we had an 'omnibus box', exactly after the pattern of the proverbial one at Her Majesty's, and occupied usually by the same distinguished noblemen. **1922** A. HADDON *Green Room Gossip* iv. 95 The passing of the green room reminds me of another effete institution of the English theatre—the omnibus box.

3. omnibus book, **volume**, etc., a book or volume having a large and occas. varied content, *spec.* one containing several reprinted works by a single author or works of the same kind and published at a price designed to place it within the reach of a wide public; **omnibus letter**, a letter intended for more than one recipient; **omnibus-sized** *a.*, of the size of an omnibus book; **omnibus ticket**, one admitting a number of persons.

1929 *Daily Tel.* 1 Jan. 6/2 It is a day of what the publishers call 'omnibus books', meaning works which carry many and varied passengers. **1933** *Mind* XLII. 525 Hume's omnibus letter addressed to Dr. Hugh Blair, and through Blair to Dr. Jardine. **1931** *Times Lit. Suppl.* 19 Nov. 918/1 This second instalment of his short stories, an almost omnibus-sized book. **1868** *Rep. Iowa Agric. Soc. 1867* 408 Some..tender hearted friends would take in their settlement [= family] and then proceed to some hole..in the fence and hand his 'omnibus ticket' to some other parent. **1928** *Times Lit. Suppl.* 12 July 514/4 The 'omnibus' volume of 'Great Short Stories of Detection, Mystery and Horror',..runs to some 1,250 pages. **1928** *Observer* 22 July 8 The four novels together make one of the most desirable of 'omnibus' volumes. **1928** *Publishers' Circular* 14 July 39/2 (*heading*) The Omnibus Wells.

Hence **'omnibus** *v.*, (*a*) ***to omnibus it***, to travel by omnibus; also *absol.*; (*b*) to place in an omnibus; (*c*) to convey by omnibus; (*d*) to publish an omnibus edition of (an author).

1833 W. C. MACREADY *Diary* 7 Nov. (1912) I. 76, I omnibused down to Drury Lane. **1836** COL. HAWKER *Diary* (1893) II. 111, I was obliged to cab it, omnibus it, and run it the whole morning. **1863** 'G. HAMILTON' *Gala-Days* 121 We were quickly omnibused to the relics of Donegana. **1886** *Tinsley's Mag.* Sept. 227 The other day I was omnibused with a bore. **1933** *Times Lit. Suppl.* 5 Jan. 1/2 For the author the possibility of becoming popular enough in his lifetime to be omnibused or to omnibus himself with profit may be looked on as a new prize in the race for fame.

omnicausality to **omni-essence**: see OMNI-.

omnicompetent (ˌɒmnɪˈkɒmpɪtənt), *a.* [f. OMNI- + COMPETENT *a.*] Competent to deal with everything; *spec.* possessing jurisdiction or authority to act in all matters. Hence **omni'competence**.

1827 BENTHAM *Logical Arrangem.* Wks. 1843 X. 561/2 Judicature undiscontinued..Judicatories omnicompetent. **1889** MAITLAND *Sel. Pleas Manorial Crts.* p. lvi, Men no longer see any objection to the King's court making itself an omnicompetent court of first instance. **1900** *Eng. Hist. Rev.* Jan. 121 That [doctrine] which would preach the omnicompetence of parliament. **1926** R. H. TAWNEY *Relig. & Rise of Capitalism* ii. 124 Recent political theory has been prolific in criticisms of the omnicompetent state. **1937** *Times Lit. Suppl.* 1 May 320 His omnicompetence dealt with the history of ideas as swiftly as with the measurement of the hide. **1943** C. S. LEWIS *Abolition of Man* iii. 30 The man-moulders of the new age will be armed with the powers of an omnicompetent state and an irresistible scientific technique. **1952** V. A. DEMANT *Relig. & Decline of Capitalism* ii. 57 The principle of the omnicompetent state and the myth of the self-sufficient individual. **1961** *Economist* 30 Dec. 1276/1 A sort of ghostly middleman between omnipurpose boroughs and omnicompetent Government departments. **1967** *Punch* 11 Oct. 541 She comes from a famous wine family..so she is omnicompetent, bullying her *maitre de chai*, [etc.]. **1971** *Mod. Law. Rev.* XXXVI. 611 Parliament as an institution must be sovereign or omnicompetent at any given moment of time. **1973** *Times Lit. Suppl.* 28 Dec. 1588/2 The computers are no longer considered even by their supporters to be omnicompetent. **1975** *Times* 25 July 13/5 Deference to professional omnicompetence is, of course, gratifying.

ˌomnidi'rectional, *a.* Also omni-directional. [f. OMNI- + DIRECTIONAL *a.*] Of equal sensitivity or power in all directions (usu., all horizontal directions).

1927 *Daily Tel.* 22 Mar. 13 The Marconi Company quoted £66,153 for the Beam system and £29,163 for a system of omni-directional communication. **1932** *Times Educ. Suppl.* 31 Dec. p. i/2 The other short-wave transmitter worked on 15,140 kc/s, using an omni-directional aerial. **1947** BUCK & PIERCE in J. S. Hall *Radar Aids to Navigation* ii. 51 The uhf omnidirectional beacons..are based primarily on the low-frequency system used for marine navigation. **1952** E. A. LAPORT *Radio Antenna Engin.* ii. 94 Experience has been gained with vertical radiators at many hundreds of broadcast stations, each employing one or more for omnidirectional or directive radiation. **1959** H. HOBSON *Mission House Murder* xxi. 140 They..fixed an omni-directional, remotely controlled microphone which transmitted on a closed circuit. **1969** R. B. FULLER *Operating Man. Spaceship Earth* vi. 88 Einstein formulated his famous equation E = M (matter's mass, explained in the terms of C²—speed of an omni-directional (radiant) surface wave's expansion, unfettered, in a vacuum). **1976** *CB Mag.* June 7/1 (Advt.), Electrical design of the long, 64 wavelength vertical radiating element plus full size radials guarantee..highest signal radiation efficiency in the desired vertical plane and omnidirectional, full coverage transmitting and receiving pattern.

Hence **ˌomnidirectio'nality**, the property of being omnidirectional; **ˌomnidi'rectionally** *adv.*, in all directions.

1950 *Jrnl. R. Aeronaut. Soc.* LIV. 279/2 By comparing the phase of the rotating radiation pattern with that of a reference signal radiated omni-directionally, the bearing of the aircraft from the beacon is determined. **1966** L. V. BLAKE *Antennas* vii. 330 In unstabilized-spacecraft applications three-dimensional omnidirectionality may be desired. **1972** *Science* 20 Oct. 273/1 In order to achieve omnidirectionality, a second array is envisaged, located at right angles to the first. **1976** *Wireless World* Mar. 44/3 Real antennas do not radiate omnidirectionally, but concentrate the power into a directional beam.

omniety: see OMNEITY.

omnifarious (ɒmnɪˈfɛərɪəs), *a.* [f. L. *omnifari-us* (f. OMNI- all: cf. *multifarious*) + -OUS.] Of all kinds or forms: exceedingly various; relating to or dealing with all kinds of things.

1653 H. MORE *Antid. Ath.* III. xv. (1712) 135 That all the Species of things..came first out of the Earth, by the omnifarious attempt of the particles of the matter upon one another. **1678** CUDWORTH *Intell. Syst.* I. i. §25. 26 The Confused Chaos of Omnifarious Atoms. **1708** J. PHILIPS *Cyder* II. 209 If Thou..omnifarious Drinks wou'dst brew. **1838–9** HALLAM *Hist. Lit.* II. II. i. §22 A mind capacious of omnifarious erudition.

Hence **omni'fariousness**.

1806 W. TAYLOR in Robberds *Mem.* II. 127 In the nude cypherableness of the story and in the omnifariousness of the language.

omniferous, etc.: see OMNI-.

omnific (ɒmˈnɪfɪk), *a.* [f. med. or mod.L. *omnific-us*, f. OMNI- + *-ficus* making.] Making all things; all-creating.

1667 MILTON *P.L.* VII. 217 Silence, ye troubl'd waves, and thou Deep, peace, Said then th' Omnific Word. **1778** *Phil. Surv. S. Irel.* 441 Who attribute to climate an omnifick influence upon the fine arts. **1868** MILMAN *St. Paul's* vi. 115 The creation of the world by one Omnific God.

Hence **om'nificness** (Bailey vol. II, 1727).

So **om'nificent** *a.* = OMNIFIC.

1677 LOCKE *Jrnl.* 8 Feb. in *Essay Draft A* (1936) 84 They who out of a great care not to admitt unintelligible things deny or question an eternall omnificent spirit run them selves into a greater difficulty by makeing an eternall and intelligent matter. **1862** MRS. SPEID *Last Yrs. Ind.* 178 Visvuarma, the carpenter of the gods, but properly the *omnificent*, in his haste cut his finger. **1929** R. BRIDGES *Testament of Beauty* iv. 177 Joyful obedience With reverence to'ard the omnificent Creator and First Cause.

om'nificence. [f. OMNIFIC *a.* + -ENCE.] The fact or quality of being omnific, or of making or doing everything.

1881 RUSKIN *Our Fathers have told Us* I. ii. 62 Unwearied in protective friendship, in meekly dextrous omnificence, in latent tutorship. **1941** *Mind* L. 297 He therefore devotes the rest of the chapter to divine 'omnificence', *i.e.* the doctrine that all that is in fact done is done by God.

omniform (ˈɒmnɪfɔːm), *a.* [ad. late L. *omniform-is*, f. OMNI- + *forma* shape, form: see -FORM.] Of all forms or shapes; taking any or every form; exhibiting or comprising every variety of form.

1647 H. MORE *Song of Soul* I. I. ix, This is that ancient Eidos omniform. **1691–8** NORRIS *Pract. Disc.* (1711) III. 155 If the Soul be united to this omni-form Essence of God. **1744** BERKELEY *Siris* §281 The living fire, the living, omniform seminary of the world, and other expressions..occurring in the ancient and Platonic philosophy. **1888** *Harper's Mag.* Apr. 760 Thou omniform and most mysterious Sea.

So **omni'formal** *a.* = OMNIFIC *a.*; †**omni'formist** [? after *conformist*], one who assumes all forms or fashions, one who conforms to all.

1683 E. HOOKER *Pref. Pordage's Mystic Div.* 59 To become all things to all men, with the Doctor of the Gentiles, that Omniformist. **1839** BAILEY *Festus* xix. (1848) 218 The stars..Stand clustered into omniformal spheres.

omniformity (ɒmnɪˈfɔːmɪtɪ). [f. late L. *omniform-is* (see prec.) + -ITY.] The quality of being omniform; the being of all forms.

1644 HARDWICK in *Toler. Disappr. & Cond.* (1670) 26 We have undertaken..the establishment of Uniformity, and how can that stand with this Omniformitie..I understand not. **1647** H. MORE *Song of Soul* III. II. xliv, The soul..By her own Centrall omniformity Brings forth in her own self when ought doth move her. **1701** NORRIS *Ideal World* I. v. 222 Containing some modal account of the Divine Ideality or Omniformity. **1816** COLERIDGE *Lay Serm.* 346 Symbolizing the unity of nature, while it represents the omniformity of her delegated functions.

'omniformness = prec. (Bailey vol. II, 1727).

omnify (ˈɒmnɪfaɪ), *v.* [f. OMNI- + -FY.]

†**1.** *trans.* To make everything of; to account as all in all. *Obs.*

1622 WARD *Serm., Christ all* (1862) 3 That he might..magnify or rather, as you see [Col. iii. 11] omnify his Lord and Master Christ. **1668** HOWE *Bless. Righteous* (1825) 89 A nullifying of self: and magnifying (I may call it omnifying) of God.

2. To render universal.

1810 COLERIDGE in *Lit. Rem.* (1838) III. 221 Omnify the disputed point into a transcendant, and you may defy the opponent to lay hold of it. **1896** *Chicago Advance* 10 Dec. 839 If, in all 'well-to-do' circles, the family wish to be omnified, to give money to real prisoners of poverty or disease.

†**omni'gatherum**. *Obs.* Also 5 **omnegadrium**, 6 **omni-gatharum**, **omnegatherum**; *Sc.* 6 **omnigatherome**, **-rine**, 7 **omnigad(d)rum**, 9 **omnegatherum**. [f. OMNI- + GATHER *v.* + *-um* after L. sbs.] = OMNIUM GATHERUM; *spec.* in Scottish burgh records, 'a name given to the unincorporated craftsmen of a burgh' (Jam. *Suppl.* 2).

14.. HOCCLEVE in *B.M. Addit. MS.* 24062 (Wks. E.E.T.S. Introd. 30 *note*) Omnegadrium. **1562** TURNER *Herbal* II. 70b, Dioscorides of whom he [Pliny] hath conueyed so much learned stuf into hys omnigatherum. **1579–80** NORTH *Plutarch* (1676) 492 They [Souldiers] were a rash confused multitude of Omnigatherum together, having no reason nor patience. **1592** G. HARVEY *3rd Lett.* in *Shaks. Allusion Bks.* I. (1874) 131 A Rayler, a beggar, an Omnigatherum, a Gay-nothing. **1603** SIR C. HEYDON *Jud. Astrol.* xxi 423 The rest of his hotch-potch and omnigatherum against Astrologie. **1604** *Burgh Records Stirling* 17 Dec. (1887) 112 Thair salbe joyned, yeirlie, to the counsall of this burgh, tua of the ald merchand bailleis, and tua of the *omnigaddrum*, as extraordiner persones of counsall. **1642** *Ibid.* 28 Nov. 184 The toun sall pay yeirlie

£4, the guild brethren £20, the crafts £20, the maltmen £10, and the omnigadrum, viz. the wrichtis, maissones, coupares, litstares, glassin-wrichtis, sklaitteris, gairdneris, the soume of ten pundis yeirlie. **1650** *Ibid.* (1889) 302 The mechanikis and omnigadrum. **1819** W. TENNANT *Papistry Storm'd* (1827) 97 And terrour garr'd them loup pell-mell.. In omne-gatherum at that bell.

om'nigener, *a. rare*⁻¹. [a. late L. *omnigener* (in *Gloss. Cyrill.*) of every kind, f. OMNI- + *genus, gener-* kind.] = next.

1857 *Nat. Mag.* I. 371 Bulwer Lytton who on the whole has achieved the omnigener ultimate success.

omnigenous (ɒm'nɪdʒɪnəs), *a.* [f. L. *omnigen-us* of all kinds (f. *omni-* all- + *genus* kind) + -OUS.] Of all kinds.

1650 B. *Discolliminium* 28, I could demonstrate it to be Heterogeneous, Heterodoxous, Incongrous, Omnigenous, Pluranimous. **1766** G. CANNING *Anti-Lucretius* III. 212 Spinoza, known too well to fame, Who dar'd a God omnigenous to frame. **1814** COLERIDGE *Lett., to J. Kenyon* (1895) 640 A miraculous combination of erudition, broad, deep, and omnigenous. **1859** *Times* 22 Mar. 9/5 National Museums and universal omnigenous collections and reservoirs of all conceivable things.

Hence **om'nigenousness** (Bailey vol. II, 1727).

omnigerent to **omniperfect**: see OMNI-.

omnipotence (ɒm'nɪpətəns). [ad. late L. *omnipotentia*, f. *omnipotent-em*: see -ENCE. Cf. F. *omnipotence* (1527 in Hatz.-Darm.).] The quality of being omnipotent; infinite or unlimited power; almightiness. **a.** *strictly*, as an attribute of deity; hence God himself, = 'the Omnipotent'.

1566 GASCOIGNE *Jocasta* III. Chorus, Who thinks that Ioue the maker of vs all,.. Hath not in hym omnipotence also To guide and gouerne all things here below? **1602** MARSTON *Ant. & Mel.* III. Wks. 1856 I. 36 Tossing up A gratefull spirit to Omnipotence. **1651** HOBBES *Leviath.* II. xxxi. 187 *margin*, The Right of Gods Soveraignty is derived from his Omnipotence. **1725** POPE *Odyss.* I. 78 And will Omnipotence neglect to save The suffering virtue of the wise and brave? **1892** WESTCOTT *Gospel of Life* 218 Omnipotence is simply the power of fulfilling the absolute law of perfection as it is realised.

b. *gen.* as an attribute of persons or things; hence *transf.* an omnipotent force or agency.

c **1590** MARLOWE *Faust.* i. 52 Oh, what a world of profit and delight, Of power, of honour, of omnipotence, Is promis'd to the studious artizan! *a* **1674** CLARENDON *Hist. Reb.* x. §123 The Omnipotence of an Ordinance of Parliament, confirmed all that was this way done. **1818** BYRON *Ch. Har.* IV. xciii, Opinion an omnipotence,—whose veil Mantles the earth with darkness, until right And wrong are accidents. **1889** *Daily News* 3 Apr. 4/8 The omnipotence of Parliament, which means its supremacy over the law.

†**om'nipotency.** *Obs.* [ad. late L. *omnipotentia*: see prec. and -ENCY.] = prec. **a.** *strictly*, as an attribute of deity.

c **1470** G. ASHBY *Active Policy* 218 God of his omnipotencie Hath brought you now forth to our grete comfort. **1555** EDEN *Decades* 311 To declare his omnipotencie & wisedome. **1684** T. BURNET *Th. Earth* II. 69 'Tis a great step to omnipotency: and 'tis hard to define what miracles, on this side creation, require an infinite power. *a* **1703** BURKITT *On N.T., Matt.* xiv. 15 All things being equally easy to omnipotency.

b. *generally*: see prec. b.

1604 JAS. I *Counterbl.* (Arb.) 107 Such is the miraculous omnipotencie of our strong tasted Tobacco, as it cures all sorts of diseases. **1639** DRUMM. OF HAWTH. *Remora* Wks. (1711) 189 It is answered, that the parliament and general assembly have an omnipotency and arbitrary power. **1675** BROOKS *Gold. Key* Wks. 1867 V. 467 Faith.. hath a kind of omnipotency in it; it is able to do all things.

omnipotent (ɒm'nɪpətənt), *a.* [a. F. *omnipotent* (11–12th c. in Littré), ad. L. *omnipotent-em*, f. OMNI- + *potens, -ent-em* able, powerful.]

1. Strictly said of God (or of a deity) or His attributes: Almighty, infinite in power.

c **1314** *Guy Warw.* (1887) p. 398 On Iesu omnipotent... He pouȝt wiþ dreri mode. *c* **1386** CHAUCER *Wife's Prol.* 423 As helpe me verray god omnipotent. *c* **1489** CAXTON *Sonnes of Aymon* i. 37 By god omnypotente I wolde lever have loste my castell. **1526** TINDALE *Rev.* xix. 6 Sayinge: Alleluya, for god omnipotent [WYCLIF, almiȝty] hath raigned. **1662** STILLINGFL. *Orig. Sacr.* III. ii. §1 A production of it by the omnipotent Will and Word of God. **1719** DE FOE *Crusoe* I. xv, I told him.. That he [God] was Omnipotent, could do every Thing for us. **1870** BRYANT *Iliad* I. II. 52 Whether the word of Jove omnipotent Be false or true.

2. *gen.* All powerful; having full or absolute power or authority; having unlimited or very great power, force, or influence; exceedingly strong or mighty.

1598 SHAKS. *Merry W.* v. v. 8 O omnipotent Loue, how nere the God drew to the complexion of a Goose. **1775** BURKE *Lett., to Dk. Richmond* (1844) II. 75 The tories and courtiers are powerful there, but not omnipotent. **1822** SCOTT *Nigel* vi, The Duke of Buckingham, the omnipotent favourite both of the King and the Prince of Wales. **1879** FROUDE *Cæsar* viii. 79 The Senate was thus made omnipotent and irresponsible.

b. *humorously.* Capable of anything; unparalleled; utter, arrant; huge, 'mighty'. (Cf. ALMIGHTY 2 ¶.)

1596 SHAKS. *1 Hen. IV*, I. ii. 121 This is the most omnipotent Villaine, that euer cryed, Stand, to a true man. **1596** NASHE *Have with you* Wks. (Grosart) III. 51 Farre more boystrous and cumbersome than a pair of Swissers omnipotent galeaze breeches.

3. *absol.* or as *sb.* An omnipotent being; *spec.* (with *the*) the Almighty, God.

1601 DOLMAN *La Primaud. Fr. Acad.* (1618) III. 639 In such sort as it pleaseth the Omnipotent to make them worthy. **1667** MILTON *P.L.* I. 49 Who durst defie th' Omnipotent to Arms. **1829** J. MILLER *Sibyl's Leaves* I. 288 What can an Omnipotent find in the possession of his power, an Omniscient in the possession of his wisdom, but that love [etc.]? **1898** G. MEREDITH *Odes Fr. Hist.* 62 The open mind, The Omnipotent's prime gift.

Hence †**omnipotentness** = OMNIPOTENCE.

1727 BAILEY vol. II.

†**omnipo'tentiary**, *a. Obs. rare*⁻¹. [f. L. *omnipotentia* OMNIPOTENCE + -ARY.] Of, belonging to, or involving omnipotence; omnipotent.

1659 D. PELL *Impr. Sea* 521 That the cessation of.. Tempests, is by, through, and from an.. uncontroulable omnipotentiary power that is in God.

om'nipotently, *adv.* [f. OMNIPOTENT + -LY².] In an omnipotent manner; with almighty or unlimited power; almightily.

a **1641** BP. MOUNTAGU *Acts & Mon.* (1642) 410 Another impious heresie of Fatall Necessity, over and upon all things, which do omnipotently come to passe. *a* **1711** KEN *Hymnotheo* Poet. Wks. 1721 III. 294 Fools, who from God omnipotence detract, Think atoms can omnipotently act. **1819** *Blackw. Mag.* IV. 396 It is perhaps on persons such as I that nature most omnipotently works.

omnipresence (ɒmnɪ'prɛzəns). [f. as next: see -ENCE.] The fact or quality of being omnipresent. **a.** *strictly*, as an attribute of God, etc.: see OMNIPRESENT a.

1601 DEACON & WALKER *Spirits & Divels* 89 An omnipresence, or.. an incorporeity, is truely in God. **1677** GALE *Crt. Gentiles* IV. 288 Next to God's Eternitie follows his Immensitie or Omnipresence, which denotes his presence in althings and al spaces. **1725** WATTS *Logic* II. iv. §2 Questions which may be raised about his own Divine Essence or Substance, his Immensity or Omnipresence. **1885** L. ABBOTT in *Chr. World Pulpit* XXVIII. 179 Most Christians do not believe in the omnipresence of God; they only believe in His ubiquity.

b. *generally*: see OMNIPRESENT b.

a **1822** SHELLEY *Tri. Life* 343 The bright omnipresence Of morning through the orient cavern flowed. **1863** GEO. ELIOT *Romola* I. ix, The omnipresence of casualties.. threatened all projects with futility. **1899** *Westm. Gaz.* 9 Aug. 3/2 The most vivid impression to which the foreigner is subjected [in England] is.. that of the omnipresence of advertising.

†**omni'presency.** *Obs.* [f. med. Schol. L. *omnipræsentia* (Du Cange), f. *omnipræsent-em*: see next and -ENCY.] = prec.

1647 H. MORE *Song of Soul* Notes 156/2 If we forsake this apprehension of the omnipresency of Ahad, God and all things else will prove mere bodies. **1664** —— *Antid. Idolatry* vii. 84 That they [images of the saints] have at least a terrestriall Omnipresency, which no.. invisible Power.. has but onely God. **1682** SIR T. BROWNE *Chr. Mor.* III. §9 Delight to be alone and single with omnipresency.

omnipresent (ɒmnɪ'prɛzənt), *a.* [f. med. Schol. L. *omnipræsent-em* (Du Cange), f. OMNI- + *præsent-em* PRESENT.] Present at the same time in all places; everywhere present. **a.** In the strict or absolute sense; chiefly said of the Deity.

1610 WILLET *Hexapla Dan.* 237 It is proper to the diuine nature to be infinite, omnipotent, omnipresent. *a* **1711** KEN *Christophil* Poet. Wks. 1721 I. 426 Thou while below wer't yet on high, By Omnipresent Deity. **1794** COLERIDGE *Relig. Musings* 105 There is one Mind, one omnipresent Mind, Omnific. **1885** L. ABBOTT in *Chr. World Pulpit* XXVIII. 179 God is not ubiquitous, but omnipresent, and never through all eternity can you and I be nearer to Him than we are at this moment.

b. In more general or weakened sense.

a **1711** KEN *Hymnarium* Poet. Wks. 1721 II. 40 A Spirit in our Bulk resides, Which all our Force corporeal guides; There omnipresent reigns. **1866** GEO. ELIOT *F. Holt* xxxi, It was a maxim which he repeated after the great Putty, that a capable agent makes himself omnipresent. **1867** BAKER *Nile Tribut.* xix. (1872) 334 The bird is omnipresent.

Hence **omnipresentness** = OMNIPRESENCE.

1727 BAILEY vol. II.

†**omnipre'sential**, *a. Obs. rare*⁻¹. [f. med.L. *omnipræsentia* (see above) + -AL¹.] Of, pertaining to, or involving omnipresence.

a **1716** SOUTH *Serm.* (1744) VII. i. 22 But his omnipresential filling all things being an inseparable property of his divine nature, always agreed to him.

omni'presently, *adv.* [f. OMNIPRESENT + -LY².] In an omnipresent manner; so as to be everywhere present.

1701 NORRIS *Ideal World* I. iii. 137 He exists every way infinitely, and therefore both eternally and omnipresently. **1863** A. B. GROSART *Small Sins* 30 No principle interpenetrates the word of God more omnipresently than this.

omniprevalent (ɒmnɪ'prɛvələnt), *a.* [f. OMNI- + PREVALENT, after L. type **omnipævalent-em.*]

1. All-prevailing; having all power or influence.

a **1661** FULLER *Worthies, Surrey* (1840) III. 210 Being chaplain to the earl of Dunbar, then omni-prevalent with King James.

2. Prevailing everywhere; universally prevalent.

a **1849** POE *Longfellow's Ballads* Wks. 1864 III. 367 The combination of the two omni-prevalent ideas. **1882** COUES *Biogen* (1884) 35 Some form of worship is omniprevalent.

omniprudent, etc.: see OMNI-.

†**omni'regency.** *Obs.* [f. OMNI- + REGENCY.] All-ruling condition; universal rule.

1616 BULLOKAR *Eng. Expos.*, *Omniregencie*, the hauing all authoritie in ones owne hands. *a* **1662** HEYLIN *Laud* (1668) 156 He could not govern there with such an absolute Omni-regency, as he had done in the Families of private Gentlemen. *a* **1670** HACKET *Abp. Williams* I. (1692) 28 The omni-regency of Divine Providence is the tree of Life in the midst of the garden of the world.

†**om'niscian.** *Obs. nonce-wd.* [f. L. *omniscius* (see OMNISCIOUS) + -AN.] One who professes to know everything.

1593 G. HARVEY *Pierce's Super.* 188 [He] would be thought to.. know all things, like Iarchas,.. and Salomon, the archpatrons of our new Omniscians.

omniscience (ɒm'nɪʃəns, -ɪəns). [ad. med. Schol. L. *omniscientia* (Du Cange), f. OMNI- + *scientia* knowledge: see -ENCE. Cf. mod.F. *omniscience* (1762 in *Dict. Acad.*).] The quality of being omniscient. **a.** Strictly: Infinite knowledge; hence *transf.* the omniscient Being, the Deity.

1612 T. TAYLOR *Comm. Titus* I. 9 His omniscience.. searcheth the heart, discouereth the thoughts. **1646** SIR T. BROWNE *Pseud. Ep.* 282 'Tis a professed and authentick obscurity, unknown to all but to the omniscience of the Almighty. **1712** ADDISON *Spect.* No. 315 ¶4 The Survey of the whole Creation.. is a Prospect worthy of Omniscience. **1836** HOR. SMITH *Tin Trump.* (1876) 271 To assist Omniscience with his Counsels, and lend a helping hand to Omnipotence.

b. Hyperbolically: Universal knowledge.

a **1845** SYD. SMITH in I. Todhunter *William Whewell* (1876) I. xxi. 410 [Said of Whewell] 'Science is his forte, and omniscience is his foible'. **1852** THACKERAY *Esmond* II. xiii, A foible of Mr. Holt's.. was omniscience. **1891** T. R. LOUNSBURY *Stud. Chaucer* II. v. 179 Men at that time thought nothing of making a specialty of omniscience.

†**om'nisciency.** *Obs.* [f. as prec., or from next + -ENCY.] = prec.

1640 FULLER *Joseph's Coat* (1867) 62 God, in the omnisciency of His wisdom, surveyed the latitude of all occurrences. **1681** GLANVILL *Sadducismus* II. (1726) 464 That Intellectual Omnisciency, which contains all the Natures and Ideas of things. **1734** E. ERSKINE *Serm.* Wks. 1871 II. 253 My eternity and omnisciency are as much in him as in myself.

omniscient (ɒm'nɪʃənt, -ɪənt), *a.* [ad. mod.L. *omnisciens, -ent-em*, substituted for med.L. *omniscius* (OMNISCIOUS) under the influence of *omniscientia* (see prec.), the substituted element being L. *sciens, -ent-em* pr. pple. 'knowing'. Grotius *De Ver. Rel. Chr.* uses both *omniscius* and *omnisciens*. So F. *omniscient* (1737 in Hatz.-Darm.).]

1. Knowing all things, all-knowing, infinite in knowledge. **a.** Strictly: esp. of God.

1604 R. CAWDREY *Table Alph.*, *Omni-scient*, knowing all things. *c* **1615** BACON *Adv. to Villiers* Wks. 1879 I. 510 By no means trust to your own judgement alone; for no man is omniscient. **1700** DRYDEN *Palamon & Arc.* III. 1054 This law the Omniscient Power was pleased to give, That every kind should by succession live. **1781** COWPER *Truth* 227 With averted eyes the omniscient Judge Scorns the base hireling. **1857** H. MILLER *Test. Rocks* iv. 154 Inspiration does not make men omniscient.

b. Hyperbolically: Having universal or very extensive knowledge.

1791 BOSWELL *Johnson* 5 Apr. an. 1776 *note*, A gentleman .. from his extraordinary stores of knowledge,.. stiled omniscient. **1871** L. STEPHEN *Playgr. Eur.* (1894) x. 251, I was roused by a very pleasant meeting with the most omniscient of mountaineers.

2. *absol.* or as *sb.* An omniscient being or person: *spec.* (with *the*), the Deity, God.

1794 COLERIDGE *Destiny of Nations* iv, Those blind omniscients. **1856** R. A. VAUGHAN *Mystics* (1860) II. 232 This divine order, which the Omniscient hath established and maintains.

Hence **omni'scientist**, one who purports to be, or is alleged to be, omniscient; **omniscientness** = OMNISCIENCE.

1727 BAILEY vol. II. **1932** R. A. KNOX *Broadcast Minds* ii. 20 (*heading*) The omniscientists. *Ibid.* 21 We are all omniscientists now, at least in ambition... It only remains that we should pride ourselves on knowing something about everything. **1948** A. O'RAHILLY *Relig. & Sci.* iv. 32 *We* stand.. opposed to the usurpations and truculent dogmatism of the omniscientists.

om'nisciently, *adv.* [f. prec. + -LY².] In an omniscient manner; with universal knowledge.

1856 WEBSTER, *Omnisciently*, by omniscience. **1889** *Univ. Rev.* Mar. 362 Both are omnisciently silly.

†**om'niscious**, *a. Obs.* [f. med. Schol. L. *omnisci-us* all-knowing (f. OMNI- + *scī-re* to know: cf. L. *nescius*, *inscius*, etc.) + -OUS.] = OMNISCIENT.

1588 J. HARVEY *Disc. Probl.* 84 Schoolemen may phantastically dreame..of..diuers putatiue wisemen, euen in that omniscious, and omnisufficient veine. **1628** BP. HALL *Old Relig.* 139 It is an Omnipresent and Omniscious God with whom wee deale. **1728** FOXTON tr. *Burnet's Re-surv. Mosaic Creat.* in Earbery tr. *Burnet's St. Dead* 47 Omniscious Providence, knowing all these things, accommodates itself to the various Orders of humane Things.

omnisciturient to **omnispective**: see OMNI-.

†**omnist** ('ɒmnɪst). *nonce-wd.* [irreg. f. L. *omnis* all + -IST.] (See quot.)

1839 BAILEY *Festus* viii. (1848) 98, I am an omnist, and believe in all Religions.

†**omnisu'fficience**. *Obs. rare*$^{-1}$. [f. as next + -ENCE.] = next.

1660 STANLEY *Hist. Philos.* IX. (1701) 383/2 *Panarceia*, omni-sufficience, endued with parts sufficient for totality.

†**omnisu'fficiency**. *Obs. rare.* [f. as next + -ENCY.] The quality of being 'omnisufficient'; all-sufficiency.

1577 FULKE *Confut. Purg.* 97 Wilt thou neuer acknowledge the omnisufficiency of the benefite of mans redemption by the sonne of God? **1622** DONNE *Serm.* xvi. 156 To find an Omnisufficiency in ourselves is an Intrusion, an Usurpation upon God. [**1876** LOWELL *Among my Bks.* Ser. II. 142 Amid the pedantic farrago of his [J. Harvey's] omni-sufficiency (to borrow one of his own words) we come suddenly upon passages whose..purity of diction reminds us of Landor.]

†**omnisu'fficient**, *a. Obs.* or *rare*. [ad. med. or mod.L. type **omnisufficient-em* all-sufficing, f. OMNI- + *sufficient-em*, pr. pple. of *sufficĕre* to SUFFICE.] All-sufficient, all-sufficing.

1543 BECON *New Year's Gift* in *Early Wks.* (1843) 342 Take me alone for thy omnisufficient Saviour. **1601** W. PARRY *Trav. Sir A. Sherley* (1863) 17 The truth thereof..is a warrant omnisufficient for the report. *a* **1625** BOYS *Wks.* (1630) 586 His passion was an Omnisufficient sacrifice for the sinnes of the whole world. *a* **1670** HACKET *Abp. Williams* I. (1693) 103 These Staffs princes must lean upon, being.. such Masters as are neither omni-sufficient, nor independent.

omnitemporal to **omnitonic**: see OMNI-.

omnitude ('ɒmnɪtjuːd). *rare.* [f. OMNI- + -TUDE, after L. type **omnitūdo*.] The fact of being all, 'allness', universality; 'the all', the whole, the total sum.

1839 BAILEY *Festus* xxviii. (1848) 329 Holding in itself the omnitude of Being. *c* **1840** SIR W. HAMILTON *Logic* App. (1866) II. 281 *Some*, though always in a certain degree indefinite, is definite so far as it excludes omnitude. **1896** *Scotsman* 25 June 6/2 He spoke..with accuracy, authority, and omnitude of knowledge.

omnium ('ɒmnɪəm). [a. L. *omnium* 'of all (things, sorts, etc.)', genitive pl. of *omnis* all. In sense 1, also, *omnium gatherum*, which may have been the original appellation.]

1. *Stock Exch.* The aggregate amount (at market price) of the parcels of different stocks and other considerations, formerly offered by Government, in raising a loan, for each unit of capital (i.e. every hundred pounds) subscribed.

'The subscribers to the Loan..are entitled not only to hold their share in the capital [the funded loan], but to an annuity for ten years, and to the right of receiving a certain number of Lottery tickets on advantageous terms. They may sell their capital to one person, their annuity to a second, and their right to the tickets to a third. The value of all these interests together is called *Omnium*: and, in order to obtain a ready subscription, it ought to amount to 102*l.* or upwards, on 100*l.* of capital. This difference is called the *bonus* to the subscribers'. (*Encycl. Brit.* (1797) s.v. *Fund*.)

1760 COLMAN *Polly Honeycomb* ii, The Omniums, eh, Miss! I like the Omniums, and don't care how large a premium I give for them. **1761** T. MORTIMER *Ev. man his own Broker* 163 Omnium is the whole subscription undivided; and is known in the Alley by the name of Omnium Gatherum, a cant phrase for, all together. **1770** C. JENNER *Placid Man* II. vi, Her head was as full with wealth, scrip, omnium, consols, and lord-mayors shews. **1783** J. ADAMS *Wks.* (1853) VIII. 117 (Stanf.) The English omnium which at first was sold for eight or ten per cent. profit, fell to one and a half. **1810** GRELLIER *Hist. Nat. Debt* 392 The Omnium of this loan was at first at a premium of $2\frac{1}{2}$ per cent. but soon fell to a discount. **1819** T. MORTIMER *Gen. Comm. Dict.* (ed. 2), *Omnium*, a term used among the Stock Jobbers to express all the articles included in the Contract between Government and the original subscribers to a loan, which of late years has consisted generally of different proportions of three, and four per cent. Stock with a certain quantity of terminable annuities. **1832–52** MCCULLOCH *Comm. Dict.* s.v., In the loan of 36,000,000*l.* contracted for in June, 1815, the omnium consisted of 130*l.* 3 per cent. reduced annuities, 44*l.* 3 per cent. consols, and 10*l.* 4 per cent. annuities, for each 100*l.* subscribed. *a* **1860** *Rules Stock Exch.* in C. Fenn *Eng. & For. Funds* (1883) 120 The settling-day in English omnium and scrip shall be two days prior to the respective days of payment of each of the several instalments.

b. Colloquially applied to other combined stocks the constituents of which are capable of being dealt with separately.

Thus 'The London Extension Stock' issued in July, 1894, by the Manchester, Sheffield, and Lincolnshire Railway, which could be divided into ordinary and preference stock, and gave a right to Debenture Stock on certain terms, was known on the Stock Exchange as 'Sheffield Omnium'.

2. (with allusion to prec.) The whole sum of what one values or is interested in; one's 'all'.

1766 COLMAN *Clandestine Marriage* IV. iii, 'Tis my only wish at present, my omnium, as I may call it. **1818** SCOTT *Rob Roy* xxii, You, that was your father's sum-total—his omnium—you that might have been the first man in the first house in the first city.

3. Applied to a large wagon (? carrying the whole of a person's possessions).

1836 A. F. GARDINER *Zoolu Country* 324 Still on the cumbrous omnium moves, By twelve or fourteen oxen towed.

4. 'A piece of furniture with open shelves for receiving ornamental articles, etc.' (*Cent. Dict.*)

omnium gatherum ('ɒmnɪəm 'gæðərəm). *colloq.* Also hyphened; and 6 **omnium githerum**, 7 **getherum**. Cf. OMNIGATHERUM. [f. L. *omnium* (see prec.) + *gatherum*, a mock-Latin form from GATHER *v.* quasi 'a gathering'.]

1. A gathering of all sorts; a miscellaneous assemblage, collection, or mixture (of persons or things); a confused medley.

1530 CROKE *Let. to Cranmer* (MS. Cott. Vit. B xiii. 123 b) Certayne subscriptions unto the kynge, wheroff sauff ij, there ys none worthe a botton, but be omnium gatherum. **1600** W. WATSON *Decacordon* (1602) 43 [The Jesuits] haue made religion..a very hotch potch of omnium githerum. **1608** MIDDLETON *Fam. Love* v. iii, A rout of omnium gatherums assembled by the title of the Family of Love. **1683** TRYON *Way to Health* 543 The Apothecary had muster'd up his several Slops and compleated the Composition of Omniumgatherum. **1776** J. ADAMS in *Fam. Lett.* (1876) 214 My letters to you are an odd mixture. They would appear to a stranger like the dish which is sometimes called *omnium gatherum*. **1830** GALT *Lawrie T.* III. vii. (1849) 107 Such an omnium gatherum as the inhabitants of a new settlement. **1863** KINGSLEY *Water Bab.* iii. 126 Odds and ends, and omnium-gatherums, and this, that, and the other, enough to fill nine museums.

†**b.** as *adv.* In a confused medley, promiscuously. *Obs.*

1648 *Merc. Acad.* No. 1. 4 Being come *omnium gatherum* into the Convocation-house. **1650** A. B. *Mutat. Polemo* 28 Whither we ganged as drunkenly reeling as the Ship, omnium getherum, all together.

†**2.** A kind of dance in vogue in the 17th c. *Obs.*

a **1652** BROME *New Acad.* v. Wks. 1873 II. 110 *Stri.* Play then Les tous ensembles. *Neh.* That's the French name on't Uncle, 'tis in Dutch call'd All-to-Mall; and I call it in English, Omnium Gatherum, 'tis the daintiest daunce. *a* **1654** SELDEN *Table-t.* (Arb.) 62 There has been nothing but French-more and the Cushion Dance, omnium gatherum, tolly, polly, hoite come toite.

†**3.** = OMNIUM 1.

1761 [see OMNIUM 1]. **1793** W. ROBERTS *Looker-on* No. 54 (1794) II. 305 With the omnium-gatherums, scrips, discounts, etc., it appeared that the funds and credit of Virtue were gradually rising.

omnivagant to **omnivolent**: see OMNI-.

omnivorous (ɒm'nɪvərəs), *a.* [f. L. *omnivorus* (f. OMNI- + *-vorus* devouring) + -OUS. Cf. F. *omnivore* (Buffon 18th c.).] All-devouring.

1. *lit.* That devours or feeds on all kinds of food. (Opposed to *carnivorous*, *herbivorous*, etc.)

1656 BLOUNT *Glossogr.*, *Omnivorous*, that devours and eats all kind of things. **1819** W. LAWRENCE *Physiol.* (1848) 143 In a similar way we conclude man to be naturally omnivorous. **1867** F. FRANCIS *Angling* i. (1880) 40 The Chub is rather an omnivorous fish. **1881** ROMANES in *Nature* No. 624. 554 Worms are omnivorous, dragging pieces of meat as well as leaves into their burrows for the purpose of eating them.

2. *fig.* (Cf. senses of DEVOUR *v.*)

1791 BURKE *Let. to Member Nat. Assembly* Wks. VI. 32 He has not observed on the nature of vanity, who does not know that it is omnivorous; that it has no choice in its food. **1863** HAWTHORNE *Our Old Home* (1879) 183 An omnivorous appetite for everything strange and rare. **1877** 'H. A. PAGE' *De Quincey* I. ix. 186 Hamilton, darkly metaphysical, omnivorous of books.

So various nonce-words: **omnivo'racity** [f. late L. *omnivorāx* (Eugenius 7th c.)], **omnivo'rosity** [f. OMNIVOROUS: see -OSITY], omnivorousness; **om'nivorant** *a.* [L. *vorānt-em* devouring], all-devouring, omnivorous; **'omnivore** [a. F., cf. *carnivore*, etc.], an omnivorous animal or person.

1889 *Spectator* 14 Dec. 856 But for the ostrich-like *omnivoracity of the wealthy collector, the Literary Stock Exchange might any day be convulsed with an ubiquitously resonant smash. **1852** C. W. H[OSKINS] *Talpa* 65 Everywhere 'The Fly' was omnipotent and *omnivorant. **1890** *Even. Post* 8 Feb., Some of the interrogated were vegetarians, and some *omnivores. **1896** JESSOPP *Frivola* viii. 143 With the *omnivorosity (what a beautiful word!) of youth I eagerly devoured them.

om'nivorously, *adv.* [f. OMNIVOROUS + -LY^2.] In an omnivorous manner (*lit.* and *fig.*).

1852 *Fraser's Mag.* XLV. 644 A fish..so omnivorously disposed. **1883** FROUDE *Short Stud.* IV. II. iii. 197 Newman had read omnivorously.

om'nivorousness. [f. as prec. + -NESS.] The quality of being omnivorous (*lit.* and *fig.*).

1727 in BAILEY vol. II. *a* **1861** MRS. BROWNING *Lett. R. H. Horne* (1877) II. lvii. 151 Do I boast of my omnivorousness of reading? **1884** *Times* 30 Dec. 7 The omnivorousness of children is balanced..by powers of digestion which seem little short of miraculous.

omnopon ('ɒmnəpɒn). *Pharm.* Also **Omnopon**. [f. L. *omn-is* all + OP(IUM *sb.* + *-on*, arbitrary ending.] A proprietary name in the U.K. for a mixture of the hydrochlorides of the opium alkaloids. Cf. PANTOPON.

1909 *Trade Marks Jrnl.* 1 Dec. 1962 Omnopon... All goods included in class 3 [*i.e.* chemical substances prepared for use in medicine and pharmacy]. The firm of F. Hoffman La Roche & Co.,..Bale, Switzerland; chemical manufacturers. **1910** *Lancet* 15 Oct. 1169/1 Pantopon is known in Great Britain as 'Omnopon'. **1922** C. T. CAMPION tr. *Schweitzer's On Edge of Primeval Forest* v. 92 He is given an injection of omnipon [*sic*]. **1957** I. MAGILL in Gillies & Millard *Princ. & Art Plastic Surg.* I. iii. 64 For premedication Omnopon and scopolamine are preferred, as their action is synergistic. **1970** *Sunday Mail* (Brisbane) 15 Mar. 4 Police took possession of a huge quantity of cannabis, opium, L.S.D., omnopon..and cocaine. **1970** PASSMORE & ROBSON *Compan. Med. Stud.* II. v. 48/2 It is widely believed that there is no therapeutic advantage in using mixed alkaloid preparations from opium, such as papaveretum (omnopon).

omo-, obs. erroneous form of HOMO-.

omo-hyoid (əʊməʊ'haɪɔɪd), *a.* (*sb.*) *Anat.* [f. Gr. ὦμος shoulder + HYOID.] Relating to, or connecting, the shoulder and the hyoid bone: applied to a long slender digastric muscle which arises from the upper border of the shoulder-blade and passes obliquely along the side and front of the neck to the lower border of the hyoid bone. Also as *sb.* the omohyoid muscle.

1840 G. V. ELLIS *Anat.* 116 Detach the process of fascia from the omo-hyoid muscle. **1876** *Clin. Soc. Trans.* IX. 121 Ligature of left common carotid, above the omo-hyoid.

So **omohy'oidean**, **omohy'oideous** *adjs.* = prec.

1855 HOLDEN *Hum. Osteol.* (1878) 144 Behind the notch is the origin of the 'omo-hyoideous' muscle. **1857** MAYNE *Expos. Lex.*, Omohyoidean.

omoio-, erron. form of HOMOIO-, HOMŒO-.

‖**omophagia** (əʊməʊ'feɪdʒɪə). [mod.L., a. Gr. ὠμοφαγία, f. ὠμός raw + -φαγία eating.] The eating of raw food, esp. raw flesh. So **omophagic** (əʊməʊ'fædʒɪk), **omophagous** (əʊ'mɒfəgəs) [f. Gr. ὠμοφάγ-ος + -IC, -OUS], eating, or characterized by the eating of, raw flesh; **omophagist** (əʊ'mɒfədʒɪst), an eater of raw flesh.

1706 PHILLIPS, **Omophagia* (Gr.)..a Feast of Bacchus, in which the mad Guests eat Goats alive, tearing their Entrails with their Teeth. **1869** BARING-GOULD *Orig. Relig. Belief* I. 407 These bloody *Omophagic feasts were celebrated every three years. **1884** *Pall Mall Gaz.* 13 Dec. 5 She cut from the victim's palm a piece of flesh and ate it raw—a literal *omophagist. **1857** MAYNE *Expos. Lex.*, *Omophagus*, living on raw food: *omophagous. **1882** *Cornh. Mag.* Nov. 569 That redoubtable friend of Mr. Freeman the omophagous Teutonic colonist.

omophore ('əʊməfɔə(r)). *rare*$^{-1}$. [ad. Gr. ὠμοφόρος one who bears on the shoulders, f. ὦμος shoulder + -φόρος bearing.] (See quot.)

1871 TYLOR *Prim. Cult.* I. 329 The world-bearing elephants of the Hindus,..the gigantic Omophore of the Manichæan cosmology, are all creatures who carry the earth on their backs or heads.

‖**omophorion** (əʊməʊ'fɔərɪən). *Gr. Ch.* [Gr. ὠμοφόριον 'a woman's tippet covering the shoulders' (Liddell and Scott), also eccl. in sense below (see *omophorium* in Du Cange); cf. prec.] A vestment resembling the pallium of the Latin church, worn by patriarchs and bishops.

1868 MARRIOTT *Vest. Chr.* 237 The Omophorion, worn (as matter of privilege) by Patriarchs and Metropolitans in the East, and, out of usage rather than theoretical right by almost all Bishops. **1888** T. W. ALLIES *Holy See* 144 He.. caused his archdeacon first to remove his omophorion, and appeared in the garb of a simple priest.

omoplate ('əʊməpleɪt). Also 9 **-plat** (-plæt). [ad. Gr. ὠμοπλάτη, f. ὦμο-ς shoulder + πλάτη broad surface, blade.] The shoulder-blade, scapula.

1597 A. M. tr. *Guillemeau's Fr. Chirurg.* 54/1 The bullet ..remayning in the inferiore angle of the foresayed Omoplate. **1653** URQUHART *Rabelais* I. xxvii, He..shook asunder their omoplates or shoulder-blade. **1833** MANTELL *Geol. S.E. Eng.* 320 The omoplate or scapula is not unlike the coracoid. **1868** BROWNING *Ring & Bk.* v. 118 There is an ailing in this omoplat May clip my speech all too abruptly short.

omoplatoscopy (,əʊməʊplæ'tɒskəpɪ). [ad. Gr. ὠμοπλατοσκοπία (Psellus), f. ὠμοπλάτη (see prec.) + -σκοπία looking: see -SCOPY.] (See quots.)

1871 TYLOR *Prim. Cult.* I. 112 Divination by a shoulder-blade, technically called Scapulimancy or omoplatoscopy. **1892** *Syd. Soc. Lex.*, *Omoplatoscopy*, the name given to a mode of divination formerly practised by some tribes of American Indians, founded on the direction of the cracks which appeared on a blade-bone when placed on a fire.

omostegite (əʊˈmɒstɪdʒaɪt). *Anat.* [f. Gr. ὦμο-ς shoulder + στέγη covering, roof + -ITE[1] 3.] The posterior part of the carapace, covering the thorax, in certain crustaceans; opp. to *cephalostegite*.

1870 ROLLESTON *Anim. Life* 91. **1877** HUXLEY *Anat. Inv. Anim.* vi. 283 The carapace presents a posterior division (omostegite), obviously developed from the anterior thoracic somites.

‖**omosternum** (əʊməʊˈstɜːnəm). *Comp. Anat.* [f. Gr. ὦμο-ς shoulder + mod.L. *sternum*, Gr. στέρνον breast.] A cartilage, or an ossification of such cartilage at the anterior extremity of the sternum.

It is probably always derived from the ventral ends of the coracoids, and is called by Gegenbaur *Epicoracoid*. The name has often been applied to the membrane bone overlying the front end of the sternum, and more properly called *episternum* or *interclavicle*.

1868 W. K. PARKER *Monograph Structure Shoulder-Girdle* (Ray Soc.) 80 The præ-coracoid bar is larger than the coracoid,.. and the 'omosternum' and true sternum have not yet made their appearance. *Ibid.* 81 In front of the bony bar a small hillock of soft new cartilage is seen..; this is the first rudiment of the 'omosternum'. **1873** MIVART *Elem. Anat.* iv. 161 The omosternum becomes amongst Mammals very conspicuous in certain Shrews and Mice. **1892** *Syd. Soc. Lex.*, *Omosternum*, the interarticular fibro-cartilage of the sterno-clavicular articulation.

Hence **omoˈsternal** *a.*, pertaining to the omosternum.

omothyroid (əʊməʊˈθaɪərɔɪd). *Anat.* Also **thyreoid.** [f. Gr. ὦμο-ς shoulder + THYROID.] A slip of muscle, of exceptional occurrence, connecting the omo-hyoid muscle with the thyroid cartilage.

1892 *Syd. Soc. Lex.*, *Omothyreoid*, a variety of the omohyoid muscle when it has an attachment to the inferior cornu of the thyreoid cartilage.

†**omphacine** (ˈɒmfəsɪn), *a.* (*sb.*) *Obs.* [f. Gr. ὀμφάκιν-ος made of unripe grapes, olives, or the like, f. ὄμφαξ unripe (grape, berry): see -INE[2].]

1. In *oil omphacine*, an oily liquid expressed from unripe olives. Also as *sb.* = oil omphacine.

[*c* **1400** *Lanfranc's Cirurg.* 137 Maad of grapis of olyue trees þat ben not ripe.. is clepid oile enfancinum (*MS. B.* Omfacinum).] **1548** tr. *Papius Conc. Apoth.* in Recorde *Urin. Physick* (1651) 216 By Olives, of which oile omphocine is made, we understand the wild boyled in oyle. **1620** VENNER *Via Recta* vi. 100 The Oyle that is made of the vnripe Oliues, which is called Oyle Omphacine, is not so grosse and fatty. **1712** tr. *Pomet's Hist. Drugs* I. 157 Hereof is made Oil of Roses, Omphacine, and Oil of Quinces.

2. Unripe. *rare*$^{-1}$.

1651 BIGGS *New Disp.* ¶ 168 Omphacine grapes.

omphacite (ˈɒmfəsaɪt). *Min.* [ad. mod.Ger. *omphazit* (Werner, 1812), f. Gr. ὄμφαξ (see prec.) + -ITE[1].] A leek-green mineral, allied to pyroxene.

1828–32 WEBSTER cites URE. **1868** DANA *Min.* (ed. 5) 223 Omphacite occurs near Hof in Baireut, Bavaria. **1879** RUTLEY *Stud. Rocks* xiii. 263 The eklogite from Eppenreuth contains about 70 per cent. of omphacite and 25 of garnet.

‖**omˈphacomel.** *rare*$^{-1}$. [L., ad. Gr. ὀμφακόμελι (Dioscorides), f. ὄμφαξ (see above) + μέλι honey.] A drink made of the juice of unripe grapes mixed with honey.

1873 in *Pallad. on Husb.* ix. 197 (E.E.T.S.) 178 *Editor's marg. note*, To make omphacomel [*text* honyonfake].

omphalic (ɒmˈfælɪk), *a. rare.* [f. Gr. ὀμφαλός navel, boss, + -IC: cf. Gr. ὀμφαλικός having a boss.] Of or belonging to the navel; umbilical.

1808 PATERSON *Orig. Hindu Relig.* in *Asiat. Res.* VIII. 52 The Argha is a vessel of copper.. in the centre of it is an oval rising embossed, and by this the Vaishnavas assert, is meant the navel of Vishnu... The Saivas, however, insist, that this Omphalic rising is meant as the emblem of the Ling. **1857** in MAYNE *Expos. Lex.*

omphalism (ˈɒmfəlɪz(ə)m). *rare*$^{-1}$. [f. as prec. + -ISM.] Centralization in government.

1868 DILKE *Greater Brit.* I. I. ix. 104 The success of this omphalism, this government from the centre, will be brought about [etc.].

omphalo- (ɒmfələʊ), before a vowel **omphal-**, combining form of Gr. ὀμφαλός navel, boss, hub. **omphaˈlectomy** [Gr. ἐκτομή a cutting out], excision of the navel. **omphaˈlitis** [-ITIS], inflammation of the umbilicus. **ˈomphaloˌcele** (-siːl) [Gr. κήλη tumour, hernia], umbilical hernia. **ˈomphaloˌmancy** [Gr. μαντεία divination], divination, by the number of knots on the umbilical cord at birth, of the number of future children of the mother. **ˌomphalo-mesaˈraic** (erron. **-meseraic**) *a.* [MESARAIC] = OMPHALO-MESENTERIC (Mivart, 1872). **ˌomphaloˈpsychic** (-ˈpsaɪkɪk) *a.*, **ˌomphaˈlopsychite** [Gr. ψυχή soul], one of a sect of quietists who practised gazing at the navel as a means of inducing hypnotic reverie. †**omphaˈlopter** [Gr. ὀπτήρ one who looks or spies], a double-convex lens (*obs. rare*$^{-0}$); so †**omphaˈloptic** [OPTIC] *sb.* = prec.; *a.*, of the form or structure of a double-convex lens. **omphaˈloscopy** [Gr. -σκοπία], contemplation of the navel. **omphaˈlotomy** [Gr. -τομια cutting], the operation of dividing the umbilical cord.

1892 *Syd. Soc. Lex.*, **Omphalectomy*, excision of the umbilicus. **1894** *Brit. Med. Jrnl. Epit.* 3 Feb. 18/1. **1876** DUNGLISON *Dict. Med. Sci.* (rev. ed.) 722/2 *Omphalitis. **1897** *Trans. Amer. Pediatric Soc.* IX. 208 Of the remaining cases.. one.. was due to pyæmia following omphalitis in the newly-born. **1974** PASSMORE & ROBSON *Compan. Med. Stud.* III. II. xlv. 22/1 The appearance [in the newborn] of non-specific signs of infection, whether or not there is liver enlargement, jaundice or evidence of omphalitis, is always an indication for culture of the umbilicus and the blood. **1706** PHILLIPS, **Omphalocele*, or *Hernia Umbilicalis*. **1836–9** TODD *Cycl. Anat.* II. 710/1 Affected with omphalocele. **1652** GAULE *Magastrom.* 165 *Omphelomancy, [divining] by the navell. **1892** *Syd. Soc. Lex.* **1892** *19th Cent.* Jan. 24 The *Omphalopsychics, with whom hypnotic reverie is obtained by steadily gazing at the umbilicus. **1882** 'BASIL' *Love the Debt* xliii, Bob has become an *Omphalopsychyte. Those thrice accursed cartoons had brought on Stomach on the brain. **1727–41** CHAMBERS *Cycl.*, **Omphalopter*, or **Omphaloptic*, in optics, a glass that is convex on both sides, popularly called a convex lens. **1819** H. BUSK *Dessert* 457 The omphaloptic stud. **1931** T. H. PEAR *Voice & Personality* iv. 35 The psychologist, unless mental *omphaloscopy contents him, must go and fetch his material. **1960** *Times* 30 Nov. 7/2 In particular he made fun of 'omphaloscopy'—gazing at the navel. **1828–32** WEBSTER, **Omphalotomy*. **1857** in MAYNE *Expos. Lex.*

omphalode (ˈɒmfələʊd). *rare*$^{-0}$. = OMPHALODIUM (in both senses).

1864 in WEBSTER.

omphalodic (ɒmfəˈlɒdɪk), *a. rare*$^{-0}$. [f. as next + -IC.] = OMPHALIC.

1891 in *Cent. Dict.*

‖**omphalodium** (ɒmfəˈləʊdɪəm). [mod.L., f. Gr. ὀμφαλώδης navel-like, f. ὀμφαλός: see -ODE[1].]

1. *Bot.* (See quots.)

1839 LINDLEY *Introd. Bot.* (ed. 3) 247 The centre of the hilum, through which the nourishing vessels pass, is called by Turpin the *omphalodium*. **1866** *Treas. Bot.* 812/1. **1870** BENTLEY *Man. Bot.* (ed. 2) 326.

2. *Anat.* The umbilicus or navel.

1892 in *Syd. Soc. Lex.*

omphaloid (ˈɒmfəlɔɪd), *a. rare.* [ad. Gr. ὀμφαλοειδής.] Resembling the navel.

1857 in MAYNE *Expos. Lex.* **1942** *Oxoniensia* VII. 47 Sandy, smoothed, dull black, well finished. Omphaloid base of medium-sized bowl.

omphalo-mesenteric (ˌɒmfələʊmɛsənˈtɛrɪk), *a. Anat.* [f. OMPHALO- + MESENTERIC.] Pertaining to, or connecting, the navel and the mesentery.

Applied to the first blood-vessels (veins and arteries) developed in the embryo of vertebrates, which pass from the umbilical vesicle into the body of the embryo; also to a duct representing the part of the yolk-sac within the body-cavity when persistent.. after birth (also called *vitelline duct*).

1727–41 in CHAMBERS *Cycl.* **1797** CRUIKSHANK in *Phil. Trans.* LXXXVII. 204 The omphalo-mesenteric artery was very distinct. **1897** *Allbutt's Syst. Med.* III. 710 The persistence of the omphalo-mesenteric or vitelline duct.

‖**omphalos** (ˈɒmfəlɒs). [a. Gr. ὀμφαλός navel, boss, centre, hub, etc.]

1. *Gr. Antiq.* **a.** A boss on a shield, etc.

1857 BIRCH *Anc. Pottery* (1858) I. 410 Some shields have their omphalos, or boss, sculptured to represent a head of Pan.

b. A sacred stone, of a rounded conical shape, in the temple of Apollo at Delphi, fabled to mark the central point of the earth.

1850 LEITCH tr. *C. O. Müller's Anc. Art* (ed. 2) 447 Apollo sitting on the tripod and with his feet on the omphalos.

2. *gen.* and *fig.* A central point or portion, centre, hub.

1855 KINGSLEY *Westw. Ho* xii, It is the very omphalos, cynosure, and soul, around which the town.. has organised itself. **1884** L. GRIFFIN in *Fortn. Rev.* Mar. 388 The centre and omphalos of a world-wide empire. **1895** *Expositor* Aug. 153 Jerusalem.. became to their imagination the spiritual omphalos of the world.

omphalotomy: see OMPHALO-.

‖**omrah** (ˈɒmrɑː). Also 7 **ombra(h, umpra, umbrawe, umbraye, 7–8 umera, umbra, omra.** [Urdū *umarā*, orig. Arab. pl. of *amīr* 'commander, lord', but used already in Urdū in sense 'lord or grandee of a court', with pl. *umarāyān* 'omrahs' (Yule).] A lord or grandee of a Muslim court, esp. that of the great Mogul.

1625 PURCHAS *Pilgrims* I. 427 Presently came a great *Ombra*. **1638** SIR T. HERBERT *Trav.* (ed. 2) 55 His Leiftenants of Provinces, and Vmbraves of Townes and Forts. **1684** J. PHILLIPS tr. *Tavernier's Trav.* I. II. i. 46 (Stanf.) A great Court, where the Omra's, that is to say, the great Lords of the Kingdom.. keep Guard in Person. **1708** *Lond. Gaz.* No. 4448/3 That Prince.. is join'd by one of the most powerful Omrahs of the Country. **1862** BEVERIDGE *Hist. India* I. III. xii. 658 The nabob had made him an omrah of the empire without a jaghire.

omul (ˈəʊmʊl). [a. Russ. *omul'*.] A fish of the salmon family, *Coregonus autumnalis*, found in Lake Baikal and regions bordering the Arctic Ocean.

1884 *Encycl. Brit.* XVII. 605/2 Only two species of fish are of any importance [in Novaya Zembla]—the goltzy (*Salmo alpinus*) in the western rivers, and the omul (*Salmo omul*) in the eastern. **1955** *Bull. Amer. Mus. Nat. Hist.* CVI. 279/2 The salmon-herring, or omul, has a spawning run of 1500 kilometers (930 miles) in the Yenesei [*sic*] River. **1969** *Nature* 13 Sept. 1091/2 Lake Baikal is particularly noted for its reserves of omul'. **1970** G. V. NIKOLSKY et al. in Lindsey & Woods *Biol. Coregonid Fishes* 257 The omul is an anadromous fish, which lives in waters of higher salinity than other coregonid fishes... Lake Baikal omul forms a separate subspecies. **1976** 'S. HARVESTER' *Siberian Road* i. 18 The Cossacks.. went after sturgeon and omul, a white-fish.

†**ˈomy,** *a. dial.* ? *Obs.* [f. dial. *oam* steam.]

1669 WORLIDGE *Syst. Agric.* (1681) 329 *Omy*-Land, mellow Land. **1674** RAY *N.C. Words*, *Omy*, mellow, spoken of Land. Hence, **1825** BROCKETT *N.C. Gloss.*

o-mys, obs. form of *amiss*: see MISS *sb.*

omyst, obs. form of OVEMEST, upmost.

omyt(te, obs. form of OMIT *v.*

on (ɒn, *unstr.* ən), *prep.* Also 1–5 **an,** 2–5 **o, a** (see AN *prep.*, A *prep.*[1], O *prep.*[1]); (3 **æn,** Orm. **onn,** 4–5 **oon,** 5 **onne,** 5–6 **one, un,** 6 **onn**). [OE. *an, on* = OFris. *an*, OS. and ODu. *ana, an* (MDu. *ane, an, aen*, Du. *aan* (dial. *an*), MLG. *an*, LG. *ân, an*), OHG. *ana, an* (MHG. *ane, an*, Ger. *an*), ON. *á* (Norw., ODa. *aa*, OSw. *å*), Goth. *ana*:—OTeut. **ana* prep. adv. = Gk. ἀνά on, upon, up, Zend *ana* upon, Oscan and Umbrian *an*. The original WGer. *an* was sometimes retained in OE. (see AN *prep.*), but the regular stressless form was *on*. Before 1200, unstressed *on* before a cons. was worn down to *o* and *a*, e.g. *o þisse wise* on this wise, *o live, a live* in life, and in this form often coalesced with the following word as *olive, alive*; when the following word began with a vowel, the enclitic form was *an*, as *an-edge, an-ende, an-hand, an-high*. See A *prep.*[1], AN *prep.*, O *prep.*[1] This form *a* (rarely *an*) survives only when its connexion with *on* is no longer felt, and usually in combination, as *ashore*, or in special constructions as *set a going*. The regular prep. and adv. is *on*. But in 16–18th c. the prep. was often colloquially, and in the dramatists, reduced to *o'*, as in *o' my life* (Shaks.), *o' my conscience* (Sheridan), a form now prevalent in north Eng. dialects: see *Eng. Dial. Dict.*]

General Sense:—The preposition expressing primarily the relation of contact with or proximity to the surface of anything, and so that of being supported or upheld by it; also, from the earliest times expressing motion to or towards such a position; these two senses being (as in the preposition IN) distinguished by the *case* of the word affected, the former taking, in OE., the *dative* (rarely the instrumental) for earlier locative, the latter the *accusative* or case of motion towards. But the OE. point of view often differed from the modern, so that the accusative was not seldom used where we should expect the dative, and *vice versa*. (See Wülfing *Syntax Alfreds des Grossen* II. §784, 801, 821). In ME., the distinction of case disappeared, but *on* continued in both uses, the sense being generally indicated by the accompanying verb (e.g. to *lie* on, to *lay* on), though not infrequently with ambiguity, to remedy which the sense of motion began in the 16th c. to be indicated in case of need by the collocation *on to*, now sometimes written *onto*, after the analogy of *into*.

From the earliest times in the Teutonic langs. this prep. has been used in reference not merely to the upper surface or top of a thing, but to the front or any surface (this being the mod.Ger. and Du. use of *an, aan*, e.g. *an der thür* at the door, *an die thür* to the door); this was also the use in OE. But here *on* received a notable extension of sense, by being used to include also the notion of 'in', almost to the elimination of the prep. *in* from W. Sax. and the dialects influenced by it. (Cf. IN *prep.*) So in Early southern ME., *on* still included the sphere of both 'on' and 'in' (sense 5); but *in* was gradually restored; not, however, without the survival of many traces of the former prevalence of *on*; thence also a difficulty, in some of the transferred senses, in determining whether the starting-point was 'on' or 'in'. Eventually, not only was this extension in the direction of 'in' given up, but the language has shown a growing tendency to restrict *on* to the upper or at least the supporting surface, = F. *sur*, so as to correspond in use rather to *auf* than *an* in German; this comes out strongly also in the transf. and fig. senses in which *on* indicates the basis or foundation of action, feeling, etc. In OE., when the upper surface was specially in view, *ofer* was sometimes used; but the notion was usually expressed by the combination *uppan*, *uppon* (= *up* + *on*: cf. ON. *upp á*). When, in course of time, *on* itself came to be more associated with the upper surface, the distinction between *on* and *upon* gradually faded away, and *upon* may now be used instead of *on*, in positions into which no notion of *up* enters (see UPON). These changes in the sense-territory covered at different times by *on* make the historical and logical order of the senses difficult; and the following arrangement is in many respects provisional. Even the primary division into senses implying position and those implying motion or direction is difficult to carry out in the figurative uses, in some of which the point of view has gradually changed since they first arose, so that what was originally felt to express a direction of the mind towards something is now felt as a static attitude or mental state.

I. Of position. [OE. *on* with dative.]

* Of local position outside of, but close to or near, any surface. Primarily of things physical, but also of non-physical things treated as having extension.

1. a. Above and in contact with, above and supported by; upon.

c **900** tr. *Bæda's Hist.* v. xvii. [xix.] (1890) 460 Wilfrið..on domsetle sittende wæs. *c* **975** *Rushw. Gosp.* Matt. xxi. 5 Sittende on [*Ags. Gosp.* uppan] eosule & on folan sunu þære teoma. *c* **1220** *Bestiary* 1 Ðe leun stant on hille. *a* **1300** *Cursor M.* 13435 (Gött.) Iohn þe godspeller, þat lai on [*Cott.* o] iesu brest at super. **1382** WYCLIF *Matt.* v. 14 A citee putt on a hill may nat be hid. *c* **1386** CHAUCER *C.T. Prol.* 370 Wel semed ech of hem a fair burgeys To sitten in a yelde-halle on a deys. *c* **1425** LYDG. *Assembly of Gods* 803 A fawcon gentyll stood on hys helme on hy. **1483** *Cath. Angl.* 259/2 On, *super*. **1588** SHAKS. *Tit. A.* II. iii. 12 The birds chant melody on every bush. **1656** S. HOLLAND *Zara* (1719) 99 He sat a long time on his Horse back in a profound study. **1697** DRYDEN *Virg. Georg.* III. 686 Scum that on the molten Silver swims. **1819** *Metropolis* III. 183 The supper on table ten minutes after our arrival. **1823** BYRON *Island* IV. iv, They rested on their paddles. **1894** J. KNIGHT *Garrick* x. 168 Garrick.. found himself on the horns of a dilemma.

b. Said in reference to (the) earth, land, ocean, sea, water, etc.; also, any part of the earth viewed as a surface, e.g. a common, moor, heath, plateau.

With *earth*, *field*, *road*, *street*, *way*, etc. usage varies, or has varied, between *on* and *in*, according as they are viewed: cf. IN *prep.*[1], and see the individual words.

c **897** K. ÆLFRED *Gregory's Past.* xvi. 102 Crist ða he on eorðan wæs. *a* **1000** *Sal. & Sat.* 583 Yldo beoð on eorðan æghwæs cræftig. **1122–31** *O.E. Chron.* an. 1122 Þær-æfter wæron feole scip-men on sæ and on wæter. *c* **1200** ORMIN 5577 Himm reoweþþ þatt he dwelleþþ her Swa swiþe lange onn eorþe. **1362** LANGL. *P. Pl.* A. I. 7 Þe moste parti of þe peple þat passeþ nou on eorþe. *c* **1400** MAUNDEV. (Roxb.) i. 3 He may wende many ways, bathe on þe see and on þe land. **1542** UDALL *Erasm. Apoph.* 254b, In battaill on the sea. *Ibid.* 170a, He tooke with hym..a greate mayny that he happely mette on yᵉ waye as he wente. **1549** *Compl. Scot.* vi. 60 Sche vas on the feildis for hyr recreatione. **1754** J. SHEBBEARE *Matrimony* (1766) II. 227 On the streets of London. **1760** GOLDSM. *Cit. W.* ii, More painful..than all the journies I ever made on land. **1797** NELSON 7 Dec. in Nicolas *Disp.* (1845) III. 188 Captain Troubridge on shore is superior to Captains afloat. **1807** CRABBE *Par. Reg.* II. 74 On life's tempestuous sea. **1849** MACAULAY *Hist. Eng.* v. I. 539 During his residence on the Continent. **1871** MORLEY *Voltaire* (1886) 29 Ideas of grace and beauty, whose forms were old on the earth. **1898** *Century Mag.* Mar. 796/1 He.. occasionally took a short stroll on the street.

c. Indicating the part of the body which supports one, being itself in contact with the ground, etc.: e.g. ***on one's feet, knees, legs, back, face, on tiptoe, on all fours.***

c **893** K. ÆLFRED *Oros.* III. ix. §14 On cneowum sittende. *c* **1000** ÆLFRIC *Gen.* iii. 14 Ðu gæst on þinum breoste. *c* **1000** *Sax. Leechd.* II. 154 ʒif mon þung ete..stande on heafde. *c* **1205** LAY. 32046 Þe king læi on cneouwen. *c* **1350** *Will. Palerne* 1766 William & þe mayde þat were white beres, gon forþ..on here foure fet. **1594** T. BEDINGFIELD tr. *Machiavelli's Florentine Hist.* (1595) 12 Constrained to come to Rome on barefoot. **1631** GOUGE *God's Arrows* I. §29. 44 Creeping..on their bare knees. **1829** MACAULAY *Ess., Civil Disabil. Jews* (1887) 145 That he should..talk about being on his legs. **1885** ANSTEY *Tinted Venus* xii. 150 Leander went down on all fours on the hearth-rug.

d. Said in reference to a means of conveyance: e.g. ***on foot, on horseback, on an ass, on the wind, on the wing***, etc.: see also the sbs. (With an enclosing carriage, ***in*** is used.) Also in reference to a means of communication, as ***on the air*** (see AIR *sb.*[1] 1 c), ***on the telephone***, etc. Hence, broadcast on a specified channel, frequency, or wavelength.

c **888** K. ÆLFRED *Boeth.* xxxvi. §6 [5] Ða cild ridað on hiora stafum. **1127–31** *O.E. Chron.* an. 1127 Hi ridone on swarte hors & on swarte bucces. **1140–53** *Ibid.* (Laud MS.) an. 1140 Scæ fleh & iæde on fote to Walingford. *c* **1205** LAY. 502 An horsen & an [*c* **1275** a] foten. *c* **1400** MAUNDEV. (1839) v. 58 Be this Desert, no Man may go on Hors back. **1539** BIBLE (Great) *1 Sam.* xxv. 20 As she rode on her asse. **1697** DRYDEN *Virg. Georg.* IV. 761 When his Head,.. Wash'd by the Waters, was on Hebrus born. **1748** *Anson's Voy.* II. viii. 218 Mackaws..wheeling and playing on the wing. **1844** MRS. BROWNING *Rom. Page* xii, Now the vision ..Wheeleth on the wind around. **1849** MACAULAY *Hist. Eng.* iii. I. 387 The bags were carried on horseback. **1886** *Century Mag.* XXXII. 471/2, I should go away on the first train. **1917** R. FRY *Let.* 23 Nov. (1972) II. 420 London's just awful for me because of the millions of people that catch me on the telephone. *c* **1928** *Ibid.* 632 I've just been talking for the second time today with Vanessa on the 'phone. **1929** *Ibid.* 5 Feb. 636, I have still two 'talks' hanging over me—one at the Athenaeum Club and one on the wireless. **1944** *Sun* (Baltimore) 7 Jan. 8/3 Common usage is unerringly correct: one does not hear a program in or even by or through the radio. He hears it on the radio. **1966** *Listener* 11 Aug. 190 Viscount Dilhorne and Lord Shawcross, Q.C., interviewed by Robin Day on B.B.C.-1. *Ibid.* 8 Sept. 363/3 Earlier, on B.B.C.-2, Rozhdestvensky was back again with the Moscow Radio Orchestra and the young pianist Nicolai Petrov. **1969** D. E. WESTLAKE *Up your Banners* xviii. 124 The beautician hollered from the living room, 'Leona, come quick! You're on the TV!' **1973** P. O'DONNELL *Silver Mistress* iv. 73 Get on the phone and book three seats..to Hong Kong. **1974** *Oxford Mail* 1 May 4/7 James Dalton, the Queen's College organist, can be heard on Radio Three on Monday. **1977** *Custom Car* Nov. 11/3 Anyone with that kind of money contact Richard on Berkhampstead 71619.

e. Said in reference to a supporting axis, pivot, or centre of revolution.

885 [see AX *sb.*]. **1635–** [see AXLE[2] 1 c, 3]. **1762** [see HINGE *sb.*]. **1832** *Prop. Reg. Instr. Cavalry* III. 55 A Line is ordered to '*Change Front*' on a flank. **1847** *Infantry Man.* (1854) 63 The sections are wheeling on their pivot men. **1859** F. A. GRIFFITHS *Artil. Man.* (1862) 32 Change front on the left company. *Ibid.* 33 To change front on a flank Company in echellon. **1868** LOCKYER *Elem. Astron.* iii. x. (1879) 56 All the planets rotate, or turn on their axes, in the same direction.

f. Indicating that on which the hands are placed in making oath; also with *conscience*, *faith*, *honour*, etc., as the basis of an oath or affirmation.

In OE. the dative was used with the material object touched, the accusative with the ideal object or absent being appealed to.

876 *O.E. Chron.*, Ond him þa aþas sworon on þam halʒan beaʒe. *c* **893** K. ÆLFRED *Oros.* IV. vi. §15 He him ʒeswor on his goda noman þæt [etc.]. *a* **1000** *Laws of Æthelred* III. ii. (Schmid), þe he durre on þam haliʒdome swerian þe him man on hand sylð. *c* **1000** *Ags. Gosp.* Matt. xxiii. 20 Witodlice seþe swereþ on weofude, he swereð on him and on eallum þam þe him ofer synt. *c* **1000** *Ags. Ps.* (Th.) lxii. 9 Ealle þa ðe on hine aðas sweriað [L. *qui jurant in co*]. *a* **1023** WULFSTAN *Hom.* xlvi. (1883) 232 Ic eow halsiʒe..on ealle Godes halʒan and on ða cyrcan, ðe ʒe to ʒelyfaþ. *c* **1330** R. BRUNNE *Chron.* (1810) 110 Þe prid poynt þei wild..þat þe Danegelde for euer suld be forgyuen,..he suore þat on þe boke. *c* **1475** *Rauf Coilʒear* 952 Thay swoir on thair swordis swyftlie all thre. **1525** LD. BERNERS *Froiss.* II. clx. [clvi.] 442 Let hym go on goddes name whider it shall please hym. **1768** GOLDSM. *Good-n. Man* I, On my conscience, I believe [it]. **1785** tr. *Fleury's Hist. Gt. Brit.* V. v. i. §1. 238 All these hostages took a solemn oath on the gospels. **1856** BOUVIER *Law Dict.* I. 589 In courts of equity peers..answer on their honor only.

g. In various elliptical and transferred uses, as (*a*) = Stationed on, at, or in charge of; (*b*) subsisting or dependent on; in the charge or care of; (*c*) on the list or staff of, employed on; (*d*) on an official list, e.g. ***on half-pay***.

1712 BUDGELL *Spect.* No. 313 ¶17 [One] endeavoured to raise himself on the Civil List, and the other..on the Military. **1761** GRAY *Lett.* Wks. 1884 III. 86 If the boy was to be on the foundation [at Eton]. **1794** NELSON 8 July in Nicolas *Disp.* (1845) I. 249, I have told Captain Stephens and Captain Wilkes, who is on the battery, that [etc.]. **1798** MILLER *ibid.* VII. p. clix, Having made one strong cable fast to the Tonnant and desired sentinels to be placed on it on board her. **1834** H. MILLER *Scenes & Leg.* xx. (1857) 296 She had to leave her mother on the care of a neighbour. **1843** *Fraser's Mag.* XXVIII. 336 A colonel on half-pay. **1855** MACAULAY *Hist. Eng.* xii. III. 205 Scarcely ever had he been on a grand jury. **1882** P. FITZGERALD *Recreat. Lit. Man* (1883) 139 A leading writer on the press. **1885** *Times* (weekly ed.) 27 Feb. 2/4 A captain on the General Staff. **1890** *Pall Mall G.* 8 Nov. 3/1 Speaking of their several avocations..I learned that So-and-so was 'on the pigs', another 'on the kitchen', and a third 'on the table'.

h. Hence arise many phrases, originally expressing physical situation, of which the sense becomes more or less figurative, as an expression of what is done or implied in such a position. Such are the following, for which see the respective sbs.:

on the bench, on the boards, on the books, on the cards, on the carpet, on 'Change, on the fence, on the field, on foot, on hand, on one's hands, on one's own hook, on one's knees, on one's legs, on the market, on the nail, on the parish, on the rack, on the shelf, on the spot, on the streets, on the stump, on tenterhooks, on the throne, on the turf, on the way, on the wing, on the world. Phrases originally literal, when thus used *fig.*, sometimes serve as models for others which never were literal, e.g. *on a level, on an equality, on a par.*

i. Indicating a musical instrument which is being played, = UPON *prep.* 25. Of a musician: playing (a specified musical instrument) *colloq.* (orig. *U.S.*).

c **1386** CHAUCER *Miller's Tale* (1885, Harl. MS. 7334) 3214 And al aboue þer lay a gay Sawtrye On which he made a nightes melodye. *c* **1400** [see PLAY *v.* 26 a]. *a* **1529** [see LUTE *sb.*[1] 1 a]. **1767, 1768** [see PIANOFORTE]. **1842, 1903** [see PERFORM *v.* 7 c]. **1926** WHITEMAN & MCBRIDE *Jazz* xii. 241 Gus Miller..was wonderful on the clarinet and saxophone. **1934** *Down Beat* Aug. 4/2 Oscar Eiler remains on cello... Hunter Kahler replaced George Frewit on piano... Milt. Chalifoux is still on drums, as is Ralph Mazza on guitar and violin. **1955** SHAPIRO & HENTOFF *Hear me talkin' to Ya* xiii. 206 Our three pieces including Sonny, Sterling Conway on banjorine, and myself. *Ibid.* 251 We went into the Little Club—Gil Rodin, myself, and Benny Goodman on saxes, Glenn Miller on trombone..; and Ben Pollack, of course, on drums. **1962** *Sunday Times* (Colour Suppl.) 10 June 3 A powerful and accomplished saxophonist—mainly on alto, originally rather too closely modelled on Charlie Parker. **1971** *Radio Times* 11 Nov. 3/4 Neither Cat Anderson on trumpet nor Lawrence Brown on trombone were able to make this tour.

j. *Math.* (Defined or expressed) in terms of (the elements of).

1934 *Ann. Math.* XXXV. 119 By an abstract ϵ p-simplex σ_p on A is meant a set of $p+1$ points of A whose sum is of diameter $<\epsilon$. **1937** R. D. CARMICHAEL *Introd. Theory Groups of Finite Order* viii. 240 Show how to form the most general group of linear homogeneous transformations on a given set of variables. **1953** BIRKHOFF & MACLANE *Survey Mod. Algebra* (rev. ed.) vi. 119 A function defined on the elements of the set S_1 with values in T. **1968** E. T. COPSON *Metric Spaces* i. 11 Suppose we have a relation $\sim$ defined on a set E. **1971** *Sci. Amer.* Aug. 94/3 The objects..will be real-valued functions f defined on some set S. In other words, f is a rule that assigns to each point s belonging to the set S a real number $f(s)$ belonging to the real-number set. **1971** *Nature* 31 Dec. 527/1 We define a pairwise dissimilarity matrix d on a set of objects P as a real-valued function on pairs of elements of P such that $d(a, b) \geqslant 0$ for all a, b in P [etc.].

k. Addicted to or regularly taking (a drug or drugs). Cf. ON *adv.* 1 b. *colloq.* (orig. *U.S.*).

1936 *Amer. Speech* XI. 124/2 *On drugs*, addicted. **1955** SHAPIRO & HENTOFF *Hear me talkin' to Ya* xxi. 333 The habit is a false crutch. Don't get on the H. *Ibid.* 335, I don't think all musicians are on junk by any means. **1971** *Lancet* 30 Oct. 985/1 A woman aged 49 received lithium carbonate 900 mg. daily... She was also on tranylcypromine 30 mg. daily. **1972** M. J. BOSSE *Incident at Naha* i. 60 Linda..asked what I was on these days. 'Pot, and not much of that,' I told her. **1972** D. SELMAN *Sudden Death* iv. 96, I suppose he didn't *truly* rape me... I mean I'm on the pill and everything. **1973** BOYD & PARKES *Dark Number* vii. 82 Julia went through a pretty bad time..after the accident—on the pills, seeing psychiatrists and what have you. **1976** P. HILL *Hunters* v. 59 He dropped his mouth to hers... 'Are you on the pill?' he asked.

l. Drinking (alcoholic liquor) in large quantities or to excess. ***on the booze***: see BOOZE *sb.* 2 b; ***on it*** (Austral. colloq.): drinking heavily, 'hitting the bottle'.

1938 E. LOWE *Salute to Freedom* 38 He knew how drink affected Brand, and he muttered to his wife, 'He's on it proper to day mother.' **1951** E. LAMBERT *Twenty Thousand Thieves* ix. 140 'They reckon Groggy's on it again,' observed Tommy. **1955** P. WHITE *Tree of Man* (1956) 141 'It is him,' she said finally. 'It is that bastard. He is on it again.' **1962** A. SEYMOUR *One Day of Year* 12 And how long was you on it before the pubs shut? *a* **1966** 'M. NA GOPALEEN' *Best of Myles* (1968) 291 Easy seen you were on the beer last night. **1966** 'J. HACKSTON' *Father clears Out* 104 When he was on it, and wanted..another drink..he never had to press the bell, but pressed the button with a bullet. **1967** H. STOREY in *Coast to Coast 1965–66* 203 One of the neighbours had ribbed him about 'being on the bottle'. **1976** *Daily Mirror* 18 Mar. 9/3 Watch that daily tipple, ladies. You could end up on the bottle.

2. Expressing contact with any surface, whatever its position; e.g. to *hang, stick on a wall*; *to border on an estate*; *a fly walking on the ceiling*; *blisters on the soles of the feet*. Also, of things that cover or clothe, as *a coat on his back, shoes on his feet, a book with a cover on it*.

c **897** K. ÆLFRED *Gregory's Past.* xxi. 152 Ealle ða hearʒas ..wæron atifred on ðæm waʒe. *a* **900** CYNEWULF *Christ* 1115 þa he on rode wæs. *c* **1205** LAY. 511 Alle heo sculden hongien On heʒe treowen. **1470–85** MALORY *Arthur* v. v, He satte atte souper gnawynge on a lymme of a man. **1508** DUNBAR *Gold. Targe* 55 And hard on burd vnto the blomyt medis..Arrivit sche. **1590** SPENSER *F.Q.* I. i. 2 On his brest a bloodie Crosse he bore. **1611** BIBLE *1 Sam.* xvi. 16 A cunning player on an harpe. **1697** DRYDEN *Virg. Georg.* III. 489 On Shrubs they browze. **1821** KEATS *Isabella* xxxvi, Isabella on its music hung. **1855** MACAULAY *Hist. Eng.* xiii. III. 361 With eight wounds on his body. **1888** W. WILLIAMS *Princ. Med.* (ed. 5) 577 A brewer's yard dog, always on the chain. **1895** *Bookman* Oct. 12/1 A small volume..printed on one side only.

3. In proximity to; close to, beside, near, by, at; on the bank of (a river or lake), on the coast of (the sea).

c **1122** *O.E. Chron.* an. 1009 (MS. E) Hi..namon him winter settl on Temesan. *c* **1200** *Trin. Coll. Hom.* 9 Bethfage ..on þe fot of þe dune þe men clepen munt oliuete. **1523** LD. BERNERS *Froiss.* I. cccxxxii. 519 The castell of Geron one the see. **1596** DALRYMPLE tr. *Leslie's Hist. Scot.* I. 15 Paslay.. is situat..onn the Riuer Carronn. *a* **1715** BURNET *Own Time* (1823) I. 74 They came up marching on the head of their parishes. **1748** *Anson's Voy.* III. viii. 379 Mr. Anson over-reached the galeon, and lay on her bow. **1816** J. WILSON *City of Plague* I. i. 399 There is a dwelling on the lone sea-shore. **1830** H. ANGELO *Reminisc.* I. 229 His residence, St. George's-row, on the Uxbridge Road. **1832** LD. MALMESBURY in *Mem. Ex-Minister* (1884) I. 50 Detained long at the Douane on the Italian frontier. **1855** MACAULAY *Hist. Eng.* xii. III. 229 Kirke and his squadron were on the coast of Ulster. *Mod.* Burton-on-Trent, Clacton-on-Sea.

4. Expressing position with reference to a place or thing: esp. with *side, hand, bow* (of a ship), and words of particular direction implying 'side', as *front, back, rear; north, south, east, west*, etc. (In OE. these took the accus. = 'looking unto or towards' the left, the north, etc.)

Hence in many *fig.* and *transf.* uses of *hand, part, side, behalf*, and in such phrases as *on the contrary, the defensive*, etc.; see these sbs. and adjs.

c **893** K. ÆLFRED *Oros.* I. i. §2 þonne on ðæm norþdæle, þæt is, Asia on þaswiþran healfe. *a* **1000** *Ags. Ps.* (Th.) xliv. 11 þær stent cwen þe on þa swyðran hand. *c* **1000** *Ags. Gosp.* Matt. xxvii. 38 An on þa swiðran healfe and oðer on þa wynstran. **1122–31** *O.E. Chron.* an. 1122 Hi sægon on norð east fir mycel & brad. *a* **1300** *Cursor M.* 13038 On oþer side was hir ful wa. **13..** *Guy Warw.* 218 (MS. A.) Gij..on hir fader half he hir grett. **1390** GOWER *Conf.* II. 183 God bad the rede See divide, Which stod upriht on either side. **1411** *Rolls of Parlt.* III. 650/1 This is the ordenance..made between William Lord the Roos on that oon partie and Robert Tirwhit..on that other partie. **1558** Q. ELIZ. in Strype *Ann. Ref.* (1824) I. App. i. 389 Not doubting on their part, but they will observe the duty. **1650** SIR T. BROWNE *Pseud. Ep.* (ed. 2) 49 The Cape *de las Agullas* hath sea on both sides near it. **1671** H. M. tr. *Erasm. Colloq.* 7, I am glad on your behalf. **1747** *Mem. Nutrebian Crt.* I. 221 It was agreed on all hands. **1748** *Anson's Voy.* I. v. 49 The Indians, lying on the back of the Portuguese settlements. **1838** THIRLWALL *Greece* (1846) III. xxiv. 338 Thucydides..does not venture to state the numbers on either side. **1883** *Law Times Rep.* XLIX. 332 Bearing about three or four points on the starboard bow of the Clan Sinclair.

** Of position *within* [OE. *on* for *in*].

†**5.** Within the limits or bounds of: = IN *prep.* 1, 9. *Obs.*

In OE. (W.Sax.) and early ME. (southern): see above.

c **900** tr. *Bæda's Hist.* Pref. ii, Se wæs biscop on Cantwara byriᵹ. *Ibid.*, Oððe on ðysse bec, oððe on oðre. *c* **1000** ÆLFRIC *Gen.* xxxvii. 13 Ðine gebroðru healdaþ scep on Sichima. *c* **1000** *Ags. Ps.* lxviii. 12 Ða him sæton sundor on portum. *c* **1175** *Lamb. Hom.* 35 Ic walde..sitten on forste and on snawe up et minne chinne. *c* **1205** LAY. 24587 þe stiward..hæxt cniht on londe. *c* **1260** *K. Horn* 653 (MS. C.) Heo sat on þe sunne. *c* **1375** *Cursor M.* 14195 (Fairf.) To ga on liȝt of day. [*c* **1485** *Digby Myst.* (1882) IV. 530 Chase he not the on his xij to bee?]

*** Of time, or action implying time.

(In OE. with dat. or accus.)

6. a. Indicating the day of an occurrence, treated as a unit of time; so with *night, morning, afternoon*, a defined date, *a time, the eve, morrow, occasion of*. ***on the instant***, instantly. Also (*dial.* and *U.S.*) used redundantly in ***on tomorrow***, ***on yesterday***, etc.

c **893** K. ÆLFRED *Oros.* II. viii. §2 þa on ðæm ilcan dæᵹe..fuhton Gallie on þa burᵹ. *a* **900** *Laws of Ælfred* Introd. §3 Wyrceað eow syx daᵹas, and on þam siofoðan restað eow. Forþam [Drihten] hine ᵹereste on þone seofoðan dæᵹ. *c* **1000** ÆLFRIC *Hom.* I..Hit ᵹelamp on sumne sæl. **1122–31** *O.E. Chron.* an. 1122 On þet dæi xi k' Apr'. *Ibid.*, þet wæs on þæs dæies xiiiº k' Nouemb'. **1137–40** *Ibid.* an. 1137 þe Iudeus..on langfridæi him on rode hengen. *c* **1250** *Gen. & Ex.* 3325 On morgen fel hem a dew a-gein. *a* **1300** *Cursor M.* 17670 Yee sperd me soth on a fridai. *c* **1420** *Anturs of Arth.* 6 (Thornton MS.) One a daye þay þam dighte to þe depe dellis. *c* **1450** *Merlin* 231 On an euen com a spie. **1542** UDALL *Erasm. Apoph.* 131 b, Anaximenes was, on a tyme, in makyng an oracion. **1556** *Chron. Gr. Friars* (1852) 14 Thys yere one sent Martyns day. **1670** LADY MARY BERTIE in *12th Rep. Hist. MSS. Comm.* App. v. 22 On Tuesday wee are to goe see the second part of it. **1764–7** LYTTELTON *Henry II* (1771) I. 17 On the eve of St. Matthew. **1766** GOLDSM. *Vic. W.* iii, The day..on which we were to disperse. **1795** *Jemima* I. 215 Rosina..taking Jemima aside on the instant. **1829** *Virginia Lit. Museum* 30 Dec. 459/2 *On.* As 'on tomorrow'; a mere expletive. Common. **1848** *Southern Lit. Messenger* XIV. 636/2 'On' yesterday, (another Southern emendation of the Queen's English, which is funny enough,) I was so unfortunate [etc.]. **1852** *N.Y. Tribune* 9 Jan. 6/1 It was the intention to send in the Treasury Report ..on yesterday. **1876** GLADSTONE *Glean.* (1879) II. 298 Croker assailed, and assailed on the instant, some of Macaulay's celebrated speeches on Reform. **1880** W. H. PATTERSON *Gloss. Words Antrim & Down* 74 *On*..is sometimes prefixed to the words to-morrow and yesterday, thus—'I'll do it on to-morrow.' **1885** *Law Times* LXXX. 112/2 On the 29th Jan. 1884 [he] absconded, and on the following day the firm suspended payment. **1899** *Pall Mall Mag.* Aug. 579 On-a-day he gravely complained in open court that [etc.]. *a* **1902** *Mod.* Presented to A. B. on the occasion of his wedding. **1914** *Dialect Notes* IV. 160 On yesterday; on last week. **1922** H. C. LODGE in *Congress. Rec.* 27 Dec. 942, I took occasion to ask the Secretary of State on yesterday. **1922** JOYCE *Ulysses* 645 Lionel's air in *Martha, M'appari*, which..he heard, or overheard, to be more accurate, on yesterday. **1944** H. W. HORWILL *Dict. Mod. Amer. Usage* (ed. 2) 214/2 The expression *on yesterday* is an example of the Am. use of *on* where it would be considered superfluous in Eng. **1977** *Irish Press* 29 Sept. 2/1 (Advt.), Removal of remains to St. Bridget's Church, Kilcurry on today (Thursday) at 6.30 o'clock.

†**b.** Formerly used of any time or period, where current usage has *in, at, during, by*. (Also before the advb. genitives *dayes, nightes*, which were perh. then taken for plurals.) *Obs.*

c **893** K. ÆLFRED *Oros.* I. i. 17 On huntoðe on wintra & on sumera on fiscaþe. *Ibid.* III. iii. §2 On þæm ilcan ᵹeare tohlad seo eorþe. *c* **1000** ÆLFRIC *Deut.* x. 1 On þære tide Drihten cwæþ to me. *Ibid.* xxviii. 29 Ðæt þu grapie on midne dæᵹ. **1127–31** *O.E. Chron.* an. 1127 Soðieste men heom kepten on nihtes. *c* **1330** R. BRUNNE *Chron.* (1810) 31 God sent him a tokenyng on nyght als he slepe. **1375** BARBOUR *Bruce* VII. 506 And fra Carlele on nychts ryd; And in cowert on dayis byd. **1377** LANGL. *P. Pl.* B. XIV. 2, I slepe þere-inne on niȝtes. *a* **1425** *Cursor M.* 12245 (Trin.) Say I neuer suche on my lyue. **1442** T. BECKINGTON *Corr.* (Rolls) II. 189 On the meane tyme. **1450–1530** *Myrr. our Ladye* 12 Also Daniel.. worshyped god thryes on the day knelynge. **1627** W. SCLATER *Exp. 2 Thess.* (1629) 137 Rome was not all built on a day. **1650** FULLER *Pisgah* III. *Zor. Temple* vii. §6 It never rained on the day-time. **1654** R. CODRINGTON tr. *Iustine* I. 19 On the break of day. **1708** SWIFT *Wks.* (1841) II. 256 Rascals that walk the streets on nights. **1779** FORREST *Voy. N. Guinea* 182 The tides rise about six inches higher on the full moon than on the change.

†**c.** Formerly also: Within the space of; = IN *prep.* 21. *Obs.*

c **893** K. ÆLFRED *Oros.* Contents v. ii, Hu on anum ᵹeare wurdon þa twa byrᵹ toworpena. *c* **897** —— *Gregory's Past.* xliii. 312 Ic fæste tuwa on wucan. *c* **1000** *Ags. Gosp.* Matt. xxvii. 40 On þrim daᵹum hyt eft ᵹetimbrað. *c* **1205** LAY. 8059 And þas dæies æn þreom wiken Wenden to Lundene. *c* **1400** MAUNDEV. (Roxb.) xiii. 57 Men may wende to Damasc on three days. **1693** *Apol. Clergy Scot.* 62 They cite the Archbishop of St. Andrews on twenty four hours to compear before them.

d. = Close upon, touching upon. Also, in ***on time*** = exactly at the (right or prescribed) time: see also TIME *sb.* 47.

1843 MRS. CARLYLE *Lett.* I. 235 It is now just on post-time. **1890** BOLDREWOOD *Miner's Right* (1899) 181/2 Anxiety about being 'on time' for the mid-day stage. **1892** *Pall Mall G.* 17 Feb. 3/3 The following are a few arrivals at Preston..September 25..2 minutes early. December 12.. On time.

7. Followed by a noun of action, etc., expressing the occasion of what is stated.

e.g. ***on reaching***.. = when I (he, &c.) reached..; ***on my return*** = when I returned; ***on hearing this*** = when (and because) I heard this, *I changed my plans*.

1593 SHAKS. *Lucr.* 186 He doth debate What following sorrow may on this arise. **1713** BERKELEY *Hylas & Phil.* I. Wks. 1871 I. 268 On second thoughts, I do not think it so evident. **1748** *Anson's Voy.* I. x. 101 A disposition to be seized with the most dreadful terrors on the slightest accident. **1761–2** HUME *Hist. Eng.* (1806) V. lxix. 186 He had ten thousand 'brisk boys'..who on a motion of his finger, were ready to fly to arms. **1793** SMEATON *Edystone L.* §68 Which would on the first blush induce one to suppose there was something culpable in this man. **1812** JEFFERSON *Writ.* (1830) IV. 178 On our arrival here. **1876** GLADSTONE *Glean.* (1879) II. 333 It attracted little notice on its appearance. **1891** *Law Times* XCII. 94/1 Milk which on analysis proved to be deficient in fatty matter.

**** Of order, arrangement, manner, state.

†**8.** Indicating physical arrangement or grouping: = *in* (a row, a heap, pieces). *Obs.* or *arch.*

a **1000–1611** [see HEAP *sb.* 5 c]. ? *a* **1400** *Morte Arth.* 238 Alle þe riche on rawe, Romaynes and oþer. **1430–40** LYDG. *Bochas* I. xiii. (1554) 25 Kepe them from tonges that been on tweine. *c* **1440** *Promp. Parv.* 364/1 On a thronge, or to-gedur ..*Gregatim.* **1575** *Brieff Disc. Troub. Franckford* 98 And others..came in suddenlie on a troupe together in to the churche. **1620** *Frier Rush* 8 They came all on a cluster. **1625** PURCHAS *Pilgrims* II. 1133 There lyeth nine little Ilands on a row. **1662** in Ellis *Orig. Lett.* Ser. III. IV. 280, I saw the monks kneeling on a row..before the altar. **1818** G. S. FABER *Horæ Mosaicæ* I. 189 Its waters stood on heaps to the right hand and to the left.

9. a. Indicating manner: = *in. Obs.* exc. in archaic phrases, as ***on this wise***. (In OE. with the accus. Cf. Ger. *auf diese weise*.) Here also belong such modern phrases as ***on the cheap, on the sly, on the square***: see CHEAP, etc.

c **888** K. ÆLFRED *Boeth.* xxxix. 10 We onᵹitaþ hwilum mon on oðre wisan, on oðre hine God onᵹit. *c* **1000** ÆLFRIC *Exod.* xii. 5 On þa ylcan wisan nymað ticcenu. *c* **1175** *Lamb. Hom.* 77 þe fader is ine þe sune on þre wise. **1258** *Procl. Hen. III* 6 Beon ilet oþer iwersed on onie wise. *Ibid.* 11 Al on þo ilche worden. ? *a* **1366** CHAUCER *Rom. Rose* 984 These arowis ..Were alle fyve on oon maneere. *c* **1380** WYCLIF *Sel. Wks.* I. 179 On two maner is Goddis word herd. **1483** *Cath. Angl.* 259/2 On Alle wyse, *omnimodo.* **1526** TINDALE *Matt.* i. 18 The byrthe off Christe was on thys wyse. *a* **1557** *Diurn. Occurr.* (Bannatyne Club) 28 Bot the lordis on na wayiss wald not aggree. **1697** J. SERGEANT *Solid Philos.* 440 To begin his search after Truth on this preposterous manner. **1864** DASENT *Jest & Earnest* (1873) II. 346 Ulf's words were on this wise.

†**b.** Indicating language: = IN 12 c. *Obs.*

(In OE., as in the other Teutonic langs., with accus.)

c **897** K. ÆLFRED *Gregory's Past.* Pref. 7 Nemned on Læden Pastoralis, and on Englisc Hierdeboc. *c* **1205** LAY. 33 An oþer he nom on Latin þe makede seinte Albin. *c* **1320** *Cast. Love* 35 On Englisch I wyl my reson shewe. **1401** *Pol. Poems* (Rolls) II. 91 Heresie, that is Grw, is divisioun on Latyn.

10. a. Of state, condition, action: (*a*) with a sb., as ***on fire, on live, on sleep, on wait, on the tap***; (*b*) with noun of action, as ***on loan, on sale, on the look-out, on the move, on the run, on the wane, on the watch***; (*c*) formerly with vbl. sb., as ***on singing, on building***. (See also 19.)

In (*b*) *on* is still normal; of those in (*a*) most have now *in*, (*in life, in wait*), some retain *on*, many have reduced it to *a*, now written in comb. (*afire, alive, asleep*: see 30); (*c*) is *obs.* or *arch.*, *on* having been first reduced to *a*-, and then omitted in mod. Standard Eng., whereby the vbl. sb. comes to function as a pres. pple. (the ark was *on building*, was *a-building*, was *building*). See A *prep.* 11–13; -ING[1, 2].

c **893** [see 6 b]. *a* **950** *Cod. Exon.* VII. 37 (E.E.T.S.) 294 Sum bið on hunþe. **971** *Blickl. Hom.* 3 þæt heo cende on sare & on unrotnesse þa hire bearn. *c* **1200** ORMIN 142 þe follc..stod þatt while onn heore bene. *a* **1300** *Cursor M.* 15649 All on slepe he fand þam fast. *c* **1325** *Body & Soul* 59 in *Map's Poems* 347 The world shal al o fure ben. *c* **1375** *XI Pains of Hell* 281 in *O.E. Misc.* 219 When I was on þerst hongyng on þe rode. **1387** TREVISA *Higden* (Rolls) V. 325 While þe masse is on syngynge. *Ibid.* 415 While þe gospel was on redynge. *c* **1435** *Torr. Portugal* 773 Whyle Torrent an huntyng wase. **1451** *Paston Lett.* I. 195, I lay on wayte up on hym. **1470–85** MALORY *Arthur* III. iii, As good a man as ony is on lyue. **1513** DOUGLAS *Æneis* V. xiii. 33 Venus, all on flocht, Amyd her breist reuoluyng mony a thocht. **1601** HOLLAND *Pliny* I. 84 When the Firth is frozen and all on yce. **1629** MAXWELL tr. *Herodian* (1635) 400 The doores (which were all on a flame). **1711** STEELE *Spect.* No. 38 ⁋1 You might see his Imagination on the Stretch. **1749** FIELDING *Tom Jones* I. ii, Her prudence was as much on the guard, as if she had all the snares to apprehend. **1808** ELEANOR SLEATH *Bristol Heiress* IV. 31 Glenn Hall, which was then advertised, and on sale. **1811** W. R. SPENCER *Poems* 211 Folly herself has long been on the wane. **1849** MACAULAY *Hist. Eng.* v. I. 608 Some men of the Horse Guards, who were on watch, heard the report. **1855** *Ibid.* xvii. IV. 92 But fortune was already on the turn. **1876** ROGERS *Pol. Econ.* ix. (ed. 3) 89 Workmen on strike. **1886** *Illustr. Lond. News* 9 Jan. 31/1 Better a dinner of herbs..than eight courses, eaten on our best behaviour.

b. Engaged in, occupied with.

1768 G. WHITE *Selborne* xx, As you have been so lately on the study of reptiles.

c. ***on it***: (*a*) *U.S. slang*, ready for, or skilled in, something; (*b*) *dial.*, preceded by an adverb or adjective: in a particular condition or situation, usu. one that is distressing.

1865 *Harper's Mag.* May 694/1 She's tolerable peert—the old 'oman is. Oh, she's on it, you bet. **1866** 'MARK TWAIN' in *Daily Union* (Sacramento) 22 May 3/4 In San Francisco sometimes, if you offend a man, he proposes to take his coat off, and inquires, 'Are you on it?' **1880** A. A. HAYES *New Colorado* (1881) v. 77 You bet he could cook. He was just *on it*. **1886** R. E. G. COLE *Gloss. Words S.-W. Lincs.* 103 Such phrases as 'Sorely on it', 'Sadly on it', for Sorely off, Sadly off; 'Two or three days ago I was strangely on it.' **1889** E. PEACOCK *Gloss. Words Manley & Corringham, Lincolnshire* (ed. 2) 886 He's sorely on it yit, 'cause his wife's runn'd awaay fra him. **1890** BARRÈRE & LELAND *Dict. Slang* II. 102/1 *On it* (American). This eccentric expression meant originally that a man was decidedly engaged in anything. It implied determination. 'I'm on it,' I understand it. **1946** F. SARGESON *That Summer* 96 He looked pretty crook on it.

***** Indicating non-material basis, ground, or footing, (fig. extension of 1).

11. a. Indicating the ground, basis, or reason of action, opinion, etc.

c **888** K. ÆLFRED *Boeth.* xi. §1 Buton he..mæᵹe ᵹebeacnian þæt he irne on his willan. *c* **1205** LAY. 3336 Ah late we hine welden His folc on his willen. *c* **1380** WYCLIF *Serm.* Sel. Wks. I. 15 3if men avysiden hem on þis resoun. **1578** WHETSTONE *Promos & Cass.* II. v, The doome was geven on cause, and not on spyte. **1594** *First Pt. Contention* (1843) 35, I do arrest thee on high treason here. **1608** SIR T. BODLEIGH *Let. to Bacon* in *Ussher's Lett.* (1686) App. 21 They turned back on their own accord. *a* **1633** AUSTIN *Medit.* (1635) 164, I think that he [St. Thomas] was absent on negligence. **1662** STILLINGFL. *Orig. Sacr.* III. i. §7 Those principles on which they deny a Deity. **1680** LUTTRELL *Brief Rel.* (1857) I. 41 Being wounded by his fellows on mistake. **1757** MRS. GRIFFITH *Lett. Henry & Frances* (1767) I. 38, I acted not on so poor a motive. **1806–7** J. BERESFORD *Miseries Hum. Life* (1826) VI. iii, Starting for a long ride on a dinner engagement. **1838** THIRLWALL *Greece* IV. xxxi. 174 The capitulation on which Athens surrendered. **1855** MACAULAY *Hist. Eng.* xiii. III. 267 He..was convicted on evidence which would not have satisfied any impartial tribunal. **1885** *Times* (weekly ed.) 8 May 15/4 A careful opinion on full knowledge. **1891** *Law Times* XCI. 21/2 We learn on good authority that arbitration has become too well established.

b. In many phrases; (e.g. ***on account (of), on design, on intent, on pretence, on purpose; on terms; on an*** (or ***the***) ***average, on the whole***; for which see the sbs. †***on less than***: see UNLESS.

12. Indicating risk, pain, or penalty; on peril of.

c **1386** CHAUCER *Knt.'s T.* 867 Arcite That fro thy lond is banysshed on his heed. **1389** in *Eng. Gilds* (1870) 10 On þe peyne of xl.*d.* to paie to þe box. **14..** *Sir Beues* 107/2031 (MS. M) The patriarke on my lyfe, Charged me, neuer to take wyfe. **1588** SHAKS. *L.L.L.* I. i. 124 On paine of loosing her tongue. **1667** MILTON *P.L.* XII. 398 Obedience to the Law of God, impos'd On penaltie of death. **1667** DRYDEN *Ind. Emperor* IV. i, On thy life secure the Prison Gate. **1755** MRS. F. BROOKE *Old Maid* No. 3 (1764) 16 [The father] charged him on his blessing to abandon all studies of that kind. **1858** O. W. HOLMES *Aut. Breakf.-t.* viii. 71 Many minds must change their key now and then, on penalty of getting out of tune or losing their voices.

13. Indicating that which forms the basis of income, taxation, borrowing, betting, profit, or loss.

1697 DAMPIER *Voy.* I. 376 We must consequently have gain'd something insensibly on the length of the particular days, but have lost on the..number. **1712** ADDISON *Spect.* No. 445 ⁋5 The Tax on Paper was given for the Support of the Government. **1745** *Col. Rec. Pennsylv.* V. 34 For raising of money on the Inhabitants. **1753** HANWAY *Trav.* (1762) II. VII. iii. 178 The king borrowed considerable sums on his jewels. **1764** *App. to Chron.* in *Ann. Reg.* 129/1 Odds at starting—Six to four on Leader. **1809** BYRON *Bards & Rev.* 675 Done!—a thousand on the..trick. **1883** *L'pool Courier* 25 Sept. 4/5 The largest procurable dividends on the outlay of capital. **1883** SIR E. E. KAY in *Law Times Rep.* XLIX. 77/2 Any charge, or lien, or equity on this particular fund. **1885** *Law Times* LXXX. 131/2 The interest on the debentures. **1891** *Law Rep.* Weekly Notes 80/1 Shewing a loss on his last year's business. *a* **1902** *Mod.* The margin of profit on the sales.

II. Of motion or direction towards a position.

14. a. To or towards the position expressed by senses 1, 2; on to.

So in reference to non-physical things treated as having physical extension, or to motion that is merely ideal.

c **900** tr. *Bæda's Hist.* I. vii. (1890) 38 Astah se..andettere ..on þa dune upp. *Ibid.* III. vii. [ix.] 178 On his hors hleop. *c* **1000** *Ags. Gosp.* Matt. v. 1 He astah on þone munt. *c* **1122** *O.E. Chron.* an. 1101 Se cyng..scipa ut on sæ sende. *c* **1205** LAY. 1228 Heo..hire hond On his heued leide. *Ibid.* 13099 He nom ane cape..On þene munec he heo dude. *a* **1300** *Cursor M.* 10393 Iesu crist was tan, And don on rode. **1382**

WYCLIF *Matt.* v. 45 That..reyneth on iust men and vniuste. *c* **1400** *Destr. Troy* 9133 Pure watur pouret vn polishet yeron. **1576** GASCOIGNE *Philomene* (Arb.) 97 They now are come on lande. **1590** SPENSER *F.Q.* I. ii. 18 'Curse on that Cross', (quoth then the Sarazin). **1697** DRYDEN *Virg. Georg.* III. 722 A Plague did on the dumb Creation rise. *Ibid.* 769 Ye Gods..turn that Impious Errour on our Foes! **1697** DAMPIER *Voy.* I. 524 A sort of a distemper that stole insensibly on them. **1807** CRABBE *Par. Reg.* I. 119–20 His shoes of swiftness on his feet he placed; His coat of darkness on his loins he braced. **1820** KEATS *St. Agnes* xxxi, These delicates he heaped..On golden dishes. **1884** W. C. SMITH *Kildrostan* 63 If in such a vacant hour He shall happen on a maiden. **1896** *Law Times* C. 488/1 The vestry served a notice on the respondent, calling upon him to repair the drain. **1897** OUIDA *Massarenes* xxvi, He has never left his card on you. *Mod.* He threw the coins on the table. They fixed placards on the walls.

b. *to* LAY *hold on*, SEIZE *on*: see these vbs.

c **897** K. ÆLFRED *Gregory's Past.* iv. 40 þæt hira nan ne durre gripan swæ orsorʒlice on þæt rice. **1399** LANGL. *Rich. Redeles* III. 49 Anoþer proud partriche..sesith on hir sete. **1551** ROBINSON tr. *More's Utop.* II. ix. (1895) 270 They layde holde on hym. **1604** SHAKS. *Oth.* I. iii. 55 Nor doth the generall care Take hold on me. **1796** *Hist.* in *Ann. Reg.* 97/2 They had seized on the citadel. **1870** ANDERSON *Missions Amer. Bd.* II. ix. 68 The natives..laid hold on the sailors.

c. Of the incidence of a blow or the like.

c **893** K. ÆLFRED *Oros.* IV. i. §5 He hiene on þone nafelan ofstang. *Ibid.* v. xv. §3 He oft unwitende sloʒ mid his heafde on þone waʒ. **13..** *Cursor M.* 21402 (Gött.) Constantine..feld fast on þat haþen lede. **1526** TINDALE *Acts* xii. 7 And he smote Peter on the syde. *a* **1548** HALL *Chron., Hen V*, 33 He strake the chiefe Iustice with his fiste on the face. **1712** ADDISON *Spect.* No. 317 ¶35 Gave Ralph a box on the Ear. *Mod.* A blow on the head.

d. In such phrases as ***heaps on heaps, company on company***, the literal sense passes into that of accumulative addition, or repetition.

a **1611** BEAUM. & FL. *Maid's Trag.* v. ii, Your curst court and you..With your temptations on temptations, made me give up mine honour. **1667** MILTON *P.L.* II. 995 With ruin upon ruin, rout on rout, Confusion worse confounded. **1726–46** THOMSON *Winter* 905 Snows swell on snows amazing to the Sky. **1839** THACKERAY *Fatal Boots* viii, I have had ill-luck on ill-luck. **1855** KINGSLEY *Plays & Puritans* 130 What Spaniard on Spaniard had been saying for fifty years.

e. Of continued motion: ***on one's way, on a journey, expedition, voyage, trip***; also ***on an errand, a message***. See these sbs., and cf. AWAY.

15. Into contact or collision with, esp. in the way of attack; against, towards.

c **893** K. ÆLFRED *Oros.* II. v. §2 Æfter þæm he wonn on Scipþie. *c* **900** tr. *Bæda's Hist.* II. viii. [ix.] (1890) 124 Sona þæs þe he on heo feaht. **1340–70** *Alisaunder* 1204 When Philip had with his folke faren on Greece. **1375** BARBOUR *Bruce* I. 140 On saracenys warrayand. *Ibid.* II. 384 On thaim! On thaim! thai feble fast! **1568** GRAFTON *Chron.* II. 294 That day he never tooke prisoner, but alwayes fought and went on his enemies. **1697** DRYDEN *Virg. Georg.* III. 140 He bears his Rider headlong on the Foe. **1796** *Instr. & Reg. Cavalry* (1813) 257 That the whole may arrive on the enemy at the same time. **1849** S. DOBELL *Roman* iii. (ed. 2) 38 He calls his blood-hounds round his gory hands, And cheers them on the prey. **1883** *Standard* 8 May 3/7 His..bowling seldom seemed to be on the wicket. **1894** BARING-GOULD *Kitty Alone* II. 170 If he drew his knife on her and attacked her.

16. a. Of aspect or direction towards; as ***to smile on, turn one's back on***.

c **888** K. ÆLFRED *Boeth.* xxxviii. §5 Hi ealle lociaþ mid bæm eaʒum on þas eorðlican ðincg. *a* **1000** *Cædmon's Daniel* 731 On þæt wundor seon. *a* **1440** *Sir Eglam.* 1225 The knyght answeryd, and on hym logh. **1592** GREENE *Philomela* (1881) 152 He spake with his eies on Philomelas face. **1726–46** THOMSON *Winter* 910 Horrid o'er the surge Alps frown on Alps. **1809** W. IRVING *Knickerb.* VII. xii. (1849) 442 He turned his back on its walls. **1844** MACAULAY *Ess., Earl Chatham* (1887) 815 The enemies..stood for a time glaring on each other. **1851** D. JERROLD *St. Giles* xxxii. 326 That melancholy, care-worn face, that..would always smile on her. **1864** TENNYSON *Enoch Arden* 727 For Philip's dwelling fronted on the street.

b. *ellipt.* Precisely in the direction of, directed towards.

1888 RIDER HAGGARD in *Harper's Mag.* July 207 Feeling that I was on him, I pulled, and..I saw the man throw up his arms.

†**17. a.** = INTO. (Cf. IN *prep.* 31.) *Obs.*

c **893** K. ÆLFRED *Oros.* I. i. §7 þa flowað buta suþ on þone Readan Sæ. *c* **897** —— *Gregory's Past.* 2 An ærendʒewrit of Lædene on Englisc areccan. *c* **900** tr. *Bæda's Hist.* IV. xxx[i]. (1890) 374 Hie woldon his ban on niwe cyste ʒedon. **971** *Blickl. Hom.* 27 þætte Hælend wære læded on westen. *c* **1000** *Ags. Gosp.* Matt. ix. 6 Aris..and gang on þin hus. **1387** *E.E. Wills* (1882) 2 Also y be-quethe iij li. to bring me on erthe.

†**b.** ***on pieces***, etc. = into (in) pieces. (Cf. IN 30 b.)

c **893** K. ÆLFRED *Oros.* I. i. §1 Ure ieldran ealne þisne ymbhwyrft þises middanʒeardes..on þreo todældon. *c* **1200** ORMIN 565 And eʒʒþerr hirrd..Todæledd wass..Onn hirdess rihht sextene. *c* **1350** *Will. Palerne* 3410 Mani a spere spacli on peces were to-broke. **1415** *E.E. Wills* (1882) 23 Y wolle hit be parted on tweyne. **1426** LYDG. *De Guil. Pilgr.* 4293 Whan the pot ys broke On pecys smale. *c* **1450** *Douce MS.* 55 (Bodleian) lf. 23 Take mary and dates, kutt on too or on thre.

18. Unto, to (a person): in reference to descent or marriage. (The latter in Sc.)

1535 STEWART *Cron. Scot.* II. 710 Richt laith he wes to wed hir on ane lord Into Ingland. *a* **1578** LINDESAY (Pitscottie) *Chron. Scot.* (S.T.S.) I. 125 The king, efter he had..ressawit this gentillwoman..marieit hir on his brother. **1631** GOUGE *God's Arrows* III. §93. 353 The Crowne and Kingdome by just..title descended on her. **1894** CROCKETT *Raiders* 280 She's marriet on saft Sammle Tamson.

19. Into, unto, to (some action, course, or condition); formerly esp. with *vbl. sb.*, as ***to go on fishing*** = a-fishing: cf. 10.

c **1000** *Ags. Gosp.* John xxi. 3 Ic wylle gan on fixað. *c* **1290** *St. Kenelm* 148 in *S. Eng. Leg.* I. 349 þat þis child scholde wende An hontingue. *c* **1350** *Will. Palerne* 2092 þai..dede hem on gate, And souʒte him. *c* **1450** *St. Cuthbert* (Surtees) 4406 And sone on slepe þai fell. **1470–85** MALORY *Arthur* II. i, A damoisel the whiche was sente on message. *c* **1530** LD. BERNERS *Arth. Lyt. Bryt.* 147 His woundes braste out agayne on bledyng. **1539** BIBLE (Great) *Acts* xiii. 36 Dauid (after he had in hys tyme fulfylled the wyll of God) fell on slepe. **1622** BACON *Hen. VII* 74 That might..set the Plough on going. **1633** LAUD *Wks.* (1857) VI. 321, I presume you will set him on work. **1635** J. HAYWARD tr. *Biondi's Banish'd Virg.* 68 He was that day rode forth on hunting. **1726** LEONI *Alberti's Archit.* II. 10/1 Very hard to stop when once it is set on going. **1828** MACAULAY *Ess., Hallam's Const. Hist.* (1887) 88 The fanaticism of Cromwell never urged him on impracticable undertakings. **1885** *Law Times Rep.* LIII. 467/2 Facts which ought to have put him on inquiry.

20. a. Indicating the person or thing to which action, feeling, etc. is directed, or that is affected by it. In the const. of many verbs and phrases.

c **1290** *Becket* 501 in *S. Eng. Leg.* I. 121 On seint Thomas heo criden faste. *a* **1300** *Cursor M.* 22474 Lauerd ha merci on all nu. *c* **1386** CHAUCER *C.T.* Prol. 300 Al þat he myghte of his freendes hente On bookes and his lernynge he it spente. *c* **1435** *Torr. Portugal* 1854 How on the dede hedys they did shoute. **1590** SPENSER *F.Q.* II. i. 52 On them she workes her will to uses bad. **1655** FULLER *Ch. Hist.* IV. ii. §2 The first on whom this cruel Law was hanselled, was William Sautre. **1657–83** EVELYN *Hist. Relig.* (1850) I. 291 Being a thing material, it should operate on immaterials. **1796** *State Papers* in *Ann. Reg.* 168/2 [He] endeavoured to recriminate on us. **1815** W. H. IRELAND *Scribbleomania* 201 She has claims on the consideration of the country. **1838** THIRLWALL *Greece* IV. xxx. 145 The title of Admiral was conferred on Aracus. **1849** MACAULAY *Hist. Eng.* v. I. 539 The effect of these reflections on his mind had been pernicious. **1883** SIR W. B. BRETT in *Law Times Rep.* (1884) L. 193/2 The decision..which is binding on us. **1885** *Law Times* LXXIX. 38/1 The magistrate may be necessary as a check on the doctor. **1885** *Manch. Exam.* 16 May 6/1 The extremely cold nights..tell very severely on the elderly members of the House.

b. Indicating the object of desire and the like. In the construction of *eager, keen, mad* (†*amorous, enamoured, fond*), *bent, determined, set, gone*, etc. Also *ellipt.* = bent on, set on.

a **1310** in Wright *Lyric P.* xi. 38 A tortle that min herte is on. *c* **1430** LYDG. *Reas. & Sens.* 113/4286 To be enamowred on a goot. **1493** *Festivall* (W. de W. 1515) 68 b, Suche thynges as mannes herte is moost on. **1623** GOUGE *Serm. God's Provid.* §10 Their mind was so on their worke. **1656** EARL MONM. tr. *Boccalini's Advts. fr. Parnass.* II. xxxvi. (1674) 189 You..having unwisely been enamoured on some one person. **1890** L. C. D'OYLE *Notches* 170 Woddell was not much on beer.

c. Indicating the bank, banker, or person to whom a cheque or draft is directed, and by whom it is payable; in ***to draw on, a cheque***, etc. ***(drawn) on***.

1671– [see DRAW *v.* 65, DRAUGHT *sb.* 35 b]. **1824** BYRON *Juan* XV. viii, A draft on Ransom. **1839** THACKERAY *Fatal Boots* x, Here..is a cheque on Child's. **1849** MARRYAT *Valerie* ix, Lionel received a cheque on the bank. **1866** CRUMP *Banking* vii. 144 The demand for bills on London at Liverpool would exceed the supply.

d. Of a joke, laugh, etc.: against or at the expense of (someone).

1866 *Harper's Mag.* July 271/2 There may be a joke about it; but if there is, it is on the Colonel, for he told me so. **1901** *Munsey's Mag.* XXV. 711/2 'It was Lanse—Lanse all the time' he exploded. 'Oh, wasn't that one on me!' **1906** *Nation* (N.Y.) 6 Dec. 478 The people rejoiced that the laugh was on those whom they consider their natural enemies. **1933** [see *B.O.* s.v. B. III]. **1936** N. COWARD *To-night at 8.30* 27 The joke is on us... We've never even been lovers. **1939** L. M. MONTGOMERY *Anne of Ingleside* vi. 33 The joke is on us... And a nice laugh he will have on me. **1967** *Listener* 11 May 634/1 The trouble is we enjoy a good laugh, especially if the joke's on us. **1977** P. HARCOURT *At High Risk* vi. 196 The joke was on me, and it left a sour taste.

e. Indicating a person, etc., who is to pay the bill, esp. for a treat of any kind. *colloq.*

1871 *Republican Rev.* (Albuquerque, New Mexico) 29 July 2/4 After the first round they said it was 'on me'. **1889**, etc. [see HOUSE *sb.*[1] 2 c]. **1902** C. J. C. HYNE *Mr. Horrocks, Purser* 78 And now come and have a bit of cheap lunch. We'll consider we've tossed for it, and it's on me. **1919** 'I. HAY' *Last Million* vii. 85 'This is on us,' Al Thompson hastened to add. **1938** L. MACNEICE *Earth Compels* 22 Five minutes spent at a bar Watching the fish coming in, as you parry and shrug This is on me or this is on me. **1973** 'P. REID' *Harris in Wonderland* iii. 26 Arbuthnot wanted to drink... I explained my financial predicament but he waved it aside. 'On me, man.'

f. To the disadvantage or detriment of (a person); so as to affect or disturb. *colloq.*

1880 W. H. PATTERSON *Gloss. Words Antrim & Down* 74 'Don't break it on me,' *i.e.* don't break that thing of mine. **1892** E. LAWLESS *Grania* I. II. iv. 184 It was the devil's own abuse he got from his wife..for letting her fine spring chickens be drowned on her, which she had been months upon months of rearing. **1907**, etc. [see DIE *v.*[1] 1 e]. **1907** J. M. SYNGE *Tinker's Wedding* II. 26 There she is waking up on us, and I thinking we'd have the job done before she'd know of it at all. **1946** K. TENNANT *Lost Haven* (1947) vii. 103, I never knew such a man for pickles—he must have eaten a bottle on me just over tea and breakfast. **1955** R. P. HOBSON *Nothing too Good for Cowboy* vii. 63 My lead cows bunched up on me and refused to face the storm. **1963**, **1966** [see GO *v.* 44 a]. **1971** M. SMITH *Gypsy in Amber* (1975) ii. 17 You're turning into a dilettante on me. **1974** M. BUTTERWORTH *Man in Sopwith Camel* iii. 34 He's passed out on me... Had some kind of seizure.

21. a. Indicating a person or thing to which hostile action is directed: against; esp. in ***to complain, inform, lie, tell, 'peach' on***; also ***an attack, assault***, etc., ***on***.

1377 LANGL. *P. Pl.* B. XIV. 144 It may nouʒt be,..or matheu on god lyeth. *c* **1400** MAUNDEV. (Roxb.) xv. 67 þai lye falsly on Mary and hir son. **1481** CAXTON *Reynard* (Arb.) 29 He made hym redy for to complayne on reynart the foxe. **1539** BIBLE (Great) *Phil.* ii. 15 That ye may be soch as no man can complayne on. **1604** SHAKS. *Oth.* v. ii. 146 Ay, 'twas he that told me on her first. **1690** LOCKE *Govt.* II. xix. §231 Attempting by force on the properties of any people. **1830** MACAULAY *Ess., Moore's Byron* (1887) 155 This degraded people had risen on their oppressors. **1849** —— *Hist. Eng.* vi. II. 113 Any attack on the civil liberties of his people. **1889** [see INFORM *v.* 7 b]. **1895** CROCKETT *Sweetheart Trav.* 14, I will tell my father on you. *Mod. Sc.* I'll no tell on ye.

b. ***to have a down on***: see DOWN *sb.*[3] 5; ***to have nothing*** (or ***something***) ***on*** (a person): see HAVE *v.* 14 h.

22. a. In regard to, in reference to, with respect to, as to.

c **888** K. ÆLFRED *Boeth.* xxxi. §1 (1864) 110 Hwæt godes maʒan we secgan on þa flæsclican unþeawas. **1456** SIR G. HAYE *Law Arms* (S.T.S.) 69 And sa was sene on thame, for thair jurisdictioun began with force and crueltee. **1470–85** MALORY *Arthur* VI. i, Some there were that..passed alle their felawes in prowesse and noble dedes and that was wel preued..on syre launcelot du lake. **1477** *Paston Lett.* III. 211 Elles it wol do you harm on your hors. **1649** J. MOYLEY in *15th Rep. Hist. MSS. Comm.* App. II. 47 There sate on him three or four judges. **1706** *Act 6 Anne*, c. 11 Art. xix, No writer to the signet [shall] be..admitted a lord of the session unless he undergo a private and publick tryal on the civil law. **1787** NELSON 13 May in Nicolas *Disp.* (1845) I. 236 To order a Court-Martial to be held on him. **1812** JEFFERSON *Writ.* (1830) IV. 176, I do not condole with you on your release. **1838** T. THOMSON *Chem. Org. Bodies* 488 *note*, This statement does not agree with my experience on the subject. **1849** MACAULAY *Hist. Eng.* ii. I. 275 He never attended the meetings of his colleagues on foreign affairs. **1885** *Manch. Exam.* 23 May 5/1 The appellants had failed on the main question.

b. Expressing the object to which mental activity is directed; after such verbs as *think, consider, remember, dream* (now usually *of*); *meditate, reflect*, etc. Also after derived sbs. as *thought, meditation, reflection*. See these words.

c **1000** *Ags. Ps.* (Th.) cxvii. 8 God ys on Dryhten ʒeorne to þenceanne. *c* **1420** *Anturs of Arthure* 192 Thynke hertly on this. *c* **1450** *St. Cuthbert* (Surtees) 8090 On his kirke was all his thoght. *c* **1470** HENRY *Wallace* I. 15 3hit we suld thynk one our bears befor. **1500–20** DUNBAR *Poems* xc. 60 And on the end hes no rememberance. **1590** GREENE *Never too late*, *M.'s Madr.*, When I at last considered on my sins. **1692** LOCKE *Educ.* §147 This being almost that alone, which is thought on, when People talk of Education. **1754** R. O. CAMBRIDGE *Intruder* 12 'Twas a plan I never dreamt on. **1816** J. WILSON *City of Plague* II. ii, Thy anxious heart will never learn To think more on thyself and less on others. **1838** THIRLWALL *Greece* II. 265 The sleepless nights in which he meditated on the trophies of Miltiades. *Mod.* Reflect on the natural results of such conduct.

c. After *speak, write*, etc., q.v.; after *book, article, essay, lecture, poem, treatise*, etc., or an author's name; also ellipt. in titles and the like.

1422 *E.E. Wills* 51, iiij quayres of Doctours on Mathewe. **1605** CAMDEN *Rem.* (1637) 411 On a childe drowned catching of an Apple. **1689** PRIOR *Ep. to Fleetwood Shepherd* 168 Critics I read on other men, And hypers upon them again. **1699** COTES tr. *Dupin's Hist. O. & N. Test.* I. I. i. 5 What he says on this Point is as follows. **1785** WILBERFORCE in *Life* I. 99 Heard Newton on the addiction of the soul to God. **1830** SCOTT (*title*) Letters on Demonology and Witchcraft. **1831** CARLYLE *Sart. Res.* III. viii, Laplace's Book on the Stars. **1884** A. R. PENNINGTON *Wiclif* ix. 290 A course of lectures on the Epistles of St. Paul. *Mod.* Coke on Littleton; Mill on Hamilton; Fenn on the Funds.

III. Other senses, obsolete, archaic, or dialectal.

(All these originally belonged to branch I.)

†**23.** After verbs of *winning, gaining, taking* (by force): = from. *Obs.* Here orig. belonged vbs. of *wreaking* or *taking vengeance, avenging, revenging*, still construed with *on*: see these.

c **893** K. ÆLFRED *Oros.* IV. vi. §6 Romane ʒenamon on him LXXXIII scipa. *c* **1000** ÆLFRIC *Num.* xxi. 1 Chananeus þa wann wiþ Israela bearn, and siʒe on him ʒewann. *c* **1330** R. BRUNNE *Chron.* (1810) 57 Magnus..chaced away Suane, & Danmark on him wan. *c* **1500** *Melusine* 219 Yf they were so bold to take on hym or on hys peuple ony thing. **1523** LD. BERNERS *Froiss.* I. cccxxxv. 525 Howe the Englysshmen recouered dyuers castelles on the frenchmen in Burdeloys. **1605** SHAKS. *Lear* v. iii. 165 But what art thou That hast this Fortune on me? **1671** MILTON *Samson* 470 All these boasted Trophies won on me.

†**24.** Indicating that to which a quality has relation: In respect of; = IN *prep.* 34, OF *prep.* 35.

c **888** K. ÆLFRED *Boeth.* i, Boetius..se wæs in boccræftum and on woruldþeawum se rihtwisesta. *Ibid.* xxxii. §1 Ðeah þu wære eallra manna fæʒrost on wlite. *c* **900** tr. *Bæda's Hist.* I. Introd. (1890) 26 Hit is weliʒ ðis ealond on wæstmum and on treowum. *a* **1175** *Cott. Hom.* 223 Se man is ece on ane dele. þat is an þer sawle. *c* **1275** *Luue Ron* 91 in *O.E. Misc.* 96 He is feir & briht on heowe. *c* **1350** *Will. Palerne* 2634 Sche had a derworþe douʒter..þe fairest on face. **1523** LD. BERNERS *Froiss.* I. cclxx. 403 He was blynde on yᵉ one eye. **1535** COVERDALE *2 Sam.* iv. 4 A sonne which was lame on his fete. **1703** *Lond. Gaz.* No. 3892/4 Robert Stephens..winks on the left Eye.

†**25.** Indicating the medium of action. *Obs.* Now expressed by *with*.

a **1375** *Joseph Arim.* 560 He seiȝ a child strauȝt þer-on, stremynge on blode. *a* **1450** *Le Morte Arth.* 1996 The chambre flore Alle ranne on blode.

26. †**a.** In uses now expressed by *at* (esp. ***on a price*** or ***rate***). *Obs.*

1477 *Paston Lett.* III. 203 He wol not selle hym..under that mony that he sette hym on. **1639** FULLER *Holy War* III. xiv. (1647) 132 Serviceable men he would purchase on any rate. *a* **1715** BURNET *Own Time* (1823) I. 150 When his matters were on that crisis. **1776** G. SEMPLE *Building in Water* 67 The Bridge must be on right Angles with the Current. **1793** JEFFERSON *Writ.* (1859) III. 510 All other of our productions are received on various duties. **1794** MRS. A. M. BENNETT *Ellen* III. 52 Ellen was walking on a slow solemn pace.

b. Used *colloq.* (chiefly *Austral.*) in locative senses, where 'at' would normally occur in standard use.

1853 *Bendigo* (Victoria) *Advertiser* 9 Dec. 1/1 We have for many months vainly endeavoured to procure suitable materials for publishing a Newspaper on Bendigo, to be devoted Exclusively to the Mining Interests. **1860** *Mining Surveyors' Rep.* (Mining Dept., Victoria) Aug. 198 This will be one of the richest claims on Ballarat. **1892** P. H. EMERSON *Son of Fens* xxv. 248 You grind my old Beccy [*sc.* scythe]; you're a better hand on it than I am. **1901** M. FRANKLIN *My Brilliant Career* iii. 17 Why, on Bruggabrong the women never had to do no outside work. **1966** BAKER *Austral. Lang.* (ed. 2) xvi. 348 A gold-seeker was never *at* a goldfield, but always *on* it. **1968** *Listener* 29 Aug. 267/2 The only reason she was on a bus stop at that un-Christian hour is that if she didn't catch that particular bus she would miss the only connection that would get her to the house in time to do a day's work. **1974** *Publishers Weekly* 5 Aug. 8/2 He began to put it all together, writing in the evenings and on weekends.

27. In senses now expressed by OF. In ***on't*** and the like, common in literary use to *c* 1750; now *dial.* or *vulgar.*

In early times generally an actual difference of idiom, but from end of 16th c. due to confusion of *of* and *on*, esp. owing to the reduction of both of these to *o'*. See OF.

1258 *Procl. Hen. III*, I Henr' þurȝ godes fultume king on Engleneloande, Lhoauerd on Yrlounde, Duk on Norm' on Aquitaine and eorl on Aniow. *c* **1325** *Poem times Edw. II* (Percy Soc.) xxii, That death that I shall on die. *c* **1420** *Avow. Arth.* xxxviii, O payn on life and on londe. *a* **1440** *Sir Eglam.* 953 Wele recovryd on hys wounde. *c* **1530** tr. *Erasmus' Serm. Ch. Jesus* (1901) 2 So this our sermon may sauer on him whiche is..the worde of the father. **1575** *Gamm. Gurton* I. iii, All th'ours on the daye. **1605** SHAKS. *Macb.* III. i. 131 The perfect Spy o' th' time The moment on't. **1611** —— *Cymb.* I. i. 164, I am very glad on't. **1641** LD. J. DIGBY *Sp. in Ho. Comm.* 21 Apr. 4 The truth on't is. **1671** H. M. tr. *Erasm. Colloq.* 545 Though I make Lay men on them all. **1709** STEELE *Tatler* No. 12 ¶7 Nay, you are in the Right on't. **1732** BERKELEY *Alciphr.* II. §6 The best on't is the World every day grows wiser. **1766** G. WILLIAMS in Jesse *G. Selwyn & Contemp.* (1843) II. 57 Those handles that the ladies make bell-ropes on. **1782** ELIZ. BLOWER *Geo. Bateman* I. 87, I know she'll take care on him. **1828** *Craven Gloss.* (ed. 2), *On't*, of it. [Still widespread in Eng. dialects.] **1829** D. JERROLD *Black-Eyed Susan* (1855) I. vi. 27 We found..three pilots' telescopes. This is one on 'em! **1848** THACKERAY *Van. Fair* li. 463 We're three on us—it's no use bolting. **1898** J. D. BRAYSHAW *Slum Silhouettes* 221 There was 'undreds on 'em, men, women, an' kids, an' most on 'em seemed ter be Total Obstinate Sons o' the Phoenix. **1916** 'TAFFRAIL' *Pincher Martin* xi. 204 'Ere's another on 'em! **1931** M. ALLINGHAM *Look to Lady* xvi. 170 Don't take no notice on 'im... 'E's as right as ever 'e was. **1937** —— *Case of Late Pig* xiv. 98, I don't know what he'll think on us—two on 'em instead of one. **1973** R. PARKES *Guardians* ix. 165 No doubt on it, mate. **1974** 'S. WOODS' *Done to Death* 41 Nobody as I knows on... It was nothing, really, to get hold on.

28. In *dial.*, *N. Amer.*, and casual contexts, used where 'in' would normally occur in standard use.

1762 BOSWELL *London Jrnl.* 13 Dec. (1950) 82, I feel a surprising change to the better on myself since I came to London. **1787** J. ELPHINSTON *Propriety* II. II. 93 Dhe Scotch can see no incongruity in meeting a person *on* dhe street,..hwaraz dhe Inglish meet a person *in* dhe street. **1892** E. G. VINCENT *Newfoundland to Cochin China* iii. 45 The City Hall in this street, or 'on', as the Canadians would say. **1900** *Times* 6 Jan. 14/5 The genuine Dorset native always says, 'I see'd it on the paper', or 'I read it on the paper'. **1924** R. MASSON *Use & Abuse of Eng.* (ed. 4) iii. 42, I will likely know a great difference on her. **1938** J. STUART *Beyond Dark Hills* vi. 139 That took lifting and skill on flipping steel. *Ibid.* x. 396 They took 14 stitches on the other fellow. **1956** A. J. LERNER *My Fair Lady* (1958) I. viii. 86 Let the time go by, I won't care if I Can be here on the street where you live. **1972** *Scholarly Publishing* III. 181 My work as assistant editor is only a sideline. Since I do it largely on my own time, I avoid extra work and correspondence. **1972** *Time* 17 Apr. 37/2 An agreement..to help finance what is now called the Barsky Unit on the grounds of the Cho Ray Hospital. **1974** H. L. FOSTER *Ribbin'* iii. 109 Terror is waiting on line at 6:30 in the morning..for the Brooklyn Paramount to open for Alan Freed's rock and roll revue. **1974** *Melody Maker* 4 May 21/1 Hospitalized not long ago with a blood clot on his leg, he entered Beth Israel hospital again last week. **1977** *Irish Press* 29 Sept. 13/1 Michael Keane..is back on the Kerry team for Sunday's All-Ireland Under 21 Football final.

IV. 29. *on* is used in the construction of many verbs, besides those mentioned under the preceding senses, e.g. *depend*; *attend, wait*; *follow*; *believe, rely*; *feed, live, subsist*; also after the direct object, in *beget, bestow, confer*; *lavish, spend, waste*; *congratulate*; *plume, pride, value* oneself; or as a second construction, e.g. to *condole, consult, with* a person *on* something. See these verbs.

30. *on* was formerly frequent in connexions in which *a-* is now usual: e.g. ***on back*** (= aback), ***on brede, on broche, on broad, on dreghe, on far, on ferrom, on fresh, on head, on live, on loft, on long, on loud, on low, on light, on new, on part, on round, on room, on side, on stray, on sunder, on thirst, on wide, on wry.*** These were usually written as two words, but have often been hyphened by modern editors, in imitation of forms in *a-*. See ABACK *sb.*, ABREDE, ABROACH, etc.; also the sbs. BACK, BREDE, BROACH, etc.

on hand, on high: see HAND 32, HIGH *a.* 18.

on (ɒn), *adv.* (*a.*, *sb.*[1]) [Orig. the same word as prec., viz. OTeut. **ana*, OS. *ana, an*, OE. *an, ǫn*. In the OE. instances almost always intimately connected with a vb. as a 'separable particle', like the Ger. separable *an* in *an-kommen*, etc.; in mod.Eng. often an elliptic use of the prep. = on something understood.]

A. *adv.* **1. a.** In the position of being in contact with, or supported by, the upper surface of something.

c **900** tr. *Bæda's Hist.* IV. iv. (1890) 274 Sume ȝerisne stowe .. mynster on to timbrenne. **1632** MILTON *L'Allegro* 132 Then to the well-trod stage anon, If Jonsons learned Sock be on. **1844** DICKENS *Mart. Chuz.* ix, The pudding-plates had been washed..while cheese was on.

b. ***to be on***: to be addicted to, or regularly taking, a drug or drugs; to be under the influence of drugs. Cf. ON *prep.* 1 k. *U.S. slang.*

1938 *Amer. Speech* XIII. 188/2 *To be on*, to be addicted or actively indulging the [drugs] habit. **1955** W. GADDIS *Recognitions* I. v. 197 She's high right now, can't you see it? She's been on for three days. **1956** B. HOLIDAY *Lady sings Blues* (1973) xiv. 121 When I was on, I was on and nobody gave me any trouble. No cops, no treasury agents, nobody. I got into trouble when I tried to get off. **1968** *Sun Mag.* (Baltimore) 13 Oct. 19/3 When I took sets, I'd do it on the way to school... I'd always be on when I had to read in speech class.

2. Into the position defined in 1 a.

c **897** K. ÆLFRED *Gregory's Past.* xvii. 124 Ðæt se se þe wunde lacnian wille ȝeote win on. *c* **1205** LAY. 311 Brutus sette on his flo. He wende to sceoten þat hea der. *c* **1475** *Rauf Coilȝear* 85 To-morne on the morning, quhen thow sall on leip, Pryse at the parting, how that thow dois. **1645** EVELYN *Diary* 11 Apr., Dashing the..whipcord over their shoulders, as hard as they could lay it on. **1824** BYRON *Juan* xv. lxv, They also set a glazed Westphalian ham on.

3. In the position of being attached to or covering any surface, esp. the body; on the body, as clothing or a limb.

c **1205** LAY. 1553 He hefde brunie on. *c* **1300** *St. Brandan* 613 None other clothes nadde he on. ? *a* **1366** CHAUCER *Rom. Rose* 1187 Largesse hadde on a robe fresh. *c* **1450** *Merlin* 191 Thei hadde on hattes of stile. **1570** B. GOOGE *Pop. Kingd.* II. 26 To weare a linnen Ephod on. **1594** SHAKS. *Rich. III*, IV. ii. 126 O let me thinke on Hastings, and be gone To Brecnock, while my fearefull Head is on. **1611** —— *Cymb.* II. i. 26 You crow Cock, with your combe on. **1711** ADDISON *Spect.* No. 128 ¶9 He had a clean Shirt on. **1850** TENNYSON *In Mem.* vi, A riband or a rose; For he will see them on to-night. **1887** 'MABEL WETHERAL' *Two North-Country Maids* xxv. 174 Her pretty buff cotton gown, which was clean on that morning. **1890** J. HILL *Unfort. Arrangem.* I. vi. 144 He had on an unobtrusive suit of dark brown tweed. *a* **1902** *Mod. slang*, Keep your hair on!

4. a. Into the position defined in 3.

a **1000** *Fate* (Cod. Exon.) 87 Sum sceal wildne fuȝel atemian, heafoc on honda..deþ he wyrplas on. *c* **1000-** [see DO *v.* 48]. **1526** TINDALE *Luke* xii. 22 Take no thought..for youre body, what ye shall putt on. **1590** LODGE *Rosalind* (Cassell) 93 And with that she slipped on her petticoat. **1605** SHAKS. *Macb.* II. ii. 70 Get on your Night-Gowne. **1712** ADDISON *Spect.* No. 311 ¶5 He immediately drew on his Boots. **1781** C. JOHNSTON *Hist. J. Juniper* II. 44 To make.. delays, by frequent tryings on, and alterations of our hero's clothes. *a* **1814** *Way to win Her* v. iii. (*New Brit. Theatre* II. 466), Mother is tying on her goloshes.

b. *ellipt.* for *go on*; ***on with*** = put on, don.

c **1485** *Digby Myst.* (1882) III. 1183 On xall my westment and myn aray. **1605** ROWLANDS *Hell's Broke Loose* 45 On with rich attire. **1753** FOOTE *Eng. in Paris* I. Wks. 1799 I. 39 I'll on with my Jemmys. **1826** DISRAELI *Viv. Grey* III. vi, I will doff my travelling cap, and on with the monk's cowl.

5. In a direction towards something, at; as ***to*** LOOK ***on.***

6. Towards something in the way of approach; approaching in space, time, or condition.

c **1400-50** [see COME *v.* 62 a, f]. **1535-** [see DRAW *v.* 86 d]. **1704** *Lond. Gaz.* No. 4054/1 The great use of their Gallies in towing on or off their great Ships. **1885** *Truth* 2 July 3/1 It was getting on for two before supper was served. **1894** LD. WOLSELEY *Life Marlborough* II. lxv. 195 How dreadful are the words 'Go on!' to the man who longs to mingle in the fray, and shout 'Come on!' instead.

7. a. Directed towards, or in a line *with*, something.

1804 NELSON Apr. in Nicolas *Disp.* (1845) V. 520 The mark for being clear of the Malora North End, is the Guard-House on the Beach..on with the last hillock of the nearest ridge of mountains. **1875** BEDFORD *Sailor's Pocket Bk.* vii. (ed. 2) 267 She will be steered with sufficient accuracy if her gunwale..be kept 'on with' the outer ends of the oars of the leader.

b. ***broadside on, face on, stem on,*** etc.: With the face, stem, or other part directed to the point of contact.

1800-40 [see BROADSIDE *sb.* 1 c]. **1856** *Leisure H.* V. 332/1 He lost his hold, and fell face on into the water. **1884** *Standard* 19 May 4 The vessels struck one another stem on.

8. *Cricket.* To the *on* side.

1882 *Daily Tel.* 24 June, This he shortly followed up by driving C. T. Studd on for 2.

9. a. Onward, forward, in space or time.

a **1000** *Andreas* 1336 Ræsdon on sona. *c* **1200** ORMIN 7717 He wollde..uss..brinngenn onn To follȝhenn þeȝȝre bisne. *c* **1230** *Hali Meid.* 17 þat mahten bringe þe on mis for to donne. *a* **1350** *Cursor M.* 5987 (Gött.) Wend on þann, siþen ȝe wil ga. **1480** CAXTON *Chron. Eng.* clv. 136 Or half a yere be go an. **1600** HOLLAND *Livy* III. liv. 124 They passe on through the cittie. **1675** HOBBES *Odyssey* (1677) 256 From that day on, centaurs and men are foes. **1809** MALKIN *Gil Blas* II. vii. ¶6 Do they get on in the world? **1820** BYRON *Mar. Fal.* III. i. 12 Seeing this Patrician pestilence spread on and on. **1831** *Blackw. Mag.* Jan. 83/2 [The police officer] possesses the power..of ordering them to 'move on'.

b. *ellipt.* = Go on, advance.

c **1425** LYDG. *Assembly of Gods* 1077 On in Pluto name! On! & all ys owre! **1592** SHAKS. *Rom. & Jul.* I. iv. 2 Or shall we on without Apologie? **1627** SANDERSON *Serm.* I. 284 Unless God kept him back, he must on. **1713** J. WARDER *True Amazons* 95 Yet on they must. **1808** SCOTT *Marm.* VI. xxxii, Charge, Chester, charge! On, Stanley, on! **1855** KINGSLEY *Plays & Purit.* 181 But no; he must on for honour's sake.

10. a. Gone onward or ahead; in advance in space or time.

17.. *Old Song* in *Burns' Works*, Oh Kenmure's on and awa, Willie! **1872** BLACK *Adv. Phaeton* xxi. 301 It was now well on in the afternoon. **1887** A. BIRRELL *Obiter Dicta* Ser. II. 91 Later on music was dragged into the fray.

b. *Cricket*, etc.: In advance of the opposite side.

1884 *Lillywhite's Cricket Ann.* 61 Notts were 392 on. **1892** *Daily News* 14 Sept. 3/6 As the game now stands the professionals with seven wickets to fall are 79 runs on.

c. *slang.* On the way to intoxication; the worse for drink.

1802 *Naval Chron.* VII. 273 The *Amelia's* men being a little on, could not bear being thwarted. **1894** WILKINS & VIVIAN *Green Bay Tree* I. 99 Pimlico, who was now slightly 'on'..was shouted down.

d. *Betting.* In favour (of a particular horse, etc., winning). Cf. AGAINST *prep.* (*adv.*) 18.

1922 JOYCE *Ulysses* 632 Betting 5 to 4 on *Zinfandel*, 20 to 1 *Throwaway* (off). **1923**, etc. [see *odds on* adv. s.v. ODDS *sb.* 8]. **1964** A. WYKES *Gambling* viii. 197 If the odds are 2 to 1 *on* and you bet $2, your total payout would be $3—your $2 stake money plus your $1 win. **1979** SETH-SMITH & MORTIMER *Derby 200* III. 97 His price was the unrewarding one of 7-2 on.

11. a. With onward movement or action; continuously; ***to speak on, hold on, work on, wait on,*** to continue to speak, hold, work, wait.

c **1000** ÆLFRIC *Saints' Lives* xxi. 236 [He] nyste butan hi sungon þone lof-sang forð on. *a* **1225** *Leg. Kath.* 434 He heold on to herien his heaðene maumez. *c* **1386** CHAUCER *Cook's Prol.* 22 Now telle on, Roger, looke that it be good. **1579** SPENSER *Sheph. Cal.* Sept. 55 Now say on Diggon. **1665** BRATHWAIT *Comm. 2 Tales Chaucer* 148 Go on with your Tale. **1795** BURKE *Regic. Peace* iv. Wks. IX. 26 Speculate on! **1858** FROUDE *Hist. Eng.* xx. IV. 235 The regent waited on, and the event came. **1891** DORA RUSSELL *Secret of River* I. xiii. 289 He sent me money regular, to keep on the house.

b. Colloq. phrases: ***to be on about***: to keep talking about, to harp on, to speak or write about (a subject); ***to be on at***: to nag or scold (a person); ***to go on about***: see GO *v.* 86 g; ***to go on at***: see GO *v.* 86 g; ***to keep*** (or ***go***) ***on and on***: to persist in speaking or questioning, to nag *at* a person.

1909 *Westm. Gaz.* 22 Sept. 8/2 Yesterday morning complainant was 'on' to him again about his religion. **1916** *Kelso Chron.* 24 Mar. 3 He was on about wa's that had ears. **1936** R. LEHMANN *Weather in Streets* viii. 348 Marda's always asking me why I don't get a divorce... Last year she was always on about it. **1938** N. MARSH *Artists in Crime* x. 145, I told him it would upset me but he went on and on. **1941** BAKER *Dict. Austral. Slang* 51 *On at (a person), to be*, to scold, reprove, nag at a person. **1952** A. BARON *With Hope, Farewell* 94 Well, now the second one's on at him to get married. **1958** N. F. SIMPSON *Resounding Tinkle* II. in *Observer Plays* 267 Fred was on at me to go up but I had my old coat on. **1966** *Listener* 22 Dec. 939/1 A reflection that brings us back to atmosphere and art forms, which I was on about some weeks ago. **1973** 'C. AIRD' *His Burial Too* iv. 40 The garage key that Ada Turvey was on about..that's still in the lock. **1974** G. BUTLER *Coffin for Canary* ii. 35 'You looked terrible yesterday,' he said. He kept on and on. He always did. **1974** 'J. MELVILLE' *Nun's Castle* ix. 214 He kept on and on at me till he got it out. I wouldn't have told him otherwise. **1975** K. BARCLAY tr. *P. Orum's Whipping-Boy* xxiii. 161 'He kept on and on at me.'.. 'I didn't do it.'.. 'Why can't you let me alone?'

12. Into action or operation: ***thrash on,*** proceed to thrash.

13.. *Gaw. & Gr. Knt.* 2300 Wy þresch on, þou þro mon, þou þretez to longe. *c* **1400** [see COME *v.* 62 c]. **1593-** [see DRAW *v.* 86 b]. **1596** DALRYMPLE tr. *Leslie's Hist. Scot.* I. 113 Thay set stoutlie onn, doubteng na danger. **1667** MILTON *P.L.* v. 233 Converse with Adam..and such discourse bring on, As may advise him of his happie state. **1745** P. THOMAS *Jrnl. Anson's Voy.* 276 The Tuffoons commonly come on.. suddenly. **1832** R. H. FROUDE *Rem.* (1838) I. 271 At last it came on to rain. **1892** *Chamb. Jrnl.* 4 June 367/1 We turned our lanterns full on.

13. a. Of persons: Engaged in some function or course of action; on the stage, the field, etc.

a **1541** WYATT *Poet. Wks.* (1861) 84 Now thus, now than, Now off, now an, Uncertain as the dice. **1640** [see OFF AND ON B.]. **1793** W. ROBERTS *Looker-on* No. 54 (1794) II. 315 Then to the Playhouses anon, If Quick or Burgess be on. **1823** MRS. CAMERON *Cleanliness next to Godliness* 3, 'I try to keep things tolerably decent, but it's a hard matter.. I am always on', replied Alice. **1883** G. R. SIMS *Lifeboat* etc. 12 She was on at the Lane last winter—She played in the pantomime. **1888** STEEL & LYTTLETON *Cricket* (Badm. Libr.) iii. 141 Supposing a slow bowler has been 'on' for some time. **1891** MRS. WALFORD *Mischief of Monica* III. 62, 'I thought he was on with Daisy', burst forth her son. *Mod. colloq.* He has been on for three years, and now retires.

b. Of things: In progress or course of action; in a state of activity. Also, of an event: arranged; going to happen. Of food or the like: placed on the stove, etc., to cook; cooking. Also ***to have nothing on***: to have no engagements, business, etc.

[**1605** SHAKS. *Lear* II. iv. 172 So will you wish on me, when the rash moode is on.] **1748**, etc. [see PUT *v.*[1] 46 k]. *c* **1825** J. WALKER *Factory Lad* I. iii. 8 Interior of Allen's House—Fire place, with saucepan on. **1830** *Examiner* 76/1 Several commissions being 'on' at the same time. **1841** DICKENS *Barnaby Rudge* xvii. 31 Hurrah! Polly put the ket-tle on, we'll all have tea. **1841** MRS. GASKELL *Let.* 23 Dec. (1966) 46 Yesterday this plan seemed quite given up—today.. it's *on* again—if all goes on well. **1873** BLACK *Pr. Thule* ii. 13 There was a considerable sea on. **1882** *Society* 18 Nov. 11/2 The schools at Oxford are 'on' once more. **1883** W. AITKEN *Lays of Line* 135 The fire's black oot, and the parrich no on. **1884** *Manch. Exam.* 3 July 5/3 There is a terrible row on between the old and the new divisions. *a* **1902** *Mod.* Is the gas on? The water was not on. **1908** R. W. CHAMBERS *Firing Line* iv. 46 If you and Virginia have nothing better on I'll dine with you tonight. **1915** R. FRY *Let.* 27 Feb. (1972) II. 383 I'm pushed away into any place and only wanted when there's nothing better on. **1938** D. RUNYON *Furthermore* vii. 129, I have nothing on of importance at the moment. **1955** M. ALLINGHAM *Beckoning Lady* ii. 21 It's still on, is it, the party? **1955** E. COXHEAD *Figure in Mist* ii. 69 'I left the potatoes on,' she muttered, and fled into the house. **1972** J. GILL *Tenant* I. iii. 25 I've nearly done, just putting the rice on. **1973** J. BURROWS *Like an Evening Gone* i. 11 Miss Limb, amazingly, had fallen in with Greta's plans. 'So it's on.' **1973** 'E. MCBAIN' *Hail to Chief* iv. 55 The television set was on, but the volume control was apparently broken. **1974** M. INGATE *Sound of Weir* xvii. 150 I'd better be getting the dinner on. We've only got sausages. **1974** *Times* 14 Mar. 16/3 It must have been the only diplomatic function on in London because many hundreds of the most notable people .. were there.

c. Having a wager on (something). Freq. in colloq. phr. ***you are*** (or ***you're***) ***on***: the bet or bargain is agreed.

1812 *Sporting Mag.* XXXIX. 23 They declared themselves off, a thing unknown in sporting, after they had been on. **1883** *Standard* 18 June 2/4 The scratching of Winchester has been a rare blow to those who were determined.. to be 'on' early. **1933** *Sun* (Baltimore) 25 Apr. 18/7 'I'll bet you a lobster dinner and all the champagne we can drink, if legal, that the dam will be filled by February 1,' said Mr. Smith... 'You're on,' said Mr. Crozier. **1961** J. SEYMOUR *Fat of Land* i. 19 'I'll let you have the two cottages .. for ten pounds a year.' 'You are on,' I said. **1967** J. BURKE *Till Death us do Part* x. 153 'I'll give it [*sc.* smoking] up if you do.'.. 'All right,' snapped Alf. 'All right, you're on.' **1969** Y. CARTER *Mr. Campion's Farthing* xvi. 156 'Just to seal the bargain,' he said... 'You're on.' **1974** L. DEIGHTON *Spy Story* xviii. 194 'A quid,' I said. 'You're on,' said Ferdy.

d. ***to be on***: to be in favour of, or willing to be a party to, something. *colloq.*

1888 'R. BOLDREWOOD' *Robbery under Arms* I. xi. 132 'What shall we do, Jim?.. go or not?'.. 'I'm half a mind to tell Warrigal to.. say we're not on.' *Ibid.* 138 Now we're here what's the play called, and when does the curtain rise? We're on. **1890** —— *Miner's Right* II. xiii. 23 'I'm on,' answered Joe, a ray of humour irradiating his honest countenance. **1898** 'H. S. MERRIMAN' *Roden's Corner* xiv. 145 If there is going to be fight.. I'm on. **1916** 'TAFFRAIL' *Pincher Martin* xiv. 270 'What about a glass of sherry to celebrate the auspicious occasion?' 'I'm on, Peter,.. but I really think it's up to me to pay for it.' **1923** WODEHOUSE *Inimitable Jeeves* xiv. 161 This jamboree is slated for Monday week. The question is, Are we on? **1939** K. TENNANT *Foveaux* IV. 350 'Are you on?' Herb asked impatiently as he began to remove his coat. 'I'll give it a go.' **1969** V. GIELGUD *Necessary End* i. 15 I'm on—if you want to play the equivalent of Twenty Questions.

e. In a state of knowledge or awareness regarding a person, state of affairs, etc. Cf. ON TO *prep.* 2. *U.S. slang.*

1885 *Santa Fé Weekly New Mexican* 9 July 2/2 He hoped to sell the cavalry a large lot of supplies, but Major Van Horn was 'on'. **1900** ADE *Fables in Slang* 68 The Preacher didn't know what all This meant,.. but you can rest easy that the Pew-Holders were On in a minute. **1902** [see NEXT *a.* 13 c]. **1909** [see DOPE *sb.* 3 a]. **1934** J. M. CAIN *Postman always rings Twice* i. 10, I seen who he was on, and quit talking about the guy in the Cadillac. **1973** R. STOUT *Please pass Guilt* (1974) xviii. 164 Wolfe, turning and seeing Saul, was on as quick as I had been. He said.. 'What?'

f. In negative contexts: acceptable, allowable; possible, likely; esp. in phr. ***it's*** (***just***) ***not on***. *colloq.*

1935 in Partridge *Dict. Slang* (1937) 587/2 The majority of amateur [snooker] players.. wildly attempt shots that are not 'on'. **1957** *Economist* 19 Oct. 200/1 This proposal is no longer 'on'. **1958** M. PUGH *Wilderness of Monkeys* 38 'I say, that's a bit much,' the military man said. 'Not on.' **1963** P. H. JOHNSON *Night & Silence* xxviii. 208 He could not conceivably go on believing in Matthew's guilt. It was just not on. **1963** *Times* 29 May 10/5 How can a ship fight effectively if a third of the crew is Portuguese, a third Belgian, and a third Danish? The thing is just not on. **1968** R. V. BESTE *Repeat Instructions* xvi. 174 'I'd like to dump the last two together next time.' 'That's not on,' King told him tersely. '.. Stick to procedure.' **1973** 'M. INNES' *Appleby's Answer* ii. 23 How, I repeat, is a fellow to come by a cathedral? It just isn't on. **1975** *Guardian* 20 Jan. 4/3 Reductions in the standard of living were not on.

g. Of an item of food: on the menu; available. Cf. OFF *adv.* 3 e. *colloq.*

1949 'M. INNES' *Journeying Boy* xx. 248 Champ is off and eggs are on. **1953** R. FULLER *Second Curtain* ix. 131, I always have the curry when it's on. **1963** 'L. BRUCE' *Crack of Doom* vi. 53 Are you going to have lunch in the hotel? They've got sheeps' hearts on today.

h. ***it was*** (or ***is***, etc.) ***on*** (***for young and old***): a description of complete disorder, a free-for-all. *Austral. colloq.*

1951 E. LAMBERT *Twenty Thousand Thieves* (1952) xvii. 258 Peter Dimmock bounded between the tents leaping into the air at every few paces and whooping: 'It's on! It's on for young and old!' **1955** J. MORRISON *Black Cargo* 77 A day come when some of our blokes in Sydney just put their coats on and walked off the job. It was on then for young and old. **1969** W. DICK *Naked Prodigal* 50 Just before closing time a brawl started when some bloke walking by spilt beer on Ackie so Ackie's young brother King hit him and the bloke's mate stepped in so Ackie hit him—and then it was on. **1971** D. MARTIN *Hughie* (1972) xi. 106 He almost forgot about it until the evening of Sunday when the party was due and when, in Harry's words, it was on for young and old.

14. Used idiomatically with many verbs: e.g. *carry, catch, come, get, go, hold, keep, look, put, send, take, try on*, etc.: see the verbs.

B. *adj.* (Cf. OFF C.)

1. a. *Cricket.* Applied to that side of the wicket on which the batsman stands, or to the corresponding side of the field (*i.e.* in the case of right-hand batting, the side on the left of the wicket-keeper). Also of a ball or hit on this side. Opp. to OFF C. 2 b.

1833 J. NYREN *Young Cricketer's Tutor* 34 The best way to play a ball, bowled as wide as your legs on the on side. **1836** [see OFF *a.* 2 b]. **1836** *New Sporting Mag.* July 196 On-balls have a greater tendency to turn in towards the wicket. **1851** LILLYWHITE *Guide to Cricketers* 20 A good general will often place three men instead of two on the 'on' side. **1854** J. PYCROFT *Cricket Field* (ed. 2) vii. 117 An angle sufficient to make Off or On hits. **1892** *Daily News* 6 May 5/2 A captain who has studied lady's play,.. will put most of her fields on the 'on' side. **1897** RANJITSINHJI *Cricket* 170 Let us now turn our attention to strokes on the on-side. **1898** K. S. RANJITSINHJI *With Stoddart's Team* (ed. 4) i. 32 For.. excellence of 'on side' play he can be compared with the best players. *Ibid.* vi. 112 Iredale.. got out to Hearne in attempting a huge 'on' hit. **1903** *Westm. Gaz.* 23 June 3/1 In all those on-side strokes.. Fry is a master. **1904** F. C. HOLLAND *Cricket* 16 The on strokes are not so often used as the off strokes. **1909** *Westm. Gaz.* 17 Apr. 16/2 A good back and on-side player.. may confidently expect to do well under these conditions. **1959** *Times* 11 June 3/5 Bold strokes, particularly on the onside.

b. ***on-verse*** [tr. G. *Anvers*]: the first half-line of a line of Old English verse. Also *attrib.* Cf. *off-verse* (OFF *a.* 2 c).

1935, 1953 [see OFF *a.* 2 c]. **1953** [see ICTUS 1]. **1970** *Jrnl. Eng. & Gmc. Philol.* LXIX. 438 Rime forces all final lifts in on-verse or off-verse into prominence.

2. In reference to the licensed sale of liquors: Short for 'on the premises'; opp. to OFF C. 5. Often hyphened, as ***on-licence***.

1891 *Daily News* 11 Mar. 3/2 The number of licensed houses mentioned in the on-licences return. **1892** W. BEATTY-KINGSTON *Intemperance* 63 It is not in the least necessary to persecute the 'on' licensee. **1896** *Westm. Gaz.* 5 Mar. 3/3 The Bill which placed off-licence holders under similar control as on-licence holders. **1899** *Daily News* 13 Apr. 6/3 The influence of the 'on' licensed houses.

3. Corresponding to the state (of an electrical device) of being on (ON *adv.* 13 b).

1899 J. PIGG *Railway 'Block' Signalling* vii. 364 When the arm is in the 'on' position, the mercury connects the two plates and completes the circuit. **1924** *Wireless World* 19 Mar. 772/2 This sort of switch is called a double-pole single-way switch, because it controls two circuits with one operation and has only one 'on' position. **1962** SIMPSON & RICHARDS *Physical Princ. Junction Transistors* vii. 142 Because the voltage across the transistor is a fraction of a volt losses in the 'on' state are small. **1962** E. G. DAVIES in G. A. T. Burdett *Automatic Control Handbk.* iii. 2 The isolator is hand operated and provided with distinct ON and OFF positions. **1967** *Electronics* 6 Mar. 133/1 With the modified circuit the relay's on-time is independent of input pulse characteristics.

4. *Physiol.* Of, pertaining to, or exhibiting the electrical activity that occurs briefly in some optic nerve fibres in vertebrates upon the commencement of illumination of the retina.

1903 F. GOTCH in *Jrnl. Physiol.* XXIX. 393 The first portion is the rise due to the sudden illumination; this I propose for brevity to term the ON effect. *Ibid.* 394 The upward movement of the image of the mercury indicates a positive (+) change in the eyeball in the ON, continuous and OFF reactions. *Ibid.* 398 The development of the ON change under these two conditions. **1937** *Brit. Jrnl. Psychol.* XXVII. 302 In the human eye the 'on effect' may occupy a time of the order of 0·1 sec. **1941** S. H. BARTLEY *Vision* xii. 286 The on-response is, in the main, duplex. **1948, 1972** [see OFF *a.* 7].

C. *sb.*[1] *Cricket.* = on side: see B. 1. *attrib.* in ***on drive, on-drive***, a drive to the on side: see also ON-DRIVE *v.*; **on-theory**, a theory that favours concentrating the fielders on the on side and bowling the ball at or outside the on stump.

1862 *Baily's Monthly Mag.* Aug. 87 A on-drive from Jackson for 5. **1881** *Daily News* 9 July 2 He then drove Moncreiffe to the on for four. *Ibid.*, Newton scored.. three for a good on drive. **1896** *Westm. Gaz.* 24 July 5/2 Wynyard then made a fine on-drive off Trumble for 3. **1896** *Badminton Mag.* Sept. 280 A few bowlers have an 'on-theory'. **1900** W. J. FORD *Cricketer on Cricket* x. 118 George Giffen.. could bowl 'off-theory' or 'on-theory'.. with equal skill. **1963** *Times* 11 June 4/6 With a powerful on-drive Barker took his score to 49 and off the next ball completed a fine half century.

‖**on** (ɒn), *sb.*[2] [Jap.] In feudal or prewar Japan, the sense of deep gratitude with an obligation or duty of service towards often highly formalized favours, as towards one's parents, teachers, lords, or the Emperor.

1946 R. BENEDICT *Chrysanthemum & Sword* (1947) v. 99 The word for 'obligations' which covers a person's indebtedness from greatest to least is *on*... *On* is in all its uses a load, an indebtedness, a burden, which one carries as best one may. *Ibid.* 101 *On* is always used in this sense of limitless devotion when it is used of one's first and greatest indebtedness, one's 'Imperial *on*'. This is one's debt to the Emperor, which one should receive with unfathomable gratitude... Every kamikaze pilot of a suicide plane was, they said, repaying his Imperial *on*. **1964** I. FLEMING *You only live Twice* iv. 56 He's acquired an ON with regard to me. That's an obligation—almost as important in the Japanese way of life as 'face'. When you have an ON, you're not very happy until you've discharged it honourably.

on (ɒn), *v.* [f. the adv.] **1.** *intr.* To go on; to move forward. Cf. ON *adv.* 9 b. *U.S. dial.*

1840 C. F. HOFFMAN *Greyslaer* II. II. x. 27 I'll see the eend of it. So with that, I ups and ons.

2. ***to on with***: to place or put on. Cf. ON *adv.* 4 b. *dial.*

1843 'R. CARLTON' *New Purchase* I. xix. 170 She bethought as how she'd render off her fat; and so she ons with the grate pot. **1899** DICKINSON & PREVOST *Gloss. Words Cumberland* 231/2 Ah on's wi' my cwoat an' off teh wark. **1960** *Forfar Dispatch* 28 Jan. 8/5, I ons w'ee porridge pot.

on, *particle*, the pref. *on-* = UN-[1], often written separately in ME.; also, in mod.Sc. dial., in sense 'without': see ON-[4].

†**on,** erron. ME. expansion of *o* = *oð*, OTH *conj.*, until: cf. O *prep.*[3]

c **1320** *Cast. Love* 472 Ich.. wole wiþ þe lede my lyf Euer on þat ilke stryf.. mowe sum ende take.

†**on,** ME. 1 and 3 sing. pres. of UNN-EN *v. Obs.*, to grant.

a **1225** *Ancr. R.* 26 ȝif me on almihti God.

on-, *prefix*[1], the prepositional adv. *on* (unstressed form of OE. *an*, *ǫn*) in combination with vbs. and their derivatives, and sometimes with other sbs. The old nominal compounds had the stressed form, as in OE. *anginn*, *ǫnginn*, beginning, *anfilt*, *ǫnfilti*, ANVIL. The compounds in *on-* belong to the following classes:

1. Old verbal compounds, as *onbídan* to ONBIDE, *oncnáw-an* to recognize, ACKNOW. Such of these as survived the OE. period appear in their alphabetical place under ON- or A-.

2. Later verbal compounds or collocations of adv. and verb. In these the union of elements is incomplete, and the adv. may be moved to another position than immediately before the vb., where however it regularly stands in the inf. and pples., so that these acquire more the character of permanent combinations. Examples are †**on-become**, to befall, happen; †**on-cry**, to cry or call upon; **on-draw**, to draw on; †**on-lace**, to lace on; †**on-look**, to look on; **on-sweep**, to sweep on; †**on-take**, to take on, assume, behave: see TAKE *v.*

c **1305** *St. Lucy* 60 in *E.E.P.* (1862) 103 To seinte Lucie norice he wende: and eschte hire faste 'What Lucie were so *onbicome'. *c* **1315** SHOREHAM *Poems* (E.E.T.S.) 146/487 Hyt on-by-come ine eche place ȝef ech [þ]yng hadde ylyche grace To ioye and blysse. **1664** *Flodden F.* IV. 40 Then each Captain he did *oncry. **1898** T. HARDY *Wessex Poems* 83 By Joidoigne, near to east, as he *onward, Dawn pierced the humid air. **1513** DOUGLAS *Æneis* XI. Prol. 102 Rays hie the targe of faith vp in thi hand, On hed the halsum helm of hop *onlace. *a* **1875** J. W. MILES in Schaff & Gilman *Libr. Relig. Poetry* (1881) 35 That all his shattered aims, his hopes bewept, Are in God's counsels deep and fathomless *onswept. **1297** R. GLOUC. (Rolls) 3548 þat hii nuste hou *on take [*v.r.* on to take], ne wat for honger do. *c* **1325** *Spec. Gy Warw.* 267 Allas! what sholen hij onne take, þat wolden here her god forsake?

3. With pr. and pa. pples. forming adjs., as '***on-carrying*** (= carrying on; hence '***oncarryingness***), ***on-marching***, ***on-rolling***, ***on-running***, ***on-surging***, ***on-sweeping***.

a **1834** COLERIDGE in *Literature* (1897) 23 Oct. 11/2 The *oncarryingness of his [Scott's] diction. **1609** DANIEL *Civ. Wars* VIII. xvi, Gather'd by th' *on-marching Enemy. **1863** *Not an Angel* I. 184 To hold by his arm for some security against the onmarching multitude. **1854** J. S. C. ABBOTT *Napoleon* (1855) I. xx. 325 The *on-rolling billow of Austrian victory. **1599** DANIEL *Musophilus* 713 To pull back th' *on-running state of things. **1884** *Chicago Advance* 31 Jan., The fury of the *onsurging barbarians. **1896** *Ibid.* 16 Apr. 553/1 The *onsweeping purposes.. of God.

4. a. With vbl. sbs. and nouns of action, forming sbs. (sometimes concrete), as ***on-bringing*** (= bringing on), ***on-carrying***, ***on-leaping***, Sc. ***-louping*** (= mounting a horse), ***on-moving***, ***on-putting***, ***on-sweeping***, etc. (which can be formed at pleasure); **on-go**, going on, progress, advance; **on-roll**, onward roll; **onsurge**, an onward surge; **on-sweep**, onward sweep; also with agent-nouns, as ***on-bearer***, ***on-goer***, ***on-pusher***, etc. See also ONLOOKER, etc.

1898 T. HARDY *Wessex Poems* 135 Changing anew my *onbearer I traversed the downland. **1658** J. DURHAM *Exp. Revelation* II. vi. (1680) 145 This inability is of her own *onbringing. **1737** E. ERSKINE *Serm.* Wks. 1871 II. 452 The *oncarrying of the designs of his glory. **1894** *Chicago Advance* 11 Oct. 58/1 As viewed in the retrospect of two years absence.. its ordinary *on-go is indeed extraordinary. **1600** *Gowrie's Consp.* in *Select fr. Harl. Misc.* (1793) 190 Maister Alexander Ruthven..haisted him fast downe to ouertake his maiestie before his *onleaping. *a* **1670** SPALDING *Troub. Chas. I.* (1792) I. 91 (Jam.) On his onlouping the earl of Argyle..and Lord Lindsay..had some private speeches with him. **1900** *Westm. Gaz.* 12 June 2/1 It is a memorable sight to witness the *on-moving of a great army. **1898** *Congregationalist* 28 Apr., The arts of diplomacy are too soon exhausted when seventy million people are the on-lookers and *on-pushers. **1599** JAS. I. *Βασιλ. Δωρον* (1682) 82 To speake of rayment, the *on-putting whereof is the ordinary action that followeth next to sleepe. **1883** *Gd. Words* 462 The steady *onroll of the mighty waves of time. **1960** J. FINGLETON *Four Chukkas to Austral.* 16 His presence allowed the English bowlers to recover from O'Neill's *onsurge. **1963** *Economist* 1 June 872/2 The real onsurge into the consumer durables revolution. **1866** *Dublin Rev.* Jan. 170 The rights of property alone..formed the basis of resistance to the *onsweep of revolution. **1893** *Chicago Advance* 26 Jan., All this prodigious swing and on-sweep of development. **1885** *Homilet. Rev.* 134 In the tremendous *onsweepings of society.

b. With sbs. used *attrib.* or as *adj.*, as **on-air**, while broadcasting; **on-axis**, situated or occuring on the axis; **on-course**, situated or taking place at a race-course; **on-demand**, done or available when demanded; **on-duty**, engaged or occupied with one's normal work; **on-farm**, occurring or used at a farm; **on-form**, that is in good form or condition; **on-street**, that is on a street; esp. of parking facilities; **on-track**, of betting: done at the race-track.

1972 *Guardian* 11 July 14/5 Parents shared what they thought about the programmes..by responding to on-air appeals to complete a questionaire. **1976** *Listener* 25 Mar. 362/1 The on-air behaviour of certain national and local disc-jockeys. **1962** A. NISBETT *Technique Sound Studio* 248 *Dead side* (of microphone), the angle within which the response of a microphone is low compared with the on-axis response. **1971** R. J. COLLIER et al. *Optical Holography* ii. 54 On-axis observation of either image is disturbed by the out-of-focus light from the other. **1964** A. WYKES *Gambling* viii. 195 These offices are in fact merely extensions of the on-course totalizators. **1973** *Times* 12 Apr. 12/4 The Tote, which does most of the on-course betting, earned a meagre profit of £100,000 last year. **1962** *Times* 9 Apr. (British Oxygen Co. Suppl.) p. v, Ready supply and on-demand delivery make sure your production goes smoothly. **1971** *Flying* (N.Y.) Apr. S5/3 Probably the most revolutionary innovation within this new system will be an on-demand capability. **1970** K. PLATT *Pushbutton Butterfly* (1971) xiv. 155 The on-duty cop outside the room. **1974** 'S. WOODS' *Done to Death* 184 His voice had..that wooden, on duty tone. **1969** *Times* 20 Jan. 2/1 There must be more integration with on-farm testing to select the bulls for central testing. **1970** *Daily Tel.* 26 Oct. 8/3 The economics of on-farm compounding with a mobile mill and mixer look fairly good. **1965** *Universe* 11 June 14/5 Mick Norman..last week..hit a convincing 70 against an on-form Sussex side. **1968** *Melody Maker* 23 Nov. 22/5 An on-form Phil Seamen is still one of the most exciting things to catch in a London jazz club or pub. **1959** *Manch. Guardian* 26 May 8 There might be strict prohibition of 'on-street parking' but 'not necessarily' of loading and unloading. **1973** D. WESTHEIMER *Going Public* iv. 64 A busy thoroughfare with no on-street parking. **1964** On-track [see *off-track* s.v. OFF- 4 b].

on-, *prefix*², the OE. unstressed form of *and-*, *ǫnd-*, against, opposite, in reply, in return (see AND *conj.*), corresp. to Gothic *anda-*, *and-*, OS. *and-*, *ant-*, Du. *ont-*, OHG. *ant-*, *ent-*, *int-*; e.g. OS. *antfâhan*, OHG. *ant-*, *intfâhan*, MHG. *entfâhen*, *enfâhen*, *enpfâhen*, Ger. *empfangen*, Du. *ontvangen*, OE. *on'fón*, pa. t. *on'feng*, to receive (cf. '*and-*, '*ǫndfenga* receiver); OE. *on'ȝitan* to understand, discern (cf. '*and-*, '*ǫndȝit* understanding, intelligence). In ME. this prefix is in form indistinguishable from ON-¹: e.g. *onfōn*, *onȝiten*.

on-, *prefix*³, the same particle originally as the prec., used with counteracting or undoing force; in early OE. *on-*, in late OE. very generally *un-* (levelled with *un-* = ON-⁴), in ME. usually *un-*, but sometimes *on-*; in mod.Eng. always *un-*. Examples: Goth. *andbindan*, OS. *antbindan*, OHG. *ant-*, *intbintan*, Ger. *entbinden*, OE. *onbindan*, *unbindan*, ME. *un-*, *on-binden*, to UNBIND; OS. *antduan*, *andôn*, OHG. *anttoan*, *intoan*, MHG. *entuon*, OE. *ondón*, *undón*, ME. *undon*, *ondon*, to UNDO; OS. *antwindan*, OHG. *intwindan*, MHG. *entwinden*, OE. *onwindan*, *unwindan*, ME. *unwinden*, *onwinden*, to UNWIND. See UN-².

on-, *prefix*⁴, frequent ME., early mod.E., and dial. variant of UN-¹, before adjs., pples., advbs. and their derivatives, as ME. *onclene* for *unclene*:—OE. *unclǽne*; ME. *onwryten*:—OE. *unwriten*. Cf. Goth. *unweis*, OS., OHG., OE. *unwis*, Du. *onwys*, *onwijs*, ME. *unwis* (*onwis*, *onwise*), UNWISE.

Formerly often written separately (see e.g. *Paston Lett.* No. 751); but generally hyphened by modern editors. In some mod.Sc. dialects written separately before pples. or vbl. sbs. as *on* (or *ohn*) in sense 'without', e.g. ***on said, ohn said***, unsaid, without there being said, without saying, ***on makin'*** without making.

-on, *suffix*¹. [f. the ending of ION (and *anion*, *cation*).] **1.** *Physics.* **a.** Used (first in ELECTRON²) to form the names of sub-atomic particles, as *hyperon*, *meson*, *neutron*, *proton*.

The example of *electron* gave rise to a few particle names in -TRON, q.v.; but *proton*, chronologically the second word of this group, has proved the dominant model.

b. Used to form the names of quanta, as *graviton*, *phonon*.

2. Used, esp. in molecular biology, to form the names of some entities conceived of as units, as *codon*, *muton*, *operon*, *pedon*.

-on, *suffix*². [f. Gr. *-ον*, neut. of *-ος*, nom. masc. sing. ending of many adjs.] The ending of the names of the noble gases other than helium, as *argon* (the earliest named), *radon*.

‖**onager** ('ɒnədʒə(r)). Pl. **-gers**, **-gri**. [L. *onager*, ad. Gr. *ὄναγρος* = *ὄνος ἄγριος* the wild ass; also both in Gr. and L. in sense 2.]

1. A wild ass; *spec.* the species *Equus onager* (*E. hemippus*) of Central Asia.

a **1340** HAMPOLE *Psalter* ciii. 12 Abyde schal onagirs in þair thirst. **1398** TREVISA *Barth. De P.R.* XVIII. lxxviii. (1495) 831 Onager is a wylde asse, and suche asses be grete and wylde in Affrica. **1774** GOLDSM. *Nat. Hist.* I. 456 The onager, or wild ass, is seen in still greater abundance than the wild horse. **1883** G. ALLEN in *Knowledge* 6 July 1/1 The various tarpans and onagers and quaggas and zebras which span the gulf [between horse and ass]. **1896** *Blackw. Mag.* May 682 Hence the difference..between a coster's donkey and an onager.

2. An ancient and mediæval engine for throwing stones in warfare.

1609 HOLLAND *Amm. Marcell.* XXIII. iv. 222 Unto which also the moderne time hath imposed the name of Onager,.. in this regard, that wild asses when they are coursed by hunters fling with their heeles stones afarre off behind their backs. **1840** L. RITCHIE *Windsor Castle* 214 Of the more powerful military engines then in use, were the scorpion or large stationary crossbow, the onager or wild ass. **1886** SHELDON tr. *Flaubert's Salammbo* xiii. 310 Catapults were as frequently called onagers, because they were like wild asses which threw stones by kicking.

‖**onagra**¹ ('ɒnəgrə). *Bot.* [L. *onagra*, a. Gr. *ὀνάγρα*, fem. deriv. of *ὄναγρος*: see prec.] A former name for the genus ŒNOTHERA.

1741 *Compl. Fam.-Piece* II. iii. 392 There are yet.. Onagra, Larkspur. **1861** MISS PRATT *Flower. Pl.* II. 289.

‖**onagra**². [pseudo-Latin, fem. of ONAGER.] A female wild ass; *humorously*, a she-ass.

1860 READE *Cloister & H.* III. 196 Gerard..had put his Onagra in harness.

onagraceous (ɒnə'greɪʃəs), *a.* *Bot.* [f. mod.Bot.L. *Onagrāceæ*, f. ONAGRA¹: see -ACEOUS.] Belonging to the Natural Order *Onagraceæ*, of which *Onagra* or *Œnothera* is the typical genus. So **onagrad** ('ɒnəgræd), Lindley's name for a plant of this order.

1845 LINDLEY *Veg. Kingd.* (1853) 724 The Onagrads..are in general tetramerous. **1866** *Treas. Bot.*, *Clarkia*, a small genus of onagrads. *Mod.* The Fuchsia, Willow-herb, and Enchanter's Nightshade are onagraceous plants.

onan, onane, obs. forms of ANON.

on and off, *adv. phr.* (*sb.*) **a.** = OFF AND ON, q.v.; also in more general sense (see ON *adv.* and OFF *adv.*).

1855 BROWNING *Bp. Blougram's Apol.* 789 It shoots.. Halfway into the next still, on and off! **1881** E. D. BRICKWOOD in *Encycl. Brit.* (ed. 9) XII. 197/2 Hedges on banks..are usually of such a size as to make flying them impossible, or at least undesirable. Horses jump them on and off. **1889** *Repent. P. Wentworth* II. 227 [He] has been working with us at Crum Street a good deal, on and off. **1889** *Dict. Nat. Biog.* XVIII. 125/2 A siege which lasted on and off for twenty years. **1892** *Times* (weekly ed.) 21 Oct. 7/3 [He] had lived with her on and off since that time.

b. *attrib.* Now usu. with hyphens. **c.** as *sb.* A putting on and taking off; intermittent action; in quot. 1852, a leap on and off a fence, a fence to be so jumped.

1852 R. S. SURTEES *Sponge's Sp. Tour* (1893) 17 They then made for a large field at the back of the house, with leaping-bars, hurdles, 'on and offs', 'ins and outs', all sorts of fancy leaps scattered about. **1854** EGERT. WARBURTON *Hunt. Songs* (1883) No. 33 xii, Which method best insures us from a fall. The Chester on-and-off step, or the Leicester clearing all? **1895** M. M. DOWIE *Gallia* 119, I love to feel the on and off of the break and to watch the way the pole seems to feel its way through the traffic. **1904** *Westm. Gaz.* 13 Jan. 2/3 The buyer resented this on-and-off policy. **1936** *Discovery* July 222/1 His left hand works an 'on-and-off' key, sounding the note when it is pressed and killing it when released. **1965** T. CAPOTE *In Cold Blood* (1966) i. 4 She had been an on-and-off psychiatric patient the last half-dozen years. **1974** *Country Life* 21 Feb. 394/3 Grazed..on a rotational or 'on and off' system. **1977** *Time* 19 Sept. 30/1 The signing of a Panama Canal treaty that was initialed last month after 13 years of on-and-off efforts through the Administrations of four U.S. Presidents.

Hence **on-and-off** *v.*, (*a*) *intr.* to sail on alternate tacks on and off the shore (see OFF AND ON 2); (*b*) *trans.* to leap on and then off; **on-and-offish** *a.*, inclined to be on and off, somewhat fluctuating (in mood, temper, or health: cf. OFF AND ON B.).

1823 BYRON *Juan* XII. lxiii, Who..keeps you on and off-ing On a lee-shore. **1852** R. S. SURTEES *Sponge's Sp. Tour* (1893) 345 'I'll have a word with you', said Sponge, on-and-offing the hedge. **1888** E. J. GOODMAN *Too Curious* xiii, As well as she ever is. Rather on-and-offish.

†**on and on** *Obs.*, one by one: see ONE.

onanism ('əʊnənɪz(ə)m). [f. proper name *Onan* (Gen. xxxviii. 9) + -ISM.] Self-abuse, masturbation. Also = *coitus interruptus*. Also *fig.*

1727-41 CHAMBERS *Cycl.*, *Onania*, and *Onanism*, terms which some late empirics have framed, to denote the crime of self-pollution. **1847-9** TODD *Cycl. Anat.* IV. 156/2 A young man excessively addicted to onanism. **1874** BUCKNILL & TUKE *Psych. Med.* (ed. 3) 760 Onanism is a frequent accompaniment of Insanity and sometimes causes it. **1892** A. K. GARDNER *Conjugal Relationships* vii. 96 This man put into practice, to calm the fears of his wife,..the best calculated refinements of conjugal onanism. **1900** L. B. SPERRY *Confidential Talks with Husband & Wife* x. 150 Another scheme for the prevention of conception is to withdraw the penis from the vagina just before the ejaculation of semen. This method is appropriately called 'Onanism'. **1939** R. CAMPBELL *Flowering Rifle* III. 96 Who sponsor Onanism and Divorce And let the birthrate flounder on its course. **1952** *Encycl. Sexual Knowl.* (ed. 2) I. 78 It is therefore not correct to attribute the practice of masturbation to Onan, though the word onanism is to-day widely accepted in this latter sense and it would be pedantic not to recognize this term. **1967** G. STEINER *Lang. & Silence* 98 The recent university experiment in which faculty wives agreed to practise onanism in front of the researchers' cameras. **1977** P. ROONEY in D. Marcus *Best Irish Short Stories* II. 141 The onanism of the language, a phrase masturbated without hope of final clear expression.

So **'onanist**, one who practises onanism; **ona'nistic** *a.*, relating to onanism.

1855 W. WHITMAN *Leaves of Grass* 70 The sick-gray faces of onanists. **1867** ROBERTSON & RUTHERFORD tr. *Griesinger's Mental Path. & Therapeutics* II. iii. 173 That hidden strife betwixt shame, repentance, good intentions, and irritation, which imperiously impels to the act, we consider, after not a little acquaintance with onanists, to be by far more important than the primary, direct physical effect. **1891** *Cent. Dict.*, *Onanist*. **1892** *Syd. Soc. Lex.*, *Onanistic*. **1926** tr. *M. von Gruber's Hygiene of Sex* vii. 120 The disturbances, which the physician so frequently finds in onanists are the same as those found in persons who indulge in extreme excesses of intercourse. **1934** F. SCOTT FITZGERALD *Tender is Night* II. ix. 199 There was something wooden and onanistic about her. **1961** D. HOLBROOK *Eng. for Maturity* iv. 45 Our essential cultural experiences are not celebrative, they are, rather, onanistic. **1962** *Listener* 20 Sept. 438/2 Quilty's fundamental childishness, his self-regarding, onanistic posing sets the tone of the whole film. **1966** *Ibid.* 22 Dec. 937/3 An uneasy childhood..Wykehamist Schooldays from the bullying horrors of which he escapes into an onanistic fantasy-world. **1973** *Daily Tel.* 23 Mar. 15/1 The onanistic aspect of these brief encounters in public places.

Onazote ('ɒnəzəʊt). Also **onazote**. A proprietary name for a type of rubber which has been expanded to a cellular condition by causing it to absorb a neutral gas under pressure during vulcanization and which is used for making life-belts and floats.

1920 *Trade Marks Jrnl.* 29 Dec. 2470 Onazote... Raw, or partly-prepared, india-rubber, balata and gutta-percha for use in manufacture. Charles Lancaster Marshall,.. London,.. manufacturer. **1940** *Jrnl. R. Aeronaut. Soc.* XLIV. 30 Onazote has a cellular structure in which each air bubble is completely separated from its neighbours. **1960** E. L. DELMAR-MORGAN *Cruising Yacht Equipment & Navigation* ix. 108 Though cork or Onazote lifejackets are well established and approved by the M.O.T. they are bulky and not very easily stowed in a yacht. **1960** *House & Garden* Aug. 46/4 Red and white lifebelt, onazote, £3 11s.

onbethink, dial. f. UMBETHINK, to consider.

†**on'bide**, *v.* *Obs.* [OE. *onbídan*, f. ON-¹ + *bídan*, BIDE.] *intr.* To abide, remain, stay on.

Beowulf 2302 Onbad..oððæt æfen cwom. *c* **1440** *Compleynt* 67 in *Lydgate's Temple of Glas* (1891) App. 60 Myn hert With ȝow onbide & nat remeuyt[h].

on board, *adv. phr.* and *a.* [f. ON *prep.* + BOARD *sb.*] **A.** *adv. phr.* See BOARD *sb.* 12 c and 14

B. *adj.* (Written *on-board*, *onboard*.) That is on board a ship, aircraft, spacecraft, or the like.

1966 *Electronics* 17 Oct. 35 In an operational launch vehicle, the signal would go to an onboard computer that would determine whether the problem was serious enough to shut down the rocket and eject the astronauts. **1967** *Technology Week* 20 Feb. 12/1 Persons who may discover the capsule are being advised that the on-board radiation source is sealed. **1969** *Jane's Freight Containers 1968–69* 433 An officially approved on-board cargo loader for Boeing 707 and 727 aircraft. **1972** *Nature* 24 Nov. 222/1 The synchronization was continuously monitored during the flight by checking the on-board clock one pulse per second against the station clock one pulse per second. **1974** HAWKEY & BINGHAM *Wild Card* xv. 128, I have to..stand by to override the on-board computer in the event of a failure.

on-bolȝen *Obs.*, enraged: see ABELȜEN.

†**on'bow**, *v. Obs.* [OE. *onbúȝan*, f. ON-¹ + *búȝan*, BOW.] *intr.* To submit, yield.

971 *Blickl. Hom.* 223 þæt he næfre næniȝum woruldricum men..swiþor onbuȝan nolde, þonne hit riht wære. *c* **1000** *Ags. Gosp.* Matt. v. 25 Beo þu onbuȝende þinum wiþerwinnan hraðe. *c* **1205** LAY. 6166 And him alle on-buȝen.

†**on'braid**, *v. Obs.* [var. of UMBRAID or ABRAID *v.*²] To upbraid.

1530 PALSGR. 646/1, I onbrayde, I twite or cast in the tethe, *Je reprouche.*

†**'oncall**, *sb. Obs.* [f. ON-¹ + CALL *sb.*] The act of calling upon: **a.** Invocation; **b.** Claim.

a **1300** *Cursor M.* 19095 (Edinb.) Þe oncalle of his hali nam. **13..** *Ibid.* 6714 (Cott.) Þis beists lauerd þan sal bi quit Of alkin oncall, and oþer wijt.

†**on'call**, *v. Obs.* [f. ON-¹ + CALL *v.*, after L. *invocāre.*] *trans.* To call upon, invoke.

1548 GEST *Pr. Masse* in H. G. Dugdale *Life* (1840) App. 117 How ought or can Christ be reverenced or oncalled as present in the sacringe. *Ibid.* 125 Those sainctes bee oncalled as advourers and ayders.

on-camera, *adv.* (*phr.*) and *a.* [f. ON *prep.* + CAMERA.] Within the range of a film or television camera; that is being filmed or televised.

1962 J. D. MACDONALD *Girl* xiii. 193 We are down here ..to do ten tropical commercials... We are surrounded by the Loyal Ones, on and off camera. Shrewd agency minds. **1971** R. PARKES *Line of Fire* ii. 26 To give chase, play the heroine. Maybe get interviewed on-camera afterwards. **1972** *Village Voice* (N.Y.) 1 June 26/3 Primo was an on-camera reporter for KDKA in Pittsburgh, went from there to Philly, then became director of local news here. **1974** *Keowee Courier* (Walhalla, S. Carolina) 24 Apr. 3/4 Peter Falk, star of the NBC-TV series 'Columbo', will serve as on-camera host. **1975** *Listener* 28 Aug. 258/2 Sheikh Mujib.. has refused all on-camera interviews.

once (wʌns), *adv.* (*conj.*, *a.*, *sb.*) Forms: see below. [ME. *ânes*, *ônes*, genitive case of *ân*, *ôn*, ONE, for the earlier *ænes*, ENES (q.v.), which took the place of the OE. instrumental-adverbial *ǽne*, ME. ENE, at the time that the genitival *-es* was taken by so many advbs. *Enes* continued in use in the south till 1500, and even later; *anes*, *ones*, are found *c* 1200, but are not frequent before 1300, from which time also *anes* is only northern. The word remained disyllabic in some dialects till 15th c., but in others was reduced to a monosyllable early in 14th. The final *s* retained its breath sound, and so began *c* 1500 to be spelt *-ce*, as in *hence*, *pence*, *fence*, *ice*, *mice*, *twice*. From this a dial. form *onst* (wʌnst) has arisen in north. midl., Ireland, etc., as in *against*, *amidst*, *amongst*, etc. The development of the initial long vowel in Standard English as *wo-*, *wu-*, in north. dial. and Sc. as *ya-*, *ye-*, is the same as in ONE.]

A. Forms. *α.* See ENES.

β. 3–5 (*Sc.* -8) **anes, 4 ans, 4–6 anys, anis;** 6 *Sc.* **aneis, ainis,** 6–7 *Sc.* **ains,** 7– *Sc.* **ance,** 8– **aince, ainse, (eance, yance, yence, yince).**

c **1200** *Trin. Coll. Hom.* 109 The sunne arist anes a dai. **13..** *Cursor M.* 7886 (Cott.) Þe king kest ans [*Gött.*, *Fairf.* anis] on hir his sight. *c* **1400** MAUNDEV. (Roxb.) xxvi. 123 Þai ete bot anes on þe day. *c* **1425** WYNTOUN *Cron.* VI. xiv. 41 Oftare yher þan anys or twys. **1570** *Tragedie* in *Scot. Poems 16th C.* (1801) II. 223 He was thy Maister ainis & ȝour Regent. *a* **1572** KNOX *Hist. Ref.* Wks. 1846 I. 357 Trew religioun now aneis begun. **1609** SKENE *Reg. Maj.* Pref. 6 Ance in the ȝere. *Ibid.* Forme of Proces 126 The execution of the principal decreit, being ains suspended. **1724** RAMSAY *Tea-t. Misc.* (1733) I. 29 Ye shall hae twa good pocks That anes were o' the tweel. **1802** R. ANDERSON *Cumbld. Ball.* (1839) 222, I yence hed sweethearts monie a yen. **1826** J. WILSON *Noct. Ambr.* Wks. 1855 I. 179 Rather..than ance to expose mysel sae. **1860** G. P. MORRIS *Poems* (ed. 15) 156, I ainse the passion slighted.

γ. 3–7 **ones,** 4–5 **oones, -is, -ys, -us, onus,** 4–6 **ons, onis, -ys, -ez, oons,** 6– **once,** (6 **onsse, onste).** 8– *dial.* and *U.S.* spellings **oncest, oncet, oncst, onct, onecest, onst.**

c **1200** [see B. 9 d]. *c* **1250** *Gen. & Ex.* 3288 Ilke dai..Ones he ðor[h] it sungen riȝt. *c* **1330** R. BRUNNE *Chron.* (1810) 3 With joy alle at ons þei went. **1340–70** *Alex. & Dind.* 735 Wiþ solepne sacrifice serue hem at onus. *c* **1350–1534** Ones [see B. 1 and 2]. *c* **1375** *Cursor M.* 2857 (Fairf.) Onys in þe woke day. *c* **1380** WYCLIF *Sel. Wks.* II. 281 Crist..entrid oonys in to heven. *Ibid.* III. 367 Oones a frere he may in no maner leeve þat. *c* **1420** *Anturs of Arth.* xii, To lette me onus haue a syȝte. *c* **1430** *Two Cookery-bks.* 44 Turne it on ȝe panne onez. *a* **1450** *Knt. de la Tour* (1868) 67 They..shalle ansuere onis. **1463** *Bury Wills* (Camden) 21 A messe oonys in yᵉ wykke. **1503** DUNBAR *Thistle & Rose* 115 All kynd of beistis..At onis cryit lawd. **1526** TINDALE *1 Cor.* xv. 6 Five hondred brethren atonce. ?**1535** STARKEY *Lett.* (1878) 30 Neuer..but onys. **1542** N. UDALL in *Lett. Lit. Men* (Camden) 3 Bee good, maister, to me this oons. **1556** *Chron. Gr. Friars* (Camden) 81 After he came onsse to Shordych. **1592** *Chester Pl.* i. 24 (MS. W.) Ever at onste [so *MS. h*] defendinge. **1593** Q. ELIZ. *Boeth.* I. met. i. 1 My groing studie ons perfourmed. *c* **1620** A. HUME *Brit. Tongue* (1865) 18 Al barked at ones. **1789** WEBSTER *Dissertations Eng. Lang.* 111 In the middle states also, many people [say]..*oncet* and *twicet*. This gross impropriety [has]..prevalence among a class of very well educated people; particularly in Philadelphia and Baltimore. **1840** C. F. HOFFMAN *Greyslaer* II. III. xiv. 255, I ups rifle at onct, and hand on trigger to cut the string with a bullet. **1847** E. BRONTË *Wuthering Heights* I. xiii. 322 Couldn't ye uh said soa, at onst? **1851** MAYNE REID *Scalp-Hunters* I. xxi. 291 He *may* shoot well; he did onecest on a time—plum centre. **1867** A. D. RICHARDSON *Beyond Mississippi* xi. 135 Even some graduates of leading universities habitually use 'oncet' and 'twicet'. **1875** W. D. PARISH *Dict. Sussex Dial.* 105, I dunno but what you'd best shun him out of the fore-door at oncest. **1878** H. ALGER *Joe's Luck* in *Street & Smith's N.Y. Weekly* 8 Apr. 2/5, I kin whip my weight in wild cats, am a match for a dozen Indians to onst, and kin tackle a lion without flinching. **1883** H. D. RAWNSLEY in *Trans. Wordsworth Soc.* VI. 164 He niver oncst said owt. Ye're well aware if he'd been fond of children he 'ud 'a spoke. **1888** G. M. FENN *Dick o' the Fens* 159 In wi' un at onced [for *onst*]. **1898** J. D. BRAYSHAW *Slum Silhouettes* 1 We was born to it, an' never expec's nuffink better; but 'e's been a real toff onct, Satan 'as. **1906** E. DYSON *Fact'ry 'Ands* viii. 95 What led me on t' wish t' be er gentleman onst more. **1909** J. MASEFIELD *Tragedy of Nan* I. 14 Why weren't I told to onst? **1913** C. E. MULFORD *Coming of Cassidy* vii. 117, I saw you onct an' I wondered if I was right. **1921** [see LAMP *v.*¹ 4]. **1922** E. O'NEILL *Hairy Ape* (1923) i. 16 But aw say, come up for air onct in a while, can't yuh? *Ibid.* v. 45, I useter go to choich onct—sure—when I was a kid. **1932** V. RANDOLPH in B. A. Botkin *Treas. S. Folklore* (1949) III. i. 453 We seen a feller in town oncet a-wearin' a coat made out'n a piedy horse-hide. **1934** C. CARMER in *Ibid.* III. ii. 506 Chillun..think twict befo' yuh speak onct. **1967** in A. Dundes *Mother Wit* (1973) 270/2 Love me and hug me oncet..again.

δ. 5 **wonus,** 6 **wons.** Also (*dial.* and *U.S.*) **wance, wancet, wanst, wonst, wunst.**

14.. *Burlesque* in *Rel. Ant.* I. 83 Ther was wonus a kyng. **1526** TINDALE *Mark* vi. 31 They had no leasur wons for to eate. **1593** Q. ELIZ. *Boeth.* I. met. ii. 4 Wons this man..used the skies to vew. **1840** *Crockett Almanac* 2 Davy Crockett got skeered wunst. *Ibid.* 14, I wonst had an old flame. **1890** KIPLING *Soldiers Three* 12 Wanst upon a time, as the childer-books say, I was a recruity. **1898** J. D. BRAYSHAW *Slum Silhouettes* 20 The poor bhoy shall be a gintleman for wance in his life. **1904** E. NESBIT *Phoenix & Carpet* v. 94, I see at wunst 'e was wuth 'is weight in flimsies. **1923** 'B. M. BOWER' *Parowan Bonanza* v. 52 Beans,..wancet they've been wrinkled wit' rain water and dried agin. **1972** L. LAMB *Picture Frame* xv. 139 Seen him wunst, I reckon. Spoke pleasant, like. **1977** *Transatlantic Rev.* LX. 152 'Lissn,' says Davey, 'Ah've beehn ower baurs duzzins a times an Ah've nivir wance goet feart anuff tae jum paff.'

B. I. Signification.

1. a. In strict sense: One time only: as distinguished from *twice*, *thrice*, *many times*. (Without any reference to *when*.)

c **1200** [see A. *β*]. *c* **1250** [see A. *γ*]. **1297** R. GLOUC. (Rolls) 7716 Þer nas so heymon non þat him enes [*v.r.* ones] wiþ sede. *a* **1300** *Cursor M.* 25744 Noght ans allan, ne tuis. **1387** TREVISA *Higden* (Rolls) VI. 121 Sche ete but ones a day. *a* **1450** *Knt. de la Tour* (1868) 85 The king sent vnto her onis, tuyes, thries. **1481** CAXTON *Reynard* (Arb.) 4 A man shal not wyth ones ouer redyng fynde the ryght vnderstandyng. **1534** WHITINTON *Tullyes Offices* I. (1540) 33 The acte of Themystocles dyd profyte but ones. **1683** D. A. *Art Converse* 110 They..think much and twice, before they speak once. **1767** GARRICK *Let. to C. Jenner* 11 May (Davey's Catal.), I took it with me and have read it more than once. **1868** LOCKYER *Elem. Astron.* ii. (1879) 40 We know that the Earth goes round the Sun once a year. **1887** *Graphic* 15 Jan. 65/2 'Once bit, twice shy', is an excellent proverb.

†**b.** At one time, on one occasion (as opposed to another time). *Obs.*

[*c* **1122** *O.E. Chron.* an. 1120 Ðises ȝeares com þet leoht to Sepulchrum..ænes to Eastron, and oðre siðe to Assumptio sancte Marie. *c* **1175** *Lamb. Hom.* 37 Enes et þam fulht-beda ..oðer siðe..et soð scrifte.] **1464** *Nottingham Rec.* II. 375 Ridyng..oons to Morley, an oþer tyme to Leycestre. **1628** GAULE *Pract. The.* (1629) 281 They once stroue to cast him down vpon the stones.

†**c.** In the first place, firstly, 'for one thing'. *Obs.*

1523 LD. BERNERS *Froiss.* I. Auth. Pref. 1 Ones the contynuall redyng therof maketh yonge men equall in prudence to olde men; and to olde fathers..it mynystreth experyence of thynges. **1596** BACON *Max. & Uses Com. Law* Ep. Ded., Your Majesty is in a double respect the life of our laws: once, because without your authority they are but *litera mortua*; and againe, because [etc.].

2. a. At any one time; on any occasion, in any contingency; under any circumstances; ever, at all, only, merely. Chiefly in conditional and negative statements. ***if once, when once***, if ever, when ever; ***not once***, not so much as once, never.

[*c* **1175** *Lamb. Hom.* 61 Ne muȝen heo nefre ufele swinken, Ne for men enes hit bi-þinken. *a* **1225** *Ancr. R.* 234 Nolde heo neuer enes bisechen ure Louerd þet he allunge deliurede hire þerof.] *c* **1350** *Will. Palerne* 195 Alle ledes him louede þat loked on him ones. **1432–50** tr. *Higden* (Rolls) I. 187 A ston callede Asbeston, whiche accendede oonys is neuer extincte. **1523** FITZHERB. *Surv.* iii. (1539) 7 After the Statute be ones declared. **1548** UDALL, etc. *Erasm. Par. Matt.* xviii. 91 He shall not once be receiued into the Kyngdome of heauen. **1611** BIBLE *Transl. Pref.* 1 It was made a capitall crime, once to motion the making of a new law. **1762** GOLDSM. *Cit. W.* xl, When once all the extent and the force of the language is known. **1795** MAR. EDGEWORTH *Lett. to Lit. Ladies* (1799) 67 If once their pupils begin to reflect upon their own hoodwinked education. **1872** BLACK *Adv. Phaeton* viii. 112 Once past the turnpike, the highway runs along an elevated ridge. *a* **1902** *Mod.* If we once lose sight of him we shall never set eyes on him again.

†**b.** In any case, at any rate. *Obs.*

a **1715** BURNET *Own Time* (1823) I. 557 Yet it was thought necessary that the prince should be once at the head of their armies. *Ibid.* II. 116 The King seemed to insist..that he would once have a peace made.

3. *emphatically.* Once for all. Hence, as a qualification of the whole statement: To sum up; in short. Now *U.S. dial.*

a **1300** *E.E. Psalter* lxxxviii. 35 Anes swore .i. in mi haligh. **1382** WYCLIF *Heb.* x. 10 In which wil we ben halewid by the offring of the body of Crist Jhesu oonys. *c* **1460** SIR R. ROS *La Belle Dame Sans Mercy* 556 Ones must it be assayd, that is no nay, With such as be of reputacioun. **1596** NASHE *Saffron Walden* To Rdr., This is once, I both can and wilbe shut of this tedious chapter of contents. **1602** CAREW *Cornwall* 59 Once certayne it is, that few men of Law, have ..growne heere to any super-eminent height of learning. **1613** PURCHAS *Pilgrimage* v. xiii. 513 Once, it yeeldeth all parts of the world to each part, and maketh the world.. known to itselfe. **1626** MASSINGER *Rom. Actor* II. Wks. (Rtldg.) 152/2 Would you'd dispatch and die once! **1667** DRYDEN *Maiden Queen* IV. i. Wks. 1882 II. 469 For if I have him not, I am resolved to die a maid, that's once, mother. **1903** S. CLAPIN *New Dict. Amer.* 294 *Once*,..in parts of Pennsylvania settled by Germans, used as an expletive: 'Sit down *once*,' i.e. once for all. **1917** *Dialect Notes* IV. 338 'Come here *once*'..among German settlers. **1948** *Amer. Speech* XXIII. 109 Give me the knife once. **1953** *Ibid.* XXVIII. 246 Will you hand me that hammer once?

4. At one time in the past; on some past occasion; formerly. Also ***once upon a time***; also as *sb. phr.* (sometimes hyphened) and *attrib.*

[*a* **1250** *Owl & Night.* 1049 Enes þu sunge ich wot wel hware Bi one bure.] **1377** LANGL. *P. Pl.* B. III. 334 A lady þat redde a lessoun ones. **1426** LYDG. *De Guil. Pilgr.* 14606 The fox Made hym oonys as he wer ded. **1551** TURNER *Herbal* I. A iv, Absinthium is named..in English wormwode..I suppose that it was ones called worme crout. **1595** G. PEELE *Old Wives' Tale* sig. B1ᵛ, Once vppon a time there was a King or a Lord, or a Duke. **1611** BIBLE *Gal.* i. 23 That he ..now preacheth the faith which once he destroyed. *a* **1656** BP. HALL *Rem. Wks.* (1660) 43, I left that my once dear Diocess. **1711** STEELE *Spect.* No. 154 ¶1 You are still what I myself was once. **1732** BERKELEY *Alciphr.* II. §19, I do not know how it might have been once upon a time. **1764** GRAY *Jemmy Twitcher* 14 When she died, I can't tell,—but he once had a wife. **1786** BURNS *Twa Dogs* 6 Twa dogs..Forgather'd ance upon a time. **1875** BRYCE *Holy Rom. Emp.* xxi. (ed. 5) 386 The once famous doctrine of divine right. **1875** JOWETT *Plato* (ed. 2) I. 134 Once upon a time there were gods only, and no mortal creatures. **1876** R. E. FRANCILLON in *Gentl. Mag.* Oct. 423 There is all the difference between 'Daniel Deronda' and 'The Mill on the Floss' that lies between Now and Once upon a Time. **1927** S. SOUTHWOLD (*title*) Once upon a time stories. **1944** BLUNDEN *Cricket Country* iv. 43 So runs this once-upon-a-time in my memory. **1959** *Listener* 22 Jan. 164/2 The horse-drawn chaises of once upon a time. **1974** J. WAINWRIGHT *Hard Hit* 173 The talk between two middle-aged has-beens about once-upon-a-time days.

5. At some future time; one day. Now *rare.*

c **1400** LANGL. *P. Pl.* C. VI. 50 (MS. F.) To be welcome whanne ich come..oonus in a monthe. *a* **1450** *Knt. de la Tour* (1868) 44 Synne, of the whiche ye shalle yelde onis acompte of. *c* **1489** CAXTON *Sonnes of Aymon* ii. 64, I promytte you ye shall ones repente for it. **1563–87** FOXE *A. & M.* (1684) III. 66 You may be once old as I am. **1618** BRATHWAIT *To his Brother* in Farr *S.P. Jas. I* (1848) 267 That ill which now seems ill, may once prove good. **1691** DRYDEN *K. Arthur* v. i, Britons and Saxons shall be once one people. *a* **1825** FORBY *Voc. E. Anglia*, *Once*, *adv.* at some time or other. **1876** MRS. WHITNEY *Sights & Ins.* vi. 70 And once—that sweet word which brings all to the blessed focus and point of promise—once, we shall find them together.

6. ***once removed***, removed by one degree.

1601 HOLLAND *Pliny* I. 162 With his nine children..with 27 nephewes the sonnes of his children, and 29 nephewes more, once remoued, who were his sons nephewes. **1650** B. *Discolliminium* 4 Which is cosen german to it once remov'd. **1653** ASHWELL *Fides Apost.* 76 Irenæus, the Apostles Scholer but once removed. **1882** J. H. BLUNT *Ref. Ch. Eng.* II. 205 The relationship of second cousin once removed. **1883** *Chr. Commw.* 6 Dec. 174/1 A condition only once removed from the lower animals.

7. a. Like other advbs. *once* is usually hyphened to a participial or other adj. standing before its sb.

a **1668** DENHAM (J.), Thereon his arms and once-loved portrait lay, Thither our fatal marriage-bed convey. **1713** POPE *Windsor For.* 314 Beside him, once-fear'd Edward sleeps. **1725** —— *Odyss.* XXIV. 328 The glory of this once-famed shore. **1809** CAMPBELL *Gertr. Wyom.* III. xxxvii, Seek we thy once-loved home? **1835** *Woman* II. 223 Virtue is taking her leave of our once-moral, once-English nation. **1865** MOZLEY *Mirac.* i. 3 To realize the past, and to see in it the once-living present. **1893** DK. ARGYLL *Unseen Found. Society* x. 285 A once-wide acceptance. **1911** KIPLING *Years Between* (1919) 7 Our ears still carry the sound Of our once Imperial seas. **1931** A. HUXLEY *Cicadas* 44 The pause and once-more fury of the gale. **1939** DYLAN THOMAS *Map of Love* 6 These once-blind eyes have breathed a wind of visions, The cauldron's root through this once-rindless hand. **1943** D. GASCOYNE *Poems 1937–42* 52 The once-met And long remembered faces. **1946** *Nature* 20 July 86/1 The once-popular 'tiger nut'. **1949** S. SPENDER *Edge of Being* 56 That past greatness and that once-willed Future Beyond the storm. **1951** W. DE LA MARE *Winged Chariot* 38 Once-green skeleton leaf. *Ibid.* 39 The angelic hierarchies Dome with their glory the once-empty skies. **1974** *Country Life* 21 Mar. 643/1 Once-popular composers..drop out of favour. **1977** J. CLEARY *Vortex* v. 135 The once-beautiful eyes, already dark with death.

b. *spec.* **once-fired** *a.*, of pottery: subjected only once to the process of firing. Also in Combs. with advs.: **once-off** *a.*, happening only once; hence as *sb.*; cf. *one off* s.v. ONE *numeral a.* B. 31 b; **once-only** *a.*, occurring only once; **once-through** *a.*, being or employing water that enters a system, flows once through it, and then leaves it.

1952 V. ELEY *Monk at Potter's Wheel* 19 **Once fired*, an expression relating to pottery that has been glazed and fired without having received a previous firing. Mediaeval English pottery was fired in this way. **1960** H. POWELL *Beginner's Bk. Pott.* II. iv. 42 If you wish to make, decorate, and glaze in one operation, this is known as once fired. **1970** *Gloss. Industrial Furnace Terms* (*B.S.I.*) 19 *Once-fired kiln*, a kiln in which the body and the glaze thereon are fired at one and the same time, instead of in two separate firings. **1965** *Math. in Biol. & Med.* (Med. Res. Council) I. 8 But in a '*once-off' job where a standard program cannot be used ..these advantages are lost. **1969** *Guardian* 1 Mar. 1/3 Steam turbines are built to a specification, often on a once-off basis or in pairs. **1973** *Times* 19 Jan. 12/1, 50 different juvenile weeklies, aside from the 'once-offs' that appear from time to time. **1976** *Gramophone* Oct. 670/3, I suppose that is the fault of once-off recordings. **1960** *Sunday Express* 28 Feb. 12/8 It is, alas, a *once-only gratuity. **1963** *Listener* 7 Feb. 263/2 A 'once only' talker can never be as good as a hardened professional. **1965** M. FRAYN *Tin Men* xxiii. 125 The open-endedness of a once-only job would require a computer so complex..that it would be cheaper to use a human being. **1971** A. PRICE *Alamut Ambush* ix. 115 They wouldn't like doing it... But for a once-only job they might stretch a point. **1940** *Chambers's Techn. Dict.* 87/1 *Benson boiler*, a high-pressure boiler of the *once-through type in which water is pumped successively through the various elements of the heating surface. **1946** J. N. WILLIAMS *Steam Generation* vi. 126 Forced circulation boilers may be divided into two classes according to whether the water is in continual circulation or is pumped through at one end of the heating surface and, making a single or 'once through' passage, leaves at the other end in the form of steam. **1978** *Environmental Conservation: Chemicals* (Shell Internat. Petroleum Co.) 2 Where sufficient surface water—lakes or rivers, for example—is available, waste heat from chemical plants has traditionally been discharged in the form of once-through (as opposed to re-used) cooling water.

II. 8. Phrases in which *once* is followed by another adv. or phrase.

a. ***once or twice***, a few times; ***once and again***, more than once, twice (or oftener).

[*a* **1225** *Ancr. R.* 70 Leaue to openen hire þurl enes oðer twies.] *c* **1369** CHAUCER *Dethe Blaunche* 665 But god wolde I had oones or twyes Y-konde and knowe the Ieupardyes. *c* **1450** tr. *De Imitatione* I. xvi. 18 If eny suche..be onys or twies amonisshed. **1597** J. KING *On Jonas* (1618) 642 By the words of his mouth once and again iterated. **1611** BIBLE *Phil.* iv. 16 Euen in Thessalonica ye sent once and againe [WYCLIF, oonys and twies also] vnto my necessitie. **1730** in B. Peirce *Hist. Harvard Univ.* (1833) 166 Inasmuch as the affair..has been once and again maturely considered by this Board. **1766** GOLDSM. *Vic. W.* ix, They once or twice mortified us sensibly by slipping out an oath. **1857** TROLLOPE *Three Clerks* ii, Once and again..a lad may be found formed of such stuff.

b. ***once again, once more.***

13.. *Coer de L.* 4881 That they scholden hye Ones more forth..To the cyte off Palestyn. **1567** *Gude & Godlie B.* (S.T.S.) 157 For I had leuer die For hir saik anis againe. **1595** SHAKS. *John* IV. ii. 1 Heere once againe we sit, once againe crown'd. **1621** QUARLES *Div. Poems, Esther* (1717) 93 That these same two should be made one again, Till singling Death this sacred knot undo, And part this new made one Once more in two. **1761** GRAY *Odin* 51 Once again my call obey. **1865** PUSEY *Truth Eng. Ch.* 268 [To] be merged in the Eighth General Council of the once-more united Christendom. **1892** TENNYSON *Akbar's Dr., Hymn to Sun*, Once again thou flamest heavenward, once again we see thee rise. *Mod.* I should like to see him once more.

c. ***once for all*** (***for always, altogether, ever***), once as a final act; once and done with; now usu. ***once and for all***; also as *sb.*, hence ***once-for-allness***; so ***once and away***. ***once in a way***, as a solitary or exceptional instance; rarely, exceptionally. ***once in*** (or irreg. ***and***) ***a while***, at long intervals; very occasionally. ***once in a blue moon***, rarely, exceptionally.

c **1489** CAXTON *Sonnes of Aymon* xix. 403 We oughte to aske it of hym ones for all. **1525** LD. BERNERS *Froiss.* II. xxxvii. 110 Ones for alwayes I defende the. **1542** UDALL *Erasm. Apoph.* 275b, Once for altogether. **1656** EARL MONM. tr. *Boccalini's Advts. fr. Parnass.* 100 These Judges have cleared the question once for ever. **1660** BOYLE *New Exp. Phys. Mech.* xxvii. (1682) 108 Give me leave to advertise your Lordship once for all. **1759** tr. *Duhamel's Husb.* I. ix. (1762) 52 It is not enough to harrow once and away. **1781** J. WITHERSPOON in *Pennsylvania Jrnl.* 23 May 1/3 He will *once in a while*, i.e. *sometimes*, get drunk. [Used in] the middle states. **1818** BENTHAM *Ch. Eng. Catech. Exam.* 115 So far as use is made of a once-for-all composed and for ever-established formulary. **1847** L. HUNT *Men, Women & B.* II. xi. 272 Fretting at corruptions, yet once and away helping to patch up one himself. **1869** MRS. STOWE *Oldtown Folks* x. 116 If he could come down here once and a while after work-hours. **1869** W. C. HAZLITT *Eng. Proverbs* 305 Once in a blue moon. **1876** Once in a blue moon [see *blue moon* s.v. BLUE *a.* 13]. **1877** SPURGEON *Serm.* XXIII. 653 Hadst thou gone into the royal presence once in a while to intercede for some special cases. **1885** J. PAYN *Luck of Darrells* vi, When a man has just once and away made up his mind to self-sacrifice. **1889** WESTGARTH *Austral. Progr.* 83 Tying up the freedom of building which a once-for-all construction of this kind might involve. **1891** J. M. DIXON *Dict. Idiomatic Eng. Phrases* 230 *Once in a way*, sometimes; at long intervals; on rare occasions. **1895** MORRIS & WYATT tr. *Beowulf* x. 23 E'en that in mind had I .., that for once and for all the will of your people would I set me to work. *a* **1902** *Mod.* I may have done it once in a way. **1922** G. R. S. MEAD in *Quest* XIII. 490 For the Jewish eschatologist it was a once for all event he expected, whereas for such men as the Stoical thinkers it was a perpetual recurrence. **1928** E. O'NEILL *Strange Interlude* II. 76 Well, then, a little truth for once in a way! **1934** G. B. SHAW *On Rocks* I. 197, I really think, father, you might for once in a way take some slight interest in the family. **1949** *Scottish Jrnl. Theol.* II. 86 A radical misunderstanding of the New Testament teaching about eschatological once-for-allness and eschatological continuity. *Ibid.* 87 The only primitive wholeness that the Reformed Churches recognise is the once-and-for-all *wholeness* of Jesus Christ in whom God and man are at one. **1951** AUDEN *Nones* (1952) 14 The once-for-all that is not seen nor said. **1955** *Times* 26 Aug. 7/4 And when, by some mischance, once in a blue moon, the bell does ring, how startled we are. **1957** *Ann. Reg. 1956* 137 The 1956 Budget..had..included a 'once-for-all' item of $961,000 for the 'Atoms for Peace' conference at Geneva. **1960** *Times* 12 Aug. 13/6 But contractile tissue as such seems to have been a once-for-all invention. **1960** V. NABOKOV *Invitation to Beheading* xvi. 159 Every once in a while he would jerk his flabby cheeks and his chin. **1963** *Times* 22 Feb. 16/7 Some absolute, once-and-for-all answer had to be found. **1970** T. LUPTON *Managem. & Social Sci.* (ed. 2) iv. 101 Pose questions like this and then try to think up once-for-all answers. **1972** *Police Rev.* 17 Nov. 1487/3 A once-and-for-all deduction from pension. **1975** J. B. HARLEY *O.S. Maps* i. 1 Before World War II..there was a tendency to regard the published large scale map as something of a 'once-and-for-all' record of fact. **1976** *National Skat & Sheepshead Q.* Mar. 18 How many of you readers 'blow' the big hand—the one that appears once in a blue moon? **1977** *Times* 12 Feb. 7/3 Try not to let the once-for-allness of the occasion tempt you to eat the whole menu.

d. ***once in a lifetime***, such as occurs only once in a person's life; freq. (with hyphens) *attrib.* and often used hyperbolically; ***once too often***, of a thing said or done: once more than necessary or tolerable; usu. implying unpleasant repercussions.

[**1854** C. PATMORE *Angel in House: Betrothal* VIII. ii. 110 Love wakes men, once a life-time each.] **1908** YEATS & GREGORY *Unicorn from Stars* III. 122 There is a fiery moment, perhaps once in a lifetime, and in that moment we see the only thing that matters. **1915** H. T. WEBSTER *Our Boyhood Thrills* 7 (*heading*) The thrill that comes once in a lifetime. **1921** G. B. SHAW *Back to Methuselah* III. 131 Havnt you said that once too often already this morning? **1929** J. B. PRIESTLEY *Good Companions* II. v. 369 Don't be a scoffer... I've known people to scoff at these things once too often. **1932** R. ALDINGTON *Soft Answers* 122 They had simply got drunk once too often and lost their money. **1934** E. O'NEILL *Days without End* II. 68 But I warned him he'd humiliate me once too often—and he did! **1962** M. SUMMERTON *Nightingale at Noon* (1963) xii. 174 Fate presented him with a once-in-a-lifetime opportunity to get rid of her. **1962** *Times* 20 June 14/6 That once-in-a-lifetime occasion. **1973** *Mad Mag.* Oct. 8/1 Now cool it and let me really ham up this once-in-a-lifetime role! **1975** P. MOYES *Black Widower* xiii. 155 I'm afraid this is a once-in-a-lifetime trip for us. **1977** *Washington Post* 18 May C 6 (Advt.), Singer. Once-in-a-lifetime sale.

e. Phr. ***once over lightly***; also (hyphenated) as *sb.* and *attrib. phr.* (chiefly *U.S.*).

1941 *Time* 12 May 55/1 Her pretty posturing, pouts, stunned, exotic stares are meaningless when she tries to do them once over lightly. **1960** WENTWORTH & FLEXNER *Dict. Amer. Slang* 364/2 *Once over lightly*, cursorily; quickly; temporarily. **1961** S. ARNE in WEBSTER s.v. *n.*, Had given political problems the once-over-lightly. **1961** S. HYMAN in *Ibid.* s.v. *adj.*, Gets the once-over-lightly treatment. **1967** M. KENYON *Whole Hog* i. 16 The young man raised the egg. ..Was it sunny-side-up..or once-over-lightly?

III. 9. *once* preceded by a preposition or demonstrative.

Arising from its equivalence to *one time*: cf. Ger. *einmal*.

a. AT ONCE: see as Main word.

b. **for once**, for one occasion. ***for once and all***, ***for once and away***, ***for once in a way*** = corresponding phrases in 8 c. ***for once in your*** (or ***his, my***, etc.) ***life***, on this single occasion in your (etc.) life.

c **1450** *Cov. Myst.* xii. (Shaks. Soc.) 118, I the forsake and from the go, For onys, evyr, and ay. **1583** GOLDING *Calvin on Deut.* i. 3 Not..for once and away, but wee haue our eares beaten with it euery day. **1640** tr. *Verdere's Romant of Rom.* II. 67 Nor is a man to put on arms for once, and ever after to let them hang ignobly rusting. **1758** GOLDSM. *Mem. Prot.* (1895) II. 132 We entreated him to risk it for once. **1791–3** in *Spirit Pub. Jrnls.* (1799) I. 43 Awake from your lethargy, Citizens, and decree, for once and all, ..that [etc.]. **1801** M. EDGEWORTH *Belinda* I. iv. 144 She has succeeded for once in her life. **1825** COLERIDGE *Aids Refl.* (1848) I. 177 Let me remark for once and all [etc.]. **1846** [see LIFE *sb.* 3 c]. **1853** MOTLEY *Corr.* (1889) I. v. 157 The opportunity of seeing what she could for once in a way. **1857** TROLLOPE *Barchester T.* III. iv. 81 And so the signora resolved..to do a good natured act for once in her life. **1859** *Blackw. Mag.* Aug. 224/2 For once in my life I agreed with my wife. **1862** W. COLLINS *No Name* I. i. ix. 115 Magdalen was caught, for once in her life, at the end of all her resources. **1881** H. JAMES *Portrait of Lady* III. xii. 189 Be a little wicked, feel a little wicked, for once in your life! **1964** 'S. WOODS' *Trusted like Fox* viii. 79 Mr. Justice Conroy..for once in his life owned himself puzzled.

c. ***this, that*** (***the***) ***once***; this or that single time, this or that time only.

13.. *E.E. Allit. P.* B. 801 Comez to your kuchiez-kote I craue at þis onez. *c* **1400** MAUNDEV. (Roxb.) xiv. 64 Þai ete bot anes on þe day..and ȝit þat anes þai ete bot riȝt lytill. **1533** J. HEYWOOD *Merry Play* (1830) 4 That I may beate her for this ones [*rime* bones]. **1561** T. HOBY tr. *Castiglione's Courtyer* (1577) Hv, Yet wil we so terme it for this once. **1603–25** *Successors of Edw. IV* in Evans *O.B.* (1784) II. xxv. 152 But when the duke of Buckingham..Began a quarrel for the once. **1611** BIBLE *Judg.* xvi. 28, I pray thee, onely this once, O God. **1758** MRS. LENNOX *Henrietta* IV. vii. (1761) I. 169 You shall be indulged this once. **1760** *Impostors Detected* I. viii. I. 72 She had not time to put on her gloves, but danced that once without them. **1822** SHELLEY *Ess.* (1852) II. 278, I think he might as well have favoured me this once. **1887** T. DARLINGTON *Folk-Speech S. Cheshire* 282 'A thing for the once'..is an unusual or unprecedented thing. **1924** A. D. SEDGWICK *Little French Girl* I. viii. 74 'He came twice afterwards.'.. 'I didn't know that. I thought it was only the once.' **1967** N. FREELING *Strike Out* 89 [He] thought he'd live for ever... He came the once for a checkup.

†**d.** ***for then once*** (***for þe nones***), for that once, for the nonce: see NONCE[1]. *Obs.*

c **1200** *Trin. Coll. Hom.* 87 Þe for þe nones was maked. *c* **1205** LAY. 17304 And comen to þan anes To fæchen þa stanes. *a* **1225** *Juliana* (Bodl. MS.) 71 Ase wunsum as þah hit were a wlech beað iwlaht for þen anes in forte beaðien. **1297** R. GLOUC. (Rolls) 5795 He adde uor þe nones [*v.r.* þan ones] tueye suerdes bi is syde.

C. as *conjunctive adv.* = When once, if once; as soon as. (So ***once that.***)

1761 MRS. F. SHERIDAN *Sidney Bidulph* II. 96 This was the master-key..and once I had got it, ..it was easy to unlock her breast. **1775** SHERIDAN *Rivals* IV. iii, Once I have stamped it there, I lay aside my doubts for ever. **1813** MOORE *Mem.* (1853) I. 334 Once I get it brilliantly off my hands, we may do what we please in literature afterwards. **1864** BROWNING *Death in Desert* 293 Will he give up fire For gold or purple once he knows its worth? [**1874** RUSKIN *Fors Clav.* xxxix. 67 Once that they were pulling together.. Hansli put himself to say.]

D. Elliptically (quasi-*adj.* and *sb.*).

1. quasi-*adj.* **a.** = Done or performed once.

With a vbl. sb. it can be explained as still an adv. qualifying the vb., e.g. ***once harrowing*** = harrowing once; cf. *thoroughly harrowing*.

1548 GEST *Pr. Masse* in H. G. Dugdale *Life* (1840) App. 90 Then is yᵉ once sacrifice of Christ utterly to be abandoned and disauthorized. **1739** TULL *Horse-Hoing Husb.* (1740) 223 Once Harrowing is generally enough. **1878** ABNEY *Photogr.* (1881) 167 Once coating is generally sufficient.

b. That once was; former.

1691 J. WILSON *Belphegor* III. i, The once generalissimo. **1757** MRS. GRIFFITH *Lett. Henry & Frances* (1767) IV. 222 But should the Heart, it's once Ally, By Falshood or by Death decay. **1880** MISS BROUGHTON *Sec. Th.* II. x. (1885) 237 Nothing remains but for the once enemies to say farewell.

2. quasi-*sb.* (ellipt. for) Doing a thing once, going once, etc.

1623 WODROEPHE *Marrow Fr. Tongue* (1625) 336 Once is no Custome. *Mod.* Once a week is enough for me.

once, oncial, obs. forms of OUNCE, UNCIAL.

'once-born, *a.* [ONCE *adv.* 7.] Designating or pertaining to someone whose attitude to life has retained a child-like simplicity and straightforwardness. (See also quot. 1942.) Cf. TWICE-BORN *a.* 3.

1849 [see TWICE-BORN *a.* 3]. **1902** W. JAMES *Var. Relig. Exper.* iv. 82 Another good expression of the 'once-born' type of consciousness, developing straight and natural, with no element of morbid compunction or crisis, is contained in the answer of Dr...Hale. **1942** BERREY & VAN DEN BARK *Amer. Thes. Slang* §325/5 *Once-born*, not regenerated or not believing in regeneration.

onceness ('wʌnsnɪs). [f. ONCE *adv.* + -NESS.] The fact or quality of happening only once, or all at once.

1866 R. & S. REDGRAVE *Century of Painters of Eng. School* I. iv. 108 [George] Barret's pictures are painted with the firm pencil and vigorous once-ness which characterize the works of the best painters of his time. **1917** E. POUND *Let.* 18 Apr. (1971) 109 H. Monroe seems to think that if her Chicago widows and spinsters will only shell out she can turn her gang of free-versers into geniuses all of a onceness. **1948** *Scottish Jrnl. Theol.* I. 141 In the Old Testament, he maintains, there is only one 'onceness' which is of theological significance, and that is the onceness of Christ. **1951** *Ibid.* IV. 3 That is to say, history is the field of relative uniqueness, but never of absolute once-ness.

once-over ('wʌnsəʊvə(r)). *colloq.* (orig. *U.S.*). [f. ONCE *adv.* + OVER *prep.*] A glance; a rapid inspection (often with an implication of cursoriness); ***to give the once-over***, to make a rapid assessment of; to give (a person) an appraising or inviting glance; to search someone (for weapons).

1915 *Recruiter's Bulletin* (U.S.) Jan. 7/2 After giving an applicant the 'once-over' the other day I told him that I was sorry but I could not take him. **1915** *Dialect Notes* IV. 234 *Once-over*, ..a glance. **1916** *Daily Colonist* (Victoria, B.C.) 27 July 6/3 Individuals whose presence on the deserted thoroughfares around the midnight hour aroused suspicions to be given what, in police parlance, is known as the 'once over'. **1926** [see JERRY *a.*[2]]. **1927** *Daily Express* 31 Oct. 4/3 You require a couple of days, as distinct from the traditional American 'once over', to see Chelsea Old Church. **1938** E. BOWEN *Death of Heart* II. ii. 190 Daphne gave the rest of the cakes a rather scornful once-over. **1948** M. ALLINGHAM *More Work for Undertaker* xix. 219 They had entered without invitation and were giving it what Luke called 'the old once-over'. **1949** *Sun* (Baltimore) 26 Aug. 10/3 Whenever travelers enter Baltimore from abroad by ship or air, they are given the onceover by Cap'n Jenks. **1951** J. D. SALINGER *Catcher in Rye* x. 85 They probably thought I was too young to give anybody the once-over..—you'd've thought I wanted to *marry* them or something. **1953** E. TAYLOR *Sleeping Beauty* ix. 152 Len was curious about Betty..and wished to give her..what he called the once-over. **1954** *Encounter* Feb. 26/2, I could feel his eyes on me even more sharply than before. He was, so to speak, giving me a professional once-over. **1972** J. PHILIPS *Vanishing Senator* (1973) III. iv. 171 Give Mr. Styles a quick once-over, Francine, but try to remember you're looking for a gun and not trying to excite him sexually. **1977** *New Yorker* 4 July 22/1 He gave his display of perfect strawberries the once-over.

oncer ('wʌnsə(r)). *colloq.* Also once-er. [f. ONCE *adv.* + -ER[1].] **1.** One who, or that which, does a particular thing only once; a thing that occurs only once; formerly *spec.* one who attends church once on a Sunday.

1892 *Review of Reviews* V. 41/2 He [*sc.* Gladstone] has a poor opinion of those whom he humorously terms 'oncers'. **1909** *Daily Chron.* 22 Apr. 4/7 A minister regretted an increasing disposition on the part of the people to become 'oncers'. **1917** *Dialect Notes* IV. 327 *Oncer*, ..he who (or that which) does a thing but once, esp. a church member who attends service but once on Sunday. **1938** *Amer. Speech* XIII. 35 For an extremely rare word..there may be only one slip, a *oncer*. **1944** AUDEN *For Time Being* (1945) 11 Could he but once see Nature as In truth she is for ever, What oncer would not fall in love? **1972** B. RODGERS *Queens' Vernacular* 143 *Oncer*, somebody who does it once, and never again with the same person; Mr. fuck 'em and forget 'em. **1973** *Shooting Times & Country Mag.* 7 July 13/3 Eventually a fish did move under an overhanging alder, but it was a 'oncer' and I had grave doubts about it rising again.

2. *slang.* A one pound note.

1931 *Police Jrnl.* IV. 502 They spieled [*sc.* played] first for stakes of a sprazey [*sc.* sixpence],..increasing it to half a tosh,..and eventually to a oncer. **1936** [see GEE *v.*[2] 1 c]. **1953** K. TENNANT *Joyful Condemned* iii. 27 Sure he took your oncer. But..here's another quid in place of it. **1968** L. DEIGHTON *Only when I Larf* vi. 80 He'd pay in used oncers, no cheques. **1970** A. ROSS *Manchester Thing* 122, I got my wallet out and let him look at a pound note... I laid a second oncer on top of the other. **1978** M. KENYON *Deep Pocket* vii. 82 They gave you an 'undred quid in oncers to see things their way.

oncest, oncet, see ONCE *adv.* A. γ.

‖**on'cethmus.** *Obs. rare.* [a. Gr. ὀγκηθμός braying.] A bray.

1656 HOBBES *Six Lessons* iii. Wks. 1845 VII. 247 You bring no argument, but fall into a loud oncethmus (the special figure wherewith you grace your oratory).

onchocercal (ɒŋkəʊ'sɜːkəl), *a.* [f. as next + -AL.] Belonging to the genus *Onchocerca* (see next); caused by worms of this genus.

1934 R. P. STRONG et al. *Onchocerciasis* I. ii. 6 Calderon.. published a monograph on the onchocercal *Filaria*. **1974** A. W. WOODRUFF *Med. in Tropics* xiv. 237/1 In the early stages of massive onchocercal infection in African adults a dark purplish-brown plaque-like skin reaction..may..be seen.

onchocerciasis (ˌɒŋkəʊsɜː'saɪəsɪs, -sɜː'kaɪəsɪs). *Path.* Also onco-. [f. mod.L. *Onchocerca* (f. Gr. ὄγκος barb + κέρκος tail), name of a genus of parasitic filarioid worms + -IASIS.] Infestation with or a disease caused by filarioid worms of the genus *Onchocerca*; in man *spec.* that caused by *O. volvulus* and transmitted by biting flies of the genus *Simulium*, common in tropical Africa and parts of Central America and marked by characteristic lesions of subcutaneous tissue and the eyes, often with blindness.

1911 R. T. LEIPER in *Rep. Local Govt. Board on Public Health & Med. Subjects* (Ministry of Health) No. 45. 6 The condition here termed Onchocerciasis is met with in frozen beef imported from Australia. **1911** STEDMAN *Med. Dict.* 604/2 *Onchocerciasis*, infestation of the ox with a species of *Onococerca*. **1912** *Jrnl. Trop. Med. & Hygiene* XV. 232/1 (*heading*) Some notes and suggestions in connection with the etiology of bovine onchocerciasis. **1934** R. P. STRONG et al. *Onchocerciasis* I. iv. 19 The limitation of the centers of onchocerciasis in Guatemala to certain zones of territory.. is very striking. **1967** A. W. JONES *Introd. Parasitol.* xiv. 184 In onchocerciasis of horses (and rarely of cattle), adult *Onchocerca* live in the tendons and ligaments of the back and neck region. **1971** *Nature* 21 May 151/3 In tropical and subtropical man-made lakes..explosive outgrowths of water weeds after filling had led to a very significant increase in the incidence of diseases carried by insects, such as malaria and onchocerciasis. **1974** *Daily Tel.* 9 Sept. 3/8 With him was.. a tropical eye disease expert from Swindon, who during the journey is to lead an investigation into onchocerciasis, a strange river blindness endemic in Central Africa. **1975** *Hansard Lords* 27 June 1706 To ask Her Majesty's Government what was the reason for the delay in presenting to Parliament the Onchocerciasis Fund Agreement 1974... Baroness Gaitskell: May I ask my noble friend to pronounce the name of the Fund? Lord Goronwy-Roberts: As if it were spelled 'Onkoserkiasis'.

onchocercosis (ˌɒŋkəʊsɜː'kəʊsɪs). *Path.* [f. as prec. + -OSIS.] = prec. Hence ˌ**onchocer'cotic** *a.* (*sb.*)

1918 P. LUNA in *Amer. Jrnl. Ophthalm.* I. 122/2 The visual disturbances which I have met with among the carriers of this filaria..and which I shall call onchocercosis. *Ibid.* 125/2 The lesions..appear in the onchocercotic, all of whom suffer disturbances of vision. **1931** *Ibid.* XIV. 518 (*heading*) Onchocercosis in Mexico. *Ibid.* 518/1 In.. Guatemala the onchocercotic infection had been demonstrated..next to the international boundary. **1972** *Biol. Abstr.* LIV. 5491/1 In none of these cases was the infestation localized to the orbital cavity as in other filarial infections (Loa-loa, onchocercosis).

onchosphere, var. ONCOSPHERE.

‖**Oncidium** (ɒn'sɪdɪəm). *Bot.* [mod.L. (Swartz 1800), f. Gr. ὄγκος barb of an arrow, angle, so called from the form of the lower petal or labellum.] A large genus of American epiphyte orchids, containing many handsome species, with few leaves and showy yellow flowers, one of the best known being the Butterfly-plant (*O. Papilio*).

1882 *Garden* 21 Jan. 48/3 Slugs are very fond both of the flower-stems and the succulent roots of this Oncidium.

oncle, obs. form of UNCLE.

onco-, combining form of Gr. ὄγκος mass, bulk, in mod.Gr. also tumour. **onco'fœtal** (*U.S.* **-fetal**) *a. Med.*, occurring in tumours and in the fœtus but not in the adult; **oncograph** ('ɒŋkəʊgrɑːf, -æ-) [-GRAPH], an instrument, used in connexion with the *oncometer*, for recording variations in the size of an organ; **'oncolite** *Petrol.* [-LITE], a small, rounded body found in sedimentary rocks that is composed of incomplete concentric layers of calcareous material and is believed to be of algal origin; hence **onco'litic** *a.*; **onco'logic** *a.* (chiefly *U.S.*) = *oncological*; **on'cologist**, an expert or specialist in oncology, now esp. one concerned with treatment by means of drugs rather than surgery or radiotherapy; **oncology** (ɒŋ'kɒlədʒɪ) [-LOGY], that part of medical science which relates to tumours (Mayne *Expos. Lex.* 1857); hence **oncological** (ɒŋkə'lɒdʒɪkəl) *a.*, pertaining to oncology; **on'cometer** (-mɪtə(r)) [-METER], an instrument for measuring variations in the size of an organ; hence **oncometric** (-'mɛtrɪk) *a.*, pertaining to or made with the oncometer; **on'cotomy** [Gr. -τομια cutting], incision into, or excision of, a tumour.

1972 P. ALEXANDER in *Nature* 21 Jan. 137/2 Table 1 is an attempt to classify the different types of *onco-foetal 'antigens' (OFAs). It seems necessary to coin this phrase because the more elegant description of carcino-embryonic antigen has been pre-empted to describe one class of these compounds. **1975** *Ibid.* 25 Dec. 734/2 In man the two best known oncofoetal antigens are the α-foetoprotein (AFP).. and the carcinoembryonic antigen (CEA) of the human digestive system. **1885** W. STIRLING in tr. *Landois' Hum. Physiol.* 209 Any variations in the size of the organ caused a variation in the amount of oil within the box, and these variations were recorded. This instrument Roy termed an '*oncograph'. **1933** R. B. YOUNG in *Trans. Geol. Soc. S. Afr.* XXXV. 32 Professor Julius Pia, in Hirmer's *Handbuch der Paläobotanik*, places the stromatolites among the *Schizophyceae* and separates them into two groups, the *Stromatolithi* and the *Oncolithi*, the latter embracing the forms..that occur as separate or individual bodies. In this paper the term '*oncolite' will be employed in the same sense, but without any implication that the bodies..differ from the rest of the stromatolites in any respect other than that generally they have formed round detached nuclei. *Ibid.* 34 When they were for a time completely stationary, the oncolitic growth became continuous, spreading over the surface of the bed to form thin but fairly extensive stromatolitic layers. **1967** *Jrnl. Sedimentary Petrology* XXXVII. 1163/2 A carbonate rock of which oncolites form a significant part may be termed oncolitic. **1972** H. BLATT et al. *Origin Sedimentary Rocks* xii. 422 Oncolites..up to 3 in. in diameter, have been found. **1974** *Nature* 22 Feb. 522/2 *Facies E.* Concentrically stacked spheroid stromatolites (oncolites). **1906** *1st Ann. Rep. Amer. Oncologic Hospital, Philadelphia* 3 The name of the Corporation shall be The American *Oncologic Hospital. **1952** A. NETTLESHIP *Basic Princ. Cancer Pract.* xix. 389 The need for a clinically useful oncologic science is clear. **1894** *Brit. Med. Jrnl.* 26 May 1131/2 The classification of new growths is carried out in accordance with modern *oncological views. **1925** H. GILFORD *Tumors & Cancers* xxvi. 574 *Oncologists in general still adhere to older methods of operative treatment, supplemented, it may be, by actinic and other remedies. **1968** BETHELL & BURG tr. *Solzhenitsyn's Cancer Ward* (1969) I. vii. 96 On top of this a society of oncologists had been started recently. **1971** *Lancet* 21 Aug. 419/2 Although the oncologist's clinical experience with malignant disease is often limited, his pharmacological background has enabled him to make a substantial contribution to the subject. **1857** R. G. MAYNE *Expos. Lex. Med. Sci.* (1860) 810 *Oncology. **1915** F. L. HOFFMAN *Mortality from Cancer* i. 1 There are few more interesting subjects for statistical analysis than cancer, or what is, perhaps, more appropriately termed the science of oncology, which comprehends tumors of all kinds, whether malignant or benign or ill-defined. **1968** BETHELL & BURG tr. *Solzhenitsyn's Cancer Ward* (1969) I. i. 3 According to the arrangement with the head doctor of the oncology clinic, the matron was supposed to wait for them at two o'clock in the afternoon. **1971** *Nature* 19 Feb. 517/3 The Imperial Cancer Research Fund (ICRF) last week announced the establishment of..a medical oncology unit. **1885** W. STIRLING in tr. *Landois' Hum. Physiol.* 581 An instrument which consists of two parts, one termed the **oncometer* or renal plethysmometer, in which the organ is enclosed, while the other part is the registering portion or oncograph. **1896** *Allbutt's Syst. Med.* I. 826 It has been demonstrated by means of Roy's onkometer. **1897** *Ibid.* IV. 316 *Oncometric observations show that such substances produce vascular dilatation of the kidneys. **1727–41** CHAMBERS *Cycl.*, **Onkotomy*, in chirurgery, the operation of opening a tumor, or abscess. **1836** SMART, *Oncotomy*.

oncocerciasis, var. ONCHOCERCIASIS.

oncogene ('ɒŋkədʒiːn). *Biol.* [f. ONCO- + GENE[1].] A gene in a virus particle held to be responsible for transforming a host cell into a tumour cell.

1969 HUEBNER & TODARO in *Proc. Nat. Acad. Sci.* LXIV. 1087 It is postulated that the viral information (the virogene), including that portion responsible for transforming a normal cell into a tumor cell (the oncogene), is most commonly transmitted from animal to progeny animal and from cell to progeny cell in a covert form. **1970** *New Scientist* 3 Sept. 465/2 Occasionally, an 'oncogene' of the virus becomes switched on, and the host cell is transformed into a cancer cell. **1971** *Nature* 6 Aug. 373/2 Attempts to analyse genetically the oncogenes in adenovirus genomes, by the isolation of temperature sensitive mutants, seem most promising. **1975** *Ibid.* 7 Aug. 498/1 The oncogene theory contends that type C viruses possess oncogenic information and that malignancy is the result of activation of this genetic information.

oncogenesis (ɒŋkə'dʒɛnɪsɪs). *Biol.* [f. ONCO- + -GENESIS.] The formation or production of a tumour or tumours.

1932 in Dorland & Miller *Med. Dict.* (ed. 16) 891/1. **1944** *Jrnl. Exper. Med.* LXXX. 122 In these cases [of rapid growth of papillomas and carcinomatoids] actual oncogenesis must have been exceedingly swift, not the drawn out process it is generally held to be. **1961** *Proc. 4th Nat. Cancer Conf.* (U.S.) 41 (*heading*) Hormones and experimental oncogenesis; mammary and mammotropic tumors. **1977** *Proc. R. Soc. Med.* LXX. 393/2 It would seem plausible to think that the susceptibility to light-induced mutations..may favour viral oncogenesis in the presence of appropriate viral elements.

So **'oncogen**, an agent that causes oncogenesis.

1969 *Jrnl. Biol. Chem.* CCXLIV. 4075/2 Present evidence does not favor 3-hydroxyuric acid as a proximate oncogen. **1971** *Nature* 5 Feb. 418/2 Hamster cells exposed to a dilute concentration of highly oncogenic compounds or to larger doses of weak oncogens can enter and pass through a complete mitotic cycle in spite of repair synthesis already in progress.

oncogenic (ɒŋkə'dʒɛnɪk), *a. Biol.* [f. ONCO- + -GENIC.] Causing the development of a tumour or tumours; of or pertaining to this effect.

1949 *New Gould Med. Dict.* 696/2 Oncogenic. **1959** *Jrnl. Nat. Cancer Inst.* (U.S.) XXIII. 277 (*heading*) The oncogenic spectrum of two 'pure' strains of avian leukosis. **1970** *New Scientist* 3 Sept. 464/2 The discovery, and confirmation, of an enzyme carried by oncogenic RNA viruses. **1971** *Nature* 29 Jan. 296/2 Both the oncogenic and protovirus hypotheses postulate that tumour viruses are escaped cellular genetic elements.

So **oncoge'nicity**, the property of being oncogenic.

1944 *Jrnl. Exper. Med.* LXXX. 119 Manifestly the real criterion is the time required to render the first cell neoplastic; for oncogenicity properly speaking is contained in that act. **1967** *Cancer Res.* XXVII. 929/2 No distinction can now be made between the oncogenicities of the 7-*N*-oxide derivatives of guanine and xanthine. **1971** *Nature* 5 Feb. 416/2 The data indicate a link between oncogenicity of a compound and its capacity to provoke DNA repair synthesis.

oncolysis (ɒŋ'kɒlɪsɪs). *Biol.* [f. ONCO- + -LYSIS.] The absorption or destruction of a tumour. So **onco'lytic** *a.*, of, pertaining to, or causing oncolysis.

1928 STEDMAN *Med. Dict.* (ed. 10) 712/2 Oncolysis. *Ibid.*, Oncolytic. **1933** *Brit. Jrnl. Ophthalm.* XVII. 754 He finds that in these animals the oncolytic power is *nil*, and thence concludes that the eye is specially susceptible to attack by new growths. **1952** *Ann. N.Y. Acad. Sci.* LIV. 945 (*heading*) Viruses with oncolytic properties and their adaptation to tumors. *Ibid.*, Oncolysis, by viral action, has not been studied very thoroughly until recently. **1972** *Nature* 30 June 486/2 (*heading*) Oncolytic viruses. **1972** *Nature New Biol.* 5 July 8/1 No oncolysis occurred when subcutaneous tumours were treated with BEV.

oncome ('ɒnkʌm), *sb.* [f. ON- + COME *v.*; cf. *to come on.*]

1. Something that comes upon one, as a calamity or visitation (*obs.*); an attack of disease (now *Sc.*).

c **1175** *Lamb. Hom.* 147 þet oðer is þe fule on-kume þa þe douel haueð þeron ibroht. **13..** *Cursor M.* 5910 (Cott.) Hard on-come [so *Fairf.*; *Gött.* sondis] sal i send him sere, Bath on him and his kingrike. *Ibid.* 5927 þat toþer on-com þat him fell. **1570** LEVINS *Manip.* 161/46 An Oncome, disease, *morbus aduentitius*. **1818** SCOTT *Br. Lamm.* xxxi, Especially in *oncomes*, as the Scotch call them, or mysterious diseases, which baffle the regular physician.

†**2.** An attack, invasion. *Obs.*

a **1340** HAMPOLE *Psalter* civ. 20 *comm.*, To gouern þe land and beware wiþ oncomys.

3. Coming on; = ONCOMING *sb.*

1898 *Allbutt's Syst. Med.* V. 1036 Evidences of the gradual oncome of chronic renal disease.

4. *Sc.* **a.** 'A fall of rain or snow': = ON-DING. **b.** 'The commencement of a business, especially of one that requires great exertion. *Fife.*' (Jamieson.)

†**on-'come**, *v. Obs.* [Not an original compound vb., but a 'separable compound' or collocation of ON *adv.* and COME *v.*; now expressed by *come on*. By ME. writers commonly written as two words.] *intr.* To come on: see COME *v.* 62.

c **1250** *Gen. & Ex.* 841 On kumen was cadalamor, King of elam, wið ferding stor. **13..** *E.E. Allit. P.* A. 644 þer on com a bote as tyt. **1382** WYCLIF *1 Kings* v. 3 For the batailis oncomynge bi enuyroun [*propter bella imminentia*].

on-coming ('ɒnˌkʌmɪŋ), *sb.* [See ON-[1].] Coming on; advance, approach, access, etc.

1861 GEO. ELIOT *Silas M.* xii, Since the on-coming of twilight. **1887** *Academy* 26 Mar. 220/2 Causally concerned in the oncoming of paralysis.

'on-'coming, *a.* Also oncoming. [See ON-[1].]

1. Coming on; advancing, approaching, etc.: see COME *v.* 62.

1844 LD. HOUGHTON *Mem. Many Scenes, Jesus & John contending for Cross* 120 A dark, dark shadow of oncoming woe. **1884** MRS. LORIMER *Sketch in Black & White* 75 Unmistakable signs of an on-coming storm.

2. Ready to be sociable; friendly, welcoming, forthcoming, sympathetic.

1925 C. P. SLATER *Marget Pow* 183 He doesna seem to be very oncomin', for he's never been in the house yet. **1938** E. BOWEN *Death of Heart* II. iv. 248 If I were a more oncoming sort of fellow I should offer you a penny, and so on. **1942** N. BALCHIN *Darkness falls from Air* vi. 109, I think we might possibly get this through... The Secretary seemed quite oncoming. **1953** M. HOPKIRK *Queen over Water* v. 102 Some people were less oncoming. *Ibid.* x. 222 At Cambridge.. he was welcomed effusively, but other places were less oncoming. **1967** N. MARSH *Death at Dolphin* v. 133 I'm not all that oncoming, even here.

oncorn, obs. form of UNCORN *Sc.*, wild oats.

oncornavirus (ɒŋˈkɔːnəvaɪərəs). *Virology.* [f. ONCO- + PICO)RNAVIRUS.] = LEUKOVIRUS.

1970 R. C. NOWINSKI et al. in *Virology* XLII. 1152/1 We ..propose the term 'oncornaviruses' to represent the oncogenic RNA viruses (following the style 'picornaviruses' for small RNA viruses). **1974** FRAENKEL-CONRAT & WAGNER *Comprehensive Virology* I. 34 Oncornavirus group. Not yet officially accepted term for leukoviruses or RNA tumor viruses, all equally imperfect names. Medium large (100 nm diameter) enveloped and ether-sensitive particles; studded in regular manner with projections and containing a dense eccentric nucleoid. **1975** *Nature* 3 Apr. 457/2 In several animal species, C-type oncogenic RNA viruses (oncornaviruses) cause malignant tumours of mesodermal origin, such as leukaemia.

Hence **on'cornaviral** *a.*

1975 *Nature* 3 Apr. 458/1 Cultures were screened for the presence of different cytoplasmic C-type oncornaviral antigens.

oncosimeter (ɒŋkəʊˈsɪmɪtə(r)). [f. Gr. ὄγκωσις swelling, increase of bulk (f. ὀγκόειν to distend, f. ὄγκος: see ONCO-) + μέτρον measure.] An instrument for measuring the variations in density of a molten metal or other substance.

1880 *Times* 7 May, Experiments with a new instrument called the 'oncosimeter' (a measurer of increase in bulk). **1881** *Nature* XXIII. 403 By means of the oncosimeter.. they had determined the density of fluid bismuth.

oncosine (ˈɒŋkəsiːn). *Min.* Also onko-, -in. [ad. G. *onkosin* (F. von Kobell 1834, in *Jrnl. f. prakt. Chem.* II. 296), f. Gr. ὄγκωσ-ις swelling (from its behaviour when heated in a blow-pipe flame): see -INE[5].] An aluminosilicate of potassium, other alkali metals, and magnesium, which is a variety of, or perhaps a mixture containing, muscovite.

1854 J. D. DANA *Syst. Min.* (ed. 4) II. 504 Onkosin... In roundish pieces, having an apple-green color; sometimes grayish or brownish. **1868** *Ibid.* (ed. 5) 480 Oncosin.. occurs in roundish masses imbedded in dolomite with mica, at Passecken near Tamsweg, in Salzburg. **1923** *Mineral. Abstr.* II. 112 Muscovite, the variety onkosine is plentiful in the salbands of the lodes. **1939** *Geol. Fören. Stockholm Förhand.* LX. 622 The vein material in the pollucite, where late muscovite occurs in the somewhat unusual form of deep mauve-coloured, compact, cryptocrystalline masses, mineralogically referred to the subspecies oncosine. **1962** *Mineral. Abstr.* XV. 393/2 Pegmatites with giant crystals of amblygonite, spodumene, and oncosine and aggregates of montebrasite.

oncosphere (ˈɒŋkəʊsfɪə(r)). *Zool.* Also oncho-. [f. ONCO- + SPHERE *sb.*] An embryonic form of certain tapeworms. Also *attrib.*

1906 P. FALCKE tr. *Braun's Anim. Parasites Man* 202 The embryo enclosed within the embryonal shell, the oncosphere, is of spheroid or ovoid form, and is distinguished by the possession of three pairs of hooklets. **1929** H. A. BAYLIS *Man. Helminthology* 65 It [*sc.* the tapeworm embryo] is frequently referred to as a 'hexacanth embryo' or 'onchosphere'. **1949** *New Biol.* VII. 114 A ripe segment, ready to fall off the end of the worm [*sc.* the pork tapeworm].. contains 30,000–40,000 eggs, each already developed into a little six-hooked embryo (onchosphere) and protected by a shell. **1962** J. D. SMYTH *Introd. Animal Parasitol.* xx. 229 In the taenioids, the embryo develops to the oncosphere stage in the uterus of mature proglottids. **1969** A. M. DUNN *Vet. Helminthology* 112/2 The embryo is called the onchosphere. **1973** T. C. CHENG *Gen. Parasitol.* xiv. 485 The oncosphere.. remains passive in the eggshell.. until the embryo is ingested by a vertebrate or invertebrate intermediate host.

oncost (ˈɒnkɒst). [f. ON *adv.* + COST *sb.*]

1. *local Sc.* **a.** Contingent cost or charge; 'extra or additional expense' (Jamieson). **b.** *attrib.* or *adj.* Applied (esp. among miners) to work done on time wages. ***oncost men*** (also *oncosts*), men who work on such terms.

(The *oncost* of a coal-mine includes all the cost of upkeep, making and maintaining shafts and roads, pumping, etc., as opposed to the amount paid for actually hewing the coal and bringing it to the surface. The latter work is paid by the piece; but engineers and others employed on the oncost work are of necessity paid by time.)

1795 J. F. ERSKINE *Agric. Survey Clackmannansh.* 401 (Jam.), [This] yields but a very small return to the coal-master, on account of the overpowering contingent expenses known in collieries by the name of *Oncost.* **1887** *Scotsman* 30 May 7/1 The oncost men, who receive fixed wages for various duties at the colliery. **1892** *Labour Commission Gloss., Oncost labour.* Enginemen, labourers, and others working for a fixed rate of wages, per day, or per hour (such as foremen), &c., who must be paid although only half the furnaces may be working. **1894** *N.B. Daily Mail* 15 Sept. 5 In Uddingston district only four oncosts worked.

2. Overhead expenses or costs. Also *attrib.*

1912 J. G. WILLIAMSON *Counting-House & Factory Organisation* 65 Oncost expenditure, such as wages of foremen, labourers, and general works supplies, etc... is dealt with in the same manner. *Ibid.* 71 Establishment Charges or Oncost is every expense in the Profit and Loss Account other than the prime cost of Productive work. **1924** J. STAMP *Stud. Current Probl. Finance & Govt.* 18 Such a tabulation.. would enable us to.. test its ratios of oncost and various kinds of unit efficiency. **1931** H. E. COLESWORTHY *Pract. Directorship* xii. 120 Overhead or running charges, such as salaries, office expenses, selling expenses, and so on, are termed 'oncost'. *Ibid.*, It is sometimes customary to divide oncost into two classes—'works oncost' and 'office oncost'. **1970** *Money Which?* Mar. 25/2 Another method is to take the figure arrived at by the first method, but add to it what is known as manufacturing 'on-cost'. This is a proportion of your manufacturing overheads, such as the rent, rates, lighting and heating of your factory or workshop. **1972** *Accountant* 23 Mar. 383/1 The problem becomes even more obscure when we look at oncost loadings—obviously the administrative backing is an essential part of running any business.

oncotic (ɒŋˈkɒtɪk), *a. Physiol.* [f. ONCO- + -OTIC.] Applied to the osmotic pressure exerted by a colloid, esp. plasma protein.

1935 C. J. WIGGERS *Physiol.* li. 802 Starling demonstrated that colloids in a sol state exert a small osmotic pressure, but this varies in uncontrollable fashion owing to the fact that colloidal molecules or aggregates called micellae vary considerably. This has tersely been called oncotic pressure. **1977** *Proc. R. Soc. Med.* LXX. 693/1 A reduction in oncotic pressure due to hypoproteinaemia.

on-cry, *sb.* [f. ON-[1] 4 + CRY *sb.*] A battle-cry or slogan.

1899 *Blackw. Mag.* Nov. 605/1 Their badge of the grey-goose feather and their on-cry of 'Cuna' were feared from Lochalsh to Cantire.

ond = *on'd*, Sc. for *on it.*

a **1584** MONTGOMERIE *Ch. & Slae* 1022, I marveld mekill ond.

‖**ondatra** (ɒnˈdætrə). [Native Canadian name: so in F. (Buffon). Adopted as a generic name in H. F. Link *Beyträge zur Naturgeschichte* (1795) I. II. 52.] The North American musk-rat, *Ondatra zibethicus*; = MUSK-RAT 1.

1774 GOLDSM. *Nat. Hist.* (1862) I. 454 The Ondatra is a native of Canada. *Ibid.* (1776) IV. 78 The Ondatra.. is about the size of a small rabbit, but has the hair, the colour, and the tail of a rat, except that it is flatted on the sides. **1867** *Amer. Naturalist* I. 400 The Musk-rat, or Ondatra (*Fiber zibethicus*), so extensively diffused over North America.

†**onde**, *sb. Obs.* Forms: 1 anda, onda, 2–5 onde, 4 ounde, 4–5 ond, 5 oonde: cf. AND(E. [OE. *anda*, *ǫnda*, cogn. w. OS. *ando*, OHG. *anado*, *ando*, *anto*; ON. *andi*, *önd* breath. The southern *onde*, *oonde* is almost confined to the OE. senses, and became obs. bef. 1500; the north. *ande*, *aynde* in the ON. sense is still in use; see ANDE.]

1. Strong feeling against a person, 'animus'; spite, ill-will, envy.

c **1000** ÆLFRIC *Gram.* 89 *Rancor*, anda. *c* **1000** *Ags. Gosp.* Matt. xxvii. 18 Hiȝ hyne for andan hym sealdon. *c* **1175** *Lamb. Hom.* 65 Hwenne we habbeð nið and onde. *a* **1225** *Ancr. R.* 194 Of prude, & of onde, & of wreððe. *c* **1320** *Cast. Love* 211 Alle þe fendes hedden onde þat he scholde come to þt blisful londe. **13..** *Guy Warw.* (A.) 3083 Toward Gij he bar gret ond. ? *a* **1366** CHAUCER *Rom. Rose* 148 Amyd saugh I Hate stonde, That for hir wrathe, yre, & onde, Semede to ben.. An angry wight, a chideresse.

2. Strong desire, longing.

c **1320** *Cast. Love* 315 Of no þing heo nedden onde Bote him to habben vnder honde.

3. Emotion, perturbation of mind.

1390 GOWER *Conf.* I. 75 Aschamed with a pitous onde Sche tolde unto her housebonde The sothe.

4. Breath. (More common in the northern form ANDE, *aynd.*)

13.. *Guy Warw.* (A.) 316 He no may sitt no stonde, No vnneþe drawen his onde. **13..** *K. Alis.* 3501 Quyk they ladde him to londe. In his body tho was litel onde. **13..** *Cursor M.* 534 (Gött.) Als onde [*Cott.* aand] wid host in brest is bred. **1390** GOWER *Conf.* II. 260 Thries on the water ther Sche gasspeth with a drecchinge onde.

†**onde**, *v. Obs.* Also oonde. [Midland and southern form of northern ANDE.] To breathe: in quot. 1393, ? To sniff, smell.

1393 LANGL. *P. Pl.* C. xxi. 257 By so þow be sobre of syght, and of tounge boþe, In ondyng, in handlyng, in alle þy fyue wittes. *a* **1425** *Cursor M.* 21075 (Trin.) And as slepyng ondeþ ofte [*Cott.* als a slepand aends oft]. *c* **1440** *York Myst.* xiv. 132 þes beestes.. oondis on hym.. to warm hym with.

‖**ondé** [F.], variant of UNDY *a. Her.*

onder, obs. form of UNDER.

‖**Ondes Martenot** (ɔ̃d martəno). Also **Ondes, Ondes Musicales, Ondium Martenot.** [After F. *ondes musicales*, lit. musical waves; named by and after Maurice *Martenot* (b. 1898), its inventor.] An electronic keyboard musical instrument, capable of producing only one note at a time.

1936 E. S. BENSINGER tr. *K. London's Film Music* IV. 177 Before all others, let us recommend the *Ondium Martenot*, the apparatus derived from Theremin's ether-wave music, but with the sound-scale anchored on a keyboard, so that no sound-fluctuations are possible. **1937** *Nature* 6 Feb. 215/1 The author's brief treatment of the comparatively new electro-musical instruments, the *Ondium Martenot*, the trautonium and the Neo-Bechstein piano, is also good. **1940** C. SACHS *Hist. Mus. Instrum.* (1942) 448 The most important monophonic instruments are Maurice Martenot's *Ondes musicales* (1928) [etc.]. **1954** *Grove's Dict. Mus.* (ed. 5) V. 591/1 Martenot.. is the inventor of a radio-electric instrument called Ondes Musicales (now usually called Ondes Martenot by composers who score for it), which he first brought out in 1928. *Ibid.* 591/2 In 1937 he organized concerts with a team of eight Ondes. **1957** MANVELL & HUNTLEY *Technique Film Music* ii. 37 Ondes Martenot: an electronic instrument of great versatility, first introduced in 1928. It combines the principle of the Thérémin with a keyboard, adding additional devices for vibrato and glissando effects. **1977** *Times Lit. Suppl.* 11 Mar. 277/2 As a music student he earned a living by playing the ondes martenot in pit orchestras.

†**ondful**, *a. Obs.* Also 2–3 ontful. [f. ONDE *sb.* + -FUL.] Spiteful, envious.

c **1175** *Lamb. Hom.* 7 þeos world is whilende and ontful and swiðe lewe. *c* **1200** *Trin. Coll. Hom.* 205 þe ondfulle feond. *a* **1225** *Ancr. R.* 68 þet te ontfule [*MS. C.* ondfule] ne muwen lien on heom. *c* **1230** *Hali Meid.* 15 þe ondfule deuel bihalt te.

ondine, variant of UNDINE, water nymph.

on-ding (ˈɒnˌdɪŋ). *Sc.* [f. ON-[1] + DING *v.*] The act of 'dinging on' (see DING *v.*[1] 5 b); esp. a persistent heavy fall (of rain or snow). Also *fig.*

1776 C. KEITH *Farmer's Ha'* xix. 9 Rain we'll hae, Or on-ding o' some kind at least. **1818** SCOTT *Hrt. Midl.* viii, 'Look out, Jock; what kind o' night is't?' 'On-ding o' snaw, father'. **1894** CROCKETT *Raiders* (ed. 3) 41 To think that she should hear all the on-ding.. of their ill tongues. **1896** BARRIE *Marg. Ogilvy* ii. (1897) 31, I have seen many weary on-dings of snow.

‖**on dit** (ɔ̃ di). [The Fr. phrase *on dit* = 'they say', 'it is said', used as a sb.] An item of gossip; something reported on hearsay.

1826 DISRAELI *Viv. Grey* II. ii, I thought it was a mere *on dit.* **1828** P. CUNNINGHAM *N.S. Wales* (ed. 3) II. 117 Our various Australian journals furnish intelligence and *on-dits.* **1899** *Daily News* 20 Sept. 5/7 How is it possible to judge a case of this sort fairly upon on dits, more or less reliable, from a distance?

ondlæt, -lett, var. ANLETH *Obs.*, countenance.

‖**ondol** (ˈɒndɒl). [Korean, ad. Chinese *wên* hot, warm + *t'u* funnel, smoke tube.] A form of domestic heating by means of a flue running underfloor from a fire or furnace, commonly used in Korea. Also *attrib.*

1964 R. RUTT *Korean Works & Days* i. 21 The famous *ondol* or hot floor, built by making flues under a floor of stone or mud. **1969** *Korean Folklore & Classics* I. 8 He found the newly-laid ondol floor.. pierced by a sharp drill in a thousand places... 'This ondol cost me a lot of money.' **1970** *Korea: its People & Culture* vii. 224/1 The people have held on to their traditional, radiant floor heating system, the *ondol.* **1972** P. M. BARTZ *S. Korea* 32/2 About six o'clock the inhabitants get up, re-stoke their *ondol* furnaces, and start charcoal fires for breakfast.

†**on'dregh**, *v. Obs.* var. ADREE, to endure.

c **1250** *Gen. & Ex.* 3319 'Stille', quað he, 'and on-dreȝ, Godes fulsum-hed is ȝu ful neȝ'.

'on-ˌdrive, *v. Cricket.* [f. ON *adv.* + DRIVE *v.*]

a. *trans.* To drive to the on: see ON *sb.*[1]

1897 *Westm. Gaz.* 18 May 9/1 R. on-drove H. for 4. **1928** *Morning Post* 7 June 16/4 Holmes attacked the bowlers after a quiet start, twice on-driving Astill for 6. **1955** *Times* 19 May 5/1 In the next over Atkinson beautifully on-drove Johnson for his 152 in 198 minutes.

b. *absol.* or *intr.* To drive the ball to the on. Hence **on-driving** *vbl. sb.*

1930 *Morning Post* 7 Aug. 13/1 Bryan on-drove and hooked most effectively. **1961** *Times* 21 Aug. 3/3 His cutting and on-driving were a delight. **1963** *Times* 13 Feb. 4/3 Pulling and on-driving with remarkable acumen, he dispatched six successive balls for a six and five fours.

'on-driving, *a.* [ON *adv.*] That drives on.

1884 A. DE VERE *Poetical Wks.* II. 435 And ever as she sang, the on-driving snow Choked the sweet strain. **1927** *Chambers's Jrnl.* Jan. 39/1 Because there was a check, there arose long on-driving shouts from the huntsmen.

ondy, variant of UNDY *a. Her.*

one (wʌn), *numeral a., pron.*, etc. Forms: see below. [Com. Teut.: OE. *án* = OFris. *ân*, *ên*, OS. *ên* (MDu., Du. *een*), OHG. (MHG., Ger.) *ein*, ON. *einn*:—*ein-r* (Da. *een*, Sw. *en*), Goth. *ain-s*:—OTeut. **ain-oz*:—pre-Teut. **oinos* = L. *ūnus* (OL. *oinos*); OIr. *óen*, OSlav. *inŭ*, Lith. *vënas* one; cf. Gr. οἶνος, οἴνη, ace. OE. *án* became in regular course in south. and midl. dial. *ôn*, exemplified before 1200. By 15th c., *ôn*, *oon*, in s.w. and west, had developed (through *ōn*, *uon*, *uōn*, *won*, *wun*) an initial *w* (cf. the s.w. *wuk*, *wuts* = *oak*, *oats*), which only occasionally appears in the spelling (see A below), but is now the standard pronunciation. The first orthoepist to refer to it was app. Jones 1701: earlier grammarians, down to Cooper 1685, give to *one* the sound that it has in *alone*, *atone*, and *only*; Dyche in 1710 has (ɒn) beside (wɒn). In the north, *ān* was retained in ME.; but through the narrowing of orig. long *ā* to (æː, ɛː, eː, ɛə, ɪə) *ân* has sunk in dialectal utterance through *āne*, to *eane*, *eän*, *yan*, *yen*, the development of (jɛn) in the north being the counterpart of that of (wʌn) in the south. In OE., *án* had the full adj.

inflexions, definite and indefinite, remains of which persisted in the south to *c* 1300, and in Kent still later (see A ζ); but, in north. and midl. Eng., the uninflected *ân*, *ôn*, with the definite form *âne*, *ône* (OE. *ána*, *âne*), is found in the accus. and dative, as well as the nom. by 1200. Already also, *ân*, *ôn* were reduced before a cons. to *â*, *ô* (*oo*), which did not die out till the 16th c.

In the north the separation of *ân* and *â* was more permanent; at the present day in Sc. the full form *ane*, *eane*, etc., is only used absolutely or in the predicate, *ae*, *eae*, is the attrib. form before cons. and vowel alike, *ae day*, *ae yeir*, *we hae ane*; so in north Eng. dial. with *yà* and *yàn*. From the early *an*, *a*, pronounced proclitically without stress, arose the 'indefinite article' AN, A, q.v. In northern dial. the numeral and article were long written alike, the stress or emphasis alone distinguishing them; in 16th c. Sc. both were written *ane*. (See A *adj.*[2], ANE.) By more or less permanent coalescence of a preceding *thet*, the collocations *thet ane*, *thet one*, *thet a*, *thet o*, became *the tane*, *the tone*, *the ta*, *the to*. (See TONE.)]

A. Illustration of Forms:

α. 1 án, 2–3 (*north.* 3–6) an, 3 en, 4–5 (*Sc.* 5–) ane (4 aun, 5 awen, *Sc.* ayne, 6 *Sc.* ain, *north. dial.* 7– yane, 8– yan, yen, *Sc.* 9 eane, yen, yin).

c **1000** *Ags. Gosp.* Matt. x. 29 An of ðam. *c* **1175** *Lamb. Hom.* 77 An child. *c* **1200** ORMIN 1352 An Godd of twinne kinde. **1340** HAMPOLE *Pr. Consc.* 4085 An sal come. *c* **1340** —— *Prose Tr.* 8 Ane es þat sche es neuer ydil. *c* **1430** *Syr Gener.* (Roxb.) 1337 Not an word ageyn he yaf. **1588** A. KING tr. *Canisius' Catech.* 124 Sic a ane as makis nocht ane man gods enimie. *Ibid.* 171 Ony of thais small ains. **1674–91** RAY *N.C. Words* 84 *Yane*, one. **1790** MRS. WHEELER *Westmld. Dial.* 95 Clock hes strucken yan. **1807** TANNAHILL *Poems* 105 A third yin owns an antique rare. **1826** J. WILSON *Noct. Ambr.* Wks. 1855 I. 177 At ane and the same time. **1855** ROBINSON *Whitby Gloss.*, *Yah* or *Yan*, one. **1860** J. G. FORSTER in Latham *Handbk. Eng. Lang.* 161 Get up, maw luiv, my bonny yen.

β. 2–7 on, 4–6 oon, 4–6 oone, (5–6 owne, un, 7 own), 5– one, (9 *colloq.* un).

c **1175** *Lamb. Hom.* 103 On is icweðen *Gula*. **1362** LANGL. *P. Pl.* A. III. 269 On cristene kyng. **1377** *Ibid.* B. III. 287 One [*v.r.* oon] cristene kynge. *c* **1380** WYCLIF *Sel. Wks.* I. 176 Oon heerde and oon flok. *c* **1425** *Cursor M.* 3444 (Trin.) Now she bredeþ two for oone. **14..** *MS. Sloane* 1986 lf. 32 in T. H. Turner *Dom. Archit.* III. 102 Un fote, y wys, hit schall be brode. **1520** in W. H. Turner *Select. Rec. Oxford* 27 The oon half therof. **1527** *Plumpton Corr.* 226 Certaine traverses depending betewt him & owne Georg Fulbarne. **1547** in *Norfolk Archæol.* (1865) VII. 23 Oon payer of challys. **1603** OWEN *Pembrokeshire* (1891) 273 Aboute on or two of the clocke. **1648** GAGE *West Ind.* xii. (1655) 46 The own toward the Cawsey, and the other toward the water. **1852** MRS. STOWE *Uncle Tom's C.* xviii. 179 It was only the young uns.

γ. 5–6 won, wone, woon(e, 6–7 wonne, 7 *dial.* wan, 9 woone.

c **1420** *Chron. Vilod.* 980 Haralde regnede byfore hym four ȝer, and won. **14..** *Burlesque* in *Rel. Ant.* I. 83 These iij kyngus ete but of wone gruell dysche. *c* **1485** *E.E. Misc.* (Warton Cl. 1855) 8 Woone myleway mornyng I came. **1517** *Domesday Inclos.* (1897) I. 220–1 Won Rychard Songer.. and won Iennis parrys. **1526** TINDALE *Rev.* xviii. 10 Att won houre is her iudgment come. **1579** *Nottingham Rec.* IV. 191 To have a good won. **1642** ROGERS *Naaman* 289 Nay not so much as the basest wonne. **1651** LD. TAAFFE in *Mrq. Ormonde's MSS.* in *4th Rep. Hist. MSS. Comm.* 568/2 He has sent two frigatts.. wan to my Black Rock and tother to my Lord of Meskery. **1863** W. BARNES *Dorset Poems* in *Sat. Rev.* 124 They had woone chile bezide.

δ. 3–5 (*Sc.* -6) a, 4 ai, 8– *north.* yaa, *Sc.* ae.

c **1200** *Trin. Coll. Hom.* 39 Ure drihten drof fele deules togedere ut of á man. *c* **1340** HAMPOLE *Prose Tr.* 32 Some ere of a tre and some ere of another. **1790** MRS. WHEELER *Westmld. Dial.* 89 Thear is monny Blanks for yaa Prize. **1791** BURNS *Farewell to Nancy*, Ae fond kiss, and then we sever! **1894** IAN MACLAREN *Bonnie Brier Bush* IV. ii. 136, I had ae son, and he is gone.

ε. 3–6 o, 4–6 oo: see O *adj.*

c **1205**–*c* **1489** [see O *adj.*]. **1521** *Notbrowne Mayde* 278 in Hazl. *E.P.P.* II. 283 Yet am I sure Of oo plesure. **1589** PUTTENHAM *Eng. Poesie* III. xix. (Arb.) 213 But o thing vvell I vvot.

ζ. *Definite form.* 1 ána, áne: 2 ana, 2–3, *north.* 4– ane, 3– one, 4–5 oone.

c **1000** *Andreas* 492 Is þys ane ma. *c* **1000** ÆLFRIC *Hom.* I. 28 God ana. *a* **1175** *Cott. Hom.* 221 þæt þes man ane beo. *a* **1225** *Juliana* 79 Beo he him ane. *c* **1340** *Cursor M.* 3052 Wandrand in wildernes hir an. **1362** LANGL. *P. Pl.* A. I. 146 Her þou miht seon ensaumple in hymselfe one. *c* **1430** in *Pol. Rel. & L. Poems* (1866) 148 Sche made hir compleynt bi hir oone.

η. *Inflected forms.*

c **1000** ÆLFRIC *Hom.* I. 12 God þa ȝeworhte ænne mannan. *c* **1000** *Ags. Gosp.* John xvi. 32 þæt ȝe.. forlæton me anne [*c* **1160** *Hatton G.* ane]. **1137–54** *O.E. Chron.* an. 1137 Twa oþer thre men hadden onoh to beron onne. *c* **1175** *Lamb. Hom.* 27 He nefde bute enne deofel. *Ibid.* 49 þe mon þe delueð ene put. *c* **1200** ORMIN 3364 3e shulenn findenn ænne child. *c* **1205** LAY. 88 Nefede he buten anne sune. **1297** R. GLOUC. (Rolls) 8266 Robert.. smot anne vpe þe helm. **1340** *Ayenb.* 102 Huanne he werreþ wyþ enne. *c* **1175** Ane [see B. 12]. *c* **1205** LAY. 2247 Nefde he bute æne dohter. *a* **1225** One [see B. 12]. *c* **1020** *Rule St. Benet* (Logeman) 52 On anum dæȝe. *a* **1175** *Cott. Hom.* 245 More blisse bið an hefene be anun synfulle man. *c* **1175** *Lamb. Hom.* 17 Beo hit of ane þinge. *c* **1205** LAY. 82 On ane daȝe. **1340** *Ayenb.* 186 Alle we byeþ of one kende. *Ibid.* 190 He acsede at onen of his diaknen. *c* **1000** *Ags. Gosp.* John xx. 7 On anre stowe. *c* **1160** *Hatton G.* ibid., On anre stowe. *a* **1200** *Moral Ode* 207 For are þare sunne. *a* **1250** *Owl & Night.* 17 In ore waste þicke hegge.

B. Signification. I. As simple numeral.

1. The lowest of the cardinal numbers; the number of a single thing without any more, the addition of another to which makes *two*.

a. In concord with a sb. expressed.

c **855** *O.E. Chron.* (Parker MS.) Introd., þa heold Seaxburȝ his cuen an ȝear þæt rice æfter him. **879** *Ibid.*, And.. aþiestrode sio sunne ane tid dæȝes. *a* **1200** *Moral Ode* 137 Hefde he bon þer enne dei oðer twa. *c* **1290** *Beket* 464 in *S. Eng. Leg.* I. 120 For o trespas: bote o Iuggement nis i-do. **1382** WYCLIF *John* vii. 21, I haue don o work, and alle ȝe wondren. **1387** TREVISA *Higden* (Rolls) I. 83 Men that haueth.. eyghte fyngres in oon honde. **1539** TAVERNER *Erasm. Prov.* (1552) 17 *One man no man*. One man lefte alone and forsaken of all the reste can do lytle good. **1545** ASCHAM *Toxoph.* I. (Arb.) 48 Except it be one day amonges .xx. or one yeare amonges .xl. **1610** SHAKS. *Temp.* III. iii. 12 Doe not for one repulse forgoe the purpose That you resolu'd t'effect. **1710** BERKELEY *Princ. Hum. Knowl.* §12 We say one book, one page, one line, etc.; all these are equally units.

b. With ellipsis of sb. (expressed in or understood from context).

a **1000** *Riddles* (Gr.) xliii. 10 þær sceal.. se torhta Æsc wesan an an linan. *c* **1200** *Trin. Coll. Hom.* 49 Turtle ne wile habbe no make bute on. *c* **1330** *Arth. & Merl.* 5771 He slough thre ogaines anne. **1382** WYCLIF *2 Cor.* xi. 24, I resceyuede of the Iewis fyue sythis fourty strokis oon lesse. **1430–40** LYDG. *Bochas* IX. (1554) 219 b, Praying the Lord, one, two, and three, Whose magnificence no clerke may comprehend. **1560** DAUS tr. *Sleidane's Comm.* 72 By mo wayes than one. **1611** BIBLE *Deut.* i. 23, I tooke twelue men of you, One of a tribe. **1784** COWPER *Task* v. 231 One eminent above the rest.. Was chosen leader. **1823** BYRON *Juan* x. xxxiii, Thermometers sunk down to.. one. **1871** *Routledge's Ev. Boy's Ann.* Mar. Supp. 1/2 The one-and-sixpenny packet contains 100 varieties.

c. esp. with ellipsis of *hour*, as in ***one o'clock***, ***half past one***, ***train due at one twenty five*** (1 hr. 25 m.). Phrase: ***like one o'clock***, vigorously, quickly; also, splendidly, excellently; readily, enthusiastically. (See *N. & Q.* 9th Ser. 1900 VI. 305, etc.).

a **1548** HALL *Chron.*, *Hen. VIII* 94 b, On Mondaie.. by one of the Clocke. **1598** SHAKS. *Merry W.* IV. vi. 19 To night at Hernes-Oke, iust 'twixt twelue and one. **1718** PRIOR *Dove* 30 St. Dunstan's, as they pass'd, struck one. **1742** YOUNG *Nt. Th.* I. 55 The bell strikes one. We take no note of time, But from its loss. **1847–78** HALLIWELL 588/2 Like one-o'clock, i.e. very rapidly, said of a horse's movement, etc. **1851** MAYHEW *Lond. Labour* (1861) I. 31 Then he trotted on like one o'clock. **1852** DICKENS *Bleak Ho.* xx, Mr. Guppy and Mr. Jobling.. find Krook still sleeping like one o'clock.. quite insensible to any external sounds, or even to gentle shaking. *Ibid.* (1853) xx. 200 He has seen him through the shop-door, sitting in his back premises, sleeping 'like one o'clock'. **1870** MISS BRIDGMAN *R. Lynne* I. xviii. 317 We pulled every one to pieces like one o'clock. **1889** E. DOWSON *Let.* 31 July (1967) 97 If I can only shake off Cursitor St I will go to the oeuvre like one oclock. **1901** M. FRANKLIN *My Brilliant Career* xix. 161 He had a taste for literature, and we got on together like one o'clock. **1924** GALSWORTHY *White Monkey* III. xv. 321 Anything about the meeting, sir? Your speech must read like one o'clock! **1970** V. C. CLINTON-BADDELEY *No Case for Police* viii. 179 It's going to rain like one o'clock. **1973** *Guardian* 27 Oct. 11/6 Hedgehogs drink beer like one o'clock.

d. *colloq.* or in *slang use*, with ellipsis of other sbs. as *blow* (also *fig.*), *kiss*, etc. With ellipsis of *glass* or *drink*; ***one for the road***, a final drink before departure. See also *quick one* (QUICK *a.* 25 b).

[? *a* **1500** *Chester Pl.* x. 334 But yet wroken I wil be: Haue here one, two, and three.] **1830** GALT *Lawrie T.* VI. i. (1849) 252, I owed him one for his shortness about family concerns. **1855** SMEDLEY *H. Coverdale* xxxvi, I certainly owe Coverdale one, for his manner to me just now was anything but nice. **1882** W. S. GILBERT *Iolanthe* 16, I heard the minx remark, She'd meet him.. And give him one! **1892** *Spectator* 7 May 646/1 To use a slang phrase borrowed from the card-table, she has 'seen Mr. D. and gone one better'. **1894** W. E. NORRIS *St. Ann's* II. 237, I venture to prophesy that, between us, we shall be one too many for the Colonel. **1894** MRS. H. WARD *Marcella* II. 276, I have owed him one for many years—now I have paid it. **1900** SIMS *In London's Heart* iv. 25 It was, in the outdoor language of Exeter Street, 'one in the eye' for her aunt. **1925** R. J. B. SELLAR *Sporting Yarns* 165 'Did I have one over the regulation number last night?' 'Not at all.. you were perfectly all right.' **1925**, **1928** [see EIGHT *sb.* 4]. **1934** WODEHOUSE *Right Ho, Jeeves* xi. 126, I.. put my feet up, sipping the mixture with carefree enjoyment, rather like Cæsar having one in his tent the day he overcame the Nervii. **1937** D. & H. TEILHET *Feather Cloak Murders* i. 20 You run off to bed like a good fellow. You've had one too many. **1943** J. MERCER (*song-title*) One for my baby (and one more for the road). **1948** 'E. CRISPIN' *Buried for Pleasure* vi. 47 How about one for the road? **1959** G. GREENE *Complaisant Lover* I. i. 20 One for the road. I insist. While I call a taxi. **1968** J. SANGSTER *Touchfeather* xiii. 140 Didn't mean to be crude. Must have had one too many. **1972** J. BLACKBURN *For Fear of Little Men* xi. 119 'What about giving me one for the road, my dear.' He gulped down the remains of the sherry. **1976** *South Notts Echo* 16 Dec. 5/4 If you are driving do not have one for the road.

†e. Ellipt. for 'one horse' (to pull a carriage, etc.). Cf. FOUR *a.* 2 c. *Obs.*

1777 P. THICKNESSE *Year's Journey* II. lv. 185 If you can find me out a sensible valetudinarian.. who will travel as we do.. in a landau and one. **1785** COWPER *Task* I. 5 Two citizens who take the air Close pack'd and smiling in a chaise and one.

f. A one-pound note or a one-dollar bill.

1846 *Illinois State Register* (Springfield) 2 Oct. 2/6 Independent of the older issues, and such as are described in the Detectors, Ones, on the Banks of 'Broome county' and 'Whitestown'.. have made their appearance. **1948** *Savings & Loan News* Mar. 18/2 My billfold had a $10 bill in it, not ten ones. **1966** O. NORTON *School of Liars* iii. 55 'Do you want this in ones, Mrs. Hetherington?' 'In ten-shillingses, dear boy.' **1967** 'A. GILBERT' *Visitor* iii. 45, I counted the notes, which took a ridiculously long time as they were mostly in ones. **1970** M. KENYON *100,000 Welcomes* iii. 18 He counted out seven one-pound notes and a five.. and selected three ones. **1976** J. WAINWRIGHT *Walther P. 38* 24 Drysdale started with five fives, followed by five ones, then he paused.. . he counted out five more singles.

g. One point or position on a scale, order, or the like; esp. in phr. ***go up*** (or ***down***) ***one***, expressing commendation (or disapprobation). *colloq.*

1909 J. R. WARE *Passing Eng.* 142/2 *Go down one*, to be vanquished. *Ibid.* 143/2 *Go up one*, applause. Derived from the school class—the scholar going one nearer the top as he goes up one. **1967** E. LEMARCHAND *Death of Old Girl* v. 59 'I was thinking maybe.. the blood on that made the mark.' 'So was I,' said Pollard. 'Go up one.'

2. a. Joined to the tens (*twenty*, *thirty*, etc.), like the other units, *one* originally always preceded (***one-and-twenty***, ***three hundred one and thirty***, etc.), but now more usually follows (***twenty-one***, etc). So with the ordinals: ***one-and-twentieth***, now more usually *twenty-first*. (See TWENTY, etc.)

c **1000** ÆLFRIC *Exod.* xii. 18 Oþ þone an and twentoȝoþan dæȝ þæs ylcan monþes. *a* **1100** *O.E. Chron.* (Laud MS.) an. 1086 On þam and twentiȝan ȝeare þæs þe Will'm weolde.. Engleland. *c* **1205** LAY. 9541 Heo wuneden inne Wincæstre an and twenti wikene. **1562** HEYWOOD *Epigr.* Y iij b, One and forty men, among one and fiftie, Would flee one and thirtie, to flee one vnthriftie. **1579** FULKE *Heskins' Parl.* 396 The one and thirtieth Chapter endeth the exposition. **1725** DE FOE *Voy. round World* (1840) 314 They were one-and-twenty days in this traverse. **1806** SURR *Winter in Lond.* (ed. 3) I. 136 Edward had attained his one-and-twentieth year. **1843** BETHUNE *Sc. Fireside Stor.* 12 A delicate.. girl, in her twentieth, or one-and-twentieth year.

b. ***one-and-thirty***: an old game of cards apparently similar to, or the same as, bone-ace: cf. quot. 1825. ***one-and-twenty***: a person of that age.

c **1554** *Interl. Youth* in Hazl. *Dodsley* II. 34, I can teach you to play, At the triump and one-and-thirty. **1611–1617** [see BONE-ACE]. **1716** *Gentl. Instructed* (ed. 6) 19 You would have thought this one and twenty came in a direct Line from Hercules, he play'd the Furioso so lively. **1728** VANBR. & CIB. *Prov. Husb.* II. i, You and I, and Sister, forsooth, sometimes, in an Afternoon, may play at One and thirty Bone-Ace, purely. **1765** *Priv. Lett. Ld. Malmesbury* I. 142 You ask me whether I play whist: very often, but oftener at one-and-thirty, which is the fashionable game among the young ladies of this country. *a* **1825** FORBY *Voc. E. Anglia*, One-and-thirty, a game at cards, much resembling Vingt-un.

c. ***one or two*** = a very few, a small number of.

1535 COVERDALE *1 Kings* xvii. 12, I haue gathered up one or two stickes. **1748** RICHARDSON *Clarissa* Wks. 1883 VI. 220 For the sake of better managing one or two executorships. *Mod.* Butterflies are coming out: I have seen one or two to-day.

3. a. Used before collective numerals (*dozen*, *score*, *hundred*, *thousand*, *million*, etc.), and fractions (*half*, *quarter*, *third*, *eighth*, etc., to which *one* is often hyphened), with more precise or definite force than the indef. article *a*, *an* (*a dozen*, *a hundred*, *a half*); and so usually in legal phraseology, and in association with other numbers. (See also the words in question.)

13.. R. GLOUC. (Rolls) App. XX. 546 Me scholde ȝiue him anon On hundred schillinges. *a* **1548** HALL *Chron.*, *Hen. VI* 150 Amountyng to the some of one thousand poundes. **1606** G. W[OODCOCKE] *Hist. Ivstine* XI. 46 In his Army were thirty two thousand footemen, foure thousand and fiue hundred horsemen, and one hundreth, fourescore, and two shippes. **1776** ADAM SMITH *W.N.* I. viii. (1869) I. 71 One-half the chidren born.. die before the age of manhood. **1809–10** COLERIDGE *Friend* (1865) 151 The price of labour.. is fully one-third less. **1876** PREECE & SIVEWRIGHT *Telegraphy* 179 No less weight than one-hundreth.. of the minimum will be reckoned. **1896** *Daily News* 30 Nov. 6/6 There was a keen competition for the three one-hundred guinea cups. *Mod.* (Statutory dating) In the year of Our Lord, One thousand, eight hundred, and ninety-nine.

†b. Formerly prefixed to other numeral expressions. Now *Obs.*

1565 CALFHILL *Answ. Treat. Crosse* (Parker Soc.) 114 When Calleis and Guines, so hardly won,.. was easily in one three days with shame lost. **1611** BIBLE *Dan.* iii. 19 That they should heat the furnace one seuen times more then it was wont to be heat.

4. a. Sometimes put for the ordinal number *first*.

Now chiefly in giving the number of the year or day of the month, or in other cases when the sb. precedes, as in *Isaiah, chapter fifty-one*, *Psalm ninety-one*, *the Æneid, book one*. ***in the year one*** (*humorous*), a long while ago, time out of mind.

1382 WYCLIF *Ezek.* xxxi. 1 In the elleuenthe ȝeer, in the thridde moneth, in oon of the moneth [1388 the firste dai of the moneth]. **1584** R. SCOT *Discov. Witchcr.* XV. xiii. (1886) 348 This psalme.. being the fiftie one psalme. **1611** BIBLE *Gen.* viii. 13 In the sixe hundredth and one yeere, in the first moneth. **1625–6** PURCHAS *Pilgrims* II. 1417 The twentie one day [we departed] from Bullomash. **1754** FOOTE *Knights* I. Wks. 1799 I. 62 A coach of his grandfather's built in the year 1. **1853** MISS MULOCK *Agatha's Husb.* II. v. 173 Fred was a very fascinating young fellow when I was a child—But all that belongs to the year One.

b. ***murder one***: see MURDER *sb.* 7.

5. *absol.* (with the abstract conception of number).

1398 TREVISA *Barth. De P.R.* XIX. cxvi. (1495) 919 One is the rote and moder of nombres, and one is not many. *c* **1440** *Promp. Parv.* 364/1 Oone, *unus*. **1583** BABINGTON *Commandm.* vii. (1637) 68 A thousand to one we forsake the Lord. **1591** SHAKS. *Two Gent.* I. i. 72 Twenty to one then, he is ship'd already. **1660** STANLEY *Hist. Philos.* IX. (1701) 378/2 They make a difference betwixt the Monad and One, concerning the Monad to be that which exists in Intellectuals; One, in numbers. *a* **1700** B. E. *Dict. Cant. Crew, One in Ten*, a Parson. **1705** VANBRUGH *Confed.* v. i, One, two, three, and away! **1719** DE FOE *Crusoe* II. vii, It would be a thousand to one but he would repent his choice. *a* **1902** *Mod.* One from twenty leaves nineteen. The quotient of one divided by nought is infinity. Twelve is to four as three is to one.

b. ***one in*** (a specified number): designating a gradient in which the height increases or decreases by one foot (or other measure) vertically for the specified number of feet, etc., horizontally; also *ellipt.* as *sb.*

1830 M. EDGEWORTH *Let.* 18 Oct. (1971) 419 The inclined plane the rise of which was one in 36. **1869**, etc. [see IN *prep.* 4]. **1910** KIPLING *Divers. Creatures* (1917) 322 It was all of a one in three gradient. **1968** N. TRANTER *Cable from Kabul* iii. 37 Down at the foot of a one-in-three hill, I found myself in some sort of village. **1971** G. HOUSEHOLD *Doom's Caravan* ii. 44 Its original builders had no objection to a slope of one in four. **1976** J. WAINWRIGHT *Bastard* i. 11, I slither and skid the car up the one-in-six.

6. a. Hence, as *sb.* with plur., Unity; a unit; a single thing, or the abstract number denoting a single thing.

1542 RECORDE *Gr. Artes* 117 The fyrste place is the place of vnities or ones, and euery counter set in that lyne betokeneth but one. **1575** LANEHAM *Let.* (1871) 54 Nor [two] it self can well bee coounted a number, but rather a freendly coniunction of too ones. **1594** BLUNDEVIL *Exerc.* I. i. (1636) 2 Number is a collection or summe of many ones or unities added together. **1659** STANLEY *Hist. Philos.* XI. (1701) 448/1 All Singulars are reduced to a One, that is, to their respective Communities.

b. A single person, thing, example, etc.

1840 THACKERAY *Catherine* i, Afterwards, sauntering by ones and twos, came the village maidens. **1889** *Pall Mall G.* 13 Feb. 3/1 Magazines..which are now sold in ones where they used to be sold in hundreds.

c. The symbol or figure (1. I. i.) denoting unity.

Mod. A row of *ones*. A Roman *one*. Your *ones* are too like *sevens*.

d. *colloq.* (now ***number one***) = Oneself, one's own interest. See also NUMBER *sb.* 5 b.

1567 R. EDWARDS *Damon & Pithias* in Hazl. *Dodsley* IV. 16 All my time at school I have not spent vainly, I can help one: is not that a good point of philosophy? **1740** tr. *De Mouhy's Fort. Country-Maid* (1741) II. 288 But my Gentleman..very silently made off, to take care of one. **1830** GALT *Lawrie T.* III. ix. (1849) 113 He had an eye awake to number one. **1849** DARWIN in *Life & Lett.* I. 369, I do not see my way clearly, beyond humbly endeavouring to reform Number one.

II. Emphatic numeral.

7. a. One in contrast to two or more: one and no more, one only; a single.

c **1000** *Ags. Gosp.* Luke xviii. 22 Ða cwæð se hælend an þing þe is wana. *a* **1225** *Ancr. R.* Pref. 23 This an Boc is todealet in eahte lesse Boke. *c* **1386** CHAUCER *Cant. T.* Prol. 304 Noght o word spak he moore than was neede. *c* **1400** *Apol. Loll.* 46 We mani are oo body, & a life þat alle taken part of oo lofe & of oo cuppe. **1482** J. PASTON in *P. Lett.* III. 290 Non oo man a lyve hathe callyd so oft upon yow as I. *a* **1548** HALL *Chron., Rich. III* 26 Bothe houseled with one hoste devided betwene theim. *Ibid., Hen. VIII* 134 Thei set not by the Frenche kyng one bene. **1551** ROBINSON tr. *More's Utop.* I. (1895) 106 The one and onlye waye to the wealthe of a communaltye. **1600** E. BLOUNT tr. *Conestaggio* Apol. A iij b, Tell me if..I have omitted any one point of importance. **1615** W. LAWSON *Country Housew. Gard.* (1626) 2 No one man is sufficient for these things. **1667** MILTON *P.L.* I. 32 And transgress his Will For one restraint, Lords of the World besides. **1818** LADY C. LAMB *Let.* in *Lady Morgan's Autobiog.* (1859) 49 So you did not vouchsafe one word to me,—what, not one? **1888** BRYCE *Amer. Commw.* II. lii. 303 Some one man must be given the power of direction.

b. Strengthened by *but, only, single, sole, alone.*

c **1175** *Lamb. Hom.* 27 Erðon he nefde bute enne deofel nu he haueð sefene. *c* **1386** CHAUCER *Sompn. T.* 143 Now sire, quod she, but o word ere I go; My child is deed. *c* **1450** *Mirour Saluacioun* 1513 Crist was noght temptid onely of o vice bot of thre. **1450–80** tr. *Secreta Secret.* 20 Truste thou neuyr in oon sool ffisiciane. **1483** CAXTON *G. de la Tour* xxiii, He is not so hardy to discouere ne say one onely word. **1579** FENTON *Guicciard.* (1618) 212 A litle rocke which is all of one onely stone. **1596** L. PIOT (Munday) tr. *Silvayn's Orator* 187 If then one alone ingratitude is punishable. **1601** BRETON *Longing Blessed Heart* in Farr *S.P. Eliz.* I. 193 Amidde the ayre one onely phœnix flies. *c* **1618** SIR W. MURE *Misc.* xix. 16 If thou wouchaife bot on smyle. **1761** HUME *Hist. Eng.* III. lx. 297 One person alone of the garrison escaped. **1845** M. PATTISON *Ess.* (1889) I. 22 He had but one voice amongst many. **1865** LUBBOCK *Preh. Times* x. (1878) 329 Only one single unworked flint.

c. Used as a more emphatic substitute for the indefinite article: (*a*) with adjs. in sense 'a very ——', 'an extremely ——'; (*b*) with sbs., esp. *hell* (see HELL *sb.* 4 d, HELLUVA). *colloq.*

1828 *Punch & Judy* I. i. 77 Toby, you're one nasty cross dog: get away with you! **1911** J. LONDON *Let.* 7 Apr. (1966) 343 Let me tell you that you have given me one hell of a time. **1920** [see HELL *sb.* 4 d]. **1925** T. DREISER *Amer. Trag.* (1926) I. xii. 82 He went out in the kitchen and blacked up an' put on a waiter's apron and coat and then comes back and serves us. That's one funny boy. **1934** [see HELLUVA]. **1948** E. POUND *Pisan Cantos* (1949) lxxviii. 66 Steele that is one awful name. **1967** 'T. WELLS' *Dead by Light of Moon* (1968) xi. 111, I wondered what Mai Farmer was doing. She was one striking girl. **1967** [see HELLUVA]. **1972** A. PRICE *Col. Butler's Wolf* xii. 132 The last two, three weeks he was one worried young man. **1973** J. DI MONA *Last Man at Arlington* (1974) II. xvi. 100 'Tell everyone I'm not Cuban,' said Medwick, hoping to get a rise out of the driver. But none came. This was one serious boy. **1976** *Publishers Weekly* 9 Feb. 85 (Advt.), Come spring, this [forthcoming book] is going to be One Hot Number.

8. a. *predicatively.* Single, individual.

a **1300** *Cursor M.* 573 (Cott.) God..es an [*v. rr.* ane, on, oon] and thre. **1382** WYCLIF *Luke* ix. 38 Maistir,..byhold in to my sone, for he is oon aloone to me. **1426** LYDG. *De Guil. Pilgr.* 248/8976 Yiff thow be on, declare to me; Yiff thow be double outher tweyne. *a* **1619** FOTHERBY *Atheom.* II. x. § 3 (1622) 305 If that word may be vsed, he is of all things, the Onest. **1722** WOLLASTON *Relig. Nat.* ix. 189 We know no such thing as a part of matter purely one (or indivisible). **1789** BELSHAM *Ess.* II. xxxvi. 300 The action is neither one, entire, nor great. **1851** ROBERTSON *Serm.* Ser. III. xi. 132 The army is one, and that is the oneness of unity. The soldier is one, but that is the oneness of the unit. **1864** BOWEN *Logic* viii. 229 The Syllogistic process in the mind is really one and undivided.

b. *absol.* or as *sb.*

c **1205** LAY. 1804 Heora nomen ne herdi neuer tellen.. Boten þes anes name, þa heore alre lauerd wes. **1587** GOLDING *De Mornay* iii. 29 The One or Vnitie wherupon all the diuine Vnities are grounded. **1598** GRENEWEY *Tacitus, Ann.* I. iv. (1622) 6 That the Common-wealth was but one body, and therefore to be gouerned by ones onely wisedom. **1744** BERKELEY *Siris* § 343 The Good or One. **1839** BAILEY *Festus* xxvii. (1852) 460 Thus spake the One again: Behold, O Earth!..it is I who gave thee birth.

9. One at least, one at any rate (as distinguished from 'none at all').

1481 CAXTON *Reynard* xxx. (Arb.) 79 Ther ben many of them that for his sake and loue wille auenture lyf and good. I know my self for one. **1638** R. BAKER tr. *Balzac's Lett.* (vol. II) 19 It sufficeth me that I have this one way left me. **1765** FOOTE *Commissary* III. (1782) 54 That's one comfort, however. *c* **1784** NELSON *Let. to Locker* in A. Duncan *Life* (1806) 321, I for one am determined. **1821** KEATS *Isabella* xliii, Sing to it one latest lullaby. **1879** MORLEY *Burke* 140 It is probable, for one thing, that the feelings of the Prince of Wales had more to do with it.

III. In pregnant senses.

10. a. One made up of many components, a united.

c **1000** ÆLFRIC *Hom.* I. 284 Ælc ðæra þreora is God, þeah-hwæðere hi ealle an God. *a* **1225** *Ancr. R.* 26 Ʒe þreo beoð o God. *c* **1385** CHAUCER *L.G.W.* Prol. 296 [They] songen with o vois. *c* **1386** —— *Merch. T.* 91 They moste nedes lyue in vnitee O flessh they been. *c* **1420** *Avow. Arth.* xxxix, Thenne sex ar atte on assente. **1526** TINDALE *Matt.* xix. 5 They twane shalbe won flese. **1568** GRAFTON *Chron.* II. 112 The chiefe Lordes..as it were in a fury cryed with one voyce, By the blood of God. **1725** WATTS *Logic* I. iv. § 1 We join simple ideas to make one complex one. **1849** MACAULAY *Hist. Eng.* vi. II. 16 One cry of grief and rage rose from the whole of Protestant Europe. **1851** [see 8 a]. **1875** JOWETT *Plato* (ed. 2) I. 196 All of them with one voice vehemently assented.

b. *pred.* (esp. = united in marriage).

1590 L. LLOYD *Diall Daies* 91 The victory of this triumphant King did much exceed all their victories being made one. **1709** STEELE *Tatler* No. 25 ¶ 7 We have been both one these two Months. **1820** LANDOR *Heroic Idylls, Thrasymedes & Ennoe* 96 He spake; and on the morrow they were one.

11. One in continuity; the same in all parts, at all times, or in all circumstances; uniformly the same; one and the same.

a **1225** *Ancr. R.* 6 For þi heo is euer on & schal beon, wiðute monglunge & wiðute chaungunge. *c* **1420** *Chron. Vilod.* 458 Bot ever stond styll in won dygre. *a* **1425** *Cursor M.* 1024 (Trin.) In oon elde shal he euer be fast. **1568** GRAFTON *Chron.* II. 155 But the weight of the ounce Troy, ..continued alwayes one. *a* **1592** H. SMITH *Serm.* (ed. Tegg) I. 169 Month after month he is all one. **1656** STANLEY *Hist. Philos.* v. (1701) 162/1 Nothing is one, constant, nor the same, because all things are in continual alteration and fluxion. **1744** BERKELEY *Siris* § 344 God remains for ever one and the same. **1869** M. PATTISON *Serm.* (1885) 188 Existence is one and uniform throughout the cognoscible.

12. One in relation to two or more things or persons; one in substance; identical; the same. ***one with***, forming part of one whole with.

c **1000** ÆLFRIC *Hom.* I. 284 Hi ealle habbað an ȝecynd, and ane godcundnysse, and ane edwiste [etc.]. *c* **1175** *Lamb. Hom.* 91 Hi alle hefden ane heorte and ane sawle. *a* **1225** *Ancr. R.* 6 Alle ne muwe nout holden one riwle. **1382** WYCLIF *Eph.* iv. 5 O Lord, o feith, o baptym, o God and fadir of alle. *a* **1425** *Cursor M.* 4246 (Trin.) Putifar..held Ioseph in menskeful lore þei her layes oon not wore. **1552** *Bk. Com. Prayer* Communion, We be one with Christ, & Christ with vs. **1632** LITHGOW *Trav.* VIII. 353 Their breaches and stockings being all one. **1697** DRYDEN *Virg. Georg.* IV. 226 Beneath one Law they live, And with one Common Stock their Traffick drive. **1799** *Med. Jrnl.* I. 170 The different earths..are modifications of one and the same simple substance, the basis of earth. **1821** SHELLEY *Adonais* xlii, He is made one with Nature. *a* **1848** R. W. HAMILTON *Rew. & Punishm.* vii. (1853) 323 The author of nature and Christianity is one.

13. a. One in kind; the same in quality or nature.

Formerly used also with *pl. sb.*

a **1300** *Cursor M.* 18845 (Cott.) Berd and hefd of a [*v. rr.* an, on] heu ware. **1377** LANGL. *P. Pl.* B. III. 237 Tho þat entren of o colour, And of on wille. *c* **1386** CHAUCER *Knt.'s T.* 154 Bothe in oon Armes wroght ful richely. *a* **1450** *Knt. de la Tour* (1868) 161 It berithe no force to do ille as for to do welle, alle passithe and vnder one thanke. **1526** TINDALE *2 Cor.* xiii. 11 Be of one mynde. **1549** LATIMER *5th Serm. bef. Edw. VI* (Arb.) 149 They are all one apples I warrante you Syr. **1868** LOCKYER *Elem. Astron.* iii. (1879) 56 All the planets revolve round the sun in one direction.

b. *predicatively.* The same; the same thing. Often strengthened by *all*: see ALL C. 5.

c **1380** WYCLIF *Serm.* Sel. Wks. I. 26 It is al oon to seie þat þese goodis ben þus sacrid. *c* **1420** *Pallad. on Husb.* IX. 204 This Aust and May in houris lengthe are oon. *c* **1430** *Pilgr. Lyf Manhode* I. xlix. (1869) 29 For j seyd not in alle places, but in alle times; and þat is not oon. **1584** R. SCOT *Discov. Witchcr.* v. ix. (1886) 87 It [witchcraft] is all one with rebellion. **1631** R. BOLTON *Comf. Affl. Consc.* vi. (1635) 36 All is One to Him, to make an Angell, or an Ant. *c* **1670** HOBBES *Dial. Comm. Laws* 50 Which is also one as if he were Judge himself. **1816** J. WILSON *City of Plague* I. iv. 371 All names are one to me. **1861** DASENT *Story Burnt Njal* II. 402 Silver by tale and silver by weight was all one.

14. One in mind, feeling, intention, or bearing; in unison, harmonious; at one.

c **1330** R. BRUNNE *Chron.* (1810) 24 At haly kirke's fayth alle on were boþe. *a* **1548** HALL *Chron., Edw. IV* 212 Rimes and poyses, whiche purported the Frenche kyng and the erle of Warwicke wer al one. **1715–20** POPE *Odyss.* III. 155 Thy sire and I were one; nor varied aught In public sentence or in private thought. **1802** CAMPBELL *Lochiel's Warning* 42 Their swords are a thousand, their bosoms are one! **1804** PITT in *G. Rose's Diaries* (1860) II. 97 Addington and I are one again. **1850** TENNYSON *In Mem.* cxxii, In all her motion one with law.

IV. In a particularizing or partitive sense.

15. One from amongst others, one of a number or of several; a particular, an individual. **a.** *attrib.*

one day, on a particular day in the past; on some undefined day in the future; see DAY 7 b.

892 *O.E. Chron.*, Ðær stent lang leoma of, hwilum on ane healfe, hwilum on ælce healfe. *a* **1300** *Cursor M.* 10180 In thrin his godes did he dele, þat godd had lent him of his lane; To pour part þan gaf he ane. *c* **1386** CHAUCER *Frankl. T.* 204 Oon of the beste farynge man on lyue. **1387** TREVISA *Higden* (Rolls) I. 83 In oo contray of Ynde. *c* **1425** *Seven Sag.* (P.) 2807 As he rode in the londe O day a toun he fande. **1483** CAXTON *G. de la Tour* K iij, [He] sayd to his moder that one tyme shold come. *c* **1489** —— *Sonnes of Aymon* x. 272 But of all Fraunce I am one of the best & truest Knyght that be in it. *a* **1548** HALL *Chron., Edw. IV* 233 One day there entered into the towne..ix M. Englishmen. **1588** J. UDALL *Diotrephes* (Arb.) 5, I hope to see them one day all put downe. **1594** T. B. *La Primaud. Fr. Acad.* II. 230 One-while we weep, and sodainly we laugh againe. **1692** E. WALKER *Epictetus' Mor.* xxxiv, One while your Hand you'll try In Wrestling. **1749** 'R. GOADBY' *Carew* (ed. 2) 214 Being feasting one Night with several of his Subjects. **1785** BURNS *Addr. to Deil* vii, Ae dreary, windy, winter night. **1856** FROUDE *Hist. Eng.* (1858) I. i. 17 Such is one aspect of these old arrangements.

b. absolutely with *of*; formerly with gen. pl., as in *úre án*, one of us; rarely without either, as in ***to make one***, to form one of a company. Also ***one of those***: a homosexual; ***one of us***: a member of our group; *spec.* (*a*) a harlot (*obs.*); (*b*) a homosexual. *colloq.*; ***one of these days***: see DAY *sb.* 7 b; ***one of those days***: see DAY *sb.* 7 b.

875 *O.E. Chron.*, Ælfred cyning..hiera an ȝefeng. *c* **1000** *Ags. Gosp.* Luke xv. 4 ȝif he for-lyst an of þam. *c* **1175** *Lamb. Hom.* 21 þah ure an heofde idon eower alre sunne. *c* **1200** *Trin. Coll. Hom.* 219 On of þo was ysaie þe prophete. *a* **1300** *Cursor M.* 19509 Philip, þat was o dekens an, þe neiest fra steuen was slan. **1340** *Ayenb.* 129 Be enne of his angles. **1485** *Nottingham Rec.* III. 233 John Wylliamson, oon of the Chaumberleyns. **1588** PARKE tr. *Mendoza's Hist. China* 399 Euerie one of them are bound to giue the king to eate. **1598** SHAKS. *Merry W.* II. iii. 48 If I see a sword out, my finger itches to make one. **1653** HOLCROFT *Procopius* II. 40 He killed on of their best men, and routed the rest. **1686** tr. *Agiatis or Civ. Wars Lacedemonians* 26 One of his Friends came and proposed to him, to make one at a Feast. **1785** GROSE *Dict. Vulgar T., One of us*, one of my cousins, a woman of the town, a harlot. **1795** *Gentl. Mag.* July 581/2 Irony..is one of those edged tools which require skilful handling. **1855** MACAULAY *Hist. Eng.* xii. III. 204 One of the wealthiest Roman Catholics in the kingdom. **1915** CONRAD *Victory* I. ii. 9 Morrison was 'one of us'. He was owner and master of the *Capricorn*, trading brig, and was understood to be doing well with her. **1933** [see NANCY[2]]. **1956** [see CAMP *a.* and *sb.*[5]]. **1961** PARTRIDGE *Dict. Slang* Suppl. 1207/1 *One of us, he's*, he is a homosexual. **1968** J. R. ACKERLEY *My Father & Myself* xvi. 185, I divined that he was homosexual, or as we put it, 'one of us'. **1976** *Times* 27 May 16/4 It would go a long way towards helping..to understand..if others would stop saying 'New Commonwealth' when they mean something like 'coffee-coloured' and 'Old Commonwealth' when they mean..'One of us'. **1977** *Gay News* 24 Mar. 18/2 Her husband..probably fits none of the stereotypes whereby she would normally identify 'one of those'.

c. ***a one***: a person who is remarkable, extraordinary, outrageous, impudent, etc.; esp. in phr. ***you are a one***; (*a*) ***one for***: a person who likes, admires, practises, supports, etc. (something) to an outstanding degree; a devotee, champion, or admirer of (something); (*a*) ***one to***: the sort of person who would (do a particular thing). *colloq.*

1880 C. M. YONGE *Bye-Words* 303 Tittering, and now and then, 'O Miss Annie, don't, pray!' 'O Miss Annie, you are a one!' **1888** —— *Our New Mistress* i. 3 Her daughters..all married, except Lady Mary, who was always such a one for schools and poor people. **1894** S. BARING-GOULD *Queen of Love* II. vi. 59, I am not one to fly in the face of Providence. **1906** E. DYSON *Fact'ry 'Ands* iii. 29 'Oh, Mr. Ellis, you are a one!' she said. **1927**, etc. [see GREAT *a.* 16 a]. **1932** N. ROYDE-SMITH *Incredible Tale* 91 She was a one for football. **1934** N. MARSH *Man lay Dead* vii. 126 'The left-hand print on the stair knob is Mr. Wilde's,' said Bailey. 'Is it?' answered Alleyn without enthusiasm. 'Aren't you a one?' **1935** G. HEYER *Death in Stocks* iii. 22 Constable Dickenson had warned the Inspector that she was not one to talk. **1948** 'G. ORWELL' *Let.* 10 July in *Coll. Ess.* (1968) IV. 438 Farm life seems to suit him, though I am pretty sure he is one for machines rather than animals. **1966** J. B. PRIESTLEY *Salt is Leaving* viii. 96 You're a bit of a one, aren't you, Dr Salt? **1973** J. THOMSON *Death Cap* vi. 86 He's never been one for the women. I think he's a bit afraid of them.

16. a. In antithesis to *one* in the sense of 'another'.

c **1000** *Ags. Gosp.* Matt. xvii. 4 þreo eardung-stowa, þe ane, moyse ane & helie ane. *c* **1330** *Arth. & Merl.* 2670 Thi child worth the noblest man Of al this world an for an. *c* **1585** R. BROWNE *Answ. Cartwright* 5 All Master Cartwrights arguments falleth from one to one, till it come to nothing at all. **1599** SHAKS. *Much Ado* II. iii. 66 One foote in sea, and one on shore. **1628** HOBBES *Thucyd.* (1822) 25 The Corcyreans.. were divided into three commands under the three commanders one under one. *c* **1700** ADDISON *To the King* 28 One Age the Hero, one the Poet breeds. **1736** GRAY *Statius* i. 12 Of Pisa one, and one from Ephyre.

b. Phrase. **one by one** (also *one after one*), formerly *one and one, by one and one*: = One after another, one at a time, singly.

a **1000** *Sal. & Sat.* 385 Ac sceal on ʒebyrd faran an æfter anum. *c* **1000** *Sax. Leechd.* I. 76 Ete.. ænne and ænne. *c* **1230** *Hali Meid.* 25 Mon.. nimeð an after an. *c* **1250** *Gen. & Ex.* 2323 He gan hem ransaken on and on. **1398** TREVISA *Barth. De P.R.* XVIII. ix. (MS. Bodl.) lf. 250/2 Nowȝt.. alle atte ones but one and one. *c* **1460** *Towneley Myst.* xxvii. 325 The tayles that he can till vs shaw, By oone and oon. *a* **1548** HALL *Chron., Hen. VIII* 140, I will examyne you one by one my self. **1575–85** ABP. SANDYS *Serm.* (Parker Soc.) 206 Reckon them up by one and one. **1607** MARKHAM *Caval.* I. (1617) 78 So must you vse the rest one after one. **1723** CHAMBERS tr. *Le Clerc's Treat. Archit.* I. 34 The Columns must only stand one by one. **1742** YOUNG *Nt. Th.* VIII. 131 Its little Joys go out by One and One. **1820** KEATS *St. Agnes* xli, By one, and one, the bolts full easy slide. **1845** WORDSW. *Love lies bleeding* 32 One after one submitting to their doom. **1865** KINGSLEY *Hereward* v, She pledged one by one each of the guests.

17. a. In antithesis to ANOTHER, OTHER, *others*: with or without *sb.* following. ***one and another***, more than one, two or more in succession.

a **1000** *Cædmon's Satan* 26 An æfter oðrum in þæt atole scref. *c* **1000** [see 18]. *a* **1300** *Cursor M.* 2409 Sai þou for-þi til an and oþer [*Trin.* to oone & oþer] þou art my sister and i þi broþer. *c* **1315** SHOREHAM I. 633 (p. 24) Wanne þer hys o þyng yked, An oþer to onder-stonde. *c* **1380** WYCLIF *Serm.* Sel. Wks. I. 28 Oon elde axiþ o manere of lyvynge and anoþir anoþir. **1484** CAXTON *Fables of Æsop* IV. vi, The bocher took him all one after another. **1513** MORE *Rich. III* (1821) 46 Knoweth anye manne anye place wherein it is lawfull one manne to dooe another wrong? **1674** N. FAIRFAX *Bulk & Selv.* 100 All stirrings one and other are nothing but gobyes or shiftings of bodies. **1711** ADDISON *Spect.* No. 34 ¶7 Taken away from me, by one or other of the Club. **1749** FIELDING *Tom Jones* VII. vii, What's one man's meat is another man's poison. **1871** BESANT & RICE *Ready Money Mortiboy* i, If one catches another's eye. *Mod.* I have heard it from one and another during the week.

b. ***one with another***: †(*a*) (also ***one and another***), Together (*obs.* or *arch.*). (*b*) One taken with another so as to deduce an average; on the average.

1429 *Rolls of Parlt.* IV. 360/1 Oone yere with anothyr. **1496** *Naval Acc. Hen. VII* (1896) 183 Ij mastes.. price oon with another—ix[li]. **1535** COVERDALE *Ps.* xlviii. [xlix.] 2 Hye & lowe, riche & poore, one with another. *c* **1550** *Decay of Eng. by Shepe* (E.E.T.S.) 101 For euery towne and vyllage, —take them one with an other throughout all,—there is one plowe decayed. **1568** GRAFTON *Chron.* II. 278 When all the Scottes were assembled, they were one and other fiftie thousand fightyng men. **1613** JACKSON *Creed* I. xxii. §4 Of which the Heathen, one and other, were altogether ignorant. **1652** EARL MONM. tr. *Bentivoglio's Hist. Relat.* 15 They contribute one year with another eight millions of Florins, for the service of their generall union. *a* **1687** PETTY *Pol. Arith.* (1690) 76 The same.. Persons do spend one with another about 18[d] per diem. *a* **1774** GOLDSM. *Surv. Exp. Philos.* (1776) II. 74 The mercury.. in the tube will sink down to about twenty-nine inches and an half, one time with another. **1809** R. LANGFORD *Introd. Trade* 125, 35 bales of silk, weighing one with another 2 cwt. 3 qr. 19 lb.

c. ***one thing***: something acceptable or satisfactory, contrasted with ***another*** (***thing***) that is unacceptable or unsatisfactory.

a **1678** H. SCOUGAL *Life of God* (1726) 392, I do not condemn all chearfulness and freedom, nor the innocent exercises of wit: but it is one thing to make use of these now and then when they come in our way, and another to search and haunt after them. **1735** BERKELEY *Defence Free-Thinking in Math.* xxxvii. 44 It is one thing when a Doctrine is placed in various lights: and another, when the principles and notions are shifted. **1828** SCOTT *Chron. Canongate* 2nd Ser. I. viii. 244 It is one thing to employ the revenues of the Church.. in the suitable and dutiful reception of your royal Majesty, and another to have it wrenched from us by the hands of rude and violent men. **1904** H. JAMES *Golden Bowl* (1905) v. 66 It was one thing to have met the girl casually at Mrs. Assingham's and another to arrange with her thus for a morning practically as private as their old mornings in Rome and practically not less intimate.

d. Ellipt. for 'one or the other'. *U.S. dial.*

1895 *Dialect Notes* I. 373 *One* seems to be superfluous or else 'or the other' is omitted. 'I will see you or send word, one.' **1926** E. M. ROBERTS *Time of Man* (1927) vii. 257, I met a parcel of travelers that owned a bear could read or tell fortunes—one, I forget which. *Ibid.* viii. 298 It was the road overseer's fault.., or the magistrate's, one. **1937** *Scribner's Mag.* Apr. 22/2 He's making it [*sc.* liquor] on my farm or your farm, one. **1938** M. K. RAWLINGS *Yearling* xv. 169 Now do things go wrong again, you or Buck, one, ride back for me. So long.

18. a. Of two things, now usually, **the one... the other** (rarely in poetry without *the*). ***the one and the other*** = both (= F. *l'un et l'autre*).

[OE. had only *án.. óþer*, but the article is found prefixed bef. 1200, of which the neuter *þæt án.. þæt óþer*, retaining the final *-t* in combination, became the reg. ME. for all genders, as *þat* or *þet an* (*one*).. *þat* or *þet oþer*, commonly divided *the tan* (*ta, tone, to*).. *the tother*, still preserved dialectally, either in full or as *tone* (*tane*).. *tother*. In course of the 16th c. *the one.. the other*, had become the literary form. *The one* (*thet o, thet on*) = one of the two, L. *alter*, is also used when *the other* is not expressed. See also TONE, TOTHER.]

[*c* **1000** *Ags. Gosp.* Luke xvii. 36 Tweȝen beoð æt æcere: án bið ȝenumen, óþer bið læfed.] *c* **1175** *Lamb. Hom.* 81 þe an is aquenched.. and þe oðer is aquenched al buten a gnast. *c* **1205** LAY. 3881 þe an sloh þene oðren [*c* **1275** Ac þe on sloh þan oþer]. **1297** R. GLOUC. (Rolls) 92 Muchedel of engelond þe on half al bi weste. *a* **1300** *Cursor M.* 3928 On þe ta [*v. rr.* þat a, þe to] side o flum jordan. **1340** *Ayenb.* 119 þe on ine þe on and þe oþer ine þe oþer. **1387** TREVISA *Higden* (Rolls) VII. 101 On þe to side and þe oþer. **1388** WYCLIF *Luke* xvii. 35 The toon shal be takun, and the tother left. **1535** COVERDALE *Prov.* xxx. 15 Y[e] one is called, fetch hither: the other bringe hither. **1594** HOOKER *Eccl. Pol.* III. viii. §10 Unless God's miracles had strengthened both the one and the other's doctrine. **1599** PORTER *Angry Wom. Abingd.* in Hazl. *Dodsley* VII. 378, I could please tone, But it is hard when there is two to one. **1622** MABBE tr. *Aleman's Guzman d'Alf.* I. 94 Reasonable men, both t'one and t'other. **1697** DRYDEN *Virg. Georg.* IV. 138 One Monarch wears an honest open Face;.. That other looks like Nature in Disgrace. **1742** RICHARDSON *Pamela* III. 193 A little awkward Piece of One-and-t'other. *a* **1774** GOLDSM. *Hist. Greece* I. 386 Both the one and the other of us equally injure justice and religion. **1816** SCOTT *Antiq.* xxvii, My lord cares as little about the tane as the tother.

b. When *the one* and *the other* refer severally to two things previously named, they are by some taken as equivalent to *the former* and *the latter*, by others as = *the latter* and *the former*.

The first of these appears to be the earlier and natural use; it is also that observed in Fr. and Ger.: see G. Duvivier *Gramm. des Gramm.* ed. 1842, I. 410; Grimm s.v. *Ander* 308. The second is probably suggested by the Lat. use of *hic* and *ille*, or Eng. *this* and *that*.

c **1320** *Cast. Loue* 631 A child.. þat þreo ffeet and þreo honden beere, And anoþer.. þat hedde ffoot or Hond forlore .. þe on hedde kuynde ouer meþ And þat oþer to luyte. **1460** *Bk. Quintessence* 9 þe maistrie of departynge of gold fro siluir.. Whanne ȝe wole drawe þe toon fro þat oþir. **1529** MORE *Dyaloge* III. i. Wks. 206. **1549** LATIMER *4th Serm. bef. Edw. VI* (Arb.) 120 The fyrste manne.. denied the matter vtterly. The seconde felowe.. acknoweleged the fault.. The one denyed the matter, and the tother confessed it. **1594** HOOKER *Eccl. Pol.* III. viii. §13 In the presence of Festus a Roman, and of King Agrippa a Jew, St. Paul omitting the one, who neither knew the Jews' religion nor the books.. speaketh unto the other of things foreshewed by Moses and the Prophets. **1599** SHAKS. *Pass. Pilgr.* 106 If music and sweet poetry agree.. Then must the love be great 'twixt thee and me, Because thou lovest the one, and I the other. **1625** BACON *Ess., Building* (Arb.) 549 A Side for the Banquet.. and a Side for the Houshold; The One for Feasts and Triumphs, the Other for Dwelling. **1668** H. MORE *Div. Dial.* II. xx. (1713) 151 Betwixt the Isopleuron and Scalenum, not so ordinate a Figure as the one, nor so inordinate as the other. **1690** LOCKE *Hum. Underst.* III. viii. §1 (R.) Our simple ideas have all abstract as well as concrete names; the one whereof is a substantive, the other an adjective, as whiteness, white. **1746** W. HORSLEY *Fool* (1748) II. 101. **1771** GOLDSM. *Hist. Eng.* I. 349 The death of John and the abdication of Lewis.. The one was brought about by accident, and the other by the prudence.. of the earl of Pembroke.

1573 L. LLOYD *Marrow of Hist.* (1653) 247 Sampson and Hercules.. the one prostrated his Club at Deianiræes foot, the other committed his strength to the beauty of Delilah. **1606** G. W[OODCOCKE] *Hist. Ivstine* II. 6 The women were accounted nothing inferior to the men. For as the one founded the Empires of the Persians and Bactrians, so the other errected the souerainty of the Amazons. **1613** PURCHAS *Pilgrimage* (1614) 695. **1685** tr. *Gracian's Courtiers Oracle* ccviii. (1694) 181 Some die because they feel, and others live because they feel not. So that the one are fools because they die not of feeling, and the others because they die of it. **1790** BURKE *Fr. Rev.* 117 The nobility and the clergy, the one by profession, the other by patronage, kept learning in existence. **1886** FAIRBAIRN *City of God* IV. iii. 356 Where the exchange and the cathedral stand together, the one for admiration, the other for business.

19. *Reciprocally*, of two or more: **one another** (formerly, of two, **one... other**, and ***the one... the other***), *one* being grammatical subject, and *another* object: they met *one another*, they spoke ***one to another***, now usually ***to one another*** (in 16–17th c. also ***to one the other***), in which the grammatical relation is lost sight of, and ***one another*** becomes a kind of reflexive pron., having like these, the object. and possess. (***one another's***), but no nominative case. (Cf. *each other*, EACH 5.)

1340 *Ayenb.* 115 We ssolle ech louye oþer, and naȝt hatie, ne harmi mid wrong on þe oþer. *a* **1450** MYRC 186 These schule neuer on wedde other. *c* **1450** *Merlin* vii. 113 Begonne for to iape oon to another. **1483** CAXTON *G. de la Tour* D viij, That they may be enamoured one of other. **1506** in *Mem. Hen. VII* (Rolls) 286 So they intersaluted the one the other and departed. **1526** TINDALE *John* xiii. 35 Yf ye shall haue loue won to another. **1548** FORREST *Pleas. Poesye* xviii. 54 b, Wone then labored another touerthrowe. **1587** GOLDING *De Mornay* xiv. 203 Without anoying the one the other. **1597** J. KING *On Jonas* (1618) 182 We should spare one the others life. **1617** MORYSON *Itin.* II. 107 Neither.. can we.. often heare one from another. **1632** LITHGOW *Trav.* v. 204 We oft fell one ouer another. **1660** BARROW *Euclid* I. Ax. 8 Things which agree together, are equal one to the other. **1745** P. THOMAS *Jrnl. Anson's Voy.* 40 They are no more one like another than an Apple is like an Oyster.

1526 TINDALE *Rom.* xii. 5 Se we beynge many are one body in Christ: and every man.. one anothers members. *Ibid.* xiii. 8 Owe no thinge to eny man; but to love one another [WYCLIF, loue to gidre]. **1590** LODGE *Rosalind* (Cassell) 154 They strained one another's hand. **1598** GRENEWEY *Tacitus, Germania* i. (1622) 258 By mutual fear of one the other. **1652** FRENCH *Yorksh. Spa* ii. 6 Elements.. mutually transmutable into one the other. **1657** R. LIGON *Barbadoes* (1673) 68 The Horses.. struck at one another. **1675** HOBBES *Odyss.* (1677) 100 The horrid winds.. toss'd me into one anothers hand. **1698** WANLEY in *Lett. Lit. Men* (Camden) 257 We never saw one another before. **1711** ADDISON *Spect.* No. 50 ¶4 These two were great Enemies to one another. **1711** BUDGELL *Ibid.* No. 161 ¶3 Cudgel-Players, who were breaking one another's Heads. **1885** *Act 48 & 49 Vict.* c. 54 §14 Churches.. within four miles of one another.

V. *Indefinite pronoun* (with genitive *one's*).

20. A person or being whose identity is left undefined; some one, a certain one, an individual, a person (L. *quidam*). A following pronoun referring to *one* is in the 3rd pers. sing., as 'One showed himself to his townsmen, who derided him'.

In this sense *one* has the stress of an independent word, which distinguishes it from the next.

†**a.** *simply* = A person; some one. *arch.* or *Obs.*

1297 R. GLOUC. (Rolls) 5864 As me him drinke tok, on was prest ynou, & þoru is wombe smot a knif. **1382** WYCLIF *John* xviii. 39 It is a custom to ȝou that I delyuer oon to ȝou in pask. *c* **1400** *Destr. Troy* 8590 'Achilles þe choise kyng', oon chaunsit to say. *c* **1425** LYDG. *Assembly of Gods* 542 Oon to Pluto roode, And told hym how Eolus was in hys daungere. *a* **1548** HALL *Chron., Rich. III* 26 Then one brought hym a cup with wine. **1607** TOPSELL *Four-f. Beasts* (1658) 145 A mad dog had suddenly tore in pieces a garment about ones body. *a* **1649** WINTHROP *New Eng.* (1853) I. 210 This month one went by land to Connecticut, and returned safe. **1759** R. BROWN *Compl. Farmer* 118 One in the Hundreds of Essex made a great improvement.

b. Defined by a sb. in apposition.

1297 R. GLOUC. (Rolls) 197 þe castel of caryl held on willam louel. **1416** *Plumpton Corr.* p. xlv, An John of Lawe, chapman, sold unto Richard Clerk [etc.]. **1484** *Surtees Misc.* (1888) 42 Ye iij[de] daye of Decembre, came oon Thomas Watson. **1521** FISHER *Serm. agst. Luther* Wks. (1876) 312 Oon Martyn luther a frere. **1526** TINDALE *Acts* xxv. 19 Certayne questions.. off their awne supersticion, and of one Iesus which was ded [**1388** WYCLIF, of oon Iesu deed], whom Paul affirmed to be alive. **1692** WASHINGTON tr. *Milton's Def. Pop.* Wks. 1738 I. 500 After his death they rebell'd again, and created one Tachus King. **1772** H. WALPOLE *Last Jrnls.* (1859) I. 2 Wilkes published an answer to one Stephens and others, who had attacked him. **1885** G. DENMAN in *Law Times Rep.* LIII. 468/2 He died in 1859, leaving the property in question to one Ann Duncan.

c. Defined by a clause or phrase. (When referring to God, written ***One***.)

1340 HAMPOLE *Pr. Consc.* 4085 Some clerkes says þat an sal come þat sal hald þe empire of Rome. *c* **1384** CHAUCER *H. Fame* II. 54 Ryght in the same vois and stevene That vseth oon I koude nevene. **1447** BOKENHAM *Seyntys* Introd. (Roxb.) 6 The.. besy preyere Of oon whom I love wyth herte entere. **1530** PALSGR. 249/2 One that spytteth moche, *crachart*. *Ibid.*, One of affinite, *affin*. **1537** CRANMER *Let. to Cromwell* in *Misc. Writ.* (Parker Soc.) II. 336 One named Dale (whom also I knew in Cambridge). *a* **1548** HALL *Chron., Edw. IV* 210 b, One to whome the common welthe was much beholden. **1560** DAUS tr. *Sleidane's Comm.* 11 b, It semeth better, to create one of our owne nation that is fit for it. **1604** SHAKS. *Oth.* V. ii. 344 One that lou'd not wisely, but too well. **1654–66** EARL ORRERY *Parthen.* (1676) 164, I will accompany my ruine with ones, whose loss you will deplore. **1741–2** GRAY *Agrip.* 88 One Who had such liberal power to give. **1825** SCOTT *Betrothed* iii, The first time that I have heard one with a beard.. avouch himself a coward. **1833** TENNYSON *May Queen* Concl. v, Now, tho' my lamp was lighted late, there's One will let me in. **1836** J. ANSTICE *Hymn*, '*O Lord, how happy should we be*' i, And feel at heart that One above,.. Is working for the best. **1871** MORLEY *Carlyle* in *Crit. Misc.* Ser. I. (1878) 198 Mr. Carlyle is as one who does not hear the question.

21. Any one of everybody; any one whatever; including (and in later language often specially meaning) the speaker himself; 'you, or I, or any one'; a person, a man; we, you, people, they (= OE. *man*, ME. *me*, G. *man*, F. *on*). Poss. *one's*, obj. *one*, reflexively ONESELF (formerly ***one's self***); but for these the third person pronouns *his, him, himself* were formerly usual, and are still sometimes used; thus, 'If one showed oneself (himself) to one's (his) townsmen, they would know one.' (The pl. prons. *their, them, themselves*, were formerly in general use on account of their indefiniteness of gender, but this is now considered ungrammatical.) In this sense *one* is quite toneless (wən), proclitic or enclitic.

1477 EARL RIVERS (Caxton) *Dictes* 57 He herde a man say that one was surer in keping his tunge, than in moche speking, for in moche langage one may lightly erre. **1530** PALSGR. 586/1, I holde, as a sycknesse holdeth one. **1587** GOLDING *De Mornay* iv. 44 It is one thing to change ones self, and another thing to will that there should be a change. **1592** SHAKS. *Rom. & Jul.* I. iv. 49 Why, may one aske? **1607** HIERON *Wks.* I. 156 When on climeth a high tower or hill, the higher he doth mount, the lesse doth euery thing appeare which is below him. **1613** PURCHAS *Pilgrimage* (1614) 748 Their wings are no bigger than halfe ones hand. *a* **1648** SIR K. DIGBY *Priv. Mem.* (1827) 239 To whom one giveth love, one giveth also their will and their whole self. *Ibid.* 255 Hereby one may take to themselves a lesson. **1650** EARL MONM. tr. *Senault's Man bec. Guilty* 355 If one propose any other end unto himself. **1652** J. WRIGHT tr. *Camus' Nat. Paradox* III. 60 At the first falling one's sure to break his neck. **1693** EVELYN *De la Quint. Compl. Gard.* II. 38, I break them off immediately, which is done with ease.. in drawing them towards one. **1794** PALEY *Evid.* (1825) II. 278 It is not what one would have expected. **1834** L. RITCHIE *Wand. by Seine* 192 One's brothers and sisters are a part of one's self.

1865 M. ARNOLD *Ess. Crit.* Pref. 9 One cannot be always studying one's works. **1886** W. W. STORY *Fiammetta* 31 One must do what his own nature prescribes. **1956** R. HENRIQUES *Red over Green* iii. 60 He meant nothing... One can't even remember his face. **1959** E. H. CLEMENTS *High Tension* ii. 19 'Do you often have your fan-mail in person?'..'Not often. One isn't in the telephone book'.

VI. Pronominal or substantival form of *a*, *an*. (With pl. *ones*.)

22. An absolute form of *a*, to avoid repetition of a sb.: A person or thing of the kind already mentioned; as 'I lose a neighbour and you gain one', 'He rents a house, but I own one'.

Formerly, *one* at the end of a clause or sentence was pleonastic or emphatic.

[**1297** R. GLOUC. (Rolls) 405 A wonder maister he was on. *c* **1330** R. BRUNNE *Chron.* (1810) 24 A gode Clerk was he one. *c* **1386** CHAUCER *Knt.'s T.* 956 For in my tyme a seruant was I oon.] *c* **1440** *York Myst.* xxvii. 170 Loke þat ȝe haue swerdis ilkone, And whoso haues non ȝou by-twene, Shall selle his cote and bye hym one. [*c* **1440** *Ipomydon* 872 A sory woman was she one.] **1611** BIBLE *Rom.* ii. 28 For he is not a Iew which is one outwardly;..But he is a Iew which is one inwardly. **1863** FR. A. KEMBLE *Resid. in Georgia* 16 The latter subject is..one sufficiently interesting in itself. *a* **1902** *Mod.* I have forgotten an umbrella, and shall be sure to want one; I think I must buy one. You need not; I can lend you one for the time.

23. Added after demonstrative and pronominal adjs., as *the*, *this*, *that*, *yon*; *any*, *each*, *every*, *many* (*a*), *other*, *such* (*a*), *what* (*a*), *what kind of* (*a*), *which*, and (in certain phrases) after *a*; also after ordinary adjs. preceded by any of these or (in plural) alone; in the sense of A thing or person, pl. things or persons, of the kind in question.

The addition of *one* or *ones* often serves as a definition of number: cf. 'Which do you choose?' with 'Which one do you choose?' 'Which ones do you choose?'; 'the good one, the good ones' = F. *le bon*, *les bons*. After *a* or *the*, *one* has weak stress; after the other words, it is enclitic ('ðɪswʌn, 'ðætwʌn, ə'gʊdwʌn, ðɪ 'iːv(ə)lwʌn). As this use began before *one* took the initial *w*, the latter is in dialect or colloquial speech often omitted, *a good 'un*, *big 'uns*, etc.

971 *Blickl. Hom.* 127 Æt æȝhwylcum anum þara hongaþ leohtfæt. *c* **1225** Euerichon [see EVERY 10 b]. *c* **1250** Euerilc on [ibid.]. **13..** *Seuyn Sages* (W.) 3035 The knight gat masons many ane. *c* **1430** *Syr Tryam.* 1449 Lordus come, as they hett, Many oon stowte and gay. **1463** *Bury Wills* (Camden) 41 To Will[a]m Sennowe oon of my short gownys, a good oon wiche as is convenient for hym. **1587** GOLDING *De Mornay* ix. 119 Let vs see what maner a ones they be. **1598** B. JONSON *Ev. Man in Hum.* III. ii, Ne'er a one to be found. **1605** SHAKS. *Macb.* III. iv. 131 There's not a one of them but in his house I keepe a Seruant Feed. **1640** LD. DIGBY in Rushw. *Hist. Coll.* III. (1692) I. 146 The concentring of all the Royal Lines in his Person, as undisputable as any Mathematical ones in Euclid. **1665** BOYLE *Occas. Refl.* Disc. IV. iv. (1848) 68 The Author aims at good things, though he does not yet perform great ones. **1736** BUTLER *Anal.* II. viii. 399 The three angles of a triangle are equal to two right ones. **1741** WATTS *Improv. Mind* I. v. §7 There is never a one of them. *a* **1864** TENNYSON *Poet's Song* 14 The nightingale thought, 'I have sung many songs, But never a one so gay.' **1868** FREEMAN *Norm. Conq.* II. App. 604 There is no reason to think that the pilgrimage was other than a self-imposed one. **1875** MAINE *Hist. Inst.* xii. 342 The examination of new materials and the re-examination of old ones. *a* **1902** *Mod.* The ones you mention. The one in the glass. That one on the table. This one will do.

b. *spec.* A story or anecdote; a joke; a lie. *colloq.*

1813, etc. [see GOOD *a.* 1 g]. **1925** WODEHOUSE *Carry On, Jeeves!* x. 254 Story? Story?..I wonder if you've heard the one about the stockbroker and the chorus-girl? **1926** D. L. SAYERS *Clouds of Witness* xiii. 240 Mr. Parker endured five stories with commendable patience, and then suddenly broke down. 'Hurray!' said Wimsey... 'I'll spare you the really outrageous one about the young housewife and the traveller in bicycle-pumps.' **1931** J. BETJEMAN *Mount Zion* 22 Each learning how to be a sinner And tell 'a good one' after dinner. **1961** 'F. O'BRIEN' *Hard Life* x. 71, I will tell you a funny one, Father, Mr Collopy said. **1967** WODEHOUSE *Company for Henry* x. 175 The low comedians of his musical comedy days who had called him 'laddie' and begged him to stop them if he had heard this one. **1977** *Listener* 24 Nov. 674/2 'Have you heard the one about the Queen Mother?' We had not heard it, and it was very funny.

24. After pronominal and other adjs., without contextual reference: = Person, body, persons; as in ***any one***, ***every one***, ***many a one***, ***some one***, ***such a one***; ***little ones***, ***the Holy One***, ***the Evil One***, etc. See further under these words.

c **1225** Everichon [see EVERY 10 c]. *a* **1300** *Cursor M.* 17994 (Gött.) Quat es he? þat sua mightful ane? [*Trin.* What is he þat so myȝty on?] *c* **1386** CHAUCER *Wife's Prol.* 606, I was a lusty oon [*v.r.* on], And faire and riche, and yonge. *a* **1425** *Cursor M.* 23720 (Tr.) Dame fortune turneþ hir whele anoon þat casteþ doun mony on. **1426** LYDG. *De Guil. Pilgr.* 398/14767, I sawh an old on, ful hydous. **1526** TINDALE *Matt.* x. 42 Whosoever shall geve vnto won of these lytle wonnes to drinke, a cuppe of colde water. **1560** BIBLE (Genev.) *Ruth* iv. 1 He sayd, Ho, such one [1611 such a one], come, sit downe here. **1580** SIDNEY *Psalms* III. i, How many ones there be That all against poor me Their numerous strength redouble. **1616** BEAUM. & FL. *Scornful Lady* III. ii, This makes you not a Baron, but a bare one. **1665** MANLEY *Grotius' Low C. Warres* 3 The Consultations of the great Ones and Governours. **1766** in *Waghorn's Cricket Scores* (1899) 61 The knowing ones were taken in. **1805** WORDSW. *Waggoner* I. 115 The evil One is left behind. **1857** HUGHES *Tom Brown* II. i. (1871) 212 Come along, young'un. **1866** CARLYLE *Inaug. Addr.* 173 And so they gathered together, these speaking ones.

†**VII.** Various obsolete uses.

†**25.** = the indef. article, *a*, *an*. **a.** In the 12th and 13th centuries, while the forms of the numeral and of the indefinite article were being differentiated, the former were sometimes used in the weakened sense of the latter. **b.** Northern writers who used the native *ane* both as numeral and indef. art. (see ANE) occasionally anglicized it as *one* in the latter sense also. *Obs.*

In quot. *c* 1420, *on* is distinct from the numeral, which in this text is *won*.

c **1000** ÆLFRIC *Hom.* I. 38 An engel bodade þam hyrdum þæs heofonlican cyninges acennednysse. **10..** ÆLFRIC *Gen.* vi. 14 Wyrc þe nu ænne arc. *a* **1175** *Cott. Hom.* 223 He ȝeworhte of þane ribbe ana wifman. *c* **1175** *Lamb. Hom.* 93 Eontas walden areran ane buruh and anne stepel. *c* **1200** *Trin. Coll. Hom.* 31 Ðo cam on angel of heuene to hem, and stod bisides hem. *c* **1200** ORMIN 3364 Ȝe shulenn finndenn ænne child. *c* **1200** *Moral Ode* 348 (Trin.) Þurh one godelease wude to one bare felde. *c* **1205** LAY. 10524 Ich æm ennes cnihtes sune [*c* **1275** on eorles sone]. *a* **1250** *Owl & Night.* 14 In one hurne of one breche. **13..** *E.E. Allit. P.* A. 9 Allas! I leste hyr in on erbere! *c* **1420** *Chron. Vilod.* 567 Of on myracule now I chulle ȝow tell. *a* **1425** *Cursor M.* 11551 (Trin.) He made oon ordinaunce in hiȝe. **1514** PACE in Ellis *Orig. Lett.* Ser. I. I. 111 My sayde lorde was oon faytheful man. **1552** LYNDESAY *Monarche* 3961 Wes neuer sene sic one multytude.

†**26. a.** *One* (like other numerals) was formerly used with superlatives, as 'one the fairest toun' = 'a town, the fairest one', 'the one fairest town'.

c **1000** ÆLFRIC *Exod.* xxxii. 21 Þis folc..hæfþ ȝeworht ane þa mæstan synne and gode þa laþustan. *c* **1330** R. BRUNNE *Chron.* (1810) 272 On þe fairest toun þat was in his pouste. *c* **1386** CHAUCER *Frankl. T.* 6 She was oon the faireste vnder sonne. **1430–40** LYDG. *Bochas* VIII. xxvi. (1588) 18 Which through Affrik was one ye best knight. *c* **1460** FORTESCUE *Abs. & Lim. Mon.* iii. (1885) 114 Yet dwellyn thai in on the most fertile reaume of the worlde. **1611** SHAKS. *Cymb.* I. vi. 165 He is one The truest manner'd. **1613** —— *Hen. VIII* II. iv. 48 Ferdinand My Father,..was reckon'd one The wisest Prince, that there had reign'd.

†**b.** ***of one***, ***of ane***, after a superlative or its equivalent, = 'of all'; after a positive = of special excellence, specially. *Sc. Obs.* (Cf. ON. *einna mestr* greatest of ones, i.e. of all.)

1375 BARBOUR *Bruce* IV. 74 The starkest man of ane. *Ibid.* v. 527 He that he trowit mast of ane. *c* **1470** HENRYSON *Bludy Serk* 18 A fowll gyane of ane. *c* **1475** *Rauf Coilȝear* 576 In ane Rob him arrayit, richest of ane. **14..** *Tale of Five Beasts* 312 in Laing's *Anc. Poet. Scotl.*, The riallest of one. **1513** DOUGLAS *Æneis* XI. vi. 100 The gret Agamemnon,..cheif ledar of on. **1535** STEWART *Cron. Scotl.* l. 35587 Of Norrowa ane grit nobill of one. *Ibid.* l. 35799 Ane fair castell of one. **1552** LYNDESAY *Monarche* 1627 Nemrod..Quhilk wes the Principall man of one.

†**27. a.** As predicate or complement following sb. or pron.: = Alone (L. *solus*). *Obs.*

Subseq. strengthened by *all*, and now written in combination with it ALONE. Often extended to two or more: 'he and she were *one*' i.e. alone.

Beowulf 1082 Nemne feaum anum. *c* **1000** *Sax. Leechd.* II. 178 ȝif of þære wambe anre þa yfelan wætan cumen. *c* **1175** *Lamb. Hom.* 111 Þu ane ne brukest naut þinra welena. *c* **1205** LAY. 23880 Þa kinges tweien ane þer wuneden. *a* **1225** *Ancr. R.* 92 Ȝif heo nis muchel one. *Ibid.* 160 Þene Louerd of heouene, þet halt up al þene world mid his ones [*v.r.* anres] mihte. **1297** R. GLOUC. (Rolls) 9448 Þere bigan a niwe bataile al vpe þe king one. *a* **1300** *E.E. Psalter* l. 6 To þe an sinned I mare. *c* **1350** *Will. Palerne* 1415 Non knew here cunseile but þei þre one. **1388** WYCLIF *Isa.* li. 2 Y clepide hym oon. **1551** ROBINSON tr. *More's Utop.* Meter 4 verses 2 b, I one of all other..Haue shaped for man a philosophicall citie.

†**b.** Single, unmarried. *Obs.*

c **1386** CHAUCER *Wife's Prol.* 66 Men may conseille a womman to been oon, Bot conseillyng is nat comandement.

†**c.** Esp. after *leave*, *let*: cf. *let alone*. *Obs.*

c **1000** *Ags. Gosp.* John xvi. 32 Ðæt ȝe forlæton me anne, and ic ne eom ana. *a* **1300** *Cursor M.* 14099 (Cott.), I am left an [*Trin.* one] to serue yow. **13..** *Guy Warw.* (A.) 525 Þe leches gon and lete Gij one. **13..** *Gaw. & Gr. Knt.* 2118 Goude syr Gawayn, let þe gome one.

†**d.** After pronouns, almost = self, selves. Hence, after the analogy of *my-*, *thy-self*, *our-*, *your-selves*, northern writers used *mine*, *thine*, *our*, *your*, *ane*, (midl. *one*). Cf. mod.Sc. *my'lane*, *our'lanes*, and see ALONE, LONE. *Obs.*

c **1200** ORMIN 1079 Whann he shollde ganngenn inn..aȝȝ him sellf himm ane. *a* **1225** *Juliana* 31 As ha þrinne wes i þeosternesse hire ane. *a* **1300** *Cursor M.* 630 (Cott.) Of þat rib he mad woman, Til adam þat was first his an [so *Gött.*; *Trin.* his oon, *Fairf.* al-ane]. *Ibid.* 2021 (Cott.) Drunken on slepe lai bi him an [so *Gött.*; *Fairf.* bi his ane, *Trin.* bi his one]. **1340** HAMPOLE *Pr. Consc.* 3109 Þe body..harder þan þe saul by it ane. **13..** *Gaw. & Gr. Knt.* 1230 Now ȝe ar here, I-wysse, and we bot oure one. **1362** LANGL. *P. Pl.* A. IX. 54 As I wente bi a wode walkyng myn one. *c* **1375** *Sc. Leg. Saints* iii. (*Andreas*) 979 We sal nocht be ws ane twa. *c* **1440** *Gesta Rom.* I. lxix. 312 Whenne þat he myȝt fynde hire by hire oone. *a* **1450** *Le Morte Arth.* 315 Whan they come by them one two. **1460** CAPGRAVE *Chron.* 162 Thei to went into a chambir al be her one.

†**28.** In this sense *one* passed into an adverb: Alone, only. *Obs.* (In early quots. it is often difficult to say whether it is adv. or adj.)

c **1175** *Lamb. Hom.* 129 Naut ane under his hond ac under his fet. *a* **1225** *Ancr. R.* 64 Al þe leor schal ulowen o teares, ..vor þe eie sihðe one. *c* **1320** *Cast. Love* 1050 Alle þing I seo, and alle þing Ich wot; But one þi þouȝt no þing I not. *c* **1380** *Sir Ferumb.* 2495 Of noþyng certis doþ(?) þay drede; bot of liflode one. *a* **1450** *Le Morte Arth.* 3111 Mordred.. Callyd hys folke, And sayd to hem One, 'Releve yow, for crosse on Rode'. **1541** R. COPLAND *Guydon's Quest. Chirurg.* E ij b, Wherof is the forheade comsed? Answere. One of the skynne & musculous flesshe.

VIII. Phrases.

29. a. one and all, every one individually and jointly.

c **1375** *Cursor M.* 2907 (Fairf.) Þaire welþe ham sloghe baþ an and al [*Trin.* oon and alle]. **13..** *Ibid.* 28036 (Cott. Galba), I say noght þis by ane ne all. **1513** [see ALL A 12 c]. **1647** WARD *Simp. Cobler* 50 He hath sounded an alarm to all the *susque deques*, pell-mels, one and alls, now harrasing sundry parts of Christendome. **1877** TYNDALL in *Daily News* 2 Oct. 2/5 Towards this great end it behoves us one and all to work.

†**b. one or other**: ? whether viewed one way or another, anyhow, altogether. *Obs.*

1704 CIBBER *Careless Husb.* v. (1705) 66, I declare 'twas a Design, one or other—the best Carry'd on, that ever I knew in my life. **1775** S. J. PRATT *Liberal Opin.* Sect. viii. (1783) I. 24 This it is which makes him [the dog], one or another, the most entertaining animal that ever crossed the Atlantic. **1796** MAD. D'ARBLAY *Camilla* I. ii, Indiana has one or other the prettiest face I ever saw.

c. ***one another***: see 19. ***one and one***, ***one by one***: see 16 b. ***all one***: see ALONE; also ALL *adv.* 5 b.

30. With following adverb.

a. one down: one point behind one's opponent in a game; inferior in one respect; disadvantaged; also (with hyphen) *attrib.* or as *adj.* Hence **one-downmanship**, the art or practice of being 'one down'; **one-downness**, the fact or state of being 'one down'. Cf. sense 30 c below.

1907 [see DOWN *adv.* 14 b]. **1952** S. POTTER *One-Upmanship* II. ii. 32 To increase the one-downness, bring in the washing-the-hands gambit immediately after touching hands with Patient. **1961** *Times* 8 Mar. 17 (*heading*) Handy guide to art of onedownmanship. *Ibid.* 22 Mar. 16/3 It is the Negroes who are educated, who 'talk posh', who go to university; the native English who are one-down, with less money and less culture. **1964** M. ARGYLE *Psychol. & Social Probl.* iii. 36 Stephen Potter has given an amusing list of techniques for making others feel 'one-down', together with counterploys for dealing with such methods when used by others. **1967** *Punch* 4 Oct. 514/3 If he were to check his facts would he not find that on the contrary the majority of Fleet Street was indulging in a form of one-down-manship towards the British public? **1976** N. POSTMAN *Crazy Talk* 44 He will naturally be one-down in the situation, a 'child' to the government agent's 'adult'.

b. one off: a single example of a manufactured product; something not repeated; a prototype. Freq. (with hyphen) *attrib.* or as *adj.* Also *transf.* and *fig.* Cf. OFF *adv.* 13, *once-off* adj. s.v. ONCE *adv.* B. 7 b.

1934 *Proc. Inst. Brit. Foundrymen* XXVI. 552 A splendid one-off pattern can be swept up in very little time. **1935** *Jrnl. R. Aeronaut. Soc.* XXXIX. 41 One off per machine does not give us much opportunity for reducing production costs. **1947** *Ibid.* LI. 308/1 With the lofting technique it is possible to cut down the time required to produce a prototype aircraft for..it is possible to reproduce full-scale layouts directly on to the material to be worked..thus cutting out what was originally the factor which absorbed the most production time in the freehand manufacture of 'one offs'. **1954** *Archit. Rev.* CXVI. 411/2 Hills built the first part of Cheshunt as a 'one off' job, with no guarantees of further business, though of course it was intended to be the first of a line. **1955** *Ibid.* CXVII. 226/2 None of the motor-cars illustrated is a standardized mass-produced model; all are expensive, specialized, handicraft one-offs which can justly be compared to the Parthenon because, like it, they are unique works of handmade art. **1958** *Listener* 25 Sept. 458/2 Both the estates of the speculative 'rush' builders and the architectural one-offs are unable to keep pace with the demand [for new houses]. **1961** *Times* 3 Oct. (Computer Suppl.) p. v/3 The centres are..even able to do a 'one-off' job, such as eliminating a production bottle-neck, very cheaply. **1965** R. B. ORAM *Cargo Handling* iv. 70 Tailor made, or 'one-off', machines, may give great satisfaction. **1968** *Sunday Times* 29 Sept. 25 Jenkins has already made a crude stab at a wealth tax with his special charge on investment incomes... But this was a one-off effort. **1970** *Times* 28 Mar. 21 All these relationships involve money and are on a continuing basis rather than a one-off purchase. **1973** *Daily Tel.* 22 Oct. 12/4 When Barry Took's *Grub Street* (BBC-2) was screened as a one-off..I rashly predicted that it could make a series. **1974** F. WARNER *Meeting Ends* II. i. 35 But we find it much harder to shake a man off afterwards, and anyway, I don't like those 'one off' dates. I need companionship, an outing, warmth. **1976** *Scottish Rev.* Spring 33 For the most part they could only produce an endless stream of one-off building prototypes. **1977** *Hot Car* Oct. 97/1 There seems to be a good deal of misunderstanding about the way the Type Approval Regulations apply to 'one-offs' or cars built by private individuals.

c. one up: scoring one point more than an opponent; ahead of another person; (fig.) maintaining a psychological advantage; also (with hyphen) *attrib.* or as *adj.* Hence **one-'upmanship**, the art or practice of being 'one up'; so **one-up** *v. trans.*, to do better than (someone); **one-upman**, an exponent of one-upmanship; **one-upness**, **-uppance**, the fact or state of being 'one up'.

1919 [see UP *adv.*[2] 13 e]. **1924** WODEHOUSE *Leave it to Psmith* i. 30 Which would make her pretty chirpy, as well as putting you one up. **1929** J. B. PRIESTLEY *Good Companions* II. vii. 449 He can give old Omar himself points in not believing in anything, for he has cut out the book of verse, most of the loaf, and the Houri stuff, and just sticks to the jug, though he has added a clay pipe and is one up on Omar there. **1952** S. POTTER (*title*) One-upmanship. *Ibid.* I. ii. 26

The establishment of one-up relations between doctor and doctor and doctor and patient and vice versa. *Ibid.* v. 64 The basic gambit is of course the achievement of the state of one-upness on the rest of the public. **1957** *Economist* 26 Oct. 295/1 This piece of applied relativity.. may go down in the annals of international one-upmanship as the sputnik ploy. **1959** N. N. Holland *First Mod. Comedies* 38 This was a perhaps pardonable attempt to retain 'one-upness' in the large eyes of a rather nasty little genius. **1959** *Times Lit. Suppl.* 6 Nov. 650/4 They are one-upmen, seen from the receiving end, and they give Mr. Gibb endless opportunities for recording sillier aspects of the contemporary social scene. **1960** *News Chron.* 14 Apr. 3/1 Will Granada deny there was an element of one-upness in its satisfaction? **1961** S. Price *Just for Record* v. 37 Stephen Potter was a square in nappies compared to these one-up graduates. **1963** *Canada Month* Mar. 10/1 John Wintermeyer.. one-upped the socialists by endorsing the Saskatchewan plan. **1964** 'C. E. Maine' *Never let Up* xvii. 172 It's a kind of one-upmanship. You thought you were smart, but he had to prove that he was even smarter. **1966** *Listener* 27 Oct. 622/1 Virginia Woolf can still show herself to be one up, in her literary judgements, on most current criticism. **1967** *Maclean's Mag.* Oct. 46 Another trap the psychiatrist must strive to avoid is the mistake of being one-up. The psychiatrist is in the perfect position to be the one-up man. **1969** D. S. Davis *Where Dark Streets Go* (1970) xviii. 162 You one-upped us there, Father. We came dead-end in a housing development. **1970** 'Jenner' & Segal *Men & Marriage* ii. 45 Marrying a doctor still gives a girl a bit of one-uppance amongst the neighbours. **1973** J. Wainwright *Touch of Malice* 87 Smithson's one-up-man-ship ploy of keeping a senior police officer waiting. **1975** *Times* 14 Mar. 14/5 There are one-upmanship entries. A power cruiser 'built for royalty' is offered. **1976** *Listener* 28 Oct. 544/4 The objects of human vituperation.. seem to be pretty well limited to people who are one up on us, and other people's pleasures. **1977** *Time* 24 Jan. 37/1 His sweet, sporting spirit as he sits trying to absorb his defeat while graciously applauding a trickster's win is something with which any weekend athlete who has been one-upped by an allegedly friendly opponent can identify.

31. Misc. phrases.

a. ***one and the same***: used as a more emphatic form of 'the same'. Cf. L. *unus et idem*.

1869 *Bradshaw's Railway Manual* XXI. 365 This modification has.. the effect of comprising in one and the same network the two lines from Paris to Lyons. **1941** H. L. Mencken *Newspaper Days* (1942) xvi. 245 His father had been, at one and the same time, a Confederate general, a French nobleman, and a graduate of both Oxford and Cambridge. **1960** C. P. Snow *Affair* v. xxxix. 364 You'd obviously got to raise the dust about Nightingale and give them an escape-route at one and the same damned time. **1973** D. Aaron *Unwritten War* iv. xi. 167 Abolitionism or Black Republicanism, to the South Carolinian, one and the same thing. **1976** G. Butler *Vesey Inheritance* iv. 117, I wonder.. whether the King and Mr Koenig could be one and the same person?

b. ***one man, one vote***: a slogan advocating that every adult man (or adult person) should have a vote; also formerly, that each voter should have only one vote; also *attrib.*

1884 A. Paul *Hist. of Reform* ii. 19 'One man, one vote', a cry which may have had a novel sound to some in 1883 was one of Cartwright's political principles. **1889** W. E. Gladstone in *Times* 13 June 7/2 The important measure which is briefly designated under the well-known phrase —one man, one vote. **1891** *Spectator* 7 Mar. 330/1 Mr. Stansfeld brought forward his resolution for an amendment of the registration law, and the adoption of the principle of 'one man one vote'. **1907** H. Lawson in Murdoch & Drake-Brockman *Austral. Short Stories* (1951) 73 The One-Man-One-Vote Bill was passed. **1964** *Punch* 15 July 74/3 To ensure that one-man-one-vote democracy is swiftly introduced. **1971** 'G. Black' *Time for Pirates* ii. 32 The government.. had declared martial law, suspending the constitution... 'So much for one man, one vote,' Russell said. **1975** D. Bagley *Snow Tiger* xiii. 115 Not so democratic as to be a one man, one vote system.

c. ***one hand for oneself and one for the ship***: a nautical proverb referring to the practice of holding on to a rope, etc., with one hand while working with the other hand; also in similar phrases (see quots.).

1799 *Port Folio* (Philadelphia) 1812 VII. 130 Always keep one hand for the owners, and one for yourself. **1902** B. Lubbock *Round the Horn* 58 The old rule on a yard is, 'one hand for yourself and one for the ship', which means, hold on with one hand and work with the other. **1924** R. Clements *Gipsy of Horn* iii. 50 One hand for yourself and one for the owners. **1938** F. A. Worsley *First Voy. in Square-Rigged Ship* 119 One hand for the Queen and one for yerself. **1968** L. Morton *Long Wake* i. 10, I did not know then the old adage 'one hand for oneself and one hand for the company'.

d. ***one and only***: one's sweetheart; one's only child or love; also *transf.* Also (with hyphens) as *attrib. phr.*, unique, unrepeatable.

1906 E. Dyson *Fact'ry 'Ands* i. 4 She's er little *boshter* ..'n' I'm 'er one 'n' only. **1933** J. D. Carr *Mad Hatter Mystery* iv. 64 He'd met some girl at a dance who was the absolute One and Only. **1961** *Times* 13 May 11/3 Artur Schnabel thought that such a one-and-only performance was obtainable. **1966** *Harper's Bazaar* Sept. 64 A coat so versatile it could be the treasured one-and-only in your life. **1967** I. Hamilton *Man with Brown Paper Face* vi. 83 Daddy wasn't too happy about his one-and-only's choice of companion. **1967** J. Wainwright *Worms must Wait* lxxvii. 201 He had the truncheon ready for what he knew was going to be a one-and-only chance. **1975** J. McClure *Snake* xii. 159 She'd been with the family since their one-and-only was five. **1977** J. van de Wetering *Japanese Corpse* (1978) xvii. 152 She had been unwilling to admit that she had ever slept with other men. Kikuji Nagai had been her one and only.

e. ***one for the (end) book***: a notable, extraordinary, or incredible event, action, saying, etc. *U.S. colloq.*

1922 H. C. Witwer *Fighting Blood* (1923) 170 Gents, this was one for the book! **1946** *Amer. Speech* XXI. 69/1 When a friend approaches with an anecdote which is strange or incredible, he often prefaces it with the remark, 'Here's one for the book'. *Ibid.*, At racetracks where parimutuel betting machines are not used.. it was customary for bookmakers to line up in a designated area... If a bettor asked unusually high odds, the bookie might comment, 'Here's one for the end book', implying that no one but a green newcomer.. would accept those odds. **1955** *Publ. Amer. Dial. Soc.* xxiv. 179 There is always someone with one for the end book, or a story that is hard to believe.

f. ***(just) one of those things***: something inevitable or inexplicable; a fact or happening that one cannot do anything about. *colloq.*

1934 J. O'Hara *Appointment in Samarra* i. 25 No, it was just one of those things. **1935** C. Porter (*song-title*) Just one of those things. **1935** *Time* 4 Mar. 17/3 Said Comedian Durante: 'Aw, it's just one of those things.' **1936** R. Lehmann *Weather in Streets* vii. 248 Oh, well... It can't be helped. It's just one of those things. **1941** C. Morgan *Empty Room* i. 46 'What is it, Carey?' She smiled. 'Nothing. One of those things.' **1951** 'J. Wyndham' *Day of Triffids* ii. 28 My inability to make any column of figures reach the same total twice caused me to be something of a mystery as well as a disappointment to him [*sc.* my father]. Still, there it was: just one of those things. **1955** A. Huxley *Let.* 16 Dec. (1969) 778 Her daughter is going to have a baby—husband twenty-one and still at college, daughter supporting the household for the moment. Which is one of those things. **1971** *Daily Tel.* 19 Nov. 3/1, I know Mr Butler is a bit choked about it, but it's just one of those things. **1974** M. Babson *Stalking Lamb* xviii. 136 The price was too high.. to be shrugged off as 'just one of those things'.

g. ***one-of-a-kind*** attrib. phr., (*a*) of only one kind; (*b*) unique.

1961 *Times* 25 Apr. 4/2 The one-of-a-kind series for racing catamarans organized last year. **1963** *New Yorker* 1 June 72 Among the one-of-a-kind mannerly materials are Paisley cotton prints. **1973** *Publishers Weekly* 23 July 66/3 A one-of-a-kind book that merits a place on the political science shelf. **1975** *New Yorker* 21 Apr. 17/3 *Children of Paradise* (1945)—A one-of-a-kind film. **1977** *Rolling Stone* 24 Mar. 48/4 Fleetwood Mac had this one-of-a-kind charm. They were gregarious, charming and cheeky onstage. *Very cheeky.*

32. After a prep.

†**a. after one**: after one and the same fashion, in the same way. *Obs.*

c **1386** Chaucer *C.T.* Prol. 341 His breed, his Ale was alweys after oon. —— *Knt's T.* 923 That lord hath litel of discrecion That.. weyeth pride and humblesse after oon.

b. at one, (atoon, aton): see at one adv. phr.

†**c. by one**: one by one; one at a time. *Obs.*

1607 Markham *Caval.* i. (1617) 35 By turning Mares single, and by one vnto the Horse.

d. in one: (*a*) In or into one place, company, or mass; together.

a **1225** *Leg. Kath.* 1524 Wit beoð ifestnet & iteiet in an. *a* **1300** *E.E. Psalter* xxxiv. 15 Ogain me þai fained and come in ane. **1390** Gower *Conf.* II. 149 Whan tuo hertes falle in on. **1526** Tindale *John* xi. 51 He shulde gadder to gedder in won the children of God. **1581** Savile *Tacitus* (1604) 31 Legions being assembled in one. **1875** J. H. Newman in Keble *Occ. Papers* (1877) p. xiv, Gathered up in one.

(*b*) In unison, agreement, or harmony.

a **1425** *Cursor M.* 20136 (Trin.) Boþe her willes was in one. **1509** Hawes *Past. Pleas.* xxxviii. (Percy Soc.) 199 We answered bothe our hertes were in one. **1589** *Triumphs Love & Fortune* in Hazl. *Dodsley* VI. 148 When the higher powers is in one, Men upon earth will fly contention. **1600** W. Watson *Decacordon* (1602) 139 Why doth not your words and deedes agree in one? **1714** tr. *à Kempis' Chr. Exerc.* iv. 233 Voices all in one agree.

†(*c*) In one course; straight on, continuously, without ceasing; = anon 3. *Obs.*

a **1250** *Owl & Night.* 356 3if me hit halt evre forth in on. *c* **1386** Chaucer *Knt.'s T.* 913 His herte hadde compassion Of wommen for they wepen euere in oon. —— *Shipman's T.* 27 A Monk.. That euere in oon was comynge to that place. **1390** Gower *Conf.* II. 29 Evere in on Sche clepede upon Demephon. *c* **1400** *Laud Troy Bk.* (E.E.T.S.) 2792 A3eyn the qwene he 3ode and stode, And loked on hir euere in on.

†(*d*) In the same state or condition. *Obs.*

a **1300** *Cursor M.* 1429 (Cott.) Euer stod þai still in an, Wit-outen wax, wit-outen wain. *Ibid.* 4278 (Cott.) Ai sco fand ioseph in ane.

†(*e*) In one action; at once. *Obs.*

1622 Bacon *Hist. Hen. VII* 48 Whereby he should in one both generally abroad veil over his ambition and win the reputation of just proceedings.

(*f*) Combined in one; in combination.

1796 Bentham *Prot. agst. Law Taxes* (1816) 11 It is robbery, enslavement, insult, homicide, all in one. **1875** Jowett *Plato* (ed. 2) III. 441 The same persons.. are husbandmen, tradesmen, warriors, all in one.

(*g*) At one stroke or attempt; esp. ***to get it in one***: to succeed at the first attempt. Cf. sense (*e*), and *hole in one* s.v. hole *sb.* 4 a. *colloq.*

1938 J. Parish *St. Michael comes to Shepherd's Bush* 11 As a matter of fact, that's just what I am. You've got there in one. **1942** 'A. Bridge' *Frontier Passage* vi. 91 'In fact, our old friend the Hidden Hand in Biarritz runs the sabotage as well as the rest—that the idea?' Crampaun enquired. 'Got it in one!' **1972** W. Garner *Ditto, Brother Rat!* xv. 106 Got it in one, old son. **1975** 'C. Aird' *Slight Mourning* iii. 26 'What we are checking on is whether someone tried to kill him...' 'Got it in one, Sloan.'

e. into one: = *in one* (*a*).

1577 tr. *Bullinger's Decades* (1592) 61 To ioyne or bring into one. **1864** J. H. Newman *Apol.* 180, I had collected into one all the strong things.

†**f. on one (on-oon, onan, onon)**: = anon.

33. ones, the old advb. genitive: see once, ones.

IX. Combinations.

34. a. Attributive phrases consisting of *one* with a substantive (= 'consisting of, having, containing, costing, lasting, measuring, characterized by, dealing with, or relating to *one* ...'); these may be formed at pleasure, and are unlimited in number; such are ***one-book, -child, -class, -clause, -colour, -crop, -culture, -day, -deck, -digit, -dollar, -drink, -electron, -family, -foot, -inch, -level, -light, -line, -member, -minute, -parent, -particle, -party, -person, -piece, -pound, -rail, -reel, -room, -sex, -star, -step, -storey*** (also ***-story***), ***-string, -tap, -term, -volume , -word, -year***, etc. **b.** Other phrases used attrib., as ***one-by-one, one-o'clock***. **c.** Compound adjectives formed by prefixing such phrases as those in **a.** to simple adjs., as ***one-year-old***. **d.** Parasynthetic formations on such phrases as those in **a.** by adding *-ed* (also unlimited in number) as ***one-ended, -flowered, -footed, -handled, -hoofed, -horned*** (in quot. *a* 1225 as sb. = unicorn), ***-leafed, -leaved, -membered, -minded, -petaled, -pointed*** (so ***-pointedness***), ***-roomed, -seeded, -sepaled, -storied, -talented, -toed, -volumed, -windowed, -winged, -worded***, etc. **e.** Parasynthetic formations in *-er* (see -er[1] 1), as ***one-decker, one-pounder, one-rater, -roomer***.

1874 J. D. Heath *Croquet Player* 31 Varieties of stroke.. divisible into '*One-ball' or roquet-strokes, in which only one ball is moved, and 'Two-ball' or croquet-strokes. **1879** tr. *Haeckel's Evol. Man* I. Pref. 21 Our *one-celled Amœba-ancestors of the Laurentian period. **1905** *Daily Chron.* 18 Nov. 6/3 It is desired to secure such a reform in the law as will bring *one-child cases within the sphere of inspection. **1971** J. Z. Young *Introd. Study Man* xxiv. 326 The effect has been an increase of 2 per cent in one-child families. **1908** *Daily Chron.* 21 Nov. 9/3 They are *one-class, one-price machines. **1909** *Westm. Gaz.* 21 Oct. 1/3 For short-distance travelling Sir Albert is in favour of one-class carriages. **1931** *Times* 5 Nov. 8/3 The sooner the 'one class' party is abolished,.. the better for the nation and Empire. **1960** Willmott & Young *Family & Class in London Suburb* viii. 97 Working Men's Clubs and other one-class organizations. **1973** A. Behrend *Samarai Affair* ii. 24 A very small one-class passenger liner. **1898** *Daily News* 28 July 3/1 The Government are being pressed to introduce a *one-clause Bill. **1965** *Language* XLI. 74 There are many one-clause sentences. **1946** *Happy Landings* (Air Ministry) July 11/3 We recall.. young pilots, chests aflame with so many medals that it made the Aurora Borealis look like a *one-colour miniature. **1842** Aiton *Domest. Econ.* (1857) 152 The butter of a *one-cow dairy is seldom good. **1942** *E. Afr. Ann. 1941–2* 85/2 Kenya.. has suffered from *one-crop farming. **1970** *Guardian* 10 Apr. 3/5 The Prime Minister, Dr Fidel Castro, [is] bent on diversifying what has been a one-crop economy based on sugar. **1962** *Times* 10 May 17/3, I decided to be a *one-culture man to make reading more enjoyable. **1763** Wesley *Wks.* (1872) III. 142, I went in the *one-day machine to Bath. **1974** *News & Press* (Darlington, S. Carolina) 25 Apr. 7/6 A one-day golf tournament.. will be held at the Tifton Golf Club in Darlington. **1975** *Cricketer* May 4/1 MCC won both their one-day matches in Hong Kong. **1977** *Times* 25 Aug. 2/7 It will not be a couple of one-day strikes. It will be a case of weeks and maybe months, but we will force the rise. **1906** *Daily Chron.* 23 Feb. 2/2 They started with the old style *one-deck buses. **1935** H. Straumann *Newspaper Headlines* 150 They.. occur in second decks or in one-deck crossheads. **1962** *Gloss. Terms Automatic Data Processing* (*B.S.I.*) 60 **One-digit adder*, a logic element with two outputs and two inputs to which may be applied signals representing a digit of a number and a single addend or carry digit. One output signal represents a digit of the sum, the other represents a digit to be carried forward. **1966** Ogilvy & Anderson *Excursions in Number Theory* 156 What we have just said means that $q(n) = x - 1$ (not x, because in the first decade none of the one-digit numbers 2, 4, 8 qualify). **1896** H. Porter in *Century Mag.* Nov. 28 A *one-dollar treasury note. **1906** *Westm. Gaz.* 13 Aug. 5/1 Most of them are '*one-drink' people, although they may have 'another'. **1909** J. Ware *Passing Eng.* 188/2 *One drink house*.., where only one serving is permitted. If the customer desire a second helping, he has to take a walk 'round the houses' after the first. **1955** H. B. G. Casimir in W. Pauli *Niels Bohr* 119, $n(\epsilon_0)$ is the density of *one-electron states per energy-interval in the neighbourhood of this maximum energy. **1970** W. G. Woodgate *Elem. Atomic Struct.* i. 1 Bohr's semi-classical theory was not general enough to describe more than the gross features of the simplest one-electron atom. **1553** Udall tr. *Geminus' Anat.* A ij/1 The blynde gutte, whiche we call in Englysh, the *one-ended gutte. **1968** *N.Y. City* (Michelin Tire Corp.) 47 There are 3000 *one-family dwellings in Manhattan. **1972** *Country Life* 28 Dec. 1781/1 They were not originally one-family houses; rather was it a case of a family a floor. **1877** Raymond *Statist. Mines & Mining* 243 A *one-foot vein of good ore. *c* **1440** *Promp. Parv.* 363/1 *O fotyd beest (*P.* or one foted best). **1922** Joyce *Ulysses* 146 Settle down on their striped petticoats, peering up at the statue of the *onehandled adulterer. *Ibid.* 564 Steel shark stone onehandled Nelson. *a* **1598** Ld. Burleigh *Adv. to Eliz.* in *Harl. Misc.* (Malh.) II. 282 A people all *one-hearted in religion. **1615** Chapman *Odyss.* xv. 63 See in chariot inclosed Their *one-hoof'd horse. *a* **1225** *St. Marher.* 7 Leose.. mi meoke mildscipe of þe *anhurnde hornes. **1849** *Sk. Nat. Hist.*, *Mammalia* III. 19 Pliny.. mentions the one-horned rhinoceros. **1865** Trollope *Belton Est.* i. 10 Low, four-wheeled, *one-horsed little phaeton. **1876** Swinburne *Erechtheus* (ed. 2) 127 Violets *one-hued with her hair. **1952** A. G. L. Hellyer

Sanders' Encycl. Gardening (ed. 22) 463 *Sophronitis*... Pseudo-bulbs usually small, *one-leafed, stout, with one or few terminal flowers. **1875** *Amer. Naturalist* IX. 17 The singular *one-leaved ash, *Fraxinus anomala*. **1946** DYLAN THOMAS *Deaths & Entrances* 29 Under the one leaved trees ran a scarecrow of snow. **1972** *Hilliers' Man. Trees & Shrubs* 507 [pinus cembroides] monophylla... 'One-leaved Nut Pine'. An unusual variety in which the.. leaves occur singly. **1957** N. FRYE *Anat. Crit.* 71 The criticism of literature can hardly be a simple or *one-level activity. **1908** A. L. FROTHINGHAM *Monuments Christian Rome* II. 192 The lower story or two had a *one-light opening. **1945** G. B. GRUNDY *55 Yrs. at Oxf.* 148 The one-light system, i.e. shading from an imaginary perpendicular light. **1655** MRQ. WORCESTER *Cent. Inv.* Index p. i, An *one-line Cypher. **1901** G. B. SHAW *Admirable Bashville* Pref. 87, I like the melodious sing-song, the clear simple one-line and two-line sayings. **1952** M. RICHERT *Reconstr. Carmelite Missal* iii. 67 A small (one-line) blue, tan, and gold letter. **1965** B. MATES *Elem. Logic* vii. 110 A derivation can begin with a tautology, as in the following one-line derivation. **1965** HUGHES & LONDEY *Elem. Formal Logic* xxix. 218 We shall usually write one-line proofs in this abbreviated form. **1884** E. W. HAMILTON *Diary* 29 Oct. (1972) II. 720 The Tory scheme leans to the *one-member principle. **1924** O. JESPERSEN *Philos. Gram.* 306 An old-fashioned grammarian will feel a certain repugnance to this theory of one-member sentences. **1963** J. LYONS *Structural Semantics* ii. 22 Some of the distributional classes will, of course, be one-member classes; but the majority will not. **1967** D. H. MONRO *Empiricism & Ethics* xvi. 201 It is not irrational to treat an individual as a one-member class. **1884** E. W. HAMILTON *Diary* 25 July (1972) II. 659 Mr. G...rather favours *one-membered constituencies. **1877** A. DOBSON *Proverbs in Porcelain* 99 We, bound with him in common care, *One-minded, celibate. **1941** L. MACNEICE *Poetry of Yeats* x. 218 If Lawrence is..an eclectic, he is..a one-minded one. **1860** PUSEY *Min. Proph.* 578 He pictures the *one-mindedness of the Church. **1883** E. P. ROE in *Harper's Mag.* Dec. 46/1 The old-fashioned *one-o'clock dinner. **1969** *Times* 7 Nov. 15/7 A committee to consider the problems of *one-parent families in society. **1974** *Evening News* (Edinburgh) 12 Apr. 7/5 An Easter holiday play scheme for children from some of Edinburgh's one-parent families ended today on the slopes of Arthur's Seat. **1976** *Times* 21 May 1/6 That benefit..is paid to fewer than half the one-parent families in Britain. **1955** W. PAULI *Niels Bohr* 32 This method is essentially based on the assumption that the theory for free particles (without interactions) holds for the so-called *one particle states. **1937** H. TINGSTEN *Political Behavior* v. 216 In certain American so-called *one party states one can hardly speak of an election campaign. **1950** 'G. ORWELL' *Shooting an Elephant* 156 The appearance of one-party régimes based on police terrorism, faked plebiscites, etc. **1964** T. B. BOTTOMORE *Elites & Society* v. 95 The possible or probable concomitants of this kind of one-party rule, dictatorship and loss of personal liberty, persecution and widespread suffering. **1971** *Guardian* 11 Dec. 10/4 India..was a benign one-party state. **1975** *Times* 11 Apr. 6/5 Independent observers had little doubt that this would be the beginning of a one-party system in Portugal. **1956** J. M. MOGEY *Family & Neighbourhood* 14 *One-person households. **1966** J. TUNSTALL *Old & Alone* xiv. 281 'Under-occupation' defined as one-person household in 4+ rooms or two-person household in 5+ rooms. **1977** G. SCOTT *Hot Pursuit* ii. 16 It's a one-person flat. **1811** *One-pointed [see BLUE GRASS 2]. **1958** *Listener* 11 Sept. 374/2 They receive an incredibly tough kind of training, which..produces 75 per cent. completely one-pointed fanatics. **1960** J. HEWITT *Yoga* xi. 153 If the mind takes one thought and holds it, one-pointed and still, time is erased, it ceases—psychologically—to exist. **1923** *Contemp. Rev.* Feb. 223 He has an innate tendency to '*onepointedness'— as it is sometimes called—to concentration on unity. **1941** A. HUXLEY *Grey Eminence* v. 120 Complete consistency comes only with complete one-pointedness, complete absorption in ultimate reality. **1960** J. HEWITT *Yoga* ix. 135 In..another method to achieve withdrawal and onepointedness, the meditator imagines that he has a diamond in each ear, [etc.]. **1896** *Rudder* VII. 245/1 Next year will see a *one-rater craze; or, correctly speaking, an epidemic of 20-foot racing-length yachts. **1920** I. P. GORE in *Stage Year Bk.* 53 Such tit-bits as..a *one-reel comedy founded on the rollicking antics of a malignant tumour. **1961** GETLEIN & GARDINER *Movies, Morals & Art* iv. 51 *The Great Train Robbery* is a one-reel film. **1897** *Daily News* 1 Nov. 5/2 There are 386,000 persons in London who are *one-room dwellers. **1934** *Archit. Rev.* LXXV. 41 (*heading*) The one-room flat. **1972** C. WESTON *Poor, Poor Ophelia* (1973) vi. 30 A hippie joint, you think? Anyhow, a bunch of one-room pads. **1854** H. MILLER *Sch. & Schm.* (1858) 355 The *one-roomed cottage which I shared with its three other inmates. **1924** D. H. LAWRENCE *Let.* 16 May (1962) II. 789 There's a two-room cabin where Mabel can come when she likes, and a *one-roomer for Brett. **1628** GAULE *Pract. The. Panegyr.* 64 Oh that I were able, or worthy to open but his *one-Sealed Booke. **1895** *Outing* (U.S.) XXVI. 422/2 He did not move from his place..in the *one-seated vehicle. **1796** W. WITHERING *Brit. Plants* (ed. 3) I. 69 Monosperma, *one-seeded. **1832** *Veg. Subst. Food* 37 One-seeded Wheat, or St. Peter's corn—*Triticum monococcum*. **1846** D. J. BROWNE *Trees Amer.* 215 *Gleditschia monosperma*, the One-seeded Gleditschia. **1964** E. J. H. CORNER *Life of Plants* xii. 208 Some normally one-seeded fruit, as acorns, avocado, palm fruits, or grass 'seed', will show considerable difference in the size of the true seed. **1888** G. ALLEN in *Gd. Words* 383 *One-seed-leaved plants. **1949** M. MEAD *Male & Female* xviii. 368 A *one-sex world would be an imperfect world. **1966** P. WILLMOTT *Adolescent Boys E. London* vii. 128 Younger boys more often belong to one-sex clubs. **1908** *Daily Chron.* 4 Nov. 3/3 In the meadows we did roam; And in the *one-star night returned Together home. **1961** *Guardian* 24 Mar. 21/4 One-star restaurants, rather slightingly dismissed by M. Michelin as 'a good restaurant for its class'. **1975** tr. *Melchior's Sleeper Agent* (1976) III. 168 The French general..was scheduled to tap four officers for the Legion of Honor, two one-star generals and two bird colonels. **1977** 'R. ROSTAND' *Killing in Rome* i. 4 A small one-star hotel. **1964** D. B. FRY in D. Abercrombie et al. *Daniel Jones* 64 He answered correctly all the items involving a *one-step difference between A and B. **1964** *English Studies* XLV. 383 The difference between a normal one-step process, beginning with Scandinavian forms and limited to names, and the multi-step process. **1833** B. SILLIMAN *Man. Sugar Cane* 64 The bagasse houses at Demerara are high *one story buildings. **1840** R. H. DANA *Bef. Mast* xiii. 29 Four lines of one-story plastered buildings. **1858** [see ONE-HORSE *a.* 2]. **1872** HOWELLS *Wedd. Journ.* (1892) 226 The little one-story dwellings. **1970** J. HANSEN *Fadeout* (1972) i. 3 The house was one-story, rambling, sided with cedar shakes. **1821** W. WIRT *Let.* 29 Aug. in J. P. Kennedy *Mem. W. Wirt* (1849) II. 132 It is a small, red, hip-roofed, *one-storied old house. **1861** in Willis & Clarke *Cambridge* (1886) III. 175 The lateral one-storied wing of the façade. **1938** *Oxf. Compan. Mus.* 591/1 The *one-string principle is also applied to the *Tromba Marina*. **1970** *Islander* (Victoria, B.C.) 8 Feb. 10/1 Occasionally from some nearby window you caught the strains of the [Chinese] one-string fiddle blending with the sing-song street cries of the vendors of lottery tickets. **1976** LD. HOME *Way Wind Blows* vii. 112 Some three hundred of them were gathered round, and he began to teach them, accompanied by a one-string banjo. **1701** BEVERLEY *Glory of Grace* 47 They who have the most, are, but as the *One Talented Man. **1952** A. COHEN *Phonemes of Eng.* 29 These two sounds (*one-tap and fricative *r*) are in no way opposed. **1845** *Congress. Globe* 28th Congress 2 Sess. 122/2 The North ..never had had any but *one-term presidents, democratic or federal. **1961** Y. OLSSON *On Syntax Eng. Verb* ii. 34 A two-term sub-system commutable with the one-term sub-system. **1966** *Philos. Rev.* LXXV. 406 Plato confuses relations with one-term predicates. **1828** STARK *Elem. Nat. Hist.* I. 353 *One-toed Eft. Feet extremely thin and short, composed of one toe, without a claw. **1888** T. T. WILDRIDGE *Northumbria* 124 The *one-tree canoe may be considered the boat of northern Europe. **1861** *Illustr. Lond. News* 17 Aug. 152/3 To visit the excesses..with the same stern and *one-voiced reprobation. **1862** MRS. GASKELL *Let.* 30 Sept. (1966) 698, I am going to publish a *one-volume story in 'All the Year Round', where..it will occupy from ten to twelve numbers. **1961** R. B. LONG *Sentence & its Parts* xix. 414 There is no possibility of doing it justice in a one-volume grammar. **1977** *Listener* 17 Nov. 651/2 The *Times* one-volume edition [of the Pentagon Papers]. **1880** GEO. ELIOT *Let.* 19 Apr. (1956) VII. 261, I prefer Muxon's *one-volumed edition of Wordsworth to any selection. **1909** *Daily Chron.* 26 July 1/1 Away it went over the cliff, that monstrous *one-winged bird. **1924** R. M. OGDEN tr. *Koffka's Growth of Mind* v. 320 Single words have been spoken as *one-word sentences. **1956** 'H. MACDIARMID' *Stony Limits* 141 The great one-word metaphors of the Enneads. **1960** W. V. QUINE *Word & Object* i. 10 'Red' as a one-word sentence usually needs a question for its elicitation. **1963** F. T. VISSER *Hist. Syntax Eng. Lang.* I. iv. 603 When a noun is the object of both a merged verb and a one-word verb. **1957** *One-worded [see *many-worded* adj. s.v. MANY *a.* 6c].

35. Special Combinations: **one-bar** *a.*, of an electric fire: having only one heating element; **one-base hit** *Baseball*, a hit that enables the batter to reach the first base; also ***one-baser***; **one-book** *a.*, of an author: having written only one book, or only one good book; **one-catch-all** *dial.*, a children's outdoor chasing game; **'one-,coloured** *a.*, of one colour, of uniform colour throughout; **one-cross** *a.*, denoting a type of tin-plate (see quot. 1890); **one-design** *a. Naut.*, designating a yacht built from a standard design, or a class of such ships which are almost identical; also *absol.* as *sb.*; hence **one-designer**, such a yacht; **one-dimensional** *a.*, having, or pertaining to, a single dimension; hence ***one-dimensionality***; **one-directional** *a.*, having, or pertaining to, a single direction; **one-egg** *a.*, (*a*) characterized by a single egg; (*b*) = MONOZYGOTIC *a.*; **one-for-one** *a.*, denoting a situation, arrangement, etc., in which one thing corresponds to, or is issued or exchanged for, each of a set of things; **'one-Goddite** (*humorous nonce-wd.*), a monotheist; †**'one-gotten** *a. Obs.* = ONE-BEGOTTEN, only-begotten; **one-inch** *a.*, measuring, or done at a distance of, one inch; *spec.* of a map: having a scale of one inch to the mile; also *ellipt.* as *sb.*; **one-liner** (chiefly *U.S.*), (*a*) a headline consisting of only one line of print; (*b*) a very short joke or witty remark; **one-lunger**, (*a*) a person with only one lung; (*b*) *slang*, an engine with a single cylinder; a vehicle or boat driven by such an engine; also *attrib.*; **'one-,man** *a.*, (*a*) consisting of, exercised, managed, or done by, one man only; also in *Comb.*; (*b*) loving, obedient, or attached to one man only; **one-man band**, a man who plays several musical instruments simultaneously; also *transf.* and *fig.*; **one-man show**, a show, entertainment etc., consisting of, or done by, one man only; *spec.* an exhibition of the work of one artist; **one-many** *a.*, applied to a correspondence or relation such that each member of one set is associated with or related to two or more members of a second set; **one-night** *a.*, lasting, residing, or used for a single night; **one-nighter**, (*a*) a person who stays at a place for a single night; (*b*) orig. *U.S.* = *one-night stand*; **one-night stand** [STAND *sb.*[1] 2e] orig. *U.S.*, a single performance of a play, show, or the like at a particular place; esp. a performance given by a touring company, band, etc.; a town, theatre, etc., where such a performance or performances take place; also *transf.* and *fig.*, *spec.* a casual sexual encounter; **one-old-cat** *U.S.*, a form of baseball in which a batter runs to one base and home again, remaining as batter until the player who puts him out succeeds him; **one-one**, at Cambridge University, a degree in the first section of the first class; **one-one** *a.* = *one-to-one* adj. (see below); **one-on-one** *a.* (*U.S. slang*), designating or pertaining to a situation in which two opponents or the like come into conflict; **one-over-one** *a.*, in Bridge, denoting a bid of one in a suit, made in response to a preceding bid of one in a suit; also *ellipt.* as *sb.*; **one-pair** *a.* (in full, ***one pair of stairs***), situated above one 'pair' or flight of stairs, *i.e.* on the first floor; †**one-penny**, name of some obsolete game; **one-piece** *a.*, made or designed in a single piece; consisting of a single piece; esp. of clothing: comprising a single garment; **one-pip** *Mil. slang* (see quot. 1919); also ***one-pipper***; **one-place** *a. Logic*, of an assertion, etc., in which only one thing is postulated or involved; **one-plus-one** *a. Computers*, applied to (the use of) an instruction that contains the address of an operand and that of the next instruction to be performed; **one-pole** *a.*, (*a*) (see quot. 1892); (*b*) consisting of a single pole; (*c*) (see quot. 1940); **one-pounder**, (*a*) a gun that fires one-pound shells; (*b*) a one-pound note; **one-reeler**, a film lasting for one reel, usu. for ten minutes or less; **one-ring circus**, a small circus containing only one ring; also *transf.* and *fig.*; **one-stop** *a.* (orig. *U.S.*), denoting a shop or the like that can supply all a customer's needs within a particular range of goods or services; **one-stress** *a.*, of a line of Old English verse, having only one stress; **one-suiter** *U.S.*, a suitcase designed to hold one suit; **one-tail** *a. Statistics* = next; **one-tailed** *a. Statistics*, applied to a test that tests for deviation from the null hypothesis in one direction only; cf. *two-tailed* adj.; **one-time** *a.*, (*a*) that was so at one time or formerly, 'sometime'; (*b*) pertaining to a single occasion; done or used only once; = ONE-SHOT *a.*; **one-time** *adv.* (*colloq.* and *dial.*), (*a*) simultaneously, at the same time; (*b*) on one occasion, once; (*c*) at once, immediately; **one-time cipher, system**, etc., a cipher in which the cipher representation of the alphabet is changed at random for each letter of the message, generating a key as long as the message; **one-time pad**, a pad of keys for a one-time cipher each page of which is destroyed after being used once, so that each message is sent using a different key; **one-to-many** *a.* = *one-many* adj. (see above); **one-to-one** *a.*, applied to a correspondence or relation such that each member of one set is associated with one member of a second set, and *vice versa*; also *adv.*, as, or by means of, a one-to-one relation; **one-track** *a.*, of a person's mind: that is concentrated on, or capable of, only one line of thought or action; obsessional; also *transf.*; **one-trip** *a.*, of a bottle or other container: that is used only once; **'one-'two**, (*a*) name of a stroke in fencing (see quot.); so ***one-two-three***; (*b*) *Boxing*, two punches in quick succession with alternate hands; (*c*) *Football, Hockey*, etc., an interchange of the ball between two players; (*d*) also *transf.* and *fig.*; also *attrib.*; **one-up, one-down** *a.*, designating a house consisting of one main room upstairs and one downstairs; **one-valued** *a.*, having one value (for each component); chiefly *Math.*, = SINGLE-VALUED *a.*; **one-while**, *a.* or *adv.* = *one-time*; see also WHILE *sb.* 6b; **one-woman** *a.*, of, pertaining to, or by one woman only; *spec.* loving, obedient to, or attached to one woman only; **one-world** *a.*, of, pertaining to, or holding the view that there is only one world, or that the world's inhabitants are or should be united; hence ***one-worlder***.

1962 L. DEIGHTON *Ipcress File* ix. 54 Dalby stood..in front of a puny *one-bar electric fire. **1972** J. MCCLURE *Caterpillar Cop* 147 The gigantic fireplace..had a one-bar electric fire poised for winter in its grate. **1909** *Collier's* 5 June 11/1 The batter..would..score only a *one-base hit, perhaps, instead of the home run. **1937** *Amer. Speech* XII. 244/1 *Bingle* is generic for a hit, but also indicates a one-base hit or single. **1880** *Chicago Tribune* 12 May 8/5 Clapp..was brought in by Anson's *one-baser. **1949** *Los Angeles Times* 13 Mar. 25/8 Unser led off with a one-baser. **1887** *Graphic* 2 Apr. 355/1 That not uncommon literary phenomenon, the *one-book man, whose endeavour to repeat a happy accident is the most imprudent thing he can do. **1890** *Pall Mall G.* 18 Sept. 2/2 One-book men are less common than they used to be. **1970** *Daily Tel.* 26 Sept. 8/6 The next book, ..certainly a better novel than the second, enjoyed more success but the feeling began to grow that Remarque was a one-book author. **1854** *One catch all [see COWARDY *a.*]. **1876** J. BURROUGHS *Winter Sunshine* VIII. i. 210, I could not only walk upon the grass, but..play 'one catch all' with children, boys, dogs, or sheep upon it. **1898** A. B. Gomme *Traditional Games* II. 25 One Catch-all. The words 'Cowardy, cowardy custard' are repeated by children playing at this game when they advance towards the one who is selected to catch them. **1861** Miss Yonge *Stokesley Secret* iii. (1862) 45 A lady with..a good-humoured, *one-coloured face. **1870** Rock *Text. Fabr.* iv. (1876) 32 A one-coloured yet patterned silk. [**1818** S. Parkes *Let.* 20 Feb. in P. W. Flower *Hist. Trade in Tin* (1880) vii. 92 The following table will show the different sizes of tin plate which are made in Great Britain, and the marks by which each kind is known in commerce... Common No. 1 [size] 13¾ × 10..CI... Cross No. 1 13¾ × 10..XI.] **1890** *Cent. Dict.*, **One-cross*, a term applied to tin-plate..having the thickness of No. 30 Birmingham wire-gage, and having an average weight of 0·5 lb. per sheet. **1897** F. C. Moore *How to build Home* viii. 120 He is to furnish all tin cellar heating-pipes of best (one cross) tin. **1902** *Encycl. Brit.* XXXIII. 906/2 What are called *one-design, or restricted classes [of yachts] have latterly become popular. **1904** *Rudder* Nov. 609/2 A one-design boat is one of a fleet built from the same plans. **1928** *Daily Tel.* 11 Sept. 15/6 The East Coast one-design class to the number of nine, started at 10.30 a.m. to sail a course of a dozen sea miles. **1933** E. A. Robertson *Ordinary Families* v. 76 My dinghy's in for the Orwell one-designs. *Ibid.*, The one-designs will be single-handed. **1949** *Sun* (Baltimore) 27 Aug. 8/8 Little Penguin Class dinghies, one of the most popular of the smaller one-design racing sailboats. **1928** *Daily Tel.* 11 Sept. 15/6 The second place on this occasion went to an Essex *one-designer. **1883** *One dimensional [see dimensional *a.* 2]. **1909** W. M. Urban *Valuation* iii. 57 All these differences are reducible to differences in intensity and duration of a one-dimensional continuum, pleasantness-unpleasantness. **1936** V. A. Demant *Christian Polity* ix. 153 History was seen as a one-dimensional continuum. **1958** M. Kennedy *Outlaws on Parnassus* ix. 141 Daniel..is as one-dimensional to her as Klesmer was. **1964** *Philos. Rev.* LXXIII. 497 A proposition is a linear or one-dimensional structure. **1970** G. K. Woodgate *Elem. Atomic Struct.* ii. 19 Equation (2.50) is in the form of a one-dimensional equation of motion. **1975** *Nature* 22 May 279/2 Fairly recently however there has been a sharp switch of attention to 'one-dimensional materials' (composed of parallel long chain molecules). **1951** S. F. Nadel *Found. Social Anthropol.* v. 90 In the order of groupings we find no exactly equivalent instances of '*one-dimensionality'. **1976** *Sci. Amer.* Dec. 105/2 These purely genetic studies were followed by cytological and biochemical work showing that the one-dimensionality of linkage maps was associated with the linear arrangement of the genes along the chromosome. **1937** *Mind* XLVI. 87 There is a *one-directional character to events, an irreversibility in their order. **1950** Auden *Enchafèd Flood* (1951) ii. 65 The determination to live in one-directional historical time rather than in cyclical natural time. **1953** N. Tinbergen *Herring Gull's World* xvi. 132 In the *one-egg phase the bird often stands a few feet away from the nest. **1959** *Listener* 29 Oct. 729/1 One-egg twins, being genetically identical, have exactly the same blood and tissue antigens. **1976** *Times* 23 Nov. 15/4 Siamese twins.. are always one-egg twins. **1955** *Times* 1 July 15/1 The capital as doubled last year by the *one-for-one capitalization issue. **1962** W. Nowottny *Lang. Poets Use* i. 4 The equivalence is more complex than a simple one-for-one relation. **1975** *Listener* 6 Feb. 162/1 Arms are to be replaced only on a one-for-one basis. **1831** Lamb *Lett., to Moxon* (1888) II. 274 Did G. D. send his penny tract..to convert me to Unitarianism?..why I am as old a *one-Goddite as himself. *c* **1425** *Orolog. Sapient.* ii. in *Anglia* X. 344/44 Myne *onegotene sone. **1886** T. P. White *Ordnance Survey of U.K.* vi. 102 On the *one-inch map, also,..are shown the foot-paths as cross-cuts between roads. **1913** M. I. Newbigin *Ordnance Survey Maps* ii. 17 The scale of the 1-inch map is too large for any rapid form of locomotion. **1929** W. E. Collinson *Spoken Eng.* 88 I've got a one-inch ordnance [survey]. **1948** *N.Y. Jrnl. American* (Sunday Mail ed.) 9 May 1/1 The Court packing plan was defeated by a one-inch punch. **1960** *Farmer & Stockbreeder* 1 Mar. 62/1 The one-inch-to-the-mile survey sheet of Carmarthenshire. **1974** G. Moffat *Corpse Road* vii. 108 'Have you got that one-inch?' he asked. Barber brought him the map. **1904** 'Mark Twain' in *Harper's Weekly* 2 Jan. 18/1 There were headings—*one-liners and two-liners—and that was good. **1969** *Harper's Mag.* May 85/2 McCarthy had a one-liner for everyone in Washington, and the reporters who found favor were those who learned to leer and feed straight lines. **1975** *New Yorker* 19 May 23/3 Gail Parent's novel is in the form of a fat girl's jokey suicide note, full of one-liners. **1976** *Times Lit. Suppl.* 11 June 688/5 His dear cousins collapse in mirth at Berry's one-liners and monologues. **1908** S. Ford *Side-Stepping with Shorty* 90 Then me and Sadie in her bubble, towin' the busted *one-lunger behind. **1911** H. Quick *Yellowstone Nights* v. 124 The Old Man..was a one-lunger. **1943** 'T. Dudley-Gordon' *Coastal Command* xiii. 125 Angus, the local boatman, came alongside in his elderly 'one-lunger' motor-boat and took us ashore. **1963** Bird & Hutton-Stott *Veteran Motor Car* 15 The 'Varsity' model, and a few of the old one-lungers. **1976** *Islander* (Victoria, B.C.) 11 Apr. 10/1 This engine, a one-lunger, as it was called, drove the Scud..at a speed of six knots. **1842** *Congress. Globe* 27th Congress 2 Sess. App. 812/3 Those whose clamors are so unceasing against what they are pleased to call the '*one-man power'. **1844** *Mechanics' Mag.* XLI. 370 A common road one-man carriage. **1882** *Daily News* 18 Jan. 5/6 To keep him in, if that may be done without erecting a One-man Government. **1894** *Ibid.* 4 Apr. 5/3 If it contains a clause establishing one-man-one-vote, they will meet it with an amendment embodying in their opinion the principle of one-vote-one-value. **1897** Mary Kingsley *W. Africa* 306 Mr. Glass and I shared a one-man canoe, and the water lapped over the edge in an alarming way. **1929** D. H. Lawrence *Lovely Lady* (1933) 99 I'm afraid Virginia is a one-man woman. **1939** L. M. Montgomery *Anne of Ingleside* xxiv. 161 There are dogs like that—one-man dogs. **1951** J. C. Fennessy *Sonnet in Bottle* vii. i. 244 Goebbels is a one-man monkey—he doesn't like anybody but me. **1956** *Railway Mag.* May 301/2 The current practice appears to be dictated..by the economics and safety of one-man operation. **1967** *Economist* 9 Dec. 1031/2 Mr Frank Cousins is facing the Government once more—this time in an attempt to keep some thousands of unnecessary bus conductors riding around on routes that could become profitable with one-man bus operation. **1975** A. Hunter *Gently with Love* xi. 32 Anne has been a one-man girl ever since she met Earle. **1976** *Dumfries & Galloway Standard* 25 Dec. 16/3 The way to make economies without too much cutting down of services is to..bring in one-man-operated buses. **1931** (*record-title*) The *one-man band. **1938** Partridge *Dict. Slang* Suppl. 1018/2 *One-man band*, a person that takes rather too much on himself..; slightly ob., as is *l'homme orchestre* supplying the origin. **1958** *Listener* 23 Oct. 663/2 The versatility..was capitally sustained. The 'one-man band' was never 'off-beat'. **1962** *Sunday Times* (Colour Suppl.) 14 Oct. 9/1 There should also be remembered the great one-man bands of the museum world: men like Sandberg of the Stedelijk Museum in Amsterdam. **1965** *Listener* 10 June 877/1 That odd one-man-band, the three-hole pipe and tabor, which is now almost entirely confined to the border lands of France and Spain. **1974** N. Bentley *Inside Information* vi. 57 We're two mechanics short and the accountant's on holiday, so I'm a one-man band at the moment. **1977** *Listener* 7 Apr. 447/1 A young antiquarian..did a one-man-band act..making lonesome horn noises with his mouth to accompany his own piano solo. **1896** G. B. Shaw *Our Theatres in Nineties* (1932) II. 287 The real objection to Cibber's version is that it is what we call a '*one man show'. **1905** *Today* 15 Mar. 211/1 One of the young artists..is now having his first 'one-man-show' in London. **1943** F. Scully *Rogue's Gallery* 132 He lectured on the drama at Columbia, and even took up painting in his middle age staging several one-man shows though he never had an art lesson in his life. **1955** *Ann. Reg. 1954* 373 The Beaux Arts Gallery..held..the first one-man show..of John Bratby. **1962** *Listener* 6 Sept. 358/3 Uncle Kweku..started singing 'Happy birthday' in English... It ..became a one-man show. **1976** 'Z. Stone' *Modigliani Scandal* i. ii. 25 'Usher's one-man show has had it.' 'I'm afraid so..it won't harm him all that much. His talent will tell in the long run.' **1910**, etc. *One-many [see *many-one* adj. s.v. many *a.* 6c]. **1945** R. G. Collingwood *Idea of Nature* i. ii. 71 The Platonic form is not a 'logical universal', and the things, in the natural world..to which it stands in a one-many relation are not instances but approximations of it. **1964** E. Bach *Introd. Transformational Gram.* iii. 35 Rules which replace a single symbol by one or more symbols (one-many rules). **1972** *Lect. R. Inst. Philos.* V. 77 Berkeley regarded the relation between the self and its ideas as a necessary one-many relation. **1900** H. Lawson *On Track* 124 But for the *one-night lodgers..I was pretty comfortable there. **1915** T. S. Eliot *Prufrock* (1917) 9 Restless nights in one-night cheap hotels. **1943** D. Gascoyne *Poems 1937–1942* 46 Dozens of one-night rooms. **1976** *New Yorker* 15 Nov. 56/3 A fund-raising one-night gala performance. **1923** U. L. Silberrad *Lett. J. Armiter* iii. 62 The people of the house follow a sort of 'sheep and goat' plan, keeping us separate; we, the maiden-lady-some-stay visitors, sit at the upper end of the table, the *one-nighters at the other end. **1937** *Amer. Speech* XII. 184/2 *One nighter*, an engagement to play for a single night. **1959** H. Hobson *Mission House Murder* iii. 22 Johnny hasn't quite become a national star yet, but he pulls in a stack of lolly doing one-nighters, mostly in the provinces. **1973** *Guardian* 28 June 15/5 Bloated, badly dressed, he was doing one-nighters with a zombie rhythm section. **1977** 'L. Egan' *Blind Search* iv. 55 We don't get so many one-nighters like we used to. **1880** D. K. Ranous *Diary of Daly Débutante* (1910) 189 This coming week..is to be what they call '*one-night stands'. **1883** *National Police Gaz.* (U.S.) 8 Dec. 3/3 One night stands are not going to be subject, if they can help it, to the experiments of one troupe of queer fakirs after another. **1896**, etc. [see stand *sb.*[1] 2e]. **1904** G. V. Hobart *Jim Hickey* i. 13 I'm too delicate for this one-night stand gag. I'm going to New York and build a theatre. **1912** Wodehouse *Prince & Betty* ii. 28 What's the use of a Republic in a place like this? For a little bit of a one-night stand like this you want something picturesque, something that'll advertise the place. **1916** G. B. Shaw *Let.* 14 May in *B. Shaw & Mrs. Campbell* (1952) 186, I told you not to do those one-night stands. **1937** *New Republic* 24 Nov. 70/2 The band plays a one-night stand in some town near. **1956** B. Holiday *Lady sings Blues* (1973) i. 3 When he went on the road with that band it was the beginning of the end of our life as a family. Baltimore got to be just another one-night stand. **1959** 'F. Newton' *Jazz Scene* xi. 185 One of the worst kinds of professional life, that of the touring artist, often passing through a succession of one-night stands. **1963** A. Heron *Towards Quaker View of Sex* iii. 23 These affairs may still be very promiscuous—'one night stands'—or mainly emotional. **1972** J. Wilson *Hide & Seek* viii. 138 Nearly everyone else he knew had had at least a few casual affairs or one-night stands. **1860** *Harper's Mag.* July 195/1 Mrs. Tyler Todd caught the toss, like a skilful player at '*one old cat', on the edge of her..bonnet. **1929** *Sun* (Baltimore) 27 Mar. 10/3 Supervised play has taken the place of 'one old cat', and hockey has replaced shinney. **1949** *Chicago Daily News* 6 July 14/7 Juvenile pirates had their hang-outs and..one-old-cat and high-button-shoe football thrived. **1974** *Amer. Speech 1971* XLVI. 84 Ball, puck, and tin-can games..one old cat baseball. **1903** B. Russell *Princ. Math.* xi. 113 This requires that there should be some *one-one relation whose domain is the one class and whose converse domain is the other class. **1922**, etc. One-one [see *many-many* adj. s.v. many *a.* 6c]. **1950** C. M. Bowra *Romantic Imagination* 33 For him [*sc.* William Blake] allegory in the good sense is not the kind of 'one-one correspondence' which we find in *Pilgrim's Progress*. **1965** Patterson & Rutherford *Elem. Abstr. Algebra* i. 3 If..f is a mapping of S_1 into S_2 such that $f(x_1) = f(x_2) \Rightarrow x_1 = x_2$, then f is called a one-one mapping or a one-one correspondence. **1972** *Lect. R. Inst. Philos.* V. 80 If there were ideas..in this sense 'simple' they would stand only in a one-one relation to minds. **1924** *Granta* 25 Apr. 361/2 Last but not least he took a '*one one' in the French Tripos last year. **1968** K. Martin *Editor* i. 3, I had taken a One-one in my Tripos at Magdalene. **1967** *Technology Week* 20 Feb. 3/1 In the *one-on-one, relatively 'simple' intercepts run during the 1962–63 test series, the 'old' *Nike-Zeus* scored on 10 of 14 attempted live ICBM intercepts. **1972** J. Gores *Dead Skip* (1973) i. 7 He had started as a field agent..three years before, when he had realized he wasn't going to be middleweight champ of the world after all; it was the only profession he knew which could give him the same one-on-one excitement he'd found in the ring. **1974** 'E. Lathen' *Sweet & Low* xi. 113 He was not in a one-on-one confrontation. There was a goodly array of..small fry present. **1932** D. Burnstine *Four Horsemen's One over One Method of Contract Bidding* i. 1 The *One-Over-One system of bidding has achieved its present fame because of its use by players who have won the majority of contract tournaments. *Ibid.* 3 The One-Over-One offers leeway in arriving at the correct contract with ease. **1934** *Amer. Speech* IX. 10/1 There are..several varieties of one-over-one bids. **1959** *Listener* 19 Mar. 530/1 Many completely minimum hands..could be hamstrung by a simple one-over-one response on the first round. **1795** *Times* 6 May in Ashton *Old Times* (1885) 317 The Name under the *one-pair-of-stairs window. **1897** *Pall Mall Mag.* Jan. 104 A big man..leaning from a one-pair window. **1585** Higins tr. *Junius' Nomenclator, Basilinda*,..The playe called *one penie, one penie: come after me. **1598** in Florio. **1677** in Holyoke. **1880** G. A. Sala *Amer. Revisited* (1882) II. 13 Slop-shops, or '*one-piece stores' overflowing with guernseys, pea jackets, sou'-wester hats. **1895** *Montgomery Ward Catal.* 501/2 Bathing suits. One-piece suits. **1912** *Woman's Weekly* 25 May 100/3 (*caption*) A One-Piece Dress, One-Piece Petticoat, One-Piece Drawers, and One-Piece Bodice. **1930** *Engineering* 7 Mar. 309/3 The housing and arm being also a one-piece casting. **1972** J. Mosedale *Football* ii. 21 The Van Buren uniform included a one-piece fiber crown replacing the sewn leather helmets of the pre-1940s. **1973** 'D. Halliday' *Dolly & Starry Bird* xiv. 203 A gorgeous one-piece black bathing suit. **1974** F. Warner *Meeting Ends* i. i. 2 Wrasse..in modern one-piece bathing costume. **1919** W. H. Downing *Digger Dial.* 37 **One-pip*, Second Lieutenant. **1937** Partridge *Dict. Slang* 589/1 *One-pipper. **1956** D. M. Davin *Sullen Bell* 181 Whatever young one-pipper it was could get a night's leave. **1974** G. M. Fraser *McAuslan in Rough* 17 Keith was a mere pink-cheeked one-pipper of twenty years, whereas I had reached the grizzled maturity of twenty-one and my second star. **1938** *Jrnl. Symbolic Logic* III. ii. 83 Chapter 2 supplements the propositional calculus..with the Boolean algebra of *one-place predicates. **1947** H. Reichenbach *Elem. Symbolic Logic* §17. 83 The term 'property'..is usually applied only to one-place situational functions. **1967** S. C. Kleene *Math. Logic* §27. 145 More essential use is made of the predicate calculus with quantification of one-place predicates in Example 19. **1974** *Canad. Jrnl. Linguistics* XIX. 151 But what I want to focus on here is the claim that *easy* is a one-place predicate with a sentential subject, while *eager* has a sentential object. **1959** J. W. Carr in E. M. Grabbe et al. *Handbk. Automation, Computation, & Control* II. ii. 58 In the *one-plus-one addressing procedure, each instruction has a basic single-address format, but also includes a second address to be used to designate the location of the next instruction to be performed. **1969** P. B. Jordain *Condensed Computer Encycl.* 351 The one-plus-one address instruction has only the power (or flexibility) of a one-address instruction, because only one operand reference is included. **1892** J. A. Ewing *Magn. Induction in Iron* ii. 40 We may distinguish this as the '*one-pole' method, seeing that the deflection of the magnetometer is mainly caused by one of the bar's poles. **1932** 'N. Shute' *Lonely Road* i. 15 From the set of her one pole mast she might have been a Thames bawley of about fifty tons. **1940** M. Miller *Harbor of Sun* xxviii. 311 When a fisherman describes the size of a school as 'one-pole tuna', 'two-pole tuna' and sometimes 'three-pole tuna', he is but saying that the size of the tuna in that special school required one, two or three men to a team for hauling in each fish. **1845** C. M. Kirkland *Western Clearings* (1846) 27 Some scattered grains of coarse powder from near the touch-hole of the *one-pounder that was fired all day by the opposition. **1893** 'Mark Twain' in *Century Mag.* Jan. 339/2 They find they've given a tramp a million-pound bill when they thought it was a one-pounder. **1916** 'B. M. Bower' *Phantom Herd* v. 69 We've made quite a haul since you left. A bunch of *one-reelers. **1976** *Listener* 23–30 Dec. 833/1 When you were making the one-reelers, did each have a lengthy script? **1922** Wodehouse *Clicking of Cuthbert* vi. 142 No human being could play golf against a *one-ring circus like that without blowing up. **1972** *Village Voice* (N.Y.) 1 June 40/3 An opera house that is not a cultural force is only a one-ring circus made up of vocal acrobats who use music as a trampoline. **1934** *Amer. Speech* IX. 112/2 Plenty of *one-stop service stations for washing, minor repairs, lubrication, etc. **1962** *Economist* 5 May 452/1 Commercial banks which are able to offer complete 'one stop' banking service—including current accounts, consumer loans and so on. **1971** *E. Afr. Jrnl.* Mar. 34 (Advt.), You will find Text Book Centre a one-stop warehouse for all your educational requirements. **1978** *Oxford Consumer* Mar. 5/1 The store will specialise in the provision of food lines at economic prices and will be backed up by a sufficient range of household goods to enable the shopping public to derive the maximum convenience from a 'one stop' shopping trip. **1958** A. J. Bliss *Metre of Beowulf* 62 We must, in fact, recognize the possibility of *one-stress verses. Sievers himself in later life envisaged such one-stress verses; Pope, too, makes one-stress verses a mainstay of his new theory. **1965** *Eng. Stud.* XLVI. 419 As examples of light, one-stress verses he gives: hu ða æðelingas. **1961** Webster, *One-suiter. **1971** 'O. Bleeck' *Thief who painted Sunlight* (1972) xx. 181 He was carrying something that looked like a one-suiter. **1947** C. Eisenhart et al. *Sel. Techniques Statistical Anal.* 459/2 (Index), One-sided or *one-tail tests of statistical hypotheses. **1954** *Brit. Jrnl. Psychol.* XLV. 174 The difference between these means is..only just significant at the 5% level, using the one-tail test. **1950** M. H. Quenouille *Introd. Statistics* v. 98 Here, since we are interested in deviations in one direction only, probabilities calculated using x^2 must be halved. We are then said to be using a *one-tailed test. **1969** R. H. Kolstoe *Introd. Statistics Behav. Sci.* x. 203 In a few situations the research worker, *before collecting his data*, decides that he is interested in one specific directional hypothesis... In this case a one-tailed test of significance would be indicated. **1971** B. Erricker *Advanced Gen. Statistics* xiv. 206 If we were only interested in whether the tensile strengths of the components of the first manufacturer are greater than those from the second we would only need a one-tailed test. **1850** W. Howitt *Year-bk. Country* vi. 179 Old Lodge, we salute thee for thy venerable antiquity; but we owe thee no respect as the *one-time resort of the boasted virgin queen! **1870** *Appleton's Jrnl.* 5 Feb. 161/2 Then you would have one brought after the other, unless accompanied by the request, 'all at the same time', or, in their [*sc.* native Liberians'] own language, '*go fetch 'em come; both two; one time*'! **1873** C. J. G. Rampini *Lett. from Jamaica* 177 Man can't smoke an' whistle one time. **1881** J. F. T. Keane *Journ. Medinah* 195-6 One very handsome pair of English..pistols..with their one-time owner's name on them. 1886 F. T. Elworthy *West Somerset Word-bk.* 537 There used to be a public-house there one time, but he bin pulled down 'is gurt many years. 1897 *Westm. Gaz.* 24 June 2/2 Prime Minister of the one-time dependency of Van Diemen's Land. 1899 C. J. C. Hyne *Further Adventures Capt. Kettle* ii. 31 He wouldn't stop for fighting-palaver. He'd be off for bush, one-time. 1924 *Time* 7 Jan. 30/2 Died. Richard Wittig, brother of Maximillian Harden, famed German publicist, onetime friend of the Kaiser, onetime Oberburgomaster of Posen. 1928 *Flynn's Weekly* 4 Feb. 436/1 Big Bill Douglas was enjoying a year's vacation from his usual haunts up at Sing Sing at the expense of the State. To his underworld associates he was doing a short bit in the Big House, or a one time loser. 1942 Z. N. Hurston in A. Dundes *Mother Wit* (1973) 225/2 A Zigaboo..asked a woman that one time. 1950 'S. Ransome' *Deadly Miss Ashley* viii. 96 Duncan Westling's onetime confidential secretary was now the secretary of Duncan Westling's onetime mistress? 1959 *Listener* 10 Dec. 1023/1 The Soviet Union has lately placed some big orders with British industry... But we have a feeling that these are, or may be, one-time orders to enable the Soviet Union to progress towards self-sufficiency. 1967 *Ibid.* 2 Feb. 157/1 S. W. Johnson-Marshall, one-time chief architect at the Ministry of Education. 1973 *N.Y. Law Jrnl.* 27 Mar. 4/5 The tenant insisted that the only increase he was obliged to pay was a one-time increase. [1955 *Gloss. Soviet Military Terminol.* (U.S. Army Technical Manual 30-544) 228/1 One-time system.] 1977 *Sci. Amer.* Aug. 120/3 It is easy to see why the *one-time cipher is uncrackable even in principle. Since each symbol can be represented by any other symbol, and each choice of representation is completely random, there is no internal pattern. 1953 *N.Y. Times Mag.* 15 Mar. 62/2 The Russians are notorious for their reliance on a device known as the '*one-time-pad'. This means..that each message is sent in a completely different code. 1966 M. R. D. Foot *SOE in France* iv. 105 By now [*sc.* 1944] the British were using a much safer.. cipher: one-time pad... The agent held a pad of silk slips, each printed with columns of random letters or figures from which any message could be enciphered or deciphered; he.. was supposed to tear each slip off and burn it after use. 1977 *Sci. Amer.* Aug. 120/3 If the one-time pad provides absolute secrecy, why is it not used for all secret communication? The answer is that it is too impractical. Each time it is employed a key must be sent in advance, and the key must be at least as long as the anticipated message. 1959 *One-to-many [see correspondence 1 b]. 1976 P. R. White *Planning for Public Transport* v. 112 In a one-to-many situation, passengers joining at the fixed point(s) request the driver to serve a destination, and no radio contact is necessary. 1873 *Proc. Lond. Math. Soc.* IV. 252 The equations..being supposed to establish a '*one-to-one' correspondence between the two integral spaces. 1882, etc. One-to-one [see correspondence 1 b]. 1903 B. Russell *Princ. Math.* xi. 113 Two classes have the same number..when their terms can be correlated one to one, so that any one term of either corresponds to one and one only term of the other. 1931 C. Fox *Mind & its Body* iii. 62 One of the most important assumptions of psychological physiology was this one-to-one correspondence between neural processes and mental processes. 1936 J. R. Kantor *Objective Psychol. Gram.* xvii. 237 There is no clear-cut one-to-one relation between a grammatical form and a definite time point. 1963 J. Lyons *Structural Semantics* iii. 37 It is not so much that one language draws a greater or less number of semantic distinctions than another which prevents the matching of their vocabularies one-to-one. 1968 C. G. Kuper *Introd. Theory Superconductivity* xii. 193 There is a one-to-one correspondence between the states of a gas of non-interacting Bosons and those of a family of harmonic oscillators. 1973 One-to-one [see nicotinic *a.* 2]. 1928 D. H. Lawrence *Lady Chatterley* xix. 363 They're all *one-track minds nowadays. 1932 *Kansas City* (Missouri) *Times* 5 May 20 The persons with the one-track mind are the ones who usually have the most collisions. 1934 H. Nicolson *Curzon: Last Phase* 18 He has been accused of possessing a 'one-track mind', of being deficient in creative, as opposed to emotional, imagination. 1935 B. Malinowski in M. Black *Importance of Lang.* (1962) 78 The advertisements emanating from such one-track remedies. 1944 'Brahms' & 'Simon' *Titania has Mother* viii. 68 Her son..had launched himself onto a one-track conversation. 1957 P. Frank *Seven Days to Never* ii. 48 The electronic machines..could distract a Russian missile's one-track mind. 1968 *National Observer* (U.S.) 3 June 15/1 It's not that I'm antisocial. It's just that I'm preoccupied. I have a very one-track mind. 1973 'H. Howard' *Highway to Murder* vii. 77 I've got a one-track mind... All this started with a man getting shot and I keep thinking along those lines. 1967 *Times Rev. Industry* May 72/2 Most containers are '*one-trip' in the sense that the product is used and the container is thrown away. 1809 Roland *Fencing* 70 In the motions of *one-two you disengage alternately, on one side of the adversary's blade, and then return on the other. *Ibid.* 89 If the adversary parries the one-two-three feint. 1811 *Sporting Mag.* XXXVIII. 140/2 He..had no difficulty at getting at his man when he chose with a *one, two.* 1815 *Pancratia* (ed. 2) 359 He fought cautiously..and whenever he closed put in his *one two* with the greatest dexterity. 1910 G. W. E. Russell *Sketches & Snapshots* xlvii. 445 A smart one-two on his smeller effectually tapped his claret. 1931 *Times Lit. Suppl.* 22 Oct. 819/1 The flawless stance and one-two punch of Peter Jackson. 1948 *Economist* 20 Mar. 454/1 His [*sc.* Stalin's] one-two play in Czechoslovakia and Finland. 1952 A. Wilson *Hemlock & After* III. i. 201 Even Ron was surprised that his 'old one two' was quite so compelling. 1960 *Times* 4 Oct. 13/4 'The old one-two', in the boxing slang of a more vulgarly robust age, indicated a quick follow-up with the right immediately after the left had landed, and the near synchronization of the two blows added immensely to their effect. 1970 *Times* 1 Oct. 10/3 Hinton came up from his position of centre back to play a one-two with Hutchinson and leave the wretched Christidis stranded. 1974 J. Gardner *Corner Men* xi. 100 Let Hart and Harvey work them over, then we can go in and do the old routine... The old one two. 1978 *Sunday Times* (Colour Suppl.) 28 May 34/4 *One-two*, using a colleague for an immediate return pass, to run on to. 1933 A. Salter in A. F. Brockway *Bermondsey Story* (1949) ii. 12 The house was *one up, one down, with a small scullery. 1968 Busby & Holtham *Main Line Kill* vi. 68 Some of the back to back terraces of poky little one-up, one-down houses had been pulled down. 1898 W. B. Smith *Infinitesimal Analysis* i. 7 When to one value of the one variable there corresponds only one value of the other, this latter is called a *one-valued or unique function of the former. 1913 *Trans. Amer. Math. Soc.* XIV. 481 None of the equivalent postulate-sets here referred to is in terms of its undefined entities one-valued ('categorical')—that is, each determines not a single algebra but a class of algebras. 1943 *Amer. Speech* XVIII. 220 The first stage of human development..is that of the savage, prelogical mentality, with a one-valued semantics (or system of evaluations), in which, as Lucien Lévy-Bruhl has said, 'everything is everything else' by ' mystic participation'. 1968 E. T. Copson *Metric Spaces* vii. 85 A function is, by definition, one-valued. 1882 *Q. Rev.* Jan. 209 Madame, the *onewhile beloved of Gibbon. 1894 Hall Caine *Manxman* I. ix. 45 I'm a *one-woman man, Kate; but loving one is giving me eyes for all. 1937 M. Hillis *Orchids on your Budget* (1938) iv. 68 We ourselves have run our one-woman ménage both with and without an office job. 1960 P. Tompkins in G. B. Shaw *To a Young Actress* 151 Thirty-five paintings for a one-woman exhibition at the Leicester Galleries. 1962 I. Murdoch *Unofficial Rose* ii. 32 He's a one-woman cat. 1974 J. Cleary *Peter's Pence* v. 156 I'm a one-woman man. 1926 A. E. Taylor *Plato* viii. 198 The epiphenomenalist is tied by his theory to a '*one-world' interpretation of human experience; morality presupposes a 'two-world' interpretation. 1947 *Collier's* 7 June 12 (*title*) Dunkirk—the one-world town. 1948 *Sun* (Baltimore) 22 June 2/1 His selection of Stassen for Taft's running mate was new and was surprising, in view of his oft-repeated denunciation of Stassen as a '*one-worlder' who would be unsafe in high office. 1958 *Spectator* 15 Aug. 228/2 'Men live and die for a flag; it is indeed the only thing for which they are willing to die in masses..' is a statement of a truth which one-worlders ignore at their peril. 1965 *Social Crediter* 31 July 2/2 The *active* Socialists, Communists, and One-Worlders.

one (wʌn), *v.* Now *rare.* Forms: 4-5 **onen, oone(n,** *north.* **ane,** 6- **one.** [ME. *onen, anen*; OE. had *ʒe-ánian*; (pa. pple. *ʒe-áned*); in OHG. *einôn*, usually *gi-einôn*, MHG. and G. *einen*; f. *án*, one. Cf. L. *ūnīre*, F. *unir*, from *ūnus, un.*]

1. *trans.* To make into one; to unite.

[*c* 900 tr. *Bæda's Eccl. Hist.* III. xiv. [xix.] (1890) 214 Oð þæt heo wæron in æn[n]e unmætne lieʒ [*MS.* læʒ] ʒeanede and ʒesomnade.] *c* 1340 Hampole *Prose Tr.* 34 To se hym in his blysse and to be anede to hym in lufe. *Ibid.* 38 Of þe soule of Iesu, whilke was aned fully to þe godhede. *c* 1386 Chaucer *Sompn. T.* 260 Ech thyng that is oned in it selue Is moore strong than whan it is toscatered. 1387 Trevisa *Higden* (Rolls) VI. 289 Egbertus onede the kyngdoms. *c* 1449 Pecock *Repr.* I. viii. 41 Forto be couplid and ooned to God. 1491 Caxton *Vitas Patr.* (W. de W. 1495) I. xlix. 98 a/1 Yf the Pryours were unyed and onyd wyth the abbayes. 1587 *Byrd's Psalms, Sonn.* etc. in Arb. *Garner* II. 93 Dead! no, no, but renowned! With the anointed oned! 1672 Cressy in Stillingfl. *Idol. Ch. Rome* (ed. 2) 225 Our soul is so fulsomely oned to God. *Ibid.*, The maker to whom it is oned. 1828 *Craven Gloss.* (ed. 2), *One*, to atone. 1839 Bailey *Festus* ii. (1852) 23 It is this which ones us with the whole and God. 1921 B. Williamson *Supernat. Mysticism* v. 45 The human race was so oned with Adam that all sinned in him.

†**2.** *refl.* and *intr.* To agree, unite; to come to terms. *Obs.*

1340 *Ayenb.* 219 Yef tuo of ous oneþ ham togidere me uor to bidde. *a* 1400-50 *Alexander* 879 He..Anes with Olympadas..And lofe hire lely, to his lyfes ende. *c* 1425 Wyntoun *Cron.* IV. xviii. *heading*, Quhen þe Kyng Antyocus anyd wyth þe Romanys.

†**one, onne,** *adv.* and *prep. Obs.* [An early ME. deriv. form from on, on the analogy of inne, etc. (Cf. offe.)] = on.

a. as *prepositional adv.*, or *prep.* after relative.

c 1200 *Trin. Coll. Hom.* 89 Swo hatte þe þrop þe preste one wunien. *Ibid.*, He..bed hem bringen a wig one te riden. *c* 1200 Ormin 3753 O þatt nahht þatt Crist wass borenn onne. *c* 1380 Wyclif *Wks.* (1880) 242 Nouȝt to liue onne. —— *Sel. Wks.* III. 207 Þat day mot periche þat I was born onne. *a* 1400 *Pistill of Susan* 164 Bi þe lord and þe lawe þat we onne leeue. *a* 1425 *Cursor M.* 676 Þat mychel murþe was onne [*earlier MSS.* on] to se. *Ibid.* 5715.

b. as ordinary *prep.*

c 1205 Lay. 4069 Cloten hauede Cornwale, þat he heold wel one griðe. *Ibid.* 6719 Þe king..nam onne [*c* 1275 on] his honde Ane wi-æxe stronge. *c* 1220 *Bestiary* 436 He billeð one ðe foxes fel. *Ibid.* 504. *c* 1400 *R. Glouc.'s Chron.* (Rolls) 1446 He biþoȝte him of felonie [*MS.* a one feloniȝe].

†**one,** app. var. of hone *sb.*[2], delay, tarrying.

1297 R. Glouc. (Rolls) 2579 Atte verste wiþoute one Castigen þe kinges broþer mid is men echone Asaylede hors & is ost.

one, obs. erron. form of own *a.*

one, rare erron. f. wone, *Obs.*, abundance, store.

-one, *suffix. Chem.* [Gr. *-ωνη* feminine patronymic.]

a. An ending used unsystematically in forming the names of chemical derivatives, as in ***acet-one*** (Gmelin 1848: see ketone), ***mellone, quinone.***

b. In the systematic nomenclature proposed by Hofmann 1866, the formative of the names of hydrocarbons of composition C_nH_{2n-4}, as in ***propone*** C_3H_2, ***quartone*** C_4H_4, ***pentone*** or ***quintone*** C_5H_6, ***sextone*** C_6H_8, etc. These are seldom used.

1877 Watts *Fownes' Chem.* II. 64 The only known member of the fatty group belonging to this series is valylene or pentone C_5H_6.

one-, obs. var. un- in many ME. words, e.g. *one-bycomelech, onecomely, onecouth, oneknowyng, oneresonable, oneshamely, one-spekable.*

one-act, *a.* [one *numeral a.* 34 a.] Denoting a short play or other production consisting of a single act. Hence as *sb.*, such a play. So **one-'acter,** a one-act play; also *fig.*

1888 *Playgoers' Mag.* Feb. 45 The story of Carton's self-sacrifice would form a touching little one-act play. 1895 *Pall Mall G.* 11 Oct. 11/2 'The Burglar and the Judge', the very clever one-acter by F. C. Philipps and C. H. Brookfield. 1905 *Athenæum* 7 Oct. 477/3 The one-act trifle which serves as *lever de rideau.* 1912 E. Nesbit *Let.* in D. L. Moore *E. Nesbit* (1933) xv. 269, I have had a one-act play accepted by a London manager. 1927 J. Pollock (*title*) Twelve one-acters. 1940 G. Marx *Let.* 5 Sept. (1967) 25 El Capitan.. has done magnificently with the Coward one-acts. 1960 A. Coren in *Introduction: Stories by New Writers* 70 The sane guy is the one who realises that life is a short one-acter. 1967 *Oxf. Compan. Theatre* (ed. 3) 223/2 The one-act play survives mainly in the productions of the amateur theatre in England and America. 1967 *Wall St. Jrnl.* 24 Apr. 18/4 The play for the evening was Lanford Wilson's 'The Madness of Lady Bright', a 45-minute one-acter. 1973 *Guardian* 23 Mar. 12/3 Tchaikovsky's seventh and last opera is a one-acter. 1976 *Scottish Rev.* Spring 17 *The Stick-Up*, a one-acter from *Fifteen Poems and a Play* (Edinburgh, 1969). 1977 L. Meynell *Hooky gets Wooden Spoon* xiii. 157 She had written a one-act play for herself.

oneale, obs. form of anneal *v.*

†**one-'ane,** obs. northern f. *onan*, anon.

c 1375 *Sc. Leg. Saints* iv. (*Jacobus*) 177 And sa parfyte mad hyme one-ane.

one argument. *Logic* [f. one *numeral a.* + argument *sb.* 3.] The variable of a function or operator of only one variable; also *attrib.*

1941 O. Helmer tr. *Tarski's Introd. Logic* 107 In order to differentiate between two-termed and three-termed functional relations, we speak, in the first case, of functions of one variable or of functions with one argument. 1951 J. Łukasiewicz in *Proc. R. Irish Acad.* LIV. A. 27 Such values are not only constant functors of one propositional argument, as *N*, negation, for example, but also complex expressions like a functor of one argument. 1955 H. Leblanc *Introd. Deductive Logic* 191 We have studied..so-called one-argument functions like the functions square of, double of, and so on. 1957 A. N. Prior *Time & Modality* 2 A system must contain a pair of one-argument operators forming statements out of statements. 1965 Hughes & Londey *Elem. Formal Logic* iii. 19 The following are *monadic operators*, (i.e. they take one argument). 1967 H. Weber tr. J. Łukasiewicz in S. McCall *Polish Logic* iii. 47 Since this proposition is valid for all functors with one argument, it is also valid for the functor '*M*'.

one-arm ('wʌnɑːm), *a.* [one *numeral a.* 34 a.] Having one arm; using only one arm; *spec.* **one-arm bandit** (orig. *U.S.*) = *one-armed bandit*; **one-arm joint** or **lunch (room)** *U.S.*, a cheap eating-house where customers sit in seats which have one arm wide enough to support plates of food, etc.; also *ellipt.* as *one-arm* sb.

1906 *Westm. Gaz.* 7 Sept. 3/2 Ordinarily I can do a one-arm press of 90 lb., but I must confess that I was almost beaten in getting hoisted some of these sheaves. 1912 M. Nicholson *Hoosier Chron.* 297 Everybody's saying 'Stop, Look, Listen!'..the white aprons in the one-arm lunch rooms say it now when you kick on the size of the buns. 1915 *N.Y. World Mag.* 9 May 14 *One arm joint*, a chair dairy lunch. 1926 *New Masses* May 9/4 Countermen in the one-arm lunches yell '*coffee-and*' not so fiercely. 1931 H. Mutschmann *Gloss. Americanisms* 43/2 *One-arm driver*, man steering auto with one arm and necking his girl with the other. 1935 J. Hargan *Gloss. Prison Lang.* 6 *One arm joint*, a cheap restaurant where one takes his food to a chair to eat. 1938 *Sun* (Baltimore) 6 Oct. 24/1 The Court of Appeals at Annapolis yesterday declared..that the so-called 'one-arm bandit' type of slot machine is illegal. 1939 *Detective Fiction Weekly* 18 Feb. 36/2 A one-arm joint is a white-tiled place that suggests a clinic. Two long rows of armchairs line the walls. The right arm of each chair is expanded into china-topped slab. You park your food on it. 1940 J. O'Hara *Pal Joey* 57 She went with me to this one-arm where I eat. 1943 *Sun* (Baltimore) 27 Jan. 5/6 Three of the [slot] machines were described by police as the 'one-arm bandit' type. 1944 B. Hope *I Never left Home* v. 63 He flew a plane back from a mission once holding his wounded copilot in his arms. That's one-arm driving that counts. 1951 E. Kefauver *Crime in Amer.* (1952) xiii. 151 The iniquitous 'one-arm bandit' slot machines sprang up in bars and cigar stores. 1956 S. Hope *Diggers' Paradise* 156 In the exclusive clubs, with few exceptions, you may see an array of 'one-arm bandits' ranged against the walls. There fruit machines—or poker machines—are usually rigged to work with shilling discs bought from the bar steward. 1960 *Times* 2 Dec. 8/4 Six fruit machines, or 'one-arm bandits', were on display at Scotland Yard.

one-armed ('wʌnɑːmd), *a.* [one *numeral a.* 34 d.] Having one arm; also *transf.*; *spec.* **one-armed bandit** (orig. *U.S.*) = *fruit machine* (see fruit *sb.* 9).

1809 *Thespiad* 10 Every subsequent comedy would have contained a weather-beaten, one-armed sailor. 1818 Cobbett *Pol. Reg.* XXXIII. 73 He cowed the one-armed Admiral. 1886 F. T. Elworthy *West Somerset Word-Bk.* 536 *One-arm'd landlord*, cant name for a pump. 1890 *Spectator* 27 Sept. 413 This writer..has great power, but of a one-armed sort. 1914 W. B. Yeats *Responsibilities* 26 A one-legged, one-armed, one-eyed man. 1938 *Time* 28 Feb. 33/1 Last fortnight, with her ax she demolished two more —as she called them—'one-armed bandits'. 1945 Baker

Austral. Lang. iv. 88 *Ned Kelly* is displacing *one-armed bandit* for a poker machine. **1948** *Richmond* (Virginia) *Times-Dispatch* 8 Apr. 5/1 He was convicted of a charge of having two slot machines, familiarly known as 'one-armed bandits', in his possession. **1959** *Times* 12 Feb. 10/7 To-day the Senators were ringed with juke-boxes, pinball tables, 'one-armed bandits', and other coin-operated devices. **1971** P. TOYNBEE *Working Life* iv. 60 You slip your card into the slot and pull down the lever which punches the time on it. 'Talk about a one-armed bandit', someone jokes.. 'Trouble is, it's never been known to pay out.' **1972** D. FRANCIS *Smokescreen* vi. 70 There's more cars parked along the streets down there than one-armed bandits in Nevada.

†'one-beˌgotten, *ppl. a. Obs.* Also oon-, on-. [tr. L. *unigenitus*.] Only begotten.

1382 WYCLIF *John* iii. 16 God so louede the world, that he ȝaf his oon bigetun sone. *c* **1425** *St. Mary of Oignies* I. xii. in *Anglia* VIII. 148/8 Þe onbygoten sone of þe hye kynge of heuene. **1571** GOLDING *Calvin on Ps.* xviii. 50 The one-begotten sonne of God.

one-berry ('wʌnˌbɛrɪ). a. Turner's name for *Paris quadrifolia* (Herb Paris); from the single berry, produced at the summit of the slender stem. (Used by later writers, but never vernacular.)

1548 TURNER *Names of Herbes* 8 Pardalianches, whiche we may call in englishe Libardbayne or one bery. **1568** —— *Herbal* III. 35 The herbe that I call one berrye hath a rounde stalke.. and in the top of the stalke about a rounde black berrye come out foure smal leaves. **1678** PHILLIPS (ed. 4), *Herb Paris*, an Herb otherwise call True Knot or One Berry, the Leaves whereof grow like a True-lovers Knot, with a Berry in the midst. **1789** G. WHITE *Selborne* (1853) II. xl. 265, I found *Paris quadrifolia* herb Paris or one-berry.

b. *U.S.* = CHECKERBERRY, *Indian turnip* s.v. INDIAN *a.* 4 b, WINTERGREEN.

1877 BARTLETT *Dict. Amer.* (ed. 4) 319 Jack-in-the-Pulpit. (*Arisæna triphyllum*)... In Connecticut, it is called One-berry. **1892** *Jrnl. Amer. Folk-Lore* V. 100 *Gaultheria procumbens*, one-berry. **1931** M. GRIEVE *Mod. Herbal* II. 766 *Mitchella repens*... Partridgeberry, Checkerberry, Winter Clover, Deerberry, One-berry.

'one-blade. [f. ONE *a.* + BLADE *sb.*, leaf.] Lyte's name for *Smilacina bifolia* (*Maianthemum bifolium*), a herb allied to the lily-of-the-valley, having a large solitary leaf springing from the root-stock, and two smaller alternate ones upon the flower-stalk.

1578 LYTE *Dodoens* III. xxvi. 178 Monophillon.. may be also called in English, one Leafe, one Blade, or Singleleafe. **1678** PHILLIPS (ed. 4), *One-blade*.. an Herb good, especially in wounds of the Nerves. **1760** J. LEE *Introd. Bot.* App. 321 One Blade, *Convallaria*.

one-eared ('wʌnˌɪəd), *a.*[1] Having one ear.

1685 *Lond. Gaz.* No. 2068/4 Two little one ear'd Pots.

† one-eared, *a.*[2] *Obs.* ? an error for *one-yeared*.

c **1645** HOWELL *Lett.* VI. xxvii, This Wine is still one-ear'd, and brisk, though put Out of Italian Cask in English Butt.

one-er, var. ONER *sb.*

† 'one-eye. *Obs.* [tr. med.L. *monoculus*.] A name for the cæcum or 'blind gut'.

1541 R. COPLAND *Guydon's Quest. Chirurg.* H iv, There as begynneth the gutte called one eye, or the bag, for it semeth yᵗ it hath but one eye.

one-eyed ('wʌnˌaɪd), *a.* **1. a.** Having only one eye; also, blind of one eye.

c **1000** ÆLFRIC *Saints' Lives* xxxiii. 321 Þa com þider sum broþor se wæs aneȝede. **13..** *E.E. Allit. P.* B. 102 Be þay hol, be þay halt, be þay on-yȝed. *c* **1440** *Promp. Parv.* 365/1 Oone eyyd, *monoculus, monotalmus*. *c* **1550** CHEKE *Matt.* xviii. 9 Better it is for ye to enter oneied into lijf. **1603** DEKKER *Grissil* (Shaks. Soc.) 3 Look how yon one-ey'd waggoner of heaven Hath.. Burst ope the melancholy jail of night. **1665** MARVELL *Char. Holland*, Among the blind the one-ey'd blinkard reigns. **1725** POPE *Odyss.* IX. 475 From all their dens the one-ey'd race repair. **1819** SHELLEY *Cyclops* 24 The one-eyed children of the Ocean God, The man-destroying Cyclopses. **1858** LYTTON *What will he do* I. xii, Waife was still one-eyed and a cripple.

†b. *U.S. slang.* Dishonest. *Obs.*

1833 *Sk. & Eccentr. D. Crockett* i. 24 In the slang of the backwoods, one swore that he would never be '*one-eyed*'.

2. a. As a general term of disapproval or contempt: small, inferior, inadequate, unimportant; = ONE-HORSE *a.* 2, esp. of a town. *colloq.* (orig. *U.S.* or *dial.*).

1871 D. G. ROSSETTI *Let.* 28 Oct. (1967) III. 1021 A little hamlet called Kelmscott, the nearest town to which is Lechlade,—that being however but a 'one-eyed' town as the Yankees say. **1881** HARDY *Laodicean* III. 246, I shouldn't care for such a one-eyed benefit as that. **1887** PARISH & SHAW *Dict. Kentish Dial.* 111 'That's a middlin' one-eyed place.' 'I can't make nothin' of these here one-eyed new-fashioned tunes they've took-to in church; why they've a'most done afore I can make a start.' **1937** G. HEYER *They found him Dead* i. 19, I wasn't born to this humdrum life in a one-eyed town. **1947** *E. Afr. Ann. 1946–7* 101/2 Some had said it was a grand little town; others, a one-eyed hole! **1977** *Times* 14 May 8/7 In its somewhat one-eyed way, it [*sc.* Tobago] is among the loveliest.. of all the Caribbean islands.

b. Narrow in outlook; prejudiced, narrow-minded. Hence *one-eyedness*.

1863 J. BROWN *Let.* Mar. (1912) 206, I do believe the man thinks he is doing God service and is honest in his way, though vain and one-eyed to ludicrosity, as you have most thoroughly and delightfully shown. **1874** SWINBURNE *Let.* July (1959) II. 302 With all his rhetorical power, he [*sc.* J. A. Froude] seems to me (even apart from his one-eyed prepossession and palpable special pleading) but a shallow reader of character. **1921** G. B. SHAW *Back of Methuselah* p. li, There is no reason to suspect Weismann of Sadism... It was a mere piece of one-eyedness; and it was Darwin who put out Weismann's humane and sensible eye. **1971** *Austral. Seacraft* June 4/2 It seems your correspondent is one-eyed so far as the southern part of Australia is concerned.

onefold ('wʌnfəʊld), *a.* [f. ONE + -FOLD.

OE. had *ánfald, -feald*, whence ME. north. *anfald*, AFALD, south. OFOLD, q.v. A single instance of *oone-fold* (perh. a scribal alteration of northern *anfald*) is recorded in 5; but the extant word seems to be a new formation.]

1. Consisting of only one member or constituent; single; simple.

[*c* **1460** *Towneley Myst.* xiv. 554 Hayll, oone-fold god in persons thre!] **1844** LINGARD *Anglo-Sax. Ch.* (1858) II. x. 122 The trial for greater crimes was called the threefold, that for smaller, the onefold ordeal. **1861** *Cornh. Mag.* III. 549 The subject ought to be onefold instead of threefold. **1897** R. H. STORY *Apost. Min. Scot. Ch.* iv. 144 The Gaelic preacher, like Origen, was not content to extract a onefold lesson from his text.

2. Simple in character; simple-minded; single-minded; free from duplicity.

1882 MACDONALD *Weighed & Wanting* II. vi. 54 Many a one imitates simplicity, but Amy was simple—one-fold.

Hence **'onefoldness**, singleness, unity; simplicity.

1674 N. FAIRFAX *Bulk & Selv.* 23 The naked essence of God is as much his all-knowingness, his all-fillingness, or his onefoldness, as his everlastingness. **1887** *Librar. Mag.* May 149 The simplicity.. which is opposed to duplicity, and which may be called one-foldness.

'one-ˌhanded, *a.*

A. *adj.* **1.** Having only one hand, or only one hand capable of use.

c **1440** *Promp. Parv.* 365/2 Oon handyd, *mancus*. **1530** PALSGR. 320/2 Onehanded, *manquet*. **1548** UDALL, etc. *Erasm. Par. John* 75, I haue restored the one handed to both.

2. Used, worked, or performed with one hand.

1611 COTGR., *Aisceau*,.. a one-handed plane-axe. **1837** *Penny Cycl.* VIII. 283/1 The one-handed [deaf-mute] alphabet was invented in Spain. **1894** *Field* 9 June 838/2 Mr. J. was.. defeated by a one-handed catch in the slips after making thirty.

B. as *adv.* Using only one hand.

1962 J. D. MACDONALD *Girl* ix. 113 You can do it okay one-handed, just push down with your thumb. **1963** *Times* 12 June 5/2 He was caught at long on, finishing his stroke one-handed. **1974** R. ADAMS *Shardik* v. 43 He crouched upon his knees, fumbling one-handed along the undulating tree-trunk. **1975** J. MITCHELL *Smear Job* v. 37 Lonely drank one-handed.

Hence **one-'handedly** *adv.*, with one hand; **one-'handedness**, the state of being one-handed; (by back-formation) **one-'hand** *v. trans.*

1972 J. ROSSITER *Rope for General Dietz* xiii. 185, I lit a cigarette one-handedly. **1973** R. STOUT *Please pass Guilt* (1974) iv. 32 Jones stretched an arm and one-handed it [*sc.* the ball], and kept it. **1975** *Times* 12 Feb. 4/3 In spite of her one-handedness, [she] had followed hobbies of gardening, paper hanging, tennis. **1977** S. COULTER *Soyuz Affair* i. 9 He.. onehandedly fingered a cigarette out of the packet.

† 'onehead. *Obs.* Forms: 4 an-, anehede, 4–5 on-, one-, oonhede, oonheed, 4–6 onhed, onehed, (4 onede, 5 ooned). [f. ONE *a.* + -HEAD.]

1. The condition of being one; oneness, unity. (In quot. *c* 1380, the number one, unity.)

a **1300** *Cursor M.* 318 Þe hali gast es tat goddhede, þat giues lijf and mas an-hede [*Fairf.* anhede; *Gött.* onede]. *a* **1325** *Prose Psalter, Athan. Creed* 34 He is on in alle, nouȝt þurȝ confusioun of substaunce, bot þurȝ onhede of persone. *c* **1380** WYCLIF *Serm.* Sel. Wks. I. 18 Two is þe first number þat comiþ after oonheed. *a* **1420** HOCCLEVE *De Reg. Princ.* 5128 Cerclelyk shappe is most perfite figure, Betokenyng in gemetrie onehede. **1450–1530** *Myrr. our Ladye* 4 The blessyd endeles Trinite in onehed of substaunce and of Godhede.

2. The condition of being united or gathered in one; union; *concr.* a communion, a community.

a **1340** HAMPOLE *Psalter* cl. 1 Þe anhede of all chosen men. *c* **1449** PECOCK *Repr.* v. iv. 505 Of Scisme making in the oonhede of Cristen bretheren. **1450–1530** *Myrr. our Ladye* 134 Ye dresse you to god, and gather you in onhed to pray in the person of holy chirche.

3. Oneness or unity of spirit, mind, or feeling; agreement, accord, concord.

1340 HAMPOLE *Pr. Consc.* 7845 Þare [in heven] es acorde ay and anehede. **1340** *Ayenb.* 79 Charite ne is non oþer þing þanne dyere onhede. **1425–6** *Rolls of Parlt.* V. 407/1 The gode onehede and accord among the Lordes. *c* **1440** *Promp. Parv.* 365/2 Onehede, or a-cord (*H., P.* ooned), *unitas*. *a* **1450** in *Eng. Gilds* (1870) 451 If the aldermen and maistres may nogth bring hem to onehede and acord.

4. The condition of being alone; solitude.

1340 *Ayenb.* 142 Þe wordle is him prisoun; onhede, paradis.

† 'onehood. *Obs.* Forms: 3 anhad, 4 on-hod, 5 one-hode, 6 onehod. [See -HOOD.] = prec.

a **1225** *Leg. Kath.* 932 Of his feader soð godd, And of his moder soð mon In anhad ba somet. *c* **1320** *Cast. Love* 10 Þat o God art and þrilli-hod, And þreo persones in on-hod. **1471** RIPLEY *Comp. Alch.* Pref. i. in Ashm. (1652) 121 One-hode in Substance. **1575** LANEHAM *Let.* 53 Whear onehod reinz, ther quiet bears rule, and discord fliez a pase.

'one-ˌhorse, *a.*

1. Drawn, or worked, by a single horse (as a vehicle, a machine, etc.); having or using only one horse.

1750 JENYNS *Mod. Fine Lady* Misc. Pieces 1761 I. 78 Severely humbled to her one-horse chair. **1795** SEWARD *Anecd.* (ed. 2) II. 367 He used to drive himself about the country in a one-horse chaise. **1839** *Planting* iii. 24 (L.U.K.) The one-horse drill. **1858** O. W. HOLMES *Aut. Breakf.-t.* xi, The Deacon's Masterpiece: or the Wonderful 'One-hoss-shay'. **1887** *Edin. Rev.* Jan. 18 'One-horse farmers'.. had to struggle with the inconvenience of borrowing and lending horses.

2. *fig.* (*colloq.*, orig. *U.S.*) On a small scale; petty; of small and limited resources or capacity. Esp. ***one-horse town***, a small or rural town; a town where nothing important or exciting happens.

1853 *Oregonian* (Portland) 19 Nov. 2/1 These *one-horse* meetings are got up by men whose capital consists in *brass*. **1855** *Knickerbocker* XLVI. 106 'In this "one-horse town",' writes a Mobile friend, 'as our New-Orleans neighbors designate it, [etc.].' **1858** O. W. HOLMES *Aut. Breakf.-t.* xi. (1891) 257, I have seen a country-clergyman, with a one-story intellect and a one-horse vocabulary. **1866** LOWELL *Biglow P.* Introd., Americanisms properly so called,.. such as *carry*, a *one-horse affair*, a *prairie*, to *vamoose*. **1883** E. E. HALE in *Harper's Mag.* Dec. 143/2 They have a one-horse sort of a tannery. **1884** *Liverpool Daily Post* 15 Oct. 5/1 The first thing it is to do is to take possession of that 'one-horsiest' of railways, from the Dock Cottages to West Kirby, and to make it into a channel of communication fit for civilised men. **1897** B. BARNATO in *Westm. Gaz.* 15 June 9/1 My company is not a one-horse show. **1933** P. FLEMING *Brazilian Adventure* III. x. 378 Doctor Amyntas was the big noise; in this one horse town he might be said to own the horse. **1940** L. A. G. STRONG *Sun on Water* 161, I was sick with I don't know what early summer passion in that one-horse store. **1969** L. KENNEDY *Very Lovely People* i. 73 Their names were Homer and Arnold and they worked in a one-horse garage down a side street in Botafogo. **1973** 'D. JORDAN' *Nile Green* viii. 39, I said, 'It's a one-horse town.' **1977** *Zigzag* June 23/2 I've a new song.. about a girl of sixteen trying to get out of a one horse town.

onehow ('wʌnhaʊ), *adv. rare.* [f. ONE *a.* + HOW (cf. *somehow, anyhow, nohow*).] In one way (as opposed to another); somehow.

1719 DE FOE *Crusoe* II. x. 440 The Seamen.. would certainly have falter'd in their Account, or onehow or other we should have seen Reason to have suspected them.

Oneida (əʊ'naɪdə). *N. Amer.* [ad. Oneida *onẽ́yoteʔ* erected stone (the name of the main Oneida settlement at successive locations, near which, traditionally, a large syenite boulder always appeared).] One of the five (later six) tribes of the Iroquois Confederacy of North American Indians commonly called the Five Nations (Six Nations), originally inhabiting upper New York state; a member of this tribe; their language. Also *attrib.*

1666 J. ALLYN *Let.* 10 July in *Mass. Hist. Soc. Coll.* (1849) 3rd Ser. X. 63 Hereof the Mohawkes and the Oneiades have given assured notice. **1722** S. SEWALL *Diary* 19 Oct. in *Ibid.* (1882) 5th Ser. VII. 311 The Messenger of the Oneidas was buried in the South Burying place. **1760** in J. W. Lydekker *Faithful Mohawks* (1938) 102 Genˡ Amherst being at the Oneida Lake on the preceeding Sunday went up as far as the Oneida town. **1823, 1933** [see CAYUGA]. **1959** [see *Five Nations* s.v. FIVE *a.* and *sb.* C. 2]. **1965** *Canad. Jrnl. Linguistics* X. 105 The structure of Pawnee as compared with Oneida. **1969** *Observer* (Colour Suppl.) 25 May 53/3 West of them were the extraordinarily fierce Oneida. **1973** A. H. WHITEFORD *N. Amer. Indian Arts* 148 Lakes area silverwork probably began when the Oneida, an Iroquois tribe, moved to northeast Wisconsin.

one-ideaed, -idea'd ('wʌnaɪ'diːəd), *a.* Also one-idead. Having, or possessed by, a single idea. So **one-idea** *a.* Hence **one-idea(d)ness**, the fact or quality of being one-ideaed.

1842 *Lancet* 12 Mar. 830 The dead superstitions, and one-idead theories, of the middle ages. **1849** THOREAU *Week Concord Riv., Tuesday* 195 Crude, and one-idea'd, like a schoolboy's theme. **1852** *Blackw. Mag.* Aug. 261/2 His absorbed one-ideadness. **1859** HELPS *Friends in C.* Ser. II. II. ix. 179 One-ideaed persons in high power. **1862** M. B. CHESNUT *Diary* 13 Mar. (1949) 199 He is a one-idea man. That idea is to get every possible man into the ranks. **1899** W. JAMES in *Talks to Teachers on Psychol.* 220 A saint in ecstasy is as.. one idea'd as a melancholiac. **1920** H. BEGBIE *Life W. Booth* I. xxii. 365 It was.. this intense singleness of view, this consuming one-ideaness of soul, which made William Booth so successful. **1934** E. BOWEN *Cat Jumps* 252 She.. was in fact a rather one-idea girl.

oneing ('wʌnɪŋ), **† 'oning**, *vbl. sb.* For early forms, cf. ONE *v.* Also one-ing. [f. ONE *v.* + -ING[1].] A making one, uniting, joining in one, union, fusion. Also as *ppl. a.*

Unlike the vb. on which it is formed, the verbal substantive appears to have become obsolete in the 15th century and to have been consciously revived in the 20th.

1340 *Ayenb.* 65 Þes meyster.. naȝt ne payþ god þet ne loueþ bote pays and onynge. *c* **1340** HAMPOLE *Prose Tr.* 38 By þe vertu of this blysfull anynge whilke may noghte be saide ne consayued. *c* **1410** LOVE *Bonavent. Mirr.* xv. 37 (Gibbs MS.)Þe oonynge and knyttynge to hyre spouse Iesu cryste. *c* **1425** WYNTOUN *Cron.* IV. xviii. *heading*, Now quhen Antiochus Kyng, Wyth þe Romanis made anyng. **1480** CAXTON *Descr. Brit.* 24 The danes regned in Northumberlond xxxvj yere vnto the oonyng of the kyngdome.

1919 D. H. LAWRENCE in *Eng. Rev.* June 488 There in the sexual passion the very blood surges into communion, in the terrible sensual oneing. **1921** B. WILLIAMSON *Supernat. Mysticism* vii. 68 Sanctity is the oneing of the soul with God. **1934** *Blackfriars* Mar. 184 Mother Julian..saw it [*sc.* pain] first and foremost as the blessed instrument of our one-ing with Christ. **1958** C. PEPLER *Eng. Relig. Heritage* IV. i. 224 In *The Cloud* the question of Christ's passion restoring all men to the oneing affection with God lost by Adam makes no reference to his sacrifice. *The Epistle*, on the other hand, speaks of this 'oneing' in terms of a continual offering of the sacrifice of a man's whole being.

oneiric (əʊˈnaɪərɪk), *a.* [f. Gr. ὄνειρος dream + -IC.] Of or belonging to dreams.

1859 *Life Eben. Henderson* vi. 378 The oneiric medium of revelation. **1953** *Scrutiny* XIX. 151 Their..dictation of the unconscious, oneiric delirium,..may be fragmentary..but they bear witness..to their determination to make all possible aspects of poetry incentives to life. **1963** T. PYNCHON *V.* xi. 335 The green light deepened, drowning the island of Malta and the island of Fausto and Elena hopelessly deeper in its oneiric chill. **1974** *Monthly Film Bull.* (Brit. Film Inst.) Apr. 84/2 Even though his film's philosophical focus may occasionally seem blurred, the images themselves..retain throughout a haunting and oneiric quality.

oneiro- (əʊnaɪərəʊ), also **oniro-**, before a vowel **oneir-**, combining form of Gr. ὄνειρος a dream. **oneiˈrocrisy**, erron. **oneirocracy** [ad. Gr. ὀνειροκρισία] = ONEIROCRITICISM; ‖**oneirodynia** (əʊnaɪrəʊˈdɪnɪə) [mod.L., f. Gr. ὀδύνη pain]: see quot. 1804; **oneirology** (ɒnɪˈrɒlədʒɪ) [Gr. ὀνειρολογία: see -LOGY], the science or subject of dreams, or of their interpretation; so **oneiˈrologist**, one versed in oneirology; **oˈneiromancy** (-mænsɪ) [see -MANCY], divination by dreams; so **oˈneiromancer**, **oˈneiromantist** [cf. Gr. ὀνειρόμαντις], one who divines by dreams; †**oneiˈropolist** [f. Gr. ὀνειροπόλος one who 'deals in' dreams, i.e. either a dreamer, or an interpreter of dreams], an interpreter of dreams; †**oneiroˈpompist** [f. Gr. ὀνειροπομπός sending dreams], a sender of dreams; **oneiroscopy** (-ˈɒskəpɪ) [Gr. ὀνειροσκόπος an interpreter of dreams], examination or interpretation of dreams; so **oneiˈroscopist**, one versed in oneiroscopy.

1653 R. SANDERS *Physiogn.* 202 This Chapter of *Oneirocracie, that is to say, the judgment of dreams. *Ibid.* 214 Oneirocracie is the prudence of presaging future contingencies by dreams, for the welfare of man. **1976** *Proc. Classical Assoc.* LXXIII. 20 Intellectual constructions such as onirocrisy and physiognomony readily degenerate into the collection of *paradoxa*, upon which the temperament of the age commonly puts a religious interpretation. **1804** T. TROTTER *Drunkenness* i. 11 *Oneirodynia, disturbed sleep, which comprehends sleepwalking and nightmare. **1822–34** *Good's Study Med.* (ed. 4) III. 49 He [Parr]..makes Vesania the genus, and arranges melancholia, mania, and even oneirodynia, as separate species under it. **1834** SOUTHEY *Doctor* lxxvi. II. 343 Artemidorus, not the *oneirologist, but the great philosopher at the Court of the Emperor Sferamond. [See also ONEIROCRITE.] **1818** MCCRIE *Life Melville* I. ii. 80 Melville was a believer in *Oneirology and expert in the interpretation of dreams. **1653** R. SANDERS *Physiogn.* 225 The Queen related the dream to an *Oneiromancer. **1952** G. SARTON *Hist. Sci.* I. xiv. 371 There are two kinds of dreams, those of divine origin, which concern oneiromancers, and those of physiologic origin. **1652** GAULE *Magastrom.* 165 *Oniromancy, [divining] by dreams. **1663** J. SPENCER *Prodigies* (1665) 297 These rude observations were at last licked into an Art (Physical Oneiromancy) in which Physicians from a consideration of the dreams proceeded to a Crisis of the disposition of the person. **1871** TYLER *Prim. Cult.* I. 108 Oneiromancy..is not unknown to the lower races. **1931** E. JONES *On the Nightmare* II. iii. 95 This cure for disease by Incubation—known as oneiromancy—was practised in Scotland and Ireland... Here the person slept in the skin of a sacrificed sheep, just as the worshippers of Ammon did in Thebes. **1935** J. S. LINCOLN *Dream in Primitive Cultures* I. 3 At Nineveh was a collection of books on oneiromancy or dream interpretation. **1653** R. SANDERS *Physiogn.* 221 The dream to the *Oneiromantist. **1652** GAULE *Magastrom.* xxvi, The dusky *oniropolist or dream-teller will affright me with nocturnall ghosts and goblins. *a* **1693** [see ONEIROCRITE]. **1652** GAULE *Magastrom.* 269 Carpocrates..used incantations..paredrials or demoniacal assessours, *oniropompists or dream-artists. **1727** BAILEY vol. II, *Oneiroscopist. **1889** MRS. LYNN LINTON in *Fortn. Rev.* Mar. 368 [He] made himself the oneiroscopist for the occasion.

oneirocrit(e, oniro- (əʊˈnaɪərəʊkrɪt). *rare.* [a. F. *onirocrite* (Rabelais), ad. Gr. ὀνειροκρίτης judge or interpreter of dreams.] = next, 1.

[**1677** GALE *Crt. Gentiles* III. 64 The Pythagoreans..had their ὀνειροκρίτης, Onirocrites, Judge and Interpreter of Dreams.] *a* **1693** URQUHART *Rabelais* III. xiii. 102 Such a one ..by the Greeks is called Onirocrit, or Oniropolist. **1837** SOUTHEY *Doctor* cxxviii. IV. 294 The Oneirocrites or Oneirologists, as they who pretended to lay down rules for the interpretation of dreams called themselves.

oneirocritic, oniro- (əʊnaɪərəʊˈkrɪtɪk), *sb.* (*a.*) [ad. Gr. ὀνειροκριτικός pertaining to the interpretation of dreams; in F. *onirocritique* (Cotgr.): cf. prec. and -IC.]

1. A judge or interpreter of dreams.

a **1652** J. SMITH *Sel. Disc.* VI. iii. (1821) 203 The Jewish doctors..constantly prefer the oneirocritics of them, to the dreamers themselves. **1668** H. MORE *Div. Dial.* II. 243 According to the sense of the ancient Onirocriticks. **1712** ADDISON *Spect.* No. 505 ¶6 An Oneirocritick, or, in plain English, an interpreter of dreams. **1819** G. S. FABER *Dispensations* (1823) I. 335 He was the first prophet and onirocritic and diviner. **1865** *Sat. Rev.* 11 Nov. 616 A second oneiro-critic modified the unpleasant answer.

2. (Usually in *pl.*) The art of interpreting dreams; oneirocriticism.

1614 SELDEN *Titles Hon.* 74 In Apomazar's.. onirocritiques out of Egyptian monuments, that name often occurres. **1724** A. COLLINS *Gr. Chr. Relig.* 89 Oneirocriticks and Hieroglyphics; and other Mystical Arts of concealment. **1740** WARBURTON *Div. Legat.* VI. vi. (R.), Now onirocritic or the art of interpreting dreams was practised in the time of Joseph. **1855** SMEDLEY *Occult Sci.* 292 Oneirocriticks.

B. *adj.* = next. *rare*$^{-0}$.

1775 ASH, *Oneirocritic*, interpretative of dreams.

oneiroˈcritical, oniro-, *a.* [f. as prec. + -AL[1].] Pertaining to, practising, or expert in, the interpretation of dreams.

1588 J. HARVEY *Disc. Probl.* 26 No dreaming Reuelations, or Onirocriticall coniectures. **1653** R. SANDERS *Physiogn.* 214 The knowledge of Oneirocritical [*printed* -cratical] precepts. **1714** BYROM *Spect.* No. 597 ¶10 My Onirocritical Correspondent has directed him. **1816** SCOTT *Antiq.* xiv, Well, I will allow for once the oneirocritical science. **1855** SMEDLEY *Occult Sci.* 248 Artemidorus..founder of the Oneirocritical science, so to call it.

Hence **oneiroˈcritically** *adv.*, in relation to the interpretation of dreams.

1816 G. S. FABER *Orig. Pagan Idol.* III. 292 He owns himself quite unable to assign any adequate cause of a temple being onirocritically symbolized by a merchant ship.

oneiroˈcriticism, oniro-. [f. ONEIROCRITIC + -ISM.] The art of interpreting dreams.

1614 SELDEN *Titles Hon.* I. iii. 63 In Oneirocriticisme, dreams of superior Deities were referd to such as had rule and command. **1672** SIR T. BROWNE *Let. Friend* §18 To dream that we are dead, was no condemnable Fantasm in old Oneirocriticism, as having a signification of Liberty, vacuity from Cares, exemption and freedom from Troubles, unknown unto the dead. **1827** G. S. FABER *Sacr. Calend. Prophecy* (1844) I. 6 The whole system of pagan onirocriticism. **1865** *Sat. Rev.* 11 Nov. 616 The science of Oneiro-criticism..appears to have always been no less vague in its principles than anomalous in its results.

oneism (ˈwʌnɪz(ə)m). *nonce-wd.* [-ISM.] A doctrine or system of which *one* is the centre.

1840 *Fraser's Mag.* XXII. 620 The oneism, the I-ism of the German, making for each individual his own mind the centre of his universe.

oneith, obs. form of UNEATH *adv.*

ˈone-leaf. ? *Obs.* = ONE-BLADE, q.v.

1578 [see ONE-BLADE]. **1884** MILLER *Plant-n.*, One-leaf, Two-leaved Lily of the Valley.

one-legged (ˈwʌnlɛgd, -ˌlɛgɪd), *a.*

1. Having only one leg.

1872 V. LUSH *Jrnl.* 6 Nov. (1975) 130 In the evening Martin took Annette to the Theatre Royal to see Donato the one-legged dancer and Zuila perform on the trapeze, &c. **1883** STEVENSON *Treas. Isl.* I. i. (1886) 7 The one-legged seafaring man. **1899** *Westm. Gaz.* 21 Mar. 10/3 The one-legged hurdy-gurdy..has obviously given way to the less mournful piano-organ.

2. *fig.* That is, or effects, only one half of what is required; that is a half-measure; one-sided.

1842 SYD. SMITH *Let. Burning alive on Railroads* Wks. 1859 II. 325/2 To pass a one-legged law, giving power over one door and not the other. **1867** MOTLEY in *Corr.* (1889) II. 255 You..have actually maintained this one-legged correspondence through all those years.

onelepy, onely: see ONLEPY, ONLY.

†**ˈonement.** *Obs.* [f. ONE *v.* + -MENT; an early instance of the addition of the Romanic suffix *-ment* to a native Eng. vb. Cf. the later ATONEMENT.] The fact of being made into one.

1. Physical union, conjunction.

1388 WYCLIF *Ezek.* xxxvii. 16 Ioyne thou tho trees oon to the tother in to o tree to thee; and tho schulen be in to onement [1382 oonyng] in thin hond.

2. Union of mind or feeling; agreement, accord, concord; reconciliation (= ATONEMENT 1, 2).

a **1450** *Le Morte Arth.* 2338 Bot onemente thar hym nevyr wene, Or eyther other herte haue sought. **1533** tr. *Erasmus' Comm. Crede* 162 He shold..reconcile hymselfe and make an onement with god. **1597–8** BP. HALL *Sat.* III. vii. 69 That sets such discord twixt agreeing parts, Which never can be set at onement more.

†**ˈonemost,** *a. Obs.* [f. ONE, after *inmost*, *hindmost*, etc.: see -MOST.] 'Most one'; absolutely the only one: applied to God.

1597 J. KING *On Jonas* (1618) 74 Our one and one-most God. *a* **1638** MEDE *Apost. Later Times* (1641) 32 As God is most one, and without all multiplicity,..the one-most God must have an one-most service. **1643** CARYL *Sacr. Covt.* 25 It make a special union of all those who shall take it with the One-most God.

onence, obs. variant of ANENT *prep.*

†**oˈnene,** *adv. Obs.* [f. ON *prep.* + ENE: cf. *at ene.*] At once: = ANON 4.

c **1450** *Mirour Saluacioun* 1039 Bot noght mankind delivred onene y^t crist was borne.

oneness (ˈwʌnnɪs). [f. ONE + -NESS: OE. had *ánnes*, which became regularly in 13th c. *onnesse* in south, *annesse* in north. (See ANNESS.) But this became obs. bef. 1300, and *oneness* was formed anew in 16th c.]

1. The quality of being one in number, singleness. (Esp. of the divine unity.)

[*c* **885**–*c* **1175**: see ANNESS 1.] **1594** HOOKER *Eccl. Pol.* I. ii. §2 Our God is one, or rather very onenesse, and meere unitie. **1652** BENLOWES *Theoph.* Pref., An eternal Being, an infinite Onenesse. **1683** PORDAGE *Myst. Div.* 11 The Holy Trinity are one, and yet three in that oneness. **1816** COLERIDGE *Lay Serm.* 339 The Science of the universal, having the ideas of oneness and allness as the two elements. **1862** DANA *Man. Geol.* 584 Man of one species.—This oneness of species is sustained by the following considerations.

b. The fact or quality of being the only one of its kind; singularity, uniqueness.

1715 J. CHAPPELON *Rt. way Rich.* (1717) 26 Here is..the singularity, oneness of this pearl, one pearl, none other like it. **1871** RUSKIN *Fors Clav.* v. 4 The thing itself being almost incredible in its oneness.

2. The fact or quality of being alone; solitariness, loneliness. *rare.*

[*a* **1000**–*a* **1300**: see ANNESS 2. *c* **1200** *Vices & Virtues* 137 Ancres and hermites ðe luuieð onnesse.] **1839** LADY LYTTON *Cheveley* (ed. 2) I. x. 212 Is my curse to be a *oneness*, both of fate and feeling? **1850** MRS. BROWNING *Early Rose* i, In her loneness, in her loneness, And the fairer for that oneness.

3. The quality of being one body or whole (though compounded of two or more parts); undividedness, integrity, unity.

[*c* **900** tr. *Bæda's Hist.* II. iv, þa ðe..ȝelumpon..to annesse þære halȝan ciricean.] **1626** JACKSON *Creed* VIII. viii. §3 The Onenesse of person in the sonne of God, Christ Jesus, God and man. **1695** LD. PRESTON *Boethius* III. 143 If by dissevering & segregating the Parts that Oneness is distracted, it is no more what before it was. **1736** BUTLER *Anal.* I. i. 17 The Simplicity and absolute Oneness of a living Agent. **1831** CARLYLE *Sart. Res.* II. x, His somewhat peculiar view of Nature, the decisive Oneness he ascribes to Nature. **18..** WHITTIER *Pr. Wks.* (1889) III. 286 It overlooks..the solidarity and oneness of humanity.

4. The fact of forming one whole (said of two or more persons or things, or of one person or thing *with* another); combination, unity, union.

1657 AUSTEN *Fruit Trees* II. 44 This Union and Onenesse between us, and God the father. **1698** *Christ Exalted* 6 Is not this taking their Persons into Oneness with himself? **1860** PUSEY *Min. Proph.* 13 The closest human oneness, of husband and wife.

5. The fact or quality of being one and the same, sameness, identity; the character of remaining the same in varying circumstances or at different times, constancy, unchangingness.

1611 W. SCLATER *Key* (1629) 339 This onenesse..of God, is not numerall,..but hath reference, either to the vnchangablenesse of God, and his keeping one steddy, and vnuaried course in iustifying all. **1869** J. MARTINEAU *Ess.* II. 175 The physical and moral oneness of existence. **1877** E. CAIRD *Philos. Kant* II. xv. 544 The numerical oneness or identity of the Soul at different times.

b. The fact or quality of being the same in kind; identity of nature or character (of two or more things).

1657 AUSTEN *Fruit Trees* II. 194 To stand for Uniformity or Oneness in the externall part of the worship of God. **1822** *Blackw. Mag.* XII. 586 All are so agreeably blended into a oneness of character. **1882** W. HUGGINS in *19th Cent.* Aug. 274 The essential oneness of the cometary stuff with the gas composed of carbon and hydrogen.

†**c.** The fact of being the same, or alike, in relation to two or more; community. *Obs. rare.*

a **1225** *Ancr. R.* 12 Me schal makien strencðe of onnesse of cloþes, & of oðer what of vttre þinges, þet te onnesse wiðuten bitocnie þe onnesse of o luue & of o wil.

6. Unity of mind, feeling, or purpose; unison, agreement, harmony, concord.

[*c* **1175**: see ANNESS 3.] *a* **1225** [see 5 c]. *c* **1555** HARPSFIELD *Divorce Hen. VIII* (Camden) 28 For the oneness & conformity of mind that both were in, touching this matter. **1647** BP. HALL *Christ Myst.* §20. 114 A spirituall oneness arising from an happy conspiration of their thoughts and affections. **1649** W. DELL *Way of Peace* 28 The members of the body can judge of the one-nesse of Spirit that is among themselves. **1850** ROBERTSON *Serm.* Ser. III. iii. (1872) 38 Have ceased to expect any other oneness for the Church of Christ than that of a sameness of spirit.

one-ˈpipe, *a.* [f. ONE *numeral a.* + PIPE *sb.*[1]]

a. Applied to a system of hot-water central heating in which radiators take water from and return it to the same pipe, which runs in a complete circuit from the boiler and back to it again.

1897 F. DYE *Hood's Pract. Treat. Warming Buildings* (ed. 3) xix. 352 It is not usual for the one-pipe system to extend to three floors above the boiler without modification. **1970** J. J. BARTON *Domestic Heating* viii. 127 Two basic circuits, the 'one-pipe' and the 'two-pipe' circuit..are commonly used in small bore heating practice.

b. Applied to a system of plumbing in which waste from sinks and the like is conveyed to the sewer by the same pipe as that from water-closets and urinals.

1910 W. P. GERHARD *Water Supply, Sewerage & Plumbing* iii. 187, I am..convinced that the one-pipe system, as I have sometimes called it, is the coming system. **1933** *Archit. Rev.* LXXIV. 54/3 The drainage and sanitary installation throughout is on the one-pipe system. **1972** T. A. TOMPSON *Guide Sanitary Engin. Services* vii. 228 Repetitive planning at each floor level of a multi-storey building favours localised application of single-stack principles of sanitation... This has led to the development of the modified one-pipe system.., achieving even greater economy than with the one-pipe system.

oner (ˈwʌnə(r)), *sb. slang* or *colloq.* Also **one-er.** [f. ONE + -ER[1].]

1. *slang.* A person or thing of a unique or very remarkable kind; *esp.* a person preeminently addicted to or expert at something; a prime one.

1840 DICKENS *Old C. Shop* lviii, Miss Sally's sich a one-er for that. **1857** HUGHES *Tom Brown* II. iii, You are a wunner for bottling the swipes. **1862** THACKERAY *Philip* (1869) II. xvi. 240 You should see her eat; she is such a oner at eating. **1884** G. ALLEN *Philistia* III. 279 You always were a one-er you know.

b. *spec.* A heavy blow.

1861 E. D. COOK *Paul Foster's Daughter* x. I. 230 'What's the matter?' 'Oh, I've got it at last—such a onener—clean off my legs—first blood—first knock down—everything.' **1885** G. ALLEN *Babylon* iii, And then paternal feeling overcame him, and he caught Hiram such a onener on his ears as he flattered himself that boy wouldn't be likely to forgit.

2. *colloq.* Something consisting of, denoted by, or in some way characterized by the number one. *spec.* one pound; one hundred pounds.

1889 *Pall Mall G.* 19 Oct. 6/1 His figures..run to anything between a fiver and two or three hundred oners. **1950** *Austral. Police Jrnl.* Apr. 116 *One-r*, £1. **1962** PARKER & ALLERTON *Courage of his Convictions* IV. i. 154 A one-er for the Guv'nor, and fifty each for me and George here, that's cut price. Two hundred all told, how's that? **1969** I. & P. OPIE *Children's Games* vii. 229 When one conker breaks another into pieces so that nothing remains on the string, the winning conker becomes a 'one-er'. *Ibid.* viii. 251 He may shout a number like 'a oner', this means that the rest of the team have to jump over the person's back from the line, taking only one step. **1970** G. F. NEWMAN *Sir, You Bastard* viii. 225 Worth a oner to you. **1974** H. R. F. KEATING *Underside* xxii. 218 You'd pay me five sovereign?.. Five golden oners?

†**ˈoner,** *v. Obs. rare.* [f. L. *onerāre*: see below; cf. *exoner.*] *trans.* To burden: = ONERATE.

1545 *St. Papers Hen. VIII*, V. 409 Who be extreme in takinge of gressoms, and oneringe of rentes. **1545** JOYE *Exp. Dan.* viii. Tj, Behold with how few single pure and easye institucyons Christ ordened & not onered his churche.

†**ˈonerable,** *a. Obs. rare*[−1]. [f. L. *onerāre* to ONERATE: see -BLE.] Burdensome, onerous.

1432–50 tr. *Higden* (Rolls) II. 143 To reherse the reasones ..hit were onerable [TREVISA, noyefulle] to vs in this tyme [*Higden* præfatis rationibus onerare nimis foret tædiosum].

†**oneˈrarious,** *a. Obs. rare*[−1]. (In quot. ono-.) [f. as next + -OUS.] = ONEROUS.

a **1548** HALL *Chron., Hen. V* 33 b, To have a rule to hym committed, not for an honor, but for an onorarious charge and daily burden.

onerary (ˈɒnərərɪ), *a.* (*sb.*) *rare.* [ad. L. *onerāri-us*, f. *onus* burden: see -ARY; cf. F. *onéraire* (Rabelais 16th c.).] **a.** *adj.* Fitted for the carriage of burdens. **b.** as *sb.* A ship of burden, transport.

1658 PHILLIPS, *Onerary*, serving for burthen or carriage. **1728** MORGAN *Algiers* I. ii. 15 Carrying with him 2000 war-like Vessels, besides oneraries. **1755** JOHNSON, *Onerary*, fitted for carriage or burthens. (Whence in mod. Dicts.)

†**ˈonerate,** *v. Obs.* (Pa. pple. in 6 **onerate.**) [f. L. *onerāt-*, ppl. stem of *onerāre* to load, burden, f. *onus, oner-* a load, burden.] *trans.* To load, burden, charge, oppress. *lit.* and *fig.*

c **1535** in Ellis *Orig. Lett.* Ser. III. II. 360 My Master.. wold..dayly onerat me with more paynes without any maner of profett. *a* **1548** HALL *Chron., Rich. III* 50 Partely onerate and vanquesshed with the faire glosynge promises. **1604** TOOKER *Fabrique Ch.* 9 Perhaps they thinke them-selves onerated in conscience for the trust reposed in them ..to bestow [etc.]. **1726** AYLIFFE *Parergon* 335 An universal Legacy happens, when the Testator onerates his Executor by obliging him to restore all his Goods and Estate unto such a Person.

†**oneˈration.** *Obs. rare.* [n. of action f. prec.: cf. med.L. *onerātio* (14th c. in Du Cange).] The action of loading or burdening; loading or filling the stomach, taking of food.

1651 HOBBES *Leviath.* I. vi. 25 Of this Kind are all Onerations and Exonerations of the body. **1658** PHILLIPS, *Oneration*, a loading or burthening. In BAILEY, JOHNSON, and in mod. Dicts.

onerative (ˈɒnərətɪv), *a. rare.* [f. as ONERATE + -IVE: cf. obs. F. *oneratif* (16th c. in Godefroy).] Conveying a charge or imposition.

1802–12 BENTHAM *Ration. Judic. Evid.* (1827) I. 312 Onerative, or say impositive..and exonerative. *Ibid.* V. 204 Self-onerative [evidence]. *Ibid.* 702 Distinctions of.. testimony,..disservitive, criminative or simply onerative.

†**oneˈrose,** *a. Obs.* [ad. L. *onerōs-us*: see below and -OSE.] = ONEROUS.

c **1450** tr. *De Imitatione* III. xxx. 100 Lo! mete, drinke, cloþe, & oþer þinges longing to þe body are onerose to a fervent spirit. **1687** N. JOHNSTON *Assur. Abby Lands* 164 By whatever contract, either Lucerative, or Onerose they have come.

oneˈrosity. *rare.* [f. as next + -ITY. Cf. obs. F. *onérosité* (15th c. in Godef.).] The quality of being onerous; in *Sc. Law*, the fact of something being for a consideration.

1874 LD. NEAVES *1 Court Sess. Cas.* 4th Ser. 481 When a cheque is presented to a bank there is no presumption of onerosity as between the drawer and the holder.

onerous (ˈɒnərəs), *a.* Also 5 **honerous.** [a. OF. *onereus, honereus* (Oresme 14th c.), F. *onéreux*, ad. L. *onerōs-us*, f. *onus, oner-* burden: see -OUS.]

1. Of the nature of a burden; burdensome; oppressive, troublesome.

c **1400** *Rom. Rose* 5633 For he nyl be importune Unto no wight, ne honerous. *c* **1450** tr. *De Imitatione* III. xx. 88 If þis lyve be onerouse and hevy, yette bi thi grace hit is fulle meritory. **1533–4** *Act 25 Hen. VIII*, c. 19 Dyuers constitucions.. ouermuch onerous to his highnes and his subiectes. **1621** BURTON *Anat. Mel.* I. ii. IV. vii. (1676) 105/1 Overcome and tormented with worldly cares, and onerous business. **1775** JOHNSON *Tax. no Tyr.* 32 Called to any onerous service. **1837** W. IRVING *Capt. Bonneville* I. 233 The duties of a wife..among Indians, are little less onerous than those of the packhorse.

b. Of the nature of a legal burden, or obligation.

1539 ELYOT *Let. to Cromwell* in Ellis *Orig. Lett.* Ser. I. II. 117 Discharged without any recompence, rewarded only with the order of Knighthode, honorable and onerouse. **1726** AYLIFFE *Parergon* 16 A banish'd Person..retains all Things onerous to himself, as a Punishment for his Crime. **1875** POSTE *Gaius* I. Introd., To enforce that performance.. from the person to whom it is onerous, that is, to whom it is commanded. **1883** *Law Times* 10 Nov. 22/2 The 23rd section..provides for disclaimer of onerous property.

2. *Sc. Law.* Done or given for value received, being for a consideration: opposed to *gratuitous*; as in ***onerous consideration, grant, property, title***, etc. (So, in Fr. law, *titre onéreux*, etc.)

1751 MACFARLANE *Genealogical Collections* (1900) 305. **1754** ERSKINE *Princ. Sc. Law* (1809) 139 If the grant be made for a valuable consideration, it is said to be onerous; if for love and favour, gratuitous. **1861** W. BELL *Dict. Sc. Law* 220/2 Where value in money, or goods, or services, has been given in return for the deed, the consideration is said to be onerous. *Ibid.* 221/1 A deed granted for a gratuitous consideration, where not struck at as a fraud against onerous creditors, is as effectual as a deed granted for a valuable consideration.

Hence **ˈonerously** *adv.*, in an onerous or burdensome manner; **ˈonerousness,** burdensomeness.

1856 WEBSTER, *Onerously.* **1866** A. L. PERRY *Elem. Pol. Econ.* (1873) 116 The comparative onerousness of the respective efforts. **1877** OWEN *Mrq. Wellesley's Desp.* Introd. 39 The position..which Wellesley was determined to compel them to recognise in all its amplitude and onerousness.

onery, var. ORNERY *a.*

†**ones,** obs. form of ONCE: used in ME. also in the sense 'at one'.

c **1386** CHAUCER *Pard. T.* 368, I make auow to goddes digne bones Herkneth felawes, we thre been al ones. *c* **1470** HENRY *Wallace* x. 225 Had thai bene gud, all anys we had ben. Be reson heyr the contrar now is seyn.

oneself (wʌnˈsɛlf), *pron.* Also 6- **ones, one's self.** [orig. *one's self* (see ONE 21 and SELF), after *my self*, etc.; afterwards assimilated to *himself, itself.*] An emphatic or distinctive equivalent of the indefinite pronoun ONE, used chiefly in the objective (after vb. or prep.) or (in sense 1) as a nominative in apposition. The corresponding possessive is *one's own*: 'occupied with oneself and one's own affairs.'

1. Emphatic use: A person's self; himself or herself (meaning or including the speaker or writer).

1621 LADY M. WROTH *Urania* 505 Griefe is felt but by one's selfe. **1837** MRS. CARLYLE *Lett.* I. 65 A letter behoves to tell about oneself. **1843** PALMERSTON in L. C. Sanders *Life* (1888) 15 If one does not know something of them oneself. **1848** DICKENS *Dombey* v, One might wear the articles one's-self. *c* **1886** *Pall Mall G.*, Oneself after all is the subject in which a man is most deeply interested. *Mod.* If it were said to oneself, one would resent it.

2. Reflexive use: objective case of ONE 21, as 'One is obliged to keep oneself by oneself.'

In this sense often stressless; e.g. *to betake oneself.*

1548 R. HUTTEN *Sum of Diuinitie* C vj b, To exalt ones selfe aboue other men. **1665** BOYLE *Occas. Refl.* IV. vi. (1848) 209 To estimate ones self not by the testimonies of ones Conscience. **1732** BERKELEY *Alciphr.* III. § 12 It were folly to sacrifice one's-self for the sake of such. **1768** BLACKSTONE *Comm.* IV. xiv. 181 The Roman law also justifies homicide, when committed in defence of the chastity either of one-self or relations. **1827** LYTTON *Pelham* xxiii, To be pleased with oneself is the surest way of offending every-body else. **1862** TROLLOPE *Orley F.* lv, To sit down to dinner all by oneself! **1881** BESANT & RICE *Chapl. of Fleet* II. ii. (1883) 129 To dress one's self in the morning to the accompaniment of sweet music. **1887** JESSOPP *Arcady* iii. 66 To project oneself at will into remote periods in the past.

†**ˈoneship.** *Obs. rare.* [f. ONE + -SHIP.] The condition of being one or alone; oneness.

1630 SANDERSON *Serm.* II. 305 From the unchangeableness, & one-ship (if I may so say) both of Priest & Sacrifice.

one-shot, *a.* and *sb.* [ONE *numeral a.* 34 a.]

A. *adj.* Achieved or done with a single shot, stroke, attempt, etc.; consisting of a single shot or try; occurring, performed, produced, used, etc., only once; single, isolated.

1907 *Westm. Gaz.* 28 Mar. 9/1 The one-shot hole..gives good play its just reward... A hole which can just, and only just, be reached from the tee by a fine driver is, therefore, an excellent hole. **1927** *Sunday Pictorial* 28 Aug. 8/4 This includes such up-to-date owner-driver features as..one-shot oiling for all other chassis points. **1948** *Sun* (Baltimore) 31 May 8/2 For this he asked a force in being fully equipped and trained. He called this 'a stop-gap, one-shot army, a plug in the dike until we rallied sufficient and effective reserves'. **1950** *N.Y. Times* 28 Dec. 3/6 A 'one-shot' insecticide system that operates when the pilot pushes a button. **1953** POHL & KORNBLUTH *Space Merchants* (1955) ii. 16 Fowler Schocken was too big for one-shot accounts. What we wanted was the year-after-year reliability of a major industrial complex. **1954** K. W. GATLAND *Devel. Guided Missile* (ed. 2) 29 The latter method is of chief interest for 'one-shot' rockets as the target plate burns away during running unless low specific impulse propellants are used. **1959** E. FENWICK *Long Way Down* xx. 155 It was hard to get anybody for a one-shot cleaning job. **1962** A. NISBETT *Technique Sound Studio* ii. 43 A 'one-shot' technique was used, i.e. the whole programme was taken as a continuous sequence. *Ibid.* xiii. 232 It is essential that the basic 'message' of a piece should be understood in a single hearing —for sound is basically a 'one-shot' medium. **1966** *Listener* 18 Aug. 234/1 Not enough one-shot original plays are presented on television. **1968** M. WOODHOUSE *Rock Baby* xvii. 163 If it had been a one-shot thing, we might have been able to do it that way... But we couldn't afford any sort of mistake. **1972** D. E. WESTLAKE *Cops & Robbers* (1973) xvi. 251 We were pitting our one-shot plan against a normal company's normal routine. **1978** *Guardian Weekly* 7 May 15/4 Copper produces 90 per cent of Zambia's foreign exchange, and the percentage is also high for the other producing countries that have what some economists call 'one-shot economies'.

B. *sb.* An event, transaction, process, etc., that occurs only once; something that is used or intended for use only once; *esp.* a single appearance by a performer, production of a play, etc.; a story or article that has no sequel. Also ***one-shotter.*** orig. *U.S.*

1937 *Printers' Ink Monthly* May 40/1 *One shot*, a single program which is not one of a series. **1942** H. HAYCRAFT *Murder for Pleasure* xi. 267 Some..magazine editors have been experimenting with novelette-length condensations ('one-shots' as they are called in the trade). **1943** *Sat. Even. Post* 20 Nov. 28/3 A one shot..is usually a charity event sponsored by a political or social organization with no professional knowledge of selling tickets. **1947** *Jrnl. Brit. Interplanetary Soc.* VI. 113 The application for which a motor is designed also has a profound effect on its design. The major variables are, magnitude and duration of thrust; fixed or variable thrust; whether for repeated use or a 'one-shot', and in the former case its total operating life. **1967** A. ARENT *Gravedigger's Funeral* (1968) iv. 44 What was it going to be? A brush-off? A friendly hint that this was just a one-shotter? **1967** WODEHOUSE *Company for Henry* ix. 172 He.. has actually sold it [*sc.* the book] as what he calls a one-shotter to a magazine. **1972** M. J. BOSSE *Incident at Naha* iii. 137 'But you'd give her *my* money?' 'Sure, because you're a one-shot. I'd never have any peace if the bread came from me.'

one-sided (ˈwʌnˈsaɪdɪd, *with shifting stress*), *a.* [Parasynthetic from *one side*: see ONE 34 d; after Ger. *einseitig.*]

1. Relating to, considering, or dealing with only one side of a question or subject; partial.

1833 DE QUINCEY *Autobiog. Sk. Opium-eater* in *Tait's Mag.* (1834) 483/1 What the Germans mean by a *one-sided* (ein-seitiger) judgment. [*Note* in Wks. 1853 I. 290 'It marks the rapidity with which new phrases float themselves into currency,..that this word *now* (1853) familiarly used in every newspaper, *then* (1833) required a sort of apology to warrant its introduction'.] **1838–9** HALLAM *Hist. Lit.* III. III. vi. § 100. 346, I think this well-written sentence a little one-sided. **1839** MRS. S. ELLIS *Women of England* xii. 297 To use a popular Germanism, it is but a *one-sided* view of the subject that we take. **1841** GEN. P. THOMPSON *Exerc.* (1842) VI. 315 A partial, or as the Germans call it a 'one-sided' view of things. **1842** MIALL in *Nonconf.* II. 1 The marriage was a one-sided one. **1850** BUSHNELL *God in Christ* 52 They can endure none but a one-sided view of truth. **1885** *Law Times* LXXVIII. 388/2 A one-sided report of a trial was not a privileged publication.

2. In physical sense. **a.** Leaning to one side; larger or more developed on one side than on the other.

a **1845** HOOD *Charity Serm.* iii, For the plaguy one-sided party wall fell in. **1857** HUGHES *Tom Brown* II. v, Tom's face begins to look very one-sided—there are little queer bumps on his forehead. *Mod.* The one-sided leaf of the elm, of the begonia.

b. Having the constituent parts (*e.g.* the flowers of an inflorescence) all on one side; unilateral.

1813 H. MUHLENBERG *Catal. Plantarum Americæ Septentrionalis* 49 One-sided Hawthorn. **1832** J. LINDLEY *Introd. Bot.* IV. 413 One-sided..; having all the parts by twists in their stalks turned one way; as the flowers of Antholyza. **1875** W. MCILWRAITH *Guide Wigtownshire* 48 On the right is a one-sided street. *a* **1902** *Mod. Bot.* The one-sided inflorescence of the lily of the valley, of the toothwort. **1945** STEP & JACKSON *Wayside & Woodland Ferns* (ed. 2) 25 Wilson's Filmy-fern... Known also as the One-sided Filmy-fern.

c. Existing or occurring on one side only.

1864 WEBSTER, *One-sided*..2. (*Bot.*) Growing on one side of a stem; as, *one-sided* flowers. **1884** BOWER & SCOTT *De Bary's Phaner.* 360 The usually one-sided sclerosis of the endodermis. **1899** *Allbutt's Syst. Med.* VI. 580 Cases in which local syncope is predominantly and perhaps exclusively, one-sided.

Hence **one-ˈsidedly** *adv.*; **one-ˈsidedness.**

1856 *Mem. Fred. Perthes* II. xvii. 272 Insisting onesidedly on the authority of the Church. **1899** SWEET *Hist. Lang.* i. 1 To look at language from a more or less onesidedly formal or logical point of view. **1831** J. S. MILL *Let.* 20–22 Oct. (1910) I. 11 The next thing that struck me was the extreme comprehensiveness and philosophic spirit which is in him [*sc.* Wordsworth]. By these expressions I mean the direct antithesis of what the Germans most expressively call one-sidedness. **1835** *Penny Cycl.* IV. 246/2 What has been aptly termed one-sidedness of mind. **1838** E. FITZGERALD *Lett.* 8 June (1889) I. 44 With a good deal of pedantry and *onesidedness* (do you know this German word?). **1893** J. ORR *Chr. View God* ii. 55 Opposite one-sidednesses correct each other. **1974** tr. *Wertheim's Evolution & Revolution* i. 20 Another factor contributing to a rather general rejection of 'evolutionism'.. was connected with a certain one-sidedness in evolutionary views, as propagated about 1900. **1977** *South China Morning Post* (Hong Kong) 13 Apr. 13/6 To avoid accusations of one-sidedness and to round out the image of his subject, Dr. Abrahamsen spoke to a number of Mr. Nixon's admirers.

†**onesprute.** *Obs. rare.* [For *onsprute, f. ON- + SPROUT.] Inspiration.
a **1300** *E.E. Psalter* xvii. 16 Fra one-sprute of gast of wreth þine.

onest(e, onestly, etc., obs. ff. HONEST, etc.

one-step ('wʌnstɛp), *sb.* Also **one step.** [f. ONE *numeral a.* + STEP *sb.*] A ballroom dance in quick time, in which the steps resemble simple walking. Hence as *v. intr.*, to dance the one-step.
1911 *Home Chat* 7 Oct. 108/1 Camilla is just mad about the 'One-step'. **1914** V. CASTLE *Mod. Dancing* 44 Simply *walk* as softly and smoothly as possible, taking a step to every count of the music. This is the One Step, and this is all there is to it. **1916** H. L. WILSON *Somewhere in Red Gap* iv. 172, I caught him.. in the deserted library later, while the rest was one-stepping in the.. ballroom. **1921** H. S. WALPOLE *Young Enchanted* III. i. 230 Bunny says I one-step better than anyone he's ever known. **1924** [see HESITATION 3]. **1938** B. SCHÖNBERG tr. *Sachs' World Hist. of Dance* vii. 445 We have shortly after 1900 the *one-step* or *turkey trot.* **1956** G. P. KURATH in A. Dundes *Mother Wit* (1973) 106/1 The one-step or turkey-trot.. was little more than a smooth walk. **1969** F. RUST *Dance in Society* x. 84 After the one-step came the fishwalk and the horsetrot—of ephemeral interest only.

oneth(e, -thes, obs. ff. UNEATH, UNEATHS, *advs.*

one-til, one-to, obs. ff. UNTIL, UNTO.

one-way, *a.* [f. ONE *numeral a.* + WAY *sb.*[1]]
†**1.** Applied to a kind of bread (see quot.). *Obs.*
1620 VENNER *Via Recta* i. 18 Sometimes onely the grosser part of the bran is by a Searce separated from the meale, and a bread made of that which is sifted, called in some places *One way bread. Ibid.* (1650) 108 Why are Oysters usually eaten a little before meales, and that with one-way-bread?
2. Applied to a plough which can turn the furrows in one direction only. Also *ellipt.*
1884 F. J. LLOYD *Sci. Agric.* 128 There is one other plough.. called the 'one-way' or 'turnwrest' plough. **1886** F. T. ELWORTHY *West Somerset Word-Bk.* 537 A two-way-zull, eens can plough vore and back in the same vore, is a handy thing like, but can't make such good work way un's can way a proper good one-way-zull. **1960** *Times* 15 Feb. 19/2 A one-way plough much lighter in weight. **1965** G. SHEPHERD *West of Yesterday* x. 77 We used a plough, for there was no 'one-way', as the modification of the disc plough was later named.
3. a. Leading, tending, pointing, thinking, or developing in one direction only.
1824 M. WILMOT *Let.* 5 Feb. (1935) 206 Our one way life, dearest Alicia, gives me so little to say. **1928** A. S. EDDINGTON *Nature Physical World* 295 The notion evidently implies that something may be born into the world at the instant Here-Now, which has an influence extending throughout the future cone but no corresponding linkage to the cone of absolute past. The primary laws of physics do not provide for any such one-way linkage. **1938** L. MACNEICE *Earth Compels* 61 Endurance of one-way thinking. **1951** KOESTLER *Age of Longing* i. 6 One-way pupils that took the light in, gave nothing out. *Ibid.* vii. 127 He put on the guarded, one-way gaze. **1953** J. S. HUXLEY *Evolution in Action* i. 12 All reality, in fact, *is* evolution, in the perfectly proper sense that it is a one-way process in time. **1960** PARTRIDGE *Charm of Words* 40 In a one-way dictionary, the explanations are made in the same language as that of the words defined. **1966** G. N. LEECH *Eng. in Advertising* v. 48 Many intonation contrasts in English signal personal attitudes and contextual presuppositions which can scarcely apply to one-way public communication. **1973** *Australian* 17 Dec. 16/7 Your child could be studying under a Miss Brooks at school and your spouse or boy-friend may well be a one-way baby (simply a term for self-centred emotional types). **1977** *Rep. Comm. Future of Broadcasting* iii. 19 Broadcasting.. is a one-way communication; viewers and listeners cannot question or express approval or disapproval.
b. *spec.* Of a ticket: entitling the holder to a journey in one direction only; 'single'. Also *fig.*
1906 *Dialect Notes* III. 148 Over three hundred negroes left Springfield, purchasing oneway tickets to many different towns. **1949** L. HUGHES (*title*) One-way ticket. **1973** *Nation Rev.* (Melbourne) 31 Aug. 1464/2 One journalist.. later earned himself further notoriety and a oneway ticket to Van Diemen's Land. **1976** J. LEE *Ninth Man* 258 You've bought yourself a one-way ticket to obscurity. **1977** *Times* 5 Oct. 17/8 On most days people are not having to queue to buy their one-way tickets to America at £59 a head.
c. Of a thoroughfare: along which traffic is permitted in only one direction; of traffic: passing only in one direction; also, of or pertaining to such traffic. Also *fig.*
1914 *World's Work* Aug. 302/1 Some little has already been done in the small streets off Piccadilly to *request* drivers to avoid some streets when going north and others when going south, thereby aiming at 'one-way' traffic, but there is no power to enforce the requests. *Ibid.* 304/1 Where streets are too narrow to permit of the rotary system the difficulty can be overcome by one-way streets. **1926** *Glasgow Herald* 11 Sept. 9 A complaint has been heard from shop-keepers against the one-way system in certain streets. **1933** [see *clover-leaf* s.v. CLOVER *sb.* 4]. **1956** B. HOLIDAY *Lady sings Blues* (1973) xxi. 171 This is a one-way street. If someone plants something on you and you're innocent, you have no way in the world to prove it. **1959** *Daily Tel.* 8 May 12 One-way study for London. *Ibid.*, The pros and cons of proposals for one-way traffic. **1961** [see DREAM *sb.*[2] 1 b]. **1961** L. VAN DER POST *Heart of Hunter* III. xv. 202 The European.. tends to believe that the consequences are only for the primitive and that he.. is immune from them. But actually there is no one-way traffic on these eventful occasions. **1963** *Traffic in Towns* (Ministry of Transport) ii. 40/2 One-way streets and the elimination of right-hand turns have been the main features that have caught public attention. **1970** P. LAURIE *Scotland Yard* iv. 96 They put up temporary one-way signs, controlled junctions. **1972** J. GORES *Dead Skip* (1973) xv. 105 Kearny entered town on one-way Howard Street. **1976** *Northumberland Gaz.* 26 Nov. 19/9 It was virtually one-way traffic in the second half as Berwick kept the visitors pinned in their own area. Heslop and Renwick added further tries and Dudgeon kicked a further three penalty goals.
d. *one-way pockets*: the pockets of a miserly person. *slang.*
1926 MAINES & GRANT *Wise-Crack Dict.* 11/2 *One-way pockets*, pockets of tightwad. **1961** WODEHOUSE *Service with Smile* (1962) ix. 143 His one-way pockets was a by-word all over England.
e. Of a window, mirror, or the like: that permits vision from one side; transparent from one side only.
a **1940** F. SCOTT FITZGERALD *Last Tycoon* (1949) ii. 31 Nowadays all chief executives have huge drawing rooms, but my father's was the first. It was also the first to have one-way glass in the big French windows. **1961** W. BROWN *Bedeviled* 40 Obscene exhibitions viewed through peepholes made of one-way glass. **1964** F. POHL in *Galaxy Mag.* Oct. 192/2 The cameras.. that the studio people had activated for me behind every one-way mirror in the room. **1967** C. DRUMMOND *Death at Furlong Post* iii. 27 What looked like a dirty bit of glass was a one-way window. **1972** *Jrnl. Social Psychol.* LXXXVIII. 153 Further, *Ss* [*sc.* subjects] were observed during the experiment through the one-way mirror for any reactions. **1975** *Times Lit. Suppl.* 7 Mar. 241/2 Two of Dizzy's aristocratic sprigs jostle at a one-way mirror watching the most high-minded statesman of all trying to reclaim a tart.
4. *Electr.* Of a switch or the like: providing only one possible path for current.
1896 W. P. MAYCOCK *Electr. Lighting* (ed. 3) I. v. 113 Fig. 49 shows a simple or one-way switch. **1925** O. RANKIN *Switches in Wireless Circuits* 56 Two ordinary 'one-way', or 'bell switches', A and B, are used to effect the usual series-parallel switching of the A.T.C. **1965** P. HONEY *Planning Electricity in House* iii. 71 Wall switches are available in one-way and two-way types, the latter being used for the control of lights from two different points (e.g. on staircases).

onewhere ('wʌnhwɛə(r)), *adv. rare.* [f. ONE + WHERE, after *somewhere, nowhere.*] In one place (as opposed to another); in one place only.
1611 BIBLE To Rdr., If we translate the Hebrew or Greek word.. onewhere *Journeying*, never *Traveiling*; if onewhere *Thinke*, never *Suppose*. **1872** L. MORRIS *Songs two Worlds* Ser. I. *Visions* 151 Not onewhere, but pervading all. **1887** G. M. HOPKINS *Poems* (1918) 65 Each limb's barrowy brawn, his thew That onewhere curded, onewhere sucked or sank.

†**oneyers.** Origin and meaning uncertain.
1596 SHAKS. *1 Hen. IV*, II. i. 84 With Nobility, and Tranquilitie; with Bourgomasters, and great Oneyers.

onez, obs. form of ONCE.

onfaithful: see UN-.

†**onfake**, in *honyonfake* (*Pallad. on Husb.* IX. 197): see OMPHACOMEL.

onfall ('ɒnfɔːl). [f. ON-[1] 4 + FALL *sb.*]
1. An attack or access of disease, plague, or calamity. Now *Sc.*
c **1000** *Saxon Leechd.* II. 104 Drenc wiþ onfealle. *a* **1300** *Cursor M.* 5943 Ful yern on godd bi-gun þai call To liuer þe folk on þat on-fall. *Ibid.* 27738 Wreth it es a brath on-fall. **1808–18** JAMIESON, *Onfall*, a disease which attacks without any apparent cause.
2. *gen.* An attack, assault, onset. (*lit.* and *fig.*)
1837 CARLYLE *Fr. Rev.* I. VII. iii, Death by starvation and military onfall. **1880** M. PATTISON *Milton* vi. 76 A violent personal onfall upon Joseph Hall. **1889** DOYLE *Micah Clarke* xxxii. 341 Who ever saw a camp so exposed to an onfall?
3. *Sc.* **a.** A fall of rain or snow. **b.** The fall of the evening.
? *a* **1800** *Old Song* (Jam.), But or the onfa' o' the nicht, She fand him drown'd in Yarrow. **1821** *Ayr Courier* 1 Feb. (Jam.) The snow lay thick.. but the on-fall had ceased.

†**on'fang**, *v. Obs.* Forms: *Inf.* 1–3 onfón, 3 (*Orm.*) onnfanngenn; *pa. t.* 1–3 onfeng, 4 onfoȝ; *pa. pple.* 1- **onfangen.** [f. ON-[2]: see FANG *v.*]
1. *trans.* To receive, accept.
c **900** tr. *Bæda's Hist.* I. iii. (1890) 30 Claudius.. mycelne dæl þæs landes on anweald onfeng. *c* **1000** *Ags. Gosp.* Matt. xxvii. 6 Ða soðlice þæra sacerda ealdras onfengon þæs seolfres. *c* **1000** *Sax. Leechd.* II. 298 Se þe þone stan on drince onfehð. *c* **1200** ORMIN 16571 Forr he ne mot nohht Cristess flæsh Ne Cristess blod onnfanngenn. *c* **1205** LAY. 1069 Nulle we noht þis on-fon.
2. To take with the mind; to conceive or understand (in a particular way).
c **1200** ORMIN 12106 þatt birrþ uss lokenn hu mann birrþ Onnfon and unnderrstanndenn.
3. To undertake.
971 *Blickl. Hom.* 155 Hwylc swa ȝelyfeþ.. þonne wile he onfon rihtre ondetnesse for Cristes naman. *c* **1200** ORMIN 8565 And ta þatt shulenn þanne onnfon To lefenn uppo Criste. *c* **1205** LAY. 21194 Mi seolf ic wullen on-fon.
4. To conceive (offspring).
a **1000** *Ags. Ps.* (Th.) l. 6 þu wast þæt ic wæs mid unrihtwisnesse onfangen. *a* **1300** *E.E. Psalter* l. 7 In wickenesses on-fanged am I, And in sinnes me on-foȝ mi modre for-þi.

onfarrand: see UN-.

†**on'fast, on'fest**, *adv.* and *prep.* Also **on uast, on væst, on uest,** (*Orm.*) **onnfasst.** [f. ON *prep.* and *adv.* + OE. *fæst*, FAST, firm, close. Known only in early ME.] Near, close on, 'fast by'.
a. *adv.* **b.** *prep.*
a. *c* **1200** ORMIN 3334 þær onnfasst i þatt illke land Wass seȝhenn mikell takenn. *Ibid.* 3358 Her onnfasst he borenn iss I Daviþþ kingess chesstre. *c* **1205** LAY. 1691 In to ane þicke wode þa þer on uest wes [*c* **1275** þat þare was anewest.]. *Ibid.* 4194 Stateres floc Iseoð ore fæire sculdes Sumen on feste.
b. *c* **1205** LAY. 9 He wonede at Ernleȝe.. On fest Radestone [*c* **1275** Faste bi Radistone]. *Ibid.* 2852 He makede an temple onfest [*c* **1275** anewest] þe baðe. *Ibid.* 30713 Forð he gon liðe In to Lundene And aneouste gunnen wende On fast Westmustre.

†**on faste, on feste**, *adv. phr. Obs.* Also 3 **on uaste, on uæste, an vest(e.** [f. ON *prep.* or *adv.* + OE. *fæste* FAST *adv.*] Swiftly, speedily, with speed; = FAST *adv.* 6.
c **1205** LAY. 1455 Balu com on ueste. *Ibid.* 10732 Sum on uæste bæh In to þere burh. *Ibid.* 22583 He on uaste iueng Fæiere his iweden. *Ibid.* 23440 Sonde he sende sone An uest touward Rome.

onfeirie, onfery: see UN-.

onfestyn, onuestne: see UNFAST, -EN.

onfilit: see UNFILED.

on flote, on-flote: see FLOAT *sb.* 1, AFLOAT.

onflow ('ɒnfləʊ). [See ON-[1] 4.] The act or fact of flowing on; onward flow.
1880 G. H. TAYLOR *Health by Exerc.* (1883) 368 The onflow [of blood] superinduced. **1883** *India's Women* Jan. 56 A constant onflow of information. **1890** H. W. MABIE *Study Fire* vii. 42 Ceaseless onflow of time.
So **'onflowing** *vbl. sb.* and *ppl. a.* Also **on-flow** *v. intr.*, to flow on.
1861 A. DE VERE *Sisters* 17 No eye Finer pursued the on-flowing line: her wheel Murmur'd complacent joy. **1862** F. HALL *Hindu Philos. Syst.* 41 As the on-flowing of the world had no beginning, so it has no end. **1879** A. DE VERE *Legends of Saxon Saints* ii. 23 Forward on-flowed in Apostolic might Augustine's strong discourse. **1905** R. DAVEY tr. *Serao's In Country of Jesus* VI. iv. 167 The rapidly on-flowing waters reflect the azure blue of the sky above. **1930** *Tablet* 26 July 107/2 The large and stately on-flowing of history.

†**on-forced**, *ppl. a. Obs. rare.* Forced upon (one), enforced.
1656 EARL MONM. tr. *Boccalini's Advts. fr. Parnass.* 437 It would be sufficient to obstruct that on-forced [*so edd.* 1669, 1674] Donative, that hath brought me to live upon bread and onions.

onforlatet, onfortune, onfoughten, onfowlit, onfreind, -frend, -friend: see UN-.

†**on'frest**, *v. Obs. rare*[-1]. [f. ON-[1] + *frest*, FRIST *v.* to delay.] *trans.* To delay, put off.
c **1300** *Havelok* 1337 Do þou nouth onfrest þis fare.

ongart, var. OGART, ANGARD *Obs.*, arrogance.

†**ongel**, obs. variant of ANGEL *sb.*
c **1250** *O. Kent. Serm.* in *O.E. Misc.* 27 An ongel of heuene.

ongentle, onglad, ongodly, etc.: see UN-[1].

onȝein, onȝen, obs. forms of AGAIN.

†**onȝenes**, obs. form of AGAINST *prep.*
1258 *Proclam. Hen. III*, l. 6 ȝif oni oþer onie cumen her onȝenes [cf. l. 5 aȝrenes alle men].

†**on'gin**, *v. Obs.* Pa. t. ongan, -gon. [OE. *onginn-an*, f. ON-[1] + a radical *-ginnan*; see BEGIN. Much used in OE.; but lost early in 13th c.; retained till 14th in form AGIN q.v.] To begin.
c **1000** ÆLFRIC *Gram.* xxiv. (Z.) 137 *Inchoo*, ic ongynne. *c* **1000** *Ags. Gosp.* Matt. iv. 17 Syððan ongan se hælend bodian. —— Mark ii. 23 His leorning-cnihtas ongunnon ða ear pluccigean. *c* **1200** ORMIN 2801 Min child i blisse sone onngann To blissenn i min wambe. *a* **1225** *Juliana* 13 Affrican feng eft on & to fondin ongon.

on-glaze, *a.* (*sb.*) *Ceramics.* [f. ON *prep.* + GLAZE *sb.*] Of, pertaining to, or designating colour, a pattern, etc., applied on top of a glaze; =

OVERGLAZE *a.* Also as *sb.*, colour, etc., applied on top of a glaze.

1897 SPARKES & GANDY *Potters* i. 56 The class of enamel colours... The name of *overglaze* or *onglaze* is borne by the whole group. **1913** J. C. WEDGWOOD *Staffordshire Pott.* viii. 131 There was something crude and hard about the effect of the on-glaze printing. *Ibid.* 133 In 1770 he [*sc.* Josiah Spode] leased Banks' works in the centre of Stoke, and began making printed cream colour. This was the old 'on-glaze', or 'black' printed ware, used to guide the enameller rather than as a decoration by itself. **1957** MANKOWITZ & HAGGAR *Conc. Encycl. Eng. Pott. & Porc.* 65/2 The development of on-glaze enamelling c.1760 by the Daniel family in Hot Lane. *Ibid.* 168/2 *On-glaze*, decoration applied after the ware has been glazed and fired. **1959** *Which?* Oct. 127/1 A good deal of decorated pottery has patterns applied on top of the glaze, because this allows a much wider range of colours to be used... With this type of decoration, known as on-glaze, the colours are directly exposed to the action of the detergent. **1961** M. JONES *Potbank* xxv. 108 On-glaze decoration, working on ware that has been glazed and then fired, is more usual [than under-glaze decoration]. **1969** *Canad. Antiques Collector* Feb. 10/1 After this glost firing the onglaze enamel paintings of birds and flowers are done. **1974** *Nature* 25 Jan. 197/2 Cadmium sulphide has been shown by x-ray diffraction to be present in the onglaze decoration.

† **'ongle.** *Obs.* [a. F. *ongle*:—L. *ungula* hoof, claw, talon, dim. of *unguis* nail.] A claw.

1484 CAXTON *Fables of Æsop* I. xviii, The lyon.. within his clawes or ongles he tooke the rat. **1643** NETHERSOLE *Parab. on Times* 13 The Eagle,.. and.. the Lyon,.. the one had parted with his tallons, the other with his teeth and ongles. **1646** HOWELL *Lewis XIII* 70 The Leopard who.. useth to teare his image with his ongles and teeth.

† **'onglet.** *Obs. rare.* [a. F. *onglet* 'ungula of a petal' dim. of *ongle* claw.] The claw of a petal.

1725 BRADLEY *Fam. Dict.* s.v. *Rose*, They cut off the Onglets with a Pair of Scissars, that is, that small white part the Roses have at the Extremity of their Leaves.

'on-glide. *Phonetics.* [f. ON *a.* + GLIDE *sb.*] A glide produced at the beginning of articulating a speech-sound. Cf. OFF-GLIDE. Hence **on-gliding** *ppl. a.*

1888 H. SWEET *Hist. Eng. Sounds* 10 All consonants consist of three elements, (1) the consonant itself, (2) the on-glide, and (3) the off-glide. **1919** E. KRUISINGA *Handbk. Present-Day Eng.* (ed. 3) I. iv. 72 The chief difference between English and Dutch voiced stops is the difference between the on-glides of initial stops. **1934** *PMLA* XLIX. 1167 In the English pronunciation of parasitic (n) before (t) in *maintenant*, the (n) is an off-glide of the nasal vowel and an on-glide of the (t). **1934** PRIEBSCH & COLLINSON *German Lang.* 385 The intermission of the breath on-glide (so noticeable in English and German). **1950** D. JONES *Phoneme* 5 The on-glide and stop of this affricate resemble those of the English t. **1954** [see OFF-GLIDE]. **1965** *Language* XLI. 478 The first allophone has a rapid palatal onglide, the second has a rapid onglide of central-vowel quality; both onglides are conditioned by the preceding consonants. **1976** *Ibid.* LII. 341 Under certain conditions of stress and sentence rhythm, syllable-final stops come to be preceded by vocalic onglides.

on-going ('ɒn,gəʊɪŋ), *sb.* [ON-[1] 4.]

1. *pl.* = Goings-on (see GOING *vbl. sb.* 5 c); proceedings, doings (esp. of a notable kind).

1825 BROCKETT *N.C. Gloss.*, *Ongoings*, conduct, doings, merriment. **1828** *Blackw. Mag.* XXIII. 362 The inner on-goings, beneath what, to our imaginations is a hallowed roof. **1856** MASSON *Ess.* iii. 57 [Milton] had to describe the ongoings of angels. **1894** CROCKETT *Raiders* 151 It breaks my heart to hear you upholding such ongoings.

2. *sing.* The action of going on; proceeding, process, continued movement or action.

1860 F. W. FABER *Precious Blood* iii. 107 Not only is the continuous preservation of all things.. an almost illimitable extension and ongoing of creation, but new souls of men are literally created out of nothing every moment of time. **1880** W. M. THOMSON *Land & Bk.* 2 The long ongoing and outworking of the Mosaic Economy. **1890** *Pall Mall G.* 28 June 4/2 The reposeful grounds.. were never more than half full, and everyone had an air of restless ongoing. **1890** *Chicago Advance* 18 Sept., The stream of tendency in the ongoing of God's spirit and providence. **1962** *Listener* 11 Oct. 559/1 Experiment must be analytical and predictive in its actual on-going. **1977** *Times* 11 Apr. 5/7 The logical conclusion of a process long in the ongoing.

'on-,going, *a.* Also **ongoing**. Going on: see GO *v.* 86. Also, continuing, continuous; that is in progress; current; proceeding, or developing. Hence **'on-,goingness**.

1877 J. BLACKWOOD *Let.* 15 Oct. in *Geo. Eliot Lett.* (1956) VI. 405 This edition.. will be a steady on-going thing, a capital leading franchise in the business. **1882** in OGILVIE. **1937** [see INTEGRATION 1 b]. **1949** M. MEAD *Male & Female* xvi. 336 American women have become.. less willing to be merely part of some on-going operation. **1951** V. BARCLAY *Challenge to Darwinians* vi. 60 Bergson.. held that an ongoing movement issued from that creative act. **1951** E. C. TOLMAN in Parsons & Shils *Toward Gen. Theory Action* III. 352 What.. would be the necessary conditions for the non-disintegration, the on-goingness, of a personality system? **1953** *Scottish Jrnl. Theol.* VI. 211 Within the time of this on-going age there would be a thousand years of political triumph for the Jews. **1954** D. RIESMAN *Individualism Reconsidered* (1955) xxii. 334 Sufficient time has elapsed since Freud built his system.. to permit.. critical re-examination of the sort undertaken here... Its aim is.. to contribute to the sociology of knowledge and to the ongoing effort. **1957** P. LAFITTE *Person in Psychol.* 59 Life.. is tense, .. as an inescapable consequence of its being rich, varied, ongoing, and creative. **1959** P. WHEELWRIGHT *Heraclitus* iii. 38 For Heraclitus the most basic ontological fact is the ongoingness of things. **1960** in L. Pincus *Marriage* 8 The worker's capacity to learn from his on-going cases. *Ibid.* I. 16 This pattern of interaction can be understood only in the context on an on-going process. **1961** R. KEE *Refugee World* vii. 73 The refugee problem in our time is an on-going problem. **1967** G. WILLS in Wills & Yearsley *Handbk. Managem. Technol.* 179 Time, in an on-going marketing situation, costs money. **1972** P. LASLETT *Household & Family in Past Time* 68 The danger of mistaking a set of coincidences for an ongoing institution. **1973** *Guardian* 13 Oct. 2/3 We have an on-going military relationship which we are continuing. **1974** *Times* 1 May 6/8 The President assigned the responsibility for the on-going investigation to Mr. Petersen. **1976** *Publishers Weekly* 16 Feb. 85/1 The ongoing polemic about the role of the atelier artist versus his university-based colleague. **1977** *Gay News* 24 Mar. 13/1 Dozens of other special relationships hold the potential of working well and of maintaining the symbiosis of ongoingness.

ongon ('ɒŋgəʊn). [Russ.] In the Shamanist religion of the Buriats of Mongolia, an image of a god or spirit supposed to be endowed with the power of the force it represents; a fetish.

1901 D. BANTZAROFF tr. J. Stadling in *Contemp. Rev.* LXXIX. 89 The dim idea of the immortality of the soul and a future life gave rise to the *Ongones*, the deified spirits of the ancestors. **1910** *Encycl. Relig. & Ethics* III. 12/1 The Turks of Yenisei call the ongon *tyus*, whereas among the Altaians it is named *Kurmes*. On the one hand, it is an image of God, and, on the other, God himself, a fetish possessed of his own power. The tyus, or ongon, reminds us of the rôle which among some Christian peoples is filled by the images of saints. **1936** V. A. DEMANT *Christian Polity* xi. 191 The Ongons of the Mongolic Buriats are effigies of dead heroes, and so are the images of Indo-China. **1950** *Funk's Stand. Dict. Folklore* II. 823/1 *Ongon*, in Buriat religion, an image embodying a god and therefore possessing the power of the god: among the Altai called *kurmes*, among certain Turks, *tyus*. **1970** *New Society* 5 Mar. 393/1 The word, 'ongon', means both a spirit and the material representation of a spirit. Drawings are made only of known spirits, each of which has particular magical powers. Since the representation *is* the spirit, the drawings themselves become magical: according to the spirit, an ongon can cure smallpox, keep young lambs healthy, give protection to fishermen and so on.

on'grouf, prone: see GROOF 1; cf. AGRUFE.

onhallow, onhalsit, etc.: see UN-.

† **onhang, onhit, onhongred:** see ANH-.

on-hanger ('ɒn,hæŋə(r)). [ON-[1] 4.] = Hanger-on: see HANGER[2] 5 a.

1848 *Blackw. Mag.* LXIV. 52 A throng of unruly onhangers. **1886** BLACKIE *What does History teach?* 14 A loose company of dependents and onhangers.

† **on'heave, on'heve,** *v. Obs.* [OE. *onhębban*, pa. t. *onhóf, onhefde*; f. ON-[1] + *hębban* to HEAVE. Cf. ANHEAVE.] *trans.* To lift up, raise.

971 *Blickl. Hom.* 149 Petrus.. onhof his stefne. *c* **1175** *Lamb. Hom.* 113 [He] on-hefð þa mildan. *Ibid.* 117 Swa swa he is on-heuene on his kine setle. *c* **1200** *Trin. Coll. Hom.* 177 Ðe water stremes on-heueden up here undes.

onhit, var. of ANHIT *v.*, to hit.

Oni ('əʊnɪ). Also with lower-case initial. [Yoruba.] The title given to the ruler of Ife, a large town now in the Western State of Nigeria.

1900 *Niger & Yoruba Notes* Sept. 19/1 The Oni of Ile Ife .. granted.. a desirable plot of ground for the Mission premises. **1904** *Jrnl. Afr. Soc.* July 472 The Oni of Ife.. has had very little political power during the present generation. **1911** *Encycl. Brit.* XXVIII. 937/1 The chief of Ife bears the title of *oni* (a term indicating spiritual supremacy). To the oni of Ife or the alafin of Oyo all the other great chiefs announce their succession. **1937** *Nigeria* XII. 4 The earliest Onis of Ife were reputed to have reigned each for as long as 200 or more years. **1967** F. WILLETT *Ife in Hist. W. Afr. Sculpture* 22 The fact that three of the heads were crowned, .. suggests that these are representations of Onis or divine kings of Ife... During this century, the Oni has appeared increasingly in public, but even the Oni Ademiluyi, who died in 1931, used to cover his mouth with a fan when he as much as took kola in public. **1974** J. R. BAKER *Race* xxi. 412 Most of the Ife bronzes are in the Oni's palace. **1976** *Daily Times* (Lagos) 8 July 11/6 Hundreds of traditional rulers including the Oni of Ife.. are attending the meeting.

† **O. Ni, oni,** *abbr. Obs.* An abbreviation of the Latin words *oneratur, nisi habeat sufficientem exonerationem* 'he is charged, or legally responsible, unless he have a sufficient discharge', with which the account of a sheriff with the King was formerly marked in the Exchequer; sometimes used subst. as a name for this phrase or the fact itself.

1644 COKE *On Litt.* IV. 116 The course of the Eschequer is, that as soon as a Sheriffe or Escheator enter into his account for issues, amerciaments and mean profits, to mark upon his head O. Ni., which is as much to say, as *Oneratur, nisi habeat sufficientem exonerationem*, and presently he is become the kings debtor, and a Debet set upon his head, and thereupon the parties peravaile are become debtors to the Sheriffe or Escheator, and discharged against the King. **1706** PHILLIPS, *Oni.* *a* **1726** GILBERT *Treat. Crt. Exchequer* (1758) 150 As to the Sheriff's Discharge first he may discharge himself by an O'ni'; (that is to say) by Order of Court, upon any particular Article, or by shewing the King's Great or Privy Seal, discharging it out of the Account.

Hence † **oni, o'ni** *v.*, *trans.* to mark with *O. Ni*; to charge to the sheriff.

a **1726** GILBERT *Treat. Crt. Exchequer* (1758) 13 The Sheriff was o' ni'd on his Account, and shewed the Book of the Clerk of the Pells in his Discharge. *Ibid.* 116 *Margin*, Rent paid on Tally to be Onied. *Ibid.* 149 The Sheriff pays in Proffers to the Value of the County Rents, because these he must Tot or O'ni' before the Cursitor Baron.

oni, onie, obs. or dial. forms of ANY.

-onic, *suffix. Chem.* [f. -ON(E + -IC, prob. after LACTONIC *a.* 1.] An ending used in forming the names of acids, esp. of carboxylic acids obtained by oxidation of aldoses, as GALACTONIC, GLUCONIC, URONIC *adjs.*, etc. (Cf. also ARSONIC *a.* (f. ARSONIUM), PHOSPHONIC *a.* (f. PHOSPHONIUM), SULPHONIC *a.* (f. SULPHONE).)

onica, oniche, onicle: see ONYCHA, ONYX, ONYCLE.

onicolo: see ONYCLE and NICOLO.

on-ido, obs. form of UNDONE.

oniȝt, obs. variant of A-NIGHT: see O *prep.*[1]

oniliche, onimete: see UN-ILIKE, UNIMETE.

onimancy: see ONYMANCY.

† **'oning,** *sb. Obs. rare.* [f. ONE *a.* + -ING[3].] An only one; a darling.

a **1300** *E.E. Psalter* xxi. 21 Out-take mi saule fra swerd to bringe, And fra hand of hunde mine oninge.

oning, obs. f. of ONEING *vbl. sb.*

onion ('ʌnjən), *sb.* Forms: α. 4–6 **unyon**, 4–8 **onyon, oynyon**, 6–7 **oynion**, 6– **onion**; also 4 **uniown, oynioun**, 4–5 **oynon**, 5 **onyounne, oynoun, oyne(u)on, onȝon, onyone, honȝon, hunyn**, 6 **unȝeon, onnyon, unyeoun**, 7 **oignion**. β. *Sc.* and *dial.* 5 **ynon**, 6 **ynion, ingowne, ingȝeon**, 7 **ynȝoin**, 8–9 **inion, ingan**, 9 **ingon, ingun**, *U.S. dial.* **ineon, ingyon**. [a. F. *oignon* (formerly also *oingnon, ongnon, ognon*) = Pr. *uignon, ignon*:—L. *ūnio*, *ūniōn-em* unity, union, a kind of large pearl, a rustic Roman name for a single onion.]

1. a. The edible rounded bulb of *Allium Cepa*, consisting of close concentric coats, and having a strong pungent flavour and smell due to a volatile oil which is destroyed by boiling; it varies much in size, and in colour from dark red to white; it has been used as a culinary vegetable from the earliest known times. **b.** The plant *Allium Cepa* itself (N.O. *Liliaceæ*), supposed to be originally a native of central Asia, but very widely cultivated in almost all climates.

1356–7 *Durham Acc. Rolls*, Unyonn [see *onion-seed* in 8]. **1382** WYCLIF *Num.* xi. 5 The leeke, and the vniowns [**1388** oynyouns] and the garlekes. *c* **1386** CHAUCER *C.T. Prol.* 634 Wel loued he garleek, oynons and eek lekes [*v. rr.* onyounnys, oynyons, onyons, oynouns]. **1398** TREVISA *Barth. De P.R.* XVII. xlii. (1495) 628 Oyneon and Ascolonia beryth leues twyes in oo yere. *c* **1475** *Pict. Voc.* in Wr.-Wülcker 785/40 *Hoc sepe*, a hunyn. **1522** SKELTON *Why not to Court* 368 What here ye of Burgonyons And the Spaniardes' onyons? **1545** BRINKLOW *Compl.* 55 b, As moch for that purpose as to lay an vnyon to my lytel fynger for the tothe ache. **1616–61** HOLYDAY *Persius* 318 A coated oignion then with salt he eats. **1717** PRIOR *Alma* I. 52 Who would ask for her opinion Between an oyster and an onion? **1875** JOWETT *Plato* (ed. 2) III. 243 They will have a relish—salt, and olives, and cheese, and onions.

β. *c* **1460** J. RUSSELL *Bk. Nurture* 569 þat ye haue ssoddyn ynons to meddille with galantyne. **1562** J. HEYWOOD *Prov. & Epigr.* (1867) 206 Wilt thow hang vp with ropes of ynions? **1596** *Compt Bk. D. Wedderburne* (S.H.S.) 71 Half a last of Ingȝeonis. **1728** Ingan [see *onion-head* in 8]. **1818** SCOTT *Leg. Montrose* ii, Our Spanish colonel, whom I could have blown away like the peeling of an ingan. **1825** J. NEAL *Bro. Jonathan* II. 84 Ingyons are proper good, when ye're sick. *a* **1845** HOOD *Lost Heir* 12 He'll be rampant.. at his child being lost; and the beef and the inguns not done!

2. With qualifying words: **a.** Applied to varieties of the above or other species of *Allium*, as **Egyptian, potato,** or **underground o.**, a variety which produces numerous small bulbs from the parent bulb; **pearl o.**, a variety or sub-species with a small bulb; **rock** or **Welsh o.**, a bulbless species (*A. fistulosum*) cultivated for its leafy tops; the Chibol; **top** or **tree o.**, a variety of Canadian origin, producing a cluster of small bulbs instead of flowers at the top of the stem; **wild o.** (U.S.), *A. cernuum*, a species with nodding rose-coloured flowers.

1552 HULOET, Onyon called a redde onyon, *pallancana*. **1581** RICH *Farew.* (1846) 218 They are sometymes rounde like to Saincte Thomas onions. **1733** MILLER *Gard. Dict.* s.v. *Onion*, Welch Onions, a sort of onions propagated by gardeners, for the use of the table in spring; they never make any bulb, and are therefore only to be eaten green in sallads. **1832** *Veg. Subst. Food* 290 The Tree, or Bulb-bearing Onion. **1855** DELAMER *Kitch. Gard.* (1861) 40 Few gardeners, if any, can say they have ever seen a potato-onion in flower. **1866** *Treas. Bot.* 40/1 The Under-ground, or Potato Onion.. has the singular property of multiplying itself by the formation of young bulbs on the parent root... The bulb-bearing Tree-Onion,.. was introduced from Canada in 1820, and is considered to be a viviparous variety of the common Onion. *Ibid.* 40/2 How this [*A. fistulosum*] obtained the name of Welsh Onion it is impossible to say, as it is a native of Siberia and certain parts of Russia.

b. Applied to plants of other genera, mostly bulbous, as **Barbados o.**, *Ornithogalum scilloides*; **bog o.**, one of several plants with roots resembling an onion, esp. the royal fern, *Osmunda regalis*; **dog's o.**, the Star of Bethlehem, *Ornithogalum umbellatum*; **French o.**: see c.

1548 TURNER *Names Herbs* (1881) 57 Ornithigalum is called in Colon Hondes vllich..after the folowynge of the duche tonge it may be called dogleke or dogges onion. **1706** PHILLIPS, *Ornithogale*, an Herb call'd Star of Bethlehem, or Dogs-Onion. **1832** W. D. WILLIAMSON *Hist. State Maine* I. 120 The Brake, of which there are several varieties, the root of which is sometimes called the 'bog-onion'. **1853** *Phytologist* (1856) V. 30 *Osmunda regalis*..is vulgarly known under the name of 'bog onion'. **1866** *Treas. Bot.* 813/2 Onion, Barbados, *Ornithogalum scilloides.* **1878** W. DICKINSON *Cumberland Gloss.* (ed. 2) 9/1 *Bog onion*, the *Osmunda Regalis* or flowering fern. **1892** *Jrnl. Amer. Folk-Lore* V. 104 *Arisæma triphyllum*, bog onion. Worcester Co.

c. sea onion, sea-onion: *Urginea* (formerly *Scilla*) *maritima*, a native of the Mediterranean region, which produces the bulbs called squills; also applied locally to *Scilla verna*.

1548 TURNER *Names Herbs* (1881) 71 Scilla is named of the Poticaries squilla, in english a sea Onion, and in some places, a french Onyon. **1597** GERARDE *Herbal* I. xciv. (1633) 171 The ordinary squill or sea onion. **1607** TOPSELL *Four-f. Beasts* (1658) 22 Pushes, or suddain boils,..are cured with the juice of asses dung, and of sea-onions beat to powder. **1807** ROBINSON *Archæol. Græca* III. iv. 211 Drawing round the person purified a squill, or sea-onion.

†**3.** *transf.* A bulb (of any plant). [= F. *oignon.*] *Obs. rare.*

1718 CHAMBERLAYNE *Relig. Philos.* (1730) II. xx. §6 Making one only Julyflower or Tulip spring out of its Onion or Bulb.

†**4.** A bunion. *Obs.*

1785 D. LOW (*title*) *Chiropodologia*, or a Scientific Inquiry into the causes of Corns, Warts, Onions and other painful or offensive cutaneous excrescences. **1802** *Hull Advertiser* 17 Apr. 2/3 He eradicates Corns, Onions, or Nails growing into the Quick. **1846** BRITTAN tr. *Malgaigne's Man. Oper. Surg.* 64 The onion has a large base, and several layers of epidermis (like the layers of an onion) adhering to the skin in several points.

5. a. A rounded projection, bulb, knob. ? *Obs.*

1825 J. NICHOLSON *Operat. Mechanic* 134 The end of the rod B..has a knob or onion on it, by which it can be moved endwise while it is turning in the box C.

b. *slang.* Head; esp. in phr. ***off one's onion***, mad.

1890 BARRÈRE & LELAND *Dict. Slang* II. 94/2 *Off his onion* (costermongers), imbecile, cracked. **1909** H. G. WELLS *Tono-Bungay* II. ii. 176 He come home one day saying Tono-Bungay till I thought he was clean off his onion. **1922** WODEHOUSE *Girl on Boat* xii. 202 When..she informed him one day that she was engaged.., he went right off his onion. **1928** *Daily Express* 11 Dec. 7/4 After four drops of beer I am properly off my onion. **1971** WODEHOUSE *Much Obliged, Jeeves* vi. 52 What on earth was the idea of inviting a fiend in human shape like that here?.. You must have been off your onion, old ancestor.

c. ***to know one's onions***, to be experienced or knowledgeable in the subject, etc., on hand; (only P. G. Wodehouse) (***not***) ***the only onion in the stew***, (not) the only person or thing to be taken into consideration.

1922 *Harper's Mag.* Mar. 530/1 Mr. Roberts knows his onions, all right. **1934** WODEHOUSE *Right Ho, Jeeves* vii. 75, I claim the right to have a pop at these problems..without having everybody behave as if Jeeves was the only onion in the hash. **1952** 'E. C. R. LORAC' *Murder in Mill-Race* v. 52 If I know my onions the woman's death has been an almighty relief to the lot of them. **1956** S. ERTZ *Charmed Circle* v. 86 'That old man,' he said, 'doesn't know his onions, luckily for you.' **1958** J. CANNAN *And be a Villain* ix. 200 Shakespeare knew his onions, didn't he? **1958** *Times* 16 June 9/4 A man 'who knows his onions' is a man wise in the ways of the world, shrewd in affairs, a tough bargainer, by no means born yesterday. **1972** WODEHOUSE *Pearls, Girls & Monty Bodkin* vii. 109 She wanted to stimulate competition. By showing you you weren't the only onion in the stew she would get your attention. **1974** J. WAINWRIGHT *Evidence I shall Give* xxxii. 166 They know their onions... They are old in wisdom and experience.

6. a. *Thieves' slang.* A seal or the like worn on a watch-chain.

1812 J. H. VAUX *Flash Dict.*, *Onion*, a watch-seal, a bunch of onions, is several seals worn upon one ring. **1829** *Blackw. Mag.* XXVI. 132 Then his ticker I set a-going..And his onions, chains and key. **1834** H. AINSWORTH *Rookwood* III. v, With my fawnied famms, and my onions gay.

b. *Naut.* A fraction of a knot.

1916 'TAFFRAIL' *Pincher Martin* v. 73 We got about six and an onion out of the old bus,..and reached there about noon. **1938** F. A. WORSLEY *First Voy. in Square-Rigged Ship* iv. 71 The speed..was 13 knots or, as Stringer put it: 'Thirteen and an onion in the squalls.' **1958** F. H. SHAW *Seas of Memory* ii. 48 'Fifteen, sir, fifteen and an onion!' called the second mate. 'That's the way I like her to move,' said Fegan.

c. = *flaming onion* (FLAMING *ppl. a.* 1 c).

1917 *Blackw. Mag.* Apr. 560/1 A line of fiery rectangles shot up... These were 'onions', the flaming rockets which the Boche keeps for..hostile aircraft. **1918** in *Amer. Speech* 1972 (1975) XLVII. 84 The airmen's pest is the 'onion', or large flaming anti-aircraft shell. **1936** 'MCSCOTCH' *Fighter Pilot* vi. 122 On heading south for the other balloon the 'onion' battery had another shot at me.

†**7.** A pearl: see UNION. *Obs.*

1688 R. HOLME *Armoury* II. 39/2 The Onion, or Unions, or Pearl, are little round Stones, white. **1750** tr. *Leonardus' Mirr. Stones* 200 The Pearl is for the most part round, and by some is called an Onion.

8. *attrib.* and *Comb.*, as ***onion bed, bulb, crop, -green*** (also as adj.), ***head, roll, salt, sauce, -seed, -seller*** (so *-selling*), ***soup, spire, steeple***; ***onion-eating, -like, onion-loving, -red, -shaped, -spired, -towered*** adjs.; †**onion asphodel**, a kind of asphodel with a bulbous root; **onion-couch**, a species of wild oat (*Avena elatior*), so called from the rounded nodes of the root-stock; **onion dome**, a dome on a church, palace, etc., shaped like an onion; so **onion-domed** *a.*; **onion-eyed** *a.*, having the eyes full of tears, as if from the effect of raw onions; **onion-fish**, a name for *Cepola rubescens* (see quot.); also (in Massachusetts) for the grenadier, *Macrurus rupestris*, from a fancied resemblance of its eyes to onions; **onion-fly**, a dipterous insect, *Delia cepetorum*, the larva of which is very destructive to onions; **onion-grass** = *onion-couch*; **onion-maggot**, the larva of the onion-fly; **onion-peel** = *onion-skin*; **onion ring**, a circular segment of an onion; **onion set** (see quots.); **onion-shell**, name for various molluscan shells of rounded form, as those of species of *Ostrea* (oyster), *Lutraria*, and *Mya*; **onion-skin**, (*a*) the outermost or any of the outer coats of an onion; (*b*) (also ***onion-skin-paper***) a very thin smooth translucent kind of paper; also (see quot. 1879) a ballot paper of very fine paper; also *attrib.*; **onion-smut**, a parasitic fungus (*Urocystis Cepulæ*) infesting onions; **onion-twitch** = *onion-couch*; †**onion-water**, a medicinal liquor prepared from onions.

1597 GERARDE *Herbal* I. lxv. 89 Of *Onion Asphodill. **1573–80** BARET *Alv.* O 91 An *onion bed, or a place planted with onions. **1826** MISS MITFORD *Village* Ser. III. (1863) 523 Most ingeniously watering her onion-bed with a new mop—now a dip, and now a twirl! **1857** *Quinland* I. I. xiii. 184, I spaded up the onion-bed after supper. **1874** *Rep. Vermont Board Agric.* II. 551 Raked as smooth as an onion bed. **1975** D. GREEN *Food & Drink from your Garden* 91 They..no longer need the special onion beds which took so many years to perfect. **1830** LINDLEY *Nat. Syst. Bot.* 274 In consequence of the free phosphoric acid which the common *Onion bulbs contain. **1880** BRITTEN & HOLLAND *Eng. Plant-names*, *Onion Couch, *Avena elatior*... It is also called Onion Grass..and Onion Twitch. **1879** *Congress Rec.* 46th Congress 1 Sess. App. 120/1 The *onion crop of South Carolina. **1956** R. MACAULAY *Towers of Trebizond* ii. 20, I dreamed too of the Crimea, of crumbling palaces decaying among orchards by the sea, of *onion domes. **1960** N. MITFORD *Don't tell Alfred* xxiv. 245 The French papers were full of lines and sidelines on Russia, no photograph without its onion dome. **1973** J. M. WHITE *Garden Game* 54 The exotic onion-dome of a church looming through the veiled whiteness. **1959** *Manch. Guardian* 26 Feb. 9/4 The Kremlin, with its three *onion-domed cathedrals. **1974** *Aiken* (S. Carolina) *Standard* 22 Apr. 6-A/1 Entering through Persian onion-domed archways, guests saw the Fermata Club in Aiken transformed into a festive pavillion of purple and orange. **1884** E. BARKER *Through Auvergne* 80 An *onion-eating or garlick-eating people. **1606** SHAKS. *Ant. & Cl.* IV. ii. 35 Looke they weepe, And I an Asse, am *Onyon-ey'd. **1753** *Stage Coach* I. 23 But your women are all onion-eyed. **1854** BADHAM *Halieut.* 232 The..*onion-fish, whose body peels into flakes like that bulb, and who zigzags through the waves like a leech. **1840** J. & M. LOUDON tr. *Köllar's Treat. Insects* II. 159 The larva very much resembles that of the *onion fly. **1882** *Garden* 4 Mar. 147/2 The well-known Onion fly. **1896** *Daily News* 17 July 6/7 Onion fly, which causes serious injuries to the onion crop. **1966** *Punch* 6 Apr. 510/2 Sets..will grow onions.. without onion fly risk. **1975** D. GREEN *Food & Drink from your Garden* 92 The main pest is the onion fly, which lays its eggs in May and June. **1906** S. W. BUSHELL *Chinese Art* II. viii. 23 The brilliant grass-greens of the Lungch'üan porcelain, called *ts'ung-lü*, or '*onion-green' by the Chinese. **1925** W. DE LA MARE *Two Tales* 71 The very ferocious onion-green dragon. **1626** BACON *Sylva* §445 It may bee tried also, with putting Onion-Seed into an *Onion-Head, which thereby (perhaps) will bring forth a larger, and earlier Onion. **1728** RAMSAY *Last Sp. Miser* v, My pouch produc'd an ingan head, To please my wame. **1713** *Phil. Trans.* XXVIII. 91 About the bigness of an *Onion-Hoe. **1811** SHELLEY *Let.* 17 May (1964) I. 76 How gets on your *onion-loving Deist. **1898** *Daily News* 10 Nov. 6/4 It is not the ordinary foreign paper, nor the '*onion peel'—so called from its transparency. **1952** M. NORTON *Borrowers* iii. 24 She [*sc.* a midget] took the *onion ring from Homily and slung it lightly round her shoulders. **1974** *Times* 21 Feb. 10 Thinly sliced onion rings. **1967** C. POTOK *Chosen* v. 100 Lunch turned out to be a massive affair, with a thick soup, fresh rye bread, *onion rolls, bagels. **1972** *New Yorker* 15 Apr. 35/3 Most of the women buy some kind of bread (a loaf of rye bread..or a few onion rolls). **1938** E. WAUGH *Scoop* III. ii. 287 A little store of seasonings..*onion salt, Bombay duck, gherkins. **1958** Onion salt [see *garlic salt*]. **1723** J. NOTT *Cook's & Confectioner's Dict.* sig. X5 (*heading*) To make *onion sauce. Cut..Onions into slices, put them into a Sauce-pan with some Veal-gravy,..simmer. **1787** J. WOODFORDE *Diary* 4 Dec. (1926) II. 356, I gave them for Dinner..a couple of Rabbitts boiled and Onion Sauce. **1877** E. S. DALLAS *Kettner's Bk. of Table* 320 (*heading*) Onion sauce.—See the Soubise sauce, the Breton sauce, and the Sauce Robert. **1939** T. S. ELIOT *Old Possum's Pract. Cats* 45 And when he's finished, licks his paws So's not to waste the onion sauce. **1356–7** *Durham Acc. Rolls* (Surtees) 558 In Cepis et *unyonnsede. **1471–2** *Ibid.* 93 Pro j lb. del vnyonsede et aliis herbis. **1626** [see *onion-head*]. **1483** *Cath. Angl.* 260/1 An *Onȝon seller, *ceparius.* **1914** W. B. YEATS *Responsibilities* 15 What th' onion-sellers thought or did. **1970** V. CANNING *Great Affair* xvi. 300 Troops..strung with hand grenades..like French onion sellers. **1915** *Daily Chron.* 23 Nov. 5/3 Onion-selling parties in England. **1886** *Harper's Mag.* Oct. 708/2 '*Onion sets'..are produced by sowing the ordinary black seed very thickly on light poor land. **1951** *Dict. Gardening* (R. Hort. Soc.) III. 1424/2 Small bulbs grown in the previous autumn and known as 'onion sets' may..be planted in spring for the raising of dry bulbs. **1975** D. & T. HOOBLER *Vegetable Gardening & Cooking* 77 Growing onions from seeds takes up to four or five months, so most home gardeners buy onion 'sets', which are the baby onion bulbs, ready to be buried in early spring, 2 inches deep, 4 inches apart, in rows 12 inches apart. **1949** R. HARVEY *Curtain Time* 97 And a brand-new wooden church, bright blue with a yellow *onion-shaped dome. **1959** J. BRAINE *Vodi* vi. 87 The chapel..was a compact red-brick building with large round-headed windows, topped rather incongruously by a tower with an onion-shaped dome. **1753** CHAMBERS *Cycl. Supp.*, *Onion-shell,..a peculiar kind of oister, which is of a roundish figure, and very thin, and transparent, and [is like] the peel of an onion. **1882** OGILVIE, *Onion-shell*, a species of oyster of roundish form; also, species of Lutraria and Mya. **1879** C. G. WILLIAMS in *Congress. Rec.* 2 Apr. 167/2 From that time to the wee small hours of the morning *onion-skin ballots went in unchallenged but not uncounted. *Ibid.* 23 June App. 120/1 The term 'onion skin' or 'tissue ballots' has obtained a generic and well-defined meaning synonymous with the 'stuffing' of ballot-boxes. **1892** *Paper & Press* July, facing p. 49 (Advt.), The Highest Grades of Typewriter Paper a Specialty. Onion Skin. Manifold Linen. **1922** *Handbk. Quality-Standard Papers* (Amer. Writing Paper Co.) 360 Onion Skin. A thin, transparent, highly glazed paper made of rag and sulphite. **1923** H. A. MADDOX *Dict. Stationery* 56 *Onion skin*, an American paper trade expression..applied to very thin and crisp typewriting or bank paper, which in texture, tear and crackle has some of the nature which characterizes the skin of an onion. **1956** S. BELLOW *Seize the Day* (1957) iv. 99 He took out a substantial bundle of onion-skin papers and said, 'These are the receipts of the transactions. Duplicates.' **1970** *New Yorker* 20 June 25/2 The shredding of a quarto of onionskin stationery, to simulate the tearing up of a billion dollars. **1973** R. THOMAS *If you can't be Good* (1974) xxii. 191 He handed me some folded sheets of onion skin..I unfolded the onion-skin sheets. **1747** H. GLASSE *Art of Cookery* ix. 77 An *Onion Soop. **1861** MRS. BEETON *Bk. Househ. Managem.* vi. 73 Onion Soup... 6 large onions,..½ pint of cream. **1942** E. PAUL *Narrow St.* xxv. 223 Most of us missed our lunch but ate onion soup and sausage with sauerkraut in midafternoon. **1966** J. B. PRIESTLEY *Salt is Leaving* xiii. 179 He..opened a tin, French and good, of onion soup. **1977** P. HARCOURT *At High Risk* i. 31 We settled for onion soup, a *filet* with a wine sauce, salad. **1966** *New Statesman* 17 June 893/1 The *onion spires of Alaska. **1959** *Times* 25 Apr. 9/5 A baroque, *onion-spired church. **1868** G. M. HOPKINS *Jrnls. & Papers* (1959) 179 The churches here have those *onion steeples nearly all. **1960** *Times* 11 June 11/6 A Church with Baroque 'onion' steeple. **1959** *Listener* 15 Jan. 131/1 Almost every little South Swabian and Bavarian village has its delightful *onion-towered church. **1875** *Gardener's Chron.* 10 Apr. 477/2 *Onion Twitch. **1694** SALMON *Bate's Dispens.* (1713) 555/2 You may make it with Parsly, Arsmart, or *Onion-water.

Hence (*nonce-wds.*) ˌ**onioˈnet** [F. *oignonet*], a small onion; ˈ**onionized** *ppl. a.*, flavoured with or smelling of onions.

1820 *Blackw. Mag.* VIII. 89 From your large, fat, yellow, insipid onion, to your little, lean, fiery, bitter onionet. **1830** *Fraser's Mag.* I. 751 The unwashed fraternity of onionized ragamuffins.

ˈ**onion**, *v.* [f. prec. sb.]

1. *trans.* To season or flavour with onions.

1755 SMOLLETT *Quix.* II. III. xvii. (1784) IV. 86 They treated him with an hachis of beef onioned.

2. To apply an onion to; to produce (tears) by application of an onion. Also *fig.*

1763 C. JOHNSTON *Reverie* I. 243 The fellow wiped his eyes which had been well onioned for the purpose. *a* **1792** WOLCOTT *Quaker & Barn* ii, When master Broadbrim.. Por'd o'er his father's will, and drop'd the onion'd tear. **1900** SHAW *Plays Purit.* p. xxix, The undertaker's handkerchief, duly onioned with some pathetic phrase.

oniony (ˈʌnjənɪ), *a.* [-Y.] Flavoured with onions; having the taste or smell of onions.

1838 T. THOMSON *Chem. Org. Bodies* 844 A fawn-coloured sediment, having a strong oniony odour. **1842** THACKERAY *Fitzboodle Papers* Wks. 1879 XVII. 210 There was the horrid familiar odour of those oniony sandwiches. **1894** *Longm. Mag.* Sept. 481 Soup very oniony and thin. **1922** JOYCE *Ulysses* 233 Armpits' oniony sweat. **1971** *Guardian* 5 May 9/4 Onions always smell oniony. **1975** L. LEE *I can't stay Long* 31 Garlic sprawls rank and oniony in the woods. **1977** *Times* 10 Dec. 9/6 An oniony omelette.

oniro-: see ONEIRO-.

onis, obs. form of ONCE.

†**onisc.** *Obs.* [Anglicized form of ONISCUS.] A wood-louse.

1661 LOVELL *Hist. Anim. & Min.* Introd., Their meat is earth and oniscs, and they live long without meate.

onisciform (əʊˈnɪsɪfɔːm), *a. Zool.* [f. L. *oniscus* wood-louse: see -FORM.] Having the form of a wood-louse or of the genus *Oniscus*; applied to certain Myriapoda, and to the larvæ of certain Lepidoptera.

1826 KIRBY & SP. *Entomol.* III. xxx. 185 An onisciform one [larva], the legs of which..are covered with a viscid skin; this produced a *Noctua.* **1843** HUMPHREYS *Brit. Moths* I. 81 The caterpillar is onisciform, naked, and green.

oniscoid (əʊˈnɪskɔɪd), *a. Zool.* [f. Gr. ὀνισκ-ος wood-louse + -OID.] Resembling or related to the wood-lice; onisciform.

‖**o'niscus.** *Zool.* [L., a. Gr. ὀνίσκος little ass, wood-louse, dim. of ὄνος ass: used in Zool. as a generic name.] A genus of terrestrial Isopod Crustacea, the type of the family *Oniscidæ*. The species are commonly known as wood-lice or slaters.

1848 S. MAUNDER *Nat. Hist.* 460 The terrestrial oniscus frequents dark and concealed places, such as cellars, caves, holes in walls [etc.].

o-nith, bad ME. spelling of *oniht*, A-NIGHT.

-onium, *suffix.* [abstracted from AMMONIUM.] **1.** *Chem.* Used in forming the names of complex cations that contain a more or less electronegative central atom, usu. bonded to a number of protons (or to other species that are regarded as substituents), as ARSONIUM, CARBONIUM, HYDRAZONIUM, NITRONIUM, OXONIUM, PHOSPHONIUM, *tetrachlorophosphonium*, etc.

1971 *Nomencl. Inorg. Chem.* (I.U.P.A.C.) (ed. 2) 20 Names for polyatomic cations derived by addition of more protons than required to give a neutral unit to monatomic anions, are formed by adding the ending -onium to the root name of the anion element.

2. *Particle Physics.* [Abstracted from POSITRONIUM.] Used in forming the names of bound states of a particle and its antiparticle, as CHARMONIUM, TOPONIUM.

onium ('əʊnɪəm), *a. Chem.* Also 'onium. [f. prec.] Applied to (compounds containing) ions of the kind named in *-onium*.

1905 *Jrnl. Chem. Soc.* LXXXVIII. I. 281 Carbon differs from other elements, which form 'onium' bases, in that it forms salts only. **1923** G. N. LEWIS *Valence* ix. 108 The formation of the typical 'onium' ion is a process which differs in no essential respect from the other processes in which hydrogen or other radicals become attached to lone pairs. **1952** KIRK & OTHMER *Encycl. Chem. Technol.* IX. 596 Several important classes of dyes, for example the cyanine dyes.., the azine dyes.., and the amino-substituted triphenylmethane dyes.., are onium compounds. **1953** C. K. INGOLD *Struct. & Mech. Org. Chem.* v. 208 It is not necessary that the anion of the 'onium salt should be the substituting agent. **1973** J. F. WILLEMS in R. J. Cox *Proc. Symposium Photogr. Processing Univ. Sussex* 227 Various onium compounds considerably accelerate the bleaching out of the silver.

onix, obs. form of ONYX.

onkosine, var. ONCOSINE.

onlace, onlase, onland, onlasse (unless), **onlawful:** see UN-.

onlap ('ɒnlæp). *Geol.* [f. ON *adv.* + LAP *v.*[2], after OFFLAP.] A progressive increase in the lateral extent of conformable strata in passing upwards from older to younger strata, so that each stratum is hidden by the one above; a set of strata exhibiting this.

1947 F. A. MELTON in *Bull. Amer. Assoc. Petroleum Geologists* XXXI. 1869 The writer proposes that the simpler name *marine-onlap*, which has already been used by various authors, be substituted for the more cumbersome term used by Grabau. Marine-onlap is thus used to describe the regular progressive pinching-out of marine strata above an unconformity..in such a way that the younger beds extend farther landward than do the older beds which lie beneath. .. The term terrestrial-onlap can be used in connection with terrestrial formations. **1955** *Sci. Amer.* Mar. 84/2 When the sea advanced, under the simplest conditions the new deposits overlapped the older in a shoreward direction—a process called onlap. **1968** R. W. FAIRBRIDGE *Encycl. Geomorphol.* 340/1 The 'Schooley Peneplain' of the Appalachians..dips unmistakably under the mid-Tertiary transgressive onlap of the Atlantic Coastal Plain.

ˌ**on'lay,** *v. Obs.* exc. as *ppl. a.* [f. ON-[1] + LAY *v.*] *trans.* To lay on (*lit.* and *fig.*): see LAY *v.*[1] 55. Hence '**onˌlaid** *ppl. a.*, laid on; †'**onˌlaying** *vbl. sb.*, laying on.

a **1300** *Cursor M.* 29162 If þe priest þat penance lais Be noght all wise in on-lainge. **1674** N. FAIRFAX *Bulk & Selv.* Contents c ij b, That two Bodies touch, somthing must needs be between; else onlay'd bodies, and inlay'd would be all one. **1830** SCOTT *Demonol.* 324 Onlaying of certain iron gauds (bars) severally one by one. **1832** J. WILSON in *Blackw. Mag.* XXXI. 173 To prepare a bed beneath the portico, and beautiful bedclothes to onlay. **1880** L. HIGGINS *Handbk. Embroidery* v. 54 'Onlaid appliqué' is done by cutting out the pattern in one or many coloured materials, and laying it down on an intact ground of another material. **1971** *Bodl. Libr. Rec.* VIII. 264 The covers are decorated with onlaid straw, a wide outer band of large stylized flowers ..with doublures bearing similar straw onlays. **1976** *Times Lit. Suppl.* 25 June 805/4 Thomas Fassam's *An Herbarium for the Fair*, 1949, onlaid with butterflies and woodruff by a new-comer, Angela James.

onlay ('ɒnleɪ), *sb.* [f. ON-[1] 4 + LAY *v.*]

a. Anything mounted upon something else or affixed to it so as to rise from its surface in relief, especially in ornamental design (*Cent. Dict.*).

1959 L. M. HARROD *Librarians' Gloss.* (ed. 2) 194 *Onlay*, a decorative panel of paper or other material glued to the cover of a book without preparing the cover to receive it. **1961** J. CARTER *ABC for Bk. Collectors* (ed. 3) 139 The technique was occasionally adapted to publisher's cloth between 1840 and 1860, when the onlays were sometimes of paper. **1971** [see prec.]. **1976** *Times Lit. Suppl.* 25 June 805/1 Technical innovations since the Second World War have greatly extended the binder's decorative range. Before then decoration was limited to gold or blind-tooling and coloured onlays.

b. *Dentistry.* An occlusal rest extended so as to cover the whole occlusal surface of a tooth.

1906 J. A. LENTZ *U.S. Pat. 833,883* 23 Oct., My objects are, first, to facilitate and expedite the reproduction or duplication in gold, gold alloy, or similar substance of a variety of forms, such as inlays, onlays, cusps, [etc.]. **1935** G. M. ANDERSON *Dewey's Pract. Orthodontia* (ed. 5) xxii. 427 If the tooth is sufficiently exposed so that one need not cut into it, an onlay may be used in conjunction with the auxiliary spring. **1973** L. BAUM *Advanced Restorative Dentistry* xi. 169 Onlays are generally more acceptable than inlays in middle-aged and older patients because the design of onlay preparations provides for a casting which will bond together the remaining tooth structure.

c. onlay graft *Surg.*: a bone graft in which a piece of bone is fixed over a fracture.

1927 *Southern Med. Jrnl.* (Nashville, Tennessee) XX. 114/2 Of the thirty-eight bones in which the onlay graft was employed, three failed to induce osseous union. **1957** ROB & SMITH *Operative Surg.* V. IX. i. 12 Fixation by on-lay graft. The technique is the same as for fixation by a metal plate except that a cortical slab graft..is used instead of the metal plate.

onleef, onleeful, onlettered, etc.: see UN-.

†'**onlepy,** *a. Obs.* Forms: α. 1 ánlépiᵹ, -lípiᵹ, -lýpiᵹ, -lépe, (ǽn-), 2 enlepi, 3 anlepiȝ, anelepi, anilepi, 3–4 anlepi, 4 anlepe, anlep, 5 anlepy, -lypy. β. 3–4 onlepi, 3–5 onlepy, 4 onelepi, -y, oonlypi, 5 oonlepye. γ. 2 ǽlpiᵹ, 2–3 elpi, 2–4 alpi, 3 ælpi. δ. 4 olepi, olepy, olupy. [OE. *ánlíepiᵹ*, *-lýpiᵹ*, *-lípiᵹ*, f. *án* one + *hlíep* leap, jump, *hléapan* to leap, run + *-iᵹ*, -Y. The first element underwent the same phonetic changes as *án*, ONE, to *ôn-*, *en-*, *ô-*, *a-*, *æ-*, *e-*, after the latter of which also *-lipiȝ*, *-lepiȝ* was reduced to *-lpi*. The form *ælpiᵹ* occurs even in late OE. ante 1120. The northern *anlep*, *-lepe* in 14th c. represents the OE. collateral form *ánlépe*: cf. ON. *einhleypr*.]

1. Only, sole, single. In quot. 1340[1] = one *with*.

α. *c* **900** tr. *Bæda's Hist.* III. xviii. [xiv.] (MS. O), Nawcht ..buton his aᵹene ᵹyrde anlipie. *c* **1000** *Ags. Ps.* (Th.) xiii. 2 Nis nan ðe eallunga wel do, no forðon anlepe. *c* **1175** *Lamb. Hom.* 75 His enlepi sune. *c* **1200** ORMIN Introd. 11 Fra þatt anlepiȝ treo. *a* **1225** *Leg. Kath.* 74 Ane kinges..anlepi dohter. *c* **1300** *Havelok* 2107 Her he spak anilepi word. **13..** *Cursor M.* 9520 He had an anlepe son.

β. *c* **1200** *Trin. Coll. Hom.* 19 Ich bileue on þe helende crist, his onlepi sune. **1340** *Ayenb.* 13 Þe holi gost..is onlepi god an[d] onlepi þing mid þe uader and þe zone. *Ibid.* 125 A grat lhord ssolde he by..þet þise onelepi uirtue hedde. **1382** WYCLIF *Luke* vii. 12 An oonlypi sone of his modir. **14..** in Maskell *Mon. Rit.* II. 241, I bileue..in Ihesu Crist his oonlepye sone.

γ. **1085–1120** *O.E. Chron.* an. 1085 Næs an ælpiᵹ hide, ne an ᵹyrde landes..þæt næs ᵹesæt on his ᵹewrite. *c* **1175** *Lamb. Hom.* 29 On enelpi luttele hwile. *Ibid.* 33 Al heo ageð on ane alpi þraȝe. *c* **1205** LAY. 3499 Mid ane alpie swein. *Ibid.* 12400 Ǽnne ælpi verde. *Ibid.* 31450 Nu hafde Oswald ..Ǽnne ælpine broðer. *c* **1300** *Vox & Wolf* 132 in Hazl. *E.P.P.* I. 62 On alpi word ich lie nelle.

δ. **13..** *Guy Warw.* (A) 2237 Here is gret scorn sikerly, When þat olepi kniȝt Schal ons do so michel vnriȝt. *a* **1400** in *Eng. Gilds* (1870) 350 þey he ne worche but o-lupy cloþ.

b. *absol.* Single one, only one; darling.

c **975** *Rushw. Gosp.* Matt. xxvi. 22 And ingunnun anlepum cweþan, ah ic hit eam dryhten. **13..** *Cursor M.* 5996 All þe fleies ware went awai..þat an-lepi þar was not sene. *a* **1400** *Prymer* (1891) 107 (Ps. xxii. 20) God delyuere my soule fro drede; and my olepy fro the howndes hond.

2. Solitary; single, unmarried.

c **900** tr. *Bæda's Hist.* IV. xxx[i.]. (1890) 376 Se þa ænlepe [*v.r.* anlypiᵹ] wunode in syndriᵹre stowe. **13..** *Cursor M.* 27939 Fornicacion..don wit anlep woman. *c* **1400** *Apol. Loll.* 38 Simple fornicacoun bi thwex an onlepy man & an onlepi womman. *c* **1440** *York Myst.* xiii. 40 Wele I might euere mare Anlepy life haue led.

3. as *adv.* Only, solely, simply.

c **1315** SHOREHAM 11 (I. 272) Olepi [me] mot hym [depe] ine the water.

Hence †'**onlepihede**, singleness, singularity; †'**onlepiliche** *adv.*, only, solely.

c **1250** *Old Kent. Serm.* in *O.E. Misc.* 28 Nacht onlepiliche to day, ac alle þo daies i þo yere. **1340** *Ayenb.* 21 Ine onlepihede, uor þe proude and þe ouerwenere weneþ more by worþ, oþer conne more þanne enie oþre. *Ibid.* 211 He waggeþ þe lippen onlepiliche, and makeþ semblont to spekene and naȝt ne zayþ.

onlete, var. ANLETH *Obs.*, countenance.

onlevene, obs. form of ELEVEN.

on-licence: see ON *a.* 2.

onlicnes, -lichnesse, var. ANLIKENESS *Obs.*, likeness, image.

onlie, var. ONLY *a.*

†**on'light,** *v.*[1] *Obs.* [OE. *onlíehtan*, *-líhtan*, f. ON-[1] 1 + *líehtan*, *líhtan* to LIGHT.]

1. *trans.* To shed light upon; to lighten, enlighten, illuminate.

c **888** K. ÆLFRED *Boeth.* xxxiv. § 5 Ealle steorran weorþaþ onlihte..of þære sunnan. **971** *Blickl. Hom.* 19 He þone blindan onlyhte. *c* **1175** *Lamb. Hom.* 97 Monnan heortan þet he onlihteð mid his ȝife.

2. To cause to shine.

a **1300** *E.E. Ps.* cxviii. 135 On-light þi face over þi hine.

†**on-'light,** *v.*[2] *Obs.* For *on light* = light on: LIGHT *v.*[1] II c.

c **1420** *Avow. Arth.* xxxviii, Is none of ȝo but he mun fele, That he may on lyȝte.

†'**onlihede.** *Obs.* [f. ONLY + *-hede*, -HEAD.]

1. Solitude: = next, 1.

1382 WYCLIF *Esther* xvi. 14 These thingus thenkende, that, hem slain, he shulde aspie to oure onlihed [1388 aloonenesse].

2. Oneness, unity.

c **1440** HYLTON *Scala Perf.* (W. de W. 1494) II. xlvi, The onelihede in substaunce, & distynccion of persones, in the blessyd trynite.

on-line (stress variable), *a.*, *adv.*, and *phr.* Also online. [f. ON *prep.* + LINE *sb.*[2]] **A.** *adj.* (Usu. stressed *'on-line*.) **1.** *Computers.* Directly connected, so that a computer receives an input from or sends an output to a peripheral device, process, etc., as soon as it is produced; carried out while so connected or under direct computer control.

1950 W. W. STIFLER *High-Speed Computing Devices* ii. 7 For some applications, of which the most prominent are those in which the reduced data are used to control the process being measured, the input must be developed for on-line operation. In on-line operation the input is communicated directly..to the data-reduction device. **1957** [see OFF-LINE *a.* 2]. **1959** [see IN-LINE *a.* 3 c]. **1964** T. W. MCRAE *Impact of Computers on Accounting* i. 17 If we are processing..a payroll,..and the output printer is directly hooked up to the computer store so that each payslip is printed immediately after it is calculated, we use the term on-line processing. **1965** *Math. in Biol. & Med.* (Med. Res. Council) VI. 295 Without time-sharing, the 'on-line' use of a fast modern machine would be unthinkably costly. **1968** *Times* 26 Oct. 4/4 It was found..by radio astronomers using the 250 ft. dish telescope connected to an on-line computer. **1971** *Computers & Humanities* V. 192 The SHOEBOX is an automatic text-processing and retrieval system implemented for on-line operation on an IBM 360/50 computer. **1972** *Accountant* 27 Apr. 549/1 A completely integrated computer data system which..through a built-in system of analysis and recording enables managers at any level to have immediate 'on-line' access to that part of the information which is relevant.

2. Occurring or effected on the current authorized routes of an airline.

1969 *Jane's Freight Containers 1968–69* 429/2 Online and interline use [*sc.* of air cargo pallets] by JAL. **1973** E. RATH *Container Systems* x. 285 Those airlines who had purchased both the 747 and either the DC-10 or the L-1011 realized that standardization of lower-deck containers would permit them to effect on-line and interline transfers of complete containers between these different types of aircraft.

3. = IN-LINE *a.* 2.

1972 *Physics Bull.* Jan. 29/3 Dr. K. A. Andrews.. described the progress which was being made with the problem of on-line ultrasonic testing of hot steel. **1976** *Gramophone* Aug. 354/2 Mass production calls for high speed working, sophisticated on-line testing and..a high degree of automation.

B. *adv.* (Usu. stressed *on-'line*.) With processing of data carried out simultaneously with its production; while connected to a computer, or under direct computer control.

1950 [see OFF-LINE *adv.*]. **1964** *Ann. N.Y. Acad. Sci.* CXV. 654 The goal of the development has been a machine which..is fast enough for simple data-processing 'on-line' while the experiment is in progress. **1966** *Economist* 23 July 382/3 Information will be available 'on-line'..to 100 BOAC centres throughout the world. **1966** *New Scientist* 27 Oct. 161/2 All the files of the users of the system are put on-line —that is, made directly accessible to the central processor. **1968** *Amer. Documentation* Jan. 72/1 Editing will be done on-line with a display scope and keyboard. **1977** *Catalogue & Index* XLVI. 8 Those who want to work on-line will be able to work in a format designed to reflect..the way the data is stored in the computer.

C. *phr.* (Written as two words.) = ON STREAM *adv. phr.* a.

1968 *Daily Colonist* (Victoria, B.C.) 28 Nov. 13/6 The Skookumchuck mill recently came on line, but none of the B.C.-produced pulp destined for Japan is in the present cardboard packages. **1975** *Nature* 9 Oct. 435/3 Domestic uranium reserves will be totally committed to those nuclear reactors which are brought on line in the next 20 years.

onliness ('əʊnlɪnɪs). Now *rare.* Forms: see ONLY. [f. ONLY *a.* + -NESS.]

†**1.** The fact or condition of being alone; solitariness, solitude. *Obs.*

c **1340** HAMPOLE *Prose Tr.* 5 Noghte emange many bot in anelynes. **1435** MISYN *Fire of Love* 30 Onelynes is nedfull with-outen noys & bodily songe. *c* **1440** HYLTON *Scala Perf.* (W. de W. 1494) II. xl, It..secheth onelynes of body: for that moche helpeth to onelynes of the soule. **1611** COTGR., *Vnisson*, an vnison..an onelynesse, or lonelynesse.

2. The fact or character of being the only one of its kind; singleness, singularity, uniqueness.

1633 D. R[OGERS] *Treat. Sacram.* I. 18 Shee hath darkned the Doctrine of the Covenant, the freedome and onelinesse of it. **1678** CUDWORTH *Intell. Syst.* I. iv. § 10. 207 It evidently appears that there can be but one such being, and that Μόνωσις, unity, oneliness or singularity is essential to it. **1682** NORRIS *Hierocles* Pref. 23 They acknowledg'd God in all his glorious attributes, that of his unity or oneliness not excepted. **1863** H. ALLON *Mem. J. Sherman* 339 It cannot be controlled by the absolute authority of the first .. its onliness renders the second impossible.

on live, *phr.* The earlier form of ALIVE: see this and LIFE.

onload, onloathsome, onlock, etc.: see UN-.

on-long(e, -en, obs. forms of ALONG.

onlook ('ɒnlʊk). [f. ON-[1] 4 + LOOK *sb.*] The act of looking on, or looking at something.

1867 MITCHELL *Rural Stud.* 158 He has no right to ignore the onlook of the world.

onlooker ('ɒn,lʊkə(r)). [f. ON-[1] 4 + LOOKER *sb.*] One who looks on; a looker on; a spectator.

1606 DRUMM. OF HAWTH. *Let. fr. Greenwich* Wks. (1711) 232 Who .. will not be an idle on-looker to such pastimes. **1615** DANIEL *Hymen's Tri.* Wks. (1717) 94 We robb'd our Looks th' Onlookers to beguile. **1833** J. RENNIE *Alph. Angling* p. xiv, So far as an on-looker and a child could learn. **1884** *Macm. Mag.* Nov. 1/1 It is the onlooker that sees most of the game.

onlooking ('ɒn,lʊkɪŋ), *vbl. sb.* [See ON-[1] 4.] The action of looking on.

1637 GILLESPIE *Eng. Pop. Cerem.* Ep. A ij b, Their carelesse and newtrall onlooking. **1876** MRS. WHITNEY *Sights & Ins.* II. xxx. 582 All chance .. of any apprehensive onlooking into what life might be to her.

'onlooking, *ppl. a.* [See ON-[1] 3.] That looks on; looking at something.

1663 BLAIR *Autobiog.* i. (1848) 8 To live always as under thy onlooking eye. **1845** A. SYMINGTON in *Ess. Chr. Union* viii. 489 Does not an onlooking world perceive the discrepancy?

[**onloðest**, *Ancr. R.* 200, error for *on loðest*: see LOATH *a.*]

only ('əʊnlɪ), *a.* Forms: 1 **ǽnlíc, ánlíc**, 3–4 **onlich, -lych**, (*superl.* **onlukest**), 4 **oonlich, onelich, -lych, -lyk**; *north.* **anli, anly, aneli**, 4–5 **anely**; 4–5 **oonli**, 4–6 **oonly, onlie**, 4– **only**, (5 **ounly, ondly, ondely, wonly, wonlych**, 5–7 **onlye**, 5–8 **onely**, 6 **onelye**, 6–7 **onelie**). [a. OE. *ánlíc* unique, solitary, only, a later form of *ǽnlíc* unique, singular, excellent, f. AN, ONE + *-líc*, -LY[1].]

1. One, without companions or society; solitary, lonely. Now only *dial.*

a **1000** *Ags. Ps.* (Spelman) xxiv. 17 ȝemildsa me, forðan ænlic and ðearfa ic eom. *c* **1000** *Ags. Ps.* (Th.) ci. 5 Ic spearuwan .. ȝelice ȝewearð, anlicum fuȝele. *a* **1225** *Ancr. R.* 90 Ancre hus, þet schulde beon onlukest stude of alle. *Ibid.* 152 So ouh ancre, hire one in onliche stude .. chirmen & cheateren euer hire bonen. *a* **1300** *E.E. Psalter* xxiv. 16 Aneli and pouer am I. **13..** *Cursor M.* 3075 (Cott.) An anli liuelade þar þai ledde. *c* **1380** WYCLIF *Serm.* Sel. Wks. I. 110 He wolde in comunalte do þis dede and not þus oonli in desert. ? *a* **1500** *Chester Pl.* ii. 129 Hit is not good man onely to be. **1582** STANYHURST *Æneis* III. (Arb.) 91 His oane light, That stood in his lowring front gloommish malleted onlye. **1642** ROGERS *Naaman* 9 Onely Denus and Demaris a poore only man and only woman, being excepted. **1828** *Craven Gloss.* (ed. 2), *Onely, Onerly*, lonely, retired. 'This is an onely platt to live in'. *a* **1865** E. WAUGH '*Come whoam to thi childer*', Mon, aw'm one-ly when theaw artn't theer.

2. a. One (or, by extension, two or more), of which there exist no more, or no others, of the kind.

Usually preceded by *the* or a *poss. pron.* or case.

c **1000** *Ags. Gosp.* Luke ix. 38 He is min anlica sunu. *c* **1160** *Hatton G.* ibid., He ys min anliche sune. *c* **1375** *Cursor M.* 26549 (Fairf.) In his sone crist ihesu, our aller anly [*Cott.* anlepi] lorde. **1526** TINDALE *Luke* vii. 12 The only sonne of his mother, and she was a widowe. **1559** *Bk. Com. Prayer* Morn. Prayer, The onely ruler of princes. **1584** POWEL *Lloyd's Cambria* 3 The onelie occasion he tooke. **1633** G. HERBERT *Temple, Aaron* iii, Christ is my onely head, My alone onely heart & breast. **1654** tr. *Martini's Conq. China* 189 The onely Southern Port .. to which Boats may have access. **1703** ROWE *Ulyss.* II. i. 801 Hear a Wretches only Pray'r. **1854** MRS. JAMESON *Bk. Th.* (1877) 347 Eve .. is the only undraped figure which is allowable in sacred art. **1875** JOWETT *Plato* (ed. 2) I. 338 These two passages are the only ones in which Plato makes mention of himself.

b. In later use, in reference to relationship, also preceded by *an*, and used with a plural; as ***an only child, an only brother, only children***; so ***only-childish*** adj., characteristic or suggestive of an only child; ***only-childishness, only-childism***, the fact or state of being an only child.

1670 DRYDEN *2nd Pt. Conq. Granada* III. ii, What cannot only sons with parents do! **1768** GOLDSM. *Good-n. Man* I. i, An only son, sir, might expect more indulgence. **1821** BYRON *Diary* in *Note* to *Juan* I. xxxvii, My wife .. and myself are .. only children. **1879** MISS BRADDON *Clov. Foot* v, This only son of the Vicar's was a thorn in his side. **1927** *Times* 29 Dec. 7/3 They might come to speak, not of drink, but of 'only-childism', as the greatest curse of this country. **1928** *Daily Tel.* 11 Sept. 11/6 Dr. Gillespie alluded to 'Only childishness'... It had been suggested that only children were peculiarly liable to become neurotic. **1938** E. BOWEN *Death of Heart* III. ii. 341 A face at a window for no reason is a face that should have a thumb in its mouth: there is something only-childish about it. **1949** —— *Heat of Day* iii. 57 Anything that savoured of only-childishness.

†**c.** *absol.* = only one, only ones; in OE. = darling.

a **1000** *Ags. Ps.* (Spelman) xxi. 19 Of handa hundes ða ænlican mine [= *unicam meam*]. **1609** BIBLE (Douay) *Song Sol.* vi. 8 She is the only to her mother, elect to her that bare her. **1678** DRYDEN *All for Love* Pref. b, It is the only of the kind without Episode, or Underplot. **1693** —— *Juvenal* Ded. (1697) 11 Suppose that Homer and Virgil were the only of their Species.

3. Single, one. † ***any only*** = any one (*obs.*); ***one only***, one single, only one, one and no more, one and no other.

1485 CAXTON *Paris & V.* 34 Wythout leuing of ony onely thynge or word. **1490** —— *Eneydos* ix. 36 Wyth one onely stroke thou haste wylled to termyne and fynysshe thy labours mortall. **1543** GRAFTON *Contn. Harding* 476 Anye onely kyndenes so sodenly contracted in an house. **1571** DIGGES *Pantom.* III. xi. R iv, I shall for breuitie sake set foorth one onely rule generall. **1604** E. G[RIMSTONE] *D'Acosta's Hist. Indies* III. xx. 183 Vpon all that coast it blowes continually with one onely winde. *c* **1630** RISDON *Surv. Devon* (1810) 13 This country hath one only deanery. **1832** MRS. F. TROLLOPE *Dom. Mann. Americans* i. (1839) 2 One only object rears itself above the eddying waters: this is the mast of a vessel long since wrecked. **1850** GLADSTONE *Glean.* (1879) II. 95 In the *Consalvo*, a dying youth .. abandoned by all but the object of his love, entreats of her the parting gift of an only kiss.

†**4. a.** Said of that of which, by itself, without anything else, something is predicated; (the thing in question) acting alone; mere, sole. *Obs.*

c **1400** *Cato's Mor.* 131 in *Cursor M.*, Sin þou art doutande .. nedderres for venim, Mare mai þou be agast of anli man vn-wrast, and warre þe for him. *a* **1425** *Cursor M.* 8439 (Trin.) Bi grace of only god of heuen Soone he coude þe artes seuen. **1483** CAXTON *Gold. Leg.* 277/1 Our only feyth shalle suffyse us. ? *c* **1523** MORE *Let. to Wolsey* in Ellis *Orig. Lett.* Ser. I. I. 206 The onely redyng therof held hym above twoo howres. **1544** PHAER *Regim. Lyfe* (1560) X v b, The onely odour of quicksilver killeth lice. *a* **1619** FOTHERBY *Atheom.* I. xv. §2 (1622) 155 All this fell vpon them, for the onely impietie of their Prince. [**1854–6** PATMORE *Angel in Ho.* II. II. i, For the sake of only love, .. he does approve, His wife entirely.]

†**b.** Placed between a demonstrative or possessive adj. or poss. case and its sb., or before a sb. followed by an *of*-phrase: referring to the sb. as thus qualified. *Obs.*

c **1449** PECOCK *Repr.* III. v. 306 Endewid into his oonli sufficience. **1509** HAWES *Past. Pleas.* XXIX. (Percy Soc.) 139, I must abyde .. Of lyfe or death your onely judgement. **1558** in *Vicary's Anat.* (1888) App. 186 To the onlye vse and behoufe of the said Thomas Vycary. *a* **1563** BALE *Sel. Wks.* (Parker Soc.) 201 At the Priest's only provocation was it. **1577** HOLINSHED *Chron., Hist. Scot.* 343 At the charges & only expenses of these .vi. abbeyes. **1653** H. COGAN tr. *Pinto's Trav.* xxx. 118 Maintained at the Kings onely charge. **1653** HOLCROFT *Procopius, Pers. Wars* I. 3 These onely Hunnes have white bodies. **1709** ADDISON *Tatler* No. 117 ¶4 She was turned into a Man, and by that only Means avoided the Danger. **1741** MIDDLETON *Cicero* I. Pref. 35 The power was retained; with this onely difference, that [etc.].

5. Unique in quality, character, rank, etc.; peerless, preëminent. In OE. in form **ǽnlíc**. In mod.Eng. from 16th c., only as hyperbolic use of 2, = 'the only one to be counted, reckoned, or considered'; with superl. **onliest** (*arch.* or *dial.*). ***onlie begetter*** [f. BEGETTER 2, quot. 1606], the sole originator.

c **888** K. ÆLFRED *Boeth.* xxxv. §6 He hæfde an swiþe ænlic wif. **1552** ASCHAM in *Lett. Lit. Men* (Camden) 12 If Lerning, Counsell, Nobilitie, Courte, and Cambridge, shold have bene all punisshed at ones by taking away .. such a general & onely man as Mr. Cheeke is. **1581** MULCASTER *Positions* (1887) 30 It was either the onely, or the onelyest, principle in learning, to learne to read Latin. **1602** SHAKS. *Ham.* III. ii. 131 Your onely Iigge-maker. **1651** LILLY *Chas. I* (1774) 224 She had been the only stately and magnificent woman of Europe. **1656** EARL MONM. tr. *Boccalini's Advts. fr. Parnass.* II. lxxv. (1674) 227 When she subscribed her name .. [she] added (as she had good reason to do) the only Unfortunate. **1691** WOOD *Ath. Oxon.* II. 486 He was .. accounted .. the onliest person to be consulted about the affairs. **1778** FOOTE *Trip Calais* I. Wks. 1799 II. 344 It is the onliest method to keep her to one's self. **1866** G. MACDONALD *Ann. Q. Neighb.* x. (1878) 173 The only man in the world ceased to be the friend of the only woman in the world. **1890** 'BOLDREWOOD' *Col. Reformer* (1891) 375 The kindest, wisest, 'onliest' thing, under the circumstances. **1907** *Yesterday's Shopping* (1969) 1136/2 Comic and humorous songs... Ma Onliest One. **1929** H. W. ODUM in A. Dundes *Mother Wit* (1973) 190 Onliest way could git him. **1937** N. MARSH *Vintage Murder* vii. 81 The Firm .. was founded and built up by Mr Meyer... He was .. the onlie begetter. **1969** *Australasian Post* 19 June 40/3 Isadora Duncan was .. the onlie begetter of all the trends in 'free dance' which are now so familiar to us. **1971** *Black World* Oct. 62/1 The onliest time I had to say something bout it was when he was playin checkers on the stoop one time and he commenst to hummin. **1972** *Daily Tel.* 30 Mar. 6/7 Stalin's onlie begetter and mentor in murder—Lenin. **1973** *Times Lit. Suppl.* 2 Mar. 228/1 The enigmatic personality of [*Citizen*] *Kane's* onlie begetter. **1975** *Times* 14 July 13/3 William Robson, Professor Emeritus of Public Administration, University of London, and 'the onlie begetter' of *The Political Quarterly*.

only ('əʊnlɪ), *adv.*, *conj.* (*prep.*) Forms: α. 3–5 **onliche**, 4 **onelych, -lyk, onlike**, 4–5 **-lyche, oon-**, 5 **won-**. β. 4 **anli, aneli, -ly**; 4–5 **oonli**, 4–6 **-ly**; 5–7 **onely**, 5– **only**, (5 **ond(e)ly**). [ME. (south. and south. midl.) *ônliche*, f. *ônlich*, ONLY *a.*, with advb. *-e* (see -LY[2]); in more northern dialects the adv. was in form indistinguishable from the adj., which from *c* 1400 became the fact also in Standard Engl. In OE. the adv. is cited only in the form *ǽnlíce* splendidly, elegantly; cf. ONLY *a.*]

A. *adv.*

1. As a single or solitary thing or fact; no one or nothing more or else than; nothing but; alone; solely, merely, exclusively. *Only* may limit the statement to a single or defined person, thing, or number (*a*) as distinguished from *more*, or (*b*) as opposed to any *other*.

a. Preceding the word or phrase which it limits.

α. **1297** R. GLOUC. (Rolls) 1513 Þe king louede is wif .. so vaste þat al is herte onliche on hire on he caste. *c* **1330** R. BRUNNE *Chron. Wace* (Rolls) 2370 He ne askede non oþer þyng, Bot onlike his doughter ȝyng. **13..** *E.E. Allit. P.* B. 1749 Heȝest of alle oþer, saf onelych tweyne. **1390** GOWER *Conf.* I. 317, I speke onliche as of the dede, Of which I nevere was coupable. *c* **1420** *Chron. Vilod.* 882 Bot duden wonlyche after þe devellys rede. *a* **1450** MYRC 656 Þer nys no mon .. þat may þat do but onlyche he.

β. *c* **1375** *Cursor M.* 13737 (Fairf.) Anli he wiþ-outen synne. *c* **1386** CHAUCER *Melib.* ¶503 (Petw.) For þat appertenеþ & longeþ oonly [*other texts* al oonly] to the Iuges. **1398** TREVISA *Barth. De P.R.* XVIII. xix. (1495) 779 The camell hath not teeth in eyther Iowe but oonli bynethe. *c* **1440** *Promp. Parv.* 366/1 Only, *solomodo.* **1447** BOKENHAM *Seyntys* (Roxb.) 53 Al this thou dost that ondly in the I schuld trust lorde. **1535** COVERDALE *Tobit* x. 5 All y[e] thinges that we haue are onely in the. **1545** in Willis & Clark *Cambridge* (1886) I. 213 Discharged of all rents .. except oonly a redd rose to be given to y[em]. *a* **1548** HALL *Chron., Edw. IV* 240 b, All these faire wordes, wer onely delaies to protracte tyme. **1596** SHAKS. *Merch. V.* IV. i. 432, I wil haue nothing else but onely this. **1611** BEAUM. & FL. *Knt. Burn. Pestle* II. ii, Now fortune, if thou be'st not only ill, Shew me thy better face. **1627** E. F. *Hist. Edw. II* (1680) 96 'Tis onely one. **1651** BAXTER *Inf. Bapt.* 5 God doth not reveal his truth onely or chiefly to the learned. **1751** JOHNSON *Rambler* No. 156 ¶14 To distinguish .. that which is established because it is right, from that which is right only because it is established. **1805** T. HARRAL *Scenes of Life* I. 194 It is true, I have been only twice. **1845** M. PATTISON *Ess.* (1889) I. 17 One of those devoted .. attachments, of which only a mother or nurse is thought capable. **1899** *Literary Guide* 1 Oct. 146/2 Certain doctrines were imparted only to initiates.

b. Following the word or phrase which it limits.

1340 HAMPOLE *Pr. Consc.* 1338 Bot þe world prayses nan, bot þa anly þat til alle worldes welthes er happy. *c* **1380** WYCLIF *Wks.* (1880) 310 To haue crist oonliche heere patroun. *c* **1485** *E.E. Misc.* (Warton Club) 25 On thi God wonly set thin herte. **1535** COVERDALE *Ecclus.* xxiv. 34, I haue not laboured for my self onely. **1548** UDALL, etc. *Erasm. Par. Matt.* vi. 47 Loke upon the best thynges, eyther onely or chiefly. **1655** MRQ. WORCESTER *Cent. Inv.* in Dircks *Life* (1865) 416 To raise Water with two Buckets onely. **1763** J. BROWN *Poetry & Mus.* vi. 104 What belongs to Nature only, Nature only can complete. **1838** LYTTON *Leila* I. iii, In one only of the casements. **1876** MOZLEY *Univ. Serm.* iv. (1877) 94 His human character is not benevolence only.

†*Only* between a numeral and sb. is now *obs.*

c **1555** HARPSFIELD *Divorce Hen. VIII* (Camden) 59 Their second counsell of Toledo .. being .. of eight only bishops. **1624** BEDELL *Lett.* vi. 92 In two onely leaues of his booke, a certaine .. Scholler did discouer thirtie .. falsifications. **1656** EARL MONM. tr. *Boccalini's Advts. fr. Parnass.* II. xiv. (1674) 152 Amidst as many .. Silver Balls as there are Sciences, three only Golden Balls are placed.

c. *Only* was formerly often placed away from the word or words which it limited; this is still frequent in speech where the stress and pauses prevent ambiguity, but is now avoided by perspicuous writers.

1483 CAXTON *Gold. Leg.* 333 b/1 Luke is only with me. *a* **1540** CROMWELL in Ellis *Orig. Lett.* Ser. II. II. 165 Unto the whiche God I have onlye commyttyd my sowlle. **1598** GRENEWEY *Tacitus, Ann.* III. iv. (1622) 69 Vipsania his mother died, onely of all Agrippas children, of a naturall death. **1660–1** MARVELL *Corr.* Wks. 1872–5 II. 51, I onely write this word to let you know that [etc.]. **1697** DRYDEN *Virg. Georg.* II. 786 When Beasts were only slain for Sacrifice. **1703** ROWE *Fair Penit.* II. ii, Brutes and boys are only taught with blows. **1721** *St. German's Doctor & Stud.* 28 The eldest son shall only inherit his father. **1833** TENNYSON *Lady Clara Vere de Vere* vii, 'Tis only noble to be good. **1875** JOWETT *Plato* I. 282, I only asked the question from habit.

d. ***not only ... but, but also.***

1340 *Ayenb.* 265 Naȝt onlyche beuore gode ac be-uore alle men. *c* **1375** *Cursor M.* 338 (Fairf.) He wroȝt noȝt anly wit his hande bot sayde wit worde. **1390** GOWER *Conf.* II. 340 Noght onliche of the wommen tho, Bot of the chaste men also. *a* **1425** *Cursor M.* 11069 (Trin.) Not only of ierusalem bourȝe But also al þe cuntre þourȝe. *a* **1548** HALL *Chron., Hen. VI* 104 b, Not onely now .. but also after. **1589–1875** [see BUT, C. 24 b].

†**2.** By or of itself alone, without anything else.

1398 TREVISA *Barth. De P.R.* III. xix. (1495) 66 By smellynge oonly he knowyth bytwene herbes good and venymous. *a* **1425** *Cursor M.* 3574 (Trin.) Whan þat [a mon] bicomeþ olde, .. Only to lyue trauail him þink. *a* **1548** HALL *Chron., Edw. IV* 232 b, He was restored to his kyngdome and made kyng onely by his ayde. *a* **1555** PHILPOT *Exam. & Writ.* (Parker Soc.) 66 Master doctor hath affirmed that these words .. spoken by the priest, only do make the Sacrament. **1624** HEYWOOD *Gunaik.* I. 30 The Phrygian pipe was onely sufficient to yeeld musicke to her sacrifices, for that was no sooner heard but they fell into a divine rapture resembling madnesse. **1760** WARTON *Idler* No. 96 ¶1 His eye was so piercing, that .. he could blunt the weapons of his enemies only by looking at them. **1801** STRUTT *Sports & Past.* I. i. 10 The see of Norwich, only, was in possession of no less than thirteen parks.

†**3.** Singularly, uniquely, specially, pre-eminently.

c **1000** ÆLFRIC *Colloq.* in Wr.-Wülcker 103 Ænlice, *eleganter*. **13..** *Chron. R. Glouc.* (Rolls) App. G. 58 Ac þe oþere were strengore & Richore oniliche [*v. rr.* vnliche, onlyche]. *c* **1394** *P. Pl. Crede* 534 Afterward anoþer onliche he blissede, þe meke of þe myddel-erde. **1554** RIDLEY *Wks.*

(Parker Soc.) 370 In them whom they only esteemed for their priests and sages. **1611** B. JONSON *Catiline* v. iv, That renown'd good man That did so onely embrace his countrey!

4. Idiomatic uses.

a. The sense 'no more than' often passes into 'as much as'; = JUST *adv.* 5c. (Cf. Ger. *nur.*)

1838 MRS. STOWE in *Life* (1889) 90 Only think how long it is since I have written to you! **1849** MACAULAY *Hist. Eng.* ix. II. 410 [They] would willingly join to effect it, if only they could obtain the help of such a force..as might secure those who should rise in arms. **1875** JOWETT *Plato* (ed. 2) III. 193 He is coming..if you will only wait. **1888** *Sunday Talk* June 345/1 If I could only give you one-half of the stories..I would make the best article I have yet written.

b. ***only not*** = all but, little else than.

1779–81 JOHNSON *L.P., Smith* Wks. II. 473, I was only not a boy. **1834** NAPIER *Penins. War* XIV. vi. (Rtldg.) II. 275 The fortresses were..only not abandoned to the enemy. **1862** NEALE *Hymn*, '*Safe home*' i, Torn sails, provision short, And only not a wreck.

c. Not before, not till. ***only just***, at a time no farther gone than the immediate past: see JUST *adv.* 4. (*Only* may precede or follow the word or phrase expressing time.)

1676 GLANVILL *Ess.* Pref. a iij, I have now only cast it into the form of a Discourse. **1791** WASHINGTON *Lett.* Writ. 1892 XII. 9 Your..letter..came to my hands the day before yesterday only. **1846** TRENCH *Mirac.* Introd. (1862) 57 The flower dropped off only as the fruit was being formed. **1898** *Westm. Gaz.* 23 Feb. 5/3 A woman..yesterday killed herself. She was only married on Saturday. *Mod.* I have only just received it; it was posted only yesterday.

†**d.** ***only but, but only***: (*a*) = only, merely; (*b*) except only. *Obs.*

1478 *Paston Lett.* III. 232 Paid..for the tythynges, ondely but in corne whan it was inned in to the barn, xxiiij *li.* **1605** CHAPMAN *All Fooles* Wks. 1873 I. 180 Now heere all are pleas'd, Onelie but Cornelio. **1678** DRYDEN *All for Love* II. i, You but only beg'd a last farewel. **1711** *Light to Blind* in *10th Rep. Hist. MSS. Comm.* App. v. 127 The first dessigne was onely but to shew the rebells, that the..garrison was watchful.

e. ***only too*** (***true, thankful***, etc.): see TOO.

f. all only, al only, an emphatic variant of *only* in various senses, at length treated as one word: see ALONELY.

B. *Conjunctive adv., conj.* (*prep.*)

1. The only thing to be added being; with this restriction, drawback, or exception only; but (*adversative*); on the other hand, on the contrary.

1382 WYCLIF *1 Cor.* vii. 39 Be she weddid to whom she wole, oonly [Gr. μόνον] in the Lord. —— *Gal.* v. 13 Britheren ȝe ben clepid in to fredom: oonli ȝeue ȝe not fredom in to occasioun of fleisch. **1579** FENTON *Guicciard.* (1618) 3 Onely the man for his integritie and soundnesse was such a one, as [etc.]. **1598** SHAKS. *Merry W.* II. ii. 242 Spend all I haue, onely giue me so much of your time in enchange of it, as [etc.]. **1625** PURCHAS *Pilgrims* II. 1117 They know not how to..refine the same [sugar-canes], onely they eat them raw. **1667** MARVELL *Corr.* Wks. 1872–5 II. 81 Onely Colonel Gilby will tell you all when he comes down. **1796** BURNEY *Mem. Metastasio* I. 64 No matter; only will there be room for us all? **1877** SPURGEON *Serm.* XXIII. 179 Many a man would have become wise, only he thought he was so already. *Mod.* The flowers are lovely; only, they have no scent.

b. ***only that***: with the exception that, except that, were it not that, but for the fact that.

1706 S. CLARKE *Let. to Dodwell* (1711) 28 That there is no real difference..only that that which the Platonists call Mind [νοῦς]..the Sacred Writers call [πνεῦμα] Spirit. **1771** T. HULL *Sir W. Harrington* (1797) II. 157 Only that I know you don't love bustle, I should wish you here. **1804** EUGENIA DE ACTON *Tale without Title* III. 241 Something like a castle in miniature, only that its windows were modern. **1845** M. J. HIGGINS *Ess.* (1875) 27, I would see and get it done at once, only that I am in doubt as to the best means.

2. Except. ***only for***, except for, but for, were it not for.

1540–1 ELYOT *Image Gov.* (1549) 40 Only by violence they coulde not be brought to theyr shippes. **1664** PEPYS *Diary* 22 Apr., My wife and I, in their coach to Hide Parke, where.. pleasant it was, only for the dust. **1668** *Ibid.* 22 Aug., It is true..that our whole Office will be turned out, only me. **1737** [S. BERINGTON] *G. di Lucca's Mem.* 295 The Project might easily take, only for the horrid Wickedness of the Fact. **1747** *Mem. Nutrebian Crt.* I. 38 Ridiculing all forms of worship..only their own. **1811** *Ora & Juliet* I. 30 Only for my tea, I should have had the head-ache. **1887** *N. & Q.* 7th Ser. III. 501 For many years the following notice was painted up at Bolton railway station: 'Do not cross the line only by the bridge'. **1888** *Poor Nellie* 245 Only for William, you would have died with her, George! **1899** T. WATTS-DUNTON *Aylwin* vii. 238 I've been a-listenin' to a v'ice as nobody can't hear on'y me. **1914** JOYCE *Dubliners* 44 And say what he would do to her only for her dead mother's sake. **1922** E. O'NEILL *Anna Christie* II. 140 And only for me,.. we'd be being scoffed by the fishes this minute! **1934** S. O'CASEY *Pound on Demand* in *Windfalls* 195 Who else could he be, only Mr. Adams? **1939** *New Yorker* 13 May 23/1 Her boy friend was working his way thru the Illinois U. and didn't get to Chi only two or three times a year. **1961** W. G. POLLARD *Physicist & Christian* (1962) 57 Yet are not we of the mid-twentieth century..just as bad off as they—only in a different way?

b. *In a clause*: Except that, were it not that, but that.

a **1766** MRS. F. SHERIDAN *Sidney Bidulph* IV. 187 And only my uncle Bidulph is fonder of my sister than he is of me, my vanity would carry me away for want of a little ballast. *a* **1774** GOLDSM. tr. *Scarron's Com. Romance* (1775) II. 162 At length their passion became so violent, that only there was no bloodshed, Pyramus and Thisbe were nothing to them for affection and sincerity. **1802** H. MARTIN *Helen of Glenross* II. 226 Only he is very melancholy, he would be agreeable. **1901** M. FRANKLIN *My Brilliant Career* iii. 16 Only I promised to stick to the missus a while I'd scoot tomorrer. **1914** JOYCE *Dubliners* 146 Only I'm an old man now I'd change his tune for him.

C. Comb. ***only-born, only-created, only-gotten***; also ONLY-BEGOTTEN.

c **1410** HOCCLEVE *Mother of God* 115 By his sone oonly-geten [*v.r.* only gottin]. **1608** WILLET *Hexapla Exod.* 126 His first borne, which also may bee his only borne. **1833** J. H. NEWMAN *Arians* II. v. (1876) 227 The Arians..explain the word *only-begotten* in the sense of *only-created.*

only (ˈəʊnlɪ), *sb.* [f. the adj.] **1.** Used *absol.* for 'the only chance'.

1878 J. H. BEADLE *Western Wilds* xxvi. 417, I seed it was my first, last and only, and I sot old Sally at a gallop for that pint.

2. An only child.

1931 J. CANNAN *High Table* ii. 17 But poor little Theodore was 'an only', said Lady Oliver. **1963** *Guardian* 22 Feb. 8/7 The 'only', on the other hand..envies her friends with brothers and sisters. **1975** C. STORR *Chinese Egg* xviii. 121 If you're an only, you're sort of a target. Everything your parents think or feel has to be worked out on you.

3. In *redupl.* form. The state of being alone. *nonce-wd.*

1946 J. B. PRIESTLEY *Bright Day* vi. 199 Left on my only-only today. Wife's had to dash over to Leeds.

'only-be'gotten, *a.* Begotten as an only child; transl. L. *ūnigenitus*, Gr. μονογενής: in OE. *áncenned*, ANKENNED.

1450–1530 *Myrr. our Ladye* 314 The only begotten sonne of god. **1526** TINDALE *John* i. 14 The glory off the only begotten sonne off the father. **1534** —— *Heb.* xi. 17 In fayth Abraham offered vp Isaac..beinge his only begotten sonne. **1833** J. H. NEWMAN *Arians* II. iii. (1876) 158 Scripture designates Him as the only-begotten or the own Son of God.

on lyfe, on-lyue, obs. forms of ALIVE.

onmeete, onmerkit, onmeuable: see UN-.

onmun (ˈɒnmʊn). [Korean, ad. Chinese *yên* say(ing) + *wên* letter, language.] = HANGUL[2].

1948 D. DIRINGER *Alphabet* 443 The Christian missionaries, who were the first to realise that Ŏn-mun was better adapted to their use than the cumbersome Chinese characters. **1950** G. M. MCCUNE *Korea Today* vi. 94 Fifteen million textbooks written in the native *Ŏnmun* alphabet for use in the elementary schools. **1951** [see HANGUL[2]].

‖**onnagata** (onaˈgata). [Jap., f. *onna* woman + *kata* figure.] In Japanese Kabuki drama and related forms, a man who plays female roles. Commonly also called *oyama*.

1901 O. EDWARDS *Jap. Plays & Playfellows* iii. 92 Peculiar attention is given to the training and discipline of *onnagata*, or impersonators of female parts. **1928** F. A. LOMBARD *Outl. Hist. Jap. Drama* xi. 294 In the earlier *Kabuki* men had often played the part of women; but now, when it had become necessary that they should do so on all occasions, a professional class of womenfolk (*onnagata*) grew into prominence. **1955** A. C. SCOTT *Kabuki Theatre of Japan* viii. 169 The good *onnagata* must symbolize feminine qualities in a way that no actress can do. **1972** *Nat. Geographic* Sept. 378 Greatest of today's *onnagata*, or male players of female roles, Utaemon Nakamura has spent a lifetime developing the charm and grace of a leading lady.

onne: see ONE *adv.* and *prep.*

onne-, obs. var. UN- *pref.*, as *onne-wyse*, unwise, etc.

onnente, obs. variant of ANENT *prep.*

onnery, var. ORNERY *a.*

onnet, variant of UNNUT *Obs.*, useless.

onnethe, -es, obs. ff. UNEATH, -S, hardly.

†**on-'netherward**, *prep. Obs. rare*[−1]. In the bottom of.

c **1200** *Trin. Coll. Hom.* 83 He ne fecheð noht þe sore siches onneðerward his heorte.

onnȝæn, onnȝæness, early ME. (Orm.) ff. AGAIN, AGAINST.

onnobeley, onnumerable, etc.: see UN-.

onnuy, obs. form of ANNOY.

onocentaur (ɒnəʊˈsɛntɔː(r)). *Mythol.* [ad. late L. *onocentaurus*, a. Gr. ὀνοκένταυρος, f. ὄνος ass + κένταυρος CENTAUR.] A fabulous creature, a centaur with the body of an ass instead of that of a horse.

[**1398** TREVISA *Barth. De P.R.* XVIII. lxxix. (MS. Bodl.) ll. 280 b/1 Onocentaurus..is a beste wonderlich schape and.. gendred bitwene an asse and a bolle. *Ibid.*, But Phisiologus ..seiþ þat Onocentaurus is compowned of þe schap of an asse and of a man.] **1567** MAPLET *Gr. Forest* 95 b, The Onocentaure is a Beast monstrous, halfe a Bull & halfe an Asse. **1601** CHESTER *Love's Mart., A Dialogue* cxxxvii, The Onocentaur is a monstrous beast; Supposed halfe a man and halfe an asse. *a* **1711** KEN *Edmund* Poet. Wks. 1721 II. 107 Gigantick Onocentaurs there he found, The tallest he in chains of darkness bound. **1845** E. H. NOEL *Richter's Flower Pieces* II. xv. 195 The true difference between hippocentaurs and onocentaurs.

†**o'nocrotal.** *Obs.* In 4–7 in Latin form. [ad. L. *onocrotalus*, a. Gr. ὀνοκρόταλος pelican, f. ὄνος ass + κρόταλον rattle, clapper. Cf. F. *onocrotale* (13th c. in Godef.).] The pelican.

1382 WYCLIF *Zeph.* ii. 14 Onocratulus [*gloss* that is, a brid with a long bill lyke a swan; 1611 cormorant; *R.V.* pelican], and the yrchoun shuln dwelle in the threshefoldis therof. **1609** BIBLE (Douay) *Lev.* xi. 18 Of birdes..which you must not eate..the swanne, and the onocratal. **1653** URQUHART *Rabelais* I. viii, A faire great blew feather, plucked from an Onocrotal. **1661** BLOUNT *Glossogr.*, *Onocrotal*, a Bird like a Swan, braying like an Ass; thought to be a Bittour.

on-off, *a.* [f. ON *adv.* + OFF *adv.*] **1.** Of a switch or the like: that turns something on or off.

1946 *Nature* 12 Oct. 501/1 In the counting and control circuits, all valves are used entirely as on-off elements, not as amplitude-sensitive elements. **1958** *Times Rev. Industry* Oct. 92/3 Photoelectric equipment designed to perform on-off switching operations. **1960** *Times* 15 Mar. 18/4 The overdrive operation is therefore more complicated than the simple on-off switch. **1973** D. FRANCIS *Slay-Ride* viii. 96 Behind me..stood my portable television... I..found the on-off switch, and turned the volume up to maximum.

2. = OFF AND ON *a.*

1953 [see HUNT *v.* 7 b]. **1962** *John o' London's* 19 July 66/2 Forget the hoo-ha, the on-off engagements. **1965** H. I. ANSOFF *Corporate Strategy* (1968) vii. 108 Concern with strategy had followed an 'on-off' cycle attuned to the appearance of major strategic opportunities. **1974** J. WAINWRIGHT *Evidence I shall Give* xxxvii. 209 The on-off pulse of the lighthouse beam. **1976** W. GREATOREX *Cassover* 119 Over the roast lamb Amberley had made fun of Galina's on-off vegetarianism.

onofrite (ˈɒnəʊfraɪt). *Min.* [Named (1845) from San Onofre in Mexico, where found: see -ITE.] A sulpho-selenide of mercury occurring in lustrous black masses.

1849 J. NICOL *Man. Min.* 471 Onofrite..occurs at St. Onofre in Mexico, with Mercury. **1892** DANA *Min.* 64.

onolatry (əʊˈnɒlətrɪ). [f. Gr. ὄνο-ς ass + λατρεία -LATRY.] Worship of the ass. Also *fig.*

1903 *Jrnl. Amer. Folk-Lore* July–Sept. 203 *Onolatry.* Reinach, S.: Le culte de l'âne... Treats of the charges of worshipping a donkey made by the pagans against the Jews and early Christians. **1953** E. SITWELL *Gardeners & Astronomers* 28 The crowd's onolatries Echo that laughter.

†**o'nology.** *Obs. rare*[−0]. [f. Gr. ὄνο-ς ass + -λογία speech: prob. repr. a mod.L. *onologia.] Foolish talking; braying.

1674 BLOUNT *Glossogr.* (ed. 4), *Onology*, vain babling, talking like an Ass. **1678** PHILLIPS (ed. 4) *List Barbarous Words*, *Onologie*, a talking like an Ass.

onoma'mania. *nonce-wd.* [irreg. f. Gr. ὄνομα name + MANIA.] A mania or rage about a name or names.

1854 W. WATERWORTH *Eng. & Rome* 120 Whilst the onomamania lasted, bickerings and divisions endured.

onomancy (ˈɒnəmænsɪ). Also in Latin form **onomantia.** [Abbreviated form of ONOMATOMANCY: = med.L. *onomantīa*, obs. It. *onomantia* (Florio), obs. F. *onomantie* 'divination by names' (Cotgr.).] Divination from names or the letters of a name, as, the number of vowels in a name, the sum of the numerical value of the letters, or the like.

1605 CAMDEN *Rem.* 35 The superstitious kinde of Divination called Onomantia, condemned by the last generall Counsell, by which the Pithagoreans iudged the even number of vowells in names to signifie imperfections in the left sides of men, and the odde number in the right. **1656** BLOUNT *Glossogr.*, *Onomancie* (*onomantia*), divination by names. **1678** PHILLIPS (ed. 4) *List Barbarous Words*, *Onomancy*, a Divination by names, or rather a Divination by some observations about an Ass, the first should seem rather to be *Onomomancy.* **1727–41** CHAMBERS *Cycl.*, *Onomancy*, or rather *Onomamancy*, the art of divining the good or evil fortune which shall befal a man, from the letters of his name. *Ibid.*, In strictness, *onomancy* should rather signify divination by asses..to signify divination by names, it should be *onomatomancy.* **1880** W. JONES *Prec. Stones* i. 5 *note*, The Rabbinical writers describe a system of onomancy,..termed Notaricon, in conjunction with lithomancy.

Hence **ono'mantic, ono'mantical** *adjs.*, of or pertaining to onomancy; practising onomancy.

1605 CAMDEN *Rem.* 35 An Onomanticall or Name-wisard Iew. **1656** BLOUNT *Glossogr.*, *Onomantical*, pertaining unto, or skilful in that kind of Divination by names. **1856** WEBSTER, *Onomantic.*

onomasiology (ˌɒnəʊmeɪsɪˈɒlədʒɪ, -zɪˈɒlədʒɪ). [f. Gr. ὀνομασί-α name + -OLOGY.] The study of the principles of nomenclature, esp. with regard to regional, social, or occupational variation. Hence **onomasio'logic, onomasio'logical** *adjs.*, **onomasi'ologist**.

1931 G. STERN *Meaning & Change of Meaning* 2 The referents..are the basis of research in onomasiology. **1937** J. ORR tr. *Iordan's Introd. Romance Ling.* iii. 248 The study of a map is..a study of the nomenclature applied to such and such an object. Studies of this kind are termed onomasiological. *Ibid.*, It should not be thought..that we are claiming onomasiology as a child of linguistic geography. **1954** *Archivum Linguisticum* VI. I. 57 Onomasiological investigation of Latin words for 'head'. **1962** Y. MALKIEL in Householder & Saporta *Probl. Lexicogr.* 18 Array of regional or temporal counterparts of each basic entry—an arrangement sometimes called 'onomasiologic' in the Central European tradition of modern-language scholarship. **1969** *Word 1967* XXIII. 578 The functional principle is useful not only in the sphere of syntax but also in the sphere of onomasiology. **1973** *Archivum Linguisticum* IV. 113 The onomasiological or semantic bases of the taxonomic principles. **1974** *Language Sciences* Aug. 28/3 Eventually the onomasiologist may be able to decide whether what we call conceptual structure is something strange of a shape we can scarcely probe by introspection. **1975** *Amer. Speech 1972* XLVII. 166 These are valid onomasiological statements (that is, statements about the relationship of extra-linguistic objects to linguistic expressions), but not structural ones.

onomastic (ɒnəʊˈmæstɪk), *a.* and *sb.* [ad. Gr. ὀνομαστικ-ός of or belonging to naming, f. ὀνομαστός named, f. ὀνομάζ-ειν to name. Cf. F. *onomastique* (c 1600 in Hatz.-Darm.).]

A. *adj.* **a.** Of, relating to, or connected with a name or names, or with the naming of something; consisting of or dealing with names.

1716 M. DAVIES *Athen. Brit.* II. 242 That most August Assembly most awful (tho' but nominal and onomastick) Synod. **1851** SIR F. PALGRAVE *Norm. & Eng.* I. 349 The nobles draw only from the most scanty family onomastic nomenclatures. **1879** *Times* 29 Aug., The Russian Grenadier regiment bearing the title of Frederick William III.. when lately celebrating its onomastic festival was [etc.]. **1880** *Contemp. Rev.* Aug. 574 The system which rests on onomastic resemblances of a highly imaginative philology.

b. Used in reference to the autograph subscription of a legal document (of which the body is in the handwriting of another person): see quots.

By Bentham an *onomastic* signature or subscription—the affixing of one's *name*—was distinguished from a *symbolic* signature, effected by a *seal* or *mark*; both of these, as mere signatures, he distinguished from *holograph*. Later writers appear to have mistaken his meaning.

1802–12 BENTHAM *Ration. Judic. Evid.* (1827) II. 449 Modes of authentication ab intrà:—1. Holography; 2. Signature (onomastic or symbolic). *Ibid.* 461 Sigillation, a succedaneum to (or rather mode of) onomastic signature. **1849** W. M. BEST *Treat. Princ. Evid.* §210 A document wholly in the handwriting of a party is said to be an autograph or holograph; where it is in the handwriting of another person and only signed by the party, the signature may be called 'onomastic'. **1850** BURRILL *Law Dict. & Gloss.*, *Onomastic*, a term sometimes applied to the signature of an instrument, where the body of it is in the handwriting of another person.

B. *sb.* †**1.** A writer of an Onomasticon; a vocabularist, a lexicographer. *Obs.*

1609 [BP. W. BARLOW] *Answ. Nameless Cath.* 330 Let all the Onomastiks, and Nomenclators, or Mathematicians, or Schoolemen be searched. **1716** M. DAVIES *Athen. Brit.* II. 349 The learned Lexicographer, Francis Pomey (who being a French-Man should understand the Nature and Names of Garlick and Shalot the best of any Onomasticks).

†**2.** An assumed name. *Obs. nonce-use.*

1653 MANTON *Smectymnuus Rediv.* Pref., I suppose the reverend authors were willing to lie hid under this onomastic ['Smectymnuus'] partly that [etc.].

3. *pl.* The study of the origin and formation of proper names, esp. of persons.

The *sing.* in quot. 1930 is unusual.

1930 T. S. ELIOT tr. *St.-J. Perse's Anabasis* x. 67 The man learned in sciences, in onomastic. **1936** *New Yorker* 8 Feb. 54 (*heading*) The advance of municipal onomastics. **1957** M. AUROUSSEAU *Rendering of Geogr. Names* i. 1 The scientific study of names as names, that is, of the human habit of naming things, is the science of onomastics. **1972** J. L. DILLARD *Black English* iii. 135 The subject has not yet been investigated, but it seems possible that the West African influence on Southern onomastics has been very great indeed. **1973** *Amer. Speech 1969* XLIV. 221 This collection of essays.. covers the nature of language, cognition, onomastics, [etc.].

†**ono'mastical**, *a. Obs.* [f. as prec. + -AL[1].] = ONOMASTIC *a.*

1609 [BP. W. BARLOW] *Answ. Nameless Cath.* 345 What is the name which the Onomasticall Censurer giueth vnto this charge? **1715** M. DAVIES *Athen. Brit.* I. Pref. 7 Pamphlets known to the learned, more by their Onomastical History than by any use that can be made of them. **1716** *Ibid.* II. To Rdr. 3 An Onomastical List of the Principal Authors.

‖**ono'masticon.** [a. Gr. ὀνομαστικόν (sc. βιβλίον) book of names, vocabulary: see ONOMASTIC.] A vocabulary or alphabetic list of proper names, esp. of persons. Formerly used more widely of a vocabulary of names or nouns, or even of a general lexicon.

Often used as a title of works of this nature, e.g. that of Jul. Pollux (180–238) which was a vocabulary arranged according to subjects and not alphabetically: cf. the Lat.-Eng. *Nominale*, and similar works of the 15th c., reprinted by Wright-Wülcker.

1710 W. HUME *Sacr. Success.* 130 What we find in all Thesaurus's, Lexicons, Glossaries, Onomasticons, etc. **1716** M. DAVIES *Athen. Brit.* III. 3 To make use of the Onomasticons, publish'd by those learned Protestant Lexicographers, H. Stephens, J. Scapula, Scrivelius and Passorius. **1877** SMITH & WACE *Dict. Chr. Biog.* Pref. 10 The intention was entertained of exhibiting a complete Onomasticon of the Christian World for the first eight centuries. **1879** CONDER *Tentwork Pal.* II. 136 The distance .. is not much greater than that given by the Onomasticon for Lachish. **1889** *Ch. Q. Rev.* XXVII. 308 The heading Joannes.. [exemplifies] the fulness of this dictionary [Christian Biography] as an Onomasticon, there being no fewer than 595 separate entries under it.

'onoma,techny. *rare*$^{-0}$. [irreg. for *onomatotechny*, f. ONOMATO- + Gr. -τεχνία f. τέχνη art.]

1730–6 BAILEY (folio) Pref., *Onomatechny*.. the Art of Prognosticating from the Letters of a Person's Name. **1846** in WORCESTER. And in mod. Dicts.

o'nomato-, = Gr. ὀνοματο-, combining form of ὄνομα, ὀνοματ-ος name: the first element of numerous derivatives: see below. **,onomato'mania** *Path.* [Gr. μανία madness], (*a*) 'morbid dread of some word, intense mental anguish at the inability to recall some word or to name a thing' (*Syd. Soc. Lex.* 1892); (*b*) a morbid preoccupation with words; a mania for word-making. **o'nomato,plasm** [Gr. πλάσμα form], a word formed by onomatopœia.

1895 tr. *M. Nordau's Degeneration* III. i. 242 Trichophobia (fear of hair), onomatomania (folly of words or names), pyromania (incendiary madness). **1919** W. OSLER in *Proc. Classical Assoc.* 28 Within the narrow compass of the primitive cell.. onomatomania runs riot.

onoma'tologist. [f. as next + -IST.] One versed in onomatology.

1695 J. EDWARDS *Perfect. Script.* 236 Dr. Skinner, a great onomatologist. *a* **1843** SOUTHEY *Doctor* clxxvi. VI. 70 What would our onomatologist have said if he had learned to read these words? **1847** WEBSTER, *Onomatologist*, one conversant with onomatology.

onomatology (ˌəʊnɒməˈtɒlədʒɪ, ˌɒnəʊmə-). *rare.* [mod. f. Gr. type *ὀνοματολογία, f. ὀνοματολόγος word-gathering: cf. F. *onomatologie* (Littré).] The science of the formation of names or terms; terminology. Hence **onomato'logical** *a.*

1847 in WEBSTER. **1919** W. DE MORGAN *Old Madhouse* 324 He therefore endeavoured to bring back the discussion from the onomatologies into which it had strayed. **1931** *Times Lit. Suppl.* 1 Oct. 747/2 'Onomatology', the ugly name which Mr. Ewen gives to this kind of research, is not an exact science. **1961** *Brno Studies in English* III. 10 Their conception of the opposition of analysis *vs.* synthesis is so wide as to include differences of lexical (more specifically onomatological) order.

†**o'nomato,mancy.** *Obs.* [ad. med.L. *onomatomantia*, F. *onomatomancie* (Rabelais 16th c.); see ONOMATO- and -MANCY.] Divination by names or the letters of a name.

1652 GAULE *Magastrom.* 165 Onomatomancy, [divining] by names. *a* **1693** URQUHART *Rabelais* III. xxv, Have you a mind.. to have the truth of the matter yet more fully and amply disclosed unto you.. by onomatomancy? How do they call thee? **1727** [see ONOMANCY].

o'nomatop, -ope (əʊˈnɒmətɒp, -təʊp). [Abbreviated from next.] A word formed by onomatopœia.

1828 in WEBSTER. **1862** M. HOPKINS *Hawaii* 70 The chances of selection in the case of onomatopes would be still greater. **1874** GODDES-LIANCOURT & PINCOTT (*title*) Primitive and Universal Laws of the Formation, and Development, of Language, founded on the natural basis of Onomatops. **1890** O. CRAWFURD *Round the Calendar* 176 Names that are not mere onomatopes, like cuckoo or peewit.

‖**onomatopœia** (əʊˌnɒmətəʊˈpiːjə, ˌɒnəʊmæt-). [a. L. *onomatopœia*, a. Gr. ὀνοματοποιία the making of words, f. ὀνοματοποιός making or coining a name, f. ONOMATO- + -ποιος making.]

1. The formation of a name or word by an imitation of the sound associated with the thing or action designated; this principle as a force in the formation of words in a language; echoism.

1577 PEACHAM *Gard. Eloquence*, Onomatopeia, when we invent, devise, fayne, and make a name intimating the sound of that it signifieth, as hurlyburly, for an uprore and tumultuous stirre. **1589** PUTTENHAM *Eng. Poesie* III. xvi[i.]. (Arb.) 192 Onomatopeia, or the New namer. **1657** J. SMITH *Myst. Rhet.* 72 Onomatopœia.. *Nominis seu nominum fictio*, the feigning of a name or names. **1727–41** CHAMBERS *Cycl.* s.v., The surest etymologies are those deduced from the onomatopœia. **1852** H. SPENCER *Philos. Style* Ess. 1891 II. 338 That frequent cause of strength in Saxon and other primitive words—their onomatopoeia. **1861** MAX MÜLLER *Sci. Lang.* 346 If this principle of onomatopoieia is applicable anywhere it would be in the names of animals. **1870** LUBBOCK *Orig. Civiliz.* ix. (1875) 410 Without.. supposing.. that all our root-words have originated from onomatopoeia.

b. A word formed by this process; a word imitating the sound of the thing or action which it signifies.

1842 BRANDE *Dict. Sci., Lit.* etc., *Onomatopœia*.. a word expressing by its sound the thing represented. **1845** STODDART *Gram.* in *Encycl. Metrop.* I. 179/1 Hout! seems to be an onomatopoeia of the same nature as the English verb, to hoot. **1875** WHITNEY *Life Lang.* vii. 120 We call such words 'onomatopœias', literally 'name-makings', because the Greeks did so.

2. *Rhetoric.* The use of naturally suggestive words, sentences, and forms for rhetorical effect.

1860 TENNYSON in *Mem.* (1897) II. 519 A good instance of onomatopoeia in 'Paradise Lost' (Bk. II. 879) 'On a sudden open fly With impetuous recoil and jarring sound The infernal doors, and on their hinges grate Harsh thunder, that the lowest bottom shook Of Erebus'. **1895** MRS. PHELPS *Chap. fr. Life* iii. 48 As much taken aback as if he had found a tribe of Cherokees studying onomatopoeia in English verse.

Hence **o,nomato'pœial** *a.*, of or pertaining to (rhetorical) onomatopœia; **o,nomato'pœian** *a.*, onomatopœic; *sb.*, an onomatope; †**o,nomato'pœious** *a. Obs. rare*$^{-0}$ (see quot.).

1880 *Academy* 28 Feb. 153/1 The technique of such work is irreproachable; the onomatopoeial sense of sound is most discriminative. **1860** FARRAR *Orig. Lang.* 108 An onomatopœian which gives rise to a large number of cognate words in the Indo-European languages. **1867** *Athenæum* 12 Jan. 58 In other instances the onomatopœian word is a verb in the one country and a noun in the other; thus the turkey which gobbles in England is a bubbly in Scotland. **1661** BLOUNT *Onomatopeious*, pertaining to the Figure Onomatopœia, which is a faining a name from any kind of sound.

onomatopœic (əʊˌnɒmətəʊˈpiːɪk, ˌɒnəʊmæt-), *a.* [f. Gr. ὀνοματοποι-ός: see prec. and -IC; cf. F. *onomatopéique* (Littré).] Of, pertaining to or characterized by onomatopœia, esp. as applied to the origin of names or words; imitative in sound; echoic.

1860 FARRAR *Orig. Lang.* i. 18 It originated from the onomatopœic character of a large part of all language. **1864** DASENT *Jest & Earnest* (1873) II. 69 What has been called that 'Bow-wow' theory of language, which would make everything 'onomatopœic'. **1875** WHITNEY *Life Lang.* xiv. 282 Where the onomatopœic or imitative element is most conspicuous. **1881** *Cornh. Mag.* July 104 Lines containing two of the finest onomatopoeic effects in our language, 'I heard the ripple washing in the reeds And the wild water lapping on the crag'.

So **o,nomato'pœical** *a.*, **onomato'pœically** *adv.*

1880 *Academy* 28 Feb. 153/3 The onomatopoeical sense of sound is most discriminative.

onomatopœics (əʊˌnɒmətəʊˈpiːɪks, ˌɒnəʊmæt-). [a. Gr. ὀνοματοποίησις the making of a name + -IC 2.] = ONOMATOPOËSIS.

1934 *Times Lit. Suppl.* 1 Feb. 73/2 It is obviously a *tour de force* in onomatopœics not quite so obvious as all the R sounds in Meredith's 'The Lark Ascending'. **1934** C. LAMBERT *Music Ho!* IV. 243 The mechanically picturesque onomatopœics of the piece [*sc. Pacific 231*]. **1978** *Language* LIV. 204 My 1969 paper on onomatopoeics in the Indian linguistic area.

‖**o,nomatopo'ësis** (-pəʊˈiːsɪs). Also **-poiesis.** [mod. a. Gr. ὀνοματοποίησις the making of a name, f. ὀνοματοποιέ-ειν to make or coin names.] The naming of a thing, etc., from the sound associated with it; onomatopœia.

1864 MAX MÜLLER *Sci. Lang.* Ser. II. (1868) ii. 63 This is one of the secrets of onomatopoësis, or name-poetry, that each name should express, not the most important or specific quality, but that which strikes our fancy. **1878** tr. *von Ziemssen's Cycl. Med.* XIV. 586 It is also certain that speech is learned only by onomatopoësis.

o'nomato,poesy. *rare.* Anglicized form of prec.

1885 W. STIRLING tr. *Landois' Hum. Physiol.* 706 The imitation of sounds by the organs of speech, constituting onomatopoesy [Ger. *onomatopoesis*], e.g., the hissing of a stream, the roll of thunder.. etc.

onomatopoetic (əʊˌnɒmətəʊpəʊˈɛtɪk), *a.* Also **onomatopoietic.** [f. Gr. ὀνοματοποίησις, after *poetic*.] = ONOMATOPŒIC.

1848 CRAIG, *Onomatopoetic*, formed to resemble the sound of the thing signified. **1860** FARRAR *Orig. Lang.* (1865) 17 Are not children invariably onomatopoetic? **1863** R. F. BURTON *Abeokuta* I. 100 The horn and the tomtom.. express to them a great complication of ideas by onomatopoetic language. **1883** *Q. Rev.* Jan. 177 An onomatopoietic explanation.

o,nomatopo'etically, *adv.* [f. prec.: see -ICALLY.] In accordance with onomatopoesis; by an onomatopoetic process; onomatopœically.

1866 *N. & Q.* 3rd Ser. IX. 497/1 An unused root, onomatopoetically imitating the sound of beating or striking. **1882** *Manchester City News* 18 Feb. 2/1 The buzzing of insects, the twittering of birds.. and the hum-drum of towns.. all contribute their quota to the onomatopoetically named phenomenon.

onomatopoietical (ɒˌnəʊmətəʊpɔɪˈɛtɪkəl), *a. rare.* [f. ONOMATO- + ποιητικός creative (see POIETIC) + -AL.] = ONOMATOPŒIC *a.* Cf. ONOMATOPOETIC *a.*

1709 W. KING *Useful Transactions in Philos.* II. 29 An Onomatopoietical Formation.

o'nomatopy. [f. L. *onomatopœia* or F. *onomatopée* (16th c. in Hatz.-Darm.).] = ONOMATOPŒIA.

1658 PHILLIPS, *Onomatopy* [edd. 1678–96 *-pæa*], the faining of a name, from any kind of sound, as *Bombarda*, i. a Gun, from the sounding of bom. **1822–34** *Good's Study Med.* (ed. 4) III. 219 The word *tic* is commonly supposed to be an onomatopy, or a sound expressive of the action it imports. *a* **1913** F. ROLFE *Desire & Pursuit of Whole* (1934) 133 'Launchchchchch' was a lovely new onomatopy for the motor-boats. **1946** *Word* Aug. 124 *Synchronic* semasiology .. deals with.. polysemantism, affective-value, onomatopy and congeners. **1947** *Ibid.* III. 9 The element of onomatopy in language is too slight to invalidate the general principle.

onomatous (əʊ'nɒmətəs), *a.* [f. Gr. ὀνόματ- (ONOMATO-) + -OUS.] Bearing the (writer's) name.

1869 *Spectator* 1 May 539 In very many cases we should as a rule prefer the anonymous to the onomatous mode of addressing the public.

†**o'nomomancy.** *Obs. rare*—⁰. Also onoma-. = ONOMANCY: see quots. 1678 and 1727–41 s.v.

'onomously, *adv. rare.* [f. *onomous (= ONYMOUS) adj. + -LY².] With the name given or stated; by name.

1800 W. TAYLOR in Robberds *Mem.* I. 346 The impropriety of using author's names in public journals, when speaking of writings not onomously claimed.

onon(e, onoon, obs. forms of ANON.

onond(e, onont, obs. variants of ANENT *prep.*

Onondaga (ɒnən'dɑːgə). [Onondaga *onǫ̃tá'ke* on the hill (the name of the main Onondaga settlement).] One of the five (later six) tribes of the Iroquois Confederacy of North American Indians commonly called the Five Nations (Six Nations), traditionally living near Syracuse, New York; a member of this tribe; their language. Also *attrib.* or as *adj.*

1684 in *Mass. Hist. Soc. Coll.* (1871) 4th Ser. IX. 187, I haue perswaded all the considerable Indians, the Maquas, Sineques, Onondages..to give up their lands. **1765** in *Documents Colonial Hist. New-York* (1856) VII. 719 The Onondaga Speaker Tyawarunt spoke as follows. **1823** [see CAYUGA]. **1826** J. F. COOPER *Last of Mohicans* I. xii. 181 The Mohawks, with their Tuscarora and Onondaga brethren. **1874** B. F. TAYLOR *World on Wheels* I. 31 The painted Senecas and the smoky Onondagas went gliding about like vanishing shadows. **1933** [see CAYUGA]. **1959** [see *Five Nations* s.v. FIVE *a.* and *sb.* C. 2]. **1971** D. HEFFRON *Nice Fire & Some Moonpennies* vii. 59 My mother is an Onondaga and my father was a Mohawk. **1974** H. WOODBURY in *Papers in Linguistics, Conf. Iroquoian Res.* 1972 2 One way of characterizing Onondaga noun incorporation is to describe its appearance in the surface structure of this language. *Ibid.* 5 In Onondaga, complex sentences are subject to special rules with respect to noun incorporation. *Ibid.* 15 Onondaga does not have relative clauses in the same sense that English does.

†**on'open,** *v. Obs.* [f. ON-¹ 2 + OE. *openian* to OPEN.] *trans.* To open up, explain.

c **1200** *Trin. Coll. Hom.* 217 Ich ne mai ne ich ne can þosse on openi. *Ibid.* 219 And nuþe biginne on opini.

onor, onour, -able, etc., obs. ff. HONOUR, etc.

†**o'norn,** *v. Obs.* Also onourn. Variant of ANORN, to deck, adorn.

1432–50 tr. *Higden* (Rolls) I. 217 An howse consecrate onornede allemoste alle with golde and precious stones. *Ibid.* III. 457 Oure women be not onournede that thei may be pleasante to man. **1545** *St. Papers Hen. VIII*, X. 681 This was in effecte his matier, which he onorned with a gret circumstaunce of wordes.

onourment, var. HONOURMENT *Obs.*, ornament.

onoy, onoynt, obs. ff. ANNOY, ANOINT.

onpacient, onperfect, onpossibill, onquart, onquemable, onquiet, etc.: see UN-.

onqwelm: see ONWHELM.

†**on'ran,** pa. t. of *on(h)rine, with changed particle, for *a(h)rine* or *at(h)rine* to touch.

a **1300** *Cursor M.* 21547 Wit aiþer tre þe cors on-ran, Bot allwais lai it still as stan.

onrebut, onreuli, onright, etc.: see UN-.

†**on'rese,** *v. Obs.* [OE. *onrǣsan*, f. ON-¹ 1 + *rǣsan* to rush: see RESE *v.*] *intr.* with *on* or *in*: To rush, make an onset.

c **825** *Vesp. Psalter* lviii. 4 Onræsdun in mec stronge. *Ibid.* lxi. 4 Hu longe onræsað ʒe on men? *a* **1300** *E.E. Psalter* lviii. 4 In me on-reseden stalworth þat ware. *Ibid.* lxi. 4 Til þat ye on-rese in man swa Yhe al unto yhe sla.

†**on'rise,** *v. Obs.* [OE. *onrīsan*, f. ON-¹ 1 + *rīsan* to RISE.] *intr.* To rise up (*against*).

c **1000** ÆLFRIC *Deut.* xxxi. 17 And min yrre onrist onʒen hiʒ on þam dæʒe. *c* **1250** *Gen. & Ex.* 1936 Hate hem on ros, in herte numen; Swilc nið & hate ros hem on, He redden alle him for to slon.

onrush ('ɒnrʌʃ), *sb.* [f. ON-¹ 4 + RUSH *sb.*] The act of rushing on; impetuous onward movement.

1844 *Fraser's Mag.* XXX. 179/2 Another hurrah and onrush made the enemy throw down their arms. **1856** MRS. BROWNING *Aur. Leigh* I. 970 In that first onrush of life's chariot-wheels. **1891** G. F. X. GRIFFITH tr. *Fouard's Christ the Son of God* I. 272 The mighty on-rush of the waters.

on'rush, *v. poet.* [f. ON-¹ + RUSH *v.*²] *intr.* To rush on. So **onrushing** *vbl. sb.*

1861 A. T. DE VERE *Sisters* 71 One through deserts drear On rushing in that race distraught. **1875** W. MORRIS tr. *Virgil's Aeneids* XII. 652 Saces on his foaming steed..onrusheth to the place. **1882** A. T. DE VERE *Foray of Queen Meave* 169, I hear the on-rushing of the car! **1887** W. MORRIS tr. *Homer's Odyssey* II. xv. 276 Grey-eyed Athene sent them a wind that blew aright through the lift on-rushing fiercely.

'on,rushing, *a.* [ON-¹ 3.] That rushes on.

1846 HARE *Mission Comf.* (1850) 145 The onrushing waves of the world. **1893** *Chicago Advance* 2 Mar., The great on-rushing train of God's kingdom.

ons, obs. form of ONCE.

onsaddle, onsatisfeit, onsavoury, etc.: see UN-.

Onsager (ʊn'sagər, 'ɒnsɑːgə(r)). *Physics.* The name of Lars *Onsager* (1903–76), Norwegian chemist, used *attrib.* and in the possessive with reference to a theorem orig. obtained for the thermodynamics of irreversible processes, but of wide applicability in physics and biophysics, as **Onsager coefficient**, a tensor coefficient expressing the degree of interference between two irreversible processes; **Onsager('s) law** or **principle**, a statement of the reciprocal nature of the interference between two irreversible processes occurring simultaneously, *spec.* that the Onsager coefficients for each direction of flow between the two processes are equal; cf. *reciprocity theorem*; **Onsager (reciprocal** or **reciprocity) relation**, a mathematical statement of the Onsager principle.

1945 *Rev. Mod. Physics* XVII. 343 (*heading*) On Onsager's principle of microscopic reversibility. **1952** *Physica* XVIII. 182 Verschaffelt has given an example of a linear transformation of flux and force variables which leaves the entropy production invariant and yet which destroys the Onsager relations. **1955** I. PRIGOGINE *Introd. Thermodynamics Irreversible Processes* iv. 46 These Onsager reciprocity relations express that when the flux, corresponding to the irreversible processes *i*, is influenced by the affinity X_k of the irreversible process *k*, then the flux *k* is also influenced by the affinity X_i through the same interference coefficient L_{ik}. **1965** W. C. REYNOLDS *Thermodynamics* xiv. 381 Some restrictions on the signs of the Onsager coefficients are provided by the requirement that the entropy-production rate be positive. **1965** KATCHALSKY & CURRAN *Nonequilibrium Thermodynamics in Biophysics* x. 120 Onsager's law provides a quantitative relation between the phenomena of ultrafiltration and osmotic flow. **1968** *Times* 31 Oct. 5/4 In the simplest terms possible, the Onsager principle or 'reciprocity theorem', as it is sometimes called, asserts that where two or more kinds of flow affect each other the equations describing them will be reciprocally related in a specific way. **1977** S. H. CHUE *Thermodynamics* ii. 248 In the Onsager coefficients the subscript *i* refers to the flux and the subscript *j* to the driving force. **1978** B. H. LAVENDA *Thermodynamics Irreversible Processes* ii. 29 The derivation of the Onsager reciprocal relations was based on an apparent analogy between the conditions of chemical equilibrium and the 'principle of detailed balance at equilibrium'.

†**onsand.** *Obs.* [f. OE. *onsond-e*, f. ON-¹ 1 + *sand(e, sond(e*, sending: see SOND(E; app. orig. transl. L. *immissio.*] Something sent or inflicted (by God) upon the people; a visitation.

c **825** *Vesp. Psalter* lxxvii[i]. 49 Onsonde ðorh englas yfle. *a* **1300** *Cursor M.* 5915 þan on-sandes he on him send. *Ibid.* 6009 þan sent drightin þe sext on-sand þe fals pharaon to faand.

†**onsaw.** *Obs.* [late OE. *onsaʒu*, f. ON-¹ 1 + *saʒu*, saying, SAW.] A charge against a person, an accusation; reproach, opprobrious language.

c **1000** *Ags. Gosp.* Matt. xxvi. 60 þa ða maneʒa mid leasum onsaʒum [*c* **1160** *Hatton Gosp.* on-sæʒen] ʒenealæhton. *c* **1250** *Gen. & Ex.* 2045 Or for misdede, or for on-saʒen, ðor woren to ðat prisun draʒen. *a* **1300** *Cursor M.* 19428 (Edin.) Fals it was, al þair onsaw [*v.rr.* onsau, onsagh]. *a* **1350** *Ibid.* 19422 (Gött.) Queþer es þis soth or vnsau.

†**'onsay.** *Obs. rare*—¹. [ON-¹ 4.] The saying of 'On!'; the signal to start.

1573 *New Custom* II. ii. Ciij, First came Newcustome, and hee gaue the onsay; And sithens, thinges haue gone worse euery day.

†**on'seek,** *v. Obs.* [OE. *onsēcan*, f. ON-¹ 1 + *sēcan* to seek.]

1. *trans.* To seek or require something of (a person). (Only in OE.)

a **800** CYNEWULF *Juliana* 679 þær .xxx. wæs and feowere eac feores onsohte þurh wæʒes wylm wiʒena cynnes.

2. To attack.

c **1205** LAY. 5657 Heo wenden to beon sikere þeo Belin heom on sohte. *Ibid.* 16254 ʒif me on-sohte him. *c* **1250** *Gen. & Ex.* 851 Fowre on-seken and fifue weren, Oc ðe fowre ðe fiue deren.

onseker, onsely, onsensible, etc.: see UN-.

‖**onsen** ('ɒnsɛn). [Jap., ad. Chinese *wênchüan* hot-spring.] In Japan, a thermal spring, esp. one thought to have medicinal properties; a hot-spring resort.

1933 *Discovery* June 189/1 The *onsen*, the native 'spa' or hot spring so dear to the heart of the folk of the *inaka*, the true countryside of this extraordinary land. **1959** R. KIRKBRIDE *Tamiko* xv. 118 At the Onsen he asked for Richi. **1965** W. SWAAN *Jap. Lantern* xvii. 197 Its *onsen* or hot-spring resorts more than came up to expectations.

†**'onsene.** *Obs.* [OE. *an-, ǫnsēon*, WS. *ansīen, -sȳn*, fem. = OS. *ansiun*, OHG. *anasiuni* (MHG. *ansiune*), neuter:—OTeut. **anasiunjo*ᵐ, f. **ana*, ON-¹ 1 + **siuni-z*, Goth. *siuns*, OS. *siun* fem., sight, from ablaut-series *sehw-, segw-, sew-*, in **sehwan*, OE. *sēon* to SEE. Cf. Ger. *ansehen, ansicht.*] **a.** Countenance, face. **b.** Look, aspect, appearance.

c **897** K. ÆLFRED *Gregory's Past.* li. 395 Ðyses middanʒeardes ansien oferʒæð. *c* **1000** *Ags. Gosp.* Matt. XVII. 2 His ansyn scean swa swa sunne [*c* **950** *Lind.* onsione; *c* **1160** *Hatt.* ansiene]. *Ibid.* John vii. 24 Ne deme ʒe be ansyne ac demað rihtne dom [*c* **950** *Lind.* onsione; *c* **1160** *Hatt.* ansyene]. *a* **1240** *Ureisun* in *Cott. Hom.* 191 Murie dreameð engles biuoren þin onsene. *a* **1250** *Owl & Night.* 1704 Vor nis of ow non so kene, That durre abide mine onsene.

onset ('ɒnsɛt), *sb.*¹ [f. ON-¹ 4 + SET *sb.*]

1. a. An act of setting on or attacking (an enemy); an attack, assault. † ***to give the onset***, to make an attack, or to commence the attack (*obs.*).

1535 STEWART *Cron. Scot.* II. 195 And in the feild syne maid ane new onset. **1631** GOUGE *God's Arrows* III. §4. 190 The Philistines came up..to prevent David by giving the first on-set, and beginning warre. **1715–20** POPE *Iliad* XVI. 949 He..thrice three heroes at each onset slew. **1855** MACAULAY *Hist. Eng.* xix. IV. 279 These troops had to bear the first brunt of the onset.

b. (Without article.) Attack, assault.

1667 MILTON *P.L.* II. 364 Achiev'd By sudden onset. **1791** COWPER *Iliad* VIII. 616 At their ships Give them brisk onset. **1871** R. ELLIS *Catullus* lxiv. 339 A son..whose back no foe, whose front each knoweth in onset.

c. *fig.* An attack, as of an opponent in argument, etc., of calamity or disease.

c **1586** C'TESS PEMBROKE *Ps.* LXXVI. iii, Whose fearelesse foote to bide Thy onsett tarieth. **1613** PURCHAS *Pilgrimage* (1614) 374 Other tables set with wine, in which they gave a new onset, as a fresh enemy. **1789** W. BUCHAN *Dom. Med.* (1790) 541 Previous to the onset of a fever. **1875** JOWETT *Plato* (ed. 2) I. 474 His argument could not sustain the first onset of yours.

2. a. The action, or an act, of beginning some operation; beginning, commencement, start. † ***to give the onset***, to make a beginning, to start (*obs.*).

1561 T. HOBY tr. *Castiglione's Courtier* I. B, I..must giue the onsett in oure pastimes this night. **1625** BACON *Ess., Delays* (Arb.) 525 There is surely no greater Wisedome, then well to time the Beginnings, and Onsets of Things. **1647** FARINGDON *Serm.* iii. 46 They had made a fair onset in Christianity,..they were forward in their way. **1860** HOLLAND *Miss Gilbert* xxi. 392 She kissed her a dozen times at the first onset, and called her dear heart.

b. *Phonetics.* (*a*) The movement of the speech-organs preparatory to, or at the start of, the articulation of a speech sound. (*b*) The initial part of a syllable; the consonant or consonants at the beginning of a syllable. Also *attrib.*

1933 L. BLOOMFIELD *Language* vii. 118 In passing from silence to a stressed vowel, we usually make a gradual onset of the voice. **1948** J. R. FIRTH *Papers in Linguistics 1934–51* (1957) ix. 131 These are the weak, neutral, or 'minimal' vowel, the glottal stop or 'maximum' consonant, aitch, or the pulmonic onset—all of which deserve the general name of laryngals. **1951** TRAGER & SMITH *Outl. Eng. Struct.* 15 Turning to the quality of the vocalic nuclei here, we find that there is an onset in raised lower high front position. **1955** C. F. HOCKETT *Man. Phonol.* 56 Onsets are *simple*, consisting of one or another of some eighteen or twenty *consonants*.., or *complex*, consisting of certain clusters of some of these consonants. **1962** [see CENTRALIZATION 3]. **1963** *Amer. Speech* XXXVIII. 57 Even if one were to agree that /h/ as an onset consonant 'is a voiceless anticipation of the following peak nucleus' [etc.]. **1966** J. C. POPE *Rhythm of Beowulf* (ed. 2) p. xix, These crests occur at or soon after the onset of the vowel. **1971** T. M. LIGHTNER in W. O. Dingwall *Survey Linguistic Sci.* 501 Word-initial voiced consonants in English begin with voiceless onset. **1973** *Canad. Jrnl. Linguistics* XVIII. 115 The onset of the back-gliding diphthong is typically slightly higher and slightly backer than the onset of the front diphthong.

¶**3.** (See quot.)

1755 JOHNSON, *Onset*..2. 'Something added by way of ornamental appendage. This sense, says Nicholson, is still retained in Northumberland, where *onset* means a *tuft*.' [No such sense in Northumbld. Glossary. As Todd notes, the quot. cited by J. does not belong to this sense, but to 2.]

onset ('ɒnsɛt), *sb.*² *Sc.* and *north. dial.* [f. ON-¹ + ? SET *sb.*: cf. OE. *set* seat, place of sitting or settling, stall, stable, or fold for beasts, *ʒe-sete* dwelling, habitation. The primary sense may have been 'dwelling-place *on* the farm or land'.] A farm-house, with its outhouses; a farmstead. Cf. ONSTEAD.

1535 *Sc. Acts Jas. V* (1597) §9 That everie man..cause everie tennent of their landes, that hes the same in tack and assedation, to plant vpon their on-set yeirly for everie marke land, ane tree. **1641** *Sc. Acts Chas. I* (1814) V. 637 All and haill the..landis of Ravelrig, with houssis, biggingis, yairdis, orcheardis, toftis, croftis, onsettis, outsettis [etc.]. **1725** RAMSAY *Gent. Sheph.* IV. i. Prol., The scene describ'd in former page, Glaud's onset. **1802** ANDERSON *Cumbld. Ball.* 36 That aw our heale onset wad be in a lowe. **1825** BROCKETT *N.C. Gloss.*, *Onset*, a dwelling house and out-buildings.

†**on'set,** *v. Obs.* [f. ON-¹ 2 + SET *v.*¹] *trans.* To make an onset upon; to set upon, attack.

1602 CAREW *Cornwall* 17 b, This for a while was hotely onsetted and a reasonable price offered, but (vpon what ground I know not) soone cooled againe. **1648** E. SPARKE *Pref. to Shute's Sarah & Hagar* A ij b, A feast where I am..doubtful which dish to on-set; where to begin of him.

onset, obs. form of UNSET.

onsetter (ˈɒnˌsɛtə(r)). [ON-[1] 4.]

†**1.** One who sets on, or urges on; an inciter. *Obs.*

1549 COVERDALE, etc. *Erasm. Par. 1 Peter* 7 Playng the intercessour and not the on settour. **1600** *Sc. Acts Jas. VI* (1814) 240 Persones makeris of the saidis tuilyeis and combattis, eftir dew tryell that they war the first onsettaris.. sall be.. apprehendit. **1619** W. SCLATER *Exp. 1 Thess.* (1630) 179 Let vs.. beware how we become on-setters to prophanenesse. **1641** EARL MONM. tr. *Biondi's Civil Warres* II. 47 The King.. knowing that Clemencie and Grace would more redound to his glory, then.. to make himselfe bee beleeved their on-setter, appeased them; pardoning all of them.

2. One who makes an onset; an assailant. *arch.*

1596 DALRYMPLE tr. *Leslie's Hist. Scot.* x. 332 Tha war not the first onsetteris. **1870** MORRIS *Earthly Par.* II. III. 500 Until the first, From midst the knot of those onsetters burst.

3. *Coal-mining.* A workman who puts the corves or tubs into the cage at the bottom of the shaft; = *hanger-on* (HANGER[2] 5 c).

1789 BRAND *Hist. Newcastle* II. 682 It is the onsetter's business to hang on the corves upon the rope to be drawn up the shaft. **1867** W. W. SMYTH *Coal & Coal-mining* 151 Keeping the total weight so moderate that.. the onsetter and banksmen can easily handle and run the tubs on the iron plates at the bottom and top of the shaft. **1883** *Athenæum* 20 Jan. 92/1 At present the light is only down to the onsetter's cabin.

So ˈ**onˌsetting** *vbl. sb.*, †(*a*) the action of placing or fixing on (*obs.*); (*b*) setting on, incitement; †an attack, assault (*obs.*); **onsetting** *ppl. a.*, attacking, assailing.

1501 in *Ld. Treas. Acc. Scot.* II. 115 For.. new girths set on the powdir barrelis, and for onsetting of thaim. **1541** *Aberdeen Reg.* XVII. (Jam.), He hes maid diuerss on-settingis & prouocaciounis on hym. **1619** W. SCLATER *Exp. 1 Thess.* (1630) 179 All the sinnes that by his on-setting and occasion haue beene committed. **1892** HENLEY *Song of Sword*, etc. Rhymes xxi. 2 The roar of onsetting waves.

on ˈshore, ˈon-shore, *adv. phr.* (*adj.*) *Naut.* [f. ON *prep.* + SHORE *sb.* Cf. IN SHORE.]

1. *adv. phr.* (*on shore*). **a.** To or on to the shore; = ASHORE 1. **b.** On the shore.

See ON *prep.* and SHORE.

2. *attrib.* or *adj.* (ˈ*on-shore*). **a.** Directed or moving towards the shore.

1875 BEDFORD *Sailor's Pocket Bk.* VI. 217 Wind blowing a hard on-shore gale. **1882** NARES *Seamanship* 258. **1932** BELLOC *Napoleon* III. 175 The.. torrid day, whose heat was barely mitigated by an on-shore wind from the west. **1961** B. FERGUSSON *Watery Maze* xiv. 342 The strong onshore wind had caused the tide to rise as much as half the hour ahead of almanac time.

b. Existing or occurring on the shore or on land.

1959 *Listener* 5 Mar. 432/3 Glances at the on-shore life. **1973** C. CALLOW *Power from Sea* ii. 67 There is a steadily growing interest in Britain's on-shore oil potential. **1974** *Daily Tel.* 5 Jan. 19/2 By comparison with some of the 20 million tons a year North Sea finds it is a drop in the ocean but encouraging when measured against other onshore finds. **1975** *Offshore* Sept. 97/1 The discovery of oil seeps along the western shore of Cook Inlet led to the drilling of several shallow onshore wells between 1900 and 1906.

on side, *phr.* In Football, Hockey, etc., One's proper side; the opposite of OFF SIDE, q.v.

18.. *Rugby School Football Rules* §5 in *Football Ann.* (1871), A player is on side when the ball has been (kicked, touched) or run with (5 yards) by any player of the opposite side. **1871** *Rugby Union Rules* §73 in *Football Ann.*, Every player when off-side is out of the game and shall not touch the ball.. until he is again on side.

onsight (ˈɒnsaɪt). *rare.* [f. ON *adv.* (*a.*, *sb.*) + SIGHT, after *insight.*] The action or faculty of looking onward or forward into the future.

1849–51 J. W. WARTER *L'Envoy to Southey's Comm.-pl. Bk.* IV. 724 Such was the continued onsight of Southey. **1869** MRS. WHITNEY *Hitherto* xi. 136 She was quick to see, not only into things, but on to what they were to be;.. to put her faculty into a single word.. you would call it onsight.

onsighty, onsilly, onslain, etc.: see UN-.

on site, on-site, *adv.* (*phr.*) and *a.* [f. ON *prep.* + SITE *sb.*[2]] On a particular site; occurring or situated at a site.

1959 *New Statesman* 17 Jan. 57/3 Russia now accepts.. on-site inspection to identify suspicious phenomena. **1960** *Farmer & Stockbreeder* 19 Jan. (Suppl.) 36/1 Calor Propane is delivered in cylinders or to bulk storage tanks on-site. **1967** A. BATTERSBY *Network Analysis* (ed. 2) xv. 271 On-site management may appear to save time and trouble through less paper-work. **1968** *Sci.-Tech. News* Fall 61/1 The librarian.. may have to visit personally a large library.. and reproduce the material on site. **1975** M. RUSSELL *Murder by Mile* viii. 84 On-site moulding.. had been thought preferable... 'But pre-casting might have been quicker?' *Ibid.* 85 He lives on site too.

onslaught (ˈɒnslɔːt). Forms: 7 **anslaight, onslat(t, onslought, anslacht,** 7, 9 **onslaught.** [Appears first early in 17th c., when also it has the forms *anslaight*, *anslacht*, and is termed by Phillips 'Dutch'; but the nearest Dutch word, *aanslag*, Ger. *anschlag* striking at, attempt, does not quite yield the required form. On the other hand, the ME. word *slaht*, *slaught*, *sleight* 'slaughter' appears to have become obs. *c* 1400.

Perh. it represents the Du. or Ger. word, modified after Eng. nouns of action such as *draught*. Cf. the following instances, which in sense closely approach the continental words: **1637** MONRO *Exped.* II. 52 The Swedens disappointed of their onslaught, retired after his Majestie to their Leaguer,.. having put a terror in the enemies Armie, by this defeat. **1683** SIR J. TURNER *Pallas Armata* 176 The noise of them [bandeliers] betray those who carry them in all Surprizals, Anslachts, and sudden enterprizes.]

Onset, attack; *esp.* a vigorous or destructive assault or attack.

(App. not used in the 18th c.: cited by J. only from Hudibras, and by Todd 1818 said to be 'not in use'. Used in 19th c. by Scott, and now common.)

a **1625** FLETCHER *M. Thomas* II. ii. (1639) D iij b, I doe remember yet that anslaight, thou wast beaten, And fledst. **1652** *News fr. Lowe-Countr.* 4 What Skermish, Battell, Onslat, Fight. **1654** GAYTON *Pleas. Notes* 19 The severall duels, onslaughts, stormes, and military performances. **1663** BUTLER *Hud.* I. iii. 422 Which was best, By Siege or Onslaught, to invest The Enemy. **1678** PHILLIPS (ed. 4), *Onslought* (Dutch), a storming, or fierce assault upon any place. **1828** SCOTT *F.M. Perth* vii, For witnesses to the onslaught. **1847** LEWES *Hist. Philos.* (1867) I. 358 The Sceptics had made an irresistible onslaught upon the two fortresses of Perception and Reason. **1859** in Trevelyan *Macaulay* (1876) II. viii. 54 The fierce onslaught upon that Government. **1874** MOTLEY *Barneveld* I. Pref. 7 Had withstood single-handed the onslaughts of Spain.

†**onˈslay**, *v. Obs.* Pa. t. onsloȝ, -slow. [f. ON-[1] 2 + SLAY.] *intr.* To strike on, make assault.

c **1205** LAY. 1529 To gadere heo comen; Hardliche heo on-sloȝen. *Ibid.* 1739 And grundliche on-slowen. *Ibid.* 14705 And mid mæine on-sloȝen [*c* **1275** on-slowe].

†**onˈslide**, *v. Obs. rare.* [f. ON-[3] + SLIDE *v.*] *intr.* ? To slide open; to unfold, open.

13.. *E.E. Allit. P.* B. 77 Of bollez as blwe as ble of ynde, As bornyst syluer þe lef onslydez.

onsned, onsonsy, onsort, onspoken, onspotted, etc.: see UN-.

onsse, obs. form, **onst**, dial. form, of ONCE.

onstable, onsteadfast, etc.: see UN-.

on stage, on-stage, *adv.* (*phr.*) and *a.* [f. ON *prep.* + STAGE *sb.*] On the stage; that is appearing or occurring on a stage. Also *transf.* and *fig.*

1927 T. S. ELIOT in *Newton's Seneca* I. p. xi, It is not at all clear whether he [*sc.* Hercules] destroys his family on-stage or off. **1944** *New Yorker* 24 June 32/1 Part of Duke's character goes well enough with the onstage Ellington who periodically throws back his head and emits a long-drawn-out 'Ah-h-h!' **1949** *Theatre Arts* XXXIII. 100/3 She might not have taken to sitting dangerously close to the onstage edge of the wings. **1952**, etc. [see OFF STAGE, OFF-STAGE *adv.* (*phr.*) and *a.*]. **1966** D. F. GALOUYE *Lost Perception* v. 52 Radcliff strode on-stage, supervised a pair of attendants as they positioned the recording camera. **1975** *New Yorker* 5 May 51/2 Everything that he did onstage was done with an excruciating and highly theatrical intensity. **1976** *Country Life* 12 Feb. 346/2 The orchestra.. are as well matched.. as the on-stage cast. **1977** *Broadcast* 7 Nov. 13/2 Dickens is very skilled at keeping mechanical dolls waiting in the wings, ready to be wound up and come on-stage.

onstand (ˈɒnstænd). *Obs.* or *dial.* [f. ON-[1] 4 + STAND *sb.*] (See quots.)

1788 W. MARSHALL *Yorksh.* Gloss., *On-stand*, the rent paid by the outgoing to the incoming tenant for such land as the former has rightfully cropped before his leaving the farm. **1812** LD. ELLENBOROUGH in East *Reports* XVI. 118 The outgoing tenant being bound by his covenant not to carry away the dung,.. but to sell it to the incoming tenant for a price to be ascertained in a certain manner, the effect of the covenant is that he must in the mean time have a right of on-stand on the farm for it. **1876** *Whitby Gloss.*, *Onstand*, that which the outgoing occupier of a farm leaves on the land for the incoming tenant, as manure, straw, etc. **1898** *Bouvier's Law Dict.* II. 547.

So ˈ**onˌstanding**, the occupation of land for a time by the crops, etc. of the outgoing tenant.

1769 *Elvington Inclos. Act* 12 The ancient owners.. shall pay to the new proprietors.. for the onstanding thereof [i.e. crops].

onstead (ˈɒnstɪd). *Sc.* and *north. dial.* [f. ON- + STEAD, place, station, place of occupation. Cf. ONSET *sb.*[2], which was app. in earlier use.] A farm-house with its attached stables, cowsheds, and other offices, a farmstead; now sometimes *spec.* the offices, as distinct from the farmer's house.

1715 PENNECUIK *Tweeddale* 25 All the Onsteads upon this Water are in the Parish of Lyne. **1787** GROSE *Prov. Gloss.*, *Onstead*, a single farm-house. N. **1816** SCOTT *Bl. Dwarf* xviii, He.. built in its stead a high narrow 'onstead' of three stories, with a chimney at each end. **1825** BROCKETT *N.C. Gloss.*, *Onstead*, *Onstid*, the buildings on a farm—a station or stay near the house for cattle or stacks. **1834** CUNNINGHAM *Life Burns* (1850) 80/1 Burns.. undertook.. to build a complete farm onstead, consisting of dwelling-house, barn, byre, stable and sheds. **1853** G. JOHNSTON *Nat. Hist. E. Bord.* I. 95 A pleasant onstead with a good farm-house roofed with slates, with houses for servants, with stables and byres. **1855** ROBINSON *Whitby Gloss.*, *Onestead*, a single farm-house.

†**onˈstell**, *v. Obs. rare.* Pa. t. onstalde. [OE. *onstellan*, f. ON-[1] 1 + *stellan* to place.] *trans.* To institute, establish, impose.

971 *Blickl. Hom.* 33 Mid his ȝeþylde he us bysene onstealde. *c* **1205** LAY. 7132 Hire nome.. þe me ærst hir' on-stalde.

onsterit, onsure, onsweet, etc.: see UN-.

on stream (stress variable), *adv. phr.* and *a.* Also as one word (see below). [f. ON *prep.* + STREAM *sb.*] **A.** *adv. phr.* (Usu. as two words.)

a. Of industrial plant and resources, etc.: in or into productive or useful operation.

1930 *Refiner* IX. I. 58/1 The problem which has been most annoying has been one of keeping the unit on stream. **1945** H. S. BELL *Amer. Petroleum Refining* (ed. 3) xvii. 262 For operating on a charge stock which produces more coke a four-case cycle may be used, with ten minutes on-stream, ten minutes for purging and valve changes, and twenty minutes for regeneration of the catalyst. **1952** *Economist* 6 Sept. 584/2 The Vacuum Company's refinery.. is expected to come on stream this autumn. **1958** *Times Rev. Industry* May 52/2 This material.. will be manufactured at Grangemouth where the plant.. is due to come on stream in 1959. **1974** *Daily Tel.* 9 Feb. 15/3 Another eight large brickmaking factories are due on stream this year raising capacity to 8,000 million. **1977** *N.Z. Jrnl. Agric.* Jan. 5/2 The dairy came on stream early in August last year.

b. *fig.*

1965 *Economist* 30 Oct. 495/1 The responsiveness of Congress to the evolution of public opinion on various questions of social, economic and fiscal change had been retarded unnaturally until 1965 and then suddenly came on stream. **1972** *Times* 14 Mar. (Hotels Suppl.) p. i/8, London had become enormously attractive to young people all over the world.. because 'le mini', Carnaby Street and the swinging set had come on stream all at more or less the same time.

B. *adj.* (Written *on-stream*, *onstream.*) Productive; done or occurring in the course of normal production.

1938 *Proc. Amer. Petroleum Inst.* XIX. III. 145/1 The catalyst activity decreases during the on-stream period of the cycle due to the accumulation of carbonaceous deposits. **1945** H. S. BELL *Amer. Petroleum Refining* (ed. 3) xvii. 260 A reduction of on-stream time per cycle has the same effect on a fixed-bed unit as an increase in catalyst-to-oil ratio on a continuous catalytic unit. **1971** *Physics Bull.* June 358/1 The main advantage of on-stream analysis is that it obviates the need for tedious sampling and separate analysis of each sample. **1975** *Petroleum Rev.* XXIX. 324/1 Among the advantages claimed for this system are.. earlier onstream production when compared with conventional offshore field developments.

onswere, obs. form of ANSWER.

ontal (ˈɒntəl), *a.* [f. Gr. ὄν, ὀντ- being: see ONTO- + -AL.] Relating to reality; comprising reality, not mere phenomena; also *absol.*

1902 J. WARD in *Encycl. Brit.* XXXII. 67/1 The former we may call the phenomenal, and the latter the ontal, meaning of 'aspect'. **1930** F. R. TENNANT *Philos. Theol.* II. i. 20 Further investigation of the regularity of Nature.. must wait on inquiry as to what the ontal things which underlie phenomena may be. **1935** *Theology* XXX. 320 A conception of experimental religion which is capable of being held in organic relation with the ontal and axiological arguments. **1970** P. BERTOCCI *Person God Is* 164 Data.. provident of fresh knowledge-contact with the ontal.

ontald, ontawght, ontellable, etc.: see UN-.

Ontarian (ɒnˈtɛərɪən), *sb.* and *a.* [f. *Ontari*(*o*, a lake and a province of Canada + -AN.]

A. *sb.* A native or inhabitant of Ontario. **B.** *adj.* Of or pertaining to Ontario.

1888 [see SEIGNEUR]. **1936** *Times Educ. Suppl.* 18 Apr. p. iv/2 Proposals.. that the Ontarian Government should acquire the house. **1967** *Economist* 30 Sept. p. v/1 A Maritimer earning three-quarters of the average income of all Canadians and only two-thirds of the average Ontarian, has a different perspective from a Quebecois. **1970** *Globe & Mail* (Toronto) 26 Sept. 5/2 After three years' striving to bring the Toronto Franco-Ontarian community together, La Chasse Galerie, a Toronto cultural organization, received official recognition from Secretary of State Gerald Pelletier yesterday. **1975** *Times Lit. Suppl.* 10 Oct. 1188/1 A majoritarian and imperialist view of the Canadian nation that was typically Ontarian. *Ibid.* 1188/5 To Ontarians especially.. it seemed to point the direction of Canada's future.

onteindit: see UNTEINDED, untithed.

†**on-ˈtelye**, *v. Obs.* [f. ON- (?) + OE. *tilian*: see TILL *v.*] *trans.* To labour for, earn by labour.

13.. *Chron. R. Glouc.* (Rolls) 944 Þat we miȝte biswinke [*v.rr.* ofswynke, tylly, on telȝe] oure mete and libbe bi oure swenche.

†**onˈtend**, *v. Obs.* [OE. *ontęndan*, f. ON-[1] 1 + **tęndan*, ME. *tenden*, TEND, = Goth. *tandjan* to kindle.] *trans.* To kindle, inflame (*lit.* and *fig.*).

c **890** *Laws of Ælfred* c. 27 ȝif fyr sie ontended ryht to bærnenne. *c* **1000** ÆLFRIC *Hom.* I. 240 Sume he [se deofol] ontent to gytsunge. *a* **1225** *Ancr. R.* 404 Þet schal.. ontenden þis fur aȝean þe brune of sunne. *a* **1240** *Ureisun* in *Lamb. Hom.* 185 Ontend me wiþ þe blase of þi leitinde loue.

ontful, var. ONDFUL, malicious, envious.

onthankful, onthrift, ontill, etc.: see UN-.

ˌon-the-ˈmakeness. *rare.* [f. phr. *on the make* (MAKE *sb.*[2] 8) + -NESS.] The fact or state of being *on the make.*

1923 GALSWORTHY *Captures* 5 In talking with Steer one never lost consciousness of his keen 'on-the-make-ness'.

onther, obs. form of UNDER.

ˌon-the-ˈspot, *a.* [SPOT *sb.*[1] 9.] Done, occurring, or located at the very place in question; observed or made by an eye-witness; immediate, instantaneous.

1886 G. M. HOPKINS *Let.* 11 Feb. (1956) 257 Some on-the-spot account of the late riots, as witnessed by yourself or friends and informants. **1955** *Astounding Sci. Fiction* Dec. 8 You'll..maybe do some on-the-spot generalling. **1955** *Times* 5 July p. iv/1 In these 'on-the-spot' laboratories routine tests are made continuously while the machines are running. **1956** *B.B.C. Handbk. 1957* 90 'On-the-spot' recordings. *Ibid.* 121 On-the-spot reports in sound and television. **1957** [see CONVECTIONAL *a.*]. **1960** *Guardian* 11 Apr. 8/1 The use of traffic wardens and on-the-spot fines. **1960** [see CASTROISM]. **1972** *Listener* 3 Feb. 159/2 The increasing use of 'voice pieces' by on-the-spot correspondents. **1977** *Herald* (Melbourne) 18 Jan. 1/1 Surgeons performed on-the-spot amputations.

ontic (ˈɒntɪk), *a.* [f. Gr. ὄν, ὀντ- being (see ONTO-) + -IC.] Of or pertaining to knowledge of the existence or structure of being in a given entity (but see quots.). Hence **ˈontical** *a.*, **ˈontically** *adv.*

1949 W. BROCK *Heidegger's Existence & Being* 31 One important difference between science and learning on the one hand and philosophy on the other seems to him [*sc.* Heidegger] to consist in the fact that every kind of scientific and scholarly knowledge was concerned with a limited set of objects, of what he called 'ontic'. **1952** *Mind* LXI. 131 The final outcome of ontically objective values. **1954** *Scottish Jrnl. Theol.* VII. 47 We have to recognise the ontic basis of our faith and obedience. **1957** M. FEAGINS tr. H. Kunz in P. A. Schilpp *Philos. K. Jaspers* II. xiii. 509 It is unavoidable to use the empirical, objectifiable data of knowledge (biological or psychological, for example) as guides to an explication of the ontic character of man as an active, experiencing and self-understanding being. **1960** W. V. QUINE *Word & Object* iii. 120 Of the three evident advantages of 'ontic' over 'ontological', in the special sense of 'as to what there is', brevity is the least. **1962** MACQUARRIE & ROBINSON tr. *Heidegger's Being & Time* i. 31 Ontological inquiry is concerned primarily with *Being*; ontical inquiry is concerned primarily with *entities* and the facts about them. *Ibid.*, The ontical inquiry of the positive sciences. **1969** A. RICHARDSON *Dict. Christian Theol.* 241/2 R. Bultmann.. argues that what is ontologically a human possibility, i.e. something which it is possible for men to know, is ontically actualised in Christian faith... It is much discussed today whether religious language..possesses ontic significance. **1970** J. W. YOLTON *Locke & Compass of Hum. Und.* i. 30 The more typical passages find Locke denying any ontic sense of 'kinds'. **1975** *Times Lit. Suppl.* 25 July 848/2 Before you can elicit the ontic commitment of a statement, you must indulge in what R. G. Collingwood contemptuously described as the scholastic pedantry of reducing to logical form. **1976** D. E. LINGE tr. *Gadamer's Philos. Hermeneutics* xi. 203 Anonymous intentionalities, that is, conceptual intentions in which something is intended and posited as ontically valid.

†**onˈtinkel,** *a. Obs. rare.* [Derivation obscure: Possibly repr. an OE. *ondþyncol, f. *on(d)-, and-* (ON-[2]) + *þyncol 'characterized by seeming', f. *þyncan* to seem, appear, look like.]

Resembling, looking like.

a **1300** *Cursor M.* 12675 (Cott.) Þis iacob..Iesu broþer cald was he..Ontinkel was him [*Gött.* ontinkel till him was] wit faciun. *Ibid.* 21132 (Cott.) Men cald him [Iacob] vr lauerd broþer, þai war ontinkel an and oþer [*Edin.* ontinkil baþe til oþir; *Gött.* ontinkil aiþer til oþer; *Fairf.* aiþer sib tille oþer; *Trin.* likely eiþer to oþer.]

on to, onto (ˈɒntuː), *prep.* and *a.* [The adv. ON + the prep. TO, used to express the notion conveyed in OE. by *on* prep. with the accusative, and often in ME. and mod.Eng. by *on* with simple objective (ON *prep.* B.), so as to remove the ambiguity of *on, upon,* after certain verbs, e.g. 'to jump on deck'. *On to* thus has the same relation to *on* that *into* has to *in.* But while *in to, into,* was in use already by 900, the need for *on to, onto* appears not to have been felt before the 16th c., while its written recognition as a combination is still quite recent and limited. Yet, in the sense in which it corresponds to *into, onto* is in speech a real compound, the *n* being shortened by its rapid passage into the allied mute *t*, while in *on to*, as two words, the *n* is long and does not glide into the *t*. But by most writers *on to* is avoided, or used only when ambiguity cannot be otherwise avoided (cf. quots. 1777, 1837, 1863, 1870, 1873, 1881).

On to, onto, in this sense, must be carefully distinguished, first, from a ME. *onto,* a frequent scribal variant of *unto*; and, secondly, from modern instances in which *on,* as the extension of a vb., is followed by *to* as a separate word, e.g. to *walk on* to the next station, to *flow on* to the sea, to *hang on* to a party, to *lead on* to another point; a ship *lies broadside on* to the waves. Here the two words are no more connected than in *up to, down to, out to, away to, back to, home to.* Some who write or print *onto* have carelessly misused it in such connexions.]

A. *prep.* **1.** To a position on or upon (or one that is expressed by these preps.). *a.* Written *on to.*

1581 RICH *Farew.* (1846) 7, I haue stept on to the stage.. contented to plaie a part. **1677** W. HUBBARD *Narrative* (1865) I. 227 Another mortally wounded, got on to an Island in the River. *c* **1681** HICKERINGILL *Trimmer* ii. Wks. 1716 I. 367 Now that I have got you on to my own ground. **1777–8** MISS C. A. BURNEY in *Mme. D'Arblay's Early Diary* (1889) II. 287 Mr. Suard tumbled on to the sopha directly, Mr. Thrale on to a chair. **1778** M. CUTLER in *Life, Jrnls. & Corr.* (1888) I. 66 This morning I crossed on to Rhode Island. **1837** DICKENS *Pickw.* ii, Assisting Mr. Pickwick on to the roof. **1863** GEO. ELIOT *Romola* lxviii, She jumped on to the beach. **1864** DASENT *Jest & Earnest* (1873) I. 75 They are.. slowly lowered, not right on to the heads of the slumbering gannets, but a little on one side. **1870** H. MAUDSLEY *Body & Mind* 13 If laid on its back, it struggles on to its legs again. **1871** MORLEY *Crit. Misc.* 219 His epithet..shoots like a sunbeam on to the matter. **1871** L. STEPHEN *Playgr. Eur.* 309 Dropping on to your knees on an ice staircase. **1873** MISS THACKERAY *Wks.* (1891) I. 70 Jumped out of window on to the water-butt. **1881** TENNYSON *Cup* II. ii. *stage direct.*, Comes forward on to step by tripod. **1888** MRS. H. WARD *R. Elsmere* xviii. II. 105 He subsided on to the music-bench obediently. **1895** *Law Times Rep.* LXXIII. 156/2 Two vessels..drifted through the violence of a storm on to the toe of a breakwater.

β. Written *onto.*

(Several early instances of this cited by Pickering, Bartlett, etc., have on examination proved to be erroneous, the originals having *on to,* in two words.)

1715 *Duxbury* (Mass.) *Rec.* (1893) 105 [A] place gutted away by the rain down onto Mr. Wiswells land. **1758** R. PUTNAM *Jrnl.* 3 June (1886) 62 Capt. Nixon's men..fell a tree onto some men as they were in another camp. **1788** J. MAY *Jrnl.* 30 June (1873) 75, I put powder-horn and shot-bag onto him, and a gun in his hand. **1819** KEATS *Otho* v. iv. (Poems, ed. Forman 1901), Please you walk forth Onto [*ed.* 1876 Upon] the Terrace. *a* **1825** FORBY *Voc. E. Anglia* Introd. 155 For the preposition *upon,* when it signifies motion to, we use *onto* (why not as good as *into*?). Ex. 'Throw some coals *onto* the fire'. **1828** *Craven Gloss.* (ed. 2), *Onto,* upon, on. 'Put it ontot' table'. **1846** in WORCESTER. **1881** B. WAUGH *Sunday Even. w. my Childr.* xxxix. 332 A steamer..was reported to be driven onto the rocks. *Ibid.*, On the cliff there were men trying to send a rope out onto the ship. **1886** C. W. STONE *Grk. Lessons* 35 An enclitic is a word which throws back its accent onto the preceding word. **1900** ANNIE E. HOLDSWORTH *Valley Gt. Shadow* v, He walked out onto the balcony. **1938** L. BEMELMANS *Life Class* II. iii. 142 Everything..can be rushed at a moment's notice onto the tables. **1954** C. S. LEWIS *Horse & his Boy* vi. 76 He jumped down onto the rubbish. **1963** *New Statesman* 24 May 781/3 Russia..has heaved itself onto the plateau of the advanced industrial powers. **1973** G. GREENE *Honorary Consul* III. iii. 132 The man was telling him to get back onto the so-called bed. **1973** [see LEAD *sb.*[2] 1 f]. **1976** D. HEFFRON *Crusty Crossed* xxviii. 175 He was hanging onto Dot as though they both might collapse to the ground if he let go.

¶ Erroneous use of *onto* for *on to.*

1888 *Amer. Jrnl. Psychol.* I. 383 Certain antecedent events that join onto the ones present. **1895** *Voice* (N.Y.) 28 Mar. 4/2 It is a very pretty game, governor, but the people are onto it.

2. Aware of or knowledgeable about (a person, state of affairs, etc.); 'wise to' (something). Cf. ON *adv.* 13 e. *colloq.* (orig. *U.S.*).

1877 *Chicago Street Gaz.* 20 Oct. 1/2 May Willard, why don't you take a tumble to yourself and not be trying to put on so much style around the St. Mark's Hotel, for very near all of the boys are on to you. **1887** *Lantern* (New Orleans) 9 July 4/3 Who is onto the rag racket. **1888** *New York Mercury* 21 July 3/3 A wife poisoner..ought to have for his wife a woman who is on to him, and who can meet his poison advances with a kerosene bath. **1899** A. H. QUINN *Pennsylvania Stories* 115 The class is about on to us, anyway, and if they find out about this deal [etc.]. **1911** J. C. LINCOLN *Cap'n Warren's Wards* xvi. 254 Everybody has been on to that for some time. **1919** WODEHOUSE *Damsel in Distress* xxi. 248 'So you're on to him, too?' said Billie. 'When did *you* get wise?' **1959** J. OSBORNE *World of Paul Slickey* I. v. 50, I can't help feeling that he's on to us... That he knows about us. **1973** G. MITCHELL *Murder of Busy Lizzie* xiii. 151 'Won't you even tell Gavin that we may be on to something?'..'You may say that I have certain suspicions, if you like.'

3. *Math.* (Written **onto.**) Used (in place of *into*) to express the relation of a set to its image under a mapping when every element of the image set has an inverse image in the first set.

1940 C. C. MACDUFFEE *Introd. Abstract Algebra* ii. 54 If a homomorphism of *A* onto *B* exists, we write $A \sim B$. **1962** B. H. ARNOLD *Intuitive Concepts Elem. Topology* vii. 113 Each of the sets *X* and *Y* is the set of all real numbers; $f(x) = 2x$. The transformation $f: X \rightarrow Y$ is onto *Y*. **1965** PATTERSON & RUTHERFORD *Elem. Abstract Algebra* i. 3 We shall denote a mapping *f* of S_1 into S_2 by $f: S_1 \rightarrow S_2$... If every element *y* of S_2 is of the form $f(x)$ for some $x \in S_1$, we call *f* a mapping of S_1 onto S_2. **1971** E. C. DADE in Powell & Higman *Finite Simple Groups* viii. 307, λ is an epimorphism of *A* onto a field *F*.

B. *adj. Math.* Used to designate a mapping of one set 'onto' another.

1942 S. LEFSCHETZ *Algebraic Topology* i. 7 If a transformation is 'onto', the inverse image of the complement of a set is the complement of the inverse image of that set. **1949** —— *Introd. Topology* 216 (Index), Onto transformation. **1951** N. JACOBSON *Lect. Abstract Albegra* I. 4 If α is a mapping of *S* into *T*, and β is a mapping of *T* into *S* such that $\alpha\beta = 1_S$ and $\beta\alpha = 1_T$, then α and β are 1–1, onto mappings and $\beta = \alpha^{-1}$. **1968** [see INTO *a.*]. **1971** E. C. DADE in Powell & Higman *Finite Simple Groups* viii. 285 By Lemma 9.5 the map is onto.

onto, on to, obs. (14–16th c.) form of UNTO.

onto-, combining form of Gr. ὄν, ὀντ- being present participle of εἶναι to be. **onˈtogony** [-γονία generation, production], the history of the production of organized beings (Mayne *Expos. Lex.* 1857). **onˈtography** [-GRAPHY], a description of the nature and essence of things (Mayne); so **ontoˈgraphic** *a.* **onˈtonomy** [-νομία distribution, arrangement] (see quot.). **onˈtosophy** [σοφία wisdom], the knowledge of being; ontology. **ontotheˈology** (see quots.); so **ontotheoˈlogical** *a.*

1803 J. STEWART (*title*) *Opus maximum*..*Ontonomy; or, the science of being. **1727–41** CHAMBERS *Cycl., Ontology,* or **Ontosophy,* the doctrine or Science *de ente,* that is, of being, in the general, or abstract. **1869** *Contemp. Rev.* X. 407 It was not to be an 'ontology' nor an 'ontosophy'. **1798** A. F. M. WILLICH *Elem. Critical Philos.* 171 *Ontotheology is the cognition of a Supreme Being from bare conceptions. **1854** GEO. ELIOT tr. *Feuerbach's Essence Christianity* ii. 38 The *ens realissimum,* the most real being of the old onto-theology. *Ibid.* 40 The *onto-theological predicates are merely predicates of the understanding.

onˈtogenal, *a. rare.* [irreg. f. ONTOGENY + -AL[1].] = ONTOGENETIC.

1890 *Nature* 6 Feb. 316/2 He has..confounded ontogenal steps of growth with phylogenal phases of plan.

ontogenesis (ɒntəʊˈdʒɛnɪsɪs). *Biol.* [mod. f. ONTO- + Gr. γένεσις birth.] The origin and development of the individual living being (as distinguished from *phylogenesis,* that of the tribe or species).

1875 tr. *Schmidt's Desc. & Darw.* 195 The phenomena of individual development or Ontogenesis admit of no other choice. **1878** G. A. SIMCOX in *Academy* 605/2 The analogy between phylogenesis and ontogenesis. **1879** tr. *Haeckel's Evol. Man* I. i. 7 Phylogenesis is the mechanical cause of Ontogenesis. The Evolution of the Tribe..effects all the events which take place in the course of the Evolution of the Germ or Embryo.

ontogenetic (ˌɒntəʊdʒɪˈnɛtɪk), *a.* [f. prec. after *genetic.*] Of, pertaining to, or characteristic of ontogenesis; relating to the development of the individual being.

1878 BELL *Gegenbaur's Comp. Anat.* 517 This union is effected during their ontogenetic development. **1883** H. DRUMMOND *Nat. Law in Spir. W.* (1884) 293 What the Germans call 'ontogenetic directive Force'. **1894** *Times* 5 May 6/6 The disappearance of a typical organ..was.. shown to be not an ontogenetic but a phylogenetic process.

So **ˌontogeˈnetical** *a. rare.* Hence **ˌontogeˈnetically** *adv.*, with reference to ontogenesis.

1872 ELSBERG in *Microsc. Jrnl.* July 185 A series of gradations..through which higher organisms have passed phylogenetically and do pass ontogenetically (embryonically). **1894** *Contemp. Rev.* Aug. 265 From a psychological as well as from an ethnological point of view (ontogenetically and phylogenetically as the biologist would say). **1965** *Sci. World* IX. iv. 4/2, I propose to classify the processes which concern biologists as molecular, physiological, ontogenetical, historical and evolutionary.

ontogenic (ɒntəʊˈdʒɛnɪk), *a.* [f. ONTOGENY + -IC.] Pertaining to or distinguished by ontogeny; = ONTOGENETIC *a.*

1893 *Proc. Boston Soc. Nat. Hist.* XXVI. 98 The product of the evolution of an ancestor into a phylum through successive independent forms or ontogenic cycles. **1944** B. MALINOWSKI *Sci. Theory of Culture* viii. 78 A new organism comes into being.. starting a partly independent career of ontogenic development. **1965** B. E. FREEMAN tr. *Vandel's Biospeleol.* xxii. 367 The information available on ontogenic evolution in the Trechinae will be given.

ontogenist (ɒnˈtɒdʒɪnɪst). [f. next + -IST.] One versed or skilled in ontogeny.

1891 in *Cent. Dict.* **1899** E. J. CHAPMAN *Drama Two Lives, Amphioxus & Ascidian* 88 Our great Ontogenist..Beheld the links his System missed.

ontogeny (ɒnˈtɒdʒɪnɪ). [f. ONTO- + Gr. -γενεια birth, production, f. -γενης born, produced.]

1. The origin and development of the individual being; = ONTOGENESIS.

1872 *Microsc. Jrnl.* July 185 'The ontogeny of every organism repeats in brief..its phylogeny', i.e. the individual development of every organism..repeats approximately the development of its race. **1892** MIVART *Ess. & Crit.* II. 337 Remarkable changes during its individual process of development, or, as it is called, during its 'ontogeny'.

2. The history or science of the development of the individual being; embryology.

1874 LEWES *Probl. Life & Mind* I. 360 Either we must know what is, or how it came to be what it is; the thing or its history: Ontology or Ontogeny. **1876** E. R. LANKESTER tr. *Haeckel's Hist. Creat.* I. i. 10 By the history of development, only one part of this science has generally been understood, namely, that of organic individuals, usually called Embryology, but more correctly and comprehensively, Ontogeny. **1879** tr. *Haeckel's Evol. Man* I. i. 24 Germ-history or Ontogeny, history of the development of the embryo of the individual organism.

ontogony, ontography: see ONTO-.

ontoˈlogic, *a.* [f. as ONTOLOGY + -IC. Cf. F. *ontologique* (1835 in *Dict. Acad.*).] = next.

1761 STERNE *Tr. Shandy* III. xix, A robbery of the Ontologic Treasury of..a jewel. **1876** M. COLLINS *Fr. Midnight to Midnight* II. ii. 223 Our ontologic poet, meditative of incisive unscannable blank verse.

ontological (ɒntəʊˈlɒdʒɪkəl), *a.* [f. as prec. + -AL[1].] Of or pertaining to, or of the nature of, ontology; metaphysical.

ontological argument, proof (for the existence of God): the *a priori* argument that the existence of the idea of God of necessity involves the objective existence of God.

1782 V. KNOX *Ess.* (1819) III. cxl. 107 Perplexing himself with ontological inquiries into the nature of angels. **1817** COLERIDGE *Biog. Lit.* I. v. 96 Any ontological or metaphysical science not contained in such..psychology was but a web of abstractions. **1825** —— *Aids Refl.* (1861) 139 We pass out of the cosmological proof, the proof *à posteriori*, and from the facts, into the ontological, or the proof *à priori*, and from the Idea. **1856** DOVE *Logic Chr. Faith* v. i. §1. 255, *I am* is the indubitable of my ontological consciousness. **1877** E. CAIRD *Philos. Kant* II. xv. 552 The ontological argument for the being of God.

b. *Path.* (See quot.)

1876 tr. *Wagner's Gen. Pathol.* (ed. 6) 5 This conception, according to which disease was a particular entity which lodged in the body, was called ontological.

Hence **ontoˈlogically** *adv.*, in the manner of, or in relation to, ontology.

1846 in WORCESTER. **1859** G. BUSH tr. *Swedenborg's Doctr. & Statem.* (1875) 9 What are these things, ontologically considered?

ontologism (ɒnˈtɒlədʒɪz(ə)m). [f. ONTOLOGIZE: see -ISM 1.] A form of mysticism, which rests on the principle that 'the order of intellectual apprehension follows the order of real being', and thus holds that 'an immediate cognition of God is essential to the human intellect, so that without this it can have cognition of nothing' (*Cath. Dict.*).

1865 *Dublin Rev.* Sept. 474 We have expressed an earnest desire for the establishment of some concordat between the two rival schools of philosophy (*Ontologism* and *Psychologism*) which now unhappily divide Catholics. **1885** *Catholic Dict.* (ed. 3), *Ontologism*..is the name, first given by Gioberti. *Ibid.*, Seven propositions, embracing the fundamental tenets of Ontologism, were censured by the Holy See..in a decree of the congregation of the Inquisition bearing date September 18, 1861.

ontologist (ɒnˈtɒlədʒɪst). [f. ONTOLOG-Y + -IST.] One who studies or is versed in ontology; a metaphysician.

1727 BAILEY vol. II, *Ontologist*, one who treats of Beings in the Abstract. **1793** BEDDOES *Math. Evid.* 12 The ontologists have mistaken the humble *posteriori* for the high *priori* road. **1825** COLERIDGE *Aids Refl.*, *Spir. Relig.* (1854) 129 The difference between the notional One of the Ontologists, and the idea of the living God. **1856** MILL *Logic* (ed. 4) I. I. iii. 65 Refutation of the Ontologists from their own premises and in their own language, which he [*sc.* Sir Wm. Hamilton] has furnished in the first paper of his *Discussions*.

onˈtologize, *v.* [f. ONTOLOGY (or its elements) + -IZE.] **a.** *intr.* To play the ontologist; to deal with or apply ontology. **b.** *trans.* To treat ontologically.

1849 tr. *Nitzsch's Chr. Doctr.* §65. 147 Whoever constructs a dogma which does not assert what God is..will afterwards endeavour to recover what has been neglected in the conceptions of his attributes, and thus ontologise in the wrong place. **1865** *Athenæum* No. 1992. 922/1 We are expected to ontologize existence.

Hence **onˈtologizing** *vbl. sb.* and *ppl. a.*

1878 S. H. HODGSON *Philos. of Reflection* I. 138 The 'too much' of ontologising philosophers. **1897** W. M. URBAN *Hist. Princ. Sufficient Reason* iv. 34 The ontologizing of this fundamental law is the Transcendental Logic of the Kantian *Kritik.* **1940** *Mind* XLIX. 118 Some categories..are 'ontological or ontologising', *i.e.*, have metaphysical import.

ontology (ɒnˈtɒlədʒɪ). [ad. mod.L. *ontologia* (Jean le Clerc 1692), f. Gr. ὀντο-, ONTO- + -λογία: see -LOGY. Cf. F. *ontologie*, 1751 in Hatz.-Darm.] The science or study of being; that department of metaphysics which relates to the being or essence of things, or to being in the abstract.

1721 BAILEY, *Ontology*, an Account of being in the Abstract. **1724** WATTS *Logic* I. vi. §9 In order to make due enquiries into all these, and many other particulars which go towards the complete and comprehensive idea of any being, the science of ontology is exceeding necessary. This is what was wont to be called the first part of metaphysics in the peripatetic schools. **1733** —— (*title*) A Brief Scheme of Ontology or the Science of Being in General. **1776** ADAM SMITH *W.N.* (1869) II. v. i. 355 Subtleties and sophisms.. composed the whole of this cobweb science of ontology, which was likewise sometimes called metaphysics. *a* **1832** BENTHAM *Fragm. Ontol.* Wks. 1843 VIII. 195 The field of ontology, or as it may otherwise be termed, the field of supremely abstract entities, is a yet untrodden labyrinth. **1865** *Reader* 8 July 30 We cordially approve and admire,.. not least, the signal demolition of Ontology, in the form of the *noumenon*, or unknowable substratum of matter and mind. **1884** BOSANQUET tr. *Lotze's Metaph.* 22 Ontology..as a doctrine of the being and relations of all reality, had precedence given to it over Cosmology and Psychology, the two branches of enquiry which follow the reality into its opposite distinctive forms.

ontonomy, ontosophy: see ONTO-.

ontoward, ontrewe, ontrusty, etc.: see UN-.

on-uppe, -n, var. forms of ANUPPE, upon.

onur, obs. form of HONOUR.

‖**onus** (ˈəʊnəs). [L. *onus* load, burden.] A burden, charge, responsibility, duty.

c **1640** J. SMYTH *Hundred of Berkeley* (1885) 89 The onus or Charge of this Burrow or market towne is in the exchequer. **1745** in J. H. Jesse *G. Selwyn & Contemp.* (1843) I. 98, I should acquiesce under the first *onus*, and stir no further. **1800** COLQUHOUN *Comm. Thames* xi. 333 Where an onus or responsibility rests there is Security. **1804** WELLINGTON *Let. to Major Shawe* in Gurw. *Desp.* (1837) II. 668 If..the onus is to fall upon the British troops, their numbers must be doubled, or even trebled. **1884** *Manch. Exam.* 23 May 5/2 On the companies would be thrown the onus of bringing forward a Bill for a new classification of maximum rates.

b. ***onus probandi*** (Latin phrase): the burden of proving; the obligation under which one who makes an assertion, allegation, or charge is of proving the same.

1722 *Act Encour. Silk Manuf.* in *Lond. Gaz.* No. 6040/5 The Onus Probandi shall lie on the Exporter, Claimer, or Owner thereof. **1793** SMEATON *Edystone L.* §79 The *onus probandi* should be upon me. **1885** SIR J. PEARSON in *Law Rep.* 29 Chanc. Div. 457 The *onus probandi* that the lease was improperly drawn would lie upon him.

onus, obs. form of ONCE.

†**oˈnust**, *a.* *Obs.* *rare*[−0]. [ad. L. *onust-us.*] Laden, loaded, burdened.

So †**oˈnusted** *a.* *rare*[−1].

1604 R. CAWDREY *Table Alph.*, *Onust*, loaden, ouercharged. **1657** TOMLINSON *Renou's Disp.* 351 It emitts ..branches onusted with small..flowers.

on uven, var. of ANOVEN *obs.*, upon.

ˈon-ˌwaiting. *Sc.* [ON-[1] 4.] The action of 'waiting on', *i.e.* waiting for, something; a tarrying for the accomplishment of what is desired or expected; an awaiting.

c **1610** SIR J. MELVIL *Mem.* (1683) 193 Continual onwaiting will be chargeable and expensive to you. **1681** R. FLEMING *Fulfill. Script.* (1801) I. 67 Prayer with quiet on-waiting in the use of means. *a* **1732** T. BOSTON *Crook in Lot* (1805) 158 A believer..may wonder 'tis come on so short on-waiting.

So **ˈonˌwaiter** *Sc.*, one who waits 'on' or for something.

c **1610** SIR J. MELVIL *Mem.* (1683) 126 About his Majesty ..sundry gentlemen began to look after service and turned onwaiters [*ed.* 1735 On-waiters].

†**ˈonwald**, *sb.* *Obs.* Forms: 1 onweald, (onwæld), 1–2 anweald, 1–3 onwald, anwald, 3 andweald, anwold, onwold. [OE. *anwald*, *ǫnweald* (cogn. w. OHG. *anawalt*), f. *an*, *on*, ON + *-wald*, *-weald* power.] Power, rule, authority.

c **893** K. ÆLFRED *Oros.* II. i. §1 Nu we witon þæt ealle onwealdas from him sindon. *Ibid.* §5 Heo..on hiere onwalde æfter þurhwunade. *c* **1000** *Ags. Gosp.* Luke xxiii. 7 He ȝecneow þæt he wæs of herodes anwalde [*Lindisf.* onwæld, *Rushw.* onwald, *Hatt.* anwealde]. *c* **1175** *Lamb. Hom.* 51 Ut of þine onwalde. *c* **1200** *Trin. Coll. Hom.* 21 He was pined on pilates andwealde. *c* **1205** LAY. 13182 Whæt heo hæfden on anwolde. *Ibid.* 25116 Þe balde þe Brutene hæfde an onwalde. *c* **1275** *Moral Ode* 264 (Jesus MS.), Heo schulleþ wunyen in helle þe ueondes onwolde.

†**onˈwald**, *v.* *Obs.* [Collateral form of AWELD *v.*] *trans.* To bring under one's power or rule; to subdue.

c **1205** LAY. 5703 Ne mihten heo Rome-wal nawiht onwalden [*c* 1275 noþing awelde].

†**on-ˈwar**, *a.*[1] *Obs.* [app. expanded form of AWARE.] = AWARE, on one's guard.

a **1310** in Wright *Lyric P.* xiv. 46 Ah feyre levedis be on-war.

onwar, *a.*[2], variant of UNWARE, unaware.

onwar: see ONWHAR.

onward (ˈɒnwəd), *adv.*, *a.* (*sb.*, *prep.*) Also 5 unward, *Sc.* onwart, 5–6 onwarde, 6 one-. [f. ON *adv.* + -WARD: formed app. in 14th c. after *inward*, *forward*, and other earlier formations.]

A. *adv.* (Formerly sometimes construed with *of*: e.g. ***onward of one's way*** or ***journey***.)

1. In the direction of what is ahead; towards the front; so as to advance or move on; forward; = ON *adv.* 9. **a.** *lit.* in space.

1532 MORE *Confut. Tindale* Wks. 409/1, I haue driuen hym onwarde one steppe down. **1568** GRAFTON *Chron.* II. 221 After the solemnitie..: this yong Queene came onward of her iourney. **1608** TOURNEUR *Rev. Trag.* Wks. 1878 II. 12 You'll bring me onward, brother? **1671** MILTON *Samson* 1 A little onward lend thy guiding hand To these dark steps, a little further on. **1761** GRAY *Odin* 13 Onward still his way he takes. **1859** TENNYSON *Enid* 251 Onward to the fortress rode the three. **1865** BARING-GOULD *Hymn*, Onward, Christian soldiers, Marching as to war.

b. in time, or in succession generally.

1667 MILTON *P.L.* x. 811 Endless miserie From this day onward. **1700** WALLIS in *Collect.* (O.H.S.) I. 327 And so onward in like proportion. **1839** I. TAYLOR *Anc. Chr.* I. ii. 148 From the apostolic age, and the times of Philo and four centuries onward. **1875** JOWETT *Plato* (ed. 2) IV. 403 Objects of sense must lead us onward to the ideas..which are contained in them.

†**2.** Towards the final settlement, provisionally; *spec.* on account, 'in advance'; as an 'earnest'.

1467 *Mann. & Househ. Exp.* (Roxb.) 406 The same day my mastyr paid to Roger Sego, unward of his werke, x.s. ? *a* **1500** *Chester Pl.*, *Christ betrayed*, Thou shalbe quite a hundreth foulde, And one warde take thou this! **1555** BONNER *Homilies* 2 To haue somethyng done onward, til God of his goodnes prouide something better.

3. In a position in advance; = ON *adv.* 10. **a.** in space, or in succession figured as space.

c **1386** CHAUCER *Knt.'s T.* 112 Onward on his wey that nyght he lay. **1523** LD. BERNERS *Froiss.* I. ccccxlv. 786 Thoughe he had knowen therof he coulde natte haue let it whan they were ones onwarde. *c* **1600** SHAKS. *Sonn.* l, My greefe lies onward and my ioy behind. **1719** DE FOE *Crusoe* I. xx, It was further onward the same way.

b. in time. Now *rare* or *Obs.*

c **1435** *Torr. Portugal* 2296 We have be here, Moche of this two yere, And onward on the thrid. **1523** LD. BERNERS *Froiss.* I. xcviii. 119 Tyll it was well onwarde in wynter.

4. *Comb.*

1832 TENNYSON *Pal. of Art* lxii, 'Mid onward-sloping motions infinite. **1881** STEVENSON *Virg. Puerisque* (1895) 172 There is always a new horizon for onward-looking men.

B. *adj.*

1. Of motion, or action figured as motion: Directed onward or forward. Rarely of a thing: Moving onward or forward, advancing.

1674 N. FAIRFAX *Bulk & Selv.* 172 This onward everlastingness which is fastned upon God Almighty, is all along made up of things which before were not, afterwards are not. **1756** HOME *Douglas* I. 14 Sincerity, Thou first of virtues, let no mortal leave Thy onward path! **1836** W. IRVING *Astoria* II. 226 Resuming his onward course. **1871** R. ELLIS *Catullus* lxiv. 249 She, as his onward keel still moved, still mournfully followed.

2. Situated in front, or in advance (in space, time, or succession generally); advanced. *rare* or *Obs.*

a **1586** SIDNEY *Arcadia* I. (1891) 46 b, [He] came to see how onward the fruites were of his friends labour. **1644** MILTON *Areop.* (Arb.) 67 To discover onward things more remote from our knowledge.

C. *sb.* (ellipt. uses of A. or B.)

†**1.** Payment towards a final settlement. ***in onward*** = A. 2. *Obs. rare.*

1496 *Acc. Ld. High Treasurer Scot.* I. 301 Item..to Dande Achinsone, in onwart of theking of the chapel of the Castel in Edinburgh, xvs. vjd.

2. (*nonce-uses.*) **a.** An onward movement. **b.** That which is on ahead, the onward time.

1654 GAYTON *Pleas. Notes* III. x. 131 A thousand stops, a thousand onwards made. **1887** G. MEREDITH *Ball. & Poems* 137 The thirsty onward waved for him no sign.

†**D.** *prep.* = ON *prep.* *Obs. rare.*

1652 LOVEDAY tr. *Calprenede's Cassandra* I. 3 Two of that Troup..conducted him onward the way to Babylon.

Hence **ˈonwarding** *vbl. sb.*, a prompting to move onward; †**ˈonwardling**, a small portion or length of time; †**ˈonwardly** *a.*, progressive; **ˈonwardly** *adv.*, with an onward motion.

1843 E. JONES *Poems, Sens. & Event* 39 The music riseth, To its voluptuous *onwardings all move. **1674** N. FAIRFAX *Bulk & Selv.* 110 For [an atome] not being a stretchling or *quid quantum*, any more than a now is an *onwardling or *quid successivum*. *Ibid.* 32 Every part of lastingness besides a now, is *onwardly as well as bounded. *Ibid.* 138 This Motion, as such, is ever onwardly or by degrees. **1850** MRS. BROWNING *Poems* II. 41 The maiden Luti watcheth Where *onwardly they float.

ˈonwardness. [f. prec. + -NESS.] The state or condition of moving onward or advancing; advance, progression, progress.

1548 UDALL, etc. *Erasm. Par. Gal.* v. (R.), Yet is she not idle, but secretly worketh a vehement onwardnes to all godlynes. **1674** N. FAIRFAX *Bulk & Selv.* 18 Gods outward or abstract is in an endless onwardness. **1844** BERESF. HOPE *Ess.* 235 We find also..great firmness and onwardness of purpose. **1856** R. A. VAUGHAN *Mystics* VI. vi. (1860) I. 207 Was a certain mystic on the side of the truth and onwardness of his time, or against it?

onwards (ˈɒnwədz), *adv.* (*prep.*) [f. ONWARD with advb. *-s*: see -WARDS.]

A. *adv.* **1. a.** = ONWARD A. 1.

c **1600** SHAKS. *Sonn.* cxxvi, If Nature..As thou goest onwards, still will pluck thee back. **1697** DRYDEN *Virg. Georg.* III. 370 The spumy Waves proclaim the watry War. .. March onwards, and insult the rocky Shoar. **1819** BYRON *Juan* II. ci, The current with a rising gale Still set them onwards to the welcome shore. **1860** TYNDALL *Glac.* I. xi. 82 Our eyes wandered from peak to peak, onwards to the remote horizon.

b. = ONWARD A. 1 b.

1732 BERKELEY *Alciphr.* VI. §27 From the first century onwards, there was never wanting the testimony of such men. **1916** G. B. SHAW *Androcles & Lion* I. 9 You may be called on to appear in the Imperial Circus at any time from tomorrow onwards. **1961** NEW ENG. BIBLE *Acts* iii. 24 So said all the prophets, from Samuel onwards. *a* **1976** A. CHRISTIE *Autobiogr.* (1977) VII. ii. 330 From then onwards I should have first-class advice.

†**2.** = ONWARD A. 2. *Obs.*

1633 BP. HALL *Hard Texts, N.T.* 15 It is not yet time.. but onwards, do ye confine your paines and preaching within the bounds of Judæa. **1637** —— *Serm. at Excester* 24 Aug., Wks. 1662 IV. [III.] 95 He..would stay Gods leisure for the possession of it, four hundred years: Onwards he takes his livery and seisin, and will purchase with money that which the great ower of heaven gave him freely.

3. = ONWARD A. 3: †*onwards of* = on towards, approaching, nearly (*obs.*).

1695 WOODWARD *Nat. Hist. Earth* II. (1723) 117 'Twas well onwards of a thousand Years before ever this Curse began to take effect.

†**B.** *prep.* = ONWARD D. *Obs.*

1588 PARKE tr. *Mendoza's Hist. China* 126 In this sort hee goeth onwards his way.

onware, onwarned, onwashed: see UN-.

[**onwhar, onwar**, error for *ouwhar*, OWHERE.]

†**onwhelm**, *v. Obs. rare.* [See ON-[3].] To overwhelm.

c **1440** *Promp. Parv.* 366/2 On-qwelmyn (*P.* onwhelmen), *desuppino.*

on wide, widely: see WIDE.

†'**onwil(l**, *a. Obs.* Also **an-**. [OE. *ánwille*, f. *án*, ONE + WILL.] Self-willed, stubborn, obstinate; persistently desirous, importunate.

c **897** K. ÆLFRED *Gregory's Past.* xlii. 305 (Hatton MS.) Ðætte on oðre wisan sint to manianne ða anwillan. *c* **1050** *Gloss.* in Wr.-Wülcker 467/30 *Pertinax*, anwille. *a* **1100** *Ags. Voc.* ibid. 337/18 *Obstinatus*, anwille. *a* **1225** *Ancr. R.* 56 ȝif eni is onwil [*C.* swa anwil] uorte iseon ou. *Ibid.* 400 ȝif þu ert so swuðe onwil, & so ut of þine witte.

onwind, onwise, onworth, etc.: see UN-.

†'**onwriting.** *Obs.* [f. ON-[1] + WRITING, after L. *inscriptio.*] That which is written on something; an inscription.

c **975** *Rushw. Gosp.* Luke xx. 24 Hwæs hæfes onlicnisse & onmercunge & onwritinge [*Lindisf. Gosp.* inn-awritting]. *c* **1550** CHEKE *Matt.* xxii. 20 He asketh yem whoos image it was, and whoos onwriting.

ony, onie, Sc. etc. forms of ANY; obs. f. HONEY.

‖**onycha** ('ɒnɪkə). Also 5 onica, 7 onicha. [L. *onycha* = Gr. ὄνυχα, accus. of ὄνυξ ONYX; in med.L. *onic(h)a*, treated as indecl. or as fem. of 1st decl. The Greek word in the accus. occurs in LXX, Exod. xxx. 34; in the nom. ὄνυξ in Ecclus. xxiv. 16; in the latter case the Vulgate renders it *ungula*, but in the former leaves *onycha* in its Greek form; this, being app. not recognized as the accus. of *onyx*, was treated by mediæval writers as a distinct word; hence in Eng. versions of the Bible.] One of the ingredients in the incense used in the Mosaic ritual; the operculum of a species of *Strombus*, or other marine mollusc, which emits a penetrating aroma when burnt.

This sense of Gr. ὄνυξ, app. due to the resemblance of the πῶμα κογχυλίου 'lid of a shell', or operculum, to a finger-nail, occurs in Dioscorides I. 2, where also mention is made of its fragrant odour 'resembling castor to some degree' when burnt.

1382 WYCLIF *Exod.* xxx. 34 Tak to thee swete smellynge thinges, stacten, and onycha [**1388** onyca], galbantum of good smel [Vulg. *sume..stacten et onycha, galbanum boni odoris*, LXX λάβε..στακτήν, ὄνυχα, χαλβάνην ἡδυσμοῦ]. **1398** TREVISA *Barth. De P.R.* XVII. clxxii. (1495) 713 Thimiama is a certen confeccyon: moost precyously ordenyd and made of Onica and of Stacten, of Galbanus of Thus. **1611** BIBLE *Exod.* xxx. 34 Take vnto thee sweete spices, Stacte, and Onicha, and Galbanum [so *R.V.* 1885; COVERDALE *had* Balme, Stacte, Galban, and pure franckencense]. **1732** tr. *Calmet's Dict. Bible, Onycha*, or *Onyx*, this Word..is put for the odoriferous Nail or Shell, and for the Stone named Onyx... The greatest Part of Commentators explain it by the Onyx, or the odoriferous Shell, which is a Shell like to that of the Shell-fish called Purpura. **1865** *Public Opin.* 7 Jan. 19 The manufacture of perfume by mingling stacte, onycha, and galbanum with pure frankincense.

‖**onychia** (əʊ'nɪkɪə). *Path.* [mod.L., f. Gr. ὄνυξ, ὄνυχ- nail.] Inflammation of the matrix of the nail, or of the adjacent part of finger or toe.

1857 MAYNE *Expos. Lex., Onychia*, term for an abscess near the nail of the fingers; otherwise called whitlow. **1861** BUMSTEAD *Ven. Dis.* (1879) 578 Affections of the nails..of two varieties: in one, called *onychia*, the disease begins in the nails themselves; and in the other, called *perionychia*, it begins in their vicinity and involves them secondarily. **1878** T. BRYANT *Pract. Surg.* I. 179 Onychia maligna is a disease of the nail matrix..far more severe and obstinate.

†'**onychin**, *a.* and *sb. Obs.* [ad. L. *onychin-us*, a. Gr. ὀνύχινος made of or like onyx.]

A. *adj.* in *onychin stone* = Onyx stone.

1382 WYCLIF *Gen.* ii. 12 Ther is foundun bdelyum, and the stoon onychynus [**1388** the stoon onychyn, *v.r.* of onychyn; Vulg. *lapis onychinus*]. **1477** NORTON *Ordin. Alch.* v. in Ashm. (1652) 56 Like in Colour to Onychyne stone.

B. *sb.* (= *onychin stone*). = ONYX 1.

(In quot. 1750 mixed up with notions of ONYCHA.)

1387 TREVISA *Higden* (Rolls) VI. 425 A maner vessel i-made of a stoon þat hatte onichinus, þat was cleer and briȝt. *c* **1400** MAUNDEV. (Roxb.) xxiii. 107 Þe ȝalow er made of topazes or crisolytez;..þe blak of onichyns or geraudes. **1563-87** FOXE *A. & M.* (1596) 134/2 A certeine uessell.. made of the pretious stone onychinus. **1750** tr. *Leonardus' Mirr. Stones* 214 *Onicinus*, tho' it is a Gum from a Tree of its own Name, is yet number'd among Stones... If put upon a live Coal, in the Manner of Incense, it gives a sweet and fragrant Smell.

†**onychite** ('ɒnɪkaɪt). *Obs.* Also in Latin form **onychites**. [ad. L. *onychītis*, a. Gr. ὀνυχῖτις (λίθος) onyx stone: see -ITE[1].] A stalagmitic limestone or marble, having a banded structure like onyx, and highly prized by the ancients; also called *onyx-marble* or *oriental alabaster*.

1568 GRAFTON *Chron.* I. 147 Of the aforesayd Iewels sent by Otto, one was a precious vessell of stone called Onychites. **1651** DAVENANT *Gondibert* II. vi. 45 From Paros' isle was brought the milky white [marble]..From Araby, the blushing onychite. **1706** PHILLIPS, *Onychites*, Alabaster, a sort of Marble. [**1868** DANA *Min.* (ed. 5) 679-80 Stalagmite is the *Alabastrites* (alabaster-stone) in part .. of Theophrastus, Pliny, and other ancient writers..It was also formerly called *onyx* and *onychites*.]

onychogryphosis (ˌɒnɪkəʊgrɪ'fəʊsɪs). *Med.* Also **-gryposis.** [f. Gr. ὀνυχο-, comb. form of ὄνυξ nail + γρύπωσις hooking of the nails.] The condition of having overgrowth, accompanied by thickening and curvature, of one or more nails (usu. of the toes).

1833 DUNGLISON *Dict. Med. Sci.* II. 104/1 Onychogryphosis, onychogryposis. **1887** *Boston Med. & Surg. Jrnl.* CXVII. 301/1 When the whole nail is affected, its free border has a tendency to curve downwards. It may occur in various directions, according as it is disturbed in the vertical or transverse way (onychogryphosis). **1901** *Encycl. Medica* VIII. 220 The subject of onychogryposis was first fully investigated by Virchow. **1972** A. ROOK et al. *Textbk. Dermatol.* (ed. 2) II. 1662/1 Nail hypertrophy implies thickening and increase in length, whilst onychogryphosis implies curvature also.

onychomancy ('ɒnɪkəʊˌmænsɪ). Also 8-9 onyco-. [f. Gr. ὀνυχο-, comb. form of ὄνυξ ONYX + -MANCY.] Divination from the finger-nails.

1652 GAULE *Magastrom.* 165 Onychomancy, [divining] by the nayles. **1727-41** CHAMBERS *Cycl.*, *Onycomancy*, or as some write it, *Onymancy*, a kind of divination by means of the nails of the fingers. **1855** SMEDLEY *Occult Sci.* 324 Chiromancers give the name of Onycomancy, likewise, to the inspection of the natural signs in the nails.

onychomycosis (ˌɒnɪkəʊmaɪ'kəʊsɪs). *Med.* Pl. **-mycoses.** [f. as ONYCHOGRYPHOSIS + MYCOSIS.] Fungal infection of a finger- or toe-nail, causing brittleness and discoloration.

1865 *Dublin Q. Jrnl. Med. Sci.* XL. 353 (*heading*) Two cases of onychomycosis. **1887** *Buck's Handbk. Med. Sci.* V. 104/2 The onychomycoses are..of only two kinds, that due to favus, and tinea tricophytina. **1954** A. C. ALLEN *Skin* xiii. 460/2 Onychomycosis is caused by many species of *Trichophyton* as well as by *Epidermophyton floccosum*, several species of *Aspergillus*, and *Candida albicans*. **1975** *Daily Colonist* (Victoria, B.C.) 5 Mar. 2/1 Onychomycosis (also called ringworm of the nails) is caused by a fungus infection.

onychopathic (ˌɒnɪkəʊ'pæθɪk), *a. rare*$^{-0}$. [f. as ONYCHOMANCY + Gr. πάθος suffering + -IC.] 'Relating to diseases of the nails' (*Syd. Soc. Lex.* 1892).

onychophagist (ɒnɪ'kɒfədʒɪst). Also erron. onygophagist. [f. Gr. ὄνυξ, ὀνυχ- nail + -φάγος eating + -IST.] One who bites his nails. So **onycho'phagia, ony'chophagy**, the habit of biting one's nails.

1834 SOUTHEY *Doctor* iii. (1862) 5 A substitute for biting the nails which I recommend to all onygophagists. **1900** DORLAND *Med. Dict.* 456/1 Onychophagy. **1900** *Daily Chron.* 10 July 5/2 'Onychophagia' is far more frequent in Parisian than in provincial schools. **1903** Onychophagist [cited as unattested correct form of *onygophagist* in *N.E.D.* (q.v.)]. **1907** *Daily News* 4 July 6/7 Dr. Didsbury..suggests that oncyophagists [*sic*] should wear his new dental apparatus, which is fastened to the lower molars and just prevents the upper and lower teeth from meeting. **1956** D. M. PILLSBURY et al. *Dermatol.* xlv. 1017 Onychophagia denotes biting of the free edge of the nail. **1977** *Woman's Jrnl.* Apr. 10 Are you an onychophagist?.. This rather long name simply means that you bite your nails.

onychophorous (ɒnɪ'kɒfərəs), *a. Zool.* [f. as ONYCHOPATHIC *a.* + Gr. -φόρ-ος bearing + -OUS.] Bearing nails or claws; applied to a group (*Onychophori*) of ophidian reptiles having rudimentary hind limbs, and to an order (*Onychophora*) of myriapods, comprising the single genus *Peripatus*, having two chitinoid claws on each limb. So **ony'chophoran** *a.* = ONYCHOPATHIC *a.*; *sb.* an onychophoran myriapod.

1857 MAYNE *Expos. Lex.*, *Onychophorus*, having nails or claws..onychophorous. **1892** in *Syd. Soc. Lex.*

†'**onycle.** *Obs.* Also 6 oynykle. [a. OF. *onicle*, perh. ad. med.L. **onyculus*, dim. of *onyx*; but cf. med.L. *onicleus* = *onycheus*, *onychinus* (Du Cange).] = ONYX 1.

a **1310** in Wright *Lyric P.* v. 25 Ase gernet in golde, ant ruby wel ryht, Ase onycle he ys on y-holden on hyht. **13..** *Owain Miles* (1837) 37 Ribes and salidoines Onicles and causteloines. *a* **1400-50** *Alexander* 5269 Onycles & orfrays & orient perles. *c* **1400** *Tundale* 2078 Amatyste and charbocull alle so, Onycull, tapas and other mo. **1548-9** *Will of J. Hall* (Somerset Ho.), My Rynge of Golde set w[t] an Oynyklestone.

onyli, obs. variant of ONLY.

onym ('ɒnɪm). [ad. Gr. ὄνυμα (stem ὀνυματ-), Æolic form of ὄνομα name: cf. *synonym.*] A proposed term for a technical name, as of a species or other group in zoology, etc., forming part of a recognized system of nomenclature. Hence **'onymal** *a.*, **'onymally** *adv.*, **'onymize** *v.*, **'onymizer, 'onymy** (see quot.).

1884 COUES *New Terms Zoöl. Nomenclature* in *Auk* Oct. 321, I would therefore suggest..as follows:—*Onym*, the tenable technical name of a species or other group in zoölogy, consisting of one or more terms applied conformably with some recognized system of nomenclature. *Onymy*, the doctrine or practice of using onyms; nomenclature in a proper sense. *Onymize*, to make use of onyms; to employ a proper nomenclature... *Onymizer*, one who, or that which onymizes; a nomenclator... *Onymal*, of or pertaining to an onym, or to onymy. *Onymally*, in an onymal manner.

'onymancy. Also 7 oni-. Shortened form of ONYCHOMANCY.

1653 R. SANDERS *Physiogn.* 69 Onimancy is commonly called the science of the nayls. *a* **1693** URQUHART *Rabelais* III. xxv. 208 By Onymancy; for that we have Oyl and Wax. **1727-41** [see ONYCHOMANCY].

onymatic (ɒnɪ'mætɪk), *a.* [f. Gr. ὀνυματ- (see ONYM) + -IC.] Relating to names: see quot.

1860 DE MORGAN *Syllabus Proposed System Logic* 48 Relations which have immediate reference to, or are directly evolved from, the application of names and the mode of thinking about names in connexion with objects named, or with other names, may be called onymatic relations. **1877** JEVONS in *Encycl. Brit.* VII. 66/1 (De Morgan) A new onymatic system of logical expression.

onyment, onymete, obs. ff. OINTMENT, UNIMETE.

onymous ('ɒnɪməs), *a. rare.* [f. Gr. ὄνυμα name (see ONYM) + -OUS: after *anonymous*, etc.] Having or bearing a name; of a writing: Bearing the name of the author; of an author: That gives his name. The opposite of *anonymous*, and usually explicitly contrasted with it.

1775 STURGES in *Lett. to Mr. Granger* 169 My daughter.. found out the anonymous character of Mr. Loveday in the preface, without having heard me read the onymous one in the advertisement. **1802** SOUTHEY in C. Southey *Life* II. 195 An onymous house too..its name is Maes Gwyn. **1864** *N. & Q.* 3rd Ser. V. 307 An opinion..that all communications ought to be onymous. **1888** *Univ. Rev.* Oct. 284 A certain class of critics (whose writings, onymous and anonymous, are to be found in many widely different journals).

So **o'nymity** (*nonce-wd.*), the condition of being 'onymous'; the opposite of *anonymity*.

1897 *Q. Rev.* July 109 With this comes the question of 'onymity' and anonymity, a matter in which all the good is not upon one side.

onymously ('ɒnɪməslɪ), *adv. rare.* [f. ONYMOUS *a.* + -LY[2], after ANONYMOUSLY *adv.*] With the writer's name given or attached.

1889 V. HORSLEY in S. Paget *Sir Victor Horsley* (1919) 86 He anonymously or onymously is not worth powder and shot.

o'nyong-nyong (əʊ'njɒŋnjɒŋ). *Med.* Also onyongnyong. [See quot. 1960.] A mosquito-borne virus disease in East Africa, similar to dengue, which is caused by an arborvirus and carried by anopheles.

1960 A. J. HADDOW et al. in *Trans. R. Soc. Trop. Med. & Hygiene* LIV. 517 (*heading*) O'nyong-nyong fever: an epidemic virus disease. *Ibid.*, The epithet 'o'nyong-nyong' originated among the Acholi, one of the first tribes to be affected, and, being the first recorded, has been selected as the definitive name of the disease. *Ibid.* 518 The Map.. shows the approximate dates at which o'nyong-nyong appeared in the various affected areas in Uganda. **1966** *Guardian* 8 Sept. 2/8 It has recently been established in Africa that a fever virus called onyongnyong is transmitted by the anopheline mosquito. **1974** A. W. WOODRUFF *Med. in Tropics* xxii. 322/1 O'nyong-nyong has caused one very major epidemic which started in Uganda in 1959 and spread to Kenya, Tanzania and Malawi involving an estimated 2 million people.

onys, obs. f. ONCE.

onywar: see UNAWARE.

onyways, onywise, Sc. ff. ANYWAYS, -WISE.

onyx ('ɒnɪks, 'əʊnɪks). Forms: α. 3-4 **oniche**; β. 4-7 **onix**, 7- **onyx**. [a. L. *onyx*, a. Gr. ὄνυξ nail, claw, onyx-stone; OF. *oniche*, *onice*, *onique*.]

1. A variety of quartz allied to agate, consisting of plane layers of different colours: much used for cameos.

a **1300** *Floriz & Bl.* 288 Jacinctes and topaces And oniche of muchel grace. *c* **1305** *Land Cokayne* 92 Beril, onix, topasiune, Ametist and crisolite. **1382** WYCLIF *Ezek.* xxviii. 13 Crisolitus, and onix, and berillus, saphirus, and carbuncle. *c* **1400** MAUNDEV. (Roxb.) xxx. 136 Ane of oniche, anoþer of cristall, anoþer of iaspre. **1567** MAPLET *Gr. Forest* 16 b, Sardonix,..by commixture of the Onix which is white and Sardus which is red. **1601** HOLLAND *Pliny* II. 615 The Indian Onyx hath certaine sparkes in it... As for the Arabian Onyches, there bee found of them blacke, with white circles. **1611** BIBLE *Job* xxviii. 16 It [wisedome] cannot be valued with the golde of Ophir, with the precious Onix, or the Saphire. **1658** PHILLIPS, *Onyx*, a certain pretious Stone,..of whitish colour, resembling the colour of a man's nail. Some say it is the congealed juyce of a Tree called Onycha. **1739** GRAY *Let.* in *Poems* (1775) 43 The glory of their collection, was a vase of an entire onyx, measuring at least five inches over, three deep, and of great thickness.

1861 C. W. KING *Ant. Gems* (1866) 11 The common Onyx has two opaque layers, of different colours, usually in strong contrast to each other.

†**2.** = ONYCHA. *Obs. rare.*

1611 BIBLE *Ecclus.* xxiv. 15, I yeelded a pleasant odour like the best mirrhe, as Galbanum and Onix [COVERD, Clowes], and sweet Storax [Gr. ὡς χαλβάνη καὶ ὄνυξ καὶ στακτή: Vulg. *quasi storax et galbanus et ungula*, whence WYCLIF *vngula*].

3. *Path.* An opacity of the lower part of the cornea of the eye, caused by an infiltration of pus behind it or between its layers, and resembling a finger-nail.

1706 PHILLIPS, *Onyx*,.. Also a Sore or gathering of Matter under the horny Coat of the Eye, the same as *Hypopyon*. **1799** R. HOOPER *Med. Dict.*, *Onyx*, an abscess, or collection of pus between the lamellæ of the cornea; so called from its resemblance to the stone called onyx. **1878** T. BRYANT *Pract. Surg.* I. 317. **1879** *St. George's Hosp. Rep.* IX. 494 One.. had an onyx involving two-thirds of one cornea.

4. *attrib.* and *Comb.*, as ***onyx-cameo***, ***stone***; **onyx-marble** = ONYCHITE.

1535 COVERDALE *1 Chron.* xxx. 2 Onix stones.. & stones of dyuerse coloures. **1611** BIBLE *Gen.* ii. 12 There is bdellium and the onyx stone. *a* **1644** SANDYS (J.), The blue-ey'd saphir, or rich onyx stone. **1866** GEO. ELIOT *F. Holt* i. (1868) 10 Her hands.. lay on her folded black-clad arms like finely-cut onyx cameos. **1892** DANA *Min.* (ed. 6) 268 In the art it is often now called Oriental Alabaster or Onyx-Marble.

oo[1], a frequent ME. spelling of long *ō*, both open and close, as in *boon*, *stoon*:—OE. *bán*, *stán*. Hence in ME. a frequent spelling of O *interj.*; and in Wyclif a name of the Greek long *ō* or Omega.

In the 16th c. *oo* was restricted to the 'close *ō*', normally representing OE. *ó*, as in *doom*:—*dóm*. In mod.Eng. this sound has been raised to (u:), of which sound therefore *oo* is the normal representative, as in *too, cuckoo, cockatoo, cooey*. In Scotch, OE. *ó*, ME. close *ō* has passed into (ø, Y, or y), which sounds are also often etymologically written *oo*, as in *toom*, otherwise *tume, tuim*, empty.

1382 WYCLIF *Rev.* i. 8, I am alpha and oo, the bigynnyng and the endyng.

oo[2], **'oo** (u:), a representation of a child-like pronunciation of *you*.

1713 SWIFT *Jrnl. to Stella* (1948) II. 644, I allow oo Six. **1900** M. CORELLI *Boy* i. 8 Oh, Poo Sing! Does 'oo feels ill? Does 'oo feels bad? **1965** *Listener* 1 July 12/2 There is now an enormous gap between a tiny avant-garde and the vast mass of viewers and listeners, between people who are happy with a painting entitled 'Won't Oo Kiss Doggie?' and the few who can accept 'sculpture' made out of old motorbikes and dustbin lids.

oo[3], **'oo** (u:), a representation of a colloq. (orig. Cockney) or vulgar pronunciation of *who*. So **'oom**, whom.

c **1870** A. LLOYD in W. Matthews *Cockney Past & Present* (1938) 91 Then left me for a feller 'oom she thought was much more grand. **1883** *Kaukneigh Awlminek* 7 People 'oo down't profit by experience is medder then moust loonatics. *Ibid.* 15 There's more then fifty thousan' pussons in Lendin oo can't write. I 'ear thet sem uv 'em is editors. **1901** G. B. SHAW *Capt. Brassbound's Conversion* II. 244 Oo a you orderin abaht, ih? **1903** KIPLING *Five Nations* 199 What *is* the sense of 'atin' those 'Oom you are paid to kill? **1950** C. S. FORESTER *Mr. Midshipman Hornblower* 232, I was wonderin' 'oo'd come to my rescue. **1970** M. MOORCOCK *Chinese Agent* x. 71 Oo's gonna pay for all me lovely china! **1973** J. LEASOR *Host of Extras* viii. 147 ''Oo're you?' he asked belligerently.

oo[4] (əʊəʊ). Also **o-o**. [Hawaiian.] Also ***oo bird***. A black and yellow bird, *Moho braccatus*, belonging to the family Meliphagidæ or honeyeaters and now believed to be extinct.

1890 S. WILSON in *Ibis* II. 179 Large numbers of the O-o must have been taken in old days. **1902** H. W. HENSHAW *Birds Hawaiian Islands* 70 The brilliant shining black body feathers of the o-o were.. in great demand for making cloaks. **1937** D. & H. TEILHET *Feather Cloak Murders* x. 181 The little Oo and Mamo birds.. from which they plucked.. the coloured feathers to make the cloaks. **1944** G. C. MUNRO *Birds Hawaii* 84 If it still exists no effort should be spared to save what would be the last of the famous Hawaiian oos. **1960** *Guardian* 3 Nov. 10/3 Robes made from the tufted feathers of the o-o bird. **1970** S. CARLQUIST *Hawaii* xi. 214 Oos were black, with tufts of yellow feathers extracted to make the yellow feather cloaks. This may well have helped to extinguish the oo. **1977** *Nat. Geographic* Nov. 588/1 (*caption*) Biologist John Sincock.. of the U.S. Fish and Wildlife Service sloshes through Alakai Swamp in hope of spying the yellow-thighed oo.. one of the world's rarest birds.

oo, *v.*: see OOH *v.*

oo, var. O *adj.*, O *adv.*, O *prep.*[1] *oo lesse than* = *on less than*, UNLESS, q.v.

oo- (əʊəʊ), before a vowel **o-**, combining form of Gr. ᾠόν egg, ovum, used in various scientific terms, chiefly biological. (See the more important of these in their alphabetical places.) **ooblast** ('əʊəblæst) [Gr. βλαστός germ], 'the primordial cell which develops into an ovule' (*Syd. Soc. Lex.*); hence **oo'blastic** *a.* **oocyan** (ˌəʊəʊ'saɪən) [Gr. κύανος a dark-blue mineral], a blue pigment occurring in the shells of birds' eggs. **oœcium** (əʊ'i:sɪəm) [Gr. οἰκίον a little house], a bud-like sac in which the ova are received and fertilized in certain Polyzoa; hence **o'œcial** *a.* **oogenesis** (ˌəʊəʊ'dʒɛnɪsɪs) [GENESIS], the production or development of an ovum; so **oogenetic** (ˌəʊəʊdʒɪ'nɛtɪk) *a.*, pertaining to oogenesis. **oogeny** (əʊ'ɒdʒɪnɪ) = *oogenesis*. **oograph** ('əʊəgrɑ:f, -æ-) [-GRAPH], a mechanical device for tracing accurately the outline of a bird's egg. **oometer** (əʊ'ɒmɪtə(r)) [-METER], a mechanical device for taking exact measurements of eggs; so **oometric** (ˌəʊəʊ'mɛtrɪk) *a.*, pertaining to an oometer, or to **o'ometry**, the measurement of eggs. **oophyte** ('əʊəfaɪt) [Gr. φυτόν plant] = OOPHORE. **oorhodeine** (ˌəʊəʊ'rəʊdi:aɪn) [Gr. ῥόδον rose], a reddish pigment found in the shells of most birds' eggs. **ooscopy** (əʊ'ɒskəpɪ) [Gr. ᾠοσκοπία], inspection of or divination from eggs. **oostegite** (əʊ'ɒstɪdʒaɪt) [Gr. στέγειν to cover: see -ITE[1] 3], an egg-case in some Crustacea, formed by an expansion of the limbs of certain somites; hence **oostegitic** (əʊˌɒstɪ'dʒɪtɪk) *a.* ‖**ootheca** (əʊəʊ'θi:kə) [Gr. θήκη case, receptacle], an egg-case in certain invertebrate animals; also, formerly, a sporangium in ferns; hence **oo'thecal** *a.* **ootype** ('əʊətaɪp) [Gr. τύπος impression, TYPE], a dilated portion of the oviduct in some Trematode worms, in which the egg is fertilized and provided with a shell. **ooxanthine** (əʊɒk'sænθaɪn, əʊəʊ'zænθaɪn) [Gr. ξανθός yellow], a yellow pigment occurring in the shells of birds' eggs.

1875 SORBY in *Proc. Zool. Soc.* 355 *Oocyan.. is.. often associated with yellow substances.. therefore the solution is of a somewhat green-blue colour. **1875** NEWTON in *Encycl. Brit.* III. 774 Some chemical relation between the oocyans and the bile. **1881** G. BUSK in *Jrnl. Microsc. Sc.* Jan. 3 The *oœcium is sub-globular and affixed to the upper and outer border of the zoœcium. **1892** *Syd. Soc. Lex.*, *Oögenesis.. *Oögeny. **1925** R. E. SNODGRASS *Anat. & Physiol. Honeybee* xii. 270 The process [of development] in the case of the egg cells involves oogenesis and maturation. **1960** *New Biol.* XXXI. 94 The process of oogenesis must not predetermine the post-fertilization history of the egg. **1974** L. B. AREY *Developmental Anat.* (ed. 7 rev.) iii. 31 The word 'egg' or 'ovum' is often used when referring to any stage in the course of differentiation of the female sex cell during oögenesis. **1895** D. SHARP in *Cambr. Nat. Hist.* V. xxii. 500 Some hypothetic rudiments they [*sc.* Weismann and others] consider to exist at the very earliest stage of the embryonic, or *oogenetic process. **1886** *Athenæum* 25 Dec. 867/1 The correlative growths may assume the characters of the *oophyte or prothallus. **1895** tr. *Kerner's Nat. Hist. Plants* II. 476 In the Fern, two stages are well shown in the life-cycle, (1) the prothallium, the sexual generation or oophyte, and (2) the fern-plant, the asexual generation (or sporophyte). **1875** SORBY in *Proc. Zool. Soc.* 354 *Oorhodeine.. occurs.. in the shells of such a great number of eggs that its entire absence is exceptional. **1875** NEWTON in *Encycl. Brit.* III. 774/2 Inclined to think that oorhodeine is in some way or other closely related to cruentine. **1727** BAILEY vol. II, **Ooscopy*, predictions made from Eggs. **1877** HUXLEY *Anat. Inv. Anim.* vi. 366 The eggs of the ordinary Edriophthalmia usually undergo their development in the chamber beneath the thorax enclosed by the *oostegites of the thoracic appendages. **1851–6** WOODWARD *Mollusca* 136 Spawn (*ootheca) vermiform, thick, semicircular. **1888** ROLLESTON & JACKSON *Forms Anim. Life* 649 In the monogenetic [Trematoda] its [the egg's] shape varies, and is determined by that of the '*ootype'. **1875** SORBY in *Proc. Zool. Soc.* 356 Emu-eggs.. are of a fine malachite green colour, due to a mixture of yellow *ooxanthine with oocyan. *Ibid.* 357 Rufous ooxanthine.. differs from yellow ooxanthine in absorbing light to a.. greater distance from the blue end.

oobit, Sc. form of WOUBIT, woolly-bear.

ooblast, -ic, oocyan: see OO-.

ooc, obs. form of OAK.

oocyst ('əʊəsɪst). [f. OO- + Gr. κύστις CYST.]

a. *Bot.* Name for a supposed reproductive cell in certain Fungi; also = OOGONIUM 1 (*Cent. Dict.*). **b.** *Zool.* A receptacle for the ova in some Polyzoa.

1875 COOKE *Fungi* 176 A distinct cell which De Bary terms an *oocyst*. **1882** OGILVIE, *Oocyst*, a chamber appended to the cells of certain of the Polyzoa, which serves as a receptacle for the eggs. Also called *Ovicell*.

oocyte ('əʊəsaɪt). *Biol.* [f. OO- + -CYTE, as ad. G. *ovocyte* (now *oozyte*) (T. Boveri 1892, in *Anat. Hefte* Abt. II. I. 446): see OVO-.] An egg mother-cell, which gives rise to a mature ovum by meiosis; the ***primary oocyte*** gives rise in meiosis I to the ***secondary oocyte*** and a small polar body; the secondary oocyte gives rise to the mature ovum and another polar body in meiosis II. Also (with some writers), a polar body so produced. Cf. OVOCYTE.

1895 *Jrnl. R. Microsc. Soc.* 511 (*heading*) Peculiar mitosis in young oocytes of salamander. **1927** [see OOTID]. **1945** W. J. HAMILTON et al. *Human Embryol.* ii. 12 The formation of the first polar spindle.. initiates the first maturation, or reduction, division, the oocyte dividing into a larger cell, the secondary oocyte, and a much smaller cell, the first polar body. **1946** B. M. PATTEN *Human Embryol.* ii. 31 The primary oöcyte divides to form two secondary oöcytes. One of these receives little cytoplasm and is called the first polar body. **1968** PASSMORE & ROBSON *Compan. Med. Stud.* I. xxxvii. 10/2 All the primary oocytes so formed begin their first meiotic division before birth, but the completion of prophase is arrested until after puberty... Meiosis restarts in individual oocytes when their follicles undergo maturation in subsequent ovarian cycles... The remainder of the first meiotic division is completed by the time of ovulation, at which time a secondary oocyte is released into the tube. The second meiotic division follows immediately and.. is not normally completed until the oocyte is penetrated by a spermatozoon. **1970** AMBROSE & EASTY *Cell Biol.* xii. 390 Only one ovum is formed from each oöcyte in contradistinction to the four sperm formed from each spermatocyte.

ood, var. OUD.

oodle (u:d(ə)l). Also **-lin** (in sense 1). [Of uncertain origin.] **1.** In *pl.*, large or unlimited quantities; abundance, 'heaps'. *colloq.*

1869 *Overland Monthly* III. 131 A Texan never has a great quantity of any thing, but he has 'scads' of it, or 'oodles', or 'dead oodles', or 'scadoodles', or 'swads'. **1887** J. C. HARRIS in *Century Mag.* Apr. 846/2 All you lack 's the feathers, and we've got oodles of 'em right here. **1892** J. BARLOW *Irish Idylls* iii. 57 A grand young pig, they'll be gettin' oodles o' money on at the fair afore Lent. **1900** ADE *Fables in Slang* 80 Jethro.. had learned Oodles of slang up in Chicago. **1904** W. N. HARBEN *Georgians* 115 An' now *you*, a man with oodlin's an' oodlin's o' pore blood kin.. are a helpin' at the job. **1919** H. L. WILSON *Ma Pettengill* iii. 78 It snowed hard. Just oodles of the most perfectly dazzling snow. **1928** *Daily Sketch* 7 Aug. 6/2 With oodles of 'Och Ayes', more Scots than ever bled with Wallace have flooded the office with caustic correspondence. **1929** D. G. MACKAIL *How Amusing!* 409 You wouldn't catch *me* coming down to the City every day, if I'd got oodles of boodle like that. **1940** O. NASH *Face is Familiar* 7 And he had one object all sublime, Which was to save simply oodles of time. **1957** *Sunday Times* 14 Apr. 13/3 Oodles for the rich, and practically nothing for the poor. **1967** *She* Dec. 95/1 The cover assures me that there are 'oodles of prizes', which indeed there are. **1975** *New Yorker* 19 May 95/2 (Advt.), Front and back yokes and oodles of shirring for fullness.

2. *Austral.* and *N.Z. slang.* Money in general. *rare.*

1941 in BAKER *Dict. Austral. Slang* 51.

oœcium: see OO-.

oo-er (u:'ɜ:(r)), *int.* Also **ooo-er**. An exclamation expressing surprise, wonder, etc.

1912 C. MACKENZIE *Carnival* ix. 104 'Oo-er!' cried Jenny. 'We aren't going to sleep in the dark?' **1926** C. BEATON *Diary* 18 Oct. in *Wandering Yrs.* (1961) 143 Everyone 'talked common'—the smart thing to do at the moment: 'That's a bit of all right; I don't mind if I do; oo-er!' **1933** D. L. SAYERS *Murder must Advertise* x. 169 When told what he had missed he merely remarked 'Oo-er!' **1934** R. FERGUSON *Celebrated Sequels* 246 Those who saunter, cry 'oo-er', bathe, knit. **1955** M. ALLINGHAM *Beckoning Lady* xvi. 223 'Oo-er.' Tonker bristled. **1958** S. HYLAND *Who goes Hang?* xvi. 73 'Oo-er,' said Alec Beasley, vulgarly. **1961** *Guardian* 20 Jan. 7/4 The reader will either dutifully say, 'Oo-er!' or ..'Come off it!' **1977** J. SAVAGE *Nemesis Club* vi. 76 Ian's mouth fell open. 'Ooo-er!'

ooes, obs. form of OOZE.

oof (u:f). *slang.* [Understood to be short for *oof-tish*, Yiddish for Ger. *auf tische*, i.e. *auf dem tische* 'on the table', i.e. (money) laid on the table, (money) down; cf. Ger. *auftischen* to table.] Money. Also in the fuller form **'ooftish**. Hence **oof-bird**, a source or supplier of money, 'the goose that lays the golden eggs'; **'oofiness**, wealth; **'oofless** *a.*, without cash; **'ooflessness**, lack of cash; **'oofy** *a.*, wealthy.

[**1882** MISS BRADDON *Mt. Royal* III. viii. 170 'It will be too lovely—too utterly oufish', exclaimed Dopsy, who had lately acquired this last flower of speech.] **1885** *Sporting Times* 28 Feb. 1/1 The subject of oof is enough to interest anybody. [With Cockney pun on *'oof = hoof*.] **1888** RIDER HAGGARD *Col. Quaritch* xxviii, Living like a fighting-cock and rolling in 'oof'. *Ibid.* II. xiv, 'Is he an oof bird?' (rich) 'Rather', answered the Tiger. **1888** *Bird o' Freedom* 10 Oct. 5/2 When Jack is on the spree His love may be termed free, And the tarts will oofless be Till his ship comes back. **1889** E. DOWSON *Let.* 18 Jan. (1967) 26, I shall be very oofless tho' & must I fear be a Pinolitic pittite on the occasion. *Ibid.* 17 Mar. (1967) 50, I foresee great—great—ooflessness—as the result of this week—much dissipation. **1891** *Daily News* 21 Dec., 'I would commit any crime for oof.' **1892** J. W. PEARCE in *Mod. Society* 16 Jan., 'Oof' as a current pseudonym for money has been in use for about seven years, but 'ooftish', which also is Whitechapel slang for coin of the realm, has been in use in England over thirty years. **1894** I. ZANGWILL *King of Schnorrers* 249 No treasury.. no oof, rhino, shiners, coin, cash, salary. **1896** *Blackw. Mag.* Dec. 727 My oofy maiden-aunt. **1899** FRYERS *Pauper Millionaire* 157 'What is oof?' 'Oof? Why ooftish, posh, money.' **1899** BINSTEAD *Houndsditch Day by Day* 33 Ooftish. **1935** WODEHOUSE *Luck of Bodkins* xvii. 211 His amazing oofiness had a tendency to slip from the mind.

oof, obs. form of WOOF.

oof, var. OUF, OUFF *int.*

oogamous (əʊ'ɒgəməs), *a. Biol.* [f. OO- + Gr. γάμ-ος marriage + -OUS.] Applied to organisms which reproduce (or to reproduction) by union of dissimilar (male and female) cells; *spec.* when one of these (the female cell or ovum) is stationary and fertilized by the motile male cell. So **oogamete** (əʊ'ɒgəmi:t), either of the two (male and female) cells in oogamous reproduction; o'**ogamy**, oogamous reproduction.

1888 *Athenæum* 29 Dec. 886/2 The sexual cells being zoogametes..its affinity is rather with Pandorineæ than with oogamous Volvoceæ. **1891** HARTOG in *Nature* 17 Sept. 484/1 True Parthenogenesis: the direct development of a facultative gamete without karyogamy..may occur in.. Oogametes. **1894** S. H. VINES *Students' Text-bk. Bot.* 225 Oogamy: the female organ is an oogonium. **1897** *Syd. Soc. Lex.*, *Reproduction, oögamous*, reproduction by means of an *ovum* or *ova*. **1933** G. M. SMITH *Fresh-Water Algae U.S.* 288 The evolution from isogamy to oögamy may be independent of any evolution in thallus structure. **1971** P. H. B. TALBOT *Princ. Fungal Taxon.* vii. 91 Oogamy, such as occurs in some of the lower fungi, is but a specialized form of gametangial contact.

oogenesis, -genetic, -geny: see OO-.

oogonial (əʊə'gəʊnɪəl), *a.* [f. OOGONIUM + -AL.] Of or pertaining to an oogonium.

1902 *Science* 21 Mar. 457/1 The protoplasm in contact with the oogonial wall. **1938** G. M. SMITH *Cryptogamic Bot.* I. ii. 74 An oögonial mother cell..may be terminal or intercalary in position. **1970** J. WEBSTER *Introd. Fungi* 73 The oogonial initial is multinucleate.

‖**oogonium** (əʊəʊ'gəʊnɪəm). *Bot.* Also rarely in anglicized form oogone. Pl. oogonia. [mod.L., dim. of Gr. *ᾠογόνος egg-layer (cf. ᾠογονία laying of eggs).] **1.** The female reproductive organ in the Thallophytes or lower Cryptogams, usually a rounded cell or sac containing one or more *oospheres*.

Usually distinguished from the flask-shaped *archegonium* of the higher Cryptogams, but sometimes including this.

1867 HOGG *Microsc.* II. i. 293 Organs similar to those long since discovered by Tulasne in *Peronospora*, which have been called *Oogonia*. **1874** COOKE *Fungi* 170 Here, as in the Algæ, the spermatozoids introduce themselves into the cavity of the oogonium, and unite with the gonospheres. **1885** KLEIN *Micro-Org.* 146 At the end of a mycelial thread a cell grows up into a spherical large ball, the *oogonium*.

2. *Biol.* [coined in Ger. as *ovogonium* (T. Boveri 1892, in *Anat. Hefte* Abt. II. I. 446): see OVO-.] A primordial female reproductive cell that gives rise to primary oocytes by mitosis.

1895 *Jrnl. R. Microsc. Soc.* 511 The oogonia show a nucleus with few chromatin fragments and a very delicate, but dense linin-framework. **1920** L. DONCASTER *Introd. Study Cytol.* v. 61 After a number of divisions..the spermatogonia and oogonia cease to divide and begin to increase considerably in size. At this stage they are called primary spermatocytes..and oocytes. **1940** G. A. BAITSELL *Human Biol.* xii. 319 The immature egg or oögonium. **1970** AMBROSE & EASTY *Cell Biol.* x. 330 In the female the oögonia, corresponding to spermatogonia, give rise to oöcytes.

oograph: see OO-.

ooh (uː), *int.* Also oo, ooohh, etc. [var. OH *int.* (*sb.*)] An exclamation of pain, surprise, wonder, disapprobation, etc. Hence as *sb.*; also **ooh-a(a)h, ooh and ah.**

1916 E. O'NEILL *Bound East for Cardiff* in *Provincetown Plays* 1st Ser. 16 It hurts like hell—here... I guess my old pump's busted. Ooohh! **1919** G. B. SHAW *Great Catherine* iv. 152 Agh!! (*She has again applied her toe*). Oh! Oo! *Ibid.* 154 Agh! Ooh! Stop! Oh Lord! **1939** JOYCE *Finnegans Wake* I. 149 Wee skillmustered shoul with his ooh, hoodoodoo! **1957** R. HOGGART *Uses of Literacy* vi. 165 A world so complex that even those who are immersed in the business of tending its more important machines can only hope to understand a little of it, is daily reduced to a local and spuriously manageable 'ooh-aah', when the paper drops on the mat. **1964** L. DEIGHTON *Funeral in Berlin* xlviii. 301 There was a great 'Ooohh' and 'Aaahh' as the rocket burst. **1975** *Times* 19 Feb. 14/1 The oohs and ahs of a 13-year-old schoolgirl contemplating the Osmonds. **1976** *New Musical Express* 12 Feb. 24/2 All that mopery and Ooooh, it's so hard and lonely at the top. **1977** F. PARRISH *Fire in Barley* ii. 19 Ooh, she's a powerful snob.

ooh (uː), *v.* Also oo. [var. OH *v.*] *intr.* To say 'ooh'; also *trans.*, to express with the sound 'ooh'. Freq. in conjunction with AH *v.* Also in reduplicated form *ooh-ooh*.

1953 POHL & KORNBLUTH *Space Merchants* (1955) x. 102 Above me the respectable Costa Rican consumers oohed and ahed at the view from the prism windows. **1957** 'P. QUENTIN' *Suspicious Circ.* i. 7 Monique was oohing and aahing about 'bone structure' and 'divinity of movement'. **1960** [see AH *v.*]. **1961** W. SANSOM *Last Hours of Sandra Lee* 112 Mouths ooed and nummed noises of appreciation. **1963** *Times* 8 May 5/6 Vociferous idiots who 'ooh' and 'ah' every time their favourites..set two feet off the stage. **1964** W. MARKFIELD *To Early Grave* (1965) iv. 75 Where do you come off with..that moaning and groaning, that ooh-ing and aah-ing? **1965** J. B. PRIESTLEY *Lost Empires* III. x. 273 People laughed and clapped and Oo'd and Ah'd. **1971** A. MORICE *Death of Gay Dog* xiii. 141 He..oohed and ahed his way through the column in quite the proper spirit. **1977** *New Musical Express* 12 Feb. 14/5 Pumping their arms in unison, pirouetting and ooh-oohing like crazy, they're very slick, very infectious and warmly humorous.

ooh-la-la ('uːlɑːlɑː), *int.* Also oo-la-la, oolala, etc. [ad. F. *ô là! là!*] An exclamation of surprise, appreciation, etc. Hence as *sb.*, (*a*) the interjection 'ooh-la-la'; (*b*) *slang*, the 'naughtiness' popularly associated with the French; 'spiciness'; (*c*) an attractive or provocative girl. Also *attrib.* or as *adj.*, and as *v. intr.*

1924 *Dialect Notes* V. 274 Exclamations in American English (*title*)..oo(h):..—la la. **1940** E. A. ROBERTSON *Summer's Lease* xx. 269 He went to France..believing that French girls were all 'Oo la la and snatch my garter'. **1943** HUNT & PRINGLE *Service Slang* 49 *Oolala*, Army French meaning O.K. or 'hot stuff'. **1950** BROOKS & WARREN *Fund. Good Writing* xii. 402 Bug-eyed young matrons oo-la-la-ing over the purchase of sheets or toothbrushes. **1952** 'J. TEY' *Singing Sands* xiii. 215 'I like my iniquity with some ooh-la-la in it.' 'Hasn't Daphne got any ooh-la-la?' 'No. Daphne's very la-di-da.' **1952** S. J. PERELMAN *Ill-Tempered Clavichord* (1953) 72 Their silken ankles a target for the ardent glances of gendarmes twirling spiked mustaches and muttering appreciative ooh-la-las. **1959** *Spectator* 24 July 102/3 The ooh-la-la French maid. **1960** I. CROSS *Backward Sex* 72 If this red-haired oo-la-la gets out of hand, I'll fix her for you. **1961** *Sunday Express* 7 May 17/2 The Swiss rely on precision..and the French on oo-la-la. **1970** S. J. PERELMAN *Baby, it's Cold Inside* 161 The playful slaps and oo-la-la's that rang through the valley reassured us that they were still alive. **1973** *Times* 10 Apr. 7/6 Those two great standbys of French fashion, quality and a little bit of ooh-la-la. **1973** A. HUNTER *Gently French* viii. 75 He gave a dirty laugh. 'I've heard about her [*sc.* a French-woman]. When do you get to the ooh la la?' **1975** J. F. BURKE *Death Trick* (1976) vii. 89 'I'll have a French Seventy-five,' she said. Cathleen said, '*Oo! La-la!*' and started a split of bubbly.

ooid ('əʊɔɪd). *Petrol.* [a. G. *ooid* (E. Kalkowsky 1908, in *Zeitschr. f. deutsch. geol. Ges.* LX. 72), f. Gr. ᾠοειδής egg-shaped.] = OOLITH.

[**1918** *Jrnl. Geol.* XXVI. 593 For an individual grain of an oölite the term 'ovulite'.. appears to be preferable to Kalkowsky's 'oöid'.] **1945** *Univ. Texas Publ.* No. 4301. 136/1 *Oöid*, the individual tiny spheroid in an oölitic rock. **1949** H. W. FAIRBAIRN *Struct. Petrol. Deformed Rocks* (ed. 2) iii. 49 Early structural studies of ooids include those of Albert Heim and Loretz. **1965** J. T. GREENSMITH *Hatch & Rastall's Petrol. Sedimentary Rocks* (ed. 4) viii. 199 A normal oolitic limestone or oolitic calcarenite is made up of an aggregate of spherical allochems called ooliths or ooids, usually about 1 mm. or less in diameter. **1974** *Nature* 15 Feb. 452/1 The formation is mainly dolomitic... It contains desiccation cracks,..oöids and algal stromatolites.

ooidal (əʊ'ɔɪdəl), *a.* [f. Gr. ᾠοειδής egg-shaped + -AL[1].] Resembling an egg; oval.

1836 PRICHARD *Phys. Hist. Man.* (ed. 3) I. II. v. §2. 281 This form of skull, I shall term..the oval or ooidal form.

oojah ('uːdʒɑː). *slang.* Also **oojar, ujah.** [Of uncertain origin.] A substitute expression used to indicate vaguely a thing of which the speaker cannot at the moment recall the name, or which he does not care to specify precisely; a 'what-you-may-call it', gadget. So in extended forms **ooja-ka-piv** ('uːdʒɑːkəpɪv), **(ujah-ka-piv), oojah-capiff** ('uːdʒɑːkəpɪf), **ooja-ka-pivi** ('uːdʒɑːkəpɪvɪ), **(ooja-ka-pivvy, oojah capivvy).** See also next word. So **oojah-cum-spiff** *a.*, all right, 'O.K.'.

1917 W. MUIR *Observations of Orderly* xiv. 229 'Oojah', anything. **1925** FRASER & GIBBONS *Soldier & Sailor Words* 215 *Oojah* (*also Ooja-ka-pivi*), a substitute expression for anything the name of which a speaker cannot momentarily think of, *e.g.* 'Pass me that h-m, h-m, oojah-ka-pivi, will you?' **1930** WODEHOUSE *Very Good, Jeeves!* i. 25 'All you have to do,' I said, 'is to carry on here for a few weeks more, and everything will be oojah-cum-spiff.' **1931** J. VAN DRUTEN *London Wall* II. ii. 73 There's a whole lot in the Oojah Capivvy now. **1933** PARTRIDGE *Words, Words, Words!* III. 192 For *thingummy*, Tommy says *oojah*, with variants *oojah-ka-piv*, *oojah-cum-pivvy*, and *oojiboo*. **1935** D. L. SAYERS *Gaudy Night* viii. 178 Oh, look! your bag's opened itself wide and all the little oojahs have gone down the steps. **1941** P. KENDALL *Gone with Draft* 118 An oojah..a gadget. **1943** HUNT & PRINGLE *Service Slang* 49 *Oojah*, sauce or custard. **1951** *Landfall* V. 89 For Pete's sake, boy, don't lose that little oojah. **1962** *Sunday Times* 4 Feb. 31/6 This was the catch-phrase in a music-hall song in use during the first world war... I remember the line and the tune: 'You cannot eat it, or see it, or hear it—you just ask for Ujah-ka-piv. *Ibid.*, 'Ujah'..was used as widely and as indiscriminately as 'gimmick' and 'gadget' are used now. **1966** 'L. LANE' *ABZ of Scouse* 78 *Whur's ther ojah-capiff?*, where is the hammer, spanner or whatever it might be? **1971** B. W. ALDISS *Soldier Erect* 94 I've seen blokes in hot countries go clean round the oojar because of the perverted practices of native women.

oojiboo (ˌuːdʒɪ'buː). *Soldiers' slang.* [Arbitrary extension of OOJ(AH, with meaningless suffix.] = prec. So (by metathesis) **oobyjiver** (ˌuːbɪ'dʒaɪvə(r)).

1918 *Daily Express* 2 Oct. 2/5 The oojiboo may be a hammer, a saw, a spanner, but Jimmy, or anyone else, knows exactly what is wanted. *Ibid.*, A laundry van bumped into me and carried away my oojiboo [*sc.* a tail lamp]. *Ibid.*, I dropped the old oojiboo [*sc.* kitbag] on the platform and nipped into the refreshment-room. Wasn't gone two minutes, but d—n me if somebody hadn't won the oojiboo [stolen the kitbag]. **1925** FRASER & GIBBONS *Soldier & Sailor Words* 215 *Oojiboo*, much the same as Oojah. **1933** [see OOJAH]. **1963** *New Society* 22 Aug. 5/2 Colourful words like 'oobyjiver', meaning 'whatsis' pop up regularly.

ook (ʊk). *slang.* [Origin unknown.] Something slimy, sticky, or otherwise unpleasant. Hence '**ooky** *a.*, slimy, viscous, repellent; also *fig.*

1964 S. BELLOW *Herzog* (1965) 277 He writes poems and reads them to Mama... He looks ooky when he says them. **1969** DISCH & SLADEK *Black Alice* viii. 81 She had been.. glad..to be here, to be anywhere so long as it marked an end, so long as she could..take a shower to wash off all this brown ook. *Ibid.* 85 'Ain't no shower,' Clara declared flatly. 'A bath, then? I want to wash this ook off of me.' *Ibid.* xiv. 158 The milk was so warm and ooky it was like yogurt.

ook, *obs.* f. OAK; obs. pa. t. of ACHE *v.*; Sc. f. WEEK.

ookroo, variant of OKRA.

‖**oolakan, -chan** ('uːləkən). Also ou-; **olachen, oolaghan, oolichan, ulichan;** and EULACHON. [f. Chinook *ûlakân*. Var. EULACHON.] The candle-fish (*Thaleichthys pacificus*) of north-western America (see CANDLE *sb.* 7). Also *attrib.*, as *oolakan oil*; **oolakan rake,** an implement used for raking these fish into the boat when in shoals.

1834 W. F. TOLMIE *Jrnl.* 16 Apr. (1963) 275 The canoes were laden with..dried herring spawn which they are to barter for Oolaghans. **1836** SIR J. RICHARDSON *Fauna Boreali-Amer.* III. 226 The Indian name of this fish is Oulachan... The oulachan spawns in the different small streams which fall into the lower part of the Columbia. **1849** A. ROSS *Adventures First Settlers Oregon River* vi. 97 There is a small fish resembling the smelt or herring, known by the name of ulichan, which enters the river in immense shoals, in the spring of the year. **1881** *Nature* XXIV. 39/2 A new medicinal oil..known as Oolachan Oil..Obtained from a fish called by the North American Indians Oolachan, or candle fish..from the fact that when dried the fish..can be used as..a candle. **1911** J. G. FRAZER *Golden Bough: Magic Art* (ed. 3) I. v. 262 The Tsimshian Indians of British Columbia believe that twins..can..call the salmon and the olachen or candle-fish. **1926** B. A. MCKELVIE *Huldowget* 2 They came today for the oolichan fishing. **1953** *Beaver* Mar. 40/2 Oolikan, olachan, eulachon, uthlecan, hollikan and hoolican—spell it as you wish. *Ibid.* 43/1 Exchange value of a large box of olachen grease equalled one caribou skin..or $1.50 in cash, a century ago. **1965** *Fisherman* (Vancouver) 19 Mar. 2/5 Robichaud said commercial exploitation of eulachons was banned by regulation. **1972** *Evening Telegram* (St. Johns, Newfoundland) 15 July 34/4 Fried and steamed clams, oysters, halibut and oolichans. **1975** H. WHITE *Raincoast Chron.* (1976) 176/2 There were oolachen oil street lamps on cross beams in front of each house.

oo-la-la, oolala, varr. OOH-LA-LA *int.*

oold, pl. ooldys, obs. form of WELD, dyer's weed.

oolie, variant of *ulyie*, Sc. form of OIL.

oolite ('əʊəlaɪt). *Min.* and *Geol.* [a. F. *oölithe* (Dict. Acad. 1762), mod.L. *oölītēs*, f. Gr. ᾠόν egg + λίθος stone: see -LITE.]

1. *Min.* A concretionary limestone composed of small rounded granules, like the roe of a fish, each consisting of carbonate of lime around a grain of sand as a nucleus; roe-stone. In later usage restricted to that of the geological formation in 2.

[**1785** HUTTON in *Trans. R. Soc. Edin.* I. (1788) 252 Among these, are different species of *oolites* marble.] **1802–3** tr. *Pallas's Trav.* (1812) I. 425 Which consists of shelly fragments and small grained oolites. **1807** AIKIN *Dict.* II. 45 Oölite..occurs in mass and is without lustre. **1833** LYELL *Princ. Geol.* III. 215 A white oolite. **1884** W. J. LOFTIE in *Pall Mall Gaz.* 18 Aug. 1/2 The railways did not yet bring oolite from the hills of Bath.

2. *Geol.* The name of an important series of fossiliferous rocks of the character described in sense 1, lying between the Chalk, or the Wealden, and the Lias; sometimes applied to the whole series of limestones, sandstones, and clays, to which these belong; now usually included, with the Lias, in the Jurassic system.

The series is generally subdivided in England into the Upper or Portland Oolite, the Middle, Great, or Oxford Oolite, and the Lower or Bath Oolite.

1816 W. SMITH *Strata Ident.* 30 Distinguished from the under Oolite. **1822** CONYBEARE & PHILLIPS *Outl. Geol.* II. ii. §1. 119 The interval between the chalk and oolites. **1842** MILLER *O.R. Sandst.* xi. (ed. 2) 253 We find..the Great Oolite uptilted against it [the gneiss] on the eastern coast of Sutherland. **1862** SMILES *Engineers* III. 315 It consisted of shale of the lower oolite. **1878** HUXLEY *Physiogr.* 36.

3. *attrib.* Pertaining to or consisting of oolite; oolitic.

1813 BAKEWELL *Introd. Geol.* (1815) 357 The coal formation..rises from under the oolite lime-stone. **1816** W. SMITH *Strata Ident.* 27 The covering of the upper Oolite rock. **1851** RICHARDSON *Geol.* i. 9 The geological site of the locality, which is about the middle of the oolite formation. **1854** RONALDS & RICHARDSON *Chem. Technol.* (ed. 2) I. 32 The limestones of the oolite group which constitute the Jura.

4. = OOLITH.

1851 H. T. DE LA BECHE *Geol. Observer* viii. 123 The little grains termed oolites, formed of concentric coatings of calcareous matter. **1907** E. H. ADYE *Mod. Lithology* xii. 60 The oolites..formed in shallow waters are cemented together by calcareous material. **1955** E. E. WAHLSTROM *Petrographic Mineral.* x. 335 Most oolites in clastic rocks contain a nucleus of organic matter, a fragment of shell, or a more or less rounded silicate or carbonate particle. **1961** J. H. JOHNSON *Limestone-Building Algae* 256 Algal pisolites are composed of more or less spherical masses ranging in sizes from that of a large oolite to spherules having a diameter as much as an inch across.

oolith ('əʊəlɪθ). *Petrol.* [f. Gr. ᾠόν egg + λίθος stone (see -LITH).]

Mod.L. *oolithus* occurs in this sense in 1721 (F. E. Brückmann *Specimen Physicum Exhibens Historiam Naturalem Oolithi seu Ovariorum Piscium et Concharum in*

Saxa Mutatorum 5) and may be the source of both this word and OOLITE (= ad. F. *oölithe*).]

Each of the small rounded granules of which oolite is composed.

1788 J. H. DE MAGELLAN *A. F. Cronstedt's Ess. Syst. Mineral.* (ed. 2 rev.) I. 76 The Stalagmites..get a mammillary form, whilst the Stalactites acquire a conic figure: the Oolithes and Pisolites belong to the same species. **1892** *Jrnl. R. Microsc. Soc.* 839 These ooliths are undoubtedly the product of a lime-separating Schizophyte; and the author believes this to be the case with the greater number of the marine calcareous ooliths with a regular zoned and radial structure. **1926** G. W. TYRRELL *Princ. Petrol.* xiii. 227 The grains are called ooliths and the rock containing them oolite or oolitic limestone. Ooliths generally show a series of concentric coats of calcareous material in which a radiating crystalline structure can often be made out. **1938** M. BLACK *Hatch & Rastall's Petrol. Sedimentary Rocks* (ed. 3) viii. 175 A normal oolite is made up of an aggregate of spherical bodies, called ooliths, usually about 1 mm. or less in diameter, cemented by some interstitial material, usually calcite. **1971** I. G. GASS et al. *Understanding Earth* i. 31/2 Ooliths are formed in environments where calcite is being precipitated and there is strong and continuous wave action.

oolitic (əʊəʊˈlɪtɪk), *a.* [f. OOLITE + -IC: in mod.F. *oölithique* (in Littré).]

1. *Min.* Of the structure of oolite or roe-stone.

1796 KIRWAN *Elem. Min.* (ed. 2) II. 179 Pisiform, or granular iron ore..Of this sort is the Oolitic Ore found at Creusot near Mount Cenis. **1878** LAWRENCE tr. *Cotta's Rocks Class.* 85 Oolitic texture is only found in limestones and ironstones, and it consists either in the entire mass being composed of small globules, or a great number..of such being contained in the mass.

2. *Geol.* Of or pertaining to the Oolite formation; Jurassic.

1832 DE LA BECHE *Geol. Man.* (ed. 2) 311 This group is.. composed of various alternations of clays, sandstones, marls, and limestones; many of the latter being oolitic, whence the name *oolitic series*. **1849** DANA *Geol.* ix. (1850) 495 The coal beds are of the Oolitic epoch. **1878** HUXLEY *Physiogr.* 118 It is the limestones of the Oolitic formations that furnish most of the springs.

ooliˈtiferous, *a.* *rare*$^{-0}$. [f. as prec. + -IFEROUS.] Producing or containing oolite.

1864 in WEBSTER.

oological (əʊəʊˈlɒdʒɪkəl), *a.* [f. as OOLOGY: see -ICAL. Cf. mod.F. *oölogique* (Littré).] Of or relating to oology.

1861 J. LAMONT *Seahorses* vi. 85 Multitudes of gulls, fulmars, eider-ducks, and alcas..in a state of great perturbation at Bruin's oological researches. **1864** *Reader* 30 Apr. 556/2 The only egg of *Æpyornis maximus* which ever came to this country..the unique oological specimen. **1875** NEWTON in *Encycl. Brit.* III. 774/1 *note*, Oological works with coloured figures.

So **ooˈlogic** *a.*; **ooˈlogically** *adv.*

In mod. Dictionaries.

oologist (əʊˈɒlədʒɪst). [f. as next + -IST.]

a. One versed in oology. **b.** A collector of birds' eggs.

1863 *Spring Lapl.* 38, I had two or three naturalist friends in the town..one of them a keen oologist. **1875** NEWTON in *Encycl. Brit.* III. 773/1 The greatest scientific triumph of oologists lies in their having fully appreciated the intimate alliance of the Limicolae with the Gaviae. **1891** *Spectator* 21 Feb., Our egg-collector calls himself an oologist..it is not a pretty name, but it enjoys a Greek derivation, and a scientific sound.

oologize (əʊˈɒlədʒaɪz), *v. rare.* [f. next + -IZE.]

a. *intr.* To collect eggs. **b.** *trans.* To take the eggs from (a nest).

1870 LOWELL *Study Wind.* I. 21 The children of a man employed about the place oologized the nest. *Ibid.* 22 The red squirrel, I think..oölogizes, I know he eats cherries.

oology (əʊˈɒlədʒɪ). [mod. f. Gr. ᾠό-ν egg + -λογία -LOGY: cf. mod.L. *oologia* (Garmann 1691); mod.F. *oölogie* (Littré).] **a.** The study of, or a description of, birds' eggs; that department of ornithology which treats of the eggs of birds, esp. in regard to their external appearance. **b.** The practice of collecting birds' eggs.

1831-7 W. C. HEWITSON (*title*) British Oology; being Illustrations of the Eggs of British Birds, with Figures of each Species. **1869** LOWELL *Wks.* (1890) III. 217 Since bird-nesting has become scientific and dignified itself as oölogy. **1883** *Nature* XXVII. 308/1 Australian birds, whose nidification and oology had previously been imperfectly known.

‖**oolong** (ˈuːlɒŋ). Also ou-. [Chinese *wulung*, f. *wu* black + *lung* dragon.] A dark variety of cured tea.

1852 MCCULLOCH *Dict. Comm.* (new ed.) 1302 Prices Current of the Various Descriptions of Teas..Ning Yong and Oolong, common to fine. **1858** SIMMONDS *Dict. Trade*, *Oolong*, a peculiar description of black tea, possessing many of the qualities of green tea. **1880** *Trade advt.*, The finest Oolong, 3*s.* a lb. This is high burnt, very pungent tea, and is an especial favourite with the tea-drinking public in America. **1898** *Westm. Gaz.* 7 May 8/1 The competition for Oolongs, some Souchongs, and flowery Pekoes is still very keen.

‖**oom** (oːm). *S. Afr.* [Afrikaans, = Du. *oom*, G. *oheim*, OE. *ēam* EME.] Uncle: often used as a respectful appellation when referring to or addressing an older or elderly man.

1822 W. J. BURCHELL *Trav. S. Afr.* I. xvii. 433 Old Lucas, or as he was more familiarly called, *Oom Hans* (Uncle Hans), now turned back with us. **1883** 'R. IRON' *Story Afr. Farm* II. xii. 227 At the farmhouses where he stopped the 'ooms' and 'tantes' remembered clearly the spider with its four grey horses. **1885** J. NIXON *Compl. Story Transvaal* vi. 116 Sir Theophilus Shepstone, by direction of the High Commissioner, applied to Paul Kruger, inviting him to help with a Boer force; but 'Oom' (uncle) Paul, as he was familiarly termed, declined. **1889** H. A. BRYDEN *Kloof & Karroo* i. 42 Mr. Pieter Maynier, familiarly called by Graaff Reinetters, 'Oom Piet' (Oom, or uncle, being a term of affection in South Africa). **1913** C. PETTMAN *Africanderisms* 349 *Oom* Paul, the ordinary designation of the President of the late Transvaal Republic. **1923** *Radio Times* 28 Sept. 8/2 'Oom Jannie', as he [*sc.* Smuts] is known among his own people. **1951** L. G. GREEN *Grow Lovely* i. 17 That lean old man..—Oom Cappy van der Westhuysen is his name. **1971** *Rand Daily Mail* 27 Mar. 5/5 Mr. Sneech, still active and still running his business, is known to almost every citizen as 'Oom Harry'. **1974** *State* (Columbia, S. Carolina) 28 Mar. 15-B/5 Why is it that man has to remain constantly at war with himself, oom Paul?

'oom: see OO^3.

oometer, -metric, -metry: see OO-.

oomiak, var. UMIAK (Eskimo boat).

oompah, oom-pah (ˈuːmpɑː). Also **oompa, umpah.** [Imitative.] A repetitive monotonous sound characteristic of a bass brass-instrument; hence, an instrument that makes such a sound. Also in reduplicated forms ***oompah-oompah***, ***oomp-pah-pah***. Also *attrib.* and as *v. trans.*

1877 *Brooklyn Monthly* Oct. 21/2 If a young lady takes her place at the piano to sing, it is your duty as a gentleman to accompany her with a very bass 'oom-pah, oom-pah, bum, bum, bum'. **1896** *Scribner's Mag.* July 16/2 And some, near the elephant, have set aside money sufficient for a day within sound of Seidl's orchestra, yet they prefer the oom-pah bands of rusted brass. **1904** ADE *True Bills* 86 He practised until he was able to crawl inside of a big Oom-pah and eat all of the Low Notes in the Blue Book. **1919** *Red Cross Mag.* Mar. 4/2 But the bands still bang and *oom-pah*. **1924** P. ROSENFELD *Port of N.Y.* 72 And the sheer noise..the 'rhythmic oompa of brasses'..saturate him, thrill grim, rough sardonic joy up in him. **1926** *Scribner's Mag.* Sept. 303/2 A genuine, imported, inimitable oompah, a horn among horns, grotesque, gigantic, inescapable. **1927** R. HUGHES *Patent Leather Kid* 224 That's the ole oompah-oompah horn... I nachelly gotta git that oompah. **1929** W. THURMAN *Blacker the Berry* 122 A brutal sliding trumpet call on the trombone..an umpah, umpah by the brass horn ..and the orchestra was playing another dance tune. **1930** I. GOLDBERG *Tin Pan Alley* 272 It was an oom-pah, oom-pah in quick tempo. **1951** AUDEN *Nones* (1952) 65 As a trombone the clerk will bravely Go oompah-oompah to his minor grave. **1958** *Spectator* 31 Jan. 135/1 A bombastic crescendo of the utmost thematic poverty and vulgarity, complete with oom-pah off-beat chords. **1959** D. COOKE *Lang. Mus.* v. 257 A grotesquely galumphing 6/8 rhythm of the 'oom-pah' kind is set up, featuring the lewd tenor saxophone. **1961** *Listener* 30 Mar. 950/3 The last movement, an erratic oom-pah of ninth chords, over which the violin sings a hymn. **1966** *Ibid.* 8 Sept. 354/1 The other night the clear air of New York City was heavy with the beat of drums and the oom-pah of brass bands. **1969** M. GILBERT *Etruscan Net* I. v. 71 They had a band..with trombones, and cornets. And a huge instrument that went oompah-oompah. **1971** *Guardian* 4 June 10/6 It was like watching a one-man band. You appreciate his oompah versatility but you don't want to hear what he's playing. **1972** J. WAIN in Cox & Dyson *20th-Cent. Mind* I. xi. 395 These newer poets favoured the woodwinds of the orchestra rather than the brass section so vigorously oompah'd by their seniors. **1974** *N.Y. Times* 23 Dec. 1/1 (*caption*) Holiday Oomp-pah-pah. **1975** *New Yorker* 3 Nov. 127/1 In place of oompah figures or tenths or clusters of offbeat chords in the left hand, he plays on-the-beat guitar chords—rump rump rump rump.

oomph (uːmf). *slang.* (orig. *U.S.*). Also **umph, umphh, oomf.** [Of imitative origin.] Sex appeal, glamour, attractiveness; vitality, enthusiasm. Also *attrib.*, esp. ***oomph girl.***

1937 *Sat. Even. Post* 10 Apr. 55/2 With actors, the 'it' quality has to do with their visual personality—sex appeal, magnetism, or whatever you care to call it. Back of the camera, we refer to the ingredient as 'umphh'. **1937** W. WINCHELL in *San Francisco Examiner* 12 Sept. 25/6 Jolson's energy gave the show most of its umph too, that gave the Gershwin memorial program its pace. **1939** *Sun* (Baltimore) 29 Apr. 10/3 The modern [girl] knows she'll make the grade if she has plenty of oomph. **1939** *Life* 31 July 2 Three cheers for the Oomph Girl—yours, *Look's* and *Collier's*—all in one week!.. This Ann Sheridan certainly must have oomph to win the attention of three such important magazines in issues which hit the newsstands at the same time. **1939** W. C. & H. S. PRYOR *Let's go to Movies* 52 'Look, Alice'—to the heroine—'try to put a little more 'umph' into your lovemaking. **1942** 'W. B. JOHNSON' *Widening Stain* 30 Lucie Coindreau, you know, is the oomph-girl of the Romance Language Department. **1943** P. CHEYNEY *You can always Duck* xii. 192 She has such allure, sex appeal, *oomph* an' what-have-you-got generally. **1951** *New Yorker* 6 Oct. 34/1 Q—What else does it [*sc.* the plot of the play] lack? A—Substance, drive, authority, emotional power, and oomph. **1960** *Guardian* 19 May 9/3 A Lhasa belle, complete with high heels, lipstick, and 'oomph'. **1970** *Daily Tel.* 20 Jan. 15/2 This strictly-tailored suit has more oomph than any see-through ever had. **1973** *Philadelphia Inquirer* (Today Suppl.) 7 Oct. 41/1 If it's on plain black and white paper it doesn't have the *oomf*. Especially to children, it just doesn't have the *oomf*. **1974** *She* Jan. 80/4 We were going to need..a fantasy element to generate enough excitement..in the children to give them the necessary *oomph*. **1974** *San Francisco Examiner* 1 May 35/1 He says I ought to use my 'oomph' to help get BART [*sc.* Bay Area Rapid Transit] finished. What 'oomph' is the man talking about? *Ibid.* 35/2 All old World War II types will remember when Annie S. was 'the oomph girl'. **1977** *Church Times* 28 Oct. 9/3 This prayer may take the form of thanks—for the fact that I am alive with enough energy and oomph to my personality to hate and lust.

oon, obs. f. ON *prep.*, ONE, OWN *a.*; dial. f. OVEN.

-oon, the form usually taken in Eng. by Fr. final *-on* in words stressed on the final syllable, esp. by those adopted during 16–18th. c., as *dragon*, *dragoon*, *Chalons*, *shalloon*; and hence by the Fr. suffix *-on*, = It. *-one*, Sp. *-on*. L. *-o*, *-ōnem*; forming in L. masculine appellatives, often contemptuous, as *balatro* jester, *calcitro* kicker, *capito* a big-headed man, *naso* a big-nosed man, etc. In It. and Sp. usually augmentative, as *donnone* big woman, *hombron* big man; but in Fr. usually diminutive, as in *aiglon* eaglet, *chaton* kitten, or after another suffix, as *ogrillon* little ogre. In Eng. in many adopted words, as *balloon*, *bassoon*, *batoon*, *buffoon*, *cartoon*, *doubloon*, *musketoon*, *quadroon*; rarely an Eng. formative, as in *spittoon*; cf. also *octoroon*.

Eng. representatives of Fr. or Romanic words in *-on*, when not stressed on the final syllable, and modern borrowings generally, have regularly *-on*, as in *baron*, *button*, *felon*, *jupon*, *chignon*, etc.

oonchook (ˈuːnʃuːk, ˈɔʊn-). Also **eunchuck, owenshook, ownshuck,** etc. [ad. Ir. *óinseach*, Gael. *òinnseach* foolish woman, clown.]

†**1.** *Newfoundland.* One of the men dressed as women who participated in a mummers' parade. *Obs.*

1885 W. WHITTLE in *Evening Telegram* (St. John's, Newfoundland) 21 Dec. (1962) 22 'Munn' Carter..was always a conspicuous 'fool'... Davey Foley was always the owner of a stylish rig, while his friend, Masey Murphy, appeared, I think, as an 'Owenshook'. The 'Owenshook' was always a terror to encounter, for he rarely was merciful to any one who made him draw upon his wind, and woe to the man who disputed his right of giving a sound castigation for the trouble incurred. **1895** D. W. PROWSE *Hist. Newfoundland* xiii. 402 Some were dressed as women, with long garments, known as 'eunchucks'. The were all masked, and ran at passengers with an Indian yell, and spoke in a falsetto voice. *a* **1930** G. J. BOND in J. R. Smallwood *Bk. Newfoundland* (1937) II. 259/1 Joined with these gaily bedecked Fools were a smaller number of veiled men in women's garments. They bore the appellation of Oonchooks, and were perhaps more persistent and punishing in their thrashing of people than their more spectacular companions. **1969** in Halpert & Story *Christmas Mumming in Newfoundland* 49 The Newfoundland eyewitnesses draw particular attention..to both the fools who belaboured the bystanders with whips and inflated bladders, and the 'oonchooks'.

2. *Newfoundland* and *Ireland.* (Also in form **oonshick** (-ʃɪk).) A person who acts foolishly, a noodle. *colloq.*

1937 P. K. DEVINE *Folklore of Newfoundland* 35 *Ownshook*, an ignorant stupid fellow. **1955** *Historic Newfoundland* (Newfoundland Tourist Devel. Office) 35 *Oonshick*, a person of low intelligence. **1961** 'F. O'BRIEN' *Hard Life* x. 83 The divil himself is in the hearts of that Corporation ownshucks. *a* **1966** 'M. NA GOPALEEN' *Best of Myles* (1968) 152 Begob if I used the word ownshuck you might take my meaning! **1975** *Globe & Mail* (Toronto) 1 Mar. 27/4 Moreover, all those jokes depicting Newfoundlanders as oonshicks—the vernacular for persons of low intelligence—are..ill-considered comment on the disintegration of 478 years of community loyalty and individual fortitude.

oonde, variant of ONDE *Obs.*

oone, obs. f. ONE.

oones, -is, -ys, oons, obs. forms of ONCE.

oonin (ˈəʊənɪn). [a. F. *oonin* (Littré), f. Gr. ᾠόν egg + -IN.] = ALBUMININ. (*Syd. Soc. Lex.*)

oonlepy, var. ONLEPY *a. Obs.*, only.

oonli, -liche, -ly, obs. forms of ONLY.

oons (uːnz), *int.* Now *rare.* Also 6 **ounes,** 8 **ouns.** [Worn-down form of *wounds* (i.e. *God's wounds! Zounds!*), *w* being dropped before (uː), and *d* after *n*, as is common in dialects.] A petty oath: = ZOUNDS.

1593 PEELE *Chron. Edw. I* 94 Ye dogs, ounes! do me a shrewd turn, and mock me too? **1687** CONGREVE *Old Bach.* v. viii, Oons how my heart aches! **1777** SHERIDAN *Trip Scarb.* III. i, Ouns! if you can't..how do you think I should do't? **1830** JAMES *Darnley* vii. 37 Oons! cried Jekin, this is magic. **1889** DOYLE *Micah Clarke* 115 'Oons! I'd as soon travel in the land of the Great Mogul!

oont (uːnt). *Indian* and *Austral. colloq.* Also **unt.** [ad. Hindi (and Urdu) *ūnt* camel.] A camel. *Comb.* **oont-wallah,** a camel-driver.

1862 MRS. J. B. SPEID *Our Last Yrs. in India* ix. 214 The Oont-wallah or camel-man. **1892** KIPLING *Barrack-room Ballads* 27 O the oont, O the oont, O the commissariat oont! With 'is silly neck a-bobbin' like a basket full o' snakes. **1894** A. G. LEONARD *Camel* 101 The baggage [camel], known as 'Gamal' and 'Unt' respectively in Egypt and India. **1900** *Pall Mall Gaz.* 1 Jan. 1/3 A mule..requires more experience in handling than the bubbling oont of India.

1902 *Chambers's Jrnl.* July 431/1 To judge from the selection of pillage, some one conversant with the interior economy of the caravan was involved, and it was significant that a number of the *oont-wallahs* (camel-drivers) were missing. **1933** *Bulletin* (Sydney) 26 Apr. 33/2 Hell! what a lot of calculation had to go into piloting a couple of smelly oonts! **1945** [see HUMPY *sb.*[2]]. **1961** PARTRIDGE *Dict. Slang* Suppl. 1207/2 *Oont*,..a camel: Australian.

oonus, obs. form of ONCE.

‖**oopak, oopack** ('u:pæk). [Chinese *u-pak*, Cantonese dialect form of *Hu-peh*, name of a central province of China (f. *hu* lake + *peh* north, in reference to the Tung-ting Lake, whence also *Hunan* from *nan* south).] A variety of black tea.

1858 SIMMONDS *Dict. Trade*, *Oopack*, a black tea. **1885** *Standard* 29 Apr. *Advt.*, Oopack. The best value in Tea.

oophore ('əʊəfɔə(r)). *Bot.* [f. Gr. ᾠό-ν egg + -φόρος bearing, bearer.] That stage, or form of a plant, in the higher Cryptogams (ferns, mosses, etc.) which, in the alternation of generations, bears male and female organs; the 'sexual generation'; also called *oophyte*. Opposed to *sporophore* or *sporophyte*.

1875 THISELTON DYER in *Encycl. Brit.* III. 692/1 For the gamogenetic generation, in which conjugation takes place, or in which special cells (*oospheres*) are fertilized by antherozoids, and become *oospores*, '*Oophore*' may be employed. **1882** VINES tr. *Sachs' Bot.* 385 The Sexual Generation (Oophore) which is developed from the spore always preserves, in Vascular Cryptogams, the form of a thallus.

oophorectomy (ˌəʊəʊfɒ'rɛktəmɪ). *Surg.* [f. mod.L. *ōophoron* ovary (f. Gr. ᾠό-ν egg, ovum + -φόρος bearing) + Gr. ἐκτομή cutting out, excision.] Excision of the ovary. So **oopho'rectomist**, one who performs oophorectomy; **ˌoopho'rectomize** *v. trans.* = OVARIECTOMIZE, OVARIOTOMIZE *vbs.*; **ˌoopho-'rectomized** *ppl. a.*

1872 PEASLEE *Ovar. Tumors* 225 Ovariotomy..to use a more distinctive term, Oöphorectomy..whose object and result is the removal of an ovarian tumor. **1889** J. M. DUNCAN *Lect. Dis. Wom.* xxvii. (ed. 4) 212 We have got some light on it from the practice of the oophorectomists. **1955** *Jrnl. Amer. Med. Assoc.* 31 Dec. 1701/2 Of 38 women with metastatic breast cancer, all of whom had previously been oophorectomized, bilateral adrenalectomy produced objective remissions in 45%. **1961** *Lancet* 7 Oct. 793/1 In one case it was found that a woman who had been oophorectomised and adrenalectomised still appeared to be excreting large amounts of œstrogens. **1972** *Jrnl. Endocrinol.* LIV. 115 Oestrogens have been shown to stimulate glycolytic activity in the uteri of oophorectomized rats.

‖**oophoridium** (ˌəʊəʊfɒ'rɪdɪəm). *Bot.* Also in anglicized form **oophorid** (əʊ'ɒfərɪd). [f. mod.L. *ōophoron* ovary + *-idium*, Gr. -ιδιον, dim. ending.] A name for the macrosporangia (or, loosely, the macrospores) of certain *Lycopodiaceæ*.

1835 LINDLEY *Introd. Bot.* (1848) II. 98 Lycopods.. Their Oophorids. **1864** T. MOORE *Brit. Ferns* 94 In the *Selaginellas*, an additional kind of spore-case is produced, which contains three or four roundish fleshy spores, many times as large as the granular spores..these larger bodies are called oophoridia. **1866** *Treas. Bot.* 815/1 *Oophoridium*, the larger form of spore-case in *Selaginella*. **1870** BENTLEY *Man. Bot.* (ed. 2) 366 The oosporangia or oophoridia are usually two-valved cases, with four lobes, each of which contains one large spore. **1870** HOOKER *Stud. Flora* 469 Lycopodiaceæ..larger capsules containing 3–4 much larger spores (macrospores or *oophoridia*).

oophoritis (ˌəʊəʊfɒ'raɪtɪs). *Path.* [f. as prec. + -ITIS.] Inflammation of the ovary.

1872 PEASLEE *Ovar. Tumors* 24 A consequence of oophoritis. **1872** F. G. THOMAS *Dis. Women* (ed. 3) 636 Ovaritis..has been described by some authors under the name of Oophoritis.

oophyte = oophore: see OO-.

ooplasm ('əʊəplæz(ə)m). *Biol.* [f. OO- + PLASM.] The cytoplasm of an egg (see also quot. 1956).

1899 *Bot. Gaz.* XXVIII. 237 There is a stage called zonation in which the nuclei, usually in metaphase, are lined up around the ooplasm. **1939** P. WEISS *Princ. Devel.* I. 78 Only that part of the egg which consists of true oöplasm is broken up into cells, while those portions which consist mainly of yolk remain either unsegmented or cleave with considerable delay. **1956** C. H. WADDINGTON *Princ. Embryol.* i. 16 The different regions of the cytoplasm of the egg may have specific properties, so that a particular region can only develop in one way. Such regions are spoken of as ooplasms; an older name was 'organ-forming substances'. **1974** *Acta Anat.* LXXXIX. 616 A granular or flocculent material, presumed to consist of blood proteins, in the intercellular spaces outside the oocyte, in the pinocytotic vesicles inside the oocyte, and in the ooplasm itself.

Hence **oo'plasmic** *a.*

1905 *Jrnl. Exper. Zool.* II. 147 The third cleavage is equatorial... The ectoplasm is now completely segregated in the four ventral cells but the other oöplasmic substances are not as yet located in separate cells. **1925** E. B. WILSON *Cell* (ed. 3) iv. 338 The enormous increase in the cytoplasmic or oöplasmic substance during the growth of the oöcyte leads to the production of the largest known forms of cells. **1961** N. J. BERRILL *Growth* xix. 483 Some insight into the ooplasmic specialization of the primitive chordate egg may be gained by a comparison among the embryonic developments in the ascidian *Styela*, the larvacean tunicate *Oikopleura*, and *Amphioxus*. **1968** F. G. GILCHRIST *Survey of Embryol.* iv. 65/2 A considerable rearrangement of the materials of the cytoplasm also takes place during meiosis... The rearrangement is termed ooplasmic segregation.

oops (u:ps, ʊps), *int.* Also o-o-o-ps, ooops, oooops. [A natural exclamation.] An exclamation expressing apology, dismay, or surprise, used. esp. after making an obvious mistake.

1933 'R. JAMES' *Worth Remembering* xiii. 423 Slap fighting —smiting one's opponent with the open hand—a method even Babe would scurn. Oops! Oops! Oops! **1937** L. B. MURPHY *Social Behavior & Child Personality* I. i. 45 Julius picked up Gregory, carried him into the bathroom and dropped him on the floor, said 'Oops!' picked him up again, then let him walk. **1939** L. M. MONTGOMERY *Anne of Ingleside* xliii. 334 She caught her foot in a croquet hoop... Gilbert only said 'O-o-o-ps!' and steadied her. **1939** D. PARKER *Here Lies* 70 Oops, I'm sorry I joggled the bed. **1944** 'P. QUENTIN' *Puzzle for Puppets* i. 5 Iris..said: 'Oops' as she ran into headlong collision with a Marine sergeant. **1960** V. NABOKOV *Invitation to Beheading* xii. 119 She..knocked the pencil off, did not catch it in time, and said 'oops!' **1961** J. HELLER *Catch-22* (1962) x. 108 'Ooops, there it goes again.' The rain began falling again. **1972** J. BURMEISTER *Running Scared* v. 80 If something went wrong you went Oops and called an expert. **1974** *Sunday Post* (Glasgow) 5 May 32/3 The 'keeper gave the ball the wet soap treatment—Oops, butter fingers! **1975** *Daily Mirror* 29 Apr. 16 Now, I'm all for new faces—oops, sorry, Hughie—appearing on talent shows on TV.

oops-a-daisy, var. UPSIDAISY.

oor, obs. f. ORE; mod.Sc. and north f. OUR.

‖**oorali** (u:'rɑ:lɪ). [One of the many forms of the word WOORALI.] A resinous substance used by the Indians of S. America as an arrow-poison; = CURARE, WOORALI.

1880 TENNYSON *Childr. Hosp.* i, And mangle the living dog..Drench'd with the hellish oorali. **1899** *Edin. Rev.* July 159 Curare, or woorali, or oorali, as it is variously called. It is the arrow poison of Guiana.

oord, oordoo, variant of ORD *Obs.*, URDU.

oore, obs. f. OAR, ORE.

oorhodeine: see OO-.

oorial, var. URIAL.

oorie, oory, var. OURIE *a. Sc.*, dreary, dingy, etc.

Oort (ʊət). *Astr.* The name of Jan Hendrik *Oort* (b. 1900), Dutch astronomer, used *attrib.* and in the possessive to designate concepts proposed by him or arising out of his work, as **Oort('s) (comet) cloud**, a cloud of small bodies that Oort proposed orbited the sun well beyond the orbit of Pluto and acted as a cometary reservoir; **Oort('s) constant**, either of two constants in the equation relating the radial velocity of a star in the galaxy to its distance from the sun (see quot. 1977).

1941 B. J. & P. F. BOK *Milky Way* v. 106 The 'Oort' constant..measures the maximum effect [of differential rotation] at a standard distance. *Ibid.* 108 The best value of Oort's constant *A* is between five and six kilometers per second for a distance of one thousand light years. **1966** *McGraw-Hill Encycl. Sci. & Technol.* VI. 12/1 The radial velocities may be closely represented by the equation Radial velocity = $rA \sin 2l$ where *r* is the distance to the object from the Sun, *l* its galactic longitude, and *A*, known as Oort's constant, depends on many factors including the mass of the galaxy and the distance of the Sun from the galactic center. Its value is approximately 18 km/(sec) (1000 parsecs). **1968** D. C. KNIGHT *Comets* 38 The American astronomer Fred L. Whipple recently proposed that a yet-to-be-seen comet belt, distinct from Oort's 'comet cloud', lies near the orbit of Pluto. **1976** *Nature* 29 Jan. 290/1 Some theories go even further and predict that, in addition to these comets in the Oort cloud, the remains of a primaeval comet belt may still exist at a distance of ~50 AU. **1976** *National Observer* (U.S.) 24 Apr. 6/1 Van Flandern's work also casts doubt on 'Oort's Cloud', one of the more cherished concepts of comet studies. **1977** J. NARLIKAR *Struct. Universe* iii. 62 Oort expressed the transverse velocity of the star in the following form $T = r\{B + A \cos 2(l - l_0)\}$. Here *r* is the distance of the star from the Sun, *l* its galactic longitude, and l_0 is the galactic longitude of the galactic centre. *A* and *B* are constants called Oort's constants.

ooscopy: see OO-.

oose, obs. form of OOZE.

oosement, corrupt f. OSMUND[1], a kind of iron.

oosi, var. OOZI.

oosite ('əʊəsaɪt). *Min.* [ad. Ger. *oosit* (Marx, 1834), f. the name of the Oos valley, in the grand-duchy of Baden, where found: see -ITE[1] 2 b.] A mineral allied to Pinite.

1868 DANA *Min.* (ed. 5) 480 *Oösite*..is white to reddish or brownish-red, and occurs in 6- and 12-sided prisms. **1878** LAWRENCE tr. *Cotta's Rocks Class.* 38 Liebnerite and Oosite are like products.

oosperm ('əʊəspɜ:m). [mod. f. Gr. ᾠό-ν egg + σπέρμα seed, SPERM.] **a.** *Zool.* A fertilized ovum. **b.** *Bot.* = OOSPORE.

1888 ROLLESTON & JACKSON *Anim. Life* Introd. 25 The ovum has now [after impregnation] become an oosperm, and it speedily undergoes fission or segmentation and gastrulation. **1892** *Syd. Soc. Lex.*, *Oosperm*..In Botany, the term is sometimes applied to the oosphere after fertilisation.

oosphere ('əʊəsfɪə(r)). *Bot.* [mod. f. Gr. ᾠό-ν egg + σφαῖρα sphere.] The female reproductive cell, esp. in the Thallophytes or lower Cryptogams, which when fertilized becomes an *oospore*.

1875 BENNETT & DYER tr. *Sachs' Bot.* 212 Oogonia are cells in which the female reproductive bodies or Oospheres are formed. **1882** THISELTON DYER in *Nature* XXV. 390 The beautiful process of division of the primary oosphere in some of the species.

‖**oosporangium** (ˌəʊəʊspɒ'rændʒɪəm). *Bot.* Also in anglicized form 'oospoˌrange. [f. OO- + SPORANGIUM.] **a.** Thuret's term for the unilocular zoosporangium of certain fucoid Algæ (Phæosporeæ). **b.** Sometimes used as = OOPHORIDIUM. **c.** A case or sac containing an oospore.

1857 BERKELEY *Cryptog. Bot.* §67. 88 In other cases, doubtless, two kinds of Zoospores are produced, as in *Leathesia* and *Mesoglœa*, as they have the two organs called Oosporangia and Trichosporangia by Thuret. **1867** J. HOGG *Microsc.* II. i. 273 Section of a lacinia of a frond, showing the stalked eight-chambered oosporanges growing on tufts with intercalated hairs. **1870** BENTLEY *Man. Bot.* (ed. 2) 365 Commonly called oosporangia or oophoridia. **1874** COOKE *Fungi* 173.

oospore ('əʊəspɔə(r)). *Bot.* [f. Gr. ᾠό-ν egg + σπόρος seed, SPORE.] The fertilized female cell or oosphere, esp. in the lower Cryptogams, which forms the germ of a future plant.

1865 COOKE *Rust, Smut*, etc. 131 After this contact of the two bodies, the gonosphere acquires a new name, and is called an 'oospore'. **1882** VINES *Sachs' Bot.* 235 The size of the antherozoids is so inconsiderable that they scarcely add ..to the mass of the oosphere, but yet produce a change in it, one consequence of which is that it becomes invested with a firm cell-wall, and then constitutes the *Oospore*.

Hence **oo'sporic, o'osporous** *adjs.*, having or producing oospores; **ˌoospo'riferous** *a.*, bearing oospores.

oost(e, oostage, obs. ff. HOST, OAST, HOSTAGE.

oostegite, -itic: see OO-.

oostman: see OSTMAN.

oostre, obs. f. HOSTRY.

oot, mod.Sc. and north. dial. f. OUT.

oothe, variant of WOOD *a. Obs.*, mad.

ootheca, -al: see OO-.

ootid ('əʊətɪd). *Biol.* [f. OO- after *spermatid*.] A haploid cell formed by the division of a secondary oocyte; by some writers restricted to the ovum, as contrasted with the polar body.

1908 F. R. LILLIE *Devel. of Chick* 14 The mature ovum (oötid) and the polar bodies are the precise equivalent of the four spermatids, but..only the ovum on the female side is functional. **1927** W. SHUMWAY *Vert. Embryol.* ii. 34 In this way four (or three, if the smaller secondary oöcyte fails to divide) oötids are produced, of which the single large cell is the ovum, while the smaller ones are known as polocytes. **1946** B. M. PATTEN *Human Embryol.* ii. 31 The secondary oöcyte..divides again, and in this division..the bulk of the cytoplasm goes to one of the two resulting oötids, which is then commonly called the 'matured ovum'. **1964** N. S. COHN *Elem. Cytol.* II. xiii. 206 The secondary oöcyte undergoes a second meiotic division, producing one large cell, the oötid, and a small second polar body. *Ibid.*, The oötid..matures into the egg or ovum. **1972** *Nature* 28 Jan. 213 It must be recalled that the sea urchin egg is an ootid whose maturation divisions..have been completed.

ootocoid (əʊ'ɒtəkɔɪd), *a.* and *sb.* *Zool.* [ad. mod.L. *Ootocoidea* (neut. pl.), f. Gr. ᾠοτόκ-ος laying eggs, oviparous: see -OID.] **a.** *adj.* Belonging to the *Ootocoidea*, a division of mammals in Dana's classification (so called from their affinity to oviparous animals), comprising the marsupials and monotremes (the latter of which have since been found to be actually oviparous). **b.** *sb.* One of the *Ootocoidea*. Also **ooto'coidean** *a.* and *sb.*

1863 *Amer. Jrnl. Sci.* XXXV. 68 The Marsupials and Monotremes constitute a natural group,..the most fundamental characteristic of which..suggests the name Oöticoids. *Ibid.* XXXVI. 315 The Oöticoid or semi-oviparous Mammals.

ootocous (əʊ'ɒtəkəs), *a.* *Zool.* [f. Gr. ᾠοτόκ-ος egg-laying + -OUS.] That lays eggs; oviparous.

In mod. Dicts.

ootus, obs. pl. of OAT.

ootype, ooxanthine: see OO-.

oouen, oous, obs. ff. OVEN, OOZE.

ooyess: see OYEZ.

ooze (uːz), *sb.*[1] Forms: α. 1 wós, 2–5 wos, (4 wus), 5–6 wose, 6 woos, 5–8 woose, 7–8 wooze. β. 6 ouse, 6–7 ouze, 6– 8 owze, 7 oose, (oze, oaze), 8– ooze. [In senses 1, 2, OE. *wós* juice, sap, expressed juice: cf. MLG. *wos(e* scum, etc. Sense 3 is a later formation from OOZE *v.*[1] (itself a deriv. of sense 1). With the loss of initial *w* in the β-forms, cf. the pronunciation of *wood, wool, woman*, in various dialects which drop *w* before (*u*, u). (Instances of *oze, oaze*, in sense 2, in 17th c., were prob. due to confusion with OOZE *sb.*[2], which had then both *oze* and *oaze*.)]

I. †**1.** Juice, sap; the liquid which flows or is obtained from a plant, fruit, or the like. *Obs.*

α. c**1000** *Sax. Leechd.* I. 178 Sume men..pæs woses synderlice brucað...wið earena sare, ȝenim ðysse ylcan wyrte..wos. **1340** *Ayenb.* 89 Uor þet hy weneþ by of gentile woze. *Ibid.* 186 Ase þe oyle op arist ine þe lompe alle þe oþre woses. **1340–70** *Alisaunder* 712 Nectanabus..laches..wortes..Hee wringes out þe wet wus. **1398** TREVISA *Barth. De P.R.* XVII. vii. (Tollem. MS.), Varro seyeþ, þat a reed of Ynde groweþ to a smal tre, and humoure is wronge oute of þe rote þerof, and no swete þinges may stryue wiþ þat wose [1535 woos] and licoure. a**1400–50** *Alexander* 413 þat Iogloure..[with] þe wose of þe wede hire wengis anoyntis. c**1440** *Tundale* 1358 He thrust hem as men dose Grapes, to wryng out the wose.

2. a. *techn.* The liquor of a tan-vat; an infusion or decoction of oak-bark, sumach, or other tannin-yielding substance in which hides are steeped.

α. **1581** LAMBARDE *Eiren.* IV. iv. (1588) 459 If any Tanner ..have tanned any rotten Hides, or wrought them negligently in the Wose, or have not renewed the Wose so oft as need was. **1603–4** *Act 1 Jas. I*, c. 22 Nor shall suffer the Hides..to lye in the Woozes any lesse tyme than Twelve Moneths at the leaste. **1638** A. READ *Chirurg.* ix. 63 You may use the red astringent wine, or tanners woose. **1726** *Brice's Week. Jrnl.* 4 Mar. 4 A large Tann-yard..furnished with Pits and Vats..full of Wooze. **1800** *Specif. Patent* No. 2409. 2 The part for raising and conveying the woose.

β. **1587** MASCALL *Govt. Cattle, Oxen* (1600) 13 Then shall ye take of sharpe Tanners owze. *Ibid.* 42 Also some doe giue them of Tanners ouse to drinke. **1601** HOLLAND *Pliny* I. 546 The filth of Tanners oose. **1614** MARKHAM *Cheap Husb.* I. xx. 55 Take a pinte of Tanners Oze. **1692** O. WALKER *Grk. & Rom. Hist.* 25 With tanners Oaze. **1725** BRADLEY *Fam. Dict.* II. 6 Cij/1 Take a Quart of Tanner's Owze. **1777** MACBRIDE in *Phil. Trans.* LXVIII. 113 The tanners prepare their bark..They..use it in the way of infusion, which is called ooze. **1852** MORFIT *Tanning & Currying* (1853) 216 Vats..two-thirds filled with a weak ooze or infusion of oak-bark. **1879** *Cassell's Techn. Educ.* v. 311 An extract of bark, technically called 'ooze'.

b. Short for *ooze leather* (see sense 4 below). Also *attrib.*

1916 *Daily Colonist* (Victoria, B.C.) 18 July 14/1 (Advt.), Ladies' 8-Inch High Laced White Ivory Ooze Boot, blind eyelets, small perforations, full Louis heel. **1922** M. B. HOUSTON *Witch Man* vi. 78 A 'gift' volume of Shakespeare, bound in dark blue ooze.

II. From OOZE *vb.*

3. The act or fact of oozing; exudation; gentle flow; also, that which oozes; a sluggish stream.

1718 PRIOR *Solomon* III. 567 From his first fountain & beginning ouze, Down to the sea each brook & torrent flows. **1821** KEATS *Isabella* lii, Divine liquids come with odorous ooze Through the cold serpent-pipe. **1822–34** *Good's Study Med.* (ed. 4) IV. 281 An outlet for the escape of the fluid, which trickles down in a perpetual ooze. **1889** *Science* XIII. 131/1 Small oozes of water issuing from the base of these slopes.

III. 4. *Comb.* (from 2) **ooze** (or **oozed**) **leather** = *ooze-calf*; **ooze-calf**, calf-skin through which the dye has been forced by mechanical means, used for the uppers of boots and shoes, and by bookbinders.

1890 in *American Mail Order Fashions* (1961) 27 Boys' Eton Caps in ooze leather. Price,..$1. **1894** *Daily News* 22 June 6/4 From Montreal comes a book in buck-skin, tanned like ooze-calf. **1895** *Times* 2 Jan. 13/4 Orders..for glacé kid, ooze calf, American red sides, and the best English tannages. **1897** *Sears, Roebuck Catal.* 324/3 A Very Good Oozed Leather Tobacco or Coin Pouch. **1928** *Publishers' Weekly* 9 June 2348 In four styles of binding..ooze leather, two colors, green or brown, $2·50. **1937** S. V. BENÉT *Thirteen O'Clock* 71, I could stomach Jeremy Jason, the homespun philosopher, whose small green ooze-leather booklets.. produced much the same sensation in me as running a torn fingernail over heavy plush. **1960** G. A. GLAISTER *Gloss. Bk.* 286/2 Ooze leather, calfskins or split sheepskins prepared to give them a suede or velvet finish on the flesh side.

ooze (uːz), *sb.*[2] Forms: α. 1 wáse; 4–6 wose, 6 woose, woes. β. 6 oous, 6–7 oes, owes; ooes, ouse; 6–8 oase, oose, owze, 7 oas, ose, owze, 7–8 oaz, oaze, oze, owse; 6– ooze. [OE. *wáse* wk. fem., cognate with ON. *veisa* wk. fem., stagnant pool, puddle, Norw. dial. *veisa* fem., mud, mud-bank. In ME. and 16th c. *wose*, rimes with *glose, disclose, repose, suppose*. The regular mod. repr. would be *ose, oase* (əʊz), as in the 16–18th c. *oas, oase, oaz, oaze, ose, oze, oes, owes*; but from 1550 there are spellings which imply (uːz), and show assimilation of this word to OOZE *sb.*[1], either through contiguity of sense, or through the tendency of OE. *wá* to pass through (wɔː, woː) to (wuː, uː), as seen in *womb, two, who*. Besides the distinct forms, there are several ambiguous spellings, so that no attempt has been made to separate the examples that appear to represent (oː) and (uː) respectively. Forms with initial *w* do not survive the sixteenth century. In popular apprehension this word is not felt to be a different word from OOZE *sb.*[1], the notions of 'moisture', 'exudation', and 'oozy soil' being naturally associated.]

1. a. Wet mud or slime; esp. that in the bed of a river or estuary.

α. c**725** *Corpus Gloss.* 386 Caenum, wase. a**1000** *Ags. Gloss.* in Wr.-Wülck. 203/45 *Cenum i.e. luti uorago, uel lutum sub aquis fetidum*, i. wase *uel* fæn. c**1050** *Glosses* ibid. 362/30 *Cænum*, wase. **1393** LANGL. *P. Pl.* C. XIII. 229 Right as weodes wexen in wose and in donge. c**1400** *Beryn* 1742 They [ships] been nat ȝit I-setelid, ne fixid in þe wose [*rime* glose]. c**1440** *Promp. Parv.* 532/2 Wose, slype of the erthe ..*gluten, bitumen.* **1555** PHAER *Æneid* II. D j b, I..in a slimy lake of mud all night lay hid in wose [*rime* disclose]. **1557** *Ibid.* v. L iv b, Hauons of Scicil woose [*rime* as I suppose]. **1582** BATMAN *On Barthol.* XIII. v. 192 He walloweth and wrappeth himselfe first in fenne and wose.

β. a**1547** SURREY *Æneid* II. 172 And lurked in a marrise all the nyght Among the ooze. **1553** BRENDE *Q. Curtius* IX. 23 Being full of mudde and ooes. **1587** FLEMING *Contn. Holinshed* III. 1539/1 Maister Ferdinando Poins would haue raised them with ouze and beach shoueled and cast togither. **1590** WEBBE *Trav.* (Arb.) 32 That she might haue gone vp to the mid leg in oes or mire. **1593** NASHE *Christ's T.* (1613) 26 The vgly oous of the channell. **1599** HAKLUYT *Voy.* II. II. 58 We sounded, and found 28 fadome water, blacke oase. **1602** CAREW *Cornwall* 27 The ose or salt water mudde. **1617** MORYSON *Itin.* III. III. iii. 136 Till it bee fatted with the Owes, or sand of the Sea. **1653** H. COGAN tr. *Pinto's Trav.* ix. 29 Having buried him in the owze. **1668** WILKINS *Real Char.* II. ii. 53 Quicksands, Drift, *Syrtis*. Oaz. **1678–1706** PHILLIPS, *Oze*, a soft slimy Ground, where a Ship cannot conveniently cast Anchor. **1680** MORDEN *Geog. Rect., Hungary* (1685) 89 By the setling of the Ouse or filth brought down by the..Danube. **1697** DRYDEN *Virg. Georg.* IV. 623 Unweildily they wallow first in Ooze, Then in the shady Covert seek Repose. **1726** G. ROBERTS *Four Years Voy.* 287 With soft Owse and Sand mix'd. **1763** W. ROBERTS *Nat. Hist. Florida* 9 The bottom, which is sandy, mixed in many places with oase, is excellent for anchorage. **1774** T. WEST *Antiq. Furness* p. xix, Manuring their land with sea-sand, or rather ouze. **1804** W. TAYLOR in *Ann. Rev.* II. 306 The strip of oose between the granite mountains of Egypt. **1859** R. F. BURTON *Centr. Afr.* in *Jrnl. Geog. Soc.* XXIX. 33 The sheet of black and fetid ooze that sends forth a surface-scum of brown tint and sickening odour.

fig. c**1440** *Jacob's Well* 174 To castyn oute ȝoure wose of synne. **1602** MARSTON *Antonio's Rev.* IV. iv. Wks. 1856 I. 128 The very ouze, The quicksand that devours all miserie. **1630** BRATHWAIT *Eng. Gentlem.* (1641) 189 Entangled by the reeds and oaze of earthly vanities. **1870** LOWELL *Among my Bks.* Ser. I. (1873) 332 Fishing a manuscript out of the ooze of oblivion.

b. A stretch or extent of mud; a mud-bank; a marsh or fen, a piece of soft boggy ground.

c**1500** *Piers of Fullham* 267 in Hazl. *E.P.P.* II. 11 Therfore know j non so redy arryvayle, As ys the redd clyfe in the warine wose [*rime* suppose]. **1568** GRINDAL *Lett., to Abp. Parker* Wks. (1843) 294 By reason of the evil air of the marshes and oozes there,..sick both of quartan and tertian agues. **1587** FLEMING *Contn. Holinshed* III. 1271/1 Twelve pirates were hanged at Whapping, in the ouze beside London. a**1598** in *MS. Map* in Royal MS. 18 D III (Lord Burghley's Atlas) lf. 63 [The Sand and Ooze, now Kilnsey Flats, in the Humber Mouth, is denominated] 'a flat and woes'. **1865** CARLYLE *Fredk. Gt.* XIX. iv. (1872) VIII. 154 There are thickets, intricacies, runlets, boggy oozes.

2. a. *Ocean-sounding.* White or grey calcareous matter, largely composed of remains of Foraminifera, covering vast tracts of the ocean-floor.

1858 J. DAYMAN *Deep Sea Soundings* 7 The sinker was detached, and the valve..full of soft ooze. *Ibid.* 9 Between the 15th and 45th degrees of west longitude lies the deepest part of the ocean, the bottom of which is almost wholly composed of the same kind of soft mealy substance, which, for want of a better name, I have called oaze. **1860** MAURY *Phys. Geog. Sea* (Low) xiv. §609 The ooze of the deep sea. **1872** NICHOLSON *Palæont.* 9 The nearest approach which we have at the present day to chalk is probably to be found in the deposit called 'ooze'. **1877** W. THOMSON *Voy. Challenger* II. i. 2 On the morning of the 16th we sounded in 2,575 fathoms with a bottom of reddish ooze containing many foraminifera.

b. A deposit or layer of ooze on the ocean floor.

1876 *Proc. R. Soc.* XXIV. 532 In the *Globigerina*, Radiolarian, and Diatom oozes we have found..only one or two shark's teeth. **1926** G. W. TYRRELL *Princ. Petrol.* xiv. 236 The oozes which cover great areas of the ocean floor are mainly calcareous and foraminiferal. **1971** *Nature* 3 Sept. 46/1 The ophiolites in those deep-sea troughs were overlain by Upper Jurassic and Lower Cretaceous radiolarian and nannofossil oozes.

3. *Comb.* **ooze-bank**, a mud-bank in a tidal river, or by the shore.

1893 J. WATSON *Conf. Poacher* 40 [We watched the ducks and geese] from behind an ooze bank.

ooze (uːz), *sb.*[3] *Obs.* or *rare*. Forms: (5 wase), 6 ouse, oase, 7 oze, 8 ouze, 8– ooze. [app. repr. a ME. *wōse (of which the northern form *wase, wayse* 'alga' is in *Catholicon Anglicum* (1483) 409/2). Like OOZE *sb.*[2], this also has been levelled under the same spelling and pronunciation as OOZE *sb.*[1]] Sea-weed.

1555 EDEN *Decades* 343 Weedes of the sea cauled reites or ouse. **1598** SYLVESTER *Du Bartas* II. i. IV. *Handie-crafts* 367 Som make their roofs with fearn, or reeds, or rushes, And some with hides, with oase, with boughs, and bushes. **1625** PURCHAS *Pilgrims* II. 1122 Great qauntitie of Oze, that growes vpon the Rockes of the Sea. **1706** PHILLIPS, *Ouze*, a sort of miry Sedge. **1770–4** A. HUNTER *Georg. Ess.* (1803) III. 559 Near the coast great quantities of sea-weed, or ooze are collected. **1833** HT. MARTINEAU *Brooke Farm* x. 120 With pannier-loads of sea ooze..to manure their little fields. [This may belong to OOZE[2].]

†**b.** The moss which forms peat bogs. *Obs.*

1665 MANLEY *Grotius' Low C. Warres* 245 Which Fuel was no other, than the muddy Oze growing in the Marishes of Holland, hardned by the Sun, and cut out into Turf.

ooze (uːz), *sb.*[4] [prob. f. *ooze, oos(e)*, plur. of *oo*, Sc. form of WOOL *sb.*] The nap or short fibres that project from yarn.

1892 J. NASMITH *Students' Cotton Spinning* 373 When thread is intended for lace purposes..it is passed several times through a gas flame at a high speed, so as to burn off the filaments or 'ooze' on its surface and leave it bare. **1909** *Engineer* 1 Oct. 352/1 The term 'gassing' is applied to the process of burning off the ends of fibres or 'ooze' on the different kinds of yarn.

ooze (uːz), *v.*[1] Forms: 4–5 wose, 5 ose, (6 oyse), 5–7 wooze, 7–8 ouse, 8 ouze, 7– ooze. [ME. *wōse-n*, f. *wōse*, OOZE *sb.*[1] 1, 2. The OE. verb was *wésan* (:—**wósjan*) with umlaut: see WEESE.]

1. a. *intr.* Of moisture: To pass slowly or in small quantities through the pores of a body; to make way gradually through small openings or interstices; to exude, to percolate.

1398 TREVISA *Barth. De P.R.* IV. xi. (Tollem. MS.), It woseþ and sweteþ oute of blood. c**1420** *Pallad. on Husb.* IX. 116 To thyn hond wol sprynge or springes ose [*scatere*]. a**1648** DIGBY *Closet Open.* (1677) 146 Ty it very close..that nothing may ouse out. **1658** ROWLAND *Moufet's Theat. Ins.* 900 Lest the rain-water..should soak and wooze into their Hives. **1697** DRYDEN *Virg. Georg.* III. 730 A wat'rish Humour swell'd and ooz'd agen. **1726** SWIFT *Gulliver* II. viii, I saw the water ooze in at several crannies. **1733** CHEYNE *Eng. Malady* II. i. §5 (1734) 121 The Solids..will suffer this thin and acrid Serum to ouze through their Substances. **1799** *Med. Jrnl.* II. 355 The spring oozes out of a rock. **1822** IMISON *Sc. & Art* I. 107 The water oozed through the gold, and stood like dew upon the surface. **1853** HERSCHEL *Pop. Lect. Sc.* i. §18 (1873) 12 When a crack takes place in ice, the water oozes up.

b. with advb. object: *to ooze its way.*

a**1849** POE *Tales* Ser. I. *Gold Bug* Wks. 1896 II. 77 A scarcely perceptible creek, oozing its way through a wilderness of reeds and slime.

c. Of a substance: To exude moisture. Also *fig.*

1398 TREVISA *Barth. De P.R.* XVII. clxxii[i]. (MS. Bodl.) lf. 233/1 þe tree þat sweteþ and woseþ thus hiȝt Libanus. **1523** FITZHERB. *Husb.* §111 The fetelockes..wyl swel in wynter tyme, and oyse of water. a**1783** BROOKE *Conrade* Poems (1810) 420/2 He the deadly wound Ere long discover'd; for it still ooz'd crimson. **1820** KEATS *Hyperion* I. 137 This passion..made..His Druid locks to shake and ooze with sweat. **1864** TENNYSON *Sea Dreams* 150 He..then began to bloat himself, and ooze All over with the fat affectionate smile That makes the widow lean.

2. *transf.* and *fig.* To pass as through pores or minute interstices, and so slowly, gradually, or imperceptibly. **a.** Of air, wind, gas, light.

1824 W. IRVING *T. Trav.* I. 46 The wind oozing through the rat-holes of the old mansion. **1871** *Echo* 13 Dec., The [sewer] gas which now oozes out into private houses. **1887** T. HARDY *Woodlanders* III. ii. 29 The breeze was oozing through the net-work of boughs as through a strainer. **1893** MCCARTHY *Red Diamonds* III. 198 No gleam of light.. oozed from its hooded windows.

b. Of internal qualities, private information, etc. Often with *out, away.*

1775 SHERIDAN *Rivals* v. iii, [My valour is certainly going! .. I feel it oozing out (as it were) at the palms of my hands.] *Ibid.*, Upon my conscience,..your valour has oozed away with a vengeance! **1840** DICKENS *Barn. Rudge* ii, Gabriel felt his firmness oozing rapidly away. **1858** LYTTON *What will he do* (L.), The ruffian felt a cold shudder—his courage oozed. **1867** A. BARRY *Sir C. Barry* vi. 147 Rumours began to ooze out. **1890** *Spectator* 11 Jan., As we understand the facts allowed to ooze out.

c. Of persons, objects. Often with *out, up, off,* etc.

1929 D. G. MACKAIL *How Amusing!* 350 Whenever I came oozing along the street, he sort of edged away. **1929** WODEHOUSE *Mr. Mulliner Speaking* ix. 313 She had planned to lure him into the thing and then ooze off and land him with these septic kids. **1930** —— *Very Good, Jeeves!* v. 122 He oozed out, leaving me to play the sparkling host. **1935** D. L. SAYERS *Gaudy Night* xi. 232 Thought I must just ooze over and pass the time of day. ?**1953** [see EEL *v.*]. **1956** N. MARSH *Off with his Head* (1957) viii. 176, I believe I oozed off before they got going. **1963** C. D. SIMAK *They walked like Men* x. 57, I oozed into the place and shut the door behind me, then slid along the wall and stood there..with my back against the wall. **1966** D. FRANCIS *Flying Finish* ii. 19 He oozed on to a bar stool, his bulk drooping around him. **1971** *Daily Tel.* 15 Sept. 9/4, 18ft 10in of gleaming black Daimler Limousine oozed up the drive and stopped outside. **1971** D. E. WESTLAKE *I gave at the Office* (1972) 127 Decrepit people ..sort of oozed out of doorways. **1977** M. RUSSELL *Dial Death* I. iii. 27 The absence of briefcase and umbrella told her that Mr Trenchard had oozed away for the night.

3. *trans.* To emit or give forth (moisture, etc.) slowly or gradually. Often with *out*. Also *fig.*

1387 TREVISA *Higden* (Rolls) I. 63 Salt veynes mulleþ and woseth oute humours and moysture. **1737** BRACKEN *Farriery Impr.* (1756) I. 314 Ulcers that lie deep and ouze out their Matter thro'..winding Passages. **1822–34** *Good's Study Med.* (ed. 4) IV. 466 A dry furfuraceous or scaly skin, often oozing a calcareous material. **1845** MRS. CARLYLE *Lett.* I. 337 His doe-skin boots were oozing out water. **1889** *Pall Mall G.* 16 Oct. 2/2 One can now hardly take up a daily paper that does not ooze Federal Home Rule at every page.

1925 E. J. P. Benn *Confessions of Capitalist* i. 21 Women over- or under-dressed, oozing money, and giving from their conversation no trace of education or of finer feeling. **1959** *Listener* 29 Jan. 228/1 The amount of charm oozed at us from the television screen. **1971** *Daily Tel.* 13 Apr. 10/7 The way he oozes bonhomie over everything from day-old chicks to old-age pensioners I find grating. **1975** B. Garfield *Death Sentence* (1976) xxix. 138 The car radio oozed wallpaper music as viscous as syrup.

ooze (uːz) *v.*[2] *rare.* [f. OOZE *sb.*[2]] *trans.* To bury or embed in ooze.

1729 Savage *Wanderer* iv. 137 The trout, that deep, in winter, ooz'd remains, Up-springs.

oozelet (ˈuːzlɪt). *nonce-wd.* [f. OOZE *sb.*[1] or *v.*[1] + -LET.] A small channel in which water oozes through bog or mud.

1865 Carlyle *Fredk. Gt.* xix. iv. (1872) VIII. 150 Wild ground..with lakelets, bushes, scrubs, and intricate meandering little runlets and oozelets.

‖**oozi** (ˈuːzɪ). Also oozie, oosi. [ad. Burmese *ù-zì* one seated at the head of an elephant or at the prow of a boat, f. *ù* head + *sì* to mount, ride on.] An elephant-driver; a mahout.

1901 G. H. Evans *Treatise on Elephants* ii. 18 Every domesticated elephant necessarily has its own particular attendant..*oo-si* (the man who rides in front), or *mahout. Ibid.*, The *oo-si* should have experience of the most approved methods of fettering, catching, subduing, and approaching unruly animals. **1905** R. T. Kelly *Burma* v. 84 It is interesting to watch the elephants at work; their sagacity is remarkable, and they hardly seem to require the direction of the 'oozis' who sit astride their necks. **1930** Mitton & Yoe *Life Story of Elephant* xiii. 205 The *oozi* who had come with me from Mandalay for some reason left me, and a new man altogether took me in hand. **1960** *News Chron.* 12 July 6/1 Working with oozies (elephant drivers) who believed in magic and nats (spirits) and every form of what we call superstition, I kept a very close hold upon myself. *Ibid.*, The drinks flowed..because they knew that very soon they would be out on trek again, alone, except for their dogs, their servants, the oozies and the elephants.

oozily, ooziness: see after OOZY.

oozing (ˈuːzɪŋ), *vbl. sb.* [f. OOZE *v.*[1] + -ING[1].] The action of the verb OOZE; also *concr.*, that which oozes. Also *fig.*

1398 Trevisa *Barth. De P.R.* xiii. ii. (Tollem. MS.), Of swetynge and wosynge [1582 wosing] of chynes and dennes of þe erþe water spryngeþ. **1495** *Ibid.* xvii. cxxi. (W. de W.) 683 Of the pyne appyll tree cometh droppyng and woosynge whyche is made harde wyth coldenesse..and soo tornyth in to a precyous stone that hyghte Electrum. **1695** tr. *Colbatch's New Lt. Chirurg. put out* 28 The ouzing out of some little Blood. **1739** Labelye *Short Acc. Piers Westm. Bridge* 50 The oozing in of the Water thro' the Pores and Interstices of the Gravel. **1820** J. Scott in *Lond. Mag.* Jan., Like natural oozings from a mind gifted with..quick..feeling. **1865** Carlyle *Fredk. Gt.* xix. iv. V. 466 Brooklets or muddy oozings wandering about.

oozing (ˈuːzɪŋ), *ppl. a.* [f. as prec. + -ING[2].] That oozes; exuding moisture, or as moisture.

1710 T. Fuller *Pharm. Extemp.* 334 The Acrimony of the owzing Serum. **1878** J. Kirkwood *Serm.* 371 It was only an oozing fountain.

oozle (ˈuːz(ə)l), *v. Austral.* and *N.Z.* (*rare*). [f. OOZE *v.*[1] + -LE.] *trans.* and *intr.* To undulate; to move slowly.

1934 T. Wood *Cobbers* xii. 153 The octopus..goggled his eyes and oozled his slimy, restless-writhing arms. **1958** *Tararua* XII. 29 The critics will no doubt note that *to oozle* and *to trickle*, which denoted much slower modes of locomotion, were comparatively little used.

oozlum bird (ˈuːzlʌm). [Fanciful.] A mythical or unrecognized bird (see quots.).

1899 W. T. Goodge *Hits, Skits, & Jingles* 6 It's a curious bird, the Oozlum, And a bird that's mighty wise, For it always flies tail-first to Keep the dust out of its eyes! **1951** Partridge *Dict. Slang* (ed. 4) 1126/1 *Oozlum bird*, 'a bird whose species you cannot recognise on sight',..: Naval. **1974** P. Cave *Dirtiest Picture Postcard* xvii. 113 The fabulous oozlum bird, which flies round in ever-decreasing circles until it disappears up its own arsehole in a puff of blue smoke.

‖**oozoa** (əʊəʊˈzəʊə), *sb. pl. Zool.* [mod.L., f. Gr. ᾠό-ν egg + ζῷα, pl. of ζῷον animal.] Carus's term for unicellular animals, as resembling the ova of higher animals; a synonym of PROTOZOA.

1881 Cleland *Evolution* i. 9 Oken appreciated the correspondence between the ovum, the beginning of life in the complex animal, and the 'oozoa' or simplest forms of animals.

Hence **ooˈzoan**, a member of the *oozoa*.

oozy (ˈuːzɪ), *a.* Also 4–5 **wosie**, 6 **woosye**, 7–8 **ouzy**; in branch II, **osie, ozie, oasy, oazy**. [In branch I, OE. *wōsiȝ*, f. *wōs* juice, OOZE *sb.*[1]; in branch II, late ME. *wosie*, f. *wose* mud, OOZE *sb.*[2]; in III a later formation related to OOZE *v.*[1]]

†**I. 1.** Full of moisture, juicy. (Only OE.)

c **1000** *Sax. Leechd.* I. 270 Ðeos wyrt..ys wel wosiȝ.

II. Related to OOZE *sb.*[2], mud.

2. Of water: Charged with ooze or mud; muddy.

1398 Trevisa *Barth. De P.R.* xiii. v. (MS. Bodl.) lf. 129/1 The Ryuer Gion..comeþ oute of Paradise..it [is] troublye erþy slymy and wosie. **1782** W. Gilpin *Observ. Wye* (1789) 53 It's waters now became ouzy, and discoloured. **1791** Cowper *Iliad* ii. 1075 Xanthus deep-dimpled rolls his oozy tide. **1870** Morris *Earthly Par.* I. i. 172 A brook..Oozy and foul, half choked with grass.

3. Composed of or resembling ooze, having the consistency of wet mud or slime. Of a sea-bottom: Consisting of ooze or fine mud.

1563 Golding *Cæsar* (1565) 113 b, Ryding at anchor in a woosye and open shore. **1610** Holland *Camden's Brit.* i. 639 Oasy mud in the botome. **1625** Purchas *Pilgrims* II. viii. ii. §2. 1367 Great flats of Osie Quagmires. **1629** Milton *Ode Nativity* 124 And bid the weltring waves their oozy channel keep. **1688** Sir R. Redding 13 Oct. in *Boate's Nat. Hist. Irel.* (1726) 189 The bottoms,..part sandy, part stony, and part ouzey, and of a black clay. **1717** Tabor in *Phil. Trans.* XXX. 802 The Lands in that Tract..are still very owzy and tender. **1730** Wriglesworth *Log Bk. of the Lyell* 2 June, Anchored in 17 Fath...in Oazy Ground. **1775** Romans *Florida* App. 71 Your first soundings will be about 80 fathom..oozy ground. **1828** Stark *Elem. Nat. Hist.* I. 298 These birds..frequent sea-shores, and the muddy and oozy margins of large rivers. **1854** Badham *Halieut.* 42 An oozy bottom does best for flat fish, such as soles, turbots, and plaice. **1890** H. H. Johnston in *Nature* 13 Nov. 45 All the oozy water-meadows are planted with rice.

fig. *c* **1440** *Jacob's Well* 68 Ȝoure body gaderyth euere more wose of synne,..þer-fore ȝoure body is a foul wosy pytt. **1617** Hieron *Wks.* (1620) II. 225 The best of Gods children are now and then to bee dashed [= to-bedashed] as they trauell thorow this oosie and muddy world. **1879** J. Cook *Marriage* 14 Any oozy region where the mere sediment of discussion settles.

b. Of a sound: Resembling that of something falling heavily on ooze.

1844 Dickens *Mart. Chuz.* xiii, It fell with an oozy, slushy sound among the grass.

III. Related to OOZE *v.*[1]

4. Exuding moisture; damp with exuded or deposited moisture.

1714 Gay *Trivia* iii. 197 The oozy Oyster. **1725** Bradley *Fam. Dict.*, *Fistula*, a hollow ouzy Ulcer in the Posteriors. **1725** Pope *Odyss.* iv. 543 The seer..Basks on the breezy shore..His oozy limbs. **1819** Shelley *Julian & Maddalo* 219 We climbed the oozy stairs Into an old courtyard. **1858** Hawthorne *Fr. & It. Jrnls.* I. 102 The floor of the dungeon oozy with wet. **1863** Woolner *My beautiful Lady* 20 Thrushes, which To feast on morsels oozy rich, Cracked poor snails' curling niche.

b. Slimy or damp: said of seaweed.

(Perhaps with some reference to OOZE *sb.*[3])

1742 Young *Nt. Th.* ix. 128 Oozy wreath And dismal seaweed crown her. **1762–9** Falconer *Shipwr.* iii. 661 By oozy tangles grappled fast. **1819** Shelley *Ode to West Wind* iii, The oozy woods [forests of seaweeds] which wear The sapless foliage of the ocean.

Hence **ˈoozily** *adv.*, **ˈooziness**.

1684 tr. *Bonet's Merc. Compit.* xix. 706 Water-furrows made to drain the ouziness of the Earth. **1745** tr. *Columella's Husb.* ii. ix, A salt and bitter ousiness. **1871** R. Ellis *Catullus* lxi. 15 Hands to the winds above Torches oozily swinging.

op[1]. A colloquial abbreviation of OPTIME, q.v.

1828 *Sporting Mag.* XXI. 426 Aspirant Senior Ops' and embryo Wranglers. **1894** *Ch. Times* 26 Jan. 84 A pleasure which he would not have exchanged for a place among the Senior Ops.

op[2] (ɒp). *Mus.* Pl. **opp, ops.** Abbrev. OPUS 1 (rarely OPUS *v.*).

In some early uses the abbreviation may be of the Italian *opera*.

1784 (*title*) A Favorite Concerto for the Harpsichord or Piano Forte with Accompanyments: Composed by Giuseppe Haydn. Op. 37. *a* **1865** Mrs. Gaskell *Let.* (1966) 817 Violet: 'Have you brought any music down Miss Gaskell?' Meta: 'No.' Violet: 'Oh—but I've brought *Op.* 7 down with me.' **1880** [see OPUS 1]. **1885** W. S. Gilbert *Mikado* ii. 36 The music hall singer attends a series Of masses and fugues and 'ops' By Bach, interwoven With Spohr and Beethoven, At classical Monday Pops. **1901** *Punch* 1 May 325/2 (*caption*) Lady (referring to programme, to friend). '"Schumann, Op. 2". What's the meaning of "Op. 2"?' 'Arry (who thinks he is being addressed, and always ready to oblige with information). 'Oh, Op. 2. Second dance; second 'op, yer know. May I 'ave the pleasure?' **1921** [see OPUS *v.*]. **1924** *Public Opinion* 12 Sept. 258/2 No longer does light and irresponsible music suffice as it did in days that are gone. The inclination of the public is towards the classical. The programmes that give the 'symphonies and ops' prove the most attractive. **1933** *Radio Times* 14 Apr. 108/2 The famous violinist, Rode, for whom Beethoven..composed this sonata for violin and pianoforte, Op. 96. **1968** *Listener* 11 July 56/2 These waltzes..differ considerably in style from the fine set of six waltzes for piano duet, Op. 22, of only a little later. **1974** *Times* 19 Oct. 9/6 Ashkenazy chooses..slow tempo for the fugues..in Op. 110. **1975** *Gramophone* July 205/1 Dvorak. Slavonic Dances, Opp. 46 and 72.

op[3] (ɒp).

1. Colloq. abbrev. OPERATION. **a.** = OPERATION 6.

1925 W. Deeping *Sorrell & Son* xviii. 273 Motor-bus ran over her..pretty hopeless. Winter has seen her,—but thought she wouldn't stand an op. **1932** A. Christie *Peril at End House* iii. 50 Just before my op... Operation. For appendicitis. **1933** Joyce *Let.* 30 May (1966) III. 281 Dangerous for operated eye which may go blind during op. because of loss of vitreous. **1934** *Punch* 11 Apr. 397/1 No need for immediate op.; right eye untouched, but he fears left may be permanently damaged. **1953** C. Day Lewis *Italian Visit* v. 59 I'd not advise you to believe There's a slick op. to end your grief. **1964** G. L. Cohen *What's Wrong with Hospitals?* iv. 74 The probationers agreed that minor ops gave the most trouble. **1973** *Guardian* 26 May 1/5 Ops on rates. Free vasectomy operations..were available in Birmingham from yesterday. **1974** O. Manning *Rain Forest* ii. i. 139 'I was so tired the evening we reached Al-Bustan, I forgot to take that damn pill.' 'If it was as long ago as that, it *is* too late, dear, unless you want a major op.'

b. Freq. pl. = OPERATION 7. Also *attrib.* and *transf.*

In quots. 1941[1], 1942[1] short for *Operations Room*.

1916 [see *night op* s.v. NIGHT *sb.* 14]. **1925** Fraser & Gibbons *Soldier & Sailor Words* 215 *Ops.*, operations. **1941** *Jrnl. Aeronaut. Sci.* (Aeronaut. Rev. sect.) Jan. 32/3 The atmosphere of the room is recreated, even to the introduction of some of the new aeronautical colloquialisms, such as 'Ops' for the operations room. **1941** *Illustr. London News* CXCVIII. 434/1 The bomber pilot is aware that his squadron is scheduled for what the Service calls 'Ops' (Operations) when his batman wakes him with an early-morning cup of tea. **1942** T. Rattigan *Flare Path* i. 112, I went up to ops. at five-thirty. **1942** *R.A.F. Jrnl.* 30 May 33 The..officer..delved into his brief-case and produced the ops log. **1942** *Tee Emm* (Air Ministry) II. 89 Make certain before going out on ops. that you have your whistle. **1944** 'N. Shute' *Pastoral* iii. 57 Each day we practise some new thing that we have learnt from the last op. **1949** *Radio Times* 15 July 38/3 Ann Scott,..gets into conversation..with an American girl who met a boy in the R.A.F. three months ago... 'Now he's starting Ops and he wants us to get married right away—he's like that!' **1967** O. Wynd *Walk Softly* xi. 171 'This is the ops room.' The place had one door and was about thirty feet square. **1970** *Daily Tel.* 16 June 7/1 A seasoned campaigner watched the campaign in awe. 'It is like a military op,' he said. **1973** 'A. Hall' *Tango Briefing* x. 120 They'd been forced to set up the op... The decision-making had been at Prime Minister level. **1973** D. Miller *Chinese Jade Affair* xviii. 173, I looked in some awe at the maps spread out in true 'Ops Room' fashion.

2. Colloq. abbrev. OPERATIVE *sb.*, OPERATOR.

a. A (private) detective (see OPERATIVE *sb.* 3 b).

1926 *Clues* Nov. 162/1 *Op*, a private detective agency operator. **1927** D. Hammett in *Black Mask* May 24/1 He says in all his fifty years of gum-shoeing he's never seen such a handsome op, besides being a fashion plate and a social butterfly and the heir to millions. **1929** —— *Dain Curse* (1930) xx. 224 'Can you spare me another op?' I asked. 'MacMan is available.' **1975** J. Gores *Hammett* viii. 60 Watching the stocky two-hundred-pound op.. Hammett felt a little ill... 'You going to take over the investigation of the police department?'

b. A radio or telegraph operator (see OPERATOR 5). (See also quot. 1970.)

1931 G. Irwin *Amer. Tramp & Underworld Slang* 138 *Op*, a telegraph operator. **1942** T. Rattigan *Flare Path* i. 94 Two bumped off—tail gunner and wireless op. **1970** *Amer. Speech 1968* XLIII. 288 *Op*, a telephone, telegraph, or teletype operator. **1973** A. Ross *Dunfermline Affair* 13 He had been a Radio Op in the R.A.F.

op[4] (ɒp), colloq. abbrev. OPTICAL *a.* 2 c. *op art*, = *optical art* s.v. OPTICAL *a.* 2 c. Also *attrib.* orig. *U.S.*

1964 *Time* 23 Oct. 78/1 No less a break from abstract expressionism than pop art, op art is made tantalizing, eye-teasing, even eye-smarting by visual researchers using all the ingredients of an optometrist's nightmare. *Ibid.*, The Museum of Modern Art is planning an op show titled 'The Responsive Eye' early next year. **1964, 1965** [see OPTICAL *a.* 2 c]. **1965** *Observer* 28 Feb. 2/6 'Op Art'—as it is known among the smart set—has taken America's contemporary art enthusiasts by storm, and made its predecessor, 'Pop Art', seem *passé*. *Ibid.* (Colour Suppl.) 23 May 23/2 Op(tical) dresses are dazzling—literally. They jar the eye with geometric billboard colour... Trad dresses are gentle and demure. Op. dresses are stark and simple. **1965** *Sun* 24 May 5/7 Then you get a blasting of Op art—that's the optical illusion art that the young artists are raving about. **1966** *Time* 28 Jan. 44 Hard on the heels of op artists, who address their work to the retina, has come a widespread number of 'kinetic' artists, who try to combine mechanics and art. **1966** *Punch* 2 Feb. 158/1 (*caption*) Or there's this op-art bowler, sir, for more formal occasions. *Ibid.* 15 June 876/3 Knee-length skirts, non-plastic fabrics, non-Op shoes; also short-haired men and neat girls in plain stockings. **1967** J. Symons *Man who killed Himself* ii. vi. 184 She was dressed now in a black and white op art dress. **1967** *Punch* 21 June 906/1 Infinite trouble is taken by op artists to produce an illusion of movement. **1967** *Spectator* 18 Aug. 194/3 With bright Op patternings, primary Pop colours and uninhibited use of synthetic materials, these designers..parallel our painters and sculptors in inventing new shapes and forms through the use of new materials. **1970** M. de Sausmarez *Bridget Riley* i. 15 Its decorative potential..has been..widely exploited commercially in 'Op' dresses, 'Op' advertising, and 'Op' packaging. **1970** W. J. Burley *To kill Cat* i. 12 A sleeveless frock in gay op-art material. **1974** *Encycl. Brit. Micropædia* VII. 545/1 The effects of Op art can be based either on perspective illusion or on chromatic tension; in painting, the dominant medium of Op art, the surface tension is usually maximized to the point at which an actual flickering is perceived by the human eye. **1974** *Listener* 24 Jan. 108/2 Artists (especially Op-artists and the like) can impose an unjustifiable authority on the observer. **1976** 'Z. Stone' *Modigliani Scandal* i. iii. 35 He..looked at the desk. .. The grain..flowed like an op-art painting.

op, ME. variant of UP *adv.*, *prep.*, and *prefix*.

op-, the form of the L. prefix OB- before *p*, as *oppilate*, *oppose*, *oppress*, *oppugn*. (Only one *p* is pronounced in Eng.)

opaac, obs. form of OPAQUE.

opacate (əʊˈpeɪkeɪt), *v. rare.* [f. ppl. stem of L. *opācāre*, f. *opāc-us* OPAQUE: see -ATE[3] 5.] *trans.* To render opaque, to dim.

1660 Boyle *New Exp. Phys. Mech.* xxxvii. 308 A whiteness which did..opacate (as some speak) the inside of the Glass. *a* **1691** —— *Hist. Air* xx. (1692) 196 The Air is..sometimes more dark, and, as it were, muddy, being clogg'd and opacated with terrestrial Streams. **1890** H. Frederic *Lawton Girl* 20 Eyes..dimmed and opacated by the effects of dissipation.

opacification (əʊˌpæsɪfɪˈkeɪʃən). [f. as next + -IFICATION.] The process of rendering or becoming opaque.

1903 *Med. Rec.* (N.Y.) LXIII. 333/2 Hyperplasia, degeneration—these are results of malnutrition and the essentials of opacification [of the lens]. **1947** *Jrnl. Soc. Glass Technol.* XXXI. Abstr. Sect. 29 A boron-free enamel might be fired to a certain degree, after which opacification decreased because the TiO_2 was dissolved. **1953** *Radiology* LX. 366/1 (*caption*) The poor opacification [to X-rays] of the liver and of the portal vein is typical of cirrhosis. **1970** *Nature* 24 Oct. 363/1 Opacification of the lens began as an increase in sheen posteriorly.

opacifier (əʊˈpæsɪfaɪə(r)). [f. next + -ER[1].] A substance which renders something opaque.

1911 *Chem. Abstr.* V. 168 Cast Iron Enamels... SnO_2 and cryolite are the best opacifiers. **1959** *Which?* Nov. 152/1 Opacifiers (which make it look opaque and creamy) make the shampoos look more attractive. **1973** *Daily Tel.* (Colour Suppl.) 12 Oct. 72/4 The developer then gets to work on the negative and the opacifier which gradually clears to reveal the dyes, now released from the negative and visible above the white pigment. *a* **1977** *Harrison Mayer Ltd. Catal.* 23/2 Tin oxide is widely used as a glaze opacifier.

opacify (əʊˈpæsɪfaɪ), *v.* [f. OPAC(ITY + -IFY; cf. F. (*s'*)*opacifier*.] **a.** *trans.* To render opaque.

1940 *Chem. Abstr.* XXIV. 4268 (*heading*) Paper opacified with calcium carbonate. **1955** P. D. TREVOR-ROPER *Ophthalm.* xxiii. 413 Post-operative uveitis may opacify the posterior corneal layers. **1957** S. D. GERSHON et al. in E. Sagarin *Cosmetics* xxiv. 615 Initially, cold-waving lotions were marketed as transparent liquids. Shortly thereafter, the advantage of marketing an opaque liquid, the milkiness connoting richness and gentleness, became evident. As a result, practically all marketed waving lotions were opacified. **1971** *Country Life* 6 May 1084/1 Milk-white glass opacified with arsenic displays a fiery opalescence if held to the light.

b. *intr.* To become opaque.

1954 S. DUKE-ELDER *Parson's Dis. Eye* (ed. 12) ii. 24 If either of these membranes [of the cornea] is disrupted, fluid is absorbed and the tissue opacifies. **1967** *Amer. Jrnl. Roentgenology* C. 410/2 The fluid-filled fundus of the stomach.. opacifies during abdominal aortography. **1971** *Nature* 12 Mar. 120/2 Corneas rapidly opacified and swelled with the first enzyme digestion after the initial irradiation.

So **oˈpacified** *ppl. a.*, **oˈpacifying** *ppl. a.* and *vbl. sb.*

1914 *Chem. Abstr.* VIII. 224 The opacifying effect of the metallic oxides of Sn, Zr, Ti and Al.. utilizable for white enamels. **1947** *Endeavour* VI. 117 The opacifying agent dissolves, leaving the glass transparent while molten, but causing it to become opaque upon cooling. **1954** *Amer. Jrnl. Roentgenology* LXXII. 592/1 In the later films the liver seems to be more opacified.. than the spleen. **1963** *Times* 25 May 11/4 These enamels were produced by fusing what amounted to opacified glass on to wafer-thin copper. **1973** *Sci. Amer.* Oct. 128/1 A talc base will often be augmented with an opacifying pigment such as zinc oxide or titanium dioxide.

opacimeter (əʊpæˈsɪmiːtə(r)). [f. OPACI(TY + -METER.] An instrument for measuring opacity, esp. by reflection.

1919 *Chem. Abstr.* XIII. 2892 (*heading*) Opacimeter designed for the estimation of the quantity of bacteria. **1944** *Paper Trade Jrnl.* 26 Oct. 27/2 The white body consists of a white standard protected by a cover glass, as is the case in the Bausch and Lomb opacimeter. **1967** *TAPPI* Feb. 59A/1 The B & L Opacimeter reads either printing opacity (as defined by Davis) or contrast ratio (as defined by TAPPI official methods).

oˈpacious, *a.* Now *rare.* [irreg. f. L. *opāc-us* + -IOUS.] = OPACOUS.

1642 *Plea for King* 4 The opacious body of the earth. *a* **1672** STERRY *Appear. God to Man* Wks. (1710) 150 Here nothing is opacious, or shady to keep out the Light. **1713** A. COLLIER *Clavis Univ.* ii. 23 Is the moon.. a luminous thing? .. No; but a dark or opacious body. **1953** S. BECKETT *Watt* III. 158, I was very fond of fences, of wire fences,..; not of walls, nor palisades, nor opacious hedges, no.

opacite (ˈəʊpəsaɪt). *Min.* [mod. (1872) f. L. *opāc-us* OPAQUE + -ITE[1].] (See quots.)

1879 RUTLEY *Stud. Rocks* x. 166 Opacite is the term applied to perfectly opaque, black, amorphous, microscopic granules, patches, or scales. **1880** *Dana's Min.* App. ii. 42 *Opacite*, a name proposed by Vogelsang for the black opaque scales or grains.. which cannot be identified with magnetite, menaccanite, or any other mineral.

opacity (əʊˈpæsɪtɪ). [a. F. *opacité* (15–16th c. in Hatz.-Darm.), ad. L. *opācitās*, f. *opācus* OPAQUE.] The quality or fact of being opaque; opaqueness.

1. a. The state of being in shadow; darkness, dimness, obscurity; also, an instance of this.

1611 COTGR., *Opacité*, opacitie, shadinesse, vmbrage [etc.]. **1646** SIR T. BROWNE *Pseud. Ep.* VI. x. (1686) 263 Others ascribe these causes to the graduality of Opacity and Light. **1656** S. H. *Gold. Law* 103 Artificial Opticks.. to amplifie thy sight, and dispel Opacity. *a* **1763** SHENSTONE *Ess.* (1806) 3 He renders the opacity of the other more discernible. **1807** KNOX & JEBB *Corr.* I. 358 When the soul emerges from the opacities of this mortal life. **1812** G. CHALMERS *Dom. Econ. Gt. Brit.* Pref. 13 The glimmering of the faintest dawn is more invigorating than the gloom of total opacity.

b. The condition of not reflecting light.

1794 G. ADAMS *Nat. & Exp. Philos.* II. xxi. 402 Opacity .. [in one sense] signifies want of transparency; in the latter, that no light comes from the body. **1862** TYNDALL *Mountaineer.* ix. 75 It was most interesting to observe.. tree after tree losing its opacity and suddenly robing itself in glory.

2. a. The quality or condition of being impervious to light: opposed to transparency or translucency; *spec.* the ratio of the intensity of the light incident on a sample or object to that of the light transmitted by it.

1634 PEACHAM *Gentl. Exerc.* III. 139 As Cristall, Ice, &c. by reason of their perspicuitie.. so are Quicksilver, Silver, Lead, Steele, Iron, Tin, and the like, by reason of their opacity. **1638** WILKINS *New World* I. (1684) 102 An Orb of thick Vaporous Air.. though it have not so great Opacity, as to terminate the Sight. **1750** tr. *Leonardus' Mirr. Stones* 35 Perspicuity, or opacity, occasion many differences in stones. **1796** HOME in *Phil. Trans.* LXXXVII. 9 A lady who had lost the sight of both [eyes], by opacities in the crystalline lenses. **1814** A. AIKIN *Man. Min.* Introd. 31 When the passage of light is entirely stopped opacity comes on. **1885** *Chamb. Jrnl.* II. 140/2 The.. milk-tester which.. owes its efficiency to the relative opacity of pure milk and milk and water. **1890** HURTER & DRIFFIELD in *Jrnl. Soc. Chem. Industry* 31 May 455/2 The inverse of that fraction, or $I/I_x = e^{kA}$ measures the opacity of the substance. **1926** J. W. T. WALSH *Photometry* xiii. 392 The opacity is then measured by placing the exposed area of the plate between a source of light and a photometer. **1939** *Q. Jrnl. Meteorol. Soc.* LXV. 417 In the case of five stations.. the summer values of opacity are higher than the winter values, owing to the prevalence of sea fogs in summer. **1966** R. J. ROSS *Television Film Engin.* iv. 169 The silver deposit and the opacity are so related that the logarithm of the opacity is directly proportional to the mass of silver.

b. *transf.* ***acoustic opacity***, imperviousness to waves of sound. Also used with reference to other forms of radiation.

1871 TYNDALL *Fragm. Sc.* (1879) I. x. 331 Here we had the acoustic opacity of the air. **1878** *Smithsonian Rep.* 510 In the cases of acoustic opacity.. if he had simultaneously made observations in an opposite direction, he would have come to a different conclusion. **1928** [see LIPIODOL]. **1971** *Jrnl. Electron. Microsc.* XX. 124/1 The pronounced electron opacity was localized especially.. on the outer membrane.

3. *fig.* **a.** Darkness or obscurity of meaning. **b.** Mental or intellectual dullness; denseness or obtuseness of intellect; *concr.* one in whom this is embodied.

α. **1560** ROLLAND *Crt. Venus* II. 497 Sa full thair warkis was of opacitie [*ed.* 1884 *pr.* oporcitie].

β. **1640** BP. HALL *Serm. 1 John* i. 5, Wks. 1837 V. 421 That gloomy and base opacity of conceit, wherewith our earthly minds are commonly wont to be overclouded. *a* **1677** BARROW *Serm.* Wks. 1716 III. 375 No Discourse could.. penetrate those Opacities of Ignorance. **1837** CARLYLE *Misc. Ess., Mirabeau* (1872) V. 202 Natural opacity being so doubly and trebly darkened by accidental difficulty and perversion. **1844** —— *Misc.* (1865) IV. 297 The Opacities have been pleased to suppress this election. **1874** LISLE CARR *Jud. Gwynne* I. iv. 111 A light dawned through the thick opacity of his brain.

c. With reference to a rule in *Phonology*: the state or quality of being opaque (sense 3 c).

1971 [see OPAQUE *a.* 3 c]. **1975** *Trans. Philol. Soc. 1974* 113, I have myself argued.. that for French the elegance of such a solution is outweighed by its disadvantages and that restructuring occurred when generalization of the loss of word-final [ə] made for opacity: the conditioning of denasalization before an intervocalic nasal was no longer discernible from surface phonetic shapes. **1977** *Language* LIII. 19 In each instance of opacity, a phonological rule which relates a large number of surface lexical items is obscured by the presence of other items in which the rule appears to fail.

opacous (əʊˈpeɪkəs), *a.* Now *rare.* [f. L. *opāc-us* OPAQUE + -OUS.] = OPAQUE *a.*

†**1.** = OPAQUE I. *Obs.*

1621-3 MIDDLETON & ROWLEY *Changeling* v. iii, What an opacous body had that moon that last chang'd on us! **1657** THORNLEY tr. *Longus' Daphnis & Chloe* 52 This Garden is thick, opacous, and shady. **1709** *Taffy's Triumph*, Trusting To the dark covert of the opacous night.

†**b.** = OPAQUE I b. *Obs.*

1712 tr. *Pomet's Hist. Drugs* I. 108 Too much of the Powder makes the Metal black and opacous.

2. = OPAQUE 2.

1625 N. CARPENTER *Geog. Del.* I. i. (1635) 11 The shadowes imitate the opacous bodies, whence they arise. **1662** MERRETT tr. *Neri's Art of Glass* xlii, The glass becomes transparent, and no more Opacous. **1755** B. MARTIN *Mag. Arts & Sc.* 36 Occasioned by an Eruption of Smoke, and other opacous Matter. **1814** CARY *Dante* (Chandos Classics) 159 Through which thou saw'st no better, than the mole Doth through opacous membrane. **1868** LOWELL *Under Willows* 201 The sound of human voice Or footfall.. Doth in opacous cloud precipitate The consciousness.

Hence **oˈpacously** *adv.*, opaquely; **oˈpacousness**, opaqueness.

1656 STANLEY *Hist. Philos.* v. (1701) 208/1 The first Mind, by its opacousness eclipsing their lustre. **1666** BOYLE *Orig. Formes & Qual.* Wks. 1772 III. 43 Gravity and levity, firmness and fluidity, opacousness.. transparency, &c. **1670** E. R. *Animadv. Glanvill's Ne Plus Ultra* 147 It seemed.. opacously red as Tent wine.

†**oˈpacular,** *a. Obs. rare*[−1]. [f. L. *opāc-us*, on some mistaken analogy.] Somewhat opaque.

1761 STERNE *Tr. Shandy* III. xx. Auth. Pref., To free it from any little motes, or specks of opacular matter.

opah (ˈəʊpə). [See quot. 1750.] A rare fish of the North Atlantic (*Lampris guttatus*), of the mackerel family, having a compressed oviform body with long single dorsal and anal fins, conspicuous for its brilliant colour, which varies from green to bright golden with azure reflexions. Also called the King-fish and Moon-fish.

1750 *Phil. Trans.* XLVI. 519 The black Prince, and his Cousin, from Anamaboe on the Coast of Guinea, and Mr. Creighton, formerly Governor of Capo Corso Castle, upon seeing this Fish immediately knew it, and said it was common on that Coast... The Natives call it Opah, and the English there call it the King-fish. **1798** T. HINDERWELL *Hist. Scarborough* II. ii. 229 The Opah or King-fish is of singular beauty. **1860-5** COUCH *Brit. Fishes* II. 134. **1899** *Dundee Advert.* 28 Sept. 7 A magnificent specimen of the rare British fish the opah has been captured in the North Sea .. the dimensions.. are, length 3 feet 7½ inches, width 2 feet 9½ inches,.. and weight 88 lbs.

opake, obs. form of OPAQUE.

opal (ˈəʊpəl). [ad. L. *opal-us* (Pliny); cf. Gr. ὀπάλλιος; according to Weigand II. 311, from Skr. *upala* 'precious stone, gem', the opal having been first brought from India. Cf. F. *opale* (16th c. *opalle* in Littré).]

1. a. An amorphous form of hydrous silica, somewhat resembling quartz, but in certain species exhibiting a delicate play of colour; these when cut are valuable as gems.

Many varieties have specific names: ***common opal***, of milk-white or bluish colour, with reflexion of green, yellow, and red; ***black opal***: see quot. 1884; ***fire*** or ***sun opal, harlequin, precious***, or ***noble opal***: see quot. 1874; ***semi-opal, wood-opal***, opaquer varieties. See also CACHOLONG, GEYSERITE, GIRASOL, HYALITE, HYDROPHANE, JASP-OPAL, MENILITE. Among the fancies formerly associated with the opal was, that when carried on the person wrapped in a bay-leaf it conferred invisibility.

[**1398** TREVISA *Barth. De P.R.* XVI. lxxii. (MS. Bodl.) lf. 179/1 Optalius hatte Opalis also and is a stone distingued with coloures of diuers precious stones.. þerein is þe firei coloure of þe Carbuncle, þe schynynge purpur of Amatistus, þe briȝt grene coloure of the Smaragdus, and as coloure schyneþ þerein wiþ a manere diuersite. **1567** MAPLET *Gr. Forest* 16 *Oppalus*.. is a stone in colour like to verie many, and those cleane contrarie gems.] **1598** FLORIO, *Opalo*, a diuers coloured precious stone called an Opale. **1601** HOLLAND *Pliny* II. 614 In the Opal you shal see the burning fire of the Carbuncle or Ruby, the glorious purple of the Amethyst, the greene sea of the Emeraud, and all glittering together. **1630** B. JONSON *New Inn* I. vi, I had No medicine, sir, to go invisible:.. nor an opal Wrapped in bay-leaf, in my left fist, to charm Their eyes with. **1690** LOCKE *Hum. Und.* IV. iii. (1695) 313 To this, perhaps, will be said, has not an Opall, or the infusion of *Lignum Nephriticum*, two Colours at the same time? **1727-46** THOMSON *Summer* 156 Thick thro' the whitening Opal play thy Beams. **1846** RUSKIN *Mod. Paint.* I. II. II. i. §14 Every one knows how capriciously the colours of a fine opal vary from day to day, and how rare the lights are which bring them fully out. **1865** G. MEREDITH *R. Fleming* xvi, A really fine opal, coquetting with the lights of every gem..; it shot succinct red flashes, and green, and yellow.. it was veined with lightning hues, and at times it slept in a milky cloud, innocent of fire, quite maidenlike. **1874** H. M. WESTROPP *Man. Prec. Stones* 38 The noble or precious opal.. exhibits a rich play of prismatic colours, which flash from minute fissures apparently striated with microscopic lines... This variety is called the Harlequin opal. *Ibid.* 39 Fire Opal is a rich hyacinth-red variety of opal, from Mexico. It is also called Girasol and Sun opal. **1884** *Encycl. Brit.* XVII. 777/2 The so-called 'black opals'.. consist of this matrix [of dark brown ironstone] penetrated in all directions by veins and spots of opal, forming a mixture sometimes known as 'root of opal'.

b. *fig.* in reference to its various and changing colours.

1591 SYLVESTER *Du Bartas* I. ii. 306 When we see Aurora passing gay, With Opals paint the Cieling of Cathay. **1601** SHAKS. *Twel. N.* II. iv. 77 The Tailor make thy doublet of changeable Taffata, for thy minde is a very Opall.

c. The colour of an opal.

1890 O. WILDE *Pict. Dorian Gray* v, in *Lippincott's Monthly Mag.* July 41 The sky was pure opal now. **1897** *Sears, Roebuck Catal.* 212/1 Dainty colorings.. baby blue, rose pink, opal, [etc.]. **1901** [see ASH *sb.*[2] I d]. **1914** R. BROOKE in E. Marsh *Rupert Brooke* (1918) vii. 142 Like an Italian town in silver-point.. with a sea and sky of opal and pearl and faint gold around. **1966** G. W. TURNER *Eng. Lang. Austral. & N.Z.* iv. 83 The sky turned into an unlucky opal.

2. A commercial appellation of semi-translucent white glass; = OPALINE *sb.* 2. Also with reference to the opalescence of the glass (rather than the colour). Also *attrib.*

1885 *List of Subscribers, Classified* (United Telephone Co.) (ed. 6) 229 (Advt.), Crystal and Demi-Crystal Table Services and Ornaments.. Opal, Flint, and Coloured Goods. **1889** *Advt.*, Photographic Views, Medallions, Etchings and Opals. **1891** W. J. DAWSON *Redempt. E. Strahan* iii. 49 Her work was to paint flowers and little landscapes on opal. **1949** W. A. THORPE *Eng. Glass* (ed. 2) ix. 226 It [*sc.* a 'nine-pin' bottle] belonged in the main to Bristol and Stourbridge manufacturers, and in.. white opal it lasted well into the nineteenth century. **1970** F. & L. SCHULER *Glassforming* vi. 50 To the commercial decorators the term 'glass color'.. means any fusible coating for glass, including both the transparent colors and the opal colors.

3. a. *attrib.* passing into *adj.* Of or resembling the opal or that of the opal, opalescent.

a **1649** DRUMM. OF HAWTH. *Poems* Wks. (1711) 26 Now an opal hew Bepaints heaven's crystal. *Ibid.* 40 Aurora.. with her opal light Night's horrours checketh, putting stars to flight. **1667** MILTON *P.L.* II. 1049 Farr off th' Empyreal Heav'n.. With Opal Towrs and Battlements adorn'd Of living Saphire. **1756** C. LUCAS *Ess. Waters* III. 307 A kind of opal color is produced. **1817** CAMPBELL *Reullura* 187 When the opal morn first flushed the sky. *c* **1865** J. WYLDE in *Circ. Sc.* I. 149/1 It should present an opal appearance.

b. *spec.* Applied to an electric light bulb made of translucent white glass.

[**1901** F. B. CROCKER *Electr. Lighting* II. xvii. 423 Lamps are made in many colors, such as red, blue, green, amber, opal, frosted, etc., besides the ordinary clear glass bulbs.] **1904** *Electr. Rev.* 19 Feb. (Suppl.) p. ix (Advt.), The 'Ideal' half opal lamp. **1926** *Gloss. Terms Electr. Engin.* (*B.S.I.*) 148 *Opal lamp*, a filament lamp, the bulb of which is made of opalescent glassware so as to enlarge the source of light with a consequent reduction in surface brightness [etc.]. **1934** *Discovery* Aug. 229/2 A hole in a screen in front of an opal lamp. **1938** [see PEARL *sb.*[1] 16 b]. **1976** *Daily Tel.* (Colour Suppl.) 25 June 15/2 Opal light bulbs are primarily suitable for use where the bulb is clearly visible, for their coating hides the filament.

4. *Comb.*, as ***opal-buyer***, ***-field***, ***-seeker***; ***opal-black***, ***-coloured***, ***-globed***, ***-green***, ***-grey***, ***-hued***, ***-like***, ***-pale***, ***-shelled***, ***tinted*** adjs.; **opal-agate** (see quot.); **opal blue**, a carefully prepared spirit-blue; **opal dirt** *Austral.*, the type of earth in which opal is found; **opal glass**, (*a*) = OPALINE *sb.* 2; (*b*) glass iridescent like the opal; also *attrib.*; **opal gouger** *Austral.*, one who digs for opal; cf. GOUGER c; **opal-jasper** = JASP-OPAL; **opal plate**, a plate of opal glass on which a photograph is taken; **opal ware**, ware made of opal glass, *spec.* a type of heat-resistant opalescent ware (now, with capital initial and as one word, a proprietary name in the U.K.).

1896 A. H. CHESTER *Dict. Names Min.*, **Opal-agate*, opal, with an agate-like structure, showing bands of different colours. *a* **1963** J. LUSBY in B. James *Austral. Short Stories* (1963) 225 The eyes *opal-black in wrinkled slits of skin. **1880** FRISWELL in *Soc. Arts Jrnl.* 445 The hydrochloride.. is known as *opal blue. **1911** C. E. W. BEAN '*Dreadnought*' *of Darling* xxv. 222 The most precious colour, the *opal-buyers told us, was 'fire'—the rich glow as of a red-hot horseshoe, which you find in the heart of the best opal. **1598** SYLVESTER *Du Bartas* II. ii. II. *Babylon* 210 Th' *Opal-colour'd Morn. **1847** EMERSON *Poems* (1857) 55 The opal-colored days. **1925** *Ann. Rep. Dept. Mines New South Wales 1924* 85/2 The '*Opal Dirt' is picking ground, being simply a layer of clay or sandy clay overlain by sandstone. **1963** Opal-dirt [see BOTTOM *v.* 5]. **1965** *Ann. Rep. Dept. Mines New South Wales 1963* 51/2 Using air compressor and jack spade on the softer opal dirt. **1902** *Chambers's Jrnl.* Aug. 496/2 There are few men on the *opal-fields who do not average five pounds per week. **1866** 'J. EASEL' in *Queen* 11 Aug. 93/2 The *opal glass, which transmits a rich and lovely iridescent light, exactly like the precious stone from which it is named. **1885** Opal-glass [see OPALOTYPE]. **1923** *Vogue* Oct. 47/1 A pair of feathered bird pictures and French opal glass bottles. **1956** L. M. ANGUS-BUTTERWORTH *Brit. Table & Ornamental Glass* iii. 10 The handle in opal glass. **1890** *Anthony's Photogr. Bull.* III. 104 For a good negative illuminator,..a duplex or other *opal-globed lamp will not be far to seek. **1931** V. PALMER *Separate Lives* 200 The bleary-eyed *opal-gougers, who spoke as if the hot winds had dried up the fountains of their speech. **1936** A. RUSSELL *Gone Nomad* vii. 57 Lured on by the uncertainty of what the next stroke of his pick will reveal, the opal-gouger never abandons hope, until, with his funds and credit exhausted, he may hope no longer. **1955** S. SPENDER *Coll. Poems 1928–53* 113 The eye is carried by the choppy tide To a shore opposite of *opal-green spaces. **1867** A. J. MUNBY *Diary* 7 June in D. Hudson *Munby* (1972) 239 All things were cool and charming, and *opal-grey, in the cool sweet morning. **1881** O. WILDE *Poems* 126 Tremulous opal-hued anemones. **1882** OUIDA *Maremma* 110 An *opal-hued light on land, and sky and sea. **1896** A. H. CHESTER *Dict. Names Min.*, **Opal-jasper*, common opal with the color of yellow jasper. **1598** SYLVESTER *Du Bartas* II. ii. I. *Ark* 495 Still (*opal-like) some changeable is seen. **1946** W. DE LA MARE *Traveller* 25 *Opal-pale..A strange and deepening lustre tinged the air. **1902** *Chambers's Jrnl.* Aug. 496/1 At that hour the *opal-seeker must cease his daily toil. **1922** V. WOOLF *Jacob's Room* i. 11 Out pushes an *opal-shelled crab. **1894** *Montgomery Ward Catal.* 520/3 Blue *Opal Ware. A new pattern, just out, made in fancy colored glass in blue opal. *Ibid.* 521/1 Opal Ware. **1929** *Encycl. Brit.* X. 412/1 In 1927 the United States had..23 manufacturers making opal ware. **1958** *Mixed Batch* (J. A. Jobling & Co.) July 47 This new glass..was a delicate pearly white; and it was given the name Opal-ware. **1964** *Trade Marks Jrnl.* 29 Apr. 688/2 Jobling Opalware... Tableware..made of opal glass. James A. Jobling & Company Limited,..Sunderland, manufacturers.

opaled ('əʊpəld), *ppl. a. rare.* [f. OPAL + -ED[2].] Made iridescent like an opal.

a **1849** POE *Al Aaraaf* I. iii, A wreath that twined each starry form around, And all the opal'd air in colour bound.

opalesce (əʊpə'lɛs), *v.* [f. OPAL + *-esce*, repr. L. *-ēscere* in *albēscĕre*, etc.: see OPALESCENT.] *intr.* To exhibit a play of colours or iridescence like that of the opal.

1819 J. G. CHILDREN *Chem. Anal.* 440 Nitrate of mercury is a very delicate test of the presence of hyposulphurous acid ..when only one hundred-thousandth is present, it opalesces on a few minutes standing.

opalescence (əʊpə'lɛsəns). [f. as next + -ENCE.] The quality of being opalescent; a play of various colours as in the opal; milky iridescence.

1805–17 R. JAMESON *Char. Min.* (ed. 3) 256 Some minerals, when held in particular directions, reflect from single spots in their interior a coloured shining lustre, and this is what is understood by opalescence. **1879** *St. George's Hosp. Rep.* IX. 647 A persistent opalescence of the urine. **1879** ROOD *Chromatics* 55 Not only liquids and solids exhibit this phenomenon of opalescence.

opalescent (əʊpə'lɛsənt), *a.* [f. OPAL + -ESCENT.] Exhibiting a play of various colours like that of the opal; having a milky iridescence.

1813 BAKEWELL *Introd. Geol.* (1815) Vocab. 488 *Opalescent*, transmitting variously coloured light combined with a milky cloudiness, as in the siliceous stone called opal. **1846** RUSKIN *Mod. Paint.* I. II. I. vii. §15 Titian hardly ever paints sunshine, but a certain opalescent twilight which has as much of human emotion as of imitative truth in it. **1868** LOSSING *Hudson* 33 The beautiful labradorite, or opalescent felspar. **1880** *Sat. Rev.* 20 Mar. 385/1 The opalescent effects manifested by specimens of glass after being long buried underground.

opalesque (əʊpə'lɛsk), *a.* [f. OPAL + -ESQUE.] Opal-like in colour or iridescence; opalescent.

1863 *Art Jrnl.* June 108 The opalesque colour, and the pearly lightening up of the jewelled dress..are magical in effect. **1877** DIXON *Diana, Lady Lyle* I. III. iii. 190 A fairy pool of water lies, fluent and opalesque, under an amber slab. **1877** BLACK *Green Past.* xxxi, [The hills] are on the contrary of a pale opalesque blue and white.

opaline ('əʊpəlɪn, -aɪn), *a.* and *sb.* [f. OPAL + -INE, after *adamantine*, *amethystine*, *crystalline*, etc. Cf. F. *opalin* (1801 in Hatz.-Darm.).]

A. *adj.* Having the colour or iridescence of an opal; opalescent. Also, resembling opal other than in colour.

1784 *Cook's 3rd Voy.* III. xiii. II. 257 Assuming various tints of blue, from a pale sapphirine, to a deep violet colour; which were frequently mixed with a ruby, or opaline redness. **1826** KIRBY & SP. *Entomol.* IV. 283 *Opaline*,.. a blueish white reflecting the prismatic colours. **1831** R. KNOX *Cloquet's Anat.* 626 By boiling, they lose their transparency, and acquire an opaque opaline tint. **1894** P. PINKERTON *Adriatica, Song for Venice*, Now shall Venezia shine In waters opaline. **1962** C. FRONDEL *Dana's Syst. Min.* (ed. 7) III. 296 Common opal. In general, opal without a play of colour... Includes..rock-forming opaline silica.

B. *sb.* **1.** 'A term sometimes applied to a variety of yellow chalcedony which presents an opaline semi-opacity' (Westropp).

1861 C. W. KING *Antique Gems* i. 8 When the stone [Calcedony] has a bright tinge of yellow, it is named the Opaline. **1874** WESTROPP *Gems* 43.

2. A semi-translucent glass, whitened by the addition of phosphate of lime, peroxide of tin, or other ingredient; also called *milk-glass*. Also, translucent glass of a colour other than white.

1875 KNIGHT *Dict. Mech.* 1561/1. **1964** [see *make-up mirror* s.v. MAKE-UP 6]. **1970** G. SAVAGE *Dict. Antiques* 296/1 The manufacture of opaline was at its most popular between 1840 and 1870, after which it declined in popularity.

3. An opaline colour, surface, or expanse.

1871 R. ELLIS *Catullus* lxiii. 88 When he saw the sexless Attis by the seas' level opaline. **1893** MRS. C. PRAED *Outlaw & Lawmaker* II. v. 33 In some places the pool was covered with a strange opaline.

opalish ('əʊpəlɪʃ), *a. rare.* [f. OPAL + -ISH[1].] Somewhat like opal in colour.

1805 *Phil. Trans.* XCV. 336 The last portion of edulcorating water dropped through the filter of an opalish hue.

opalite ('əʊpəlaɪt). Also **Opalite**. [f. OPAL + -ITE[1].] Opal glass made in the form of tiles or bricks suitable for building purposes. (Formerly a proprietary name.)

1903 *Science* 13 Feb. 266/2 The feature of this building is the treatment of the interior of the cages with light-green opalite tile. **1940** *Archit. Rev.* LXXXVII. 19 The walls and counter fronts are faced with black and white opalite glass. **1975** HUNTINGTON & MICKADEIT *Building Construction* (ed. 4) x. 520 Structural glass is available in the form of tile or slabs..for use as a finish on exterior and interior wall surfaces. It is known by various trade names such as *Carrara Glass*, *Vitrolite*, and *Opalite*.

opalize ('əʊpəlaɪz), *v.* [f. OPAL + -IZE.]

1. *intr.* To exhibit a play of colours like the opal; to opalesce.

1811 PINKERTON *Petral.* I. 580 A coal..in which crimson, green, blue, and yellow, perfectly opalise or interchange; so that the substance has more splendour than even the noble opal.

2. *trans.* To make iridescent like an opal. Chiefly in **'opalized** *ppl. a.*, converted into opal, made opaline or opalescent.

1811 PINKERTON *Petral.* I. 159 The beautiful opalised kind of felspar, called Labrador stone. **1838** T. THOMSON *Chem. Org. Bodies* 99 Either not at all or only very slightly opalized by caustic ammonia. **1842** BRANDE *Dict. Sci.* etc., *Opalized wood*, petrified by silica, and acquiring a structure resembling common opal.

opaloid ('əʊpəlɔɪd), *a.* [f. OPAL + -OID.] Resembling an opal in appearance; having a milky translucence.

1882 *Dredge's Electr. Illum.* I. 643 Each lamp being enclosed within a ground [glass] or opaloid shade.

'opalo,type. [f. L. *opal-us* OPAL + TYPE.] A positive photograph on opal glass. Also *attrib.*

1885 *Spon's Workshop Appliances* 294 Opalotype pictures. Opalotypes by the wet process. It is only necessary to use opal glass instead of patent plate.

opan, obs. form of UPON.

opaque (əʊ'peɪk), *a.* (*sb.*) Forms: 5–9 **opake**, (7 opace, 7–8 opac), 8 **opaac**, 7– **opaque**. [ad. L. *opāc-us* shaded, darkened, dark, whence also It., Sp., Pg. *opaco*, F. *opaque* (*c* 1500 in Hatz.-Darm.); hence the current Eng. spelling, which is rare before the 19th c.]

A. *adj.* †**1. a.** Lying in shadow; not illuminated, darkened, obscure. *Obs.*

c **1420** *Pallad. on Husb.* II. 262 They honge hem vp in place opake and drie. **1647** H. MORE *Poems* 53 The Nights nimble net That doth encompasse every opake ball, That swims in liquid air. **1696** WHISTON *Th. Earth* (1722) 37 The Opake and obscure parts were..perfectly inconsiderable. **1775** *Chron.* in *Ann. Reg.* 110/1 The light of the sun was somewhat opake, by the shadows, as if two or three digits were eclipsed.

b. Of a body or surface: Not reflecting or emitting light; not shining or lustrous, dull, dark.

1794 G. ADAMS *Nat. & Exp. Philos.* IV. xxxvii. 11 The planets are all opake, or dark bodies. **1800** tr. *Lagrange's Chem.* I. 293 It has an opake colour, interspersed with yellowish spots. **1826** KIRBY & SP. *Entomol.* IV. 284 *Opaque*,..a surface which does not reflect the light at all. **1847** EMERSON *Poems* (1857) 154 Thou, in our astronomy An opaker star. **1877** BLACK *Green Past.* xxxvii, An opaque, solid green—not unlike sealing-wax.

2. a. Impermeable to light, not transmitting light, not transparent; hence, impenetrable to sight; *spec.* of glass which is not translucent.

1641 FRENCH *Distill.* v. (1651) 168 If you would have this masse not to be transparent but opac. **1664** POWER *Exp. Philos.* II. 103 These Luminous and Opace Bodies (I mean the Starrs and Planets). **1667** MILTON *P.L.* III. 619 Whence no way round Shadow from body opaque can fall. **1697** J. PETIVER in *Phil. Trans.* XIX. 678 Its Leaves are stiff..and opake (i.e.) not to be seen through. **1727** A. MORETON *On Apparitions* 26 They are habitable bodies, solid, opaac as this earth. **1818** FARADAY *Exp. Res.* vii. 19 Exposed to the air these crystals became opake. **1836** E. W. LANE *Acct. Manners & Customs Mod. Egyptians* II. 368 There is a very common kind [of bracelet]..of opaque, coloured glass, generally blue or green. **1867** BAKER *Nile Tribut.* xii. 314 The lions..having the advantage of thick and opaque jungle. **1869** TYNDALL *Notes Lect. Light* 21 It is the frequency of the reflexions at the limiting surfaces of air and water that renders foam opaque. **1878** A. NESBITT *Descr. Catal. Glass Vessels S. Kensington Mus.* p. ii, It can be produced either wholly devoid of colour or tinted with any hue, and either opaque or transparent, without loss of brilliancy. **1907** E. DILLON *Glass* xvii. 291 Much opaque white glass was made in Germany..in the first years of the eighteenth century... At South Kensington may be seen a covered beaker of this *milchglas* elaborately painted. **1926** W. BUCKLEY *European Glass* ii. 11 The Venetians in the 14th century made an opaque red glass resembling jaspar. **1961** E. M. ELVILLE *Collector's Dict. Glass.* 145/1 Nine out of every ten glasses with opaque-twist stems will show an unknopped stem.

b. *transf.* Not transmitting heat, sound, etc.

1876 TAIT *Rec. Adv. Phys. Sc.* viii. (ed. 2) 205 Extremely opaque to radiant heat. **1903** PUSEY & CALDWELL *Pract. Application Röntgen Rays* vi. 133 It will be a great help to the radiographer if the dressings are of a material which is not opaque to the ray. **1937** I. C. C. TCHAPEROFF *Man. Radiol. Diagnosis* iv. 167 The emphysematous area remains transparent in the radiograph of full expiration, whereas the normal areas become more opaque on expiration. **1972** *Jrnl. Ultrastruct. Res.* XXXIX. 580 The transverse..tubules and sarcoplasmic reticulum..of *Limulus* myocardium have been examined by infusing hearts with materials which either produce electron-opaque reaction products..or which are inherently electron opaque.

3. *fig.* **a.** Hard to understand or make out; not clear, lucid, or distinct; obscure.

1761 STERNE *Tr. Shandy* III. xx. Auth. Pref., To darken your hypothesis by placing a number of tall, opake words.. betwixt your own and your readers' conception. **1789** BURNEY *Hist. Mus.* (ed. 2) I. II. 242 An opake expression, upon which they are utterly unable to throw a single ray of light. **1845** CARLYLE *Cromwell* (1871) I. 94 Whoever wishes ..may consult the opaque but authentic Commons Journals.

b. Impervious to reason, unintelligent, dense, obtuse, dull.

[**1755** YOUNG *Centaur* vi. Wks. 1757 IV. 260 We have in abundance..lunar great men. Men in themselves opaque, who borrow beams, from their circumstances, or situation.] **1850** CARLYLE *Latter-d. Pamph.* i, A fund of purblind obduracy, of opaque flunkeyism grown truculent and transcendent. **1882** MRS. OLIPHANT *Lit. Hist. Eng.* III. 227 Too opaque to understand her husband's jeers.

c. *Phonology.* Of a rule: that cannot be extrapolated from every occurrence of the phenomenon; in which not every context implies the rule.

1971 P. KIPARSKY in W. O. Dingwall *Survey Linguistic Sci.* 621 Define the concept *opacity of a rule* as follows:..A rule A→B/C–D is opaque to the extent that there are surface representations of the form (i) A in environment C–D or (ii) B in environment other than C–D... Let us refer to the converse of opacity as *transparency*. **1974** S. R. ANDERSON *Organization of Phonol.* xii. 209 Kiparsky gives examples.. in which historical change can be seen to operate on nontransparent (or *opaque*) rules so as to make them more transparent or to eliminate them from the grammar. *Ibid.* xiii. 250 If we disregard the second possible application instead, we derive *djalum* + *ba*: + *daŋ* + *be*:, which is not opaque because the long vowels are not adjacent. **1977** *Language* LIII. 18 Palatalization is opaque to the extent that there are, on the surface, some palatalized consonants not in the environment of a following *i*.

4. *Comb.*, as ***opaque-souled*** adj.

1793 BURNS *Let. to Ainslie* 26 Apr., If any opaque-souled lubber of mankind complain.

B. *sb.* **1. a.** Something opaque; a medium or space through which light cannot pass. Also *fig.*

1742 YOUNG *Nt. Th.* I. 43 Thro' this opaque of nature, and of soul, This double night, transmit one pitying ray, To lighten, and to chear. **1814** SOUTHEY *Roderick* XXI. 429, I watch'd..And deem'd the deep opake would blot her beams. **1822** W. TENNANT *Thane of Fife* i. 10 That arrowed through th' opaque their forky fire. **1824** MISS FERRIER

Inher. xxxvi, The light began to penetrate the dim opaque of his understanding. **1903** *Westm. Gaz.* 20 Aug. 4/1 A red batiste of voile or open canvas is more lovable than a red face-cloth or serge or tweed or linen; and, again, it is to be noted how of these red opaques the linen is better than the others. **1969** *Earth & Planetary Sci. Lett.* VII. 237/1 All the samples showed some effects—oxidation of the opaques and reddening of the silicates. **1976** *Nature* 22 Jan. 196/1 The Santiago lavas contain up to 10% phenocrysts of olivine and plagioclase in a matrix of plagioclase laths, clinopyroxene, olivine and opaques.

b. A shade for the eyes.

1900 *Westm. Gaz.* 21 Jan. 1/2 Mr. B., who has suffered by a lamp explosion, appeared with an opaque stuck over his forehead for the protection of his eyes from the rays of electric light.

2. *Photogr.* **a.** A water colour or other substance for producing opaque areas on negatives, as in retouching.

1908 SCHRIEVER & CUMMINGS *Compl. Self-Instructing Libr. Pract. Photogr.* IV. xl. 322 To make the opaque, add one ounce of No. 1 to four ounces of No. 2. **1943** *Chem. Abstr.* XXXVII. 1946 (*heading*) Removing opaque from photographic negatives. **1953** A. SUSSMAN *Amat. Photographer's Handbk.* (ed. 4) xiv. 254 To spot a negative you can use a little India ink or you can buy a cake of opaque.

b. A print made on opaque paper.

1959 *Recomm. for Density & Contrast Range of Monochrome Films (B.S.I.)* 5 Prints of black-and-white photographic opaques should be made in such a way that a middle tone.. will have a reflection density within the range 0·5 to 0·7. **1969** *Focal Encycl. Film & Television Techniques* 518/1 *Opaque*, term contrasting with transparency, such as a lantern slide, to denote a printed picture on opaque paper.

o'paque, *v.* [f. OPAQUE *a.*: cf. L. *opācāre* to OPACATE.] *trans.* To render opaque. Hence **o'paqu(e)ing** *ppl. a.* and *vbl. sb.*

1880 S. LANIER *Poems, Crystal* 23 Not one but winks His ray, opaqued with intermittent mist. **1888** *Sci. Amer.* LIX. 235/3 The most.. practical way of opaqueing the backgrounds on negatives of furniture. **1912** E. HEILMANN *Brit. Pat.* 26,498, Materials which cannot be used alone as opaquing substances for enamel, yield good opaquing effects when heated so highly as to form spinels. **1913** *Chem. Abstr.* VII. 2460 Opaqueing agents for white enamels. **1967** E. CHAMBERS *Photolitho-Offset* v. 52 Opaquing is used for spotting out pinholes, edge lines and other undesirable marking on the negatives. **1967** KARCH & BUBER *Offset Processes* v. 195 Paint out these holes and scratches.. with an opaquing solution.

opaquely (əʊ'peɪklɪ), *adv.* [f. as prec. + -LY^2.] In an opaque manner, so as to be opaque.

1746 BADCOCK in *Phil. Trans.* XLIV. 191 'Tis opaquely of a clear White. **1858** CARLYLE *Fredk. Gt.* v. i. (1872) II. 58 Raised into a kind of cloudy narcotic Olympus, and opaquely superior to the ills of life. **1860** *All Year Round* No. 42. 362 Glass.. opaquely steamed with youthful breath.

opaqueness (əʊ'peɪknɪs). [f. as prec. + -NESS.] The quality of being opaque; opacity.

1647 H. MORE *Song of Soul* II. i. II. xxxi, The Earths opakeness enemie to Light. **1742** H. BAKER *Microsc.* I. xiii. 53 The Transparency or Opakeness of an Object. **1855** tr. *Labarte's Arts Mid. Ages* iv. 159 Giving.. complete opaqueness to the colours. **1893** *Columbus* (O.) *Disp.* 12 Jan., We are often the victims of our own opaqueness or prejudice. **1897** HUGHES *Medit. Fever* ii. 44 [It] gives rise to a general and increasing opaqueness.

opard, obs. f. UPWARD.

op art: see OP^4.

opassom, obs. f. OPOSSUM.

opbigge, opbraid, etc.: see UP-.

op. cit. (ɒp sɪt). Abbrev. of L. *opus citatum*, the work quoted, or *opere citato*, in the work quoted.

1883 *Nineteenth Century* Feb. 213 *Op. cit.* vol. ii pp. 200, 201. **1966** *Listener* 1 Sept. 305/1 Van Bath (*op. cit.*) has drawn attention to the relation between urban prosperity and agricultural improvement in the Netherlands. **1970** J. NEEDLEMAN *New Religions* 233 J. G. Bennett, op. cit., p. 53.

ope (əʊp), *a.* and *sb.* [Reduced from *open*, the *n* being dropped as in pa. pples.: cf. *awake* for *awaken*, *wove(n*, *bespoke(n*, etc.]

A. *adj.* = OPEN *a.* in various senses. (Only *pred.* or after the sb.) Now *arch.* and *poet.*

a **1250** *Owl & Night.* 168 Vor swikedom haved schome and hete, ȝif hit is ope and under-ȝete. *c* **1290** *S. Eng. Leg.* I. 28/66 He leide ope him þis bok. **1426** LYDG. *De Guil. Pilgr.* 4841 The large wonde vp-on my syde Al hope, I geue hem to refut. **1549–62** STERNHOLD & H. *Te Deum*, Thou heavens kingdom didst set ope. **1595** SHAKS. *John* II. i. 449 The mouth of passage shall we fling wide ope. **1678** BUNYAN *Pilgr.* I. 186 To keep ope their drowsie slumbring eyes. **1820** KEATS *Ode to Psyche* 66 A casement ope at night, To let the warm Love in! **1873** BROWNING *Red Cott. Nt.-cap* 211 With both eyes wide ope.

B. *sb.* [Cf. OPEN *sb.*]

†**1.** = OPEN *sb.* 2, OPENING *vbl. sb.* 5. *Obs.*

1611 W. SCLATER *Key* (1629) 293 What an ope I should giue to aduersaries. **1627** —— *Exp. 2 Thess.* (1629) 167 Its fearefull when God.. intercludes all possibility or ope for returne out of errour.

2. = OPEN *sb.* 1, OPENING *vbl. sb.* 2.

a. *Arch.*

1845 PETRIE *Round Towers Irel.* 371 Pointed opes, splayed reveals. **1878** MᶜVITTIE *Ch. Ch. Cathedral* 59 The central ope of each triplet having a trefoiled head.

b. *local.* (See quot. 1880.)

1866 *N. & Q.* 3rd Ser. IX. 320/1 At the street corner, where the name of the street is usually painted, you find Charles' Ope, Chapel street Ope. **1880** *W. Cornwall Gloss.*, *Ope*, a narrow covered passage between two houses; an opening. **1893** Q. [COUCH] *Delect. Duchy* 227 Her window yonder, over the ope.

ope (əʊp), *v.* [Reduced from OPEN *v.* after prec.] = OPEN *v.* in various senses. (Chiefly, and since 17th c. exclusively, *poet.*)

c **1430** *Two Cookery-bks.* 18 Take þe hennys & skalde hem & ope hem. **1573** TUSSER *Husb.* (1878) 210 Which opte his doore to rich and poore. **1577** WHETSTONE *Remembr. Life Gascoigne* xii, The windowes of my muse, then straight I ope. **1607** SHAKS. *Timon* v. iv. 47 Set but thy foot Against our rampyr'd gates, and they shall ope. **1610** —— *Temp.* I. ii. 37 The howr's now come The very minute byds thee ope thine eare. **1664** WOOD *Life* Jan. (O.H.S.) II. 4 Going to his study doore and oping it. **1741–2** GRAY *Agrip.* 451 Oped his young eye to bear the blaze of greatness. **1807** CRABBE *Par. Reg.* I. 662 He opes his ample jaws, And lets a frog leap down, to gain applause. **1849** WHITTIER *Leg. St. Mark* 80 Lord, ope their eyes that they may see!

ope = HOOP *sb.*^{3} 2, bullfinch; cf. OLPH.

1669 WORLIDGE *Syst. Agric.* (1681) 266 Kill the Opes or Bull finches that feed on the buds of Fruit-trees.

ope, obs. f. HOPE; UP, UPON *prep.*

[**opeagha**, a misreading or misprint for *quagha*, QUAGGA.

1776 MASSON in *Phil. Trans.* LXVI. 297. **1797** *Encycl. Brit.* VI. 713 1: etc.]

Op-Ed (ɒp'ɛd). *U.S.* [Abbrev. *op*posite *ed*itorial.] In full *Op-Ed page*. A page of a newspaper, opposite the editorial page, devoted to personal comment, feature articles, etc.

1970 *Time* 10 Aug. 32 The Op-Ed page—so named because it runs opposite a newspaper's editorial page—became a journalistic tradition with the rise of the personal column. Pioneered by the Pulitzers in the old New York morning *World*, the Op-Ed provides a variety of viewpoints in dozens of major metropolitan dailies. **1970** *N.Y. Times* 21 Sept. 42/2 Through the new page opposite the Editorial Page that we inaugurate today, we hope that a contribution may be made toward stimulating new thought and provoking new discussion on public problems... The two pages together—Editorial and Op. Ed.—are designed to create an intellectual forum. **1974** *Verbatim* Dec. 6/1 The Op-Ed Page of *The New York Times*. **1977** G. V. HIGGINS *Dreamland* i. 8 If you don't get a regular fix of the stuff that goes on the front page, you're not going to have anything to be insightful about on the Op Ed page.

ope-head: see OPENHEAD, quot. 1297.

opeidoscope (əʊ'paɪdəskəʊp). [f. Gr. ὤψ, ὀπ- voice + εἶδο-ς form, image + -SCOPE.] An instrument invented by Prof. A. E. Dolbear (West Virginia), consisting of a tube closed at one end by a tense membrane, having attached to its centre a small mirror, to show the musical vibration caused by speaking or singing at the open end.

1873 A. E. DOLBEAR in Prescott *Sp. Telephone* (1879) 262 While engaged in making a manometric flame capsule, I invented the opeidoscope.

†**ope-land.** *local. Obs.* [f. OPE *a.* + LAND.] *lit.* Open ground: see quot.

1674 RAY *S. & E.C. Words* 74 *Ope lande*, ground plowed up every year, ground that is loose or open, *Suff.* **1726** *Dict. Rust.* (ed. 3), *Hook-Land*, or *Ope-land*, Land ploughed and sowed every Year.

opelet ('əʊplɪt). [f. OPE *a.* + -LET.] A name of a sea-anemone, *Anemonia sulcata*, so called because the tentacles cannot be retracted.

1860 GOSSE *Actinologia Britannica* 162 The English name (Opelet) I have formed for it.. alludes to the habitually open condition of the disk. *Ibid.* 165 No very special care is required to maintain the health and vigour of the Opelet in captivity.

†**'opely**, *adv. Obs.* [f. OPE *a.* + -LY^2.] = OPENLY *adv.*

a **1250** *Owl & Night.* 853 Hit is alre wnder mest, þat þu darst liȝe so opeliche. *c* **1250** *Gen. & Ex.* 2583 Ðo bad ðis king al opelike.. Euerilc knape child of ðat kin, ben a-non don ðe flod wið-in. **1460** *Paston Lett.* I. 511 He seyd opely to the prior, hevyng myche folk in the church.

open ('əʊp(ə)n), *sb.* [Partly vbl. sb. f. OPEN *v.*; partly ellipt. use of OPEN *a.*]

I. 1. a. = OPENING *vbl. sb.* 2; an aperture.

c **1470** HENRY *Wallace* VIII. 1065 The fyr brak in at all opynnys about. **1483** *Cath. Angl.* 260/2 Þe Opyn of yᵉ hede, *calvaria*. **1686** BURNET *Lett. Trav. Switzerland*, etc. iv. (1750) 233 At the Top there is an Open left of thirty Foot in Diameter. **1726** LEONI tr. *Alberti's Archit.* II. 41/1 The height of the Open of that door is divided into three parts. **1782** A. MONRO *Anat. Bones, Nerves*, etc. 66 The.. unossified.. part of the cranium [in] new-born children, called by the vulgar the *open of the head*. **1885** MRS. C. PRAED *Head Station* 21 Other dusky forms.. sprawled on red blankets at the open of their gunyahs.

b. The mouth or estuary of a river.

1710 *Lond. Gaz.* No. 4655/3 The Dunwich.. gave Chace to a French Privateer.. in the open of Humber, and.. took her, and brought her into the River.

c. *local.* (Lincolnsh.) A gap in the sand dunes through which a road passes to the shore.

Mod. We drove through Theddlethorpe Open [or Opening].

d. *Mining.* (See quot.)

1881 RAYMOND *Mining Gloss.*, *Opens*, large caverns.

2. = OPENING *vbl. sb.* 5.

1711 SHAFTESB. *Charac.* (1737) III. 293 The poor.. shadow of an adversary has said as little for his cause as can be imagin'd, and given as many opens and advantages as cou'd be desir'd. **1757** MRS. GRIFFITH *Lett. Henry & Frances* (1767) II. 230 Perhaps this may leave an open to sarcasm. **1866** TROLLOPE *Claverings* xxx, Down he went, and not finding a good open for a hazard, again waxed himself to the cushion.

II. sb. use of OPEN *a.*

†**3.** Open, unconcealed, or plainly seen condition. Phr. ***in open***, (*a*) in public, openly; (*b*) clearly, plainly; ***into open***, into public view, etc. *Obs.*

1382 WYCLIF *Wisd.* xiv. 17 These whom in opene men myȝten not wrshipen. **1388** —— (Purvey) *Luke* viii. 17 Nether hid thing, which schal not be knowun, and come in to open. **1390** GOWER *Conf.* I. 62 He seith in open, fy! to Sinne, And in secre ther is no vice Of which that he nis a Norrice. **1430–40** LYDG. *Bochas* I. vi. (1554) 9 Their piteous fate in open to expresse. **1613** SHAKS. *Hen. VIII*, III. ii. 405 The Lady Anne.. This day was view'd in open as his Queene. **1646** BP. MAXWELL *Burd. Issach.* in *Phenix* (1708) II. 285 You shall have them anon in open contemning Sovereign Authority.

4. a. ***the open***: the open space. (*a*) The part of the country not fenced or enclosed; (*b*) Clear space; ground without buildings, trees, or other 'cover'; (*c*) The open water, in sea or river; (*d*) The open air.

1624 CAPT. SMITH *Virginia* III. 65 Presently from each side the river came arrowes.. whereat we returned to get the open.. we seised on all their canowes, and moored them in the midst of the open. **1732** POPE *Ess. Man* I. 10 Try what the open, what the covert yield. **1858** KINGSLEY *My Hunting Song* in *Andromeda*, etc. 128 One more fence and we're out on the open. **1859** LAWRENCE *Sword & Gown* v. 53 [The clergyman] had never had the satisfaction of a 'shot in the open' at that stout-hearted sinner. **1875** WOLSELEY in Bedford *Sailor's Pocket Bk.* vii. (ed. 2) 248 In tropical climates it is pleasant at night to bivouac in the open. **1880** *Daily Tel.* 16 Feb., The soldier is taught how to attack in the open. **1883** *Harper's Mag.* Aug. 445/2 The *Vindex*.. beat in the open the.. schooner.., both being reefed down. **1893** *Daily Tel.* 3 Oct. 5/3 A quantity of ripe raspberries.. grown in the open.

(*e*) Public knowledge or view, *spec.* in phrs. ***to come (out) into the open***: to reveal one's plans, acts, thoughts, etc.; ***to bring*** (something) ***(out) into the open***, to bring into public notice or view.

1942 T. BAILEY *Pink Camellia* v. 35 We may as well come into the open, Miss Merryman. **1965** *New Statesman* 30 Apr. 670/2 The Tory Party statement which last year brought immigration into the open as a Birmingham election issue. **1965** *Listener* 16 Sept. 399/2 The Peking *People's Daily* came out into the open, supporting Pakistan's version of events. **1976** K. ROYCE *Bustillo* iv. 45 They both had something to hide... It would be better out in the open.

b. An open or clear space.

1796 *Hist. Ned Evans* I. 193 He was astonished to see so extensive an open in the midst of a populous city. **1846** J. W. WEBB *Altowan* I. ii. 42 All openings or natural clearings are called 'opens' by the half-breeds of the Indian country. *Ibid.* viii. 201 They cautiously entered where there seemed no indication of an open. **1880** *Encycl. Brit.* XIII. 603/1 Living in herds of from fifty to one hundred in the grassy 'opens'. **1958** *Edmonton* (Alberta) *Jrnl.* 28 July 4/3 The animal seemed to distrust the bald opens of the marsh.

5. a. *Stock Exchange.* The open market.

1898 *Daily News* 9 May 2/3 In the open, bar gold remained in strong demand for America at about 77s. 9⅝d. per ounce.

b. *Electr.* An accidental break in the conducting path for a current.

1913 T. CROFT *Amer. Electricians' Handbk.* i. 55 Open circuits in multiple wiring installations are usually readily located... The lamps on the generator side of the 'open' will.. burn while those on the far side will not. **1933** F. F. FOWLE *Stand. Handbk. Electr. Engineers* (ed. 6) iii. 193 Open-circuit faults or 'opens' are produced by breaks in the conductors. **1967** *Electronics* 6 Mar. 320/2 The D200's.. identify shorts or opens and the polarity of diodes. **1977** *Sci. Amer.* Feb. 88/1 (Advt.), That's the beauty of the TDR, it's not limited to identifying shorts or opens—it points out any disturbances.

c. An open competition, tournament, or the like; cf. OPEN *a.* 14.

1926 WODEHOUSE *Heart of Goof* iv. 128 'After all, there is always golf.' He nodded. 'Yes... Who knows?.. The Amateur Championship—' 'The Open!' I cried... 'The American Amateur,' said Chester, flushing. 'The American Open,' I chorused. **1930** *Daily Express* 8 Sept. 11/4 Miss Brazier also has played in 'opens'. **1972** *Country Life* 7 Dec. 1600/3 Jack White who, in 1904, was the first man to break 300 in the Open. **1973** *Guardian* 28 June 13/3 The World Open is a ten-round [chess] championship open to all-comers.

d. ***the Open***: the Open University. *colloq.*

1970 *Guardian* 29 Aug. 9/6 Along with Jennie Lee, Mrs Thatcher has a right to be seen as the saviour of the Open. **1972** *Ibid.* 15 June 9/5 Pupils in schools.. had to wait until 21 to qualify for the Open or 23 to enter other universities as 'mature' students.

6. *Comb.*, as **open-grown** *a.*, grown in the open air or ground.

1894 *Daily News* 7 Apr. 5/4 Open-grown rhubarb costs 4*d.* the bundle.

open ('əʊp(ə)n), *a.* (*adv.*) Forms: 1– open; also 3 (*Orm.*) openn, 4 -in, -ine, -ene, -enne, -one, -oun, (hop(p)yne), 4–5 opun, -on, 4–6 -yn, -yne; 5 oppyn, -on, 6 oppin, -ine, -en, (*Sc.* appin). [A Com. Teut. adj.: OE. *open* = OS. *opan* (MDu.,

Du. *open*), OFris. *epin*, OHG. *offan* (MHG., Ger. *offen*), ON. *opinn*, *opin*, *opit* (Da. *aaben*, Sw. in comb. *öppen-*); not recorded in Gothic; OTeut. type **upano-*, **upino-*, app. from the root of UP *adv.* In all the langs., the word has the form of a strong pa. pple., as if meaning 'set up', 'put up', but no corresponding vb. exists. Cf., however, for the sense, the obs. or dial. 'put up the door', 'set up the door' (Ger. *macht die thür auf*), 'the door is up, put it to'. The *o*, orig. short, was lengthened in ME. at the end of the stressed syllable, as in *stolen*, *woven*, etc.]

A. *adj.* I. Physical senses.

1. Of a door, gate, or the like: Not 'put to' the place which it fits, not closed or shut; 'up', set up, standing up, so as to allow free passage through. (Cf. *do up* (Early ME. *up dōn*), *dup*, to put 'up', to open.) Also said of the doorway, gateway, or other passage.

*c*888 K. ÆLFRED *Oros.* III. v. §4 þonne andydan hie þa duru þe on þa healfe open wæs. **971** *Blickl. Hom.* 239 Hie ȝemetton þæs carcernes duru opene. *c* **1200** ORMIN 15536 þatt heffness ȝate uss openn be Att ure lifess ende. *c* **1380** WYCLIF *Last Age Ch.* p. xxviii, Every lettre in the abece may be souned wiþ opyn mouþ saue .m. lettre one. *c* **1400** MAUNDEV. (Roxb.) xxxiii. 150 þer es nane entree open in to it. **1477** *Paston Lett.* III. 212 There arn wyndownes blow opyn in the place. *a* **1548** HALL *Chron.*, *Hen. VI* 158 b, And to set open the fludde gates of these devises. **1549** *Compl. Scot.* vi. 60 He sal be fundin dede, and his ene appin. **1697** DRYDEN *Virg. Georg.* III. 407 The Sluces of the Sky were open spread. **1726** SWIFT *Gulliver* I. iv, The windows..were left open on purpose. **1749** FIELDING *Tom Jones* x. ii. The door burst open. **1859** TENNYSON *Enid* 328 The voice of Enid..rang Clear thro' the open casement of the Hall, Singing. **1884** BLACK *Jud. Shaks.* xxxiv, The door was open an inch or two.

2. a. Of a containing space, a house, box, etc.: Having its gate, door, lid, or some part of its enclosing boundary drawn aside or removed so that there is free access to its interior; not shut up.

971 *Blickl. Hom.* 239 þin carcern open we ȝemetton. *c* **1000** *Ags. Gosp.* John i. 51 ȝe ȝe-seoð opene heofonas. **1388** WYCLIF *Rom.* iii. 13 The throte of hem is an opyn sepulcre. *c* **1400** MAUNDEV. (Roxb.) xxvi. 121 þai er open at þe sydes and laced togyder with lacez of silke. **1593** SHAKS. *2 Hen. VI*, IV. iii. 18 Breake open the Gaoles, and let out the Prisoners. *a* **1682** SIR T. BROWNE *Tracts* 45 The granaries were made open, the country being free from rain. **1799** *Med. Jrnl.* II. 422 Hectic fever arises only from the matter of an open ulcer. **1816** JAS. SMITH *Panorama Sc. & Art* II. 318 Keep the open end of the tube immersed. **1859** JEPHSON *Brittany* v. 56 A pianoforte..lying open, for show, not use. **1882** OUIDA *Maremma* I. 200 The earth had yawned open in many places. **1887** *Dict. Nat. Biog.* IX. 335/2 His head was split open with a blow. **1900** EVA C. E. LÜCKES *Gen. Nursing* xi, If it is desired to keep the blister 'open'. *a* **1902** *Mod.* Standing beside the open grave. They found the drawer open and its contents strewed about the floor.

b. Hence, Free of entrance or admission to all (or *to* persons specified).

971 *Blickl. Hom.* 61 Se ȝifra helle bið á open deoflum. **1784** COWPER *Let.* 19 July, When Bedlam was open to the cruel curiosity of holiday ramblers. **1816** J. WILSON *City of Plague* III. i. 100 Even the house of God Was open to the Plague. **1891** *Speaker* 2 May 534/1 The old universities are open to all, without distinction of rank or creed.

c. Of a shop, public house, etc.: accessible to use by customers (at a particular time); available for business; ***they are open***: the public houses are open.

1824 E. WEETON *Let.* 8 June in *Jrnl. of Governess* (1969) II. 287 As I go to any place of Worship, fruit stalls are in the road, and confectioners shops open, as on any other day. **1836** DICKENS *Sunday under Three Heads* i. 5 In streets like Holborn and Tottenham Court Road, which form the central market of a large neighbourhood, inhabited by a vast number of mechanics and poor people, a few shops are open at an early hour of the morning. **1942** 'S. CAMPION' *Bonanza* 19 It was eleven—'they' were open. **1952** E. O'NEILL *Moon for Misbegotten* III. 152 There'll be a speak open, and some drunk laughing. *Ibid.* IV. 173 The bar at the Inn won't be open for hours. **1961** 'E. FENWICK' *Friend of Mary Rose* (1962) i. 16, I was talking to Mrs. Rudd... I wanted to be sure she was open. **1965** J. PORTER *Dover Three* ii. 30 Just one question, laddie... Are they open yet? **1973** A. MANN *Tiara* xiii. 118 Piccoli's will still be open. Shall I nip down and get pictures of all these types?

d. Designating a prison, borstal, or the like where the inmates are seldom or never locked up.

1946 *Rep. Commissioners of Prisons 1939–41* 47 in *Parl. Papers 1945–6* (Cmd. 6820) XIV. 281 All were now required to pass straight from the restraint of a prison wall to associated life in buildings designed as a perfectly open Borstal. **1950** *Prisons & Borstals* (Home Office) 20 The first prison camp in England was started in connection with the training prison at Wakefield in 1933... The open prison is therefore beyond the stage of experiment: it is a well-established feature of this as of many other prison systems. **1957** *Economist* 2 Nov. 397/3 Miss Size's last job was as Governor of the first open prison for women, at Askham Grange, near York, a pleasant Victorian mansion where there are neither high walls nor keys. **1964** M. ARGYLE *Psychol. & Social Probl.* v. 69 Open borstals had a higher success rate than closed borstals, at all levels of expected failure. **1972** P. D. JAMES *Unsuitable Job* vii. 210 Perhaps they would send her to an open prison. Open. It was a contradiction in terms.

e. ***open heart***, a practically bloodless heart that has been temporarily by-passed and cut open for examination or surgery; usu. *attrib.*

1950 *Surgery* XXVIII. 474 Recent rapid strides in the field of vascular surgery are leading inevitably to the point where a direct surgical attack on the open heart is possible. **1960** *Sci. Amer.* Feb. 84/1 The cardiac surgery group at Minnesota has now performed nearly 1,000 open-heart operations with the aid of the heart-lung machine or other methods of by-pass. **1977** *Private Eye* 1 Apr. 5/3 As he recovers from open-heart surgery (new valves) Sir Christopher Soames is confident of an early return to Parliament.

3. a. Of a space: Not shut in or confined, not surrounded by barriers; to which there is free access or passage on all or nearly all sides; unenclosed, unwalled, unconfined. See also OPEN AIR.

c **825** *Kent. Gloss.* in Wr.-Wülcker 82/9 *Urbs patens*, open burh. *c* **1330** R. BRUNNE *Chron.* (1810) 110 For comon þe folk it wan, wod open & forest. *c* **1400** MAUNDEV. (Roxb.) x. 38 It es noȝt lang sen þe sepulchre was all open, þat men myȝt kisse it and touche it. Bot..þe sowdan has gert make a wall aboute þe graue. *a* **1548** HALL *Chron.*, *Hen. VIII* 139 b, The people would not assemble..in no houses, but in open places. **1611** BIBLE *Gen.* i. 20 Foule that may flie..in the open firmament of heauen. **1622** BACON *Hen. VII*, Mor. & Hist. Wks. (Bohn) 332 The fields then being open and champain. **1704** *Lond. Gaz.* No. 3991/2 The Enemy..sent a strong Party into an open Village. **1745** P. THOMAS *Jrnl. Anson's Voy.* 20 A vast open Ocean. **1789** *Times* 28 June 4/4 The House is open and airy backwards. **1818** JAS. MILL *Brit. India* II. v. iv. 429 He was obliged to abandon the open country, and to depend upon his forts. **1885** *Law Rep.* 14 Queen's Bench Div. 918 The footpath ran over an open moor.

b. Hence, of a battle: Fought in the open (and not in a fortress or stronghold), and so with full forces.

a **1548** HALL *Chron.*, *Hen. VI* 110 b, To avoyde open ioynyng,..force to force. *Ibid.*, He determined never..to fight in open battaill with the Englishmen, nor by a feld to adventure. **1706** PRIOR *Ode to Queen* 206 We our forts and lines forsake, To dare our British foes to open fight. **1765** SMOLLETT *Hist. Eng.* (1804) V. 263 Generally speaking, their parties declined an open engagement. **1865** KINGSLEY *Herew.* xix, What men they could afford him, in case of open battle.

4. a. Not covered over or covered in; having no roof, lid, or other covering; esp. in ***open boat***, ***open car***, ***open carriage***; ***open crown***, a crown without the arched-over top (considered in modern heraldry to symbolize sovereignty); a coronet; also, a badge or ornament resembling a coronet.

971 *Blickl. Hom.* 125 Seo myccle cirice..seo is ufan open & unoferhrefed. **1535** COVERDALE *Num.* xix. 15 Euery open vessel that hath no lydd nor couerynge is vncleane. **1573–80** BARET *Alv.* O 109 Open aboue: not couered ouer. **1720** *Lond. Gaz.* No. 5898/7 Four Hundred open Boats. **1756** C. LUCAS *Ess. Waters* I. 145 They let the water stand in a large open bason. **1771** [see *open-top* in 22 a]. **1797** LADY NEWDIGATE *Let.* 30 July in A. E. Newdigate-Newdegate *Cheverels* (1898) xiv. 200, I have never felt yᵉ Downs too hot for my open Carriage till yesterday, when I was forced to put up yᵉ Head to shade me from yᵉ Sun. **1803** A. DUNCAN *Mariner's Chron.* IV. 255 The poor fellow and his dumb companion, in an open boat, were left to the mercy of this immense ocean. **1803** M. WILMOT *Let.* 6 Aug. in *Russ. Jrnls.* (1934) i. 36 We drove about in an open Carriage, the night was lovely. **1854** LD. HOUGHTON in *Life* (1891) I. xi. 497 A drive in an open carriage and four. **1878** *Act 41 & 42 Vict.* c. 14 §5 No covered or open swimming-bath when closed may be used for music or dancing. **1882** CUSSANS *Heraldry* xvii. (ed. 3) 238 The earliest coins struck by Henry the Seventh bear an open Crown with fleur-de-lys on the rim. **1948** M. LASKI *Tory Heaven* ix. 123 An open car..ceases to be a source of pure pleasure after a certain age. **1976** *Times* 1 Mar. 13/6 Having read the correspondence for and against ..seat belts, it seems that no one has put forward the case for the driver of the open car. **1977** G. V. HIGGINS *Dreamland* xii. 139 A small four-passenger open car with a canvas roof.

b. Of a fire: that is not enclosed in a stove or the like; also of a fireplace.

1876 B. CHAMPNEYS *Rep.* in Willis & Clark *Cambridge* (1886) III. 238 A large open-fire ventilating grate. **1886** [see *flue-curing* s.v. FLUE *sb.*³ 6]. **1894** *Country Gentlemen's Catal.* 117/1 The Nautilus dog grate... A cheerful open fire. **1926** *Daily Colonist* (Victoria, B.C.) 24 Jan. 20/1 He used to be heard singing..at night, beside his open fire. **1931** E. O'NEILL *Homecoming* II, in *Mourning becomes Electra* (1932) 51 At rear, centre, is an open fireplace. **1949** M. LASKI *Little Boy Lost* x. 150 'How nice to see an open fire,' he said tritely. Madame Mercatel laughed... 'One finds open fireplaces in many old French houses.' **1965** in P. Jennings *Living Village* (1968) 122 It looks as if open coal fires are on the way out in England at last. **1976** 'TREVANIAN' *Main* xiii. 249 He enjoys fiddling with open fires... The bark has begun to crackle and flutter with blue flame.

5. a. Not covered so as to be concealed or protected; bare, exposed. See also *wide open* s.v. WIDE *adv.* 3 b. ***open jet***: see sense 22 c.

Beowulf 2271 Hord-wynne fond eald uht-sceaða opene standan. **1390** GOWER *Conf.* II. 260 With open hed and fot al bare. *c* **1449** PECOCK *Repr.* I. xx. 124 Noone wommen weriden thanne..keuercheefis, but weriden her open heer. **1526** *Pilgr. Perf.* (W. de W. 1531) 254 He thus lyenge wyde open, & they goynge ouer hym & bestrydynge hym. **1604** E. G[RIMSTONE] *D'Acosta's Hist. Indies* v. viii. 348 When any one dyed, they layd him open in a chamber, vntill that all his kinsfolkes and friends were come. **1664** EVELYN *Kal. Hort.*, *Feb.* (1729) 193 Sow Alaternus Seeds in Cases, or open Beds. **1826** KIRBY & SP. *Entomol.* IV. 309 Upper Jaws..Open, when they are not quite concealed by the upper lip. **1840** *Jrnl. R. Agric. Soc.* I. III. 323 They will probably require to be laid open with the knife. **1962** *Newnes Conc. Encycl. Electr. Engin.* 728/2 The majority of switchgear manufactured up to 11 kV is of the metal-enclosed type and above this the trend is towards outdoor open type switchgear. **1968** *Gloss. Terms Offset Lithogr. Printing* (*B.S.I.*) 12 *Open arc*, an arc lamp in which the electrodes burn in free air.

†**b.** ***with open face***: with uncovered face; hence, confidently, frankly; also, brazenly. *Obs.*

1388 WYCLIF *2 Cor.* iii. 18 We that with open [1382 schewid, Vulg. *revelata*] face seen the glorie of the Lord. **1474** CAXTON *Chesse* 31 We may goon with open face and good conscience. **1650–3** tr. *Hales' Dissert. de Pace* in *Phenix* (1708) II. 384 Men..who..did..with open face, as they say, vent Blasphemies and Impieties. **1761** LLOYD *Ep. to Churchill* 11 Critics of old, a manly liberal race, Approv'd or censur'd with an open face.

c. Of a telephone line or other transmission line: above ground.

1876 PREECE & SIVEWRIGHT *Telegraphy* 158 Telegraph lines are..1st. Those in which open, that is overground, wires are employed. **1909** *Trans. Amer. Inst. Electr. Engin.* XXVIII. 1079 Even the best cable circuit is much less efficient than an open-wire circuit. **1925** *Bell Syst. Techn. Jrnl.* IV. 524 Practically all long toll circuits were in open wire construction; that is, individual wires mounted..on poles. **1966** *McGraw-Hill Encycl. Sci. & Technol.* XIV. 48/1 Open-wire construction is used for communication or power transmission wherever practical and permitted, as in open country.

d. *Med.* Communicating with or exposed to the air; involving the deliberate exposure of an interior part of the body, esp. a fracture, so as to make it directly accessible.

1894 J. C. DA COSTA *Man. Mod. Surg.* xviii. 307 Compound fracture is an open fracture, or one in which an open wound admits air to the seat of bone-injury. **1897** STIMSON & ROGERS *Man. Operative Surg.* (ed. 3) v. 257 (*heading*) Suture of the patella. I. Open Method. **1944** C. A. PANNETT *Surg.* xliii. 541 Union of the fracture after open operation always takes longer than if a closed method has been employed. **1949** P. KIELY *Text-bk. Surg.* xxvi. 700 Injuries to the Bowel. These may be subcutaneous or open. **1969** F. T. HOAGLAND in S. I. Schwartz *Princ. Surg.* xlvi. 1658/2 Open reduction [of a fracture] carries the risk of local infection. **1975** *Nature* 10 Apr. 529/1 Human liver obtained by open biopsy.

e. *Med.* Of (a case of) tuberculosis: accompanied by the discharge of infectious material from the body.

1930 J. A. MYERS *Tuberculosis among Children* ii. 9 The source of infection is found to be cases of open tuberculosis in the homes. **1939** *Brit. Encycl. Med. Pract.* XII. 288 The rapid decline in the number of open cases of tuberculosis.. have reduced the sources of infection. **1961** *Times* 30 June 15/3 Infectious (or 'open') tuberculosis. **1974** PASSMORE & ROBSON *Compan. Med. Stud.* III. I. xiv. 2/2 Occasionally outbreaks have occurred in young tuberculin-negative adults who have been heavily exposed to open cases [of tuberculosis].

6. Not having the marginal parts drawn, folded, or rolled together; unclosed, expanded, spread out.

c **1470** HENRY *Wallace* XI. 1399 To lat him haiff his Psaltyr buk in sycht. He gert a preyst it oppyn befor him hauld. **1513** W. DE WORDE *Bk. Keruynge* in *Babees Bk.* 278 All maner of fowles hauynge open clawes as a capon. **1549** *Compl. Scot.* vi. 57 Helytropium..hes the leyuis appin as lang as the soune is in our hemispere. **1611** BIBLE *1 Kings* vi. 32 Caruings of..palme trees, and open flowers. **1857** MRS. CARLYLE *Lett.* II. 331 With..the open sheet in her hand. **1865** TROLLOPE *Belton Est.* ii. 15 Having an open letter in his hand.

7. a. Of a line, texture, etc.: Having apertures or spaces between its parts; containing interstices, gaps, holes, or unoccupied spaces; perforated; porous.

open order (*Mil.*), a formation in which the individual men are three or more yards apart; (*Naval*), a formation in which the individual ships are more than a cable's length apart. ***open harmony*** (*Mus.*), a harmony in which the chords are separated by wide intervals.

1625 MARKHAM *Soldier's Accid.* 12 In Files..Open Order is sixe foote betweene person and person..in Rankes..to stand or march at Open-Order, is ever twelue foote. **1663** GERBIER *Counsel* 29 A ranck of open teeth. **1686** W. HARRIS tr. *Lemery's Course Chym.* I. vi. (ed. 3) 150 You had better use Verdegreese..because it is more open and disposed for solution by the acids of Vinegar. **1796** *Instr. & Reg. Cavalry* (1813) 54 Changes of position in open column, are in general movements of previous disposition. **1805** ADM. STIRLING in *Naval Chron.* XV. 81 The signal for sailing in open order. **1820** SCORESBY *Acc. Arctic Reg.* I. 229 *Open ice*, or *sailing-ice*, is where the pieces are so separate as to admit of a ship sailing conveniently among them. **1879** *Cassell's Techn. Educ.* IV. 182 Unless a very open and porous collodion be used. **1880** GRAY *Struct. Bot.* iv. §2 (ed. 6) 134 The æstivation is said to be *Open* or Indeterminate when the parts do not come into contact in the bud, so as to cover those within.

b. *Chem.* and *Metallurgy.* (See quot. 1938).

1938 HUME-ROTHERY & RAYNOR in *Phil. Mag.* XXVI. 130 A rough indication of the nature of a metal or alloy may be obtained by comparing the interatomic distances in the crystal with the suitably defined ionic radii of the atoms concerned. In brief, if the ionic radius is small compared with the interatomic distance, we shall have a metal of what may be called the 'open' type, whilst if the ionic radii are nearly equal to the interatomic distances we shall have a metal of the 'full' type, with many different properties. **1967** A. H. COTTRELL *Introd. Metall.* xix. 322 In open metals we need consider only the valency electrons, for the electrons in the ionic shells are negligibly disturbed by the metallic binding.

8. a. Of a passage or space: Not occupied by anything that prevents passage or view; free from obstructions; unobstructed, clear. Of a country: Free from wood, buildings, etc. Of a river, port, etc.: Not frozen over, free from ice. Esp. in ***open space***; *spec.* an area without buildings in a city or town; a small park or the like for public recreation; also ***great*** (or ***wide***) ***open spaces***: large tracts of open country.

c **1400** *Destr. Troy* 1575 The Stretis were..of stronge brede, For ymur & aire opon in þe myddis. *a* **1548** HALL *Chron., Rich. III* 57 Makyng open passage by dent of swerde. **1587** GOLDING *De Mornay* xiv. 214 He is made to come foorth into an opener place, where he may haue what to see and to behold. **1681** *Lond. Gaz.* No. 1587/2 The Empress and her Court will remain till the River be open, so that she may go by Water. **1709** STEELE *Tatler* No. 7 ⁋21 The Ice being broke, the Sound is again open for the Ships. **1725** DE FOE *Voy. round World* (1840) 319 The country was all open, with very little wood, and no trees. **1809** KENDALL *Trav.* III. lxxii. 129 The road..is over very rocky land, recently laid open by burning the trees. **1827** J. S. BUCKINGHAM *Trav. Mesopotamia* I. xi. 375 Attached to it are extensive stables, and a Maidan, or open space, where the horses are kept in the air. **1850** *Household Words* 3 Aug. 451/2 Suburban open spaces are being entombed in brick-and-mortar mausoleums. **1869** A. MACKENZIE (*title*) The parks, open spaces and thoroughfares of London. **1876** FREEMAN *Norm. Conq.* (ed. 3) IV. xviii. 157 The besieged must have had the river and the sea open to them during.. the siege. **1896** SIR R. HUNTER (*title*) The Preservation of Open Spaces and of Footpaths and Other Rights of Way. **1910** H. G. WELLS *New Machiavelli* (1911) I. iv. 131, I recall as if I had been there the wide open spaces, the ragged hillsides [of South Africa]. **1913** C. B. PURDOM *Garden City* viii. 112 An open space in a city has come to mean..even a disused churchyard... In the Garden City the characteristics of the open space belong to the town as a whole. **1924** WODEHOUSE *Leave it to Psmith* viii. 138 You will find me somewhere out there in the great open spaces where men are men. **1942** *Ann. Reg. 1941* 286 Mr. G. E. Hatfield ..bequeathed to the National Trust Marden Hall estate,.. for preservation as an open space. **1943** *Our Towns* (Women's Group on Public Welfare) p. xvi, The special town conditions of overcrowding, lack of open spaces, smoke and noise. **1944** [see *closed book* s.v. CLOSED *ppl. a.* 3]. **1965** K. GILES *Some Beasts no More* i. 12 A phony passport, maybe, and life anew in the great open spaces. **1969** S. COULTER *Embassy* xiv. 159 The big huskies, the boys from the wide open spaces. **1971** *Daily Tel.* 13 July 2/8 The Wimbledon centre court was not an open space within the meaning of the 1936 Public Order Act. **1974** *Guardian* 28 Mar. 19/3 What do people want today—apart from open space? **1975** *Times* 8 Feb. 10/4 If you seek clean fresh air and the wide open spaces (cliche though it is, that phrase is exactly right), this is the place.

b. Of the bodily passages: Not obstructed; *esp.* of the bowels: Not constipated.

1562 J. HEYWOOD *Prov. & Epigr.* (1867) 215 When folke be most open,.. Then go they to stooles that be made most close. **1710** FLOYER *Physic. Pulse-Watch* 427 Oil, Butter, and course Bread, and Hony-drinks keep the Body open. **1812** J. BAILLIE *Advice to Mothers* x. 142 *Magnesia alba*,..a lenient purgative, and keeps the body gently open. **1823–4** *Lancet* (ed. 3) 447 Bowels not open.

9. a. Of the soil: Unbound by frost or heat; loose, permeable. **b.** Of weather or season: Free from frost, as ***an open winter***; also *Naut.*, free from fog or mist.

1615 W. LAWSON *Country Housew. Gard.* (1626) 19 In winter..open, calme, and moist weather is best. **1647** A. ROSS *Mystag. Poet.* xv. (1675) 376 Sometimes she [the earth] is open, as in the Summer and Spring. **1697** DRYDEN *Virg. Georg.* I. 98 That while the Turf lies open, and unbound, Succeeding Suns may bake the Mellow Ground. **1714** SWIFT *Corr.* Wks. 1841 II. 523 Hay will certainly be dear unless we have an open winter. **1769** FALCONER *Dict. Marine* (1789) M b, The weather is said to be clear when it is fair and open. **1812** *Sporting Mag.* XXXIX. 107 The meetings shall be held the first open week in or after November. **1884** D. C. MURRAY in *Graphic* Christm. No. 20/2 The weather being fine and open and dry.

10. *Naut.* †**a.** Looking unobstructedly *upon* or *to*; in full view (*obs.*). **b.** Seen with an opening between; clear, detached. Cf. OPEN *v.* 8.

1478 BOTONER *Itin.* (Nasmith 1778) 110 Insula Sancti Michaelis de Loo jacet anglice opyn upon villæ Loo. *Ibid.*, Le forland de Raume opyn upon Plymmouth. **1530** PALSGR. 573 Our shyppe wente to wrake open upon Donkyrke (..*tout deuant Donkyrke*). **1670** NARBOROUGH *Jrnl.* in *Acc. Sev. late Voy.* I. (1711) 62 When you are at the West-part of this Narrow, you will see three Islands come open, which shew to be steep up Cliffs. **1686** *Lond. Gaz.* No. 2112/4 They are to keep the Great Light a little open to the Eastward of the Small One, to avoid their coming ashore upon the Main. **1719** DE FOE *Crusoe* I. x, I found myself open to the northern shore. **1772–84** COOK *Voy.* (1790) V. 1863 As we stood off, the most westerly of the two hills.. came open off the bluff point, in a N.W. direction. **1858** *Merc. Marine Mag.* V. 227 Until you observe the spire..its breadth open of Bradley's head.

11. In various technical uses: **a.** *Music.* Of an organ-pipe: Not closed or shut at the top. Of a string: Not stopped by a finger. Of a brass instrument: not muted. Of a cymbal: left free to vibrate. Hence, of a note, Produced by such a pipe or string, or by the lip of a performer on a wind-instrument without the aid of a slide, key, or piston.

1674 PLAYFORD *Skill Mus.* II. 93 Tune it till it agree in sound with your Treble open. *Ibid.* 104 The open shake. **1811** BUSBY *Dict. Mus.* s.v. **1852** SEIDEL *Organ* 80 We call a pipe open, if its upper end or aperture is not shut up. **1856** MRS. C. CLARKE tr. *Berlioz' Instrument.* 4 Keeping the majority of his strings open. **1880** W. H. STONE in Grove *Dict. Mus.* II. 757 Depressing the open note a tone and a semitone. **1888** *Murray's Mag.* III. No. 14 The transition from open to closed tones should not be quite abrupt. **1926** *Melody Maker* Mar. 30 Nothing is better suited to obtain a highly successful result than the beautiful, sweet full tone of the open instrument, and I advise all artistes to try a few 'open' solos. **1927** *Ibid.* June 609/3 The cymbal must be 'open' when it is struck and must remain 'open' for practically the full length of the beat being played, only being choked out just before the next beat. **1955** KEEPNEWS & GRAUER *Pict. Hist. Jazz* xiii. 141 Cootie Williams,.. strictly an open-horn stylist until he took over Bubber Miley's chair and produced a fine, muted 'jungle' sound. **1956** B. EDWARDS in S. Traill *Play that Music* vi. 60 Short-damped cymbal beats or loud and frequently aimless open ones. **1967** *Crescendo* Apr. 7/2 The Les Brown trick of trumpets in tin mutes playing above open trombones. **1972** *Jazz & Blues* Nov. 11/3 Razor-sharp riffs, and sweeping, open-horn statements.

b. *Entom.* (See quot.)

1826 KIRBY & SP. *Entomol.* IV. 341 *Open.* Areolets that terminate in the margin of the wing, or that are not surrounded on all sides by nervures.

c. *Bot.* (See quot.)

1875 BENNETT & DYER tr. *Sachs' Bot.* 93 There are.. bundles devoid of and bundles containing cambium; the former may be termed closed, the latter open... The open fibro-vascular bundle..continues to produce new layers of permanent tissue on both sides of its cambium.

d. Of sounds: Uttered with the mouth open. *spec.* Of vowels: Produced with a wider opening of the oral cavity than those called *close*; e.g. ***open*** *o* and *e* (= ɔ, ɛ), close *o* and *e* (= o, e).

1485 in *Rutland Papers* (Camden) 16 My lord Cardinall.. shall syng with open voice iij tymes *Vt presentem famulum tuum.* **1503** DUNBAR *Thistle & Rose* 59 The birdis did with oppin vocis cry. **1611** FLORIO *Ital. Dict.* 618 The Italians haue two very different sounds for the two vowels, E. and O. which for distinctions sake, they name the one close and the other open. **1709** POPE *Ess. Crit.* 347 These equal syllables alone require, Tho' oft' the ear the open vowels tire. **1867** A. J. ELLIS *E.E. Pronunc.* I. iii. 65 Ben Jonson's conception of the French sound [of *a*] must have been opener than the English. **1889** B. H. KENNEDY *Rev. Lat. Prim.* 3 The most open sound is *a*; the closest sharp sound is *i*.

e. Of a syllable: Ending in a vowel, as opposed to a *closed* (*close, shut*) syllable which ends in a consonant.

1845 W. E. JELF *Gram. Greek Lang.* I. iii. 30 When a syllable ends with a vowel it is called an open, when with a consonant, a close syllable. **1871** *Public Sch. Lat. Gram.* 6 An inner syllable is called *open*, if it ends with a vowel, *close* if it ends with a consonant. **1891** LAURA SOAMES *Introd. Phonetics* 74 The short accented vowels never occur in open syllables. *a* **1902** *Mod.* A Latin short vowel in an open stressed syllable is long in Romanic; e.g. L. *bŏ-nus*, It. *buô-no*, Sp. *bue-no*, Eng. *bō-nus*. An original short *a, e, o* in a stressed open syllable became long in ME.; e.g. OE., Early ME. *ŏ-pen*, later ME., mod.Eng. *ō-pen*. Welsh, unlike modern Teutonic, Romanic, and Greek, retains a short stressed vowel in an open syllable, as in *Bă-lă* (distinct from Eng. *Bā-lā*, or *Băl-ă*).

f. *Electr.* Having a break in the conducting path for an electric current; esp. in ***open circuit*** (see sense 22 c).

1827, etc. [see *open circuit*]. **1869** *Phil. Mag.* XXVIII. 2 When the shunt is open the battery is unable to send a steady current through the voltameter. **1884** S. P. THOMPSON *Dynamo-Electr. Machinery* vii. 133 Dynamos..which leave the circuits of some of the armature coils open during part of the rotation, are sometimes termed 'open-circuit' dynamos. **1901** *Chambers's Jrnl.* Sept. 617/2 If a new machine, the switches should be left open, the brushes lifted, and the machine allowed to run without load for a little time. **1962** J. P. GREGORY in G. A. T. Burdett *Automatic Control Handbk.* ii. 21 With the initiating switch open, the timing capacitor..is charged to the peak value of the a.c. voltage. **1975** I. CLUCAS *Reed's Electr. for Deck Officers* vii. 212 The inductance in the circuit..tries to maintain the current once the switch is open.

g. Of a game of chess: developed either by gambits or by opening up the files. Cf. CLOSE *a.* 2 c.

1856 C. TOMLINSON *Chess-Player's Ann.* 75 He was a very accomplished player, and generally preferred open games, gambits, &c. **1890** R. F. GREEN *Chess* v. 14 An Open Game is one in which the development is effected chiefly in advance of the pawns. P to K4 as a first move on both sides, leads generally to an open game; and formerly all games begun in this way were called open—other openings being treated as close. **1917** J. DU MONT tr. *Lasker's Chess Strategy* (ed. 2) iv. 43 We find an early break-up of the centre, and concurrently the opening of the Ks or Qs file for the Rooks. That is why games opened in this fashion have been classed very generally as 'open', whilst all the other openings are called 'close games'. **1936** W. WINTER *Chess for Match Players* ii. 24 In the category of Open games come the vast majority of the King's side openings. **1959** H. GOLOMBEK *Mod. Opening Chess Strategy* 11 Certain openings suit certain people—some like an open type of game, others prefer a close.

h. *Med.* Applied to methods of administering anæsthetics in which the patient's respiratory tract is in communication with the air so that exhaled air is not rebreathed.

1888 D. W. BUXTON *Anæsthetics* v. 78 The open method. .. A common towel is arranged so as to form a square of six folds, and enough choloroform is poured upon it to wet an area the size of a hand's palm. **1922** *Encycl. Brit.* XXX. 137/2 The induction of anaesthesia by the open method is liable to be somewhat prolonged. **1972** J. C. SNOW *Anesthesia* v. 39 The Ayre T-tube system is another example of an open or semi-open system.

i. *Math.* Of a set of points: not containing any of its boundary points. Of an interval in the real line: not containing either of its end points.

1902 *Proc. Lond. Math. Soc.* XXXIV. 289 Open sets of points. **1939** M. H. A. NEWMAN *Elem. Topology of Plane Sets of Points* ii. 25 The sum of any set of open sets is an open set. **1956** E. M. PATTERSON *Topology* ii. 23 An example of a set which is not open is the set defined by $0 \leq x < 1$; no ϵ-neighbourhood of $x = 0$ lies entirely in the set, for every ϵ-neighbourhood of $x = 0$ contains a point whose coordinate is negative. **1968** P. A. P. MORAN *Introd. Probability Theory* iv. 185 An open interval in R_n is defined to be a set of points whose coordinates satisfy the inequalities $a_i < x_i < b_i$..*where the* a_i may be $-\infty$ and the b_i, $+\infty$. An open interval is clearly an open set.

j. *Logic* and *Math.* Of a statement or equation: containing at least one free variable or undetermined quantity.

1937 A. SMEATON tr. *Carnap's Logical Syntax of Lang.* I. 21 If a variable which is free in $\mathfrak{U}_1$ occurs in $\mathfrak{U}_1$, then $\mathfrak{U}_1$ is called open; otherwise it is called closed. *Ibid.*, Our classification into closed and open sentences corresponds to the usual classification into sentences and sentential functions. **1952** S. C. KLEENE *Introd. Metamath.* vii. 151 Let A be a formula containing free exactly the distinct variables $x_1, \ldots, x_n$ in order of first occurrence. According as $n > 0$ or $n = 0$, we call A open or closed. **1963** W. V. QUINE *Set Theory* I Imagine a sentence about something. Put a blank or variable where the thing is referred to. You have no longer a sentence..but an open sentence, so called, that may hold true of each of various things and be false of others. **1967** M. L. TOMBER *Introd. Contemporary Algebra* ii. 63, $5 \cdot 3^{-1} = \frac{5}{3}$ is a solution of the open equation $3x = 5$. **1971** *Sci. Amer.* Mar. 55 The technique of long division represents a decision procedure for the predicate '*x* is divisible by *y*', where *x* and *y* can be any natural numbers. (A predicate is an open sentence: one that can be completed by assigning names to its variables.)

k. *Astr.* Of the universe: having a negative or zero radius of curvature; spatially infinite and always expanding.

1937 E. HUBBLE *Observational Approach Cosmol.* iii. 55 The radius [of curvature] in our universe might be positive, negative, or zero, and might be large or small... A negative curvature implies open space, an infinite universe. **1965** J. D. NORTH *Measure of Universe* vi. 135 The logical advantages of an open model were generally thought to be fewer than those of a model with positive curvature. **1976** *New Scientist* 2 Dec. 514/1 Indirect evidence for a low-density (or 'open') Universe—one which will expand for ever—comes from the recent discovery that deuterium (heavy hydrogen) exists in interstellar space. **1978** *Daily Tel.* 27 Mar. 7/2 This question of whether the universe will prove to be 'open' or 'closed' raises an important philosophical question about the existence of God. If the cosmos is going to expand for ever,..for countless thousands of millions of years of its future history, life anywhere will be impossible.

II. Non-physical senses.

12. Exposed to the mental view, brought to light; patent, evident, plain, clear, easy to understand. Now only in ***to lay open***, to lay bare, reveal, explain, 'expose'.

c **888** K. ÆLFRED *Boeth.* xxxvi. §3 Ða cwæþ ic: ʒenoȝ open hit is. *c* **1200** ORMIN 731 Þatt wass wurrþshipe inoh til menn, & ec full openn takenn þatt heore streon wass Drihhtin leof. *a* **1340** HAMPOLE *Psalter* xxxvi. 31 Þis has na nede of expounynge for it is opon ynoghe. **1382** WYCLIF *Matt.* xxvi. 73 Treuly and thou art of hem, for whi and thi speche makith thee opyn. **1395** PURVEY *Remonstr.* (1851) 51 It is opin at ighe that the bisshop of Rome hath not so greet power in worchyng of miracles..as Petir and Paul hadden. **1450–1530** *Myrr. our Ladye* 18 Yf eny worde seme derke: yt is lefull to make yt more open by more esy translacion. **1588** J. UDALL *Diotrephes* (Arb.) 8 Laye open your former speches that I may vnderstand your meaning. **1611** BIBLE *Prov.* xiii. 16 A foole layeth open his folly. **1706** HEARNE *Collect.* 7 Feb. (O.H.S.) I. 180 He lays open some sort of People in..too lively Colours. **1799** MACKINTOSH *Stud. Law Nat.* Wks. 1846 I. 379, I shall next endeavour to lay open the general principles of civil and criminal laws. **1836** W. IRVING *Astoria* I. 68 They..laid open to him the whole scheme of Mr. Astor..and inquired whether they..could lawfully engage in it.

13. a. Exposed to general view or knowledge; existing, performed or carried on without concealment or so that all may see, hear, or take cognizance; public; †also, declared in public or by public authority. Of persons: Acting in public or without concealment. *spec.* Designating administration or government in which the public is kept well-informed and is invited to participate.

c **893** K. ÆLFRED *Oros.* v. xiii. §2 Antonius him selfum onbead ʒewin and openne feóndscipe. *c* **1000** *Ags. Gosp.* John vii. 4 Ne deð nan man nan þing on diʒlum ac secþ þæt hit open sy. *c* **1200** ORMIN 10352 Wiþþ all full openn spæche. **13..** *Cursor M.* 27355 (Cott.) Þat he ne mak opine knaulage of all his sak. **1386** *Rolls of Parlt.* III. 225/1 Wronges subtiles, and also open oppressions, ydo to hem. *c* **1400** *Destr. Troy* 11565 Hit was ordant of all men by oppon assent. *c* **1425** *Found. St. Bartholomew's* (E.E.T.S.) 59 Anooyn the godly myracle was made opyne. **1548** GESTE *Serm.* in H. G. Dugdale *Life* (1840) 190 Which sentence.. he caused to be wryten in his palace and all other open workes [public buildings]. **1558** *Act 1 Eliz.* c. 2 §4 Mattens, Euensong, administration of the Sacraments or other open Prayers..(Open Prayer in and throughout this Act, is meant that Prayer which is for other to come vnto, or hear..). **1712** ARBUTHNOT *J. Bull* I. viii, This affair between Hocus and Mrs. Bull was now so open, that all the world were scandalized at it. **1844** THIRLWALL *Greece* VIII lxii. 144 Cleombrotus he treated with open contempt. **1884** *Law Times Rep.* L. 255/2 He took his notes in the most open manner possible, sitting in one of the front seats. **1968** R. M. NIXON in *N.Y. Times* 20 Sept. 33/2 It's time we once again had an open administration—open to ideas from the people, and open in its communication with the people—an administration of open doors, open eyes, and open minds. **1971** J. AITKEN *Officially Secret* xv. 211 The absence of effective checks and controls on the activities of the contemporary Civil Service has recently led to demands for 'more open government'. **1973** *Public Administration* LI. 428 'Open government' and 'greater public participation' were becoming increasingly fashionable political slogans at this time. **1975** *Times* 11 Jan. 12/2 The need for 'open government', in which people are informed about what is being decided and have a chance to make their own suggestions. **1976** LD. HOME *Way Wind Blows* vii. 115 That this crisis was averted was in the greatest part due to the instinct for fair play and open government practised by the Tunku Abdul Rahman. **1977** *Time* (Overseas ed.) 17 Jan. 13/1 The coalition's goal, explained Dowiyogo in an interview with the *Australian*: to replace DeRobert's increasingly personal rule with 'open government—that is, to tell the people what we plan to do and why'. **1978** *Times* 17 Mar. 6/5 The Civil Service Department has refused a formal request from *The Times*, arising from the Prime Minister's open-government policy announced last July, that background material used in the preparation of the White Paper on the Civil Service published on Wednesday should be disclosed.

b. Of a place of work: in which both union and non-union workers are employed, esp. ***open-shop*** (cf. *closed shop*); also *attrib.* orig. *U.S.*

1896 *Typogr. Jrnl.* IX. 445 Our next efforts were directed to the Morning Leader, also an 'open' office. **1901** *World's Work* (N.Y.) July 914/2 The shop had previously been an 'open' one—that is, union and non-union men were employed without distinction. **1904** *N.Y. Even. Post* 15 Aug. 2 The Exposition is conducted along the lines of an 'open shop', by permitting the employment of both union and non-union labor. **1906** *Daily Colonist* (Victoria, B.C.) 1 Jan. 133 What is all this talk that's in the papers about the open shop? **1909** *Daily Chron.* 3 May 1/5 The strike has originated in the intention..to enforce an 'open shop' on the lake boats. **1939** *Sun* (Baltimore) 18 Apr. 22/7 As a direct result of the shutting down of union mines.., 'open-shop' mines in Garret county..were working at maximum capacity. **1964** E. H. POWELL in I. L. Horowitz *New Sociol.* 333 The open-shop crusade of the 'twenties was known as the 'American plan'.

14. Not confined or limited to a few, generally accessible or available; that may be used, shared, or competed for without restriction.

open champion, one who has been successful in a competition or 'championship' thus open. ***open communion***: see COMMUNION 7.

1460 CAPGRAVE *Chron.* (1858) 113 This man [K. Alfred].. mad an open Scole of divers Sciens at Oxenford. **1493** in Poulson *Hist. Beverley* (1829) I. 256 So that he kepe no oppyn shopp in retayling. **1642** *Vindic. King* p. i, Since the Times hath given an open Presse to cleere every imagination which is not stifled in this Dampe. *c* **1750** in *Westm. Gaz.* (1901) 5 Dec. 1/3 Upon the Foot of a Free and Open Trade to all His Majesty's Subjects. **1861** HUGHES *Tom Brown at Oxf.* i. 3 There were a large number of open fellowships. **1870** E. PEACOCK *Ralf Skirl.* III. 213 The mystery was now an open secret. **1884** *Pall Mall G.* 21 Aug. 9/1 Claret Open Hunters' Stakes (Two miles). **1884** G. ALLEN *Philistia* I. 44 He got..an open scholarship..at the college. **1896** *Daily News* 27 Apr. 4/6 Professional competition—Victory of the open champion.

15. a. Without defence or protection, esp. of a mental or spiritual kind; exposed, liable, or subject *to*.

c **1450** tr. *De Imitatione* I. xxv. 37 The religiose man þat is wiþoute discipline is open to a greuous falle. **1509** HAWES *Past. Pleas.* XL. (Percy Soc.) 202 The youth is open to all fraylte. **1561** T. HOBY tr. *Castiglione's Courtyer* II. (1577) Lvb, A daungerous place that lay open uppon gunshot. **1597** SHAKS. *2 Hen. IV*, v. ii. 8 The seruice..Hath left me open to all iniuries. **1782** PRIESTLEY *Corrupt. Chr.* I. II. 158 Dangerous constructions to which they are now too much open. **1865** *Ch. Times* 18 Nov., Whether they really beat ours..may be open to question. **1891** *Law Times* XC. 250/2 It seems open to doubt.

b. *to lay* (one) ***open to***: to render (one) liable to (something), to expose (one) to.

1853 C. BRONTË *Villette* I. viii. 149, I shall make blunders that will lay me open to the scorn of the most ignorant. *Ibid.* x. 183 There was something in it that pleased, but something too that brought surging up into the mind all one's foibles and weak points: all that could lay one open to a laugh. **1931** T. R. G. LYELL *Slang* 455 Judging by the people he knows and the books he reads and recommends, he certainly lays himself open to the suspicion of being one [*sc.* a Communist].

16. Not given to concealing one's thoughts or feelings; free in conversation; unreserved, frank, candid. Of persons; also of qualities, attributes, or manner showing or marked by candour.

1513 MORE in Grafton *Chron.* (1568) II. 781 A good knight and a gentle,..plain and open to his enemies, and sure and secret to his friend. **1609** B. JONSON *Sil. Wom.* I. Wks. (Rtldg.) 210/1 Come, you are a strange open man, to tell everything thus. **1667** MILTON *P.L.* VI. 610 To entertain them fair with open Front And Brest. **1697** DRYDEN *Virg. Georg.* IV. 138 One Monarch wears an honest open Face. **1709** ADDISON *Tatler* No. 97 ¶6, I will be open and sincere with you. **1805** WORDSW. *Waggoner* IV. 147 With careless air and open mien. **1885** HOWELLS *Silas Lapham* (1891) I. 283, I wish Tom would be a little opener with me.

17. Free in giving or communicating; liberal, generous, bounteous. Now chiefly in ***open hand, open-handed***.

1597 SHAKS. *2 Hen. IV*, IV. iv. 32 Hee hath a Teare for Pitie, and a Hand Open (as Day) for melting Charitie. **1607** —— *Timon* V. i. 61 Sir: Hauing often of your open Bounty tasted. **1696** TATE & BRADY *Ps.* cxlv. 16 With open hand he gives. *c* **1764** GRAY *Owen* 8 Liberal hand and open heart. **1884** W. C. SMITH *Kildrostan* I. ii. 180 How could he Have aught to leave..? You know his hand was open.

18. †Of a term or period of time: Not finished or closed (*obs.*). Of a matter, discussion, etc.: Not finally settled, or determined; undecided, undetermined; that may be decided according to circumstances or at will; hence, uncertain. See also *open question* (sense 22 c). *open* POLICY, VERDICT: see these words.

1562 *Act 5 Eliz.* c. 1 §3 Justices..shall certify every Presentment..in..the King's Bench within forty Days..if the Term be then open. **1818** CRUISE *Digest* (ed. 2) IV. 555 The other question as to..power of leasing was still left open. **1848** ARNOULD *Mar. Insur.* (1866) I. I. v. 218 An open policy is one in which the value of the subject assured..is left to be estimated in case of loss. **1892** *Law Times* XCII. 156/1 Lord Justice Cotton..left the matter open for future consideration.

19. Of a thing, course of action, etc.: Not closed or shut against access; that can be used or reached without hindrance; accessible, available. Const. *to* (a person).

1526 TINDALE *Acts* xix. 38 The lawe is open, and there are ruelars. **1644** HUNTON *Vind. Treat. Monarchy* vi. 48 He.. sayes 'here the way is open enough to rebellion'. No opener then himselfe makes it. *a* **1770** JORTIN *Serm.* (1771) I. v. 85 In the Holy Scriptures every thing necessary for general practice is open to all. **1860** MRS. CARLYLE *Lett.* III. 38 Whether the invitation..which I..declined for this year, be still open to me. **1867** FREEMAN *Norm. Conq.* I. App. 633 It is open to any one to reject both stories. **1883** *Manch. Exam.* 29 Nov. 5/1 There are three, or perhaps four, courses open to us.

20. Of a person: Accessible to appeals, offers, emotions, or ideas; ready to receive impressions, to respond to sympathy, or to entertain ideas or arguments; amenable *to* (pity or reason). ***open mind***, a mind accessible to all arguments or points of view, esp. in phr. ***to keep an open mind***. See also *open-minded* adj. (sense 22 c).

1672 G. FOX *Jrnl.* in Weeks *South. Quakers & Slav.* 39 The people being generally tender and open. **1782** MISS BURNEY *Cecilia* v. v, She seems so open..to reproof..that I should hope in a short time she may also be open to conviction. **1822** HAZLITT *Table-t.* II. vi. 140 He was.. open to impressions. **1841** MYERS *Cath. Th.* III. §41. 149 A mind open to all theories. **1865** M. ARNOLD *Ess. Crit.* ii. (1875) 56 Those whose intelligence is quickest, openest, most sensitive. **1898** *Westm. Gaz.* 10 Feb. 3/1, I..hope some open-to-conviction employer will happen on it. *a* **1902** *Mod.* I will not name a price, but I am open to offers. **1911** G. B. SHAW *Doctor's Dilemma* I. 6 *Schutzmacher.* Oh, in my case the secret was simple enough... I'm afraid youll think it rather infra dig. *Ridgeon.* Oh, I have an open mind. What was the secret? **1914** —— *Misalliance* 29 *Lord Summerhays.* Giving the show away is a method like any other method... I should keep an open mind about it. *Johnny.* Has it ever occurred to you that a man with an open mind must be a bit of a scoundrel? **1974** 'M. ALLEN' *Super Tour* vi. 210 We'd rather you go into all this with an open mind. **1976** *Star* (Sheffield) 29 Oct. 1/3 Senior detectives said they were keeping an open mind whether the attacker is the same man who has committed several rapes in the Barnsley area.

III. Phrases and Combinations.

21. Phrases. ***with open arms*** (sense 6), with arms outspread to receive; hence, with great willingness or eagerness of reception. ***open book***, a person or thing that can be readily understood; a person who conceals nothing; also in phr. ***to read*** (someone) ***like an open book*** (cf. READ *v.* 5 d). ***in open court***, in the public court of justice, before the judge and the public. ***open ear***, a listening or attentive ear. ***open eye***, an unclosed, hence an observant or watchful eye; used esp. in phr. ***with open eyes*** to denote clear perception. ***open hand*** (see 17). ***open letter***, a letter, esp. one written in protest against something, addressed to a particular person or persons but made public by being printed, e.g. in a newspaper. ***with open mouth***, with mouth open to speak; also, gaping with wonder, etc.; open-mouthed. ***open question*** (see 18). ***to keep open doors, house***, (†***household***) or ***table***, to provide hospitality or entertainment for visitors generally; ***open house***, welcome or hospitality for all visitors; also *attrib.* (see also HOUSE *sb.*[1] 18 b). See also OPEN-TIDE, TIME.

1735 POPE *Prol. Sat.* 142 And St. John's self..With *open arms receiv'd one Poet more. **1783** MAD. D'ARBLAY *Diary* 19 Nov., To Bolt Court..I went, and with open arms was I received. **1849** tr. *Hamilton's Fairy Tales* (ed. Bohn), She instantly flew towards him with open arms. **1853** G. H. BOKER *Bankrupt* IV. ii, in *Amer. Lost Plays* (1940) 105, I read your black heart like an *open book. **1919** WODEHOUSE *Damsel in Distress* iv. 53 There's no mystery about me. I'm an open book. **1934** A. G. STREET *Endless Furrow* xv. 254 Talk about old Nicholas Crawford's art and mystery in grocerin', why, that's an open book compared to farmin'. **1944** Open book [see *closed book* s.v. CLOSED *ppl. a.* 3]. **1973** 'S. WOODS' *Enter Corpse* 60 'You haven't tried to shake them off?' 'What would be the good?.. My life is an open book.' **1530** PALSGR. 249/2 *Opyn courte, *court planiere*. **1596** SHAKS. *Merch. V.* IV. i. 338 He hath refus'd it in the open Court, He shall haue meerly iustice and his bond. **1614** TAILOR *Hog hath lost his Pearl* IV. in Hazl. *Dodsley* XI. 478 He'd spend his judgment in the open court As now to me, without being once sollicited In his private chamber. *a* **1225** *Ancr. R.* 424 Habbe euer hire *earen opene touward hire dame. *a* **1548** HALL *Chron., Hen. VII* 12 b, To give open eare to his request. **1879** CALDERWOOD *Mind & Br.* 227 There is something additional in the open eye and open ear. *c* **1200** *Trin. Coll. Hom.* 53 Ure *eȝen ben eure opene to biholde ure helende. **1713** BERKELEY *Hylas & Phil.* i. Wks. 1871 I. 288 Directing your open eyes towards yonder part of the heaven. **1796** JANE AUSTEN *Pride & Prej.* II. v, But she had chosen it with her eyes open. **1878** (*title*) *Open letter to the English nation from Berlin. **1890** R. L. STEVENSON (*title*) Father Damien. An open letter to the Reverend Doctor Hyde of Honolulu. **1917** *Fortn. Rev.* Nov. 748 (*heading*) Problems of finance: an open letter to Lord Milner. **1966** *Listener* 6 Oct. 506/1 There are three open letters in the memorial volume. **1977** *Time* 21 Mar. 49/1 In 1972 he attacked the Black Muslims in an open letter, an act that is thought to have led to the execution of his family. *a* **1548** HALL *Chron., Hen. VI* 169 With *open mouthes and fierce corages, thei came to Quene Margaret. **1595** SHAKS. *John* IV. ii. 195, I saw a Smith..With open mouth swallowing a Taylors newes. **1530–1849** To *keep open house [see HOUSE *sb.*[1] 18 b]. *a* **1548** HALL *Chron., Hen. VIII* 146 But the Cardinall..kept open housholde, to lordes, ladies, and all other. **1720** *Lond. Gaz.* No. 5870/1 Most of the Presidents are to keep open Table. **1824** BYRON *Don Juan* XVI. lxviii. 98 Though not exactly what's called 'open house'. **1836** T. POWER *Impressions Amer.* II. 71 Mr. Oliver was one of a class of excellent open-house men, of which class there are specimens to be found in every part of this Union. **1841** CATLIN *N. Amer. Ind.* (1844) I. xvii. 118 A chief, who must be liberal, keep open doors, and entertain. **1907** *Westm. Gaz.* 30 Dec. 8/1 On the seventieth anniversary there was an 'open-house' reception. **1921** *Daily Colonist* (Victoria, B.C.) 23 Oct. 15/1 Victoria's three great laundries will hold 'open house' daily from 9 a.m. to 4.30 p.m. **1971** *Daily Tel.* 11 Oct. 15/2 Clarksons has an 'open house' hospitality suite at the Majestic where free liquor is flowing almost round the clock.

22. *Comb.* **a.** With a sb., forming an *attrib.* phrase, as ***open-cell, -class, -crib, -deck, -face, -frame, -hand, -house, -letter, -sand, -seam, -view, -web***: see also OPEN-AIR, OPEN-DOOR, OPEN-HAIR, OPEN-MOUTH, etc.

1933 *Amer. Speech* VIII. III. 30 **Open-cell wing*, division of the main prison building in which there were no bars on the front of the cells. **1957** *N.Z. Timber Jrnl.* Dec. 59/2 *Open-cell process*, a means of impregnating wood under pressure. The preservative is retained in the cell walls only, and the cells left empty. **1971** C. BONINGTON *Annapurna South Face* App. B. 243 A thin layer of open-cell foam in the sleeves. *Ibid.* 249 Open-cell foam mattresses. **1949** R. K. MERTON *Social Theory* II. iv. 136 Despite our persisting *open-class-ideology, advance toward the success-goal is relatively rare..for those armed with little formal education. **1954** F. C. AVIS *Boxing Reference Dict.* 79 *Open class contest*, an amateur contest consisting of four 3-minute rounds, with 1-minute intervals. **1974** *Times* 26 Oct. 12/3 P & O..the last [line] to operate two-class cruises, decided.. to..revert to 'open-class' cruising. **1881** RAYMOND *Mining Gloss.*, **Open-crib timbering*, shaft timbering with cribs alone, placed at intervals. **1886** *Harper's Mag.* June 18/2 In vessels of this class it is usual to have an *open-deck battery. **1906** 'H. MCHUGH' *Skiddoo!* v. 75 The Human Hog was invented long before the *open-face street car began to stop for him. **1931** *Amer. Speech* VII. 51 Custard [in lumberjack lingo] is 'open face pie'. **1942** BERREY & VAN DEN BARK *Amer. Thes. Slang* §91/27 *Open-face pie*, pie without an upper crust. **1946** *Sun* (Baltimore) 13 Mar. 22/7 The proposed serving of 'open-face' pies and sandwiches. **1940** *Chambers's Techn. Dict.* 595/2 **Open-frame girder*, a girder consisting of upper and lower booms connected at intervals by (usually) vertical members, and not braced by any diagonal members. **1969** *Jane's Freight Containers 1968–69* 477/2 Tilt covered open-frame containers are available. **1875** KNIGHT *Dict. Mech.*, **Open-sand Molding*, heavy beams, foundations, and bed-plates are sometimes molded in the floor of the foundry, without any cope or top part. **1910** *Installation News* Jan. 4/1 The much abused *open-seam conduit and the socket joint conduit. **1968** E. MCCOURT *Saskatchewan* iii. 36 The most fascinating by-products of open-seam mining are the miniature mountain ranges formed of the clay stripped away to expose the coal seams. **1899** *Westm. Gaz.* 10 Nov. 4/2 An *open-view balcony with balustrades in the roof. **1871** T. CARGILL *Strains Bridge Girders* 63 The lattice, or *open web girder.

b. Parasynthetic combinations in *-ed* (unlimited in number); such are, ***open-armed, -bladed, -chested, -collared, -countenanced, -flowered, -fronted, -grained, -housed*** (hence ***-housedness***), ***-jointed, -kneed, -lined, patterned, -roofed, -sided, -sleeved, -spaced, -spoken, -throated, -topped, -windowed*** (hence ***open-windowedness***).

1862 T. C. GRATTAN *Beaten Paths* II. 309 The two Sicilies only waited *open-armed for their deliverer. *c* **1890** W. H. CASMEY *Ventilation* 7 The *open-bladed fan is useful in moving large volumes of free air. **1828** TYTLER *Hist. Scot.* (1864) I. 159 He was broad-shouldered and *open-chested. **1945** DYLAN THOMAS *Let.* 30 July (1966) 277 Such lovely ladies and gentlemen.., *open-collared and wild-haired in the photographers' wind. **1966** R. ELLMANN *Lett. of J. Joyce* II. p. liii, The open-collared eloquence of D. H. Lawrence. **1890** BOLDREWOOD *Miner's Right* xxxiv. (1899) 146/2 A respectably-dressed, *open-countenanced miner. **1874** LUBBOCK *Wild Flowers* iii. 68 An interesting series commencing with *open-flowered species. **1796** PEARSON in *Phil. Trans.* LXXXVI. 448 Its fractured..surface was *open-grained, and crystallized. **1804** ANNA SEWARD *Mem. Darwin* 6 *Open-housed hospitality. **1874** THEARLE *Naval Archit.* 22 When they are *open-jointed, the timbers are kept in their correct relative position by placing blocks of the required thickness between the two tiers composing the frame. **1878** HUXLEY *Physiogr.* 36 So porous and open-jointed are some of the rocks of this series. **1719** DE FOE *Crusoe* I. iv, My breeches..were only linen, and *open-knee'd. **1845** *Athenæum* 11 Jan. 42 *Open-lined engravings like Albert Durer's. **1647** A. ROSS *Mystag. Poet.* ix. (1675) 219 Juno's temple was *open-roofed. **1714** *Lond. Gaz.* No. 5248/3 A Person in an *Open-Sleev'd Gown. **1863** S. L. J. *Life in South* II. ii. 49 A plain *open-spoken body. **1891** 'L. MALET' *Wages of Sin* II. IV. iii. 81 The north wind blew piercing, strong and tonic... Colthurst drank it down *open-throated. **1962** K. ORVIS *Damned & Destroyed* 111 A loud, open-throated sports-shirt. **1904** *Westm. Gaz.* 9 Dec. 7/2 The sight should be adjustable with *open-topped hood. **1964** W. L. GOODMAN *Hist. Woodworking Tools* 93 It is in effect an open-topped steel box. **1859** G. A. SALA *Tw. round Clock* (1861) 8 Shops wide open, staringly open,..yawning with a jolly ha! ha! of *open-windowedness on the bye-strollers.

c. Special combs.: **open access**, a system whereby users of a library have direct access to the bookshelves; also *attrib.*; **open admission** *U.S.* = *open enrolment*; **open-and-shut** *a.* (orig. *U.S.*), (*a*) simple, straightforward; esp. of a legal case in which there is no doubt as to the outcome; (*b*) of weather: characterized by alternating sunny and cloudy conditions; hence as *sb.*, (*a*) a simple or straightforward operation, case, etc.; also in phr. *as* (or *like*) *open and shut*: easily, straightforwardly; (*b*) alternately sunny and cloudy conditions; **open back** (see quot. 1923); †**open-bellied** *a.*, ruptured; **open bite** *Dentistry*, lack of occlusion of the front teeth when the jaw is normally closed; **Open Board** *U.S.*, an association formed in cities of the U.S. to transact dealings in options on a small scale not permitted by the local board of trade; **Open Brethren**, a branch of the Plymouth Brethren which does not practise extreme separatism; **open-cast, -cut**, in *Mining*, an open working; also, a method of mining coal, ore, etc., by removing surface layers and working from above, not from shafts; hence as *adj.*, of, pertaining to, or designating this method of mining; also quasi-*advb.*; **open-casting**, open-cast mining; **open chain** *Chem.* (see CHAIN *sb.* 5 g); freq. *attrib.*; **open cheque**, (*a*) an uncrossed cheque (see CROSS *v.* 7 c); (*b*) a cheque for an unstated amount; also *fig.*; **open circuit**, a circuit, esp. an electric circuit, that is incomplete; freq. *attrib.*; applied to breathing apparatus in which air is exhaled into the atmosphere and so lost; hence **open-circuited** *a.*, consisting of or containing an open circuit; (as a back-formation) **open circuit** *v. trans.*; **open city**, an undefended city; *spec.* a city declared to be unfortified and undefended, and hence, under international law, exempt from enemy bombardment; **open classroom**, a classroom in which instruction is informal, individual, and free-ranging; **open community** *Ecology*, an area in which the plant cover is not dense; **open compound** *Linguistics*, a compound in which there is a space (i.e. no hyphen) between the component elements; **open cover**, marine insurance that covers all the shipments made by a person or firm without specification in advance of the details of each shipment; **open credit** *Finance*, a credit free from restrictions; **open cycle**, a cycle of operations in which a working fluid, coolant, etc., is used only once (cf. *closed cycle*); **open day**, a day when a place, e.g. a school, which is normally closed to the public is made accessible to visitors (in quot. 1892, a day kept as a holiday at Durham University); **open end** *a.* = *open-ended* adj.; *spec.* (*a*) of an investment trust (see quot. 1940); (*b*) *Spinning* (see quot. 1975); **open-ended** *a.*, having an open end; freq. *fig.*, having no predetermined limit or boundary as to time, extent, size, etc.; *spec.* of a question or test: to which the respondent frames his own answer, as opp. to selecting one or two or more pre-phrased answers; hence **open-endedness**; **open enrolment** *U.S.*, the unrestricted enrolment of students at schools, colleges, etc., of their choice; **open-faced** *a.*, having a frank or ingenuous face; †also, having the face uncovered; also of a sandwich, pie, etc.: without an upper layer of bread or pastry; hence *openfacedness*; **open floor** (see quot. 1932); †**open-founded** *a.*, based on plain or obvious facts; **open-front** (see quot.); **open go** *Austral. colloq.*, an unimpeded opportunity; a 'fair go' (see GO *sb.*[1] 4 d); **open-hearth**, a hearth of the reverberatory type: see HEARTH[1] 3; also *attrib.*; **open housing** *U.S.*, property that can be rented or bought without restriction on racial grounds; also *attrib.*; **open jet**, a stream of air in a wind-tunnel which is not bounded by rigid walls in the working section; **open juncture** *Linguistics*, the type of juncture (sense 2 c) found at word boundaries or marked syllable division within the word; **open learning** *Educ.*, any system of learning which is based on independent study or initiative rather than formal classroom instruction; *spec.* = *distance learning* s.v. DISTANCE *sb.* 12; **open line**, (*a*) a telephone line on which conversations can be overheard or intercepted by others; (*b*) used *attrib.* to denote a radio or television programme in which the public can participate by telephone; **open loop**, a control loop (LOOP *sb.*[1] 4 l) without feedback, each operation or activity being affected only by those earlier in the sequence; **open market**, a market in which any buyer or seller may trade freely and where prices are determined by supply and demand; also *attrib.*; **open marriage**, a marriage in which partners are by agreement free to have sexual relations with persons other than each other; **open-minded** *a.*, having an open mind, accessible to new arguments or ideas, hence *open-mindedness*; **open-mindedly** *adv.*, in an open-minded manner; **open-neck**, a collar of a kind that leaves the neck unrestricted; *spec.* as *adj.*, of a shirt, that is worn with the collar unbuttoned, without a tie; also *fig.*; hence **open-necked** *a.*; **open occupancy** *U.S.*, occupancy of housing available to persons of any race; **open-pit** *a.* chiefly *N. Amer.* = *open-cast* adj.; **open plan**, an architectural style allowing for no (or few) internal walls or partitions within a building, esp. an office or a school; freq. *attrib.*; hence **open-planned** *a.*, **open-planning**; **open question**, a matter on which differences of opinion are legitimate; **open range**, (*a*) *N. Amer.*, a range or tract of land that is not intersected with fences; also *attrib.*; (*b*) used *attrib.* or as *adj.* = *free range* (*b*) s.v. FREE *a.* D. 2; also *fig.*; **open-reel** *a.*, employing or having tape reels of such a kind that they and the tape they carry are accessible (in contrast to cassettes and cartridges); **open road**, (*a*) *U.S.*, a road that is not private; (*b*) a country road or a main road outside urban areas; (somewhat sentimentally) a road or route along which one can travel without care or hindrance; also *attrib.*; **open roof** (see quot. 1932); **open sandwich**, a sandwich without a top slice of bread; **open score** *Mus.* (see quot. 1899); **open season**, the season when hunting or fishing is allowed; also *transf.* and *fig.*, a time when something, esp. criticism, is unrestricted; **open shed** *N.Z.* (see quots.); **open shelf**, a bookshelf that is not enclosed behind a door or the like; in a library: one of any number of shelves from which the readers can take books themselves; freq. *attrib.* or as *adj.*; **open-side**, in *Rugby Football*, the side of the scrum on which the main line of the backs is ranged; opp. *blind side* (BLIND *a.* and *adv.* 2 c); also *attrib.*; **open skies**, used, chiefly *attrib.*, to designate a system whereby aircraft of any nation are allowed to fly over a particular territory; *spec.* of a system whereby two or more nations permit surveillance of one another from the air; also *open sky*; **open society**, a society characterized by its flexible structure and beliefs; one having much contact with other peoples or tolerant of change or of diversity in its existing order and traditions; opp. *closed society* (CLOSED *ppl. a.* 3); **open stage** (see quots.); also *attrib.*; **open-step** *sb.* used *attrib.*, of the sight of a gun, arranged with parallel bars after the fashion of a ladder; **open-stitch**, *Sc.* **open-steek**, a style of openwork stitching; also *attrib.*; **open-stock** (*N. Amer.*), goods that are always kept in stock by a shop, etc.; esp. a crockery set for which items can be bought separately at any time; also *attrib.*; **open subroutine** *Computers*, a routine that is written, in full, directly into a program wherever it occurs; **open system**, a material system in which the total mass or energy fluctuates; an incomplete or alterable system (of ideas, doctrines, things, etc.); **open texture** *Philos.* (see quots.); hence **open-textured** *a.*; **open-texturedness**; **open toe(d)** *a.*, designating a shoe that is open at the front to reveal the toes; **open-top** *a.*, having an open top; also as *sb.* (*U.S. colloq.*), a vehicle, trailer, or the like with an open top; hence **open-topped** *a.*; **open town**, (*a*) *U.S.*, a town characterized by a lack of restrictions on drinking and gambling places and the like; (*b*) = *open city*; **open tread** *a.*, of a staircase: having no risers; **open university**, a university having few if any restrictions on admission, *spec.* (with capital initials) a university founded in Great Britain in 1969 to provide courses for adult working people based on correspondence and radio and television broadcasts; also *fig.*; **open vegetation** = *open community*; †**open-visaged** *a.* = *open-faced*; **open ward**, a hospital ward designed to accommodate several patients; also *attrib.*; **open water** (chiefly *Canad.*), the melting of the ice on rivers and lakes in spring, or the time when this happens or has occurred; a stretch of water in which there is little or no ice; **open window unit** *Acoustics* (see quot. 1968[1]); **open wood, woodland** (see quot. 1889); **open woods** *N. Amer.*, a patch of woodland in which there is no undergrowth; cf. OPENING *vbl. sb.* 3.

1894 *Library* VI. 344 There is absolutely no novelty about the principle of *open-access. **1899** (*title*) Account of the safe-guarded open-access system in public lending libraries. **1934** *Archit. Rev.* LXXVI. 168/1 The new library has one important feature that distinguishes it from most large libraries in this country and elsewhere; I refer to the system of 'open access'. *a* **1956** A. ESDAILE in D. Lodge *Brit. Mus. is falling Down* (1965) vi. 96 Free or open access can hardly be practised in so large a library as this. **1977** *Times Lit. Suppl.* 30 Dec. 1532/2 The long-standing fight about open access..is won now... Behind lay a deep-seated fear..in some librarians..of anyone from the outside world actually having the run of the shelves. **1969** *Sat. Rev.* (U.S.) 20 Dec. 54/1 (*heading*) The challenge of *open admissions. Will Everyman destroy the university? **1970** *Time* 28 Sept. 36 Under its new 'open admissions' policy, CUNY [*sc.* the City University of New York] was taking such students despite their academic shortcomings. **1973** E. TAYLOR *Serpent under It* (1974) xii. 176 The kinds of things that stir them [*sc.* students] up these days are parietal hours and open admissions and black studies. **1976** *Times* 13 Jan. 7/4 There were three basic principles at [New York's] City University: quality education, free tuition and open admission. **1977** *Time* 28 Mar. 13/2 The country's enduring recession and unlimited open-admissions policies have turned Italian universities into what students call 'unemployment factories' or 'jobless parking lots'. **1841** *Picayune* (New Orleans) 11 Mar. 2/3 The contest between *Humming Bird* and *Maria Collier* was considered all but a 'dead *open and shut game'. **1848** G. P. BURNHAM in F. A. Durivage *Stray Subjects* 128 That chap's snoring beat *all* the high-pressures he *ever* heerd—jest as easy as open and shet! **1890** *Dialect Notes* I. 19 The common New England maxim is 'Open and shet's a sign of wet'. **1893** *Harper's Mag.* May 975/2 The case was a dead open-and-shut one. **1904** W. H. SMITH *Promoters* x. 162 It seems as if it was a dead open and shut that we've got to stay with 'em. **1930** KIPLING *Limits & Renewals* (1932) 262 Like broken water, with the sun tipping it. Like Portland Race in open-and-shut weather. **1936** M. ALLINGHAM *Flowers for Judge* ix. 139 They [*sc.* the police] feel they've got an open-and-shut case. **1966** T. H. RADDALL *Hangman's Beach* III. xv. 230 It was what fishermen call an open-and-shut day, with patches of black cloud, and occasional showers of rain. **1971** 'D. SHANNON' *Ringer* (1972) ix. 163 This was such an open-and-shut thing. **1974** A. MORICE *Death of Heavenly Twin* xiii. 138 What's the hurry if it's as open and shut as you make out? **1975** 'E. LATHEN' *By Hook or by Crook* iii. 28 It's an open-and-shut case. There's no doubt. **1976** *Encounter* June 12/2 'No sweat, Mr Dennie,' said the police chief... 'It's an open and shut. The lady must have fell asleep smoking a cigarette.' **1923** H. A. MADDOX *Dict. Stationery* 56 **Open back*, a bookbinding term alternatively described as hollow back, spring back, or extra... Letter-press books are either 'fast back' (in which case the leather is pasted directly on the folded sections) or 'open back' (in which case the book has a false back or is actually cased). **1961** Open back [see *loose back* s.v. LOOSE *a.* 9]. **1598** FLORIO, *Gualloroso*, burst, *open bellied. **1893** SMALE & COLYER *Dis. & Injuries Teeth* ii. 14 Lack of anterior occlusion, or *open bite may be caused in several ways—by thumb, finger, lip or tongue sucking [etc.]. **1975** W. J. B. HOUSTON *Orthodontic Diagnosis* iv. 36 A skeletal open bite can not be satisfactorily treated by attempting to extrude the anterior teeth which have already grown as much as possible. Nor should posterior teeth be ground or extracted. **1870** J. K. MEDBERY *Men & Mysteries Wall St.* 16 The consolidation of the Government and the *Open Boards with the old historic Stock Exchange. **1902** G. H. LORIMER *Lett. Merchant* ix. 113 If she is the daughter of old Job Dashkam, on the open Board, I should say..that she was a fine girl to let some other fellow marry. **1879** A. MILLER *Brethren* v. 66 The new motto on the standard of the *Open Brethren was, 'The blood of the Lamb is the union of the saints'. **1883** J. S. TEULON *Hist. & Teaching of Plymouth Brethren* ii. 18 Henceforth the Brethren parted into two hostile camps. The followers of Messrs. Müller and Craik, under the name of Open Brethren, adhered to the principles which had animated the movement in its earliest days. **1909** *Encycl. Relig. & Ethics* II. 845/2 The 'Open' Brethren..fraternize freely with other Christians. **1968** F. R. COAD *Hist. Brethren Movement* x. 159 Those who refused to apply his decree against Bethesda... Commonly called 'Open Brethren', but in this book referred to hereafter by the more accurate name of independent Brethren. **1713** in *Sc. Nat. Dict.* (1965) VI. 487/3, 33½ fadoms wrought of closs Mynding besyds what is wrought of a flagged Mynd, and *oppen cast. **1789** J. WILLIAMS *Nat. Hist. Mineral Kingdom* I. II. 272 This open-cast has been worked to a great length upon the bearing and the old works now exhibit a horrid and frightful gulph of great length. **1802** J. MAWE *Mineral. of Derbyshire* 207 *Opencast*, when a vein is worked open from the day. **1811** [see OPEN-WORK 2]. **1851** GREENWELL *Coal-trade Terms Northumb. & Durh.* 37 *Opencast*, a cutting in stone, coal, &c., at the top or bottom of an excavation already made, and open to that place. **1903** *Copper Handbk.* III. 260 Veins are stripped and worked open-cast. **1944** *Times* 8 Apr. 2/4 The movement of opencast coal has been increased by 80,000 tons a week. **1955** *Times* 27 May 19/1 We are in process of pumping the water out of this opencast. *Ibid.* 1 July 17/3 Your company has taken a leading part in the operations of opencast mining and has dug, during the year under review, over a quarter of a million tons of coal. **1974** *Country Life* 14 Feb. 284/2 Development and exploitation, ranging from housing estates to open-cast mining. **1886** J. BARROWMAN *Gloss. Scotch Mining Terms* 48 **Open-casting*, holing above the seam: working as a quarry. **1976** *Ilkeston Advertiser* 10 Dec. 11/1 Mr Alex Eadie, Parliamentary Under-Secretary of State for Energy, praised the council for its 'exceptional foresight' by co-operating with the Coal Board in planning and restoring land after opencasting. **1884** M. M. P. MUIR *Treat Princ. Chem.* ii. 164 In an *open chain molecule the action does not return to the carbon atom at which it started. **1928** [see CHAIN *sb.* 5 g]. **1968** O. R. C. NORMAN *Princ. Org. Synthesis* i. 23 Organic reactions frequently lead to the formation of cyclic compounds from open-chain (alicyclic) compounds. **1882** R. BITHELL *Counting-House Dict.* 212 **Open cheque*, an *uncrossed* cheque, payable to Bearer or to Order on presentation. **1977** J. WAINWRIGHT *Nest of Rats* I. iii. 17 'I'll pay... Just name it.'.. 'An open cheque. That makes it very big.' **1827** J. Cumming *Man. Electro. Dynamics* iv. 164 In all cases of continued rotation, one of the conductors forms an *open circuit. **1876** Preece & Sivewright *Telegraphy* iv. 105 Where many intermediate stations are fixed on one wire worked on the Morse principle, the closed circuit system offers considerable advantages over the open circuit system. **1893** S. R. Bottone *How to manage Dynamo* 42 This line of conductors is said to form an open circuit when there is any gap in the way; and then no current can flow. **1904** *Electrician* 13 May 139/2 If the field winding on one of the limbs of a Manchester-type dynamo is open-circuited, this limb will magnetically short-circuit the remaining limb. **1907** J. Erskine-Murray *Handbk. Wireless Telegr.* 5 Modern wireless telegraphy is, in general, open circuit telegraphy. **1927** A. E. Claxton *Performance & Design D.C. Machines* xii. 269 An open-circuited coil prevents the passage of current in its circuit. **1939** *Jrnl. Exper. Zool.* LXXXII. 420 The method employed for measuring the rate of metabolism was an open-circuit respiration system modified from the system originally developed by Haldane. **1953** [see *closed circuit* s.v. closed *ppl. a.* 3]. **1954** *Induction Motor* (Brook Motors Ltd.) xii. 184 If one phase is open-circuited, the motor will make a humming noise when switched on. **1956** C. Evans *Kanchenjunga* ix. 92, I planned that every European going above Camp 3 should..climb with an open-circuit oxygen set. **1957** *Practical Wireless* XXXIII. 539/1 The input resistance with open-circuited output, and output resistance with short-circuited input, remain the same. **1962** J. P. Gregory in G A. T. Burdett *Automatic Control Handbk.* ii. 7 The timing of the relay is brought about by delaying the decay of the flux in its magnetic circuit after switching off the supply to the coil, either by short-circuiting or open circuiting it. **1977** G. V. Higgins *Dreamland* vi. 59 If I don't touch an open circuit.. it'll be a cave-in, or a blast. **1914** Duchess of Sutherland *Six Weeks at the War* p. xii, Unfortunately Namur is not an *open city so she suffered for a short time from horrors worse than 'moral effect'. **1938** *Newsweek* 4 July 9/3 A pact restricting bombing of 'open' cities. **1944** *Ann. Reg. 1943* 57 The Government had been urged in Parliament to treat Rome as an open city. **1965** H. Kahn *On Escalation* ix. 178 Military disengagement on the open-city model. **1971** *N.Y. Times* 8 June 39 An *open classroom means nothing to me unless it means that a child learns in that classroom that learning is not dependent at every level on the presence of a teacher. **1973** *Britannica Bk. of Year 1972* 732/3 *Open classroom*, a system of education in which activities involving multidisciplinary skills replace traditional subject courses. [**1909** Groom & Balfour tr. *Warming's Oecol. Plants* xxxv. 137 In some communities the soil is densely covered,.. but in others the vegetable covering is so open that the colour of the soil imparts to the landscape its hue.] **1923** A. G. Tansley *Pract. Plant Ecol.* ix. 126 We get an *open community in stable equilibrium with its habitat. **1929** Weaver & Clements *Plant Ecol.* vii. 142 Open communities are invaded readily. **1975** O. Rackham *Hayley Wood: Hist. & Ecol.* iii. 124 It is an open community: these plants do not form a carpet, and there is plenty of bare ground. **1961** Webster, *Open compound. **1965** *Amer. Speech* XL. 41 An enterable open compound like *threshing machine*. **1884** D. Owen *Marine Insurance* (ed. 2) 56 (*heading*) Agreement to execute policies. (Off *open cover.) **1895** W. Gow *Marine Insurance* xiv. 229 In every case with which the writer is acquainted the open cover is a mere document of honour. **1928** F. W. S. Poole *Marine Insurance of Goods* iv. 59 Open covers provide the merchant with continuous protection, enabling him to calculate the insurance charges for shipments ahead. **1960** *Times* 24 Oct. (Finance. Rev.) p. xiii/2 It was to meet this convenience that the 'open cover' type of policy was developed. **1903** *Pitman's Business Man's Guide* 326 **Open credit*. This is the name given to a letter of credit which contains an unconditional request to pay money to another person. **1920** J. Stephenson *Princ. & Pract. Commerc. Corr.* iii. iv. 186, I..now beg to inquire whether you would be inclined to open an Account Current with me, granting me an open credit of £875. **1881** Raymond *Mining Gloss.*, **Open cut*, a surface-working, open to daylight. **1950** *Nucleonics* Mar. 47/1 The *open cycle system is generally practical only with a plentiful and inexpensive coolant like air or water, except in the case of a rocket drive. **1957** *Gloss. Terms Nuclear Sci.* (Nat. Res. Council, U.S.) 114 *Open cycle*, cycle of operation of a heat engine in which the power fluid is used only once... Also applicable to a cooling system in which the coolant is used once and then discarded. **1958** M. J. Zucrow *Aircraft & Missile Propulsion* II. vi. 13 An open-cycle power plant is a continuous-flow prime mover using atmospheric air as the working fluid. **1971** M. M. El-Wakil *Nuclear Energy Conversion* vii. 200 In designing open cycles, the extent of induced radioactivity in the coolant and its effects on plant and surroundings should be carefully evaluated. **1973** Kettani & Hoyaux *Plasma Engin.* viii. 243 In the open cycle system, fuel is burned with the oxidiser to which seed is added without preheating. **1892** *Durham Univ. Calendar* 6 February 22..M. *Open Day. **1941** H. G. Stead *Mod. School Organisation* xv. 261 Open Days..let parents and other interested friends have an opportunity of seeing the school in action. **1953** A. K. C. Ottaway *Educ. & Soc.* vi. 117 Whenever 'open days' for visitors are possible these are appreciated by parents. **1971** *Guardian* 23 Aug. 4/1 Tours or 'open days' are being held..on sites within the Roman 'colonia' at Lincoln. *Ibid.* 12 Nov. 7/3 It was like most school open days. The women questioned the staff about how the teaching would help John's or Simon's career. **1975** B. Meyrick *Behind the Light* xi. 143 Open Days on local Trinity service vessels were an annual event. **1908** *Daily Chron.* 13 Feb. 6/2 The *open-end garden-seated light car.. might be trailed as a relief car. **1940** *Sun* (Baltimore) 26 Apr. 23/9 Open-end trusts are those in which shares are redeemable at their asset value at any given time. **1945** Webster Add., *Open-end*, of a contract calling for the filling by a particular contractor of all government needs for a specific product during a specified period. **1952** W. J. H. Sprott *Social Psychol.* vi. 102 The questions..may be 'open-end' questions which allow of a more elaborate answer. **1953** *Economist* 21 Feb. 500/1 An open-end trust is in all major respects similar to a flexible unit trust. It holds a portfolio of securities and cash, against which units are issued to the public, and the managers have a wide discretion in their investment policy. *Ibid.* 500/2 The principle of the open-end fund is sound. **1954** [see *closed-end* s.v. closed *ppl. a.* 3]. **1955** T. H. Pear *Eng. Social Differences* iii. 110 Questionnaires, 'closed or open-end', might lead to interviews and written personal and private communications. **1966** *Listener* 23 June 926/1 This was what happened in the open-end discussion. **1972** *Guardian* 21 July 16/1 There was a considerable debate in financial quarters about the wisdom of open-end funds, or unit trusts, which invest in property. **1972** *Sci. Amer.* Dec. 55/1 Open-end spinning has been the subject of intense development during the past five years. Commercial frames of Czechoslovakian and Japanese design have recently become available. **1974** *Times* 22 Mar. 21/1 The demand background is there and with its lead in 'open end' and 'self twist' machines Stone should be able to exploit it whilst it lasts. **1975** A. J. Hall *Stand. Handbk. Textiles* (ed. 8) iii. 170 In an open-end spinning a sliver of, say, cotton is fed into a relatively small device..in which the fibres under air pressure are impelled by centrifugal action and an existing air vortex on to the internal surface of a high speed (up to 40000 rev/min) rotating cylinder and are therefore carried forward with their twisting together to an exit point from which they are drawn in the form of yarn having an appropriate degree of twist. **1976** *National Observer* (U.S.) 13 Mar. 10/6 (Advt.), A managed diversified Open-end Investment Trust. **1825** J. Nicholson *Operat. Mechanic* 172 The disadvantages attending the *open-ended cylinder. **1935** [see *hydraulic gradient* s.v. hydraulic *a.* 1]. **1940** M. Mead *Male & Female* ii. 47 The problem will be whether.. those who read can keep such words as 'men', 'women', and 'children' open-ended words. **1952** *Newsweek* 26 May 39/2 This program..is bound to fail if it is looked upon as a final step. Like the original Union of our States, it should be 'open-ended'. **1952** *Sat. Even. Post* 25 Oct. 150/3 Unlike the atomic bomb, the hydrogen bomb is an 'open-ended' weapon. In theory, if you want to make it more powerful, you just shovel in more of the heavy-hydrogen mixture. **1953** E. G. Williamson in *Ann. Rev. Psychol.* IV. 344 The open-ended interviews were concerned with the manner in which an individual was currently dealing with his problem of occupational choice. **1953** K. Cobb in *Ibid.* 367 A study of visually handicapped school children, tested with an open-ended adjustment inventory printed in large print or Braille. **1957** R. K. Merton *Student-Physician* 314 Questions marked with an asterisk were initially asked in open-ended form. **1964** *Ann. Reg. 1963* 401 This at least was suggested by their answers to questions in standard intelligence tests, which tended to an alarming degree to be of the closed rather than open-ended type. **1967** M. Argyle *Psychol. Interpersonal Behaviour* ii. 39 Questions vary in the extent to which they are open or closed—an open-ended question requires a lengthy explanation rather than a choice between alternatives; the best way to get someone to talk is to ask this kind of question. **1970** D. Goldrich et al. in I. L. Horowitz *Masses in Lat. Amer.* v. 177 It seemed desirable to use mainly open-ended interviewing techniques. **1973** *Daily Tel.* 2 Mar. 2/5 Powers of punishment for contempt are open ended as no maximum prison sentence or fine is laid down. **1953** W. H. McNeill *Amer., Brit., & Russia* i. i. 63 It was almost irresistible to look at the war-time history in the light of what had come after, to search for signs and portents of the strained situation which had prevailed since 1946 or 1947, and to forget or minimize the '*open-endedness' of Allied relationships during the war years. **1973** *Amer. Speech 1969* XLIV. 289 The seeming 'open-endedness' of the set of sentences of a language presents a challenge to transformational theory. **1974** G. F. Newman *Price* vii. 218 The open-endedness of the situation worked as well for her. She was as free as Sneed to quit. **1964** *N.Y. Times* 12 Jan. E11/1 The New York system in 1960 inaugurated a policy of '*open enrollment' which permitted youngsters from designated predominantly non-white schools to apply for transfer to designated predominantly white schools. **1970** *Ibid.* 7 Jan. 42 The open enrollment policy for the city universities will be a mistake. **1974** *Florida FL Reporter* XIII. 80/3 If indeed the phrase is not to become a meaningless slogan as many people regard the term 'open enrollment' in the City University of New York. **1610** Guillim *Heraldry* vi. v. (1611) 265 This fashion of sidelong helmet and *openfaced with gardensure over the sight. **1897** *Daily News* 31 Mar. 6/3 A typical, tall, broad-shouldered, open-faced, English gentleman. **1934** Webster, *Open-faced* ..Of pies, etc., without top crust. **1946** *Sun* (Baltimore) 26 Apr. 6/1 A spokesman for the Case-Moody Pie Corporation ..said it expected to realize a one fourth savings in flour by bringing out an 'open-faced' pie in which the top crust is eliminated. **1970** *Islander* (Victoria, B.C.) 22 Feb. 14/2 This little book tells you exactly how to make..toppings for world famous and eye-appealing Open-Faced Sandwiches. **1976** *National Observer* (U.S.) 14 Feb. 7/2 They can be fried and covered with goodies, thus becoming a pre-Columbian open-faced sandwich. **1649** H. Lawrence *Some Considerations* 41 As much as betweene *openfacednesse, and vailing. **1932** T. Corkhill *Conc. Building Encycl.* 146 **Open floor*, one with exposed joists, not covered by a ceiling. **1571** Golding *Calvin on Ps.* xlix. 10 An *openfounded doctrine, that cannot escape the knowledge even of the rudest. **1881** Raymond *Mining Gloss.*, **Open-front*, the arrangement of a blast furnace with a forehearth. **1919** W. H. Downing *Digger Dial.* 36 **Open go*, see *fair go*. **1959** H. P. Tritton *Time means Tucker* ii. 15/1 The sergeant said we were putting on a better show than the professionals. He said we could have an open go the following night. **1973** *Bulletin* (Sydney) 25 Aug. 24/1 This intimidatory behavior, the company charges, contrasts with the 'open go' policy being afforded two other major prawning operators in the region. **1885** *Daily News* 17 Sept. 5/7 The duel is between wrought or puddled iron and Bessemer, or its rival '*openhearth' steel. **1897** *Times* 18 Oct. 12/1 The growing importance of open hearth and the diminishing relative value of Bessemer steel. *Ibid.*, To-day the open hearth system has completely asserted its supremacy. **1966** *Guardian* 29 Aug. 7/2 The agreement provides for stronger enforcement of *open-housing regulations. *Ibid.*, Labour leaders agree to support open housing. **1971** *N.Y. Times* 1 June 28 The Suburban Citizens for Open Housing, an organization pushing for integration of the outer city. **1976** *National Observer* (U.S.) 8 May 6/2 The Rev. James E. Groppi, the Roman Catholic priest who led open-housing marches in the '60s. **1932** *Jrnl. R. Aeronaut. Soc.* XXXVI. 999 In a tunnel of any sort the provision of an *open jet calls for rather more power than a walled-in jet would need. **1947** A. Pope *Wind-Tunnel Testing* ii. 34 For propeller and rotor tests..the open jet offers considerable advantage. **1971** D. C. Bain et al. *Wind Tunnels* ii. 1/2 Open jet tunnels are mainly used for air flow observations and have the advantage of easy access to the model for modifications and an unobstructed view for observation and photography. **1941** *Open juncture [see juncture 2c]. **1942** Bloch & Trager *Outl. Ling. Analysis* iii. 47 In a phonemic transcription, external open juncture is marked by leaving a space between symbols, internal open juncture by a hyphen. **1966** [see junctural *a.*]. **1970** D. Rockey *Phonetic Lexicon* 43 Spanish permits no clusters before final pause and open juncture. **1974** *Amer. Speech 1969* XLIV. 57 The liquids occur only immediately before open juncture. **1970** R. A. Anderson in *Educational Technol.* June 15/2 Open-planning is merely a tool which makes the solution to an educational problem possible. Since the educational program is father to the plan, we must call these schools, then, '*open-learning places'. **1980** *Economist* 21 June 47 Open learning, beamed from the Gulf to the Mediterranean, will have the great advantage of drawing the Palestinian diaspora together. **1985** *Times* 12 Dec. 31/5 Self-study—or 'open learning' as it is so often called— is a proven technique in technical training. **1963** 'W. Haggard' *High Wire* xiv. 151 He..booked a call to London. It would be an *open line, but he didn't have access to another. **1966** 'G. Black' *You want to die, Johnny?* iii. 47 Perhaps I should tell you, even on an open line, that I've just had a summons, from Ministerial level. **1970** *New York* 16 Nov. 5/2 Her over-involvement with the Renaissance Project and the Open-Line Program present an unbalanced image. **1972** *Gaurdian* 25 Sept. 4 Open-line radio shows, during which the visitor sits in..a radio studio and answers questions in amplified telephone conversations with local people. **1973** 'D. Jordan' *Nile Green* xliv. 223 They had also given me an open line to London. **1947** *Jrnl. Inst. Electr. Engin.* XCIV. IIA 5/3 (*heading*) Examples of *open-loop and closed-loop control. **1954**, **1962** [see loop *sb.*[1] 4l]. **1966** *New Scientist* 30 June 830 Almost all skilled muscular activities seem to exhibit many 'open-loop', pre-programmed characteristics. An open-loop system (one that draws little or no information from the thing it governs) can always be operated more effectively than a closed-loop one, provided that its task is well defined and not subject to major disturbances. **1967** *Electronics* 6 Mar. 306/2 Typical open-loop voltage gain is greater than 200,000. **1766** Blackstone *Comm.* II. xxx. 449 Our Saxon ancestors prohibited the sale of any thing above the value of twenty pence, unless in *open market. **1838** W. Bell *Dict. Law Scotl.* 627 The law of Scotland differs from that of England as to the legal effect of a sale in open market. **1870** J. K. Medbery *Men & Mysteries Wall St.* 18 The stock which has occasioned the default is sold or bought in the open market under the rule. **1930** *Economist* 22 Mar. 630/1 The failure of the Reserve Bank's buying rate to go down as fast as the open-market rate. **1933** R. McKenna *Speech Midland Bank* 10 During the period of open market buying bank deposits continued to decline, though only slightly. **1934** [see berry *sb.*[1] 1c]. **1961** *Wall St. Jrnl.* 24 Mar. 26 This was a departure from its open market activities in the previous four weeks, in which the System extended these operations to securities in the medium-term range, with maturities up to ten years. **1972** *Times* 26 Jan. 6/2 To have the said rent reviewed at the said time by reference to the open market rental value of the demised premises. **1972** N. & G. O'Neill (*title*) *Open marriage. *Ibid.* 9 We began to synthesize and delineate those qualities and conditions that seemed most necessary for growth for a man and woman living together in today's world. In writing a preliminary draft on the subject in 1968, we defined such a relationship as *open marriage*. **1975** M. Bradbury *History Man* iii. 52 It is an adult, open marriage. They are both having affairs. **1985** J. Epstein in D. J. Enright *Fair of Speech* 60 Stripped of its psychological sham, an open marriage is one in which the partners in a conventional marriage have agreed to give way to the need to copulate with anyone else who will agree to copulate with them. **1828** Carlyle in *Foreign Rev.* II. 115 To *open-minded, truth-seeking men, the deliberate words of an open-minded, truth-seeking man can in no case be wholly unintelligible. **1861** T. Hughes *Tom Brown at Oxf.* III. xii. 223 In fact, he is a wonderfully open-minded man for his age, if you only put things to him the right way. **1903** G. B. Shaw *Let.* 6 Mar. (1972) II. 316 You can't feel at home with anything that is strange, no matter how open-minded you may be. **1969** *Jane's Freight Containers 1968–69* 31/3 CN will be open-minded about participating. **1976** P. Donovan *Relig. Lang.* iv. 43 The words..would appear to have little relevance to testing which stems from belief and faith, or even from openminded enquiry. **1909** H. G. Wells *Tono-Bungay* ii. iv. 230 'Your aunt makes Game of people,' was Marion's verdict, and, *open-mindedly; 'I suppose it's all right..for her.' **1832** Carlyle in *Fraser's Mag.* V. 386/1 Boswell wrote a good Book.. because of his free insight, his lively talent, above all, of his Love and childlike *Open-mindedness. **1865** Masson *Rec. Brit. Philos.* 9 An open-mindedness that should even solicit contrary impressions. **1914** *Jrnl. Iron & Steel Inst.* LXXXIX. 184 Whilst he could not but admire the authors' eloquence and open-mindedness, he certainly considered that they had not proved the theory which they had set out to expound. **1972** *Science* 16 June 1209/2 Much conventional scientific training..tends to produce rigidity and avoidance of personal involvement with subject matter, rather than open-mindedness and flexibility. **1939–40** *Army & Navy Stores Catal.* 656/3 All-Wool Sweaters... V-shape *open neck, plain or cable stitch. **1949** *Penguin New Writing* XXXVIII. 14 The sleeves of his open-neck shirt were rolled up. **1971** D. Bagley *Freedom Trap* vii. 152 She looked too damned fetching in stretch pants, open-neck shirt and short jacket. **1976** *Daily Mirror* 16 July 13/1 An elaborately casual outfit of trousers and jacket, in man-made fibre and worn with an open-neck shirt. **1959** E. H. Clements *High Tension* v. 83 His step-cousin's [neck] rose, long and boyish-looking, from an *open-necked shirt. **1973** P. Moyes *Curious Affair of Third Dog* iii. 32 A slim, fair-haired girl in corduroy trousers and an open-necked shirt. **1975** N. Luard *Robespierre Serial* xv. 131 The burly men in open-necked shirts. **1976** *Listener* 10 June 751/1 Australia?.. A free-and-easy, no-nonsense, open-necked continent. **1953** *Open Occupancy in Public Housing* (U.S. Housing & Home Finance Agency) i. 3/1 When a shifting is made from a policy of enforced segregation to one of *open occupancy, clear-cut policy..is found to be mandatory. **1966** *Economist* 28 May 962/2 The landlords' association, which Core blames in part for the persistent refusal of the City Council to pass an open-occupancy law. **1968** M. Harrington *Toward Democratic*

Left x. 289 And study after study documents a correlation between high educational attainment and libertarian views on civil liberties, capital punishment, open occupancy—and the war in Vietnam. **1913** *Amer. Year Bk. 1912* 421/2 The eight-hour day in Arizona..has been extended to all open-cut workings and *open-pit workings. **1959** *Times* 12 June 17/4 It [*sc.* British capital] has pioneered in the new technique of open-pit borate mining. **1971** *Daily Colonist* (Victoria, B.C.) 19 Feb. 11/3 H. M. Wright..says open-pit mines in British Columbia are 'a beautiful sight'. **1975** *New Yorker* 3 Mar. 74/2 Copper was hardly worth taking out of the ground, and times were hard in Bisbee. In 1951, Phelps Dodge began a new open-pit mine—the Lavender Pit. **1938** *Archit. Rev.* LXXXIII. 90/2 The *open plan is almost universal but perhaps less easy to work than it looks. **1954** *Ibid.* CXV. 213 A few are more experimental, influenced either by the pre-war work of Arne Jacobsen and Mogens Lassen or, more recently, by the open-plan American house. **1960** M. SPARK *Ballad of Peckham Rye* iii. 38 We used to have an open-plan... So that you could see everyone in the office without the glass. **1973** 'R. MACLEOD' *Burial in Portugal* ii. 41 An open-plan stairway curved..towards the upper floor. **1975** in Cox & Boyson *Black Paper 1975* 30/2 The education hierarchy..doubt the wisdom of having an open-plan school in a difficult area. *Ibid.* 31/1 For children from a less fortunate environment open plan is disaster. **1958** *Washington Post* 16 Aug. B 10/1 *Open-planned kitchens have been described by designers as 'one of the most desirable areas in the home'. **1960** *Guardian* 24 Feb. 12/5 Comparatively few people have really lived in modern, open-planned houses. **1976** *Ilkeston Advertiser* 10 Dec. 12/5 (Advt.), Front shop (ideal lounge), open-planned living kitchen. **1958** *Washington Post* 16 Aug. B 10/1 The welcome theme of this architect-designed House of The Week is '*open planning'. **1958** *Listener* 25 Sept. 459/1 The trend towards open planning favours development of this method. **1859** MASSON *Milton* I. 630 The summary decision of what had hitherto been an *open question in the Church. **1863** COX *Instit.* I. x. 255 Certain questions brought before Parliament are treated as 'open' questions; that is, questions on which Ministers in Parliament are allowed to take opposite sides without resigning. **1972** *Guardian* 2 Feb. 7/4 A sixth-form general studies unit..was designed to promote discussion of 'open' questions, to which there may be no known or agreed answers. **1976** *Howard Jrnl.* XV. I. 17 What brought about this change is an open question. **1890** *Stock Grower & Farmer* 15 Mar. 6/3 The cow men of the *open ranges will make money. **1905** *Bull. Bureau of Forestry* (U.S. Dept. Agric.) No. 62, 9 The great bulk of the western stockmen are definitely in favor of the Government control of the open range. *Ibid.* 52 Under the open-range system the honest and law-abiding cattleman was at a great disadvantage. **1958** *Spectator* 11 July 60/1 Occasionally they [*sc.* the chickens] have been a little flavourless, probably because these were not open-range birds. **1959** *Times Lit. Suppl.* 6 Nov. 639/1 After the..novels laid by American and western European novelists in their batteries or deep litter, it is pleasant to discover a Greek novel as tasty as an open range egg. **1962** W. STEGNER *Wolf Willow* (1963) II. ii. 45 Last survival of the open-range cattle industry, booby prize in a belated homestead rush, this country saved each stage of the Plains frontier long past its appointed time. **1970** *High Fidelity* Nov. 77/1 Here we encounter what may well be a very significant parting of the ways between cassettes and open-reel tapes. **1971** *Gramophone* Dec. 1125/1 An 8-track cartridge machine capable of recording and reproducing and a sophisticated recorder covering open-reel, cassette and cartridge recording and reproducing. **1977** *Rolling Stone* 7 Apr. 6/1 (Advt.), A cassette, unlike its open-reel counterpart, actually becomes an integral part of your system the instant you put it in your cassette deck. **1817** E. P. FORDHAM *Jrnl.* 31 July in *Pers. Narr. Trav.* (1906) vi. 100 This state [*sc.* Indiana] is one vast forest, intersected by a few Blaze roads and two or three *open roads. **1856** W. WHITMAN *Leaves of Grass* (ed. 2) 223 Afoot and light-hearted I take to the open road! **1920** E. O'NEILL *Beyond Horizon* III. ii. 162 So I thought I'd try to end as I might have—if I'd had the courage to live my dream. Alone—in a ditch by the open road—watching the sun rise. *a* **1930** D. H. LAWRENCE *Phoenix II* (1968) 220 Some of these sonnets are very fine: they stand apart in an age of 'open road' and Empire thumping verse. **1968** L. DEIGHTON *Only when I Larf* i. 16 I'm for the open road, the jet routes, Cannes, Nice, Monte; where the pickings are rich and the living is easy. **1975** *Country Life* 16 Oct. 1007/1 Open-road motoring is inhibited by ever-lower speed limits. **1976** *Southern Even. Echo* (Southampton) 2 Nov. 15/2 Yet on the open road a new virtue is revealed, and the VX becomes an admirable companion for covering long distance in comfort. **1932** T. CORKHILL *Conc. Building Encycl.* 146 **Open roof*, one in which the principals are on view. No ceiling. **1946** *Sun* (Baltimore) 13 Aug. 2/8 Some lunch counters were serving 'the *open sandwich', a single slice affair. **1959** *Listener* 15 Jan. 136/2 The simplest open sandwich or even everyday platter of roast meat. **1973** D. BAGLEY *Tightrope Men* xxv. 172 The open sandwiches of Scandinavia. **1899** BRIDGE & SAWYER *Course Harmony* ii. 8 There are two methods of writing harmony—viz., in *open score and short score. In open score each voice is written on a separate staff. **1979** *Early Music* Oct. 531/1 The..music examples..are offered in open score to avoid the congestion inevitable with reduction to short score. **1896** *Outing* Sept. 596/2 The first day of September marks the beginning of the *open season on pheasants, grouse, and quail in Oregon. **1914** 'HIGH JINKS, JR.' *Choice Slang* 16 *Open season*, time when a person may expect no mercy or protection. **1918** [see BEE[1] 5 b]. **1948** *Chesterton* (Indiana) *Tribune* 28 Oct. 6/4 A brief open season on pheasants will enhance this autumn's pleasure for Hoosier sportsmen. **1958** *Listener* 18 Sept. 416/1 The open season for tropical storms is declared in the last week in August. **1969** 'J. MORRIS' *Fever Grass* i. 10 He remembered those thirty years, before the island became independent and open season on its security tacitly declared. **1974** *Times* 18 Feb. 14/7 Any appearance of open season for pay could spark off an explosion. **1977** D. ANTHONY *Stud Game* xxviii. 189 It happened to be a year the state allowed open season on does, to thin out the herd. **1872** M. A. BARKER in D. M. Davin *N.Z. Short Stories* (1953) 37 Brown and Wetherby's was an '*open shed', where any shearers that came were taken on until there were hands enough. *a* **1948** L. G. D. ACLAND *Early Canterbury Runs* (1951) vii. 169 Clayton was an 'open shed', that is, the shearers were not engaged beforehand, but turned up and took their chance of a pen on the advertised starting day. **1821** M. EDGEWORTH *Let.* 12 Dec. (1971) 290 They live in the library—*open shelves—mixture of half bound and bound books. **1897** *Library Jrnl.* Jan. 44/1 The adoption of the open-shelf system. **1910** A. E. BOSTWICK *Amer. Publ. Library* 38 Practically all small and moderate sized American libraries are now 'open-shelf', which means that the user is allowed to go personally to the shelves and select his book. **1906** GALLAHER & STEAD *Compl. Rugby Footballer* xi. 145 (*heading*) Tactics—combined attack on the *open side. **1960** E. S. & W. J. HIGHAM *High Speed Rugby* vii. 71 Break to the openside and close to the scrum if the openside flank is going straight for your fly-half. **1945** *Richmond* (Virginia) *Times Dispatch* 10 Feb. 12 (*heading*) U.S. accepts agreements on aviation pact. Will exchange '*open skies' rights. *Ibid.*, Today's action confirmed the position taken by the United States delegation in favor of 'open skies' or virtually unlimited freedom of the air. **1956** *Friends Jrnl.* 18 Feb. 103/2 The United States position is that until the scientists have solved the problem of detecting stocks, priority should be given to the Eisenhower 'open skies' plan and other measures designed to create confidence rather than to affect disarmament. **1957** *Daily Mail* 7 Oct. 6/2 The day when the Communists gave an ironic answer to President Eisenhower's plea for 'Open Skies'—by creating just that. **1965** D. D. EISENHOWER *White House Yrs.* (1966) II. v. xx. 470 The Open Skies proposal was criticized by the Soviets because, they said, it covered only the territories of our two homelands and would fail to cover territory where United States forces were stationed overseas. **1973** *Times* 31 Jan. (Mediterranean Suppl.) p. iv/3 To attain their ambitious targets the Greek authorities proclaimed an 'open skies' policy for charter flights. **1944** *Sun* (Baltimore) 30 Nov. 7/2 The British apparently now have the choice of going along with the '*open sky' program or facing the development of a large bloc of nations which want something along the lines of the United States. **1955** *Ibid.* 11 Nov. 1/7 Vyacheslav M. Molotov buried President Eisenhower's 'open-sky' plan for disarmament under a five-point indictment here tonight. **1935** R. AUDRA et al. tr. *Bergson's Two Sources Morality & Relig.* iv. 230 Never shall we pass from the closed society to the *open society, from the city to humanity, by any mere broadening out. **1940** *Mind* XLIX. 116 Bergson's distinction of 'open' and 'closed' societies, when applied to the society of all mankind, leads to the conclusion that this all-inclusive society will be 'quantitatively closed'. **1945** K. POPPER (*title*) The open society and its enemies. **1954** P. MASON *Ess. Racial Tension* xvii. 119 The painful transition from a society based on status to an open society in which contract and competition play a part. **1973** *Listener* 17 May 635/1 Mill's..overriding goal of maintaining an open society..in which might be realised..the flowering of human individuality in all its diversity. **1953** R. SOUTHERN *Open Stage* 41 The name '*open stage' cannot be given merely on the grounds of there being a platform free on three sides... Those three sides must be occupied by audience. **1960** *Times* 15 July 16/4 A cynic might regard the crude..Riviera settings as a powerful argument in favour of open-stage methods. **1962** *Listener* 8 Nov. 771/3 It is I think now widely accepted that the term 'open stage' is conveniently used to include not only the three-sided open stage of which Dr Southern was primarily writing in his book, but all forms of theatre where the acting area is in the same room as the audience. **1818** SCOTT *Rob Roy* xix, Nane o' yere..*opensteek hems about it. **1884** *Harper's Mag.* Aug. 365/1 The ordinary *open-step sight attached to the barrel. **1897** *Sears, Roebuck Catal.* 681 Decorated dinner-ware. Patterns sold in *open stock. **1911** *Daily Colonist* (Victoria, B.C.) 23 Apr. 4/4 We are in receipt of the latest open stock pattern in Limoges China... You can always replace a broken piece at any time. **1970** *Globe & Mail* (Toronto) 26 Sept. 13/1 (Advt.), 30% off makers' suggested retail prices on open stock dinnerware patterns. **1976** *Columbus* (Montana) *News* (Joliet Suppl.) 17 June 2/4 'Open stock' is the term for piece-by-piece sales instead of sales by the place setting category. The theory behind open stock sales is that you can buy just the pieces you need as you wish them, and you can replace items as you need. **1951** M. V. WILKES et al. *Preparation of Programs for Electronic Digital Computer* 22 The simplest form of subroutine consists of a sequence of orders which can be incorporated as it stands in a program... This type of subroutine is called an '*open' subroutine. **1958** [see INLINE *a.* 3 a]. **1969** P. B. JORDAIN *Condensed Computer Encycl.* 353 Typically, an open subroutine will convert floating-point numbers to fixed-point numbers or fixed-point to floating-point (four to six instructions), find the next larger integer value, or find the absolute magnitude. The advantages of open subroutine [*sic*] consist of simple usage.., faster execution, and if used sparingly, conservation of memory. **1939** F. H. MACDOUGALL *Thermodynamics & Chem.* (ed. 3) x. 134 When a transfer of matter to or from a system is also possible, the system may be called an *open system. **1962** P. STREVENS *Papers in Lang.* (1965) xii. 152 The study of closed-system items is what we conventionally call 'grammar', while the open systems constitute 'lexis'. **1963** A. K. RICE *Enterprise & its Environment* IV. xx. 184 Open systems exist and can only exist by the exchange of materials with their environment... An open system can achieve a time-independent steady state. **1971** J. Z. YOUNG *Introd. Study Man* ii. 26 Organisms are not stable systems..but 'open' systems maintained in a steady state by continual expenditure of energy. **1945** F. WAISMANN in *Aristotelian Soc. Suppl. Vol.* XIX. 121 The failure of the phenomenalist to translate a material object statement into terms of sense data..is due to..the '*open texture' of most of our empirical concepts... I owe this term to Mr. [W. C.] Kneale who suggested it to me as a translation of *Porosität der Begriffe*, a term coined by me in German. *Ibid.* 123 It is not possible to define a concept like gold with absolute precision, *i.e.* in such a way that every nook and cranny is blocked against entry of doubt. That is what is meant by the open texture of a concept. **1956** J. HOLLOWAY in A. Pryce-Jones *New Outl. Mod. Knowl.* 35 Waismann's term for this pervasive quality of language [*sc.* its ineradicable fluidity] was 'open texture'... The view is that the meanings of most words and expressions in common use are not precisely and exhaustively fixed, and..that it would be very inconvenient if they were. **1965** *Amer. Philos. Q.* II. 112/2 There are *practical* reasons independent of vagueness, open-texture and the like for refusing to equate names with descriptions. **1966** *Ibid.* III. 116/2 There is a certain 'open texture' about Christian beliefs. **1950** *Mind* LIX. 159 Straightway we have a case of a vague and *open textured criterion. **1965** *Amer. Philos. Q.* II. 120/1 The concepts they express are open-textured. **1974** T. E. WILKERSON *Minds, Brains & People* 7 A concept is too open-textured, so we tighten it up a little. **1966** *Jrnl. Linguistics* II. 243 The ordinary language philosopher..emphasizing the intricacy, variety and '*open-texturedness' of language. **1938** *Chatelaine* Mar. 32/3 *Open-toe shoes will be more popular than ever. **1942** *Sun* (Baltimore) 12 Aug. 10/7, I don't understand window dressing, but it looks to me that some of the 'girls' displaying fur coats in Charles street windows are standing in the snow with open-toe shoes on. **1942** R. CHANDLER *High Window* (1943) v. 43 She wore..blue and white *open-toed sandals. **1965** 'M. NEVILLE' *Ladies in Dark* viii. 80 The shoe was none too new, open-toed and with a strap round the heel. **1973** 'R. MACLEOD' *Burial in Portugal* iv. 91 She had simple open-toed sandals. **1771** *Connect. Col. Rec.* (1885) XIII. 514 Every open chair and other *open top riding wheel-carriage [shall be rated] three pounds. **1856** *Trans. Mich. Agric. Soc.* VII. 61 John Patton..[exhibited an] open top buggy. **1935** *Discovery* June 163/1 The tin can has gradually developed into the present day open top or 'sanitary' can, with the ends rolled on by machine, and made airtight by a rubber gasket. **1955** *Amer. Speech* XXX. 92 *Open top*, a rig with sides but no permanent top. **1972** D. E. WESTLAKE *Bank Shot* ii. 17 Open-top cartons full of paperback books. **1974** 'J. ROSS' *Burning of Billy Toober* ix. 89 A veteran open-top Bentley in racing dark-green. **1964** L. DEIGHTON *Funeral in Berlin* xix. 111 The *open-topped Mercedes that drove lazily past. **1977** L. GORDON *Eliot's Early Years* v. 99 He walked across London Bridge amidst horse-drawn carts, open-topped buses. [**1901** 'J. FLYNT' *World of Graft* 11 The City Hall gang went into office on the promise that the town was to be open, an' they've kept it open.] **1915** *Amer. Mag.* Sept. 51/2 On an '*open town' platform Gill was elected mayor in March, 1910. **1938** H. NICOLSON *Diary* 22 Sept. (1966) 364 It may mean surrender..in return for such quite valueless concessions as..'no bombing of open towns'. **1939** R. CAMPBELL *Flowering Rifle* VI. 148 Keep safe his bomb-dump while our patience lasts While from its store our open towns he blasts. **1946** *Reader's Digest* July 96/2 Amarillo is the most open-town in the country. **1975** J. GORES *Hammett* vi. 43 They form a Committee to clean up San Francisco, and as chairman they take the man who's been running it as an open town for sixteen years. **1960** *Guardian* 11 Mar. 8/7 Modern architects are known to favour *open-tread stairs. **1972** *Daily Tel.* 29 Nov. 24/3 A circular, opentread hardwood stairway gives on to a galleried landing. **1966** *New Statesmen* 14 Oct. 548/3 The *Open University..is the latest and most impressive offspring of the founders of ACE (Advisory Centre for Education). **1968** *Listener* 12 Dec. 806/1 (Advt.), January 1971 is the starting date for the transmission of the BBC radio and television programmes which form part of the Open University foundation year courses. **1969** *Radio Times* 27 Nov. 12 Originally named 'the University of the Air', the Open University offers an exciting new opportunity for adults throughout the country to study for degree qualifications through the media of integrated television, radio and specially-designed correspondence courses. **1973** *Listener* 17 May 634/1 [John Stuart] Mill..set out to be a public thinker, a one-man Open University. **1977** *R.A.F. News* 11–24 May 2/3 Gp Capt Frank Rice (Retd).. played a major part..in setting up the Cyprus Open University scheme. **1960** N. POLUNIN *Introd. Plant Geogr.* xiv. 447 Cacti in the New World and cactus-like Euphorbias in the Old World frequently form a characteristic feature of the usually *open vegetation [in semi-deserts]. **1971** D. W. SHIMWELL *Descr. & Classification of Vegetation* ii. 106 Where there is space between individuals which can be colonized.., the term open vegetation is applied. **1494** FABYAN *Chron.* VII. 568 He was..*opyn vysaged layed in the mynster of Pounfrayt, so y[t] all men myght knowe and see that he was dede. **1960** A. HUXLEY *Let.* 27 Dec. (1969) 901 Maxwell Jones..pioneered the *Open Ward system in English mental hospitals. **1965** *Nursing Times* 5 Feb. 183/2 The staff kept her under as close observation as was possible in an open ward. **1922** *Beaver* Jan. 33/1 We remained at Mountain House until *open water in the spring. *Ibid.* Sept. 9/1 When the open water came, I got one hundred and thirty-two beaver. **1930** L. MUNDAY *Mounty's Wife* iii. 50 We had to keep him at Cumberland until he could be taken to Prince Albert at open water. **1956** H. S. M. KEMP *Northern Trader* (1957) x. 130 When open-water came..we were able to pitch-off to our private trapping grounds. **1956** *Polar Record* Jan. 8 *Open water*, a relatively large area of water free of ice. **1971** T. BOULANGER *Indian Remembers* 4 The people came home after open water at Oxford House. **1900** W. C. SABINE in *Amer. Architect* LXVIII. 22/1 [Hereafter all results..will be expressed in terms of the absorbing power of open windows.] *Ibid.*, The absorbing power was found to be ·73 of *open-window units. **1957** D. H. FENDER *Gen. Physics & Sound* xii. 398 The area of material multiplied by its absorption coefficient measures its total absorption in 'open window units'. **1968** *Punch* 11 Sept. 364/2 An Open Window Unit (o.w.u.) is a unit of sound absorption... It is equal to the absorption by an open window of one square foot in area. **1968** R. C. STANLEY *Light & Sound for Engineers* xvi. 308 If the area of the surface is expressed in square feet, then the absorption is expressed in open window units or sabins. **1889** W. SCHLICH *Man. Forestry* I. 9 Thin Wood, or *open wood, means a wood in which the crowns of the trees do not interlace. **1926** TANSLEY & CHIPP *Study of Vegetation* x. 210 Open woodland consists of open woodland without a closed and thickly interlaced canopy. **1790** J. ARMSTRONG *Jrnl.* in *Ohio Archaeol. & Hist. Q.* (1911) XX. 82 A course a little to the N. of W., passing through several small prairies and *open woods. **1799** J. SMITH *Acct. Remarkable Occurrences* 13 About the lick was clear, open woods, and thin white-oak land. **1823** C. VIGNOLES *Obs. Floridas* 77 Instead of the clear open woods generally seen, masses of young pine saplings are thickly spread over the rocky ground. **1824** D. E. BURCH *Let.* 30 Oct. in *Florida Hist. Q.* XIV. 105 In the open woods, especially in the pine barrens, these [*sc.* fallen trees] can always be avoided by turning out. **1939** *Canad. Hist. Rev.* XX. 282 The general results..would seem at first sight to point to the 'groves', 'open woods', 'oak openings', parklands, or whatever name one may give them, being more pronounced on the western borders of this huge territory than on the Atlantic slope.

B. *adv.* = OPENLY (in various senses).

a **1300** *Cursor M.* 26215 His penance open most be schaun. **1482** *Monk of Evesham* (Arb.) 26 [He] lernyd and knewe an ordir of euery thing synglerly, more opynner and fullyor than he knewe afore. **1533** More *Apol.* 100 Some they say be playne and open false. **1601** Shaks. *Twel. N.* iii. iii. 37 Do not then walke too open. **1780** J. Woodforde *Diary* 24 Oct. (1924) I. 293 He..spoke very open and ingenuous about it. **1921** E. O'Neill *Diff'rent* ii, in *Emperor Jones* 252 Tell me all about 'em. You needn't be scared—to talk open with me.

open (ˈəʊp(ə)n), *v.* Forms: 1 openian, 2 openien, 3–5 opene(n, 4– open. (Also 3 hopen, 3–4 opon, 3–7 opne(n, 4 apon, hopne, upon, 5–6 opeyne, 6 *Sc.* apen; 3 *Orm.* oppnenn; 3–5, 9 *dial.* oppen, 4–6 -yn, 5 -ene.) [OE. *openian* = OS. *opanôn*, *oponôn* (MDu. *openen*, Du. *openen*), OHG. *offanôn*, (MHG. *offenen*):—OTeut. **opanôjan*, f. *opan-* open *a.* Cf. also Ger. *öffnen*.]

I. Transitive senses.

1. a. To move or turn (a door, gate, or the like) away from its closed position, so as to admit of passage.

Cf. the dial. 'put up' or 'set up' (the door); also Ger. *aufmachen*, *aufthun*, Du. *opmaken*, lit. to do or make up, put up, open.

c **1000** *Ags. Psalms* (Spelm.) cxvii. 19 Opnyað me gatu rihtwisnysse. *c* **1205** Lay. 19486 Duȝeðe scal arisen & oppenien [*c* **1275** hopeni] ure castel-ȝæten. *a* **1225** *St. Marher.* 12 Paraises ȝeten aren ȝarewe iopenet þe nu. *a* **1300** *Cursor M.* 1881 (Cott.) Þan opind noe his wyndou, Lete vte a rauen. *c* **1375** *Ibid.* 19788 (Fairf.) Wiþ þat ho openid hir eye-lid. *c* **1400** *Destr. Troy* 11308 Ne to pas of þis place, ne no port opun. *c* **1420** *Chron. Vilod.* 949 Upon þe durre, my lady. **1588** A. King tr. *Canisius' Catech.* 168 b, Knok, and it sall be apened vnto ȝou. **1629** Milton *Ode Nativity* 148 Heav'n..Will open wide the Gates of her high Palace Hall. **1786** tr. *Beckford's Vathek* (1883) 106 The Angel of death had opened the portal of some other world. **1855** Macaulay *Hist. Eng.* xx. IV. 404 Huy had opened its gates to the French. **1894** W. E. Norris *St. Ann's* I. 177 He opened his lips, as if with the intention of putting some further question.

b. *absol.* (In sense 1 or 2.)

1382 Wyclif *Matt.* xxv. 12 Lord, lord, opene to vs. *c* **1386** Chaucer *Pars. T.* ¶215 He that openeth to me,.. I wol entre in-to hym by my grace. *c* **1400** *Apol. Loll.* 16 He closiþ, & þan no man opunniþ; He opunniþ, & þan no man closiþ. *c* **1470** Henry *Wallace* v. 1018 Opyn, he bad, the captayne cummand was. **1535** Coverdale *Sol. Song* v. 6 When I had opened vnto my beloued, he was departed, and gone his waye. **1793** *Arabian Nights* IV. 125 Their captain.. pronounced these words distinctly, Sesame (which is a sort of corn), open. **1841** Lytton *Nt. & Morn.* iii. x, Open, in the King's name!

2. a. To make (a building, box, or enclosed space of any kind) open (open *a.* 2), as by moving or turning a door, gate, lid, by removing part of the walls, or clearing away anything that obstructs passage in or out; to break open, unclose, undo; to obtain or provide free access to or egress from.

c **1200** Ormin 7357 Þurrh þatt te kalldewisshe follc Oppne-denn þeȝȝre maddmess,..i þatt hus. **1297** R. Glouc. (Rolls) App. II. 15 His tumbe was yopened. **13..** *Cursor M.* 24423 (Cott.) Al opind war þair graues sen. **1382** Wyclif *Judg.* iv. 19 The which openyde a botel of mylk, and ȝaf to hym to drynk. **1387** Trevisa *Higden* (Rolls) VIII. 83 In his comynge prisouns were i-oponed. *c* **1400** Maundev. (Roxb.) v. 14 He went and opned þe grafe. **1535** Coverdale *Gen.* xlii. 35 When they opened their sackes, euery man founde his boundell of money in his sacke. ? *a* **1550** *Freiris of Berwik* 373 in *Dunbar's Poems* (1893) 297 Ga belyfe vnto ȝone almerie, And oppin it. **1598** Shaks. *Merry W.* ii. ii. 2 Why, then the world's mine Oyster, which I, with sword will open. **1712–14** Pope *Rape Lock* iv. 126 He first the snuff-box open'd, then the case. **1885** *Law Times* LXXIX. 173/2 As soon as C— and Co.'s office was opened on the morning of the 19th. *Mod.* Shall we open another bottle?

b. In figurative expressions.

a **1300** *Cursor M.* 26118 (Cott.) Opins to your lauerd your hert. **1523** Ld. Berners *Froiss.* I. cccxlvi. 547 Clement opyned his graces to all clerkes. **1613** Shaks. *Hen. VIII*, iii. ii. 184 My hand ha's open'd Bounty to you.

c. With the purpose as the main notion: To give access to; to render accessible *to* (persons or to the public) or *for* (some purpose); to make freely accessible; to establish for the entrance of the public, of customers, etc., as ***to open a shop, store, branch of a bank, registry office***, etc. With various qualifications implied by the context.

1560 Daus tr. *Sleidane's Comm.* 346 That no man open his house unto privy conventicles. **1647** Boyle *Let. to Dury* 3 May, Wks. 1772 I. p. xxxix, Either to bolt heaven against, or open Newgate for all those, that believe [error]. **1791–1823** D'Israeli *Cur. Lit., Libraries* 1 This library..Julius Cæsar once proposed to open for the public. **1855** Macaulay *Hist. Eng.* xiii. III. 378 The Government..ventured to open the Courts of Justice which the Estates had closed. *Ibid.* xviii. IV. 125 That the House of Lords and the House of Commons should be open to men to whom he would not open a guild of skinners. **1865** Mill in *Morn. Star* 6 July, Everyone who gets into Parliament..by opening the public-houses, goes there to represent the vices of the constituency. *fig.* **1813** Mar. Edgeworth *Patron.* I. iii. (1832) 40 Attempts were made to open the borough.

d. To declare (a building, park, etc.) open, and introduce to public use by a formal ceremony. (Passing into sense 13.)

1865 W. Howitt *Hist. Discovery in Austral.* I. xiii. 207 Measures were..instituted to construct a high road through the whole distance already gone... It was then, in modern phraseology, opened by the governor, attended by Mrs. Macquarie, and an escort on horseback. **1889** *Bury Times* 20 July 8/6 Prince Albert Victor visited Harrogate..and opened the new Buildings of the Bath Hospital. **1896** *Eastern Morn. News* (Hull) 22 Feb. 1/2 St. Thomas's Church. Opening of the New Lectern. **1898** *Oxford Directory*, The new Town Hall, Courts and Municipal Buildings..were opened by H.R.H. the Prince of Wales on ..the 12th May, 1897.

3. a. To spread apart, widen, expand, unfold, unroll, extend. (Sometimes with combination of sense 2, as in *to open a letter*.) Also *absol.* with ellipsis of object, as 'to open (*sc.* a book) at a page, on a part', etc.

c **1000** *Ags. Psalms* (Spelm.) cxliv. 17 Openast [*aperis*] þu hand þine. *a* **1240** *Ureisun* in *Cott. Hom.* 201 Bitweonen þeo ilke ermes so swiðe wiðe to-spredde and i-openeð. *c* **1375** *Sc. Leg. Saints* xxiv. (*Alexis*) 396 We pray þe, opyne þi hand, & lat ws se þat closyt wryt. **1387** Trevisa *Higden* (Rolls) VI. 37 Whan þe book was i-opened. **1423** Jas. I *Kingis Q.* xxi, The tender flouris opnyt thame and sprad. **1480** Caxton *Chron. Eng.* ccxxi. 213 He opened the letter that he had folden afore togeder. *a* **1548** Hall *Chron., Hen. VIII* 135 b, It was not well ment to the Emperor, to stop his packet with letters and to open them. **1570** *Satir. Poems Reform.* xv. 8 Ȝe Mariguildis, forbid the sune To oppin ȝow euerie morrow! **1602** Carew *Cornwall* 136 b, A little beyond Foy, the land openeth a large sandie Bay, for the sea to ouerflow. **1657** *North's Plutarch* (1676) Add. Lives 35 With his hands he [Charlemaine] would open and extend four Horse-shoes being joyned together. **1711** Addison *Spect.* No. 115 ¶8 This opens the Chest. **1783–9** T. Day *Sandford & Merton, Cure of Gout* (1851) 143 He too had a library, although he never opened a book. **1839** I. Taylor *Anc. Chr.* I. iii. 411 Nor can we do better than open Chrysostom. **1882** *Daily Tel.* 24 June, Three overs later B—opened his shoulders in tremendous style.

absol. **1817** Coleridge *Biog. Lit.* xviii. (1882) 172, I will take the first stanza, on which I have chanced to open, in the Lyrical Ballads. **1883** *Daily Tel.* 15 May 2/7 U—then opened out, and..drove the captain..for 3.

b. To expand, enlarge (a hole or aperture).

1703 Moxon *Mech. Exerc.* 52 To open a Hole, is in Smith's Language, to make the Hole wider.

4. a. To make an opening in; to cut or break into; to make a hole or incision in, †to make a breach in (a wall or fortification). ***to open ground***, to break up the surface of ground, as by ploughing, digging trenches, etc.

c **1175** *Lamb. Hom.* 147 Weren his side mid speres orde iopened. *c* **1205** Lay. 27556 Opened wes his breoste þa blod com forð luke. *a* **1300** *Cursor M.* 17140 Bi-hald and se mi blodi side, þat for þi luue es opend wide. **1306** *Exec. Sir S. Fraser* xxiv. in *Pol. Songs* (Camden) 221 He wes y-opened, is boweles ybrend. **1486** *Bk. St. Albans* E vij, With his feete he opynys the erth ther he gooth a way. **1568** Grafton *Chron.* I. 148 The Speare wherewith Longeus opened Christes side. **1667** Milton *P.L.* viii. 465 Who stooping op'nd my left side, and took From thence a Rib. **1748** *Anson's Voy.* ii. xiv. 286 A battery of five or six pieces of cannon..would have opened it [the rampart] in a short time. **1794** *Hist.* in *Ann. Reg.* 39 They did not..yield to the first summons, but waited until the French General had opened ground. **1807** Vancouver *Agric. Devon* (1813) 305 The old moorland..had not been opened for time immemorial. **1897** *Allbutt's Syst. Med.* IV. 252 If a localised abscess be discovered in the liver, it should be opened and drained.

b. To make, produce, or cause (an opening or open space of some kind). ***to open trenches***, to dig trenches in besieging: see trench.

a **1240** *Lofsong* in *Cott. Hom.* 211 Þurh þine fif wunden iopened o rode. **1382** Wyclif *Isa.* xli. 18, I shall opene in heȝe hillis flodys, and in the myddel of feeldis welles. *a* **1548** Hall *Chron., Hen. VII* 29 But the Italians her awne.. chyldren opened the gappe, and made the waye of her destruccion. **1667** Milton *P.L.* i. 688 Soon had his crew Op'ned into the Hill a spacious wound. **1684** J. Peter *Siege Vienna* 3 He had resolved to leave the Place, where he had not yet opened the Trenches. **1820** Shelley *Arethusa* ii, Alpheus bold..With his trident..opened a chasm In the rocks. **1853** Stocqueler *Mil. Encycl.* s.v. *Trenches*, To *open the Trenches* is to break ground for the purpose of carrying on approaches towards a besieged place.

†**c.** To penetrate by force, break through. *Obs.*

1523 Ld. Berners *Froiss.* I. cxxx. 158 Certayne frenchemen..perforce opyned the archers of the princes batayle, and came and fought with the men of armes hande to hande. *Ibid.* clx. 195 To the entent they somwhat to breke and to opyn the archers.

5. a. To loosen (that which is tight, compact, close together, dense, stiff, etc.). (In various shades of meaning.) †**b.** To dissolve, decompose (*obs.*).

1683 Moxon *Mech. Exerc., Printing* xxii. ¶2 By Opening, you must now understand removing the Quoins, till they stand loose. **1686** W. Harris tr. *Lemery's Course Chym.* i. vi. (ed. 3) 150 Verdegreese is nothing but a Copper opened. **1727–41** Chambers *Cycl.* s.v. *Purgative*, The saline part is set loose by preparation, and opening the sulphur. **1765** A. Dickson *Treat. Agric.* (ed. 2) 366 All kinds of manures open the soil. **1796** *Instr. & Reg. Cavalry* (1813) 245 The leading troop..opens its ranks, at which time the officers..move into the front of the troop. **1833** *Regul. Instr. Cavalry* i. 38 The ranks will then be opened. *Ibid.* 154 From the centre open your Files.

6. a. To clear of obstruction or hindrance; to make (a road) free for passage. Chiefly *fig.*

1387 Trevisa *Higden* (Rolls) IV. 163 Þe way was opened forto take wreche of al olde wreþþe. **1560** Daus tr. *Sleidane's Comm.* 70 It opened the waye to rebellion, sedition, and to civile warres. **1573** *Life Frith* in *Wks.* (1829) 73 Wherewithal he might have opened an easy way unto honour and dignity. **1667** Milton *P.L.* ix. 809 Thou op'nst Wisdoms way, And giv'st access, though secret she retire. **1852** Mrs. Stowe *Uncle Tom's C.* xxxiii. 297 Not without hope that some way of escape might yet be opened to him. **1891** T. Hardy *Tess* (1892) 110 The field had already been 'opened'; that is to say, a lane a few feet wide had been hand-cut through the wheat..for the first passage of the horses and machine.

b. To make (the passages of the body) clear; to clear away (obstructions) in the bodily passages.

1574 Newton *Health Mag.* 55 Filberdes..are aperitive and open oppilations and obstructions. **1653** Culpepper *Lond. Disp.* i. 6 [Endive] opens obstructions and provokes urine. **1727–41** Chambers *Cycl.* s.v. *Hellebore*, Sternutatory powder, to clear and open the head. **1755** Johnson, *Aperitive*, that..has the quality of opening the excrementitious passages of the body. **1897** *Allbutt's Syst. Med.* IV. 420 The bowels should be well opened at the onset by a brisk purgative.

c. *Electr.* To break or interrupt (an electric circuit); to put (a switch or the like) into a condition in which there is no path through it for an electric current.

In quot. 1834 the meaning is the opposite, viz. 'to create, close' (close *v.* 10 e).

[**1834** M. Faraday in *Phil. Trans. R. Soc.* CXXIV. 429 The presence of a piece of platina touching both the zinc and the fluid to be decomposed, opens the path required for the electricity.] **1836** *Ann. Electr., Magn., & Chem.* I. 71 The shock is never produced only at the moment of opening the voltaic circuit. **1876** Preece & Sivewright *Telegraphy* iv. 103 If B wishes to communicate with A he..opens the switch. **1924** Wedmore & Trencham *Switchgear for Electr. Power Control* xxiii. 252 A smart operator can open a medium-voltage circuit safely with a plain lever switch. **1962** *Newnes Conc. Encycl. Electr. Engin.* 735/1 The circuit-breaker contacts are held closed by springs and the contacts are opened in the event of a fault by the overcurrent in a series solenoid coil. **1975** M. Mandl *Basics of Electr.* vi. 123 When voltage is applied to the coil, the flexible section is pulled down..., opening the switch.

7. To uncover, lay bare, disclose to sight, expose or exhibit to view, display.

a **1000** *Beowulf* 3056 Nefne God sylfa..sealde þam ðe he wolde..hord openian. *c* **1315** Shoreham 54 The croune of clerke yopened hys, Tokneth the wyl to hevene. **1382** Wyclif *Isa.* xxvi. 21 The erthe shal opene [1388 schewe] his blod. **1573–80** Baret *Alv.* O 96 Opening their naked pappes. **1667** Milton *P.L.* vii. 318 Herbs of every leaf.. Op'ning their various colours. **1671** —— *P.R.* ii. 294 Alleys brown That open'd in the midst a woody Scene. **1746–7** Hervey *Medit.* (1818) 206 The boughs, rounded into a set of regular arches, opened a view into the distant fields. **1879** *Cassell's Techn. Educ.* IV. 95/1 The torch which..opened new prospects to his eager views. **1899** *Newcastle Even. Chron.* 14 Mar., The hopper opened her red light and sounded a short blast.

8. *Naut.* To come in sight of, get an open view of, by rounding or passing some intervening object.

1748 *Anson's Voy.* i. vii. 75 We opened Streights Le Maire, and soon after..entered them with fair weather and a brisk gale. *Ibid.* ii. ii. 130 We were..surprized..to see her open the N.W. point of the bay. **1768** J. Byron *Narr. Patagonia* (ed. 2) 94 As soon as we opened the headland to the westward of us. **1837** T. Hook *Jack Brag* xiv, The breeze, which blew right in his face..as he 'opened' the sea between Weston's shop and the library. **1858** *Merc. Marine Mag.* V. 227 Taking care not to open the Obelisk on the slope of the North Head. **1898** R. Kipling *Fleet in Being* v. 46 The tide's setting us up a little... We shall open Dunboy House in a minute round the corner.

9. †**a.** To lay bare or make manifest to the (mental or spiritual) view; to reveal, disclose, declare, make known. *Obs.* exc. as in b.

c **900** tr. *Bæda's Hist.* i. vii. (1890) 36 Albanus..cyðde and openade..þæt he cristen wære. *c* **1175** *Lamb. Hom.* 127 Of þere heouenliche blisse þe us wes iopenad. *c* **1200** *Vices & Virtues* 27 Min fader on heuene hit openede in to (þine) herte. *a* **1325** *Prose Psalter* xlviii[i]. 4 Y..shal open in þe sauter myn purpose. *c* **1450** tr. *De Imitatione* i. xiii. 15 Temptacion openiþ what we be. **1526** Tindale *Matt.* xi. 27 Nether knoweth eny man the father, save the Sonne, and he to whome the Sonne will open hym. **1548** Udall, etc. *Erasm. Par. Matt.* xvi. 87 Nor open it to others that he was Messias. **1598** Greneway *Tacitus, Ann.* ii. xviii. (1622) 59 Semius openeth that by letters to Piso; warning him not to go about to tempt the army with corrupters. **1647** Evelyn *Diary* 9 Nov., My sister open'd to me her marraige. **1771** *Antiq. Sarisb.* Pref. Biog. 121 Striking incidents..which, if preserved, would open their real characters. **1804** *Europ. Mag.* XLV. 42/2 The plan of the work is fully opened in the Preface.

b. *esp.* To disclose or divulge (one's mind, feelings, designs, etc.); *refl.* to communicate one's intentions or feelings, to unbosom oneself.

c **1400** *Destr. Troy* 553 He onswared hir onestly opynond his hert. **1533** in W. H. Turner *Select. Rec. Oxford* (1880) 115 That we should friendly open our minds each to other. **1545** Brinklow *Compl.* 36 b, There may he open his matter hymself. *a* **1548** Hall *Chron., Hen. VI* 152 Before his purpose was openly published, and hys frendes opened theim selfes. **1682** Bunyan *Holy War* Wks. 1768 II. 7, I have opened my mind unto you. **1711** Steele *Spect.* No. 240 ¶1 When he was grown familiar with me he opened himself like a good Angel. **1761** Hume *Hist. Eng.* I. xv. 366 The king began with opening his intentions to the Count of Hainault. **1849** Macaulay *Hist. Eng.* ix. II. 406 Russell opened the design to Shrewsbury. **1860** Ruskin *Mod. Paint.* V. ix. vii. §8. 269 To them, he can open himself, by a word, or syllable, or a glance.

†**c.** To announce, declare; to make public, promulgate. *Obs.*

1433 *Rolls of Parlt.* IV. 423/2 For oþer diverse causes, openyd and alleggid. *a* **1548** Hall *Chron., Hen. VIII* 138 b, When this matter was opened through Englande, howe the greate men toke it..the poore curssed, the riche repugned. **1562** in Strype *Ann. Ref.* (1709) I. xxxi. 310 That the sum of mony by him given be opened by the parson, vicar or curate, to the parish. **1656** *Burton's Diary* (1828) I. 57, I cannot but dissent from the gentlemen that have opened it to be blasphemy.

10. To unfold the sense of; to expound, explain, interpret. *Obs.* or *arch.*

c **1200** *Trin. Coll. Hom.* 217 On þesse fewe litele wored lotied fele gode wored ȝif hie weren wel iopenen. *a* **1225** *Ancr. R.* 242 Euerichon of þeos wordes habben longe hwule uorte beon wel iopened. *a* **1340** HAMPOLE *Psalter* Prol., þou sall fynd þaim oppynd in þaire stedis. **1382** WYCLIF *Luke* xxiv. 32 Wher oure herte was not brennynge in vs, while he..openyde scripturis to vs? *c* **1449** PECOCK *Repr.* Prol. 1 First openyng or doing to wite, thanne next blamyng, and aftirward biseching. **1535** COVERDALE *2 Esdras* xiii. 21, I will open vnto the, the thinge yt thou hast requyred. **1571** DIGGES *Pantom.* III. xii. Rivb, Your quotient openeth how many times the lesser vessell is conteyned in the greater. **1642** W. AMES *Marrow of Divinity* title-p., A table opening the hard words. **1720** WATERLAND *Eight Serm.* 233 The force of these Expressions I have elsewhere open'd and explain'd.

11. To make more intelligent or sympathetic; to expand, enlarge, enlighten (the mind or heart).

a **1310** in Wright *Lyric P.* xxv. 71 Ihesu, my saule drah the to, Min heorte opene ant wyde un-do. **1382** WYCLIF *Acts* xvi. 14 A womman Lidda bi name..whos herte the Lord openyde. **1526** TINDALE *Luke* xxiv. 45 Then opened he their wyttes, that they myght vnderstond the scriptures. **1605** BACON *Adv. Learn.* I. vi. §16 Not only opening our understanding..but chiefly opening our belief. **1713** BERKELEY *Guardian* No. 39 ¶8 His Understanding wants to be opened and enlarged. **1886** RUSKIN *Præterita* I. ix. 305 My eyes had been opened, and my heart with them.

12. To render accessible or available for settlement, use, intercourse, etc.; as ***to open land, to open a country to trade.*** Usually *open up*: see 24.

1617 ABP. ABBOT *Descr. World* (1634) 292 The English.. did adventure farre to open the North parts of America. **1816** BRACKENRIDGE *Jrnl. Voy. Missouri* (ed. 2) 28 We stopped..at the cabin of an old Frenchman, who is beginning to open a plantation, according to the phraseology of the western country. **1863** ALFORD in *Gd. Words* Mar. 199 We are to understand that a communication is to be opened between two places.

13. a. To begin, start, commence; to set in action, initiate, set on foot (any proceedings, operations, or business). ***to open an account, open the ball or the campaign, open fire, open parliament***, etc.: see the sbs. (Allied to 2 d.)

1693 [see CAMPAIGN *sb.* 3]. **1709** STEELE *Tatler* No. 17 ¶5 The Allies hasten their Preparations for opening the Campaign. **1712** ADDISON *Spect.* No. 267 ¶2 He..opens his Poem with the Discord of his Princes. **1731** *Gentl. Mag.* Dec. 538/2 The Duke gave a Ball, which..his Highness open'd with the Princess Mary. **1735** BERTIN *Chess* v, Never play your Queen, till your game is tolerably well opened. **1762–71** H. WALPOLE *Vertue's Anecd. Paint.* (1786) IV. 162 The pictures were..exhibited to the public, and the subscription opened. **1781** *Hist. Eur.* in *Ann. Reg.* 24/2 On the 12th of March the Spaniards opened their battery. **1787** JEFFERSON *Writ.* (1859) II. 316 They are about to open a loan of one hundred millions. **1827** ROBERTS *Voy. Centr. Amer.* 54 To open a trade with the Indians in the interior. **1833** *Act 3 & 4 Will. IV*, c. 46 §61 An account to be opened in the name of the Commissioners. **1833** HT. MARTINEAU *Manch. Strike* ix. 92 Opening the weekly meetings. **1839** THIRLWALL *Greece* VI. 15 Ptœodorus..had opened a correspondence with him. **1840** *Penny Cycl.* XVII. 274/2 It is the practice for the lord chancellor, with other peers appointed by commission..to open the parliament by stating 'that her Majesty will [etc.]'. **1849** MACAULAY *Hist. Eng.* ii. I. 205 A negotiation was opened. **1889** BOLDREWOOD *Robbery under Arms* xxxiv, We opened fire at them directly. *Mod.* The Queen will open Parliament in person.

b. *Bridge.* To commence (the bidding); to offer (a particular bid).

1958 *Listener* 6 Nov. 753/1 What should West open, assuming that he is playing a Two Club system? **1964** N. SQUIRE *Bidding at Bridge* ii. 17 When you open the bidding with a *suit* your strength may be absolutely minimum. *Ibid.* 21 You should open One Diamond, as your hand is unsuitable for you to be declarer in no-trumps. **1977** *Times* 10 Dec. 13/5 North has opened One Spade at game and 30. **1977** *Harpers & Queen* Dec. 26/2 West opened the bidding with one of those..artificial Two Diamond calls.

14. *Legal.* To state (a case) to the court, preliminary to adducing evidence; esp. to speak first in a case, a privilege belonging to the affirmative side. ***to open pleadings***, in a trial before jury, to state briefly the substance of the pleadings. Also, To state or bring forward (an argument, assertion, etc.) in opening a case.

1621 ELSING *Lords' Debates* App. (1870) 134 The breefes of the whole abuses read in open Court, w[hi]ch Sir Randolph Crew in divers poyntes opened to their Lordships... Mr. Atturney Generall opened divers poyntes to their Lordships touching these abuses. **1631** *Star Chamb. Cases* (Camden) 6 The Complainants Counsell having made their charge, and opened all their proofes, the defendants Counsell having also made their defence. *c* **1645** HOWELL *Lett.* (1655) IV. viii. 24 She may make Her self your Client, and so employ you to open her Case, and recover her Portion. **1682** DRYDEN *Medal* Ep. to Whigs ¶4 You retained him only for the opening of your cause,..your main lawyer is yet behind. **1891** *Daily News* 8 Dec. 7/5 Sir H. D. was opening the case for the respondents when the Court rose.

15. To undo, recall, or set aside (a judgement, settlement, sale, etc.), so as to leave the matter open to further action, discussion, or negotiation.

1792 in Vesey, jr. *Reports* I. (1801) 453 The Court gives its assistance to open biddings, for the benefit of the suitor and the estate, not of the purchaser. **1806** LD. ERSKINE *ibid.* XIII. 204 The true Equity and Justice of the Case seem to be, that Foreclosure is opened by the Action [brought by the mortgagee]. **1848** ARNOULD *Mar. Insur.* (1866) I. I. vi. 292 The policy was to be opened. By this, these writers understood that the agreed valuation was to be set aside as the standard and basis of the underwriter's liability. **1867** *Act 30 & 31 Vict.* c. 48 §7 It is the long settled practice of courts of equity in sales by auction of land under their authority to open biddings even more than once. *Ibid.*, That the practice of opening the biddings..be discontinued.. unless..on the ground of fraud or improper conduct. **1877** SIR G. JESSEL in *Law Rep.* 7 Ch. Div. 175 The mortgagor is entitled to open the foreclosure on the usual terms.

II. *intr.* (Sometimes for *refl.*, sometimes *ellipt.* or *absol.* use of the trans.)

16. a. To become open, unshut, or unclosed: (*a*) of a door or other means of entrance; (*b*) of the passage or doorway; (*c*) of the space or enclosure to which this gives access. Hence, (*d*) generally, to come apart or asunder, so as to admit of passage, disclose a gap or vacant space, display the interior or contents. (*e*) Of an abscess, To burst and discharge.

c **1000** ÆLFRIC *Hom.* II. 258 Byrȝenu openodon mid deadum banum. *c* **1250** *Gen. & Ex.* 3772 Erðe..opnede vnder [h]ere fet. *c* **1375** *Cursor M.* 3783 (Fairf.) Him þoȝt þe ȝate opened of heyuen. **1393** LANGL. *P. Pl.* C. xxi. 368 For eny wye oþer warde wyde openede þe ȝates. **1526** *Pilgr. Perf.* (W. de W. 1531) 289 b, The herte hoppeth and lepeth in the body: and now openeth & now closeth. **1573–80** BARET *Alv.* O 112 The skie openeth, or goeth asunder. **1592** SHAKS. *Rom. & Jul.* v. iii. 47 Thus I enforce thy rotten Iawes to open. **1647** A. ROSS *Mystag. Poet.* x. (1675) 236 The Marigold..opens or shuts with the Sun. **1724** DE FOE *Mem. Cavalier* (1840) 14 My wound opened again with riding. **1774** GOLDSM. *Nat. Hist.* (1776) VI. 170 The bony covers open and give it a free passage. **1828** SCOTT *F.M. Perth* iv, They were scarce gone ere the door of the glover's house opened. **1864** E. A. PARKES *Man. Pract. Hygiene* 107 The windows should open at the top, and in case the wind has a high velocity, means should be taken to distribute it. **1870** E. PEACOCK *Ralf Skirl.* III. 157 Law offices opened at eight o'clock in those days. **1871** L. W. M. LOCKHART *Fair to See* I. iii. 103 'A Cameron of Aberlorna!' exclaimed the host, in a tone of unaccountable astonishment, his eyes opening wide upon Bertrand. **1893** M. E. MANN *In Summer Shade* I. x. 238 Claude's eyes opened slowly upon his brother's face. **1912** *Chambers's Jrnl.* Feb. 82/1 Suddenly the great eye of the lighthouse opened. **1952** M. ALLINGHAM *Tiger in Smoke* iv. 68 It was just when we were opening... I was just getting my keys for the spirits.

b. Of the weather: To become clear of frost.

1678 LADY CHAWORTH in *12th Rep. Hist. MSS. Comm.* App. v. 45 As soone as the weather opens to allow travelling.

c. Of things non-physical, the way to them, etc.

1845 STEPHEN *Comm. Laws Eng.* (1874) I. 390 The heir to an estate..when the succession to it opens or becomes vacant upon the death of the proprietor.

d. *Electr.* Of a circuit or device: to become open (OPEN *a.* 11 f); to suffer a break in its conducting path.

1836 *Ann. Electr., Magn., & Chem.* I. 71 If there is a spark ..it is..feeble when compared to that seen when the circuit is opening. **1924** WEDMORE & TRENCHAM *Switchgear for Electr. Power Control* ii. 14 The circuit breaker..is designed to open freely and quickly. **1975** I. CLUCAS *Reed's Electr. for Deck Officers* vii. 215 A second pair of contacts..are the first to close and the last to open... They take the full brunt of the spark when opening. *Ibid.* 224 When the main switch is closed the buzzer should sound..and the individual circuits open.

17. a. Of a door, etc.: To serve as a passage *to* or *into*; to give access to. **b.** Of a room or space: To have an opening or passage *to, into, out of*, etc. Also **c.** To have its opening, or outlet *towards*, to lie open *to*.

a. 1760–72 H. BROOKE *Fool of Qual.* (1809) IV. 124 A door that opened into a garden; and..another door that opened to the street. **1832** *Act 2 & 3 Will. IV*, c. 64 Sched. O. 45 The gate..opens into an occupation road leading to Penrallt. **1885** *Law Times* LXXX. 5/1 The rooms have an outer door opening on to a common staircase.

b. 1615 BEDWELL *Arab. Trudg.* Mj. Babe'lmandeb,..is the mouth of the Arabian gulfe [i.e. Red Sea], by which it openeth and falleth into the Red sea [i.e. Indian Ocean]. **1722** DE FOE *Plague* (1884) 171 The back Road..opened into the said great Road. **1801** *Lusignan* III. 155 A library, opening through a greenhouse on to a lawn. **1817** J. EVANS *Excurs. Windsor* 268 The house, an old one, opens upon seven acres of ground.

c. 1697 DRYDEN *Virg. Georg.* III. 472 A Cote that opens to the South prepare. **1825** COBBETT *Rur. Rides* (1885) II. 25, I saw a lane opening in the right direction. **1839** YEOWELL *Anc. Brit. Ch.* xii. 140 A valley opening to the sea shore.

18. a. To expand, extend, spread apart. Of a collective body or its units: To move apart so as to present openings or wider interstices. Also *open out*: see 23.

1398 TREVISA *Barth. De P.R.* v. xliv. (MS. Bodl.) lf. 24/1 For drawyng and by fonging of winde þe bladder openyth and sprediþ. **1667** MILTON *P.L.* VI. 481 They shoot forth.. op'ning to the ambient light. **1675** tr. *Machiavelli's Prince* (1883) 242 His horse,..opening to the right and left,..made room for the foot. **1856** KANE *Arct. Expl.* II. xxix. 297 The little flag..opened once more to the breeze.

b. *fig.* To expand in intellect or sympathy.

1709 FELTON *Classics* (1718) 38 To repeat his Grammar over, two or three Years before his Understanding opens enough to let him into the Reason..of the Rules. **1713** STEELE *Englishm.* No. 55. 354 All Hearts begin to open.

19. a. To become disclosed or revealed, to begin to appear; to expand to the view, to become more and more visible, esp. on nearer approach or change of position.

1708 J. PHILIPS *Cider* II. 86 Joy and Pleasure open to the View. **1782** COWPER *Table-t.* 265 The varied fields of science, ever new, Opening and wider opening on her view. *a* **1822** SHELLEY *Summer* 6 The stainless sky Opens beyond them like eternity. **1842** LYTTON *Zanoni* v. 29 Mournful Campagna, thou openest on us in majestic sadness. **1844** MRS. BROWNING *Lay Brown Rosary* III. ii, Down through the wood..Till the chapel-cross opens to sight. **1875** JOWETT *Plato* (ed. 2) I. 420 Plato had the wonders of psychology just opening to him.

b. *Naut.* To appear distinct or separate.

1745 P. THOMAS *Jrnl. Anson's Voy.* 56 The Town of Payta ..began to open in a direct line with it [the Point that forms the Bay]. **1854** MOSELEY *Astron.* i. (1874) 2 The lights..will appear to separate, or in the nautical phrase, they will open. **1858** *Merc. Marine Mag.* V. 226 The..Lighthouse has opened its own breadth north of the..Obelisk below it.

20. To disclose or declare one's knowledge, thoughts, or feelings in speech, to speak out; to speak explicitly, explain.

a **1641** BP. MOUNTAGU *Acts & Mon.* (1642) 300 His enemies..would soone be quashed and not once dare to open, if hee were at Court. **1753** FOOTE *Eng. in Paris* II. Wks. 1799 I. 44 It will be impossible for me to divine: but come, open a little. **1775** T. HUTCHINSON *Diary* 9 Nov. I. 555 He opened very largely on the state of affairs. **1809** MALKIN *Gil Blas* XII. xiii. ¶7 He did not open on the subject of Seraphina, nor did we attempt to draw him out. **1830** COBBETT *Rur. Rides* (1885) II. 304 When I opened, I found that this man was willing to open too. **1841** J. T. HEWLETT *Parish Clerk* I. 231 If he opens upon it I'll give him a sound thrashing.

21. Of hounds: To give tongue, to begin to cry when in pursuit on a scent; hence, contemptuously, of men.

1565–73 COOPER *Thesaurus, Circumspecti canes*..good hounds that open not but where they finde. **1573–80** BARET *Alv.* O 114 To vent, or open as an hound or spaniel doth, when he hath the sent of anie thing. **1598** SHAKS. *Merry W.* IV. ii. 209 If I cry out thus vpon no traile, neuer trust me when I open againe. **1657** THORNLEY tr. *Longus' Daphnis & Chloe* 68 The deep-mouth'd dogs open'd loud. **1735** SOMERVILLE *Chase* I. 110 To chear the Pack Op'ning in Consorts of harmonious Joy. **1836** *Penny Cycl.* V. 7/2 When in pursuit..the hound opens with a voice deep and sonorous.

22. To begin; to start or commence operations. In theatrical parlance, To make a début, to begin a season or tour. Often elliptical, for *open fire*. Also, to begin to speak (occas. with the quoted words as quasi-obj.).

1716 ADDISON *Free-holder* No. 22 ¶2 Our Conversation opened, as usual, upon the Weather. **1761** FOOTE *Liar* I. Wks. 1799 I. 282 Where do we open?.. Let us see—one o'clock—..the Mall will be crouded. **1803** MRQ. WELLESLEY *Desp.* (1877) 366 The batteries of the British army opened against the fort. **1827–39** DE QUINCEY *Murder* Wks. 1862 IV. 52 In spite of all I could do or say, the orchestra opened. **1828** *Lights & Shades* I. 254 W. Settle opened in 'Liberty Hall'. **1851** C. CIST *Sk. Cincinnati in 1851* 296 They [*sc.* strawberries] usually open at 20 to 30 cents per quart. *c* **1871** J. ALBERY *Apple Blossoms* I, in *Dramatic Wks.* (1939) I. 244 Come and see me open to-night. **1876** TREVELYAN *Macaulay* II. xv. 469 When the year 1859 opened. **1880** *Daily News* 1 Mar. 3/3, I open in this piece, providing myself the company, and superintending the rehearsals. **1883** *Manch. Guard.* 3 Nov. 6/6 Lard opened active at higher prices. **1884** *Ibid.* 22 May 5/2 The summer session of the French Chambers opened on Tuesday. **1894** WOLSELEY *Marlborough* II. 175 A battery of eight guns opened on the fleet. *a* **1902** *Mod.* Our school opens next Monday. **1926** A. BENNETT *Lord Raingo* I. xiii. 63 'I quite agree with you, Clews,' Sam opened immediately. **1972** *Time* 17 Apr. 28/1 Joey and Sina, whose young daughter opened in the Broadway play *Voices* last week, soon became a part of the theater-going, nightclubbing celebrity set. **1976** B. FREEMANTLE *November Man* iv. 47 'Jocelyn is still the big tycoon,' he opened predictably. **1977** A. MORICE *Murder in Mimicry* I. i. 11 Gilbert is our new lead... His name alone ensures a sell-out for the entire run..before we even open.

III. With adverbs.

23. open out. *trans.* **a.** To render visible or accessible by the removal of that which envelopes or conceals; to unfold, unpack. **b.** To develop. **c.** To disclose, reveal, display or offer to mental view. *intr.* **d.** To expand, extend, move apart: = sense 18. **e.** To give vent to one's feelings or thoughts: to speak out, speak freely; = sense 20.

a. 1861 CLOUGH *Poems*, etc. (1869) I. 248 In one spot some lesser ruins have been opened out. **1882** DE WINDT *Equator* 99 Coal is found..here, and Government has opened out a small mine for the use of its vessels. **1883** J. W. SHERER *At Home & in India* 112 We..had got our tin travelling cases inside, and were opening out some necessary things.

b. 1826 SOUTHEY in *Corr. w. C. Bowles* (1881) 93 Whether the studied deference which is now assumed toward me,.. will open out anything like a frank and easy intercourse time must show. **1878** GLADSTONE *Glean.* (1879) I. 206 The work of searching the soil and the bowels of the territory, and opening out her enterprise throughout its vast expanse.

c. *c* **1814** COLERIDGE *Lett., to D. Stuart* (1895) 631 Having for the very first time..opened out my whole feelings and thoughts concerning my past fates and fortunes. *a* **1834** —— in *Lit. Rem.* (1836) II. 96 The perfect probability of the moment chosen by Prospero..to open out the truth to his daughter. **1865** *Ch. Times* 28 Oct., The newly-formed diocese opened out a magnificent opportunity for a Bishop whose training fitted him for his work.

d. 1833 *Regul. Instr. Cavalry* I. 154 The left wing open out. **1859** F. A. GRIFFITHS *Artil. Man.* (1862) 30 A Battalion in Close column should first open out to quarter-distance. **1871** L. STEPHEN *Playgr. Eur.* iv. III. 245, I was glad when the trees began to open out..and we came upon the.. meadow.

e. 1855 COSTELLO *Stor. Screen* 89 She now opened out a little, and told me [etc.]. **1861** HUGHES *Tom Brown at Oxf.*

v. (1889) 42 Tom..[was] very much astonished at himself for having opened out so freely.

f. *trans.* and *intr.* To open the throttle of (an engine); to accelerate. *colloq.* Cf. sense 24e below.

1906 *Punch* 19 Sept. 200/1 'Open her out!' my host had said; And on the instant word The mobile monster flew ahead Like a prodigious bird. **1918** 'Q' *Foe-Farrell* 105 There was a certain amount of outcry in the rear. But I opened-out down the slope and soon had it well astern. **1922** *Encycl. Brit.* XXX. 41/1 Such a 'light' engine would not withstand being opened out fully near the ground.

24. open up. (*Up* is added to *open* in many of its senses, often merely with the effect of strengthening or giving emphasis, but esp. in the following.) **a.** *trans.* To open to view, access, use, passage, or traffic (usually implying the removal of obstructions to sight or access); to lay open (a question previously untouched); to bring to light, disclose, raise and leave open or unsettled. Also *absol.*; *spec.* to open a door or the like.

1582-8 *Hist. Jas. VI* (1804) 180 To oppin up the meanes for the mair facill atteening to a gude peace. **1793** *Monthly Rev.* XI. 159 The place which is first opened up. **1827** Carlyle *Germ. Rom.* IV. 149 By Miracles and Similitudes, a new world is opened up. *c* **1829** Coleridge in *Sterling's Ess. & Tales* (1848) I. *Life* 23, I..detected two errors; one of them the phrase *open up a subject*, which, I suppose, is an innovation of the sectarian pulpits. **1844** Mill *Ess. Pol. Econ.* 97 The views of political economy which his [Ricardo's] genius was the first to open up. **1851** Dixon *W. Penn* i. (1872) 3 Opening up a new and tempting branch of trade. **1852** Gladstone *Glean.* (1879) IV. 191 This inquiry, however, opens up and detects the master fallacy. **1884** *Times* (weekly ed.) 19 Sept. 6/2 Each turn of the road.. opened up new effects in the enchanting landscape. **1884** *Pall Mall G.* 29 Aug. 11/2 He would begin by opening up, say, twenty-five acres his first year, clearing, draining, and planting. **1895** *Manch. Guard.* 14 Oct. 5/6 The Isker Valley line..will open up this country for the first time. **1935** M. M. Atwater *Murder in Midsummer* xxii. 210 Why didn't you open up when I knocked? **1976** 'H. Carmichael' *False Evidence* i. 14 Someone knocked at the door... 'Open up, Miss Crawford.'

b. *intr.* To become open to passage, view, enterprise, etc. (by the removal of obstructions).

1857 Livingstone *Trav.* xx. 407 Avenues of wealth opening up so readily. *Mod.* Hoping a way will open up.

c. *trans.* and *intr.* To shear wool from (a particular area, esp. the neck, of a sheep). *Austral.* and *N.Z.*

1882 Armstrong & Campbell *Austral. Sheep Husbandry* xiv. 167 The fleece should be opened up the neck, commencing at the brisket. **1904** 'G. B. Lancaster' *Sons o' Men* 81 A big Maori was making the [shearing] pace; opening up in a scientific fashion with a clean-run cut over the ear-root. **1914** H. B. Smith *Sheep & Wool Industry Australasia* vi. 37 The machine is then driven up the front of the neck several times till the neck wool is well opened up. **1956** G. Bowen *Wool Away!* (ed. 2) iii. 32 Three short sharp blows are essential here to open up the neck for clean shearing.

d. *intr.* To talk; to speak openly; to cease to be secretive.

1921 *Sat. Even. Post* 12 Feb. 61/4 We had a drink and we had another and a couple more. Finally he opened up... It took him two hours to tell his story. **1949** B. Wolfe in A. Dundes *Mother Wit* (1973) 534 How much did the Negroes tell him when they 'opened up'? Just how far did they really open up? **1952** 'N. Shute' *Far Country* 244 It's just possible she might open up with me. *a* **1953** E. O'Neill *Hughie* (1959) 23 At first, he wouldn't open up. Not that he was cagy about gabbin' too much. But like he couldn't think of nothin' about himself worth saying. **1970** M. Braithwaite *Never sleep Three in a Bed* xvi. 197 Although he never answered—or perhaps because of it—I opened up to him completely, telling him things I'd never told anyone. **1976** J. Crosby *Nightfall* xii. 66 You're not being very helpful... You must have a few ideas. Open up!

e. *trans.* and *intr.* To open the throttle of (an engine); to accelerate. Cf. sense 23f above.

1922 *Encycl. Brit.* XXX. 41/1 At height, however, it [*sc.* an aircraft engine] could be fully opened up, and the increased power..taken advantage of. **1926** T. E. Lawrence *Let.* 27 Sept. (1938) 500 It's my great game on a really pot-holed road to open up to 70 m.p.h. or so and feel the machine gallop. **1942** *Tee Emm* (Air Ministry) II. 95 On no account ..should the engine be opened up during the final stages of ditching. **1970** K. Benton *Sole Agent* vii. 78 She's a nice car, the Chevvy. She'd do ninety if I opened her up. **1973** 'D. Halliday' *Dolly & Starry Bird* ix. 131 As soon as he's got a clear stretch of road, he'll open up and you'll lose him.

f. *intr.* To start shooting (*at* or *on* someone). Also *fig.*

1939 H. L. Ickes *Diary* 30 July (1954) II. 688 Two or three days ago John L. Lewis, before the Labor Committee of the House, opened up savagely on Garner. **1974** *Black Panther* 16 Mar. 16/4 Frelimo guerrillas opened up on the train from both sides 'creating panic among the passengers', according to the report. **1974** J. Cleary *Peter's Pence* i. 25 Someone had fired a shot at the Tans and the latter had opened up as if on a duck shoot.

IV. Phrases. ***to open a*** (or ***the***) ***door to***: see door 3. †***to open one's ears***, to give ear, listen willingly or attentively. ***to open one's eyes***, to take notice, regard, look; to stare with astonishment. ***to open a person's eyes***, to cause him to see, to make him aware of facts. ***to open one's mouth***, i.e. in order to swallow or eat, or (also ***one's lips***) to speak; ***not to open one's lips***, to be absolutely silent.

c **1200** *Trin. Coll. Hom.* 35 Hie openeden his earen to luste þe defles lore. *a* **1300** *Cursor M.* 19941 Petre opend þan his muth..he said [etc.]. *a* **1340** Hampole *Psalter* xxi. 12 þai oppynd on me þaire mouth. *c* **1375** *Sc. Leg. Saints* i. (*Petrus*) 705 In þat howre god hopnyt þar ewyn. **1393** Langl. *P. Pl.* C. xii. 61 (Rawlinson MS.) For god is def now a dayes and deyneth [see dain *v.*] his heres to opne. **1545** Brinklow *Lament.* 20 He must open his mouthe agaynst Antichriste. **1711** Budgell *Spect.* No. 77 ⁋6 He..thinks a great deal, but never opens his Mouth. **1712** Steele *ibid.* No. 427 ⁋1 Too ill-natur'd to open their Lips in Conversation. **1849** Macaulay *Hist. Eng.* ii. I. 247 In the House of Lords he never opened his lips. **1874** *Q. Rev.* CXXXVI. 131 Already the eyes of her prelates..are being opened to the hollowness of the plea. **1879** Escott *England* I. 360 The door is opened to a host of frauds.

Hence **'opened** *ppl. a.*, made open.

14.. *Voc.* in Wr.-Wülcker 564/35 *Apertus*, openyd. *a* **1568** in *Bannatyne MS.* (1879) 673/17 Hir hair wes lyk the oppynnit silk. **1765** *Universal Mag.* XXXVII. 236/1 A.. quantity of this poison is dropped into an opened vein. **1837** Marryat *Dog-Fiend* ix, Beer was foaming from the mouths of the opened bottles. **1859** F. A. Griffiths *Artil. Man.* (1862) 40 The escort will be drawn up..with opened ranks. **1889** *Pall Mall G.* 1 Jan. 4/3 In the present opened-up condition of Central Africa.

openable ('əʊpənəb(ə)l), *a.* [f. prec. + -able.] Capable of being opened.

1823 *New Monthly Mag.* VII. 417 It is worse than useless to leave box-doors openable from behind. **1881** J. G. Fitch *Lect. Teach.* 68 All pigeon-holes and covered spaces.. should be open or easily openable.

open air, open-air.

1. *'open 'air*: The unconfined atmosphere; hence, the unconfined space outside buildings, usually more or less exposed to the weather: cf. air *sb.* 3b.

1526 *Pilgr. Perf.* (W. de W. 1531) 2b, Her naturall inclynacyon is to be abrode in the open ayre. **1653-1756** [see air *sb.* 3b]. **1659** Lovelace *Poems* (1864) 177 Now he takes the open air, Drawes up his wings with tactick care. **1717** Berkeley *Jrnl. Tour Italy* 24 Jan., Wks. 1871 IV. 534 A Jesuit preaching in the open air. **1851** *Beck's Florist* 148 A leaf of the Victoria regia, said to be grown in the open air at Chelsea.

2. *attrib.* (usually *'open-,air*). Existing, carried on, performed in, or characteristic of the open air. Also *transf.* and *fig.*

1830 *New Baptist Misc.* Aug. 331/1 (*heading*) Open air preaching in the villages. **1842** W. Howitt *Rural & Dom. Life Germany* xvii. 237 Those open-air concerts, walks and other amusements. **1860** G. H. K. *Vac. Tour.* 143, I never heard a complete silence in the open-air world yet. **1864** *Chambers' Bk. of Days* 10 Mar. 355 Open air Preaching is sometimes heard from a great distance. **1878** Tait & Stewart *Unseen Univ.* i. §48. 67 They have an open-air look about them. **1896** *Allbutt's Syst. Med.* I. 297 The hygienic and dietetic arrangements and especially the open-air treatment. **1926** C. Connolly *Let.* Jan. in *Romantic Friendship* (1975) 111 It is nice being able to sit out or go.. to open air cinemas full of fireflies. **1949** Koestler *Promise & Fulfilment* iii. i. 296 A people living underground must be single-minded..; but these qualities when carried over into open-air politics, become a grave handicap. **1958** *Times* 25 Oct. 10/7 His editorial influence was always exerted towards purity and strength [in music]... His songs..are animated by the same open-air kind of ideals. **1960** C. Day Lewis *Buried Day* x. 219 It was decided we should hold an open-air meeting. **1973** 'R. MacLeod' *Burial in Portugal* ii. 36 Brightly lit open-air cafés. **1975** J. Rathbone *Kill Cure* i. ii. 17 This hotel..overlooked..an open air cinema.

Hence **,open-'airish** *a.*, marked by open-air characteristics, so **,open-'airishness**; **,open-'airism**; **,open-'airness**, open air quality, coolness and freshness.

1881 *Daily News* 30 Aug. 5/2 Wholesome and almost moral in their healthy downright tone and the breezy open-airishness of them. **1891** *Ibid.* 14 Oct. 5/1 A fastidious age.. trying for all sorts of refinements of the art—for impression, for 'open airism', for values, for good workmanship as such. **1896** *Q. Rev.* July 201 The coolness and freshness, the open-airness of English life and art.

'open-,arse. Now *dial.* [In reference to the large open disk between the persistent calyx-lobes.] An old name of the Medlar, fruit and tree.

c **1000** Ælfric *Gloss.* in Wr.-Wülcker 137/36 *Mespila*, openærs. *c* **1386** Chaucer *Reeve's Prol.* 17, I fare as dooth an Openers; That ilke fruyt is euer leng the wers, Til it be roten in Mullok or in stree. *c* **1425** *Voc.* in Wr.-Wülcker 646/29 *Hec sorbus*, opynharstre. **1544** Phaer *Bk. Childr.* (1553) U ij b, Take the kernels or stones that are founde in the fruite, called openers. **1663** Killigrew *Parson's Wedd.* ii. ii. in Hazl. *Dodsley* XIV. 414 As useless as open-arses gathered green. **1877** *N.W. Linc. Gloss.*, *Oppen-arses*, medlars. **1886** Elworthy *W. Somerset Word-bk.*, *Open-ass*..the common and usual name among the working class.

'open-beak. = next.

1838 *Penny Cycl.* XII. 165/1 The open-beak, *Bec-ouvert* (Anastomus of Illiger).

'open-bill. A bird of the genus *Anastomus*, allied to the Stork, found in Africa and Asia; so called because the mandibles of its bill when shut are in contact only at the ends, leaving an open space in the middle.

1837 Swainson *Nat. Hist. Birds* II. 174 The tufted umbre ..is obviously allied to the open-bills (*Anastomus*, Ill.), a singular form, remarkable for a thick and very powerful bill gaping in the middle. **1894** Newton *Dict. Birds* s.v.

'open-'breasted, *a.*

1. Having the breast exposed. Of a garment: Not covering the breast or bosom.

1599 Marston *Sco. Villanie* ii. vii. 203 Mean'st thou him that walks all open brested? **1666** Pepys *Diary* 20 June, A thin silke waistcoate..open-breasted. **1709** Steele *Tatler* No. 95 ⁋1, I could scarce keep him this Morning from going out open-breasted. **1829** Lytton *Devereux* iv. v. 103 Even in June, one could not go open-breasted in those regions of cold and catarrh.

†**2.** Not concealing thoughts or feelings, frank.

a **1616** Beaum. & Fl. *Cust. Country* v. iii, Thou art his friend..And therefore I'le be open breasted to thee. **1650** R. Stapylton *Strada's Low C. Warres* iii. 67 Count Egmont a blunt souldier, open-breasted in his love and hatred.

open door.

1. a. A door standing open to give access or admission; hence used *fig.* to typify free admission or access, freedom of admission.

1526 Tindale *Rev.* iii. 8 Beholde I have set before the an open doore and no man can shutt hit. **1865** Lowell *Ode Harvard Commem.* xi, She of the open soul and open door, With room about her hearth for all mankind.

b. *Internat. Politics.* Admission to a country, esp. for purposes of commercial intercourse, open to all upon equal terms. Used esp. *c* 1898 with reference to Chinese ports.

1856 Emerson *Eng. Traits, Result* Wks. (Bohn) II. 134 England keeps open doors, as a trading country must, to all nations. **1898** Sir M. Hickes Beach *Sp. Swansea* 17 Jan., If we wanted to keep open doors for our commerce..we must be prepared in savage countries to incur territorial responsibilities. [*Ibid.*, [As to China] The Government were absolutely determined, at whatever cost,..that that door should not be shut.] **1898** *Daily News* 25 Jan. 4/7 Why should Russia object to the policy of the open door which has been proclaimed..as the essence of British policy? **1898** *Times* 1 Mar. 9/5 The incidents which suggest doubts as to the adoption of the policy of the open door by our rivals in the Far East. **1898** Sir E. Monson *Sp.* 6 Dec., Although we cannot insist upon that 'open door' which has latterly become a household word in our mouths.

attrib. **1898** *Atlantic Monthly* LXXXII. 438/1 Coöperation between this republic and Great Britain as to the furtherance of the open door policy. **1900** *Daily News* 22 Oct. 5/3 Both Governments agree in maintaining the open door principle in all regions where they can exert any influence. **1927** *New Republic* 21 Sept. 108/1 There is some merit in the general plea for 'most-favored nation' treatment, if only under the open-door policy. **1964** *Listener* 1 Oct. 492/2 Not only Americans, but almost everyone else thinks of the 'open-door' doctrine as American. **1974** *Times* 14 Dec. 13/5 Israel's open door policy to Jewish refugees from all parts of the world. **1976** *Listener* 9 Sept. 302/3 The Americans stood by their own open door policy—that China, just like every other part of the world except the United States, should be wide open to everybody's trade.

2. *Sc. Law.* ***letters of open doors***: see quots.

[**1693** Stair *Inst. Law Scot.* iv. xlvii. §40 Letters for making patent Doors, when Parties keep themselves or their Goods within locked Doors, and do not give access thereto, for executing of Caption or Poynding.] **1861** W. Bell *Dict. Law Scot.* s.v., Letters of Open Doors..authorise the messenger to break open the doors of those places in which the goods of the debtor are lodged.

3. *attrib.* **a.** (*'open-,door*). Done with open doors, public.

1899 *Westm. Gaz.* 9 Aug. 2/2 The open-door proceedings are hardly less puzzling.

b. Designating a mental hospital in which patients are allowed the maximum freedom of movement and communication.

1958 *Spectator* 11 July 49/1 All over the country mental hospitals have been converting to the 'Open Door' system. **1969** *Daily Tel.* 1 Nov. 2 The modern vogue for open-door mental hospitals, far from improving conditions for some patients, has led to reprehensible methods of restraining them. *Ibid.*, Plain common sense..required that such patients be managed in a secure environment and not in an open-door system. **1977** *Lancet* 18 June 1302/1 A total open-door policy is considered to be progressive; but in practice it means that mentally ill people who lack insight and are troublesome..cannot be contained there for treatment.

Hence **,open-'doored** *a.*, having the door open; hence, ready to take in or receive; keeping open house, hospitable.

1839 Bailey *Festus* ix. (1852) 97 The open doored cottages and blazing hearth. **1842** Sir H. Taylor *Edwin the Fair* iv. i. (D.), Some, Whose ears are open-doored to phantoms. **1859** Tennyson *Enid* 302 A house Once rich, now poor, but ever open-door'd.

opener ('əʊp(ə)nə(r)). [f. open *v.* + -er[1].]

1. a. One who or that which opens, in the senses of the verb. Also ***opener-up***.

1548 Udall *Erasm. Par.* Pref. 11 An opener and teller of the trueth. *a* **1555** Ridley *Brief Declar.* Wks. (Parker Soc.) 29 An opener of high mysteries in Scripture. **1637** R. Humphrey tr. *St. Ambrose* i. 1 An opener of the way to obtaine blessednesse. **1732** Berkeley *Alciphr.* v. §17 Divers to the bottom of things, fair inquirers, and openers of eyes. **1872** A. J. Gordon *In Christ* iii. (1889) 55 Opener of the prison doors to them that are bound. **1883** *Law Times* 27 Oct. 434/2 The opener having replied, the question was put, and carried in the affirmative. **1911** *Chambers's Jrnl.* Mar. 149/2 Carl Mauch, another German opener-up of South Africa. **1946** *Mind* LV. 102 The great philosopher is an opener-up of *new* paths for the mind of man.

b. An opening medicine, an aperient. Now *U.S. slang.*

1610 Markham *Masterp.* ii. clxxiii. 491 Iuy is a great drawer, and opener. **1626** Bacon *Sylva* §555 It is also an excellent Opener for the Liver. **1787** Withering *Brit.*

Plants (ed. 2) I. 320 A gentle opener and promotes perspiration. **1931** G. IRWIN *Amer. Tramp & Underworld Slang* 139 *Openers*, cathartic pills. **1942** BERREY & VAN DEN BARK *Amer. Thes. Slang* §91/5 Laxative food, *loosener, opener. Ibid.* §874/14 *Openers*, cathartic compound pills.

c. An implement or device for opening tins, cases, etc. See also *bottle-opener*, *can-opener*, *tin-opener*.

1906 *Daily Chron.* 15 Aug. 5/2 An ordinary packing-case opener had been used to force the door of the case. *Ibid.*, When the robbery was discovered the iron opener was found lying on the floor. **1912** *Chambers's Jrnl.* Feb. 144/1 The man who invented an opener for tins did well. **1942** BERREY & VAN DEN BARK *Amer. Thes. Slang* §75/6 *Opener*.., a jimmy. *Ibid.* §259/2 Key, *opener*. **1951** T. STERLING *House without Door* x. 113 She turned the bright red handle of her opener and the squat tin spun around under the knife. **1964** G. LYALL *Most Dangerous Game* i. 13 He had a bottle in one hand and an opener in the other. **1970** *Which?* Jan. 27/2 The tin which the openers found hardest to manage was the squared one. **1977** S. COULTER *Soyuz Affair* x. 110 You have a cold beer, Jim?.. There an opener someplace?

d. The first of a series of events, etc.; *spec.* in *U.S.*, the first game in a baseball match. Also ***opener-upper***. orig. *U.S.*

1941 in Wentworth & Flexner *Dict. Amer. Slang* (1960) 368/2 A patriotic opener-upper, 'Under the Double Eagle'. **1942** BERREY & VAN DEN BARK *Amer. Thes. Slang* §9/1 *Opener, starter-offer*, that which comes first. *Ibid.* §9/2 *Opener*, an opening remark. *Ibid.* §590/16 First act,.. *opener*. *Ibid.* §675/5 First game of a 'double-header' [at baseball], ..*opener*. **1949** *Down Beat* 11 Mar. 15 *Frost* is a simple but fairly bright arrangement with a good opener. **1962** *John o' London's* 19 Apr. 388/4 *Measure for Measure*..is a little lacking in lustre for a Stratford opener. **1967** [see DOUBLE-HEADER c]. **1967** *Crescendo* June 10/3 The opener, Lennie's composition 'Morning Stroll', should please all stride piano fans. **1970** *Globe & Mail* (Toronto) 28 Sept. 23/3 Queen's Golden Gails and the..Mustangs struggled through three quarters of the Ontario–Quebec Athletic Association football opener here. **1974** *Cleveland* (Ohio) *Plain Dealer* 26 Oct. 5-D/3 Vaclav Nedomansky, the hulking center iceman from Czechoslovakia who will do his skating for the Toronto Toros, in town for the Coliseum opener Sunday night. **1976** *Daily Tel.* 21 June 8 The opener of the present trilogy from Granada's 'The State of the Nation'..did little to allay worries about the unaccountable power exercised by Whitehall over Westminster. **1977** A. C. H. SMITH *Jericho Gun* vi. 80 I'll tell you what's going to win the opener. You see that bay gelding? **1978** *Rugby World* Apr. 25/2 It was draftsman Bertranne's tackle, after half-an-hour in Paris, in the championship opener on January 21, that put Maxwell out of the game.

e. *Cricket.* One of the two batsmen who open an innings.

1950 R. G. STRUTT *Schoolboy Cricket* vi. 81 No. 3..can get on better with his brilliant scoring strokes if the openers have taken the shine off the ball. **1959** *Listener* 19 Mar. 517/1 The breakdown of our batting, chiefly of the openers. **1974** *Observer* 9 June 24/6 The other opener, Geoff Greenidge, had just flicked Lever for two fours round his legs. **1976** DEXTER & MAKINS *Test Kill* 83 The Australian batting had collapsed on a wicket that the England openers found tolerably easy.

f. Colloq. phr. ***for*** (or ***as***) ***openers***: to begin with; for a start.

1967 *Boston Sunday Herald* 2 Apr. (T.V. Mag.) 6/2 Joey hosts Danny Thomas for openers. **1970** K. PLATT *Pushbutton Butterfly* (1971) xvi. 176 'Didn't they tell you at the plant? I quit.' That was good enough for openers. **1970** E. TIDYMAN *Shaft* (1971) xi. 152 Shaft decided to tear the trap apart. He killed Caroli as openers, then went plunging through the door. **1971** J. SANGSTER *Your Friendly Neighbourhood Death Pedlar* viii. 106 It was Walpole calling from London. 'I thought you were being hanged,' he said for openers. **1974** P. ERDMAN *Silver Bears* iv. 54 I'd like to ask you a few simple questions..for openers, what's with this place here? **1976** *Word 1971* XXVII. 58 These suggestions and observations call for professional reconsideration, not only of a fundamental definition of Speech per se, but of phonology, idiolect, lexicon, and Child Language as well, just for openers.

2. A machine for opening or loosening the tussocks of cotton as it comes from the bales and separating dust and other impurities.

1875 *Ure's Dict. Arts* III. 965 Perhaps the most common description of Opener in use is known as the Scutcher. **1890** G. B. SHAW *Fab. Ess. Socialism* 72 A machine called an opener, by which 15,000 lbs. of cotton can be opened in 56 hours. **1895** *Oracle Encycl.* II. 189/2 From the willow the [cotton] fibres pass to the opener or scutching machine.

3. *Poker.* (*pl.*) Cards on which a player can open the betting. Also *fig.*

1902 *Out West* Mar. 291 'I got openers, this pot,' says he, tapping the rifle. **1909** R. A. WASON *Happy Hawkins* 114, I didn't hold openers, an' yet if I didn't draw some cards an' see it out, I stood to lose entirely. **1920** C. E. MULFORD *Johnny Nelson* ii. 25 A round or two had been played when Big Tom drew his first openers. **1946** MOREHEAD & MOTT-SMITH *Penguin Hoyle* 122 If the opener cannot prove to the satisfaction of other players that he held openers, his hand is dead and cannot win the pot.

open-eyed (əʊp(ə)n'aɪd), *a.*

1. Having the eyes open; awake, vigilant.

1601 HOLLAND *Pliny* I. 27 Whosoeuer is smitten [by lightning] sleeping, is found open eied. **1610** SHAKS. *Temp.* II. i. 301 While you here do snoaring lie, Open-ey'd Conspiracie His time doth take. **1883** F. M. PEARD *Contradict.* xi, Gina was all open-eyed amazement. **1886** RUSKIN *Præterita* I. x. 338 A..just open-eyed puppy, disconsolate at the existence of the moon.

b. Done with the eyes open.

1876 GEO. ELIOT *Dan Der.* liv, An open-eyed dream that the world has done with sorrow. **1892** EMILY LAWLESS *Grania* I. iii. 17 His comfortable perch and open-eyed afternoon snooze.

2. Having the mental 'eyes' or perceptive powers open.

1648 BP. HALL *Sel. Th.* §12 A Christian..can be, at once, open-eyed to nature and blind to lust. **1873** SYMONDS *Grk. Poets* i. 25 The result of open-eyed wisdom. **1888** WESTCOTT *Vic. Cross* 6 The soul open-eyed to all the facts of the world.

Hence **open'eyedly** *adv.*, with open eyes.

1894 F. T. PALGRAVE in *Jrnls.* (1899) 246 He [A. P. Stanley], perhaps open-eyed-ly,..backs men he only half or not at all agreed with, from pure charity.

open field. An unenclosed field; undivided arable land. Chiefly *attrib.* in ***open-field system***, a system by which the arable land of a village was planned out into a number of unenclosed portions or strips and distributed among the villagers.

1780 A. YOUNG *Tour Irel.* 130 The mischiefs of our open field system in England. **1808** FORSYTH *Beauties Scotl.* V. 220 Land inclosed and subdivided is reckoned worth from a fourth to one-half more rent than in an open-field state. **1884** SEEBOHM *Eng. Vill. Comm.* (ed. 3) i. 7 The most.. important feature of the open field system..is the fact that ..the several holdings were made up of a multitude of strips scattered about on all sides of the township. *Ibid.* 8 Under the English system the open fields were the common fields —the arable land—of a village community or township under a manorial lordship. **1900** JENKS *Hist. Politics* vi. (ed. 2) 50 There were practically no hedges in the medieval village. The arable land of the village lay in great open fields, many hundreds of acres in extent.

†**'open-,hair,** *a. Obs. rare*⁻¹. With hair uncovered, bareheaded. Cf. OPEN *a.* 5.

c **1380** *Sir Ferumb.* 1943 Al open-her, & eke oungerte.. Wyþ a rop aboute þy nekke.

'open-'handed, *a.* [Parasynthetic f. *open hand*: see OPEN *a.* 22 b.] *lit.* Having an open hand.

a. Free in giving, liberal, generous, bountiful.

1601 B. JONSON *Poetaster* III. i, Is he open-handed? bountiful? **1632** MASSINGER *City Madam* I. iii, Let me yield my reasons why I am No opener-handed to him. **1705** STANHOPE *Paraphr.* II. 409 The Liberality of the Wealthiest and most Open-handed Man. **1863** A. BLOMFIELD *Mem. Bp. Blomfield* II. ix. 204 He did it with an open-handed generosity. **1882** MISS BRADDON *Mt. Royal* I. i. 17 He was open-handed, and had no petty vices.

†**b.** Ready to receive gifts. *Obs.*

1701 DE FOE *True-born Eng.* I. 325 So open-handed England, 'tis believ'd, Has all the Gleanings of the World receiv'd. **1785** TRUSLER *Mod. Times* III. 14 Biddy,..always open-handed, more ready to receive, than people to give.

Hence **,open'handedly** *adv.*, **-'handedness.**

1873 L. WALLACE *Fair God* v. iv. 281 He struck openhandedly at the page, but with such good-will [etc.]. **1628** JACKSON *Creed* XI. xlv. §2 Mercy, bounty, and openhandedness to the poor. **1844** J. T. HEWLETT *Parsons & W.* i, They appreciate the open-handedness that keeps him poor.

†**'open-,head,** *a.* and *adv. Obs.* [See OPEN *a.* 22: cf. *barehead*, *bareback*, *barefoot*, etc.] = next.

a **1225** *Ancr. R.* 424 No mon ne i-seo ham unweawed, ne open heaued. **1297** R. GLOUC. (Rolls) 6967 Þe king ligginge hii founde Wepinde & ope heued [*v.rr.* open heued, open-hefd, openhede]. *c* **1400** *Chron. Eng.* lxxxv. in Herrig *Archiv* LII. 23 Key and Bedewere..founde a wedowe oppin hede sitting by syde a tombe. ? *c* **1513** in *Three 15th Cent. Chron.* (Camden) 110 He shall be open hede, and shall bere yᵉ swerd of yᵉ esquire yᵉ poynt downwarde.

†**'open-'headed,** *a.* and *adv. Obs.* [Parasynthetic f. *open-head*: see OPEN *a.* 22 b.] With head uncovered, bare-headed.

c **1386** CHAUCER *Wife's Prol.* 645 Open-heueded [*so Hengwrt MS.*; *Corp.* openhede, *Harl.* open heedid] he hir say Lokynge out at his dore vpon a day. **14..** *Siege Jerus.* (E.E.T.S.) 19/346 Y bidde hem be boun,..To morow or vndren open-heded alle, Vp her ȝates to ȝelde, with ȝerdes an hande. **1480** CAXTON *Chron. Eng.* lxxvi. 61 Ladyes open heded come byfore kyng Arthur and cryed hym mercy.

'open-'hearted, *a.* [Parasynthetic f. *open heart*: see OPEN *a.* 22 b.]

1. Disposed to communicate thoughts or feelings; not reserved, frank.

1611 COTGR., *Rond*,..free, blunt, plaine, open-hearted, sincere. **1653** WALTON *Angler* i. 3, I will be as free and open-hearted as discretion will warrant me to be with a stranger. **1701** DE FOE *True-born Eng.* II. 21 They're so open-hearted, you may know their own most secret Thoughts, and others too. **1864** PUSEY *Lect. Daniel* vi. 370 Their chiefs, in their openhearted character, fell into snares.

2. Accessible to noble emotions, especially those of generosity or pity; full of kindly feeling.

a **1617** HIERON *Wks.* I. 27 There be..few that are open-hearted and handed to releeue. **1680** HICKERINGILL *Meroz* 26 Neither make open hearted nor open handed their close-fisted Disciples. **1768–74** TUCKER *Lt. Nat.* (1834) I. 257 The generous open hearted man sees a thousand bright spots in the prospect around him. **1855** KINGSLEY *Heroes* Pref. 13 He loves to see men and children open-hearted, and willing to be taught.

Hence **,open'heartedly** *adv.*, **-'heartedness.**

1611 COTGR., *Vivre à la Carlonne*..to deale open-heartedly. *Ibid.*, *Honnesteté*, freedome of nature, open-heartednesse, a noble disposition. **1768–74** TUCKER *Lt. Nat.* (1834) I. 260 Craft, cunning, and artifice stand opposed to fair dealing, sincerity, and open-heartedness. **1883–4** J. G. BUTLER *Bible-Work* II. 118 That open-heartedness that searches, and ponders, and receives God's word.

opening ('əʊpnɪŋ, 'əʊp(ə)nɪŋ), *vbl. sb.* [f. OPEN *v.* + -ING¹.]

1. a. The action of the verb OPEN in various senses; making free of passage, drawing apart, unclosing, unfolding, uncovering, disclosing to the view, etc. Also with adv. as ***opening out***, ***opening up***.

c **1175** *Lamb. Hom* 49 þurh heorte bireusunke þurh muðes openunge. *a* **1225** *Ancr. R.* 60 þu schalt ȝelden þet best vor þe puttes openunge. *c* **1380** WYCLIF *Serm.* Sel. Wks. II. 8 In openyng of hevene ȝatis. **1486** *Naval Acc. Hen. VII* (1896) 13 The..openyng and newe leying of old Ropes. **1530** TINDALE *Answ. More* Wks. 252/1 If stories be true, wemen haue preached sence the openyng of yᵉ new Testament. **1543** BALE *Course Rom. Fox* title-p., A dysclosynge or openynge of the manne of synne. **1611** BIBLE *Transl. Pref.* 2 If it pertaine..to the opening and clearing of the word of God. **1706** PHILLIPS, *Opening of Trenches*,..the first breaking of Ground made by the Besiegers, in order to carry their Approaches to the place besieged. **1732** BERKELEY *Alciphr.* v. §1 We heard a confused noise of the opening of hounds, the winding of horns, and the roaring of country squires. **1850** CLOUGH *Dipsychus* II. v. 43 A painful opening out Of paths for ampler virtue. **1887** *Spectator* 4 June 759/1 The opening-up of a market almost as great as India itself.

b. An action of the bowels.

1799 M. UNDERWOOD *Treat. Dis. Childr.* III. 192 They should..not [be] suffered to play until they have had an opening.

c. *Cotton Manuf.* (See quots.)

1888 C. P. BROOKS *Cotton Manuf.* i. 17 *Opening* or passing the matted pieces of the bales through a series of armed beaters..separating the material into small flakes and removing the heavier impurities. **1901** T. THORNLEY *Cotton Spinning* I. iii. 64 *Q.* Give a statement of the objects aimed at in the operation of opening... *A.* This process first opens out the matted masses of fibres to a very fleecy, soft condition; secondly, it extracts the major portion of the impurities present in the cotton..and also much seed that has escaped the ginning process; thirdly it almost now always makes a lap. **1963** A. F. W. COULSON et al. *Man. Cotton Spinning* II. II. vi. 129 Better opening and cleaning will be obtained if the machines can be kept working and operating on the cotton continuously in a rather small quantity.

2. a. A vacant space between portions of solid matter; a gap, hole, or passage; an aperture. In *local* use: = OPEN *sb.* 1 b.

a **1225** *Ancr. R.* 276 Mon, þi flesch, hwat frut bereð hit, in all his openunges? **1382** WYCLIF *Amos* iv. 3 By opnyngis ȝe shuln go out. **1398** TREVISA *Barth. De P.R.* XVIII. i. (MS. Bodl.) lf. 240/1 Þe openynge of þe owle [iȝe] is meche: and þe openynge of þe Egle iȝe is litel. **1632** J. HAYWARD tr. *Biondi's Eromena* 51 A..hood which covers the face, saving the eyes; for whose use there is an opening. **1725** DE FOE *Voy. round World* (1840) 261 Climbing up the rocks in the opening on the right hand. **1769** FALCONER *Dict. Marine* (1789), *Opening*, a passage, or streight, between two adjacent coasts or islands. **1774** GOLDSM. *Nat. Hist.* (1862) I. 159 The blood..goes through the heart, by an opening called the *foramen ovale*. **1858** LARDNER *Hand-bk. Nat. Phil.*, *Hydrost.*, etc. 141 This lateral circular opening is surrounded by a horizontal wheel.

b. A bay, gulf or other more or less wide indentation of the land.

1719 DE FOE *Crusoe* II. iv, Entering that opening of the sea. **1725** POPE *Odyss.* II. 440 Full in the openings of the spacious main It [a vessel] rides. **1796–7** H. HUNTER tr. *St. Pierre's Stud. Nat.* (1799) I. 159 These bays, or openings, are formed in the ice, merely by the influence of the nearest adjacent lands.

c. The width of an arch between its pillars.

1739 LABELYE *Short Acc. Piers Westm. Bridge* 44 The lower an Arch is, in proportion to its Opening. **1881** RAYMOND *Mining Gloss.*, *Openings*, the parts of coal mines between the pillars, or the pillars and ribs.

d. Two pages of a book, etc., that face one another.

1906 E. JOHNSTON *Writing & Illuminating* vi. 110 Parchment sheets should have their smooth sides so placed together that each 'opening' of the book has both its pages rough or both smooth. **1914** *Trans. Bibliogr. Soc.* XII. 239 A line of type at the top of a page, above the text, is called a 'head-line'; or, if it consists of the title of the book (or of the section of the book) on every page or every 'opening' (*i.e.*, two pages facing one another), sometimes a 'running-title' or 'running-head'. **1963** *Listener* 21 Mar. 522/1 A good example of his elaborate book-production is *The Book of Ruth*, with alternate openings in full colour and in golds and greys.

3. *U.S.* A tract of ground over which trees are wanting or thinly scattered in comparison with adjoining forest tracts. Cf. *oak-opening* s.v. OAK *sb.* 8.

1704 *Providence R.I. Records* (1893) IV. 178 On the south side of the place in the swamp..which is called the first opening. **1745** P. THOMAS *Jrnl. Anson's Voy.* 35 Hills.. covered with..Groves of Trees, interspersed with many Openings and ever-green Valleys. **1824** LONGF. *April Day* iv, The forest openings. **1839** MARRYAT *Diary Amer.* Ser. I. II. 46 The term used here to distinguish this variety of timber land from the impervious woods is oak openings. **1851** MAYNE REID *Scalp Hunt.* xxxii, We debouched through the mountain pass into a country of 'openings'.

4. a. The action of beginning, starting or setting on foot; the first steps or commencement; the part, act, words, etc., with which anything opens; the initial steps or stage in a course of action.

1712 ADDISON *Spect.* No. 412 ¶3 In the opening of the Spring. **1782** MISS BURNEY *Cecilia* VI. iv, She came running into Cecilia's room, saying she had very good news for her, 'A charming opening!' cried Cecilia, 'pray tell it me.' **1789** GOUV. MORRIS in Sparks *Life & Writ.* (1832) I. 306 At the opening of the States-General. **1849** MACAULAY *Hist. Eng.*

iv. I. 509 The days which..preceded the opening of the session. **1887** *Grove's Dict. Mus.* IV. 415 The opening of the opera was originally intended to be quite different from what it is now. *Mod.* The King's Speech at the opening of Parliament.

b. *spec.* The statement of the case made by counsel to a court of law preliminary to adducing evidence.

1660 *Trial Regic.* 77 [We] cannot hear you to speak that upon your opening which is treason. **1818** CRUISE *Digest* (ed. 2) VI. 132 Lord Chief Justice Eyre said, it was manifest from the opening, that it was intended to be insisted on, that ..Sir T. C. lost his old estate. **1881** *Spectator* 30 Apr. 573 Like the opening of an advocate who has not mastered his brief.

c. The introductory or burlesque part of a pantomime preceding the harlequinade.

The two portions of the pantomime were not separated before the year 1800.

1825 P. EGAN *Life of Actor* vii. 264 To get up splendid Spectacles; write openings for Pantomimes. **1838** *Mem. Grimaldi* II. xxii, He played Fribble in the opening, and afterwards the Lover. **1859** *Illustr. Lond. News* 8 Jan. 34/1 The introduction or opening, which, but for the comic masks, differs little from the burlesque or extravaganza. **1894** J. A. CAVE *Jubilee Dramatic Life* (ed. 2) xix. 177 For the openings of my pantomimes I was able, as opportunity occurred, to secure the services of such inimitable burlesque performers as the Vokes family.

d. *Chess.* A mode of beginning a game; *spec.* a definite sequence of moves for the purpose of establishing a line of defence or attack.

1735 BERTIN *Chess* iv, Particular instructions..how the player may make the proper openings, to attack, or defend. **1871** M. COLLINS *Mrq. & Merch.* III. iv. 120 She remembered it was an evening for chess, and wondered what opening Miss Griffin would choose. **1889** *Chambers's Encycl.* 166 All openings of repute have distinctive titles, often being named after their inventors.

e. *Theatr.* The first performance of a play or entertainment; a première. *U.S.*

1855 W. B. WOOD *Pers. Recoll. Stage* ix. 191 The loss we sustained was less important in a pecuniary view..than in rendering our opening still more embarrassing. **1916** *Variety* 27 Oct. 12/1 Openings here next week include Marie Tempest in 'A Lady's Name' (Plymouth); 'Sybil' (Colonial); [etc.]. **1923** H. RUBY *Let.* 16 Aug. in G. Marx *Groucho Lett.* (1967) 183 The out-of-town opening.. occurred in Fairmont, West Virginia. **1959** J. THURBER *Years with Ross* xv. 247 I'm having dinner with Aleck and he's taking me to an opening. **1977** J. AIKEN *Last Movement* i. 37 'What about your opening?'..'Big success. I'll show you our press notices.'

f. The start of an art exhibition, fashion show, or the like.

1905 E. WHARTON *House of Mirth* II. ix. 428 Beings without definite pursuits of permanent relations, who drifted on a languid tide of curiosity from restaurant to concert-hall, from palm-garden to music-room, from 'art exhibit' to dress-maker's opening. **1952** D. AMES *Murder, Maestro, Please* xxxv. 255 Geoffrey insists on taking me to Paris for the autumn dress openings. **1969** D. S. DAVIS *Where Dark Streets Go* (1970) ix. 89 There was a showing of Tchelitchew drawings at the Burns Gallery... 'Not everybody who goes to an opening signs in. Especially when it's not new work.' **1972** P. MARKS *Collector's Choice* ii. 62 He never went to museums except for openings.

5. An opportunity; a circumstance or combination of circumstances which offers a chance of advantage, success or gratification; a vacant place in connexion with any business or profession, which admits of being occupied.

1793 BURKE *Lett., to Sir G. Elliot* Corr. 1844 IV. 153 Here is an opening which, if neglected by our government,..they will one day sorely repent. **1855** FITZJ. STEPHEN in *Cambr. Ess.* 178 She might have made him miss one or two openings in life. **1889** RUSKIN *Præterita* III. ii. 69 D'Israeli saw his opening in an instant. **1898** *Times* 17 Oct., In his early years of promise in the tennis court L—— relied mainly on his wonderful return, his accuracy for the openings, and his activity.

6. *Comb.* **opening-machine**, any machine for opening; *spec.* = OPENER 2; **opening night**, the first night of a theatrical play, entertainment, etc.; **opening-time**, (*a*) the time at which a place, esp. a public house, is opened; (*b*) the time that a device takes to open.

1875 KNIGHT *Dict. Mech.* 1561/2. *Opening-machine. *c* **1814** (*play-title*) The *opening night; or, the manager hoax'd. **1828** J. EBERS *Seven Yrs. King's Theatre* 210 The interest felt by the public in the arrival of the gran maestro, on the opening night. **1929** Opening night [see DOODAH 1]. **1975** P. G. WINSLOW *Death of Angel* 9 The milkman finds a body dressed up for opening night. **1927** D. L. SAYERS *Unnatural Death* xii. 136 Within, a cheerful bustle in the bar announced the near arrival of *opening time. **1943** *Gloss. Terms Electr. Engin.* (*B.S.I.*) 66 *Opening time*, applied to a circuit-breaker: the time interval from the instant of application of the tripping power when in the closed position to the instant of separation of the arcing contacts. **1971** 'H. CALVIN' *Poison Chasers* i. 7 We got back around opening time... I said to Dai, 'I'll get drinks while you're telephoning.'

opening ('əʊpnɪŋ, 'əʊp(ə)nɪŋ), *ppl. a.* [f. as prec. + -ING².] That opens.

1. a. That renders open; *spec.* that opens the bowels or other bodily passages; aperient.

1398 TREVISA *Barth. De P.R.* VII. lxx. (MS. Bodl.) lf. 74/2 Openyng medicyn..openeth weyes that beþ stopped and makeþ þynne humours þat be cleymye þikke. **1620** VENNER *Via Recta* vi. 94 Vinegar that is made of White-wine, is more opening, and that which is made of Claret, more binding. **1727** BRADLEY *Fam. Dict.* s.v. *Almond*, Bitter-Almonds are of an opening and detersive nature. **1783** [see CHELTENHAM 1]. **1804** ABERNETHY *Surg. Obs.* 192 She took some gentle opening medicine. **1912** *More Secret Remedies* (B.M.A.) x. 157 Do the bowels act regularly without opening medicine? **1965** A. NICOL *Truly Married Woman* 72 Magnesium sulphate for opening-medicine.

b. That opens, or forms the commencement of, a discourse, entertainment, or proceeding; initial; introductory. (The opposite of CLOSING *ppl. a.* b.) Esp. in *Cricket*, designating or pertaining to the batsmen who open the innings, or the bowlers who open the attack.

1851 WILLMOTT *Pleas. Lit.* iv. (1857) 15 It contained the opening letter of Junius. **1882** *Daily Tel.* 4 May, It was the opening day of the exhibition. *a* **1902** *Mod.* His opening remarks were eagerly listened to. The opening event was won by the Dark Blues. **1929** P. G. H. FENDER *Turn of Wheel* iii. 92 Hendry..had a habit of..retreating when facing Larwood, and that would never do, especially in an opening batsman. **1952** J. H. MORGAN *Glamorgan County Cricket* facing p. 64 (*caption*) Arnold Dyston, a stylish opening bat. **1955** A. E. R. GILLIGAN *Urn Returns* 36 The pace attack of Statham and Tyson keeps Rutherford and Sawle, the opening pair, strictly on the defensive. **1971** *Times* 15 Feb. 8/2 Their opening partnerships for the seven Test matches have averaged as much as 75. **1976** J. SNOW *Cricket Rebel* 25 Tony Buss, his opening partner, was far more dangerous to face than he looked from the ringside. **1977** *Times* 29 Nov. 12/5 Geoffrey Arnold's two for 95 were the best figures by a recognized opening bowler in three Tests.

2. That becomes open; unclosing, unfolding, expanding, widening out, developing, beginning, giving tongue, etc.: see the verb.

1637 MILTON *Lycidas* 26 The opening eyelids of the morn. **1667** —— *P.L.* XI. 277 From the first op'ning bud. **1702** ROWE *Tamerl.* I. i. 108 Watchful they stood expecting op'ning day. **1754** J. LOVE *Cricket* (1770) 5 The Ball, close cushion'd, slides askew, And to the op'ning Pocket runs, a Cou. **1805** Z. ALLNUTT *Navig. Thames* 23 A Plan of an opening Weir across the Thames. **1810** SCOTT *Lady of L.* I. iii, Yelled on the view the opening pack. An hundred dogs bayed deep and strong. **1872** W. R. GREG *Enigmas Life* v. (1882) 184 To the opening mind..it [Life] seems like a delicious feast.

3. *Comb.*, as **opening-bit**, a tapering tool for widening an aperture; a broach or reamer.

1875 KNIGHT *Dict. Mech.* 1561.

† **'openly**, *a. Obs.* [f. OPEN *a.* + -LY¹.] Open to sight, manifest, public.

c **1050** *Ags. Gloss.* in Wr.-Wülcker 343/28 *A puplicis*, openlecum. *Ibid.* 466/4 *Puplica*, openlecre. *c* **1200** *Trin. Coll. Hom.* 5 Ure louerd ihesu cristes openliche tocume. *c* **1200** ORMIN 2909 Þærr þurrh he ȝaff ȝuw, læwedd follc, Full opennlike bisne. *a* **1225** *Ancr. R.* 426 Þauh þe ancre on hire meidenes uor openliche gultes legge penitence.

openly ('əʊp(ə)nlɪ), *adv.* [f. OPEN *a.* + -LY².] In an open manner.

1. Without concealment; so that all may see, hear, or take cognizance; in public, publicly.

971 *Blickl. Hom.* 193 Hie openlice þæt ȝesetton. *c* **1020** *Rule St. Benet* (Logeman) 55 He si ȝeþread openlice toforan eallum. *c* **1200** ORMIN 13630 Opennliȝ biforenn man. *a* **1300** *Cursor M.* 175 Iesu crist..openlik [*v.rr.* opinli, openly] bigan to preche. **1375** BARBOUR *Bruce* XI. 633 The Erll of murreff oppynly Takis playne feld with his menȝhe. **1480** CAXTON *Chron. Eng.* ccxxi. 213 He opened the letter..and red it openly word by word. **1549** *Compl. Scot.* xv. 133 [We] dar neuyr pray appynly to send sic vengeance on ane euil prince. **1597** SHAKS. *2 Hen. IV*, IV. ii. 76 My loue to ye, Shall shew it selfe more openly hereafter. **1774** GOLDSM. *Nat. Hist.* (1776) IV. 69 The dog..openly declares his alacrity to pursue them. **1856** FROUDE *Hist. Eng.* (1858) I. ii. 158 The words had been repeated to Wolsey, who mentioned them openly at his table. **1885** *Spectator* 30 May 714/2 The lady..flirts openly and unblushingly.

† **b.** By people generally, commonly, publicly.

1154 *O.E. Chron.* an. 1137 §5 Hi sæden openlice ðæt christ slep & his halechen. **1473** *Rolls of Parlt.* VI. 83/1 In the paryssh of Seynt Michell, openly called Pater noster church, otherwise called Weritynton college. *a* **1548** HALL *Chron., Hen. VI* 149 It was openly knowen, that the French kyng, was ready..to make open warre.

2. Without concealment of thought or feeling; without reserve; frankly, unreservedly.

1340 HAMPOLE *Pr. Consc.* 531 Þar-for Iob þus openly sayse; *Homo, natus de muliere* [etc.]. *c* **1375** *Sc. Leg. Saints* iii. (*Andreas*) 241 He bad þame opynly þat þai suld hold þar way in hy. *a* **1548** HALL *Chron., Hen. VIII* 249 b, Who should seme secretly to wyll more, than in the commission he did openly professe. **1828** SCOTT *F.M. Perth* vii, I speak among neighbours and friends, and therefore I speak openly.

† **3.** In a way easy to see or understand; evidently, manifestly; clearly, plainly. *Obs.*

c **888** K. ÆLFRED *Boeth.* xix, Cato, se wæs eac Romana heretoȝa, se wæs openlice uþwita. *c* **1200** ORMIN Pref. 55 Þiss iss to seggenn opennliȝ þe Laferrd Cristess Karrte. *a* **1225** *Ancr. R.* 8 Hwar he ifinde in holi write religiun openluker descriued & isuteled þen in sein Iames canoniel epistle? **1340** *Ayenb.* 73 Ine hevene þou sselt yzy openliche hou uirtues and guode dedes byeþ heȝliche yolde. *c* **1400** MAUNDEV. (Roxb.) xxx. 135 Þare er fewles also spekand of þaire awen kynde; and þai will hails men..spekand als openly as þai ware men. **1484** CAXTON *Fables of Æsop* v. xiii, He that can or shalle proue more openly that he hath the most parte. **1682** NORRIS *Hierocles* Pref. 34 Many things might have been deliver'd more openly and clearly.

† **4.** In an open, not closed, state or condition; so as to admit of entrance or passage. *Obs.*

? *a* **1366** CHAUCER *Rom. Rose* 502 If that the passage opunly Hadde be unto me free. **1387-8** T. USK *Test. Love* Prol. (Skeat) l. 1 Men..that, with eeres openly sprad.. swalowen the deliciousnesse of iestes and of ryme.

† **5.** With wide spaces or interstices. *Obs. rare.*

c **1790** IMISON *Sch. Art* II. 48 For your first practice, copy such prints as are openly shaded.

† **'open-mouth**, *a. Obs.* [OPEN *a.* 22.] = next.

1692 R. L'ESTRANGE *Josephus, Antiq.* VI. iv. (1733) 134 They went presently Open-Mouth to the Father,..with a grievous complaint against his Sons. **1786** O'KEEFE in *Roxb. Ball.* (1887) VI. 383 On Effingham's squadron, though all in abreast, Like open-mouth curs they came bowling.

open-mouthed ('əʊp(ə)n'maʊðd), *a.* [Parasynthetic f. *open mouth*: see OPEN *a.* 22 b.]

1. Having the mouth open; having an open mouth: hence rapacious, in full cry, etc.

c **1532** DU WES *Introd. Fr.* in Palsgr. 899 Ye shal pronounce your *a* as wyde open-mouthed as ye can. **1709** STEELE *Tatler* No. 62 ¶2 A fine open-mouthed Dog. **1801** STRUTT *Sports & Past.* III. iv. 182 Hounds running at them open-mouthed. **1900** *Westm. Gaz.* 28 Aug. 2/3 An open-mouthed army, like an open-mouthed individual, does not strike one as particularly intelligent.

b. Of a vessel or the like: Having a wide mouth.

1660 BOYLE *New Exp. Phys. Mech.* xxii. 177 The open-mouth'd Glass was by this means almost replenished. **1830** R. KNOX *Béclard's Anat.* 186 Each molecule of the organs is in a manner placed between two open-mouthed vessels.

2. Gaping, as with astonishment or surprise.

1593 DRAYTON *Pastorals* v. Poems (1810) 437/1 This fond gentility, Whereon the fool world open-mouthed gazes. **1786** tr. *Beckford's Vathek* (1883) 118 The poor peasants.. remained open-mouthed with surprise. **1840** DICKENS *Old C. Shop* xiii. Mr. Swiveller looked, as he was, all open-mouthed astonishment. **1870** MORRIS *Earthly Par.* III. IV. 56 Yet did the shipmen stay their speech And open-mouthed upon her stare.

3. With mouth open to speak; speaking freely, clamorous, vociferous.

1599 MASSINGER, etc. *Old Law* v. i, Justice, indeed, Should ever be close-eared, and open-mouthed. *a* **1602** W. PERKINS *Cases Consc.* (1619) 367 What is that makes men to be open mouthed in declaring and censuring our faults? **1802** JEFFERSON *Writ.* (1830) III. 500 Officers who are active or open-mouthed against the government. **1849** MACAULAY *Hist. Eng.* viii. II. 367 Zulestein..found all the people whom he met open-mouthed about the infamous fraud just committed by the Jesuits.

Hence ˌ**open-'mouthedness**.

1882-3 SCHAFF *Encycl. Relig. Knowl.* II. 973 He confessed, with his usual incurable open-mouthedness.

openness ('əʊp(ə)nnɪs). [f. OPEN *a.* + -NESS.]

1. The quality or condition of being open; unclosed, unenclosed, uncovered, unsheltered, or unobstructed condition; exposedness, etc.

1530 PALSGR. 249/2 Opynnesse, *ouuerture*. **1577** HARRISON *England* I. x. in Holinshed I. 26/2 There is nothing to be discommended in this ryuer, but the openesse thereof..to the weather. **1610** HEALEY *St. Aug. Citie of God* XV. iv. (1620) 507 Mans opennesse to aduersity. **1748** *Anson's Voy.* III. ii. 309 Aided by the openness of the woods. **1791** NEWTE *Tour Eng. & Scot.* 239 The openness of the fields makes this improvement impracticable or unprofitable. **1876** STAINER & BARRETT *Dict. Mus. Terms* s.v. *Notation*, *Ut* was also changed to *Do* for the sake of the openness of the vowel.

b. The condition of being open to impressions or ideas.

1671 J. BURNYEAT *Jrnl.* in *Friends' Library* xi. 144, I found a great openness in the country [Virginia], and had several blessed meetings. **1874** MORLEY *Compromise* (1886) 41 [That] which..clogs their intellectual energy and mental openness.

2. Absence of dissimulation, secrecy, or reserve; frankness, candour, sincerity.

1611 SHAKS. *Cymb.* I. vi. 88 Deliuer with more opennesse your answeres To my demands. **1711** ADDISON *Spect.* No. 119 ¶2 An unconstrained Carriage, and a certain Openness of Behaviour, are the Height of Good-breeding. **1796** MORSE *Amer. Geog.* I. 669 [Chicasaws] have an openness in their countenances and behaviour, uncommon among savages. **1828** D'ISRAELI *Chas. I*, I. xi. 308 There is an apparent openness in the speech, which gives a favourable idea of the man. **1875** JOWETT *Plato* (ed. 2) I. 115 He considers openness to be the best policy.

3. Of weather: Absence of frost; †freedom from cloud, clearness (*obs.*).

1611 COTGR., *Serenité*, serenitie, cleerenesse,.. calmenesse, or opennesse of weather. **1856** KANE *Arct. Expl.* I. iv. 42 The known openness of the season of 1852 and the probable mildness of the following winter. **1882** *Gd. Words* Apr. 252 The openness of the weather during the past winter.

open sesame ('əʊp(ə)n 'sɛsəmiː). Also 9 **open sesamum.** [See SESAME.] The magic words by which, in the tale of Ali Baba and the Forty Thieves, the door of the robbers' cave was made to fly open; hence, any marvellous or irresistible means of securing immediate admission.

[**1793** *Arab. Nts.* IV. 125 [Ali Baba] went among the shrubs, and perceiving the door, he said, Open Sesame; and the door flew wide open.] **1826** SCOTT *Diary* 14 Sept. in *Lockhart*, A laudatory copy of French verses sent up the evening before by way of Open Sesamum, I suppose. *a* **1837** MRS. MARKHAM *Hist. France* xxxiii. (1855) 416 She tried that universal key, that *open sesame*, a bribe. **1882** MRS. OLIPHANT *Lit. Hist. Eng.* I. 185 Genius was understood, and poetry a sort of 'open Sesame' to every noble door.

† **'open-tail.** *Obs. rare*$^{-1}$. A light, indelicate, or unchaste woman.

a **1618** DAVIES *Scourge of Folly* xxiii. (1878) 10 Kate still exclaimes against great medlers, A busie-body hardly she abides..I muse her stomacke now so much shoulde faile To loath a medlar, being an open-taile.

†**'open-,tide.** *Obs.* = next.

c **1440** *Anc. Cookery* in *Househ. Ord.* (1790) 472 This potage may be made in Lenten, and also in opentyde, on this same manere, withouten eyren. *Ibid.*, Appeluns for a Lorde, in Opyntide. *a* **1700** KENNETT in *MS. Lansd.* 1033 (Halliwell) The time between Epiphany and Ash-Wednesday, wherein marriages were publicly solemnized, was on that account formerly called *open-tide*; but now in Oxfordshire and several other parts, the time after harvest, while the common fields are free and open to all manner of stock, is called open-tide. **1744** JACOB *Law Dict.*, *Open-tide*, i.e. when Corn is carried out of the Common Fields.

'open ,time. The time during which anything specified is open: *spec.* †**a.** The time after harvest when cattle might be turned into the open fields. †**b.** The time out of Lent when no fast is imposed. **c.** That which is not close-time for fish, etc.

[**1293** *Notit. ann. 21 Edw. I Glouc.* rot. 14 in *Abbrev. Placit.* 232 Habeant communiam pasturæ per omnes terras suas in Shenington Tempore Aperto et post fena et blada collecta.] **1483** *Rolls of Parlt.* VI. 257/1 Aswell in opyn tyme called Averes tyme, as all other tymes. **1523** FITZHERB. *Surv.* 6 b, If their commen feldes lye toguyder vnclosed in opyn tyme whan haruest is in. *a* **1529** SKELTON *Col. Cloute* 861 Their dewtyes..That they ought by the lawe..In open tyme and in Lent. **1635** PAGITT *Christianogr.* I. iii. (1636) 150 They fast not upon Saturdaies in open time but onely Wensdaies and Fridaies.

'open-,work. [See OPEN *a.* 7.]

1. Any kind of work so made or constructed as to show openings or interstices in its substance, as in open-work of iron or other metal; *esp.* such work in knitting, netting, lace, embroidery, or the like, introduced for ornament in any textile fabric.

1598 FLORIO *Worlde of Wordes* 460/2 *Zeganélla*, such small fine net worke or open worke as gentlewomen use to make and weare vpon their heads in caules. **1782** T. PENNANT *Journey Chester to London* 264 The fronts are of most elegant gothic open work. **1819** SHELLEY *Cenci* Pref. p. xiv, With balcony over balcony of open work. **1847** TENNYSON *Princ.* IV. 185 Betwixt were valves Of open-work. **1863** HAWTHORNE *Our Old Home* 77 There is an iron gate, through the rusty open-work of which you see a grassy lawn. **1872** J. H. INGRAHAM *Pillar of Fire* 68 The chariot was gorgeously decorated at the sides with ornaments of light open-work. **1894** *Daily News* 10 Sept. 6/5 On the bodice a saddle-shaped yoke repeated the openwork with its warm red lining.

attrib. **1812–16** J. SMITH *Panorama Sc. & Art* I. 160 The whole interior is one series of open-work pannels laid on the Norman work. **1890** *Daily News* 24 Mar. 6/1 Open-work stockings will be the only wear when the weather gets a little warmer.

2. *Mining.* Excavation open to the surface.

1811 J. FAREY *Gen. View Agric. & Minerals Derbyshire* I. 359 The sinking was further continued, and the heaps on the sides of these *open-works*, or open-casts, increased. **1881** RAYMOND *Mining Gloss.*, *Open-work*, a quarry or *open cut.*

So **'open-,worked** *a.*, **'open-,working** *sb.*

1835 *Court Mag.* VI. p. xiii/2 White open-worked silk gloves. **1836–9** DICKENS *Sk. Boz*, *Characters* iv, Down came J'mima herself soon afterwards in..Denmark satin shoes, and open-worked stockings. **1886** BURTON *Arab. Nts.* I. 75 Open-worked tarts and fritters scented with musk. **1896** *Westm. Gaz.* 25 June 3/2 The bolero of embroidered lawn very much openworked. **1844** G. DODD *Textile Manuf.* vii. 225 The working round of the outline [of lace] is called 'running', while the filling up of the interior parts is termed either 'fining' or 'open-working'.

openyoun, obs. form of OPINION.

opepe (əʊ'piːpiː). Also **epepe.** [Yoruba.] A West African tree, *Sarcocephalus diderrichii*, of the family Rubiaceæ, or its hard yellowish-brown wood; also (see quot. 1908) occasionally used for an evergreen tree of the genus *Terminalia*.

1891 *Kew Bull.* 43 Names of Yoruba Timbers... 4. Opepe. **1908** *Ibid.* 193 An unnamed species of Terminalia.. is also likely to furnish timber suitable for the home markets. .. The Yoruba name of the tree is 'Epepe'. **1920** *Nature* 29 July 692/1 Other heavy constructional woods [in the Empire Timber Exhibition]..are..the gamboge-coloured Opepe.. and Apa. **1936** J. D. KENNEDY *Forest Flora S. Nigeria* 217 The accepted trade name for this timber in England is Opepe. **1956** *Archit. Rev.* CXX. 229 The board room [has] an opepe wood block floor. **1972** *Timber Trades Jrnl.* 13 May 40/2 Opepe, an early substitute for greenheart, was originally thought to be a bottomless pit, but..the bottom of the pit had been reached about two years ago. So they were already interested in a substitute for a substitute.

opera ('ɒpərə), *sb.*[1] [a. It. *opera*, a. L. *opera* labour, pains, exertion, a work produced, f. *opus*, *oper-* work; cf. F. *opéra* (17th c. in Hatz.-Darm.).]

1. a. A dramatic performance in which music forms an essential part, consisting of recitatives, arias, and choruses, with orchestral accompaniment and scenery; also, a dramatic or musical composition intended for such performance, a libretto or score.

1644 EVELYN *Diary* 19 Nov., It is the work of Bernini,.. who, a little before my coming to the citty [Rome], gave a publiq Opera (for so they call shews of that kind) wherein he painted the scenes [etc.]. **1656** BLOUNT *Glossogr.*, *Opera*..In Italy it signifies a Tragedy, Tragi-Comedy, Comedy or Pastoral, which (being the studied work of a Poet) is not acted after the vulgar manner, but performed by Voyces in that way, which the Italians term *Recitative*, being likewise adorned with Scenes by Perspective, and extraordinary advantages by Musick. **1659** EVELYN *Diary* 5 May, I went to visite my brother in London, and next day to see a new Opera, after the Italian way, in recitative music and sceanes, much inferior to the Italian composure and magnificence. **1661** PEPYS *Diary* 2 July, Went to Sir William Davenant's Opera. **1685** *Lond. Gaz.* No. 2042/4 The Opera of Albion and Albanius..is to be Printed. **1685** DRYDEN *Albion & Albanius* Pref., An Opera is a poetical Tale or Fiction, represented by Vocal and Instrumental Musick, adorn'd with Scenes, Machines and Dancing. **1711** ADDISON *Spect.* No. 18 ¶2 Arsinoe was the first Opera that gave us a Taste of Italian Musick. **1740** CIBBER *Apol.* (1756) I. 277 The scheme was to have but one theatre for plays, and another for operas. **1819** BYRON *Juan* I. cciii, If any person doubt it, I appeal..To plays in five, and operas in three acts. **1880** W. S. ROCKSTRO in Grove *Dict. Mus.* II. 526/2 Wagner..has written the Libretti as well as the Music of all his later Operas.

fig. **1693** NORRIS *Pract. Disc.* (1707) IV. 207 We may.. expect towards the latter end of this Great Opera, that the Scenes will thicken..and the Fashion of this World will pass yet more swiftly away.

b. *at* or *to the opera* includes the notion of the place: cf. *at the play*.

1645 EVELYN *Mem.* June, This night [at Venice]..we went to the Opera where comedies and other plays are represented in recitative musiq.., with variety of sceanes painted.., and machines for flying in the aire,.. one of the most magnificent and expensive diversions the wit of man can invent. **1880** W. S. ROCKSTRO in Grove *Dict. Mus.* II. 518/2 If we would know what Mozart really meant, we must study him, not at the Opera, but in his own delightful Scores.

2. (Usually ***the opera.***) As a branch of dramatic art. (Cf. *the drama*, *tragedy*, *comedy*, etc.)

1759 GOLDSMITH *Bee* No. 8 Some years ago the Italian opera was the only fashionable amusement among our nobility. **1763** J. BROWN *Poetry & Mus.* xii. 201 Venice was the Place where the Opera first appeared in Splendor. **1789** BURNEY *Hist. Mus.* IV. 18 This [end of 16th c.] seems the true æra whence the opera, or drama, wholly set to Music.. should be dated. **1881** BARING-GOULD *Germany* ix. 249 It is in the Opera and the Oratorio that the most flourishing descendants of the old Mystery Plays are to be met with. **1884** G. A. MACFARREN in *Encycl. Brit.* XVII. 87/2 The masques performed at Whitehall and at the Inns of Court were of the nature of opera.

3. With qualification denoting a particular branch or kind; as ***ballad-opera*** (see BALLAD *sb.* 6); ***comic opera*** (see COMIC A. 1), also in Fr. form ***opéra comique***; ***grand opera*** (see GRAND A. 8 b); ***opera bouffe*** (= F. *opéra bouffe*, also ellipt. ***bouffe***, and in It. form ***opera buffa***), comic opera, esp. of a farcical character, an operatic extravaganza; also *attrib.* or as *adj.*; (hence (*nonce-wds.*) ***opera-'bouffer***, an actor in opera bouffe; ***opera-'bouffeish*** adj., having the character of opera bouffe); ***opera magica*** (*rare*), opera with a fantastic or supernatural subject; ***opera semiseria***, seriocomic opera; ***opera seria***, serious or tragic opera, *spec.* a type of Italian opera flourishing in the 18th century, usually with a classical or mythological subject; ***horse opera***: see HORSE *sb.* 28 a; ***soap opera***: see as main entry.

1711 ADDISON *Spect.* No. 18 ¶1 It is my Design in this Paper to deliver down to Posterity a faithful Account of the Italian Opera. **1802** C. WILMOT *Let.* 31 Jan. in *Irish Peer* (1920) 39 We have been to the Opera Buffa or the Italian Opera. **1817** *Examiner* No. 486. 253 This lady at the Italian Opera is respectable: on the English stage she was formidable. **1879** GROVE *Dict. Mus.* I. 617 Grand Opera.. may contain any number of acts, and ballets or divertissements, but if spoken dialogue is introduced it becomes a 'comic' opera. **1870** D. J. KIRWAN *Palace & Hovel* xvi. 235 Mademoiselle Helena Schneider, the opera bouffe singer. **1878** L. W. M. LOCKHART *Mine is Thine* I. iii. 58 Offenbach outdoes himself in a new opera-bouffe—'Suzanne et les Vieillards'. **1895** G. B. SHAW *Let.* 31 Aug. (1965) I. 553 Such are the opera bouffe depths to which I have descended. **1937** *New Statesman* 25 Dec. 1102/2 The *opéra-bouffe* Jupiter who attempts to cuckold him [*sc.* Amphitryon] by assuming his form. **1970** W. APEL *Harvard Dict. Mus.* (ed. 2) 187/2 A special type of comic opera is represented by the *opéras bouffes* of Offenbach. **1882** J. J. JENNINGS *Theatr. & Circus Life* 76 There is something so indescribably funny in the costumes, in the facial make-up, and all that, of the happy opera-bouffer or festive burlesquer. **1888** *Pall Mall G.* 29 Nov. 14/1 The opera bouffers from the Gaiety Theatre. **1889** T. A. GUTHRIE *Pariah* I. vi, One of the opéra-bouffeish cabanes came creaking..over the sand. **1801** F. BURNEY *Jrnls. & Lett.* 22–24 Apr. (1975) V. 267 Madᵉ d'henin made a party for us all to meet again the next day, & go to the Opera Buffa. **1842** *Ainsworth's Mag.* II. 78 It is satisfactory to see the Italian Opera..returning to the opera buffa of Fioravanti. **1880** W. S. ROCKSTRO in Grove *Dict. Mus.* II. 9 The period in which the history of the Intermezzo merges permanently into that of the Opera Buffa, its legitimate heir. **1963** AUDEN *Dyer's Hand* 184 For Falstaff, time does not exist, since he belongs to the *opera buffa* world of play and mock action. **1965** C. HIBBERT *Garibaldi & his Enemies* I. i. 13 He [*sc.* Mazzini] joined the Carbonari..but the *opera buffa* ceremony of the ritualistic initiation, in which he was required to swear allegiance to unknown leaders on a bared dagger..struck him as absurd. **1968** S. TOWNELEY in *New Oxf. Hist. Music* IV. xv. 837 Cavalieri divides the work into three acts. And he suggests the *intermedii* should intersperse them—a practice which a century later helped in the creation of *opera buffa*. **1744** H. WALPOLE *Let.* 22 July (1903) II. 40 Young Churchill has got a daughter by the Frasi; Mr. Winnington calls it the *opéra comique*; the mother is an opera girl; the grandmother was Mrs. Oldfield. **1765** H. WALPOLE *Lett.*, *to G. Montagu* 22 Sept., The Italian comedy, now united with their *opera comique*, is their most perfect diversion. **1866** G. H. LEWES *Jrnl.* 30 Dec. in *Geo. Eliot Lett.* (1956) IV. 328 A wretched opera comique—*Cartouche*. **1879** J. HULLAH in Grove *Dict. Mus.* I. 379 The renascence of 'opera comique' in France dates from the latter part of the 17th century. **1897** R. KIPLING *Captains Courageous* 133 The opera-comique crew..greeted him as a brother. **1955** *Times* 6 May 14/7 It was doubtful whether, had it not been for Grétry, we should have had some of the striking later developments of *opéra comique*. **1976** *New Yorker* 16 Feb. 110/3 In 1870, Verdi was toying with the idea of writing an opéra comique. **1956** AUDEN & KALLMAN *Magic Flute* Pref. p. xiv, We have written the dialogue in verse, because it seemed to us the right medium for the spoken word in an *opera magica*. **1963** AUDEN *Dyer's Hand* 484 *Die Zauberflöte*..stylistically, an *opera magica*. **1947** A. EINSTEIN *Mus. Romantic Era* xvi. 290 The stereotyped insipidity of the Italian *opera semiseria* since Rossini. **1959** *Times* 21 Aug. 13/2 The world première of Heimo Erbse's *Julietta*, an *opera semiseria*. **1970** W. APEL *Harvard Dict. Mus.* (ed. 2) 601/2 *Opera semiseria* is a serious opera including comic elements, e.g., Mozart's *Le Nozze di Figaro*. **1876** STAINER & BARRETT *Dict. Mus. Terms* 392/2 *Seria* (*It.*), serious, grave, tragic, as, *Opera seria*, a tragic opera. **1880** GROVE *Dict. Mus.* II. 513/2 The gradual development of the Opera Buffa from the Interludes which were formerly presented between the Acts of an Opera Seria, or Spoken Drama. **1892** G. B. SHAW *How to become Mus. Critic* (1960) 211 The public had been educated by Gluck to expect at least a show of seriousness in an *opera seria*. **1911** *Encycl. Brit.* XX. 124/2 *Opera seria* is classical Italian opera with secco-recitative; almost always..on a Greek or Roman subject, and,..with a happy ending.. The only great classic in *opera seria* is Mozart's *Idomeneo*. **1951** M. COOPER *Russian Opera* i. 14 The Empress Catherine,..favoured the opéra comique—the opera of social comment and ideas—rather than the more exclusively musical opera seria. **1975** *New Yorker* 31 Mar. 82/1 Sometime in mid-1780, Mozart was commissioned to write the principal work, an *opera seria*, for the Munich carnival season.

4. *attrib.* and *Comb.* **a.** general, as ***opera ballet***, ***band***, ***bill***, ***-book***, ***-box***, ***chorus***, ***company***, ***-dancer***, ***-goer***, ***-going***, ***hero***, ***-maker***, ***-master***, ***-night***, ***repertory***, ***-singer***, ***-song***, ***stage***, ***ticket***; ***opera-going***, ***-mad*** adjs.

1899 *Daily News* 23 May 5/6 As Lumley truly prognosticated, 1845 saw 'the culminating point in the History of the *opera ballet in England.' Now, in opera, the ballet is a mere divertissement. **1955** *Times* 1 July 7/4 In the production at the Louvre on Tuesday the piece was given in the form of an 'opera-ballet'. **1964** *Conc. Oxf. Dict. Opera* 23/1 So popular did the opera ballet become in Paris that Wagner had to rewrite and develop the opening scene of *Tannhäuser*..to meet the demands of the Parisians. **1798** T. HOLCROFT *Diary* 14 Oct. in *Mem.* (1816) III. 48 Gave young Watts the letters of recommendation for the *opera band. **1814** J. MAYNE *Jrnl.* 2 Sept. (1909) 30 The orchestra consists of nearly sixty performers, whereas our opera band seldom musters forty. **1712** ADDISON *Spect.* No. 405 ¶1 The *Opera Bills for this Day. **1879** GROVE *Dict. Mus.* I. 196 Like Mendelssohn he [Beethoven] was in earnest in pursuit of an *opera-book. **1811** *Times* 21 Jan. 3/2 You have permitted an anonymous paragraph to appear in your columns, reflecting on a noble young lady, and accusing her of..authorising an act of..injustice, by the improper disposal of an *Opera Box... It is a gross..falsehood; neither is it true that this was the cause that induced Mr. Taylor to deprive the Portland family of their Opera box. **1828** J. EBERS *Seven Yrs. King's Theatre* iv. 82 It had been customary with my predecessors to publish, at the commencement of every season, a little book, specifying that boxes were taken for the season by the different subscribers—a sort of Opera-box directory. **1831** PEACOCK *Crotchet Castle* 302, I think an opera box a very substantial comfort. **1865** D. G. ROSSETTI *Let.* 28 June (1965) II. 560 Couldn't you work up the Opera-box design? **1840** H. COCKTON *Life Valentine Vox* xi. 72 His real name is Growlaway. He's in the *Opera chorus, and a regular trump he is too. **1947** A. EINSTEIN *Mus. Romantic Era* xvi. 275 It is an Italian opera chorus; one ought not to think of Handel in connection with it. **1827** W. CLARKE *Every Night Bk.* 146 There are several persons in the *opera-company besides those we have mentioned. **1880** ROCKSTRO in Grove *Dict. Mus.* II. 512/2 A rival Opera Company was established at the 'Little Theatre, in Lincoln's Inn Fields'. **1759** GOLDSM. *Voltaire* Wks. 1881 IV. 11 A kept mistress, an actress, or an *opera dancer generally compose the society. **1853** LYTTON *My Novel* x. xxiv, The walls were covered with..the portraits of opera-dancers. **1710–11** SWIFT *Lett.* (1767) III. 107, I..dined with Ford upon his *Opera-day. **1712** OLDISWORTH *Odes of Horace* VIII. 35/1 Unless some unexpected Copy should step forth like an *Opera God out of a flying Chariot. **1850** 'J. TIMON' *Lorgnette* (ed. 2) i. 21 A prim clergyman, who, though he is not an *Opera-goer, has yet a good ear for a fiddle. **1854** H. MORLEY *Jrnl.* 15 July (1866) 91 The opera-goer who enjoyed that musical farce..now finds the enjoyment of it trebled by the addition of Ronconi's.. drolleries. **1883** *Harper's Mag.* Nov. 887/1 The opera-goer, that is to say, the citizen in an opera hat and an opera frame of mind. **1947** A. EINSTEIN *Mus. Romantic Era* xix. 358 The bourgeois opera-goer of 1880 had not only the opportunity of hearing an international repertory. **1955** P. VINCENT in H. Van Thal *Fanfare for E. Newman* 177 It appears that each opera-goer has his own preference for a particular 'school' of opera. **1975** *Country Life* 13 Nov. 1312/1 For Russian audiences, memories of the book [*sc.* War and Peace] may perhaps give the opera a sort of unity which it lacks for most English opera-goers. **1833** MACAULAY in *Life & Lett.* (1880) I. 359 *Opera-going damsels. **1876** GEO. ELIOT *Dan. Der.* I. II. xviii. 359 It was enough for them to go on in their old way, only having a grand treat of opera-going (to the gallery) when Hans came home on a visit. **1947** A. EINSTEIN *Mus. Romantic Era* xvi. 239 In it the most intimate experience of the soul is made into an *opera* and presented to the opera-going public, to the mass. **1949** *Penguin Music Mag.* VIII. 16 The beginning of my opera-going was marked by outstanding failure. **1955** P. VINCENT in H. Van Thal *Fanfare for E. Newman* 175 The first years of opera-going are among our most stately memories. **1834** J. R. PLANCHÉ *Deep, Deep Sea* in *Extravaganzas* (1879) I. 164 To sing a song—As *Opera heroes choose Always to do, when they've no time to lose. **1855** W. B. WOOD *Pers. Recoll. Stage* v. 113 As the representative of opera heroes..he had no superior. **1768–74** TUCKER *Lt. Nat.* (1834) I. 493 Had I run *opera-mad..or election-mad, I might have found companions enow to keep me in countenance. **1776** J. WALLACE in D. Garrick *Private Corr.* (1832) II. 140 She had objections to both: Saturday was *Opera-night; Monday degraded her. **1716** POPE *Lett. to Jervas* 7 July (1735) I. 253 Some Italian Chymists, Fidlers, Bricklayers, and *Opera-makers. **1813** SIR R. WILSON *Priv. Diary* II. 186 The Crown Prince was still in Leipsic..dressed like an *opera-master. **1822** DE QUINCEY *Confess.* 107 Tuesday and Saturday were the regular *Opera nights. **1898** STAINER & BARRETT *Dict. Mus. Terms* (rev. ed.) 329/2 Their works are still part of every *Opera repertory. **1870** LOWELL *Study Wind.* (1886) 17 The bobolink's..*opera-season is a short one. **1742** FIELDING *Miss Lucy in Town* Wks. 1882 X. 312 One is an *opera-singer. **1737** POPE *Hor. Ep.* II. ii. 11 A perfect genius at an *Opera-song. **1763** D. GARRICK *Let.* in R. B. Peake *Mem. Colman Family* (1841) I. 90 The famous Gabrielli pleased me much; she has a good person, is the best actress I ever saw on an *opera stage, and has the most agreeable voice I ever heard. **1948** *Penguin Mus. Mag.* VII. 58 Wagner..in the end..had to sell out to the commercial opera-stage. **1755** LADY W. W. MONTAGUE in *Poems by Eminent Ladies* II. 170 There was a time (oh! that I could forget!) When *opera-tickets pour'd before my feet. **1820** BYRON *Let. to Murray* 12 Nov., I happened to have a spare Opera ticket.

b. Special combs.: **opera-cloak**, a cloak of rich material worn by ladies at the opera or in going to or returning from evening parties (hence *opera-cloaked* adj.); **opera-girl**, (*a*) a girl or woman who dances in the ballet of an opera; (*b*) *pl.* a greenhouse plant, *Mantisia saltatoria*, called also DANCING-GIRLS; **opera-glass, -glasses**, a small binocular for use at theatres, concerts, etc.; **opera-hat**, a hat suitable for use at the opera; *spec.* a tall hat which folds flat, and when open is kept in shape by springs; a crush-hat; **opera-hood**, a lady's hood for use at operas, or in going to evening parties, etc.; **opera-house**, a theatre for the performance of operas.

1835 DICKENS *Sk. Boz* (1836) 1st Ser. II. 47 There..was the young lady, wrapped up in a *hopera-cloak. **1872** BLACK *Adv. Phaeton* xxvi. 363 Maidens in white with scarlet opera-cloaks. **1760** FOOTE *Minor* I. Wks. 1799 I. 243 An *opera girl is as essential a piece of equipage for a man of fashion as his coach. **1848** THACKERAY *Van. Fair* xvi, Her mother was an opera-girl. **1866** *Treas. Bot.* 815/2 Opera-girls, *Mantisia saltatoria.* **1738** R. SMITH *Optics* 377 There is an instrument sold in the shops which some call an *opera-glass, others a diagonal perspective; it is properly a reflecting perspective, so contrived for viewing a person in a publick place that no one can distinguish who it is you look at. **1842** BRANDE *Dict. Sci.* etc. s.v., The common opera-glass is nothing else than the Galilean telescope, invented by Galileo in 1609. **1810** *Irish Mag.* III. 226 Strutting as gentlemen, by aid of..silk stockings, *opera hats. **1813** *Love Sick Frog* (song) (B.L. Mus. Libr. G. 383. h. (37)) 3 Off he set with his Opera Hat. .. On the road he met with a Rat. **1827** SIR J. BARRINGTON *Pers. Sk.*, I found mine host decked out in his best jacket and a huge opera-hat. **1720** *Lond. Gaz.* No. 5839/3 The *Opera-House in the Hay-Market. **1976** *New Yorker* 9 Feb. 81/1 The decision to present this production in the large opera house of the Academy instead of in the pleasant new theatre downstairs did it no good.

c. Applied to styles of women's underclothing suitable for wearing with evening dress, characterized by low tops and narrow shoulder-straps, as *opera combinations, shape, top.*

1923 *Weekly Dispatch* 18 Feb. 14 (Advt.), Pure Wool Opera Combinations... Ribbon shoulder straps. **1928** *Daily Mail* 31 July 1/1 (Advt.), Artificial silk vest..opera shape. **1921** *Daily Colonist* (Victoria, B.C.) 18 Oct. 19/1 (Advt.), Women's 'Turnbull's' Mixture Combinations, with low neck, short or no sleeves, with opera tops and ankle length. **1923** *Daily Mail* 17 Feb. 4 (Advt.), Ladies' Pure Wool Combinations,..opera tops, ribbon straps. **1968** J. IRONSIDE *Fashion Alphabet* 72 *Vest*..sometimes with shoulder-straps, and known as 'Opera top'.

Hence **'opera** *v.*, to take to the opera.

1853 READE *Chr. Johnstone* 318 He will fête you, and opera you.

‖**opera** (ˈɒpərə), *sb.*[2] pl. of OPUS *sb.* 'work', q.v.

In this sense *operas* is used by Southey, perh. after It. *opera* (sing.) a work (pl. *opere* works).

1808 SOUTHEY *Lett.* (1856) II. 16 The two volumes are in the printer's hands,..one reason..was..to have all my operas in the same size. **1834** *Ibid.* IV. 374 Allan Cunningham has sent me his 'Burns'... My own operas will come into this form when I am gone.

operability (ɒpərəˈbɪlɪtɪ). [f. next + -BILITY.] The state of being operable; *spec.* in *Med.*, suitability for surgical treatment.

1905 *Jrnl. Nerv. & Mental Dis.* XXXII. 481 (*heading*) Brain tumors: a study of clinical and post-mortem records bearing on their operability. **1910** *Practitioner* Jan. 84 The question of operability or otherwise is a matter in which surgeons differ considerably. **1922** *Ann. Surg.* LXXVI. 396 In estimating the final value of any operative procedure for the cure of cancer, the operability rate is the crux of the situation. **1952** *Sci. Amer.* Sept. 104/2 The gun parts could be interchanged among all 10 without affecting the guns' operability. **1972** *Brit. Jrnl. Dis. Chest* LXVI. 162 (*heading*) The value of mediastinoscopy in assessing operability in carcinoma of the lung. **1975** J. HOWLETT *Christmas Spy* III. vi. 96 Zürich had been correct about the operability of two-way traffic.

'operable, *a.* and *sb.* [f. L. type **operābilis*, f. *operārī* to OPERATE: cf. F. *opérable.*]

A. *adj.* **1.** That may or should be operated or done; practicable.

1646 SIR T. BROWNE *Pseud. Ep.* I. iii. 9 Being uncapable of operable circumstances..they onely gaze upon the visible successe. **1911** H. S. HARRISON *Queed* xiii. 160 How could this principle be..reduced to an operable law? **1961** *Medicine in Nat. Defense* (Final Rep. Office of U.S. Asst. Secretary of Defense) vi. 69 Visual and operable training aids..were used in support of Army Medical Service mass casualty exercises.

2. *Med.* Capable of being treated by an operation.

1904 *Arch. Middlesex Hosp.* III. 163 Patients..are admitted in practically all cases for operable cancer. **1925** W. DEEPING *Sorrell & Son* xxxviii. 381 'But, my dear sir, if the thing is operable—' 'No, thank you. Besides, it is only a question of a few days. If you can help me to fight the pain.' **1925** H. GILFORD *Tumours & Cancers* xxvi. 580 Of operable uterine cancers as large a number can be destroyed by the [radium and X-]rays as by surgical operation. **1973** *Cancer* XXXI. 180/2 Patients with carcinoma of the cervix are admitted..only if..the tumor is considered operable and the patient potentially curable by surgery.

†**B.** *sb.* Something that may or should be done; a matter or point of practice. *Obs.*

1677 GALE *Crt. Gentiles* II. IV. 6 So Aquinas 'Synesis or sensate judgment imports a right judgment about particular operables'.

operameter (ɒpəˈræmɪtə(r)). *Mech.* [irreg. f. L. *opera* works + Gr. μέτρον measure.] A device for registering the number of revolutions made by a shaft, axle, or wheel, the strokes of a piston, the copies delivered from a printing-press, etc.

1829 *Patents* in *Ann. Reg.* 548/2 S. Walker, Beeston, Leeds, for an improved apparatus which he denominates 'an operameter'. **1839** URE *Dict. Arts, Operameter*,..It consists of a train of toothed wheels and pinions enclosed in a box, having indexes attached to the central arbor, like the hands of a clock, and a dial plate; whereby the number of rotations of a shaft projecting from the posterior part of the box is shown. **1875** KNIGHT *Dict. Mech.* 1562/1.

operance (ˈɒpərəns). *rare.* [f. as OPERANT *a.* + -ANCE.] The action of operating; operation.

1612 *Two Noble K.* I. iii, The elements That..do effect Rare issues by their operance. **1825** COLERIDGE in *Lit. Rem.* (1836) II. 344 An agency antecedent in order of operance. **1840** J. H. GREEN *Vital Dynam.* 23 The same power is at work under different conditions of operance.

operancy (ˈɒpərənsɪ). *rare.* [f. as prec. + -ANCY.] The quality or condition of being operant; operance, operation.

1810 COLERIDGE in *Lit. Rem.* (1838) III. 303 Taylor..is always too shy of this 'Grace of God': he..never admits it any separate operancy *per se.* **1847–9** TODD *Cycl. Anat.* IV. 511/2 Function..implying by that word an immediate organic operancy. **1878** DOWDEN *Stud. Lit.* 127 When all intellection and all operancy of will seem to be suspended.

operand (ˈɒpərænd). *Math.* [ad. L. *operandum*, neuter gerundive of *operārī* to OPERATE.] A quantity or symbol to be operated on.

1886 ALDIS *Solid Geom.* xiv. (ed. 4) 238 The operation of multiplication by a vector is distributive both as regards the operator and the operand. **1956** BERKELEY & WAINWRIGHT *Computers* II. 37 The first two registers receive the operands, or numbers operated on. **1965** *Language* XLI. 377 There is also a zero (and affix) causative in which the *W* contains no new verb, but the *N* and *V* of the operand sentence are permuted: *The children sat → He seated the children.* **1969** P. B. JORDAIN *Condensed Computer Encycl.* 354 In the mathematical operation of division, the dividend and divisor are two operands. *Ibid.*, Most digital computer instructions have one or more operands, each indicated by a field within the instruction. **1973** D. U. WILDE *Introd. Computing Probl.* v. 106 The *or* operation is said to be true if either or both of its operands are true; otherwise, it is false. The *and* operation is true if both operands are true; otherwise, it is false.

operant (ˈɒpərənt), *a.* and *sb.* [ad. L. *operāntem*, pr. pple. of *operārī* to OPERATE.]

A. *adj.* **a.** That operates, works, or produces effects; in operation, operative; †powerful in effect (*obs.*).

1602 SHAKS. *Ham.* III. ii. 184 My operant Powers my Functions leaue to do. **1607** —— *Timon* IV. iii. 25 Sawce his pallate With thy most operant Poyson. **1677** GALE *Crt. Gentiles* IV. 427 This efficacious medicinal grace..they terme it sometimes..'the operant and cooperant grace'. **1810** COLERIDGE in *Lit. Rem.* (1838) III. 305 The Roman doctrine, that the priest's absolution is operant, and not simply declarative. **1894** G. MACDONALD *Lilith* xvi. (1895) 119 No conscious courage was operant in me.

b. *Psychol.* Involving the modification of behaviour by the reinforcing or inhibiting effect of its consequences; opp. *respondent.* Cf. INSTRUMENTAL *a.* 7.

1937 [See B. 1 b below]. **1938** B. F. SKINNER *Behavior of Organisms* xiii. 439 Comparing conditioning of Type S (which is largely, if not wholly, respondent) with Type R (which is apparently wholly operant). **1941** *Amer. Jrnl. Psychol.* LIV. 568 (*heading*) An automatic device for providing motivation and reinforcement in operant conditioning. **1959** *Jrnl. Exper. Analysis of Behavior* II. 57 Young and Boycott (1955) describe behavior in the octopus which is almost certainly operant in nature, i.e., not elicited, but maintained by its consequences. **1963** P. SWARTZ *Psychol.* x. 208/2 In contrast to respondent conditioning, in which the reinforcing agent is coupled with the conditioned stimulus, in operant learning the appearance of the reinforcer is dependent upon the occurrence of the response. **1964** RATNER & DENNY *Compar. Psychol.* xi. 566 A common distinction between instrumental and operant learning, at least in the laboratory, is that the animal is free to respond at any time in the operant situation but is usually given discrete trials when the learning is labeled instrumental. **1968** *Listener* 29 Aug. 265/2 The sickest man in the hospital was selected to be..the first experiment in 'operant conditioning' therapy on a severely regressed and catatonic schizophrenic in Britain. **1970** HINSIE & CAMPBELL *Psychiatric Dict.* (ed. 4) 150/2 It has been suggested that many forms of psychotherapy are applications of operant conditioning... The patient learns what the therapist expects or wants to hear, and he modifies his own speech and behavior accordingly. **1975** *Nature* 20 Mar. 219/1 Behaviourism..puts us in a position to alter and improve the condition of mankind if only we will apply its commanding insights..into the agency of such cardinal notions as reinforcement and operant behaviour.

B. *sb.* **1. a.** One who, or that which, operates, works, or exerts force or influence.

1700 S. PARKER *Six Philos. Ess.* 96 Where the Operation is essentially one, the Operant cannot be more. **1871** G. MACDONALD *Wilf. Cumb.* I. x. 89 Cupboard love is not..always the most powerful operant on the childish mind.

b. *Psychol.* An item of behaviour that is held to be not a response to a prior stimulus but something which is initially spontaneous on the part of the organism, 'operating on' or affecting the environment so as to produce consequences which may reinforce or inhibit its recurrence.

1937 B. F. SKINNER in *Jrnl. Gen. Psychol.* XVI. 274 There is also a kind of response which occurs spontaneously in the absence of any stimulation with which it may be specifically correlated... It does not mean that we cannot find a stimulus that will elicit such behaviour but that none is operative at the time the behaviour is observed. It is the nature of this kind of behaviour that it should occur without an eliciting stimulus, although discriminative stimuli are practically inevitable after conditioning... I shall call such a unit an operant and the behavior in general, operant behavior. **1938** —— *Behavior of Organisms* i. 21 If the occurrence of an operant is followed by presentation of a reinforcing stimulus, the strength is increased. **1941** *Amer. Jrnl. Psychol.* LIV. 568 Aversion drives..offer certain advantages which other drives, *e.g.* hunger and thirst, do not... Reinforcement can follow immediately the emission of the operant; under hunger motivation several responses may intervene between the operant that is measured and its subsequent reënforcement. **1967** KOESTLER *Ghost in Machine* i. 8 Operant strength is usually measured, for technical reasons, by the 'rate of extinction'—how long the rat will persist in pressing the lever after the supply of pellets has been stopped. **1972** *Jrnl. Social Psychol.* LXXXVI. 11 Recent analyses have conceived of conforming behavior as an instrumental response directed toward the attainment of functional goals... It can be considered a kind of social operant, which should change..with changes in the characteristics of reinforcement.

2. A workman: = OPERATIVE B. 2. *rare.*

1831 LAMB *Elia* Ser. II. *Newsp. 35 Yrs. Ago*, No fractious operants ever turned out for half the tyranny which this necessity exercised upon us.

†**ope'rarious**, *a. Obs. rare*$^{-0}$. = next.

1656 BLOUNT *Glossogr.*, *Operarious*,..pertaining to the workman, done with labor.

†**'operary**, *a. Obs.* [ad. L. *operāri-us*, f. *opus, oper-* work: see -ARY.] Pertaining to or based on manual operations or practice (as opposed to scientific theory); practical.

1612 COTTA *Disc. Dang. Phys.* I. v. 36 Esteeming themselues deserueing well for the operary uses of a skillfull and well exercised hand in wounds. **1640** G. WATTS tr. *Bacon's Adv. Learn.* III. v. 167 A Mechanicall Knowledge, which is meerely empericall, and operary not depending on Physique.

'ope,ratable, *a. rare.* [f. OPERAT(E *v.* + -ABLE.] Capable of being operated (on); operable.

1895 *Funk's Stand. Dict.*, *Operatable*, that can be operated or worked; operable. **1932** JOYCE *Let.* 12 July (1966) III. 248 The right eye was still operatable 20 months ago. Now the cataract is total.

operate (ˈɒpəreɪt), *v.* [f. L. *operāt-*, ppl. stem of *operārī* to work, labour, take pains, bestow pains on; in late L., also, to have effect, be active, produce by working, cause, f. *opus, oper-* work.]

I. Intransitive senses.

1. To be in working, exercise force or influence, produce an effect, act, work.

1606 SHAKS. *Tr. & Cr.* v. iii. 108 Th' effect doth operate another way. **1611** —— *Cymb.* v. v. 196 Mine Italian braine Gan in your duller Britaine operate Most vildely. **1671** BLAGRAVE *Astrol. Physic* 21 The..Influence of the Moon unto any planet doth begin to operate when she is within ten degrees aspecting any planet. **1794** PALEY *Evid.* (1825) II. 418 Religion operates most upon those of whom history knows the least. **1818** JAS. MILL *Brit. India* II. v. ix. 713 The whole force of the motives,..which operate to their appointment, must operate likewise to connivance at their faults. **1849** MACAULAY *Hist. Eng.* iii. I. 407 The revolutionary spirit, ceasing to operate in politics. **1874** MORLEY *Compromise* (1886) 119 Though themselves invisible to the outer world, they [convictions] may yet operate with magnetic force..upon other parts of our belief.

2. Of persons: To bring force or influence to bear *on* or *upon*; †formerly also simply, to exert oneself *to do* something.

1650 HOWELL *Giraffi's Rev. Naples* I. 82 The Archbishop ..did desire His Excellence wold operate to bring to a period that solemn ceremony. **1783** WATSON *Philip III* (1793) II. v. 100 They endeavoured to counteract its effects by operating upon his natural ambition. **1790** BEATSON *Nav. & Mil. Mem.* I. 246 He knew the Highland chieftans well, and how to operate on them. **1833** *Act 3 & 4 Will. IV*, c. 46 §61 An account to be opened in the name of the commissioners, and to be operated upon by the treasurer for the time.

3. To produce the intended or proper effect; esp. of drugs and medicines, as cathartics, etc.: To act.

1706 PHILLIPS, *To operate*, to work or stir the Humours of the Body, as Physick does. **1783** J. C. SMYTH in *Med. Commun.* I. 142 The bolus has operated four or five times. **1793** SMEATON *Edystone L.* §307 Everything, regarding the light, operated in a proper manner. **1804** ABERNETHY *Surg. Obs.* 186 He had taken purging medicine..which had operated. **1849** MACAULAY *Hist. Eng.* v. I. 582 The Act of Attainder was a remedy which could not operate till all danger was over.

4. a. To perform a practical operation or series of operations: see OPERATION 5. Const. *on*, *upon*.

1674 R. GODFREY *Inj. & Ab. Physic* Pref., I by diligent observance, by Operating,..having gain'd the knowledg of some Injuries in Physick. **1832** PORTER *Porcelain & Gl.* ix. 239 It is necessary to operate upon both sides of the plate. **1870** JEVONS *Elem. Logic* ii. 9 Instruments with which we must operate in reasoning. **1882** *Rep. to Ho. Repr. Prec. Met. U.S.* 271 An arrastra is now being built to operate upon the ores of the Wayup.

b. *Surg.*: see OPERATION 6.

1799 *Med. Jrnl.* II. 157 Vesalius,..in his 'Chirurg. magn.' ..describes the whole process of operating. **1826** A. C. HUTCHISON *Pract. Obs. Surg.* 314 *note*, A boy was operated upon in Haslar hospital, and recovered. **1894** *Westm. Gaz.* 4 July 2/3 The phrase 'When in doubt, operate', was, I believe, first made use of by Sir William Lawrence with regard to the methods to be adopted in treating cases of strangulated hernia.

c. *Mil.* and *Naval.* To carry on warlike operations: see OPERATION 7. Also *transf.*, of a gambler, criminal, etc.

1808 [see OPERATING *ppl. a.*]. **1863** P. BARRY *Dockyard Econ.* 137 Against no Power whatever could we operate successfully on the coast with our *Minotaurs*, our *Valiants*, or our *Warriors*. **1883** SWEET & KNOX *On Mexican Mustang through Texas* (1884) i. 16 This high-toned and honorable desperado 'operated' in one of the inland cities of Texas two years ago. **1885** *Manch. Exam.* 22 June 5/4 A Russian army operating against India..could be assailed on the flank. **1901** 'J. FLYNT' *World of Graft* 19 The West Side grafters.. who have 'operated' in Chicago. **1955** D. W. MAURER in *Publ. Amer. Dial. Soc.* XXIV. 30 There are the *lone wolves*, who are professionals, but who operate predominantly alone, without the support of a mob,..for example, jewel thieves of some types, swindlers, expert forgers. **1975** T. ALLBEURY *Special Collection* xi. 73, I set up a network for him dealing with industrial espionage. It operated into West Germany.

d. To deal or speculate in stocks or shares; to buy and sell commodities as a broker.

1859 *Athenæum* 23 July 113 A bull in the same jargon, is one who operates for a rise. **1868** SEYD *Bullion* 480 If between these he sees profits he operates. **1889** *Harper's Mag.* Aug. 448/1 Do you think all men who are what you call operating around are like that? **1961** in WEBSTER.

e. To function, to fulfil a function, to act. (Closely related to sense 4 a.)

1931 J. T. ADAMS *Epic of Amer.* viii. 221 There were..a thousand boats operating regularly on the Mississippi. **1932** [see CYLINDER *sb.* 6]. **1932** N. M. BUTLER *Looking Forward* xi. 117 Government officials operating in all parts of the country. **1971** *Gloss. Electrotechnical, Power Terms (B.S.I.)* I. iii. 13 A relay operates when it completes its designed function in a specified output circuit(s). **1972** *Daily Tel.* 16 Nov. 7/1 Extra buses and Underground trains will operate on most routes. **1976** *National Observer* (U.S.) 2 Oct. 18/3 Rudderless and without a keel, the 195-foot craft operates similar to a flat-bottomed fishing boat.

II. Transitive senses.

5. To effect or produce by action or the exertion of force or influence; to bring about, accomplish, work.

1637 SALTONSTALL *Eusebius' Constantine* 160 Tis an generall position that that which..hath no being cannot operate, or effect any thing. **1642** MILTON *Argt. conc. Militia* 12 Now plotting to operate the ruine of the Protestant Religion. **1799** N. DRAKE in Beddoes *Contrib. Phys. & Med. Knowl.* 478 The digitalis was supposed to have operated a cure. **1889** *Nature* 19 Sept. 510/2 Energy in the form of light operates changes in the surface of bodies.

6. To cause or actuate the working of; to work (a machine, etc.). Chiefly *U.S.*

1864 WEBSTER s.v., To operate a machine. **1872** *Omaha Bee* in *Times* 28 Nov. 7/3 The monster [steam snow plough] ..will be operated by three of the heaviest engines on the road. **1876** PREECE & SIVEWRIGHT *Telegraphy* 285 Every current sent on that circuit operates each instrument alike and simultaneously. **1886** *Troy (U.S.) Daily Times* 24 Dec. 3 Estimates of the cost of operating the cars..by the motor will be furnished. **1888** *Scribner's Mag.* Aug. 187/1 The number of arc lamps which are nightly operated by the different electric lighting companies in the city of New York is probably over five thousand.

7. To direct the working of; to manage, conduct, work (a railway, business, etc.); to carry out or through, direct to an end (a principle, an undertaking, etc.). orig. *U.S.*

1880 *Travellers' Off. Guide U.S. & Canada* July 91 The Roads owned and operated by the Pennsylvania Railroad. **1883** F. A. WALKER *Pol. Econ.* 432 State railways and private companies' lines were operated side by side. **1887** *Lit. World* (U.S.) 6 Aug. 248/1 How long is it to be before the government of the United States will operate the telegraph system of the country as it operates the mails? **1891** *Leeds Merc.* 19 Sept. 11 The..Company operate a large foundry. **1948** 'N. SHUTE' *No Highway* i. 19 C.A.T.O. are operating five or six of them [*sc.* aircraft] on the Atlantic route. **1971** D. POTTER *Brit. Eliz. Stamps* xii. 130 Cambrian Airways.. took over the operation of some internal routes previously operated only by BEA. **1974** *Anderson* (S. Carolina) *Independent* 20 Apr. 2A/1 Joe King, who operates a hardware store 13 miles south of Greenville on S.C. 25, fired four bullets into their car as they fled.

8. *Surg.* To operate on. (See sense 4 b.)

1908 *Practitioner* Sept. 423, I know of two cases of pyelitis which were operated in mistake for appendicitis. **1915** W. OWEN *Let.* 1 Mar. (1967) 324 Dr Denucé (who operated Sarah Bernhardt—and Charlie). **1925** SIMMONS & FISHBEIN *Art & Pract. Medical Writing* v. 43 'Operate' means, and is generally synonymous with, 'to work': the terms nearly always may be used interchangeably. The surgeon who would hesitate to say 'I worked this patient' says, without a blush, 'I operated this patient.' **1930** *Amer. Speech* V. 289 Of those questioned 26½ per cent used 'operated him', 40 per cent used 'operated on', and 33⅓ per cent used 'operated upon him'.

operatee (ˌɒpərəˈtiː). [f. OPERATE + -EE[1].] One who is operated on, the subject of an operation.

1831 TRELAWNEY *Adv. Younger Son* xxx, Not only the operator, but the operatee, is bountifully compensated. **1883** FR. GALTON *Hum. Faculty* 36 The tests..give an approximate measure of the discrimination with which the operatee habitually employs his senses.

operatic (ɒpəˈrætɪk), *a.*[1] and *sb.* [irreg. f. OPERA, app. after *dramatic.*] **A.** *adj.* Pertaining to, or of the nature of, opera.

1749 in *Priv. Lett. Ld. Malmesbury* I. 74 My sister went with me last night to hear the Oratorio,..it is in the light operatic style. **1858** GLADSTONE *Homer* III. 512 Homer has the full force and play of the drama, Virgil is essentially operatic. **1861** *Sat. Rev.* 14 Dec. 610 The plot..affords opportunities for effective operatic treatment.

B. as *sb. pl.* The production or performance of operas.

1907 N. MUNRO *Daft Days* xvi. 142 He says he could never die a Christian death if he had to listen to them at their operatics through the wall. **1920** *Punch* 10 Mar. 197/1 Operatics. It has been suggested before now that Opera might be improved if the singing were done behind the scenes and the performance on the stage were carried out in dumb show by competent actors. **1928** *Daily Express* 6 Nov. 9/3 This is a real event in London's amateur operatics.

ope'ratic, *a.*[2] *rare.* [f. L. *operāt-*, ppl. stem of *operārī* to OPERATE + -IC.] = OPERATIVE *a.* 6.

1823-27 T. ARNOLD *Later Rom. Commw.* (1882) II. 446 The place of our labourers and operatic manufacturers being almost entirely supplied by slaves.

†ope'ratical, *a. Obs.* [See -ICAL.] = OPERATIC *a.*[1]

1730-36 BAILEY (folio), *Operatical*, of or belonging to an opera. **1758** *Herald* No. 25 (1758) II. 155 So pretty a farcical, operatical, pantomimical tragedy. **1807** *Director* I. 233 The operatical Beau is constantly seen at the King's Theatre on the evening preceding the Sabbath. **1826** *Examiner* 179/1 A new operatical play was produced.

ope'ratically, *adv.* [f. prec. + -LY[2].] In an operatic manner; from an operatic point of view.

1821 *Examiner* 1 Apr. 204/2 Were we to speak, operatically..we should observe that [etc.]. **1883** *My Trivial Life* I. v. 85 [She] made the great mistake of dressing herself and her daughter operatically.

operating (ˈɒpəreɪtɪŋ), *vbl. sb.* [f. OPERATE + -ING[1].] **a.** The action of the vb. OPERATE; an instance of this, an operation.

1674 R. GODFREY *Inj. & Ab. Physic* 39 After long, tedious, and chargeable Operatings to no purpose, he pulls down his Laboratory. **1913** ROBERTS & SMITH (*title*) Practical locomotive operating.

b. *attrib.* and *Comb.*, as ***operating altitude, box, control, costs, expenses, height, revenue, room***; **operating crew** (see quot.); **operating system** *Computers*, a set of programs for organizing the resources and activities of a computer; **operating-table** (see quot.); **operating-theatre**, a room constructed for surgical operations before a class.

1956 D. E. CHARLWOOD *No Moon Tonight* 15 Where the planes were circling, climbing steadily to *operating altitude. **1918** 'Q' *Foe-Farrell* 117, I..found..the *operating box and the gallery, switched on the lights, and shinned down a pillar to the stalls. **1930** *Daily Express* 6 Sept. 5/5 The '*operating control' can be readily grasped from the sketch. **1913** ROBERTS & SMITH *Pract. Locomotive Operating* 26 *Operating costs. **1972** *Lebende Sprachen* XVII. 34/1 US *operating costs, operating expenses*—BE working expenses. **1975** 'D. JORDAN' *Black Account* xi. 54 Condon said, 'Let's settle the truck like this, then,' and wrote... Initial operating costs and interest: $85 million. **1965** *Operating crew [see *flight crew* s.v. FLIGHT *sb.*[1] 15]. **1869** *Bradshaw's Railway Manual* XXI. 417 The *operating expenses are about 51 per cent. of the gross earnings. **1909** *Daily Chron.* 25 Feb. 3/5 At the same time the operating expenses had gone down from 67·9 per cent. of gross receipts in 1907 to 54·5 in 1908. **1948** 'N. SHUTE' *No Highway* iv. 111 I'm prepared to shut down the inboard engines after climbing up to *operating height. **1930** *Daily Express* 9 Sept. 10/2 *Operating revenues show a gain of about 40 per cent. at £556,936, compared with £389,518, and while profit on sales of securities is lower, the gross earnings have expanded by nearly £80,000 to £740,582. **1889** *Anthony's Photogr. Bull.* II. 305 It is just in the *operating room..that the skill of the photographer comes into play. **1961** *Computer Jrnl.* IV. 222 (*heading*) The Manchester University Atlas *operating system. **1963** GREGORY & VAN HORN *Automatic Data-Processing Syst.* (ed. 2) xii. 477 Operating Systems are programs that increase machine operating efficiency by controlling the compilation and execution of programs, supervising input and output operations, converting data from one medium to another, testing programs to debug them, and simulating the operation of one processor on another. **1973** D. U. WILDE *Introd. Computing* ii. 43 When a computer system is under the control of a monitor or operating system, the computer operator loads programs into the card reader, mounts tape reels onto tape drives, and removes results from the printer while the monitor schedules the work flow and keeps the CPU busy. **1875** KNIGHT *Dict. Mech.* 1562/1 *Operating-table (*Surgical*), one on which the patient is placed to expose prominently the portion to be operated upon. **1861** *Times* 23 Aug., The weekly board of the hospital ..will also provide a convenient *operating theatre.

'operating, *ppl. a.* [f. as prec. + -ING[2].] That operates (in senses of the vb.).

1808 WELLINGTON *Let. to Castlereagh* 5 Sept. in Gurw. *Desp.* (1837) IV. 142 This army..would be the operating army against what I have supposed to be the French operating army. **1825** J. NICHOLSON *Operat. Mechanic* 10 The operating force at A acting in the direction of A D. **1897** *Allbutt's Syst. Med.* III. 975 Both to the physician and the operating surgeon. **1904** *Daily Chron.* 16 July 7/3 The operating company is to take over the tunnel before the end of the month.

operation (ɒpəˈreɪʃən). [a. OF. *operation*, *-cion* action, deed (14th c., Oresme), ad. L. *operātiōn-em*, n. of action f. *operārī* to OPERATE.]

†1. Action, performance, work, deed. *Obs.*

c **1386** CHAUCER *Wife's T.* 292 Folk ne doon hir operacion Alwey as dooth the fyr lo in his kynde. **1432-50** tr. *Higden* (Rolls) VII. 155 Everyche operacion or dede of man awe to be ponderate after the intencion of the doer. **1483** CAXTON *G. de la Tour* H j b, To nourysshe the orphanes or faderles.. is an operacion of mysericorde. **1564-78** BULLEYN *Dial. agst. Pest.* (1888) 35 Election goeth before operation or worke. **1567** *Triall Treas.* (1850) 6 To horrible besides is thy operation.

2. a. Working; exertion of force, energy, or influence; action, activity, agency; manner of working, the way in which anything works.

1390 GOWER *Conf.* III. 118 Of this constellacioun The verray operacioun Availeth. **1432-50** tr. *Higden* (Rolls) II. 177 A man and the worlde be assimilate..in operation virtualle. **1526** TINDALE *1 Cor.* xii. 6 There are divers manners off operacions and yet but one God which worketh all thynges. **1553** EDEN *Treat. Newe Ind.* (Arb.) 14 His [a diamond's] vertue is to bewray poisons, and to frustrate thopperacion therof. **1611** TOURNEUR *Ath. Trag.* v. i. Wks. 1878 I. 133 The Starres whose operations make The fortunes and the destinies of men. **1744** HARRIS *Three Treat.* i. (1765) 20 Can there possibly be Operation, without Motion and Change? **1818** CRUISE *Digest* (ed. 2) I. 465 The statute 29 Cha. II. did not extend to trusts raised by operation of law. **1824** R. STUART *Hist. Steam Engine* 118 The operation of the condenser pump is very simple. **1860** TYNDALL *Glac.* I. xxvii. 213 Suggesting the operation of intelligence amid that scene of desolation.

b. The condition of being operative or in working. Chiefly in the phrases ***in operation, to come into operation.***

1818 JAS. MILL *Brit. India* II. v. ii. 349 The operation of the new constitution..was ordained to commence. **1836** P. M. LATHAM *Lect Clin. Med.* xiii. (L.), It displays a power different in kind from that of blood letting, and coming into operation..after blood-letting has done all it can. **1878** HUXLEY *Physiogr.* 80 Many other natural and artificial processes in daily operation. **1885** *Manch. Exam.* 16 Sept. 5/2 The sixpenny telegram rate will come into operation in the course of a fortnight.

3. a. Power to operate or work; capacity of producing effects or a particular effect; efficacy, influence, virtue, force. Now chiefly of legal instruments.

1509 HAWES *Past. Pleas.* I. (Percy Soc.) 9 An olde antiquitie,..When..nature..More stronger had her operacion Than she had nowe in her digression. **1542-3** *Act 34 & 35 Hen. VIII*, c. 8 §1 Endued with the knowledge of the nature kinde, & operacion of certein herbes, rootes, & waters. **1606** SHAKS. *Ant. & Cl.* IV. xv. 26 If Knife, Drugges, Serpents haue Edge, sting, or operation. **1607** TOPSELL *Four-f. Beasts* (1658) 199 Goats fat is better then Swines, not because it hath more operation in it to expell the grief, but by reason it is thick. **1660** N. INGELO *Bentivolio & Urania* II. (1682) 91 Toads are sometimes found in the midst of a firm stone, and give it Operation. **1796** BURKE *Regic. Peace* i. Wks. VIII. 161 That heartless and dispirited people, whom Lord Somers had represented..as dead in energy and operation. **1884** LD. SELBORNE in *Law Times Rep.* L. 3/1 He cannot..enlarge, in his own favour, the legal or equitable operation of the instrument.

b. The effect or result produced; influence *on* something. Now *rare* or *Obs.*

1605 BACON *Adv. Learn.* I. iii. §4 Studies have an influence and operation upon the manners of those that are conversant in them. **1655** FULLER *Ch. Hist.* I. i. §4 The Bards..played excellently to their Songs on their Harps; whereby they had great Operation on the Vulgar. **1656** EARL MONM. tr. *Boccalini's Advts. fr. Parnass.* I. xiv. (1674) 17 Though many remedies had been applyed..yet none of them had procured the desired operation. **1770** *Junius Lett.* xxxix. 199 We should..have..felt the operation of a precedent. **1831** BREWSTER *Nat. Magic* ii. (1833) 29 Among the affections of the eye which..deceive..those also who witness their operation, may be enumerated the insensibility of the eye to particular colours.

4. a. A particular form or kind of activity; a mode of action; an active process, vital or natural.

1594 HOOKER *Eccl. Pol.* I. xvi. § 5 The actions of men are of sundry distinct kinds..There are in men operations, some natural, some rational. **1677** GALE *Crt. Gentiles* IV. 30 Every thing manifestes its life by that operation which is most proper to it. **1697** POTTER *Antiq. Greece* II. xiii. (1715) 304 The Animal Spirits, which are the Instruments of Sensation, and all other Animal Operations. **1785** REID *Intell. Powers* I. i. 221 By the operations of the mind we under-stand every mode of thinking of which we are conscious. **1878** HUXLEY *Physiogr.* 76 During the operation of rusting, something must be absorbed by the metal. **1878** BROWNING *La Saisiaz* 500 Would'st thou live now, regularly draw thy breath! For suspend the operation, straight law's breach results in death.

b. *Psychol.* A mental activity whereby the effect of actions or ideas is logically understood or predicted, esp. with reference to the supposed stages of a child's development; also ***concrete operations, formal operations*** (see esp. quots. 1960, 1963). Cf. PREOPERATIONAL *a.*

1930 M. GABAIN tr. *Piaget's Child's Concept. Phys. Causality* IV. 301 At each stage of intellectual development we can distinguish roughly two groups of operations. **1953** MAYS & WHITEHEAD tr. *Piaget's Logic & Psychol.* ii. 8 Psychologically, operations are actions which are internalizable, reversible, and coordinated into systems characterized by laws which apply to the system as a whole. **1960** J. S. BRUNER *Beyond Information Given* (1974) xxiii. 415 Concrete operations, though they are guided by the logic of classes..are means for structuring only immediately present reality. **1963** J. H. FLAVELL *Developmental Psychol. J. Piaget* iii. 86 The period of formal operations (11–15)... The adolescent can deal effectively not only with the reality before him..but also with the world of pure possibility. **1975** J. W. BRUNK *Child & Adolesc. Devel.* vi. 252 In the period of concrete operations (approximate ages 7–11), the child becomes capable of logical thought processes that can be applied to concrete problems.

5. a. The performance of something of practical or mechanical nature, esp. as a practical application of a science or art, or as a scientific experiment or demonstration.

c **1386** CHAUCER *Sqr.'s T.* 122 He wayted many a constellacion Er he had doon this operacion. *c* **1420** *Pallad. on Husb.* VII. 115 Ek in this mone is maad castracion Of calues..Therynne is subtil operacion. **1555** EDEN *Decades* 181 They..vsed certeine secreate magicall operations. **1646** RECORDE, etc. *Gr. Arts* 83 For your further practise..behold these operations, which I have wrought to prime minutes. **1674** DRYDEN *Prol. to Univ. Oxford* 12 Your theories are here to practice brought; As in mechanic operations wrought. **1828** J. H. MOORE *Pract. Navig.* (ed. 20) 236 If the latitude found thus differs considerably from the latitude by account, it will be proper to repeat the operation. **1873** HAMERTON *Intell. Life* x. iii. (1875) 353 We ought to remember what a slow and painful operation reading is to the uneducated. **1927** P. W. BRIDGMAN *Logic Mod. Physics* i. 5 To find the length of an object, we have to perform certain physical operations. The concept of length is therefore fixed when the operations by which length is measured are fixed. **1935** *Psychol. Rev.* XLII. 517 Only those constructs based upon operations which are public and repeatable are admitted to the body of science. **1967** *Encycl. Philos.* V. 544/1 By the end of the nineteenth century, however, scientists had accepted the view that if we cannot devise operations which would disclose whether or not space was Euclidean, then no definite geometrical properties can be assigned to space.

b. A business transaction, esp. one of speculative character: cf. OPERATE 4 d. Also more generally, a business activity or enterprise. Also *transf.* orig. *U.S.*

1832 *Reg. Deb. Congress U.S.* 22nd Congress 2 Sess. App. 107/1 The liability to be called upon for large advances, for the above operation,..makes it absolutely necessary that the limit should be strictly attended to. **1848** W. ARMSTRONG *Stocks* 11 We conceive that this operation [*sc.* betting] is too well understood to need any particular explanation. **1851** C. CIST *Sk. Cincinnati in 1851* 236 Such is the extent of the operations of this firm. **1863** *All the Year Round* VIII. 499 Just now there's an operation coming off West, in which you could try your wings. **1876** HOLLAND *Sev. Oaks* xi. 142 It was all an acute business operation with him. **1889** *Harper's Mag.* Aug. 448/1 One is an operation, and the other is embezzlement. **1911** J. C. LINCOLN *Cap'n Warren's Wards* xi. 178, I judged..that you were well enough acquainted with Wall Street to know that queer operations take place there. **1928** F. A. BRADFORD *Money* xv. 283 The open market operations of the reserve banks. **1938** J. B. WILLIAMS *Theory of Investment Value* ii. 10 The rate of operations never precedes stock prices. **1960** 'E. MCBAIN' *Give Boys Great Big Hand* iv. 30 A photo of the bag on the front pages ..might not be bad for our operation... You can't buy that sort of advertising space, now can you? **1977** 'J. LE CARRÉ' *Hon. Schoolboy* xviii. 442 The spearhead of the operation will be handled by ourselves.

6. *Surg.* An act or a series of acts performed upon an organic body either with the hand alone or by means of an instrument, with the object of remedying deformity or injury, curing or preventing disease, or relieving pain.

Surgical operations frequently bear the name of the person who first performed or described them, indicating the particular mode of treatment introduced by him for a special disease: e.g. *Batley's, Buchanan's, Lister's operation.*

1597 A. M. tr. *Guillemeau's Fr. Chirurg.* 1 b/2 This worde operatione is an artificialle and normaticke applicatione wrought by the handes on mans bodye, wherwith the decayed health is restored. **1655** CULPEPPER *Pract. Phys.* I. ii. 11 Manual Operations, or Chyrurgery. **1707** *Reflex. upon Ridicule* 67 What Curses might not the Physician expect, who should perform so wonderful an Operation? **1806** *Med. Jrnl.* XV. 313 The Rev. M. Le François..having become an expert inoculator, instructed them how to perform the operation. **1863** *Macm. Mag.* May 25 [He] knew how to treat a patient after an operation as well as antecedently to it.

7. a. *Mil.* and *Naval.* A series of warlike or strategic acts; a movement. Also, the strategic movement of troops, ships, etc.; the people concerned with such movements. Freq. *attrib.* See also *combined operation.*

1749 FIELDING *Tom Jones* IX. v, She again began her operations. **1781** GIBBON *Decl. & F.* xxiv. (1869) I. 683 Their subsequent operations were left to the discretion of the generals. **1811** WELLINGTON *Let. to Earl Liverpool* 11 Sept. in Gurw. *Desp.* (1838) VIII. 270, I had detained the 85th..in consequence of..the prospect of an early operation. **1839** ALISON *Hist. Europe* (1850) VII. xlii. §37. 119 Not in regular battles with the English fleet, but in detached operations in smaller armaments. **1867** SMYTH *Sailor's Word-bk.*, *Line of operations*, in strategy, the line an army follows to attain its objective point. **1885** U. S. GRANT *Pers. Mem.* xxi. I. 286 The true line of operations for us was up the Tennessee and Cumberland rivers. **1915** R. W. CAMPBELL *Private Spud Tamson* xiii. 167 Any chapter on training must also refer to night operations, generally called Night Attacks. These operations are never popular in times of training. They interfere with social engagements. **1939** *War Pictorial* 22 Dec. 9 (*caption*) The gallery above is the Operations Section of the R.A.F. Fighter Command. **1941** N. MACMILLAN *Air Strategy* iv. 30 We must perforce ignore ..the layout of an Operations Room which functions as the brain to the body, the body in this case being the operational aircraft. **1943** J. S. HUXLEY *TVA* 108 The operations crew ..get their orders from the control room. **1946** *R.A.F. Jrnl.* May 170 Now, in a world at peace, operations are but a faint memory for the men. **1968** R. L. ACKOFF in *Internat. Encycl. Social Sci.* XI. 291/1 British military executives turned to scientists for aid when the German air attack on Britain began... These teams of scientists were usually assigned to the executive in charge of operations. **1975** A. BEEVOR *Violent Brink* vii. 167 In the Operations Room..two members of the Security Committee had advocated that the two sides should be left to fight it out.

b. Used as first element of the code-name for a military or civil campaign.

1938 'TAFFRAIL' *Operation 'M.O.'* iii. 58 It's stuffed full of secret papers that I was going to work on at home! Operation 'M.O.' **1941** *New Statesman* 26 Apr. 443/2 In this brief workmanlike account of the Evacuation from Dunkirk, Mr. Masefield..brings back a plain exact narrative of The Operation Dynamo (as the lifting was officially called). **1945** *News Chron.* 1 June 1/4 This is the first picture to be released of Operation 'Fido'. **1946** T. DRIBERG in *Reynolds News* 28 Apr. 4 Note to sub-editors and others: please cooperate in killing..the most overworked of current clichés—the whimsical application to a variety of topics of the military locution 'Operation —'. **1950** *Nat. Geographic Mag.* Sept. 367/1 'Operation Link', they call the project because when completed, the 4-mile bridge will link Maryland's eastern and western shores. **1968** *Listener* 23 May 656/2 Between Tet and the 'second wave', General Westmoreland launched 'Operation Final Vietcong' to sweep the enemy from the surroundings of Saigon. But this enterprise, nicknamed 'Operation Final Solution', failed. **1973** *Guardian* 25 Jan. 2/1 The operation to return the..prisoners of war..Operation Homecoming, as the Pentagon has called it.

8. *Math.* **a.** The action of subjecting a number or quantity to any process whereby its value or form is affected. (The general term including addition, subtraction, multiplication, division, involution, evolution, differentiation, integration, etc.) In connection with *Computers* freq. identical with sense 5; also = FUNCTION *sb.* 3 d.

1713 J. WARD *Introd. Math.* III. vi. (ed. 2) 347 If the whole Æquation..be now taken, and we proceed to a Second Operation, the Value of *a* may be increas'd with twelve Places of Figures more, and those may be obtain'd by plain Division only. **1743** EMERSON *Fluxions* 39 The Series is $Ay + B + Cy^{-1} + Dy^{-2}$ &c. and the Operation will be as follows. **1817** H. T. COLEBROOKE *Algebra*, etc. 286 Operations, subservient to the eight investigations, have been thus explained. **1885**, etc. [see *logical operation* s.v. LOGICAL *a.* (and *sb.*) 7]. **1893** J. EDWARDS *Diff. Calc.* ii. 25, $\frac{d}{dx}$ is a symbol of operation which, when applied to *y*, denotes the result of taking the limit of the ratio of the small quantities δy, δx. **1946** *Ann. Computation Lab. Harvard Univ.* I. 50 Since the control tapes deal with operations only, they represent the solution of a mathematical situation independent of the values of the parameters involved. **1947** *Math. Tables & Other Aids to Computation* II. 356 Provision is planned for squaring, taking the reciprocal, and the maximum or minimum of two quantities, but these operations are not yet available. **1953** A. D. & K. H. V. BOOTH *Automatic Digital Calculators* vi. 35 It is customary, in *all* existing computers, to have circuits which will perform the operations of addition and subtraction. *Ibid.* 37 The left shift operation is more complex. **1956** BERKELEY & WAINWRIGHT *Computers* II. 38 The arithmetical operations of a computer..include addition, counting, subtraction,.. truncating, rounding off, [etc.]. **1969** P. B. JORDAIN *Condensed Computer Encycl.* 358 In general, an operation is a single irreducible step in the performance of a computer program... In some higher-level languages, an operation is a single higher-level step (such as finding a square root). **1972** GROSS & BRAINERD *Fund. Programming Concepts* ix. 248 The first hexadecimal digit is called the operation code and specifies which operation is to be performed, such as add, subtract, print, etc.

b. In the numerical solution of simultaneous linear equations by relaxation, the process of changing the trial value of one of the unknowns in order to reduce the magnitude of one of the residuals.

[**1935** R. V. SOUTHWELL in *Proc. R. Soc.* A. CLI. 65 In the operation considered, B is held fixed and A is moved.] **1940** —— *Relaxation Methods in Engin. Sci.* i. 1 The Relaxation Method takes it farther by devising methods of systematic adjustment: we apply a series of operations, each one an indirect solution of a particularly simple kind, and in this way we 'tune up' a trial solution..until it conforms with some imposed standard of accuracy. **1957** L. FOX *Numerical Solution Two-Point Boundary Probl.* iii. 38 The computations are embodied in Tables 1 and 2, showing respectively the possible operations and details of the relaxation process. **1969** W. A. WATSON et al. *Numerical Anal.* I. vi. 160 Usually the operation which reduces the magnitude of the largest residual is used at any stage of the working.

†**9. a.** The action of making or producing something. *Obs. rare*⁻¹. **b.** Something made; a product, work. *Obs.*

? *a* **1500** *Chester Pl.* i. 46 The blessing of my benignitie I geue to my first operacion. **1616** R. C. *Times' Whistle* III. 878 It then did please High Iove ('ere he began mans operation) To give vnto the Angels their creation. **1774** J. BRYANT *Mythol.* I. p. xiv, The whole was the operation of one and the same people.

10. The action of operating or working a machine, engine, railway, business, etc.: see OPERATE 6, 7.

1872 J. RICHARDS (*title*) Treatise on the Construction and Operation of Wood-working Machines. **1895** *Westm. Gaz.* 12 Jan. 3/2 Electricity has been used for the operation of the *Montauk's* turrets for some time. **1898** *Times* 22 Feb. 13 In America..what with us is a single department [on Railways] is split into 'traffic' and 'operation'.

11. *attrib.* and *Comb.* (chiefly in sense 6), as ***operation-room, wound***, etc.; **operation code** *Computers*, a character or set of characters that when put into the operation part of an instruction specifies the operation that is performed; **operation part** *Computers*, the part of an instruction that receives the operation code; **operations research** *U.S.* = *operational research* (OPERATIONAL *a.* 1 b); so ***operations researcher***; **operations table** *Math.*, in the numerical solution of simultaneous linear equations by relaxation, a table showing the changes in the values of the residuals that result when each unknown in turn is increased by one; **operation-table**, an operating-table (see OPERATING *vbl. sb.*).

1949 E. C. BERKLEY *Giant Brains* vi. 103 Division has the code 76 and multiplication the code 761, and so the difference is essentially an operation code not in the third or *C* field. **1972** C. B. GERMAIN *PL/1 for IBM 360* ii. 14/2 The general format of 360 instructions is an operation code.. specifying the operation to be performed followed by two addresses to specify the data, or operands, involved in the operation. **1879** *St. George's Hosp. Rep.* IX. 471 An operation list is appended. **1957** D. D. MCCRACKEN *Digital Computer Programming* ii. 14 Instruction Format... The first two digits..are called the operation part, and tell the machine what to do. The next four digits are termed the address part. **1969** P. B. JORDAIN *Condensed Computer Encycl.* 359 The operation part is usually at the left end of the instruction, and is of fixed length. **1945** E. J. KING in G. C. Marshall et al. *War Rep.* (1947) 719 The application, by qualified scientists, of the scientific method to the improvement of naval operating techniques and material, has come to be called operations research. **1956** BERKELEY & WAINWRIGHT *Computers* VII. 281 Much operations research can be carried out with pencil, paper, and a desk calculating machine. **1969** J. ARGENTI *Managem. Techniques* 81 The same problem occurs in Operations Research, i.e. in those management techniques that depend largely upon mathematics. **1970** P. M. MORSE in G. J. Kelleher *Challenge to Syst. Analysis* iii. 23 Operations research has emerged as a unified area of applied science..designed to influence policy. **1953** *Operational Research Q.* IV. 51 The operations researcher's competence stops. **1806** FORSYTH *Beauties Scot.* III. 239 The operation-room is a large circular apartment. **1940** R. V. SOUTHWELL *Relaxation Methods in Engin. Sci.* i. 8 Having completed the calculations we can present their results in an operations table. **1957** L. FOX *Numerical Solution Two-Point Boundary Probl.* iii. 40 The full number of figures is used for the calculation of residuals, but the coefficients can be rounded-off to convenient numbers for use in the operations table. **1969** W. A. WATSON et al. *Numerical Anal.* I. vi. 159 For ease of reference during the working it is convenient to summarise the effects on the residuals of unit changes in the unknowns in a table, usually referred to as the operations table. **1896** *Westm. Gaz.* 5 Mar. 3/2 Smoking his cigar..until he mounted the operation table. **1876** *Clin. Soc. Trans.* IX. 308 The discharge from the operation wound was intense.

operational (ɒpəˈreɪʃənəl), *a.* [f. OPERATION + -AL.] **1. a.** Of or pertaining to operation or operations; *spec.* engaged in or connected with active military operations as distinct from being under training, in reserve, etc.

1922 *Edin. Rev.* Oct. 212 The development of..air communications..ensuring the maintenance of a large and flourishing constructional and operational aircraft industry. **1928** C. F. S. GAMBLE *Story N. Sea Air Station* x. 146 They were placed in various groups for disciplinary and operational purposes. **1940** *War Illustr.* 5 Jan. 568/2 Each balloon can be raised to its operational ceiling in a very few minutes. **1941** *Economist* 19 Apr. 521/2 The new status is not intended merely to prevent wastage. There are operational reasons. The range of women's duties in the Army and the Air Force is extending. **1943** B. J. HURREN *Eastern Med.* xii. 129 The air forces moved up their advanced aerodromes (technically known as Operational Landing Grounds). **1962** A. NISBETT *Technique Sound Studio* 246 The soundproof room equipped with control desk, gramophone and tape reproducers and high quality loudspeaker, which is occupied by production and operational staff. *a* **1963** J. LUSBY in B. James *Austral. Short Stories* (1963) 222 They were young, quiet, and looked tired. Operational men, instructing for a 'rest'. **1963** C. W. BARY (*title*) Operational economics of electric utilities. **1964** *Ann. N.Y. Acad. Sci.* CXV. 683 The problems of achieving adequate operational flexibility..underline the need for more appropriate computer systems. **1974** M. BABSON *Stalking Lamb* II. xvii. 127 He intended to make the mews house his operational headquarters... It would be safe, quiet, unsuspected. **1977** *R.A.F. News* 11–24 May 3/4 The real test lies in our operational efficiency.

b. ***operational research***: a method of mathematically based investigation for providing a quantitative basis for management decisions (orig. for military planning); abbrev. O.R., OR (O 5 d); so ***operational researcher***.

1941 P. M. S. BLACKETT in *Advancement of Sci.* (1948) V. 27/1 The work of an Operational Research Section should be carried out at Command, Groups, Stations or Squadrons as circumstances dictate. *Ibid.* 29/1 One of the tasks of an Operational Research Section is to make possible..a numerical estimate of the merits of a change over from one device to another. **1945** *World Rev.* June 49 The Operational Research Section..is a new element in the organisation of the Royal Air Force which has been evolved during the war. **1948** *Nature* 13 Mar. 377/1 In war, operational research was applied to the use of weapons, to tactics, and to strategy. In the peace-time applications of operational research, studies are directed, for example, to the use of equipment and man-power, to operating procedures, and to the solution of those many problems faced by management..or by Government authorities. **1948** *Advancement of Sci.* IV. 320/1 The operational researcher was visualised as requiring dual ranges of knowledge; on the one hand a wide and fairly detailed knowledge of technical possibilities..; on the other..a close personal knowledge of the working conditions. **1953** *Economist* 15 Aug. 465/1 This technique is called 'operational research'; and under it, teams that may include engineers, mathematicians, statisticians, economists and sociologists combine together. **1959** *Birmingham Mail* 11 Mar. 1/5 London Transport has set up an operational research team to investigate the desirability of increasing the non-smoking accommodation in Tube coaches. **1964** M. ARGYLE *Psychol. & Social Probl.* xvi. 194 The kind of research done by social scientists working for organizations can be divided into trend analysis, operational research and experiments. **1967** R. WHITEHEAD in Wills & Yearsley *Handbk. Managem. Technol.* 70 The operational researcher seeks to control the situation by making a model of the outside factors from which he can to some extent predict and form a plan of production. **1967** E. DUCKWORTH in *Ibid.* 99 The purpose of operational research is..to assist a manager to take decisions and to help him to take fewer decisions. **1971** D. C. HAGUE *Managerial Econ.* (rev. ed.) 6 Managerial economics is a background subject which both the line manager and the operational researcher must understand if they are to be successful.

c. In a condition of readiness to perform some intended (esp. military) function.

1944 H. ST. G. SAUNDERS *Per Ardua* xvii. 270 Only the Martinsyde F.4, not then operational, was superior to them. **1948** 'N. SHUTE' *No Highway* i. 19 'Could you..find out how many hours flying these machines have done?'..'They can't have done much. They've only been operational for about a month.' **1963** R. M. HARE *Freedom & Reason* iii. 46 We are to make morality again (as the military writers say) 'operational'. **1965** *New Statesman* 14 May 758/1 The new Russian weapon is clearly operational. **1974** *Nature* 22 Nov. 279/2 The Cambridge group operates the majority of operational catenary instruments.

d. Of, or pertaining to, mental operations (see OPERATION 4 b).

1953 MAYS & WHITEHEAD tr. *Piaget's Logic & Psychol.* p. xviii, The structures which emerge in the analysis of the operational mechanisms of thought. **1963** J. H. FLAVELL *Developmental Psychol. J. Piaget* v. 168 The operational systems of middle childhood have certain definable properties. **1975** M. D. SMITH *Educ. Psychol.* ii. 40 When a learner becomes able to deal with things that are not actually present..and to relate images and memories to predict and control the future, then he is in the formal operational stage of thought.

2. a. *Math.* Of, involving, or employing operators.

1927 H. JEFFREYS (*title*) Operational methods in mathematical physics. **1937** E. STEPHENS (*title*) The elementary theory of operational mathematics. **1957** L. FOX *Numerical Solution Two-Point Boundary Probl.* ii. 8 We easily produce the operational equivalents $E = e^{hD}$, $E - 1 = \Delta$... With few restrictions these operators can be manipulated according to the rules of ordinary algebra. **1973** L. E. EDWARDS *PL/1 for Business Applications* ii. 55 An expression may consist of a single variable or a single constant or a combination of these using operators, and is then referred to as an operational expression.

b. Electronics. ***operational amplifier***: an amplifier with a very high open-loop gain and a very low output impedance that is used (usu. with negative feedback) as the basis of a circuit for performing a particular mathematical operation on an input voltage with high accuracy, the relation of output to input being effectively determined solely by the arrangement and magnitude of the other, passive, circuit elements.

1947 J. R. RAGAZZINI et al. in *Proc. IRE* XXXV. 444/2 As an amplifier so connected can perform the mathematical operations of arithmetic and calculus on the voltages applied to its input, it is hereafter termed an 'operational amplifier'. **1962** SIMPSON & RICHARDS *Physical Princ. Junction Transistors* xiii. 309 The operational amplifier is also valuable as a linear adder. Because the input and output resistances are very low, the base voltage may be made accurately proportional to the sum of a number of separate input voltages each 'weighted' by its own summing resistor. **1963** B. FOZARD *Instrumentation Nucl. Reactors* xii. 152 The basic unit of an electronic analogue computer is the operational amplifier. **1972** VASSOS & EWING *Analog & Digital Electronics* v. 139 Deviations from ideality in operational amplifiers are very often negligible. For this reason the input-output relation is independent of the characteristics of the particular amplifier. This property brings about a unique simplicity of design, which is the key to the extensive use of operational amplifiers in instrumentation and control systems.

3. Of, pertaining to, or in accordance with operationalism.

1927 P. W. BRIDGMAN *Logic Mod. Physics* i. 8 Einstein, in thus analyzing what is involved in making a judgment of simultaneity..is actually adopting a new point of view as to what the concepts of physics should be, namely, the operational view. **1935** *Psychol. Rev.* XLII. 517 Operational doctrine makes explicit recognition of the fact that a concept, or proposition, has empirical meaning only if it stands for definite, concrete operations capable of execution by normal human beings. **1937** *Harper's Mag.* Dec. 51/1 Some deductions may still be sound, but all are suspect pending operational check in modern America. **1941** A. HUXLEY *Grey Eminence* iii. 48 That 'operational philosophy' which contemporary scientific thinkers have begun to apply in the natural sciences. **1952** G. SARTON *Hist. Sci.* I. xvi. 404 It [*sc.* the Platonic method] is sterile because it is unworkable, or, to use our modern terminology, it is not 'operational'. **1955** A. HUXLEY *Genius & Goddess* 21 'Wouldn't he have lived to eighty-seven without the pills?'..'We can never know how his self-medication was related to his longevity. And where there's no possible operational answer, there's no conceivable sense in the question.' **1971** *Brit. Med. Bull.* XXVII. 37/2 The operational definition of hypertension in the population should be flexible.

operationalism (ɒpəˈreɪʃənəlɪz(ə)m). [f. prec. + -ISM.] A theory or system which accepts only such concepts as can be described in terms of the operations necessary to determine or prove them.

1931 *Jrnl. Philos.* XXVIII. 545 Operationalism must be understood to state that a concept has no meaning unless its definition formulates performable operations. **1941** P. FRANK *Between Physics & Philos.* 5 Professor Bridgman's views have..been labelled 'operationalism', although he himself is not pleased by this name. **1950** *Mind* LIX. 571 Pragmatism and its modern offspring operationalism. **1965** N. CHOMSKY *Aspects of Theory of Syntax* 194 Perhaps this loss of interest in theory..was fostered by certain ideas (i.e., strict operationalism or strict verificationism) that were considered briefly in positivist philosophy of science..in the early nineteen-thirties. **1965** [see OPERATIONALLY *adv.*]. **1968** M. BLACK *Labyrinth of Lang.* vi. 142 Operationalism may rank with Freudianism as one of the major intellectual forces in the Western world between the first two World Wars. **1972** *Language* XLVIII. 418 It would appear that the appeal of various forms of operationalism, positivism, and behaviourism,..had a great deal to do with the emergence of a new professional identification on the part of a small group of young men.

Hence **opeˈrationalist** *sb.* and *a.*

1931 *Jrnl. Philos.* XXVIII. 545 When the operationalist defines a concept in terms of operations, the meaning of the concept thus defined is not restricted to performed operations or to operations which are actually going to be performed. **1934** *Mind* XLIII. 201 This Mead wants to prove by following the operationalist argument about the concepts of physics. **1941** A. HUXLEY *Grey Eminence* iii. 48 Buddha was not a consistent operationalist. **1965** J. D. NORTH *Measure of Universe* xv. 335 One of the biggest objections to the operationalist philosophy is that it appears to deny meaning even to such apparently harmless dispositional words as 'imperceptible', 'movable', and so on. *Ibid.* 336 But (runs the operationalist's argument) even where D_1 and D_2 turn out to be more or less the same and even where, as a matter of convenience, one assimilates the two concepts, in any careful or philosophical account they must always be distinguished. **1977** *Language* LIII. 170 In the period when a strictly behaviorist and operationalist philosophy dominated American linguistics, constraining the linguist to discount any data beyond the 'physical' record, Hoijer delivered a paper at the 8th International Congress of Linguists on the importance of 'Native reaction as a criterion in linguistic analysis'.

operationality (ˌɒpəreɪʃəˈnælɪtɪ). [f. OPERATIONAL *a.* + -ITY.] The property of being operational.

1972 *Computers & Humanities* VII. 81 First, how well have the available [computer] programs served the current generation..? Second, considering basic design tensions—flexibility and uniformity, elegance and operationality—what directions should future design and dissemination efforts take? **1973** *Nature* 21/28 Dec. 532/1 Piaget's insistence on 'operationality' makes his experiments indirect and complicated.

operationalizable (ɒpəˌreɪʃənəˈlaɪzəb(ə)l), *a.* [f. next + -ABLE.] Capable of being operationalized.

1975 *Cooperation & Conflict* (Oslo) X. 35/1 As it consists of transactions, the transactor profile characteristic is more easily operationalizable. **1976** *Brit. Jrnl. Sociol.* XXVII. 35 However, my goal is to develop a single, broad operationalizable interpretation from the philosophical sources and to test the contemporary usages against that standard.

operationalize (ɒpəˈreɪʃənəlaɪz), *v.* [f. OPERATIONAL *a.* + -IZE.] *trans.* To express or determine in operational terms. Also **opeˈrationalizing** *vbl. sb.*

1954 *Jrnl. Abnormal Psychol.* XLIX. 460 Once the codability variable..had been operationalized, it remained to relate this variable to some nonlinguistic behavior. **1964** [see CODABILITY]. **1966** HUGHES & PINNEY in E. L. Pinney *Compar. Politics & Polit. Theory* 67 Most of these interpretations are exercises in conceptualization, rather than efforts to operationalize the concept. **1972** *Jrnl. Social Psychol.* LXXXVII. 30 Previous studies have operationalized panic in terms of average time of group escape. **1975** *Gen. Systems* XX. 116/2 By accommodating evolution, class exploitation, and industrialism, cultural materialism helps operationalize anthropology.

Hence **ˌoperationaliˈzation**, the process of operationalizing.

1966 HUGHES & PINNEY in E. L. Pinney *Compar. Politics & Polit. Theory* 67 The problem which must be solved in order to exploit the usefulness of the concept is basically one of operationalization. **1969** P. WORSLEY in Ionescu & Gellner *Populism* 235 The formulation and operationalization of policy..is thus a function of many other things than simply adhesion to some kind of ideology. **1973** *Sociol. Rev.* XXI. 419 The term 'operationalisation' is usually reserved for the process of trying to turn hypotheses into testable postulates, and for the problems of selecting or creating techniques to test them. **1975** *Political Stud.* XXIII. 75 That Deutsch himself is aware of the limitations of his operationalization is indicated by his calling a 'politicized people' a 'nationality', and not inhabitants of a society featuring a large public sector.

operationally (ɒpəˈreɪʃənəlɪ), *adv.* [f. as prec. + -LY[2].] In terms of, or as regards, operation(s), esp. the operations required to define a concept or term (cf. OPERATIONALISM).

1927 *Jrnl. Philos.* XXIV. 663 Every concept must henceforth be defined operationally, i.e., we know what a concept means when we know what operations must be performed in order to produce an instance of that concept. **1934** *Times* 26 June (Air Suppl.) p. xvii/2 It was decided, therefore, shortly after the War ended that the third Service, the Royal Air Force, should be operationally responsible for the units..engaged in the air defence of the country. **1948** *Jrnl. Abnormal Psychol.* XLIII. 143/1 There remains the evanescent residual category of 'personality', at once too broad to be operationally useful..and too ubiquitous to be neglected. **1951** [see OPERATIONIST *a.* and *sb.*]. **1965** J. D. NORTH *Measure of Universe* viii. 152 The belief that any theory must be provided with a 'sound conceptual foundation' is..often closely allied to the doctrine of operationalism, coinciding with that variant form according to which *every* concept must be explicitly 'operationally defined', even if only hypothetically so. **1972** *Science* 5 May 545/3 It is operationally impossible to distinguish between selection at a single locus and selection for closely linked genes. **1975** *Daily Tel.* 30 May 2/3 Operationally, the occasion on which the drop of a complete parachute brigade would be required and feasible has for long seemed remote.

operationism (ɒpəˈreɪʃənɪz(ə)m). [f. OPERATION + -ISM.] = OPERATIONALISM.

1935 *Psychol. Rev.* XLII. 517 The principles of operationism provide a procedure by which the concepts of psychology can be cast in rigorous form. **1942** D. D. RUNES *Dict. Philos.* 219/2 Operationism makes explicit the distinction between *formal* and *empirical* sentences. **1970** *Jrnl. Gen. Psychol.* LXXXII. 113 About 25 years ago, during the period that I may call rampant operationism, a great many psychologists were misled into believing that here at last..was the long-needed panacea for guaranteeing useful scientific terms. **1975** *New Left Rev.* Nov.–Dec. 53 Baihelard's concept of the transitive dimension of science is flawed by operationism and an unrelenting hostility to the role of the imagination in science.

Hence **opeˈrationist** *a.* and *sb.* = OPERATIONALIST *sb.* and *a.*

1950 *Brit. Jrnl. Psychol.* XL. 112 An unwarranted assumption is..that a person who is frustrated in a behaviourist or operationist sense, necessarily feels frustrated. **1951** *Mind* LX. 46 The operationist school in psychology. *Ibid.* 53 All operationists are rationalistic in the sense that they maintain that unless scientists define their terms operationally they will not uncover Nature's secrets. **1956** E. H. HUTTEN *Lang. Mod. Physics* ii. 62 The operationist theory of meaning..is not acceptable.

†**operatist.** *Obs. rare*[−1]. [See -IST 4.] One who operates professionally; an operator.

1651 WITTIE tr. *Primrose's Pop. Err.* I. vi. 24 Manual Operatists..such as couch the cataract.

operative (ˈɒpərətɪv), *a.* and *sb.* [a. F. *opératif, -ive* (14th c., Oresme), or immed. ad. late L. *operātīv-us* creative, formative, f. ppl. stem of *operārī* to OPERATE: see -IVE.]

A. *adj.* **1. a.** Characterized by operating or working; active in producing, or having the power to produce, effects; exerting force, energy, or influence; productive *of* something; in operation; *spec.* in legal use, applied to those words in a document which express the intention to effect the transaction concerned.

1603 HOLLAND *Plutarch's Mor.* 847 Animals which are called unreasonable and brute beasts, are endued with reason; howbeit they are not operative with that reason, neither can they actuate it. **1654** BRAMHALL *Just Vind.* iii. (1661) 31 Whether the Act or Statute of Separation were operative or declarative, creating new right, or manifesting or restoring old right. *c***1705** BERKELEY *Commonplace Bk.* Wks. 1871 IV. 478 Enquiring and judging are actions which depend on the operative faculties. **1792** N. CHIPMAN *Rep.* (1871) 72 Words operative at common law to convey. **1865** GROTE *Plato* I. iv. 135 The motive to preserve the Platonic MSS. would still be operative. **1872** in J. Russell *Rep. Cases High Court of Chancery* V. 344 If the operative part of a deed be doubtfully expressed, there the recital may safely be referred to as a key to the intention of the parties; but where the operative part of the deed uses language which admits of no doubt, it cannot be controlled by the recital. **1879** G. MACDONALD *P. Faber* II. ix. 164 The strongest and most operative sense of duty would not satisfy you. **1925** G. C. CHESHIRE *Mod. Law Real Property* 601 We will now turn to the operative words of the conveyance. **1951** *Times* 27 Nov. 7/4 Something to prevent that should be put into the operative part of the treaty.

b. Of words, sentences, etc.: containing the main point or key, essential to the meaning of the whole.

1926 *Sat. Rev.* 3 July 12/1 Every English sentence has an operative word. **1954** KOESTLER *Invis. Writing* ii. 28 The tendency of the novel had to be 'operative', that is, didactic; each work of art must convey a social message. **1963** N. MARSH *Dead Water* (1964) ii. 43 'It was nice getting your occasional letters,' Patrick said, presently. 'Operative word "occasional".' **1973** O. LANCASTER *Littlehampton Bequest* 24 He was known..to have trailed a pike in the Low Countries when there were those..who loudly proclaimed that in his case 'trailed' was the operative word.

c. Of political ideas or principles: (*a*) capable of being put into effect; likely to be beneficial; (*b*) (see quot. 1954).

1938 H. G. WELLS *Brothers* iii. 46 Are you lot over there really giving it an operative form? That's one of my phrases, brother—*operative form*... *Competent receiver* and *operative form*; two phrases for two problems that Socialism and Communism ought to have tackled forty years ago. **1954** KOESTLER *Invis. Writing* xx. 224 It is called the 'operative principle'. It means that you cannot write about the strategy of Communism without having worked in a factory, or Party cell, or underground organisation.

d. In weakened sense (without reference to specific activity or production): significant, important.

1955 J. L. AUSTIN *How to do Things with Words* (1962) i. 7 But 'operative'..is often used nowadays to mean little more than 'important'. **1977** 'D. CORY' *Bennett* ii. 74 After all, she *didn't* bring the boy on that operative Saturday.

2. Productive of the intended or proper effect; effective, effectual, efficacious.

1598 BACON *Let. to Ld.-Keeper Puckering* 28 Sept., That your lordship may perceive how effectual and operative your lordship's last dealing with her Majesty was. **1660** JER. TAYLOR *Worthy Commun.* ii. §2. 137 If these desires be..as operative as they are inquisitive..then we shall perceive the blessings and fruits of our holy desires. **1818** JAS. MILL *Brit. India* II. IV. viii. 277 Fraud was an operative instrument in the hands of this aspiring general. **1879** TROLLOPE in *19th Cent.* Jan. 38 The judgment..is not operative against the reading of novels.

3. Concerned with manual or mechanical work; practical.

1624 WOTTON *Archit.* 1, In Architecture, as in all other Operative Arts, the End must direct the Operation. **1785** REID *Intell. Powers* V. iv. 401 In every operative art, the tools, instruments, materials..must have general names. **1827** STEUART *Planter's G.* (1828) 480, I should wish to see them employ, for the operative part, none but the most experienced Foresters that can be had. **1899** *Whitaker's Alm.* 163/2 Mint..Superintendent Operative Department.

4. Pertaining to surgical operations.

1783 P. POTT *Chirurg. Wks.* II. 7 The operative part of the arts. **1845** J. SAUNDERS *Cab. Pict. Eng. Life* 181 Serapion Senior..treats of diseases as curative solely by medicine and diet, omitting operative surgery. **1899** *Allbutt's Syst. Med.* VIII. 31 The prospect of much benefit from treatment other than operative is practically nil.

5. Of a person: Engaged in work or production, putting forth activity, active.

1824 SOUTHEY *Sir T. More* (1831) I. 369 The active,..or, in the phraseology of the present day, the operative clergy. **1825** LAMB *Elia* Ser. II. *Superann. Man*, Man..is out of his element as long as he is operative. I am altogether for the life contemplative. **1835** *Court Mag.* VI. 51/1 Mr. Pl. is not a little proud at finding himself..the..head and front of the operative dramatists of the day.

6. Engaged in production as a workman or artisan, working. (Now perh. the sb. (B. 4) used *attrib.*)

1831 *Mechanics' Mag.* XIV. 106 To the Operative Printers of London. **1849** C. BRONTË *Shirley* xxii, Most of these were not members of the operative class. **1854** H. MILLER *Sch. & Schm.* xxiii, I was still an operative mason.

B. *sb.*

†**1.** *ellipt.* An operative mood or condition. *Obs.*

1608 D. PRICE *Chr. Warre* 6 The Imperatiue in God begets an Optatiue in man, not an Operatiue.

†**2.** That which operates or works. *Obs.*

†**a.** An agent, efficient means.

1672 PENN *Spir. Truth Vind.* 24 If Water and Spirit be the only operative to Regeneration, and Regeneration the only Way to the Kingdom of God.

†**b.** A drug or medicine that operates.

1716 M. DAVIES *Athen. Brit.* II. 353 The most immediate Operative upon a dangerous Flux, is a Scruple or two of the Flower of Sulpher, with a proportionable *quantum sufficit* of Alkermes, to make it into a Bolus.

3. a. One who operates or works; one who is engaged in any branch of industry, trade, or profession; a worker.

1809–10 COLERIDGE *Friend* (1863) II. 130 The remaining mass of useful labourers and operatives in science, literature, and the learned professions. **1832** GEN. P. THOMPSON *Exerc.* (1842) II. 38 (*Doctrine de Saint-Simon*) Priests, 'savans', operatives—there you have the whole of society. **1838** HAWTHORNE *Amer. Note-bks.* (1883) 206 He was the operative of a scientific person in Boston. **1898** J. E. C. BODLEY *France* III. ii. 64 Lawyers and other unproductive operatives.

b. A detective or agent employed by a detective agency; a secret-service agent.

1905 *N.Y. Press* 23 Oct. 6/4 The word 'detective' became so offensive..that it was dropped by some successful [detective] agencies. The word chosen by the Pinkertons to take its place was 'operative'. **1930** *Sat. Even. Post* 26 July 142/2 Riding on the train with him was another operative who had spent that day following Castagara. **1934** A. CHRISTIE *Murder on Orient Express* II. ix. 137 That's not to say he'll remember me from a crowd of other operatives. **1937** *N.Y. Times* 22 Dec. 22/5 *Operative*, a spy employed by an agency. Usually has a secret designation. An operative may be a hooked man or a professional spy. **1954** W. TUCKER *Wild Talent* (1955) xiv. 184 Paul wondered if this new woman in the adjoining apartment would be a plant... Slater might be playing it doubly safe and ringing in another operative on him. **1966** J. PORTER *Sour Cream* iii. 36, I thought..you might just care to make your will. I advise all my operatives to do it. **1977** J. CROSBY *Company of Friends* viii. 56 Sascha looked at her, pierced with reluctant admiration. What an operative!

4. A workman in any industrial art, esp. one employed in a mill or factory; an artisan, mechanic; a mill-hand.

1827 *Westm. Rev.* VII. 279 A few dozens of operatives at two or three shillings a-day. **1833** HT. MARTINEAU *Loom & Lugger* II. i. 9 It belongs equally to the sinewy miner, the stout ploughman, and the withered operative. **1872** YEATS *Techn. Hist. Comm.* 272 The Spanish persecutions in the Low Countries drove hither many skilful operatives. **1879** *Cassell's Techn. Educ.* IV. 214/2 The cotton operatives have ..gained very much.

attrib. **1832** *Blackw. Mag.* Jan. 115/1 To keep up these operative electors over the whole country. **1858** GREENER *Gunnery* 411 The reluctant operative shooters employed to carry out the experiment. **1890** *Daily News* 9 June 7/6 The anniversary of Garibaldi's death has been commemorated at Nice, a large number of operative societies taking part in the ceremony.

'operatively, *adv.* [f. prec. + -LY².] In an operative manner; so as to operate, work, or produce effects; effectively, practically.

1601 DOLMAN *La Primaud. Fr. Acad.* III. (1618) 733 The first qualities of cold and dry, wherewith the earth is actually, and the moone operatiuely replenished. **1625** USSHER *Answ. Jesuit* 132 [They] doe discharge that part of their function which concerneth forgivenesse of sinnes, partly operatively, partly declaratively. **1782** PAINE *Let. Abbé Raynal* (1791) 24 The one was as operatively his tax as the other. **1843** *Blackw. Mag.* LIV. 62 Probably the ancient Persian satraps..have much more truly been operatively present to the describers than any thing..amongst the realities of England.

b. By or in respect of surgical operation.

1879 *St. George's Hosp. Rep.* IX. 512 Closed pupil.. treated operatively.

'operativeness. [f. as prec. + -NESS.] The quality or condition of being operative; power to work or produce effects; effectuality, efficacy.

1627 W. SCLATER *Exp. 2 Thess.* (1629) 62 The cessation of sensible Operativeness of Grace. **1656** R. ROBINSON *Christ all* 316 It hath not lost..that liveliness and operativeness which it once had. **1880** MUIRHEAD *Gaius* Dig. 597 The operativeness of the substitutions depended..upon the consideration whether the institute and substitutes were nominated with or without cretion.

,opera'tivity. *rare*⁻⁰. [f. as prec. + -ITY.] = prec.

In recent Dicts.

operatize ('ɒpərətaɪz), *v.* [irreg. f. OPERA + -IZE, after *dramatize*; cf. *operatic*.] *trans.* To turn into an opera, put into operatic form.

1865 *Pall Mall G.* 25 Mar. 9 Mr. Charles Kenney's excellent translation of the operatized version of the comedy. **1891** J. W. HALES in *19th Cent.* Dec. 922 The play ..has been freely modified by somebody, who augmented the lyrical parts and the dances—operatised it, in short.

operator ('ɒpəreɪtə(r)). [a. late L. *operātor*, agent-n. f. *operārī* to OPERATE: cf. F. *opérateur* (14th c., Oresme).] One who or that which operates.

1. One who does or effects something; a worker, an agent; †a maker, producer, creator (*obs.*).

1611 COTGR., *Operateur*, an Operator, a worker; also, a Quacksaluer, Cheater, Imposter (called so at Tours). **1632** *Star Chamb. Cases* (Camden) 173 Mr Deane is falsely accused, the maine operator is Mr Travers. **1696** EDWARDS *Demonstr. Exist. God* II. 39 So admirably fenced and guarded is this curious piece of workmanship by the celestial operator of it. *a* **1716** SOUTH *Serm.* (1744) X. i. 21 This is the philosophy of the popish operators in all their religious performances. **1772** *Char.* in *Ann. Reg.* II. 31 He is recorded as operator of all these gaudy works, in a large inscription over the tribune. *a* **1843** SOUTHEY *Comm. Pl. Bk.* Ser. II. 75 Prince Hohenlohe is the operator in this cure.

2. a. One who performs the practical or mechanical operations belonging to any process, business, or scientific investigation; a person professionally or officially engaged in doing this; *spec.* a secret-service agent. Cf. OPERATIVE *sb.* 3.

1597 A. M. tr. *Guillemeau's Fr. Chirurg.* 50b/2 The Mechanicall operatours, or handyecraftes men. **1646** SIR T. BROWNE *Pseud. Ep.* 165 Culinary operators observe that flesh boyles best, when the bones are boyled with it. **1667** BOYLE in *Phil. Trans.* II. 594 This..Trial..you may get reiterated by the Society's Operator. **1683** WOOD *Life* 22 May (O.H.S.) III. 55 Mr. Christopher White, the skilfull and industrious operator of the University. **1726** LEONI tr. *Alberti's Archit.* Pref. 2 The manual Operator being no more than an Instrument to the Architect. **1756–7** tr. *Keysler's Trav.* (1760) III. 302 In calcining this stone over a fire..the operator must take care not to hang his head over the effluvia arising from it. **1831** BREWSTER *Nat. Magic* x. (1833) 246 Accompanied by..his own mechanical operator. **1866** CRUMP *Banking* x. 226 The operators [of the Mint] were formed into a corporation by charter of Edward III. **1966** J. PORTER *Sour Cream* iii. 36, I'm sure you won't find any snags. She's a most experienced operator. *Ibid.* viii. 101 I'll know by mid-morning if Feodorov's side of the operation has been successful... He's a very experienced operator. **1977** S. COULTER *Soyuz Affair* vii. 73 He keeps a close watch on his things... He's a trained operator.

†**b.** (See quot.) *Obs.*

1731 *Gentl. Mag.* I. 25 The following List of Officers established in the most notorious Gaming-Houses... 3. An Operator, who deals the cards at a cheating Game called Faro.

3. a. One who performs a surgical operation or operations; an operating surgeon or dentist.

1597 A. M. tr. *Guillemeau's Fr. Chirurg.* *iiij, The rigoure and severitye of the first Operatours or Chyrurgians. *Ibid.* 38/1 Because the Ioynct may be præsented the stedyer and faster to the Operator. **1706** PHILLIPS, *Operatour for the Teeth*, one skill'd in drawing and cleansing the Teeth, and in making Artificial ones. **1813** J. THOMSON *Lect. Inflam.* 537 There are..cases in which this mortification supervenes.. without any fault being attributable to the operator. **1869** RUSKIN *Q. of Air* §146 A great operator told me that his hand could check itself within about the two-hundredth of an inch, in penetrating a membrane.

†**b.** A name given to a quack manufacturer of drugs, etc. (cf. quot. 1611 in 1); one who lives by fraudulent operations. *Obs.*

1674 R. GODFREY *Inj. & Ab. Physic* 10 Such perverse Mercurial and Antimonial preparations as are made by Mercenary Operators. **1696** PHILLIPS (ed. 5), *Operator*,.. more particularly it signifies an Empyric or Mountebank that sells his Drugs and his Remedies in publick upon a Theatre. **1704** SWIFT *T. Tub* x, He deals in a pernicious Kind of Writings, called Second Parts,..under the Name of the Author of the First... As soon as I lay down my Pen, this nimble Operator will have stole it. **1710** ADDISON *Tatler* No. 131 ¶1 There is in this City a certain Fraternity of Chymical Operators... They can squeeze Bourdeaux out of the Sloe, and draw Champagne from an Apple.

4. One who carries on financial operations in stocks, shares, or commodities, or who works a speculative business. Also now freq. with a stronger implication of speculativeness or shrewdness; one who acts in an underhand manner. (Cf. OPERATE 4 d.)

1828 *Examiner* 138/1 The principal operator for a rise is supposed to be getting rid of his stock. **1875** *N. Amer. Rev.* CXX. 157 An operator in Wall Street, and a professional gambler. **1883** *Manch. Guard.* 3 Nov. 6/7 The great operator whose movements had become almost as potent an influence on [cotton] markets as the size of a crop or the state of trade. **1895** *Daily News* 30 Dec. 7/5 The market declined early on large receipts, but eventually improved, due to local operators covering. **1951** [see HOLE *sb.* 11]. **1955** D. W. MAURER in *Publ. Amer. Dial. Soc.* XXIV. 35 Also, unlike many if not most other types of underworld operator, he tends to take his woman on the road with him. **1959** N. MAILER *Advts. for Myself* (1961) 399 He spent years hob-nobbing with gentlemanly shits and half-ass operators. **1964** A. W. GOULDNER in I. L. Horowitz *New Sociol.* 209 The whole world may be seen as one of marks and operators. **1970** *New Yorker* 6 June 132/3 He is what we call nowadays an 'operator', and completely unscrupulous and unashamed. **1971** D. POTTER *Brit. Eliz. Stamps* i. 15 Stamps were solemnly discussed in the financial columns,..and get-rich-quick operators joined in the *mêlée*. **1974** *Times* 4 Feb. 12/6 One almost expects him to say, with J. K. Galbraith, that modesty is a much over-rated virtue, but he is far too smooth an operator to be trapped into such an admission.

5. a. One who operates or works a machine, telegraph, etc.: cf. OPERATE 6; *spec.* one who works at the switchboard of a telephone exchange (now the usual sense). Also in *Comb.*

1847 *Commerc. Rev. of South & West* Nov. 138 Its receipt [was] acknowledged by the Montreal operator in 30 minutes. **1858** E. E. HALE *If, Yes, & Perhaps* (1868) 119 It is not the business simply of 'operators' in telegraphic dens to know this Morse alphabet. **1865** *Harper's Mag.* July 169/2 Here they gathered a new force.., a telegraph operator, and workmen. **1870** F. L. POPE *Electr. Tel.* viii. (1872) 103 To become an expert operator requires much time and patience. **1873** J. RICHARDS *Wood-working Factories* 103 The following rules..are recommended to operators when they have occasion to determine the angle and bevel of wood cutters. **1884** *List of Subscribers* (London & Globe Telephone Co.) 2 The Special Telephone Exchange Switchboard is so constructed, that the operators ..do not overhear the conversation between Subscribers. **1887** *Pall Mall G.* 19 Aug. 3/2 A machine operator, making nine shirts a day. **1891** *Pearson's Weekly* II. 39 From being a telegraph operator..he rose to the position of superintendent of that branch. **1921** [see DIAL *v.* 4]. **1927** HALDANE & HUXLEY *Animal Biol.* vi. 140 The human cerebrum contains more than a thousand million nerve-cells each connected by fibres with scores or hundreds of others, ..so we can get some idea of its complexity by imagining a telephone exchange in which the whole human race were acting as operators. **1972** B. F. CONNERS *Don't embarrass Bureau* (1973) II. 201 Operator, I'd like to call person to person to Officer Dolan. **1976** *Norwich Mercury* 10 Dec. 10/2 Bookings for operator-connected international telephone calls over Christmas will be accepted by the Post Office from Monday. **1977** G. MARKSTEIN *Chance Awakening* xix. 55 He dialled 100. He gave the operator the number. 'What seems to be the trouble?' asked the operator.

b. *U.S.* One who is licensed to drive a motor vehicle.

1967 *Boston Sunday Herald* 7 May III. 1/1 Several witnesses to the accident have supplied police pieces of information, which, when put together, revealed the involvement of this other car—and male operator, who stopped at this point, without knowing his car—and he—had actually been involved in the tragedy. **1972** *N.Y. Law Jrnl.* 24 Oct. 18/6 At the time involved defendant was a resident of the State of New Jersey and the holder of a New Jersey operator's license. It also appears from a Motor Vehicle Bureau exhibit..that defendant's New York license had been cancelled.

6. One who works a business, undertaking, etc. Also in wider use, of companies, corporations, etc.

1838 *Niles' Reg.* 13 Oct. 112/2 Our trade..is brought nearly to a stand again, by a collision between the dealers, operators and boatmen, as regards the price of freight. **1851** C. CIST *Sk. Cincinnati in 1851* 170 The largest operators in this line [manufacturing alcohol], are Lowell Fletcher & Co. **1857** *Harper's Mag.* Sept. 459/1 The leases of the operators usually covered a 'run' upon the out-crop..of from fifty to seventy yards. **1875** *Chicago Tribune* 30 Sept. 2/4 The operators on the Pan-Handle Railroad have been paying 2¼ cents per bushel for mining over 1¼ inch screen. **1877** RAYMOND *Statist. Mines & Mining* 238 Messrs. P. S. and J. C. were the principal operators in gold-veins last season. **1881** —— *Mining Gloss.*, *Operator*,..the person, whether proprietor or lessee, actually operating a colliery. **1884** *Sat. Rev.* 5 July 4/2 The skilful operators who controlled the Chicago Convention. **1891** *Daily News* 9 Feb. 6/4 If the coke-workers in several counties in Pennsylvania carry out their threat to strike work..the operators intend to bank the ovens and stop all production. **1897** *Outing* (U.S.) XXX. 170/1 A yeast and spirit distillery..where owner and operator divide the result of the year's working. **1953** *Manch. Guardian Weekly* 19 Nov. 9 The State, through a new sort of BBC is to own the new system and will hire it out to commercial 'operators'. **1962** *Listener* 8 Mar. 401/1 Though they [*sc.* the nationalized industries] were to be regarded partly as commercial operators, partly as public services, the relation between these two functions was not defined in the legislation that set them up. **1972** *Lebende Sprachen* XVII. 134/1 The official body representing the majority of independent operators is the British Independent Air Transport Association. **1977** *Times* 23 Mar. 14/3 Exporters have turned increasingly to road haulage for cargoes... This traffic..has attracted a large number of operators who are not equipped for the job. **1977** *Offshore Engineer* May 42/1 The results of the four wells are being closely studied by the operator Elf Aquitaine and partners ETAP and STEG.

7. *Math.* A symbol indicating an operation or series of operations, and itself subject to algebraical operation. Also, a sign or symbol which effects other types of operation, as logical, phonological, syntactic, etc.

1855 CARMICHAEL *Calculus of Operations* 3 The indetermination is due to a source quite independent of the character of the functional operator. **1925** BRYANT & CORRELL *Alternating-Current Circuits* iii. 74 The operator, $j = \sqrt{(-1)}$, turns the vector through 90 degrees in a counterclockwise direction each time it is used. **1936** *Jrnl. Symbolic Logic* I. 60 The formal system..employs material implication, propositional negation, universal quantification, and operators analogous to the combinatory operators *I, B,* and *C.* **1937** A. SMEATON tr. *Carnap's Logical Syntax of Lang.* I. §6. 21 The expressions which occur at the beginning of the sentences above..are called the *unlimited* universal operator, the *unlimited* existential operator, the *limited* universal operator, and the *limited* existential operator respectively. **1952** *Eng. & Gmc. Stud.* IV. 12 We may regard Modern English *stone* as the result of operating with an operator that I shall write {AS. ā > MnE. [ou]} on Anglo-Saxon *stān.* **1952** S. C. KLEENE *Introd. Metamath.* iv. 73 Let us call an expression of one of these ten forms an operator. In particular, ⊃, &, ∨, ¬ are *propositional connectives,* and operators of the forms ∀x and ∃x are *quantifiers*..; these six are *logical operators.* **1957** L. FOX *Numerical Solution Two-Point Boundary Probl.* ii. 8 In the theory of finite differences we carry this farther, introducing first the operator *E,* the effect of change of position, and defined by the equation $y(x + ph) = E^p y(x)$. **1964** E. BACH *Introd. Transformational Gram.* v. 113 The concatenation operator +. **1965** PHILLIPS & WILLIAMS *Inorg. Chem.* I. i. 12 Wave mechanics sets up, as postulates, equations of the type $H\psi = X\psi$, where ψ is the wave function, and *X* some observed property such as the energy, momentum, etc. *H* is a mathematical instruction (e.g. differentiate with respect to *x*) or set of instructions..called an operator. **1966** A. KOUTSOUDAS *Writing Transformational Gram.* i. 6 The rules of a transformational grammar consist of three types of symbols: (1) vocabulary symbols, (2) operators, and (3) abbreviators. Vocabulary symbols are symbols used to represent syntactic classes and other linguistic units; operators, as their name indicates, symbolize certain operations; and abbreviators are devices used to conflate the listing of rules. **1968** CORLETT & TINSLEY *Pract. Programming* ii. 14 Numbers and variables may be combined by the arithmetic operators + − × ÷ / ↑ to form an arithmetic expression. **1969** V. J. CALDERBANK *Course on Programming in FORTRAN IV* iii. 28 Another very common form of logical expression..is the relational expression. This has the general form $e_1 r e_2$ where e_1 and e_2 are arithmetic expressions..being compared by one of the following relational operators, *r*: .EQ. Equal to (=); .LT. Less than (<); [etc.]. **1969** P. A. M. SEUREN *Operators & Nucleus* iv. 116 Our hypothesis of operators as a deep structure category in grammar thus has a philosophical pedigree leading back to both the theory of quantifiers and the logic of modalities. **1976** A. R. LACEY *Dict. Philos.* 148 A logical operator is any expression whose function is to affect in a specific way the logical properties (e.g. the entailments) of an expression or expressions to which it is attached, e.g. 'and' operates on two propositions by joining them into a whole, which has entailments neither of them has separately.

8. a. In 'Basic English', an article, particle, preposition, etc., or one of certain words used as substitutes for verbs; a 'superverb'.

1929 C. K. OGDEN in *Psyche* IX. III. 1 The number of necessary names is 400, of qualifiers (adjectives) 100, of operators, particles, etc., 100. **1930** —— *Basic English* iii. 60 In conversation, the operators are frequently shortened to more convenient forms. Thus *I will* becomes *I'll.* **1946** H. JACOB *On Choice of Common Lang.* iii. 104 Three analogical extras, *say, see,* and *send*..provide a useful link between the operators and the verb-system proper. **1966** M. PEI *Gloss. Ling. Terminol.* 188 *Operator,* one of the verbal forms, prepositions, articles, etc. (about one hundred in number) in Basic English.

b. *Linguistics.* = *form-word* s.v. FORM *sb.* 22, *function word* s.v. FUNCTION *sb.* 3 c.

1938 B. L. WHORF *Lang. Thought & Reality* (1956) 128 Predication..operators (words specialized for predication, otherwise lexical meaning blank ('be, become, cause, do') or vague ('make, turn, get,' etc.)). auxiliary verbs. **1957** S. POTTER *Mod. Linguistics* vii. 143 Operators are..forms like articles, prepositions, conjunctions and conjunction adverbs ..which perform syntactic functions. **1967** [see FUNCTOR 2].

9. *Biol.* [tr. F. *opérateur* (Jacob & Monod 1959, in *Compt. Rend.* CCXLIX. 1284).] A segment of chromosomal DNA which is thought to control the activity of the structural gene(s) of an operon, protein synthesis occurring when it is uncombined with a repressor (or is absent altogether).

1961 *Cold Spring Harbor Symp. Quant. Biol.* XXVI. 194/1 The synthesis of messenger RNA is supposed to be a sequential and oriented process which can be initiated only at certain regions, or operators, on the DNA strands. **1969** *New Scientist* 28 Aug. 416/1 In the presence of substrate, the repressor is altered, so that it can no longer bind to the operator, and enzymes are synthesized freely. **1971** D. J. COVE *Genetics* xi. 165 A mutation in the operator gene prevents the recognition of the structural genes by the repressor. **1973** *Nature* 16 Nov. 133/1 The sites on DNA to which repressors bind are called operators.

†**,opera'torious,** *a. Obs. rare*$^{-1}$. [f. as next + -OUS.] = next.

a **1555** BRADFORD *Serm. Lord's Supp.* Wks. (Parker Soc.) I. 86 No less..their words spoken of the bread are operatorious and mighty to transubstantiate the bread.. which thing is absurd.

†**'operatory,** *sb.*[1] *Obs.* [ad. med.L. *operātōrium,* neut. sb. from *operātōrius* adj.; see prec.] A workshop, laboratory.

1651 HOBBES *Leviath.* IV. xlvii. (1839) 699 In what shop, or operatory the fairies make their enchantment, the old wives have not determined. **1663** COWLEY *Ess., College* (1669) 44 The House and Gardens, and Operatories, and Instruments. **1666** MRQ. WORCESTER in Dircks *Life* xvii. (1865) 286 A house called Fauxhall, for an operatory for engineers.

†**'operatory,** *a.* (*sb.*[2]) [ad. late L. (*a* 400) *operātōrius* creating, forming, f. ppl. stem of *operārī* to OPERATE: see -ORY.] Producing, or capable of producing, an effect; effectual; concerned with action, practical: = OPERATIVE A. 1-3.

a **1556** CRANMER *Wks.* (Parker Soc.) I. 36 When this true believing man..receiveth the bread..and drinketh the wine ..to him the words of our Saviour Christ be effectuous and operatory. **1638** FEATLEY *Transubst.* 179 That [these words] are not at all operatorie. **1674** JEAKE *Arith.* (1696) 421 The Operatory Part consists in the Invention of the Divisor.

B. *sb.*[2] An efficient agent: = OPERATIVE B. 2.

1660 JER. TAYLOR *Worthy Commun.* i. §2. 41 The whole progression of mysteries in his body, was still an operatory of life and spiritual being to us.

'operatress. *rare*$^{-1}$. [f. OPERATOR + -ESS.] A female operator.

1841 *Fraser's Mag.* XXIV. 712 He..had hired an excellent cook; but the said operatress found such difficulties in pleasing herself at the cottage fireplace, that [etc.].

†**'opera,trice.** *Obs. rare*$^{-1}$. [f. F. *opérateur* OPERATOR, after fem. forms from F. in *-rice.*] = prec.

1531 ELYOT *Gov.* III. xxiii, That hygher sapience whiche is the operatrice of all thynges.

‖**ope'ratrix.** *rare*$^{-1}$. [late L., fem. of *operātor* OPERATOR.] A female operator.

1792 *Chron.* in *Ann. Reg.* 21/1 Mr. Maden, husband to the celebrated operatrix on the teeth.

opercle (əʊ'pɜːk(ə)l). [ad. L. *operculum* cover, covering, lid: see -CULE.]

†**1.** A cover, covering. *Obs.*

1597 A. M. tr. *Guillemeau's Fr. Chirurg.* 12/1 A farre better opercle for the braynes, then that newe incarnated fleshe. *Ibid.* 36/2 A cleane linnen clothe, to be an opercle or coveringe to the woman.

2. *Nat. Hist.* = OPERCULUM.

1840 HALDEMAN *Freshwater Shells,* Shell conoid,.. aperture closed with a thin corneous opercle. **1879** LE CONTE *Elem. Geol.* IV. 331 The want of an opercle or gill-cover, growing backward over..the gill-slits. **1880** GÜNTHER *Fishes* 2.

Hence **o'percled** *a.* = OPERCULATE *a.*

1819 [see OPERCULATE *a.*].

opercular (əʊ'pɜːkjʊlə(r)), *a.* (*sb.*) [f. L. *operculum* (see below) + -AR[1].]

1. *Nat. Hist.* Of, pertaining to, or of the nature of an operculum; characterized by the presence of an operculum; see also quot. 1857[1].

opercular apparatus, the gill-cover of fishes, consisting of four pieces, the *præoperculum, operculum, suboperculum,* and *interoperculum.*

1830 LINDLEY *Nat. Syst. Bot.* 265 Anther terminal, opercular. **1835-6** TODD *Cycl. Anat.* I. 308/1 The opercular flap is largely developed in our common Barn-owl. **1849** MURCHISON *Siluria* x. 238 The opercular plate in Limulus. **1854** WOODWARD *Mollusca* II. 251 In the extinct genus Radiolites, both adductors were attached to large toothlike processes of the opercular valve. **1857** MAYNE *Expos. Lex.,* *Opercular,*..term applied by Prof. Owen, in his Homologies [1848], to the diverging appendages of the tympano-mandibular arch... In bivalve shells, of which the two valves are unequal, as the *Ostrea,* applied to the smaller. **1857** HENFREY *Elem. Bot.* I. ii. 116 Opercular dehiscence results from the partial separation of a portion of the wall of the loculus. **1875** HUXLEY in *Encycl. Brit.* I. 751/2 The gill apertures are closed by the growing over them of an opercular membrane.

2. Furnished with a lid. *rare.*

1884 *Health Exhib. Catal.* 50/1 Sanitary Stoneware of every description, including..opercular pipes.

B. *sb.* The opercular bone; an operculum.

1893 in *Funk's Stand. Dict.*

operculate (əʊ'pɜːkjʊlət), *a.* (*sb.*) *Nat. Hist.* [ad. L. *operculāt-us,* pa. pple. of *operculāre* to furnish or cover with a lid, to cover, f. *operculum* cover, lid.] **A.** *adj.* Furnished with or having an operculum; effected by means of an operculum.

1775 ASH, *Operculate,* covered, close-covered. **1819** *Pantologia* s.v. *Operculum,* Such a capsule is said to be operculate, opercled, or covered with a lid. **1826** KIRBY & SP. *Entomol.* IV. 315 *Operculate,* when the eyes are covered by an *operculum.* Ex. *Noctua conspicillaris.* **1835** LINDLEY *Introd. Bot.* (1848) I. 327 The calyx is said to be operculate, if it falls off without any lateral rupture of its cap, as in Eucalyptus. **1856** WOODWARD *Mollusca* 132 Shell minute,.. operculate. **1857** HENFREY *Elem. Bot.* 364 The peculiar operculate dehiscence of the anthers distinguishes this Order. **1879** W. PHILLIPS tr. E. Boudier in *Grevillea* VIII. 46, I would call the first section [of Discomycetes] by the name of *Operculate Discomycetes,* or simply *Operculæ,* because in this section the opening of the asci takes place by the elevation of a little lid at its summit. **1913** *Trans. Brit. Mycol. Soc.* IV. 402 The asci in the operculate series are generally larger. **1929** *Ibid.* XIV. 275 The material for this study has been gathered in great part from the accounts which have already been given by other investigators, chiefly on operculate species. **1971** P. H. B. TALBOT *Princ. Fungal Taxon.* xi. 160 The dehiscent types [of ascus], both operculate and inoperculate, become turgid and discharge their ascospores forcibly.

B. *sb.* An operculate mollusc. In the pl. the L. form **operculata** is commonly used.

1856 WOODWARD *Mollusca* 174 Class II. Gasteropoda. Order II. Pulmonifera... Section B. Operculata. **1895** *Edin. Rev.* Oct. 366 In one aberrant operculate, respiration is conducted by means of a lung-cavity.

†**o'perculate,** *v. Obs.* [f. ppl. stem of L. *operculāre:* see prec.] *trans.* To cover.

1623 COCKERAM, *Operculate,* to couer with a couering. **1657** TOMLINSON *Renou's Disp.* 501 Keep the first..in a glass well operculated.

operculated (əʊ'pɜːkjʊleɪtɪd), *ppl. a. Nat. Hist.* [-ED[1].] = OPERCULATE *a.*

[**1657** *Physical Dict., Operculated,* close-covered.] **1676-** in COLES. **1776** DA COSTA *Conchol.* 102 Operculated, or covered with a lid. **1849** MURCHISON *Siluria* x. 222 Several of these operculated fossils. **1854** WOODWARD *Mollusca* II. 169 One large division of the land-snails is furnished with an operculated shell. **1897** *Allbutt's Syst. Med.* II. 1023 The liver-fluke pours its large brown operculated eggs..into the bile.

opercule (əʊ'pɜːkjʊl). *Nat. Hist.* [a. F. *opercule* (1752 in Hatz.-Darm.), ad. L. *opercul-um:* see -CULE.] = OPERCULUM.

1835-6 TODD *Cycl. Anat.* I. 685/1 The opening in the summit of the cone is closed by an opercule. **1862** ANSTED *Channel Isl.* II. ix. (ed. 2) 210 Lower part of opercule somewhat toothed.

operculi-, combining form of L. *operculum,* as in **opercu'liferous** *a.* [-FEROUS], having an operculum, operculate; **o'perculiform** *a.* [-FORM], having the form of a lid or operculum; **opercu'ligenous** *a.* [-GEN + -OUS: cf. *alkaligenous*], producing an operculum: said of the metapodium of gastropods; **opercu'ligerous** *a.* [-GEROUS] = *operculiferous, operculigenous.*

1857 MAYNE *Expos. Lex., Operculiferus,*..provided with a horny opercule, serving to close the cells which they inhabit: *operculiferous. **1828** STARK *Elem. Nat. Hist.* II. 76 *Radiolites*... Shell inequivalve..lower valve turbinated.. the upper..*operculiform. **1836** *Penny Cycl.* V. 311/1 The opposite valve generally smaller, flatter, and sometimes operculiform. **1882** OGILVIE s.v. *Metapodium,* The posterior lobe of the foot in mollusca, often called the *operculigenous lobe, because it develops the operculum when this structure is present. **1856** WOODWARD *Mollusca* 47 *Trochus Ziziphinus* ..exhibits..an *operculigerous lobe.

operculum (əʊ'pɜːkjʊləm). Pl. -la. [a. L. *operculum* cover, covering, lid, f. *operīre* to cover, close: see -CULUM.] An organ or structure forming or resembling a lid or cover; *spec.*

1. *Zool.* **a.** The gill-cover of a fish; esp. the hindmost and uppermost bone of this.

1752 SIR J. HILL *Hist. Anim.* 225 They are in great part covered by the opercula of the gills. **1849** THOREAU *Week Concord* Sat. 31 There is also another species of bream.. without the red spot on the operculum. **1880** GÜNTHER *Fishes* 38 The operculum, forming the posterior margin of the gill-opening.

b. The calcareous, horny, or fibrous plate secreted by some gastropods and other molluscs, which serves to close the aperture of the shell when the animal is retracted; also, the flap or lid closing the aperture of the shell in sessile cirripeds.

1777 PENNANT *Zool.* IV. 61 Lepas..Common English Barnacle,..the lid or operculum sharp pointed. **1777** G. FORSTER *Voy. round World* I. 434 The round operculum, or cover of a shell. **1856** WOODWARD *Mollusca* 47 Most spiral shells have an operculum, or lid, with which to close the aperture when they withdraw for shelter. **1866** J. G. MURPHY *Comm. Exod.* xxx. 34 Onycha is probably the operculum..or lid of the shell of a strombus.

c. Applied to various other parts and organs covering or closing an aperture: *spec.*

(*a*) In aquatic mammalia, as the water-vole, a part of the ear, which acts as a valve to prevent the entrance of water. (*b*) In birds, the ear-conch or feathered flap of the ear of the owl; also, the nasal scale, a small horny or membranous lid or flap which in some birds closes the nostril. (*c*) In insects, the covering of each of the two spiracles on the sides of the metathorax. (*d*) In the king-crab (*Limulus*), the eighth pair of appendages which are conjoined into a single broad plate covering the succeeding appendages. (*e*) In spiders, each of the small scales covering the branchial and tracheal stigmata or breathing-orifices. (*f*) In *Chilostomata* and some other *Polyzoa,* the movable lid of the cell of the polypid which is shut down when the zooid is withdrawn within. (*g*) In

Infusoria, as *Vorticella*, the lid of the lorica or protective sheath.
1713 DERHAM *Phys.-Theol.* VII. ii. 382 *note*, This Bottom or Base of the Columella [in the inner ear of a bird], I call the Operculum. *Ibid.*, In the Conclave, at the Side opposite to the Operculum, the tender Part of the Auditory Nerve enters. **1794** G. ADAMS *Nat. & Exp. Philos.* I. vi. 239 The moveable operculum on the pipe of the human throat, which is imitated by the reed of the organ. **1816** KIRBY & SP. *Entomol.* (1818) II. xxiv. 405 The drum-covers or opercula [of the cicada] from beneath which the sound issues. **1826** *Ibid.* III. 383 *Opercula*, plates that cover the vocal spiracles in humming insects. **1840** *Penny Cycl.* XVIII. 366/1 *Myriapora*. Animals cylindrical, terminating anteriorly in a tubular extensible proboscis..; on one side of this body is a cartilaginous round operculum. **1842** *Ibid.* XXIII. 117/2 The aperture of the ear.. is large, measuring,.. in the Brown Owl, more than an inch in length. This is protected by an operculum. **1843** *Ibid.* XXVII. 629/1 In each half of this operculum [in the king-crab] are to be distinguished one or two basilary pieces and two terminal laminæ. **1888** ROLLESTON & JACKSON *Anim. Life* 234 The mouth so-called .. is crescentic in outline, and its proximal edge or lip is thickened, forming the operculum, a structure from which the suborder *Cheilostomata* takes its name. *Ibid.* 523 *Limulus* has six pairs of limbs on the abdominal mesosoma, of which the first pair fuse to form a genital operculum. **1894** NEWTON *Dict. Birds* 675 In *Asio*,.. the conch is enormously exaggerated,.. and is furnished in its whole length with an operculum. **1897** *Allbutt's Syst. Med.* II. 1017 The shell [of the egg of Bothriocephalus latus] is simple, brown, and closed in at one end with an operculum.

2. *Bot.* **a.** The lid of the capsule in mosses, and of certain circumscissile capsules in phanerogams; also, the lid of the pitcher in *Nepenthes*, and the concail limb of the calyx of *Eucalyptus*.
1788 LEE *Introd. Bot.* (ed. 4) Gloss. 422 *Operculum*, a Cover, as in the Mosses. **1830** LINDLEY *Nat. Syst. Bot.* 64 In Eucalyptus.. the sepals are consolidated into a cup-like lid, called the operculum. **1840** *Penny Cycl.* XVI. 9/2 The urn itself [of mosses] is closed by a lid, or *operculum*. *Ibid.* 446/1 *Operculum*.. this term.. has also been applied to the lid which covers in the Pitcher of Nepenthes, where it is the lobe of a modified leaf. **1857** BERKELEY *Cryptog. Bot.* 483. **1867** J. HOGG *Microsc.* II. I. 310 These spore-capsules are closed on their summit by opercula or lids.

b. The lid of the ascus or sporangium of certain fungi.
1879 W. PHILLIPS tr. E. Boudier in *Grevillea* VIII. 46 After the examination of a considerable number of Discomycetes, I am able to call the attention of mycologists to the necessity of separating this family into two very natural sections, according as to whether the mode of dehiscence is with or without an operculum. **1887, 1888** [see ASTROPYLE]. **1971** P. H. B. TALBOT *Princ. Fungal Taxon.* xi. 160 Operculate asci have an operculum at the apex: a hinged lid-like opening.

3. *Anat.* In the brain, the principal covering of the insula or island of Reil, which overlaps the gyri operti from above.
1892 *Syd. Soc. Lex.*

4. *gen.* A cover. Also *fig.*
1837 *Civil Eng. & Arch. Jrnl.* I. 58/1 They carry small square bits of black paper, which project in front of the screen, and serve as opercula or covers to conceal the letters. **1866** BLACKMORE *Cradock Nowell* xxiv. (1883) 116 Noble wine deserves not to be the mere operculum to a stupidly-mixed hot meal.

operetta (ɒpəˈrɛtə). [a. It. *operetta*, dim. of *opera*.] A short opera, usually of light and humorous character, consisting originally and properly of one act, but now sometimes of two or more.
1770 HOOPER in *Monthly Rev.* 280 They sometimes give operattas that are charming. **1817** *Examiner* No. 505. 554 The new Operetta produced here, called *Fire and Water*. **1865** DUTTON COOK in *Once a Week* XII. 235 *Operetta*, a coinage which was first introduced at the Lyceum, or English Opera House. **1884** *St. James's Gaz.* 10 Apr. 5/2 On Monday a comic opera or operetta.. is to be brought out.

operette (ɒpəˈrɛt). Also ‖**opérette** (ɔperɛt). English (with accent, French) form of OPERETTA. Also *transf.*
1890 E. DOWSON *Let.* 19 May (1967) 149 Playing snatches of opérette—Gilbert & Sullivan, Sultan of Mocha etc. **1928** *Observer* 15 Apr. 21/2 Few operettes launched on the public nowadays can compare with the delicious music of Pongrác Kacsoh. **1935** *Discovery* July 211/2 The Estonians have some charming 'operettes', too, which.. without being heavy have much more in them than our average musical comedies. **1938** N. COWARD (*title*) Operette. **1961** *Times* 7 Mar. 8/4 On the borderline between *opera bouffe* and *opérette*. **1977** *Listener* 30 June 867/1 Joan Aiken's *Lost Movement*, an entirely enjoyable story, offers.. a pretty and melodramatic operette.

operettist (ɒpəˈrɛtɪst). [f. OPERETTA + -IST.] A writer or composer of operettas.
1922 *Blackw. Mag.* June 717/2 There are a mass of Hungarian operettists.

†**oˈperiment.** *Obs. rare.* [ad. L. *operīmentum* covering, cover, f. *operīre* to cover.] A covering.
1650 BULWER *Anthropomet.* 212 [It] was only for beauty; yet in another place he adds for an operiment. **1656** BLOUNT *Glossogr.*, *Operiment*, a covering.

†**ˈoperish,** *a. Obs. nonce-wd.* Of, pertaining to, or having the character of opera.
1742 FIELDING *Miss Lucy in Town* Wks. 1882 X. 316 This is certainly one of those operish singers Miss Jenny used to talk of.

operon (ˈɒpərɒn). *Biol.* [ad. F. *opéron* (F. Jacob et al. 1960, in *Compt. Rend.* CCL. 1729), f. *opér-* (in *opérer* to effect, work, *opération* OPERATION, etc.): see -ON¹.] A unit of co-ordinated gene activity which is believed to account for inducible and repressible enzymes in bacteria and hence for the regulation of protein synthesis, and is usu. conceived as a linear sequence of genetic material comprising an operator, a promoter, and one or more structural genes.
1961 JACOB & MONOD in *Jrnl. Molecular Biol.* III. 344 This genetic unit of co-ordinate expression we shall call the 'operon'. **1969** *Nature* 18 Jan. 219/2 Essentially, Grodzicker and Zipser's experiment was to take strongly polar nonsense mutants of the lactose operon of *E. coli*. **1969** A. M. CAMPBELL *Episomes* ix. 116 The genes of one operon are all transcribed onto the same messenger molecule. **1971** J. Z. YOUNG *Introd. Study Man* iii. 59 Each operon is controlled by one or more regulator genes. **1973** B. J. WILLIAMS *Evolution & Human Origins* vi. 91/1 The model of genetic control receiving the most attention today is that of the operon.

operose (ˈɒpərəʊs), *a.* [ad. L. *operōs-us*, f. *opus*, *oper-* work.]
1. Made or done with, attended by, or involving, much labour; laborious; tedious; elaborate.
1678 CUDWORTH *Intell. Syst.* 884 An Operose, Cumbersom, and Moliminous Business. **1683** CAVE *Ecclesiastici*, *Ambrose* 371 His Arguments.. do not deserve an operose Confutation. **1756** JOHNSON *Introd. Browne's Chr. Mor.* p. xix, Browne might himself have obtained the same conviction by a method less operose. **1841** STEPHEN *Comm. Laws Eng.* (1848) I. I. iii. 241 The indirect and operose expedient of a fine or recovery. **1855** GEO. ELIOT *Let.* 25 June (1954) II. 206 Such sentences.. make a style seem operose and unwieldy. **1959** *New Scientist* 19 Nov. 983 Operose and scholarly collected editions.
2. Of a person: Laborious; industrious, busy.
1670 BLOUNT *Glossogr.* (ed. 3), *Operose*, busie, diligent in labour, laborious. *a* **1734** NORTH *Exam.* I. iii. §3 (1740) 126 We cannot think such an operose Compiler of History.. should be ignorant of so remarkable a Passage. **1883** SYMONDS *Ital. Byways* 100 The atmosphere of operose indolence.

ˈopeˌrosely, *adv.* [f. prec. + -LY².] In an operose manner: laboriously, busily; elaborately.
1668 H. MORE *Div. Dial.* II. xviii. (1713) 148, I take his Sophistry to be so conspicuous, that I think it not needful.. more operosely to confute it. **1792** A. YOUNG *Trav. France* 411, I have seen, in the operosely cultivated parts of France, labour comparatively dear, and ill performed, amidst swarms of half idle people. **1836-7** SIR W. HAMILTON *Metaph.* (1877) II. xxviii. 168 The petty and recondite objections they have so operosely combated.

ˈopeˌroseness. [f. as prec. + -NESS.] Operose character or quality, laboriousness, elaborateness.
1664 H. MORE *Exp. 7 Epist.* Pref. c v b, They.. have not that operosenesse of Synchronisms necessarily hanging on them. **1699** BENTLEY *Phal.* xv. 487 All that.. affects you, is a stillness and stateliness and operoseness of Stile. **1817** H. T. COLEBROOKE *Algebra*, etc. 80 The objection to this mode of finding the diagonals is its operoseness. **1856** *Titan Mag.* Nov. 392/2 Sully, in the midst of his operoseness, evinces many really beautiful.. qualities.

operosity (ɒpəˈrɒsɪtɪ). [ad. L. *operōsitās*, n. of quality f. *operōsus* OPEROSE.] Operoseness, laboriousness, painstaking endeavour.
1623 COCKERAM, *Operocitie*, great paines or labor. **1648** BP. HALL *Sel. Th.* §65 There is a kinde of operosity in sin, in regard whereof sinners are stiled, The workers of iniquity. **1885** *Sat. Rev.* 22 Aug. 248/2 This troublesome and polypragmatic operosity.

†**ˈoperous,** *a. Obs.* [ad. L. *operōsus* OPEROSE: see -OUS.] = OPEROSE.
1641 W. TWISSE *Pref. Mede's Apost. Later Times* 5 Some things, whereof he had written.. in more operous and large discourses. **1657** TOMLINSON *Renou's Disp.* 607 There is nothing.. in this preparation, either difficult or operous. **1783** POTT *Chirurg. Wks.* II. 81 An operous, expensive process.
Hence †**ˈoperously** *adv.*, operosely.
1668 HOWE *Bless. Righteous* x. 170 Operously to insist in proving that [etc.]. **1696** WHISTON *Th. Earth* IV. i. 257 The Creator.. had so operously and so liberally provided for the well-being.. of Mankind.

†**operˈtaneous,** *a. Obs. rare*⁻⁰. [f. L. *opertāneus*, f. *opert-us* covered + *-āne-us* 'belonging to the class of'.] Of secret, hidden, or covert nature.
1656 BLOUNT *Glossogr.*, *Opertaneous*, done within doors, in secret or in cover. **1775** in ASH; and in some mod. Dicts.

ˈope-tide. Now *arch.* = OPEN-TIDE.
1597 BP. HALL *Sat.* II. i. 13 So lavish ope-tyde causeth fasting lents. **1641** —— *Serm. bef. King in Lent* Rem. Wks. (1660) 69 There is an Ope-tyde by his allowance, as well as a Lent. **1911** BEERBOHM *Zuleika D.* iii. 28 Her soul was as a flower in its opetide. She was in love.

opeynyon, oph, obs. forms of OPINION, OAF¹.

‖**ophannim, ophanim** (əʊˈfænɪm). [Heb. *ōfannīm* wheels.] The 'wheels' mentioned, in Ezekiel i and x, as accompanying the living creatures or cherubim: treated in the 'Book of Enoch' as an order of angels.
1821 R. LAURENCE *Bk. of Enoch* (1838) 83 Then the Seraphim, the Cherubim, and Ophanin surrounded it. **1839** BAILEY *Festus* vi. (1852) 80 Not where the anteformal seraphs beam, Nor cherubim, with winged countenance, but Where roll the bright Ophanim. **1892** A. B. DAVIDSON *Ezekiel* 9 In the Book of Enoch 'wheels' (Ophannim) are a class of angels named along with Seraphim and Cherubim.

Ophelian (ɒˈfiːlɪən), *a.* [f. the name of the heroine of Shakespeare's play *Hamlet*: see -AN.] Resembling or characteristic of Ophelia.
1903 'MARJORIBANKS' *Fluff-Hunters* 101 Some time ago I felt so moody and sad that I sought out a pretty pool, with an Ophelian resolution. **1928** *Observer* 18 Mar. 15/3 One can hardly fail to hear this play's Shakespearean echoes... The Gaoler's Daughter is of pure Ophelian stock. **1929** D. H. LAWRENCE *Pansies* 6 Its transience, its breath, its maybe mephistophelian, maybe palely ophelian face. **1962** *John o' London's* 25 Jan. 91/4 Miss Maclaine would be well advised to drop her Ophelian aspirations.

ophelimity (ɒfɪˈlɪmɪtɪ). *Econ.* [f. F. *ophélimité* (also used), ad. Gr. ὠφέλιμος useful, serviceable.] (See quots.)
[**1896** V. PARETO *Cours d'Économie Politique* I. 3 Nous emploierons le terme *ophélimité*, du grec ὠφέλιμος, pour exprimer le rapport de convenance qui fait qu'une chose satisfait un besoin ou un désir, légitime ou non.] **1896** *Political Sci. Q.* XI. 750 The term utility, for example, has its ambiguities; and Professor Pareto substitutes the word ophélimité, meaning capacity to satisfy any want, whether rational or irrational. **1920** A. C. PIGOU *Econ. of Welfare* ii. 23 Several writers have endeavoured to get rid of the confusion.. by substituting for 'utility'.. some other term such, for example, as Professor Pareto's 'ophelimity'. **1935** BONGIORNO & LIVINGSTON tr. *Pareto's Mind & Society* I. i. 29 In pure economics my hypothesis of 'ophelimity'.. remains experimental so long as inferences from it are held subject to verification on the facts. **1966** D. MIRFIN tr. *Pareto's Sociol. Writings* 99 We shall employ the term *ophelimity*.. to designate the relationship of convenience which makes a thing satisfy a need or desire, whether legitimate or not... *Utility* will be required for use in its ordinary accepted sense as the property which makes a thing favourable to the development and well-being of an individual, a community or the whole human species.

opherion (ɒˈfiːrɪən). Used by T. S. Eliot, perhaps in error for ORPHARION.
a **1922** T. S. ELIOT *Waste Land Drafts* (1971) 99 (*title*) Song. For the opherion.

Ophian (ˈɒfɪən). *Ch. Hist.* [ad. Gr. Ὀφιαν-οί (Clemens Alex.).] = OPHITE *sb.*²
1678 TENISON *Idolatry* viii. 153 The sect of the Ophians, a kind of Spawn of the Gnostics. **1882-3** SCHAFF *Encycl. Relig. Knowl.* II. 880 This class of Gnostics, called by Hippolytus Ophites, by Clement of Alexandria Ophians.

ophic (ˈɒfɪk), *a. rare.* [irreg. f. Gr. ὄφι-ς serpent + -IC: the Gr. adj. is ὀφιακός.] Of or relating to serpents.
1865 *Athenæum* No. 1986. 679/2 The ophic or serpent worship. **1866** *Fortn. Rev.* No. 22. 474 There is.. no proof of Ophic worship ever having been practised in this island.

ophicalcite (ɒfɪˈkælsaɪt). *Min.* [f. Gr. ὄφι-ς serpent + CALCITE. In Fr. *ophicalce* (Brongniart 1813), Ger. *Ophicalcit*.] A species of rock composed of a mixture of serpentine and crystalline limestone (calcite); calcitic ophiolite.
1846 WORCESTER, *Ophicalcic*, n. (*Min.*). **1866** CARPENTER in *Q. Jrnl. Geol. Soc. Lond.* XXII. 227 A specimen of Ophicalcite from Cesha Lipa in Bohemia, which gave on decalcification a form of *Eozoon*. **1869** PHILLIPS *Vesuv.* viii. 238 Three tall columns, which as being calcareous with magnesian veins may be called Ophicalcite. **1875** DAWSON *Dawn of Life* vi. 147 A beautiful variety of ophicalcite or serpentine-marble.

ophicleide (ˈɒfɪklaɪd). Also -cleid. [a. F. *ophicléide* (*Moniteur Universel* 19 Ap. 1811) f. Gr. ὄφις serpent + κλείς, κλειδ- key.] A musical wind-instrument of powerful tone, a development of the ancient 'serpent', consisting of a conical brass tube bent double, with keys, usually eleven in number, forming the bass or alto to the key-bugle; also, a performer on this instrument.
1834 *Times* 21 June 6/1 (Westminster Abbey Festival) Ophicleides.—Messrs. Hubbard & Ponder. **1835** *Court Mag.* VI. 23/2 One of the Ophicleides was incompetent to the task he had undertaken. **1849** A. J. SYMINGTON *Harebell Chimes* 119 The ophicleid rich and deep With soft cornopion. **1879** GROVE *Dict. Mus.* I. 497 From the gradual disuse of the Serpent and Ophicleide, the Euphonium is becoming the chief representative of the eight-foot octave among the brass instruments.
b. Name for a powerful reed-stop on the organ, now usually called *tuba*.
1842 in BRANDE *Dict. Sci.* etc. 857/1. **1843** *Mech. Mag.* XXXIX. 208 The Ophicleide is the name given by Mr. Hill .. to a new stop of his invention. **1880** GROVE *Dict. Mus.* II. 601, 1840. [Organ at] Town Hall, Birmingham... This was the first organ that had the 'Great Ophicleide', or 'Tuba', on a heavy wind.
Hence **ophiˈcleidean** *a.*, pertaining to or resembling an ophicleide; **ˈophiˌcleidist**, a performer on the ophicleide.
1881 *Century Mag.* XXIII. 489/1 The mighty ophicleidean roll of the.. organ.

‖**Ophidia** (əʊˈfɪdɪə), *sb. pl. Zool.* [mod.L. deriv. of Gr. ὄφι-ς serpent: app. an arbitrary formation to provide a term in *-ia*, analogous to *Reptilia*, *Sauria*, *Crocodilia*, etc. (It can hardly represent Gr. ὀφίδια pl. of ὀφίδιον, OPHIDIUM.)] An order of Reptiles containing the snakes or serpents.

1848 in CRAIG. **1854** OWEN *Skel. & Teeth* in *Circ. Sc.*, *Organ. Nat.* I. 199 The vertebræ also are..always fewer in number than in the typical ophidia. **1878** BELL *Gegenbaur's Comp. Anat.* 418 The scales of the Saurii and Ophidii are..processes of the whole cutis. **1892** *Chambers's Encycl.* IX. 531 The fossil remains of Ophidia are scarce.

ophidian (əʊˈfɪdɪən), *a.* and *sb.* [f. prec. + -AN.]

A. *adj.* **1.** *Zool.* Belonging to the order *Ophidia*.

1826 KIRBY & SP. *Entomol.* III. xxxvi. 717 The fangs of one tribe of Ophidian reptiles. **1854** OWEN *Skel. & Teeth* in *Circ. Sc.*, *Organ. Nat.* I. 192 The osteology of the..Ophidian reptiles differs from that of the batrachians. **1939** T. S. ELIOT *Family Reunion* I. ii. 56 The dead stone is seen to be batrachian, The aphyllous branch ophidian.

2. Pertaining or relating to, or resembling that of, a snake or serpent; snake-like.

1883 D. COOK in *Time* No. 53. 186 The prominent ophidian forehead of the great French actress. **1885** E. C. STEDMAN in *Century Mag.* XXIX. 509 An Elsie Venner, tainted with the ophidian madness.

B. *sb.* (*Zool.*) A reptile of the order *Ophidia*; a snake or serpent.

1832 LYELL *Princ. Geol.* II. 104 The larger ophidians may be themselves transported across the seas. **1872** NICHOLSON *Palæont.* 551 The Ophidians make their first appearance in the Eocene.

‖**ophidiarium** (əʊˌfɪdɪˈɛərɪəm). *rare.* Also **ophidarium.** [f. OPHIDIA, after *aquarium*, *vivarium*, etc.] A place where snakes are kept; a snake-house.

1882 MISS HOPLEY *Snakes* Introd. 16, I now invite my readers to accompany me in imagination to the Ophidarium. **1891** *Cent. Dict.*, *Ophidiarium.*

oˈphidioid, *a.* (*sb.*) *Zool.* [f. *Ophidi-um* + -OID.]

a. *adj.* Belonging to the group *Ophidioidea* of gadoid fishes, of which *Ophidium* is the typical genus. **b.** *sb.* A fish of this group.

oˈphidious, *a. rare.* = OPHIDIAN *a.*

1846 WORCESTER, *Ophidian*, *Ophidious*, relating to serpents or snakes.

‖**Ophidium** (əʊˈfɪdɪəm). *Zool.* Also 8 **ophidion.** [med.L., ad. L. *ophidion* (Pliny), a. Gr. ὀφίδιον 'a fish resembling the conger', dim. of ὄφις serpent.] A genus of gadoid fishes with elongated bodies; a fish of this genus.

1706 PHILLIPS, *Ophidion*, a sort of Sea-fish resembling a Serpent or Eel. **1752** SIR J. HILL *Hist. Anim.* 238-9 The Ophidion, with four beards on the lower jaw..is frequent in the Mediterranean... The Ophidion, without beards..is frequent in the Baltic, and some other seas. **1774** GOLDSM. *Nat. Hist.* (1862) II. III. i. 295 The Ophidium, or Gilt-head.

ophido- in comb., erroneous form of OPHIO-.

ophio-, combining form of Gr. ὄφι-ς serpent, used in various words, chiefly scientific.

ophiobaˈtrachia *pl. Zool.* = *Ophiomorpha*: see OPHIOMORPH. †**ophioˈcephale** *a. Obs.* [ad. Gr. ὀφιοκέφαλος, f. κεφαλή head], having a serpent's head. ˌ**ophioˈcephaloid** (*Zool.*), *a.*, allied to or resembling the fishes of the genus *Ophiocephalus* (walking-fishes), which have a long body and snake-like head, and are capable of breathing air and of travelling considerable distances overland; *sb.* a fish of the family *Ophiocephalidæ*, of which *Ophiocephalus* is the typical genus. ‖**ophiogenes** (-ˈɒdʒɪniːz), *pl.* [Gr. ὀφιογενής serpent-gendered]: see quot. ‖**Ophioˈglossum** *Bot.* [Gr. γλῶσσα tongue], the genus of ferns containing the adder's-tongue, the type of the sub-order *Ophioglossaceæ*. **ophiˈography** [-GRAPHY], a treatise on, or the description of, serpents (Mayne *Expos. Lex.* 1857). †ˈ**ophiomach** [ad. L. *ophiomachus*, Gr. ὀφιομάχος 'fighter with serpents', a name of the ichneumon, and a kind of locust]: see quot. **ophiˈophilist** [Gr. -φιλος loving], a lover of snakes; so **ophiˈophilism,** love of snakes. ˈ**ophiosaur** [ad. mod.L. *ophiosaurus*, f. Gr. σαῦρος lizard], a lizard of the genus *Ophiosaurus* or family *Ophiosauridæ*, limbless and of snake-like form; a glass-snake; so **ophioˈsaurian** (used in quot. 1882 for a hypothetical reptile combining the characteristics of a lizard and a snake).

1608 TOPSELL *Serpents* (1658) 608 Some of the Heathen had their *Ophiocephale Beasts with Serpents heads, which they did worship. **1601** HOLLAND *Pliny* I. 154 Crates..saith, That in Hellespont about Parium there was a kind of men (whom he nameth *Ophiogenes) that if one were stung with a serpent, with touching only, will ease the paine. **1871** TYLOR *Prim. Cult.* II. 218 The Ophiogenes, or Serpent-race of the Troad, kindred of the vipers, whose bite they could cure by touch. **1881** *Sat. Rev.* 19 Mar. 374/2 The genus *ophioglossum, or adder's tongues, which are to the races of ferns what the lampreys are to the race of fishes. **1609** BIBLE (Douay) *Lev.* xi. 22 As is the bruke after his kind, the attake, and the *ophiomach [**1611** beetle, *Rev. V.* cricket] and the locust. **1883** *Daily News* 19 Feb. 5/2 *Ophiophilism is by no means an ugly word..but it may be doubted whether Miss Catherine C. Hopley..will succeed in persuading her readers to become ophiophilists. **1882** MISS HOPLEY *Snakes* xxiii. 429 A meaning which may be worth seeking by a philologist, should he be also an *ophiophilist. **1857** MAYNE *Expos. Lex.*, *Ophisaurus*,..a Family..of saurian reptiles, having the *Ophisaurus* or *Ophiosaurus* for their type: *ophisaurian. **1882** MISS HOPLEY *Snakes* xv. 263 Suspected species of reptiles, compound *ophiosaurians, or saurophidians, or who shall say what, in those inaccessible depths.

ophiolater (ɒfɪˈɒlətə(r)). [f. OPHIO- + Gr. -λάτρης worshipper.] A serpent-worshipper.

1895 ELWORTHY *Evil Eye* ix. 315 That our Celtic forefathers were Ophiolaters.

Hence **ophiˈolatrous** *a.*, given to serpent-worship; **ophiˈolatry,** serpent-worship.

1887 A. B. ELLIS *Tshi-speak. Peoples* vii. 95 It has been inferred that the Tshi-speaking tribes are ophiolatrous. **1862** *St. James's Mag.* Oct. 279 On the plains of Wiltshire still remain the traces of ophiolatry. **1864** R. F. BURTON *Dahome* I. 96 Ophiolatry..is mostly confined to the coast regions; the Popos and Windward races worship a black snake of a larger size. **1894** *Nation* (N.Y.) 13 Sept. 204/1 Instead of assuming it to be a form of ophiolatry, we now recognize it..as an elaborate prayer for rain.

ophiolite (ˈɒfɪəlaɪt). [f. OPHIO- + -LITE.]

a. *Min.* A name for serpentine (*obs.*) or a mixture of serpentine with other minerals (= *verd-antique*): see quots.

1848 in CRAIG. **1862** DANA *Elem. Geol.* viii. 82 Ophiolite (or verd-antique marble). A variegated mixture of serpentine and either carbonate of lime (*calcareous ophiolite*), dolomite (*dolomitic ophiolite*), or carbonate of magnesia or magnesite (*magnesitic ophiolite*). **1876** PAGE *Adv. Text-bk. Geol.* viii. 158 The name serpentine, or its learned equivalents—ophite and ophiolite.

b. *Geol.* Any of a group of basic and ultrabasic igneous rocks, including serpentinite and serpentinized peridotite, gabbro, and diabase, which occur associated with pillow lava and radiolarian chert in a characteristic pattern of layers in the Alps and certain other regions and are thought to have been formed as a result of the submarine eruption of oceanic crustal and upper mantle material; so **ophiolite suite** or **association,** the assemblage of ophiolites, pillow lava, and radiolarian chert.

This use originated in Ger. with the recognition of the association by G. Steinmann (*Ber. d. naturforsch. Ges. zu Freiburg i. Br.* (1906) XVI. 18-49).

1937 A. L. DU TOIT *Our Wandering Continents* viii. 168 There is a wide development in Morocco, Spain and the Alpine region of the so-called greenstones or 'ophiolites'. **1963** *Spec. Papers Geol. Soc. Amer.* No. 73. 204 Throughout the Alpine-Himalayan system extensive lavas occur in close association with coarse mafic and ultramafic rocks... This assemblage is the ophiolite suite of Alpine writers. It seems to represent long pre-orogenic extrusion of ultramafic magma. **1970** J. C. MAXWELL in Johnson & Smith *Megatectonics of Continents & Oceans* viii. 181 The assemblage of igneous rocks which Europeans call ophiolites seems incompatible with the dominantly sedimentary melange in which it typically occurs. **1971** I. G. GASS et al. *Understanding Earth* iv. 132/2 The former is dominantly volcanic (a thick sequence of ophiolites with subsidiary cherts, carbonates and pelites). **1972** *Sci. Amer.* May 65/3 Within the Alpine-Himalayan mountain belt are narrow zones characterized by a distinctive assemblage of rocks, known as the ophiolite suite. *Ibid.* 66/3 The Ural and Appalachian-Caledonian mountain belts..have narrow zones where ophiolites are found... This implies that the Urals, for example, were created by the collision of two continental masses and that the ophiolites were generated by sea-floor spreading at a ridge axis before the continents were brought together. **1977** A. HALLAM *Planet Earth* 166 The whole assemblage of sea-floor basalts and associated upper-mantle peridotites is known as the ophiolite association.

ophioˈlitic, *a.* [f. OPHIOLITE + -IC.] Of, pertaining to, or composed of ophiolite.

1909 H. B. C. & W. J. SOLLAS tr. *Suess's Face of Earth* IV. v. 153 The sheet of the green-rocks (Ophiolitic, Rhaetic, Vindelician sheet; Steinmann). **1911** *Geol. Mag.* Decade V. VIII. 243 The constant association of dialase (spilite), serpentine, and gabbro in the northern Alps with radiolarian cherts has led Steinmann..to regard these 'ophiolitic eruptives' as the typical volcanic rocks of abysmal depressions. **1963** D. W. & E. E. HUMPHRIES tr. *Termier's Erosion & Sedimentation* xvii. 341 Radiolarites associated with the rocks of the ophiolitic suite (of geosynclines), demonstrate the subordinate role of living organisms in comparison to that played by transported material. **1971** *Nature* 3 Sept. 46/2 One of the most significant drilling results..was the discovery of a Lower Cretaceous and Upper Jurassic pelagic sequence above an ophiolitic oceanic basement, almost identical to the coeval Alpine sequences.

ophiology (ɒfɪˈɒlədʒɪ). (Erron. ophidology). [f. OPHIO- + -LOGY.] That branch of zoology which treats of serpents. Hence **ophioˈlogic, ophioˈlogical** *adjs.*; **ophiˈologist,** one versed in the natural history of serpents.

1817 *Blackw. Mag.* May 187/1 Reserving the history of the serpent tribes for the article *Ophiology.* **1828** WEBSTER, *Ophiology, Ophiologic, Ophiological, Ophiologist.* **1882** MISS HOPLEY *Snakes* Introd. 19 To enrich ophiological literature. **1882** STRADLING in *Nature* XXV. 378/1 Which motion..has, singularly enough, been very little commented upon by ophiologists. **1896** *Academy* 26 Dec. 604/2 The reason..which precludes the appointment of an official ophiologist in Iceland. ['There are no snakes in Iceland'.]

ˈ**ophioˌmancy.** *rare.* [ad. mod.L. *ophiomantīa*, f. OPHIO- + Gr. μαντεία -MANCY.] Divination by means of serpents.

[**1683** HOFFMANN *Lex. Univ.*, Ophiomantia, Græcè ὀφιομαντεία, divinatio ex serpentibus est, cujus exempla passim obvia.] **1753** CHAMBERS *Cycl. Supp.*, *Ophiomancy*, Ὀφιομαντεία, in antiquity, the art of making predictions from serpents. **1877** W. JONES *Finger-ring* 101 The serpent held by the female figure refers to ophiomancy, the art which the ancients pretended to, of making predictions by serpents.

ophiomorph (ˈɒfɪəmɔːf). *Zool.* [mod. f. OPHIO- + Gr. μορφή form.] An amphibian of the order *Ophiomorpha* or *Ophiomorphæ* (also called *Apoda*, *Gymnophiona*, and *Ophiobatrachia*); a limbless, serpentiform amphibian; a cæcilian. So **ophioˈmorphic, ophioˈmorphous** *adjs.*, having the form of a serpent or snake; *spec.* of or pertaining to the *Ophiomorpha*; **ophioˈmorphite,** an old name for fossil ammonite shells, from their snake-like appearance; a snake-stone.

1677 PLOT *Oxfordsh.* 110 Other Ophiomorphit's there are, that have only straight single ribs. **1828** WEBSTER, *Ophiomorphous.* **1909** LD. BALCARRES *Ital. Sculpture* i. 16 In the Celtic art of the North..these ophiomorphic meanderings of line bewilder the eye by their complexity.

ophiˈophagous, *a.* [f. Gr. ὀφιο-φάγ-ος serpent-eating + -OUS.] Eating or feeding upon serpents.

1650 SIR T. BROWNE *Pseud. Ep.* VI. xxviii. (ed. 2) 151 Ophiophagous nations and such as feed upon Serpents. **1881** STRADLING in *J. W. Ogle's Harveian Orat.* 93 Man is casually ophiophagous. **1886** *Sat. Rev.* LXI. 430/2 The Revolution is the ophiophagous reptile, and gradually but steadily eats up all the other reptiles.

‖**ophiˈophagus.** Pl. -gi. [L., a. Gr. ὀφιοφάγος: see prec.] A serpent-eater.

1555 EDEN *Decades* 14 *marg.*, Ophiophagi. (*text*) There is nothing amonge theyr delicate dysshes, that they esteeme so muche as these serpentes. **1601** HOLLAND *Pliny* I. 143 The Candei, whom they call Ophiophagi, because they are wont to feed on serpents.

2. *Zool.* A genus of very venomous serpents allied to the cobra, inhabiting the East Indies, and feeding upon other snakes. One species is *O. elaps*, the HAMADRYAD, q.v.

1883 MRS. BISHOP in *Leisure Ho.* 195/2 The *Ophiophagus*, a snake-eating snake over eighteen feet long, whose bite they say is certain death.

†ˈ**ophiouch.** *Obs. rare*[−1]. [ad. L. *Ophiūchus*, Gr. ὀφιοῦχος serpent-holder.] A (figure of a) man holding a serpent.

a **1697** AUBREY *Surv. Wilts.* in *Misc.* (1714) 27 A Bass relieve of an Ophiouch [*mispr.* Optriouch].

Ophir (ˈəʊfə(r)). [Heb. *ōphīr.*] The name of a place or region mentioned in the O.T., whence fine gold was obtained, the locality of which is still uncertain; hence ***gold of Ophir, Ophir-gold,*** and *Ophir* alone (as in Heb. Job xxii. 24), in the sense 'fine gold'.

1614 SYLVESTER *Bethulia's Rescue* IV. 40 Adorn'd with Ophir-Gold. **1630** *Evans' Almanac* in *Brit. Q. Rev.* LVI. 350 It is not wealth, nor Ophir-gold that can enrich our need. **1682** SIR T. BROWNE *Chr. Mor.* I. §28 There is Dross, Alloy, and Embasement in all human Temper; and he flieth without Wings, who thinks to find Ophyr or pure Metal in any.

Ophism (ˈɒfɪz(ə)m). *rare.* [f. as OPHITE *sb.*[2] + -ISM.] The doctrine or worship of the Ophites: see OPHITE *sb.*[2]

1865 *Chambers's Encycl.* s.v. *Ophites*, Their singular attempt to engraft 'Ophism' on Christianity.

ophite (ˈɒfaɪt), *sb.*[1] *Min.* Also 7 **ophit.** [ad. L. *ophītēs* (Pliny), a. Gr. ὀφίτης (sc. λίθος) serpentine stone, f. ὄφι-ς serpent: see -ITE[1] 2 b.] Name for various eruptive or metamorphic rocks, usually green, and having spots or markings like a serpent; serpentine; serpentine marble.

[**1398** TREVISA *Barth. De P.R.* XVI. lxviii. (1495) 574 Marbyl is callyd Ophites for it is speclyd lyke an adder. **1567** MAPLET *Gr. Forest* 15 That kinde of Marble which is called Ophites, which hath spottes like a Serpent.] **1644** EVELYN *Diary* 22 Oct., A column of ophite on which [is] a statue of Justice..cut out of porphyrie. **1703** T. S. *Art's Improv.* p. xix, It consists of one solid Stone, a kind of an Ophite or Spotted Marble. **1740** DYER *Ruins Rome* 77 Cærulean ophite, and the flow'ry vein Of orient jasper. **1868** DANA *Min.* (ed. 5) 468 The names *Serpentine*, *Ophite*, *Lapis colubrinus*, allude to the green serpent-like cloudings of the serpentine marble.

attrib. **1644** EVELYN *Diary* 25 Oct., A columne of ophite stone. **1694** MOTTEUX *Rabelais* v. xxxvii, A hard well-polish'd Ophits Stone.

Ophite (ˈɒfaɪt), *sb.*[2] *Eccl. Hist.* [a. late L. *Ophītæ* (Isidore *Orig.* VIII. v.), a. Gr. Ὀφῖται (Hippolytus, etc.), pl. of Ὀφίτης, f. ὄφι-ς serpent: see -ITE[1] 1.] A member of a sect which arose about the 2nd century, who paid reverence to the serpent as an embodiment of divine wisdom.

1692 W. WOTTON tr. *Dupin's Eccl. Writers* I. 127 [Origen] attacks the Ebionites,..the Ophites, and the Sabellians. **1727** H. HERBERT tr. *Fleury's Eccl. Hist.* I. 194 The Ophites, who said that Wisdom had turned itself into a Serpent. **1855** PUSEY *Doctr. Real Presence* Note S. 326 Even the Ophites, who worshipped the serpent as Christ 'introduced him to bless their Eucharist'. **1871** TYLOR *Prim. Cult.* II. 220 The cultus which tradition..declares the semi-Christian sect of Ophites to have rendered to their tame snake.

attrib. **1793** W. HOLWELL *Mythol. Dict.* 306 The Ophite priests were very learned. **1888** E. HATCH *Infl. Grk. Ideas* iii. (1890) 70 The Ophite writer, Justin.

Hence **'Ophitism** = OPHISM.

1875 LIGHTFOOT *Colossians* 98 Phrygia reared the hybrid monstrosities of Ophitism.

'ophite, *a. rare.* [ad. Gr. ὀφίτης of or like a serpent.] Of the nature of or resembling a serpent; of a sinuous form; serpentine.

1828 WEBSTER, *Ophite*, pertaining to a serpent. **1851** *Murray's Hand-bk. Devon & Cornwall* p. xxiv, The avenues ..run invariably in straight lines, and thus differ from those which have a true ophite character.

ophitic (əʊˈfɪtɪk), *a.*[1] *Min.* [f. OPHITE *sb.*[1] + -IC.] Of the nature of ophite; serpentine; used of the structure of certain rocks in which crystals of feldspar are interposed between plates of augite. By some writers restricted to textures in which augite predominates and the feldspar laths do not in general touch each other.

1875 G. H. KINAHAN in *Proc. R. Irish Acad.* II. 118 The passage-rock..may be called ophitic hornblende-rock or amphibolic-ophyte, according to the mineral predominating. **1881** *Jrnl. Chem. Soc.* XL. 697 The ophitic rocks of the Pyrenees are characterised by the development of microliths of triclinic felspar embedded in elongated layers of pyroxene. *Ibid.*, The labradoric ophite..showed the passage from trachytoidal to ophitic structure. **1889** *Pall Mall G.* 20 Aug. 3/1 A boulder..composed of sub-ophitic dolerites. **1897** GEIKIE *Anc. Volcanoes Gt. Brit.* I. 21 A specially characteristic feature of many basic rocks is..what is termed an ophitic structure. **1970** K. C. JACKSON *Textbk. Lithology* v. 300 Diabasic texture... Composed of tabular plagioclase with smaller interstitial granular pyroxene crystals. Ophitic texture... Small tabular plagioclase embedded in larger anhedral pyroxene crystals. **1973** G. J. H. MCCALL *Meteorites* xiii. 174 (*heading*) Eucrite showing ophitic intergrowth of narrow plagioclase laths.

Hence **o'phitically** *adv.*, with an ophitic texture.

1908 *Q. Jrnl. Geol. Soc.* LXIV. 491 [The biotite] is moulded ophitically on these minerals. **1971** *Nature* 3 Dec. 265/1 The plagioclase-phyric basalts contain abundant pyroxene.., most of which has crystallized ophitically with the small calcic plagioclase laths.

O'phitic, *a.*[2] *Eccl. Hist.* [f. OPHITE *sb.*[2] + -IC.] Of or belonging to the sect of the Ophites.

1865 tr. *Strauss' New Life Jesus* I. II. xi. 84 Expressions.. brought forward from an Ophitic work. **1867** LIDDON *Bampt. Lect.* v. (1872) 217 We find Ophitic Gnostics.. appealing to passages in St. John's Gospel.

†**o'phitical,** *a. Obs.* [f. as OPHITIC *a.*[1] + -AL[1].] = OPHITIC *a.*[1]

1611 CORYAT *Crudities* 346 This piece of marble may be very properly called Ophiticall. **1657** TOMLINSON *Renou's Disp.* 421 The ophytical or serpentine-marble.

‖**Ophiuchus** (ɒfɪˈ(j)uːkəs). [L., a. Gr. ὀφιοῦχος, f. ὀφιο- OPHIO- serpent + -εχος -holding, -holder.] One of the ancient constellations, figured as a man holding a serpent; also called *Serpentarius*.

1658 PHILLIPS, *Ophiuchus*, a constellation in Saggittary. **1667** MILTON *P.L.* II. 708 And like a Comet burn'd, That fires the length of Ophiuchus huge In th' Arctick Sky. **1727-8** CHAMBERS *Cycl.*, *Serpentarius*, in astronomy a Constellation of the northern hemisphere called also Ophiuchus, and anciently Aesculapius. **1870** PROCTOR *Other Worlds* xi. 254 To account for the appearance of the Milky Way between Centaurus and Ophiuchus.

ophiuran (ɒfɪˈ(j)ʊərən), *a.* and *sb. Zool.* [f. mod.L. *Ophiūra*, f. Gr. ὄφις serpent + οὐρά tail, in reference to the long snake-like arms.]

a. *adj.* Belonging to the genus *Ophiura*, family *Ophiuridæ*, or class *Ophiuroidea* of Echinoderms, comprising starfishes with well-defined slender arms (simple or branched) covered with plates or spines. **b.** *sb.* A starfish of this genus, family, or class; a brittle-star or sand-star. So **'ophiure** (= b); **ophi'urid** *a.* and *sb.*; **ophi'uroid** *a.* and *sb.*

1836-9 TODD *Cycl. Anat.* II. 45/1 The Ophiura has..ten ovaries..in the central part of the animal. **1864** *Reader* No. 85. 204/2 Starfishes, echinoids, or ophiurans. **1874** LUBBOCK *Orig. & Met. Ins.* iii. 61 Among the Ophiurans.. we find two well-marked types of development. **1877** HUXLEY *Anat. Inv. Anim.* ix. 566 The mouth of the Echinopaedium becomes that of the *ophiurid. **1877** W. THOMSON *Voy. Challenger* II. iv. 202 A viviparous ophiurid occurred in considerable numbers. **1888** *Chambers' Encycl.* II. 467 The technical title *Ophiuroid describes the snake-like coils of their 'arms'. **1888** ROLLESTON & JACKSON *Anim. Life* 549 The Echinoid and Ophiuroid larva is known as *Pluteus*.

‖**ophryon** (ˈɒfrɪɒn). *Anat.* [mod.L., f. Gr. ὀφρύς eyebrow.] That point in the forehead at the middle of the line joining the upper margins of the orbits of the eyes.

1878 BARTLEY tr. *Topinard's Anthrop.* II. ii. 234 Supra-orbital point, or supra-nasal, or ophryon. **1880** *Nature* XXI. 223/1 A point..immediately above the projection of the glabella, to which Broca has given the name ophryon.

‖**Ophrys** (ˈɒfrɪs). *Bot.* [a. Gr. ὀφρύς eyebrow; a. L. *ophrys* (Pliny) some bifoliate plant, adopted by Linnæus 1737 as a generic name.] A genus of terrestrial *Orchidaceæ*, containing the Bee-, Fly-, and Spider-orchis. Also popularly extended to allied genera, as *Neottia* or *Spiranthes* (Ladies'-tresses).

1785 MARTYN *Rousseau's Bot.* xxvii. (1794) 419 The Spiral Ophrys, commonly called Triple Ladies Traces..on heaths and dry pastures. **1829** A. JAMIESON *Dict. Mech. Sc.* s.v. *Ophrys*, Bee Ophrys ranks among the few plants that are more generally admired than all the Orchideae for their singular beauty. **1844** S. R. in *Church Poetry* (ed. 2) 291 There amid many weeds I see,..That curious plant, the Ophrys Bee.

ophthalm- bef. a vowel, = OPHTHALMO-: as in ‖**ophthal'malgia** *Path.* [Gr. ἄλγος pain], pain in the eye; neuralgia of the eye-ball; hence **ophthal'malgic** *a.* ‖**ophthalma'trophia, ophthal'matrophy** *Path.* [Gr. ἀτροφία atrophy], atrophy of the eye-ball; shrivelling or wasting of the eye.

1892 in *Syd. Soc. Lex.*

‖**ophthalmia** (ɒfˈθælmɪə). *Path.* Forms: 4-6 **obtalmia,** 5 **obtolmia,** 6 **op-, ophtalmia,** 6- **ophthalmia.** See also the anglicized form OPHTHALMY. [late L. (Boethius), a. Gr. ὀφθαλμία f. ὀφθαλμός eye.] Inflammation of the eye, esp. of the conjunctiva of the eye; ophthalmitis.

1398 TREVISA *Barth. De P.R.* VII. xvi. (1495) 235 A rewme rennyth to the eyen, and therof comyth an euyll that highte Obtalmia, a shrewde blerinesse and ache. *c* **1400** *Lanfranc's Cirurg.* 241 Oþere maner sijknes of þe i3e,..as obtolmia & blere i3ed. **1541** R. COPLAND *Guydon's Formul.* Yj b, Thyrdly is admynystred colirium de thutia..in the ende of optalmia. **1562** BULLEYN *Bk. Simples* 2 Ophthalmia..is a sicknes of the eye. **1597** LOWE *Chirurg.* (1634) 155 Ophthalmia..is an inflammation of the whole eye, but chiefly of the membraine called conjunctiue. **1794** E. DARWIN *Zoon.* (1801) I. 30 Light is as intolerable in this kind of ophthalmia, as pressure is to the finger in the paronychia. **1821** SHELLEY *Lett.* Pr. Wks. 1880 IV. 197, I have had a severe ophthalmia. **1878** BOSW. SMITH *Carthage* 225 Hannibal, himself tortured with ophthalmia, rode on the one elephant which had survived the last year's campaign.

b. *fig.* Disordered mental vision.

1831 CARLYLE *Sart. Res.* II. vii, Mechanical Profit-and-Loss Philosophies, with the sick ophthalmia and hallucination they had brought on. **1883** E. J. MOERAN in *Time* No. 53. 215 A temporary attack of mental ophthalmia.

oph'thalmiac. *rare.* [f. prec. + -AC.] A person suffering from ophthalmia.

1884 J. PAYNE *1001 Nights* VIII. 129 As slumber on eyes of ophthalmiac shed.

ophthalmi'ater. *rare.* [f. Gr. ὀφθαλμός eye + ἰατήρ healer.] An ophthalmic surgeon, an oculist.

1761 (*title*) Adventures of Chevalier John Taylor, ophthalmiater, written by himself. **1852** JERDAN *Autobiog.* II. 71 A glorious quack oculist, or 'opthalmiater', as he styled himself. **1892** in *Syd. Soc. Lex.*

So **ophthalmi'atric** *a.*, relating to the treatment of eye-diseases. (*Syd. Soc. Lex.* 1892.)

ophthalmic (ɒfˈθælmɪk), *a.* and *sb.* [ad. L. *ophthalmic-us* (in Martial as sb. 'an oculist'), a. Gr. ὀφθαλμικ-ός of or pertaining to the eye, f. ὀφθαλμός eye: see -IC.]

A. *adj.* **1.** Pertaining or relating to the eye, ocular; connected with the eye, as a nerve, artery, etc.; affecting the eye, as a disease.

1727-41 CHAMBERS *Cycl.*, *Ophthalmic Nerves.* **1741** A. MONRO *Anat. Nerves* (ed. 3) 44 This ophthalmic Branch.. supplies the *Glandula lacrymalis.* **1831** R. KNOX *Cloquet's Anat.* 453 The ophthalmic artery. **1852** DANA *Crust.* I. 27 The first antennary and the ophthalmic segments. **1858** J. MARTINEAU *Stud. Chr.* 304 Ophthalmic epidemics. **1877** [see OPHTHALMITE 2]. **1881** MIVART *Cat* 208 The ophthalmic artery passes along the inner side of the orbit.

2. Good for diseases or disorders of the eye; that treats such maladies; that performs, or is used for, operations on the eye.

1605 TIMME *Quersit.* III. 155 An excellent ophthalmick matter for the eyes. **1725** BRADLEY *Fam. Dict.* s.v. *Eye-water*, A choice Ophthalmick Water to preserve the Eyes and Sight. **1830** LINDLEY *Nat. Syst. Bot.* 91 The seeds are considered..as ophthalmic and cephalic. **1871** HAMMOND *Dis. Nerv. Syst.* p. xiii, A competent ophthalmic surgeon.

3. Affected with ophthalmia; ophthalmious.

1845 E. WARBURTON *Cresc. & Cross* I. 144 An ugly ophthalmic set..drest in blue shirts and red caps. **1897** *Westm. Gaz.* 25 Jan. 2/3 Ophthalmic, feeble-minded, ailing, and neglected children.

4. *ophthalmic acid*, a tripeptide found in the lenses of various mammals (see quot. 1958).

1956 S. G. WALEY in *Biochem. Jrnl.* LXIV. 715/1 The work..deals only with acidic peptides. One such peptide (for which the name ophthalmic acid is proposed) is particularly abundant. **1958** *Ibid.* LXVIII. 192/1 The electrophoretic mobility of ophthalmic acid, a tripeptide isolated from calf lens, shows that the glutamic acid residue is γ-linked, and hence that ophthalmic acid is γ-glutamyl-α-amino-n-butyrylglycine. **1962** R. VAN HEYNINGEN in H. Davson *Eye* I. v. 237 Although liver contains but little ophthalmic acid, extracts of liver will synthesize ophthalmic acid from the amino-acids. **1970** J. F. R. KUCK in C. N. Graymore *Biochem. Eye* iii. 206 An interesting feature of the relationship between glutathione and ophthalmic acid is that the former is a specific co-enzyme for glyoxalase while ophthalmic acid is a potent inhibitor of this same enzyme.

B. *sb.* (absolute uses of the adj.)

1. A medicine or remedy for diseases of the eye.

1653 CULPEPPER *Pharm. Londin.* v. 306 Such Medicines as are appropriated to the Eyes... I would have called them Ophthalmics had not the word been troublesom to the reading. **1693** SIR T. P. BLOUNT *Nat. Hist.* 292 The Liquor of Ants is commended by Schroder for a most Excellent Ophthalmick. *a* **1800** COWPER in Hayley *Life* (1809) II. 381 One would suppose that reading Homer were the best ophthalmic in the world. **1870** TALMAGE *Crumbs Swept Up* 124 Hepatics,..stomachics, ophthalmics.

2. The ophthalmic or orbital nerve.

1727-8 CHAMBERS *Cycl.* s.v. *Eye*, The first branch of the fifth pair, called ophthalmicks. **1872** HUMPHRY *Myology* 45 Soon after entering the orbit, the ophthalmic detaches a large branch which runs beneath the eye.

oph'thalmious, *a.* [f. OPHTHALMI-A + -OUS.] Affected with ophthalmia.

1859 W. H. GREGORY *Egypt* I. 12 Fellahs..with their blue-shifted veiled spouses and ophthalmious children.

oph'thalmist. *rare.* [f. Gr. ὀφθαλμός eye + -IST.] One versed in the structure and functions of the eye; an ophthalmologist.

1696 J. EDWARDS *Demonstr. Exist. God* II. 33 The fourth and last Membrane..though some Ophthalmists have talk'd of a Fifth..is the Retina.

ophthalmite (ɒfˈθælmaɪt). [f. Gr. ὀφθαλμός eye + -ITE[1] 2 b and 3.]

†**1.** *Min.* (See quot.) *Obs.*

1811 PINKERTON *Petral.* II. 63 Miagite..has by some been called Corsican granite, or Corsican granitel; and by others, from some resemblance to the eye, ocular granite, or, as it more properly may be expressed from the Greek, ophthalmite... It consists of concentric but irregular circles of white felspar and black siderite.

2. *Zool.* The stalk on which the eye is borne in podophthalmous Crustacea; the ophthalmic peduncle, eye-stalk.

1877 HUXLEY *Anat. Inv. Anim.* vi. 305 The moveable stalks, which support the eyes,..'the ophthalmic peduncles' or 'ophthalmites'. **1887** *Athenæum* 4 June 741/2 The assumption of antenniform characters by the left ophthalmite.

ophthalmitic (ɒfθælˈmɪtɪk), *a.*[1] *Path.* [f. OPHTHALMIT-IS + -IC.] (See quot.)

1857 MAYNE *Expos. Lex.*, *Ophthalmiticus*, of or belonging to *Ophthalmitis*; ophthalmitic.

ophthal'mitic, *a.*[2] *Zool.* [f. OPHTHALMITE 2 + -IC.] Of or pertaining to an ophthalmite or eye-stalk in Crustacea.

‖**ophthalmitis** (ɒfθælˈmaɪtɪs). [mod.L., f. Gr. ὀφθαλμός eye + -ITIS. (Gr. had ὀφθαλμῖτις as epithet of Athena).] Inflammation of the eye, ophthalmia; *spec.* inflammation involving all the structures of the eye.

1822-34 *Good's Study Med.* (ed. 4) III. 177 Amongst the local complications are to be noticed cataract.. ophthalmitis, &c. **1878** T. BRYANT *Pract. Surg.* I. 385 Ophthalmitis is usually the result of injuries. **1892** *Syd. Soc. Lex.*, *Ophthalmitis*, inflammation of all the structures of the eye... Also, the same as *Ophthalmia.*

ophthalmo- (ɒfˈθælməʊ), combining form of Gr. ὀφθαλμός eye, used in various scientific terms: the more important are entered in their alphabetical places as main words.

‖**oph,thalmoblenno'rrhœa** *Path.* [mod.L.: see BLENNORRHŒA], discharge of mucus from the eyes. ‖**oph,thalmocarci'noma** *Path.* [mod.L.: see CARCINOMA], cancer of the eye. **oph'thalmocele** *Path.* [Gr. κήλη tumour, hernia], 'protrusion or excessive prominence of the eyeball' (*Syd. Soc. Lex.* 1892). **oph,thalmodia'stimeter** [DIASTIMETER], an instrument for adjusting the distance between two lenses (as in a pair of spectacles) to that between the eyes. ‖**ophthalmodynia** (-əʊˈdɪnɪə) [Gr. ὀδύνη pain], pain in the eyeball; neuralgia of the frontal nerve in the orbit (Craig, 1848). **ophthal'mography** [-GRAPHY], description of the eye. **oph'thalmolith** [Gr. λίθος stone], a lacrimal concretion (*Syd. Soc. Lex.*). **oph'thalmophore** *Zool.* [Gr. -φορος bearing], a specialized portion of the head in Gastropod molluscs, which bears an eye (*e.g.* the 'horn' of a snail); an ommatophore; so **ophthal'mophorous** *a.*, eye-bearing, or pertaining to an ophthalmophore. ‖**ophthal'mophthisis** *Path.* [mod.L.: see PHTHISIS], 'wasting or shrivelling of the eyeball'

(*Syd. Soc. Lex.*). **oph'thalmo,plasty** *Surg.* [Gr. πλαστός fashioned], 'the application of an artificial eye' (*ibid.*). ‖**ophthalmo'plegia** *Path.* [mod.L., f. Gr. πληγή stroke], **oph'thalmoplegy**, 'paralysis of one or more of the muscles of the eye' (*Syd. Soc. Lex.*); hence **ophthalmo'plegic** *a.* **oph'thalmostat** [Gr. στατός standing], an instrument for holding the eyeball in a fixed position for an operation. **ophthal'motomy** *Anat.* and *Surg.* [Gr. τομή cutting], the dissection, or the excision, of the eye (Dunglison *Med. Lex.*, 1842). **oph,thalmoto'nometer** [Gr. τόνος stretching, tension; μέτρον measure], an instrument for measuring the tension of the eyeball; so **oph,thalmoto'nometry**, the measurement of this. **oph'thalmotrope** [Gr. τρόπος turning], an instrument devised to measure the muscular shortening in strabismus; also an apparatus for rendering manifest ocular movements. **oph,thalmotro'pometer**, an instrument for measuring the lateral movements of the eye.

Other compounds, given in the medical dictionaries, in which *ophthalmo-* 'of' or 'for the eye', 'eye-', is prefixed to known words, are *oph,thalmo-dyna'mometer*, *-mela'nosis*, *-'microscope*, *-my'otomy*, *-no'sology*, *-pa'ralysis*, *-phle'botomy*, *-spasm*, *-thera'peutics*, *-'therapy*, *-xyster*.

1842 DUNGLISON *Med. Lex.*, **Ophthalmoblennorrhœa.* **1846** DAY tr. *Simon's Anim. Chem.* II. 80 The mucus in ophthalmoblennorrhœa..is of a deep yellow colour. **1842** DUNGLISON, **Ophthalmo-carcinoma*,..**Ophthalmocele.* **1875** KNIGHT *Dict. Mech.*, **Ophthalmodiastimeter*, an instrument contrived by Landsberg, a Hanoverian optician, ..for adjusting the optical axes of lenses to the axis of vision. **1713** DERHAM *Phys. Theol.* (1727) 87 *note*, That accurate Surveyor of the Eye, Dr. Briggs, whose *Ophthalmography I have met with since penning this part of my Survey. [W. BRIGGS Ophthalmographia, sive Oculi, ejusque Partium descriptio anatomica, 1676.] **1896** *Natural Sci.* VIII. 340 [G. A. Boulenger] has, too, for the first time, utilized the development or want of an *ophthalmophorous shelf to the second suborbital as a family character. **1853** DUNGLISON *Med. Lex.*, **Ophthalmophthisis.* **1842** *Ibid.*, **Ophthalmoplegia.* **1848** CRAIG, **Ophthalmoplegy.* **1875** H. WALTON *Dis. Eye* 185 Paralysis of the orbital muscle, ophthalmoplegia. **1899** *Allbutt's Syst. Med.* VI. 893 In the etiology of chronic ophthalmoplegia. *Ibid.* VII. 380 Accompanied by *ophthalmoplegic symptoms. **1857** MAYNE *Expos. Lex.*, An *ophthalmostate. **1876** *Catal. Sci. App. S. Kens.* 552 *Ophthalmotropometer. An apparatus for determining the movements to right and left of each eye.

ophthalmo'logic, *a.* Chiefly *U.S.* [f. as next + -IC.] Of or belonging to ophthalmology.

1846 in WORCESTER. **1901** [see HOMATROPINE]. **1972** ARONSON & ELLIOTT *Ocular Inflammation* xiv. 314/2 Ophthalmologic examination was requested because she complained of intermittent blurring of vision in her right eye.

ophthalmological (ɒfθælməʊ'lɒdʒɪkəl), *a.* [f. as OPHTHALMOLOGY + -IC + -AL[1].] Belonging to or dealing with ophthalmology.

1839–47 TODD *Cycl. Anat.* III. 85/1 In their ophthalmological works. **1873** (*title*) Report of the Ophthalmological Congress. **1891** *Pall Mall G.* 31 Aug. 1/3 A test..which is absolutely unimpeachable if carried out by an ophthalmological expert.

Hence **ophthalmo'logically** *adv.*, in relation to ophthalmology.

1876 tr. *Wagner's Gen. Pathol.* (ed. 6) 233 Engorgement of the optic papilla, ophthalmologically..important.

ophthalmology (ɒfθæl'mɒlədʒɪ). [f. OPHTHALMO- + -LOGY.] The scientific study of the eye; that branch of science which treats of the structure, functions, and affections of the eye.

1842 in DUNGLISON *Med. Lex.* **1865** *Pall Mall G.* 30 Nov. 4 It is proposed to establish a chair of ophthalmology in the medical faculty of Paris. **1881** *Nature* XXIV. 349/1 Modern ophthalmology has scarcely a single point of similarity with that of the last century.

Hence **ophthal'mologist**, one versed in ophthalmology.

1834 *Good's Study Med.* (ed. 4) III. 166 No ophthalmologist..has paid so much attention to this subject as Professor Beer. **1900** *Edin. Rev.* Oct. 393 Von Graefe, the great ophthalmologist, first surveyed the fundus of the living human eye.

ophthalmometer (ɒfθæl'mɒmɪtə(r)). [f. OPHTHALMO- + -METER.] **a.** See quot. 1842. **b.** An instrument devised by Helmholtz for measuring the curvatures of the (living) eye by means of images reflected in it.

1842 DUNGLISON *Med. Lex.*, *Ophthalmometer*,..An instrument of the nature of compasses, invented by F. Petit, for measuring the capacity of the..chambers of the eye in anatomical experiments. **1864** tr. *Donders' Anom. Accommod. Eye* 17 Helmholtz constructed a peculiar instrument, called by him the ophthalmometer for the purpose of determining the magnitude of the reflected images. **1895** *Daily News* 27 Feb. 6/5 Before Helmholz's inventions of the ophthalmoscope and the ophthalmometer, 'no one had ever seen a living retina at its task'.

So **ophthalmo'metric** *a.*, relating to measurement of the eye; **ophthal'mometry**, measurement of the eye.

1899 *Daily News* 23 Feb. 5/1 The 'Dioptric and Ophthalmometric Review'. **1883** *Contemp. Rev.* Mar. 407 The startling and unexpected results of ophthalmometry.

ophthalmophore, -plegy: see OPHTHALMO-.

ophthalmoscope (ɒf'θælməʊskəʊp), *sb.* [f. OPHTHALMO- + Gr. -σκοπος viewing, viewer, see -SCOPE.] An instrument for inspecting the interior of the eye, esp. the retina.

1857 *Dunglison's Med. Lex.* 656 An ophthalmoscope..has been invented, which by reflecting the light on the retina enables the condition of the interior of the eye to be appreciated. **1867** BRANDE & COX *Dict. Sci.*, etc. [The] ophthalmoscope..invented by Helmholtz in 1851, for the examination of the interior of the living eye. **1878** T. BRYANT *Pract. Surg.* I. 293 The ophthalmoscope since its introduction has undergone innumerable modifications, both in principle and detail.

Hence **oph'thalmoscope** *v. intr.*, to inspect the eye by means of the ophthalmoscope; **ophthalmo'scopic, -'scopical**, *adjs.*, of or pertaining to the ophthalmoscope or its use; **ophthalmo'scopically** *adv.*, by means of ophthalmoscopy.

1857 in MAYNE *Expos. Lex.* 820/2 Ophthalmoscopic. **1861** BUMSTEAD *Ven. Dis.* (1879) 719 A gummy tumor of the ciliary body, which ophthalmoscopically..was seen and taken by others for a sarcoma. **1871** HAMMOND *Dis. Nerv. Syst.* p. xiii, Ophthalmoscopic examinations require the observer to possess a very thorough acquaintance with the anatomy of the eye, and also with the science of optics. **1879** J. H. JACKSON *Ophthalmoscope* 3 Extremely abnormal ophthalmoscopical appearances may exist when sight is good.

ophthalmoscopy (ɒfθæl'mɒskəpɪ). [f. as prec. + Gr. -σκοπια looking, viewing.]

1. A branch of physiognomy, by which character is inferred from the appearance of the eyes. ? *Obs.*

[**1727–41** CHAMBERS *Cycl.*, *Ophthalmoscopia*, that branch of physiognomy which considers a person's eyes, and looks; to deduce thence the knowledge of his temperament, humour, and manners.] **1730–6** BAILEY (folio), *Ophthalmoscopy.* **1828** in WEBSTER; and in later Dicts.

2. Inspection of the interior of the eye; the use of the ophthalmoscope.

1864 *N. Syd. Soc. Year-bk. Med.* 240 Atlas of ophthalmoscopy. **1866** A. FLINT *Princ. Med.* (1880) 104 Works which treat..of ophthalmoscopy. **1899** *Allbutt's Syst. Med.* VI. 760 The chapter on medical ophthalmoscopy.

Hence **ophthalmoscopist** (-'ɒskəpɪst), one skilled in ophthalmoscopy.

1866 A. FLINT *Princ. Med.* (1880) 104 The student or practitioner who desire to become a skilful ophthalmoscopist.

ophthalmostat, -trope: see OPHTHALMO-.

ophthalmy ('ɒfθælmɪ). Now *rare* or *Obs.* Forms: 6 **optalmie, ophthalmye**, 7 **ophthalmie**, 7–9 **ophthalmy**. [a. F. *ophtalmie* (Oresme 14th c. *obtalmie*), ad. L. *ophthalmia.*] = OPHTHALMIA.

1543 TRAHERON *Vigo's Chirurg.* 51 b/1 An optalmie caused of grosse matter. **1597** A. M. tr. *Guillemeau's Fr. Chirurg.* 32 b/2 Agaynst payne in the heade,..ophthalmye and payne in the teeth. **1650** TRAPP *Comm. Deut.* xxviii. 28 God, we trust, will,..cure them of this spiritual ophthalmy and phrensie. **1755** WALL in *Phil. Trans.* XLIX. 466 He had a scrophulous ophthalmy in each eye. **1865** *Englishman's Mag.* Aug. 145 He had..suffered from an obstinate ophthalmy of both eyes.

-opia, formative element [a. Gr. -ωπία, f. ὤψ, ὠπ- eye, face: see -IA[1].] of terms denoting visual disorders and abnormalities, as AMBLYOPIA, MYOPIA, POLYOPIA. Occas. anglicized as **-opy** [cf. -Y[3]].

opiammone ('əʊpɪəməʊn). *Chem.* [f. OPI(AN- + AMMONIA.] An amide of opianic acid $C_{20}H_{19}NO_8$, obtained by evaporating a solution of opianic acid in ammonia.

1845 *Penny Cycl.* Suppl. I. 348 Opiammon. **1866–77** WATTS *Dict. Chem.* IV. 207 Opiammone is a pale yellow crystalline powder.

opiane. [f. OPI-UM + *-ane* as var. of *-ine.*] An obsolete synonym of narcotine. Hence numerous chemical terms in *opian-*:

opianate ('əʊpɪəneɪt), a salt of opianic acid. **opianic** (əʊpɪ'ænɪk) *a.*, formed from narcotine; as in ***opianic acid*** ($C_{10}H_{10}O_5$), crystallizing in thin colourless prisms of bitter taste, produced, together with cotarnine, by the oxidation of narcotine; ***opianic ether*** ($C_{10}H_9.C_2H_5.O_5$) crystallizing in inodorous brilliant white needles of bitter taste. **'opianine**, a base resembling narcotine, and not certainly distinct from it. **opi'ano-**, comb. form of *opianic*, as in ***opiano-sulphurous acid***, an acid derived from opianic and sulphurous acid, forming a transparent crystalline mass. **'opianyl**, $C_{10}H_9O_4$, the radical of opianic acid and its derivatives.

1842 DUNGLISON *Med. Lex.*, *Opiane*, Narcotine. **1845** *Penny Cycl.* Suppl. I. 348 Opianate of ammonia. *Ibid.*, Opianic acid. **1857** MILLER *Elem. Chem.* III. 277 Opianine has hitherto only been found in Egyptian opium, and has been but imperfectly examined. *Ibid.* 284 The opianyl yields opianic and hemipinic acids. **1866–77** WATTS *Dict. Chem.* IV. 206 Opianates. **1873** —— *Fownes' Chem.* (ed. 11) 739 Opianic Acid is a monobasic acid.

opiate ('əʊpɪət), *a.* and *sb.* Also 7–8 **opiat**. [ad. med.L. *opiāt-us*, *-um*, pa. pple. of **opiāre*: see next.] **A.** *adj.* **a.** Made with or containing opium; hence, inducing sleep; narcotic, soporiferous.

1543 TRAHERON *Vigo's Chirurg.* VIII. xviii. 215 Opiate medicines swage payne, howbeit it is onely after the maner of palliation. **1579–80** NORTH *Plutarch* (1676) 800 They gave Dionysius the elder..a strong Opiat-drink to cast him in a sleep. **1626** BACON *Sylva* §903 And for the particular ingredients..it is like they are opiate, and soporiferous. **1667** MILTON *P.L.* XI. 133 Charm'd with Arcadian Pipe, the Pastoral Reed Of Hermes, or his opiate Rod. **1732** ARBUTHNOT *Rules of Diet* 267 Such things as are endued with an opiate Quality. **1887** BOWEN *Virg. Æneid* VI. 420 Morsels..of meal, and of honeyed opiate cakes.

b. *fig.* Inducing drowsiness or inaction.

a **1626** BP. ANDREWES *Serm.* (1856) I. 321 Have a little opiate divinity ministered to our souls. **1754** H. WALPOLE *Lett.* (1846) III. 56 Even in France the squabbles of the parliament and clergy are under the same opiate influence. *a* **1845** HOOD *To Sylv. Urban* vi, Confessions dozing from an opiate pen.

B. *sb.* **1. a.** Any medicine containing opium and having the quality of inducing sleep; a narcotic.

1603 B. JONSON *Sejanus* i. ii, More comforting Than all your opiates, juleps, apozems. **1674** R. GODFREY *Inj. & Ab. Physic* 195 Instances..of such who with Opiates slept to Death. **1742** YOUNG *Nt. Th.* VIII. 67 A pillow, which, like opiates ill-prepar'd, Intoxicates, but not composes. **1828** SCOTT *F.M. Perth* xvii, Compelled to sleep in spite of racking bodily pains, by the administration of a strong opiate. **1887** FENN *Master Cerem.* ii, The old woman took her opiate every night. **1948** *Arch. Internal Med.* LXXXII. 387 These men were..again offered the choice of either an opiate or methadon.

b. *fig.* Anything that causes drowsiness or inaction, or that dulls or quiets the feelings. See also OPIUM *sb.* 1 b.

1641 MILTON *Animadv.* ii. Wks. (1851) 209 If men should ever bee thumming the drone of one plaine Song, it would bee a dull Opiat to the most wakefull attention. **1751** JOHNSON *Rambler* No. 171 ¶3, [He] began to lull my conscience with the opiates of irreligion. **1866** GEO. ELIOT *F. Holt* i, Mrs. Transome..found the opiate for her discontent in the exertion of her will about smaller things. **1927** C. CONNOLLY *Let.* 4 Mar. in *Romantic Friendship* (1975) 276, I find covering ground rather an opiate. **1942** *R.A.F. Jrnl.* 30 May 24 There's no more beautiful feeling than the opiate of unguarded sleep on a sunny boat deck. **1960** D. EISENHOWER in W. Safire *New Lang. Politics* (1968) 309/1 Hundreds of millions behind the Iron Curtain are daily drilled in the slogan: 'There is no God, and religion is an opiate'. But not all the people within the Soviet accept this fallacy; and some day they will educate their rulers, or change them. **1968** tr. M. de Unamuno in *Bartlett's Familiar Quotations* (ed. 14) 870/1 One of those leaders of what they call the social revolution has said that religion is the opiate of the people. **1975** *Gen. Systems* XX. 109/1 The European revolutionary found religion an opiate to be abolished. **1976** C. DEXTER *Last seen Wearing* xxi. 158 The heady, heavy opiate of the gambling game.

2. Any drug having similar addictive effects to those of the opium alkaloids morphine and cocaine. Freq. *attrib.*

1954 *Ann. Rev. Med.* V. 318 Another interesting field of usefulness for nalorphine is in the detection of opiate addiction. Administration of 5 mg. nalorphine to individuals addicted to morphine or methadon induces abstinence symptoms within 15 min. **1960** *Federal Register* (U.S.) 5 Aug. 7351/2 The word 'opiate'..shall mean any drug..found by the Secretary or his delegate..to have an addiction-forming or addiction-sustaining liability similar to morphine or cocaine. **1961** *Jrnl. Pharmacol. & Exper. Therap.* CXXXIII. 371/1 Codeine accounts for at least 80% of the natural opiates sold on prescription. **1970** *Nature* 14 Apr. 323/1 Methadone itself is an addictive opiate. **1974** M. C. GERALD *Pharmacol.* xiii. 242 In 1973 evidence was presented demonstrating the existence of an opiate receptor in the brain. *Ibid.* 251 Although acute opiate withdrawal is thought to be a very dangerous and often fatal process, there is no evidence to support this belief.

opiate ('əʊpɪeɪt), *v.* [app. f. a med.L. **opiāre* to form or treat with OPIUM, It. *oppiare* (Florio).]

1. *trans.* To stupefy or put to sleep by means of opium; to narcotize.

1611 FLORIO, *Oppiare*, to oppiate, to stupefie the senses. **1659** TORRIANO, *Alloppiare*, to opiate, to bring asleep, by art, by drugs..as with Opium. **1668** in *7th Rep. Hist. MSS. Comm.* 486/2 He opiated the mother and daughter and then ravished the daughter. **1717** FENTON *Ep. to Lambard* Poems 209 Tho' no lethargick fumes the brain invest, And opiate all her active pow'rs to rest.

b. *fig.* To dull the sense or sensibility of.

1762 GOLDSM. *Cit. W.* c. [ciii.] II. 153 We..in that pleasing expectation opiate every calamity. **1764** —— *Hist. Eng. in Lett.* (1772) I. 190 Happy in his natural imbecility, which seemed to opiate all his afflictions. **1800** SOUTHEY in C. Southey *Life* II. 72 One who can let his feelings remain awake, and opiate his reason.

2. To mix or impregnate with opium. Chiefly in **opiated** *ppl. a.*

1611 FLORIO, *Alloppiáto vino*, wine opiated. **1683** KENNETT tr. *Erasm. on Folly* Pref. Verses, The opiated milk glews up the brain. **1857** D. MACMILLAN *Mem.* viii. (1882) 299 The ulcer was..treated with opiated caustic.

opiatic (əʊpɪ'ætɪk), *a.* (*sb.*) [f. med.L. *opiātum* + -IC.] Of or pertaining to opiates or their use; of the nature of or resembling an opiate.

1678 CUDWORTH *Intell. Syst.* I. v. 795 Soporated with the dull steams and opiatick vapours of this gross body. **1684** tr. *Bonet's Merc. Compit.* XIX. 749 Concerning the right use of Opiatick Pharmacy. **1882** O'DONOVAN *Merv Oasis* I. xxvi. 455 To combat the terrific opiatic reaction.

B. *sb.* An opiatic agent; = OPIATE B. *rare.*

1847 GILFILLAN in *Tait's Mag.* XIV. 768 Either a lulling, soothing opiatic, or a rousing and stimulating gratification.

† **'opiative**, *a. Obs. rare.* [f. med.L. *opiat-*, ppl. stem of *opiāre* to OPIATE + -IVE.] = OPIATE A.

1674 R. GODFREY *Injuries & Ab. Physic* 191 An Opiative Medicine..that has not so bad and malevolent tricks, but is by far better corrected than the Laudanum.

† **'opie.** *Obs.* Also opy(e, opi. [f. L. *opi-um* (see OPIUM).] Opium; an opiate.

c **1385** CHAUCER *L.G.W.* 2670 *Hypermnestra*, The narcotykis & opijs [*v. rr.* opies, apies, epies] ben so stronge. *c* **1386** —— Knt.'s T. 614 A Clarree maad of a certeyn wyn Of Nercotikes and Opie [*v. rr.* opy, opye] of Thebes fyn. *c* **1420** *Pallad. on Husb.* IV. 143 Her seede yf me reclyne In baume, or narde, or opi [*L.* opio] daies thre.

† **'opier.** *Obs.* [a. obs. F. *opier*, 'the Ople, water Elder, Dwarfe plane, Whitten tree' (Cotgr.); mod.F. *obier*; app. related to L. *opulus*, It. *oppio*, but of obscure formation.] The Guelder Rose or Water Elder (*Viburnum Opulus*): cf. OPLE.

1548 TURNER *Names of Herbes* (1881) 57 Opulus is a tree ..called in frenche as Gesnere sayeth opier, and so maye it be also called in englishe tyl we fynde a better name. [**1578** LYTE *Dodoens* VI. lxxii. 752, I think this not to be the right *Opulus*; but the very tree whiche we cal Witche, and Witche Hassel: in Frenche *Opier*... Reade more of Opier in the LXXX Chapter of this booke. *Ibid.* lxxx. 760 Of Marris Elder, Ople, or Dwarffe Plane tree... In Frenche *Obiere*, or *Opiere*... This is not *Opulus* as some do thinke.]

† **opiet.** *Obs.* App. an error for prec.

1601 HOLLAND *Pliny* I. 512 The Opiets or Wich-Hazels are sown of seed after the same maner as Elme. *Ibid.* II. 205 Touching the tree (in manner of an Opiet or Poplar) called Rumbotinus.

† **o'piferous**, *a. Obs. rare*$^{-0}$. [f. L. *opifer* help-bringing, f. *op-em* help + *-fer*: see -FEROUS.]

1656 BLOUNT *Glossogr.*, *Opiferous*, which aids or helps, succoring. Hence in Phillips, Bailey, and some mod. Dicts.

† **opifex.** *Obs.* [a. L. *opifex* (*opific-em*), f. root *op-* of *opus* work + *-fex*, *-fic-*, doer, f. *fac-ĕre* to do.] A worker, maker, framer, fabricator.

1649 BULWER *Pathomyot.* Pref. 11 The Soule only is the Opifex of all the movings of the Muscles. **1678** CUDWORTH *Intell. Syst.* I. iv. §15. 273 The Opifex of the World, the Fountain of Good.

† **'opifice.** *Obs.* [ad. L. *opifici-um* a working, f. as prec. + *-ficium* doing, making. Cf. OF. *opifice* 16th c., *opifisse* (13th c. in Godef.).] The doing or making of a work; construction, workmanship; *concr.* a fabric, a work.

1616 R. C. *Times Whistle* I. 104 Look on the heavens.. look, I say, Doth not their goodly opifice display A power 'bove Nature? **1635** GELLIBRAND *Variation Magn. Needle* 20 This admirable opifice of God or frame of the world. **1657** TOMLINSON *Renou's Disp.* 393* Bees..suppeditate both aliments and medicaments to man by their own opifice. **1677** GALE *Crt. Gentiles* IV. 302 God so manifestes himself in the whole opifice of the Universe.

† **o'pificer.** *Obs.* [f. L. *opifex*, *opific-em* + Engl. suffix -ER: cf. *artificer*, *officer*.] One who makes or constructs a work; a maker, framer, fabricator; a workman.

1548 FORREST *Pleas. Poesye* xviii. 57 The highe Opificer sendethe not his giftes too wone pertycularlye. **1660** *Char. Italy* 84 If you respect either Artificers or Opificers, all Nations have been benefited thereby. **1692** BENTLEY *Boyle Lect.* ii. 67 Considering the infinite distance betwixt the poor mortal Artist, and the Almighty Opificer. **1761** STERNE *Tr. Shandy* III. xxiv. ¶2 So many play-wrights, and opificers of chit-chat have ever since been working upon..my uncle Toby's pattern.

opignorate, etc.: see OPP-.

opihi (ɒ'piːhɪ). [Hawaiian.] A limpet belonging to the genus *Helcioniscus*, or its shallow shell. Also *attrib.*

1915 W. A. BRYAN *Nat. Hist. Hawaii* xxxv. 466 To the old-world limpets belongs the opihi of the natives. It is a favorite food with the Hawaiians... This knee-cap or umbrella shell is roughly though evenly ribbed without and pearly white within. **1976** *National Observer* (U.S.) 10 Apr. 17/2 Legend has it that when the highly prized Opihi Shell is given to one's sweetheart, the love between them becomes eternal. Thus, wearing the Opihi around the neck assures that the shell—and their love—is preserved forevermore!

opiism ('əʊpɪɪz(ə)m). [f. OPI-UM + -ISM.] The intoxication induced by taking opium; the habit of taking opium as an intoxicant or stimulant. So **'opiize** *v. trans.*, to affect or intoxicate with opium.

1889 *Leisure Hour* 438 Experience had taught him to know all the stages of the opiised state. *Ibid.* 440 Unmistakable tokens of the torpor of opiism. **1894** *Westm. Gaz.* 23 July 3/2 A very short time suffices for the establishment of 'opiism'.

opilate, etc.: see OPP-.

† **o'pime**, *a. Obs.* [ad. L. *opīm-us* rich, sumptuous, etc. Cf. F. *opime* (1762 in *Dict. Acad.*), It., Sp. *opimo.*] Rich, abundant, sumptuous, splendid.

1533 BELLENDEN *Livy* IV. (1822) 339 Na spuleyeis may be callit opime, bot onelie thay quhilkis ar takin be ane duke fra ane uthir. **1664** H. MORE *Myst. Iniq.* 426 Those great and opime Preferments and Dignities which thy ambitious and wordly minde so longingly hankers after. **1681** —— *Exp. Dan.* vi. 183 He had taken the more easie and opime places. **1694** MOTTEUX *Rabelais* V. (1737) 232 Th' Opime you'd linquish for the Macerated.

Opimian (əʊ'pɪmɪən), *a.* (*sb.*) *Rom. Antiq.* [ad. L. *Opīmiān-us* of or belonging to Opimius.] In *Opimian wine* (L. *vīnum Opīmiānum*), or absol. *Opimian*, a very celebrated ancient Roman wine of the vintage of A.U.C. 633, when Opimius was consul.

1601 HOLLAND *Pliny* I. 419 That there were wine sellars at Rome..appeareth plaine by a good proofe of the Opimian wine. **1863** SHIRLEY in *Fraser's Mag.* Feb. 241 The cry for light will not be silenced though we..pour the hundred-yeared Opimian before the shrine of Apollo.

† **o'pimous** *a. Obs. rare*$^{-0}$. = OPIME.

1656 BLOUNT *Glossogr.*, *Opimous*, fat, gross, in good liking or plight; rich, plentiful.

opinable (əʊ'paɪnəb(ə)l, †'ɒpɪnəb(ə)l), *a.* Now *rare* or *Obs.* [ad. L. *opīnābil-is*, f. *opīnārī* to OPINE: see -BLE. Cf. F. *opinable* (15.. in Godef.).]

†**1.** That is a matter of opinion; not certain, disputable, conjectural. *Obs.*

1456 *Paston Lett.* I. 369 My Lord Bedford wylle was made yn so bryeff and generall termys..but all wey new to constrew and oppynable. **1471** RIPLEY *Comp. Alch.* Ep. iii. in Ashm. (1652) 111 This Scyence is not opinable, But very true by Raymond and others determynate. *c* **1530** *Remedie of Loue* 62 The matter is doubtfull and opinable To a certain you I woll my self enable. **1546** *Confut. Nicholas Shaxton* C iij b, Opinable matters and disputable.

2. That is the object of opinion; capable of being opined or held as an opinion.

1603 HOLLAND *Plutarch's Mor.* 1117 How..he should admit and leave unto us sense and opinion, and not withall allow that which is sensible and opinable, a man is not able to shew. **1678** CUDWORTH *Intell. Syst.* I. iv. §36. 571 Not properly knowable, but opinable only or the object of opinion.

Hence **opina'bility** (Bailey 1721), **o'pinably** *adv.* (in quot. *opiniably*).

1655 in Hartlib *Ref. Commw. Bees* 31, I speak not opiniably, but what I know, and that experimentally.

opinant ('ɒpɪnənt). *rare*$^{-1}$. [a. F. *opinant* 'celui qui opine', pr. pple. of *opiner* to OPINE, used subst.] One who opines or forms an opinion.

1860 THACKERAY *Round. Pap., Late Great Victories*, The opinions differ pretty much according to the nature of the opinants.

† **opinate**, *a. Obs.* [ad. L. *opīnāt-us* pa. pple. of *opīnārī* to OPINE.]

1. Opined, supposed.

c **1450** tr. *De Imitatione* III. li. 123 þi copiose mercy is better to me for getinge of indulgence, þan myn opinate riȝtwesnes, for defending of myn hid conscience.

2. Obstinate in opinion; opinionated.

1491 CAXTON *Vitas Patr.* (W. de W. 1495) II. 265 b/1 He had condescended to make it to that other whiche was opynate [*i.e.* as said *ante*, 'obstynate in an ylle opynyon'].

† **'opinate**, *v. Obs. rare.* [f. ppl. stem of L. *opīnārī* (also *opīnāre*) to be of opinion, think.] *intr.* To give an opinion; to pronounce a formal or authoritative opinion; = OPINE I.

1625 W. B. *True School War* 55 There is not a matter of State in which..they haue not opinated and decreed.

† **'opinated**, *ppl. a. Obs. rare.* [f. OPINATE *a.* or *v.* + -ED.] Having a (specified) opinion; *to be opinated* = to be of opinion.

1610 MARKHAM *Masterp.* II. clix. 467 Wee are strongly opinated, that [it] doth make the horses chine or backe a great deale the stronger.

† **opi'nation.** *Obs.* [ad. L. *opīnātiōn-em*, n. of action from *opīnārī* to OPINE: cf. obs. F. *opination* (1590–95 in Montaigne).] The action of opining or forming an opinion, supposition; the mental result of this, an opinion, a supposition.

1611 COTGR., *Opination*, an opination, opining, opinion-delivering. **1656** STANLEY *Hist. Philos.* v. (1701) 216/2 Errour, temerity, ignorance, opination, suspicion, and.. whatsoever is not of firm and constant assent. **1687** RYCAUT *Knolles' Hist. Turks* II. 258 The occasion of this..caused many roving guesses and opinations of the reasons of it.

† **o'pinative**, *a.* (*sb.*) *Obs.* Also 6 -itive, -ytyve. [ad. late and med.L. *opīnātīv-us* (Priscian 6th c.), f. L. *opīnāt-*, ppl. stem: see -IVE. Perh. immed. a. obs. F. *opinatif*, *-ive* (Oresme 14th c.); cf. It. *opinativo* (Florio 1598).]

1. Stiff in opinion; adhering obstinately to one's own opinion; opinionative.

1530 TINDALE *Answ. More* III. xiii. Wks. (Parker Soc.) III. 159 They rail on him..and call him opinative, self-minded, and obstinate. **1550** J. COKE *Eng. & Fr. Heralds* v. (1877) 58 The Frenchemen..be opynatyfe, thynkyng Fraunce to be of more greater valure than any other realme. **1621** BURTON *Anat. Mel.* II. iii. VII, Speake truth. Be not opinatiue, maintaine no factions. **1660** tr. *Amyraldus' Treat. conc. Relig.* III. iv. 372 There is no Jew so opinative, as to account them proper for the government of all sorts of Nations in all Ages.

2. Of or belonging to opinion; of the nature of, or expressing, opinion; conjectural, not certain.

1588 J. HARVEY *Disc. Probl.* 16 A probable surmize, and opinitiue collection. **1593** BILSON *Govt. Christ's Ch.* Pref. 25 The coniecturall and opinatiue ghesses of some. **1610** HEALEY *St. Aug. Citie of God* v. xix. (1620) 214 He that contemneth their opinative praise contemneth also with it their vnaduised suspect. **1656** STANLEY *Hist. Philos.* v. (1701) 162/1 All this part of things, they called Opinative: Science they affirmed to be no where but in the Reasons and Notions of Mind. **1816–30** BENTHAM *Offic. Apt. Maximized, Extract Const. Code* (1830) 6 Judicially augmented will natural honour be by two conjunct and correspondent appropriate judicial decrees; the first opinative, the other imperative. **1829** —— *Justice & Cod. Petit.* 181 Opinative [functions], exercised by declaration made of opinion.

B. *sb.* An opinionated person.

1639 DRUMM. OF HAWTH. *Speech of Author's* Wks. (1711) 219 Such men..prove themselves to be altogether seditious and factious, malicious opinatives.

† **o'pinatively**, *adv. Obs.* [f. prec. + -LY^{2}.] In an 'opinative' manner, in the way of opinion; with obstinate adherence to opinion.

1533 MORE *Apology* xlviii. Wks. 925/1 He wyll not holde it opinatiuely, and therefore yet agayne it may be no heresie. **1536** *Theolog. Tracts, Hen. VIII* I. lf. 213 (P.R.O.) To stonde in it opynytyuely it is heresie agenst scripture. **1630** LENNARD tr. *Charron's Wisd.* III. iii. (1670) 359 If Vices gather not strength, and men grow not opinatively obstinate in them. **1696** [see OPINATOR].

† **'opinator.** *Obs.* [a. L. *opīnātor*, agent-n. from *opīnārī* to OPINE.] One who opines or holds an opinion; a thinker; a theorist.

1626 LAUD *Wks.* (1847) I. 143 If they had not been opinators..that God could never have maintained His cause against them. *a* **1641** BP. MOUNTAGU *Acts & Mon.* (1642) 228 Banded up and downe, by different Opinators many wayes. **1663** BLAIR *Autobiog.* vi. (1848) 86 Mr. Freeman, a strong opinator. **1696** LORIMER *Goodwin's Disc.* iv. 10, I will ..only ask him..Whether he holds that God is an Opinator, that he hath an Opinion of things, and knows them opinatively?

opine (əʊ'paɪn), *v.* [ad. L. *opīn-ārī* (also *-āre*) to be of opinion, think, judge; cf. F. *opiner*, in 15th c. *oppiner* (Littré), It. *opinare* (Florio 1598).]

1. *intr.* or *obj. cl.*: To express an opinion; to say that one thinks (so and so).

1598 DALLINGTON *Meth. Trav.* M ij b, Where hee opineth of the maner of seruice, he sayth: of Archers, the English are the flower. **1609** HOLLAND *Amm. Marcell.* 53 Some opined, That they must goe by Arborosa. **1628** LE GRYS tr. *Barclay's Argenis* 209, I cannot tell who they are against whom I haue opined. **1633** EARL MANCH. *Al Mondo* (1636) 3 All opining, that some one is to be chosen. **1797** J. LAWRENCE in *Monthly Mag.* XLVI. 215 The answerer.. opines that the old enmity and rivalship subsisting between France and this country..are beneficial to both. **1838** DICKENS *Nich. Nick.* vii, Mr. Squeers yawned fearfully, and opined that it was high time to go to bed. **1884** *Athenæum* 6 Dec. 725/3 Without pain, he opines, there would be no gratitude to God, no pity towards man.

b. *esp.* To express or pronounce a formal or authoritative opinion; to give one's opinion in council, etc. Now *rare.*

1581 SAVILE *Tacitus, Hist.* II. xxvii. (1591) 106 Once by fortune Heluidius Priscus Prætor elect had opined against a matter which Vitellius affected. **1589** PUTTENHAM *Eng. Poesie* III. ii. (Arb.) 154 In all deliberations of importance where counsellours are allowed freely to opyne and shew their conceits. **1600** HOLLAND *Livy* XLVIII. 1237 Cornelius Nasica opined and said, That hee saw as yet no iust and sufficient cause of warre. **1744** ARMSTRONG *Preserv. Health* (1807) 36 Thus the Coan sage opin'd. **1846** MRS. GORE *Eng. Char.* (1852) 45 The stability of the administration is opined upon, according to the indications of the barometer of that variable atmosphere, the breath of Kings. **1866** FREER *Regency of Anne of Austria* I. i. 31 [They] all opined for the Regency. **1891** *Law Times* XCI. 224/1 Lord Coleridge opined that even brokers and dealers are not exempt from the general regulations imposed by the Ten Commandments.

2. To form a judgement on grounds insufficient for positive proof; to hold an opinion, or to hold as one's opinion; to think, suppose. **a.** *trans.* (usually with *obj. cl.*).

1611 BEAUM. & FL. *Philaster* I. i, And from you..do I Opine myself most happy. **1654** H. L'ESTRANGE *Chas. I* (1655) 133 Men were left at liberty to opine what they pleased. **1694** MOTTEUX *Rabelais* v. (1737) 232 Opining to revise a Structure new. *a* **1711** KEN *Hymnarium* Poet. Wks. 1721 II. 95 Both the same thing opine, Both have the same Design. **1865** TROLLOPE *Belton Est.* ix. 99 The clergyman would opine that he was simply a reprobate. **1871** RUSKIN *Fors Clav.* vi. 4 You fancy, doubtless, that I write my 'opinions'—..You are much mistaken. When I only opine things, I hold my tongue; and work till I more than opine —until I know them.

b. *intr.*

1656 [? J. SERGEANT] tr. *T. White's Peripat. Inst.* 106 They, whose brain is of a thin, and hot constitution,..opine rashly and changeably. **1676** G. TOWERSON *Decalogue* 302 We should..choose to opine with them. **1881** M. PATTISON in *Academy* 12 Feb. 110 You may opine upon everything under the sun.

opiner (əʊ'paɪnə(r)). Also 7 -or. [f. OPINE *v.* + -ER. = F. *opineur.*] One who opines; one who holds or expresses an opinion.

1611 COTGR., *Opineur*, an opinor, one that delivers his opinion. 1652 GAULE *Magastrom.* 115 The opinors or opinionists (old and new) each of them contending. 1656 *Artif. Handsom.* 157 Others who are weak and wilfull opiners, but not just arbitraters. 1736 *Disc. Witchcraft* 42 A probable Argument that they were the first Opiners of Dæmons. 1881 *Oracle* No. 133. 324/3 An opinion—presuming the opiner is not a fool—is a coin with a current value.

† **o'pinial**, *a. Obs. rare*$^{-1}$. [f. stem *opīni-* (see OPINIATE *a.*) + -AL[1].] = OPINIONAL.

c 1450 PECOCK *Treat. Rule Faith* (1688) 3 There ben two maners of feith: oon is opinial feith... Another feith is sciencial feith.

opiniaster, -astre, -ty: see OPINIATRE, -TY.

† **opini'astrous**, *a. Obs. rare*$^{-1}$. [f. F. *opiniastre* (see OPINIATRE) + -OUS.] Opinionated; = OPINIATRE *a.*

1645 MILTON *Colast.* Wks. (1847) 222/2 The Laws of England, wherof you have intruded to be an opiniastrous subadvocate, and are bound to defend them.

† **o'piniate**, *a.* and *sb. Obs.* [In this and the following words to *opiniatry*, the stem *opini-* appears either to be shortened from L. *opīnio*, OPINION, or due to the influence of that word upon *opīn-* in *opinate, opinative*, etc.; they are not confined to Eng., for *opini-ato, opiniativo* occur in It. (Florio), *opini-atico* in Sp. (Minsheu), *opiniatif, opini-âtre* in Fr. etc.; but Eng. has more of them. They have mostly parallel forms in *opinion-* and *opin-*: see *opinial, opinional*; with *opiniate*, cf. *opinate, opinionate.*]
a. *adj.* = OPINIATED 3. **b.** *sb.* An opiniated person.

1597 J. PAYNE *Royal Exch.* 7 Sory to behoulde suche blynd opiniates so farr to outrun very many professors.

Hence † **o'piniately** *adv.*; † **o'piniateness.**

1645 *City Alarum* 18 Must the free horse alwayes be spurgalled, and the dull Asse favoured in his opiniatness? 1647 *Sectary Dissected* 27 Contumacie, obstinate opiniatnesse, sedition, pertinacity in speaking evill of dignities. 1658 T. WALL *Comm. Times* 22 It makes the knowing more learnedly ignorant, and the ignorant more opiniately knowing.

† **o'piniate**, *v. Obs.* [Cf. *opiniate* adj., and the vbs. *opinate, opinionate.*]
1. *trans.* To hold as an opinion, or to hold an opinion concerning; to suppose, think, opine.

1624 HEYWOOD *Gunaik.* I. 25 These Goddesses.. as they are opiniated, have the government of children in their infancie. 1656 BRAMHALL *Replic.* I. 10 This present age.. doth not know what it self beleeveth, or rather opiniateth.

2. To fix (a person) in an opinion; *refl.* to adhere obstinately to an opinion. (Cf. OF. *s'opinionner.*)

1603 FLORIO *Montaigne* I. xiv. (1632) 24 Men are punished by too-much opiniating themselves in a place without reason.

3. To pronounce an opinion upon.

a 1797 H. WALPOLE *Mem. Geo. III.* (1845) II. vii. 138 Rose Fuller said he would not opiniate the point, but declared he was against the precedent.

opiniated (əʊ'pɪnɪeɪtɪd), *ppl. a.* [f. as OPINIATE *a.* + -ED. Cf. *opinated* and *opinionated.*]
† **1.** Holding the opinion; of opinion (*that*...).

1610 MARKHAM *Masterp.* I. lxxiii. 152, I am confidently opiniated, that bots are euer bred in the stomacke.

† **2.** Having a conceited opinion *of*; thinking much *of*. *Obs.*

1589 *Late Voy. Sp. & Port.* (1881) 47 It may be you will thinke me.. too much opiniated of the Voiage, or conceited of the commanders. 1719 DE FOE *Crusoe* II. xii, Not being able to put the old Man out of his Talk, of which he was very opiniated or conceited.

3. Obstinately attached to one's own opinion; opinionated.

1597 J. PAYNE *Royal Exch.* 29 Whosoever ys so styffly opiniated as so stande in there owne conceite. 1627 SIR S. D'EWES *Jrnl.* (1783) 63 He being proud and self-opiniated, tooke his owne way. 1740 WESLEY *Wks.* (1872) I. 294 Positive and opiniated to the last degree. 1796 MRS. M. ROBINSON *Angelina* I. 109 A vain opiniated idiot. 1870 DISRAELI *Lothair* xiii. 56 The gardener, like all head-gardeners, was opiniated.

Hence **o'piniatedly** *adv.*

1651 HOBBES *Govt. & Soc.* Author's Pref., [I] Would rather chuse to brooke with patience some inconveniences.. then selfe opiniatedly disturb the quiet of the publique.

opiniater: see OPINIATRE.

opiniative (əʊ'pɪnɪətɪv), *a.* Now *rare.* [In obs. F. *opiniatif, -ive* (15th c. in Godef.); also It. *opiniativo* (in Florio 1598). See OPINIATE *a.*]
1. = OPINATIVE 1, OPINIONATIVE 2.

1574 HELLOWES *Gueuara's Fam. Ep.* (1584) 371 Ye are too too much obstinate, and in the maner of disputation extremely opiniative. 1621 BP. MOUNTAGU *Diatribæ* 416 It maketh men idle, and yet opiniatiue, and well conceited of themselues. 1690 LOCKE *Toleration* ii. Wks. 1727 II. 268 They.. grow so opiniative and so stiff in their Prejudice. 1707 *Reflex. upon Ridicule* 220 Lysias is only Opiniative because he wants Sense. 1835 *Fraser's Mag.* XII. 466 He may be suspicious or opiniative. 1885 J. MARTINEAU *Types Eth. The.* II. 94 There is something here manifestly beyond the play of opiniative despotism.

† **2.** = OPINATIVE 2, OPINIONATIVE 1. *Obs.*

1592 G. HARVEY *Pierce's Super.* in *Archaica* (1815) II. 88 Opiniative and prejudicate assertions, that strive for a needless and dangerous innovation.

Hence **o'piniatively** *adv.*; **o'piniativeness.**

1600 F. WALKER *Sp. Mandeville* 36 b, Trusting opiniatiuely to their owne wit. 1611 COTGR., *Opiniastreté*, opiniatiuenesse. a 1618 RALEIGH *Arts of Empire* xiv. (1658) 34 The first obstacle to good Counsel is Pertinacy or Opiniativeness. 1715 tr. *à Kempis' Chr. Exerc.* III. xviii. 154 To speak.. with Opiniativeness is the part of one that is a stranger to Wisdom. 1807 EARL MALMESBURY *Diaries & Corr.* III. 363, I am.. not surprised with the opiniativeness of Lord Grenville.

† **o'piniator.** *Obs.* Also 7 -our. [agent-n. in L. form from OPINIATE *v.* In 17–18th c. app. often identified with *opiniater*, OPINIATRE B.] One who holds or maintains an opinion (= OPINATOR); *esp.* one who obstinately adheres to his opinion: = OPINIATRE B.

1523 [COVERDALE] *Old God & New* (1534) R ij, With syxe hundreth opiniators & questionistes braulynge and striuyng among them selues. 1638 MAYNE *Lucian* (1664) A iv, I do not wonder that such Opiniators should be sick of this Disease. 1670 H. STUBBE *Plus Ultra* 42 He wished that first these Opiniatours would go to both Poles. 1714 SAVAGE *Art of Prudence* 182 All Fools are Opiniators.

So † **o'piniatory** *a. Obs.* = OPINIATRE A.

1626 SIR D. CARLETON *Sp.* in Rushw. *Hist. Coll.* (1659) I. 359 In my opinion, the greatest and wisest part of a Parliament are those that use the greatest silence, so as it be not opiniatory, or sullen.

† **opini'atre, opini'astre**, *a.* and *sb. Obs.* Also 7 -aster, 6–7 -ater. [a. F. *opiniastre* (R. Estienne 1539), later *opiniâtre*, It. *opiniastro* (Florio 1598), a Romanic formation on L. *opīnio*: see -ASTER.]
A. *adj.* Stiff or stubborn in opinion; obstinate in adhering to or maintaining one's opinion; opinionated.

α. 1606 R. WHYTE in Nichols *Progr. Jas. I* (1828) II. 98 They are the same opiniastre in their humors. 1641 MILTON *Animadv.* xiii. Wks. (1851) 240 Spare your selfe, lest you bejade the good galloway, your owne opiniastre wit. 1666 PEPYS *Diary* 3 July, A man of excellent.. learning, but most passionate and opiniastre. 1692 O. WALKER *Grk. & Rom. Hist.* 330 He seems also to have been very Opiniastre in his Paganism.

β. 1591 *Garrard's Art Warre* 291 The strong Fortresse had beene lost, a thing to be noted of such as be Opiniatre [*printed* Opiniatro]. 1594 A. HUME *Hymns*, etc. (1832) 64 Be not opiniater and wilfull in trifill maters. 1668 DRYDEN *Even. Love* II. (1671) 13 If she begins to fly before me, I grow opiniatre as the Devil. 1692 LOCKE *Educ.* §189 An insignificant Wrangler, Opiniater in Discourse.. or questioning every Thing. 1716 LADY BOLINGBROKE in *Swift's Wks.* (1841) II. 530 Silly, obstinate, opiniatre friends.

B. *sb.* A person obstinately attached to his own opinion. (In the form *opiniater*, this fell together with the agent-n. OPINIATOR, q.v.)

α. 1603 SIR C. HEYDON *Jud. Astrol.* ii. 108, I onely exempt Ptolemie out of the number of these superstitious opiniasters. 1653 GAUDEN *Hierasp.* To Rdr. 9 A Prophecy; which every opiniaster is prone to imagine strongly portendeth the advancement of his opinion. 1684 tr. *Agrippa's Van. Arts* xcv. 326 A monstrous heap of Opiniasters.

β. a 1677 BARROW *Serm.* (1686) III. 378 A clownish singularist, or non-conformist to ordinary usage, a stiff opiniatre. 1710 *Acc. Last Distemp. Tom Whigg* I. 6 Tom was ever an Opiniatre and a Hobbist. a 1716 SOUTH *Serm.* (1744) X. 304 Sovereignty itself must be forced.. to give way to every religious opiniater.

Hence † **opini'atreness**, † **opini'atreship.**

1689 HARVEY *Curing Dis. by Expect.* vii. 53 They continue in the use of [the remedies].. with that opiniatreness and brazen Confidence. 1704 N. N. tr. *Boccalini's Advts. fr. Parnass.* II. 51 Deprav'd Judgment, Opiniatreship, blind Zeal, Folly, boundless Pride and Ambition.

† **opini'atre**, *v. Obs.* Also -ater. [a. F. *opiniâtrer*, f. *opiniâtre* adj.: see prec.] **a.** *trans.* To maintain or persist in obstinately. **b.** *intr.* To persist obstinately in an opinion, or in a course of action; to 'insist hard'.

1652 LOVEDAY tr. *Calprenede's Cassandra* I. 32 Some of the Enemy.. finding Resistance had opiniater'd the fight. *Ibid.* 222 Whilst my Master opiniaters the making himself a passage to him, his horse is kild under him. 1678 MARVELL *Def. John Howe* Wks. 1875 IV. 183 But if The Discourse shall still opiniatre in this matter, let It.. strike efficacious. a 1734 NORTH *Exam.* III. ix. §4 (1740) 649 Dr. Short might differ from what Opinion prevailed, but, in the Case of a King, must not *opiniatre*. 1777 *Evelyns in Amer.* (1881) 248 Whether.. L[ord] G[ermaine] will have strength enough to opiniatre this business for another year, must soon be determined.

† **opini'atred**, *ppl. a. Obs.* Also -ter'd. [f. prec. + -ED.] Obstinately attached to one's opinion: = OPINIATRE *a.*

1641 EARL MONM. tr. *Biondi's Civil Warres* III. 123 Opiniatred onely in odde fancies. a 1668 DAVENANT *Rutland House* Wks. (1673) 351 My most opiniater'd Antagonist.

† **opini'atreture.** *Obs. rare*$^{-1}$. [irreg. or erron. f. OPINIATRE.] = next.

1699 C. GILDON *Ep. Ded. Langbaine's Dram. Poets*, Wit without Opiniatreture, but balanc'd with a true and penetrating Judgment.

† **opini'atrety, -'astrety.** *Obs.* Also 7 **a-strete, -atrete (-té, -tie,** *mispr.* **-atrecy, -cie, -atricy, -atracy), 7–8 -atrity, (8 -té).** [a. F. *opiniastreté* (c 1560 in Hatz.-Darm.), later *opiniâtreté*, f. *opiniastre*: see OPINIATRE *a.* and -TY.] The character of being 'opiniatre'; obstinate adherence to or maintenance of one's own opinion; stubbornness of mind.

α. 1648 J. BEAUMONT *Psyche* XVI. cciii, Whene'er her proud Opiniastrete Against Ecclesiastick Sanctions swells. 1656 BRAMHALL *Replic.* i. 73 The Romanists.. whose opiniastrety did hinder an uniform Reformation of the western Church. 1684 T. GODDARD *Plato's Demon* 290 Arguments.. sufficient to convince *opiniastrete* and wilful ignorance it self.

β. 1619 SIR D. CARLETON in *Hales' Gold. Rem.* (1673) II. 177 The Remonstrants being excluded from further conference, by reason of their Opiniatrity. 1639 DRUMM. OF HAWTH. *Prophecy* Wks. (1711) 181 Why should our opiniatrete be the overthrow of the state? 1649 EARL MONM. tr. *Senault's Use Passions* (1671) 345 Upon such an occasion Opiniatrecy is commendable. 1650 —— tr. *Senault's Man bec. Guilty* 30 Is not opiniatrecie a furious love to be always victorious? 1654 —— tr. *Bentivoglio's Warrs Flanders* 130 By this opiniatracy of the adverse party. 1690 LOCKE *Hum. Und.* I. iv. (1695) 38 What in them was Science, is in us but Opiniatrity. 1717 W. REEVES tr. *Justin Martyr's Apol.* I. lxx, Not carried away with opiniatrety and passion. a 1734 NORTH *Exam.* I. ii. §176 (1740) 123 The *opiniatrité* of his Party misled him.

† **opini'atry, -'astry.** *Obs.* [a. F. *opiniastrie* (16th c.), f. *opiniastre*: see prec.] = prec.

α. a 1643 SUCKLING *Lett.* Wks. (1646) 96 Opiniastrie is a sullen Porter and.. shuts out often-times Better things than it lets in. 1663 SIR G. MACKENZIE *Relig. Stoic* vi. (1685) 47 The mad hands of bigot opiniastry.

β. 1651 BIGGS *New Disp.* 203 'Tis not therefore an inference in our opiniotry only. 1692 LOCKE *Educ.* §98 The other teaches Fallacy, Wrangling, and Opiniatry. 1765 STERNE *Tr. Shandy* VII. xxvii, The scrapes which we were perpetually.. getting into in consequence of his [my father's].. opiniatry.

† **opinicus.** *Her.* A term of uncertain origin and meaning, given in modern heraldic works.

The word appears to be corrupt; the suggestion has been made that it is an error perh. for *Ophinicus* or *Ophiuchus.*

1780 EDMONDSON *Heraldry* II. Gloss., *Opinicus*, a fictitious beast, of heraldic invention. Its body and fore legs are said to be those of a lion, the head and neck like those of the eagle; to the body are affixed wings, like those attributed to the griffin; and it hath a short tail, resembling that of a camel... The Opinicus is the crest to the arms belonging to the Company of the Barber Surgeons of the City of London. 1863 BOUTELL *Eng. Heraldry* x. (ed. 5) 141 Opinicus a fabulous heraldic monster, a dragon before, and a lion behind with a camel's tail.

o'pining, *vbl. sb.* [f. OPINE *v.* + -ING[1].] The formation or expression of opinion; an opinion, a notion.

1656 *Artif. Handsom.* 131 Very few examine the marrow and inside of things, but take them upon the credit of customary opinings. 1716 M. DAVIES *Athen. Brit.* II. 333 Scarce one ever suffer'd under him for any opining. 1875 JOWETT *Plato* (ed. 2) IV. 85 This was the source of false opinion and opinings.

opinion (əʊ'pɪnjən), *sb.* Also 4–6 opp-, and with the usual interchange of *i* and *y*, *-on, -oun*, and *-one*; 4 openyoun, 5 opeynyon, (a-penyon, 6 *Sc.* apenion); *Sc.* 4 opunion, -yon(e, 6 -ȝoun. [a. F. *opinion* (12–13th c. in Hatz.-Darm.), ad. L. *opīniōn-em*, f. stem of *opīn-ārī* to be of opinion, think: cf. *oblivion, religion*, and see -ION[1].]
1. a. What one thinks or how one thinks about something; judgement resting on grounds insufficient for complete demonstration; belief of something as probable, or as seeming to one's own mind to be true, though not certain or established. (Distinguished from *knowledge, conviction*, or *certainty*; but sometimes = *belief.*)

in my opinion: according to my thinking; as I think, as it seems to me. ***a matter of opinion***: a matter about which each may have his own opinion; a disputable point.

1387–8 T. USK *Test. Love* III. i. (Skeat) l. 60 Opinion is while a thing is in non certaine, & hidde from mens very knowleginge, and by no parfite reason fully declared. 1390 GOWER *Conf.* III. 368 Of hem that walken up and doun Ther was diverse opinioun. 1483 LD. DYNHAM in Ellis *Orig. Lett.* Ser. II. I. 157 In myn openion it shuld be gretly for the wele of that toune and marches. 1538 STARKEY *England* I. i. 11 Saying ther ys no dyfference betwyx vyce and vertue but strong opynyon. a 1628 PRESTON *Breastpl. Faith* (1630) 118 The object of opinion is something in its own nature uncertain. 1644 MILTON *Areop.* (Arb.) 69 Opinion in good men is but knowledge in the making. 1704 NORRIS *Ideal World* II. ii. 130 What we call opinion, which is an imperfect assent or judgment. 1814 JANE AUSTEN *Mansf. Park* I. xviii, To see such an undersized, little, mean-looking man, set up for a fine actor, is very ridiculous in my opinion. 1852 MRS. STOWE *Uncle Tom's C.* xv. 141 Well, the position may be a matter of opinion. 1875 JOWETT *Plato* (ed. 2) IV. 23 Opinion is based on perception, which may be correct or mistaken.

b. Qualified by *common, general, public, vulgar*, etc.: Such judgement or belief on the part of a number, or the majority, of persons; what is generally thought about something. Also in attrib. phrases, as ***public opinion investigation***, ***poll*** [POLL *sb.*[1] 7 d], ***polling***, ***survey*** (see *opinion poll*, *survey*, sense 9 below), etc.

c **1425** LYDG. *Assembly of Gods* 1739 From Adam to Moyses, was idolatry Thorow the world vsyd in comon opynyoun. **1689–90** TEMPLE *Ess.*, *Popular Discontents* Wks. 1731 I. 258 Nothing is so easily cheated, nor so commonly mistaken, as vulgar Opinion. **1735** BOLINGBROKE *On Parties* (ed. 2) p. xxxi, Let them stand, or fall in the publick Opinion, according to their Merit. **1751** tr. *Rousseau's Discourse Arts & Sci.* 36 They only hate all publick opinions. **1763** CHESTERFIELD *Duke of Newcastle* in *Lett.* (1845) II. 463 The public opinion put him below his level: for though he had no..eminent talents, he had a most indefatigable industry, a perseverance. **1769** BURKE *Let.* 30 July (1844) I. 181 We must strengthen the hands of the minority within doors, by the accession of the public opinion, strongly declared to the court. **1781** GIBBON *Decl. & F.* xxxi. III. 257 Even this story is some evidence of the public opinion. **1801** JEFFERSON in Tucker *Life* II. 101 The mighty wave of public opinion which has rolled over our republic. **1871** *Daily News* 20 Apr. 5 That is a question..in which 'general opinion must assume the ultimate arbitrement'. **1892** *Pall Mall G.* 29 Nov. 5/1 When the court has pronounced its decision, then let it be freely commented upon; but until then parties must not attempt to influence public opinion. **1939** G. GALLUP (*title*) Public opinion in a democracy. **1952** W. J. H. SPROTT *Social Psychol.* 87 It is difficult to put into exact terms what is meant by 'public opinion'... We might, of course, define 'public opinion' on any particular issue..in terms of the people who actually have an 'opinion' on that issue. **1961** L. VAN DER POST *Heart of Hunter* I. v. 88 Tom refused to let public opinion create a sense of shame in him. **1964** GOULD & KOLB *Dict. Social Sci.* 477/2 *Public opinion* is a nebulous concept; it is not the simple aggregate of the opinions of the members of a public, but depends on the society's power structure, the mass media, channels of influence, etc.

attrib. **1936** L. DENNING *Coming Amer. Fascism* 299 A score of great corporations can raise ten million dollars for anti-social purposes of price-fixing or public-opinion manipulation. **1937** *Sociometry* I. I. II. 155 (*title*) Public opinion polls. **1939** G. GALLUP *Public Opinion in Democracy* 3 The development during the last few years of the public-opinion survey or unofficial poll has raised..a host of new and far-reaching questions. **1940** GRAVES & HODGE *Long Weekend* xxiii. 401 From the United States came public opinion investigation. *Ibid.*, Public opinion investigation was first started on a large and permanent scale by the American Dr. Gallup. **1941** J. S. HUXLEY *Uniqueness of Man* xi. 231 The modern scientific public opinion poll, indeed, is developing such uncanny accuracy that it is infringing upon practical politics. **1944** G. GALLUP *Guide to Public Opinion Polls* lxix. 91 The chief function of public opinion polls, and their chief value, is to report the *trend* of opinion. **1958** *Listener* 20 Nov. 813/1 Public-opinion polls... Public-opinion surveys. **1963** *Rep. Comm. Inquiry Decimal Currency* 5, in *Parl. Papers* 1962–3 (Cmnd. 2145) XI. 195 We considered going to further than this by commissioning a public opinion survey. **1964** *Ann. Reg. 1963* 5 His dominance of the parliamentary party was soon apparent in the major debates of the next five months, assisted, no doubt, by Labour's soaring lead in the public opinion polls. **1967** M. ARGYLE *Psychol. Interpersonal Behaviour* ix. 153 Public opinion polls are more closed questions, research surveys make more use of open-ended ones. **1972** *Jrnl. Social Psychol.* LXXXVII. 136 The sealing methodology employed was discussed and suggested as a possibly new public opinion polling device.

c. Also, in same sense, without qualification.

1603 FLORIO tr. *Montaigne* (1634) 133 Opinion is a powerfull, bould, and unmeasurable party. **1638** R. BAKER tr. *Balzac's Lett.* (vol. II) 96 It is not onely that opinion governs the world. **1753** HANWAY *Trav.* (1762) II. I. i. 4 Those..who offer incense to this..stupid idol, opinion. **1837** HT. MARTINEAU *Soc. Amer.* III. 7 The worship of Opinion is, at this day, the established religion of the United States. **1841** D'ISRAELI *Amen. Lit.* Pref. (1867) 3 Authors are the creators or the creatures of opinion.

2. a. (With *an* and *pl.*) What one thinks about a particular thing, subject, or point; a judgement formed or a conclusion reached; a belief, view, notion.

(Sometimes distinguished from a *conviction*; but in other cases denoting a systematic or definitely-held belief—e.g. an item of one's (religious, political, etc.) creed, or sometimes (in earlier use) the whole distinctive belief of a sect, etc.—and then practically identical with *conviction*.)

a **1300** *Cursor M.* 8843 þus sais sum opinion. **1340** *Ayenb.* 69 Ofte hi uallep ine errour, and ine ualse opinions, and ine eresye. *c* **1380** WYCLIF *Serm.* Sel. Wks. II. 287 Alle þes newe sectis..have newe opynyouns. *c* **1386** CHAUCER *Knt.'s T.* 622 Ffor shortly this was his opinion That in that groue he wolde hym hyde al day. *c* **1485** *Digby Myst.* III. 1463 Iesu! Iesu! qwat deylle is him? þat? I defye þe and þyn a-penyon! **1560** DAUS tr. *Sleidane's Comm.* 37 b, What time he was yet in Spaine, he hearde muche of Luthers false opinions. **1579** E. K. *Gloss. Spenser's Sheph. Kal.* June 25 The opinion of Faeries and elfes is very old, and yet sticketh very religiously in the myndes of some. **1596** SHAKS. *Merch. V.* III. v. 90 Nay, but aske my opinion to of that? **1611** BIBLE *1 Kings* xviii. 21 How long halt ye between two opinions? **1665** BOYLE *Occas. Refl.* IV. xi. (1848) 233 As for my Opinions, whether of Persons, or things, I cannot in most cases command them my self, but must suffer them to be such as the Nature of the things I judge of requires. **1705** STANHOPE *Paraphr.* III. 312 No Opinion truly good can promote any Moral Evil. **1789** BELSHAM *Ess.* II. xli. 526 It is not to controul opinions, but actions, that Government is instituted. **1844** DISRAELI *Coningsby* VIII. iii, As for your opinions, you have no business to have any other than those I uphold. You are too young to form opinions. **1876** GLADSTONE *Glean.* II. 361 Dr. Macleod had always the courage of his opinions. **1877** MORLEY *Crit. Misc.* Ser. II. 89 Our opinions are less important than the spirit and temper with which they possess us.

b. ***pious opinion*** (*R.C. Ch.*): a belief commonly accepted, but not enjoined as a dogma or matter of faith. Hence *transf.* (in general use): A belief cherished in the mind, but not insisted on or carried out in practice.

1865 PUSEY *Truth Eng. Ch.* 127 The Bishop..'could not dare'..to decide that there was evidence enough to erect the 'pious opinion' into a matter of faith, or that then was the best time to define it.

3. Phrase. ***to be of opinion***: to hold the belief or view; to think (in a specified way) about something; to opine. (Often with defining clause: ***I am of opinion that..*** = I think that..)

1485 CAXTON *Chas. Gt.* 103 Thyery and the other were of thoppynyon of Rolland. *a* **1548** HALL *Chron.*, *Rich. III* 50 Noble men..whiche amongest theim selfes were not of one opinion. **1589** PUTTENHAM *Eng. Poesie* I. xviii. (Arb.) 52 Some be of opinion..that the pastorall Poesie..should be the first of any other. **1623** BINGHAM *Xenophon* 49 All, that are of the same opinion, let them hold vp their hands. **1702** J. PURCELL *Cholick* (1714) 93, I am of Opinion..that the hitherto unknown use of the Spleen, is to interrupt the Fermentation of the Blood. **1818** CRUISE *Digest* (ed. 2) VI. 455 He was clearly of opinion they were both liable. **1856** EMERSON *Eng. Traits*, *Manners* Wks. (Bohn) II. 46 They require you to dare to be of your own opinion.

4. The formal statement by a member of an advisory body, an expert, or professional man, or the like, of what he thinks, judges, or advises upon a question or matter submitted to and considered by him; considered advice; as a ***legal*** or ***medical opinion***, ***to get an opinion of counsel***, etc. Phr. ***a second*** (or ***another***) ***opinion***, the opinion of a second medical adviser; also in *transf.* and extended uses.

c **1470** HENRY *Wallace* III. 332, 'I gif consell, or this gud knycht be slayne, Tak pes a quhill, suppos it do ws payne'. So said Adam the ayr of Rycardtoune; And Kneland als grantyt to thar opynyoun. *a* **1533** LD. BERNERS *Huon* xlix. 164 Whan Iuoryn vnderstode his lordes, he sayd, 'Syrs, I parseyue well your opynyon is good'. *Ibid.* lxxxii. 254, I desyre you all..to shew me your opynyons. **1598** *Let. to Stowe* (Ashm. MSS.), Your oppinioun in wrytinge or otherwise is expected. The question is, Of the antiquitie..of parishes in Englande. **1696** PHILLIPS (ed. 5), *Opinion*, the Thought of him who gives his Advice upon any thing that is debated or consulted upon. **1818** JAS. MILL *Brit. India* II. v. v. 496 The Supreme Council..came to an opinion..that [etc.]. **1861** MAINE *Anc. Law* ii. (ed. 6) 33 Collections of opinions interpretative of the Twelve Tables. **1885** C. M. YONGE *Nuttie's Father* II. xvii. 201 Dr. Brownlow became very grave over the injury. He said it was a surgical case, and he should like to have another opinion. **1888** *Chambers's Encycl.* s.v. *Barrister*, Barristers in England advise on the law by giving an opinion on a case stated. **1899** *Westm. Gaz.* 9 Nov. 1/2 The three clergymen..who have refused obedience to the Archbishops' 'Opinion' on the legality of incense and processional lights. **1924** J. BUCHAN *Three Hostages* xvi. 237 There's no cause to worry about Peter John... But if you want another opinion, why not get it? *Ibid.* 238, I think a second opinion would please Dr. Greenslade, for he too looked rather anxious. **1954** M. SHARP *Gipsy in Parlour* xxiv. 228 So my father and Miss Jones agreed... I didn't think my father would be quite so pleased to know of this second opinion, so to speak. **1966** J. B. PRIESTLEY *Salt is Leaving* xvi. 213, I have quite a competent doctor... He's never suggested a second opinion. **1970** P. LOVESEY *Wobble to Death* v. 52 Herriot sought for words to influence the doctor... 'Perhaps—another opinion. Your colleague..may see the possibility of a faster recovery.' **1971** A. PRICE *Alamut Ambush* x. 124 So he..wanted a second opinion on what he had seen—that made sense. **1972** J. WAINWRIGHT *Night is Time to Die* 121 You're not here *as* a solicitor... Therefore, you're entitled to call some other solicitor... You might need advice—a second opinion.

5. a. What one thinks *of* a person or thing; estimation, or an estimate, of character, quality, or value.

c **1375** *Sc. Leg. Saints* xx. (*Blasius*) 9 Sume men gud opunyone Has..Quhat man he was. *c* **1510** MORE *Picus* Wks. 14/2 Ye haue not knowen the opinion, ye philosophers haue of them self. **1605** SHAKS. *Macb.* I. vii. 33, I haue bought Golden Opinions from all sorts of people. **1638** R. BAKER tr. *Balzac's Lett.* (vol. II) 203 It is impossible for mee to expresse the high opinion I conceive of you. **1771** *Junius Lett.* xlviii. 253 Their constituents would have a better opinion of their candour, and..not a worse opinion of their integrity. **1897** MARY KINGSLEY *W. Africa* 12 The Coast..formed an even higher opinion of my folly than it had formed on our first acquaintance, which is saying a good deal.

b. *spec.* Good, high, or favourable estimate; esteem. (Now only with negative, or such adjs. as *great*.)

1597 MORLEY *Introd. Mus.* 115 Those who stande so much in opinion of their owne sufficiencie. **1672** PETTY *Pol. Anat.* (1691) 94 They have a great Opinion of Holy-Wells, Rocks, and Caves, which have been the reputed Cells and Receptacles of..Saints. **17..** LAW (J.), If a woman had no opinion of her own person and dress. **1796** JANE AUSTEN *Pride & Prej.* ii, She is a selfish, hypocritical woman, and I have no opinion of her.

†**c.** Favourable estimate of oneself or one's own abilities; either in bad sense (self-conceit, arrogance, dogmatism), or in good sense (self-confidence). *Obs.*

1588 SHAKS. *L.L.L.* V. i. 6 Your reasons haue beene..witty without affection, audacious without impudency, learned without opinion, and strange without heresie. **1596** —— *1 Hen. IV*, III. i. 185 Pride, Haughtinesse, Opinion, and Disdaine. **1606** —— *Tr. & Cr.* I. iii. 353 What heart from hence receyues the conqu'ring part To steele a strong opinion to themselues.

†**6.** What is thought of one by others; the estimation (esp. good estimation) in which one stands; standing; reputation, repute, character, credit (*of* being so and so, or *of* possessing some quality). *Obs.*

1551 ROBINSON tr. *More's Utop.* II. vi. (1895) 196 Which for the opinion of nobilitie reioyse muche in their owne conceite. **1596** SHAKS. *1 Hen. IV*, V. iv. 48 Thou hast redeemed thy lost opinion. **1605** CAMDEN *Rem.* 121 The change of names, hath most commonly proceeded from a desire to avoyd the opinion of basenes. **1637** SHIRLEY *Gamester* (Dodsley *O. Pl.* IX. 16, N.) I mean you have the opinion of a valiant gentleman. **1685** COTTON tr. *Montaigne* I. 222 These fellows to make parade and to get opinion..are perpetually perplexing and entangling themselves in their own nonsense. **1705** STANHOPE *Paraphr.* II. 65 Every Counterfeit supposes something, not only of Reality but of Excellence too, which it hopes to gain the Opinion of, by such artful Dissimulation.

†**7.** The thought of what is likely to happen; expectation; apprehension. *Obs.*

a **1548** HALL *Chron.*, *Hen. VI* 108 b, [He] thought now, that al thynges succeeded, accordyng to opinion and good hope. **1568** SKEYNE *The Pest* (1860) 27 Quhay..most remoue the opinione of dethe, but not the dredour of God. **1601** R. JOHNSON *Kingd. & Commw.* (1603) 197 The warre continuing beyonde opinion, the State was inforced to procure pay for the armie. **1658** SIR T. BROWNE *Hydriot.* Ep. Ded., Having no old experience of the Duration of their Relics, [Men] held no opinion of such After-considerations.

†**8.** Report, rumour. [A Latinism of transl.]

c **1380** WYCLIF *Sel. Wks.* II. 23 And opynyoun of Crist wente þourȝ al þe lond of Siry. [*Vulg.* Matt. iv. 24 Et abiit opinio eius in totam Syriam.] **1382** —— *Matt.* xxiv. 6 ȝe ben to heere bateyls, and opynyouns [*Vulg.* opiniones] of bateyls.

9. *attrib.* and *Comb.*, as ***opinion-former***, ***leader***, ***maker***, etc.; ***opinion-forming***, ***-making*** (also vbl. sb.), ***-tapping*** ppl. adjs.; **opinion poll**, the assessment of the opinion of all, or of a section of, the general public by questioning a random or representative sample; hence ***opinion polling***, ***pollster***; (see also sense 1 b above); **opinion survey** = *opinion poll*.

1875 W. CORY in *Lett. & Jrnls.* (1897) 375 Morbid combination of piety with opinion-breeding. **1906** G. W. E. RUSSELL *Social Silhouettes* xiii. 90 A Journalist of this type once said to me, with all imaginable gravity, 'I should, I confess, resent any change which interfered with my position as chief opinion-former in the neighbourhood of'—Leeds or Plymouth, or whatever was the name of his town. **1962** *Times Lit. Suppl.* 24 Aug. 633/4 To hear well over half the electors of Britain talk, or read or listen to their favourite opinion-formers, one would conclude that it would be best..if no profits were made by any business. **1967** *Economist* 22 Apr. 338/1 The opinion-formers have begun their debunking. **1977** *Private Eye* 13 May 14/2 He has a fine independence of outlook and a contemptuous disregard for whatever is smart or fashionable among opinion-formers. **1959** *Encounter* Nov. 66 Literary parties..the opinion-forming fringe of the United States. **1969** *Guardian* 28 Aug. 11/6 One section of Oxfam has argued that the organisation should abandon direct aid and devote itself wholly to an opinion-forming rôle. **1974** *Broadcast* 9 Dec. 17/1 The advertising industry has few friends in the educational and opinion-forming strata. *c* **1449** PECOCK *Repr.* 87 Summe..ben clepid Doctour-Mongers and summe ben clepid Opinioun-holders. **1949** LAZARSFELD & STANTON *Communications Res.* II. vii. 217 The opinion-leaders are not identical with the socially prominent people in the community. **1968** *Internat. Encycl. Soc. Sci.* III. 51 The hard-core noncommissioned officers constituted a cadre of 'opinion leaders' who supported the control structure. **1975** *Times* 25 Feb. 14/1 His audience of nearly 200 were predominantly..people whom the Wessex area office staff would describe only as opinion leaders. **1952** *Time* 27 Oct. 20/1 To intellectuals and other 'opinion makers', Eisenhower was infinitely preferable to the other two. **1957** *Economist* 28 Sept. 1005/1 The reactions of..professional opinion makers were more precise, but just as personal. **1975** S. RANGANATHAN in H. M. Patel et al. *Say not the Struggle Nought Availeth* 297 There are limits to growth as world opinion-makers are trying to explain. **1909** *Westm. Gaz.* 16 June 1/3 The Conference at the Foreign Office..exceeded expectations. The question that outshadowed all others at this council of 'opinion-making power' was..Imperial Defence. **1956** C. W. HILLS *Power Elite* xiii. 310 The means of opinion-making..have paralleled in range and efficiency the other institutions of greater scale. **1867** WHITTIER *Tent on Beach* 85 One..Who ..Had left the Muses' haunts to turn The crank of an opinion-mill, Making his rustic reed of song A weapon in the war with wrong. **1937** Opinion poll [implied in *public opinion poll*, sense 1 b above.] **1946** *Vogue* Aug. 2/2 Try a little opinion-poll for yourself. Ask a representative sample of Englishmen the following question: [etc.]. **1951** M. McLUHAN *Mech. Bride* (1967) 46/2 Opinion polls function as educational rather than fact-finding agencies. **1965** *New Statesman* 30 Apr. 670/3 The substantial pro-Labour swing indicated by the opinion polls. **1971** *Guardian* 10 July 11/8 Mr Heath..interprets every unfavourable opinion poll as a clear signal that the public is one hundred per cent behind him. **1976** *Times* 27 Feb. 14/4 It is clear from opinion polls that the very large majority of people in Scotland wish to remain part of Britain. **1963** *Economist* 7 Dec. 1094/1 Opinion-polling is still a young..art in Spain. **1970** *Times* 2 June 1/2 The increase has no statistical significance when allowance is made for the tolerance limits of opinion polling. **1977** *Times* 18 Oct. 16/4 One of the weaknesses of much opinion-polling is that..it must exclude..extended questioning. **1951** M. McLUHAN *Mech. Bride* (1967) 47/1 The cabdriver tends to be the opinion-pollster hero. **1970** *Times* 19 June 1/6 (*heading*) Opinion pollsters admit to wide margin of error. **1977** *News of World* 17 Apr. 1/1 Its existence is unknown to two out of every three women in the country, according to opinion pollsters. **1939** G. GALLUP *Public Opinion in Democracy* 12 If elections themselves do not impose clôture on debate, is it likely that opinion surveys will? **1958** *New Statesman* 23 Aug. 213/3 The first would entail many interviews with people by the well-tried opinion-survey methods. **1948** J. TOWSTER *Political Power in U.S.S.R.* vii. 153 The Party conference..is primarily..an opinion-tapping and effort-mobilizing agency. **1808** BENTHAM *Sc. Reform* 23 On the part of the non-lawyer, conscious ignorance, thence consultation and advice (opinion-trade).

† **o'pinion**, *v. Obs.* [f. OPINION *sb.*, prob. after obs. F. *opinionner* (in Froissart). There may have been a med.L. *opīniōnārī, -āre.*] *trans.* To hold the opinion, or hold as an opinion; to think, suppose, opine. (With obj. clause, or equivalent obj.)

1555 in Strype *Eccl. Mem.* (1721) III. App. xliii. 121 Whosoever they be..[they] may opinion with themselves that they be none of God's children. **1609** HEYWOOD *Brit. Troy* To Twofold Rdrs., These indeed know no other meanes to have themselves opinioned in the ranke of understanders. **1643** SIR T. BROWNE *Relig. Med.* I. §50 Philosophers that opinioned the worlds destruction by fire. **1646** —— *Pseud. Ep.* I. xi. 46 If any other opinion there are no antipodes. **1661** GLANVILL *Van. Dogm.* 191 We opinion a more certain efficiency. *a* **1825** FORBY *Voc. E. Anglia*, *Opinion*, to opine.. 'I opinion so', is, 'I am of that opinion'. **1839** MARRYAT *Diary Amer.* Ser. I. II. 224, I opinion quite the contrary.

† **o'pinionable**, *a.* (*sb.*) *Obs. rare.* [f. OPINION *v.* or *sb.* + -ABLE.] That is a matter of opinion, disputable, uncertain; that is the object of opinion: = OPINABLE. Also as *sb.* An object of opinion.

1615-20 C. MORE *Life Sir T. More* (1828) 317 A marvellous opinionable problem of Sheep. **1656** STANLEY *Hist. Philos.* v. (1701) 184/2 If Intellect differ from true Opinion, that which is Intelligible differeth from that which is Opinionable; and if so, there are Intelligibles distinct from Opinionables.

opinional (əʊˈpɪnjənəl), *a. rare.* [f. OPINION *sb.* + -AL[1].] Belonging to, of the nature of, or grounded upon opinion.

(Erroneously attributed by various writers to Bp. Pecock *c* 1450, whose word was OPINIAL.)

1725-44 LEWIS *Pecock* 200 Shewing that faith in this life is only probable or opinional not sciential, which, the Bishop says, is had in the blisse of heaven. **1868** H. BUSHNELL *Serm. Liv. Subj.* 84 No mere body of opinional truths or doctrines. **1889** J. M. ROBERTSON *Ess. Crit. Meth.* 68 Our notional and opinional relation to the total environment.

opinionaster, -astry: see OPINIONATRE, -ATRY.

† **o'pinionate**, *a. Obs.* [f. OPINION + -ATE; perh. as a latinized form of *opinioned*, OF. *opinionné*: see -ATE *suff.*[2]]

1. Based on opinion, or held in the way of opinion; conjectural, uncertain; supposed, fancied.

1553 EDEN *Treat. Newe Ind.* (Arb.) 10 Erringe, wyth hys lyghte and opinionate argumentes. *a* **1586** SIDNEY *Arcadia* (1622) 450 Wisedome being an essentiall and not an opinionate thing. **1627-47** FELTHAM *Resolves* I. lxi. 188 Nor is their misery merely opinionate, but truly argued from the measure of pity, that it meets with from others. **1661** *Sir H. Vane's Politics* 1 To cloath vice be it never so ugly, with an opinionate tinct of beauty.

2. Unduly attached to one's own opinion; conceited; obstinate in belief; = OPINIONATED 3. (In quot. 1576 *gen.* Obstinate, self-willed.)

1576 TURBERV. *Venerie* iii. 8 These fallow houndes..are more opinionate and harder to be taught than the whyte houndes. **1603** SIR C. HEYDON *Jud. Astrol.* xx. 410 It were more then an opinionate singularitie in M. Chamber to contradict it. **1640** QUARLES *Enchirid.* III. lxix, In holding of an Argument, be neither chollericke, nor too opinionate. **1658** SLINGSBY *Diary* (1836) 204 Arguments springing from the brains of those ambitious and opinionate Sectaries.

opinionate (əʊˈpɪnjəneɪt), *v.* Now *rare.* [f. L. *opīniōn-em* OPINION + -ATE[3]: perh. after OF. *opinionner*, or med.L. **opīniōnārī, -āt-us.*]

1. To form or hold an opinion; to believe, suppose, think; = OPINE *v.* 2, OPINION *v.*

a. *trans.* (also with *compl.* or *obj. cl.*).

1621 LADY M. WROTH *Urania* 532 As rude and ill manner'd a company..though much opinionated to bee well-behaued creatures. **1622** MABBE tr. *Aleman's Guzman d'Alf.* II. 204 Opinionating them to be principall persons. **1643** R. O. *Man's Mort.* iii. 10 Pythagoras opinionated it [the Soul] a Number moving of it selfe. **1678** R. R[USSELL] *Geber* II. I. iii. 28 We also find many who have a Soul easily opinionating every Phantasie. **18..** ELIZA LESLIE *That Gentleman*, I opinionate that he was one of the gentlemen.

b. *intr.*

1653 R. SANDERS *Physiogn.* 260 Amongst..Authors thus opinionating, I find Haly Abenragel the Arabian. **1656** STANLEY *Hist. Philos.* v. (1701) 223/1 A wise Man may consent to that which is not perceived; that is, he may opinionate. **1891** 'M. O'RELL' *Frenchm. in Amer.* 140, I have always gone my own quiet way, philosophising rather than opinionating.

† **2. a.** *trans.* To express as a formal opinion; **b.** *intr.* To state or deliver one's opinion formally; = OPINE *v.* 1. *Obs.*

1651 N. BACON *Disc. Govt. Eng.* II. xxxvii. (1739) 167 To subject the Consciences of all the people to the opinion of one Metropolitan, that might opinionate strange things. **1677** NEEDHAM *2nd Packet Advices to Men of Shaftesbury* 72 Nor was it to be supposed, that the Judges would have undertaken to opinionate about so Supreme a Question.

† **3.** *refl.* To become or be opinionated or obstinate. *Obs.* exc. in pa. pple.: see next.

1603 FLORIO *Montaigne* (1634) 183 Even good Authors doe ill..wilfully to opinionate themselues about framing a constant and solide contexture of us. **1622** A. COURT *Constancie* I. 38 Wee retaine still their griefe, and opinionate our selues to rumenate and continually bring them into our memory.

† **4.** To bring *into* some condition, by force of thought or imagination. *Obs.*

1650 H. BROOKE *Conserv. Health* 66 They..opinionate themselues into Sickness.

opinionated (əʊˈpɪnjəneɪtɪd), *ppl. a.* [f. prec. + -ED.]

† **1.** Possessed of or holding a (specified) opinion; of opinion (*that*...); = OPINIONED 1. *Obs.*

1602 FULBECKE *1st Pt. Parall.* 94 The Romans it seemeth were in this strangly opinionated: for the Græcians and others did approue such medicines. **1635** BARRIFFE *Mil. Discipl.* lxii. (1643) 164 Divers men are diversly opinionated. **1645** PAGITT *Heresiogr.* (1661) 196 Mr. Trask towards his end fell to Antinomian opinions: He died at one of his friends houses, whose wife was that way somewhat opinionated.

† **2.** Possessed of a particular opinion or estimate *of* a person or thing; *esp.* having a favourable opinion, thinking highly *of*. *Obs.*

1601 MUNDAY *Downf. Robt. Earl of Huntington* II. ii. in Hazl. *Dodsley* VIII. 139 How are you, sir, of me opinionated? *a* **1656** USSHER *Ann.* (1658) 559 The Citizens ..being highly opinionated of the mans integrity. **1739** WESLEY *Wks.* (1830) I. 68 As opinionated of their own parts and wisdom, as either modern Chinese or ancient Romans.

3. Thinking too highly of, or adhering too persistently to, one's opinion; conceited; obstinate in opinion, dogmatic, opinionative.

1601 CORNWALLIS *Ess.* II. li. (1631) 325 With our lives delivered to the censure of opinionated ignorance. **1754** RICHARDSON *Grandison* I. v. 20 A young gentleman lately married; very affected, and very opinionated. **1805** LUCCOCK *Nat. Wool* 219 The cynical sneer of self-opinionated folly. **1889** TRAILL *Strafford* 201 The mere high-handed violence of the opinionated and self-willed autocrat.

b. Obstinate, self-willed (in general sense).

1649 EARL MONM. tr. *Senault's Use Passions* (1671) 31 Of these two Passions..the more mild is the less tractable, and the more furious the less opinionated. **1677** GILPIN *Demonol.* (1867) 388 They..are opinionated in sin because of his mercy. **1840** DICKENS *O.C. Shop* (C.D. ed.) 172 The most obstinate and opinionated pony.

Hence **o'pinionatedness**.

1860 S. WILBERFORCE *Addr. Ordination* 229 The quickened religious life..is exposed to all the temptations of religious self-will, party-spirit, self-opinionatedness, and division. **1889** *Sat. Rev.* 18 May 619/2 Angouleme..had all the obstinacy and opinionatedness, of the Bourbons.

† **o'pinionately**, *adv. Obs.* [f. OPINIONATE *a.* + -LY[2].] **a.** In the way of opinion; in one's own opinion. **b.** In an opinionated manner; obstinately.

1627-77 FELTHAM *Resolves* I. lxxxv. 131 Where either are only opinionately wise. **1647** *Sectary Dissected* 14 If you opinionately persecute the house of Abimelech, a fire may issue thence..and consume you. **1704** *Faction Display'd* x. 151 A gay, pragmatical, pretending Fool, Opinionately wise, and pertly dull.

opinionation (əʊˌpɪnjəˈneɪʃən). [f. OPINION *sb.* + -ATION.] The state or condition of persisting in holding a dogmatic opinion or opinions.

1925 *Inner Life* x. 184 Self-expression in the immature stages may become mere self-opinionation, with an unwillingness to heed advice or guidance. **1957** R. HOGGART *Uses of Literacy* vi. 167 It can be said, with some justice, that this is an age of 'opinionation', that though few people take the trouble thoroughly to understand any problem, a great many assume that their opinions on almost every general issue will have weight. **1960** *Times Lit. Suppl.* 27 May 339/1 What is expected of him is to..advise and comment on public affairs—..to add his mite to the flood of opinionation which is slopping over the world, obscuring the inner world of values.

† **o'pinionatist.** *Obs.* [f. as OPINIONATELY *adv.* + -IST.] An opinionated person; an obstinate dogmatist.

1634 SIR T. HERBERT *Trav.* 222 None save detracting opinionatists can justly oppose such worthy testimonies. **1651** BAXTER *Inf. Bapt.* 146 Meer talking censorious Opinionatists. **1720** FENTON *Serm. bef. Univ. Oxford* 11 The pernicious Counsels of some such Opinionatists.

opinionative (əʊˈpɪnjəneɪtɪv), *a.* (*sb.*) [f. assumed L. stem **opīniōnāt-* + -IVE; or simply f. OPINION + -ATIVE: cf. *talkative*.]

† **1.** Based upon, or of the nature of, opinion; fancied, imaginary; conjectural, speculative (as distinguished from *real* or *certain*). = OPINATIVE 2, OPINIATIVE 2, OPINIONATE *a.* 1. *Obs.*

c **1555** [implied in OPINIONATIVELY 1]. **1610** HEALEY *St. Aug. Citie of God* 546 This opinionative suspicion every one may take as he please. **1627-77** FELTHAM *Resolves* I. xciv. 147 If this be not rather opinionative than real. **1702** C. MATHER *Magn. Chr.* III. ii. (1852) 364 He declined a settlement in some other, which he thought more opinionative, and so more contentious and undesireable places.

b. Relating to, or consisting in, opinion or belief; doctrinal (as distinguished from *practical*).

a **1638** MEDE *Wks.* (1672) 115 The difference between a saving Faith which joyns us to Christ, and that which is true indeed, but not saving, but dogmatical and opinionative only. **1684** BUNYAN *Pilgr.* II. 144 We will deny ourselves of some things, both Opinionative and Practical, for your sake. **1869** H. BUSHNELL *New Life* iv. 49 So far what is done is merely opinionative or notional, and there is no transactional faith.

c. Of the nature of an opinion. *rare.*

1894 *Pall Mall G.* 24 Dec. 1/2 The Board to have..the option of refraining from making any award, and of publishing an opinionative report on the dispute instead.

2. Unduly attached to, or persistent in adhering to, one's own opinion; conceited, or obstinately dogmatic; = OPINATIVE 1, OPINIATIVE 1, OPINIONATE *a.* 2, OPINIONATED 3.

1547 BOORDE *Introd. Knowl.* xvii. (1870) 167 The people of Boeme be opinionatyue, standyng much in theyr owne conceits. **1621** BURTON *Anat. Mel.* To Rdr. 19 He was an illiterate idiot,..an opinionative ass, a caviller, a kind of pedant. **1751** JOHNSON *Cheynel* Wks. IV. 504 Too young to teach, and too opinionative to learn. **1817** MAR. EDGEWORTH *Bores* (1832) 314 The common female blue is intolerable, opinionative and opinionated. **1897** *Westm. Gaz.* 9 Nov. 1/3 An opinionative Anglo-Indian, who spoke as one whose words were officially authoritative, was of the party.

† **b.** Holding too high an opinion *of*; proud or conceited *of*. *Obs. rare.*

1621 BP. MOUNTAGU *Diatribæ* 9 Your Selfe, very Opinionatiue of your knowledge.

† **B.** *sb.* An 'opinionative' or speculative point.

1659 STANLEY *Hist. Philos.* III. IV. 11 The Sceptick's is, in opinionatives, indisturbance; in impulsives, moderation.

o'pinioˌnatively, *adv.* [f. prec. + -LY[2].]

† **1.** In the way of opinion; as an expression of opinion; in relation to opinion or belief. *Obs.*

c **1555** HARPSFIELD *Divorce Hen. VIII* (Camden) 122 It was not spoken asseverantly but opinionatively. **1685** BAXTER *Paraphr. N.T., James* i. 21 [To] receive God's Word, not only opinionatively, but as the Graff is taken into the Tree.

2. In an opinionative manner; with undue attachment to or persistence in one's own opinion; conceitedly; obstinately.

1725 tr. *Dupin's Eccl. Hist. 17th C.* I. VI. ii. 228 He was confident in his Sentiments, and maintain'd them obstinately and opinionatively.

o'pinioˌnativeness. [f. as prec. + -NESS.] The quality or character of being opinionative; undue attachment to or persistence in one's own opinion; conceit; obstinate dogmatism.

1599 SANDY'S *Europæ Spec.* (1632) 179 Such as not to interrupt the common Concord with private opinionativenesse. **1639** HORN & ROBOTHAM *Gate Lang. Unl.* lxxxiii. §812 As over-hasty giving credit is hurtfull,.. much more stiffenesse or opinionativeness. **1742** MRS. DELANY *Autobiog. & Corr.* II. 166 Conceit or opinionativeness becomes no sex or age. **1872** TULLOCH *Ration. Theol.* I. iii. 100 [Lord Falkland] especially detested ..the dogmatic opinionativeness so prevalent in his time.

o'pinionator. Also 8 -er. [f. OPINIONATE *v.* after L. agent-nouns.] One who holds an opinion, a theorist; = OPINATOR, OPINIATOR.

1677 GALE *Crt. Gentiles* III. 83 Such..are to be called Philosophers not opinionators or lovers of opinion. *a* **1716** SOUTH *Serm.* (1744) X. i. 9 The Pharisees, and the Opinionaters of their own holiness. **1930** *New Statesman* 8 Nov. 147/1, I can only regret that Mr. West devotes so much of his space to Mr. Wells the opinionator instead of to Mr. Wells the artist. **1960** *Times Lit. Suppl.* 27 May 339/1 The opinionators..are quite ready to sign petitions and organize meetings, and to these the artist is supposed to contribute his ration of right-feeling and right-thinking. **1973** *Ibid.* 16 Mar. 294/2 A pleasure that ought never to be tasted by the professional opinionator. **1974** *Ibid.* 7 June 610/2 The age demands superstars, intellectual acrobatics, personality cults, instant opinionators.

opinionatre, -atry, (**-astry**), erroneous ff. OPINIATRE, -ATRY (-ASTRY), conformed to *opinion*.

1662 J. HEATH in *Pagitt's Heresiogr.* Ded. to Sir J. Frederick, The opinionastry of these sects. **1689** HICKERINGILL *Modest Inq.* ii. 11 Mad with self-love, Opinionatry and Bigotism. **1693** W. FREKE *Sel. Ess.* 39 The Dogmatical Opinionatre, and the Morose Cynick.

opinioned (əʊˈpɪnjənd), *a.* Now *rare.* [f. OPINION *sb.* + -ED.]

1. Having a (specified) opinion; holding the opinion, or of opinion (*that*...). Also in parasynthetic comb., as ***ill-opinioned***, ***strange-opinioned***.

1584 R. SCOT *Discov. Witchcr.* I. vii. (1886) 11 How diverslie people be opinioned. **1631** *Star Chamb. Cases* (Camden) 42 The court was opinioned the words were spoken. **1650** SIR. R. STAPYLTON *Strada's Low C. Warres* x. 6 Nor was Don John otherwise opinioned of a Truce. **1890** *Pall Mall G.* 10 Mar. 2/3 Is it so, that England as a whole is ..so opinioned as to prefer a high order of eloquence to the principles of the Reformation?

2. Holding a particular opinion or estimate, esp. a favourable one, *of* a person or thing; usually, Thinking highly *of* oneself or one's own qualities, conceited *of*.

1612 W. SCLATER *Sick Souls Salve* 23 Was ever hypocrite thus opinioned of himselfe? **1667** DRYDEN *Sir Martin Mar-*

all I. i, He's so opinion'd of his own Abilities, that he is ever designing somewhat. **1707** NORRIS *Humility* vi. 282 A man well opinioned of himself.

3. Unduly attached to one's own opinion; opinionated.

1649 MILTON *Eikon.* xiii. Wks. (1851) 443 Uzziah..was thrust out with a Leprosie for his opinion'd zeale, which he thought judicious. *a* **1716** SOUTH *Serm.* I. 298 (T.) He may cast him upon a bold self-opinioned physician, worse than his distemper.

Hence **o'pinionedness** (*self-o'pinionedness*).

1879 *Daily News* 22 Oct. 6/5 A peculiar kind of religious self-opinionedness sprang up, which tended to make each man more and more a law to himself.

opinionist (əʊ'pɪnjənɪst). [f. as prec. + -IST.]

†**1.** A holder or maintainer of some opinion or doctrine at variance with the general belief (or that of the speaker); a sectary, a faddist. *Obs.*

1623 COCKERAM II, An Opinionist, *Sectarie.* **1634** SIR T. HERBERT *Trav.* 160 The Mahometan Doctours..bended themselves against this late Opinionist. **1661** RAY *Three Itin.* II. 161 There are few or no sectaries or opinionists among them. **1692** T. W. *Short Story Antinomians New Eng.* Pref. 9 Now you might have seen the Opinionists rising up, and contemptuously turning their backs upon the faithful Pastors of that Church. **1760** T. HUTCHINSON *Hist. Mass.* (1765) I. 68 This general agreement struck a damp upon the opinionists.

b. *Ch. Hist.* One of a sect in the 15th century who held that only those Popes who practised voluntary poverty were true vicars of Christ.

1693 tr. *Emilianne's Hist. Monast. Ord.* xix. 219 They were called also Opinionists. **1707** *Glossogr. Angl. Nova, Opinionists*, a Name given in Pope Paul's time, to a Sect that boasted of affected Poverty, and held there could be no Vicar of Christ on earth that did not practice this Vertue.

2. The holder of any specified opinion.

1630 WESTCOTE *Devon* (1845) 44 Every hearer and author hath his private opinion, and every opinionist his peculiar judgment and censure. **1647** *Thomasson Tracts* (Br. Mus.) CCCXXXVI. No. 22. 2 Whether have you any general rule of good education..which may be admirable to all opinionists? **1813** SOUTHEY in *Life* (1850) IV. 24 In league with all varieties of opinionists. **1820** CLARE *Rural Life* (ed. 3) 111 On receiving a damp from a genteel opinionist in poetry. **1845** DISRAELI *Sybil* II. xv, In estimating the accuracy of a political opinion, one should take into consideration the standing of the opinionist.

3. One whose business it is to give a professional opinion.

1802–12 BENTHAM *Ration. Judic. Evid.* (1827) IV. 289 Hence comes an appropriate branch of made business, the trade of the law-adviser or opinionist; the opinion trade. *Ibid.* 38, 413.

o'pinionless, *a.* [f. OPINION *sb.* + -LESS.] Having no opinion of one's own.

1830 *Examiner* 644/2 Other opinionless journals that inundate the country. **1881** *19th Cent.* Sept. 341 Souls who had otherwise existed as opinionless dead weights.

opinionnaire (əʊˌpɪnjə'nɛə(r)). Also opinionaire. [f. OPINION *sb.* + *-aire*, after QUESTIONNAIRE.] A series of questions designed to gauge (public) opinion on a specific issue; a questionnaire.

A word of doubtful usefulness.—R. W. B.

1949 R. K. MERTON *Social Theory* II. 207 Interview techniques in all their numerous variety..questionnaires, opinionnaires and attitude tests. **1955** M. REIFER *Dict. New Words* 148 *Opinionaire*, a questionnaire to be filled in by various persons, for polling public opinion. **1964** P. MEADOWS in I. L. Horowitz *New Sociol.* 450 Researchers, equipped with pencils, pads, and opinionnaires, sought to throw on the screen of national attention the bright beams of percentages and averages of mass opinions. **1973** *Jrnl. Genetic Psychology* Mar. 56 Compliance was defined as correspondence between the child's report on an opinionnaire and the parent's report. **1975** *Bull. Canad. Assoc. Univ. Teachers* Feb. 7/3 The report..admonishes its reader not to rely on student opinionnaires in the evaluation of university teaching.

†**o'pinionous,** *a. Obs. rare.* [f. OPINION *sb.* + -OUS.] Of or belonging to opinion.

1666 G. ALSOP *Maryland* 16 Steering the Actions of State quietly, through the multitude and diversity of Opinionous waves that diversely meet.

†**o'pinious,** *a. Obs. rare.* [f. L. type **opīniōs-us*, f. *opīnio*: cf. *religiōsus*.] Of opinion, opinioned. Hence †**o'piniousness**, opiniativeness.

1632 LITHGOW *Trav.* VI. 275 Leauing it to be searched, by the pregnancy of riper iudgements then mine, howsoeuer opinious. **1688** in *Ellis Corr.* II. 35 Rather than the Christian cause against the Turks should longer suffer by his opiniousness and absence.

†**opinitive,** erron. f. OPINATIVE. *Obs.*

opinor, obs. form of OPINER.

opio-, combining form of Gr. ὄπιον poppy-juice, OPIUM, occurring in a few rare technical words. **opiology** (əʊpɪ'ɒlədʒɪ) [-LOGY], 'the account of the nature and qualities of opium' (*Syd. Soc. Lex.*). **opiomania** (əʊpɪəʊ'meɪnɪə) [MANIA], an insane or excessive craving for opium; hence **opio'maniac**, a person affected with opiomania. **opiophagy** (əʊpɪ'ɒfədʒɪ) [Gr. -φαγια eating], opium-eating.

1681 tr. *Willis' Rem. Med. Wks.* Vocab., *Opiologie*, the doctrine of opium. **1882** *Sat. Rev.* 29 July 160/2 Dr. Hubbard's treatise on what he calls Opiumania and Dipsomania. **1889** *Leisure Hour* 371 Young, rich, with a good position in the county..in love with her, and—an opiomaniac. **1878** tr. *von Ziemssen's Cycl. Med.* XVII. 875 Chronic opium-poisoning, opiophagy,..belong to the category of diseases which are almost incurable.

opioid ('əʊpɪɔɪd). [f. OPI(UM *sb.* + -OID.] = OPIATE *sb.* 2.

1957 *Pharmaceutical Jrnl.* CLXXIX. 321/1 Acheson has suggested that the morphinans and other synthetic morphine substitutes should be called opioids. **1972** R. D. DRIPPS et al. *Introd. Anesthesia* (ed. 4) xxv. 347 Opioids administered intravenously..may be followed by hypotension. **1974** M. C. GERALD *Pharmacol.* xiii. 237 Synthetic narcotic agents or opioids, which bear only highly subtle similarities to the structure of morphine. **1974** *Nature* 20 Dec. 708/2 Antiserum obtained after immunisation with morphine-6-hemisuccinyl-bovine serum albumin..has highest and approximately equal affinity for morphine and heroin and progressively less for opioids of decreasing structural similarity.

O. Pip: see O 5 d.

†**o'piparous,** *a. Obs. rare.* [f. L. *opipar-us* richly furnished, sumptuous, f. *op-em* wealth, means + *par-āre* to prepare, furnish, equip + -OUS.] Rich, sumptuous. Hence †**o'piparously** *adv.*

1621 BURTON *Anat. Mel.* II. ii. IV. (1676) 170/2 Sweet odours and perfumes, generous wines, opiparous fare. **1653** WATERHOUSE *Apol. Learn.* 93 Not men meanly bred, or loosly seen in Arts, but opiparously accomplished. **1694** MOTTEUX *Rabelais* v. (1737) 229 Your Opiparous or Aureous Charms. **1824** LANDOR *Imag. Conv., Southey & Porson* Wks. 1853 I. 75/1 We rather send these dismal dainties to his chamber, and treat our heartier friends opiparously.

opisometer (ɒpɪ'sɒmɪtə(r)). [f. Gr. ὀπίσω backwards + μέτρον measure.] An instrument for measuring curved lines, as on a map, consisting of a small wheel turning on a screw fixed in a rod or frame; the wheel is rolled along the line to be measured, and then rolled back on a straight scale until it reaches its former position on the screw.

1872 BLACK *Adv. Phaeton* iii. (1878) 33 The women were found in a wild maze of maps..and Bell had armed herself with an opisometer.

opisthe (əʊ'pɪsθiː, əʊ'piːst). *Biol.* [a. F. *opisthe* (Chatton & Lwoff 1936, in *Arch. de Zool. expér. et gén.* LXXVIII. 85), f. Gr. ὄπισθεν behind.] In ciliate protozoa, the posterior of the two organisms formed by transverse fission. Cf. PROTER.

1950 A. LWOFF *Probl. Morphogenesis Ciliates* xi. 74 (*caption*) The peristome of the opisthe is formed from one kinetosome. **1961** MACKINNON & HAWES *Introd. Study Protozoa* iv. 214 At fission the organism [*sc.* a ciliate] divides to produce 2 daughters, an anterior proter and a posterior opisthe. **1977** *Jrnl. Protozool.* XXIV. 23/2 There is a need for enlargement or formation of oral parts such as..enlargement of oral structures in young opisthes.

opisthion (əʊ'pɪsθɪən). *Anat.* [a. F. *opisthion* (P. Broca 1875, in *Bull. de la Soc. d'Anthrop. de Paris* X. 345), f. Gr. ὀπίσθιον hinder part.] (See quot. 1878.)

1878 R. T. H. BARTLEY *G. Topinard's Anthropol.* II. ii. 234 *Opisthion*, the posterior border of the occipital foramen at the median line. **1933** *Jrnl. R. Anthrop. Inst.* LXIII. 403 The remainder, which includes the opisthion, is missing. **1971** *Nature* 20 Aug. 568/1 Of the seven available specimens of *Homo erectus*, the positions of opisthion were uncertain in Java 1 and 6 and have been estimated in the literature.

opistho- (əʊpɪsθəʊ), before a vowel **opisth-**, combining form of Gr. ὄπισθεν behind, used in various scientific terms; for the more important of which see their alphabetical places.

o'pisthodont (-ədɒnt) *a. Zool.* [Gr. ὀδούς, ὀδόντ- tooth], having back teeth only. **opisthogastric** (-'gæstrɪk) *a. Anat.* [ad. F. *opisthogastrique* (Chaussier): see GASTRIC], situated behind the stomach. **opisthoglossal** (-'glɒsəl), **-glossate** (-'glɒsət) *adjs. Zool.* [f. mod.L. *Opisthoglossa* neut. pl., f. Gr. γλῶσσα tongue], belonging to Günther's division *Opisthoglossa* of batrachians, having the tongue free behind and attached in front. **opisthognathous** (-'ɒgnəθəs) *a.* [Gr. γνάθος jaw], (*a*) *Anthropol.* having retreating jaws or teeth; (*b*) *Ichthyol.* having the maxillary bones prolonged backwards, as fishes of the genus *Opisthognathus*. **opisthomous** (-'əʊməs) *a. Ichthyol.* [f. mod.L. *Opisthōmī* (pl.), f. Gr. ὦμος shoulder], belonging to the division *Opisthomi* of teleostean fishes, having the scapular arch separate from the skull. **opisthopulmonate** (-'pʌlmənət) *a. Zool.* [L. *pulmo, pulmōn-* lung], applied to those pulmonate or air-breathing gastropod molluscs which have the pulmonary sac behind the heart (cf. OPISTHOBRANCHIATE).

1857 MAYNE *Expos. Lex.*, **Opisto-Gastric*, applied by Chaussier to the cœliac artery, from its situation. **1892** *Syd. Soc. Lex., Opisthogastric artery.* **1864** HUNT *Vogt's Lect. Man* ii. 53 Welcker distinguishes the extremely orthognathous as *opisthognathous (or with retreating teeth), a distinction which does not seem to me quite justifiable. **1877** HUXLEY *Anat. Inv. Anim.* viii. 514 When the pulmonary sac is posterior, and the pallial region small, the ventricle of the heart is anterior,..and the animal may be said to be *opisthopulmonate.

opisthobranch (əʊ'pɪsθəbræŋk), *sb.* (*a.*) *Zool.* [f. mod.L. *Opisthobranchia* neut. pl., f. OPISTHO- + Gr. βράγχια gills.] An opisthobranchiate gastropod: see next. **b.** *adj.* = next.

1851–6 WOODWARD *Mollusca* 50 The sexes are..united in the (monœcious) land-snails, pteropods, opisthobranchs, tunicaries, and in part of the conchifers. **1877** HUXLEY *Anat. Inv. Anim.* viii. 511 No Opisthobranch possesses a large visceral sac of this kind.

Hence **o'pistho,branchism**, the condition of being opisthobranchiate.

opisthobranchiate (-'bræŋkɪət), *a.* (*sb.*) *Zool.* [ad. mod.L. *Opisthobranchiāta* = *Opisthobranchia*: see prec.] Belonging to the order *Opisthobranchiata* or *Opisthobranchia* of gastropod molluscs, comprising aquatic forms having the gills behind the heart. (Also said of the heart in other orders of molluscs when placed as in the *Opisthobranchia*, i.e. so as to have the gills behind it.) **b.** *sb.* = prec.

1854 WOODWARD *Mollusca* II. 169 *Oncidium Typhæ*:.. Animal oblong, convex;..heart opistho-branchiate. **1877** HUXLEY *Anat. Inv. Anim.* viii. 506 Strictly speaking, no Odontophoran is other than opisthobranchiate. **1889** *Athenæum* 13 July 67/1 Dr. Pelseneer..maintains..that it is a mistake to regard the Pteropoda as a 'class' at all. He considers them as forming two sub-orders of the opisthobranchiate gastropods.

opisthocœlian (-'siːlɪən), *a.* (*sb.*) *Zool.* and *Comp. Anat.* [f. as next + -IAN.] = next; also, having opisthocœlous vertebræ. Also as *sb.* An opisthocœlian animal, esp. (extinct) reptile.

1854 OWEN *Skel. & Teeth* in *Circ. Sc., Organ. Nat.* I. 202 Vertebræ of the 'opisthocœlian' type. **1870** ROLLESTON *Anim. Life* Introd. 62 The vertebrae..show, ordinarily, the procoelian, though, sometimes, the opisthocoelian arrangement of the articular ends of their centra. **1888** ROLLESTON & JACKSON *Anim. Life* 383 Opisthocoelian.. centra are found in exceptional instances [in *Reptilia*].

opisthocœlous (-'siːləs), *a. Comp. Anat.* [f. OPISTHO- + Gr. κοῖλ-ος hollow + -OUS.] Hollow behind; applied to vertebræ the bodies of which are concave posteriorly: distinguished from *procœlous* and *amphicœlous*.

1872 NICHOLSON *Palæont.* 308 In the Bony Pike, the vertebral column is composed of opisthocœlous vertebræ. **1888** ROLLESTON & JACKSON *Anim. Life* 340 The vertebral centrum may be biconcave (amphicœlous), biconvex, concave in front or behind (= pro- and opisthocœlous), or flat.

opisthocome (əʊ'pɪsθəʊkəʊm). *Ornith.* [ad. mod.L. *Opisthocomus*, ad. Gr. ὀπισθόκομος wearing the hair long behind, f. OPISTHO- + κόμη hair.] The bird *Opisthocomus hoazin* (*O. cristatus*), characterized by an occipital crest of feathers; the hoactzin. So **opisthocomine** (əʊpɪs'θɒkəmaɪn), **opis'thocomous** *adjs.*, allied in character to the hoactzin; having an occipital crest.

[**1895** *Pop. Sci. Monthly* Apr. 763 *Opisthocomus* has a size about equal to the chachalaca of our Texan border.] *Ibid.* 764 No fossil forms of opisthocomine birds are known.

‖**opis'thodomos.** *Gr. Antiq.* Also in anglicized form **o'pisthodome.** [Gr., f. ὀπισθο- behind + δόμος house, room, chamber.] An apartment at the back of an ancient Greek temple, corresponding to the πρόδομος, πρόναος, or vestibule in front.

[**1697** POTTER *Antiq. Greece* (1715) I. viii. 31 On the Backside of Minerva's Temple, was the publick Treasury, call'd from its Situation Ὀπισθόδομος.] **1706** PHILLIPS, *Opisthodomos.* **1776** R. CHANDLER *Trav. Greece* 29 They deified him, and lodged him in the Opisthodomos or the back part of the Parthenon. **1846** WORCESTER, *Opisthodome*, an apartment, or place, in the back part of a Grecian house. **1846** ELLIS *Elgin Marb.* I. 71 An apartment called the *opisthodomos* which contained the treasures of the temple.

opisthoglyph (əʊ'pɪsθəʊglɪf), *sb.* (*a.*) *Zool.* [a. F. *opisthoglyphe*, mod.L. *Opisthoglypha* (A. H. A. Dumeril 1853, in *Mém. Acad. Sci.* XXIII. 412) f. OPISTHO- + Gr. γλυφή carving.] A snake belonging to a group characterized by grooves in the upper back teeth. Also *attrib.* or as *adj.* So **opistho'glyphic, opis'thoglyphous** *adjs.*

1895 *Athenæum* 7 Dec. 795/3 In the opisthoglyphous snakes the poison-gland is very variable. *Ibid., Opisthoglyphic.* **1896** *Proc. Zool. Soc.* 615 The grooved teeth in the Opisthoglyphs vary in number from one to three. **1923** *Nature* 14 Apr. 579/1 A comparative study of the buccal glands and teeth of opisthoglyph snakes, and a discussion of the evolution of the order from Aglypha. **1965** R. & D. MORRIS *Men & Snakes* viii. 177 The aglyphs and the opisthoglyphs do not release their prey, once they have bitten it. **1968** R. D. MARTIN tr. *Wickler's Mimicry in Plants & Animals* xii. 112 The fangs may possess a groove that connects with the outlet of a poison gland. If the hind teeth in the upper jaws are grooved, they are called opisthoglyph.

Snakes with grooved hind teeth are weakly to moderately poisonous. **1969** A. BELLAIRS *Life of Reptiles* I. v. 186 Each of the big teeth generally has a groove down its anterior face for carrying the venom into the prey. Snakes showing this condition are called 'back-fanged' or opisthoglyphous.

opisthograph (əʊ'pɪsθəʊgrɑːf, -æ-), *sb.* (*a.*) *Gr.* and *Rom. Antiq.* [ad. Gr. ὀπισθόγραφος written on the back or cover, f. ὀπισθο- + -γραφος written.] A manuscript written on the back as well as the front of the papyrus or parchment; also, a slab inscribed on both sides. **b.** *adj.* = *opisthographic*.

1623 COCKERAM, *Opistograph*, a booke written on the backe side. *a* **1693** URQUHART *Rabelais* III. Prol., Giving to one of his old acquaintance his Wallet, Books and Opistographs away went he [Diogenes] out of Town towards a little Hill or Promontory. **1876** VENABLES in *Encycl. Brit.* V. 209/2 Not a few of the slabs..bearing a pagan inscription on one side, and a Christian one on the other. These are known as *opisthographs*. **1885** W. M. LINDSAY in *Athenæum* 5 Sept. 304/2 The fragments are opisthograph.

So †**opis'thographal** (*obs.*), **opistho'graphic, -ical** *adjs.*, written or inscribed on the back as well as the front; **opis'thography**, the practice of writing on both sides of a papyrus, slab, etc.; *concr.* writing of this kind.

1684 H. MORE *Answer* 38 To write that which is last in the inside, and that which is first on the outside, [is] quite contrary to the mode of Opisthographal Writings. **1813** J. FORSYTH *Rem. Excurs. Italy* 315 The opisthographic manuscripts required, I apprehend, a double leaf so glued that the fibres crossed. **1816** SINGER *Hist. Cards* 124 It is Opisthographic, or printed on both sides of the vellum. **1656** BLOUNT *Glossogr.*, *Opisthographical*. **1715** tr. *Pancirollus' Rerum Mem.* I. III. iv. 138 Some Poems of the Ancients were tedious with Opistography, or endors'd Prolixity.

opisthotic (ɒpɪs'θɒtɪk, -əʊtɪk), *a.* (*sb.*) *Comp. Anat.* [f. OPISTH(O- + Gr. οὖς, ὠτ- ear, ὠτικ-ός of the ear.] Epithet of one of the otic or periotic bones, situated at the back of the ear; separate, or fused with one of the occipital bones, in Fishes, Reptiles, and Birds; in Mammals, fused with the other otic bones, and forming that part of the petrosal bone which contains the auditory chamber. **b.** as *sb.* The opisthotic bone.

1870 ROLLESTON *Anim. Life* 43 A glenoid cavity which is formed by the squamosal, opisthotic and prootic bones. **1872** MIVART *Elem. Anat.* 106 The Opisthotic constantly anchyloses with the lateral part of the occipital before it unites with the pro-otic in all Vertebrates below Mammals. **1892** *Syd. Soc. Lex.*, *Opisthotic centre*, the ossification centre of the opisthotic bone.

opisthotonic (əʊpɪsθəʊ'tɒnɪk), *a. Path.* [ad. Gr. ὀπισθοτονικ-ός, f. ὀπισθοτονία: see next and -IC.] Affected with, or pertaining to, opisthotonos.

1623 COCKERAM, *Opisthotonicke*, one hauing his necke drawne into his shoulders, by shrinking vp of the sinews. **1748** tr. *Renatus' Distemp. Horses* 315 An Horse..is said to be *Opisthotonic* when the Disease is seated in his hinder Parts. **1879** *St. George's Hosp. Rep.* IX. 681 Signs..soon followed by frequent opisthotonic spasms.

‖**opisthotonos** (ɒpɪs'θɒtənɒs). *Path.* Also **-us.** [Gr. ὀπισθότονος drawn backwards, f. OPISTHO- + -τονος stretched, stretching, τείνειν to stretch.] Spasm of the muscles of the neck, back, and legs, in which the body is bent backwards; a form of tetanus.

1657 *Physical Dict.*, *Opisthotones.* **1706** PHILLIPS, *Opisthotonus*, a kind of Cramp or stretching of the Muscles of the Neck backwards. **1807** *Med. Jrnl.* XVII. 213 A universal rigidity of the dorsal muscles..with a strong retraction of the head, assuming the marks of a true opisthotonos. **1860** H. SPENCER *Phys. Laughter* Ess. 1891 II. 460 The head is thrown back and the spine bent inwards; there is a slight degree of what medical men call opisthotonos.

opisthure ('ɒpɪsθjʊə(r)). *Ichthyol.* [f. OPISTH(O- + Gr. οὐρά tail.] The posterior end of the caudal axis in the embryonic stage of some fishes, which is ultimately absorbed into the caudal fin. Hence **opis'thural** *a.*, pertaining to the opisthure.

1891 *Cent. Dict.* cites J. A. RYDER.

†**o'pitulate**, *v. Obs.* [ad. L. *opitulārī* to bring aid, to assist, f. *op-em* aid + **tul-* to bring.] *trans.* To help, assist, aid.

1597 A. M. tr. *Guillemeau's Fr. Chirurg.* *iiij, A Manuall for my selfe, to opitulate & addresse my memorye. **1599** —— tr. *Gabelhouer's Bk. Physicke* 29/2 Administer to him of this water, for it opitulateth the perloqutione exceedingelye.

So †**opitu'lation** *Obs.* [ad. late L. *opitulātio*], help, aid, assistance; †**o'pitulator** *Obs.* [a. late L. *opitulātor*], a helper.

1597 M. BOWMAN in *Guillemeau's Fr. Chirurg.* *ij, Benefites which through your ayde & opitulatione we reape. **1624** F. WHITE *Repl. Fisher* 343 *heading*, Papists make Saints speciall opitulators. **1651** BIGGS *New Disp.* 148 Speedy opitulation. **1724** R. SUTTON *Let. to Sir T. Parkyns* (1726) 4, I received such Opitulation from your Dicæology.

opium ('əʊpɪəm), *sb.* Also 6 oppium. [a. L. *opium* (Pliny), a. Gr. ὄπιον 'poppy-juice, opium', dim. of ὀπός vegetable juice. Cf. F. *opium*, also *opion* (13th c. in Hatz.-Darm.).]

1. a. The inspissated juice of a species of poppy (*Papaver somniferum*), obtained from the unripe capsules by incision and spontaneous evaporation, worked into cakes, balls, or sticks, of a reddish-brown colour, heavy smell, and bitter taste; valuable as a sedative and narcotic drug, and much used as a stimulant and intoxicant, esp. in the East.

1398 TREVISA *Barth. De P.R.* XVII. cxxviii. (1495) 687 Of popy comyth iuys that physycyens callyth Opium other Opion. *c* **1400** *Lanfranc's Cirurg.* 41 It is not yuel to putte a litil opium [*v.r.* opin] to þe oile of þe rosis. **1525** tr. *Jerome of Brunswick's Surg.* F iiij a/2 Whan the payne is grete, then it is nedefull to put therto a lytell Opium. **1551** TURNER *Herbal* I. E ij, Agaynste the poyson of the iuice of poppye, called oppium. **1615** G. SANDYS *Trav.* 66 The Turkes are also incredible takers of Opium. **1751** H. WALPOLE *Lett.* (1846) II. 397 Lady Stafford used to say to her sister, 'Well, child, I have come without my wit to-day'; that is, she had not taken her opium. **1838** T. THOMSON *Chem. Org. Bodies* 268 Opium yields at an average about $\frac{1}{15}$th of its weight of pure morphina. **1875** H. C. WOOD *Therap.* (1879) 221 Death occurs from opium, in the great majority of cases, by failure of the respiration.

b. *fig.* Applied to any stupefying agent or agency. Freq. referring to religion, esp. in phr. ***the opium of the people*** (see quot. 1844); also in *transf.* and allusive uses.

1608 T. MORTON *Preamb. Encounter* 33 Stupified with that Opium of implicit faith and blinde deuotion. **1658** SIR T. BROWNE *Hydriot.* v. 43 There is no antidote against the Opium of time. **1742** H. WALPOLE *Corr.* (1837) I. lviii. 225 Whist has spread an universal opium over the whole nation. [**1840** HEINE *Ludwig Börne* IV. 287 Für Menschen, denen die Erde nichts mehr bietet, ward der Himmel erfunden... Heil dieser Erfindung! Heil einer Religion, die dem leidenden Menschengeschlecht in den bittern Kelch einige süsse, einschläfernde Tropfen goss, geistiges Opium. **1844** MARX 'Zur Kritik der Hegel'schen Rechts-Philosophie' in *Deutsch-Französische Jahrbücher* Feb. 72 Die Religion ist der Seufzer der bedrängten Kreatur, das Gemüth einer herzlosen Welt, wie sie der Geist geistloser Zustände ist. Sie ist das *Opium* des Volks.] **1848** *Politics for People* 27 May 58 We have used the Bible as if it was a mere special constable's handbook—an opium-dose for keeping beasts of burden patient while they were being overloaded—a mere book to keep the poor in order. **1860** GEO. ELIOT *Let.* 26 Dec. in J. W. Cross *George Eliot's Life* (1885) II. xi. 283, I have faith in the working out of higher possibilities than the Catholic or any other Church has presented... The 'highest calling and election' is to *do without opium*, and live through all our pain with conscious, clear-eyed endurance. **1881** T. S. EGAN tr. *Heine's Ludwig Börne* IV. 169 For these people, to whom this world had nothing more to offer, Heaven was invented. .. Hail to this invention! Hail to that religion which could pour a few sweet soporific drops into the bitter cup of the suffering human race, spiritual opium. **1926** H. J. STENNING tr. *Marx's Selected Ess.* 12 Religion is the moan of the oppressed creature, the sentiment of a heartless world, as it is the spirit of spiritless conditions. It is the opium of the people. **1939** G. B. SHAW *Geneva* I. 28 Karl Marx—Antichrist—said that the sweet and ennobling consolations of our faith are opium given to the poor to enable them to endure the hardships of that state of life to which it has pleased God to call them. **1951** N. ANNAN *Leslie Stephen* vii. 201 Kingsley might protest that religion was being used as opium for the people. **1957** tr. *M. de Unamuno's San Manuel Bueno* 39 One of those leaders of what they call the social revolution has said that religion is the opium of the people. Opium... opium... opium, yes. Let us give them opium and let them sleep and dream. **1968** *Daily Tel.* (Colour Suppl.) 13 Dec. 43/4 Drink, in other words, is becoming the opium of the people. **1971** G. STEINER *In Bluebeard's Castle* iv. 93 A good deal of classical music is, today, the opium of the good citizen. **1974** *Times Lit. Suppl.* 28 June 692/5 A revue like *Here is the News* only shows politics becoming the opium of the people.

2. †**a.** [tr. L. *opium.*] A vegetable juice in general. *Obs. rare.* **b.** [*transf.* from 1.] A juice resembling opium in composition or properties (in quot. *lactucarium* or *lactucin*). *rare.*

c **1420** *Pallad. on Husb.* III. 1140 And in is kest This opium Quirinaik (the Greek So nameth hit).. In water first this opium relent, Of sape vntil hit ha similitude. **1815** *Sporting Mag.* XLVI. 63 A valuable paper on the opium obtained from the inspissated white juice [of the lettuce].

3. *attrib.* and *Comb.* **a.** *attrib.* in *fig.* sense: Soporific, stupefying, producing drowsiness. *rare.*

1635 A. STAFFORD *Fem. Glory* (1869) 91 Nothing..is so irksome to me, as to heare their cold Opium Sermons. **1797–1803** FOSTER in *Life & Corr.* (1846) I. 196 There is an opium sky stretched over all the world, which continually rains soporifics.

b. General Combs.: attrib., as ***opium cellar, cigarette, haul, house, lamp, liniment, -pipe, plaster, shop, war***; obj. and obj. gen., as ***opium addict, -dealer, -drinker, -drinking, -eater, -eating, -smoker, -smoking, -smuggler, -taker, -taking***; instrumental, as ***opium-drowsed*** adj., ***-fumed*** adj., ***-poisoning, -shattered*** adj. **c.** Special Combs.: **opium den**, a public room, of low or mean character, kept as a resort of opium-smokers; **opium dream**, a dream during an opium-induced sleep; also in extended use; **opium habit**, the habit of eating or smoking opium as a stimulant or intoxicant; **opium joint** (*U.S.*), a place illegally kept for opium-smoking (see JOINT *sb.* 14); **opium plant, opium poppy**, the white poppy, *Papaver somniferum*; **opium-smoke** *v.* (*nonce-wd.*) *trans.*, to bring by opium-smoking (*into* some condition); **opium war**, a war waged by Britain against China (1839–42) following China's attempt to prohibit the importation of opium into China; also, a later war (1856–60) against China by Britain and France.

1974 *Times* 2 Dec. 8/7 Charles was a charming *opium addict and rural clergyman. **1911** O. ONIONS *Widdershins* 278 He took me into an *opium-cellar within a stone's throw of Oxford Street. **1920** *Opium cigarette [see HEROIN]. **1841** J. STURGE *Let.* 30 Sept. in *Visit to U.S. in 1841* (1842) p. lxiv, Waging a murderous war to compel them to make restitution to the contraband *opium dealers. **1977** 'J. LE CARRÉ' *Hon. Schoolboy* xviii. 451 By afternoon he was airborne, and..chatting merrily to a couple of friendly opium dealers. **1882** J. D. MCCABE *New York* 590 Here are the headquarters of the Mongolians, their..*opium dens. **1897** *Daily News* 1 Nov. 6/5 Mr. Ganthony's opium den ruffian and Mr. Blinn's doctor are noteworthy instances. **1921** *Daily Colonist* (Victoria, B.C.) 25 Mar. 6/4 Lee Fong was charged in the City Police Court yesterday with being the keeper of an opium den at 536 Cormorant Street; and also with being in unlawful possession of opium. **1969** Opium-den [see CHINATOWN]. **1821** BYRON *Don Juan* IV. xix. 201 This is in others a fictitious state, An *opium dream of too much youth and reading. **1922** W. S. MAUGHAM *Writer's Notebk.* (1949) 202 Singapore: Opium Dream. I saw a road lined on each side with tall poplars. **1974** J. PHILIPS *Power Killers* (1975) I. ii. 18 What about his theory? It sounds like an opium dream. **1975** *Listener* 11 Sept. 343/2 *Who Am I Now?*, a fantasy based..on the opium dreams of George Crabbe. **1804** W. TAYLOR in Robberds *Mem.* I. 484 Poor Burnett! Rickman writes me word he is turned *opium-drinker. **1883** *Harper's Mag.* Nov. 961/2 The.. husband of an *opium-drinking wife. **1895** *Daily News* 27 Sept. 6/5 The *opium-drowsed and terror-stricken Dr. Marshall. **1821** DE QUINCEY (*title*) Confessions of an English *Opium-Eater. *Ibid.* (1822) 125 From this date [1813] the reader is to consider me as a regular and confirmed opium-eater. **1974** *Evening News* 27 June 1/7 (*headline*) £250,000 *opium haul. **1888** KIPLING *Plain Tales from Hills* 233 It was a *pukka*, respectable *opium-house, and not one of those stifling, sweltering *chardoo-khanas*. **1966** 'A. HALL' *9th Directive* vi. 54 The opium house at the Phra Chao. **1882** H. H. KANE *Opium-Smoking* 5 The principal places, known as '*opium joints', are in Mott, Pell, and Park streets. **1884** *New York paper*, Twenty-two males and four females were captured in an opium joint on Crosby street, New York, on Saturday night. **1897** HOWELLS *Landlord at Lion's Head* 85 Secret visits to the Chinese opium-joints in Kingston Street. **1926** *Daily Colonist* (Victoria, B.C.) 4 July 6/2 Charged with being inmates of an opium joint in Theatre Alley, Lee and Jim, Chinese, were each fined $15. **1897** *Allbutt's Syst. Med.* II. 885 Engaged in rolling and heating in their *opium-lamps treacly pellets of opium. **1890** KIPLING *City of Dreadful Night* (1891) vi. 40 The lamp for the *opium-pipe is the only one in the room. **1976** M. BUTTERWORTH *Festival!* i. 12 A crude photo print of a naked youth..carrying an opium pipe. **1899** *Allbutt's Syst. Med.* VI. 402 *note*, The myosis of *opium-poisoning.. appears, according to Dr. Ogle never to have been definitely referred to till 1818. **1863** *Opium poppy [see POPPY *sb.* 3]. **1880** BENTLEY & TRIMEN *Medicinal Plants* I. 18 It cannot be said that the opium poppy is known anywhere in a thoroughly wild condition. **1921** A. HUXLEY *Crome Yellow* xxii. 247 They passed a bed of opium poppies, dispetaled now. **1931** M. GRIEVE *Mod. Herbal* II. 651 The Opium Poppy..is indigenous to Asia Minor, and is cultivated largely in European and Asiatic Turkey, Persia, India and China for the production of Opium. **1975** *Times* 31 May 5/3 (*caption*) Peasant women tilling an opium poppy field in Turkey. **1849** DE QUINCEY *Eng. Mail Coach* Wks. 1897 XIII. 313 My frail *opium-shattered self. **1841–4** EMERSON *Ess.*, *Prudence* Wks. (Bohn) I. 98 The pitiful drivellers..at evening, when the bazaars are open, slink to the *opium-shop. **1870** DICKENS *E. Drood* i, The woman has *opium-smoked herself into a strange likeness of the Chinaman. **1860** H. GREELEY *Overland Journey* 259 [The Chinaman] is ..an *opium-smoker. **1921** *Daily Colonist* (Victoria, B.C.) 1 Apr. 6/4 The magistrate said that the accused had admitted ownership of the opium smoking paraphernalia, and to being an opium smoker himself. **1971** *Listener* 11 Nov. 644/1 A large existing market of opium-smokers. **1840** MALCOM *Trav.* 43/1 Another disciple, who has now fallen into the deadly habit of *opium-smoking. **1938** N. MARSH *Artists in Crime* (U.S.) xiii. 202 Fox had found Malmsley's opium-smoking impedimenta. **1976** *Times* 4 Sept. 7/4 What are the pros and cons of opium smoking? **1841** J. STURGE *Let.* 30 Sept. in *Visit to U.S. in 1841* (1842) p. lxii, To take under his protection one of the most extensive *opium smugglers. **1966** J. CLEARY *High Commissioner* iii. 50 The Chinese opium smugglers he had met before he had gone on to the Murder Squad. **1975** M. STERN in L. M. Alcott *Behind Mask* p. xxi, William Henry Thomes..had sailed aboard an opium smuggler that plied between China and California, and was himself a mine of suggestions for authors whose thrilling romances he would publish. **1792** D. STEWART *Philos. Hum. Mind* I. v. i. v. (1853) 181 Account of the *Opium-takers at Constantinople. **1821** DE QUINCEY *Confess.* (1822) II. 90 The whole art and mystery of *opium-taking. **1836** H. C. ROBINSON *Diary* 29 Aug. (1967) 161 A letter written by Coleridge..in which he gives an account of his sad habit of opium-taking. **1892** *Dict. Nat. Biog.* XXIX. 18/1 He..fell a victim to opium-taking. **1840** MALCOM *Trav.* 50/1 No person can describe the horrors of the *opium trade. **1841** J. STURGE *Let.* 30 Sept. in *Visit to U.S. in 1841* (1842) p. lxi, *Opium War with China. **1917** *Encycl. Sinica* 406/1 The action which forced the foreign merchants at Canton to deliver up their stocks of opium, which was destroyed by the Commissioner, and the subsequent events which led to war with Great Britain. This has been called the 'Opium War'. **1969** V. G. KIERNAN *Lords of Human Kind* v. 148 The West resorted to force, and the Opium Wars of 1840–42 and 1856–60..inducted China into..the comity of nations. **1974** *Listener* 8 Aug. 175/1 The Opium War totally destroyed Chinese confidence.

Hence **'opium** *v. trans.*, to treat with opium; **'opiumate**, one addicted to the use of opium; **'opiumist**, a person in favour of opium (opp. to *anti-opiumist*); so **'opiumite**; **'opiumy** *a.*, containing or resembling opium; **'opiumless** *a.*

1825 HONE *Every-day Bk.* 3 July I. 900 The bitten person, unless opiumed to death,.. will.. die in unspeakable agony. **1894** *Westm. Gaz.* 23 July 3/2 The opiumate, if accused of the habit, usually pleads guilty. **1893** *Ibid.* 29 June 1/3 The Anti-Opium Crusade. Fad or Fact?—By an Opiumist. **1891** MISS DOWIE *Girl in Karp.* xv. 196 Poppies, from whose sleepy heads an opiumy oil is made.

†**ople.** *Obs.* [ad. L. *opulus*: app. formed by Turner. Cf. OPIER.] The Guelder Rose or Water Elder (*Viburnum Opulus*).

1551 TURNER *Herbal* II. (1562) 69 Opulus,.. Conradus Gesnerus tolde me that it is called in Frenche *vn opier.* I neuer saw it in England, but it may be called in English an ople tre. **1578** LYTE *Dodoens* VI. lxxx. 760 Of Marris Elder, Ople, or Dwarffe Plane tree. **1611** COTGR., *Obier*, the Ople, water Elder, marsh Elder, Dwarfe plane, Whitten tree. **1706** PHILLIPS, *Ople*, a Shrub otherwise call'd Water-elder.

oplitic, oplophorous, erron. ff. HOPL-.

1854 BADHAM *Halieut.* 493 Then the oplitic troop to goad, Who bend beneath their chargers' load.

opo, obs. form of UPON.

opobalsam (ɒpəʊ'bɔːlsəm), anglicized f. next.

1658 PHILLIPS, *Opobalsame*, the gumme, or liquor that distilleth from the Balm-tree. **1730** *Phil. Trans.* XXXVI. 285 All Sorts of Oils, Pitch, Turpentine, Opobalsams. **1860** *Chambers' Encycl.* s.v. *Balsam*, The finest balsam, called Opobalsam or Balm of Mecca.

‖**opobalsamum** (ɒpəʊ'bælsəməm). [L., a. Gr. ὀποβάλσαμον juice of the balsam tree, f. ὀπός juice + βάλσαμον the balsam-tree.] The balsam or oleoresin called Balm of Gilead or Balm of Mecca: see BALM *sb.* 10.

1398 TREVISA *Barth. De P.R.* XVII. xviii. (1495) 613 Balsamum is a tree lyke to a vine,.. yf the rynde of the stocke is smyten wyth yren combes, thenne droppyth therof noble Opobalsamum. **1616** BULLOKAR *Eng. Expos.*, *Opobalsamum*, a precious iuice or liquor. **1725** BRADLEY *Fam. Dict.*, *Balm of Gilead*,.. Opobalsamum, the finest Balsom we know of, and being brought to us chiefly from Mecca, some call it the Balm of Mecca. **1844** LINGARD *Anglo-Sax. Ch.* (1858) II. x. 113 The ignorance or experience of antiquity had ascribed to the opobalsamum the most salutary virtues.

b. The tree producing this, a species of *Balsamodendron.*

1737 WHISTON *Josephus, Antiq.* IX. i. §2 In that place grows.. the opobalsamum.

opodeldoc (ɒpə'dɛldɒk). Also 7 -toch, -doch, 8 -dock, opp-. [Believed to be invented by Paracelsus; perh. containing Gr. ὀπο- vegetable juice.]

†**1.** *orig.* The name given in the works of Paracelsus to medical plasters of various kinds. *Obs.*

[*a* **1541** PARACELSUS *Chirurg. Min., De Apostem.* xxiii. (1603) 90 Descriptio oppodeltoch. ♃. De quatuor seminibus incarnatiuis ℨ f. Ceræ Colophoniæ ana ℨ ij. Picis naualis ℨ iij. Reduc in emplastrum. *Ibid.* xxxiii. 97 Descriptio oppodeltoch. ♃. Colophoniæ lib.j. puluerum chelidoniæ, aranciarum ana ℨ iiij. Visci de botin, quantum satis est ad incorporationem.] **1656** tr. *Paracelsus' Dispens.* 305 Now you must apply the Oppodeltoch Plaister. *Ibid.* 308 Then apply the Plaister Oppodeltoch. **1658** A. FOX *Wurtz' Surg.* II. vi. 62 In case the Wound doth not bleed.. lay a Headplaister to it, after the manner of an Opodeldoch. **1733** ALLEYNE *Dispensatory*, *Emplastrum opodeldoc.* [**1857** MAYNE *Expos. Lex.*, *Opodeltoch*, the name of a plaster.. referred to by Paracelsus.]

2. Now applied to various kinds of soap liniment.

a. Commonly applied to that (*Linimentum saponis*) of the British Pharmacopœia. 'The original opodeldoc of the Pharmacopœias was a soft ointment composed of soap 3 oz. dissolved in a pint of alcohol, and an ounce of camphor, with a drachm each of oils of origanum and rosemary added' (*Syd. Soc. Lex.* 1892). This was the *Unguentum opodeldoch* of the Edinr. Pharmacop. of 1722. 'In 1744 the Edinr. *Unguentum* took the name *Balsamum saponaceum* vulgo *oppodeldoch*; and in 1745 it appeared in the London Pharmacop. under the name *Linimentum saponaceum.* Of this preparation, the *Linimentum Saponis* of the present British Pharmacopœia is the lineal descendant' (C.C.B. in *N. & Q.* (1902) 1 Mar. 166).

b. As described in Merchant Shipping Act 1867, a liniment composed of equal parts of soap liniment (as in a) and tincture of opium; liniment of opium.

c. *Steer's opodeldoc*, 'a preparation composed of Castile soap, camphor, oils of marjoram and rosemary, rectified spirit, and solution of ammonia' (Mayne).

[**1650** *Chemical Dict. Paracelsus, Oppodeltoch* in Paracelsus is an ointment.] **1733** CHEYNE *Eng. Malady* II. xii. §3 (1734) 243 Warm and active Oils and Ointments, especially the Opodeldoc. **1746** SIR A. WESTCOMB in *Mrs. Delany's Autobiog. & Corr.* II. 440 Tell my aunt that I use oil of earthworms with opodeldoc to endeavour to dispel the lump. **1785** J. COLLIER *Mus. Trav.* App. (ed. 4) 22 He rubbed it with opodeldock or arquebusade water. **1826** SCOTT *Jrnl.* 25 Dec., By dint of abstinence and opodeldoc I passed a better night. **1842** BARHAM *Ingol. Leg., Bl. Mousquet.*, Her delicate fingers are charred With the Steer's opodeldoc, joint oil, and goulard. **1857** HUGHES *Tom Brown* I. vi. (1871) 111 Leaving East better for those few words than all the opedeldoc in England would have made him. **1890** *Chambers's Encycl.* VI. 644 Soap Liniment, or Opodeldoc, the constituents of which are soap, camphor, and spirits of rosemary. **1902** C. C. B. in *N. & Q.* 9th Ser. IX. 166 Steers's Opodeldoc, a famous nostrum of the eighteenth century,.. an imitation of the old Edinburgh *Unguentum opodeldoch*, with the addition of ammonia.

Hence **opo'deldoc** *v.*, to treat with opodeldoc.

1797 J. WARTON in *Wilkes' Corr.* (1805) IV. 333, I was blooded, oppodeldoc'd, &c. and got home as I could.

-opolis, combining form of -POLIS, Gr. πόλις city.

opon, op on, obs. forms of UPON.

opopanax (əʊ'pɒpənæks). Also 5 opopanac, appoponak, 6 oppopanac(k, 6- opoponax, opp-. [a. L. *opopanax* (Pliny), a. Gr. ὀπόπαναξ, f. ὀπός juice + πάναξ (also πανακές, neut. of πανακής adj. all-healing: cf. PANACEA), name of a plant.]

1. A fetid gum-resin obtained from the root of *Opopanax Chironium*, a yellow flowered umbelliferous plant, resembling a parsnip, a native of Southern Europe; formerly of repute in medicine. Also applied to the juice (***English opopanax***) obtained from Lovage (*Levisticum officinale*).

c **1400** *Lanfranc's Cirurg.* 60 Opopanac [*v.r.* Appoponak] ys wondirful, þe leuys of a Gourde, & þe rote of ffynegreke, þe gele of fyssches, & amptes y-stampyde. **1563** T. GALE *Antidot.* 31 b, Dissolue the Opopanax and Galbanum, in some part of the wyne. **1569** R. ANDROSE tr. *Alexis' Secr.* IV. I. 6 Of Galbanum, of Oppopanack, of ech half an ounce. **1616** BULLOKAR *Eng. Expos.*, *Opopanax*, a sappe or liquor flowing in some hot Countries out of a Plant called Panax. It is brought hither dry, being of a yellow colour on the outside, and white within. **1732** ARBUTHNOT *Rules of Diet* i. 250 The plant from which Apopanax is taken, is a sort of Parsnip. **1857** MAYNE *Expos. Lex.*, *Opopanax, English*, a common name for the juice yielded by the *Ligusticum levisticum*, or lovage plant. **1876** HARLEY *Mat. Med.* (ed. 6) 603 Opopanax was formerly imported into this country from Turkey.

2. In *Perfumery*, applied to a gum-resin obtained from *Balsamodendron Kataf.*

1867 *Gardeners' Chron.* 29 June 690/1 New Perfumes.—Opoponax. **1895** E. M. HOLMES in *Pharm. Jrnl.* Ser. III. XXV. 501 The oil of opoponax of perfumery is obtained from a gum-resin which has a totally different origin, being derived from [*Balsamodendron*] *Commiphora Kataf*, Engl. It is the 'Bissabol' of Pharmacographia,.. and the perfumed bdellium of Dymock... In appearance it resembles opopanax.. but it has a slightly pleasant and quite distinctive odour. **1913** [see MIGNONETTE 1 d]. **1924** GALSWORTHY *White Monkey* I. vii. 55 A profiteer who dropped his aitches and reeked of opoponax.

3. Short for *opopanax-tree* (see 4).

4. *attrib.* and *Comb.*, as **opopanax soap**, soap perfumed with opopanax (sense 2); **opopanax-tree** (*Acacia Farnesiana*), the Sponge-tree of the Southern United States, West Indies, etc., having fragrant yellow flowers; †**opopanax wine**, wine medicated with opopanax (sense 1).

? **1540** tr. *Vigo's Lyt. Pract.* A iij, Take Oppoponac wyne. **1811** HOOPER *Med. Dict.* s.v. *Opopanax*, The plant from whence the gum is produced is known by the names of.. Hercules all heal, and opoponax-wort. **1889** *Boston* (Mass.) *Jrnl.* 30 Nov. 2/3 The opoponax tree is not only a very pleasant but a profitable one to the ladies of Charleston, S.C... The Flowers are made up in tiny button-hole bouquets.. to sell. **1897** *Blackw. Mag.* Nov. 685/2 Opoponax trees filling the air with the fragrance of their yellow blossoms. **1897** OUIDA *Massarenes* xviii, She came straight from her bath and its oppoponax soap and eau de verveine.

‖**oporice** (əʊ'pɔərɪsiː). *Pharm.* [L *opōricē* (Pliny), a. Gr. ὀπωρική of fruit, f. ὀπώρα late summer, fruit-time, fruit.] A medicine composed of autumnal fruits and wine, formerly employed as a remedy in dysentery, etc. (Dunglison).

1753 CHAMBERS *Cycl. Suppl.*, *Oporice*, a name given by the antients to a medicine composed of the autumnal fruits, and extolled for its great virtues against weaknesses of the stomach and dysenteries. **1811** HOOPER *Med. Dict.*, *Oporice*, a conserve made of ripe fruit. **1846** in WORCESTER; and some mod. Dicts.

†**opo'ropolist.** *Obs. nonce-wd.* [f. Gr. ὀπωροπώλης fruit-seller + -IST.] A fruit-seller.

1671 H. M. tr. *Erasm. Colloq.* 276 A woman that sold fruit, or if you would rather have it in Greek, an Oporapolist. **1725** BAILEY *Erasm. Colloq.* 309.

Oporto (wine): see PORT (wine).

oportune, opose, etc., obs. forms of OPP-.

opossum (ə'pɒsəm). Forms: 7 opassom, opossom, 8 opassum, oposon, 8–9 oppossum, 8– opossum. See also POSSUM. [American Indian name in Virginia, given by early writers as *aposon, apossoun, oposon, opassom.*]

1. General name of the small marsupial mammals of the American family *Didelphyidæ*, mostly arboreal, some (genus *Chironectes*) aquatic, of nocturnal habits, with an opposable digit (thumb) on the hind foot, and tail usually prehensile; esp. *Didelphys virginiana*, the common opossum of the United States. (Colloq. shortened to POSSUM, q.v.)

1610 *True Declar. Col. Virginia* (1844) 13 There are Arocouns, and Apossouns, in shape like to pigges, shrowded in hollow roots of trees. **1612** CAPT. SMITH *Map Virginia* 14 An Opassom hath an head like a Swine, and a taile like a Rat, and is of the bignes of a Cat. Vnder her belly she hath a bagge, wherein shee lodgeth, carrieth, and sucketh [1624 suckleth] her young. **1613** PURCHAS *Pilgrimage* 636 [*erron.*] The Ouassom [etc. (quoting Smith)]. *c* **1615** W. STRACHEY *Hist. Trav. Virginia* (Hakl. Soc. 1849) 123 An opussum is a beast as big as a pretty beagle, of grey cullour. *Ibid.* Glossary Indian Wds. 183, *Aposon*, a beast in bignes like a pig and in tast alike. **1635** SWAN *Spec. M.* ix. §1 (1643) 439 [*erron.*] A beast called Ovassom [etc. (quoting Purchas)]. **1688** J. CLAYTON in *Phil. Trans.* XVIII. 122 An Opossom, as big, and something shaped like our Badgers, but of a lighter Dun colour. **1719** OZELL tr. *Misson's Mem.* 280 The Oposon is of the Bigness of a Pig of a Fortnight old. **1763** WESLEY *Compend. of Nat. Philos.* (1784) I. II. i. § 10. 236 The tender young of the Opossum are delicate morsels. **1769** PENNANT *Brit. Zool.* III. 19 As the young of the oppossum retire into the ventral pouch of the old one. **1859** THACKERAY *Virgin.* xxxviii, Like the fabled opossum.. who when he spied the unerring gunner from his gum-tree said 'It's no use, Major, I will come down'. **1880** HAUGHTON *Phys. Geog.* vi. 267 Seven species of Opossum have been found, fossil, in caves of Brazil.

2. Extended to various other small or moderate-sized marsupials; *esp.* the common name in Australia and Tasmania of those of the sub-family *Phalangistinæ*, more properly called Phalangers. (Now normally replaced in Australian usage by ***possum*** but still the more usual form in New Zealand.)

'The name opossum is applied in Australia to all or any of the species belonging to the genera, which together form the sub-family *Phalangerinæ*... The commoner forms are as follows:—Common Dormouse O., *Dromicia nana.* Common Opossum, *Trichosurus vulpecula.* Common Ring-tailed O., *Pseudochirus peregrinus.* Greater Flying-O., *Petauroides volans.* Lesser Dormouse O., *Dromicia lepida.* Lesser Flying-O., *Petaurus breviceps.* Pigmy Flying-O., *Acrobates pygmæus.* Short-eared O., *Trichosurus caninus.* Squirrel Flying-O., or Flying-Squirrel, *Petaurus sciureus.* Striped O., *Dactylopsila trivirgata.* Tasmanian, or Sooty O., *Trichosurus vulpecula*, var. *fuliginosus.* Tasmanian Ring-tailed O., *Pseudochirus Cooki.* Yellow-bellied Flying-O., *Petaurus australis*'. (Morris *Austral Eng.* (1898) s.v.)

[**1770** *Capt. Cook's Jrnl.* 4 Aug. (1893) 294 Here [at Endeavour River] are Wolves, Possums, an animal like a ratt, and snakes.] **1777** COOK *Voy.* (1784) I. 109 The only animal of the quadruped kind we got, was a sort of opossum, about twice the size of a large rat. **1789** A. PHILLIP *Voy. Botany Bay* xxii. 297 Black Flying Opossum. **1793** J. HUNTER *Voyage* 68 The opossum is also very numerous here, but it is not exactly like the American opossum. **1802** BARRINGTON *Hist. N.S. Wales* i. 23 The females.. wear a little apron, made from the skin of the opposum. **1847** LEICHHARDT *Jrnl.* v. 146 The Black-fellows told us, that they had caught a ring-tailed opossum. **1862** G. T. LLOYD *30 Yrs. Tasmania* iv. 47 The large sable and gray opossums, when disturbed, will either await death in their dark nest or at once spring to the earth. **1875** *Melbourne Spectator* 10 July 118/2 A snow-white opossum has been captured on a tree at the Murray. **1911** C. E. W. BEAN *'Dreadnought' of Darling* xvii. 162 Australia, at one time, along with its harmless marsupial kangaroos, opossums.. and the rest, had its own beasts of prey. **1911** E. M. CLOWES *On Wallaby* ii. 19 The only possible chance visitor is an occasional opossum on the roof. **1944** *Living off Land* iii. 57 To improvise a water container, copy the blacks, who used the skins of opossums. **1968** *Wanganui* (N.Z.) *Chron.* 15 Nov. 10/6 (Advt.), Opossum skins. Good prices, wanted immediately for overseas contract. **1973** *Massey Ferguson Rev.* (N.Z.) Mar.–Apr. 8/3 Intensive control measures around the farms by the New Zealand Forest Service and local pest destruction boards have reduced opossum numbers with the aim that this will break the cattle infection cycle and stop Tb-tested cattle from becoming re-infected.

3. *attrib.* and *Comb.*, as ***opossum kind, skin, tribe***; **opossum-mouse**, the Pygmy Flying Phalanger of Australia, *Acrobates pygmæus*; **opossum-shrew**, an insectivorous mammal of the West Indian genus *Solenodon*, outwardly resembling an opossum; **opossum-shrimp**, a shrimp of the genus *Mysis* or family *Mysidæ*, so called from the brood-pouch in which the female carries her eggs; **opossum-tree**, an Australian timber-tree, *Quintinia Sieberi.*

1770 J. BANKS *Jrnl.* 26 July (1896) 291 While botanising to-day I had the good fortune to take an animal of the opossum (*Didelphis*) tribe. **1789** A. PHILLIP *Voy. Botany Bay* xv. 147 A small animal of the opossum kind. **1832** J. BISCHOFF *Van Diemen's Land* 28 The opossum mouse is about the size of our largest barn mouse. **1844** CARPENTER *Zool.* §790 The curious genus *Mysis*, or Opossum-Shrimp. **1859** CORNWALLIS *New World* I. 161 Beating their stretched opossum-skin rugs as a drum accompaniment. **1862** WHYTE MELVILLE *Ins. Bar* 343 What I believe Mr. Poole terms the 'opossum pocket' of his shooting-jacket. **1894** LYDEKKER *Marsupialia* 118 The Flying Mouse, or Opossum Mouse,.. is one of the most elegant of the Australian Marsupials.

o'possuming, *vbl. sb.* [-ING[1].] Opossum-hunting.

1917 'H. H. RICHARDSON' *Fortunes R. Mahony* III. iv. 211 There is to be opossuming and a moonlight picnic to-night.

opotherapy (ɒpəˈθɛrəpɪ). *Med.* [f. Gr. ὀπός juice + THERAPY.] = ORGANOTHERAPY.

1897 *Index Medicus* XIX. 899/2 Opotherapy. **1899** *Ann. Rep. Board of Regents Smithsonian Inst. 1897–98* 696 An entire new method, designated under the name of opotherapy, or treatment by organic extracts. **1902** *Brit. Med. Jrnl.* 12 Apr. 909/1 (*heading*) Placentophagy and placental opotherapy. **1908** *Practitioner* Mar. 412 The many different substances recently utilised in opotherapy. **1915** [see *ketogenetic* adj. s.v. KETO- a].

† **ˈoppicate**, *v. Obs. rare*⁻⁰. [f. ppl. stem of L. *oppicāre*, f. *ob-* (OB- 1 c) + *picāre* to pitch, f. *pix, pic-* pitch.] (See quot.) Hence † **oppiˈcation**.

1623 COCKERAM, *Oppicate*, to pitch. **1656** BLOUNT *Glossogr.*, *Oppication*, a covering with pitch.

oppidan (ˈɒpɪdən), *a.* and *sb.* [ad. L. *oppidānus* belonging to a town (other than Rome); as sb., a townsman, f. *oppidum* town.]

A. *adj.* Of or belonging to a town, or to the town (as opposed to the country); civic; urban.

1643 NETHERSOLE *Parables refl. on Times* 11 They so inchanted..all the common sort of Oppidan, rurall, and Sea-birds. *c* **1645** HOWELL *Lett.* I. 72 Touching the Temporall Government of Rome and Oppidan Affairs. **1845** R. W. HAMILTON *Pop. Educ.* viii. (ed. 2) 182 Such great abodes of the oppidan population. **1878** GLADSTONE in *19th Cent.* Jan. 204 Between the rural peasant and the oppidan artisan.

† **b.** Pertaining to a university town, as opposed to the university itself. (Cf. B. 2.)

1655 FULLER *Hist. Camb.* (1840) 179 These oppidane animosities..continued all this king's reign. **1831** SIR W. HAMILTON *Discuss.* (1852) 407 The oppidan schools then everywhere established.

B. *sb.* **1.** An inhabitant of a town, a townsman.

c **1540** *Order in battayll* B iv, Vpon a vyctory, oftentymes the opidanis be necligent. **1613** R. CAWDREY *Table Alph.*, *Oppidane*, a townesman. **1859** *Times* 24 Nov. 8/5 It will be a metamorphose which was never contemplated by any orthodox mind,—the conversion of nature into an oppidan.

† **2.** A 'townsman', as opposed to a 'gownsman' or member of a unversity; also, a student not resident in a college. *Obs.*

c **1645** HOWELL *Lett.* I. I. viii. (1726) 28 Here [in Leyden] are no Colleges at all,..nor scarce the face of an University, only there are general Schools where the Sciences are read by several Professors, but all the Students are Oppidanes. *a* **1696** WOOD *Hist. Univ. Oxford* (1796) II. 33 The Oppidans in the mean time were not wanting to trouble us, and particularly the Baillives.

3. At Eton College: A student not on the foundation (who boards in the town): distinguished from *colleger*. Formerly also at other great schools.

1557–8 *Eton Audit Bk.* in Lyte *Hist. Eton Coll.* 136 *note*, Two newe chandlestycks for the opydans in the Churche ijs. vjd. *a* **1661** FULLER in *Etoniana* 31 There be many oppidanes there maintained at the cost of their friends. **1706** PHILLIPS, *Oppidan*, a School-word for a Townsboy, particularly such as do belong to the College of Queen's-Scholars at Westminster. **1809** SHELLEY *Lett.* Pr. Wks. 1880 III. 329, I am..prosecuting my studies as an Oppidan at Eton. **1882** *Standard* 1 Dec. 7/2 The time-honoured match at the Wall between the Oppidans and Collegers was played in the Eton fields yesterday.

† **oppie**. *Obs. rare*⁻¹. [ad. It. *oppio* 'Poppy, Piet or Wich-hazell..*Oppio nero*, the blacke Poplar' (Florio, 1611), 'a kind of poplar tree' (Baretti): cf. OPIER.] Some tree: ? the Witch Hazel.

1592 R. D. *Hypnerotomachia* 5 Poplars, wilde Oliue, and Oppies [orig. *opio*] disposed some hyer then other.

† **oˈppignorate, oˈppignerate**, *v. Obs.* [f. ppl. stem of L. *oppignorāre, -erāre* to pledge, f. *ob-* (OB- 1 b) + *pignorāre, -erāre*, f. *pignus, pignor-* (also *pigner-*) pledge.] *trans.* To pawn, pledge.

1622 BACON *Hen. VII* 99 Ferdinando..merchanded at this time..for the restoring of the Counties of Russignon and Perpignian, oppignorated to the French. **1625** —— *Apophthegms* § 148. 167 [Henry, duke of Guise] had sold and oppignerated all his Patrimonie. **1822** SCOTT *Nigel* xxxi, We opignorated in your hands certain jewels of the crown. **1857** *Chamb. Jrnl.* VII. 406, I had been constrained..to..oppignerate, or hypothecate, or effect a mortgage by way of wadset.

† **oppignoˈration**. *Obs.* [a. OF. *oppignoration*, ad. med.L. or L. type **oppignorātiōn-em*, n. of action f. *oppignorāre*: see prec.] Pledging or giving of security; a pawning.

1592 ANDREWES *Serm.* (1843) V. 74 The..swearing..by oppignoration or engaging of some good which we would not lose. **1622** MALYNES *Ancient Law-Merch.* 220 Returning..to the said matter of Oppignorations, let vs note the questions of Ciuilians. *a* **1677** MANTON *On Job* xvii. 6 The Elect are made over to Christ, not by way of alienation, but oppignoration.

ˈoppilant, *a. Med.* [ad. L. *oppīlānt-em*, pr. pple. of *oppīlāre*: see next.] Obstructing, hindering.

1857 in MAYNE *Expos. Lex.* **1892** in *Syd. Soc. Lex.*

† **ˈoppilate**, *ppl. a. Med. Obs.* Also 5 oppilat. [ad. L. *oppīlāt-us*, pa. pple. of *oppīlāre*: see next.] Stopped up, obstructed.

? *a* **1412** LYDG. *Two Merch.* 325 His vryne was remys, attenuat..The veyne ryueeres, for they wern oppilat, It was ful thynne. **1610** BARROUGH *Meth. Physick* I. xxxii. (1639) 52 The nerves optick be oppilate and mortified. **1612** WOODALL *Surg. Mate* Wks. (1653) 200 The right gut..being oppilate or stopped.

oppilate (ˈɒpɪleɪt), *v. Med.* Also 6–7 opilate. [f. ppl. stem of L. *oppīlāre* to stop up, f. *ob-* (OB- 1 b) + *pīlāre* to ram down.] *trans.* To stop or block up, fill with obstructive matter, obstruct.

1547 BOORDE *Brev. Health* xv. 12 b, A reumatike humour opylatinge the celles of the brayne. **1620** VENNER *Via Recta* vi. 95 It openeth the passages, and dissipateth..the humours oppilating the nerues. **1706** PHILLIPS, *To Oppilate*. **1832** J. P. KENNEDY *Swallow B.* x. (1860) 93 The pipes become oppilated with crudities.

Hence **ˈoppilated, ˈoppilating** *ppl. adjs.*

1577 FRAMPTON *Joyful Newes* II. 50 They did remaine opilated, and with euill colour of the face. **1620** VENNER *Via Recta* v. 88 The property of all Cheese to breede grosse and oppilating humors. **1822–34** *Good's Study Med.* (ed. 4) IV. 84 Characterised by a rich and oppilated habit.

oppilation (ɒpɪˈleɪʃən). *Med.* Also 5–7 opi- [ad. L. *oppīlātiōn-em*, n. of action f. *oppīlāre*: see prec. Cf. F. *opilation* (14th c. in Hatz.-Darm.).] The action of stopping up or obstructing, or condition of being obstructed; an obstruction.

c **1400** *Lanfranc's Cirurg.* 251 It is opilacioun of þe nerue, þat comeþ fro þe brain. **1539** ELYOT *Cast. Helthe* II. vii. 196 Fygges..profyt moch to them which haue oppilations. **1601** HOLLAND *Pliny* XX. xxii, If one drinke the wilde Thyme with water, it is excellent good for the opilation..of the liver. **1727** BRADLEY *Fam. Dict.* s.v. *Barley*, It opens Oppilations of the Bladder by its abstersive Faculties. **1822–34** *Good's Study Med.* (ed. 4) IV. 316 Accompanied with oppilation or indurated enlargement of one or more of the abdominal viscera. **1849** J. A. CARLYLE tr. *Dante's Inferno* 292 As one who falls..through force of Demon which drags him to the ground, or of other oppilation that fetters men. [*Note*] 'Obstruction' of the vital spirits, 'that binds a man in fits', like those of Epilepsy or 'possession'.

oppilative (ˈɒpɪleɪtɪv), *a. Med.* Also 6–8 opilative. [f. as OPPILATE *v.* + -IVE; cf. F. *oppilatif, -ive* (1425 in Hatz.-Darm.).] Tending to stop up or obstruct, obstructive, constipating.

1528 PAYNEL *Salerne's Regim.* P ij, At suche tymes as folkes vse grosse and opilatiue meatis. **1620** VENNER *Via Recta* (1650) 116 Eggs..made hard are oppilative, of hard digestion. **1725** BRADLEY *Fam. Dict.* s.v. *Rye*, This Bread is of a viscous, opilative Nature.

Hence **ˈoppilativeness** (Bailey 1727).

† **oppin**. *Sc. Obs. rare.* [? for *opine*] = OPINION.

1456 SIR G. HAYE *Law Arms* (S.T.S.) 179 Me think this the rycht oppin, and the best way.

oppinion, -oun, obs. forms of OPINION.

† **oˈpplete**, *ppl. a. Med. Obs.* Also 6 opplet. [ad. L. *opplēt-us*, pa. pple. of *opplēre*: see next.] Filled up, crowded.

1545 RAYNOLD *Byrth Mankynde* P j, The cotilidons be opplete, stopped, & stuffed with yll humours. **1578** BANISTER *Hist. Man* I. 34 The posteriour part [of the leg] is opplet, and filled with much store of flesh. **1646** J. HALL *Horæ Vac.* 134 How should they not be opplete with grosse humours?

† **oˈpplete**, *v. Med. Obs. rare.* [f. ppl. stem of L. *opplēre* to fill up, f. *ob-* (OB- 1 d) + *plēre* to fill.] *trans.* To fill up, fill to repletion.

1620 VENNER *Via Recta* ii. 41 They..opplete their bodies with waterish, crude, and windy humors. *Ibid.* iv. 71 That it be not..oppleted with much fat.

† **oˈppletion**. *Med. Obs.* [ad. med.L. or L. type **opplētiōn-em*, n. of action f. *opplēre*: see prec.] The action of filling or condition of being filled up; undue fullness of habit or of an organ or part.

1615 CROOKE *Body of Man* 506 In the oppletion or filling of the ventricles by any humor. **1713** *Gentl. Instructed* (ed. 5) 183 An Imposthume calls for a Lance, and Oppletion for unpalatable Evacuatories. **1764** *Characters* in *Ann. Reg.* 42/2 He..had..an oppletion of the whole habit.

oppo (ˈɒpəʊ). *slang* (orig. Forces'). Abbrev. of *opposite number*.

1939 *Airman's Gaz.* Dec., Get an oppo to relieve you for 'break'. **1942** *Gen* 1 Sept. 13/2 A sweetheart or companion in the navy is an 'oppo'. **1948** PARTRIDGE *Dict. Forces' Slang* 133 *Oppo*, ... In the Navy and Air Force; a companion..or even one's wife. **1955** P. WILDEBLOOD *Against Law* 99 Me and my oppo was in the Royal Navy. **1961** F. H. BURGESS *Dict. Sailing* 154 *Opposite number, oppo*, one of two hands who perform similar duties alternately; he may be on another ship or station. **1962** K. DOBBS *Running to Paradise* 49 My oppo, my best friend in the mess, was a former Sussex poacher. **1967** D. REEMAN *Deep Silence* iii. 48 Me an' the kid is oppos, see? **1971** B. W. ALDISS *Soldier Erect* 101 He's dotty on them Wog gods, aren't you, Stubby, me old oppo? **1973** *Times* 24 May 18/4 He was Mr. Justice Lawson,..and what is more he was accompanied by his oppo, Mr. Justice Mais.

oppon, obs. form of UPON.

† **oˈppone**, *v. Obs.* [ad. L. *oppōn-ĕre* to set against, f. *ob-*, OB- b + *pōn-ĕre* to place.] = OPPOSE (of which vb. in the modern sense it was the precursor; cf. Sc. legal *depone* and Eng. *depose*).

1. *trans.* To set over against or opposite (in quot., in an entry).

1610 W. FOLKINGHAM *Art of Survey* IV. Concl. 87 These are opponed, Residence, Species, Habitude, Crassitude, Inuesture.

2. = OPPOSE *v.* 5, 6.

1570 *Henry's Wallace* I. 14 Thocht all Leidis wald have yis land in thrall, Oppone his power God can aganis yame all. **1671** *True Nonconf.* 62 You proceed, to oppone to us our Saviours Sermons,..I will not contend with your Mockeries.

3. *refl.* and *intr.* = OPPOSE *v.* 7.

1513 DOUGLAS *Æneis* XII. xiii. 191 Be quhat slycht May I oppone me to resist or stryve With sik a monstre? *c* **1555** HARPSFIELD *Divorce Hen. VIII* (Camden) 205 Many other ..men..opponing themselves..against this divorce. **1640** *Consid. touching Ch. Eng.* 5 Two opinions, which doe directly confront and oppone to reformation.

4. *trans.* = OPPOSE *v.* 9.

1610 B. JONSON *Alch.* III. ii, What can you not doe, Against lords spirituall, or temporall, That shall oppone you? **1629** SIR W. MURE *True Crucif.* 3014 To suffer, rather than by armes oppone The Lawfull Magistrat. *a* **1641** BP. MOUNTAGU *Acts & Mon.* (1642) 531 Whosoever shall [so] teach..opponeth the Apostle and divine Scripture.

opponency (əˈpəʊnənsɪ). [f. OPPONENT *a.* and *sb.*: see -ENCY.]

1. The action of an opponent or of something opposing; antagonism, opposition.

1727 BAILEY, *Opponency*, opposition. **1826** J. GILCHRIST *Lecture* Pref. 4 Which affinity might have been assisted..by the very nature of the opponency to be contended with. **1834** *New Monthly Mag.* XL. 402 A fierce and unyielding opponency is rising upon the point between manufacture and agriculture. **1857** J. W. DONALDSON *Chr. Orthod.* 256 'Oppositions of science falsely so called'..(i.e. opponencies of the misnamed Gnosis).

2. The action or position of the opponent in an academical disputation as an exercise for a degree. (Cf. OPPONENT B. 1.) *Obs.* exc. *Hist.*

1730–6 BAILEY (folio), *Opponency*, the maintaining a contrary argument. **1767** J. BALGUY *Let. to Parr* 14 Feb. in *Parr's Wks.* (1828) VII. 177 Colston has kept a third opponency in the schools with a perquam. **1841** PEACOCK *Stat. Cambr.* 9 When they had kept..two opponencies.. they were presented..as candidates for admission *ad respondendum quæstioni*. **1892** A. G. LITTLE *Grey Friars Oxf.* (O.H.S.) iii. 50 We have no means of checking them [figures] with regard to opponency [for the B.D. degree].

opponens (əˈpəʊnɛnz), *a. Anat.* [L., pr. pple. of *opponere* to set against.] Used, ellipt. as sb. (L. *musculus* being usu. omitted), in the names of four pairs of small muscles of the hands and feet: the ***opponens pollicis***, which helps to draw the thumb across the palm; the ***opponens digiti minimi***, which helps to raise the little finger when the palm is stretched out flat; the ***opponens digiti minimi***, of the foot; and (seldom distinguished) the ***opponens hallucis*** of the foot. Cf. OPPONENT *a.* 3.

1797 J. BELL *Anat. Bones* II. iii. 280 The opponens pollicis, is often called the metacarpal of the thumb. **1836–9** R. B. TODD *Cycl. Anat. & Physiol.* II. 519/2 Flexor ossis metacarpi or opponens pollicis..of a rhomboidal form. *Ibid.* 521/1 Adductor ossis metacarpi or opponens minimi digiti. **1902** D. J. CUNNINGHAM *Text-bk. Anat.* 329 The opponens minimi digiti..arises from the anterior annular ligament and the hook of the unciform bone. **1967** G. M. WYBURN et al. *Conc. Anat.* ii. 68/2 The opponens..is inserted into the shaft of the 1st metacarpal bone. **1973** *Gray's Anat.* (ed. 35) 582/2 Part of the muscle [*sc.* the adductor hallucis] may be attached to the first metatarsal, constituting an opponens hallucis.

opponent (əˈpəʊnənt), *a.* and *sb.* [ad. L. *oppōnent-em*, pr. pple. of *oppōnĕre*: see OPPONE, OPPOSE *v.*]

A. *adj.*

1. Standing over against: opposing, opposite.

1728–46 THOMSON *Spring* 665 Her sympathizing lover takes his stand High on th' opponent bank. **1735** SOMERVILLE *Chase* III. 95 Then up th' opponent Hill..we mount aloft. **1871** M. COLLINS *Mrq. & Merch.* II. vi. 182 They are the opponent poles of a cycle.

2. Antagonistic, adverse, contrary, opposed. Const. *to*, †*against*.

1647 F. BLAND *Souldiers March* 25 We are to consider enemies as men opponent to peace and justice. **1670** *Conclave wherein Clement VIII was elected Pope* 20 To forgive all them that had been opponent against his Exaltation. **1725** POPE *Odyss.* XIX. 524 The savage..springs impetuous with opponent speed! **1730** FIELDING *Temple Beau* I. iii, Sir, I desire to deliver my reasons opponent to this match. **1857** RUSKIN *Two Paths* iv. 185 The artist, when his pupil is perfect, must see him leave his side that he may declare his distinct, perhaps opponent, skill.

3. *Anat.* Said of a muscle (*opponens*) of the hand in man and some quadrumana, which opposes a lateral digit to one of the other digits. Also of the digit itself: cf. OPPOSABLE 2.

1842 BLACKW. MAG. LI. 424 The thumb or fifth finger.. in the latter..is opponent, or antagonizing. **1857** MAYNE *Expos. Lex.*, *Oppōnens, Anat.*,..opponent; applied to muscles, etc.

B. *sb.*

1. One who maintains a contrary argument in a disputation; esp. the person who opens an academical disputation by proposing objections to a philosophical or theological thesis: correlative to *respondent*. (Cf. OPPOSE *v.* 2.) *Obs.* exc. *Hist.*

1588 FRAUNCE *Lawiers Log.* II. ix. 101 b, The opponent who defendeth the contrary. **1670** G. H. tr. *Hist. Cardinals* I. II. 39 The Father being himself both Opponent and Respondent, there was no answer given to that position. **1705** HEARNE *Collect.* 25 Nov. (O.H.S.) I. 98 He..was

Prior-Opponent in ye Divinity Schoole, Mr. Entwistle.. being respondent. **1846** McCulloch *Acc. Brit. Empire* (1854) II. 351 (*Univ. Cambr.*), The 'previous examination' is followed by the 'exercises'.. These relics of old scholastic fashion consist of Latin theses (generally on subjects of moral philosophy), which are propounded by the student who is candidate for the degree of B.A. (the respondent), and answered by others, styled 'opponents', in syllogistic form, in Latin.

2. One who opposes or contends against; one who takes the opposite side in a controversy, struggle, or contest; an antagonist, adversary.

1615 *Stow's Ann.* 833/2 The second day, the foure opponents brought in their complaints. **1645** Bp. Hall *Peace Maker* xxiv. 211 He met with feeble opponents, and such as his nimble wit was easily able to over-turn. **1759** Robertson *Hist. Scot.* v. Wks. 1813 I. 363 The most violent opponents of the king's government were forfeited. **1794** Sullivan *View Nat.* I. 7 He searches about for opponents to his doctrine. **1829** Lytton *Devereux* II. xi, I had already run my opponent through the sword arm. **1874** Green *Short Hist.* viii. §7. 531 The proposal found stubborn opponents among the moderate Royalists.

† **o'pportunate**, *a.* *Obs.* [irreg. f. L. *opportūn-us* fit, suitable, opportune + -ATE[2]; cf. *importunate.*] Fit, suitable, proper, opportune.

1541 R. Copland *Galyen's Terapeut.* 2 G iij b, It is profytable yt the blode be leten flowe many tymes from the inueterate vlceres (in what soeuer maner yt shall be seen opportunate). **1630** Brathwait *Eng. Gentlem.* (1641) 6 Speech.. is.. an apt composing and an opportunate uttering of words.

Hence † **o'pportunately** *adv.*, opportunely.

1552 Huloet, Oportunatlye, *in tempore, oportune, tempestiue.* **1590** Burrough *Meth. Physick* 236 That it be opportunatly, and done in due time. **1620** Brathwait *Five Senses* in *Archaica* (1815) II. 10 A salve.. opportunately ministered.. affords comfort to the patient.

opportune (ɒpə'tjuːn, 'ɒpətjuːn), *a.* (*adv.*) Also 5–6 opor-. [a. F. *opportun, -une* seasonable, timely; formerly also, exposed, liable (14–15th c. in Hatz.-Darm.) = It., Pg. *opportuno*, Sp. *oportuno*, ad. L. *opportūn-us* fit, suitable, convenient, seasonable; advantageous, serviceable; adapted; exposed, liable, f. *ob-* (OB-): cf. *Portūnus* the protecting god of harbours, f. *portu-s* harbour, PORT. The same stem is found in *importūn-us* IMPORTUNE.]

1. Adapted to an end or purpose or the circumstances of the case; fit, suitable, appropriate; convenient. **a.** Of a time.

1412–20 Lydg. *Chron. Troy* I. v. (MS. Cott. Aug. IV) lf. 13 b/2 Whan sche cauȝte opportune space, To his desire.. Toward Jason anoon sche gan hir dresse. *c* **1430** —— *Reason & Sens.* 1840 Whan I espyed by her chere Tyme opportune and best leysere. **1568** Grafton *Chron.* II. 395 When time oportune will serve, ye shall doe well to advertise him therof. **1676** G. Towerson *Decalogue* 464 That part of the day.. is the most opportune for business. **1780** Burke *Lett., to T. Burgh* Wks. 1842 II. 411 There never seemed a more opportune time for the relief of Ireland than that moment. **1868** E. Edwards *Ralegh* I. xxiv. 568 He had the unfortunate quality of showing his teeth before the opportune moment for using them.

† **b.** Of a place. *Obs.*

a **1548** Hall *Chron., Rich. III*, 49 b, That his adversaries in no wise should have any place apte or oportune easely to take lande. **1610** Shaks. *Temp.* IV. i. 26 The murkiest den, The most opportune place.. shall neuer melt Mine honor into lust. **1665** Boyle *Occas. Refl.* II. xiii. (1848) 137 The great mistake of those that think a Death-bed the fittest and opportunest place to begin Repentance in. **1796** Burke *Lett. Regic. Peace* iii. Wks. VIII. 301 We know that they meditated the very same invasion.. upon this kingdom; and, had the coast been as opportune, would have effected it.

2. Of an event, action, or thing: Fitting in regard to time or circumstances, seasonable; now chiefly in more restricted sense, Meeting the requirements of the time or occasion, timely, well-timed.

c **1425** [implied in OPPORTUNELY]. *a* **1548** Hall *Chron., Hen. VII*, 40 b, With all diligence prepared oportune remedies to resist and withstand. **1611** Shaks. *Wint. T.* IV. iv. 511 Most opportune to her neede, I haue A Vessell rides fast by. **1670** Milton *Hist. Brit.* II. Wks. (1847) 485/2 The Romans now over-matched and terrified, Cæsar with opportune aid appears. **1784** Cowper *Task* VI. 470 Prophet as he was, he might not strike The blameless animal.. Her opportune offence Saved him. **1837** Landor *Pentameron* iv. Wks. 1853 II. 337/1 These are better thoughts and opportuner than such lonely places formerly supplied us with. **1856** Max Müller *Chips* (1880) III. vii. 184 The opportune death of Philip alone prevented the breaking out of a rebellion.

† **3.** Advantageous, serviceable, useful. *Obs.*

1432–50 tr. *Higden* (Rolls) II. 231 Thei were religious men, and oportune exhibicion was ȝiffen to theyme. ? *c* **1470** G. Ashby *Active Policy* 357 Kepe secretnesse as a secretarye,.. But vnto suche persones oportune As may be furthering to youre fortune. *c* **1510** Barclay *Mirr. Gd. Manners* (1570) G j, Despise thou no person although thou purer be Of clothing, of cunning.. or ought els oportune then is he. **1658** Sir T. Browne *Hydriot.* Ep. Ded., It is opportune to look back upon old Times, and contemplate our Forefathers.

† **4.** Conveniently exposed; liable or open (*to* attack or injury). *Obs.*

c **1450** tr. *De Imitatione* III. lxiv. 149, I may fully truste in noon þat may helpe me in oportune necessities, but allone in þe, my god. **1667** Milton *P.L.* IX. 481 Behold alone The Woman opportune to all attempts.

5. Adopted with a view to present expediency: cf. OPPORTUNISM. *rare.*

1851 Thackeray *Eng. Hum.* iii, Marlborough's.. opportune fidelity and treason.

† **B.** quasi-*adv.* = Opportunely. *Obs.*

1667 Milton *P.L.* IX. 85 [He] Consider'd every Creature, which of all Most opportune might serve his Wiles. **1760–72** H. Brooke *Fool of Qual.* (1809) IV. 151 How opportune has our Jesus sent us to us on this occasion!

† **oppor'tune**, *v.* *Obs. rare.* [f. prec.]

1. *trans.* To be well adapted or convenient to; to suit, accommodate.

a **1637** R. Clerke *Serm.* 483 The Pronoune opportunes *us.* Some Copies have *vobis*; but the most and best, have *Nobis.*

2. *intr.* ? To have opportunity, to get the chance.

1606 Warner *Alb. Eng.* XV. xcviii. 390 Not sticking cautilously the hier of Filthinesse to purse, For, may she opportune for Pence, liues not like lurching Blaine.

† **oppor'tuneful**, *a.* *Obs.* [irreg. f. OPPORTUNE *a.* + -FUL.] Affording opportunity; seasonable.

1605 *1st Pt. Jeronimo* (1901) II. iv. 68 The euening to begins to slubber day, Sweet, oportunefull season. *a* **1626** Middleton *Mayor of Queenborough* IV. iii, If we let slip this opportuneful hour, Take leave of fortune.

opportunely (see the adj.), *adv.* [f. OPPORTUNE *a.* + -LY[2].] In an opportune manner; suitably in respect of time, place, or circumstances; conveniently; now always, At an opportune time or juncture, seasonably.

c **1425** *Found. St. Bartholomew's* (E.E.T.S.) 25 He mevid hym.. with goode and honeste wordes, opportunely and importunely. **1602** Warner *Alb. Eng.* XIII. lxxvii. (1612) 319 Sathan.. opportunely there did Oracles begin. **1629** Davenant *Albovine* Wks. (1673) 436 Thou art far more opportunely stor'd with time and place for thy revenge, then we i' th' midst of day. **1774** J. Bryant *Mythol.* I. 380 The land of Canaan lay.. opportunely for traffic. **1836** Marryat *Midsh. Easy* xxv, How opportunely he had frightened away the robbers, just as they were about to murder her relation. **1884** *Law Times* LXXVII. 62/1 [He] has written a good book and published it opportunely.

opportuneness (see the adj.). [f. as prec. + -NESS.] The quality of being opportune; fitness of time or occasion; seasonableness, timeliness.

1727 Bailey vol. II, *Opportuneness*, seasonableness. **1862** R. H. Patterson *Ess. History & Art* 378 The opportuneness of these revelations of the Past cannot but strike one as remarkable. **1884** *Manch. Exam.* 16 Oct. 5/2 The only suspicious thing about this telegram is its opportuneness.

opportunism (ɒpə'tjuːnɪz(ə)m, 'ɒpətjuːnɪz(ə)m). [f. OPPORTUNE, after It. *opportunismo*, F. *opportunisme*: see -ISM.]

1. a. The policy of doing what is opportune, or at the time expedient, in politics, as opposed to rigid adherence to party principles; often used to imply sacrifice of principle or an undue spirit of accommodation to present circumstances.

A term first of Italian, and then of French politics, which in English use has been extended to characterize any method or course of action by which a party or person adapts himself to, and seeks to make profitable use of, the circumstances of the moment. (The introduction of the word has often been erroneously ascribed to Gambetta.)

1870 *Contemp. Rev.* XV. 389 To lead the [Italian] people away from the idea of unity as Utopian, and induce them [*i.e.* Cavour and others in 1844] to enter upon the path of compromise, or '*opportunism*', to use their own term. **1880** *19th Cent.* Apr. 632 Among Nonconformists there is not.. one who has less of the spirit of opportunism than Mr. Illingworth. **1881** *Standard* 27 May, He [Gambetta] is likewise a master of effect, an adept in the craft of Opportunism in a wider sense than he himself has ever publicly ascribed to a word of his own invention. **1882** A. W. Ward *Dickens* iii. 69 The Daily News was to rise superior to the opportunism.. of the Times. **1885** Ld. Granville *Sp. at Hanley* 6 Nov. (*Times* 7 Nov.), I asked an Englishman, I asked a Frenchman, I asked an Italian what was opportunism... The Englishman said that he thought opportunism was the preference of expediency to principle. The French gentleman said he thought it was the coquetting with principles which you do not approve in your heart. The Italian said it was adapting yourself to those circumstances which were most fitted to get you into power and to maintain you there. **1886** G. Allen *Darwin* vii. 124 The dry and cautious French intelligence, ever inclined to a scientific opportunism. **1898** Bodley *France* II. IV. vi. 407 Opportunism in its wholesome sense is the art of adapting one's self to changing circumstances.

b. *Socialism* and *Communism.* A policy of concessions to bourgeois elements of society in the development towards socialism.

1902 *Social-Democrat* Aug. 232 Bernstein's position leads him straight to opportunism, the denial of the class war, reform-politics, classes working together for the common good.., &c. **1903** [see MARXISM[1]]. **1921** in J. Degras *Communist Internat. Documents* (1956) I. 247 The parties of the Communist International will become revolutionary mass parties only if they overcome opportunism, its survivals and traditions, in their own ranks. **1930** M. J. Olgin tr. *Lenin's Conference of Foreign Sect. of R.S.-D.L.P.* in *Coll. Wks.* XVIII. 148 The collapse of the Second International is the collapse of Socialist opportunism. *Ibid.*, The crisis created by the war has exposed the real substance of opportunism, revealing it in the role of a direct aid to the bourgeoisie against the proletariat. **1934** tr. Lenin in *Lenin on Britain* IV. i. 149 To explain to the masses the inevitability and the necessity of breaking with opportunism, to educate them for revolution by a merciless struggle against opportunism,.. is the only Marxian line to be followed in the world labour movement.—*Autumn* 1916. **1942** M. J. Olgin tr. *Lenin's Imperialism* in *Coll. Wks.* XIX. 194 That bond between imperialism and opportunism, which revealed itself first and most clearly in England. **1957** R. N. C. Hunt *Guide to Communist Jargon* 101 Opportunism stood for that disposition of mind which rejected Marx's revolutionary teaching, with its insistence upon the total destruction of the capitalist system, in favour of concessions made by the bourgeoisie within its framework. **1974** tr. *Sniečkus's Soviet Lithuania* 26 In its relentless struggle against reformism, opportunism and Trotskyism, it [*sc.* the Lithuanian Communist Party] became even more Bolshevik in character.

2. Opportunistic state or activity.

a. *Med.* (See OPPORTUNISTIC *a.* 3.)

1962 *Laboratory Investigation* XI. 1073/1 The concept of microbial opportunism as an important occasional factor in the etiology of infectious disease has been generally recognized and its validity has been accepted.

b. *Ecol.* (See OPPORTUNISTIC *a.* 2.)

1967 G. E. Hutchinson *Treat. Limnol.* II. xxii. 366 There is reason to believe that the same sort of lognormal distribution may arise by a process of evolutionary opportunism among competitive species. **1973** P. A. Colinvaux *Introd. Ecol.* xxvii. 392 If you are small and short-lived, opportunism is probably the only satisfactory strategy for life in unstable places, but if you are big, and with a low metabolic rate,.. you may just sit tight through the bad times, living on your reserves and reducing your life processes to the minimum.

opportunist (ɒpə'tjuːnɪst, 'ɒpətjuːnɪst), *sb.* (and *a.*) [f. as prec. + -IST; in F. *opportuniste.*]

1. a. One who professes or practises opportunism in politics, or in any sphere of action; *spec.* in French politics, a member of the party led by Gambetta (see quot. 1881); also, one who, at the Vatican Council of 1870, held that the time was opportune for the promulgation of the doctrine of Papal Infallibility (cf. INOPPORTUNIST), and in Socialism and Communism, an advocate of opportunism (sense 1 b).

1881 *Contemp. Rev.* Oct. 624 The term Opportunist was first applied to him [Gambetta] by Rochefort, in an article in the *Droits de l'homme*, published in February, 1876. **1881** Auberon Herbert in *Times* 29 Sept. 3/6 The opportunist is .. the man who says 'I would not, but I must'. He yields to what he condemns, to what he thinks neither right nor just .. but what, as he claims, is justified and forced upon him by .. circumstances. **1882–3** Schaff *Encycl. Relig. Knowl.* II. 1077 Called inopportunists, as distinct from the opportunists. **1886** M. Creighton in *Academy* 27 Feb. 139/3 It is a conceivable view to take of him [Cranmer] that he concealed a good deal of firmness under the guise of an opportunist. **1889** *Athenæum* 16 Feb. 205/2 Mr. Gosse.. considers him [Dryden].. to be a sort of literary opportunist. **1898** *Daily News* 8 Nov. 6/2 Mr. Gladstone was, in the best sense of the word, an opportunist. Like Prince Bismarck, he held that a statesman should serve his country as circumstances require, rather than as his own opinions, which are often prejudices, dictate. **1902** *Fortn. Rev.* Jan. 128 The mountain of the [German Social Democratic] party joined hands with the Opportunists. **1903** *Social-Democrat* VII. 87 It is constantly being brought as a reproach against the German Party that they were more severe with the revolutionary dissenters from the party theory than they have been with the opportunists. **1909** M. Epstein tr. *Sombart's Socialism & Social Movement* II. iii. 217 All authoritative Revisionists, Opportunists, Reformers .. stand firm for the class war, and.. desire the total abolition of the capitalist system, and not merely its reformation. **1919** Trotsky in J. Degras *Communist Internat. Documents* (1956) I. 41 The opportunists, who before the world war appealed to the workers to practise moderation for the sake of the gradual transition to socialism. **1930** M. J. Olgin tr. *Lenin's Conference of Foreign Sect. of R.S.-D.L.P.* in *Coll. Wks.* XVIII. 149 It would be a harmful illusion to hope to restore a real Socialist International without drawing a clear line of organisational demarcation between real Socialists and opportunists. **1934** tr. Lenin in *Lenin on Britain* IV. i. 142 The *opportunists* (social-chauvinists) are working together with the imperialist bourgeoisie.. in the direction of creating an imperialist Europe on the backs of Asia and Africa;.. the *opportunists* are a section of the petty bourgeoisie [etc.]... *Autumn* 1916.

b. *attrib.* or as *adj.*

1881 Seeley *Bonaparte* in *Macm. Mag.* July 164/1 All serious governments alike, that of Bonaparte, that of the Restoration,.. that of Louis Napoleon and the present opportunist Republic, have adhered to the principles of 1789. **1887** *Spectator* 27 Aug. 1144 The present [French] Cabinet is in essentials an Opportunist Cabinet. **1895** F. M. Crawford *Ralstons* v. 68 A man of fine principles and opportunist practice. **1902** *Fortn. Rev.* Jan. 129 Where Marx is fatalistic, Bernstein is opportunist. **1903** *Social-Democrat* VII. 86 To turn.. to the German Party, the opportunist tendency has naturally always existed. **1929** J. Fineberg tr. *Selections from Lenin* I. 177 Axelrod and Martov.. have dropped into the opportunist wing of our Party... They have to repeat opportunist phrases.. to seek .. some kind of justification for their position. **1934** tr. Lenin in *Lenin on Britain* v. iv. 212 The victory of the revolutionary proletariat is impossible.. unless the opportunist social-traitor leaders are exposed, disgraced and driven out... *April–May* 1920. **1974** tr. *Sniečkus's Soviet Lithuania* 12 A reformist opportunist trend.. had developed on the basis of the petty-bourgeois nationalistic ideology. **1974** J. White tr. *Poulantzas's Fascism & Dictatorship* IV. i. 147 The 'left opportunist' elements bore a very grave responsibility in the advent of fascism.

2. *Med.* An opportunistic fungus or micro-organism (see OPPORTUNISTIC *a.* 3). Also *attrib.* or as *adj.*

1937 M. Frobisher *Fund. Bacteriol.* xiv. 138 These organisms.. do not initiate the rot. They are opportunists.

1967 *Jrnl. Hygiene* LXV. 575 (*heading*) Classification of *Mycobacterium avium* and related opportunist mycobacteria met in England and Wales. *Ibid.*, Overt opportunist infection. **1973** *Amer. Jrnl. Med.* LV. 862/1 As an opportunist, its ability to produce human disease depends not on its intrinsic virulence but on abnormalities of host defenses. **1976** *Lancet* 27 Nov. 1169/1 There was no evidence of opportunist infection.

3. *Ecol.* An opportunistic species (see OPPORTUNISTIC *a.* 2). Also *attrib.* or as *adj.*

1970 *Lethaia* III. 70 Even in habitats of low physico-chemical stress and great stability, opportunists may participate in occasional invasions of an otherwise stable fauna. **1973** P. A. COLINVAUX *Introd. Ecol.* xvii. 392 It is opportunist animals..which, exposed to hazard of weather in their normal lives, are most likely to have their numbers curbed by accident of weather. *Ibid.* 393 Opportunists, being specialists at dispersion, are likely to get there first but, since the fresh bare ground may be in a place of generally stable climate, the equilibrium species will not be far behind. The opportunists enjoy the new land only briefly, after which they are eliminated by competition. **1975** *Nature* 20 Nov. 197/1 These data suggest that birch is behaving as an opportunist in the composition of the forest.

opportu'nistic, *a.* [f. OPPORTUNIST + -IC.]

1. Pertaining to or characteristic of an opportunist.

1892 *Speaker* 5 Mar. 292/2 He attempts to apologise for them..on the opportunistic ground that the fecundity of the black races threatens the 'political effacement of the European population'. **1958** J. BALDWIN in W. King *Black Short Story Anthol.* (1972) 284 Their religion was strongly mixed with an opportunistic respectability and with ambitions to better society and their own place in it. **1976** *Brit. Jrnl. Sociol.* XXVII. 89 The common man is portrayed as the innocent and helpless victim of opportunistic and self-serving politicians who must be replaced by enlightened and benign rulers. **1976** *Publishers Weekly* 15 Mar. 118/3 An opportunistic TV programmer brings him to New York and takes an exploitation piece. **1977** *Listener* 20 Oct. 515 The ebullient..Furnivall comes out of it badly (vain, unprincipled,..opportunistic, unscholarly—though no one contributed more quotations for the dictionary).

2. *Ecol.* Of a species: especially suited to unexploited or newly formed habitats and occurring in populations whose size is not determined primarily by their density, being characterized by poor competitiveness in relation to other species and an ability to increase rapidly in numbers and to disperse readily.

1960 R. MACARTHUR in *Amer. Naturalist* XCIV. 33 A distinction is made between opportunistic and equilibrium species. **1974** *Jrnl. Marine Res.* XXXII. 267 *Capitella capitella* and the other relatively opportunistic species discussed may be continuously present if the environment is unpredictable or may disappear as in the case of recovery following the oil spill.

3. *Med.* Of a fungus or micro-organism: not normally pathogenic but becoming so in certain circumstances, as when the body is rendered vulnerable by other agencies. Of an infection: caused by such an organism.

[**1955** *Sci. Amer.* May 31/2 Was it not possible, they argued, that the bacteria were only the secondary cause of disease—opportunistic invaders of tissues already weakened by crumbling defenses?] **1962** *Ann. N.Y. Acad. Sci.* XCVIII. 617 (*heading*) Experiences with and diagnosis of diseases due to opportunistic fungi. **1962** *Laboratory Investigation* XI. 1073/1 Opportunistic infections by bacteria, viruses, and protozoa are known. **1970** C. W. EMMONS et al. *Med. Mycol.* (ed. 2) 3 The fungi which cause systemic and subcutaneous mycoses have been called 'opportunistic fungi' to emphasize the aspect of a normally saprobic fungus which can suddenly become parasitic and pathogenic when it is introduced by inhalation or traumatic implantation into the human body... It has also been used to designate fungi which cause disease only in a patient with a concurrent disease which increases his susceptibility, or in one whose innate immunity has been otherwise impaired. **1973** *Chest* LXIII. 4/1 Even more striking is the rise of opportunistic fungal infections accompanying: transplantation, immunosuppression, heart surgery and intravenous hyperalimentation. Today one can no longer accept a culture report of 'nonpathogenic fungus isolated', for indeed there may be no truly nonpathogenic fungus.

Hence ˌ**opportu'nistically** *adv.*, in an opportunist manner.

1958 *Times* 27 Dec. 2/4 In one brief interlude Phillips nearly scored opportunistically at the other end. **1960** W. V. QUINE *Word & Object* v. 188 We can vacillate between two, opportunistically enjoying their incompatible advantages. **1972** *Maclean's Mag.* Sept. 10/1 He will act with expediency but not often, I think, opportunistically. **1976** *Sci. Amer.* Apr. 117/2 At the same time the adults will feed opportunistically on lesser prey: frogs, crabs and small fish.

opportunity (ɒpəˈtjuːnɪtɪ). Also 4–6 opor-, 4 opar-, 6 oppur-, 7 opper-; 4–6 -ite, -yte, (4 -ytee), 6–7 -itie. [a. F. *opportunité* (13th c. in Hatz.-Darm.), ad. L. *opportūnitās*, f. *opportūn-us* OPPORTUNE: see -ITY.]

1. The quality or fact of being opportune; seasonableness, timeliness; opportuneness. Now *rare*, and chiefly with reference to the L. phrase 'felix opportunitate mortis'.

1531 ELYOT *Gov.* I. xviii, Exercises whiche be nat utterly reproued of noble auctours, if they be used with oportunite and in measure. **1581** SAVILE *Tacitus, Agricola* (1622) 202 Thrice happie then maiest thou..be counted, not onely for the renowne of thy life, but..for the opportunitie of thy decease. **1660** MILTON *Free Commw.* Wks. (1851) 434 Thir business is..oft-times urgent; the opportunity of Affairs gain'd or lost in a moment. **1873** PATER *Renaissance* viii. 167 A death which, for its swiftness and its opportunity, he might well have desired. **1878** SEELEY *Stein* III. 559 How much suffering had been saved them by the opportunity of their deaths.

2. a. A time, juncture, or condition of things favourable to an end or purpose, or admitting of something being done or effected; occasion, chance.

Orig. without article or pl. = 'convenience of time'; the individualized notion 'a convenient time', with pl., appears in 1560: cf. sense-development of *circumstance*, *conscience*.

1375 BARBOUR *Bruce* v. 523 He..vatit opportunite For to fulfill hys mawite. **1388** WYCLIF *Matt.* xxvi. 16 Fro that tyme he souȝte oportunyte [1382 couenablete] to bitraye hym. *c* **1450** *St. Cuthbert* (Surtees) 1005 Oportunite when he gatt, He was anker and sole satt. **1560** DAUS tr. *Sleidane's Comm.* 271 b, Many goodly oportunities, through disceptation were omitted. *Ibid.* 310 b, In these eight hondreth yeares past, chaunced never so good an opportunitie. **1605** SHAKS. *Lear* IV. vi. 268 You haue manie opportunities to cut him off. *c* **1645** HOWELL *Lett.* (1650) II. 103 That Almighty Majesty who useth to draw..strength out of weaknes, making mans extremity his opportunity. **1709** STEELE *Tatler* No. 10 ⁋1, I am not a little pleased with the Opportunity of running over all the Papers. **1736** BUTLER *Anal.* I. ii. Wks. 1874 I. 42 The natural course of things affords us opportunities for procuring advantages to ourselves at certain times. **1875** STUBBS *Const. Hist.* II. xvii. 511 In national history opportunity is as powerful as purpose. **1890** BOLDREWOOD *Col. Reformer* (1891) 161 Neuchamp had been sufficiently awake to his opportunities.

†**b.** A time when there is occasion or need for something. *Obs. rare.*

1526 *Pilgr. Perf.* (W. de W. 1531) 120 Somtyme he maketh as though he herde vs not, in oportunite and tyme of nede. **1683** MOXON *Mech. Exerc., Printing* ii. ⁋2 He also provides..some of these, as he reckons his opportunities may be to use them.

c. ***equality of opportunity***: equal chance and right to seek success in one's chosen sphere regardless of social factors such as class, race, religion, and sex.

1891 *Econ. Rev.* I. 474 It will possibly, however, be contended that here the ideal is equality of Opportunity. **1920** M. BEER *Hist. Brit. Socialism* II. xiv. 295 By 'equality of opportunity' Fabian women do not necessarily mean 'similarity of opportunity'. **1920** H. G. WELLS *Outl. Hist.* II. IX. xli. 754/2 A sufficient measure of social justice, to ensure health, education, and a rough equality of opportunity. **1930** W. K. HANCOCK *Australia* ix. 183 Equality of opportunity implies free scope for natural talent, which must create new inequalities; whereas what Australian democracy desires is equality of enjoyment. **1950** G. B. SHAW *Farfetched Fables* 67 Democratic civilization is impossible, because equality of opportunity is impossible. **1973** R. R. PALMER in P. P. Wiener *Dict. Hist. Ideas* II. 146/2 The key words are fair competition, equality of opportunity, reward for merit, and careers open to talent. **1976** R. WILLIAMS *Keywords* 102 *Equality of opportunity*..can be glossed as 'equal opportunity to become unequal'.

†**3.** Convenience or advantageousness of site or position. In quot. 1730 app. advantage afforded by position. *Obs.*

1555 EDEN *Decades* 284 This is the most famous citie in Moscouia..for the commodious oportunitie of ryuers, multitude of houses [etc.]. **1649** MILTON *Eikon.* viii. Wks. (1851) 390 Hull, a town of great strength and opportunitie both to sea and land affaires. **1673** RAY *Journ. Low C.* 22 Flushing..a Town..very considerable for..the opportunity of its Situation and convenience of its Harbour. **1730** A. GORDON *Maffei's Amphith.* 378 The Opportunity they had of its Harbour, incited them..to make it the Staple-Port for Merchandize of the East. **1781** GIBBON *Decl. & F.* xxx. III. 158 Augustus, who had observed the opportunity of the place, prepared..a capacious harbour.

†**4.** Fitness, aptitude, competency, 'faculty'. *Obs.*

c **1374** CHAUCER *Boeth.* II. pr. iii. 25 (Cambr. MS.) Thow were ryht weleful..with the castete of thi wyf And with the oportunite and noblesse of thi masculyn chyldren. **1535** COVERDALE *Eccl.* ii. 20 For so moch as a man shulde weery himself with wysedome, with understondinge and oppurtunite, and yet be fayne to leave his labours vnto another. **1607** TOPSELL *Four-f. Beasts* (1658) 341 Although the swiftness or other opportunity of the Dogs helpeth them to flie away from her, yet if she can but cast her shadow upon them, she easily obtaineth her prey.

†**5.** Fitness of things, need. *Obs. rare.*

(Its use here is app. due to association with L. *oportet.*)

1432–50 tr. *Higden* (Rolls) IV. 435 That man is a cowarde that wille not dye when oportunite requirethe hit [*Higden*, quando oportet; *Trevisa*, whannse it nedeth].

¶**6.** *erroneously.* = IMPORTUNITY 4. *Obs.*

1598 SHAKS. *Merry W.* III. iv. 20 Yet seeke my Fathers loue, still seeke it sir, If opportunity and humblest suite Cannot attaine it, why then harke you hither. **1653** HOLCROFT *Procopius, Vandal Wars* II. 50 John the son of Sisinniolus, at the Africans opportunity, raised Forces and went against them. *a* **1667** JER. TAYLOR (W.), He that entreats us to be happy, with an opportunity so passionate, as if not we, but himself, were to receive the favor.

7. Phr. ***opportunity knocks*** (***but once***): an opportunity presents itself (but once).

1942 WODEHOUSE *Money in Bank* (1946) xv. 134 Opportunity knocks but once, and he had allowed it to knock in vain. **1946** *Calif. Folklore Q.* July 241 A number of sayings surely not peculiar to Oregon; rather, trite and obvious, but still effective:..Opportunity knocks but once. **1970** *Computers & Humanities* V. 16 From the earliest English settlements to the closing of the frontier and the advent of industrialism, opportunity knocked for young men of high and low social status at fairly regular alternate intervals. **1970** *Globe & Mail* (Toronto) 28 Sept. 29/4 (Advt.), Opportunity knocks for a fluently bilingual representative over 25 with a B.Sc. **1972** *Accountant* 21 Sept. p. xvii/1 (Advt.), Opportunity knocks for an experienced qualified man.

8. *attrib.* and *Comb.* **opportunity cost** *Econ.* (see quots.); **opportunity state**, a country which offers many opportunities for advancement.

1911 H. J. DAVENPORT in *Amer. Econ. Rev.* Dec. 725 These displacements of possible products, these foregoings of alternative openings, these sacrifices of some second thing in the process of getting some particular thing, are perhaps best indicated under the term *opportunity cost.* To go without fish to get game..may be taken as illustrative of one of the simplest aspects of the doctrine. **1926** L. D. EDIE *Econ.* III. viii. 121 The opportunity cost is the sacrifice of foregoing some alternative utility. **1936** AULT & EBERLING *Princ. & Probl. Econ.* xiii. 217 Opportunity or alternative costs play a very important part in determining the nature and direction of industrial development... The principle of opportunity cost is effective in bringing about great changes in the field of production. **1951** J. R. WINTON *Dict. Econ. Terms* (ed. 3) 63 *Opportunity cost.* In economic life, decisions are constantly being made which involve a choice between alternatives... One particular alternative must be chosen,..the 'opportunity-cost' of which is represented by the alternatives foregone. **1964** GOULD & KOLB *Dict. Social Sci.* 143/2 The determination of implicit cost, as well as other managerial decisions, must be based on the concept of alternative or opportunity costs, which measures cost in terms of alternatives or opportunities that are foregone. **1965** SELDON & PENNANCE *Everyman's Dict. Econ.* 312 To answer the question, 'Should good agricultural land be built over?' requires a comparison of the opportunity costs for society of the various alternatives. **1971** D. C. HAGUE *Managerial Econ.* (rev. ed.) II. v. 121 A very useful concept is that of 'opportunity cost'... If the businessman would have invested the money at 10 per cent interest, had he not put it into the business, then the 'opportunity cost' of investing in his own business is the 10 per cent interest he has foregone. **1974** *Guardian* 27 Aug. 14/7 Couples in the United States..are well aware of the opportunity cost of having children. **1957** Opportunity state [see CONTRACT *v.* 2 d]. **1958** *Listener* 26 June 1068/3 The mental distance between himself and his appalling younger daughters, products of the opportunity state, is brilliantly suggested.

†**oppor'tunous**, *a. Obs. rare*$^{-1}$. [f. L. *opportūn-us* OPPORTUNE + -OUS.] = OPPORTUNE.

1609 HEYWOOD *Brit. Troy* XII. x. 305 The opportunous night friends her complexion.

opposability (əpəʊzəˈbɪlɪtɪ). [f. next + -ITY.] The quality of being opposable.

1863 HUXLEY *Man's Place Nat.* II. 86 The great toe,..in uncivilized and barefooted people,..retains a great amount of mobility, and even some sort of opposability. **1882** A. R. WALLACE in *Contemp. Rev.* Mar. 430 The large size and complete opposability of the thumb.

opposable (əˈpəʊzəb(ə)l), *a.* [f. OPPOSE *v.*² + -ABLE.]

1. Capable of being opposed, withstood, or placed in opposition (*to*). *rare.*

1667 [implied in UNOPPOSABLE]. **1802–12** BENTHAM *Ration. Judic. Evid.* (1827) IV. 151 The application is either opposable or unopposable. **1829** —— *Justice & Cod. Petit.* 195 No arguments will be found opposable to it other than ungrounded assertions.

2. Of a digit, esp. the thumb: Capable of being opposed to, or applied so as to meet, another.

1833 *Penny Cycl.* I. 442/2 Those [monkeys] of Africa and Asia have completely opposable thumbs on the fore-feet as well as on the hind. **1854** OWEN *Skel. & Teeth* in *Circ. Sc., Organ. Nat.* I. 253 A freedom of the digits, with some opposable faculty in them. **1894** H. DRUMMOND *Ascent Man* 129 A thumb is..a finger so arranged as to be opposable to the other fingers.

†**o'pposal.** *Obs.* Also 5 opposaylle, -ayle, -aile. [f. OPPOSE *v.* + -AL¹: I and II were independently formed on the two branches of the verb.]

I. 1. The putting of posing questions; examination, interrogation; a posing question, a puzzle; = APPOSAL 1.

1426 LYDG. *De Guil. Pilgr.* 10397, I..for fer, be-gan to quake, What Answere I sholde make Vn-to hys vnkouthe opposaylle. **1436** *Pol. Poems* (Rolls) II. 204 Go furthe, libelle,..And pray my lordes the to take in grace In opposaile. **1607** NORDEN *Surv. Dial.* II. 40 Sith you will needs diue into my poore skill, by your opposall,..I will as briefly as I can, satisfye your desire.

II. 2. = OPPOSITION 5.

1654–66 EARL ORRERY *Parthen.* (1676) 121, I should have found a strong opposal in my obedience. **1665** SIR T. HERBERT *Trav.* (1677) 81 The Castle gates opened, fearless of any further opposal.

3. = OPPOSITION 2, 3.

1686 GOAD *Celest. Bodies* II. iv. 199 An opposal of ♂ and the ☉ very seldom fails of its warm thawing Breath. **1839** BAILEY *Festus* xxxi. (1852) 516 No sooner came I to the seat, in right opposal placed, To that despotic empress.

†**opposant.** *Obs. rare*$^{-0}$. [a. F. *opposant* (R. Estienne, 1539), pr. pple. of *opposer* OPPOSE *v.*]

1611 COTGR., *Opposant*, an Opposant or Opponent.

oppose (əˈpəʊz), *v.* [a. F. *opposer*, in 12th c. *oposer* (Hatz.-Darm.), f. L. *ob-* (OB- 2) + *poser* to place, put down, taken as representing L. *pōnĕre* to place (see POSE, COMPOSE, DEPOSE, etc.). In OF. chiefly used in the mediæval sense of L. *oppōnĕre* 'to oppose in argument, question, examine', and in this sense alone found in ME., in which also it varied with *apose*, APPOSE, which later became the established form: see APPOSE *v.*¹, POSE *v.* For the more literal senses of *oppōnĕre*, which appear in the 16th c., OPPONE was at first used, but before 1600 *oppose* prevailed, as in *compose*, *depose*, *dispose*, *expose*, and other assumed representatives of L. *pōnĕre*. Branches I and II are thus of distinct history in Eng., though both repr. L. *oppōnĕre*.]

I. ME. uses, in mediæval sense of L. *oppōnĕre*.

†**1.** *trans.* To confront with objections or hard question; to pose; to examine, interrogate, question; = APPOSE *v.*[1] 1. *Obs.* (or merged in 9).

c **1386** CHAUCER *Friar's T.* 297 And answere there by my procutour To swich thyng as men wole opposen me [*so* 3 *MSS.*; *v.rr.* oposen, apposen, aposen]. **1390** GOWER *Conf.* II. 72 Of tuo pointz sche him opposeth. *c* **1425** *Found. St. Bartholomew's* (E.E.T.S.) 56 He was callid yn of the preyste, and opposid. **1530** PALSGR. 647/1, I oppose one, I make a tryall of his lernyng, or I laye a thyng to his charge, *je apose.* **1570** T. NORTON tr. *Nowel's Catech.* (1853) 109 The master opposeth the scholar to see how he hath profited. **1607** NORDEN *Surv. Dial.* II. 39 You seeme to oppose me farre, and the thing you demaund, will require a longer time.

2. *absol.* and *intr.* To put objections or hard questions; *spec.* to put forward objections to be answered by a person maintaining a philosophical or theological thesis, esp. as a means of qualifying for a degree, etc.; = APPOSE *v.*[1] 2. *Obs.* exc. *Hist.*

1390 GOWER *Conf.* III. 332 This king unto this maide opposeth, And axeth ferst what was hire name. *c* **1500** [implied in OPPOSER 1]. **1581** E. CAMPION in *Confer.* IV. (1584) F f b, Let me oppose. Is it not reason that I shoulde oppose? **1581** W. CHARKE *ibid.*, I will..suffer you to oppose and make an argument in this matter. **1690** E. GEE *Jesuit's Mem.* 176 To the end that fit men may prepare themselves to oppose for the same [scholarships, fellowships, etc.]. **1716** M. DAVIES *Athen. Brit.* II. 296 He was admitted to the reading of the Sentences, having a little before oppos'd in Divinity, in 1533.

†**3.** To examine and check (accounts), to audit; = APPOSE *v.*[1] 3. *Obs.*

a **1483** *Liber Niger* in *Househ. Ord.* (1790) 58 Suche parcelles of pourveyaunces as shal be brought in..and duly opposed in the countynghouse monethly. *Ibid.* 61 To helpe oppose all the partycular accomptes of offycers.

II. Modern uses.

4. *trans.* To set (a thing) over against, place directly before or in front. Const. *to*, †*against*.

1593 SHAKS. *2 Hen. VI*, IV. x. 48 Oppose thy stedfast gazing eyes to mine, See if thou canst out-face me with thy lookes. **1613** —— *Hen. VIII*, IV. i. 67 Her Grace sate downe ..opposing freely The Beauty of her Person to the People. **1778** SIR J. REYNOLDS *Disc.* viii. (1876) 449 If one figure opposes his front to the spectator. **1781** COWPER *Conversat.* 269 The emphatic speaker dearly loves to oppose, In contact inconvenient, nose to nose. **1812–16** J. SMITH *Panorama Sc. & Art* II. 180 When two equal magnets oppose their contrary poles to each other. **1842** TENNYSON *Ulysses* 48 My mariners..That ever with a frolic welcome took The thunder and the sunshine, and opposed Free hearts, free foreheads.

†**b.** To hold out for acceptance; to offer. *Obs.*

1598 CHAPMAN *Blinde Beg. Alexandria* I. i, Let his true picture through your land be sent, Opposing great rewardes to him that findes him.

†**c.** To expose, subject. *Obs.*

1589 NAHSE *Ded. Greene's Manaphon* (Arb.) 9 And count it a great peece of arte in an inkhorn man..to oppose his superiours to envie. **1605** SHAKS. *Lear* IV. vii. 32 Was this a face To be oppos'd [*Qos.* exposed] against the iarring windes?

5. To set (something) against or on the other side, as a counterpoise or contrast; to bring forward or adduce by way of counterbalance; to contrast; to put in rhetorical or ideal opposition (*to*).

1579 FULKE *Heskins' Parl.* 23 He thinketh Alphonsus good ynough to oppose against Erasmus. **1594** T. B. *La Primaud. Fr. Acad.* II. 193 When the flesh is opposed and set against the spirite in man, wee vnderstand thereby, not the body only, but also the soule of man. **1652** BP. HALL *Invis. World* II. iii, Opposing our present condition to the succeeding. **1751** JOHNSON *Rambler* No. 139 ¶6 The tragedy of *Samson Agonistes* has been..opposed with all the confidence of triumph to the dramatick performances of other nations. **1875** JOWETT *Plato* (ed. 2) IV. 275 Memory and imagination, though we sometimes oppose them, are nearly allied.

6. To set (something) against by way of hindrance, check, or resistance; to place as an obstacle; also, to set or place (a person) as an antagonist.

1596 SHAKS. *Merch. V.* IV. i. 10, I do oppose My patience to his fury. **1607** —— *Timon* III. iv. 80 What, are my dores oppos'd against my passage? **1704** SWIFT *Batt. Bks.* Misc. (1711) 255 Nor could the Modern have avoided present Death, if he had not luckily oppos'd the Shield that had been given him by Venus. **1794** GODWIN *Cal. Williams* 195 The door was no longer opposed to my wishes. **1847** MRS. A. KERR *Hist. Servia* 438 Michael was determined..to oppose force to force. **1868** FREEMAN *Norm. Conq.* II. ix. 422 There was now no such unexceptionable rival to oppose to the Norman.

7. *refl.* and *intr.* To set oneself in opposition, contend *against*, act in opposition or other resistance *to*. **a.** *refl. Obs.* or *arch.*

1590 MARLOWE *Edw. II*, I. iv, Leave now t' oppose thyself against the King. **1591** SHAKS. *Two Gent.* III. ii. 26 Thou art not ignorant How she opposes her against my will? **1676** HOBBES *Iliad* I. 183 Others fear t'opose themselves to me. **1717** POPE *Eloisa* 282 Oppose thyself to heav'n; dispute my heart.

†**b.** *intr. Obs.*

1599 SANDYS *Europæ Spec.* (1632) 41 To all such..as should oppose against his Soveraigntie. **1623** BINGHAM *Xenophon* 77 Aske them againe, quoth he, why they oppose against vs in armes. **1640** HABINGTON *Edw. IV* 83 Warwicke opposed against their feare both with language and example.

†**c.** *intr.* Of a thing: To be repugnant or contrary *to*. *Obs.*

1605 BACON *Adv. Learn.* II. xi. §3 If it be admitted that imagination hath power, and that Ceremonies fortify imagination, ..yet I should hold them unlawful, as opposing to that first edict which God gave unto man.

d. With *inf.* To forbid. *rare.*

1813 BYRON *Corsair* II. iv, My stern vow and order's laws oppose To break or mingle bread with friends or foes.

8. *trans.* To stand or lie over against (something); to look towards, face, front. Now *rare.*

1608 [see OPPOSING *ppl. a.* 1]. **1615** G. SANDYS *Trav.* 160 The Frontispice opposing the South, of an excellent structure. **1668** CULPEPPER & COLE *Barthol. Anat.* I. xxxiii. 75 They are so situate that each possesses a corner, and oppose one another in manner of a quadrangle. **1820** SHELLEY *Hymn to Merc.* xxxv, He walked..From one side to the other of the road, And with his face opposed the steps he trod.

9. To set oneself against (a person or thing); to contend against with physical force, by exertion of influence, or by argument; to endeavour to hinder, thwart, or overthrow; to withstand, resist, combat; to stand in the way of, obstruct.

1596 SHAKS. *1 Hen. IV*, IV. iv. 33 He shall be well oppos'd. **1607** —— *Timon* III. v. 20 With a Noble Fury..He did oppose his Foe. **1667** MILTON *P.L.* II. 419 Awaiting who appeer'd To second, or oppose, or undertake The perilous attempt. **1774** GOLDSM. *Nat. Hist.* (1776) IV. 342 With these arms alone, it has often been found to oppose the dog, and even the Jaguar. **1792** *Anecd. W. Pitt* I. xx. 309 Pitt communicated to the Cabinet his resolution of attacking Spain. Lord Bute was the first person who opposed it. **1823** F. CLISSOLD *Ascent Mt. Blanc* 21 After some hundred feet of ascent, we found ourselves opposed by a parapet of congealed snow. **1834** J. H. NEWMAN *Par. Serm.* (1837) I. xxiv. 357 The world does not oppose religion as such. **1860** TYNDALL *Glac.* I. ii. 19 They opposed the idea of ascending further.

absol. **1602** SHAKS. *Ham.* III. i. 60 Or to take Armes against a Sea of troubles, And by opposing end them. *a* **1830** TIERNEY in *Westm. Gaz.* (1900) 22 Oct. 2/3 The duty of an Opposition is threefold: always to oppose, never to propose, and to turn out the Government.

b. To contest. *rare.*

1822 SHELLEY *Calderon's Magico Prodigioso* i. 100, I Had so much arrogance as to oppose The chair of the most high Professorship, And obtained many votes.

opposed (ə'pəʊzd, *poet.* -zɪd), *ppl. a.* [f. OPPOSE *v.* + -ED[1].]

1. a. Placed or set over against; facing, opposite.

[**1552** HULOET, Opposed, *oppositus.*] **1596** SHAKS. *1 Hen. IV*, III. i. 110 Gelding the opposed Continent as much, As on the other side it takes from you. **1725** POPE *Odyss.* XIX. 660 The gate opposed pellucid valves adorn. **1827** ELLIS *Orig. Lett.* Ser. II. II. 218 (tr. *Rep. to Venet. Sen.*) The Island of England..is situated in the Ocean..opposed on the east to the coast of Lower Germany. **1885–94** R. BRIDGES *Eros & Psyche* Mar. xxvi, High in the opposed west the wondering moon All silvery green in flying green was fleec't.

b. *Mech.* (Having pistons) arranged in pairs moving in opposite directions along the same straight line.

1910 W. A. TOOKEY tr. *Mathot's Construction & Working Internal Combustion Eng.* v. 71 In Europe, the two-cylinder 'twin' engine soon displaced the type with opposed or *vis-à-vis* cylinders, because the latter gave a great deal of trouble in practical work. **1925** A. W. JUDGE *Automobile Engines* iii. 87 Although the balance and torque of the opposed two-cylinder engine are excellent, the overall length and the cylinder dimensions limit it to power units of about 12 to 15 H.P. (maximum) for car use. **1932** A. F. EVANS *Hist. Oil Engine* ii. 71 In the 'seventies we had engines with opposed pistons in one cylinder. **1966** G. F. ALLEN *Brit. Rail after Beeching* iv. 115 English Electric took an intricate but compact 18-cylinder opposed-piston engine originally applied to fast, small naval craft..and with it achieved a six-axle 3,300 h.p. diesel-electric unit. **1977** *Lancashire Life* Jan. 79/1 The horizontally opposed engine is air cooled.

2. Standing in opposition, contrast, or conflict; contrasting, conflicting; contrary or opposite *to*.

1588 SHAKS. *L.L.L.* v. ii. 768 Fashioning our humors Euen to the opposed end of our intents. **1596** —— *Merch. V.* II. ix. 62 To offend, and iudge are distinct offices, And of opposed natures. **1736** BUTLER *Anal.* II. vii. Wks. 1874 I. 253 Supposition, and possibility, when opposed to historical evidence, prove nothing [etc.]. **1849** MACAULAY *Hist. Eng.* vi. II. 129 They had different national characters as strongly opposed as any two national characters in Europe.

3. a. Of persons: Hostile, inimical, at variance, adverse (*to*, †*against* a person).

1584 R. SCOT *Discov. Witchcr.* XIII. xxx. (1886) 277 Laie a wager with your confederate (who must seeme simple, or obstinatlie opposed against you). **1615** BEDWELL *Moham. Imp.* III. §101 An opposed aduersary to God. **1865** PUSEY *Truth Eng. Ch.* 6 Common zeal for faith could alone bring together those who were opposed.

b. Adverse *to* a measure, practice, system, etc.

1789 FRANKLIN *Let. to Webster* 26 Dec., During my late absence in France, I find that several..new words have been introduced into our parliamentary language..The word *opposed*, though not a new word, I find used in a new manner, as, 'The gentlemen who are opposed to this measure; to which I have also myself always been opposed'. **1844** H. H. WILSON *Brit. India* III. 134 The sense of the nation was strongly opposed to the prolongation of the war. **1874** J. H. NEWMAN *Lett.* (1891) I. 151 He was especially opposed to young men being compelled..to go terminally to communion.

Hence **o'pposedness** (-ɪdnɪs).

1876 EADIE *Thessalonians* 87 This opposedness to all men the apostle could not condemn.

o'pposeless, *a. poet.* and *rhet.* [f. OPPOSE *v.* + -LESS.] Not to be opposed, resistless, irresistible.

1605 SHAKS. *Lear* IV. vi. 38 If I could beare it longer, and not fall To quarrell with your great opposelesse willes. **1789** tr. *Klopstock's Messiah* II. 51 The wide seas feel the power of his opposeless foot. **1887** *Cornh. Mag.* Oct. 442 Not gainsaying the great opposeless will of his patron.

o'pposer. Also 6 -ier. [f. OPPOSE *v.* + -ER[1].]

I. 1. a. One who 'opposes' the defender of a thesis in an academical disputation. Cf. OPPOSE *v.* 2, OPPONENT B. 1. *Obs.* exc. *Hist.*

c **1500** in Peacock *Stat. Cambridge* App. A. p. xlv, There shall wayte on hym [the Doctor] all the Opposers. **1574** *Ibid.* p. xiv, Mr Vichauncellor, Mr Proctours, the Father, the Opposiers, the Bachiler awnsweryngе and the Bedels.

b. (Usu. with capital initial.) One of two examiners formerly appointed to carry out at Winchester College the elections to New College, Oxford. Cf. POSER[1] 1.

Rarely used, in preference to *poser*, even before 1901 (P. Yeats-Edwards, Fellows' librarian, Winchester College, private communication 28 Jan. 1977).

1891 R. G. K. WRENCH *Winchester Word-bk.* 32 *Poser*, an examiner. A very old word: also still used at Eton. *Apposer* and *opposer* are other old forms of it. **1901** RASHDALL & RAIT *New College* vi. 132 The Warden and Opposers are not to take bribes.

†**2.** One who checks accounts: cf. OPPOSE *v.* 3.

a **1483** *Liber Niger* in *Househ. Ord.* (1790) 51 The Chamberlayne is this clerke's auditor & opposer.

II. 3. One who opposes or contends against a person, doctrine, argument, cause, scheme, etc.: = OPPONENT B. 2.

1601 SHAKS. *All's Well* III. i. 6 Holy seemes the quarrell Vpon your Graces part: blacke and fearefull On the opposer. **1607** —— *Cor.* I. v. 23 Now the faire Goddesse Fortune, Fall deepe in loue with thee, and her great charmes Misguide thy Opposers swords. **1764** *Mem. G. Psalmanazar* 195, I had a much greater number of opposers to combat with. **1776** NIMMO *Stirlingshire* (1817) I. vi. 125 He had been a strenuous opposer of the Reformation. **1884** *Kendal Mercury* 31 Oct. 5/2 The opposers of the scheme were a minority.

o'pposing, *vbl. sb.* [f. OPPOSE *v.* + -ING[1].]

†**1.** Confronting with hostile or hard questions; interrogation. *Obs.*

c **1440** *Promp. Parv.* 368/2 Opposynge, *opposicio.* **1570** T. NORTON tr. *Nowel's Catech.* (1853) 109 The Bishop..in his whole manner of opposing useth such form as here..the *Catechumenus* or child is prepared unto.

2. Acting against; opposition.

1624 LD. E. MOUNTAGU in *Buccleuch MSS.* (Hist. MSS. Comm.) I. 259 There will be no opposing of your son. **1656** *Artif. Handsom.* 52 No..crossings or opposings of his will. *a* **1716** SOUTH *Serm.* (1744) XI. x. 253 Those exact bills of our accounts relating all our opposings even of the smallest motions of the Spirit.

opposing (ə'pəʊzɪŋ), *ppl. a.* [f. as prec. + -ING[2].] That opposes.

1. That stands or lies over against, or comes in front of (something else, or each other); fronting, opposite; confronting.

1608 SHAKS. *Per.* III. Prol. 17 By the four opposing coigns Which the world together joins. **1792** WORDSW. *Descr. Sketches* 96 As up the opposing hills they slowly creep. **1860** TYNDALL *Glac.* I. xvii. 119 Ground between the opposing surfaces of the masses of ice.

2. Acting against or in opposition; withstanding, resisting; adverse, conflicting, contrary.

1634 MILTON *Comus* 600 Against th' opposing will and arm of Heav'n May never this just sword be lifted up. **1793** BURKE *Conduct Minority* Wks. VII. 275 All these parts of our constitution, whilst they are balanced as opposing interests, are also connected as friends. **1844** H. H. WILSON *Brit. India* III. 91 They succeeded in persuading the opposing party to permit the despatch of an embassy.

Hence **o'pposingly** *adv.*, in the way of opposition.

1842 G. S. FABER *Prov. Lett.* (1844) II. 150 The novel system..as adopted by Mr. Knox and the Council of Trent, opposingly replies. **1885** G. MEREDITH *Diana* II. iii. 77 Lady Dunstane's opposingly corresponding stillness provoked Miss Paynham to expatiate.

opposit (ə'pɒzɪt), *v.* Also 7 **opposite**. [f. L. *opposit-*, ppl. stem of *oppōnĕre*: see OPPONE.]

†**1.** *trans.* To oppose, resist. *Obs. rare*$^{-1}$.

1657 J. SERGEANT *Schism Dispach't* 607 To think they were separated from the Church for oppositing those more rigorous pretences.

2. *Metaph.* To posit as a contradictory. *rare.*

1881 ADAMSON *Fichte* 159 If there is to be op-positing at all, that which is opposed to A can only be Not-A... It only becomes plain from much later developments of the system, what is the precise nature of the act of oppositing or negating.

opposite ('ɒpəzɪt), *a.*, *sb.* (*adv.*, *prep.*) Also 4–8 **opposit**, (5 **-yt**), 5 **oposyte**, (5–6 *erron.* **apposite**). [a. F. *opposite* adj. and sb. (13th c. in Godef.

Compl.), ad. L. *opposit-us*, pa. pple. of *oppōnĕre*: see OPPONE, OPPOSE.]

A. *adj.*

1. a. Placed or lying over against something on the other or farther side of an intervening line, space, or thing; contrary in position. Const. *to*, *from*, †*against*.

Said of the two ends or sides of a line in relation to each other, and of two points on these sides, the line joining which would intersect the given line at right angles; also, of the two sides of a quadrilateral or elongated figure which are more or less parallel, or of any object having such a figure, and of two points in these sides, the line joining which would intersect the axis of the figure at right angles. In a quadrilateral, *opposite sides* are distinguished from *adjacent sides* which meet in an angle; *opposite angles* are at the two ends of a diagonal. In a circle *opposite points* are at the ends of any diameter. *Opposite sides* of a street, courtyard, or the like, face each other, but opposite sides of a building face directly away from each other; the *opposite angles* formed by two intersecting straight lines also lie in contrary directions; hence the notion of *opposite directions* in 2.

c **1391** CHAUCER *Astrol.* II. §6 The nadir of the sonne is thilke degree þat is opposit to the degree of the sonne. **1474** CAXTON *Chesse* IV. ii. Kj, On the lifte side the foure holden the places opposite. **1549** [see OPPOSITION 3]. **1551** RECORDE *Cast. Knowl.* 153 Then are they [the sun and moon] right opposite, the one against the other. **1652** NEEDHAM tr. *Selden's Mare Cl.* Advt., A large Bay which..in the end receives a stop..by an opposite shore. **1660** BARROW *Euclid* I. xv, If two right lines cut thro' one another, then are the two angles which are opposite equal one to the other. *Ibid.* xxxiv, In parallelograms the opposite sides are equal each to other; and the opposite angles are also equal. **1706** PHILLIPS, *Opposite Cones* (in *Geom.*), two Cones of the like Quality, that are vertically opposite, and have the same common Axis. *Opposite Sections*, are the two *Hyperbola's*, made by a Plane cutting both those Cones. **1756–7** tr. *Keysler's Trav.* (1760) III. 145 It is quite round,..two persons directly opposite to each other, and whispering close to the wall, may converse with each other, without being over-heard by the company in the middle. **1796** MRS. E. PARSONS *Myst. Warning* III. 147 A larger apartment, that overlooked the opposite side of the Castle from that which he had entered at. **1840–1** F. E. PAGET *Tales of Village* 58 Upon the opposite side of the river from that on which [etc.]. **1860** TYNDALL *Glac.* I. vii. 50 At the opposite side of the glacier was the Aiguille Verte.

b. *Bot.* (*a*) Situated, as similar parts or organs, in pairs on opposite sides of an axis or intervening body, as leaves on a stem; (*b*) Situated in front of an organ, so as to come between it and its axis, as a stamen in front of a sepal or petal. Opposed to *alternate*.

1707 *Curios. in Husb. & Gard.* 87 Plants that have opposite Leaves, as the Sensitive has. **1776–96** WITHERING *Brit. Plants* (ed. 3) II. 490 Cistus..anglicus:..leaves hairy, opposite, oblong. **1866** *Treas. Bot.* 817/2 *Opposite*, placed on opposite sides of some other body or thing and on the same plane. Thus, when leaves are opposite, they are on opposite sides of the stem; when petals are opposite, they are on opposite sides of the flower; and so on.

2. Turned or moving the other way; contrary, reverse.

1594 R. ASHLEY tr. *Loys le Roy* 8 b, The inhabitants on the one side and the other haue their shadowes opposite. **1801** CHARLOTTE SMITH *Lett. Solit. Wand.* I. 72 Which..led..in an opposite direction from that which she had before followed. **1868** LOCKYER *Elem. Astron.* iv. (1879) 144 When we travel in an express train, the objects appear to fly past us in the opposite direction to that in which we are going. *Mod.* Standing together but looking in opposite directions. Two trains coming from opposite directions met in collision. We started in opposite directions.

3. a. Contrary in nature, character, or tendency; diametrically different. Const. *to*, *from* (¶ *than*).

1580 LYLY *Euphues* (Arb.) 236 So began we to be more opposit in opinions: He graue, I gamesome: he studious, I carelesse. **1604** SHAKS. *Oth.* IV. ii. 91 You Mistris, That haue the office opposite to Saint Peter, And keepe the gate of hell. **1650** EARL MONM. tr. *Senault's Man bec. Guilty* 31 Self love takes a clean opposite way, from that of charity. **1754** J. HILDROP *Misc. Wks.* I. 91 They imploy their Wealth and Interest to quite opposite Purposes than were intended by the Grant. **1794** PALEY *Evid.* (1825) II. 229 There are two opposite descriptions of character, under which mankind may be classed. **1831** BREWSTER *Optics* xxxvi. 305 The accidental colour of any particular colour will be the colour exactly opposite that particular colour. Hence the two colours have been called opposite colours. **1870** FREEMAN *Norm. Conq.* (ed. 2) I. App. 724 His authority will hardly bear up against so many opposite witnesses. **1887** M. ARNOLD *Ess. Crit.* Ser. II. viii. (1888) 296 But he is an opportunist of an opposite kind from those who in politics..give themselves this name.

b. With *the*: that is opposed to something else; the contrary, the other (of two related things of different character).

1638 R. BAKER tr. *Balzac's Lett.* (vol. II.) 12 Finds never any fault in their owne side, nor vertue in the opposite. **1711** ADDISON *Spect.* No. 99 ¶ 3 Nothing makes a Woman more esteemed by the opposite Sex than Chastity. **1849** JAMES *Woodman* xiii, After the king's death, you continued in office under the opposite faction.

†4. a. Opposed in will or action, hostile, antagonistic, adverse. Const. *to*, *against*. *Obs.*

1577 HANMER *Anc. Eccl. Hist.* (1663) 226 The adversary, who sets himself opposite against the truth. **1589** WARNER *Alb. Eng.* Prose Add. (1612) 331 Æneas, supposing the Gods to bee yet opposite to the Troians. **1601** SHAKS. *Twel. N.* II. v. 162 Be opposite with a kinsman, surly with seruants. **1620** E. BLOUNT *Horæ Subs.* 490 You shall finde some to flatter.. most, when they shew to be most opposite against it. **1716** M. DAVIES *Athen. Brit.* II. 110 He was opposit to the Monopoly of Warwick's Power. **1737** WHISTON *Josephus, Antiq.* XVIII. vi, But God proved opposite to his designation.

†b. Of things: Antagonistic, adverse, repugnant. *Obs.*

1595 SHAKS. *John* III. i. 254 All forme is formelesse, Order orderlesse, Saue what is opposite to Englands loue. **1684** N. D. (*title*) A Rich Treasure at an Easie Rate:..Shewing how Inconsistent Riches is with Piety usually, and how Opposite Poverty is often. **1726–31** TINDAL tr. *Rapin's Hist. Eng.* (1743) II. XVII. 67 Preachers exclaimed..against these worldly vanities, as very opposite to true Religion.

5. *Comb.*, as ***opposite-leaved*** adj.; ***opposite number***, a person or thing similarly placed in another set, etc., to the given one; a partner, a counterpart; an opponent.

1871 KINGSLEY *At Last* I. vii. 253 Stems..opposite-leaved, alternate-leaved, leafless, or covered with leaves of every conceivable pattern. **1884** MILLER *Plant-n.* 179/1 Opposite-leaved Golden Saxifrage. **1906** KIPLING *Actions & Reactions* (1909) 202 'And your Opposite Number?' Penfentenyou described him. **1915** 'BARTIMEUS' *Tall Ship* iv. 84 We were 'opposite numbers' at your brother's wedding. **1917** *Times* 7 May 6/2 The establishment of personal contact between Sir William Robertson and his opposite number, General Pétain. **1917** E. WALLACE *Kate plus Ten* (1919) vi. 107 Pick up Mr. Pretherston and don't lose him—you may choose your own opposite number. **1927** *Observer* 24 July 4/6 The 'A.A.'s' opposite number..the Automobile Association of America..has issued a very interesting map of the United States. **1969** *Times* 13 Mar. 25/2 (*caption*) The model bison the papermakers' association got from its Polish opposite numbers. **1973** J. ROSSITER *Manipulators* xiii. 134 Before leaving for B Division he should have telephoned his opposite number there, clearing his proposed incursion on to another's territory.

B. *sb.* [The adj. used *absol.*, and in some uses scarcely a sb.]

†1. a. = Opposite point, esp. of the heavens. *Obs.* (Cf. OPPOSITION 3.)

c **1386** CHAUCER *Knt.'s T.* 1036 Estward ther stood a gate of Marbul whit, Westward right swich another in the opposit [*Corpus MS.* in opposite]. **1490** CAXTON *Eneydos* xxix. 111 The fayre Iris descendynge..at the oposyte of the sonne. **1604** E. G[RIMSTONE] *D'Acosta's Hist. Indies* III. v. 133 In eight notable poyntes of heaven, which are the two Poles, the two Equinoxes, the two Solstices, and their opposites in the same Circle.

†b. = Opposite aspect, OPPOSITION 3. *Obs.*

1667 MILTON *P.L.* x. 659 Planetarie motions and aspects In Sextile, Square, and Trine, and Opposite.

2. a. That which is opposite or contrary; an object, fact, or quality that is the reverse of something else; often in *pl.*, things the most different of their kind. †***in opposite***, on the contrary, on the other hand.

1549 *Compl. Scot.* iv. 30 In opposit, Osias vas bot aucht ȝeir of aige quhen he vas vnctit kyng..ȝit he gouuernit veil the cuntre. **1606** SHAKS. *Ant. & Cl.* I. ii. 130 The present pleasure, By reuolution lowring, does become The opposite of it selfe. *a* **1735** ARBUTHNOT *State Quacks* Misc. Wks. 1751 I. 159 This is that Oedipus, whose Wisdom can reconcile inconsistent Opposites. **1863** COWDEN CLARKE *Shaks. Char.* xi. 280 Ariel is the extreme opposite of Caliban. **1875** JOWETT *Plato* (ed. 2) I. 145 The most extreme opposites have some qualities in common.

b. *Logic.* An opposite term or proposition; †a contrary argument (*obs.*).

1588 FRAUNCE *Lawiers Log.* I. x. 46 b, Opposites are disagreeable argumentes which disagree both in respect and in matter it selfe. **1656** BLOUNT *Glossogr.* s.v., Aristotle makes four kinde of Opposites. **1727–38** CHAMBERS *Cycl.* s.v., Contraries are positive opposites... Such are cold and heat. **1864** BOWEN *Logic* vi. 162 The logical doctrine of Opposition shows us what can be immediately inferred as to the truth or falsity of one Judgment, from positing or sublating..one of its Opposites. *Ibid.* 164 Sub-Contraries can be called 'opposites' only in a qualified and technical sense.

3. A person who stands in a relation of opposition to another; an antagonist, adversary, opponent. (Very common in 17th c.: now *rare* or *Obs.*)

1423 JAS. I *Kingis Q.* clxx, Though thy begynnyng hath bene retrograde, Be froward opposyt. **1593** SHAKS. *2 Hen. VI*, v. iii. 22 Our foes..Being opposites of such repayring Nature. **1625** COOKE *Pope Joan* in *Harl. Misc.* (Malh.) IV. 56 If their opposites writings were not extant..we had never heard of such an objection. **1675** BROOKS *Gold. Key* Wks. 1867 V. 5 Aurelianus..brought Tetricus his opposite, and the brave Queen Zenobia of Palmyra, in triumph to Rome. **1751** JOHNSON *Cheynel* Wks. IV. 504 Had Cheynel been equal to his adversary in greatness and learning, it had not been easy to have found either a more proper opposite. **1821–30** LD. COCKBURN *Mem.* 159 He would have gone..as far as anybody to tread down his opposites politically. **1874** SWINBURNE *Bothwell* IV. v. 397 The task was hard with Knox for opposite To bend the council.

C. quasi-*adv.*

†1. In opposition, by way of counterpoise. *Obs.*

1523 LD. BERNERS *Froiss.* I. cclii. 374 In lykewyse, opposit to this dede, the kynge of Englande shewed his quarel in Almaygne, and in other places.

2. In an opposite position or direction.

[**1667** MILTON *P.L.* VI. 128 From his armed Peers Forth stepping opposite, half way he met His daring foe. *Ibid.* VII. 376 Less bright the Moon, But opposite in leveld West was set His mirror.] **1817** SHELLEY *Pr. Athanase* II. i. 38 And Athanase, her child,..sate opposite and gazed. **1896** *Daily News* 5 June 5/4 Several hon. gentlemen opposite.

D. quasi-*prep.* [ellipt. for *opposite to.*] Over against; facing or fronting on the other side. (Cf. L. *adversus*, *adversum* prep.) Phr. *to play* etc. *opposite*: to have (a specified actor or actress) as one's leading man or lady; also ***to play opposite to*** (cf. C. above).

1758 GOLDSM. *Mem. Prot.* (1895) I. 226 Opposite this Chamber was another. **1771** MRS. GRIFFITH *Hist. Lady Barton* III. 97, I was sitting..opposite the door of the room. **1834** LANDOR *Citation Shakespeare* Wks. 1853 II. 274/1 We knelt down opposite each other, and said our prayers. **1892** *Law Rep. 2 Queen's Bench* 535 A number of questions..with a blank opposite each question for the answer. *a* **1903** *Mod.* In a building opposite the Town Hall. **1926** J. AGATE in *Sunday Times* 7 Feb. 6/1 'Opposite him', as they say, was Miss Ilise Marvenga, who..made Kathie into a semblance of one of those expensive mechanical dolls with a staccato utterance. **1931** P. MACDONALD *Crime Conductor* II. iv. 178 Mary Wheelwright—England's Première Leading Lady—was not to play 'opposite' Kristania in *Harlequin's Holiday*. **1936** *Times Lit. Suppl.* 31 Oct. 894/3 He was to play 'opposite to' Anna Kenney, a very famous figure on the stage.

oppositely ('ɒpəzɪtlɪ), *adv.* [f. prec. + -LY².]

1. In an opposite position or direction; so as to be opposite (†*to*, †*against*); on opposite sides.

oppositely pinnate: see quot. 1753.

1593 *Rites & Mon. Ch. Durh.* (Surtees) 49 Oppositlie & firste to Sᵗ Marie is placed yᵉ picture of Thom's Langley. **1602** CAREW *Cornwall* (1723) 154 The watch-towre, mencioned by Orosius, and oppositely placed to such another in Galitia. **1753** CHAMBERS *Cycl. Supp.* s.v. *Leaf* (*Pinnated*), The oppositely pinnated [leaves]..when the folioles stand opposite to one another on the common petiole. **1830** LINDLEY *Nat. Syst. Bot.* 154 Calyx 4-leaved, inferior, oppositely imbricated in æstivation. **1862** ELLACOMBE in *Church Bells* (1883) 15 Sept. 808/1 The bells would be pulled to follow each other oppositely. *c* **1864** E. DICKINSON *Poems* (1955) II. 695 A Suspicion..That I am looking oppositely For the site of the Kingdom of Heaven—. **1929** R. BRIDGES *Testament Beauty* iii. 129 Thatt other hath the arm bent down and oppositely nerved.

2. a. In an opposite or contrary manner; †in reverse order; in opposition or contrast (*obs.*).

1567 MAPLET *Gr. Forest* 11 Iris..being..stricken of the Sunne his beames..doth represent..both the figure and colours of the Rainebow upon the wall next to it, and that oppositely. **1649** *Bounds Publ. Obed.* 63 Have not our Antagonists..observ'd them..to have as oppositly, yet as peremtorily differ'd from one another, as people of any family ever did? **1792** *Anecd. W. Pitt* I. iv. 81 His country and he are..equally, though oppositely, concerned. **1843** MILL *Logic* III. ix. §2 (1856) I. 449 The..body which is to be oppositely electrified is the surrounding atmosphere.

b. On the contrary, contrariwise; conversely.

1681 FLAVEL *Meth. Grace* xxiv. 410 This sin against the Spirit is..the deadly stop to the whole work of salvation: oppositely, when the spirit is received..into that soul the eternal love of God [etc.]..run freely. **1909** *Bodleian* Mar. 3/1 'You can have a dead rat,..but not a dead artist.' But oppositely, and appositely, a dead rat has no signification. **1972** *Science* 27 Oct. 425/1 Or oppositely, should we encourage economic growth.

oppositeness ('ɒpəzɪtnɪs). [f. as prec. + -NESS.] The quality of being opposite or opposed; contrariety, antagonism; †repugnance (*obs.*).

1645 W. JENKYN *Stil-Destroyer* 5 An..out-going of affection after our own things which we make our aime..in a way of oppositnesse even to the things of Christ. **1658** DURHAM *Exp. Revelation* I. viii. (1680) 50 Notwithstanding his great oppositnesse thereto, [Ambrose] was at length so pressed as he was made to yield. **1824** *Blackw. Mag.* XVI. 664 The same oppositeness to the accustomed opinions of decent Englishmen prevails in a hundred other points.

o,ppositi-, combining form of L. *oppositus* opposite, used in scientific (chiefly botanical) adjs., often adaptations of modern Latin terms, as **oppositi'florous**, having opposite peduncles or inflorescences; **oppositi'folious**, (*a*) having opposite leaves, (*b*) situated opposite a leaf (as a peduncle or tendril); **oppositi'pinnate**, oppositely pinnate; **oppositi'petalous**, situated opposite a petal; **oppositi'polar**, having poles situated at opposite ends (as certain nerve-cells); **oppositi'sepalous**, situated opposite a sepal (as a stamen).

1760 J. LEE *Introd. Bot.* III. xxi. (1765) 217 *Oppositifolious*, such as come out opposite to the Leaves. **1857** MAYNE *Expos. Lex.*, *Oppositiflōrus*, having opposing peduncles,..oppositiflorous. *Ibid.*, *Oppositipennātus*, applied to pennate leaves, of which the folioles are opposite: oppositipennate. **1880** GRAY *Struct. Bot.* 422/2 *Oppositipetalous*, placed before a petal. *Oppositisepalous*, situated before a sepal.

opposition (ɒpə'zɪʃən). [ad. L. *oppositiōn-em*, n. of action f. *oppōnĕre*: see OPPONE, OPPOSE *v.* Cf. F. *opposition* (12th c. in Hatz.-Darm.).

The specific senses 3, 4 b, and 7, appear earlier than the more general senses.]

†1. a. The action of setting opposite or against. (In quot., offering for combat.) *Obs.*

1602 SHAKS. *Ham.* v. ii. 178, I meane my Lord, the opposition of your person in tryall.

b. *spec.* Cf. OPPOSABLE 2.

1899 *Allbutt's Syst. Med.* VII. 209 Two principal movements, namely, abduction of the thumb, and opposition of the thumb... By opposition we mean the power of touching the tips of all the fingers in succession with the tip of the thumb.

2. Position over against something; opposite situation or direction; ***in opposition*** (*to*), facing, fronting.

1667 MILTON *P.L.* II. 803 Before mine eyes in opposition sits Grim Death my Son and foe. **1845** STODDART *Grammar* in *Encycl. Metrop.* (1847) I. 134/1 When any two visible objects are nearly connected, in local situation, they must appear to be placed in opposition to each other, if both be viewed from a distant point; but if one be viewed from the other, it will appear to be placed in opposition. **1854** DE QUINCEY *Autobiog. Sk., Wordsworth* II. v. 230 In one quarter, a little wood..; more directly in opposition to the spectator, a few green fields.

3. *Astrol.* and *Astron.* The relative position of two heavenly bodies when exactly opposite to each other as seen from the earth's surface, their longitude then differing by 180°; *esp.* the position of a heavenly body when opposite to the sun.

c **1386** CHAUCER *Frankl. T.* 329 Now next at this opposicion Which in the signe shal be of the leon As preieth hire [the moon] so greet a flood to brynge. **1549** *Compl. Scot.* vi. 55 Sum tyme the mune is in opposition, that is, quhen the mune & the soune are in apposite degreis. **1594** BLUNDEVIL *Exerc.* IV. xliv. (1636) 502 You shall find the Moone to be.. in an opposition with Saturne. *a* **1658** CLEVELAND *Gen. Poems* (1677) 165 The Moon when she is Eclipsed is always in Opposition with the Sun. **1701** SWIFT *Contests Nobles & Comm. Athens* Wks. 1755 II. I. 35 Pompey and Caesar, two stars of such a magnitude, that their conjunction was as likely to be fatal, as their opposition. **1881** *Athenæum* No. 2829. 61 The planet was in opposition..on the 27th of December.

4. a. The action of placing one thing in contrast with another; the condition of being opposed or contrasted; contrast, contradistinction, antithesis.

1581 MULCASTER *Positions* xxxviii. (1887) 173 Oppositions of vertues by way of comparison is their chiefe commendation. **1641** HINDE *J. Bruen* xxxiii. 105 How great is the opposition betwixt that assembly and this company? **1712** J. JAMES tr. *Le Blond's Gardening* 46 Their Verdure serving as a Ground to the Figures,..improves them by the Opposition it produces. **1846** RUSKIN *Mod. Paint.* (1848) I. II. v. iii. §9. 355 What was made above bright by opposition to blue, being underneath made cool and dark by opposition to gold. **1867** FREEMAN *Norm. Conq.* I. App. 599 In the English Chronicles..the opposition is made between 'French' and 'English'. **1876** J. PARKER *Paracl.* II. xix. 351 Enmity is set in opposition to love, and carnality in opposition to spiritual-mindedness.

†**b.** *Rhet.* A contrast of positions or arguments; a contrary position or argument; a proposition opposed to a thesis, counter-proposition, objection. (Cf. ANTITHESIS 1, 2.) *Obs.*

1412–20 LYDG. *Chron. Troy* III. xxviii. (MS. Digby 230) lf. 133 b/1 There may be made noon opposicioun Aboue þe grounde ȝif þe body lye þat of Resoun it mote putrifye. **1526** TINDALE *1 Tim.* vi. 20 Avoyde..opposicions of science falsly so called. **1577** VAUTROUILLIER *Luther on Ep. Gal.* 137 It containeth this invincible opposition: that is, if the sinnes of the whole world be in that one man Iesus Christ, then are they not in the world. But if they be not in him, then are they yet in the world. **1678** PHILLIPS (ed. 4), *Opposition*,.. In Rhetorick is a figure of Sentence, the same with Objection.

c. *Logic.* The relation between two propositions which have the same subject and predicate but differ in quantity or quality or both.

The recognized kinds of opposition are four, viz. *contradictory, contrary, subcontrary, subaltern*: see these.

1697 tr. *Burgersdicius' Logic* I. xxxiii. 128 True Opposition afore-mentioned is either Contrariety or Contradiction. **1788** REID *Aristotle's Log.* i. §3. 11 The four kinds of opposition of terms are explained. **1844** WHATELY *Logic* II. ii. §3 (ed. 8) 72 'Contradictory-opposition' is the kind most frequently alluded to, because..to deny,—or to disbelieve,—a proposition, is to assert, or to believe, its Contradictory. **1860** ABP. THOMSON *Laws Th.* 148 Opposition of Judgments is the relation between any two which have the same matter, but a different form. **1864** BOWEN *Logic* vi. 162 Opposition..was first applied only to the relations between two Contraries, or two Contradictories. **1866** FOWLER *Deduct. Logic* III. ii. (ed. 2) 74 It is only in a Contradictory Opposition (where the opposed terms differ both in quantity and quality) that from the truth or falsity of one proposition we can invariably infer the truth or falsity of another.

†**d.** *concr.* That which is opposite or contrary; that which contrasts or counterbalances. *Obs.*

1596 SHAKS. *1 Hen. IV*, II. iii. 15 The purpose you vndertake is dangerous,..and your whole Plot too light, for the counterpoize of so great an Opposition. **1703** *Rules Civility* 137 The Opposition of the Pleasant Stile, is the dull Burlesque that consists in mean Ironies.

e. *Semantics.* The state or condition of being opposite in meaning; the relationship between antonyms.

1870 [see ANTONYM]. **1925** P. RADIN tr. *J. Vendryès's Language* III. iii. 218 Among animal names the same opposition is frequent. Latin had *equus* and *equa*... In English *horse* is apposed to *mare*. **1932** C. K. OGDEN *Opposition* i. 8 The theory of opposition offers a new method of approach not only in the case of all those words which can best be defined in terms of their opposites..but also to *any* word whose use may give rise to controversy. **1963** J. LYONS *Structural Semantics* iv. 68 The polarity of a term is a function of its opposition to its antonym, and not vice versa. **1967** R. A. WALDRON *Sense & Sense Devel.* v. 107 *Black* and *white* are often two ends of a scale but in 'people are inclined to see things in black and white'..the pair is taken as the type of all 'either/or' antonymic opposition. **1976** F. R. PALMER *Semantics* iv. 82 A quite different kind of 'opposite' is found with pairs of words which exhibit the reversal of a relationship between items... Lyons suggests the term *converseness* for these, but I am more concerned to point out their essentially relational characteristics, and would thus prefer *relational opposition*.

f. *Linguistics.* A functional, or potentially functional, contrast between partially similar linguistic elements.

[**1931** *Travaux Cercle Ling. Prague* IV. 311 *Opposition phonologique*..—Différence phonique susceptible de servir, dans une langue donnée, à la différenciation des significations intellectuelles.] **1936** *Amer. Speech* XI. 110 A 'phonological system' is defined as the ensemble of phonological oppositions proper to a given language. **1953** [see BINARY *a.* k]. **1963** J. LYONS *Structural Semantics* iv. 68 In Russian or German..there is an opposition to be recognized, in word-initial and word-medial position, between the voiced and the voiceless plosives. **1970** G. C. LEPSCHY *Survey Struct. Ling.* iii. 58 In order to have distinctive function, speech sounds must be opposed to each other (distinction presupposes opposition). An opposition can be either *distinctive* (or *phonological*), or non-distinctive. Only sounds which may occur in the same context (i.e. that are permutable) can be in opposition. **1972** M. L. SAMUELS *Ling. Evol.* viii. 171 In the fifteenth and sixteenth centuries there are signs that the opposition /ɛ ~ ɑ/ in class III verbs is no longer adequate. **1978** *Jrnl. Lancs. Dial. Soc.* Jan. 20 The opposition between the reflex of ME ui/oi and ME ī is preserved.

5. a. Contrary or hostile action, antagonism, resistance; the fact or condition of being opposed, hostile, or adverse.

1588 SHAKS. *L.L.L.* v. ii. 743 That you vouchsafe..to excuse, or hide, The liberall opposition of our spirits. **1663** GERBIER *Counsel* 10 Nature of Aire being to ascend, and when it meets with a sudden opposition it spreads. **1747** BUTLER *Serm. Ho. Lords* Wks. 1874 II. 300 Opposition..to measures which he sees to be necessary, is itself immoral. **1771** GOLDSM. *Hist. Eng.* I. 11 They made a brave opposition against the veteran army. **1868** HELPS *Realmah* xvii. (1876) 487 A disagreeable man will often dissent from you from the mere love of opposition. **1876** MOZLEY *Univ. Serm.* x. (1877) 211 A life of enmities is greatly in opposition to growth in holiness.

†**b.** Encounter, combat. *Obs.*

1596 SHAKS. *1 Hen. IV*, I. iii. 99 On the gentle Seuernes sedgie banke, In single Opposition hand to hand. **1604** —— *Oth.* II. iii. 184 Tilting one at others breastes, In opposition bloody. **1610** SELDEN *Duello* 2 That single opposition, which the French cal Combate *seul à seul*,..our English single fight. **1655** E. TERRY *Voy. E. Ind.* 48 Our Charles in this opposition made at her adversary..three hundred seventy and five great Shot.

c. *Fencing.* See quot. 1879. (A Gallicism.)

1809 ROLAND *Fencing* 77 The old system of Fencing recommends to use the left hand, when you make the flanconade as an opposition to the adversary's blade from the line of your body. **1879** *Encycl. Brit.* IX. 70/2 In fencing, 'opposition' signifies the art of covering the body at the time of delivering a thrust, on that side where the foils happen to cross, in order to prevent an antagonist exchanging hits.

d. ***in opposition***, in the position of being opposed to the administration; said of one of two political parties, or a member of that party, when the other is in office. (Cf. 6.)

1793 BURKE *Conduct Minority* Wks. VII. 286 The authors ..of the American war, with whom I have acted, both in office and in opposition. **1847** EMERSON *Repr. Men, Goethe* Wks. (Bohn) I. 386 How can he be honoured, when..he must sustain with shameless advocacy some bad government, or must bark all the year round, in opposition? **1895** *Westm. Gaz.* 15 Aug. 1/2 They are in Opposition and not in office.

6. *concr.* **a.** A political party opposed to that in office; *esp.* the party opposed to the administration in the British Parliament or other legislative body.

1704 DAVENANT in Ellis *Orig. Lett.* Ser. II. IV. 244 They who shall form Oppositions hereafter will be thought to be bribed by France. **1744** M. BISHOP *Life & Adv.* 263 There is no Senate without an Opposition, nor no Party of Men without different Opinions. **1817** EVANS *Parl. Deb.* 136 Hear, hear, from the Opposition, and laughter from the Ministerial benches. **1826** J. CAM HOBHOUSE *Sp. Ho. Comm.* 10 Apr. (Hansard XV. 135), It was said to be very hard on his majesty's ministers to raise objections to this proposition. For his own part, he thought it was more hard on his majesty's opposition (a laugh) to compel them to take this course. [The phrase was at once taken up and was used in the course of the same debate by Canning and Tierney.] **1850** HT. MARTINEAU *Hist. Peace* (1877) II. v. xii. 378 These French formed the first political Opposition ever known in Canada. **1856** W. H. SMYTH *Rom. Fam. Coins* 55 He [Lentulus] relapsed to the opposition, with the appointment of proprætor in Asia.

b. *transf.* Any party or body of opponents.

1781 J. MOORE *View Soc. It.* (1790) II. lxvii. 319 Every system of philosophy, like every Minister of Great Britain, has an opposition. **1869** ROGERS *Hist. Gleanings* I. 44 In those days the Opposition was not only hungry but desperate.

†**7.** [from OPPOSE *v.* I.] **a.** Inquisition, inquiry, examination. **b.** = APPOSITION¹. *Obs.*

c **1540** tr. *Pol. Verg. Eng. Hist.* (Camden) I. 97 Now let us returne to the opposicion of those things which concerne the state of Brittaine. **1660** PEPYS *Diary* 9 Jan. (1825) I. 4, I rose early..and looked over and corrected my brother John's speech, which he is to make the next opposition [i.e. Apposition at St. Paul's School].

8. *attrib.* (esp. in sense 6), as ***opposition benches, cheer, newspaper, party, spokesman,*** etc.

1795 tr. *C. P. Moritz's Trav.* 60 They tell me, that at these elections when there is a strong opposition-party, there is often bloody work. **1801** SURR *Splendid Misery* II. 14 Scowling in opposition minorities. **1815** N. W. WRAXALL *Hist. Mem.* II. 167 The Treasury Bench, as well as the Places behind it, had been for so many years occupied by Lord North and his friends, that it became difficult to recognize them again in their new Seats, dispersed over the Opposition Benches, in great coats, frocks, and boots. **1817** COLERIDGE *Biog. Lit.* 89 If..he will compare the opposition newspapers. **1819** KEATS *Cap & Bells* in R. M. Milnes *Life, Lett., & Lit. Remains J. Keats* (1848) II. 221 I'll make the opposition-benches wince. **1824** J. S. MILL in *Westm. Rev.* I. 505 The Edinburgh Review..has really exhibited the vices, which we described as likely to characterize a periodical publication attached to the Opposition party. **1860** FORSTER *Gr. Remonstr.* 27 That was in February, 1234. In April..the opposition barons were in power. **1867** FREEMAN *Norm. Conq.* I. iv. 197 The election of Robert.. Count of Paris, as an opposition King. **1888** *Daily News* 18 Dec. 2/6 Mr. Gladstone, who was received with Opposition cheers, said [etc.]. **1930** G. B. SHAW *Apple Cart* p. xxiii, Nothing has any sense or reality in it except the vituperation of the opposition party. **1974** *Times* 12 June 2/5 Mr Heseltine, Opposition spokesman on trade, said..yesterday [etc.]. **1976** *Hansard Commons* 7 Dec. 252 The Government ..cannot accept views expressed from the Opposition Benches... I object strongly to that. *Ibid.* 8 Dec. 570, I am far more concerned about the measures that would be enacted by the rabble sitting on the Opposition Benches if they were in Government.

oppositional (ɒpəˈzɪʃənəl), *a.* [f. prec. + -AL¹.]

†**1.** Of or pertaining to astronomical opposition.

1686 GOAD *Celest. Bodies* II. iv. 199 The Quincunx of Sol, a Sign distant from the Oppositional Line. *Ibid.* xiv. 354 This seems a Conjunctional Comet..it may be reckoned Oppositional, in respect of the Fixed Stars.

2. Pertaining to, or having the character of, opposition or hostile action; belonging to, or connected with, the parliamentary opposition.

1829 *Examiner* 754/1 It [the revenue] loses its oppositional, grim, taxing-man aspect. **1857** *Chamb. Jrnl.* VII. 97, I saw the premier,..and other people, ministerial and oppositional. **1885** tr. *Wellhausen's Proleg. Hist. Israel* IV. i. 138 Their extraordinary and oppositional action.

oppositionary (ɒpəˈzɪʃənərɪ), *a. rare.* [f. OPPOSITION + -ARY¹.] = OPPOSITIONAL *a.* 2.

1926 *Contemp. Rev.* Sept. 276 Petrograd ('Leningrad') became the centre of Zinoviev's oppositionary activity.

oppoˈsitionist, *sb.* (and *a.*) [f. OPPOSITION + -IST.]

a. One who professes or practises opposition; *esp.* a member of the parliamentary opposition.

1773 J. BOUCHER *Amer. Revol.* (1797) 297 Like modern oppositionists..they seem to have thwarted David..[as] the best way to promote some indirect purpose of their own. **1786** *Europ. Mag.* IX. 296 Ministers and Oppositionists vie with each other who shall be most frugal and saving of the public money. **1809–10** COLERIDGE *Friend* (1837) II. 191 The oppositionists to 'things as they are', are divided into many and different classes. **1881** MRS. C. PRAED *Policy & P.* I. 294 The various ministers, the Oppositionists, and officials walked in. **1965** A. NOVE in B. Pearce tr. *Preobrazhensky's New Economics* p. xiv, Like other former oppositionists he came to the Congress to apologize for past misdeeds and to denounce Trotsky. **1971** I. DEUTSCHER *Marxism in our Time* (1972) vi. 113 In June 1957, exactly twenty-five years will have elapsed since I was expelled from the Party as an oppositionist. **1973** *Sunday Advocate-News* (Barbados) 16 Dec. 4/3 The Consul-General attributed the rumours to be the work of 'oppositionists' who he said are trying to embarrass the Government.

b. *attrib.* or as *adj.*

1812 SHELLEY *Lett., to E. Hitchener* (1888) II. 90 The public papers are either oppositionist or ministerial. **1881** MRS. C. PRAED *Policy & P.* III. 220 The grave nature of the Oppositionist attack. **1962** S. E. FINER *Man on Horseback* xii. 231 The members of the nationalist movement have been reared in an oppositionist mentality. **1963** *Cambr. Rev.* 4 May 405/2 An individual perception of reality—as distinguished from a conformist perception, whether it be 'official' or 'oppositionist'—is of value and interest.

oppoˈsitionless, *a.* [f. OPPOSITION + -LESS.] Having no opposition.

1758 H. WALPOLE *Lett. to Montagu* ciii, The parliament is met, but empty and totally oppositionless.

oppositious (ɒpəˈzɪʃəs), *a. rare.* [f. OPPOS(ITE *a.* + -ITIOUS².] Inclined to oppose; recalcitrant.

1923 *Blackw. Mag.* Aug. 176/2 He became oppositious on leaving truly delectable posadas to left and right.

oppositive (əˈpɒzɪtɪv), *a.* (*sb.*) [f. *opposit-*, ppl. stem of L. *oppōnĕre* to oppose, OPPONE + -IVE; cf. F. *oppositif, -ive* (Littré).]

†**1.** = OPPOSITE A. 1, 1 b. *Obs.*

1632 LITHGOW *Trav.* VI. 281 A little foure-squared Roome, oppositiue to the duelling side of..Syon. **1857** MAYNE *Expos. Lex.*, *Oppositīvus*, applied to stamens when situated opposite the divisions of a simple perianth, as in the *Lilium*; or to a corol, as in the *Primula*;..to petals when placed before the divisions of the calyx, as in the *Berberis*: oppositive.

2. Characterized by opposing or contrasting; expressive of contrariety or antithesis; adversative.

1622 [implied in OPPOSITIVELY]. **1634** BP. HALL *Contempl., N.T.* IV. *Prosec. Transfig.*, Not without some oppositive comparison; not Moses, not Elias, but this: Moses and Elias were servants; this a Sonne. **1845** STODDART *Grammar* in *Encycl. Metrop.* I. 50/1 In most Languages there are negative or oppositive verbs, as *volo* or *nolo* in Latin; to *do* and *undo* in English; *fier* and *mefier* in French. **1865** LIGHTFOOT *Galatians* (1874) 76/1 *Εἰ μή* seems always to retain its proper exceptive sense, and is not simply oppositive.

3. Inclined to opposition, contentious. *rare.*

1865 G. MACDONALD *A. Forbes* lxxxiii. 394 Neither was the duty so unpleasant to Thomas's oppositive nature.

†**B.** *sb.* = OPPOSITE B. 2. *Obs. rare*⁻¹.

1651 *Stowe's Chaucer, Astrol.* 268 b/2 Then haste thou East and West, and per consequens the oppositife, that is Southe and North. [Cf. *Astrol.* II. §38.]

Hence **o'ppositively** *adv.*, in an oppositive manner; also **o'ppositiveness**.

1622 T. STOUGHTON *Chr. Sacrif.* xv. 205 The will of God ..is here said to be perfect. This also I understand oppositiuely and comparatiuely. Oppositiuely, because the old Testament was imperfect: comparatiuely, because this therefore is more perfect. **1633** T. ADAMS *Exp. 2 Peter* iii. 18 Oppositively, as it is opposed to that external duration after this world, when time shall be no more. **1824** *Blackw. Mag.* XV. 225, I had the organ of 'oppositiveness'.

† **o'ppositor.** *Obs.* [agent-n. from L. *oppōnĕre, oppositum* to oppose: see -OR. Cf. It. *oppositore* and obs. F. *oppositeur* (16th c. in Godef.).] One who opposes, an opponent.

1598 FLORIO, *Oppositore*, an oppositor, an opponent. **1604** A. SERLE in *Buccleuch MS.* (Hist. MSS. Comm.) 52 My oppositors are so many..that I have submitted all to the Archbishop. **1641** EARL MONM. tr. *Biondi's Civil Warres* IV. 80 For the Constable no man names him but Chartier, who ..hath as some that live in these dayes his oppositors.

o'pposive, *a. rare.* [irreg. f. OPPOSE *v.* + -IVE.] Inclined to oppose, contradictory.

1676 *Acc. L. Muggleton* in *Harl. Misc.* (Malh.) I. 610 An obstinate, dissentious, and opposive spirit. **1911** W. DE MORGAN *Likely Story* 107 He had an opposive or lazy disposition.

oppossum, obs. form of OPOSSUM.

† **o'pposure.** *Obs.* [f. OPPOSE *v.* + -URE: cf. *exposure*.] The action of opposing, opposition.

1611 HEYWOOD *Golden Age* III. Wks. 1874 III. 48 Wee'l stand their fierce opposure. **1615** CHAPMAN *Odyss.* XI. 127 Neptune still will his opposure try. **1692** LEIGHTON *Serm.* Wks. (1868) 358 In the heat of dispute and opposure to the unjust imputations of his friends.

oppress (ə'prɛs), *v.* Forms: *α.* 4–5 **oppres(e**, 4–6 **opress(e**, 4–7 **oppresse**, 4– **oppress**. *β.* 4 **apresse**, 5 **appres**, **appress(e**. [a. OF. *oppresser, apresser* (13th c. in Hatz.-Darm.) = It. *oppressare* (Florio), ad. med.L. *oppressāre*, freq. of L. *opprimĕre* to press against, press or bear down; to put down, crush, overwhelm, check; to fall upon, take by surprise; to suppress, conceal; in late L., to force (a woman), f. *ob-* (OB- 1 b) + *premĕre* to press.]

† **1.** *trans.* To press injuriously upon or against; to subject to pressure with hurtful or overpowering effect; to press down by force; to crush, trample down, smother, crowd. *Obs.*

1382 WYCLIF *Mark* iii. 9 Iesus seith to his disciplis, that the litil boot shulde serue hym, for the cumpanye of peple, lest thei oppressiden hym. *c* **1420** *Pallad. on Husb.* III. 499 Yef euery kynde an order by hymselve, Lest myghty treen the smale adoun oppresse. **1460** CAPGRAVE *Chron.* (Rolls) 266 He was sleyn at Caleys, oppressed betwix to fedir bedis. **1490** [see OPPRESSION 1]. **1597** BEARD *Theatre God's Judgem.* (1612) 230 Brennus..when hee entred the citie so loaded her with gold, that hee couered and oppressed her therewith. **1642** R. CARPENTER *Experience* II. vii. 162 The upper part of a Church fell..and..the women sitting in the body of the Church, many of them were oppressed. **1741** RICHARDSON *Pamela* (1824) I. cii. 493 Fear to put on his hat, lest he should oppress his foretop. **1781** GIBBON *Decl. & F.* xxxv. (1869) II. 298 The wounded king was oppressed in the general disorder, and trampled under the feet of his own cavalry.

b. *esp.* To bear down or crush in battle; to overwhelm with numbers. Now *rare.*

c **1400** *Destr. Troy* 5889 [Thai] woundit hom wikkedly, walt hom to ground, Oppresset hom with pyne, put hom abake. *a* **1548** HALL *Chron., Hen. VI* 130 The Englishe-men ..beyng oppressed with so greate a multitude, thei wer compelled to flie into the Abbaye. **1655** STANLEY *Hist. Philos.* III. (1701) 86/2 Enclosed by the Enemy who exceeded them in number; they gave back and were in the end opprest, and all kill'd. **1713** ADDISON *Cato* IV. iv, Opprest with multitudes, he greatly fell. **1827** SCOTT *Tales of Grandfather* Ser. I. viii. (1841) 29/2 He resolved to avoid fighting at that time, lest he should be oppressed by numbers.

c. *fig.* Of sleep, etc.: To press upon, overpower, weigh down. (Chiefly *poet.*)

1582 N. T. (Rhem.) *Acts* xx. 9 A certaine yong man..was oppressed with heauy sleepe. **1667** MILTON *P.L.* IX. 1045 Till dewie sleep Oppress'd them, wearied with thir amorous play. **1697** DRYDEN *Alexander's Feast* v, With love and wine at once oppressed. **1715–20** POPE *Iliad* XIV. 405 With love and sleep's soft power oppress'd. **1820** KEATS *Eve St. Agnes* xxvii, Until the poppied warmth of sleep oppress'd Her soothed limbs. **1820** SHELLEY *Witch of Atlas* lxix, The grave Of such, when death oppressed the weary soul, Was as a green and over-arching bower.

2. To affect with a feeling of pressure, constraint, or distress; to lie heavy on, weigh down, burden, crush (the feelings, mind, spirits, etc.).

c **1374** CHAUCER *Troylus* III. 1040 (1089) Euery spirit his vigour yn knette, So þey a-stoned & oppressed were. *c* **1477** CAXTON *Jason* 35 Hit semeth that he hath his herte oppressed with aspre dueil and sorowe. *a* **1533** LD. BERNERS *Huon* xxii. 65 Hunger opressyd hym more than it dyde to them of gretter age. **1667** MILTON *P.L.* VII. 129 Knowledge is as food, and needs no less Her Temperance over Appetite, ..Oppresses else with Surfet. **1719** DE FOE *Crusoe* I. vi, These Reflections oppress'd me for the second or third Day of my Distemper. **1783** CRABBE *Village* I. 226 Thus groan the old, till by disease oppress They taste a final woe. **1822** LAMB *Elia* Ser. I. *Dist. Corresp.*, The Weary World of Waters between us oppresses the imagination. **1894** HALL CAINE *Manxman* III. xix. 188 He was oppressed with a sense of meanness never felt before.

† **3.** To put down, suppress; to crush, quell, subdue, overwhelm (a person); to check, extinguish, or put an end to (a thing or state of things, feeling, disposition, etc.). *Obs.*

c **1340** HAMPOLE *Prose Tr.* 42 'Scrutator maiestatis opprimetur a gloria'.. Raunsaker of þe myghte of Godd and of His Maieste..sall be ouerlayde and oppresside of Hym-selfe. *c* **1386** CHAUCER *Sec. Nun's T.* Prol. 4 Ydelnesse..To eschue and by hire contrarie hire oppresse That is to seyn by leueful bisynesse. *c* **1398** —— *Fortune* 60 (Camb. MS.) Whi sholdys thow my realte apresse [*v.r.* opresse]. **1413** *Pilgr. Sowle* (Caxton 1483) IV. xxxiv. 83 Stronge and myghty for to oppressen brybours and extorcioners. **1560** DAUS tr. *Sleidane's Comm.* 41 b, That the trueth should be oppressed, and the lyght of the Ghospell extinguisshed. **1579** FENTON *Guicciard.* v, To areare a sufficient strength to oppressse the conspirators. **1603** KNOLLES *Hist. Turks* (1621) 745 He.. determined..to passe over into Affricke,..in hope to oppresse that rebellion in the beginning. **1647** A. ROSS *Mystag. Poet.* viii. (1675) 167 He [Hercules] oppressed Cacus. **1709** *Tatler* No. 32 ⁋6 An Enormity which has been revived (after being long oppressed) and is called Punning. **1829** MACKINTOSH *Case Donna Maria* Wks. 1846 II. 412 England..who had the power of rapidly succouring Portugal, without the means of oppressing her independence.

† **b.** To suppress, keep out of sight, conceal.

1538 STARKEY *England* I. i. 17 Man, yf he be brought vp in corrupt opynyon, hath no perceyueance of thys natural law, but suffryth hyt by neclygence to be oppressyd, as ther wer no such sedys plantyd in hym. **1539** TONSTALL *Serm. Palm. Sund.* (1823) 20 His godly nature coulde not be hydde, nor kepte vnder, nor oppressed by any humilitie. **1560** DAUS tr. *Sleidane's Comm.* 153 This is alwayes theyr facion, that..they wyll in suche maner of assemblies, oppresse Christ and his ueritie.

† **c.** *intr.* To be crushed or overwhelmed. *rare*$^{-1}$.

c **1485** *Digby Myst.* III. 2111 Now I know well I xall not opprese.

4. To trample down or keep under by wrongful exercise of authority or superior power or strength; to load or burden with cruel or unjust impositions or restraints; to tyrannize over.

1382 WYCLIF *Exod.* iii. 9 Y haue seen the affliccioun of hem, with the which thei ben oppressid of the Egipcyens. —— *Jas.* ii. 6 Wher riche men oppresen not ȝou bi power? *c* **1430** *Goddis Compl.* 201 in *Pol. Rel. & L. Poems* (1866) 181 Þe poore peple þou doist oppresse Wiþ sleitis and wilis. **1596** DALRYMPLE tr. *Leslie's Hist. Scot.* I. 114 Thay ar frie of al custumes, with quhilkes ar opprest the subiectes of vthiris princes. **1620** E. BLOUNT *Horæ Subs.* 309 Euery great man ..seuerally oppresseth the common people. **1737** POPE *Hor. Epist.* I. i. 182 That Man divine whom Wisdom calls her own;..Rich ev'n when plunder'd, honour'd while oppress'd. **1844** THIRLWALL *Greece* lxii. VIII. 147 The powerful citizens oppressed the weak. **1849** MACAULAY *Hist. Eng.* ii. I. 180 She had been pillaged and oppressed by the party which preached an austere morality.

absol. **1611** BIBLE *Ps.* x. 18 To judge the fatherless & the oppressed, that the man of the earth may no more oppress.

† **5.** Of an enemy, external circumstances, etc.: To press or bear heavily on; to reduce to straits; to molest, trouble, harass, distress. *Obs.*

1382 WYCLIF *Judg.* x. 12 Whether not the Egipciens, and Amorreis,..and Amalech, and Chanaan oppressiden ȝou? *c* **1460** FORTESCUE *Abs. & Lim. Mon.* iii. (1885) 115 The Scottes and the Pyctes, so bete and oppressid this lande, þat the peple therof sought helpe of the Romayns. **1555** EDEN *Decades* I. 20 Fewe of the inhabitantes..kepte theyr promyse, bycause they were sorer oppressed with famine then any of the other. **1560** DAUS tr. *Sleidane's Comm.* 37 b, The fury of the Turkes, and the Heresie of Luther oppresse us both at once. **1611** BIBLE *Num.* x. 9 If ye go to war in your land against the enemy that oppresseth you, then ye shall blow an alarm with the trumpets.

† **6.** *trans.* To fall upon, come upon unexpectedly, take by surprise. *Obs.* (So L. *opprimĕre.*)

1382 WYCLIF *Prov.* xx. 13 Wile thou not looue slep, lest thee nedynesse opresse [Vulg. *opprimat*]. *a* **1555** RIDLEY *Wks.* (Parker Soc.) 145 Woe be unto us, if he can oppress us at unawares. **1603** KNOLLES *Hist. Turks* (1621) 673 Hoping ..to steale into the campe undiscovered, and there so to oppresse Solyman sleeping in his tent.

† **7.** To force, violate, ravish. *Obs.* (So L. *opprimĕre.*)

1382 WYCLIF *2 Sam.* xiii. 32 Fro the day that he oppresside Thamar, his sister. *c* **1386** CHAUCER *Frankl. T.* 657 She..Chees rather for to dye than assente To been oppressed of hir maydenhede. **1432–50** tr. *Higden* (Rolls) V. 39 The abbote..was accusede..that he hade oppressede that woman callede Melancia. **1613** HAYWARD *Will. I* in *Harl. Misc.* (Malh.) III. 157 If a man oppressed any woman, he was deprived of his privy parts.

† **8.** To press, force, urge; *refl.* to force or exert oneself. *Obs.* (So OF. *oppresser*, Godef.)

c **1400** *Destr. Troy* 3390, I shall appres me with pyne your prayer to here. *Ibid.* 9450 Oppresse the with payn, & present hym dethe! **1523** LD. BERNERS *Froiss.* I. cxxxv. 162 If I wolde sore oppresse you I am sure ye wolde gladly pay x. thousand crownes.

† **9.** To press close; to close, shut up. *Obs.* (Cf. L. *opprimere ora, oculos.*)

1583 *Exec. for Treason* (1675) 46 Persons that have.. stopped their ears against the sound of Justice, and oppressed their hearts against the force of reason.

10. *Her.* = DEBRUISE *v.* 2.

Chiefly in *pa. pple*: see OPPRESSED *ppl. a.* 2.

† **o'ppress**, *sb. Obs.* Also 6 oppresse. [a. OF. *oppresse*, ad. L. *oppressa*, fem. of *oppressus*, pa. pple. of *opprimĕre*: see prec.] = OPPRESSION 2.

c **1470** HENRY *Wallace* VII. 144 The gret oppress off wer. **1502** *Ord. Crysten Men* (W. de W. 1506) IV. xxix. 331 Suche oppresse of paynes and of temptacyon. **1577** DEE *Relat. Spir.* I. (1659) 399 He became in a great oppresse of mind to find us coupled with so ungodly a man.

oppressed (ə'prɛst, *poet.* ə'prɛsɪd), *ppl. a.* Also 6–8 **opprest**. [f. OPPRESS *v.* + -ED[1].]

1. Pressed down or weighed down physically or mentally; burdened, troubled, depressed; reduced to straits or difficulties; *esp.* harassed or crushed down by tyranny or unjust treatment; downtrodden.

1382 WYCLIF *Isa.* i. 17 Helpeth to the opressid. *c* **1511** *1st Eng. Bk. Amer.* (Arb.) Introd. 31/2 Ye opprest pope of ye schole of Rome. **1605** SHAKS. *Lear* v. iii. 5 For thee oppressed King I am caste downe. *a* **1687** SIR W. PETTY *Pol. Arith.* (1690) 21 The Hollanders were one hundred years since a poor and oppressed People. **1767** GOOCH *Treat. Wounds* I. 280 He was seized with a lethargy, and other usual symptoms of an oppressed brain, and expired soon after. **1871** FREEMAN *Norm. Conq.* IV. xxi. 618 There is not a word to hint that that oppressed nation was what it is now the fashion to call an oppressed nationality.

2. *Her.* = DEBRUISED.

1572 BOSSEWELL *Armorie* II. 132 b, The fielde is de Azure, two winges iointly en Lewre de Argent, oppressed wᵗ a barre Gules. **1868** CUSSANS *Her.* vi. (ed. 3) 86 When an Ordinary surmounts, or is placed over, a Lion, or other animal, it is said to be *Debruised*, or *Oppressed*, by that Ordinary.

† **o'ppresser.** *Obs. rare.* [f. OPPRESS *v.* + -ER[1].] One who oppresses; = OPPRESSOR.

1388 WYCLIF *Gen.* x. 9 Huntere [*gloss*, that is, oppressere]. **1607** HIERON *Wks.* I. 185 The young man will bee loose,.. the oppresser cruell. *a* **1617** *Ibid.* 2 The Lord was pleased to call Paul, who before..was a persecutor and a blasphemer and an oppresser.

† **o'ppressful**, *a. Obs. rare.* [f. OPPRESS + -FUL.] Oppressive.

1606 G. W[OODCOCKE] *Hist. Ivstine* VIII. 39 Bewailing.. the oppresseful estate wherein themselues liued. *Ibid.* XXI. 78 What taxes how oppressfull soeuer imposed vpon them-selues, they account it their duty to obey them.

oppressing (ə'prɛsɪŋ), *vbl. sb.* [-ING[1].] The action of OPPRESS *v.*; oppression. Now *gerundial.*

1388 [see OPPRESSION 2]. **1395** PURVEY *Remonstr.* (1851) 24 Spoilinge pore men with vniust axingis, oppressingis, extortions. **1460** *Rolls of Parlt.* V. 383/1 Ride to the oppressyng of any of the said rebellions. **1483** *Cath. Angl.* 260/2 An Oppressynge, *oppressio.* **1762** WOOLMAN *Wks.* (1840) 220 In many ways they corrupted the law,..the oppressing of the stranger was one.

o'ppressing, *ppl. a.* [f. as prec. + -ING[2].] That oppresses (in senses of the vb.).

1611 BIBLE *Zeph.* iii. 1 Woe..to the oppressing citie. **1649** LILBURN *Liberties People Eng.* (ed. 2) title-p., Who, although they have beheaded the King for a Tyrant, yet walk in his oppressingest steps. *a* **1732** T. BOSTON *Crook in Lot* (1805) 129 They prove an oppressing load. **1820** J. BROWN *Hist. Brit. Ch.* I. VII. 228 The oppressing managers. *Mod.* The oppressing hand of sickness.

o'ppressingly, *adv. rare.* [-LY[2].] So as to oppress or be oppressive; oppressively.

1925 *Glasgow Herald* 17 May 7/1 That it [*sc.* the cost] is oppressingly large no one will deny.

oppression (ə'prɛʃən). Also 4–5 **opression**. [a. F. *oppression* (12th c.), ad. L. *oppressiōn-em*, n. of action f. *opprimĕre* to OPPRESS.] The action of oppressing or condition of being oppressed.

1. The action of pressing or weighing down; pressure, weight, burden. (Chiefly *poet.*)

1490 CAXTON *Eneydos* xxvii. 96 The tourment & flagitacyon wherof the see was bette in righte grete violence, by opressions of the shippes, that opressid her in their saillyng. **1593** SHAKS. *Rich. II*, III. iv. 31 Yond dangling Apricocks, Which like vnruly Children, make their Syre Stoupe with oppression of their prodigall weight. **1667** MILTON *P.L.* VIII. 288 There gentle sleep..with soft oppression seis'd My droused sense. **1727–46** THOMSON *Summer* 360 Infant hands..with the fragrant load O'ercharged, amid the kind oppression roll.

2. † **a.** The action of weighing down or bearing heavily on a person, the mind, feelings, etc.; pressure of outward circumstances, or of grief, pain, or trouble; the condition of being pressed hard by misfortune, distress. *Obs.* **b.** The feeling of being oppressed or weighed down; bodily or mental uneasiness or distress.

1382 WYCLIF *Ecclus.* xl. 9 Deth, blod, strif, and two bitende swerd, opressiouns [1388 oppressyngis], hungres, and to-treding, and scourges. *c* **1430** LYDG. *Min. Poems* (Percy Soc.) 69 Over salt mete doth grete oppressioun To fieble stomakes. **1593** SHAKS. *Rich. II*, I. iv. 13 My hart.. taught me craft To counterfeit oppression of such greefe, That word seem'd buried in my sorrowes graue. **1710** STEELE *Tatler* No. 168 ⁋6 He..who performs nothing through the Oppression of his Modesty. **1719** YOUNG *Busiris* IV. i, Fainting beneath th' oppression of her grief. **1748** HARTLEY *Observ. Man* I. ii. 167 Dreams, Agitations, and Oppressions, that Excess in Diet occasions in the Night. **1853** MAURICE *Proph. & Kings* iv. 62 With this oppression ..came the drying up of all the moisture and freshness of life, the parching heat of fever.

3. Exercise of authority or power in a burdensome, harsh, or wrongful manner; unjust

or cruel treatment of subjects, inferiors, etc.; the imposition of unreasonable or unjust burdens.
1340 HAMPOLE *Pr. Consc.* II. 1175 Þe world is..a sted of mykel wrechednes,..Of violence and of oppression. **1386** *Rolls of Parlt.* III. 225/1 Many wronges subtiles, and also open oppressions, ydo to hem. *a* **1420** HOCCLEVE *De Reg. Princ.* 2541 Ministres to seelde hem wel gouerne: Oppressioun regneth in euery herne. **1599** SHAKS. *Hen. V*, II. ii. 172 You would haue sold your King to slaughter,..His Subiects to oppression, and contempt. **1656** STANLEY *Hist. Philos.* IV. (1701) 139/2 She was in danger of oppression by the Magistrates. **1729** BUTLER *Serm. Self-deceit* Wks. 1874 II. 126 There is not a word in our language which expresses more detestable wickedness than *oppression.* **1796** BURKE *Lett., to Hussey* Corr. 1844 IV. 397 You and I hate Jacobinism as we hate the gates of hell. Why? Because it is a system of oppression. **1822** MONTGOMERY *Hymn, 'Hail to the Lord's Anointed'* i, He comes to break oppression, To set the captive free. **1858** FROUDE *Hist. Eng.* III. xiii. 95 The law itself had been made an instrument of oppression.

†**4.** Forcible violation of a woman, rape. *Obs.*
c **1385** CHAUCER *L.G.W.* 1868 *Lucrece*, Openly [he] let cary her on a bere Thurgh al the tovne, that men may see and here The horryble dede of hir oppressyon. *c* **1386** —— *Wife's T.* 33.

†**5.** The action of forcibly putting down or crushing, repression. *Obs.*
c **1385** CHAUCER *L.G.W.* 2591 *Hypermn.*, With Wenus, and other oppressyoun Of houses, Mars hys venym ys adoun. **1545** *Primer Hen. VIII*, Prayers of Passion, That they may..judge..to the oppression of wickedness. **1553** BRENDE *Q. Curtius* D d viij, The Musicans..rebelled, for the oppression of whom, Python was sent thither.

†**6.** *Astron.* Obscuration of the light of a planet or star by proximity to the sun. *Obs.*
1551 RECORDE *Cast. Knowl.* (1556) 196 The darkenynge or hidynge of the starre, whiche chaunce happeneth commonly to any starre being within 15 degrees of the Sonne,..is called of many men Combustion. Other contract the name of combustion to syxe degrees, and call this Oppression.

Hence **o'ppressionist**, one who practises or approves of oppression.
1828 BENTHAM *Wks.* (1843) X. 581 The enemies of the people may be divided into two classes. The *depredationists*, whose love of themselves is stronger than their hatred to others; and the *oppressionists*, whose hatred to others is stronger than their love of themselves.

oppressive (ə'prɛsɪv), *a.* [ad. med.L. *oppressīv-us*, f. ppl. stem of *opprimĕre* to OPPRESS: see -IVE. Cf. F. *oppressif, -ive* (1480 in Godef. *Compl.*).]
1. Of the nature of oppression or tyrannous treatment of subjects, inferiors, etc.; unjustly burdensome, harsh, or merciless; tyrannical.
1627-77 FELTHAM *Resolves* II. lxii. 290 Those sins, that grate, and scratch, and gall,..Plunders, Perjuries, and oppressiue Murthers. **1729** BUTLER *Serm. Self-deceit* Wks. 1874 II. 125 An hard and oppressive course of behaviour.. is most certainly immoral and vicious. **1861** WRIGHT *Ess. Archæol.* I. v. 73 One of the great vices of the Roman rule was the oppressive taxation of the provinces.
2. Characterized by oppressing, disposed to oppress, tyrannical. Also with *of*.
1712 BERKELEY *Pass. Obed.* §41 Calamities and devastations which oppressive governments bring on the world. **1738** WESLEY *Ps.* I. i, The Persecutor's Guilt to share Oppressive in the Scorner's Chair. **1845** S. AUSTIN *Ranke's Hist. Ref.* III. 637 In the Danish cities..there were civic bodies impatient of the yoke of an oppressive aristocracy. **1972** *Times* 10 Mar. 9/1 The art world is so international today that it is not oppressive of a world-renowned art dealer living in France to have an action against him tried in England.
3. Having the quality of oppressing or weighing heavily on the mind, spirits, or senses; burdensome, depressing; overpowering, overwhelming.
1712 STEELE *Spect.* No. 429 ¶12 By reason of his luxuriant Health he is oppressive to Persons of composed Behaviour. **1796** H. HUNTER tr. *St.-Pierre's Stud. Nat.* (1799) III. 113 The maladies of the mind, so oppressive in a state of solitude. **1835** LYTTON *Rienzi* VI. ii, It was a bright, oppressive, sultry morning. **1858** DICKENS *Lett.* (1880) II. 55 My cold has been oppressive. **1880** OUIDA *Moths* II. 160 Paris became very oppressive to her.

o'ppressively, *adv.* [f. prec. + -LY².] In an oppressive manner, crushingly.
1. With unjustly harsh exercise of authority or power; tyrannically.
1769 BURKE *Late St. Nation* 40 Her taxes are more injudiciously and more oppressively imposed. **1832** LEWIS *Use & Ab. Pol. Terms* viii. 68 The rulers govern oppressively. **1860** DICKENS *Uncomm. Trav.* v, I should be very slow to interfere oppressively with Dark Jack.
2. So as to oppress or weigh heavily on the mind, spirits, or senses.
1859 MILL *Liberty* 157 Opinions similar..to these.. prevail widely among the artizan class, and weigh oppressively on those who are amenable to the opinion chiefly of that class. **1894** *Outing* (U.S.) XXIV. 351/1 Although..we were at an altitude of fully ten thousand feet ..it was oppressively hot.

o'ppressiveness. [f. as prec. + -NESS.] The quality or fact of being oppressive.
1701 *Jura Pop. Anglic.* Pref. 5 If upon the account of its Oppressiveness and Illegality, the Voice of the People be everywhere against it. **1863** H. COX *Instit.* I. x. 240 Records of the oppressiveness of their jurisdiction. **1883** SCHAFF *Hist. Ch.* I. vi. 393 The oppressiveness of the Roman yoke increased every year.

†**o'ppressment.** *Obs. rare.* [f. OPPRESS *v.* + -MENT.] Oppression; crushing.
c **1537** in Ellis *Orig. Lett.* Ser. III. III. 78 To the encrease of vertewe and oppressmentt of syne. **1592** WYRLEY *Armorie, Ld. Chandos* 60 Whilst this good king in England made his stay, Him sicknes took with..strong oppresment.

oppressor (ə'prɛsə(r)). Also 5-8 -our, (5 -ur). [a. AF. *oppressour* = F. *oppresseur* (14th c. in Godef. *Compl.*), ad. L. *oppressor*, agent-n. from *opprimĕre* to OPPRESS.]
1. One who oppresses; *esp.* one who harasses with unjust or cruel treatment.
c **1425** LYDG. *Assembly of Gods* 676 Oppressours of pepyll, and myghty crakers. **1432-50** tr. *Higden* (Rolls) II. 251 Nemproth the bostuous oppressor of men. **1531** ELYOT *Gov.* III. iv, He is..a valiaunt man, sauynge that he is an oppressour, an extorcioner. **1621** BACON in *Four C. Eng. Lett.* (Camden) 42, I have been no avaricious oppressor of the people. **1704** POPE *Windsor For.* 74 Th' Oppressor rul'd tyrannic where he durst. **1874** MORLEY *Compromise* (1886) 14 The patriots of Hungary are now in possession of their rights and have become friends of their old oppressors.
2. Anything that oppresses the mind or spirits.
1723 DIGBY *Let. to Pope* 14 Aug., Sickness is a great oppressor.

†**o'ppressure.** *Obs.* [f. OPPRESS *v.* + -URE: cf. It. *oppressura.*] The action of oppressing; oppression; distress, trouble.
c **1600-8** B. JONSON in *Four C. Eng. Lett.* (Camden) 64 You that counsel me to a silence in these oppressures. **1658** CLEVELAND *Rustick Rampant* Wks. (1687) 457 He complains ..of the oppressures of the Commons, of withholding the Wages of poor Labourers. *a* **1670** HACKET *Abp. Williams* II. 222 The Oppressures that in Three and twenty years.. exercis'd the Defence and Patience of one man, made him stand the stronger.

†**oppro'bration.** *Obs. rare.* (In quot. erron. -bation.) [ad. L. *opprobrātiōn-em*, n. of action f. *opprobrāre* to reproach, taunt, f. *ob-* (OB- 1 b) + *probrum* infamous act, infamy.] Reproaching, taunting, reviling.
c **1616** CHAPMAN *Hymn to Hermes* Poems (1875) 296 Such a one In all the art of opprobation As not in all the Deities I have seen. **1623** COCKERAM, *Opprobation*, rebukefull, sprightfull.

†**'opprobratory**, *a.* *Obs. rare*⁻¹. (In quot. erron. -batory.) [f. ppl. stem of L. *opprobrāre*: see -ORY.] Conveying reproach or detraction.
1833 *Fraser's Mag.* VII. 505 Some observation, either approbatory or opprobatory, touching this portico.

†**o'pprobre.** *Obs.* Also 5-6 obprobre, 6 oprobre, opprobe. [a. OF. *ob-*, *opprobre*, *obprobe*, *oprobe* (12th c. in Godef. *Compl.*), ad. L. *opprobrium.*] = OPPROBRIUM, OPPROBRY.
1490 CAXTON *Eneydos* xxvii. 96 She..reputed it to be doon in opprobre and confusion inhomynyouse. **1502** *Ordinary of Crysten Men* (W. de W. 1506) IV. xxii. 296 Hym ..to delyuer from opprobe whan there was place or tyme. **1512** *Helyas* in Thoms *Prose Rom.* (1828) III. 37, I was wel borne in an unhappie houre for to se nowe this obprobre. *c* **1532** DU WES *Introd. Fr.* in Palsgr. 1017 Fulfyller of oprobre & of detraction.

opprobriate (ə'prəʊbrɪeɪt), *v.* [f. med.L. *opprobriāt-*, ppl. stem of *opprobriāre*, f. L. *opprobrium*: see OPPROBRIUM.] *trans.* To cover with opprobrium; to speak abusively or contemptuously of or to. Hence **o'pprobriated** *ppl. a.*
1649 G. DANIEL *Trinarch., Rich. II*, cccxlvi, What they writt Hee Read T' opprobriate himselfe. **1840** *Tait's Mag.* VII. 167 [They] would never dream of thus opprobriating the great names stamped current by the universal voice. **1842** *Ibid.* IX. 563 Known only by his ill repute in the world, —under the opprobriated name of A.O. **1846** MRS. GORE *Eng. Char.* (1852) 42 She will probably come in time to be opprobriated as a coquette.

opprobrious (ə'prəʊbrɪəs), *a.* Forms: 4- opprobrious, (5 obprobryes, 6 obprobrious(e, -yous(e, -yus, 6-7 approbrious, 7 opproprious). [ad. OF. *ob-*, *opprobrieux*, or late L. *opprobriōs-us*, f. L. *opprobrium*: see OPPROBRIUM.]
1. Of words, language, etc.: Conveying opprobrium or injurious reproach; attaching, or intended to attach, disgrace; contumelious, vituperative, abusive. Rarely of persons: Using contumelious or abusive language.
1387 TREVISA *Higden* (Rolls) VII. 167 Prayeng a opprobrious a reprevynge name unto þaym but if they drank. **1483** CAXTON *Gold. Leg.* (1892) 1079 After many obprobryes wordes..they ladde hym forthe vnto a tree. *a* **1548** HALL *Chron., Edw. IV*, 198 b, A man contumelious, opprobrious, and an iniurious person. *Ibid., Hen. VIII*, 144 These with many approbrious wordes, were spoken against the Cardinall. **1602** ROWLANDS *Greene's Ghost* 3 The name of Conicatchers is..vsed for an opprobrious name for euerie one that sheweth the least occasion of deceit. **1715-20** POPE *Iliad* VII. 108 Stern Menelaus first the silence broke, And, inly groaning, thus opprobrious spoke. **1831** MACAULAY *Ess., Hampden* (1887) 228 The multitude pressed round the King's coach, and insulted him with opprobrious cries. **1839** I. TAYLOR *Anc. Chr.* I. IV. 548 The opprobrious epithet, hypocrite..is the world's rough judgment.
†**b.** Of actions, feelings, etc.: Offering or disposed to offer indignity; insulting, insolent. *Obs.*
1630 QUARLES *Div. Poems, Sion's Sonn.* XI. iv, The Bridall bed, which Time, or Age Durst never warrant from th' opprobrious rage Of envious fate. **1701** ROWE *Amb. Step-Moth.* IV. iii, Whom that fell Dog..With most opprobrious Injuries has loaded.
2. Attended by or involving shame or infamy; held in dishonour; associated with disgrace; infamous, shameful, disgraceful. Now *rare.*
c **1510** MORE *Picus* Wks. 15/2 The opprobriouse death of the crosse. **1597** HOOKER *Eccl. Pol.* v. lxxxi. §15 Neither did any thing seeme opprobrious out of which there might arise commoditie and profit. **1667** MILTON *P.L.* I. 403 The wisest heart Of Solomon he led..to build His Temple right against the Temple of God, On that opprobrious Hill. **1784** COWPER *Task* v. 379 Opprobrious more To France than all her losses and defeats,..Her house of bondage,..the Bastille. **1860** PUSEY *Min. Proph.* 81 The reproachful words of the enemies of God are but the echo of the opprobrious deeds of His unfaithful servants.
b. Subject to opprobrium. *rare.*
1804 EUGENIA DE ACTON *Tale without Title* II. 133 To see their emoluments arise from some other source than tithes, the collection of which frequently renders them very opprobrious to their parishioners.

o'pprobriously, *adv.* [f. prec. + -LY².] In an opprobrious manner; with opprobrium.
1. With opprobrious language, abusively.
1494 FABYAN *Chron.* VI. clxxxvi. 187 He rebuked hym otherwyse than was syttynge with his honour, and called hym obprobriously. **1578** *Chr. Prayers* in *Priv. Prayers* (1851) 453 The immaculate Lamb,..who being opprobriously railed at, opened not his mouth. **1645** MILTON *Tetrach.* Introd., It serv'd him..to inveigh opprobriously against the person, branding him with no lesse then impudence. **1761-2** HUME *Hist. Eng.* (1806) V. lxvii. 67 The king, whom they opprobriously called the Black Bastard. **1843** J. MARTINEAU *Chr. Life* (1867) 184 The world (as divines opprobriously term it). **1855** MACAULAY *Hist. Eng.* xvii. IV. 82 He had, at Versailles, spoken opprobriously of the Irish nation.
†**2.** In a way involving shame or disgrace; with indignity, contumeliously, ignominiously. *Obs.*
1602 T. FITZHERBERT *Apol.* 39 The Iewes finding it [an image of Christ], vsed it most opprobriously, & pearced it with a lance. *a* **1682** SIR T. BROWNE *Tracts* (1684) 105 The Fish, whereby Fornicatours were so opprobriously and irksomely punished.

o'pprobriousness. [f. as prec. + -NESS.] The quality or fact of being opprobrious; reproachfulness, scurrility; †opprobrium, shame, disgrace.
a **1540** BARNES *Wks.* (1573) 344/1 A righteous man is better that hath none Images, for he shall be free from obprobriousnes. *c* **1540** *Pilgr. T.* 368 in *Thynne's Animadv.* (1875) App. i, Oure closters ner farmeris,..wher we were wont to work the workes of falsnes, is now obiect to oure opprobryusnes. **1711** SHAFTESB. *Charact.* III. *Misc.* v. iii. The Opprobriousness and Abuse of those naturally honest Appellations of Free-Livers, Free-Thinkers, Latitudinarians.

†**o'pprobrity.** *Obs. rare*⁻¹. [f. OPPROBROUS + -ITY.] = prec.
1751 *Female Foundling* I. 53 It is by Ignominies and Opprobrity that your Redeemer calls you to himself.

opprobrium (ə'prəʊbrɪəm). [a. L. *ob-*, *opprobrium* disgrace, infamy, reproach; abusive language or word; cause of reproach, f. *ob-*, *opprobrāre* to reproach, taunt: see OPPROBRATION.]
1. The disgrace or evil reputation attached to conduct considered shameful; the imputation or expression of this disgrace; infamy, reproach.
1683 J. SCOTT *Serm. bef. Ld. Mayor* Wks. 1826 IV. 86 Persecuted with all the reproach and opprobrium that the most inveterate rancour can invent. **1696** PHILLIPS (ed. 5), *Opprobrium*, a Latin word become English, the Shame that sticks continually to a leud and vicious Act. **1769** *Junius Lett.* xxix. 134 [He] will assert his natural right to the modesty of the quotation, and leave all the opprobrium to his grace. **1858** BUCKLE *Civiliz.* (1869) II. viii. 573 Spain.. has been plundered and oppressed, and the opprobrium lights on the robbers, not on the robbed. **1862** TROLLOPE *Orley F.* xxvii, Great opprobrium has been thrown on her name.
2. An occasion or cause of reproach or reprobation; something that brings disgrace.
1656 in Clarendon *Hist. Reb.* xv. §113 That opprobrium of Mankind..who now calls himself our Protector. **1704** F. FULLER *Med. Gymn.* (1711) 140 This Distemper..is become the Opprobrium both of the Patient and Physician. **1861** TULLOCH *Eng. Purit.* I. 45 The May-pole..on the village green became a standing opprobrium to his conscience. **1869** J. MARTINEAU *Ess.* II. 253 A maxim absolutely groundless..the opprobrium of philosophy.

†**o'pprobrous**, *a.* *Obs. rare*⁻¹. [a. OF. *ob-*, *opprobreux*, *-euse* (15th c. in Godef.), f. *opprobre*: see OPPROBRE and -OUS.] = OPPROBRIOUS.
c **1530** *Remedie of Loue* xli, That opprobrous name cokold.

†**o'pprobry.** *Obs.* Forms: 5-6 obprobry(e, 5-7 opprobrie, 5-8 opprobry, (7 appropry); also 6 opprobie, 6-7 opproby. [ad. L. *ob-*, *opprobrium*: see OPPROBRIUM.]
1. A condition of infamy, shame, disgrace, or reproach; = OPPROBRIUM 1.
1432-50 tr. *Higden* (Rolls) IV. 365 Gaius putte Pilate to exile in to Vienna of Fraunce..in opprobry of his kynrede, for he was borne in those partes. **1542** BECON *Pathw. Prayer* in *Early Wks.* (Parker Soc.) 132 In like manner Anne, the

wife of Helcana..prayed God that he would take away from her the opprobry and shame, and give her children. **1597** BEARD *Theatre God's Judgem.* (1612) 98 By the just vengeance of God he was abased lower than hell, and put in euerlasting shame and opprobrie. **1656** EARL MONM. tr. *Boccalini's Advts. fr. Parnass.* 172 That those nobly descended Souldiers may be freed from that shameful opprobry. **1732** *Hist. Litteraria* IV. 122 Not being able to endure the Opprobry of so infamous a Name.

2. The imputation of shameful or infamous conduct; the utterance of contumelious reproach.

1432–50 tr. *Higden* (Rolls) VIII. *Harl. Contin.* 469 The kynge rehersede mony wordes of obprobry to the archebischop. **1491** CAXTON *Vitas Patr.* (W. de W. 1495) v. xiv. 344 a/1 He..concluded in hym selfe..to endure pacyently all Iniuryes and obprobryes that he wolde saye to hym. **1535** *Goodly Primer* Dirige Ps. xlii, They cast into my teeth this grievous opprobry. **1667** *Naphtali* (1761) 201 The curate had calumniated him by such vile opprobies. **1702** C. MATHER *Magn. Chr.* VI. vi. (1852) 432 Some have not scrupled to stigmatize the Indians with greatest opprobry. **1765** JOHNSON *Notes Shaks.* Mids. N.D. III. ii. 9 Patch was in old language used as a term of opprobry.

b. Contumelious treatment; an indignity, insult.

1569 STOCKER tr. *Diod. Sic.* I. xix. 29 He dyd him all the opprobries he knewe or could deuise. **1617** *French Jubile* 5 What French-man was there, whose heart did not bleed to see these opprobies?

3. An occasion, cause, or object of reproach; 'a reproach', 'a disgrace'; = OPPROBRIUM 2.

1535 *Goodly Primer* Prayer of Daniel, Jerusalem and thy people are brought into an opprobry to all that dwell round about us. **1650** EARL MONM. tr. *Senault's Man bec. Guilty* 254 Poverty is no more the opprobrie of men, but the glory of Christians. **1675** J. SMITH *Chr. Relig. App.* II. 18 Hyperbolus..whom Pliny, Thucidides, and Lucian report to have been banish'd the City as its disgrace and opprobry.

b. Conduct that brings or merits infamy or disgrace; a shameful act.

1563–87 FOXE *A. & M.* (1596) 283/1 They cannot doo too much to detect your so detestable opprobrie. **1599** *Broughton's Let.* v. 17 He is fallen into Chams opprobrie, accusing his father. **1795** SOUTHEY *Joan of Arc* III. 89 Doom'd to be the scene of blacker guilt, Opprobry more enduring, crimes that call'd For heavier vengeance.

oppugn (ə'pjuːn), *v.* Also 6 **oppung, opponge,** 7 **opugn.** [ad. L. *oppugnāre* to fight against, attack, assail, besiege, f. *ob-* (OB- 1 b) + *pugnāre* to fight. Cf. obs. F. *oppugner* (16th c. in Godef.).]

†**1.** *trans.* To fight against, attack, assail, assault, besiege. *Obs.*

1432–50 tr. *Higden* (Rolls) III. 269 Furius Camillus oppugnede the walles in an oþer parte of the cite. **1563–87** FOXE *A. & M.* (1596) 220/2 This Town of Achon..as it was mightilie oppugned by the Christians, so it was stronglie defended by the Saracens. **1597** BEARD *Theatre God's Judgem.* (1612) 174 He was induced..to oppugne the Emperor Henry by armes. **1643** PRYNNE *Sov. Power Parl.* III. 3 The Parliament..may not onely lawfully resist, but oppugne, suppresse all Forces raised against it. **1860** MRS. BROWNING *Italy & World* xii, That nation still is predominant Whose pulse beats quickest in zeal to oppugn or Succour another, in wrong or want.

†**b.** To withstand, resist (attack). *Obs. rare*$^{-1}$.

1636 HEYWOOD *Lucrece* III. iv. Wks. 1874 V. 205 The walles made to oppugne Hostile incursions.

2. *fig.* To assail or oppose actively by speech, writing, action, or influence of any kind; *esp.* to call in question (a state of things), controvert (a statement, belief, or the like).

1529 MORE *Dyaloge* IV. ix. 107 b/1 That wolde..so enemyously blaspheme and oppugne yᵉ chyrch of Cryst. **1549** COVERDALE, etc. *Erasm. Par. 2 John* 53 He doeth wittynglye throughe malyce opponge them, whome God woulde well vnto. **1596** DALRYMPLE tr. *Leslie's Hist. Scot.* x. 414 ȝe wald in ane and the same crime oppung the Maiestie of God, and my authoritie. **1634** T. JOHNSON *Parey's Chirurg.* XXVI. xx. (1678) 641 The simple medicine alone, hath not strength enough to oppugn the disease. *a* **1683** SIDNEY *Disc. Govt.* i. §5 (1704) 10 He that oppugns the publick Liberty, overthrows his own. *a* **1734** NORTH *Lives* (1826) II. 54 Then and afterwards he openly oppugned Popery. **1817** COLERIDGE *Biog. Lit.* iii. (1882) 26 In promiscuous company no prudent man will oppugn the merits of a contemporary in his own supposed department. **1882** *Knowledge* No. 16. 334 Inviting the officials whose judgment was oppugned to say whether they were mistaken.

b. Of things: To be opposed to, come in conflict with, run counter to. Now *rare.*

1584 R. SCOT *Discov. Witchcr.* XVI. viii. (1886) 408 Certeine parts thereof..doo not directlie oppugne my purpose. **1615** in *Buccleuch MSS.* (Hist. MSS. Comm.) I. 169 A contract so..unjust, as nothing doth more oppugn the Law of Nature. *c* **1670** HOBBES *Dial. Com. Laws* 62 When Law and Conscience, or Law and Equity seem to oppugne one another, the written Law should be preferr'd.

c. *intr.* and *absol.* To fight, contend, oppose.

1591 *Troub. Raigne K. John* II. (1611) 81 Vnworthy man ..That do'st oppugne against thy mother Church. **1616** R. C. *Times Whistle* 3 Every one..can doe nothing if the prohibition Of the Almighty doe oppugne. **1714** MACKY *Journ. thro' Eng.* (1724) I. viii. 142 A Youth..before he can be a Batchelor of Arts..must publickly oppugn for several Days.

†**3.** *trans.* To prevail upon, win over. *Obs. rare*$^{-1}$.

1596 DALRYMPLE tr. *Leslie's Hist. Scot.* IV. 213 The King of Peychtes..sum of the Peychtes he oppugnes for money, quha figurand thame selfes Britonis, walde..throuch deceit put doun Constantine King of Britannie.

†**4.** To oppose (a statement, argument, or the like) *to* another; to maintain in opposition. *Obs.*

1781 C. JOHNSTON *Hist. J. Juniper* I. 126 To this opinion it is oppugned with equal verisimilitude, that [etc.]. **1849** *Tait's Mag.* XVI. 296/1 Lord Kaimes thinks it sufficient to oppugn that musical proportions and those of architecture are addressed to different senses.

Hence **o'ppugning** *vbl. sb.*, attacking, assailing.

1535 [see OPPUGNER]. **1611** CORYAT *Crudities* 460 Martin Luthers oppugning of the venale indulgences. **1654** EARL MONM. tr. *Bentivoglio's Warrs Flanders* 183 Trenches may easily be made, or any thing else which the necessity of oppugning requires.

oppugnance (ə'pʌgnəns). [ad. late L. *oppugnāntia*, f. L. *oppugnānt-em* OPPUGNANT: see -ANCE.] The fact or action of oppugning or opposing; opposition; oppugnancy.

1855 MILMAN *Lat. Chr.* III. v. I. 355 The conflicting decisions of the lawyers, the oppugnance of the laws themselves seemed to demand this ultimate organisation of the whole. *Ibid.* VII. ii. (1864) IV. 63 The decrees were received with the most vigorous or stubborn oppugnance.

oppugnancy (ə'pʌgnənsɪ). [f. as prec.: see -ANCY.] The quality or state of being oppugnant; opposition, antagonism, contrariety, conflict.

1606 SHAKS. *Tr. & Cr.* I. iii. 111 Vn-tune that string, And harke what Discord followes: each thing meetes In meere oppugnancie. **1711** SHAFTESB. *Charac.* (1737) III. VI. v. 373 Such a Confusion, Oppugnancy, and Riot of Colours. **1824** COLERIDGE *Aids Refl.* (1848) I. 227 Whatever is placed in active and direct oppugnancy to the good is, *ipso facto*, positive evil. **1892** W. WATSON in *Academy* 9 Apr. 341/2 Involving no strife of ideas, no oppugnancy of principles.

oppugnant (ə'pʌgnənt), *a.* (*sb.*) [ad. L. *oppugnānt-em*, pr. pple. of *oppugnāre* to OPPUGN.] Opposing, antagonistic, contrary, repugnant.

1513 BRADSHAW *St. Werburge* II. 1868 To infringe theyr fraunchis..By fals recordes oppugnant to ryght. **1651** WITTIE tr. *Primrose's Pop. Err.* I. iv. 12 From thence we may gather, that the curing of diseases in it self..is not oppugnant to the Ecclesiasticall office. **1751** WARBURTON *Notes Pope* III. 86 By overthrowing the oppugnant principle of *no natural justice.* **1890** *Q. Rev.* Oct. 294 One to whom anything approaching inaccuracy and unthoroughness were ..oppugnant.

B. *sb.* One who opposes, an opponent. *rare.*

a **1834** COLERIDGE in *Lit. Rem.* (1838) III. 165 A new sect naturally..sets another portion into activity as alarmists and oppugnants.

†**o'ppugnate,** *v. Obs. rare.* [f. ppl. stem of L. *oppugnāre* to OPPUGN.] = OPPUGN.

1749 LAVINGTON *Enthus. Meth. & Papists* II. (1754) 90 We have a List of those upon whom the Judgments of God ..fell for oppugnating St. Francis and his Order. **1804** FESSENDEN *Democr.* (1806) II. 35 Will e'er oppugnate this morality Of such a pretty genteel quality.

oppug'nation. Now *rare.* [ad. L. *oppugnātiōn-em*, n. of action f. *oppugnāre* to OPPUGN. Cf. obs. F. *oppugnation, -cion* (16th c. in Godef.).]

1. The action of attacking or assaulting; attack, assault.

1533 BELLENDEN *Livy* IV. (1822) 341 To defend the vane oppugnacioun and segeing of thare wallis. **1586** FERNE *Blaz. Gentrie* 129 To the oppugnacion of Turkishe and infidell enemyes. **1654** EARL MONM. tr. *Bentivoglio's Warrs Flanders* 185 Hither was the greatest bulk of the oppugnation brought.

2. *fig.* Opposition in spirit, word, argument, or manner of action.

1553 T. WATSON in Crowley *Soph. Dr. Watson* ii. (1569) 78 To the oppugnation of it they neuer yet to this houre alledged any direct scripture. **1610** BP. HALL *Apol. Brownists* xxx. 75 [They] spend their liues and labours in oppugnation of him. **1716** M. DAVIES *Athen. Brit.* II. 387 An open and profess'd Contradiction or Oppugnation. **1795** J. SULLIVAN *Hist. of Maine* 54 The Spaniards and Portuguese..considered all attempts of this nature..as a vile oppugnation of ecclesiastical authority. **1874** H. W. BEECHER in *Chr. World Pulpit* V. 393 Do you think I feel oppugnation toward them?

†**oppugnator.** *Obs. rare*$^{-0}$. [a. L. *oppugnātor*, agent-n. from *oppugnāre* to OPPUGN: cf. obs. F. *oppugnateur* (1488 in Godef.).] = next.

1611 COTGR., *Oppugnateur*, an oppugnator; assaulter, batterer, besieger; resister; wrong-doer.

oppugner (ə'pjuːnə(r)). [f. OPPUGN + -ER[1].] One who oppugns; an assailant, opposer, opponent.

1535 G. BROWNE *to Ld. Privy Seal* in *Hist. Coll. Ch. Irel.* (1681) 2 Your humble Servant..hath endeavoured..to procure the Nobility and Gentry of this Nation to due obedience, in owning of his Highness their supream Head as well Spiritual as Temporal, and do find much oppugning therein, especially by my Brother Armagh, who hath been the main oppugner. **1599** SANDYS *Europæ Spec.* (1632) 217–8 The Græcians are..perpetuall oppugners of the Papall right and authority. **1641** EARL MONM. tr. *Biondi's Civil Warres* v. 161 Whilest the oppugners and defendors were in their chiefest heate, the Lord Talbot came thither with the Lord Scales and 1800 Souldiers. **1791** BENTHAM *Panopt.* 130[They would] find more advocates among the patrons, than among the oppugners, of that measure. **1853** MERIVALE *Rom. Rep.* i. (1867) 10 The tribuneship.. afforded..a ground of vantage to the oppugners of rank and authority.

oppurtenance, opreption, erron. ff. APPURTENANCE, OBREPTION.

oppynyon, -oun, etc., obs. ff. OPINION.

opress(e, obs. f. OPPRESS.

opright, -riȝt, -ryȝt, oprising, oprist: see UP-.

oprobre: see OPPR-.

opry ('ɒprɪ), representation of a U.S. dial. pronunc. of OPERA; also *attrib.* ***Grand Ole Opry***: a concert of country music broadcast on radio from Nashville, Tennessee; the type of music performed there.

Grand Ole Opry is registered as a proprietary name in the U.S.

1914 R. GRAU *Theatre of Science* 23 The local manager could not see any future in exhibiting films, so he went back to the town where he had his 'op'ry house'. **1950** *Official Gaz.* (U.S. Patent Office) 18 Apr. 723/1 WSM, Incorporated, Nashville, Tenn. Grand Ole Opry. For radio program broadcasting services. **1957** *Time* 15 Apr. 49/1 Donegan..often..sounds like *Grand Ole Opry* cornball recorded at 33⅓ r.p.m. played at 78. **1961** A. BERKMAN *Singers' Gloss. Show Business* 64 *Opry*,..opera. **1968** *Rolling Stone* 24 Aug. 17/3 Roy Acuff tried unsuccessfully to give the audience a taste of Grand Ole Opry. He was too corny for most people's taste. **1974** *New Yorker* 6 May 46/1 They asked me where I was going. I said, To Nashville to see the Grand Ole Opry. Friday is the last show..before the Opry moves out to Opryland U.S.A. **1976** *Time* 27 Sept. 98/1 For the mass market, cruder Southern products flooded the land: hillbilly music, gospel music, the Grand Ole Opry. **1977** *Parade* (*Washington Post*) 9 Oct. 12/3 Grand Ole Opry began in 1925 almost incidentally, when Nashville station WSM put on an hour-long program featuring a country fiddler named Uncle Jimmy Thompson. The show happened to follow a broadcast of Walter Damrosch's music appreciation hour from New York, so announcer George D. Hay started out by saying: 'For the past hour you've listened to grand opera, now you're going to hear some grand *ole* opry.'

ops. (= military operations): see OP[3] 1 b.

opseche: see UP-.

opsigamy (ɒp'sɪgəmɪ). *rare.* [ad. Gr. ὀψιγαμια, f. ὀψίγαμ-ος late-married, f. ὀψέ, ὀψι- late + γάμος marriage.] Marriage late in life.

1824 MCCULLOCH *Scotland* III. 287 Nor is there any danger of Donald's being flogged for opsigamy by the Highland nymphs as the Spartans were of old.

'opsimath. [ad. Gr. ὀψιμαθής: see next.] One who begins to learn or study late in life.

1883 *Ch. Times* 9 Feb. 97 Those who gave the name were not simple enough to think that even an opsimath was not something better than a contented dunce. **1883** *Sat. Rev.* 3 Feb. 159/1[He] is what the Greeks called an *opsimath*; not ignorant, but a laggard in learning.

opsimathy (ɒp'sɪməθɪ). *rare.* [ad. Gr. ὀψιμαθία, f. ὀψιμαθής late in learning, f. ὀψέ, ὀψι- late + μάθη learning.] Learning or study late in life; learning acquired late.

a **1656** HALES *Gold. Rem.* (1673) I. 218 Therefore Opsimathie, which is too late beginning to learn, was counted a great vice, and very unseemly. **1656** in BLOUNT *Glossogr.* **1872** F. HALL *Rec. Exempl. False Philol.* 73 Whatever philological learning he possesses is..in all seeming, the latest of opsimathies. **1889** *Harper's Mag.* Sept. 508/2 The figures alone betray the inevitable weakness of opsimathy.

opsin ('ɒpsɪn). *Biochem.* [Back-formation from *rhodopsin* s.v. RHODO-.] A protein liberated from rhodopsin by the action of light.

1951 G. WALD in *Science* 15 Mar. 287/2 Rhodopsin and porphyropsin are carotenoid-proteins—proteins bearing carotenoid prosthenic groups to which they owe their color and sensitivity to light... The protein probably varies from one animal to another; it may be called *opsin*, and named for the animal of origin. **1956** *Nature* 28 Jan. 174/1 When opsin is in excess.., the synthesis of rhodopsin removes neo-*b* retinene almost entirely from solution. **1970** R. W. MCGILVERY *Biochem.* xxvi. 644 The interaction of the conjugated hydrocarbon chain with the opsins creates the particular absorption spectrum of the visual pigments, and therefore the spectral sensitivity of the eye.

opsiometer (ɒpsɪ'ɒmɪtə(r)). [mod. f. Gr. ὄψι-ς sight + -O)METER.] = OPTOMETER.

1842 BRANDE *Dict. Sci.* etc., *Opsiometer*, an instrument for measuring the extent of the limits of distinct vision in different individuals, and consequently for determining the focal lengths of lenses necessary to correct imperfections of the eye. **1888** *Public Opin.* (Washington) 31 Mar., The 'opsiometer' is a new instrument for testing the eyesight. It consists of a mahogany case with two front eyeholes, behind which are two traveling bands mounted on rollers.

‖**opsit** ('ɒpsɪt), *v. S. Afr.* [f. Du. *opzitten* to sit up.] (See quot. 1955.)

1887 RIDER HAGGARD *Jess* viii. 72 How often do you 'opsit' (sit up at night) with Uncle Croft's pretty girl, eh? **1899** —— *Swallow* i. 6 After we had 'opsited' together several times according to our customs, and burnt many very long candles, we were married. **1900** H. A. BRYDEN *From Veldt Camp Fires* 195 Tobias meant to make a bit of a splash today, ..although he was not prepared for the solemnity of an 'opsitting' (that all-night form of courtship, dear to the heart of the Boer). **1913** C. PETTMAN *Africanderisms* 351 *Opsit*.., in Cape Dutch this word is descriptive of the peculiar method of courting which in earlier days was in vogue among the Dutch farming population. **1939** S. CLOETE

Watch for Dawn 377 Why, if you wanted to court her, could you not opsit like a Burger in the sit-Kamer with a candle between you? **1955** W. ROBERTSON *Blue Wagon* xix. 181 'In my young days I had to *opsit* for weeks.' He referred to the Boer custom of two young people sitting up by the light of a candle after the elders had gone to bed. When the candle burned out it was time for the young man to go, and if the girl did not favour him she would produce a candle-end instead of a long one as a hint she preferred his going to his company.

‖**opsomania** (ɒpsəʊˈmeɪnɪə). [mod.L., a. Gr. ὀψομανία, f. ὄψον cooked meat, relish, rich fare, dainties, etc. + μανία madness.] A morbid longing for dainties, or for some particular food. Hence **opsoˈmaniac**, one affected with opsomania.

1842 DUNGLISON *Med. Lex.* (ed. 3), *Opsomaniac*... One who loves some particular aliment to madness. **1857** MAYNE *Expos. Lex.*, *Opsomania*. **1892** *Syd. Soc. Lex.*, *Opsomania*,.. *Opsomaniac*.

†**opsoˈnation**, variant of OBSONATION *Obs.*

1658 in PHILLIPS. **1755** in JOHNSON. Hence in mod. Dicts.

opsonic (ɒpˈsɒnɪk), *a.* *Bacteriology.* [f. as next + -IC.] Of or pertaining to opsonins; produced by or involving opsonins.

1903 [see next]. **1906** *Practitioner* Dec. 750 A doubling of the opsonic index means that the quantity of opsonin present has been increased in a far greater proportion. **1911** G. B. SHAW *Doctor's Dilemma* Pref. p. xxxviii, A few doctors have now learnt the danger of inoculating without any reference to the patient's 'opsonic index' at the moment of inoculation. **1929** TOPLEY & WILSON *Princ. Bacteriol. & Immunity* I. vi. 175 Normal serum loses almost all its opsonic action when diluted 15 times with saline. **1950** C. J. WITTON *Microbiol.* xxii. 297 Opsonic test. If the patient's white blood cells show unusual ability to engulf the bacteria, it indicates the presence of specific opsonins. **1969** H. I. WINNER *Microbiol. in Mod. Nursing* xiii. 154 Yet another serological test, not much used today, is that to determine the opsonic index of a serum. **1972** *Pediatrics* XLIX. 225 (*heading*) Fatal familial Leiner's disease: a deficiency of the opsonic activity of serum complement.

opsonin (ˈɒpsənɪn). *Bacteriology.* Formerly also -ine. [f. L. *obs-*, *opsōn-āre* to buy provisions, cater (f. Gr. ὀψωνεῖν) + -IN[1].] A substance (usu. an antibody) in blood serum which combines with bacteria or other foreign cells and renders them more susceptible to phagocytosis.

1903 WRIGHT & DOUGLAS in *Proc. R. Soc.* LXXII. 366 We may speak of this as an 'opsonic' effect (opsono—I cater for; I prepare victuals for), and we may employ the term 'opsonins' to designate the elements in the body fluids which produce this effect. **1904** [see *saturation experiment* s.v. SATURATION 5]. **1906** *Practitioner* Dec. 750 We know.. that the presence of opsonins is necessary for phagocytosis. **1911** G. B. SHAW *Doctor's Dilemma* 10 Opsonin is what you butter the disease germs with to make your white corpuscles eat them. **1937** R. W. FAIRBROTHER *Text-bk. Med. Bacteriol.* ix. 116 There seems to be little doubt that opsonins are quite distinct from complement. **1950** [see prec.]. **1970** W. H. PARKER *Health & Dis. in Farm Animals* ix. 116 Polymorphs ..will consume many times more bacteria of a particular species if the right opsonin is present, i.e. if the animal concerned is immunised against that species.

Hence **ˈopsonist** (*nonce-word*), an advocate of the therapeutic use of opsonins; **opsoniˈzation**, the process of opsonizing; **ˈopsonize** *v. trans.*, to render (a bacterium or other particle) more susceptible to phagocytosis.

1906 G. B. SHAW *Let.* 18 Nov. (1972) II. 661 A vaccine opsinises [*sic*] your disease germs—to opsinize = à rendre friande—so that the white blood corpuscles pitch into them with an appetite. **1907** *Practitioner* Apr. 581 The hungry phagocyte is supposed to have its diet daintily opsonized for it. **1907** *Science* 13 Sept. 346/1 An alkalinity.. prevented opsonization. **1911** G. B. SHAW *Doctor's Dilemma* Pref. p. xci, Add to the newly triumphant homeopathist and the opsonist that other remarkable innovator, the Swedish masseur. **1936** *Med. Rec.* (N.Y.) CXLIII. 16/1 It seems wise.. to divide the reactions occurring with antigen and antibody into three groups: A. Protective. These include neutralization.., lysis.., killing.. and opsonization. **1970** HARRIS & SINKOVICS *Immunol. Malignant Dis.* i. 6 Antibody may have opsonized the antigen before it reaches the lymph node. **1973** *Sci. Amer.* Nov. 64/3 Antibody and complement render bacteria susceptible to phagocytosis, a process called opsonization.

opsonocytophagic (ˌɒpsənəʊsaɪtəʊˈfædʒɪk), *a.* *Bacteriology.* [f. OPSON(IN + -O + CYTO- + Gr. -φαγία eating (sb.) + -IC.] = OPSONIC *a.*

1910 GLYNN & COX in *Jrnl. Path. & Bacteriol.* XIV. 92 We have expressed the result of comparing the combined action of leucocytes plus serum of two persons by the term Opsono-cytophagic Index. Such an index denotes.. the total phagocytic power of any blood. **1940** SCHAUB & FOLEY *Methods Diagnostic Bacteriol.* viii. 219 The opsonocytophagic test in brucellosis determines the immunity status of the individual toward Brucella. **1950** C. J. WITTON *Microbiol.* xxii. 297 This figure is called the opsonic index, or opsonocytophagic index. *Ibid.* xxv. 338 The presence of antibrucella antibodies.. may be tested by agglutination tests and by opsonocytophagic tests. **1969** WILSON & MIZER *Microbiol. in Nursing Pract.* xix. 447/2 Opsonins also develop, as recognized by tests that demonstrate increased phagocytosis of brucellae in the presence of the patient's serum (opsonocytophagic test).

†**ˈopsony.** *Obs. rare*[−1]. [ad. Gr. ὀψώνιον or L. *opsōnium* (*obs-*) provisions, viands, esp. anything eaten as a relish with bread.] Anything eaten along with bread to give it relish; in ancient Greece and Rome, chiefly applied to fish; = mod.Sc. 'kitchen'.

1657 TOMLINSON *Renou's Disp.* 333 Grateful to eat, and much celebrated in opsonies. [**1881** W. R. SULLIVAN in *Encycl. Brit.* XIII. 257/1 The opsonia were very limited—onions and watercresses.]

opsophagy (ɒpˈsɒfədʒɪ). *nonce-wd.* [ad. Gr. ὀψοφαγία, f. ὀψοφάγ-ος an eater of dainties; f. ὄψον (see OPSOMANIA) + -φάγος eating, eater.] The eating of dainties, esp. of fish. So **opˈsophagist**, an eater of dainties; **opˈsophagize** *v. intr.*, to eat dainties.

1854 BADHAM *Halieut.* 331 A favourite *mets* at most opsophagists' tables. *Ibid.* 519 Opsophagy again was necessarily confined to the rich. *Ibid.*, At Corinth.. the law enacted that none should 'opsophagize' but such as could prove their income sufficient to support the extravagance.

opster (ˈɒpstə(r)). *U.S.* [f. OP[4] + -STER.] A practitioner of op art. *Temporary.*

1965 *Sat. Rev.* (U.S.) 29 May 29/3 It would seem that two older artists have been curiously misunderstood—Albers by the 'opsters' and Duchamp by the 'popsters'. **1967** *N.Y. Times* 18 Mar. 25 The intricate light-and-shadow wall reliefs of the opster Ben Cunningham.

opstropolous, erron. f. OBSTREPEROUS *a.*

opt (ɒpt), *v.* [ad. F. *opte-r* to choose, ad. L. *optāre* to choose, wish, desire: cf. *adopt*.]

1. *intr.* To choose, make choice (*between* alternatives); to decide (*for* one or other of two alternatives).

1877 *World* 25 Apr., The Paris correspondent of the *Times*, about a month ago.. was allowed to speak of Alsatians *opting* between France and Germany. **1879** SALA *Paris Herself Again* I. x. 151 He was supposed to be a native of Alsace-Lorraine, who had 'opted' to become a French subject. **1885** *Pall Mall G.* 31 Jan. 8/2 If.. returned for more than one borough he should be permitted to opt for the borough of Northampton. **1890** GLADSTONE in *Leeds Mercury* 25 July 7 The present Heligolanders opting to be British subjects. **1899** *Speaker* 15 Apr. 433/1 The two boys 'opted' for the Navy.

2. Phr. *to opt out of*: to choose not to do or participate in (something); also *absol.* So, **opter-out**, one who opts out (of something). Hence phr. *to opt into*: to choose to do or participate in something; also *absol.* as *to opt in*. See also OPTING *vbl. sb.*

1922 [see OPTING *vbl. sb.*]. **1951** *Ann. Reg. 1950* 82 It became clear that many of the older and larger schools.. were likely to opt out [of the Education Act]. **1966** 'A. HALL' *9th Directive* i. 12 A man wants to opt out; they have to give him an incentive that will make him opt in again. **1966** *Maclean's Mag.* 20 Aug. 43 Morgan has no cures for society so he opts out, even if his Mum does call him a class traitor. **1968** *Globe & Mail* (Toronto) 17 Feb. 1/1 Pierre Trudeau opted into the Liberal leadership race yesterday. **1968** *Listener* 20 June 790/3 But the problem is compounded if one section of the affluent majority now decides to avert its eyes from the whole sordid business of material betterment. The opters-out may not realise it, but they will make it harder to remove the remaining pockets of real poverty. **1970** *New Scientist* 30 Apr. 226/1 It is clearly impossible for the UK to opt out of the microelectronics race. **1971** 'G. BLACK' *Time for Pirates* v. 85, I looked at the princely opter-out conscious of how much I liked him. **1973** C. BONINGTON *Next Horizon* xii. 174, I did not intend to go to the top, having already opted out on grounds of risk. **1976** *Country Life* 26 Feb. 496/3 Her group of rather dim students.. are all determined pre-adolescents. Neither drop-outs, nor opter-outs, they have simply refused to opt in. **1977** *Church Times* 29 Apr. 2/4 The OCU said that mercy-killing extended to cases in which there was no dissent from the victim was even more permissive than the recommendations of voluntary euthanasia Bills—'in these at least the victim has to 'opt in' to be killed. Should these recommendations become law it will not easily be possible to 'opt out' of being killed.'

optable (ˈɒptəb(ə)l), *a.* [ad. L. *optābil-is*, f. *optāre*: see prec. and -BLE.] To be wished for, desirable.

1569 NEWTON *Cicero's Olde Age* 54b, After death, the sence is eyther suche as is blessed and optable, or else it is none at all. **1623** in COCKERAM. **1716** M. DAVIES *Athen. Brit.* II. 242 Furnish'd with even such an Ideal, optable or designable Arianizing Library.

Hence **ˈoptableness**; **ˈoptably** *adv.*, desirably.

1657 TOMLINSON *Renou's Disp.* 497 With this [method].. their Theorems [are] more optably read, and easily learned. **1727** BAILEY vol. II, *Optablenes*, desirableness.

Optacon (ˈɒptəkɒn). Also **optacon**. [f. OP(TICAL *a.* + TA(CTILE *a.* + CON(VERTER.] A device for enabling a blind person to recognize printed characters by touch, the fingertip being placed on an array of many tiny rods certain of which vibrate in accordance with the pattern of light from the characters.

1970 *N.Y. Times* 24 July 33/2 Another technique—that of turning symbols and letters into touch—has also become a practical reality recently because of a light-weight, portable transistor device developed by Prof. John Linvill.. and Prof. James Bliss... This device, called the Optacon, consists of a tactile stimulator and an optical scanner, connected together electronically. **1973** *Times* 26 May 16/5 Mr Richard Dufton, director of research for St Dunstan's, said.. that the Optacon imposed a severe learning task because the reader's right hand had to track the camera accurately across the page, picking up the print letter by letter. **1975** *Telegraph* (Brisbane) 18 May 22/3 The optacon is being used successfully in Washington, U.S., by a blind radio announcer.

optain(e, obs. erron. form of OBTAIN.

optant (ˈɒptənt). [G. and Da. *optant*, f. L. *optant-*, *optans*, pr. pple. of *optāre* to choose.] A person who, when the territory of which he is a citizen changes its sovereignty, has a choice between retaining his former citizenship, and accepting a new one.

1914 W. R. PRIOR *North Sleswick under Prussian Rule* 9 Nearly 40,000 of the Sleswick Danes had become optants... The peril to which their optant relatives and neighbours were exposed. **1927** *Daily Tel.* 8 Mar. 11/5 This arbitral tribunal pronounced in favour of the Hungarian optants. **1930** *New Statesman* 10 May 138/2 Both sides have made considerable concessions, especially with regard to the difficult problem of the dispossessed Hungarian optants. **1937** V. BARTLETT *This is my Life* x. 143 The Hungarian optants—Hungarians in Transylvania who had the right to choose between Hungarian and Roumanian nationality after the territory had been transferred to Roumanian rule.

optate (ˈɒpteɪt), *v. rare.* [f. L. *optāt-*, ppl. stem of *optāre* to choose.] *intr.* To choose: = OPT.

1611 COTGR., *Opter*, to chuse, optate, elect. **1694** MOTTEUX *Rabelais* v. (1737) 231 O most infaust who optates there to live! **1895** *Tablet* 28 Dec. 1029 He optated for this title in exchange for that of San Callisto at the recent public Consistory.

optation (ɒpˈteɪʃən). [ad. L. *optātiōn-em* a wishing (also in rhetorical sense), n. of action from *optāre* (see OPT). Cf. F. *optation*, in rhetoric.]

1. a. The action of wishing; a wish or desire. **b.** *Rhet.* The expression of a wish under the form of an exclamation.

1577 PEACHAM *Gard. Eloquence* Piij, To this.. belong.. Optation, Obtestation, Interrogation. **1609** R. BARNERD *Faithf. Sheph.* 67 Optation; when we fall to wishing, to declare our desire and good will towards them: it procureth good will. **1646** SIR T. BROWNE *Pseud. Ep.* 48 Regulating their determined realityes unto their private optations. **1651** BIGGS *New Disp.* 200 To which she hath had a strong optation. **1922** E. POUND *Let.* 4 May (1971) 177 As you have been so explicit in yr. optation of undisturbed solitude I hesitate to offer to prolong my sojourn in Italy.

2. A choice or preference.

1874 WARD *Ess.* (1884) I. 290 His inclination towards the immediate leaving school may be called (if you will) an 'optation'; but it cannot be called a desire.

optative (ˈɒptətɪv, ɒpˈteɪtɪv), *a.* and *sb.* [a. F. *optatif*, *-ive* (15th c. in Littré), ad. late L. *optātīv-us*, f. *optāre* to wish: see -ATIVE. The first pronunciation above is the normal one (cf. *ablative*, *precative*, *relative*), recognized by orthoepists generally, but the second prevails in Eng. grammar school and college use.]

A. *adj.* **1.** *Grammar.* Having the function of expressing wish or desire.

optative mood or ***mode***, *optātīvus modus* of the Latin grammarians, Priscian, etc., representing εὐκτικὴ ἔγκλισις (ἡ εὐκτική, τὸ εὐκτικόν) of the Greek grammarians: That mood or form of the verb, of which a prominent function is the expression of wish or desire, as in Gr. μὴ γένοιτο, 'may it not happen!' It is an original feature of the vb. in Aryan or Indo-European (where its sign was the element *iē*, unaccented *ī*, *i*, *j*, inserted between the tense-sign and the personal endings). It is retained most fully in Sanskrit and Greek, and in the so-called Subjunctive of the Teutonic langs. The name has also been applied to syntactical forms expressing the sense of the Greek Optative Mood, as in L. *utinam essem*, *fuissem*.

1530 PALSGR. 84 The optative mode whiche they use whan they wisshe a dede to be done, as *bien parle il*, wel speke he or well myght he speke. *Ibid.* 85 The optative mode borroweth also his II tenses of the subjunctive. **1571** GOLDING *Calvin on Ps.* lx. 6 Some transpose the pretertence of the verb into the optative moode, that it may be a continual prayer. **1603** HOLLAND *Plutarch's Mor.* 1355 Thus you see, how in this little word EI there is an optative power sufficiently declared. **1751** HARRIS *Hermes* I. ii. (1786) 16 To speak Sentences interrogative, imperative, precative, or optative. **1845** STODDART *Grammar* in *Encycl. Metrop.* (1847) I. 53/1 We should not be inclined to separate the optative mood from the imperative, were it not that various Languages, and particularly the Greek, distinguish it by a separate inflection. **1879** ROBY *Lat. Gram.* II. xxi. 282 Use of the subjunctive mood to express desire: Optative and jussive subjunctive.

2. Characterized by desire or choice; expressing desire. **b.** *Rom. Law.* = OPTIVE.

1611 W. SCLATER *Key* (1629) 126 It is eyther optatiue in the wish, or desire of the heart, or occasionall. **1651** HOBBES *Leviath.* I. vi. 29 The language of Vain-Glory, of Indignation, Pitty and Revengefulness, Optative. **1850** MCCOSH *Div. Govt.* III. i. (1874) 264 The Will or Optative Power, choosing or rejecting among the objects presented to the mind. **1875** POSTE *Gaius* I. §154 A guardian nominated by the testator is called a dative guardian; one selected by the widow is called an optative guardian.

B. *sb.* **1.** *Gram.* The optative mood.

1530 PALSGR. Introd. 36 Some want theyr present and indiffinit optatyve, savyng onely the thyrde parson synguler. **1612** BRINSLEY *Pos. Parts* (1669) 31 How know you the optative? *A.* It wisheth or desireth. **1614** T. ADAMS in Spurgeon *Treas. Dav.* Ps. cxix. 4, 5 [Verse 4] is God's imperative.. [Verse 5] this should be our optative. **1869** J. EADIE *Galatians* 108 The first verb in the present subjunctive, where perhaps an optative might have been expected.

†**2.** Something to be desired, a desirable thing.

1605 BACON *Adv. Learn.* II. viii. §3 That by these optatives and potentials mans enquirie may be the more awake. **1703** T. S. *Art's Improv.* p. xiii, By Optatives is to be understood, all those Perfections, that being desirable, are rather very difficult, than absolutely impossible to be obtained.

Hence **optatively** *adv.*, in an optative manner or sense, in expression of a wish; in the optative mood.

1625 J. HALL *Thanksgiv. Serm. 29 Jan.*, God blesseth man imperatively, and man blesseth God optatively. **1657** TRAPP *Comm. Job* xvi. 4 Some read it optatively, as.. Would to God your soul were in my souls stead. **1832** *Fraser's Mag.* VI. 291 They all, *unâ voce*, declaratively or optatively, condemned the conduct of the council. **1890** *Blackw. Mag.* CXLVIII. 88/1 The only persons even optatively addicted to it belong to a species of miser vanished long since.

optayne, -teigne, etc., obs. ff. OBTAIN.

optic ('ɒptɪk), *a.* and *sb.* Forms: (6 obtyke, 7 obtick), 6–7 opticke, -ike, 6–8 -ique, 7–8 -ick, 7– optic. [a. F. *optique* (*obtique*, *c* 1300 in Littré) = OIt. *optico*, It. *ottico*, ad. med.L. *opticus* (see Note to sense 2), a. Gr. ὀπτικ-ός of or pertaining to sight, f. ὀπτός seen, visible, f. stem ὀπ- (cf. ὄψ, ὀπ- eye, face, ὄψομαι I shall see, etc.).

1656 BLOUNT *Glossogr.* To Rdr., There is a liberty in most Adjectives, whether you will say *Optique* (after the French), *Optick*, *Opticous*, or *Optical*.]

A. *adj.* **1.** Of or pertaining to sight; visual. (Now *rare* or *Obs.* in general sense.)

1599 B. JONSON *Ev. Man out of Hum.* II. iii, Dazle, you organs to my optique sense. **1616** BULLOKAR *Eng. Expos.*, *Optike*, belonging to the sight. **1637** HEYWOOD *Dial.* xviii. Wks. 1874 VI. 249, I hardly can withdraw myne Optick sence. **1657** TRAPP *Comm. Job* ix. 11 God is all window, and he, like the Optike vertue in the eye, seeth all, and is seen of none. **1805** T. HARRAL *Scenes of Life* II. 44 His optic senses were somewhat awakened by the brilliant appearance. **1831** CARLYLE *Sart. Res.* III. x, May we not well cry shame on an ungrateful world... which will waste its optic faculty on dried Crocodiles, and Siamese Twins?

2. *Anat.* Pertaining to or connected with the eye as the organ of sight, or with the sense of sight as a function of the brain; esp. in the names of bodily parts or structures. (Also used in *Path.* of diseases affecting, and in *Surg.* of operations performed on, such parts.)

optic chiasm, o. commissure, the commissure of the right and left optic nerves at the base of the brain. **optic cup**, a cup-like depression in the front of the optic vesicle of the embryo; also that in the centre of the optic disc. **optic disc**, the roundish slightly prominent disc on the retina at the entrance of the optic nerve. **optic foramen**, the opening in the sphenoid bone through which the optic nerve passes. **optic ganglion** = *optic lobe* (esp. when small, as in the higher animals). **optic groove**, a groove on the upper surface of the sphenoid bone, in which the optic commissure lies. **optic lobe**, each of the two (right and left) lobes of the dorsal part of the mid-brain, from which in part the optic nerves arise; in lower vertebrates large, and forming two hollow bulbs (*corpora bigemina*); in mammals small, covered in by other parts, and marked each by a cross-furrow, so as to form four protuberances (*corpora quadrigemina*). **optic nerve**, the second cranial nerve on each side (esp. that part in front of the optic commissure), which enters the eyeball and terminates in the retina; they are the nerves of the special sense of sight. **optic neuritis** (*Path.*), inflammation of the optic nerve. **optic neurotomy** (*Surg.*), division of the optic nerve. **optic pad**, an eye-bearing protuberance at the end of an arm of a star-fish. **optic papilla** = *optic disc*. **optic peduncle**, (*a*) *Zool.* the eye-stalk of a crustacean (= OPHTHALMITE 2); (*b*) *Embryol.* the narrow tube connecting the *optic vesicle* with the fore-brain, from which the *optic tract* is developed. †**optic sinew**, old name for the optic nerve. **optic stalk** = *optic peduncle* (*a* and *b*); also the ommatophore of a snail or other mollusc. **optic thalamus**, each of two large masses of nerve-matter in the brain, one on each side of the third ventricle, lying upon the *crura cerebri*, and forming with the *corpora striata* the basal ganglia of the brain; from them in part the optic nerves arise. **optic tract**, that part of the optic nerve between its origin in the brain and the optic commissure. **optic tubercle**, each of the *corpora quadrigemina* (see *optic lobe* above). **optic vesicle**, a vesicle connected with the fore-brain of the embryo, from which the optic nerve and retina are developed.

[The earliest of these is *optic nerves* (in 16th c. *optique sinews*), OF. *les ners obtiques* (*c* 1300), med.L. *nervi optici*: cf. 1100–25 ADELARD OF BATH c. xxiii Habet autem [spiritus visibilis] egressum per diversos nervos concavos, quos Greci vocant opticos; also *a* 1300 in ROGER BACON.]

1541 R. COPLAND *Guydon's Quest. Chirurg.* E iij, Wherfore are the synewes obtykes perced? Answere. For to be the waye of the spyryte vysyble. **1543** TRAHERON *Vigo's Chirurg.* I. ii. 3 That they might receave the visible spirite by the synnowe called Optique. [**1548–77** VICARY *Anat.* v. (1888) 37 These senews be called *Nerui optici*.] **1615** CROOKE *Body of Man* 530 The Opticke Nerues stood in neede to bee very short. **1633** P. FLETCHER *Purple Isl.* v. 56 *note*, The eye hath two nerves, the Optick or seeing nerve, and moving. **1717** PRIOR *Alma* I. 34 Two optic nerves, they say, she ties, Like spectacles, across the eyes. **1842** E. WILSON *Anat. Vade M.* (ed. 2) 27 Passing outwards and forwards from the olivary process, are the optic foramina, which transmit the optic nerves and ophthalmic arteries. **1854** OWEN *Skel. & Teeth* in *Circ. Sc.*, *Organ. Nat.* I. 176 The alisphenoids protect the sides of the optic lobes. **1869** TYNDALL *Notes Lect. Light* §275 When light of any particular colour falls upon the eye the optic nerve is rendered less sensitive to that colour. **1872** Optic chiasma, optic commissure [see CHIASMA]. **1876** *Clin. Soc. Trans.* IX. 133 By far the greater number of cases of optic neuritis so complete as this are followed by almost total extinction of vision. **1881** MIVART *Cat* 268 The optic thalami are thickenings in the outer walls of the third ventricle. **1882** *Syd. Soc. Lex.* s.v. *Commissure*, The greater number of the fibres of each optic tract cross in the optic commissure to the opposite optic nerve. **1899** *Allbutt's Syst. Med.* VII. 66 The occurrence of optic atrophy did not escape the observation of Charcot.

3. Of, pertaining to, or skilled in the science of sight and light (optics); = OPTICAL 2, 3. *Obs.* or *arch.*

1569 J. SANFORD tr. *Agrippa's Van. Artes* 34 Nexte after Geometrie, is the Arte Opticke which is called Perspectiue. **1624** WOTTON *Archit.* in *Reliq.* (1672) 26 We have an Optique Rule, that the higher they [Pillars] are,.. the less should be alwayes their diminution aloft. **1635** SWAN *Spec. M.* (1670) 292 The Optick Masters confess and prove that the forms of the Stars are comprehended of the sight reflectly, and not rightly. **1656** BLOUNT *Glossogr.* s.v., The Optick Science is that by which the reason of sight is known. **1709** BERKELEY *Th. Vision* §6 Another way, mentioned by optic writers.

4. Constructed to assist the sight; acting by means of light; = OPTICAL 4. Chiefly in the phrases (now *arch.*) ***optic glass***, a lens, or an instrument having a lens, esp. a telescope; ***optic tube***, a telescope; ***optic square***: see OPTICAL 4.

1607 WALKINGTON (*title*) The Optick Glasse of Humors. **1611** CORYAT *Crudities* Kirchner's Orat. Praise Trav., This Counsellor is like that opticke-glasse wherein not onely the space of three or tenne miles but.. of the whole world it selfe may be represented. *a* **1626** BP. ANDREWES *Serm.* (1856) I. 42 We shall need no prospective glasses, or optic instruments, to make it visible. **1633** P. FLETCHER *Purple Isl.* Ded. Ep., Some Optick-Glasses, if we look one way, increase the object; if the other, lessen the quantity. **1648** BOYLE *Seraph. Love* (1660) 59 A difference resembling that where-with Children and Astronomers consider Galileo's Optick Glasses. **1651** DAVENANT *Gondibert* v. ii. 16 Others with Optick Tubes the Moons scant face.. Attract through Glasses. **1748** LADY LUXBOROUGH *Lett. to Shenstone* 11 Sept., Mr. Sanders speaking of the dimension of his Optic Glasses.. put me in mind of measuring mine. It is near three inches and a half diameter, convex on one side, and flat on the other. **1809** *Farmer's Mag.* X. 489 By means of the optic square.. a right-lined figure of any size can be measured with the utmost accuracy. **1827** POLLOK *Course T.* VI, Survey With optic tube the systems circling round. **1884** *Guardian* 3 Sept. 1293/3 The general.. with whom he was in communication by optic telegraph. **1889** BROWNING *Asolando* Prol. iii, Did you need an optic glass, Which were your choice?

5. Of or pertaining to sight in relation to light, or to light as the medium of sight or generally; = OPTICAL 2.

optic angle, (*a*) the angle between the two lines from the extremities of an object to the eye, being the angle under which it is seen, or the visual angle; (*b*) the angle between the optic axes of the eyes when directed to the same object; (*c*) the angle between the optic axes of a biaxial doubly-refracting crystal. **optic axis**, (*a*) the straight line through the centres of the pupil and crystalline lens, the axis of the eye; (*b*) a line in a doubly-refracting crystal such that a ray of light passing in the direction of it suffers no double refraction.

1664 POWER *Exp. Philos.* I. 80 Take a fresh Eye.. cut it with a plain Parallel to the Optick Axis. **1710** J. CLARKE *Rohault's Nat. Phil.* (1729) I. 247 We turn our Eyes to it in such a manner, that the two Optick Axes meet at the Point which we fix our Attention principally upon. **1727–41** CHAMBERS *Cycl.* s.v. *Angle*, *Visual*, or *Optic angle*, is the angle included between the two rays drawn from the two extreme points of an object to the centre of the pupil. **1781** HERSCHEL in *Phil. Trans.* LXXII. 96 It has been observed, that objects grow indistinct when the principal optic pencil at the eye becomes less than the 40th or 50th part of an inch in diameter. *c* **1790** IMISON *Sch. Art* I. 210 Easy to apprehend, by any person who understands the nature of the optic angle. **1881** *Syd. Soc. Lex.*, *Optic axis*, the axis of the dioptric system of the eye... It is not identical with the visual line or axis. Also, in a doubly refracting crystal, a line which represents a direction in which the double refraction does not occur.

B. *sb.* **1. a.** The organ of sight, the eye: chiefly in *pl.* (Formerly the learned and elegant term; afterwards pedantic, and now usually humorous.)

1620 BRATHWAIT *Five Senses* Table in *Archaica* (1815) II. p. v, By that elevating muscle by which it is distinguished from the optic in all other creatures, it [the eye] is taught to be on that subject only fixed, where it may be wholly and solely satisfied. **1642** HOWELL *For. Trav.* (Arb.) 88 Not by hear-say only, or through the mist of other mens breaths, but through the cleere casements of his own optiques. **1661** GLANVILL *Van. Dogm.* 5 The acuteness of his natural Opticks. **1713** SWIFT *Elegy on Partridge*, Partridge made his opticks rise From a shoe-sole to reach the skies. *a* **1734** NORTH *Lives* (1826) III. 286 He surveyed it with all his optics. **1775–82** J. TRUMBULL *McFingal* I. 67 But optics sharp it needs, I ween, To see what is not to be seen. **1781** COWPER *Truth* 3 Far as human optics may command. **1790** MRS. A. M. JOHNSON *Monmouth* I. 22 Giving that relief in perspective so necessary to the otherwise fatigued optic. **1818** *Q. Rev.* XVIII. 133 *note*, An advantage.. which has escaped the optics of former writers. **1850** HAWTHORNE *Scarlet L.* (1883) II. 80 Yet those same bleared optics had a strange, penetrating power.

fig. *c* **1650** DENHAM *Friendsh. & Single Life agst. Love & Marriage* ii, Our corporeal eyes, we find, Dazzle the optics of our mind. **1790** J. WILLIAMS *Shrove Tuesday* 28 Example clears the optics of the soul. **1844** LD. BROUGHAM *Brit. Const.* viii. (1862) 97 The error common to our moral and our natural optics, of mistaking near objects for great ones.

†**b.** Short for *optic nerve*; *fig.* visual power. *Obs.*

1615 CROOKE *Body of Man* 485 The first coniugation there-fore of the nerues of the braine are the Opticks. **1643** SIR T. BROWNE *Relig. Med.* I. §44 Nor is it in the Opticks of these eyes to behold felicity. **1657** W. RAND tr. *Gassendi's Life Peiresc* II. 97 The Optic, or the middle of the Retina. **1687** *Death's Vis.* (1713) 15 Will He come Teach an Unfledg'd Soul to Fly, To see, without the Opticks of an Eye? **1718** D'URFEY *Grecian Heroine* v. i, On this with covetous Eyes I us'd to gaze, 'till I even crackt their Opticks.

2. †**a.** An 'optic glass'; an eye-glass, lens, magnifying glass; a microscope or telescope. *Obs.*

a **1631** DONNE *Div. Poems, To Mr. Tilman* 46 If then, th' astronomers, whereas they spy A new-found star, their opticks magnify. **1640** NABBES *Bride* IV. i, A.. stone with an inscription That is not legible but through an optick Tells us its age. **1673** *Lady's Call.* II. iii. §16 She that can make her mourning veil an optic to draw a new lover neerer to her sight. **1745** ELIZA HEYWOOD *Female Spect.* No. 17 (1748) III. 268 The telescope was again unscrewed,.. when.. they were obliged to draw in the optic, and make fast the window, against which it had been placed. *c* **1800** K. WHITE *Childhood* II. 109 Which bright through Hope's deceitful optics beam'd. [**1886** *Daily Tel.* 7 Apr. 5/4 One of the two places.. where alone these gigantic 'opticks' can be properly perfected.]

b. *pl.* The optical components of an instrument or apparatus.

1942 J. MITCHELL *Ilford Man. Photogr.* xiv. 297 (*heading*) Optics of the condenser enlarger. **1948** *Rev. Sci. Instruments* XIX. 153/2 Now that better optics and energy detectors are more generally available.. polarization work will undoubtedly increase. **1962** *Analyt. Chem.* XXXIV. 242/2 A double-beam infrared microspectrophotometer employing a double-beam-in-time system and reflecting optics having 8 × magnification. **1972** *Physics Bull.* Mar. 155/2 It is easy to arrange the x ray optics so that the diffracted beams from a selected set of parallel crystal planes form an image of the crystal.

†**3.** One skilled in optics; = OPTICIAN 1. (In quot. 1636, one who has a 'good eye' or well-trained sight.) *Obs.*

1636 FEATLY *Clavis Myst.* xxxi. 410 Artificiall pictures drawne by the pencill of a skilful Opticke. **1656** HEYLIN *Surv. France* 180 A tablet.. such as would infinitely delight an optick. **1675** *Phil. Trans.* X. 501 Mr. Newton had no reason to tax P. Pardies of Hallucination... For that learned optike very well saw [etc.].

†**4.** The science of sight and light; OPTICS. *Obs.* (= F. *optique*, OIt., Sp., Pg. *optica*, It. *ottica*, in 16th c. L. *optica*, sing. fem. as well as pl. neut.)

1611 FLORIO, *Ottica*, the science whereby the reason of sight is knowen, the optike. **1621** BURTON *Anat. Mel.* II. ii. IV. (1651) 279 Arithmetick, Geometry, Perspective, Optick, Astronomy. **1634** PEACHAM *Gentl. Exerc.* III. 140 The extreame parts of a perspicuous body shine and yeeld a more faint light than the middle, as appeareth by Opticke. **1646** SALTMARSH *Some Drops* i. 18 Bringing in Christ by Obtick or sense, and making conversion to be by perspective. **1869** *Eng. Mech.* 17 Dec. 329/1 Can they be explained according to the laws.. of optic and perspective?

5. (Properly with capital initial.) The proprietary name of a device fastened to the neck of a bottle for measuring out spirits, etc.; also ***optic measure***.

1926 *Trade Marks Jrnl.* 22 Sept. 2158 *Optic*, an apparatus included in Class 8, for delivering a measured quantity of Spirits or other Liquids. Gaskell & Chambers Limited. **1953** *Word for Word: Encycl. Beer* (Whitbread & Co.) 27/2 *Optic*, a measuring and dispensing device widely used for spirits. It is usually inserted into the neck of an inverted bottle. **1967** *Guardian* 18 Feb. 3/1 Overnight, with the drop in temperature, a small amount of the alcohol in optics is lost... Now the Licensed Victuallers Association has told the landlords to take the bottles down each morning and allow the liquor in the optics to flow back into the bottle. **1968** 'P. BARRINGTON' *Accessory to Murder* i. 16 Joe, the landlord, was surprised to see him... 'Going to a sale somewhere, then?' he asked genially, holding a small glass under the optic measure. **1968** 'A. HAIG' *Sign on for Tokyo* 58 Joe could see his face reflected in the glass behind the bar, between the spirits bottles on their optic measures. **1970** V. CANNING *Great Affair* xii. 215 A row of shining optics under the whisky and gin bottles. **1974** P. CAVE *Dirtiest Picture Postcard* xiii. 85 She swung at her empty glass, sending it flying across the smooth bar-top to smash against a row of optics.

optical ('ɒptɪkəl), *a.* and *sb.* [f. prec. + -AL[1].]

A. *adj.* **1.** Of, pertaining or relating to, the sense of sight; visual; ocular. (Now chiefly in special connexions, e.g. ***an optical illusion***.) Also *fig.*

In *Astron.* used of double stars which appear so only because the two components are nearly in the same line of sight, as distinguished from those physically connected (binary).

1570 DEE *Math. Pref.* 20 By demonstration Opticall, the ..Cause thereof, is certified. **1723–24** CHAMBERS tr. *Le Clerc's Treat. Archit.* I. 41 The most perfect Arches.. consist of a Semicircle; and the Imposts are usually placed on a level with their Centre. There are some Architects, however, who from an Optical consideration, place them a few Minutes lower. **1794** [see ILLUSION 4]. *c* **1806** D. WORDSWORTH *Jrnl.* (1941) I. 253 Right before us.. were several small single trees.. but some optical delusion had detached them from the land on which they stood, and they had the appearance of.. little vessels sailing along the coast of it. **1812** WOODHOUSE *Astron.* xvii. 184 Divest an observation of any optical or illusory inequality. **1844–57** G. BIRD *Urin. Deposits* (ed. 5) 354 This appearance.. has always appeared to me to be an optical delusion. **1859** *Rep. Brit. Assoc. Adv. Sci. 1858* II. 14 (*heading*) On an apparatus for exhibiting optical illusions of spectral phenomena. **1868** LOCKYER *Elem. Astron.* i. (1879) 20 Optical couples, in which the component stars are really distant from each other, and have no real connection. **1911** *Rep. Labour & Social Conditions in Germany* (Tariff Reform League) III. 193 It may have been an optical illusion, but it certainly did seem to me that Germany was in a state of abounding prosperity. **1922** JOYCE *Ulysses* 370 Looks like a phantom ship. No. Wait. Trees are they? An optical illusion. Mirage. **1937** K. BLIXEN *Out of Africa* v. 386 Between.. the mellow English landscape and the African mountain ridge, ran the path of his life: it is an optical illusion that it seemed to..

swerve—the surroundings swerved. **1961** C. Greenberg *Art & Culture* 77 Flatness may now monopolize everything, but it is a flatness become so ambiguous and expanded as to turn into illusion itself—at least an optical if not, properly speaking, a pictorial illusion. **1971** D. Francis *Bonecrack* xiii. 169 Don't be tempted by the optical illusion that the winning post is much nearer than it really is. **1976** *Times* 20 Feb. 14/4 But it will be said, surely the growth of public spending has..been arrested... Not, alas, so. This is an optical illusion.

2. a. Of or pertaining to sight in relation to the physical action of light upon the eye; hence, Pertaining or relating to light, as the medium of sight, or generally in relation to its physical properties; belonging to optics. Also used with specific reference to visible light as contrasted with other electromagnetic radiation; *spec.* operating in or employing the visible part of the spectrum.

optical axis = *optic axis* (see optic A. 5). **optical centre**, that point in the axis of a lens so situated that all rays passing through it remain unrefracted. **optical density**, (*a*) the degree in which a refractive medium retards transmitted rays of light; (*b*) the logarithm to the base 10 of the opacity.

1570 Dee *Math. Pref.* 48 The chief Science of the Archemaster..is an other (as it were) Optical Science. **1663** Boyle *Usef. Exp. Nat. Philos.* I. 96 An eye thus frozen, may be cut along that which Optical Writers call the Optical Axis, and then it affords an instructive Prospect. **1736** Butler *Anal.* I. i. 29 Common optical Experiments. **1831** Brewster *Optics* ii. §23. 16 The image..cannot be used for any optical purpose. **1869** Tyndall *Notes Lect. Light* §117 Hence the all-important optical law: 'the sine of the angle of incidence divided by the sine of the angle of refraction is a constant quantity'. **1891** W. Abney in *Jrnl. Soc. Chem. Industry* 31 Jan. 20/1 From the colour of the negatives..the photographic and optical densities were very nearly alike. **1953** J. W. T. Walsh *Photometry* (ed. 2) v. 161 The reciprocal of the transmission factor of a plate is sometimes termed the opacity of the plate and the logarithm to base 10 of the opacity is often known as the optical density of the plate. **1958**, etc. [see maser]. **1960** [see laser[2] 1]. **1966** S. D. Rockoff in G. D. Whedon et al. *Progress in Devel. of Methods in Bone Densitometry* 7/1 The mean optical density of the bone, obtained from densitometric scanning of the radiographic image of the bone is expressed in terms of thickness of calibration wedge material which gives the same optical density. **1967** *Listener* 27 Apr. 544/2 Before the radio telescope made its impact..the optical telescopes were able to photograph galaxies. **1970** *Sci. Jrnl.* Mar. 14 The first machine to automate completely one of the important processes of optical astronomy. **1974** *McGraw-Hill Yearbk. Sci. & Technol.* 11/2 The VLA will allow scientists to see, study, and map the radio sky at wavelengths of 1 cm or greater, with detail even greater than that possible for earthbound optical telescopes.

b. Used with reference to electromagnetic radiation other than light, and to beams of particles analogous to light: relating to the transmission of such radiation.

1933 [see *electron-optical* adj. s.v. electron[2] 2b]. **1938** Maloff & Epstein *Electron Optics in Television* i. 38 The electron optical problem of the electron microscope is to obtain electrostatic or magnetostatic lenses of short focal lengths capable of producing high magnifications with low image distortions. **1944** R. A. Sawyer *Exper. Spectroscopy* xi. 277 Infrared spectroradiometers differ from those used in the ultraviolet, or visible, regions chiefly because of the optical characteristics of the infrared region. **1964** *Jrnl. Optical Soc. Amer.* LIV. 15/2 A recent study of optical properties in the extreme ultraviolet.

c. Designating a form of abstract art and visual decoration in which optical effects are used to provide illusions of movement in the patterns produced. Chiefly as ***optical art, artist, painting***, etc. Abbrev. op[4]. orig. *U.S.*

1964 *Time* 23 Oct. 78/1 Preying and playing on the fallibility in vision is the new movement of 'optical art' that has sprung up across the Western world. **1964** *Life* 11 Dec. 133 Op-art is short for 'optical art', a paradoxical movement dedicated to the practice of fascinating deceptions. **1965** *Reporter* (N.Y.) 14 Jan. 46/3 They [*sc.* Israeli artists] do have the beginnings of Pop Art and Op Art (Optical Art). **1965** *Listener* 4 Feb. 196/3 To pass..to the American optical painter Edward Avedisian, and thence to the British Patrick Caulfield, is to realize the impossibility to trying to apply consistent standards to modern art. **1965** *Observer* 28 Feb. 2/6 The occasion was the private viewing of the most important show of the New York art season—an exhibition called 'The Responsive Eye', which has gathered together, for the first time, a comprehensive international collection of optical art. **1965** *New Scientist* 20 May 491 Leaving aside the question of the contemporary fashion for 'optical' painting, Vasarely's work shows—indeed it largely created—two important trends in abstract art today. **1968** N. Weston *Kaleidoscope of Mod. Art* xv. 220 The public has taken to Optical art in a big way, and it has spread rapidly from the art galleries to the Press. **1969** *Time* 7 Feb. 4 The Manhattan optical artist [*sc.* Josef Levi] has devised several new dizzying exercises with illuminated shadow boxes superimposed on black and white perforated metal screens. **1969** *New Yorker* 1 Nov. 12/3 Optical paintings by a leading Latin-American artist. **1970** C. Barrett *Op Art* i. 7/1 The evolution of abstract art was a preliminary step towards the development of optical painting. **1973** J. Lancaster *Introducing Op Art* ii. 28 Optical art is a method of painting concerning the interaction between illusion and picture plane, between understanding and seeing.

3. Treating of, or skilled in, optics.

1570 Dee *Math. Pref.* 48 The Astronomer, and the Opticall Mechanicien. **1605** Camden *Rem.* 203 Pecham that Opticall Archbishop of Canterbury who writte *Perspectiva Communis*. **1704** Norris *Ideal World* II. vii. 359 So..we are told by the optical men. **1815** D. Stewart *Dissert. Progr. Philos.* I. ii. (1858) 132 The various signs of it, enumerated by optical writers.

4. Constructed to assist the sight, or to enable one to see objects otherwise invisible; acting by means of sight or light; devised on the principles of optics. ***optical square***: see quot. 1875.

1610 H. Wotton *Let.* 13 Mar. in L. P. Smith *Life & Lett. Sir H. Wotton* (1907) I. 486 The Mathematical Professor at Padua, who by help of an optical instrument..hath discovered four new planets. *a* **1666** Evelyn *Diary* an. 1641 (1955) II. 64 Those spotts in the Moone, attributed to the seas there &c according to our new Philosophy & the Phænomenas by optical Glasses. **1748** Lady Luxborough *Lett. to Shenstone* 17 Apr., It would give me pain to see St. James's, Vauxhall, Ranelagh &c. &c., represented in so lively a manner as I see them through an optical glass, which I have lately purchased, now that I am absent from them. **1839** G. Bird *Nat. Philos.* 381 Description of Optical Apparatus, and of the Eye considered as an Optical Instrument. **1875** Knight *Dict. Mech.*, *Optical Square*, a reflecting instrument used by surveyors and others for laying off lines at right angles to each other. *Ibid.*, *Optical Telegraph*, a semaphoric telegraph. One whose signals are formed by altering the relative position of its indicators or by differing combinations of colors. **1891** *Anthony's Photogr. Bull.* IV. 100 Nothing has done more to popularize the optical lantern, or magic lantern, as it is more commonly called, than the introduction of mineral oil lamps.

5. ***optical bleach, brightener, white***: a substance applied to textiles which produces a whitening effect by absorbing ultraviolet light and re-emitting it as blue light; so ***optical bleaching, brightening, whitening***.

1947 *Jrnl. Textile Inst.* XXXVIII. A 521 'Optical bleaching' is defined as the physical alteration of a white fabric in such a way as to make it reflect, in addition to white light, a certain amount of blue light, and thereby producing a much 'bluer' and also brighter white than before. **1948** *Amer. Dyestuff Reporter* XXXVII. 432/3 Whereas 'bluings' improve the appearance of white products by absorbing red light, and 'bleaches' improve their appearance by destroying the yellow color, 'optical bleaches' operate on the entirely different principle of transforming ultra-violet and violet radiation into visible blue light. **1959** *Which?* Sept. 107/2 If a detergent with optical white is used on a white fabric too generously or too often, the fabric can get a blue or mauve tint which is not particularly pleasing. **1961** Cohen & Linton *Chem. & Textiles for Laundry Industry* v. 79 Optical bleaches will give blue by light emission and consequently improve brightness both psychologically and actually—that is, a 'whiter' white is obtained. **1964** Kirk & Othmer *Encycl. Chem. Technol.* (ed. 2) III. 739 The principle of optical bleaching was described in 1929 by Krais, but the industrial use of optical brightening began about ten years later. **1964** *Ibid.* XIX. 13 The majority of optical brighteners that are commercially available are based on stilbene derivatives. **1971** A. K. Sarkar *Fluorescent Whitening Agents* i. 1 Fluorescent whitening agents are known under various names, e.g. optical whitening agents, optical bleaching agents or optical bleaches, fluorescent bleaching agents, whiteners, brighteners, etc. **1974** *Encycl. Brit. Macropædia* XVI. 916/2 Now an integral part of all washing powders, optical brighteners are dye-stuffs absorbed by textile fibres from solution but not subsequently removed in rinsing. *Ibid.*, The chemical structures of optical brightening agents are complicated.

6. Special collocations: **optical activity**, the ability of a substance to produce optical rotation; **optical axis, centre**: see sense 2; **optical bench**, a straight, rigid bar, usu. graduated, along which supports for lenses, light sources, and the like can be slid and to which they can be clamped; **optical character reader**, a device which performs optical character recognition and produces coded signals corresponding to the characters identified; **optical character recognition**, identification of printed characters using photoelectric devices; **optical comparator**, an instrument for facilitating comparisons of two objects by projecting shadows or transparencies of them on to a screen; **optical disc** *Computing*, a smooth non-magnetic disc with a special coating that allows data to be recorded on it by means of a laser beam and read by a laser scanner, providing a large storage capacity; **optical fibre**, a fibre that will act as a light guide in fibre optics; **optical flat** (see flat *sb.*[3] 2 f); **optical glass**, glass of specially high homogeneity manufactured for use in optical components (see also sense 4); **optical isomer**, each of two isomeric compounds whose molecules are enantiomorphs and which are distinguishable by their equal but opposite optical rotations; so **optical isomerism**; †**optical length** = *optical path* below; **optical model** *Nuclear Physics*, a model of the atomic nucleus in which it is treated as having a potential well with an additional negative imaginary component, so that its behaviour with respect to incident particles is somewhat analogous to that of a partially absorbing body with respect to incident light waves; **optical path**, the distance which in a vacuum would contain the same number of wavelengths as the actual path followed by a ray of light, equal to the product of the actual path-length and the refractive index of the medium if the latter is homogeneous; **optical printer** = *projection printer* s.v. projection 10; **optical pumping** [tr. F. *pompage optique* (A. Kastler 1950, in *Jrnl. de Physique et la Radium* XI. 257/2)], the production of an inversion in the population of certain energy levels in the atoms of a gas by the absorption of optical (visible) resonance radiation of suitable polarization; **optical pyrometer**, a device for measuring the temperature of an incandescent body by comparing its brightness with that of a heated filament in the instrument; **optical rotation**, the rotation of the plane of polarization of plane-polarized light by a substance through which it passes; *spec.* = *specific rotation*; **optical scanner** = *optical character reader* above; **optical scanning**, scanning in which the light reflected or transmitted by the area being scanned is detected, esp. as used in optical character recognition; **optical sound** *Cinemat.*, sound recorded by optical (photographic) means on a film.

1877 *Chem. News* 23 Nov. 230/1 The optical activity disappears in those derivatives of active bodies, by the formation of which the so-called asymonetry [*sic*] of the carbon atoms ceases. **1883** *Athenæum* 29 Dec. 871/1 A series of sugars, having the composition of $C_6H_{12}O_6$, is formed, of gradually decreasing optical activity, which the author names α, β, γ, and δ arabinose. **1967** K. B. Krauskopf *Introd. Geochem.* xi. 295 If a natural material containing carbon compounds can be shown to possess optical activity, the conclusion seems inescapable that living organisms played a role in its formation. **1883** R. T. Glazebrook *Physical Optics* v. 113 The experiment is usually made on an optical bench. **1974** *Sci. Amer.* Apr. 28/3 An optical laboratory needs a large optical bench that is typically 20 feet long. **1962** *Proc. Symposium Optical Character Recognition* I. 133 The IBM 1418 Optical Character Reader..provides an example of the maximum tolerance for several of these variables that can be obtained in today's commercially available character readers. **1968** *Amer. Documentation* Jan. 74/2 Typed pages are transferred to magnetic tape by an optical character reader. **1974** *Encycl. Brit. Macropædia* XIV. 892/1 The U.S. Post Office has had an alpha-numeric optical character reader in operation on live mail since 1965. **1962** *Proc. Symposium Optical Character Recognition* I. 93 A research and development program was initiated..to create a wide-tolerance optical character recognition system. **1970** O. Dopping *Computers & Data Processing* iii. 64 In optical character recognition (OCR), the reader responds to the darkness of the ink, just as the human eye does. **1935** O. W. Boston *Engin. Shop Pract.* II. ix. 452 An optical comparator or Optimeter is a gage used for comparing the size of various parts with that of master gages. **1967** *Economist* 14 Oct. 4 (Advt. suppl. following p. 176), The image of the gauge, magnified to 50 times its size, is projected on the screen of the Optical Comparator so that the finest details of the thread can be examined and checked. **1976** M. Maguire *Scratchproof* iii. 40 Perhaps the boys at forensic had made a gaff. Perhaps the optical comparator was malfunctioning. **1977** *Computer & Information Syst.* XVII. 514/1 The objective of the program is to develop an inexpensive optical disk recorder suitable for minicomputer applications. **1981** *New Scientist* 29 Oct. 310 One optical disc can store up to 200 million bytes of information. **1985** *Personal Computer World* Feb. 196/3 The optical disk is 12in in diameter, double-sided, and its tracks are made up of a series of micron-sized pits illuminated by a low-power, helium-neon laser. These are read by a photodiode. **1970** *Sci. Jrnl.* Dec. 68 Nobody has yet produced glass which meets all the challenging requirements of optical fibres. **1974** *McGraw-Hill Yearbk. Sci. & Technol.* 27/1 Optical fibers that act as 'light pipes' have been around for some years, serving in a variety of ways—in medical instruments, in photocopying machines, in automobile instrument panels. **1840** *Mem. R. Astron. Soc.* XI. 165 (*heading*) On the optical glass prepared by the late Dr. Ritchie. **1879** *Encycl. Brit.* X. 665/1 Optical glass is of two principal kinds—flint and crown. **1922** L. Bell *Telescope* iii. 60 The fundamental difference between the making of optical glass and the ordinary commercial varieties lies in the individual treatment of each charge necessary to secure uniformity and regularity. **1973** D. G. Holloway *Physical Prop. Glass* iv. 107 The characteristics of optical glasses are customarily represented by quoting the refractive index for one of the sodium D lines and the constringence. **1892** Optical isomer [see enantiomorph]. **1974** *Encycl. Brit. Macropædia* V. 138/2 Optical isomers differ from the other isomeric coordination compounds in that their physical and chemical properties are identical. **1894** *Jrnl. Chem. Soc.* LXVI. I. 422 (*heading*) Optical isomerism of closed chain compounds. **1968** R. O. C. Norman *Princ. Org. Synthesis* v. 156 Optical isomerism in biphenyls is possible because the conformation..which possesses a plane of symmetry is strained with respect to non-coplanar conformations. **1894** *Phil. Mag.* XXXVII. 515 The time it takes for an impulse at G to pass completely through F will be that required by light to go over a space equal to the difference in optical length of the extreme rays GBF and GAF. **1934** W. H. A. Fincham *Optics* ii. 26, *nl* is termed the optical length of a path *l* in medium of refractive index *n*. **1952** Le Levier & Saxon in *Physical Rev.* LXXXVII. 40/1 There is an energy range for which the problem of nucleon-nuclei scattering is somewhat analogous to the scattering of light by a conducting glass sphere... Such a medium is conventionally described by introducing a complex index of refraction... We have investigated an optical model for nucleon-nuclei scattering in which a complex square well potential is used, this being equivalent to a complex index of refraction. **1963** P. E. Hodgson *Optical Model Elast. Scattering* i. 3 The initial development of the optical model was due to Fernbach, Serber, and Taylor (1949). **1970** I. E. McCarthy *Nuclear Reactions* i. iii. 70 A mechanistic description of a non-elastic reaction..involves an optical model description of the system while it is in the entrance channel and another one while it is in the exit channel. The transition between these channels is described by a model which includes details of nuclear structure. **1893** *Phil. Mag.* XXXV. 471 The phenomenon is due to the interference of two parallel gratings... Their distance, which is virtually constant, is the optical path, *2ne*, *e* being the thickness, and *n* the index of the gelatine. **1923** GLAZEBROOK *Dict. Applied Physics* IV. 216/1 The differences of optical paths are a direct measure of the distortion from true spherical form of the waves emerging from a lens system. **1957** G. E. HUTCHINSON *Treat. Limnol.* I. vi. 391 Poole and Atkins computed *b*, the mean optical path per meter, as 1·19. **1944** *Jrnl. Soc. Motion Pict. Engin.* XLII. 204 The use of the optical printer to enhance the value of the modern motion picture is demanded increasingly by studios with foresight enough to give a free hand to the man in charge of the optical department. **1953** L. J. WHEELER *Princ. Cinematogr.* v. 144 Figure 61 shows in outline the layout of the intermittent or 'stop' optical printer. **1974** L. LIPTON *Independent Filmmaking* i. 39 Optical printers are used to make dissolves, special effects, frame line corrections, freeze-frame printing and so on. The optical printer is also ideal for the preparation of master printing material printed from original camera film. **1952** *Physical Rev.* LXXXV. 1051/2 The net result is an optical 'pumping' as Kastler suggests, from $m = -\frac{1}{2}$ to $m = +\frac{1}{2}$, or a tendency in the direction of nuclear orientation. This is in competition with a disorienting tendency caused by collisions. **1959** [see MULTILEVEL *a.*]. **1970** G. K. WOODGATE *Elem. Atomic Struct.* ix. 191 Recently.. the methods of optical pumping, double resonance, and level-crossing spectroscopy have begun to provide data on the hyperfine structure of excited states. **1901** G. K. BURGESS tr. *Le Chatelier & Boudouard's High-Temperature Measurements* viii. 155 The optical pyrometer, by reason of the uncertainty of emissive powers.., cannot give as accurate results as other pyrometric methods. **1922** GLAZEBROOK *Dict. Appl. Physics* I. 649/1 It is possible to calibrate optical pyrometers by direct observations of freezing- or melting-points. **1958** BUSSARD & DELAUER *Nuclear Rocket Propulsion* viii. 303 The optical pyrometer has been built around the frequency-response characteristics of the human eye. **1895** C. S. PALMER tr. *Nernst's Theoret. Chem.* II. v. 288 The connection with constitution is shown in no other physical property so clearly as it is in this of optical rotation. **1929** R. A. GORTNER *Outl. Biochem.* xxi. 473 Naturally-occurring tartaric acid is the *d* form, and its purity is usually determined by the optical rotation of a solution of the acid. **1967** *Oceanogr. & Marine Biol.* V. 190 Suzuki and Suzuki.. have demonstrated that ovalbumin has an optical rotation of − 27·6° in the native state. **1962** *Proc. Symposium Optical Character Recognition* I. 16 (*caption*) An example of the actual printed output which optical scanners are required to read. **1975** *McGraw-Hill Yearbk. Sci. & Technol.* 201/1 An optical scanner.. reads a symbol printed on the product as it is passed over a slit in the checkout counter. **1958** J. MOIR *High Quality Sound Reproduction* xviii. 540 Optical scanning of the sound track takes place while the film is held in contact with the drum and rotating with it. **1971** *Computers & Humanities* V. 282 Optical scanning of printed texts (avoiding the need for keypunching the material). [**1933** B. BROWN *Amat. Talking Pict.* vii. 146 The optical sound system of the R.C.A. portable is shown diagrammatically.] **1960** *McGraw-Hill Encycl. Sci. & Technol.* III. 124/2 The magnetic sound track is.. 26 frames ahead [of the picture] on 16-mm film, the same as optical sound. **1970** *New Yorker* 29 Aug. 22/1 Here we have to use optical sound—printed down the side of the film.

B. *sb.* **1.** *Cinematogr.* and *Television.* (See quots.)

1953 K. REISZ *Technique Film Editing* 281 *Optical*, any device carried out by the optical department of a laboratory requiring the use of the optical printer, e.g., dissolve, fade, wipe. **1959** HALAS & MANVELL *Technique Film Animation* 340 *Opticals*, mixes, fades, wipes, etc., which are made by the processing laboratories on an optical printing machine after the scenes have been photographed, instead of in the camera during photography. **1959** *Punch* 28 Oct. 366/2 Many amateurs are clearly of the opinion that this [*sc.* the subject matter] is of minor importance, their chief concern being to demonstrate their skill at devising star-burst wipes and other trick opticals. **1969** C. O. RASPOR in W. R. R. Park *Plastics Film Technol.* iv. 94 It has become customary to distinguish three properties of films which are generally categorized as 'opticals': gloss, haze, and transparency. **1970** A. FOWLES *Dupe Negative* xiv. 192 'I've got four hundred feet of 35 mm. ECO original here,' I said, 'how long will it take to strike a master positive?'.. 'You can have it by five this evening,' he said, 'but wouldn't you rather have an optical?' **1974** L. LIPTON *Independent Filmmaking* vi. 273 When printed with an optical printer, the image can have the same orientation as it had on the camera film. If we used a contact printer to make the fades and dissolves, and then cut them into the master, we'd wind up with release prints with flopped opticals.

2. An example of optical art.

1966 *New Statesman* 5 Aug. 208/2 A sizzling red-blue optical by Ellsworth Kelly.

optically ('ɒptɪkəlɪ), *adv.* [f. prec. + -LY[2].] In an optical manner, or by optical means; by means of or in relation to sight, light, or optics.

1593 R. HARVEY *Philad.* 21 Brute presently upon his Arriual searched this Iland optically and throughly. **1656** W. D. tr. *Comenius' Gate Lat. Unl.* ¶528 They measure distances optically, by visible lines, with the help of a Quadrant. **1833** LAMB *Elia* Ser. II. *Barrenn. Imag. Fac. Mod. Art*, Not all that is optically possible to be seen, is to be shown in every picture. **1834** MRS. SOMERVILLE *Connex. Phys. Sc.* xxxvii. (1849) 421 Instances of these optically double stars. **1871** TYNDALL *Fragm. Sc.* (1879) II. xiii. 304 The air.. was proved by the luminous beam to be optically pure.

optician (ɒp'tɪʃən). [ad. F. *opticien* (*c* 1640 Hatz.-Darm.), f. med.L. *optica* OPTICS: see -ICIAN.]

1. One versed in optics; an opticist. (So also in Fr.) Now *rare* or *Obs.*

1687 *Death's Vis.* (1713) 15 Dr. Cheyne shows from the same Great Optician [Newton] that all Bodies attract the Rayes of Light towards them in Lines perpendicular to their Surfaces. **1738** *Med. Ess.* (ed. 2) IV. 143 Whether Physician, Anatomist, or Optician. **1837** GORING & PRITCHARD *Microgr.* 101 Of what description should such persons be —should they be profound opticians or microscopists?

2. A maker of or dealer in optical instruments; *spec.* one who makes up and dispenses spectacles and corrective lenses (sometimes also testing the eyes and providing a prescription).

1737 J. CHAMBERLAYNE *Pres. St. Gt. Brit., List Offices* 254 Officers and Servants attending.. the Prince of Wales.. Tradesmen.. Optician, Nathaniel Adams. **1804** YOUNG in *Phil. Trans.* XCIV. 14 The blue glass sold by the opticians. **1868** LOCKYER tr. *Guillemin's Heavens* (ed. 3) 494 That.. our modern opticians contrive to admit more light by means of a superior polish imparted to the surfaces of the object glass. *Mod.* I must go to an optician's to get an eye-glass. **1892** *Keystone* (Philadelphia) June 578/2 Some persons are unkind.. enough, after the optician has spent a great deal of time testing their eyes, to ascertain from him the proper number of the glasses they need, and then.. go around the corner to some street peddler of spectacles. **1897** *Sears, Roebuck Catal.* 462/1 Opticians make a practice of imposing on their customer.. and give as an excuse for the prices charged, 'that the lenses were ground to order'. **1912** L. LAURANCE *Visual Optics* p. vii, I have endeavoured to cover .. all that is essential for the sight-testing optician. *Ibid.*, No apologies are needed for mentioning some indications of pathological conditions, since a person with defective sight may go to the optician when he should go to the oculist. **1928** S. DUKE-ELDER *Practice of Refraction* xxiii. 333 The ophthalmologist has no more valuable and essential asset than a reliable optician with whom to co-operate. **1951** R. L. STIMSON *Ophthalmic Dispensing* vi. 140 An ophthalmic dispenser's First Commandment is, an optician shall never express an opinion pertaining to a patient's vision or eye health. **1969** *Which?* Feb. 43/1 Ophthalmologist. He is a qualified doctor who has had a further training in eye disease... He will give you a prescription for your spectacles... He will not make up the spectacles... Ophthalmic Opticians are opticians who do sight tests... After giving you a prescription for your spectacles, an Ophthalmic Optician will usually expect to make them up herself. *Ibid.*, A Dispensing Optician does not do sight tests but makes up your spectacles to your prescription, wherever you have got it. **1975** *Nature* 8 May 151/1 It has sometimes been noted by opticians involved in the fitting of contact lenses that the sensitivity of the cornea seems to vary, depending on whether the patient has blue or brown eyes.

opticist ('ɒptɪsɪst). *rare.* [f. OPTIC + -IST: cf. *physicist*.] One who studies or is versed in optics.

1884 *Pop. Sci. Monthly* XXIV. 814 The real cause.. is now thoroughly understood by physiological opticists.

opticity (ɒp'tɪsɪtɪ). [ad. F. *opticité* optical quality: see OPTIC *a.* and *sb.* and -ITY.] In the brewing and food industries, the degree of optical activity of a solution, as a measure of its concentration.

1900 *Jrnl. Federated Inst. Brewing* VI. 219 The pyridine solutions of osazones are.. very suitable for determinations of opticity. **1924** J. GRANT *Chem. of Breadmaking* (ed. 4) xiii. 197 Two instruments in common use for the determination of the opticity of sugars and other optically active carbohydrates are the Laurent.. and the Schmidt-Haensch.

optico- (ˌɒptɪkəʊ), combining form of Gr. ὀπτικός OPTIC; used variously in a few scientific terms, as **optico-'chemical** *a.*, relating to optics and chemistry conjointly; **optico-'ciliary** *a.*, relating to the optic and ciliary nerves; **ˌopticoki'netic** *a.* = OPTOKINETIC *a.*; **optico-'papillary** *a.*, belonging to the optic papilla.

1875 tr. *Vogel's Chem. Light* xii. 133 The optico-chemical difficulties often frustrate his best endeavours. **1892** *Syd. Soc. Lex.*, *Optico-ciliary.. neurotomy*, division of the optic and the ciliary nerves. **1899** *Allbutt's Syst. Med.* VI. 756 It seems probable that the optico-papillary fibres differ in appearance from the visual fibres. **1950** F. H. ADLER *Physiol. Eye* x. 372 Opticokinetic nystagmus is induced in a subject using wide alternating stripes on a rotating drum. **1965** F. W. NEWELL *Ophthalm.* xxvi. 442/2 Opticokinetic nystagmus arises from looking at constantly moving objects, such as telegraph poles, from a moving automobile or train.

optics ('ɒptɪks). [A pl. of OPTIC *a.*, used subst. to render med.L. *optica* pl. neut., a. Gr. τὰ ὀπτικά, optical matters, optics (Aristotle, Ptolemy, etc.): see -ICS. Besides this, Greek had also ἡ ὀπτική (sc. θεωρία) the theory of the laws of sight, whence L. *opticē* in Vitruvius.

The med.L. *optica* occurs *c* 1160 in the Sicilians, Henricus Aristippus who speaks of *Euclidis Optica*, and Eugenius who translated from Arabic the Ὀπτικά of Ptolemy under the title *Optica Ptolomæi*. *Optica* appears later as a fem. sing., and still in 16th c.; thence OIt., Sp., Pg. *optica*, It. *ottica*, F. *l'optique* sing. fem., also Eng. *optic* sb. sing. In the 16th c. was also used L. *opticē* after Gr.]

The science of sight, or of the medium of sight, i.e. light; that branch of physics which deals with the properties and phenomena of light. Plural in origin and form, and formerly so construed ('the Optics'); but now always as singular; less usually made singular in form (like F. *l'optique*, OIt., Sp., Pg. *optica*): see OPTIC *sb.* 4.

1579 T. DIGGES *Stratioticos* 189 Such was his Fœlicitie and happie successe.. also in the Optikes and Catoptrikes, that he was able by Perspectiue Glasses.. to discouer euery particularitie in the Countrey rounde aboute. **1625** N. CARPENTER *Geog. Del.* I. xi. (1635) 244 The Optickes teach vs, all things are seene in the places opposite to the eye. **1646** SIR T. BROWNE *Pseud. Ep.* 374 Alhazen cognominall unto him that wrote his history;.. he was contemporary unto Avicenna, and hath left sixteene bookes of Opticks. **1666** PEPYS *Diary* 17 Oct., I do not see that he minds optickes or mathematiques of any sort. **1726** BUTLER *Serm. Rolls Chap.* ii. 27 The Science of Opticks, deduced from ocular Experiments. **1812–16** J. SMITH *Panorama Sc. & Art* I. 407 Optics treats of the mechanical properties of light. **1831** BREWSTER *Nat. Magic* i. (1833) 4 Of all the sciences Optics is the most fertile in marvellous expedients. **1872** RUSKIN *Eagle's N.* §97 To-day we are to speak of optics, the science of seeing.

optigraph ('ɒptɪgrɑːf, -æ-). [irreg. f. Gr. ὀπτ-ός seen + -GRAPH.] A contrivance for copying landscapes, consisting of a telescope placed in a vertical position so that the rays from the object are reflected from an inclined mirror through the object-glass and then from another through the eye-glass, in the focus of which is placed a movable plane glass having at its centre a small dot, which can be moved over the outline of the image.

1864 in WEBSTER. **1875** in KNIGHT *Dict. Mech.*

optimacy ('ɒptɪməsɪ). Now *rare.* [ad. 16th c. L. *optimātia*, f. L. *optimās*, pl. *optimātēs*: see OPTIMATE and -ACY. Much used between 1579 and 1688, when it yielded to *aristocracy*. In mod.F. *optimatie* (Littré).]

1. Government, or a government, by the nobles or upper classes in a state; aristocracy; also, a state so governed.

[**1579–80** NORTH *Plutarch* (1676) 417 Cimon.. set up the Government of the Nobility (called *Optimatia*) that was established in the time of Clisthenes.] **1594** T. BEDINGFIELD tr. *Machiavelli's Flor. Hist.* To Rdr., By this.. appeareth how both the optimacie and Popular gouernments are subiect to mutation. **1598** DALLINGTON *Meth. Trav.* D iv b, The State of Venice, which, at this day, is the most perfect Optimacy in the world. **1644** HEYLIN *Stumbling-block* Tracts (1681) 682 Till the Romans had expulsed their Kings,.. Monarchy being changed to an Optimatie. **1649** HOWELL *Pre-em. Parl.* 6 A wholsom mixture 'twixt Monarchy, Optimacy, and Democracy. **1681** NEVILE *Plato Rediv.* 43 Aristocracy, or Optimacy, is a Common-wealth, where the better sort.. have the chief Administration of the Government. **1776** J. ADAMS *On Govt.* Wks. 1851 IV. 473 Where the noble or the rich held all the power, they called their own government *aristocracy*, or government of the better sort, or *optimacy*, government of the best sort.

2. The upper classes in the state; the nobility or aristocracy.

1579–80 NORTH *Plutarch* (1676) 839 The City of Sicyone, after it fell from her first government of the Optimacy and Nobility. **1613–18** DANIEL *Coll. Hist. Eng.* (1626) 63 The Londoners, who are.. as among the optimacy of England. **1644** H. PARKER *Jus Pop.* Milton's Wks. (1851) 59 Bloody disputes between the Optimacy and Populacy. **1682** tr. *Erastus' Treat. Excommun.* 17 Though they had a Leader, yet were they govern'd by the Optimacy or Nobility.

fig. **1883** F. W. H. MYERS in *Cornh. Mag.* Feb. 222 A member of that new aristocracy.. that optimacy of passion and genius.. which is coming into existence as a cosmopolitan gentility among the confused and fading class-distinctions of the past.

†**3.** The best or highest place. *Obs. rare*[−1].

1651 BIGGS *New Disp.* 173 Which of all these generall remedies hath the principality of verity and vertue, and the optimacy in sanation, is not worth the dispute.

optimal ('ɒptɪməl), *a.* orig. *Biol.* [f. L. *optim-us* best + -AL[1]: cf. *proximal*.] Best or most favourable, most satisfactory: cf. OPTIMUM.

1890 SIBLEY in *Nature* 20 Nov. 70/1 (*Rep. Brit. Assoc.*) There is probably an optimal temperature, or one at which the process proceeds most rapidly or most favourably. **1900** A. L. LOEB tr. *J. Loeb's Compar. Physiol. Brain* xv. 223 The greatest happiness in life can be obtained only if all the instincts—that of workmanship included—can be maintained at a certain optimal intensity. **1935** ADAMS & ZENER tr. *Lewin's Dynamic Theory of Personality* iii. 110 Optimal environmental conditions.. vary considerably with different individuals. **1935** *Mind* XLIV. 359 There might be *optimal* sense-data, such as the one which a man senses when he observes a penny head on, from a short distance, in a good light, with a normal eye, etc. **1956** AMOS & BIRKINSHAW *Television Engin.* II. xv. 222 The constants of a feedback circuit can be proportioned to give an optimally-flat response, i.e., one with an equation having no terms in frequency. Such feedback is termed optimal and gives the widest possible frequency coverage. **1961** *Atlantic Monthly* Apr. 42/2 Students.. have often told me that it doesn't pay to be too interested in anything, because then one is tempted to spend too much time on it, at the expense of that optimal distribution of effort which will produce the best grades. **1970** *Sci. Jrnl.* Jan. 25/1 A controller.. automatically adjusts the speed and feedrates of the drill so as to maintain optimal performance as the drill wears. **1971** D. C. HAGUE *Managerial Econ.* (rev. ed.) i. 11 An optimal decision is the one which comes as close as possible to achieving a given objective.

Hence **'optimally** *adv.*, in the best or most advantageous way.

1933 *Proc. R. Soc.* B. CXII. 505 The animal's tissues were not optimally hydrated. **1950** D. HALLIDAY *Introd. Nucl. Physics* ix. 340 Phase-defocused atoms are not optimally accelerated and do not contribute to the useful beam. **1956** [see above]. **1972** *Sci. Amer.* Sept. 148/3 The time of physicians is not always optimally employed. **1976** *Lancet* 13 Nov. 1039/1 In the absence of bacteria the nitrosation reaction proceeds optimally at an acid pH.

optimality (ɒptɪ'mælɪtɪ). [f. OPTIMAL *a.* + -ITY.] The state or quality of being optimal.

1944 VON NEUMANN & MORGENSTERN *Theory of Games* iii. 162 (*heading*) Mistakes and their consequences. Permanent optimality. **1961** W. J. BAUMOL *Econ. Theory & Operations Analysis* ix. 184 Our condition..is a geometric representation of the following basic optimality rule. **1964** GOULD & KOLB *Dict. Social Sci.* 573/2 The rational consumer of formal economic theory maximizes his expected utility, and the rational entrepreneur maximizes his expected profit. If a distinction is wanted between this very strict species of rationality and more general forms, the former may be termed optimality, the latter adaptiveness or functionality. **1970** P. A. SAMUELSON *Economics* (ed. 8) IV. xxxii. 609 Graduate treatises call this a case of 'Pareto optimality', named after Pareto's work at the turn of the century. **1971** *Nature* 31 Dec. 527/2 Jardine and Sibson showed that the single-link method is the only hierarchic cluster method which satisfies certain invariance and optimality conditions. **1974** *Times Lit. Suppl.* 22 Feb. 172/3 A model of the city which achieves Pareto optimality (ie, a condition in which no one can get richer through moving without making someone else poorer).

optimalization (ˌɒptɪməlaɪˈzeɪʃən). [f. OPTIMAL *a.* + -IZATION.] = OPTIMIZATION.

1965 *Economist* 31 July 446/3 A mechanistic commentary on optimalisation theory and resource allocation. **1971** *Nature* 15 Jan. 150/3 The council pulled its punch, and decided to 'limit itself to searching for optimalization within the possibilities existing in the present constitutional situation'. **1975** *Gen. Systems* XX. 108/2 Allen Johnson.. found that legends of agricultural affinity well befitted ecological optimalization in northeastern Brazil. **1977** *Language* LIII. 327 We have seen that 'optimalization of phonotactic structure' (i.e. the *C + *h* constraint) wins out over 'paradigm coherence' (i.e. the invariable prefixation of pronouns) in Hua.

optimate (ˈɒptɪmət), *sb.* (*a.*) [ad. L. *optimās*, as adj. 'belonging to the best or noblest, aristocratic', as sb. pl. *optimātēs* aristocrats; f. *optim-us* best. Chiefly in pl., which is now generally pronounced as Latin (ɒptɪˈmeɪtiːz).]

A. *sb.* **1. a.** A member of the patrician order in Rome; in wider sense, A noble or aristocrat.

[**1572** WHITGIFT *Def. Answ.* III. Wks. (Parker Soc.) I. 393 Though they might be counted *optimates*, yet, because most things..were done by the consent of the people, therefore the state..was 'popular'. **1606** HOLLAND *Sueton.* 88 All the Claudii..were alwaies *Optimates*, the onely maintainers or patrons of the dignitie and power of the Patritians.] *c* **1611** CHAPMAN *Iliad* IX. 322 Other to optimates and kings he gave. **1635** HEYWOOD *Hierarch.* II. 67 But where a Principalitie (misguided) Is amongst seuerall Optimates diuided. **1650** HOBBES *De Corp. Pol.* 82 It is impossible, that the People, as one Body Politick, should covenant with the Aristocracy or Optimates. **1793** GODWIN *Pol. Just.* (1796) II. 85 In..Cicero..this order of men is styled the 'optimates', the 'virtuous'. **1850** GROTE *Greece* VIII. II. lxiv. 216 'Chastising the high-handed oppressions of the optimates'. **1865** MERIVALE *Rom. Emp.* VIII. lxiv. 84 The free spirit of the Optimate has been repressed, and he has been constrained to cringe and flatter. **1954** I. MURDOCH *Under Net* xvii. 234 The editor was calling on the *optimates* to exercise..strong measures. **1966** AUDEN *About House* 20 As Nietzsche said they would, the *plebs* have got steadily Denser, the *optimates* Quicker still on the uptake.

†**b.** In literal sense: One who is the best. *Obs.*

1635 HEYWOOD *Hierarch.* II. 103 The world..gouerned by One who is the best, and..that one Optimate is God himselfe.

†**2.** = OPTIME. *Obs.*

1792 COLERIDGE *Lett., to G. Coleridge* (1895) 25 Middleton is fourth senior optimate.

B. *adj.* (or *attrib.*) Of or pertaining to the optimates, patrician.

a **1846** *Eclectic Rev.* cited in WORCESTER.

†**opti'matical**, *a. Obs. rare.* [f. as OPTIMATE + -ICAL, after *monarchical*, etc.] Conducted by an optimacy or aristocracy; aristocratical.

1652 EARL MONM. tr. *Bentivoglio's Hist. Relat.* 55 The Government is of three sorts; Monarchical, Optimatical, and Popular. **1657** —— tr. *Paruta's Pol. Disc.* 58 If the Form be Optimatical, wherein vertue is esteemed above all things.

optimatie, obs. form of OPTIMACY.

optime (ˈɒptɪmiː). [a. L. *optimē* adv., 'best', 'very well', originating in the phrase *optimē disputāsti* 'you have disputed very well' (Wordsw. *Scholæ Acad.* 1877, 37–8).] One who has been placed in the second or third division, called respectively senior and junior optimes, in the Mathematical Tripos at Cambridge.

proctors' optimes, 'degrees [formerly] granted without examination, by the prerogative of the vice-chancellor, proctors and moderators' (Wordsw. *Sch. Ac.* 57–8, 358).

[**1709–10** RENEU *Let. to Strype* 10 Feb. (Wordsw. *Sch. Ac.* 305), He took his degree very honourably, and I believe will have an *optimé*.] **1755** in *Cambridge Univ. Cal.* (1797) 157 Apthorpe, Jes. Col. V. C., and Proctor's S. Opt. **1764** *Ibid.* 169 Ds More Trin. 1st Sr. Optime..Ds Love Caii 1st Jun. Optime. **1840** *Encycl. Brit.* (ed. 7) XXI. 505/1 Their names are..classed in three divisions, viz. wranglers, senior optimes, and junior optimes, which constitute the three orders of honour.

optimific (ɒptɪˈmɪfɪk), *a. Philos.* [f. L. *optim-us* best + -FIC.] Producing the maximum good consequences.

1930 W. D. ROSS *Right & Good* 34 No one *means* by 'right' just 'productive of the best possible consequences', or 'optimific'. **1933** *Mind* XLII. 181 The 'Maximalist' Theory (this designation suggests quantity better than 'Optimific'). **1940** —— XLIX. 230 The first half of Universalistic Ethical Hedonism, to wit the theory that being optimific is the one and only right-making characteristic.

optimism (ˈɒptɪmɪz(ə)m). [a. F. *optimisme*; in mod.L *optimism-us*, f. L. *optim-us* best: see -ISM.]

1. A name given to the doctrine propounded by Leibnitz, in his *Théodicée* (1710), that the actual world is the 'best of all possible worlds', being chosen by the Creator out of all the possible worlds which were present in his thoughts as that in which the most good could be obtained at the cost of the least evil. Also applied to doctrines of earlier or later thinkers to a like effect.

Leibnitz, in his *Théodicée*, uses *optimum* as a technical term, on the model of *maximum* and *minimum*. Hence the Jesuits who conducted the *Mémoires de Trévoux*, in the number for Feb. 1737, gave to his doctrine the name *optimisme*. It appears in the *Dict. Trévoux* 1752. It owes its general diffusion to the attack upon the doctrine by Voltaire in *Candide ou l'Optimisme* 1759; and was admitted into the *Dict. Acad.* in 1762.

[**1737** *Mém. de Trévoux* (Fév.) 207 En termes de l'art, il l'appelle *la raison du meilleur* ou plus savamment encore, et Theologiquement autant que Géométriquement, le systême de l'*Optimum*, ou l'*Optimisme*.]

1759 WARBURTON in *W. & Hurd's Lett.* (1809) 289 The professed design is to ridicule the Optimisme, not of Pope, but of Leibnitz. **1782** WARTON *Ess. Pope* (ed. 4) II. IX. 124 That this Platonic scheme, of *Optimism*, or the *best*, sufficiently accounts for the introduction of moral and physical evil into the world. [The words 'Optimism, or' are not in the previous edd.] **1791** BOSWELL *Johnson* an. 1759 Voltaire's Candide, written to refute the system of optimism, which it has done with brilliant success. **1793** D. STEWART *Outl. Mor. Philos.* II. ii. (1801) 213 By some modern authors the scheme of optimism has been proposed in a form..which leads to a justification of moral evil, even with respect to the delinquent. **1842** BRANDE *Dict. Sc.*, etc., s.v., The optimism of Leibnitz was based on the following trilemma:—If this world be not the best possible, God must either, 1. not have known how to make a better, 2. not have been able, 3. not have chosen. The first proposition contradicts his omniscience, the second his omnipotence, the third his benevolence.

b. More generally applied to any view which supposes the ultimate predominance of good over evil in the universe.

1841–4 EMERSON *Ess.*, *Prudence* Wks. (Bohn) I. 95 One might find argument for optimism in the abundant flow of this saccharine element of pleasure in every suburb. **1878** T. SINCLAIR *Mount* 18 The optimism that may well be considered fanciful is that of Hegel, Buckle, republicans like Hugo,..Whitman, and the development men generally. **1880** GOLDW. SMITH *Pessimism* in *Atlant. Monthly* No. 268. 196 Besides optimism, which affirms the definitive ascendency of good, and pessimism, which affirms the definitive ascendency of evil, a third hypothesis is possible. **1888** MRS. H. WARD *R. Elsmere* VI. xlii, The young reformer's social simplicity, his dreams, his optimisms. **1889** S. ALEXANDER *Moral Ord. & Progr.* II. v. §37. 227 Morality is therefore of itself and necessarily a kind of optimism. **1900** W. L. COURTNEY *Idea of Tragedy* 67 A shallow optimism is the last theory of all to which a thinking man ought to consent.

2. The character or quality of being for the best.

1795 SOUTHEY in Cottle *Early Recoll.* (1837) II. 3 Of all things it is most difficult to understand the optimism of this difference of language. **1821** BYRON *2nd Let. Bowles' Strict.* Wks. 1832 VI. 403 It may be wrong, but it does not assume pretentions to Optimism.

b. The quality of being the best; 'bestness'.

1796 SOUTHEY *Lett. fr. Spain* (1799) 228 Portugal is the best part of Spain... So much for the beauty and optimism of Portugal.

3. Disposition to hope for the best or to look on the bright side of things; general tendency to take a favourable view of circumstances or prospects.

1819 SHELLEY *Ess.* (1852) II. 188 Let us believe in a kind of optimism, in which we are our own gods. **1859** WRAXALL tr. *R. Houdin* xix. 277 His disposition to look at the bright side of everything. He was the incarnation of optimism. **1872** *Pall Mall G.* 6 Apr. 1 Mr. Disraeli's optimism has a great deal too much the air of inviting his party to confine itself to the cultivation of cabbages. **1881** BLACK *Sunrise* III. ix. 143 'Let it be cheerful' said he, with his gay optimism. **1893** LIDDON, etc. *Life Pusey* I. viii. 158 Pusey's optimism as to the existing state of German Protestantism.

optimist (ˈɒptɪmɪst), *sb.* (*a.*) [f. as prec. + -IST. Cf. F. *optimiste* (1752 in *Dict. Trévoux*, 1762 in *Dict. Acad.*).]

1. One who holds or believes in the metaphysical principle of optimism.

1783 T. TWINING in *Recreat. & Stud.* (1882) 119 Oh, commend me to the gentle philanthropists and optimists.. who think all well while they are well themselves! **1791** CHARLOTTE SMITH *Celestina* IV. 112 You must learn to be more of an Optimist, and to believe that whatever happens could not, nor ought not, to have been otherwise. **1792** MARY WOLLSTONECR. *Rights Wom.* i. 19 Rousseau became enamoured of solitude; and, being at the same time an optimist, he labours with uncommon eloquence to prove that man was naturally a solitary animal. **1832** PUSEY in Liddon, etc. *Life* (1893) I. x. 224 A true Christian can be the only real Optimist, for he alone can feel that happen what may, it must be best since it comes from a Father's love. **1878** GEO. ELIOT *Coll. Breakf. P.* 496, I am no optimist whose faith must hang On hard pretence that pain is beautiful.

2. One who is inclined to practical optimism; a person who looks on the bright side of things; one disposed, with or without sufficient reason, to hope for the best or think favourably of circumstances.

1766 MRS. GRIFFITH *Lett. Henry & Frances* IV. 217, I am a perfect Optimist. I rejoice in a Lottery, when the five thousand Prize passes me by,..I immediately conclude that Fortune has palmed the Ten Thousand for me. **1819** *Gentl. Mag.* 529 On the subjects of revenue, commerce, and finance, he was a decided optimist. **1833** W. F. HOOK in Stephens *Life* iv. 258, I am a bit of an optimist, I always look to the bright side of things. **1895** SIR W. HARCOURT in *Daily News* 23 May 2/1, I have always observed that good physicians are optimists.

B. *adj.* (*attrib.* use of *sb.*) Characterized by optimism; optimistic.

1863 DICEY *Federal St.* I. 283 The objection to this optimist view is, that it does not take into account the extraordinary social influence of slavery. **1865** *Sat. Rev.* 11 Mar. 287 We are reminded of the optimist governess..who, when the weather was very bad, was still thankful because it was better than none at all. **1880** T. HUGHES in *Academy* 24 Jan. 62 His view is somewhat too optimist.

optimistic (ɒptɪˈmɪstɪk), *a.* [f. OPTIMIST + -IC.] Of or pertaining to optimism; characterized by optimism; inclined to take a favourable view of circumstances, and to hope for the best.

1848 M. ARNOLD *To a Republican Friend* 5 The barren optimistic sophistries Of comfortable moles. **1874** MORLEY *Compromise* (1886) 26 The optimistic or sentimental hypothesis that wickedness always fares ill in the world. **1887** *Pall Mall G.* 17 Feb. 6/1 The director is ever energetic, optimistic, and full of new plans and ideas.

optimistical (ɒptɪˈmɪstɪkəl), *a.* [f. as prec. + -AL[1].] = prec.

1834 *Fraser's Mag.* IX. 42 The magnificent schemes of optimistical theorists.

Hence **opti'mistically** *adv.*

1882 *Athenæum* 29 Apr. 537/1 Political aspirations, which may be described as optimistically Liberal. **1882** J. HAWTHORNE *Pr. Saroni's Wife* iii. (1884) 18 'You will come to it [love for wife] afterward', I affirmed, optimistically.

optimity (ɒpˈtɪmɪtɪ). [ad. late L. *optimitās* (Mart. Capella 6th c.), f. *optim-us* best: see -ITY.]

1. The quality or fact of being the best or very good; excellence.

1656 BLOUNT *Glossogr.*, *Optimitie*, utility, great profit, excellency. **1866** *Guide Elgin Cathedral* Introd. 8 Originality necessarily implies optimity.

2. The fact of being for the best.

1885 *Faith of the Unlearned* 103 No necessity other than the Creator's can order his creation;..it follows that the bugbear Necessity must either become optimity or, within the scope of finite freedom, must disappear.

optimi'zation. [f. OPTIMIZE *v.* + -ATION.] The making the best (of anything); the action or process of rendering optimal; the state or condition of being optimal. Freq. *attrib.*

1857 L. HUNT *Let. to Browning* in *Athenæum* (1883) 7 July 17/1 Wisdom, you know, is the optimization of knowledge, the turning it to its best and therefore least sad account. **1951** PARSONS & SHILS *Toward Gen. Theory Action* II. ii. 123 An important superordinate problem concerning mechanisms which depend entirely on the learning—performance distinction (when this is taken as relevant to the over-all problem of the system—the optimization of gratification). **1959** *Times Rev. Industry* June 39/2 Optimization problems (e.g. minimization of costs or maximization of profits). **1961** *Aeroplane* CI. 725/1 These desiderata were then used in what the Americans delight in calling 'optimization' studies, to find the best of some 300 helicopter configurations. **1966** S. BEER *Decision & Control* x. 211 Given this framework, the process of reaching the best decision is known as optimization. **1968** *Brit. Med. Bull.* XXIV. 242/1 This resulted in a major advance known as optimization of treatment..which in essence is for the computer to give the radiotherapist a number of alternative plans, and for the radiotherapist to decide which he considers to be the most suitable. **1974** COOPER & STEINBERG *Methods & Appl. Linear Programming* i. 1 In an optimization problem we seek values of the..variables which do not violate the several constraints imposed on them, but which lead to an optimal (maximal or minimal) value of the function which is to be optimized. **1976** *Daily Times* (Lagos) 22 Sept. 3/3 The socio-economic development of any nation depended on the optimisation and maximisation of land use.

optimize (ˈɒptɪmaɪz), *v.* [f. L. *optim-us* best + -IZE, after *optimism*.]

1. *intr.* To act as an optimist; to take favourable views of circumstances.

1844 GLADSTONE *Glean.* (1879) V. 118 Neither are we of those who pretend to optimise upon the present condition of the Church.

2. a. *trans.* To make the best or most of; to develop to the utmost.

1857 *Sat. Rev.* III. 306/1 This is an incomplete view..but it is so far borne out by fact that both parties to the suit accept it, and endeavour to optimize it. **1894** *Westm. Gaz.* 20 Mar. 2/3 We have the two optimised in the blundering and bad taste of this wanton act.

b. To render optimal.

1946 [see BEAM *sb.*[1] 24]. **1958** *New Scientist* 17 July 410/1 They could optimise the designs to be submitted..for the first three nuclear power stations to be built in Britain. **1965** *Economist* 15 May 788 The shape of the aircraft, i.e. its geometry, can be optimised for what ever it happens to be doing. **1966** T. LUPTON *Managem. & Social Sci.* II. 44 To optimize any one of these elements does not necessarily result in a set of conditions optimal for the system as a whole. **1974** [see prec.]. **1975** *Nature* 10 Apr. 498/2 If the expected signal wavelength is known there are specialised methods which can optimise the sensitivity of such an experiment. **1978** *N.Y. Times* 30 Mar. C 11/4 As a small businessman, you never really understand the importance of optimizing time and effort.

3. *intr.* To become optimal.

1971 *Nature* 23 July 251/1 The eight radii model quoted cannot optimize to the two layer model above. **1972** *Physics Bull.* Feb. 91/3 The bonding of p electrons in the broadside on (π) arrangement optimizes at shorter distances than that in the end on (σ) position.

Hence **'optimizing** *vbl. sb.* and *ppl. a.*

1877 GLADSTONE *Glean.* (1879) I. 160 The optimising side of the question. **1880** W. CORY *Mod. Eng. Hist.* 128 The theories fabricated by their optimising defenders.

optimum ('ɒptɪməm), *sb.* (*a.*) orig. *Biol.* [L. *optimum* the best, that which is best, neuter of *optimus* best.]

A. *sb.* That degree or amount of heat, light, food, moisture, etc. most favourable for growth, reproduction, or other vital process. Hence, the best, or the most favourable or advantageous, condition, situation, etc.

1879 tr. *Semper's Anim. Life* 43 This may be briefly designated as the optimum of food. **1882** VINES tr. *Sachs' Bot.* 747 An increase of the amount of carbonic acid present in the air, up to a certain limit (optimum), increases the evolution of oxygen. **1885** GOODALE *Phys. Bot.* (1892) 210 For the most rapid circulation of protoplasm there must be a definite amount of water,—the optimum. **1955** SCHULTZ & CLEAVES *Geol. in Engin.* xvii. 416 It can be seen from the shape of the curves near optimum that moisture content is extremely critical in the compaction of soils. **1970** O. DOPPING *Computers & Data Processing* xxii. 340 In many planning programs..time limitations make it impossible to reach the optimum and provide proof that this has been reached. **1971** *Marriage, Divorce & Church* iii. 50 In principle the State need not encourage more children when population growth appears to be reaching, or to have passed, an optimum.

B. *adj.* (*attrib.* use of *sb.*) Best or most favourable: = OPTIMAL.

1885 VINES *Lect. Physiol. Plants* 276 The minimum or zero point is the point at which the performance is just possible; the optimum point, at which it is carried on with the greatest activity. **1896** *Allbutt's Syst. Med.* I. 513 Experience alone can tell us the optimum temperature for a given kind of micro-organism. **1926** RIDEAL & TAYLOR *Catalysis* (ed. 2) v. 113 Most of the statements concerning promoter action by added substances have no information which would indicate what the optimum concentration of promoter is for the given reaction. **1929** S. LESLIE *Anglo-Catholic* iii. 34 How shall we strike the so-called optimum density, which is best for both the health and the soul of London, and keep the population there? **1930** *Economist* 1 Nov. (Russ. Suppl.) 13/1 The question of the optimum size of such a farm is not quite settled. **1935** *Planning* 18 June 8 It is a problem of maintaining the numbers and balance of population in such a manner as to enable optimum social and economic activity. **1949** E. W. KIMBARK *Electr. Transmission* xiii. 279 Another matching device is used at the sending end of the line..in order to obtain optimum power output from the transmitter. 'Optimum' signifies a compromise between maximum output and other considerations. **1950** G. B. SHAW *Farfetched Fables* Pref. 98 While the time lag lasts the future remains threatening. The problem of optimum wealth distribution..will not yield to the well-intentioned Utopian amateurs. **1954** H. M. CORLEY *Successful Commerc. Chem. Devel.* ix. 152 The question of the optimum production rate for a new plant is not easy to answer. **1967** E. DUCKWORTH in Wills & Yearsley *Handbk. Managem. Technol.* 110 When the optimum order quantities have been decided, problems may occur in scheduling these through factories in the optimum manner. **1975** *New Yorker* 21 Apr. 92/2 These drivers are deviant only in that they depart from ideal or optimum behavior.

'opting, *vbl. sb.* [f. OPT *v.* + -ING[1].] The action of the verb OPT. Freq. const. *out.* So **opting-in** *vbl. sb.*, **opting-out** *vbl. sb.*

1922 *Glasgow Herald* 13 Apr. 6 The opting of Australia out of the chain..does..impair the symmetry of the Imperial chain plan. **1958** [see APOLITICAL *a.*]. **1966** *Guardian* 17 Oct. 1/5 An opting out of the Church's duty. **1969** *Daily Tel.* 19 Aug. 20/1 On the crucial question of when doctors should be allowed to use the hearts of accident victims, the weight of opinion is that an 'opting in' principle should apply—only people who have signed a legal document stating that this can be done should be used as heart donors. **1970** *Globe & Mail* (Toronto) 28 Sept. 1/6 The provincial cabinet will study a proposal from Dr. Robillard for an entirely new opting-out scheme for the plan. **1973** D. AARON *Unwritten War* III. viii. 125 Howells neither extenuated nor deprecated his opting out in his reminiscences. **1977** *Jrnl. R. Soc. Arts* CXXV. 639/2 'Alienation'..too often..is used as an alibi for inaction, lack of imagination or a sort of 'opting out' (another dangerous expression).

option ('ɒpʃən), *sb.* [a. F. *option* (16th c. in Littré), also rare OF. (12–13th c. in Godef. *Compl.*), ad. L. *optiōn-em* choosing, choice, f. root *op-* of *optāre* to choose.]

1. a. The action of choosing; choice. Also *transf.* a thing that is or may be chosen; an alternative, a choice. ***soft option***: a choice which entails no difficult or strenuous actions or decisions; also (with hyphen) *attrib.*

1604 R. CAWDREY *Table Alph.*, *Option*, choosing or wishing. *c* **1615** BACON *Adv. Sir G. Villiers* vii. §2 Plantation ..must proceed from the option of the people, else it sounds like an exile. **1650** in Swayne *Sarum Churchw. Acc.* (1896) 222 Certeyne houses and options lying in the Close of Sarum. *a* **1660** HAMMOND (T.), He decrees to punish the contumacy finally, by assigning them their own options. *a* **1711** KEN *Hymnarium* Poet. Wks. 1721 II. 73 Since, Lord, thou Man didst free create, That Heav'n might Option be, not Fate. **1790** BURKE *Fr. Rev.* 346 They seem then to have made their option. **1854** TOULMIN SMITH *Parish* 118 This Act may, according to option, be put into operation in any parish, or in any defined part of any parish. **1885** *Guardian* 544/1 Under this influence the State University introduced theological options into its arts course. **1923** *Granta* 2 Mar. 315/1 It follows that our Tripos must be difficult; that we have little use for 'duds', for Tutors who misconceive it as being a soft option. **1953** R. LEHMANN *Echoing Grove* II. 42 The lifelong consequences of a choice that, once made, is made to be adhered to with no soft option. **1957** M. K. JOSEPH *I'll soldier no More* (1958) xiii. 238 Odd bods from various HQs and soft-option types with vague jobs. **1967** *Technology Week* 23 Jan. 11/1 (Advt.), Everything is modular—memory, input/output processors, peripherals, central processor options, software. **1967** *Listener* 6 July 5/2 There is a tendency for many prospective students to regard social studies as a soft option. **1969** *Guardian* 14 May 1/2 Mr. Callaghan..is understood to have reserved his decision —or, in the current jargon, 'kept his options open'. **1971** J. B. CARROLL et al. *Word Frequency Bk.* p. xv, This decision was guided by the results of a pilot test undertaken to try out various procedural options for the eventual work on the AHI Corpus. **1972** D. DELMAN *Week to Kill* 139 This cut down my options. **1973** 'M. INNES' *Appleby's Answer* xxi. 183 You've been most fiendishly clever... You've kept your options open. **1976** K. THACKERAY *Crownbird* v. 94 Gould had tremendous self-assurance, the ability to cope when all the options were running out. **1977** *Times* 22 Apr. 18/8 The British electorate have a powerful instinct for the soft option and a quiet life.

b. *spec.* in *Amer. Football*, a play in which a quarter- or half-back chooses whether to pass or to run with the ball; also *attrib.*

1954 *Sun* (Baltimore) 25 Nov. 15/4 We couldn't pass enough from it and our quarterbacks couldn't take the pounding on the option play as a steady diet. **1966** ROTE & WINTER *Lang. Pro Football* III. 127/2 *Option*, play where ball carrier has choice of running or passing; option pass play. **1974** *Cleveland* (Ohio) *Plain Dealer* 13 Oct. 1-C/3 He baffled the Badgers with the option run, gaining 146 yards and scoring on runs of 11 and six yards. **1976** *Webster's Sports Dict.* 291/2 When a halfback is running the option play, it is commonly called the *halfback option*.

2. a. Power or liberty of choosing: opportunity or freedom of choice. ***local option***: see LOCAL.

1633 BP. HALL *Occas. Medit.* (1656) 81 Might I have my option, O God, give mee rather a little, with peace and love. **1697** POTTER *Antiq. Greece* II. xi. (1715) 295 He gave them their option of two things. **1755** YOUNG *Centaur* vi. Wks. 1757 IV. 272 It is, indeed, in man's option, which of these revelations he will admit. **1850** HT. MARTINEAU *Hist. Peace* II. v. i. 206 He [Peel] had no option about accepting [office] —his sovereign sent for him, and he must come. **1881** HUXLEY *Hume* i. 7 Hume's option lay between a travelling tutorship and a stool in a merchant's office.

b. Alternative; esp. in phr. ***with*** (or ***without***) ***the option*** (***of a fine***).

1901 *Chambers's Jrnl.* Sept. 582/2 A third [conviction] should result in imprisonment without the option of a fine. **1903** 'T. COLLINS' *Such is Life* (1944) iii. 106 Yet he has thoughts that glow, and words that burn, albeit with such sulphurous fumes that, when uttered in a public place, they frequently render him liable to fourteen days without the option. **1908** *Daily Chron.* 16 Sept. 4/6 A Suffragette who has been offered the option of a fine. **1914** E. PANKHURST *My Own Story* 71 They were given the option of a fine. **1925** WODEHOUSE *Carry on, Jeeves!* vii. 159 He will serve a sentence of thirty days in the Second Division without the option of a fine.

3. The right which an archbishop formerly had on consecration of a bishop, of choosing one benefice within the see of the latter, to be in his own patronage for the next presentation. (Abolished by Act of Parliament in 1845.)

1701 in *Cowell's Interpr.* **1706** HEARNE *Collect.* 3 Apr. (O.H.S.) I. 217 He got to be precentor of Chichester (that being an Option of ye Archbishop's). **1763** BURN *Eccl. Law* I. 172 s.v. *Bishops*. **1765** BLACKSTONE *Comm.* I. xi. 381. **1818** BENTHAM *Ch. Eng.* 286 The valuable rectory of Almondsford, on the Severn, in the patronage of the Bishop of Bristol, having just become vacant, but the presentation to it devolving to his Grace, as an option, he has liberally waved his right, on condition that it be annexed to the See in perpetuity.

4. The privilege (acquired on some consideration) of executing or relinquishing, as one may choose, within a specified period a commercial transaction on terms now fixed; esp. that of calling for the delivery, or making delivery, or both, within a specified time, of some particular stock or produce at a specified price and to a specified amount.

The first kind of option is usually termed a *call*, and the second a *put*: the right to either is a ***double option***. See also FUTURE *sb.* 6.

1755 MAGENS *Insurances* I. 401 The Sum given is called Premium, and the Liberty that the Giver of the Premium has to have the Contract fulfilled or not, is called Option, and the Contracts are made to the Bearer. **1817** W. SELWYN *Law Nisi Prius* (ed. 4) II. 980 The effect of the whole contract..was only to give the insured an option to continue the insurance or not, during fifteen days after the expiration of the year. **1857** *Hunt's Merchant's Mag.* XXXVII. 134 A purchase of stocks at the brokers' board, buyers' option, thirty, sixty, or ninety days, can call for the stock any day within that time... He pays interest at the rate of 6 per cent up to the time he calls. *Ibid.*, *Seller's option.* This gives the seller the option to deliver any time within the time of his contract, or at its maturity... The buyer..pays interest up to delivery. **1881** *Spectator* No. 2761. 695 Millions a year are lost on the Stock Exchange in buying and selling Options alone, just because the keenest of mankind think everything will remain as it was for one more fortnight. **1882** *Truth* 13 Apr. 515 An option or call of stock means this—a person thinks..some particular stock will go up, he therefore buys the right to take it, if he pleases, at a fixed price at the next account, or at some still more distant account. **1909** D. LLOYD GEORGE in *Hansard Commons* 29 Apr. 519 'Option notes' will be charged at similar rates, calculated upon the value of the securities to which the option relates. **1928** *Daily Mail* 25 July 18/5 None of the shares of the Company are under option. **1976** *Listener* 29 Apr. 533/3 You had bought the option for a book that they hadn't yet written. **1976** L. ST. CLAIR *Fortune in Death* iii. 25 'And the stocks you are interested in?' 'Just one. Aglia Petroleum. Thought I might pick up some calls on it.' '"Options" is our term.' **1977** *Gay News* 7–20 Apr. 22/1 WH Allen, who have the option on it here, are wary of libel suits. **1977** A. MORICE *Scared to Death* i. 7 One condition of this guarantee is an option on each of the plays.

†**5.** A wish or desire. *Obs.*

1604 [see sense 1]. *a* **1626** BP. ANDREWES *Serm.* (1856) I. 60 For this adoption is the fulness of our option, we cannot extend our wish..any farther. **1662** GURNALL *Chr. in Arm.* (1669) 376/2 He adds his holy option, O that men would praise the Lord for his goodness. *c* **1730** *Layman's Def. Christ.* 23 (T.), I shall conclude this epistle with a pathetick option, O that men were wise.

6. *attrib.* and *Comb.* (from 4), as ***option day, market, money, note, plan, pool, price, -taker, time***, etc.; also ***options exchange***.

1865 *Shareholders' Guardian* 8 Nov. 847/2 If at the expiration of the 'option' time the price be the same as the 'option' price, the person who paid the money has the right to buy, sell, or neither, as he thinks proper. **1881** *Daily News* 1 Sept. 3/1 At Paris this was option day, but that fact had no influence upon the Bourse, all options having been previously abandoned. **1889** *Ibid.* 7 Oct. 2/1 'Option-pools' ..imply that a number of persons club together for the purchase of a large option for the put or call of specific securities... To give away money in the purchase of options is bad policy on the whole; and..those who take option money are on the right side of the hedge as a rule. **1899** *Westm. Gaz.* 27 Sept. 9/1 A little option business..is now being done in the shares, £1 being given for the call of the shares at £10 each for six weeks. **1909** Option note [see prec. sense]. **1930** *Daily Express* 30 July 10/3 (*heading*) The option market. **1961** 'E. LATHEN' *Banking on Death* (1962) xv. 123 He had 10 per cent of the stock already as part of an option plan. **1973** *N.Y. Law Jrnl.* 4 Sept. 7/5 (Advt.), The Chicago Board Options Exchange opened in late April.

b. (gen.) **option mortgage** (see quots.).

1966 *New Statesman* 4 Mar. 312/1 People will be free in future to choose between taking an ordinary mortgage and an 'option' mortgage. **1971** *Reader's Digest Family Guide to Law* 61/1 The Option Mortgage Scheme..gives the borrower the choice of foregoing tax relief in return for a Government subsidy which reduces the interest on his mortgage loan. *Ibid.* 61/2 The Option Mortgage Scheme was devised to lower the cost of home ownership to people who do not pay enough tax to obtain full advantage from tax relief on mortgage repayments. **1975** in R. Crossman *Diaries* I. 343 The Minister had announced the new option-mortgage scheme, providing subsidies on mortgages whatever the ruling interest rate if mortgagors would forgo tax relief at the standard rate. **1976** *Star* (Sheffield) 3 Dec. 6/4 Our mortgage is an Option Mortgage, therefore we get no tax relief.

'option, *v.* Chiefly *U.S.* [f. the sb.] *trans.* To buy or sell under option; also, to have an option on.

1934 in WEBSTER. **1947** *Sun* (Baltimore) 3 Apr. 20/1 It was necessary for the Flock to purchase him inasmuch as Cleveland could not option him out again. **1966** E. V. RICKENBACKER *Rickenbacker* (1968) viii. 127, I also optioned the land around the company for future expansion. **1968** R. LOCKRIDGE *Murder in False Face* (1969) v. 68 A friend of his had had a musical optioned a dozen times. 'Lived on options for years,' he said. **1973** *Publishers Weekly* 26 Feb. 121/2 She has written a first novel and had it optioned for films. **1975** *Bookseller* 11 Oct. 2038/3 With [the book] *Saladin* already optioned by the film makers for 150,000 dollars. **1977** *Ottawa Citizen* 8 Feb. 17/2 Irwin Meyer and Stephen R. Friedman..heard the score for Annie. They liked it; they optioned it.

optional ('ɒpʃənəl), *a.* [f. OPTION *sb.* + -AL[1].]

1. That is a matter of choice; depending on choice or preference; that may be done or left undone according to one's will or pleasure.

1792 D. STEWART *Hum. Mind* iv. §2 (1802) 173 In the former case the use of words is, in a great measure, optional; whereas, in the latter, it is essentially necessary. **1818** JAS. MILL *Brit. India* II. v. viii. 625 Even this burthen was optional, not compulsory. **1884** *Law Times Rep.* LI. 667/1 It was perfectly optional with the defendants whether they treated the cheques..as their own or not. **1934** *Language* X. 120 Occasionally one finds free variants, that is, non-conditional or optional variants. **1964** E. PALMER tr. *Martinet's Elem. Gen. Linguistics* iii. 68 In the case of the actor who 'rolls' his r's on the stage but uses the 'throaty' pronunciation elsewhere, we may rather speak of 'optional' variants. **1971** *Good Motoring* Sept. 18/2 Rubber mats are standard; carpets are an optional extra at £10·88. **1972** BERMAN & SZAMOSI in *Language* XLVIII. 313 In the above examples, the phenomenon of 'optional' stress placement does not seem to correlate with significant differences in meaning or sense.

2. Leaving something to choice. ***optional clause***, see quot. 1776. ***optional writ***, see quot. 1809.

1765 *Hist.* in *Ann. Reg.* 90 No bank..can issue notes after the 15th of May 1766, containing optional clauses: but such optional notes as are then in the circle may freely pass from hand to hand during any after period. **1768** BLACKSTONE *Comm.* III. xviii. 274 Original writs are either optional or peremptory. **1776** ADAM SMITH *W.N.* II. ii. (1869) I. 327 Inserting into their banknotes..an Optional Clause, by which they [Scotch Banks] promised payment to the bearer, either as soon as the note should be presented, or, in the option of the directors, six months after such presentment, together with the legal interest for the said six months. **1809**

TOMLINS *Law Dict.* s.v., The *præcipe* was an optional writ, i.e. it was in the alternative, commanding the defendant to do the thing required, or show the reason wherefore he had not done it. **1930** [see ARTIFICIAL *a.* 3 b]. **1962** *Gloss. Terms Automatic Data Processing* (*B.S.I.*) 39 *Optional stop instruction*, an instruction which includes the possibility of stopping the operation of the program immediately before or after the instruction is obeyed, there being some means of permitting or inhibiting this facility as required. **1967** *Technology Week* 23 Jan. 11/1 (Advt.), Input/output is managed independently by one built-in and five optional I/O processors, with up to 160 automatic I/O channels. **1970** D. DODGE *Hatchetman* i. 17 'Underwriters..are being tapped for U.S. dollar payoffs under an airtight optional-money clause.' 'What's an optional-money clause?'.. 'Most major insurers in international trade write it... You put a clause in your insurance policy giving you an option to take payment in another money of your choice.'

Hence **'optionally** *adv.*, in an optional way, at choice.

1846 in WORCESTER.

'optional, *sb.* orig. *U.S.* [f. the adj.] An optional subject or course of study; a group of students constituting a class devoted to an optional subject.

1855 *Songs Biennial Jubilee Class of '57* (Yale Univ.) 3/2 For optionals will come our way. **1857** *Yale Lit. Mag.* XXII. 291 What was never known before, since the establishment of optionals, the number pursuing the study of Hebrew is nine. **1900** *Dialect Notes* II. 47 *Optional.* 1. An optional course selected by a student in addition to his regular work. 2. A student who elects only optional or special courses. **1930** *Times Educ. Suppl.* 12 Apr. 167/3 The advanced mathematics paper set as an 'optional' by London University. **1934** *Times Lit. Suppl.* 8 Mar. 162/2 *Optional.* —An optional subject of study. One example, of 1857, is given from Yale. For over 40 years at St. Paul's School the word has meant the class studying such a subject—e.g., the Spanish optional.

optio'nality. [f. OPTIONAL *a.* + -ITY.] Optional quality; opportunity or freedom of choice.

1880 *Scotsman* 24 Jan. 6/3 How much optionality there may be in an option which is allowed to opt only in one direction may yet be a question for the learned. **1972** *Language* XLVIII. 337 (*heading*) Stress Optionality and the Global Alternative. *Ibid.* 340 The second case of optionality concerns questions. **1975** *Amer. Speech 1973* XLVIII. 39 Even so, the number of implicational relationships remains huge, suggesting..that at least some optionalities are '*not* learned by the child, but [are] predictable from exactly the kinds of substantive constraints..[and] general functional considerations..as those discussed' in Kiparsky's article and suggested to him on quite independent grounds. **1975** *Language* LI. 1015 Generative grammar has no way of formalizing optionality.

'optionalize, *v.* [f. OPTIONAL *a.* + -IZE.] *trans.* To make optional.

1921 *Proc. Classical Assoc.* XVIII. 43 Scotland, where the disastrous results of optionalising Greek in the Universities ..have had time to manifest themselves.

'optionless, *a. poet.* [-LESS.] Without choice, without an option.

1908 HARDY *Dynasts* III. I. i. 328 The hunger for embranglement That gnaws this man, has left us optionless, And haled us recklessly to horrid war.

optique, obs. form of OPTIC.

†**optist.** *Obs. rare*⁻¹. [f. stem of OPT-IC + -IST: cf. *chemic, chemist*, etc.] = OPTICIAN.

1639 HORN & ROBOTHAM *Gate Lang. Unl.* lxxvi. §769 An Optist sercheth into raies (sun-beams) that are for sight, and any thing set before the eye, that may be seen;..and accordingly he frameth spectacles and perspective glasses.

optive ('ɒptɪv), *a.* [ad. L. *optīv-us*, f. stem *opt-* of *optāre* to choose.] Pertaining to or characterized by option; constituted by choosing; elective. In *Rom. Law*: see quotations.

1656 BLOUNT *Glossogr.*, *Optive*, see *Adoptive*. [**1876** MEARS *Rom. Law* 128 The wife might have the right..of choosing the tutor herself..and hence this kind of tutor was called *Tutor optivus*.] **1880** MUIRHEAD *Gaius* I. §154 Tutors appointed in a testament by express nomination are called tutors dative; those selected in virtue of a power of option, tutors optive.

opto-, from Gr. ὀπτός 'seen, visible' and related words in ὀπτ-, used to form modern derivatives and compounds with the notion of 'sight, vision', or 'optic'. See the following words.

optoacoustic (ˌɒptəʊə'kuːstɪk), *a.* Also **opto-acoustic.** [f. OPTO- + ACOUSTIC *a.*] Involving or being the effect whereby a light beam periodically interrupted at an audio frequency produces an audible sound when made to irradiate an enclosed body of gas.

[**1959** *Science Progress* XLVII. 459 (*heading*) The optic-acoustic effect in gases.] **1971** *Jrnl. Appl. Physics* XLII. 2934/1 This technique uses the optoacoustic effect which was discovered by Bell, Tyndall, and Röntgen. **1976** *Nature* 19 Aug. 681/2 Opto-acoustic detection was discovered by Bell nearly a century ago, but was recently revived as a means of monitoring low concentrations of pollutant molecules.

optochin ('ɒptəʊtʃɪn). *Pharm.* Also **optoquine.** [ad. mod.L. *optochinum* (coined in Ger. by M. Goldschmidt 1913, in *Klin. Monatsbl. f. Augenheilkunde* LI. II. 449), f. OPTO- (from its use in treating eye infections) + G. *chin-in* QUININE.] = *ethylhydrocuprein(e* s.v. ETHYL.

1914 *Chem. Abstr.* VIII. 3692 (*heading*) Chemotherapy of the pneumococci infections of the eye, particularly of the ulcus serpens by means of optochin ointment (ethylhydrocuprein). **1925** [see *ethylhydrocuprein(e* s.v. ETHYL]. **1957** J. H. BURN *Princ. Therapeutics* xxvii. 225 When by 1918 it was agreed that, clinically, optochin was dangerous, hope of treating bacterial infections seemed to fade away. **1959** *Acta Path. et Microbiol. Scand.* XLVII. 315 The optochin test is more reliable than the bile test in differentiating between pneumococci and streptococci. **1970** *Jrnl. Gen. Microbiol.* LXI. 138 Assays were made..for the single transformant, to erythromycin, streptomycin, and optochin resistances.

optoelectronic (ˌɒptəʊɪlɛk'trɒnɪk), *a.* Also **opto-electronic.** [f. OPTO- + ELECTRONIC *a.*] Involving or pertaining to the interconversion or interaction of light and electronic signals.

1955 *Proc. IRE* XLIII. 1906/1 The opto-electronic characteristics of electroluminescent and photoconductive transducers make them suitable for..devices and functional networks capable of light amplification, light switching, and light storage. **1959** *RCA Rev.* XX. 742 The simplest class of optoelectronic devices consists of converters. One of the earliest optoelectronic converters is the photovoltaic cell. **1969** *Sci. Jrnl.* Jan. 72/1 The integration of the semiconductor lamp into a microcircuit is a logical step towards opto-electronic applications. **1976** *Pract. Electronics* Oct. 838 (Advt.), This catalogue..offers items from advanced opto-electronic components to humble (but essential) washers.

optoelectronics (ˌɒptəʊɪlɛk'trɒnɪks). *sb. pl.* (const. as *sing.*). Also **opto-electronics.** [f. OPTO- + ELECTRONICS.] The study and application of optoelectronic effects.

1959 *RCA Rev.* XX. 742 Solid-state optoelectronics concerns the use and control of numerous relations among optical and electronic phenomena in solids. **1963** T. E. BRAY in D. K. Pollock et al. *Optical Processing of Information* xvi. 216 Much of the interest in optoelectronics stems from its low cost potential. **1968** *Brit. Universities Ann.* 20 Courses in Man-Machine Systems Engineering and Opto-Electronics. **1973** *Electronics & Power* 5 Apr. 117/4 The use of an optoelectronics transmitter as a means of transmitting quantity and price data from self-service petrol pumps to garage cash desks. **1976** *Pract. Electronics* Oct. 803/3 With over 150 pages the catalogue is broken down into seven sections; Transistors; Integrated Circuits; Diodes and Rectifiers; Opto Electronics; Resistors; Capacitors and Accessories.

optogram ('ɒptəgræm). [f. OPTO- + -GRAM.] Kühne's term for the image formed on the retina by the action of light, which may be rendered permanent by chemical means. So **optography** (ɒp'tɒgrəfi), 'the fixation of a visual image on the retina' (*Syd. Soc. Lex.*).

1878 FOSTER *Phys.* III. ii. 416 In this way Kühne succeeded in obtaining promising 'optograms'. **1890** C. LLOYD MORGAN *Anim. Life & Intell.* 276 If a rabbit be killed at the moment when the image, say, of a window, is formed on the retina, and the membrane at once plunged in a solution of alum, the image may be fixed, and an 'optogram' of the window may be seen on the retina.

optokinetic (ɒptəʊkɪ'nɛtɪc, -kaɪ'nɛtɪk), *a.* [f. OPTO- + KINETIC *a.*] Pertaining to or designating a form of nystagmus produced by attempting to fixate objects which are rapidly traversing the visual field; also, more widely, = OPTOMOTOR *a.*

1925 H. W. STENVERS in *Acta Otolaryngologica* VIII. 545 (*heading*) On the optic (opto-kinetic, opto-motorial) nystagmus. **1947** *Jrnl. Neurol., Neurosurg. & Psychiatry* X. 110/1 When the patient watched a revolving drum the direction of which was reversed, the optokinetic nystagmus obtained to the left side was greater than that obtained to the right. *Ibid.* 116/2 The optokinetic responses..suggest an epileptogenic zone in the left temporal zone. **1966** *New Scientist* 2 June 598/1 Many animals move their eyes or their head if they see something move, and this 'optokinetic' response is often useful as an indication..that an animal has perceived a movement. **1974** *Nature* 8 Feb. 403/1 Newborn infants showed optokinetic nystagmus to a 4 cycles per degree pattern. **1975** *Ibid.* 22 May 330/2 If the visual surround of a walking animal is rotated, the animal turns in a characteristic way. With arthropods, this optomotor (optokinetic) response has usually been described in terms of the angular velocity of the body or eyestalks.

Hence **optoki'netically** *adv.*

1959 *Experientia* XV. 443/2 The question..seems to be whether the nystagmic movements observed..are optokinetically released by the movements of images along the photosensitive surface of the eye. **1965** *Proc. R. Soc. B.* CLXI. 243 The seeing eye is brought artificially instead of optokinetically to the same position.

optometer (ɒp'tɒmɪtə(r)). [OPTO- + -METER.] A name of instruments of various kinds, for measuring or testing vision, in respect of range, acuteness, perception of form or colour, etc.; *esp.* one for measuring the refractive power of the eye and thus testing long- or short-sightedness.

1738 W. PORTERFIELD in *Med. Ess. & Observ.* (ed. 2) IV. 185 The Instrument formerly mentioned; which..I have called an Optometer. **1801** YOUNG in *Trans. R. Soc.* 34. **1801** HOME in *Phil. Trans.* XCII. 5 Dr. Young..constructed an optometer, upon the principle of that of Dr. Porterfield. **1879** *Handbk. Univ. Oxford* 59 In this apartment are being collected instruments of Diagnosis, Ophthalmoscopes, Optometers [etc.]. **1886** *Leeds Merc.* 15 Feb. 5/6 The spectroscopic optometer is available for the study of flames in the Bessemer converter.

optometry. [f. OPTOMETER: see -METRY.] The measurement of the visual powers; the use and application of the optometer; also, the occupation concerned with the measurement of the refractive power of the eyes and the prescription of corrective lenses.

1886 C. M. CULVER tr. *Landolt's Refraction & Accomm. of Eye* iii. 259 One important matter to consider is the point of the retina to be chosen in optometry. **1903** *Optical Jrnl.* Nov. 658 Kindly let me know..if there is any law in New York State governing 'optometry'. **1923** GLAZEBROOK *Dict. Appl. Physics* IV. 287/1 Optometry is a term sometimes applied to all ocular methods of estimating the refraction of the eye. We confine the application here to that generally accepted in Europe, *i.e.* to instruments where an adjustment of lenses is made by the patient in order to obtain the image of an object. **1948** H. W. HOFSTETTER (*title*) Optometry: professional, economic and legal aspects. **1971** *Optometry Today* (Amer. Optometric Assoc.) 15 One such program, which the profession of optometry has encouraged..is the Model Reporting Area for Blindness.

Hence **opto'metric, -ical** *adjs.*, of or pertaining to optometry; **opto'metrically** *adv.*, by means of optometry; **op'tometrist** (chiefly *U.S.*), one who practises optometry; an ophthalmic optician.

1864 W. D. MOORE tr. *Donders' Anomalies Accomm. & Refraction of Eye* i. 71 It was extremely important to see how far these results of measurement and calculation agreed with those of the simple optometrical investigation in the same persons. *Ibid.* (*heading*) Comparison of R and P, deduced from measurements on the eye and optometrically determined. **1886** C. M. CULVER tr. *Landolt's Refraction & Accomm. of Eye* iii. 252 To determine this degree of the ametropia, we may use all the above-mentioned optometric methods. **1903** *Optical Jrnl.* Oct. 558/2 The word 'optometrist'..coined by Mr. Eberhardt [President of the American Association of Opticians], is a popular one, and likely to be adopted by the American Association at its Milwaukee Convention in 1904. **1923** GLAZEBROOK *Dict. Appl. Physics* IV. 287/2 This optometric system is the best if one can rely upon the accurate judgment of comparison by the patient. **1945** *Amer. Jrnl. Ophthalm.* XXVIII. 669/1 It seems obvious that optometrists will continue to perform a large percentage of the refractions in America and will always be interested in matters that concern ophthalmologists also. **1957** A. HUXLEY *Let.* 12 Jan. (1969) 815 The medical and optometrical lobby has gone to work in the various state legislatures. *Ibid.*, What is happening in the US is that optometrists—a breed superior to opticians, in as much as they get a long training, but not fool [*sic*] blown oculists..are steadily adopting..Batesian procedures. **1965** *Amer. Jrnl. Optometry* XLII. 50 Optometry has taken on a brighter public image in those areas where optometric educational institutions exist. **1971** 'D. SHANNON' *Murder with Love* (1972) v. 79 Nearly every tenant..was a professional of some kind: doctors, dentists, optometrists. **1976** *Casper* (Wyoming) *Star-Tribune* 29 June 6/1 Members voted to assist Dr. James Lane, an optometrist, with the Vision Day program on July 19. Children who will attend first grade in the fall are given a free eye examination to rule out serious problems with their vision.

optomotor ('ɒptəməʊtə(r)), *a.* [f. OPTO- + MOTOR *a.*] Pertaining to or characterized by turning of the eyes or body in response to the visual perception of a moving object.

1926 *Brain* XLIX. 333 This nystagmus has been termed 'railway nystagmus', 'optomotor nystagmus' or simply 'optic nystagmus'. **1932** *Arch. Neurol. & Psychiatry* (Chicago) XXVIII. 1024 Interruption of the optomotor pathway at any point in its course would disturb the ocular adaptation to a certain direction of movement of the visual field. **1961** H. SCHÖNE in T. H. Waterman *Physiol. Crustacea* II. xiii. 492 The fine adjustment of turning movements in locomotion is checked by optomotor mechanisms. **1971** *Nature* 9 July 128/1 In the classical optomotor experiment an animal is placed inside a rotating striped drum. **1975** [see OPTOKINETIC *a.*].

optophone ('ɒptəfəʊn). Also **Optophone.** [ad. G. *optophon* (E.E.F. d'Albe 1912, in *Physikal. Zeitschr.* XIII. 942/2), f. *opto-* OPTO- + Gr. φωνή voice, sound.] An instrument designed to enable blind persons to read, in which a photoelectric cell is employed to scan a text and produce electrical signals that are converted into audible ones corresponding to the different characters.

1913 E. E. F. D'ALBE in *Electrician* 24 Oct. 103/1 The reading optophone consists essentially of a selenium preparation illuminated by a line of light broken up into dots. **1923** *Glasgow Herald* 3 Oct. 6 Messrs Barr and Stroud ..by the invention and manufacture of their 'Optophone' have supplied the blind with a practical means of reading almost any printed type. Every letter sounds a tiny musical-motive up in the treble region. **1960** *Daily Tel.* 18 Oct. 15/1 She used an optophone, an experimental instrument developed from an invention of the late Dr Fournier d'Albe. **1973** *Nature* 27 Apr. 591/1 A device for converting letters into auditory signals, the 'Optophone' of E. F. d'Albe, allowed a trained blind person to read ordinary print.., but never met the ultimate criterion of success because reading ..was slow, and learning to do it was very difficult.

optoquine, var. OPTOCHIN.

opto-striate (ɒptəʊ'straɪət), *a. Anat.* [f. OPTO- + STRIATE.] Pertaining to, or consisting of, the optic thalamus and corpus striatum together.

1892 *Syd. Soc. Lex.*, *Opto-striate body*, the conjoined *Optic thalamus* and *Corpus striatum*. **1899** *Allbutt's Syst.*

Med. VI. 305 On several occasions I have found obliterative endarteritis of the opto-striate branches.

optotype ('ɒptəʊtaɪp). [f. OPTO- + TYPE. First formed as mod.L. *optotypus* (H. Snellen 1875, in *Klin. Monatsbl. f. Augenheilkunde* XIII. 479).] A type or letter of definite size used for testing acuteness of vision; a test-type.

[**1886** C. M. CULVER tr. *Landolt's Refraction & Accomm. of Eye* iii. 229 These tables of type figures, 'optotypi', as Snellen calls them, are what we use in optometry.] **1892** in *Syd. Soc. Lex.* **1905** *Trans. Amer. Ophthalm. Soc.* X. 648 Attempts have been made..to construct special optotypes adapted to the limited capacity and observing powers of young children and illiterates. **1963** *Arch. Ophthalm.* LXX. 113/2 Amblyopic eyes required more light to read optotypes than did normal eyes. **1970** A. H. KEENEY *Ocular Exam.* iii. 29/1 Letters and numbers in the patient's own language most closely relate to his daily seeing requirements and therefore are the most practical optotypes.

'opt-out, *sb.* [f. *to opt out* (OPT *v.* 2).] A radio or television programme broadcast by a regional station for local consumption (in preference to one distributed nationally). Also *attrib.* or as *adj.*

1962 *B.B.C. Handbk.* 27 The regions have concentrated on providing themselves with facilities for putting out television programmes which have either been fed into the national programme or have provided special programmes for local consumption on an 'opt out' basis. *Ibid.* 38, I think it would probably be convenient and sensible to place most of the regional programmes, the opt-outs as we call them, in one channel. **1964** *Listener* 31 Dec. 1049 An 'opt-out' programme is one broadcast only on a regional wavelength. **1970** *Daily Tel.* 9 Nov. 6/5 At present in Birmingham there is one weekly opt-out time slot. **1972** P. BLACK *Biggest Aspidistra* I. ii. 24 The regional listeners preferred London to their local station, though..you could sometimes tune in to the local opt-out as well as the net-worked programme. **1975** *Listener* 6 Feb. 166/3 The BBC in the North-East has to divide its ration of opt-out time. **1977** *Private Eye* 1 Apr. 4/2 Moreover, a mere 250,000 viewers watch *Tonight* at the best of times and it's only a regional opt-out programme anyway.

opugn, obs. form of OPPUGN.

opulence ('ɒpjʊləns). [ad. L. *opulentia*, f. *opulens, -ent-em* or *opulent-us*: see OPULENT and -ENCE. Cf. F. *opulence* (R. Estienne 1549).] Wealth, riches, affluence.

c **1510** BARCLAY *Mirr. Gd. Manners* (1570) D iiij, No giftes nor treasure of greatest opulence. **1668** WILKINS *Real Char.* II. viii. 201 Riches, Wealth, Opulence, Pelf, Means, Fortunes, Estate. **1742** YOUNG *Nt. Th.* VI. 529 How Few can rescue Opulence from Want!.. Who lives to Fancy, never can be rich. **1776** ADAM SMITH *W.N.* II. iii. (1869) I. 349 It is this effort..which has maintained the progress of England towards opulence. *a* **1806** C. J. FOX in Emerson *Cond. Life* Wks. (Bohn) II. 419 The most meritorious public services have always been performed by persons in a condition of life removed from opulence. **1838** THIRLWALL *Greece* xxi. III. 203 Citizens who had more recently risen to opulence.

b. *fig.* Abundance of resources or power.

1791 MACKINTOSH *Vindic. Gallicæ* Wks. 1846 III. 4 Argument..aided by the most pathetic and picturesque description, speaks the opulence and the powers of that mind. **1847** EMERSON *Repr. Men, Plato* Wks. (Bohn) I. 297 He has that opulence which furnishes, at every turn, the precise weapon he needs.

c. *transf.* 'Wealth', abundance (e.g. of hair); plumpness of person [from mod. Fr.].

1878 B. TAYLOR *Deukalion* III. vi. 129 The loose golden opulence of her hair These clouds untangle. **1896** A. MORRISON *Child Jago* 131 Leary, in his heavy opulence of flesh.

†**'opulency.** *Obs.* [ad. L. *opulentia*: see prec. and -ENCY.] = prec.

1607 SHAKS. *Timon* V. i. 38 A Discouerie of the infinite Flatteries That follow youth and opulencie. **1692** tr. *Sallust* 9 Envy sprung from Opulency. **1753** HOGARTH *Anal. Beauty* viii. 47 An air of opulency and magnificence.

opulent ('ɒpjʊlənt), *a.* Also 7 oppulent. [ad. L. *opulens, -ent-em* or *opulent-us* rich, wealthy, splendid, f. *op-s, op-em* power, might, resources, wealth: see -ULENT. Cf. F. *opulent* (14th c. in Littré), It. *opulente, -ento*, Sp., Pg. *opulento*.]

1. Rich, wealthy, affluent.

1601 J. WHEELER *Treat. Comm.* 72 The Hanses should growe opulent, and possesse the whole trade of the realme. *c* **1645** HOWELL *Lett.* (1650) I. 394 The potentest monarchies, the proudest republicks, the opulentest cities have their growth, declinings, and periods. *a* **1704** T. BROWN *Two Oxford Scholars* Wks. 1730 I. 10, I shall be strangely unfortunate if I meet not with some opulent widow. **1761** HUME *Hist. Eng.* I. viii. 168 His way of life was splendid and opulent. **1852** MRS. STOWE *Uncle Tom's C.* i. 1 The arrangements of the house, and the general air of the house-keeping, indicated easy and even opulent circumstances.

b. Yielding great wealth, lucrative.

1664 EVELYN *Sylva* (1679) 6 The richest and most opulent Wheat-lands. **1818** JAS. MILL *Brit. India* I. I. i. 12 So opulent and brilliant a commerce.

2. *transf.* and *fig.* Rich or wealthy in some respect; abounding or profuse in some property: **a.** in mental wealth; **b.** in material possessions or qualities; **c.** in physical development; plump [from Fr.].

1791–1823 D'ISRAELI *Cur. Lit., Libraries*, Grollier, whose library was opulent in these luxuries. **1851** CARLYLE *Sterling* I. xiv. (1872) 82 The certain prefigurement..of an opulent, genial and sunny mind. **1863** WOOLNER *My Beautiful Lady* 32, I wonder whether She now her braided opulent hair unlace. **1867** J. H. STIRLING in *Fortn. Rev.* Oct. 380 The injustice of applying the epithet 'destructive' to such an opulent and affirmative soul. **1896** *Westm. Gaz.* 10 Mar. 2/1 Although a little short for her build, and somewhat opulent for statuary, she is superbly modelled.

3. Of flowers, etc.: Having a wealth of blossom, tint, or fragrance; splendid.

1863 B. TAYLOR *H. Thurston* xiv. 181 The hyacinths.. filling the walk with their opulent breath. **1868** TENNYSON *Lucretius* 248 Or beast or bird or fish, or opulent flower. **1886** WOOLNER *Nelly Gray* 5 Our pathway..So rich with blossom, and opulent Successive honeysuckle scent.

Hence **'opulently** *adv.*, in an opulent manner or degree; richly, affluently, splendidly. **'opulentness**, wealthiness (Bailey vol. II, 1727).

1611 COTGR., *Richement*, richly, wealthily, opulently. **1727** BAILEY vol. II, *Opulently*. (Hence in Johnson, etc.) **1871** A. AUSTIN *Golden Age*, We turned away, and opulently cold, Put back our swords of steel in sheaths of gold!

‖**opulus** ('ɒpjʊləs). *Bot.* [L. *opulus*, a kind of maple; taken in Bot. as a generic or specific name.] The Guelder Rose, *Viburnum Opulus.*

1706 PHILLIPS, *Opulus*, a kind of Shrub, which some call Witch-hasel. **1751** J. BARTRAM *Observ. Trav. Pennsylv.* 27 A hill covered with spruce, oak spruce, lawrel, opulus, yew.

opunion, -yon(e, -ȝoun, obs. Sc. ff. OPINION.

‖**Opuntia** (ɒ'pʌnʃɪə). [L. *Opuntia* (sc. *herba*), a plant growing, according to Pliny, about the Locrian city Opus (acc. *Opunt-em*) in Greece; taken by Tournefort, 1700, as a generic name.] A large genus of cactaceous plants; also, the fruit of a plant of this genus; the Prickly Pear or Indian Fig.

Opuntia vulgaris, the Common Prickly Pear or Barbary Fig, a native of America, is now naturalized on both shores of the Mediterranean, in the Canary Islands, etc.

1601 HOLLAND *Pliny* II. 99 About the city Opus there is an herb called Opuntia, which men delight to eat: this admirable gift the leafe hath, That if it be laied in the ground, it will take root. **1765** in W. Stork *Acc. East Florida* (1766) 79 The third sort of soil produces the cabbage-tree, ..the plumb-tree, and opuntia. **1785** MARTYN *Rousseau's Bot.* xxi. (1794) 287 Opuntias are composed of flat joints connected together. **1878** HOOKER & BALL *Marocco* 277 Enclosed within massive hedges of Opuntia.

Hence **o'puntioid** *a.*, resembling the Prickly Pears.

1857 BERKELEY *Cryptog. Bot.* 408 Remarkable for the opuntioid constriction of the subfastigate branches.

‖**opus** ('ɒpəs, 'əʊpəs), *sb.* [L. *opus* work, pl. *opera.*]

1. A work, a composition; *esp.* a musical composition or set of compositions as numbered among the works of a composer in order of publication. Abbreviated *op.* Also attrib., as ***opus number***.

1809 SOUTHEY *Lett.* (1856) II. 162, I shall do it volume by volume in my great 'Opus'. **1815** *Ibid.* 404, I have found out another opus for you when you have completed the 'West Indies'. **1880** *Grove's Dict. Mus.* II. 135 No opus-number is given on the English copy. *Ibid.* 532/2 No rule is observed as regards the size of an opus: for instance, Beethoven's op. 1 consists of three pianoforte trios, while Schubert's op. 1 is only the song 'Erlkönig'.

2. The Latin expression ***opus magnum*** or ***magnum opus*** 'great work', is frequent in Eng. use, esp. in reference to a large or important literary work.

1704 SWIFT *T. Tub* v. 116 His Account of the *Opus magnum* is extremely poor and deficient. **1791** BOSWELL *Let. to Rev. W. Temple* (1857) 406 My *magnum opus*, the 'Life of Dr. Johnson'..is to be published on Monday, 16th May. **1843** MILL *Logic* v. iii. §1 To determine what these propositions are, is the *opus magnum* of the more recondite mental philosophy. **1892** *Nation* (N.Y.) 29 Dec. 500/2 When an author's *magnum opus* is his only work, we have no right to complain if we sometimes detect tentative efforts in it. *Mod.* 'How goes the *magnum opus*? What letter are you working at now?'

3. Applied to slighter productions, compostions, etc.

1957 J. D. SALINGER *Zooey* in *New Yorker* XXXIII. 93/1 The most courageous goddam offbeat television opus you ever read. **1959** P. BULL *I know Face* ix, 147 'B' films and other ghastly opuses. **1967** *Crescendo* May 8/2 'When Lights Are Low' is the old Benny Carter opus—one of my favourites. **1967** *Telegraph* (Brisbane) 30 June 12 Nine young couples are determined to go ahead with New York's latest open air opus—a 'wed-in'. **1976** *Publishers Weekly* 15 Mar. 49/3 A spooky chiller of a first novel, this will have readers waiting impatiently for the next Ryder Brady opus to come along.

opus ('ɒpəs, 'əʊpəs), *v.* [f. the sb.] *trans.* To include and number among the works of a composer of music. Abbreviated *op.*

1900 W. A. ELLIS *Life Wagner* I. 376 This negligence in 'opus-ing' his musical works. **1921** A. B. SMITH in *Music & Lett.* II. 364 A large class of composers..write pieces solely for the pleasure of opusing them. *Ibid.*, Every piece of his [Gurlitt] is Op.-ed.

‖**opus alexandrinum** ('ɒpəs ˌælɛksɑːn'draɪnəm, -æ-). Also with capital initials. [med.L., lit. 'Alexandrian work'.] A type of pavement mosaic work consisting of coloured stone, glass, and semiprecious stones arranged in intricate geometric patterns. It was much used in Byzantium in the 9th century and is later found in Italy.

1852 *Murray's Handbk. N. Italy* (ed. 4) 546/1 A mosaic.. of that kind which is called 'opus Alexandrinum'. **1854** WYATT & WARING *Byzantine & Romanesque Court in Crystal Palace* 38 The *Opus Alexandrinum*——we may describe it generally as tessellated marble-work..an arrangement of small cubes, usually of porphyry or serpentine. **1875** F. E. HULME *Princ. Ornamental Art* i. 10 The *opus Alexandrinum* was a marble tessellation generally composed of porphyry..and serpentine..arranged into geometric patterns that were cut into the white marble slabs that composed the groundwork of the pavement. **1897** J. WARD *Historic Ornament* vii. 345 Another kind of mosaic used in pavement is that known as *opus Alexandrinum.* **1904** L. F. DAY *Ornament* v. 122 But for the economic instinct prompting men always to find use for a waste product, nothing like Opus Alexandrinum might ever have been done. **1955** *Times* 18 May 12/4 The sacristy lost the whole of its contents, but still retains part of the ancient pavement of *opus alexandrinum.* **1974** *Encycl. Brit. Micropædia* I. 228/3 In the 12th century several variations of *opus Alexandrinum* evolved at local centres in Italy, including the well-known Cosmati work..of Rome.

‖**opus anglicanum** ('ɒpəs æŋglɪ'kɑːnəm). Also with capital initials. [med.L., lit. 'English work'; see ANGLICAN *a.* and *sb.*] The name given to the fine pictorial embroidery produced in England in the Middle Ages, esp. between *c* 1250 and *c* 1350, and used esp. for ecclesiastical vestments.

[**1277–81** in A. G. I. CHRISTIE *Eng. Medieval Embroidery* (1938) 2 Unum pretiosissimum pluviale ad ymagines Sanctorum contextum de opere Anglicano. *c* **1840** LADY WILTON *Art of Needlework* vii. 66 So celebrated was the English work, the Opus Anglicum, that other nations eagerly desired to possess it.] **1848** C. H. HARTSHORNE *Eng. Medieval Embroidery* 11 English embroidery has consistently enough been called the *opus Anglicanum*, from being a manufacture extensively and skilfully pursued in our own country. **1870** D. ROCK *Textile Fabrics* 281 This invaluable and matchless specimen of the far-famed 'Opus Anglicanum', or English needlework. **1909** L. DE FARCY in *Embroidery* VI. 168/2, I hope that..soon I may applaud their [*sc.* that of the English] success in the revival of their *opus Anglicanum.* **1922** *Daily Tel.* 12 June 20/6 (Advt.), The collection of XV Century vestments from Whalley Abbey, including some magnificent examples of 'Opus Anglicanum', the property of the Right Hon. Lord O'Hagan. **1936** *Burlington Mag.* Oct. 182/1 The rich collection of *Opus Anglicanum* at the Victoria and Albert Museum. **1954** M. RICKERT *Painting in Brit.: Middle Ages* v. 128 The fineness of quality which is to give to English embroidery, the so-called *opus anglicanum*, its wide reputation during the late thirteenth and early fourteenth centuries. **1960** D. M. WILSON *Anglo-Saxons* v. 155 In the twelfth century, embroideries of 'English work' (*opus anglicanum*) were to become famous throughout Europe. **1964** tr. *A. Geijer's Textile Treasures of Uppsala Cathedral* 23 Technical similarities to recognized examples of *opus anglicanum*, the famous English art of the High Middle Ages, have caused some scholars..to attribute this work to England. **1974** *Encycl. Brit. Micropædia* VII. 557/1 Opus anglicanum has..survived all over Europe wherever historic vestments are treasured.

‖**opus anglicum** ('ɒpəs 'æŋglɪkəm). Now *rare.* [med.L., lit. 'English work'; see ANGLIC *a.* and cf. prec.] A type of manuscript illumination regarded as characteristically English (see quot. 1860).

1860 F. DELAMOTTE *Primer of Art of Illumination* 11 When the graceful and luxuriant curves of foliage begin to steal into the pages of the MS. they are to be found also forming the capital of the column,..a style of illumination generally known as the *opus Anglicum.* **1901** J. W. BRADLEY *Hist. Introd. Coll. Illum. Lett. & Borders V. & A. Mus.* vi. 81 So excellent is the work and so famous did it become that it was considered on the Continent as typical of our national art and received the appellation of 'opus Anglicum'.

‖**opus araneum** ('ɒpəs æ'rɑːnɪəm). [med.L., lit. 'spider's work'.] Darned netting; a type of delicate embroidery done on a ground of net. Also called *spiderwork* (SPIDER *sb.* 11).

1865 F. B. PALLISER *Hist. Lace* ii. 17 Distinct from all these geometric combinations was the Lacis of the sixteenth century, done on a network ground (réseau), identical with the 'opus araneum', or spider-work of continental writers. **1870** D. ROCK *Textile Fabrics* 162 This is a good specimen of a kind of cobweb weaving, or 'opus araneum', for which Lombardy..earned such a reputation at one time. **1874** [see *spiderwork* s.v. SPIDER *sb.* 11]. **1882** CAULFEILD & SAWARD *Dict. Needlework* 233/1 During the Middle Ages this Network was called Opus Araneum, Ouvrages Masches, Punto a Maglia, Lacis, and Point Conté. **1900** F. N. JACKSON *Hist. Hand-Made Lace* 185 *Opus araneum*, Spider Work. The ancient name for Cluny Guipure Lace and Darned Netting.

opuscle (əʊ'pʌs(ə)l). *rare.* [ad. L. *opusculum.*] = OPUSCULE.

1658 PHILLIPS, *Opuscle*, a little work, or labour. **1862** WRAXALL *Hugo's 'Misérables'* I. v. 3 The various opuscles published in the last century.

‖**opus consutum** ('ɒpəs kɒn'suːtəm). [med.L., lit. 'work sewn together'.] = APPLIQUÉ *sb.*

1870 D. ROCK *Textile Fabrics* p. cii, *Our old English opus consutum, or cut work*, in French, 'appliqué', is a term of rather wide meaning, as it takes in several sorts of decorative accompaniments to needlework. **1882** CAULFEILD & SAWARD *Dict. Needlework* 7/2 This work was anciently known as *Opus Consutum* or cut work. **1899** E. T. MASTERS *Bk. of*

Stitches i. 1 The average woman feels no interest in knowing that when she is working an *appliqué* panel.. she is executing the classical *opus consutum*. **1972** *Country Life* 6 Jan. 24/1 Pieced work, or the sewing together of different materials for ornamentation—the *opus consutum* of the convents—was a common form of fabric adornment in the Middle Ages.

opuscular (əʊˈpʌskjʊlə(r)), *a.* [f. L. *opuscul-um* (see next) + -AR.] Of, belonging to, or of the nature of a small work.

1802 *Edinb. Rev.* I. 116 (*Mrs. Opie's Poems*) The verses of *feeling*.. are certainly among the best in our opuscular poetry.

opuscule (əʊˈpʌskju:l). [a. F. *opuscule* (14th c.), ad. L. *opuscul-um*: see next and -CULE.] A small work; esp. a literary or musical work of small size.

1656 BLOUNT *Glossogr.*, *Opuscule*, a little work, a little labor. *a* **1851** in Thackeray *Christmas Bks.* (1872) 127 To put forth certain opuscules, denominated 'Christmas Books'. **1876** MORLEY *Crit. Misc.* (1888) III. 361 In this opuscule he points out that Modern Society is passing through a great crisis. **1885** *Bookseller* July 649/1 His customers refused to pay a shilling for a tiny opuscule which should have been sold for sixpence.

‖**opusculum** (əʊˈpʌskjʊləm). Pl. **-ula**. [L., dim. of *opus* work.] = prec.

1654 GAYTON *Pleas. Notes* 33 Many more eminent *Opuscula* of that nature. **1657** EVELYN *Memoirs* (1857) III. 90 Dr. Andrews, Grotius, Dr. Hammond, in a particular opusculum.. have all treated on this subject. **1782** V. KNOX *Ess.* cvi. (1819) II. 249 Pretty and pleasing opuscula. **1886** *Athenæum* 14 Aug. 208/2 Hitherto undescribed opuscula, both in prose and verse, printed before 1539.

‖**opus Dei** (ˈɒpəs ˈdeii:). [med.L. (attributed to St. Benedict).] **1.** *Eccl.* The work of God, *spec.* the Divine Office, or liturgical worship in general, seen as man's primary duty to God.

[*c* **530–540** *Rule of St. Benedict* (1952) xliii. 102 Ad horam divini Officii mox auditum fuerit signum, relictis omnibus quaelibet fuerint in manibus, summa cum festinatione curratur... Ergo nihil operi Dei praeponatur.] **1887** F. C. DOYLE *Teaching of St. Benedict* xix. 141 An 'opus Dei'—namely, the 'care of souls', which, according to the teaching of theologians, is even more the 'work of God' than psalmody. **1896** F. A. GASQUET in C. F. De Montalembert *Monks of West* I. p. xiii, The Divine Office was the daily service and formal homage rendered to the Divine Majesty. This, the *opus Dei*, was the crown of the whole structure of the monastic edifice. **1907** *Cath. Encycl.* II. 469/2 This public worship of God, the *opus Dei*, was to form the chief work of his monks. **1921** J. MCCANN tr. *Delatte's Commentary on Rule of St. Benedict* viii. 133 Our Holy Father and other ancient writers are well inspired when they call the liturgy in its totality the *Opus Dei* (Work of God). **1929** R. EATON *Benedictines of Colwich* iv. 47 The nuns were desolate of all spiritual help.. their one consolation being to continue the 'Opus Dei' as best they could in the dismantled chapel. **1939** J. CHAPMAN *St. Benedict & Sixth Cent.* v. 86 St. Gregory the Great follows St. Benedict in the habitual use of *opus Dei*. **1969** R. GODDEN *In this House of Brede* ii. 71 'Everything we do..,' said Dame Clare, 'our work, our reading, our private prayer, even our meals.. are simply pauses, meant to prepare ourselves for real work, the Opus Dei.' **1977** *Church Times* 5 Aug. 10/4 The complete *Opus Dei*—Mattins, Solemn Eucharist and Evensong—is sung at Edington Priory Church.. from Sunday evening, August 21, until the following Sunday morning by cathedral and collegiate choristers.

2. (With capital initials.) The name of a Roman Catholic organization of laymen and priests founded in Spain in 1928 with the purpose of re-establishing Christian ideals in society through the implementation of them in the lives of its members. So **Opusde'ista**, a member of this organization.

1954 V. S. PRITCHETT *Spanish Temper* v. 99 The infiltrations of the members of Opus Dei who work, exactly in communist fashion, to frustrate professional groups. **1960** *Spectator* 25 Nov. 803 The organisation.. is known as *Opus Dei*; the Jesuits call it 'The White Freemasonry'. **1961** *Ibid.* 9 June 830 A group of *Opus Dei* economists within the Spanish Government. **1967** G. HILLS *Franco* xv. 432 Ullastres and Navarro Rubio were known to be.. members of a religious society, *Opus Dei*, men pledged by a solemn vow to the dedication to God of all their professional talents. **1968** K. BIRD *Smash Glass Image* vi. 79 Hostile to the Government.. were monarchists, liberals, Christian Democrats, Communists, anarchists, the Opus Dei. **1970** J. W. D. TRYTHALL *Franco* ix. 226 Members of Opus Dei, like freemasons, form the sort of semi-secret, loosely organised body that everybody who is not a member regards as a conspiracy. **1973** L. MACKENZIE in *Govt. & Opposition* VIII. 72 The Opus Dei was founded as a religious organization in 1928 by Father Escrivá de Balaguer in Spain. **1974** *Encycl. Brit. Micropædia* VII. 557/2 The two economic ministries were entrusted to Opusdeistas, and since that time [*sc.* 1956] other members of Opus Dei have held ministerial posts and other positions in government.

‖**opus filatorium** (ˈɒpəs fɪləˈtɔərɪəm). [med.L., lit. 'work of threads'.] An early name for darned netting or spiderwork. Cf. OPUS ARANEUM above.

1882 CAULFEILD & SAWARD *Dict. Needlework* 233/1 In this lace [*sc.* Guipure d'Art].. we have the modern revival of the Opus Filatorium, or Darned Netting, or Spiderwork, so much used in the fourteenth century. **1883** J. W. MOLLETT *Illustr. Dict. Art. & Archæol.* 235/2 *Opus filatorium*, a kind of embroidery, 14th century; modern 'filet brodé'.

‖**opus sectile** (ˈɒpəs ˈsɛktɪleɪ). [L., lit. 'cut work'.] A form of floor decoration dating from Roman times and made up of pieces shaped individually to fit the pattern or design, in which respect it differs from mosaic which is an arrangement of regularly shaped pieces.

1852 *Murray's Handbk. N. Italy* (ed. 4) 491/1 This Florentine mosaic seems to be the 'opus sectile' of the Romans. **1854** WYATT & WARING *Byzantine & Romanesque Court in Crystal Palace* 39 'Opera di commesso'—that is, a mosaic formed by slices of marble, arranged somewhat on the principle of the ancient 'opus sectile', the projections of one piece being so cut as to enter into the recesses of another. **1935** E. W. ANTHONY *Hist. Mosaics* iii. 48 The work which the Romans designated as *opus sectile* does not come under the head of mosaic, although it has sometimes been thus classified. **1948** *Antiquity* XXII. 77 Opus sectile floors at the major sites of Cyrene and Tolmeita. **1950** O. DEMUS *Mosaics of N. Sicily* III. i. 369 There existed.. a technique of decoration somewhat akin to mosaic, the Saracenic *opus sectile*. **1971** P. FISCHER *Mosaic* 80 Earthenware pieces are specially cut to the individual shapes required by the design .. rather in the manner of the second type of Roman *opus sectile*. **1978** *Sci. Amer.* Jan. 116/2 This kind of pavement is known as *opus sectile* (the Latin phrase for cut work), and the example in our house is the first Byzantine *opus sectile* floor found in a private house in Carthage that can be confidently dated.

‖**opus signinum** (ˈɒpəs sɪgˈni:nəm). [L. *opus* work + *signinum* Signian, of or pertaining to Signia.] A flooring material used by the Romans and consisting of broken tiles and other fragments mixed with lime mortar, being named after Signia (modern Segni), a town in Latium which was famous for its tiles.

References to *opus signinum* occur in the works of Columella, Vitruvius, and Pliny: see Lewis and Short *Lat. Dict. s.v.* Signinus. A description of the making of *opus signinum* is found in Vitruvius *De Architectura* VII. vi. §14.

1745 *Columella's Husbandry* I. vi. 34 They, it seems, contrived a plaister or flooring made with bruised tiles, or sheards of earthen vessels, and lime, tempered together. With this composition they made very durable floors, &c. and this they called *opus Signinum*. **1899** R. GLAZIER *Man. Hist. Ornament* 75 *Opus Signinum*, small pieces of tile. **1937** *Discovery* July 208/1 A [Roman] floor of bits of stone and tile bound together with cement (*opus signinum*). **1967** *Antiquaries Jrnl.* XLVII. 269 The two northern cells retained their floors of *opus signinum* which, in both cells, had been once renewed. **1971** P. FISCHER *Mosaic* 45 The humblest mosaic-type floor decoration, *opus signinum* (named after Signia, a town in Latium), is a levelled surface made up from odd fragments of stone or pottery of different colours, set at random in lime mortar rather like raisins in a cake. **1974** *Encycl. Brit. Micropædia* VII. 557/3 *Opus signinum* was the prevalent form of pavement in Roman houses from the 1st century BC to about the 2nd century AD when it was rapidly replaced in main rooms by patterned pavement mosaics of the tessellated variety.

opy(e, variant of OPIE *Obs.*, opium.

O'quassa. The name of one of the Rangeley Lakes in western Maine, used *attrib.* or *absol.* to designate a small trout, the blue-back trout, *Salvelinus oquassa*, found in these lakes.

1883 J. J. LALOR *Cycl. Polit. Sci.* II. 215/2 The oquassa, or blue-backed trout (*Salvelinus oquassa*) of the lakes of Maine is a noteworthy American form. **1884** *Bull. U.S. Nat. Mus.* No. 27. 427 Oquassa Trout; Blue-Back Trout. Lakes in western Maine. **1888** G. B. GOODE *Amer. Fishes* 93 Tautog, chogset,.. oquassa and namaycush are among the best of them [*sc.* aboriginal American fish names]. **1902** JORDAN & EVERMANN *Amer. Food & Game Fishes* 217 Oquassa Trout; Blueback Trout... The blueback trout is the smallest and one of the most handsome of the charrs... Formerly this fish was very abundant.

oque, oquea, oqui, obs. ff. OKA, OKE.

or (ɔ:(r)), *sb. Her.* [a. F. *or*:—L. *aurum* gold.] The tincture gold or yellow in armorial bearings.

1562 LEIGH *Armorie* (1597) 1 b, I will begin with the most pretious mettall Golde: Or. **1591** SYLVESTER *Du Bartas* I. v. 973 Azure they bear three Eaglets Argentine, A Cheuron Ermin grailed Or between. **1646** G. DANIEL *Poems* Wks. 1878 I. 44 And tell you how they beare Gules, or, vert, azure, —heathen words for Red, Yellow, green, blue. **1766** PORNY *Heraldry* (1787) 20 Or, which signifies gold, and in colour yellow, is expressed by points, pricks, or dots... The precious Stone to which it is compared is Topaz, and the Planet Sol. **1875** FORTNUM *Maiolica* ix. 79 These arms are paly gules and or, on a fess argent a dog in the act of bounding sable.

b. *or moulu*, *or molu*: see ORMOLU.

or (ɔ:(r), ə(r)), *adv.*[1] (*prep.*, *conj.*[1]) *arch.* and *dial.* Forms: see below, and cf. AIR *adv.* [OE. *ár* adv. (late Northumb.): cf. ON. *ár*, Goth. *air*, OE. *ǽr*, OTeut. **air* (?) and **airi*: see ERE. In early ME. *ār*, *are*, later *ōr*, *ore*, *oore*. But in all the uses exc. A. 1 the sense is that of the comparative, OE. *ǽr*, Goth. *airis*, OHG. *ēr* earlier, sooner, before.

The solitary O.Northumb. instance of adv. *ár* in A.I., with Ormin's *ār*, the *ār*, *āre* of Cursor M., and Sc. *are*, AIR, can only be from the ON. positive adv. *ár* 'early'. To the same origin must be assigned, so far as *form* goes, the Early ME. and north. *ār*, midl. *ōr*, in A. II (*ōre* having assumed an adverbial *-e*, as in *there*, *where*, etc.). But the *sense* here is that of the OE. comparative *ǽr*, ME. *ēr*, *ēre*: as *ār* existed side by side with *ēr* in the positive, it may have intruded also into the comparative, in which *ēr*, ERE, from OE. *ǽr*, was the only etymological form. In this sense Sc. still has AIR. B. and C. have, beside *er*, *ere*, the form *or* in midl. (before 1225). In 13–14th c. *ar* (*are*) is found in the north, but appears soon to have been displaced by the midl. *or*, which is still the ordinary northern word. The northern texts of *Cursor M.* have the prepositional and conjunctive *ar* (*are*); but *or* occurs also in the Cott. text, and is frequent in Fairf. In Sc., Bearder finds the prep. *or* at first only in Barbour (*Ueber den Gebrauch der Präpositionen in der altschott. Poesie*, Halle 1894, p. 43). *Ar* (*are*) occurs also in 13–14th c. southern writings; there it may have originated in an unstressed form of OE. *ǽr*. The relations between the positive and comparative of this adv. present complications in all the cognate langs. In all the WGer. group, also, the comparative has developed prepositional and conjunctive uses, as in English.]

A. *adv.* **I.** As a positive (1 **ár**, 2–3 **ār**; *Sc.* 4–6 **are**, 5– **air**: see AIR *adv.*).

†**1.** Early, at an early hour; = AIR *adv.* 2, ERE. *Obs.*

c **950** *Lindisf. Gosp.* Matt. xx. 1 Qui exiit primo mane, *glossed* seðe foerde ærist *vel* ár in merne. *c* **1200** ORMIN 6242 Beon ar & lāte o ȝunnkerr weorrc. *a* **1300** *Cursor M.* 19033 (Edin., Cott., Gött.) Desseli baþe late and are. **1300–** [see AIR *adv.* 2].

II. As comparative (3–4 **ār**, 4 **aar**, 5–6 *Sc.* **air**; 3– 4 **ōr**, 4–5 **ore**, 5 **oore**, **hoore**, **ȝore**).

†**2.** At an earlier time; earlier, sooner; = ERE A. 2.

c **1330** R. BRUNNE *Chron. Wace* (Rolls) 10147 Cador & hyse.. to þe hauen wel raþer [*v.r.* ore] cam Er any Saxon to schipe nam. *c* **1400** *Ywaine & Gaw.* 1061 Bitwene this and the thrid night, And ar if that it are myght be.

†**3.** At a former time, on a former occasion; formerly, before; = AIR *adv.* 1, ERE A. 4. *Obs.*

c **1205** LAY. 28687 þa at þan fehte ar weoren. *a* **1300** *Cursor M.* 511 (Cott.) Als i tald ar [*F.* are, *Gött.* or]. *Ibid.* 870 (C., F., G.) þis said i are [*Tr.* ere]. *c* **1330** R. BRUNNE *Chron.* (1810) 8 He sette þe Inglis to be þralle, þat or was so fre. **13..** *Guy Warw.* (A.) 425 Mi sore þat is dedeliche, as y seyd ore. *c* **1440** CAPGRAVE *Life St. Kath.* III. 410 If she fayr and bryght were hoore [= ore], It is a-mended an hundird part more As to his sight. *a* **1450** *Le Morte Arth.* 2202 He thought on thyngis that bene ore. *a* **1500** *Childe of Bristowe* 342 in Hazl. *E.P.P.* I. 123 Into the chamber he went that tide.. And knelid, as he dud ore.

†**b.** Before something else, in the first place. *Obs.*

c **1220** *Bestiary* 139 Oc he speweð or al ðe uenim ðat in his brest is bred. *Ibid.* 208 Oc or sei ðu in scrifte to ðe prest sinnes tine [= þine]. *c* **1250** *Gen. & Ex.* 88 Fro ðat time we tellen ay, Or ðe niȝt and after ðe day. *a* **1300** *Cursor M.* 916 (Cott., F., Gött.) For i most couer mi tinsal are [*Tr.* furst]. *c* **1300** *Havelok* 728 But or he hauede michel shame.

B. *prep.* (3–5 **ar**, (4 **are**), 3– **or**).

1. Before (in time); = ERE B. 1.

c **1250** *Gen. & Ex.* 645 So ðe flod flet de dunes on; fowerti ȝer or domes-dai. *a* **1300** *Cursor M.* 11383 (Cott.) A tuel-month ar [*Gött.* are, *Tr.* or] þe natiuite. **1375** BARBOUR *Bruce* xx. 607 It wes neuir led or his day So weill. *a* **1425** *Cursor M.* 9830 (Tr.) Neuer ar þis. **1467–8** *Rolls of Parlt.* V. 622/2 Which had been doon or that tyme. **1509** BARCLAY *Shyp of Folys* (1570) 167 To dye or their day. **1564** GRINDAL *Fun. Serm.* 3 Oct., Wks. (Parker Soc.) 16 So should we have had the Turk, or this day, to have come to our own doors. **1632** LITHGOW *Trav.* IV. 141 He came.. in the morning ouer to Constantinople; and long or midday turned Turke. *Mod. Sc.* Ye'll be ower the hill lang or nicht.

b. In the following there appears to be confusion with the conjunctive *or ere* (C. 1 e), for *or e'er*, *or ever*, but used simply as = ere, before.

1629 MILTON *Ode Christ's Nativity* 86 The Shepherds on the Lawn, Or ere the point of dawn, Sate simply chatting in a rustick row. **1811** WORDSW. *Ep. to Sir G. H. Beaumont* 95 And long or ere the uprising of the Sun O'er dew-damped dust our journey was begun.

2. Before an adv. of time taken subst., as *long*, *now*, etc., forming an advb. phrase: cf. *erelong*, *erenow*, etc.; = ERE B. 2.

a **1450** *Cursor M.* 17785 (Laud) Ye wold nevir yt leve or now. *c* **1460** *Towneley Myst.* vi. 4, I cam neuer or now where I am. **1559–60** *MS. Cott. Cal.* B. ix, The mater had bene lang or now compounded. **1786** BURNS *Earnest Cry & Prayer* xv, I'll wad my new pleugh-pettle, Ye'll see't or lang. *Mod. Sc.* He'd been there oft or than, Ise warran'. I've seen him lang or now.

C. *conj.* (or *conjunctive adv.*). (3–4 **ar**, (4 **are**), 3– **or**.)

1. Of time: Before (= L. *priusquam*, F. *avant que*). †**a.** in a conjunctional phrase: (*a*) *or than*, (*b*) *or that*: see ERE C. 1 a. *Obs.*

(*a*) *c* **1250** *Gen. & Ex.* 2435 Or ðan he wiste off werlde faren, He [Jacob] bade hise kinde to him charen. **1382** WYCLIF *Gen.* xxvii. 10 Whan.. he etith, he blisse to thee or than [Vulg. *priusquam*, 1388 bifore that] he die. **1465** *Paston Lett.* II. 199 They were delyveryd owt of pryson or than the massenger come ageyn. **1506** GUYLFORDE *Pilgr.* (Camden) 39 Or than we rose from the borde the warden rose.

(*b*) *a* **1300** *Cursor M.* 2810 Are þat [*Gött.* ar þan, *F.* or þat, *Tr.* ar þat] hit be sunken don. *Ibid.* 4976 Ar þat [*F.* or]. *c* **1386** CHAUCER *Knt.'s T.* 2212 (Harl. MS.) Or [*v.r.* er] þat we departe fro þis place. **1542** BOORDE *Dyetary* vii. (1870) 242 He must prouyde for necessarye thynges or that he begyn howsholde. **1548–9** (Mar.) *Bk. Com. Prayer* Consecr. Bishops, Our savioure Christe continued the whole night in praier, or euer that [1662 before] he did chose and sende furth his xii Apostles. **1721** *St. German's Doctor & Stud.* 102, I would here.. ask thee another question, or that I make answer to thine.

b. *Or* alone, in same sense.

c **1220** *Bestiary* 91 Or he bicumeð cristen. *Ibid.* 94 Or he it biðenken can, hise eȝen weren mirke. **13..** *Cursor M.* 710 (Cott.) Ar [*F.* or] Adam had fordon þe grith. *Ibid.* 5578 (Cott.) Born er he þis werld wroght [*F.* or þis werlde was wroȝt]. *c* **1330** *Owain Miles* 32 Now turn oȝain or to late, Ar we the put in at helle gate. *c* **1340** HAMPOLE *Pr. Consc.* 1051 Yhit wil I mare say, Ar I pas fra þis mater away. *c* **1489** CAXTON *Sonnes of Aymon* i. 41 Lete us ryde hastely towarde Troy or it be take. **1535** COVERDALE *Prov.* iv. 19 Wherin men fall or they be awarre. 1553 T. WILSON *Rhet.* 108 Wil you drink or you go, or wil you go or you drinke? 1562 J. HEYWOOD *Prov. & Epigr.* (1867) 169 Leaue it or it leaue you. 1665 HOWARD & DRYDEN *Ind. Queen* v. i, We must go meet them or it be too late. 1725 RAMSAY *Gent. Sheph.* v. ii, Ye intend to..take your leave of Patrick or he gang. 1870 MORRIS *Earthly Par.* II. III. 119 Yet or fell the night He rose. 1886 STEVENSON *Kidnapped* xviii. 173 Ye shall taigle many a weary foot, or we get clear.

†**c.** With redundant *or*, or equivalent adv.; = ERE C. 1 c. *Obs.*

c1250 *Gen. & Ex.* 1506 Ðe firme sune..sulde auen ðe bliscing Or or ðe fader dede his ending. 1303 R. BRUNNE *Handl. Synne* 650 ȝyf þou trowyst þat he was noghte Before or þe worlde was wroghte. c1330 —— *Chron.* (1810) 74 Or Roberd wist, or þouht on suilk a dede, Ore was his hous on fire, þer Sir Robert lay. ?a1366 CHAUCER *Rom. Rose* 864 Hir yen greye..That laughede ay in hir semblaunt, First or the mouth, by covenaunt. c1400 MAUNDEV. (1839) viii. 83 Before or þei resceyue hem, þei knelen doun. 1485 CAXTON *Paris & V.* 30 Tofore or he wente to hys bedde.

d. with the addition of *ever*, *e'er*: cf. ERE C. 1 d.

Ever adds emphasis: *or ever* = before ever, before even, before..at all, or in any way; see EVER 8 c. But, in many early instances, *or ever* does not perceptibly differ from the simple *or*, *ere*, or *before*, whence perh. the later spelling *or ere*; see e.

1423 JAS. I *Kingis Q.* v, Or euer I stent, my best was more to loke Upon the writings of this nobil man. 1450 *Rolls of Parlt.* V. 202/2 Make the aweners..paye, or ever they can gete deliveraunce. 1526 TINDALE *John* iv. 49 Syr come awaye or ever that my chylde deye. 1599 HAKLUYT *Voy.* II. 101, I was two dayes after or ever I could get in. 1606 G. W[OODCOCKE] *Hist. Ivstine* III. 20 They..put forth to sea, or euer the Lacedemonians got knowledge of them. 1611 BIBLE *Dan.* vi. 24 And the Lyons..brake all their bones in pieces or euer they came at the bottome of the den. 1752 WESLEY *Wks.* (1872) X. 223 Thou accursed Spirit! damned or ever thou wert born! 1784 COWPER *Task* I. 67 Long time elapsed or e'er our rugged sires Complain'd. 1846 KEBLE *Lyra Innoc.* (1873) 76 Stay thee, sad heart, or e'er thou breathe thy plaint. 1879 CHR. ROSSETTI *Seek & F.* 246 Or ever He ascended up where he was before. *Mod. Sc.* An' or ever I wust, there I was i' the mids o' them!

e. *or ere*, for *or e'er*, or ever: see d, and B. 1 b.

1568 FULWEL *Like Will to Like* in Hazl. *Dodsley* III. 349 Thou shalt have somewhat of me, or ere I go. 1605 SHAKS. *Lear* II. iv. 288 But this heart shal break into a hundred thousand flawes Or ere Ile weepe. 1674 N. FAIRFAX *Bulk & Selv.* To Rdr., Forthwith or ere I could well help it, I fell a Roving. 1823 LOCKHART *Span. Ball., Calaynos* xiii, For his soul shall dwell with him in hell, or ere yon sun go down! 1851 MRS. BROWNING *Casa Guidi Wind.* I. 133 That not a letter of the meaning fall Or ere it touch and teach His world's deep heart.

2. Of preference: Sooner than, rather than; = ERE C. 2.

a1300 *Cursor M.* 9815 (Cott.) His hert aght ar at-brest in thrin Ar fra his comamentes tuin [*Gött.* Or aght his herte brest o thrinne, Or fra his comandementis tuinne]. 1377 LANGL. *P. Pl.* B. xv. 502 þe red noble Is reuerenced or [C. xviii. 201 by-fore] þe Rode. c1470 *Golagros & Gaw.* 511 Or thay be dantit with dreid, erar will thai de. 1514 EARL WORCESTER in Ellis *Orig. Lett.* Ser. II. I. 244 Never man..better loved his wife than he did, but or he wold have suche a woman abought hur, he hadde lever be without hur. 1567 DRANT *Horace, Epistles* Ep. xvii. Fj, Or he would weare a suite of silke the winter should him kil. 1814 SCOTT *Wav.* xlii, He wald scroll for a plack the sheet, or she kenn'd what it was to want. *Mod. Sc.* I wad sterve or I wad be obleig't to the like o' him.

†**3.** After a comparative or *other*: = Than. *Obs.*

Northern, and in later use only Sc.

c1250 *Gen. & Ex.* 1510 And hauen mete ðan, at is mel, More or ðe ȝungere twinne del. *Ibid.* 2928 Ðoȝ deden wiches ðo men to sen On oðere wise or soðe ben. 13.. *Gaw. & Gr. Knt.* 1543 To yow þat..weldez more slyȝt Of þat art..or a hundreth of seche As I am. 1513 DOUGLAS *Æneis* v. viii. 88 Felis thow nocht ȝit, quod he, Othir strenth or mannis force has delt with the? 1567 *Gude & Godlie B.* (S.T.S.) 135 Rather or thow suld ly in paine. 1637-50 ROW *Hist. Kirk* (Wodrow Soc.) 500 The Marques of Hunteley obtained more subscriptions..in the toune and shyre of Aberdeen and Bamff or any other.

†**4.** = Lest. *Sc. Obs. rare.*

c1470 HENRY *Wallace* I. 272 That gud man dred or Wallace suld be tane; For Suthroun ar full sutaille euirilk man.

†**or**, *adv.*[2] *Obs. rare.* [? a. Fr. *or* now.] As an introductory particle: = Now.

1413 *Pilgr. Sowle* (Caxton) IV. xxix. (1859) 61 Or this ymage signyfyed the kynge Nabugodonosor. c1450 *Mirour Saluacioun* 1165 Or Salomones throne had greces sex, als I saide toforne.

or (ɔː(r), ə(r)), *conj.*[2] (*adv.*[3]) Forms: see below. [A phonetically reduced form of the obs. OTHER *conj.*, which, when disyllabic, Ormin wrote *operr*, when monosyllabic and unstressed, *oþþr* before a vowel, *orr* before a cons. The e. midl. dial. had *or* c1250; and c1300 *or* was in common use in north midl. and northern writers; though the fuller *oþer*, *other* continued in use, esp. in the south, till late in the 16th c. *Or* is properly the conjunction, not the associated adv. (see sense 2), which continued to be *other*, or *outher*, in modern Standard Eng. *either* (i.e. *either..or*); though *or..or* also occurs: see sense 3. Forms parallel to *or* are *ar* (reduced from *aþer*), ER (from EITHER); *our*, treated here, may be reduced from *outher*.]

A. Illustration of the evolution of *or* out of *other*, and of some variant forms.

α. 3 **oþer, oþþr, orr, or.**

c1200 ORMIN 6480 Her iss litell oþerr nohht I þiss land. *Ibid.* 16100 [þa] þatt sellenn Haliȝ Gast..Att fullhtninng, oþerr att hanndgang, Oþþr att hadinng, forr mede. *Ibid.* 7588 þatt lac..Wass tweȝȝenn cullfre briddess..Oþþr itt wass tweȝȝenn turrtless. *Ibid.* 10882 Hofenn upp and hadedd Till bisscopp orr till unnderrpreost. *Ibid.* 11843 To don ohht orr to spekenn ohht off ifell. c1250 [see B. 2 c] queðer ..or. ?a1300 [see B. 2] oþer..or. c1300 *Havelok* 977 King or cayser forto be.

β. 4 **our, ouer, ouir,** 4-5 **ore.**

13.. *Cursor M.* 19523-25 (Edinb.) Godis uirtu our [*other MSS.* or] grete prophete, our angel ellis þai him lete, our godis sune ellis þai him helde. *Ibid.* 19715 Nichte ouir [*other MSS.* or] dai. *Ibid.* 23425 Wit þi fot to ouircast a fel, ouer [*other MSS.* or] al þis erþe. c1375 *Sc. Leg. Saints* ii. (*Paulus*) 737 How hard panis, ore how sar His modir tholit. a1400-50 *Alexander* 2260 (Ashm. MS.) Of sum threuyn gome Of were ore [*Dubl. MS.* or] of wristilling.

B. Signification.

I. 1. *generally.* A particle co-ordinating two (or more) words, phrases, or clauses, between which there is an alternative. ***or otherwise***: see OTHERWISE *sb. phr., adv., a.* A. c; ***or something***: see SOMETHING *sb.*, (*a.*), and *adv.*

Things so co-ordinated may differ in nature, or quality, or merely in quantity, in which case the one may include the other, as in 'it will cost a pound or thirty shillings', 'two or three minutes', 'a word or two'. The second member may also express a correction or modification of the first, which may be strengthened by expanding *or* to *or even, or rather, or at least*.

c1200 [see above in A. a]. c1300 *Havelok* 573-4 Leoun or wulf, wuluine or bere Or oþer best þat wolde him dere. *Ibid.* 612-13 He shal him hangen, or quik flo, Or he shal him al quic graue. *Ibid.* 2101 þan birþe men casten hem in poles, or in a grip, or in þe fen. c1330 R. BRUNNE *Chron.* (1810) 154 If werre or wo had risen. 1382 WYCLIF *Matt.* xviii. 20 Where two or three shulen be gedrid in my name. c1386 CHAUCER *Knt.'s T.* 813 Be it of werre or pees, or hate or loue. 1483 *Cath. Angl.* 260/2 Or, *aut, vel, sev, que*. 1513 DOUGLAS *Æneis* VI. Prol. 39 Twichand our faith mony clausis he fand, Quhilk bene conforme, or than collaterall. a1548 HALL *Chron., Edw. IV* 232 b, No man hathe sene a better counterfaytor or player in any Comedie or Tragedie. 1667 MILTON *P.L.* I. 583 And all who since, Baptiz'd or Infidel, Jousted in Aspramont or Montalban. 1709 STEELE *Tatler* No. 45 ¶1, I took a Walk a Mile or Two out of Town. 1766 GOLDSM. *Vic. W.* i, The year was spent in moral or rural amusements. 1776 *Trial of Nundocomar* 61/2 Did you send a verbal or a written message? 1816 J. WILSON *City of Plague* I. i. 439 He heeded not Me or my sorrow. 1818 CRUISE *Digest* (ed. 2) III. 485 The possession of the others or other of them. 1835 *Chambers' Informat.* II. 282/1 It is generally flat or but slightly undulating. 1861 M. PATTISON *Ess.* (1889) I. 45 A vine or two. *Mod.* You may walk ten or even twelve miles without finding one.

b. When singular subjects (sb. or pron.) are co-ordinated by *or*, strict logic and the rules of modern grammarians require the vb. and following pronouns to be singular; but at all times there has been a tendency to use the plural with two or more singular subjects when their mutual exclusion is not emphasized.

When the subjects differ in number or person, the rule is that the vb. and pronouns should agree with the last or nearest, e.g. 'I or thou art to blame', 'I, or thou, or he is the author of it' (Lindley Murray); but such constructions are apt to seem stiff and pedantic, and are consequently avoided. The question of gender causes further complication—esp. the want of a 3rd pers. pron. of common gender. To say either 'if he or she has his friends with him' or 'if he or she has her friends with her' may be misleading, while 'if he or she has his or her friends with him or her' is clumsy and pedantic, which is avoided by saying 'have their friends with them'; so 'Your brother or sister will lend their aid'. These difficulties appear to have been felt at all times, and have been sometimes avoided by making the verb immediately precede or follow the first subject, and agree with it.

[13.. *K. Alis.* 75 Whan kyng, other eorl, cam on him to weorre.] 1601 B. JONSON *Poetaster* II. i, As soon as ever your maid or your man brings you word. 1621 HAKEWILL *David's Vow* 328 A great towne or a great Personages house, if they bee good, do much good to the Countrey. 1749 FIELDING *Tom Jones* XIII. vi, Among whose vices ill-nature or hardness of heart were not numbered. 1813 SCOTT *Rokeby* II. xxiv, Wilfrid, or Bertram raves, or you! a1822 SHELLEY *Ess.*, etc. II. 249 *note*, Tacitus, or Livius, or Herodotus, are equally undelightful and uninstructive in translation. 1823 SYD. SMITH *Mem.* (1855) II. 234 Friendship, or propriety, or principle are sacrificed. 1849 RUSKIN *Sev. Lamps* 126 If Tintoret or Giorgione are at hand. 1855 FITZJ. STEPHEN in *Cambr. Ess.* 176 Scott or Sir E. Lytton have generally some funny man. 1867 M. ARNOLD *Celtic Lit.* 162 Novalis or Rückert, for instance, have their eye fixed on nature. 1873 L. STEPHEN *Ess. Freespeak.* 127 The Pope, or the Archbishop of Canterbury, or even Mr. Spurgeon, are much more satisfactory guides than the prophets of the revolution. 1874 —— *Hours in Library* Ser. I. 273 Mr. Darwin or Barnum would claim him as their own. 1875 GLADSTONE *Glean.* VI. 179 Why should we expect of the Bishop,..or of the Judge,..that they should be adepts in historical research? 1879 GEO. ELIOT *Theo. Such* 339 The *corpus vile* on which rage or wantonness vented themselves with impunity.

c. In modern colloq. use *or* can introduce an emphatic repetition of a rhetorical question.

1939 P. CHEYNEY *Poison Ivy* vii. 122 Just then Mirabelle comes through [on the telephone]. Has that dame gotta a swell voice or has she? *Ibid.* xii. 198, I blew in here a coupla hours ago on the *Minnetonka*, an' directly I read the papers an' saw that you was stuck here, did I run here or did I? 1946 'BRAHMS' & 'SIMON' *Trottie True* vii. 201 'Well,' said Bradford, torn between pride and regret, 'she may be going to marry a Lord, but can I pick 'em or can I pick 'em?'

2. a. The alternative expressed by *or* is emphasized by prefixing to the first member, or adding after the last, the associated adverb EITHER, formerly OTHER or OUTHER (the latter still in dialect use): e.g. 'you may have either an apple or a pear'; 'I could eat an apple or a pear either'.

The primary function of *either*, etc., is to emphasize the perfect indifference of the two (or more) things or courses; e.g. 'you may take either the medal or its value' = the medal and its value are equally at your option, you may take either; but a secondary function is to emphasize the mutual exclusiveness, = either of the two, but not both. For full illustration, see EITHER, OTHER, OUTHER; the following are early examples of the various forms:

?a1300 *Cursor M.* 5855 (Cott.) þat I suld oþer [*Gött.* ethir] here his saand, Or lat þe folk vte o mi land. *Ibid.* 9838 (Cott.) þat wanted oiþer [*Gött.* eyder, *Fairf.* ethir, *Trin.* ouþer] fote or hand. c1300 *Havelok* 94-5 Oþer he refte him hors or wede, Or made him sone handes sprede. c1385 CHAUCER *L.G.W.* Prol. 5 Eythir [*Tanner* either]..in heuene or in helle.

¶**b.** *Or* occurs also after *neither*, where the normal conjunction is *nor*. See these words.

1523 LD. BERNERS *Froiss.* I. xxvi. 37 We fynd nat aunciently, that..Scotlande shulde..be subgiet to the realme of Ingland, nother by homage, or any other wayes. 1597 BEARD *Theatre God's Judgem.* (1612) 129 There is neither scepter, crowne, stay, or strength of man that is able to hinder and turne aside the hand of the Almightie. a1648 LD. HERBERT *Hen. VIII* (1683) 221 From which they saw neither profit or honour likely to ensue. 1691 WOOD *Ath. Oxon.* II. 516 An horse that had neither good eyes or feet. 1713 STEELE *Guard.* No. 5 ¶4 Neither strict piety, diligence in domestick affairs, or any other avocation, have preserved her against love. 1757 BURKE *Abridg. Eng. Hist.* Wks. (1812) 4 Neither on the one side or on the other. 1812 SOUTHEY *Omniana* I. 310 Morality can neither be produced or preserved in a people..without true religion. 1822 HEBER *Life Jer. Taylor* p. clxxxvi. 1864 RUSKIN *Fors Clavig.* xlviii. 267 Neither rabbits at Coniston, road-surveyors at Croydon, or mud in St. Giles's. 1882 FREEMAN in *Life & Lett.* (1895) II. 267 Neither Reformers in the sixteenth century or Puritans in the seventeenth century strove in any sense for 'religious liberty'.

c. *Or* is used after *whether*: see WHETHER.

Here *oðer*, *or*, took the place of the earlier disjunctive particle, OE. *þe* (OS. *the*, OFris. *tha*, Goth. *þau*). The following examples show the introduction of *or*:—

[c1205 LAY 9464-5 Heo..axeden wheðer he wolde grið þe he wolde unfrið [c1275 oþer fiht ȝam wiþ]. c1200 ORMIN 528 Wheþþr..i þe firrste lott Oþþr i þatt comm þæraffterr. a1225 *Leg. St. Kath.* 2313 Loke nu..hweðer þe beo leuere don þat ich leare..oðer þis ilke dei..deien. c1250 *Gen. & Ex.* 3272 Egipcienes woren in twired wen, queðer he sulden folȝen or flen. 13.. *Cursor M.* 22167 (Edinb.) Queþir þate he be criste ouir [*other MSS.* or] nai. 1382 WYCLIF *Gen.* xxvii. 21 Whethir [1388 wher] thow be my sone Esau, or noon. c1440 *Ipomydon* 1844 Whethyr will ye come or nay?

3. a. *or..or* is sometimes used in the sense of *either..or*: this is now poetic.

Formerly, sometimes a literalism of translation (cf. L. *aut ..aut*, F. *ou..ou*), but perh. sometimes an actual phonetic reduction of *other..other, other..or*: cf. *wher..or* for *whether..or*.

a1300 *Cursor M.* 494 þan fell þai depe, or lesse or mare. —— *Ibid.* 10490 Allas! allas! þat i or born or geten was! c1325 *Poem times Edw. II* (Percy Soc.) iv, Or he shal sing *si dedero*, or all gaineth him nouht. c1380 WYCLIF *Serm.* Sel. Wks. I. 124 ȝif he heere treuthe or o tyme or oþer. 1390 GOWER *Conf.* I. 182 And alle tho that hadden be Or in appert or in prive. 1474 CAXTON *Chesse* 7 Or thou art a god or a man or nought. 1576 GASCOIGNE *Steele Gl.* (Arb.) 76 Who would never take or bribe or rich reward. 1590 SHAKS. *Com. Err.* I. i. 137 Loth to leaue vnsought Or that, or any place. 1615 DAY *Festivals* xii. 325 You are not all of you, or Husbands, or Parents, or Maisters; or Wives, or Children, or Servants; or Virgins, or Widowes. 1715-20 POPE *Iliad* xxi. 396 Or let us glory gain, or glory give! 1798 COLERIDGE *Anc. Mar.* VI. iv, Without or wave or wind. 1867 JEAN INGELOW *Story of Doom* VII. 266 Learn that to love is the one way to know Or God or man.

†**b.** *or..or* occurs with alternative questions, direct or indirect; = *whether..or*. (*Or* alone = 'whether' is rare, and prob. only repr. L. *an.*)

1382 WYCLIF *Ecclus.* xlvi. 5 Or not in wrathefulnesse of hym is lettid the sunne? [*Vulg.* an non; 1388 Whether the sunne was not lettid in the wrathful?] 1510 *Virgilius* in Thoms *E.E. Rom.* 23 He asked the lordes..or they wolde thereforre warre. 1579 SPENSER *Sheph. Cal.* Mar. 29 Or hast thy selfe his slomber broke? Or made preuie to the same? 1596 SHAKS. *Merc. V.* III. ii. 64 Tell me where is fancie bred, Or in the heart, or in the head? c1600 —— *Sonn.* cxiv, Or whether doth my mind..Drink up the monarch's plague, this flattery? Or whether shall I say [etc.]? 1611 —— *Cymb.* IV. ii. 356 How? a Page? Or dead, or sleeping on him? 1623 WEBSTER *Devil's Law Case* II. iii, Denied Christian burial! I pray, what does that? Or the dead lazy march in the funeral? Or the flattery in the epitaphs? 1734 POPE *Ess. Man* IV. 245-6 Alike or when, or where, they shone, or shine, Or on the Rubicon, or on the Rhine.

4. After a primary statement, *or* appends a secondary alternative, or consequence of setting aside the primary statement: = otherwise, else; in any other case; if not.

c1330 R. BRUNNE *Chron.* (1810) 44 He said..He wild haf treuage, or brenne alle þat he fond. c1386 CHAUCER *Miller's T.* 95 Loue me al atones, Or I wol dyen. a1440 *Sir Degrev.* 156 He preyd hem to do him ryght, Ar telle hyme whereffore. 1601 SHAKS. *Twel. N.* II. iv. 38 Then let thy Loue be yonger then thy selfe, Or thy affection cannot hold the bent. 1667 MILTON *P.L.* I. 330 Awake, arise, or be for ever fall'n. 1703 ROWE *Fair Penit.* I. i. 273 Waking I dream, or I beheld Lothario. 1791 COWPER *Iliad* I. 95, I judge amiss, or he who rules the Argives..will be incensed. 1820 KEATS *Eve St. Agnes* xxvi, But dares not look behind or all the charm is fled. 1840 *P. Parley's Ann.* 82 Leave off, sir, or I will cane you again. 1860 ABP. THOMSON *Laws Th.* Introd. 2 [This] was an experimental discovery, or why did the discoverer sacrifice a hecatomb? *Mod.* It is my brother, or I'm a Dutchman!

5. *or else* (also formerly as one word *orels, or(r)ellis*): = or if not, or otherwise; = sense 4: see ELSE 4 b. †Formerly also = senses 1, 2. See also ELSE *adv.* 4 b.

a **1300**- [see ELSE 4 b]. **1475** *Bk. Noblesse* (Roxb.) 30 And takethe theire congie and licence..orellis they departethe bethout licence. **1477** EARL RIVERS (Caxton) *Dictes* 21 To dye in their propre lande orellis ferre from thens. **1513** BRADSHAW *St. Werburge* I. 956 Is now orels shalbe. **1523** FITZHERB. *Surv.* xxv. (1539) 48 Orels to tye a rope faste. **1526** TINDALE *Matt.* xvi. 27 Whatt shall hit proffet a man yf he shulde wyn all the whoole warlde: so he loose hys owne soule? Or els what shall a man geve to redeme hys soule agayne with all? *a* **1548** HALL *Chron., Edw. IV* 233 If either yᵉ Constable had bene faithfull to.., or els had kept his promes. **1577** WHETSTONE *Life Gascoigne* xl, In wo orels in endles blis.

6. *Or* connects two words denoting the same thing: = otherwise called, that is (= L. *vel. sive*).

c **1200** ORMIN 480 An hæfedd prest..þatt ta [= þa] bi name nemmnedd wass Abyuþþ oþþr Abyas. **1382–1420** WYCLIF *Gen.* iii. 19 In the swoot of thi chere, or face, thou shalt ete þi brede. **1548** TURNER *Names of Herbes*, Asplenum or asplenium named in greke asplenon, or Scolopendrion. *Ibid.*, Helxine or pardition is called in englishe Parietorie or Pelletorie of the wal. *Ibid.* s.v. *Rumex*, With a sharper toppe or ende of the leafe. **1578** LYTE *Dodoens* II. xcvi. 276 The tame or garden Nigella is agayne parted into two sortes. *Ibid.* 277 Small knops or heads. **1608** TOPSELL *Serpents* (1658) 777 Of the Tame or House Spider. **1671** GREW *Anat. Plants* iv. §8 These Vascular Threds or Fibres. **1842** *Act 5 & 6 Vict.* c. 79 §17 From the centre of the track of the right or off wheel to the centre of the track of the left or near wheel. **1857** *Chambers' Informat.* II. 297/1 Australia or New Holland..Papua or New Guinea..Van Diemen's Land or Tasmania. *Mod.* Using a common or garden spade.

7. *Or* introduces questions which, in the character of an afterthought, cast doubt on a preceding assertion or on the presuppositions behind a preceding statement or question.

c **1907** W. B. YEATS *Let.* 4 July (1954) 483, I suppose the matter is technically your concern as well as mine, or is it? **1924** R. MACAULAY *Orphan Island* xvi. 212 Matilda had the laugh of the bees after all. Or did she? I'm not so sure! **1930** E. WAUGH *Vile Bodies* iv. 59 It really would serve him right if..he lost his job, don't you think so, Sir James..or don't you? *Ibid.* x. 203 They shouldn't put up symbols like that in the middle of the road, should they, or should they? **1935** V. MARKHAM *Deadly Jest* xi. 138 They couldn't have come from the servants' quarters or you'd have heard. Or would you? You were dropping off. **1937** W. FAULKNER *Monk* in *Scribner's Mag.* May 22/2 You force me to do what, for all you know, may be against my own principles too—or do you grant me principles? **1937** D. SAYERS *Busman's Honeymoon* xii. 251 These spiky cactus-affairs didn't like too much damp. Or did they? **1950** A. WHITE *Lost Traveller* IV. iv. 186 'Don't let's speak of falling in love, even as a joke.' 'Ah, but I want to speak of it,' he said... 'Or do I? I was certain I did when I ran into you this afternoon. Now I'm not so sure.' **1954** 'H. CECIL' *According to Evidence* i. 16 But you didn't need any help, did you? Or *did* you? **1956** H. MCCLOY *Two-Thirds of Ghost* (1957) i. 8 Vera must know how everyone who cared for Amos felt about her. Or did she? Probably not. **1962** I. MURDOCH *Unofficial Rose* I. 12 She must surely, he reminded himself, be fourteen now. Or was she? **1971** *Times* 20 Oct. (Motoring Suppl.) p. ii/7 The connoisseur needs taste, a limitless cheque book and the ability to differentiate at the level of an expert. Or does he? He can be impulsive, illogical and tasteless. Or can he?

II. 8. As *sb.*[2] or *adj.* A Boolean function of two or more variables that has the value unity if at least one of them is unity, and is otherwise zero; also called ***inclusive or*** (= L. *vel*); also (*exclusive or*), a function that has the value unity if at least one, but not all, of the variables are unity; (= L. *aut*). Usu. *attrib.* and in capitals, esp. designating devices for realizing this function.

[**1938** C. E. SHANNON in *Trans. Amer. Inst. Electr. Engin.* LVII. 718/1 There are many special types of relays and switches... The operation of all these types may be described with the words 'or', 'and', 'if', 'operated', and 'not operated'. **1940** W. V. QUINE *Math. Logic* i. 12 When 'or' is used in the inclusive sense..joint truth of the components verifies the compound. An 'or'-compound in this sense can be expressed more clearly by adding the words 'or both'. *Ibid.* 13 The exclusive use of 'or' is not frequent enough in technical developments to warrant a special name and symbol.] **1947** *Proc. IRE* XXXV. 758/1 The 'or' operation is performed by a 'buffing' circuit. **1949** E. C. BERKELEY *Giant Brains* ix. 149 The 'or' (as in statement 7) that is defined in the truth table is often called the inclusive 'or' and means 'and/or'. Statement 7, '1 or 2', is considered to be the same as '1 or 2 or both'. There is another 'or' in common use, often called the exclusive 'or', meaning ' or else'. **1950** [see NOT *sb.* 3]. **1959** *Electronic Engin.* XXXI. 591/2 The two input lines are fed into an 'or' circuit,..which gives out a pulse whenever a pulse is received on one or both inputs. **1969** J. J. SPARKES *Transistor Switching* iv. 100 OR gates in one logic system are AND gates in the other. **1970** O. DOPPING *Computers & Data Processing* i. 25 Several functions can be combined in one and the same equation... The order in which different operations are taken is important. The normal order is NOT, AND, OR in decreasing order of priority. **1971** J. H. SMITH *Digital Logic* iv. 45 OR units are not extensively employed because they are usually constructed with components such as diodes, which have no amplification. **1972** [see NOT *sb.* 3].

or, var. *hor*, HER *Obs. poss. pron.*, 'their'.

or, obs. form of ORE, *o'er* (OVER), YOUR.

or-, *pref.*, frequent in OE., retained in a few words in ME., now *obs.* exc. in ORDEAL, and perh. ORT-S, where it is no longer recognized as a significant element. OE. *or-* was the stressed form (used in nominal compounds), corresp. to Goth. *us-*, *ur-*, ON. *ór-*, *ör-*, OHG., Ger. *ur-*, OS. *ur-*, *or-*, MDu. *or-*, *oor-*, Du. *oor-*, orig. an adv. and prep., meaning 'out'. The unstressed form (in verbal compounds) was in OHG. *ur-*, *ar-*, *ir-*, MHG., MLG., MDu., Ger., Du. *er-*, OS., OE. *a-*. Thus OE. *ordál*, OS. *urdêli*, MDu. *ordeel*, MLG. *ordêl*, OHG. *urteili*, Ger. *urteil* decision, judgement; OE. *adǽlan*, OS. *adêljan*, OHG. *arteilen*, Ger. *erteilen* to decide, allot, share. The primary sense was 'out', as in Goth. and OHG. *úrruns* 'outrunning, exit, exodus', ON. *órför* out-going, departure; thence various derived senses, of which OE. had 'out, completely, to an end', as in *orþanc* 'thinking out, contrivance, skill, intelligence'; 'out and out', 'extreme', in *orię̄lda* 'extreme old age'; 'outwardly, manifestly', in *orcnǽwe* 'recognizable', *orȝiete* 'clearly perceptible, manifest'; and esp. 'without, void of, bereft of', as in the adjs. *ormǽte* 'measureless, immense', *ormód* 'bereft of courage, despairing', *orsáwle* 'lifeless', *orwēne* 'without hope, desperate', *ortréowe* 'without trust, faithless', *orsorȝ* 'without anxiety, secure'. (Cf. L. adjs. in *ex-*, as *exanimis, excors, exossis, exsanguis.*) In this last sense the prefix survived in early ME.: see ORMETE, ORMOD, ORRATH, ORTROW.

-or, a termination of words, and form of various suffixes, of Latin origin.

Latin long *ō* in early OF. was represented by a close sound between (*ō*) and (*ū*), written variously *o* and *u*, as in L. *honōrem*, OF. *onor, onur*. In AngloFr. the sound sank into (*ū*) and came *c* 1300 to be written *ou* (*onour*). In continental Fr., on the other hand, the sound passed at length into *eu* = *ö* (*oneur, honneur*). The earliest adopted words in ME. had *o* or *u* (*onor, onur*), but the regular representation after 1300 was that of AngloFr. *ou* (*onour, honour*). In many instances this is still retained; but, at the Renascence, many of the *-our* words, which in other respects were like their L. originals, were conformed to the L. in *-or*; and nearly all words taken then or later directly from L. were spelt *-or*, though, even in these words, there was at first a considerable vacillation between *-or* and *-our*. In Great Britain the traditional *-our* is still written in many of the words in which it was retained in the 16th c., though not a few of these, as *ancestor, author, error, horror, prior, senator, tailor*, are now spelt with *-or*, which spelling is extended in American usage to all the *-our* words.

This termination appears in the following suffixes:

1. *-or* (formerly often *-our*), representing ultimately L. *-or*, *-ōrem*, in nouns of condition from intr. vbs. in *-ēre*, less usually from other vbs., as *error, horror, liquor, pallor, stupor, tenor, terror, torpor, tremor*, etc. Such of these as existed in ME. were formerly spelt with *-our*, e.g. *errour, horrour, licour, tenour*. In other words of the same class, as *ardour, favour, fervour, humour, labour, rigour, valour, vigour*, as also in some words not directly connected with extant L. verbs, as *colour, honour, odour*, *-our* is generally retained in British usage, but American usage spells these also with *-or*: *ardor, favor, labor, color, honor*, etc.

2. *-or* (formerly often *-our*), repr. L. *-or*, *-ōrem* of agent-nouns, formed on stems identical with the ppl. or 'supine' stems of verbs. Of these there are three varieties:

a. Those repr. L. agent-nouns other than those in *-ātor, -ētor, -itor, -ītor*; as *actor, assessor, author, captor, censor, confessor, doctor, elector, extensor, factor, flexor, inventor, lictor, oppressor, pastor, possessor, professor, rector, sculptor, sponsor, successor, transgressor, tutor, victor*. These are of different ages, going back to OF. words in *-or*, *-ur*, AF. in *-our* = F. *-eur*, or L. in *-or*. So far as they existed in ME., they were then spelt *-our*, e.g. *actour, assessour, authour, censour, confessour, dettour, doctour*, etc.; they are now all conformed to the L. spelling in *-or*.

b. Agent-nouns in L. *-ātor, -ētor, -itor, -ītor*, in coming down in living use into OF., were regularly reduced from *-ātōr-em*, etc., through *-edor* to *-eör*, *-eür*, AF. *-eour*, which became in ME. *-our*, and in F. *-eur*, and thus fell together with those from simple *-ōr-em* in a. Such are *barrator, cessor*, (:—*cessatōr-em*), *conqueror, donor, emperor* (*imperātōr-em*), *governor, juror, lessor, solicitor, vendor, visitor* (*visitātōr-em*). To this group also belongs *saviour* (AF. *sauveöur*:—OF. *salveör, salvedor*, L. *salvātōr-em*), which has preserved the vowel before *-our*. To these may be added agent-nouns formed in Fr. or AF. on the vb. stem, in imitation of those in *-eör, -eur, -our*, repr. L. *-ātōrem*, etc., as *purveyor, surveyor, tailor, grantor, warrior* (AF. *werreyour*, f. *werreier* to war). From want of evidence it is sometimes uncertain whether the agent-noun was already formed in late L. in *-ātor, -itor*, or in Fr. after these suffixes had been reduced to *-eör* and *-eur*, AF. *-our*.

c. Agent-nouns in *-ātor, -ētor, -itor, -ītor, -ūtor*, adopted in later times in Fr., or in Eng., retain *t*, appearing in French as *-ateur, -iteur*, etc., and have now in Eng. the same written form as in L., e.g. *administrator, agitator, creator, curator, dictator, equator, gladiator, imitator, legislator, navigator, spectator, translator, vindicator*; *orator, procurator, senator*; *auditor, creditor, editor, janitor, monitor, servitor*; *executor*. These are of different ages: some from OF. or AF. (in which case they formerly had *-our*, as *creatour, creditour, dictatour, oratour, servitour*); some of later formation immediately from L., which have had the *-or* form from the first. The pronunciation varies greatly, the stress being sometimes as in the L. nominative (*cre'ator*, *'creditor*), sometimes on the second syllable before the stressed vowel of the AF. and L. accusative (on which a secondary stress fell originally in ME.), as in *'auditor* (*ˌaudi'tour, ˌaudī'tōrem*), *'orator* (*ˌora'tour, ˌōrā'tōrem*), *'senator* (*ˌsena'tour, ˌsēnā'tōrem*), *'servitor* (*'servi'tour, ˌservī'tōrem*), *e'xecutor* (*eˌxecu'tour, eˌxecū'tōrem*), sometimes corresponding with that of the Eng. vb., as *ad'ministrator, 'agitator, 'imitator, 'prosecutor*, or otherwise shifted, as *'procurator*. In some cases two forms exist, as *cu'rator* after L. nom., *'curator* after *ˌcura'tour, ˌcūrā'tōrem*.

d. *-or* is sometimes an alteration of another suffix, as of L. *-ārius*, F. *-ier*, AF. *-er*, in *bachelor, chancellor, heritor*, or of Eng. *-er*:—OE. *-ere*, in *sailor, bettor*.

The frequent occurrence of ME. *-our*, mod. *-or*, in legal terms denoting the person acting, as opposed to the person acted upon in *-é*, *-ee*, e.g. *lessor lessee, grantor grantee, mortgageor mortgagee*, has imparted a kind of technical or professional character to the ending, and explains the differentation of *sailor*, one who sails professionally, from *sailer*. In ME. there was a tendency to confuse the endings *-er* and *-our* (helped prob. by the OF. declension nom. *-ère*:—L. *-ātor*, acc. *-or, -ur, -eur*, L. *-ātōrem*); thus *butcher, dicer, fletcher, jailer, jester, juggler, porter*, etc. are found also with the ending *-our*. On the other hand, in a large number of words, the original *-our, -or* has, since the 15th c., been exchanged for the -ER of agent-nouns of English derivation; such are *barber, broker, chanter, diviner, labourer, pleader, preacher, robber, rimer* or *rhymer*, in all which the earlier *-our, -or*, is the etymological form.

3. *-or* (*-our*) sometimes represents F. *-oir*, from various sources, as *manor*, OF. *manoir, maneir*, L. *manēre*; *mirror*, F. *miroir*, L. **mīrātorium*; so with *-our*, *parlour*, F. *parloir*, L. **parabolātōrium*.

4. *-or*, repr. ME. and AF. *-our*, F. *-eur*, L. *-or, -ōrem*, a variant of *-ior*, suffix of the comparative degree of adjs., in *major, minor*. See -IOR[2].

ora[1] ('ɔərə). *Hist.* [OE., app. ad. ON. *øyrir* or its pl. *aurar*: commonly regarded as ad. L. *aure-us* golden; but the sense-history is not clear. Cf. ORE[4].]

1. A Danish money of account, introduced into England with the Danish invasion.

In the Laws of Edward the Elder and Guthrun, it is reckoned as equivalent to 2½ shillings, in Domesday book as equal to 20*d*.

c **920** *Laws of Edw. & Guthr.* c. 7 (Schmid) þolie..twelf orena mid Denum, and xxx scill. mid Englum. *c* **950** *Lindisf. Gosp.* Luke xix. 13 Woeron ȝeceȝid ðonne teno ðrælas his, salde ðæm tea oro vel libras, & cuoeð to ðæm, ceapiȝas oð þ ic cymo. *c* **1000** *Laws of Æthelred* III. c. 1 (Schmid) Bete man þæt æt deadum menn mid vi healf-marce, and æt cwicon mid xii oran. **1706** PHILLIPS, *Ora*, a Saxon Coin of the value of one Shilling and four Pence. **1838** *Encycl. Brit.* (ed. 7) XVI. 514/2 Dr. Hickes observes, that the mode of reckoning money by marcs and oras was never known in England until after the settlement of the Danes. **1851** D. WILSON *Preh. Ann.* (1863) I. II. vi. 445 Upon the altar was placed a ring without any joint of the value of two oras. **1875** JEVONS *Money* viii. 71 The mark, the ora, and the thrimsa were other moneys of account used by the Anglo-Saxons.

2. A measure of weight: see quot. 1838.

1610 HOLLAND *Camden's Brit.* I. 519 This Citie payd yeerely to the King 30 pounds by tale, and twenty in ora (or in ore) that is by weight. **1707** FLEETWOOD *Chron. Prec.* (1745) 25 So that 15 oræ make a pound. **1838** *Encycl. Brit.* (ed. 7) XVI. 514/2 In Doomsday-book the ora is used for the ounce, or the twelfth part of the nummulary Saxon pound, and the fifteenth of the commercial.

‖**ora**[2] ('ɔərə). [L., = border, brim, coast, shore.]

1. *Entom.* The inflexed or inferior lateral margin of the prothorax.

1826 KIRBY & SP. *Entomol.* III. 368 *Prothorax*,..called by way of eminence the *Thorax*. It includes the *Ora, Patagia, Umbones*, and *Phragma*.

2. 'The edge or border of an ulcer' (*Syd. Soc. Lex.* 1892).

3. ora serrata *Anat.* [L. *serrātus* SERRATE *a.*], the serrated edge of the retina, just behind the ciliary body.

1839 K. GRANT *Hooper's Lexicon Medicum* (ed. 7) 963/2 *Ora serrata*, the posterior serrated edge of the ciliary processes is so called. **1849** S. G. MORTON *Illustr. Syst. Human Anat.* 606 The retina.. terminates behind the ciliary body in an irregular border, ora serrata. **1908** L. LAURANCE *Eye* i. 17 The sensibility of the retina to light diminishes rapidly from the macula ring to the ora serrata. **1973** *Brain Res.* LXIII. 285 Such new cells as are added after this period are added at the margin of the *ora serrata*.

ora, variant of ORRA *Sc.*, odd.

orabill, orace, obs. ff. HORRIBLE, ORRIS.

orach, orache (ˈɒrətʃ). Forms: 5–6 **arage**, 5–8 orage, 6 **arech(e**, oreche, (aretch), 6–7 **arach(e**, 7 **a-**, orrage, 7–8 **a-**, orrach, 6– **orach(e**. [In 15th c. *arage*, 16th c. *arache*, a. Anglo-F. *arasche* (*c* 1265 in *Vocab. Plant-n.*, Wr.-Wülcker 559), F. *arroche* (Paré 16th c.), Norman-Picard form (Berry *arrosse*, Walloon *ârase*, Namur *aurause*) = It. *atrepice*:—L. *atriplic-em*, in nom. *atriplex*, ad. Gr. ἀτράφαξυς, -ις (ἄδρα-, ἀνδράφαξις).]

A plant of the genus *Atriplex*, N.O. *Chenopodiaceæ*; esp. the ***garden orach*** or Mountain Spinach (*A. hortensis*).

wild orach, *A. patula* (including several sub-species), a weed in gardens and cultivated ground in Great Britain.

c **1430** *Two Cookery-bks.* I. 5 Take Borage,.. Bete, Auence, Longebeff, wyth Orage an oþer. *c* **1440** *Anc. Cookery* in *Househ. Ord.* (1790) 426 Take cole.. and betes, and arage.. and sethe hom. *c* **1440** *Promp. Parv.* 13/2 Arage, herb, *attriplex*. **1551** TURNER *Herbal* I. E v b, Areche is of two kyndes: the one is garden areche,.. the other kynde is called in englyshe, wyld areche: and it groweth abrode in the corne feldes. **1563** HYLL *Art Garden.* (1593) 48 The hearbe named Orach or Arage. **1579** LANGHAM *Gard. Health* (1633) 34 Arache vsed in pottage, openeth the belly. **1586** BRIGHT *Melanch.* xxxix. 251 Rocket and taragon are not to be refused; no more is aretch. **1657** C. BECK *Univ. Character* I iv, Orage herb. **1769** SIR J. HILL *Fam. Herbal* (1812) 12 There is another kind of arrach.. called garden arrach, it is an annual raised from seed, for the use of the kitchen. **1837** C. A. WHEELWRIGHT *Transl. Aristophanes* I. 321 Full of calumnies, that grow like orrache. **1855** DELAMER *Kitch. Gard.* (1861) 94 Orache, or Mountain Spinach—*Atriplex hortensis*. Of this handsome plant there are two principal varieties.

b. Comb., as ***orach-like*** adj.: **orach-moth**, *Hadena atriplicis*, a noctuid moth, the caterpillar of which feeds on the orach.

1712 J. PETIVER in *Phil. Trans.* XXVII. 423 Its thick Orach-like jagged Leaves. **1869** NEWMAN *Brit. Moths* 417 The Orache Moth.. The caterpillar.. feeds on various species of orache, goosefoot,.. and many other low plants.

oracle (ˈɒrək(ə)l), *sb.* [ME. *o'racle*, a. F. *oracle* (12th c. in Hatz.-Darm.), ad. L. *ōrācul-um* (*ōrāclum*), f. *ōrāre* to speak, plead, pray, with suffix *-culo-* of material instrument.]

I. Originally.

1. a. In *Gr.* and *Rom. Antiq.* The instrumentality, agency, or medium, by which a god was supposed to speak or make known his will; the mouthpiece of the deity; the place or seat of such instrumentality, at which divine utterances were believed to be given.

c **1400** tr. *Secreta Secret., Gov. Lordsh.* 48 To þe tyme þat y cam to þe Oracle of þe sone þat Esculapides mad for hym, where y fand oon solitarye man abstinente ful wys of Philosophie. *c* **1477** CAXTON *Jason* 4 And they visyted temples and oracles unto the consummation of their dayes. **1574** HELLOWES *Gueuara's Fam. Ep.* (1577) 174 Amongst all the oratories that.. they had in Asia, the most famous was the Oracle of Delphos: for to that place from all partes of the worlde they did concurre. **1611** SHAKS. *Wint. T.* II. iii. 194 Please' your Highnesse, Posts From those you sent to th' Oracle, are come An houre since. **1629** MILTON *Hymn Nativity* 173 The Oracles are dumm. **1692** DRYDEN *St. Euremont's Ess.* 284 He speaks like the Oracles to puzzle the World. **1814** WORDSW. *Laodamia* viii, The Delphic oracle foretold That the first Greek who touched the Trojan strand Should die. **1835** THIRLWALL *Greece* I. vi. 205 The Gods.. had a great variety of agents and vehicles at their disposal, for conveying the secrets of their prescience... Sometimes they attached it to a certain place, the seat of their immediate presence, which is then termed an oracle. **1884** J. TAIT *Mind in Matter* (1892) 255 The great Oracles of antiquity belonged to the Greeks.

b. Hence, allusively, ***to work the oracle***, to influence the agency or medium; to obtain an utterance in one's favour, or to procure a favourable issue in a matter, by influence or manœuvring behind the scenes; also (*slang*), to raise money.

1863 *All Year Round* 10 Oct. 168 He has a double, who.. worked the oracle for him. **1886** *Pall Mall G.* 1 Sept. 1/3 Every reader will be able to form his own judgment of the methods which [certain publishers] adopt to 'work the oracle' in their favour. **1891** J. NEWMAN *Scamping Tricks* xiv. 116 With.. big local loan-mongers to work the oracle and swim with them.

2. A response, decision, or message, given usually by a priest or priestess of a god, and, as was supposed, by his inspiration, at the shrine or seat where the deity was supposed to be thus accessible to inquirers. These responses were for the most part obscure or ambiguous; to which allusion is made in later senses of the word and its derivatives.

1598 GRENEWEY *Tacitus, Ann.* III. xiii. (1622) 83 The Smyrnæans alleaged an oracle of Apollo, by which they were commanded to dedicate a temple to Venus Stratonicis. **1611** SHAKS. *Wint. T.* III. ii. 119 Therefore bring forth (And in Apollo's Name) his Oracle. **1647** A. ROSS *Mystag. Poet.* xvi. (1675) 388 The seat from whence she [Sibyl] gave her Oracles. **1791** COWPER *Iliad* v. 78 Unskill'd to spell aright The oracles predictive of the woe. **1838** THIRLWALL *Greece* III. 59 An oracle was procured exactly suited to the purpose of the leaders of the expedition. **1847** PRESCOTT *Peru* (1850) II. 89 The temple of Pachacamac continued to maintain its ascendancy; and the oracles, delivered from its dark and mysterious shrine, were held in no less repute among the natives.. than the oracles of Delphi obtained among the Greeks. **1885–94** R. BRIDGES *Eros & Psyche* Apr. x, The chanting Pythoness gave oracle, And thus in priestly verse the sentence ran.

II. Transferred to Jewish, Christian, or other religious use.

3. A vehicle or medium of divine communication.

a. That part of the Jewish Temple where the divine presence was manifested; the holy of holies; also, the mercy-seat within it.

c **1440** *Wyclif's Exod.* xxv. 18, 19 Thou schalt make on euer eithir side of Goddis answeryng place [*Bodl. MS.* 277 the oracle] twei cherubyns of gold.. o cherub be in o syde of Goddis answeryng place [*Bodl.* the oracle]. **1483** CAXTON *Gold. Leg.* 72 b/2 The preestes sette the Arke in the hows of our lord in the oracle of the temple *in sancta sanctorum* under the wynges of cherubyn. **1609** BIBLE (Douay) *Exod.* xxxvii. 6 He made also the Propitiatorie, that is, the Oracle, of the purest golde. **1611** BIBLE *Ps.* xxviii. 2 When I lift vp my handes toward thy holy Oracle. **1667** MILTON *P.L.* I. 12 Sion Hill.. and Siloa's Brook that flowd Fast by the Oracle of God. **1838** *Encycl. Brit.* (ed. 7) XVI. 514 Oracle is in sacred history sometimes used for the mercy-seat, or the cover of the ark of the covenant; and by others it is taken for the sanctuary, or the most holy place, in which the ark was deposited.

b. Applied to the breastplate of the Jewish High Priest, the Urim and Thummim, by which divine messages were believed to be communicated.

1868 MARRIOTT *Vest. Chr.* 5 On the breastplate (or 'Oracle') are set twelve stones of unusual size and beauty.

c. One who or that which expounds or interprets the will of God; a divine teacher.

a **1548** HALL *Chron., Hen. VI* 109 In his company Ione the Puzel, whom he used as an oracle and a southsaier. **1671** MILTON *P.R.* I. 460 God hath now sent his living Oracle Into the World, to teach his final will. *a* **1711** KEN *Div. Love* Wks. (1838) 307, I adore thee, O heavenly Oracle of Love, for contriving this prayer in that admirable method. **1833** J. H. NEWMAN *Arians* I. iii. (1876) 82 In the history of Balaam .. a bad man and a heathen is made the oracle of true divine messages. **1863** E. V. NEALE *Anal. Th. & Nat.* 129 Bacon had brought man to the feet of nature, as to a Divine oracle.

4. Divine revelation; a declaration or message expressed or delivered by divine inspiration; also, *pl.* the sacred scriptures (from Rom. iii. 2).

c **1384** CHAUCER *H. Fame* I. 11 Why this a dreme, why that a swevene, And noght to euery man lyche evene, Why this affaintome, why these oracles. **14..** in *Tundale's Vis.* (1843) 93 Whos vertue was to Kyng Saloman Full long aforon in dyuyne oracle As I fynd schewed by myracle. **1548** UDALL, etc. *Erasm. Par. Matt.* ii. 26 The oracles or sayinges of God. **1557** N. T. (Geneva) *Acts* vii. 38 This is that Moses.. who receaued the lyuely oracles to geue vnto vs. **1611** BIBLE *Transl. Pref.* 3 The forme [of Scripture being] Gods word, .. Gods oracles. **1613** PURCHAS *Pilgrimage* x. ii. 133 First had divine mercy by Oracle removed the Christians to Pella out of the danger. **1737** POPE *Hor. Epist.* II. i. 28 Whose Word is Truth, as sacred and rever'd, As Heav'n's own Oracles from Altars heard. **1746–7** HERVEY *Medit.* (1818) 106 By Him, says the Oracle of inspiration, all things consist. **1844** STANLEY *Arnold* I. iv. 213 In the Bible, he [Arnold] found and acknowledged an oracle of God—a positive and supernatural revelation made to man, an immediate inspiration of the Spirit.

†**5.** An injunction or command of the Pope. *Obs.* (Cf. late L. *oraculum* 'an imperial rescript' (Just. *Inst.*).)

1579 FULKE *Confut. Sanders* 551 The Frenchmen deposed their King Childericus by the Oracle of Pope Zacharie, which discharged them of their.. othe of obedience. **1625** tr. *Camden's Hist. Eliz.* I. (1688) 21 A commandment given vivâ voce by the Oracle of the most Holy Lord the Pope, in the virtue of his holy Obedience, and under pain of the greater Excommunication.. not to depart the City.

III. Figurative senses.

6. a. Something reputed to give oracular replies or advice.

1625 HART *Anat. Ur.* I. v. 47 This Parson being.. reputed famous in vromancie, this Gentlewoman had recourse to his oracle. **1713** POPE *Windsor For.* 382, I see.. a new Whitehall ascend! There mighty Nations shall inquire their doom, The World's great Oracle in times to come. **1831** BREWSTER *Newton* (1855) II. xxvii. 404 The oracle which he had himself established refused to give its responses.

b. Something regarded as an infallible guide or indicator, esp. when its action is viewed as recondite or mysterious, as a chronometer, a compass.

1726 SWIFT *Gulliver* I. ii, He called it [a watch] his oracle, and said it pointed out the time for every action of his life. **1738** —— *Pol. Conversat.* i. 108 Pray, my Lord, what's a Clock by your Oracle? **1762** FALCONER *Shipwr.* II. 105 And by the oracle of truth below, The wondrous magnet, guides the wayward prow. **1837** W. IRVING *Capt. Bonneville* III. 97 This little, whining, feast-smelling animal, is, therefore, called among Indians the 'medicine wolf'; and such was one of Buckey's infallible oracles.

7. A person of great wisdom or knowledge, whose opinions or decisions are generally accepted; an authority reputed or affecting to be infallible.

1596 SHAKS. *Merch. V.* I. i. 93, I am sir Oracle, And when I ope my lips, let no dog barke. **1632** LITHGOW *Trav.* VII. 303 He straight sent for a Iewish Phisitian, his familiar Oracle. **1647** CLARENDON *Hist. Reb.* III. §26 He [Lord Say] had for many years been the Oracle of those who were call'd Puritans in the worst sense, and steer'd all their counsels and designs. **1705** STANHOPE *Paraphr.* III. 526 The Oracles of the Law being called together to consult, the demand made of them is Where Christ should be born. **1852** TENNYSON *Ode Death Dk. Wellington* iv, O friends, our chief state-oracle is mute. **1858** O. W. HOLMES *Aut. Breakf.-t.* vi. 56 It is a fine thing to be an oracle to which an appeal is always made in all discussions.

8. An utterance of deep import or wisdom; an opinion or declaration regarded as authoritative and infallible; undeniable truth.

1569 J. SANFORD tr. *Agrippa's Van. Artes* 12 For that cause the Auncientes surnamed Homer his Oracles, of the verses of Homer. **1610** *Histrio-m.* III. 38 Are not you Lawyers, from whose reverend lippes Th' amazed multitude learne Oracles? **1632** MASSINGER *City Madam* II. ii, *Lady Frugal* [after Stargaze has given an astrological exposition]. Kneel, and give thanks. *Sir Maurice.* For what we under-stand not?.. *Lady F.* Be incredulous: To me, 'tis oracle. **1701** W. WOTTON *Hist. Rome, Marcus* vi. 101 His Words were received as Oracles. **1842** ABDY *Water Cure* (1843) 175 Such epithets.. pronounced with a grave face by those whose looks are omens, and whose words are oracles.

9. a. An oracular reply; a wise or prudent answer.

1638 *Penit. Conf.* (1657) 343 It was the glory of Queen Elizabeth.. that wise answer or Oracle she returned to a Pragmatick Petition.

b. A prognostication, such as those in almanacs.

1596 BP. W. BARLOW *Three Serm.* i. 11 One of their owne late Prophets.. hath very fitlie prefixed before his yearely false oracles, I would say Almanacks [etc.].

10. (With capital initial.) The proprietary name of a type of teletext system. [See quot. 1976[2].]

1973 *IBA Technical Rev.* III. 61 Oracle—broadcasting the written word. Engineers of the IBA have recently developed and demonstrated an experimental data system, Oracle, capable of providing a continuous public information service on conventional television transmitting networks. With this system the public could receive up to 50 different 'pages' of information 'written' on their television screens, each page containing up to 880 characters, or roughly 120 words. These messages can be displayed or superimposed on the screen of a domestic television receiver without in any way affecting the reception of normal television programmes. *Ibid.* 62/1 Experimental Oracle transmissions are being made on the IBA's London television stations. *Ibid.* 63/2 The domestic television set requires adaptation for Oracle either by means of an independent add-on unit or,.. by an internal modification. **1974** *Trade Marks Jrnl.* 17 July 1295/2 Oracle... Apparatus for the transmission or reception of television signals and apparatus for the transmission of, processing of, or visual display of alphanumeric characters and/or characters for defining parts of diagrams. Independent Broadcasting Authority.., London,..; manufacturers and merchants. **1975** *Spectator* 19 July 86/3 Within a year or two.. 'teletext'—the generic term for the system used by both Ceefax and Oracle—will take its place in the ordinary person's vocabulary. **1976** *Times* 19 May 1/8 At present experimental Teletext services are being broadcast by both the BBC and the Independent Broadcasting Authority, under the names Ceefax and Oracle respectively. **1976** P. R. HUTT in *IBA Technical Rev.* IX. 4/2 The author hit on the idea of the name 'ORACLE' one Sunday while lunching with friends. Being a classical source of advice and information the name seemed to be very apposite, and it was not long before it was made into an acronym for 'Optional Reception of Announcements by Coded Line Electonics'.

11. *attrib.* and *Comb.*, as ***oracle-monger***, ***-shop***; ***oracle-like*** adj.; ***oracle-wise*** adv.; **oracle bones**, bones used in ancient China for divination (see quot. 1970).

1611 COTGR., *Oraculeux*, Oracle-like, true as the Gospell. **1625** K. LONG tr. *Barclay's Argenis* I. xx. 64 Meleander's Thoughts runne upon that, that Oracle-wise was uttered by her. **1663** GERBIER *Counsel* d iv, Your Apollo's Oracle-like Arcenall. **1673** CAVE *Prim. Chr.* I. i. 7 The Impostor setting up for an Oracle-monger. **1675** COTTON *Scoffer Scoft* 114 He sets up Oracle-shops in Greece. **1860** RAWLINSON tr. *Herodotus* VII. vi. IV. 6 Onomacritus of Athens, an oracle-monger.. who set forth the prophecies of Musæus. **1915** *Encycl. Relig. & Ethics* VIII. 262/1 During recent years a very interesting discovery of 'oracle bones' and tortoise-shell fragments was made in the province of Honan. **1934** K. S. LATOURETTE *Chinese* I. ii. 40 Inscriptions on the 'oracle bones', used for divination. **1970** BRAY & TRUMP *Dict. Archaeol.* 167/2 *Oracle bones.* Animal bones, particularly ox shoulder-blades and tortoise shells, were employed by the ancient Chinese for divination purposes. A groove was cut in the bone, after which a hot point was applied nearby, and the shape of the resulting cracks determined the answer. **1977** G. W. HEWES in D. M. Rumbaugh *Lang. Learning by Chimpanzee* i. 31 He found evidence for this theory in ancient Egyptian hieroglyphs, and in the most ancient form of Chinese writing, on the Shang oracle-bones and bronzes.

ˈ**oracle**, *v. rare.* [f. prec. sb.]

1. *trans.* To utter or pronounce as an oracle; to proclaim as by divine inspiration or authority.

c **1595** R. SOUTHWELL *St. Peter's Compl.* Ded., The Heathen, whose Gods were chiefely canonized by their Poets, and their paynim Diuinitie oracled, in verse. **1600** W.

WATSON *Decacordon* (1602) 356 We finde this difference.. to be oracled from those diuine lips that knew best how to terme them. **1645** MILTON *Colast.* Wks. (1851) 343 A by-blow from the Pulpit.. more beholding to the authority of that devout place.. then to any sound reason which it could oracle. **1922** JOYCE *Ulysses* 183 All these questions are purely academic, Russell oracled out of his shadow. **1952** C. DAY LEWIS tr. *Virgil's Aeneid* III. 58 This is not the land which Delian Apollo Oracled for you.

2. *intr.* To speak as an oracle.

1654 WHITLOCK *Zootomia* 254 If it Oracle contrary to our Interest, or Humour, we will create an Amphiboly.. and make it speak our meaning. **1790** *Bystander* 159 He augured—or Oracled, if Mr. Bell likes it better—very greatly of the prodigious improvements he would make. **1812** W. TENNANT *Anster F.* VI. xxxiv, Nor deem that some dumb beldam.. Hath oracling deceiv'd me like a fool.

Hence **ˈoracling** *vbl. sb.* and *ppl. a.*

1656 T. ADY *Candle in Dark* 77 A hollow feigned voyce which those Witches or Deceivers used in their Oracling Divinations. **1671** MILTON *P.R.* I. 455 No more shalt thou by oracling abuse The Gentiles.

†**ˈoracler.** *Obs.* [f. ORACLE *sb.* or *v.* + -ER[1].] The giver of oracular responses; the priest or priestess of an oracle; any one claiming to be a medium of divine or diabolic communications.

1584 R. SCOT *Discov. Witchcr.* VII. v. (1886) 109 Ye shall see.. the cousenage of these oraclers. **1591** SYLVESTER *Du Bartas* I. vi. 823 Pyrrhus (whom the Delphian Oracler Deluded). **1736** *Disc. Witchcr.* 12 It is certain that Oraclers, when they pronounced their Oracles, did use to counterfeit strange Kinds of Voices.

†**ˈoraclist.** *Obs.* [f. ORACLE *sb.* + -IST.] One whose utterances are esteemed as oracular.

1603 HARSNET *Pop. Impost.* Pref., Your Popes being proclaimed by your own Oraclists to the worlde, one to be an Asse, another a Foxe.

†**ˈoraclize,** *v. Obs. rare.* [f. as prec. + -IZE: cf. ORACULIZE.] *trans.* To pronounce or predict like an oracle. **b.** *intr.* To speak as an oracle.

1648 EARL OF WESTMORELAND *Otia Sacra* (1879) 57 Then shall Thy Conscience Oraclise thy Fate. **1709** *Brit. Apollo* II. No. 12. 3/1 For as you Orac'lize in Verse.

oracular (ɒˈrækjʊlə(r)), *a.* [f. L. *ōrācul-um* ORACLE + -AR. (L. had a rare *ōrāculāri-us*, the Eng. repr. of which would be **oraculary*.)]

1. Of or pertaining to an oracle; that is the seat or medium of an oracle, or of direct divine communications.

1678 PHILLIPS (ed. 4), *Oracular*, belonging to, or having the authority of an Oracle. **1742** YOUNG *Nt. Th.* IX. 1044 The breast-plate of the true High-priest, Ardent with gems oracular, that give, In points of highest moment, right response. **1774** J. BRYANT *Mythol.* I. 254 Its guardian Deity, whose orgies were there celebrated; and whose shrine was oracular. **1781** COWPER *Truth* 389 Once the blest residence of truth divine,.. Where, in his own oracular abode, Dwelt visibly the light-creating God. **1853** FELTON *Fam. Lett.* xxxvi. (1865) 282 An hour more brought us in sight of Delphi,—one of the richest oracular sites in the world. **1856** EMERSON *Eng. Traits, Stonehenge* Wks. (Bohn) II. 126 The fable that the ship Argo was loquacious and oracular.

2. Of the nature of an oracle, or of an inspired, divinely authoritative, or infallible utterance.

1631 BRATHWAIT *Whimzies* 20 The vulgar doe admire him, holding his novels oracular. **1664** H. MORE *Myst. Iniq.* 206 He has left some Oracular Records wherein a man may read.. the State and Condition of the Church. **1702** S. PARKER tr. *Cicero's De Finibus* II. 137 He had stamp'd it upon your minds for an Oracular Truth, that nothing after Death can have any effect upon us. **1855** MACAULAY *Hist. Eng.* xix. IV. 353 Whatever he said or wrote was considered as oracular by his disciples.

b. Resembling the ancient oracles in the mystery, ambiguity, or sententiousness of their answers.

1736 BOLINGBROKE *Patriot.* (1749) 240 Such expressions were often used,.. and I believe these oracular speeches were interpreted, as oracles used to be, according as every man's inclinations led him. **1845** JAMES *A. Neil* ii, He opened his lips, with an oracular shake of the head. **1845** DISRAELI *Sybil* v. x, 'The deuce!' said the Dandy, who did not clearly comprehend the bent of the observation of his much pondering.. friend, but was touched by its oracular terseness.

c. Of mysterious portent; ominous, portentous.

1820 BYRON *Mar. Fal.* IV. ii. 182 Where swings the sullen huge oracular bell, Which never knells but for a princely death. **1820** SHELLEY *Œdipus* II. ii. 64 These prodigies are oracular, and show The presence of the unseen Deity.

3. Of a person: That delivers oracular responses; *transf.* that speaks or writes in the character or manner of an oracle.

1821 D. STEWART *Dissert. Progr. Philos.* II. v. 352 In his [Dr. Law's] original speculations, he is weak, paradoxical, and oracular. **1829** LYTTON *Devereux* I. xi, Morton, you are quite oracular. **1863** W. PHILLIPS *Speeches* xiv. 299 The oracular press lays down the law. **1865** GROTE *Plato* II. xxi. 11 Like prophets and oracular ministers.

4. Delivered, uttered, or decreed by an oracle.

1820 SHELLEY *Hymn to Mercury* lxxx, Understood.. by thee the mystery Of all oracular fates. **1863** MARY HOWITT *F. Bremer's Greece* II. xvi. 157 Some oracular replies show great political wisdom. **1873** SYMONDS *Grk. Poets* vii. 190 When Oedipus slays his father, he does so in contempt of oracular warnings. **1876** SWINBURNE *Erechtheus* 55 For the note Rings as of death oracular to thy sons.

Hence **oˈracularness,** oracularity.

1717 in BAILEY II. **1886** *American* XII. 189 Their oracularness is merely an opinion. **1891** *Illustr. Lond. News* Christm. No. 2/3 'He's sure to wear a big beard'.. said Amos Gunn, with Metropolitan oracularness.

oracularity (ɒˌrækjʊˈlærɪtɪ). [f. prec. + -ITY.] The quality or character of being oracular.

a. The quality of being the medium or seat of an oracle, or of making divine communications.

1816 G. S. FABER *Orig. Pagan Idol.* III. 260 Agreeably to the notion which ascribed oracularity to the sacred grotto. **1818** —— *Horæ Mosaicæ* I. 130 The mouth relates to the supposed oracularity of the diluvian ship, which was feigned to direct its votaries in an audible voice what course they ought to take. **1842** —— *Prov. Lett.* (1844) II. 36 To invest the Clergy with some dreamy and mysterious oracularity.

b. The quality of being laconic, obscure, and of veiled meaning; with *pl.* an instance of this.

1840 *Blackw. Mag.* XLVIII. 365 This we conceive to be in the purest style of the hieroglyphics, and to establish Coleridge's oracularity beyond all question. **1845** THACKERAY *Picture Gossip* Wks. 1900 XIII. 458 Stanfield has no mysticism or oracularity about him. *a* **1849** POE *Whipple* Wks. 1864 III. 383 The quips, quirks, and curt oracularities of the Emersons [etc.].

oracularly (ɒˈrækjʊləlɪ), *adv.* [f. ORACULAR + -LY[2].] In an oracular manner.

a. In the solemn, authoritative, or sententious manner of an ancient oracle.

1771 BURKE *Powers Juries in Libels* Wks. 1877 VI. 162 A timid jury will give way to an awful judge delivering oracularly the law. **1788** REID *Aristotle's Log.* i. §1. 3 He delivers his decisions oracularly. **1884** *Truth* 13 Mar. 380/2 Mr. Justice Stephen, speaking oracularly, declared that there was no law against human cremation 'if effected without nuisance to others'.

b. With the obscurity or ambiguity of the responses of the ancient oracles; enigmatically.

1864 *Daily Tel.* 17 May, Utterances even more oracularly ambiguous are ascribed to him at Washington.

oˈraculate, *v. rare.* [f. L. *ōrācul-um* (see ORACLE *sb.*) + -ATE[3].] *trans.* and *intr.* To say or speak oracularly.

1822 E. NATHAN *Langreath* II. 315, I think I behold you shaking your wise head.. as you would oraculate, 'the simple Madelina little suspects' [etc.]. **1919** J. BUCHAN *Mr. Standfast* I. i. 32 He boomed and oraculated and the Misses Wymondham prattled. **1930** —— *Castle Gay* viii. 134 The Professor oraculated on letters, with an elephantine deference to his hearers' opinions.

†**oˈraculist.** *Obs.* [f. L. *ōrācul-um* ORACLE + -IST.] A professed communicator of oracles.

1652 GAULE *Magastrom.* 310 It was answered by the divining Oraculists that Augustus had onely a hundred dayes to live. *Ibid.* 363 And thus was it shuffled up betwixt the astrologers and the oraculists.

†**oˈraculize,** *v. Obs. rare.* [f. L. *ōrācul-um* ORACLE + -IZE.] *trans.* To make an oracle of; to render, or hold as, oracular.

1593 NASHE *Christ's T.* (1613) 127 That of Terence is oraculiz'd, *Patres aequum censere nos adolescentulos* [etc.].

Hence †**oˈraculizer,** one who constitutes himself an oracle, or plays the oracle.

1634 SIR T. HERBERT *Trav.* 169 But he that sits on high.. in foure and twenty houres after proved this great Oraculizer a compleat lier.

oraculous (ɒˈrækjʊləs), *a.* Now *rare* or *Obs.* [f. L. type **ōrāculōs-us*, f. *ōrācul-um*: cf. obs. F. *oraculeux* (Cotgr. and Godef.), and *miraculous*.] Of the nature of, or pertaining to, an oracle. (Formerly common; now superseded by ORACULAR.)

1. = ORACULAR 1.

1610 HEALEY *St. Aug. Citie of God* 596 This [counting the sands] the oraculous device of Delpho's ascribed to himselfe. *a* **1658** CLEVELAND *Answ. Pamph.* (1677) 130 Reason.. why Jupiter, when he was most Oraculous, was called Jupiter Ammon. **1660** INGELO *Bentiv. & Ur.* II. (1682) Pref., Where the Oraculous Tripos stands. **1671** MILTON *P.R.* III. 14 Urim and Thummim, those oraculous gems On Aaron's breast. **1776** MICKLE tr. *Camoens' Lusiad* 179 When.. Orac'lous Argo sail'd from wondering Greece. **1849** tr. *Ct. A. Hamilton's Fairy T.* 174 [He] soon left the oraculous wood a full league behind him.

†**2.** = ORACULAR 2. *Obs.*

1612 DRAYTON *Poly-olb.* x. 162 That what he spake, was held to be oraculous So true his writings were. **1647** WARD *Simp. Cobler* 59 Is no Bishop no King, such an oraculous Truth? **1751** JOHNSON *Rambler* No. 172 ¶10 He.. expects that.. his opinion be received as decisive and oraculous.

†**b.** = ORACULAR 2 b. *Obs.*

1625 BACON *Ess., Simulation* (Arb.) 509 As for Equiuocations, or Oraculous Speeches, they cannot hold out long. *a* **1720** SHEFFIELD (Dk. Buckhm.) *Wks.* (1753) II. 125 To guess.. what the meaning of this oraculous clause should be.

3. = ORACULAR 3.

1617 MIDDLETON & ROWLEY *Fair Quarrel* II. ii, Like a conjuror, One of our fine oraculous wizards. **1647** CRASHAW *Poems* 117 The oraculous doctors' mystic bills, Certain hard words made into pills. **1725** POPE *Odyss.* IV. 519 The oraculous seer [Proteus] frequents the Pharian coast. **1750** JOHNSON *Rambler* No. 61 ¶4 He grows on a sudden oraculous and infallible. **1818** T. L. PEACOCK *Nightmare Abbey* xii, He.. asked Mr. Flosky, whom he looked up to as a most oraculous personage, whether any story of any ghost.. was entitled to any degree of belief.

†**4.** = ORACULAR 4. *Obs.*

1615 G. SANDYS *Trav.* 61 Deliuer him in writing the state of the question; who in writing briefly returnes his oraculous answer. **1624** HEYWOOD *Gunaik.* II. 99 Who.. sung many oraculous cautions to the people of Sparta, yet could they not predict their owne disaster. **1624** GATAKER *Transubst.* 197 As the oraculous predictions of the Prophets and expresse promises of God himselfe describe it.

b. (With allusion to ORACLE *sb.* 5.)

1626 DONNE *Serm.* lxxxviii. 793 One whose books are dedicated to the Pope.. and so hath had an oraculous refining by an allowance *oraculo vivæ vocis.*

Hence **oˈraculously** *adv.*, by or in manner of an oracle; as if by an oracle; oracularly; **oˈraculousness,** oracularity.

1632 BROME *North. Lasse* I. ii. Wks. 1873 III. 6 My Cosins counsel, which hath ever been oraculously good. **1646** SIR T. BROWNE *Pseud. Ep.* I. vi. 21 The testimonies of Antiquity and such as passe oraculously amongst us. **1697** DRYDEN *Virg. Georg.* II. 22 The branching Beech and vocal Oke, Where Jove of Old Oraculously spoke. **1755** JOHNSON *Oraculous.—Oraculousness*, the state of being oracular.

‖**oraculum** (ɒˈrækjʊləm). [L.: see ORACLE.]

1. = ORACLE.

1719 SWIFT *To Sheridan* 14 Dec., But I doubt the oraculum is a poor supernaculum. **1899** WATTS-DUNTON *Aylwin* (1900) 88/2 'You seem to be the Oraculum of the hay-fields, sir.. Have you any other Delphic utterance?'

2. = ORATORY[1] 1.

1845 PETRIE *Eccl. Archit. Irel.* II. iii. 2. 352 Such oratories are often designated by the term *oraculum*, a word which was also sometimes applied to oratories in Ireland.

oracy (ˈɔərəsɪ). [f. L. *ōs, ōr-* mouth + -ACY, after LITERACY.] The capacity or ability to express oneself fluently in speech. Also, oral transmission of poetry, etc.

1965 A. WILKINSON *Spoken Eng.* 14 The term we suggest for general ability in the oral skills is *oracy*; one who has those skills is *orate*, one without them *inorate*. **1965** *New Society* 12 Aug. 4/2 A new qualification has been proclaimed: oracy, 'general ability in the oral skills'. The coiner of word and concept is Andrew Wilkinson, lecturer in education at Birmingham. **1967** *Daily Mirror* 16 Oct. 18 The team is making a three-year investigation into oracy.. with a £15,000 grant from the Schools Council. **1971** *Daily Tel.* 20 Apr. 14 An additional year.. of the schooling.. will not.. benefit them unless it has been preceded by.. a successful learning of literacy and of oracy. **1972** T. A. SHIPPEY *Old Eng. Verse* iv. 89 Though literacy and the fixed text may have killed 'oracy' in the long run, the change need not have happened as quickly as in the present century.

ˈorad, *adv. rare.* [f. L. *ōs, ōr-* mouth + *-ad*: see DEXTRAD.] Towards the mouth.

1891 in *Cent. Dict.*

†**oˈrafle.** *Obs. rare*[−1]. [a. OF. *orafle*: see GIRAFFE.] A giraffe.

c **1400** MAUNDEV. xxviii. (1839) 288 There also ben many Bestes, that ben clept Orafles.

‖**oˈrage.** [a. F. *orage* (ɔraʒ):—popular L. *aurātic-um*, f. *aura* breeze: see -AGE.]

†**1.** A violent or tempestuous wind; a storm. Also *fig. Obs.*

c **1477** CAXTON *Jason* 56 b, Whiche knightes beyng.. upon the see, were sore vexid.. with great orages and tempestes. **1483** —— *Gold. Leg.* 137/2 Sodenly descended fro heuen suche a tempest of rayne and of orage that it couerd alle the montayne. **1611** COTGR., *Orage*, a storme, tempest, orage. *a* **1734** NORTH *Lives* (1826) I. 183 His gains.. were much greater by his practice; for that flowed in upon him like an orage. —— *Exam.* III. viii. §63 (1740) 632 But there was then enough of the Church and Loyal Party.. to stem that Orage of Faction.

2. An organ-stop designed to produce an imitation of the noise of a tempest.

1891 in *Cent. Dict.*

orage, obs. form of ORACH.

oragious (ɒˈreɪdʒəs), *a. rare.* [a. Anglo-F. *orageus*, F. *orageux* stormy, f. *orage* storm.] Stormy, tempestuous. *lit.* and *fig.*

c **1590** *Burel's Pilgr.* in Watson *Coll. Poems* (1706) II. 19 The storme wes so outragius, And with rumlings oragius, That I for fear did gruge. **1855** THACKERAY *Newcomes* xxxi. 303 M. d'Ivry, whose early life may have been rather oragious, was yet a gentleman.

†**oraˈguella.** *Obs.* A kind of fabric: see quot.

1719 J. ROBERTS *Spinster* 346 Woollen stuffs, and stuffs mixed with silk.. quite lost, and thrown out of sale, such as.. sattinets and chiverets, oraguella's.

oraison, obs. form of ORISON.

‖**oraison funèbre** (ɔrɛzɔ̃ fynɛbr). [Fr.] A funeral oration.

1874 H. L. FARRER *Bossuet* vii. 313 [On] the occasion of the Queen's death,.. Louis XIV requested him [*sc.* Bossuet] to preach her Oraison Funèbre. This was in 1683. **1876** *Encycl. Brit.* IV. 70/2 In the *Oraisons Funèbres* Bossuet is unapproachable.. Nowhere does his genius take such wing as at the grave's mouth. **1907** G. MEREDITH *Let.* 22 Dec. (1970) III. 1620 You will not care for an *oraison funèbre.* **1953** W. STEVENS *Let.* 16 Nov. (1967) 802 An *oraison funebre* is not in my line. **1957** N. FRYE *Anat. Crit.* 296 The corresponding form in oratorical prose is the *oraison funèbre*, which survives in some forms of modern obituary.

oral (ˈɔərəl), *a.* (*sb.*) [f. L. *ōs, ōr-* mouth + -AL[1]. Cf. F. *oral* (18th c. in Hatz.-Darm.).]

A. *adj.* **1. a.** Uttered or communicated in spoken words; transacted by word of mouth; spoken, verbal. *oral history*: (the collection or study of) tape-recorded historical information concerning matters from the personal knowledge of the speaker; such a taped record; ***Oral Law, oral law***: the part of Jewish religious law passed down by oral tradition before being collected in the Mishnah.

1638 *Penit. Conf.* iv. (1657) 43 Opened by himself in orall confession to the principal party wronged. *c* **1680** in Somers *Tracts* I. 211 How often have they formerly urged us to an Oral or Pen Combat. **1733** tr. *B. Picart's Ceremonies & Relig. Customs* I. 46 A Man who hath made the Oral Law his principal Study.. is looked upon by the Generality amongst them as a Doctor. **1751** JOHNSON *Rambler* No. 87 ¶12 Temptations to petulance..which occur in oral conferences. **1797** *Encycl. Brit.* XVIII. 303/2 The Mishna is divided into six parts... In the fourth..are named those by whom the oral law was received and preserved. **1874** GREEN *Short Hist.* v. §4. 239 Disputes were easily settled by the steward of the manor..on oral evidence of the custom at issue. **1879** FARRAR *St. Paul* I. 155 To throw discredit even upon the Oral Law would not be without danger. **1907** Oral law [used s.v. MISHNAH, MISHNA]. **1962** *New Jewish Encycl.* 362/1 At present, most Jews, though they may deviate from certain of its practices, believe the Oral Law to be divinely inspired. **1971** WEBSTER Add., Oral history. **1976** C. BERMANT *Coming Home* I. vii. 93 The Talmud incorporates the Oral Law, and..the Oral Law was dictated with the written Law by God to Moses on Sinai, and..the Oral Law was received intact by the Rabbis. **1977** *Times* 16 May 7/7 Oral history..enables the historian to put the questions he wants. **1977** *Program Announcement 1977–78* (U.S. Nat. Endowment for Humanities) 11 (*caption*) Oral history taping sessions, and a more informal jam session took place as part of..an NEH Division of Research Grants project that brought together these St. Louis jazz musicians to recount their experiences... Taping sessions..produced an oral history which will be made available to music historians and centers of research through the University's Learning Resources Center. **1978** P. THOMPSON *Voices of Past* ii. 19 The term 'oral history' is new, like the tape recorder; and it has radical implications for the future.

b. (Of poetry, etc.) delivered or transmitted orally; of or pertaining to such poetry. Also *transf.* So **oral-formulaic** *a.*, of or pertaining to (usu. early) poetry belonging to a spoken tradition which is characterized by the use of poetic formulae as an aid to memory.

1628 BP. HALL *Old Relig.* xvi. §3. 167 As for orall Traditions, what certaintie can there be in them? **1767** PERCY *Ess. Anc. Eng. Minstrels* (Notes) 44 He [*sc.* Asser] has however particularly recorded Alfred's fondness for the oral Anglo-Saxon poems and songs. **1774** T. WARTON *Hist. Eng. Poetry* I. Diss. i p. l, That scalds were common in the Danish armies when they invaded England, appears from a stratagem of Alfred; who, availing himself of his skill in oral poetry and playing on the harp, entered the Danish camp habited in that character, and procured a hospitable reception. **1777** J. BRAND *Observations Pop. Antiq.* p. iv, These [ceremonies],..though erazed by public Authority from the *written Word*, were committed as a venerable Deposit to the keeping of *oral Tradition.* **1892** J. EARLE *Deeds of Beowulf* p. xlvi, Müllenhoff had discovered six different authors, of which the first two were oral poets, but the third had a written copy of the rudimentary work as it then existed. *Ibid.* p. xlviii, The oral Epic was simple in outline and plain in style, and therefore the contradictions, irregularities, inversions..and intolerable repetitions..can only be explained by the gradual accretion of heterogeneous elements in the process of transmission. **1898** S. A. BROOKE *Eng. Lit. fr. Beginning to Norman Conquest* ii. 42 This was the origin of the early unhistoric sagas, like that of Beowulf, and such a saga was the highest form of the oral literature of the German tribes. **1906** G. P. KRAPP *Andreas* 75 The poem opens with the conventional epic formula, citing the authority of oral tradition for the story. **1928** W. W. LAWRENCE *Beowulf & Epic Trad.* 289 A written version of *Beowulf* might conceivably have served as a guide for oral recitation. **1929** W. E. LEONARD in Malone & Ruud *Stud. Eng. Philol.* 1 The intrinsic nature..of oral or chanted verse as inevitably emphasizing an organic metrical pattern. **1953** S. A. BROWN in A. Dundes *Mother Wit* (1973) 40/1 The Negro was contributing..through what we call oral literature—folk literature. **1953** F. P. MAGOUN in *Speculum* XXVIII. 446 (*heading*) Oral-formulaic character of Anglo-Saxon narrative poetry. **1970** *Jrnl. Eng. & Gmc. Philol.* LXIX. 72 Even contemporary criticism has tended to damn with faint praise by suggesting that Old English poems were largely collections of formulae indicative of oral composition... The conclusion that the presence of formulae is an indication of oral composition has been attacked as illogical. *Ibid.* 439 It would have been possible to use [in the OE *Riming Poem*] some of the oral formulae of other elegies and add a second half-line that rimed. **1972** T. A. SHIPPEY *Old Eng. Verse* iv. 89 The theory claims that much classical and modern poetry has been composed by an 'oral-formulaic' process. **1973** *Black World* Nov. 10/2 Black music..as a basically oral-tradition music, is lacking in the kind of documentation that..would clarify these aspects.

2. a. Using speech only; communicating instruction, etc. by word of mouth. *rare.*

1870 ARBER *Introd. Ascham's Scholem.* 6 The influence of simply Oral Teachers rests chiefly in the hearts and minds of the Taught.

b. Using ordinary speech or 'lip-language' in the instruction of the deaf and dumb.

1880 *Daily News* 11 Nov. 6/2, I understand that under the oral system both signs and finger-speaking are prohibited. *Ibid.*, If I [a deaf mute] had been sent to an oral school I should have made little or no progress whatever.

3. a. Of or pertaining to the mouth, as a part of the body.

oral cavity, (*a*) the cavity of the mouth; (*b*) in haustellate insects, the hollow on the lower surface of the head, from which the haustellum or sucking-mouth protrudes.

1656 BLOUNT *Glossogr.*, *Oral*, pertaining to the mouth, visage, face, look, favor or voyce. **1816** KIRBY & SP. *Entomol.* (1843) I. 89 The acute pain which attends the insertion of their oral stings. **1826** *Ibid.* xlvii. (ed. 1) IV. 379 Their oral organs..are of a Neuropterous type. **1888** ROLLESTON & JACKSON *Anim. Life* 503 Salivary glands..open into the oral cavity, the most important pair belonging to the labium.

b. Involving or being sexual activity in which the genitals of one partner are stimulated by the mouth of the other; freq. in *Comb.*, as ***oral-genital*** adj. Cf. CUNNILINGUS, FELLATIO.

1948 A. C. KINSEY et al. *Sexual Behavior Human Male* II. x. 373 Most prostitutes are from the lower social levels, and consequently..few of them engage freely in oral activities. **1953** —— et al. *Sexual Behavior Human Female* vii. 257 Oral stimulation of the male genitalia by the female occurs somewhat less frequently. **1958** G. S. SPRAGUE et al. in C. Berg *Homosexuality* II. i. 213 At one end..would stand the most primitive oral pattern, fellatio. **1961** *Encounter* XVI. v. 77 His short paragraph on oral-genital techniques. **1969** 'J' *Sensuous Woman* (1970) xi. 79 A few minutes of oral-genital play was a small price to pay. **1973** S. FISHER *Female Orgasm* vii. 209 Most of the women..received manual and often oral stimulation of the clitoral region. **1973** *Sunday Times* (Colour Suppl.) 11 Mar. 20 Her main discovery is that oral sex is fun. **1977** *Time Out* 17–23 June 45/3 There's more erotic charge from two seconds of Damiano's close-up oral sequences than in Ms Richmond's entire oeuvre.

4. a. Done or performed with or by the mouth, as the organ of eating and drinking.

1625 USSHER *Answ. Jesuit* 71 This grosse opinion of the orall eating and drinking of Christ in the Sacrament. *a* **1655** VINES *Lord's Supp.* (1677) 382 The guiltiness of Christs Body is not by the oral eating. **1888** *Ch. Times* 13 July 613 Attendance at the Holy Eucharist without oral communion on every occasion.

b. Administered or taken through the mouth; involving such administration.

1957 *Amer. Jrnl. Med. Sci.* CCXXXIV. 28/1 The purpose of this study was to evaluate the efficacy of an oral alcohol-water solution of theophylline in terminating acute asthmatic attacks. **1959** *Science* 10 July 81/1 This property ..led to the experimental testing of a norethyn-odrel-estrogen combination as an oral contraceptive. **1959** K. H. BEYER in Waife & Shapiro *Clin. Eval. New Drugs* ii. 18 Oral efficacy..is certainly a limiting factor in the acceptance of a new drug for systemic use. **1962** *Lancet* 22 Dec. 1315/2 Oral contraception is now a matter of practical politics. **1967** *Proc. Soc. Exper. Biol. & Med.* CXXIV. 483/1 The acute oral toxicity of sodium selenite in the rat does not seem to have been investigated. **1970** W. J. BURLEY *To kill Cat* i. 24 A sachet of oral contraceptives. **1974** PASSMORE & ROBSON *Compan. Med. Stud.* III. I. xxviii. 34/1 A number of women ..experience amenorrhoea after discontinuing oral contraception.

5. *Psychol.* In psychoanalysis, characterized by having the mouth as the main focus of infantile sexual energy and feeling.

[**1910** *Amer. Jrnl. Psychol.* XXI. 316 In infantile sexuality the oral and anal-urethral erogeneous zones..as well as sadistic and masochistic impulses rule.] **1925** J. RIVIERE tr. *Freud's Infantile Neurosis* in *Coll. Papers* III. v. 587, I have been driven to regard as the earliest recognizable sexual organization the so-called 'cannibalistic' or 'oral' phase. **1954** R. W. PICKFORD *Analysis of Obsessional* iii. 68 In general the oral stages are concerned with taking in of objects and ideas, or introjection. **1972** ROSEN & GREGORY *Abnormal Psychol.* (ed. 2) 53/2 The child's relationship with his parents as established during the oral period.

6. *Phonetics.* Of a sound: that is articulated with the velum raised, so that there is no nasal resonance. Cf. NASAL *a.* 2. So ***oral-nasal*** adj.

1919 E. KRUISINGA *Handbk. Present-Day Eng.* (ed. 3) I. I. i. 14 We see therefore that sounds can be produced..with the nose-passage shut: *oral* sounds. **1924** J. S. KENYON *Amer. Pronunc.* 36 (*heading*) Oral and nasal consonants. **1933** L. BLOOMFIELD *Language* vi. 96 Most sounds of speech are purely *oral*; the velum is completely raised and no breath escapes through the nose. **1955** P. STREVENS *Papers in Lang. & Lang. Teaching* (1965) ix. 114 In rapid speech the consonant may be omitted, leaving a nasalized vowel where Received Pronunciation would have an oral vowel followed by a nasal consonant. **1961** H. A. GLEASON *Introd. Descriptive Linguistics* (ed. 2) xv. 250 If only the mouth is open, the sound is an oral resonant. **1962** *Amer. Speech* XXXVII. 228 Differences between oral and nasal vowels. **1965** *Language* XLI. 478 The oral-nasal contrast is neutralized after a nasal; such vowels are written in this paper as oral. **1970** *Ibid.* XLVI. 81 There are eight consonants in Maxakalí, comprising an oral-nasal pair at each of four points of articulation. **1975** P. LADEFOGED *Course in Phonetics* i. 3 Note that the air passages that make up the vocal tract may be divided into the oral tract within the mouth and the pharynx and the nasal tract within the nose.

B. as *sb.* **a.** Short for *oral sound*, *oral plate*, etc.

1885 *Athenæum* 11 Apr. 475/2 A ring of plates which are the homologues of the five oral plates... These orals are the actinal representatives of the basals. **1887** BENSON *Univ. Phonography* 11 The vowels [may be divided] into Five Pharyngals: Five Orals: Five Diphthongs. *Ibid.* 12 The Orals, short or long, in Feel, Fill, Tulle, Full, Fool.

b. Short for *oral examination.*

1876 G. H. TRIPP *Student-Life Harvard* 18 Do something splendid on the mathematics and the 'orals', and I will wage any thing you will pass clear. **1927** W. E. COLLINSON *Contemp. Eng.* 124 In regard to teaching within the University the only terms worthy of notice are the use of Oral (where some universities use Viva for Viva Voce)..and tutorials. **1973** D. MAY *Laughter in Djakarta* xii. 194 Examiners told candidates their marks immediately at the end of the oral. **1974** B. JOHNSTON *It's been a Lot of Fun* vi. 45 One of the dons pointed this out to me during my oral.

‖**orale** (ɒˈreɪliː, ɒˈrɑːleɪ). *Eccl.* [med.L., = 'veil', neuter of **ōrāl-is* adj., f. *ōs, ōr-* face, countenance, mouth. See Du Cange.] A veil, covering the face and breast and falling upon the shoulders, worn by the Pope at certain solemn ceremonials.

1844–49 [see FANON 2].

oralism (ˈɔərəlɪz(ə)m). [f. ORAL + -ISM.] The method of instructing deaf-mutes by ordinary speech or 'lip-language', instead of by the manual alphabet.

1883 *Amer. Ann. Deaf & Dumb* Apr. 90 So far as oralism ..is concerned.

oralist (ˈɔərəlɪst). [f. as prec. + -IST.]

1. One practised in oral delivery; a correct or model speaker. *rare.*

1867 A. M. BELL *Vis. Speech* 109 A comparison of the independent pronunciations of two or three such selected oralists to fix the alphabet for Visible Speech printing.

2. One who uses oral teaching or 'lip-language' for the instruction of the deaf and dumb.

1880 *Daily News* 11 Nov. 6/2 The oralists say that under the French system signs only are taught. **1882** *Amer. Ann. Deaf & Dumb* July 154 An ardent oralist.

oˈrality. [f. ORAL + -ITY.] **1.** The quality of being oral, or orally communicated. Also, preference for or tendency to use spoken forms of language.

1666 J. SERGEANT *Letter of Thanks* 108 The Orality of the Rule of Faith. **1946** *Hansard Commons* 17 Oct. 1055 Does the right hon. Gentleman not appreciate that it is the uncertainty about the date when written Questions will be answered which promotes orality? **1967** A. L. LLOYD *Folk Song in England* i. 25 Orality is a most important characteristic..and we have every right to speak of the grandeurs of oral tradition. **1973** *Times Lit. Suppl.* 26 Oct. 1323/2 A synthesis of Black orality with White literacy and technocracy. *Ibid.* 1323/3 The Black man enslaved took his African orality with him.

2. In sense of ORAL *a.* 5.

1934 LEWIN & ZILBOORG tr. *Fenichel's Outline Clin. Psychoanal.* x. 372 Our findings then are:—ambivalence, turning against the ego, orality. **1951** W. & J. MCCORD in *Jrnl. Mental Sci.* XCVII. 765 (*title*) The problem of 'orality' and of its origin in early childhood.

3. *Phonetics.* With reference to a sound: the quality or state of being oral (see ORAL *a.* 6).

1949 *Word* V. 158 Nasality vs. Orality. **1952** A. COHEN *Phonemes of Eng.* ii. 36 Features that are not actually relevant in distinguishing two phonemes, e.g. alveolarity, plosion, orality..must be taken into account all the same as contributing to the existence of both phonemes. **1964** R. H. ROBINS *Gen. Linguistics* iv. 155 Orality and voicelessness being regarded as the absence of a feature, nasality and voice, respectively.

orally (ˈɔərəlɪ), *adv.* [f. ORAL + -LY².]

1. By, through, or with the mouth as the organ of eating and drinking.

1608 BP. HALL *Epist.* I. v. 30 The priest did sacrifice, and orally devour it whole. **1625** USSHER *Answ. Jesuit* (1631) 48 That which is externally delivered in the Sacrament, and orally received by the Communicant. **1893** *Ch. Times* 17 Feb. 164/4 It is the duty of every Catholic to be present every Lord's Day at the offering of the Eucharist, whether he communicates orally or in the prayers only.

2. By or with the mouth as the organ of speech; by word of mouth; verbally. Also in *Comb.*

1666 TILLOTSON *Rule of Faith* III. ix. §2 The faith of the Jews was not delivered to them orally, but by writing. **1786–1805** H. TOOKE *Purley* 32 Without..Language mankind would have nothing but Interjections with which to communicate, orally, any of their feelings. **1838** THIRLWALL *Greece* xix. III. 109 The votes, according to Spartan usage, were given orally. *a* **1859** MACAULAY *Hist. Eng.* xxiii. V. 28 An Act..forbidding English subjects to hold any intercourse orally, or by writing, or by message, with the exiled family. **1957** R. HOGGART *Uses of Literacy* iv. 86 These views usually prove to be a bundle of largely unexamined and orally-transmitted tags. **1966** C. M. SIMPSON *Brit. Broadside Ballad* p. ix, The orally circulating ballad of tradition. **1967** A. L. LLOYD *Folk Song in England* iii. 144 Orally-diffused amateur composition. *Ibid.* v. 368 There is the anonymous, orally-spread, firmly traditional kind of song. *Ibid.* v. 381 The text is from a broadside... The orally-transmitted versions are not so complete.

3. With the mouth, as a means of sexual stimulation. Cf. ORAL *a.* 3b.

1951 FORD & BEACH *Patterns Sexual Behaviour* (1952) iii. 54 Alorese men occasionally stimulate the woman's genitals orally. **1953** A. C. KINSEY et al. *Sexual Behavior Human Female* vii. 258, 16 per cent had stimulated the male genitalia orally.

-orama, -(r)ama, *suffix.* [a. Gk. ὅραμα view, as in the second element of CYCLORAMA, PANORAMA.] As a suffix suggestive of considerable size or expanse, in commercial use to form nouns the nature of which is indicated by the first element. Cf. DIORAMA, CINERAMA.

1824 E. WEETON *Jrnl.* 17 July (1969) II. 306 Visited the Cosmorama... I had now seen many of the -ramas in London, Ignoramus' and all. **1896** E. MARRIAGE tr. *Balzac's Old Goriot* 54 The diorama, a recent invention,..had given rise to a mania among art students for ending every word with *rama*... 'Well, Monsieur-r-r Poiret,..how is your health-orama?' *Ibid.* 'There is an uncommon *frozerama* outside!'... 'Why do you say *frozerama*?..it should be *frozenrama*.' **1954** *Amer. Speech* XXIX. 157 Audiorama, a display of acoustic instruments;..*striporama*, a burlesque movie. **1962** *Word Study* Dec. 6/2 An exhibition of automobiles known as Motorama,..a Launderama (coin-operated automatic washers with dryers). **1963** *Guardian* 24 Aug. 6/3, I observe from your London Letter..that a fresh verbal monstrosity is to be inflicted on the defenceless English population—something called a 'scent-a-rama'. **1973** *Advocate-News* (Barbados) 15 Dec. 6/1 With all the 'ramas' like cyclerama, brassorama, musicrama and laugharama, why can't we call this one ugly-o-rama?

Doesn't it sound great? **1977** *Radio Times* 29 Oct. 20/3 *Swaporama* with Keith Chegwin.

orang (ɒˈræŋ), abbreviated f. ORANG-OUTANG.
1778 CAMPER in *Phil. Trans.* LXIX. 145, I had an opportunity of seeing seven Orangs. **1854** OWEN *Skel. & Teeth* in *Circ. Sc., Organ. Nat.* I. 299 Both chimpanzees and orangs differ from the human subject in the order of the development of the permanent series of teeth.
attrib. **1882** DE WINDT *Equator* 106 Our last attempt at orang shooting.

orange (ˈɒrɪndʒ), *sb.*[1], *a.* Forms: 4–8 orenge, (6 orr-, -ndge, -(n)che, 7 oreng); 5– orange, (5 hor-, oronge, 6–7 -inge, 7 -ynge; 5 *Sc.* oreynze). [ME. *orenge*, *orange*, a. OF. *orenge* (13th c.), *orange*, = It. *narancia* (Florio), now *arancia* (Venet. *naranza*, Milan. *naranz*), Sp. *naranja*, Pg. *laranja*, also med. Gr. *νεράντζιον*. The Sp. and Gr. are ad. Arabic *nāranj*, in Pers. *nārang*, *nāring*: cf. late Skr. *nāranga*, Hindī *nārangī*; also Pers. *nār* pomegranate.
The native country of the orange appears to have been the northern frontier of India, where wild oranges are still found, and the name may have originated there. The loss of initial *n* in Fr., Eng., and It. is usually ascribed to its absorption in the indef. article in *une narange*, *una narancia*. Med.L. had also the forms *arangia*, *arantia* (Du Cange), whence *aurantia* by popular association with *aurum* gold, from the colour. So perh. OF. *orenge* for *arange*, after *or* gold.]

A. *sb.* **1. a.** The fruit of a tree (see sense 2), a large globose many-celled berry (HESPERIDIUM) with sub-acid juicy pulp, enclosed in a tough rind externally of a bright reddish yellow (= orange) colour.
The common variety is variously called the ***China***, ***coolie***, ***Lisbon***, ***Portugal***, or ***sweet*** *o.*; the name *China orange* was especially common in 17–18th c. Other varieties or species are known as ***blood(-red)***, ***Malta*** or ***Maltese*** *o.*, a red-pulped variety; ***Jaffa*** or ***Joppa*** *o.*, a lemon-shaped and very sweet kind; ***navel*** *o.*, a nearly seedless variety from Brazil, etc., having the rudiment of a second fruit imbedded in its apex; ***clove*** (in Ogilvie 1882), ***noble***, or ***mandarin*** *o.* = MANDARIN; ***tangerine*** *o.*: see TANGERINE. The fruit of the *Citrus Bigaradia* is called the ***bitter***, ***horned***, or ***Seville*** *o.*; and that of the *C. Bergamia*, ***bergamot*** *o.* or BERGAMOT.
13.. *E.E. Allit. P.* B. 1044 As orenge & oþer fryt. *a* **1387** *Sinon. Barthol.* (Anecd. Oxon.) 15 *Citrangulum pomum*, orenge. *c* **1425** *Voc.* in Wr.-Wülcker 647/40 *Hoc masuclum*, orange. *c* **1440** *Promp. Parv.* 371/1 Oronge, fruete. *c* **1490** *Paston Lett.* III. 364 Halfe a hondryd orrygys. **1497** in *Acc. Ld. High Treas. Scot.* (1877) I. 330 For bering of the appill oreynzeis..fra the schip. **1538** TURNER *Libellus*, *Malum medicum*, an oreche. *c* **1550** LLOYD *Treas. Health* (1585) Sj, The sede of Orenche. **1587** GOLDING *De Mornay* x. 141 The rinde of the Orrendge is hot, and the meate within it is cold. **1598** *Epulario* Cij, Take the iuice of an Oringe, or else Vergice. **1698** A. BRAND *Emb. Muscovy to China* 87 Grapes, Apples..China-Oranges,..and other fruits. **1796** STEDMAN *Surinam* II. xxix. 375, I found a crystal phial filled with essential oil of orange..extracted from the rind or peel of the oranges. *c* **1830** *Cries of York* 18 Sweet China Oranges. St. Michael's Oranges I vend At one or two a penny. **1841** *Mann. & Househ. Exp.* (Roxb.) Pref. 48 In the 18th of Edward the first [1290] a large Spanish ship came to Portsmouth; out of the cargo of which the Queen bought..fifteen citrons and seven oranges [*Poma de orenge*]. **1866** *Treas. Bot.* 292 Oranges were unknown in Europe, or at all events in Italy, in the eleventh century, but were shortly afterwards carried westward by the Moors. *Ibid.*, The Noble or Mandarin Orange is a small flattened and deep orange..it is exceedingly rich and sweet. **1870** YEATS *Nat. Hist. Comm.* 179 The rind of the orange yields by distillation a fragrant oil much used in perfumery.

b. Phrase: ***to squeeze*** or ***suck an orange***, to extract all the juice from it; *fig.* to take all that is profitable out of anything.
1685 *Gracian's Courtier's Orac.* 4 So soon as the Orange is squeezed, it's thrown upon the ground. **1822** G. CANNING in *G. Canning & his Times* 364 For fame, it is a squeezed orange; but for public good there is something to do. **1884** HAWLEY SMART *From Post to Finish* I. vii. 108 It is rather rough on the boy..to suddenly discover that his father had sucked the orange, and that he has merely inherited the skin. **1891** in Dixon *Dict. Idiom. Eng. Phr.*, By this time Dibdin was a sucked orange; his brain was dry.

c. ***oranges and lemons***, a nursery game, in which a ditty beginning with these words is sung, and the players take sides according to their answer to the question 'Which will you have, oranges or lemons?'.
1873 *Young Englishwoman* Mar. 154/2 Could you..give me the words in full of 'Oranges and Lemons'; 'I wrote a Letter to my Love'; 'Kiss in the Ring'; and any other of the old games? **1887** E. D. BOURNE *Girls' Games* 48. **1939** [see *London bridge*]. **1969** I. & P. OPIE *Children's Games* viii. 236 Players..are invited to be an 'orange' or a 'lemon' in the game of 'Oranges and Lemons'.

d. *absol.* = Orange squash, orange juice.
1950 [see GIN *sb.*[2] 2 a]. **1968** T. KINSELLA *Nightwalker* 45 A small jug of orange. **1972** *Guardian* 20 June 4/6 And so, back to fizzy orange and the ritual conference. **1977** N. SLATER *Crossfire* iii. 60 'What can I get you?' 'Fresh orange. At least I can..set you an example.'

2. (More fully ORANGE-TREE, q.v.). An evergreen tree (*Citrus Aurantium*), a native of the East, now largely cultivated in the South of Europe, the Azores, and in most warm, temperate, or subtropical regions; it produces fragrant white flowers, and the fruit mentioned in sense 1. (Also applied to allied species or subspecies, as *C. nobilis*, *C. Bigaradia*, *C. Bergamia*: see 1.)
Otaheite orange, a hardy shrubby variety used as an ornamental plant and as a stock for dwarfing other varieties (*Cent. Dict.* 1891).
1615 G. SANDYS *Trav.* (1621) 3 Groues of Oranges. **1785** MARTYN *Rousseau's Bot.* xxv. (1794) 371 The Orange and Lemon may be distinguished by pointed leaves from the Shaddock. **1866** *Treas. Bot.* 292/1 It is said that St. Dominic planted an orange for the convent of St. Sabina in Rome, in the year 1200. **1886** G. MEREDITH *Ball. Yng. Princess* IV. i, The soft night-wind went laden to death With smell of the orange in flower.

3. a. Applied, with qualifying word prefixed, to plants of various families, or their fruit, mostly from some apparent resemblance in flower or fruit to the orange-tree.
Jamaica orange, the fruit of the *Glycosmis citrifolia* (*Treas. Bot.* 1866); **native orange** (*Australia*), (*a*) the orange-thorn (see quot. 1889); (*b*) the small native pomegranate, *Capparis mitchelli*; **Quito orange**, the berry of *Solanum Quitoënse*, a species of nightshade, in colour, fragrance, and taste resembling an orange; **Sumatra orange**, *Murraya sumatrana* (Miller *Plant-n.* 1884); **wild orange**, (*a*) of the West Indies, *Drypetes glauca* (*Treas. Bot.*); (*b*) the Carolina cherry-laurel, *Prunus Carolina*; (*c*) an Australian rubiaceous timber-tree, *Canthium latifolium*, also called wild lemon (Morris 1898). See also MOCK-ORANGE, OSAGE ORANGE.
1866 *Treas. Bot.* 290/1 The plants [of the genus *Citriobatus*] are called the Native Orange and Orange Thorn by the Australian colonists. **1889** J. H. MAIDEN *Useful Native Plants* 12 'Small Native Pomegranate', 'Native Orange'..The fruit is from one to two inches in diameter, and the pulp, which has an agreeable perfume, is eaten by the natives. *Ibid.* 16 'Native Orange', 'Orange Thorn'. The fruit is an orange berry with a leathery skin, about one inch and a half in diameter... It is eaten by the aboriginals.

b. Applied to varieties of apples or pears, resembling the orange in colour; cf. *orange-bergamot*, *-musk*, *-pear*, *-pippin* (see B. 2 c below).
1731–3 MILLER *Gard. Dict.* s.v. *Pyrus*, The Villain of Anjou. It is also called..The Tulip Pear, and..The Great Orange. **1767** J. ABERCROMBIE *Ev. Man his own Gard.* (1803) 673/1 Pears..Summer orange, Winter orange, Swiss bergamot. **1884** *Pall Mall G.* 15 Aug. 2/1 'Cox's orange pippin' and 'Blenheim orange', are certain to repay liberally for careful cultivation.

4. = SEA ORANGE, a large orange-coloured holothurian (*Lophothuria fabricii*) of globose shape.
1753 CHAMBERS *Cycl. Suppl.* s.v. *Orange*, *Sea Orange*, in natural history, a name given by Count Marsigli to a very remarkable species of sea plant,..it is round and hollow, and in all respects resembles the shape of an orange. **1838** *Encycl. Brit.* (ed. 7) XVI. 518/1 The body of the orange, as it is called, is fastened by them [fine filaments] to the rock, or other solid substance.

5. (More fully ORANGE-COLOUR.) The reddish-yellow colour of the orange; one of the so-called seven colours of the spectrum, occupying the region between red and yellow. Also, a pigment of this colour; usually, with defining words, as trade names for various shades, often indicating chemical origin, as ***cadmium***, ***Chinese***, ***diphenylamina***, ***gold***, ***Mars***, ***zinc orange***, etc.
a **1600** MONTGOMERIE *Misc. Poems* xxiv. 66 O wareit orange! willed me to weir. **1776–96** WITHERING *Brit. Plants* (ed. 3) IV. 327 Pileus frequently tinged with orange. **1832** TENNYSON *Mariana in the South* 26 Till all the crimson changed, and past Into deep orange o'er the sea. **1851** MAYNE REID *Scalp Hunt.* I. 10 Yonder the orange predominates in the showy flowers of the *asclepia*.

6. *Her.* A roundel tenné (tawny-coloured).
1562 LEIGH *Armorie* (1597) 88 The seuenth He beareth Argent, vij Orenges. **1610** GUILLIM *Heraldry* IV. xix. (1660) 352 If they [Roundles] be Tenne then we call them Orenges. **1727–41** in CHAMBERS *Cycl.* **1868–82** in CUSSANS *Her.* iv.

7. *attrib.* and *Comb.* **a.** simple attrib.: of an orange or oranges, as ***orange-bloom***, ***-grove***, ***-juice***, ***kernel***, ***leaf***, ***-pip***, ***-plant***, ***-plantation***, ***-room***, ***salad***, ***-thicket***, ***-tribe***, ***-wood***; employed or used in the orange trade, as ***orange-box***, ***-chest***, ***-crate*** (also fig.), ***-girl***, ***-man***, ***-merchant***, ***-wench***, ***-wife***, ***-woman***; flavoured with orange-juice or peel, as ***orange bitters***, ***cream***, ***crush***, ***Curaçao***, ***-custard***, ***gravy***, ***-pudding***, ***sauce***, ***squash***, ***-wine***. **b.** objective or obj. genitive, as ***orange-grower***, ***-seller***, ***squeezer***, ***-throwing***. **c.** parasynthetic, as ***orange-shaped*** adj.
c **1870** in H. W. Allen *Number Three St. James's St.* (1950) vii. 186/2 *Orange bitters. **1877** E. S. DALLAS *Kettner's Bk. of Table* 328 Parfait Amour is made of the bitter zest of limes,..syrup,..spirit of roses, and..spicy odours. It is in fact a kind of orange bitters spoilt. **1958** A. L. SIMON *Dict. Wines* 121/1 *Orange bitters*, the most popular form of bitters used for flavouring cocktails and other mixed drinks. It is made from the bitter Seville orange. **1977** *Sunday Times* (Colour Suppl.) 6 June 63/2 (Advt.), Sherry..with a dash of orange bitters. **1713** C'TESS WINCHELSEA *Misc. Poems* 16 The *Orange-bloom, that with such sweetness blows. **1968** 'J. LE CARRÉ' *Small Town in Germany* xiv. 229 An old lady dropped a two-Mark piece into an *orange-crate. **1972** L. ANDERSON *Let.* 20 June in *Amer. Speech 1972* (1975) XLVII. 38 In pilots training, we called the planes..'orange crates'. **1977** M. KENYON *Rapist* ix. 107 [He] sat on an orange crate in the storeroom. **1723** J. NOTT *Cook's & Confectioner's Dict.* sig. L5 **Orange Cream.* Take..Oranges, grate the Peels into..Water; beat..Eggs..sweeten..set it on the Fire, stir till it is as thick as Cream. **1861** MRS. BEETON *Bk. Househ. Managem.* 736 Orange cream... 1 oz of isinglass, 6 large oranges, 1 lemon, sugar to taste, water, ½ pint of good cream... Squeeze the juice from the oranges and lemon; [etc.]. **1939–40** *Army & Navy Stores Catal.* 31/2 Kia-Ora *Orange Crush—bot. 1/6. **1952** [see CRUSH *sb.* 4 e]. **1973** D. MAY *Laughter in Djakarta* iii. 54 What was almost the national drink of the Indonesian middle classes, orange crush. **1907** *Yesterday's Shopping* (1969) 100/2 *Curaçao..Orange..3/6. **1951** E. DAVID *French Country Cooking* 27 Grand Marnier, Mirabelle and Orange Curaçao are particularly good for soufflés and for omelettes. **1965** *House & Garden* Dec. 90/2 *Bols.* This old-established Dutch firm covers almost every liqueur—best known for Kummel, Apricot and Orange Curaçao. **1977** *Times* 9 July 10/7 A little brandy..or orange curaçao may be added. **1769** MRS. RAFFALD *Eng. Housekpr.* (1778) 256 To make *Orange Custards. **1787** SIR J. HAWKINS *Life Johnson* 195 One poet feigns, that the town is a sea, the playhouse a ship,..and the *orange-girls powder-monkies. **1842** *Knickerbocker* XX. 472 The orange-girl is generally allowed to enter [an auction-store], for auctioneers are mortal, and sometimes eat oranges. **1939** G. B. SHAW *In Good King Charles's Golden Days* I. 60, I never was an orange girl; but I have the gutter in my blood all right. **1963** M. FRAYN in Sissons & French *Age of Austerity* 336 The orange-girls, dressed up as replica Nell Gwyns. **1845** E. ACTON *Mod. Cookery* iii. 109 **Orange Gravy, For Wild Fowl.* Boil.., in ..Espagnole, half the rind of a Seville orange,..and a small strip of lemon-rind... Strain it off, add to it..port or claret. **1877** Orange gravy [see BIGARADE]. **1766** J. BARTRAM *Jrnl.* 30 Jan. in Stork *Acc. E. Florida* 56 We..encamped at a great *orange-grove. **1877** E. S. DALLAS *Kettner's Bk. of Table* 340 The present practice over the Continent is to stew them [*sc.* perch] in vinegar, fresh grape, *orange-juice, or other sour sauce. *a* **1901** C. M. YONGE *Autobiogr.* in C. Coleridge *C. M. Yonge* (1903) iii. 85, I did not like to eat orange juice out of a pewter spoon. **1960** F. RAPHAEL *Limits of Love* I. i. 10 Think I'll have an orange juice. **1977** J. ARCHER *Shall we tell President?* x. 130 'An orange juice for me. I'm watching my weight.' Doesn't he know that orange juice is the last thing to drink if you're dieting? **1838** C. GILMAN *Recoll. Southern Matron* iii. 25 An *orange leaf..was laid on every finger bowl. **1877** E. S. WARD *Story of Avis* 408 The splendor slept..upon the green pulses of the orange-leaves. **1880** G. W. CABLE *Grandissimes* ii. 15 Perfumed ad nauseam with orange-leaf tea. **1858** *Punch* 13 Mar. 103/1 There have bawled..in his street, sweeps, *orangemen, dustmen. **1707** *Lond. Gaz.* No. 4344/4 Thomas Martin, late of London, *Orange-Merchant. **1719** D'URFEY *Pills* I. 349 The *Orange-Miss, that here Cajoles the Duke. **1821** KEATS *Isabella* xvi, Fair *orange-mounts Were of more soft ascent than lazar stairs. **1897** *Allbutt's Syst. Med.* III. 885 It is impossible to understand how a cherry-stone or..an *orange-pip could enter the appendix. **1729** FENTON in *Waller's Wks.* Observ. p. xlvi/2 When this Poem was written, the *orange-plantations of this island were in good repute. **1769** MRS. RAFFALD *Eng. Housekpr.* (1778) 171 An *Orange-Pudding. Boil the rind of a Seville orange very soft [etc.]. **1845** E. ACTON *Mod. Cookery* xxv. 629 **Orange Salad.* Take off the outer rinds,..from some fine China oranges; slice them thin,..strew over them..white sifted sugar, and pour on them a glass or more of brandy. **1973** 'I. DRUMMOND' *Jaws of Watchdog* ix. 123 Elaborate spreads of cold duck and orange salad. **1867** *Common Sense Cook Bk.* 28 *Orange Sauce for Game. **1977** *Vogue* Feb. 114/3 Scallops in orange sauce. **1926–7** *Army & Navy Stores Catal.* 34/1 *Orange squash..Kia Ora..Schweppes'. **1936** *Discovery* June 192/1 Fruit Squashes..were analogous to the well-known orange and lemon squashes. **1975** J. MCCLURE *Snake* iii. 42 A uniformed sergeant..was drinking orange squash..because he was on duty. **1949** M. MEAD *Male & Female* xii. 247 Idly turning the pages of a catalogue that shows the best type of *orange-squeezer. **1962** L. DEIGHTON *Ipcress File* ii. 21 Stainless steel orange squeezers. **1665** PEPYS *Diary* 21 Feb., Mrs. Jenings..the other day dressed herself like an *orange wench. **1711** STEELE *Spect.* No. 141 ¶7 A Poet..neglects the Boxes, to write to the Orange-Wenches. **1607** SHAKS. *Cor.* II. i. 78 A cause betweene an *Orendge wife, and a Forset-seller. **1675** *Phil. Trans.* X. 256 Casks of *Orenge-wine. **1772** HEY *ibid.* LXII. 260 He drank a bottle of orange-wine in the course of this day. **1678** OTWAY *Friendship in F.* IV. i, At the Play whisper it to the *orange-women. **1801** MAR. EDGEWORTH *Good French Governess* (1832) 108 Carts and wheel-barrows, and vulgar looking things, fit for orange-women's daughters. **1884** G. W. CABLE *Dr. Sevier* lvii. 437 He moved his *orange-wood staff an inch. **1889** *Harper's Mag.* Dec. 106/2 Strangers..were detained by eager vendors of flowers and orange-wood walking-sticks. **1910** *Daily Chron.* 23 Apr. 7/3 Dilute peroxide with one-half water and apply under nails with cotton on an orangewood stick.

d. Special comb.: **orange-aphis**, a black aphis (*Siphonophora citrifolii*) that infests the orange-tree; †**orange-apple**, an orange; **orange-bead**, an orange-pip formed into a bead; **orange-berry**, an immature orange; **orange-bird**, a bird of Jamaica: see quot.; **orange-brandy**, brandy flavoured with orange-peel; **orange-butter** (see quot.); **orange-butterfly**, a large black and white butterfly, *Papilio cresphontes*, the larva of which feeds on the orange-tree; **orange-chip**, a slice of orange-peel prepared for eating; **orange-dog**, the larva of the orange-butterfly; **orange-fly**, a name of several small flies, whose larvæ burrow in the orange; **orange-jelly**, (*a*) a jelly flavoured with orange-juice and orange-peel; (*b*) a variety of swede turnip; (*c*) popular name of a fungus, *Tremella mesenterica*; **orange-maggot**, the larva of the orange-fly; **orange-marmalade**: see MARMALADE *sb.*; **orange-oil**, the essential oil obtained from the rind of the orange; **orange-pea**, a young unripe fruit of the curaçoa or other orange, used as an issue pea and to flavour liqueurs; **orange-quarter**, (*a*) one of the natural divisions of an orange; (*b*) a fourth part of an orange; **orange-scale**, any scale-insect which infests the orange-tree; esp.

Aspidiotus aurantii (*Cent. Dict.*); **orange-skin**, (*a*) orange-peel; (*b*) an orange tint of the skin; (*c*) ***orange-skin surface***, a name given to the slightly rough glaze of certain varieties of Oriental porcelain; **orange skin food**, a type of moisturizer for the skin; **orange stick**, a short stick, usu. of orange-wood, used for manicuring the nails; **orange-strainer**, a utensil for straining the juice of an orange.

1561 HOLLYBUSH *Hom. Apoth.* 35 Yalow as an *Orenge appel. **1626** BACON *Sylva* §962, I commend also Beads of Harts-Horne,..also *Orenge-Beads; also Beads of Lignum Aloes, Macerated first in Rose-water, and Dryed. **1886** *Guide Kew Mus. Econ. Bot.* No. 1. 29 The small immature fruits which drop from the trees, when collected and dried, form the *Orange berries of pharmacy. **1847** GOSSE *Birds Jamaica* 231 Cashew-bird... About Spanish Town, it is called the *Orange-bird..from the resemblance of its plump and glowing breast to that beautiful fruit. **1894** NEWTON *Dict. Birds, Orange-bird*, a name in Jamaica for *Spindalis* (prop. *Spindasis*) *nigricephala*, wrongly identified ..with *Fringilla zena*..one of the Tanagers. **1700** CONGREVE *Way of World* IV. v, I banish all foreign forces, all auxiliaries to the tea-table, as *orange-brandy [etc.]. **1769** MRS. RAFFALD *Eng. Housekpr.* (1778) 337 To make Orange Brandy. Pare eight oranges very thin, and steep the peels in a quart of brandy forty-eight hours in a close pitcher [etc.]. **1706** *Closet of Rarities* (N.), The Dutch way to make *orange-butter.—Take new cream two gallons, beat it up to a thickness, then add half a pint of orange-flower water, and as much red wine, and so being become the thickness of butter, it retains both the colour and scent of an orange. **1675** E. WILSON *Spadacr. Dunelm.* 80 He must eat some *Orange Chips. *c* **1730** *Royal Remarks* 52 Tea in the Boxes, and Orange-Chips 2*s.* 6*d.* **1769** [see CHIP *sb.*[1] 2b]. **1896** *Cassell's Dict. Cookery, Orange Chips.*—Take the rinds of some large oranges. Cut into quarters, and weigh them... Put the chips on a sieve in the sun. **1890** JULIA P. BALLARD *Among Moths & Butterfl.* 142 The common name in Florida for this caterpillar is 'the *orange dog', from a fancied resemblance of its most curious head to that animal. **1769** MRS. RAFFALD *Eng. Housekpr.* (1778) 210 To make *Orange Jelly. Take half a pound of hartshorn shavings, and two quarts of spring water,..and the rind of three oranges pared very thin, and the juice of six. **1893** *Times* 11 July 4/1 Some of the following:—The late swede, hardy swede, the orange jelly, golden ball turnip,..or the grey stone turnip. **1863–72** WATTS *Dict. Chem.* I. 1003 Oil or Essence of Mandarin..has an agreeable odour, different from that of lemon or *orange-oil, and a not unpleasant taste, like that of orange-oil. **1857** MAYNE *Expos. Lex.*, **Orange Peas*, common name for issue peas, made from the *Aurantia Curassaventia*, or Curassoa apples or oranges when dried and hardened. **1718** *Mrs. Mary Eales's Receipts* 98 Take it off the Fire, and put in your *Orange-Quarters. **1822–34** *Good's Study Med.* (ed. 4) IV. 540 *Epichrosis Aurigo.* *Orange skin. **1926–7** *Army & Navy Stores Catal.* 492 An Elizabeth Arden treatment is based on ..Cleansing..Toning..Nourishing, with **Orange Skin Food* or the delicate *Velva Cream.* **1939–40** *Ibid.* 438/3 Seymour[,] Jane..Orange Skin Food—2/9. **1944** M. LASKI *Love on Supertax* iii. 36 She slapped the Orange Skin Food on to her face. **1974** D. GRAY *Dead Give Away* xv. 144 She now patted Elizabeth Arden's Orange Skin Food into her face. **1911** H. S. HARRISON *Queed* vii. 89 *Orange-stick in mouth, he went around like a museum guide. **1922** F. COURTENAY *Physical Beauty* 46 You may use an orange stick ..to push back the cuticle from the nails. **1966** [see CUTICLE 1 d]. **1688** *Lond. Gaz.* No. 2316/4 A set of Casters, and an *Orange-Strainer, all of Silver. **1705** *Ibid.* No. 4154/4 A silver Orange-strainer.

B. *adj.* **1. a.** Of the colour of an orange (see A. 5).

Orig. an attrib. use of the sb., as in OLIVE *adj.*; so in quot. 1542, 'orange hue'; but in 1620, 'orange velvet', an adj.

For the political or party use of the colour (quots. 1723, 1849, 1884), see ORANGE *sb.*[2] 1 note.

1542 *Inv. R. Wardr.* (1815) 104 Item thrie peces of courtingis for the chepell of oringe hew. **1620** *Unton Inv.* 22 Two low stooles of black and oringe wrought velvett. **1723** HIGGONS *Short View Eng. Hist.* (1736) 350 His daughter Denmark [afterwards Queen Anne], with her great favourite (lady Churchill), both covered with Orange ribbands,.. went triumphant to the playhouse. **1799** WORDSW. *Infl. Nat. Objects* 46 In the west The orange sky of evening died away. **1831** BREWSTER *Optics* vii. 72 We have therefore, by absorption, decomposed..orange light into yellow and red. **1849** MACAULAY *Hist. Eng.* ix. (1856) II. 530 The whole High Street [of Oxford, in 1688] was gay with orange ribands. **1884** *Encycl. Brit.* XVII. 813/1 (*Orangemen*), The orange flowers of the *Lilium bulbiferum* are worn in Ulster on the 1st and 12th July, the anniversaries of the Boyne and Aughrim.

b. *spec.* Applied to a variety of opal.

1902 *Chambers's Jrnl.* Aug. 494/1 The miners..say, one stroke of the pick may lay bare a seam of 'pin-fire' opal or break in two a rich band of 'orange'. **1971** J. S. GUNN *Opal Terminol.* 32 *Orange*, name given to opal with this distinctive colour.

2. Combinations. **a.** With other adjs. of colour, expressing modification by orange, as ***orange-brown***, ***-buff***, ***-chestnut***, ***-cinnamon***, ***-cream***, ***-crimson***, ***-fiery***, ***-flesh***, ***-gold***, ***-pink***, ***-rufous***, ***-scarlet***, ***vermilion*** adjs. (sbs.); also in names of pigments, as ***orange-chrome***, ***-lake***, ***-lead***. **b.** parasynthetic, as ***orange-flowered*** (having orange flowers), ***-headed*** (having an orange-coloured head), ***-hued***, ***-keyed***, ***-quilled***, ***-spiked***, ***-spotted***, ***-tailed***, ***-winged***, etc., adjs.; **orange-fuming** *a.*, that produces orange-coloured fumes; **orange-legged**, **-thighed** *adjs.*, of birds: having the shank or thigh orange-coloured, as the Orange-legged Hobby, *Falco vespertinus*, the Orange-thighed Falcon, *Falco fuscocærulescens* (*List Anim. Zool. Soc.* (1896) 398).

1799 G. SMITH *Laboratory* II. 305 *Orange brown Body. **1866** ODLING *Anim. Chem.* 153 The bromine floats on the surface as an orange-brown layer. **1882** *Garden* 26 Aug. 183/2 Another with a sort of an *orange-buff tint. **1875** *Ure's Dict. Arts* III. 460 **Orange-chrome*, a subchromate of lead; a fine orange-coloured pigment. **1882** *Garden* 14 Jan. 16/2 The flowers ranging in colour from yellow to a bright *orange-cinnamon. **1862** R. H. PATTERSON *Ess. Hist. & Art* 27–8 A wall of an *orange-cream colour. **1882** *Garden* 16 Dec. 534/2 A glowing *orange-crimson, very bright and effective. **1922** JOYCE *Ulysses* 296 The orangefiery and scarlet rays. **1887** W. PHILLIPS *Brit. Discomycetes* 108 The colour varies from reddish-brown to pale *orange-flesh or salmon-colour. **1853** W. GREGORY *Inorg. Chem.* (ed. 3) 89 Along with pure nitric acid, it forms the *orange-fuming nitric acid of the shops, often called nitrous acid. **1885–94** R. BRIDGES *Eros & Psyche* Mar. xxv, Broad and low down, where late the sun had been, A wealth of *orange-gold was thickly shed. **1881** RITA *My Lady Coquette* iii, Miss Skipton, in her radiant *orange-hued garments. **1922** JOYCE *Ulysses* 715 *Orangekeyed ware..consisting of basin, soapdish and brushtray.., pitcher and night article. **1825** J. NICHOLSON *Operat. Mechanic* 717 The *orange-lake above-mentioned ..was used with great success by a considerable manufacturer. The colour it produces is that of the vinegar-garnet. **1865–72** WATTS *Dict. Chem.* III. 552 When the temperature is properly regulated, another pigment is obtained, called *Orange Lead. **1865** *Reader* No. 123. 521/1 The *orange-quilled porcupine (*Hystrix Malabarica*). **1956** D. BARNHAM *One Man's Window* vi. 67, I am enveloped in a world of luminous *orange-pink. **1967** O. RUHEN in *Coast to Coast 1965–6* 189 The orange-pink of its desert sand. **1894** R. B. SHARPE *Handbk. Birds Gt. Brit.* I. 37 Under surface pale *orange-rufous, the abdomen white. **1824** MISS MITFORD *Village* Ser. I. (1863) 139 Tulip, poppy, lily,—something orange or scarlet, or *orange-scarlet. **1861** MISS PRATT *Flower. Pl.* VI. 57 *Orange-spiked Fox-tail. **1802** BINGLEY *Anim. Biog.* (1813) III. 290 The *orange-tailed bee... This is one of the largest of the British Bees. **1895** *Montgomery Ward Catal.* 253/1 Special colors... *Orange Vermilion. **1951** R. MAYER *Artist's Handbk.* ii. 56 *Orange vermilion*, a variety of real vermilion. **1865** *Sat. Rev.* 5 Aug. 182 The beautiful grakle, familiar to visitors at the Convent of Marsaba as the '*orange-winged blackbird'.

c. In names of orange-coloured varieties of apples or pears, as ***orange-bergamot***, ***-musk***, ***-pear***, ***-pippin***; also in names of plants, animals, etc. of this colour (more or less), as **orange bat**, the *Phinonycteris aurantia*, inhabiting northern Australia, the male of which has fur of a bright orange (*Cassell's Encycl. Dict.* 1886); **orange book**, a report of the Ministry of Agriculture and Fisheries dealing with marketing questions and published in orange covers; **orange-cowry**, a large handsome cowry (*Cypræa aurantia*), of a deep yellow colour; **orange dove**, a Fijian bird (*Chrysœnas victor*), the male of which has bright orange plumage; **orange-fin**, a variety of trout found in the Tweed; **orange-fly**, a fishing-fly (see quot.); **orange fungus**, a fungus which attacks roses; **orange grass**, (*a*) *Hypericum Sarothra*, having minute deep-yellow flowers (Miller *Plant-n.* 1884); (*b*) *U.S.* = NIT-WEED; **orange gum**, an Australian myrtaceous tree, *Angophora lanceolata* (Morris); **orange-leaf**, (*a*) an evergreen shrub of New Zealand, *Coprosma lucida* (Miller *Plant-n.*); (*b*) a quality of shellac; **orange lightning**: see quot.; **orange lily**, *Lilium croceum*; also *L. bulbiferum*, var. *aurantium*; **orange-list**, a kind of wide baize; **orange mine**, **mineral**, an oxide of lead of similar composition to red lead, but of brighter colour, formed by oxidizing white lead; † **orange-mint**, a species of mint; **orange moth**, a geometrid moth (see quot.); **orange paste** (*Dyeing*), a paste for producing an orange colour; **orange pekoe**, a type of black tea; **orange-quit**, a bird of Jamaica, *Glossoptila ruficollis*; **orange-root**, a North American ranunculaceous plant, the golden-seal; **orange-sallow**, a night-moth, *Xanthia citrago* (Cassell); **orange-slip clay**, a clay used in Staffordshire, of a grey colour, having mixed with it reddish nodules, which impart an orange colour to the 'slip' or tempered mass; **orange thorn**: see A. 3, quot. 1889[2].

1664 EVELYN *Kal. Hort.* (1729) 232/2 Fruit-Trees..for a moderate Plantation..Pears..*Orange Bergamot [etc.]. **1928** *Daily Express* 30 Apr. 7/4 The report is one of the Ministry's famous '*orange' books—those scientific farming pamphlets for the education of English farmers. **1932** *N. & Q.* 30 Jan. 73/2 We were glad to have a note of the reception of the Orange Books on Marketing which the Ministry of Agriculture has been putting forth. **1875** E. L. LAYARD in *Ibis* 435 In the same locality he procured the '*Orange Dove', and found..that the female and young male were green. **1834** SELBY in *Proc. Berw. Nat. Club* I. No. 2. 36 A trout..analogous to the *Orange fin of the Tweed. **1787** BEST *Angling* (ed. 2) 105 The *Orange fly..Dubbed with orange coloured wool; the wings off the feather of a blackbirds wing. **1882** *Garden* 25 Feb. 133/1 There is..no disease to which the Rose is liable that is so destructive in its effects as a virulent attack of *Orange fungus. **1837** W. DARLINGTON *Flora cestrica* (ed. 2) 324 Ground Pine. Nit-Weed. *Orange-grass. **1882** E. K. GODFREY *Island of Nantucket* 36 The orange grass with its fragrance now greeting us at every turn. **1907** Orange-grass [see NIT-WEED]. **1883** *Cassell's Fam. Mag.* Oct. 683/2 Shell-lac..is known..as 'button', '*orange-leaf',..and 'reddish orange-leaf'. **1884** MILLER *Plant-n., Coprosma lucida*, Otago Orange-leaf, or Looking-glass bush. **1881** GREENER *Gun* 501 The captain..loaded with Dittmar powder in the first and *orange lightning, No 6, in the second barrel. **1856** DELAMER *Fl. Gard.* (1861) 38 The *Orange Lily, *L. croceum*, a native of Austria, may be found in almost every cottage plot of flowers. **1880** BRITTEN & H. *Plant-n., Orange Lily*, the common name in gardens for *Lilium bulbiferum.* **1830** BOOTH *Anal. Dict.* I. 182 A wide Baize, dyed in fancy colours, is exported, chiefly to Spain, under the name of *Orangelist. **1839** URE *Dict. Arts* s.v. *Minium*, The best minium, however, called *orange mine, is made by the slow calcination of good white lead (carbonate) in iron trays. **1699** EVELYN *Acetaria* 39 The gentler Tops of the *Orange-Mint, enter well into our Composition. **1869** NEWMAN *Brit. Moths* 92 The *Orange Moth (*Angerona prunaria*). The wings of the male generally rich orange. **1731–3** MILLER *Gard. Dict.* s.v. *Pyrus*, The *Orange Musk. **1664** EVELYN *Kal. Hort.*, *Orch.* July (1729) 210 Pears..green Chesil Pears, *Orange Pear [etc.]. **1731–3** MILLER *Gard. Dict.* s.v. *Pyrus*, The Green Orange Pear. **1877** *Cassell's Dict. Cookery* 961/1 One pound of Moning Congo, a quarter of a pound of Assam, and a quarter of a pound of *Orange Pekoe. **1911** *Encycl. Brit.* XXVI. 480/2 They [*sc.* the leaves] are now broken apart and sorted by mechanical sifters into the various grades or qualities, which are described as Orange Pekoe, [etc.]. **1960** A. E. BENDER *Dict. Nutrition* 123 Orange Pekoe [is made] from the first opened leaf. **1823** J. BADCOCK *Dom. Amusem.* 48 The female flower of the *orange pippin. **1884** [see A. 3b]. **1894** NEWTON *Dict. Birds* s.v. *Quit*, Thus the *Orange-Quit is *Glossoptila ruficollis*, one of the *Cærebidæ.* **1866** *Treas. Bot.* 605/1 *Hydrastis canadensis* is the only species of a genus of *Ranunculaceæ*, found in damp places in woods, in the Northern United States and Canada, where it is called Yellow Puccoon, *Orange root, or Canadian Yellow root. *Ibid.* 818/2 **Orange-thorn*, a colonial name for *Citriobatus.*

Orange ('ɒrɪndʒ), *sb.*[2]

1. a. The name of a town on the river Rhone in France, formerly the capital of a small principality of the same name, which passed in 1530 into the possession of the House of Nassau, and so to the ancestors of William III of England, styled princes of Orange-Nassau. On the death of William III, the territory of Orange was acquired by Louis XIV, and added to France; but the title continued to be held by the cousin of William and his descendants, who now constitute the royal line of Holland. In Eng. Hist., 'William of Orange' is an appellation of William III.

The accidental coincidence of this name with that of the fruit and colour (ORANGE *sb.*[1]), made the wearing of orange ribbons, scarfs, cockades, orange-lilies, etc., a symbol of attachment to William III, and to the principles of the Revolution settlement of 1689, and led to their use by the Orange lodges and Orangemen.

1558–9 CLOUGH *Descr. Funeral Chas. V* in Burgon *Life Gresham* I. 254 A nobellman..(so far as I coulde understand it was the Prince of Orange), who standing before the herse, strucke with the hand uppon the chest, and sayd—'He is ded'. **1665** MANLEY *Grotius' Low C. Warres* 86 Many of the prime Nobility, that did not heartily love the Prince of Aurange. **1680** *True Copy Let. for Holland*, For his..never Failing Friend Roger Le Strange, at the Oranges Court, with Care and Speed, hast, hast, post hast. **1848** W. H. KELLY tr. *L. Blanc's Hist. Ten Years* I. 325 What are these treaties?.. Those of 1814? But these assure the possession of Belgium to the house of Orange.

b. *attrib.* Of or belonging to the Orange family or dynasty in Holland.

1647 G. WHARTON *Bellum Hybernicale* 27 But this is Wormwood to an Orange Scarff and Feather. **1840** *Penny Cycl.* XVI. 98/2 William (IV) Henry Friso..was raised by the Orange party to the stadtholdership in 1747.

2. *Eng. Hist.* (*attrib.*) Applied to the ultra-Protestant party in Ireland, in reference to the secret Association of Orangemen formed in 1795: cf. ORANGEMAN.

The exact origin of this use of 'Orange' is somewhat obscure. But it is supposed that 'the two Copes' of quot. 1795 were members of a celebrated lodge of Freemasons then existing in Belfast, styled 'The Orange Lodge', and that thence their adherents were known as 'Orange boys' and 'Orangemen'. The name of this lodge probably had reference to William of Orange, or to the use of orange badges at the anniversaries at which his memory was celebrated; and it was, no doubt, in this sense that the term became perpetuated as a party name. Also freq. as ***Orange Order***. The first two quots. which follow refer to the Orange Lodge of Freemasons.

[**1783** in Joy *Hist. Coll. Belfast* (1817), The procession was conducted by the Orange Lodge, so confessedly acknowledged to be the first in Europe, being composed of 150 gentlemen..noblemen and commoners of the very first distinction. The Orange Lodge was first revived in Sept. 1780, at which time it consisted merely of the present Past-Master and two other gentlemen. **1791** C. T. BOWDEN *Tour through Ireland* 236, I was introduced to the Orange-lodge by a Mr. Hyndeman... Mr. H. informed me this lodge was founded by a Mr. Griffith, who held a lucrative employment here under Government.]

1795 JEPHSON *Let. to Ld. Charlemont* 9 Oct. in *13th Rep. Hist. MSS. Commiss.* App. VIII. 266 It is impossible..to disavow the absolute necessity of giving a considerable degree of support to the Protestant party, who, from the activity of the two Copes, have got the name of the 'Orange boys'. *Ibid.*, My brother William told me he rode through three hundred well armed ' Orange boys' in the middle of the night. **1796** GRATTAN *Sp. in Ho. Comm.* 22 Feb., Those insurgents, who called themselves Orange Boys, or Protestant Boys—that is, a banditti of murderers, committing massacre in the name of God. **1797** in *13th Rep. Hist. MSS. Comm.* App. VIII. 303 We had a display here yesterday morning of the whole force the 'Orange boys', 'Orange' wenches, and 'Orange' children could muster.

1798 *Ibid.* 341 The Orange system spreads in many parts of this country. **1808** G. MOORE (*title*) Observations on the Union Orange Association. **1813** *Gen. Hist.* in *Ann. Reg.* 93/2 It appeared that Orange lodges met regularly in London, Manchester [etc.]. **1844** *Regul. & Ord. Army* 382 Officers, Non-commissioned Officers, and Soldiers, are forbidden to institute, countenance, or attend Orange-Lodges or any other Meetings whatever, for Party or Political Purposes. **1868** HOLME LEE *B. Godfrey* l. 281 The orange candidate's wife. **1884** *Pall Mall G.* 16 Sept. 2/1 Of south-west Lancashire..the Toryism is more orange than bucolic in the lower grades, and very much coloured by Liverpool in the upper strata. **1885** *Encycl. Brit.* XVIII. 453/2 (*Peel, Sir Robt.*) Peel became, by the necessity of his situation, 'Orange Peel', and plied the established engines of coercion and patronage with a vigorous hand. **1902** C. L. FALKINER *Stud. Irish Hist.* 52 On the morrow of that affair [Battle of the Diamond], September 22, 1795, the first Orange Lodge was formed in the house of a farmer named Sloan. **1940** L. MACNEICE *Last Ditch* 28 A framed Certificate of admission Into the Orange Order. **1975** *Irish Times* 10 May 9/3 Mr. Thomas Passmore, grand master of the Orange Order in Belfast, said yesterday that while Britain would be simply a small member in an exclusive club if she remained in Europe, outside it she could once again earn the title of Great Britain. **1977** P. CARTER *Under Goliath* i. 5 To make sure that the Protestant religion stays on top of the league in Northern Ireland, is what the Orange Order is all about.

orangeade (ɒrɪn'dʒeɪd). [f. ORANGE + -ADE, after *lemonade*.] A beverage composed of orange and lemon juice diluted with water and sweetened with sugar. Now also applied to an aerated water, similar to lemonade but of an orange tint.

1706 in PHILLIPS. **1727** BRADLEY *Fam. Dict.* s.v. *Fever*, Let him drink Ptisan..or else Lemonade or Orangeade. **1869** SIR S. NORTHCOTE in *Life* (1890) I. x. 348 Oranges which though too acid to eat will make capital orangeade.

†**oran'geado.** *Obs.* Also oreng-, orang-, oringado, -eado, -iado. [Cf. Sp. *naranjada* conserve of oranges, F. *orangeat*.] Candied orange-peel.

1599–1600 in Nichols *Progr.* III. 457 One pye of orengado. **1604** DEKKER *Honest Wh.* Wks. 1873 II. 61 Provide no great cheare, a couple of Capons, some Fesants, Plovers, an Oringeado-pie, or so. **1635** SHIRLEY *Lady of Pleasure* I. i, The gallant..That carries oringado in his pocket, And sugar-plums, to sweeten his discourse. *a* **1648** DIGBY *Closet Open.* (1677) 139 A little sliced oringiado from which the hard candy-sugar hath been soaked. **1796** MRS. GLASSE *Cookery* xiv. 259 Pare twelve pippins..and pour on them some orangeado syrup.

'orange-,blossom. **1. a.** The white fragrant blossom of the orange-tree. Worn by brides in wreaths, trimmings, etc., or carried in bouquets at the marriage ceremony.

This custom appears to have been introduced from France *c* 1820–30. According to Littré, 'Women at their marriage wear a crown of orange buds and blossoms; hence the orange-blossom is taken as a symbol of marriage'. (Thackeray's explanation of the symbolism appears to be his own.)

1786 tr. *Beckford's Vathek* (1883) 114 The ground strewed over with orange blossoms and jasmines. **1855** TENNYSON *The Daisy* 3 O Love, what hours were thine and mine,..In lands of palm, of orange-blossom..and vine.

c **1835** HAYNES BAYLY *Song*, '*She wore a wreath of roses*', A wreath of orange blossom upon her head she wore. **1848** THACKERAY *Van. Fair* xii, Had orange blossoms been invented then (those touching emblems of female purity imported by us from France..) Miss Maria..would have assumed the spotless wreath. **1853** MISS MULOCK *Agatha's Husb.* I. ix. 237 So for two long hours Agatha sat in her wedding-dress..sometimes playing with the wreath of orange-blossoms which her lover had sent her. **1857** T. S. ARTHUR (*title*) Orange Blossoms, a Gift Book for all who have worn, are wearing, or are likely to wear them. *a* **1891** W. E. NORRIS (Dixon *Dict. Idiom. Eng. Phrases* 1891), 'What has he come to this lovely retreat for? To gather orange-blossoms?' [get a bride]. **1971** K. WHEELER *Epitaph for Mr. Wynn* (1972) xxvii. 355 Orange blossoms and murder trials don't mix.

b. In England applied also to the blossom of the Mock-orange, *Philadelphus*.

2. A cocktail flavoured with orange juice. Also *attrib.*

1930 *Savoy Cocktail Bk.* 117 Orange Blossom Cocktail. ½ Orange Juice. ½ Dry Gin. Shake well. **1938** L. BEMELMANS *Life Class* (1939) II. ii. 134 Waiters stand about with trays of cocktails, the favourite being Orange Blossoms, a mixture of gin and orange juice. **1960** B. KEATON *Wonderful World of Slapstick* (1967) 158 After taking a couple of orange blossoms, a cocktail made of orange juice and gin, Virginia got sick. **1963** I. FLEMING *On H.M. Secret Service* x. 105 A sprinkling of feminine cocktails—Orange Blossoms, Daiquiris. **1965** T. CAPOTE *In Cold Blood* (1966) iv. 223 We'd brought a bottle of ready-mix Orange Blossoms—that's Orange pop and vodka.

orange colour, 'orange-,colour. = ORANGE *sb.*[1] 5; also *attrib.*

1512 *Will of Cater* (Somerset Ho.), Orenge colour. **1578** LYTE *Dodoens* I. xix. 29 At the top..groweth fayre Orenge-colour floures. **1686** *Lond. Gaz.* No. 2158/4 Four new Coats lin'd with Orange-colour. **1865** J. H. INGRAHAM *Pillar of Fire* (1872) 193 A gorgeous fan of radiant beams, of a pale orange-colour, spread itself over the sky.

So **'orange-,coloured** *a.*

1678 T. JORDAN *Triumphs Lond.* 11 An Orange-colour'd Mantle edg'd and fring'd with Silver. **1686** *Lond. Gaz.* No. 2115/4 A Blue Livery lined with Orange-coloured Stuff. **1849** D. CAMPBELL *Inorg. Chem.* 283 This salt precipitates as an orange-coloured powder.

oranged ('ɒrɪndʒd), *a. rare.* [f. ORANGE *sb.*[1] + -ED[2].] Coloured orange, tinted with orange.

1862 THORNBURY *Turner* I. 48 The boy still went on washing in blue skies for Grecian temples..with semi-circular oranged gravel walks.

'orange-,flower.

1. The white flower of the orange-tree; = ORANGE-BLOSSOM.

1626 BACON *Sylva* § 18 And the like I conceive of Orenge-Flowers. **1757** A. COOPER *Distiller* II. vi. (1760) 128 Take twelve Pounds of Orange-flowers, and twenty four Quarts of Water. **1842** LONGF. *Quadroon Girl* iii, Odours of orange-flowers..Reached them. **1850** TENNYSON *In Mem.* xl, As on a maiden in the day When first she wears her orange-flower.

2. ***Mexican orange-flower*** (*tree*), a handsome white-flowered shrub, *Choisya ternata*, N.O. *Rutaceæ* (Miller *Plant-n.* 1884).

3. Short for *orange-flower water* (or ? *cordial*).

1712 ADDISON *Spect.* No. 328, I cannot undertake to recite all her medicinal Preparations, as Salves,..Cordials, Ratafia, Persico, Orange-flower, and Cherry-Brandy.

4. *Comb.*: **orange-flower bread, -cake,** that made or flavoured with orange-flowers; **orange-flower oil,** the fragrant oil distilled from orange-flowers, neroli oil; **orange flower skin food** = *orange skin food*; **orange-flower tree,** (*a*) *dial.* the Syringa or Mock-orange; (*b*) (see sense 2 above); **orange-flower water,** the aqueous solution of orange-flowers; the fragrant watery distillate left over in the preparation of neroli oil.

1750 MRS. DELANY *Autobiog. & Corr.* (1861) II. 571 Making *orange-flower bread, of my own orange flowers. **1718** *Mrs. Mary Eales's Receipts* 68 Wet it..with Orange-Flower Water, for the *Orange-Flower-Cakes. **1838** T. THOMSON *Chem. Org. Bodies* 461 *Orange-flower oil, is extracted by the distillation of the flowers of the orange-tree. **1908** *Sears, Roebuck Catal.* 798/1 *Orange Flower Skin Food..acts as skin nourisher and wrinkle remover. **1877** *N.W. Linc. Gloss.*, **Orange-flower tree*, the Syringa. **1880** BRITTEN & H. *Plant-n.*, Orange-flower Tree, *Philadelphus coronarius*..from its perfume resembling that of orange-blossoms. It is also called Mock Orange. **1595** COPLEY *Wits, Fits, & Fancies* 79 He sent her two bottles of *Orange flower water by his page. **1839** URE *Dict. Arts* 908 The oil of orange-flowers, called neroli, is extracted from the fresh flowers of the *citrus aurantium*... The aqueous solution, known under the name of orange-flower water, is used as a perfume.

Orangeism, Orangism ('ɒrɪndʒɪz(ə)m). [f. ORANGE *sb.*[2] + -ISM.] The system and principles which the Orange Association was formed to uphold; the principle of Protestant political ascendancy in Ireland.

1823 *Orange System exposed* 42 Evidence..of the nature, spirit and extent of Orangism at that time [28 Dec. 1795]. **1847** *Fraser's Mag.* XXXVI. 104 The most rancorous..champion of Orangeism and landlordism in the British parliament. **1850** HT. MARTINEAU *Hist. Peace* II. v. v. 268 In 1828, on the accession of the Duke of Cumberland to the throne of Orangeism. **1890** LECKY *Eng. in 18th C.* VIII. xxix. 93 Every Protestant who was not well known..lay under the suspicion of Orangism.

Orangeman ('ɒrɪndʒmən). [f. ORANGE *sb.*[2] + MAN.] A member of a political society formed, in 1795, for the defence of Protestantism and maintenance of Protestant ascendancy in Ireland: see ORANGE *sb.*[2]

1796 GRATTAN *Sp. Ho. Comm.* 22 Feb., A magistrate of the county of Armagh..has spoken of the use of what he calls Orange-men, of the services rendered by these murderers. **1796** E. HUDSON *Lett.* 29 May in *13th Rep. Hist. MSS. Comm.* App. VIII. 273 A report was circulated that a number of 'Orangemen'..were to be there in order to fall upon the C[atholic]s. **1803** E. HAY *Insurr. Wexf.* 38 To these succeeded, in the summer of the same year (1795), a description of public disturbers, calling themselves orangemen, who now made their first appearance in the county of Armagh. **1813** *Jrnl. Ho. Comm.* 29 June, That a Committee be appointed to enquire into the existence of certain illegal Societies under the denomination of Orange Men. **1842** S. C. HALL *Ireland* II. 465 In 1836 the number of Orangemen in England was stated to have been between 120,000 and 140,000. **1844** MACAULAY *Let.* 4 July (1977) IV. 202 If the letters were opened, it was not by any authority from the late government, but by some rascally Orangemen in the Post Office. **1894** W. B. YEATS *Let.* 16 Dec. (1954) 242, I lectured..on Fairy lore to an audience of Orangemen. **1921** *Daily Colonist* (Victoria, B.C.) 12 Mar. 2/4 Orangemen from all over the world will convene in Winnipeg in 1923, according to an announcement made today. **1975** *Irish Times* 24 May 9/4 Mr. William Douglas, Official Unionist (U.U.U.C.) Convention member for Derry said that as an Orangeman, Unionist and Loyalist he was convinced that all Ulster people who loved their country should say no to the Common Market. **1976** *Daily Record* (Glasgow) 29 Nov. 17/4 Orangeman [*name given*], from Edinburgh, will face 400 delegates from Scottish lodges at Govan next Saturday over remarks on TV about leading the Ulster Defence Association in Scotland.

'orange-,peel. **1. a.** The rind of an orange, esp. when separated from the pulp.

1615 MARKHAM *Eng. Housew.* (1668) 114 Four or five Orange-peels dry and beaten to powder. **1626** BACON *Sylva* § 21. **1646** SIR T. BROWNE *Pseud. Ep.* 90 The distilled water of Orange pilles. **1712** tr. *Pomet's Hist. Drugs* I. 151 Candied Orange Peel. **1838** DICKENS *O. Twist* xiv, I've been lamed with orange-peel once, and I know orange-peel will be my death. **1899** *Westm. Gaz.* 13 June 4/1 One of them [Republican journals] compares the events of Sunday simply to a piece of orange-peel on which M. Dupuy slipped.

b. *attrib.*, as ***orange-peel cutter, oil*** (= orange-oil), ***water***.

1757 A. COOPER *Distiller* II. xvi. (1760) 142 Recipe for one Gallon of Orange-peel-Water. **1858** SIMMONDS *Dict. Trade*, *Orange-peel Cutter*, a slicer of Seville orange-peel, for drying or candying. **1875–9** WATTS *Dict. Chem.* 2nd Suppl. 877 Orange-peel oil..The essential oil of orange-peel consists mainly of a hydrocarbon $C^{10}H^{16}$, called hesperidene.

2. Used, usu. *attrib.*, to designate a suspended bucket or grab composed of a number of curved, pointed segments that are hinged at the top and come together to form a container.

1905 C. PRELINI *Earth & Rock Excavation* x. 129 Excavator-buckets are usually either clam-shell or orange-peel buckets. **1912** C. G. ELLIOTT *Engin. for Land Drainage* (ed. 2) xiv. 209 The orange-peel is particularly useful in building levees. **1922** POWERS & TEETER *Land Drainage* xvi. 170 (*caption*) A small dry land excavating outfit with orange-peel bucket. **1959** *Micropaleontol.* V. 218/1 Two sampling devices were used, the Hayward standard orange-peel grab and a snapper sampler. **1967** *Oceanogr. & Marine Biol.* V. 527 The samples were taken with an orange-peel bottom sampler. **1975** B. FELL *Introd. Marine Biol.* iii. 21 An orange-peel grab..has four valves that appear to form the four segments of an orange when cut along its meridians.

'oranger. *rare.* [f. ORANGE *sb.*[1] + -ER[1].] A sailing-vessel employed in the orange trade.

1880 SIR S. LAKEMAN *What I saw in Kaffir-land* xii. 149 Nothing afloat, from a St. Michael oranger to a fifty-gun frigate, could stand with her in a gale.

'orange-'red, *a.* (*sb.*) A shade of red approaching orange.

1776–96 WITHERING *Brit. Plants* (ed. 3) IV. 210 Gills buff, ..pileus orange red, flat, border turned down. **1859** GEO. ELIOT *A. Bede* vii, Rich orange-red rust on the iron weights and hooks and hinges.

orangery ('ɒrɪndʒrɪ, 'ɒrɪndʒərɪ). Also 7–8 -erie, 8 -arie. [In sense 1, a. F. *orangerie* (1603 in Hatz.-Darm.), f. *oranger* orange-tree: see -ERY 2. The etymology of sense 2 is not clear.]

1. A place appropriated to the cultivation of orange-trees; *spec.* a structure or building in which orange-trees are reared and kept, where the climate does not allow them to be cultivated in the open.

1664 EVELYN *Diary* 14 July, The orangerie and aviarie handsome, and a very large plantation about it. **1705** *Lond. Gaz.* No. 4098/4 The..Mansion-House, called Belsize,.. ..with..a fine Orangarie, is to be Lett. **1744** MRS. DELANY *Lett., to Mrs. Dewes* 315 A sort of parterre, that will make the prettiest orangery in the world. **1848** W. H. KELLY tr. *L. Blanc's Hist. Ten Years* II. 512 The dilapidation of that fine staircase in the orangery [of Versailles]. **1861** DELAMER *Fl. Gard.* 124 Large Orange-trees, in cubical boxes,..wintered in an orangery, and placed in conspicuous positions in the pleasure-ground during summer.

2. A scent or perfume extracted from the orange-flower; also, snuff scented with this. Also *attrib.*

1676 ETHEREDGE *Man of Mode* III. ii, Orangerie: you know the smell, ladies. **1698** FARQUHAR *Love in a Bottle* II. ii, O Lard, sir! you must never sneeze; 'tis as unbecoming after orangery as grace after meat. **1706** T. BAKER *Tunbr. Walks* IV. i, A nice snuff box, with the best orangery. **1744** ELIZA HEYWOOD *Female Spect.* (1748) I. 83 Another..dies for some fresh orangerie and bergamot.

'orange-'tawny, *a.* and *sb.*

A. *adj.* Of a dull yellowish brown colour; tan-coloured or brownish-yellow with a tinge of orange.

1590 SHAKS. *Mids. N.* III. i. 129 The Woosell cocke, so blacke of hew, With Orenge-tawny bill. **1594** *Acc.-bk. W. Wray* in *Antiquary* XXXII. 346, j pece of Oringe Taunie buffing. **1625** BACON *Ess., Usury* (Arb.) 541 That Vsurers should haue Orange-tawney Bonnets, because they doe Iudaize. **1826** SCOTT *Woodstock* xxx, A..boy, in an orange-tawney doublet. **1865** *Daily Tel.* 12 Dec. 7/2 Each pair of orange-tawny tyrants [tigers] had their district, with leopards, panthers, and jackals for the aristocracy.

B. *sb.* As the name of a colour or a fabric.

1602 *Narcissus* (1893) 298 Thou shalt dye whyte, and Ile dye oreng tawnye. *a* **1662** HEYLIN (T.), Baronets, or knights of Nova Scotia, are commonly distinguished from others by a ribbon of orangetawny. *c* **1800** R. CUMBERLAND *John De Lancaster* (1809) II. 45 The domestics of the castle were arrayed in their gala-liveries of orange-tawney.

b. *Comb.*, as ***orange-tawny-coated*** adj.

1633 B. JONSON *Tale Tub* IV. iii, Thou scum of man; Uncivil, orange-tawney-coated clerk!

'orange-tip. [f. ORANGE A. 5, B. 1 + TIP.] In full ***orange-tip butterfly***, a butterfly having wings tipped with orange, esp. *Anthocharis cardamines* and (in America) *E. genutia*. Also **orange-tipped** *a.*

Only the male has orange tips on the wings.

1819 G. SAMOUELLE *Entomol. Compend.* 236 Orange tip butterfly inhabits pathways in woods. **1845** *Zoologist* III. 991, I took one beautiful orange-tip on the 2d of June. **1829** *Glover's Hist. Derby* I. 174 *Papilio Cardamines*, Orange-tipped Butterfly. **1906** R. SOUTH *Butterflies Brit. Isles* 43 The Orange-tip..has a large patch of orange colour on the outer third of its white, or creamy white, fore wings. **1930** *Times Educ. Suppl.* 4 Oct. p. iv/4 The little orange-tip flickering along the hedgeside. **1973** T. G. HOWARTH *South's Brit. Butterflies* 58 The Orange-tip is essentially a butterfly of lanes, hedgerows and rough fields. **1973** *Shooting Times & Country Mag.* 7 July 20/2 An orange-tip butterfly went fluttering by.

'orange-tree. The tree which bears oranges.
1530 PALSGR. 249/1 Orenge tree, *orengier.* **1553** EDEN *Treat. Newe Ind.* (Arb.) 8 No more wyll the Orange tree bringe foorth fruit in Englande. **1588** DRAKE in *Four C. Eng. Lett.* (1880) 32 He shall wish hymselff at Sainte Marie Porte among his orynge trees. **1756–7** tr. *Keysler's Trav.* (1760) III. 375 A covered walk of cedar and orange-trees planted alternately. **1856** BRYANT *Child's Funeral* iv, Currents of fragrance, from the orange tree. **1866** *Treas. Bot.* 293/1 The Orange tree at the convent of St. Sabina at Rome is thirty-one feet high.

b. ***New Zealand orange-tree***, a name given to the Tarata, from the aromatic odour of its leaves when crushed (Morris *Austral Engl.*).

'orangey, *a.* Also **orangy.** [f. ORANGE *sb.*[1] + -Y.]
a. Resembling an orange in colour, taste, etc. Also, covered in orange; suggestive of oranges.
1778 W. MARSHALL *Minutes Agric.* Observ. 129 The Sun rose orangey. *Ibid.* 137 Sun. Rising orangey; Rain. *a* **1903** *Mod. colloq.* It tastes rather orangey. **1913** H. S. WALPOLE *Fortitude* I. xii. 165 My fingers are all over orange... I always have an orange before dinner... I am orangy, but then I was late and couldn't finish it. **1919** C. ORR *Glorious Thing* xx. 245 A delicious, warm, orangy smell hung about the kitchen walls. **1966** *New Statesman* 6 May 663/1 Olivier's blue-black face and frame, Maggie Smith's pink-pallid Desdemona move for too much of the time against a dreadful orangey back-cloth. **1974** N. GORDIMER *Conservationist* 199 A sun as pale as last night's.. moon was orangey, is stiffening the topmost leaves of that tree. **1977** C. FREMLIN *Spider-Orchid* iv. 32 The orangy glow of the standard lamp.

b. *Comb.*, as ***orangey-blue, -brown, -buff, -red, -yellow*** adjs.
1977 A. SCHOLEFIELD *Venom* III. 118 Eyes weeping, knuckles orangey-blue. **1968** H. R. F. KEATING *Inspector Ghote hunts Peacock* i. 8 Its hideous orangey-brown colour, masquerading as the tan of leather. *a* **1973** 'G. ASHE' *Herald of Doom* (1974) v. 49 An orangey-brown kilted suit. **1976** H. R. F. KEATING *Filmi, Filmi* xiii. 123 A sportingly cut orangey-buff suit. **1977** E. W. HILDICK *Loop* iv. 17 Fashionable orangey-red blush make-up. **1974** *Times* 2 May 8/7 This year's recommended colour..is a warm orangey-yellow.

'orange-'yellow, *a.* (*sb.*) A shade of yellow approaching orange.
1838 T. THOMSON *Chem. Org. Bodies* 518 Nitric acid acts upon the balsam with energy, and gives it an orange-yellow colour when assisted by heat. **1879** ROOD *Chromatics* iii. 42 Not only the pure yellow rays, but also the orange-yellow and greenish-yellow. **1882** *Garden* 14 Oct. 347/1.

Orangism: see ORANGEISM.

†**'orangist**[1]. *Obs. rare*[−1]. [a. F. *orangiste* (La Quintinie, 1690), f. *orange* ORANGE *sb.*[1]] A cultivator of oranges.
1693 EVELYN *De la Quint. Compl. Gard.* Dict. 4 *Orangist*, is a Gard'ner that cultivates Oranges, or any person that understands and delights in the Culture of them.

Orangist[2] ('ɒrɪndʒɪst). Also **Orangeist.** [f. ORANGE *sb.*[2]] **a.** A supporter of the House of Orange in the Netherlands. (Also *attrib.*) **b.** An Orangeman.
c **1800** *Pelham MS.* in Lecky *Hist. Eng. in 18th C.* (1890) VIII. 363 *note*, Some of the most violent Orangists have opposed the measure. **1822** *Examiner* 817/1 The Irish Orangists. **1848** W. H. KELLY tr. *L. Blanc's Hist. Ten Years* I. 371 An Orangist movement which broke out in Ghent was attributed to the English ambassador.

orangite ('ɒrɪndʒaɪt). *Min.* [Named, 1851, from its colour.] An orange variety of thorite.
1851 *Amer. Jrnl. Sc.* XII. 387 The mineral orangite which contains the metal thorium. **1865–72** WATTS *Dict. Chem.* V. 788 The variety [of thorite] called orangite, found in the zircon-syenite near Brevig, is yellowish or yellow to brown, yields an orange-yellow powder.

'Orangize, *v. rare.* [f. ORANGE *sb.*[2] + -IZE.]
a. *trans.* To render 'Orange' in form or character. **b.** *intr.* To play the part of William of Orange.
1825 LOCKHART in *Scott's Fam. Lett.* (1894) II. 306 The Protestants..call St. Patrick's, Patrick's, and St. Stephen's Green has been Orangeized into Stephen's. **1840** THACKERAY *Catherine* i, When the seventeenth century, after a deal of..Oliver Cromwellizing, Stuartizing, and Orangizing, had sunk into its grave.

orang-outang (ɒˌræŋuː'tæŋ), more correctly **orang-utan** ('ɔːrəŋ'uːtæn). *Zool.* Forms: 7– orang-, 8–9 ourang-, 8 oerang-, ouran-, 8–9 oran-; 7–9 -outang, 9 -utang, -otang, -outan, -otan, -oatan, -utan. [Ultimately ad. Malay *'ōrang 'ūtan* 'man of the woods', found in similar forms in most European langs., e.g. Du. *orang-outang* (also 18th c. *oerang-oetan*), Ger., Da., Sw. *orangutang*, F. *orang-outang*, It., Pg. *orangotango*, Sp. *orangután*. The last (exc. as to the place of the stress) comes nearest to the Malay; in the other langs. *ūtan* 'woods' has been corrupted to jingle with the first.
It is stated that the name is not (now, at least) applied to the animal in Malay; but that it was in use in Java in the 17th c. is stated by Bontius (a Dutch East Indian physician), the first to record the name. Moreover, the Kayan of Borneo are said, in *Jrnl. Ind. Archipel.* (1850) IV. 186, to know it as *orang-tuan*, meaning 'man of the woods' or 'wild man'.
1631 BONTIUS *Hist. Nat. et Med. Ind. Orient.* v. xxxii. (1658) 85 Iavani..Nomen ei induunt Ourang Outang, quod hominem silvæ significat.]

An anthropoid ape, *Simia satyrus*, of arboreal habits, inhabiting Borneo, Sumatra, and formerly Java; the male exceeds 4 feet in height, and has very long arms. The ***lesser orang-utan*** is *S. morio* of Borneo. (The name has been incorrectly applied to the Chimpanzee or other large African ape.)
1699 E. TYSON (*title*) Orang-Outang, sive Homo Sylvestris: or, the Anatomy of a Pygmie, Compared with that of a Monkey, an Ape, and a Man. *Ibid.* Pref., The Orang-Outang imitates a Man more than Apes and Monkeys do. **1727** A. HAMILTON *New Acc. E. Ind.* II. 131 As there are many Species of wild Animals in these Woods [of Java], there is one in particular, called the Oran Outang. **1774** GOLDSM. *Nat. Hist.* II. 343 The foremost of the ape kind is the ourang-outang or wild man of the woods. **1777** MILLER in *Phil. Trans.* LXVIII. 170 The oerang oatan, or wild man (for that is the meaning of the words) I have heard much talk of, but never seen. **1802** BINGLEY *Anim. Biog.* (1813) I. 55 The difference betwixt the Chimpanzee and Oran Otan is chiefly in size and colour. **1803** T. WINTERBOTTOM *Sierra Leone* I. xii. 201 Some writers of eminence have asserted that man originally walked upon four feet, and was in fact the same with the oran outang. **1819** BOWDICH *Mission to Ashantee* II. xiii. 440 The African Ourang-outan (*Pithecus Troglodites*) is found here. **1836** *Penny Cycl.* V. 188/1 The variety of the ape and monkey tribes is endless [in Borneo]; and among them is the orang-outang, or the 'man of the woods', as the name implies. **1889** A. R. WALLACE *Darwinism* 69 Among the nine adult male Orang-utans, collected by myself in Borneo, the skulls differed remarkably in size and proportions.
attrib. **1851** TRENCH *Stud. Words* i. (1882) 13 The 'urang-utang theory', as it has been so happily termed..according to which the primitive condition of man was the savage one.

orans ('ɔːrənz). Also **orant.** [ad. L. *ōrāns, ōrānt-em*, pr. pple. of *ōrāre* to pray.] (See quot. 1900). Also *attrib.*
1900 W. LOWRIE *Chr. Art & Archaeol.* (1901) 201 The name *orans* or *orant* designates a figure in the attitude of prayer, with arms outstretched in the manner which was common to both Jews and Gentiles, and was accounted by the Church particularly significant, because it recalled the position of the Saviour upon the cross. **1937** *Burlington Mag.* July 25/2 Though the Trecento type, the seated Virgin with clasped hands, persists in the Quattrocento, it is the Virgin derived from the old 'orans' type, of which the Antwerp *Assumption* is the earliest Italian example. **1949** O. DEMUS *Mosaics Norman Sicily* 309 The Orans was seen 'spreading out her pure hands to ensure the Emperor's triumph over his enemies'.

Oraon (əʊ'rɑːɒn). [Indian name, of undetermined origin.
The following are among numerous explanations of the meaning of the name: **1900** F. HAHN *Kurukh Gram.* p. iii, The Hindus, who are supposed having invented the name *Urāõ* or *Orāõ* for the *Kurukh* people, might have concluded that the whole nation was called by the name of this sept, *i.e. Orgorā*; this word means hawk or cunny bird, and educated Urāõs believe that the foreign designation *Orāõ* or *Orā* is derived from this totemistic word. **1906** G. A. GRIERSON *Linguistic Survey India* IV. II. 406 Hindūs say that the word 'Orāõ' is simply the Indo-Aryan *urāū*, spendthrift, the name being an allusion to the alleged thriftless character of the people to whom it is applied. **1915** S. C. ROY *Orāons of Chōtā Nāgpur* i. 14 The name [of a monster-king] Rāwan, pronounced, as some people do, with an arrested 'O' sound at the beginning gave us the present form 'O-rāwan' or Orāon.]

(A member of) an aboriginal tribe, which calls itself *Kurukh*, dwelling in the state of Bihar in northern India; the Dravidian language of this tribe. Also *attrib.* or as *adj.*
1872 E. T. DALTON *Descriptive Ethnol. Bengal* VIII. i. 245 The Khurũkh or Orāons of Chútiá Nágpúr are the people best known in many parts of India as 'Dhángars', a word that from its apparent derivation (*dang* or *dhang*, a hill) may mean any hillmen... According to the traditions I have received from the most venerable and learned of my Oráon acquaintances, the tribe has gradually migrated from the western coast of India... Oráon appears to have been assigned to them as a nickname, possibly with reference to their many migrations and proneness to roam. **1892** H. H. RISLEY *Tribes & Castes Bengal: Ethnogr. Gloss.* II. 138 *Oráon, Uráon, Kunokh, Kunrukh*, a Dravidian cultivating tribe of Chota Nagpur, classed on linguistic grounds as Dravidian, and supposed to be closely akin to the Málés of the Rájmahál hills. **1908** [see KORKU]. **1915**, etc. [see MALER *sb.* and *a.*]. **1917** *Encycl. Relig. & Ethics* IX. 501/2 The Orāons..call themselves Khurũk or Kūṛukh, a Dravidian term of uncertain origin, connected by some with the word *horo*, 'man', or with *kuruk*, 'a crier', or one capable of speaking, in contradistinction to the other races, whose language is not intelligible to them... This word *horo* is probably the origin of the name Orāon. **1939** L. H. GRAY *Foundations of Lang.* 386 Kurukh, consisting of Kurukh or Orāōn in the western part of the Bengal Presidency and the neighbouring parts of the Central Provinces, and Malto in the Rajmahal Mountains of Bengal. **1972** W. B. LOCKWOOD *Panorama Indo-European Lang.* 224 Kurukh and Malto. The former, also termed Oraon, is used by 150,000 persons in the western ranges of the Chota Nagpur Hills, in the districts of Raigarh and Sambalpur. **1974** *Encycl. Brit. Micropædia* VII. 563/1 Speakers of Oraon number about 1,140,000, but in urban areas, and particularly among Christians, many Oraon speak Hindi as their mother tongue.

orarian (ɒ'rɛərɪən), *a.* and *sb. rare.* [f. L. *ōrārius* of or belonging to the coast, f. *ōra* border, coast + -AN.] **a.** *adj.* Of, pertaining to, or dwelling on the coast. **b.** *sb.* A dweller on the sea-shore.
1870 *Pall Mall G.* 24 Dec. 12 The three tribes of Innuits, Aleutians, and Asiatic Eskimo;..Mr. Dall proposes to confer on them the generic appellation of Orarian, dwellers by the sea-shore.

orarion (ɒ'rɛərɪɒn). *Eccl.* [late Gr. ὠράριον, ad. L. *orarium* ORARIUM.] = ORARIUM.
1772 J. G. KING *Rites & Cerem. Gk. Ch. in Russia* 36 Plate III. represents a deacon officiating in his..Orarion which is a sort of tippet thrown over his left shoulder. **1850** J. M. NEALE *Hist. Holy Eastern Ch.* I. 310 The stole was frequently called the orarion in the Western Church. **1907** A. FORTESCUE *Orthod. Eastern Ch.* 408 Other clerks wear a shorter sticharion and an orarion wound around them.

‖**orarium** (ɒ'rɛərɪəm). *Eccl.* [L., a napkin, handkerchief, f. *ōs, ōr-* mouth, face: see -ARIUM.] The earlier name of the stole; *spec.* in the Greek Church, that worn by deacons.
1706 PHILLIPS, *Orarium*, a kind of Priest's Vestment. **1720** BRETT *Liturgies* 298 The *Orarium* was a long narrow Towel, which the Deacon hung on his left Shoulder;..the primary Use of it was to wipe the Mouth or the Fingers as there was occasion. **1885** *Catholic Dict.* (ed. 3) s.v. *Stole*, The Council of Braga in 563 (can. 9) speaks of the orarium as worn by deacons. *Ibid.*, The Greeks have always regarded the orarium as a vestment peculiar to deacons. *Ibid.*, Hefele acknowledges his failure after much search to find the reason why the word 'stole' came to be used for orarium.

orary ('ɔərərɪ). [ad. L. *ōrāri-um.*] = prec.
1814 SOUTHEY *Roderick* XVIII, Not in his alb and cope and orary Came Urban now. **1826** —— *Vind. Eccl. Angl.* 87 [He] told him to fetch a little box, in which he kept a few precious things, such as pepper, incense, and oraries.

ora serrata: see ORA[2] 3.

orason, -oun, obs. forms of ORISON.

orate ('ɔəreɪt, ɒ'reɪt), *v.* [f. L. *ōrāt-*, ppl. stem of *ōrāre* to speak, plead, pray.
This word is occasionally instanced since *c* 1600, but has only recently come into more common use, as a back-formation from *oration*, app. first in U.S. *c* 1860; in Dictionaries it is recorded in Webster *Supp.* (1879).]

1. *intr.* †**a.** To pray; to plead. *Obs.* **b.** To deliver an oration; to act the orator; to hold forth, 'speechify'. Now usually humorous or sarcastic.
c **1600** *Timon* II. iv. (1842) 32 O let it bee lawfull for mee ..to orate and exorate. **1669** GALE *Crt. Gentiles* I. Introd. 4 A Rhetorician, whose businesse is to orate and persuade. **1780** *Town & Country Mag.* June 294/1 Four actresses, who ..obtained better salaries for orating at Carlisle-house. **1828** SOUTHEY *Ess.* (1832) II. 269 Write, and orate, and legislate as we will upon the principles of free trade. **1864** SALA in *Daily Tel.* 18 Nov., General Banks..has been 'orating' in New York. **1876** C. M. DAVIES *Unorth. Lond.* (ed. 2) 430, I ..passed on, and left him orating. *a* **1881** J. L. DIMAN in Caroline Hazard *Mem.* xi. (1887) 231 Last week I went to Andover and repeated my address, and next week do the same at Burlington; so you see my time this summer is much taken up with 'orating'.

2. *trans.* To address in a harangue. *rare.*
1885 W. RYE *Hist. Norfolk* v. 71 A turbaned boy on a platform orated her for the fourth time.

‖**oratio** (ɒ'reɪʃ(ɪ)əʊ). [L. *ōrātiō, ōrātiōn-em*: see ORATION *sb.*] Speech, language. Only in phrases: **oratio obliqua** [L. fem. of *oblīqu-us*: see OBLIQUE *a.* 5 b], indirect speech; **oratio recta** [L. fem. of *rect-us* straight, direct], direct speech.
1842 W. E. JELF *Gram. Greek Lang.* II. iv. 508 The infin. and acc. follows the verb in the *oratio obliqua*, and then follows a dependent clause in which the verb stands in the *oratio recta.* **1876** Oratio obliqua, oratio recta [see ORATION *sb.* 3]. **1929** R. HUGHES *High Wind in Jamaica* i. 35 Then she put it into Oratio Recta, told it as a story, beginning with that magic phrase, 'Once I was in an Earthquake.' **1957** R. SPEAIGHT *Life H. Belloc* ix. 175 Belloc would have been on safer ground if he had covered his quotation by making it clear that he was only giving the sense of Robespierre's words, or if he had abridged them in *oratio obliqua.* **1962** *Times Lit. Suppl.* 26 Oct. 826/2 This involves questions of phraseology, idiom, *oratio obliqua*, and the adjustment of dialogue to the pace and mood of the narrative. **1968** *Listener* 25 July 120/2 The stilted *oratio obliqua* of court reportage.

oration (ɒ'reɪʃən), *sb.* Also 4–5 oracion(e. [ad. L. *ōrātiōn-em*, n. of action f. *orāre*: see ORATE *v.* Cf. rare F. *oration* in Godefroy and Cotgr.; the ordinary Fr. is *oraison* ORISON.]

1. A prayer, petition, or supplication to God; orison. Now only *Hist.*
c **1375** *Sc. Leg. Saints* xxxvi. (*Baptista*) 840 He mekly knelit done, makand to god his oracione. **1483** CAXTON *Gold. Leg.* 72 b/2, I haue herde thy prayer and thyn oracion that thou hast prayed tofore me. **1593** B. BARNES *Sonn.* lii, O let us use and have in readinesse Those sweet orations, prostrate at his feete. **1894** R. C. HOPE *Mediæval Music* vi. 58 The Collectarium, the collects, orations, capitula or short lessons used at all the Hour Services.

2. A formal speech or discourse delivered in elevated and dignified language; *esp.* one delivered in connexion with some particular occasion, as an anniversary celebration, a funeral, etc.
1502 ATKYNSON tr. *De Imitatione* I. iii. 156 Elegant oratours with theyr oracions garnisshed with eligancy. **1526** TINDALE *Acts* xii. 21 Apon a daye apoynted, the kynge..set

hym in his seate and made an oracion vnto them. **1605** BACON *Adv. Learn.* II. xiii. §7 Demosthenes..had ready framed a number of prefaces for orations and speeches. **1796-7** HUNTER tr. *St. Pierre's Stud. Nat.* (1799) II. 379 What a funeral oration for a wife and a mother! **1844** LD. BROUGHAM *Brit. Const.* App. iii. (1862) 450 The greatest orations of the two first orators of any age, Demosthenes and Æschines.

3. Speech, language; now only in *Gram.* as rendering L. *oratio recta* and *obliqua*, 'direct' and 'oblique oration', or use of language (see ORATIO).

1669 GALE *Crt. Gentiles* I. I. x. 52 Oration was given to man, as a companion, or organ of Reason. **1876** B. H. KENNEDY *Pub. Sch. Lat. Gram.* §190 Oratio Obliqua (in distinction from Oratio Recta, *direct oration*) is a term especially applied to Substantival Clauses, and, above all, to the Infinitive Clause and its substitutes.

4. *dial.* A noise or hubbub; a fuss.

1828 *Craven Gloss.* (ed. 2) s.v., 'For seur, barns, what an oration ye mak'. **1869** *Lonsdale Gloss., Oration*, noise, uproar. **1875** *Sussex Gloss.*, 'He makes such an oration about anything'.

5. *attrib.*, as *oration-hall*.

1855 THACKERAY *Newcomes* II. 332 Before marching from the oration-hall.

o'ration, *v. colloq.* [f. prec. sb.] *intr.* To make a speech or oration; to 'speechify'. (In quot. 1802 *trans.* To get (*into*) by 'speechifying'.) Hence **o'rationing** *vbl. sb.*

1633 J. DONE *Hist. Septuagint* 79-80 They..had marvailous promptitude both for orationing and giving Judgment. **1764** FOOTE *Mayor of G.* II. i, You have heard him oration at the Adam and Eve..about Russia and Prussia. **1802** H. MARTIN *Helen of Glenross* I. 233 A symptom..much more unequivocal, than those my uncle orations himself into a fever about. **1876** G. MEREDITH *Beauch. Career* I. iii. 45 Now you get out of that trick of prize-orationing. I call it snuffery, sir!

o'rational, *a. rare.* [f. as prec. + -AL[1].] Of or pertaining to prayer in religious worship.

1889 *Ch. Times* 11 Jan. 29/3 A course of different services for the several Sundays in each month, as in some of the orational books of Family Prayer which we have in use in England.

o'rationer. *rare.* [f. ORATION *v.* + -ER[1].] One who makes an oration; an orator or speaker.

1765 FOOTE *Commissary* II. i, Why it is the famous orationer that has publish'd the book. **1881** *St. James's Gaz.* 2 Mar. 3 The whole pack of Radical scribes and orationers.

[The sense 'Petitioner' in *Cent. Dict* (and Funk), founded on a quot. from Dixon's *Hist. Ch. Eng.* I. 111 *note*, has no existence; the word in the original is *oratours*. See ORATOR 2, quot. 1532.]

oratist ('ɒrətɪst). *rare.* [f. ORATE *v.* + -IST.] One given to orating.

1887 SWINBURNE in *Fortn. Rev.* XLII. 173 The orotund oratist of Manhattan.

oratiuncle (ɒreɪʃɪ'ʌŋk(ə)l). *rare*[-1]. [ad. L. *ōrātiuncula*, dim. of *ōrātio*.] A short oration.

1832 J. WILSON *Noct. Ambr.* in *Blackw. Mag.* XXXII. 393 In a short, plain, unvarnished oratiuncle, [he] told the company that the thing must be done.

orator ('ɒrətə(r)). Also 4-8 **-our**, 5 **-ur(e**. [ME. a. AFr. *oratour* = OF. *orateur* (14th c. in Littré), ad. L. *ōrātōr-em* speaker, orator, beseecher, agent-n. from *ōrāre*: see ORATE.]

†**1.** One who pleads or argues in favour of a person or cause; an advocate, a spokesman; *spec.* a professional advocate. *Obs.*

c **1374** CHAUCER *Boeth.* IV. pr. iv. 100 (Camb. MS.) Thise oratours or aduocats don al the contrarye for they enforcen hem to commoeue the Iuges to han pite of hem þat han suffred. **1382** WYCLIF *Acts* xxiv. 1 Tercull, sum oratour [*gloss* or fair speker, or avocat], whiche wenten to the presedent aȝeyns Poul. **1592** WARNER *Alb. Eng.* VIII. xxxix. (1612) 193 Take you no Orators for them, but that they hang or starue. **1593** SHAKS. *Lucr.* 30 Beautie it selfe doth of it selfe perswade, The eies of men without an Orator. **1650** FULLER *Pisgah* v. 202 But oh! remember the Oratour on thy right hand, Christ Jesus our Lord.

†**2.** One who offers a prayer or petition; a petitioner or suppliant. (Commonly used in subscribing a letter or petition to a superior.) *Obs.*

1433 *Rolls of Parlt.* IV. 458/1 To the Kyng..sheweth.. your devoute Oratours. ?**1449** ROBERT, PRIOR OF BROMHOLM in *Paston Lett.* I. 79 Writtin in hast,..Your Orator, Robt., P. of B. **1532** *Submiss. of Clergy to Hen. VIII* (MS., P.R.O.), We your most humble subjectis dayly oratours and beadismen of your clergye of England [etc.]. **1535** COVERDALE *Bible* Ded., Youre graces humble subiecte and daylye oratour, Myles Couerdale. *a* **1677** BARROW *Serm.* (1687) I. x. 136 Devout oratours and humble solicitours at the Throne of grace. **1700** P. LORRAIN *Let.* 12 Oct. in *Pepys' Corr.* V. 395 Who with profound respect beg leave to subscribe myself..your Honour's most humble and most obed[t] Serv[t] and daily Orator, Paul Lorrain. **1727** in Quincy *Hist. Harvard Univ.* (1840) I. 565 Your Honors' most humble orators shall ever pray for the prosperity and happiness of this government.

†**b.** *Law.* The plaintiff or petitioner in a bill or information in Chancery. *Obs.*

1594 WEST *2nd Pt. Symbol., Chancerie* §77 But of his further malyce agaynst your said Orator, he doth threaten your Orator in such sort, that your Orator for want of the said Evidences,..dareth not make his just and lawfull entrie. **1623** *Bill of Complaint* in *N. Shaks. Soc. Trans.* (1885) 495 Humbly complayning, Sheweth vnto your good Lordshipp, your dayly oratours Ellis Worth, of London, gentleman, John Cumber, of the same, gentleman, and John Blany, of London aforesaid. **1768** BLACKSTONE *Comm.* III. xxvii. 442 The first commencement of a suit in chancery is by preferring a bill to the lord chancellor, in the stile of a petition; 'humbly complaining sheweth to your lordship your orator A. B. that, &c.'

3. One who delivers a speech or oration in public; a public speaker, esp. one distinguished for oratorical ability; an eloquent public speaker.

c **1430** LYDG. *Min. Poems* (Percy Soc.) 87 In Rome, by soverayne excellence, Of rethoriques Tullius fonde the floures, Plee and defence of sotyl oratours. **1555** EDEN *Decades* 92 Vsinge also thoffice both of an oratoure and preacher. **1601** SHAKS. *Jul. C.* III. ii. 221, I come not (Friends) to steale away your hearts, I am no Orator, as Brutus is. **1667** MILTON *P.L.* IX. 670 As when of old som Orator renound In Athens or free Rome,..to some great cause addresst, Stood in himself collected. **1752** HUME *Ess. & Treat.* (1777) I. 105 The vehemence of action, observed in the ancient orators. *a* **1862** BUCKLE *Misc. Wks.* (1872) I. 254 The vulgar are always unwilling to believe that a great orator can be a profound thinker.

†**b.** An eloquent writer. *Obs. rare.*

1587 *MS. Robert Leng* (Brit. Mus.), Whereas yt hath bene th'order of all antiant orators..to regester..in cronicle all such worthye persons..as..have deserved perpetuall remembraunce.

†**4.** One sent to plead or speak for another; an ambassador, envoy, or messenger. *Obs.*

1494 FABYAN *Chron.* v. cxxxii. 115 The sayd Sclauons hauyng knowlege of ye kynges great hoost, aggreed, by oratours to hym sent, to contynue the trybute that they before tyme payde. **1502** ARNOLDE *Chron.* (1811) 162 Whan my noble prince the Soudan of Babilone had decerned to sende me his oratour to Fraunce. **1600** HOLLAND *Livy* XXVIII. xvii. 680 Scipio..sent C. Lælius with rich gifts and presents, as an Orator to treat with him. **1673** RAY *Journ. Low C., Venice* 174 Audience is given to publick Oratours and Embassadours.

fig. **1592** S. DANIEL *Compl. Rosamond* liii, He daily Messages doth send, With costly Jewels (Orators of Love).

5. ***Public Orator***: an officer of the Universities of Oxford and Cambridge, whose functions are to speak in the name of the University on state occasions; to go in person, when required, to plead the cause of the University; to write suitable addresses, letters of congratulation or condolence; to introduce candidates for certain honorary degrees, and to perform other duties of a like kind.

'Orators' were in early times sent by the universities, as special envoys, when occasion required, e.g. to Councils of the Church, as that of Basel in 1430. A permanent Public Orator was appointed at Cambridge in 1522, and at Oxford in 1564.

1614 J. CHAMBERLAIN in *Crt. & Times Jas. I* (1848) I. 305 The University Orator, Nethersole..is taxed for calling the prince *Jacobissime Carole*. **1622** J. MEADE in Ellis *Orig. Lett.* Ser. I. III. 126, I shall not tell you..how our Orators fathered the foundation of our University [Cambridge] upon the Spanyards out of the old Legend of Cantaber. **1642** WOOD *Life* 29 Oct. (O.H.S.) I. 68 Dr. Gardiner prebend of Christchurch makinge a speech to his majestie, as Dr. Strode the orator's deputy. **1645** *Ibid.* Mar. 116 William Strode..public orator of the University, died, M., 10 Mar. anno 1644/5. *a* **1734** NORTH *Lives* (1826) I. 168 Dr. Henry Paman, sometime orator of the university of Cambridge. **1899** *Oxford Univ. Cal.* 1 Public Orator. 1880 William Walter Merry, D.D. Rector of Lincoln.

6. *Comb.*, as **'orator-like** *a.* and *adv.*, like or after the manner of an orator.

1553 T. WILSON *Rhet.* 13 It were wel done and Oratour-like. **1579** G. HARVEY *Letter-bk.* (Camden) 63 The Commendation of an eloquente and oratorlike stile. **1647** TRAPP *Comm. 2 Thess.* iii. 4 Here the Apostle, Oratour-like, entereth their bosoms. **1673** O. WALKER *Educ.* 161 What is well, and Orator-like written or spoken.

oratorial (ɒrə'tɔərɪəl), *a.* Now *rare.* [In sense 1, f. L. *ōrātōri-us* of or belonging to an orator + -AL[1]. In sense 2, referred to ORATORIO.]

1. Of, pertaining to, or proper to an orator.

1546 LANGLEY *Pol. Verg. de Invent.* I. x. 20 Aristotle affirmeth that Empedocles was first aucthor of the Oratoriall Arte. **1619** HALES *Gold. Rem.* (1673) II. 92 The manner of his discourse was oratorial. **1760-72** H. BROOKE *Fool of Qual.* (1809) I. 172 The auctioneer mounted his oratorial eminence. **1852** BLACKIE *Stud. Lang.* 34 Imitative outbursts of oratorial argument. **1886** *Argosy Mag.* May 351 Paul.. began in an oratorial tone.

2. Of or pertaining to an oratorio.

1811 BUSBY *Dict. Mus.* (ed. 3), *Oratorial*, an epithet derived from the word *Oratorio*, and consequently applicable to that species of composition. **1819** —— *Hist. Mus.* II. 462 His oratorial choruses..exhibit well-worked fugues. **1923** *Daily Mail* 8 Aug. 8/1 The very front rank of our oratorial singers.

ora'torially, *adv.* [f. prec. + -LY[2].]

1. After the manner of an orator.

1553 GRIMALDE *Cicero's Offices* (1558) Ep. iiij, So conningly and oratorially treated and endited.

2. In the manner of an oratorio.

1889 *Harper's Mag.* Dec. 109/2 Rubinstein's proposal to dramatize oratorially the Old Testament.

oratorian (ɒrə'tɔərɪən), *a.* and *sb.* [f. L. *ōrātōri-us* of or pertaining to an orator, *ōrātōri-um* place of prayer, ORATORY *sb.*[1]]

A. *adj.* †**1.** Of or pertaining to an orator; = ORATORIAL 1, ORATORICAL 2. *Obs.*

1644 BULWER *Chiron.* 132 Oratorian Action must varie according to the diversitie of people and Nations. *a* **1734** NORTH *Exam.* II. v. §163 (1740) 420 A Reverend Parson who relates the Fact of a Conspiracy in a good Method..and beautiful English; in a Word, in an oratorian Way.

2. Of or pertaining to the ORATORY (5 a).

1862 in *Dublin Daily Express* 30 Dec., The youths from all lands, whom the Oratorian Father paints like doves flying over the blue seas to the windows. **1876** FOX BOURNE *Locke* II. ix. 31 Father Simon, an oratorian priest. **1882** *Athenæum* 30 Dec. 895/2 His life of quiet study among the Oratorian brotherhood.

B. *sb.* A father or priest of an oratory; *spec.* (with capital initial) a member of one of the societies mentioned s.v. ORATORY *sb.*[1] 5, esp. of the Oratory of St. Philip Neri. Cf. F. *oratorien*.

1656 BLOUNT *Glossogr., Oratorians*, a Religious Fraternity or Order Instituted the last age by St. Phillip Nerius, a Florentine Priest. **1679** PRANCE *Add. Narr. Pop. Plot* 47 Monks have a great feud..against Fryars..Oratorians against Jesuits. **1710** SMITH in Hearne *Collect.* 18 Mar. (O.H.S.) II. 361 The Convent of the Oratorians at Paris. **1850** MRS. JAMESON *Leg. Monast. Ord.* Introd. (1863) 33 The black habit is worn by the Augustines, the Servi, the Oratorians and the Jesuits.

Hence **Ora'torianism**, the system, principles, or practice of the Oratorians; **Ora'torianize** *v. intr.* to follow the method of the Oratorians.

1847 J. H. NEWMAN *Let.* 31 Dec. (1962) XII. 140, I am anxious you should [try] if you have fully mastered *what* Oratorianism is. **1848** F. W. FABER in R. Chapman *Father Faber* (1961) viii. 172 There is nothing in what you say about oratorianism which takes any of us by surprise. *Ibid.* ix. 182 It seems you have not captivated him, and he won't Oratorianize. **1851** BERESF. HOPE in *Chr. Remembrancer* XXI. 151 Being more than anything else the germ of Oratorianism, that of multiplying altars in the same church. **1852** *Ecclesiologist* XIII. 352 When Oratorianism arose in his own communion. **1883** BERESF. HOPE *Worship & Ord.* 126 Whatever faults may be found with the Eastern Church, it certainly does not Oratorianize.

ora'toric, *a.* [f. L. *ōrātōr-em* ORATOR + -IC, after Gr. formations like *historic*, *rhetoric*.] = next.

1656 CROMWELL *Sp.* 17 Sept. in *Carlyle*, Not discoursively, in the oratoric way; but to let you see the matter of fact. **1848** LYTTON *K. Arthur* VIII. iii, The oratoric Knight Regained the vantage. **1891** S. S. CURRY (*title*) The Province of Expression..methods of developing Dramatic and Oratoric Delivery.

oratorical (ɒrə'tɒrɪkəl), *a.* [f. as prec. + -AL[1].]

†**1.** = ORATORIAN *a.* 2. *Obs.*

1619 FAVOUR *Antiq. Tri. over Nov.* xiii. 339 He that hath written the tales of Nereus, Cardinall Baronius his oratoricall patron.

2. Of, pertaining to, or characteristic of an orator or oratory; rhetorical; also, according to the rules of oratory; characteristic of a professional orator or advocate.

1634 W. TIRWHYT tr. *Balzac's Lett.* (vol. I) A iij, Wee are therefore to confesse Oratoricall treatises to have no other subject than Letters. **1702** H. DODWELL *Apol.* §5 in S. Parker *Cicero's De Finibus*, The use he had made of his Philosophical Notions in his Oratorical Discourses. **1861** CRAIK *Hist. Eng. Lit.* II. 351 Burke..by his wonderful oratorical displays on the impeachment of Hastings. **1872** MINTO *Eng. Prose Lit.* Introd. 9 The long sentence..would universally be designated oratorical.

transf. **1878** PROUT in Grove *Dict. Mus.* I. 15 That which is sometimes called the oratorical accent..the adaptation in vocal music of the notes to the words, of the sound to the sense.

3. Given to the use of oratory.

1801 MAR. EDGEWORTH *Angelina* iv. (1831) 79 'Your friend!' pursued the oratorical lady, detaining Miss Warwick with a heavy hand. **1898** *Daily News* 16 Aug. 4/4 Americans are an oratorical race, and it is as natural for an American to speak as for an Englishman to be silent.

ora'torically, *adv.* [f. prec. + -LY[2].] In the manner of an orator, or in the way of oratory.

1682 *2nd Plea for Nonconformists* A ij b, I say nothing in this Opposition Oratorically, but truly and upon Proof. **1813** L. HUNT in *Examiner* 15 Feb. 102/2 This is oratorically spoken. **1840** CARLYLE *Heroes* v. (1872) 162 Chatham.. forgets..that he is acting the sick man; in the fire of debate, snatches his arm from the sling, and oratorically swings and brandishes it!

oratorio (ɒrə'tɔərɪəʊ). [a. It. *oratorio*:—eccl. L. *ōrātōrium*, ORATORY *sb.*[1] In the extant sense 1, named from the musical services held in the church of the Oratory of St. Philip Neri in Rome in the latter half of the 16th century; these being virtually examples of the older Mystery Play improved and adapted to a religious service: see Grove *Dict. Mus.* s.v. Cf. F. *oratorio* (1739 in Hatz.-Darm.).

1644 EVELYN *Diary* 8 Nov. [see ORATORY *sb.*[1] 5 a]. **1670** LASSELS *Voy. Italy* II. 227 The house of these good Priests [of S. Philip Neri] deserves also to be seen..for the great Oratoryes sake, where there is every Sunday and Holyday in winter at night, the best Musick in the world.]

1. A form of extended musical composition, of a semi-dramatic character, usually founded on a Scriptural theme, sung by solo voices and a chorus, to the accompaniment of a full orchestra, without the assistance of action, scenery, or dress.

1727-38 CHAMBERS *Cycl.* s.v. *Opera*, At Rome they have a kind of spiritual opera's, frequent in Lent... The Italians

call them oratorio's. **1742** FIELDING *Amelia* IV. viii, She had a present of a ticket for the oratorio. **1756–7** tr. *Keysler's Trav.* (1760) I. 470 In the church of St. Philippo Neri, belonging to the fathers of the oratory..Every Sunday evening, during the winter, an oratorio, or religious opera, is performed in this church, which is founded on some scripture history. **1789** MRS. PIOZZI *Journ. France* I. 176 [They] performed an oratorio with..deserved applause. **1880** W. S. ROCKSTRO in Grove *Dict. Mus.* II. 534/1 The year 1600 witnessed the first performance, in Rome, of Emilio's 'Rappresentazione' and, in Florence, of Peri's 'Euridice'—the earliest examples of the true Oratorio and the true Opera ever presented to the public. **1881** BARING-GOULD *Germany* ix. 249 It is in the Opera and the Oratorio that the most flourishing descendants of the old Mystery Plays are to be met with.
fig. **1818** T. MOORE *Fudge Fam. Paris* x. 43 Vulgar Pall Mall's oratorio of hisses! **1838** EMERSON *Addr., Literary Ethics* Wks. (Bohn) II. 210 By Latin and English poetry, we were born and bred in an oratorio of praises of nature. **1899** ABP. ALEXANDER in *Times* 31 Oct. 9/5 The oratorio of the cannonade Rolls through the hills sublime.

†**2.** A pulpit. (So It. *oratorio* in Florio.) *rare.*
1631 *High Commission Cases* (Camden) 230 The turning of God's oratorio, the pulpit, into a place to vent his malice upon the poore people.

3. *attrib.* and *Comb.* (from 1), as ***oratorio style***; ***oratorio-frequenting*** adj.
1828 *Lights & Shades* I. 255 Certain oratorio-frequenting people have censured O'Carrol. **1861** WOODS *Pr. of Wales in Canada* 140 The Montreal Oratorio Society performed..a grand Cantata specially composed. **1900** *Daily News* 8 Feb. 6/3 The later choral compositions of Elgar..and others, which, if secular as to story, practically follow the oratorio style.

†**ora'torious**, *a.* *Obs.* [f. L. *ōrātōri-us* of or belonging to an orator + -OUS.] Of or pertaining to an orator; of the nature of oratory; oratorical.
1563 [implied in ORATORIOUSLY]. **1607** R. CRAKANTHORP *Serm.* (1608) 35 Pietie, zeale, and godlinesse, which are the most oratorious and perswading reasons with Almightie God. **1656** *Artif. Handsom.* 29 What Error is so rotten and putrid, which some Oratorious varnish hath not sought to colour over? **1689** EVELYN *Mem.* (1857) III. 310 Gentlemen and scholars bring their essays, poems, and other oratorious productions upon a thousand curious subjects.
Hence †**ora'toriously** *adv.*, after the manner of an orator; rhetorically; eloquently. *Obs.*
1563 FOXE *A. & M.* 1188/1 Addinge oratoriously Amplifications, to moue the said Bradford to yelde. **1597** BROUGHTON *Ep. to Nobility* Wks. III. 573 Moses saith.. Saint Peter translateth him most oratoriously. **1656** *Artif. Handsom.* 115 Nor do they..oppose things of this nature argumentatively, so much as Oratoriously.

'oratorize, *v.* [f. ORATOR *sb.* + -IZE.] *intr.* To play the orator; to deliver an oration. Now usually humorous or contemptuous: to 'speechify'.
1620 SIR S. D'EWES in *Coll. Life Jas. I* (1851) 107 Dr. Collins oratorized, as his manner was, most excellently. *a* **1654** WEBSTER *App. & Virg.* v. iii, To hear me concionate, And oratorize. **1837** DICKENS *Pickw.* xxiv, Mr. Pickwick oratorizing, and the crowd shouting. **1853** *Blackw. Mag.* LXXIII. 508 Lecturers..have of late years been perambulating the country oratorising on this subject.
b. *trans.* To set forth with oratory. *rare.*
1853 *Blackw. Mag.* LXXIV. 503 You knew, the while these your words were awakening detestation of Swift, you were oratorising a very great sham—all nonsense—stuff.

'oratorship. [See -SHIP.] The position or office of orator; esp. in ***Public Oratorship***, the office of Public Orator in a University.
1592 G. HARVEY *Foure Letters* (1969) iii. 17, I was supposed not vnmeet for the Oratorship of the vniuersity. **1869** R. C. JEBB *Let.* 3 Nov. (1907) 98, I was standing for the Public Oratorship.

oratory ('ɒrətərɪ), *sb.*¹ [ad. L. *ōrātōri-um* place of prayer (prop. adj. 'for prayer', sc. *templum*); f. *ōrāt-*, ppl. stem of *ōrāre* to speak, pray, etc.: see -ORY. In OF. *oratur* (12th c.) whence Sc. ORATOUR, and *oratoire* (14th c. in Littré).]
1. A place of prayer; a small chapel or shrine; a room or building for private worship, esp. one in or attached to a house, monastery, church, etc. Also in reference to Jewish or Pagan worship.
13.. *Creatio Mundi* in Horstm. *Altengl. Leg.* (1878) 227 ȝit liggen þe tables in þat ilke stude in Adames oratorie þer he bad his beodes. **1382** WYCLIF *Judith* ix. 1 Judit wente in to hir oratorie, and..putte askes vp on hir hed. *c* **1386** CHAUCER *Knt.'s T.* 1047 In worshipe of Venus goddesse of loue, Doon make an Auter and an Oratorie. —— *Wife's Prol.* 694 If wommen hadde writen stories As clerkes han with-Inne hire oratories. **1387** TREVISA *Higden* (Rolls) I. 365 At Glyndalkan aboute þe oratorie of Seint Keynewyn, wilewys bereþ apples as it were appel treen. *a* **1400–50** *Alexander* 1651 He offird in þat oratori [Solomon's temple] & honourd oure lorde. *c* **1450** *St. Cuthbert* (Surtees) 291 In his oratory he lay, Mikel o the nyght to pray. **1527** *Lanc. & Chesh. Wills* (Chetham Soc.) 20 The maynteynyng of devyne service off the chapell or orrotorye of Saynt Savyoʳ off Stretton. **1597** HOOKER *Eccl. Pol.* v. lxi. §2 In Temples hallowed for publique vse and not in priuate Oratories. **1662** STILLINGFL. *Orig. Sacr.* II. iv. §5 So at Gibeah at the Oratory there, we find a company of Prophets coming down from the high place..prophecying. **1756** NUGENT *Gr. Tour* II. 405 The way to it is full of chapels in the manner of oratories. **1816** SCOTT *Old Mort.* xix, 'Where is Lady Margaret?' was Edith's second question. 'In her oratory', was the reply,—a cell adjoining to the chapel. **1885** *Catholic Dict.* (ed. 3) s.v., An oratory is public or private, according as it has or has not a door opening into the public road.
fig. **1526** *Pilgr. Perf.* (W. de W. 1531) 103 b, For streyght waye he gothe in to yᵉ chambre or oratory of his conscyence, which god hath buylded in his soule. **1880** J. THOMSON *City of Dreadf. Nt.* 27 The inmost oratory of my soul, Wherein thou ever dwellest quick or dead.

†**2.** A faldstool at which a worshipper kneels in prayer. *Obs.*
1697 tr. *C'tess D'Aunoy's Trav.* (1706) 150 When a Person of Quality, or a strange Lady comes in, the Sexton spreads a large Carpet before 'em, upon which he either sets an Oratory with Cushions, or else he leads 'em to certain little Closets..with Glass windows round. *a* **1771** GRAY in *Corr.* (1843) 205 In St. John's Library is what I take for the original of Lady Margaret, kneeling at her oratory under a state.

†**3.** = ORACLE 1: cf. ORATOUR 2. *Obs.*
1513 DOUGLAS *Æneis* VII. v. 173 Responsis, schaw Furth of my faderis oratoury law.

†**4.** A place for public speaking. *Obs.*
1613 T. GODWIN *Rom. Antiq.* (1658) 11 It may be Englished, the great Oratory or place of common-plea. **1729** POPE *Dunc.* III. 199 *note*, John Henley the orator..set up his Oratory in Newport-Market, Butcher-row.

5. The name of certain religious societies in the Roman Catholic Church.
a. (Originally and etymologically.) The ***Oratory of St. Philip Neri*** or ***Congregation of the Fathers of the Oratory***, a society of simple priests without vows, for plain preaching and popular services, constituted at Rome in 1564 and recognized by the Pope in 1575; so named from the small chapel or oratory built over one of the aisles of the Church of St. Jerome, in which the founder and his followers, 'Fathers of the Oratory', carried on their work for six years before 1564. In 1577 the congregation removed to the new church (*Chiesa Nuova*) of the Valicella, in which were conducted the musical services thence called, in Italian, ORATORIO, q.v. Also, a local branch or house of this congregation, as the Oratory at Birmingham, the Brompton Oratory.
1644 EVELYN *Diary* 8 Nov., This evening I was invited to heare rare musiq at the Chiesa Nova; the black marble pillars within led us to that most precious Oratory of Philippus Nerius their founder, they being of the oratory of secular priests, under no vow. **1693** J. EDWARDS *Author. O. & N. Test.* 59 The learned Father of the Oratory. **1885** *Catholic Dict.* (ed. 3) s.v., The Oratory was introduced into England in 1847 by Dr...Newman, who, during his long sojourn in Rome..had studied closely the work of the holy founder. *Ibid.*, The Oratory at Birmingham has remained under the direction..of its illustrious founder.
b. *transf.* The ***French Oratory*** or ***Congregation of the Oratory of Our Lord Jesus Christ in France***, founded by Cardinal Bérulle in Paris, in 1611, in order to strengthen ecclesiastical discipline, and deepen devotion among the secular clergy and the population generally. This congregation was dissolved at the Revolution. **c.** The ***Oratory of the Immaculate Conception***, a congregation founded at Paris in 1852, the members of which have the same aims as the former French Oratory, and follow its rules. **d.** Also in the titles of other societies.
1815 D. STEWART *Dissert. Progress Philos.* (1854) I. ii. 151 *note*, Malebranche belonged to the Congregation of the Oratory; a society much more nearly allied to the Jansenists than to the Jesuits. **1885** *Catholic Dict.* s.v., Among the eminent men whom the French Oratory produced were Thomassin,..Lejeune, Richard Simon, Malebranche, Quesnel, Pouget, Massillon [etc.].

oratory ('ɒrətərɪ), *sb.*² [ad. L. *ōrātōria* (sc. *ars*) the oratorical art, oratory.]
1. The art of the orator or of public speaking; the art of speaking eloquently according to definite rules, so as to please or persuade; rhetoric.
1593 SHAKS. *Lucr.* 815 The orator, to deck his oratory, Will couple my reproach to Tarquin's shame. **1596** DALRYMPLE tr. *Leslie's Hist. Scot.* VII. 14 Bot this.. sumthing hindirit his prais, that his language was nocht mair illustre, conforme to the Romane oratrie. **1691** WOOD *Ath. Oxon.* II. 308 He applied himself to Oratory and Philosophy. **1719** SWIFT *To a Young Clergyman*, That part of oratory, which relates to the moving of passions.
2. The exercise of eloquence; oratorship; the delivery of orations or speeches; rhetorical or eloquent language.
1588 SHAKS. *Tit. A.* v. iii. 90 Nor can I vtter all our bitter griefe, But floods of teares will drowne my Oratorie. **1667** MILTON *P.L.* XI. 8 Sighs..Unutterable, which the Spirit of prayer..wing'd for Heav'n with speedier flight Than loudest Oratorie. *a* **1745** SWIFT *Will. II*, Lett. 1768 IV. 265 A notable mark of the force of oratory in the churchmen of those ages. **1847** JAMES *J. Marston Hall* viii, The state of insanity to which all this oratory raised the populace may easily be imagined. **1849** MACAULAY *Hist. Eng.* ii. I. 259 It is seldom that oratory changes votes.
b. *fig.*
a **1586** SIDNEY *Arcadia* I. (1590) B vij, The prety lambs with bleting oratory craued the dams comfort. **1642** FULLER *Holy & Prof. St.* I. ix. 23 His first care is for his cattell, where dumbenesse is oratory to a conscientious man. **1726** SWIFT *Gulliver* II. i, A child..began a squall,..after the usual oratory of infants, to get me for a plaything. **1858** LYTTON *What Will He do* I. i, Quintilian in his remarks on the oratory of fingers.

†**'oratory**, *a.* *Obs.* [ad. L. *ōrātōri-us*, f. *ōrātōr-em* ORATOR.] Of or pertaining to an orator; oratorial, oratorical; rhetorical.
1534 WHITINTON *Tullyes Offices* I. (1540) 1 In exercyse of oratory crafte. **1589** PUTTENHAM *Eng. Poesie* III. xviii. (Arb.) 197 Either in the Poeticall or oratorie science. **1652** GAULE *Magastrom.* 296 Epaminondas..commanded that those that promised victory should be layd on the right hand the oratory chaire, and the other on the left.

†**ora'tour.** *Obs.* Forms: 4 oratore, 4–6 oritore, 5–6 orature, 6 oratour, oriture. [a. OF. *oratour*, earlier *orator*, *-tur* oratory = Pr. *oratori*, Sp., It. *oratorio*, mod.F. *oratoire*, ad. L. *ōrātōrium*. A northern and chiefly Sc. doublet of ORATORY *sb.*¹]
1. = ORATORY *sb.*¹ 1.
13.. *Gaw. & Gr. Knt.* 2150 Þis oritore is vgly, with erbez ouer-growen. *c* **1375** *Sc. Leg. Saints* xviii. (*Egipciane*) 127 Þai entryt in þare oratore..& kneland, maad þare oracione. *c* **1480** HENRYSON *Test. Cresseid* 8 Within myn orature I stude. *a* **1578** LINDESAY (Pitscottie) *Chron. Scot.* (S.T.S.) I. 116, I will pas to my orature and pray to god for yow... Than this bischop..led him to his oriture. **1596** DALRYMPLE tr. *Leslie's Hist. Scot.* I. 123 Altaris, Kirkes dedicat to sanctes, Images, oratouris.
2. = ORACLE 1. *rare.*
1513 DOUGLAS *Æneis* VII. ii. 127 The kyng..gan to seik belive His fader Fawnus oratour and answair, Quhilk couth the fatis for to cum declair.

oratour, obs. form of ORATOR.

†**ora'tourly**, *adv.* *Sc. Obs. rare.* [f. *oratour*, ORATOR + -LY². Corresp. to L. *ōrātōriē*, and F. *oratoirement*.] Oratorically.
1549 *Compl. Scot.* x. 82 Quhou beit that the said poietical beuk be dytit oratourly.

oratress ('ɒrətrɪs). Also 7–9 **-toress.** [f. ORATOR + -ESS¹.] A female orator.
†**1.** A female pleader, petitioner, or plaintiff. *Obs.*
1586 WARNER *Alb. Eng.* II. ix. (1589) E ij, Because I see Loues Oratresse pleads tediouslie to thee. **1613–16** W. BROWNE *Brit. Past.* II. i. 587 Had such an Oratresse beene heard to plead For faire Polixena. **1660** *Charac. Italy* 14 Provided the Lady Pecunia be your Suada or Oratress. **1848** [see ORATRIX 1].
2. A female public speaker.
1595 *Polimanteia* (1881) 58 Conceiued with teares, accented with sighes; and vttered by truethes naked oratresse. **1747** *Gentl. Mag.* 98 (*School of Rhetorick*) To each fair oratress this school Its rhet'ric strong affords. **1819** MOORE *Mem.* (1853) II. 354 The oratoress gave her opinion pretty freely of the family. **1868** W. WHITMAN *Poems* 83 Listening to the orators and the oratresses in public halls.

†**'oratrice.** *Obs.* [a. AFr. *oratrice*, ad. L. *ōrātrīc-em*, in nom. *ōrātrix*: see ORATRIX.]
1. A female pleader, plaintiff, petitioner, or offerer of prayers.
1432 *Rolls of Parlt.* IV. 396/2 Graunted be his Lettres Patentz to youre seide Oratrice. **1447** *Let.* in *Ep. Acad. Oxon.* (1898) I. 250 Yowr ful devoute oratrice, þe Universite of the study of Oxenford. **1513–14** *Act 5 Hen. VIII*, c. 12, *Preamble*, Your true and feithfull Subgiet and daily Oratrice Margaret Pole. **1559** *Reg. St. Andrews Kirk Sess.* (1889) I. 20 Your wisedome's maist humil and obedient oratrice Elizabeth Gedde. **1594** WEST *2nd Pt. Symbol., Chancerie* §145 Execution against your said poore Oratrices husband.
2. = ORATRESS 2.
1653 *Nissena* 115 Being admired by the people, she came into the Senat, nor needed this fairest Oratrice to win their attention by any artificial Rhetorick.

†**o'ratricle.** *Obs. rare*⁻¹. In 6 orratrycle. [dim. of ORATOR after words in *-cle*: see -CULE.] A little or insignificant petitioner.
1574 in W. H. Turner *Select. Rec. Oxford* 354 Yoʳ pore orratrycles good name and fame.

oratrix (ɒ'reɪtrɪks, 'ɒrətrɪks). Pl. oratrices (-siːz). [a. L. *ōrātrix*, pl. *-trīcēs*, fem. of *ōrātor* ORATOR.] A female orator.
†**1.** A female petitioner or plaintiff: see quot. 1848. *Obs.*
1464 *Rolls of Parlt.* V. 551/2 To graunte unto youre said Oratrices youre moost gratious Lettres Patentes. **1534–5** in C. More *Life Sir T. More* (1828) 373 Your poure contynuall Oratryx Dame Alis More. **1594** WEST *2nd Pt. Symbol., Chancerie* §145 It chaunced the husband of your said Oratrix ..to be bounden in a Recognisance. **1747** *Mem. Nutrebian Crt.* I. 107 The king, raising the princess, said to the queen, Your little oratrix has pleaded too well, not to succeed. **1848** WHARTON *Law Lex.*, *Oratrix*, or *Oratress*, a female petitioner; a female plaintiff in a bill in Chancery [*ed.* **1872** *adds* was formerly so called].
2. = ORATRESS 2.
1592 KYD *Sol. & Pers.* I. iii. 69, I fight not with my tongue; this is my Oratrix. (*Laying his hand vpon his sword.*) **1651** CHARLETON *Eph. & Cimm. Matrons* II. (1668) 5 There needed not much of Rhetorick on the part of this Oratrix. **1842** THACKERAY *Miss Tickletoby's Lect.* i, That magic spell of poesy, which the elegant oratrix flung round her audience. **1865** *Pall Mall G.* No. 210. 5/2 The well-known secularist oratrix.

orayson, obs. form of ORISON.

orb (ɔːb), *sb.*¹ [ad. L. *orb-is* ring, circle, round disc: cf. F. *orbe* (13th c. in Littré). In Eng. the general sense appears later than some of the special ones, e.g. 6, 7.]
I. A circle, and derived senses.
1. A circle, or anything of circular form, as a circular disc or wheel, or (less usually) a ring. Now *rare* or *Obs.* (exc. as in 9).
1590 SHAKS. *Mids. N.* II. i. 9 And I serue the Fairy Queene, To dew her orbs vpon the green. **1658** CLEVELAND *Rustic Rampant* Wks. (1687) 433 The Wheels, or Orbs, upon which Providence turns. **1667** MILTON *P.L.* VI. 254 The rockie Orb Of tenfold Adamant, his ample Shield. **1727–46** THOMSON *Summer* 901 Lo! the green serpent..gathers up his train In orbs immense. **1812** WOODHOUSE *Astron.* xxiii. 240 Day after day, the [moon's] crescent increases, till it is

changed into a full orb. **1821** BYRON *Sardan.* III. i. 91 The Bactrians..fighting inch by inch, and forming An orb around the palace.

2. *Astrol.* The space on the celestial sphere within which the influence of a planet, star, or 'house' is supposed to act.

1727–41 CHAMBERS *Cycl.*, *Orb*, in astrology. An orb of light is a certain sphere or extent of light, which the astrologers allow a planet beyond its centre... The orb of Saturn's light they make to be 10 degrees; that of Jupiter 12°,..that of the Sun 17°,..that of the Moon 12° 30'. **1819** J. WILSON *Dict. Astrol.* s.v., Stars of the first magnitude have 7° 30' for their orbs.

†**3.** *Astron.* The plane of the orbit of a planet, etc.; also, the orbit or path. Also *fig. Obs.*

1726 tr. *Gregory's Astron.* I. 7 The Orbs of the Planets (that is, the Planes of their Orbits) are inclin'd to the Ecliptic in the following Manner. **1732** POPE *Ess. Man* II. 21 Instruct the planets in what orbs to run. **1755** B. MARTIN *Mag. Arts & Sc.* v. 23, I observe you have made the Orbs of the Planets circular, but the Orbit of a Comet..a very long Oval. **1768–74** TUCKER *Lt. Nat.* (1834) II. 605 Whenever we venture to move in an eccentric orb.

†**4.** A kind of fish, of a round form (= L. *orbis*, Pliny). *Obs. rare.*

1740 R. BROOKES *Art of Angling* II. lxxviii. 200 The Orb.. is taken in the Mouth of the River Nile.

†**5.** A cyclical period, a cycle.

1658 J. HARRINGTON *Prerog. Pop. Govt.* I. xii. (1700) 322 The eight years Orb of the Embassadors. **1667** MILTON *P.L.* v. 862 When fatal course Had circl'd his full Orbe. **1697** DRYDEN *Virg. Past.* IV. 8 Mighty Years, begun From their first Orb, in radiant Circles run. **1742** YOUNG *Nt. Th.* II. 208 Not on those terms..From old eternity's mysterious orb, Was Time cut off.

†**6.** *Eccl.* A division of the office of matins: see quot. *Obs. rare.*

1526 *Pilgr. Perf.* (W. de W. 1531) 248 In matyns be communly iii orbes, otherwyse called iii nocturnes..euery orbe conteyneth iii psalmes, iii lessons, and iii responsories.

II. A sphere, and derived senses.

7. *Old Astron.* Each of the concentric hollow spheres supposed to surround the earth and carry the planets and stars with them in their revolution: see SPHERE. *Obs.* exc. *Hist.*

1526 *Pilgr. Perf.* (W. de W. 1531) 188 Y[e] planetes..hath.. an other [motion] by the mouyng of the fyrst orbe, which draweth them with him in his circle euery day. *a* **1548** HALL *Chron., Hen. VIII* 74 b, Set with starres of gold foyle, and the Orbes of the heavens by the crafte of colours in the roffe. *a* **1628** SIR J. BEAUMONT *Dial.* in Farr *S.P. Jas. I* (1848) 153 As waters in a chrystall orbe contain'd Aboue the starry firmament, are chain'd To coole the fury of those raging flames Which eu'ry lower spheare by motion frames. *a* **1677** HALE *Prim. Orig. Man.* II. iv. 152 In matters Astronomical ..we find the old Hypothesis of the Heavenly System called since in question by Copernicus, Galilæus, and Kepler; the solidity of the Orbs detected to be untrue, by the plain discovery of Tycho Brahe and others. **1877** MASSON *Introd. to Par. Lost* in *Milton's Poems* (Globe Ed.) 27 The World or Mundane Universe, as Milton keeps it in his mind's eye.. consisting within itself of ten Orbs or hollow Spheres in succession, wheeling one within the other, down to the stationary nest of our small Earth at the centre.

8. A sphere or globe (in general); anything of spherical or globular shape.

1597 SHAKS. *Lover's Compl.* 289 What a hell of witchcraft lies In the small orb of one particular tear! **1696** WHISTON *Th. Earth* II. (1722) 76 All these..shall rise up, and make a confus'd cloudy Orb. **1736** GRAY *Statius* i. 15 Another orb upheaved his strong right hand. **1796** MORSE *Amer. Geog.* I. 37 By the celestial sphere is meant the apparent concave orb which invests the earth. **1830** TENNYSON *Isabel* iii, Ambrosial orbs Of rich fruit-bunches.

9. a. Used as a general name for the heavenly bodies (sun, moon, planets, or stars); with reference either to their actual form (= globe), or their apparent form (= disc: cf. 1). Chiefly *poet.* or *rhet.*

1596 SHAKS. *Merch. V.* v. i. 60 There's not the smallest orbe which thou beholdst But in his motion like an Angell sings. **1667** MILTON *P.L.* VII. 361 Of Light by farr the greater part he took..and plac'd In the Suns Orb. **1712** ADDISON *Hymn*, '*The spacious Firmament on high*' iii, What tho' nor real Voice nor Sound Amid their radiant Orbs be found? **1757** GRAY *Bard* 136 Think'st thou yon sanguine cloud, Rais'd by thy breath, has quench'd the Orb of Day? **1838** THIRLWALL *Greece* II. xiii. 165 They worshipped the elements, the heavens, and the orbs of day and night. **1871** R. ELLIS *Catullus* lxii. 2 Hesper his orb long-look'd for aloft 'gins slowly to kindle.

†**b.** *spec.* The earth, the world: cf. Lat. *orbis* (*terrarum*), Ger. *Erdkreis*. *Obs.*

1601 SHAKS. *Twel. N.* III. i. 43 Foolery sir, does walke about the Orbe like the Sun, it shines euery where. **1607** —— *Cor.* v. vi. 127 The man is Noble, and his Fame folds in This Orbe o' th' earth. [**1667** MILTON *P.L.* IX. 82 Thus the Orb he [Satan] roam'd With narrow search; and with inspection deep Consider'd every Creature.]

10. The globe of the eye, the eye-ball; the eye. *poet.* and *rhet.*

16.. DRUMMOND *Sonn.*, Poems (1656) 64 And her bright Eyes (the Orbes which Beauty move). *c* **1655** MILTON *Sonn.*, *To C. Skinner on his Blindness*, These eys..thir seing have forgot, Nor to thir idle orbs doth sight appear. **1719** YOUNG *Revenge* v. ii, But, O those eyes!.. Whence didst thou steal their burning orbs? **1822** LAMB *Elia* Ser. I. *Decay Beggars*, Old blind Tobits..casting up their ruined orbs to catch a ray of pity. **1871** R. ELLIS *Catullus* lxiii. 56 Yet an eyeless orb is yearning ineffectually to thee.

11. The globe surmounted by a cross forming part of the regalia; also called *mound*, formerly *globe*, *ball*.

1702 *Lond. Gaz.* No. 3804/1 The Duke of Somerset Lord President with the Orb. **1761** *Brit. Mag.* II. 503 His majesty was then invested with the armill, the purple robe or imperial pall, and orb. **1838** *Office Coron. Q. Victoria* in Maskell *Mon. Rit.* III. 115 Then the Orb with the Cross is brought from the Altar by the Dean of Westminster, and delivered into the Queen's Right Hand by the Archbishop. **1872** O. SHIPLEY *Gloss. Eccl. Terms* s.v., The mound or orb signifies the dominion, and the cross the faith of the king.

12. *fig.* †**a.** A 'sphere' or region of action or activity; rank, station. (Often with immediate reference to sense 7.) *Obs.*

1609 TOURNEUR *Fun. Poem Sir F. Vere* 183 In that mooving orbe of active warre His high command was the transcendant starre. **1644** JESSOP *Angel of Eph.* 27 Evangelists of an higher Orbe then..Bishops. **1649** G. DANIEL *Trinarch., Rich. II*, ccxxxiv, Richard is now in Orbe; or, if you will, In his Meridian Glorie. **1665** GLANVILL *Scepsis Sci.* xii. 66 Whenever we are within the Orb of its activity. *a* **1713** ELLWOOD *Autobiog.* (1714) 1 My Station, not being so Eminent..as others who have moved in higher Orbs. **1747** *Scheme Equip. Men of War* 4 Objects, situated in a quite different Orb, and as far beyond the Sphere of our Capacities as the World in the Moon. **1757** FOOTE *Author* Prol., Those, who adorn the orb of higher life.

b. (from 8 or 9.) An organized or collective whole: a rounded mass; a 'world'.

1603 DANIEL *Def. Rhime* Wks. (1717) 14 For the Body of our Imagination being as an unform'd Chaos,..it be wrought into an Orb of Order and Form. **1606** WARNER *Alb. Eng.* XV. xcviii. (1612) 388 What are these but the mapped Orbs of all Hypocrisie? **1849** SEARS *Regeneration* I. vii. (1859) 57 He regards the race in its totality, as an organic whole, as making one orb of being. **1866** G. MACDONALD *Ann. Q. Neighb.* xiii. (1878) 249 So is the great shining orb of witness-bearers made up of millions of lesser orbs.

13. *attrib.* and *Comb.*, as **orb-like** adj.; **orb-fish**, an East Indian fish (*Chætodon* or *Ephippius orbis*) of a circular form; **orb-weaver**, a spider of the family Argiopidæ, which builds an orb-web; so **orb-weaving** *a.*; **orb-web**, a web formed of lines radiating from a central point, produced by a spider of the family Argiopidæ; also *attrib.*; so **orb-webbed** *a.*

1864 WEBSTER, *Orb-fish. **1886** PROCTOR in *Longm. Mag.* VII. 269 We have in the sun an example of an orb in that particular stage of *orb-life. **1820** SHELLEY *Prom. Unb.* IV. i. 210 An *orblike canopy. **1925** T. DREISER *Amer. Trag.* I. II. xxxi. 367 Her eyes, which were now fixed on him in round orblike solemnity. **1935** W. DE LA MARE *Poems, 1919 to 1934* 335 The white dews drip untrembling down, From bough to bough, orb-like, unblown. **1889** H. C. MCCOOK *Amer. Spiders* I. iii. 53 The round web of the *Orbweaver probably deserves the distinction of having given the popular name cobweb to the whole spinningwork of spiders. **1889** *Science* 23 Aug. 136/2 The spinning habits of the great group of spiders known as orb-weavers. **1941** W. S. BRISTOWE *Comity of Spiders* II. 244 Most orb-weavers renew their webs, other than the framework, daily. **1885** H. C. MCCOOK *Tenants Old Farm* 203 Cocoons spun by an *orbweaving spider. **1889** —— *Amer. Spiders* I. iii. 53, I define an *orbweb as a snare constructed of right lines radiating from a common centre. **1971** *Oxf. Bk. Invertebr.* 150/1 *Meta* is a common orb-web spinner. **1958** W. S. BRISTOWE *World of Spiders* xix. 256 A series of papers..is opening the door to clearer understanding of the unhesitating route pursued by the *orb-webbed spiders in the course of completing their webs.

orb, *sb.*[2] *Arch.* [Derivation: see below.] An architectural term in use from 14th to 17th c., as to the meaning of which modern writers on architecture have expressed different opinions; the view now prevalent being that of: Blank or blind window; hence plain stone panel, blank panel.

Other inferred or suggested senses are: An arched window; a circular boss; a quatrefoil. The early instances follow in a; quots. from modern authors in b. Of the latter the full context should be consulted, esp. that of Willis 1844.

a. [**1395** in Rymer *Fœdera* VII. 795 (Tomb of Rich. II and queen) Et les ditz Masons serront Measons pur xii. Images ..vi. a l'une coste, & vi. al'autre coste..& le remenaunt du dite Toumbe Serra fait ove orbes, accordantz & semblables as dites Measons pur Ymages. *a* **1490** BOTONER (William of Worcester) *Itin.* (1778) 282 Et habet 4 storyes..In superiori historia tres orbæ in qualibet panella. *Ibid.* 283 In secunda et tercia historia sunt duæ orbæ in qualibet panella 4 panellarum. In inferiori historia [*text has* panella] sunt in duobus panellis in qualibet panella south et west fenestræ, in aliis duobus panellis ex parte boriali et orientali [*text has* occidentali] sunt duæ archæ.] **1500–1** *Acc. Louth Steeple* in *Archæol.* X. 71 There is coming home stone to the broach 10 score foot and 5, and to the gallery within the steeple, 40 foot grofts and 10 orbs. **1512–13** *King's Coll. Contract* in Willis & Clark *Cambridge* (1886) I. 610 Fynyalles, ryfant gablettes, Batelmentes, orbys, or Crosse quaters,..and euery other thyng belongyng to the same. *a* **1548** HALL *Chron.* (1809) 639 A mightie buildyng of tymber w[t] towers set in carbles forced with arches buttand & al abilamentes embossed, & the lynterelles inhaunsed with pillers quadrant & the vautes in orbes with crobbes dependyng & monsters bearyng vp the pillers. **1669** SIR C. WREN in *Parentalia* (1750) 304 (Salisbury Cathedral) The whole Church is vaulted with Chalk between Arches and Cross-springers only, after the ancienter Manner, without Orbs and Tracery, excepting under the Tower, where the Springers divide, and represent a wider Sort of Tracery.

b. **1838** BRITTON *Dict. Archit.* s.v. *Orb*, In *William of Worcester's Itinerary*, p. 282, the arched windows of St. Stephen's church, Bristol, are called *orbæ*... The two latter quotations [i.e. 1395 and 1512–13 above] induce the supposition that *orbs* were similar to what we now term quatrefoils. **1842** GWILT *Encycl. Archit.* Gloss., *Orb* (Lat. *Orbis*), a knot of foliage or flowers placed at the intersection of the ribs of a Gothic ceiling or vault to conceal the mitres of the ribs. **1844** WILLIS *Archit. Nomencl. Mid. Ages* 53, I shall proceed to shew that these panels were termed 'orbs'. *Ibid.* 54 In all these examples the word [*orb*] plainly applies itself to a blank or blind window... The fact that stone pannelling was first called by a name that implies a blank window, would explain the history of its introduction into mediæval architecture. **1850** PARKER *Gloss. Archit.*, *Orb*,.. a blank window or panel. See Willis' *Nomencl.* 53. [edd. 1840–45 had explained *Orbs* as 'plain circular bosses'.] *Ibid.* [referring to quot. 1395], The tomb has tabernacles at the sides, between which are placed blank panels (*orbs*) corresponding to them, as may be seen from the drawing of the tomb of Edward the Third (which is exactly similar). **1877** *Archit. Publ. Soc. Dict.*, *Orb*, a mediæval word for a blind window. Also the panels in Third Pointed wall-work; so called because they were as it were blank windows. **1886** WILLIS & CLARK *Cambridge* I. 56 The window in the south wall..is a genuine orb window. [Note] 'Orb' is a blank window or panel.

[*Note.* In med.L. (quot. 1490) *orba*, in AngloFr. (q. 1395) *orbe*, as if for med.L. **orba fenestra* blind window: cf. *orbus luminis* bereft of light, blind, Ovid *Met.* iii. 518, and F. *orbe* 'blind, sightless,..hence also, darke, obscure, without light' (Cotgr. 1611); *mur orbe* a blind or blank wall, 'un mur qui n'a ni portes ni fenêtres' (Laveaux 1828). The explanation 'circular boss', goes with a conjectured derivation from L. *orbis* circle, ORB[1]; but this does not suit med.L. *orba*.]

†**orb**, *a. Obs.* [ad. L. *orb-us* without or bereaved of parents or children: thence F. *orbe* (13th c.) bereft of sight, blind.] Bereaved, childless.

1607 BP. ANDREWES *Serm.* (1856) 59 No father adopts, unless he be orbe, have no child. **1660** G. FLEMING *Stemma Sacrum* 21 Edward the Confessor, who dyed Orb or Childless.

orb (ɔːb), *v.* [f. ORB *sb.*[1]]

1. *trans.* To enclose in, or as in, an orb or circle; to surround, encircle, encompass with a rim or tire.

1645 QUARLES *Sol. Recant.* vii. 32 This span of frailty, plung'd, and orb'd about With floods of Bitternesse. **1673** MILTON *Nativity Ode* xv, Yea Truth, and Justice then Will down return to men, Orb'd in a Rain-bow. **1717** ADDISON tr. *Ovid* Wks. 1753 I. 153 The wheels were orb'd with gold. **1847** TENNYSON *Princess* VI. 153 Remain Orb'd in your isolation.

†**b.** *to orb out*, to shut out as by an orb. *Obs.*

1649 G. DANIEL *Trinarch., Hen. IV*, ccclxxi, The earth of misreport, Knitt vp a Bodie, t' interpose that hight Might Orbe him out.

2. To form or gather into an orb, disk, or globe; to make circular or globular; to round out.

1600 FAIRFAX *Tasso* IX. xciv, To orb their scattered troops, and in firm rank retire. **1635** QUARLES *Embl.* III. i. (1718) 129 And with her circling horns..orbs her silver face. **1649** G. DANIEL *Trinarch., Hen. V*, lxxxii, Princes are still Secure, where they..by Sage fore-cast, orbe themselves about Impenetrable Spheres. **1820** L. HUNT *Indicator* No. 22 (1822) I. 175 Orbing their blood-fed bellies in and out. **1858** O. W. HOLMES *Aut. Breakf.-t.* xii. 264 Two large tears orbed themselves beneath the Professor's lids.

b. *intr.* To form itself into an orb.

1850 TENNYSON *In Mem.* xxiv, [Is it] that the past will always..orb into the perfect star We saw not, when we moved therein?

3. *trans.* To carry in its orb (see ORB *sb.*[1] 7); to cause to move in an orbit. *rare.*

1641 MILTON *Ch. Govt.* I. i, That our happinesse may orbe it selfe into a thousand vagancies of glory and delight, and with a kinde of eccentricall equation be as it were an invariable Planet of joy and felicity. **1863** *All Year Round* VIII. 396 Orbing with motion slow or fleet Their small but perfect fires.

b. *intr.* To move in an orbit (or ? as a heavenly orb). *rare.*

1819 KEATS *Otho* IV. i. 79 O, thou golden Crown, Orbing along the serene firmament Of a wide empire, like a glowing moon. **1842** TENNYSON *Two Voices* 138 To carve out Free space for every human doubt, That the whole mind might orb about.

†ˈ**orbal**, *a. Obs. rare.* [irreg. f. ORB *sb.*[1] + -AL[1].] Of, or of the nature of, an orb; circular.

1603 DRAYTON *Bar. Wars* VI. xxxi, An orbal form with pillars small composed.

†ˈ**orbate**, *a. Obs.* [ad. L. *orbātus*, pa. pple. of *orbāre* to bereave.] Orphaned, bereaved, destitute.

1525 *St. Papers Hen. VIII*, VI. 481 [A realm] orbate and destitute of an hed and governour. **1557** PAYNEL *Barclay's Jugurth* B j b, Departing he lefte hym orbate wihoute lande or lyuelode.

†**orˈbation.** *Obs.* [ad. L. *orbātiōn-em*, n. of action from *orbāre* to bereave.] Bereavement, deprivation (of parents, children, or the like).

1623 BP. HALL *Contempl.*, *O.T.* XIX. vii, How much more easie had the want of a sonne been than the mis-cariage? Barrennesse than orbation? **1798** W. TAYLOR in *Monthly Rev.* XXVII. 517 A conspiracy..conferring on orbation a triple crown.

orbed (ɔːbd, *poet.* ˈɔːbɪd), *a.*[1] [f. ORB. *sb.*[1] and *v.* + -ED.]

1. Formed into, or having the form of, an orb; circular or spherical; rounded; arched.

1597 SHAKS. *Lover's Compl.* 25 The orbed earth. **1601** —— *Twel. N.* v. i. 278 That Orbed Continent, the fire That seuers day from night! **1649** G. DANIEL *Trinarch., Hen. IV*, ccxxvii, To make his Crescent Orbed in an Hower. **1667** MILTON *P.L.* VI. 543 Let each..Fit well his Helme, gripe fast his orbed Shield. **1820** SHELLEY *Cloud* iv, That orbed maiden with white fire laden, Whom mortals call the moon. **1861** *Press Newspaper* IX. 889/2 An orbed mass of the electric fluid. **1871** R. ELLIS *Catullus* lxiv. 65 Binds not a cincture smooth her bosom's orbed emotion.

2. *fig.* Fully rounded like a perfect circle.

1864 LOWELL *Fireside Trav.* 3 An orbed and balanced life.

3. In parasynthetic combinations, as ***full-orbed*** (having a full orb), ***half-orbed***, ***gold-orbed***.

1667 MILTON *P.L.* v. 42 Now reignes Full Orb'd the Moon. **1807** J. BARLOW *Columb.* I. 32 Her half orb'd moon declining to the main. **1839** BAILEY *Festus* xxxi. (1852) 487 Where..the gold orbed orange glows.

†**orbed**, *a.*[2] *Obs. rare*[−1]. [f. L. *orbāre* + -ED[1], after L. *orbātus* ORBATE.] Bereaved.

1616 DRUMM. OF HAWTH. *Niobe* Wks. (1711) 22 Wretch'd Niobè I am,..Seven daughters..And sons as many, which one fatal day, (Orb'd mother!) took away.

†'**orbell**. *Obs. rare.* [a. OF. *orbelle* (15th c.), dim. of *orbe*, ORB *sb.*[1]] A circular surface or plot.

1635 BRATHWAIT *Arcad. Pr.* II. 148 In the lowest part of the garden I might see a curious orbell all of touch wherein the Syracusan tyrants were..artfully portrayed.

'**orbic**, *a. rare.* [ad. *orbic-us*, a former reading of L. *orbēt-us* circular, f. *orbis* circle.] Of the form of an orb; round, orbicular.

1619 SIR A. GORGES tr. *Bacon's De Sap. Vet.* 24 How the bodie of this Orbicque frame From tender infancy so bigg became [transl. Virg. *Ecl.* VI. 34 ipse tener mundi concreuerit orbis]. **1892** *Sat. Rev.* 4 June 652/1 [He] gazes up with rapturous orbic eyes.

†'**orbical**, *a. Obs.* [f. as prec. + -AL[1].] = prec.

1582 STANYHURST *Æneis* III. (Arb.) 91 Thee mone three seasons her passadge orbical eended Sence I heere..dyd harboure. **1688** R. HOLME *Armoury* III. 366/1 Any Cilindrick or Orbicall body.

†'**orbicle**. *Obs.* or *rare.* [ad. L. *orbicul-us*, dim. of *orbis* circle: see *-cle*, -CULE.] A small orb, globe, or ball; a globule.

1610 G. FLETCHER *Christ's Vict.* II. lix, Such watry orbicles young boyes doe blowe Out from their sopy shells. **1657** TOMLINSON *Renou's Disp.* 117 Till they acquire the consistency of pills and then they are formed into orbicles. **1840** GALT *Demon Destiny* III. 23 Orbs and orbicles exploding, burst Like havoc shells.

orbicular (ɔːˈbɪkjʊlə(r)), *a.* (*sb.*) [ad. L. *orbiculār-is*, f. *orbiculus*: see ORBICLE and -AR. Cf. F. *orbiculaire* (14th c. in Hatz.-Darm.).] Of the form of a circle or orb; circular, round.

A. *adj.* **1. a.** Round as a circle or disc; circular, or of circular plan or section.

c **1420** *Pallad. on Husb.* III. 230 Vpbounde, orbiculer and turned rounde. **1447** BOKENHAM *Seyntys* (Roxb.) 182 The hevenys orbiculer revolucyoun From est to west wyth oute cessacyoun. **1596** FITZ-GEFFRAY *Sir F. Drake* (1881) 14 Enclaspeth with her winged eminence The worlds orbicular circumference. *c* **1611** CHAPMAN *Iliad* VII. 222 Quite through his bright orbicular targe. **1664** EVELYN *Sylva* (1776) 504 The trunk or bough of a Tree being cut transversely..sheweth several circles or rings more or less orbicular..one without the other. **1731** *Gentl. Mag.* I. 238 Signing their Names in an orbicular manner, which they call a *round Robin.* **1851** D. WILSON *Preh. Ann.* (1863) I. II. iv. 399 Shields,..some oblong and oval, and some orbicular.

b. *Anat.* and *Zool.* Applied to various organs or structures of circular, discoidal, or ring-like form; *spec.* to those muscles (*sphincters*) surrounding, and having the function of closing, natural apertures of the body, as the sphincters of the mouth, eyelids, iris, anus, bladder, vagina, etc. (Also in L. form *orbiculāris.*)

orbicular spot (*Entom.*), a circular spot on the fore-wings of most noctuid moths.

1615 CROOKE *Body of Man* 165 The naturall motion, which the Ancients called περισταλτικὸν is accomplished by transuerse and orbicular Fibres contracting the guts. **1691** RAY *Creation* II. (1692) 49 The Arteries consist of a quadruple Coat, the Third of which is made up of Annular or Orbicular carneous Fibres. **1761** STERNE *Tr. Shandy* III. vi, Directing..the o[r]bicular muscles around his lips to do their duty,—he whistled Lillabullero. **1840** G. V. ELLIS *Anat.* 64 The orbicular muscle of the eyelids. **1872** NICHOLSON *Palæont.* 212 In Discina, the shell is generally circular or orbicular in shape.

c. *Bot.* Applied to leaves, or the like, of circular outline.

1753 CHAMBERS *Cycl. Suppl.* s.v. *Leaf*, Orbicular Leaf, one of a round figure, the breadth of which is equal to its length. **1785** MARTYN *Rousseau's Bot.* xxiv. (1794) 333 The leaves are almost orbicular. **1835** LINDLEY *Introd. Bot.* (1848) II. 354 *Orbicular*; perfectly circular. **1845** —— *Sch. Bot.* iv. (1858) 35 Seeds in one row in each cell, oval or orbicular.

2. Round as a sphere or globe; spherical, globular. Sometimes *loosely*, Having a rounded or convex (as opp. to a flat) form or surface.

c **1420** *Pallad. on Husb.* III. 891 The meles [= apples] rounde, ycald orbiculer. **1578** BANISTER *Hist. Man* I. 33 This same head [of thigh bone] is almost wholly affourmed by an orbicular Appendaunce. **1622** MIDDLETON *Honour & Virtue* Wks. (Bullen) VII. 367 Here fix my foot on this orbicular ball. **1782** A. MONRO *Anat. Bones, Nerves*, etc. 203 A round head of one bone plays in the orbicular socket of another. **1853** RUSKIN *Stones Ven.* II. viii. §117. 357 Having roses set, instead of orbicular ornaments, between the spandrils.

3. *fig.* Full-orbed, rounded, complete.

1673 MARVELL *Reh. Transp.* II. 395 The ends of your publick government will at last excuse if not hallow, the most orbicular untruth. **1827–39** DE QUINCEY *Murder* (1862) 76 The household ruin was thus full and orbicular. **1841** —— *Plato's Repub.* Wks. 1858 IX. 215 An orbicular system, or total body of philosophy.

4. *Nat. Hist.* Combined with other adjs. of form, to express a combination of the two or an intermediate form; (*esp.* in *Bot.* of leaves), as ***orbicular-cordate***, ***-crenate***, ***-ovate***, etc.

1847 W. E. STEELE *Field Bot.* 116 *Villarsia Nymphæoides.* Leaves orbicular-cordate. **1870** HOOKER *Stud. Flora* 37 *Lepidium ruderale*..pod orbicular-oblong notched. *Ibid.* 346 *Betula nana*..leaves short-petioled orbicular-crenate. *Ibid.*, *Alnus glutinosa*, L.; leaves..orbicular-cuneate.

5. ***orbicular bone*** (***os orbiculare***), a very small bone of the middle ear, at the end of the process of the incus (with which it is united in the adult), and articulating with the stapes.

1706 PHILLIPS, *Orbicular Bone* (in *Anat.*), one of the little Bones of the inner part of the Ear, which is fasten'd by a slender Ligament to the sides of that called *Stapes.* **1892** *Syd. Soc. Lex.*, *Orbicular bone*, a very minute bone of the middle ear, like to a grain of sand..; it is a separate bone in childhood, but by some is looked upon as an epiphysis of the incus.

6. *Petrol.* Containing orbicules.

1824 H. T. DE LA BECHE tr. *Sel. Geol. Mem. in Annales des Mines* p. ix. Diabase... Orbicular D. Spheres with concentric zones of hornblende and compact felspar in a diabase of moderately sized grains. (Orbicular granite of Corsica.) **1857** J. B. JUKES *Student's Man. Geol.* iii. 73 (*heading*) Globular diorite, orbicular greenstone, Corsican granite. **1873** *Proc. Geol. Assoc.* II. 267 The so-called 'orbicular silica'. **1954** H. WILLIAMS et al. *Petrogr.* vii. 132 A few granites have an orbicular texture. **1970** K. C. JACKSON *Textbk. Lithology* v. 280 Orbicular granite... Very commonly, the orbicules show abnormal concentration of the ferromagnesium minerals.

B. *sb.*

†**1.** ? Orbicular course, orbit (or ? Orb, sphere).

1523 SKELTON *Garl. Laurel* 4 When Mars retrogradant reuersyd his bak, Lorde of the yere in his orbicular.

2. *Anat.* An orbicular muscle: see A. 1 b. Also in L. form *orbiculāris.*

1872 DARWIN *Emotions* vi. 149 For the sake of brevity these muscles will generally be spoken of as the orbiculars. **1899** *Allbutt's Syst. Med.* VIII. 39 Where the orbicularis is thus affected the earliest manifestations may..resemble that quivering of muscles [in the eyelid or other facial muscle] popularly spoken of as 'live blood'.

3. *Entom.* Short for *orbicular spot*: see A. 1 b.

orbicularis (ɔːˌbɪkjʊˈlɑːrɪs), *a.* (*sb.*) *Anat.* Pl. orbiculares. [L., = ORBICULAR *a.*] **a.** In full (***musculus***) ***orbicularis oris*** [L. *ōs*, *ōr-* mouth]. A muscle surrounding the lips that is partly responsible for moving the lips and the mouth.

1681 J. BROWNE *Compl. Treat. Muscles* 31 There is also another Constrictive Muscle, which hath gotten the name of orbicularis common to the upper lip. **1733** G. DOUGLAS tr. *Winslow's Anat. Expos. Struct. Human Body* II. x. 136 The Semi-Orbiculares are commonly looked upon as one Muscle, surrounding both Lips, from whence it is called Orbicularis. **1797** J. BELL *Anat. Human Body* (ed. 2) I. II. i. 200 The orbicularis oris, or muscle round the mouth, is often named constrictor oris, sphincter, or osculator. **1906** *Practitioner* Dec. 726 The muscles..which..soon become implicated by the disease when cancer begins in this region [*sc.* the angle of the mouth] are: the orbicularis oris, risorius, buccinator, [etc.]. **1970** *Language* XLVI. 315 Electromyographic data were obtained from the cricothyroid and orbicularis muscles of a female speaker of American-English.

b. In full (***musculus***) ***orbicularis palpebrarum*** [L. *palpebra* eyelid] or (now more commonly) ***oculi*** [L. *oculus* eye]. A flat muscle that surrounds the orbit and occupies the upper and lower eyelids, responsible for closing the lids (voluntarily or involuntarily).

In quot. 1967 *palpebræ* is the gen. sing. rather than the more usual gen. pl. of *palpebra.*

1681 J. BROWNE *Compl. Treat. Muscles* 14 There is held a Dispute whether that these two Muscles be not properly one, and that *Orbicularis* being so generally received; though the one doth depress, and the other..lift up..to make a perfect close over the eye. **1733** G. DOUGLAS tr. *Winslow's Anat. Expos. Struct. Human Body* II. x. 89 The Muscles of the Palpebræ are commonly reckoned to be two, one peculiar to the upper Eye-Lid, named Levator Palpebræ Superioris; the other common to both, called Musculus Orbicularis Palpebrarum. *Ibid.* 91 The Supercilia..may be moved..downward by the Orbiculares. **1797** J. BELL *Anat. Human Body* (ed. 2) I. II. i. 194 Orbicularis oculi, or palpebrarum, is a neat and regular muscle, surrounding the eye. **1887** J. TOMES *Syst. Dental Surg.* (ed. 3) 573 The spasm of the orbicularis was so great that the right eye could only be opened by great effort. **1902** D. J. CUNNINGHAM *Text-bk. Anat.* 376 The orbicularis palpebrarum (m. orbicularis oculi) is a transversely oval muscle surrounding and occupying the eyelids. **1967** G. M. WYBURN et al. *Conc. Anat.* v. 131/1 Incise the fibres of the orbicularis palpebrae and expose the tarsal plates. **1968** PASSMORE & ROBSON *Compan. Med. Stud.* I. xxi. 17/1 Paralysis of the orbicularis oculi abolishes the blinking response, so that the affected eye is totally unprotected from direct injury.

orbicularity (ɔːbɪkjʊˈlærɪtɪ). [f. ORBICULAR *a.* (*sb.*) + -ITY. Cf. obs. F. *orbicularité* (16th c. in Godef.).] Orbicular form or character.

1650 BULWER *Anthropomet.* i. (1653) 16 These Nations distending the orbicularity of their Heads. **1831** DE QUINCEY *Whiggism* Wks. 1857 VI. 175, I have questioned the systematic perfection—the orbicularity (so to speak) of Dr. Parr's classical knowledge. **1883** G. ALLEN in *Nature* 15 Mar. 466/2 Intermediate types between these two extremes of entire orbicularity and minute subdivision.

or'bicularly, *adv.* [See -LY[2].] In an orbicular manner; in a circle or ring, round about; in a circular or spherical form.

1519 *Interl. 4 Elem.* in Hazl. *Dodsley* I. 14 About the earth and water jointly they [air and fire] go, And compass them everywhere orbicularly. **1631** HEYWOOD *London's Jus Hon.* Wks. 1874 IV. 278 It imitates the Spheres swift agitation, Orbicularly, still mouing to Saluation. **1724** J. MACKY *Journ. thro. Eng.* II. xii. 201 A most graceful Arch,..jutting out somewhat orbicularly. **1822** T. TAYLOR *Apuleius* 97 Her garments..orbicularly expanding. **1843** DE QUINCEY *Ceylon* Wks. 1859 XII. 13 The flesh of the peach..is massed orbicularly around a central stone. **1860** ADLER *Fauriel's Prov. Poetry* xviii. 408 They took each other by the hand and danced around orbicularly.

or'bicularness. *rare.* [-NESS.] The quality of being orbicular; orbicularity.

1611 COTGR., *Circularité*, circularitie, roundnesse, orbicularnesse. **1727** in BAILEY vol. II. **1755** in JOHNSON; thence in mod. Dicts.

orbiculate (ɔːˈbɪkjʊlət), *a.* Chiefly in *Nat. Hist.* [ad. L. *orbiculāt-us*, f. *orbicul-us*: see ORBICLE and -ATE[2] 2. Cf. F. *orbiculé* (Godef.).] Rounded; ORBICULAR.

1760 J. LEE *Introd. Bot.* I. xiv. (1765) 36 *Orbiculate*, rounded. **1785** MARTYN *Rousseau's Bot.* xxiv. (1794) 342 Dwarf Mallow has..orbiculate leaves hollowed next the petiole. **1846** HARDY in *Proc. Berw. Nat. Club* II. No. 14. 174 Pileus convex, orbiculate. **1892** *Gardeners' Chron.* 27 Aug. 239/2 The leaves are orbiculate.

b. In *Comb.* = ORBICULATO-.

1843 *Penny Cycl.* XXV. 380/1 Shell orbiculate-convex.

or'biculated (-eɪtɪd), *a.* [f. as prec. + -ED.] = prec.

1656 BLOUNT *Glossogr.*, *Orbiculated*, made round in the form of a circle or compass. **1694** MOTTEUX *Rabelais* V. xliii, On the middle..stood a Pillar orbiculated. **1752** SIR J. HILL *Hist. Anim.* 89 The body of the Medusa is of an orbiculated figure.

or'biculately, *adv.* [-LY[2].] In an orbiculate manner or form.

1856 W. CLARK *Van der Hoeven's Zool.* I. 801 *Cyclostoma*..Aperture regular, rotund, with margins connected orbiculately, reflected by age.

†**orbicu'lation**. *Obs.* [n. of action f. L. *orbiculāt-us* rounded, circular: see -ATION.] The formation of an orb (circle or sphere); rounding.

1647 H. MORE *Poems* Interpretation Generall 424 The circling of water, when a stone is cast into a standing pool, ..might have been more significantly called orbiculation. **1676** SHADWELL *Virtuoso* IV, It comes first to Fluidity, then to Orbiculation, then Fixation. **1788** T. TAYLOR *Proclus* I. Dissert. 97 An orbiculation agrees to the soul, through intellect; but progression and rectitude according to her own proper nature.

or,biculato-, used as combining form of L. *orbiculāt-us*, ORBICULATE, in sense 'orbiculately —', as ***orbiculato-cordate***, ***-elliptical***: cf. ORBICULAR *a.* 4.

1852 DANA *Crust.* I. 264 The..abdomen is very large orbiculato-elliptical. *Ibid.* 289 The form of the sternum is orbiculato-cordate.

orbicule (ˈɔːbɪkjuːl). *Petrol.* [back-formation from ORBICULAR *a.*; cf. L. *orbiculus* (see ORBICLE).] A spheroidal inclusion, esp. one composed of a number of concentric layers.

1931 A. JOHANNSEN *Descr. Petrogr. Igneous Rocks* I. ii. 17 In many glassy rocks there are found certain more or less spherical bodies varying in size from pellets visible only under the microscope..to huge spheres ten feet or more in diameter. These rounded bodies are called spherulites when the constituents are arranged radially..and orbicules when these constituents are in concentric shells. **1956** L. E. SPOCK *Guide to Study of Rocks* iii. 26 A few igneous rocks contain orbicules. These are close spherical concentrations of amphibole arranged radially or of biotite in concentric-tangential pattern. **1970** [see ORBICULAR *a.* 6].

orbific (ɔːˈbɪfɪk), *a. rare*[−1]. [f. L. *orbi-s* circle, ORB *sb.*[1] + -FIC, L. *-ficus* making.] Orb-making, orb-forming.

1855 BAILEY *Mystic* 67 Instant impulse to begin The work orbific.

†'**orbing**. *Arch. Obs.* [f. ORB *sb.*[2] + -ING[1].] The making of 'orbs': see ORB *sb.*[2]

1426 *Contract for Steeple* in Gardner *Hist. Dunwich* (1754) 157 The Walles, the Wallyng, the Tabellyng, and the Orbyng sewtly, after the Stepil of Dunstale.

orbit (ˈɔːbɪt), *sb.* [ad. L. *orbita* wheel-track, orbit, f. *orbis* wheel, circle: 'orbita vestigium carri, ab orbe rotæ dicta' Isidore XV. xvi. 13. The sense 'orbit' of the moon, etc., was also class. L.; that of 'eye-cavity' med.L., also Fr., 14th c.]

1. a. *Anat.* The bony cavity of the skull containing the eye and its appendages (muscles, glands, etc.); the eye-socket.

[*c* **1400** *Lanfranc's Cirurg.* 241 He goiþ out of þe scolle boon, & entriþ into orbitam, þat is þe holow place þat þe yȝe sitt on.] **1548–77** VICARY *Anat.* iii. 27 The Coronal bone, in which is yͤ Orbyts or holes of the Eyes. **1725** POPE *Odyss.* IX. 391 In the broad orbit of his monstrous eye. **1767** GOOCH *Treat. Wounds* I. 331 A patient..who..had a piece of wood forced into the orbit of one of his eyes. **1879** HARLAN *Eyesight* ii. 21 The orbit, in which the ball is lodged, is a hollow cone of bone with the base directed forwards and outwards.

b. *Zool.* The border, or part surrounding the eye in a bird, insect, etc.

1774 PENNANT *Tour Scotl. in 1772.* 109 The orbits of the eyes are black. **1825** WATERTON *Wand. S. Amer.* III. iii. 256 The orbits scarlet and the irides white. **1892** *Syd. Soc. Lex.*, *Orbit*.. In Zoology, the skin surrounding the eye of a bird.

¶ **c.** (By confusion with ORB *sb.*[1] 10.) The eye-ball; the eye.

1728 YOUNG *Love Fame* v. 7 Or roll the lucid orbit of an eye; Or, in full joy, elaborate a sigh. **1850** TENNYSON *In Mem.* lxxxvii, When we saw The God within him light his face,..and glow In azure orbits heavenly-wise; And over those ethereal eyes The bar of Michael Angelo. **1873** BROWNING *Red Cott. Nt.-cap* III. 738 That man will.. through each black Castilian orbit, see into your soul.

2. *Astron.* The path or course of a heavenly body; the curved path described by a planet or comet about the sun, by a satellite about its primary, or by one star of a binary system about the other. (Rarely applied to the (apparent) course of the sun in the heavens, usually called the *ecliptic*.) More recently also of artificial satellites and spacecraft. Also, one complete passage around the orbited body.

1696 PHILLIPS (ed. 5), *Orbit*, is properly the Tract left by a Wheel in the Road; but Astronomers use the word to signifie the way or course of the Sun, particularly called the Ecliptick, as also of any other Planet moving on according to the Circle of its Latitude. **1726** tr. *Gregory's Astron.* 174 Every Planet describes an Orbit about the Sun. **1812–16** PLAYFAIR *Nat. Phil.* II. 91 Apparent Orbit of the Sun. **1871** TYNDALL *Fragm. Sci.* (1879) I. i. 20 The earth's orbit is an ellipse. **1951** *Jrnl. Brit. Interplanetary Soc.* X. 219 He predicted the establishment of 'Earth satellite vehicle' rockets in orbits 25,000 miles from the Earth within about 10 years. **1951** A. C. CLARKE *Sands of Mars* vii. 82 They were now floating round Mars in a free orbit. **1962** J. GLENN in *Into Orbit* 144 Al would also give me the exact times at which the retro-rockets would have to be fired to start bringing the capsule home at the end of one, two and three orbits. **1974** *Sci. Amer.* Jan. 115/1 In its polar orbit it swings close to the North Pole, then moves south across the Equator and finally, having traversed Antarctica, returns north for the next orbit. **1977** J. SCOTT *Hot Pursuit* x. 90 Tracking stations..spotted it straight away when the orbit altered.

b. *fig.* and *transf.*

1759 STERNE *Tr. Shandy* I. xxi, The backslidings of my aunt Dinah in her orbit did the same service in establishing my father's system. **1829** I. TAYLOR *Enthus.* x. 266 In the remotest orbits of religious feeling. **1831** —— *Edward's Freed. Will* Introd. iv. 69 The young horse that, free a-field, makes large orbits over the level mead. **1880** *Academy* 18 Sept. 195 Under 'rights at rest' he considers the 'orbit' and infringement of each right.

¶ **c.** Confused with *orb*: see ORB *sb.*[1] 7, 9, 12.

1727 DE FOE *Syst. Magic* I. i. (1840) 15 Made immortal at his death, and..exalted to shine in a higher orbit. **1815** SCOTT *Guy M.* iii, The planets, each, by its own liquid orbit of light, distinguished from the inferior or more distant stars. **1875** JOWETT *Plato* (ed. 2) III. 536 He put the moon in the orbit which was nearest to the earth.

d. In extended use: An approximately circular or elliptical path traced by something in motion (e.g. round an atomic nucleus, in a surface wave in a liquid, or in a particle accelerator).

1827 [see *planet-wheel* s.v. PLANET *sb.*[1] 5]. **1864** W. J. M. RANKINE in *Phil. Trans. R. Soc.* CLIII. 131 The centres of the orbits of the particles in a given surface of equal pressure stand at a higher level than the same particles do when the liquid is still. **1891** *Sci. Trans. R. Dublin Soc.* IV. 599 The dominant orbit of the electron..as affected during the subsequent flight of the molecule by an apsidal perturbation. **1904** *Phil. Mag.* VII. 454 If the spectra of the elements be due to the motion of electrons revolving in circular orbits, as above supposed, several rings of orbits must exist where there are different series of spectra. **1913** BOHR in *Ibid.* XXV. 11 The forces which keep the electrons in their position—or their orbits—inside the atom. **1942** J. D. STRANATHAN *'Particles' of Mod. Physics* xi. 426 A magnetic field between two peculiarly shaped pole faces serves to guide the electron repeatedly around an orbit in this field. **1962** *Newnes Conc. Encycl. Nucl. Energy* 169/1 As the particle energy rises the radius of curvature of the path in the magnetic field increases and so the particles execute approximately spiral orbits. **1962** I. R. & M. W. WILLIAMS *Basic Nucl. Physics* i. 15 The physical significance of ψ.. means that the exact position of electrons in an atomic orbit or indeed the exact location of the orbit cannot be precisely defined. **1972** M. G. GROSS *Oceanography* ix. 243 In deep water..the water parcels move in nearly stationary circular orbits... The diameter of these orbits at the surface is approximately equal to the wave height.

e. The state of being or moving in an orbit; also *fig.*; chiefly in ***in, into orbit*** (also with intervening qualifier).

1958 *Spectator* 22 Aug. 263/2 The US satellite now in orbit. **1959** *Economist* 21 Feb. 706/2 One observer.. describes the stock market as being 'in orbit', released from the gravitational pull of the bond market. **1959** *Daily Tel.* 21 Nov. 1/2 The United States put a satellite into orbit from Vandenberg Air Force base in California today. *Ibid.*, Recovery from orbit has never been accomplished by us or Russia. **1961** L. MUMFORD *City in Hist.* (1966) xvi. 580 Our descendants will perhaps understand our curious willingness to expend billions of dollars to shoot a sacrificial victim into planetary orbit. **1967** W. R. HINDMARSH *Atomic Spectra* ii. 9 If an ion..has, like hydrogen, a single electron in orbit about the nucleus. **1969** R. AIRTH *Snatch!* x. 99 Morland..said they were great, which sent Giorgio approximately into orbit. **1971** *Nature* 17 Sept. 160/3 A Salyut spacecraft is already in Earth orbit. **1973** R. BUSBY *Pattern of Violence* v. 81 So Charlie's an acid head... He's probably in orbit by now.

†**3.** ? An outer flat ring. *Obs.*

1726 AYLIFFE *Parergon* 483 To the end that a Seal may be called an Authentick Seal, it ought to have an Orbit and some Impression thereon.

4. *attrib.* and *Comb.*

1862 H. SPENCER *First Princ.* II. x. §83 A slow change in the position of the orbit-plane. **1875** KNIGHT *Dict. Mech.*, *Orbit-sweeper*, [a telescope and bearings] invented by Airy, to follow the inclined path of a comet or planet.

orbit ('ɔːbɪt), *v.* [f. the sb.] **1.** *trans.* To revolve round in an orbit; to travel round.

1946 *R.A.F. Jrnl.* May 169 Orbiting the target at low level, Pathfinders' Master Bomber assessed the T.I. markers. **1949** *Jrnl. Brit. Interplanetary Soc.* VIII. 3 The way to overcome this difficulty is to have the object circle the earth at a greater distance. It might, in fact, be convenient to have it orbit the earth at a distance of 22,200 miles up. **1951** A. C. CLARKE *Sands of Mars* xi. 141 Orbiting Saturn was Titan, the largest satellite in the Solar System. **1954** *N.Y. Times* 29 Aug. 39/1 If there are satellites orbiting the earth fairly close to it, the Army Office of Ordnance Research will locate them. **1959** D. BEATY *Cone of Silence* xiv. 154 He had been slowly cruising round Mayfair in the car, orbiting huge squares. **1960** *Daily Tel.* 22 Aug. 1/6 (*caption*) Television pictures received from space by the Russians of their dogs..as they orbited the earth in a 4½-ton space ship. **1963** *Ann. Reg. 1962* 399 Orbiting the moon, and finally landing from a parking orbit round the earth. **1973** *Sci. Amer.* Dec. 47/1 One cannot be sure that real galaxy pairs orbit each other in the parabolas or elongated ellipses demanded by our models. **1975** *Times* 11 Aug. 10/5 In 1971 and 1972, the next Mariner spacecraft to orbit the planet revealed a new..face of Mars.

2. *intr.* **a.** To move in an orbit. Const. various preps.

1951 [see ORBITAL *a.* 2]. **1955** *Time* 14 Feb. 112/3 When Allingham sketched a sun with planets orbiting round it on a pad, he says, the visitor smiled and pointed to the fourth planet and then to his own space-suited figure. **1957** *Times* 7 Oct. 9/2 The satellite..is orbiting too high to be of maximum value for observations. **1962** F. I. ORDWAY et al. *Basic Astronautics* i. 3 Manned space capsules have orbited several hundred miles above the Earth. **1970** *Nature* 3 Oct. 11/1 American spy satellites orbiting over the Soviet Union have spotted 18 new sites. **1972** *Sci. Amer.* Nov. 105/3 Earlier investigations..showed..how muonic atoms behave when the muons orbit within the nucleus.

b. To fly in a circle.

1952 *Sat. Even. Post* 27 Dec. 26/3 Clapp broke off and flew south to drop a flare. I orbited just north of the bridge. **1957** R. WATSON-WATT *Three Steps to Victory* 315 Dive-bombers and fighters were to orbit as required till they were joined by the slower torpedo-bombers. **1969** I. KEMP *Brit. G.I. in Vietnam* iii. 68 We had been orbiting in our helicopter for about forty-five minutes.

c. To go into orbit. Also *fig.*

1958 *Times* 30 Aug. 6/1 The Vanguard satellite which failed to orbit on May 27 probably travelled 7,500 miles into the south Atlantic. **1970** *Daily Tel.* 8 June 16/1 The company suspended dealings in March..and they should be resumed by the end of July. The shares should orbit in next to no time. **1970** *Toronto Daily Star* 24 Sept. 22/1 There is no velocity test on the British ball. So, in effect, the manufacturers could improve it to the point where it orbits.

3. *trans.* To put, send, or place in orbit.

1958 *Spectator* 14 Feb. 192/1 Soon after Explorer was orbited the air below it was filled by television stations with five-minute talks. **1961** *Listener* 20 Apr. 684/1 The news of the first man to be orbited and brought to earth. **1962** F. I. ORDWAY et al. *Basic Astronautics* ii. 25 By 1962 the two countries had orbited over a hundred objects into space. **1970** *Nature* 13 June 1011/1 France has been orbiting modest satellites with her own launcher. **1973** *Sci. Amer.* Oct. 75/3 Coronagraphs orbited in space can be constructed differently from their ground-based counterparts.

Hence **'orbited** *ppl. a.*, **'orbiting** *vbl. sb.* See also ORBITING *ppl. a.*

1956 *Spaceflight* I. 6/2 Whether we can land on all of them is improbable, but orbiting trips will be made to get a closer look. **1958** *Engineering* 28 Feb. 270/1 A vehicle weighing 2,000 lb. would expend only a further 70 lb. of propellent in accelerating from an orbiting speed of 18,000 m.p.h. to the escape speed of 25,000 m.p.h. **1966** *Aviation Week & Space Technol.* 5 Dec. 22/3 The separately orbited satellite modules could be mothballed in space—fully equipped with all experiments, however—until ready for use.

orbital ('ɔːbɪtəl), *a.* and *sb.* [prob. ad. med. or mod.L. *orbitāl-is*, f. *orbita* ORBIT *sb.*: see -AL[1].]

A. *adj.* **1. a.** *Anat.* and *Zool.* Of, belonging to, or connected with the orbit or eye-socket.

1541 R. COPLAND *Guydon's Quest. Chirurg.* E iij, The eyes ..are set within the bone arbytall that is a party of the coronall, & the bones of the temples. **1828** STARK *Elem. Nat. Hist.* I. 44 The Active Gibbon..forehead very low; orbital arches very prominent. **1870** ROLLESTON *Anim. Life* 7 The temporal is never separated from the orbital fossa. **1878** A. M. HAMILTON *Nerv. Dis.* 168 The anterior lobe of the brain is composed of two divisions, the one inferior, or orbital, formed by the several convolutions called orbital.

b. *Anthrop.* ***orbital index*** [tr. F. *indice orbitaire* (P. Broca 1875, in *Mém. de la Soc. d'Anthrop. de Paris* II. 172)], one hundred times the ratio of the height of an orbit to its width.

1879 A. DE QUATREFAGES *Human Species* xxx. 388 The smallest orbital index known is that of the old man of Cro-Magnon, which we have seen to be 61·36. **1904** W. L. H. DUCKWORTH *Stud. from Anthrop. Lab. Anat. Sch. Cambridge* xvii. 104 The mean orbital index of thirty-one skulls is 82·6: that of twenty-four males 81·2; of three females 87·4. **1955** *Chambers's Encycl.* I. 460/2 Similar conventional divisions of the orbital index..are: chamaeconchic ('low orbits') *x*–75·9, mesoconchic ('medium orbits') 76·0–84·9, and hypsiconchic ('high orbits') 85·0– *x*.

2. Of, belonging to, or of the nature of the orbit of a heavenly body; moving in an orbit; pertaining to such motion; taking place in an orbit, as ***orbital motion, revolution*** (as distinguished from rotation on an axis).

1839 BAILEY *Festus* xxxi. (1852) 533 Its æras are all cycles; its events, How strange soe'er, are ever orbital. **1875** TAIT & STEWART *Unseen Univ.* (ed. 2) 126 That our earth will gradually lose its orbital energy and approach the sun by a slow spiral motion. **1932** [see sense B below]. **1949** W. LEY *Conquest of Space* (1950) 48 Probably the manned moonship will have to be postponed until there is an orbital station. **1951** A. C. CLARKE *Exploration of Space* 47 'Orbital refuelling'..is the key to interplanetary flight. It depends simply on the fact that once a spaceship had reached circular velocity outside the atmosphere, it would continue to orbit indefinitely without the use of power. **1961** *Guardian* 6 May 1/4 The Mercury programme itself could be used as a means of sending men into substantially protracted orbital flights. **1961** *New Scientist* 27 July 203 The advent of *Midas* in orbit raises the whole question of orbital warfare. Either manned or unmanned orbital bombers are an obvious starting point for such conceptions. **1962** I. R. & M. W. WILLIAMS *Basic Nucl. Physics* i. 9 The innermost orbital electrons are the most tightly bound to the atom. **1970** G. K. WOODGATE *Elem. Atomic Struct.* iv. 55 A single-electron atom has a magnetic moment associated with the orbital motion of the electron. **1972** M. G. GROSS *Oceanography* ix. 243 (*caption*) Orbital motion and displacement of a water particle during the passage of a wave.

3. Designating a road, railway, or rail or road system encircling a large town; cf. RING-ROAD. Also *ellipt.* as quasi-*sb.*, an orbital road.

1933 *Archit. Rev.* LXXIV. 166/2 Orbital road system around London. **1937** *Times* 13 Apr. (British Motor Suppl.) p. x/2 The plan may provide for orbital and radial roads, parkways, viaducts and tunnels, communications to aerodromes, railway stations, and docks. **1939** *N. & Q.* 1 July 1/2 The proposal to thrust an orbital road through land belonging to the National Trust. **1967** *Times Rev. Industry* Apr. 50/2 Essential features are good car parking space.. and good communications. Orbital roads, motorways and similar positions are popular. **1970** *Times* 3 Feb. 2 First priority for roads, after the orbitals outside Greater London, is Ringway 2 (North and South Circular Roads). **1975** *Country Life* 16 Oct. 970 (*caption*) Near Great Warley. The London Orbital will pass across the fields in the middle distance. *Ibid.*, The London Outer Orbital Route—a far-flung bypass..running around London. **1976** *Conservation News* Nov./Dec. 7/2 Conservationists..are already presently split on their views of the proposed extension of the M25, London Outer Orbital Motorway. **1977** *Modern Railways* Dec. 459/3 This would effectively establish one of the north orbital routes discussed in the Barran Committee's *London Rail Study* three years ago.

B. *sb.* *Physics* and *Chem.* A possible pattern of electron density in space which can be realized by two electrons at the most in an atom or molecule; the wave function of a single electron corresponding to any such pattern.

1932 R. S. MULLIKEN in *Physical Rev.* XLI. 50 From here on, one-electron orbital wave functions will be referred to for brevity as orbitals. The method followed here will be to describe unshared electrons always in terms of atomic orbitals but to use molecular orbitals for shared electrons. **1956** *Nature* 11 Feb. 275/1 The resultant *g* values..will yield data on the orbitals involved in the chemical binding of the central iron atom. **1964** J. W. LINNETT *Electronic Struct. Molecules* i. 6 In quantum mechanics the orbits of the Bohr-Sommerfeld semi-classical methods are replaced by orbitals. *Ibid.* 9 Since each spatial orbital is defined by the three quantum numbers *n*, *l* and *m*, this [*sc.* the Pauli Principle] is equivalent to saying that each orbital can accommodate two electrons. **1970** *Sci. Amer.* Apr. 54/2 Each orbital is characterized by a set of 'quantum numbers', denoting various properties of the electrons in that orbital (for instance their spin, angular momentum and the probability of finding the electrons in various regions of space). **1971** J. Z. YOUNG *Introd. Study Man* ii. 26 They are atoms able to receive electrons in the orbitals of their outer shell.

orbitale (ɔːbɪ'teɪliː, -'ɑːliː). [neut. of med.L. *orbitālis* cyclic, f. L. *orbita* ORBIT.] The lowest point on the lower edge of the orbit.

1920 H. H. WILDER *Lab. Man. Anthropometry* I. i. 47 *Orbitale*, the lowest point in the margin of the orbit; one of the points used in defining the Frankfort Horizontal. **1933** *Jrnl. R. Anthrop. Inst.* LXIII. 30 The orbitales..are found, with the aid of the scriber, by rotating the cranium round its auricular axis until the lowest point on the inferior margin of whichever orbit is being considered is at the same height above the drawing-board supporting the instruments as is the auricular axis. **1974** *Nature* 8 Mar. 165/1 Six bilateral and four single roentgenographic landmarks were delineated... The bilateral landmarks were: orbitale; centre of condylar shadow; [etc.].

†**'orbitant.** *Obs. rare.* [f. L. *orbita* (in med.L. sense) + -ANT[1]. The significance of the suffix is not apparent.] = ORBIT *sb.* 1.

1541 R. COPLAND *Guydon's Quest. Chirurg.* D iv b, The fyrst bone..called Coronall, that dureth and compryseth fro the myddes of the orbytauntes vnto the commyssure that trauerseth the Crane or skull.

orbitar ('ɔːbɪtə(r)), *a.* (*sb.*) *Anat.* [ad. F. *orbitaire* (Paré 16th c.), perh. repr. a med. or mod.L. **orbitāri-us*, f. *orbita*: see -AR.] = ORBITAL 1.

1741 MONRO *Anat. Bones* (ed. 3) 79 Which Parts may justly enough be called Orbitar Processes. **1831** R. KNOX *Cloquet's Anat.* 47 Internal orbitar canals. **1877** HUXLEY *Anat. Inv. Anim.* vi. 344 A strong pointed process, the external orbitar lobe.

B. *sb.* The suture between the zygomatic process and the malar bone; the zygomatic suture.

1782 A. MONRO *Anat. Bones, Nerves,* etc. 92 The two external orbitars are continued, each from the end of the internal orbitar, to the under and fore-part of the cheek.

orbitary (ˈɔːbɪtərɪ), *a. Anat.* [f. as prec.: see -ARY.] = prec.

1827 ABERNETHY *Surg. Wks.* II. 42 The orbitary process of the frontal bone. **1831** R. KNOX *Cloquet's Anat.* 45 Forming the internal orbitary holes.

orbitelous (ɔːbɪˈtiːləs), *a. Zool.* [f. mod.L. *orbitēl-us*, F. *orbitèle*, f. L. *orbis* circle, ORB + *tēla* web.] 'Orb-weaving'; applied to those spiders which spin orbicular or circular webs, as the garden-spider. So **orbiˈtelar** *a.* = prec.; **orbiteˈlarian** *a.* (= prec.) and *sb.* (= next); **ˈorbitele**, an orbitelous spider, an 'orb-weaver'.

1857 MAYNE *Expos. Lex., Orbitelus*, applied by Latreille to a tribe (*Orbitelæ*) of the *Araneidæ*, comprehending those which make their webs in regular network, composed of concentric circles crossed by straggling rays which proceed from the centre: orbitelous.

orbiter (ˈɔːbɪtə(r)). *Astronautics.* [f. ORBIT *v.* + -ER[1].] A spacecraft in orbit or intended to go into orbit, esp. one that does not subsequently land.

1958 C. C. ADAMS et al. *Space Flight* 140 It is not inconceivable that variations of Project Farside, or Kurt Stehling's proposal Saloon (balloon-launched satellite) may hold the key to economy-type orbiters. **1961** *Life* 3 Mar. 33 The Russians will follow their manned orbiter..with a multi-manned moon orbiter..and space station. **1969** *Times* 4 Feb. 13/4 Maps drawn from orbiter photographs can differ by nearly two km., depending on the position assumed for the satellite when the photographs were taken. **1971** *Daily Tel.* (Colour Suppl.) 12 Nov. 12/4 While the Viking orbiter continues to survey Mars from space, the lander will start a robot examination of its surroundings. **1976** *Times* 4 Sept. 4/3 He explained that the failure occurred just after the lander separated from the orbiter and prepared to fire a crucial rocket blast that would knock it out of orbit towards Mars.

orbiting (ˈɔːbɪtɪŋ), *ppl. a.* [f. ORBIT *v.* + -ING[2].] That is moving in or into an orbit.

1957 *Observer* 20 Oct. 14/4 Such tricky problems as traffic regulations for orbiting satellites. **1960** *Eng. Lang. Teaching* XIV. 85 The orbiting prices also smooth the road to merger. **1962** *Newnes Conc. Encycl. Nucl. Energy* 37/2 The number *Z* of orbiting electrons equals the number of protons. **1965** *Newsweek* 20 Dec. 57 After weeks inside an orbiting laboratory, the physiological changes may be so profound that Earth becomes the alien environment. **1969** *Guardian* 17 Jan. 1 Russia yesterday created the first orbiting space station. **1971** *Nature* 23 Apr. 494/2 The orbiting Explorer 42 satellite is beginning to oust rocket and balloon borne X-ray experiments from their position of prime importance. **1976** *Field* 18 Nov. 979/1 Orbiting satellites..can tell quickly and comprehensively what is happening on earth at the present, particularly in the matter of temperatures and wind.

orbito-, used as combining form of L. *orbita* ORBIT *sb.*, in anatomical terms, usually in sense 'relating to the orbit along with (some other part)', as ***orbito-alveolar, -basilar, -malar, -nasal, -occipital, -pineal, -rostral, -temporal*** adjs. (See these words.)

1842 E. WILSON *Anat. Vade M.* 20 It is divisible into a superior or frontal portion, and an inferior or orbito-nasal portion. **1883** MARTIN & MOALE *Vertebr. Dissect.* 104 The large orbito-temporal fossa. **1888** *Amer. Nat.* XXII. 917 A process similar to that which enters the orbitopineal canal. **1892** *Syd. Soc. Lex., Orbito-malar*, relating to the orbit and the malar bone.

orbitoid (ˈɔːbɪtɔɪd). [f. mod.L. *orbitoīdes*, f. *orbita* ORBIT *sb.*; see -OID.] The flat round fossil shell of a Foraminifer of the genus *Orbitoides*, occurring in tertiary limestones in N. America, etc.

1885 *Amer. Jrnl. Sc.* XXX. 70, I found..a small specimen of an Orbitoid.

orbitoidal (ɔːbɪˈtɔɪdəl), *a. Geol.* [f. as prec. + -AL[1].] Applied to (N. American) limestones containing shells of the genus *Orbitoides*.

1850 LYELL *2nd Visit U.S.* II. 91 The bluff was..formed of an aggregate of corals..called by A. D'Orbigny orbitoides. I had seen the same 'orbitoidal' limestone in the interior of Clarke county. **1876** PAGE *Adv. Text-bk. Geol.* xix. 363 The nummulitic and orbitoidal limestones, mainly composed of coin-shaped and globular foraminiferal shields, are undoubtedly the most important of tertiary strata.

orbitoline (ɔːˈbɪtəlaɪn), *a.* (*sb.*) [irreg. f. next: see -INE[1].] Belonging to the genus *Orbitolites*; as *sb.* a Foraminifer of this genus.

1883 CARPENTER in *Athenæum* 15 Dec. 780/2 Absence of any distinguishable differentiation in the parts of the sarcodic body of even the most complex orbitolines.

orbitolite (ɔːˈbɪtəlaɪt). [In mod.L. *orbitolītēs*, f. *orbita* ORBIT *sb.* + Gr. λίθος stone: see -LITE.]

a. The fossil shell of a Foraminifer of the genus *Orbitolites*. **b.** A fossil coral of the genus *Orbitolites* or *Chætites*.

1865 CARPENTER in *Intell. Observer* No. 40. 297 Internal casts of an Orbitolite.

orbitosphenoid (ˌɔːbɪtəʊˈsfiːnɔɪd), *a.* and *sb. Anat.* [f. ORBITO- + SPHENOID.] **a.** *adj.* Belonging to the orbit and the sphenoid bone; applied to a small bone or bony process forming part of the eye-socket, and (in man) constituting the lesser wing of the sphenoid bone; in some lower animals it is a separate bone. **b.** *sb.* The orbitosphenoid bone or process.

1854 OWEN *Skel. & Teeth* in *Circ. Sc., Organ. Nat.* I. 177 The neurapophyses, called 'orbitosphenoids',..are small semi-oval plates, protecting the sides of the cerebrum. *Ibid.* 193 The smooth orbitosphenoid plate of the frontal joins the outer margin. **1872** MIVART *Elem. Anat.* 110 Each of the lesser wings of the sphenoid is termed in Zootomy an orbito-sphenoid.

So **ˌorbitospheˈnoidal** *a.* = prec. a.

1872 MIVART *Elem. Anat.* 83 A pair of lesser-wings, or orbito-sphenoidal parts.

orbitual (ɔːˈbɪtjuːəl), *a.* ? *Obs.* [irreg. f. ORBIT *sb.*, as if f. an assumed L. *orbitu-s + -AL[1]; ? after *habitual.*] = ORBITAL 2.

1828–32 in WEBSTER. **1833** HERSCHEL *Astron.* v. 199 Having learned to attribute an orbitual motion to the earth. **1877** NICHOL in Dawson *Orig. World* vi. 119 In the same direction with the orbitual motion.

orˈbituary, *a. rare*⁻⁰. [irreg. f. as prec. + -ARY[1].] = prec.

1864 in WEBSTER.

†**ˈorbitude.** *Obs. rare*⁻⁰. [ad. L. *orbitūdo*, f. *orbus* bereaved: see -TUDE.] = next.

1623 COCKERAM, *Orbitude*, the lacke of what wee loue, when a wife hath lost her husband. **1818** in TODD. Hence in mod. Dicts.

†**ˈorbity.** *Obs.* [ad. L. *orbitās* bereavement, f. *orbus* bereaved, orphaned: see -ITY. Cf. F. *orbité, orbeté* (Godef.).] The condition of being bereaved, bereavement, esp. of children; also more widely, Childlessness.

1597 J. KING *On Jonas* (1618) 579 Hee hath smitten..thy family with orbities and priuations. **1637** HEYWOOD *Dialogues* ii. Wks. 1874 VI. 127 Wretched is that Orbitie And deprivation, which yet never had, Or euer shall haue issue. **1750** JOHNSON *Rambler* No. 69 ¶6 Nothing seems to have been more universally dreaded by the ancients than orbity or want of children. **1804** W. TAYLOR in *Crit. Rev.* Ser. III. I. 11 In opulent families, where the means of maintenance..are profusely supplied, orbity is common.

orbivirus (ˈɔːbɪvaɪərəs). *Biol.* [f. L. *orbis* ring, circle (see quot. 1971) + VIRUS.] Any of a group of arthropod-borne RNA viruses which cause disease chiefly in higher animals and are similar to reoviruses.

1971 E. C. BORDEN et al. in *Jrnl. Gen. Virol.* XIII. 269 The authors suggest as a name for the distinctive group of viruses described, *orbiviruses* (from *orbis*, (L.), ring or circle). This name reflects the especially large, doughnut-shaped capsomeres seen on the surface of virus particles in negative contrast preparations. It is proposed as a 'genus' name, equal in hierarchy to *reoviruses*. **1974** W. K. JOKLIK in Fraenkel-Conrat & Wagner *Comprehensive Virology* II. v. 236 Since very few orbiviruses have yet been characterized with respect to the structure of their RNA or the polypeptide constitution of their capsids, and since they are serologically very diverse.., the principal criterion for admission to this genus is morphology. *Ibid.*, Although only few orbiviruses have been isolated from vertebrates, antibodies to them are widely distributed. **1976** FENNER & WHITE *Med. Virol.* (ed. 2) xxii. 407 Colorado tick fever virus is the only orbivirus so far recognized as a human pathogen.

orble, obs. form of HORRIBLE.

orbless (ˈɔːblɪs), *a.* [f. ORB *sb.*[1] + -LESS.] Without an orb; destitute of orbs.

1820 MOIR in *Blackw. Mag.* VII. 272 Far—far, within the orbless blue, A tiny lustre twinkles thro'. **1891** *Temple Bar Mag.* 250 Then shall our orbless eyes Behold realities.

orblet (ˈɔːblɪt). [-LET.] A little orb.

1839 BAILEY *Festus* xx. (1852) 351 Natural luxury, and joy and love, Those secondary orblets of our life. **1841** *Fraser's Mag.* XXIII. 461 Flung rudely on the boards which this orblet's stage affords.

orby (ˈɔːbɪ), *a. rare.* [-Y.] **a.** Of the form of an orb; orbicular, circular. **b.** Moving as in a circle, revolving, 'coming round'. **c.** Of the nature of, or pertaining to, an orb or heavenly body.

c **1611** CHAPMAN *Iliad* III. 357 It smote Atrides' orby targe. **1615** —— *Odyss.* x. 588 The world was with the spring, and orby hours Had gone the round again through herbs and flowers. **1818** KEATS *Endym.* III. 180[To the Moon] Thine orby power Is coming fresh upon me.

orc, ork (ɔːk). Also 6–7 orque, orke, (7–8 orch). [In sense 1, a. F. *orque* (16th c. in Hatz.-Darm.), ad. L. *orca*, a kind of whale, taken as a specific or generic name in Zoology. Cf. also ON. *orkn, örkn*, a kind of seal.]

1. A cetacean of the genus *Orca*, family *Delphinidæ*; esp. the killer (*Orca gladiator* Gray, *Delphinus Orca*, Linn.). By earlier authors applied, after the mediæval L. writers, to more than one vaguely identified ferocious sea-monster.

[*c* **1520** L. ANDREWE *Noble Lyfe* in *Babees Bk.* 236 Orchun is a monster of the se..& he is mortal ennemye to the balene, & tereth asonder the bely of the balene.] **1611** COTGR., *Epaular*, an Orke; a great sea-fish mortall enemie vnto the Whall. **1612** DRAYTON *Poly-olb.* ii. 25 The uglie Orks that for their Lord the ocean wooe. **1638** RAWLEY tr. *Bacon's Hist. Life & Death* (1650) 11 Touching that monstrous bulk of the Whale, or Orke, how long it is weilded by vitall spirit, we have received nothing certain. **1667** MILTON *P.L.* XI. 835 The haunt of Seales and Orcs, and Sea-mews clang. **1822** W. TENNANT *Thane of Fife* v. vi, Whole herds of sea-cows and of orcs appear. **1827** tr. *Cuvier's Anim. Kingd.* IV. 455 There are two varieties of the Delphinus Orca, the Orc and the Grampus. **1869** BROWNING *Ring & Bk.* IX. 972 Near and nearer comes the snorting orc.

2. Sometimes more vaguely (perh. derived from or influenced by L. *Orcus*, Romanic *orco*: see OGRE, and cf. OE. *orcþyrs oððe heldeofol* 'orc-giant or hell-devil', also *orcneas* in Beowulf: see ORKEN), A devouring monster, an ogre. Used by J. R. R. Tolkien (1892–1973) in his tales: one of an imaginary warlike people in whom are combined human and ogreish characteristics. Also *attrib.* and *Comb.*

1598 SYLVESTER *Du Bartas* II. i. III. *Furies* 51 Insatiate Orque, that even at one repast Almost all Creatures in the World would waste. **1656** S. HOLLAND *Zara* (1719) 5 Who at one Stroak didst pare away three Heads from off the shoulders of an Orke, begotten by an Incubus. **1865** KINGSLEY *Herew.* I. i. 71 But beyond, things unspeakable—dragons, giants, orcs [etc.]. **1937** J. R. R. TOLKIEN *Hobbit* vii. 149 Before you could get round Mirkwood in the North you would be right among the slopes of the Grey Mountains, and they are simply stiff with goblins, hobgoblins, and orcs of the worst description. **1954** —— *Fellowship of Ring* 15 The last battle..was beyond living memory: the Battle of Greenfields, S.R. 1147, in which Bandobras Took routed an invasion of Orcs. *Ibid.* 23 With the help of the ring he escaped from the orc-guards at the gate and rejoined his fellows. *Ibid.* 339 The orcs were dismayed by the fierceness of the defence. *Ibid.* 346 There was a guard of orcs crouching in the shadows behind the great door-posts towering on either side. *Ibid.* 350 The cut is not poisoned, as the wounds of orc-blades too often are. **1954** —— *Two Towers* 48 Orc-speech sounded at all times full of hate and anger. *Ibid.* 138 There the hugest Orcs were mustered, and the wild men of the Dunland fells. *Ibid.* 171 He was not so obviously orc-like as most of these were. **1955** —— *Return of King* 279 No welcome, no beer, no smoke, and a lot of rules and orc-talk instead. *Ibid.* 412 But Orcs and Trolls spoke as they would, without love of words or things; and their language was actually more degraded and filthy than I have shown it. *a* **1973** —— *Silmarillion* (1977) x. 96 And when Thingol came again to Menegroth he learned that the Orc-host in the west was victorious.

†**3.** A large cask or vessel for liquor, etc.; a butt. (So L. *orca.*) *Obs.*

1638 WHITING *Hist. Albino & Bellama* E v b, One bad them fill an Orke of Bacchus water. **1658** PHILLIPS, An *Orch*, or *Ork*, a monstrous fish,..also a Butt for wine, or figs.

4. *Comb.* (from 1), as ***orc-catcher, -killer***.

1631 P. FLETCHER *Sicelides* F ij b, Because a lover, therefore an Orkekiller. *Ibid.*, That Orke-catcher Ataches. *Ibid.* I ij, That Orke mouth of thine did crumme thy porridge with my grandsires braines.

Hence **ork** *v. nonce-wd.*, to make an orc or monster of.

1631 P. FLETCHER *Sicelides* F ij b, I Orkt you once, and now Ile fit you for a Cupid.

orca (ˈɔːkə). [a. L. *orca* a kind of whale, adopted as a generic name by J. E. Gray in Richardson & Gray *Zool. Voy. Erebus & Terror* (1846) I. 33.] The killer whale, *Orcinus orca* (formerly *Orca gladiator*); cf. ORC, ORK 1.

1866 tr. D. F. ESCHRICHT in W. H. Flower *Recent Mem. Cetacea* ii. 172 The teeth of the Orcas are of quite a different kind from those of the cachalots. **1906** *Windsor Mag.* Sept. 469/2 A school of killers or orcas had quietly come up. **1964** E. P. WALKER et al. *Mammals of World* II. 1121/1 Killer Whales; Orcas. **1977** *N.Y. Rev. Bks.* 14 July 26/1, I was called out on deck by excited voices to gaze on a pod of orcas, or killer whales, that flanked and followed our boat as if in escort.

Orcadian (ɔːˈkeɪdɪən), *a.* and *sb.* [f. L. *Orcadēs* the Orkney Islands + -IAN.] **a.** *adj.* Of or pertaining to Orkney. **b.** *sb.* A native or inhabitant of Orkney.

1661 LOVELL *Hist. Anim. & Min.* 234 Quawiuers..the poor Orcadians eate them for hunger. **1814** SCOTT *Diary* 17 Aug. in *Lockhart*, For this slovenly labour the Orcadians cannot plead the occupation of fishing. **1821** —— *Pirate* Note Q. The Orcadian traditions allege the work to be that of a dwarf. **1860** MRS. EDKINS *Chinese Scenes & People* (1863) 114 She knew I was an Orcadian.

Orcagnesque (ɔːkəˈnjɛsk), *a.* [f. the nickname *Orcagna* Archangel, of Andrea di Cione (active *c* 1308–*c* 1368): see -ESQUE.] Resembling in subject-matter, style, or quality the work or manner of Andrea di Cione, Florentine painter, sculptor, and architect.

1910 W. J. LOCKE *Simon* xix. 261 Call it the Valley of the Shadow, if you like. But don't you think the attendant circumstances were rather mediæval, gargoyley, Orcagnesque? **1933** *Burlington Mag.* Oct. 173/1 He builds upon the remnants of the Orcagnesque tradition and upon Gothic sculpture. **1938** *Ibid.* Dec. 238/1 Lorenzo [Monaco]..may..have been impressed by the decorative style and the pretty colours of Jacopo [di Cione]..because of the very Sienese features which, together with the Orcagnesque basis of the forms, produce a pleasant effect.

orcall, obs. form of ORCHIL.

orcanet (ˈɔːkənɪt). Forms: 6–7 **orchanet**, 7–8 **orcanet**, 8 **orkanet**, 8–9 **orcanette**. [a. OF. *orcanette*, altered from *arcanette*, dim. of *arcanne* (Cotgr.), for OF. *alcanne* (15th c. in Hatz.-Darm.), ad. med.L. *alkanna*, whence the parallel form ALKANET.] The plant *Alkanna tinctoria*, or the dye obtained from it: = ALKANET.

1548 TURNER *Names Herbes, Anchusa*.. may be named in englishe wilde Buglos or orchanet, as the french men do. **1567** [see ALKANET 2]. **1601** HOLLAND *Pliny* I. 381 But those that haue the root of Orcanet in them, need no salt. **1712** tr. *Pomet's Hist. Drugs* I. 48 We have brought to us often-times, from the Levant, a kind of Orcanette. **1736** BAILEY *Househ. Dict.* 446 Orkanet. **1861** MISS PRATT *Flower. Pl.* IV. 50 The Common Alkanet, or Orcanette, used by druggists.

orcein (ˈɔːsiːɪn). *Chem.* [Altered from ORCIN.] A red colouring-matter ($C_7H_7NO_3$) obtained from orcin by the action of ammonia and oxygen, and existing in the dye called orchil.

1838 T. THOMSON *Chem. Org. Bodies* 404 To the substance into which orcin is converted by the joint action of oxygen, ammonia, and water, Robiquet has given the name of orcein. **1876** HARLEY *Mat. Med.* (ed. 6) 363 The blue colouring matter called orcein, which is the essential constituent of these dyes.

orcelite (ɔːˈsɛlaɪt). *Min.* [ad. F. *orcélite* (also used) (S. Caillère et al. 1959, in *Compt. Rend.* CCXLIX. 1773), f. the name of Jean *Orcel* (b. 1896), French mineralogist: see -ITE[1].] An arsenide of nickel, Ni_2As, found as bronze-coloured hexagonal crystals.

1960 *Amer. Mineralogist* XLV. 753 Orcelite... The mineral has a rose bronze color, browner than that of niccolite. **1962** *Mineral. Abstr.* XV. 352/1 Orcélite.. occurs as a bronze mineral making up a large part of a vein in serpentinized harzburgite in the Trebaghi massif, New Caledonia.

orch, obs. (erron.) form of ORC.

orch, var. ORK.

orchal(l, orchanet, obs. ff. ORCHIL, ORCANET.

orchant, obs. or dial. form of URCHIN.

orchard (ˈɔːtʃəd). Forms: see below. [orig. OE. *ort-ȝeard*, parallel to Goth. *aurti-gards* garden, the first element of which is considered to be L. *hortus* (in late and med.L. *ortus*, It. *orto*) garden. Cf. Goth. *aurtja* gardener, and OHG. *orzôn* (:—**ortôjan*) to cultivate. Already in 9th c., OE. *ortȝeard* passed into *orcȝeard*, *orceard*, whence ME. *orchard*; also, with recognition of the second element *orch-yard*, *ort-yard*, or, with later conformation to L. *hortus*, *hort-yard*.]

A. Illustration of Forms.

α. 1 **ortȝeard, ordceard, 4 ortyerd, 6 ortyerde, ortȝard, ortiard,** (ortesyerde), **6–7 ortyard, 7 ort-yard.**

c **897** K. ÆLFRED *Gregory's Past.* xl. 292 To plantianne.. swæ se ceorl deð his ortȝeard. *Ibid.* xlix. 380 Hlyst hider, ðu þe eardast on friondes ortȝearde [*Hatt.* orcȝearde]. **1042** *Charter* in Kemble *Cod. Dipl.* IV. 72 Ða haȝawon porte ðæt is se ordceard æt mærdice. *c* **1450** *Cursor M.* 10473 (Laud) In-to hir ortyerd [*Cott.* orchard] she yede anon. **1506** *Will of Duckworth* (Som. Ho.), The orte ȝarde. **1532** in Willis & Clark *Cambridge* (1886) II. 54 The Garden or ortȝard ouer ageinst the College. **1563** *Ibid.* I. 160 The gardeynes and ortesyerdes belonging to Gonevill. **1579** STUBBES *Gaping Gulf* F iij, Our Ortyards must be measured by the foote. **1693** EVELYN *De la Quint., Orange Trees* 1 In our Ort-yards and Olitorie Gardens.

β. 1 **orcȝeard, -ȝyrd, 1–2 orceard,** (1 orcird, -yrd, -erd), **3 orchærd,** (horechard), **3–6 orcharde, 3– orchard;** (4 **orichard, 4–6 orcherd(e, 5** *Sc.* **orchart, 6 ortchard,** *north.* **orchert, -erit).**

c **897** Orcȝearde [see α]. *c* **1000–1100** Orceard, etc. [see B. 1 a]. *a* **1100** *Gerefa* in *Anglia* IX. 261 Timber cleofan, orceard ræran and mænige inweorc wyrcean. *c* **1205** LAY. 12955 Heo comen in ænne orchærd [*c* 1275 horechard]. *a* **1225** *Ancr. R.* 378 Ȝe beoð ȝunge impen iset in Godes orcharde. *c* **1300** *Thrush & Nightingale* 98 in Hazl. *E.P.P.* IV. 54 Ich habbe leue to ben here, In orchard and in erbere. *a* **1440** *Sir Degrev.* 615 In at an orcherd thei lepe, Y-armede as thei ware. *c* **1470** HENRY *Wallace* VIII. 740 Gud gardens gay, and orchartis gret thai spill. **1535** COVERDALE *Eccl.* ii. 4, I made me ortchardes and gardens of pleasure.

γ. 4 **orchiard, orcheȝerde, -ȝarde, -yerde, 4–6 orcheyarde, 5 orche-ȝerd, orcheyerd, 6 orchiarde, orchyarde, orcheyard, 6–7 ortchyard, 7–8 orchyard.**

13.. *Cursor M.* 8200 (Cott.) Wit-in his aun orchiard. *c* **1394** *P. Pl. Crede* 166 Orcheȝardes and erberes euesed well clene. *c* **1400** tr. *Secreta Secret., Gov. Lordsh.* 108 Lekyn þanne þi subgitz to oon orche-ȝerd. **1523** FITZHERB. *Husb.* §122 Set in a garden or an orchyarde. **1555** EDEN *Decades* 11 To make gardeynes and orchiardes.

δ. 6 **horteyarde, hortyeard, 6–7 hort(e)yard, 7 hort-yard:** see HORTYARD.

B. Signification.

1. An enclosed piece of ground for the purposes of horticulture. †**a.** Formerly, in general sense, A garden, for herbs and fruit-trees. *Obs.* **b.** Now, An enclosure for the cultivation of fruit-trees.

a. *c* **1000** ÆLFRIC *Gram.* viii. (Z.) 28 *Ortus*, orceard [*v.rr.* orcird, orcyrd, orcȝyrd, ordceard] oððe wyrtun. *c* **1000** ÆLFRIC *Gen.* ii. 8 God þa aplantode wynsumnisse orcerd.. on þam he ȝeloȝode þone man þe he ȝeworhte. *a* **1100** *Ags. Voc.* in Wr.-Wülcker 333/24 *Ortus*, orcyrd. *Ortulanus*, orcerdweard. **1387** TREVISA *Higden* (Rolls) I. 115 In þat orcheȝerde Crist was i-take [L. *in quo horto captus fuit*]. *Ibid.* VI. 31 [Mahomet's] paradys þe orchard of likynge [L. *paradisum hortum scilicet deliciarum*]. **1388** WYCLIF *Isa.* i. 30 Whanne ye schulen be.. as an orcherd [1382 gardyn, *Vulg.* hortus] with out watir.

b. *c* **1000** *Sax. Leechd.* III. 252 Beoð.. hyra orcerdas mid æpplum afyllede. **1388** WYCLIF *Eccl.* ii. 5, Y made ȝerdis and orcherdis [1382 gardynes and appil gardynes, *Vulg.* hortos et pomaria]. *c* **1440** *Promp. Parv.* 368/2 Orcherde, *supra in* appull-yerde, *pomerium*. *c* **1475** *Pict. Voc.* in Wr.-Wülcker 810/5 *Hoc pomerium*, a norchard. **1522** *Test. Ebor.* (Surtees) V. 149 The new ortyerde with the gardyns. **1600** HOLLAND *Livy* XXII. xv. 441 Standing upon Hortyards [L. *arbustum*] and Vineyards. **1657** TRAPP *Comm. Job* ii. 11 Their trees suddenly withered in their Ort-yards. **1796** C. MARSHALL *Garden.* iii. (1813) 44 An orchard is a spot to plant standard fruit in which are forbidden a place in the garden. **1838** *Murray's Hand-bk. N. Germ.* 285 Güls.. is surrounded by orchards, which furnish cherries and walnuts in large quantities. **1845** *Florist's Jrnl.* 7 Orchards are portions of ground appropriated to the growth of fruit trees only.

2. *attrib.* and *Comb.*, as ***orchard-bird, bounds, -close, door, -fruit, ground, -land, side, tree, wall***; ***orchard-circled, -fresh*** adjs.; ***orchard-breaker, -maker, -robber***; **orchard grass**, any grass grown in an orchard, *esp.* in U.S., the Cock's-foot Grass, *Dactylis glomerata*; **orchard-house**, a glass house for the protection of fruit that is either too delicate to be grown in the open air, or required to ripen earlier; **orchard oriole**, a North American oriole (*Icterus spurius*) which suspends its nest from the boughs of fruit and other trees.

1876 LANIER *Poems, Psalm of West* 446 We heard the *orchard-bird's small song. **1725** POPE *Odyss.* XXIV. 260 Sets of flow'ry thorn, Their *orchard-bounds to strengthen and adorn. **1818** SCOTT *Guy M.* vi, He detected poachers, black-fishers, *orchard-breakers, and pigeon-shooters. **1889** W. B. YEATS *Wanderings of Oisin* 90 They will lead her home again To the *orchard-circled farm. **1844** E. B. BROWNING *Lost Bower* in *Poems* II. 100 In the pleasant *orchard closes, 'God bless all our gains,' say we. **1881** O. WILDE *Poems* 116 Past sombre homestead and wet orchard-close. **1922** E. K. CHAMBERS in *Poems of Today* 2nd Ser. 101, I like to think how Shakespeare.. ate his pippin in his orchard close. **1900** *Daily News* 12 Sept. 5/1 A visit to the *orchard country in the garden of England is a revelation. *a* **1847** ELIZA COOK *Birds* 11 The *orchard-deck'd land. **1535** COVERDALE *Susanna* 17 Shut the *orcharde dore. **1971** *Countryman* Autumn 201/2 (Advt.), Direct delivery in own transport to most areas (south of and incl. Glasgow) to reach you in *orchard-fresh condition. **1664** EVELYN *Kal. Hort.* (1729) 222 Now.. gather your last *Orchard-Fruits. **1765** *Ann. Reg.* II. 144/2 A seed of the plant which they call *orchard grass. **1882** *Garden* 8 Apr. 244/1 Orchard Grass should never be made into hay. **1884** MILLER *Plant-n.*, Orchard Grass, *Dactylis glomerata*. **1858** GLENNY *Gard. Every-day Bk.* 206/1 These *Orchard Houses, as they are called, may answer well where there is no lengthened frost after April comes in. **1687** *Southampton Rec.* (1877) II. 55 One acre for his *orchard land. **1903** *Daily Chron.* 4 Mar. 7/1 In the orchard-land of Normandy the privately distilled liquor is.. a recognized medium of exchange. **1938** [see *grain-land* s.v. GRAIN *sb.*[1] 18 a]. **1977** P. G. WINSLOW *Witch Hill Murder* II. 126 The Brewster land was orchard land. **1721** STRYPE *Eccl. Mem.* I. lii. 393 Many gardiners and *orchyard makers. **1868** WOOD *Homes without H.* xiii. 242 The *Orchard Oriole, or Bob-o'-link.. is equally notable for its skill in nest-building. **1562** TURNER *Herbal* II. 108 Dioscorides writeth of.. the *ortiard Peartre.. and of the wyld Pere tre. **1859** SMILES *Self Help* 63 Scapegrace, *orchard-robber, shoe-maker, cudgel-player, and smuggler. *c* **1345** *Orpheo* 64 [She] walked in the undertyde To pley in hur *orchardsyde. **1627** tr. *Bacon's Life & Death* (1651) 4 Wilde trees, in comparison of *Orchard-trees. **1876** J. SAUNDERS *Lion in Path* i, The murmur of orchard trees brushing together softly. **1592** SHAKS. *Rom. & Jul.* II. ii. 63 The *Orchard walls are high, and hard to climbe. **1633** P. FLETCHER *Purple Isl.* I. ii, Where by the orchyard walls The learned Chume with stealing water crawls.

ˈorcharded, *a.* [f. prec. + -ED[2].] Furnished with orchards; planted with fruit-trees.

1757 *Boston News-Letter* 17 Mar. 2/2 To be sold.. Thirteen Acres of Land, well orcharded. **1791** J. BYNG *Torrington Diaries* (1935) II. 350 Most religious houses have the same kind of low sequester'd situation; and were well orcharded, and well supplied with ponds. **1968** G. JONES *Hist. Vikings* III. iii. 231 Its one perdurable asset was its rich and orcharded soil.

ˈorcharding. [f. as prec. + -ING[1].]

1. The cultivation of fruit-trees in orchards.

1664 EVELYN *Pomona* v. (1729) 67 All land is not fit for Orcharding. **1804** *Ann. Reg.* 842/1 This example probably induced orcharding in Herefordshire.. on a much larger scale. **1892** *Boston* (Mass.) *Jrnl.* 16 Jan. 1/4 An address.. upon 'The Advances of Orcharding in New England'.

†**2.** *concr.* Land laid out or planted with fruit-trees. *Obs.* (Chiefly American.)

1654 in C. W. Manwaring *Digest of Early Connecticut Probate Rec.* (1904) I. 155 One halfe of all my howsing, Barnes and orcharding. **1721** *Lond. Gaz.* No. 5951/4 Five Acres of Orcharding. **1788** *Massachus. Spy* 19 June 4/3 Said Farm consists of mowing, pasturing, and orcharding, and is well watered. **1818** *Ibid.* 25 Feb. 1/2 [A farm] is well proportioned into Mowing, Pasturing, Ploughland, Woodland and Orcharding. **1863** *Rep. Maine Board Agric.* 142 One acre of orcharding on suitable soil.. will produce three times the amount in value of any other crop.

ˈorchardist. [f. as prec. + -IST.] One who cultivates an orchard or orchards; a fruit-grower.

1794 T. S. D. BUCKNALL in *Trans. Soc. Arts* XII. 211 As I have long wished to introduce the name of orchardist, I here desire it may take place. **1862** THOREAU *Excurs., Wild Apples* (1863) 292, I wonder all orchardists do not get a scion from that tree. **1890** *Chamb. Jrnl.* 27 Sept. 614/1 An enormously augmented consumption of fruit, for which the British orchardist.. was not prepared.

ˈorchardman. [f. as prec. + MAN *sb.*] = prec.

1885 *Athenæum* 14 Feb. 220/1 Some of the chief prizes were gained by English orchardmen. **1892** *Standard* 12 July 5/2 Between the orchardman of East Kent and the householder in London, intervene the salesman and the greengrocer.

†**ˈorchat.** *Obs.* Affected form for ORCHARD, after Gr. ὄρχατος row of trees, garden.

(*Orchat*, *orchet*, or *worchet* is also a northern dialect form (Cumbld., Roxb.) for Sc. *orchart*, ORCHARD.)

1708 J. PHILIPS *Cyder* I. 9 His Fruit.. in Summer's Pride, When other Orchats smile, abortive fail. *Ibid.* 18 Wouldst thou, thy Vats with gen'rous Juice should froth? Respect thy Orchats. [**1802** in Anderson *Cumbld. Ball.* 39 The throssle.. Aye in our worchet welcomes spring.]

orchel(l, orchella: see ORCHIL, ORCHILLA.

†**orcheˈmatical**, *a.* *Obs. rare.* [f. Gr. ὀρχηματικ-ός (f. ὀρχηματ- dancing, f. ὀρχέεσθαι to dance: see -IC) + -AL[1].] Pertaining to dancing; in quot. *fig.* Characterized by 'skipping' or omission of intermediate numbers.

1583 T. WATSON *Centurie of Loue* lxxx, The foote of the piller [of verses] is Orchematicall, yat is to say, founded by transilition or ouer skipping of number by rule and order, as from 1 to 3, 5, 7, and 9.

orchen, orcherd(e, obs. ff. URCHIN, ORCHARD.

orchesography (ɔːkɪˈsɒgrəfɪ). *rare.* ? *Obs.* [ad. F. *orchésographie* (title of a book by J. Tabourot, publ. in 1589), irreg. f. Gr. ὄρχησις, ὀρχησε- dancing + -O-GRAPHY.] The description or notation of dancing by means of diagrams, etc.

1706 J. WEAVER (*title*) Orchesography, or the Art of Dancing by Characters and Demonstrative Figures. *a* **1843** SOUTHEY *Comm.-pl. Bk.* IV. 566 The art of Orchesography, or denoting the several steps and motions in dancing by characters, was invented by M. Beauchamp.

orchester, variant of ORCHESTRE.

orchestic (ɔːˈkɛstɪk), *a.* and *sb.* [ad. Gr. ὀρχηστικ-ός, f. ὀρχηστ-ής dancer: see -IC.]

A. *adj.* Of or pertaining to dancing.

1850 LEITCH tr. *C. O. Müller's Anc. Art* §44 That feeling for what is significant and beautiful in the human form.. found its gratification in the food afforded to it by the orchestic arts. **1869** W. SMITH *Dict. Gr. & Rom. Antiq.* (ed. 2) 1061 The athletic and orchestic arts attained about Ol. 50 a high degree of perfection.

B. *sb.* (more freq. in pl. **orchestics**.) The art of dancing.

1850 LEITCH tr. *C. O. Müller's Anc. Art* §20 This series of arts reaches its highest point in mimic orchestics. *Ibid.* §77 Gymnastics and orchestics, arts which were exercised with the greatest zeal. **1864** J. HADLEY *Ess.* (1873) 81 The silent art of orchestic has its arses and theses, its trochees and iambi,.. not less truly than music and poetry.

orchestra (ˈɔːkɪstrə). [a. L. *orchēstra*, a. Gr. ὀρχήστρα the space on which the chorus danced, f. ὀρχέεσθαι to dance, ὀρχηστήρ, -τής dancer. Formerly stressed *or'chestra*, e.g. by Byron.]

1. a. In the ancient Greek theatre, A large semicircular space in front of the stage, where the chorus danced and sang.

In the Roman theatre, the orchestra was reserved for the seats of senators and persons of distinction.

1606 HOLLAND *Sueton.* 17 He passed directly from the Stage by the Orchestra, to take up his place among the Knights. **1611** CORYAT *Crudities* 299 It [Theatre of Vicenza] hath an Orchestra made in it according to the imitation of the Roman Orchestraes. **1647** SIR R. STAPYLTON *Juvenal* 121 To furnish the orchestra, next the stage. **1734** tr. *Rollin's Anc. Hist.* (1827) I. 126 The orchestra.. amongst the Greeks was the place assigned for the pantomimes and dancers. **1900** W. L. COURTNEY *Idea of Tragedy* 15 A huge semi-circle of seats, perhaps first made of wood, afterwards of stone, looked down upon a central portion, called the orchestra, and allotted to the chorus.

fig. **1658** SIR T. BROWNE *Hydriot.* iv. 39 They may sit in the Orchestra, and noblest Seats of Heaven.

b. Dancing; title of a poem on dancing.

1596 DAVIES (*title*) Orchestra, or a poeme of Dauncinge. **1599** MARSTON *Sco. Villanie* III. xi. 225 Praise but Orchestra and the skipping Art, You shall command him, faith you haue his hart Euen capring in your fist.

c. In modern use, a section of the auditorium of a theatre, now usually the forward part or all of the main floor. Chiefly *U.S.*

1768 STERNE *Sentimental Journey* I. 192 At the end of the orchestra.. there is a small esplanade... Though you stand, as in the parterre, you pay the same price as in the orchestra. **1786** *Independent Jrnl.* (N.Y.) 5 Aug. 2 The Pit is very large, and the Theatrum and Orchestra elegant and commodious. **1872** *Chicago Tribune* 28 Mar. 5/4 The interior will contain an orchestra and three circles. **1911** *World's Work* (N.Y.) Sept. 14840/1 They were accustomed, when they went to the theatre, to pay an extra half dollar for seats in the front rows of the orchestra. **1924** D. LAWRENCE *True Story Woodrow Wilson* 117 A President..cannot sit in the orchestra or in the balcony. **1927** *Amer. Speech* Oct. 23 In the early days of the English theatre what we know as the 'orchestra' or parquet floor of the house, was called the 'pit'. **1961** BOWMAN & BALL *Theatre Lang.* 242 *Orchestra* 1. The seating area on the main level of an auditorium.

2. a. That part of a theatre or other public building assigned to the band of performers on musical instruments (and, in a concert-room, to the chorus of singers). **b.** A building or structure for a band of instrumental performers; a band-stand.

1724 *Short Explic. For. Wds. Mus. Bks., Orchestra*, is that Part of the Theater, where the Musicians sit with their Instruments to perform. **1787** P. BECKFORD *Lett. Italy* (1805) I. 283 Orchestras were erected in different parts, and the common people danced in the center, having the sky for a canopy. **1817** MAR. EDGEWORTH *Harrington* vii, The impatient sticks in the pit, and shrill catcalls in the gallery, had begun to contend with the music in the orchestra. **1880** W. S. ROCKSTRO in Grove *Dict. Mus.* II. 560 In modern theatres the normal position of the Orchestra is in front of the Stage, but on a level with the floor of the Stalls and Pit. .. In concert-rooms, the Orchestra is usually placed at one end of the apartment, at such a height above the general level of the floor that the full length figure of a Performer, standing in front, may be visible to a seated audience.

3. a. The company of musicians themselves; a company of performers of concerted instrumental music in a theatre, concert-room, etc. (either alone, or as accompaniment to voices). *fig.*

More restricted in use than *band*; the 'strings' or instruments of the viol class being always present and usually of fundamental importance in an *orchestra*.

1720 GAY *To W. Pulteney* 191 But, hark! the full orchestra strike the strings. **1753** HANWAY *Trav.* (1762) I. VII. xc. 413 The orchestra consists of about fifty musicians. **1811** BYRON *Hints fr. Hor.* 308 The pert shopkeeper, whose throbbing ear Aches with orchestras which he pays to hear. **1880** W. S. ROCKSTRO in Grove *Dict. Mus.* II. 561 The term Orchestra is also applied, collectively, to the body of Instrumental Performers officiating at a Theatre, in a Concert-room, or on a Stage or raised Platform in the open air. **1880** 'VERN. LEE' *Stud. Italy* III. ii. 100 The singular effect produced by the sight of an orchestra entirely composed of women.

fig. **1742** YOUNG *Nt. Th.* IV. 650 High heav'n's orchestra chaunts amen to man. **1927** CHESTERTON *Coll. Poems* 40, I salute your three violinists... They play my accompaniment; but I shall take no notice of any accompaniment; I myself am a complete orchestra. **1958** M. KENNEDY *Outlaws on Parnassus* v. 77 Writers using an orchestra of minds to tell their story for them were obliged to consider..the variety of language, as used by different minds.

b. *transf.* The set of instruments played by such a company of musicians.

1834 MRS. SOMERVILLE *Connex. Phys. Sc.* xvii. (1849) 168 The sounds of an entire orchestra may be transmitted and reciprocated. **1880** W. S. ROCKSTRO in Grove *Dict. Mus.* II. 561 We constantly hear of 'an Orchestra consisting of thirty stringed Instruments, with a full complement of Wind'. **1888** MISS A. K. GREEN *Behind Closed Doors* iv, Hearing the bewildering tones of an orchestra mingling with the hum of many voices.

4. *attrib.* and *Comb.*, as ***orchestra chair, leader, pitch***, etc.; **orchestra pit**, the space in front of, and below, the stage, where the orchestra plays; **orchestra seat** (*U.S.*), **stall**, a seat in a theatre in the orchestra; also, a seat in a theatre next to the orchestra and stage.

1836 DUBOURG *Violin* ix. (1878) 269 Old Baumgarten, who was orchestra-leader at Covent Garden. **1849** *Theatrical Programme* 11 June 22 New Strand Theatre... In order to add to the convenience of the Audience, the Orchestra Stalls have been made more commodious. **1852** J. J. SEIDEL *Organ* 22 The so-called chamber-pitch..at this time agreed with the orchestra-pitch. **1856** *Porter's Spirit of Times* 20 Dec. 262 Laura Keene's Theatre..Reserved Orchestra Seats, 75 cents... Seats in orchestra stalls, $1 each. **1872** *Chicago Jrnl.* 18 July 3/1 The house is divided into an orchestra circle, which includes the entire main floor, Mr. McVicker having decided to discard the names parquet and parquet circle, orchestra and orchestra chairs, and dress circles of first and second balcony circle. **1874** W. LENNOX *My Recoll.* II. 108, I was ensconced in a snug orchestra stall. **1895** *N.Y. Dramatic News* 19 Oct. 3/4 You wouldn't know the orchestra seats were $1,..the scale 75, 50, 25 being displayed everywhere. **1901** Orchestra stall [see STALL *sb.*[1] 5 c]. **1903** *Smart Set* IX. 57/1 There would be a modest little dinner at a quiet French restaurant..and an orchestra-chair at the Metropolitan. **1923** G. SELDES in *Vanity Fair* (N.Y.) Jan. 57/2 It [*sc.* the revue] corresponds to those de luxe railway trains which are always exactly on time..; jazz or symphony may sound from the orchestra pit, but underneath is the real tone of the revue, the steady, incorruptible purr of the dynamo. **1932** *Times Lit. Suppl.* 24 Nov. 888/3 The only other playbill reference..is a King's Theatre bill for July 13 [1831], which advertised stalls and orchestra places at a guinea each for a concert. **1940** M. DE LA ROCHE *Whiteoak Chron.* II. vii. 241 He had got orchestra chairs for a Russian vaudeville. **1952** GRANVILLE *Dict. Theatr. Terms* 128 *Orchestra stalls*, the seats nearest the orchestra. **1956** G. DURRELL *My Family* viii. 109 Two of them were thrown into the orchestra pit before someone had the sense to lower the curtain. **1977** R. BARNARD *Death on High C's* xv. 155 The opening chords of *Rigoletto* were sounding from the orchestra pit. **1977** *Times* 24 Sept. 12/7 Two sweeping shell-like roofs..cover all but 10 rows of orchestra seats... The opera house sits on a hillside.

orchestral (ɔːˈkɛstrəl, ˈɔːkɪstrəl), *a.* [f. prec. + -AL[1].] Pertaining or relating to, composed for, or performed by, an orchestra (sense 3). Also *transf.* in ***orchestral effects***.

orchestral-accompanied in quot. 1844 = having an orchestral accompaniment, orchestrally accompanied.

In names of organ-stops, indicating similarity in tone to the instrument used in the orchestra, as ***orchestral flute***.

1811 BUSBY *Dict. Mus.* (ed. 3), *Orchestral*, an epithet given to music intended for the orchestra. **1844** J. T. HEWLETT *Parsons & W.* viii, With..orchestral-accompanied imitations. **1869** OUSELEY *Counterp.* xxiii. 182 Until the student had gone through a course of instrumentation and orchestral scoring. **1888** KIPLING *In Black & White* 66 It [*sc.* the Religion] added an air-line postal *dak*, and orchestral effects. **1889** W. H. STONE in Grove *Dict. Mus.* IV. 181 The modern orchestral or slide Trumpet..is made of brass, mixed metal, or silver. **1898** STAINER & BARRETT *Dict. Mus. Terms* s.v. *Flute* (4), Titles appended to flute-stops... Implying that the quality of tone is similar to the modern flute,..as orchestral flute,..concert-flute. **1918** *Sphere* 9 Feb. 125/1 The orchestral effects of Monday night's raid.

Hence **orˈchestrally** *adv.*

1880 E. PROUT in Grove *Dict. Mus.* I. 387 These are treated orchestrally rather than as solo instruments. **1897** [see ORCHESTRATION b].

orchestralist (ɔːˈkɛstrəlɪst). [f. ORCHESTRAL *a.* + -IST.] A writer of orchestral music; an orchestrator.

1899 F. J. CROWEST *Beethoven* 221 The enharmonic change in the first movement..again illustrates the wonderful resources of this king of orchestralists.

†**orˈchestran**, *a. Obs. rare*[−1]. = ORCHESTRAL.

1765 *Meretriciad* 48 Then, solus, hops a dull Orchestran flute.

orchestrate (ˈɔːkɪstreɪt), *v.* [f. ORCHESTRA + -ATE 3, perh. after mod.F. *orchestrer* (1878 in *Dict. Acad.*).] **a.** *trans.* To compose or arrange for an orchestra; to score for orchestral performance. Also *absol.* Hence **ˈorchestrated** *ppl. a.*

1880 *Daily Tel.* 19 Feb., This brief and cleverly orchestrated symphony is instinct with profound melancholy. **1882** *Standard* 27 Nov. 3/6 The..song..is capitally written, and orchestrated with notable skill. **1889** *Pall Mall G.* 4 June 2, I got into the way of orchestrating and writing for every instrument. **1896** *Times* 28 Aug. 4/3 A composer who can write sparkling tunes and knows how to orchestrate.

b. *fig.* To combine harmoniously, like instruments in an orchestra.

1883 *Blackw. Mag.* Oct. 437 A symphony of accordant and orchestrated spirits. **1956** H. WHITEHALL in *Kenyon Rev.* XVIII. 418 The traditional 'ideal' metrical patterns..have been 'orchestrated' since Marlowe. **1957** *Times Lit. Suppl.* 6 Dec. 789/2 *Nostromo*, greatest and most splendidly orchestrated of all his fictions. **1967** C. L. WRENN *Word & Symbol* 11 Swinburne's poem *Dolores*. Here there is a kind of orchestrated language which conveys a mood of meaning but no clearly describable sense. **1969** *Daily Tel.* 25 Nov. 30 Russia and America yesterday ratified the treaty banning the spread of nuclear weapons. They chose the same day by a diplomatic agreement typical of the way the two super-Powers are 'orchestrating' their moves in this front. **1974** *Guardian* 23 Jan. 2/8 The White House deployed its heavy artillery today... The counter-attack was well orchestrated. **1975** *N.Y. Times* 31 Oct. 11/6 Planning and organization were particularly striking today, when three busloads of foreign journalists were brought to the staging camps on an officially sponsored visit. The enthusiasm that greeted them was as carefully orchestrated as is the march itself. **1977** *Time* 7 Mar. 8/2 Owen helped to orchestrate the European Community's fishing agreement with the Soviet Union.

orchestration (ɔːkɪˈstreɪʃən). [f. prec., or its source: see -ATION. Cf. mod.F. *orchestration* (1878 in *Dict. Acad.*).] **a.** The action or art of composing or arranging music for an orchestra; the style in which a piece of music is orchestrated; instrumentation of orchestral music.

1864 in WEBSTER. **1864** *Reader* 17 Sept. 364 The reveries of Lorenzo and Jessica are set to soft dreamy strains, with orchestration of no less delicate texture. **1876** *Athenæum* 7 Oct. 472/1 The setting of the vocal parts is as splendid as the orchestration is picturesque and powerful. **1889** *Ibid.* 5 June 10/2 No master of orchestration has had a clearer insight into the individual character and colour of each instrument.

b. *fig.* Harmonious combination, as of the parts or instruments in an orchestra.

1888 F. T. MARZIALS *Victor Hugo* 98 Music will make them immortal, a kind of superb verbal orchestration that for variety and power, for 'sonority' and brilliance of effect, has no equal in French dramatic verse. **1897** DOWDEN *Fr. Lit.* 378 His soul echoed orchestrally the orchestrations of nature and of humanity. **1900** G. ILES *Flame, Electr. & the Camera* 252 A new orchestration of inquiry is possible by means of the instruments created for him by the electrician. **1905** *Smart Set* Sept. 113/1 Suddenly there was developed a terrific orchestration of chromatic odors. **1936** *Essays & Stud.* XXI. 150 *The Wreck of the Deutschland* has a completeness, an intellectual and emotional unity, a subtlety and variety of verbal orchestration which are unique not only in English but in the literature of the world. **1953** J. S. HUXLEY *Evolution in Action* vi. 138 The world community which we envisage and hope to bring to the birth is a variety-in-unity. In the useful phrase of the American writer, L. K. Frank, it involves an orchestration of cultures. **1956** H. WHITEHALL in *Kenyon Rev.* XVIII. 418 Yet 'orchestration' is affected by another feature of English. **1959** [see BUILD-UP c]. **1966** *Economist* 2 Apr. 17/2 What is required is the orchestration of the western countries' common interest in reaching an arrangement with Russia. **1975** *Country Life* 16 Jan. 139/2 Braque..achieved a marvellous orchestration of colours and forms. **1975** *New Yorker* 5 May 132/2 Each night, the great orchestration of the evening news went on. **1977** *Time* 17 Oct. 22/1 A conference that collapsed because of poor orchestration was even worse than no conference at all.

c. An overcoat. *U.S. slang.*

1940 *Music Makers* May 37/3 *Orchestration*, an overcoat. **1970** in C. MAJOR *Dict. Afro-Amer. Slang.*

orchestrator (ˈɔːkɪstreɪtə(r)). [f. ORCHESTRATE *v.* + -OR.] One who composes or arranges music for an orchestra, band, etc. Also *fig.*

1907 E. WALKER *Hist. Mus. Eng.* 306 As an orchestrator he [*sc.* Elgar] is among the very greatest in musical history. **1927** *Observer* 20 Nov. 14/4 Liszt, as an orchestrator, seems to overtop the other. **1954** *Grove's Dict. Mus.* (ed. 5) VII. 56/2 Although he [*sc.* Ravel] is a born orchestrator and his command of the medium is unsurpassed, hardly any of his works were originally conceived for the orchestra. **1974** *Times Lit. Suppl.* 1 Nov. 1226/3 An effort was made..to smooth away the more absurd elements of 'crusade' historiography... The orchestrator of this campaign was to be Ricardo de la Cierva, a dynamic and prolific historian. **1976** *Gramophone* May 1750/2, I had no idea what a superb orchestrator he was before I heard that record.

orchestre, -ter (ˈɔːkɪstə(r), *formerly* ɔːˈkɛstə(r)). [a. F. *orchestre* (1547 in Hatz.-Darm.), f. L. *orchestra*: see above.] = ORCHESTRA.

1623 COCKERAM, *Orchester*, a Scaffold. **1658** PHILLIPS, *Orchester*, that part of the Scene in a Theater, where the Chorus useth to dance; it is also sometimes taken for the place where the Musicians sit. **1740** CIBBER *Apol.* (1756) I. 230 The flat ceiling that is now over the orchestre was then a semi-oval arch. **1770** LANGHORNE *Plutarch* (1879) I. 183/2 As Pericles, a whole orchestre [he] bears. **1857** *Chamb. Jrnl.* VIII. 48 Whose golden blossoms waved above my head—A fragrant orchester, where hymns were said..By myriad bees.

orchestrelle (ˈɔːkɪˌstrɛl). [f. ORCHESTR(A + Fr. dim. suffix *-elle*.] (See quot. 1961.)

a **1910** 'MARK TWAIN' in *Harper's Mag.* (1911) Jan. 215/1 Paine began playing on the orchestrelle Schubert's *Impromptu*. **1912** A. B. PAINE *Mark Twain* III. 1227 He added..a great Æolian Orchestrelle, with a variety of music. **1925** T. DREISER *Amer. Tragedy* (1926) I. II. xviii. 288 Fox-trots and one-steps were being supplied by an orchestrelle of considerable size. **1961** E. AMES *Daughter of House* (1963) I. vi. 95 The orchestrelle..was a kind of organ which could either be played manually, or—by switching to electrical controls—could be made to play perforated rolls like a player piano.

orchestric (ɔːˈkɛstrɪk), *a.* [f. ORCHESTRE, -TER + -IC.]

1. Of or pertaining to dancing: more properly ORCHESTIC, q.v.

1786 GILLIES *Hist. Greece* I. iii. 104 Their sedentary studies were relieved by the orchestric and gymnastic exercises. **1850** BLACKIE *Æschylus* I. Pref. 41 The author of the Prometheus really was a professor of the orchestric art. **1888** BURGON *Lives 12 Gd. Men* I. II. 228 Rose's father, who had sent [his boys] to be instructed by him in the orchestric art.

2. Belonging to an orchestra; orchestral.

1839 *Blackw. Mag.* XLV. 461 We ourselves may boast to have introduced the word *orchestric*, which we regard with parental pride, as a word expressive of that artificial and pompous music which attends, for instance, the elaborate hexameter verse of Rome and Greece. **1892** *Edinb. Even. Disp.* 13 Feb. 3/1 The orchestric playing was not all that might have been wished.

orchestrina (ɔːkɪˈstriːnə). Also -ino. [f. ORCHESTR-A + -INA[1], after *concertina*, etc.]

†**a.** An instrument of the key-board kind constructed so as to imitate various other musical instruments. *Obs.* **b.** A mechanical instrument, resembling a barrel-organ, but of more elaborate construction, intended to imitate the effect of an orchestra. So **orˈchestrion** [cf. *accordion*], **orˈchestrionette**, names of similar instruments. (See quots.)

1838 *Encycl. Brit.* (ed. 7) XVI. 519/1 *Orchestrino*, a modern musical instrument..shaped like a piano-forte... It imitated the tones of the violin, the viola, the violoncello, the viol d'amour, the double bass, etc. *Ibid.*, *Orchestrion*, a musical instrument invented by the Abbé Vogler about 1789. It was a kind of portable organ, about nine feet in height, breadth, and depth... Another instrument of the same name, invented in 1796,..consisted of a piano-forte, combined with some organ-stops. **1842** DICKENS *Amer. Notes* vi, Are there no Punches..Conjurers, Orchestrinas, or even Barrel-organs? **1880–1** *Libr. Univ. Knowl.* (U.S.) X. 63 *Organo-Lyricon*,..piano-forte combined with 12 kinds of wind-instruments..the first of a number of similar inventions, such as the orchestrion. **1882** C. W. WOOD *In Black Forest* 115 The Black Forest is famous for these mechanical organs—*orchestrions*, as they are called.

orcheyard(e, -iard(e, etc., obs. ff. ORCHARD.

orchic (ˈɔːkɪk), *a. Anat.*, etc. *rare*[−0]. [a. mod.L. *orchic-us*, a. Gr. ὀρχικ-ός, f. ὄρχις testicle.]

1857 MAYNE *Expos. Lex.*, *Orchicus*, of or belonging to the testicles: orchic.

orchid (ˈɔːkɪd). [Introd. by Lindley, 1845, as an Eng. repr. of mod.L. *Orchideæ* or *Orchidaceæ*: see ORCHIDEOUS, and -ID *suff.*[2]] **1. a.** Any plant of the orchis family (*Orchidaceæ* or *Orchideæ*), a large and widely distributed Natural Order of monocotyledons, distinguished by having one, or rarely two, sessile anthers, united with the pistil (*gynandrous*) into a central body called the *column*, and containing pollen coherent in masses (*pollinia*); the flowers have three sepals and three petals (one petal, called the *lip* or *labellum*, being usually much larger than the other two, and of special colour or shape), and vary greatly in appearance, being often remarkable for brilliancy of colour or grotesqueness of form, in some cases resembling various insects and other animals. Orchids are often epiphytes; many exotic species are now cultivated for their beauty.

1845 LINDLEY *School Botany* (ed. 3) 131 Order lxv. Orchidaceæ.. Orchids. **1848** in CRAIG. **1858** GLENNY *Gard. Every-day Bk.* 111/1 When orchids are in the common hot-house, they should be in the most shady part, and be more frequently syringed than any other plants. **1859** DARWIN *Orig. Spec.* vii. (1873) 172 The flowers of orchids present a multitude of curious structures. **1885** *Pall Mall G.* 12 May 4/2 The popularity of orchids is a growth of the present century. **1885** *Pop. Guide to Ho. Comm.* Pall Mall G. Extra No. 21, Everybody knows Mr. Chamberlain... His eye-glass and his orchids are as well known as Mr. Gladstone's collars.

b. *attrib.* and *Comb.*

1852 B. S. WILLIAMS (*title*) The orchid-grower's manual. **1861** TYLOR *Anahuac* iv. 89 The fantastic shapes and brilliant colours one sees in English orchid-houses. **1884** *Encycl. Brit.* XVII. 818/1 Orchid-lovers have better reasons to support their fancy than had the speculative growers and barterers of tulips. **1888** *Pall Mall G.* 1 Feb. 5/1 The extent ..[of] the so-called orchid mania can be estimated from the frequency of public orchid sales, the quantity of orchids now imported. *Ibid.*, Mr. Chamberlain's orchid collection, if not the largest in the country, is at least the best known. **1893** DK. ARGYLL *Unseen Found. Soc.* xv. 492 Sending out orchid-hunters. **1903** *Daily Chron.* 9 Nov. 3/5 One can never tell what the orchid-seed of enterprise may blossom into. **1908** *Westm. Gaz.* 28 May 12/1 The dangers of orchid-hunting. **1909** *Chambers's Jrnl.* July 430/2 Many an orchid-hunter has sacrificed his life to his daring. **1935** N. MITCHISON *We have been Warned* I. ii. 24 Joyce's dress was long and diaphanous, orchid-coloured. **1974** *Country Life* 18 Apr. 950/4 Already my alpine house and orchid house have been shaded and humidity increased in the latter. **1974** *Encycl. Brit. Macropædia* XIII. 648/1 Discussions about orchids, whether among professional botanists or amateur orchid enthusiasts, often leave the impression that orchids are 'somehow different' from other plants. **1977** A. WILSON *Strange Ride R. Kipling* iii. 136 Singapore's orchid garden.

2. A purplish colour or tint.

1923 *Daily Mail* 15 Jan. 1 Shades of Navy, Bisque, Rust, Champagne, Orchid, Flesh, Silver, Nattier Blue, Black, Jade & Ivory. **1936** *Times* 6 Jan. 11/3 A model Court gown in orchid morganza. **1971** *Guardian* 28 Sept. 11/2 Quilted raincoat... In sand, orchid, or damson. **1975** D. RAMSAY *Descent into Dark* ii. 78 He wore orchid pyjamas of real silk.

orchidacean (ɔːkɪˈdeɪʃ(ɪ)ən). *rare.* [f. as next + -AN; but improperly used: cf. *crustacean*.] One who devotes himself to the cultivation of orchids; an orchid fancier.

1887 *Sat. Rev.* 26 Nov. 727 There are men famous over the civilized world for their zeal as orchidacians. **1888** *Longm. Mag.* Feb. 432, I am not old enough as an orchidacean to judge.

orchidaceous (ɔːkɪˈdeɪʃəs), *a.* [f. mod.Bot. L. *Orchidace-æ*, substituted by Lindley (*Veget. Kingd.* 173) for the earlier *Orchideæ*: see ORCHIDEOUS, and -ACEOUS.]

1. Belonging to the Natural Order *Orchidaceæ*: see ORCHID.

1838 *Penny Cycl.* XI. 511/2 Gynandria.. The principal part of the class consists of Orchidaceous plants. **1859** DARWIN *Orig. Spec.* iii. (1878) 57 Nearly all our orchidaceous plants absolutely require the visits of insects.. to fertilise them. **1882** *Garden* 20 May 348/3 Cattleya gigas ..is now within the reach of all who grow Orchidaceous plants.

2. Resembling an orchid in some way, esp. in being showy.

1864 MISS YONGE *Trial* I. 84, I have read of a woman with an orchidaceous face. **1894** R. LE GALLIENNE *Prose Fancies* 34 The simple old type of manhood is lost long since in endless orchidaceous variation. **1897** *Sat. Rev.* 13 Feb. 170 Engaged to be orchidaceous and flamboyant as the Improper Person of Babylon.

orchidacity (ɔːkɪˈdæsɪtɪ). [f. ORCHID + -ACITY.] The quality of being ' orchidaceous' (sense 2).

1897 *Sat. Rev.* 13 Feb. 169, I have power and passion, orchidacity and flamboyancy. **1933** *Times Lit. Suppl.* 2 Nov. 747/3 He [*sc.* Kenneth Grahame].., sheltered within the sinister orchidacity of the *Yellow Book*, wrote 'pagan' papers full of the fresh air.

orchideal (ɔːˈkɪdiːəl), *a. rare.* = next.

1848 in CRAIG. **1885** H. O. FORBES *Nat. Wand. E. Archip.* ii. 93 The rostellum.. retains the more natural orchideal form of a broad flat floor to the anther.

orchidean (ɔːˈkɪdiːən), *a. rare.* Also orchidian. [f. mod.L. *Orchide-æ* (see ORCHIDEOUS) + -AN.] Belonging to the *Orchideæ*, orchidaceous; pertaining to or characteristic of an orchid.

1857 MAYNE *Expos. Lex.*, Orchideous: orchidean. **1862** DARWIN *Fertil. Orchids* vi. 271 This single genus [Cypripedium], now widely disseminated, as a record of a former and more simple state of the great Orchidean Order. **1914** C. A. MERCIER *Astrol. in Med.* 4 One eminent physician discovered.. the elixir of life in orchidian extract.

orchidectomy (ɔːkɪˈdɛktəmɪ). *Surg.* [Improperly for *orchiectomy*, f. Gr. ὄρχι-ς + ἐκτομή cutting-out.] Excision of one or both of the testicles; castration. Cf. ORCHIECTOMY.

1870 *Austral. Med. Jrnl.* XV. 277 Dr. [D. J.] Thomas said, 'I look upon it as a case of strumous sarcocele, requiring operation, which I have taken upon myself to call Orchidectomy. Notices appearing in the daily papers of the operations to take place at this hospital, I thought, that excision of the testicle, or the word castration, would not look well.' **1894** *Columbus* (O.) *Disp.* 7 Nov. 9/1 Orchidectomy might be resorted to as a punishment. **1900** *Brit. Med. Jrnl.* No. 2046. 645 After orchidectomy diminution in the size of the prostate followed in every one of the author's cases. **1947** *Nature* 4 Jan. 15/1 Cancers of the male breast yield to orchidectomy. **1967** *Med. Ann.* LXXXV. 217 In cases of male pseudohermaphroditism with testicular feminization, orchidectomy is carried out after puberty.. and oestrogen therapy given. **1977** BLACK & BISHOP *Sisterhood* viii. 74 An orchidectomy involves the removal of the testicles.

Hence **orchiˈdectomize** *v. trans.*, to perform orchidectomy on; to castrate; **orchiˈdectomized** *ppl. a.*

1942 *Amer. Jrnl. Anat.* LXXI. 456 One castrate member ..had been orchidectomized when 12 years of age. **1965** *Endocrinology* LXXVI. 1220/1 An intact group and an orchidectomized group were given ·9% saline. *Ibid.* 1222 (*heading*) Orchidectomized rat given saline.

orchideous (ɔːˈkɪdiːəs), *a.* [f. mod. Bot.L. *Orchide-æ* (Linnæus, 1751) an improperly-formed deriv. of Gr. ὄρχις, L. *orchis* (the stem of which, *orchi-*, was erroneously taken by early botanists as *orchid-*): cf. *orchidis*, *orchides*, in Bauhin *Hist. Plant.* (1650) II. 772).] Belonging to the *Orchideæ* or natural order of plants akin to the genus *Orchis*; orchidaceous: see ORCHID. (In quot. 1851, erron., for the cultivation of orchids.)

1818 COLEBROOKE *Import Colonial Corn* 130 Coagulated mucilage.. from.. arrow-roots, cassada, smilax, orchideous roots and scitamineous. **1830** LINDLEY *Nat. Syst. Bot.* 263 The singularities of Orchideous plants. **1833** *Penny Cycl.* I. 242/2 Orchideous air-plants have become comparatively common in the hot-houses of the lovers of beautiful flowers. **1851** GLENNY *Handbk. Fl. Gard.* 38 The moist atmosphere of an orchideous house.

orchidist (ˈɔːkɪdɪst). [f. ORCHID + -IST.] A cultivator of orchids; an orchid fancier.

1881 *Gard. Chron.* XVI. 748 An English orchidist. **1888** *Pall Mall G.* 25 July 5/1 What has been done by an amateur orchidist in a small suburban garden.

orchidize (ˈɔːkɪdaɪz), *v.* [f. ORCHID + -IZE.] *trans.* To make like an orchid. (In quots. *fig.*)

1918 A. BENNETT *Pretty Lady* xxxi. 222 In the right environment she would become another being, that was to say, the same being, but orchidised. **1922** JOYCE *Ulysses* 418 Jesified orchidised polycimical jesuit!

orchid-like (ˈɔːkɪdlaɪk), *a.* [f. ORCHID + -LIKE.] Like or resembling an orchid.

1881 W. ROBINSON *Wild Garden* xii. 93 The German Irises, with their great Orchid-like blossom. **1918** C. W. BEEBE *Jungle Peace* (1919) viii. 180 And later, orchid-like, violet, butterfly peas which at first flowered among the ashes on the ground, but climbed as soon as they found support. **1923** D. H. LAWRENCE *Birds, Beasts & Flowers* 39 What would I not give To bring back the rare and orchid-like Evil-yclept Etruscan?

orchido-, assumed combining form of Gr. ὄρχις (the etymological form being *orchio-*); usually taken as if repr. ORCHID; as in **orchiˈdologist**, one versed in orchidology; **orchiˈdology**, that branch of botany, or of horticulture, which deals with orchids; **ˌorchidoˈmania**, a craze for orchids; **ˈorchidopexy** *Surg.* [-PEXY], fixation of a testicle, esp. of an undescended testicle in the scrotum; **orchiˈdophilist**, a lover of orchids. Also in terms of Pathology, etc., as **ˈorchidoˌcele**, **orchiˈdotomy**: see ORCHIOCELE, ORCHOTOMY.

1842 DUNGLISON *Med. Lex.*, *Orchidocele, Hernia humoralis. **1881** BENTHAM in *Jrnl. Linn. Soc.* XVIII. 338 Neglected by subsequent *orchidologists. **1886** *Academy* 3 July 12/3 A work called *Reichenbachia*—after the famous orchidologist of Hamburg. **1885** B. S. WILLIAMS *Orchid Grower's Man.* 2 *Orchidology being then in its infancy. **1849** *Fraser's Mag.* XL. 135 We catch the prevailing *orchido-mania. **1893** W. H. A. JACOBSON *Dis. Male Organs* I. ii. 83 (*heading*) Transplantation of a retained or misplaced testicle into the scrotum.—*Orchidopexy. **1974** PASSMORE & ROBSON *Compan. Med. Stud.* III. I. xxvii. 8/1 The operation of choice [for imperfect descent of the testis] before puberty is orchidopexy, and after puberty orchidectomy. **1882** *Gard. Chron.* XVII. 300 Such flowers.. as would delight and astonish even the best-informed *orchidophilist. **1892** *Syd. Soc. Lex.*, *Orchidotomy, see *Orchotomy*.

orchiectomy (ɔːkiːˈɛktəmɪ). *Surg.* [See ORCHIDECTOMY.] = ORCHIDECTOMY.

1894 in GOULD *Dict. Med.* 938/1. **1948** BAILEY & LOVE *Short Pract. Surg.* (ed. 8) III. xxxiii. 602 Orchiectomy is indicated when the other testis is normal, and the cord too short to allow replacement of the maldescended organ in the scrotum. **1963** *Lancet* 5 Jan. 21/1 In four cases where the testicle was regarded as non-viable the operation was orchiectomy. Orchiopexy was carried out in the rest though it was not always thought that the organ would function. **1974** *Acta Endocrinol.* LXXVI. 237 A progressive decrease in the pituitary FSH level was observed up to 72 h after orchiectomy.

orchil (ˈɔːtʃɪl). Forms: 5–8 orchell, 6–8 orchel, 6–9 orchall, (6 orcheall, orcall), 7–9 orchal, (8 orcheil, orselle, oricelle, 9 orseille), 9 orchil, -ill. See also ARCHIL. [a. OF. *orchel*, *orcheil* (late *orseil*), mod.F. *orseille*, in It. *orcello*, earlier *oricello*, OSp. *orchillo*, mod.Sp. *archilla*. Origin uncertain: see ARCHIL.]

1. A red or violet dye prepared from certain lichens, esp. *Roccella tinctoria*.

1483 *Act 1 Rich. III*, c. 8 Preamble, The Colours made with the which Orchell.. faden away. *Ibid.* §15 Orchell or Cork called Jarecork [Fr. *Orchel ou Cork appellez Jarecork*]. **1502** ARNOLDE *Chron.* (1811) 188 The Crafte to make Orchell. **1532–3** *Act 24 Hen. VIII*, c. 2 With good and sufficient corke or orchall. **1695** *Lond. Gaz.* No. 3086/4 He also manufactures the Blue-Cake-Orchal.. and the Blue Liquid Orchal for Scotland. **1771** WOULFE in *Phil. Trans.* LXI. 129 Cochineal, Dutch litmus, orchel,.. and many other colouring substances. **1866** *Treas. Bot.* 820/2 *Orchil, Archil, Orchal*, or *Orchill*, various names for the dye prepared from Orchella-weed. **1897** *Allbutt's Syst. Med.* II. 86 *note*, The clubs are best stained with orseille or orange rubine.

2. The lichen *Roccella tinctoria*, or other species from which the dye is obtained.

1758 *Phil. Trans.* L. 653 The orchel, or Canary-weed. **1813** E. BANCROFT *Philos. Perm. Colours* (ed. 2) I. Introd. 42 That species of lichen which is now called orchall. **1877** MAJOR *Discov. Pr. Henry* ix. 123 Others went.. to gather orchil for dyeing.

orchilla (ɔːˈtʃɪlə), **orchella** (ɔːˈtʃɛlə). Also 8–9 orchelia. [ad. It. *orcello*, OSp. *orchillo* (mod.Sp. *archilla*): see ORCHIL.]

1. = prec. 1.

1703 *Lond. Gaz.* No. 3917/4 The Loading.. consisting of Canary Wines, Orchilla, Rosewood, and some few Water-Stones. **1722** *Act Encour. Silk Manuf.* in *Lond. Gaz.* No. 6040/7 Orchelia the Hundred Weight,.. twenty Shillings. **1800** tr. *Lagrange's Chem.* II. 283 The orchilla used in dyeing is under the form of a violet-red paste. **1881** *Daily News* 21 Jan. 6/8 Orchella.. 100 packages sold at 45*s*.

2. (usually ***orchilla-weed.***) = prec. 2.

1772–84 COOK *Voy.* (1790) IV. 1224 This, like all the other Canary Islands, affords orchilla weed in great plenty. **1813** E. BANCROFT *Philos. Perm. Colours* (ed. 2) I. 294 The orchella was discovered growing abundantly.. at the Cape de Verd islands. **1857** LIVINGSTONE *Trav.* xv. 266 We came upon groups of lofty trees as straight as masts, with festoons of orchilla-weed hanging from the branches.

orchiocele (ˈɔːkɪəʊsiːl). *Path.* Also orche-. [f. Gr. ὄρχι-ς testicle + κήλη tumour, rupture.] A tumour or hernia of the testicle.

1842 DUNGLISON *Med. Lex.*, *Orchiocele*, a tumour of the testicle. **1848** CRAIG, *Orchecele*, hernia of the scrotum; also, swelling of the testis. **1892** in *Syd. Soc. Lex.*

orchiopexy (ˈɔːkiːəpɛksɪ). *Surg.* [f. Gr. ὄρχι-ς testicle + -O + -PEXY.] = *orchidopexy* s.v. ORCHIDO-.

[**1909** F. TOREK in *N.Y. Med. Jrnl.* XC. 952/2, I had to present one of my cases of orcheopexy before this section of the Academy.] **1931** —— in *Ann. Surg.* XCIV. 97 My original spelling, orcheopexy, should therefore be changed to orchiopexy. **1938** BAILEY & LOVE *Short Pract. Surg.* (ed. 4) xxix. 544 If this treatment fails, orchiopexy should be advised. **1963** [see ORCHIECTOMY]. **1974** *Investigative Urol.* XI. 303 Nephropexy and orchiopexy using tissue adhesives were performed on rats and rabbits.

orchiotomy, variant of ORCHOTOMY.

orchis (ˈɔːkɪs). [a. L. *orchis* (Pliny), the plant, a. Gr. ὄρχις testicle, also the plant orchis (so called from the shape of the tubers in most species: cf. BALLOCKS, DOGSTONES). For the pl. *orchises*, *orchids* is often substituted.] The typical genus of *Orchidaceæ* or Orchids, comprising terrestrial herbs of temperate regions, with tuberous root (having usually two tubers), and erect fleshy stem bearing a spike of flowers, usually purple or red, with spurred lip; any plant of this genus, or (popularly) of several other genera having similar characters.

1562 TURNER *Herbal* II. 152 There are diuers kindes of orchis.. yᵉ other kindes ar in other countrees called fox stones or hear stones, and they may after yᵉ Greke be called dog-stones. **1653** H. MORE *Antid. Ath.* II. vi. §4. 57 All your orchisses that they have given names unto from some beasts or other as cynosorchis [etc.]. **1725** BRADLEY *Fam. Dict.* s.v., In the Culture of the Orchis the Gardener must give it a moist Earth and a Northern Exposition. **1850** TENNYSON *In Mem.* lxxxiii, Bring orchis, bring the foxglove spire, The little speedwell's darling blue. **1856** MRS. BROWNING *Aur. Leigh* I. 1085 Such nooks of valleys, lined with orchises. *attrib.* **1753** CHAMBERS *Cycl. Supp.*, Orchis root, in the materia medica, is otherwise named *salep*. **1807** J. E. SMITH *Phys. Bot.* 272 In the Orchis family.. the pollen is of a glutinous nature.

b. With defining word (sometimes denoting an insect, or other animal, or thing, to which the flower bears some resemblance, actual or fancied): as

BEE O., BIRD'S-NEST O., BUTTERFLY O., CUCKOO O., FINGER O., FLY O., FROG O., GREEN-MAN, or GREEN MAN-O., HAND O., LIZARD O., MEDUSA'S-HEAD O., MONKEY O., REIN O., SPIDER O., q.v. Also **bog o.**, *Malaxis paludosa*; **crane-fly o.**, *Tipularia discolor* of N. America; **dwarf o.**, *O. ustulata*, also the genus *Spiranthes*; **female o.**, an old name for *O. Morio*; **fen o.**, *Liparis Lœselii*; **fringed o.**, several N. American species of *Habenaria* with fringed lip; **male, man o.**, old name of *O.*

mascula; **musk o.**, *Herminium Monorchis*; **sweet o.**, *Spiranthes*; etc.

1785 Martyn *Rousseau's Bot.* xxvii. (1794) 416 Two very common species..are the *broad-leaved and spotted Orchis, generally found in moist meadows. **1597** Gerarde *Herbal* I. cxiii. (1633) 212 *Butter fly Orchis or Satyrion. **1578** Lyte *Dodoens* II. lix. 225 The floures..speckled with smal speckes of a deeper purple, like to *Cuckow Orchis, or fooles ballockes. *Ibid.* lvi. 222 The fifth kinde is called..sauerie Standel-wurte, or sweete Ballocke, and *Dwarffe Orchis. *Ibid.* 219 The second kinde of Orchios..is of twoo sortes *Male and *Female. **1785** Martyn *Rousseau's Bot.* xxvii. (1794) 414 Two of the most common sorts with double bulbs, are called Male and Female Orchis foolishly, because there is no distinction of sexes. **1884** Miller *Plant-n.*, Orchis, Great *Fringed,..Purple Fringed, *Habenaria fimbriata*,..Ragged Fringed, *Habenaria lacera*. *a* **1824** Holdich *Ess. Weeds Agric.* (1825) 65 *Man-orchis, Red-lead, and Frogwort, are the only English names we have heard given to these weeds in damp pastures. **1866** *Treas. Bot.* 585 The *Musk Orchis..is occasionally found in southern and eastern England. **1785** Martyn *Rousseau's Bot.* xxvii. (1794) 413 *Pyramidal Orchis, found in pastures where the soil is chalky. **1578** Lyte *Dodoens* II. lvi. 222 The *sweete Orchis, or Ladie traces are moste commonly to be found..vpon hilles and Downes.

‖**orchitis** (ɔːˈkaɪtɪs). *Path.* [mod.L., f. Gr. ὄρχις testicle + -ITIS.] Inflammation of the testicle.

1799 in Hooper *Med. Dict.* **1822–34** *Good's Study Med.* (ed. 4) II. 190 *note*, The first symptoms of orchitis. **1878** T. Bryant *Pract. Surg.* (1879) II. 199 Orchitis or inflammation of the seminal gland.

Hence **orchitic** (ɔːˈkɪtɪk) *a.*, pertaining to or affected with orchitis.

1857 in Mayne *Expos. Lex.*

orchotomy (ɔːˈkɒtəmɪ). *Surg.* Also orchio-. [ad. Gr. ὀρχοτομία, f. ὄρχις testicle + -τομία cutting.] Excision of the testicles; castration.

1753 in Chambers *Cycl. Supp.* **1842** Dunglison *Med. Lex.*, Orcheotomy. **1848** Craig, *Orchiotomy*, castration; removal by surgical operation of one or both of the testes.

orchyard(e, obs. form of ORCHARD.

orcin (ˈɔːsɪn). *Chem.* Also **-ine**. [mod. f. mod.L. *orc-ina*, It. *orc-ello*, ORCHIL: see -IN.] A former name for ORCINOL. Cf. ORCEIN.

1840 *Penny Cycl.* XVI. 480/2 *Orcin*, a peculiar matter obtained by Robiquet from a species of lichen (*variolaria orcina*). *Ibid.*, These crystals are orcin, which become, as already stated, of a reddish violet colour by the action of the air and alkalis. **1873** Watts *Fownes' Chem.* (ed. 11) 805 Orcin appears to exist ready-formed in all the lichens.

orcinol (ˈɔːsɪnɒl) [f. ORCIN + -OL 2.] A colourless crystalline substance ($C_7H_8O_2$ + H_2O) obtained from the various kinds of orchilla-weed, turning red, brown, or yellow, in contact with air or when treated with various compounds, which gives a purple colour with ribose and is used in estimating nucleic acids.

1880 *Jrnl. Chem. Soc.* XXXVIII. 113 (*heading*) Resorcinol and orcinol derivatives. **1892** *Syd. Soc. Lex.*, *Orcinol*, a dihydric phenol, present in the lichens used in the preparation of archel and litmus. **1921** W. T. K. Braunholtz tr. *Moureu's Fund. Princ. Org. Chem.* vii. 372 An ammoniacal solution of orcinol undergoes oxidation in the air, giving orcein,..which is a red dyestuff. **1922** *Chem. Age* VII. 709/1 The various orders of *Variolaria*.., *Rocella* and *Lecanora* all contain orcinol in the free state, and these lichens are now used for the production of the two substitution products, litmus and archil. **1969** *Phytochem.* VIII. 2223 Orcinol (5-methylresorcinol) has been detected for the first time in higher plants, in ten species of the Ericaceae. **1973** N. C. Mishra et al. in Niu & Segal *Role of Ribonucleic Acid* 261 DNA and RNA were determined chemically by diphenylamine and orcinol reactions respectively.

orciprenaline (ɔːsɪˈprɛnəliːn). *Pharm.* [f. ORCI(NOL + ISO)PRENALINE.] A sympathomimetic amine, $C_6H_3(OH)_2CH(OH)CH_2NHCH(CH_3)_2$, that is closely related to isoprenaline in structure and is taken (usu. as the sulphate, a white, bitter-tasting powder) for the relief of bronchitis and asthma, usu. in an inhaler or as tablets or a syrup.

1963 *Med. Digest* VIII. 95/1 Alupent (orciprenaline) is a recently introduced synthetic drug, 1-(3,5-dihydroxyphenyl)-2-isopropylamino-ethanol sulphate. **1964** *Brit. Med. Jrnl.* 18 Apr. 1017/2 Orciprenaline ('alupent'), an analogue of isoprenaline was..effective in the relief of airways obstruction..whether taken by mouth or by inhalation. **1971** *Brit. Med. Bull.* XXVII. 27/1 Death might be caused by the excessive use of aerosol inhalers containing..orciprenaline. **1974** *Times* 12 Jan. 1/3 Her pregnancy..lasted 37 weeks aided by a muscle-relaxant drug called Orciprinaline [*sic*].

orcloud, orcome: see OVER-.

†**ˈorcost.** *Obs. rare*⁻¹. [ad. ON. *ǫrkosta* penury, want, f. *ǫr-* privative + *kostr* means.] Want of means, penury, indigence.

a **1225** *Leg. Kath.* 1724 ȝef þu ȝet witen wult..ȝef þer is orcost oðer eni ahte.

†**ord.** *Obs.* Also 2–4 **hord**, 3 **ort**, 4 **oord**, 4–5 **word(e**. [OE. *ord* = OS. *ord* point (MLG. *ord* point, edge, corner, MDu. *oort, ort, ord* point, beginning, Du. *oord* place, country, *oort* quarter), OHG., MHG. *ort* point, edge, corner, beginning (Ger. *ort* point, edge, corner, place), ON. *oddr* point of a weapon, front, leader (Da. *odd, od* point, Sw, *udd* point, pick):—OTeut. **ozdo-z*: cf. ODD.]

1. A point, esp. of a weapon; hence, a pointed weapon, a spear.

(With first quot. cf. ON. *oddr ok egg* point and edge.)

Beowulf 1549 Breost-net broden þæt ȝe-bearh feore wið ord ond wið ecge. *c* **897** K. Ælfred *Gregory's Past.* xl. 297 Ne ofstong he hiene no mid ðy speres orde. *c* **1000** Ælfric *Hom.* II. 480 He..sette his swurdes ord toȝeanes his innoðe, and feol him on uppon. *c* **1205** Lay. 20658 Turnden heo heore ordes, Strikeden & sloȝen. *a* **1300** *Cursor M.* 7770 (Cott.) Þan drogh saul self his suord And ran him-self a-pon the ord [*Gott.* hord]. *Ibid.* 10626 (Gött.) Hir witt, hir vertu, hir loue word, May na man write wid pennys ord [*Fairf.*, *Tr.* point]. *a* **1400** *Disp. Mary & Cross* 149 in *Leg. Rood* (1871) 136 Þi fruit is prikked with speres ord.

2. Point of origin, beginning; esp. in ***ord and end***.

c **897** K. Ælfred *Gregory's Past.* xlix. 385 Ðebid ðu..oð ðu wite ðæt ðin spræc hæbbe æȝðer ȝe ord ȝe ende. *c* **1000** Ælfric *Hom.* II. 220 Se leahter is ord and ende ælces yfeles. *a* **1200** *Moral Ode* 85 He is hord buten horde and ende buten ende. *c* **1200** Ormin 18620 Godess Sune ankennedd Wass aȝȝ occ aȝȝ wiþþutenn ord. *a* **1225** *Juliana* 24 Iesu crist godes sune þe is ort ant ende of al. *c* **1410** *Chron. Eng.* 174 in Ritson *Metr. Rom.* II. 277 Y schal telle, ord and ende, The rihte sothe.

‖**orda**, variant of HORDE (Tartar *horda*).

ordain (ɔːˈdeɪn), *v.* Forms: 3 **orden-i**, 3–7 **ordeine, ordeyne**, (3–4 **hordeyne**); 4–5 **ordeigne, -eygne, orden, -an, -yne**, 4–6 **ordene**, 4–7 **ordein, -eyn, -ayn(e, -aine, -ine**; 4– **ordain**, (5 **wordeyn(e, horden**, 6 **ordenne**). [a. OF. *ordene-r* (3rd sing. *ordeine, -daine, -deigne*), later *ordone-r*, mod.F. *ordonner*, AFr. *ordeiner, -deigner*, ad. L. *ordinā-re*, f. *ordo, ordin-em* ORDER. Originally the stress was on first syllable (from OF. infin. ˌ*ordeˈner*) but at length was fixed on the second (as in OF. *orˈdeine*). A ME. form ORDONNE, after later Fr., is rare.]

I. To put in order, arrange, make ready, prepare.

†**1.** *trans.* To arrange in rows or ranks, or other regular order; esp. to draw up in order of battle; to set in array; to array, marshal, order. *Obs.*

c **1290** *S. Eng. Leg.* I. 72 He liet ordeinie is fierd wel. **13..** *K. Alis.* 2024 Let arme the Affrigauns,..And al thyn ost ordeyn anone. **1375** Barbour *Bruce* XI. 304 Thair four battalis ordanit thai. *Ibid.* 351 [Bruce] ordanit his men for the fechting. **1387** Trevisa *Higden* (Rolls) III. 375 [The] ledere of þe Sampnites..hadde i-ordeyned his oost bysides Fucule Caudynes. **1484** Caxton *Fables of Æsop* III. iv, Whanne the batylle was ordeyned on bothe sydes. **1523** Ld. Berners *Froiss.* I. xli. 23 b/2 The frenchemen ordayned thre great batayls; in eche of them fyftene thousand men of armes .xx. M. men a fote. **1581** Styward *Mart. Discipl.* II. 134 In what manner thy men are to bee ordeined and placed.

†**2.** To set in proper order or position; to arrange; to keep in due order; to regulate, govern, direct, manage, conduct. *Obs.*

c **1300** *Beket* (Percy Soc.) 144 He ordeyned wel his hous, and his meyné also. **1390** Gower *Conf.* III. 184 Richesse upon the comun good And noght upon the singuler Ordeigned was. *c* **1400** *Rule St. Benet* 1676 Þat euer-ilkon in þer degre Be ordand als þam aw to be. **1422** tr. *Secreta Secret., Priv. Priv.* 216 Al bodely thyngis be gouernyd and ordaynyd by the Planetes and Sterris. **1450–1530** *Myrr. our Ladye* 270 Resonably ordenynge all her wordes and warkes to the worshyp of god. *c* **1489** Caxton *Sonnes of Aymon* xxiv. 511 Whan they had sported theymselfe ynough they ordened the watche.

†**3.** To settle the order or course of; to arrange.

a **1300** *Cursor M.* 8202 To-quils wald he mak him bun At [*v.r.* to] ordain þar procession. *c* **1470** Henry *Wallace* IX. 895 His assailȝe he ordannys wondyr sayr Ws for to harm. **1523** Ld. Berners *Froiss.* I. 468 Whiche voyage had ben ordayning & imagenynge thre yere before. **1681** Dryden *Abs. & Achit.* 729 Who now begins his progress to ordain With Chariots, Horsemen, and a num'rous Train.

4. To set up (something) to continue in a certain order; to establish or found by ordinance; to institute. *arch.*

c **1315** Shoreham 151 Here hys o justyse..dampneth theves for to ordeyne Peys in londe. **1387** Trevisa *Higden* (Rolls) IV. 101 Þis pleyes þat were i-cleped Ludy scenici were first i-ordeyned by excitinge of þe devel. **1422** tr. *Secreta Secret., Priv. Priv.* 193 Thereas Seint benet ordeyned the monken rull, and Seinte Austeyn chanoun Rull in erth. **1477** Earl Rivers (Caxton) *Dictes* 66 There he ordeigned ij scoles. **1482** *Monk of Evesham* (Arb.) 81 He hordende there an hospitalle for pilgrimmys. **1584** Powel *Lloyd's Cambria* 53 Ordeining three sorts of lawes. **1697** Dryden *Virg. Past.* v. 45 Daphnis did rites to Bacchus first ordain.

†**5.** To plan, devise, contrive. *Obs.*

a. a material structure.

1340 *Ayenb.* 7 Ine þe zix dayes..ine huichen he made the worlde an ordaynede [*v.r.* diȝte]. **13..** *Cursor M.* 8311 (Gött.) Suilke a werke..þu sal it ordaine in þi thoght, Thoru salamon it sal be wroght. **1377** Langl. *P. Pl.* B. xix. 315 Ordeigne þe an hous, Piers, to herberwe in þi cornes. *a* **1400–50** *Alexander* 3680 Of Euor & of Olifants was ordand þe ȝatis. **1481** Caxton *Reynard* xxxii. (Arb.) 89 Alle this..was made & wrought in this glasse. The maister that ordeyned it was a connyng man. **1526** Tindale *Mark* xii. 1 A certayne man planted a vyne yarde..and ordeyned a wyne presse, and bilt a toure.

b. something immaterial or abstract.

c **1330** R. Brunne *Chron.* (1810) 141 Fayn I wild purueie for Acres, þat cite Ordeyned wer som weie, how it moucht be saued be. **1390** Gower *Conf.* III. 43 What lust it is that he ordeigneth. *c* **1440** *Generydes* 10 What pleasure he cowde for her ordeyne, That shuld be do. **1485** Caxton *Paris & V.* 53 And anone ordeyned two letters.

c. with clause or infinitive.

c **1400** *Gamelyn* 798 Ordeigne how it shal be & it shal be do. **1450–80** tr. *Secreta Secret.* 38 If thou maiste not reve hem her watir, loke that thou ordeyne forto envenyme it. **1480** Caxton *Chron. Eng.* ccxiii. 199 They caste and ordeyned both by nyght and day how they myght breng hym out of prison.

†**6.** To put in order (for a purpose); to prepare, make ready, equip; to furnish, provide. *Obs.*

1375 Barbour *Bruce* XVII. 626 Engynys alsua for till Cast Thai ordanit and maid redy fast. *c* **1400** Maundev. (Roxb.) xxiii. 106 Þis hall es nobilly and wirschefully araid and ordaynd in all thinges... Vp at þe hie deesse..es ordained þe trone for þe emperour. *c* **1475** *Rauf Coilȝear* 325 Agane the morne airly He ordanit him ane laid. **1500–20** Dunbar *Poems* lxxii. 242 Ordane for Him ane resting-place, That is so werie wrocht for the. **1535** Coverdale *Ps.* vii. 13 He hath..ordeyned his arowes to destroye. *a* **1548** Hall *Chron., Hen. VIII* 74 Chimnayes, Ranges, and suche instrumentes that there was ordained.

†**b.** To fit out, equip, or furnish (a person, etc.) *with* (*in, of*) something. *Obs.*

c **1380** Wyclif *Serm.* Sel. Wks. I. 26 To take from hem cause of her synne, and ordeyne þe Churche in temporal goodis. **1387** Trevisa *Higden* (Rolls) I. 5 But þe mercy of God had i-ordyned vs of lettres. *c* **1400** *Three Kings Cologne* 39 Þan þei ordeyned hem anoon wiþ greete and riche ȝiftis. *c* **1450** Lonelich *Grail* xliv. 399 The Castel with-Inne wel Ordeyned was Of Men of strengthes In Every plas. **1548** Bodrugan (Adams) *Epit. King's Title* Hj, Nature..ordeined all beastes with some natural municion, as horne, spurre, tothe or naile.

†**7.** To put into a particular mental condition or disposition, esp. into a right or fitting frame of mind; to dispose (aright). *Obs.*

1340 *Ayenb.* 24 Þe uirtues of kende, huerby som ys kendeliche more þanne oþer,..oþer gracіouser, oþer atempre and wel y-ordayned. *Ibid.* 125 Þise þri uirtues armeþ an[d] ordayneþ and agrayþeþ man ase to þri deles of þe herte. **1380** *Lay Folks Catech.* (Lamb. MS.) 956 Yf þou wilt ordeyne þy wil to haue for-ȝefnesse. **1502** *Ord. Crysten Men* (W. de W. 1506) II. xv. 122 In accomplysshynge these thre commaundementes we be ordeyned towarde all the blessyd trynyte. *Ibid.* 123 By these .vii. yᵉ last commaundementes we be perfytely and iustely ordeyned ayenst our neyghboures.

†**8.** *refl.* To prepare oneself, make ready; to set or apply oneself (*to do* something). *Obs.*

13.. *Seuyn Sag.* (W.) 2790 And bad tham fast..Ordain tham vnto batayl. **1377** Langl. *P. Pl.* B. x. 242 Austin..hym-self ordeyned to sadde vs in bileue. *a* **1425** *Cursor M.* 20403 (Trin.) Oure lady..ordeyneþ hir to fare vs fro. **1493** *Festivall* (W. de W. 1515) 78 Afterwarde he ordeyned hymself & went into the holy londe.

†**9.** *intr.* To make preparation, prepare, arrange.

c **1350** *Will. Palerne* 4848 Þe clerk..fond..how þe king of poyle prestli hade ordeyned, at swich a certayn day his semliche douȝter wedde. **1375** Barbour *Bruce* XVII. 259 Valter steward..He left in berwik..And ordanit fast for Apparaill, Till defend gif men vald assaill. **1470–85** Malory *Arthur* I. xxvii, Doubte ye not he wille make warre on you..wel said Arthur I shall ordeyne for hym in short tyme. **1523** Ld. Berners *Froiss.* I. viii. 6 Than the quene..ordeyned for her voyage, and made her purueyaunce. *a* **1533** —— *Gold. Bk. M. Aurel.* (1546) E v b, Wyse men ought..to ordein for that that is present.

II. To appoint, decree, destine, order.

†**10.** *trans.* To appoint (a person, etc.) to a charge, duty, or office. (With the official name or position as simple object or complement.) *Obs.*

a **1300** *Cursor M.* 11403 At þe last þai ordeind tuelue,..And did þam in a montain dern Desselic to wait þe stern. **13..** *Coer de L.* 239 He let ordeyne, aftyr hys endynge, His sone Rychard to be kyng. *c* **1386** Chaucer *Sqr.'s T.* 169 With certeine officers ordeyned [*v.r.* yordeyned] therfore. **1464** *Rolls of Parlt.* V. 532/2 Our Lettres Patentes..by the which we ordande the same John to be Clerk of the then Sheref. **1549** Latimer *Ploughers* (Arb.) 26 Wherefore are magistrates ordayned, but that the tranquillitie of the commune weale maye be confirmed. **1568** Grafton *Chron.* I. 93 According to promess made, he was ordeyned king. *a* **1645** Habington *Surv. Worcs.* in *Worcs. Hist. Soc. Proc.* I. 49 The curate of thys chappell is ordeygned by the Vicar of St. Andrewes in Pearshore. **1652** Needham tr. *Selden's Mare Cl.* 103 An Officer was ordained for that purpose. **1809** *Will of J. Kellett* in Dow *Rep.* (1816) III. 250 And I also ordain, appoint, and devise the said..W.K.,..G.H., and F.H.H., executors to this my last will and testament.

†**b.** Const. *to do* something; *to* (*on, upon*) some office, etc. *Obs.*

c **1330** R. Brunne *Chron. Wace* (Rolls) 12531 He ordeynd messegers to wende, To þe Emperour. **1382** Wyclif *Matt.* xxiv. 47 Vpon [1388 on] alle his goodis he shal ordeyne hym. **1387** Trevisa *Higden* (Rolls) VIII. 19 He was y-ordeyned to þe service of oþere men. *c* **1400** Maundev. (Roxb.) vii. 25 Certayne persones er ordaynd to kepe þat ilke hous. **1535** Coverdale *Josh.* Contents iii, The Leuites are ordeyned to go before with the Arke. **1676** Hobbes *Iliad* I. 308 Two publick servants of the king were these Ordained to carry his commandments.

11. *Eccl.* To appoint or admit to the ministry of the Christian Church; to invest with a ministerial or sacerdotal character by the laying on of hands or other symbolic action; to confer holy orders upon. Formerly, and still in a general sense, used of any sacred office, including that of bishop, but now, in the Ch. of

England, used esp. of admission to the orders of deacon and priest; in other churches, of ceremonial admission to the ministry; in Presbyterian churches, lay elders also are ordained.

c **1290** *Beket* 336 in *S. Eng. Leg.* I. 116 He was in grete fere, For-to Ordeinen ani Man: bote he þe betere were. a **1300** *Cursor M.* 21246 Men sais þat of his thumb he smate..þat he ne preist suld ordeind be. **1387** Trevisa *Higden* (Rolls) IV. 347 þat ȝere about Pentecoste..þe apostles ordeyned þe lasse Iames..bisshopp of Ierusalem. **1588** J. Udall *Demonstr. Discipl.* (Arb.) 20 The Apostles ordayned bishops euery where. **1638** Chillingw. *Relig. Prot.* ii. §109 He cannot be a true Pope, unless he were rightly ordained Priest. **1641** Milton *Ch. Govt.* I. iv. Wks. (1847) 34/1 The pope is not made by the precedent pope, but by cardinals, who ordain and consecrate to a higher and greater office than their own. **1718** *Freethinker* No. 93 ¶6, I am a young Clergyman, Ordained the very Last Ember-Week. **1782** Priestley *Corrupt. Chr.* II. x. 227 They were..ordained to their office by prayer. **1845** H. J. Rose in *Encycl. Metrop.* (1847) II. 884/1 It is shown..that the Apostles did ordain ministers by the imposition of hands, and did give them authority to ordain others. **1861** Stanley *East. Ch.* v. 187 Melitius was to retain his title and rank but not to ordain. **1870** Arnot *Life Jas. Hamilton* iv. 168 He was ordained as minister of Roxburgh Church by the Presbytery of Edinburgh on the 21st Jany. 1841.

†**12.** To appoint or assign (*to* or *for* a special purpose, etc.). *Obs.*

1303 R. Brunne *Handl. Synne* 854 þe satyrday ys specyaly Ordeynede to wurschyp oure ladye. **1390** Gower *Conf.* III. 265 The king, which herde..How that this Maide ordeigned is To Mariage. c **1400** Maundev. (Roxb.) xiii. 58 In steed of messangers..þai ordayne dowfes for to bere lettres. **1541** R. Copland *Galyen's Terapeut.* 2 H ij b, All medicamentes..ordeyned to the vlcere of the Thorax. **1584** Cogan *Haven Health* clxxvi. (1636) 159 One halfe of the yeare is ordeyned to eat fish in. **1596** Dalrymple tr. *Leslie's Hist. Scot.* x. 319 Of the quhilkes horsses he ordaynet for the Erle ane. a **1618** Raleigh *Mahomet* (1637) 19 That day was ordayned by him to be their Sabbaoth.

†**b.** To assign (*to* any one) as a share, portion, or allowance; to allot. *Obs.*

1375 Barbour *Bruce* xvii. 298 And till gret lordis, ilkane syndri, Ordanit ane felde for thar herbry. **1483** Caxton *G. de la Tour* H v b, Of suche goodes..ye must ordeyne and departe to the poure folke a parte of them. **1495** *Act 11 Hen. VII*, c. 36 *Preamble*, Londes..of the yerely value of M^1 marč ordeyned to her by the last Will of the same late Duke. **1596** Dalrymple tr. *Leslie's Hist. Scot.* I. 106 To thame for thair trauel publiklie is ordayned thair sustentatione, steddings directed, houses appoynted.

13. Of the Deity, fate, or supernatural power: To appoint as part of the order of the universe or of nature; to decree, predestine, destine.

a **1300** *Cursor M.* 285 (Cott.) þat he ordaind [*Gött.* ordained, *Fairf.* ordenet, *Trin.* ordeyned] wit his witte He multiplis and gouerns itte, þerfor is he cald trinite. **1393** Langl., *P. Pl.* C. iv. 241 As hus werdes were ordeined by wil of oure lorde. **1450–80** tr. *Secreta Secret.* 16 God suffrith the planetis forto make and holde her cours in the rewle and ordir as he ordeynyd hem. **1582** Stanyhurst *Æneis* II. (Arb.) 57 So Gods ordayned thee chaunce. **1611** Bible *Isa.* xxvi. 12 Lord, thou wilt ordaine peace for vs. **1700** Dryden *Pal. & Arc.* III. 964 And laurels, which the gods for conquering chiefs ordain. **1792** in *Anecd. Pitt* III. xliv. 205 It is your duty..if fate should so ordain it. **1865** Lightfoot *Galatians* (1874) 165/2 The moment..which God had ordained from the beginning.

b. With *obj. cl.*, or *inf.* or other *compl.*

c **1330** R. Brunne *Chron.* (1810) 68 If it so betide, That God haf ordeynd so I after him abide. **13..** *Cursor M.* 1198 (Gött.) Vr lauerd had ordained ȝeit A child to rise in his ospringe. c **1400** *Apol. Loll.* 25 God wordeyniþ him for þis synne to be putte to peyn, and out of comyn. **1477** Earl Rivers (Caxton) *Dictes* 1 Borne & ordeigned to be subgette and thral. c **1560** A. Scott *Poems* (S.T.S.) xxx. 45 As grund is ordand to beir seid. **1667** Milton *P.L.* VIII. 297 Rise First Man, of Men innumerable ordain'd First Father. **1728** Young *Love Fame* II. 264 But fate ordains that dearest friends must part. **1837** Lytton *E. Maltrav.* I. xvi, He goes with us in the path we are ordained to tread.

†**c.** To destine to a lot or fate. *Obs.*

a **1300** *Cursor M.* 23745 To trauail ordeint is þis liue. c **1340** Hampole *Prose Tr.* 12 Men and wymmene þat er ordaynede to þe joye of heuene. **1482** *Monk of Evesham* (Arb.) 36 The doers of al synnes ordente to dyuers kyndes of peynes. **1508** Kennedy *Flyting w. Dunbar* 508 Tak the a fidill, or a floyt and geste, Wndought, thou art ordanyt to not ellis.

d. *absol.* or *intr.*

1340 Hampole *Pr. Consc.* 7632 Ilk ane þair course obout ay mase..als God ordaynd hase. c **1430** Lydg. *Min. Poems* (Percy Soc.) 7 As grace list to ordeyne, Upon his heede to were crownys tweyne. **1700** Dryden *Pal. & Arc.* II. 360 But Love, their lord, did otherwise ordain. **1855** Kingsley *Heroes, Perseus* I. 2 So the Gods have ordained, and it will surely come to pass.

14. To appoint authoritatively as a thing to be observed; to decree, to enact.

1297 R. Glouc. (Rolls) 3025 After viftene dawes þat he adde y-ordeined þis To Londone he wende uor to amende þat þer was amys. **1389** in *Eng. Gilds* (1870) 9 These ben þe poyntes & þe articles ordeigned of the brotherheed of seint ffabian and sebastian. c **1400** *Sowdone Bab.* 615 He ordeyned assaute anone in haste. **1568** Grafton *Chron.* II. 110 He also ordeyned auriculer confession. **1654** Bramhall *Just Vind.* iii. (1661) 41 Fisher Bishop of Rochester, and Sir Thomas Moor..in prison..for opposing the Kings Marriage, and the succession of his Children to the Crown, after it was ordained in Parliament. **1710** Prideaux *Orig. Tithes* iii. 152 The Canons of Egbert..ordain the same thing. **1875** Jowett *Plato* (ed. 2) III. 229 That which is ordained by law they term lawful and just.

b. with *obj. cl.* or *inf.*

c **1375** *Cursor M.* 14879 (Fairf.) þai ordent him to hange on rode. **1375** Barbour *Bruce* XVI. 288 How scho furth suld caryit be, Or euir he fure, than ordanit he. **1387** Trevisa *Higden* (Rolls) V. 41 It was i-ordeyned þat Esterday schulde be i-holde þe firste Sonday from þe fourtenþe day of þe mone of þe firste monthe. a **1533** Ld. Berners *Huon* xx. 58 He ordened a grete shyppe to be made redy. **1697** Dryden *Virg. Georg.* III. 245 To shun this Ill, the cunning Leach ordains ..To feed the Females, e'er the Sun arise. **1702** Rowe *Tamerl.* IV. i. 1553 She ordains, the fair should know no Fears. **1855** Prescott *Philip II*, II. i. (1857) 197 By this edict ..it was ordained that all who were convicted of heresy should suffer death 'by fire, by the pit, or by the sword'.

†**c.** To determine, settle, resolve. *Obs.*

1375 Barbour *Bruce* v. 305 Syne emang thame preualy Thai ordanit, that he still suld be In hyddillis and in preuate. **1377** Langl. *P. Pl.* B. VIII. 98 Dowel and dobet amonges hem ordeigned To croune one to be kynge to reule hem bothe. c **1477** Caxton *Jason* 19 After the soupper it was ordeyned that on the morn the siriens..sholde reste them.

d. *absol.* or *intr.* To appoint, direct, command.

c **1380** Wyclif *Serm.* Sel. Wks. I. 13 Yet þei turneden agen, as Crist himsilf ordeynede, to lyve in þe world. **1718** Prior *Pleasure* 398 Mine to obey; thy part is to ordain.

†**15.** To order, command, bid (a person *to do* something, or *that* a thing be done); = order *v.* 7. *Obs.* or *arch.*

1375 Barbour *Bruce* XIII. 53 King Robert..Ordanit..His marschall with a gret menȝe..For to prik emang the archeris. a **1425** *Cursor M.* 11189 (Trin.) Al þe world ordeyned he þat þei shulde vndir him be. **1526** Tindale *Mark* iii. 14 And he ordeined the twelve that they shulde be with him. **1540–1** Elyot *Image Gov.* (1549) 144 For so God hath ordeined you, nature commaundeth you, and philosophie beadeth you. **1633** Bp. Hall *Hard Texts* 525 In that day will I ordaine..all creatures, that they shall be helpfull unto them. **1887** Bowen *Virg. Æneid* IV. 270 Jove himself ordains me to bear these words on the breeze.

†**16.** To order (a thing) to be made or furnished; = order *v.* 8. *Obs.*

1390 Gower *Conf.* III. 167 Of what Ston his sepulture Thei scholden make, and what sculpture He wolde ordeine therupon. **1486** *Naval Acc. Hen. VII* (1896) 18 Okum and other stuffe ordeyned and bought for the same Ship. **1599** Hakluyt *Voy.* II. II. 1 Afterward he ordeined a boat made of one tree..and went to sea in it. **1621** R. Bolton *Stat. Irel.* 37 (*An.* 5 *Edw. IV*) To ordeyne one payre of Butts for shooting within the towne or well neere.

Hence **ordained** (-'eɪnd) *ppl. a.* (esp. in sense 11).

c **1440** *Promp. Parv.* 368/2 Ordeynyd, *ordinatus, constitutus.* **1552** Huloet, Ordeyned, *comparatus, constitutus, institutus, status.* **1588** J. Udall *Demonstr. Discipl.* (Arb.) 43 The ordeyned when he feeleth a calling and charge from God..sensiblie comming vpon him. **1849** Thackeray *Pendennis* xxix, A well-ordained workhouse or prison. **1876** J. Parker *Paracl.* I. xv. 237 He is an ordained minister of Jesus Christ.

or'dain, *sb. rare.* [f. prec.] = ordinance.

1804 *Something Odd* II. 225 Providence, in whom we trust, whose high ordains we strive to follow.

or'dainable, *a. rare.* [f. ordain *v.* + -able.] Capable of being ordained.

a **1656** Bp. Hall *Rem.* (1660) 377 The nature of man is ordeinable to life.

or'dainer. Forms: 3–4 ordenour(e, ordeinour, 4–5 ordeynour, -owr, -ere, 5 ordyner, 5–6 -eyner, 6–7 -einer, 6– ordainer. [ME. a. AF. *ordenour, -inour, -einour*, f. OF. *ordener* to ordain; the stem and suffix subseq. conformed to the Eng. vb. and suffix -er[1].]

1. One who ordains: in various senses of the vb. †**a.** One who puts or keeps in order; a manager, director, ruler. *Obs.* **b.** One who appoints or institutes. **c.** One who admits to holy orders; an ordaining bishop, priest, or minister.

c **1290** *Beket* 269 in *S. Eng. Leg.* I. 114 In his warde he let do His eldeste sone sire henri..þat he were is wardein, and as is ordeinour. **1303** R. Brunne *Handl. Synne* 6310 He ches hym þre executours, Of al hys godys ordeynours. **13..** *St. Augustin* 610 in Horstm. *Altengl. Leg.* (1878) 72 To him þat schulde bisschop ordeynd be Alle þe constituciouns..his ordeynours Schuld him furst schewe wiþ honours. c **1374** Chaucer *Boeth.* IV. pr. i. 86 (Camb. MS.) So mochel a fader and an ordenoure of meyne. **1422** tr. *Secreta Secret., Priv. Priv.* 193 For the auctorite of almyghty god, ordyner of matremony. **1586** T. B. *La Primaud. Fr. Acad.* I. (1594) 553 Those first rectors and ordainers of civill societie. **1631** Gouge *God's Arrows* III. §36. 246 The Authour of Government, and Ordainer of Governours. **1653** Baxter *Chr. Concord* 67 You cannot shew all the succession of Orders from the Apostle to your Ordainer. **1736** Chandler *Hist. Persec.* 92 All..accused him of coming to his bishoprick by the perjury of his ordainers. **1879** Chr. Rossetti *Seek & F.* 62 Frost and cold..are invoked to render blessing, praise, and magnification, to the Lord their Ordainer.

2. (*Eng. Hist.*) ***Ordainers***: The name applied to a commission of twenty-one barons and bishops appointed on 20 March, 1310, in the third year of Edward II, to draw up ordinances for the better administration of the kingdom.

Styled in contemporary documents in Anglo-Fr., *ordinours, ordeinours*; in Latin, *ordinatores*; but this was originally only a descriptive designation, as in sense 1, not a specific title. The English *Ordainers*, or ***Lords Ordainers*** of modern historians, has not been found in contemporary writings, and was apparently unknown to the 16th c. chroniclers.

[**1309–10** *Annal. London.* 17 Mar. (Rolls 1882), Qe lour poer des ordinours quant as ordinances faire ne dure outre le terme avant dit. **1312** *Rolls of Parlt.* I. 281/1 Que nul Doun de Terre [etc.] se face a nul des ditz Ordeinours durant lour poer del dit ordeinement, ne a nul autre saunz consail et assent des ditz Ordeinours. c **1325** in *Chron. Edw. II* (Rolls 1883) 164 Electi sunt igitur ordinatores de potentioribus et descretioribus totius regni.]

1750 Carte *Hist. Eng.* II. 314 An instrument was signed ..by eleven bishops, eight earls and thirteen barons, in whom..the power of electing the ordainers was vested. **1839** Keightley *Hist. Eng.* I. 256 A committee of eight earls, seven bishops and six barons, who under the title of ordainers were to regulate his household and redress the national grievances. **1875** Stubbs *Const. Hist.* II. xvi. 329 The Ordainers had not loitered over their work. Six Ordinances had been published and confirmed by the king as early as August 2, 1310. **1882** —— *Chron. Edw. I & II* (Rolls) I. 172 Names of the lords ordainers. **1896** T. F. Tout *Edw. I.* iv. 77 That extraordinary combination of power which Earl Thomas, as the head of the Lords Ordainers, was able to bring to bear against Edward II.

or'daining, *vbl. sb.* [See -ing[1].] The action of the verb ordain in its various senses; ordination. Now only gerundial and *attrib.*

c **1315** Shoreham *Poems* (E.E.T.S.) 6 Of harder stat god grauntep, Wel tokne þrowȝ his ordininge. **1375** Barbour *Bruce* XIX. 26 Scho tald all to the king Thair purpos and thair ordanyng. **1509** Hawes *Past. Pleasure* xxxiii. (Percy Soc.) 168 For me my suppour was in ordeyning. **1560** Daus tr. *Sleidane's Comm.* 457 b, [They] reiecte the Sacramentes of the churche, and contemne the ordeining of priestes. **1643** Milton *Divorce* Pref., In the first ordaining of mariage. **1662** (*title*) The Book of Common Prayer,..with..the Form and Manner of Making, Ordaining and Consecrating of Bishops, Priests and Deacons.

attrib. **1875** Stubbs *Const. Hist.* II. xvii. §292 The ordaining power of the crown in council became distinguishable by very definite marks from the enacting power of the crown in parliament.

or'dainment. [a. AF. *ordeinement*; see ordain *v.* and -ment.]

1. The action or fact of ordaining; appointment; authoritative order; institution; ordinance.

13.. *Coer de L.* 1144 Kyng Rychard they afftyr sente, For to her that ordeynemente. **1645** Milton *Tetrach.* Wks. (1851) 224 (Matt. xix. 7) Tutelage, an ordainment then which nothing more just, being for the defence of Orfanes. **1649** —— *Eikon.* xvii. ibid. 464 Bishops rather by custom, then any ordainment of Christ, were exalted above Presbyters. **1881** G. Macdonald *Mary Marston* III. vii. 119 According to the sweet inexorability of musical ordainment.

2. Divine or superhuman appointment; an ordinance of the Deity, of fate, etc.

1605 Bacon *Adv. Learn.* I. iii. §6 A true or worthy end of their being and ordainment. **1824** Hood *Two Swans* x, Redeem'd from sleepy death, for beauty's sake, By old ordainment. **1851** Ruskin *Stones Ven.* III. i. §26. 19 It is an illustration of an ordainment to which the earth and its creatures owe their continuance, and their Redemption. **1895** *Eclectic Mag.* Mar. 297 The divine ordainment of kingship was an article of faith with him.

†**or'dalian**, *a. Obs.* [f. med.L. *ordāli-um* (see next) + -an.] Of or pertaining to ordeal.

1608–11 Bp. Hall *Epist.* IV. ii. Wks. (1625) 339 Why put wee not men as well to the old Saxon, or Liuonian, Ordalian tryals of hot yrons, or scalding liquors? **1656** Blount *Glossogr.*, *Ordalian Law*, was that Law which instituted the *Ordael*..and was long before the Conquest, but did continue of force in England till the time of King John. **1670** Milton *Hist. Eng.* VI. Wks. (1851) 281 She offerd to pass blindfold between certain Plow-shares red hot, according to the Ordalian Law.

‖**or'dalium.** The med.L. adaptation of the word *ordál*, ordeal; in English use in the 17th c.

1599 [see ordeal 1]. a **1614** Donne *Βιαθανατος* (1644) 138 With us both the species of Ordalium lasted evidently till King Johns time. **1643** Milton *Divorce* II. xviii. Wks. (1851) 112 As uncertaine of effect, as our antiquated law of Ordalium. a **1654** Selden *Table-t., Trial* (Arb.) 112 Ordalium was a Trial; and was either by going over Nine red hot Plough-Shares..or [etc.].

ordeal ('ɔːdiːəl, 'ɔːdiːl, ɔː'diːl). Forms: 1 ordál, -dél; (4 ordal), 6–7 ordale, ordell, (6 ordele, 7 ordael, -deale), 7– ordeal. [A mod. (16th c.) repr. of OE. *ordál, -dél*, a Comm. Teutonic word: in OFris. *ordêl, urdêl*, OS. *urdêli* (MDu. *ordeel*, MLG. *ordêl*, Du. *oordeel*), OHG. *urteili* (MHG. *urteile, urteil*, mod.Ger. *urteil*) (all neut., but in OHG., MHG. also fem.) judgement, judicial decision; thence med.L. *ordālium, ordēla*, OF. *ordel* (Diez), F. *ordalie*. The sb., of which the OTeut. type would be **uzdailjo^m*, is a nominal compound, belonging to a compound vb. of Goth. type **uzdailjan*, in OHG. *artailan, irteilan*, MHG. and Ger. *erteilen*, OS. *adêljan*, OE. *adǽlan*, lit. 'to deal out', 'allot in shares'; hence 'to allot or adjudge to one his share, decide, give judgement'. The sb. has come down in the cognate langs. in the general sense of 'judgement, judicial decision', but in OE. had become restricted, in historical times, to ancient modes of trial which survived from an earlier stage of society.

The word has not been found in ME., except in a single instance in Chaucer's *Troylus* (perh. from Latin or French). Its modern historical use began c 1575, partly as an Englishing of med.L. *ordālium*, partly as an adaptation of the OE. word. The true repr. of OE. *ordál* would be *ordole*;

the received spelling *ordeal* appears 1605 in Verstegan, who associates the word with *deal* 'part' (OE. *dǣl*). '*Or* is heer vnderstood for due or right, *deal*, for parte, as yet wee vse it, so as *ordeal*, is asmuch as to say as due-parte, and at this present it is a word generally vsed in Germanie, & the Netherlands, in stede of dome or iudgement' (*Dec. Intell.* iii. 63). Ignorance of the etymological relationship has led to the pronunciation *or-de-al*, as in *boreal, cereal, lineal.*]

1. An ancient mode of trial among the Teutonic peoples, retained in England till after the Norman Period, in which an accused or suspected person was subjected to some physical test fraught with danger, such as the plunging of the hand in boiling water, the carrying of hot iron, walking barefoot and blindfold between red-hot ploughshares, etc., the result being regarded as the immediate judgement of the Deity. Hence applied to analogous modes of determining innocence or guilt, still practised in various parts of the East, and in traditional societies generally.

With the exception of wager of battle, which is sometimes included in the class, the various forms of ordeal were abolished in England 1215–19.

c **915** *Laws of Edward* I. c. 3 Eac we cwædon be þam mannum, þe man-sworan wæran.. þæt hy siððan að-wyrðe næron, ac ordales wyrðe. *c* **920** *Laws of Edw. & Guthr.* c. 9 Ordel and aðas syndan tocwedene freols-dagum and riht fæsten-dagum. *c* **1000** *Laws of Æthelred* III. c. 4 Gange to anfealdum ordale oþþe ʒilde iii-ʒylde. *c* **1374** Chaucer *Troylus* III. 997 (1046) Wher so yow lyste by ordal or by oth. **1570–6** Lambarde *Peramb. Kent* (1826) 278 A new church, that he had erected.. for the execution of iudgments by the Ordale. **1596** Spenser *F.Q.* v. i. 25 This.. right Can hardly but by Sacrament be tride, Or else by ordele, or by blooddy fight. **1599** Thynne *Animadv.* 66 A tryall by fyre, whiche is but a species of the ordell; for ordalium was a tryall by fyre and water. **1647** N. Bacon *Disc. Govt. Eng.* I. xxxvii. (1739) 55 A second sort of Evidence was that of Ordeale. **1660** R. Coke *Power & Subj.* 158 The trial of the Ordal. **1769** Blackstone *Comm.* IV. xxvii. 342 The most antient species of trial was that by ordeal; which was peculiarly distinguished by the appellation of *judicium Dei.* **1828** Scott *F.M. Perth* xx, If any one of the suspected household refuse to submit to the ordeal of bier-right? **1865** Tylor *Early Hist. Man.* iii. 50 During the administration of the ordeal by poison in Madagascar.

2. *fig.* Anything to which recourse is had as a test, or which itself severely tests character or endurance; a trying experience, a trial.

1658 Cleveland *Rustick Ramp.* Wks. (1687) 391 The Ordale of the Sword justified Cæsar, and condemned Pompey, not his Cause. **1807** *Med. Jrnl.* XVII. 149 One fifth of the whole number vaccinated has been subjected to this severe ordeal. **1809** W. Irving *Knickerb.* VII. vi. (1849) 407 Adversity.. has been wisely denominated the ordeal of true greatness. **1864** Tennyson *Aylmer's Field* 561 Then ensued A Martin's summer of his faded love, Or ordeal by kindness. **1892** 'F. Anstey' *Voces Pop.* Ser. II. 80 The ladies in the carriages bear the ordeal of public inspection.

3. *attrib.* and *Comb.*, as ***ordeal fire, trial***, etc.; **ordeal-bean**, the poisonous calabar-bean.

1647 Cowley *Mistr., Written in Juice of Lemon* iv, Be not discourag'd, but require A more gentle Ordeal Fire. **1678** Butler *Hud.* III. i. 52 Who might, perhaps, reduce his Cause To th' Ordeal Tryal of the Laws. **1774** J. Adams *Wks.* (1854) IX. 339 Politics are an ordeal path among red hot ploughshares. **1861** Wilson & Geikie *Mem. E. Forbes* i. 26 The ordeal rocks, on which nuns suspected of breaking their vows had their innocence tested, or rather their guilt prejudged. **1885** *Chambers' Jrnl.* 3 Oct. 626 The ordeal or Calabar bean of Africa. **1897** Mary Kingsley *W. Africa* 490 The intelligent native.. squares the common-sense factor by bribing the witch-doctor who makes the ordeal drink.

ordelf, variant of oredelf, *Obs.*

†**ordene**, *a. Obs.* Also 4 ordenee, -dine, -ee, 4–5 -deyne, -ee, 5 -dein, -dain. [a. OF. *ordené*, pa. pple. of *ordener* to ordain; the final *e* became subseq. mute as in *assigne, costive*, etc.] Ordained, ordered, regulated; orderly, regular.

1340 *Ayenb.* 259 Hit becomþ wel to man of worssipe.. þat he by wel ordine and amesured ine alle his dedes. *c* **1374** Chaucer *Boeth.* III. pr. xii. 80 (Camb. MS.) The certeyn ordre of nature ne sholde nat brynge forth so ordene [*Add. MS.* ordinee] moeuynges. *c* **1430** *Pilgr. Lyf Manhode* I. cxxiii. (1869) 65 Whan þou seest þe thouht gon out of good wey and ordeynee.

Hence †**ordenely** *adv.*, in an ordered or orderly manner; according to rule; in proper order.

1340 *Ayenb.* 125 Riʒtvolnesse makeþ þane man ordeneliche libbe amang oþren. *c* **1374** Chaucer *Boeth.* IV. pr. vi. 109 (Camb. MS.) þat they ne ben don ryhtfully and ordenely [*Add. MS.* ordeinly]. **1422** tr. *Secreta Secret., Priv. Priv.* 129 That grete hoste.. was ouercome.. of few Pepil, ordaynly gouernyd. **1447** Bokenham *Seyntys* Introd. (Roxb.) 1 If he procedyn wyl ordeneely.

order ('ɔːdə(r)), *sb.* Forms: 3–6 ordre, 4– order, (4–5 -ir, -yr, 4–6 -our, -ur, 5 wordre). [ME. a. OF. *ordre* (11th c.):—**ordne*, ad. L. *ordin-em* (nom. *ordo*) row, series, course, order, array, etc.

Many senses of the word had been developed before it was adopted in OF. and Eng. The order of the appearance of the senses here is consequently not that of their logical development in L., ancient and mediæval. The specific senses of 'order of angels' and 'monastic order' appear in the Ancren Riwle; nearly all the ecclesiastical uses, with that of 'a rank of the community', are found by 1300; but the primary sense of 'row or rank' appears first in the 16th c. The arrangement here followed is in many points merely provisional.]

I. Rank generally; a rank, grade, class.

1. A rank, row, series; one of several parallel series behind or above one another. *Obs.* or *arch.*

1563 W. Fulke *Meteors* (1640) 26 b, Thick cloudes over us, and commonly a double order of cloudes, one above an other. **1565** Cooper *Thesaurus* s.v. *Consurgo, Terno consurgunt ordine remi*, thei rowed with three orders of oars on a side. **1607** Topsell *Four-f. Beasts* (1658) 459 It beareth three orders or rows of horns on the head. **1608** A. Willet *Hexapla Exod.* 851 Euerie side had these fiue orders or rankes of barres. **1745** P. Thomas *Jrnl. Anson's Voy.* 197 [It] hath no other Ornament besides one Single Order of Columns. **1863** P. S. Worsley *Poems & Transl.* 9 And wheels, a countless order, each like each.

b. *Arch.* A series of mouldings. (See also 9.)

1845 Paley *Gothic Mouldings* 10 An arch of two or more orders, is one which is recessed by so many successive planes or retiring arches, each placed behind and beneath the next before it. **1879** Sir G. Scott *Med. Archit.* I. 224 This suggested the system of sub-ordinating the rims, or recessing them, one behind the other, so as to divide the arch into what are called orders.

c. *Physics.* Each of a successive series of spectra formed by the interference or diffraction of light; hence, a positive number characterizing a particular spectrum or interference fringe, now recognized as equal to the number of wavelengths by which the optical paths of successive contributing rays differ.

1704 Newton *Opticks* II. 6 The third Circuit or Order was purple, blue, green, yellow, and red. **1722** *Phil. Trans. R. Soc.* XXXI. 244 We had here four Orders of Colours, and perhaps the beginning of a fifth, for what.. I call the Purple, is a Mixture of the Purple of each of the upper Series with the Red of the next below it. **1831** Brewster *Optics* xii. 103 Seven rings, or rather seven circular spectra or orders of colours. **1874** *Phil. Mag.* XLVII. 194 In considering the influence of the number of lines (n) and the order of the spectrum (m), we will suppose that the ruling [of the diffraction grating] is accurate. **1953** Spink & Feigl tr. *Pinsker's Electron Diffraction* ii. 26 We obtain.. $n\lambda = 2d \sin \theta$, n being the order of the reflection [*sc.* of electrons from a crystal]. This gives the number of whole wave-lengths corresponding to the path difference for waves scattered by two neighbouring parallel planes of the direct lattice. **1967** W. H. Steel *Interferometry* viii. 139 Observation of the interference fringes yields only the excess fraction ϵ of the order of interference, the amount by which the order exceeds some unknown integer.

2. A rank of the community, consisting of persons of the same status (esp. in relation to other ranks higher or lower); a social division, grade, or stratum; esp. in the phrases ***higher, lower orders.***

a **1300** *Cursor M.* 25268 Yong and ald, bath mare and less, of alkin ordre þat here es. **1538** Starkey *England* I. iii. 77 Al statys, ordurys, and degres.. in our cuntrey. **1596** Dalrymple tr. *Leslie's Hist. Scot.* I. 105 The Scottis peple is deuydet in thrie ordouris. **1712** Steele *Spect.* No. 436 ⁋1 A Place of no small Renown for the Gallantry of the lower Order of Britons, namely.. the Bear-Garden. **1749** Fielding *Tom Jones* VI. ix, Controversies that arise among the lower orders of the English Gentry, at Horse-races, Cock matches, and other public Places. **1776** Foote *Bankrupt* III. Wks. 1799 II. 132 All orders concur to give up a great public benefit, for the sake and security of private honour and peace. **1822** G. Hornby *Serm. Establ. Savings bank at Bury*, The young women amongst the lower orders. **1823** H. Ravelin *Lucubr.* 317 By all classes of society, and by the middle orders in particular. **1893** J. Adderley *S. Remarx* i. 2 That part of the Catechism is written for the lower orders.

b. A definite rank in the state.

c **1374** Chaucer *Boeth.* I. pr. iv. 19 (Add. MS.) The kyng.. caste hym to transporten vpon al þe ordre of þe senat þe gilt of his real maieste. **1683** *Britanniæ Speculum* Pref. 2, The most High and Sacred Order of Kings, which is the Ordinance of God himself. **1845** Disraeli *Sybil* II. ii, I made a speech to the order [of baronets of England] at the Clarendon; there were four hundred of us.

c. Rank or position in the abstract.

1667 Milton *P.L.* I. 506 These were the prime in order and in might. **1784** Cowper *Task* IV. 586 All the graduated scale Of order, from the chariot to the plough. **1842** Tennyson *Vision of Sin* 86 What care I for any name? What for order or degree?

3. A body of persons of the same profession, occupation, or pursuits, constituting or regarded as a separate class in the community, or united by some special interest.

c **1380** Wyclif *Sel. Wks.* III. 417 To grounde soche ordiris of beggers. **1597** Hooker *Eccl. Pol.* v. lxxvii. §2 Ministerial power.. seuereth them that haue it from other men, and maketh them a speciall *order* consecrated unto the service of the Most High... Their difference therefore from other men, is in that they are a distinct *order*... And St. Paul himself dividing the body of the Church.. nameth the one part ἰδιώτας,.. the Order of the Laity, the opposite part wherunto we in like sort term the Order of God's Clergy. **1613** Shaks. *Hen. VIII*, IV. i. 26 The Archbishop Of Canterbury, accompanied with other Learned, and Reuerend Fathers of his Order. **1776** Gibbon *Decl. & F.* (1869) I. xii. 243 A generous though transient enthusiasm seemed to animate the military order. **1849** Macaulay *Hist. Eng.* vi. II. 92 The spirit of the whole clerical order rose against this injustice.

4. A class, group, kind, or sort, of persons, beings, or things, having its rank in a scale of being, excellence, or importance, or distinguished from others by nature or character.

1736 Butler *Anal.* I. iii. 87 Good men may naturally unite, not only amongst themselves, but also with other orders of virtuous Creatures. **1751** Harris *Hermes* Wks. (1841) 172 Verbs, participles, and adjectives, may be called attributives of the first order. The reason.. will be better understood, when we have more fully discussed attributives of the second order. **1774** Goldsm. *Nat. Hist.* (1776) V. 2 Every order and rank of animals seems fitted for its situation in life. **1794** Burke *Let. to Dk. Portland* Corr. IV. 236 Three or four of the senior fellows are men of the first order. **1796** H. Hunter tr. *St.-Pierre's Stud. Nat.* (1799) II. 233 If we consider the vegetable Order.. we shall find it divided.. into three great classes, namely, into herbs, into shrubs, and into trees. **1798** Ferriar *Illustr. Sterne* iv. 134 There may be as many different orders of beauty as of architecture. **1826** Disraeli *Viv. Grey* III. i, He possessed talents of a high order. **1877** 'H. A. Page' *De Quincy* I. i. 1 All literature that comes under the order of pure phantasy. **1888** Bryce *Amer. Commw.* III. cii. 429 Cornell.. is an instance; Johns Hopkins [College] in Baltimore is another of a different order.

II. Rank in specific departments.

5. Each of the nine ranks or grades of angels, according to mediæval angelology. Also, any analogous class of spiritual or demonic beings.

The nine orders of angels are enumerated first in the Pseudo-Dionysius (4th c.), according to which there are three hierarchies, each including three orders: these are seraphim, cherubim, thrones; dominations, principalities, powers; virtues, archangels, angels. (The names are derived from the mention of cherubim and seraphim in the O.T., and from words used by St. Paul in enumerating things in heaven and in the earth, in Coloss. i. 16, Ephes. i. 21.)

a **1225** *Ancr. R.* 30 þer beoð niene englene ordres. *a* **1300** *Cursor M.* 430 Of angels wald he serued be, þat suld of ordres [*v.r.* ordoures] haf thris thre. *c* **1400** *Prymer* 47 Alle ordris of holi spiritis, preie ʒe for us! **1500–20** Dunbar *Poems* xxv. 31 Of angellis all the ordouris nyne. **1621** Burton *Anat. Mel.* I. ii. I. ii. (1676) 26/1 Those orders of good and bad Devels, which the Platonists hold. **1667** Milton *P.L.* VI. 885 As they went, Shaded with branching Palme, each order bright, Sung Triumph, and him sung Victorious King. *a* **1711** Ken *Hymns Evang.* Poet. Wks. 1721 I. 35 Nine heavenly orders enter one by one, The lowest shin'd much brighter than the sun. **1860** Pusey *Min. Proph.* 515 A subordinate order in the heavenly Hierarchy. **1872** A. de Vere *Leg. St. Patr., Striving St. P.*, Down knelt in Heaven the Angelic Orders Nine.

6. *Eccl.* **a.** A grade or rank in the Christian ministry, or in an ecclesiastical hierarchy.

The orders of the unreformed Western Church are those of bishop, priest, deacon, subdeacon, acolyte, exorcist, reader, and *ostiarius* or door-keeper, variously counted as eight or seven, according as bishop is or is not considered a distinct order from priest. Those of bishop, priest, deacon, and (since 13th c.) subdeacon, are the greater, sacred, or holy orders; the others are the minor orders. The Anglican Church recognizes only the three holy orders of bishop, priest, and deacon. In most branches of the Eastern Church the orders recognized are those of bishop, priest, deacon, subdeacon, and anagnost or reader, to which some add that of singer (ψαλτής). In the Roman Catholic Church, the orders of subdeacon, exorcist, and *ostiarius* were suppressed in 1972.

a **1300** *Cursor M.* 26151 (Cott.) For-qui þat kay es giuen to nan bot preist þat has þis order [*Fairf.* ordour] tan. *c* **1375** *Sc. Leg. Saints* viii. (*Philepus*) 90 þane prestis & deknys þare mad he.. al þe remaynyne to do, þat efferyte þare ordyr to. *c* **1440** *Jacob's Well* 162 þe x. fote depthe is betwen a womman & a man of ordre. & þe heyere ordre, þe deppere synne. **1552** *Bk. Com. Prayer* Ordering of Deacons, Diuerse orders of ministers in the churche. **1563–87** Foxe *A. & M.* (1684) II. 86 And so orderly proceeding unto all the other Orders, degraded him from the Order of Benet and Collet, from the Order of Exorcist, from the Lectorship, and last of all, from the Office of Door-keeper. **1709** Strype *Ann. Ref.* I. xi. 138 Divers having been made deacons, after long and good tryal.. were admitted into priests orders. **1844** Lingard *Anglo-Sax. Ch.* (1858) II. xii. 230 The clergy were divided into two classes, one of inferior clerks in minor orders, and employed as lectors, cantors, acolythists, exorcists, and doorkeepers; and the other of clerks in holy orders. **1845** Stephen *Comm. Laws Eng.* (1874) II. 660 Holy orders, which are the orders of bishops (including archbishops), priests, and deacons.

b. The rank, status, or position of a clergyman or ordained minister of the Church. Now always *pl.*, more fully ***holy orders.*** Hence the phrases ***to take orders***, to enter the ministry of the Church, to be ordained; ***in orders***, in the position of an ordained clergyman or minister of the Church; ***in deacon's orders, in priest's*** or ***full orders.***

This has some affinities with sense 3 (see quot. 1597 from Hooker there). But the pl. form in *holy orders, to be in orders, to take orders*, etc. evidently refers to the different orders *within* the ministry, rather than to the ministerial or clerical order as a class or body of men.

sing. **13..** *Cursor M.* 27252 If he in hali order [*Fairf.* ordour] be. *c* **1386** Chaucer *Pars. T.* ⁋817 Folk that been entred in-to ordre as subdekne or preest or hospitaliers. *Ibid.* ⁋819 Sooth is that hooly ordre is chief of al the tresorie of god. **1426** Audelay *Poems* 34 Here hole order when that thai toke, Thai were exampnyd apon a boke. **1580** Hay *Demandes Chr. Relig.* §52 Quhy deny the ordoure to be ane Sacrament. **1620** Bp. Hall *Hon. Mar. Clergy* I. xxi. Wks. (1625) 743 Continency is not of the substance of order, nor by Diuine Law annexed to it.

pl. **13..** *Cursor M.* 28365 In dedly sin i tok vnscriuen, myn orders sua war þai me giuen. **1592** Nashe *P. Penilesse* (ed. 2) 25 b, Let him straight take orders, and bee a Churchman. **1666** Pepys *Diary* 21 Feb., My brother John.. is to go into orders this Lent. **1713** Steele *Englishm.* No. 50. 326 Persons, even in Holy Orders,.. have stood unconcerned. **1719** Swift *To a Young Clergyman*, When they have taken a degree.. they get into orders as soon as they can. **1814** Jane Austen *Mansf. Park* I. ix, Yes, I shall take orders soon after my father's return. **1833** Ht. Martineau *Three Ages* III. 107 A master of arts, in full orders, is desirous of a curacy. *Mod.*

The Pope has pronounced against the validity of Anglican orders.

c. The conferment of holy orders, the rite of ordination; in the Latin Church reckoned one of the seven sacraments.

Letters of Order(s (also ellipt. *Orders*), a certificate of ordination given by a bishop to a priest or deacon.

c **1290** *Beket* 335 in *S. Eng. Leg.* I. 116 Of is ordres he was ful streit: and he was in grete fere, For-to ordeinen ani an: bote he þe betere were. c **1315** SHOREHAM 7 Cristendom, and bisschoppynge, Penauns, and eke spousinge, Godes body ine forme of bred, Ordre, and aneliinge, Thes sevene Heth holi cherche sacremens. **1550** BALE *Eng. Votaries* II. Oj, None were admytted to cure whych had not the letters of hys orders. **1560** DAUS tr. *Sleidane's Comm.* 24 Sacramentes of the Church,..the other foure, confirmation, order, Matrimony, and Unction. **1699** BURNET 39 *Art.* xxv. (1700) 284 The third Sacrament rejected by this Article, is Orders. **1699** GOV. NICHOLSON in Perry *Hist. Coll. Amer. Col. Ch.* I. 66 Acquaint the minister or ministers..that they bring with them their priests and Deacons Orders. **1706** HEARNE *Collect.* 20 Mar. (O.H.S.) I. 206 A friend..has lost his letters of Order. **1780** COWPER *Progr. Err.* 120 Go, cast your orders at your Bishop's feet. **1852** HOOK *Ch. Dict.* (1871) 444 Letters of orders are the bishop's certificate of having ordained a clergyman, either as priest or deacon. **1873** E. E. ESTCOURT *Question of Anglican Ordinations* i. 4 Holy Order is a Sacrament, requiring a certain matter and form. **1875** MANNING *Mission H. Ghost* i. 17 In the sacrament of Orders there is given a grace, whereby a priest will always have a perpetual assistance for the discharge of his office. **1977** *Christian* IV. 31 There are two priesthoods... One is conferred on all, in baptism; the other on some, in the sacrament of holy order. *Ibid.* 34 The sacrament of order is a direct participation in the mystery of Pentecost.

†**d.** Applied to matrimony, as a condition of life into which men enter, or as a sacrament. *Obs.*

c **1386** CHAUCER *Merch. T.* 103 O blisful ordre of wedlok precious Thou art so murye and eek so vertuous.

7. A body or society of persons living by common consent under the same religious, moral, or social regulations and discipline; especially, **a.** A monastic society or fraternity: as ***an order of monks*** or ***friars, the Benedictine*** or ***Franciscan order***. Sometimes applied to the rule or distinguishing constitution of such a fraternity, or to monasticism as an institution.

a **1225** *Ancr. R.* 8 Gif eni unweote acseð ou of hwat ordre ȝe beon..onswerieð & siggeð þet ȝe beoð of seint Iames ordre þet was Godes apostle. c **1290** *S. Eng. Leg.* I. 57/138 He þare bi-gan þe ordre of frere Menours. c **1305** *St. Dunstan* 49 in *E.E.P.* (1862) 35 þer was ordre of monekes er seint patrik com And er seint Austyn to Engelonde brouȝte cristendom. **1362** LANGL. *P. Pl.* A. Prol. 55, I font þere Freres, all þe Foure Ordres. c **1400** MAUNDEV. (Roxb.) x. 40 Chanouns of þe ordre of saynt Austyne. c **1470** HENRY *Wallace* XI. 1241 A ȝong monk als with him in ordour stud. **1560** DAUS tr. *Sleidane's Comm.* 47b, The order of Monkes is the invention of man. a **1596** in Shaks. *Tam. Shr.* IV. i. 148 It was the Friar of Orders gray. **1669** WOODHEAD *St. Teresa* II. i. 2 To follow the Call..from his Divine Majesty unto this Order. **1756** NUGENT *Gr. Tour, France* IV. 274 The famous abbey of La Trappe, of the Cistercian order. **1769** ROBERTSON *Chas. V*, VI. Wks. 1813 VI. 104 The Jesuits, as well as the other monastic orders, are indebted for the existence of their order, not to the wisdom of their founder, but to his enthusiasm. **1873** DIXON *Two Queens* I. I. i. 8 The Friends of Light..were not an order, and still less a Church.

b. A fraternity or society of knights bound by a common rule of life, and having a combined military and monastic character; such as those formed in the Middle Ages for the defence or propagation of Christianity, or the defence of the Holy Land, e.g. the Knights Templars, Knights Hospitallers, Knights of the Teutonic Order, the legendary Knights of the Round Table, etc.

1387 TREVISA *Higden* (Rolls) VII. 465 Aboute þis tyme bygan þe ordre of Templeres. **1550** BALE *Eng. Votaries* II. 103 The hospytelers and Templars were two fygtinge orders, instituted firste in the countreye of Palestine..for the only defence of Christen pylgrymes goyng to and fro. **1568** GRAFTON *Chron.* I. 106 That king Arthure first builded the Castle of Windsour, and there founded the order of the round Table. **1645** FULLER *Good Th. in Bad T.* (1841) 43 Martin De Golin, master of the Teutonic order, was taken prisoner. **1727-41** CHAMBERS *Cycl.* s.v. *Malta*, Knights of Malta, an order of military religious, who have bore various names; as..Knights of Rhodes, order of Malta, religion of Malta, etc. **1839** *Encycl. Brit.* (ed. 7) XVIII. 670/1 Pope Celestine III..conferred on them the title of Knights of the Teutonic Order. *Ibid.* 670/2 The Teutonic order continued in Prussia until the year 1531. **1859** TENNYSON *Guinevere* 460 That fair Order of my Table Round, A glorious company, the flower of men.

8. An institution, partly imitated from the mediæval and crusading orders of military monks, but generally founded by a sovereign, or prince of high rank, for the purpose of rewarding meritorious service by the conferring of a dignity.

1429 *Rolls of Parlt.* IV. 346/2 The honourable Ordre of the Gartier. **1508** DUNBAR *Poems* vii. *heading*, Lord Barnard Stewart, lord of Aubigny..consaloure..to..Loys, King of France, Knight of his ordour, Capitane of the kepyng of his body. **1530** PALSGR. 236/2 Knight of the order of saynt Michaell. **1560** DAUS tr. *Sleidane's Comm.* 25 The maner is, that kynges with the swordes drawen, shall strike softely, the shoulders of them that desyre the ordre. **1591** SHAKS. *1 Hen. VI*, IV. vii. 68 Knight of the Noble Order of S. George, Worthy S. Michael, and the Golden Fleece. **1645** PAGITT *Heresiogr.* (1647) 6 He..wore a great chaine like the Collar of some Order. **1762-71** H. WALPOLE *Vertue's Anecd. Paint.* (1786) IV. 121 He..painted the portraits of the knights of the Bath, on the revival of that order. **1813** WELLINGTON *Let. to Sir Isaac Heard* 9 June in Gurw. *Desp.* (1838) X. 429 Different titles and orders of Knighthood..conferred upon me by the Spanish and Portuguese governments. **1855** PRESCOTT *Philip II*, I. i. (1857) 5 The order of the Golden Fleece, of Burgundy; the proudest and most coveted, at that day, of all the military orders of knighthood.

b. ***Order of Merit***; hence ***Order-of-Merited*** adj. (*nonce*).

1799 *Public Characters of 1799-1800* II. 164 The King of Poland..also conferred on him the honours of knighthood of the Order of Merit. **1842** T. CAMPBELL *Frederick the Great* II. xv. 71 If the order of the Black Eagle was conferred on any of the members of the order of Merit, he had to send back the latter to the king. **1880** DISRAELI *Endymion* II. xv. 150 Now you tell your master..that if he wants to strengthen the institutions of this country, the government should establish an order of merit. **1902** *Pall Mall Gaz.* XXVIII. 71/1 The King's new Order of Merit would have attracted more attention if the list had appeared alone, and not at the tail of the honours bestowed at the Coronation. **1912** G. W. E. RUSSELL *Afterthoughts* xxxix. 325 An 'Order of Merit'—as far as History goes, *the* Order of Merit—was founded by Frederick the Great in 1740; and the name was copied in turn by Hesse Cassel, Baden, Bavaria, Saxony, Oldenburg, Würtemberg, and Belgium. **1929** A. HUXLEY *Swift* in *Holy Face & Other Ess.* 64 If Swift were alive to-day, he would be the adored..the Order-of-Merited author, not of *Gulliver*..but of *A Kiss for Cinderella* and *Peter Pan.* **1959** *Chambers's Encycl.* X. 228/2 The Order of Merit (O.M.) was instituted in 1902 and is awarded to officers of the fighting services and civilians for conspicuous service. **1970** C. L. CLINE *Lett. George Meredith* I. p. xxix, In 1905 came official recognition: he became the twelfth member of the recently founded Order of Merit.

c. The badge or insignia of such a dignity.

1539 *Inv. Habiliments, etc. Jas. V. Scot.* (1815) 49 Item the ordoure of the Empriour with the goldin fleis. **1673** *Lond. Gaz.* No. 780/1 The Ceremony of investing the Prince Savelli..with the Order of the Golden Fleece. **1710** *Ibid.* No. 4650/2 To whom he will carry the Order of the Black Eagle. **1753** HANWAY *Trav.* (1762) I. VI. lxxxii. 374 This lady wears the order of St. Andrew, which is a blue ribbon. **1818** KEATS *Let.* 14 Oct. (1958) I. 396 No sensation is created by Greatness but by the number of orders a Man has at his Button holes. **1874** HELPS *Soc. Press.* i. (1875) 3 A distinguished foreigner. Lots of orders on his coat; an Austrian, I think. a **1885** ANNE GILCHRIST *Century Guild Hobby Horse* (1887) 15 He stands there in gloomy black doublet with the order of the golden fleece round his neck.

d. ***order of the boot***: see BOOT *sb.*³ 1 c.

9. *Arch.* A system or assemblage of parts subject to certain uniform established proportions, regulated by the office which each part has to perform; esp. in *Classical Arch.* applied to modes of architectural treatment founded upon the proportions of columns and the kind of their capitals, with the relative proportions and amount of decoration used in their entablatures, etc.

These constitute the ***Five Orders of Classical Architecture***, rising above each other in relative height, lightness, and decoration, viz. the Tuscan, Doric, Ionic, Corinthian, and Composite; of which the Doric, Ionic, and Corinthian are the original Greek orders, the Tuscan and Composite, Roman modifications or varieties.

1563 SHUTE *Archit.* Fjb, These three orders of pillers Dorica, Ionica, Corinthia, to be vsed as folowith. **1624** WOTTON *Archit.* in *Reliq.* (1651) 225 There are five Orders of Pillars, according to their dignity and perfection. **1697** POTTER *Antiq. Greece* I. viii. (1715) 31 The Chapters seem to be a mixture between that [the Ionick] and the Dorick Order. **1731** *Gentl. Mag.* I. 123 A Colonade of 48 Corinthian Pillars supporting the upper part of the Building which is to be adorn'd with the like Number of Pilasters of the same Order. **1782** GILPIN *Wye* (1789) 82 There are orders of architecture in mountains as well as in palaces. **1823** P. NICHOLSON *Pract. Build.* 451 The Orders of Architecture constitute the basis upon which, chiefly, the decorative part of the science is built. **1856** FROUDE *Hist. Eng.* (1858) I. i. 2 Just as the last orders of Gothic architecture were the development of the first.

†**b.** A system of disposal of columns in or about a building in respect of their distance apart or 'intercolumniation'. *Obs.*

1563 SHUTE *Archit.* Ajb, The placing of the fiue orders, namely, *areostylos, diastylos, eustylos, sistylos,* and *picnostylos. Ibid.* Fjb, The fifth and last order is that which Vitruuius calleth Picnostylos.

10. a. *Math.* The degree of complexity of any analytical or geometrical form, equation, expression, operator, or the like, as denoted by an ordinal number (first, second, third,..., *n*th). Also in *Comb.* with preceding ordinal number.

The order of a plane curve corresponds to the degree of its equation, or to the number of points (real or imaginary) in which it can be cut by a straight line. ***a fluxion of the second order*** is a fluxion of a fluxion; ***an infinitesimal of the second order*** is one infinitely smaller than one of the first order, etc.; ***of the same order***, said of two variables whose ratio tends to a finite number as they both tend to zero or to infinity; ***to the first*** (or ***second***, etc.) ***order***, neglecting quantities of higher order than the first (or second, etc.).

1706 DITTON *Fluxions* 22 An Infinitesimal of another Order or Degree. *Ibid.* 123 These sorts of [Exponential] Quantities are of several Orders or Degrees. **1726** E. STONE *New Math. Dict.* s.v., Order of Curve-Lines. Sir I. Newton ..gives an Enumeration of Geometrical Lines of the third Order, as thus. **1727-41** CHAMBERS *Cycl.* s.v. *Curve*, Algebraic Curves of the same kind or order, are those whose equations rise to the same dimension. **1743** EMERSON *Fluxions* 3 In any Fluxionary Equation, a Quantity of the first Order is that which has only one first Fluxion in it; a Quantity of the second Order has either one second Fluxion or two first Fluxions: Quantities of the third Order, are third Fluxions, product of three first Fluxions, product of a first and second Fluxion, etc. **1758** LYONS *Fluxions* iv. §99 A line of the first order, or which is the same thing, the locus of a simple equation is always a right line. *Ibid.* §100 A line of the second order is always a conic section. **1820** BABBAGE *Functional Equations* 4 To find periodic functions of the *n*th order, or to solve the equation $\psi^n x = x$. **1834** MRS. SOMERVILLE *Connex. Phys. Sc.* xxxviii. (1849) 453 The curves in which the celestial bodies move by the force of gravitation are only lines of the second order. **1838** *Penny Cycl.* XII. 472/2 A succession of infinitely small quantities, each of which is infinitely smaller than the preceding, is said to be a series of infinitesimals of different orders. Such a series is x, x^2, x^3, &c. **1843** *Scientific Mem.* III. 172 It follows ..that for an infinitely small ρ, a/ρ must itself be infinitely small; but the two values will be of the same order only if there is a finite radius of curvature. *Ibid.*, If we assume a/ρ to be of the same order as ρ^μ,..then $a/(\rho^{1+\mu})$ represents a finite quantity varying continuously. **1880** *Encycl. Brit.* XIII. 14/1 Two infinitesimals α, β are said to be of the same order if the fraction β/α tends to a finite limit. If β/α^n tends to a finite limit, β is called an infinitesimal of the *n*th order in comparison with α. **1895** E. B. ELLIOTT *Algebra of Quantics* 1 The degree of a quantic in the variables x, y, z..is generally spoken of as its order. **1908** G. H. HARDY *Course Pure Math.* v. 169 We shall say that $\phi(x)$ is of the *k*th order of greatness when x is small if $\phi(x)/x^{-k} = x^k\phi(x)$ tends to a limit different from zero as x tends to 0. **1922** *Phil. Mag.* XLIII. 945 Both Sommerfeld and Epstein have obtained the value of W..by slightly different methods to the first order in F... We shall proceed to a second approximation. **1937** E. C. KEMBLE *Fund. Princ. Quantum Mech.* xi. 384 In order to get the second-order corrections to E_k and Ψ_k we differentiate Eq. (47·2) twice with respect to λ and then set λ equal to zero. *Ibid.* 386 These second-order formulas are so complicated that they are seldom used and the corrections of the third and higher order [*sic*] are still more complex. **1952** D. R. HARTREE *Numerical Anal.* ix. 192 If $a_1 \neq 0$..the number of additional correct significant figures obtained from each repetition of such a process (or..the number of repetitions required to obtain each new correct significant figure) is the same, however many figures have been obtained. Such a process is called 'first-order'. But if $a_1 = 0$, $a_2 \neq 0$..the successive errors ξ_n are ultimately related by $\xi_{n+1} = a_2\xi_n^2$... The number of correct significant figures is approximately doubled for each repetition of the iterative process... Such a process is called 'second-order'. **1962** SIMPSON & RICHARDS *Physical Princ. Junction Transistors* vi. 110 This discussion shows that h_{rb} and h_{ob} arise in such an indirect manner that they might almost be regarded as second-order effects. Their magnitudes confirm this impression. **1971** *Nature* 19 Feb. 522/2 Talk of the eclipse being an unusual strain to the Earth is idle nonsense when eclipse type conditions prevail to first order twice every lunar month.

b. ***of the order of***: (*a*) *Math.* (also ***of order***), having a ratio to (the quantity specified) that tends in the limit to a finite number, or that is neither a large number nor a small fraction; (*b*) *gen.* (also ***in*** or ***on the order of***), in the region of; somewhere about.

1903 O. LODGE *Mod. Views Matter* 7 Their mass is of the order one-thousandth of the atomic mass of hydrogen. **1913** *Rep. Brit. Assoc. Adv. Sci. 1912* 398 The change of weight ..should have been of the order of 1 in 10^7 per 1°C. **1927** N. V. SIDGWICK *Electronic Theory of Valency* ii. 20 The accuracy of spectroscopic measurements (of the order of one in a million). **1937** MICHELL & BELZ *Elem. Math. Analysis* I. i. 94 A number is said to be of order 10^n if its ratio to 10^n is neither large nor small. *Ibid.*, The function $f(x)$ is said to be of the order of x^n as x converges to zero, or to be of the *n*th order with respect to x, if the ratio $f(x)/x^n$ has two focal bounds of the same sign. *Ibid.* 95 The notation $f(x) = O(x^n)$ is sometimes used to express that the function $f(x)$ is of the order of x^n, that is, of the *n*th order, when x converges to zero. **1947** R. L. WAKEMAN *Chem. Commercial Plastics* xxvi. 786 Concentrations of catalyst in the order of 1 per cent. **1955** D. A. QUADLING *Math. Analysis* xi. 178 We may write ..$|E/h^n| \leqslant K$, where K is independent of h. In such a case we say that E is 'of order h^n', or 'of the *n*th order of small quantities'. **1958** *Times* 10 Dec. 10/4 Their radioactivity was of the order of tens of millicuries. **1962** F. I. ORDWAY et al. *Basic Astronautics* x. 422 Specific impulses on the order of 3000 lb-sec/lb are possible. **1963** R. A. RANKIN *Introd. Math. Analysis* vii. 455 The statement $f(n) = O\{\phi(n)\}$ as $n \to \infty$, or for large n, means that there exist real numbers $K \geqq 0$ and $X \geqq X_0$, which are independent of n, and are such that $|f(n)| \leqq K\phi(n)$ for all $n > X$... The statement..may be read as '$f(n)$ is a quantity of the order of $\phi(n)$'. **1970** *Daily Tel.* 3 Dec. 21/1 (Advt.), A salary in the order of £1,500 is envisaged. **1971** *Sci. Amer.* June 24/1 Pulses lasting on the order of a nanosecond or longer can be reliably produced. **1975** *Nature* 10 Apr. 478/1 The average flow through the gorge is of the order of 2,000–3,000 cubic metres per second.

c. ***order of magnitude***: approximate number or magnitude in a scale in which equal steps correspond to a fixed multiplying factor (usu. taken as 10); a range between one power of 10 and the next; also, the order (ORDER *sb.* 10) of an infinitesimal or an infinite number. Also *attrib.* (with hyphens).

1875 *Jrnl. Anthrop. Inst.* IV. 143 The number of surnames extinguished becomes a number of the same order of magnitude as the total number at first starting in N. **1891** *Phil. Mag.* XXXII. 296 The electrochemical equivalent of gas atoms is of the same order of magnitude as that of the same atoms in electrolytes. **1903** D. A. MURRAY *First Course Infinitesimal Calculus* iii. 31 When the limiting value of the ratio m/n is a finite number, m and n are said..to be of the same order of magnitude. *Ibid.* 32 Infinite numbers, being reciprocals of infinitesimals, also have different orders of magnitude. **1909** J. P. IDDINGS *Igneous Rocks* I. vi. 193 The grains..are not all of the same order of magnitude, since one may be nine or ten times larger than another. **1937** MICHELL & BELZ *Elem. Math. Analysis* I. i. 94 Two numbers (or quantities) are of the same order of magnitude when their ratio is neither a large number nor a small fraction... It is often convenient to make a comparison of a number with a power of 10. **1941** COURANT & ROBBINS *What is Math.?* viii. 469 We shall say that b_n tends to infinity faster than a_n, or has a higher order of magnitude than a_n, if the ratio a_n/b_n (numerator and denominator of which both tend to infinity) tends to zero as n increases. **1968** R. A. LYTTLETON *Mysteries Solar Syst.* v. 157 The general size..would be expected to be of the order of the width of the stream. An order-of-magnitude estimate of this can be made in the following way. **1971** I. G. GASS et al. *Understanding Earth* iv. 78/2 The dynamo theory seems natural and unforced, and order-of-magnitude arguments are encouraging. **1971** *Physics Bull.* Oct. 586/1 The width of the second line of the hydrogen Balmer series, Hβ, is now considered to be a reliable measure of electron density to better than 10% over four orders of magnitude (say 10^{14}–10^{18} cm^{-3}). **1974** *Sci. Amer.* June 27/1 These processes multiply the power per unit area by 14 orders of magnitude from 10^5 watts per square centimeter..to 10^{19} watts per square centimeter.

d. *Math.* (i) The number of elements in a group.

1878 A. CAYLEY in *Amer. Jrnl. Math.* I. 51 A set of symbols α, β, γ..such that the product $\alpha\beta$ of each two of them..is a symbol of the set, is a group... When the number of the symbols (or terms) is $= n$, then the group is of the nth order. **1941** [see next sense]. **1965** PATTERSON & RUTHERFORD *Elem. Abstr. Algebra* ii. 36 The set of all permutations of 1, 2, 3, ..., n forms a group with respect to multiplication... It is a finite group of order $n!$ and it plays an important part in the theory of finite groups.

(ii) The smallest positive integer m for which g^m is equal to the identity element of a group, g being any given element.

1897 W. BURNSIDE *Theory of Groups of Finite Order* ii. 14 Let S be an operation of a group of finite order N... If S^{m+1} is the first of the series [*sc.* $S, S^2, S^3, \ldots$] which is the same as S,..then..$S^m = 1$... The integer m is called the order of the operation S. **1941** BIRKHOFF & MACLANE *Survey Mod. Algebra* vi. 147 Every element of a finite group G has as order a divisor of the order of G. **1968** I. D. MACDONALD *Theory of Groups* iii. 45 A periodic group is a group in which every element has finite order.

e. Each of the ranks or levels in a (non-mathematical) hierarchy in which every member save those in the lowest rank is a function of members of the next lower rank; *spec.* in *Logic* (see quot. 1908) and *Psychol.* (see quot. 1947). Freq. in *Comb.* with preceding ordinal number.

In *Math.* this sense is identical with 10.

1908 B. RUSSELL in *Amer. Jrnl. Math.* XXX. 238 A proposition containing no apparent variable we will call an elementary proposition... Elementary propositions together with such as contain only individuals as apparent variables we will call first-order propositions... We can thus form new propositions in which first-order propositions occur as apparent variables. These we will call second-order propositions... Thus, *e.g.*, if Epimenides asserts 'all first-order propositions affirmed by me are false', he asserts a second-order proposition. *Ibid.*, Propositions of order n.. will be such as contain propositions of order $n - 1$, but of no higher order, as apparent variables. **1929** A. W. WHITEHEAD *Process & Reality* II. ix. 285 We must provide a reason.. why one 'ground' is selected rather than another... We are thus driven back to a second-order 'ground' of probability. **1936** *Mind* XLV. 170 Necessary propositions are, thus, second-order propositions, which implicitly define 'proposition' by stating the properties of anything that is a proposition. **1941** J. S. HUXLEY *Uniqueness of Man* xi. 245 Cells are first-order individuals, bodies second-order ones, and human societies (like hydroid colonies or beehives) third-order ones. **1947** L. L. THURSTONE *Multiple-Factor Analysis* xviii. 411 Factors that are obtained from the test correlations will be called first-order factors... Factors that are obtained from correlations of the first-order factors will be called second-order factors. **1954** I. M. COPI *Symbolic Logic* 336 The hierarchy of orders prevents us from speaking about all functions or properties of a given type, permitting us to speak only about all first order functions of a given type, or all second order functions of a given type, etc. *Ibid.* 337 A proposition is of order $n + 1$ if it contains a quantifier on a propositional variable of order n but contains no quantifier on any propositional variable of order m where $m \geqslant n$. **1961** J. B. WILSON *Reason & Morals* i. 4 Philosophers themselves are accustomed to speak of philosophical statements as being 'second-order' statements. **1971** *Sci. Amer.* Aug. 98/1 All the axioms of a complete ordered field are first-order sentences except for the completion axiom.., which talks about a property of *all* subsets. **1977** A. HALLAM *Planet Earth* 75/3 In this system, fingertip tributaries are described as first-order; when two first-order streams combine the result is a second-order stream. Two second-orders give a third-order, and so on.

f. *Chem.* The sum of the exponents of the concentrations of reactants, or the exponent of any particular reactant, in the expression for the rate of a chemical reaction. Freq. in *Comb.* with preceding ordinal number.

1902 H. C. JONES *Elem. Physical Chem.* ix. 465 Although there are only two substances, there are three molecules involved in the reaction, and we would expect it to be a reaction of the third order. **1933** E. A. MOELWYN-HUGHES *Kinetics of Reactions in Solution* vii. 219 Ionic reactions have occasionally been found to be of a higher kinetic order than is now regarded as possible. **1950** W. J. MOORE *Physical Chem.* xvii. 514 This is also a second-order reaction. It is said to be *first-order with respect to* C_2H_5Br, *first-order with respect to* $(C_2H_5)_3N$, and *second-order over-all*. **1968** R. O. C. NORMAN *Princ. Org. Synthesis* iii. 78 The decarbonylation of acetaldehyde is of non-integral order but contains both unimolecular and bimolecular steps.

g. *Physics* and *Chem.* An integer (usually 1 or 2) characterizing a change of phase of a substance, equal to the order of the lowest-order derivatives of the free energy that exhibit a discontinuity at the change. [After the similar use of G. *ordnung* introduced by P. Ehrenfest 1933 (see quot. 1933).]

1933 *Proc. Sect. Sci. Kon. Akad. Wetensch. Amsterdam* XXXVI. 152 G may be a function of p and T which suffers along a λ-curve (Fig. 3) a discontinuity of the second order[1], so that along that curve..$\Delta G = 0$, whereas the differential coefficients of G make a jump. [[1]*Note*] Cf. P. Ehrenfest. Proceedings of this meeting. [i.e. *Ibid.* 153–7 (in Ger.)]. **1946** *Nature* 28 Dec. 924/2 At low temperatures both crystalline and amorphous states [of rubber] give place to the glass-hard condition. The transition to the glassy state —the so-called second-order transition—is discussed. **1948** *Jrnl. Chem. Physics* XVI. 665 (*heading*) Note on a relation between the order of a phase transition and discontinuities in the distribution functions of molecules. **1967** A. H. COTTRELL *Introd. Metall.* xiv. 220 First-order changes such as melting and polymorphic changes of crystal structure. **1968** C. G. KUPER *Introd. Theory Superconductivity* ii. 23 The superconducting transition in the absence of a magnetic field is of second order (Ehrenfest 1933). In other words, the specific heat is discontinuous but there is no latent heat.

11. *Nat. Hist.* One of the higher groups in the classification of animals, vegetables, or minerals, forming a subdivision of a *class*, and itself subdivided into families, or into genera and species.

Natural Order (of plants), a group consisting of genera or families naturally allied in general structure, as opposed to an Order in an artificial system (such as the Sexual system of Linnæus), the members of which agree only in some single characteristic which may or may not be important.

1760 J. LEE *Introd. Bot.* II. i. (1765) 74 The first general Division of the whole Body of Vegetables is into twenty-four Classes; these are again subdivided into Orders, the Orders into Genera, the Genera into Species, and the species into Varieties, where there are any worthy of Note. **1803** R. A. SALISBURY in *Trans. Linn. Soc.* (1807) VIII. 7 All the Natural Orders which agree in that respect [perigynous insertion of the stamens] may be arranged in one continuous series. **1828** STARK *Elem. Nat. Hist.* I. 32 Since the publication of the *Régne Animal*, Latreille and others have made a separate order of the Cheiroptera. **1830** LINDLEY *Introd. Nat. Syst. Bot.* 1 *heading*, The Natural Orders of Plants. **1859** DARWIN *Orig. Spec.* xiii. (1866) 488 All these genera descended from *A* form an order distinct from the genera descended from *I*. **1862** HUXLEY *Lect. Wrkng. Men* 49 If you divide the Animal Kingdom into Orders you will find that there are above one hundred and twenty. **1897** WILLIS *Flowering Pl.* I. 147 He will be able to classify..any new order that may be presented to him.

III. Sequence, disposition, arrangement, arranged or regulated condition.

12. a. Disposition of things in which one thing, or each of a number of things, duly succeeds another; sequence or succession in space or time; succession of acts or events; the mode in which this occurs, course or method of occurrence or action.

c **1320** *Cast. Love* 741 A trone..Seuene steppes þer beoþ þer-to, þat so feire wt ordre i-tized beoþ, Feiror þing in world no mon seoþ. **1382** WYCLIF *Luke* i. 8 Whanne Sacharie was set in presthod, in the ordre of his sort bifore God [**1388** in the ordir of his cours to fore God]. *a* **1548** HALL *Chron., Rich. III*, 25 b, In this ordre they passed throughe the palayce. **1596** DALRYMPLE tr. *Leslie's Hist. Scot.* VI. 317 S. Margaret buir to King Malcolme..Edgar, Alexander and Dauid; quhilkes all conforme to thair ordour war kingis. **1605** SHAKS. *Macb.* III. iv. 119 Stand not vpon the order of your going, But go at once. **1613** —— *Hen. VIII*, IV. i. *stage-direct.*, The Order of the Coronation. 1. A liuely Flourish of Trumpets. 2. Then, two Iudges. 3. Lord Chancellor, with Purse and Mace before him [etc.]. **1667** MILTON *P.L.* XI. 736 Of everie Beast, and Bird, and Insect small Came seavens, and pairs, and enterd in, as taught Thir order. **1737** POPE *Hor. Epist.* II. i. 316 Pageants on Pageants, in long order drawn. **1799** MACKINTOSH *Stud. Law Nature*, etc. Wks. 1846 I. 354 His method is inconvenient and unscientific: he has inverted the natural order. **1833** CRUSE *Eusebius* III. iv. 85 Now let us pursue the order of our history. **1846** MILL *Logic* I. v. §6 Instead of Co-existence and Sequence, we shall sometimes say, for greater particularity, Order in Place, and Order in Time.

b. ***order of battle***, the arrangement or disposition of sections of an army or naval force; now *spec.* the organization, movements, weaponry, etc., of an enemy force; the discovery of this; a tabular record of this. Also *attrib.*

1769 [see BATTLE *sb.* 12]. **1797** *Encycl. Brit.* III. 81/1 A Roman legion, ranged in order of battle, consisted of *hastati*, placed in the front; of *principes*, who were all old experienced soldiers, placed behind the former; and of *triarii*, heavy armed with large bucklers, behind the *principes*. **1889** H. R. GALL *Mod. Tactics* ii. 11 A practical and experienced soldier, seeing his enemy get under arms and form up in order of battle, will rapidly gather a lot of valuable information regarding his numbers, artillery positions [etc.]. **1924** W. C. SWEENEY *Military Intelligence* viii. 172 Enemy Order of Battle. This section is charged with maintaining the battle order of the enemy located within the area of responsibility of the commander. **1928** H. M. D. PARKER *Roman Legions* ix. 251 Arrian, in his order of battle against the Alani, shows that the legions were drawn up as a phalanx eight deep. **1934** WEBSTER s.v., *Order of battle*.., a tabular compilation by unit showing organization, commanders, movements, etc. over an extended time. **1946** CHANDLER & ROBB *Front-Line Intelligence* xii. 137 O/B (Order of battle) is a military science whose mission is to determine: (1) How strong the enemy is. (2) How he is organized. (3) What kind of weapons he has. (4) Experience of his troops. (5) Leadership of his troops. (6) Where his units are located. **1948** F. R. COWELL *Cicero & Roman Republic* ii. 36 The Greeks..were the first to invent an order of battle in which drilled man acting together as a unit..were able to overcome unorganised enemies many times more numerous. **1950** *Tactics & Techniques Infantry* (U.S.) II. ii. 312 When a new enemy unit is identified, order of battle records will indicate its last known strength and special equipment such as tanks, armored cars, and artillery; its combat record; or any quirks of its commander. A new operation is contemplated; order of battle data will provide information as to the strength, equipment, location, mobility, and combat efficiency of the specific units the enemy can employ. *Ibid.* 313 Strategic order of battle deals with all enemy military units, regardless of location. **1966** D. G. CHANDLER *Campaigns of Napoleon* (1967) 1099 Order of battle of the Army of Italy, April 12, 1796. **1971** *Combat Intelligence* (U.S. Dept. of Army, Field Manual 30-5) vii. 7-1 In determining enemy capabilities and probable courses of action, commanders must consider order of battle intelligence together with other intelligence pertaining to the enemy, weather, and terrain. **1975** T. ALLBEURY *Special Collection* ii. 11 There were daily situation reports from both the west and east fronts including Wehrmacht orders-of-battle. **1977** S. COULTER *Soyuz Affair* v. 42 The spy..who brought you the cypher table or the enemy order of battle.

13. Formal disposition or array; regular, methodical, or harmonious arrangement in the position of the things contained in any space or area, or composing any group or body.

c **1374** CHAUCER *Boeth.* IV. pr. vi. 105 (Camb. MS.) By the whiche disposicion the puruyance knytteth alle thinges in hir ordres. *a* **1400–50** *Alexander* 27 Þai..Of þe ordere of þat odde home þat ouer þe aire hingis Knew þe kynd. *c* **1425** LYDG. *Assembly of Gods* 250 A dew ordre in euery place ys expedyent. *c* **1450** HOLLAND *Howlat* 578 Gif I sall schewe The order of thar armis. *a* **1533** LD. BERNERS *Huon* lix. 205 Than paynyms on euery parte..ranne thether he that best myght, without kepynge of any good ordre. **1594** *Mirr. Policy* (1599) 49 Order is the due disposing of al things. **1695** WOODWARD *Nat. Hist. Earth* III. i. (1723) 165 A broken and confused Heap of Bodyes, placed in no Order to one another. **1712–14** POPE *Rape Lock* III. 168 When num'rous wax-lights in bright order blaze. **1860** TYNDALL *Glac.* II. xvii. 315 The crevasses are..apparently without law or order in their distribution. **1875** BEDFORD *Sailor's Pocket Bk.* I. (ed. 2) 22 The formation or disposition of a fleet is termed its Order.

b. In wider sense: The condition in which everything is in its proper place, and performs its proper functions.

1382 WYCLIF *Job* x. 22 The erthe of wrecchidnesse and of dercnessis; wher shadewe of deth, and noon order. **1423** JAS. I *Kingis Q.* cxxv, The strenth, the beautee, and the ordour digne Off his court riall, noble and benigne. **1599** SHAKS. *Hen. V*, III. Prol. 9 Heare the shrill Whistle, which doth order giue To sounds confus'd. **1667** MILTON *P.L.* III. 713 Till at his second bidding darkness fled, Light shon, and order from disorder sprung. **1734** POPE *Ess. Man* IV. 49 Order is Heav'n's first Law. **1882** A. W. WARD *Dickens* iv. 90 His love of order made him always the most regular of men.

†**c.** Form, shape (as resulting from arrangement). *Obs. rare.*

1578 LYTE *Dodoens* I. lxxxvii. 130 Nettell leaues..reduced to the order of a Pessarie..prouoketh the floures.

d. Equipment, uniform, etc., for some purpose, as ***drill order, field-day order, review order; marching order***: see MARCHING *vbl. sb.* d. Also with sbs. descriptive of appearance, as ***shirt-sleeve order***. (Orig. and chiefly *Mil.*)

1852 R. BURN *Naval & Milit. Techn. Dict. French Lang.* (ed. 2) II. 176/2 *Drill order*, tenue d'exercise, petite tenue. **1874** *Queen's Regulations Army 1873* 162 Review-order; to be worn when the Sovereign is present, for Royal escorts and guards of honour. *Ibid.* 163 Field-day-order; to be used generally for summer field-days, divisional and brigade drills,..[etc.]. *Ibid.*, Drill-order; to be used at ordinary drills and in riding-schools. **1876** Review order [see REVIEW *sb.* 3]. **1968** J. LOCK *Lady Policeman* viii. 60 My serge skirt feels heavy, my feet feel hot and sticky. Still, we are lucky to have shirt-sleeve order—the PCs haven't and look as if they are about to expire. **1973** R. HILL *Ruling Passion* II. vii. 138 The warm weather..had returned..it would be shirt-sleeve order before the day was out. **1977** 'D. MACNEIL' *Wolf in Fold* v. 49 Behind them, dressed in review order, marched the infantry of the British Army.

14. Disposition of measures for the accomplishment of a purpose; suitable action in view of some particular end; ***to take order***, to take measures or steps, to make arrangements. *Obs.* or *arch.*

1546 in Strype *Eccl. Mem.* (1721) II. II. App. C. 20 Preying you al to take order, that every commissioner in that shire may have a double or copy of this lettre. **1557** *Order of the Hospitalls* D vij, Bring them before a Court, that order may be taken therein. **1568** GRAFTON *Chron.* I. 176 When the king had thus taken order with his affayres in Denmarke, he returned shortly into England. **1603** SHAKS. *Meas. for M.* II. ii. 25 Let her haue needfull, but not lauish meanes, There shall be order for't. **1612** L. MUNCK in *Buccleuch MSS.* (Hist. MSS. Comm.) I. 115, I pray you therefore to take order to send it away with convenient speed. **1652** NEEDHAM tr. *Selden's Mare Cl.* 497 Certain orders made to make our Fishing prosperous, and successful. **1709** STRYPE *Ann. Ref.* I. I. ix. 129 After they had taken order to meet there again by eight of the clock in the morning, they shifted them, and departed. **1827** SOUTHEY *Hist. Penins. War* xxiv. II. 418 Even for this inevitable necessity no order having been taken by the Spanish authorities.

†**15.** Regular or customary mode of procedure; a method of action; a customary practice, an established usage. *Obs.*

1461 *Rolls of Parlt.* V. 494 After the olde ordre of their accomptes. **1526** *Pilgr. Perf.* (W. de W. 1531) 18 b, To make hym partener of his glory by a certeyn meane, and certeyn order. *a* **1548** HALL *Chron., Hen. VIII*, 143 b, To se a reformacion in the ordre of the kynges housholde. **1575** SERJT. FLEETWOOD in Ellis *Original Lett.* Ser. II. III. 29 It is harde to cause a Northeren Tanner, or any other in his old daies, to lerne a newe order of Tanning. *c* **1592** MARLOWE *Jew of Malta* IV. ii, He..sleeps in his own clothes,..'tis an order which the friars use. **1597** HOOKER *Eccl. Pol.* v. lxxii. §8 It came afterward to be an order, that even as the day of

Christs resurrection, so the other two, in memory of his death and buriall, were weekly. **1653** HOLCROFT *Procopius* I. 26 Belisarius seeing the Enemies order with their Engins, fell into a laughing. *a* **1715** BURNET *Own Time* (1823) I. 401 The constant order of that matter was, to set all the pipes a-running on Saturday night, that so the cisterns might be all full by Sunday morning.

16. A method according to which things act or events take place; the fixed arrangement found in the existing constitution of things; a natural, moral, or spiritual system in which things proceed according to definite laws. Chiefly in such phrases as ***order of nature, of things, of the world, moral order, spiritual order***, etc. (In quot. 1340–70, A particular instance of such method or arrangement, a law.)

1340–70 *Alex. & Dind.* 327 Bi an ordre of oure kinde whan we holde waxen,.. We schulle for-leten oure lif. **1553** EDEN *Treat. Newe Ind.* (Arb.) 5 No lesse confoundinge the order of thinges, than he whiche cloteth an ape in purple, and a king in sackecloth. **1558** KNOX *First Blast* (Arb.) 11 God by the order of his creation hath spoiled woman of authoritie and dominion. *Ibid.* 26, I haue proued.. by the ordre of Goddes creation.. that [etc.]. **1604** E. G[RIMSTONE] tr. *D'Acosta's Hist. Indies* III. xii. 158 Agreeing with the wisdom of the Creator, and the goodly order of nature. **1709** POPE *Ess. Crit.* 157 Objects.. Which out of nature's common order rise. **1785** PALEY *Mor. Philos.* Wks. 1825 IV. 13 The laws of custom are very apt to be mistaken for the order of nature. **1842** TENNYSON *Morte d'Arthur* 240 The old order changeth, yielding place to new, And God fulfils Himself in many ways. **1853** CARPENTER *Princ. Hum. Phys.* (ed. 4) 814 The belief in the stability of the order of nature, or in the invariable sequence of similar effects to similar causes. **1855** PRESCOTT *Philip II*, II. ix. (1857) 312 A craving, impatient spirit, which naturally made them prefer any change to the existing order of things. **1865** R. W. DALE *Jew. Temple* xix. (1877) 219 Christ's death is the foundation of new spiritual order. **1871** MORLEY *Voltaire* (1886) 3 More than two generations of men had almost ceased to care whether there be any moral order or not. **1875** MAINE *Hist. Inst.* ii. 28 The Druids, whom the Brehon lawyers regarded as having belonged altogether to the old order of the world. **1878** STEWART & TAIT *Unseen Univ.* i. §42. 60 The existence of an invisible order of things.

17. *Eccl.* In liturgics, A stated form of divine service, or administration of a rite or ceremony, prescribed by ecclesiastical authority; also the service so prescribed.

c **1400** *Apol. Loll.* 68 þis haue we seid schortly of þe wordre of lowsing, þat schepherdis of þe kirk ow to bind & lowse vnder gret moderacoun. **1548–9** (Mar.) *Bk. Com. Prayer* 1 An ordre for Mattyns dayly through the yere. **1563** WINȜET *Four Scoir Thre Quest.* Wks. 1888 I. 72 The doctrine and ordour laitlie set furth at Geneua. **1662** *Bk. Com. Prayer*, The Order of Confirmation. **1827** HALLAM *Const. Hist.* (1876) I. vi. 298 He had already.. enjoined the bishops to proceed against all their clergy who did not observe the prescribed order. **1872** E. W. ROBERTSON *Hist. Ess.* 209 The service for consecrating a Northumbrian sovereign.. is the oldest 'Order' on record.

18. *spec.* (from 15.) The prescribed or customary mode of proceeding in debates or discussions, or in the conduct of deliberative or legislative bodies, public meetings, etc., or conformity with the same; as ***order of business, to rise to a point of order, the speaker*** or ***motion is not in order***, or ***is out of order***. See also ***order of the day***, in 25.

a **1751** in *Camden Miscellany* (1969) XXIII. 170 His vanity will make him constantly puzzling our Speaker and our Chairmen of Committees, in points of order, which in reality he will know better than they. **1781** *Parl. Reg.* 27 Nov. 46 After some debate on the point of order, respecting the right of reply, claimed by those who had made a motion. **1782** *Gentl. Mag.* LII. 622 Here the House was all in a roar, to order! to order! On which Mr. Speaker rose. **1812** *Parl. Deb.* in *Examiner* 4 May 280/1 Here Gen. Manners called Sir Francis to order. **1817** *Parl. Deb.* 1849 Mr. Brougham spoke to order, and submitted, that these were expressions which were not consistent with the decorum and dignity of their proceedings. **1837** DICKENS *Pickw.* i. **1849** in Ht. Martineau *Hist. Peace* I. v. 51 A breach of order by some individual of warm temperament. **1888** BRYCE *Amer. Commw.* II. III. lxix. 545 Business begins by the 'calling of the convention to order' by the chairman of the National Party committee. **1898** *Daily News* 25 Mar. 2/3, I wish to ask you whether your privilege as Speaker is not limited to excluding questions which transgress order.

19. (= ***civil*** or ***public order***.) The condition in which the laws or usages regulating the public relations of individuals to the community, and the public conduct of members or sections of the community to each other, are maintained and observed; the rule of law or constituted authority; law-abiding state; absence of insurrection, riot, turbulence, unruliness, or crimes of violence.

1483 *Rolls of Parlt.* VI. 240/2 The ordre of all poletique Rule was perverted, the Lawes.. broken, subverted and contempned. **1500–20** DUNBAR *Poems* lxvi. 30 Gude rewle is banist our the Bordour, And rangat ringis but ony ordour. *a* **1548** HALL *Chron., Hen. VIII* 251 People without order or civilitie. **1558** KNOX *First Blast* (Arb.) 11 The subuersion of all good order, of all equitie and iustice. **1683** *Col. Rec. Pennsylv.* I. 76 Constables should go to publick houses to see good Ord^{rs} kept. **1712** STEELE *Spect.* No. 270 ¶1 Order is the Support of Society. **1784** COWPER *Task* II. 785 He graced a college, in which order yet Was sacred. **1861** M. PATTISON *Ess.* (1889) I. 47 Peace and order were maintained by police regulations of German minuteness and strictness. *Mod.* These riotous proceedings were at length suppressed and order restored.

20. a. State or condition generally (qualified as *good, bad*, etc.); normal, healthy, or efficient condition (in phrases ***in order, out of order***: see 27 b, 30).

1568 GRAFTON *Chron.* I. 133 This schoole.. newely repayred, and set it in much better order than before it had bene. **1667** MILTON *P.L.* IX. 402 All things in best order to invite Noontide repast, or Afternoon's repose. **1743** BULKELEY & CUMMINS *Voy. S. Seas* 1 The Ships were all in prime Order, all lately rebuilt. **1799** J. ROBERTSON *Agric. Perth* 153 Land may be said to be in good order, when it is clean of weeds [etc.]. **1836** *Backwoods of Canada* 162 The ducks are in the finest order during the early part of the summer. **1885** SIR W. R. GROVE in *Law Rep.* 15 Queen's Bench Div. 320 To see that the machinery of the truck is apparently in good order. *Mod.* The land is in bad order. *humorously.* **1809** MALKIN *Gil Blas* III. iv. ¶9 We.. drank as we liked, so that the servants'-hall and the dining-room were in equally high order when we took our leave. **1829** SCOTT *Jrnl.* 17 July (1890) II. 319 Her husband, being in good order [i.e. drunk] also, did not miss her till he came to Prestonpans.

b. *spec.* of tobacco. Cf. CASE *sb.*[1] 5 b.

1897 M. WHITNEY in *U.S. Dept. Agric. Farmers' Bull.* No. 60. 4 'Order' or 'case' in tobacco curing means a mint condition in which the tissue will not break. **1966** *Pubn. Amer. Dial. Soc.* XLV. 18 The tobacco has to be in order before it can be properly stripped.

21. *Mil.* The position in which a rifle is held as a result of the command to 'order arms': see ORDER *v.* 1 b.

1847 *Infantry Man.* (1854) 40 b, A company.. can load from the order with the same ease as from the shoulder. **1879** *Martini-Henry Rifle Exerc.* 6 When the rifle has been placed at the Order, the recruit will be instructed always to fall in with it in that position. **1938** J. CARY *Castle Corner* 435 The sentry threw his gun to the order and shouted in one word, 'alt-oo-go dar. Pass, friend'.

IV. The action or an act of ordering; regulation, direction, mandate.

†**22.** The action of putting or keeping in order; regulation, ordering, control. *Obs.*

a **1548** HALL *Chron., Edw. IV* 239 The French kyng, which then claymed to have the order and mariage of the yonge lady, as a pupille, ward and orphane. *Ibid., Hen. VIII*, 240 b, The Graunde Master Hostoden, which had the conduyte and ordre of the performaunce of her maryage. *c* **1550** CHEKE *Matt.* xxiv. 47 Truli J sai unto iou, he wil give him ye order of all y^t he hath. **1627** BP. HALL *Heaven vpon Earth* vii. Wks. 80 If excesse of passions be naturall to vs as men, the order of them is naturall to us as Christians. **1690** NORRIS *Beatitudes* (1694) I. 2 To give Laws and Precepts for the Instruction and Order of his Disciples.

23. a. An authoritative direction, injunction, mandate; a command, oral or written; an instruction. Cf. ***under starter's orders*** s.v. STARTER. Esp. in phr. ***under orders***.

a **1548** HALL *Chron., Hen. VIII* 94 The Ambassador was commaunded to kepe his house in silence,.. which ordre sore abashed the Frenche. **1596** SHAKS. *Tam. Shr.* IV. iii. 118–9 *Tail...* Grumio gaue order how it should be done. *Gru.* I gaue him no order, I gaue him the stuffe. **1646** BP. MAXWELL *Burd. Issach.* in *Phenix* (1708) II. 291 The Scotish Pope's Sermon, preach'd at Westminster, and printed by Order of the House. **1648** *Hamilton Papers* (Camden) 242 Commanded to obey the orders of the Committee of Estats. **1725** POPE *Odyss.* III. 414 Thy ship and sailors but for orders stay. **1799** WELLINGTON *Let. to Lieut-Gen. Harris* in Gurw. *Desp.* (1837) I. 30, I have not heard anything of the 12 pounders ordered to a new situation by the general orders of yesterday. **1835** DICKENS *Let. c* 29 Dec. (1965) I. 113, I regret to say that my being under orders from The Chronicle will prevent my enjoying the pleasure of seeing you tomorrow. **1859** TENNYSON *Enid* 152 Then the good king gave order to let blow His horns for hunting. **1884** *Times* (weekly ed.) 31 Oct. 15/1 The Agamemnon was under orders to strengthen the China fleet. **1969** H. R. F. KEATING *Inspector Ghote plays Joker* iii. 55 This authoritative figure took the microphone.. and made an announcement that the horses were under orders. **1977** A. C. H. SMITH *Jericho Gun* iv. 52 The PA commentary told him when they were under orders, and off.

b. ***Order in Council***: an order issued by the British sovereign (†or the governor of a British colony) on the advice of his or her privy council; also, an order issued by a government department under powers bestowed by Act of Parliament.

[**1674–5** (*title*) His Majesties Declaration for enforcing a late Order made in Council.] **1746** in *New Jersey Archives* (1882) 1st Ser. VI. 369 An Embargo on all Vessels in this Province for the Space of one Month unless his [*sc.* the president's] Order in Council shall be first Obtained for the Sailing of any Vessel. **1785** [see COUNCIL *sb.* 6 a]. **1809** *Ann. Reg. 1807* xii. 227/2 English commerce.. was not only greatly cramped, but lay prostrated on the ground, and motionless, before a protecting and self-defensive system was interposed by our orders in council. **1867** A. TODD *On Parl. Govt. in Eng.* I. v. 287 The crown has no right, by a mere Order in Council,.. to sanction a departure from the requirements of an existing law. **1892** W. R. ANSON *Law & Custom of Constitution* II. i. 47 An Order in Council is practically a resolution passed by the Queen in Council, communicated by publication or otherwise to those whom it may concern. **1911** *Encycl. Brit.* XX. 187/2 At the present day orders in council are extensively used by the various administrative departments of the government, who act on the strength of powers conferred upon them by some act of parliament. **1928** A. FITZROY *Hist. Privy Council* iv. 85 The Orders in Council in reply to Napoleon's Milan and Berlin decrees. **1961** *Halsbury's Laws Eng.* (ed. 3) XXXVI. 477 Proclamations and Orders in Council are instruments made by the Crown, the latter, by which the great majority of powers conferred on the Crown are required to be exercised, being orders expressed to be made by and with the advice of the Privy Council. **1964** *Mod. Law Rev.* XXVIII. III. 335 His Majesty could by Order in Council provide.. that the registers of a particular country.. should be deemed to be 'a public register'. **1973** *Trinidad & Tobago Overseas Express* 28 May 4/2 If the initiative came from Britain then the Order-in-Council method would be applied. **1977** *Gay News* 24 Mar. 1/3 Mr. Mason is expected to draw up an Order in Council.

c. ***doctor's orders***: instructions from one's physician; *fig.*, any injunctions which cannot be evaded.

1841 DICKENS *Let.* 18 Jan. (1969) II. 189, I have been obliged to make up my mind—on the doctor's orders—to stay at home this evening. **1886** H. MUNBY *Let.* 12 Mar. in D. Hudson *Munby* (1972) 410 Oh the miserable & false step you took when you separated me from you, by the doctor's orders. **1932** A. CHRISTIE *Peril at End House* ix. 104 No one .. will be admitted... 'Doctor's orders,' they will be told. A phrase very convenient and one not to be gainsayed. **1940** W. FAULKNER *Hamlet* 73 He returned to the gallery offering his candy about. 'Doctor's orders,' he said. 'He'll probably send me another bill now for ten cents for advising me to eat a nickel's worth of candy.' **1970** *Guardian* 26 Nov. 3/4 The absence of East German leader, Herr Ulbricht, whose official explanation of 'doctor's orders' failed to convince a Communist journalist. **1976** *Sci. Amer.* Mar. 127/2 'Doctor's orders' excuse almost any behaviour, yet they are mere advice.

d. Phr. ***orders are*** (also vulg. or joc. ***is***) ***orders***: commands must be obeyed.

1852 H. MELVILLE *Pierre* XVI. ii. 323, I am sorry, sir, but orders are orders:.. I can't disobey him. **1933** 'HAY' & 'ARMSTRONG' (title of play) Orders are orders. **1939** A. RANSOME *Secret Water* i. 18 I'm awfully sorry, you people. It just can't be helped. Orders is orders. **1973** *Times* 2 June 12/3 The delicious ridiculousness of the telegram perhaps has to be explained... But orders were orders.

e. *Computers.* = INSTRUCTION 4 c, COMMAND *sb.* 1 d; *esp.* one in machine language or another low-level language.

1946 GOLDSTINE & VON NEUMANN in J. Von Neumann *Coll. Wks.* (1961) V. 26 In performing a multiplication one usually performs about 3 or 4 associated additions or subtractions or comparisons; hence at least 4–5 orders must be given and at least that many numbers transferred—it is assumed that an order specifies only one basic operation, together with its transfers. *Ibid.*, We agree to store our orders in the same place as our numbers. **1948** [see INPUT *sb.* 2 d]. **1958** [see INSTRUCTION 4 c]. **1967** KLERER & KORN *Digital Computer User's Handbk.* I. i. 10 Machine-language coding uses the machine order code, which is directly interpreted by the instruction register. **1970** O. DOPPING *Computers & Data Processing* vi. 98 The detailed information sent to the input/output units from the local control units can be called orders.

24. *spec.* **a.** *Law.* A decision of a court or judge, made or entered in writing; in the Supreme Court, a direction of the court or a judge other than a final judgement.

a **1726** GILBERT *Cas. Law & Eq.* 137 Two Justices made an Order, that upon Sight thereof the Overseers should [etc.]. **1845** M^{c}CULLOCH *Taxation* II. vi. (1852) 264 Property sold by order of the Courts of Chancery and Exchequer. **1846** —— *Acc. Brit. Empire* (1854) II. 651 Relief.. treated as a loan.. may be recovered, under an order of justices, by attachment of the party's wages in his master's hands. **1883** *Law Rep.* 11 Queen's Bench Div. 591 An order nisi was afterwards obtained for a new trial, on the ground of misdirection. **1884** SIR H. COTTON in *Law Rep.* 12 Q.B.D. 345 The Orders under the Judicature Act provide that every order may be enforced in the same manner as a judgment, but still judgments and orders are kept entirely distinct. *Mod. Newspr.* A committal order was refused, but, by consent, a new order to pay 2*s.* a month was made.

b. *Banking* and *Commerce.* A written direction to pay money or deliver property, given by a person legally entitled to dispose thereof; a postal order.

1673 LD. SHAFTESBURY *Parl. Speech* in *Coll. Poems* 238 He saw.. the difference through all His Business between Ready Money and Orders. **1682** SCARLETT *Exchanges* 53 Its unadvisedly done for a Drawer.. to make his Bills payable to order. **1709** STEELE *Tatler* No. 60 ¶2 Pray pay to Mr. Tho. Wildair, or Order, the Sum of One Thousand Pounds, and place it to the Account of Yours, Humphrey Wildair. **1846** MRS. CARLYLE *Lett.* I. 366, I will send a Post-Office order, in repayment. **1866** CRUMP *Banking* iv. 90 By the Act of 1853 the drawer is allowed to make a stamped cheque payable to 'order'. **1883** LD. BLACKBURN in *Law Times Rep.* (1884) XLIX. 687/1 The bills of lading also were made out in the name of D. and Co., deliverable to their order. **1891** YEATS *Let.* Dec. (1954) 186, I had intended to return the £1 at once... Some days passed by.. the order which I enclose being all the time on my table awaiting posting. **1913** W. OWEN *Let.* 16 Dec. (1967) 221, I have cashed the Order long ago.

c. *Business.* A direction to make, provide, or furnish anything, at the responsibility of the person ordering; a commission to make purchases, supply goods, etc. ***a large order*** (*slang*), a large requirement, demand, request, proposal, etc. Also, ***a big order, a strong order***; ***a tall order***: see TALL *a.* 8 d.

1837 LONGF. in *Life* (1891) I. 262 He writes the piece to order, for Miss Clifton, who gives him a thousand dollars. **1845** DISRAELI *Sybil* III. vii, 'If it's an order, let us have it at once.' 'It is not an order', said Morley. **1855** BAGEHOT *Lit. Stud.* I. 29 Poets indeed are not made 'to order'. **1879** H. GEORGE *Progr. & Pov.* v. i. (1881) 242 Manufacturers find their orders falling off. **1880** TROLLOPE *Duke's Children* I. xxiv. 284 In her opinion it would be best that the Duke should.. give them money enough to live upon. 'Is not that a strong order?' asked the Earl. **1884** *Pall Mall G.* 24 July 5/1 That is, to employ an agreeable piece of slang, a very large order. **1892** W. S. GILBERT *Mountebanks* 1, Exchange all the beautiful things I've got inside?.. It's a large order. *a* **1903** *Mod.* 'Boots and shoes ready made, or to order.' **1907**

G. B. SHAW *Major Barbara* I. 210 *Barbara*. Yes. Give us Onward, Christian Soldiers. *Lomax*. Well, thats rather a strong order to begin with, dont you know. **1919** V. WOOLF *Night & Day* xxiv. 340 Well, Greek may be rather a large order. I was thinking chiefly of English. **1923** H. G. WELLS *Men like Gods* II. ii. 174 'You mean to jump this entire Utopian planet?' said Mr. Hunter. 'Big order,' said Lord Barralonga. **1927** *Sunday Times* 6 Mar. 23/3 There is no technical necessity now for the spark system, but it would be a rather big order to ask that all ships should abolish it. **1958** 'A. BRIDGE' *Portuguese Escape* viii. 125 This is quite a large order, isn't it? Suppose you tell me a bit more.

d. A pass for admission, without payment or at a reduced price, to a theatre or other place of entertainment, or to any place which is not unrestrictedly open to the public, as a museum, library, park, private establishment, etc.

1763 JOHNSON in *Boswell* 16 May, He has refused me an order for the play for Miss Williams, because he knows the house will be full. **1779** SHERIDAN *Critic* I. i, On the first night of a new piece they always fill the house with orders to support it. **1838** DICKENS *Nich. Nick.* ii, And about the box-office in the season,..when they give away the orders. **1855** *London as it is to-day* 134 During the session of Parliament, admission to hear the debates may be obtained by an order from a member. *Ibid.* 243 Museum of the Royal Institution. Admission by member's order. **1899** *Whitaker's Alm.* 378/1 Mansion House..Admission by order and a small fee. *Ibid.* 379/2 The *Times* and the *Daily Telegraph* Printing Offices. .. By special orders only. *Ibid.* 379/1 Woolwich..Royal Arsenal..admission..by order obtained at War Office.

e. *colloq.* A request for refreshments or food, e.g. in a restaurant or public house; a portion or helping of a dish or article of food or drink served in a restaurant, snack-bar, etc.

1836 DICKENS in *Bell's Life in London* 17 Jan. 1/1 'Pray give me your orders gen'lm'n—pray give me your orders'.. and demands for 'goes' of gin, and 'goes' of brandy, and pints of stout, and cigars of peculiar mildness, are vociferously made. *c* **1863** T. TAYLOR in M. R. Booth *Eng. Plays of 19th Cent.* (1969) II. 90 Now then James! Jackson, take orders. Interval of ten minutes allowed for refreshment. Give your orders, gents. **1898** A. BENNETT *Man from North* v. 29 A waitress, who approached and listened condescendingly to his order. **1904** 'O. HENRY' in *N.Y. World Mag.* 27 Mar. 10/4 And all this while she [*sc.* the waitress] would be performing astounding feats with orders of pork and beans, pot roasts, [etc.]. **1905** —— in *N.Y. World* 16 July (Oregon Fair Suppl.) 3/2 The screaming of 'short orders'..and all the horrid tumult of feeding man. **1934** G. B. SHAW *Village Wooing* 120 *Z*... Will you take a string bag? *A*. Yes. *Z*. Thanks very much. Shall I put the rest of the order into it? *A*. Of course. What else do you suppose I am buying it for? **1934** *Punch* 8 Aug. 158/3 The publican wanted to call on his clients with orders. 'What orders?'.. 'Beer.' **1949** *Crisis* (N.Y.) Nov. 305/2 They looked like the best tasting flapjacks in the world. They went inside and had an order. **1963** V. NABOKOV *Gift* v. 302 One could already hear the energetic '*psst, psst*' of Shahmatov, who had been served the wrong order. **1973** J. SHUB *Moscow by Nightmare* xiv. 165 Two orders of stuffed vine leaves, please. **1978** K. O'HARA *Ghost of T. Penry* xiii. 112 The pub sign was swinging furiously in the wind..inside..they were taking last orders.

f. *order to view*: a requisition from a house or estate agent to an occupier to allow a client to inspect his premises.

1911 W. J. LOCKE *Glory of Clementina Wing* xxiii. 337 A caretaker took the order-to-view given by the estate agents and conducted the party over the place. **1922** E. H. YOUNG *Bridge Dividing* III. xi. 301 It's to let. I've got an order to view. **1940** L. MACNEICE (*title of poem*) Order to view. **1967** C. DRUMMOND *Death at Furlong Post* iv. 36 Vacant these fourteen years... There have been many orders to view. **1971** M. TRIPP *Five Minutes with Stranger* II. v. 125 I'll call in personally tomorrow and get an order to view.

V. Phrases and Combinations. See also 10, 23, 24, etc.

25. order of the day.

a. In a legislative body, the business set down for debate on a particular day (= F. *l'ordre du jour*). **b.** Specific commands or notices issued by the commanding officer to the troops under his command. **c.** *colloq.* The prevailing rule or custom of the time.

1698 *House of Commons Jrnl.* 8 Apr. (1742–62) XII. 198/2 The House, according to the Order of the Day, resolved itself into a Committtee of the whole House to consider further of Ways and Means for raising the Supply granted to his Majesty. **1729** E. KNATCHBULL *Parliamentary Diary* (1963) 95 The orders of the day were moved for and so this day's debate ended. **1779** *Parl. Reg.* 5 May 401 The order of the day was read for the House to resolve itself into a committee of supply. **1792** A. YOUNG *Trav. France* 551 *note*, Writers who wish to spread the taste of revolutions, and make them every where the *order of the day*. **1795** WASHINGTON in Sparks *Life & Writ. Gouv. Morris* (1832) III. 66 Peace has been (to borrow a modern phrase) the order of the day. **1840** R. H. DANA *Bef. Mast* xxvi. 87 Industry was the order of the day. **1842** BRANDE *Dict. Sci.* etc. 895/2 The motion *for reading the order of the day* has equally [with a motion to adjourn] the effect of superseding the existing question. **1863** COX *Inst. Eng. Gov.* I. ix. 137 Orders of the day..relate to business for which by orders of the House particular days are appointed. **1897** *Pall Mall Mag.* Dec. 583 November's dark hours and gloomy fogs were once more the order of the day. **1959** *Times* 19 Sept. 7/7 The restorers are at work: *anastylosis* is the order of the day. **1976** *Abingdon Herald* 9 Dec. 5/2 The removal of ice from the moving parts and sheets was the order of the day. The light air and bright cold conditions required a high degree of concentration.

26. by order.

†**a.** = *in order*: see 27. *Obs.*

13.. *Coer de L.* 2961 Be order they comen in her maneres. *c* **1380** WYCLIF *Sel. Wks.* III. 352 He is dettour to eche man but bi ordre. *c* **1385** CHAUCER *L.G.W.* 2514 *Phyllis*, But al hire lettere wryte I ne may By ordere. **1604** E. G[RIMSTONE] *D'Acosta's Hist. Indies* III. xxvi. 199 All these notable Earthquakes..have succeeded one an other by order. **1649** JER. TAYLOR *Gt. Exemp.* Exhort. §11 What he abated by the order to his intendment and design. **1655** STANLEY *Hist. Philos.* I. (1701) 24/1 Every Citizen according to his age, should..by and in order declare his judgement.

b. By authoritative direction or command; see 23 and 24.

27. in order.

a. In proper sequence or succession, according to rank, importance, seniority, size, position, date, affinity, etc.

c **1400** *Destr. Troy* 9797 All þai toldyn hym tale,.. Of þaire answare, in ordur. *c* **1500** *How Plowman lerned Paternoster* 113 in Hazl. *E.P.P.* I. 213 In ordre folowed them other thre. *a* **1548** HALL *Chron., Rich. III* 29 After whome marched in order quene Anne his wife likewyse crouned. **1667** MILTON *P.L.* II. 507 Forth In order came the grand infernal Peers. **1791** COWPER *Retired Cat* 94 The lowest first, and without stop The rest in order to the top. **1871** R. ELLIS *Catullus* xxxvii. 2 Ninth post in order next beyond the twins cap-crown'd. *Mod.* Are the letters in order?

b. In a condition in which the elements or constituents are properly disposed with reference to each other, or to their purpose; in proper condition; in obedience to constituted authority or usage.

c **1380** WYCLIF *Wks.* (1880) 349 þe fendes of helle trowen alle þat we trowen, but hem failen charite to bynde her schelde in order. **1526** TINDALE *1 Cor.* xi. 34 Wother thynges will I set in order when I come. **1535** COVERDALE *2 Kings* xx. 1. **1566** PAINTER *Pal. Pleas.* II. 213 Havinge set all thinges in order for that voyage. **1709** POPE *Ess. Crit.* 672 Thus useful arms in magazines we place, All rang'd in order, and dispos'd with grace. **1772** *Test Filial Duty* II. 219 Their house is putting in order. **1878** E. JENKINS *Haverholme* 28 Why should we spend a hundred thousand men and millions of money in setting that part of the world in order? **1897** MARY KINGSLEY *W. Africa* 525 One of the chief duties of these societies is to keep the women in order.

c. Appropriate to or befitting the occasion; suitable; called for; also, in fashion, current, correct. orig. *U.S.*

a **1861** T. WINTHROP *John Brent* (1862) viii. 85 If the gent has made a remark what teches you, apologies is in order. **1878** J. H. BEADLE *Western Wilds* xxv. 399 One week sufficed to conclude my business in Oregon, but before leaving a few general notes are in order. **1903** *N.Y. Times* 4 Sept. 2/3 Good byes were in order on the Erin last night. **1931** G. T. CLARK *Leland Stanford* xiv. 457 It was quite in order..that when this bill was before the Senate, he should express himself upon it. **1973** 'M. INNES' *Appleby's Answer* xv. 128 A confidential and man-to-man note will be in order. **1977** N. MARSH *Last Ditch* vi. 151 Is it in order for us to ring up your father and ask him to dine?

d. *in* (or *at, on*) *short* (or *quick*) *order*: without delay, immediately, summarily. orig. *U.S.*

1834 W. G. SIMMS *Guy Rivers* I. 204 Be off now in a hurry, or I shall fire upon you in short order. *a* **1852** F. M. WHITCHER *Widow Bedott Papers* (1856) xxv. 307 If ever you dew it agin you'll git your walkin'-ticket on short order. **1892** *Outing* Apr. 19/1, I was so thoroughly comfortable that I went to sleep in short order. *a* **1916** H. JAMES *Ivory Tower* (1917) III. iv. 198 Your solution, is marriage to a wife at short order. **1932** N. HODGKINS *Some Canad. Ess.* 202 We had made a sailor of him in short order. **1973** E. BERCKMAN *Victorian Album* 180 The woman checked... This doesn't mean she failed to tally, because she did in short order—and all the more savagely. **1976** *Publishers Weekly* 24 May 58/3 Linda descends on twenties London to become, in short order, a model, the toast of lords [etc.].

28. in order to.

†**a.** In regard or respect to, in reference to; for the sake of. *Obs.*

1526 *Pilgr. Perf.* (W. de W. 1531) 6 The rychesse of y[e] worlde hath no goodnes, but in order to man. **1646** H. LAWRENCE *Comm. Angells* 56 Wee come to their punishment, which..is necessary for us to know, in order to this subject. **1656** JEANES *Fuln. Christ* 393 That which Paul speaketh of himselfe, and Timothy, in reference unto the Corinthians, 2 Cor. 6. 11 is applicable unto Christ in order unto all Christians. **1669** R. MONTAGU in *Buccleuch MSS.* (Hist. MSS. Comm.) I. 427, I gave..an account in my last of what I had done in order to his Majesty's commands.

b. (*a*) With a view to the bringing about of (something), for the purpose of (some prospective end).

1655 *Clarke Papers* (Camden) III. 33 Col. Jones and Col. Penruddock are sent downe into the west in order to theire tryall. **1672** EVELYN *Diary* 1 Sept., After this I returned home, in order to another excursion to the sea side. **1711** SPOTSWOOD in Perry *Hist. Coll. Amer. Col. Ch.* I. 188 To meet me next week on our frontiers in order to a treaty. **1773** BURKE *Corr.* (1844) I. 428 A meeting ought..to be called.. in order to a regular opposition in parliament. **1837** HT. MARTINEAU *Soc. Amer.* II. 229 In order to shoemaking, there must be tanning. **1869** GOULBURN *Purs. Holiness* viii. 67 In order to the existence of love between two parties, there must be a secret affinity between them.

(*b*) with *infinitive* object.

1711 STEELE *Spect.* No. 48 ¶2, I shall next Week come down..in order to take my Seat at the Board. **1774** GOLDSM. *Nat. Hist.* (1776) II. 336 They then incur every danger, in order to rescue their young. **1818** CRUISE *Digest* (ed. 2) II. 584 Lord Mansfield rightly said, it was not necessary to show actual force, in order to prove an ouster. **1868** *Chambers' Encycl.* III. 142/1 In order to support the roof.. a second row of columns was introduced.

†**c.** Formerly also **in order for**: = b. *Obs.*

1746 ELIZA HEYWOOD *Female Spect.* No. 24 (1748) IV. 281 The various stratagems to which she was obliged to have recourse, in order for this discovery. **1749** FIELDING *Tom Jones* VIII. xi, There was scarce a Wickedness which I did not meditate, in order for my Relief.

29. in order that: With the aim or purpose that, to the end that.

1711 ADDISON *Spect.* No. 62 ¶2 In order..that the Resemblance in the Ideas be Wit [etc.]. **1832** HT. MARTINEAU *Hill & Valley* viii. 126 In order that you may see that we cannot help doing so. **1875** JOWETT *Plato* I. 123, I have come to you now, in order that you may speak to him.

30. out of order: Not in proper sequence, orderly arrangement, or settled condition; in disorder or derangement; unsettled; not in proper or normal condition of action, mind, bodily health, etc. Now freq. of mechanical and electrical devices. (In the sense 'indisposed' very common in 18th c.) Also (sometimes hyphenated) *attrib.*

a **1548** HALL *Chron., Hen. VIII* 70 The kyng beyng infourmed, that his realme of Irelande was out of ordre. **1596** DALRYMPLE tr. *Leslie's Hist. Scot.* I. 31 Ky, nocht tame ..bot lyke wylde hartes, wandiring out of ordour. **1608** TOPSELL *Serpents* (1658) 771 The patient is much disquieted, vexed, and too much out of order. **1611** BIBLE *Transl. Pref.* 3 If out of order, they [the Scriptures] will reforme vs. **1661** BOYLE *Style of Script.* (1675) 113 To mend a watch, that's out of order. **1666** PEPYS *Diary* 6 Aug., Find my wife mightily out of order, and reproaching of Mrs. Pierce and Knipp as wenches. **1722** *Lond. Gaz.* No. 6098/1 His..Majesty being out of Order, by reason of a Cold. **1772** JOHNSON *Let. to Mrs. Thrale* 4 Nov., Since I came to Ashbourne I have been out of order. I was well at Litchfield. **1859** DARWIN *Orig. Spec.* iv. (1866) 145 A high organisation would be..more liable to be put out of order and thus injured. **1882** *Daily Tel.* 28 Oct. 2/4 Waters in Sheffield district still out of order, and angling at a standstill. **1926** E. O'NEILL *Great God Brown* III. i. 70, I forgot to tell him something important this morning and our phone's out of order. **1928** D. L. SAYERS *Unpleasantness at Bellona Club* xii. 141 The telephone cabinet..was so annoyingly labelled 'Out of Order'. **1950** T. WALSH *Nightmare in Manhattan* III. 82 A phone booth behind the news-stand—it has an out-of-order sign on it. **1971** R. THOMAS *Backup Men* xxii. 190 The two elevators wore *out of order* signs. **1977** A. SCHOLEFIELD *Venom* IV. 172 She had also telephoned the house..and had received an out-of-order tone.

31. *attrib.* and *Comb.*, as ***order-maker, system***; ***order-making*** vbl. sb. and adj.; ***order-disorder, -loving*** adjs.; **order clerk**, a clerk who enters business orders; **order form**, a partially blank form to be filled up in giving a business order; **order man, orderman**, a man who takes or makes out orders; **order mark** (see quot. 1963); **order pad**, a pad (PAD *sb.*[3] 4) of order forms; **order-paper**, (*a*) a paper on which questions, etc., coming in the order of the day, in a legislative assembly, are entered; (*b*) in the House of Lords, a publication of questions, etc., for the remainder of the session; **order wire** *Teleph.*, a wire used to communicate verbal information about the setting up of a connection for a customer, or between operators at different manual exchanges, or between a customer and an operator in establishing a data link; **order-word** (F. *mot d'ordre*), the military pass-word of the day, a watchword.

1938 *Nature* 9 Apr. 643/1 Fröhlich has tried to interpret the λ-phenomenon of liquid helium as an order-disorder transition. **1964** *Discovery* Oct. 65/2 The theory of order-disorder transformations in alloys. **1894** *Country Gentlemen's Catal.* 3 We hope..that subscribers..will use our Enquiry and Order Forms. **1929** *Radio Times* 8 Nov. 114/2 Note in Order Form below the extra saving made by ordering 500 or 1000 [cigarettes] at a time. **1972** *Accountant* 26 Oct. 504/1 The phrase 'order forms' is to be understood to mean forms which the company makes available for other persons to order goods or services from the company. **1890** 'R. BOLDREWOOD' *Miner's Right* (1899) 81/1 His order-loving soul was daily vexed by reason of the irregularities. **1906** W. JAMES *Mem. & Stud.* (1911) ix. 222 Not only in the great city, but in the outlying towns, these natural ordermakers, whether amateurs or officials, came to the front immediately. **1902** —— *Var. Relig. Exper.* viii. 170 Unhappiness is apt to characterize the period of order-making and struggle. **1963** *Times* 22 Feb., The order-making machinery in the Bill. *a* **1951** A. C. HEADLEY in Murdoch & Drake-Brockman *Austral. Short Stories* (1951) 367 It was the rent and the order man, and a new pair of shoes. **1977** *N.Z. Herald* 5 Jan. 2-11/5 (Advt.), An experienced timber orderman is required for timber yard in western suburbs. **1912** A. BRAZIL *New Girl at St. Chad's* vi. 99 By general custom all pencils..or other stray possessions were put into what was known as the forfeit tray, whence their owners might reclaim them by paying the penalty of the loss of an order mark. **1963** BARNARD & LAUWERYS *Handbk. Brit. Educ. Terms* 141 *Order mark*, a punishment (usually confined to girls' schools) for offences of a comparatively trivial kind. **1936** L. C. DOUGLAS *White Banners* x. 226 She pushed the order-pad and pencil towards him. **1972** M. KAYE *Lively Game of Death* (1974) i. 4 Manufacturers..whip out order pads and hope to sell enough merchandise. **1896** *Times* (weekly ed.) 19 Jan. 52/2 There were as many as 70 questions on the order paper. **1946** *May's Treat. Parliament* (ed. 14) II. xii. 245 Together with the Minutes of Proceedings is printed the Order Paper, consisting of a programme of future business so far as appointed. **1829** *Censor* 224 Render it incumbent on him to adopt the Shilling Order system. **1912** THIESS & JOY *Toll Telephone Pract.* xiv. 214 (*caption*) Phantom circuit used as an order wire. **1948** J. ATKINSON *Herbert & Procter's Telephony* (new ed.) I. xvii. 345/1 The out-going order-wires are multiplied throughout all positions at the originating exchange. **1973** R. N. RENTON *Data Telecommunication* ix. 211/1 Communication with the customer for setting up and clearing connections is effected over telephone circuits (order wires) via the normal telephone exchange. **1898** T. HARDY *Wessex Poems* 71 Marmont against the third gave the order-word.

order ('ɔːdə(r)), *v.* Forms: 3–7 ordre, 5 ordyr, 6 ordour, -ur, 4– order. [ME. *ordre-n*, f. *ordre*, ORDER *sb.*: cf. OF. *ordreer*, f. *ordre*, and L. *ordināre*, f. *ordin-em*, whence OF. *ordener*, mod.F. *ordonner*; Eng. *to order* is thus the equivalent in sense of L. *ordināre* and F. *ordonner*, and so in part a doublet of ORDAIN.]

I. 1. a. *trans.* To give order or arrangement to; to put in order; to arrange or dispose in a particular order; to arrange methodically or suitably, place in right order; *spec.* to draw up in order of battle, to array, marshal. *arch.*

a **1240** *Sawles Warde* in *Lamb. Hom.* 261 Nihe wordes þer beoð, ah hu ha beoð iordret ant sunderliche isette..were long to tellen. **1514** BARCLAY *Cyt. & Uplondyshm.* (Percy Soc.) 20 In what maner were ordred theyr offrynges. *a* **1533** LD. BERNERS *Huon* lviii. 197 Kyng yuoryn..ordred them in batayle. *a* **1548** HALL *Chron., Hen. VI*, 99 b, He ordred his battail, like a man expert in marciall science. **1611** BIBLE *Transl. Pref.* 2 When he corrected the Calender, and ordered the yeere according to the course of the Sunne. **1652–62** HEYLIN *Cosmogr.* III. (1673) 114/1 The news came to her as she was ordering her hair. **1683** *Apol. Prot. France* i. 3, I..found him ordering his Books, and loose Papers. **1719** DE FOE *Crusoe* I. v, Boards like a dresser, to order my victuals upon. **1762** *Ann. Reg.* 142 The officiating clerk..observing..a genteel couple standing in the aile, ordered them into a pew..being afterwards thanked for his civility. **1842** TENNYSON *Day-Dream* 74 Here all things in their place remain, As all were order'd, ages since. **1875** HOWELLS *Foregone Concl.* 216 Ordering her hair, some coils of which had been loosened by her flight.

b. *Mil.* ***to order arms (a gun)***, to bring a firearm into a position in which it is held vertically against the right side, the butt on the ground.

1826 SCOTT *Woodst.* viii, Order your musket. **1844** *Regul. & Ord. Army* 260 The Commanding Officer is then to direct the Parade to Order Arms. **1847** *Infantry Man.* (1854) 40 b, Arms are to be ordered without the word Order arms.

†**c.** To class, to rank. *Obs. rare.*

1662 PETRIE *Ch. Hist.* ii, Despising the legions of Angels (socially ordered with him). *Ibid.*, All these..are ordered among the Members of the Church.

2. a. To set or keep in order or proper condition; to adjust, dispose, or carry on according to rule; to regulate, direct, conduct, rule, govern, manage; to settle. (In quot. 1593, to regulate the conveyance of (troops).)

1509 FISHER *Fun. Serm. C'tess Richmond* Wks. (1876) 296 Her owne houshold with meruayllous dylygence and wysdome this noble prynces ordred. *a* **1548** HALL *Chron., Rich. III*, 52 b, While he was thus ordrynge his affaires, tydinges came that the Earle of Richemond was passed Severne. **1593** SHAKS. *Rich. II*, v. iii. 140 Good Vnckle helpe to order seuerall powres To Oxford. **1599** —— *Hen. V*, v. Prol. 39 To order peace betweene them. **1673** TEMPLE *Obs. United Prov.* Wks. 1731 I. 57 Each of the Provinces was left to order the Matter of Religion, as they thought fit. **1710** PHILIPS *Pastorals* v. 76 At that he wound The murm'ring Strings, and order'd ev'ry Sound. **1739** LABELYE *Short Acc. Piers Westm. Br.* 72 A small Arch, which is order'd to be turned under each of the Abutments. **1768** STERNE *Sent. Journ.* I. 1 They order, said I, this matter better in France. **1886** MRS. LYNN LINTON *Paston Carew* iii, 'Carpe diem' was the motto by which he ordered his days. **1893** FAIRBAIRN *Christ in Mod. Theol.* II. II. iii. 437 The father so rules..as to order and bless his home.

†**b.** with clause: To settle, determine. *Obs.*

1523 FITZHERB. *Husb.* §3 The ploughe fote..is as a staye to order of what depenes the ploughe shall goo. **1581** SIDNEY *Apol. Poetrie* (Arb.) 63 One verse did but beget another, without ordering at the first, what should be at the last.

c. *refl.* To conduct oneself, behave. *arch.*

1535 COVERDALE *Prov.* xxiii. 1 Ordre thy self manerly with yᵉ thinges that are set before yᵉ. —— *2 Macc.* x. 23 When they had ordred them selues manly with their weapens & hondes. **1548–9** (Mar.) *Bk. Com. Prayer, Catechism*, To ordre myselfe lowlye and reuerentlye to al my betters.

d. Of the Deity, etc.: To regulate or determine (occurrences, events, etc.); to ordain.

1642 ROGERS *Naaman* 41 Lo, how doth the Lord order the meanes unto it? **1671** MILTON *Samson* 30 Why was my breeding order'd and prescrib'd As of a person separate to God, Design'd for great exploits? **1719** DE FOE *Crusoe* I. ix, If the good providence of God had not wonderfully ordered the ship to be cast up nearer to the shore. **1819** SHELLEY *Cenci* v. ii. 121 So my lot was ordered. **1856** FROUDE *Hist. Eng.* (1858) I. ii. 91 It was ordered otherwise, and doubtless wisely.

†**3.** To put in order or readiness (for a purpose); to make ready, prepare. *Obs.*

1526 *Pilgr. Perf.* (W. de W. 1531) 1 Shewynge how the pilgrym of yᵉ waye of religyon sholde prepare and order hymselfe. *a* **1533** LD. BERNERS *Huon* lxiii. 219 Than the couent..orderyd themselues & so went out of the abbay to mete Huon. **1616** SURFL. & MARKH. *Country Farme* 279 That manner of ordering things, whereby they are stamped and beaten verie small. **1657** *Burton's Diary* (1828) II. 10 Read your votes..and so order your way for an explanatory Bill. **1662** PEPYS *Diary* 26 Apr., They brought us also some caveare, which I attempted to order. **1722** DE FOE *Plague* (1756) 167 Some Kitchen-ware for ordering their Food.

†**4.** To bring into order or submission to lawful authority; hence, to inflict disciplinary punishment on; to correct, chastise, punish. *Obs.*

1526 *Pilgr. Perf.* (W. de W. 1531) 219 An incorrigyble persone that wyll not be ordered. *a* **1533** LD. BERNERS *Huon* lxxxi. 250 Syn that he is one of my peers I wyll ordre hym by iugement. **1642** T. LECHFORD *Plain Dealing* (1867) 91 One master Doughty, a Minister,..spake so in publique,..which was held a disturbance, and the Ministers spake to the Magistrate to order him. **1667** PEPYS *Diary* 9 Dec., This Lord is a very proud and wicked man, and the Parliament is likely to order him.

†**5.** To take a certain 'order' or course with (a person or thing); to treat, deal with, manage (in a specified manner). *Obs.*

1513 MORE *Rich. III* (1883) 34 Yet is there none that..knoweth better to order him, then I that so long haue kept him. **1562** in *Child-Marriages* 12 He was ordred worse then any seruaunt in her fathers house. **1660** SHARROCK *Vegetables* 18 Many..being thus ordered..will bear flowers the second year after the sowing. **1681** GLANVILL *Sadducismus* II. 105, I..was assured that he had been well fed, and ordered as he used to be. **1721** *St. German's Doctor & Stud.* 278 To take such persons..that they may be ordered according to the law. **1760** BROWN *Compl. Farmer* II. 45 The way of ordering marle must be according to the nature of it. **1799** G. SMITH *Laboratory* I. 401 Hang it to dry, and order it as you do other coloured silks.

II. 6. a. To give orders for (something to be done, etc.); to enjoin, bid, command, direct; to prescribe medically. Const. with simple obj., obj. clause, or obj. and inf. pass., expressing the thing enjoined; more rarely with obj. and complement. Also with ellipsis of *to be* (chiefly *U.S.*)

a **1550** *Freiris of Berwik* 489 in *Dunbar's Poems* (1893) 301 That he compeir in to our habeit quhyt, Vntill I ordour it, wer a grit dispyte. **1637** *Star Chamb. Decree* §11 in *Milton's Areop.* (Arb.) 14 It is further Ordered and Decreed that no Merchant, Bookseller [etc.]. **1667** D. ALLSOPP in *12th Rep. Hist. MSS. Comm.* App. v. 8 They passed the Bill..and ordered it to be reported the next day. **1706** A. BEDFORD *Temple Mus.* vii. 143 Moses had ordered the Kings a Copy of the Law. **1749** FIELDING *Tom Jones* XIV. ii, I have ordered to be at Home to none but yourself. **1781** J. WITHERSPOON in *Pennsylvania Jrnl.* 9 May. 1/2 These things were ordered delivered to the army. **1794** J. SMITHEMAN *Let. to Parr* 19 Mar. in *Parr's Wks.* (1828) VIII. 567, I have..to beg that you will have the goodness to order a proper monument erected to his memory. **1799** in *Essex Inst. Hist. Coll.* (1877) XIII. 61 But the wind growing faint, I ordered the signal taken in. **1809** MALKIN *Gil Blas* II. v. ¶2 He ordered my companions to be handcuffed. **1841** LANE *Arab. Nts.* I. 102 Who ordered again that four hundred pieces of gold should be given to him. **1873** J. H. BEADLE *Undevel. West* xi. 191 My bill was introduced by Senator Williams of Oregon, read by title, and ordered printed. **1875** J. G. HOLLAND *Sevenoaks* in *Scribner's Monthly* Sept. 599/1 He went out,..jumped into Mr. Talbot's waiting coupe, and ordered himself driven home. **1891** E. PEACOCK *N. Brendon* I. 228 The doctor had ordered as much fresh air as possible. **1938** W. T. WALSH *Philip II* xxi. 423 The Duchess ordered ships fitted out to meet and escort him. **1972** *Sci. Amer.* July 76/1 Frederick ordered the children raised in silence, so that they would not hear one spoken word. **1976** M. MACHLIN *Pipeline* l. 510 Coutts ordered the ship's speed reduced to six knots. **1977** *Time* 19 Dec. 9/2 When the local military commander was ordered removed after having congratulated the throng on its patriotic singing, Lagoa angrily summoned the marchers back on the pavement.

†**b.** To appoint (a day) for some purpose, by a parliamentary order. *Obs.*

1669 MARVELL *Corr.* Wks. 1872–5 II. 292 To-morrow is..ordered for the motion of the King's supply. **1676** *Ibid.* 514 They rose, ordering Friday next to resume this consideration.

7. a. To give orders to, command, authoritatively direct (a person or agent, *to do* something, etc.).

1628 HOBBES *Thucyd.* (1822) 79 The Lacedemonians were orderd to furnish..so many more. **1749** FIELDING *Tom Jones* I. ii, He ordered an elderly Woman to rise..and come to him. **1855** PRESCOTT *Philip II*, I. iii. (1857) 103 He..ordered them to prepare to march on the following night. *absol.* **1824** MRS. CAMERON *Marten & Scholars* iv. 26 Like some little boys, who, when they are hearing other children say their lessons,..order about them as if they were grown men. **1883** FROUDE *Short Stud.* IV. II. i. 176 He belonged himself to the class whose business was to order rather than obey.

b. *ellipt.* To command or direct (a person) to go or come *to*, *into*, *upon* (a place, etc.), *away*, *here*, *home*, *out*, etc. ***to order about***, to order hither and thither in a peremptory manner, domineer over, treat as a subordinate.

1667 *Ormonde MSS.* in *10th Rep. Hist. MSS. Comm.* App. v. 58 The two soldiers ordered upon him. **1723** *Pres. St. Russia* I. 157 The Czar ordered him for Astracan. **1727** SWIFT *Country Post* Wks. 1755 III. I. 177 This day a jackdaw..was ordered close prisoner to a cage. **1747** *Gentl. Mag.* 246 A bill is order'd into parliament for vesting the forfeited estates of certain traytors in his majesty. **1853** C. BRONTË *Villette* I. iv. 74, I refused to be ordered about and thrust from him. **1855** MACAULAY *Hist. Eng.* xv. III. 607 He was exasperated by the thought that he was ordered about and overruled by Russell. **1898** RIDER HAGGARD *Dr. Therne* i. 5 He..was ordered to a warmer climate. **1942** R. G. COLLINGWOOD *New Leviathan* 201 For a man of weak or undeveloped will nothing is so pleasant as being ordered about.

c. ***to order up***, in the game of euchre: to order (the suit of the card turned up by an opponent who is dealing) to be adopted as trumps; also *absol.*

1847 J. S. ROBB *Streaks of Squatter Life* 129 His antagonist ordered the king up. **1878** [see ASSIST *v.* 7 c]. **1950** *Hoyle's Games Modernized* (ed. 20) 88 If the non-dealer thinks his hand good enough, with the suit of the turn-up card as trumps, to make three tricks, he says..'I order it up'. **1963** G. F. HERVEY *Handbk. Card Games* 184 The elder hand (non-dealer) may either order up or pass. If he orders up, the suit of the exposed card becomes the trump suit, and the dealer must take up the exposed card and discard..a card.

8. To give an order or commission for; to direct (a thing) to be furnished or supplied. Also const. *up* and *absol.*

1763 J. WOODFORDE *Diary* 3 Sept. (1924) I. 31 Mrs. Bacon pressed me to drive with her, but I had ordered in Hall, and I could not. **1836** BP. WILSON *Diary* in *Life* (1860) II. xv. 108 We ordered our ponies and johnpons. **1868** DICKENS *Uncomm. Trav.* xxii, 'What would you..do, if you ordered one kind of wine and was required to drink another?' **1880** MRS. FORRESTER *Roy & V.* I. 63 Shall I order you a cab? **1895** *Montgomery Ward Catal.* Spring & Summer 1 Please read remarks and rules before ordering. *Ibid.*, How to order. Commence your order similar to the sample heading on page 2. *a* **1903** *Mod.* What have you ordered for dinner? **1930** A. BENNETT *Imperial Palace* II. liv. 400 The waiter wrote and vanished. When Gracie returned, Evelyn said: 'I've ordered.' **1946** D. STIVENS *Courtship Uncle Henry* 197 We all drank together and ordered again. **1967** 'L. EGAN' *Nameless Ones* xvi. 212 'Would you like to order, sir?' Obsequious waiter. **1973** J. GORES *Final Notice* (1974) xxvi. 166 We'll have some more sparkling burgundy and then we can order. **1976** B. LECOMBER *Dead Weight* vi. 72, I..ordered up two toasted ham sandwiches. **1976** J. M. BROWNJOHN tr. *Kirst's Time for Payment* vi. 134 Order up, ladies and gentlemen, and don't worry about the breath test.

III. 9. *Eccl.* To admit to holy orders; to ordain; formerly also, to admit ceremonially into a monastic order; to admit or institute to a benefice. *arch.*

1303 [see ORDERED *ppl. a.* 1]. *c* **1315** SHOREHAM 47 The bisschop, wanne he ordreth thes clerekes, Takth hym the cherche keyȝe. **13..** *Guy Warw.* (A.) 5288 He made him a croun brod þere As a monke þat orderd were. **1496** *Dives & Paup.* (W. de W.) VII. xvi. 303/2 Some frende of him that shall be ordred gyueth the bysshop some gyft. **1552** *Bk. Com. Prayer* Ordering of Deacons, The Bisshoppe shal surcease from ordering that person. **1565** JEWEL *Repl. Harding* (1611) 211 That the Bishop of Rome ordered and admitted all the Bishops thorowout the World..hath no possibilitie, or colour of truth in it selfe. *a* **1610** BABINGTON *Comf. Notes Num.* viii. 11. §4 Note how fit it is to order Ministers in the face of the Church. **1895** BESANT *In Deacon's Orders* i. 2 One who has thus been ordered.

ˈorderable, *a. rare.* [f. ORDER *v.* + -ABLE.]

a. Capable of being ordered or directed (*to* an end or result); amenable to direction or control. **b.** That may be arranged in series. **c.** That may be ordered (at a snack bar, etc.).

1641 J. SHUTE *Sarah & Hagar* (1649) 27 No act of sin is in its nature orderable to any good end. **1655** FULLER *Ch. Hist.* x. vii. §22 The King..being very orderable in all His sicknesse. **1656** [? J. SERGEANT] tr. *T. White's Peripat. Inst.* 216 It makes a body orderable to all possible Action. **1949** *Mind* LVIII. 194 Recently it was realised that it was not necessary to regard satisfactions as additive; all previous conclusions about economic behaviour could still be deduced if they were merely regarded as orderable. **1962** C. O. FRAKE in J. A. Fishman *Readings Sociol. of Lang.* (1968) 438 Some, but apparently not all, orderable items at a lunch counter are distinguished by the term *something to eat.*

ˈorder-book. [f. ORDER *sb.* + BOOK.] A book in which orders are entered. *spec.* **a.** In the army, a book (of which there is one for each company) in which the orderly sergeants enter general and regimental orders. **b.** In the navy, a book kept on a man-of-war for recording occasional orders of the commander. **c.** In the House of Commons, a book in which motions to be submitted to the House must be entered. **d.** In business, a book in which the orders of customers are entered. Also *transf.*, the amount of orders to be fulfilled; also *fig.*

1771 J. WEDGWOOD *Let.* 10 Apr. (1965) 105, I had immediate recourse to the order book where I did not doubt of finding some of the Vases we had ordered unmade. **1833** MARRYAT *P. Simple* liv, Captain Hawkins came on board and gave me an order-book saying, 'Mr. Simple, I have a great objection to written orders, as I consider that the articles of war are quite sufficient to regulate any ship.' **1844** *Regul. & Ord. Army* 55 To see that all General Orders and Regulations are carefully and accurately entered in the Order Books of the Regiments composing their Brigades. **1844** ERSKINE MAY *Law of Parl.* viii. 168 Each member..rises and reads the notice he is desirous of giving, and afterwards..delivers it..to the second clerk assistant, who enters it in the Order Book. **1856** *National Rev.* III. 354 Passions are contending; life is a discipline; there is a reference every moment to the directory of the discipline—the order-book of the passions. **1893** *Daily News* 26 June 2/5 Directly their order books get at all full they are certain to put quotations up. **1910** A. BENNETT *Clayhanger* II. i. 161 I've shown him he's wrong by our order-book, but he wouldn't see it. **1929** G. F. M. CAMPION *Introd. Proc. House of Commons* ii. 65 The Order Book, which is also coloured white, is issued each day before the meeting of the House. **1955** *Times* 13 May 19/2 The order book at the year-end was satisfactory, comparing very favourably with the position at the end of 1953. **1958** *Times Rev. Industry* Sept. 79/1 Order-book position is patchy. **1964** ABRAHAM & HAWTREY *Parl. Dict.* (ed. 2) 128 The Order Book of the House of Commons is published in the afternoon of each sitting day. It contains a complete list of all the orders, notices and questions for the following and subsequent days up till the end of the session. **1971** *Daily Tel.* 4 Aug. 13/3 Much of the industry remains pessimistic, with many companies still facing stagnant or declining order books. **1974** *Listener* 24 Oct. 531/3 You would think there was a boom on, from our order book.

ordered ('ɔːdəd), *ppl. a.* [f. ORDER *v.* + -ED[1].]

†**1.** In holy orders, ORDAINED. (Also, Belonging to a religious order.) *Obs.*

1303 R. BRUNNE *Handl. Synne* 1540 By þese ordryde men, y mene, Here wurdys owtȝ to be feyrer and clene. *c* **1325** *Poem Times Edw. II* 124 in *Pol. Songs* (Camden) 329 Nu is pride maister in everich ordred hous. *c* **1386** CHAUCER *Pars. T.* ¶708 If he be ordred he is irreguleer. **1615** WADSWORTH in *Bedell's Lett.* 13 Neither doe the Orderer nor the Ordered giue nor receiue the Orders as a Sacrament.

2. a. Set in order, arranged, disposed; disciplined, regulated, controlled; †made ready, prepared (*obs.*).

1579 TOMSON *Calvin's Serm. Tim.* 70/2 The verie Barbarians..haue a more ordered state in truth and justice. **1612** T. TAYLOR *Comm. Titus* ii. 14 Pure hands, chast eyes, an ordered tongue. **1712** ADDISON *Spect.* No. 417 ¶5 Like a well ordered Garden. **1850** BLACKIE *Æschylus* II. 230 Strong in the ordered ranks of war Forth they went. **1872** WHITTIER *Brewing of Soma* 79 And let our ordered lives confess The beauty of Thy peace.

b. *Mil.* in ***ordered arms***: see ORDER *v.* 1 b.

1847 *Infantry Man.* (1854) 40 b, Any movement can take place from ordered arms.

c. *Math.* Of a set: having the property that there is a transitive binary relation, >, such that for any elements a, b of the set $a > b$, $b > a$, or $b = a$; ***ordered pair***, a pair of elements (a, b) such that $(a, b) = (u, v)$ if and only if $a = u$ and $b = v$; similarly ***ordered triple***, *n-**tuple***.

1901 *Bull. Amer. Math. Soc.* VII. 225 Consider the ordered assemblage $1, 2, \ldots, n', \ldots, n, \ldots n''$, where n', n and n'' are definite and subject to the condition that, in (*S*), n' comes before n and the latter before n''. **1906** W. H. & G. C. YOUNG *Theory of Sets of Points* vi. 121 A set in given order will be called an ordered set... Its components..may be distinguished as ordered components. **1941** BIRKHOFF & MACLANE *Survey Mod. Algebra* ii. 55 There are many other ordered fields: the field of real numbers, the field..of numbers $a + b\sqrt{2}$.., and other subfields of the real number field. **1953** *Mind* LXII. 541 A notion so little abstruse as that of an ordered pair. **1963** H. J. RYSER *Combinatorial Math.* i. 5 Let S be a set and let $(a_1, a_2, \ldots, a_r)$ be an ordered r-tuple of not necessarily distinct elements of S. **1966** MEYER & HANLON *Fun with New Math* vii. 90 To each point in 'the Cartesian Plane'..there corresponds a unique ordered pair of real numbers. **1968** E. T. COPSON *Metric Spaces* i. 5 The set of all ordered triples (x, y, z) of real numbers.

3. Commanded, bidden, prescribed, ordained.

1780 COWPER *Table-t.* 560 Thus genius rose and set at ordered times. **1796** *Instr. & Reg. Cavalry* (1813) 137 The divisions of squadrons make their ordered degree of wheel. **1892** *Daily News* 14 June 5/3 Leave hawks and owls, even.. the weasel, to play their ordered parts. **1898** *Ibid.* 23 Apr. 8/2 The ordered business of the day was Committee of Supply on the Civil Service Estimates.

Hence **'orderedness**, the quality or fact of being ordered or regulated. *rare.*

1724 R. WODROW *Life Jas. Wodrow* (1828) 183 The orderedness, sureness and everlasting nature of the Covenant. **1935** *Jrnl. Theol. Stud.* XXXVI. 314 The belief that the world's orderedness or knowability is an expression of mind. **1974** *Sci. Amer.* Mar. 43/1 (Advt.), In liquid-crystal work, one deals with the different forms and degrees of orderedness among molecules.

'ordered, *a. rare.* [f. ORDER *sb.* + -ED[2].] Decorated with the badge of an order of knighthood, merit, etc.

1817 LADY GRANVILLE *Lett.* (1894) I. 107 A number of little black starred and ordered Frenchmen.

orderer ('ɔːdərə(r)). Also 5 -our. [f. ORDER *v.* + -ER[1].] One who, or that which, orders (in senses of the vb.).

1496–7 *Act 12 Hen. VII*, c. 13 §1 The seid orderours and assessours in the seid Shires. **1532** HERVET *Xenophon's Househ.* (1768) 1 A good husband, and a good orderer of an house. **1595** DANIEL *Civ. Wars* I. xcv, Thou but as an vpright orderer, Sought'st to reform th' abused Kingdome here. **1615** [see ORDERED 1]. **1644** DIGBY *Nat. Bodies* i. (1658) 6 Aristotle..the most judicious orderer of notions, and director of mens conceptions, that ever lived. **1754** EDWARDS *Freed. Will* IV. ix. 252 The first Cause and supreme Orderer of all Things. **1889** H. F. WOOD *Englishm. Rue Caïn* xx. 318 How all these terrible orderers of other men were to be twisted round one's little finger!

ordering ('ɔːdərɪŋ), *vbl. sb.* [-ING[1].] The action of the vb. ORDER: ordination, arrangement, regulation, direction, management, preparation, treatment, etc.

c **1315** SHOREHAM (E.E.T.S.) 56 Þe bisschopes blessynge, Forþ myd þe admynystracioun þat he deþ atte ord[r]ynge. **1494** FABYAN *Chron.* v. ci. 76, I passe ouer..the orderynge of the yongest sone called Clodoaldus. **1547** BOORDE *Introd. Knowl.* i. (1870) 123 There meate..is marde and spylt for lacke of good ordring & dressynge. **1561** T. NORTON *Calvin's Inst.* IV. xix. (1634) 729 Laying on of hands, which I grant in true and lawfull Orderings to bee a Sacrament. **1667** C. MERRET in *Phil. Trans.* II. 455 The other two Trees, left without this ordering, had most of their fruit withered. **1732** BERKELEY *Alciphr.* III. §13 We want laws,..in one word, for the whole ordering of life. **1828** SCOTT *F.M. Perth* xxxiii, Directions about the encampment..and such other instructions as might be necessary to the proper ordering of the field. **1895** BESANT *In Deacon's Orders* i. 2 This ordering, once accepted, is a life-sentence like a peerage.

'ordering, *ppl. a.* [-ING[2].] That orders, arranges, directs, etc.: see ORDER *v.*

1678 CUDWORTH *Intell. Syst.* I. i. §25. 26 An Ordering and Disposing Mind that was the Cause of all things. **1898** G. MEREDITH *Odes Fr. Hist.* 28 His ordering fingers point the dials to time their ranks.

orderless ('ɔːdəlɪs), *a.* [f. ORDER *sb.* + -LESS.] Devoid of order, arrangement, regularity, or method; disorderly.

1569 J. SANFORD tr. *Agrippa's Van. Artes* 72 b, The Italiane is cleane in his fare, the Spaniarde delicate, the Frencheman aboundaunt, the Germane orderlesse. **1575** *Hist. Troubles Frankfort* (1642) 50 Their orderlesse thrusting themselves into the Church. **1595** SHAKS. *John* III. i. 253 All forme is formelesse, Order orderlesse, Saue what is opposite to Englands loue. **1660** N. INGELO *Bentivolio & Urania* I. (1682) Pref., An orderless rabble of troublesome Chimeras. **1868** LOCKYER *Guillemin's Heavens* (ed. 3) 369 Are the stars..spread orderless on the celestial vault?

orderliness ('ɔːdəlɪnɪs). [f. ORDERLY *a.* + -NESS.] The quality or condition of being orderly.

1. Conformity to order or method; regularity.

1571 GOLDING *Calvin on Ps.* viii. 6 Then is that perfection of orderlinesse decayed. **1667** J. CORBET *Disc. Relig. Eng.* 17 The Reformation in England, for its Legality and Orderliness, is unquestionable. **1711** SHAFTESB. *Charac.* (1737) II. II. ii. i. 132 He is made to pay dear..by losing his natural good Disposition, and the Orderliness of his Kind or Species. **1894** *Law Times* XCVII. 387/2 A court in which speed was considered rather than orderliness.

b. Observance of, or regard for, order; methodicalness.

1830 GALT *Lawrie T.* III. xiii. (1849) 127 To see how the habits of orderliness..were daily slackening. **1871** R. H. HUTTON *Ess.* II. 14 Goethe..seems to have inherited..from his father..the nervous orderliness..by which he was always distinguished.

2. Orderly quality of conduct or behaviour.

1581 MARBECK *Bk. of Notes* 655 Who then would not wonder at such behauiour and orderlinesse? **1676** TOWERSON *Decalogue* 318. **1740–87** MISS TALBOT, etc. *Lett.* (1808) 201, I never saw a more perfect orderliness; we had no crowd going or coming, and our places were excellent. *a* **1864** HAWTHORNE *Amer. Note-bks.* (1879) I. 116 He bears testimony to the orderliness of the crowd.

orderly ('ɔːdəlɪ), *a.* and *sb.* [f. ORDER *sb.* + -LY[1].]

A. *adj.* **1. a.** Arranged or disposed in order; characterized by regular sequence, arrangement, or disposition; exhibiting system or method; regular.

a **1577** GASCOIGNE *Maske for Visc. Montacute* Wks. 1869 I. 80 Vpon the waltring waues his Foistes and Gallies fleete, More forrest-like than orderly. *a* **1653** BINNING *Serm.* (1845) 11 If your intention be once right established, all your course will be orderly. **1686** PLOT *Staffordsh.* 423 These Symbols..have a more rational orderly texture than the Runae upon the Danish Rimestocks. **1860** TYNDALL *Glac.* I. xxv. 183 We were..tied together, and thus advanced in an orderly line. **1861** CRAIK *Hist. Eng. Lit.* I. 455 Where the chief thing demanded in a tragedy was a certain orderly pomp of expression.

b. Of persons, their temperament, etc.: Observant of, or having regard for, order, system, or method; regular, methodical.

1830 [implied in ORDERLINESS 1 b]. **1852** MRS. STOWE *Uncle Tom's C.* xxvi. 249, I thought you were one of the orderly sort, that liked to lie in bed in a Christian way. **1858** MRS. OLIPHANT *Laird of Norlaw* II. 94 Desirée..was of a womanly and orderly temper.

†**c.** ***orderly in years***: ? of mature years. *Obs.*

1583 B. RICH *Phylotus & Emelia* (1835) 11 An auncient Citizen, whose name was Phylotus, a man very orderly in yeares, and wonderfully aboundyng in goodes.

†**2.** Conformable to established order or rule; regular. *Obs.*

1581 MARBECK *Bk. of Notes* 481 To expresse by orderly definition what thing maketh an Heretike..is either impossible or verie hard. **1597** HOOKER *Eccl. Pol.* v. lxxvii. §12 A proude vsurpation without any orderly calling. **1614** MARKHAM *Cheap Husb.* v. i. (1668) 101 The orderliest feeding of swine is, in the morning early. **1637** *Star Chamb. Decree* §20 in *Milton's Areop.* (Arb.) 18 For want of orderly imployment for Iourneymen printers.

3. Observant of order, rule, or discipline; disposed to observe good order; not unruly or tumultuous; well-conducted, well-behaved.

1598 SHAKS. *Merry W.* II. i. 59 Hee..gaue such orderly and wel-behaued reproofe to al vncomelinesse. **1622** BACON *Hen. VII* Wks. 1879 I. 768 Observing their orderly, and not tumultuary arming. **1799** MACKINTOSH *Stud. Law Nat.* etc. Wks. 1846 I. 368 The firmest bands of a peaceable and orderly intercourse. **1844** H. H. WILSON *Brit. India* III. 338 Compensation for the losses inflicted on the orderly portion of the population. **1884** *Manch. Exam.* 26 May 6/2 Elections are now conducted in an orderly manner.

4. *Mil.* Pertaining to orders or their issue; charged with the conveyance or execution of orders.

orderly book, a book kept in a regiment, or each company of a regiment, for the entry of general or regimental orders; ***orderly buff*** (slang) = *orderly sergeant* (*b*); (see also quot. 1948); ***orderly corporal***, (*a*) a corporal who attends upon an officer to carry orders or messages; (*b*) a corporal whose turn it is to attend to the domestic affairs of his corps or regiment; ***orderly dog*** (slang) = *orderly corporal* (*b*); (see also quot. 1948); ***orderly man*** = B. 1, 2; see also, in other sense, quot. 1731; ***orderly officer***, (*a*) = B. 1; (*b*) the officer whose turn it is to superintend the domestic economy of his corps or regiment, the officer of the day; ***orderly pig*** (slang) = *orderly officer* (*b*); (see also quot. 1948); ***orderly room***, a room in barracks in which the business of a company is carried on; †***orderly sergeant***, (*a*) the first sergeant of a company, whose duties formerly included the conveyance of orders; (*b*) a sergeant whose turn it is to act as officer of the day.

1723 BLACKMORE *True Hist.* 49 If their Orderly Men.. should bring them intelligence..that the King was gone to Richmond. **1727** H. BLAND *Treat. Milit. Discipl.* xix. 286 All Orders, Subsequent to those at Orderly-time, which the Generals of the Day shall receive from the General in Chief, they are to send by their Aid-de-Camps to the Majors of Brigade of the Day for the Whole... Upon their receiving such Orders, they are to send them in Writing to the National Majors of Brigade of the Day by their Orderly Serjeants. **1731** *Gentl. Mag.* I. 25 Officers established in the most notorious Gaming-houses... An Orderly Man who walks up and down the outside of the Door to give notice to the Porter, and alarm the House, at the approach of the Constables. **1757** LOUDOUN & LYMAN *Gen. Orders of 1757* (1899) 126 Each Corp is to have an Orderly Searj[ean]t Ready. **1771** *Hist.* in *Ann. Reg.* 235, I receive by my orderly officer, two letters of yours upon the same subject. *a* **1798** *Army Med. Board* in W. Blair *Soldier's Friend* 85 Every regimental hospital will be provided with a steady serjeant; with one orderly man, or more,..and one woman nurse. **1799** CAPT. HAMILTON in *Naval Chron.* I. 529, I sent an orderly dragoon to the admiral. **1802** C. JAMES *New Mil. Dict.* s.v., *Orderly Officer*. See Officer of the Day. *Ibid.*, Orderly serjeants when they go for orders are sashed. Orderly corporals and orderly men wear their side arms. **1806** H. BURRARD *Let.* 26 Mar. in *Circumstantial Rep. Charges against Duke of York* (1809) 269 Your messenger knows where to find me, as I am at this Orderly Room for two or three hours most days. **1812** *Examiner* 7 Dec. 781/1 Sir E. Paget..had but one orderly man with him. **1815** J. W. CROKER in *C. Papers* 27 July (1884), [She] made me a present of the orderly book of one of the French regiments. **1833** *Mirror of Parliament* 11 June 2216/2 They (often from connexion or friendship with the Orderly-room clerks) got their ages entered as eighteen. **1844** *Regul. & Ord. Army* 147 A Private Soldier is to be employed as Regimental Orderly-Room Clerk. *Ibid.* 273 Officers Commanding the Out-Guards are to send guides or Orderly-men to the Major of Brigade of the Day..in order to conduct the new Guards, and to carry such orders as may be necessary. **1867** J. M. CRAWFORD *Mosby* 121 Horace Johnson of Warrenton..was appointed orderly sergeant. **1873** *Act 36 & 37 Vict.* c. 77 §28 Affixing the same at the orderly room or other room where the business is carried on of the corps..to which he belongs. **1890** *Illustr. Lond. News* Christm. No. 2/3 Porter tore a leaf from his orderly book. **1917** A. G. EMPEY *Over Top* 302 *Orderly-corporal*, a non-commissioned officer who takes the names of the sick every morning. **1918** E. S. FARROW *Dict. Mil. Terms* 420 *Orderly Officer*, the officer of the day, or that officer of a corps or regiment whose turn it is to supervise for the day the arrangements for food, cleanliness etc. **1925** FRASER & GIBBONS *Soldier & Sailor Words* 216 *Orderly buff*, orderly sergeant. *Ibid.*, *Orderly dog*, orderly corporal. **1934** V. M. YEATES *Winged Victory* 224 Grey..was censoring the men's letters, being orderly dog for the day. **1943** C. H. WARD-JACKSON *Piece of Cake* 45 *Orderly buff*, orderly corporal. *Ibid.*, *Orderly dog*, orderly sergeant. *Ibid.*, *Orderly pig*, orderly officer. **1948** PARTRIDGE *Dict. Forces' Slang* 132 *Orderly buff, dog, pig*. Strictly speaking, *dog* seems to have been officer or corporal, *buff* sergeant, and *pig* corporal. The non-regular Army, however,..used all three phrases indiscriminately. **1953** K. TENNANT *Joyful Condemned* xviii. 163 David..was signed into the care of an orderly sergeant. **1964** A. POWELL *Valley of Bones* i. 31 Tell the Orderly Corporal Mr Bithel is reporting sick this morning. **1971** S. MILLIGAN *Adolf Hitler* III. 51 Oh those military meals!.. Visits from orderly officers did little to help. **1974** G. M. FRASER *McAuslan in Rough* 39 When I was..doing my recruit training..there was a villainous orderly sergeant who used to get us up in the mornings. **1977** J. TARRANT *Rommel Plot* xviii. 187 He asked the operator to put him through to the Orderly Room.

5. Pertaining to the system of keeping the streets constantly clean by continual sweeping and removal of dirt; see B. 3.

orderly-bin, box, a street box for the reception of refuse.

1851–61 MAYHEW *Lond. Labour* II. 259 The streets of Windsor..are now in the course of being cleansed upon the orderly plan. **1894** *Daily News* 24 Jan. 5/3 The street orderly bins are still occasionally taken for letter boxes. **1904** *Daily Chron.* 18 Mar. 6/3 They had..been seen bearing up documents and throwing them into orderly boxes.

B. *sb.* **1.** A non-commissioned officer or private soldier attending upon a superior officer to carry orders or messages.

1781 *Calendar Virginia State Papers* (1875) I. 452 The orderly, his wife and negro woman at York..have never received one single shilling. **1800** *Asiat. Ann. Reg., Chron.* 44/1 The garrison..marched down to the number of 2 killedars, 1 sippadar,..2 orderleys, 1 colour bearer [etc.]. **1814** WELLINGTON *Let. to Junta of Bilbao* 12 Jan. in Gurw. *Desp.* (1838) XI. 439 In the house as the servant or orderly of the officer in question. **1877** A. B. EDWARDS *Up Nile* xvi. 438 An orderly comes in haste to bring him news of the battle. **1966** [see BATMAN[2]].

2. An attendant in a military or other hospital, charged with the care of the patients and the maintenance of order and cleanliness.

1809 WELLINGTON *Let. to Col. Peacocke* 29 Sept. in Gurw. *Desp.* (1837) V. 200 The men of one regiment must not be employed as orderlies to men of other regiments in the hospital. **1854** MISS MITFORD in L'Estrange *Life* (1870) III. xiv. 297 The worst of surgeons and hospital dressers and orderlies.

3. A man whose constant work it is to keep the streets clean.

1851–61 MAYHEW *Lond. Labour* II. 260 The orderlies.. keep the streets free from mud in winter, and dust in summer. **1895** *Times* 28 Mar. 4/6 E. B. and J. L. street orderlies in the employ of the St. Giles's Board of Works.

4. One who is orderly or a supporter of order.

1832 HT. MARTINEAU *Ireland* iv. 63 If the orderlies chose to try their strength against the desperates, there should be a fair battle.

Hence (*nonce-wds.*) **'orderlyism**, the system of keeping the streets clean by means of orderlies; **'orderlyship**, the office of an orderly.

1851–61 MAYHEW *Lond. Labour* II. 256 Orderlyism, or the employment of the poor in the promotion of public cleanliness. **1900** *Daily News* 7 Sept. 3/2 The young soldier ..is then placed in charge of a ward, where..he may in a year or so attain to the culmination of orderlyship.

orderly ('ɔːdəlɪ), *adv.* [f. ORDER *sb.* + -LY².]

1. In order; in due order or regular succession; with proper arrangement, disposition, or distribution; methodically. Now *rare*.

1477 NORTON *Ord. Alch.* Proem in Ashm. (1652) 10 The effect is here set out Orderly. **1535** COVERDALE *Luke* i. 3, I thought it good..to wryte the same orderly vnto the (good Theophilus). **1599** NASHE *Lenten Stuffe* (1871) 58 He enquired of every one orderly, What he had eat? **1654** VILVAIN *Epit. Ess.* II. 61 Of Antoni's blood..issued three, Caius, Claudius, and Nero orderly. **1728** MORGAN *Algiers* II. iv. 282 The 18 Galeots and 2 Brigantines advanced, very orderly. **1847** LONGF. *Evang.* I. iii. 69 Orderly all things proceeded, and duly and well were completed.

†**b.** In conformity with order; properly in regard to place in a series; in due course, duly. *Obs.*

1548 GEST *Pr. Masse* in H. G. Dugdale *Life* (1840) App. i. 98 Be it the sayd sacrifice were a thankesgeving; yet it shall not orderlye hereupon ensue that it were an acceptable..thankesgeving. **1628** EARLE *Microcosm., Formall man* (Arb.) 31 Hee..laughes orderly himselfe, when it comes to his turne. **1657** SPARROW *Bk. Com. Prayer* (1661) 16 We begin our Service with Confession..And that very orderly. *a* **1677** HALE *Prim. Orig. Man.* IV. viii. 359 As in a curious piece of Landskip there are orderly interspersed Clouds.

2. According to established order or rule; regularly, properly, duly; in conformity with good order or discipline; in a well-conducted or well-behaved manner. Now *rare*.

1509 BP. FISHER *Fun. Serm. C'tess Richmond* Wks. (1876) 309 Yf the sacramentes of the chirche orderly taken..be auaylable. **1583** STUBBES *Anat. Abus.* II. (1882) 100 The church hath no absolute power..to elect their pastor, to choose him, to cal him orderly. **1611** BIBLE *Acts* xxi. 24 That ..all may know..that thou thyself also walkest orderly and keepest the law. *a* **1715** BURNET *Own Time* (1766) I. 394 As long as they lived orderly. **1727** *Philip Quarll* (1816) 24, I..let him go with me, which he did very orderly. **1817** SOUTHEY *Wat Tyler* III. i, Comporting ourselves orderly, As peaceful citizens.

†**3.** *Arch.* (Cf. ORDER *sb.* 9 b.) *Obs.*

1563 SHUTE *Archit.* E iv b, The chaunge of the five pillers orderly to be vsed, eche of them in his kynde, whiche order of buildings be named of Vitruuius as followeth ***picnostylos, sistylos, diastylos, ariostylos, eustylos.***

orderly-man: see ORDERLY *a.* 4.

†**ordina'bility.** *Obs.* [f. next: see -ITY.] The quality of being ordinable; capability of being ordained or directed to an end or purpose.

1677 GALE *Crt. Gentiles* IV. 484 That God is the prime efficient cause of the material entitative act of sin, may be demonstrated..from the ordinabilitie of al evil to some good. *a* **1710** BP. BULL *Serm.* ix. Wks. 1827 I. 222 Our obedience to God ought to be such, as that it may have, though not a merit of condignity to deserve everlasting bliss ..yet an ordinability (as a great doctor of our church expresseth it)..that is, a meetness, fitness, and due disposition toward the obtaining of it.

†**'ordinable,** *a. Obs.* [ad. med.L. *ordinābil-is*, f. *ordināre* to ORDAIN. Cf. OF. *ordenable, ordonable* (Godef.).] Capable of being ordained, ordered, or directed *to* an end, purpose, or destiny.

1387-8 T. USK *Test. Love* II. xiii. (Skeat) l. 29 Euery thing though it be good, it is not of hymself good, but it is good by that it is ordinable to the greate goodnes. **1650** *Vind. Hammond's Addr.* xiv. §33 The Killing my self is no way ordinable to good. *a* **1677** HALE *Prim. Orig. Man.* I. i. 5 The knowledge..is not much ordinable or applicable to the use and benefit of the Man that knows them.

‖**ordinaire** (ordinɛr), *sb.* [Fr.] Short for VIN ORDINAIRE. Also as *adj.*

1861 THACKERAY *Roundabout Papers* xiv, in *Cornh. Mag.* July 123 A sound genuine ordinaire, at 18*s.* per doz. let us say. **1888** MRS. H. WARD *R. Elsmere* II. III. xxii. 215 He ate his boiled mutton and drank his *ordinaire* like a man. **1906** *Daily Chron.* 24 July 6/5 What is 'ordinaire' as applied to wine?.. That is a local term which has existed for two centuries in France. **1920** [see BOURGEOIS *a.* 4]. **1936** H. G. WELLS *Croquet Player* ii. 11 He..ordered another half litre of wine. Either out of ignorance or preference he was drinking red ordinaire. **1959** *Good Food Guide* 32 Spanish ordinaires at 1/6 a glass. **1960** *House & Garden* July 13/1 Two decent, slightly better than *ordinaire* wines. **1972** *Ibid.* Feb. 100/4 Roodeberg is an honest wine, distinctly better than an *ordinaire*.

ordinal ('ɔːdɪnəl), *a.* (*sb.*¹) [ad. late L. *ordināl-is* denoting order or place in a series (as a number), f. *ordo, ordin-* ORDER: see -AL¹. Cf. F. *ordinal*, used by Oresme, 14th c., but not in Cotgr., nor in common use till 17th c.]

†**1.** Conformable to order, rule, or custom; regular, ordinary, orderly. *Obs.*

c **1380** WYCLIF *Serm.* Sel. Wks. I. 180 þis suynge stondiþ most in ordynal love of man. **1496** *Dives & Paup.* (W. de W.) II. vi. 115/1 To kepe obedyence and ordynall subgeccion of the subgettes to theyr soueraynes.

2. Marking position in an order or series; applied to those numbers which refer an object to a certain place in a series of such objects (*first, second, third*, etc.), as distinguished from the CARDINAL numbers (*one, two, three*, etc.).

1599 MINSHEU *Sp. Gram.* 12 *marg.*, Ordinall Numerals. **1607** BP. ANDREWES *Serm.* II. 212 'Primus' is an ordinal number. *a* **1677** HALE *Prim. Orig. Man.* I. iv. 109 Number ..whether Collective, as three, six, nine; or Ordinal, as the second, third, or fourth. **1711** J. GREENWOOD *Eng. Gram.* 277 Third is an Adjective, and is call'd an Ordinal Number, as Three is a Cardinal Number. **1892** SWEET *Short Hist. Eng. Gram.* 126 Most of the ordinal numerals are derivatives of the cardinal ones.

3. *Nat. Hist.* Of or pertaining to an order of animals or plants, or to natural order in general.

1822-34 *Good's Study Med.* (ed. 4) II. 1 The ordinal name made choice of is Phlogotica. **1830** LINDLEY *Nat. Syst. Bot.* 182 The dehiscence of their capsule; a character which is not now esteemed as of ordinal importance. **1874** COUES *Birds N.W.* 294 Specific, or generic, or ordinal lines of distinction.

4. Of or pertaining to holy orders. *rare.*

1842 G. S. FABER *Prov. Lett.* (1844) I. 240 Such an arrangement evidently supposes the ordinal identity of Bishops and Presbyters.

5. Relating to, or consisting of, a row or rows.

1892 *Classical Rev.* 460/1 All the pieces move both in an ordinal or straight line..or in a diagonal line. **1897** F. THOMPSON *New Poems* 139 Hand in hand in ordinal dances.

B. *sb.* An ordinal number: see 2.

1591 PERCIVALL *Sp. Dict.* B iij, The ordinals are, which declare the order of place or time. **1674** JEAKE *Arith.* (1696) 42 The Denominators are best pronounced by the Ordinals, as halves, thirds..etc. **1862** R. G. LATHAM *Elem. Comp. Philol.* II. iv. 742 The cardinals as compared with the ordinals are certainly abstract, and, as such, ought, at the first view, to be the newer terms.

Hence **'ordinalism**, the quality of being ordinal.

1864 WEBSTER cites LATHAM.

ordinal ('ɔːdɪnəl), *sb.*² [ad. med.L. *ordināle*, sb. use of neuter of *ordinālis* adj.: see prec. Cf. F. *ordinal* (15th c. in Godef.).]

†**1.** A book containing rules, or a body of rules or regulations. *Obs.*

1390 GOWER *Conf.* III. 117 To every Monthe..He hath after his Ordinal Assigned on [signe] in special. **1532** *Fortescue's Abs. & Lim. Mon.* xv. (1714) 119 (Digby MS.) A Boke..kept..as a Registre or an Ordynal, how they schal do, and be orderyd. **1674** BLOUNT *Glossogr.* (ed. 4), *Ordinal* is..sometimes used for a Book, containing the Orders and Constitutions of a Religious House or Colledge.

2. A book setting forth the order of the services of the Church, or of any one of them, as they existed before the Reformation; a service-book.

1387 TREVISA *Higden* (Rolls) VII. 295 He made þe ordynal of þe service of holy chirche, and cleped it þe Consuetudinarius. *c* **1449** PECOCK *Repr.* 203 As Y haue red in dyuerse oolde Ordinalis of Cathedrall Chirchis and of Monasteries in Ynglond. **1549** *Act 3 & 4 Edw. VI*, c. 10 §1 All Books called..Couchers, Journals, Ordinals..shall be..abolished. *a* **1746** LEWIS in Gutch *Coll. Cur.* II. 169 An Ordinal; in which was ordained the manner of saying and solemnizing divine offices. **1846** MASKELL *Mon. Rit.* I. p. xliii, Other Churches equally with that of Sarum would have had their Ordinals.

3. A book prescribing the rules to be observed, and containing the form of service to be used, in the ordination of deacons and priests, and the consecration of bishops.

1658 BRAMHALL *Consecr. Bps.* 112 Their exceptions..were..either against our English Ordinall, or against the Legality of our Bishops. **1732-8** NEAL *Hist. Purit.* (1822) I. 64 The new Common Prayer-book was brought into the house, with an ordinal or form of ordaining bishops, priests, and deacons. **1876** *Prayer-book Interleaved* 339 This prayer is in the Roman Ordinal preceded by an exposition of the duties of a priest.

ordinance ('ɔːdɪnəns), *sb.* Also 4-6 orden-, ordyn-, (4 ordren-, 5 ordeyn-), 5-8 ordon-, (6 ordonn-), 6-8 ordn-; 4-5 -aunse, 4-6 -aunce, -ans, 5 -auns, -anse, -awnce. [a. OF. *ordenance, ordren-, ordenn-, ordon-*, mod.F. *ordonnance*, ad. med.L. *ordinantia*, f. *ordinant-em*, pr. pple. of *ordināre* to ORDAIN: cf. the variants ORDNANCE, ORDONNANCE.] The action of ordaining, ordering, or arranging; the fact or condition of being ordered or arranged.

†**1.** Arrangement in ranks or rows; esp. in order of battle; battle-array or a mode of battle-array; also, a display of military force; a host in array.

c **1330** R. BRUNNE *Chron.* (1810) 178 Alle þe Sarazins conseile in þe schaft was writen, & alle þer ordinance, kyng R. it wiste. **1375** BARBOUR *Bruce* XVII. 101 Soyn thar ordinans brak thai. **1456** SIR G. HAYE *Law Arms* (S.T.S.) 112 We fynd be ancient custumis of weris thre ordynancis of bataillis. *c* **1477** CAXTON *Jason* 29 He assembled alle his folke and putte hem in fayr ordenaunce of bataylle. **1552** LYNDESAY *Monarche* 5424, I was Pape Iulius manfullye Passe to the feilde.., With ane rycht aufull ordinance. **1601** HOLLAND *Pliny* I. 455 A whole troupe..of horsmen may ride vpright vnder them in ordinance of battell.

2. Arrangement in regular sequence or proper relative position; disposition (of things or matters) according to rule; ordered, arranged, or regulated condition; order. *Obs.* exc. as in b.

c **1374** CHAUCER *Boeth.* IV. pr. vi. 105 (Camb. MS.) Destine is the disposicion and ordinaunce clyuynge to moeuable thinges. *c* **1386** —— *Clerk's T.* 905 The chambres for tarraye in ordinance After my lust. *a* **1450** *Knt. de la Tour* (1868) 154 She kepte her astate so noble, and of so good ordenaunce. **1450-80** tr. *Secreta Secret.* 21 Astronomye is divided in foure parties..In the ordinaunce of the sterres; In disposicioun of þe signes [etc.]. **1535** COVERDALE *1 Chron.* xxvi[i]. 12 This is the ordinaunce of the dorekepers..to mynister in the house of the Lorde. **1699** LISTER *Journ. Paris* 36 The Ordinance and Design of most of the Royal and great Gardens in and about Paris are of his Invention.

b. Arrangement of literary material, or collocation of parts, as in architecture, in accordance with some plan or rule of composition or artistic production; also, a characteristic series of architectural parts: = ORDONNANCE 1.

1460 CAPGRAVE *Chron.* 315 Vhech vere ageyn the ordinauns of oure Book. **1485** CAXTON *Chas. Gt.* 39 To devyde the mater by chapytres in the best ordynaunce that I shal conne. **1523** LD. BERNERS *Froiss.* I. i. 1, I..haue enterprysed this hystory on yᵉ forsaid ordynaunce and true fundacion. **1683** EVELYN *Diary* 16 May, Verrio's invention is admirable, his ordnance full and flowing. **1706** PHILLIPS, *Ordnance*, In Architecture, the giving to all the parts of a Building, the just Dimensions and Quantity, which are requisite, according to the Model. **1850** LEITCH tr. *C. O. Müller's Anc. Art* §108 (ed. 2) 75 With regard to the columnar ordinances, the Doric was at this period cultivated to a higher degree of grace. **1862** FERGUSSON *Hist. Mod. Archit.* 185 It is not easy to ascertain how far the ordinance of the present building was influenced by his designs. **1885** *Academy* 1 Aug. 69/2 Want of ordinance has led Major T. to perpetual repetition.

†**3.** The arranging of plans; devising, contriving, planning; a device, contrivance, plan. *Obs.*

a **1330** *Otuel* 49 þei..maden alle here ordenaunce, To werren uppon þe king of France. *c* **1374** CHAUCER *Troylus* II. 461 (510) In with þe paleys gardyn..Gan he and I wel half a day to dwelle Right for to speken of an ordenaunce How we þe Grekes myghte disauaunce. *a* **1472** *Eng. Chron.* (Camden 1856) 39 Certayn Lollardes..hadde purposid..to haue slayn the kyng..but the king..was warned of their fals purpos and ordenaunce. **1480** CAXTON *Chron. Eng.* ccxix. 209 Commune loos sprong in englond thurgh coniectyng and ordynaunce of the frere prechours, that sire Edward of Carnariuan was alyue.

†**b.** Institution, foundation (*of* anything). *Obs.*

1382 WYCLIF *Heb.* iv. 3 Sotheli the werkis maad parfyt fro the ordynaunce of the world.

†**4.** The action or process of making ready, preparing, or providing; preparation, provision, equipment; a preparatory step or measure; hence, the result of such, provision *of* (something). *Obs.*

c **1374** CHAUCER *Troylus* III. 486 (535) And Troylus þat al þis puruyaunce Knew at þe fulle..Hadde here-vp-on ek made gret ordenaunce. *c* **1400** MAUNDEV. (1839) xxx. 300 Whan men passed..unto that yle men maden ordynance for to passen by Schippe, 23 dayes or more. **1450-80** tr. *Secreta Secret.* 12 That he may wisely purveye and make contrary ordynaunce ayens hem. *c* **1500** *Bat. Egyngecourte* 70 in Hazl. *E.P.P.* II. 96 Great ordynance of gunnes the kynge let make, And shypte them at London all at ones. *c* **1534** *MS. Additional* 6113, lf. 106 The counterpoynte clothe of golde, the curteyns of whyte sarcenette..were of the quenes owne ordonnance. **1580** BARET *Alv.* D 1166 The first ordinaunce, or first draught, which is done with a cole, *adumbratio.* **1612** DAVIES *Why Ireland*, etc. (1747) 126 But there was..no ordinance, no provision made for the abolishing of their barbarous customs and manners.

b. Material adjuncts, apparatus, furniture. *Obs.*

1475 *Rolls of Parlt.* VI. 133/1 The Tynne, Stuff and Ordenaunce to the same myne belongyng. **1512** in Willis & Clark *Cambridge* (1886) I. 608 Cynctours, moldes, ordynaunces, and euery other thyng concernyng the same vawtyng. **1552** *Inv. Ch. Goods St. Andrew's, Norwich* in *Norfolk Archæol.* (1865) VII. 52 Itm the ordynance of the sepulcre prised at vˢ. **1611** BIBLE *1 Kings* vi. 38 *marg.*, [Was the house finished] with all the appurtenances therof, and with all the ordinances therof.

†**c.** *spec.* Warlike provision, equipment, or stores: now ORDNANCE, q.v.

5. The action of ordering or regulating; regulation, direction, management; authoritative appointment or dispensation; control, disposal. *arch.*

c **1330** R. BRUNNE *Chron.* (1810) 83 His doughter Custance was wedded to Bretayn, With William's ordinance, vnto the erle Alayn. *c* **1386** CHAUCER *Melib.* ¶759, I putte me hoolly in youre disposicion and ordinaunce. *c* **1410** HOCCLEVE *Mother of God* 43 Thou schapen art by goddis ordynance To preye for vs. *a* **1548** HALL *Chron., Edw. IV* 222 b, Committyng the lyfes..whole to the dukes discrecion and ordinaunce. **1549** *Compl. Scot.* i. 19 Stablit be the infinite diuyne ordinance. **1669** GALE *Crt. Gentiles* I. i. 5 That Ordinance of God, whereby every creature is governed and guided. **1885** RUSKIN *Pleas. Eng.* 139 Unless music exalt and purify, it is not under St. Cecilia's ordinance.

b. That which is ordained or decreed by the Deity or by Fate; a dispensation, decree, or appointment of Providence or of Destiny.

a **1340** HAMPOLE *Psalter* cxliv. 18 Godis wayes ere his ordynaunce & willis. *c* **1450** *St. Cuthbert* (Surtees) 619 He wist it was goddis ordenaunce. **1554** J. BRADFORD in Strype *Eccl. Mem.* (1721) III. II. App. xxix. 82 By thy most just ordinance yea by thy merciful ordinance also. **1611** SHAKS. *Cymb.* IV. ii. 145 Let Ord'nance Come as the Gods fore-say it. **1688** SHADWELL *Sqr. Alsatia* v, Great souls are above ordinances. **1842** TENNYSON *Tithonus* 30 Why should a man desire..To..pass beyond the goal of ordinance Where all should pause?

†**c.** Ordained or appointed place, condition, course, etc. *Obs.*

1456 SIR G. HAYE *Law Arms* (S.T.S.) 141 [He] passis till his ordinaunce quhare he is ordanyt tobe. **1601** SHAKS. *Jul. C.* I. iii. 66 If you would consider the true cause,..Why all these things change from their Ordinance, Their Natures, and pre-formed Faculties.

6. Authoritative direction how to proceed or act; established rule or body of principles; system of government, polity, or discipline. *Obs.* or *arch.*

c **1330** R. Brunne *Chron.* (1810) 101 Of Godes ordinance he forsoke þe schap. *c* **1380** Wyclif *Serm.* Sel. Wks. I. 26 For þis ende shulden clerkes.. preie God þat his ordrenance [*v.r.* ordenaunce] were kepte in his strengþe. *c* **1400** Maundev. (Roxb.) xiii. 58 After þe constitucioun and ordinaunce of þe rewmes whare þai dwell. **1538** Starkey *England* I. i. 16 Cyuyle ordynance ys but as a mean to bryng man to obserue thys law of nature. **1641** Milton *Ch. Govt.* I. ii. Wks. (1851) 102 At the returne from the Captivity things were only restor'd after the ordinance of Moses and David. **1784** Cowper *Task* I. 743 She has presum'd t'annul And abrogate.. The total ordonance and will of God. **1847** Tennyson *Princ.* VI. 352 Then the voice Of Ida sounded, issuing ordinance.

7. An authoritative direction, decree, or command; in more restricted sense, a public injunction or rule of narrower scope, less permanent nature, or less constitutional character than a *law* or *statute*, as a decree of a sovereign, an enactment of a municipal or other local body, etc.

As to the distinction between *ordinance* and *statute*, see Hallam *Mid. Ages* (1878) III. VIII. iii, Stubbs *Const. Hist.* II. xvii. §292. In Eng. Hist. the decrees of the Ordainers (with the king's assent) in 1310 were 'ordinances'; the name is also given to the ***Ordinance of the Forest*** (33 & 34 Ed. I), and the ***Ordinance of the Staple*** (27 Ed. III, st. 2), etc. The Acts of the Long Parliament after 1641 were at first called *Ordinances*; one of these was the ***Self-denying Ordinance*** of 1645, ordaining that no member of parliament should thenceforth hold any civil or military office. After 1649 the name 'act' was officially used; but as all these 'acts' were expunged from the Statute-book at the Restoration, they are usually referred to as 'ordinances'. In reference to French History, 'the Ordinances' are esp. those of Charles X in 1830, overthrowing the constitution, and suspending the liberty of the press. See also ordonnance 2, 2 b.

1303 R. Brunne *Handl. Synne* 1460 Swyche ys Goddys ordynaunce, 'For veniaunce to take veniaunce'. **1389** in *Eng. Gilds* (1870) 80 þeise ben ye ordynaunse of þis gilde. **1413** *Pilgr. Sowle* IV. xxix. (1859) 61 Ordynaunces of pryuate lawes in Reames and in comynaltees ben cleped 'statutes'. **1477** *Presentm. Juries* in *Surtees Misc.* (1888) 27 Rychard Dyschforth.. toke & selld j stranges man heirreng.. agans ordonans of the ton. **1562** *Act 5 Eliz.* c. 12 §5 Every Person .. that shall take any License contrary to this Ordinance. **1577–87** Holinshed *Chron.* II. 320/1 This yeare [1310] also there were ordinances made for the state and gouernement of the realme, by the prelats, earles, and barons, which were confirmed with the sentence of excommunication against all them that should go about to breake the same. **1598** Barret *Theor. Warres* II. i. 30 He shall obey the ordinances of the Sergeant Maior. **1622** Callis *Stat. Sewers* (1647) 230 An Ordinance is a word having a more private and less powerful signification then the word Law hath; for it is a Law but of a secundary power, enacted by a Corporation, Company or Commission. **1647** Clarendon *Hist. Reb.* IV. §199 They should have an Ordinance of Parliament for their Indemnity. **1767** A. Young *Farmer's Lett. to People* 185 Laws and ordonances, which are framed according to the aspect of the day. **1827** Hallam *Const. Hist.* (1876) II. x. 180 The most popular justification for the self-denying ordinance.. was soon found at Naseby. **1830–1** *Hist.* in *Ann. Reg.* 182/1 On the 25th of July, the king [Ch. X.] signed three Ordinances which superseded the Constitution. **1830** Amelia Opie *Jrnl.* 23 Dec., This gentleman.. is the editor of a journal, and wrote against the Ordinances. **1875** Stubbs *Const. Hist.* II. xvii. §292 The Statute is primarily a legislative act, the ordinance is primarily an executive one; .. the enacting process incorporates the statute into the body of the national law, the royal notification of the ordinance simply asserts that the process enunciated in the ordinance will be observed from henceforth.

8. A practice or usage authoritatively enjoined or prescribed; *esp.* a religious or ceremonial observance, as the sacraments.

1388 Wyclif *Titus* Prol., He warneth Tite, and enfourmeth hym of the ordynaunce of presthod, and of spiritual conuersacioun. *a* **1425** *Cursor M.* 11292 (Trin.) þei bare þe childe.. into þe temple For to do of him þat day þat ordenaunce [*Cott.* settenes] was of þe lay. **1643** T. Case *Serm.* in Kerr *Covenants & Covenanters* (1895) 265 This service, being an ordinance of God. **1648** *Shorter Catech.* §92 A sacrament is an holy ordinance instituted by Christ, wherein, by sensible signs, Christ and the benefits of the new covenant are represented, sealed, and applied to believers. *a* **1649** Winthrop *New Eng.* (1853) II. 376 Private members making speeches in the church assemblies to the disturbance and hindrance of the ordinances. **1704** Nelson *Festivals & Fasts* II. vii. (1720) 542 Candidates of this sacred Ordinance [Confirmation]. **1785** Paley *Mor. Philos.* Wks. 1825 IV. 59 Civil society is but the ordinance and institution of man. **1861** Stanley *East. Ch.* ii. 72 Reciting the Nicene creed.. before the administration of the Eucharist, to guard that ordinance against Arian intruders. **1865** Seeley *Ecce Homo* i. (1868) 3 Many.. presented themselves as candidates for his baptism in implicit faith that the ordinance was divine.

b. Applied esp. to the sacrament of the Lord's Supper.

1830–40 'To observe the Ordinance' [a usual expression with Independents and Baptists]. *a* **1892** Spurgeon *Autobiog.* iv. (1897) 26 The table, on which were spread the bread and the wine on days when they had the ordinance; I think that was the correct phrase when our good folks intended 'the communion'.

†**9.** The decree of an umpire settling a matter in dispute; the authoritative settlement of relations between parties. *Obs.*

1375 Barbour *Bruce* I. 79 This ordynance thaim thocht the best. **1411** *Rolls of Parlt.* III. 650/1 This is the ordenance that Thomas Archebisshop of Canterbury, and Richard Lord the Grey.. haven made betwen William Lord the Roos on that oon partie and Robert Tirwhit.. on that other partie. **1569** J. Rogers *Gl. Godly Loue* (1876) 182 The ordinance that God made betweene man and wife.

†**10.** Appointment to office; *esp.* admission to office in the Church; = ordination 2. *Obs.*

1387 Trevisa *Higden* (Rolls) II. 141 His successour schal come to þe primat of Caunterbury, and he schal take his ordynaunce [L. *ordinationem*, 1432–50 ordinacion] of hym. **1450** *Rolls of Parlt.* V. 184/1 To make or ordeine ony Officer .. of whom the makyng and ordenaunce.. longed to you.

†**11.** Rank, order (in the state). *Obs. rare*$^{-1}$.

1607 Shaks. *Cor.* III. ii. 12 Things created.. to.. be still, and wonder, When one but of my ordinance stood vp To speake of Peace, or Warre.

†**12.** = *company of ordinance*: see ordonnance 2 b. *Obs.*

†**'ordinance,** *v. Obs. rare.* [f. *ordinance*, ordnance *sb.*] *trans.* To furnish with ordnance or military equipment, esp. artillery.

1531 Elyot *Gov.* II. ii, A shippe of wonderfull beautie, well ordinanced and manned for his defence and saulfe conducte. *a* **1548** Hall *Chron., Hen. VIII* 22 Foystes and Rowgalies so well ordinaunced and with such peces as was not seen in shippes before. *Ibid.* 119 This was a strong toune well walled, dyched and ordinaunced but not manned.

ordinand ('ɔːdɪnænd). [ad. L. *ordinānd-us*, gerundive of *ordināre* to ordain.] One who is about to be ordained, a candidate for ordination.

1842 Brande *Dict. Sci.*, etc., *Ordinand*,.. in Ecclesiastical Antiquities, one about to receive orders. **1885** Dixon *Hist. Ch. E.* III. 191 The only dress prescribed to the ordinands.

ordinant ('ɔːdɪnənt), *a.* and *sb. rare.* [In 15th c. a. OF. *ordinant*, pr. pple. of *ordiner*; in modern use ad. L. *ordinānt-em*, pr. pple. of *ordināre*: see ordain *v.*]

A. *adj.* That orders, arranges, regulates, or directs; †able to order or direct (*obs.*).

c **1400** tr. *Secreta Secret., Gov. Lordsh.* 109 Be þy comandour swyfte, & qweynte, & ordinant. **1602** Shaks. *Ham.* V. ii. 48 (Qos.) Euen in that was Heauen ordinant. **1870** Ruskin *Lect. Art* iii. 72 The instantaneously selective and ordinant energy of the brain.

B. *sb.* One who ordains or confers holy orders.

1842 Brande *Dict. Sci.*, etc., *Ordinant*, a prelate conferring orders. **1882–3** Schaff *Encycl. Relig. Knowl.* II. 1701 The Council of Trent declares.. that the words of the ordinant, 'Receive ye the Holy Ghost', have efficacy.

†**ordi'nantial,** *a. Obs. rare*$^{-1}$. [f. med.L. *ordinantia* ordinance + -al^1.] Of or pertaining to ordinances; of the nature of an ordinance.

1657 Trapp *Comm. Ps.* xxv. 10 All the passages and proceedings, both ordinantiall and providentiall whereby he cometh and communicateth himself to his people.

'ordinar, *a.* and *sb.* Chiefly *Sc.*; now only *dial.* Forms: 5 ordonnayre, 5–6 **ordiner, ordynare,** 6–9 **ordinare,** 6– **ordinar,** (9 **ordnar**). [a. OF. *orden-*, *ordinaire* adj. and sb., ad. L. *ordinārius*: see ordinary *a.* and *sb.*]

A. *adj.* = ordinary *a.*

Judge Ordinar: see ordinary *a.* 2.

1508 Dunbar *Poems* vii. *heading*, Consaloure, and chamerlane ordinare to.. Loys, King of France. **1517** Torkington *Pilgr.* (1884) 62 The Maryoners brake the ordinar takele of the shippe. **1563–7** Buchanan *Reform. St. Andros* Wks. (1892) 6 The ordinar expensis of the college of humanite. **1614** Wither *Sat. to King* in *Juvenilia* (1633) 338, I speak not this because I think there be More than the ordinarest gifts in me. *c* **1670** *Bond* in G. Hickes *Spirit of Popery* (1680) 44, I shall take, or apprehend any Person or Persons guilty thereof, and present them to the Judge Ordinar. **1692** Sir W. Hope *Fencing-Master* 156 The ordinar Complement of all Fencing-Schools. **1826** J. Wilson *Noct. Ambr.* Wks. 1855 I. 179, I wad rather get fou five hunder times in an ordinar way.

b. ***by ordinar***, adjectival and advb. phr. (*Sc.*): Beyond what is usual; unusual, unusually.

1823 Galt *R. Gilhaize* II. 126 They were by ordinare obedient and submissive. *Ibid.* 181 With a calm voice, attuned to by ordinare solemnity.

B. *sb.* = ordinary *sb.*, in various senses.

1405 *Bidding Prayer* in *Lay Folks Mass Bk.* 64 For al prelates and ordiners. **1465** *Paston Lett.* II. 186 He was chef Justic of the Peas and hys ordynare. **1485** Caxton *Chas. Gt.* 20 Ye shal byleue in holy chyrche our catholyque moder, & her ordonnayre. **1553** *Reg. Privy Council Scot.* I. 142 The exhorbitant prices takin.. for thair ordinar, viz., dennar, supper and bedding. *a* **1578** Lindesay (Pitscottie) *Chron. Scot.* (S.T.S.) I. 262 Feild peaceis witht all thair ordinaris of poullder and bullat. **1600** *Burgh Recs. Glasgow* (1876) I. 207 That nane of thame have nather boy nor doig with thame quhair thai eit thair ordiner. **1818** Scott *Hrt. Midl.* xviii, Our minnie's sair mis-set, after her ordinar, sir. **1887** Stevenson *Merry Men* v. 55 There's nae soberer man than me in my ordnar.

Hence †**'ordinarly** *adv.* = ordinarily.

1557 N.T. (Genev.) *John* xii. 20 Among them, that ordinarely came to worshyp. **1596** Dalrymple tr. *Leslie's Hist. Scot.* x. 286 As fell thame ordinarlie. *a* **1649** Drumm. of Hawth. *Irene* Wks. (1711) 168 Such.. are ordinarly afraid and stand in awe of false scorns.

ordinarily ('ɔːdɪnərɪlɪ), *adv.* [f. ordinary *a.* + -ly^2.] In an ordinary manner or degree.

†**1.** In conformity with rule or established custom or practice; according to settled method; as a matter of regular practice or occurrence. *Obs.*

1532 More *Confut. Tindale* Wks. 588/2 As.. god.. calleth vpon al people both electes and reprobates to come to him, so doth he after both twaine.. gone awaye by sinne againe, call ordinarily vpon them both of hys lyke mercy still. **1540** *Act 32 Hen. VIII*, c. 7 §2 The same ordinarye.. shall.. procede.. ordinarylye or summarilye, accordynge to.. the sayd ecclesiasticall lawes. **1695** Woodward *Nat. Hist. Earth* III. i. (1723) 135 Springs and Rivers.. do [not] derive the Water, which they ordinarily refund, from Rains.

2. In the ordinary or usual course of events or state of things; in most cases; usually, commonly.

1555 Eden *Decades* 176 We ought not to iudge of that whiche chaunceth seldome, but of that which happeneth most ordinarily. *c* **1645** Howell *Lett.* (1650) I. 169 In.. Madrid.. there are ordinarily 600,000 souls. **1691** T. H[ale] *Acc. New Invent.* 18 Of a more blew colour than Lead ordinarily is. **1712** J. James tr. *Le Blond's Gardening* 150 The Trees and Shrubs that are ordinarily made use of. **1849** Macaulay *Hist. Eng.* iv. I. 432 The gates of Whitehall, which ordinarily stood open to all comers, were closed.

3. In an ordinary degree; to the usual extent. Esp. in phr. ***more than ordinarily*** = unusually, exceptionally: cf. ordinary *a.* 3 c.

1697 Locke *2nd Vind. Reas. Chr.* 255 If they were but ordinarily fair and prudent Men. **1709** *Tatler* No. 81 ¶1, I am more than ordinarily anxious to do Justice to the Persons. **1876** Miss Yonge *Womankind* viii. 65 The ordinarily intelligent child, with a healthy appetite for books.

4. In the ordinary way; as is normal or usual.

1831 Brewster *Optics* xviii. 161 Ray D G ordinarily refracted by the first rhomb will be extraordinarily refracted by the second. **1873** J. H. Newman *Hist. Sk.* II. Pref. 11 Materials.. to be found in any ordinarily furnished library.

ordinariness ('ɔːdɪnərɪnɪs). [f. as prec. + -ness.] The quality or condition of being ordinary; usual or commonplace character; (with *an* and *pl.*) an instance of this quality.

1619 Hieron *Wks.* II. 8 Let profanenesse and poperie cast reproches vpon diligence and ordinarinesse. *a* **1665** J. Goodwin *Filled w. the Spirit* (1867) 397 Whereas the persons yet under reproof are wont to pretend.. lowness and ordinariness of matter, or of teaching, in the ministry which they have a mind to quit. **1807** W. Taylor in *Monthly Mag.* XXIV. 332 An idiomatic ordinariness of diction, which has been praised for its simplicity. **1871** H. B. Forman *Living Poets* 247 The eight verses work through a variety of ordinarinesses to the final.

ordinary ('ɔːdɪnərɪ), *sb.* Also 4–7 **ordyn-**, 5–6 **orden-**, 7 **ordn-**. [In earlier senses, a. early OF. and Anglo-F. *ordinarie*, ad. med.L. *ordinārius* (sc. *judex*, *liber*, etc.) and as neut. sb. *ordinārium*; in some senses prob. immediately from the L. words; later senses are partly native developments of the earlier, partly translations of F. *ordinaire*, and largely, elliptical uses of ordinary *a.*, sometimes after F. types.]

I. Applied to a person or staff of persons.

1. *Eccl.* and *Common Law.* One who has, of his own right and not by special deputation, immediate jurisdiction in ecclesiastical cases, as the archbishop in a province, or the bishop or bishop's deputy in a diocese.

[**1292** Britton III. xxii. §3 En tel cas covendra de ceo estre certifié par le Evask et par les ordinaries.] *c* **1380** Wyclif *Sel. Wks.* III. 384 Freris.. ben exempt fro bischopis and oþer ordinaries. **1480** *Bury Wills* (Camden) 60 The ordenary, afore whom this myn testament schall be prouyd. **1529** Rastell *Pastyme, Hist. Brit.* (1811) 193 Clerkes indyted of felonye shalbe delyvered to the ordynaryes. **1590** Swinburne *Testaments* 205 The executor which deriueth his authoritie from the lawe, is the Bishop or Ordinarie of euerie diocesse. **1607** Cowell *Interpr.*, *Ordinarie* (*Ordinarius*), though in the ciuil lawe, whence the word is taken, it doth signifie any iudge that hath authoritie to take knowledge of causes in his owne right, as he is a magistrate, and not by deputation; yet in our common lawe, it is most commonly.. taken for him, that hath ordinarie Iurisdiction in causes ecclesiasticall. **1687** Bp. Cartwright in *Magd. Coll. & Jas. II* (O.H.S.) 115 The King.. is Supreme Ordinary of this Kingdom. **1767** Blackstone *Comm.* II. xviii. 277 If the bishop be both patron and ordinary, he shall not have a double time allowed him to collate in. **1875** Stubbs *Const. Hist.* III. xviii. 98 It was agreed that all Lollards.. should be handed over to the ordinaries to be tried.

2. *Civil Law.* A judge having authority to take cognizance of cases in his own right and not by delegation; *spec.* in Scotland, one of the five judges of the Court of Session who constitute the Outer House (= *Lord Ordinary*, ordinary *a.* 2); in *U.S.*, a judge of a court of probate.

1607 [see prec. sense]. **1641** *Termes de la Ley* 212. **1658** in Phillips. **1834** *Tait's Mag.* I. 724/1 From Mr. Hope's statement.. the Ordinaries fare worse than the Judges of the Inner-House, as they must sometimes read manuscript.... I do not know a more laborious life than that of one of the Lords Ordinary. **1861** W. Bell *Dict. Law Scot.* 755/2 The junior or last appointed Ordinary of the First Division is appointed to sit as junior of the two permanent Lords Ordinary of the Second Division.

3. An officer in a religious fraternity having charge of the convent, etc.: = med.L. *ordinārius* (Du Cange). *Obs.* exc. *Hist.*

1481 *Bury Wills* (Camden) 68 The Secresten of the Monasterie of Bury Seynt Edmund, Ordinarie of the same place.

4. a. A diocesan officer appointed to give criminals their neck-verses, and to prepare them for death; more fully *o. **of assize and sessions***. **b.** The chaplain of Newgate prison, whose duty it was to prepare condemned prisoners for death. *Obs.* exc. *Hist.*

1696 Phillips (ed. 5), *Ordinary*,.. Also the Bishop of the Diocesses Sub at Sessions and Assizes, to give Malefactors their Neck-verses, and to judge whether they read or no. **1700** Congreve *Way of World* III. xiii, The Ordinary's paid for setting the psalm, and the parish-priest for reading the ceremony. **1754** Fielding *Jon. Wild* IV. i, In Newgate.. the ordinary himself.. declared that he was a cursed rogue, but no conjurer. **1818** Hazlitt *Eng. Poets* v. (1870) 187 He is a kind of Ordinary, not of Newgate, but of nature. **1900** Sir W. Besant in *Daily News* 3 Sept. 6/2 The prisoner was conveyed to the spot in a cart beside his own coffin, while the ordinary sat beside him and exhorted him.

†**5.** A stage prompter. *Obs.*

1602 Carew *Cornwall* 71 b, The players.. are prompted by one called the Ordinary, who followeth at their back with the booke in his hand.

†**6.** A courier conveying dispatches or letters at regular intervals; hence, post, mail. *Obs.* (= F. *ordinaire*, 17th c. in Littré.)

1667 Temple *Lett. to Gourville* Wks. 1731 II. 32 By the last Ordinary from Spain, it appears that they dream no more of War there than they do of Fire. **1704** Swift *Operation of Spirit* Wks. 1768 I. 202, I have not had a line.. these three last ordinaries. **1730** Owen Swiny in G. Colman *Posth. Lett.* (1820) 26, I have rec^d no answer, as yet,.. but hope to have one by ye next week's ordinary.

†**7.** A staff of officers in regular attendance or service: cf. ordinary *a.* 3 b. *Obs.*

1526 in *Househ. Ord.* (1790) 165 The ordinary of the King's chamber which have bouche of Court & also their dietts within the Court. [Here follows a list of officers of the Household.]

8. *Naut.* †**a.** (See quot. 1769.) *Obs.*

a **1642** Sir W. Monson *Naval Tracts* III. (1704) 323/1 He is to take care to pay the Ordinary of the Navy every Quarter. **1702** Luttrell *Brief Rel.* (1857) V. 230 Resolv'd, that 129,314£. 18*s.* 03*d.* be allowed for the ordinary of the navy. **1757** Robertson in *Phil. Trans.* L. 31 They were all labouring men, belonging to the ordinary of Portsmouth yard. **1769** Falconer *Dict. Marine* (1789), *Ordinary*, the establishment of the persons employed by the government to take charge of the ships of war, which are laid-up in.. harbour. These are.. composed of the warrant-officers of the said ships,.. and their servants. There is besides a crew of labourers enrolled in the list of the ordinary.

b. (See quot. 1863.) Chiefly in phr. ***in ordinary*** (of a ship), laid up or out of commission (also *fig.*).

1754 *Ess. Manning Fleet* 24 Warrant-Officers doing Duty on Board any Ships in Ordinary. **1847** J. Wilson *Chr. North* (1857) I. 242 The crutch is laid up in ordinary. **1863** P. Barry *Dockyard Econ.* 192 Dockyard ordinaries is merely another name for reserves of ships of war. When ships of war are said to be in ordinary, the meaning is that they are in one of three stages of readiness for commission and active service. **1898** J. K. Laughton in *Trans. R. Hist. Soc.* XII. 89 'In ordinary' at that time [1805] meant being repaired, or waiting to be repaired, but certainly not fit for service.

II. Rule, ordinance, ordinal. (= med.L. *ordinārius, ordinārium.*)

†**9. a.** A formula or rule prescribing a certain order or course of action; an ordinance, regulation, prescript. **b.** A prescribed or customary course or procedure; regular custom or wont. *Obs.*

1303 R. Brunne *Handl. Synne* 10910 Wyþ þese prestes hyt shulde fare so Whan here parysshenes oghete mysdo, Wyþ feyre techyng, gode spelles,.. And wyþ ordynaryys of holy cherche. *c* **1450** *Cov. Myst.* ix. (Shaks. Soc.) 87 To obey the ordenaryes of the temple echeon. **1526** in *Househ. Ord.* (1790) 140 The Serjeant of the bakehouse.. to make & bake the bread.. according to the auntient ordinary of the household. **1594** Carew *Huarte's Exam. Wits* (1616) 193 Oft times they procure the feauer, and their ordinarie is to make melancholie by adustion.

10. A rule prescribing, or book containing, the order of divine service, esp. that of the mass; the established order or form for saying mass; the service of the mass, or that part preceding and following the canon. Usu. with capital initial, in the Roman Catholic rite, those parts of a service, esp. the mass, which do not vary from day to day; *spec.*, those unvarying parts which form the mass as a musical setting (Kyrie, Gloria, Credo, Sanctus, Benedictus and Agnus Dei). Also *transf.*, of other rites.

1494 Fabyan *Chron.* VII. ccxxii. 245 Bokes, that were occupyed in the deuyne seruyce of the Churche, as the Ordynall or Consuetudynary, the whiche.. is nowe named Salysbury vse, or the ordinary after Salysbury vse. **1655** Fuller *Ch. Hist.* III. i. §23 Osmund, Bishop of Salisbury, devised that Ordinary or form of service, which hereafter was observed in the whole kingdom. *a* **1832** Mackintosh *Revol. 1688* Wks. 1846 II. 263 The judicial determinations, which recognised his [the King's] right.. to make ordinaries for the outward rule of the Church. **1905** Proctor & Frere *New Hist. Bk. Common Prayer* (rev. ed.) i. 12 In the Liturgy, the 'Canon' or central prayer.. was the Roman canon, and in fact the rest of the invariable framework of the public service (or 'Ordinary') was that adopted from Rome. **1929** E. C. Thomas *Lay Folks' Hist. Liturgy* I. v. 22 These Nestorian Liturgies differ in the Anaphora, but the Ordinary of the Mass is the same in all. **1944** W. Apel *Harvard Dict. Mus.* 427/2 Around 500, the Mass consisted only of the chants of the Proper, alternating with lections from the Epistles, etc. Gradually, the chants of the Ordinary were introduced, probably in the following chronological order: Sanctus, Kyrie, Gloria, Agnus Dei, Credo. *Ibid.* 523/2 Other services [than the Mass].. also comprise invariable and variable portions. For instance, the Magnificat forms a part of the Ordinary of Vespers. **1974** *Daily Tel.* 20 July 7/8 Surely the way Haydn in his 70s appears tormented by sudden doubts at the word 'mortuorum' belies the confidence of the preceding 'Et expecto resurrectionem', uniquely so in any setting of the Ordinary. **1976** *Gramophone* Apr. 1653/3 It is found in ninth-century manuscripts and may well be connected with two well-known items of the Ordinary, Sanctus I and Sanctus XI.

†**11.** A devotional manual containing instructions for the conduct of life. *Obs.*

1502 *Ord. Crysten Men* colophon, Here endeth the booke named the Ordynarye of Crysten Men,.. enprynted in Flete Strete by Wynken de Worde. **1578** Scoloker (*title*) The Ordenarye for all faythfull Chrystians to leade a Vertuous and Godly lyfe.

III. Something ordinary, regular, or usual. (From the adj. in Fr. or Eng.)

†**12.** A lecture read at regular or stated times.

1432–50 tr. *Higden* (Rolls) VIII. 219 Hit happede seynte Edmunde to forgete that impression.. by studyenge for an ordinary to be redde in the morowe foloynge. *c* **1500** in Peacock *Stat. Cambridge* (1841) App. A. p. xliv, The Bedellys shall sett the Doctor from hys place to the commyn Scolys to rede his Ordinarye.

†**13.** Customary fare; a regular daily meal or allowance of food; by extension, a fixed portion, an allowance of anything (= F. *ordinaire*). *Obs.*

1481 Caxton *Myrr.* III. xvi. 173 They.. reteyne and kepe more goodes and richesses than [*printed* that] they nede for their ordynarye. **1577–87** Holinshed *Chron.* II. 20/2 Albeit.. his house is frequented.. of the nobilitie.. yet his ordinarie is so good, that a verie few set feasts are provided for them. **1616** Surfl. & Markh. *Country Farme* 129 Giue him rather some Hay to eat, than to lead him to water, and after that to giue him his ordinarie of Oats. **1667** *Decay Chr. Piety* viii. §44 Nor is he now to be lookt on as a gentleman, whose single ordinary costs not as much as would be.. a fair exhibition for some whole families. *a* **1668** Sir W. Waller *Div. Medit.* (1839) 45 Behemoth is satisfied with that ordinary which the mountaines bring him forth.

14. a. A public meal regularly provided at a fixed price in an eating-house or tavern; also, formerly, the company frequenting such a meal, the 'table'.

1589 Nashe *Ded. Greene's Menaphon* (Arb.) 17 They might have.. dinde everie daie at the pease porredge ordinarie with Delphrigus. **1650** Fuller *Pisgah* III. vi. 328 He kept a daily Ordinary (thanks being the only shot his guests were to pay). **1678** *Yng. Mans Call.* 58 Civil and loving society.. is natures table of ordinary. **1709** Steele *Tatler* No. 135 ¶6 In the presence of the whole Ordinary that were now gathered about him in the Garden. **1771** Mackenzie *Man Feel.* xix. (1886) 41 A board hung out of a window signifying, 'An excellent Ordinary on Saturdays and Sundays'. **1887** H. Smart *Cleverly won* v, Joe.. played a very good knife and fork at the farmers' ordinary. **1908** G. B. Shaw *Lett. to Granville Barker* (1956) 114 Charlotte at a farmers' ordinary at Towcester was immense. **1928** *Daily Chron.* 9 Aug. 4/4 Lord Beaconfield [*sic*] was accustomed to make some of his most important pronouncements at the farmers' ordinary at Aylesbury. **1976** N. Roberts *Face of France* xv. 157 The establishment in an English market town which still does a good farmers' ordinary.

fig. **1750** W. Kenrick (*title*) The Kapélion, or Poetical Ordinary; consisting of Great Variety of Dishes in Prose and Verse. **1816** Coleridge *Lay Serm.* 327 The two public ordinaries of literature, the circulating library and the periodical press.

b. An eating-house or tavern where public meals are provided at a fixed price; a dining-room in such a building.

In the 17th cent. the more expensive *ordinaries* were frequented by men of fashion, and the dinner was usually followed by gambling; hence the term was often used as synonymous with 'gambling-house'.

1590 Payne *Descr. Irel.* (1841) 8 A man may be as well and cleanely tabled at an English house in Ireland.. as at the best ordinarie in England. **1631** T. Powell *Tom All Trades* (1876) 141 The unwholsome ayre of an Eightpenny Ordinarie. **1712** Swift *Let. Eng. Tongue* Wks. 1755 II. I. 189 All the odd words they have picked up in a coffee-house or a gaming ordinary. **1812** *Sporting Mag.* XXXIX. 278 The plaintiff had no right to insist upon going into the ordinary or any other particular room. **1883** J. Hawthorne *Dust* III. 286 In one of the narrow streets leading towards Cheapside she noticed a small inn or ordinary.

c. In parts of the United States, as Virginia: A tavern or inn of any kind.

1637 in *Essex Inst. Hist. Coll.* (1869) IX. 55 Mr. John Holgraue.. hath undertaken to keep an ordinary for the entertainment of strangers. **1650** *Archives of Maryland* (1883) I. 294 Wine or other Provisions to bee expended in any Ordinaries within this Province. **1680** in *New Hampsh. Hist. Soc. Coll.* (1866) VIII. 15 What person soever.. shall profane ye Lord's Day.. by Dining at ordinarys in time of publique worship.. shall forfeite 10*s.* **1774** P. Fithian *Jrnl.* in *Amer. Hist. Rev.* V. 315 All Taverns they [Virginians] call 'Ordinary's'. **1775** A. Burnaby *Trav.* 83 When he went into an ordinary [*Note*, Inns are so called in America]. **1866** Whittier *Marg. Smith's Jrnl.* Pr. Wks. 1889 I. 19 Sir Thomas.. excused himself for the time.. and rode on to the ordinary.

†**d.** A gambling game carried on at an ordinary.

1684 *Lond. Gaz.* No. 1950/4 Rafflings, Ordinaries, and other publick Games.

15. *Her.* **a.** A charge of the earliest, simplest, and commonest kind, usually bounded by straight lines, but sometimes engrailed, wavy, indented, etc.

The principal charges so classed are the Chief, Pale, Bend, Bend-sinister, Fess, Bar, Chevron, Cross, and Saltire.

1610 Guillim *Heraldry* II. iii. (1660) 53 Those Charges.. which.. do peculiarly belong to this Art, and are of ordinary use therein, in regard whereof they are called *Ordinaries*. *Ibid.* III. xxvi. (1611) 182 Sometimes you shall find this bird borne in the forme of some Ordinary, [as] displaied in Pale, three of them one aboue another. **1882** Cussans *Handbk. Her.* (ed. 3) iv. 56 Armorists usually divide the Ordinaries into Honourable Ordinaries and Sub-ordinaries.

b. Hence, ***Ordinary of Arms***, applied (*erron.*) to a book or work of reference in which heraldic bearings are arranged in some methodical order and referred to the persons or families who bear them; the converse of an *Armoury*, arranged in the order of the names of the persons.

This appears to have originated in a misunderstanding (perh. through a colloquial *Ordinary Book*) of the appellation *Book of Ordinaries* properly applied in 1628 by John Withie to the MS. work of R. Glover, Somerset Herald (1571–88). R. Glover's own MS., Brit. Mus. Tib. D. x, has no title.

1628 J. Withie *Harl. MS.* 1459 This is a true coppie of a booke of Armes; (otherwise called a booke of Ordinaries) wch was trickt and written by the hands of the late worthy gent: Robert Glouer Esquire Somerset-Herauld. *a* **1726** H. Wanley *Descr. Harl. MS.* 1078 A large collection of the Arms of English Families disposed by way of Ordinary... But a table shewing the Order of this Ordinary is wanting. **1780** Edmondson *Heraldry* title-p. [contains *inter alia*] Glover's Ordinary of Arms, augmented and improved. *Ibid.* Contents, A Copious Ordinary of Arms, originally compiled by Robert Glover, Somerset Herald, and now enlarged and improved.

16. a. Ordinary condition, course, run, degree; ordinary state of health, etc. (In quots. 1672, 1710 = ordinary or regular course of reading.) ***the ordinary***, what is customary or usual. Now *colloq.*

1581 Savile *Tacitus, Hist.* IV. xiii. (1591) 177 Of a crafty and suttle wit, aboue the ordinary of those barbarous people. **1600** Shaks. *A.Y.L.* III. v. 42, I see no more in you then in the ordinary Of Natures sale-worke. **1672** J. Fraser in *Sel. Biol.* (Wodrow Soc.) II. 152 Reading in my ordinary, I read these words Hag. ii. 17. **1710** Col. Blackader *Diary* 2 July in *Life* xvi. (1834) 397 In reading the Scripture in my Ordinary I got both reproof and instruction. **1846** J. Hamilton *Mount of Olives* vii. 150 If he is in his 'frail ordinary' he is content. **1893** *Chicago Advance* 14 Sept., Something out of the ordinary was anticipated. **1909** *Times Lit. Suppl.* 20 May 185/2 Shakespeare introduces the ordinary, whether in characters or in events, only as a foil to the extraordinary. **1977** 'D. Cory' *Bennett* iv. 121 The case I'm engaged on.. is rather out of the ordinary. **1978** *Atlanta Jrnl. & Constitution* 14 Jan. 23T (Advt.), Tapas. When you're fed up with the ordinary... Our European chef proudly presents over 40 delightfully different hot and cold appetizer treats.

b. An ordinary thing or person; something of usual or commonplace character. *rare.*

1624 Bacon *Cons. War w. Sp.* Wks. 1879 I. 542/2 At that time Spain had no other wars save those of the Low Countries, which were grown into the ordinary. **1647** Ward *Simp. Cobler* 17, I would not have.. my Animall Spirits purged any way but by my Naturall, and those by my bodily humours, and those by such Ordinaries as have the nearest vicinage to them. **1897** *Chicago Advance* 2 Sept. 314/1 To touch and lift the common life about him, till its veriest ordinaries should feel the thrill of the new life.

c. One of a class of inmates in a poor-house.

1910 *Daily Chron.* 14 Jan. 8/5 The 'ordinaries' (whom we should call able-bodied) were able to roam all over the building.

17. Applied to various things of the more or most usual class or type, to distinguish them from others of some special sort.

†**a.** A particular make or variety of kersey. *Obs.* **b.** An ungeared bicycle of the earlier type, with one large and one very small wheel. So called for some years after the introduction of the 'Safety' type, *c* 1885. **c.** An ordinary share (as distinguished from preference shares, etc.).

a. **1552** *Act 5 & 6 Edw. VI*, c. 6 §12 Kersies called Ordinaries.. being well scowred, thicked, milled, dressed and fully dried, shall weigh xx. li. at the least.

b. **1888** *Cycl. Tour. Club Gaz.* Sept. 369 A youth who, on sighting us.. forthwith mounted his ordinary, rode out of the yard [etc.]. **1898** *Cycling* 84 Osmond at his best on the Ordinary was riding when the rear-driver began to establish itself as a racing cycle.

c. **1898** *Westm. Gaz.* 9 Mar. 8/2 The market values the ordinaries at over 115–16. **1900** *Ibid.* 21 Aug. 7/3 Last year the ordinaries were divided into £1 shares. **1964** *Financial Times* 23 Mar. 12/3 Plans are being considered to fund back indebtedness through.. a 1-for-1 rights issue of 5s Ordinary at par.

†**18.** *Phrases.* **a.** (These might equally be placed under the adj.) ***of, for, in ordinary*** (= F. *d'ordinaire, pour l'ordinaire*), in the ordinary course, as a regular custom or practice, ordinarily. *Obs.*

1556 J. Heywood *Spider & F.* lii. 17 Spiders of ordinarie haue store Of all municion, for warrs redie rated. **1589** Puttenham *Eng. Poesie* III. xviii. (Arb.) 202 In his Oration which ye know is of ordinary to be made before the Prince at the first assembly of both houses. **1596** Danett tr. *Comines* (1614) 344 Twise that weeke, once of ordinarie, and once for those that came to be cured of the Kings euill. **1762** Kames *Elem. Crit.* (1763) I. ii. 87 May we not with equal reason derive from self-love the affection a man for ordinary has to them [children]? **1808** Jefferson *Writ.* (1830) IV. 112 We shall man them, in ordinary, but with their navigating crew of eight or ten good seamen.

b. ***in ordinary*** added to official designations: app. an expansion of *ordinary* (see ordinary *a.* 3 b), and like it opposed to *extraordinary*, as ***chaplain-in-ordinary*** to his Majesty, ***physician-in-ordinary*** to the Prince of Wales.

a **1639** Wotton *Life Dk. Buckingham* in *Reliq.* (1651) 78 There is conveyed to Master Villiers an intimation of the Kings pleasure.. to be.. his Cup-bearer at large; and the Summer following he was admitted in Ordinary. *a* **1683** Walton *Angler* i. (1886) 14 Therefore I think my eagle is so justly styled 'Jove's servant in ordinary'. *a* **1686** Fell (T.), He.. was soon after made chaplain in ordinary to his majesty. **1707** J. Chamberlayne *St. Gt. Brit.* III. 550 (List of Queen's Officers and Servants), Physicians in Ordinary to her Majesty's Person. **1737** *Ibid.* II. III. 245 (Establishmt. of her Majesty's Household), Ladies of the Bed-Chamber in Ordinary,..Ladies of the Bed-Chamber Extraordinary. *Ibid.* 247 Upholster in Ordinary. **1934** *Burlington Mag.* Oct. 182/2 In this very year, January 1431, the King's painter to Charles IX of France was Henry Mellein, and his painter-in-ordinary was Conrad de Vulcop. **1944** *Ibid.* Dec. 307/1 Jacques d'Arthois, painter-in-ordinary of the Forêt de Soignes, is one of the leading figures of the Brussels landscape school of the seventeenth century.

19. *attrib.* and *Comb.* **a.** in sense 14, as ***ordinary supper***, ***-keeper***, ***-keeping***, etc.; **ordinary table**, the table at which an ordinary was served and which was afterwards cleared for gambling; hence, a gambling-table or gambling-house.

1579 LYLY *Euphues* (Arb.) 152 Frequent not those ordinary tables, wher..yee both spend your money vainely, and your time idly. **1635** BRERETON *Trav.* (Chetham Soc.) 93 We were well used: 6*d.* ordinary supper, and 4*d.* breakfast. **1645** in *Essex Inst. Hist. Coll.* (1869) IX. 136 To provide for a ordinarie keeper. **1662** *Archives of Maryland* (1883) I. 447 All Ordinary Keepers debts either upon bill or accompt..shall be allowed due. **1681** *Connect. Col. Rec.* (1859) III. 78 He shall give publique notice..at a town meeting or by a writing set up upon the ordinary or mill dore. **1685** *Col. Rec. Pennsylv.* I. 166 That Ordinary Keepers within Philadelphia should bring in their Lycences on this day. **1710** *Providence Rec.* (1896) X. 113 Anne Tirpin tooke a licence for Ordinary Keeping and gave bond. **1883** CROFT in *Elyot's Gov.* 274 *note*, 'Hells' in England..were previously known as 'Ordinary-Tables'.

b. in sense 8, as ***ordinary ship***, etc.; †**ordinary-man** (see quot. 1769).

a **1642** SIR W. MONSON *Naval Tracts* III. (1704) 325/2 The Victualling of the Ordinary Ship keepers. **1769** FALCONER *Dict. Marine* (1789), *Matelots-gardien*, the ordinary-men attending a royal dock-yard, and it's harbour or dock.

Hence **'ordinaryist**, one who rides an 'ordinary' bicycle: see 17 b. **'ordinaryship**, the quality, dignity, or personality of an ordinary.

1889 *Pall Mall G.* 10 May 1/1 Taken altogether, the riding of the safety men was infinitely better than that of the *ordinaryists. **1891** *Wheeling* 4 Mar. 426 On a wet day a safety rider is simply coated with mud, while the ordinaryist is comparatively clean. *a* **1661** FULLER (Webster), The same ..doth not destroy his *ordinaryship, but only showeth that he was made an ordinary in an extraordinary manner. **1830** *Westm. Rev.* XIII. 451 His Ordinaryship sitting in three new characters at once.

ordinary ('ɔːdɪnərɪ), *a.* (*adv.*) Also 5–6 orden-, -yn-, 7 ordn-. [ad. L. *ordinārі-us* regular, orderly, customary, usual, f. *ordo, ordin-*, ORDER: see -ARY[1]. Cf. F. *ordinaire* (OF. *ordenaire*, 13th c.), whence some of the uses are taken.]

A. *adj.* †**1.** Conformable to order or rule; regular; orderly, methodical. *Obs.*

1529 MORE *Dyaloge* II. Wks. 183/2 Yf it were thus, God hadde lefte none ordinarye waye for his ghospell and fayth to be taught. **1555** W. WATREMAN *Fardle Facions* App. 314 Those [lawes] that he left written by piecemeale..we haue framed togeather into one ordenarie treatise. **1638** R. BAKER tr. *Balzac's Lett.* (vol. II.) 37 Stay your selfe within the bounds of ordinary justice. **1639** I. W. tr. *Guibert's Charit. Physic.* title-p., The advice of the best and ordinariest physitians.

2. Of a judge: Having regular jurisdiction, i.e. exercising authority by virtue of office and not by special deputation; *esp.* empowered *ex officio* to take cognizance of ecclesiastical or spiritual cases: now only in special collocations (cf. ORDINARY *sb.* 1, 2). Of jurisdiction, ecclesiastical power, etc.: Exercised *ex officio* (now merged in 3).

Judge Ordinary: (*a*) the judge of the Court for Divorce (formerly a branch of ecclesiastical judicature); (*b*) in Scotland, the sheriff of a county. ***Lord Ordinary***: see quot. 1861.

1483 CAXTON *Cato* A viij, To understonde the sentence of thy Iuge competent and ordynarye. **1534** *Act 26 Hen. VIII*, c. 3 §7 Archebysshoppes and bysshoppes, and all other hauing iurisdiction ordinary. *a* **1600** HOOKER *Eccl. Pol.* VIII. viii. §3 Our judges in causes ecclesiastical are either ordinary or commissionary: ordinary, those whom we term ordinaries, and such, by the laws of this land, are none but prelates only. **1656** BRAMHALL *Replic.* v. 200 They have yet another evasion, that the highest ecclesiasticall power was given..to Saint Peter as an ordinary Pastor to descend from him to his Successors. **1834** [see ORDINARY *sb.* 2]. **1861** W. BELL *Dict. Law Scot.* 600/1 Lord Ordinary. In the Court of Session, the judge before whom a cause depends in the Outer-House is called the Lord Ordinary in that cause. And the judge who officiates in the Bill-Chamber is called the Lord Ordinary on the Bills. **1872** *Wharton's Law Lex.* (ed. 5), *Judge Ordinary*, the judge of the Court for Divorce.

3. a. Belonging to the regular or usual order or course; having a place in a fixed or regulated sequence; occurring in the course of regular custom or practice; regular, normal, customary, usual.

ordinary ray: see quot. 1831 (cf. EXTRAORDINARY 1 d).

c **1460** FORTESCUE *Abs. & Lim. Mon.* vi. (1885) 120 Ordinance ffor the Kynges ordinarie charges. **1577** HARRISON *England* II. vi. (1877) I. 148 The servants haue their ordinarie diet assigned. **1607–12** BACON *Ess.*, *Atheism* (Arb.) 330/1 God never wrought miracle to convince Atheistes because his ordinary workes convince them. **1756** C. LUCAS *Ess. Waters* I. 145 It proves a very useful, good water for the ordinary purposes of families. **1831** BREWSTER *Optics* xvii. §90. 146 The ray..is refracted according to the ordinary law of refraction..[and] is therefore called the ordinary ray. **1875** JEVONS *Money* (1878) 250 In ordinary life we use a great many words with a total disregard of logical precision.

b. Of officials, persons employed, etc.: Belonging to the regular staff or to the fully recognized class of such. Cf. EXTRAORDINARY 2. Now mostly represented by *-in-ordinary*: see ORDINARY *sb.* 18.

[**1508** Chamerlane ordinare: see ORDINAR *a.*] **1555** W. WATREMAN *Fardle Facions* II. x. 231 The Emperour..neuer speaketh to any foreine ambassadours,..excepte bothe thei and their giftes..bee purified by the ordenarie women. **1577–87** HOLINSHED *Chron.* III. 1136/1 There were in the towne of Calis fiue hundred English souldiors ordinarie,.. and of the townesmen not fullie two hundred fighting men. **1592** GREENE *Disput.* 21, I was an ordinary dauncer. **1621** BURTON *Anat. Mel.* I. ii. III. vi, A grave and learned Minister, and an ordinary Preacher at Alcmar in Holland. **1737** J. CHAMBERLAYNE *St. Gt. Brit.* II. III. 117 Military Branch of the Ordnance..Engineer-Ordinary, Joseph Day.

c. Phr. ***more than ordinary***: (*a*) more in number or amount than is usual; (*b*) with adj. or sb; to a greater degree than is usual, unusual, exceptional; also *advb.* unusually, exceptionally. *Obs.*, *arch.*, or *dial.* So ***greater, better, worse*** (etc.) ***than ordinary***.

1560 DAUS tr. *Sleidane's Comm.* 339 b, He that taketh yerely of his subjectes more than ordinarye, .iii. C. M. Ducates. **1589** PUTTENHAM *Eng. Poesie* III. xx. (Arb.) 264 Surplusage..lieth not only in a word or two more than ordinary, but in whole clauses. **1644** MILTON *Areop.* (Arb.) 57 Though a licencer should happ'n to be judicious more then ordinary. **1662** STILLINGFL. *Orig. Sacr.* III. iv. §9 There was a more than ordinary multiplication of the world from the Sons of Noah after the Flood. **1670** EACHARD *Cont. Clergy* 122 The clouds being more than ordinary thick. *a* **1704** LOCKE (J.), This designation of the person our author is more than ordinary obliged to take care of. **1748** RICHARDSON *Clarissa* (1811) I. ii. 11 When she aimed to be worse tempered than ordinary. **1852** MRS. STOWE *Uncle Tom's C.* xix. 197 If Eva, now, was not more angel than ordinary, she would be ruined.

d. Of language, usage, discourse, etc.: that most commonly found or attested, *spec.* as contrasted with logical symbolism or a specialized terminology.

1685 tr. *Arnauld & Nicole's Logic* II. x. 221 As when I say, *All Men have two Arms.* This Proposition ought to pass for true, according to ordinary use. *Ibid.* III. xv. 70 Whereas it is the method of the Schools to propound the Argument entire, and afterwards to prove the Proposition which receives the difficulty, that which is usual in ordinary discourse, is to join to doubtful propositions the Proofs that confirm 'em. **1690** LOCKE *Essay Hum. Und.* II. xxi. 121 Philosophy it self,..must have so much Complacency, as to be cloathed in the ordinary Fashion and Language of the Country. **1828** J. S. MILL in *Westm. Rev.* IX. 145 Arranging all these propositions in that *order*, which (so strongly does ordinary language corroborate our view of the case) is termed their *logical* order. **1843** —— *Logic* I. I. i. 25 We must begin by recognising the distinctions made by ordinary language. *Ibid.* II. IV. v. 268 These changes, by which words in ordinary use become more and more generalized. **1874** W. WALLACE tr. *Hegel's Logic* 43 The deeper and philosophical meaning of truth can be partially traced even in the expressions of ordinary language. **1892** —— *Ibid.* (ed. 2) 52 The deeper and philosophical meaning of truth can be partially traced even in the ordinary usage of language. **1902** W. JAMES *Var. Relig. Exper.* ii. 36 Trifling, sneering attitudes even towards the whole of life... It would strain the ordinary use of language too much to call such attitudes religious. **1906** B. RUSSELL in *Mind* XV. 256 One of the objects to be aimed at in using symbols is that they should be free from the ambiguities of ordinary language. **1909** W. M. URBAN *Valuation* ii. 33 Our ordinary usage, at least, makes a clear distinction between feeling and will. **1932** H. H. PRICE *Perception* viii. 256 We also stick to common sense and the ordinary usage of language. **1939** *Mind* XLVIII. 62 While it is true that a formal calculus frequently assists in detecting errors which are unnoticed in ordinary language, each formal calculus carries with it new sources of confusion. **1949** *Mind* LVIII. 147 The redefinitions which are implicit in philosophical paradoxes do quite often.. receive a certain backing from ordinary usage. **1951** J. HOLLOWAY *Lang. & Intelligence* viii. 123 Ordinary language is the language of persons unacquainted even with the idea of conforming to a dictionary. **1957** J. PASSMORE *100 Yrs. Philos.* xviii. 438 Not all ex-students of Wittgenstein look with kindness on the 'ordinary language' philosophies which have latterly dominated the philosophical scene at Oxford. **1977** *Oxford Times* 9 Dec. 5/3 He is the leading exponent of ordinary language philosophy, and became a fellow of the British Academy in 1960.

†**4. a.** Of common or everyday occurrence; frequent: abundant. *Obs.*

1597 SHAKS. *2 Hen. IV*, IV. iv. 115 Be patient (Princes) you doe know, these Fits Are with his Highnesse very ordinarie. **1675** tr. *Camden's Hist. Eliz.* III. (1688) 324 Tobacco-Shops are now as ordinary in most Towns as Tap-houses and Taverns. **1725** SLOANE *Jamaica* II. 323 These are very ordinary here, but thrive not..for want of water.

†**b.** Commonly practised or experienced; common, customary, usual. Chiefly predicative, in phr. ***it is ordinary***, or ***an ordinary thing*** (*with* a person *to do* something, etc.). *Obs.*

1605 BACON *Adv. Learn.* I. ii. §3 It hath been ordinary with politique men to extenuate and disable learned men by the names of pedantes. **1670** BAXTER *Cure Ch.-Div.* 167 It is very ordinary with poor fanciful women..to take all their deep apprehensions for revelations. **1709** STEELE *Tatler* No. 5 ¶2 Her Eyes are intent upon one who looks from her; which is ordinary with the Sex. *Ibid.* No. 27 ¶6 It is ordinary for Love to make Men Poetical. **1794** PALEY *Evid.* I. v. §4 (1817) 98 This proves that a morality, more pure and strict than was ordinary, prevailed..in Christian societies.

5. a. Of the usual kind, such as is commonly met with, not singular or exceptional. Often in depreciatory use: Not above, or somewhat below, the usual level of quality; commonplace, somewhat inferior; also (now *dial.* or *colloq.*) ordinary-looking, 'plain', 'ugly, not handsome' (Johnson).

ordinary seaman: see quot. 1769.

1590 WEBBE *Trav.* (Arb.) 18 We were set to wipe the feet of the kings horses, and to become ordinarie slaues in the said Court. **1607** TOPSELL *Four-f. Beasts* (1658) 220 A common name for ordinary Hackney-horses. **1661** RUST *Origen's Opin.* in *Phenix* (1721) I. 81 They were Men of ordinary Intellectuals. **1667** PRIMATT *City & C. Build.* 71 There is those that do it for four shillings a peece; but very ordinary work. **1710** HEARNE *Collect.* (O.H.S.) III. 52 His Books are very mean and ordinary. **1752** HUME *Ess.* I. i. (1788) 20 The most ordinary machine is sufficient to tell the hours, but the most elaborate alone can point out the minutes and seconds. **1769** FALCONER *Dict. Marine* (1789), *Ordinary*..is likewise used to distinguish the inferior sailors from the more expert... The latter are rated *able* on the navy-books. *a* **1847** MRS. SHERWOOD *Lady of Manor* III. xx. 148 Lady Anne was..remarkable for her ordinary appearance, her person being clumsy, and her face spoiled by the small-pox. **1848** C. BRONTË *J. Eyre* v, Miss Miller was more ordinary; ruddy in complexion. **1879** *Paper & Print. Trades Jrnl.* No. 29. 5 The get-up and printing of both works being of the most ordinary character. **1883** *Knowledge* 10 Aug. 95/1 In Cambridgeshire..'An ordinary child' was 'a plain child'.

b. ***ordinary wine*** (Fr. *vin ordinaire*). Cf. ORDINAIRE *sb.*

1814 M. BIRKBECK *Notes Journey through France* 102 Such is the habitual temperance..that the inns..seldom have any liquor stronger than their ordinary wine. If you call for brandy, they are obliged to send for it to the Caffé. **1860** DICKENS *Uncomm. Trav.* (1861) vii. 92, I was in the dear old France of my affections. I should have known it, without the well-remembered bottle of rough ordinary wine.

c. *Comm.* Of shares, stock, etc.: forming part of the common stock and without 'preference'; also applied to shareholders holding such stock.

1869 *Bradshaw's Railway Manual* XXI. 10 No dividend was declared in March on the ordinary stock. *Ibid.* 42 An obligation..to pay to the ordinary shareholders a dividend ..at the rate of 2 per cent. **1878** [see PREFERENCE 8]. **1891** [see SHARE *sb.*[2] 2]. **1955** *Times* 12 May 17/7 The issue of three shares to Ordinary shareholders for every five which they hold at present.. *Ibid.* 1 July 16/5 The balance-sheet shows the increase in ordinary share capital arising from this capitalization and the manner in which the reserves have been applied. **1974** *Terminol. Managem. & Financial Accountancy* (Inst. Cost & Managem. Accountants) 60 *Ordinary shares*, shares which entitle the holders to the remaining divisible profits (and, in a liquidation, the assets) remaining after prior interests (e.g. preference shareholders) have been satisfied. **1977** *Times* 1 Dec. 20/7 Earning per Ordinary Share 4.44p... Ordinary Dividend 3.4914p.

d. Of people: typical of a particular group; average; without exceptional experience or expert knowledge.

1855 GEO. ELIOT *Let.* 12 May (1954) II. 201, I really think a taste for descriptive writing is the rarest of all tastes among ordinary people. **1902** G. B. SHAW *Mrs. Warren's Profession* Pref. p. xvii, The ordinary Briton thinks that if every other Briton is not under some form of tutelage..he will abuse his freedom viciously. **1903** —— *Man & Superman* III. 76 But I am well aware that the ordinary man—even the ordinary brigand, who can scarcely be called an ordinary man (Hear, hear!)—is not a philosopher. **1922** M. A. VON ARNIM *Enchanted April* iii. 50, I don't think references are nice things at all..between ordinary decent women. **1952** A. CHRISTIE *Mrs McGinty's Dead* ii. 21 It's not the sort of thing that an ordinary man—or a jury—can believe. **1971** *Listener* 28 Oct. 566/1 The language of everyday speech is used in verse..because the role of the poet is an ordinary-man role. **1974** *Times* 11 Oct. 14/8 A government claiming that it wants to involve ordinary people in decision-making. **1975** T. HEALD *Deadline* ii. 19 The *Globe*..made its appeal to 'the man in the street'. Leader writers were instructed..to spice their texts with frequent references to 'ordinary folk'.

e. ***ordinary level***, the lowest of the three levels of the General Certificate of Education; abbrev. *O level* (O 5 d).

1947 *Examinations Secondary Schools* (Secondary Schools Exam. Council) 8 An examination at 'Ordinary', 'Advanced' and 'Scholarship' levels should be available each year to candidates who are at least sixteen on Sept. 1st. **1959** *Listener* 29 Jan. 195/2 The arts sixth former who has perhaps 'done' a little science to 'ordinary level'. **1960–1** *Where* Winter 14/1 Ordinary (O) level is normally taken at 16 after a 5-year course. **1963** BARNARD & LAUWERYS *Handbk. Brit. Educ. Terms* 99 In 1951 the *School* and *Higher School Certificate* examinations in secondary schools were replaced by a General Certificate of Education..examination at three levels—ordinary, advanced, and scholarship. **1978** *Nature* 27 Apr. 784/1 Asimov carefully explains the inverse-square law of force in a manner that should be comprehensible to a pupil considered incapable of taking ordinary level school physics.

†**6.** Not distinguished by rank or position; belonging to the commonalty; of low degree; pertaining to, or characteristic of, the common people; common, vulgar; unrefined, low, coarse. Cf. ORNERY *a.* *Obs.*

1659 PEARSON *Creed* (1839) 117 The ordinary Jews had lost the exact understanding of the old Hebrew language. **1722** DE FOE *Plague* (1756) 79 Expressions, such as..even the worst and ordinariest People in the Street would not use. **1741** CHESTERF. *Lett.* (1792) I. 209 To speak of Mr. What-d'ye-call-him, or Mrs. Thingum,..is excessively awkward and ordinary. *Ibid.*, They are the distinguishing marks of the ordinary people. *Ibid.* 255 Most women and all the ordinary people in general speak in open defiance of all

grammar. **1800** *Aurora* (Philadelphia) 1 May 2/3 This ordinary drunken wretch is supposed to be the perpetrator.
7. *Phrases*: see ORDINARY *sb.* 18.

†**B.** *adv.* In an ordinary manner; according to, or as a matter of, regular practice; in ordinary cases, commonly, ordinarily. *Obs.*

1596 DANETT tr. *Comines* (1614) 24 My selfe was resident there,.. being lodged at the Tournelles, and ordinary eating and lodging in the Court. **1607** TOPSELL *Four-f. Beasts* (1658) 241 They mounted without other stirrop.. not only when they were ordinary attired in common garments, but then also when they were armed. **1697** tr. *C'tess D'Annoy's Trav.* (1706) 56 Their Sword oftentimes hangs by their side tied with a bit of Cord, and ordinary without a Scabbard. **1798** *Invasion* I. 276 When you are quite ordinary dressed, so that no one could guess you for ladies.

C. *Comb.*, as ***ordinary-looking***, ***-sized*** adjs.

1818 SCOTT *Rob Roy* xx, One or two starched and ordinary-looking mechanics stood beside and behind me. **1831** BREWSTER *Nat. Magic* xi. (1833) 274 It is capable of accommodating an ordinary-sized man. **1891** S. MOSTYN *Curatica* 2 That other young man, who.. had a turned-up nose, and was quite ordinary looking.

ordinate ('ɔːdɪnət), *a.* and *sb.* Also 4–7 **-at.** [ad. L. *ordināt-us*, pa. pple. of *ordināre* to ORDAIN.]

A. *ppl. a.* and *adj.* Now *Obs.* or *rare.*

I. †**1. a.** Construed as *pa. pple.* Ordered, arranged, disposed; ordained, destined, appointed. *Obs.*

1398 TREVISA *Barth. De P.R.* v. v. (1495) 108 The curtelles or webbes of the eye ben.. so ordynat togyders that four ben in the formest partyes. **1509** HAWES *Past. Pleas.* XXXVII. (Percy Soc.) 194 The serpent venimous, Which by sorcery was surely ordinate You for to sle. **1649** JER. TAYLOR *Gt. Exemp.* Pref. §34 Taking such proportions of their objects which are ordinate to their end.

II. Construed as *adj.*

†**2.** Conformed to order or rule; reduced to order, ordered, regulated; orderly, regular. *Obs.*

ordinate power (of God), the divine power as exhibited in the order of mundane things. (Opposed to *absolute*.)

c **1400** *Apol. Loll.* 28 Crist, þat is God Almiȝty, & of his absolut power may al þing.. ȝet may not of his ordinat power ȝele þe folk for þer ontrowþ. **1455** *Rolls of Parlt.* V. 279/1 An ordinate and a substantiall rule. **1534** WHITINTON *Tullyes Offices* I. (1540) 2 With comly gesture.. with ordynate eloquence, to make an oracyon. **1668** CULPEPPER & COLE *Barthol. Anat.* III. v. 138 The Brain hath sundry Circumvolutions without any Method or Order; the Brainlet hath circular and ordinate ones.

†**3.** Observant of order, keeping within orderly limits; orderly, regular, moderate, temperate. *Obs.*

c **1374** CHAUCER *Boeth.* I. met. iii. 7 (Camb. MS.) Cleer of vertu, sad, and wel ordinat of leuynge. *c* **1386** —— *Merch. T.* 40 Ther as a wedded man.. Lyueth a lyf blisful and ordinaat. **1483** CAXTON *Gold. Leg.* 178/2 He was wel ordynate in hym self. **1563** MAN *Musculus' Commonpl.* 35 b, Where as men saye, that ordinate charitie beginneth of it self, if it be meante of the charite of God, it is true. **1678** R. L'ESTRANGE *Seneca's Mor.* (1702) 124 His life is Ordinate, fearless, Equal, Secure.

†**4.** *Geom.* Of a figure: Having all its sides and angles equal; regular. *Obs.*

1625 N. CARPENTER *Geog. Del.* II. ii. (1635) 21 An Ordinate figure wee defined to bee that which commeth neerest to an equality of Sides and Angles. **1709** V. MANDEY *Syst. Math., Geom.* (1729) 142 In Triangles only the Equilateral is Ordinate or Regular.

†**5.** *Math.* ***ordinate proportion***, a proportion or statement of equality of ratios in which the terms are in regular order. ***ordinate line*** = B.

1570 BILLINGSLEY *Euclid* v. def. 18. 136 This ordinate proportionalitie may be extended as farre as ye list. **1656** HOBBES *Six Lessons* Wks. 1845 VII. 288 The increasing impetus.. will be designed by the ordinate lines in the parabola. **1862** TODHUNTER *Euclid* 280 In 19 he defines *ordinate proportion*.

6. *Entom.* Arranged in a row or rows.

1826 KIRBY & SP. *Entomol.* IV. 292 Ordinate. When spots, puncta, &c. are placed in rows. *Ibid.* 313 Ordinate. When simple eyes are arranged in a certain order.

B. *sb. Geom.* **a.** Any one of a series of parallel chords of a conic section, in relation to the diameter which bisects each of them; now usually applied to half the chord (i.e. the line from the curve to the bisecting diameter), originally called the *semi-ordinate*. Hence, **b.** Formerly, a straight line drawn from any point parallel to one of the co-ordinate axes, and meeting the other: see CO-ORDINATE *sb.* 2. (Correlative to ABSCISSA.) In mod. use, the distance of a point from the left-to-right (x) axis measured parallel to the other (y) axis; the y co-ordinate of a point.

The name *ordinate*, formerly more fully *ordinate applicate*, is derived from the Latin phrase [*linea*] *ordinate* (or *ordinatim*) *applicata*, used in the 16th c. Latin translation of Apollonius of Perga.

[**1537** *Apollonii Pergæ Conicorum* I. xvi. Definitio 4, Ducta autem per centrum ordinate applicata,.. Secunda Diameter vocetur.] **1676** COLLINS in Rigaud *Corr. Sci. Men* (1841) II. 7 The angle that an ordinate in a known ellipsis makes with either of the axes. **1706** PHILLIPS, *Ordinate* or *Ordinate Applicate* (in Conick Sections) is a Line drawn at Right Angles to the Axis, (which cuts it into two equal Parts) and reaching from one side of the Section to the other. The Half of this Line is properly the *Semi-Ordinate*, but is now commonly called the *Ordinate*. **1706** DITTON *Fluxions* 31 'Tis required to find the relation of the Fluxion of the Ordinate to the Fluxion of the Abscisse. **1726** E. STONE *New Math. Dict.* s.v. *Order* (transl. Newton 1704), If any Right and Parallel Lines be drawn and terminated on both sides by one and the same Conic-Section, and a Right Line bisecting any two of them, shall bisect all the rest.. All the Right Lines so bisected, are called Ordinate Applicates to that Diameter [*ordinatim applicatæ ad Diametrum*]. **1748** HARTLEY *Observ. Man* I. iii. 339 The Ordinates of any unknown Curve. **1807** HUTTON *Course Math.* II. 95 An Ordinate to any diameter, is a line parallel to its conjugate, or to the tangent at its vertex, and terminated by the diameter and curve. **1855** I. TODHUNTER *Treat. Plane Co-ordinate Geom.* i. 2 *OM* is called the abscissa of the point *P*; and *ON*, or its equal *MP*, is called the ordinate of *P*. **1861** SMILES *Engineers* II. VII. vi. 183 Transverse timbers,.. laid across the whole of the ribs, set out to the exact form of the curve by ordinates from the main or longitudinal axis of the ellipsis. **1879** PRESCOTT *Sp. Telephone* 246 We let fall perpendiculars, or, in mathematical language, ordinates to it, on either side. **1880** *Proc. R. Soc.* XXX. 511 The horizontal ordinates give the stress.., the vertical ordinates give the elongation. **1891** C. TAYLOR *Elem. Geom. Conics* 8 The Principal Ordinate, or briefly the Ordinate, of any point is the perpendicular drawn from it to the axis. **1896** *Min. Proc. Inst. Civil Engin.* CXXVI. 233 The area of the loop, with the magnetizing force as abscissas, and the magnetization as ordinates, represents the energy dissipated. **1948** *Electronic Engin.* XX. 10/1 This apparatus was constructed to produce a trace on a cathode ray tube in which the ordinates were proportional to shutter opening and the abscissa to time. **1951** R. M. GARRELS *Textbk. Geol.* 470 In order to graph these changes, it is customary to begin by drawing two lines at right angles to each other. One is usually drawn horizontally (the *X* axis or abscissa), the other vertically (the *Y* axis or ordinate). **1971** NILES & HABORAK *Calculus with Analytic Geom.* i. 14 The directed distance *OM* is the x-coordinate or abscissa of point *P* and is denoted by x. The directed distance *ON* is the y-coordinate or ordinate of point *P* and is denoted by y.

ordinate ('ɔːdɪneɪt), *v.* [f. L. *ordināt-*, ppl. stem of *ordināre*: cf. prec.]

†**1.** *trans.* To appoint authoritatively to any office; *spec.* to appoint or admit to holy orders; = ORDAIN *v.* 11. *Obs.*

1562 WINȜET *Cert. Tractatis* Wks. 1888 I. 15 As the Apostolis ordinatit St. Paule and Barnabas. **1565** JEWEL *Def. Apol.* (1611) 568 As for that ye say, Your Bishops be duly Ordinated and Consecrated. **1595** DANIEL *Civ. Wars* IV. xxii, Richard.. this man did ordinate The heyre apparent to the Crowne and Land. **1597** A. M. tr. *Guillemeau's Fr. Chirurg.* 8/1 Monsr de la Tour, ordinated and chosen gentleman of the kinges chamber of presence.

2. To order, regulate, control, govern, direct. Now *rare* or *Obs.*

1595 DANIEL *Civ. Wars* I. lxix, He.. That best knowes how a Realme to ordinate. **1646** BP. HALL *Balm Gilead* 113 That over-ruling hand of the Almighty, who ordinates all their motions to his owne holy purposes. **1701** BEVERLEY *Glory of Grace* 24 Even those Great Links, and Branches of Salvation, that are within us,.. Are yet so Ordinated, that they are to the Praise of the glory of grace. **1823** DE QUINCEY *Lett. Yng. Man* Wks. 1860 XIV. 86 He did no more than regulate and ordinate the evident nisus and tendency of the popular usage into a severe definition.

3. To institute, establish, ordain, predestine. Now *rare* or *Obs.*

1610 BP. CARLETON *Jurisd.* 292 The publike good is peace, whereunto justices and just warres are ordinated. **1660** N. INGELO *Bentivolio & Urania* I. (1682) 168 The Precepts and Actions of Vertue are.. all ordinated to one End. **1850** L. HUNT *Autobiog.* xxxv. (1860) 399 Providence, by the like reasoning, ordinates dreadful revenge and retribution.

4. To place side by side in a series, to co-ordinate.

1882 FARRAR *Early Chr.* II. 385 The sentences are ordinated by simple conjunctions, not subordinated to each other by final particles. **1882** HARDY *Two on a Tower* I. xii. 208, I have never ordinated two such dissimilar ideas.

5. *Statistics* and *Ecology*. To subject to the mathematical operation of ordination (sense 1 c).

1962 *Ecol. Monogr.* XXXII. 137 (*heading*) Ordinating forest communities by means of environmental scalars and phytosociological indices. **1969** E. C. PIELOU *Introd. Math. Ecol.* xx. 255 When we wish to ordinate vegetation by means of a principal components analysis, there are four decisions to make.

Hence '**ordinated** *ppl. a.*, ordained.

1652 GAULE *Magastrom.* 152 To an ordinated destiny of an unfortunate end comes in, inordinately, fire, water, a fall, a gun, a sword.

†'**ordinately**, *adv. Obs.* [f. ORDINATE *a.* + -LY².]

1. In an ordinate, ordered, or regulated manner; in due order, in regular succession or sequence; according to order or rule, regularly; properly, duly, temperately.

1382 WYCLIF *1 Macc.* vi. 40 Thei wenten warly, and ordynatly. *c* **1425** LYDG. *Assembly of Gods* 203 Pluto.. gan to declare euen by and by Bothe her compleyntes ordynatly. **1549** LATIMER *1st Serm. bef. Edw. VI* (Arb.) 27, I wyll make a durable lawe, whyche shal compell the to walke ordinatlye, and in a plain way. **1603** SIR C. HEYDON *Jud. Astrol.* xxiii. 548 God worketh ordinately, not preposterously. **1651** *Raleigh's Ghost* 100 It is impossible, that a thing should particularly and ordinately in its own operation aim at one certain end, except it.. knoweth the end.

2. *Math.* **a.** With equality of sides and angles. **b.** So as to form an ordinate; as an ordinate. Cf. ORDINATE A. 4, 5, B.

1653 H. More *Antid. Ath.* II. v. §5 (1712) 54 If it be but exactly round.. or ordinately Quinquangular. **1655–87** —— *App. Antid.* (1712) 192 To be ordinately figured, is an undoubted Perfection of a Body. **1763** PEMBERTON in *Phil. Trans.* LIII. 525 If *DK* be not ordinately applied to *LM*, let *DO* be ordinately applied to *LM*.

ordination (ɔːdɪ'neɪʃən). [ad. L. *ordinātiōnem*, n. of action f. *ordināre* to ORDAIN. Cf. F. *ordination* (12th c.).] The action of ordaining.

I. 1. a. The action of ordering, arranging, or disposing in ranks or order; the condition of being ordered or arranged; an arrangement or disposition.

(This, the primary sense in L., appears to have been the last to be adopted in Eng.)

1658 SIR T. BROWNE *Gard. Cyrus* i. 36 Disposing his trees like his armies in regular ordination. *Ibid.* iii. 53 Quincuncial forms and Ordinations are also observable in animall figurations. **1703** T. N. *City & C. Purchaser* 85 He meaneth by Ordination, nothing but a well setling of the Model or Scheme of the whole Work. **1823** BYRON *Juan* VII. l, The first Detachment of three columns took its station,.. the second's ordination Was also in three columns. **1863** COWDEN CLARKE *Shaks. Char.* i. 18 We must bear in mind the different ordination of ceremony.. in that early and rude stage of society.

b. Arrangement in orders or classes; classification in orders.

1656 tr. *Hobbes' Elem. Philos.* (1839) 28, I would not have any man think I deliver the forms above for a true and exact ordination of names. **1885** P. MACOWAN *Rep. Cape Town Bot. Gard. for 1884.* 11 The ordination of the *Orchideæ*.

c. *Statistics* and *Ecology*. [tr. G. *ordnung*.] The arrangement of a set of points, given as in a multidimensional space, into a space of fewer dimensions with minimal distortion.

1954 D. W. GOODALL in *Austral. Jrnl. Bot.* II. 323 Factor analysis does not result in a classification of vegetation in the ordinary sense, but in an arrangement of the vegetational data in a multi-dimensional series. For such an arrangement, there appears to be no word in English which one can use as an antonym to classification; I would like to propose the term 'ordination'. **1969** E. C. PIELOU *Introd. Math. Ecol.* xx. 250 As a method of summarizing the results of a survey, ordination has two great advantages over classification: it obviates the need for setting up arbitrary criteria for defining the classes and there is no need to assume that distinct classes (if there are any) are hierarchically related. **1971** BLACKITH & REYMENT *Multivariate Morphometrics* xvi. 229 Proctor.. found that ordinations of some British liverworts gave readily interpretable polarities.

II. 2. a. The action of ordaining, or conferring holy orders; appointment or admission to the ministry of the Church; the fact of being ordained.

1432–50 tr. *Higden* (Rolls) II. 141 If the archebischop of Yorke dee, his successor shalle comme to Caunterbury to receyve his ordinacion [*ordinationem ab eo accipiet*]. **1641** MILTON *Animadv.* xiii. Wks. (1851) 229 As for Ordination, what is it, but the laying on of hands, an outward signe or symbol of admission? it creates nothing, it conferres nothing. **1660** R. COKE *Power & Subj.* 87 Bishops have power of ordination of presbyters in every city, Tit. 1. 5; 1 Tim. 5. 22. **1766** BLACKSTONE *Comm.* II. iii. 23 That, where the benefice was to be conferred on a mere layman, he was first presented to the bishop, in order to receive ordination. **1842** G. S. FABER *Prov. Lett.* (1844) I. 241 Many of our best .. divines hold presbyteral ordination to be valid in cases of necessity.

attrib. **1879** ASHWELL *Life Bp. Wilberforce* I. viii. 334 The reforms in regard to Ordination work, for which the Church is indebted to him. *Ibid.* 339 The features of a Cuddesdon Ordination week.

†**b.** Appointment to any office or position. *rare.*

1650 HOBBES *De Corp. Pol.* 152 An Election or Ordination, howsoever made.

III. 3. a. The action or fact of ordaining or decreeing, esp. as a divine action.

1460 CAPGRAVE *Chron.* (Rolls) 10 The sexte cause is of Goddis ordinacioun. **1552** ABP. HAMILTON *Catech.* (1884) 33 To quhome he was.. subjeckit be the ordinatioun of God. **1659** PEARSON *Creed* (1839) 233 From hence those which are subject learn to obey the powers which are of human ordination. **1794** ADAMS *Nat. & Exp. Philos.* II. xx. 384 The quality of transparency is given, by a wise ordination of Providence, to the fluid substance of water. **1849** R. I. WILBERFORCE *Holy Bapt.* (1850) 149 That such a decree would go forth.. had been known beforehand to the Supreme Intelligence and had been part of His ordination.

†**b.** Destination (*to* an end or purpose); destined or ordained function or disposition. *Obs.*

1607 TOPSELL *Four-f. Beasts* (1658) 63 An ox.. is called a plower,.. slow, and ill-favoured; with many other such notes of their nature, ordination, and condition. **1678** NORRIS *Coll. Misc.* (1699) 184 Whatsoever has such a Natural Ordination to, or Connexion with, the well or ill Being of mankind. **1829** J. L. KNAPP *Jrnl. of Naturalist* 332 The same propensity, or ordination, for removing decayed matters.

†**4.** That which is ordained; an ordinance, decree, statute, law; a prescribed observance. *Obs.*

1526 TINDALE *Luke* i. 6 Booth.. walked in all the lawes and ordinacions of the lorde. **1651** *Life Father Sarpi* (1676) 101 A constant tenacity and an habited custom to observe ordinations with all exquisiteness. **1656** HOBBES *Lib., Necess., & Chance* (1841) 157 If he intended.. that unjust laws are not genuine laws,.. because they are not the ordinations of right reason.

ordinative (ˈɔːdɪnətɪv), *a.* and *sb.* [ad. late L. *ordinātīvus* (Tertull.), f. ppl. stem. of *ordināre* to ORDAIN: see -ATIVE.]

A. *adj.* Having the character or function of ordaining, ordering, determining, or regulating; of the nature of ordination or ordering. Now *rare.*

1605 TIMME *Quersit.* III. 142 These internal beginnings of things they called hypostatical, vertual, and ordinatiue beginnings. **1652** GAULE *Magastrom.* 156 For these, being but the executive only, may either be directed or diverted by the intellectuall and ordinative. **1677** GALE *Crt. Gentiles* IV. 481 The holy God, in al his..gubernation about sin, whether it be permissive or ordinative, is gloriosely vindicated from being the Author..of sin.

B. *sb.* A particle which ordinates clauses. *rare.* (Cf. L. *ordinativa adverbia* in Priscian.)

1845 STODDART *Gram.* in *Encycl. Metrop.* I. 172/1 'Where' is an ordinative of place in the following passage. 'He rails Even there, where merchants most do congregate.'

ordinato-, combining form of L. *ordinātus* arranged in a row or rows, as **ordiˌnato-ˈliturate, -ˈmaculate, -ˈpunctate** *adjs.*, having lituræ (or indistinct spots), maculæ, or punctures, in rows.

ˈordinator. [a. L. *ordinātor*, agent-n. f. *ordināre* to ORDAIN.] One who ordains.

1. One who orders, regulates, directs, or governs. *rare.*

1615 T. ADAMS *Two Sonnes* 83 The wise ordinator of all things. **1615** —— *Eng. Sickness* ii. Wks. 1861 I. 424 Nature, and her ordinator, God. **1680** H. DODWELL *Two Lett.* (1691) 162 The necessity of an universal ordinator of the second causes both to their own ends..and..to that of the Universe. **1818** R. P. KNIGHT *Symb. Lang.* (1876) 127 His name signified the Ordinator or Regulator, as it does still in the modern Coptic. **1929** R. BRIDGES *Testament of Beauty* i. 134 And wouldst thou play Creator and Ordinator of things. **1952** G. SARTON *Hist. Sci.* I. xvi. 421 The world artificer (*dēmiurges*) is not a creator but, like the *nus* of Anaxagoras, an ordinator.

†**2.** One who ordains to the Christian ministry. *Obs. rare.*

1609 SKENE *Reg. Maj.* 24 Gif he [a bondman] be ordered without the knawledge of his maister, and of his ordinator, ..he sall be called back againe to bondage, and sall be randered to his maister.

ordinee (ɔːdɪˈniː), *a.* and *sb.* Forms: 4 **ordine**, 5 **ordane**, 9 **ordinee**. [In ME. a. OF. *ordiné*, pa. pple. of *ordiner* to ORDAIN; in mod. use formed anew: see -EE.]

†**A.** *adj.* Admitted to holy orders, or into a religious order or fraternity; ordained. *Obs.*

c **1330** R. BRUNNE *Chron.* (1810) 225 Þan went þis Ottobone þorghout þe cuntre, & quaynted him with ilkone, lewed & ordine. *c* **1400** *Rule St. Benet* (E.E.T.S.) 22/7 Princlike sal she sende an ordane nunne till her þat is in sentence.

B. *sb.* An ordained clergyman or minister; now, usually, a newly-ordained deacon.

c **1330** R. BRUNNE *Chron.* (1810) 210 [To] þat holy kirke, & alle þe ordinez, & bisshop wo þei wirke & clerkes of dignitez. **1863** A. BLOMFIELD *Mem. Bp. Blomfield* I. iv. 106 In addressing his ordinees on the subject of amusements, he has deprecated fox-hunting. **1884** *Ch. Times* 428/4 There was a falling-off in the number of ordinees at the beginning of the decennium.

ordnance (ˈɔːdnəns). [A syncopated variant of *ordenance*, ORDINANCE, established since the 17th c. in a certain group of senses. The complete historical illustration of these is given here, although every sense begins with forms spelt *ordinance.*]

†**1.** Military materials, stores, or supplies; implements of war; missiles discharged in war: = ARTILLERY 1. Also in pl. *ordinaunces. Obs.* in general sense.

1390 GOWER *Conf.* II. 195 That thei..beholde myhte Here enemys..With al here ordinance there, Which thei ayein the Cite caste. **1432-50** tr. *Higden* Harl. Contin. (Rolls) VIII. 485 His ordinaunce and trussynge cofres were taken þer. **1497** *Naval Acc. Hen. VII* (1896) 82 By the first part is declared the..Receiptes of ordinaunces..By the secunde part is declared ordenaunces Retorned and deliuered. *a* **1548** HALL *Chron., Rich. III* 51 Armoure, weapons, vitayle and all other ordinaunces expedient for warre. **1549** *Compl. Scot.* ix. 78 He brocht sa mony schipis to grece vitht al ordonnance. **1644** VICARS *Jehovah-Jireh* 143 For hast they left their Ordnance behind them.

2. Engines for discharging missiles.

†**a.** Formerly including catapults, slings, bows, etc.: = ARTILLERY 2a. *Obs.* **b.** Now, Mounted guns, cannon: = ARTILLERY 2b.

Formerly often distinguished as *great* or *small*, now usually as *heavy* or *light o. piece of ordnance*: see PIECE.

a. *c* **1430** *Syr Gener.* (Roxb.) 7811 He purveid for maygnelles and belfrayes And othre ordinaunce at al assayes. **1535** COVERDALE *2 Sam.* xx. 15 All the people.. layed to their ordynaunce, and wolde haue cast downe the wall. **1600** HOLLAND *Livy* XXIV. XXXIII. 532 They approched with all their fabrickes, engines, and ordinance of batterie against the walls.

b. *c* **1489** CAXTON *Blanchardyn* liv. 215 As fire giuen to the ordinance, tis to late to recall the shot. **1497** *Naval Acc. Hen. VII* (1896) 99 Wheles for grete ordinaunce..iiij pair. *a* **1548** HALL *Chron., Hen. VI* 105 Thei laied gonne against gonne, ..and laied a pece of ordynaunce directly against the wyndowe. *Ibid., Hen. VIII* 136b, The goodly ordinance whiche were .xij. greate Bombardes of brasse, and .xxiv. greate Canon peces [etc.]. **1653** H. COGAN tr. *Pinto's Trav.* ix. 28 Small Ordnance, as Falcones and Bases. **1672** *Essex Papers* (Camden) 12, I Desyer Yr Exs Licence to keepe thes six small Iron Ordnance in my Castell of Ballemartin. *a* **1715** BURNET *Own Time* (1766) II. 212 The King and the Duke came to the Tower..to see some invention about the ordinance. **1861** W. H. RUSSELL in *Morn. Chron.* 3 Aug., Another work..mounts three pieces of heavy ordnance. **1879** *Cassell's Techn. Educ.* III. 267 Rifled ordnance was used freely by the French in the campaign in Italy in 1859.

†**c.** With *pl.* An engine for discharging missiles; a large gun, piece of ordnance. *Obs.*

1480 *Waterf. Arch.* in *10th Rep. Hist. MSS. Comm.* App. v. 315 No marchaunt..shall bryng none of the saide ordenaunces oute of no countre beyonde the see. *a* **1548** HALL *Chron., Hen. VIII* 160 The Romaynes shot great ordinaunces, handgonnes, quarrels. **1626** CAPT. SMITH *Accid. Yng. Seamen* 24 Gunners spunge your Ordinances. **1629** WADSWORTH *Pilgr.* 35 They replying so stoutly, made our Marriners quickly..fly to their Ordnances vnderneath.

†**d.** The artillery as a branch of the army. *Obs.*

1665 MANLEY *Grotius' Low C. Warres* 293 Here was kill'd ..Charles Levinus Famarsh, who..at this time was General of the Ordnance. **1786** W. THOMSON *Watson's Philip III*, VI. (1839) 343 Mansveldt marched into Bohemia, where he was ..honoured with the charge of general of the ordnance.

3. The public establishment, or branch of the public service, concerned with the supply of military stores and materials, the management of the artillery, etc.

Board of Ordnance, a board, partly military and partly civil, which had the management of all affairs relating to the artillery, engineers, and the matériel of the Army; it was under the direction of a Master-General, assisted by a Lieutenant-General, a Surveyor-General, a Principal Storekeeper, Clerks of the Ordnance, and various other officers. After having existed from the reign of Henry VIII, it was dissolved in 1855, most of its functions as regards matériel being now discharged by the ***Army Ordnance Department***.

The organization of the Ordnance Department has undergone numerous transformations since 1855. From 1870 to 1887, the ***Surveyor-General of Ordnance*** was (with the Commander-in-Chief, and the Financial Secretary) one of three officers to whom the actual army adminstration was then delegated, his province being all civil administrative duties except the Pay Department, with the purchase, construction, and charge of matériel. After 1887 these duties were divided among various officials, e.g. the Commissary-General of Ordnance Stores, Director-General of Ordnance Factories, etc. In 1895 they were once more grouped under an ***Inspector-General of Ordnance***, for whom a ***Director-General*** was substituted by an Order in Council of 7 March, 1899. (*N.E.D.*, 1903)

1485 *Rolls Parlt.* VI. 354/2 Maister of oure Ordinaunce and maister of oure Armery. **1548** PATTEN *Exp. Scotl.* E j b, Syr Fraunces Flemynge knight, master of the ordinaunce. **1679** WOOD *Life* 30 Apr. (O.H.S.) II. 449 He was lieftenant of the ordinance. **1737** J. CHAMBERLAYNE *St. Gt. Brit.* II. III. 117 Military Branch of the Ordnance... Gentleman of Ordnance, John Palmer. **1810** WELLINGTON in Gurw. *Desp.* (1838) VI. 22, I should have thought..that the Duke would have gone to the Ordnance, which he would have liked. **1863** H. COX *Instit.* III. viii. 710 The Master-General of the Ordnance directed..all those matters with reference to the Corps of Artillery and Engineers, which, as to the rest of the army, belonged to the Commander-in-Chief. **1875** *Encycl. Brit.* II. 572 The Surveyor-General of the Ordnance is [1870-87] charged with 'providing, holding, and issuing, to all branches of the army and reserve forces, food, forage.. and all other stores necessary for the efficient performance of their duties,' etc.

†**4.** Occas. var. of ORDINANCE in other senses.

5. *attrib.*, as ***ordnance carriage, hospital, officer, park, stores, store-keeper***, etc. **Ordnance Board** = *Board of Ordnance*: see 3; **ordnance datum**, the datum-line or level, to which all heights are referred in the Ordnance Survey, being 12½ feet below Trinity High-water mark, and 4½ feet above Trinity Low-water mark; **ordnance map**, a map prepared by the Survey; also ***ordnance sheet***; **Ordnance Survey**, the official survey of Great Britain and Ireland, undertaken by Government, and originally carried out under the direction of the Master-General of the Ordnance; also *fig.*

1800 WELLINGTON *Let. to Major Gen. Braithwaite* in Gurw. *Desp.* (1837) I. 276 The ordnance and military stores to be sent from Fort St. George. **1803** —— *Let. to Col. Murray* 30 Apr. *ibid.* 529 Wheels for ordnance carriages. **1833** W. DYOTT *Diary* Nov. (1907) II. 170 On the 17th Captain Gosset, who had been employed last year stationed at Lichfield on the ordnance survey service called. **1839** C. FOX *Jrnl.* 8 Oct. (1972) 59 Sir H. Vivian was chuckling over the admirable Ordnance map. **1840** *Encycl. Brit.* (ed. 7) XXI. 354/2 In 1791 the Ordnance survey was begun. *Ibid.* 360/1 Ordnance Maps..are not only drawn, but also engraved and printed, at the Ordnance Map Offices in the Tower, and at Dublin. **1841** LEVER *C. O'Malley* lxxxviii. 421 In front of an old ordinance marquee. **1845** MCCULLOCH *Acc. Brit. Empire* (1854) I. 229 Ben Macdhu, ascertained, by the Ordnance survey, to be the highest mountain in the United Kindgom. **1853** STOCQUELER *Mil. Encycl., Ordnance Store-keeper*, a civil officer in the artillery, who has the charge of all the stores. **1868** *Rep. to Govt. U.S. Munitions War* 143 After a time these coil guns..find their way to the ordnance hospital at Woolwich. **1869** J. MARTINEAU *Ess.* II. 156 Do they set their ordnance officers to ball-practice? **1878** HUXLEY *Physiogr.* 11 Maps of the Ordnance Survey are constructed on the scale of one inch to the mile. **1886** T. P. WHITE *Ordnance Survey of U.K.* vi. 106 The Ordnance datum for Ireland is not the same as for Great Britain. **1889** G. W. USILL *Pract. Surveying* ix. 177 The ordnance datum of this country was determined by the ordnance authorities to be 'the approximate mean water at Liverpool'. **1893** FORBES MITCHELL *Remin. Gt. Mutiny* 146 The whole of his ordnance park, containing a large quantity of ammunition and thirty-two guns. **1934** C. LAMBERT *Music Ho!* 11 This book makes no attempt to be an ordnance survey of modern music. **1956** Ordnance datum [see O.D. s.v. O 5d]. **1972** L. ALCOCK *By South Cadbury* ii. 24 The summit is a little over five hundred feet above Ordnance Datum, with the hill itself standing about two hundred and fifty feet above the surrounding countryside. **1973** *Times* 13 Aug. 4/1 Mounting pressure from country walkers..may save the popular 2½ in. Ordnance Survey map.

ordnary, obs. form of ORDINARY.

‖**ordo** (ˈɔːdəʊ). [L., = row, series, order.]

a. *Eccl.* An ordinal, directory, or book of rubrics; an office or service with its rubrics. **b.** In old Latin school-books, (*ordo verborum*) The arrangement of words required in translating into English. **c.** *Pros.* = COLON[2] 1.

1849 ROCK *Ch. of Fathers* I. i. 10 The 'Ordo', or priest's Directory for finding the Mass and the Divine office for every day in the year. **1867** (*title*) Catholic Directory and Ordo for Ireland. **1885** *Catholic Dict.* (ed. 3) 265 *note*, The *Catholic Directory*, familiar to English Catholics, contains besides the Ordo a list of clergy, churches, etc.

ordoñezite (ɔːdəˈnjeɪzaɪt). *Min.* [f. the name of Ezequiel *Ordoñez* (1867-1950), Mexican geologist + -ITE[1].] An antimonate of zinc, $ZnSb_2O_6$, which is found as brown tetragonal crystals at Guanajuato, Mexico.

1954 *Mineral. Abstr.* XII. 303 (*heading*) Ordoñezite, zinc antimonate, a new mineral from Guanajuato, Mexico. **1955** *Amer. Mineralogist* XL. 66 Ordoñezite occurs as drusy or stalactitic masses of repeatedly twinned tetragonal crystals having a maximum size of 2 mm. **1968** I. KOSTOV *Mineral.* II. iv. 264 To this [byströmite] group are referred the following oxides, which are isostructural with rutile and tapiolite. ($P4_2/mnm$): byströmite.., ordoñezite.., and tripuhyite.

ordonnance (ˈɔːdənəns, or, as F., ɔrdɔnɑ̃s). [a. mod.F. *ordonnance*, for OF. *ordenance*: see ORDINANCE.]

1. Systematic arrangement, esp. of literary material, architectural parts or features, or the details of any work of art; a plan or method of literary or artistic composition; an order of architecture.

1644 EVELYN *Diary* 20 Nov., A Church..for outward forme not comparable to St. Peter's, being of Gotiq ordonance. **1712** STEELE *Spect.* No. 552 ¶1, I found his spacious warehouses fill'd and adorn'd with tea, China and Indian ware. I could observe a beautiful ordonnance of the whole. **1723** CHAMBERS tr. *Le Clerc's Treat. Archit.* I. 22 Columns that have Pedestals, are in a more stately Ordonnance than those which have none. *Ibid.* 140 Two Ordonnances of Architecture shou'd never be placed within one another. **1776** SIR J. REYNOLDS *Disc.* vii. (1876) 413 Disproportionate ordonnance of parts. **1817** COLERIDGE *Biog. Lit.* xviii. (1882) 174 [Difference] between the ordonnance of poetic composition and that of prose. **1885** *Athenæum* 22 Aug. 246/2 The ordonnance of the typography ..is at once simple, perspicuous, and compact.

2. In reference to France and other continental countries: An ordinance, decree, law, or by-law; *spec.* in France, (*a*) under the monarchy, a decree of the king or the regent; applied esp. to the partial codes issued by Louis XIV and his successors; (*b*) an order of a criminal court.

For the *ordonnances* of Charles X, 1830, see ORDINANCE 7.

1756 JOHNSON *K. of Prussia* Wks. IV. 551 The ordonance of 1667, by which Lewis the Fourteenth established an uniformity of procedure. **1761** *Hist.* in *Ann. Reg.* 67 An ordonance was issued at Copenhagen..prohibiting the importation of foreign tobacco. **1815** HOBHOUSE *Substance Lett.* (1816) I. 78 Only three days after the publication of the charter, the director-general of the police issued two ordonnances in open contradiction to the fifth and sixty-eighth articles. **1839** JAMES *Louis XIV*, III. 208 The criminal code did not appear till 1670; though an ordonnance affecting the marine had been promulgated in the preceding year. **1878** *Grove's Dict. Mus.* I. 7 The 'vagrants' met each new ordonnance with a new evasion.

b. (In full, ***company of ordonnance***, (†*ordinance*), F. *compagnie d'ordonnance*). A name applied to organized companies of men-at-arms which formed the beginnings of a standing army in France. So called from the ***ordonnance royale*** of 2 Nov. 1437 by which they were created.

'*Gensdarmes des Ordonnances.* The ordinary men of Armes of France; first reduced by Charles the seuenth into certaine Companies, and under particular Orders' (Cotgr.).

[**1601** R. JOHNSON *Kingd. & Commw.* (1603) 17 Charles the seventh reduced these Ordinances to perfection, made the number certaine, appointed their wages. *Ibid.* 18 He likewise devided these Ordinances into men at armes and archers.] **1752** CARTE *Hist. Eng.* III. 47 If Scotland was attacked, Francis was to aid them with 100,000 crowns, 1500 lance-quenets and 200 archers of ordonnance. **1823** SCOTT *Quentin D.* v, Here are my companies of ordonnance—here are my French Guards. **1843** PRESCOTT *Mexico* VI. ii. (1864) 340 The famous ordonnance of Charles the Bold, the best-appointed cavalry of their day.

†**3.** Occasional early spelling of ORDNANCE.

ordonnant, *a. rare*[−1]. [a. F. *ordonnant*, pr. pple. of *ordonner* to ORDAIN.] That arranges, or disposes in order.

1820-30 COLERIDGE in *Lit. Rem.* (1838) III. 32 An ample and most ordonnant Conceptionist, to the tranquil empyrean of ideas he had not ascended.

†**ordonne**, *v.*, a 15th c. variant of ORDAIN, after later F. *ordonner*.

1440 in *Wars Eng. in France* (Rolls) II. 591 Ordonne notable capitaines unto the keping of the same placis. *c* 1500 *Melusine* xii. 44 (*heading*) How they that were ordonned camme. *Ibid.* xix. 80 The kinge..ordonned men armed to kepe euery man therfro.

Ordovician (ɔːdəʊˈvɪʃ(ɪ)ən), *a. Geol.* [f. L. *Ordovic-es*, name of an ancient British tribe in North Wales + -IAN.] Of, pertaining to, or designating the second earliest period of the Palæozoic era, following the Cambrian and preceding the Silurian. Also *absol.*, the Ordovician period or its rocks.

1879 C. LAPWORTH in *Geol. Mag.* Decade II. VI. 14 The whole of the great Bala district where Sedgwick first worked out the physical succession among the rocks of the intermediates or so-called Upper Cambrian or Lower Silurian system..lay within the territory of the *Ordovices*; a tribe as undaunted in its resistance to the Romans as the Silures... Here, then, we have the hint for the appropriate title for the central system of the Lower Palæozoics. It should be called the Ordovician System. 1887 *Athenæum* 29 Jan. 163/3 Mr. Jukes-Browne..gets over the difficulty of nomenclature by adopting Prof. Lapworth's name of 'Ordovician' for the 'Lower Silurian' of Murchison. 1888 *Daily News* 24 Sept. 6/2 Strata representing ordovician, silurian, and carboniferous times. 1902 A. J. JUKES-BROWNE *Student's Handbk. Stratigr. Geol.* viii. 118 In Ayrshire..the Ordovician has the ordinary facies of a formation accumulated at no great distance from a continental coast-line. 1955 *Times* 4 June 8/5 It is a site of great geological interest for its variety of Ordovician volcanic lavas, with intrusive igneous rocks interbedded with fossiliferous mudstones and slates. 1967 D. H. RAYNER *Stratigr. Brit. Isles* iv. 80 In the British Isles the first fragmental remains of vertebrates are known from the Silurian beds, although bony plates have been found in the Ordovician of the United States.

ordure (ˈɔːdjʊə(r)). Also 5 ordoure, 5–6 ordur, 6 urdeur. [a. F. *ordure* (12th c. in Godef. *Compl.*), f. *ord* filthy, foul:—L. *horridus* HORRID.]

1. Filth, dirt. Formerly also in *pl. arch.*

13.. *E.E. Allit. P.* B. 1092 By nobleye of his norture he nolde neuer towche O3t þat watz vngoderly oþer ordure watz inne. 1430–40 LYDG. *Bochas* IX. vii. 24 Fret with olde rust gadreth greate ordure. 1528 PAYNELL *Salerne's Regim.* O iij b, Water..where into ronneth no vrdeurs of cites. 1558 WARDE tr. *Alexis' Secr.* (1568) 70 b, Boile this together..and if there bee any ordure or fylth at the bottom, you must take it away. 1727 BRADLEY *Fam. Dict.* s.v. *Ear*, An Ulcer often ..is occasion'd by a Wound, some Hurt, or some Ordure that is corrupted in the Ear. 1887 BOWEN *Virg. Æneid* v. 332 The youth..Fell, in the victim's gore and the ordure meeting with ill.

2. Excrement, dung. Formerly also in *pl.*

1388 WYCLIF *Deut.* xxviii. 27 The Lord smyte the part of bodi wherbi ordures ben voyded. 1480 CAXTON *Chron. Eng.* VII. (1520) 104 b/1 In the same place he made his ordure. 1581 MULCASTER *Positions* xv. (1887) 70 They will.. disburden themselues one waie or other, by ordure, vrine, or some other matter. 1658 ROWLAND tr. *Moufet's Theat. Ins.* 911 Mingle Attick honey with the first ordure the Infant makes. 1774 WARTON *Hist. Eng. Poetry* xlix. (1840) III. 209 Dante represents some of his criminals rolling themselves in human ordure. 1865 LIVINGSTONE *Zambesi* viii. 181 Ordure is deposited around countless villages.

3. *fig.* Applied to that which is morally filthy or defiling, or to foul language 'cast' or 'thrown' at a person. (Cf. DIRT *sb.* 6 b, FILTH *sb.* 3 c.)

c 1374 CHAUCER *Troylus* v. 385 Allas! allas! so noble a creature As is a man shal drede swich ordure! *c* 1386 —— *Pars. T.* ¶83 In the stynkynge ordure of synne. 1430–40 LYDG. *Bochas* VII. viii. (1554) 171 b, With such rebukes and casting of ordure..blotted was his visage. 1509 BARCLAY *Shyp of Folys* (1570) 61 Knowing their owne vice, and life full of ordure..Yet sinne they still. 1682 DRYDEN *Medal* 188 Those let me curse; what vengeance will they urge, Whose ordures neither plague nor fire can purge? 1814 JEFFERSON *Writ.* (1830) IV. 224 These ordures are rapidly depraving the public taste. 1870 LOWELL *Among my Bks.* Ser. I. (1873) 49, I have been forced to hold my nose in picking my way through these ordures of Dryden.

Hence †**'ordured** *a.*, defiled with ordure, polluted; †**'orduring** *vbl. sb.*, the voiding of ordure: in quot. *concr.* excrement; †**'ordurous** *a.*, of the nature of ordure, filthy.

1593 DRAYTON *Ecl.* viii. 77 The rude times their ord'rous matter fling, Into the Sacred and once hallowed Spring. *c* 1595 SOUTHWELL *St. Peter's Compl.* viii, A sea will scantly rince my ordur'd soule. 1614 C. BROOKE *Ghost Rich. III* Poems (1872) 110 A filthy carpet fits an ordur'd thought. 1654 GAYTON *Pleas. Notes* I. iii. 8 These high thoughts brought the Don to his Knees, happily on a Cushion of Rosinantes own orduring.

†**ore**[1]. *Obs.* Forms: α. 1–4 ár, 1–5 áre, (3 ære, aore). β. 2–5 ore, 3–5 hore, 5 ȝore. [OE. *ár* str. fem. = OFris. *êre*, OS. *êra* (MDu. *êre*, Du. *eer*), OHG. *êra* (MHG. *êre*, Ger. *ehre*), ON. *eir* clemency (Icel. *æra*, Sw. *ära*, Da. *áre*, are from Ger.):—OTeut. **aizā* (wanting in Gothic, which has the related vb. *ais-t-an* to regard, respect, with which cf. L. *æs-tum-āre* to esteem, value). The primary sense seems to have been 'esteem, regard, respect', whence the senses of 'honour (glory, dignity), reverence, respect, favour, sparing, mercy, help', etc., found in the various languages. The derived vb. OE. *árian* to regard, reverence, honour, = ON. *eira* to spare, OHG. *êren*, Ger. *ehren* to honour, is found in Early ME. as ARE *v.*[1]]

1. Respect, reverence; honour, glory.

α. *c* 900 tr. *Bæda's Hist.* II. xvi. [xx.] (1890) 148 Ond þeah þe he Cristen beon sceolde, ne wolde he æniȝe aare weotan on þære Cristnan æfestnisse. *a* 1000 *Cædmon's Gen.* 1580 Cam..on his aȝenum fæder are ne wolde ȝesceawian. *a* 1000 *Phœnix* 663 Ar and onwald in þam up-lican Rodera rice. *a* 1225 *St. Marher.* 5 For he ne alið neauer, ah lueð a in are. *a* 1300 *Cursor M.* 4245 (Cott.) Putifer..held ioseph in mensk and are. *Ibid.* 8770 (Cott.) Þat men it suld sua hald in ar [*Gött.* are]. *c* 1320 *Sir Tristr.* 1816 Ysoude he loued in are. *c* 1375 *Sc. Leg. Saints* xxx. (*Theodera*) 134 Þu..has rentis fare & til haf mare has perans of are.

2. Grace, favour, mercy, pity, clemency.

Of common use in ME. in appeals to the Deity, entreaties for a hearing, help, etc., esp. in the parenthetic *thine ore* = of thy grace, F. *de grâce*, which tended to become a mere precatory phrase.

α. *Beowulf* (Z.) 2607 He..ȝemunde ða ða are þe he him ær forȝeaf, wicstede weliȝne. *a* 1000 *Andreas* 1131 (Gr.) Ne mihte earmsceapen are findan. *a* 1200 *Moral Ode* 53 (Lamb. MS.) For habben godes are. *a* 1240 *Ureisun* in *Cott. Hom.* 187 A ihesu, þin aore! hwet deþ þanne þi blod isched on þe rode? *a* 1300 *Cursor M.* 2749 (Cott.) Lauerd, said abraham, þi nare [so *Fairf.; Gött. & Trin.* þin are] Sal þou þine auin sua-gat for-fare? *a* 1400–50 *Alexander* 5361 Candace.. pleynes 'Lord Alexander, þine are, quare is þi wittis?' *a* 1500 *Kyng & Hermit* 180 in Hazl. *E.P.P.* I. 20 The kyng seyd: Be Gods are, And I sych an hermyte were.

β. *a* 1200 *Moral Ode* 298 (Lamb. MS.) Nis noþer inne helle, ore ne forȝiuenesse. *a* 1225 *Ancr. R.* 26 Swete Iesu þin ore! *a* 1300 *Floriz & Bl.* 173 'Sire', he sede, 'bi godes ore, So god in nauede ihc wel ȝore'. *c* 1386 CHAUCER *Miller's T.* 540 Lemman, thy grace, and sweete bryd, thyn ore. 1412–20 LYDG. *Chron. Troy* (MS. Helmingham) lf. 64 a, Ay, Sir, she said, for Goddes ore What ye ar tel me more. *c* 1420 *Chron. Vilod.* st. 1236 He sayde, Blessude Virgyn! y crie ȝow mercy and hore. *c* 1450 *Erle Tolous* 226 Yschall be trewe, be goddys ore.

3. The condition of being spared; security from danger, peace.

c 1205 LAY. 26266 And lete we þat folc wræcche, wunien an ære. 1297 R. GLOUC. (Rolls) 9771 Alle þe avowes of þis churche, in was ore ich am ido. *c* 1320 *Sir Tristr.* 276 Now haþ rohand in ore Tristrem and is ful bliþe.

Hence †**'oreful, 'areful** *a.* [OE. *árful*], honourable, venerable; merciful, compassionate; †**'oreless, 'areless** *a.* [OE. *árléas*], void of reverence, mercy, or pity; merciless, cruel.

743–5 in Thorpe *Dipl. Angl.* (1865) 28 Ic Æðelbald..wæs beden from þæm *arfullan bisceope Milrede. *c* 1000 *Ags. Ps.* (Spelm.) cii. 3 Se ðe arfull biþ eallum unrihtwisum ðinum. *c* 1200 ORMIN 1460 3iff þin herrte iss arefull, & milde, & sofft, & nesshe. *c* 900 tr. *Bæda's Hist.* IV. xix. [xvii.] (1890) 312, & eahtatyne wið þæm *arleasum Arreum eretici & his lare. *a* 1000 *Juliana* 4 Maximianes se ȝeond middan-ȝeard arleas cyning, eahtnysse ahof. *a* 1200 *Moral Ode* 216 (Lamb. MS.) Ac helle king is are-les [*Trin. MS.* ore-leas, *Egert.*[1] *oreles, Jesus* ore-les] with þa þe he mei binden. *c* 1200 *Trin. Coll. Hom.* 123 Þat orelese mennisse, þe ne haueð ore of him seluen. *c* 1200 ORMIN 9881 Arelæs, & grimme, & grill.

ore[2] (ɔə(r)). Forms: α. 1 óra, 4 ore, 5–7 oore, 5–6 oure, 6 (ower, owre), ur, 6–7 ure; β. (1 ár), 3 or, 4 oor, 5– ore, (6 wore, 6–8 oare, 7–8 oar.) [Two types of this word are found from 14th to 17th c.: viz. (1) *oor(e, oure, owre, ur(e*, of which (as shown by spelling and by rimes) the regular mod. repr. would be *oor* (ʊə(r)), and which corresponds to OE. *óra* wk. masc. 'unwrought metal', 'ore', corresp. to Du. *oer*, LG. (E. Fris.) *ûr*, of uncertain origin; (2) ME. *ōr*, in 17–18th c. *oar*, mod. *ore*, which answers phonetically to OE. *ár* (also *ǽr*) 'brass' = OS. *ēr* (in *ērin* 'brazen'), MDu. *eer*, OHG., MHG. *êr*, ON. *eir*, Goth. *aiz* str. neut. 'brass' = L. *æs*, *ær-* 'brass', Skr. *ayas* 'metal'. It would appear that, about the 12th c., OE. *ár* began to be identified in sense with OE. *óra*, and that forms descended from both continued side by side until the 17th c., when the forms from *óra* became obs., or were levelled under those from *ár*. Thus the mod.Eng. word appears to derive its sense from OE. *óra*, but its form from OE. *ár* 'brass', which may have been extended to the sense 'metal', and thus to 'ore'. It is possible that, in very modern Eng., the form *oor* might itself have passed into (ɔə(r)), as in the spoken forms of *door*, *floor*, and southern pronunc. of *moor*, *poor*; but this would not explain the double forms from 13th to 17th c., nor the 16th c. *oar*.]

1. a. A native mineral containing a precious or useful metal in such quantity and in such chemical combination as to make its extraction profitable. Also applied to minerals mined for their content of non-metals.

Sometimes, esp. formerly, applied also to a mixture of a native metal with a rock or vein-stone, or to metal in an unreduced or unworked state.

[Cf. *a* 1000 *L. & Ags. Glosses* in Wr.-Wülcker 237/20 *Ferri fodina, in quo loco ferrum foditur*, isern ore.]

α. *a* 1000 *Ags. Ps.* (Th.) xi. 7 Swa þæt seolfor,..syþþan se ora adolfen byð. *c* 1000 ÆLFRIC *Voc.* in Wr.-Wülcker 142/34 *Metallum*, ælces kynnes wecg, *uel* ora oþðe clyna. *c* 1386 CHAUCER *Wife's T.* 208 For al the metal ne for oore [*v. rr.* ore, oure, oer; *rime* poore, pore, poure, pouer]. 1436 *Pol. Poems* (Rolls) II. 186 Of sylvere and golde there is the oore Amonge the wylde Yrishe, though they be pore. *c* 1505 *Mem. Ripon* (Surtees) III. 197, iiijor foder de vr non ignit. 1513 DOUGLAS *Æneis* X. iii. 52 Quhar the goldin riveir Pactolus warpys on grund the gold vre cleir. 1552 EDW. VI *Jrnl.* in *Lit. Rem.* (Roxb.) 416 The oure that the Almaines had diged in a mine of silver. 1552 HULOET, Oore of golde, siluer, or other mettall. *Vide in* owre. *Ibid.*, Ower, or oore of brasse, *cadmia*. 1555 EDEN *Decades* 331 Where they saw the vre or myne shewe it selfe. 1567 *Wills & Inv. N.C.* (Surtees 1835) 274, ij lods of lead vre pric xxviijs. 1570 LEVINS *Manip.* 175/3–6 [riming with *A Floore*, *A Moore* heath, *A Moore* Maurus] Oore of brasse. Oore of siluer [etc.]. 1590 SPENSER *F.Q.* III. iv. 18 The gravell mixt with golden owre [*rimes* an howre, in her powre]. 1625 BACON *Ess.*, *Plantations* (Arb.) 532 If there be Iron Vre. 1626 —— *Sylva* §33 A Lump of Ure in the Bottome of a Mine.

β. (In OE. in sense 'brass'; in 1225 = 'metal'.)

[*c* 725 *Corpus Gloss.* (O.E.T.) 255 *Aurocalcum* groeni aar. *c* 897 K. ÆLFRED *Gregory's Past.* xxxvii. (Sw.) 267 Hie wurdon ȝehwierfde inne on ðam ofne to are & to tine, & to iserne & to leade. *c* 1000 ÆLFRIC *Gram.* vi. (Z.) 15 *Aes* bræs oððe ár, *aeneus* bræsen oþþe æren.] *a* 1225 *Ancr. R.* 284 Nis þet iren acursed [*v.r.* or (*note in C.* Golt, seluer, stel, irn, copper, mestling, breas: al is icleopet or)]. 1297 R. GLOUC. (Rolls) 16 Vor engelonde is vol inoȝ..Of seluer or & of gold, of tyn & ek of lede, Of stel, of yre, & of bras. 1340–70 *Alex. & Dind.* 525 Þere þe grauel of þe ground was of gold ore. 1387 TREVISA *Higden* (Rolls) II. 17 Þe erþe of that lond is copious of metal ore & of salt welles. *Ibid.* 79 Salt welles, metal, and oor [*mineras et metalla*]. 14.. *Voc.* in Wr.-Wülcker 596/12 *Mineria, anglice* a myne *vel* Ore, *vel minera secundum quosdam et anglice* ore.., as goold ore, syluer ore, etc. 1519 *Interlude Four Elem.* in Hazl. *Dodsley* I. 30 They have none iron, Whereby they should in the earth mine, To search for any wore [*rime* therefore]. 1562 *Act 5 Eliz.* c. 4 §30 A..Burner of Oare and Wood-Ashes. 1631 JORDEN *Nat. Bathes* x. (1669) 70 For Iron, we have the Oar in abundance. 1667 DRYDEN *Ind. Emperor* I. i, Where golden Ore lyes mixt with common Sand. 1728 T. SHERIDAN *Persius* ii. (1739) 35 To run the Gold from its Oar. 1853 W. GREGORY *Inorg. Chem.* (ed. 3) 242 This is the common ore of antimony. 1886 A. WINCHELL *Walks Geol. Field* 124 Each of these layers is called a comb, and the whole is styled the gangue. The metalliferous layer is the ore. 1910 J. F. KEMP in *Jrnl. Canadian Mining Inst.* XII. 357 Sometimes..in the mining of the non-metallic substance sulphur, the output of the mine is called 'sulphur-ore', although no metal is involved at all. Yet while we may not especially controvert this usage, it cannot be said to seriously affect the general and large conception of ore as limited to the metalliferous minerals. 1913 W. LINDGREN *Mineral Deposits* i. 4 The use of the term 'ore' is not quite consistent. Ordinarily it implies a metal, but the expression 'sulphur ore', meaning pyrite, is sometimes seen, and occasionally such terms as 'sapphire ore' are found. 1939 G. A. ROUSH *Strategic Mineral Supplies* xiv. 401 The deposits of ore, or caliche, are highly irregular. 1951 A. F. TAGGART *Elem. Ore Dressing* i. 2 The miner was principally responsible for making ore of the low-grade California gravels by discovering ways to mine them that are ..cheap. 1970 *Materials & Technol.* III. ii. 97 There are no fundamental differences between the treatment of metalliferous ores and other types of ore.

b. with *an* and *pl.* A quality or kind of ore.

α. *c* 900 tr. *Bæda's Hist.* I. i. (1890) 26 Swylce hit is eac berende on wecga orum ares & isernes, leades & seolfres. 1454 *Rolls of Parlt.* V. 272/1 Many Mynes of Silver Oures. β. 1666 BOYLE *Orig. Formes & Qual.*, Melting the Oares to reduce them into perfect metal. 1768 PENNANT *Zool.* I. Pref., Silver is found in great abundance in our lead ores. 1826 HENRY *Elem. Chem.* II. 583 Ores of manganese. 1874 RAYMOND *Statist. Mines & Mining* 449 Foreign ores, which contain on an average 1 per cent. of silver. About half of these are 'dry ores', i.e. ores containing no appreciable amount of lead.

c. *fig.*

a 1628 F. GREVIL *Mustapha* Chorus iii. Poems (1633) 124 Whom I choose As my Anointed, from the Potters oare. 1642 FULLER *Holy & Prof. St.* II. xviii. 116 The good Yeoman is a Gentleman in Ore. 1711 SHAFTESB. *Charac.* (1737) III. 255 From the rich oar of our early poets. 1801 W. GODWIN *Chaucer* (1804) I. xv. 477 Mandeville, Wicliffe and Gower..did not begin so early to work upon the ore of their native language. 1861 CLOUGH *Mari Magno* 828 An intellect so charming in the ore.

2. Metal, esp. precious metal. Chiefly *poetic*.

1639 G. DANIEL *Ecclus.* i. 6 He did repaire the Cisternes, and restore Salomon's Ruines, in the Sea of Ore [? the molten sea, *1 Ki.* vii. 23]. 1709 ADDISON *Tatler* No. 116 ¶9, I consider Woman as a beautiful Romantick Animal, that may be adorned with Furs and Feathers, Pearls and Diamonds, Ores and Silks. *a* 1763 SHENSTONE *Elegies* ix. 49 Let others toil to gain the sordid ore. 1830 TENNYSON *Arab. Nts.* xiv, A rich Throne of the massive ore.

3. *attrib.* and *Comb.* a. simple attrib., as ***ore brokerage***, †***debt***, ***extraction***, ***freight***, ***impregnation***, ***market***, ***shipment***, ***supply***, etc.; consisting of or containing ore, as ***ore-band***, ***-bed*** (BED *sb.* 13 b), ***-channel***, ***-chimney***, ***-deposit***, ***-dump***, ***-ground***, ***-mass***, ***-pit***, ***-pocket***, ***-shoot***, ***-stope***, ***-streak***, ***-vein***, etc.; used in the gaining or working of ore, as ***ore-apparatus***, ***-bin***, ***-bucket***, ***-car***, ***-chute***, ***-dish***, ***-furnace***, ***-house***, ***-mill***, ***-pass***, ***-stamp***, etc. b. objective and obj. gen., as ***ore-bearing***, ***-buying***, ***-calcining***, ***-carrying***, ***-crushing***, ***-dressing***, ***-extracting***, ***-milling***, ***-roasting***, ***-smelting***, etc., vbl. sbs. and ppl. adjs.; ***ore-assorter***, ***-breaker***, ***-carrier***, ***-crusher***, ***-dresser***, ***-drier***, ***-feeder***, ***-hauler***, ***-separator***, ***-sorter***, ***-washer***, etc. c. Special combs.: **ore body**, a body or connected mass of ore in a mine, as a vein, bed, pocket, etc.; **ore-breast**, the face or breadth of the working of a body of ore; †**ore-coal**, ? a name for coal in thick seams; **ore-concentrator** = CONCENTRATOR 3; **ore-hearth**, a form of small reducing furnace made of cast-iron, used in lead-smelting; a Scotch or blast hearth; **ore-shoot** = SHOOT *sb.*[1] 7. Also OREDELF.

1881 *Rep. Geol. Expl. N. Zealand* 5 A trench cut to intersect the *ore-band at about 20 feet from the outcrop. **1877** RAYMOND *Statist. Mines & Mining* 174 The principal *ore-bearing deposits in this mine. **1796** MORSE *Amer. Geog.* I. 441 At this *ore-bed are a variety of ores. **1935** *Economist* 8 June 1334/1 It will be necessary .. to sink the shaft .. below the reef and to cut stations and *ore bins. **1962** R. B. FULLER *Epic Poem on Industrialization* 197 The magnificent horizontal and vertical lines of its highways, .. ore bins, and skyscrapers. **1872** RAYMOND *Statist. Mines & Mining* 25 This vein has shown thus far three separate *ore bodies. **1955** *Times* 12 July 15/6 Difficulties being met are the poor bearing quality of the ground .. and the presence of unconsolidated footwall beds associated with considerable volumes of water in No. 1 shaft area—which is holding up the advance towards the orebody. **1971** *Wall St. Jrnl.* 19 Feb. 20/5 Bad weather during the past three weeks delayed stripping of the overburden of the Black Cub orebody. **1977** *Bulletin* (Sydney) 22 Jan. 42/1 But a mineral deposit doesn't become an orebody unless the mineral concerned can be extracted and sold at a profit. **1877** RAYMOND *Statist. Mines & Mining* 447 From the *ore-breaker the ore went through a chute to the first set of steel rolls below. *Ibid.* 48 On the 800-foot level the *ore-breasts are about 100 feet in width, with but little waste-rock. **1912** *Chambers's Jrnl.* Dec. 784/2 The men .. had begun to send the *ore-buckets down empty. **1893** GUNTER *Miss Dividends* 189 There are two *ore-cars running on tracks in this shaft, to the lower level of the mine. **1936** *Atlantic Monthly* CLVII. 164/2 Our great .. *ore-carriers .. are no exception, because their existence is due to the State's primary intervention in granting monopoly rights to the rental value of the .. ore-fields they tap. **1975** 'D. JORDAN' *Black Account* viii. 46 Ore shipping studies comparing the capacity of Japanese ore carriers with the proposed berthing and loading facilities. **1909** *Westm. Gaz.* 29 Nov. 8/2 During the storm three *ore-carrying steamers were beached near the entrance to the harbour. **1874** RAYMOND *Statist. Mines & Mining* 517 None had, however, struck the *ore-channel. **1882** *Rep. to Ho. Repr. Prec. Metals U.S.* 195 The *ore chimney is from 250 to 300 feet in length, and the ore is all taken out above the tunnel. **1874** RAYMOND *Statist. Mines & Mining* 32 The entire product of the mine will be run out through this tunnel .. to the *ore-chute. **1603** OWEN *Pembrokeshire* (1891) 91 An *ore Coale .. the oare is the best and is a great vayne spreadinge euery way and endureth longest. **1882** *Rep. to Ho. Repr. Prec. Metals U.S.* 597 There have been in California many inventions in *ore crushing. *Ibid.*, There should be no mistakes made as to the value of new ore-crushing machines. **1653** MANLOVE *Customs Lead-Mines* (E.D.S.) 106 If they such sutes in other Courts commence, They lose their due *oar-debt for such offence. **1709** J. WARD *Introd. Math.* I. iii. (1734) 36 The Miners bought and sold their Lead Ore by a Measure which they call'd an *Ore Dish. **1974** *Encycl. Brit. Micropædia* IV. 194/2 This ability of the *ore dresser to modify the flotability of minerals made possible many seemingly magical separations. **1862** *Dublin Rev.* Nov. 18 The degrading toil of *ore-dressing or nail-making. **1909** H. LOUIS *Dressing of Minerals* i. 4 It appears better to treat coal-washing and ore-dressing as one and the same subject. **1914** S. J. TRUSCOTT tr. *Beyschlag's Deposits Useful Minerals* I. 72 There should be at least sufficient iron present .. to cover the costs of ore-dressing and of metallurgical treatment. **1946** *Nature* 27 July 140/1 To provide an information service dealing with publications concerning all branches of geology, mineralogy, .. ore-dressing and production metallurgy. **1895** *Westm. Gaz.* 28 Sept. 4/2, I took three samples, and also one from the *ore dump. **1877** RAYMOND *Statist. Mines & Mining* 48 Automatic *ore-feeders are coming into general use. **1884** *Pall Mall G.* 13 Sept. 5/1 That the process of *ore-forming still goes on beneath the earth's surface at the present day. **1874** J. H. COLLINS *Metal Mining* (1875) 53 Shafts are sunk until the *ore-ground is reached. **1825** J. NICHOLSON *Operat. Mechanic* 356 The smelting of the [lead] ore is performed by either a blast-furnace, called an *ore-hearth, or a reverberatory-furnace. **1862** *Times* 9 Sept., The smelting of lead in the 'ore-hearth'. **1886** A. WINCHELL *Walks Geol. Field* 126 The *ore-masses are huge lenticular accumulations. **1878** *Encycl. Brit.* XVI. 453/2 E the main lode, H permanent levels, and K *ore-pass reserved amidst the rubbish (*deads*) D. **1877** RAYMOND *Statist. Mines & Mining* 177 Within a foot of the surface, and covered only by the remains of the disintegrated *ore-shoot. **1884** J. A. PHILLIPS *Treat. Ore Deposits* 50 As a general rule, all the ore-shoots in a given vein dip in the same direction. **1944** *Q. Jrnl. Geol. Soc.* C. 251 A mineral vein may carry several ore-shoots, separated by barren stretches. **1877** RAYMOND *Statist. Mines & Mining* 26 The *ore-sorters constitute quite a large force. *Ibid.* 23 An *ore-stope was opened and a considerable amount of ore extracted. **1872** *Ibid.* 331 An *ore-streak 2 feet wide, composed of lead, zinc, gray copper, and iron sulphurets. **1882** *Rep. to Ho. Repr. Prec. Metals U.S.* 584 A patent has recently been granted .. for an *ore-washer which has some peculiarities. **1906** *Chambers's Jrnl.* Feb. 159/2 A few digs with the shovel laid bare the outcropping of the *ore-vein.

†**ore**[3]. *Obs. rare.* [OE. *ór*, beginning, origin, front, van.] Beginning.

Beowulf (Z.) 2407 Se ðæs orleȝes or on-stealde. *a* **1000** *Andreas* 649 Secȝan or and ende. *a* **1200** *Moral Ode* 179 (Lamb. MS.) þer hi sculen wunien a buten are [*Trin.*, *Egert.*, *Jesus* ore] and ende.

ore[4] (ɔə(r)). **1.** A modern adaptation of OE. *óra*, ORA[1], sometimes used by historical writers.

1610 HOLLAND *Camden's Brit.* I. 256, I have observed thus much, that twentie Ores are worth two Markes of silver. **1650** ELDERFIELD *Tythes* 85 For every ceorle or husbandman twelve ores. **1817** SCOTT *Harold* I. xv, And you, you cowl'd priests, who have plenty in store, Must give Gunnar for ransom a palfrey and ore. **1872** E. W. ROBERTSON *Hist. Ess.* 134 The two ores of 16*d.* which were paid to the king from the Lancashire carucate.

‖**2.** Properly *öre* (ørə): The smallest denomination in the coinage of Denmark, Norway, and Sweden, the hundredth part of a KRONE, about equal to a German *pfennig*; a copper coin of this value.

1716 *Lond. Gaz.* No. 5439/3 A Silver Coin called 15 Ore Pieces are advanced to 16 Ore. **1756** ROLT *Dict. Trade, Ore* .. a copper coin of Sweden; being 7-12ths of an English penny; and 96 of them make the rix-dollar, or 4*s.* 8*d.* sterling. **1899** *Whitaker's Almanack* 701 Silver coins .. Denmark .. 1 krone of 100 ore. **1899** *Westm. Gaz.* 29 Aug. 8/2 In Copenhagen .. a premium of ten ore per rat is being paid for every one of the rodents produced whole but dead.

ore[5] (ɔə(r)). *local.* Also 7 **wore, woore, oore,** 8 **oare.** [For earlier *wore*, *woore*:—OE. *wár* seaweed, whence the more frequent northern form WARE, q.v.] Seaweed, esp. such as is cast on the shore and gathered for manure: also called ***sea-ore***, †***float-ore***, and ORE-WEED.

1592 in J. Lewis *Hist. Thanet* (1736) App. 89 To forbid and restraine the burning or takinge up of any Sea Oare within the Ile of Thanet. **1602** CAREW *Cornwall* 27 b, To this purpose also serueth Orewood, which is a weed growing vpon the rockes vnder high water marke... His vse serueth for barly land. Some accustomed to burne it on heapes... This Floteore is now and then found naturally formed like rufs, combs, and such like. **1674–91** RAY *N.C. Words, Weir, Waar*, sea-wrack... The Thanet men (saith Somner) call it wore or woore. **17..** DR. T. MORE in *Ray's S. & E. Words* (1874), *Oore*, sea-wrack. **1841** S. C. HALL *Ireland* I. 73 His little car, which was filled with sea ore. **1847–78** HALLIWELL, *Ore*, sea-weed, used for manure. *South.* **1875** *Sussex Gloss.*, *Ore*, sea-weeds washed on shore by the tides.

Hence **'ore-stone** (*local*), a rock covered with seaweed; **'ory** *adj. dial.*, seaweedy. Also ORE-WEED, q.v.

1854 *N. & Q.* 1st Ser. X. 359 (*Gloss. Polperro in Cornwall*) *Orestone*, the name of some large single rocks in the sea, not far from land. Some fishes when cooked are said to taste *ory*, some things to smell *ory*; that is, like the sea-beach.

†**ore**[6]. *Obs. rare.* [ad. L. *ōra*: see ORA[2].] Shore, coast.

1652 HOLYDAY *Horace Odes* I. i, That other, if he in his garnier Stores Whatever hath been swept from Lybian ores. **1661** [see next].

†**ore**[7]. *Obs.* [Of unascertained origin. (Blount *Glossogr.* appears to explain it from ORE[6].)] In ***Lemster*** (i.e. ***Leominster***) ***ore***, a name for a fine kind of wool.

1612 DRAYTON *Poly-olb.* vii. 104 To whom did neuer sound the name of Lemster Ore? That with the Silke-wormes web for smalness doth compare. **1648** HERRICK *Hesper.*, *Oberon's Palace* 28 A bank of mosse .. farre more Soft then the finest Lemster ore. *a* **1661** FULLER *Worthies* 33 As for the wooll in this county, it is best known to the honour thereof by the name of Lempster ore, being absolutely the finest in this county, and indeed in all England. [**1661** BLOUNT *Glossogr.* (ed. 2), *Ore* (*ora*), the end or extreme part; a Region Land or Country: Thus Lempsters Ore is that fertile part of Herefordshire, which lyes about two miles round that Town.]

ore, var. *hor*, HER *Obs.* their; obs. f. HORE, HOUR, OAR, OR, OUR.

ore, o're, ore-, obs. ff. *o'er*, OVER, OVER-.

oread ('ɔəriːæd). *Gr.* and *Lat. Mythol.* [ad. L. *Orēas*, *Orēad-*, a. Gr. *'Ορειάς*, *'Ορειαδ-* mountain-nymph, f. *ὄρος* mountain: see -AD.] A nymph supposed to inhabit mountains; a mountain-nymph.

c **1586** SPENSER *Past. Aeglogue* 64 The Nymphs and Oreades her round about Do sit lamenting on the grassie grene. **1667** MILTON *P.L.* IX. 387 Like a Wood-Nymph light Oread or Dryad. *a* **1763** SHENSTONE *Wks.* (1764) I. 273 The oreads lik'd the climate well. **1795–1814** WORDSW. *Excursion* IV. 882 Fleet Oreads sporting visibly. **1844** MRS. BROWNING *Dead Pan* viii, Have ye left the mountain places, Oreads wild, for other tryst?

†**oreb.** *Obs. rare.* [perh. misprint for *orob* = F. *orobe*, L. *orobus*: cf. OROBE.] The Bitter Vetch, *Vicia Orobus*, or some allied leguminous plant.

1587 MASCALL *Govt. Cattle, Horses* (1596) 112 Sore eies which may be heald with the meale of wild tares, cald Oreb.

orebear, -burden, -cast, etc.: see OVER-.

orebil, obs. form of HORRIBLE.

‖**orecchion.** *Obs. rare.* [ad. It. *orecchione* (Florio 1598), 'large ear', augm. of *orecchio* ear.

1611 FLORIO, *Orecchione*, a great eare, but properly that part of a bulwarke which enginers call the pome, the gard, the shoulder or eares to couer the casamats.]

= ORILLION.

1589 IVE *Fortif.* 16 The best way into it, were some 40 foote distant from the Bulwarke Orechion or Cullion. **1598** BARRET *Theor. Warres* V. i. 125 The point or front of the Orecchion shall alwayes ende with two .. obtuse Angles.

orecharge, orecome, etc.: see OVER-.

oreche, obs. form of ORACH.

orectic (ɒ'rɛktɪk), *a.* (*sb.*) [ad. Gr. *ὀρεκτικός* (Aristotle) appetitive, f. *ὀρεκτός* stretched out, longed for, f. *ὀρέγ-ειν* to stretch out, grasp after, desire.]

A. *adj.* **a.** *Philos.* Of, pertaining to, or characterized by appetite or desire; appetitive. **b.** *Med.* Having the quality of stimulating appetite or desire.

1779 LD. MONBODDO *Anc. Metaph.* I. II. vii. 110, I come now to a division of the powers of the human mind... The division I mean, is into Gnostic and Orectic .., by the second, we desire or incline. **1836–7** SIR W. HAMILTON *Metaph.* xli. (1870) II. 415 In the Peripatetic School .. the mental modifications were divided into Gnostic or Cognitive, and Orectic or Appetent. **1881** SYMONDS *Renaiss. Italy* (1898) V. xvi. 407 That blending of the reason with the orectic soul which we call will. **1890** M. MAHER *Psychology* 217 Orectic faculty .. is too unfamiliar. **1892** *Syd. Soc. Lex.*, *Orectic*, exciting, or having power to excite, the appetites. **1947** [see AFFECTIVE *a.* 7 b]. **1952** C. P. BLACKER *Eugenics* 216 We may perhaps be on the threshold of a period when similar advances will be made in tests of the so-called 'orectic' functions; these comprise the qualities which make up what is commonly called character. **1970** G. GREER *Female Eunuch* 67 For, no matter which theory of the energy of personality we accept, it is inseparable from sexuality... Flügel called it orectic energy.

†**B.** *sb.* A stimulant for the appetite. *Obs.*

1671 SALMON *Syn. Med.* 357 Orecticks or Stomachicals, are Medicines appropriated to the Ventricle or Stomach.

Hence **orec'tivity**.

1906 S. S. LAURIE *Synthetica* I. 161 Let us rather call it Orectivity or Conation.

ored (ɔəd), *a. nonce-wd.* [f. ORE[2] + -ED[2].] Covered or adorned with ore or metal.

1627–47 FELTHAM *Resolves* I. xx. 70 Obscene scurrilities, that the Stage presents us with, .. or'd and spangled in their gawdiest tyre.

†**'oredelf, 'ordelf.** *Law. Obs.* [f. ORE[2] + DELF, digging, excavation, quarry, mine.] The digging of mineral ore; the right to dig minerals.

1579 *Expos. termes of Lawes*, *Oredelfe* is where one claimes to haue the ore that is founde in his soile or ground. **1617** in MINSHEU *Duct. Ling.*

oredrive, oreflow, etc.: see OVER-.

orefraye, orefrye, obs. forms of ORPHREY.

oreful, *a. Obs.*: see ORE[1].

oregano (ɒrɪ'gɑːnəʊ, ɒ'rɛgənəʊ). [Sp. and Amer. Sp. var. of ORIGANUM.] The dried leaves of wild marjoram, *Origanum vulgare*, or, esp. in North and Central America, the dried leaves of a shrub of the genus *Lippia*, esp. *L. graveolens*; both are used as seasonings for food, the latter having a stronger flavour.

1771 J. R. FORSTER tr. *Osbeck's Voy. to China* I. 33 *Origanum Creticum*, Spanish *Oregano*, known by the name of Spanish hops, is used to make anchovies and other meats more palatable. **1889** S. WATSON in *Proc. Amer. Acad. Arts & Sci.* XXIV. 67 *Lippia* (*Zapania*) *Palmeri*... 'Origano'; with a strong sage-like odor and used as a pot-herb. **1899** *Contrib. U.S. Nat. Herbarium* V. 226 Lippia spp. Oregano. The leaves of oregano are very much used to flavor food. *Ibid.* 227 The name 'oregano' seems to be a generic term applied to the leaves thus used of several species of Lippia. **1959** *Listener* 2 Apr. 601/2 The hallway smelled of herbs, of oregano and basil. **1969** F. ROSENGARTEN *Bk. Spices* 276 The pungent Mexican oregano, indigenous to the warmer areas of the Western Hemisphere, is of the genus *Lippia*... The milder European oregano .. is of one of several species of *Origanum* native to the Mediterranean region, principally *Origanum vulgare* L. The perplexing confusion between marjoram and oregano, and between the two types of oregano, is not limited to botanists. **1972** M. J. BOSSE *Incident at Naha* i. 17, I rolled some grass from the oregano jar where we keep ours and smoked the joint. **1976** *National Observer* (U.S.) 2 Oct. 11/4 Cook the meat loaf for 15 minutes, and then sprinkle the top with seasoning mixture of oregano, cinnamon, and sugar.

oregel(e, var. ORGEL *Obs.*, pride, proud.

Oregon ('ɒrɪgɒn). The name of one of the United States of America, situated on the Pacific coast, used *attrib.* to designate plants and animals found in the region, as **Oregon ash**, a species of ash, *Fraxinus oregana*, or its wood; **Oregon cedar** = *Lawson cypress* (LAWSON); **Oregon fir** = *Douglas fir* (DOUGLAS[1]); **Oregon grape**, an evergreen shrub, *Mahonia aquifolium*, bearing racemes of yellow flowers followed by dark berries resembling grapes; also, the berry itself; **Oregon junco**, a small black, brown, and white bunting, *Junco oreganus*; **Oregon lily**, one of the hybrid lilies produced by Jan de Graaff at the Oregon Bulb Farms; **Oregon pine** = *Oregon fir*.

1869 *Amer. Naturalist* III. 407 Oregon Ash... This first appears at the Dalles. **1969** T. H. EVERETT *Living Trees of World* 287/1 Other American ashes worthy of note include the Oregon ash .. most important of Western species, which grows to a height of 80 feet and may have a trunk 4 feet in diameter. **1872** F. F. VICTOR *All over Oregon & Washington* xxvii. 279 The Oregon cedar .. grows very abundantly near the coast. **1971** F. H. TITMUSS *Commercial Timbers of World* (ed. 4) 94 Alternative names for the timber [of Lawson cypress] include Oregon Cedar and White Cedar. **1904** E. O. WOOTON *Native Ornamental Plants of New Mexico* 15 The Douglas Spruce or Oregon Fir .. and the Bull Pine .. would well repay the care necessary to getting them established. **1851** *Oregon Statesman* (Oregon City) 27 June 3/1 Oregon Grape, so called, is not a grape, but resembles the grape in size and appearance. **1873** G. M. GRANT *Ocean to Ocean* 283 A dark green prickly-leaved bush like English holly, called the Oregon grape. **1949** *Jrnl. N.Y. Bot. Gdn.* July 153/1 In one bed is Oregon grape and beauty-berry. **1971** *Daily Colonist* (Victoria, B.C.) 27 May 53/3 The meat is then placed in the pit and covered with kelp, seaweed, Oregon grape and other wild plants. **1974** J. E. UNDERHILL *Wild Berries* 69 Still other people are devotees of Oregon

Grape wine. **1917** T. G. PEARSON *Birds Amer.* III. 47 Maybe the handsomest is the Oregon Junco..with a black head and breast sharply defined against a mahogany-brown back, white under parts, and pinkish-brown sides. **1964** A. WETMORE *Song & Garden Birds N. Amer.* 364/2 In winter flocks of Oregon juncos roam western foothills, canyons, and suburbs. **1971** *Islander* (Victoria, B.C.) 13 June 13/3 Oregon junco..come from the north during winter. **1964** *Horticulture* Dec. 49/1 (Advt.), *World Famous Oregon Lilies*, Higo Iris, Hardy Cyclamen and Exbury Azaleas. Send for free catalog. Rex Bulb Farms..Newburg, Oregon. **1967** J. DE GRAAFF *Lilies* 31 Those [lilies]..are becoming known as the Oregon lilies because they are bred and raised in Oregon. **1845** *N. Amer. Rev.* LX. 166 One of those gigantic Oregon Pines..whose prostrate trunk Douglas found to be two hundred and fifty feet in length. **1888** *Encycl. Brit.* XXIV. 386/2 The principal timber is yellow and red fir, ordinarily known as 'Oregon pine', which constitutes the bulk of the forests. **1889** [see *Nootka fir* s.v. NOOTKA B. *adj.* 2]. **1947** R. PEATTIE *Sierra Nevada* 148 Douglas fir..is known in the trade as Oregon pine. **1964** *House & Garden* Oct. 95/1 Her kitchen units, in Oregon pine.

Hence **Orego'nese**, the people of Oregon; **Ore'gonian** *a.*, belonging to Oregon; as *sb.*, a native or inhabitant of Oregon; **'Oregonly** *adv.*, after the manner of an Oregonian.

1848 E. BRYANT *California* xv. 197, I think the Oregonese had a little the advantage of us in this respect. *a* **1861** T. WINTHROP *John Brent* (1862) xxii. 243 Armstrong's opinion was only my own, expressed Oregonly. **1863** *Harper's Mag.* Sept. 570/2 If one does not know the 'lingo', he will often be troubled in conversing with the Oregonians. **1873** J. H. BEADLE *Undevel. West* xxxv. 762 There is a distinctively Oregonian look about all the natives and old residents. *Ibid.* xxxvi. 772 No Oregonians will eat of salmon caught above the mouth of the Willamette. **1974** *New Yorker* 25 Feb. 88/3 Oregonians, in whatever part of the state they reside, tend to be small-town-ish.

oregonite ('ɒri:gənaɪt). *Min.* [ad. G. *oregonit* (Ramdohr & Schmitt 1959, in *Neues Jahrb. f. Min. Monatshefte* 247), f. prec.: see -ITE[1].] An arsenide of nickel and iron, Ni_2FeAs_2, which occurs as white hexagonal crystals with a metallic lustre in Oregon and has been made artificially.

1960 *Mineral. Abstr.* XIV. 500/1 A new nickel-iron arsenide from Josephine Creek, Josephine County, Oregon, is named *oregonite*. **1968** *Ibid.* XIX. 285/2 By heating at 470°C under a pressure of 1600 kg/cm² mixtures of arsenic ground with iron and nickel or with Fe–Ni alloys (36, 50, and 77% Ni) oregonite,..was obtained.

oreide ('ɔəri:ɪd). [a. F. *oréide*, f. *or* gold: see -IDE.] A name given to a kind of brass with golden brilliancy, used for imitation jewellery, etc.

The composition apparently varies; that given in quot. 1875 is app. identical with that of OROIDE.

1875 *Ure's Dict. Arts* III. 461 *Oreide* is the name given by MM. Meurier and Valient, of Paris, to an alloy which has a golden brilliancy. It is composed of copper 100, zinc 17, magnesia 6, sal-ammoniac 3·6, quick-lime 1·8, and tartar of commerce 9. *Ibid.*, The oreide..is malleable, takes a most brilliant polish, and, if it tarnishes, its lustre is restored by acidulated water. **1881** *Metal World* No. 6. 89 Oreide must not be confounded with oroide. *Ibid.*, Oreide, zinc 13 parts, nickel 6 parts, copper 80 parts.

†**oreille.** *Obs. rare.* [erron. ad. F. *oreiller* pillow, f. *oreille* ear.] A pillow.

1523 LD. BERNERS *Froiss.* I. lxxiv. 95 Therle of Moret bare in his armour, syluer, thre oreylles goules. [Froissart *Un escu d'argent à trois oreillers de gueules*.] **1568** GRAFTON *Chron.* II. 249. **1881** STODART *Scot. Arms* II. 18.

oreillet ('ɒrɪlɛt), ‖**oreillette** (ɔrɛjɛt). Forms: 6 orrelette, orrellet, orilyeit, 7 aurielet, 9 oreillet(te. [a. F. *oreillette* fem. (formerly also *oreillet* masc.), a little ear, earlet, covering or ornament for the ear, auricle of the heart, etc. (12th c. in Hatz.-Darm.), dim. of *oreille* ear: see -ET[1].]

†**a.** A part of a head-dress covering the ears. †**b.** A covering or defence for the ears. **c.** The ear-piece of a helmet.

a **1548** HALL *Chron.* (1809) 519 Ye orrelettes [Holinshed (1587) III. 808/2 orrellets] were of rolles wrethed on lampas douck holow, so that the golde shewed thorow. **1578** *Inv. R. Wardrobes* (1815) 232 Ane quaiff with a orilyeit of holane claith sewit with crammosie silk. **1603** HOLLAND *Plutarch's Mor.* 52 That children should have certaine aurielets [Amyot in Littré, *aureillettes de fer*] or bolsters to hang about their eares for their defence. **1834** PLANCHÉ *Brit. Costume* 195 Sometimes the oreillets themselves [temp. Hen. VI] have spikes projecting from their centres.

oreillon: see ORILLION.

oreison, -soun, obs. forms of ORISON.

ore-jade, orelay, orelead, etc.: see OVER-.

orelege, obs. f. HOROLOGE, time-piece.

oreless, *a. Obs.*: see ORE[1].

†**orell.** *Obs.* (See quot.)

1614 MARKHAM *Cheap Husb.* I. (1668), Red-Oker, is a hard red stone, which we call Raddle, Orell, Marking-stone.

orellin (ɒ'rɛlɪn). *Chem.* [f. *Orell-ana*, name of the Amazon river, as used in the specific name (*Bixa orellana*) of the plant from which anatta is obtained + -IN[1].] A yellow colouring matter contained in anatta, used in dyeing alumed goods.

1857 MILLER *Elem. Chem.* III. 517 *Annatto.*—This colouring matter..appears to contain an orange-red colouring substance, called *bixin*, and a yellow termed *orellin*. **1863–72** WATTS *Dict. Chem.* I. 600.

orellis, orels, obs. ff. *or else*: see OR *conj.*

‖**oremus** (ɒ'reɪmʊs). [L. *orēmus* 'let us pray': so F. *orémus* (17th c. in Hatz.-Darm.).] A liturgical prayer introduced by the word *oremus* (in the service of the R.C. Church).

1795 tr. *Mercier's Fragm. Pol. & Hist.* II. 462 The monks made their purchases with oremuses, and good passports to heaven. **1888** *Blackw. Mag.* Dec. 794 The canticles he knew, Oremuses, and prayers and collects not a few.

orenche, orendge, orenge, obs. ff. ORANGE.

orenda (ɒ'rɛndə). [Iroquoian.] (See quots.)

1902 J. N. B. HEWITT in *Amer. Anthropologist* IV. 33 (*title*) Orenda and a definition of religion. *Ibid.* 37 This subsumed magic power is called..*manitowi* by the Algonquian, *pokunt* by the Shoshonean, and *orenda* by the Iroquoian tribes. And it is suggested that the Iroquoian name for the potence in question, *orenda*, be adopted to designate it. **1911** *Encycl. Brit.* XVII. 306/2 Everything in nature, and particularly all animate objects, have their *orenda*; so have gods and spirits... *Orenda* is above all the power of the medicine man. **1917** *Encycl. Relig. & Ethics* IX. 556/1 The term *orenda* is, in fact, only one of a large group of terms, members of which are found in most, if not all, Indian languages, which have the same general meaning—invisible power or energy. **1920** [see MANA]. **1947** C. S. LEWIS *Miracles* xi. 100 It [*sc.* pantheism] may even be the most primitive of all religions, and the *orenda* of a savage tribe has been interpreted by some to be an 'all-pervasive spirit'.

orendron, var. UNDERN *Obs.*, forenoon.

Oreo ('ɔəriːəʊ). *U.S. slang.* Also **oreo.** [See quot. 1973.] A derogatory term for an American Black who is seen (esp. by other Blacks) as part of the white establishment.

1968–70 *Current Slang* (Univ. S. Dakota) III–IV. 89 *Oreo, n.*, a black who thinks like a white or tries to join white society. (Blacks on the outside but whites on the inside). **1969** *Harper's Mag.* Mar. 61 Trouble is Negroes been programmed by white folks to believe their products are inferior. We've developed into a generation of Oreos—black on the outside, white on the inside. **1970** H. E. ROBERTS *Third Ear* 11/1 *Oreo*, a black person with white-oriented attitudes. **1971** *Black World* June 31/1 Every Black man or woman who refers to his Black brother or sister by a derogatory label such as *Tom*, *nigger*, or *oreo*..is deliberately walking into the enemy's trap. **1973** A. DUNDES *Mother Wit* 596 One term of derision is 'oreo' for such an individual [*sc.* a Negro with 'white' mentality]. The term comes from a standard commercially prepared cookie which has two disc-shaped chocolate wafers separated by sugar cream filling. An 'oreo' is thus brown outside but white inside, hence, a Negro who has internalized white values. **1975** *Amer. Speech 1972* XLVII. 151 Black educators are sometimes included in this hostile cosmos, for they are labeled *Oreos*.

‖**Oreodon** (ɒ'riːədɒn). *Palæont.* [mod.L. f. Gr. ὄρος, ὀρε-ος mountain + ὀδούς, ὀδοντ- tooth: named by Leidy in 1851.] A genus of extinct ruminant mammals, typical of the family *Oreodontidæ*, the remains of which are found in the miocene tertiary formations of the western United States. Hence **o'reodont, oreo'dontine** *adjs.*, of or pertaining to the *Oreodontidæ*.

1877 LE CONTE *Elem. Geol.* (1879) 505 The Oreodon is another very remarkable animal, intermediate between the hog, the deer and the camel, which at this time inhabited the whole Continent from Nebraska to Oregon.

oreography, -ology, etc., var. OROGRAPHY, etc.

orepass, orepeer, oreperch, etc.: see OVER-.

†**o'rere,** obs. var. of ARREAR *v.*, to fall back.

c **1450** HOLLAND *Howlat* 909 Gif ony nech wald him neir He bad tham rebaldis orere, With a ruyne. *Ibid.* 984 Bot thow reule the richtuiss, thi rovme sall orere.

orerotund: see OROTUND.

‖**ore rotundo** ('ɔəri: rəʊ'tʌndəʊ), *adv. phr.* [L. abl. of *ōs* mouth + abl. of *rotundus* round.] Lit. 'with round mouth'; with round, well-turned speech. Cf. OROTUND *a.* (*sb.*)

[HORACE *Ars Poetica*, Grais ingenium, Grais dedit ore rotundo Musa loqui]. **1720** SWIFT *Let.* 1 Dec. in *Works* (1859) II. 300/1 Is taught there to mouth it gracefully, and to swear, as he reads French, *ore rotundo*. **1845** R. FORD *Hand-bk. for Travellers Spain* I. 82 The Castilian speaks with a grave distinct pronunciation, *ore rotundo*; he enunciates every letter and syllable. **1922** BLUNDEN *Bonadventure* 144 Replying You. Big. Stiff *ore rotundo*. **1931** M. SUMMERS *Supernatural Omnibus* 7 In his fine stage voice *ore rotundo* he would declaim some half a dozen wilting lines and demand applause.

orerule, orerun, oreset, oreshoote, oreslip, orespread: see OVER-.

oreson(e, -soun, -sun, obs. ff. ORISON.

†**'orest,** obs. variant of ERST, first: cf. OR *adv.*

c **1250** *Gen. & Ex.* 2061 A win-tre..Orest it blomede, and siðen bar ðe beries ripe.

oresyle, var. OVERSILE *Obs.*, to cover, hide.

oretake, -throw, -thwart, -top: see OVER-.

‖**'ore'tenus.** *Law.* The med.L. phrase *ore tenus* by word of mouth; hence as *sb.* (*nonce-wd.*), A sentence by word of mouth.

a **1639** CAREW *Cœl. Brit.* Wks. (1824) 159 Vulcan was brought to an Oretenus and fined for driving in a plate of iron into one of the Sunne's chariot-wheeles.

ore-weed, oar-weed ('ɔəwi:d). *local.* Forms: 6–9 ore-, 7 or-, 8– oar-; 6 -wad, 7–8 -wood, 7– -weed. [f. ORE[5] + WEED. The forms in *wad*, *wood*, app. arose from the second element being unaccented, and may have been popularly associated with other words.] Seaweed; = ORE[5], LAMINARIA.

α. **1586** J. HOOKER *Hist. Irel.* in Holinshed II. 183 The common people..had a long time liued on limpets, orewads, and such shelfish as they could find. **1602** CAREW *Cornwall* 27 Orewood, which is a weed growing vpon the rockes vnder high water marke, or..cast vpon the next shore by the wind and flood. **1610** W. FOLKINGHAM *Art of Survey* I. x. 30 They vse both Orewood, Sea-sand, and Sea-slubbe for soylings. **1725** BRADLEY *Fam. Dict.* s.v. *Sea Weed*, That call'd Ore-Wood is much used in Cornwall.

β. **1622** R. HAWKINS *Voy. S. Sea* (1847) 108 He shall meete with bedds of oreweed, driving to and fro in that sea. **1669** WORLIDGE *Syst. Agric.* (1681) 68 In Cornwal there is also a Weed called Ore-weed. **1892** QUILLER-COUCH *I saw three Ships* 80 Manure better than the ore-weed you gather down at the Cove.

γ. **1755** *Gentl. Mag.* XXV. 447 A sea weed, called oarweed, is also sometimes used, but principally for gardens. **1855** KINGSLEY *Glaucus* ii. 57 Tangle (oar-weed, as they call it in the south). **1884** *West. Morn. News* 20 June 2/5 For Sale, Boat, suitable for oar-weed. **1917** *Chambers's Jrnl.* July 473/1 The 'oar weed' variety of seaweed..contains considerable supplies of potash. **1922** JOYCE *Ulysses* 45 He climbed over the sedge and eely oarweeds. **1954** *New Biol.* XVII. 102 The broad oar-weeds, the Laminarias,..occupy the shore at low-water mark of spring tides and at greater depth. **1971** C. L. DUDDINGTON *Beginner's Guide to Seaweeds* iii. 47 The oarweeds (genus *Laminaria*) are large seaweeds that grow in the sublittoral zone, from just below low-tide mark down to a depth of about fifteen feet. The oarweeds are perennial plants. *Ibid.*, The oarweeds have a varied history of usefulness, first in the old kelp burning industry..and later as a source of alginic acid and alginates.

orewhelm, orework: see OVER-.

orexin (ɒ'rɛksɪn). *Chem.* [f. as next + -IN[1].] The hydrochlorate of phenyl-dihydro-quinazolin, a colourless, odourless crystalline substance, very irritating to the nose, and of nauseous bitter taste, having some repute as a stomachic.

1891 *Lancet* 24 Jan. 211/2 Orexin given in quantities of from five to twelve grains daily..increases the assimilation of fat in diseased subjects. **1892** *Syd. Soc. Lex.*, *Orexin*..has been recommended for the purpose of increasing the appetite, but its efficacy is very doubtful. **1893** *Brit. Med. Jrnl.* (Epit.) 20 May 84/1 Paal has discovered that the base of orexin, phenyldihydro-chinazolin ($C_{14}H_{12}N_2$), is almost free from taste, and..acts as well as the raw drug.

‖**orexis** (ɒ'rɛksɪs). [a. Gr. ὄρεξις desire, appetite.] A desire or longing. Now *techn.* in *Med.*

1619 H. HUTTON *Follie's Anat.* 22 Motives his Orexis to provoke. **1675** J. SMITH *Chr. Relig. App.* III. i. §4. 9 This *Orexis* after dirty Puddings. **1842** DUNGLISON *Med. Lex.*, *Orexis*, appetite. **1857** MAYNE *Expos. Lex.*, *Orexis*,..term for desire or appetite; orexy.

orey, oreyson, obs. forms of ORY, ORISON.

†**orf,** *sb.*[1] *Obs.* Also 3 oref, orve, oreve, horf. [OE. *orf*, not exemplified in the cognate langs., but corresp. to an OTeut. **orbo*ᵐ-:—**urbo*ᵐ, from weak grade of ablaut series *erb-*, *arb-*, *urb-*, whence Goth. *arbi*, OHG. *erbi*, OE *ęrfe*, *ierfe*, *yrfe*, possession, esp. cattle, inheritance: see ERF.]

Cattle, live stock.

960–975 *Laws of Edgar* (Schmid) IV. c. 2 §8 ȝif hit cuce orf bið. *Ibid.* §11 þæt forstolene orf and þæs orfes ceap-ȝyld. *c* **1000** ÆLFRIC *Gen.* xii. 16 He hæfde þa on orfe and on þeawum, on olfendum and on assum micele æhta. —— *Exod.* xii. 38 On ælces cynnes orf. **10..** *O.E. Chron.* an. 1010 (MS. F) Menn and orf ofsloȝan eal þæt hi to comon [*Laud MS.* menn and yrfe hi sloȝon]. *a* **1100** *Ibid.* an. 1041 (Laud MS.) Swa mycel orfes wæs ðæs ȝeares forfaren. *c* **1200** *Trin. Coll. Hom.* 31 Herdes..wittende here oref. *Ibid.* 39 Ac þe gode herdes wakieð..ouer here orf. *c* **1205** LAY. 15316 Heo nomen orf, heo nomen corn. *Ibid.* 31809 þat quale com on orue. *a* **1250** *Owl & Night.* 1155 Thu bodest cualm of oreve. **1297** R. GLOUC. (Rolls) 7765 Orf failede & eke corn. **1390** GOWER *Conf.* I. 17 Schepherdes..Into the breres thei forcacche Her Orf, for that thei wolden lacche With such duresce.

b. *Comb.*: †**orf-gild**: see quots.; †**orf-qualm**, cattle-plague, murrain.

[LAMBARD *Archaionomia* (1568) 126, to the words 'quod dicitur ceapgeld' in *Stat. Will. I*, c. 3 §14, adds in margin 'al. orfgyld, quod idem est'; ed. 1644 omits this.]

1607 COWELL *Interpr.*, **Orfgild*, alias *Cheapegild*, is a restitution made by the Hundred or Countie, of any wrong done by one that was *in plegio*. **1708** *Termes de la Ley* 402 *Orfgild* signifies a payment or restoring the Cattel. **1014** WULFSTAN *Serm. ad Anglos* in *Hom.* (1883) 159 Stalu and cwalu, stric and steorfa, *orfcwealm and uncoðu. *a* **1100** *O.E. Chron.* an. 1054 On þisum ȝeare wæs swa mycel orfcwealm. *c* **1200** *Trin. Coll. Hom.* 61 Ure louerd binimeð us ure aȝte, oðer þurh fur, oðer þurh þiefes, . . oðer þurh orf qualm.

orf (ɔːf), *sb.*[2] [Var. of dial. *hurf*, prob. f. ON. *hrufa* crust or scab on boil; cf. dial. *reef* skin eruption, dandruff.] A virus disease of sheep, cattle, and goats, characterized by a secondary infection with the bacillus *Fusiformis necrophorus*, which causes ulcers and scabs in and around the mouth and on the feet or other parts of the body; also called scabby mouth, contagious ecthyma, or contagious pustular dermatitis.

1868 J. C. ATKINSON *Gloss. Cleveland Dial.* 362 Orf... Scurf on an animal's skin. **1876** C. C. ROBINSON *Gloss. Mid-Yorks.* 95/1 Orf.., applied to a running sore on cattle. **1948** *Brit. Jrnl. Dermatol.* LX. 405 The virus of orf could produce lesions in man. **1959** *News Chron.* 9 July 5/5 Live sheep.. have been found to be suffering from orf, a skin disease. **1972** *Country Life* 30 Mar. 812/3 The flock is then dipped, vaccinated against orf and allowed to scavenge.

orf (ɔːf), *prep.* and *adv.* Representing a 'phonetic' spelling of a vulgar or affected pronunciation of OFF *adv.*, *prep.*, *a.*, and *sb.*[1]

1889 [see GREEN *a.* 1 j]. **1901** B. PAIN *De Omnibus* i. 2 Pressintly a gint calls 'im an' orf 'e goes. **1916** [see COBBER *sb.*[2]]. **1937** N. MARSH *Vintage Murder* xx. 226 She tells 'im orf a treat. **1955** M. ALLINGHAM *Beckoning Lady* iv. 55 Just then orf come 'is 'at, and lord luvaduck! **1976** M. BUTTERWORTH *Remains to be Seen* v. 82 Do you mind awfully if I push orf? There's a point-to-point. **1978** A. PRICE '*44 Vintage* xxiii. 260 Everyone had scarpered—cleared orf.

orfarian, obs. form of ORPHARION.

orfe (ɔːf). [a. Ger. *orfe*, F. *orfe*, *orphe*; cf. L. *orphus* (Pliny), a. Gr. ὀρφός a kind of sea-perch.] A golden yellow variety of the ide (*Leuciscus idus*), long domesticated in Germany, acclimatized in England in the 19th c.

[**1706** PHILLIPS, *Orphus*, the Sea-rough; a kind of fish.] **1879** WEBSTER Supp., *Orf*, a European semi-domesticated fish of the carp family. **1884** *Century Mag.* Apr. 904/1 The gold-orfe or golden-ide [is] a fish bred for both ornament and the table. **1886** *Athenæum* 8 May 619/1 The orfe and the golden tench have been acclimatized in England.

orferay, orferes: see ORPHREY.

†**orfever**. *Obs. rare*$^{-1}$. [a. F. *orfèvre* (13th c. in Littré):—pop. L. *aurifabr-um* workman in gold, goldsmith.] A goldsmith.

1415 in *York Myst.* Introd. 21 Orfeuers, Goldbeters, Monemakers.

‖**orfèvrerie** (ɔrfɛvrəri). Now only as French. Forms: 5 orfeverye, 9 orféverie, orfevery, orfèvrerie. [a. F. *orfèvrerie*, in 12th c. *orfaverie*, f. *orfèvre*: see prec.] Goldsmith's work.

1423 JAS. I *Kingis Q.* xlviii, A gudely cheyne of smale orfeuerye. **1840** BARHAM *Ingol. Leg.*, *St. Dunstan*, To indulge in a little *orfevrerie*. **1842** *Ibid.*, *St. Cuthbert* ii, Plate of *orféverie* costly and rare. **1860** READE *Cloister & H.* I. 16 He offered prizes for the best specimens of 'orfévrerie' in two kinds, religious and secular.

Orford ('ɔːfəd). The name of the *Orford* Copper Company of New Jersey, U.S.A., used *attrib.* to designate a process it developed for separating nickel from copper by making use of the difference in the solubilities of their sulphides in molten sodium sulphide.

1895 *Mineral Industry* III. 458 The Orford Copper Company was employed some time ago by the United States Navy Department to separate copper from nickel in a large quantity of Canadian matte purchased by the department, and to deliver nickel in the form of an oxide for use in alloying steel. In order to do this the company employed a new process, which may fairly be called the Orford process, and this has been from time to time improved until there is now produced from the Canadian mattes by a fire process metallic nickel which is from 99% to 99·3% pure. **1923** U. R. EVANS *Metals & Metallic Compounds* III. 183 Copper sulphide is soluble in fused sodium sulphide; nickel sulphide is not (the principle of the Orford process). **1967** J. R. BOLDT *Winning of Nickel* 276 Inco completed replacement of the Orford method by the matte separation process at the Copper Cliff smelter in 1948.

orfray, orfrays, etc.: see ORPHREY.

orful ('ɔːfʊl), *a.* Representing a 'phonetic' spelling of an affected or emphatic pronunciation of AWFUL *a.*

1890 KIPLING *Courting of D. Shadd* (ed. 2) 166 'Got any money?' 'On'y a little—orful little.' **1901** A. H. RICE *Mrs. Wiggs of Cabbage Patch* ix. 123 He coughs all the time... Other day he had an orful spell. **1946** A. CHRISTIE *Hollow* iv. 34 'Feel pretty bad, don't you?'.. 'Orful, I feel.'

org (ɔːg). colloq. abbrev. of ORGANIZATION. Also in *Comb.*

1936 *Esquire* Sept. 160/3 The Joe Breen (Hays org) influence on pix. **1951** GREEN & LAURIE *Show Biz* 570/2 *Org*, organization. **1970** *Harper's Mag.* Apr. 86 They [*sc.* White Anglo-Saxon Protestants] drew the institutions around themselves, moved to the suburbs, and became org-men. **1973** R. HAYES *Hungarian Game* xxi. 129 A private C and D org? **1976** *Times Lit. Suppl.* 5 Mar. 273/5 Systems theorists wish, unlike biologists, to 'explain' the brain.. in cybernetic terms of the global properties of organizations ('orgs' as Mr Serebriakoff calls them). **1977** *Time* 6 June 48/2 Many are anti-org types and hard to count.

orgal(l, obs. variant of ARGOL[1].

1616 BULLOKAR *Eng. Expos.*, *Orgall*, the lees of Wine dried. [So in COCKERAM, BLOUNT, PHILLIPS.]

†'**orgament**. *Herb. Obs.* [Corrupt ad. L. *origanum*.] = ORIGAN, marjoram.

1552 ELYOT, *Amomis*.. hath a flower like to Orgament. **1601** HOLLAND *Pliny* II. 64 Orgament, which in tast.. resembleth Sauery, hath many kinds, & all medicinable. **1607** TOPSELL *Four-f. Beasts* (1658) 103 Herb-dragon, orchanes, orgament, and mastick. **1657** C. BECK *Univ. Char.* I iv b, Orgament herb.

Also †'**orgamy** *Obs.* (cf. ORGANY[2]).

1609 HEYWOOD *Brit. Troy* IV. xiv. 81 The Storke hauing a branch of Orgamy Can.. the Adders sting eschew.

organ ('ɔːgən), *sb.*[1] Forms: 1 organon, *pl.* -na, organe *wk. fem.*; 4 orgne, orgoyn, 4- organ (4-5 orgene, -gyn, -gun, 4-6 orgon(e, -gen, 4-7 organe, 6-7 -gayne, -gaine). [ad. L. *organum*, pl. *organa*, a. Gr. ὄργανον, pl. -να, instrument, organ, musical instrument. Used in OE. in Gr. form, also *organe* wk. fem. (so OHG. *organa*, -*ina*, MHG. *orgen(e*, MDu. *orghene*). In early ME. forms, from OF. *organe*, *orgene* (12th c.), *orghene*, *orguine* (15th c.), also *orgre* (13th c. from *orgne*), mod.F. (14th c.) *orgue*; all going back to *organa*, treated as a fem. sing. See also the by-form ORGLE.

In Greek, orig. 'that with which one works' (ablaut formation from 'ἐργ- work), tool, instrument, spec. musical instrument, surgical instrument, also bodily organ as instrument of sense or faculty. In L., instrument, engine, musical instrument generally, pipe, in Christian writers also 'church-organ'. Augustine (*c* 400), on Ps. lvi, says 'All musical instruments are called *organa*. Not alone is that called *organum*, which is large and inflated by bellows, but whatever is fitted to accompany singing, and is corporeal, which he who sings uses as an instrument, is called *organum*.' To the same effect Isidore *Orig.* II. xx. In Eng. adopted first in the musical sense; in OE. in the more general sense of 'musical instrument', including, no doubt, that of 'church-organ'.]

I. A musical instrument.

†**1.** Applied vaguely in a general sense to various musical (esp. wind) instruments; chiefly in versions of Scripture or allusions thereto (often understood in sense 2). *Obs.* (exc. as a verbal rendering of Gr. or L.)

c **1000** ÆLFRIC *Gen.* iv. 21 Iubal.. wæs fæder herpera and þæra þe organan macodan [Vulg. *canentium cithara et organo*]. *c* **1000** *Ags. Ps.* cxxxvi. 2 On saliȝ we sariȝe.. ure organan [*organa*] up-ahengan. *c* **1000** *Apollonius* 25 Ða organa wæron ȝetoȝene, and ða biman ȝeblawene. *a* **1300** *Cursor M.* 1521 Cubal.. Organis harp and oþer gleu, He drou þan oute o musik neu. *a* **1340** HAMPOLE *Psalter* cxxxvi. 2 In þe wylghes in þe myddis of hit, we hang vp our orgoyns. **1382** WYCLIF *Job* xxi. 12 They.. ioȝen at the soun of the orgne. **1388** —— *Ps.* cxxxvi. 2 In salewis in the myddil therof; we hangiden vp oure orguns [1382 instrumens]. ?*c* **1475** *Sqr. lowe Degre* 1072 With rote, ribible and clokarde, With pypes, organs and bumbarde. **1539** BIBLE (Great) *Gen.* iv. 21 Iubal, which was the father of such as handle harpe & organe. **1602** SHAKS. *Ham.* III. ii. 385 Will you play vpon this Pipe?.. There is much Musicke, excellent Voice, in this little Organe. **1611** BIBLE *Ps.* cl. 4 Praise him with stringed instruments and organs. **1667** MILTON *P.L.* VII. 596 The Harp.. the solemn Pipe, And Dulcimer, all Organs of sweet stop.

2. *spec.* **a.** A musical instrument (in its modern form the largest and most comprehensive of all), consisting of a number of pipes, supplied with *wind* or compressed air by means of bellows, and sounded by means of keys, which on being pressed down admit the wind to the pipes by opening valves or *pallets*.

In the modern organ the pipes are distributed into sets or *stops* of various qualities of tone, the admission of wind to the several stops being controlled by handles or *draw-stops*, drawn in and out by hand or by mechanism worked by special pedals (*combination-pedals*); and the stops are arranged in groups, each separate group forming a *partial organ* (see d) and being controlled by a separate keyboard; these are usually from two to five in number, one of the keyboards consisting of *pedals* played with the feet, the rest being *manuals* played with the hands; these can be connected in various ways by *couplers* so as to sound together.

From its power and dignity of tone the organ has been distinctively the church instrument from early Christian times, and in modern times is also used in concert-halls and other buildings.

The instrument has of course undergone immense changes since the 4th c., when it is first referred to in L. writers, and even since the date of the earliest Eng. references. According to Grove's *Dict. Mus.* II. 576, 'At the commencement of the 8th c. the use of the organ was appreciated, and the art of making it was known in England'. But although mentioned from that period in Latin documents, no English quots. specifically in this sense are known in OE. or Early ME.

c **1386** CHAUCER *Nun's Pr. T.* 31 His voys was murier than the murie orgon, On Messedayes that in the chirche gon. **1483** *Cath. Angl.* 261/1 An Organ, *organum*. To synge or to play (on þe) Organ, *organizare*. *a* **1661** FULLER *Worthies* IV. (1662) 33 The first Organ which was ever seen in the West of Europe, was, what was sent Anno 757 from Constantine the Grecian Emperor to Pipin King of France. **1667** MILTON *P.L.* I. 708 As in an Organ from one blast of wind To many a row of Pipes the sound-board breaths. **1687** DRYDEN *Song St. Cecilia's Day* 44 What human Voice can reach The sacred Organ's praise? **1721** BAILEY, *Cabinet Organ*, a small portable Organ. **1756-7** tr. *Keysler's Trav.* (1760) III. 334 It is furnished with two fine organs, erected opposite to each other. **1782** PRIESTLEY *Corrupt. Chr.* II. VIII. 123 Marinus Sanutus introduced organs into churches. **1837** WHEWELL *Hist. Induct. Sc.* (1857) I. 353 Ctesiphon.. is said to have invented a.. hydraulic organ. **1898** STAINER & BARRETT *Dict. Mus. Terms* 336/1 The so-called hydraulic organ owed its utility and consequent fame to the fact, that in it water was used in such a manner as to counterbalance the hitherto variable pressure.

†**b.** Formerly in *pl.* denoting a single instrument. (After med.L. *organa* (Du Cange) similarly used, app. to express its composite character: the L. sing. *organum* had also the sense 'pipe'. With '*the organs*' cf. *the bagpipes*, *the pipes*.)

c **1330** R. BRUNNE *Chron. Wace* (Rolls) 11266 Þo þat couþe orgnes blowe. *a* **1340** HAMPOLE *Psalter* cl. 4 Orgyns, þat is made as a toure of sere whistils. *c* **1386** CHAUCER *Sec. Nun's T.* 134 And whil the Organs [*v. rr.* Orgues, Organes, Orgles, Orgels, orgens] maden melodie To god allone in herte thus sang she. *c* **1430** LYDG. *Min. Poems* (Percy Soc.) 54 Thi organys so hihe begynne to syng ther messe. **1488** *Croscombe Churchw. Acc.* (Som. Rec. Soc.) 17 Payd to Thomas Rogg for pleyng at orgons iij[s] iiij[d]. *c* **1591** *Vestry Bks.* (Surtees) 267 The long stall in the South porche before the Orgaines. **1601** F. GODWIN *Bps. of Eng.* 452 He.. could not only sing, but play very well vpon the organs. **1647** CLARENDON *Hist. Reb.* IV. §113 Many Dissolute and Prophane People, went into the Abbey at Westminster, and would have pull'd down the Organs. **1683** KENNETT tr. *Erasm. on Folly* 68 No more skill .. than a Pig playing upon the Organs. **1708** POPE *Ode St. Cecilia* 11 The deep, majestic, solemn organs blow. **1746** WESLEY *Wks.* (1872) II. 21 Then the organs began to play amain.. The curate endeavoured to stop them. *a* **1825** FORBY *Voc. E. Anglia*, *Organs*, an organ, the musical instrument.

†**c.** Also called ***a pair***, or ***set, of organs***. *Obs.* (*Pair* here means 'set', not couple.)

1501 *Bury Wills* (Camden) 84, I wyll ther be bougth on peyr of orgonys to the chyrche of Wulpett. **1530** PALSGR. 183 *Vnes orgues*, a payre of organs, an instrument of musyke. **1594** T. B. *La Primaud. Fr. Acad.* II. 95 Al the pipes and flutes of a paire of organs being set together. **1678** WOOD *Life* (O.H.S.) II. 407 The church.. containing a good set of organs before the warr time. **1686** *Lond. Gaz.* No. 2141/4 Two pair of very fair Organs to be sold.. One pair of Seven Stops, the other Four. **1714** MANDEVILLE *Fab. Bees* (1725) I. 97 With one pair of organs they can make the whole house ring.

d. Applied, with distinctive epithets, to the separate groups of stops (***partial organs***), each with its own keyboard, which make up an organ.

Of these the chief is the ***great organ***, containing stops mostly of powerful tone; the others are the ***choir organ***, containing lighter stops used for accompanying a choir (see CHOIR ORGAN); the (formerly used) ***echo organ***, inclosed in a case, for producing a soft and distant effect, and its successor the ***swell organ***, inclosed in a *swell-box* capable of being opened or shut by a *swell pedal* so as to produce crescendo or diminuendo effects; the ***solo organ***, in which each stop is of special quality of tone, adapted for playing a solo melody accompanied by other stops; and the ***pedal organ***, containing the stops of lowest pitch, forming a bass to the manuals.

1606-7, etc. [see CHOIR ORGAN]. **1613** *Organ Specif. Worcester Cathedral*, The particulars of the great organ. **1660** *Specif. Organ Banqueting Room, Whitehall* in Grove *Dict. Mus.* II. 590 Great Organ, 10 stops... Eccho Organ, 4 stops. **1876** HILES *Catech. Organ* i. (1878) 3 The fourth manual, the Solo Organ, contains pipes of a particular species, on a high pressure of wind and voiced specially for Solo playing. **1898** STAINER & BARRETT *Dict. Mus. Terms* 337/2 A complete organ may be said to consist of five parts: choir organ, great organ, swell organ, solo organ, and pedal organ... A large organ therefore consists of a number of small organs differing in quality of tone, and so arranged as to be under the control of one performer.

3. a. Applied to other musical instruments, as in ***Dutch organ***.

1825 HONE *Every-day Bk.* I. 1248 A band.. consisted of a double drum, a Dutch organ, the tambourine.

fig. **1844** *Zoologist* II. 727 The croaking.. being so loud and shrill, as to have obtained for these frogs the name of 'Cambridgeshire nightingales', and 'Whaddon organs'!

b. = BARREL-ORGAN: cf. *organ-grinder* in 8.

1840 DICKENS *Old C. Shop* xviii, 'You must be more careful, sir', said Jerry, walking coolly to the chair where he had placed the organ, and setting the stop. **1849** RUSKIN *Sev. Lamps* v. §24 He.. would also, if he might, give grinding organs to God's angels to make their music easier.

c. A keyboard wind-instrument with metal reeds, bellows mostly worked by treadles, and (usually) a number of stops; an instrument of the harmonium class; a reed-organ. ***American organ***: a reed-organ in which the air is drawn inwards to the reeds, instead of being driven outwards as in the harmonium proper.

1876 STAINER & BARRETT *Dict. Mus. Terms* 25/1 *American Organ*, an instrument having one or more manuals, and registers which control series of free reeds. **1880** E. PROUT in Grove *Dict. Mus.* I. 61 The American organ under its present name.. was first introduced by Messrs. Mason and Hamlin of Boston, about the year 1860. **1880** A. J. HIPKINS *ibid.* I. 667 He was induced to secure to himself the sole privilege of using the name Harmonium in France, thus forcing other makers to use the name Organ, and thus to add another stone to the cairn of confusion in musical instrument nomenclature.

†**4.** *Mediæval Mus.* = ORGANUM 2. *Obs.*

c **1380** WYCLIF *Wks.* (1880) 91 Wiþ knackynge of newe song, as orgen or deschant. **1393** LANGL. *P. Pl.* C. XXI. 7 And how osanna by orgone olde folk songe.

II. An instrument generally.

5. a. A part or member of an animal or plant body adapted by its structure for a particular vital function, as digestion, respiration, excretion, reproduction, locomotion, perception, etc.

c **1420** *Chron. Vilod.* 2480 Alle þe remanent of my body.. Excepte þe organys of þe lemys þe whyche gouernede my wyttus fyue. **1529** MORE *Dyaloge* I. Wks. 132/1 The bodye, kepyng yet stil his shappe & his organis not much perished. **1578** BANISTER *Hist. Man* VIII. 108 The hand, beyng.. the organ of organes, and an organ before all other organs. **1596** SHAKS. *Merch. V.* III. i. 62 Hath not a Iew hands, organs, dementions, sences, affections, passions? **1656** tr. *Hobbes' Elem. Philos.* (1839) 390 The parts of our body, by which we perceive any thing, are those we commonly call the organs of sense. **1668** WILKINS *Real Char.* 375 That Configuration which there is in the Organs of speech upon the framing of several Letters. **1759** B. STILLINGFLEET tr. *Biberg's Econ. Nature* in *Misc. Tracts* (1762) 59 The organs of generation are contained in the flower. **1773** HUNTER in *Phil. Trans.* LXIII. 486 Two branches, which pass to the electric organ through the gills. **1855** BAIN *Senses & Int.* I. ii. §25 (1864) 65 The organ of mind is not the brain by itself: it is the brain, nerves, muscles, organs of sense and viscera. **1878** HUXLEY *Physiogr.* 221 In the centre of each flower is found a hollow organ, the pistil.

b. The human organs of speech or voice collectively; the larynx and its accessories as used in speaking or singing. (Somewhat *rare*; perh. associated with sense 1 or 2.)

1601 SHAKS. *Twel. N.* I. iv. 33 Thy small pipe Is as the maidens organ, shrill, and sound. **1732** LEDIARD *Sethos* II. VII. 102 Uttering cries.. deeper than was in the power of any human organ. **1860** TYNDALL *Glac.* II. i. 226 The boy's organ vibrates more rapidly than the man's. **1860** READE *Cloister & H.* lv. (1896) 151 A little muttering was heard outside; Denys's rough organ and a woman's soft and mellow voice.

c. *Phrenology.* One of the regions of the brain held to be the seat or material centre of particular mental faculties or tendencies.

1806 *Med. Jrnl.* XV. 210 His organ for thieving is very visible; he has likewise the organ of representation. **1836** JAS. GRANT *Random Recoll. Ho. Lords* xiv. 332 The organ of combativeness is most prominently developed. **1860** DICKENS *Uncomm. Trav.* v, Such vigilant cherub would.. have that gallant officer's organ of destructiveness out of his head.

d. Used in the names of special structures in the animal body, denominated after their discoverers, as:

organ of Bojanus, the nephridium or urinary apparatus in molluscs; ***organ of Corti***, a complicated structure in the cochlea of the ear, supposed to be the essential auditory apparatus; ***organ of Giraldes***, the remnant of the Wolffian body in the male, the parepididymis; ***organ of Rosenmüller***, the remnant of the Wolffian body in the female, the parovarium.

1877 HUXLEY *Anat. Inv. Anim.* 478 The renal organs, or organs of Bojanus, are usually two in number. **1882** *Syd. Soc. Lex.*, s.v. *Corti*, The organ of Corti is developed from the epiblast cells lining the canalis cochlearis. **1885** *Ibid.*, *Giraldes, organ of*, the three or more small irregular masses situated in front of the spermatic cord, just above the head of the epididymis. **1888** ROLLESTON & JACKSON *Anim. Life* 133 Organ of Bojanus or nephridium [in the Mussel]. **1897** *Syd. Soc. Lex.*, *Rosenmüller, organ of*, the *Parovarium*.

†**6.** Applied to certain mechanical contrivances, esp. fire-arms of more or less elaborate construction, machine-guns, etc.: see quots. Cf. ORGUE. *Obs.*

a **1548** HALL *Chron., Hen. VI* 91 b, And shot.. great gonnes.. The citezens of Mauns muche merveilyng at these newe orgaynes. **1603** KNOLLES *Hist. Turks* (1621) 1033 Wee tooke thirteene field pieces, whereof foure were greater than the rest, which they called organes. **1729** SHELVOCKE *Artillery* v. 312 Cannons, Mortars, Petards &c. might be more properly called Organs than Machines. **1769** FALCONER *Dict. Marine* (1789), *Orgues*, an organ, or machine, some-times used in a sea-fight by privateers: it contains several barrels of small arms, fixed upon one stock, so as to be all fired together.

III. An instrument. *fig.*

7. a. A means of action or operation, an instrument, a 'tool'; a person, body of persons, or thing by which some particular purpose is carried out or some function is performed. *arch.*

a **1548** HALL *Chron., Hen. VI* 113 b, An enchanteresse, an orgayne of the deuill, sent from Sathane. *Ibid.* 158 b, He was noted to be the very organ, engine, and diviser of the destruccion of.. the good duke of Gloucester. **1675** BAXTER *Cath. Theol.* II. II. 28 God knoweth all Names, Notions, Propositions and Syllogisms, with their modes; as they are the measures, organs or actings of Humane Understandings. **1801** A. HAMILTON *Wks.* (1886) VII. 225 To provide a faithful and efficient organ for carrying into execution the laws of the United States, which otherwise would be a dead letter. **1849** MACAULAY *Hist. Eng.* ix. II. 529 James.. afraid that his enemies might get this organ of his will [the great seal] into their hands. **1888** BRYCE *Amer. Commw.* I. ix. 116 The functions which these officials discharge belong in America to the State Governments or to the organs of local governments.

b. A mental or spiritual faculty regarded as an instrument of the mind or soul; sometimes as compared to a bodily organ (sense 5).

1656 STANLEY *Hist. Philos.* v. (1701) 180/2 That is Intellect; this the natural Organ accommodated for Judgment. **1809–10** COLERIDGE *Friend* (1865) 96. **1836–7** SIR W. HAMILTON *Metaph.* xxxviii. (1870) II. 374 Faith,—Belief,—is the organ by which we apprehend what is beyond our knowledge. **1850** MCCOSH *Div. Govt.* III. (1874) 298 The conscience is not the law itself, it is merely the organ which makes it known to us—the eye that looks to it.

c. An instrument, means, or medium of communication, or of expression of opinion; *spec.* applied to a newspaper or journal which serves as the mouthpiece of a particular party, denomination, cause, movement, or pursuit.

1788 REID *Aristotle's Log.* iv §3. 76 The silly and uninstructive reasonings.. brought forth by this grand organ of science. **1806** M. CUTLER in *Life, Jrnls. & Corr.* (1888) II. 336, I am now, in compliance with the order of this ecclesiastical council, and as their organ, to address you. **1826** E. IRVING *Babylon* II. 385 Not only.. the men, but.. the organs of the men, the distempered newspapers which they pour in amongst you. **1853** BRIGHT *Sp. India* 3 June, A newspaper which was generally considered throughout India to be the organ of the Government. **1882** *Athenæum* 11 Mar. 309/1 The various branches of natural science.. have their special organs, by means of which their votaries can communicate with one another.

8. *attrib.* and *Comb.*, as (sense 2) ***organ-bench***, ***-blast***, ***-case***, ***-curtain***, ***-harmony***, ***-key***, ***-music***, ***-note***, ***-peal***, ***-prelude***, ***recital***, ***-seat***, ***-song***, ***-tone***, ***-voice***; ***organ-like***, ***-toned*** adjs.; (sense 5) ***organ albumin***, ***current***, ***proteid***, ***regeneration***, ***transplant***, ***transplantation***; **organ-beater** (tr. med.L. *pulsator organorum*), a player on a mediæval organ, with large keys struck with the fist; **organ-bird**, a name for the South American *Cyphorhinus cantans* and a Tasmanian species of *Gymnorhina*, from their notes; **organ-blower**, a person who works the bellows of an organ; also a mechanical contrivance for the same purpose; **organ-builder**, one who 'builds' or constructs organs; so ***organ-building***; **organ-cactus**, the giant cactus or saguaro, *Carnegiea gigantea*, found in south-western North America and so called from its resemblance to the pipes of an organ; **organ clock** (see quot. 1962); **organ-coral** = ORGAN-PIPE *coral*; **organ-fish**, a name for *Sciæna ocellata* of the Southern U.S., also called *drum-fish* (see DRUM *sb.*[1] 11); **organ-gallery**, a gallery in a church or other building, in which the organ is placed; **organ-grinder**, an itinerant street musician who turns the handle of a barrel-organ (see GRIND *v.*[1] 7); so ***organ-grinding*** adj. and sb.; **organ-gun**, a firearm having several charged chambers set side by side like organ-pipes (cf. 6); **organ-harmonium**, a large harmonium of elaborate construction or powerful tone, adapted to take the place of an organ; **organ-loft**, a loft or gallery in which an organ is placed; **organ-maker** (now *rare*), a maker of organs, an organ-builder; **organ-man**, (*a*) a man employed in building or repairing an organ; (*b*) = *organ-grinder*; † **organ-metal**, metal used for the pipes of an organ; **organ-piano**, a pianoforte with a special contrivance for producing a sustained tone as in the organ; also called *melopiano*; **organ-player** (now *rare*), one who plays an organ, an organist; **organ pleat** = ORGAN-PIPE 3 c; **organ-point** (*Mus.*) = PEDAL-POINT; **organ-rest** (*Her.*) = CLARION *sb.* 2 (1846 in Worcester); **organ-screen**, an ornamental screen on which an organ is placed in a cathedral or other church; †**organ-soler** *Obs.* [see SOLER], an organ-loft or organ-gallery; **organ specificity** *Biol.*, specificity towards a particular organ, esp. as exhibited by an antigen, so **organ-specific** *a.*; **organ-stop**, a stop, or set of pipes of the same quality of tone, in an organ (see 2); also *fig.* (see STOP *sb.*[2]). See also ORGAN-PIPE.

1892 *Syd. Soc. Lex.*, **Organ albumin*, the albumin which constitutes part of a tissue in contradistinction from the circulating albumin of the fluids. **1877** HOPKINS & RIMBAULT *Organ* 33 They [the keys] were struck down by the fist of the player.. whence.. arose the expression *organ-beater. **1880** HOPKINS in Grove *Dict. Mus.* II. 580 There were probably nearly as many springs for the organ-beater to overcome as there were pipes to sound. **1863** BATES *Nat. Amazon* xiii. (1864) 448, I frequently heard.. the 'realejo' or *organ-bird.., the most remarkable songster, by far, of the Amazonian forests. **1893** NEWTON *Dict. Birds* 404 Tasmania has.. the Organ-bird of the colonists, *G. hyperleuca*,.. or *organica*. **1837** CARLYLE *Fr. Rev.* III. VII. i, The rushing of a mighty *organ-blast. **1540** *Ludlow Churchw. Acc.* (Camden) 4 Payd to the *organ bloere for his yeares wages.. ijs. viijd. **1719** in Willis & Clark *Cambridge* (1886) II. 214 Chamber for ye Organ-blower. **1725** *Lond. Gaz.* No. 6347/3 Renatus Harris, of London, *Organ-Builder. **1859** GEN. P. THOMPSON *Audi Alt.* II. lxxxviii. 60, I have, as you know, a weakness for *Organ-building. **1883** W. H. BISHOP in *Harper's Mag.* Mar. 502/2 We made haste.. to cut down an example of the.. saguaras, the *organ-cactus. **1947** *Time* 10 Mar. 18/2 The two Presidents rode between rows of organ cacti. **1644** in Willis & Clark *Cambridge* (1886) I. 513 Solut' Ashley pro taking downe the *Orgaine case, o. 3. o. **1956** G. H. BAILLIE et al. *Britten's Old Clocks & Watches* (ed. 7) 155 Musical and *organ-clocks became more popular during the last half of the eighteenth century. **1962** E. BRUTON *Dict. Clocks & Watches* 126 *Organ clock*, clock playing a small pipe organ every three hours. Popular in the second half of the eighteenth century. **1973** *Times* 2 Jan. (Europe Suppl.) p. xii/2 The centrepiece of the show will be an organ clock by Charles Clay. **1892** *Syd. Soc. Lex.*, **Organ current*, the current existing in the electrical organ of certain fishes. **1766** ENTICK *London* IV. 213 The *organ-gallery is supported with Corinthian columns. **1806–7** BERESFORD *Miseries Hum. Life* 73 While an *organ-grinder, or ballad-singer.. are exhausting their whole stock of dissonances. **1887** *Spectator* 26 Mar. 412/2 The Italian fruit-vendor or organ-grinder is often a retired workman. **1806** WOLCOTT (P. Pindar) *Tristia* Wks. 1812 V. 305 The *organ-grinding Girl, whose discords kill. **1881** *Macm. Mag.* XLIII. 436/1 The organ-grinding branch of the musical profession. **1883** *Daily News* 19 Sept. 3/3 After passing between two fine old '*organ guns', cannons with half-a-dozen or more barrels. **1864** WEBSTER, **Organ-harmonium*, an harmonium of large capacity and power, designed as an economical substitute for the organ. **1842** TENNYSON *Sir Galahad* 75 A rolling *organ-harmony Swells up. **1878** B. TAYLOR *Deukalion* II. i. 54 Cecilia, sitting at her *organ keys. **1543** *Aberdeen Reg.* (1844) I. 190 In the *organe loft. **1664** in Willis & Clark *Cambridge* (1886) I. 156 The doore beneath the organ loft. **1867** LADY HERBERT *Cradle L.* iii. 100 The panels of the organ-loft and the screen are all beautifully painted. **1431** in *Test. Ebor.* (Surtees) V. 22 *note*, John Gyse, *organe maker. **1542** in Glasscock *Rec. St. Michaels* (1882) 43 Item for fetching of the orgon makers toolis viijd. **1809–10** in Willis & Clark *Cambridge* (1886) I. 521 Paid Mr. Elliot Organ-Maker for repairing and compleating the Organ. **1626** *Vestry Bks.* (Surtees) 296 Imprimis geven to the *organman for goinge to Durham about wood, xijd. **1868** HELPS *Realmah* xvii. (1869) 468 The polka which the organman was grinding out. **1578** in Kerry *St. Lawrence Reading* (1883) 62 Solde to Rocke 37 li. of leade which was *organ metall, viijs. vjd. **1869** G. MEREDITH *Let.* 25 June (1970) I. 382 He [*sc.* Poe] gave the idea shape in a fine roll of *organ music. **1934** Organ music [see MIMSEY *a.*]. **1422** tr. *Secreta Secret.*, *Priv. Priv.* 243 The nyghtyngall shewyth his *organe notis. **1921** A. HUXLEY *Let.* 8 Sept. (1969) 204 Papini.. one can read with much pleasure... Great sharpness and clarity and wit combined with melody and organ notes and sweeping gesture. **1942** *R.A.F. Jrnl.* 3 Oct. 26 The organ-note of four engines hoisting the flying boat into the air. **1958** WODEHOUSE *Cocktail Time* iii. 29 A good bishop, denouncing from the pulpit with the right organ note in his voice. **1804** J. GRAHAME *Sabbath* 76 Again the *organ-peal, loud, rolling, meets The hallelujahs of the choir. **1544** *Churchw. Acc. St. Giles, Reading* 70 The *Organ player for his yeres wages, iij[li] x[s]. *a* **1640** J. BALL *Answ. Art. Can* I. (1642) 143 Squealing choristers, organ-players.. vergerers. **1886** *Pall Mall G.* 3 June 8/1 The train is slightly rounded, and falls in two *organ pleats. **1897** R. KIPLING *Captains Courageous* 250 The skipper lurched into his seat as an *organ-prelude silenced him. **1896** *Allbutt's Syst. Med.* I. 186 An increase in destruction of *organ proteid. **1881** *Harper's Mag.* May 814/1 Piano and *organ recitals have long been fashionable. **1923** *Radio Times* 28 Sept. 9/1 3.0.—Organ recital at Steinway Hall, London. **1974** *Times* 12 Nov. 15/2 No one would be happier than I to have Sunday afternoon organ recitals once again at the Palace. **1927** HALDANE & HUXLEY *Animal Biol.* ix. 174 Among reptilia, lizards are the only animals which possess even the power of *organ-regeneration. **1972** L. V. POLEZHAEV *Organ Regeneration in Animals* i. 3 It is conventional to divide all animals into.. those which are capable of organ regeneration and those which are not. **1540** *Ludlow Churchw. Acc.* (Camden) 4 Mendynge of the locke on the *organ-soler dore. *c* **1425** *St. Elizabeth of Spalbeck* in *Anglia* VIII. 109/31 A wrast, þat is an instrument of *organ-songe. **1936** K. LANDSTEINER *Specificity Serol. Reactions* iii. 64 Upon injection of the *organ specific substances. **1971** J. Z. YOUNG *Introd. Study Man* xvii. 210 Organ-specific inhibitors are known from many tissues. **1911** *Jrnl. Exper. Med.* XIV. 48 Absolutely no *organ specificity is demonstrable as regards the agglutination experiments. **1968** H. HARRIS *Nucleus & Cytoplasm* iv. 78 It has been contended that the pattern of puffing shows organ specificity but the evidence for this does not seem to be at all conclusive. **1644** MILTON *Educ.* Wks. (1847) 101/2 Sometimes the lute or soft *organ stop waiting on elegant voices. **1880** HOPKINS in Grove *Dict. Mus.* I. 403 *Cornet.* This name is given to several kinds of organ stops. **1955** A. L. ROWSE *Expansion Eliz. Eng.* 27 The Queen.. was furious... At once all the organ-stops are out. **1971** P. WORSTHORNE *Socialist Myth* iii. 37 The Tory Party has.. a liking for the language of togetherness, and real patriotic fervour. These are the organ-stops it can pull out with genuine faith and zest. **1819** KEATS *Hyperion* I, in *Lamia & other Poems* (1820) 148 She spake In solemn tenour and deep *organ tone. **1894** 'MARK TWAIN' in *Century Mag.* Mar. 773 There was nothing weak in the deep organ tones that responded. **1895** *New Age* 12 Sept. 372/2 An organ-toned voice of prodigious depth. **1901** *Q. Rev.* July 122 Milton could not have produced his organ-tones on a 'scrannel pipe'. **1922** JOYCE *Ulysses* 454 The strains of the *organtoned melodeon. **1968** *Listener* 18 July 90/2 Idea-transplants are as difficult as *organ-transplants: in both cases human beings have a built-in mechanism for rejection. **1970** *Memorandum Organtranspl.* (Netherlands Red Cross) §5c Should an organ transplant be considered.. it will be desirable not to have the diagnosis of the donor's death made by one physician only. **1971** *Essentials from Rep. Organtranspl.* (Netherlands Red Cross) 3 It was considered necessary, in the context of organtransplantations, to establish a precise.. criterion of.. death. **1864** TENNYSON *Milton* 3 God-gifted *organ-voice of England, Milton, a name to resound for ages.

†**organ**, *sb.*[2] *Obs.* exc. *dial.* Also 6 **organe**, 7 **orgaine**. [Corrupt ad. L. *origanum*, Gr. ὀρίγανον.] = ORIGAN; penny-royal.

c **1000** *Sax. Leechd.* I. 236 Ðeos wyrt þe man origanum & oðrum naman.. organan nemneþ is hattre ʒecynde. *c* **1265** *Vocab. Plant-n.* in Wr.-Wülcker 557/19 *Organum*, organe. **1548** TURNER *Names of Herbes* 57, I neuer sawe the trewe organ in England.. our commune organ.. is called *origanum syluestre* in latin, and in some places in England wylde mergerum. **1620** VENNER *Via Recta* ii. 44 Take of the tops of Rosemary, of Sage, of Marioram, of Orgaine,.. of each one handfull. **1640** PARKINSON *Theat. Bot.* 30 *Pulegium angustifolium sive Cervinum*.. Wee in English [call it] Penny-royall, Pudding grasse, and Pulioll-royall, and in the West parts, as about Exeter, Organs. **1640** G. H. *Witts Recreations* C vj b, A good wife, once a bed of Organs set, The pigs came in and eate up every whit. **1886** ELWORTHY *W. Somerset Word-bk.*, *Organ*,.. the plant Penny-royal (*Mentha pulegium*)... It is chopped small and put into a mess called 'Tea-kettle broth',.. often called 'Organ broth'.

organ, short for ORGAN LING, a kind of fish.

'organ, *v. rare.* [f. ORGAN *sb.*[1]]

†**1.** *trans.* To furnish with an organ or organs; to organize. *Obs.*

1652 BENLOWES *Theoph.* IV. lvii. 59 While lungs my Breath shall organ I'l press still Th' Exinanition of my o'regrown will. **1681** MANNINGHAM *Disc.* 89 Alas!.. thou art Elemented and Organ'd for other Apprehensions.

2. To play on an organ (*intr.* and *trans.*). ***organ out*** (quot. 1837), to dismiss by playing on an organ, to 'play out'.

1827 CARLYLE *Germ. Rom.* III. 301, I organed, my gossip managing the bellows. **1837** —— *Fr. Rev.* I. III. iii, As in a kind of choral anthem, or bravura peal, of thanks.. the Notables are, so to speak, organed out, and dismissed to their respective places of abode. **1844** E. FITZGERALD *Lett.* (1889) I. 141 There is a dreadful vulgar ballad.. which is sung and organed at every corner in London. *c* **1870** BLACKIE in W. McIlwraith *Guide Wigtownshire* (1875) 57 Anthems organed from rich cloistered halls.

Hence **'organing** *vbl. sb.*, organ-playing.

1827 CARLYLE *Germ. Rom.* II. 302 There was such a piping and organing. **1878** STEVENSON *Inland Voy.* (1896) 173 Laboriously edified with chaunts and organings.

†**'organal**, *a. Obs. rare.* Also 6 -onall. [a. OF. *organal*, *orguenal*, f. L. *organ-um* + -AL[1].]

1. ***organal vein*** [OF. *veine organal*]: the 'vital' or jugular vein.

1523 LD. BERNERS *Froiss.* I. ccclxxiv. 621 The speare heed dyd entre into his throte, and dyd cutte asonder the orgonall vayne.

2. Of or pertaining to a musical organ.

1633 AMES *Agst. Cerem.* II. 404 His denying of Organall musicke to have beene significant or typicall, is without reason.

3. Of or pertaining to the medieval style of part-singing known as organum. (Cf. ORGANUM[1].)

1916 STANFORD & FORSYTH *Hist. Mus.* 128 At this time the organal voice had.. become finally fixed in its position above the plain-song. **1932** *Music & Lett.* XIII. 190 The melody has a long reciting note on b, which, as he [*sc.* Otker] says, 'has no proper organal response.' **1977** *Early Music* July 337/1 The upper voice seems rather like an ornamented organal voice.

organcine, obs. form of ORGANZINE.

organdie ('ɔːgəndɪ). Also -dy, -di. [a. F. *organdi* (1723 in Hatz.-Darm.), of uncertain origin.] A very fine and translucent kind of muslin.

1835 *Court Mag.* VI. p. ii/2 The most elegant [bonnets] are composed of organdy of the clearest kind. **1861** *Eng. Wom. Dom. Mag.* III. 117/1 The skirt of a very pretty blue and white Organdie. **1892** *Pall Mall G.* 26 May 1/3 The organdi muslins with French flower-patterns.

organed ('ɔːgənd), *ppl. a. rare.* [f. ORGAN *sb.*[1] + -ED.]

1. Furnished with organs; organized.

1586 BRIGHT *Melanch.* xii. 61 Life lyeth rather in the essence.. of the soule, giving it to a fit organed body. **1669** COKAINE *Fletcher's Plays* Poems 101 Whilst his well organ'd Body doth retreat To its first matter. **1689** SWIFT *Ode to Temple* Wks. 1755 IV. I. 242 Methinks, when you expose the scene, Down the ill-organ'd engines fall.

2. *nonce-use.* Having an organ (musical).

1834 FONBLANQUE *Eng. under 7 Administ.* (1837) III. 19 It should be seen whether the men of Caius, organless, are better than those of organed Colleges.

organelle (ɔːgə'nɛl). *Biol.* Formerly also **organella**. [mod.L. *organella* (see ORGAN *sb.*[1] and -EL[2]), after earlier *organulum* (K. Möbius 1884, in *Biol. Centralbl.* IV. 392; O. Bütschli *H. G. Bronn's Klassen und Ordnungen des Thier-Reichs* (1888) I. III. 1412), dim. of ORGANUM[1] (see -ULE).] Any of various specialized structures of an individual cell, analogous to the organs of multicellular organisms.

1909 H. M. WOODCOCK in E. R. Lankester *Treat. Zool.* I. I. 212 A Trypanosome was merely described as possessing an unmistakable nucleus, and also a small deeply-staining element.. situated at the root of the flagellum, and termed variously 'blepharoplast', centrosome, or micronucleus. It is to Schandinn that we are indebted for the revelation of the essential nuclear nature of the latter organella. **1912** E. A. MINCHIN *Introd. Study Protozoa* i. 1 However complex the structure and functions of the body [of Protozoa], the organs that it possesses are parts of a cell ('organellæ'), and are never made up of distinct cells. **1924** HEGNER & TALIAFERRO *Human Protozool.* vi. 233 Division of the trophozoite is by longitudinal fission, the posterior end of the animal splitting before the anterior organelles are completely divided. **1926** L. W. SHARP *Introd. Cytol.* (ed. 2) iii. 59 It is also frequently urged that 'organelle' rather than 'organ' should be used for intracellular differentiations. **1955** *New Biol.* XIX. 27 Essentially similar organelles, cilia, cover many membranes ..of animals. **1969** F. E. ROUND *Introd. Lower Plants* ii. 19 Within the outer cytoplasmic membrane occur all the normal organelles—chloroplast, nucleus, dictyosome(s) (Golgi body), endoplasmic reticulum, granules, and vacuoles. **1974** *Sci. Amer.* Oct. 45/1 Bacteria also have flagella, but these are an entirely different organelle.

Hence **orga'nellar** *a.*

1970 *Genetics* LXVI. 305 (*heading*) Organellar damage and revision as a possible basis for intraclonal variation in *Paramecium*. **1975** *Nature* 13 Mar. 160/2 If this were the case in my wild carrot protoplasts, about 20% (the approximate proportion of organellar DNA in these cells) of the dimers would have remained after maximum excision.

†**'organer**. *Obs.* Also 5 -our. [ad. L. *organārius*, or OF. *orgenere*, *organeor* organist. OF. had also *organier* (14th c.) as title of a book on the organ; mod.F. has *organier* organ-maker.] **a.** An organ-maker. **b.** An organ-player, organist.

1413 LYDG. *Pilgr. Sowle* IV. xxxvii. (1483) 84 More helply is a Carpenter or a potter, than an Organer, a peynter or an ymager. **1442** in *Lincoln Cath. Stat.* II. 482 [Five marcs to be paid.. to one Arnald] organor' de Civitate Norwyc. *a* **1485** *Promp. Parv.* 369/1 (MS.S.), Organer, *Orgonista, organicus*.

orga'nette. [f. ORGAN[1] 2 + -ETTE.] A small 'organ': a trade name for various musical instruments: cf. ORGAN *sb.* 3. In q. 1892 = ORGUINETTE.

1889 *Daily News* 15 Nov. 5/5 A peculiar sort of photographer's camera.. not unlike an American organette of about a foot square. **1892** *Pall Mall G.* 21 Sept. 6/3 At Milan yesterday the International Literary and Artistic Congress.. the use of perforated cards for organettes was declared to be an act of piracy. **1893** *Mission. Herald* (Boston) Aug. 324 When the organette was played, the crowd soon began to gather. **1898** *Westm. Gaz.* 30 Dec. 9/2 An organette has also been purchased for use in the school block of the workhouse.

organetto (ɔːgə'nɛtəʊ). [It.] A small portative organ used in the Middle Ages.

1876 STAINER & BARRETT *Dict. Mus. Terms* 340/2 *Organetto (It.)*, a little organ. **1952** W. L. SUMNER *Organ* iii. 58 Francesco Landini.. was an excellent player on several instruments, but he preferred the portative or organetto. **1959** *Collins Mus. Encycl.* 474/1 *Organetto*.., small portative organ of the Middle Ages. **1960** D. J. GROUT *Hist. Western Mus.* (1962) iv. 129 In addition to the portative organ or organetto, there were positive organs. **1976** D. MUNROW *Instruments Middle Ages & Renaissance* ii. 16/1 The *organetto*, usually known today as the portative organ, was one of the most popular instruments, regularly illustrated from the thirteenth to the sixteenth centuries.

organic (ɔː'gænɪk), *a.* and *sb.* [ad. L. *organic-us*, a. Gr. ὀργανικός of or pertaining to an organ, instrumental, f. ὄργανον ORGAN *sb.*[1]; in L. in senses 'mechanical', and 'pertaining to a musical instrument'. Cf. F. *organique* 14–15th c. in Anatomy.]

A. *adj.* **1.** Serving as an organ, instrument, or means; acting as an instrument, of nature or art, to a certain end; instrumental. *rare.*

1517 WATSON *Shyppe of Fooles* I. i, Approche you vnto this doctryne and it reuolue in your myndes organyques. **1541** R. COPLAND *Guydon's Quest. Chirurg.* C j b, Which are the membres compostes, and wherfore are they called organykes & instrumentalles? **1644** MILTON *Educ.* Wks. (1851) 389 Those organic arts which enable men to discourse and write. **1645** —— *Tetrach.* Wks. (1851) 168 With that organic force that logic proffers us. **1667** —— *P.L.* IX. 530 He.. with Serpent Tongue Organic, or impulse of vocal Air, His fraudulent temptation thus began. **1883** T. H. GREEN *Proleg. Ethics* §85 The animal system is not organic merely to feeling of the kind just spoken of as receptive, to impressions.. conveyed by the nerves of the several senses.

†**2. a.** Relating to an organ, instrument, or means. (Cf. ORGANON 2.) *Obs. rare.*

1697 tr. *Burgersdicius his Logick* I. i. 2 A System of Logical Precepts consists of two Parts, Thematick and Organick... [The latter] converses about the Organs themselves, with which the Understanding entreats of Themes.

b. Done by means of instruments; mechanical: = ORGANICAL *a.* 2 b.

[**1646** SCHOOTEN (*title*) De organica conicarum sectionum in plano descriptione tractatus. **1704** NEWTON *Enumeratio Linearum* VI. Theor. i, De Curvarum descriptione Organica.] **1885** LEUDESDORF *Cremona's Proj. Geom.* 297 This theorem is due to Newton, and was given by him under the title of *The Organic Description* of a conic.

†**c.** Of or pertaining to musical instruments; instrumental. *Obs.*

1811 BUSBY *Dict. Mus.* (ed. 3), *Organic*, the epithet applied by the ancients to that part of practical music which concerned instrumental performance. **1825** DANNELEY *Encycl. Mus.*, *Organic*, according to the Greeks, that part of music which was executed upon instruments.

3. *Phys.* Of or pertaining to the bodily organs; vital; *spec.* in *Path.* of a disease, Producing or attended with alteration in the structure of an organ; structural (opp. to *functional*). So ***organic pulse*** (F. *pouls organique*), a pulse of such a character as to indicate organic disease.

1706 PHILLIPS, *Organical* or *Organick*, belonging to the Organs of the Body. *a* **1711** KEN *Hymnotheo* Poet. Wks. 1721 III. 212 Hymnotheo's Soul, which while he slept remain'd From its Organick Drudgery unchain'd. **1801** *Med. Jrnl.* V. 441 If the powers of an agent should.. induce a decided influence on the organic motions of life. **1809** *Ibid.* XXI. 302 Great organic affections often excite the disease. **1822–34** *Good's Study Med.* (ed. 4) I. 546 He [M. Bordeu] describes.. an overwhelming multiplicity of organic pulses. **1835** T. S. SMITH *Philos. Health* i. 15 The organic actions consist of the processes by which the existence of the living being is maintained. **1842** BRANDE *Dict. Sci.*, etc. 857/1 Tuberculated induration of the liver is an organic or structural disease of that viscus.

4. a. Having organs, or an organized physical structure; having the characteristics of, belonging to, derived from, or relating to, organized or living beings (animals or plants). (Opp. to *inorganic*.)

1778 J. R. FORSTER (*title*) Observations made during a Voyage round the World.. on 1. The Earth and its Strata.. 5. Organic Bodies, and 6. The Human Species. **1808** GOOD (*title*) On the general Structure and Physiology of Plants, compared with those of Animals, and the mutual convertibility of their Organic Elements. **1813** SIR H. DAVY *Agric. Chem.* i. (1814) 18 Organic substances as soon as they are deprived of vitality begin to pass through a series of changes. **1813** BAKEWELL *Introd. Geol.* Pref. (1815) 5 These rocks contain no organic remains. **1835** KIRBY *Hab. & Inst. Anim.* I. iii. 139 The animal derives this nutriment from organic matter, the vegetable from inorganic. **1851** CARPENTER *Man. Phys.* (ed. 2) 206 The Muscular tissue of Organic Life.. exists under two forms; that of fibres and that of cells. **1862** HUXLEY *Lect. Orig. Spec.* i. 7 In speaking of the causes which lead to our present knowledge of organic nature, I have used it almost as an equivalent of the word 'living'. **1878** —— *Physiogr.* xx. 337 The matter of the organic world.

b. *Chem.* (i) Applied to a class of compound substances which naturally exist as constituents of organized bodies (animals or plants), or are formed from compounds which so exist, as in ***organic acid***, ***base***, ***compound***, ***molecule***, ***radical***; all these contain or are derived from hydrocarbon radicals, hence ***organic chemistry***, that branch of chemistry which deals with organic substances, is the chemistry of the hydrocarbons and their derivatives.

1827 FARADAY *Chem. Manip.* ii. 42 In the processes of organic analysis. **1831** R. KNOX *Cloquet's Anat.* 2 By the mutual combination of these principles are formed the organic elements, which exist only in living beings, and are the exclusive product of organization... These organic elements are, gelatine, albumen, fibrin, fat, mucus, and certain other substances less generally distributed. **1849** D. CAMPBELL *Inorg. Chem.* 295 Sulphuric and several organic acids do not cause a precipitate, even in strong solutions. **1869** KIRKES *Physiol.* (ed. 7) 16 The term *organic* has long ceased to imply a substance that is formed only by organized living tissues, and now signifies only matter with a certain degree of complexity of composition. **1871** ROSCOE *Elem. Chem.* 289 Organic Chemistry is defined as the chemistry of the carbon compounds. **1894** SCHORLEMMER *Rise & Devel. Organ. Chem.* v. 88 We define, therefore, that part of our science which is commonly called organic chemistry as the *Chemistry of the Hydrocarbons and their derivatives*.

(ii) Of an element: contained in an organic compound.

1868 *Jrnl. Chem. Soc.* XXI. 87 Estimation of the carbon and nitrogen contained in the organic portion of the solid constituents (organic carbon and nitrogen). **1900** [see NITRIFYING *ppl. a.*]. **1924** L. DONCASTER *Introd. Study Cytol.* (ed. 2) ii. 20 Practically the whole of the organic phosphorus in the nucleus is contained in.. nucleic acid. **1957** G. E. HUTCHINSON *Treat. Limnol.* I. xii. 735 There is no information available as to the fraction constituting the soluble or colloidal organic phosphorus of lake waters. **1972** *Limnol. & Oceanogr.* XVII. 349/2 Dissolved organic carbon .., particulate organic carbon.., and particulate nitrogen.. were measured to determine the distribution of organic matter.

†**c.** ***organic molecules***: (*a*) Particles of matter supposed by Buffon to exist in living bodies, and to which he attributed the power of reproduction; †(*b*) 'Spallanzani's term for the *spermatozoa*' (*Syd. Soc. Lex.*).

1790 BURKE *Fr. Rev.* Wks. V. 59 They acted by the ancient organised states in the shape of their old organisation, and not by the organick moleculæ of a disbanded people. **1815** J. SCOTT *Vis. Paris* (ed. 2) 293 His theory of the Earth, now forgotten, and his organic molecules, on which he attempted to raise a system of materialism.

d. Of a fertilizer or manure: produced from natural substances, usually without the addition of chemicals.

1869 S. R. HOLE *Bk. about Roses* vi. 76, I made anxious experiment of a multiplicity of manures—organic and inorganic, animal and vegetable. **1942** *Organic Farming & Gardening* I. 3/2 Compost fertilizer is a purely organic material as distinguished from mineral fertilizers (chemicals). **1952** C. E. L. PHILLIPS *Small Garden* iii. 18 Compared with the chemical fertilizers, the organic ones are slow in action but enduring in effect. *Ibid.* 19 Of other forms of organic manure, the following are valuable. **1960** *Times* 27 Feb. 9/2 A good organic-based general fertilizer. **1975** D. GREEN *Food & Drink from your Garden* v. 38 There is probably something in the theory that vegetables have their quality improved by the use of organic fertilizers.

e. ***organic soil***: (see quot. 1928).

1928 *Bull. Amer. Soil Survey Assoc.* IX. 33 *Organic soils*, soils composed mainly of organic material; the organic content being sufficient to dominate the soil characteristics. **1943** MILLAR & TURK *Fund. Soil Sci.* ii. 63 Deposits of organic soils are of common occurrence in the northern border states of Minnesota eastward. **1966** *McGraw-Hill Encycl. Sci. & Technol.* XII. 423/1 Organic soils such as peats and mucks may contain as much as 95% carbonaceous material.

f. Of farming or gardening: growing plants without the use of chemical fertilizers, pesticides, etc., adding only organic fertilizers to the soil.

1942 J. I. RODALE in *Organic Farming & Gardening* I. 3/1 What is claimed roughly for these organic methods of farming is that they increase the fertility of the soil, produce much better tasting crops,.. reduce weeds, do away with the necessity of using poisonous sprays, improve the mechanical structure of the soil. **1948** *Sci. Monthly* June 482/1 Considerable success is claimed in the humid tropics with 'organic farming' where labor is plentiful.. and where fertilizers are very expensive or difficult to obtain. *Ibid.*, The organic devotees are primarily interested in production. *Ibid.* 482/2 Great claims have been made for soil improvement by earthworms, usually as a special phase of 'organic' gardening. **1971** *Islander* (Victoria, B.C.) 13 June 14/2 An organic gardener uses natural mineral and organic fertilizers to build his soil. **1973** *Country Life* 6 Dec. 1986/4 Organic farming community. Six professional couples with children wish to purchase . . large country residence with small-holding acreage. **1975** *Listener* 14 Aug. 203/2 The great thing about organic farming is that you . . build up life in the soil, using natural organic manures such as compost and farmyard manure.

g. Of food: produced without the use of chemical fertilizers, pesticides, etc.

1972 *Daily Tel.* 12 Feb. 6/7 The organic food market is booming. *Ibid.*, 'Ninety per cent of the ''organic'' apple juice being sold in California is not made from organically grown apples,' said a spokesman for one of the country's biggest organic food wholesalers. **1972** R. Bloch *Night-World* (1974) xiv. 93 Past the organic-food hangouts for the health freaks. **1975** *Times* 5 Sept. 14/8 Another great interest was the growing of food organically, which resulted in a number of books on organic food . . in the late 1940s and early 1950s.

5. a. Belonging to or inherent in the organization or constitution (bodily or mental) of a living being; constitutional; fundamental. **b.** Belonging to the constitution of an organized whole; structural.

1796 Burney *Mem. Metastasio* II. 415, I have, perhaps, a little indulged my organic indolence. **1844** Emerson *Lect., New Eng. Ref.* Wks. (Bohn) I. 266 We believe that the defects of so many perverse and so many frivolous people . . are organic. —— *Yng. Amer.* ibid. II. 306 There still remains an organic simplicity and liberty, which . . redresses itself. **1880** Disraeli *Endym.* xxii, The bow of Waldershare was a study. Its grace and ceremony must have been organic. **1884** J. Tait *Mind in Matter* (1892) 58 The work of plausible writers in minimising organic difference is easy. **1895** E. B. Titchener tr. *Külpe's Outl. Psychol.* I. ii. 140 By 'organic sensations' we mean the sensations adequately stimulated by changes in the condition of the bodily organs,—muscles, joints, etc. **1901** W. James *Let.* 10 July (1920) II. 158 What I *crave* most is some wild American country. It is a curious organic-feeling need. **1933** G. Murphy *Gen. Psychol.* viii. 124 From what has been said about hunger and thirst it seems reasonable to believe that these organic sensations depend partly upon the compounding of simple sense qualities.

c. *Philol.* Belonging to the etymological structure of a word; not secondary or fortuitous.

Mod. In *these* (ME. *þise*) final *e* is organic, in *those* (ME. *þás, þôs*) it is inorganic.

d. ***organic selection*** (see quot. 1942).

1896 J. M. Baldwin in *Amer. Naturalist* XXX. 444 We may simply . . apply the phrase, 'Organic Selection', to the organism's behavior in acquiring new modes or modifications of adaptive function. **1942** J. S. Huxley *Evolution* vi. 304 We have here a beautiful special case of the principle of organic selection, . . according to which modifications repeated for a number of generations may serve as the first step in evolutionary change. **1970** T. Dobzhansky *Genetics Evol. Process* ix. 303 The term organic selection has been coined to describe the parallelism between racial genotypic and environmental phenotypic variability.

6. a. Of, pertaining to, or characterized by systematic connexion or coordination of parts in one whole; organized; systematic.

1817 Coleridge *Biog. Lit.* I. xii. 237 The fairest part of the most beautiful body will appear deformed and monstrous, if dissevered from its place in the organic whole. **1847** W. Smith tr. *Fichte's Characteristics Present Age* 94 What this organic unity of a work of Art . . really is,—will be asked by no one to whom it is not already known. **1850** Carlyle *Latter-d. Pamph.* vi. (1872) 210 [They] bound it up into organic masses. **1855** Brimley *Ess., Tennyson* 54 After all that philosophical critics have talked of organic unity. **1870** S. H. Hodgson *Theory of Practice* II. 166 Rome . . was unequal to . . incorporating into an organic whole the nations included in her empire. **1874** W. Wallace tr. *Hegel's Logic* 19 The truths of philosophy are valueless, apart from their interdependence and organic union. **1880** J. Caird *Philos. Relig.* x. 307 Consciousness is not a mere collection or aggregate of 'faculties' existing side by side, . . but a membered or organic whole, every part of which exists only in and through its relation to the rest. **1923** *Psychol. Rev.* XXX. 371 Thinking is not an isolated fact . . . It is the final step in an organic learning process. *a* **1943** R. G. Collingwood *Idea of Hist.* (1946) 123 Marx . . conceived this unity not as an organic unity.

b. Organizing, constitutive. (Cf. F. *loi organique.*) *rare.*

1849 *Congress. Globe* 30th Congress 1 Sess. App. 47 [The origin of a Territorial Government] is not from *such people*, but from the law of Congress, usually styled the 'organic law', establishing it. **1857** in Bartlett *Dict. Amer.* (1860) 304 The powers of the corporation of Washington are only those which are conferred by the organic law, the charter. **1883** G. T. Curtis *Buchanan* II. ix. 202 His official duty under the organic Act by which the Territory was organized. **1963** M. Khadduri *Mod. Libya* vii. 184 Both the Tripolitanian and Fazzanese organic laws permit the amendment of any provision during the first session of the legislative assemblies by a simple majority of all the members.

c. Phr. ***organic composition of capital*** (Econ.): see esp. quot. 1887.

1887 Moore & Aveling tr. *Marx's Capital* II. xxv. 625 The composition of capital is to be understood in a twofold sense. On the side of value, it is determined by the proportion in which it is divided into constant capital or value of the means of production, and variable capital or value of labour-power, the sum total of wages. On the side of material, as it functions in the process of production, all capital is divided into means of production and living labour-power. . . I call the former the *value-composition*, the latter the *technical composition* of capital. Between the two there is a strict correlation. To express this, I call the value-composition of capital, in so far as it is determined by its technical composition and mirrors the changes of the latter, the *organic composition* of capital. Wherever I refer to the composition of capital, without further qualification, its organic composition is always understood. **1937** M. Dobb *Pol. Econ. & Capitalism* i. 14 The important simplifying assumption that the ratio of labour to capital employed in different lines of production was everywhere equal: what Marx termed equality in the 'organic composition of capital' or what later economists would have called uniformity of the 'technical coefficients'. **1966** J. Robinson *Essay Marxian Econ.* ii. 7 We can avoid ambiguity, without falsifying Marx's meaning, if we use symbols *c*, *v* and *s* only for rates per unit of time of depreciation and raw material lost, wages and profit, and speak of the organic composition of capital, not as *c*/*v* but as capital per man employed. **1972** G. C. Harcourt *Some Cambr. Controv. Theory Capital* 8 The assumption . . is akin to that of Marx . . , namely, a uniform organic composition of capital for the processes . . of each technique. **1974** M. B. Brown *Econ. of Imperialism* iii. 54 With the increasing application of machinery to production the organic composition of capital would rise. **1975** *Chinese Econ. Studies* VIII. iv. 84 Capital accumulation and capital concentration inevitably increase the organic composition of capital.

7. a. Resembling an organ (musical instrument), or the tones of an organ; organ-like.

1609 Donne *1st Elegy Mistress Boulstred*, He rounds the aire, and breakes the hymnique notes In birds, heaven's choristers, organique throats. **1818** L. Hunt *Foliage* Pref. 31 The long organic music of Homer. **1832** —— *Poems* Pref. 29 Hear young Milton practising his organic numbers.

†**b.** *Mediæval Mus.* Pertaining to the organum: see organum[1] 2. *Obs.*

1782 Burney *Hist. Mus.* II. ii. 138 In some French churches, where the organizing the plain chant at a close has ceased, the organic, or additional part, has frequently been retained in the melody instead of the original notes.

†**8.** ***organic vein***: an old name for the jugular vein. *Obs.* Cf. organal *a.* 1.

[*c* **1400** *Lanfranc's Cirurg.* 149 Boþe on þe riȝt side and on þe lift side of þe caane of þe lungis þer ben ij. greete veynes þat ben clepid organice or ellis guydes.] **1597** A. M. tr. *Guillemeau's Fr. Chirurg.* xii. b/2 The Iugulare or organicke vayne.

B. *sb.* An organic compound. Usu. *pl.*

1953 R. E. Grim *Clay Mineral.* iv. 62 Studies of the methylation of certain organics during their adsorption by montmorillonite. **1970** *Nature* 11 July 149/1 Small samples . . of the meteorite . . were ground with a small chisel previously heated to a dull red to remove organics. **1974** *Sci. Amer.* May 75/1 The biological material in Dean's recipe . . represents 2,000 times the amount of organics normally present in seawater.

†**or'ganical**, *a. Obs.* [f. as prec. + -al[1].]

1. Of music: Performed on an instrument, instrumental; = organic *a.* 2c.

1521 J. T. in *Bradshaw's St. Werburge* Prol. 1 Honour, ioye, and glorie, the toynes organicall, Endeles myrthes wt melodies! **1609** Douland *Ornith. Microl.* 2 Organicall Musicke (as Cælius writeth) is that which belongeth to artificiall Instruments. **1698** Stillingfl. *Eccl. Cases* 382 The use of organical musick in the publick service. **1700** Wallis in *Collect.* (O.H.S.) I. 317 Consorts of musick (vocal and organical).

2. Of the nature of, or pertaining to, an instrument or machine; mechanical. (In quot. 1729 used specifically.)

1579–80 North *Plutarch* (1676) 261 To frame Instruments and Engines (which are called mechanicall, or organicall). **1729** Shelvocke *Artillery* v. 311 The Action or Motion of some of these [Machines] is Mechanical, and of others Organnical . . the latter operate by the slight artful Touch of a single Person.

b. = organic 2 b.

1726 E. Stone *New Math. Dict.*, *Organical* Description of Curves, is the Description of them upon a Plane, by means of Instruments. [**1819** in Rees *Cycl.*]

3. Serving as an instrument, instrumental.

1605 Timme *Quersit.* I. v. 22 As organical and instrumental causes. **1649** Jer. Taylor *Gt. Exemp.* I. Disc. i. 37 It is not fitted with an instrument apt and organical to the faculty. **1668** Wilkins *Real Char.* 1 The third Part shall treat concerning such helps and Instruments, as are requisite, . . which may therefore be stiled the Organical or Instrumental Part. **1681** Baxter *Acc. Sherlocke* vi. 210 The Pastors Office was made as the organical Office to make the rest; As Nature maketh the Heart and other noble organical parts, before the rest of the Body.

b. *Phys.* Applied to parts of the body having particular functions: = organic *a.* 3. ***organical part*** = organ *sb.*[1] 5.

c **1450** Lydg. & Burgh *Secrees* 2543 Fle his presence, Which acomplysshed in membrys Organychall Is not. **1594** *Mirr. Policy* (1599) N ij, Eies (which are the organicall instruments of sight). **1659** Pearson *Creed* (1741) 277 The hands of man are those organical parts which are most active and executive of our power. **1707** *Curios. in Husb. & Gard.* 49 Plants have . . some organical Parts, that are . . like some . . we may observe in Animals. **1733** Cheyne *Eng. Malady* I. x. §2 Is not every Animal a Machine of an infinite Number of organical Parts? [**1819** Rees *Cycl.*, Organical Part.]

4. Furnished with or consisting of organs, physically organized, as an animal or plant body; pertaining to or having the characteristics of an organized being: = organic 4.

1563–87 Foxe *A. & M.* (1684) III. 39 Organical, is called that which is a perfect body, having all the members and parts compleat belonging to the same. **1597** J. King *On Jonas* (1618) 624 The organicall body of a little Ant, is no lesse to bee wondred at, than the huge body of Behemoth. **1656** Stanley *Hist. Philos.* vi. (1701) 256/1 The Intellect is not confined to any part of the Body, as not being corporeal, nor organical, but immaterial and immortal. **1775** Reid *Let.* in Wks. I. 52/1 The result of such an organical structure as that of the brain. **1802** *Eng. Encycl.* VIII. 26/1 Our organical frame we call our *body*.

b. Dealing with the 'organic molecules' of Spallanzani; dealing with organized bodies.

1770 *Monthly Rev.* 531 The organical or molecular hypothesis. **1837** Whewell *Hist. Induct. Sc.* III. xvii. Introd. 378 The sciences which thus consider organization and vital functions may be termed organical sciences.

5. Pertaining to the bodily organs; belonging to the bodily or mental constitution, constitutional.

1643 R. O. *Man's Mort.* vi. 49 In man it is some organicall deficiency . . that is the cause, that some men are lesse rationall then others. **1669** Holder *Elem. Speech* 115 Deprived of Speech, not by any immediate Organical Indisposition. **1811** *Edin. Rev.* XVIII. 39 It is indeed much clearer that there is such an organical delight. [**1819** Rees *Cycl.*, Organical or Organic Diseases.]

6. Of the nature of, or pertaining to, an organized structure; organized; structural; = organic 6.

1659 Baxter *Key Cath.* II. iii. 427 He that is baptized into the Church, is baptized into an Organical body. **1674** Owen *Holy Spirit* (1693) 112 This various Distribution of Gifts makes the Church an Organical Body. **1786–1805** H. Tooke *Purley* (1829) I. Introd. 14 *B.* Where will you begin? *H.* Not with the organical part of language. **1802** *Eng. Encycl.*, That [judgment] which considers nature as one vast organical structure.

b. ? Making up the structure of something; constituent.

1794 G. Adams *Nat. & Exp. Philos.* IV. xlix. 351 These particles then are the organical parts of water.

7. ***organical vein***: the jugular vein (cf. prec. 8).

1607 Topsell *Four-f. Beasts* (1658) 223 The Organical vein of the neck, is the best letting of bloud, both in stoned and gelded Horses.

organically (ɔːˈgænɪkəlɪ), *adv.* [f. prec. + -ly[2].] In an organic or organical manner.

1. a. In relation to bodily organs or their functions; in the manner of an organized or living being; vitally. **b.** *Path.* In relation to the structure of an organ (opp. to *functionally*). **c.** From organic or organized matter (quot. 1882).

1681 Baxter *Acc. Sherlocke* vi. 211 If the Head, or Heart, . . be gone, the Soul will be gone, because the Body is not organically capable Matter. *a* **1704** Locke *Elem. Nat. Philos.* viii. (1754) 32 All stones, metals, and minerals, are real vegetables; that is, grow organically from proper seeds, as well as plants. **1857** *G. Bird's Urin. Deposits* (ed. 5) 155 When the kidneys are . . organically diseased, or even merely in a state of congestion. **1861** Bentley *Man. Bot.* 85 The bark . . surrounding the wood, to which it is organically connected by means of the medullary rays and cambium-layer. **1879** Miss Braddon *Vixen* III. 281 Do you mean that Mrs. Winstanley has heart disease—something organically wrong? **1882** Geikie *Text-bk. Geol.* II. II. §4. 106 Most of the organically derived detrital rocks are calcareous.

d. In relation to the constitution of a living being; constitutionally; structurally.

1862 H. Spencer *First Princ.* I. v. §32 (1875) 118 Were it not . . that we have been rendered in a considerable degree organically moral . . disastrous results would ensue from the removal of those strong and distinct motives. **1880** Disraeli *Endym.* xlii, Perhaps he was organically of that cheerful and easy nature, which is content to enjoy the present, and not brood over the past. **1887** Mrs. M. L. Woods *Village Tragedy* 216 Nothing's the matter—everything's the matter. She's organically weak.

e. Without the use of chemical fertilizers, pesticides, etc.

1971 *Countryman* Autumn 203/1 (Advt.), Homely atmosphere, quality food, organically grown vegetables, log fires. **1972** *Guardian* 3 Apr. 7/3 Apple pie . . . Wash apples (don't peel if organically grown). **1975** *Listener* 14 Aug. 204/2 Their last crop of the season, hand-grown, organically-manured leeks.

2. As parts of an organized whole.

1841 Myers *Cath. Th.* III. §11. 42 Though the two Testaments may justly be considered as organically connected into one living whole. **1880** R. W. Dale *Evangelical Revival* xiii. 277 The third chapter of John's Gospel and the fifth chapter of Matthew's Gospel are organically one.

†**3.** By means of instruments, mechanically. *Obs.*

1797 Brougham in *Phil. Trans.* LXXXVIII. 396 This curve may be described (organically) by drawing one end of a given flexible line . . along a straight line, whilst the other end is urged by a weight towards the same straight line.

or'ganicalness. *rare.* [f. as prec. + -ness.] The quality of being 'organical' or organic.

1675 Brooks *Gold. Key* Wks. 1867 V. 169 Christ's body had all the essential properties of a true body; such as are organicalness, extension, local presence, . . &c. **1727** in Bailey vol. II. **1755** in Johnson. Hence in mod. dicts.

organicism (ɔːˈgænɪsɪz(ə)m). [See -ism.]

1. a. The doctrine that organic structure is merely the result of an inherent property in matter to adapt itself to circumstances.

1883 *Church Times* XXI. 154/2 The objection that organicism excludes design, on the ground that the living creature has properties necessary to the fulfilment of its functions, and that all is explained by these properties, which produce the organs and set them to work.

b. The doctrine that everything in nature has an organic basis or explanation; that everything in nature is part of an organic whole (in sense of organic *a.* 6 a).

1912 A. Tridon tr. *Delage & Goldsmith's Theories Evol.* 163 In that respect, organicism is the perfect antithesis of Weismannism. **1928** *Jrnl. Philos. Stud.* Jan. 39 This is the reason why modern organicism, the organic theory of nature, seems so important for modern biology. **1945** [see HOLISM]. **1960** *Encounter* XV. II. 73 Mr. Tate and his friends ..were accused of sentimental organicism, of naïvely hoping to revive the virtues of the antique world by restoring its economic forms. **1969** *Times Lit. Suppl.* 20 Nov. 1341 Organicism..holds that some organic properties are not reducible to those of smaller parts. **1976** *Nature* 3 June 439/1 Reductionism rests on the belief that the whole can be fully explained in terms of the parts whereas organicism (biological holism) asserts that the whole cannot be fully explained in this way.

2. *Path.* 'The doctrine or theory which refers all disease to a material lesion of an organ' (*Syd. Soc. Lex.*).

1853 DUNGLISON *Med. Lex.*, *Organicism*,..The doctrine of the localization of disease. **1893** VIRCHOW in *Standard* 17 Mar., In the second period..they endeavoured to find in a certain region the actual organ which might be considered as the seat of disease. On this foundation arose the Parisian school of organicism, which, until late in this century, held a dominant position in pathology.

Hence **or'ganicist**, one who maintains a theory of organicism; also *attrib.* or as *adj.*; **organi'cistic** *a.*

1879 LEWES *Study Psychol.* 36 The two antagonistic schools of spiritualists and organicists, the one referring insanity to disease of the soul, the other to disease of the body. **1912** A. TRIDON tr. *Delage & Goldsmith's Theories Evol.* 164 Roux and the other organicists lay special stress on the factors of individual evolution. **1928** *Jrnl. Philos. Stud.* Jan. 29 That which was common to the organicists, said Delage, was that they regarded..life, the form of the body ..as resulting from the reciprocal play or struggle of all its elements. *Ibid.* 39 The organicistic schema formerly covered the living world, and now covers also the world of the non-living. **1941** J. NEEDHAM in P. A. Schilpp *Philos. A. N. Whitehead* 251 About the historical origins of the organicistic viewpoint in biology a great deal could be said. **1941** W. M. URBAN in *Ibid.* 304 Bergson from whom..the organicist philosophy has got its main insights. **1954** D. RIESMAN *Individualism Reconsidered* vi. 401 All such 'organicistic' analogies are..dangerous. **1969** P. A. ROBINSON *Freudian Left* 164 He [*sc.* Marcuse] argued that the Fascist conception of the state was in fact heir to the organicist tradition in political theory. **1971** *Nature* 24 Dec. 490/1 These factors are added to a resurgence of organicist philosophy and a revulsion against Jensenism. **1974** D. L. HULL *Philos. Biol. Sci.* 125 Exchanges between the so-called mechanists and organicists, materialists and vitalists, reductionists and holists, to mention but a few of the terms used to characterize the two sides of this perennial dispute. **1976** *Times Lit. Suppl.* 15 Oct. 1301/1 Extending the organicist thinking of his 'master', the Scottish planner and regionalist Patrick Geddes.

organicity (ɔːgəˈnɪsɪtɪ). [f. ORGANIC *a.* + -ITY.] The quality or state of being organic.

1936 V. A. DEMANT *Christian Polity* ix. 161 Instead of a return to true organicity, we have Collectivism, both in the patchwork of decaying Capitalism and in Russian Communism. **1945** *Mind* LIV. 53 This fourth and last of the distinctively mental properties..might be called 'organicity' as well as 'integration'. **1970** *Jrnl. Gen. Psychol.* July 110 Concepts relating to organicity and psychosis were excluded in order to limit the population of concepts. **1977** A. SHERIDAN tr. *J. Lacan's Écrits* vi. 213 Freud first threw light on the evolution itself of the process, thus making it possible to illuminate its own determination, by which I mean the only organicity that is essentially relevant to this process.

organie, variant of ORGANY.

organific (ɔːgəˈnɪfɪk), *a.* [f. L. *organ-um* ORGAN *sb.*[1] + -FIC.] Having the property or power of forming organs or organized structures; formative, organizing.

1840 J. H. GREEN *Vital Dynamics* 36 To..concentrate the organific energies. **1886** E. G. ROBINSON in *Chr. World Pulpit* XXX. 254/1 The vegetable seed in the ground decays, but the organific life-principle within it..organizes to itself a new body.

organification (ɔːˌgænɪfɪˈkeɪʃən). [f. ORGANI(C *a.* + -IFICATION.] Incorporation into an organic compound.

1937 *Nature* 15 May 836/1 (*heading*) Rate of 'organification' of phosphorus in animal tissues. **1966** WRIGHT & SYMMERS *Systemic Path.* II. xxxi. 1099/1 Thiocarbamide and aniline derivatives..impair organification of iodine in the thyroid. **1976** *Lancet* 27 Nov. 1191/2 Congenital goitres and hypothyroidism have been caused by maternal ingestion of iodides, presumably because the iodides had blocked the organification of iodine and induced pituitary-dependent thyroid hyperplasia.

organify (ɔːˈgænɪfaɪ), *v. Photogr.* [f. *organi(c* adj. + -FY.] In old collodion dry-plate processes, To impregnate with organic matter (such as albumen, gelatin, gum arabic, etc.) by means of a weak solution applied to the sensitized plate, in order to keep open the pores and increase the sensitiveness and durability of the plate. Hence **or'ganifier**, a solution used in this way.

1873 E. SPON *Workshop Receipts* ser. I. 264/1 The plate is not to be exposed immediately after it is organified. *Ibid.*, The Organifier must be applied after the removal of the plate from the rain-water pan... For the usual organifier employ albumen, 1 part; distilled water, from 3 to 6 parts.

organigram (ɔːˈgænɪgræm). Also **organogram**. [f. ORGANI(ZATION + -GRAM.] = *organization chart* (ORGANIZATION 4).

1962 A. SAMPSON *Anat. Brit.* xxvii. 437 (*caption*) The organogram of Shell October 1959. *Ibid.* xxx. 490 The aircraft companies, built up by brilliant pioneers like de Havilland or Sopwith, are passing painfully into an era of accountants and organograms. **1967** *Economist* 22 Apr. 392/2 A current joke is that Montedison is drawing up, not an organigram, but a 'baronigram'. **1975** A. BEEVOR *Violent Brink* iii. 64 Many notes had been taken..and doodles drawn. The CGS had a complicated organigram sketched in front of him. **1977** *Official Jrnl.* (Patent Office) 23 Nov. 3791 The first issue of the Official Journal of the European Patent Office will appear in December 1977. The contents will include..an organigram of the European Patent Organisation.

organism (ˈɔːgənɪz(ə)m). [f. ORGANIZE *v.*: see -ISM. Cf. F. *organisme* (1729 in Hatz.-Darm.).]

1. Organic structure; organization. Now *rare*.

1664 EVELYN *Sylva* (1776) 648 So astonishing and wonderful is the Organism, parts and functions of plants and trees. **1701** GREW *Cosm. Sacra* II. iii. §11 It is the advantagious Organism of the Eye, by which that is procured. **1890** J. MARTINEAU *Seat Author. Relig.* II. ii. §3. 245 From the complexion of the language and the organism of the style.

2. a. An organized or organic system; a whole consisting of dependent and interdependent parts, compared to a living being.

1768–74 TUCKER *Lt. Nat.* (1834) I. 474 When an artist has finished a fiddle to give all the notes in the gamut, but not without a hand to play upon it, this is an organism. **1840** CARLYLE *Heroes* vi. (1858) 365 To bridle-in that great devouring, self-devouring French Revolution; to tame it, so ..that it may become organic, and be able to live among other organisms and formed things, not as a wasting destruction alone. **1860** MOTLEY *Netherl.* (1868) I. vi. 299 The weight of the strong Protestant organism..might have balanced the great Catholic League. **1889** *Spectator* 16 Mar., An army is not a crowd of men, but a vast organism, travelling with indispensable baggage of enormous weight. **1900** J. D. ROBERTSON *Holy Spirit* iii. 53 Paul first taught us to speak of society as an organism.

b. *Philos.* The theory that in science everything is eventually an organic part of an integrated whole.

1925 A. N. WHITEHEAD *Sci. & Mod. World* (1926) 112 This doctrine involves the abandonment of the traditional scientific materialism, and the substitution of an alternative doctrine of organism. **1928** *Jrnl. Philos. Stud.* III. 33 He [*sc.* Lloyd Morgan] saw no reason why the term organism should not be applied to all those 'natural entities', as he called them, existing throughout the universe in emergent degrees of complexity. **1959** A. W. LEVI *Philos. & Mod. World* xii. 486 The 'philosophy of organism'..suggests the synthesis of incompatibles. **1965** E. E. HARRIS *Foundations of Metaphys. in Sci.* xiv. 282 The appropriate philosophy for contemporary science must be..a philosophy of organism.

3. a. An organized body, consisting of mutually connected and dependent parts constituted to share a common life; the material structure of an individual animal or plant.

Sometimes treated as something possessed by an animal or plant; sometimes, as in *minute organisms, a fossil organism*, identified with the animal or plant itself.

1842 H. MILLER *O.R. Sandst.* i. (ed. 2) 40 There are formations which yield their organisms slowly to the discoverer. **1858** LEWES *Sea-side Stud.* 157 The simplest organisms breathe, exhale, secrete, absorb, and reproduce by their envelopes alone. **1882** A. W. WARD *Dickens* vii. 205 A mental and moral vigour supported by a splendid physical organism. **1889** A. R. WALLACE *Darwinism* 11 The total number of living organisms in the world does not, and cannot, increase year by year. **1894** H. NISBET *Bush Girl's Rom.* 60 Wounded and insulted in the most sensitive part of his organism.

b. Organized existence in the mass.

1887 RUSKIN *Præterita* II. 336 That quality of beauty which I now saw to exist through all the happy conditions of living organism.

4. organism-environment, designating the relationship between an animal and its surroundings.

1946 C. MORRIS *Signs, Lang. & Behavior* iii. 84 One action rather than another..is 'required' by the organism-environment situation. **1958** *New Biol.* XXVI. 84 His [*sc.* man's] social, mental, and technological achievements do not make his 'organism-environment' relationship less important than that of other animals. **1969** *Listener* 13 Nov. 655/1 What lemmings are supposed to do when they get too many has become almost apocryphal and the simile has been used often enough to prophesy courses of human behaviour by people who have no understanding of lemmings or their environment or of the organism-environment relation.

Hence **orga'nismal** *a.*, of, pertaining, or relating to organisms.

1861 WILSON & GEIKIE *Mem. E. Forbes* iv. 125 The power of organic chemistry to alter and extend the organismal sciences was felt and acknowledged by all. **1887** *Athenæum* 7 May 611/3 The internal or organismal [explanation of evolution] as naturally commences with the fundamental rhythm of variation in the lowest organism in nature.

organismic (ɔːgəˈnɪzmɪk), *a.* [f. ORGANISM + -IC.] Of or pertaining to an organism; applied esp. to theories, etc., relating to interdependence or organic unity. Hence **orga'nismically** *adv.*

1886 J. C. BURNETT (*title*) Diseases of the skin, from the organismic standpoint. **1921** C. M. CHILD *Origin & Devel. Nervous Syst.* i. 3 The problem..is the problem of the nature and origin of the pattern which constitutes the organism as a whole, whether it consists of one cell or many, in short, the problem of organismic pattern. [*Note*] In view of the fact that the word 'organism', which implies the existence of a unity and order in the entity so designated, is universally accepted and employed, the word 'organismic' is not only biologically and etymologically justified but fills a need which is becoming more and more apparent. **1923** *Psychol. Bull.* XX. 684 (*heading*) The organismic vs. the mentalistic attitude toward the nervous system. **1934** *Jrnl. Philos. Sci.* I. 474 Having thus given, in organismic terms, a brief over-view of the nature and content of thought, we may now consider for a moment its logical aspect. **1943** C. L. HULL *Princ. Behavior* ii. 28 The basic principles of organismic behavior are to be viewed against a background of organic evolution. **1948** M. SHERIF *Outl. Social Psychol.* I. ii. 29 The perfectly defensible organismic position..holds that typical reactions of the organism are not fragmentary and that the conceptual or abstract level of psychological functioning is the level of human functioning in the normal conditions of civilized life. **1951** E. E. EVANS-PRITCHARD *Social Anthropol.* iii. 54 Professor Radcliffe-Brown has.. clearly and consistently stated the functional, or organismic theory of society. **1961** WEBSTER, Organismically. **1967** *Encycl. Philos.* V. 549/1 The term 'organismalism' was coined by the zoologist W. E. Ritter in 1919 to describe the theory that..'the organism in its totality is as essential to an explanation of its elements as its elements are to an explanation of the organism'. Subsequent writers have largely replaced 'organismal' with..'organismic' as a title for this theory. **1971** *Jrnl. Gen. Psychol.* LXXXV. 230 This finding suggests that cognitive style is organismically based. **1975** *Nature* 27 Mar. 370/2 Luria emphasises molecular aspects of biology, but not to the exclusion of organismic aspects.

organist (ˈɔːgənɪst). [f. ORGAN *sb.*[1] + -IST, after med.L. *organista*, or F. *organiste* (15th c. in Hatz.-Darm.).]

1. One who plays an organ; *spec.* a person appointed to play the organ at the services in a church or other place of worship.

1591 in *Gentl. Mag.* (1779) XLIX. 85 She gaue a newe name unto one of their Pauans, made long since by Master Thomas Morley, then Organist of Paules Church. **1597** MORLEY *Introd. Mus.* 154 This point..might well enough be left out, though it be very usuall with our Organists. **1640** in Rushw. *Hist. Coll.* III. (1692) I. 165 Sir Nathanael Brent, and Sir John Lamb, Summoned for laying a Tax upon the Town of Hodsden in the County of Bucks, contrary to Law, for the maintaining a pair of Organs and an Organist. **1712** STEELE *Spect.* No. 503 ¶2 The organist observed it, and he thought fit to play to her only. **1835** WILLIS *Melanie* 364 The organist play'd out the hymn.

b. A player on a street- or barrel-organ.

1793 *Trial T. Muir at Edinb.* 38 That she has been sent by Mr. Muir to an organist in the streets of Glasgow, and desired him to play *ça ira*.

†**2.** A maker of organs; an organ-builder. *Obs.*

1594 T. B. *La Primaud. Fr. Acad.* II. 96 How much more ..ought wee to admire that great and diuine organist, that hath made those goodly organs of mans body, and giuen them such a good sound? **1609** HOLLAND *Amm. Marcell.* 327 Sericus an Organist [*Organarius*] or maker of instruments. **1653** URQUHART *Rabelais* I. xxiv, Looking-glasse-framers, Printers, Organists, and other such kinde of artificers.

†**3.** *Mediæval Mus.* = ORGANIZER 2. *Obs.*

1782 BURNEY *Hist. Mus.* II. ii. 75 *note. Ibid.* 136 The four singers of the Alleluja are called Organists of the Alleluja, because they *organize* the melody of it. **1819** [see ORGANIZE *v.* 3].

4. A West Indian song-bird, a species of *Euphonia*, esp. *E. musica*. [F. *organiste* Buffon.] Also ***organist tanager***.

1882 OGILVIE, *Organist tanager*, a species of finch of the genus Tanagra, peculiar to the New World, so called from its musical powers. **1894** NEWTON *Dict. Birds*, *Organist*, the English rendering of the *Organiste* of Buffon (*Hist. Nat. Ois.* iv. p. 290), though it may be questionable whether all the information he cites really refers to this species.

†**organister, -tre.** *Obs.* [a. OF. *organ-*, *orguenistre*, earlier form of *organiste*: see -ISTER.] = prec. 1.

c **1314** *Guy Warw.* (A.) (1887) p. 396 Organisters and gode stiuours, Minstrels of mouþe, and mani dysour, To glade þo bernes bliþe. **1387** TREVISA *Higden* (Rolls) II. 227 Tubal þat was fadre of organistres and of harpores [L. *canentium in cithara et organo*]. *c* **1440** *Promp. Parv.* 369/1 Orgonyster (*S.* organer), *orgonista*, *organicus*.

orga'nistic, *a. rare.* [f. as ORGANIST + -IC.]

a. Of or pertaining to organists or the organ.

1840 BUSBY *Dict. Mus.*, *Organistic*, an adjective indicating that the music to which it refers, is composed for the organ.

b. Of or pertaining to an organism; based on organisms.

1910 *Fabian News* XXI. 16/1 He adopts the organistic view of society—that society is a being. **1953** *Essays in Crit.* III. 429 Is it speech about individual things..or speech about their feeling of being related, a Whiteheadian organistic 'feeling'?

organistrum (ɔːgəˈnɪstrəm). [a. med.L. *organistrum*, f. *organum* organ.] A name for the earliest form of hurdy-gurdy (see quots. 1954, 1974.)

[*c* **1350** *Nova Legenda Anglie* (1901) II. 310 Tundalus.. uidit quasi castrum et papiliones plurimas..in quibus chordas et organa, timpana et citharas cum organistris et cymbalis canentes..audierat.] **1870** C. ENGEL *Descr. Catal. Mus. Instrum. S. Kensington Mus.* 38 The *organistrum* had three strings, producing three different tones, which appear to have consisted of the tonic, fifth, and octave. **1940** C. SACHS *Hist. Mus. Instruments* (1942) xiv. 272 The hurdy-gurdy then [*sc.* in the 13th century] was no longer called *organistrum*, but *symphonia* in Latin (or rather Greek), *chifonie* in French and *cinfonia* in Spanish. **1954** *Grove's Dict. Mus.* (ed. 5) IV. 416/1 In the 12th century the organistrum was about five feet in length, and two executants were required, one of them to turn the handle which moves the wheel (*rotulus*) and the other to manipulate the key-mechanism (*plectra*). There were three strings, the outer tuned in octaves, the middle one a fourth or fifth below the highest string. **1960** *Times* 10 June 4/5 The New York performers [of the *Ludus Danielis*], however, have added an orchestra consisting of a trumpet, soprano recorder, oboe, carillon, handbells, viola, hurdy-gurdy (organistrum), [etc.]. **1974** *Encycl. Brit. Macropædia* X. 437/1 The organistrum, a large medieval hurdy-gurdy operated by two players: one turned a crank rotating a wheel that rubbed against one or more strings to make them sound, while the other produced different notes by turning the key-shaped levers that stopped the strings at various points.

organistry (ˈɔːgənɪstrɪ). *rare.* [f. ORGANIST + -RY.] The post of organist.

1890 *Peel City Guardian* 19 July 4/1 He..held the local town hall organistry.

ˈorganistship. [f. ORGANIST + -SHIP.] The position or office of organist.

1889 *Grove's Dict. Mus.* IV. 594 He resigned the organistship of St. Patrick's in 1810.

orˈganity. *rare.* [irreg. f. ORGAN *sb.*[1]: see -ITY.] †**1.** The condition of having organs, or of being organic; organization. *Obs.*

1647 H. MORE *Song of Soul* II. I. II. xxiv, In their ethereall corporeity, Devoid of heterogeneall organity.

2. An organized whole or organism.

1929 R. BRIDGES *Testament of Beauty* iv. 801 These perfected unify'd organities..all act in response to external stimulants.

organizable (ˈɔːgənaɪzəb(ə)l), *a.* [f. ORGANIZE *v.* + -ABLE. So mod.F. *organisable* (Littré).] Capable of being organized; *spec.* in *Biol.* Capable of being converted into organized or living tissue.

1679 M. RUSDEN *Further Discov. Bees* 6 An organizable or animable matter extracted by the Honey-Bees from Trees, Plants, Flowers, &c. **1806** KNIGHT in *Phil. Trans.* XCVII. 111 A pulpous organisable mass. **1875** BENNETT & DYER *Sachs' Bot.* 619 They mainly form the organised and organisable part of the plant and of every individual cell.

Hence **ˌorganizaˈbility**, capability of being organized; or of being formed into living tissues.

1839–47 TODD *Cycl. Anat.* III. 754/1 A fluid..entirely destitute of organizability. **1847–9** *Ibid.* IV. 507/2.

†**orgaˈnizate**, *ppl. a. Obs. rare*⁻¹. [ad. med.L. *organīzātus*, pa. pple. of *organīzāre* to ORGANIZE.] Furnished with organs; organized.

1647 H. MORE *Song of Soul* III. App. xxi, Death our spirits doth release From this distinguish'd organizate sense.

organization (ˌɔːgənaɪˈzeɪʃən, ɔːgənɪˈzeɪʃən). [ad. med.L. *organīzātio*, n. of action from *organīzāre*.]

1. a. The action of organizing, or condition of being organized, as a living being; connexion and co-ordination of parts for vital functions or processes; also, the way in which a living being is organized; the structure of an organized body (animal or plant), or of any part of one; bodily (*rarely* mental) constitution.

1432–50 tr. *Higden* (Rolls) II. 213 The body of man was.. so proporcionate to the sawle that equalite of complexion was in hit, conformite of organizacion. **1664** POWER *Exp. Philos.* I. 82 The several wayes and Organization of the Body [are] inscrutable. **1690** LOCKE *Hum. Und.* II. xxvii. 179 That being then one Plant, which has such an Organization of Parts in one coherent Body. **1706** PHILLIPS, *Organization*, a forming of Organs or Instrumental Parts. **1807** J. E. SMITH *Phys. Bot.* 7 Their curious crystallization bears some resemblance to organization, but performs none of its functions. **1882** VINES *Sachs' Bot.* 904 Only in a few plants of low organisation does a fertile union take place between sister-cells.

b. The fact or process of becoming organized or organic; in *Path.* conversion into living tissue.

1804 ABERNETHY *Surg. Obs.* 12 Its [a tumour's] organization depends upon actions begun and existing in itself. **1873** T. H. GREEN *Introd. Pathol.* (ed. 2) 326 A thrombus which is undergoing a process of organization gradually diminishes in size,..and ultimately it becomes converted into a fibro-cellular cord.

c. *concr.* An organized structure, body, or being; an organism.

1707 *Curios. in Husb. & Gard.* 27 The Contexture of Plants; whose structure is an Organization compos'd of Fibres. **1768–74** TUCKER *Lt. Nat.* (1834) II. 283 In the worst-formed bodies, and most untoward organizations, there lies an immortal spirit. **1860** DICKENS *Uncomm. Trav.* vi, I must stuff into my delicate organisation, a currant pin-cushion which I know will swell into immeasurable dimensions when it has got there. **1876** GEO. ELIOT *Dan. Der.* II. III. xxiii. 97 Choice organisations—natures framed to love perfection.

2. a. *gen.* The action of organizing or putting into systematic form; the arranging and co-ordinating of parts into a systematic whole.

1816 J. SCOTT *Vis. Paris* (ed. 5) 255 In the organization of forms, Rubens was a most extraordinary being. **1841** W. SPALDING *Italy & It. Isl.* II. 131 To gain strength..by self-dependence and internal organization. **1862** HELPS (*title*) On Organization in Daily Life. **1897** MARY KINGSLEY *W. Africa* 364 The organisation of a service of transport was then proceeded with.

b. The condition of being organized; the mode in which something is organized; co-ordination of parts or elements in an organic whole; systematic arrangement for a definite purpose.

1790 BURKE *Fr. Rev.* 30 They acted by the ancient organized states in the shape of their old organization and not by the organic moleculæ of a disbanded people. **1832** tr. *Sismondi's Ital. Rep.* xi. 240 The Turks arrived in Europe with an organization wholly military. **1849** MACAULAY *Hist. Eng.* vi. II. 129 Compensated by a great superiority of intelligence, vigour, and organization. **1875** JEVONS *Money* (1878) 257 The organization of the Clearing House will be described in the next chapter.

c. *concr.* An organized body, system, or society. Esp. as ***social organization*** in *Sociol.* and *Anthropol.*

1829 J. S. MILL *Let.* 7 Nov. in *Wks.* (1963) XII. 40 Several great steps should be taken in the improvement of the social organisation. **1865** —— *Auguste Comte* 88 In constructing.. a theory of society, all the different aspects of the social organization must be taken into consideration at once. **1873** H. SPENCER *Study Sociol.* vii. 175 Sentiments and beliefs in ..harmony with the social organization in which they are incorporated. **1880** McCARTHY *Own Times* IV. liv. 169 This vast organisation had apparently sprung out of the ground. **1882** L. STEPHEN *Sci. of Ethics* iii. 109 This vast social organization is the work of a vast series of generations unconsciously fashioning the order which they transmit to their descendants. **1894** *Durh. Univ. Jrnl.* 15 Dec. 104 We now have in the University..somewhere about fifty-three different 'Organizations', athletic, intellectual, literary, social, and religious. **1914** W. H. RIVERS *Kinship & Social Organisation* 1 The aim of these lectures is to demonstrate the close connection which exists between methods of denoting relationship or kinship and forms of social organisation. **1937** R. H. LOWIE *Hist. Ethnol. Theory* xii. 225 Most important of all..is Radcliffe-Brown's contribution to Australian social organization. **1944** *Mind* LIII. 352 Social organisation should be designed to encourage change in desirable directions. **1951** E. E. EVANS-PRITCHARD *Social Anthropol.* i. 12 The social organization of the Yao of southern Nyasaland. **1952** GERTH & MARTINDALE tr. *Weber's Anc. Judaism* I. i. 15 In Israelite antiquity, social organization is usually articulated in terms of father houses. **1967** M. ARGYLE *Psychol. Interpersonal Behaviour* iv. 73 A great deal of social behaviour takes place against a background of social organization—in families, industry, hospitals, and elsewhere. 'Social organization' means the existence of a series of ranks, positions or offices—such as father, foreman, hospital sister, etc. which persist regardless of particular occupants. **1974** R. J. SMITH (*title*) Social organization and the applications of anthropology.

d. Phr. ***organization and methods*** (see quot. 1968).

1959 *Listener* 10 Dec. 1020/1 Organization and Methods may indeed prove that the central principles of local government are irrational. **1963** *Ibid.* 28 Feb. 389/2 The Old English state was a ramshackle..affair, lying in 1066 wide open to a take-over bid from William the Conqueror and certain to benefit both spiritually and materially from the brisk and ruthless operations of his Organization-and-Methods men. **1968** JOHANNSEN & ROBERTSON *Managem. Gloss.* 97 *Organisation and Methods* (*O & M*), 1. An advisory service for management specifically designed to assist in obtaining maximum efficiency and accuracy in organisation and procedures. 2. The application of work study and other management techniques to administration procedures and systems within a company. **1969** J. ARGENTI *Managem. Techniques* 189 Organisation and Methods is a group of techniques rather similar to Work Study but applied usually to office work. **1971** K. GOTTSCHALK in B. de Ferranti *Living with Computer* v. 46 Groups concerned with efficiency in the office are sometimes called organization and methods (O & M) groups.

3. *Mediæval Mus.* The singing of the ORGANUM.

1782 BURNEY *Hist. Mus.* II. ii. 135 There can be no doubt but that some instrument had been used in the singing schools to teach this *organization*. **1880** W. S. ROCKSTRO in *Grove's Dict. Mus.* II. 609 Hucbaldus,..who died..in the year 930,..prefers no claim to be regarded as the orginator of the new method of Singing, but speaks of it as a practice 'which they commonly call organization'.

4. Special comb.: **organization centre** *Embryol.* [tr. G. *organisationszentrum* (H. Spemann 1921, in *Arch. f. Entwicklungsmech. d. Organismen* XLVIII. 568)], a region of an embryo that acts as an inductor (INDUCTOR 5); **organization chart**, a graphic representation of the structure of an organization showing the relationships of the positions or jobs within it; **organization man** orig. *U.S.*, a man who subordinates his individuality and his personal life to the organization he serves.

[**1927** H. SPEMANN in *Proc. R. Soc.* B. CII. 180 The region of the early gastrula where these organizers lie may be called for the present a 'centre of organization'.] **1928** *Biol. Abstr.* II. 1320/2 Experiments..confirm the assumption that the organization centers are localized in the 2 cell stage. **1935** *Discovery* May 136/2 If..an organisation centre is grafted out of its usual place..it will cause these new surroundings to develop into a complete embryo or complete organ. **1956** C. H. WADDINGTON *Princ. Embryol.* x. 177 The extent of the organisation centre was examined by inserting small fragments of one gastrula into the blastocoel cavity of another. **1941** P. E. HOLDEN et al. *Top-Managem. Organization* 5 A good organization chart for the company as a whole, with auxiliary charts for each major division, is an essential first step in the analysis, clarification, and understanding of any organization plan. **1958** L. A. ALLEN *Managem. & Organization* III. xiii. 289 The organization chart is a graphic means of showing organization data. **1967** *Harper's Mag.* Jan. 38 (*title*) How to Read an Organization Chart for Fun and Survival. **1970** *Time* 10 Aug. 8 According to the tidy White House organization charts, the key influence on presidential decisions in all but foreign affairs ought to be the Domestic Affairs Council, headed by John Ehrlichman. **1956** W. H. WHYTE (*title*) The organisation man. **1958** J. K. GALBRAITH *Affluent Society* xviii. 208 Our liberties are now menaced by the conformity exacted by the large corporation and its impulse to create..the organization man. **1958** A. HUXLEY *Let.* 16 Feb. (1969) 847 It justifies the Organization Men and the dictators in satisfying their urge for tidiness. **1958** *Economist* 4 Oct. 27/1 Are we gradually getting our equivalents of the 'organisation man', smooth, able, well-adjusted, unexceptionable—and unexceptional? **1960** KOESTLER *Lotus & Robot* 277, I loathe crooners and swooners..the Organization Man and the *Reader's Digest*. **1966** N. FREELING *King of Rainy Country* 27 Canisius is just an accountant, an organisation man. A nobody. **1972** 'J. QUARTERMAIN' *Rock of Diamond* xiii. 74 He's expendable, an organisation man and a useful commodity in America.

Hence **organiˈzationist**, one who advocates or practises organization in any department.

1881 *Temperance Record* 14 July 433/1 It may be desirable to consider..whether some organisational change could not with advantage be made. **1885** *Pall Mall G.* 29 May 3/1 Two of the largest cities in the States advertised for a skilled 'charity organizationist'. **1895** *Westm. Gaz.* 23 Sept. 3/3 A convinced Charity Organisationist.

organiˈzational, *a.* [f. ORGANIZATION + -AL[1].] Of or pertaining to organization.

1938 I. KUHN *Assigned to Adventure* xxx. 315 Fox itself went through three complete organizational changes in less than two years. **1960** *Guardian* 12 July 1/7 The high noon of the twentieth century 'organisational man'. **1962** A. BATTERSBY *Guide to Stock Control* vii. 62 Such organizational problems are combined with investigations of the nervous systems of animals and the design of servo-mechanisms in the new studies called cybernetics. **1964** M. ARGYLE *Psychol. & Social Probl.* xiv. 171 *Organizational pathology* refers to the tendency for organizations to become ineffective in several characteristic ways. The most familiar trouble is the over-elaboration of formal rules and procedures, seen by the outsider as 'red-tape'. **1965** *New Society* 22 Apr. 14/3 Industry has its problems. Can organisational psychology help? **1969** J. ARGENTI *Managem. Techniques* v. 22 *All* organisations..have organisational problems. **1970** T. LUPTON *Managem. & Social Sci.* (ed. 2) iii. 71 The organizational environment for maximum performance and human satisfaction. **1973** A. DUNDES *Mother Wit* p. xiii, Having explained the organizational plan of the book, I should like to add a final word about the title.

Hence **organiˈzationally** *adv.*

1933 *Times Lit. Suppl.* 15 June 415/3 This is a moment for fresh, organizationally detached and sympathetically cooperative thinking. **1959** *Internat. Jrnl. Appl. Radiation & Isotopes* VI. 305/1 Even were technical feasibility successfully achieved, the firms organizationally capable of using the process and exploiting its marginal advantages are few. **1962** *B.B.C. Handbk.* 94 Organizationally, the External Services are an integral part of the BBC. **1976** *Nature* 8 July 88/3 'Organisationally,' it says, 'OTA lacks the minimum of orderly structure.'

organizator (ˈɔːgənaɪˌzeɪtə(r)). *Embryol.* [ad. G. *organisator* organizer (given this sense by H. Spemann 1921, in *Arch. f. Entwicklungsmech. d. Organismen* XLVIII. 568).] = ORGANIZER 2, INDUCTOR 5.

1924 *Nature* 23 Feb. 276/2 Spemann has proved that the dorsal-lip region is a differentiator (or 'organisator' as he styled it). **1928** *Biol. Abstr.* II. 1320/2 Embryos with 1 axis are harmonically built, developing from germs in which 'organizators' lie close beside each other. **1939** E. E. JUST *Biol. Cell Surface* xi. 290 By experiment it is possible to analyze the factors which set up the conditions for differentiations in a more normal or natural manner than.. in experiments with transplantations involving conceptions of 'organizators' and the like.

ˌorganiˈzatory, *a.* [f. med.L. *organizat-*, ppl. stem of *organizāre*, see ORGANIZE *v.* + -ORY[2].] Of or pertaining to organization.

1921 *Public Opinion* 17 June 560/1 The merely organisatory work of delivering wooden houses and materials to France. **1926** *Ibid.* 2 July 15/3 If the question of women's professions was a theoretical and ethical problem in the beginning, it must be regarded as an intellectual and organisatory one nowadays.

organize (ˈɔːgənaɪz), *v.* [ad. med.L. *organīzāre*, *-izāre*, f. *organ-um* ORGAN *sb.*[1]: see -IZE. Cf. F. *organiser*, *-izer* (14th c. in Hatz.-Darm.).]

1. a. *trans.* To furnish with organs; to render organic; to give the structure and interdependence of parts which subserves vital processes; to form into a living being, or living tissue. Usually in *pa. pple.*; see also ORGANIZED 1.

1413 *Pilgr. Sowle* (Caxton 1483) IV. xxv. 70 The body was organysed kyndely in power for to receyuen the sowle withynne hym. **1597** HOOKER *Eccl. Pol.* v. lviii, Even as the soul doth organize the body, and give unto every member thereof that substance, quantity, and shape, which nature seeth most expedient. **1664** POWER *Exp. Philos.* I. 16 Some Cheese Mites we could see (as little..as a Mustard-seed) yet perfectly shap'd and organiz'd. **1707** *Curios. in Husb. & Gard.* 319 Can a meer Vegetable become organiz'd to form it self into a flying Animal like a Duck? **1873** T. H. GREEN *Introd. Pathol.* (ed. 2) 326 The thrombus when once formed either becomes organized or softens. **1874** LUBBOCK *Orig. & Met. Ins.* i. 7 In the perfect state they are highly organized.

b. *intr.* for *refl.* To become organic, be formed into living tissue.

1880 MACCORMAC *Antisept. Surg.* 147 The coagulum left behind undisturbed will presently organise.

2. a. *gen.* To form into a whole with mutually connected and dependent parts; to co-ordinate parts or elements so as to form a systematic whole (with either the whole or the parts as object); to give a definite and orderly structure to; to systematize; to frame and put into working order (an institution, enterprise, etc.); to arrange or 'get up' something involving united action.

1632 LITHGOW *Trav.* x. 488, I Organize the Truth, you Allegate the Sense. **1791** BURKE *App. Whigs* Wks. VI. 231 The several orders..so organized and so acting..they were the people of France. **1799** WELLINGTON in Gurw. *Desp.* I. 42 Col. Wellesley was long occupied in..organizing the civil as well as the military establishments. **1855** MILMAN *Lat. Chr.* IX. viii. (1864) V. 380 No philosophising Christian ever organised or perpetuated a sect. **1874** GREEN *Short Hist.* ii. §6. 86 A vast conspiracy was organized to place Stephen of Albemarle..upon the throne. *Mod.* To organize a picnic, a procession, a disturbance, opposition.

b. *intr.* for *refl.*

1887 *Amer. Jrnl. Philol.* VIII. 187 The men organize and, as Choros of old men, approach with hostile intent, but are worsted in the encounter that ensues. **1904** 'MARK TWAIN' *$30,000 Bequest* (1906) 7 When we organize, we'll get three shares for one. **1966** *McGraw-Hill Encycl. Sci. & Technol.* II. 614/2 They may organize into complex structures such as plastids. **1976** *Spare Rib* Nov. 26/4 This is not the first time women have organised for peace.

c. *trans.* With a person as obj.: to provide for; to make (special) arrangements for. Also *refl.*

1892 'MARK TWAIN' *Amer. Claimant* ii. 35 I'll get you organized in no time. **1952** M. TRIPP *Faith is Windsock* iv. 72 'Where's Arthur?' asked Bergen. 'Gone off with a Waaf, I think. Jake's organised too.' **1959** 'M. CRONIN' *Dead & Done With* viii. 122 There were going to be official complaints reaching the office in the morning about his activities... He felt he could organize himself out of most of it. **1977** B. PYM *Quartet in Autumn* v. 46 She was the kind of person who liked to keep herself to herself and must not be organized in any way.

d. *trans.* To arrange (personally); to take responsibility for providing (something); to 'fix up'. *colloq.*

1952 M. LASKI *Village* ix. 141 Martha organized a scratch meal. **1972** G. DURRELL *Catch me a Colobus* ix. 179 We spent the rest of the day organizing a car to take us to Mexico City the following morning. **1976** P. HILL *Hunters* v. 55 Got a big job fer you, son... Organize some sandwiches from the pub.

3. *Mus.* To sing the ORGANUM or accompaniment to a plain-song. (*intr.* and *trans.*)

[= Med.L. *organizāre*, 13th c. in Du Cange '4 clericis qui organizabunt Alleluya, cuilibet 6 den'.]

1782 BURNEY *Hist. Mus.* II. ii. 132 About the time that the organ was received in churches and convents, the Gregorian chant began to be *organized* by voices, in the manner which was afterwards called *Discant*. *Ibid.* 135 Hubald and Odo.. as well as Guido, speak frequently, in their treatises, of *organizing*. **1819** *Pantologia, Organists*, the old name applied to those Romish priests who organized, or sung in parts... Certain priests or clerks,..generally four of them,..sung in parts, i.e. they organized the melody; particularly that applied to the word Hallelujah, by adding to it other parts, and thence were called Organists of the Hallelujah.

4. *trans.* To acquire deviously or illicitly; to obtain cleverly (orig. *Mil. slang*). Cf. G. *organisieren* Mil. slang in same senses.

1941 *New Statesman* 30 Aug. 218/3 *Organise*, to acquire illicitly. (A new R.A.F. equivalent for the last-war word 'win', meaning to 'scrounge'). **1942** *R.A.F. Jrnl.* 16 May 12 Even the plugs in the washbasins are replaced. Why do people like to 'organize' those plugs? They just fade away.. and have to be replaced; but what use they are to the lads who make them souvenirs, few know. **1957** H. ROOSENBURG *Walls came tumbling Down* ii. 53 The verb 'to organize' had been widely in use in the [Nazi] prisons and camps and simply meant to acquire what one needed by stealing, bamboozling, or any other means at one's disposal. *Ibid.* iii. 73 Those Frenchwomen..were busy organizing some sausages from a reluctant butcher.

Hence **'organizing** *vbl. sb.* and *ppl. a.*

1599 MINSHEU *Sp. Dict.*, *Organizo*, the organizing or drawing the body into his parts and members. **1856** FROUDE *Hist. Eng.* (1858) I. i. 11 The feudal system was still the organizing principle of the nation. **1861** STANLEY *East. Ch.* i. 43 The organising centralising tendency which prevailed in the West. **1865** MILL in *Evening Star* 10 July, Mr. Hare's was the most practical and organizing head that he knew. **1876** STAINER & BARRETT *Dict. Mus. Terms* 131 The first step towards harmony was to allow the organizing voices to have a choice of intervals. **1880** E. H. DONKIN in Grove *Dict. Mus.* I. 324 A rude style of part-singing, called 'organising', had been known for centuries before the Reformation.

organized ('ɔːgənaɪzd), *ppl. a.* [-ED¹.]

1. Furnished with organs; composed of parts connected and co-ordinated for vital functions or processes; that is, or has been, endowed with physical life, as an animal or plant body, or any part of one; living; organic.

1598 FLORIO, *Organizzato*, well proportioned, organised. **1647** H. MORE *Poems* 86 Here dare I not define't, th' Entelechie Of organized bodies. **1665–6** *Phil. Trans.* I. 200 The Body of the Chick seems but a little Organized Gelly. **1733** CHEYNE *Eng. Malady* I. x. §4 (1734) 94 There may be *Animalcula* or Organised living Bodies of all Sizes. **1802** PALEY *Nat. Theol.* xxiii. (1819) 373 Plants or animals, i.e. organized bodies, with parts bearing strict and evident relation to one another and to the utility of the whole. **1874** ROSCOE *Elem. Chem.* xxvii. 290 Such an organized structure is seen in the simple cell, the germ of living organisms.

2. a. *gen.* Formed into a whole with interdependent parts; co-ordinated so as to form a system or orderly structure; systematically arranged.

1817 WYNN in *Parl. Debates* 357 Until it was necessary to meet the organized rebels in the field of battle. **1874** MORLEY *Compromise* (1886) 40 All other organised priesthoods..move within formularies even more inelastic.

b. Acquired deviously, illicitly, or cleverly. (Cf. ORGANIZE *v.* 4.) *slang.*

1957 H. ROOSENBURG *Walls came tumbling Down* v. 127 They had moved in..with a few organized mules and removed all the stores.

3. Made like an organ, or like the sound of an organ.

1603 FLORIO *Montaigne* I. xx, Tunable and organized ones. **1819** *Pantologia, Organized Piano-forte*, an instrument of modern invention, consisting of an organ and piano-forte, so conjoined that the same set of keys serve for both. **1889** A. J. HIPKINS in Grove *Dict. Mus.* IV. 795 Two claviorgans or organized clavecins.

4. Of or pertaining to a coordinated criminal organization directing operations on a large or widespread scale, esp. in phr. ***organized crime***.

1929 J. LANDESCO *Organized Crime in Chicago* ii. 25 Organized crime is not, as many think, a recent phenomenon in Chicago. *Ibid.* ix. 205 Newspaper writers,.. interested in establishing the national and international ramifications of organized criminals. **1931** F. D. PASLEY *Muscling In* iii. 94 Next to beer and booze, organized prostitution yielded the heaviest profits. **1941** H. ASBURY *Underworld of Chicago* ix. 299 During the last few months of Mayor Harrison's final term Chicago was probably as free from organized vice as at any time in its history. **1952** TURKUS & FEDER *Murder, Inc.* i. 9 In all the history of crime, there has never been an example of organized lawlessness to equal the Syndicate. **1973** *Black Panther* 5 May 2/2 It is widely known that Inman is himself a kingpin in the city's organized crime and racket rings, as is Atlanta Mayor Sam Massell. **1975** *Globe & Mail* (Toronto) 3 June 1/9 He was named in police evidence before the Quebec organized crime inquiry as one of the four top lieutenants of the Godfather of organized crime in Montreal.

5. Special combs.: **organized games**, athletics or sports as organized in a school, college, etc.; **organized labour**, workers affiliated by membership in trade or labour unions.

1933 D. L. SAYERS *Murder must Advertise* xviii. 304 In Brotherhood's régime of bread and circuses, organised games naturally played a large part. **1944** L. P. HARTLEY *Shrimp & Anemone* i. 16 The world of day-schools and organized games. **1974** *Times* 5 Jan. 10/3 At modern Oxbridge there has been a decline in the participation by undergraduates in organized games. **1885** in C. Evans *Hist. United Mine Workers of Amer.* (1918) I. 131 To organized labor..and to the generous and sympathetic public..we return our sincere and heartfelt thanks. **1924** L. WOLMAN *Growth of Amer. Trade Unions* 82 The number of wage earners..would not be considered by some a thoroughly fair base for measuring the achievement in size of an organized labor movement. **1926** *Brit. Worker* 10 May 2/4 The fight to maintain the workers' standard of living will be won by the united forces of organised labour. **1948** *Time* 15 Mar. 27/2 He thought of himself as the leader of all the people, not just of organized labor. **1975** *Times* 7 Jan. 12/8 The rise of both organized labour and high management around the turn of the century.

organizer ('ɔːgənaɪzə(r)). [f. as prec. + -ER¹.]

1. a. One who organizes; one who arranges systematically (see ORGANIZE 2); sometimes (with qualifying adj.), one skilled in organization. Also *spec.*, one who 'organizes' criminal activity (cf. ORGANIZE *v.* 4).

1849 GROTE *Greece* II. xliii. V. 304 An organizer of that systematic espionage which broke up all freedom of speech. **1853** *Ibid.* II. lxxxvi. XI. 295 The ablest organiser and the most scientific tactician of his day. **1864** BURTON *Scot Abr.* I. i. 16 Wallace..an organiser..of his fellow-men. **1884** *Manch. Exam.* 22 Mar. 4/7 The organisers of obstruction. **1945** C. BURNEY *Dungeon Democracy* I. 19 He was an admirable 'organiser' at worst,..and succeeded in building up a private stock of those luxuries which did not come on the standard lists of the canteen. **1976** E. WARD *Hanged Man* iii. 15 Gold was now an organizer—setting up criminal work on commission.

b. *Mediæval Mus.* (See ORGANIZE 3.)

1880 W. S. ROCKSTRO in Grove *Dict. Mus.* II. 609 Nothing could be more natural than..that the choristers who practised that method of vocalisation should be called Organizers, though..they sang without any instrumental accompaniment whatever. **1881** *Ibid.* III. 61 *Quintoyer* (Old Eng. *Quinible*) To sing in Fifths—a French verb, in frequent use among extempore Organizers during the Middle Ages.

2. *Embryol.* [tr. G. *organisator* (see ORGANIZATOR).] = INDUCTOR 5.

1925 H. SPEMANN in *Brit. Jrnl. Exper. Biol.* II. 500, I have given the name of 'organisers' to cells capable of inducing the formation of new anlagen. **1927** —— in *Proc. R. Soc.* B. CII. 177 (*heading*) Organizers in animal development. **1934** [see EVOCATOR b]. **1946** [see INDUCTOR 5]. **1970** A. M. WINCHESTER *Concepts Zool.* xviii. 474/1 The transplanted dorsal lip acted as an organizer. **1975** *Nature* 13 Nov. 129/2 The organiser for the axial pattern of the whole body [of *Xenopus*] during amphibian development is a small group of cells at the dorsal lip of the blastopore.

'organless, *a.* [f. ORGAN *sb.*¹ + -LESS.]

1. Having no (bodily) organs.

1864 HUXLEY *Elem. Comp. Anat.* i. 11 It is structureless and organless and without definitely formed parts. **1898** *Pop. Sci. Monthly* LII. 490 Those organless organisms out of which the true cell only develops.

2. Having no organ (musical instrument).

1834 [see ORGANED 2]. **1897** *Daily News* 15 July 5/3 On the at present organless orchestra.

†**organ ling.** *Obs.* Also abbreviated **organ**. [Corrupted from *orgas ling*, comb. of *orgas*, ORGAYS, q.v. *Orkney ling* was an etymological conjecture.] A large kind of ling (fish).

1499– in Rogers *Agric. & Prices* III. 320, VI. 392– [Earlier entries have *orgays, orkays, orgas, orgas ling*: see ORGAYS.] Organ ling (many entries from Cambridge, Sion, Worksop, 1499–1593), orgayn ling (Camb. 1526); Organs (Camb. 1507–1623), organ (Camb. 1550–1627). **1526** *Ord. Hen. VIII* in *Househ. Ord.* (1790) 175 Organe Lyng—1 mess —3*d*. **1603** OWEN *Pembrokeshire* (1891) 42 Differinge as much from other people..as the Stockefishe or poore Johns doe from the lardge organ lynge. **1607** COWELL *Interpr.*, *Orgeis*..is the greatest sort of North sea-fish, now adaies called *Organ ling* [1672 *adds*: corruptly from *Orkney Ling*, because the best are near that Island]. **1655** MOUFET & BENNET *Health's Improv.* (1746) 245 Standing every Fish-day as a cold Supporter at my Lord Mayor's Table, yet is it nothing but a long Cod, whereof the greater sized is called Organ-Ling, and the other Codling, because it is no longer than a Cod, and yet hath the Taste of Ling. [**1887** ROGERS *Agric. & Prices* V. 419 Ling, sometimes called organ or great ling.]

†**'organly,** *a.* *Obs.* [f. ORGAN *sb.*¹ + -LY¹.] Pertaining to an organ or musical instrument, or resembling the sound of an organ.

1435 MISYN *Fire of Love* II. xii. 103 Gude ihesu, gyf me orgonly & heuenly songe of aungels.

organo-. Combining form of Gr. ὄργανον ORGAN, used in various technical terms, chiefly of Biology, etc. (ORGAN *sb.*¹ 5), rarely of Music (ORGAN *sb.*¹ 2). In many compounds a secondary stress may be given as ˌ*organo-* or *orˌgano-*, and is not indicated in the individual words listed below. **ˌorgano'leptic** *a.* [F. *organoleptique* (Chevreul), f. Gr. ληπτικός, f. λαμβάνειν to apprehend by the senses], said of the properties by which bodies act upon the senses and bodily organs (1857 Mayne); also, involving the use of the senses; hence **organo'leptically** *adv.*, as regards organoleptic properties; **ˌorganome'tallic** *a. Chem.*, 'a term applied to chemical compounds in which an organic radical is directly combined with a metal' (*Syd. Soc. Lex.*); also *absol.*, an organometallic compound; **ˌorgano'morphic** *a.* [*nonce-wd.* after ANTHROPOMORPHIC] (see quot.); **or'ganophone**, a musical instrument: see quot.; **ˌorgano'phonic** *a.* [Gr. φωνή voice], epithet assumed by a band of musicians who imitated various instruments with the voice; **orga'nophyly** [Gr. φῦλον race, tribe], the tribal history of the organs of living beings; **'organoˌplastic** *a.* [Gr. πλαστικός PLASTIC], having the property of forming or producing the bodily organs; so **'organoˌplasty**, the formation or development of the organs; †**ˌorganopoi'etical** *a. Obs.* [Gr. ποιητικός capable of making, productive: cf. Gr. ὀργανοποιικός of or for instrument-making] = *organoplastic*; **orga'noscopy** [Gr. -σκοπια looking, examination], examination of the organs; *spec.* a name for PHRENOLOGY; **organosedi'mentary** *a. Geol.*, produced by or involving sedimentation as affected by living organisms.

1852 T. R. BETTON tr. *Regnault's Elem. Chem.* I. 13 (*heading*) Of the different physical and *organoleptic characters by which bodies are distinguished. *Ibid.*, The organoleptic characters are those impressions produced on the organs of taste, smell, and touch. **1940** *Nature* 21 Dec. 796/1. Unimpeachable organoleptic evidence exists for the statement that even under modern conditions cheese-making is not by any means a fully controlled industrial process. **1963** W. SUMMER *Methods Air Deodorization* iii. 228 Science has failed, so far, to conceive of an instrument which might be called an artificial nose and which would allow comparisons..between organoleptic sensations and instrumental measurements. **1970** *Daily Tel.* (Colour Suppl.) 25 Sept. 32/2 Each morning he must check the contents of the 50 vats to ensure they are suitable for bottling. His responsibilities there are organoleptic, that is, he is concerned with the qualities of the senses—sight, taste and smell. **1976** *Daily Colonist* (Victoria, B.C.) 30 May 4/7 The U.S. Food and Drug Administration would be crippled without its organoleptic analysts. **1959** *Proc. Florida State Hort. Soc.* LXXII. 145/1 Celery air-expressed from California was compared with freshly harvested Florida celery in April and May of 1957. The samples were rated *organoleptically and analyzed chemically for several constituents. **1970** H. E. NURSTEN in A. C. Hulme *Biochem. Fruits & Products* I. x. 246 (*heading*) Organoleptically significant components of specific fruits. **1852** *Phil. Trans. R. Soc.* CXLII. 417, I have continued my researches upon the *organo-metallic bodies. **1857** MILLER *Elem. Chem.* III. 214 Several polymeric forms, besides other compounds of these organo-metallic bodies may be obtained. **1880** CLEMINSHAW *Wurtz' Atom. The.* 270 In organo-metallic radicals properly so called we find properties of the same order, which we interpret in the same manner. **1938** H. GILMAN *Org. Chem.* I. iv. 463 They [*sc.* organomercurials] are the only organo-metallics in the first two groups which can be manipulated in water. **1965** *New Scientist* 2 Dec. 658/1 Organometallics have already amply proved their worth as catalysts. **1974** *Encycl. Brit. Macropædia* XIII. 716/1 The syntheses of many specific organometallics are dictated by the particular properties or reactions of a single compound or group of compounds. **1976** *Nature* 4 Mar. 11/1 Thus, so far as σ-bonded transition metal organometallics are concerned, the realisation of the difference between their kinetics and thermodynamic stabilities has led several research groups to design stable molecules. **1886** *Kernel & Husk* 62 Some metaphors..

which describe Him [God] by reference to implements (such as a shield) may be called *organomorphic. **1880** *Advertisement*, *Organophone. (Debain, Inventor.) A close imitation of the brilliant and broad effects produced by a well-balanced pipe organ. **1890** *Stratford-on-Avon Herald* 19 Dec. 8/1 He joined an *organophonic band which travelled throughout the district, and gave variety entertainments. **1879** tr. *Haeckel's Evol. Man* I. i. 24 *Organo-phyly. **1864** WEBSTER, **Organoplastic*. **1879** tr. *De Quatrefages' Human Species* 122 Under the influence of the organo-plastic or evolutive force there were formed proto-organisms of a very simple structure. **1892** *Syd. Soc. Lex.*, *Hygienic *Organoplasty*, Roger-Collard's term for the art of developing organs by appropriate exercise of them. **1664** POWER *Exp. Philos.* I. 71 The Soul is in full exercise of her Plastick and *Organo-Poïetical Faculty. **1864** WEBSTER, **Organoscopy*,..phrenology. **1892** *Syd. Soc. Lex.*, *Organoscopy*, the examination of the several organs of the body in order to form an opinion concerning the..faculties ..and other endowments of the person. Also, a synonym of *Cranioscopy*. **1964** *Jrnl. Geol.* LXXII. 81/2 Algal stromatolites are laminated *organosedimentary structures formed by the activity of algal mats in binding fine particulate sediment. **1972** *Ibid.* LXXX. 592/1 'Molar tooth' structure..most likely resulted from organosedimentary processes similar to those forming algal stromatolites.

2. *Chem.* **a.** Prefixed to the names of elements to form adjs. designating compounds in which an atom of the element is bound to an organic radical; as ***organochlorine***, ***-lead***, ***-lithium***, ***-magnesium***, ***-mercury***, ***-phosphorus***, ***-silicon***, ***-tin***, ***-zinc***. These may also be used *absol.*

1961 *Jrnl. Econ. Entomol.* LIV. 636/1 The..effectiveness of six organochlorine insecticides applied to soil were determined in the field against *Hippelates* gnats. **1970** *Motor Boat & Yachting* 16 Oct. 25/2 Two serious disadvantages about the early organochlorines such as D.D.T. were that they were..concentrated in certain tissues of the bodies of successive predators. **1974** *Country Life* 26 Dec. 1984/2 The gradual decline in the use of organochlorine pesticides has allowed predatory birds..to re-establish themselves. **1861** *Q. Jrnl. Chem. Soc.* XIII. 228 Organo-lead compounds are arranged under the types of sesquioxide and peroxide of lead. **1974** *Physics Bull.* May 180/1 Lead alkyl petrol additives provide virtually the only source of organolead compounds in the environment. **1932** *Jrnl. Amer. Chem. Soc.* LIV. 1957 It is possible to prepare many organolithium compounds by the direct interaction of lithium with an RX compound in ether or benzene. **1974** *Chem. & Pharm. Bull.* XXII. 1711 Many reports have been published so far on the reactions between organolithiums and open chain compounds. **1901** *Jrnl. Chem. Soc.* LXXX. I. 263 The organo-magnesium compound produced crystallises in colourless, flattened needles. **1968** R. O. C. NORMAN *Princ. Org. Synthesis* vi. 202 Organomagnesium compounds, known as Grignard reagents after their discoverer, are the most widely used of organometallic reagents. **1860** *Chem. News* 30 June 26/1 At present the representatives of the organo-mercury series all belong to the mercuric type. **1963** A. J. HALL *Textile Sci.* v. 263 Shirlan is also much used for protecting cotton against mildew attack. A number of complex organo-mercury compounds are also effective for this purpose. **1974** *Nature* 20 Sept. 236/2 The ability of organo-mercury compounds, particularly methylmercury, to concentrate in tissues of fish and other animals at levels which are toxic for human consumption, is of increasing environmental concern. **1950** G. M. KOSOLAPOFF *Organophosphorus Compounds* i. 7 In many classes of organophosphorus compounds we find mixtures that are inseparable by fractional distillation. **1962** *Brit. Birds* LV. 431 Certain organophosphorus sprays were used on Brussels sprouts. **1971** *Homes & Gardens* Aug. 89/3 A servicing company can apply a long-lasting organo-phosphorus insecticide to pendant fittings. **1941** *Jrnl. Amer. Chem. Soc.* LXIII. 1194/1 The lack of a clear understanding of the behavior of the substituted organo-silicon compounds and the possibility of producing useful resinous polymers for them led to an investigation of some of the disubstituted compounds. **1955** BROWN & DEY *India's Mineral Wealth* (ed. 3) x. 391 The resultant organosilicon chlorides are hydrolised [*sic*] to silanols which condense into the polysiloxanes or silicones. **1974** *Encycl. Brit. Macropædia* XIII. 716/1 The organosilicon halides..are prepared by a special reaction using copper as catalyst. **1866** WATTS *Dict. Chem.* IV. 220 No organo-tin compounds containing only one equivalent of positive radicle, have hitherto been produced. **1960** *Times Rev. Industry* Apr. 83/3 Among the new chemicals are..organotin compounds of germicidal.. nature. **1860** *Chem. News* 30 June 26/1 Organo-zinc compounds are decomposed by water, oxide of the metal and hydride of the radical being produced. **1966** *McGraw-Hill Encycl. Sci. & Technol.* IX. 403/1 For many years organo-zinc compounds were used for synthetic purposes.

b. Prefixed to the names of various types of compounds to form sbs., indicating the presence of an organic radical in the molecule, as ***organoalkali***, ***-borane***, ***-mercurial***, ***-metal***, ***-phosphate***, ***-siloxane***; these may also be used *attrib.* Also **organocompound**, an organometallic compound.

1932 *Jrnl. Amer. Chem. Soc.* LIV. 1958 A corresponding simpler technique might be used with organoalkali compounds like phenyl-lithium. **1968** G. E. COATES et al. *Princ. Organometallic Chem.* iii. 34 A large class of charge-delocalized organoalkali compounds consists of the addition compounds between alkali metals and bi- or poly-nuclear aromatic hydrocarbons. **1957** Organoborane [see HYDROBORATION]. **1971** J. D. ROBERTS et al. *Org. Chem.* xix. 536 The boron halides and the organoboranes (BR_3) are Lewis acids. **1976** *Nature* 15 Jan. 163/2 Chapters 4–6.., on four-coordinate organoboranes, organodiboranes, and other polyboranes, are particularly welcome. **1866** WATTS *Dict. Chem.* IV. 224 Aluminium series.—The only known organo-compounds of this series are aluminic methide, Al'''(CH^3)^3, and aluminic ethide, Al'''(C^{2}H^5)^3. **1974** *Nature* 13 Dec. p. x (Advt.), Each chapter provides a complete review of all aspects of the organocompound in question. **1972** *Ibid.* 25 Feb. 414/3 The dumping of substances likely to find their way into the food chains is completely prohibited—these include organohalogen and organosilicon compounds. **1977** *Offshore Engineer* May 29/1 The real villains on the 'blacklist' are certain organohalogens (for example the extremely toxic and readily absorbed printing by-product PCB), mercury and cadmium. **1866** WATTS *Dict. Chem.* IV. 221 A brisk action with considerable elevation of temperature attends the formation of the organo-mercurial compound. **1938** H. GILMAN *Org. Chem.* I. iv. 463 Organomercurials are the least active organometallic compounds of the first two groups. **1961** *Times* 27 Mar. 5/3 It is comparable with the organo-mercurials against apple scab. **1971** *Nature* 23 July 222/1 Only inhaled elemental mercury vapour is comparable with the above organo-mercurials in inducing intoxication. **1866** WATTS *Dict. Chem.* IV. 230 Arsenic Series.—This series.. contains the first discovered organo-metal, cacodyl. **1971** *Nature* 31 Dec. 518/1 The use of metal complexes as organo-metal catalysts for the synthesis of industrially important organic intermediates and polymers. **1958** *Jrnl. Econ. Entomol.* LI. 714 (*heading*) New organophosphate insecticides developed on rational principles. **1974** M. C. GERALD *Pharmacol.* vii. 133 Medically, organophosphate compounds are used for the treatment of glaucoma. **1946** E. G. ROCHOW *Introd. Chem. Silicones* i. 2 The period since 1940 has seen rapid development of the organosiloxanes or silicone polymers. **1970** *Sci. Jrnl.* Feb. 21/3 Cement and plaster can be made water repellent by incorporating into the mix small quantities of organosiloxanes which have a large proportion of silicon bonded hydroxyl groups.

organogenesis (ˌɔːgənəʊˈdʒɛnɪsɪs). *Biol.* [mod. f. ORGANO- + -GENESIS; cf. F. *organogénésie* (Littré).] = ORGANOGENY a. So **ˌorganogeˈnetic** *a.* = ORGANOGENIC.

1859 TODD *Cycl. Anat.* V. 130/2 Organogenetic changes known under the general term of development. **1866** *Treas. Bot.*, *Organogenesis*, the gradual formation of an organ from its earliest appearance. **1894** H. DRUMMOND *Ascent Man* i. 93 Human Organogenesis is a transitory comparative Anatomy.

organoˈgenic, *a.* [f. as ORGANOGENY] **a.** *Biol.* Of or pertaining to organogeny. **b.** *Petrol.* = ORGANOGENOUS *a.* Hence **organoˈgenically** *adv.*

1852 DANA *Crust.* II. 1030 The positions have rather a relation to the length or organogenic nature of the organ. **1934** WEBSTER, *Organogenic* Petrog., derived from organic substances. **1949** F. J. PETTIJOHN *Sedimentary Rocks* x. 301 These crinoidal limestones may be termed 'organogenic conglomerates'. **1967** *Oceanogr. & Marine Biol.* V. 550 The coralligenous biocoenosis..is particularly well developed.. on rocky as well as on organogenically fixed bottoms.

organogenous (ˌɔːgənəʊˈdʒɛnəs), *a. Petrol.* [f. ORGANO- + -GENOUS.] Of a rock: formed from organic materials.

1881 E. RENEVIER in *Proc. Geol. Assoc.* VI. 426 (*table*) Organogenous.—Sedimentary by organic means. **1967** *Oceanogr. & Marine Biol.* V. 503 The soft substrata of the circalittoral zone are made up of terrigenous sediments.. and organogenous remnants.

organogeny (ɔːgəˈnɒdʒɪnɪ). *Biol.* [mod. f. ORGANO- + -GENY; in F. *organogénie* (Littré).] **a.** The production or development of the organs of an animal or plant. **b.** That department of biology which deals with this.

1844 DUNGLISON *Dict. Med. Sc.*, *Organogeny*..The doctrine of the formation of the different organs. **1854** H. SPENCER *Ess.* (1858) 166 (*Genesis of Science*) [Oken] says.. Biology, therefore, divides into Organogeny, Phytosophy, Zoosophy. **1857** BULLOCK tr. *Cazeaux' Midwif.* 211 A few interesting particulars of organogeny. **1888** *Athenæum* 18 Aug. 227/3 Organogeny, or the study of development, then showed that these types were not wholly imaginary.

So **orgaˈnogenist**, one versed in organogeny.

1895 *Athenæum* 27 July 134/2 He..became a pupil of Payer, whose work as an organogenist he greatly admired.

organography (ɔːgəˈnɒgrəfɪ). [mod. f. ORGANO- + -GRAPHY; in mod.F. *organographie*.]

†**1.** A description of instruments. *Obs.*

1559 W. CUNNINGHAM *Cosmogr. Glasse* Contents, 4 Organographia, Lib. iij. *Ibid.* 40, I wyll reserue the making of the Sphere, vntyll I shewe you the composition of other instrumentes required in this Art, in my Organographie. **1674** *Phil. Trans.* IX. 215 The Authors thought of the Astronomical Organography of the Excellent Hevelius.

2. The description of the organs of living beings; structural anatomy, esp. of plants.

1806 WADDINGTON *Goldbeck's Metaphysic Man* title-p., The Organography of Man. **1829** *Edin. Rev.* L. 147 The Organography [*Organographie Végétale*] of M. De Candolle ..is almost entirely anatomical. **1832** LINDLEY *Introd. Bot.* I *heading*, Organography; or, the structure of plants. **1895** M. C. COOKE (*title*) Introduction to the Study of Fungi, their organography, classification, and distribution.

3. The description of the organ (musical).

1825 DANNELEY *Encycl. Mus.*, *Organography*, or the description of that musical instrument.

So **ˌorganoˈgraphic**, **-ical** *adjs.* [in F. *organographique*], relating to organography; **orgaˈnographist**, one versed in organography.

1828 WEBSTER, *Organographic*, *Organographical*. **1835** LINDLEY *Introd. Bot.* (1848) I. 385 Describing..the phenomena..without investigating, so as to render complete their organographic meaning. **1848** CRAIG, *Organographist*, one who describes the organs of animal or vegetable bodies.

organoid (ˈɔːgənɔɪd), *a.* and *sb.* [a. mod.L. *organoïdes*: see ORGANO- and -OID.]

A. *adj.* Resembling an organ or organism in structure; having an organic appearance.

1857 in MAYNE *Expos. Lex.* **1876** BRISTOWE *The. & Pract. Med.* (1878) 51 Tumours..organoid or such as are characterised by greater complexity and an approach to the structure of organs. *Ibid.* 73 'Organoid tumours'.. composed of a fibrous framework, or stroma, so arranged as to form a series of loculi, and of groups of cells which are contained in dense masses within them.

B. *sb. Biol.* = ORGANELLE.

1930 MAXIMOW & BLOOM *Text-bk. Histol.* i. 5 The constituents of the cytoplasm..may be classified as the organoids and the inclusions. The organoids are structures ..which are probably endowed with the ability to divide.. in contrast to the inclusions which are passive, lifeless, temporary constitutents of the cell. The organoids comprise the mitochondria, the Golgi apparatus, the centrioles, and fibrils. [*Changed to* organelle *in ed.* 7 (1957).] **1956** *Anatomical Rec.* CXXV. 481 The presence of mitochondria in smooth muscle was described by Cowdry ('34), long after these organoids had been studied in other tissues. **1957** H. S. D. GARVEN *Student's Histol.* i. 19 The centrosome... Not infrequently this organoid is found lying embedded in the skein of the Golgi body.

organology (ɔːgəˈnɒlədʒɪ). [mod. f. ORGANO- + -LOGY: in F. *organologie* (Littré).]

1. The department of biology which treats of the organs of living beings, in reference to their structure and functions.

1842 in DUNGLISON *Med. Lex.* **1856** W. L. LINDSAY *Pop. Hist. Brit. Lichens* 108 A knowledge of the embryology or organology of the simplest plants is a necessary prelude or key to that of higher vegetables. **1861** BENTLEY *Man. Bot.* I Organology or Physiological Botany; this treats of plants, and their organs, in a state of life or action.

2. The study of the supposed organs of the mental faculties, etc. indicated by regions of the cranium (see ORGAN *sb.*[1] 5 c); phrenology.

1814 T. FORSTER (*title*) Essay on the application of the Organology of the Brain to Education. **1836–7** SIR W. HAMILTON *Metaph.* App. (1870) I. 407 The organology of Gall and his followers. **1880** BASTIAN *Brain* xxv. 518 The use of this convolutional grey matter being altogether differently estimated by the Phrenologist from what it is at present, their 'System' was devised, and their organology defined with no special reference thereto.

3. The study of anything as an organ or means.

1840 DE QUINCEY *Style* Wks. 1860 XI. 201 The science of style, as an organ of thought, of style in relation to the ideas and feelings, might be called the organology of style. **1877** MORLEY *Crit. Misc.* Ser. II. 377.

4. The study of the history of musical instruments.

1959 *Times Lit. Suppl.* 17 July 428/4 More specialized aspects of 'organology' (to use the term proper to the study of old instruments) formed the topics of the fifteen papers read by members of the Galpin Society. **1960** *Times* 18 Mar. 4/6 Organology..pursues one branch of ethnomusicology, the comparative study of instruments as they are found in the various communities. **1971** *Times Lit. Suppl.* 19 Nov. 1453/5 (Advt.), Studies in keyboard organology. **1977** *Early Music* July 405/2 Only one thing is lacking to help the student of organology: a photograph of each instrument.

So **ˌorganoˈlogical** *a.* [in F. *organologique*], relating to organology; **orgaˈnologist**, one versed in organology.

1857 MAYNE *Expos. Lex.*, Organological. **1878** BELL tr. *Gegenbaur's Comp. Anat.* 2 Special Anatomy takes for its object the organological composition of the animal body. **1869** J. HUNT in *Eng. Mech.* 19 Mar. 578/1 Bonnet must.. be considered as an organologist. **1976** *Early Music* July 293/1 Munrow's emphasis on the musical use of instruments reflects a refreshing and welcome new departure in organological studies. **1976** *Jrnl. Amer. Mus. Instrument Soc.* II. 120 He must be counted among the finest organologists of our generation.

‖**organon** (ˈɔːgənɒn). [a. Gr. ὄργανον instrument, bodily organ, etc.; the title of Aristotle's logical treatises; = 'instrument' of all reasoning: cf. ORGANUM. Formerly naturalized in sense 1, with pl. *-ons* (so F. *organon*, *-ons*); now treated as alien in sense 2 with pl. in *-a*.]

†**1.** A bodily organ, esp. as an instrument of the soul or mind: = ORGAN *sb.*[1] 4, 6. *Obs.*

1590 MARLOWE *2nd Pt. Tamburl.* v. iii, The soul, Wanting those organons by which it moves, Cannot endure, by argument of art. *a* **1597** PEELE *David & Bethsabe* Wks. (Rtldg.) 484/1 A more than human skill May feed the organons of all my sense. **1629** HUBERT *Hist. Edw. II*, lxvi, Our Mother Nature..By whom we haue our apt Organons assign'd.

2. An instrument of thought or knowledge; a means by which some process of reasoning, discovery, etc., is carried on; *esp.* a system of rules or principles of demonstration or investigation; spec. title of the logical writings of Aristotle.

a **1643** LD. FALKLAND, etc. *Infallibility* (1646) 193 It is easy to impugne the Organon of faith, or Doctrinall principles, but not easy to compose it. [*c* **1645** HOWELL *Lett.* v. x. 11 When you have devour'd the *Organon*, you will find Philosophie far more delightfull and pleasing to your palat.] **1823** DE QUINCEY *Lett. Educ.* ii. Wks. 1860 XIV. 26 An *organon* of the human understanding is as much above it. **1845** GLADSTONE *Glean.* (1879) VII. 156 A sound view of it [probability] is not indeed ethical knowledge itself, but is the organon, by means of which that knowledge is to be rightly handled. **1864** BOWEN *Logic* ii. 40 It [Logic] is not an organon of discovery. **1884** J. PARKER *Apost. Life* III. 346 Human intellect ..as the organon by which we are to acquaint ourselves with God.

orgaˈnonomy[1]. [mod. f. ORGANO- + *-o)nomy*, as in *astronomy*, *economy*, etc.; but here associated in sense with νόμος law.] The study of the laws of organic life. So ˌ**organo'nomic** *a.*, pertaining to organonomy.

1801 *Med. Jrnl.* V. 369 *Elementarlehre*; i.e. Elementary Doctrine of Organic Nature, by Dr. F. J. Schelver, Vol. I. Organomy. **1857** MAYNE *Expos. Lex.*, *Organonomia*,..a declaration of the laws which regulate the activity of the organism, or organic life: organonomy. *Ibid.*, Organonomic.

orga'nonomy[2], variant of ORGANONYMY.

1881 WILDER in *Proc. Amer. Philos. Soc.* XIX. 533 The Names of the Parts—Organonomy.

organonym (ɔːˈgænəʊˌnɪm). *Biol. rare.* [f. Gr. ὄργανον ORGAN + ὄνυμα, ὄνομα name: cf. ONYM.] The technical name of an organ. So **orga'nonymal**, ˌ**organo'nymic** *adjs.*, pertaining to organonyms, or of the nature of an organonym; **orga'nonymy** [= F. *organonymie*], the nomenclature of organs, or of a system of organonyms.

1885–9 *Buck's Handbk. Med. Sci.* VIII. 515 (Cent.) The terms..are the names of parts, organ-names, or organonyms, and their consideration constitutes organonymy. **18..** COUES (Cent.), Organonymal. **18..** WILDER (Cent.), Organonymic.

organosol (ɔːˈgænəsɒl). [a. G. *organosol* (E. A. Schneider 1892, in *Ber. d. Deut. Chem. Ges.* XXV. 1164): see ORGANO- and SOL *sb.*[6]] A dispersion in which the dispersion medium is an organic liquid; *spec.* one of particles of a synthetic resin in a liquid consisting of plasticizer and volatile components, which can be converted into a solid plastic simply by heating (cf. PLASTISOL).

1892 *Jrnl. Chem. Soc.* LXII. 775 Organosol Ag ([in] ethyl alcohol) is formed by the dialysis of the hydrosol in absolute alcohol. **1931** E. S. HEDGES *Colloids* xiv. 192 When the organosols are treated with a liquid which is soluble in the dispersion medium, but does not dissolve the disperse phase, the latter is precipitated. **1946** *Mod. Packaging* Mar. 262/2 Conversion..from solution coating to an organosol dispersion more than doubled the unit output of one modern coating plant. **1960** *Times Rev. Industry* May 23/2 The best known of the organosol coatings are the vinyl synthetic resin types. **1963** H. R. CLAUSER *Encycl. Engin. Materials* 454/2 Several plants are using spread coaters for the application of organosols and plastisols to strip steel to provide materials competitive with the light metals and plastics. **1972** *Materials & Technol.* V. xi. 338 Organosols are easier to spray in conventional equipment, and give thinner films with a greater range of flexibility and hardness.

organotherapy (ˌɔːgənəʊˈθɛrəpɪ). *Med.* [f. ORGANO- + THERAPY.] Treatment by the administration of preparations made from animal organs, esp. glands.

1896 *Med. Times & Hosp. Gaz.* XXIV. 545/2 The belief ..that diseases arising from a lack of the normal secretion of a certain gland, may at times be treated with benefit by administering the secretion of that gland from lower animals ..forms the basis of modern organotherapy. **1915** [see KETONE 2]. **1939** M. A. GOLDZIEHER *Endocrine Glands* i. 1 Organotherapy is as old as mankind and is used by primitive peoples to-day. **1958** *Internat. Jrnl. Fertility* III. 315 It is difficult to determine the incidence of endocrine disorders in studies of sterility. It is largely for this reason that organotherapy is either neglected or applied empirically. **1968** *Guardian* 27 Apr. 7/6 Organotherapy—the use of organs, animal or human, as a form of treatment.

Hence ˌ**organothera'peutic**, **-'therapic** *adjs.*, of or pertaining to organotherapy; ˌ**organothera'peutics** *sb. pl.* = ORGANOTHERAPY.

1900 *Lancet* 25 Aug. 610/2 Dr. J. G. Soutar..regarded the subject of organo-therapeutics as one of great importance. **1905** *Ibid.* 19 Aug. 554/2 Tests whereby organo-therapeutic substances might be recognized. **1908** *Practitioner* Sept. 428 All forms of medical treatment of this affection, whether hygienic, dietetic, medicinal, organo-therapic, or electrical in nature, are unsatisfactory. **1911** *Encycl. Brit.* XXVI. 798/2 The success which has been achieved has led to the use of many other organs in a raw or compressed form, or as extracts, in other diseases... To this method of treatment the name of organo-therapeutics or opo-therapy has been given. **1923** H. R. HARROWER *Index of Organotherapy* 26 Measures that I know have been unusually effective..are not necessarily organotherapeutic. **1928** F. W. BRODERICK *Dental Med.* xi. 223 There may exist..certain definitely recognisable conditions in which appropriate organotherapeutic and other measures will be extremely useful. **1934** *Q. Cumulative Index Med.* XV. 934/2 Action of certain organotherapeutic preparations on coronary vessels of isolated heart of animals and of man.

organ-pipe. [f. ORGAN *sb.*[1] + PIPE *sb.*]

1. a. One of the pipes of an organ: see ORGAN *sb.*[1] 2.

c **1440** *Promp. Parv.* 369/1 Orgon pype, or pype of an orgon. **1530** PALSGR. 250/1 Organ pype, *fleute dorgre.* **1588** *Nottingham Rec.* IV. 224 The orgayne pypes is in number xij. score and xv. **1832** TENNYSON *Pal. Art* xxv, Near gilded organ-pipes..slept St. Cecily. **1842** BRANDE *Dict. Sci.*, etc. 856/1 Organ pipes are of two sorts, mouth pipes and reed pipes, of each..there are several species.

b. *fig.*

1595 SHAKS. *John* v. vii. 23 This pale faint Swan, Who chaunts a dolefull hymne to his owne death, And from the organ-pipe of frailety sings His soule and body to their lasting rest. **1611** —— *Temp.* III. iii. 98 The Thunder (That deepe and dreadfull Organ-Pipe) pronounc'd The name of Prosper.

2. *transf.* Applied to things resembling the pipes of an organ. †**a.** Some kind of fire-arm. *Obs.*

1594 BARWICK *Disc. Weapons of Fire* 10 b, Fauconits, Robinets and Organpipes, all these be but light peeces.

b. *pl.* Applied to basaltic columns, closely-placed, like a row of organ-pipes.

1861 E. T. HOLLAND in *Peaks Passes & Glaciers* Ser. II. I. 68 High up in the cliffs of this mountain is a very singular-looking group of red basaltic organ-pipes, arranged with great regularity of structure.

c. 'In costume, a large piping; a rounded flute' (*Cent. Dict.*).

d. = *organ-cactus* (ORGAN *sb.*[1] 8).

1854 *Colburn's United Service Jrnl.* Feb. 274 A specimen of [cactus]..which from its shape is commonly called 'the organ pipe' rose to the height of about twenty feet. **1957** J. KEROUAC *On Road* (1958) IV. v. 276 We began to see the ghostly shapes of yucca cactus and organ-pipe on all sides.

3. organ-pipe cactus = sense 2 d above; **organ-pipe coral**: see CORAL *sb.*[1] 1 b.

1833 MANTELL *Wonders Geol.* (1838) II. 478 Tubipora: Organ-pipe coral. **1890** *Athenæum* 216/2. **1908** W. T. HORNADAY *Camp-Fires on Desert* 352 The mines are quite the northern limit of the organ-pipe cactus. **1977** *Times* 21 Apr. 16/8 Organ-pipe cacti still grow alongside..golf course greens [in Arizona].

organry (ˈɔːgənrɪ). *nonce-wd.* [f. as prec. + -RY.] Organ-music; musical matter.

1850 D. G. MITCHELL *Reveries of Bachelor* 71 Such manly verse as Pope's, or..such sound and ringing organry as Comus.

‖**organum**[1] (ˈɔːgənəm). [L. *organum*, a. Gr. ὄργανον: see ORGANON, ORGAN *sb.*[1]]

1. a. An instrument; = ORGANON 1.

1614 RALEIGH *Hist. World* I. ii. 16 He maketh the Phantasie in representing the Object to the Understanding to be a 'corporal Organum'.

b. An instrument of thought or knowledge; = ORGANON 2. Esp. in the title of Bacon's work called, with reference to the Ὄργανον of Aristotle, *Novum Organum*, i.e. New Instrument or set of principles for scientific investigation.

[**1620** BACON (*title*) Instauratio Magna, sive Novum Organum, accedit Parascue ad Historiam Naturalem et Experimentalem.] **1856** R. A. VAUGHAN *Mystics* (1860) I. 80 It is the heaven-given organum, in the hands of the wise and holy.

2. *Mediæval Mus.* A part sung as an accompaniment below or above the melody or plain-song, usually at the interval of a fourth or fifth; also, *loosely*, this method of singing in parts, the most primitive form of counterpoint or harmony. (Also called DIAPHONY.) Also *attrib.*

1782 BURNEY *Hist. Mus.* II. ii. 75 Organum..consisted in singing a part under the plain-song, or chant. *Ibid.* 136 Organum..was a general term for a single part, or second voice, added to the melody of a chant. **1880** HELMORE in Grove *Dict. Mus.* I. 509 The first kind of variation from strictly unisonous singing in the Middle Ages was the 'Organum' or simple aggrandisement of multitudinous choral effect by the additions of octaves above and below the Plain Song or Melody. **1880** W. S. ROCKSTRO *ibid.* II. 610 Guido d'Arezzo..objects to the use of united Fourths, and Fifths, in an Organum of three parts, on account of its disagreeable harshness. **1884** W. H. FRERE *Winchester Troper* p. xxi, He [*sc.* Notker] first tried his hand with the melody known as Organa. *Ibid.* p. xxxix, The Organum became not a mere mechanical repetition of the principalis, but another part more or less independent of it. **1932** *Music & Lett.* XIII. 185 This singing in two parts..was also popularly called 'Organum'. *Ibid.* 189 The alto and bass have the melody, the others the organum. **1965** *Listener* 20 May 756/3, I specially liked the alternating plainchant and two-part polyphony in *organa* style of the Kyrie. **1977** *New Yorker* 23 May 126/3 The 'Hymn for a New Age' is an antiphonal chant given out by the children in organum fourths, accompanied by oboes and English horn.

organum[2] = ORGANY[2], ORGAN[2], ORIGANUM.

a **1450** *Trevisa's Barth. De P.R.* XVIII. ix. (MS. Bodl.) lf. 250/1 He sechep Organum [*ed.* 1495 Origanum] and findeþ bi taste remedye. **1533** ELYOT *Cast. Helthe* (1541) 9 b, Thynges makynge the stomake stronge: Mirabolanes: Nutmygges: Organum. **1552** HULOET, Organum and organye herbe [= *origanum*].

†**'organy**[1]. *Obs. rare.* Also 4 orgonye. [a. OF. *organie* 'organ', a deriv. of *organ*, the formation of which is not clear.]

1. An organ; a musical instrument.

1377 LANGL. *P. Pl.* B. XVIII. 9 Of gerlis and of *gloria laus* gretly me dremed, And how osanna by orgonye olde folke songen [*v. rr.* organye, orgene, organ; *C-text has* orgone].

2. An instrument, means; = ORGAN *sb.*[1] 7.

Perh. a mispr. for *organes*.

1605 CHAPMAN *All Fooles* Plays 1873 I. 135 Since youth and love Were th' vnresisted organies to seduce you.

†**'organy**[2]. ? *Obs.* Also 6 organ(n)ye, 6–7 organie. [Corrupt ad. L. *origanum.*] = ORIGAN.

1545 RAYNOLD *Byrth Mankynde* 122 Sethe organnye or myrhe with oyle olyfe. **1546** LANGLEY *Pol. Verg. De Invent.* I. xvii. 32 The Wesil in chasing the Serpent preserueth her self with Rue, and the Storke with Organie. **1578** LYTE *Dodoens* II. lxv. 232 This herbe is called..in English Penny Royall..and Organie. **1647** LILLY *Chr. Astrol.* ix. 64 Organy or Wild Marjorane. **1706** PHILLIPS, *Organy* or *Orgain*, wild or bastard Marjoram. **1861** MISS PRATT *Flower. Pl.* IV. 173 Common Marjoram... The plant is sometimes called Wild Organy.

organza (ɔːˈgænzə). [ad. F. *organsin*, It. *organzino*: see ORGANZINE.] A thin stiff transparent dress-fabric of silk or synthetic fibre.

1820 M. EDGEWORTH *Let.* 4 June in C. Colvin *M. Edgeworth in France & Switz.* (1979) 144 The distinguishing characteristic is a silk organza handkerchief. **1934** *Times* 22 June 17/4 The latter in checked organza in red, white and black colourings. **1956** 'R. CROMPTON' *Matty & Dearingroydes* x. 93 The dress was egg-shell blue organza. **1964** D. FRANCIS *Nerve* xvi. 210 Alice front-view in spotted organza at a Hunt Ball. **1973** *Country Life* 19 Apr. 1114/2 The pink and green flowers used for the cap sleeves..are cut from the exquisite organza fabric.

organzine (ˈɔːgənziːn), *sb.* Also 7–8 organcine, 8 organsine. [a. F. *organsin* (1667 in Littré), ad. It. *organzino*, of unknown origin.] The strongest and best kind of silk thread, formed of several strands twisted together in the contrary direction to that in which their component filaments are twisted. Also ***organzine silk***.

1699 *Phil. Trans.* XXI. 184 The Goodness of Silk is distinguished by its lightness,..the Organcine is Superfine, it being the best sort. **1732–7** CHAMBERLAYNE *St. Gt. Brit.* I. I. iii. 9 Upon the Derwent..were erected in the late Reign, by Sir Thomas Lombe, those Mills which work the three capital Italian Engines for making Organzine or Thrown Silk. **1759** PULLEIN in *Phil. Trans.* LI. 23 The French were desirous of making raw silk fit for organcine or warp among themselves. **1835** URE *Philos. Manuf.* 235 There are three kinds of raw silk, organzine, tram, and floss. **1893** *Dict. Nat. Biog.* XXXIV. 96 The machinery had rendered the manufacturers of this country independent of Italy for the supply of organzine.

1732 *Lond. Mag.* I. 36 Three Italian Engines for making Organzine Silk. **1831** G. R. PORTER *Silk Manuf.* 203 Organzine silk is of the nature of rope, where the combined strands are twisted in an opposite direction to that given to the separate threads.

'organzine, *v.* [ad. F. *organsine-r* (1762 in *Dict. Acad.*), f. *organsin*: see prec.] *trans.* To make into organzine; *intr.* To twist threads of silk so as to form organzine. Chiefly in **'organzined** *ppl. a.* and **'organzining** *vbl. sb.*

1779 *Chron.* in *Ann. Reg.* 198/1 Fine Italian organzined thrown silk. **1789** PILKINGTON *View Derbysh.* II. 172 Organzining or preparing the silk for the manufactures of Spitalfields. **1831** G. R. PORTER *Silk Manuf.* 210 The expense of organzining in France..is said not to exceed two shillings and ninepence to three shillings per pound.

orgasm (ˈɔːgæz(ə)m), *sb.* [ad. mod.L. *orgasmus*, a. Gr. type *ὀργασμός, f. ὀργά -ειν to swell as with moisture, be excited or eager. Cf. F. *orgasme* 'an extreame fit or expression of anger' (Cotgr. 1611).]

1. Immoderate or violent excitement of feeling; rage, fury; a paroxysm of excitement or rage.

[**1646** SIR T. BROWNE *Pseud. Ep.* 145 It may be onely some fast retention or sudden compression in the Orgasmus or fury of their lust.] *a* **1763** SHENSTONE *Economy* I. 159 Vain, ah vain the hope Of future peace, this orgasm uncontroul'd! **1806** W. TAYLOR in *Ann. Rev.* IV. 604 So the poetic orgasm, when excited, glows but for a time. **1875** LOWELL *Wordsworth* Prose Wks. 1890 IV. 365 He saw man such as he can only be when he is vibrated by the orgasm of a national emotion.

2. *Physiol.* **a.** Excitement or violent action in an organ or part, accompanied with turgescence; *spec.* the height of venereal excitement in coition.

1684 tr. *Bonet's Merc. Compit.* XIX. 809 When there appears an Orgasm of the humours, we rather fly to bleeding as more safe. **1771** T. PERCIVAL *Ess.* (1777) I. 200 A kind of nervous orgasm, or spasm on the vitals. **1802** *Med. Jrnl.* VIII. 236 Many viviparous animals are subject to periodical venereal orgasm. **1899** *Hutchinson's Archives Surg.* X. 129 The state of vascular turgescence which attends the sexual orgasm.

b. *attrib.*

1936 H. M. & A. STONE *Marriage Manual* viii. 276 Orgasm incapacity is more frequent. **1949** *Orgone Energy Bull.* Apr. 94 *Orgasm reflex*, the unitary involuntary contraction and expansion of the total organism in the acme of the sexual embrace. **1965** P. & E. KRONHAUSEN *Sexual Response in Women* II. i. 64 The kind of 'orgasm anxiety' to which our informant referred is very common among women. **1967** P. S. CATLING *Experiment* xxxvi. 228 You might have expected higher I.Q. levels to mean..an enhanced orgasm yield. **1968** R. KYLE *Love Lab.* xxiv. 322 With his help, she had broken through into orgasm country. **1973** S. FISHER *Female Orgasm* i. 31 The amount of time spent by the husband stimulating his wife does not correlate with her orgasm frequency.

Hence **or'gasmal** *a.* = ORGASMIC *a.*

1964 *Brit. Jrnl. Med. Psychol.* XXXVII. 63 Failure to achieve normal adult heterosexual adjustment was shown.. by frigidity, and sometimes promiscuity with orgasmal disappointment. **1969** C. ALLEN *Textbk. Psychosexual Disorders* (ed. 2) iv. 71 Castration seems to have little effect on the desire or orgasmal capacity of the woman.

'orgasm, *v.* [f. the sb.] To experience a sexual orgasm.

1973 S. FISHER *Female Orgasm* vii. 207 It often takes me as much as 15 minutes of stimulation before I can orgasm. **1974** *New Direction* IV. IV. 5/3 He stroked my clitoris until I orgasmed. **1977** *Observer* 25 Sept. 23/7 Approved wisdom has it that women should orgasm from that which achieves male orgasm and reproduction—penile thrusting; not from direct clitoral stimulation.

orgasmic (ɔːˈgæzmɪk), *a.* [f. ORGASM + -IC.] Of or pertaining to sexual orgasm; in a state of sexual orgasm. Also *transf.* and *fig.*

1935 R. V. STORER *Sexual Technique* xxi. 278 The orgasmic contractions of the uterus act as a kind of suction pump. **1946** M. PEAKE *Titus Groan* 368 What had gone wrong? The orgasmic moment [of murder] he had so long awaited was over. **1947** J. STEINBECK *Wayward Bus* xiv. 197 Back in the bus he had felt, in anticipation, a bursting, orgasmic delight of freedom. **1953** A. C. KINSEY et al. *Sexual Behavior Human Female* ix. 390 It had acquainted the girl with the nature of an orgasmic response. **1966** MASTERS & JOHNSON *Human Sexual Response* ix. 131 The female is capable of rapid return to orgasm immediately following an orgasmic experience. **1968** *New Statesman* 16 Aug. 208/1 The Trojans meet the Greeks like lovers, almost naked, agog for the dark orgasmic flutter of killing or being killed. **1969** *Daily Tel.* (Colour Suppl.) 7 Mar. 7/2 She lay naked on the floor doing the standard orgasmic heaving. **1971** *Daily Tel.* 3 Apr. 14 Television commercials are often blatantly erotic, so that even the simple act of eating a chocolate bar is turned into an orgasmic experience. **1971** 'V. X. SCOTT' *Surrogate Wife* 13 Women do *not* ejaculate any sort of fluid.., but they *do* have an orgasmic reaction that is physiological, not just mental. **1976** L. DEIGHTON *Twinkle, twinkle Little Spy* xviii. 186 From Katerina came a long orgasmic whimper.

Hence **orˈgasmically** *adv.*

1972 D. F. BARBER *Pornography & Society* iii. 93 The orgasmically satisfied man or woman is unlikely to throw a bomb. **1974** *Forum* VII. 30/2 While she is still glowing orgasmically, he should enter her.

orgasmist (ɔːˈgæz(ə)mɪst). *rare*$^{-1}$. [f. ORGASM + -IST.] One who delights in sexual excitement.

1938 DYLAN THOMAS *Let.* 6 July (1966) 205 It's a crack at young Georgians, not at New-Versers, intellectual muckpots leaning on a theory, post-surrealists and orgasmists, tit-in-the-night whistlers, [etc.].

orgastic (ɔːˈgæstɪk), *a.* [f. Gr. type *ὀργαστικός, f. ὀργάειν: see ORGASM *sb.* and cf. *sarcasm, sarcastic,* etc.] Of, pertaining to, or characterized by orgasm.

1822–34 *Good's Study Med.* (ed. 4) III. 392 An orgastic state of the genital organs. *Ibid.* IV. 92 The frequency of the orgastic paroxysms. **1930** *Internat. Jrnl. Psycho-Anal.* XI. 439 In many cases the trauma of punishment falls upon children in the midst of some erotic activity, and the result may be a permanent disturbance of what Reich calls 'orgastic potency'. **1942** T. P. WOLFE tr. W. Reich in *Internat. Jrnl. Sex-Econ. & Orgone Res.* Mar. 33/2 Psychic as well as somatic disturbances are due to the *stasis* (damming-up) of energy in the organism. This stasis is due to *orgastic impotence*; only *orgastic potency*, i.e. biologically correct discharge of sexual energy, guarantees a normal energy household (sex-economy). **1963** H. I. SCHNEER *Asthmatic Child* vi. 78 She said that it was often impossible to have an orgastic response with her husband. **1969** P. A. ROBINSON *Freudian Left* 17 Orgastic potency was *defined* in economic terms; it was 'the capacity for complete discharge of all dammed-up sexual excitation through involuntary pleasurable contractions of the body'.

Hence **orˈgastically** *adv.*

1941 *Internat. Jrnl. Psycho-Anal.* XXII. 215 The patient was also orgastically potent in Reich's sense of the term. **1953** W. REICH *Murder of Christ* 189 Orgastically impotent physicians in the realm of medical orgonomy will mess up the medical techniques to establish the orgonotic streaming in sick organisms or will forget them. **1973** S. FISHER *Female Orgasm* i. 32 The more a woman is capable of responding orgastically to her spouse,.. the happier their marriage will be.

Orgatron (ˈɔːgətrɒn). [f. ORGA(N *sb.*[1] + ELEC)TRON(IC *a.*] A kind of electronic organ.

Registered as a trade mark in the U.S. in 1935 but this mark was later cancelled. It was re-registered as a trade mark in 1975.

1935 *Official Gaz.* (U.S. Patent Office) 16 July 518/2 Everett Piano Company, Chicago, Ill... Orgatron.. For Musical instruments—Namely, Key-Board Instruments for Producing Pipe Organ Tones through Electronic Means. Claims use since Apr. 12, 1935. **1935** *Piano Trade Mag.* May 8 The Everett Piano Co., South Haven, Mich., this month announces its new musical instrument, the Orgatron, an electronic instrument with the tone of a fine pipe organ. **1937** *Sun* (Baltimore) 12 Nov. 19/4 The feature of the entertainment program will be a recital each afternoon and evening on 'The Orgatron', one of the latest developments of the electric organ. **1940** *Chambers's Techn. Dict.* 599/1 *Orgatron* (*Acous.*), an electronic musical instrument using the pneumatic action of a reed organ. The electrical current for the operation of radiating loudspeakers is obtained by electrostatic pick-ups operated by the motion of the languids of the air-operated reeds, using adequate amplifiers. **1959** *Collins Mus. Encycl.* 218/1 The Everett Orgatron.. amplifies the vibration of harmonium reeds. **1975** *Official Gaz.* (U.S. Patent Office) 1 Apr. TM 23/1 GTR Products, Inc., Cranford, N.J... Orgatron. For Electronic Organs.. First use Oct. 29, 1973.

orgayne, obs. form of ORGAN.

†**orgays.** *Obs.* Forms: 4 orgeis, 5–6 orgays, orgas, (5 orkays). [a. OF. *orgeis*, of uncertain origin.] A kind of fish; = ORGAN LING.

[**1357** *Act 31 Edw. III* Stat. III. c. 2 En cas que nul orgeis, cestascauoir pesson pluis graunde que lob soit troue en niefe appelle lodeship. *Ibid.*, Eyent les meister & maryners toutes les orgeis. *transl.* And in case that no Orgeys, that is to say Fish greater than Lobbe be found in a Ship called a Lode ship... The Masters and Mariners shall haue all the Orgeys.] **1427–1524** in Rogers *Agric. & Prices* III. 312–Orgays (many entries in Cambridge Accts. 1427–51, 1508–15), Orkays (1438), Orgas (Sion Coll. Accts. 1489–94, Camb. 1506–24); Orgas ling (Sion 1460, -89). [Later 1499–1593 Organ ling, orgayn ling, 1507–1627 organs: see ORGAN LING.]

orgeat (‖ɔrʒa, ˈɔːdʒiːət). Also 8 orgeate. [a. F. *orgeat* (15th c. in Hatz.-Darm.), ad. Pr. *orjat, ourjat* (in 17th c. Fr. also *orgée, orgeade,* It. *orgiata* (obs.) Florio, *orzata*), f. F. *orge*, Pr. *ordi*, It. *orzo*:—L. *hordeum* barley.] A syrup or cooling drink made originally from barley, subsequently from almonds, and orange-flower water.

1754 *Connoisseur* No. 38 Whatever orgeat or capillaire can inspire. **1769** BARETTI *Manners of Italy* II. xxx. 203 Their servants attend with lemonade, orgeate,.. and other cooling drinks. **1786** HAN. MORE *Bas Bleu* 229 Nor be the milk-white streams forgot, Of thirst-assuaging, cool orgeat. **1843** THACKERAY *Misc. Ess.* (1885) 45 Pulling a queer face over a glass of orgeat (pronounced *orjaw*). **1864** SALA in *Daily Tel.* 21 Sept., Light refreshments, such as ices, coffee, orgeat, and lemonade, were handed about.

orgeilus, obs. form of ORGULOUS.

orgeis, variant of ORGAYS, *Obs.*

†**orgel, orghel, orhel**, *sb.* and *a. Obs.* Forms: 1 orgel, orgol, 3 orȝel (*Orm.* orrȝhell), oregel, oreȝel, orhel, horhel, horel. [OE. *orgel, orgol, orȝol* (whence *orȝel-líc, -líce* in Ælfred; etymology uncertain, as is the question of its relationship to the OHG. word which gave OF. *orgoill*, F. *orgueil*, 'pride', by which ME. *orȝel, orhel, orel* was superseded in the 13th c.: see ORGUEIL.]

A. *sb.* Pride, haughtiness.

a **1023** WULFSTAN *Hom.* (Napier) 148 Hwær ys.. heora prass and orgol, buton on moldan beþeaht and on witum ȝecyrred? *c* **1200** *Trin. Coll. Hom.* 43 Woreldes richeise wecheð orgel on mannes heorte. *Ibid.* 191 þe heȝe sete on heuene, þe he fel of þurgh is oreȝel. *a* **1225** *St. Marher.* 11 Ichabbe isehen his ouergart, ant his egede orhel ferliche afallet. *a* **1225** *Ancr. R.* 176 Horhel wolde awakien. *Ibid.* 210 þe prude beoð his bemares.. uorte makien noise—lud dream to scheauwen hore horel.

B. *adj.* Proud, haughty, presumptuous.

In *orȝel mod* haughty mind, written in comb.

c **1200** *Trin. Coll. Hom.* 35 Ne to none heȝe, ne oreȝele men on þe wurelde wið to spekende. *Ibid.* 37 Alle oreȝel men, þe telleð hem seluen heiȝe. *c* **1200** ORMIN 6262 3iff þatt he þurrh orrȝhellmod Forrhoȝheþþ þe to wurrþenn. *c* **1250** *Gen. & Ex.* 3767 Ne wulde he.. For orȝel pride forð ðor cumen.

Hence †**ˈorgelness, orȝelness**, pride, haughtiness, hauteur.

a **1000** *Aldhelm Glosses* (Napier, 31, 1108), *Elationis*, orgelnesse, creasnesse. *c* **1200** *Trin. Coll. Hom.* 215 þare telde ðe werse þe grune of oreȝelnesse.

orgel: see ORGLE.

‖**orgia** (ˈɔːdʒɪə), *sb. pl.* [L. *orgia*, Gr. ὄργια neuter pl., 'orgies'.] = Orgies: see ORGY. (Sometimes erron. as sing., with pl. *orgiaes, -ay's,* in 7.)

1570–6 LAMBARDE *Peramb. Kent* (1826) 331 Then they fell afresh to their orgia. **1584** R. SCOT *Discov. Witchcr.* III. iii. (1886) 34 Those feasts of Bacchus which are named *Orgia*. **1621** BP. MOUNTAGU *Diatribæ* 553 From him are the Sabasia, old Pagan Orgiaes and Mysteries deriued. **1660** N. INGELO *Bentivolio & Urania* II. (1682) 174 The Triennial Orgiay's of Bacchus. **1675** OTWAY *Alcibiades* I. i, When last Night the youth of Athens late Rose up the Orgia to celebrate. **1749–51** LAVINGTON *Enthus. Meth. & Papists* (1820) 288 While they are celebrating the orgia. **1830** GALT *Life Byron* xxxix. 256 The return of the mourners from the burning, is the most appalling orgia.

orgiac (ˈɔːdʒɪæk), *a.* and *sb. rare.* [f. Gr. type *ὀργιακ-ός, f. ὄργια orgies: cf. *cardiac, maniac.*]

a. *adj.* Pertaining to orgies or an orgy. **b.** *sb.* (*pl.*) = Orgies: see ORGY 1.

a **1859** DE QUINCEY *Posth. Wks.* (1891) I. 42 He is acquainted with.. the Orgiacs.. and all the great ceremonies and observances practised at Olympia. **1890** *Harper's Mag.* Oct. 885/2 The writhing dance of naked black forms, the orgiac round circling in and out of shadows and light.

†**ˈorgial.** *Obs. rare*$^{-1}$. [f. L. *orgia* + -AL[1].] A song sung at the orgies.

1610 G. FLETCHER *Christ's Vict.* II. l, The jolly priest.. Chaunted wild orgials, in honour of the feast.

orgiasm (ˈɔːdʒɪæz(ə)m). *rare.* [ad. Gr. ὀργιασμός, f. ὀργιάζ-ειν to celebrate orgies.] Properly, The celebration of orgies; but in quot. A state of excited or exalted feeling, as of a worshipper at the orgies (? confused with *orgasm*).

1840 MILMAN *Hist. Chr.* II. 213 The Orgiasm, the inward rapture, the working of a divine influence upon the soul.

orgiast (ˈɔːdʒɪæst). [ad. Gr. ὀργιαστής, agent-n. from ὀργιάζ-ειν: see prec.] One who celebrates orgies.

1791–3 in *Spirit Pub. Jrnls.* (1799) I. 269 The main objection of the governing powers to the Orgiasts of Bacchus, was, that their meetings were by night. **1939** JOYCE *Finnegans Wake* 254 Orion of the Orgiasts. **1957** M. SPARK *Comforters* iv. 87 'He's an orgiast on the quiet.' 'A what?' 'Goes in for the Black Mass.' **1967** *Punch* 8 Nov. 723/2 That's why orgiasts have to be slightly tight And orgiate in the middle of the night. **1975** R. H. RIMMER *Premar Experiments* (1976) ii. 194 Sorry, love bug. I'm not an orgiast.

orgiastic (ɔːdʒɪˈæstɪk), *a.* [ad. Gr. ὀργιαστικός, f. ὀργιαστής: see prec. and -IC.] Belonging to, or characterized by, orgies; of the nature or character of orgies; marked by extravagance, licentiousness, or dissolute revelry. (In quot. 1698, app. of or pertaining to the flute or wind instrument: cf. next.)

1698 FRYER *Acc. E. India & P.* 376 For Instrumental [Musick], they [Persians] have little regard to Stringed, but the Orgiastick they are very expert at. **1846** GROTE *Greece* I. xii. I. 314 The orgiastic worship of Zeus. **1879** *Athenæum* 27 Dec. 829 After the orgiastic confusion of the revolution. **1896** BRINTON in *Science* 6 Nov. 695/1 The 'ecstasy' and prophetic 'manteia' which played such a large part in the orgiastic rites of Greece.

orgiˈastical, *a. rare.* [f. as prec. + -AL[1].] Of orgiastic character or tendency.

a **1871** GROTE *Eth. Fragm.* vi. (1876) 228 The flute which he considers as not ethical, but orgiastical—calculated to excite violent and momentary emotions. **1930** *Observer* 26 Jan. 10 The Greek Tragedy up to date includes a number of ballads, revolutionary songs, and orgiastical dances.

Hence **orgiˈastically** *adv.*

1930 A. BENNETT *Imperial Palace* xliii. 310 A grand climacteric of display designed orgiastically to receive the New Year into the infinite succession of years. **1934** [see COLOURISTIC *a.*]. **1961** J. HELLER *Catch-22* (1962) xxiii. 238 Yossarian and Dunbar were busy in a far corner pawing orgiastically at four or five frolicsome girls and six bottles of red wine. **1965** *Eng. Stud.* Feb. 28 We may get nearer the truth by seeing Venus.. as having fused orgiastically with Adonis.

orgic (ˈɔːdʒɪk), *a. rare.* [irreg. f. ORGY + -IC.] = ORGIAC.

1789 T. TWINING *Aristotle's Treat. Poetry* (1812) II. 10 After the celebration of the orgic rites. **1885** R. F. LITTLEDALE in *Encycl. Brit.* XIX. 91/1 They [Egyptian pilgrims] landed at every town along the river to perform orgic dances.

orgies, *sb. pl.*: see ORGY.

orgillous, var. ORGULOUS *a.*, proud.

†**orgion.** *Obs. rare*$^{-1}$. [a. Gr. ὄργιον (rare), sing. of ὄργια ORGIA, orgies.] = ORGY.

1613 SIR E. HOBY *Countersnarle* 2 If they refuse to dance a round in her Orgions antick, she will be sure they shall not passe without a broken head.

ˈorgiophant. *Gr. Antiq. rare.* [ad. Gr. ὀργιοφάντ-ης, he who shows or expounds the orgies: cf. HIEROPHANT.] (See quot.)

1886 LEWIS & SHORT *Lat. Dict.*, *Orgiophanta*,.. a presider over the orgies, an orgiophant.

†**ˈorgle.** *Obs.* Also 4–5 orgel. [OE. *orgel* (in comb. *orgel-dréam*), ME. *orgel, orgle* = OHG. *orgela* fem., MHG. *orgel(e*, Germ. *orgel*, MDu. *orghele*, Du. *orgel*, Sw., Da. *orgel*: in its origin an alteration of L. *organa*, pl. of *organum* ORGAN.] = ORGAN *sb.*[1] 1 or 2.

a **1100** *Blickl. Gloss.*, Orgeldreame, *organo.* **13..** *K. Alis.* 191 Orgles, tymbres, al maner gleo, Was dryuen ageyn that lady freo. **1386** Orgels, orgles [see ORGAN *sb.*[1] 2 b]. **1426** AUDELAY *Poems* 16 He con harpe, he con syng, his orglus ben herd ful wyd.

†**orgmount.** *Sc. Obs.* [app. a corruption of F. *orge mondé* 'pilled and cleansed Barlie; also.. Barlie pottage' (Cotgr.). Cf. Littré, *orge mondé ou amandé.*] Boiled pearl-barley.

1596 DALRYMPLE tr. *Leslie's Hist. Scot.* I. 98 Vpon fleshe, milk, and cheis, and sodne beir or orgmount [L. *hordeoque cocto*], principallie thay lyue.

orgne, orgon, -e, obs. forms of ORGAN.

orgoil, -oile, variants of ORGUEIL, *Obs.*

orgone (ˈɔːgəʊn). [f. ORG(ANISM, ORG(ASTIC *a.* + *-one* as in HORMONE.] In the psychoanalytical theory of Wilhelm Reich (1897–1957), a vital energy or life force which supposedly informs the universe and can be collected and stored in an ***orgone accumulator*** or ***box*** for subsequent use in the treatment of mental and physical illnesses. Also *attrib.*

1942 T. P. WOLFE tr. *Reich's Discovery of Orgone* I. ix. 341 This energy, which is capable of charging non-conducting substance, I termed *orgone*. *Ibid.*, The orgone energy can be demonstrated visually, thermically and electroscopically in the soil, the atmosphere and in plant and animal organisms. **1942** —— tr. W. Reich in *Internat. Jrnl. Sex-Econ. & Orgone Res.* July 138/2 Our orgone therapy experiments with cancer patients consist in their sitting in an orgone accumulator. *Ibid.* 143/2 The patient left the orgone box. **1948** —— tr. *Reich's Discovery of Orgone* II. iv. 95 The orgone accumulator consists of an outer wall of organic material such as wood or celotex and an inner wall of sheet metal. **1949** *Orgone Energy Bull.* Apr. 95 *Physical orgone therapy*, application of physical orgone energy concentrated in an orgone accumulator to increase the natural bio-energetic defenses of the organism against disease. *Ibid.*, *Psychiatric orgone therapy*, mobilization of the orgone energy in the organism, i.e., the liberation of biophysical emotions from muscular and character armorings and the establishment of orgastic potency. **1952** M. MCCARTHY *Groves of Academe* (1953) ii. 24 A senior girl's voice, plaintive, 'Dr. Mulcahy, really, do we have to believe in orgones?' **1955** W. GADDIS *Recognitions* I. v. 194 Max was discussing orgone boxes as though he had lived in one all of his life. **1957** J. KEROUAC *On Road* (1958) 152 Why don't you fellows try my orgone accumulator? **1959** N. MAILER *Advts. for Myself* (1961) 295 God who is It, who is energy, life, sex, force, the Yoga's *prana*, the Reichian's orgone. **1973** A. S. NEILL *Neill! Neill!*

Orange Peel! II. 141, I could not understand Reich's theory of Orgone Energy... He had a small motor which was charged by an orgone accumulator. **1973** *Sat. Rev. World* (U.S.) 6 Nov. 4/1 Reichian orgone therapy.

orgonity (ɔːˈgɒnɪtɪ). [f. ORGON(E + -ITY.] (See quot. 1949.) So **orgoˈnotic** *a.*, **orgoˈnotically** *adv.*

1942 T. P. WOLFE tr. *Reich's Discovery of Orgone* I. ix. 342 Many biologists.. have observed the blue coloration of frogs in sexual excitation, or a bluish light emanating from flowers; we are dealing here with the biological (orgonotic) excitation of the organism. **1942** —— tr. W. Reich in *Internat. Jrnl. Sex-Econ. & Orgone Res.* Nov. 205/2 Mix on a microscopic slide biologically (i.e., orgonotically) weak blood with rot bacteria or T-bacilli. **1945** —— in *Ibid.* Apr. 19/2 Protozoa form in the organism only in the case of orgonotic weakness in the respective organs, and that they disappear with strong orgonity. **1949** *Orgone Energy Bull.* Apr. 95 *Orgonity*, the condition of containing orgone; the quantity of orgone contained. **1953** W. REICH *Murder of Christ* ii. 17 The qualities of the freely functioning orgonotic living system.. bear out this mystified religious inkling of a basic truth.

orgonomy (ɔːˈgɒnəmɪ). [f. as prec. + -NOMY.] The study or investigation of 'orgone'. Hence **orgoˈnomic** *a.*, pertaining or relating to orgonomy; **orˈgonomist**, one who practises orgonomy.

1949 *Orgone Energy Bull.* Jan. 23 (*heading*) The First Orgonomic Conference at Orgonon, August 30 to September 3, 1948. *Ibid.*, On Sunday evening, Aug. 29, 1948, 35 physicians, educators, and laboratory workers gathered in the laboratory at Orgonon, Rangeley, Maine, for a 4-day conference in the field of orgonomy. *Ibid.* 27 Reich concluded by saying.. orgonomy represented a new way of thinking and a new science. **1950** *Ibid.* Apr. 93 It happens again and again that a physician who has not finished his training in medical orgonomy, or has never even entered training, poses as a trained medical orgonomist. **1953** W. REICH *Murder of Christ* 200 Orgonomy.. is the factual comprehension of the universal 'Cosmic Orgone Energy'. **1964** *Parade* (Austral.) Mar. 47/2 Indeed they came in such numbers that the Austrian [*sc.* Wilhelm Reich] was forced to put on a staff of orgonomists—regular doctors who saw quick profits in this new branch of medicine. **1969** P. A. ROBINSON *Freudian Left* 59 The student who has immersed himself in Reich's early work will find the science of Orgonomy curiously familiar.

‖**orgue.** *Obs.* [F. *orgue* organ, instrument, warlike machine, etc., as in quots.]

1. *Fortification.* (See quot. 1706.)

1706 PHILLIPS, *Orgues*.. in *Fortification*, long and thick pieces of Wood, armed with Iron-Plates at the end, and hung up separately by a Cord, over a Gate; being ready upon any surprize, to be let fall in the Way, to stop it up instead of a Portcullice. **1762** STERNE *Tr. Shandy* VI. xxii, These [portcullises] were converted afterwards into orgues, as the better thing. **1853** STOCQUELER *Mil. Encycl.* 204/1 Orgues.. are now disused.

2. *Old Artillery.* (See quot.)

1706 PHILLIPS, *Orgues* is also taken for a Device, consisting of many Harquebusses linked together, or of several Musket-Barrels set in a row within one wooden Stock, to be discharged either all at once, or separately.

3. An organ: in quot. a series of basaltic columns like organ-pipes.

1836 G. DARLEY *Nepenthe* in *Q. Rev.* July (1902) 191 Where his vast orgue, high-fluted, stands Basaltic, swept with billowy hands.

‖**orgueil,** †**orguil, orgul,** *sb.* and *a.* Forms: 3 orguil, 4 -uyl, 5 -uille, -ueyl, 5–6 orgul(e, -oil, -oill, 6 -uell, *Sc.* -weill, (‖9 orgueil). [a. AF. *orguil* (Gower), OF. *orgoill*, *orguill* (11th c.), *orgoil* (11–12th c.), *orguel*, *orgueil* (12th c.) = Pr. *orgolh*, *-guelh*, Cat. *orgull*, Sp. *orgullo*, It. *orgoglio*, a Com. Romanic sb., supposed ad. OHG. **urguolî*, f. *urguol* renowned. (See Diez.) In Early ME. this superseded *orȝhel*, *orhel*, ORGEL; it became obs. itself in 16th c. When used now (as in quot. 1833) it is only as an alien mod.F. word (ɔrgœj). The adj. use is not French: in ME. it was a continuation of that of *orȝel*, ORGEL.]

A. *sb.* Pride, haughtiness. *Obs.* exc. as alien.

c **1200** *Trin. Coll. Hom.* 63 To temien þe lichames orguil. *Ibid.* 137 Wiðteo þi lichame fro orguil. **13..** *Coer de L.* 1821 For all your bost and your orguyl. *c* **1430** *Pilgr. Lyf. Manhode* II. 107, I hatte orgoill the queynte. **1456** SIR G. HAYE *Law Arms* (S.T.S.) 172 [They] makis unrychtwis weris for pride or orguille of thair hertis. **1470–85** MALORY *Arthur* XXI. xi, Whan I remembre me how by my defaute & myn orgule and my pryde, that they were bothe layed ful lowe. **1474** CAXTON *Chesse* 46 The mynystres by theyr pryde and orgueyl subuerte iustyce. **1521** *St. Papers Hen. VIII*, I. 88 It shall so rebaite his high lookes and orgule. **1563–87** FOXE *A. & M.* (1596) 348/1 Not upon any orgoile, presumption or pride. [**1833** LYTTON *England* I. ii, Our reserve, and that *orgueil*, so much more expressive of discontent than of dignity, which is the.. proverb of our continental visitors.]

†**B.** *adj.* Proud, haughty, presumptuous. *Obs.*

a **1275** *Prov. Ælfred* 286 in *O.E. Misc.* 121 Idilscipe and orgul prude, þat lerit ȝung wif leþere þewes. **1470–85** MALORY *Arthur* XXI. i, The bysshop.. dyd the cursyng in the moost orgulist wyse that myght be doon. **1560** ROLLAND *Crt. Venus* II. 614 Sic orgweill mynde to suffer it not docht.

orguinette (ɔːgɪˈnɛt). [f. F. *orgue*, or OF. *orguine*, var. of *organe* ORGAN (in sense 'lyre' (Godef.) + -ETTE.] A mechanical musical instrument, consisting of a set of reeds and a bellows, the wind from which is admitted to the reeds through holes in a strip of paper which is moved along by turning a crank.

1885 *Church Bells* July 3 *Advt.*, Orguinette Music, 1½ per foot. **1885** *Bazaar* 30 Mar. 1264/1 Orguinette, with music, quite new.

†**orˈgulity.** *Obs.* In 5 orgulyte. [f. *orgul* adj. (see ORGUEIL) + -ITY.] Pride, haughtiness.

1470–85 MALORY *Arthur* x. i, Thurgh our orgulyte we demaunded bataille of you. *Ibid.* x. lxiv, For pryde and orgulyte he wold not smyte sire Palomydes.

orgulous (ˈɔːgjʊləs), **orgillous** (ˈɔːgɪləs), *a. arch.* Forms: 3 orgeilus, 4–6 (9 *arch.*) orgulous, 5 orguillous, -eux, orguylleus, 5–6 orguyll-, 6 orguly-, orgueil-, orguell-, orgyllous, orgullows, 6 (9 *arch.*) orgullous, 7 (9 *arch.*) orgillous. [a. OF. *orguillus*, *-goillus* (11th c.), *orguilleus* (12th c.), AF. *orguillous* (Gower), mod.F. *orgueilleux* = Pr. *orguelhos*, *orgoillos*, Sp. *orgulloso*, It. *orgoglioso*, f. *orgueil*, etc., 'pride': see ORGUEIL and -OUS. Used once by Shaks., and retained in the 1634 modernization of Malory's *Morte Arthur*, but app. obs. from 16th c., until employed as a historical archaism by Southey and Scott, and affected by late 19th c. journalists.]

a. Proud, haughty.

c **1250** *Old Kent. Serm.* in *O.E. Misc.* 30 Of þo euele manne good man, of þe orgeilus umble. *c* **1330** *Arth. & Merl.* 9344 Thai to driuen four kingis orgulous. *a* **1450** *Knt. de la Tour* (1868) 84 Thorugh her orguylleus port.. throwen doune of her worshippe and astate. **1470–85** MALORY *Arthur* XX. xvii, And I were as orgulous sette as ye are. **1481** CAXTON *Reynard* xvii. (Arb.) 36 He was so prowde and orguillous. *a* **1529** SKELTON *Replyc.* Wks. 1862 II. 234 Odyous, orgulyous, and flyblowen opynions. **1529** *Art. agst. Wolsey* in Ld. Herbert *Hen. VIII* (1683) 294 The Lord Cardinal of York.. of his high, orgullous, and insatiable mind. **1592** WYRLEY *Armorie* 150 The English orgulous words did say Gainst Lord Cowcie. **1606** SHAKS. *Tr. & Cr.* Prol. 2 From Iles of Greece The Princes Orgillous, their high blood chaf'd, Haue to the Port of Athens sent their shippes. **1808** SOUTHEY *Chron. Cid* 239 They are of high blood and full orgullous, and I have no liking to this match. **1820** SCOTT *Monast.* xxi, Punished for your outrecuidance and orgillous presumption. **1848** LYTTON *Harold* v. iii, This our orgulous Earl shall not have his triumph. **1890** *Sat. Rev.* 12 July 29/2 Lord Rosebery tore things to shreds.. in the best and most orgillous fashion. **1922** JOYCE *Ulysses* 383 Then spoke young Stephen orgulous of mother Church that would cast him out of her bosom. **1928** V. WOOLF *Orlando* i. 46 There was an orgulous credulity about him which was pleasant enough. *Ibid.* iv. 151 A covey of swans floated, orgulous, undulant, superb. **1929** WYNDHAM LEWIS *King Spider* (1930) iv. 227 Charles, baffled here, turns his eyes elsewhere, filled with orgulous dreams. His imagination and his early successes have turned his head. **1941** AUDEN *New Year Let.* 187 That the orgulous spirit may while it can Conform to its temporal focus with praise. **1946** E. LINKLATER *Dark of Summer* 60 Coloured prints.. all were bright, fantastic, orgulous—and serenely defiant of war and the cold Atlantic. **1976** M. SPARK *Takeover* x. 147 This confidence.. frequently over-rides with an orgulous scorn any small blatant contradictory facts.

b. *fig.* Splendid. c. Swelling, violent.

13.. *Coer de L.* 272 His atyre was orgulous. **1484** CAXTON *Curiall* 2 Better in humble tranquillyte than in orguyllous myserye. **1525** LD. BERNERS *Froiss.* II. cii. [xcviii.] 297 They wyst nat how to passe yᵉ ryuer of Derne, which was full and orgulous at certayne tymes. **1610** BARROUGH *Meth. Physick* VI. iii. (1639) 363 These most orgueilous and extreme paines are caused of a very moist and maligne vapour.

Hence †**ˈorgulously** *adv.*

c **1475** *Partenay* 3543 Off A fers behold, orgulously wrought, Als with the behold of his eyes twain.

orgun, orgweill, obs. ff. ORGAN, ORGUEIL.

orgy, orgie (ˈɔːdʒɪ); chiefly in pl. **orgies** (ˈɔːdʒɪz). [in pl. *orgies*, a. F. *orgies* ('les orgies de Bacchus', *c* 1500 in Hatz.-Darm.), ad. L. *orgia*, a. Gr. ὄργια pl., 'secret rites', esp. 'a nocturnal festival in honour of Bacchus', also, in L. 'secret frantic revels'. The singular *orgie*, *orgy* (F. *orgie*) is later and comparatively rare, exc. in sense 3.]

1. *Gr.* and *Rom. Antiq.* Secret rites or ceremonies practised in the worship of various deities of Greek and Roman mythology; *esp.* those connected with the festivals in honour of Dionysus or Bacchus, or the festival itself, which was celebrated with extravagant dancing, singing, drinking, etc.

1589 WARNER *Alb. Eng.* VI. xxxi. (1612) 152 The Goteheards of Hyrcania hild their Orgies vnto me [Pan]. **1697** DRYDEN *Virg. Georg.* IV. 756 The Thracian Matrons,.. With Furies, and Nocturnal Orgies fir'd. **1763** J. BROWN *Poetry & Mus.* v. 59 The Orgys of Bacchus.. were famed through all the Ages of Antiquity. **1846** GROTE *Greece* (1851) I. 29 Diffusion of special mysteries, schemes for religious purification, and orgies (I venture to anglicise the Greek word, which contains in its original meaning no implication of the ideas of excess to which it was afterwards diverted) in honour of some particular god.

b. *sing.*

1665 SIR T. HERBERT *Trav.* (1677) 118 It would have resembled an Orgy to Bacchus. **1871** R. ELLIS *Catullus* lxiii. 24 To a barbarous ululation the religious orgy wakes. **1887** BOWEN *Virg. Æneid* IV. 302 In triennial orgy [L. *orgia*] the Bacchus cry and the choir Peal.

c. *attrib.*

1866 CONINGTON *Æneid* VI. 196 An orgie dance she chose to feign.

2. *transf.* Applied to any rites, ceremonies, or secret observances, religious or otherwise; with or without implication of extravagance or licence.

1598 DRAYTON *Heroic. Ep.* v. 60 Grac'd with the Orgies of my Bridall Feast. *a* **1667** COWLEY *Agric.* Verses & Ess. (1687) 108 The Birds above rejoyce with various strains, And in the solemn Scene their Orgies keep. **1667** MILTON *P.L.* I. 415 Yet thence his lustful Orgies he [Peor] enlarg'd Even to that Hill of scandal, by the Grove Of Moloch homicide, lust hard by hate. **1746** MORELL *Judas Maccabæus* (Air), Pious orgies, pious airs, Decent sorrow, decent prayers, Will to the Lord ascend. **1850** MRS. JAMESON *Leg. Monast. Ord.* (1863) 78 On this night.. the witches held their orgies on the Blockberg. **1894** *19th Cent.* July 63 Edward Colston, of Bristol, in whose honour pious orgies are still annually celebrated in that city.

¶**b.** Misused by Daniel in sense 'panegyric'.

1646 G. DANIEL *Poems* Wks. 1878 I. 63 What Numbers bring T' empassionate, and worthy Orgies Sing? **1646–8** *Ibid.* 199 To bring His Praise in Catalogue, were but to Singe A forced orgie.

3. Feasting or revelry, esp. such as is marked by excessive indulgence or licence; wild or dissolute revels; debauchery; often in *sing.* A drunken or licentious revel.

1703 ROWE *Ulyss.* I. i. 199 These rude licentious Orgyes are for Satyrs. **1740** SOMERVILLE *Hobbinol* II. 463 The frolic Crowd.. Their Orgies kept, and frisk'd it o'er the Green Jocund, and gay. **1798** W. TAYLOR in *Monthly Rev.* XXVII. 521 Friends of stability or rather of retrogression.. describing every private supper as an orgie. **1828** SCOTT *F.M. Perth* xi, The effect of the Bacchanalian orgies. **1840** BARHAM *Ingol. Leg.* Ser. I. *Spectre of Tapp.*, Heated and inflamed from his midnight orgies. **1850** W. IRVING *Goldsmith* 37 He dreaded the ridicule of his fellow-students for the ludicrous termination of his orgie. **1870** DISRAELI *Lothair* lxxvii, The worship of the beautiful always ends in an orgy.

fig. **1883** F. HARRISON *Choice Bks.* (1886) 400 That orgy of blood and arrogance—the European tyranny of Bonaparte.

orgyllous, orgyn, obs. ff. ORGULOUS, ORGAN.

orhel, variant of ORGEL *Obs.*, pride.

-orial, a compound suffix, consisting of the suffix -AL[1], L. *-āl-is*, added to L. *-ōri-*, in *-ōri-us*, *-a*, *-um* (see -ORY). The termination is originally adjectival (substantival only by ellipsis), and app. arose in connexion with sbs. in *-ōrium*, *-ōrius*, Eng. -ORY; thus late L. had *territōri-āl-is* from *territōrium*. But it has been extended in Eng. to form derivatives from L. adjs. in *-tōrius*, *-sōrius*, from agent-nouns in *-tor*, *-sor*, as *cursori-al*, *dictatori-al*, *pictori-al*, *piscatori-al*, *procuratori-al*, *professori-al*, *sartori-al*, *senatori-al*, and others formed directly on agent-nouns themselves or on the cognate ppl. stem of the vb., as *equatorial*, *mediatorial*. In sense, these adjs. in *-orial* are usually identical with those in *-ory*, and the two forms are not rarely found side by side (e.g. *piscatorial*, *piscatory*); but the former is preferred for the adj. when there is a sb. in *-ory* (*purgatory*, *purgatorial*). Words in *-orial* from agent-nouns are chiefly of Eng. formation, the compound suffix being rare in Fr.

oribatid (ɒˈrɪbətɪd), *sb.* and *a.* [f. mod.L. family name *Oribatidæ*, f. generic name *Oribata* (P. A. Latreille in C. N. S. Sonnini *Buffon's Hist. Nat. Insectes* (1802) III. 65), perh. f. Gr. ὀρειβάτης mountain-ranging: see -ID[3].] **A.** *sb.* A small, oval, dark-coloured mite belonging to the family Oribatidæ or the order Oribatoidea, which includes non-parasitic mites with a thickened integument, giving them a leathery appearance. **B.** *adj.* Of or pertaining to this group of mites.

1875 *Encycl. Brit.* II. 276/1 The Oribatides in general live on vegetable matter. **1914** *Brit. Mus. Return* 170 in *Parl. Papers* LXXI. 193 Thirty-three Oribatid Mites from Hawaii. **1924** *Glasgow Herald* 12 Jan. 4/2 The hard-shelled 'beetle-mites', or Oribatids feed on decaying vegetable matter. **1967** M. E. HALE *Biol. Lichens* vii. 101 The lichens .. are in turn infested with oribatid mites that appear to be lichenivorous. **1972** J. BALOGH *Oribatid Genera of World* 9 The Oribatid mites are one of the richest soil Arthropodan groups. *Ibid.* 14 Permanent mounts with framing are wholly unsuitable for the study and conservation of Oribatids. *Ibid.* 15 The Oribatid specimen to be studied is carefully lifted from the lactic acid.

‖**oribi, orebi** (ˈɒrɪbɪ). Also 9 orabie, ourebi, oribé. [Cape Dutch, app. from Hottentot.] A small species of South African antelope (*Antilope scoparia* or *Scopophorus ourebi*), inhabiting open plains.

1795 THUNBERG in *Pinkerton's Voy.* (1808) XVI. 95 A very small and extremely scarce goat called Orebi. **1801** SIR J. BARROW *Trav. S. Africa* 138 Orabie. **1827** GRIFFITHS tr. *Cuvier's Anim. Kingd.* V. 339, *A. scoparia*, the Orebi, adult male, 22 to 24 inches high, four feet long, head eight inches. **1834** PRINGLE *Afr. Sk.* 11 By valleys remote where the oribi plays. **1834** *Penny Cycl.* II. 76/2 The Ourebi,.. called *bleekbok* or *palebuck* by the Dutch colonists at the Cape... The ourebi inhabits the open plains of South Africa. **1887**

RIDER HAGGARD *She* vi. 80 A tanned hide of a small red buck, something like that of the oribé. **1893** SELOUS *Trav. S.E. Africa* 74, I shot a fine oribi antelope.

orible, -bull, obs. ff. HORRIBLE.

orice, oricelle, obs. ff. ORRIS, ORCHIL.

orichalc ('ɒrɪkælk). Also 6 oricalche, 7 -chalch; and in Lat. form **orichalcum** (also 7 aurichalc(h)um). [ad. L. *orīchalc-um*, a. Gr. ὀρείχαλκον, lit. 'mountain-copper', f. ὄρος, ὀρε- mountain + χαλκός copper, applied to a yellow copper ore or brass. In later L. made into *aurichalcum*, after L. *aurum* gold, as if 'golden copper'.] Some yellow ore or alloy of copper, highly prized by the ancients; perhaps brass.

Applied by Strabo to brass, though some Greek writers treated ὀρείχαλκον as a fabulous metal; in the Middle Ages, *aurichalcum* is often mentioned as a very precious metal known only by report.

1590 SPENSER *Muiopot.* 78 The metall was of rare and passing price; Not Bilbo steele, nor brasse from Corinth fet, Nor costly Oricalche from strange Phœnice. **1646** SIR T. BROWNE *Pseud. Ep.* II. iv, Their electrum,..a substance now as unknown as true *aurichalcum*, or Corinthian brass. **1661** DARNELL *Corr. I. Basire* (1831) 195 Several boxes of Orichalch. **1670** *Phil. Trans.* V. 2036 Of Copper,..together with a discourse of the Native and Factitious Orichalchum. **1785** BP. WATSON in *Mem. Lit. & Phil. Soc. Manch.* II. 47 On Orichalcum. **1855** SINGLETON *Virgil* II. XII. 485 Then he..dons his coat of mail, With gold and sheeny orichalcum crisp. **1867** J. B. ROSE tr. *Virgil's Æneid* 348 Breastplate.. rough with mingled orichalc and gold.

orichalceous (ɒrɪ'kælsiːəs), *a.* [f. med. or mod.L. *orichalce-us* (f. *orichalcum*, after *aureus*, *argenteus*, etc.): see prec. and -EOUS.] (See quot.)

1826 KIRBY & SP. *Entomol.* IV. 283 Splendour... b. Metallic...3. Orichalceous (*Orichalceus*). A splendour intermediate between that of gold and brass.

orichalcite (*Min.*): see AURICHALCITE.

orichard, obs. variant of ORCHARD.

oriel ('ɔərɪəl). Also 5 **oryel, oriell**, 5-6 **oryall**, 6-8 **oriall**, 7 **orial, oryal**, 7-8 **oriol**, (9 **oriole**). [ME. a. OF. *oriol* (*eurieul*, *oeurieul* (in Godefroy) 'porch, passage, corridor, gallery', med.L. (? from Fr.) *oriolum* (in Matt. Paris, *a* 1259) 'porch, entrance-hall, antechamber'.

Of unknown origin: for the conjecture that the F. or med.L. might be altered from L. *aureolum* 'golden, gilded', in sense 'gilded chamber', there is no historical foundation; the Fr. forms in *eu*, *œu* point to an original *ō* not *au*.]

Although much research has been expended upon the history of this word, and esp. upon the development of the current use in *oriel window*, the sense-history remains in many points obscure and perplexed. Mr. W. Hamper in an exhaustive article in *Archæologia* XXIII. (1831) 114, asserts, and app. proves, for *oriel* the senses, penthouse, porch (attached to an edifice), (detached) gatehouse, loft, upper floor, gallery (for minstrels). It is also shown in Parker's *Domest. Archit.*, that the name was applied to a gallery or upper chamber in the west end of a domestic chapel, or to a small private apartment having a window looking into the chapel (see also *Bentley's Qu. Rev.* 1860 Jan. 497). The earliest sense known is that of 'portico, passage, corridor, gallery', assured from OFr. (Godef.) and med.L., and it is probable that 'oriel window' meant at first 'window in a gallery or balcony'. Most of the earlier senses claimed by Mr. Hamper are found only in L. context, examples in Eng. being scarce. The modern Cornish use of *orrel* is however an important link.

†**1.** A portico, corridor, gallery, balcony, etc. *Obs.*

[*a* **1259** MATT. PARIS *Vitæ Abbat. S. Albani* (an. 1251) (1681) 1071 Adjacet Atrium nobilissimum in introitu; quod porticus vel Oriolum appellatur.] **1385** *Durham Acc. Rolls* 265 In mundacione del Oriel, iij *d.* **1448** *Roll 27 Hen. VI* in *Archæologia* XXIII. 113 Pro sperres, postibus, et gradubus, de eisdem fiendis pro uno Oriell supra Stabulam ibidem. **1450-51** *Roll 30 Hen. VI, ibid.*, Pro novo Oreyell pro Trumpetes Domini in Aula ibidem. *c* **1450** *Erle Tolous* 307 When ye here the Mas-belle, Y schall hur brynge to the Chapelle,..Be the Oryall syde stonde thou stylle, Then schalt thou see hur at thy wylle. *a* **1490** BOTONER (William of Worcester) *Itin.* (1778) 89 Altitudo dictæ turris, cum le ovyrstorye vocat' an Oriell. *a* **1500** *MS. Chron.* (an. 1424) in Blakeway & Owen *Hist. Shrewsbury* (1825) II. 257 He..laft behynde hym a doughter of hys namyd Blase Tuptun, who cam by chance to be a leeper, and made the oryell which goythe allong the west side of the sayde churche-yarde [St. Chad's], throughe which she cam aloft to heare serveys.. and so passyd usually uppon the leades unto a glasse wyndowe, throughe which she dayly sawe and hard dayly serveys as longe as shee lyvyd.

b. In Cornwall (*orrel*), A porch or balcony at the head of an outside stair.

1880 *E. Cornwall Gloss.* s.v., The ground-floor of a fisherman's house is often a fish-cellar, and the first floor serves him for kitchen and parlour, which is reached by a flight of stone steps ending in an *orrel* or porch (Polperro). **1880** MRS. PARR *Adam & Eve* xxxii. 435 The steps which led up to the wooden oriel, or balcony—at that time a common adornment to the Polperro houses.

2. A large recess with a window, of polygonal plan, projecting from the outer face of the wall of a building, usually, in an upper story, and either supported from the ground or on corbels. Formerly sometimes forming a small private apartment attached to a hall, or the like.

c **1440** *Promp. Parv.* 369/2 Oryel of a wyndowe, ..*cancellus*,..*intendicula*. ? *c* **1475** *Sqr. lowe Degre* 97 In her oryall there she was Closed well with royall glas, Fulfylled it was with ymagery, Euery wyndowe by and by, On eche syde had there a gynne, Sperde with many a dyuers pynne. **1655** FULLER *Ch. Hist.* VI. ii. (1840) III. 305 Sure I am, that small excursion out of gentlemen's halls in Dorsetshire (respect it east or west) is commonly called an orial. **1814** SCOTT *Ld. of Isles* III. ii, In an oriel's deep recess. **1828** MACAULAY *Hist.* in *Misc. Writ.* (1860) I. 280 The oriels of Longleat and the stately pinnacles of Burleigh. **1841** MOTLEY *Corr.* (1889) I. iv. 86 We marched back through the hall with the oriel into a suite of two or three rooms filled with pictures. **1844** F. A. PALEY *Church Restorers* 42 She was pleased..that they had condescended to visit her little oriel which she had not hoped ever to see thus highly honoured.

b. for *oriel window*. (Sometimes vaguely put for *stained-glass window*.)

1805 SCOTT *Last Minstr.* II. xi, The moon on the east oriel shone, Through slender shafts of shapely stone. **1832** TENNYSON *Pal. Art* xli, Thro' the topmost Oriels' colour'd flame Two godlike faces gazed below. **1842-76** GWILT *Encycl. Archit.* §415 Near to the high table, a projecting or bay window, termed an *oriel*, was introduced [i.e. in English halls, *c* 1300-1460]. **1886** WILLIS & CLARK *Cambridge* II. 28 The gallery..has one large and two small oriels on the side next to the court.

fig. **1845** LONGF. *Evening Star* 1 Lo! in the painted Oriel of the West..shines the Evening Star.

3. *attrib.* and *Comb.* (from 2).

1542 *Will of John Tynte of Wraxall* 22 June (MS.), A fether bedde in the oriall chamber. **1843** LYTTON *Last Bar.* I. vii, There was a large oriel casement jutting from the wall. **1872** BROWNING *Fifine* xxx, No tinted pane of oriel sanctity Does our Fifine afford. **1883** OUIDA *Wanda* I. 97 The painted panes of the oriel casements.

b. oriel window, the window of an 'oriel'; a projecting window in an upper story.

1765 H. WALPOLE *Otranto* v. (1798) 78 Calling her aside into the recess of the oriel window of the hall. **1824** DIBDIN *Libr. Comp.* 590 The vast bay and auriol windows of the larger apartments. **1836** LOUDON *Encycl. Archit.* Gloss. 1129 An oriel window is a projecting window in an upper story; a bay window is a similar one on the ground floor. **1879** SIR G. SCOTT *Lect. Archit.* I. 265 The oriel window or bay window was another Mediæval invention.

c. ***Oriel College*** (Oxford) derives its name from a messuage previously occupied by Seneschal Hall, but called, in the reign of Henry III, *La* (or *Le*) *Oriole*, the origin of which name is unknown.

This was granted to St. Mary's College at its foundation in 1326, and occupied by the provost and fellows; the society being consequently known as 'of the Oriole'. In a deed of 1349 they are styled 'the Master and Scholars of the Hall of the Blessed Mary, called the Oriole'.

1450 *Rolls of Parlt.* V. 187/2 Oure Collage in Oxford, called the Oriell.

†**orielle.** *Obs.* Some precious stone: see quot.

c **1400** MAUNDEV. (1839) v. 48 And his Nekke is ȝalowe, aftre colour of an Orielle, that is a Ston well schynynge. [Fr. *e ad col tout iaune de la colour dun oriel bien luisant.*]

'**orielled**, *a. rare.* [f. ORIEL + -ED².] Provided with oriels (sense 2).

1905 *Westm. Gaz.* 4 Nov. 6/2 Tawny sunlight works bright wizardries In orielled cloisters.

oriency ('ɔərɪənsɪ). Now *rare*. Also orience. [f. ORIENT *a.*: see -ENCY.] 'Orient' quality (see next, B. 2 b); brilliancy, lustre. (*poet.*)

1652 CULVERWELL *Lt. of Nat.* Rep. 20 The picture has lost its gloss and beauty, the oriency of its colours. **1693** BEVERLEY *True St. Gosp. Truth* 5 Every Link of the Golden Chain..hath in it self the Oriency, and Riches of all the Other. *c* **1865** G. M. HOPKINS *Poems* (1967) 120 Once it was scarce perceived Lent For orience of the daffodil. *Ibid.* 139 The heightening dawn with milky orience Rounds its still-purpling centreings of cloud. **1896** *Daily News* 4 Jan. 5/3 The delicate oriency of his pearls is lost in the strong hues.

Orient ('ɔərɪənt), *sb.* and *a.* Also orient. [a. F. *orient* (11th c. in Littré), ad. L. *oriens*, *orient-em* rising sun, east, sb. use of *oriens* 'rising', pr. pple. of *orī-rī* to rise. Opposed, in senses A. 1, 2, B. 1, to OCCIDENT.]

A. *sb.*

1. That region of the heavens in which the sun and other heavenly bodies rise, or the corresponding region of the world, or quarter of the compass; the east. Now *poetic* or *rhet.*

c **1386** CHAUCER *Knt.'s T.* 636 And firy Phebus riseth vp so brighte That al the Orient laugheth of the lighte. **1390** GOWER *Conf.* II. 247 He shulde make his sacrifice..on knees down bent Thre sithes toward orient. **1420**, **1483** [see OCCIDENT A. 1]. **1509** HAWES *Past. Pleas.* XXVIII. (1845) 134 Seynge the cloudes rayed fayre and rede Of Phebus rysinge in the orient. **1578** T. N. tr. *Conq. W. India* 349 The Mexicans..sawe flames of fire toward the Orient, where now Vera Cruz standeth. *c* **1600** SHAKS. *Sonn.* vii, Lo! in the orient when the gracious light Lifts up his burning head. **1725** POPE *Odyss.* VIII. 2 All the ruddy Orient flames with day. **1847** TENNYSON *Princ.* III. 2 Morn..Came furrowing all the orient into gold.

2. That part of the earth's surface situated to the east of some recognized point of reference; eastern countries, or the eastern part of a country; the East; usually, those countries immediately east of the Mediterranean or of Southern Europe, which to the Romans were 'the East', the countries of South-western Asia or of Asia generally (cf. ORIENTAL A. 3); occas., in mod. American use, Europe or the Eastern Hemisphere. Now *poetic* or *literary*.

13.. *E.E. Allit. P.* A. 3 Perle plesaunte..Oute of oryent I hardyly saye, Ne proued I neuer her precios pere. *c* **1386** CHAUCER *Monk's T.* 324 They conquered manye regnes grete In the Orient. *a* **1450** *Le Morte Arth.* 2057 A fulle Ryche Aparaylmente..That wroght was in the oryente. **1535** STEWART *Cron. Scot.* II. 296 Tua Saxone kingis of the Orient Of Ingland. **1552** LYNDESAY *Monarche* 4257 For Orient and Occident To thame were all obedient. **1612** BREREWOOD *Lang. & Relig.* i. 9 The diocess of the orient.. contained Syria, Palestine, Cilicia, and part of Mesopotamia and of Arabia. **1676** CUDWORTH *Disc. Lord's Supper* ii. 15 Another sect..famous in the orient. **1849** CLOUGH *Amours de Voy.* v. 7 Sicily, Greece, will invite, and the Orient. **1864** LOWELL *Fireside Trav.* 40 Annual voyages to that vague Orient known as Down East. **1890** *Century Mag.* 103/1 He was sent as consul to the Orient.

b. ***pearl of orient***: = orient pearl, oriental pearl; a pearl from the Indian seas, as distinguished from those of less beauty found in European mussels; hence, a brilliant or precious pearl: see quot. 13.. above; cf. B. 2 and ORIENTAL A. 4.

a **1440** *Sir Degrev.* 650 A front endent With peyrl of orient. **1700** CONGREVE *Way of World* I. ix, As dim by thee, as a dead whiting's eye by a pearl of orient.

3. Rising (of the sun, or the daylight); sunrise, dayspring, dawn; also *fig.* Now *rare* or *Obs.*

1582 N. T. (Rhem.) *Luke* i. 78 In which the Orient from on high hath visited vs. *a* **1649** DRUMM. OF HAWTH. *James II* Wks. (1711) 37 His life having set in the orient of his age and hopes. **1651** C. CARTWRIGHT *Cert. Relig.* I. 28 In whose light the people should walke, and kings in the brightnesse of her Orient. **1842** MRS. BROWNING *Grk. Chr. Poets* (1863) 109 From the orient of the sun. **1850** NEALE *Med. Hymns* (1867) 171 Draw nigh Thou Orient, Who shalt cheer And comfort by Thine Advent here.

4. Short for 'pearl of orient' or 'orient pearl': see 2 b.

1831 CARLYLE *Sart. Res.* I. ii. (1858) 5 A very Sea of Thought..wherein the toughest pearl-diver may dive..and return not only with sea-wreck but with true orients. **1840** BROWNING *Sordello* III. 258 What spoils an orient like some speck Of genuine white, turning its own white grey?

5. The colour or peculiar lustre of a pearl of the best quality: see quot. 1755. *rare.*

1755 *Gentl. Mag.* XXV. 32 Orient, the fine naker or mother of pearle colour, which is seen on some shells. **1861** *Templebar Mag.* III. 391 The British pearls are from the mussel, not the oyster; as are also the Bohemian, which are likewise deficient in brilliancy and 'orient'.

6. Orient Express, the name of a train which ran (from 1883 to 1961) between Paris and Istanbul and other Balkan cities, via Vienna, and of its successors (see quots. 1961, 1977). Also *attrib.* in *fig.* sense, in allusion to its association with espionage and intrigue.

1883 *Times* 2 Nov. 10/1 A small folded card,..the back giving the timetable of the journey up to Constantinople,.. and the front, under the heading 'Orient Express', the direction 'M.—is requested to take his seat, in carriage—, bed No.—'. **1904** A. E. HOUSMAN *Let.* 23 Sept. (1971) 75, I *can* pay the sum they ask, but I very much object to, as Constantinople and the Orient Express are both pretty expensive. **1920** *Cornh. Mag.* Jan. 23 From Paris onwards, my three days journey was happily in the diplomatic train, the one-time Orient Express. **1925** C. CONNOLLY *Let.* May in *Romantic Friendship* (1975) 81, I was thinking of.. vanishing on the orient express. **1937** E. AMBLER *Uncommon Danger* i. 24 He could see a destination board on..one of the sleeping cars—Wien, Buda-Pesth, Belgrade, Sofia, Istanbul. The Orient Express looked warm and luxurious inside. **1960** O. MANNING *Great Fortune* i. 5 The day before had been spent on familiar territory, even if the Orient Express had kept to no schedule. **1961** *Guardian* 29 May 11/3 The Orient Express is no more. After 78 years of existence the train..is today [May 28] on its last journey from the Gare de l'Est station here [Paris] to Bucharest. **1965** *Observer* 16 May 9/1 Amateurish-sounding Orient Express techniques..are widely used... Master agent Lonsdale passed messages via drawing pins stuck..in a Lyons Corner House. **1977** *Daily Tel.* 2 May 6 (Advt.), Thursday, 19th May, 1977, will mark the death of a legend. .. On that day..*The Orient Express*..will begin its final run... On 22nd May the great train comes to rest in Istanbul's Sirkeci Station. **1977** *Ibid.* 19 May 10/8 The train, known since 1969 as the 'Direct-Orient', goes..to Belgrade, where first- and second-class coaches, including sleepers, separate. One section then heads for Athens and the other for Istanbul. After tonight there will be no through coaches to Athens or the Bosphorus... All that will be left..will be the Simplon Express from Paris Gare de Lyon to..Belgrade. The sole survivor of the original northern route, still wistfully and only symbolically labelled 'Orient Express', will run from the Gare de l'Est in Paris to Budapest and Bucharest.

B. *adj.*

1. Situated in or belonging to the east; eastern, oriental. Now *poet.*

a **1450** *Knt. de la Tour* xciv. 122 She came from the parties orientys. **1589** R. BRUCE *Serm.* (1843) 61 The Latine and Orient Kirks. **1629** MILTON *Nativity* 231 When the Sun.. Pillows his chin upon an Orient wave. **1817** COLERIDGE *Zapolya* IV. iii A richer dowry Than orient kings can give! **1827-44** WILLIS *Ermengarde* 38 The Danube..seeks an orient sea!

2. Applied to pearls and precious stones of superior value and brilliancy, as coming anciently from the East; often a vague poetic epithet: Precious, excellent; brilliant, lustrous, sparkling.

c **1400** MAUNDEV. (Roxb.) xxi. 97, ccc. precious stanes, grete and orient [*Fr.* ccc perles dorient]. *Ibid.*, A ruby, fyne and gude and orient. **1494** FABYAN *Chron.* v. cxvii. 93 He nowe shyneth as doth an orient stoone. **1555** EDEN *Decades* 39 Many of these perles were as bygge as hasell nuttes, and oriente (as we caule it), that is, lyke vnto them of the Easte partes. **1611** SPEED *Hist. Gt. Brit.* v. viii. 3 These Pearles, though not altogether so orient as they in India. *a* **1661** FULLER *Worthies* (1840) I. 306 It is possible that the Cornish diamonds..may be pure and orient. **1713** YOUNG *Force Relig.* II. (1757) 62 When orient gems around her temples blazed. **1862** TYNDALL *Mountaineer.* ii. 12 The grass..was sown with orient pearls [*i.e.* dewdrops].

b. Hence, of other things: Brilliant, lustrous, shining, glowing, radiant, resplendent (also *fig.*); sometimes (after A. 3), Shining like the dawn, bright red. *arch.*

1430–40 LYDG. *Bochas* I. i. (1554) 1 b, The rivers were so orient and so fine Like quicksilver upboyling on the pleyne. **1526** *Pilgr. Perf.* (W. de W. 1531) 183 b, Whyte set by blacke, appereth more oryent whyte than yf it stode by it selfe. **1578** LYTE *Dodoens* II. ix. 158 The floures [of rose campion]..be of an excellent shining or orient redde. *a* **1600** HOOKER *Eccl. Pol.* VIII. ii. §8 To make the countenance of truth more orient. **1650** FULLER *Pisgah* IV. v. 99 A shrub, whose red berries, or grains, gave an orient tincture to cloth. **1667** MILTON *P.L.* I. 546 Ten thousand Banners..With Orient Colours waving. *a* **1703** BURKITT *On N.T.* (1818) 355 The several graces and virtues, which were so orient in the life of Christ. *a* **1881** ROSSETTI *House of Life* Introd. Sonnet, Its flowering crest impearled and orient.

3. Rising, as the sun or daylight; also *fig.*

1598 YONG *Diana* 99 Behold a Nymph more faire then orient sunne. **1646** J. COOKE *Vind. Law* 32 That spirit of Reformation which I see orient in that court. **1728** POPE *Dunc.* III. 74 Far eastward..from whence the Sun And orient Science at a birth begun. **1822** SHELLEY *Hellas* 266 The orient moon of Islam. **1831** CARLYLE *Sart. Res.* II. v, A many-tinted, radiant Aurora,..this fairest of Orient Light-bringers.

orient (ˈɔərɪɛnt, ˌɔərɪˈɛnt), *v.* [a. F. *orient-er* to place facing the east, f. *orient* east.]

1. *trans.* To place or arrange (anything) so as to face the east; *spec.* to build (a church) with the longer axis due east and west, and the chancel or chief altar at the eastern end; also, to bury with the feet to the east.

1727–41 CHAMBERS *Cycl.* s.v. *Orienting*, In most religions, particular care has been taken to have their temples oriented.—St. Gregory Thaumaturgus is said to have made a mountain give way, because it prevented the orienting of a church he was building. **1896** JEVONS in *Classical Rev.* Feb. 22/1 The primitive Aryan in taking his bearings literally oriented himself and turned to the east.

b. By extension: To place with the four faces towards the four points of the compass; to place or adjust in any particular way with respect to the cardinal points or other defined data; to place or arrange the parts of a structure in any particular relative position; also, to ascertain the position of (anything) relatively to the points of the compass, etc.; to determine the bearings of.

1842 BRANDE *Dict. Sci.* etc. 857/2 In surveying, to orient a plan signifies to mark its situation or bearing with respect to the four cardinal points. **1866** *Boys' Wonder Bk.* 34 To tell him if she saw the Pole-star directly opposite the end of it, so that he might orient his stake. **1882** PROCTOR in *Knowledge* No. 13. 266 We are certain that the builders of the Pyramid wanted to orient it very carefully. **1882** GEIKIE in *Nature* XXVII. 123/2 The minute flakes interspersed through the ground-mass..are oriented in the same direction. **1892** J. T. BENT *Ruined Cit. Mashonaland* vi. 161 To orient it towards the setting sun. **1896** *Science* 3 July 11 We are now at a loss to orient the several parts of the cranium. **1926** C. E. MULFORD *Cassidy's Protégé* xiii. 170 Hesitating for a moment while he oriented the report, he started toward the edge of the hill-top. **1953** E. LYNAM *Mapmakers' Art* ii. 48 All early maps were oriented with the East at the top (whence our words 'to orient'). **1965** *Orienteering* ('Know the Game' series) 31 Once a map has been 'set' or oriented an orienteer should be aware of his position at all times by relating the map to the ground over which he is moving. **1972** N. J. W. THROWER *Maps & Man* vii. 102 A network of fundamental survey lines oriented predominantly in cardinal directions.

2. *fig.* To adjust, correct, or bring into defined relations, to known facts or principles; *refl.* to put oneself in the right position or relation; to ascertain one's 'bearings', find out 'where one is'. Also, to assign or give a specific direction or tendency to.

1850 T. PARKER *Let.* 9 Sept. in *Life H. Mann* (1865) 325 It seems to me you might, in this way, *orient* yourself before the public. **1864** E. SARGENT *Peculiar* I. 141 He tried to orient his conscience as to his duty under the extraordinary circumstances in which he found himself. **1867** O. W. HOLMES *Guardian Angel* xxix. (1891) 338 Mistress Kitty accepted Mrs. Hopkins's hospitable offer, and presently began orienting herself, and getting ready to make herself agreeable. **1883** WARD *Dynamic Sociology* II. 44 Men must orient themselves before they can expect to go right. **1940** W. FAULKNER *Hamlet* 223 So he held himself still.., trying to orient himself by looking back up the slope, to establish whether he was above or below the tree, to the right or left of it. **1952** G. SARTON *Hist. Sci.* I. xxii. 579 The orator's art consist[s] in shaping and orienting the passions of the people who listen to him. **1972** *Sci. Amer.* Dec. 6/2 The program is oriented toward the long-range goal of providing small power sources, automobiles included, with nonpolluting synthetic fuels. **1977** D. BENNETT *Jigsaw Man* iv. 88 He had recognised the lie of the land... He was fully oriented.

3. *intr.* To turn to the east, or (by extension) towards any specified direction.

1896 JEVONS in *Classical Rev.* Feb. 23/1 The primitive Aryan undoubtedly oriented east.

4. *Chem.* **a.** *intr.* Of a substituent in a ring: to direct atoms and groups to a specified position in the ring when they enter it as substituents.

1924, 1937 [implied in ORIENTING below]. **1949** ENGLISH & CASSIDY *Princ. Org. Chem.* vi. 106 Why should one group orient predominantly ortho and para, and another predominantly meta? **1971** [see ORTHO *a.* (*adv.*) 1].

b. *trans.* To ascertain the relative positions of the substituents in (a ring or a cyclic compound).

1941 F. E. RAY *Org. Chem.* xv. 375 To prove the structure (orient the ring) of an unknown di-substituted compound. **1958** READ & GUNSTONE *Text-bk. Org. Chem.* xxiv. 419 After sound methods of orienting substituted benzenes had been devised it became possible to study more satisfactorily the substitution reactions concerned.

5. *trans.* To cause the molecules of (a plastic or other material) to assume a position in which their axes are parallel.

1958 W. D. PAIST *Cellulosics* xi. 252 Considerable enhancement of the physical properties of many resin films has been realized on biaxially orienting the formed film. **1969** W. R. R. PARK *Plastics Film Technol.* ii. 26 Virtually any thermoplastic material can be oriented.

Hence **ˈorienting** *vbl. sb.* and *ppl. a.*; *spec.* in *Chem.* (cf. sense 4 a).

1727–41 [see sense 1 a above]. **1924** *Jrnl. Chem. Soc.* CXXV. 1377 (*heading*) The orienting influence of the thiocyano-group in aromatic compounds. **1937** F. C. WHITMORE *Org. Chem.* III. 723 Benzotrichloride and other meta orienting compounds. **1962** F. I. ORDWAY et al. *Basic Astronautics* iv. 159 (*caption*) Magnetic field measuring devices carried by Soviet Sputniks, showing orienting apparatus. **1965** *Orienteering* ('Know the Game' Series) 32 The engraved arrow inside the compass housing points to the top of the map and the orienting lines lie parallel to the grid lines. **1977** 'A. STUART' *Snap Judgement* 167, I did some orienting..by looking out of the [helicopter] window.

orientable (ˈɔərɪəntəb(ə)l), *a.* [f. ORIENT *v.* + -ABLE.] Capable of being oriented; in *Math.* [tr. G. *orientierbar*], applied to a surface for which it is possible, if each point is regarded as surrounded by a small closed curve, to assign a sense (clockwise or anticlockwise) to each curve so that they are the same for all points sufficiently close together; not non-orientable; also used analogously of spaces of higher dimension.

1935 A. P. HERBERT *What a Word!* iii. 85 One of our great motor-manufacturers advertises 'A very neat orientable anti-glare visor.' **1949** S. LEFSCHETZ *Introd. Topology* ii. 82 Two orientable connected closed surfaces are homeomorphic if they have the same genus. **1952** P. NEMENYI tr. *Hilbert & Cohn-Vossen's Geom. & Imagination* vi. 306 It can be demonstrated that all two-sided surfaces are orientable. **1960** L. PICKEN *Organization of Cells* vii. 265 Cleveland's material suggests only that in hypermastigine flagellates the centrioles utilize all orientable material. **1965** tr. *Lietzmann's Visual Topology* 120 A one-sided surface is not orientable. **1968** A. H. WALLACE *Differential Topology* vi. 79 The sphere is orientable but the projective plane is not. **1975** W. M. BOOTHBY *Introd. Differentiable Manifolds* v. 215 A manifold *M* is orientable if and only if it has a covering..of coherently oriented coordinate neighborhoods.

Hence **ˌorientaˈbility**, the property of being orientable.

1949 S. LEFSCHETZ *Introd. Topology* ii. 76 Orientability implies that the triangles of *K* may be 'oriented' (in an intuitive sense) so that adjacent triangles always have their orientations disposed as in Fig. 37. **1956** E. M. PATTERSON *Topology* i. 9 The idea of orientability is derived from the physical idea of two-sidedness. **1972** *Nature* 13 Oct. 387/1 Within general relativity it is necessary to impose time orientability on the E_4 manifold such that the arrows placed on timelike world lines agree in sign.

oriental (ɔərɪˈɛntəl), *a.* and *sb.* Also **Oriental.** [a. F. *oriental* (12th c. in Hatz.-Darm.), ad. L. *orientāl-is*, f. *orient-em* ORIENT: see -AL[1]. Opposed in all uses to OCCIDENTAL.] **A.** *adj.*

1. Belonging to, or situated in, that part or region of the heavens in which the sun rises; of or in the east, eastern, easterly; *spec.* in *Astrol.* said of a heavenly body when in the eastern part of the sky, *esp.* of a planet when seen in the east before sunrise (or, by extension, when seen before sunrise in any part of the sky).

c **1391** CHAUCER *Astrol.* I. §5 Whiche lyne..is cleped the Est lyne, or elles the lyne Orientale. **1590** SPENSER *F.Q.* I. v. 2 The golden orientall gate Of..heaven gan to open..And Phoebus..Came dauncing forth. **1646** SIR T. BROWNE *Pseud. Ep.* 305 His [the sun's] ascendent and orientall radiations. **1647** LILLY *Chr. Astrol.* xix. 114 To be Orientall is no other thing then to rise before the ☉. **1794** [see OCCIDENTAL A. 1]. **1835** ZADKIEL *App. to Lilly's Chr. Astrol.* 340 Planets found between the fourth house and the mid-heaven, rising, are in the eastern half of the figure, and said to be oriental.

†**2.** Belonging to or situated in the east of a country or place, or of the earth; eastern. *Obs.*

c **1528** R. THORNE *to Hen. VIII* in Hakluyt *Voy.* (1589) 251 All the Indies which we call Orientall. **1576** TURBERV. *Venerie* 26 A kennell ought to be placed in some orientall parte of a house. **1610** WILLET *Hexapla Daniel* 67 The diuision of the Romane Empire into the Occidentall and Orientall. **1669** GALE *Crt. Gentiles* I. I. xii. 81 Mount Hermon..the most oriental part of al Canaan.

3. *spec.* Belonging to, found in, or characteristic of, the countries or regions lying to the east of the Mediterranean or of the ancient Roman empire; belonging to south-western Asia, or Asiatic countries generally; also, belonging to the east of Europe, or of Christendom (as ***the Oriental Empire***, or ***Church***); Eastern.

c **1477** CAXTON *Jason* 53 In the parties orientall is an ile. *a* **1540** BARNES *Wks.* (1573) 365/1 Priests in yᵉ orientall Church. **1586** MARLOWE *1st Pt. Tamburl.* III. iii, The Persian fleet..Sailing along the oriental sea, Have fetch'd about the Indian continent. **1630** BRATHWAIT *Eng. Gentlem.* (1641) 143 The Alexandrian and all the Orientall Histories. **1679** RICAUT *Pres. State Grk. Ch.* Pref., The four Oriental Patriarchs. **1712** ADDISON *Spect.* No. 512 ¶5 A Turkish tale, which I do not like the worse for that little Oriental extravagance which is mixed with it. **1777** SIR W. JONES *Poems* Pref. 12 A comparison between the Oriental and Italian poetry. **1815** ELPHINSTONE *Acc. Caubul* (1842) I. 253 The Pushtoo..is..not unpleasing to an ear accustomed to Oriental tongues.

b. In names of natural products, diseases, etc. occurring specially in the East; as ***oriental alabaster, arbutus, hyacinth, plane-tree***, etc., ***oriental leprosy***; **oriental poppy**, a perennial poppy, *Papaver orientale*, with large scarlet flowers, native to western Asia; **oriental sore**, an ulcerous skin-disease occurring in the East, also called *Aleppo boil*, *Aleppo ulcer*, etc. (See also 4.)

1578 LYTE *Dodoens* II. xlviii. 206 The Oriental Hyacinthes do flower before the common sort. **1664** EVELYN *Kal. Hort.*, Jan. in *Sylva* etc. (1729) 192 Oriental Jacinth, Levantine Narcissus. **1731** P. MILLER *Gardeners Dict.* s.v. Papaver. *Papaver; Orientale...* Very rough Oriental Poppy, with a large Flower. **1756–7** tr. *Keysler's Trav.* (1760) II. 428 A very grand urn of oriental alabaster. **1803** *Med. Jrnl.* IX. 564 The oriental leprosy, of which Egypt seems to have been the native land. **1878** T. BRYANT *Pract. Surg.* I. 173 The Oriental sore seems to be due to the use of brackish hard well-water. **1882** *Garden* 8 Apr. 230/3 The large Oriental Poppy. **1963** W. BLUNT *Of Flowers & Village* 139, I think the oriental poppy..is the most exciting of them all.

c. ***oriental stitch***: a long straight stitch tied down with a short diagonal stitch in the centre.

c **1890** *Weldon's Pract. Needlew.* VI. No. 68. 6 Oriental stitch..closely resembles herringbone in the method of working, and forms a solid plait upon the surface of the material. **18..** *Pract. Jrnl. Decorative Needlework* [Manchester] No. 12. 14 If the design is to be worked solidly I would suggest the oriental stitch. **1899** W. G. P. TOWNSEND *Embroidery* vi. 98 A sort of Oriental or herring-bone in alternate colours. **1900** DAY & BUCKLE *Art in Needlework* 66 Oriental-stitch, sometimes called 'Antique-stitch', is a stitch in three strokes, just as feather-stitch is a stitch in four.

d. Other Special Combs.: ***oriental carpet, rug***: a hand-knotted carpet or rug made to one of various designs in the Orient; a carpet or rug made to a similar design elsewhere; ***oriental Jew***, a Jewish person from the Middle or Far East, esp. from Yemen, Ethiopia, Iraq, or India; ***Oriental languages***, Eastern languages; these as a subject of university study; ***oriental-looking*** ppl. adj.; ***Oriental Lowestoft***: name given to oriental porcelain erron. thought to have been made or decorated at Lowestoft, England; see sense B. 4.

1868 C. L. EASTLAKE *Hints Household Taste* 267/2 Oriental carpets. **1894** *Country Gentlemen's Catal.* 114 *Oriental carpets and rugs.* In Selected Designs and Colourings, Imported direct. **1972** *Guardian* 8 Sept. 11/5 You'll find an Aladdin's cave crammed full of authentic, handmade Oriental and Persian carpets. **1938** R. T. FEIWEL *No Ease in Zion* xxi. 298 One-fifth of Tel Aviv consists of Oriental Jews. **1961** L. FINKELSTEIN *Jews* II. xxv. 1179 Shakespeare's *Comedy of Errors*,..appealed greatly to the imagination of the Oriental Jew. **1968** MRS. L. B. JOHNSON *White House Diary* 7 Feb. (1970) 628 Some interesting excerpts: Between 60 and 65 percent of the people of Israel are 'Oriental' Jews. **1822** M. EDGEWORTH *Let.* 23 Jan. (1971) 334 We have just walked to see Hertford College... There are eight professors—two for classical literature—three Oriental languages, [etc.]. **1970** M. KELLY *Spinifex* i. 23, I went up to Cambridge, doing Oriental Languages. **1972** 'J. BELL' *Death of Poison-Tongue* i. 8, I have come to Polford to do Oriental languages. **1869** 'MARK TWAIN' *Innoc. Abr.* viii. 79 A ragged, oriental-looking negro. **1964** P. F. ANSON *Bishops at Large* viii. 281 This long-bearded, oriental-looking prelate. [**1866** W. CHAFFERS *Marks Pott. & Porc.* (ed. 2) 317 There is such a peculiarity in the form and quality of the Lowestoft porcelain that we are surprised any one at all conversant with..collections of china, could ever mistake it for Oriental.] **1949** G. SAVAGE *Ceramics for Collector* ii. 41 The former belongs to the 'Oriental Lowestoft' or 'East Indian China' group. **1971** L. A. BOGER *Dict. World Pott. & Porc.* 67/1 It [*sc.* Chinese Lowestoft] is also called Chinese Export Porcelain and Oriental Lowestoft. **1974** SAVAGE & NEWMAN *Illustr. Dict. Ceramics* 208 *Oriental Lowestoft*, an erroneous term, first given currency by W. Chaffers.., for the enormous quantity of porcelain made in the 18th century in China for export to Europe. **1881** C. C. HARRISON *Woman's Handiwork* III. 138 Oriental rugs are so generally used. **1931** A. U. DILLEY (*title*) Oriental rugs and carpets. **1966** M. G. EBERHART *Witness at Large* (1967) vii. 95 The wide hall upstairs had faded oriental rugs placed at spots almost sure to trip anybody. **1976** J. VAN DE WETERING *Corpse on Dike* ii. 20 A table, covered with a thick oriental rug.

4. Of pearls and precious stones, and hence (formerly) of other things: = ORIENT B. 2, 2 b.

In some names of precious stones, denoting a stone different from, but resembling in colour, that bearing the simple name; as ***oriental amethyst, o. emerald, o. topaz*** (respectively purple, green, and yellow varieties of sapphire).

c **1385** CHAUCER *L.G.W.* Prol. 221 Of oo perle, fyne, oriental, Hire white coroune was ymaked al. *c* **1400** LYDG. *Æsop's Fab.* Prol. 26 Perlis white, cliere, and oriental Bien oft founde in muskle shellis blake. **1596** *Edward III*, II. i. 12 But no more like her oriental red Than brick to coral. **1599**

HAKLUYT *Voy.* II. 279 Some dozen of very faire Emeraulds orientall. **1693** SIR R. REDDING in *Phil. Trans.* XVII. 661 The in-sides of the shells are of an Oriental and Pearly Colour. **1747** [see OCCIDENTAL A. 3]. **1796** KIRWAN *Elem. Min.* (ed. 2) I. 289 Those that possess this varying splendor are called *Oriental opals*, though they are not found in the East. **1868** DANA *Min.* 138 Corundum.. Var. 1. Sapphire.. Includes the purer kinds of fine colors,..true *Ruby*, or *Oriental Ruby*, red; *O. Topas*, yellow; *O. Emerald*, green; *O. Amethyst*, purple.

B. *sb.* (Often with capital initial.)

†**1.** An oriental pearl or other gem; see A. 4. *Obs.*

1377 LANGL. *P. Pl.* B. II. 14 Diamantz of derrest pris, and double manere safferes, Orientales and ewages. **1750** tr. *Leonardus' Mirr. Stones* 84 Cornelian is a stone of a reddish or ruddy colour, and such are Orientals.

†**2.** *pl.* Oriental languages; see A. 3. *Obs.*

1680 H. DODWELL *Two Lett.* (1691) 155 Those tongues.. derived from the Hebrew Tongue, as most of the Orientals are. **1712** STEELE *Spect.* No. 473 ¶1, I heard a young Man ..comfort himself in his Ignorance of Greek, Hebrew, and the Orientals. *a* **1734** NORTH *Lives* (1826) III. 322 Latin, and the vernaculars westward,..carry nearly the same idiom; but the Orientals and Greek partake not so much of them.

3. A native or inhabitant of the East; i.e. usually, an Asiatic; cf. A. 3.

1701 GREW *Cosm. Sacra* IV. i. §26 The Jews, and all the Orientals, took all those Prophecies..in a Literal Sense. **1850** ROBERTSON *Serm.* Ser. III. iii. (1872) 38 The Oriental prostrates himself on the ground. **1864** BURTON *Scot. Abr.* I. ii. 97 A solemn, bearded, turbanded, and robed Oriental.

b. Name of a fancy variety of pigeon.

1897 *Daily News* 6 Jan. 3/3 The show presents..barbs, Antwerps, homers, Modenas, magpies, Archangels, orientals, and other varieties of the columbarian family.

4. Denoting a variety of porcelain imported from China by European countries from *c* 1700 to *c* 1835; also known as *Oriental Lowestoft, Chinese Lowestoft, Chinese Export Porcelain.* Also *attrib.*

1863 W. CHAFFERS *Marks Pott. & Porc.* 134 Brameld. This mark is in red, on porcelain vases, in imitation of Oriental. **1873** C. SCHREIBER *Jrnl.* (1911) I. 201 A collection of choice specimens of Oriental. **1926** [see MINTON].

5. Used *ellipt.* for *oriental carpet, pattern, rug*, etc.

1897 *Sears, Roebuck Catal.* 220/2 *Extra Fine Lace Back Suspenders*... A magnificent assortment of patterns. Persians, Orientals, Dresdens. **1938** I. GOLDBERG *Wonder of Words* v. 91 The noun *oriental* has ceased, or half-ceased, to mean a rug woven in the Orient; it has come to mean a rug of a certain design and coloring. **1969** M. G. EBERHART *Message from Hong Kong* xvii. 152 The rugs in the hall were old Orientals, worn thin too, but still glowing in reds and blues. **1972** E. BERCKMAN *Fourth Man on Rope* i. 19 On its polished floor-boards lay a thin faded Oriental, once a very good one. **1977** C. MCFADDEN *Serial* (1978) xxx. 67/2 Martha..began to pull Kate unsteadily across the Oriental.

orientalia (ɔərɪɛnˈteɪlɪə), *sb. pl.* Also **Orientalia.** [mod.L., neut. pl. of L. *orientālis* oriental.] Things, esp. books, relating to or characteristic of the Orient.

1916 *Asiatic Rev.* VIII. p. iii, (*Index*) Orientalia. **1928** H. CRANE *Let.* 28 Mar. (1965) 322, I enjoyed your historical notes and orientalia. **1932** *N. & Q.* 16 Jan. 35 (Advt.), *Books, prints, autographs*... No. 534. Orientalia. **1973** *Country Life* 20 Sept. (Suppl.) 73 19th Century Orientalia. **1975** *Sat. Rev.* (U.S.) 22 Mar. 57/2 Gumps, San Francisco —celebrated for *objets d'art*, orientalia, china, glass, jade.

†**orienˈtalian.** *Obs. rare*⁻¹. [f. L. *orientālia* (neut. pl. of *orientālis*) in mod.L. 'oriental studies' + -AN.] = ORIENTALIST 3.

1691 WOOD *Ath. Oxon.* II. 432 Mr. Sam. Clark an eminent Orientalian.

oriˈentalism. [f. ORIENTAL *a.* + -ISM.] Oriental character, style, or quality; the characteristics, modes of thought or expression, fashions, etc. of Eastern nations; with *pl.* an oriental trait or idiom.

1769 HOLDSWORTH *On Virgil* 265 There are frequent instances of the very same orientalism in Homer. **1774** WARTON *Hist. Eng. Poetry* (1775) I. i. 17 Dragons are a sure mark of orientalism. **1807** F. WRANGHAM *Serm. Transl. Script.* 25 The sublime orientalisms of Job. **1862** MERIVALE *Rom. Emp.* (1865) VI. xlix. 123 The Orientalism which had pervaded the court. **1877** OWEN *Wellesley's Desp.* p. xliv, The beauty of the style, unimpaired..by the amalgam of infusible Orientalisms.

b. Oriental scholarship; knowledge of Eastern languages.

1811 BYRON *Ch. Har.* II. *note*, Mr. Thornton's frequent hints of profound Orientalism.

oriˈentalist. [f. as prec. + -IST.]

†**1.** A member of the Eastern or Greek Church.

1683 CAVE *Ecclesiastici, Hilary* 205 He found..the Western Prelates..vex'd into compliance, and the Orientalists forc'd to go the same way.

†**2.** = ORIENTAL B. 3. *Obs.*

1738 WARBURTON *Div. Legat.* I. 423 Thinking that the Orientalists had a genius more subtile and metaphysical than the Greeks. **1791–1823** D'ISRAELI *Cur. Lit.* (1858) III. 311 He..supposed, like orientalists, they wrote from the right to the left.

3. One versed in oriental languages and literature.

1779–81 JOHNSON *L.P., Smith* Wks. II. 465 The great Orientalist, Dr. Pocock. **1879** *Addr. Pres. Philol. Soc.* 4 The Congress of Orientalists at Florence.

orienˈtality. [f. L. *orientāl-is* + -ITY.] The quality or condition of being oriental.

1. The state of being in the eastern part of the sky, or of being visible before sunrise, as a planet.

1646 SIR T. BROWNE *Pseud. Ep.* VI. vii. 308 The Sunne.. hath no power nor efficacie peculiar from its orientality. **1731** [see OCCIDENTALITY 1]. **1819** WILSON *Dict. Astrol.* s.v., Orientality is generally meant with respect to the ☉.

2. Eastern style or character.

1761 STERNE *Tr. Shandy* III. xii, There is an orientality in his [curses] we cannot rise up to. **1890** *Longm. Mag.* July 292 The scene [was] most striking in its thorough Orientality.

oriˈentalize, *v.* [f. ORIENTAL *a.* + -IZE.]

1. *trans.* To make oriental; to give an oriental character to.

1823 MOORE *Mem.* (1853) IV. 41 [He] disapproves of my idea of orientalising the 'Angels'. **1853** CLOUGH in *Longfellow's Life* (1891) II. 258 He had not Orientalized himself in the least. **1880** L. WALLACE *Ben-Hur* II. vii, Groves of palm-trees orientalized the landscape.

¶**b.** Badly used to render F. *orienter*: = ORIENT *v.*, ORIENTATE. *Obs.*

1823 W. TAYLOR in *Monthly Mag.* LVI. 18 Capt. Kennedy will not have the same difficulty..to orientalize himself (*s'orienter*) in this book.

2. *intr.* **a.** To become oriental in character. **b.** To play the Oriental; to act, speak, or think as an Oriental.

1829 LANDOR *Imag. Conv., Emp. China* Wks. 1853 II. 146/2 The occidental world orientalises rapidly. **1870** *Contemp. Rev.* XIV. 338 He will perhaps intimate that St. Paul 'orientalizes' in ascribing to the personal agency of Christ what he would, had he been used to our more discriminating western analysis, have ascribed only to the fascination exercised by his own thought of Christ.

Hence **oriˈentalized** *ppl. a.*; also **orientaliˈzation.**

1846 GROTE *Greece* I. xvi. I. 564 Congenial to their orientalised turn of thought. **1874** MAHAFFY *Soc. Life Greece* xi. 345 The fine-drawn subtleties of the Orientalised Hellenist. **1886** R. F. BURTON in *Academy* 23 Oct. 277/3 Thus what I may call the Orientalisation of the French 'Nights' has been done for me.

oriˈentalizing, *vbl. sb.* and *ppl. a.* [f. ORIENTALIZE *v.* + -ING¹.] *spec.* designating a style of Greek art, or the period to which it is dated (*c* 750–*c* 650 B.C.), in which influences from the art of the Near East are discernible.

1847 GROTE *Greece* II. xxxvii. IV. 534 The orientalising tendency—then beginning to spread over the Grecian and Roman world. **1879** CONDER *Tentwork Pal.* II. 89 A very marked improvement..in what might be called the orientalising of the Bible. **1902** *Encycl. Brit.* XXV. 574/2 From Ionia the style of vase-painting which,..may best be termed the 'orientalizing', spread to Greece proper. **1939** J. D. S. PENDLEBURY *Archaeol. Crete* vi. 335 Courby, in his study of such vases, divides them into three groups... Orientalizing, which he dates from 750 to 650. *Ibid.* 336 In the Orientalizing Period a number of important works of art in bronze was produced in Crete. **1948** [see *black-figure* s.v. BLACK a. 19]. **1950** H. L. LORIMER *Homer & Monuments* ii. 74 Late Geometric and Early Orientalizing graves. **1960** T. BURTON-BROWN *Early Mediterranean Migrations* iii. 74 There was a group which..knew the same kinds of procedure in architecture and sculpture, as the Greeks used from the Orientalizing Period. **1973** P. GREEN *Conc. Hist. Anc. Greece* 55 (*caption*) The domestication of mythical and other beasts was typical of 'Orientalizing' art.

orientally (ɔərɪˈɛntəlɪ), *adv.* [f. ORIENTAL *a.* + -LY².] In an Oriental manner or position; in the east; after the Eastern fashion; like, or in favour of (quot. 1847) what is Oriental.

1796 BURNEY *Mem. Metastasio* I. 363 Believe me orientally, and with the most sincere..esteem [etc.]. **1824** *Examiner* 69/1 The people..are mercenary and orientally ignorant. **1847** LD. LINDSAY *Chr. Art* I. 140 The populace ..at Venice, always orientally disposed. **1852** WILLIS *Summer Cruise in Medit.* xliv. 265 Our appointments were orientally simple.

orientate (ɔərɪˈɛnteɪt, ˈɔərɪənteɪt), *v.* [f. F. *orient-er*: see -ATE³ 6.]

1. a. *trans.* = ORIENT *v.* 1.

1849 *Ecclesiologist* IX. 153 It was always thought preferable to orientate rightly where possible. **1880** JEFFERIES *Gr. Ferne F.* ix. 218 'Don't disturb the skeleton!' cried Felix, anxious to make scientific notes..whether the grave was 'orientated' [etc.].

b. *fig.* = ORIENT *v.* 2.

1866 *Ecclesiologist* XXVII. 158 Gaining the knowledge requisite for practical working..and orientating himself in general. **1884** *World* 26 Mar. 12/2 To orientate exactly his present mode of thought.

2. *intr.* To face towards the east, or in some specified direction; to turn to the east.

1850 NEALE *East. Ch.* I. 222 [The church] of Haghios Georgios..in Crete..orientates north, and [that] of the Asomatoi..in the Morea..orientates south. **1877** J. D. CHAMBERS *Div. Worship* i. 1 The Church should Orientate, that is, should be built from West to East, the entrances.. being at the West end. **1883** *Ch. Times* XXI. 673/4 The choir..do not fail to orientate.

3. *trans.* (*Chem.*) = ORIENT *v.* 4 b.

1924 E. J. HOLMYARD *Outl. Org. Chem.* xix. 368 When several compounds have been orientated in this way, the constitution of other substances may be ascertained by converting them into substances of known constitution. **1926** J. READ *Text-bk. Org. Chem.* xxiv. 550 Such multitudes of benzene derivatives have been orientated that it is a comparatively simple matter to apply this method.

ˈorientated, *ppl. a.* [f. ORIENTATE *v.* + -ED¹.]

1. = ORIENTED *ppl. a.* 1.

1886 WILLIS & CLARK *Cambridge* III. 278 A properly orientated chapel. **1900** L. FLETCHER in *Brit. Mus. Return* 156 Exactly orientated sections [of crystals] have been.. optically examined.

2. = ORIENTED *ppl. a.* 3 (and similarly hyphenated).

1967 *Indexer* V. 162/2 We must, as far as possible, be customer- or user-orientated. **1968** *Listener* 1 Aug. 153/1 Stravinsky's Webern-orientated style. **1971** *Guardian* 18 Oct. 8/1 Polytechnics..are too big, too static, too institutional, too degree-orientated. **1972** C. JONES *Introd. Middle English* 4 Earlier works on the subject of medieval English language..have tended to be performance-orientated. **1974** *Cape Times* 1 Aug. 1/8 The highest percentage of votes appeared to be recorded at the Progressive Party-orientated..polling districts. **1975** *Daily Tel.* 26 July 11/3 His attitude..has been condemned as 'irresponsible and politically orientated'.

ˈorientating, *ppl. a.* [f. as prec. + -ING².] That orientates or orients; *spec.* in *Chem.* (cf. ORIENT *v.* 4 a).

1876 *Jrnl. Chem. Soc.* XXIX. 240 The author closes this section with some remarks on the value of the 'orientating' influence exercised by various radicles. **1920** *Christian World* 19 Aug. 7/1 Upon these young men and women the lecture must have had a great orientating effect. **1921** E. HERMAN *Creative Prayer* 104 For that world of reality..is.. Love, and its highway—the great orientating path that gives it coherence—is Christ. **1952** *Mind* LXI. 484 The use of warning, priming or orientating signals. **1966** G. P. ELLIS *Mod. Textbk. Org. Chem.* v. 101 The substituent A possesses a specific directing or orientating effect on the incoming group.

orientation (ɔərɪənˈteɪʃən). [n. of action from ORIENTATE or ORIENT *v.*: see -ATION. So in mod.F. (1878 in *Dict. Acad.*).] The action of orienting, or the condition of being oriented or orientated.

1. The placing or arranging of something so as to face the east; *spec.* the construction of a church with the longer axis east and west, and the chancel or chief altar at the eastern end; also, the burying of a corpse with the feet towards the east.

1849 *Ecclesiologist* IX. 153 The primitive tradition of orientation. **1855** FERGUSSON *Handbk. Archit.* 516 *note*, The orientation of Churches, by turning their altars towards the east, is wholly a peculiarity of the Northern or Gothic races; the Italians never knew or practised it. **1881** STANLEY *Chr. Instit.* xi. 209 The orientation of churches is from the rites of Etruscan augury. **1883** BERESF. HOPE *Worship & Order* 126 Orientation, we should add, is exploded by the Oratorians.

2. a. Hence, by extension, The placing or construction of a church, temple, house, tomb, or other structure, so as to face in any specified direction; adjustment in some particular way with respect to the points of the compass.

1839 *Hints Study Eccles. Antiq.* (Cambr. Camd. Soc. 1842) 17 *Orientation.* It is important to notice the deviation of a church from east, because it is supposed that the chancel points to that part of the horizon where the sun rises on the Feast of the Patron Saint. **1871** TYLOR *Prim. Cult.* II. 382 A series of practices concerning the posture of the dead in their graves and the living in their temples..which may be classed under the general heading of Orientation. **1871** E. H. PALMER *Desert of Exodus* 7 The Orientation of the chapel ..had been altered at a later date. **1885** ADLER *Schliemann's Tiryns* Pref. 18 The orientation, towards the South, of the rooms most used.

b. Position or arrangment (of a natural object or formation) relatively to the points of the compass or to other parts of the same structure; the 'lie' of a thing. In *Chem.*, the relative position of the atoms or radicals in complex molecules.

1875 *Wonders Phys. World* I. ii. 75 This arrangement of the ridges is simply a result of the orientation. **1877** WATTS *Fownes' Chem.* II. 420 The higher [benzene] derivatives formed by replacement of two or more hydrogen-atoms in the molecule exhibit isomeric modifications, which are supposed to depend upon the relative position or *orientation* of the substituted radicals. **1881** —— *Dict. Chem.* 3rd Suppl. 1187 'Optical orientation' denotes the order in which the axes of elasticity correspond to the right-angled crystallographic axes. **1884** BOWER & SCOTT *De Bary's Phaner.* 319 The orientation of collateral bundles is in the usual cases..such that the xylem is turned towards the middle, and the phloem towards the periphery of the whole organ.

c. Transference eastward. Also, = ORIENTALIZATION.

1884 *Pall Mall G.* 26 Aug. 1/1 That orientation of the *entente cordiale* from Paris to Berlin which was one of the cherished hopes of Lord Ampthill's life. **1914** G. K. CHESTERTON *Flying Inn* viii. 81 He also wants to drive a tunnel—between East and West—to make the British Empire more Indian; to effect what he calls the orientation of England and I call the ruin of Christendom.

3. The action of turning to or facing the east, *esp.* in acts of worship, as at the recitation of the Creed or the celebration of the Eucharist; the eastward position.

[Cf. quot. from Tylor, 1871, in 2.]

1875 GLADSTONE *Glean.* VI. viii. 147 The case in favour of what we may be allowed to call orientation. **1888** *Ch. Times* 339/1 Orientation at the Creed was observed.

4. a. The action or process of ascertaining, or fact of knowing, the position of anything or of oneself in relation to the points of the compass or to objects in general; determination of (one's) bearings or relative position; *spec.* in *Zool.* the faculty by which birds and other animals find their way back to a place after going or being taken to a place distant from it (as in homing pigeons and migratory birds).

1868 AIRY *Pop. Astron.* iii. 122 We have no term for expressing that peculiar act of determining the direction of a side of a triangle, or the direction of a chain of triangles, and therefore we have adopted a word from the French, 'orientation'; it is, however, a bad word, used only for the want of a better. **1887** *Amer. Jrnl. Psychol.* I. 510 Tympanic sensibility plays no role in auditive orientation. **1897** tr. *Flammarion's Lumen* 212 Another sense with which I was still more struck.. I found on a second world. This was the sense of orientation. **1899** *Allbutt's Syst. Med.* VI. 342 Psychical disturbance, marked by apathy, dulness of comprehension, variable temper, delusions, imperfect orientation.

b. *Chem.* The process of ascertaining the relative positions of the substituents in a ring.

1891 *Jrnl. Chem. Soc.* LX. 1199 The method employed by Claus and Runschke.. for the orientation of 4:6-dichlorometaxylene. **1903** WALKER & MOTT tr. *Holleman's Text-bk. Org. Chem.* II. 473 Oxidation is another important aid in their orientation, and is employed to determine whether the substituents are attached to the same or to different rings. **1953** ASTLE & SHELTON *Org. Chem.* xxii. 420 (*heading*) Korner's absolute method of orientation.

5. *fig.* (from various senses): Adjustment, position, or aspect with respect to anything; determination of one's 'bearings' or true position in relation to circumstances, ideas, etc.

1870 BARING-GOULD *Orig. Relig. Belief* (1878) II. ii. 31 The double orientation, one towards God, the other towards the world. **1890** *Ch. Q. Rev.* XXX. 19 It may be well to make a few remarks by way of orientation. **1893** in Barrows *Parl. Relig.* I. 759 That is the best education which gives a man, so to speak, the best orientation; which most clearly defines his relations with society and with his Creator.

b. An introduction to some subject or particular situation; a briefing. Also *attrib.*, as (U.S.) ***orientation course, program*** (see quots.).

1942 in Partridge *Usage & Abusage* 226/2 *Orientation course*, American pedagoguese for an introductory, general or historical study, usually of the social sciences, designed for college freshmen or sophomores. **1953** K. REISZ *Technique Film Editing* II. viii. 140 Had we, for instance, opened the sequence with the long continuous scene of the bearded forest (as an *orientation* scene of the locale in which the tale was set) we would have no preparation to understand and appreciate its charms and mysteries. **1968** *Globe & Mail* (Toronto) 17 Feb. B6 (Advt.), Selected applicants will be offered a comprehensive orientation program in branch banking. **1968** *N.Y. Times* 23 July 41/1 Mr. Mailer was giving an 'orientation' (or was it a sophisticated party game?) for nearly 100 participants in his third film venture. **1970** *Toronto Daily Star* 24 Sept. 2/2 A student orientation program at the University of British Columbia. **1972** D. DELMAN *Sudden Death* (1973) iii. 73 'I needed.. an insight into the way you tennis cats think.' 'In other words I've just delivered what amounts to an orientation lecture.' **1976** *Columbus* (Montana) *News* 10 June 4/2 Four prospective LABO host families met Sunday evening at the home of Mr. and Mrs. Bill Wright to go over an orientation program and participate in a Japanese style dinner. **1976** J. CROSBY *Nightfall* xxxviii. 231 Hawkins had read Wittgenstein only because Theresa had. Her books were his orientation course.

6. *Chem.* The orienting effect of a substituent in a ring on other atoms or groups (see ORIENT *v.* 4 a).

In quot. 1890 the word could be interpreted in sense 2 b.

1890 *Jrnl. Chem. Soc.* LVIII. 484 The study of substitution phenomena, especially in the aromatic series, shows that the so-called orientation rules are dependent on the atomic or molecular weight of the atom or radicle which dominates or directs the position taken up by the substituting-group. **1946** A. A. MORTON *Chem. Heterocyclic Compounds* ii. 33 Replacement reactions are unique in that the position of the entering group is largely determined by the nature of the reactant, not by any orientation by groups. **1971** J. D. ROBERTS et al. *Org. Chem.* xx. 574 When the two substituents have opposed orientation effects, it is not always easy to predict what products will be obtained.

7. Special Comb.: **orientation triad** (see quot. 1962).

1953 H. HABER *Man in Space* 155 If all three components of the orientation triad are intact, the human body is fully equipped to reckon with the force of gravity, to keep its balance and to remain properly aligned relative to the vertical. **1962** F. I. ORDWAY et al. *Basic Astronautics* xii. 475 The center of the body's orientation system is located in the inner ear; the system, however, consists of three elements, often called the orientation triad. The first component is sight, and the second is the system of mechanoreceptors or nerve endings.. that are sensitive to pressure. But the vestibular apparatus of the inner ear is the heart of the system since it contains the mechanism that senses acceleration.

orientational (ɔərɪən'teɪʃənəl), *a.* [f. ORIENTATION + -AL.] Pertaining to or involving orientation, esp. of variable elements in a specified context.

1952 [see COGNITIVE *a.*]. **1962** CORSON & LORRAIN *Introd. Electromagn. Fields* iii. 113 We then considered orientational polarization in which molecules with a permanent dipole moment tend to be aligned by an external field. **1968** J. LYONS *Introd. Theoret. Linguistics* vii. 275 The notion of *deixis*.. is introduced to handle the 'orientational' features of language which are relative to the time and place of utterance. **1974** R. JESSOP *Traditionalism, Conservatism & Brit. Pol. Culture* i. 17 Most political scientists employ 'political culture' as a mere catchword.. for all sorts of influences.. that include both structural and orientational factors. **1976** *Nature* 23 Sept. 353/2 An extraordinary orientational relationship between the rhombohedral green rust.. and magnetite.. has been reported.

Hence **orien'tationally** *adv.*

1975 *Nature* 31 Jan. 310/2 The molecules are positionally ordered but orientationally disordered and mobile.

'orien,tator. *rare.* [agent-n. f. ORIENTATE *v.*] A contrivance for determining orientation.

1844 (*title*), The Orientator, a contrivance for ascertaining the orientation of churches.

oriented ('ɔərɪɛntɛd), *ppl. a.* [f. ORIENT *v.* + -ED[1].] **1.** Having a definite or specified orientation; *spec.* in *Math.*

1918 O. VEBLEN *Projective Geom.* II. ix. 426 If two oriented points are similarly oriented with respect to a line *l*, they are similarly oriented with respect to a line *m* if and only if *l* and *m* do not separate the two points. **1950** D. J. STRUIK *Lect. Classical Differential Geom.* i. 6 The sense of increasing arc length is called the positive sense on the curve; a curve with a sense on it is called an oriented curve. **1951** C. PALACHE et al. *Dana's Syst. Min.* (ed. 7) II. 181 From Tsumeb.. as a secondary mineral associated with smithsonite (in part as oriented growths thereon). **1960** L. PICKEN *Organization of Cells* vii. 265 Once we admit.. that the centromeres.. are 'sticky' to oriented proteins, we may have conceded all that is necessary for them to figure as centres of orientation. **1970** A. GOETZ *Introd. Differential Geom.* i. 6 The space with a chosen ordered triple e_1, e_2, e_3 of independent vectors is called an oriented space. **1975** *Nature* 29 May 389/1 A shipboard palaeomagnetic reconnaissance of 295 vertically oriented basement samples.

2. Of a plastic or other material: having the constituent molecules oriented with their axes parallel to one another.

1947 R. NAUTH *Chem. & Technol. Plastics* viii. 195 Table 32.. indicates the qualities of 'oriented' and 'unoriented' vinylidene chloride plastics. **1950** V. STANNETT *Cellulose Acetate Plastics* i. 17 If a poorly oriented fibre is loaded only those chains lying parallel to the axis take the load. **1969** L. S. MOUNTS in W. R. R. Park *Plastics Film Technol.* v. 139 Oriented polystyrene films have excellent clarity, sparkle, and gloss.

3. Having an emphasis, bias, or interest indicated by a preceding sb. (usu. joined by a hyphen) or advb.

1950 *Psychiatry* XIII. 181 Our language patterns.. are adult-oriented. **1957** *Jrnl. Nervous & Mental Dis.* CXXV. 459/2 The 'disease-oriented' physician and his 'person-oriented' fellow commonly encounter difficulties in agreeing. **1960** R. K. WEBB *Harriet Martineau* x. 295 Our psychologically oriented, relativistic age. **1968** *Globe & Mail* (Toronto) 17 Feb. B7 (Advt.), Multi-faceted and expansion oriented company with operations in Eastern Canada and United States. **1971** *Computers & Humanities* VI. 30 SIMS will provide a user-oriented language, making it easy for the user to define, validate, interrogate, and analyze the data. **1971** M. MCCARTHY *Birds of America* 269 Why are you so art-oriented, all of a sudden? **1972** *Lebende Sprachen* XVII. 134/1 Environmentally oriented research. **1974** *Times* 12 Feb. 11/5 We simply must produce managers in the future who are design oriented. **1978** *Jrnl. R. Soc. Arts* CXXVI. 744/2 To move away from performance-oriented drama towards more reflective drama.

orienteering (ɔərɪən'tɪərɪŋ). [ad. Sw. *orientering* orienteering; cf. ORIENT *v.*] The competitive sport of finding one's way on foot across rough country with the aid of map and compass; this sport as undertaken on horseback or by car, canoe, etc. Also *attrib.* So **orien'teer**, one who engages in orienteering; also as *v. intr.* and *fig.*

1948 *Amer. Ski Ann.* 1949 146/1 Senior Scouts representing 15 Boy Scout Councils from New York and New Jersey met at Snow Ridge Ski Center last winter to compete in the first official Ski Orienteering race to be held in America. **1949** *Univ. Mass. Executive Bull.* 8 Dec., Dr. Bjorn Kjellstrom, from Sweden, and instigator of the new sport of Orienteering will show a new colored film on training for Cross-Country and Touring Skiing. **1954** *Time* 1 Nov. 58 Known officially as 'orienteering', the sport dates back to 1918 when the first Swedish club was formed to hold formal competitions. **1956** *Official Gaz.* (U.S. Patent Office) 10 Apr. TM92/2 Bjorn Kjellstrom, d.b.a. American Orienteering Service, New York, N.Y... *Orienteering.* For Instructing in Map and Compass Reading Through Lectures Delivered in Person With or Without Illustrations by Means of Film. Use since August 1946. **1965** *Orienteering* ('Know the Game' series) 10 The orienteer must remember that peat hags can be very rough pasture. *Ibid.* 36 Ankle support is very important in rough orienteering country. *Ibid.* 40 There are fascinating opportunities to orienteer by canoe, cycle, pony or ski. **1971** 'D. HALLIDAY' *Dolly & Doctor Bird* v. 60 You were supposed to be treating my blisters, not orienteering all over my torso. **1971** *Sunday Times* 10 Oct. 30 Furthermore, Swedish orienteers bled their way into medical history a few years ago following an epidemic of the disease. **1973** *Whole Earth Catal.* 23/1 Within recent years, Orienteering as a sport, in the form of 'Orienteering Races' has swept Europe. ..Orienteering events have become regular features in many athletic and outdoor clubs. **1976** *Observer* 26 Sept. 16/3 Egil Johansen, asked to single out the most compelling attraction of orienteering, says simply: 'It is the fellowship of the other orienteers.'

orientite (ɔə'rɪɛntaɪt). *Min.* [f. *Orient-e*, the name of the province in Cuba where it was first found + -ITE[1].] A hydrated silicate of calcium and manganese, $Ca_4Mn^{III}{}_4Si_5O_{20}.4H_2O$, found as light brown or pink orthorhombic crystals.

1921 HEWETT & SHANNON in *Amer. Jrnl. Sci.* CCI. 491 As the mineral is known to occur in two localities in Oriente Province, where many manganese deposits are found, and it may be widespread in the region, it is appropriate that the geographic relation be perpetuated in the name *orientite*. **1961** *Amer. Mineralogist* XLVI. 227 The largest known crystals of orientite do not exceed 1 mm. in length.

'orientize, *v.* *rare*[−1]. [See -IZE.] *trans.* = ORIENT *v.* 1.

1881 SMYTH & CHAMBERS *Celestial Cycle* (ed. 2) 35 They [the Arabians] looked to Polaris, and could thereby readily orientize themselves.

†**'oriently,** *adv. Obs.* [f. ORIENT *a.* + -LY[2].] In an 'orient' manner; brilliantly, lustrously; clearly.

1515 BARCLAY *Egloges* v. (1570) Div/1 Their crownes glistering bright and oriently. **1603** DEKKER *Wonderfull Yeare* F j b, Chrisolites and Carbunckles, which glistened so oriently. **1664** H. MORE *Myst. Iniq.* ix. 139 Such an Ecclesiastick Polity as will appear most oriently Luciferian and Antichristian.

†**'orientness.** *Obs.* [f. as prec. + -NESS.] The quality of being 'orient'; lustre, brilliancy.

1519 HORMAN *Vulg.* 105 Pearlis wyll abyde no crafte: but anone theyr orientnes flytteth. **1548** RECORDE *Urin. Physick* xi. (1651) 105 The orientness and the beauty of the Colour. **1627–77** FELTHAM *Resolves* II. lxviii. 303 The orientness of that Fame which their Fore-Fathers left them. *a* **1661** FULLER *Worthies* I. (1662) 215 Pearls.. far short of the Indian in Orientness.

orifacial (ɒrɪ'feɪʃəl), *a. Craniometry.* [f. L. *ōri-* comb. form of *ōs*, *ōr-* mouth + *facial.*] In ***orifacial angle***: the angle which the facial line of Camper makes with the plane of mastication, i.e. of the grinding surfaces of the upper molars.

1890 in *Cent. Dict.*

†**ori'facture.** *nonce-wd.* [f. L. *ōs*, *ōr-* mouth, after *manufacture*.] Making with the mouth.

1673 MARVELL *Reh. Transp.* II. Wks. 1776 II. 269 From the manufacture—he will criticise because not orifacture—of soape-bubbles.

†**'orifex,** obs. erron. form of ORIFICE.

1590 MARLOWE *2nd Pt. Tamburl.* III. iv, All my entrails bath'd In blood that straineth from their orifex. **1606** SHAKS. *Tr. & Cr.* v. ii. 151 Yet the spacious bredth of this diuision, Admits no Orifex. **1624** MIDDLETON *Game at Chess* III. i, I strike deep in, And leave the orifex gushing.

orifice ('ɒrɪfɪs). Also 6 **orifis, oryfice, -fyce.** [a. F. *orifice* (14th c. in Hatz.-Darm.), ad. late Lat. *ōrificium*, f. *ōs*, *ōr-* mouth + *facĕre*, in comp. *-ficĕre*, to make.] An opening or aperture, which serves as, or has the form of a mouth, as of a tube, of the stomach, bladder or other bodily organ, of a wound, etc.; the mouth of any cavity, a perforation or vent. (Formerly including larger openings than now, e.g. the mouth of a cave, a mine, etc.)

1541 R. COPLAND *Guydon's Quest. Chirurg.* H j, And ouer the thre oryfyces of the sayde thre ventrycles there be thre pellycles. **1596** SPENSER *F.Q.* IV. xii. 22 That same former fatall wound of his.. closely rankled under th' orifis. **1614** MARKHAM *Cheap Husb.* (1668) i. Table Hard Words, Orifice is the mouth, hole, or open passage of any wound or ulcer. **1623** HART *Arraignm. Ur.* I. ii. 4 Both the bladders together with their orifices and concavities. **1671** J. WEBSTER *Metallogr.* vi. 108 It guided me to the orifice of a Lead Mine. **1682** GREW *Anat. Leaves* I. iv. §2 Certain open Pores or Orifices. **1700** ADDISON *Æneid* III. Misc. Wks. 1726 I. 62 There gap'd The spacious hollow where his eye-ball roll'd, A ghastly orifice. **1713** —— *Guard.* No. 103 ¶6 The mountain resembled Ætna, being bored through the top with a monstrous orifice. **1858** LARDNER *Hand-bk. Nat. Phil.* 80 The squares of the velocities of the liquid in passing through the orifice are proportional to the depth. **1862** DARWIN *Fertil. Orchids* iii. 125 The orifice into the nectar-receptacle lies.. close to the lower side of the flower. **1878** HUXLEY *Physiogr.* 189 The solid matters.. fall in showers around the mouth of the orifice.

ori'ficial, *a.* [f. L. *ōrifici-um* opening, orifice + -AL[1]. (But the word meant was perh. *orificall*.)]

†**1.** Mouthmaking; hence high-sounding, bombastic. *Obs. rare*[−1].

1594 NASHE *Unfort. Trav.* 69 O orificiall rethorike, wipe thy euerlasting mouth.

2. Of or pertaining to an orifice or orifices; in *Med.* used *spec.* with reference to a theory that many pathological conditions arise from irritation of the orifices of the rectum and urogenital system and can be relieved by surgery or other treatment of these areas.

1887 E. H. PRATT *Orificial Surg.* i. 14, I believe that all forms of chronic diseases have one common predisposing cause, and that cause is a nerve-waste occasioned by orificial irritation at the lower openings of the body. **1926** *Spectator* 25 Sept. 473/1 With a fine inconsistency, they belong to societies of so-called 'orificial surgery' and follow strange cults of electrical healing. **1960** [see CLITORIDECTOMY]. **1973** *Biol. Abstr.* LV. 6287/1 This.. revealed an orificial pulmonary stenosis which clinical investigation had failed to detect.

oriflamme ('ɒrɪflæm). Forms: 5 **oriflam, -flame, -flamble,** (**aurisflambe**), 5–6 **oriflambe,** 7 auriflambe, (oiliflame), 7– oriflamme, (9 oriflamb). [a. F. *oriflamme*, OF. *oriflambe* (11th c.); also *ori-*, *oli-*, *-flamble*, *-flam*, *-flan*, *-flant*, in Pr. *auriflamma*, *-flan*, *-flor*, It. *oriflamma*, med.L. *auriflamma*; f. L. *aur-um*, F. *or* gold + *flamma* flame.]

1. The sacred banner of St. Denis, a banderole of two or (according to some accounts) three points, of red or orange-red silk, attached to a lance, which the early kings of France used to receive from the hands of the abbot of St. Denis, on setting out for war.

'*Oriflambe*: the great and holie Standerd of France; borne at first onely in warres made against Infidells; but afterwards vsed in all other warres; and at length vtterly lost in a battell against the Flemings' (Cotgrave).

1475 *Bk. Noblesse* (Roxb.) 13 Ser Geffrey Chauny that bare the baner of the oriflamble. *c* **1489** CAXTON *Sonnes of Aymon* xx. 452 Whan Reynawd sawe the oryflame of France com. **1494** FABYAN *Chron.* v. 72 Whan this precyous Relyke or Aurisflambe was borne agayne Cristen Princes, the vertue therof seasyd, and lastly was lost, but yet the lyke therof is kept at Seynt Denys. *Ibid.* VII. 467 Sir Reynolde Camyan baneret..bare the oryflambe, a speciall relyke that the Frenshe kynges vse to bere before them in all battayles. **1523** LD. BERNERS *Froiss.* I. ccccxii. 720 It is nedefull that we..apoynt..who shall beare the Oriflambe of France. **1611** SPEED *Hist. Gt. Brit.* IX. xii. §92. 689 An hallowed Banner of red silke, whereof the French had a wonderfull high conceit, as of that which was sent from heauen, and called Oreflame or Auriflames. **1794** J. GIFFORD *Reign Louis XVI* 503 The oriflamme, or grand standard of the king. **1822** K. DIGBY *Broadst. Hon.* (1846) 63 *note*, The Oriflamme..was the banner of the abbey [of St. Denis]. The last that we hear of it is in the inventory of the treasury of this church in 1534. **1865** NICHOLS in *Herald & Genealogist* III. 7 At a later period, the Oriflamme was sometimes powdered with golden flakes of fire, as it is represented in the *Indice Armorial* of Louvain Geliot. **1871** LONGF. *Wayside Inn*, *Baron St. Castine* 69 The Curate..draws from the pocket of his gown A handkerchief like an oriflamb.

2. *transf.* and *fig.* **a.** Something which serves the purpose of the Oriflamme of St. Denis; any banner or ensign, material or ideal, that serves as a rallying point for a struggle, etc.

1600 W. WATSON *Decacordon* A iij b, Did not then the primitives of the East Church..carry away the auriflambe of all religious zeale. **1824** MACAULAY *Ivry* 30 And be your oriflamme to-day the helmet of Navarre! **1853** LYTTON *My Novel* VIII. i, If his heart match his head, and both proceed in the Great March under a divine Oriflamme. **1864** *Sat. Rev.* 14 Sept. 262 The North has not hoisted for its oriflamme the Sacred Symbol of Justice to the negro. **1880** WEBB *Goethe's Faust* I. i. 47 All Hell displays its oriflamme. **1885** *Standard* 26 May 5/5 [There] will be reared masts bearing the oriflammes of the town [Paris].

b. Something which suggests the Oriflamme of St. Denis by its golden, bright, or conspicuous colouring, position, etc.

1862 WHITTIER *Waiting*, The golden spears uprise Beneath the oriflamme of day! **1868** GEO. ELIOT *Sp. Gypsy* I. 17 The new-bathed Day With oriflamme uplifted o'er the peaks. **1879** HELEN RICH *Invocation* in *Poems of Places, Br. America.* etc. 84 All the azure archway streams With oriflamme of gems and gold. **1895** MATHILDE BLIND *Birds of Passage, Agnostic* ii, Spring's Oriflamme of flowers waves from the Sod.

origami (ɒrɪˈgɑːmɪ). Also **origame**. [Jap., f. *ori* fold + *kami* paper.] The Japanese art of folding paper into intricate designs. Also *attrib.*

[**1922** F. STARR in *Japan* (San Francisco) Oct. 43/1 Their book on paper-folding in schools compares favorably with any we have. It is entitled *shikaka origami dzukai*, paper-folding explained with figures.] **1956** 'R. HARBIN' *Paper Magic* 14 The art of *origami* has been handed down from father to son through countless generations. **1959** R. CONDON *Manchurian Candidate* (1960) ii. 56 While they had light he..amused them or startled them or flabbergasted them with the extent of his skill at *origami*. **1961** E. KALLOP in S. Randlett *Art of Origami* (1963) 16 Apart from origami as an art in the sense of the individually unique, folded paper has a role in the ceremonial etiquette of Japanese life. **1963** 'R. HARBIN' *Secrets of Origami* 11 If you can obtain a supply of Japanese Origami paper, so much the better. **1968** R. V. BESTE *Repeat Instructions* vii. 67 You should try origame.. Paper-folding. It's a Jap word. **1972** C. FREMLIN *Appointment with Yesterday* xi. 83 The Origami cut-outs they'd had such a craze for over Christmas, they were on the bed too. **1973** M. CROWELL *Greener Pastures* 101 There are ..paper stars and origami birds.

origan (ˈɒrɪgən). Now *rare*. Also 5 origon, 5–6 (9) origane. [a. F. *origan* (13th c. in Hatz.-Darm.), *origane* (14th c. in Godef.), ad. L. *origan-um*: see next. Also found in numerous other forms, as ORIGANY, ORGAMENT, ORGAMY, ORGAN, ORGANY, q.v.] A plant of the genus *Origanum*, esp. Wild Marjoram (*O. vulgare*); formerly also applied to other aromatic labiates, as Pennyroyal (*Mentha Pulegium*).

c **1420** *Pallad. on Husb.* I. 902 Kest origane ystamped with brimstoon Vppon their hole. *Ibid.* 1024 Of tymbra, peletur and origon. **1567** MAPLET *Gr. Forest* 110 In their iourneying they eate of Origan, to sharpe their teeth. **1578** LYTE *Dodoens* II. lxix. 236 Origan is of three sortes,..garden Origan, wilde Origan, and that kinde which they call *Origanum Onitis*. *Ibid.* 238 Of Tragorigan, or Goates Origan. **1590** SPENSER *F.Q.* I. ii. 40, I chaunst to see her in her proper hew, Bathing her selfe in origane and thyme. **1699** *Phil. Trans.* XXI. 248 They put Origan, and other Herbs, powder'd, into it. **1819** H. BUSK *Banquet* I. 17 The tufted origan and vulgar heath. **1886** BURTON *Arab. Nts.* I. 140 Origane and the winter gilliflower carpeted the borders.

ˈorganize, *v. rare.* [f. prec. or next + -IZE.] *trans.* To flavour with marjoram.

1853 *Fraser's Mag.* XLVIII. 480 An organized anchovy atmosphere proceeds, always offensive, but in hot weather worse..than the potent garlic.

‖**origanum** (ɒˈrɪgənəm). *Bot.* [L. *orīganum*, *-us*, 'wild marjoram' (Lewis & Short), a. Gr. ὀρίγανον, -ος, 'an acrid herb like marjoram' (L. & S.); in appearance, a compound of ὄρος mountain + γάνος brightness, joy, pride, whence the scribal alteration ὀρείγανος. Also ORGANUM, q.v.; and in many anglicized forms: see ORIGAN.] A genus of labiates, comprising herbs and low shrubs, with flowers in clustered heads, and aromatic leaves; as Wild Marjoram (*O. vulgare*), Sweet Marjoram (*O. Marjorana*), Pot M. (*O. Onites*), Dittany of Crete (*O. Dictamnus*), etc. In the old herbals, including Pennyroyal, and other labiates.

[*c* **1265** *Voc. Names Plants* in Wr.-Wülcker 557/20 *Origanum, i.* puliol real, *i.* wdeminte.] **1398** TREVISA *Barth. De P.R.* XVIII. vii. (MS. Bodl.) lf. 246/2 ʒif þe pointes of his [boar's] tuskes beþ blonte..he secheþ an herbe þat hatte Origanum and gnawiþ & chewiþ it. **1540** ELYOT *Image Gov.* xxi. 39 The grounde was thicke couered with Camomyle, Origanum, and other lyke grasses. **1583** *Rates of Customs* D v, Origanum the pound viij*d*. **1683** TYRON *Way to Health* 562 [It] is said of the Stork when she has eaten Snakes, she seeks for the same Herb Originum, and finds a Remedy. **1757** COOPER *Distiller* II. ii. (1760) 120 Plants which long retain their natural Fragrance, such as Balm, Hyssop,.. Origanum, Pennyroyal, Rosemary, etc. **1897** *Allbutt's Syst. Med.* II. 522 Oil of Cloves, origanum, and aniline oils must be avoided.

†**oˈrigany.** *Herb. Obs.* = ORIGAN, ORIGANUM.

1741 *Compl. Fam.-Piece* I. i. 85 Take also of Grains of Paradise,..Origany, Osier of the Mountain, of each 1 Dram. **1757** COOPER *Distiller* III. xxxiii. (1760) 197 Origany, and Thyme, of each one Pound. **1760** J. LEE *Introd. Bot.* App. 321 Origany, *Origanum*.

origen (Wyclif, Coverdale): see ORYX.

Origenist (ˈɒrɪdʒɪnɪst). [-IST.] A disciple or follower of the famous Greek Christian Father Origen of Alexandria (*c* 185–253), or a holder of some one of the special doctrines attributed to Origen, among which were a threefold sense (literal, moral, and mystical) in Scripture, the pre-existence of souls, and the probable ultimate salvation of all men and of the fallen angels.

1546 GARDINER *Declar. Joye* xvi, Then shuld no man be dampned, but al saued at the last, as the Origenistes sayed. **1796** BURKE *Regic. Peace* iv. Wks. IX. 43 He is an Origenist, and believes in the conversion of the Devil. **1858** R. A. VAUGHAN *Ess. & Rem.* I. 43 Many of the Origenists held opinions which the departed Origen would never have sanctioned.

attrib. **1874** BLUNT *Dict. Sects* s.v., A very able defence of Origenist opinions was printed anonymously, in the year 1661, by Rust, bishop of Dromore.

b. See quot. 1874.

1647 A. ROSS *Mystag. Poet.* iii. (1675) 77 The Encratites, Or[i]genists, Manicheans, and all other Hereticks, who hath condemned Matrimony. **1874** J. H. BLUNT *Dict. Sects* s.v., From Epiphanius it appears that there was a sect of Origenists who were followers of some unknown Origen... These Origenists are spoken of as given to shameful vices.

So †**Oriˈgenian** *sb.* (= prec.) and *a.* (= next); †**Oriˈgenic**, **Oriˈgenical** *adjs.*, pertaining or attributed to Origen; **ˈOrigenism**, the doctrines held by or attributed to Origen; **ˌOrigeˈnistic** *a.*, pertaining or relating to Origenism or the Origenists; **ˈOrigeˌnize** *v. intr.*, to follow Origen, maintain Origenistic opinions.

1661 G. RUST *Origen* 19 A perfect explication of the Trinity after the *Origenian way. **1666** S. PARKER (*title*) Account of the Nature and Extent of the Divine Dominion and Goodnesse, especially as they refer to the Origenian Hypothesis, concerning the Pre-existence of Souls. **1727–41** CHAMBERS *Cycl.*, *Origenians*,..a sect of ancient heretics, who even surpassed the abominations of the Gnostics. St. Epiphanius speaks of them as still subsisting in his time... They rejected marriage. **1879** R. ORNSBY in *Dubl. Rev.* July 64 A fourth branch of the Origenian evidence is prophecy and its fulfilment. **1678** CUDWORTH *Intell. Syst.* I. v. 810 The *Origenick Hypothesis..That in Angels, there is a Complication of Incorporeal and Corporeal Substance both together. *Ibid.* 819 This Origenick Opinion in Photius. **1600** ABBOT *Exp. Jonah* 2 To follow the letter of the text, and to lay down the doctrine of it..without allegories *Origenicall. **1727–8** CHAMBERS *Cycl.* s.v. *Origenist*, *Origenism spread itself chiefly among the monks of Egypt. **1833** J. H. NEWMAN *Arians* I. i. (1876) 6 Origenism has been assigned as the actual source from which Arianism was derived. **1903** W. BRIGHT *Age of Fathers* II. xxix. 54 Anastasius.. condemned Origenism in a Roman synod. **1908** L. B. RADFORD (*title*) Three Teachers of Alexandria: Theognostus, Pierius and Peter. A Study in the Early History of Origenism and Anti-Origenism. **1960** H. C. GRAEF tr. *Altaner's Patrology* v. 242 He [*sc.* Methodius] is important principally as a successful opponent of Origenism. **1966** H. CHADWICK *Early Christian Thought & Classical Tradition* iv. 120 In judging the system of Origen as a whole it is important to remember that some of the most characteristic features of 'Origenism' are not his personal invention. **1853** J. C. ROBERTSON *Hist. Chr. Ch.* III. vi. §3 (1874) 299 Theodore Ascidas, a monk of *Origenistic opinions. **1880** FARRAR *Hist. Interpr.* 205 Origenistic allegory and Philonian methods. *Ibid.* 202 The most *Origenising of all the Fathers.

origes, pl. of *orix*, ORYX.

origin (ˈɒrɪdʒɪn), *sb.* (*a.*) Also 5 -yne, 7–8 -ine. [app. a. F. *origine*, ad. L. *orīgin-em* rise, beginning, source, f. *orī-rī* to arise.

F. *origine* took the place of the popular form *orine*; although cited by Hatz.-Darm. only from 1512, it appears to be the immediate source of the Eng. word. The instance from *Alexander* in 1 b is, from its date, suspicious.]

1. The act or fact of arising or springing from something; derivation, rise; beginning of existence in reference to its source or cause. ***certificate of origin***, a custom-house document certifying the place of origin of a commodity imported.

[**1387** TREVISA *Higden* (Rolls) V. 223 þe book of þe comynge forþ of þe soule; **1432–50** the begynnynge of the saule = *libellum de origine animæ*.] **1563** *Homilies* II. *Peril of Idolatry* II. (1859) 183 Lactantius..in his book of the Origin of Error. **1602** SHAKS. *Ham.* III. i. 185 Yet do I beleeue The Origin and Commencement of this greefe Sprung from neglected loue. **1663** GERBIER *Counsel* E viij, The Antiquity and Origine of Herauldry. **1741** T. ROBINSON *Gavelkind* ii. 9 The better ascertaining the Origin of Gavelkind. **1796** H. HUNTER tr. *St.-Pierre's Stud. Nat.* (1799) II. 390 Man alone ..bears upon his countenance the impress of a celestial origin. **1850** McCOSH *Div. Govt.* III. ii. (1874) 377 The origin of evil, like every other beginning, shrouds itself in darkness. **1886** *Pall Mall G.* 4 Sept. 2/2 Under the existing Spanish Customs regulations, certificates of origin are required.

b. In reference to a person: The fact of springing from some particular ancestor or race; descent, extraction, parentage, ancestry.

[*a* **1400–50** *Alexander* 92 þe Arrabiens and all þa of þat origyne.] **1605** SHAKS. *Lear* IV. ii. 32 That nature, which contemns its origin, Cannot be border'd certain in itself. **1695** LD. PRESTON *Boeth.* III. 118 And doth his noble Origine forget. **1738** GLOVER *Leonidas* I. 17 Their kings, who boast an origin divine. **1838** LYTTON *Leila* I. iii, Why cannot I learn thine origin, thy rank, thy parents? *Mod.* A distinguished man of humble origin.

2. That from which anything arises, springs, or is derived; source.

1604 T. WRIGHT *Passions* v. §2. 163 What are those dolefull tunes..but offsprings of pensiue furies, and origens of more vehement melancholie fits? **1696** WHISTON *Th. Earth* II. (1722) 83 Mountains are the principal Source and Origin of Springs and Fountains. **1824** R. HALL *Wks.* (1832) VI. 354 To be alienated from the Great Origin of being.. must be a calamity. **1860** TYNDALL *Glac.* I. ii. 18 We hoped ..to be able to examine the glacier to its origin. **1870** LOWELL *My Study Wind.* 242 It is to the North of France.. that we are to look for the true origins of our modern literature.

b. *Anat.* The place or point at or from which a muscle, nerve, etc. arises; the proximal or more fixed end or attachment of a muscle; the root of a nerve in the brain or spinal cord.

1691 RAY *Creation* II. (1692) 119 The very strong Ligaments..which in drawing it back towards its Origine, do fold it up. **1831** R. KNOX *Cloquet's Anat.* 275 Between these two origins [of the Abductor Oculi] pass the third pair of nerves, sixth pair, and nasal branch of the ophthalmic. **1840** E. WILSON *Anat. Vade M.* (1851) 238 A good view of the whole extent of origin of the flexor sublimis digitorum.

c. *Math.* A fixed point from which measurement or motion commences; *spec.* the point of intersection of the axes in Cartesian co-ordinates, or the pole in polar co-ordinates. [= F. *origine*.]

1723 E. STONE *Con. Sect.* [tr. *Marquis de l'Hospital's Sections Coniques*] 5 The Parabola infinitely extends itself more and more on each Side the Axis AP, beginning from the Origin. **1873** B. WILLIAMSON *Diff. Calc.* xii. §180 If on any radius vector.., drawn from a fixed origin.., a point.. be taken, such that [etc.]. *Ibid.* §182 If the focus [of a conic] be the origin of inversion, the inverse is a curve called the Limaçon of Pascal. *Ibid.* xiv. §202 If the absolute term be wanting in the equation of a curve, it passes through the origin.

†**B.** *attrib.* or *adj.* = ORIGINAL A. 1. *Obs. rare.*

1632 SANDERSON *Twelve Serm.* 217 The origine story it selfe..is written at full by Moses in Numb. 25.

Hence †**ˈorigin** *v. trans. Obs.* = ORIGINATE *v.* 1.

a **1661** FULLER *Worthies, Cardigan* IV. (1662) 28 We must remember this Proverb was origined whilest England and Wales were at deadly Feude.

oˈriginable, *a. rare*⁻⁰. [f. ORIGIN-ATE + -ABLE: cf. *penetrate*, *penetrable*.] Capable of being originated.

1864 in WEBSTER.

†**oˈriginacy.** *Obs. rare*⁻¹. [irreg. f. ORIGINATE *v.*: see -ACY 3, and cf. conspiracy.] The fact of originating; origination.

1658–9 *Burton's Diary* (1828) III. 512 Let those..have right to sit in the other House, not upon any old account, but to have originacy from this House.

original (ɒˈrɪdʒɪnəl), *a.* and *sb.* [a. F. *original* (13th c. in Hatz.-Darm.), ad. L. *orīgināl-is*, f. *orīgin-em*: see ORIGIN. Cf. F. *originel*, used in some of the senses, e.g. *péché originel* original sin.]

A. *adj.* **1. a.** Of or pertaining to the origin, beginning, or earliest stage of something; that belonged at the beginning to the person or thing in question; that existed at first, or has existed from the first; primary, primitive; innate; initial, first, earliest.

1390 Gower *Conf.* III. 106 The lawe original, Which he hath set in the natures. **1592** H. Chettle *Kinde-harts Dr.* To Rdr., I am as sory, as if the originall fault had beene my fault. **1597** Hooker *Eccl. Pol.* v. lii. §3 The very first originall Element of our nature. **1697** Dryden *Virg. Georg.* I. 91 This is th' Orig'nal Contract; these the Laws Impos'd by Nature, and by Nature's Cause. **1751** Johnson *Rambler* No. 156 ¶1 The re-establishment of its original constitution. **1794** Paley *Evid.* I. §1 (1817) 15 Persons professing to be original witnesses of other miracles. **1849** Macaulay *Hist. Eng.* ii. I. 237 Oates..soon added a large supplement to his original narrative. **1879** Harlan *Eyesight* ii. 15 The original color of the iris is blue, and depends not upon a pigment, or coloring matter, but upon what opticians call an 'interference phenomenon'. **1900** *Bookseller's Catal.*, Sm. folio,..in the original calf.

b. ***original sin*** (*Theol.*): the innate depravity, corruption, or evil tendency of man's nature, in all individuals of the human race, held to be inherited from Adam in consequence of the Fall. Opposed to *actual sin*: see ACTUAL 1, quots. 1315–1534. (The earliest use of the word in English.)

c **1315** Shoreham (E.E.T.S.) 102/105 Oryginale þys senne hys cleped, For man of kende hyt takeþ. *a* **1340** Hampole *Psalter* l. 6, I am haldyn wiþ þe filth of originall syn. **1390** Gower *Conf.* III. 1 The grete Senne original, Which every man in general Upon his berthe hath envenymed. **1471** Ripley *Comp. Alch.* IV. iii. in Ashm. (1652) 144 Clensyd from hys orygynall Syn. **1562** *Articles of Religion* ix, Of Original or Birth-sin. **1577** Northbrooke *Dicing* (1843) 5 The lambe that taketh away our sinnes, original and actual. **1647** Cowley *Mistress, Innocent Ill* ii, Though in thy Thoughts scarce any Tracks have been, So much as of Original Sin. **1702** tr. *Le Clerc's Prim. Fathers* 27 The Pagans knew nothing of what was called since, *Original Sin.* **1888** Bryce *Amer. Commw.* (1889) II. xciv. 464 Experience, ..whether it talks of Original Sin or adopts some less scholastic phrase, will recognize that the tendencies to evil in human nature are..as various and abiding even in the most civilised societies, as its impulses to good.

c. *transf.* That is such from the beginning, or by birth; 'a born ...'. *rare.*

1720 De Foe *Capt. Singleton* x. (1840) 172, I..was..an original thief, and a pirate..by inclination. **1722** —— *Col. Jack* (1840) 4 He was an original rogue. **1894** Ian Maclaren *Bonnie Brier Bush* IV. iv. 159 Elspeth,..div ye ken that ye're an oreeginal sinner?

†**2. a.** ? Having the same origin; sprung from the same stock, or native of the same place. *rare*$^{-1}$.

14.. *Sir Beues* (MS. M) 104/2138 He louid me moste ouer alle, Wyth him I am oryginall.

†**b.** With *upon*: Having its origin in, originating from. *Obs. rare*$^{-1}$.

1679 Kid in Hickes *Spir. Popery* (1680) 9 Not only Prelacy, Popery, Malignancy and Heresie, but Supremacy, and every thing Original upon and derivate from it.

3. a. That is the origin or source of something; from which something arises, proceeds, or is derived; primary; originative. (Now usually associated with or merged in 1.)

1398 Trevisa *Barth. De P.R.* XVIII. i. (1495) 737 An vnresonable beest..the face therof boweth towarde the erthe, that is the origynall and materyall matere wherof it comyth. **1509** Hawes *Past. Pleas.* VIII. (Percy Soc.) 32 For you therof were fyrst originall ground. **1551** Bible *Rom.* Prol., The rote and orygynall fountayne of all synne. **1664** H. More *Myst. Iniq.* ix. 27 There is another fraud, and indeed the more principal and original one, in the distribution of these Excellencies immediately into three. **1741–2** Gray *Agrip.* 92 Shake her own creation To its original atoms. **1861** M. Pattison *Ess.* (1889) I. 30 A writer ..who goes back beyond the printed annalists to original and documentary authorities. **1872** *Wharton's Law Lex.* (ed. 5), *Original and derivative estates.* An original is the first of several estates, bearing to each other the relation of a particular estate and a reversion.

†**b.** ***original writ*** (in *Law*): a writ issuing from the Court of Chancery, which formed the beginning or foundation of a real action at common law; also applied to certain writs for other purposes.

[**1334** *Rolls Parlt.* II. 82 Le Brief originall n'est my meinteinable par Ley saunz nomer son Baron.]

1467–8 *Rolls of Parlt.* V. 633/1 That Information so gyven, stand and be in place of Bille or Writte oryginall. **1641** *Act 17 Chas. I*, c. 10 By Process made by Writ Original at the Common Law. **1727–41** Chambers *Cycl.* s.v. *Writ*, *Original Writs* are those sent out of the high court of chancery, to summon the defendant in a personal, or tenant in a real action; either before the suit begins, or to begin the suit thereby. **1848** Wharton *Law Lex.* s.v., Original writs differ from each other in their tenor, according to the nature of the plaintiff's complaint, and are conceived in fixed and certain forms.

c. *spec.* Applied to anything in relation to that which is a representation or reproduction of it; *e.g.* said of a writing or drawing in relation to a copy or translation of it, of an object in relation to a picture of it, etc. (Cf. B. 3.)

1631 Gouge *God's Arrows* I. §41. 66 The originall word translated *wrath*, signifieth a fervor, fiercenesse, or vehemency of anger. **1659** Bp. Walton *Consid. Considered* 14 The Original Texts are not corrupted either by Jews, Christians, or others. **1688** *Col. Rec. Pennsylv.* I. 231 As to yᵉ Delivery of yᵉ Originall Letters or Instructions. *Mod.* It may be a misprint; you had better examine the original document. This is only a copy; the original picture is in ——'s collection.

4. Produced by or proceeding from some thing or person directly; not derivative or dependent:

a. Proceeding immediately from its source, or having its source in itself; not arising from or depending on any other thing of the kind; underived, independent.

1792 R. Guy *Pract. Obs. Cancers* 27 When these..arise from no apparent Cause, they may be deemed original Affections. **1822–34** *Good's Study Med.* (ed. 4) I. 441, I mean where the hooping-cough is original. **1877** E. R. Conder *Bas. Faith* ix. 400 In an original (that is, independent) and perfect moral being—such as we conceive God to be.

b. Made, composed, or done by the person himself (not imitated from another); first-hand.

1700 Dryden *Pref. Fables* (Globe) 495, I have added some original papers of my own. **1818** Hallam *Mid. Ages* (1872) I. ii. 205 The exclusive exercise of original judicature in their dominions. **1857** Ruskin *Pol. Econ. Art* i. (1868) 54 There is a certain quality about an original drawing which you cannot get in a woodcut. **1900** G. C. Brodrick *Mem. & Impr.* 182 Apostles of 'mature study and original research'.

c. ***original print***, a print made directly from a master image on wood, stone, metal, etc., which is executed by the artist himself, printed by him or under his supervision and, in recent times, usually signed by him.

1961 *What is an Original Print?* (Print Council of Amer.) 9 An *original print* is a work of graphic art, the general requirements of which are: 1. The artist alone has made the image in or upon the plate, stone, wood block or other material, for the purpose of creating a work of graphic art. 2. The impression is made directly from that original material, by the artist or pursuant to his directions. 3. The finished print is approved by the artist. *Ibid.* 12 The difference in the price commanded by an original print and a reproduction acknowledged as such is largely a reflection of the difference in their aesthetic qualities. **1965** Zigrosser & Gaehde *Guide to Collecting Original Prints* ii. 14 When we speak of an *original* print, we mean that the artist both conceived and executed it. **1970** P. Gilmore *Mod. Prints* 7 Several committees between 1960 and 1965 tried variously to define, protect, and elevate the 'original' print, always equating it with artist handwork. **1970** *Studio Internat.* June 283/3 These [assemblage] prints look just as individual as most original prints. **1972** J. Heller *Printmaking Today* (ed. 2) p. v, The 'original' print has become a significant feature of contemporary life.

5. a. Having the quality of that which proceeds from oneself, or from the direct exercise of one's own faculties, without imitation of or dependence on others; such as has not been done or produced before; novel or fresh in character or style.

1756–82 J. Warton *Ess. Pope* I. III. 192 Dante wrote his sublime and original poem, which is a kind of satirical Epic. **1808** *Med. Jrnl.* XIX. 209, I send you the following observations, not because they are new or original, but because I conceive them to be useful. **1882** H. C. Merivale *Faucit of B.* I. vi. 97 Even on the perplexing mysteries of Aristotle's Ethics he could throw an original light.

b. *transf.* Of a person: Capable of original ideas or actions; given to the direct and independent exercise of the faculties in thinking or acting; that does things not known to have been done before; inventive, creative.

1803 Syd. Smith *Wks.* (1859) I. 35/2 There are very few original eyes and ears. The great mass see and hear as they are directed by others. **1840** Carlyle *Heroes* ii. (1858) 219 Such a man is what we call an original man; he comes to us at first hand. A messenger he, sent from the Infinite Unknown with tidings to us. **1875** Jowett *Plato* (ed. 2) V. 192 A great original genius struggling with unequal conditions of knowledge.

¶**6.** ***original vein***: ? error for ORGANICAL *vein.*

1486 *Bk. St. Albans* C iv b, Do let hir [a hawk] blode in the Origynal vayne, and after that yeue hir a frogge for to eete, and she shall be hooll.

7. *Comb.*, as ***original-minded*** (see 5 b).

1801 Southey in Robberds *Mem. W. Taylor* I. 384 For financial..subjects, I think Rickman might be put down, a most original-minded and strong-headed man.

B. *sb.*

1. a. The fact of arising or being derived from something; origination, derivation; = ORIGIN *sb.* 1. Now *rare* or *arch.*

1432–50 tr. *Higden* (Rolls) II. 153 Englische men other Saxones toke theire originalle of Germanye. **1560** Daus tr. *Sleidane's Comm.* 94 The cause and originall of that sedition, was declared also foure yeares synce. **1646** Evelyn *Mem.* (1857) I. 243 It is from these sources that the Rhone and the Rhine..derive their originals. **1726** Leoni tr. *Alberti's Archit.* II. 69/2 The Circus and Amphitheatre..all owe their original to the Theatre. **1818** Hallam *Mid. Ages* (1872) I. ii. 315 *note*, Some word of barbarous original. **1873** Rogers *Orig. Bible* (1875) App. 445 The first verse simply ascribes the original of all things to the will of God.

b. Of persons: Descent, extraction, parentage; = ORIGIN *sb.* 1 b. Now *rare* or *arch.*

1555 Eden *Decades* 27 The people are verye fierse and warlyke men, hauing theyr original of the canybales. **1682** Bunyan *Holy War* 5 We will..discourse of the Original of this Diabolus. *c* **1730** in Skene *Highlanders* (1837) I. 156 These are subdivided into smaller branches of fifty or sixty men, who deduce their original from their particular chieftains. **1784** J. Potter *Virtuous Villagers* I. 147 Notwithstanding his mean original, he was not satisfied with upwards of three hundred pounds a year.

†**c.** *Anat.* The fact of springing or arising (as a nerve, vein, etc.) from some part; also *concr.* = ORIGIN *sb.* 2 b. *Obs.*

1578 Banister *Hist. Man* VIII. 105 Their [the nerves] originall is from the seate or foundation of the brayne. **1612** Woodall *Surg. Mate* Wks. (1653) 20 All veins have their original in the liver. **1668** Culpepper & Cole *Barthol. Anat.* II. iv. 93 The Pleura having taken its Original about the Back.

†**d.** Beginning, commencement, earliest stage (without reference to source or derivation). *Obs.*

1526 Skelton *Magnyf.* 120 By measure all thynge is wrought As at the first orygynall. **1570–6** Lambarde *Peramb. Kent* (1826) 247 Touching the originall, proceeding, and event of these wars, I willingly spare to speake muche. **1690** Locke *Hum. Und.* III. x. §2 Words, that .. will be found, in their first Original..not to stand for any clear..Ideas. **1753** E. Carter (*title*) The History of the University of Cambridge from its Original to the Year 1753.

†**e.** Applied by Wyntoun to his chronicle or history: see quot. *Obs.*

c **1425** Wyntoun *Cron.* I. i, The tytil of this tretis hale I wyll be caulde Orygynale; For that begynning sall mak clere Be playne proces owre matere.

2. a. The thing (or person) from which something else arises or proceeds; a source, cause; = ORIGIN *sb.* 2; an originator, author. Now *rare* or *arch.* in general sense: see 3.

c **1386** Chaucer *Pard. T.* 172 O cause first of oure confusion, O original of oure dampnacion. **1443** *Pol. Poems* (Rolls) II. 209 *Misericordia*, ground and original Of this processe, *Pax* is conclusioun. **1535** Coverdale *Ecclus.* x. 13 Pryde is the origenall of all synne. **1658** Sir T. Browne *Hydriot.* Introd. (1736) 3 Of the Opinion of Thales, that Water was the Original of all Things. **1712** Addison *Hymn, 'The Spacious Firmament'*, Spangled Heav'ns, a Shining Frame, Their great Original proclaim. **1893** Stevenson *Catriona* iv. 44 A fomenter of discontent, and..the unmistakeable original of the deed in question.

b. *Law.* = *original writ*: see A. 3 b.

[**1354** *Rolls of Parlt.* II. 259/1 A receivre les Briefs, si bien Originals de la Chauncellerie come Judicials souz les Seals des Justices.] **1450** *Ibid.* V. 201/1 Such juggement..as they shuld have upon eny originall sued ayenst hym by the cours of the comon lawes. **1523** *Act 14 & 15 Hen. VIII*, c. 1 The person..that will first sue for the same, by originall of dette. **1848** Wharton *Law Lex.* s.v. *Process*, In other cases their processes or modes of commencing the suits were as follows:—..By original..By bill.

3. A thing (or person) in relation to something else which is a copy, imitation, or representation of it; the pattern, archetype.

a. A writing or literary work (less commonly, a phrase or word) in its relation to another which is a translation of it, or (quot. 1869) which reproduces, or is founded upon, its statements.

c **1385** Chaucer *L.G.W.* 1558 *Hypsip.*, Ye get no more of me, but ye wol rede The original that telleth al the case. **1412–20** Lydg. *Chron. Troy* I. v, Though my makyng be the same in all As Guido wryteth in his oryginall. **1595** Copley *Wits, Fits, & Fancies* 79 Your selfe being the Originall, what would you doe with the translation? **1611** Bible *Luke* xvi. 7 *marg.*, The word here interpreted measures, in the originall conteineth about foureteene bushels and a pottle. **1790** Paley *Horæ Paul.* vi, The resemblance is more visible in the original than in our translation. **1869** J. Martineau *Ess.* II. 99 He would..sustain himself by continual appeal to his originals. **1873** Lodge *Note Pallad. on Husb.* v. 118 The original is '*proximam tenui atque jejunæ*'.

b. The primary or earlier writing or document of which another is a copy or transcript.

1494 in Sharp *Cov. Myst.* (1825) 15 *note*, Paid to John Harryes for berying of þe Orygynall þat day, vj*d.* **1591** Lambarde *Archeion* (1635) 48 The Chancellor hath also the Seale of simple Justice and keepeth (as it were) the Forge and Shop of all Originals. **1604** E. G[rimstone] *D'Acosta's Hist. Indies* III. xiii. 161 They carried the copie to the King of Spaine, and the original to their viceroy of Peru. **1776** *Trial Nundocomar* 98/2, I never shewed him the original, before I shewed him the copy. **1875** Scrivener *Lect. Text N. Test.* 5 When several transcripts have to be taken from the same original.

c. The object or person represented by a picture or image; a picture or other work of art in its relation to a copy of it.

1624 Gataker *Transubst.* 82 Of the Image there must needs be some originall. **1726** Leoni *Alberti's Archit.* III. 25/2 Copying other mens work, as being originals more constant..than any living object. **1781** Cowper *Charity* 433 Such was the portrait an apostle drew, The bright original was one he knew. **1855** Prescott *Philip II*, I. iii. (1857) 52 She has sent her a portrait of the prince from the pencil of Titian, which she was to return so soon as she was in possession of the living original.

d. *gen.* and *fig.*

1670 Cotton *Espernon* III. ix. 443 There can be no so dreadful Original, from whence pleasant Copies are not to be taken. **1692** Dryden *Eleonora* 300 And, could there be A copy near the original, 'twas she. **1730** A. Gordon *Maffei's Amphith.* 149 An Original for the others to copy from. **1892** Gardiner *Student's Hist. Eng.* 12 Cunobelin, the original of Shakspere's Cymbeline.

e. An image or impression produced during an actual photographing or recording session from which copies may subsequently be made.

1918 H. Seymour *Reprod. Sound* 16 At first, every record sold to the public was an original, or what is technically described as a 'master', but means were soon found by which copies could be secured from the master. **1949** Frayne & Wolfe *Elem. Sound Recording* xiv. 266 Making the master from the original is a process involving several operations. **1970** A. Fowles *Dupe Negative* xiv. 196 This type of film doesn't have a negative... The piece of film that actually runs through the camera is called the original..

from which all subsequent prints are struck. **1971** L. B. HAPPÉ *Basic Motion Picture Technol.* ix. 277 (*caption*) Duplicates from reversal originals.

4. a. A writing, picture, or other work produced first-hand by the author or maker; a work of literature or art that is not a copy or imitation; an original portrait.

1683 D. A. *Art of Converse* Pref., Of this Treatise, I shall only add, 'tis an Original. **1762–71** H. WALPOLE *Vertue's Anecd. Paint.* (1786) III. 221 He sold many of his pieces for originals by Italian hands. **1825** SCOTT *Diary* 20 Nov. in *Lockhart*, Both these great connoisseurs were very nearly.. agreed that there are no absolutely undoubted originals of Queen Mary.

b. *spec.* in Fashion and *haute couture*, a garment specially designed by a couture house for exhibition in a collection, or a copy of such a garment made to order. Also *Mus.* (usu. jazz), a piece written by the performer(s).

1946 B. G. CHAMBERS *Keys to Fashion Career* x. 86 Partner and designer of the firm of Young Originals. **1957** M. B. PICKEN *Fashion Dict.* 238 *Original*, a garment designed in and produced by a couture house, bearing the label of the house. It is usually a duplication made to order of the model shown in the collection. Each order is called a 'repeat' by the couture house. **1966** *Crescendo* Oct. 22/3 The Monk Quartet was playing originals—'Hackensack', 'Rhythm-A-Ning' and 'Epistrophy'. **1967** *Melody Maker* 28 Jan. 15/5 The material is a nice mixture of originals, blues and ballads. **1975** R. H. RIMMER *Premar Experiments* (1976) ii. 195 My sister, wearing Pucci originals. **1976** *Observer* 22 Feb. 32/5 (Advt.), Anna Belinda announce that until February 28th they will continue to add a further distinction to their hand-made originals in silks, velvets and Liberty prints.

5. a. A person who acts in an original way; one who does things such as have not been done before or are not commonly done (esp. of a ridiculous kind); a singular, odd, or eccentric person.

1676 WYCHERLEY *Pl. Dealer* II. i, I hate imitation, to do anything like other people. All that know me do me the honour to say, I am an original. **1741** RICHARDSON *Pamela* (1824) I. xlix. 379, I may be looked upon as an original in my way. **1771** SMOLLETT *Humph. Cl.* 8 Nov., But my aunt and her paramour.. formed, indeed, such a pair of originals, as I believe, all England could not parallel. **1824** SCOTT *St. Ronan's* xvii, A friendship.. was therefore struck up hastily betwixt these two originals. **1865** M. ARNOLD *Ess. Crit.* iv. 131 This boy is a real original.

b. A thing of singular or unique character; a specimem or example of originality. *rare.*

1727 POPE, etc. *Art of Sinking* 86 Our next instance is certainly an original. **1850** SCORESBY *Cheever's Whalem. Adv.* i. (1859) 12 In adventures.. almost every whaleman's voyage is an original.

6. †**a.** *pl.* Original elements. *Obs.*

c **1400** tr. *Secreta Secret., Gov. Lordsh.* 95 Of hem ys maad by lenghthe of tyme all maner of kynde of composisiouns þat originals, minerals, vegitables, & bestyals. And originals er what þyng ys engelyd yn þe entrailles of þe erthe, and yn þe depnesse of þe sees, & in Cauees of hilles, & in fumositez stoppyd & from vapours vpsteyinge. **1616** CAPT. SMITH *Descr. New Eng.* 15 Her treasures hauing yet neuer beene opened, nor her originalls wasted, consumed, nor abused. **1667** MILTON *P.L.* VI. 511 Up they turn'd Wide the celestial soil, and saw beneath Th' originals of nature in their crude Conception.

b. *pl.* Original inhabitants, settlers, etc. *rare.*

1703 PENN in *Pa. Hist. Soc. Mem.* IX. 205 If the coming of others shall overrule us that are the originals. *Mod. colloq.* They are only recent members; we're the originals.

Hence **o'riginalist** *nonce-wd.* = ORIGINAL B. 5.

1846 WORCESTER cites *Month. Rev.* Hence in later Dicts.

originality (ɒrɪdʒɪ'nælɪtɪ). [ad. F. *originalité* (1699 in Hatz.-Darm.), f. ORIGINAL: see -ITY.] The quality or fact of being original.

1. The fact or attribute of being primary or first-hand; authenticity, genuineness.

1742 H. WALPOLE *Let.* 14 July (1903) I. 256 It is one of the most engaging pictures I ever saw. I have no qualms about its originality. **1776** H. SWINBURNE *Trav. Spain* xliii. 397 One of the most valuable pictures in the world. I do not know how Amiconi came to doubt of its originality. **1881** WESTCOTT & HORT *Grk. N.T.* II. 9 An unsafe guide in the discrimination of relative originality of text.

2. a. The quality of being independent of and different from anything that has appeared before; novelty or freshness of style or character.

1787 SIR J. HAWKINS *Life Johnson* 383 His [Richardson's] sentiments were his own; and.. he was so sensible.. of the originality and importance of many of them, that he would ever be talking of his writings. **1861** M. PATTISON *Ess.* (1889) I. 31 These essays have a character of originality beyond their companions. **1882** SCHAFF *Encycl. Relig. Knowl.* II. 1204/1 Origen.. urges the originality of the person of Christ.

b. with *pl.* An original trait, act, remark, etc.

1854 EMERSON *Lett. & Soc. Aims, Quot. & Orig.* Wks. (Bohn) III. 213 Whoso knows Plutarch, Lucian, Rabelais, Montaigne.. will have a key to many supposed originalities. **1855** W. H. MILL *Applic. Panth. Princ.* (1861) 96 Our author's sagacity has effectually removed all such apparent originalities here.

3. As an attribute of persons: Exhibition of original thought or action; the character of independently exercising one's own faculties; the power of originating new or fresh ideas or methods.

1742 T. GRAY *Let.* 24 May (1935) I. 206 My Lady of Queensbury is come out against my Lady of Marlborough; & she has her Spirit too, & her Originality, but more of the Woman, I think, than t'other; as to the Facts it don't signify two pence, who's in the right. **1787** SIR. J. HAWKINS *Life Johnson* 269 Of singularity it may be observed, that, in general, it is originality; and therefore not a defect. **1822** HAZLITT *Table-t.* I. v. 103 Originality is the seeing nature differently from others, and yet as it is in itself. **1839** HALLAM *Hist. Lit.* III. vi. 617 Shirley has no originality, no force in conceiving or delineating character. **1880** A. H. HUTH *Buckle* I. iv. 218 Originality as understood by the vulgar is independence of the labours of others. *Mod.* A preacher of great originality.

originally (ɒ'rɪdʒɪnəlɪ), *adv.* [-LY[2].]

1. In respect of origin, derivation, or causation; by extraction or descent; indigenously.

1490 CAXTON *Eneydos* iv. 19 The haboundaunce of bloode whiche thou haste seen yssue oute of the trees.. is not orygynally of thyse trees. **1509–10** *Act 1 Hen. VIII*, c. 18 §2 The Quene [shall] have like Habilitie.. as though she had orygynally ben borne within this Realme. *a* **1619** FOTHERBY *Atheom.* II. i. §7 (1622) 185 Though instrumentally they be wrought by the Sun; yet are they originally wrought, onely by God. **1648** MILTON *Tenure Kings* (1650) 19 The power of kings was and is originally the peoples, and by them conferr'd in trust, with liberty and right to reassume it. **1698** A. BRAND *Emb. Muscovy to China* 88 He is originally a Mongul Tartar, of a brown Complexion. **1711** ADDISON *Spect.* No. 69 ¶5 Natural Historians tell us, that no Fruit grows Originally among us. **1794** SULLIVAN *View Nat.* I. 121 Matter is supposed, originally, to consist of minute divisible, or indivisible atoms. *Mod.* He is originally German, but has long been naturalized in England.

2. In the first place, primarily.

1533 MORE *Confut. Tindale* Wks. 734/1 Originally y[e] scripture is knowen as Tindall hymselfe confesseth by none other churche, as the faythe is originallye learned by none other scripture. **1646** SIR T. BROWNE *Pseud. Ep.* 117 Though it originally respected the generation of man, yet is it applyable unto that of other animalls. **1783** HAILES *Antiq. Chr. Ch.* iv. 118 'Dust to dust', which we consider as originally a denunciation of the divine displeasure, was in the Stoical system, a chief topic of consolation. **1875** JOWETT *Plato* (ed. 2) IV. 497 Education is originally to implant in men's minds a sense of truth and justice.

b. In its origin, beginning, or earliest stage; at first, at the beginning, initially.

1651 HOBBES *Leviath.* I. vii. 30 As for the Knowledge of Fact, it is originally, Sense; and ever after, Memory. **1711** STEELE *Spect.* No. 78 ¶4 The Club of Ugly Faces was instituted originally at Cambridge. **1774** PENNANT *Tour Scotl. in 1772.* 251 Originally.. here were three noble globes. **1840** DICKENS *Barn. Rudge* i, The bricks.. had originally been a deep dark red. **1881** BESANT & RICE *Chapl. of Fleet* I. 156 My station, originally, was not lofty.

3. From the beginning, from the first.

1654 BRAMHALL *Just Vind.* iii. (1661) 32 First, England is, that is, originally, not shall be by vertue of this act. *a* **1871** GROTE *Eth. Fragm.* i. (1876) 14 The indefinite power which each man originally possesses of hurting his neighbours.

†**4.** By the person or author himself; not in a copy or transcript. *Obs.*

1661–2 MARVELL *Corr.* Wks. 1872–5 II. 77 Two.. petitions, both alike originally subscribed.

5. In a manner or style that comes fresh from the author; with originality. *rare.*

1882 OGILVIE, *Originally.* 1. In an original manner; as, the author treats this subject very originally.

o'riginalness. *rare*[−1]. [f. as prec. + -NESS.] The quality or fact of being original; originality.

1727 in BAILEY vol. II. **1761** *Acc. of Books* in *Ann. Reg.* 279/2 It would be extremely hard to conclude against the general originalness of the performance.

originant (ɒ'rɪdʒɪnənt), *a.* (*sb.*) [f. ORIGIN-ATE *v.* + -ANT; cf. *militate, militant.*] Originating.

a. That gives origin to something else.

1647 M. HUDSON *Div. Right Govt.* II. ix. 129 The originant principall end.. is the glory of God. **1825** COLERIDGE *Aids Refl.* (1848) I. 209 No natural thing or act can be called originant, or be truly said to have an origin in any other. **1832** *Fraser's Mag.* VI. 336 In virtue of this originant power of his will. **1868** W. G. T. SHEDD *Homiletics* V. (1869) 119 Not equal in true productive force, in real originant and influential power.

b. Arising, taking its origin; = ORIGINARY 3.

1825 COLERIDGE *Aids Refl.* (1873) 226 Sin originant, underived from without.

B. as *sb.* Originating agent or influence.

1892 TRAILL *Mrq. Salisbury* xii. 187 The real originant of Irish disorder.

originary (ɒ'rɪdʒɪnərɪ), *a.* (*sb.*) Now *rare.* [ad. late L. *originārius* original, aboriginal, f. *origin-em* ORIGIN: see -ARY. Cf. F. *originaire* (1365 in Hatz.-Darm.).] **A.** *adj.*

†**1.** That originates or springs *from* (*of*) the thing or place in question; derived, sprung, or having one's extraction *from*; aboriginal, native; cf. ORIGINAL A. 2. *Obs.*

1594 *Mirr. Policy* (1599) L liij, In such honors, offices and dignities of a cittie, the originarie cittizens are to be preferred before strangers. **1633** R. ASHLEY tr. *Barri's Cochin China* B, Cochin China.. is called in the language of the originarie inhabitants Anam, which is the West. **1685** BOYLE *High Veneration*, etc. §18 This heteroclite mineral scarce seems to be originary of this world of ours. **1716** M. DAVIES *Athen. Brit.* III. *Diss. Drama* 25 John Bird, who was a Natif of Coventry, tho' originary of Cheshire.

2. That is the origin or source; from which something originates; = ORIGINAL A. 3.

1638 SANDYS *On Job* 15 Remember I am built of clay; and must Resolve to my originary Dust. **1678** NORRIS *Coll. Misc.* (1699) 44 Take wing (my soul) and upwards bend thy flight, To thy Originary fields of Light. **1862** F. HALL *Hindu Philos. Syst.* 69 The originary atoms of earth, water, fire, and air.

†**3.** Arising directly; primary, underived; = ORIGINAL A. 4a. *Obs.*

1679 LOCKE *Jrnl.* 15 Nov. in Fox Bourne *Life* (1876) I. viii. 451 After October no more originary agues, but such as returned. **1716** M. DAVIES *Athen. Brit.* III. 33 The very Objections of the Arians against Christ's Originary Divinity.

4. 'Productive, causing existence'. (J.)

1705 CHEYNE *Philos. Princ.* (J.), The production of animals in the originary way requires a certain degree of warmth.

5. Arising from or founded upon origin. *rare.*

18.. *New Princeton Rev.* I. 34 (Cent.) Without originary title to Palestine, they conceived that it became theirs by his arbitrary bestowment.

†**B.** *sb.* An aboriginal, a native. *Obs.*

1594 R. ASHLEY tr. *Loys le Roy* 33 The Indians.. did boast, that they were the true Originaries. **1694** FALLE *Jersey* v. 144 And the Originaries, or Natives of the Isle, shall be preferred before others to the Ministery. **1716** M. DAVIES *Athen. Brit.* III. *Diss. Physick* 38 Melampus is said also to have been an Originary of Pylos and a Travellour into Egypt.

Hence †**o'riginarily** *adv.*, originally, primarily.

1610 DONNE *Pseudo-martyr* 181 Originarily, and fundamentally, the Scriptures of God informe vs, what our subiection to the Church ought to be. **1611** COTGR., *Originairement*, originarily, originally.

†**o'riginate**, *ppl. a.* *Obs. rare.* [As if f. L. **orīgināt-us*, pa. pple. of **orīgināre*. F. had the corresponding pa. pple. *originé* in 16th c. (Godefroy). See next and ORIGINATION.] Originated, founded, having its origin. (Const. *upon* = from: cf. ORIGINAL A. 2b, also *founded upon*.)

1679 J. KID in *Last Sp. J. King & J. Kid* (1680) 23 My Testimony to and Abhorrence of every Invasion.. against Christs Royal prerogative,.. Originate upon and derivate from that which they call the Supremacy.

originate (ɒ'rɪdʒɪneɪt), *v.* [As if f. ppl. stem **orīgināt-* of a L. vb. **orīgināre* (f. *orīgin-em* ORIGIN), not in ancient L., but perh. used in med. or mod.L.; cf. It. *originare* 'to fetch his beginning or originall' (Florio, 1598), Sp. and Pg. *originar*; also obs. F. *originé* (16th c. in Godef.) and ORIGINATION.]

1. *trans.* To give origin to, give rise to, cause to arise or begin, initiate, bring into existence.

1657–83 EVELYN *Hist. Relig.* (1850) I. 54 The soul, as seated more conspicuously in the brain, does by the originated Neurology, give intercourse to the animal spirits. **1667** FLAVEL *Saint Indeed* (1754) 23 Christ is.. the originating root; and grace,.. a root originated, planted and influenced by Christ. **1767** T. HUTCHINSON *Hist. Mass.* (1768) II. 335 The exclusive right of the house in originating grants. **1796** MORSE *Amer. Geog.* I. 273 The bishops of the church.. form a separate house, with a right to originate and propose acts for the concurrence of the house of deputies. **1840** I. TAYLOR *Anc. Chr.* (1842) II. vi. 212 Poetry does not originate, but it adorns. **1878** R. W. DALE *Lect. Preach.* iv. 100 Men.. who have originated remarkable religious movements.

†**b.** To trace the origin or derivation of; to derive or deduce *from* a specified source. *Obs. rare.*

1653 WATERHOUSE *Apol. Learn.* 9 The Holy Story originates skill & knowledg of arts, from God.

2. *intr.* To take its origin or rise; to arise, come into existence, have its beginning, commence; to spring, be derived. Const. *from, in, with.*

1775 *Tender Father* II. 50 The scandal.. which I thought must certainly originate from Mr. Selby. **1790** *Norman & Bertha* II. 71 Lord Osgood.. well knew with whom this happy alteration of manners originated. **1816** J. SMITH *Panorama Sc. & Art* II. 253 On the supposition that the commotion originates entirely within the earth. **1846** WRIGHT *Ess. Mid. Ages* II. xvii. 173 A cycle of poetry.. which originated with the people, and rested with the people. **1885** *Manch. Exam.* 10 July 4/7 The fire originated in the chemical room.

b. *Anat.*, etc. To have its origin (locally); to arise, spring (*in* or *from*): cf. ORIGIN *sb.* 2b.

1799 *Med. Jrnl.* II. 167 Galen's opinion, that the veins originated in the liver, had been exploded. **1874** CARPENTER *Ment. Phys.* I. ii. §76 (1879) 79 The points whence the legs and wings originate.

Hence **o'riginated** *ppl. a.* (whence **o'riginatedness**), **o'riginating** *ppl. a.*

originating notice, a notice originating legal proceedings.

1657–83 Originated, **1667** Originating [see 1]. **1829** BENTHAM *Justice & Cod. Petit., Abr. Petit. Justice* 61 On the part of the judge, of the originating judicatory. **1830** COLERIDGE *Table-t.* 29 July, Every intellectual act, however you may distinguish it by name in respect of the originating faculties. **1835** I. TAYLOR *Spir. Despot.* III. 89 A divinely originated economy. **1862** F. HALL *Hindu Philos. Syst.* 53 The soul's will, &c. cannot be eternal; for their originatedness is evidenced by consciousness. **1881** *Daily News* 22 Nov. 5/7 The number of originating notices served in this district is believed to be larger than in any other part of Ireland. **1886** *Pall Mall G.* 10 Apr. 2/1 The solicitor's costs for all proceedings—from originating notice to final orders—are limited by the rules of the Land Commissioners to ten shillings when the rent is under five pounds.

origination (ɒrɪdʒɪ'neɪʃən). [a. obs. F. *origination* (15th c. in Godefroy), ad. L. *orīginātio* 'derivation of words, tracing of origin'

(Quintil.), n. of action, as if f. a vb. *orīgināre, orīgināt-: see ORIGINATE v.] The action or fact of originating.

1. a. Coming into existence, commencement (in reference to its cause or source); rise, origin. **1647** JER. TAYLOR *Lib. Proph.* vii. 129 That promise.. which did not pertaine to Peter principally and by origination, and to the rest by communication. **1649** —— *Gt. Exemp.* I. Ad §5. 59 Here is origination enough for sin.. without charging our faults upon Adam. *a* **1661** FULLER *Worthies* I. (1662) 47, I begin with War, because Arms..had a military Origination. *a* **1832** BENTHAM *Anarch. Fallacies* Wks. 1843 II. 500 The origination of governments from a contract is a pure fiction. **1885** SIR E. FRY in *Law Times Rep.* LII. 67/2 The proceeding..had, therefore, its proper origination in the petition which the statute requires.

b. *Anat.* The fact of arising or springing from some place or part; also *concr.*, = ORIGIN *sb.* 2 b. **1666** J. SMITH *Old Age* x. 65 Those muscles.. notwithstanding their origination may be..from the back. **1717** J. KEILL *Anim. Oecon.* (1738) 170 Muscles whose Originations are as far distant as the *Ischium.* **1870** ROLLESTON *Anim. Life* 107 The origination of the post-abdominal ganglia.

2. The giving of origin; bringing into existence; original production or causation. **1837** CARLYLE *Fr. Rev.* III. v. v, That old Scotch Body named Lords of the Articles, without whose origination.. the so-called Parliament could introduce no bill. **1851** CARPENTER *Man. Phys.* (ed. 2) 236 The origination of the change by an impression acting on the central organ. **1856** FROUDE *Hist. Eng.* (1858) I. iii. 254 His notorious activity.. may have easily connected him with the origination of the plan.

†**3.** *spec.* Derivation (of a word), etymology. *Obs.* (The only recorded sense of L. *orīginātio.*) **1614** SELDEN *Titles Hon.* Pref. d ij, How currant went that idle Deduction of the Persian Sophi from Wollen Tulipants? It hauing origination in the Sophilar, Sophi, or Suffi. **1658** W. BURTON *Itin. Anton.* 24 We may by no means out of our old British Tongue seek the Originations also of Townes names in Africk. *a* **1716** SOUTH *Serm.* (1744) XI. 92 The origination of which word some take from the Hebrew. **1741** FIELDING *Conversation* Wks. 1784 IX. 362 Deduced from the origination of the word itself.

originative (ɒˈrɪdʒɪneɪtɪv, -ətɪv), *a.* [f. ORIGINATE *v.* or its source: see -ATIVE, -IVE.] Having the quality or power of originating; productive, creative, inventive. **1827** I. TAYLOR *Transm. Anc. Bks.* xv. (1875) 205 The imitative, more than originative turn of the Roman mind. **1862** F. HALL *Hindu Philos. Syst.* 26 Consideration and meditation thereon, are originative of a knowledge of the true nature of the soul. **1886** SHORTHOUSE *Sir Percival* 79 Persons of a not very originative habit of mind.

Hence **oˈriginatively** *adv.* **1858** BUSHNELL *Nat. & Supernat.* iv. (1864) 110 Left to act originatively.

originator (ɒˈrɪdʒɪneɪtə(r)). [agent-n. in L. form from ORIGINATE *v.*] One who (or that which) originates something; an initiator, beginner, creator, author. **1818** LADY MORGAN *Fl. Macarthy* IV. iii. 140 An author, an inventor, or an originator. **1871** TYLOR *Prim. Cult.* I. 34 A progressive movement in culture spreads, and becomes independent of the fate of its originators. **1874** L. STEPHEN *Hours in Library* (1892) I. vii. 253 He is an interpreter, not an originator of thought.

So **oˈrigiˌnatress**, a female originator. **1860** WALT WHITMAN *Broadway Fragm.* iv. 6 The Originatress comes, The land of Paradise..the nest of birth.

‖**origines** (ɒˈrɪdʒɪniːz), *sb. pl.* [L., pl. of *orīgo* ORIGIN.] The original facts or documents on which any historical or other work is founded. **1892** *Nation* (N.Y.) 15 Dec. 451/3 If a controversy had not arisen at once as to the *origines* of the volumes.

†**oˈriginist.** *Obs. rare.* [f. ORIGIN *sb.* + -IST.] One who treats of the origin or beginning of things. **1675** R. BURTHOGGE *Causa Dei* 380 A Custom bottomed upon the Great Originist, and that account he gives us of the Genesis and Rise of things. **1694** —— *Reason* 104 The great Originist, Moses.

originist, obs. form of ORIGENIST.

†**oˈriginize**, *v. Obs. rare.* [f. ORIGIN *sb.* + -IZE.] *trans.* = ORIGINATE *v.* 1. **1657** J. SERGEANT *Schism Dispach't* 186 To renounce reason, because it is not originiz'd from his own invention, but proposed first by another. **1665** —— *Sure Footing* 161 How the Revolt..comes to be originiz'd. **1697** —— *Solid Philos.* 218 Originized from some Pure Spirit or Angel.

†**oˈriginous**, *a. Obs. rare*⁻¹. Native, natal; = ORIGINAL A. 1. (? intended as a blunder.) **1633** B. JONSON *Tale Tub* I. ii, What, wisps on your wedding-day, zon! this is right Originous Clay, and Clay o' Kilborn too!

origlion, obs. variant of ORILLION.

‖**orignal** (ɒˈrɪnjəl). [Canadian Fr., alteration of Basque *oregna* stag, pl. *oregnac* (Hatz.-Darm.). Littré cites from Lescarbot *Hist. de la Nouvelle France* (1615) xx, that the Basques landing on the American coasts gave to the American elk the name *orenac*, and that *orenac* in Basque meant 'stag'.]

A Canadian name of the American moose. **1775** J. ANDERSON *Ess. Agric.* 462 In North America they have a species of deer, called by the natives Orignial or Aurignial..probably the Moose-deer. **1787** JEFFERSON *Notes on Virginia* 88 The animals called..grey and black moose, caribou, orignal, and elk.

‖**orihon** (ˈɒrɪhɒn). [Jap., f. *ori* fold + *hon* book.] A book formed by folding a printed roll alternately backwards and forwards between the columns, and usu. fastening it with cord down one side. **1907** C. DAVENPORT *Book* ii. 28 The Chinese and Japanese ..by help of the ancient device of 'stabbing' the flattened roll along one of its sides,..produce a form called an 'Orihon', easy to consult, strong. **1910** *Encycl. Brit.* IV. 216/2 A roll [of vellum, paper, etc.] of this kind can be folded up, backwards and forwards, the bend coming in the vacant spaces between the columns of writing. When this is done it ..becomes a book, and takes the Chinese and Japanese form known as *orihon*—all the writing on one side of the roll or strip of paper and all the other side blank... The earliest fastening of such books consists of a lacing with some cord or fibre run through holes stabbed right through the substance of the roll, near the edge. Now the *orihon* is complete, and it is the link between the roll and the book. **1951** S. JENNETT *Making of Bks.* xi. 155 This form of book was much used throughout the East, and was known as an orihon. **1960** G. A. GLAISTER *Gloss. Bk.* 287 *Orihon*, a manuscript roll on which the writing was done in columns running the short way of the paper with margins between each. The roll was then folded, the margins having the effect of a closed fan. **1968** E. G. TURNER *Greek Papyri* 173 It has been suggested that the codex evolved out of an intermediate form of leather or skin roll in which stitches were inserted in the spaces between every second column, the skin being folded on itself at the intervening column, so that the whole roll was folded concertina-fashion. Books of this kind (termed *orihon*) are still in everyday use in China and Japan.

‖**oˈrillion, oreillon.** *Fortif.* Also 7 orillioune, origlion, 7– orillon. [a. F. *orillon* (ɔrijɔ̃), *oreillon* ear-shaped appendage, 'ear' of any vessel, etc., deriv. of *oreille* ear: cf. ORECCHION.] In obsolete methods of fortification: A part of the defence of a bastion, etc.; see quots. **1647–8** COTTERELL *Davila's Hist. Fr.* (1678) 524 *marg.*, Orillons are the round shoulders at the ends of the faces of Bastions next the Flanks, which cover the covered Flanks; little used in Holland, but much in Italy and France. **1654** EARL MONM. tr. *Bentivoglio's Warrs Flanders* 325 A half Bulwark was thrust out from the Citadel with a great Orillioune. *Ibid.*, The abovesaid Orillion. **1658** —— tr. *Paruta's Wars Cyprus* 116 Origlion. **1696** PHILLIPS (ed. 5), *Orillon*, a mass of Earth lin'd with a Wall, built upon the shoulder of Bastions with Casemates to secure the Canon in the retir'd Flank, and hinder it from being dismounted. **1723** *Pres. St. Russia* I. 302 Of four Bastions every one has one Oreillon. **1853** STOCQUELER *Mil. Encycl.*, *Orillon*,..a projecting tower at the shoulder of a bastion, covering the flank from exterior view.

oriloge, -lage, obs. forms of HOROLOGE.

orilyeit, obs. form of OREILLET.

orinasal, var. ORONASAL *a.* (*sb.*)

O-ring: see O 6.

oringado, oringe, obs. ff. ORANGEADO, ORANGE.

oringo, obs. corrupt form of ERYNGO. **1658** *Songs Costume* (Percy Soc.) 164 Madam, here are pistachie nuts, Strengthening oringo roots.

oriol, obs. form of ORIEL.

oriole (ˈɔːrɪəʊl). [ad. med. and mod.L. *oriolus* (13th c. *oryolus*), in OF. *oriol*, OPr. *auriol* and *auriola*, mod.Pr. *auriou*, Sp. *oriol*:—L. *aureol-us* golden.]

1. A bird of the genus *Oriolus*, esp. *O. galbula* (the Golden Oriole), a summer visitor to Europe and the British Islands, with plumage of a rich yellow contrasted with black; also extended to any bird of the family *Oriolidæ*, comprising various species of Europe, Asia, Africa, and Australia. [*c* **1250** ALBERTUS MAGNUS *De Animal.* XXIII. xxiii, Oryoli aues sunt a tono vocis vulgariter sic vocati vt dicit Plinius.] **1776** PENNANT *Zool.* (ed. 3) II. 532 The oriole..This beautiful bird is common in several parts of Europe. **1839** *Penny Cycl.* XV. 121/1 The genus *Oriolus* or true Oriole of the present day. **1840** *Ibid.* XVII. 17/1 In our own country the Golden Oriole has been found in Hampshire, Devonshire, Cornwall, near Manchester, near Lancaster. **1848** *Life Normandy* (1863) I. 131 Another very pretty bird that is uncommon in England—I mean the oriole. **1894** NEWTON *Dict. Birds* s.v., Another genus which has been referred to the *Oriolidæ*..is *Sphecotheres*, peculiar to the Australian Region, and distinguishable from the more normal Orioles by a bare space round the eye.

2. A bird of the genus *Icterus*, as the Baltimore Oriole (*I. baltimore*), the Orchard Oriole (*I. spurius*); or any bird of the family *Icteridæ* and subfamily *Icterinæ*, peculiar to America, mostly with yellow (or orange) and black coloration; also called *hangnests* or *hangbirds*. [**1791** W. BARTRAM *Carolina* 302 Both species of the Baltimore bird (*oriolus*, Linn. *icterus*, Cat.) are spring birds of passage, and breed in Pennsylvania.] **1792** MARIA RIDDELL *Voy. Madeira* 57 Two kinds of orioles..are found in Antigua. **1845** LONGF. *To a Child* 109 An oriole's pendent nest. **1850** WHITTIER *Sabbath Scene* 96 With golden bosom to the sun, The oriole was singing. **1894** R. B. SHARPE *Handbk. Birds Gt. Brit.* 27 The so-called 'Orioles' of America belonging to a totally different family of birds, viz., the *Icteridæ*.

Orion (ɒˈraɪən). *Astron.* [L. *Ōrīon* = Gr. Ὠρίων (ῑ or ῐ), name of one of the Giants of Greek mythology, a mighty hunter, slain by Artemis, and of the constellation by which he was represented.] Name of a large and brilliant constellation south of the zodiac, figured as a hunter with belt and sword. ***Orion's hound***, the dog-star, Sirius (S.E. of Orion). **1398** TREVISA *Barth. De P.R.* VIII. xxiv. (1495) x v/2 Orion is a moost notable Constellacyon by cause of hugenesse and also of fayrnesse, and it is shape in the ordre of sterres as knighte gyrde wyth a swerde. **1490** CAXTON *Eneydos* xii. 46 The sygne of Oryon rendreth the watres to be proude and cruelle. **1590** SPENSER *F.Q.* I. iii. 31 Scorching flames of fierce Orions hound. **1674** MOXON *Tutor Astron.* (ed. 2) II. 70 The most Northerly Star in the Girdle of Orion doth yet decrease in Declination. **1842** TENNYSON *Locksley Hall* 8 Great Orion sloping slowly to the West. **1868** LOCKYER *Elem. Astron.* i. 33 The great nebula of Orion is situated in the part of the constellation occupied by the sword-handle. *Mod.* The three stars of second magnitude in Orion's Belt.

Orionid (ɒˈraɪənɪd). *Astron.* [f. ORION + -ID, female patronymic: cf. LEONID.] One of a system of meteors whose radiant point is in Orion. **1876** G. F. CHAMBERS *Astron.* 799 The example [of *Leonid*] has been followed in designating other meteor showers by the constellations in which their radiant-points are situated; so that we have the..Orionids of October 18–20. **1899** *Edin. Rev.* Oct. 325 The well-known Orionid centre.

-orious, a compound suffix forming adjs., consisting of -OUS (L. *-ōsus*), added to L. *-ōri-* in *ōri-us, -a, -um* (see -ORY). Instances of this occur in med.L., as in *victōri-ōs-us*, F. *victori-eux* victorious, f. *victōria* victory; but most of the Eng. examples are directly formed upon L. adjs., actual or possible, in *-ōri-us*; e.g. *censorious, meritorious, notorious, proditorious.* The sense is either the same as, or closely akin to, that of adjs. in -ORY.

oripore (ˈɔːrɪpɔə(r)). *Zool.* [f. L. *ōs, ōri-* mouth + PORE.] A pore or small opening representing a mouth. **1846** DANA *Zooph.* (1848) 338 Indistinct seriate oripores.

oririme (ˈɔːrɪraɪm). *Zool.* [f. as prec. + L. *rīma* cleft, chink.] A cleft or narrow opening representing a mouth. **1846** DANA *Zooph.* (1848) 284 A central pore or puncture (oririme), marking the position of the mouth.

oris, obs. form of ORRIS.

Orisha (ɒˈrɪʃə). [Etym. obscure (see quot. 1926).] A name given to a number of native deities of Southern Nigeria. Also *attrib.* **1926** P. A. TALBOT *Peoples S. Nigeria* II. iii. 29 A hierarchy of Orisha (derived perhaps from 'ri', see, and 'sha', select—or from the Edo word Oyisa). **1929** A. C. M. BURNS *Hist. Nigeria* ii. 39 A number of minor deities (Orishas) who are more directly interested in mundane matters. **1937** M. PERHAM *Native Admin. Nigeria* II. xii. 189 The House of the Orishas or sacred images stands in the market outside the official residence of the Ataoga. *Ibid.*, The visits to Orisha-houses and consultations of oracles. **1949** G. PARRINDER *West Afr. Relig.* ii. 16 The chief divinities, generally non-human spirits, often associated with natural forces (called *abosom, vodũ, orisha*). **1961** J. JAHN in A. Dundes *Mother Wit* (1973) 97/1 Without the drums it was impossible to call the orishas. *Ibid.* 98/2 The procedure which in the African orisha cult evokes ecstatic immobility..produces, in the Negro churches, 'mass ecstasy'. **1974** *Afr. Encycl.* 548/3 Many Yoruba people are Christians or Muslims, but still follow the traditional religion, which has several powerful Gods..and many less important ones called 'orisha'. **1976** *Wilson Q.* Autumn 77 The African deities (*orishas*) became identified with various Christian saints.

orismology (ɒrɪzˈmɒlədʒɪ). *rare.* [For *horismology, f. Gr. ὁρισμός definition + -LOGY.] A name for the explanation of technical terms, or for such terms collectively; terminology. **1816** KIRBY & SP. *Entomol.* (1856) I. Pref. 13 The Terminology..to avoid the barbarism of a word compounded of Latin and Greek; they would beg to call the Orismology of the science. **1839–47** TODD *Cycl. Anat.* III. 548/2 The orismology of any particular branch of zoological science.

Hence **orismoˈlogic, orismoˈlogical** *adjs.*, pertaining to orismology. **1826** KIRBY & SP. *Entomol.* III. Advt. p. iv, The Anatomical and Orismological Tables. **1852** J. FREEMAN *Life William Kirby* 311 Criticising and perfecting our anatomical and orismological terms. **1882** OGILVIE, *Orismologic.*

orison (ˈɒrɪzən, -sən). *arch.* Forms: α. 2–3 ureisun, 3–5 oreison, etc. (5 uresun, *Caxton* oroyson), 3–6 oreson, etc., 6 orayson, orasoun, 6–7 orason, 6–9 oraison, 7 oraizon; β. 3– orison, (3–7 -oun, oryson, etc., 4–6 urison, etc., 4–7 horison, 5 orisson, urrysone, 6 *Sc.* wrisoun, wriesone, 6–8 orizon, 6 -one): with interchanges in 3–7 of *i* and *y*, and of *-on, -un, -onn, -unn, -oun,*

-own, with or without final *e*. [a. OF. *oreisun*, *orison* (12th c.), now *oraison* (16th c. in Littré) = Pr. *orazon*, Sp. *oracion*, It. *orazione*:—L. *ōrātiōn-em* speech, oration, in Christian L. an address to God, a prayer (Vulgate); n. of action f. *ōrāre* to utter words, speak, pray, f. *ōs*, *ōr-* mouth. Etymologically a doublet of *oration*.]

1. A prayer. (In later use chiefly in *pl.*: cf. *say one's prayers*.)

α. *c* **1175** *Lamb. Hom.* 51 Þe halie ureisuns þe me singeð in halie chirche. *a* **1225** *Ancr. R.* 16 Siggeð so al ðe imne.. & te oreisun, 'Deus qui corda'. *c* **1290** *S. Eng. Leg.* I. 64/375 Al one in is oresones: þere he lai wel stille. **1340** *Ayenb.* 51 He begynþ his matyns and his benes and his oreysones. **1490** CAXTON *How to Die* 1 Certayn oreysons and deuoute prayers that they oughte to saye. *a* **1533** LD. BERNERS *Huon* xliii. 146 Whan he had made his oreson ther came a sarazyn to Huon. **1615** G. SANDYS *Trav.* 36 The Captain Bassa.. performing appointed oraisons and ceremonies. **1740** DYER *Ruins of Rome* Poems (1761) 21 The pilgrim oft..'mid his oraison hears Aghast the voice of time.

β. **1297** R. GLOUC. (Rolls) 7196 As þis holiman adde is orison ydo þere. *c* **1320** R. BRUNNE *Medit.* 361 Þe same orysun þat he preyd byfore. **1382** WYCLIF *Dan.* ix. 17 Now forsothe, oure God, heere the orisoun of thi seruaunt. *c* **1386** CHAUCER *Pars. T.* ¶965 Of whiche orisons certes in the orison of the Pater noster hath Ihesu crist enclosed moost thynges. **1387-8** T. USK *Test. Love* III. ix. (Skeat) I. 92 Devoute horisons & praiers to God. *c* **1420** *Chron. Vilod.* st. 582 Wiþ certeyne urrysones for hurre prayng. **1474** CAXTON *Chesse* 33 They wake alle the nyght in prayers and orisons. *a* **1578** LINDESAY (Pitscottie) *Chron. Scot.* (S.T.S.) I. 349, I teichit thame the dominicall wrisoun quhilk we call the Lordis prayer. **1589** GREENE *Menaphon* (Arb.) 50 Manie orizons [she made] to Hymæneus. **1602** SHAKS. *Ham.* III. i. 89 Soft you now, The faire Ophelia? Nimph, in thy Orizons Be all my sinnes remembred. **1667** MILTON *P.L.* XI. 137 When Adam and first Matron Eve Had ended now thir Orisons. **1797** MRS. RADCLIFFE *Italian* xv, Remember me in your orisons. **1812** BYRON *Ch. Har.* I. xli, Three tongues prefer strange Orisons on high. **1868** MILMAN *St. Paul's* vii. 144 Provided for the due celebration of these inestimable orisons.

Comb. **1653** URQUHART *Rabelais* I. xxi, To the same place came his orison-mutterer.

b. Without *an* or *pl.*: The action of praying, prayer. Now *rare*.

c **1250** *O. Kent. Serm.* in *O.E. Misc.* 28 Stor, for holy urisun. Mirre, for gode werkes. *a* **1300** *Cursor M.* 15623 To-quils he lai in orisun. **1483** CAXTON *Cato* F iv, There by the space of twenty dayes as he was in oryson. **1572** *Lament. Lady Scotl.* in *Scot. Poems 16th C.* II. 246 Thus to disdane the hous of orisoun. **1860** PUSEY *Min. Proph.* 19 The soul hath in orison familiar converse with God.

†**2.** A speech, oration. Chiefly *Sc. Obs.*

1430-40 LYDG. *Bochas* VI. xv. (1554) 161 b, Through his language, this sayd Tullius Reconciled by his soote Orisons. **1549** *Compl. Scot.* vi. 43 The principal scheiphirde maid ane orison tyl al the laif of his conpanyȝons. **1603** *Philotus* lxv, Ȝovr Orisoun sir sounds with sic skil In Cupids Court as ȝe had bene vpbrocht.

orison, -soun, -sont(e, obs. ff. HORIZON.

Orissi (ɒˈrɪsɪ). *India.* [f. *Orissa* a state of eastern India.] = ODISSI.

1960 C. FABRI in *Mārg* (Bombay) XIII. II. 5 Orissi.. bears great resemblance not only to Bharata Natya, but also to Kuchipudi, in Andhra, which may be described as 'next door'. **1962** B. GARGI *Theatre in India* 51 Orissi dance, practised in Orissa in South-East India, is recognised by scholars as an authentic classical dance... This dance style ..claims to be over two thousand years old. **1965** E. BHAVNANI *Dance in India* vi. 50 The Orissi dance has its roots in devotional ritual. **1971** *Femina* (Bombay) 2 Apr. 9/1 The first part of the programme was in Bharat Natyam, the second and third in the Kuchipudi and Orissi styles of dancing. **1974** *Encycl. Brit. Macropædia* XIII. 741/1 The classical dance of Orissa, known as the *orissi* dance, has survived for more than 700 years.

oristic (ɒˈrɪstɪk), *a. rare.* [ad. Gr. ὁριστικ-ός of or for defining.] Determinately expressed. So **oˌristicoseˈmeiotic** *a.* [Gr. σημειωτικ-ός observant of signs].

1811-31 BENTHAM *Logic* App. B. Wks. 1843 VIII. 287 Oristic, and aoristic, or more expressively, oristicosemeiotic and aoristicosemeiotic, determinately and indeterminately expressed.

-orium, *suffix*, the neuter sing. ending of L. adjs. in *-ōrius* (see -ORIOUS, -ORY), used sbst. in the sense 'place for or belonging to, thing used for, requisite', as in *auditōrium* place for hearing, *prætōrium* general's tent, *promontōrium* headland, *repositōrium* dumb-waiter, *scriptōrium* writing-room, *sensōrium* organ of sensation (Boethius). The Eng. form of these words, taken through Norman Fr. *-ori*, is -ORY; but some of the Latin words have been taken into historical or learned use in the L. form, as *auditorium*, *prætorium*, *sanatorium*, *scriptorium*, *sensorium*, and after these others, as *haustorium*, *inclinatorium*, *inductorium*, etc., have been formed as scientific terms.

b. Now used, esp. in America, in many, often hybrid, formations, as *barbatorium*, *bobatorium*, *healthatorium*, etc.

1925 *Amer. Speech* I. 38/2 *Barbatorium*, a barber shop. *Bobatorium*, a place where hair is bobbed. *Healthatorium*, synonymous for *sanatorium*. *Infantorium*, a sanatorium for infants... *Motortorium*, an automobile repair shop... *Suitatorium*, a place where suits are cleaned and pressed. [etc.]. **1943** *Ibid.* XVIII. 71/1 Perhaps the following forms on the *-orium* ending have not previously been noted: *furnitorium* (a furniture store), *hairitorium* (a store dealing in wigs and hair goods), and *puritorium* (a Hebrew ritual bath). **1957** *Journal des Traducteurs* II. 49 In recent decades advertisers intent on catching the public eye have freely exploited such suffixes as *-orium*..to form *hairorium*, *meatorium*, *sportorium*. **1959** *Times* 28 Oct. 13/4 A market gardener in New South Wales..keeps a lonely stall bearing the notice 'Potatorium'. *Ibid.* 31 Oct. 7/7 Lubritorium (United States) is, inevitably, not Latin. *Ibid.* 2 Nov. 13/4 Thirty years ago there was a 'pantatorium' in Cambridge (Mass.), which pressed pants..rapidly. **1963** R. I. MCDAVID *Mencken's Amer. Lang.* 221 The former [*-orium*] has given *lubritorium* (the lubricating rack in a filling station), *printorium*, *corsetorium*, *hotdogatorium*, *parentorium* (a parent guidance center), *puritorium* (a Jewish ritual bath) and *eatatorium*.

orix, obs. form of ORYX.

Oriya (ɒˈriːjə), *a.* and *sb.* Also **Ooreah, Ooriya, Uriya**, etc. [f. Skr. *Odra* name of a region of India.] **A.** *adj.* **a.** Of or pertaining to Odra, an ancient region of India corresponding to the State of Orissa. **b.** Of or pertaining to the State of Orissa, which takes its name from Odra. **B.** *sb.* **a.** A native of Odra. **b.** The Indo-European language of Odra, which is spoken widely in Orissa.

1801 *Asiatick Researches* VII. 225 Utcala or Ódradésa is co-extensive with the Subá of Órésá... The language of this province, and the character in which it is written, are both called Uriya... The Bráhmens of this province use the Uríya character in writing the Sanscrit language. **1831** A. SUTTON *Introd. Gram. Oriya Lang.* p. vii, The Oriyas speak every word with the bold rusticity of an English countryman... A Bengallee can scarcely be met with who speaks Oriya, but he may instantly be detected by his peculiar mode of pronunciation. **1848** J. H. STOCQUELER *Oriental Interpreter* 177/2 The *Ooreahs* are, in some respects, excellent servants; they are very careful of furniture. *Ibid.* 179/1 The language of the Oreeah nation is a dialect of the Sanscrit, much resembling the Bengalee, and called the Ooreah. **1855** H. H. WILSON *Gloss. Indian Terms* p. xxii, The Telugu..meeting on the north with Uriya, on the west with Maráthí and Karnáta. **1866** G. CAMPBELL in *Jrnl. Asiatic Soc. Bengal* XXXV. II. (Suppl.) 52 They [*sc.* the 'Bhooyas']..speak Oorya on the Ooriah borders..and Hindee farther north. *Ibid.* A resemblance in appearance to the Ooryahs, among whom high cheek bones seem to prevail. **1872** W. W. HUNTER *Orissa* I. v. 171 The Uriyá language held its own for centuries, almost to the walls of Kalingapatnam itself. **1873** E. BALFOUR *Cycl. India* (ed. 2) IV. 266/1 A monster snake.. was worshipped by the Ooryah as a deity. *Ibid.* 267/1 In Vizianagram, Telugu is only spoken in the open country, and Urya in the mountains. **1903** G. A. GRIERSON *Linguistic Survey India* V. II. 367 It is called Oṛiyā, Ōḍrī, or Utkalī, that is to say the language of Ōḍra or Utkala, both of which are ancient names of the country now known as Orissa. *Ibid.* 368 The Oṛiyā verbal system is at once simple and complete. **1930** R. D. BANERJI *Hist. Orissa* I. x. 136 The average Oriya ..is usually dwarfish in stature and brownish black in complexion. **1954** PEI & GAYNOR *Dict. Linguistics* 155 *Oriya*, an Indic language (also called *Odri*) spoken in Orissa, Bihar, Bengal, the eastern regions of the Central Provinces and in the northern part of the Madras Presidency, by a total of about 13,000,000 native speakers. **1971** *Femina* (Bombay) 30 Apr. 29/1 A student of Hindustani classical music, she knows many Oriya songs. **1972** W. B. LOCKWOOD *Panorama Indo-European Lang.* 206 Oriya is the state language of Orissa, where it is the native medium of sixteen and a half millions. *Ibid.*, The Oriyas reached their present seats after advancing from the west.

orizon(t, orizunt, obs. forms of HORIZON.

ork (ɔːk). *slang.* (orig. and chiefly *U.S.*). Also orch. [abbrev. of ORCHESTRA.] An orchestra, *spec.* a jazz or dance band.

1936 *Metronome* Feb. 61/3 Orville Knapp and ork back in town... Curly Riggs and ork home from the Santa Rita Hotel, Tucson engagement. **1937** in *Variety* 10 Nov. 58/3 Philly Orch on Thursday (11) night will preem..'Mystic Pool'. **1950** *Down Beat* 1 Dec. 13 (*title*) Ina Ray Ork looks good on TV; plays well, too. **1959** C. MACINNES *Absolute Beginners* 136 The Dickie Hodfodder ork, led by Richard H. in person, playing away merrily. **1977** *Zigzag* June 41/4 'Weeping Willow'—recorded in London backed..by Georgie Fame, Colin Green and the Norrie Paramour Ork!

ork(e, orkanet, obs. var. ORC, ORCANETTE.

orken, an adaptation of **orcen* assumed as sing. of *orcneas* in Beowulf, (?) monsters or sea-monsters.

a **1000** *Beowulf* 112 Eotenas and ylfe and orcneas. **1855** THORPE tr. *Beowulf* 225 Thence monstrous births all sprang forth, eotens, and elves, and orkens.

†**ˈorkey.** *Obs.* [Corruption of Du. *oortken*, dim. of *oort*, a small coin: cf. ORKYN.] (See quot.)

1660 HEXHAM, *Een Oort, ofte Oortken*, An Orkey, or the fourth part of a stiver, or two Doits. **1708** T. WARD *Eng. Ref.* (1710) I. 131 The poorest of 'em Could scarcly wrest an Orkie from him.

Orkney (ˈɔːknɪ). The name of a group of islands off the north coast of Scotland, applied *attrib.* to various local animals and products; **Orkney sheep**, a small feral sheep distinguished by horns curving backwards and a brown, white, or speckled fleece; **Orkney vole**, a larger subspecies of the European vole, *Microtus arvalis orcadensis*, found only in the Orkney Islands.

[**1805** G. BARRY *Hist. Orkney Islands* III. i. 319 The Sheep (*ovis aries*, Lin. Syst.) here is a peculiar breed, and, from some features in its character, seems to have sprung from the same stock with those of Iceland, the Ferroes, and Shetland.] **1861** MRS. BEETON *Bk. Househ. Managem.* 320 The Leicestershire breed [of sheep] is the best example of this lymphatic and contented animal, and the active Orkney, who is half goat in his habits, of the restless and unprofitable. **1905** J. G. MILLAIS *Mammals Gt. Brit. & Ireland* II. 279, I have noticed that both the Orkney and the Water Voles often possess a white tip to the end of the tail. **1912** H. J. ELWES in *Scottish Naturalist* 6 Orkney Sheep. Sheep never seem to have been as important here as in Shetland. **1926** *Daily Colonist* (Victoria, B.C.) 7 Jan. 5/3 A group of smartly designed coats of the popular Orkney cloth in half a dozen beautiful shades. **1935** *Discovery* June 168/2 All our voles, including the Orkney and Skomer voles, seem as numerous as they have ever been. **1952** L. H. MATTHEWS *Brit. Mammals* vi. 155 In captivity the Orkney vole is noticeable for its pugnacious disposition and its readiness to bite. **1965** T. FITZGIBBON *Art Brit. Cooking* 133 Orkney cheese is a creamy Cheddar type cheese made in the Orkney Islands, but exported to England. **1971** [see *inverted pleat* s.v. INVERTED *ppl. a.* 9]. **1972** *Country Life* 3 Aug. 273/2, I shall be grateful if you can give me any information regarding Orkney chairs... As the name suggests, this is a traditional Orkney kind of furniture. **1973** *Scotsman* 21 Feb. 10/1 Cheese straws made from Orkney cheese. **1974** J. M. DONEY et al. in P. A. Jewell et al. *Island Survivors* iv. 124 The litter size of these [Soay] lambs was 1·28, which is the same as.. the Orkney sheep on North Ronaldshay. **1978** *Vole* No. 6. 54/2 Orkney is distinguished in having its own special vole, the Orkney vole, larger than its mainland cousin.

Orkneyman (ˈɔːknɪmən). = ORCADIAN *sb.*; a native or inhabitant of the Orkney Islands.

1775 HEARNE & TURNOR *Jrnls.* (1934) 191, I have interfered so far as to ask what encouragement they required to which the Orkneymen seem'd to intermate that 12L per annum would enduce them to be active & useful. **1842** *Trans. Lit. & Hist. Soc. Quebec* iv. 1333 The animals frequenting this country [include]..the Common Hare of Canada, called Rabbits, by the Orkney men in the service of the Hudson's Bay Company. **1936** *Beaver* (Winnipeg) Dec. 4/1 In the year 1799 about five hundred and thirty persons were employed by the Hudson's Bay Company, at their fur trade posts in North America, of whom four hundred and sixteen..were Orkneymen. **1956** V. FISHER *Pemmican* 30 He had heard that..there were..a few red-faced Orkneymen, a few Moravian sisters and brothers. **1961** J. W. ANDERSON *Fur Trader's Story* i. 1 For nearly two hundred years Orkneymen played a prominent part in the fur trade of Canada. **1969** G. M. BROWN *Orkney Tapestry* 26 Hardly a thing is known about these first Orkneymen.. apart from the monuments they left behind them.

†**ˈorkyn.** *Obs. rare*[−1]. = ORKEY.

1542 UDALL *Erasm. Apoph.* (1877) 91 They that goo about to bye an yerthen potte, or vessell for an orkyn, dooe knocke vpon it with their knuccle.

orl, dial. form of *olr*, *alr*, ALDER, the tree.

[*c* **1440**: see ORYELLE.] **1747** R. BOWLKER *Art of Angling* 27 This Hedge ought to be made chiefly of Orls. **1804** DUNCUMB *Hist. Hereford* I. Gloss. (E.D.S.), *Orl*, the wood alder.

Hence **orl-fly** (*ellipt.* orl), the alder-fly, *Sialis lutarius*, used by anglers.

1747 R. BOWLKER *Art of Angling* 69 The Orle Fly..is the best Fly to Fish with after the May Flyes are gone. **1787** BEST *Angling* (ed. 2) 115 The Orl fly comes on the latter end of May and continues on till the latter end of June. **1875** W. HOUGHTON *Brit. Insects* 64 The well-known orl or Alder-fly (*Sialis lutarius*).

orl (ɔːl), *a.* and *adv.* Representing a 'phonetic' spelling of a vulgar pronunciation of ALL *a.* and *adv.*

1864 [see O.K. *a.* a]. **1898** J. D. BRAYSHAW *Slum Silhouettes* 14, I could 'ear the plates abreakin' pretty nigh orl night. **1923** 'R. CROMPTON' *William Again* xiv. 240 That ..looks a bit of orl *right*. **1939** [see O.K. *a.* a]. **1955** M. ALLINGHAM *Beckoning Lady* ii. 31 Orl right, orl right, I'll go. **1971** *Listener* 9 Sept. 342/2 To use her own quaint phraseology *May bien*, she was a bit of orlright. **1972** *Buster & Jet* 15 Jan. 33 Orl right, you ol' Scrooge! I'm meetin' some real tightwads today, it seems!

orlache, -age, -ager, obs. ff. HOROLOGE, -ER.

orle (ɔːl). Also 6 urle. [a. F. *orle*, OF. *urle*, *ourle*:—late L. type **ōrulum*, dim. of *ōra* border; It. *orlo* border, hem. Cf. URLE *v.*]

1. *Her.* A narrow band of half the width of the bordure, following the outline of the shield, but not extending to the edge of it.

1610 GUILLIM *Heraldry* II. vii. (1611) 65 The Orle..is an ordinarie composed of a threefold line duplicated admitting a transparencie of the field thorowout the innermost area or space therein enclosed. **1830** ROBSON *Hist. Her.* Gloss., *Orle*, an inner bordure of the same shape as the escutcheon itself... The field being seen within and round it, on both sides. **1872** RUSKIN *Eagle's N.* §235 The Orle, a narrow band following the outline of the shield midway between its edge and centre, is a more definite expression of enclosure or fortification by moat or rampart.

b. A band of small charges arranged round the shield orlewise. Hence ***in orle***, said of subordinate charges thus borne.

1572 BOSSEWELL *Armorie* II. 43 K. beareth Or, a Lyon Seiante, Sable, within an Orle d'Ogresses. **1587** FLEMING *Contn. Holinshed* III. 1370/1 He beareth azure, a crosse forme fiche or, within an vrle of stars or. **1610** GUILLIM *Heraldry* III. iii. (1611) 88 These stars are said to bee borne in Orle or Orle waies. **1786** W. BOYS *Coll. Hist. Sandwich* (1792) 797 The same legend of St. Martin within a quatrefoil, with four demi-ships conjoined with four demi-lions in orle. **1864** BOUTELL *Her. Hist. & Pop.* vii. 32 Sometimes a series of separate charges form an Orle.

c. The chaplet or wreath round the helmet of a knight, bearing the crest.

1834 PLANCHÉ *Brit. Costume* 186 A bascinet..having.. the lining or cap within, and the orle or chaplet without.

2. The metal rim of a shield.

In mod. Dicts.

†**3.** *Arch.* See quots. and cf. ORLO. *Obs.*

1706 PHILLIPS s.v., In Architecture, Orle is the same with Plinth. **1727–41** CHAMBERS *Cycl.*, *Orle*..in architecture, a fillet under the ovolo, or quarter-round of a capital.

Hence **'orlewise, -ways,** *advs.*, in orle: see 1 b.

1610 GUILLIM *Heraldry* II. vi. (1611) 66 Borne Orlewaise or in Orle.

Orleanian (ɔːˈliːənɪən). [f. *Orlean*(*s* + -IAN.] An inhabitant of New Orleans in the United States.

1946 *New Orleans Times-Picayune* 23 Mar. 17/4 (*heading*) Orleanian tells of Jap tortures. **1947** in B. A. Botkin *Treas. S. Folklore* (1949) III. ii. 535 Perhaps the most famous of romantic Mardi Gras stories that Orleanians tell is that one concerning the 'ghost dinners' served each Shrove Tuesday. **1948** *Highway Traveler* Dec. 18/1 Because Orleanians at one time depended upon the duel as a means of settling disputes, the extensive display of dueling pistols and swords on the second floor has special interest. **1952** B. ULANOV *Hist. Jazz in Amer.* (1958) v. 46 The dance-music instrumentation familiar to most Orleanians.

Orleanist ('ɔːliːənɪst), *sb.* (and *a.*) [a. F. *Orléaniste*, f. local name *Orléans*: see next and -IST.] In French politics: An adherent of the princes of the house of Orleans, descended from the Duke of Orleans, younger brother of Louis XIV, whose descendant Louis Philippe reigned as King of the French, 1830–1848. Also *attrib.* or as *adj.*

1834 tr. *C. M. Catherinet de Villemarest's Life Prince Talleyrand* II. ix. 184 The letter of the Abbé Maurice [*sc.* Talleyrand]..proves to me, that after having been an anarchist, an Orleanist, and not having been able to become a Robespierrist..he has now become a Directorist. **1848** W. H. KELLY tr. *L. Blanc's Hist. Ten Y.* I. 235 It had been the focus of Orleanist and Bonapartist conspiracies. **1870** *Standard* 16 Nov., The Legitimists, the Orleanists, the Republicans, the Napoleonists, are arrayed in one rank. **1976** W. GÉRIN *E. Gaskell* xiv. 155 Mary Anne Clarke..an Orleanist to the backbone..had the good fortune to charm Chateaubriand.

So **'Orleanism**, the political principles of the Orleanists; **Orlea'nistic** *a.*, pertaining to or of the nature of the Orleanists.

1865 tr. *Strauss' New Life Jesus* II. II. liii. 10 Possessed, so to say, with an Orleanistic spirit.

Orleans ('ɔːliːənz). [Name of a city in France, giving the title to a dukedom.]

1. A variety of plum.

1664 EVELYN *Kal. Hort.* (1729) 233 Fruit-Trees..for a moderate Plantation:..Newington, excellent. Orleans, Persique. **1770** FOOTE *Lame Lover* III. Wks. 1799 II. 86 The green gages, or the orleans. **1860** PIESSE *Lab. Chem. Wonders* 121 Orleans, greengages, damsons, and all plums.

attrib. **1761** FITZGERALD in *Phil. Trans.* LII. 71 The main arms of an Orleans plumb-tree. **1771** MAD. D'ARBLAY *Early Diary, Let. to M. Allen*, I..desire that I may have a boil'd Orlean plomb pudding for my dinner.

2. A fabric of cotton warp and worsted weft, brought alternately to the surface in weaving.

According to Beck, *Draper's Dict.*, introduced in 1837, and the first fabric of the kind known in England.

1844 G. DODD *Textile Manuf.* iv. 137 There are two kinds of stuff now made, called 'Orleans' and 'Paramatta' (why so named, it would probably be difficult to say) apparently formed of worsted, but the weft only is of worsted, the warp being cotton.

orlege, orleger, obs. ff. HOROLOGE, -ER.

‖**orlo** ('ɔːləʊ). *Arch.* [It. *orlo* border, brim, hem, etc.: see ORLE.] **a.** The fillet between the flutings of a column. **b.** The plinth of the base of a column.

1613–39 I. JONES in Leoni *Palladio's Archit.* (1742) II. 50 The Orlo, Brim, or Spaces are $\frac{1}{4}$ of the Fluting. **1715** LEONI *Palladio's Archit.* (1742) I. 21 Orlo, or Plinth of the Base.

orloge, orloger: see HOROLOGE, HOROLOGER.

Orlon ('ɔːlɒn). Also **orlon.** A proprietary name of a man-made polyacrylonitrile fibre which makes a soft, warm yarn for textiles and knitwear. Freq. *attrib.*

1948 *N.Y. Times* 25 Aug. 43/3 The DuPont Company announced today it had adopted the trade mark 'Orlon' for a synthetic textile fiber on which it has been conducting research for several years and which previously has been known as Fiber A. **1950** *Official Gaz.* (U.S. Patent Office) 17 Oct. 677/1 E. I. DuPont de Nemours and Company... *Orlon.* For yarns of synthetic fibers. Claims use since Aug. 3, 1948. **1952** *Trade Marks Jrnl.* 9 Jan. 31/1 *Orlon*... Raw or partly prepared synthetic textile fibres. E. I. DuPont De Nemours and Company..Wilmington, State of Delaware, United States of America; manufacturers. **1952** [see ACRILAN]. **1956** A. HUXLEY *Let.* 17 Nov. (1969) 811 It is interesting to find ruffles coming back—in orlon and nylon, no ironing, no starch. **1957** P. WILDEBLOOD *Main Chance* 36 His smiling teeth looked as expensively synthetic as his orlon shirt and dacron suit and nylon socks. **1969** 'J. MUNRO' *Innocent Bystanders* vii. 98 The journey was a gruelling one, and by the end of it the yellow Orlon dress had lost its glitter. **1973** *Materials & Technol.* VI. 327 Polyacrylonitrile, best known under the trade names of 'Courtelle', 'Acrilan' and 'Orlon'.

orlop[1] ('ɔːlɒp). Forms: α. 5–6 **over-loppe,** (*Sc.* 5 **ou(e)r-lop**), 6–7 **-lop,** 7 **-loop, -lope.** β. 6 **orloppe, or(e)loope, oarlop,** 7 **orelop, orlopp, arloup,** 7–8 **orlope;** 8 **horlop;** 7– **orlop.** γ. *Sc.* 5–7 **ou(e)rloft.** [a. Du. *overloop* a covering, '*ouer-loop van t'schip*, fori, tabulata nauium constrata, per quæ nautæ feruntur' (Kilian, 1599), f. *overloopen* to run over: see OVER and LEAP *v.*] Originally, the single floor or deck with which the hold of a ship was covered in, which, by the successive addition of one, two, or three complete decks above, became the lowest deck of a ship of the line; sometimes applied to the lowest deck of a steamer or ship with three or more decks.

The orlop was not usually reckoned in nomenclature as a 'deck'; when a ship had two complete floors these were called orlop and deck; when three floors, they were orlop, lower, and upper deck; when four floors, orlop, lower, middle, and upper deck. See DECK *sb.*[1] But sometimes *orlop* is found in the general sense of 'deck', and applied in the pl. to both (or all) the decks present at the time.

1467 *Sc. Acts Jas. III* (1814) 87 And at the maisteris fure na guidis vpon his ouerlop [**1597** § 14 ouer-loft] the quhilk & he do, tha gudis sall pay na fraucht, nor na gudis vnder the ourlop [ouer-loft] to scot nor lot with tha gudis in cas thai be castin. **1496** *Naval Acc. Hen. VII* (1896) 176 Tymbre.. under the Ovyloppes & Alawe in the seid Ship. *Ibid.*, Forcastell, the overloppe, the somercastell, the dekke ovyr the somercastell, & the pope. **1578** T. N. tr. *Conq. W. India* 23 Other three ships..All the residue were small without overloppe, and vergantines. **1578** BOURNE *Inventions* 3 You may make a plaine Decke or Orloppe, that hath but plaine hatches. **1598** W. PHILLIPS *Linschoten* (Hakluyt Soc.) II. 179 One side of the upper part of the ship, between both the upper Oarlops, where the great boat lay, burst out. **1611** COTGR., *Tillac*, the Orelop or Arloup; or, more generally, the hatches of a ship. **1627** CAPT. SMITH *Seaman's Gram.* ii. 3 When they are planked vp to the Orlop they make the ships Howle. *Ibid.* 5 The first Orlop..is the first floore to support the plankes doth couer the Howle. *Ibid.* 6 The third Decke or Orlop, or the third Decke which is neuer called by the name of Orlop, and yet they are all but Decks. **1658** PHILLIPS, *Orlop*, a Term in Navigation, signifying the second and lower deck of a ship. **1741** WATSON in *Phil. Trans.* XLII. 67 Bringing Air from the Bread-room, Horlop and Well of the Ship at the same time. **1859** *Merc. Marine Mag.* (1860) VII. 16 The stream anchor..was stowed in the after orlop. **1878** BESANT & RICE *Celia's Arb.* xxii. (1887) 164 To roam about in the dim silences of the lower deck, the twilight of the orlop;..and to gaze down the impenetrable Erebus of the hold.

γ. *c* **1470** HENRY *Wallace* x. 882 Wallace..A man he straik our burd in to the se; On the our loft he slew son othir thre. **1513** DOUGLAS *Æneis* v. xi. 122 The flamb wpkendling blesis braid at large Throw hechis, ouerloft, air, and payntit targe. *c* **1614** SIR W. MURE *Dido & Æneas* III. 278 O that I had their shipps once set on fire And ov'rlofts all with flaming firebrands fill'd.

b. *attrib.*

1623 WHITBOURNE *Newfoundland* 76 Two thousand of good Orlop nailes. **1758** J. BLAKE *Plan Mar. Syst.* 3 If more room be wanted the orlop deck may be enlarged. **1869** SIR E. REED *Shipbuild.* xix. 423 Vessels over 24 feet in depth are required by Lloyd's to have orlop beams on every sixth frame. **1892** *Daily News* 24 Feb. 6/8 It is believed that by battening down the orlop deck in the after part of the ship they will succeed in floating her.

†**orlop**[2]. *Obs.* [? for *overlap.*] The turned-up edge of a sheet of lead, bent over the edge of the adjoining sheet in making a joint.

1703 T. N. *City & C. Purch.* 192 The Orlop is about $3\frac{1}{2}$ Inches of the edge, (next to the Stander) of the other Sheet, rais'd up in the same manner as the Stander.

orly, orely, obs. forms of EARLY.

†**'ormasi.** *Sc. Obs.* See also ARMOSIE. A fabric, prob. the same as ARMOZEEN, and orig. identical with ORMUZINE.

1566–7 *Prec. Treas.* in Chalmers *Mary* (1818) I. 207 Of Ormaise taffatis to lyne the bodeis and sclevis of the goune, and velicotte. **1566** in Hay Fleming *Mary Q. of Scots* (1897) 505 Item of ormasi taffatis vj elle. **1567** *Ibid.* 511 Of blak ormasi i elle.

†**orme.** *Obs. rare.* (See quot.)

1688 R. HOLME *Armoury* II. 85/1 The Orme, is the same to husk. *Ibid.* 117/1 Orme or husk [is] the thing Flowers grow out off.

ormer ('ɔːmə(r), ‖ɔrmɛr), *sb.* [Jersey and Guernsey Fr., = F. *ormier*, contracted from *oreille-de-mer*, or ad. L. *auris maris* sea-ear, from its resemblance to the ear (Littré).] The Sea-ear; a species of univalve mollusc, *Haliotis tuberculata*, specially abundant in Guernsey, where it is used as food. Hence extended to all species of *Haliotis*.

1672 SIR C. LYTTELTON in *Hatton Corr.* (Camden) 81 Ye ormers were thought most excellent meate. **1694** FALLE *Jersey* ii. 74 We have also the Ormer, which is a Fish scarce known out of these Islands. *Ormer*..is a Contraction of *Oreille de Mer*... It has no Under-shell like the Oyster, but the Fish clingeth to the Rock with the Back, and the Shell covers the Belly. **1837** M. DONOVAN *Dom. Econ.* II. 169 The ormer, a shell-fish, has been compared to veal-cutlet. **1856** WOODWARD *Mollusca* III. 425 Ormers..may be removed from the rocks to which they adhere by throwing a little warm water over them. **1873** M. COLLINS *Squire Silchester* II. xvi. 201 The ormer is the most delicious of univalves.

b. *attrib.*

1755 H. WALPOLE *Lett., to Bentley* 31 Oct. (1846) III. 167, I shall thank you for the Ormer shells and roots.

'ormer, *v. Channel Islands.* [f. the sb.] To collect ormers. Chiefly as **'ormering** *vbl. sb.*; also *attrib.*

1903 *Eng. Dial. Dict.* IV. 359/2 He's gone ormering. **1953** W. D. HOOKE *Channel Islands* iv. 110 Ormering is another important amusement. A very low tide is always referred to in the Islands as 'an Ormering tide'. **1953** S. P. B. MAIS *Channel Islands* 67 It was a full moon and a spring tide, 'ormering' time. **1953** M. PEAKE *Mr. Pye* x. 71 'Where are you going, Tintagieu?' 'Ormering.'.. 'I d-didn't know there was an ormer tide.' **1965** 'J. CHRISTOPHER' *Wrinkle in Skin* vi. 77 Matthew had walked out occasionally, on an ormering tide. **1968** R. M. LOCKLEY *Channel Islands* 74 Even hard-hearted employers have forgiven employees absent from work over a low tide when the excuse has been 'ormering'. **1976** W. RUTHERFORD *Jersey* iii. 40 The land and the sea were exploited to the utmost for the islanders' subsistence, and from them came the traditional customs: the ormering parties, held when the *oreille-de-mer* were gathered.

†**'ormete,** *a. Obs.* [OE. *or-mǽte*, f. OR-, without, beyond + *mǽte* moderate, mean, f. *metan* to measure.] Measureless, immense, excessive.

c **1000** ÆLFRIC *Hom.* II. 164 þær læȝ ða sum ormæta stan. *a* **1100** *O.E. Chron.* an. 1001 (Laud MS.) þa ȝesomnode man þær ormæte fyrde of Defenisces folces. *c* **1200** ORMIN 238 þuss hafeþþ Drihhtin don wiþþ me þurrh hiss orrmete millce. *Ibid.* 13687 And shulenn unnderrfon..Orrmete pine inn helle.

orming ('ɔːmɪŋ), *a. dial.* [The same word as HAWM *v.*] Ungainly and clumsy in movement, tall and awkward; (quot. 1913) (standing about) gawping and staring.

E.D.D. Hawm v.[1] cites from 'Sc., Yks., Chs., Der., Not., and Lin.'.

1903 *Eng. Dial. Dict.* IV. 359/2 *Orming*, ppl. adj... Notts. Tall and awkward. **1913** D. H. LAWRENCE *Love Poems* 52 Niver a baby had eyes As sulky an' ormin' as thine. **1922** —— *England, my England* 261 Mrs. Goodall..fairly hated the sound of correct English. She *thee'd* and *tha'd* her prospective daughter-in-law, and said: 'I'm none as ormin' as I look, seest ta.' Fanny did not think her prospective mother-in-law looked at all orming.

†**'ormod,** *a. Obs.* [OE. *or-mód* (= OHG. *urmuot*), f. OR-, without + *mód*, mind, courage, MOOD.] Without spirit; despondent, despairing.

c **888** K. ÆLFRED *Boeth.* viii, Se ðe hine forþencð se beð ormod. *c* **1000** *Joshua* ii. 9 (Heptat.) Ðis folc is ȝeirȝed and ormod onȝean eow. *c* **1175** *Lamb. Hom.* 105 þet we on unilimpan to ormode ne beon.

ormolu ('ɔːməluː). [a. F. *or moulu*, lit. 'ground gold'.] Originally, Gold or gold-leaf ground and prepared for gilding brass, bronze, or other metal; hence, gilded bronze used in the decoration of furniture, etc. Now, An alloy of copper, zinc, and tin, having the colour of gold.

1765 H. WALPOLE *Lett., to H. S. Conway* 6 Oct. (1846) V. 82 A large funnel of bronze with *or moulu*, like a column. **1778** *Eng. Gazetteer* (ed. 2) s.v. *Birmingham*, Their ornamental pieces in Or-Moulu are highly esteemed all over Europe. **1819** *Act 59 Geo. III*, c. 52. §36 Any Articles.. ornamented with or manufactured wholly or partly of Or Moulu. **1831** CARLYLE *Sart. Res.* I. iv, A whole immensity of Brussels carpets, and pier-glasses, and or-moulu. **1852** MOTLEY *Corr.* (1889) I. v. 138 Cabinets and caskets of every age, of mother-of-pearl, agate, amber, ivory, buhl and ormolu. **1875** *Ure's Dict. Arts* III. 461 *Or-molu*, a brass in which there is less zinc and more copper than in the ordinary brass; the object being to obtain a nearer imitation of gold than ordinary brass affords.

b. *attrib.* and *Comb.*, as *ormolu clock*; **ormolu-varnish**, a copper, bronze, or imitation-gold varnish, also called 'Mosaic gold'.

1825 C. M. WESTMACOTT *English Spy* I. 334 Enriched with ormolu chasings. **1842** BARHAM *Ingol. Leg.*, *Bloudie Jacke* xiv, To gaze at your vases, Your pictures and or-molu clocks.

†**ormu'zine.** *Obs.* A fabric brought from Ormuz, near the entrance of the Persian Gulf, a famous mart of the Portuguese in the 16th c. Probably the same originally as ARMOZEEN; see also ORMASI.

1625 PURCHAS *Pilgrims* II. 1432 Very good Ormuzenes, and Persian Carpets of a wonderfull finenesse.

†**orn, ourn**(**e,** *v. Obs.* [ME. *ourne* corresponds in form to an OF. **ourner*:—L. *ornāre* to fit out, equip, adorn; but as the simple vb. is not cited in OF., which had the compound *aourner* (see ADORN), the ME. word was app. either an aphetic form of *aourne*, or directly from L. with the vowel conformed to *ournement*, ORNAMENT, and the earlier *aourne*, *anourne*. It is noticeable that the orig. Wycliffite version of 1382, in the O.T. portion, often has the fuller *anourne*, *enourne*, which Purvey changes to *ourne*. The 15–16th c. *orn* is conformed to F. *orner* or L. *ornare*.]

trans. To adorn, ornament.

1382 WYCLIF *Tit.* ii. 10 That thei ourne [1388 onoure] in alle thingis the doctryn of oure sauyour God. —— *1 Pet.* iii. 5 Holy wymmen..not in ournement of clothinge ourneden ..hem silf. **1388** —— *Gen.* xxiv. 47 Y hangide eere ryngis to ourne his face [1382 to honoure (*v.r.* anoure) the face of hir]. —— *Prov.* xv. 2 The tunge of wise men ourneth [1382 enhourneth] kunnyng. *c* **1440** *Gesta Rom.* I. lxvi. 305 (Harl.

MS.) Sepulcris..ben maade faire withoute, And rially ornyd with precious clothing of silke and of palle. *c* **1449** PECOCK *Repr.* 193 Eny unquyk stok or stoon graued and ourned with gold and othere gay peinting. **1545** JOYE *Exp. Dan.* ii. Argt. (R.), God stered vp prophetes and orned his chirche with great glory. **1588** A. KING tr. *Canisius' Catech.* Kivb, Was orned in Christ Iesus..with ane croune of iustice.

Hence †'**orned, ourned** *ppl. a.*, adorned; †'**orning, ourning** *vbl. sb.* and *ppl. a.*, adorning.

1382 WYCLIF *1 Pet.* iii. 3 Not with..curious ournyng of heer..or ournyng of clothinge. **1545** JOYE *Exp. Dan.* iii. D vij b, The preciouse decent orned ymage.

orn, obs. pa. t. of OE. *yrnan, rinnan*, to RUN.

orna'bility. *rare.* [f. *ornable (f. L. *ornāre* to fit out, equip, adorn: see -BLE) + -ITY.] Capability of being adorned or used ornamentally.

1811-31 BENTHAM *Fragm. Univ. Gram.* Introd., Properties..desirable..in every language..Ornability, i.e. facility of being made subservient to the purpose of ornament. —— *Ess. Lang.* iv. §6 Of Ornability or Decorability.

†'**ornacy.** *Obs.* [f. ORNATE *a.*: see -ACY[3].] The quality of being ornate, ornateness.

1526 SKELTON *Magnyf.* 1549, I am supprysed Of your language..Pullyshyd and fresshe is your ornacy. **1540** MORYSINE *Vives' Introd. Wysd.* F v b, This worlde, is..an house, or a temple of God, which of nought be brought forth into this shappe and ornacy, that it now is in. **1606** BIRNIE *Kirk-Buriall* (1833) 28 Under these three conditions (to wit, of amplitude, ornacy, and vnprostitude chastity to any other use) it becomes a Kirk.

ornament ('ɔːnəmənt), *sb.* Forms: 3-4 **urnement**, (4 **vrnment**), 4-5 **ournement**, 4-6 **ornement**; 5 **ournament**, 5- **ornament**. [a. OF. *ournement, ornement*, ad. L. *ornāment-um* equipment, trapping, ornament, f. *ornāre*: see ORN *v.*]

†**1. a.** Any adjunct or accessory (primarily for use, but not excluding decoration or embellishment); equipment, furniture, attire, trappings. *Obs.*

a **1225** *Ancr. R.* 302 And makede hire ueir..mid alle þe ueire urnemenz þet bitocneð blisse. **1340** *Ayenb.* 140 Hy hise agrayþeþ and azet mid alle hire ournemens. *c* **1386** CHAUCER *Clerk's T.* 202 And eek of othere aornementes [*v.rr.* aournementes, ornamentes] alle That vn-to swich a weddyng sholde falle. **1398** TREVISA *Barth. De P.R.* v. xxviii. (1495) 137 The hande is a grete helpe and ornament of the body. **1565-73** COOPER *Thesaurus, Aphistre*,..the tackling or ornaments of a ship. **1591** SHAKS. *1 Hen. VI*, v. i. 54 The summe of money which I promised..For cloathing me in these graue Ornaments. *c* **1611** CHAPMAN *Iliad* XI. 450 A surgeon is to be preferr'd, with physic ornaments, Before a multitude. **16..** R. JOHNSON *Seven Champions* II. iv. (1670) Ej, All attired in black and mournful Ornaments. **1682** R. BURTON *Admir. Curios.* (1684) 3 Most of her [England's] other Plenties and Ornaments are expressed in this old verse following. *Anglia, Mons, Pons, Fons, Ecclesia, Fœmina, Lana.* **1747** GOULD *Eng. Ants* 50 The Head with its Ornaments, and the Legs regularly placed, first make their Appearance.

b. *Eccl.* The accessories or furnishings of the Church and its worship: see quot. 1857.

13.. *E.E. Allit. P.* B. 1284 Wyth alle þe vrnmentes of þat hous [the Jewish Temple]. *Ibid.* 1799 þe fylþe of þe freke..defowled hade þe ornementes of goddez hous þat holy were maked. *c* **1400** MAUNDEV. (Roxb.) xi. 43 With many oþer ournementz and clething of Aaron and of þe tabernacle. **1470-85** MALORY *Arthur* XVII. xv, The other held a crosse and the ornementys of an aulter. **1482** *Monk of Evesham* (Arb.) 49 Thoo thyngys that were necessarye to the ornamentys of alle the chyrche, as yn lyghtys or any othyr thyngys. **1486** *Act 3 Hen. VII*, c. 9 Chalice, Books, Vestments, and other Ornaments of holy Church. **1559** *Act 1 Eliz.* c. 2 §25 (*Act Uniformitie Com. Praier*), That suche ornaments of the Churche, and of the ministers therof, shalbe reteined and be in vse as was in this Churche of England, by auchthority of Parliament, in the second yere of the raygne of Kyng Edward the vi. vntil other order shalbe therin taken. **1565** in *Eng. Ch. Furniture* (Peacock 1866) 60 Thinventarie of all the popishe ornamentes that remaynid in the Church of Calsterworth at anie tyme sens the deathe of the late Quene Marie. **1857** *Decis. Privy Council* in Blunt *Annot. Prayer-bk.* p. lxx, The term 'ornaments' in Ecclesiastical law is not confined, as by modern usage, to articles of decoration or embellishment, but it is used in the larger sense of the word 'ornamentum'... In modern times, Organs and Bells are held to fall under this denomination.

c. ***ornaments rubric***, the rubric which stands immediately before the Order for Morning and Evening Prayer in the Book of Common Prayer; so called as referring to the 'ornaments' to be used in the Church. (Cf. 1559 in b.)

1872 *Law Rep.* Adm. & Eccl. Crts. III. 69 The ornament rubric in the prayer book set forth by authority of the statute. **1888** GLADSTONE in *19th Cent.* Nov. 767 They [Q. Eliz. and Govt.] suffered the ornaments rubric to lie partially dormant, but they kept it in force.

2. a. Something employed to adorn, beautify, or embellish, or that naturally does this; a decoration, embellishment.

1388 WYCLIF *Judith* x. 3 And sche took ournementis [1382 onournemens] of the armes, and lilies..and ournede hir silf with alle hir ournementis. *c* **1460** FORTESCUE *Abs. & Lim. Mon.* vii. (1885) 125 Rich stones..and oþer juels and ornamentes conuenyent to his estate roiall. **1495** *Trevisa's Barth. De P.R.* v. xv. (W. de W.) hj b/2 The berde is the hyghnes and ournament of mannes face. **1591** SHAKS. *1 Hen. VI*, IV. i. 29 Or whether that such Cowards ought to weare This Ornament of Knighthood [the garter], yea or no? **1665** BOYLE *Occas. Refl.* IV. iv, The Blossoms are in themselves great Ornaments to a Tree. **1751** JOHNSON *Rambler* No. 170 ⁋3 My mother sold some of her ornaments to dress me in such a manner as might secure me from contempt. **1833** L. RITCHIE *Wand. by Loire* 178 Formerly the châteaux were the ornaments of France. **1851** D. WILSON *Preh. Ann.* (1863) II. III. v. 140 Torcs, head-rings, armlets, and other personal ornaments. **1875** JOWETT *Plato* (ed. 2) III. 130 Mere narration, when deprived of the ornaments of metre.

b. *fig.* A quality or circumstance that confers beauty, grace, or honour.

1560 DAUS tr. *Sleidane's Comm.* 4 b, Amonge other ornamentes of the house of Saxony, this was ever propre unto it, greatly to favour Religion. **1611** BIBLE *1 Pet.* iii. 4 The ornament of a meek and quiet spirit.

c. A person who adorns or adds lustre to his sphere, time, etc.

1573 G. HARVEY *Letter-bk.* (Camden) 53 Thos singular men, the late ornaments of Cambridg and the glori of Pembrook Hal. **1595** SPENSER *Col. Clout* 500 She is the ornament of womankind. **1681** PRIDEAUX *Lett.* (Camden) 110 An ornament to the University. **1774** WARTON *Hist. Eng. Poetry* Diss. ii. (1840) I. p. cxx, A most distinguished ornament of this age was John of Salisbury. **1896** *Law Times* C. 488/2 Like so many other ornaments of the Scotch Bench and Bar, John Inglis was a son of the manse.

d. *Mus.* A grace note; a decorative figure used to embellish a melodic line.

1664 J. PLAYFORD *Introd. Skill of Musick* (ed. 4) I. 58 There is made now adayes an indifferent and confused use of those Excellent Graces and Ornaments to the good manner of Singing, which we call Trills, Grapps, [etc.]. *c* **1779** W. WARING tr. *Rousseau's Dict. Mus.* 185 *Graces in Singing*. By this term are called, in the French music, certain turns and shakes in the throat, and other ornaments joined to the notes, which are in such or such a position, according to the rules prescribed by a taste in singing. **1801** BUSBY *Dict. Mus.* p. xxx, Of the graces in music... To these ornaments may be added the *Slur*,..the *Staccato*. **1885** G. B. SHAW *How to become Mus. Critic* (1960) 67 Her voice is not yet quite solid, and..she appended a dreadful 'ornament' to Hark, those Chimes. **1962** *Listener* 17 May 885/2 The important indications of Rameau's ornaments were either unnecessarily simplified or omitted, regrettably since ornaments are not optional embellishments in music of this period; they form an integral part of the harmony, frequently devised to prepare or resolve dissonance. **1969** *Ibid.* 26 June 904/3 The ornaments are not frequent, and only come on emotional words.

3. a. The action of adorning or fact of being adorned; adornment, embellishment, decoration (*lit.* or *fig.*); that in which this is embodied or consists.

1596 SPENSER *F.Q.* IV. ii. 39 Courage..Approved oft in perils manifold, Which he achiev'd to his great ornament. **1611** TOURNEUR *Ath. Trag.* I. ii. Wks. 1878 I. 15 Accomplements are more for ornament Then use. **1667** MILTON *P.L.* v. 280 The pair that clad Each shoulder broad, came mantling o're his brest With regal Ornament. **1739** HUME *Hum. Nat.* (1874) I. Introd. 307 The improvement or ornament of the human mind. **1817** J. SCOTT *Paris Revis.* (ed. 4) 245 There was no beauty..either of artful ornament, or natural wildness. **1883** L. F. DAY *Every-Day Art* i, Ornament is the Art of every Day.

b. Mere adornment; outward show or display.

1596 SHAKS. *Merch. V.* III. ii. 74 So may the outward showes be least themselues: The world is still deceiu'd with ornament. *Ibid.* 97 Thus ornament is but..The seeming truth which cunning times put on To intrap the wisest.

ornament (ˌɔːnə'mɛnt, 'ɔːnəˌmɛnt), *v.* [f. ORNAMENT *sb.* Cf. mod.F. (19th c.) *ornementer.*] *trans.* To furnish with ornament, to make ornamental; to adorn, deck, embellish, beautify.

1720 POPE *Iliad* XVIII. Observ. 1457 The Divisions, Projections, or Angles of a Roof are left to be ornamented at the Discretion of the Painter. **1740** DYCHE & PARDON, *Ornament*, to set off, beautify, enrich, make handsome. **1758** BLACKSTONE *Study of Law* in *Comm.* Introd. I. 26 It will ornament and assist them all. **1797** MRS. RADCLIFFE *Italian* i, Some copies from the antique, which ornamented a cabinet of the Vivaldi palace. **1816** SCOTT *Old Mort.* xxix, A man, formed to ornament, to enlighten, and to defend his country. **1840** DICKENS *Barn. Rudge* iii, He had ornamented his hat with a cluster of peacock's feathers. **1875** JOWETT *Plato* (ed. 2) V. 332 The fountains..shall be ornamented with plantations and buildings for beauty.

Hence **ornamented** *ppl. a.*

1736 THOMSON *Liberty* v. 347 That very Portion, which..might make the smiling Public rear Her ornamented Head. **1769** *Junius Lett.* xxxi. 141 The ornamented style he has adopted. **1838** THIRLWALL *Greece* xxxvi. IV. 405 The prizes ..consisted of ornamented armour and weapons.

ornamenta'bility. [f. **ornamentable* (f. ORNAMENT *v.*) + -ITY.] Capability of being adorned: = ORNABILITY.

1811-31 BENTHAM *Ess. Lang.* iv. §1 Properties desirable in a language... Decorability, or ornamentability, as opposed to baldness.

ornamental (ɔːnə'mɛntəl), *a.* (*sb.*) [f. L. *ornāment-um* ORNAMENT + -AL[1].]

A. *adj.* **a.** Of the nature of an ornament, serving as an ornament or decoration; adding beauty and attractiveness; decorative.

1646 SIR T. BROWNE *Pseud. Ep.* To Rdr. a vj, Digressions, Corollaries, or ornamentall conceptions. **1664** H. MORE *Myst. Iniq.* 257 The ornamental Pompousness in Idolatry. **1701** ROWE *Amb. Step-moth.* Ded., Men..Useful and Ornamental to the Age they live in. **1703** T. N. *City & C. Purchaser* 54 By the word Ornamental work, is to be understood in Bricklayers Work; all kind of Brick-work, that is hewed with an Ax, or rubbed on a Rubbing-stone, or of Stone wrought with Chissels, or rubbed with Stones, or Cards. **1796** C. MARSHALL *Garden.* xix. (1813) 319 These ornamental trees are proper to plant at the back of shrubberies. **1855** *London as it is to-day* 112 A large piece of ornamental water. **1876** J. SAUNDERS *Lion in Path* vi, The male dress of the time, is more or less ornamental. *Mod.* It may be useful, it certainly is not ornamental.

b. ***ornamental-leaved*** adj.

1870 B. S. WILLIAMS (*title*) Choice stove and green-house ornamental-leaved plants. **1952** A. G. L. HELLYER *Sanders' Encycl. Gardening* (ed. 22) 122 Ornamental-leaved kinds [of coleus] require to have points of their shoots pinched off in early stage of their growth to ensure dwarf or well-shaped plants.

B. *sb.* **1.** *pl.* Things that are ornamental; adornments, embellishments, as opposed to *essentials*.

1650 H. BROOKE *Conserv. Health* 240 The other two are Ornamentals that adde to its perfection but not to its essence. **1659** GAUDEN *Tears Church* I. xi. 86 Seeking to deface the Pinnacles and Ornamentalls of Religion, but not capable to shake the foundations of it. **1761** *Ann. Reg.* 242 On the table between each service was placed near 100 cold ornamentals. **1863** S. L. J. *Life in South* II. ii. 63 French, music and the ornamentals.

2. A tree or shrub grown for the sake of its attractive appearance.

1903 *Pop. Sci. Monthly* Jan. 277 It could be done more easily with strawberries, or with some of the common ornamentals that do not reproduce true to seed. **1972** *House & Garden* Feb. 24/2 When planting ornamentals, plant fruit trees and bushes too.

Hence **ornamen'tality**, condition of being ornamental; *concr.* that which is ornamental; **orna'mentalize** *v.*, to make ornamental; **orna'mentalness** (Bailey, vol. II. 1727).

1842 MRS. CARLYLE *Lett.* I. 152 Her picture..looks very fine indeed in its gilt ornamentality. **1865** CARLYLE *Fredk. Gt.* III. xix. (1872) I. 263 This doubled wish..first set the poor man thinking of expensive ornamentalities. **1892** L. F. DAY *Nature in Ornament* v. 76 Such undergrowth must be ornamentalised accordingly.

orna'mentalism. [f. prec. + -ISM.] The principle or practice of being ornamental.

1862 W. M. ROSSETTI in *Fraser's Mag.* Aug. 195 The Belgian sculpture verges towards ornamentalism. **1866** *Illustr. Lond. News* 1 Dec. 526/3 The intentional ornamentalism of execution.

orna'mentalist. [f. as prec. + -IST.] One who occupies himself with ornamental art.

1837 *Blackw. Mag.* XLI. 184 The ambitious ornamentalist who will be half artist, will issue but tasteless, displeasing, incongruous productions. **1868** C. C. PERKINS *Italian Sculptors* vi. 234 After his [*sc.* Piero Giacomo Illario's] day Mantuan sculptors are few, and are generally ornamentalists in marble or stucco. **1888** *Pall Mall G.* 9 June 5/2 Mr. Walter Crane, who followed, spoke on behalf of the designer and ornamentalist. **1925** *Daily Tel.* 13 May 20/6 Pastrycooks.—First hand required. Must be first-class decorator and ornamentalist.

orna'mentally, *adv.* [f. as prec. + -LY[2].] In an ornamental manner; with a view to ornamentation.

1711 SHAFTESB. *Charact., Misc.* v. ii. 280 Other politer Tracts ornamentally writ, for publick use. **1787** M. CUTLER in *Life, Jrnls. & Corr.* (1888) I. 273 They are neither placed ornamentally nor botanically, but..jumbled together in heaps. **1879** *Cassell's Techn. Educ.* v. 277/2 However ornamentally or beautifully formed it may be.

†**orna'mentary**, *a. Obs. rare.* [f. L. *ornāment-um* ORNAMENT + -ARY: cf. *documentary*, etc.] = ORNAMENTAL.

1715 M. DAVIES *Athen. Brit.* I. 332 Which might serve as a sort of Index supplementary, or as an Ornamentary Appendix to those Annals.

ornamentation (ɔːnəmən'teɪʃən). [f. ORNAMENT *v.* + -ATION: cf. mod.F. *ornementation.*]

1. The action or process of ornamenting; the state of being adorned; the subordinate branch of art which deals especially with ornament.

1860 MILL *Repr. Govt.* (1861) 49 To the amusement and ornamentation of private life. **1861** BERESF. HOPE *Eng. Cathedr. 19th C.* vii. 249 The philosophy of architectural ornamentation is continually being more deeply sifted. **1866** *Cornh. Mag.* May 544 In the comparatively petty art of ornamentation, in rings, brooches, croziers, relic-cases, and so on, he has done just enough to show his delicacy of taste, his happy temperament.

2. That in which the process of ornamenting is embodied; the ornaments which adorn a thing collectively; ornament in general.

1851 WILSON *Preh. Ann.* (1863) II. III. v. 135 A great similarity is traceable in the ornamentation of the whole northern races of Europe. **1879** LUBBOCK *Sci. Lect.* v. 160 The ornamentation on the arms, implements, and pottery..consists of geometrical patterns.

3. *Mus.* The use of grace notes to provide embellishment of a melodic line.

1879 [see ARABESQUE *sb.* 5]. **1938** *Oxf. Compan. Mus.* 675/1 Ornamentation in the old Italian vocal style had become so much second nature with them that nothing he could say would induce them to keep to the copies before them. **1947** A. EINSTEIN *Mus. Romantic Era* xvii. 310 The ornamentation of the Russo-Oriental folk song. **1962** *Listener* 2 Aug. 189/3 Her ornamentation is always designed to stress dissonances at crucial points. **1963** *Ibid.* 3 Jan. 45/3 Should we not consider carefully whether, say, spread piano chords are not as obligatory in playing Ravel as correct ornamentation in playing Bach?

orna'menter. [f. ORNAMENT *v.* + -ER[1].] One who (or that which) ornaments; an artist who devotes himself to decoration.

1825 in Hone *Every-day Bk.* I. 1492 This..profuse ornamentor of whatever is permitted to afford it support [the ivy]. **1852** WRIGHT *Celt, Rom. & Sax.* (1861) 218 The ornamenter would proceed by dipping the thumb, or a round mounted instrument, into the slip. **1884** *Birmingham Daily Post* 24 Jan. 3/3 Bedstead Ornamenters.—Good Workmen used to Flowers.

orna'mentist. [f. ORNAMENT *sb.* + -IST.] A professional decorator; a designer of ornaments.

1845 W. B. SCOTT (*title*) The Ornamentist, or Artisan's Manual in the Various Branches of Ornamental Art. **1864** *Daily Tel.* 29 June, Manufacturers want the services of good ornamentists. **1888** F. G. JACKSON *Decor. Design* iv. 88 Shapes..worth the attention of the ornamentist.

ornate (ɔː'neɪt, 'ɔːnət), *ppl. a.* Also 5–6 **ornat.** [ad. L. *ornāt-us*, pa. pple. of *ornā-re*: see ORN.]

†**1.** as *pa. pple.* Adorned, ornamented (*with*).

1432–50 tr. *Higden* (Rolls) III. 317 A fowle man did schewe..to Diogenes his place ornate with riche apparaile. **1530** ELYOT *Gov.* I. iii, A sufficient nombre, ornate with vertue and wisedome. **1771** *Antiq. Sarisb.* 187 An image of God the Father..ornate with red stones.

2. as *adj.* Ornamented; elaborately adorned; highly decorated or embellished. Also *fig.*

1503 HAWES *Examp. Virt.* VII. xxix, Lyke a vessell chosen and made ornat. **1538** STARKEY *England* II. i. 178 Our cuntrey..wyl not suffur to be so ornat and so beutyful in euery degre as other cuntreys be. **1671** MILTON *Samson* 712 Femal of sex it seems, That so bedeckt, ornate, and gay, Comes this way sailing Like a stately Ship Of Tarsus. **1829** COLERIDGE *Sibyl. Leaves* II. 329 Thou brightest star of star-bright Italy! Rich, ornate, populous, all treasures thine. **1882** *Contemp. Rev.* XLII. 681 If we go to churches where the services are ornate, we see a far larger proportion of women than we wish to see.

b. Of literary or oratorical style: Embellished with choice language or flowers of rhetoric.

a **1420** HOCCLEVE *De Reg. Princ.* 1973 Bookes of his ornat endyting, That is to al þis land enlumynyng. **1538** *Songs Costume* (Percy Soc.) 71 Because the mater bene so vyle, It may nocht have an ornate style. **1564** BECON *Wks.* Gen. Pref., The eloquent orators with their sugared and ornate eloquence. **1816** *Gentl. Mag.* LXXXVI. I. 51 The ornate style of poetry. **1858** GLADSTONE *Homer* III. 531 In diction Virgil is ornate and Homer simple.

†**or'nate,** *v. Obs.* [f. L. *ornāt-*, ppl. stem of *ornāre*: see prec. and -ATE[3].] *trans.* To ornament, adorn, embellish.

1495 *Trevisa's Barth. De P.R.* XVII. cxvi. (W. de W.) S j b/1 Palma is a tree of vyctory, for therwyth the vyctours honde is ornatyd. **1508** FISHER 7 *Penit. Ps.* cii. Wks. (1876) 181 Yf thou wolde edyfy and ornate thy chyrche on this maner. **1611** SPEED *Hist. Gt. Brit.* IX. xxi. §134. 1037 All these foresaid figures, stories, and ornaments shall be made to garnish and ornate the two Pillars of the Church. **1651** *Fuller's Abel Rediv., Piscator* (1867) II. 313 I' th' German tongue the Bible he translated, And it with learn'd Analysis ornated.

Hence †**or'nated** *ppl. a.*, †**or'nating** *vbl. sb.*

1491 CAXTON *Vitas Patr.* (W. de W. 1495) II. 176 b/2 Som-tyme ornatynge of wordes maketh the proposycion to be withdrawen fro the trouthe. **1630** J. TAYLOR (Water P.) *Wks.* (N.), Had I that admir'd ornated stile Of Petrark.

ornately (see the adj.), *adv.* [f. ORNATE *a.* + -LY[2].] In an ornate manner; with ornate language; ornamentally, elegantly; with decoration.

c **1460** G. ASHBY *Dicta Philos.* 434 A king sholde enfourme his sone..to speke ornatly with equite. *a* **1548** HALL *Chron., Hen. VIII*, 94 b, A solempne oracion, to whom the Emperors Secretary answered ornatly. **1611** SPEED *Hist. Gt. Brit.* IX. xviii. (1623) 922 He rehearsed them the same matter againe..so well and ornately, so euidently and plaine. **1854** H. MILLER *Sch. & Schm.* (1858) 342 Some of the ornately sculptured foliage.

or'nateness. [f. as prec. + -NESS.] The quality of being ornate.

1668 WILKINS *Real Char.* II. i. 36 Ornateness, adorn, set out, Deck, beautifie, embellish, trimm. *a* **1849** POE *R. Dawes* Wks. 1864 III. 153 A well-disciplined ornateness of language.

ornation (ɔː'neɪʃən). *rare.* [ad. L. *ornātiōn-em*, n. of action from *orn-āre* to adorn.] The action of adorning; the condition of being adorned; adornment, ornament, †equipment; ornamentation.

1483 CAXTON *Gold. Leg.* 37/1 Thus in sixe dayes was heven and erthe made and alle the ornation of them. **1675** tr. *Machiavelli's Prince* Ded. (1883) 10 Nor have I beautified..it with rhetorical ornations. **1879** [LINGHAM] *Sci. Taste* i. 6 The extravagant floridity of Genoese ornation.

†**ornative,** *a. Obs. rare.* [f. ppl. stem of L. *ornāre* to adorn: see -ATIVE.] Tending or serving to adorn; decorative.

1660 STANLEY *Hist. Philos.* III. I. 54 An ornative and exemplary reason.

‖**ornatrix** (ɔː'neɪtrɪks). [L. *ornātrīx* female adorner.] A woman who adorns, a tire-woman.

1834 LYTTON *Pompeii* III. vii, The ornatrix (i.e. hairdresser) slowly piled, one above the other, a mass of small curls.

ornature ('ɔːnətjʊə(r)). *rare.* [a. F. *ornature* (1530 in Godef.) = It. *ornatura*, ad. late L. *ornātūra* ornament, ornamentation, f. ppl. stem of L. *ornāre*, see -URE.] Ornamentation, adornment, decoration: embellishment; ornament.

1538 LELAND *Itin.* I. New Years Gift p. xxi, A thing that desired to be sumwhat large, and to have ornature. **1601** B. JONSON *Poetaster* III. i. 45 A mushroom, for all your other ornatures. **1658** PHILLIPS, *Ornature*, a setting forth, trimming, or adorning [ed. 1706 substitutes *Ornament*]. **1814** SOUTHEY *Roderick* XVIII. 113 Vestments..stiff With ornature of gold. **1886** BLACKIE in *19th Cent.* Apr. 531 The Gothic Castle with its..grotesque ornature of all kinds.

orndern, orndorn, dial. ff. UNDERN *Obs.*

†**orne,** *a.*[1] *Obs. rare.* [Origin and sense uncertain.] ? Careful, particular.

a **1225** *Ancr. R.* 370 Bute þe on..was ornure of mete & of drunche þen þe twei oðre. *c* **1315** SHOREHAM *Poems* (E.E.T.S.) 77/2214 Þe syxte onleke swete ihesus, Of ordre noþyng orne.

†**orne,** *a.*[2] *Obs. rare*[−1]. [app. a. OF. *orné*, with mutescent *e* as in *assign* (sb.[2]), etc.] Ornate.

c **1430** *Freemasonry* (ed. Halliw. 1840) 569 Rethoryk metryth with orne speche amonge.

‖**orné,** *a.*[3] Erron. **ornée.** F. = 'adorned', in *cottage orné*: see COTTAGE 4. Also, decorated, ornate.

1781 J. BYNG *Torrington Diaries* (1934) I. 48 The place ..[*sc.* a garden bower] is not sufficiently ornée. **1781**, etc. [see COTTAGE 4 a]. **1811** SHELLEY *St. Irvyne* xi. Pr. Wks. 1888 I. 207 A cottage ornée, which I possess at some little distance hence. **1864** TROLLOPE *Small House at Allington* I. i. 9 A solitude in the centre of a wide park is now the only site that can be recognized as eligible. No cottage must be seen, unless the cottage orné of the gardener. **1951** N. MITFORD *Blessing* I. ii. 22 If she could propose an 18th-century mausoleum..or cottage orné as the object for a walk, he would accompany her.

†**ornel.** *Obs. rare.* [a. F. *ornel*, pl. *ornaulx* (14th–15th c. in Godef.).] A kind of rather soft white building stone.

1442 in Willis & Clark *Cambridge* (1886) I. 386 Fraughtage of x tonne of Ornell fro london vn to ye College. **1443** *Ibid.* 388 Fraught of Cj quarter and a-half of Ornel.

ornement, obs. form of ORNAMENT.

†**orneo-,** repr. Gr. ὀρνεο-, comb. form of ὄρνεον = ὄρνις bird, in numerous compounds; hence the obs. †**orneo'scopic,** †**orne'oscopist**: see quot.

1727 BAILEY, vol. II, *Orneoscopicks*, Omens or Predictions given from the Flight, etc. of Birds. *Ibid.*, *Orneoscopists*, Augurs or Diviners by Birds. [So **1730–6** (folio).]

orneriness ('ɔːnərɪnɪs). Chiefly *U.S.* [f. ORNERY *a.* + -NESS.] Meanness, cussedness, contrariness.

1899 B. TARKINGTON *Gentleman from Indiana* iv. 45 They ..let loose their deviltries just for pure orneriness. **1927** W. R. JAMES *Cow Country* 229 The bronk's orneriness had come to the top, and that pony..begin to get sort of desperate and to looking for a way out. **1957** *Economist* 9 Nov. 469/2 Some of these groups are based on geography, like Indonesia's island dissidents, some on tribal differences, like Ghana's Ashantis, and some arise out of pure political orneriness. **1959** J. THURBER *Years with Ross* v. 75 Some orneriness of mood aggravated by..peptic ulcers. **1973** W. H. AUDEN in *Listener* 22 Feb. 238/2, I out of sheer orneriness said: 'I'll drive cars for the TUC.'

ornery ('ɔːnərɪ), *a. dial.* and *colloq.* Also **onery, onnery, o'n'ry, ornary.** [dial. var. of ORDINARY *a.* 5.] Commonplace, of poor quality, coarse, unpleasant; low, mean, cantankerous. (Now chiefly *U.S.*)

1816 U. BROWN *Jrnl.* in *Maryland Hist. Mag.* (1915) X. 369 The Land is old, completely worn out, the farming extremely ornary in general. **1849** J. J. HOOPER *Night at Ugly Man's* in *Spirit of Times* 24 Nov. 471/2 We had an old one-horned cow, mighty onnery (ordinary) lookin'. **1860** M. J. HOLMES *Maude* v. 63 She pronounced her 'not quite so *onery* a white woman as she at first took her to be.' *a* **1861** T. WINTHROP *John Brent* (1862) vii. 71 Good company betters the orneriest sort er weather. **1875** C. M. YONGE *My Young Alcides* II. ix. 261 If I refused, he should think..that I couldn't take that 'ornary object', as he had overheard himself described that day. **1887** E. CUSTER *Tenting on Plains* ix. 286 He's a good enough fellow, only he's an onery scamp of a Republican. **1905** *Dialect Notes* III. 63 The *onriest* critter. **1913** H. KEPHART *Our Southern Highlanders* viii. 169 'What sort of men are they?' 'Torn down scoundrels, every one.' 'Oh, come now!' 'Yes, they are; plumb onery.' **1924** GALSWORTHY *White Monkey* II. ix. 196 A low-down thought—mean and ornery. **1937** P. K. DEVINE *Folklore of Newfoundland* 35 *Ornery*, ugly or plain; no good. **1938** I. KUHN *Assigned to Adventure* xiv. 128 If he had not mentioned the clothes I should not have become ornery. But these clothes were a sore point with me. I was on the defensive at once. **1938** *Sun* (Baltimore) 28 Jan. 10/3 We are forced to spend all this money solely because mankind up to now is too ornery to organize international life on some more sensible basis. **1939** *Nat. Geogr. Mag.* Aug. 144/1 Wild sweet williams in the wood lot were much more alluring than the 'o'n'ry' weeds. **1941** J. FAULKNER *Men Working* 201 Mules is the orneriest critters. **1943** *Pocahontas Times* (Marlinton, W. Va.) 4 Mar. 2/1 That onery cuss of a jay bird. **1944** T. D. CLARK *Pills, Petticoats & Plows* xvi. 28 Not a thing, you ornery cuss do you have to do. **1958** M. SAKEL *Epilepsy* (1959) 40 He may, contrary to his usual behavior, become argumentative, pugnacious or 'ornery' in behavior. **1962** G. MACEWAN *Blazing Old Cattle Trail* xxi. 143 There the sheep were in one of their orneriest moods, determined not to get their nice Merino wool wet. **1962** W. STEGNER *Wolf Willow* III. i. 135 No Canadian steer would ever be angry or stubborn; he would be o'nery or ringy or on the prod. **1972** *Newsweek* 10 Jan. 18/3 The public as a whole might turn ornery if some semblance of prosperity were not found just around the corner.

†**orni-,** an irregular substitute for ORNEO- or ORNITHO- in †**orni'scopic,** †**or'niscopist,** †**or'niscopy**: see quots., and cf. ORNEO-.

1775 ASH, **Orniscopics*, the omens or predictions drawn from the observation of birds. **1755** JOHNSON, **Orniscopist*, one who examines the flight of birds, in order to foretel futurity. **1775** in ASH. **1828** in WEBSTER, and in some mod. Dicts. **1890** *Century Dict.*, **Orniscopy*, same as ornithoscopy.

†'**ornify,** *v. Obs.* Also 6 **ornefy.** [irreg. f. F. *orner* or L. *ornā-re* to adorn + -FY.] *trans.* To adorn, ornament.

1594 T. BEDINGFIELD tr. *Machiavelli's Florentine Hist.* (1595) 48 They likewise ornefied their city with new buildings. **1602** SEGAR *Hon. Mil. & Civ.* I. xxi. 27 Permitting them also to ornifie their weapons with siluer and gold. **1633** J. DONE *Hist. Septuag.* 58 As the Maister-workemen had shewed their Arte in imbellishing and ornifying every thing. **1671** BRYDALL *Law Nobil. & Gentry* 8 A Duke is Ornified with a Surcoat Mantle and Hood at his Creation.

‖**ornis** ('ɔːnɪs). [a. Ger. *Ornis*, a. Gr. ὄρνις bird. (Introd. *c* 1859.)] A collective term for the birds or bird life of a region or country; = avifauna.

1861 *Ibis* 292 (*heading*) On the Diversity of the Estimate of the European Ornis and its causes [tr. Ger. paper by Dr. J. H. Blasius]. **1882** in *Edin. Rev.* Apr. 474 An ornis more anomalous in its admixture of forms, but poorer as regards species. **1893** *Proc. Somerset Arch. & Nat. Hist. Soc.* 102 This number appears inadequate to represent the Ornis of so large a county as Somerset.

ornithian (ɔː'nɪθɪən), *a. rare.* [f. Gr. ὀρνīθίας the north wind which brought the birds of passage, f. ὄρνις, ὀρνīθ- bird; hence χειμὼν ὀρνιθίας (Arist. *Acharn.*), a tempest of birds, an 'Ornithian gale'.] Bringing birds; laden with birds.

1830 tr. *Aristophanes, Acharnians* 36 *D.* What bring you? *B.* Ducks, jackdaws, woodcocks, tufted-ducks, landrails, divers. *D.* Marry then, like an Ornithian gale, you have come to the market.

ornithic (ɔː'nɪθɪk), *a.* [ad. Gr. ὀρνīθικός bird-like, f. ὄρνις bird. So mod.F. *ornithique* (1875 in Littré).] Of, or pertaining to, birds; characteristic of birds; of the bird kind; avian.

1854 OWEN in *Circ. Sc., Organ. Nat.* I. 226 Retaining its ornithic type. **1865** *Reader* 29 July 123/3 The ornithic character of the cast of the brain-cavity. **1896** NEWTON *Dict. Birds* Introd. 21 The ornithic portion of the Fauna of any particular country.

b. Dealing with or skilled in birds.

a **1876** M. COLLINS *Th. in Garden* (1880) II. 99 A point I am not ornithic enough to explain. **1881** RUSKIN *Love's Meinie* I. iii. 126 You will scarcely find in any ornithic manual more than a sentence..about their hearing.

ornithichnite (ɔːnɪ'θɪknaɪt). [ad. mod.L. *ornīthichnītēs*, f. Gr. ὄρνις, ὀρνīθ-, bird + ἴχνος track: see -ITE[1] and ICHNITE. Often used in the L. form.] A fossil footprint of a bird, or bird-like reptile; applied orig. to those found in Triassic deposits in Connecticut, now attributed to dinosaurs.

1836 HITCHCOCK in *Amer. Jrnl. Sci.* XXIX. 315, I include all the varieties of tracks under the term *Ornithichnites*;.. signifying *stony bird tracks*. *Ibid.* 324 Some of the specimens of Ornithichnites, which I regard as produced by a three toed bird, may have been made by one with four toes. **1845** LYELL *Trav. N. Amer.* I. 93 Red sandstone..remarkable for its ornithichnites. **1848** LOWELL *Biglow P.* 12 Apr. (1867) 93 The Runes resemble very nearly the ornithichnites or fossil bird-tracks of Dr. Hitchcock.

So ˌ**ornithich'nology** [see -OLOGY], the branch of palæontology which deals with ornithichnites.

1836 HITCHCOCK in *Amer. Jrnl. Sci.* XXIX. 315 Since this is a department of oryctology hitherto unexplored..I should call it ornithichnology.

ornithine ('ɔːnɪθaɪn). *Chem.* [f. Gr. ὀρνīθ- bird + -INE[5].] A base, $C_5H_{12}N_2O_2$, which enters into the composition of ORNITHURIC *acid*, q.v.

1881 WATTS *Dict. Chem.* VIII. 1446 [see ORNITHURIC].

ornithischian (ɔːnɪ'θɪskɪən), *a.* and *sb.* [f. mod.L. order name *Ornithischia* (H. G. Seeley 1887, in *Proc. R. Soc.* XLIII. 170), f. ORNITH(O- + ISCHIUM: see -IA[2], -IAN.]

A. *adj.* Of, pertaining to, or designating an ornithischian. **B.** *sb.* A herbivorous dinosaur of the order Ornithischia, which includes forms having a pelvic structure resembling that of birds.

1901 H. G. SEELEY *Dragons of Air* xvii. 199 In some at least of the..Ornithischian Dinosaurs, there is no antorbital vacuity. **1933** A. S. ROMER *Vertebrate Paleontol.* ix. 195 It is probable that few ornithischians were entirely bipedal in habits. **1965** E. H. COLBERT *Age of Reptiles* i. 19 The ornithischian dinosaurs, in which the rod-like pubic bone of the pelvis had rotated backwardly to run parallel to the ischium,..were..of late Triassic origin. **1967** *New Scientist* 16 Mar. 534/2 [In Lesotho] they also found a fair proportion of ornithischians, a group with an elongated bird-like pelvis. **1971** *Nature* 12 Nov. 75/1 Before 1962 the genus

Geranosaurus, which is represented by a single jaw, was the only undisputed Triassic ornithischian on record, but since that date knowledge of the earliest ornithischian dinosaurs has increased considerably. **1977** *Radio Times* 17 Dec. 45 One of the liveliest of these disputes concerns the two great groups of dinosaurs, the saurischians (with hip-bones like those of lizards) and the ornithischians (in which they were more bird-like).

orni'thivorous, *a. rare.* [irreg. f. Gr. ὀρνῑθ- bird- + L. *-vor-us*: see -VOROUS.] Bird-devouring.

1857 in MAYNE *Expos. Lex.* **1884** J. E. TAYLOR *Sagacity of Plants* 276 The larger and peculiarly-constructed *nepenthes*, therefore, may be ornithivorous as well as insectivorous.

ornitho-, bef. vowel **ornith-**, repr. Gr. ὀρνῑθο-, ὀρνῑθ-, combining form of ὄρνις bird, as in ὀρνῑθο-θήρας bird-catcher, ὀρνῑθο-φάγος bird-eating, etc., used in Eng. to form numerous scientific terms: see the following, and the Main words below.

The pronunciation varies with the place of the stress; when the primary stress falls on the following element, there must be a secondary stress on *ornitho-*, which according to the etymology ought to be *or,nītho-*, and is so pronounced by most English scholars in learned words; but conformation to *,orni'thology*, *,orni'thologist*, has established *,ornītho'logical* (instead of *or,nītho'logical*), the analogy of which has introduced *,ornītho-* into other words in popular use.

or,nithobi'ography, the life-history of a bird or birds; hence **or,nithobio'graphical** *a.* **or,nithoce'phalic, or,nitho'cephalous** *a.* [Gr. κεφαλή head], shaped like a bird's head (Mayne *Expos. Lex.* 1857). **or,nitho'coprolite**, an avian coprolite, fossil birds' dung. **,ornithoco'prophilous** *a.* [cf. *coprophilous* (s.v. COPRO-)] (see quot. 1928). **or,nitho'copros**, the dung of birds, guano. **or,nitho'leucism** [Gr. λευκός white], albinism in birds (Mayne). **or,nitho'melanism** [Gr. μέλαν black], melanism in birds (Mayne). **or,nitho'myzous** *a.* [Gr. μυζάειν to suck], living parasitically on birds (Mayne). ‖**or,nitho'pappi** *pl.* [πάππος grandfather, ancestor], an order of Jurassic birds of archaic type, represented by the genus *Archæopteryx*; hence **or,nitho'pappic** *a.* **orni'thopterous** *a.* [Gr. πτερόν feather, wing], bird-winged, having wings like a bird. **or'nithotrophe** *nonce-wd.* [Gr. τροφός feeder], a place to which birds are attracted by food, so as to come under observation.

1928 B. D. JACKSON *Gloss. Bot. Terms* (ed. 4) 454/1 Ornithocoprophilous.., applied to lichens, which benefit by the excreta of birds. **1958** J. J. BARKMAN *Phytosociol. & Ecol. Cryptogamic Epiphytes* ii. 104 *Xanthoria candelaria* is highly ornithocoprophilous on rocks in Sweden. **1967** [see NITROPHILOUS *a.*]. **1826** DOVASTON in *Bewick's Brit. Birds* (ed. 6) I. Pref. 5, I examined..no less than twenty three sorts of birds in and about my Ornithotrophe, as I humourously denominate it.

‖**Ornithodelphia** (ɔːnaɪθəʊ'dɛlfɪə), *sb. pl. Zool.* [mod.L. (De Blainville 18..), f. ORNITHO- + Gr. δελφ-ύς womb + -IA[2].] De Blainville's name for the lowest of the three sub-classes of the Mammalia, identical with the *Prototheria* of later zoologists. The sub-class, deriving its name from the ornithic character of the reproductive organs, consists of a single order, the *Monotremata*, containing the two genera *Echidna* and *Ornithorhynchus*. Hence **ornitho'delphian, ornitho'delphic, ornitho'delphid, ornitho'delphous**, *adjs.*, of, belonging to, or of the nature of the *Ornithodelphia*.

1871 HUXLEY *Anat. Verteb. An.* 114. **1872** MIVART *Elem. Anat.* 18 The 3rd sub-class is called Ornithodelphia, and the animals comprised within it are termed Ornithodelphous mammals. **1879** D. M. WALLACE *Australas.* iii. 57 The lowest group of mammals—the sub-class Ornithodelphia or Monotremata, consisting of two of the most remarkable animals on the globe.

‖**Ornithogæa** (ɔːnaɪθəʊ'dʒiːə, -'giːə). *Zoogeog.* [mod.L., f. Gr. ὀρνῑθο- bird- + γαῖα land.] A proposed term for a division of the land surface of the earth, characterized by the existence of many peculiar birds, including formerly some gigantic species, and by the absence of Mammalia, except bats, seals, and whales. It corresponds to the New Zealand region of some authors. Hence **ornitho'gæan** *a.*

1874 P. L. SCLATER in *Manchester Sci. Lect.* Ser. vi. v. 79 We may divide our earth..into four divisions..IV... *Ornithogæa*—Bird-land. **1899** W. L. & P. L. SCLATER *Geogr. Mammals* Introd. 11 Mr. Gill..has proposed a division of the Earth into nine 'realms'... (8) The Ornitho-gæan (= New Zealand).

†**or'nithogal.** *Obs.* Also 8 **-gale**. [ad. L. *ornithogalē*, or Gr. ὀρνῑθόγαλον: see next.] = next.

1578 LYTE *Dodoens* II. xlvii. 205 Dioscorides writeth of Ornithogal that the bulbus or round roote thereof may be eaten. **1706** PHILLIPS, *Ornithogale*, an Herb call'd Star of Bethlehem, or Dogs-Onion. **1725** BRADLEY *Fam. Dict.* s.v. *Star of Bethlehem*, The Arabick..and that call'd the Indian Ornithogale, are most esteem'd.

ornithogalum (ɔːnɪ'θɒgələm). [mod.L., ad. L. *ornithogalē* (Pliny), Gr. ὀρνιθόγαλον, f. ὀρνιθο- bird + γάλα milk, adopted as the name of a genus by Linnæus (*Hortus Cliffortianus* (1737) 124) and earlier botanists.] A bulbous plant of the genus so called, belonging to the family Liliaceæ, native to Europe, Asia, or Africa, and usually bearing racemes of white flowers; *Ornithogalum umbellatum*, = ORNITHOGAL, *star of Bethlehem* (STAR *sb.*[1] 22 c).

1664 EVELYN *Kal. Hort.* (1729) 208 June... Flowers in Prime or yet lasting..Pinks,..Ornithogalum. **1755** [see *Star of Bethlehem* s.v. STAR *sb.*[1] 22 c]. **1792** *Curtis's Bot. Mag.* VI. 190 (*heading*) Golden ornithogalum. **1825** *Greenhouse Comp.* I. 116 Tunicate bulbs, as some of the Ornithogalums. **1901** L. H. BAILEY *Cycl. Amer. Hort.* III. 1174/2 Ornithogalums may be divided into hardy and tender groups, and each of these may be subdivided into dwarf and tall. **1931** M. GRIEVE *Mod. Herbal* II. 770/1 Only one [species] is truly native to Great Britain, the spiked Ornithogalum, *O. pyrenaicum* (Linn.), and is not common, being a local plant, found only in a few counties. **1966** E. PALMER *Plains of Camdeboo* xvii. 284 Milk-white Ornithogalums of various species grew here and there, Chinkerinchees to us all.

ornithoid ('ɔːnɪθɔɪd), *a.* [f. Gr. ὀρνῑθ- bird + -OID.] Resembling a bird; approaching birds in structure: *esp.* applied to certain reptiles.

1858 HITCHCOCK *Ichnol. New Engl.* 105, I attach the Typopus to the ornithoid Lizards. **1895** *Pop. Sci. Monthly* Sept. 693 Ornithoid lizards or batrachians.

ornitholeucism: see ORNITHO-.

ornitholite (ɔː'nɪθəlaɪt). [f. ORNITHO- + -LITE.] A fossil of a bird or fragment of a bird.

1828 in WEBSTER. **1836** HITCHCOCK in *Amer. Jrnl. Sci.* XXIX. 307 For this paucity of ornitholites, geologists have ..assigned probable reasons. **1869** GILLMORE tr. *Figuier's Reptiles & Birds* Introd. 3 Traces had been discovered..of certain Ornitholites. **1876** PAGE *Adv. Text-bk. Geol.* xix. 370 Many unknown fragments of bird-bones are..ranked under the general term ornitholites.

Hence **ornitho'litic** *a.*, as in 'ornitholitic remains'.

ornithologer (ɔːnɪ'θɒlədʒə(r)). *rare.* [f. ORNITHOLOG-Y + -ER[1].] = ORNITHOLOGIST.

1661 LOVELL *Hist. Anim. & Min.* 134 Savonarola preferreth it before the Bustard or Thrush, so Bapt Fier. Yet the Ornithologer and Volateranus deny it.

ornitho'logic, *a. rare.* [f. Gr. ὀρνιθολόγ-ος speaking or treating of birds + -IC.] = next.

1846 in WORCESTER.

ornithological (,ɔːnɪθəʊ'lɒdʒɪkəl), *a.* [f. as prec. + -AL[1].] Of or pertaining to ornithology; relating to the study of birds. (In quot. 1875 *catachr.* Of or pertaining to birds, avian, ornithic.)

1802 MONTAGU (*title*) Ornithological Dictionary; or Alphabetical Synopsis of British Birds. **1812** *Pennant's Zool.* II. 88 Mr. Montagu..has given a very detailed description of it in his..ornithological dictionary. **1824** MISS MITFORD *Village* Ser. I. (1863) 204 The ornithological ear of the master..was struck by a regular and melodious call, the note, as he averred, of a sky-lark. **1875** MISS BRADDON *Strange World* II. i. 9 A marvellous specimen of the ornithological race.

Hence **ornitho'logically** *adv.*, according to ornithology, from an ornithological point of view.

1862 *Ibis* 87 The country..is rather poor ornithologically. **1970** *Daily Tel.* 2 May 11/4 This month is quite the best for the ornithologically minded. **1977** *Listener* 30 June 867/1 A superb setting, a marshy bird reserve in Southern Spain where..the..narrator's ornithologically outrageous mania which traps him into seeing too much, forces him into flight among sordid tourist development.

ornithologist (ɔːnɪ'θɒlədʒɪst). [f. as ORNITHOLOGY + -IST.] One who studies or is versed in ornithology; a student of birds.

1677 PLOT *Oxfordshire* 177 She may be placed amongst them by future Ornithologists. **1766** PENNANT *Zool.* (1768) I. 135 This is the gyrfalco of all the ornithologists except Linnæus. **1874** COUES *Birds N.W.* Introd. 11 No one, not an ornithologist, has contributed more to the advance of our knowledge of the birds of the West.

So **orni'thologize** *v.*, to pursue the study of birds.

1872 *Amer. Naturalist* VI. 268 At Topeka..we also tarried for ten days, devoting the time almost exclusively to ornithologizing. **1892** *Gd. Words* Apr. 238/2 One day in early summer, whilst ornithologizing amongst the mountains.

ornithology (ɔːnɪ'θɒlədʒɪ). [ad. mod.L. *ornīthologia* (Aldrovandus, 1599), f. Gr. ὀρνῑθολόγος treating of birds, f. ὀρνῑθο- bird + -λόγος speaking. Cf. F. *ornithologie* (1690 in Hatz.-Darm.).] The branch of zoology which deals with birds, their nature and habits. (By Fuller used otherwise.)

[**1655** FULLER (*title*) Ornitho-Logie: or, the Speech of Birds. Hence 1670 in BLOUNT.]

[**1676** WILLUGHBY (*title*) Ornithologiæ Libri tres, recognovit..J. Raius.] **1678** RAY (*title*) Ornithology, translated into English and enlarged [tr. of prec.]. **1706** PHILLIPS (ed. Kersey), *Ornithology*, a Discourse or Description of the several kinds and natures of Birds. **1755** in JOHNSON. **1828** MISS MITFORD *Village* Ser. III. (1863) 15 The lectures on ornithology, with which..he had thought fit to favour Fanny. **1893** NEWTON *Dict. Birds* Introd. 20 The other work to the importance of which on Ornithology in this country allusion has been made is Bewick's *History of British Birds* (1797–1804).

ornithomancy (ɔː'naɪθəʊ,mænsɪ). [ad. med. or mod.L. *ornīthomantīa*, a. Gr. ὀρνῑθομαντεία divination from birds, augury, f. ὀρνῑθο- bird- + μαντεία divination: see -MANCY.] Divination by means of the flight and cries of birds; augury.

1652 GAULE *Magastrom.* 165 Ornithomancy [divining] by Birds. **1727–41** CHAMBERS *Cycl.* s.v., Ornithomancy, among the Greeks, was the same with augury among the Romans. **1840** DE QUINCEY *Mod. Superst.* Wks. 1862 III. 317 Ornithomancy, or the derivation of omens from the motions of birds, grew into an elaborate science.

So **ornitho'mantic** *a.*, of or pertaining to ornithomancy; **ornitho'mantist**, a diviner by birds (Bailey vol. II. 1727).

ornithomelanism, etc.: see ORNITHO-.

ornitho'morphic, *a.* [f. Gr. ὀρνῑθόμορφ-ος bird-shaped (μορφή form) + -IC.] Having the form and appearance of a bird; birdlike.

1887 LANG *Myth, Ritual & Relig.* II. 4 Between these two ornithomorphic creators the strife was..fierce. **1893** *National Observer* 11 Mar. 418/2 The 'oof-bird' is the ornithomorphic aspect of the tutelary genius of wealth.

ornithophile ('ɔːnɪθəʊfaɪl). [f. ORNITHO- + -PHILE.] **1.** = ORNITHOPHILIST.

1963 *Punch* 10 July 69/3 Irresistible to ornithophiles.

2. *Bot.* A plant pollinated by birds.

1970 *Watsonia* VIII. 67 Mountain regions..are..also regions where ornithophiles from diverse plant genera congregate.

ornithophilist (ɔːnɪ'θɒfɪlɪst). [f. ORNITHO- + Gr. φίλ-ος lover + -IST.] A lover of birds.

1876 *World* V. 5 Like a true ornithophilist, Mr. Spurgeon likes birds, but likes them wild.

So **orni'thophilite** *sb.* = ORNITHOPHILIST (also *attrib.*). **orni'thophilous** *a.*, bird-loving; in Botany, applied to flowers fertilized by the agency of birds, chiefly humming-birds, which visit them for honey.

1859 L. F. SIMPSON *Handbk. Dining* vii. (ed. 3) 73 *note*, He never omitted this ornithophilite excursion. **1880** GRAY *Struct. Bot.* 217 Ornithophilous—i.e. bird-fertilized—flowers are to be ranked with entomophilous. **1890** G. F. SCOTT-ELLIOTT in *Ann. Bot.* IV. 265 (*title*) Ornithophilous flowers in South Africa. **1906** J. R. A. DAVIS tr. *Knuth's Handbk. Flower Pollination* I. 76 The following Cape plants are ornithophilous. **1975** *New Phytologist* LXXIV. 366 There are species [of giant lobelia] which are ornithophilous.

ornithophily (ɔːnɪ'θɒfɪlɪ). [f. ORNITHO- + -PHILY.] **1.** Love of birds.

1884 'BASIL' *Wearing of the Green* I. iii. 44 Summers's opinion both of her practice and of her preaching of ornithophily.

2. *Bot.* [cf. mod.L. *Ornithophilæ*, name of a group of plants pollinated by birds (F. Delpino in H. Müller *Die Befruchtung der Blumen* (1873) 15).] Pollination by birds.

1903 W. R. FISHER tr. *Schimper's Plant-Geogr.* I. vi. 121 The ornithophily of a species of Erythrina was also established by Belt. **1970** *Watsonia* VIII. 67 The plates (75 colour photographs, mainly of birds visiting flowers) are.. illustrative of the importance of ornithophily in the U.S.A. **1975** *New Phytologist* LXXIV. 368 Ornithophily is replaceable by autogamy.

ornithopod (ɔː'nɪθəʊpɒd), *a.* and *sb.* [ad. mod.L. *Ornithopoda* (O. C. Marsh 1881, in *Amer. Jrnl. Sci.* 3rd Ser. XXI. 423), neuter pl., f. ORNITHO- + Gr. πούς, ποδ- foot.] **a.** *adj.* Having feet like those of a bird; belonging to the *Orni'thopoda*, a group or sub-order of extinct saurians, containing herbivorous *Dinosauria*, whose hind feet closely resembled those of birds in their structure. **b.** *sb.* A member of this group. So **orni'thopodous** *a.*

[**1888** ROLLESTON & JACKSON *Anim. Life* 392 Two of the sub-divisions [of Dinosaurs] (*Stegosauria* and *Ornithopoda*) show ornithic characters, especially in the hind-limb.] **1888** LYDEKKER in *Q. Jrnl. Geol. Soc.* (1889) XLV. I. 41 Vertebræ of an Ornithopodous Dinosaur from the..Green-sand. **1933** A. S. ROMER *Vertebrate Paleontol.* ix. 196 (*caption*) Dorsal and lateral views of the ornithopod dinosaur *Camptosaurus*. *Ibid.* 197 The arch of the back was stiffened in ornithopods by a latticework of tendons. **1975** *Nature* 23 Oct. 668/1 We describe here ornithopod dinosaur remains from the Lower Cretaceous of western North America. **1977** A. HALLAM *Planet Earth* 275 Larger ornithischians, known as ornithopods, had appeared in the middle Jurassic.

ornithopter ('ɔːnɪθɒptə(r), ɔːnɪ'θɒptə(r)). *Aeronaut.* Also †**-ptere**. [ad. F. *ornithoptère* (P. Renard 1908, in *L'Aérophile* 15 Jan. 35), coined to replace *orthoptère* (ORTHOPTER 2) because of the latter's etymological inappropriateness and its entomological meaning; see ORNITHO-.] A machine designed to achieve flight by means of flapping wings.

1908 *Aeronautics* I. 86/1 *Ornithoptere* denotes a machine in which the means of sustentation and propulsion consist of beating-wings. **1909** *Flight* I. 99/2 There are many who watch most anxiously for the success of artificial flapping flight by the aid of machines which have been variously named 'orthopters' and 'ornithopters'. **1933** *Jrnl. R. Aeronaut. Soc.* XXXVII. 205 This gentleman.. produced a machine of the ornithopter type for military observation. **1957** *Listener* 19 Dec. 1021/2 Where the aeroplane was concerned, Leonardo gave most of his attention almost obsessionally to the flapping wing ornithopter. **1960** *Observer* 17 Apr. 17/1 A Tass announcement said that the ornithopter—apparently powered by a motor-cycle engine —was flown 'for several yards' in Moscow. **1973** *Nature* 16 Nov. 173/3 A book largely concerned with a theoretical synthesis of man-powered ornithopters. **1976** *Globe & Mail* (Toronto) 4 Aug. 2/6 Mr. Newell, 64, has built five of his airplanes, called ornithopters, in the past 12 years.

ornithopterous: see ORNITHO-.

ornitho'rhynchous, *a. Zool.* [f. as next + -OUS.] Having a beak like that of a bird.
1857 in MAYNE *Expos. Lex.*

‖**ornithorhynchus** (ˌɔːnɪθəʊˈrɪŋkəs, ɔːnaɪθəʊ-). [mod. f. ORNITHO- + Gr. ῥύγχος bill.] An aquatic mammal of Australia, the duck-billed platypus or duck-mole (*O. paradoxus* or *anatinus*), the only species of its genus and family in the order *Monotremata*; it has glossy dark-brown fur, webbed feet and bill like a duck's; it lays eggs like a bird.
1800 *Phil. Trans.* XC. 432 My opportunities of examining the *Ornithorhynchus* were procured through Sir Joseph Banks. **1820** J. OXLEY *Jrnl. 2 Exp. N.S. Wales* 284 We saw numbers of the ornithorynchus, or water mole, in the river. **1864** OWEN *Power of God* 46 The anomalous Ornithorhynchus, with the tail of a beaver, the skin of a mole, the beak of a duck, and the spurs of a cock. **1870** COURTHOPE *Paradise of Birds* 70 For he gave to the Earth the first animal birth, and conceived the Ornithorhyncus. **1892** J. A. THOMSON *Outlines Zool.* 566 The mammary glands in the female Ornithorhynchus open on a flat patch.

or'nithosaur. [f. as next.] = next, b.
1882 in OGILVIE (Annandale). **1887** H. G. SEELEY in *Phil. Trans. R. Soc.* B. CLXXVIII. 191 This osseous condition approximates to that which characterises the bones of Ornithosaurs and Birds. **1913** *Q. Jrnl. Geol. Soc.* LXIX. 372 An Ornithosaur from the Wealden Shales of Atherfield (Isle of Wight).

ornithosaurian (-ˈsɔːrɪən), *a.* (*sb.*) *Palæont.* [f. mod.L. *Ornīthosauria*, neut. pl. f. ORNITHO- + Gr. σαῦρος lizard: see SAURIAN.] **a.** Of, belonging to, or having the character of, the *Ornithosauria*, an extinct order of flying reptiles, including the pterodactyl; more usually called *Pterosauria*. **b.** *sb.* A member of this order.
1888 R. LYDEKKER *Catal. Fossil Reptilia Brit. Mus.* I. 24 Considerable portion of the skeleton of a large Ornithosaurian.. from the Wealden of Brook, Isle of Wight. **1901** H. G. SEELEY *Dragons of Air* xvi. 187 In many ways the Ornithosaurian animals are like Birds. **1913** *Q. Jrnl. Geol. Soc.* LXIX. 372 The late Rev. W. D. Fox.. discovered.. many associated ornithosaurian bones.

ornithoscelidan (-ˈsɛlɪdən), *a.* (*sb.*) *Palæont.* [f. mod.L. *Ornīthoscelida* pl. (f. ORNITHO- bird + Gr. σκέλ-ος leg + *-ida*) + -AN.] Of or belonging to the *Ornithoscelida*, a sub-class or order of extinct reptiles of Mesozoic and Tertiary age, which approached birds in the form of the hinder legs and the pelvic arch. **b.** *sb.* A member of this order.
The *Ornithoscelida* are sometimes reckoned as identical with the *Dinosauria* (in a wide sense), sometimes as containing the *Dinosauria* and *Compsognatha*.
1876 HUXLEY *Amer. Addr., Lect. Evolution* ii. (1877) 61 Hind limbs of a crocodile, a three-toed bird, and an ornithoscelidan. *Ibid.* 64 The ornithoscelidan limb is comparable to that of an unhatched chick. **1880** HAUGHTON *Phys. Geog.* vi. 265 The Archæopteryx is a connecting link between the true birds and the Ornithoscelidan reptiles.

ornithoscopy (ɔːnɪˈθɒskəpɪ). [ad. Gr. ὀρνιθοσκοπία, n. of quality f. ὀρνιθοσκόπ-ος observing (and divining by) birds, auguring, sb. = augur, f. ὀρνιθο- bird + -σκοπος viewing.] Observation of birds for the purpose of divination; augury.
1840 DE QUINCEY *Mod. Superst.* Wks. 1862 III. 321 Speaking of ornithoscopy in relation to Jews. **1897** A. DRUCKER tr. *Ihering's Evol. of Aryan* 374 The original meaning, therefore, of Ornithoscopy cannot possibly have been the mere watching of birds.
So **orni'thoscopist**, one who professes or practises ornithoscopy; an augur. (Ogilvie, 1882.)

ornithosis (ɔːnɪˈθəʊsɪs). [f. ORNITHO- + -OSIS.] A disease affecting birds, certain small mammals, and man, caused by a micro-organism belonging to the genus *Chlamydia*, and producing severe, sometimes fatal, pneumonitis in man and respiratory or generalized infection in birds and other animals. Cf. PSITTACOSIS. Hence **orni'thotic** *a.*
1939 K. F. MEYER et al. in *Proc. Soc. Exper. Biol. & Med.* XLI. 173 (*title*) Complement-fixation test.. as aid in recognizing latent avian psittacosis (ornithosis). **1947** W. P. BLOUNT *Dis. Poultry* xliii. 388 There are, however, other allied virus infections of birds, such as that under investigation.. in the pigeon, which is equally ornithotic. **1951** *Lancet* 29 Sept. 572/2 This monograph is essentially a review of present knowledge of the clinical features [etc.].. and treatment of psittacosis and ornithosis. **1959** *Times* 25 Mar. 8/6 A generalized virus infection known as psittacosis or ornithosis. **1966** *Daily Tel.* 4 Nov. 13/4 A much bigger danger.. is the wood pigeon, which.. suffers from ornithosis, more usually associated with budgerigars, that can give man a form of pneumonia. **1973** *Observer* 4 Nov. 5/3 A steadily increasing number of people.. catch psittacosis—or ornithosis, as it is known in humans—from imported parrot-like birds.

ornithotomy (ɔːnɪˈθɒtəmɪ). [f. ORNITHO- + Gr. -τομια cutting: see -TOMY.] Dissection of birds; the anatomy of birds.
1854 OWEN *Skel. & Teeth* in *Circ. Sc., Organ. Nat.* (1865) II. 73/1 An additional specific term in ornithotomy.
So **ornitho'tomical** *a.*, of or pertaining to ornithotomy; **orni'thotomist**, one who practises the dissection, or studies the anatomy, of birds.
1875 W. K. PARKER in *Encycl. Brit.* III. 728/1 The merest abstract of our present ornithotomical knowledge. **1885** NEWTON *Ibid.* XVIII. 41/2 To harmonize the views of ornithotomists with those taken by the ornithologists who only study the exterior.

ornithuric (ɔːnɪˈθjʊərɪk), *a. Chem.* [f. ORNITH(O- + URIC.] In ***ornithuric acid***, $C_{19}H_{20}N_2O_4$, an acid extracted from the excrement of birds whose food has been mixed with benzoic acid; it crystallizes in small colourless anhydrous needles.
1881 WATTS *Dict. Chem.* VIII. 1446 In constitution ornithuric acid is analogous to hippuric acid, being formed by the union of 2 mol. benzoic acid and 1 mol. ornithine, with elimination of 2 mol. water.

ornithurous (ɔːnɪˈθjʊərəs), *a. Zool.* [f. mod.L. *Ornithūræ*, fem. pl., f. ORNITH(O- + Gr. οὐρά tail.] *lit.* Bird-tailed; of or pertaining to the *Ornithuræ* or ordinary birds having a tail terminated by a pygostyle, as opposed to the *Saururæ* or lizard-tailed birds, represented by the fossil *Archæopteryx*.

†**'ornomancy**. *Obs.* [irreg. f. Gr. ὄρνις bird + μαντεία divination.] = ORNITHOMANCY.
c **1420** LYDG. *Assembly of Gods* 869 These folowyd Konnyng.. Adryomancy, Ornomancy, with Pyromancy. **1656** BLOUNT *Glossogr.*, *Ornomancy*, divination by the moving of birds.

oro-, formative element repr. Gr. ὄρος mountain (as in *orometric* (1774), *orology* (1781)). For the var. oreo- see etym. of OROGRAPHY.

oro-anal (ˌɔərəʊˈeɪnəl), *a.* [irreg. f. L. *ōs, ōr-* mouth + ANAL.]
1. That serves both as mouth and anus, as the single orifice of the digestive system of the star-fish.
1872 NICHOLSON *Palæont.* 131 The question is narrowed to its being the anus alone, or an 'oro-anal' orifice.
2. Extending in the direction from mouth to anus.
1885 RAY LANKESTER in *Encycl. Brit.* XIX. 434/2 A new long axis is.. established at right angles to the original oro-anal axis.

‖**Orobanche** (ɒrəʊˈbæŋkɪ). [L. (Pliny), a. Gr. ὀροβάγχη, f. ὀροβ-ος OROBUS + ἄγχ-ειν to throttle.] A genus of leafless plants (Tournefort, 1700), parasitical on the roots of other plants, chiefly *Leguminosæ*; the broomrape. Also *attrib.*
1562 TURNER *Herbal* II. 71 b, It choketh and strangleth them [pulses] where of it hath the name of Orobanche, that is chokefitche or strangletare. **1601** HOLLAND *Pliny* II. 145 A weed there is which we named Orobanche, for that it choketh Eruile and other pulse. **1873** TRISTRAM *Moab* xiii. 249 Splendid orobanches, of two species.. thrive on the roots of the *Atriplex halimus*. **1890** *Athenæum* 21 June 805/2 Specimen of an orobanche parasitic upon a pelargonium.
Hence **oro'bancheous** *a.*, of or pertaining to the Natural Order *Orobancheæ* or *Orobanchaceæ*.
1857 in MAYNE *Expos. Lex.*

†**'orobe**. *Obs. rare.* [a. F. *orobe* (1545 in Hatz.-Darm.), ad. L. *orobus*, by mod. Fr. botanists applied to *Orobus tuberosus*, now *Lathyrus macrorhizus*: see OROBUS.] Some species of vetch or other leguminous plant.
1714 *Fr. Bk. of Rates* 95 Orobes per 100 weight. **1756** ROLT *Dict. Trade*, *Orobe*, a plant, whose seed and root are of some use in medicine and dying.
b. *Comb.* †**orobe-strangler** = OROBANCHE.
1562 TURNER *Herbal* II. 72 It hath gotten the name Orobanche, that is Orobstrangler.

Orobus (ˈɒrəʊbəs). *Bot.* [L. (Pliny), a. Gr. ὄροβος some kind of vetch; adopted by Linnæus (*Genera Plantarum* (1737) 325) and earlier botanists as the name of a genus.] A herb of the genus so called, belonging to the family Leguminosæ and now usually included in the genus *Lathyrus*; = *bitter-vetch* (BITTER- *a.* 2).
Usually Englished from Turner onward as *bitter vetch*, an appellation founded by Turner upon a passage in Galen; though the early herbalists admit that the identity of Galen's ὄροβος was unknown to them.
1551 TURNER *Herbal* I. P iij b, Galen.. and Aetius with one consent hold that the black orobus is bitter. **1562** *Ibid.* II. 77 b, Opium.. taken in the quantite of a bitter fich, called eruum or orobus. **1688** R. HOLME *Armoury* II. 91/2 Wood, or wild Orobus [hath] the Flowers white, the cod black. **1703** tr. *van Oosten's Dutch Gardener* II. cv. 135 Of the Orobus. This is a small blue purplish Flower, bears plentifully; it is a sort of Vetches. **1801** *Curtis's Bot. Mag.* XV. 521 (*heading*) Early-flowering Orobus. **1894** W. ROBINSON *Wild Garden* (ed. 4) vi. 53 Among the plants that are suitable for hedgerows and lanes, &c. are.. May Apple, Orobus in variety, many Narcissi. **1903** *Flora & Sylva* I. 202/1 The name 'Orobus' is useful, for it expresses a race of plants.. distinct from the climbers to which the name 'Lathyrus' was formerly exclusively applied. These Orobi .. supply some of the most beautiful of spring and early summer flowers.

orocentral (ɔərəʊˈsɛntrəl), *a.* [irreg. for **oricentral*, f. L. *ōs, ōr-* mouth + CENTRAL.] Occupying the centre of the oral side (of an echinoderm).
1884 P. H. CARPENTER in *Challenger Rep., Zool.* XXXII. 158, I propose to call it [a plate of calcareous matter] the 'orocentral'. **1885** *Athenæum* 11 Apr. 475/2 The orocentral plate corresponds with the centrodorsal. **1888** ROLLESTON & JACKSON *Anim. Life* 545 (*Echinodermata*) In its typical form .. there is an orocentral surrounded by five interradial oral plates, and these in their turns by circles of oral radials and interradials.

orocline (ˈɒrəʊklaɪn). *Geol.* [f. ORO- + κλίνειν to bend.] (See quot. 1955.)
1955 S. W. CAREY in *Papers & Proc. R. Soc. Tasmania* LXXXIX. 257 For an orogenic system which has been flexed in plan to a horse-shoe or elbow shape, the name *orocline* is proposed. **1970** LINTON & MOSELEY in *Cambr. Anc. Hist.* (ed. 3) I. I. i. 21 Carey recognizes six oroclines in the orogenic belt in Europe. **1972** *Nature* 13 Oct. 389/2 The orocline concept is incompatible with strong plates and offers no reason why arcs should be circular.

orocratic (ɒrəʊˈkrætɪk), *a. Geol.* [f. ORO- + κράτ-ος strength + -IC.] Characterized by an increase in the roughness of relief as a result of crustal upheaval.
1924 W. RAMSAY in *Geol. Mag.* LXI. 155 Only after the orogenic phases was the relief comparable to that of the present day, or still higher and more broken. For such a condition I will use the term *orocratic*. **1929** L. J. WILLS *Physiogr. Evol. Brit.* vi. 71 The Carbo-Permian times witnessed.. one of the greatest orocratic phases that is known. **1961** *Times* 28 Aug. 9/4 A 'pediocratic period' is a relatively quiet one between two 'orocratic periods'.

orogen (ˈɒrədʒən). *Geol.* Also **orogene**. [a. G. *orogen* (L. Kober *Der Bau der Erde* (1921) i. 21): see ORO- and -GEN.] An orogenic belt.
1923 *Bull. Geol. Soc. Amer.* XXXIV. 167 Geanticlines and orogens may remain as dry lands or may sink into the depths of the oceans. **1934** *Geogr. Jrnl.* LXXXIII. 517 The orogen on the west North American Cordillera. **1953** [see *mountain system* s.v. MOUNTAIN 9 a]. **1964** L. V. DE SITTER *Struct. Geol.* (ed. 2) xxxi. 424 The Pyrenees are essentially a Hercynian orogene reactivated in the Alpine Period. **1970** *Nature* 28 Nov. 838/2 The width of the orogen is anomalously great in the region of the central United States. **1975** *Ibid.* 20 Feb. 599/2 The effects are restricted to the western seaboard of Scandinavia and within overthrust masses on the respective sides of the Caledonian orogene.

orogenesis (ɒrəʊˈdʒɛnɪsɪs). *Geol.* [f. Gr. ὄρος mountain + -GENESIS.] The formation of mountains.
1886 W. B. TAYLOR in *Proc. Amer. Assoc. Adv. Sc.* XXXIV. 202 Does not this impartial testimony form a most suggestive.. indication of the secret cause of orogenesis? **1925** [see EPEIROGENESIS]. **1970** *Nature* 9 May 498/1 Basaltic dykes have been used to separate chronologically two principal periods of orogenesis.

orogenetic (ɒrəʊdʒɪˈnɛtɪk), *a. Geol.* [f. ORO(GENESIS + -GENETIC.] = OROGENIC *a.*
1888 J. J. H. TEALL *Brit. Petrogr.* 441 *Orogenetic*, that which relates to the formation of mountains. **1925** J. JOLY *Surface-Hist. Earth* i. 24 The orogenetic movements which developed the Appalachians. **1956** *Nature* 28 Jan. 156/2 The rate of cooling [of the earth] was greater in the past.., and this suggests that orogenetic activity may have decreased. **1970** R. J. SMALL *Study of Landforms* iii. 89 Over much of the earth compressive forces in the crust, stemming mainly from orogenetic movements of diverse age, have produced folding of sedimentary strata.
Hence **oroge'netically** *adv.*
1923 *Bull. Geol. Soc. Amer.* XXXIV. 158 There must have been another crustal element orogenetically connected with it. **1949** *Ibid.* LX. 1756/2 He is.. strongly convinced.. that the anorogenetic periods were of long duration, as against the short orogenetically active phases.

orogenic (ɒrəʊˈdʒɛnɪk), *a.* [f. as OROGENY (see OROGENESIS) + -IC. Cf. F. *orogénique* (Littré).] Mountain-forming; concerned in the formation of mountains; ***orogenic belt***, a strip of the earth's surface which has been subjected to folding or other deformation during an orogeny.
1886 *American* XII. 351 The old belief that earthquakes are generally volcanic; they are more commonly orogenic. **1898** J. E. MARR *Princ. Stratigr. Geol.* 32 Inversion is a frequent accompaniment of the more local orogenic or mountain-forming movements. **1942** M. P. BILLINGS *Structural Geol.* v. 95 Some geologists, however, believe that entire orogenic belts are due to gigantic terrestrial couples. **1944** A. HOLMES *Princ. Physical Geol.* xviii. 378 It is.. essential to discriminate carefully between the geographical

concept of a mountain range or system and the geological concept of an orogenic belt: the one refers to the height and relief of the land; the other to the structure of the rocks, whether the region be high, low, or submerged. **1969** *Sci. Jrnl.* Feb. 52/2 The entire orogenic belt bordering the eastern margin of the Pacific may have been caused by sea floor spreading and the consequent underthrusting along the eastern Pacific margin.

Hence **oro'genically** *adv.*, by orogenesis.

1935 *Geogr. Jrnl.* LXXXVI. 76 Neither in the orogenically nor in the isostatically affected areas. **1971** I. G. Gass et al. *Understanding Earth* xxii. 323/2 The ancient diamondiferous sediments of the Ivory Coast were orogenically deformed some 2000 million years ago.

orogenital (ˌɔərəʊˈdʒɛnɪtəl), *a.* [irreg. for *origenital*, f. L. *ōs*, *ōr-* mouth + GENITAL *a.*] = ORAL *a.* 3 b.

1963 A. Heron *Towards Quaker View of Sex* 56 In the U.S.A. (and probably in this country) orogenital contact seems much less common in what are often called the lower social classes. **1971** *Nature* 16 Apr. 433/1 Human sex play has a large, though tabooed, orogenital component. **1974** E. Rosen et al. *Abnormal Psychol.* (ed. 2) xv. 277/2 The technical terms for oro-genital activity are cunnilingus.. and fellatio.

o'rogeny. [cf. F. *orogénie* (Littré), and see -GENY.] **a.** = OROGENESIS.

1890 [see EPEIROGENY]. **1950** F. E. Zeuner *Dating Past* (ed. 2) xi. 349 The periods of regression and orogeny result in intensified erosion on the continent. **1972** *McGraw-Hill Yearbk. Sci. & Technol.* 305/1 Orogeny results from interactions of this global, continuously evolving system of oceanic ridges and trenches, according to the concepts of.. lithosphere plate tectonics.

b. A geological period of mountain-building.

1914 *Jrnl. Geol.* XXII. 647 Throughout its range the Laramide orogeny was marked by great volcanic activity. **1940** *Geogr. Jrnl.* XCVI. 51 The conception of the orogenic cycle.. gets little support from a study of the Variscan orogeny of Central Europe. **1974** *Nature* 5 Apr. 471/2 Is it generally correct to associate all previous Chinese orogenies with times of rapid seafloor spreading?

orographic (ɒrəʊˈɡræfɪk), *a.* [f. OROGRAPHY + -IC: see -GRAPHIC.] **a.** Of or pertaining to orography; connected with the physical character, features, and relative position of mountains.

1846 in Worcester. **1864** *Reader* 5 Mar. 303/1 The two chains repeat each other in all their primary orographic conditions. **1880** F. R. & G. R. Conder *Handbk. to Bible* vii. 333 Such being the orographic features of the site. **1888** J. D. Whitney *Names & Places* 85 It needs but little orographic study to find out that a single entirely isolated mountain is something of comparatively rare occurrence.

b. *Meteorol.* Applied to precipitation which results from moist air being forced upwards by mountains, and to the action of mountains in producing such precipitation.

1915 *Q. Jrnl. R. Meteorol. Soc.* XLI. 41 These considerations at once brought into prominence the distinction between orographic and cyclonic rainfall, which was perhaps one of the most puzzling features in British meteorology. **1938** E. G. Bilham *Climate Brit. Isles* v. 101 Thunderstorm rains.. do not often produce total amounts of rainfall.. of the same order of magnitude as are observed when intense cyclonic rains are augmented by orographic action. **1955** W. J. Saucier *Princ. Meteorol. Analysis* x. 324/2 To the windward of the Appalachians.. orographic lifting of the moist and turbulent air is sufficient to produce precipitation without needing convergence in surface flow. **1968** *Jrnl. Appl. Meteorol.* VII. 857/1 Orographic precipitation has long been considered to be an attractive target for cloud seeding. **1976** B. Lecomber *Dead Weight* iii. 41 It's the same pattern on all the West Indian Islands:.. on the high ground, where the orographic clouds form and double or treble the rainfall, you find the jungles.

oro'graphical, *a.* [f. as prec. + -AL[1].]

a. Relating to or connected with orography.

1802–3 tr. *Pallas's Trav.* (1812) II. 100 In an orographical respect.. Tshorguna deserves every attention. **1880** Haughton *Phys. Geog.* v. 205 An Orographical Map of Africa. **1894** *Nation* (N.Y.) 23 Aug. 142/2 An orographical and geological description of the Cordilleras.

b. *Meteorol.* = OROGRAPHIC *a.* b.

1909 H. R. Mill in *Geogr. Teacher* V. 75 Placing this established fact of the dependence of the annual rainfall on the height or the configuration of the land side by side with the equally established fact of the complete independence of heavy cyclonic or thunderstorm rains on terrestrial conditions, we are obliged to divide rain into two classes; one greater in intensity but shorter in duration, and, in aggregate, trifling in amount, which we may call meteorological rain (in thunderstorms and cyclones), and the other kind of rain, of less intensity but greater frequency and duration, we may call orographical rain. **1921** *Geofysiske Publikationer* II. iii. 9 The effects of orographical rain are strongly restricted by the tendency of all stable air currents to curve round the mountains horizontally. **1947** *Q. Jrnl. R. Meteorol. Soc.* LXXIII. 16 The orographical rain was well developed over North Wales and the English Lake District.

Hence **oro'graphically** *adv.*, in accordance with, or by, orography; by the action of mountains.

1873 *Q. Jrnl. Geol. Soc.* XXIX. 389 These two lakes.. are separated by a prolongation of the parallel ridges of the Schaffberg massif, so that orographically the Wolfganger See lies in a synclinal trough which may be traced along a line of lakeless valleys, and is separated from the head of the Foschelsee by a narrow ridge. **1877** *Ibid.* XXXIII. 143 The part of North Greenland here described can be geologically and orographically divided into three districts. **1902** D. G. Hogarth *Nearer East* 14 Here is a continuous parting of waters, but not, orographically, a continuous mountain range. **1947** *Q. Jrnl. R. Meteorol. Soc.* LXXIII. 13 Warm front rain is intensified orographically, but not so much as warm sector rain. **1971** *Nature* 23 Apr. 504/1 The development of ice fog in relatively still, orographically protected areas.

orography (ɒˈrɒɡrəfɪ), **oreography** (ɒrɪˈɒɡ-). [f. Gr. ὄρος, ὀρε- mountain + -GRAPHY. Greek compounds of ὄρος are formed in ὀρει-, ὀρο-, and ὀρε(ο-; hence the two forms, of which *orography* is now the more usual. So in Fr., *orographie* (*Dict. Acad.* 1878) has displaced *oréographie*.] That branch of physical geography which deals with the formation and features of mountains; the description of mountains. Also, the orographical features of a region.

1846 Worcester, *Orography*. **1853** E. Hitchcock *Outl. Geol. Globe* 10 A knowledge of the Hydrography of a country aids as much in determining its geology as does its Orography,—that is, a description of its mountains. **1856** A. K. Johnston (*title*) Physical Atlas of Natural Phenomena, Geology and Orography. **1865** *Sat. Rev.* 11 Feb. 163 He has made an addition to oreography. **1873** *Q. Jrnl. Geol. Soc.* XXIX. 382 As the general circumstances of climate and orography are fairly similar throughout the great Alpine chain, it may reasonably be expected that any explanation suggested for the lake-basins of one district should apply also to another. **1881** Pinto *How I crossed Africa* II. i. 107 The oreography of that region. **1883** *Athenæum* 29 Sept. 407/1 A detailed description of the orography.. of one of the most complex mountain systems on the face of the earth. **1904** *Geogr. Jrnl.* XXIII. 183 How the system of orography of Eastern Siberia accords with the orography of Asia altogether, such as it now appears from the recent explorations in Central Asia. **1923** *Q. Jrnl. R. Meteorol. Soc.* XLIX. 226 The 'normal' orographical distribution of rainfall depends of course not only on the orography of the country but on the constancy of the prevailing wind. **1955** W. J. Saucier *Princ. Meteorol. Analysis* x. 304/1 Local circulations due to convection or orography may.. cause discrepancy between local winds and the flow pattern of the surroundings. **1975** *Weather* XXX. 141 Orography has the main influence in mountainous regions while the latitude effect is most important in regions with small orographies.

‖**Orohippus** (ɒrəʊˈhɪpəs). [mod.L., f. Gr. ὄρος mountain + ἵππος horse.] A genus of fossil quadrupeds found in the Eocene beds of North America, having four toes on the fore feet and three on the hind feet; held to be an ancestral form of the horse and its congeners. The animals were only about the size of a fox.

1877 Dawson *Orig. World* x. 227 The earliest of them, the Orohippus, would require, on the theory, to have been preceded by a previous series. **1879** Le Conte *Elem. Geol.* 504 First of all.. appears.. the Eohippus,.. then.. the Orohippus.

orohydrography (ˌɒrəʊhaɪˈdrɒɡrəfɪ). [f. ORO- + HYDROGRAPHY.] (See quot. 1967.) Hence ˌ**orohydro'graphic, -'graphical** *adjs.*

1892 *Syd. Soc. Lex.*, *Orohydrography*, a description of the water sheds of mountains. **1900** *Geogr. Jrnl.* XVI. 35 The oro-hydrographic conformation of the Andine region extending southwards of Mount Tronador is extremely complex. **1908** C. R. Enock *Peru* i. 2 A glance at the map will show the remarkable series of parallel topographical—or rather oro-hydrographical—features which exist, due to this agency. **1936** *Geogr. Jrnl.* LXXXVIII. 268 There are.. maps, geological and orohydrographical, covering the whole region. **1967** E. Vollmer *Encycl. Hydraulics* 208 *Orohydrography*, the branch of hydrography which deals with the relation of mountains to drainage. **1970** *Soviet Hydrology: Selected Papers* No. 1. 19 As an example of one of the most ancient orohydrographic discrepancies we can mention the crossing of the Penzhina Range by the Talovka River.

oroide (ˈɔərəʊɪd). [f. Fr. *or*, It. *oro* (L. *aurum*) gold + Gr. εἶδος form: cf. -OID.] An alloy of copper and zinc, having the colour of gold. Also *attrib.* (See also OREIDE.)

1875 Knight *Dict. Mech.*, *Oroide*,.. an alloy resembling gold in appearance. **1879** Webster Suppl., *Oroide*. (Also written *oreide*.) **1880** *Sat. Rev.* 7 Feb. 175/2 Oroide gold. **1881** *Metal World* No. 6. 89 Oreide must not be confounded with oroide, which consists of 12 parts of caustic lime, 360 of sal-ammoniac, 600 of magnesia, 900 of tartar, 10,000 of copper, and 1,700 of zinc.

orolingual (ɔərəʊˈlɪŋɡwəl), *a.* [irreg. for **orilingual*, f. L. *ōs*, *ōr-* mouth + *lingua* tongue + -AL[1].] Connected with the mouth and tongue.

1899 *Allbutt's Syst. Med.* VII. 287 Unilateral extirpation of the oro-lingual or of the laryngeal centres.

orologe, orologge, obs. forms of HOROLOGE.

orology (ɒˈrɒlədʒɪ), **oreology** (ɒriːˈɒl-). [f. Gr. ὄρος, ὀρε- mountain + -LOGY. As to the two forms see OROGRAPHY.] The scientific study of mountains; the branch of geology or of physical geography which treats of mountains.

1781 J. T. Dillon *Trav. through Spain* 245 We are not therefore to wonder, that orology, or the science of mountains, is so little understood. **1860** Maury *Phys. Geog. Sea* (Low) xiv. §582 Equally important is it.. to present its orology, by mapping out the bottom of the ocean. **1892** *Daily News* 26 Mar. 2/1 Originally Mr. Whymper intended to pursue his studies in Oreology.. in the cloud-capped region of the Himalaya.

Hence **oro'logical, oreo-,** *a.* [cf. F. *orologique*], of or pertaining to orology (1828 in Webster); **o'rologist, ore'ologist,** one skilled in orology.

1802 Playfair *Illustr. Hutton. Th.* 114 If the Oreologist would trace back the progress of waste, till he come in sight of that original structure.

orology, obs. variant of HOROLOGY.

orometer (ɒˈrɒmɪtə(r)). [f. Gr. ὄρος mountain + μέτρον measure; see -METER.] An instrument for measuring the altitudes of mountains.

1879 *Cassell's Techn. Educ.* IV. 92/1 The clinometer or orometer for levelling and finding altitudes.

orometric (ɒrəʊˈmɛtrɪk), *a.* [f. as prec. + -IC.] Of or pertaining to the measurement of mountains; †(in quot. 1774) = trigonometrical with mountain summits as the points of triangulation.

1774 M. Mackenzie *Maritime Surv.* p. xxi, An Orometric Survey is, when one long Base-line is exactly measured, and the Distance of the Summits of two, or more, high Mountains in the Neighbourhood found from thence trigonometrically. **1945** *Q. Jrnl. R. Meteorol. Soc.* LXXI. 44 At the other end of the orometric scale it seems pretty evident that the British mountains which only exceptionally reach an altitude of even 4,000 feet are neither high enough nor compact enough to produce the maximum amount of orographic rainfall.

orometry (ɒˈrɒmɪtrɪ). *Geogr.* [f. ORO- + -METRY.] The measurement of forms of relief.

1898 *Geogr. Jrnl.* XI. 205 As the geoid is treated in geodesy, he treats the *oroid* in orometry. **1972** P. Tilley tr. *Hettner's Surface Features of Land* 160 Ideas used in analytical geometry to express geometrical figures arithmetically have been copied in orometry.

oronasal (ɒrəˈneɪzəl), *a.* (*sb.*) Also **orinasal**. [f. *oro-*, altered f. L. *ōri-*, comb. form of *ōs*, *ōr-* mouth + NASAL.] **A.** *adj.* Pertaining to the mouth and the nose; *spec.* of a vowel: Pronounced with the oral and nasal passages both open, so as to resound in the mouth and in the nose simultaneously, as the 'nasal' vowels in French.

B. *sb.* An oronasal vowel.

1867 A. J. Ellis *E.E. Pronunc.* i. iii. 67 It is very difficult to determine what is the oral basis of the orinasal vowel, so strangely is it modified by the nasal vibration. **1882** *Brit. Med. Jrnl.* 1 July 13/1 Metal Respirators. 1. The principal forms made by Jeffries.. are three: one for the mouth only ..; a second.., for the mouth, with a scarf; and a third, for the mouth and nose (ori-nasal). **1887** A. J. Ellis in *Encycl. Brit.* XXII. 383/2 If the nasal passage is left open at all the vowel is 'nasalized', and as it resounds partly in the nose and partly in the mouth it becomes an 'orinasal'. **1888** Martindale *Extra Pharmacopœia* (ed. 5) 163 (*heading*) Oro-nasal inhalations. **1892** *Syd. Soc. Lex.*, *Orinasal fistula*, a communication between the nose and the mouth by means of a false passage through the arch of the palate. **1898** *Allbutt's Syst. Med.* V. 235 Creasote.. used for inhalation in an orinasal respirator. **1926** Jordan & Kindred *Textbk. Embryol.* xx. 407 The oronasal groove is obliterated by the fusion of the median nasal and maxillary processes to form the upper lip. **1938** *Jrnl. Aviation Med.* IX. 184/2 Since most aviators breathe through the nose, it would be necessary to use an oronasal type of mask only in the presence of nasal obstruction. **1960** J. J. Sharry in W. L. McCracken *Partial Denture Construction* xxi. 468 The palatal repair itself may look adequate, and yet we find that there may be an oronasal perforation in the labial mucobuccal fold. **1970** *Jrnl. Physiol.* CCVI. 22P (*heading*) Oronasal distribution of inspiratory flow during various activities.

Hence **oro'nasally** *adv.*, by means of the mouth and nose.

1970 *Science* 15 May 858/2 In the course of previous experiments, more than 100,000 newborn.. mice received reovirus 3 oronasally.

oronge: see ORANGE.

oronoco, oronooko (ɔərəʊˈnəʊkəʊ, -ˈnuːkəʊ). Also 8 Oranoco, Oronoko, 8–9 **Oroonoko, -ka,** 9 Oronokoo, Orinoco. [Origin uncertain: app. a proper name, but stated in *A Paper on Tobacco* 118 by J. Fume 1839 to be unconnected with the river Oronoco in South America.] Name of a variety of tobacco.

1706 Phillips, *Oranoco* (i.e. bright and large), a Name given to the common sort of Tobacco in the Plantations of Virginia. **1708** E. Cook *Sot-weed Factor* (1865) 23 Broad Oronooko bright and sound, The growth and product of this ground. **1760** J. Lee *Introd. Bot.* App. 321 Oroonoka, *Nicotiana*. **1800** in *Spirit Pub. Jrnls.* IV. 365 Bursting from the effluvia of train-oil, salt-cod, and oroonoko. **1889** Doyle *Micah Clarke* 34 Smoking his evening pipe of Oronooko. **1896** P. A. Bruce *Econ. Hist. Virginia* I. 436 Between the sweet-scented and the Oronoco.. there were several varieties.

orontiaceous (ɒrɒntɪˈeɪʃəs), *a. Bot.* [f. mod.L. *Orontiăceæ* + -OUS.] Of or belonging to the *Orontiaceæ*, a Natural Order or tribe of Endogens closely allied to *Araceæ*, of which the genus *Orontium* is the type; represented in Britain by the Sweet Flag, *Acorus Calamus*.

1857 in Mayne *Expos. Lex.*

So **o'rontiad**, a plant of the N.O. *Orontiaceæ*.

1876 Harley *Mat. Med.* (ed. 6) 385 Orontiads differ from the Arums in having hermaphrodite flowers and usually a scaly perianth.

oropendola (ɒrəʊˈpɛndələ). [a. Sp. *oropendola* golden oriole.] Any of several birds belonging to one of the species of the family Icteridæ, found in tropical regions of south and central America. Also *attrib.*

1898 *Auk* XV. 327 (*heading*) Cassin's Oropendola. **1912** BRABOURNE & CHUBB *Birds S. Amer.* I. 431 Swainson's Oropendola. **1955** *Sci. News Let.* 23 July 64/3 Nests of the oropendola, or 'giant oriole', are narrow bags two to three feet long, woven of straws and weeds. **1968** *Sci. Jrnl.* Nov. 11/3 Nests of oropendolas—a bird found in the Republic of Panama—containing also one or two young of the cowbird.. often produce more oropendola fledglings than 'unparasitized' ones. **1970** R. MEYER DE SCHAUENSEE *Guide Birds S. Amer.* 352 This family [*sc.* Icteridæ] comprises an assortment of birds ranging from forest-inhabiting oropendolas and caciques to the more familiar grackles, cowbirds and meadowlarks. **1974** *Nat. Geographic* Nov. 687 Oriole-like oropendolas were building their hanging nests in nearby trees.

Oropesa (ɒrəʊˈpiːzə). The name of the vessel first used to test the apparatus, used *attrib.* to designate a minesweeping device first developed during the war of 1914–18.

1939 *War Illustr.* 9 Dec. 399/2 Minesweepers work in pairs, with each unit 300 to 500 yards apart. Between them, sometimes suspended from two sets of apparatus called Oropesa floats, is drawn the sweep wire, which has a series of steel cutters. Should this come into contact with a mooring cable, the mine will rise to the surface and it can then be destroyed by gunfire. *Ibid.* 29 Dec. 538/1 *Oropesa*, a type of minesweeping float. The name originated from that of a trawler in which the newly-invented gear was first tested. **1940** *Manch. Guardian Weekly* 12 Apr. 297 A little farther on a minesweeper was being reconditioned, grim-looking with bristling gun, and oropesa sweeps. **1949** J. S. COWIE *Mines, Minelayers & Minelaying* vi. 105 The spread of an Oropesa type of sweep. **1965** K. LANGMAID *Approaches are Mined!* II. vii. 138 The introduction of.. the Oropesa Float made it possible for a *single* vessel to sweep a wide area in a reasonably short time.

oro-pharyngeal (ɔərəʊfəˈrɪndʒiːəl), *a.* [f. next: see PHARYNGEAL.] Of or pertaining to the oropharynx.

1885 *N.Y. Med. Jrnl.* XLII. 376/1, I experimented with regard to the isolation of the temperature sense in the nasal and oro-pharyngeal cavities. **1897** *Allbutt's Syst. Med.* IV. 742 The abscess is generally confined to the oro-pharyngeal region. *Ibid.* 775 Owing to the enlarged tonsils encroaching on the oro-pharyngeal space. **1967** *Nursing Times* 8 Sept. 1196/2 An oropharyngeal airway will help, but the proper position of the attendant's fingers is far more important.

oropharynx (ɔərəʊˈfærɪŋks). [irreg. f. L. *ōs, ōr-* mouth + PHARYNX.] That part of the throat immediately continuous with the mouth; the pharynx proper, as distinct from the nasopharynx.

1887 L. BROWNE *Throat & its Dis.* (ed. 2) iii. 53 (*heading*) Inspection of the mouth, fauces, and oro-pharynx. **1894** P. W. WILLIAMS *Dis. Upper Respiratory Tract* ii. 12 For clinical purposes the pharynx is divided into three regions, the naso-pharynx, the oro-pharynx and the laryngo-pharynx. **1935** R. S. STEVENSON *Rec. Adv. Laryngol. & Otol.* ii. 38 Norman Patterson is of opinion that at the present time a combination of diathermy and radiation is usually best in the treatment of malignant disease of the oro-pharynx. **1976** *Lancet* 4 Dec. 1248/1 There was diffuse ulceration in the oropharynx.

orosomucoid (əˈrəʊsəʊˈmjuːkɔɪd). *Biochem.* [f. Gr. ὀρός serum + -O + MUCOID *sb.*] A glycoprotein which forms the major component of seromucoid.

1955 R. J. WINZLER in *Methods Biochem. Analysis* II. 281 The major component in human seromucoid is an electrophoretically and ultracentrifugally distinct acidic glycoprotein which has been crystallized and quite well characterized by chemical, physical, and immunological methods... It is appropriate to assign to this protein the name orosomucoid.. to indicate its source and nature. **1965** *Biochim. & Biophys. Acta* CI. 336 The human and bovine orosomucoids had molecular weights of 41 600 and 37 300 respectively by the sedimentation diffusion method. **1972** *Res. Communications Chem. Path. & Pharmacol.* III. 663 Important increases in the level of orosomucoid accompany exudative inflammatory processes.

orotic (ɒˈrɒtɪk), *a.* *Chem.* [ad. It. *orotico* (Biscaro & Belloni 1905, in *Ann. della Soc. Chim. di Milano* XI. 18), f. Gr. ὀρό-ς serum, whey + It. *-otico* -OTIC.] ***orotic acid***, a colourless crystalline heterocyclic acid, $C_4HN_2(OH)_2COOH$, which is found in milk and is a growth factor for some micro-organisms.

1905 *Jrnl. Chem. Soc.* LXXXVIII. I. 672 The occurrence of small crystals of an organic compound in the mother liquor of lactose has led to the discovery of a new acid, orotic acid, which has been found to be a normal constituent of milk. **1944** *Nature* 26 Feb. 251/2 Four out of five of the strains of Group *C* streptococci of various types which were tested also needed uracil or orotic acid for optimal growth. **1965** T. L. V. ULBRICHT *Introd. Nucleic Acids* vi. 70 Studies with bacterial mutants showed that orotic acid.. was an effective precursor of both DNA and RNA pyrimidines.

Hence **oˈrotate** [-ATE¹ c], the anion, or an ester or salt, of orotic acid; **oˈrotidine** [-IDINE d], a nucleoside containing an orotic acid residue, the phosphate of which is a precursor of pyrimidine nucleotides.

1905 *Jrnl. Chem. Soc.* LXXXVIII. I. 672 Methyl orotate, .. a white, crystalline powder with a somewhat bitter taste, melts at 248–250° and dissolves in water or alcohol, forming faintly acid solutions. **1973** HENDERSON & PATERSON *Nucleotide Metabolism* xi. 182 Under certain circumstances, the carbamyl phosphate product from the liver enzyme may be diverted.. into the orotate pathway. **1951** A. M. MICHELSON et al. in *Proc. Nat. Acad. Sci.* XXXVII. 396 (*heading*) A new ribose nucleoside from Neurospora: 'orotidine'. **1963** A. M. MICHELSON *Chem. Nucleosides & Nucleotides* ii. 44 Periodate oxidation and enzymatic synthesis.. and conversion into uridine show that orotidine is 3-β-D-ribofuranosylorotic acid. **1973** J. R. BRONK *Chemical Biol.* xii. 465 The resulting orotidine 5′-phosphate is then decarboxylated to give.. uridine 5′-phosphate.

orotic aciduria (ɒˌrɒtɪk æsɪˈdjuːrɪə). *Path.* Also as one word. [f. *orotic acid* (see prec.) + -URIA.] A rare genetic disorder in which an enzyme deficiency impairs the metabolism of orotic acid, resulting in anæmia and excessive amounts of the acid in the blood and urine. Hence **oˌrotic aciˈduric** *a.*

1959 SMITH & BAKER in *Jrnl. Clin. Invest.* XXXVIII. 798/1 Only recently has a 'pyrimidine disease', orotic aciduria, been described. **1961** *Ibid.* XL. 662/2 No large survey has.. been undertaken to document the true incidence of the orotic aciduric defect. **1962** *Jrnl. Laboratory & Clin. Med.* LIX. 852 The family of an infant with congenital oroticaciduria excreted normal amounts of pseudouridine. **1972** F. NOUR-ELDIN *Haematol.* xxi. 218/2 Hereditary orotic aciduria is a rare disorder of the pyrimidine metabolism with megaloblastic anaemia, refractory to vitamin B_{12} but responding to uridine.

orotund (ˈɔərəʊtʌnd), *a.* (*sb.*) [f. L. phrase *ore rotundo* 'with round, well-turned speech' (*lit.* 'with round mouth') Horace *A.P.* 323, with contraction of *ore ro-* to *oro-*. This some have essayed to alter to *ororotund*, for *ore-* or *orirotund.*] Characterized by greater fullness, clearness, and strength than ordinary speech: applied to the voice or utterance proper to good public speaking, recitation, or reading; also contemptuously to an inflated or pompous style of eloquence: magniloquent.

1792–9 T. GOSSE *Autobiog.* (MS. penes E. Gosse), In the winter evenings (1792) my brother Harry's wife.. would read aloud therein in a manner both emphatic and orotund. **1827** RUSH *Philos. Hum. Voice* viii. (1833) 121 The Qualities of voice employed as the means of expression, are those of the Whispering, the Natural, the Falsette and the Orotund voices. **1840** *Penny Cycl.* XVI. 472/1 The name of orotund .. is given to that natural or improved manner of uttering the elements, which exhibits them with a fulness, clearness, strength, smoothness, and a ringing or musical quality rarely heard in ordinary speech. **1871** 'M. LEGRAND' *Camb. Freshm.* xxii. 365 Mr. Chutney would have.. ejaculated, in orotund voice, 'Alas!' **1881** FLOR. MARRYAT *Sister the Actress* I. xviii. 149 Dreaming.. of natural, falsetto and orotund voices. **1887** LOWELL *Old Eng. Dram.* (1892) 90. **1891** T. R. LOUNSBURY *Stud. Chaucer* III. vii. 196 In place of simple language we had a succession of orotund phrases.

b. *ellipt.* as *sb.* (*sc.* voice, utterance).

1827 RUSH *Philos. Hum. Voice* viii. (1833) 121 Few persons have by nature, a pure orotund. **1888** *Cassell's Fam. Mag.* Dec. 12/1 The deep-orotund is a very pleasing and effective acquisition, and may be cultivated with surprising success. **1889** J. M. ROBERTSON *Ess. Crit. Method* 245 Such an exclusive cultivation of the orotund as makes the bulk of his work a mere weariness of the flesh.

Hence **oroˈtundity** (also **oro-rotundity**); **ororotundoism** *nonce-wd.*

1831 CROKER *Boswell's Johnson* I. 196 *note*, The number of syllables, and oro-rotundity.. of the sound of a word, can never add much. **1840** G. RAYMOND in *New Monthly Mag.* LIX. 248, I.. exclaimed, in all the ororotundoism I could summon to my aid, 'Hear me' [etc.]. **1892** *Blackw. Mag.* Sept. 395 There is a pomposity, an ororotundity. **1909** *Cent. Dict.* Suppl., Orotundity. **1922** J. M. MURRY *Probl. Style* 20 Wordsworthians were there to discover the hallmark of genius on his most insignificant orotundities. **1936** 'M. INNES' *Death at President's Lodging* ix. 167 D.C. was absorbed in his narrative now: the self-consciousness, the orotundity were gone. **1960** *Spectator* 2 Sept. 347 Those thudding clichés, those meaningless orotundities. **1963** *Punch* 16 Jan. 105/3 An orotundity which isn't meant to be funny.

Oroya fever (ɒˌrɔɪə ˈfiːvə(r)). *Path.* [f. La *Oroya*, the name of a town in central Peru + FEVER *sb.*¹] An acute, frequently fatal, febrile and hæmolytic disease which occurs in Peru as the first stage of infection with the bacterium *Bartonella bacilliformis*, the second, chronic, stage being verruga peruana.

1873 T. J. HUTCHINSON *Two Yrs. in Peru* II. xx. 61 The 'Oroya fever', as it was called, from the simple circumstance of its having occurred on this line [*sc.* the Callao-Lima-Oroya railway line] (although more than a hundred miles distant from the terminus at the little town of Oroya), caused a dreadful mortality here during the years of 1870 and 1871. **1903** *Encycl. Medica* XIII. 326 Death ensues without any appearance of eruption, constituting the grave form or Oroya fever. **1949** M. A. JENNINGS in H. W. Florey et al. *Antibiotics* II. xxxi. 1033 *Bartonella bacilliformis*, the organism of Carrion's disease—known also in its acute stage as Oroya fever, and in its chronic stage as verruga peruana —is highly sensitive to penicillin. **1962** GORDON & LAVOIPIERRE *Entomol. for Students of Med.* xx. 138 In addition to being a severe biting nuisance, sandflies are responsible for the transmission to man of several forms of leishmaniasis, a sand-fly fever and Oroya fever or Carrion's disease. **1974** PASSMORE & ROBSON *Compan. Med. Stud.* III. I. xii. 86/2 In those who survive Oroya fever, after an interval.. the dermal lesions of verruga peruana develop.

oroyson, obs. form (in Caxton) of ORISON.

orp, *v.* *Sc.* [Origin obscure: cf. ON. *verpa* to throw, pa. pple. *orpin* thrown: cf. Sc. *thrawn* in sense 'cross-grained, perverse, ill-humoured'.] *intr.* To fret, to murmur discontentedly; 'to weep with a convulsive pant' (*Glossary to Ramsay*).

1725 RAMSAY *Gent. Sheph.* I. ii, Like dawted wean.. That for some feckless whim will orp and greet. **1836** M. MACKINTOSH *Cottager's Dau.* 191 They bood aye keep the neath-most in, To orp wi' grief.

Hence **ˈorping** *vbl. sb.*, fretting, murmuring; **ˈorpit** *ppl. a.*, fretful, discontented.

1599 JAS. I Βασιλ. Δῶρον (1603) 46 Feare not their orping or being discontented, as long as yee rull well. **1609** BP. W. BARLOW *Answ. Nameless Cath.* 116 Notwithstanding all the perswasions, orpings, threats, yea Treasonable assaults. **1614** BP. COWPER *Dikaiologie* 143 You seeme to be very earnest here, but all men may see it is but your Orpit or Ironic conceit. **1871** W. ALEXANDER *Johnny Gibb* xiv. (1873) 84 'Benjie was an orpiet, peeakin, little sinner'.

†**ˈorped**, *a.* *Obs.* Also 6 *Sc.* orpit. [OE., of obscure origin.] Stout, strenuous, valiant, bold.

10.. in *Anglia* VIII. 324 Swa ʒedafenaþ esnum ðam orpedan, ðonne he god weorc ongynþ, ðæt he ðæt ʒeornlice beswynce. *Ibid.* 325 La orpeda cleric ʒif ðu wylle witan ða terminos ðe we ymbe spræcon, wite hwylc ʒer hyt sy ðæs monan ðæt man hæt *lunaris.* **13..** *Guy Warw.* (A.) 6062 Wiþ hem fif hundred kniȝtes, Orped men & gode in fiȝtes. **1340** *Ayenb.* 183 Aze þe guode kniȝt and orped þet heþ guod herte and hardi. **1390** GOWER *Conf.* I. 129 Som orped knyht to sle this lord. *c* **1440** *Promp. Parv.* 371/1 Orpud,.. *audax, bellipotens.* **1480** CAXTON *Chron. Eng.* VII. (1520) 103 b/2 As thou hast ben orped in thy dedes he dyde to the moche honoure. **1587** FLEMING *Contn. Holinshed* III. 1339/2 See you this orped giant here, so huge of limme and bone?

b. Of a beast: Fierce, furious.

1567 GOLDING *Ovid's Met.* VIII. (1593) 194 Yet should this hand.. confound this orped swine. **1594** CONSTABLE *Venus & Adonis* vii, For an orped swine Smit him in the groyne.

Hence †**ˈorpedly** *adv.*, stoutly, bravely; †**ˈorpedness**, †**ˈorpedship**, valour, bravery.

c **1330** *Arth. & Merl.* 1729 *Orpedlich thou the bi-stere And the lond thou fond to were. **1387** TREVISA *Higden* (Rolls) V. 231 Þe emperour dede noþing orpedliche [L. *strenue*]. *c* **1400** *Chron. Eng.* lxxiii. in Herrig *Archiv* LII. 14 They defendede hem welle and orpydly ayens hem. **1398** TREVISA *Barth. De P.R.* IX. xxxii. (MS. Bodl.) lf. 99 b/2 Aboute pentecoste is tyme of cheualry and of *orpudnesse. **13..** *K. Alis.* 1413 His folk ful of *orpedschype, Quicliche leputh to hepe.

orpement, orpent, obs. ff. ORPIMENT, ORPINE.

orphaline, variant of ORPHELIN *Obs.*

orphan (ˈɔːfən), *sb.* and *a.* Also 5–7 **-ane**, 6–7 **-ant**. [ad. late L. *orphan-us* (Vulg.), a. Gr. ὀρφανός without parents, bereaved; cf. OF. *orfene* (13th c.), It. *orfano*. See also ORPHENIN, ORPHELIN.]

A. *sb.* **1.** One deprived by death of father or mother, or (more generally) of both parents; a fatherless or motherless child.

Orphan's Court, a probate court in some states of the United States, having jurisdiction over the estates and persons of orphans.

[**13..** *K. Alis.* 4948 Another folk woneth there biside; Orphani hy hatteth wide.] **1484** CAXTON *Chivalry* 31 Thoffyce of a knyght is to mayntene and deffende wymmen widowes and orphans. **1547–64** BAULDWIN *Mor. Philos.* (Palfr.) 126 Innocent persons, orphants, widdowes, & poore men. **1603** DRAYTON *Heroic. Ep.* iv. 95 Mak'st me an Orphan ere my Father die. **1632** HEYWOOD *2nd Pt. Iron Age* v. Wks. 1874 III. 429 Sweet Orphant do; thy fathers dead already. **1715–20** POPE *Iliad* XXII. 629 The day, that to the shades the father sends, Robs the sad orphan of his father's friends. **1848** WHARTON *Law Lex.* s.v. *Orphan*, In London the Lord Mayor and Aldermen have the custody of the orphans of deceased freemen, and also the keeping of their lands and goods. **1849** STEPHENS *Bk. of Farm* (ed. 2) I. 596/2 When a lamb is left an orphan.. [it is necessary] to mother it.. upon another ewe.

2. a. *fig.* One bereft of protection, advantages, benefits, or happiness, previously enjoyed.

1483 CAXTON *Gold. Leg.* 242 b/2 Thenne he assembled twelue freres of the Couent of Bouloyne and to thende that he wold not leue them and disheryted and orphanes he made his testament. **1844** MRS. BROWNING *Cry of Childr.* xii, They.. Are orphans of the earthly love and heavenly.

b. *slang.* A discontinued model of a motor vehicle.

1942 BERREY & VAN DEN BARK *Amer. Thes. Slang* §81/7 *Orphan*, a discontinued make. **1948** MENCKEN *Amer. Lang.* Suppl. II. 724 *Orphan, or off-breed*, an obsolete model. **1967** W. & M. MORRIS *Dict. Word & Phr. Origins* II. 280 *Load, orphan, pig*,.. and *iron* all designate poor cars.

3. *attrib.* and *Comb.*, as ***orphan-like*** adj.; **orphan asylum, -hospital, -house**, an orphanage.

a **1649** DRUMM. OF HAWTH. *Poems* Wks. (1711) 15 When .. bravest minds live orphan-like forlorn. **1711** C. MATHER *Diary* 25 Mar. in *Harv. Stud.* (1897) V. 58 A present of Gold for his orphan-house. **1769** *Chron.* in *Ann. Reg.* 65/2 The children of the orphan-hospital.. were ranged in two lines. **1792** S. ROGERS *Pleas. Mem.* 40 Orphan-sorrows drew the ready tear. **1811** *Freemason's Mag.* (Philadelphia) Nov. 97 The other proclaims its benevolent character in its name, 'The Orphan Asylum Society'. **1832** G. DOWNES *Lett. Cont. Countries* I. 159 The Preachers' Church, and that of the Orphan-house. **1833** J. B. PURCELL in *Catholic Hist. Rev.* (Washington) (1919) V. 241 There was a benefit at the L. [Louisville] Theatre for the Orphan-Asylum, at this time.

1857 MAYNE *Expos. Lex.* 831/2 An orphan-hospital, or institution for bringing up orphaned children in. **1878** GEO. ELIOT *Coll. Br. P.* 294 Love forsaken sends out orphan cries. **1921** E. O'NEILL *Diff'rent* II, in *Emperor Jones* 281 He'll go and leave all he's got to some lousey orphan asylum. **1964** D. OWEN *Eng. Philanthropy* (1965) II. v. 159 This London Orphan Asylum at Clapton, opened in 1825... Again..a movement was launched which, by the early 1840's, had established the Infant Orphan Asylum at Wanstead. **1978** E. HEALEY *Lady Unknown* ii. 60 Faraday's earliest letters to her..were..mostly requests for proxy votes for his protégés at the Orphan Asylum of which they were both patrons.

B. *adj.* **1. a.** Bereaved of parents; fatherless or motherless, or both; *fig.* bereft of protection analogous to that of a parent.

1483 CAXTON *Gold. Leg.* 409b/2 Whan Machomete was orphane of fader & moder he was under the gouernaunce of his uncle. *c* **1586** C'TESS PEMBROKE *Ps.* LXVIII. ii, Prepare his path, who..Doth sitt a father to the orphan sonne. **1589** WARNER *Alb. Eng.* VI. xxxii. (1612) 161 Queene mother and her kindred hild the Orphant King a while. **1755** SMOLLETT *Quix.* II. III. xvi. (1784) IV. 83 And I beg your worship will consider the orphan state of my daughter. **1814** SCOTT *Ld. of Isles* IV. xvii, Thou art a patron all too wild And thoughtless, for this orphan child. **1847** GROTE *Greece* II. x. III. 87 An orphan girl might be claimed in marriage of right by any member of the gens.

fig. **1660** N. INGELO *Bentivolio & Urania* II. (1682) 65 [God] doth not abandon the Orphan World to..blind Chance. **1883** SCHAFF *Hist. Church* II. vii. §42. 425 It was probably the martyrdom of Peter and Paul that induced John to take charge of the orphan churches.

b. ***Orphan Annie***: see *little Orphan(t) Annie* (LITTLE *a.* 13).

2. *Path.* **orphan virus**, any virus that is not known to be the cause of a disease.

1954 J. L. MELNICK in *Amer. Jrnl. Publ. Health* XLIV. 572/1 The remainder of this report is concerned with...3. The detection of new viruses, provisionally called 'orphan viruses' (as we know so little to what diseases they belong) from patients suspected of having nonparalytic poliomyelitis. **1955** [see ECHO VIRUS]. **1961** P. L. CARPENTER *Microbiol.* ix. 110 A considerable number of viruses recently isolated from the feces of healthy as well as ill individuals are not known to produce disease... These viruses..are called orphan viruses, and those isolated from humans are known as ECHO viruses.

orphan ('ɔːfən), *v.* [f. prec. sb.] *trans.* To make an orphan of; to bereave of parent or parents.

1814 SOUTHEY *Roderick* III. 290 One hour hath orphaned me and widowed me. **1832-4** DE QUINCEY *Cæsars* i. Wks. 1860 X. 34 It is, or it is not, according to the nature of men, an advantage to be orphaned at an early age. **1876** EADIE *Thessalonians* (1877) 92 This orphaning separation had been for 'the season of an hour'.

orphanage ('ɔːfənɪdʒ). [f. prec. sb. + -AGE.]

1. The state or condition of being an orphan.

1579-80 NORTH *Plutarch* (1676) 185 Orphanage bringeth many discommodities to a Child. *a* **1631** DONNE *Lett.* (1651) 108 There can fall no..Orphanage upon those Children, to whom God is Father. **1748** RICHARDSON *Clarissa* (1811) VII. 321 A desolate creature she suffered under the worst of orphanage. **1876** LOWELL *Among my Bks.* Ser. II. 207 His early orphanage was not without its effect in confirming a character naturally impatient of control.

b. Orphans collectively.

1845 W. H. MAXWELL *Hints Soldier on Service* I. 34 He will talk of widowed wives and unprotected orphanage.

†**2.** The guardianship formerly exercised by the Lord Mayor and Aldermen of London over the persons and property of orphan children within the City under 21 years of age. *Obs.*

1538 in Strype *Eccl. Mem.* (1721) I. II. App. xc. 252 Al and syngler the porcyons..to be ordered according to the custome of the orphanage of the citie of London. *a* **1734** NORTH *Lives* (1826) II. 19 The common serjeant in London, an office of considerable account, especially in the orphanage.

3. An institution or home for orphans.

1865 *Even. Standard* 7 Feb., There is..an orphanage, in which there are at present 40 children being educated at a low charge. **1871** *Daily News* 16 Dec., The Chinese Government demands the suppression of the foreign orphanages.

4. *attrib.* (chiefly in sense 2).

1641 *Termes de la Ley* 88 b, His successor may in his owne name have execution of a Recognisance acknowledged to his predecessor for Orphanage money. **1767** BLACKSTONE *Comm.* II. xxxii. 519 In London the share of the children (or orphanage part) is not fully vested in them till the age of twenty-one, before which they cannot dispose of it by testament:..but after the age of twenty-one it is free from any orphanage custom. **1818** CRUISE *Digest* (ed. 2) VI. 423 In that part of the will relating to the orphanage share.

orphancy ('ɔːfənsɪ). [f. ORPHAN *sb.* + -CY.] The condition of being an orphan; orphanhood.

a **1586** SIDNEY *Arcadia* III. (1590) K k iij, Yet did not thy orphancie, or my widowhood, depriue vs of the delightfull prospect. **1592** WARNER *Alb. Eng.* VII. xxxiv. (1612) 164 Nor can Æneas Offsprings now of Orphansie complaine. **1839** LANDOR *Andrea of Hungary* I. iv. 115 The worst Of orphancy, the cruellest of frauds. **1866** J. B. ROSE tr. *Ovid's Fasti* III. 225 Shall we Elect for widowhood or orphancy?

'orphandom. *rare.* [See -DOM.] = prec.

1892 *Leisure Hour* Jan. 195/1 To softly cradled childhood ..had succeeded orphandom.

orphaned ('ɔːfənd), *a.* [f. ORPHAN *sb.* or *v.* + -ED.]

1. a. Made or left an orphan; bereaved.

1631 *Celestina* xx. 195, I, even this very day, have left many servants orphaned, and quite destitute of a master. **1757** MRS. GRIFFITH *Lett. Henry & Frances* (1767) II. 134 He is orphan'd both of father and mother. **1827** PRAED *Arminius* vii, The sobs of orphaned infancy. **1874** DIXON *Two Queens* III. 64 To save the orphaned girl from trouble.

b. *fig.* Bereaved, destitute and unprotected.

a **1649** DRUMM. OF HAWTH. *Poems* Wks. (1711) 46 Religion orphan'd waileth o're thy urn. **1827** KEBLE *Chr. Y.* 3rd Sund. Lent, The orphan'd realm threw wide her gates. **1898** W. K. JOHNSON *Terra Tenebr.* 148 Ye shall not long live orphaned of the light!

2. *transf.* Of or pertaining to an orphan.

1799 SHERIDAN *Pizarro* II. iv, To dry the widowed and the orphaned tear of those Whose brave protectors have perished in their country's cause. **1882** *Mrs. Raven's Temptation* III. 43 Could he presume on Alice's orphaned loneliness.

3. *slang.* Of a motor vehicle: discontinued as a model. Cf. ORPHAN *sb.* 2 b.

1920 F. B. SCHOLL *Automobile Owner's Guide* 3 Orphaned cars may run as well..as anybody could ask for, but when a company fails or discontinues to manufacture a model, the car immediately loses from one-third to one-half of its natural value.

†**'orphaner.** *Obs.* An unexplained by-form of ORPHAN *sb.*

c **1461** tr. *Oath Recorder Lond.* in *Lett.-Bk. D.* lf. 7 *Calr.* (1902) 34 Ye schall attende to save (and mayntene) the Right of the Orphaners aftir þe lawes and usagis of the Cite [Cf. *a* **1399** *Sacram. Record* in *Lib. Albus* lf. 208 b (Rolls) I. 309 Et qe tendre serrez dez drotures dez orphanyns sauvere et meintener, solonc lez leyes et usagez de la citee.]

†**'orphanet.** *Obs.* [-ET[1].] A little orphan.

1591 DRAYTON *Harmony Ch., Finding of Moses*, Calling her maids this orphanet to see.

orphanhood ('ɔːfənhʊd). [f. ORPHAN *sb.* + -HOOD.] The condition or position of an orphan.

1824 DAVISON *Disc. Prophecy* vi. (1861) 219 The captivity, devastation, and public orphanhood of the Jewish Church was a far more perplexing phenomenon. **1856** LEVER *Martins of Cro' M.* 5 The girl, over whom the dark shadow of orphanhood passed as she spoke. **1869** *Pall Mall G.* 11 Oct. 2 It provides for sickness, age, widowhood, orphanhood.

†**'orphanism.** *Obs. rare.* [See -ISM.] The condition of being an orphan; orphanhood.

1598 FLORIO, *Orfanita*, Orphanisme. **1611** COTGR., *Orbité*, Orphanisme. **1790** ANNA SEWARD *Lett.* (1811) II. 345 It is an anxious and alarmed life,..better, however,.. than that of lonely orphanism. **1834** *Tait's Mag.* I. 43 To feign convulsions, starvation, orphanism, widowhood.

†**or'phanity.** *Obs.* [a. OF. *orphanité, orfanité*, earlier *orfenté*:—late L. *orphanitās* (6th c. in Quicherat *Addenda*), f. *orphan-us* ORPHAN: see -ITY.] The condition of an orphan, orphanhood.

c **1430** *Pilgr. Lyf Manhode* III. lii. (1869) 163, I haue brouht thee the burdoun ayen, to deliuere thee from orphanitee. **1480** CAXTON *Ovid's Met.* XIII. ix, Now I am fallen in orphanyte of parents & of my lorde. *c* **1500** *Melusine* 147 The land were in grete orphanite of bothe lord & of lady.

orphanize ('ɔːfənaɪz), *v.* [f. ORPHAN *sb.* + -IZE.] *trans.* To make (any one) an orphan.

1797 ANNA SEWARD *Lett.* (1811) V. 17 Women and children, widowed and orphanized, alas! by the obstinacy of Dutch resistance. **1851** LIVINGSTONE *Let.* in *Life* vi. (1885) 97 To orphanize my children, will be like tearing out my bowels. **1879** P. LORIMER tr. *Lechler's Wiclif* I. 43 The parish was spiritually orphanised.

†**orpha'notrophism.** *Obs. rare*[−1]. [f. Gr. ὀρφανοτρόφ-ος bringing up orphans (-τρόφος feeding) + -ISM.] The support and rearing of orphans. So †**orpha'notrophy** [ad. L. *orphanotrophīum*, a. Gr. ὀρφανοτροφεῖον], a hospital or asylum for orphans.

1711 C. MATHER *(title)* Orphanotrophism; or, Orphans well provided for. **1727** BAILEY vol. II, *Orphanotrophy.* **1730-6** —— (folio). Hence in JOHNSON, etc. **17..** *(title)* A Memorial concerning the Erecting an Orphanotrophy or Hospital for the Reception of Poor Cast-off Children or Foundlings.

'orphanry. *rare.* [f. ORPHAN *sb.* + -RY.] A home for orphans, an orphanage.

1882 in OGILVIE (Annandale).

'orphanship. *rare.* [See -SHIP.] The position or fact of being an orphan; orphanhood.

1832 *Fraser's Mag.* V. 524 [Parents] of such habits and temper as would have rendered orphanship a blessing.

orphant, obs. corrupt form of ORPHAN.

†**orphany**[1] ('ɔːfənɪ). *Obs. rare.* [f. ORPHAN + -Y.] The condition of an orphan, orphanhood.

1539 CRANMER *Let. to Crumwell* in *Misc. Writ.* (Parker Soc.) II. 389 My heart is much moved with pity towards the young lord of Bargavenny..by cause he is within orphany.

†**orphany**[2], app. an error for *orphery*, ORPHREY.

1501 DOUGLAS *Pal. Hon.* I. 543 In vestures quent of mony sindrie gyse,..Satine figures champit with flouris and bewis, Damisflure, tere, pyle quhairon thair lyis Peirle, Orphany quhilk euerie stait renewis.

orphanyne, orpharas, orphare: see ORPHENIN, ORPHREY.

orpharion (ɔːfə'raɪən). Also 6 **orpheryon**, 7 **Orph-Arion, orpharyon, -erion, -erian, -irian, orfarian**, (9 **orph(e)oreon**). [Composed of the names of Orpheus and Arion, mythical musicians of antiquity. Cf.

1601 B. JONSON *Poetaster* IV. ii, Another Orpheus! an Arion riding on the back of a dolphin.]

A large instrument of the lute kind with from six to nine pairs of metal strings played with a plectrum: much used in the 17th century.

Said to have been invented *c* 1560 by John Rose, citizen of London, living in Bridewell. See Grove *Dict. Mus.* II. 612.

1593 DRAYTON *Eclogues* iii. 111 Set the Cornet with the Flute, The Orpharion to the Lute. **1601** P. ROSSETER *(title)* A Booke of Ayres, set foorth to be song to the Lute, Orpherian and Base Violl. *c* **1620** W. LAUSON in J. D[ennys] *Secr. Angling* (ed. 2) 153 Wind them on two or three of your fingers, like an Orph-Arion's string. **1626** BACON *Sylva* §146 It maketh a more Resounding Sound than a Bandora, Orpharion or Cittern, which have likewise Wire-strings. **1655** tr. *Com. Hist. Francion* v. 20 To one he Petitioned for a Violl, to another for a Lute, to this Man for an Orfarian. **1825** DANNELEY *Encycl. Mus., Orpheoreon or Orphoreon.* [**1878** *Grove's Dict. Mus.* II. 612 A larger orpheoreon was called Penorcon, and a still larger one Pandore: Prætorius spells this Pandorra or Bandoer.]

Orphean (ɔː'fiːən), *a.* and *sb.* Also 7 **Orphæan.** [f. L. *Orphē-us*, (a. Gr. Ὀρφεῖος, f. Ὀρφεύς Orpheus, the famous mythical musician and singer of Thrace, in later times accounted a philosopher and adept in secret knowledge, whence the Orphic mysteries and Orphic doctrines) + -AN.]

A. *adj.* **1.** Of or relating to Orpheus, as musician and singer, who was said to move rocks and trees by the strains of his lyre; hence, melodious, musical, entrancing, like his music.

1593 *Tell-Troth's N. Y. Gift* (1876) 45 Charme more then the Orphean musicke. **1660** HICKERINGILL *Jamaica* (1661) 99 His soul engross'd th' Monopoly of Arts, And thy Orphæan skill could ravish Hearts. **1667** MILTON *P.L.* III. 17 With other notes then to th' Orphean Lyre I sung of Chaos and Eternal Night. **1870** LOWELL *Among my Bks.* Ser. I. (1873) 157 Refractory feet, that will dance to Orphean measures.

2. = ORPHIC *a.* 1.

1657-83 EVELYN *Hist. Relig.* (1850) I. 330 The most zealous abettors of the Orphean and Gentile philology, Porphyry, Hierocles, Celsus, and the rest.

B. *sb.* An adherent of the Orphic philosophy.

1818 R. P. KNIGHT *Symbolic Lang.* (1876) 5 *note*, The Orpheans endeavored to express divine things by Symbols. **1827** G. HIGGINS *Celtic Druids* 33 Mr. Davies is of opinion that the Orpheans were Druids.

So **'Orpheist** = ORPHEAN *sb.*

1678 CUDWORTH *Intell. Syst.* I. iv. §20. 374 The reason of this difference betwixt the Orpheists and Plato..proceeded only from an equivocation in the word Love.

†**orphelin** ('ɔːfəlɪn), *a.* and *sb. Obs.* Forms: 4-6 **orphelyn**, 6 **-line, -len, -ling, orphiline**, 7 **orphaline, orphling.** [a. OF. *orphelin, orfelin* (13th c. in Littré), arising by dissimilation from OF. *orphenin*: see ORPHENIN.]

A. *adj.* Orphaned; bereaved.

c **1374** CHAUCER *Boeth.* II. pr. iii. 25 (Camb. MS.) Wan thow weere orphelyn of fadyr and modyr. **1512** *Helyas* in Thoms *Prose Rom.* (1828) III. 105 Shall I abide orpheline in my yonge dais.

B. *sb.* An orphan.

a **1450** *Knt. de la Tour* (1868) 112 For to norisshe orphelyns and for to endoctrine hem in vertu and science. **1483** CAXTON *Gold. Leg.* 260b/1 Leue us not orphelyns. *a* **1533** LD. BERNERS *Huon* lx. 210 He distroyeth the burgesses and marchauntes, wedous and orphelyns. *a* **1572** KNOX *Hist. Ref.* (1732) 109 The Blind, Crooked, Bedralis, Widowis, Orphelingis, and all uther Pure. **1630** J. LEVETT *Ord. Bees* Ded., Of your..love to the deceased Author, or your charity to this posthume Orphling. **1652** J. WRIGHT tr. *Camus' Nat. Paradox* III. 51 To preserve it for the Orphaline.

orphenadrine (ɔː'fɛnədriːn). *Pharm.* [f. OR(THO- + *-phenadrine* (contraction of DI)PHENHYDRAMINE).] A bitter-tasting ortho-methyl derivative of diphenhydramine used (as its white crystalline citrate or hydrochloride) as an antispasmodic, esp. in the treatment of Parkinsonism; $(CH_3C_6H_4)CH(C_6H_5){\cdot}O{\cdot}CH_2CH_2N(CH_3)_2$.

1957 *Jrnl. Amer. Med. Assoc.* 13 Apr. 1352/1 The new drug, orphenadrine (Disipal) hydrochloride..has proved exceptionally beneficial in the control of..symptoms of Parkinsonism, without increasing tremor. **1963** *Practitioner* Nov. 646 Two cases are recorded in which the distressing symptoms of persistent hiccup were relieved by orphenadrine citrate. **1977** *Lancet* 16 Apr. 858/2 He was put on orphenadrine but because of progressive extra-pyramidal disability levodapa with benserazide ('Mado-par') was prescribed.

†**orphenin**, *sb.* and *a. Obs.* Also **-anin, -yne.** [a. OF. *orphenin, -anin* (12th c.), deriv. of L. *orphan-us* ORPHAN, subseq. *orphelin*: see ORPHELIN *a.* and *sb.*]

A. *sb.* = ORPHAN A. 1.

c **1375** *Sc. Leg. Saints* xxxi. (*Eugenia*) 446 Namly it þat mycht ryne til wydow or til orphanyne. *c* **1430** *Pilgr. Lyf Manhode* I. lxi. (1869) 37, I am norishe of orphanynes, osteleer to pilgrimes. *c* **1500** *Melusine* 187 They oughte to helpe and susteyne the wydowes an orphenyns.

B. *adj.* Bereaved (in quot. of children).

1480 CAXTON *Ovid's Met.* XIII. xii, I am put to this Exille, that of one sone & foure doughters, I am orphenyn.

orpheonist ('ɔːfiːənɪst). [a. F. *orphéoniste*, f. *Orphéon*, name of a school of vocal music established at Paris in 1833, and named from Orpheus.] A member of an *Orphéon*; a choral singer.

1860 GEN. P. THOMPSON *Audi Alt.* III. cxxiii. 72 Ask the Orpheonistes how near this is to the truth. **1888** *Times* 21 Sept. 3/2, 2000 Orpheonists will attend and sing one of the composer's choruses.

attrib. **1882** *Athenæum* 8 Apr. 455/2 A grand festival and competition of orpheonist societies and military bands. **1884** *Ibid.* 9 Aug. 187/3 The fourth general meeting of the Orpheonist societies at Paris is postponed.

orpheoreon, orpherian, -on: see ORPHARION.

Orpheotelest (ɔːfiː'ɒtɪlɛst). *Corruptly* orphetulist, orpheotellist. [ad. Gr. Ὀρφεοτελεστής.] An initiator into Orphic mysteries; a professor of Orphic magic.

a **1610** HEALEY *Theophrastus* (1636) 61 To the end he may be initiated in holy Orders, he goes often unto the Orphetulists. **1839** *Fraser's Mag.* XX. 31 He [Orpheus] is represented.. as the founder of a school of magic, whose students were termed 'Orpheotellists'.

orpheray, -ry, obs. forms of ORPHREY.

Orphic ('ɔːfɪk), *a.* (*sb.*) [ad. Gr. Ὀρφικ-ός (in L. *Orphic-us*), f. Ὀρφεύς Orpheus: see -IC.]

A. *adj.* **1. a.** Of, belonging or attributed to, or connected with Orpheus, the mysteries associated with his name, or the writings or doctrines subsequently attributed to him (see ORPHEAN); hence, oracular.

1678 CUDWORTH *Intell. Syst.* I. iv. §14. 250 According to the Orphick Tradition, this Love which the Cosmogonia was derived from, was no other than the Eternal Vnmade Deity. **1701** NORRIS *Ideal World* I. iii. 177 That Orphic sentence mentioned by Ficinus, Ζεὺς εἶδος πάντων, Jupiter is the form, species, or idea, of all things. **1813** SHELLEY in Dowden *Life* (1887) I. 396, I intend.. to reason in my preface concerning the Orphic and Pythagoric system of diet. **1816** D. STEWART *Dissert. Progr. Philos.* II. iii. (1858) 304 *note*, The old Orphic verses, quoted in the treatise Περὶ κόσμου, ascribed to Aristotle. **1852** HAWTHORNE *Blithedale Rom.* xvi. (1883) 483 'No summer ever came back, and no two summers ever were alike', said I, with a degree of Orphic wisdom that astonished me. **1880** *Athenæum* 20 Nov. 680/3 They are founded on the mystic Orphic doctrine, and seem to be part of the sacred book of the initiated in those mysteries. **1880** F. W. H. MYERS *Stanzas on Shelley* in *Macm. Mag.* No. 245. 392 Yet, with an Orphic whisper blent, A Spirit in the west-wind sighs.

b. ***Orphic egg***, a term applied to the earth or world, as being held to be egg-shaped.

1684 T. BURNET *Th. Earth* I. 280 The opinion of the oval figure of the earth is ascrib'd to Orpheus and his disciples; and the doctrine of the mundane egg is so peculiarly his, that 'tis call'd by Proclus the Orphick egg. **1696** WHISTON *Th. Earth* III. (1722) 233 Nothing was more celebrated than the Original.. Orphick Egg, in the most early Authors. **1789** MRS. PIOZZI *Journ. France*, etc. I. 228 The mundane, or as Proclus calls it, the orphick egg, is possibly the earliest of all methods taken to explain the rise, progress, and final conclusion of our earth and atmosphere.

2. Of the nature of the music of Orpheus, or the verses attributed to him; melodious, entrancing, ravishing.

1817 COLERIDGE *Sibyl. Leaves* (1862) 204 An orphic song indeed, A song divine of high and passionate thoughts, To their own music chaunted! **1820** HAZLITT *Lect. Dram. Lit.* 18 To pass over the Orphic hymns of David. **1821** SHELLEY *Prometh. Unb.* IV. i. 421 Language is a perpetual orphic song. **1853** KINGSLEY *Hypatia* xxv, Homer and Hesiod, and those old Orphic singers, were of another mind.

3. Of, pertaining to, or characteristic of Orphism (ORPHISM 2).

[**1913** G. APOLLINAIRE *Méditations Esthétiques* vii. 25 *Le cubisme orphique* est l'autre grande tendance de la peinture moderne. C'est l'art de peindre des ensembles nouveaux avec des éléments empruntés non à la réalité visuelle, mais entièrement créés par l'artiste. **1914** A. J. EDDY *Cubists & Post-Impressionism* (1915) v. 69 *Cubism Orphique* is created entirely by the artist; it takes nothing from visual, objective realities, but is derived wholly from the painter's imagination; it is pure art.] **1950** D. COOPER tr. *Raynal's Hist. Mod. Painting* III. 52 Apollinaire used to distinguish between 'scientific Cubism', 'physical Cubism', 'instinctive Cubism' and 'Orphic Cubism'. **1959** *Listener* 19 Nov. 869/1 He [*sc.* Apollinaire] distinguished two kinds of pure Cubism —scientific and Orphic... Orphic Cubism.. dealt with the universe of mind and imagination, the inner world. **1974** *Encycl. Brit. Micropædia* VII. 594/3 Apollinaire's use of the word 'Orphic' recalls both the Symbolist painters' use of the term 'Orphic Art'.. and the poetry of Orpheus.

B. *sb.* **1.** An Orphic song or hymn: chiefly in *pl.*

1855 KINGSLEY *Heroes, Argon.* IV. 108 They call them the Songs of Orpheus, or the Orphics, to this day.

2. A member of the Orphic school of philosophy.

1897 *Edin. Rev.* Apr. 461 These tablets were buried with the deceased Orphic. **1899** R. H. CHARLES *Eschatol.* iii. 149 This doctrine first appears among the Orphics.

So **'Orphical** *a.* = ORPHIC; **'Orphically** *adv.*, after the manner of the Orphic writings, doctrines, mysteries, etc.; **'Orphicism** = ORPHISM.

1678 CUDWORTH *Intell. Syst.* I. iv. §17. 294 Aristotle seems to have meant no more than this, that there was no such Poet as Orpheus Senior to Homer, or that the Verses vulgarly called *Orphical, were not written by Orpheus. *Ibid.* 300 We cannot believe all that to be genuine which is produced by ancient Fathers as Orphical. *Ibid.* 307 The whole Produced or Created Universe, with all its Variety of things in it; which yet are *Orphically said to be God also, in a certain other sence. **1816** I. TAYLOR in *Pamphleteer* VIII. 477 Hence Socrates calls the multitude Orphically Thyrsus-bearers. *a* **1849** POE *W. E. Channing* Wks. 1864 III. 239 More profound than the *Orphicism of Alcott.

†or'phion. *Obs.* [ad. Gr. Ὀρφεῖον, neuter of Ὀρφεῖος ORPHEAN.] A musical instrumen invented by Thomas Pilkington, who died in 1660.

1660 COKAINE *Elegy T. Pilkington* 6 Mastring all Musick that was known before; He did invent the Orphion, and gave more.

Orphism ('ɔːfɪz(ə)m). [f. ORPH-IC + -ISM.]

1. The system of mystic philosophy embodied in the Orphic poems, and taught to the initiated in the Orphic mysteries.

1880 *Ch. Q. Rev.* 244 The whole system of what M. Girard designates under the name of Orphism, which.. inculcated the strict necessity on the part of man to shake off the low elements of his nature. **1884** W. M. RAMSAY in *Encycl. Brit.* XVII. 128/2 The spirit of Orphism was that of the Oriental Phrygian cultus.

2. A movement within Cubism, identified by Guillaume Apollinaire (1880–1918) and pioneered by a group of French painters calling themselves *Le Section d'Or*, which emphasized the lyrical use of colour in pure abstract designs.

1914 A. J. EDDY *Cubists & Post-Impressionism* (1915) xiv. 207 Superficial Impressionism leads naturally to the painting of pure color effect—*color music, orphism, compositional* painting. **1915** *Forum* (N.Y.) Dec. 663, I have always held that Orphism and Simultaneism are merely extended Impressionism. **1959** H. READ *Conc. Hist. Mod. Painting* III. 91 Robert Delaunay.. was responsible for another deviation from orthodox Cubism... This deviation Apollinaire christened Orphism. **1959** BROWN & SLATER tr. *Pasternak's Safe Conduct* xi. 259 In its symbolism, that is to say, in everything in the imagery verging on orphism,.. the romantic view of life is devastatingly vivid and it is incontrovertible. **1971** J. WILLETT in A. Bullock *20th Cent.* x. 235/1 Expressionism.. was an all-absorbent force which sucked up every other new tendency since Fauvism (Cubism, Futurism and Delaunay's near-abstract Orphism). **1976** *Telegraph* (Brisbane) 20 Oct. 2/3 Apart from orphism, futurism and several other arty isms, the doc is an expert on early Australian painters.

Hence **Orphist** (less commonly **Orphiste**) *sb.* and *a.*

1914 A. J. EDDY *Cubists & Post-Impressionism* (1915) v. 60 Today we have the 'Neo-Impressionists', .. the 'Futurists', the 'Orphists', [etc.]. *Ibid.* 64 A form of dramatic representation that is essentially Cubist, Futurist, and Orphist in its expression. **1915** *Blast* July 41 Less interesting.. is the Orphiste movement. Delaunay is the most conspicuous Orphiste. **1959** J. GOLDING *Cubism* i. 39 Léger,.. whose art was now becoming more obviously divergent, is also sometimes referred to as an Orphist. **1959** *Listener* 13 Aug. 253/2 After 1911.. he [*sc.* Chagall] begins to place his figures among arbitrary arcs of colour which are like caricatures of *Orphist* forms. **1970** C. BARRETT *Op Art* i. 9/2 Delaunay.. and.. other Orphists were familiar with Chevreut's theory of simultaneous contrast.

'orphizing, *ppl. a.* [From an implied vb. **orphize* to practise Orphism: see -IZE.] Practising or following the Orphic doctrines and worship.

1884 W. M. RAMSAY in *Encycl. Brit.* XVII. 128/2 The Orphizing mystic cultus of Phyla.

orphling, variant of ORPHELIN *Obs.*

orphrey, orfray ('ɔːfreɪ, -frɪ). Forms: α. 4–5 orfreis, -eys, -ais, -ays, 4–6 orfraies, -ayes, -eyes, 5 orpharas, -is, 6 orefrayes, orferaus, orfris, -ys, (orpheis, orphis, offreis). β. 5 oferay, orpheray, orpharé, orffrey, 5–6 (9) orfrey, 6 orphery, (orfer), 9 orfray, orphrey. [ME. *orfreis*, a. OF. *orfreis* = Pr. *aurfres*, OSp. *aurofres* :—*aurifrisium* (med.L. *aurifrisum*, *aurifrisia*, *aurifresus*, *aurifrixium*, *aurifrigium*, *-ia*) for L. *auriphrygium* gold embroidery, f. *aurum* gold + *Phrygius* Phrygian: cf. *Phrygiæ vestēs* Phrygian (gold-embroidered) garments. The final *-s*, belonging etymologically to the singular, is now treated as the plural suffix; so mod.F. *orfroi*, formerly *orfrois*. The Eng. historical spelling is *orfrey* or *orfray*; *orphrey* combines Fr. *or* with the *ph* of L. *phrygium*.]

1. Gold embroidery, or any rich embroidery; with *an* and *pl.*, a piece of richly embroidered stuff. Now only *Hist.* or *arch.*

[**1222** *Ornam. Eccl. Sarum* in *Osmund Reg.* (Rolls) II. 132 Stola una de aurifris. cum manipulis tribus.] **13..** *K. Alis.* 179 With mony bellis, of selver schene, Y-fastened on orfreys of mounde. *c* **1330** R. BRUNNE *Chron.* (1810) 117 A hede þat was of smyten.. in an orfreis [he] it wond. ? *a* **1366** CHAUCER *Rom. Rose* 562 Of fyn orfrays hadde she eke A chapelet. *c* **1425** *Thomas of Erceld.* 62 Hir payetrelle was of irale fyne, Hir cropoure was of Orpharе. *c* **1483** CAXTON *Dialogues* 36/9 Ther was therin many orfrayes and rybans of silke. **1599** THYNNE *Animadv.* (1875) 35 Yoᵘ.. see that 'orefryes' was 'a weued clothe of golde', and not 'goldsmythe woorke'. **1706** PHILLIPS s.v., The Coat-Armours of the King's Guards were also termed Orfraies, upon account of their being adorned with Gold-smith's Work. **1851** SIR F. PALGRAVE *Norm. & Eng.* I. 158 [Charlemagne] clad in his silken robes, ponderous with broidery, pearls, and orfray. **1890** W. MORRIS in *Eng. Illustr. Mag.* July 767 The King's pavilion.. wrought all over.. with orphreys of gold and pearl and gems.

2. An ornamental border or band, esp. on an ecclesiastical vestment, sometimes richly embroidered.

c **1400** MAUNDEV. xxii. 233 Clothes dyapred of red selk all wrought with gold, and the orfrayes sett full of gret perl and precious stones. **1440** in *Eng. Ch. Furniture* (ed. Peacock 1866) 182 One vestment of whitе silke with a read orferay. **1485** *Churchw. Acc., St. Mary Hill, London* (Nichols 1797) 99 A childe's cope of clothe of golde and the orpharis of blue veluet. **1503** in Kerry *St. Lawrence, Reading* (1883) 113 The orfrey on the bak a narrow crose with warks. *a* **1548** HALL *Chron., Hen. VIII*, 73 b, All the Coopes and Vestementes so riche.. the Orfrys sette with pearles and precious stones. **1844** F. A. PALEY *Ch. Restorers* 21 The orphrey or border of the chasuble. **1877** J. D. CHAMBERS *Div. Worship* 66 The orfrays.. are broad and elaborately chased. **1882** *Contemp. Rev.* Nov. 679 The rochets and the orfreys, worn in the second year of King Edward the Sixth. **1894** *Athenæum* 3 Mar. 282/1 A splendid cope of green bawdekyn, with orphreys embroidered with six scenes from the life of St. John Baptist, of late fifteenth century Flemish work.

3. *Comb.*, as ***orphrey-web, -work***.

1876 ROCK *Text. Fabr.* iii. 21 On a piece of German orphrey-web. **1890** STOCKS & BRAGG *Market Harborough Parish Rec.* 53 *note*, In the fifteenth century Cologne became famous for the manufacture of orphrey-web.

orphreyed, orfrayed ('ɔːfreɪd, -frɪd), *a.* [f. prec. + -ED².] Embroidered with gold; adorned with 'orphrey'; bordered with an orphrey.

c **1400** MAUNDEV. (1839) xiv. 153 Arrayed in clothes of gold, orfrayed and apparayled with grete perles & precyous stones. **1480** CAXTON *Ovid's Met.* XIV. viii, He was clad with a mantel of purple orfrayed. **1546** *Invent. Ch. Goods* (Surtees) 137 Two copes of white damask, orfraid with red damask. **1865** *Direct. Angl.* (ed. 2) 20 The Orphreyed Mitre.

orpiment ('ɔːpɪmənt). Also 5–7 **orpement**, 5 **-mynt, orpyment**, 6–7 **orp(e)mente, (orpinent)**, 6–8 **orpment**. See also AURIPIGMENT. [a. OF. *orpiment* (12th c. in Hatz.-Darm.), also *or pieument, or pigment* (Godef.), ad. L. *auripigmentum* (Vitruv.) gold pigment. Cf. It. *orpimento*, Sp. *oropimiento*.] A bright yellow mineral substance, the trisulphide of arsenic, also called Yellow Arsenic, found native in soft masses resembling gold in colour; also manufactured by the combination of sulphur and arsenious oxide; used as a pigment under the name of King's Yellow.

Orpiment is the original ARSENIC, ἀρσενικόν, of the ancients. Also called ***yellow orpiment*** to distinguish it from the so-called ***red orpiment*** = REALGAR, disulphide of arsenic: see ARSENIC 1 a, b.

[**1310** *Acc. Exors. T. Bp. of Exeter* (Camden) 8 De xxd. de iiij libris de orpiment venditis.] *c* **1386** CHAUCER *Can. Yeom. Prol. & T.* 270 The firste spirit quyk siluer called is, The seconde Orpyment [*v. rr.* orpement, orpemynt, orpiment]. *a* **1387** *Sinon. Barthol.* (Anecd. Oxon.) 12 *Auripigmentum*, orpiment, quando simpliciter de citrino intelligitur. **1486** *Bk. St. Albans* B v, Powdre of orpement blowen uppon an hawke. **1545** *Rates of Customs* c j, Orpmente the C. pounde xs. **1577** HARRISON *England* III. x. (1878) II. 67 We haue in England great plentie of quicke siluer, antimonie, sulphur, blacke lead, and orpiment red and yellow. **1646** SIR T. BROWNE *Pseud. Ep.* 90 Arsenick red and yellow, that is, Orpement and Sandarach may perhaps doe something. **1683** MOXON *Mech. Exerc., Printing* xxiv. ¶17 Orpment, Pinck, Yellow Oaker, for Yellow. **1777** *Phil. Trans.* LXV. 393 The other colours I tried were orpiment, gamboge,.. and a few others. **1831** BREWSTER *Optics* xvi. 140 A thin plate of native yellow orpiment absorbs the violet and refrangible blue rays very powerfully. **1969** R. L. S. BRUCE-MITFORD *Art of Codex Amiatinus* 3 The third leaf, a purple-stained folio with text written in yellow orpiment (not gold), carried on its recto and verso respectively a prologue and a table of contents.

Hence **orpi'mental** *a.*, of the nature of orpiment.

1685 BOYLE *Salubr. Air* 62 Orpimental or other noxious Minerals.

orpine, orpin ('ɔːpɪn). Also 7 **orpent**. [a. F. *orpin* (14th c. in Hatz.-Darm.), in same senses, app. some kind of altered form of *orpiment*.]

†**1.** = ORPIMENT. *Obs.*

1548 ELYOT, *Auripigmentum*,.. a coulour lyke golde, in englysshe Orpine. **1582** STANYHURST *Æneis* II. (Arb.) 66 Eech path was fulsoom with sent of sulphurus orpyn. **1675** E. WILSON *Spadacr. Dunelm.* 36 There's no smell of Sulphur, as is when Antimony, Orpin, or Marcasites, are calcin'd. **1725** BRADLEY *Fam. Dict.* s.v. *Rabet*, Take some Powder of Orpine and Brimstone.

fig. **1656** EARL MONM. tr. *Boccalini's Advts. fr. Parnass.* II. xcii. (1674) 246 With a little Orpine of affected goodness, they can cover.. wicked vices.

2. A succulent herbaceous plant, *Sedum Telephium*, with smooth fleshy leaves and corymbs of numerous purple flowers; a native of Britain, and also a well-known inmate of the cottage garden, being esteemed as a vulnerary. From its tenacity of life, one of its popular names is *live-long*.

The connexion between this and the preceding sense is not clear; it has been conjectured that the name *orpine* was given first on account of their colour to one or more of the yellow stonecrops, was extended to the genus *Sedum* as a whole, and was subseq. restricted to *S. Telephium*. In support of this, Littré gives *orpin* as a generic name for *Sedum*, and calls *S. Telephium, orpin reprise*, and *S. acre* (Wall Pepper) *orpin âcre*; but Hatzfeld and Darmesteter know only the former as *orpin*.

a **1387** *Sinon. Barthol.* (Anecd. Oxon.) 17 *Crassula major*, aurum valet, *anglice* orpin. *c* **1440** *Promp. Parv.* 371/1 Orpyn, herbe, *crassula major, et media dicitur* howsleek *et minima dicitur* stoncrop. **1530** PALSGR. 250/1 Orpyn an herbe, *orpyn*. **1555** EDEN *Decades* 135 An herbe muche lyke vnto that which is commonly cauled Sengrene or Orpin. **1590** SPENSER *Muiopotmos* 193 Coole Violets, and Orpine growing still. **1615** MARKHAM *Eng. Housew.* II. i. (1668) 37 Take of Orpents, Smallage, Ragwort,.. of each a good handful. **1647** C. HARVEY *Schola Cordis* xxx. 44 Orpin never waxing old. **1727** BRADLEY *Fam. Dict.* s.v. *Fly*, Put some Hellebore with Orpin into Milk, and moisten the Place the Flies pitch upon. **1854** S. DOBELL *Balder* xi, Livelong orpine that cannot die.

'Orpington. [From *Orpington* in Kent.] Name of a breed of poultry.

189. F. A. MCKENZIE *Pop. Poultry-Keeping* 56 Mr. Cook, a poultry farmer then living in the village of Orpington.. introduced the single-combed Black Orpington to the poultry world in the autumn of 1886. **1897** K. B. B. DE LA BERE *New Poultry Guide* I. 18 He stocks.. the other house with Dorkings, or Orpingtons, as being at once good layers, table fowls, and sitters.

orpit, orpment: see ORP, ORPED, ORPIMENT.

orque, obs. form of ORC.

orquhelm, obs. Sc. form of OVERWHELM.

orra ('ɒrə), *a. Sc.* Also 8 **ora, orrow.** [Of unascertained origin.] = ODD *a.*, in various senses: esp. 4, 7, 8. ***orra man*** (also *orraman*) = odd man: see ODD 8 d.

1728 RAMSAY *Twa Cut-purses* 5 And lay out ony orabodles On sma' gimcracks that pleas'd their noddles. *a* **1774** FERGUSSON *Leith Races* Poems (1845) 30 Their orra pennies there to ware. **1791** J. LEARMONT *Poems* 188 Come an' spend a' ye're orrow hours 'Mang groves an' glades. **1802** J. SIBBALD *Chron. Scot. Poetry* IV. (Gloss.), *Orrow man*, a day labourer. **1814** SCOTT *Wav.* ix, May-be catching a dish of trouts at an orra-time. **1864** *Cornh. Mag.* Nov. 615 After sixty.. he continues to work as what is called an orra man, that is, he does all sorts of odd jobs about the farm. *a* **1867** E. SMITH *Mem. Highland Lady* (1898) ix. 161 Orraman means the jobber or Jack-of-all-trades. **1886** STEVENSON *Kidnapped* xxvii. 285, I daresay you would both take an orra thought upon the gallows. **1937** F. NIVEN *Staff at Simson's* xxv. 243 Of his return the cashier was made aware by the arrival in his office of the odd-job man—the 'orra man'. **1955** in *Sc. Nat. Dict.* (1965) VI. 494/2 (Advt.), Orraman (married) or Orrawoman required for Hillhead, attend some cattle in winter. **1973** *Courier & Advertiser* (Dundee) 14 Feb. 1/3 (Advt.), Tractor-Orraman wanted for intensive livestock and cropping.

orrace, obs. variant of ORRIS².

orrach(e, orrage, obs. forms of ORACH.

† **'orrath,** *a. Obs.* [f. OR- *pref.* 'without' + *raþ*, RATH, counsel.] Doubtful, perplexed, irresolute. Hence † **orrathness,** doubt, indecision.

c **1200** ORMIN 3145 Forr he wass þa brohht ut off all Orrtrowwþe & orraþnesse. *Ibid.* 3150 All orraþ whatt he mihhte don. *Ibid.* 6593 And iss all alls he wære blind & orraþ butenn lade.

Orrefors ('ɒrɪfɔːz). The name of the town in Sweden where glass is manufactured, used to designate glassware produced there and the style of decoration characteristic of it.

1928 T. PALM tr. *Wettergren's Mod. Decorative Arts Sweden* 23 The relation between the figures of the Orrefors glasses and these daughters of the Renaissance and of the baroque style proves to be a result of the material.. and of the technique. **1929** *Encycl. Brit.* X. facing p. 404 (*caption*), Modern cut and engraved European glass. 1. 'Fashion' vase of engraved Orrefors glass designed by Edvard Hald. **1931** G. JANNEAU *Mod. Glass* ii. 21 The Orrefors production is not entirely limited to this style. **1935** N. MITCHISON *We have been Warned* IV. 427 The Orrefors mirror and the linen sheets on the bed. **1961** E. M. ELVILLE *Collector's Dict. Glass* 174/2 The examples.. are illustrative of the vigorous, muscular figures which have established the Orrefors tradition. **1970** *House & Garden* May 41/1 Scandinavian elegance of design.. is, literally, crystallized in Orrefors glass. **1970** W. WAGER *Sledgehammer* (1971) iii. 13 He put down the Orrefors pitcher.

orrelegge, orrellet(te: see HOROLOGE, OREILLET.

orrells, obs. spelling of *or else*: see OR B. 5.

orrenge, obs. form of ORANGE.

orrery ('ɒrərɪ). [Named after Chas. Boyle, Earl of Orrery, for whom a copy of the machine invented by George Graham *c* 1700 was made by J. Rowley, an instrument-maker.] A piece of mechanism devised to represent the motions of the planets about the sun by means of clockwork.

1713 STEELE *Englishm.* No. 11 Mr. John Rowley.. calls his Machine the *Orrery*, in Gratitude to the Nobleman of that Title. **1720** W. STUKELEY in *Mem.* (1882) I. 50 A machine.. in the nature of what we since call Orrerys. **1742** YOUNG *Nt. Th.* IX. 787 [It] dwarfs the whole, And makes an universe an Orrery. **1833** HERSCHEL *Astron.* viii. 287 Those very childish toys called orreries. **1854** LOWELL *Jrnl. Italy* Pr. Wks. 1890 I. 191 When that is once done, events will move with the quiet of an orrery.

† **'orrest.** *Obs.* [ad. ON. *orrosta, orrasta* battle. See EARNEST *sb.*¹] Battle, contest.

c **1100** *O.E. Chron.* an. 1096 [Gosfrei] hit him on gefeaht, and him on orreste ofer com. *c* **1200** ORMIN 12539 In all þatt time þatt he wass Inn orresst ȝæn þe deofell.

orrho- (bef. a vowel **orrh-**), comb. form of Gr. ὀρρό-ς serum, in a few rarely used terms of pathology, etc., as **'orrhocyst, -'cystis,** a serous cyst; **orrhyme'nitis,** inflammation of a serous membrane; also, **'orrhoid** *a.*, of the appearance or nature of serum (Mayne *Expos. Lex.* 1857); **'orrhous** *a.*, serous (*Syd. Soc. Lex.* 1892).

orribel, -bil, -ble, obs. variants of HORRIBLE.

orright (ɔː'raɪt), repr. a vulgar or colloq. pronunciation of *all right* s.v. RIGHT *a.* 15 c.

1941 M. TREADGOLD *We couldn't leave Dinah* iii. 58 Thomas gave a little sigh of relief. 'Orright,' he said. **1969** E. MCGIRR *Entry of Death* v. 89 It's orright, yer money's on. **1971** J. WAINWRIGHT *Dig Grave* 54 'Here, have another toffee, Billy.' 'Orright. Ta.' **1971** 'J. RIPLEY' *Davis doesn't live Here* 18 'You wanna say summat?'.. 'Orright. Say it.' **1978** J. WAINWRIGHT *Jury People* xxiii. 68 'I'll do orright.' 'On social security?' 'Aye.'

orris¹ ('ɒrɪs). Forms: 6 **oreys, oris, arras,** 7 **orace,** 7–8 **orrice,** 7– **orris.** [Apparently an unexplained alteration of IRIS: cf. also IREOS.]

1. A plant of the genus *Iris*, esp. *Iris germanica* and *I. florentina* (Mayne); the flower-de-luce.

1626 BACON *Sylva* §863 The nature of the orrice is almost singular: for there are but few odoriferous roots. **1656** RIDGLEY *Pract. Physick* 96 The Juyce of our Orris with Honey. **1718** QUINCY *Compl. Disp.* 120 Orris, or Flower-de-luce, Flowers in April and May. **1824** LANDOR *Imag. Conv.*, *Abbé Delille & Landor* Wks. 1853 I. 106/2 *note*, The Florentines used the iris as the symbol of their city... We call it *orris*, corruptly.

2. Short for *orris-root, -powder*: see 3.

1545 *Rates of Customs* c j, Oreys the C. pounde xiij.*s.* iiii.*d.* **1587** HARRISON *England* II. vi. (1877) I. 159 She addeth to hir brackwoort.. halfe an ounce of arras. **1721** C. KING *Brit. Merch.* I. 301, 200 lib. Red Orrice. **1888** MARG. DELAND *John Ward* 319 He lifted a bit of lace,.. noting the faint scent of orris which it held.

3. *Comb.* **orris-pea,** an issue-pea made of orris-root; **orris-powder,** powdered orris-root.

1602 PLAT *Delightes for Ladies* IV. ii, Take.. some orace powder, and foure ounces of Beniamin. **1611** *Churchw. Acc., St. Margaret's, Westminster* (Nichols 1797) 30 Paid for a pound of Orris-powder to put among the church linen. **1861** *Our Eng. Home* 118 The choicest linen, smelling sweetly of orris powder.

b. orris-root. The rhizome of three species of Iris (*I. florentina, I. germanica, I. pallida*), which has a fragrant odour like that of violets; it is used powdered as a perfume and in medicine.

orris-root oil, oil of orris-root, a crystalline oil of pearly lustre obtained from orris-root; also, in commerce, a solid crystallizable substance distilled from orris-root.

1598 FLORIO, *Irios*, a kinde of sweete white roote called oris-roote. **1736** BAILEY *Househ. Dict.* 503 Put some Iris or Orris root, or bay leaves, or origanum.. into the vessel with it; and the ale will recover its natural taste. **1830** LINDLEY *Nat. Syst. Bot.* 261 The violet-scented Orris root, the produce of *Iris Florentina*. **1855** BROWNING in Collingwood *Life Ruskin* I. 202 Why don't you [Ruskin] ask the next perfumer for a packet of orris-root? Don't everybody know 'tis a corruption of iris root?

orris² ('ɒrɪs). Forms: 8 **orice, orrice, orace, orrace, orras,** 9 **orris.** [Origin obscure: in sense akin to *orfrays* (ORPHREY); but the phonetic relation to that word is not clear.] A name given to lace of various patterns in gold and silver; embroidery made of gold lace; see also quots. 1858 and 1882.

1701 *Lond. Gaz.* No. 3716/4 A Scarlet Coat with Gold Orras. **1703** *Ibid.* No. 3984/4 A Scarlet Cloth Petticoat, with a Silver Orrice; a white Cloth Petticoat with a Gold Orrice. **1772** *Test Filial Duty* I. 127 His coat was wonderfully laced with gold orace. **1858** SIMMONDS *Dict. Trade, Orris*, a peculiar pattern, in which gold and silver lace is worked. The edges are ornamented with conical figures placed at equal distances, with spots between them. **1882** BECK *Draper's Dict., Orris*.. the name is still in use, but is given a wider application, so as to include nearly every description of upholstery galloons.

b. *attrib.* and *Comb.*, as ***orris-lace, -weaver, -work***; **orris-pattern:** cf. quot. 1858 above.

1705 *Lond. Gaz.* No. 4154/4 A Calimanco Petticoat.. a Silver Orace-Lace upon it. *c* **1710** CELIA FIENNES *Diary* (1888) 103 A broad tissue border of orrace work gold and silver. **1769** *Chron.* in *Ann. Reg.* 123/2 Mr. W. Dell, an orrice-weaver, in Bridewell-hospital. **1790** UMFREVILLE *Hudson's Bay* 59 The suit is ornamented with orris lace. **1851** in *Illustr. Lond. News* (1854) 5 Aug. 119 Occupations of the people, orris-weaver.

† **orris**³, variant of ARRAS.

1634 *Unton Invent.* (1841) 32 Fyve peces of Orrisse hangings. *c* **1710** CELIA FIENNES *Diary* (1888) 167 Very fine orris hanging in wᶜʰ was much silk and gold and silver.

orrour, orrybel, obs. ff. HORROR, HORRIBLE.

ors, obs. f. OURS.

ors, orse, obs. ff. HORSE.

orsade, -sady, -sede, etc. obs. varr. ORSIDUE.

† **orsadine, orsden,** var. forms of ARSEDINE.

1614 CHAPMAN *Commem. C. Brooke's Ghost Rich. III*, Tis Pageant orsadine, That goes for gold in your barbarian rate.

orschadow, obs. Sc. var. of OVERSHADOW *v.*

orsell, os(s)el, ossil, oz(z)el, etc. varr. NORSEL *sb.*

orselle, orseille, variants of ORCHIL, ARCHIL.

orseller, var. NORSELLER.

or'sellic, *a. Chem.* [f. med.L. *Orsella* ORCHIL + -IC.] In ***orsellic acid***, a crystalline solid, $C_{16}H_{14}O_7$ + $2H_2O$, obtained from South African and South American lichens.

1857 MILLER *Elem. Chem.* III. 542 *note*, Lecanoric acid, according to Gerhardt, is identical with the alpha and beta orsellic acids of Stenhouse. **1868** WATTS *Dict. Chem.* IV. 235.

So **'orsellate,** a salt of orsellic acid; **orse'llinic acid,** a crystalline substance, $C_8H_8O_4$ + H_2O, obtained by the action of baryta water on erythrin; also called **orse'llesic** *acid.* **or'sellinate,** a salt of orsellinic acid.

1857 MILLER *Elem. Chem.* III. 543 Orsellesic Acid. *Ibid.*, Lecanoric ether, more properly orsellesic ether. **1873** WATTS *Fownes' Chem.* (ed. 11) 805 Orsellinic acid, when boiled with baryta-water, splits up into carbon dioxide and orcin.

† **orsidue** ('ɔːsɪdjuː). *Obs.* Forms: 6 **orsade, -dy, orsede,** 6–7 **orsdew(e,** 8 **orsedeu,** 9 **-dew, orsidue.** See ARSEDINE. [Derivation uncertain.

The first element appears to be *or* gold, but it is doubtful whether this is original, or altered from *ar-*.]

A gold-coloured alloy of copper and zinc, rolled into very thin leaf, and used to ornament toys, etc.; 'Dutch gold', 'Mannheim gold'.

1502 ARNOLDE *Chron.* (1811) 234 Orsady, at x. d'. the ll'. **1527** *Acc. Gibson, Master of Revels* (P.R.O.), For v score and ijˡⁱ of orsade. **1545** *Rates of Customs* c j, Orsede the pounde vj. d. **1583** *Ibid.* D v, Orsdew the xij. pound xiij *s.* iiij *d.* **1812** J. SMYTH *Pract. of Customs* (1821) 176 Orsedew, or Manheim Gold, sometimes called Dutch Gold, Dutch Leaf, and Dutch Metal, is, properly speaking, Leaf Brass, from.. the ingredients of which it is made being the same as those employed in the manufacture of Brass. **1833** J. HOLLAND *Manuf. Metal* II. 16 The tortoise-shell,.. placed over a foil of orsidue, to give a yellow lustre to the lighter part, is a rich and curious mounting [for knives].

ort (ɔːt). Usually in pl. **orts;** also 5 **ortys,** 7 **ortes,** 8 **oughts.** [First found in 15th c. in pl. *ortys, -us*, but not usual till end of 16th c.; app. cognate with early mod.Du. *oor-aete, oor-ete* remains of food (Kilian), LG. *ort* (Brem. Wbch.), Sw. dial. *oräte, uräte* refuse fodder; cf. N. Fris. *ôrte* to leave fragments; f. *or-, oor-*, privative + *etan* to eat. There may have been an unrecorded OE. **or-æt*, cognate with the continental forms, but the absence of OE. and ME. examples is noteworthy.] Fragments of food left over from a meal; fodder left by cattle; refuse scraps; leavings, broken meat: also *fig.* ***to make orts of***, to treat with contempt, undervalue.

c **1440** *Promp. Parv.* 371/2 Ortus, releef of beestys mete. **1483** *Cath. Angl.* 262/1 Ortys, *forrago* (A. *farrago*), *ruscus*. **1593** SHAKS. *Lucr.* 985 Let him haue time a beggers orts to craue. **1598** T. BASTARD *Chrestoleros* (1880) 93 She hath the orts and parings of our time. **1607** SHAKS. *Timon* IV. iii. 400 It is some poore Fragment, some slender Ort of his remainder. **1675** CROWNE *Country Wit* II. i. 23 Those poor creatures.. swim after men of wit and sense for the scraps and orts of wit that fall from them. **1678** RAY *Eng. Prov.* (ed. 2) 133 Evening orts are good morning fodder. *a* **1722** LISLE *Husb.* (1752) 258 The graziers buy lean oxen to eat up the oughts. **1828** *Craven Gloss.* (ed. 2), *Orts*, the refuse of hay left in the stall by cattle. **1861** GEO. ELIOT *Silas M.* iii. 18 Besides, their feasting caused a multiplication of orts, which were the heirlooms of the poor. **1886** F. HARRISON *Choice Bks.* 187 These pots and pans, where the eminent writer flung the orts of his ill-digested meals. **1913** D. H. LAWRENCE *Love Poems* 50 Then what art colleyfoglin' for?—I'm not havin' your orts and slarts. **1917** —— *Look! We have come Through!* 60 To me it seems the seed is just left over From the red rose-flowers' fiery transience; Just orts and slarts. **1922** BLUNDEN *Shepherd* 44 With hungry hubbub begging crusts and orts. **1940** V. WOOLF *Writer's Diary* 30 May (1953) 334 Scraps, orts and fragments. **1946** K. TENNANT *Lost Haven* (1947) xi. 169 'Orts and leavings, that's what pigs eat.' The idea of a set of pigs fattening on what Bee-Bonnet left from his scanty meal amused the loungers. **1950** R. MOORE *Candlemas Bay* 223 Neal took the orts out to the hens and hurled them, dish and all, over the henyard wall. *Ibid.* 224 Neal started back to the house, kicking the orts dish along the gravel walk in front of him. **1972** J. METCALF *Going Down Slow* iv. 61 When you've eaten every last ort and scrap, would you like dessert? Coffee? Brandy? **1976** 'M. INNES' *Gay Phoenix* iv. 54 A waiter.. wheeled up a trolley of elaborately bedized scraps, orts and broken meats.

ort, variant of ORD *Obs.*, beginning.

ortalan, ortalon, ortelan, var. ORTOLAN.

ortanique (ɔːtə'niːk). [f. OR(ANGE *sb.*¹ + TAN(GERINE *sb.* 2 + UN)IQUE *a.*] A citrus fruit resembling a slightly flattened orange, produced by crossing an orange and a tangerine and cultivated in the West Indies. Also *attrib.*

1937 *Times* 16 Feb. 11/2 Jamaica shows ortaniques, a cross between the usual orange and a tangerine. **1961** *Spectator* 9 June 857 The West Indian experimental ortaniques, a cross between a tangerine and an orange. **1969** 'J. MORRIS' *Fever Grass* viii. 72 I've got to risk turning fifty acres of certain sugar into avocadoes, ortaniques and Bombay mangoes. **1969** *Harrod's Summer Food News* 6/2 Canadian Ortanique Juice 19 oz. tin 3/3.

ortch(y)ard, orte(s) yerde: see ORCHARD.

‖**orteguina** (ɔːtɛˈgiːnə). [Sp., f. the name of Domingo *Orteg(a* (born 1906), Spanish bullfighter, who practised it + *-uina.*] In bullfighting, a decorative pass made with the muleta; = MANOLETINA.

The more usual term is *manoletina*.

1957 A. MACNAB *Bulls of Iberia* viii. 86 Domingo Ortega introduced a variant in which the man.. passes his left arm behind his back and grips the lower edge of the cloth with his left hand. This was called the *orteguina* but is now generally called *manoletina* owing to its having been popularised by the late Manolete. **1959** [see MANOLETINA]. **1962** B. CONRAD *Encycl. Bullfighting* 174/1 *Orteguina*, a cape pass attributed to Domingo Ortega in Spain... Also may refer to a *muleta* pass similar to the *manoletina*. **1967** MCCORMICK & MASCAREÑAS *Compl. Aficionado* iv. 147 The manoletina is another embellishment... Formerly, it was called the *orteguina*, after Domingo Ortega, who took it from the nineteenth-century repertoire and refurbished it. Manolete picked it up and further refined (i.e. vulgarized) it.

orter, var. OUGHTA, OUGHTER.

‖**orterde** (ˈɔrtɛrdə). *Soil Sci.* [G.] (See quot. 1939.)

1930 *Bull. Wisconsin Geol. & Nat. Hist. Surv.* LXXVIIA. 86 Dark rusty brown sandy loam containing coffee-brown cemented lumps (the orterde of the Podsol). **1936** J. S. JOFFE *Pedology* vi. 132 These chemical compounds are responsible for the condition of ortstein and orterde (hard-pan). **1939** *U.S. Dept. Agric. Yearbk. 1938* 1173 *Ortstein*, hard irregularly cemented, dark-yellow to nearly black sandy material formed by soil-forming processes in the lower part of the solum. Similar material not firmly cemented is known as orterde. **1965** B. T. BUNTING *Geogr. Soil* xiii. 152 Modal iron podsols are the true forest podzol, usually under spruce, with deep F1, 2, 3 layers, and deep orterde rather than pan.

†**orth.** *Obs.* In 1 oroð, oruð, 1–2 orð, orþ. [OE. *oroð, -uð*, shortened from *or-óð*:—OTeut. **uz-anþ* out-breathing; cf. Goth. *uz-anan* to breathe out, expire. (Sievers *Ags. Gram.* ed. 3, §43. 4.) Cf. also OE. *éðian*:—**anþjōjan* to breathe, and L. *an-imus*, Gr. ἄν-εμος, etc.] Breath, breathing; hence, wrath.

a **1000** *Guthlac* 1245 He oroþ stundum teah. *a* **1000** *Hymns* ix. 55 Ðu him on dydest oruþ and sawul. *a* **1000** *Life St. Guthlac* xx. (1848) 84 He þa.. mid langre sworetunge þæt orð of þam breostum teah. *c* **1175** *Lamb. Hom.* 13 Iswica þenne þe orð þa iswingla.

†ˈ**orthangle.** *Obs.* [f. Gr. ὀρθ-ός right, straight + ANGLE.] A rectangle.

1603 HOLLAND *Plutarch's Mor.* 88 The Numbers, Orthangles and Triangles of Plato [Greek had ὀρθογώνιος right-angled, rectangular].

orthaxial (ɔːˈθæksɪəl), *a. Ichthyol.* [f. ORTHO-, ORTH-, straight + AXIAL.] Having the vertebral axis straight, as the tail of a diphycercal fish.

1886 J. A. RYDER in *Rep. U.S. Comm. Fisheries 1884* 985 The word orthaxial is used to designate the archaic straight type of vertebrate axis which is not bent upwards at its posterior extremity.

orthesis (ɔːˈθiːsɪs). *Med.* [f. Gr. ὀρθ-ός straight, right + *-esis*, after PROSTHESIS.] = ORTHOSIS.

1956 R. L. BENNETT in *Physical Therapy Rev.* XXXVI. 721/1 To my knowledge, the words, 'orthesis', 'orthetics', and 'orthetic devices', have not been used before... The word 'orthesis' may be defined as a medically prescribed device applied to or around a weakened bodily segment to give support and increased function. **1963** *Med. Electronics & Biol. Engin.* I. 511/1 Prehensile motion of the hand.. is to be performed by an externally powered orthesis, but is not to be preprogrammed and is to be completely controlled by the patient. **1971** *Rand Daily Mail* 4 Sept. 14/1 He has developed various aids for the disabled. The most useful, perhaps, is the motorised orthesis or hand splint which can be connected to a blow-and-suck pipe or any other control system.

orthian (ˈɔːθɪən), *a.* [f. Gr. ὄρθι-ος upright, high-pitched + -AN.] Applied to a style of singing, or tune, of very high pitch: rendering Gr. ὄρθιος.

1751 SMOLLETT *Per. Pic.* xxxi. I. 239 His empress singing the loud Orthyan song among the servants below. **1820** T. MITCHELL *Aristoph.* I. 15. **1830** tr. *Aristophanes, Acharnians* 5 Chæris came shuffling on to chaunt the Orthian strain. **1872** BROWNING *Fifine at Fair* lxxviii, Sing, unalloyed by meaner mode thine own The Orthian lay. **1883** LIDDELL & SCOTT *Gr. Lex.* s.v. ὄρθιος, The νόμος ὄρθιος or *orthian strain* was in so high a pitch that few voices could reach it.

orthic (ˈɔːθɪk), *a. Min.* [f. Gr. ὀρθ-ός straight + -IC.] Having the cleavage-planes at right angles to one another: = ORTHOCLASTIC.

1877 LE CONTE *Elem. Geol.* (1879) 204 *note*, In this case syenite would differ from diorite only in the form of the feldspar, which in the former is orthic (orthoclase), and in the latter clinic (plagioclase).

orthicon (ˈɔːθɪkɒn). [abbrev. of next.] A kind of television camera tube similar to the iconoscope but having a transparent target plate, so that the scanning beam can be made to strike normally the opposite side to that on which the image is projected, and employing low-speed electrons for the beam, resulting in increased sensitivity and an absence of the spurious signals associated with the iconoscope. See also *image orthicon* (IMAGE *sb.* 8).

The term was registered in the U.S.A. as a proprietary name in 1940, but it is now a generic term in the public domain.

1939 [see next]. **1942** *Electronic Engin.* XV. 127 Because of the greater light sensitivity of the orthicon it is expected that the equipment will fill a need for lightweight equipment to be used under adverse light conditions. **1955** G. M. GLASFORD *Fund. Television Engin.* iv. 98 The disadvantages of the orthicon have encouraged the search for better tubes in spite of the improvement over the iconoscope in the matter of increased sensitivity. The orthicon suffers from a very poor contrast scale with a very small range of intermediate grays as compared with the iconoscope. **1968** *Brit. Med. Bull.* XXIV. 261/2 Tubes such as.. orthicons integrate the light energy incident upon each part of the tube over the entire frame-scanning interval.

orthiconoscope (ɔːθaɪˈkɒnəskəʊp). Now *rare* or *Obs.* [f. ORTH(O- + ICONOSCOPE; see quot. 1939.] = prec.

1939 *Electronics* July 11/1 On June 7th Albert Rose and Harley Iams of the RCA Manufacturing Company Research Laboratories at Harrison, revealed.. the details of a new developmental television pick-up tube which.. is one of the most significant advances in television electronics since the advent of the iconoscope itself. The new tube's formal name is 'Orthiconoscope' ('Orthicon' for short) from the Greek root ortho meaning 'straight' and iconoscope for 'image-viewer'. The name derives from the fact that the curve between input light and output current is a straight line, in contrast to the similar curve of the iconoscope which is not linear. **1940** D. G. FINK *Princ. Television Engin.* iii. 111 The orthiconoscope displays no spurious signal, and there is accordingly no background shading defect to be compensated. **1953** AMOS & BIRKINSHAW *Television Engin.* I. 81 The orthicon (orthiconoscope in full) was developed by Rose and Iams in America and used in that country immediately before the Second World War for outside broadcasts.

orthid (ˈɔːθɪd). [f. mod.L. *Orthidæ*, f. *Orthis*, f. Gr. ὀρθός straight: see -ID[2].] A member of the *Orthidæ*, or genus *Orthis*, of fossil bivalves.

1873 DAWSON *Earth & Man* iii. 43 Lamp-shells of another type.. the *Orthids*, these have the valves hinged along a straight line, in the middle of which is a notch for the peduncle.

orthite (ˈɔːθaɪt). *Min.* [= Ger. *orthit* (Berzelius, 1817), f. Gr. ὀρθός straight: see -ITE[1].] A variety of ALLANITE, found in long slender crystals, or straight masses.

1817 in T. Thomson *Ann. Philos.* IX. 160 Orthite so named because it always forms straight radii. **1868** DANA *Min.* (ed. 5) 289 Orthite occurs in acicular crystals sometimes a foot long at Finbo near Fahlun, and at Ytterby in Sweden.

Hence **or'thitic** *a.*, of the nature of orthite.

1843 HUMBLE *Dict. Geol.*, *Allanite*, an orthitic melane-ore.

ortho-, before a vowel sometimes **orth-**, combining form of Gr. ὀρθός 'straight, right', an element of various words, chiefly scientific or technical, sometimes in the physical sense 'straight', sometimes in the ethical sense 'right, correct, proper'.

1. In technical words generally (for the more important of which see their alphabetical places): **'ortho-axis** *Cryst.* = *orthodiagonal*; **ortho'basic** *a. Cryst.* [BASIC], applied to those systems of crystallization in which the axes are at right angles; **ortho'carpous** *a. Bot.* [Gr. καρπός fruit], having straight fruit; **ortho'chronograph** (see quot.); **orthocœlic** (-ˈsiːlɪk), **ortho'cœlous** *adjs. Zool.* [Gr. κοιλία belly], having a straight intestine (as an infusorian), or the intestines arranged in straight or parallel folds (as a bird: opp. to *cyclocœlic*); **'orthocone**, the conical shell of certain fossil nautiloid cephalopods or a fossil characterized by a shell of this shape; hence **ortho'conic** *a.*, of or pertaining to a fossil or a shell of this type; **'ortho-cousin**, one of cousins whose related parents are of the same sex (cf. *cross-cousin* s.v. CROSS- B); **'orthocycle** (-saɪk(ə)l) *Geom.* [Gr. κύκλος circle], the circle that is the locus of intersections of tangents to a conic at right angles to each other; the director circle; **orthodi'agonal** *Cryst.*, (*a*) *sb.*, that lateral axis in the monoclinic system which is at right angles to the vertical axis; (*b*) *adj.*, belonging to or in the line of this axis (opp. to *clinodiagonal*); **ortho'digita** (see quot. 1939); hence **ortho'digital** *a.*; **'orthodome** *Cryst.* [DOME *sb.* 5 b], a dome parallel to the orthodiagonal in the monoclinic system; hence **,orthodo'matic** *a.*, pertaining to an orthodome; **ortho'ferrite**, any of the compounds with the formula $AFeO_3$, where A is a trivalent metal ion (usu. a rare earth), which have an orthorhombic crystal structure and exhibit weak ferromagnetism at room temperature; **'orthoform** *Pharm.* [after CHLOROFORM *sb.*], methyl *m*-amino-*p*-hydroxybenzoate, $C_8H_9NO_3$, a crystalline compound with anæsthetic properties which has been used as a dusting powder for wounds and ulcers and in dentistry; **or'thogamy** *Bot.* [Gr. γάμος marriage] (see quot.); **'orthogeo'syncline** *Geol.* [ad. G. *orthogeosynklinale* (H. Stille 1935, in *Sitzungsber. d. preuss. Akad. d. Wissensch.* (*Phys.-mat. Kl.*) 182)], a linear geosyncline between a continental and an oceanic kratogen (craton), typically comprising a miogeosyncline and an adjacent eugeosyncline; hence **,orthogeosyn'clinal** *a.*; **'orthoglossy** *nonce-wd.* [Gr. γλῶσσα tongue, after *orthography*], correct pronunciation; **'orthogneiss** *Petrogr.* [a. G. *orthogneiss* (H. Rosenbusch *Elem. d. Gesteinlehre* (1898) 467)], gneiss derived from igneous rocks; **orthoki'nesis** *Zool.* [KINESIS 2], a kinesis in which linear movement is shown; hence **orthoki'netic** *a.*; **,orthoper'cussion** *Med.*, very light diagnostic percussion of the chest by means of one finger striking the knuckles of another bent at right angles and with its tip resting in an intercostal space; **orthophony** (ɔːˈθɒfənɪ) [Gr. φωνή voice, sound], the art of correct speaking or enunciation; hence **ortho'phonic** *a.*, pertaining to orthophony; reproducing sounds correctly; **ortho'phoria** *Ophthalm.* [Gr. φορός bearing], the state of perfect oculomotor balance, in which the visual axes tend towards being parallel in the absence of a fusion stimulus; hence **ortho'phoric** *a.*; **'ortho,photo, ortho'photograph**, an image produced optically or electronically from aerial photographs by eliminating distortions of angles and scales so as to give a result corresponding to a planimetric map; **ortho'photomap**, a map made up from an assembly of orthophotographs on which relief has been indicated by contours or shading; **'orthophyre** *Petrogr.* [a. F. *orthophyre* (H. Coquand 1856, in *Mém. de la Soc. d'Émulation du Dép. du Doubs* I. 64)], porphyry in which the phenocrysts are chiefly of orthoclase; **ortho'phyric** *a. Petrogr.* [ad. G. *orthophyrisch* (H. Rosenbusch *Mikrosk. Physiogr.* (ed. 2, 1887) II. 594)], (of the groundmass of porphyritic rocks) containing short, stout feldspar crystals of rectangular or quadratic cross-section; **ortho'pinacoid** *Cryst.* [PINACOID], one of the principal planes in the monoclinic system, parallel to the vertical axis and the orthodiagonal; hence **orthopina'coidal** *a.*; **'orthoploid** *a. Cytology* [a. G. *orthoploid* (H. Winkler 1916, in *Zeitschr. Bot.* VIII. 422)], having a complete or balanced set of chromosomes: with most authors = EUPLOID *a.*; **'orthoprism** *Cryst.*, a prism in a monoclinic crystal, the faces of which are parallel to the vertical axis; **ortho'pyramid** *Cryst.*, in the monoclinic system a pyramid for which the ratio of the intercept made by it upon the orthodiagonal to that made upon the clinodiagonal is greater than the corresponding ratio for the primary pyramid; **orthopy'roxene** *Min.* [ad. G. *orthopyroxen* (E. Düll, at the suggestion of F. Rinne, in *Zeitschr. f. Krystallogr. und Mineral.* (1902) XXXVI. 654)], any orthorhombic pyroxene; **or'tho(r)rhaphous** *a. Ent.* [f. mod.L. *Orthorhapha* (later *Orthorrhapha*) (F. Brauer *Monographie der Oestriden* (1863) 33), f. Gr. ῥαφή seam], belonging or pertaining to the suborder Orthorrhapha, a group of dipterous insects in which the adult emerges from the puparium through a straight or T-shaped split; cf. *cyclorrhaphous* adj. (CYCLO-); **'orthostyle** *Arch.* [Gr. στῦλος column], a straight row of columns; **orthotec'tonic** *a. Geol.* [ad. G. *orthotektonik* sb. (H. Stille *Einführung in den Bau Amerikas* (1940) i. 9)] formed by, or of the nature of, a deformation which produces complicated and crowded systems of fold belts such as the Alps and is characterized by much magmatism and lateral thrusting (believed to be characteristic of orthogeosynclines); cf. *paratectonic* adj. (*b*) s.v. PARA-[1] 1; **ortho'topic** *a. Med.* and *Biol.* [Gr. τοπικ-ός of place], involving transplantation of a structure to the same site in the recipient as it occupied in the donor; also said of the transplanted structure; hence **ortho'topically** *adv.*; **or'thotypous** *a. Min.* [Gr. τύπος TYPE], 'having a perpendicular cleavage' (Webster, 1864); **'orthovoltage** *Med.*, a voltage (in an X-ray tube) of the size used in conventional deep therapy (200–400 kilovolts); usu. *attrib.*; **'orthowater** = POLYWATER.

1857 MAYNE *Expos. Lex.*, *Orthobasicus*, applied by Naumann to systems of crystallization that are coördinate, orthagonal or rectangular, viz., the tessular, prismatic, pyramidal and rhombohedrical: *orthobasic. **1881** WEST in *Jrnl. Bot.* X. 115 This species belongs to the *orthocarpous leiophyllous Hypnaceae. **1844** *Mech. Mag.* XLI. 337 At the late meeting of the British Association, Dr. Robinson exhibited and explained the *Orthochronograph, an ingenious instrument recently introduced..[for] the ascertaining of correct time. **1882** W. A. FORBES in *Rep. Challenger Exp.* IV. 10 The arrangement of the intestinal folds is '*orthocœlic', the intestine being disposed in light folds lying close to and parallel with each other. **1857** MAYNE *Expos. Lex.*, *Orthocelous. **1892** *Syd. Soc. Lex.*, *Ortho-cœlous*, having a straight or longitudinally ranged intestine. **1900** A. HYATT in C. R. Eastman tr. *von Zittel's Textbk. Paleont.* I. 573 An *orthocone is the young of the straight as well as many of the coiled forms [of fossil cephalopod]. **1935** TWENHOFEL & SHROCK *Invertbr. Paleontol.* ix. 368 Early cephalopod shells were dominantly straight or but slightly coiled... Among the Nautiloidea this type of shell is known as an orthocone. **1969** BENNISON & WRIGHT *Geol. Hist. Brit. Isles* iv. 88 In the Durness sequence..the commonest fossils are gastropods..together with orthocone cephalopods. **1970** R. M. BLACK *Elements Palaeont.* viii. 78 *Orthoceras* and similar orthocones range in length from about 3 cm to possibly 460 cm. **1926** A. F. FOERSTE in *Jrnl. Sci. Lab. Denison Univ.* XXI. v. 304 (*heading*) *Orthoconic genera. *Ibid.* 310 The specimen is figured as having its ventral side ribbed and fluted vertically in a manner very similar to that of *Kionoceras*, a form of ornamentation unknown in any other orthoconic triangular cephalopod. **1935** TWENHOFEL & SHROCK *Invertbr. Paleontol.* ix. 367 (*caption*) Idealized diagram of an orthoconic cephalopod. **1974** *Nature* 8 Feb. 396/1 Glaciomarine beds..in South West Africa have yielded..an orthoconic nautiloid. **1918** J. G. FRAZER *Folk-Lore in Old Testament* II. II. vi. 98 It has become customary to call the marriageable cousins *cross-cousins*, because..the related parents are of opposite or cross sexes. There has hitherto been no special name for the unmarriageable cousins, the children of two brothers or of two sisters, but for convenience I propose to call them **ortho-cousins* to distinguish them from cross-cousins. In the case of ortho-cousins the related parents are of the same sex. **1932** [see *cross-cousin* s.v. CROSS- B.]. **1937** R. STOUT *Red Box* iii. 38 Ortho-cousins are..the children of two brothers or of two sisters. **1972** D. DAVIES *Dict. Anthropol.* 141 *Ortho-Cousin*, a term little used now,..can be a synonym for parallel cousin.. or for a parallel cousin of the same unilineal descent..group as the person concerned. **1891** TAYLOR *Elem. Geom. Conics* iv. §31 The locus of the point of concourse of a pair of tangents at right angles will be shewn to be a circle, which we shall term the **Orthocycle. Note*, It has also been named the *Director Circle*, since in the parabola it degenerates into the directrix and the line infinity. **1858** THUDICHUM *Urine* 123 The *ortho-diagonal is shorter than the clino-diagonal. **1868** DANA *Min.* Introd. (ed. 5) 27 The orthodiagonal section. **1879** RUTLEY *Stud. Rocks* ix. 80 Sections lying in the zone of the orthodiagonal. **1937** *Fiopian Footprints* VIII. 3/2 Let us hope that the history of *orthodigita will in time be replete with names of those who will..have illuminated Podiatry. **1939** H. A. BUDIN in *Jrnl. Exper. Podiatry* I. 19 In his first lecture on this subject, delivered at a local society meeting in February 1934, the writer introduced some of the appliances and the technic which he had devised... For the purpose of designation of this newer phase of therapeusis, the author.. chose the term Orthodigita... Orthodigita may be defined as the amelioration or correction, by non-surgical means, of toe deformities or malalignments. *Ibid.* (*heading*), New and improved *orthodigital appliances in the non-surgical correction of deformities of the..toes. **1968** FISHER & WHITNEY in F. Weinstein *Princ. & Pract. Podiatry* xii. 265/1 Although permanent orthodigital correction is sought in adults also,..the patient may need to wear the appliance continually in order to keep the toes in proper alignment. **1978** *Chiropodist* XXXIII. 105 Although I personally favour the qualities (for most orthodigita) of KE 20 silicone rubber, I have found that Otoform provides..an inexpensive and effective method of introducing removable silicone appliances to patients. **1895** STORY-MASKELYNE *Crystallogr.* §328 This variety of dome is termed the *ortho-dome, because, like the ortho-prisms, it has an ortho-symmetrical character. **1956** *Jrnl. Chem. Physics* XXIV. 1239 (*heading*) Magnetic properties of a gadolinium *orthoferrite, $GdFeO_3$, crystal. **1966** *McGraw-Hill Encycl. Sci. & Technol.* V. 219/2 Many of the orthoferrites are strongly ferromagnetic at liquid helium temperatures. **1971** *Sci. Amer.* June 83/2 The first magnetic materials found to have the desired properties for studying the new bubble technology were orthoferrites, a special class of ferrites with the chemical formula $RFeO_3$, where R represents yttrium or one or more rare-earth elements. Samarium terbium orthoferrite is a good example. **1897** *Lancet* 18 Sept. 738/1 It has been found by Dr. Einhorn and Dr. Heintz, of Munich, that the compound methylic ether of amidoxybenzoic acid is possessed of remarkable anæsthetic, or rather analgesic, properties when locally applied. To this substance the name of '*orthoform' has been given. **1940** F. R. DAVISON *Synopsis Materia Medica* xi. 383 Orthoform.. has also been used in dentistry, nasal catarrh, hay fever, and in similar conditions. **1965** FAULCONER & KEYS *Foundations Anesthesiol.* II. iv. 806 In the light of these considerations it is understandable that the Orthoform group anesthetizes better than the corresponding benzoyl combinations. **1874** R. BOWN *Man. Bot.* 418 The typical and orthodox method, which may be styled **Orthogamy*, or direct ('straight') fertilisation. **1941** *Orthogeosynclinal [see *parageosyncline* s.v. PARA-¹ 1]. **1945** *Bull. Geol. Soc. Amer.* LVI. 1172 Marginal geosynclines gaining principal detritus from uplifts in orthogeosynclinal belts. **1975** *McGraw-Hill Yearbk. Sci. & Technol.* 223/1 The orthogeosynclinal belts of Stille and Kay have come to be understood as an assemblage of crustal features related to continental shelf subsidence. **1936** tr. H. Stille in *Bull. Amer. Assoc. Petroleum Geologists* XX. 853 Although the orogenic movements took place at the same time in different areas, they were strong (Alpine type) only in certain mobile belts which had developed as *orthogeosynclines. **1951** *Mem. Geol. Soc. Amer.* XLVIII. 88 The later Devonian and Carboniferous are of argillite and graywacke when detritus could reach the subsiding structural basin from distant highlands of rocks laid in orthogeosynclines. **1968** Orthogeosyncline [see *foredeep* s.v. FORE- 5]. **1877** *Fraser's Mag.* XVI. 565 The discrepance between our orthography and our *orthoglossy gravely discourages foreigners. **1902** *Orthogneiss [see *paragneiss* s.v. PARA-¹ 1]. **1932** A. HARKER *Metamorphism* xvii. 271 The more or less distinctly banded crystalline rocks which are conveniently styled orthogneisses (in contradistinction to paragneisses, which are highly metamorphosed sediments) attain in some countries a vast development. **1962** *Mineral. Abstr.* XV. 553/2 Alkaline syenitic orthogneisses form a lenticular body 5 km in length in biotite gneisses in the Cevadais area, near Ouguela, Alto Alentejo, Portugal. **1937** D. L. GUNN et al. in *Nature* 18 Dec. 1064/2 Variations in generalized, undirected, random locomotory activity..are kineses... We propose to divide kineses into (*a*) *ortho-kineses..variations in linear velocity (previously called simply kineses), [etc.]. **1940** FRAENKEL & GUNN *Orientation of Animals* II. ii. 17 Woodlice aggregate in moist air..by means of an ortho-kinesis. **1971** J. D. CARTHY in J. E. Smith et al. *Invertebr. Panorama* xii. 251 This behaviour, consisting of changing rates of movement with different levels of stimulation, is known as an orthokinesis. **1958** —— *Introd. Behaviour Invertebr.* xii. 317 When the stones are beneath the surface ..they [*sc.* chitons] do not tend to congregate by a simple *orthokinetic response. **1973** *Nature* 16 Nov. 168/1 An orthokinetic effect may serve to influence adult movements, as their rate of progress over the reefs is almost certainly affected by the ease with which they can find adequate food and shelter from day-light. **1907** *Practitioner* Apr. 530 The chief disadvantage of Goldscheider's *ortho-percussion is that it requires an absolutely silent room. **1916** L. F. BARKER *Monographic Med.* II. 499 In orthopercussion, the force of the blow is directed exactly perpendicular to the surface. **1966** *Lancet* 31 Dec. 1469/1 The technique of percussion (ortho-percussion) of the patient's abdomen in order to recognise peritoneal irritation is shown. **1926** *Daily Colonist* (Victoria, B.C.) 2 July 6/6 (Advt.), The genuine His Master's Voice Victrola is the only true *orthophonic. **1927** *Gramophone* V. 309/2 The gramophone part of it contains an improved form of orthophonic horn. **1954** PEI & GAYNOR *Dict. Linguistics* 155 *Orthophonic*, relating to orthophony..; conformable with the standard or accepted rules of pronunciation. **1969** *John Edwards Mem. Foundation Q.* V. II. 81 This valuable discographic aid lists all Victor Recordings..starting with the introduction of the electrical 'orthophonic' recording system in February, 1925. **1845** W. RUSSELL (*title*) *Orthophony, or Vocal Culture, a Manual of elementary Exercises for the Cultivation of the Voice in Elocution. *Ibid.* p. xiii, The term orthophony is used to designate the art of cultivating the voice. The systematic cultivation of the vocal organs..is a branch of education for which our own language furnishes no appropriate designation. The compiler of this manual has ventured to adopt, as a term convenient for this purpose, the word *orthophony*—a modification of the corresponding French word '*orthophonie*', used to designate the art of training the vocal organs. **1954** PEI & GAYNOR *Dict. Linguistics* 155 *Orthophony*, Correct pronunciation or articulation. **1886** *Orthophoria [see *exophoria* s.v. EXO-]. **1907** J. H. PARSONS *Dis. Eye* xxviii. 563 In cases of latent squint the position of rest is not orthophoria, with the visual axes parallel, but heterophoria, with some deviation of the axes. **1950** F. H. ALDER *Physiol. Eye* x. 386 It is unfortunate that the implication is frequently made that orthophoria is the normal condition and heterophoria an abnormal one. This is not true. **1888** *Arch. Ophthalm.* XVII. 159 In the *orthophoric state the eyes are able to unite images when a prism of 2° to 3° is introduced with its base up or down before one of the eyes. **1954** S. DUKE-ELDER *Parsons' Dis. Eye* (ed. 12) xxix. 483 Since the position of rest is usually one of slight divergence, few people are orthophoric and some degree of heterophoria is almost universal. **1965** *Photogrammetric Engin.* XXXI. 223/1 Several stereo aerial models from test areas were successfully compiled into contour maps and *orthophotos. **1972** *McGraw-Hill Yearbk. Sci. & Technol.* 245 The orthophoto, like any good map, allows the engineer to lay out a proposed highway with accurate scale, direction, and curvature. **1955** *Photogrammetric Engin.* XXI. 529/2 Given an *orthophotograph, the engineer, surveyor, forester, geologist,..can correlate points imaged on the orthophotograph with points observed on the ground, and ..can make direct measurements on the orthophotograph to determine distances between points. **1970** J. A. HOWARD *Aerial Photo-Ecol.* xii. 136 No doubt orthophotographs will have a wide application in natural resource studies not requiring a stereoscopic examination. **1967** *Photogrammetric Engin.* XXXIII. 274/1 The altitude contours derived from the height measured can then be added, along with any desired annotations, to form an accurate '*orthophotomap' of the area of interest. **1974** *Geo Abstr.* G. 520 The Topographic Division of the U.S. Geological Survey produces a series of orthophoto products ranging from separate photos for in-house use..to the multicoloured orthophotomap. **1890** *Cent. Dict.*, *Orthophyre. **1895** A. HARKER *Petrol.* viii. 102 The most usual type of orthoclase-porphyry (orthophyre of Rosenbusch) is exemplified by dykes and sills in the Carboniferous of Thuringia. **1930** PEACH & HORNE *Geol. Scotl.* iv. 108 Examples of dykes of orthophyre occur on Sgonnan Mòr. **1947** E. E. WAHLSTROM *Igneous Minerals & Rocks* x. 301 Orthophyre is a porphyritic trachite consisting largely of orthoclase. **1895** A. HARKER *Petrol.* viii. 102 Other porphyrites have the '*orthophyric' type of ground-mass (with short felspar-prisms), as in the porphyries. **1964** G. A. JOPLIN *Petrogr. Austral. Igneous Rocks* v. 65 Most trachytes are porphyritic with phenocrysts of anorthoclase in an orthophyric and/or trachytic ground-mass. **1879** RUTLEY *Stud. Rocks* x. 88 When the light falls obliquely either on the basal plane, the *ortho-pinakoid, or the hemidome of a monoclinic felspar. **1889** *Q. Jrnl. Geol. Soc.* XLV. II. 299 The Augite is almost colourless, and gives the usual eight-sided sections. Prismatic, *ortho- and clinopinacoidal cleavages are present. [**1920** *Svensk Bot. Tidskr.* XIV. 301, I have in my material found the following numbers: 14, 21, 28, 35 and 42. Further, in some specimens, I met with numbers not being a multiple of 7 (anorthoploid forms).] **1932** *Proc. 6th Internat. Congr. Genetics* II. 63 The ratios between *orthoploid and aneuploid gametes in the cases studied were found to be 1·4:1. **1937** T. DOBZHANSKY *Genetics & Origin of Species* ix. 268 In a translocation heterozygote at least six classes of sex cells can be produced. .. Classes 1 and 2 carry normal gene complements..; 1 and 2 are termed regular or orthoploid. **1963** *Portugaliae Acta Biol.* A. VII. 8 The unfortunate terms orthoploid and anorthoploid have been used in various senses also by more recent writers. *Ibid.* 9 There is no doubt that euploid and aneuploid should be maintained and orthoploid and anorthoploid definitely dropped. **1895** STORY-MASKELYNE *Crystallogr.* §328 The *vertical* or **ortho-prism*.., usually distinguished as the *prism-form*, the faces of which lie in the zone [100, 010]. **1903** *Mineral. Mag.* XIII. 374 Following Rinne, E. Düll..proposes the terms *ortho-pyroxene and klinopyroxene. **1940** *Amer. Mineralogist* XXV. 282 Orthopyroxenes of plutonic igneous rocks normally show well developed diopsidic lamellae. **1963** W. A. DEER et al. *Rock-Forming Min.* II. 33 Many orthopyroxenes can be distinguished from clinopyroxenes by their characteristic pink to green pleochroism. **1970** *Science* 28 Aug. 866/2 (*heading*) Orthopyroxene-plagioclase fragments in the lunar soil from Apollo 12. **1890** *Cent. Dict.*, *Orthorhaphous. **1899** D. SHARP in *Cambr. Nat. Hist.* VI. vii. 458 In the Mesozoic epoch the Order [*sc.* Diptera] is found as early as the Lias, the forms being exclusively Orthorrhaphous. **1946** *Nature* 2 Nov. 636/2 Against the orthorrhaphous Diptera, 'Gammexane' shows a high degree of activity. **1961** Orthorrhaphous [see *cyclorrhaphous* adj. s.v. CYCLO- 1]. **1892** DANA *Min.* Introd. p. xxxi, *Ortho-pyramids. **1898** *Ibid.* 101 The pyramids may be unit pyramids (*hhl*), orthopyramids, (*hkl*) when $h > k$, or clinopyramids, (*hkl*) when $h < k$. **1831** *Encycl. Brit.* (ed. 7) III. 468/2 **Orthostyle*, any straight range of columns. **1956** L. V. DE SITTER *Struct. Geol.* i. 16 A later uplift, separated from the last orogenic paroxysmal phase by a period of erosion, is typical of *orthotectonic regions. **1969** *Earth & Planetary Sci. Lett.* VI. 189 The orthotectonic orogens forming island arcs such as Japan lie entirely within ocean basins. **1969** J. F. DEWEY in M. Kay *N. Atlantic* xxiv. 309/1 Strata ranging in age from late Precambrian through early Ordovician constitute a northern orthotectonic belt, characterized by complex recumbent and commonly triclinic fold geometry and high-grade metamorphism. **1921** *Jrnl. Exper. Zool.* XXXII. 7 Limb bud placed in natural location—*orthotopic transplantation. **1958** *Immunology* I. 46 The survival times of successive sets of orthotopic scale (skin) homografts revealed that increasing systematic immunity develops rapidly in stepwise fashion. **1968** *National Observer* (U.S.) 29 Jan. 4/4 Dr. Starzl performed the first orthotopic liver transplant, in which the diseased liver is removed and another implanted, in 1963. **1921** *Jrnl. Exper. Zool.* XXXII. 61 The shoulder-girdle in *orthotopically grafted limbs is derived in part from the host and in part from the transplanted tissue. **1974** *Nature* 11 Oct. 553/1 When solid tissue allografts are transplanted orthotopically to alien hosts they are rejected with a characteristic tempo and vigour that depends primarily on the immunogenetic disparity between donor and host. **1976** *Ibid.* 22 Jan. 209/1 We used a standardised H-test procedure in which tail-skin grafts were orthotopically exchanged in a 'reciprocal circle' among syngeneic mice. **18..** SHEPARD cited by Webster (1864) for *Orthotypous. **1967** M. E. J. YOUNG *Radiological Physics* (ed. 2) xi. 372 Superficial therapy..60–120 kVp. Medium voltage therapy... 120–140 kVp. Deep therapy or *orthovoltage therapy..200–400 kVp. Megavoltage therapy... Above 1 MV. **1972** BARNES & REES *Conc. Textbk. Radiotherapy* iii. 63 In recent years there has been a tendency for deep X-ray therapy (orthovoltage radiation) to be largely superseded by megavoltage therapy as the advantages of the higher energy radiation become more generally appreciated. **1976** *Lancet* 6 Nov. 1031/2 All patients received induction treatment..for 4 weeks followed by 2400 rad of orthovoltage cranial irradiation plus five intrathecal injections of methotrexate. **1966** B. V. DERJAGUIN in *Discussions Faraday Soc.* XLII. 118 The usual state of water and certain other liquids is thermodynamically metastable... It would be convenient to call 'usual water' metawater, and the anomalous columns —*orthowater. **1969** *Nature* 27 Dec. 1293/1 Water condensed into glass or quartz capillaries has unusual properties, which have been ascribed to the formation of a new polymer termed 'orthowater', 'anomalous' water or 'polywater'. **1970** *Compton Yearbk.* 176/2 The substance, variously called orthowater, anomalous water, polywater, and super-water, differs radically from ordinary water.

2. In *Chemistry*. **a.** *Ortho-* is used to distinguish one class of acids and their salts from another denoted by the prefix *meta-*, which contain the same elements in different proportions, the *meta-* acid containing a molecule of H_2O less than the *ortho-* acid, the *ortho-* salt being also the more basic and the *meta-* salt the less basic. Thus *orthophosphoric acid* H_3PO_4, *metaphosphoric acid* HPO_3; *sodium orthophosphate* Na_3PO_4, *sodium metaphosphate* $NaPO_3$. So *orthosilicic*, *orthotungstic*, *orthosilicate*, *orthotungstate*, etc. This use of *ortho-* originated with Prof. Odling in 1859, *meta-* having been introduced by Graham in 1833. **b.** With the names of isomeric benzene di-derivatives, *ortho-* is applied to those in which two consecutive hydrogen atoms are replaced by another element or radical, as distinguished from *meta-* and *para-* derivatives, in which the two atoms are not consecutive, but unsymmetrically or symmetrically dispersed respectively. Examples: *orthodibromobenzene*, *orthobromotoluene*, *orthopropylphenol*; **ortho-'xylene**, an isomer of xylene that is a colourless mobile liquid and is now obtained from petroleum naphtha for use esp. as a source of phthalic anhydride. (This was introduced by Körner, 1867, in *Brussels Acad. Sc. Bull.* XXIV. 166–185.)

As *ortho-*, although usually prefixed without a hyphen, has always its own distinct meaning, chemical names in *ortho-* are not separately treated in this Dictionary.

1859 ODLING in *L.E. & D. Philos. Mag.* Ser. IV. XXVII. 368 On Ortho- and Meta-silicates. Intermediate between common or orthophosphates and metaphosphates we have several varieties of compounds, among which the best defined are the pyrophosphates, salts which result from the union of an atom of orthophosphate with an atom of metaphosphate. **1868** WATTS *Dict. Chem.* IV. 238 The prefixes *ortho-* and *meta-* have been introduced..to denote two classes of salts..the more basic salts being called ortho- and the less basic, meta- salts. **1872** *Jrnl. Chem. Soc.* XXV. 893 (*heading*) Preparation of orthoxylene from liquid bromotoluene. **1873** WATTS *Fownes' Chem.* (ed. 11) 225 The aqueous solution..deposits orthophosphoric acid in prismatic crystals. **1876** HARLEY *Mat. Med.* (ed. 6) 66 Neutral solutions of the orthophosphates..give precipitates with salts of lime and baryta. **1877** WATTS *Fownes' Chem.* II. 422 The di-derivatives of benzene..exhibit three such modifications which are distinguished by the prefixes *ortho*, *meta*, and *para*: thus..Orthodichlorobenzene, 1:2, $C_6ClClHHHH$, Metadichlorobenzene, 1:3, $C_6ClHClHHH$; Paradichlorobenzene, 1:4, $C_6ClHHClHH$. **1968** *Economist* 14 Dec. 63/3 Both BP Chemicals and ICI have existing plants for phthalic anhydride. ICI's 20,000 ton plant at Wilton manufactures from naphthalene, an older method being replaced by the ortho-xylene method as oil supersedes coal tar as a source of raw materials for the chemical industry.

3. *Physics* and *Chem.* Of, pertaining to, or designating the form of some homonuclear diatomic molecules in which (as in orthohydrogen) the two nuclei have parallel spins (see also quot. 1940[2]); also more widely, characterized by the presence of parallel spins. Also as an independent word.

1927 T. VERSCHOYLE tr. *Haas's Atomic Theory* v. 182 No spectroscopic transition between the normal para-term and the lowest (two-quantum) ortho-term is possible. **1939** J. W. T. SPINKS tr. *Herzberg's Molecular Spectra* I. iii. 150 The modification with the *greater* statistical weight is usually called the ortho modification and that with the smaller weight the para modification. **1940** GLASSTONE *Text-bk. Physical Chem.* i. 79 From the spectrum of helium it is known that the ortho-levels have less energy than the par-levels with the same values of the quantum numbers *n* and *l*. *Ibid.* 96 Symmetrical polyatomic molecules, such as water, deuterium oxide, cyanogen and acetylene, exist in ortho- and para-forms; they behave in a manner similar to hydrogen, deuterium and nitrogen molecules, since the other atoms, viz., carbon and oxygen, have no nuclear spins. **1966** D. H. WHIFFEN *Spectroscopy* ix. 114 The best-known example is hydrogen where the ortho states with odd *J* have three times the degeneracy of the even *J* or para states. **1970** P. J. WHEATLEY *Chem. Consequences Nucl. Spin* xi. 50 The hydrogen molecule, $^1H_2$... The rotation levels with *J* odd are associated with symmetric nuclear states, that is with ortho states, and..the rotational levels with *J* even are associated with antisymmetric nuclear states, that is with para states. *Ibid.* 51 The deuterium molecule, $^2D_2$... Ortho-D_2 will be associated with rotational levels having even values of *J*, and para-D_2 with those having odd values of *J*. **1977** *Sci. Amer.* Oct. 66/3 The parallel quark spins combine to give each meson one unit of spin. This arrangement of spins is known in atomic physics as the 'ortho' configuration.

ortho (ˈɔːθəʊ), *a.* (*adv.*) [f. ORTHO-.]

1. *Chem.* (Now usu. italicized.) Characterized by or relating to (substitution at) two adjacent carbon atoms in a benzene ring; at a position adjacent *to* some (specified) substituent in a benzene ring. Also as *adv.*

1876 *Jrnl. Chem. Soc.* I. 240 An influence is exercised by the NO_2-group in favouring the displacement of Cl, Br, ..&c., *only* when it is in the ortho (1:2) or para (1:4) position relatively to one or other of these radicles. **1903** WALKER & MOTT tr. *Holleman's Text-bk. Org. Chem.* II. 347, 1:2 = 1:6 substitution-products are called *ortho*-compounds. **1920** *Conquest* Apr. 260/3 The ortho acid is the one of use to the Saccharin manufacturer, the para form producing a compound of very slight sweetening power. **1924** [see META *a.*]. **1938** L. F. FIESER in H. Gilman *Org. Chem.* I. ii. 73 The ortho coupling and ortho bromination of phenols involve substitution at the carbon atom connected to that carrying the hydroxyl group by a double linkage. **1949** [see ORIENT *v.* 4 a]. **1968** G. E. COATES et al. *Princ. Organometallic Chem.* ii. 26 Contrast the effect of heat on mercuric benzoate, when substitution of the aromatic ring *ortho* to the carboxyl group occurs. **1971** J. D. ROBERTS et al. *Org. Chem.* xx. 573 Halogen substituents..strongly orient *ortho* and *para* through conjugation of the unshared electron pairs.

2. *Photogr.* [f. ORTHO(CHROMATIC *a.*] Orthochromatic. Also *ellipt.*, an orthochromatic plate.

1904 G. B. SHAW *Let.* 26 July (1972) II. 435, I have..a box of half-plate extra-rapid Ortho plates which I got 6 months ago. **1906** *Westm. Gaz.* 17 May 14/2 The Barnet medium ortho is about half the speed of the well-known extra-rapid Barnet ortho-plate... For the best results the Barnet ortho screen is recommended. **1921** *Glasgow Herald* 27 Apr. 9, I have said something in previous articles about ortho plates. **1956** E. MYTUM *Introd. Photogr. Materials* iii. 58 If the emulsion is optically sensitized by a dye which absorbs green and yellow light, it is said to be orthochromatic, often abbreviated to 'ortho'.

3. See ORTHO- 3.

orthocentre (ˈɔːθəʊˌsɛntə(r)). *Geom.* [f. ORTHO- + CENTRE.] The point at which the perpendiculars from the angles of a triangle on the opposite sides intersect.

1869 BESANT *Conic Sect.* 131 If a rectangular hyperbola circumscribe a triangle, it passes through the orthocentre. **1885** LEUDESDORF *Cremona's Proj. Geom.* 273 The directrices of all parabolas inscribed in a given triangle meet in the same point, viz. the orthocentre of the triangle.

orthocephalic (ˌɔːθəʊsɪˈfælɪk), *a.* *Ethnol.* [f. ORTHO- 'right, correct' + Gr. κεφαλή head + -IC: cf. *cephalic.*] Applied to skulls of which the breadth is from about $\frac{3}{4}$ to $\frac{4}{5}$ of the length (intermediate between *brachycephalic* and *dolichocephalic*); or, according to some, of which the height is from $\frac{7}{10}$ to $\frac{3}{4}$ of the length, or of which the height is $\frac{4}{5}$ of the breadth.

1865 LUBBOCK *Preh. Times* v. (1869) 129 Now if we class those skulls in which the relation of the breadth to the length is from 74–79 to 100 as medium heads,..Orthocephalic. **1866** HUXLEY *Prehist. Rem. Caithn.* 88 The skull is orthocephalic, the cephalic index being 0·76.

So **orthocephalous** (-ˈsɛfələs), *a.* = prec.; **orthoˈcephaly**, the condition of being orthocephalic.

1874 DAWKINS *Cave Hunt.* vi. 191 In the round barrows ..they belong mainly to the third division, although some are ortho-cephalous. **1892** *Syd. Soc. Lex.*, *Orthocephaly*, the condition of a skull which, according to the Frankfort agreement, possesses a vertical index of from 70·1° to 75°. According to Welcker, an orthocephalous skull is one whose height is to its width as 10 to 8.

‖**Orthoceras** (ɔːˈθɒsəræs). *Palæont.* Pl. **orthocerata** (ˌɔːθəʊsəˈreɪtə). [f. ORTHO- 'straight' + Gr. κέρας, pl. κέρᾱτα horn.] An extinct genus of cephalopods, having long straight (or nearly straight) chambered shells; a fossil shell of this genus.

1830 LYELL *Princ. Geol.* I. 101 The gigantic orthocerata of this era being, to recent multilocular shells, what the fossil ferns, equiseta, and other plants of the coal strata, are in comparison with plants now growing within the tropics. **1863** —— *Antiq. Man* xx. 404 It is said truly that the ammonite, orthoceras, and nautilus of these ancient rocks were of the tetrabranchiate division.

Hence **orthoceran** (ɔːˈθɒsərən) *a.*, belonging to the *Orthocerata.*

1884 *Science* III. 127/1 Evidence..that the Ammonoidea, with their distinct embryos, arose from the orthoceran stock.

orthoceratite (ɔːθəʊˈsɛrətaɪt). Also in Lat. form **orthoceratites** (ˌɔːθəʊsɛrəˈtaɪtiːz). [f. as prec. + -ITE[1] 2.] A fossil shell of the genus *Orthoceras* or family *Orthoceratidæ*; also, an animal of this genus or family.

1754 *Phil. Trans.* XLVIII. 804 The orthoceratites is a strait concamerated shell, ending in a point. **1786** *Ibid.* LXXVI. 445 Belemnites, orthoceratites, and so on, are all sea animals. **1871** HARTWIG *Subterr. W.* ii. 18 In the more ancient Palæozoic seas flourished the Orthoceratites, or straight-chambered shells, resembling a nautilus uncoiled. *attrib.* **1853** TH. ROSS *Humboldt's Trav.* III. xxxii. 376 The orthoceratite limestone of the Alleghanies.

Hence **orthoceratitic** (ˌɔːθəʊsɛrəˈtɪtɪk) *a.*, pertaining to or resembling an orthoceratite. So also **orthoceratoid** (-ˈsɛrətɔɪd) *a.* = *orthoceratitic*; *sb.* = *orthoceratite.*

orthochoanite (ɔːθəʊˈkəʊənaɪt). *Palæont.* Also Ortho-. [f. ORTHO- + Gr. χοάν-η funnel + -ITE[1] 2 a.] A nautiloid cephalopod having a straight, very short septal neck; also, a member of the obsolete sub-order Orthochoanites, of which such necks were characteristic.

1898 A. HYATT in *Proc. Amer. Assoc. Adv. Sci.* XLVII. 364 The suborders..are as follows:..IV. Orthochoanites. The siphuncles small except in primitive forms and without deposits, or, if present, these are irregular and are gathered around the funnels. No endosiphuncles. The funnels are straight and the siphuncle is apt to be tubular. **1944** E. O. ULRICH et al. *Ozarkian & Canad. Cephalopods III* (Geol. Soc. Amer. Spec. Papers, No. 58) 27 Some of the Canadian nautilicones have lamellar deposits within the camerae... Apparently they are not present in the holochoanites, but they are being found in many orthochoanites and cyrtochoanites of the Paleozoic and the Triassic. **1952** R. C. MOORE et al. *Invertebr. Fossils* ix. 342/1 The Cyrtochoanites have been found to include a very diverse assemblage of which some are closely related to 'Holochoanites' and others to 'Orthochoanites'.

Hence **orthochoaˈnitic** *a.*

1905 [see HOLOCHOANITIC *a.*]. **1944** E. O. ULRICH et al. *Ozarkian & Canad. Cephalopods III* (Geol. Soc. Amer. Spec. Papers, No. 58) 26 In all the coiled Canadian cephalopods, the siphuncle is orthochoanitic in structure, the septal necks being short and straight. **1964** C. TEICHERT in R. C. Moore *Treat. Invertebr. Paleont.* K. 95/2 Kuhn.. separated the straight, orthochoanitic nautiloids as a new 'suborder' termed Orthoceracea. *Ibid.* 174/2 Siphuncle large..; septal necks very short, orthochoanitic.

orthochromatic (ˌɔːθəʊkrəʊˈmætɪk), *a.* *Photogr.* [f. ORTHO- 'correct, proper' + Gr. χρωματικός relating to colour, CHROMATIC.]

1. Representing colours in their correct relations, *i.e.* without exaggerating the deepness of some and the brightness of others (as in ordinary photography). In mod. use, having a sensitivity which is more nearly uniform throughout the visible range than that of silver halide used alone, but which is relatively low in the red and high in the blue part of the spectrum (cf. PANCHROMATIC *a.*).

The emulsions, etc., orig. called 'orthochromatic' were in fact orthochromatic in this mod. sense.

1887 *Athenæum* 26 Mar. 421/1 The colours were purposely selected to test as severely as possible the capacity of the plate used—a Dixon's orthochromatic. **1889** *Pall Mall G.* 21 Aug. 7/1 We want photography to be orthochromatic, or colour-correct. **1890** AGNES M. CLERKE *Syst. Stars* 30 'Orthochromatic' plates absolutely free from colour-preferences can be produced by special processes. **1903** A. PAYNE *Pract. Orthochromatic Photogr.* vi. 88 Orthochromatic plates possessing additional sensitiveness to the yellow and green rays only may be handled in a red light possessing abrupt absorption... Plates..sensitive to the whole of the spectrum..require to be treated in darkness. Such plates are occasionally termed panchromatic. **1919** *Conquest* Nov. 24/1 Plates known as 'orthochromatic' or 'isochromatic' are sensitive to some of the greens and yellows... Nevertheless, even with these plates, the delicate greens of springtime, the yellow of the gorse, and many other colours in nature, are rendered unsatisfactorily, while the red leaves of autumn photograph as black [*sic*]. **1920** *Jrnl. Franklin Inst.* CLXXXIX. 25 In the commercial orthochromatic (sensitive to green and yellow) and panchromatic (sensitive to all colors) plates, the dyes are incorporated in the emulsion and the mixture flowed over the glass plate. **1944** *Electronic Engin.* XVI. 326/1 It is essential to use either an orthochromatic or panchromatic emulsion. **1970** *Amat. Photographer* 11 Mar. 60/1 As positive film is orthochromatic (that is, it is not sensitive to the red component of the visible spectrum), it can be handled under a red photographic safelight.

2. *Biol.* Exhibiting or characterized by the same colour as that of the stain used.

1899 *Jrnl. R. Microsc. Soc.* 379 Orthochromatic macrocytes which are without nuclei and appear late in embryonic life and in anæmia. **1930** MAXIMOW & BLOOM *Text-bk. Histol.* v. 114 In this way erythroblasts arise in which the protoplasm is purely acidophil, and stains a bright pink with the Romanowsky mixture. These cells are called orthochromatic erythroblasts or normoblasts. **1971** *Cancer Res.* XXXI. 505/1 This behavior was paralleled by a shift in the pH of the transition from orthochromatic to metachromatic staining of the nucleus after methanol fixation.

So **orthochromatism** (-ˈkrəʊmətɪz(ə)m), the condition of being orthochromatic; **orthoˈchromatize** *v.* *trans.*, to render orthochromatic; **orthoˈchromatized** *ppl. a.*, **orthoˈchromatizing** *vbl. sb.*

1889 *Anthony's Photogr. Bull.* II. 315 In order to obtain true orthochromatism it is always necessary..to interpose a transparent yellow screen somewhere between the object and the plate in order to cut off a certain proportion of the blue and violet rays, to which the plates still remain relatively too sensitive. **1890** *Ibid.* III. 220 We will give an easy method by which any gelatine dry-plate can be orthochromatized. **1892** W. J. STILLMAN in *Nation* (N.Y.) 15 Dec. 448/3 'Orthochromatism' avoids the glaring contrasts which used to be made by photography between the color-values of blues, yellows, and reds. **1902** P. H. MELL *Biol. Lab. Methods* xii. 175 M. Monpillard says that, for scientific purposes, he prefers ready orthochromatized plates. **1903** A. PAYNE *Pract. Orthochromatic Photogr.* iv. 46 This process is termed orthochromatising, and plates so treated are known as orthochromatic or isochromatic plates. **1956** E. MYTUM *Introd. Photogr. Materials* iii. 59 Sometimes the word *isochromatic*..was applied to the earlier orthochromatised emulsions.

orthoclase (ˈɔːθəkleɪs). *Min.* [mod. (Breithaupt, 1823) f. ORTHO- 'straight, right' + Gr. κλάσ-ις breaking, cleavage.] Common or potash feldspar, a silicate of aluminium and potassium, occurring in crystals or masses of various colours, characterized by two cleavages at right angles to each other.

1849 NICOL *Min.* 119 All orthoclase from trachyte contains soda along with the potash. **1863** S. R. GRAVES *Yacht. Cruise Baltic* 142 The felspar of this quarry is of two kinds, orthoclase and oligoclase, in large masses, the former pink, and the latter quite white. **1900** SILLMAN *Min.* 87 Ground orthoclase is extensively used as a glaze.

b. *attrib.* Consisting of or containing orthoclase.

1849 MURCHISON *Siluria* i. (1867) 11 Four separate stages of orthoclase-gneiss. **1869** BRISTOW tr. *Figuier's World bef. Deluge* ii. 33 Alongside these orthoclase crystals, quartz is implanted. **1881** GEIKIE *Geol. Sketches* 219 The grains of which are mainly of pink cleavable orthoclase felspar.

orthoclastic (ɔːθəʊˈklæstɪk), *a.* *Min.* [f. ORTHO- + Gr. κλαστ-ός broken, cloven + -IC.] Having cleavages at right angles to each other.

1878 LAWRENCE tr. *Cotta's Rocks Class.* 8 We distinguish two principal kinds of felspar, the orthoclastic (monoclinic) ..and the plagioclastic (triclinic). **1879** RUTLEY *Stud. Rocks* x. 91 The orthoclastic (rectangular cleavage) or that in which the chief cleavages are mutually situated at right angles.

orthocœlic, orthodome, etc.: see ORTHO-.

†**orthodiagraphy** (ɔːθəʊdaɪˈægrəfɪ). *Med. Obs.* [ad. G. *orthodiagraphie* (F. Moritz 1900, in *Münch. med. Wochenschr.* 17 July 992/2): see ORTHO-, DIA-[1], and -GRAPHY.] A technique for producing sketches showing the exact sizes of organs by projecting the shadow formed by a narrow beam of X-rays on to a fluorescent screen perpendicular to the beam and drawing round the shadow.

1904 C. Beck *Röntgen Ray Diagnosis* iii. 44 (*heading*) Orthodiagraphy. **1907** *Practitioner* Apr. 524 By means of orthodiagraphy..the exact size and shape of an organ or tumour can be ascertained. **1930** D. A. Rhinehart *Roentgenographic Technique* 382/1 (Index), Orthodiagraphy of heart.

Hence **ortho'diagram**, a sketch produced by orthodiagraphy; **ortho'diagraph**, an instrument for orthodiagraphy; **orthodia'graphic** *a.*, of or pertaining to orthodiagraphy; performed by means of orthodiagraphy; **ˌorthodia'graphically** *adv.*

1904 C. Beck *Röntgen Ray Diagnosis* iii. 44 The orthodiagraph made by Hirschmann permits direct tracing by the aid of a movable screen. *Ibid.*, The fact that the size of all skiagraphs is larger than that of the objects they represent, led to the construction of orthodiagraphic apparatus, by the aid of which the exact size of a body is determined. **1907** *Practitioner* Apr. 526 Changes in the size of the heart..can be determined by the system..of measuring orthodiagrams which have been taken direct on paper. **1930** D. A. Rhinehart *Roentgenographic Technique* xvii. 305 With certain types of fluoroscopes or with special attachments that may be fastened to other kinds, orthodiagraphic tracings of the cardiac outlines, giving nearly the exact dimensions of the heart shadow, can be made. **1931** P. Kerley *Rec. Adv. Radiol.* iv. 76 When screening the heart at 2 metres' distance, it takes only twenty seconds for the operator to map out an outline with a pencil, and this measurement is as accurate as that of an orthodiagram. **1938** K. C. Clark *Positioning in Radiogr.* xviii. 290/2 As an alternative to teleradiography,..the orthodiagraph may be used to record the size of the heart, a short anode-film distance being employed. **1938** *Jrnl. Amer. Med. Assoc.* 14 May 1718/1 Trimani found the parapericardial triangular shadow at the left lower arch of the roentgen silhouette of the heart in fifty-seven of 3,568 teleroentgenograms and 400 orthodiagrams which he studied. **1938** *Brain* LXI. 118 Measured Orthodiagraphically, the transverse diameter of his chest was 26 cm.

orthodontia (ɔːθəʊ'dɒntɪə). *Dentistry.* [f. as next + -ia[1].] Orthodontics.

1849 C. A. Harris *Dict. Dent. Sci.* 554/2 Orthodontia. **1850** —— *Princ. & Pract. Dental Surg.* (ed. 4) i. xi. 149 Fauchard and Bourdet were among the first who turned their attention to orthodontia. **1908** *Practitioner* Dec. 858 A case showing the importance of moving the roots of the teeth in orthodontia. **1939** S. J. Bregstein *Dentist & his Control of Pract.* v. 155 Preventive orthodontia, however, is regarded..as more commendable than corrective realignment of teeth and jaws. **1970** *Biol. Abstr.* LI. 3601/2 Surgery and orthodontia in 'retained teeth'.

orthodontic (ɔːθəʊ'dɒntɪk), *a.* and *sb. Dentistry.* [f. ortho- + Gr. ὀδοντ-, ὀδούς tooth + -ic.]

A. *adj.* Serving to correct the positions of the teeth; of or pertaining to orthodontics.

1905 *Brit. Dental Jrnl.* XXVI. 993 (*heading*) Where extraction is justifiable in connection with orthodontic operations. **1939** S. J. Bregstein *Dentist & his Control of Pract.* v. 155 Speech defects, psychiatric disturbances, personality changes, rhinological pathoses all are correctable through orthodontic measures. **1962** Blake & Trott *Periodontology* xiv. 148 More permanent and more satisfactory immobilization can be obtained by fitting stainless steel orthodontic bands to each individual tooth. **1974** *Trans. European Orthodontic Soc. 1973* 403 A practitioner undertakes treatment in co-operation with the fully-trained orthodontic specialist.

B. *sb. pl.* The branch of dentistry concerned with the treatment and prevention of irregularities of the teeth and jaws. Usu. const. as *sing.*

1909 *Trans. Brit. Soc. Study Orthodontics* II. 86 The President..said that it was decided..that some change should take place in the name of the society. The council..thought it desirable..the name of the society should be 'The British Society for the Study of Orthodontics'. He said..they had had the opinion of Dr. Murray the great philologist, of Oxford, to guide them. Mr. [C.] Schelling, as the originator of the suggested new title, here explained why he introduced the word Orthodontics. Mr. Schelling proposed..that the title of the society should be changed to the above, and..the motion was carried. **1939** L. B. Higley in Higley & Boyd *Dentistry for Children* ix. 218 Many difficult problems confronting the general dentist and orthodontist could be eliminated if preventative orthodontics were more thoroughly understood and practiced by all dentists who do work for children. **1941** J. D. McCoy *Appl. Orthodontics* (ed. 5) 6 Orthodontics has an abundant literature. **1955** G. M. Anderson *Dewey's Pract. Orthodontics* (ed. 8) ii. 89 Does orthodontics today differ from the practice of forty..years ago? **1971** *Daily Tel.* 24 Sept. 11/5 Unknown to many mothers, orthodontics (correction of irregularities in teeth) are available on the National Health Service.

Hence **ortho'dontically** *adv.*, with regard to orthodontics.

1935 G. M. Anderson *Dewey's Pract. Orthodontia* (ed. 5) xxii. 458 Cases which though completed orthodontically were never satisfactory esthetically. **1940** M. G. Swenson *Complete Dentures* xxvi. 436 Orthodontically any movement of a tooth or teeth..will cause a change in the relationship of the inclines of the moved teeth to the remainder of the teeth. **1972** *Biol. Abstr.* LIV. 4614/2 An orthodontically interesting pair of twins.

orthodontist (ɔːθəʊ'dɒntɪst). *Dentistry.* [f. orthodont(ic *a.* and *sb.* + -ist.] One who practises orthodontics.

1903 *Dental Ann.* 130 Orthodontist, a newly-coined word, already considerably used in the United States to signify one who studies and practises orthodontia, or the treatment of irregularity, malposition, or malocclusion of the teeth. **1939** [see orthodontic *sb.*]. **1969** *Daily Tel.* 7 Feb. 22 (*caption*) Mr. Lewis, an Australian orthodontist, is returning to Sydney as he is dissatisfied with working under the National Health Service.

orthodox ('ɔːθədɒks), *a.* and *sb.* [Ultimately ad. Gr. ὀρθόδοξ-ος right in opinion, f. ὀρθό-ς + δόξα opinion. Cf. late L. *orthodox-us* (Jerome *Codex Just.*), and F. *orthodoxe* (*a* 1488 in Godef. *Compl.*), which may have been the proximate sources.]

A. *adj.*

1. Holding right or correct opinions, i.e. such as are currently accepted as correct, or are in accordance with some recognized standard:

a. in theology.

1611 Cotgr., *Orthodoxe*, orthodox, orthodoxall; of a right faith, true beliefe, sound opinion. *c* **1615** Bacon *Adv. Villiers* Wks. 1879 I. 510/2 The church of England; which doubtless is as sound and orthodox in the doctrine thereof [i.e. of the true protestant religion], as any christian church in the world. **1636** Prynne *Unbish. Tim.* (1661) 45 None of the Orthodoxest or most Judicious Writers. **1722** Sewel *Hist. Quakers* (1795) I. iv. 287 Men falsely called orthodox and divines. **1850** W. Irving *Mahomet* viii. (1853) 40 We follow, says the Koran, the religion of Abraham the orthodox who was no idolater. **1861** Stanley *East. Ch.* vii. (1869) 246 To be called 'orthodox'..implies, to a certain extent, deadness of feeling; at times rancorous animosity; narrowness, fixedness, perhaps even, hardness of intellect.

b. Hence in reference to other subjects.

c **1645** Howell *Lett.* i. v. x. (1650) 145 Of Authors, two is enough upon any Science, provided they be plenary and orthodox. **1690** Locke *Hum. Und.* iii. xi. §5 Obscure and equivocal Terms,..capable to make the most Attentive or Quick-sighted, very little..more knowing or orthodox.

2. Of opinions or doctrines: Right, correct, true; in accordance with what is accepted or authoritatively established as the true view or right practice; **a.** *orig.* in theological and ecclesiastical doctrine.

1581 Hamilton (*title*) Certane orthodox and catholik conclusions vith yair probations. **1616** Jas. I *Remonstr. Right of Kings* Wks. 440 To maintaine the precepts of the orthodox faith. **1710** Steele *Tatler* No. 187 ¶1 The Doctrine is received amongst you as Orthodox. **1865** Max Müller *Chips* (1880) I. vi. 135 The received and orthodox view of..Christian divines.

b. Hence in general application.

1730 Swift *Vind. Ld. Carteret* Wks. (1761) 186, I am well aware, how much my sentiments differ from the orthodox opinions of one or two principal patriots. **1804** Jefferson *Writ.* (1830) IV. 20 Every word of mine..however innocent, however orthodox even, is twisted, tormented, perverted. **1888** H. Sidgwick *Scope Econom. Sci.* 3 This kind of political economy is sometimes called 'orthodox', though it has the characteristic unusual in orthodox doctrines of being repudiated by the majority of accredited teachers of the subject.

3. In accordance with what is regarded as proper or 'correct'; conventional; approved.

1838 Lytton *Alice* 124 Then the orthodox half-hour had expired. **1877** Freeman *Norm. Conq.* (ed. 3) II. App. 553 The orthodox thing was to condemn William and Harold alike.

4. Also **Orthodox.** The specific epithet of the Eastern Church, which recognizes the headship of the Patriarch of Constantinople, and of the various national churches of Russia, Serbia, Romania, etc., which hold the same 'orthodox' creed, and recognize each other as of the same communion; the historical representative of the churches of the ancient East, commonly called the *Greek Church.*

The full ancient designation is ἡ ἁγία ὀρθόδοξος καθολικὴ ἀποστολικὴ ἀνατολικὴ ἐκκλησία, 'the holy, orthodox, catholic, apostolic, Eastern church'. The epithet 'Orthodox' was originally assumed to distinguish it from the various divisions of the Eastern Church, e.g. the Jacobite or Monophysite, Nestorian, etc., which separated on points of doctrine, and have not accepted all the decrees of the successive general councils; but it is sometimes used by historical writers as opposed to 'Catholic'. Also combined with national names, as ***Greek Orthodox, Russian Orthodox, Serbian Orthodox***, etc.

[**1679** Ricaut *Pres. State Gk. Ch.* xviii. 331 That which they call, The Orthodox Confession of the Anatolian Church.] **1772** J. G. King *Rites Gk. Ch.* Pref. 18 They are read at the grave to testify to the people that the party died in the true faith of the orthodox church. **1850** Neale *East. Ch.* I. 69 An Union has often been proposed between the Armenian and Orthodox Eastern Communions. **1861** Stanley *East. Ch.* i. (1864) 3 By whatever name we call it —'Eastern', 'Greek', or 'Orthodox'—it carries us back more than any other existing Christian institution, to the earliest scenes and times of the Christian religion. **1881** Freeman *Hist. Geog. Eur.* I. vii. 170 Till a new patriarchate of Moscow arose in Russia, to mark the greatest spiritual conquest of the Orthodox Church.

5. Also **Orthodox.** Of Judaism or Jews: adhering to the rabbinical interpretation of Biblical law and its traditional observances.

1853 *Jewish Chron.* 15 July 326/2 In all affairs of this kind, concessions are expected only on the orthodox side. **1858** *Manch. Guardian* 26 Mar. 3/4 He would not limit himself to a mere apology for their position, but confidently proclaim their right to the title of 'The truly orthodox Manchester Hebrew congregation'. **1876** Geo. Eliot *Dan. Der.* III. vi. xlvi. 308 He is not a strictly orthodox Jew, and is full of allowances for others. **1898** W. J. Locke *Idols* iv. 38 An elderly..Jewess of the most orthodox faith. **1904** *Jewish Encycl.* VII. 368/1 The stability and the immutability of the Law remained from the Orthodox standpoint one of the cardinal principles of Judaism. **1938** *Time & Tide* 12 Mar. 343/1 Peggy Simon, who was Jewish too, didn't have to bother about prayers..because Peggy's father and mother weren't Orthodox. **1960** 'E. McBain' *Give Boys Great Big Hand* iv. 31 The family was..practising Orthodox Judaism. **1966** *Guardian* 28 July 6/5 The traditionalist right flank of Orthodox Judaism. **1973** *Jewish Chron.* 19 Jan. 22/2 It is..unlikely that he would have been allowed to speak in an Orthodox pulpit in this country. **1974** *Encycl. Brit. Macropædia* X. 301/1 For many, the foreign designation 'orthodox' (used by Reform Jews for traditionalist Jews) makes little if any sense. **1973** J. Ryder *Trevayne* (1974) xxxii. 247 It is the Hebrew Sabbath... This house is Orthodox. **1975** *Nature* 6 Nov. 9/2 For an Orthodox woman, sexual intercourse is only permitted during a limited period each month. **1977** *Rolling Stone* 21 Apr. 72/2 Conversation among Orthodox Jews never strays far from questions of ethics, points of law, one's religious activities.

6. Applied to sleep characterized by the absence of rapid eye-movements and probably of dreams and by lesser physiological activity as compared with 'paradoxical' or REM sleep.

1967 W. P. Koella *Sleep* ii. i. 16 Subjects after being aroused from..'orthodox' sleep stages rarely recalled dreams. **1971** U. J. Jovanović *Normal Sleep in Man* ii. 75 We shall..use the Kleitman (1963) and Jouvet classification (1961, 1965, 1968), and divide up the entire polygraphic period of sleep in man into normal (orthodox) sleep and paradoxical sleep (periods of dream phases). *Ibid.* vii. 259 A phase of orthodox sleep lasts for about one-and-a-half hours.

B. *sb.* **1.** An orthodox person. **b.** A member of the Orthodox Eastern Church.

1587 Harrison *Descr. Brit.* i. ix. 27 The Pelagian heresie, which not a little molested the orthodoxes of that Iland. *a* **1641** Bp. Mountagu *Acts & Mon.* (1642) 169 Was he an Heretick, or an Orthodoxe? **1797** W. Johnston *Beckmann's Invent.* III. 406 In the altercation between a Luciferan and an Orthodox. **1888** *Pall Mall G.* 26 Sept. 2/1 Punctual..in discharging all the functions of a Greek Orthodox.

c. An orthodox Jew (see sense A. 5).

1889 I. Zangwill in *Jewish Q. Rev.* I. 391 With the 'unintelligently orthodox', this mental attitude is generally associated with ignorance of our history and of the fluidity of ceremonial forms. **1892** I. Zangwill *Childr. Ghetto* II. 296 Now at last we poor orthodox will have a voice. **1914** *Encycl. Relig. & Ethics* VII. 608/2 The choice of method, unpleasing though it be to the orthodox, must be left to the conscience and judgment of the liberals themselves. **1927** E. O'Neill *Lazarus Laughed* i. ii. 35 Their former distinctions of Nazarenes and Orthodox are now entirely forgotten. *Ibid.* 42 The Nazarenes and the Orthodox separate and slink guiltily apart. **1964** E. E. Klein in W. Berkowitz *Ten Vital Jewish Issues* 48 The Conservative Jew always keeps one [*sc.* a yarmulke] in his pocket, and the Orthodox wears it on his head.

†**2.** An opinion generally accepted as right; an orthodox opinion. *Obs.*

a **1619** Fotherby *Atheom.* i. xiv. §3 (1622) 150 It is indeed an Orthodoxe; though it be numbred as a Paradoxe; that *Omnes Stulti insaniunt.* **1646** Buck *Rich. III*, i. 4 The Sirname and Sobriquet of Plantagenest, or Plantagenet after the vulgar Orthodoxe.

†**'orthodoxal**, *a. Obs.* [f. as prec. + -al[1].]

1. = orthodox A. 1.

1592 G. Harvey *Pierce's Super.* in *Archaica* (1815) II. 94 The works of the fathers and doctors, howsoever ancient, learned, or orthodoxal, are little or nothing worth. **1635** Pagitt *Christianogr.* (1636) 89 Things..set downe in the Creed, and unanimously received by all Orthodoxall Christians. **1689** *Sovereign Right of People over Tyrants* 7 Mosaical, Christian, and Orthodoxal Authors.

2. = orthodox A. 2.

1585-7 T. Rogers *39 Art.* (1607) 336 All churches Protestant and reformed subscribe unto this doctrine, as both apostolical and orthodoxal. **1641** Milton *Prel. Episc.* Wks. (1851) 90 Who willingly passe by that which is Orthodoxall in them, and studiously cull out that which is Commentitious. **1656** B. Hubbard (*title*) Orthodoxal Navigation; or the admirable and excellent Art of Arithmetical Great Circle Sailing. **1819** Shelley *P. Bell 3rd* Prol. 12 Shielding from the guilt of schism The orthodoxal syllogism.

Hence †**orthodo'xality**, †**ortho'doxalness**, orthodox quality or condition; †**ortho'doxally** *adv.*, orthodoxly.

1660 H. More *Myst. Godl.* x. ii. 494 They be but neatly & elegantly trimm'd up in these fine ornaments of *Orthodoxality. **1726** *Penn's Wks.* I. Life 43 Denying with them the Authority, Antiquity, and Orthodoxality of the Romish Church. **1606** W. Crashaw *Rom. Forgeries* 15 Ferus soundly and *orthodoxally teacheth in plaine words, that Christs iustice is our iustification. **1834** *Fraser's Mag.* X. 608 A very excellent and worthy young fellow, who drinks brandy pawnee as orthodoxally as if he were a Christian. **1654** Hammond *Answ. Animadv. Ignat.* iii. §3. 67 The *Orthodoxalness of Damas in this, and the like of other Bishops.

†**orthodo'xastical**, *a. Obs. rare.* [f. Gr. ὀρθοδοξαστικ-ός according to right opinion, orthodox (f. ὀρθοδοξαστής an orthodox person) + -al[1].] = orthodox A. 1, 2.

1563-87 Foxe *A. & M.* (1596) 258/1 Persisting..in the ancient and true orthodoxasticall faith immooveable. **1577** tr. *Bullinger's Decades* (1592) 602 Synods not hereticall, but orthodoxasticall and catholike.

orthodoxian (ɔːθəʊ'dɒksɪən). Now *rare.* Also 7 **orthodoxan.** [f. late Gr. ὀρθοδοξία, or med.L. *orthodoxia* + -an.] A professor of orthodoxy.

1621 Molle *Camerar. Liv. Libr.* iv. x. 263 The Arrian refused the match, but the Orthodoxan without delay went into the fire. **1716** M. Davies *Athen. Brit.* II. 253 Arianism was concluded by those severe Orthodoxians to be the very Sin against the Holy Ghost. **1887** *Daily Tel.* 16 Aug. 5/1 To this *modus vivendi*, which gave great umbrage to strict orthodoxians, he steadfastly adhered.

orthodoxical (ɔːθəʊˈdɒksɪkəl), *a.* Now *rare*. [f. as prec. + -ICAL.] Characterized by orthodoxy; orthodox.

1577 tr. *Bullinger's Decades* (1592) 828 It [the Church] is called Orthodoxicall, because it is sound of iudgement, opinion and faith. **1644** MILTON *Judgm. Bucer* To Parlt., In the public confession of a most orthodoxical church and state in Germany. **1810** BENTHAM *Packing* (1821) 124 In possession of orthodoxical truth. *a* **1860** H. H. WILSON *Ess. & Lect.* (1862) I. 262 They..usually adopt the outward worship of any other division, whether orthodoxical or heretical.

Hence **orthoˈdoxically** *adv.*, orthodoxly.

1834 LANDOR *Exam. Shaks.* Wks. 1853 II. 293/2 Those who discourse orthodoxically on theology. **1896** *Chicago Advance* 21 May 741/2 The Divinity School [Chicago University] is regularly and orthodoxically Baptist.

orthodoxism (ˈɔːθədɒkˌsɪz(ə)m). [-ISM.]

†**1.** The quality of being orthodox; orthodoxy.

1644 J. GOODWIN *Innoc. Triumph.* (1645) 33 Mr. Prynne's judgement in questioning the Orthodoxisme, yea, the tolerablenesse of the premised Doctrine.

b. In derogatory sense: The treating orthodoxy of creed or doctrine as the important feature of religion; the making of orthodoxy one's special *-ism*.

1828 PUSEY *Hist. Enq.* 69 Enemies he had..from his undervaluing the mere intellectual orthodoxism of his day. **1854** —— *Colleg. Teach.* 53 'An orthodoxism, uninfluential on life'. I ventured to coin this word to designate a lifeless spurious claim to orthodoxy. **1882** FARRAR *Early Chr.* II. xxxvi. 500 There is too much reason to fear that to the end of time the conceit of orthodoxism will claim inspired authority for its own conclusions, even when they are most antichristian.

So **ˈorthodoxist**, one who professes or lays claim to a rigid orthodoxy.

1857 BADEN-POWELL in *Oxford Ess.* 180 In these views of the High Orthodoxists.

orthodoxly (ˈɔːθədɒkslɪ), *adv.* [f. ORTHODOX *a.* + -LY[2].] In an orthodox manner or fashion; in accordance with what is accounted the right opinion or doctrine; **a.** in theology.

c **1615** BACON *Adv. Villiers* Wks. 1879 I. 510/2 Concerning the doctrine of the church of England expressed in the thirty-nine articles..that is so soundly and so orthodoxly settled, as cannot be questioned without extreme danger to the honour and stability of our religion. **1723** WATERLAND *2nd Vind.* 123 He there speaks as orthodoxly of the Blessed Trinity as a man can reasonably desire. **1885** A. J. C. HARE *Russia* iv. 168 A primitive old lady..orthodoxly crossed herself whenever the carriage gave a jolt.

b. in general application: Correctly, properly.

a **1643** W. CARTWRIGHT *Ordinary* III. v, You err most orthodoxly, sweet Sir Kit. **1708** OZELL tr. *Boileau's Lutrin* IV. (1730) 296 Twenty large Hogsheads, fill'd by my Command, Rang'd Orthodoxly in my Cellar stand. **1721** AMHERST *Terræ Fil.* No. 21 (1754) 106, I..firmly and orthodoxly believe that Aristotle, as by law establish'd, is the best author. **1885** WINGFIELD *Barb. Philpot* II. i. 35 My lord ..offered the extreme tips of his white attenuated fingers with orthodoxly filbert nails to Mrs. Barbara.

ˈorthodoxness. [f. as prec. + -NESS.] The quality of being orthodox; orthodoxy.

1644 *Observ. Prynne's 12 Quest.* 5 The mischiefes of Presbytery are vailed with Orthodoxnesse. **1709** CHANDLER *Eff. agst. Bigotry* 12 What will a Man's Orthodoxness.. contribute to the healing of his Pride, Passion, or Worldliness?

orthodoxy (ˈɔːθədɒksɪ). [ad. Gr. ὀρθοδοξία (*c* 180 in L. & S.), n. of quality f. ὀρθόδοξ-ος ORTHODOX; prob. through med.L. *orthodoxia*. Cf. mod.F. *orthodoxie* (Furetière 1701).] **a.** The quality or character of being orthodox; belief in or agreement with what is, or is currently held to be, right, esp. in religious matters.

1630 PRYNNE *Anti-Armin.* 261 Dying men, especially of such orthodoxie, worth and fame as he, speake truth. **1756-78** [see DOXY[2]]. **1768-74** TUCKER *Lt. Nat.* (1834) II. 255 Orthodoxy lies in rectitude of sentiment upon all branches of our duty, not in the characteristic doctrines of any church, however infallible. **1823** LINGARD *Hist. Eng.* VI. 355 By these Articles Henry had now fixed the landmarks of English orthodoxy. **1869** FREEMAN *Norm. Conq.* III. xii. 105 Lanfranc was again present as the champion of orthodoxy.

b. With *pl.* An orthodox belief or opinion.

1871 MORLEY *Voltaire* (1886) 9 The free-thinker [would fain pass] for a person with his own orthodoxies if you only knew them. **1874** H. R. REYNOLDS *John Bapt.* iv. §4. 254 The fruitless lives, the barren orthodoxies..are at once to undergo the most searching scrutiny.

c. *Feast of Orthodoxy*, in the Greek Church, a festival celebrated on the first Sunday in Lent, called *Orthodoxy Sunday*: see quots.

1727-41 CHAMBERS *Cycl.*, *Orthodoxy*, or, *Feast of Orthodoxy*, denotes a solemn feast in the Greek church, instituted by the empress Theodora; still held on the first Sunday in Lent, in memory of the restoration of images in churches, which had been taken down by the Iconoclastes. **1850** TORREY tr. *Neander's Ch. Hist.* (Bohn) VI. 371 The 19th of February, the first Sunday of Lent in the year 842, was the day appointed for this celebration... This day was ever afterwards observed in the Greek church as a high festival, called the Feast of Orthodoxy. **1850** NEALE *East. Ch.* I. 732 Orthodoxy Sunday = First Sunday in Lent. *Ibid.* 867. **1891** *Tablet* 8 Aug. 211/2 Heresies which are solemnly anathematised on 'Orthodoxy Sunday'.

d. The orthodox practice of Judaism; the body of orthodox Jews.

1888 *Jewish Q. Rev.* I. 55 The Rabbis..would have either suspected the man's orthodoxy, or would have denied that his views were really what he professed them to be. **1892** *Ibid.* IV. 215 Let us..hope that Dr. Friedländer's conception is by no means Orthodoxy's last word. **1899** B. DRACHMAN *Nineteen Lett. Ben Uziel* p. xvii, Hirsch set up that view of Judaism called in Germany 'Denkgläubigkeit', which we may translate as 'intellectual or enlightened Orthodoxy'. **1955** M. SKLARE *Conservative Judaism* i. 25 It would be desirable to conclude this historical introduction with some statistics about the growth or decline of Orthodoxy, Conservatism and Reform. **1966** H. KEMELMAN *Saturday the Rabbi went Hungry* (1967) viii. 51 Some of the older congregants brought up in Orthodoxy. **1975** *Times* 13 Aug. 12/4 The mayor of Hackney..says: 'I never travel by car on Saturdays or Jewish festivals.'.. Now the mayor aims to combine his orthodoxy with a little money-making by getting people to sponsor his walks.

orthodromic (ɔːθəʊˈdrɒmɪk), *a.* [f. Gr. type *ὀρθόδρομ-ος (cf. ὀρθοδρομεῖν to run straight, ἀνάδρομ-ος running up, etc.) + -IC.] **1.** (See quot. 1775.) Also, representing great circles as straight lines. So **ˈorthodrome**, a great circle or a route forming part of one. **orthoˈdromics** *sb.*, **orˈthodromy** (see quots.).

1704 J. HARRIS *Lex. Techn.* I, *Orthodromiques*,..the Art of sailing in the Ark of some great Circle. **1706** PHILLIPS, *Orthodromy*, such a Course, which is the most direct and shortest distance between any two Points on the Surface of the Globe. **1775** ASH, *Orthodromic*, sailing on the arch of a great circle, sailing the most direct course. **1855** J. PRYDE *Treat. Pract. Math.* 455 The arc of a great circle, which is the shortest distance between two places, is called the orthodrome. **1922** R. KEEN *Direction & Position Finding by Wireless* iv. 103 A chart on which all Great Circles are represented as straight lines is known as orthodromic. **1928** L. S. PALMER *Wireless Princ. & Pract.* xii. 487 This type of projection is the orthodromic projection and the map of the district surrounding the tangent point is termed a Gnomonic chart. **1935** *Geogr. Jrnl.* LXXXV. 466 The equation of the orthodrome (geodesic line). **1956** *McGraw-Hill Yearbk. Sci. & Technol.* VI. 267/2 The longer the distance, the greater the deviation between loxodromes and orthodromes.

2. *Physiol.* Being or involving a nerve impulse that is propagated in the normal direction.

1943 *Jrnl. Neurophysiol.* VI. 143 (*heading*) The interaction of antidromic and orthodromic volleys in a segmental spinal motor nucleus. **1954** *Jrnl. Physiol.* CXXVI. 501 (*heading*) Interaction between direct current and orthodromic stimulation. **1972** *Science* 2 June 1043/1 The prolonged inhibition of the monographic excitation of motoneurons by orthodromic volleys in muscle and cutaneous afferent fibers.

Hence **orthoˈdromically** *adv.*

1954 PENFIELD & JASPER *Epilepsy & Functional Anat. Human Brain* v. 203 Distant projection of the impulses from a local after-discharge has been shown to be conducted only orthodromically (not antidromically) over transcortical bundles of fibers. **1976** *Nature* 4 Mar. 56/2 When the interval between the two spikes was reduced progressively, the antidromic response eventually disappeared because it collided with the direct spike travelling orthodromically along the same nerve fibre.

orthoepic (ɔːθəʊˈɛpɪk), *a.* [f. as ORTHOEPY + -IC: cf. *epic*.] Pertaining to orthoepy; relating to correct or accepted pronunciation. So **orthoˈepical** *a.*; hence **orthoˈepically** *adv.*

1859 G. P. MARSH *Lect. on Eng. Lang.* (1863) xxii. 470 It is often impossible to suggest any explanation of *orthoepic mutations. **1882** SCUDDER *Webster* ii. 38 The basis of orthoepic canons. **1969** *Computers & Humanities* III. 259 The authors aimed at producing a broad phonetic transcription similar to the phonetic transcription already established for orthoepic French. **1803** T. CARPENTER (*title*) The Scholar's Orthographical and *Orthoepical Assistant. **1809** T. BATCHELOR (*title*) An Orthoepical Analysis of the English Language. *Ibid.* title-p., Illustrated and exemplified by the use of a New Orthoepical Alphabet or Universal Character. **1867** A. J. ELLIS *E.E. Pronunc.* I. iv. 405 Final *e* in the 16th century..had come to be regarded mainly as an orthoepical symbol. **1864** WEBSTER, **Orthoepically*, in an orthoepical manner; with correct pronunciation. **1975** *Amer. Speech 1973* XLVIII. 113 Being perhaps abnormally tenacious orthoepically and considerably past middle age, I use [æ] in all these words, but scholars and laymen alike have been seen to wince at the crudity of my speech.

orthoepist (ˈɔːθəʊiːpɪst, ɔːˈθəʊɪpɪst), *sb.* (and *a.*) [f. ORTHOEPY + -IST.] One versed in orthoepy; one who treats of the pronunciation of words. Used esp. of those 16th- and 17th-century writers whose aim was to describe a 'correct' pronunciation of English, to reform the spelling system to make it reflect such a pronunciation more accurately, etc. Also *attrib.* or as *adj.*

1791 J. WALKER *Crit. Pronouncing Dict.* s.v., *Orthoepist*,.. one who is skilled in Orthöepy. **1796** S. JONES (*title*) Sheridan Improved. A general pronouncing and explanatory Dictionary of the English Language:..the discordances of that celebrated orthoepist being avoided, and his improprieties corrected. **1861** *Proc. Amer. Phil. Soc.* VIII. 376 A great disagreement prevails among the orthoëpists and grammarians on the subject of syllabification. **1882** [see ORTHOGRAPHIST]. **1909** O. JESPERSEN *Mod. Eng. Gram.* I. ix. 248 Up to quite recent times, most orthoepists have disregarded natural pronunciation. **1917** J. M. CLARK *Vocab. Anglo-Irish* 18 It is a well-known fact that in Tudor English a much more open *ō* was pronounced than is the case today. Apart from the testimony of orthoepists, the proof is to be found in contemporary American and Irish usage. **1920** H. C. WYLD *Hist. Mod. Colloq. Eng.* iv. 115 Hitherto writers upon the history of Modern English have relied mainly upon the Orthoepists. **1927** R. E. ZACHRISSON *Eng. Pronunc. at Shakespeare's Time* p. x, The old-fashioned types of pronunciation were, as a rule, taught by English orthoepists. **1957** E. J. DOBSON *Eng. Pronunc. 1500–1700* I. ii. 193 The tendency to regard the spelling reformers as primarily interested in teaching 'correct pronunciation'..may be due to the difficulty of finding a term to cover all the sixteenth- and seventeenth-century writers on pronunciation; 'grammarians' is clearly inexact except in a few cases, and so the term 'orthoepists' has been widely accepted. **1969** A. C. PARTRIDGE *Tudor to Augustan English* viii. 173 On their own admission, orthoepists were students of language who sought to establish the principles of correctness in speech. **1972** M. L. SAMUELS *Linguistic Evol.* vii. 144 For Early Modern English, there is much orthoepist, phonetic and other evidence. **1975** *Language* LI. 747 It would be of great value if a presumably accurate report of upper-class speech of the period [*sc.* Early Modern English] could be carefully analysed and related to witnesses such as Hunt and the other orthoepists.

Hence **orthoeˈpistic** *a.*, pertaining to or characteristic of orthoepists; **orthoeˈpistical** *a.*

1867 A. J. ELLIS *E.E. Pronunc.* I. 223 Attempting to shew that formerly *h* was not pronounced in English, and that it was altogether an orthoepistic fancy to pronounce it. **1913** R. E. ZACHRISSON *Pronunc. Eng. Vowels 1400–1700* 3 Statements in early grammars and spelling-books (= the orthoepistical evidence). **1957** E. J. DOBSON *Eng. Pronunc. 1500–1700* I. i. 36 There is no other orthoepistical evidence for this pronunciation. **1972** *Eng. Studies* LIII. 506 This type of pronunciation was vulgar or dialectal..but at least in some words it must have infiltrated educated speech, as is shown by its frequent occurrence in orthoepistic works. **1972** P. M. WOLFE *Linguistic Change* iii. 31, I have in general limited myself to English orthoepistical works.

orthoepy (ˈɔːθəʊiːpɪ, ɔːˈθəʊɪpɪ). [ad. Gr. ὀρθοέπεια correctness of diction, f. *ὀρθοεπής speaking correctly, f. ὀρθό-ς ORTHO- + ἔπος, ἐπε- word.]

1. That part of grammar which deals with pronunciation; phonology. Also, the study of the relationship between pronunciation and a writing system.

1668 WILKINS *Real Char.* III. i. 298 Parts of Grammar.. Concerning the most convenient marks or sounds for the expression of such names or words; whether by writing, *Orthography*; or by speech, *Orthoepy*. **1711** J. GREENWOOD *Eng. Gram.* 35 Orthoepy..ought to have been reckon'd as a Part of Grammar before Orthography, since Speech preceeds Writing. **1784** R. NARES (*title*) Elements of Orthoepy, containing a Distinct View of the whole Analogy of the English Language. **1832-4** DE QUINCEY *Cæsars* i. Wks. 1862 IX. 51 The grammar and orthoepy of the Latin Language. **1915** D. AGATE in H. C. O'Neill *Guide to Eng. Lang.* I. v. 74/1 To these four divisions of grammar many grammarians have added Orthoëpy, which treats of pronunciation generally. **1957** E. J. DOBSON *Eng. Pronunc. 1500–1700* I. ii. 193 In spite of his title *Orthoepia Anglicana* ..what he [*sc.* Daines] sets out to teach is orthography, not orthoepy. **1969** A. C. PARTRIDGE *Tudor to Augustan English* viii. 181 Though his was not the last shot fired in the hundred years' war of English orthoepy, Cooper's *Grammar* established that the criterion of correct Standard English rests firmly on its pronunciation. **1976** *Visible Language* X. 20 Phonetization of the alphabet and other writing systems is a province of orthoepy.

2. Correct, accepted, or customary pronunciation.

[**1773** W. KENRICK (*title*) A new Dictionary of the English Language: containing not only the explanation of words.. but likewise their orthoepia or pronunciation in speech.] **1801** CHENEVIX in *Phil. Trans.* XCI. 195 *note*, Without offending the radical orthoepy of our language. **1830** D'ISRAELI *Chas. I*, III. viii. 177 Formerly they regulated their orthography by their orthoepy. **1875** WHITNEY *Life Lang.* iii. 37 Changes which have altered the whole aspect of our orthoëpy and orthography.

orthogamy: see ORTHO-.

orthogenesis (ɔːθəʊˈdʒɛnɪsɪs). *Biol.* [a. G. *orthogenesis* (W. Haacke *Gestaltung und Vererbung* (1893) ii. 31), f. ORTHO- + -GENESIS.] A series of similar variations in successive generations, leading to evolutionary change produced by these mutations. Also **orthogeˈnetics** *sb. pl.*

1895 *Nature* 3 Oct. 554/2 Prof. Eimer, of Tübingen, spoke ..on the subject of orthogenesis. **1897** *Jrnl. R. Microsc. Soc.* 108 The causes of orthogenesis are to be found in the action of environment upon the constitution of the organism. **1911** *Encycl. Brit.* XXVII. 912/1 Many successful series,..as they have survived, must inevitably display orthogenesis to some extent. **1930** G. R. DE BEER *Embryol. & Evolution* iv. 32 This incorrigible tendency to produce larger and larger horns, to vary continuously in the same direction, has been given the name of orthogenesis. **1937** A. HUXLEY *Ends & Means* xiv. 261 Neither Lamarckism nor the orthogenetics theory seems to be compatible with the fact that most mutations are demonstrably deleterious. **1956** *Nature* 18 Feb. 309/1 His [*sc.* Arthur Trueman's] contributions to the more philosophical aspects of palæontology ranged..from lineage and orthogenesis, to a reconsideration of the species concept. **1965** R. HOWARD tr. *de Beauvoir's Force of Circumstance* x. 500 They talked, not about birth control but about the joys of maternity, not about contraception but about orthogenesis. **1970** *Watsonia* VIII. 178 A telling argument in favour of mutation pressure (orthogenesis) rather than natural selection. **1973** *Nature* 10 Aug. 375/1 A non-Darwinian orthogenesis had sealed the fate of *Megaloceros* under the oppressive weight of its own enlarging antlers.

orthogenetic (ˌɔːθəʊdʒɛˈnɛtɪk), *a.* [f. prec.; see -GENETIC.] Of, pertaining to, or characterized by orthogenesis. Also *transf.* Hence **orthoge'netically** *adv.*

1899 H. GADOW in *Proc. Cambr. Philos. Soc.* X. 35 (*title*) Orthogenetic variation in the shells of Chelonia. *Ibid.* 37 Since these variations all lie in the direct line of descent.. I call this kind of atavistic variation orthogenetic. **1911** J. WARD *Realm of Ends* xvii. 383 Can we conceive this world evolving orthogenetically, as a biologist would say? **1927** HALDANE & HUXLEY *Animal Biol.* xi. 253 The orthogenetic series can be perfectly well explained by natural selection. *Ibid.*, The extinct cephalopod molluscs..often evolved orthogenetically into the most bizarre forms. **1930** W. R. INGE *Christian Ethics & Mod. Probl.* i. 13, I shall not maintain that the evolution of Christianity has been.. orthogenetic. **1965** B. E. FREEMAN tr. *Vandel's Biospeleol.* xiii. 198 Biospeleologists..are more interested in orthogenetic evolution which proceeds in a parallel manner, in different phyletic lines. **1973** *Jrnl. Genetic Psychol.* CXXIII. 231 In its most general sense, Werner's theory of development centers on his orthogenetic principle.

orthoglossy: see ORTHO-.

orthognathic (ɔːθəʊ'gnæθɪk), *a.* [f. as ORTHOGNATH-OUS + -IC.] = ORTHOGNATHOUS.

1849–52 TODD *Cycl. Anat.* IV. 1321/1 The front teeth meet at an angle, instead of being..in parallel planes, as in those skulls which are termed orthognathic. **1874** DAWKINS *Cave Hunt.* v. 187 Their skulls are orthognathic, or not presenting a lower jaw advancing beyond the vertical line dropped from the forehead.

orthognathism (ɔː'θɒgnəθɪz(ə)m). [f. as next + -ISM.] The condition of being orthognathous.

1871 DAWKINS *Cave Hunt.* vi. 201 They are remarkable for..the delicacy of their features, and the orthognathism of their faces. **1896** A. H. KEANE *Ethnol.* 181 Prognathism is naturally regarded as characteristic of the lower, orthognathism of the higher races.

orthognathous (ɔː'θɒgnəθəs), *a. Ethnol.* [f. ORTHO- 'straight' + Gr. γνάθ-ος jaw + -OUS; in mod.F. *orthognathe.*] Straight jawed; having the jaws not projecting beyond the vertical line drawn from the forehead; having a facial angle of about 90°. Said of the skull; also of persons.

1853 in DUNGLISON *Med. Lex.* **1863** *Q. Rev.* CXIV. 383 No law..will give us the relative dates of brachycephalous, and dolichocephalous, thick-skulled or thin-skulled, orthognathous or prognathous men. **1877** DAWSON *Orig. World* 428 Culture tends to the elevation of the nasal bones, to an orthognathous condition of the jaws. **1881** TYLOR *Anthropol.* 62 The European is orthognathous or upright jawed.

†**'orthogon.** *Obs. rare.* Also in L. form **ortho'gonium** and Gr. **-'gonion.** [ad. late L. *orthogōnium*, neuter of *orthogōnius*, a. Gr. ὀρθογώνιος right-angled; so F. *orthogone* (16th c. in Godef. *Compl.*). Cf. L. *orthogōnium* a rectangle (Isidore III. xii. 2).] A right-angled triangle.

1570 BILLINGSLEY *Euclid* I. def. xxvii. 5 An Orthigonium or a rightangled triangle, is a triangle which hath a right angle. **1612** PEACHAM *Gentl. Exerc.* 17 The square will make you ready for all manner of compartments..your Cylinder for valted turrets, and round buildings; your Orthogonium and Pyramis, for sharp steeples. **1653** H. MORE *Conject. Cabbal.* (1713) 221 The Orthogonion what a foundation it is of Trigonometry..every body knows that knows any thing at all in Mathematicks.

orthogonal (ɔː'θɒgənəl), *a. Geom.* [a. F. *orthogonal*, f. *orthogone*: see prec. and -AL[1]; and cf. *hexagonal*, etc.] **1.** Having or of the nature of a right angle, right-angled (*obs.*); pertaining to or involving right angles; at right angles to something else, or to each other; rectangular.

orthogonal projection, projection in which the rays are at right angles to the plane of projection. ***orthogonal trajectory***, a curve intersecting each of a family of curves at right angles.

1571 DIGGES *Pantom.* I. Elem. Bj b, Of straight lined angles there are three kindes, the Orthogonall, the Obtuse and the Acute Angle. *Ibid.*, Eche of those Angles is an Orthogonall or right Angle. **1612** SELDEN in *Illustr. Drayton's Poly-olb.* Aiij, Pythagoras's sacrifice after his Geometricall Theorem in finding the squares of an Orthogonall triangles sides. **1694** MOTTEUX *Rabelais* v. (1737) 235 An Orthogonal Line. **1816** tr. *Lacroix's Diff. & Int. Calculus* 403 The trajectories in which the angle *TMt* is a right angle, are called orthogonal trajectories. **1878** GURNEY *Crystallogr.* 37 If two symmetral planes intersect at right angles the line in which they cut is called an axis of orthogonal symmetry. **1878** BARTLEY tr. *Topinard's Anthrop.* II. iii, Orthogonal projections are the only ones which give exact measurements applicable to craniometry.

2. *Math.* **a.** Of a linear transformation: preserving lengths and angles; leaving unchanged quantities of the form $x_1^2 + x_2^2 + \ldots + x_n^2$ and the inner product of any two vectors.

1859 G. SALMON *Lessons Introd. Mod. Higher Algebra* xv. 125 What we may call the orthogonal transformation is to transform simultaneously a given quadratic function, and $x^2 + y^2 + z^2 + w^2$ + &., so that the latter remaining of the same form, the former may become $Ax^2 + By^2 + Cz^2 + Dw^2$ + &. **1893** L. G. WELD *Short Course Theory Determinants* ix. 227 The transformation, in analytical geometry, from one set of axes to another, without changing the origin, is orthogonal. **1941** BIRKHOFF & MACLANE *Survey Mod. Algebra* ix. 222 A linear transformation *T* is orthogonal if it preserves the absolute value of every vector ξ, so that $|\xi T| = |\xi|$. **1972** F. E. HOHN *Introd. Linear Algebra* viii. 237 An orthogonal transformation of $\mathscr{E}^n$ maps orthogonal vectors onto orthogonal vectors and nonorthogonal vectors onto nonorthogonal vectors.

b. Applied to the group of all orthogonal matrices of a given order.

1898 *Bull. Amer. Math. Soc.* IV. 196 A linear substitution *S* on the marks of a Galois Field of order p^n..will be called orthogonal if it leaves absolutely invariant $\xi_1^2 + \xi_2^2 + \ldots + \xi_m^2$... The order of the orthogonal group *G* on *m* indices in the $GF[2^n]$ is thus [etc.]. **1941** BIRKHOFF & MACLANE *Survey Mod. Algebra* ix. 225 This subgroup of the full linear group..is called the orthogonal group O_n; it is isomorphic to the group of all orthogonal transformations of the given Euclidean space. **1972** F. E. HOHN *Introd. Linear Algebra* viii. 252 Show that the set of all linear operators on $\mathscr{E}_n$ of the form $Y = UX$, where *U* is orthogonal, constitute a group (the orthogonal group).

c. Of a square matrix: representing an orthogonal transformation; such that the rows (and likewise the columns) are orthonormal when considered as vectors; equal to the inverse of its transpose; (these three properties are equivalent).

1907 M. BÔCHER *Introd. Higher Algebra* xi. 154 An orthogonal transformation. [*Note*] The matrix of such a transformation is called an orthogonal matrix. **1964** N. N. HANCOCK *Matrix Anal. Electr. Machinery* ii. 18 The value of the determinant of an orthogonal matrix is necessarily ± 1, but the converse is not true.

d. Of two vectors or functions: perpendicular; having an inner product equal to zero. Of a set of vectors or functions: such that the inner product of any two is zero if and only if the two are distinct.

1913 *Proc. London Math. Soc.* XII. 297 The theory of Fourier series and of other series of orthogonal functions. **1926** E. W. HOBSON *Theory of Functions of Real Variable* (ed. 2) II. x. 754 If $\{\psi_n(x)\}$ be a complete sequence of linearly independent functions for the interval (*a*, *b*), a normal orthogonal and complete system of functions $\{\phi_n(x)\}$ can be so determined that $\phi_n(x)$ is a linear function of $\psi_1(x), \psi_2(x), \ldots \psi_n(x)$. **1941** R. V. CHURCHILL *Fourier Series* iii. 45 The functions $e^{inx} = \cos nx + i \sin nx$ ($n = 0, \pm 1, \pm 2, \ldots$) form a system which is orthogonal on the interval $(-\pi, \pi)$. **1967** A. A. GOLDSTEIN *Constructive Real Analysis* iii. 112 We define an inner product space *I*[*a*, *b*] by introducing an inner product..defined by $[f, g] = \int_a^b f(t)\, g(t)dt$. Two functions *f* and *g* in *I*[*a*, *b*] are said to be orthogonal if $[f, g] = 0$. *Ibid.* 115 Two points *x* and *y* of [a Hilbert space] *H* are orthogonal if $[x, y] = 0$. Similarly, two subspaces *M* and *N* of *H* are said to be orthogonal if $[M, N] = 0$. **1968** C. G. KUPER *Introd. Theory Superconductivity* i. 3 Bardeen, Cooper and Schrieffer (1957) constructed a variational wave function for a ground state with complete electron pairing, and orthogonal functions for low-lying excited states having only a few such pairs broken.

3. *Statistics.* Of a set of variates: statistically independent. Of an experimental design: such that the variates under investigation can be treated as statistically independent.

1933 *Jrnl. Agric. Sci.* XXIII. 110 In an ordinary replicated field experiment of the randomised block or Latin square type the differences of the means of plots receiving the same treatments are taken without hesitation to be true measures of treatment differences, but this is only so because the experiment has been specially arranged so as to be orthogonal. **1950** M. H. QUENOUILLE *Introd. Statistics* iv. 59 If we are comparing a series of..measurements on people to determine the effect of age, these comparisons may be complicated by the effect of sex... The only manner in which we can assume that sex does not enter into the comparison is to choose the same proportion of each sex in each age group. The effect of sex is then said to be 'orthogonal' to the effect of age. **1967** *Word* XXIII. 219 Another model which provides a relevant comparison to phonological distinctive features is the mathematical method of factor analysis... The various mathematical methods employed lead to the positing of a number of independent 'orthogonal' factors and each test or other set of responses is described in terms of positive or negative loadings on each factor. **1973** *Jrnl. Genetic Psychology* CXXII. 45 Implicit in the work..is the concept that creativity and intelligence are relatively orthogonal (i.e., unrelated statistically) at high levels of intelligence.

orthogonality (ɔːθɒgə'nælɪtɪ). [f. ORTHOGONAL *a.* + -ITY.] The property of being orthogonal. Freq. *attrib.*

1892 O. HEAVISIDE *Electr. Papers* II. 583/2 (Index), Orthogonality of electric and magnetic forces. **1930** P. A. M. DIRAC *Princ. Quantum Mech.* iii. 50 The orthogonality theorem. **1933** *Jrnl. Agric. Sci.* XXIII. 108 Orthogonality is that property of the design which ensures that the different classes of effects to which the experimental material is subject shall be capable of direct and separate estimation without any entanglement. **1935** PAULING & WILSON *Introd. Quantum Mech.* 441 (*heading*) Proof of orthogonality of wave functions corresponding to different energy levels. **1962** CORSON & LORRAIN *Introd. Electromagn. Fields* iv. 158 This property of orthogonality of the Legendre polynomials is important in evaluating the coefficients of Eq. 4-139. **1970** G. K. WOODGATE *Elem. Atomic Struct.* ii. 17 The spherical harmonics have the orthogonality property. **1972** A. W. F. EDWARDS *Likelihood* vi. 106 Such cases may be expected to be rather rare..and the most important application of the concept of orthogonality is to the quadratic support surface. **1973** *Jrnl. Genetic Psychol.* CXXII. 202 The correlations between the E and N dimensions are low enough to justify the assumption of orthogonality of these two dimensions of personality.

or,thogonali'zation. *Math.* [f. as prec. + -IZATION.] The procedure of constructing an orthogonal set of functions or vectors from ones that are linearly independent but not orthogonal.

1922 *Proc. London Math. Soc.* XXI. 97 We have now only to derive from $\{\chi_n(t)\}$ a new set $\{\psi_n(t)\}$ by the 'orthogonalisation method' of Mr. E. Schmidt to get a complete, orthogonal, and normalised set possessing the property (3). **1966** G. ARFKEN *Math. Methods for Physicists* ix. 342 Consider two (nonparallel) vectors **A** and **B** in the *xy*-plane. We may normalize **A** to unit magnitude and then form **B′** = *a***A** + **B** so that **B′** is perpendicular to **A**. By normalizing **B′** we have completed the Schmidt orthogonalization for two vectors.

So **or'thogonalize** *v. trans.*, to render orthogonal (and, often, to normalize); **or'thogonalized** *ppl. a.*

1930 RUARK & UREY *Atoms, Molecules & Quanta* 747 Other systems of polynomials often used in wave mechanics are obtained by orthogonalizing the system, $p^{1/2}$, $xp^{1/2}$, $x^2p^{1/2}$,..where *p*(*x*) is a so-called 'weight function'. **1937** MICHELL & BELZ *Elem. Math. Analysis* II. xvii. 914 If the set of functions $\phi_k(x)$..is orthogonalized by means of the function $\psi(x)$. **1939** C. H. GOULDEN *Methods Statistical Analysis* xii. 192 If the number of varieties is 21, the numbers would be written out as below..and we would have to use a completely orthogonalized 4 × 4 square..to which the remaining numbers would be added as described above. **1948** BROWN & CAMPBELL *Princ. Servomech.* iii. 66 After the initial transformation, certain manipulations enable us to orthogonalize the mathematical forms. **1966** *McGraw-Hill Encycl. Sci. & Technol.* II. 93/1 Several techniques exist for solving the wave equation, at least for certain states, notably the Wigner-Seitz method and the orthogonalized-plane-wave method.

or'thogonally, *adv.* [f. ORTHOGONAL *a.* + -LY[2].] In an orthogonal manner; at right angles.

1571 DIGGES *Pantom.* I. xviii. Fj, *E* is the fourth staffe running sydewise orthogonally or in a squire from the third. **1669** STURMY *Mariners Mag.* v. 52 Divide it into 4 Quadrants, with 2 diamet. cutting each other in the Centor orthogonally. **1797** BROUGHAM in *Phil. Trans.* LXXXVIII. 382 The parabola shall cut the logarithmic orthogonally. **1881** MAXWELL *Electr. & Magn.* I. 241 Case of two spheres cutting orthogonally. **1887** R. A. ROBERT *Integr. Calc.* I. 359.

†**ortho'gonial,** *a. Obs.* [f. L. *orthogōni-us* (see ORTHOGON) + -AL[1].] = ORTHOGONAL I.

1653 H. MORE *Conject. Cabbal.* (1713) 142 All which refer to Five, as it is the Hypotenusa of the first Orthogonial Triangle, that has its sides including the right Angle, rational. **1660** COKE *Justice Vind.* 22 An orthogonial triangle.

†**orthogonion, -gonium**: see ORTHOGON.

orthograde ('ɔːθəʊgreɪd), *a.* [irreg. f. ORTHO- + L. *-gradus* walking: see GRADE *sb.*] Holding the body upright.

1902 A. KEITH in *Jrnl. Anat. & Physiol.* XXXVII. 18 He [*sc.* the author] regards the primates as divided into two very distinct groups—those which carry the axis of the body in a horizontal position—the Pronograde Primates..; and those which carry the axis of the body in an upright position—the Orthograde Primates, into which group fall the gibbon, orang, chimpanzee, gorilla, and man. *Ibid.* 19 It is now generally recognised that the anthropoids, in their natural habitat, carry their bodies in an upright position, i.e. are orthograde. **1925** J. LAIRD *Our Minds & their Bodies* 46 An orthograde (or erect) animal, like man. **1940** *Nature* 6 July 27/1, I regarded the Gibbon as a representative of the pioneers of the orthograde stock. **1973** B. J. WILLIAMS *Evol. & Human Origins* viii. 112/2 Many features of this arboreal primate life..predisposed primates to a more orthograde, upright posture. *Ibid.* 114/1 Man being completely orthograde has a recurved spine that bends back sharply in the lumbar region.

'orthograph. [f. ORTHOGRAPH-IC, after *autograph, chirograph*, etc.: see -GRAPH.] An orthographic projection or vertical elevation; = ORTHOGRAPHY 2 b.

1875 in KNIGHT *Dict. Mech.*; and in mod. Dicts.

orthographer (ɔː'θɒgrəfə(r)). [f. Gr. ὀρθογράφ-ος correct writer (see ORTHOGRAPHY) + -ER.] One skilled in orthography; one who spells in accordance with accepted usage.

1598 FLORIO, *Ortographista*, an ortographer, or teacher.. of orthographie. **1599** MINSHEU, *Ortografo*, an Orthographer. [**1599** SHAKS. *Much Ado* II. iii. 21: see ORTHOGRAPHY I c.] **1706** PHILLIPS, *Orthographist* or *Orthographer*, one skilled in Orthography. **1757** MRS. GRIFFITH *Lett. Henry & Frances* (1767) III. 167 Frances is a remarkable Orthographer, and, unless that Letter [k] is expunged from Johnson's Dictionary, I am afraid we shall not be able to wrest it from her. **1850** GROTE *Greece* II. lxviii. VIII. 624 The former..comes nearer to the good orthographer or arithmetician than the latter. **1887** *Athenæum* 5 Mar. 305 Rapid writer and correct orthographer.

orthographic (ɔːθəʊ'græfɪk), *a.* [In sense 1, f. ORTHO- 'straight, right' + Gr. -γραφος written, γραφικός of or pertaining to writing. In sense 2, f. ORTHOGRAPHY + -IC: see -GRAPHIC.]

1. Applied to a kind of perspective projection, used in maps, elevations of buildings, etc., in which the point of sight is supposed to be at an infinite distance, so that the rays are parallel.

1668 *Phil. Trans.* III. 892 The Orthographick Projection, by Perpendiculars falling from the respective Points of the Circles of the Spheare, on the Projecting Plain: Such a Projection, if the Plain be the Meridian, Ptolemy called the Analemma. **1796** MORSE *Amer. Geog.* I. 56 If the eye be supposed to be placed at an infinite distance, it is called the orthographic projection. **1802** JAMES *Milit. Dict.* s.v. *Bridge, Elevation*, the orthographic projection of the front of a bridge, on the vertical plane, parallel to its length. **1866** *Athenæum* No. 2002. 339/2 The orthographic delineation of the skull. **1867** DENISON *Astron. without Math.* 11 That mode of projecting a hemisphere or any part of it on a plane is called the orthographic, because it shews the surface as it would be seen straight by parallel lines of sight from an infinite distance.

2. = ORTHOGRAPHICAL 1.

1868 *Pall Mall G.* 23 July, This last is likely to be modern, and to have got in through orthographic influence on speech among a generally cultivated..people. **1882–3** SCHAFF *Encycl. Relig. Knowl.* III. 2568 There are some orthographic peculiarities; but in the main the Hebrew is pure.

orthographical (ɔːθəʊˈgræfɪkəl), *a.* [f. as prec. + -AL[1]: see -ICAL.]

1. Pertaining to orthography; belonging to correct spelling, or to spelling in general; correct in spelling.

1589 PUTTENHAM *Eng. Poesie* III. x. (Arb.) 172 That I might with better warrant haue vsed in their steads these words, orthographicall or syntacticall, which the learned Grammarians left ready made to our hands. *c* **1629** MEDE *Wks.* (1672) 784 Could I have gotten an orthographical Scribe, I would have sent your Lordship all ere this. **1653** BROME *Mad Couple well Match'd* I. i. Wks. 1873 III. 5 His ..Orthographicall speaking friend..that cals People Pe-o-ple. **1712** ADDISON *Spect.* No. 499 ¶1 Having rectified some little orthographical mistakes. **1747** JOHNSON *Plan Eng. Dict.* Wks. 1787 IX. 172 The great orthographical contest has long subsisted between etymology and pronunciation. **1867** *Nation* (N.Y.) 3 Jan. 9/1 In a majority of our words, orthographical changes have disguised or affixes have smothered the radical.

2. = ORTHOGRAPHIC 1.

1706 PHILLIPS, *Orthographical Projection of the Sphere*, is a drawing the Surface of a Sphere on a Plane which cuts it in the middle; the Eye being vertically plac'd at an infinite distance from one of the Hemispheres. *Ibid.* s.v. *Orthography, Orthographical Section*, is a Profil or Draught, which shews the thickness, breadth, depth and height of any Work, as it would appear, if perpendicularly cut off from the highest to the lowest part of it. **1864** BURTON *Scot Abr.* II. i. 126 Excellently well skilled in..the orthographical projections.

orthoˈgraphically, *adv.* [f. prec. + -LY[2].]

1. In accordance with correct spelling; in relation to spelling or orthography.

1617 *Janua Ling.* 140, I haue writ out my theame orthographically. **1802** W. TAYLOR in *Monthly Mag.* XIII. 10 When two words of distinct parentage and meaning become orthographically identical, the less usual of the two should be traced back to its original form, and employed in some one of its more antique but more distinguishable appearances. **1817** COLERIDGE *Biog. Lit.* 67 They could write orthographically, make smooth periods, and had the fashions of authorship almost literally at their fingers' ends.

2. On the principle of orthographic projection.

1669 STURMY *Mariners Mag.* VI. 107 So have you the Sphere Orthographically in Right-Lines in the Convex-Sphere. **1835** POE *Adv. Hans Pfaall* Wks. 1864 I. 35 The entire northern hemisphere lay beneath me like a chart orthographically projected. **1866** PROCTOR *Handbk. of Stars* 22 *note*, The earth viewed from the sun would be seen orthographically projected.

orthographist (ɔːˈθɒgrəfɪst). [f. ORTHOGRAPHY + -IST.] One versed in orthography.

1616 BULLOKAR *Eng. Expos.*, *Orthographist*, hee that professeth or is skilfull in Orthographie. **1704** (*title*) The Expert Orthographist, teaching to write English exactly according to the Doctrine of Sounds. **1882** SCUDDER *Webster* vii. 256 The orthoepists had elaborated their system more than the orthographists.

orthographize (ɔːˈθɒgrəfaɪz), *v. rare.* [f. as prec. + -IZE.]

a. *intr.* To follow or apply the rules of orthography. **b.** *trans.* To spell (a word) correctly.

1611 COTGR., *Ortographier*, to ortographise; to write, or vse, true ortographie. **1821** *Sporting Mag.* VIII. 134 The omission of a useless letter will certainly not detract from the value of the substances orthographized. **1833** *Fraser's Mag.* VII. 501 Our amiable Quaker..does not orthographise over correctly. **1880** MRS. WHITNEY *Odd or Even* xlii. 429 She had orthographized correctly.

orthography (ɔːˈθɒgrəfɪ). Forms: 5–7 orto-, 6– ortho-, 5–6 **-grafy(e**, 6 **-graphye**, 6–7 **-graphie**, 6– **-graphy**, (7 **ortagriphie, authography**). [a. OF. *ortografie* (13th c.), later *ortographie*, mod.F. *orthographie* (16th c. in Littré), ad. L. *orthographia* (Suet.), a. Gr. ὀρθογραφία, n. of quality f. ὀρθογράφ-ος writing correctly, a correct writer, orthographer, f. ὀρθό-ς + -γράφος that writes, writer: see -GRAPHY. The earlier pronunciation, as in Fr., is shown by the spelling *orto-*.]

1. a. Correct or proper spelling; spelling according to accepted usage; the way in which words are conventionally written. (By extension) Any mode or system of spelling.

c **1450** *Cov. Myst.* xx. (Shaks. Soc.) 189 Loke what scyens ȝe kan devyse, Of redynge, wrytynge, and trewe ortografye. **1509** HAWES *Past. Pleas.* v. (Percy Soc.) 22 In all good ordre to speke directly, And for to wryte by true ortografy. **1530** PALSGR. Introd. 16 For kepyng of trewe orthographie. **1573** J. TYRIE in *Cath. Tract.* (S.T.S.) 11/2 We keip his awin wordis and orthographie. **1582** STANYHURST *Æneis* Pref. (Arb.) 13 Althogh thee ignorant pronounce Impératiue, Cosmógraphie, Ortógraphy, geeuing the accent too thee therd syllable, yeet that is not thee true English pronuntiation. **1588** SHAKS. *L.L.L.* v. i. 22 Such rackers of ortagriphie, as to speake dout sine [B], when he should say doubt. **1631** WEEVER *Anc. Fun. Mon.* 803 In our later English Ortography (I know not with reason) some write it Whore. **1645** MILTON *Colast.* Wks. (1851) 346 If these Greek Orthographies were of his licencing; the boyes at School might reck'n with him at his Grammar. **1750** CHESTERF. *Lett.* (1774) III. 80, I come now to..the orthography, if I may call bad spelling orthography. **1824** J. JOHNSON *Typogr.* I. 540 The singular orthography used in the foregoing legend. **1873** EARLE *Philol. Eng. Tongue* (ed. 2) §187 When we use the word 'orthography', we do not mean a mode of spelling which is true to the pronunciation, but one which is conventionally correct.

b. That part of grammar which treats of the nature and values of letters and of their combination to express sounds and words; the subject of spelling.

1588 W. KEMPE *Educ. Children* sig. F 3[v] Orthographie.. teacheth with what letters euery syllable and word must be written, and with what points the sentence and parts thereof must be distinguished... Which expressing and skill of the hand, belongeth properly to the Arte of Painting, and not vnto Grammar. **1616** BULLOKAR *Eng. Expos.*, *Orthographie*, the art of writing words truely; as sonne of man, with an o: sunne that shineth, with the vowell v. *a* **1619** FOTHERBY *Atheom.* II. xiii. §1 (1622) 348 *Orthographie*, the second part of Grammer, teaching the Arte of writing. **1824** L. MURRAY *Eng. Gram.* (ed. 5) I. 26 Orthography teaches the nature and powers of letters, and the just method of spelling words.

¶**c.** app. an error of some kind for *orthographer*.

1599 SHAKS. *Much Ado* II. iii. 21 Now is he turn'd orthography [*Qo.* ortography] his words are a very fantasticall banquet, iust so many strange dishes [*Rowe* (1714) *read* orthographer; *Capell* (1767) *conjectured* orthographist].

2. a. Orthographic projection. **b.** A representation in orthographic projection or section; a vertical elevation.

1645 N. STONE *Enchirid. Fortification* 6 Orthographie or Profile. **1664** EVELYN *Architects & Architect.* (R.), *Orthography*, or the erect elevation of the same in face or front, describ'd in measure upon the former idea, where all the horizontal lines are parallels. **1683** *Lond. Gaz.* No. 1820/4 Mr. John Spilberg has finished the Banqueting-house in Whitehal in Ortography, for the sole Printing and Publishing whereof,..His Majesty has been pleased to grant him his Royal License. **1772** C. HUTTON *Bridges* 95 *Orthography*, the elevation..or front view as seen at an infinite distance. **1823** P. NICHOLSON *Pract. Build.* 589 *Orthography*, an elevation, showing all the parts of a building in true proportion.

orthohelium (stress variable). [f. ORTHO- + HELIUM, as an antonym of the earlier *par(a)helium*.] The form of helium whose spectrum exhibits a fine structure of triplets owing to the spins of the two orbital electrons being parallel.

1922 A. D. UDDEN tr. *Bohr's Theory of Spectra* III. iii. 86 Helium was at first assumed to be a mixture of two different gases, 'orthohelium' and 'parhelium', but now we know that the two spectra simply mean that the binding of the second electron can occur in two different ways. *Ibid.* 87 The metastable state..is the final stage of the process giving the orthohelium spectrum. **1961** POWELL & CRASEMANN *Quantum Mech.* xii. 458 Spectroscopically, the singlet and triplet systems are independent of one another, and have been given the names *parahelium* (singlets) and *orthohelium* (triplets). The ground state of the orthohelium system..is therefore stable with respect to optical transitions of the usual kind, and has a correspondingly long lifetime.

orthohydrogen (stress variable). Also **ortho hydrogen** and with hyphen. [f. ORTHO- + HYDROGEN as tr. G. *orthowasserstoff* (Bonhoeffer & Harteck 1929, in *Naturwissenschaften* XVII. 182/1), coined on the analogy of *orthohelium* (see quot. 1935).] The form of molecular hydrogen in which the two nuclei in the molecule have parallel spins, so that the spectrum exhibits a hyperfine structure of triplets; it differs slightly in physical properties from the other form (PARAHYDROGEN) and forms 75 per cent of hydrogen in equilibrium at room temperature.

1929 *Chem. Abstr.* XXIII. 2614 (*heading*) Experiments on para- and ortho-hydrogen. **1935** A. FARKAS *Orthohydrogen, Parahydrogen & Heavy Hydrogen* ii. 4 The parahydrogen molecules have antiparallel nuclear spins and even rotational quantum numbers, while the orthohydrogen molecules possess parallel nuclear spins and odd rotational quantum numbers. *Ibid.*, The names orthohydrogen and parahydrogen were chosen by Bonhoeffer and Harteck on analogy with the nomenclature for the helium atom (orthohelium and parahelium), but it must be emphasized that the distinction between the hydrogen modifications is based on the different orientations of the nuclear spins, while in the case of helium it depends on the orientation of the electron spins. **1962** P. J. & B. DURRANT *Introd. Adv. Inorg. Chem.* xiii. 368 Ordinary hydrogen gas is a tautomeric mixture of orthohydrogen and parahydrogen. **1966** D. H. WHIFFEN *Spectroscopy* ix. 114 In the absence of magnetic materials non-equilibrium mixtures of ortho and para hydrogen are stable for many months. **1969** H. T. EVANS tr. *Hägg's Gen. & Inorg. Chem.* xviii. 452 At 0°K..only parahydrogen exists at equilibrium.

orthology (ɔːˈθɒlədʒɪ). *rare.* [ad. Gr. ὀρθολογία correctness of language, f. *ὀρθολόγος speaking correctly, f. ὀρθό-ς + -λόγος speaking. So mod.F. *orthologie*.] Correct speaking; that part of grammar which deals with the correct use of words.

a **1619** FOTHERBY *Atheom.* II. xiii. §1 (1622) 346 The natural, and as it were the homogeneal, parts of grammar be two; orthology, and orthography:..orthology..teaching men the right imposition of names. **1884** A. J. PATTERSON in *13th Addr. Philol. Soc.* 42 The struggle between the respective partizans of 'orthology' and 'neology'.

So **orˈthologer**, **orthologian** (ɔːθəʊˈləʊdʒɪən), one who speaks correctly, or who treats of the correct use of words; **orthoˈlogical** *a.*, relating to correct speaking.

1844 L. A. J. MORDACQUE (*title*) French Orthologer: or Complete Course of Theory and Practice on the French Language. **1884** A. J. PATTERSON in *13th Addr. Philol. Soc.* 43 Even at the outset of Kazinczy's career as a 'neologian', there was an opposition on the part of those who called themselves 'orthologians'. **1873** FORSTER *Life of Dickens* II. 241 Victims of orthological impropriety.

orthometric (ɔːθəʊˈmɛtrɪk), *a. Cryst.* [mod. f. ORTHO- + Gr. μέτρον measure: cf. *isometric*.]

1. Belonging to those systems of crystallization (the isometric, tetragonal, and orthorhombic) in which the axes are mutually at right angles.

1854 J. D. DANA *Syst. Min.* (ed. 4) I. 23 In Crystallography there are three axes employed,..and these axes are either at right angles with one another, producing orthometric forms, or oblique, producing clinometric forms. **1864** WEBSTER cites DANA. **1883** *Encycl. Brit.* XVI. 349/2 All crystals may be divided into 'orthometric' or erect forms and 'clinometric' or inclined forms.

2. *Surveying.* Of, pertaining to, or being a height measured from the geoid.

1919 G. L. HOSMER *Geodesy* x. 254 The United States Coast Survey has adopted the method of applying to ordinary elevations the correction for convergence, called Orthometric Correction. **1923** D. CLARK *Plane & Geodetic Surveying* II. v. 205 A line of constant orthometric elevation is parallel to the mean sea level surface. **1967** HEISKANEN & MORITZ *Physical Geodesy* iv. 172 Orthometric heights are the natural 'heights above sea level', that is, heights above the geoid. **1974** *Encycl. Brit. Macropædia* XVII. 832/2 To correct these distortions, orthometric corrections..must be applied to long lines of levels at high altitudes that have a north-south trend.

Hence **orthoˈmetrically** *adv.*

1952 G. BOMFORD *Geodesy* iv. 155 If no error of observation is made, Bb and aA will be measured orthometrically.

orthometry (ɔːˈθɒmɪtrɪ). *rare.* [f. ORTHO- + Gr. -μετρία (in comb.) measurement.] The art of correct versification.

1775 PERRY *Gram. Eng. Tongue* in *Dict.* p. xliv, Prosody comprises orthoepy..and orthometry, or the art of making verse. **1893** R. F. BREWER (*title*) Orthometry. A treatise on the Art of Versification and the Technicalities of Poetry.

orthomolecular (ˌɔːθəʊməʊˈlɛkjʊlə(r)), *a. Psychol.* [f. ORTHO- + MOLECULAR *a.*] (See quot. 1968.)

1968 L. PAULING in *Science* 19 Apr. 265/1, I have reached the conclusion..that another general method of treatment, which may be called orthomolecular therapy, may be found to be of great value... Orthomolecular psychiatric therapy is the treatment of mental disease by the provision of the optimum molecular environment for the mind, especially the optimum concentrations of substances normally present in the human body. **1970** [see *megavitamins* s.v. MEGA- a]. **1971** *Nature* 15 Oct. 452/2 The term 'orthomolecular psychiatry' introduced by Professor L. Pauling in 1968 has taught American psychiatrists to appreciate a principle well known to scientists. **1972** *Daily Colonist* (Victoria, B.C.) 16 July 25/3 Heavy doses of certain vitamins..correct biochemical imbalances. It's called the orthomolecular approach. **1977** *National Observer* (U.S.) 22 Jan. 11/5 Megavitamin, or orthomolecular therapy, is sometimes used to treat mental retardation, psychoses, hyperactivity, autism, dyslexia, and other learning disorders.

orthomorphic (ɔːθəʊˈmɔːfɪk), *a.* [f. ORTHO- + Gr. μορφή form + -IC.]

†**1.** *Biol.* (See quots.) *Obs. rare.*

1866 BRANDE & COX *Dict. Sci.*, etc., *Orthomorphic*.., that period in the developement of organised beings in which their full perfection is attained, prior to the formation of spermatic and germinal elements. **1892** *Syd. Soc. Lex.*, *Orthomorphic*, term applied to animals which attain their full size before the development of the generative organs.

2. Preserving the true or original shape of infinitesimal parts: applied to a class of map-projections in which small areas retain their correct shapes.

orthomorphic transformation, or **orthomorˈphosis** (*Math.*), a functional transformation which expresses the representation of one geometrical plan by another of which the infinitesimal parts retain their accurate form.

1882 T. CRAIG (U.S. Coast Survey) *Treatise on Projections* 33 It will be convenient to use the term given by Germain to such projections, and so we shall call them *orthomorphic*. **1891** CAYLEY *Wks.* XIII. 191 The author [Schwartz] considers the orthomorphic transformation (or, as I call it, the orthomorphosis) of a square into the infinite half-plane, or into a circle. *Ibid.*, It is easy to deduce the orthomorphosis of the rectangle into a circle. **1900** C. F. CLOSE *Sketch of Map Projections* 10, *Orthomorphic* (or *conform* or *conformable*): in these the scale is the same in all directions round a point in its immediate neighbourhood. *Ibid.* 17. **1910** [see CONFORMAL *a.* 2]. **1937** *Jrnl. Optical Soc. Amer.* XXVII. 338/2 The only telescope with orthomorphic object and image spaces is the unit power telescope. **1938**, **1957** [see CONFORMAL *a.* 2]. **1971** *Jrnl. Photographic Sci.* XIX. 24/2 A slit width of ¼ in. was used for orthomorphic copying.

Hence **ortho'morphism**, the property of being orthomorphic.

1919 *Wireless World* May 69/2 Orthomorphism.. may be possessed by many different types of graticule. **1940** *Geogr. Jrnl.* XCV. 381 It is well to preserve orthomorphism, if only for its help in solving great circle problems. **1975** J. B. HARLEY *O.S. Maps* ii. 19 The projection stretched the topography equally in all directions, rather than only in a north-south direction, and this gave it the property of conformality or orthomorphism, in which there is a minimal distortion of shape over small areas and the scale.. is likewise equal in all directions at any one point.

‖**orthoneura** (ɔːθəʊˈnjʊərə), *pl.* [mod.L., f. Gr. ὀρθό-ς ORTHO- 'straight' + νεῦρον nerve.] In Gegenbaur's system of classification, a series of prosobranchiate gastropods, in which the commissure to the abdominal or visceral ganglion takes a straight course backwards.

1878 BELL tr. *Gegenbaur's Comp. Anat.* 348.

Hence **ortho'neural**, **ortho'neurous** *adjs.*, of or pertaining to the *Orthoneura*.

orthonormal (ɔːθəʊˈnɔːməl), *a. Math.* [f. ORTHO(GONAL *a.* + NORMAL *a.*] Both orthogonal and normalized.

1932 M. H. STONE *Linear Transformations in Hilbert Space* i. 7 Two elements *f*, *g*, of 𝔥 are said to be orthogonal if (*f*, *g*) vanishes... A subset 𝔖 of 𝔥 is said to be an orthonormal set if, when *f* and *g* are elements of 𝔖,

$$(f, g) = \{{}^{1,\, f = g}_{0,\, f \neq g}.$$

1941 R. V. CHURCHILL *Fourier Series* iii. 35 The symbol $\{\phi_r\}$ will be used to denote an orthonormal set whose vectors are ϕ_1, ϕ_2, and ϕ_3. The simplest example of such a set is that consisting of the unit vectors along the three coordinate axes. **1965** PATTERSON & RUTHERFORD *Elem. Abstr. Algebra* v. 173 It is frequently desirable to choose an orthonormal basis: that is, a basis of which each vector is of unit length.. and such that any two basic vectors are orthogonal. **1968** G. LUDWIG *Wave Mech.* I. iii. 33 The degree of such a complete orthonormal system can be called the dimension of a Hilbert space.

Hence **orthonor'mality**, the property of being orthonormal.

1949 L. I. SCHIFF *Quantum Mech.* 401 (Index), Orthonormality. **1959** G. TROUP *Masers* ii. 16 This orthonormality is an expression of the independence of the stationary states. **1971** *Amer. Jrnl. Physics* XXXIX. 498/1 The $\{c_n'\}$ must satisfy the orthonormality relation.

orthonormalize (ˌɔːθəʊˈnɔːməlaɪz), *v. Math.* [f. prec. + -IZE.] *trans.* To make (a set of vectors or functions) orthonormal by orthogonalizing them and then multiplying each by an appropriate factor. Hence ˌ**orthonormali'zation**.

1935 *Trans. Amer. Math. Soc.* XXXVII. 309 When we orthonormalize $\{T^n - {}^1\chi_i\}$ we obtain $\{\phi_i\}$. **1968** B. KRIPKE *Introd. Anal.* iii. 57 Orthonormalize the functions 1, x, x^2 with respect to the inner product $[f, g] = \int_0^1 f(x)g(x)dx$ on $\mathscr{C}([0, 1])$. **1972** A. KYRALA *Appl. Functions Complex Variable* xiii. 318 Establish the orthonormalization relations.. for the associated Legendre functions. **1974** ADBY & DEMPSTER *Introd. Optimization Methods* iv. 89 Rosenbrock's method with linear search does not exhibit quadratic termination, due to the orthonormalization of the search directions in the second part of each iteration and the alignment of one of them towards the minimum.

orthopædic, -pedic (ɔːθəʊˈpiːdɪk), *a.* [ad. F. *orthopédique* (Dict. Acad. 1835), f. *orthopédie*: see ORTHOPÆDY.] Relating to or concerned with the cure of deformities in children, or of bodily deformities in general. ***orthopædic bed***, a bed in an orthopædic ward; normally one individually designed to relieve specific skeletal symptoms; ***more generally***, a bed with a very firm mattress or board; also ***orthopædic bedding***, ***divan***, etc.; ***orthopædic shoe***, a shoe designed to ease or correct deformities of the feet (cf. quot. 1842 s.v. ORTHOPÆDICAL *a.*); also ***orthopædic boot***, ***footwear***.

1840 *Prospectus*, The Royal Orthopædic Hospital for Club Foot, Spinal and other Deformities. **1847** tr. *Dupuytren's Injuries Bones* 56 Much benefit is derived from orthopedic means in this latter class of affections. **1879** HARLAN *Eyesight* ix. 134 A distinguished orthopaedic surgeon, Eulenberg, has stated that ninety per cent. of curvatures of the spine.. are developed during school-life. **1943** FUNSTEN & CALDERWOOD *Orthopedic Nursing* iv. 90 Orthopedic beds may be made with top linen placed over the end of the bed, rather than by tucking it in at the end of the mattress. **1971** B. MALAMUD *Tenants* 214 The tall mother.. wears a plain white dress, orthopedic shoes, and a blue cloche hat that hides her eyes. **1974** N. GORDIMER *Conservationist* 241 She.. turns a foot on the heel of one of those clogs, like orthopaedic shoes, the women are wearing these days. **1976** *P.O. Teleph. Directory: London Postal Area* June, Orthopaedic Bedding Centre. **1976** P. VAN RJNDT *Tetramachus Collection* (1977) i. 11 A cripple, obliged to wear a heavy orthopedic boot on his right foot. **1977** *Evening Post* (Nottingham) 27 Jan. 19/1 (Advt.), Modern single bed with mattress £15. Single bed base £10. Single orthopædic mattress as new £30. *Ibid.*, Orthopædic 4 ft divan complete. As new. £130. **1977** *Daily Express* 1 Feb. 29 (Advt.), OBC orthopædic beds.. look like any good quality bed... The big difference is this: They are designed with medical help and hand-assembled in thousands of different versions to give correct individual support to back sufferers whatever their weight or type of build. **1977** *Observer* 13 Feb. 18/6 (Advt.), Beds, soft, firm, extra firm, orthopædic. **1977** *Times* 14 May 25/7 (Advt.), Orthopaedic footwear our speciality.

So **ortho'pædical, -ped-**, *a.* = ORTHOPÆDIC *a.*; **ortho'pædics, -ped-** = ORTHOPÆDY.

1842 BARHAM *Ingol. Leg.*, *St. Medard* xliii, It at last came down Plump upon Nick's Orthopedical shoe! **1853** DUNGLISON *Med. Lex.*, Orthopædics. **1880** G. H. TAYLOR *Health by Exerc.* (1883) 372 Mechanical divulsion.. of the highest value in orthopaedics. **1900** *Pop. Sci. Monthly* 510 Hypnotism.. its application to general pedagogy and mental orthopaedics.

ˌ**ortho'pædist, -pedist.** [f. next: see -IST: cf. mod.F. *orthopédiste.*] One who cures deformities; an orthopædic surgeon.

1853 DUNGLISON *Med. Lex.*, *Orthopedist*,.. one who practises orthopædia. **1869** tr. *Hugo's By the King's Command* I. ii. 20 Let an orthopedist be imagined in the inverse sense.

orthopædy, -pedy (ˈɔːθəpiːdɪ). [ad. F. *orthopédie* (1741 in Hatz.-Darm.), mod.L. *orthopædia*, f. Gr. ὀρθό-ς ORTHO- + παιδίον child, παιδεία rearing of children.] The curing or correcting of deformities in children, or in persons generally; orthopædic surgery.

1840 *Prospectus of Royal Orthopædic Hospital*, Orthopædy,.. the art of remedying deformities of children. The term is extended to the art of curing distortions in general. **1863** KINGSLEY *Water Bab.* viii. 302 There cobblers lecture on orthopedy.. because they cannot sell their shoes.

orthopantomography (ˌɔːθəʊpæntəˈmɒgrəfɪ). *Med.* [f. ORTHO- + PANTOMOGRAPHY.] A modification of pantomography in which the X-rays are made to be more nearly normal to the line of the jaws, so that a radiograph can be obtained showing all the teeth and adjacent tissue in a straight line.

1959 Y. V. PAATERO in *Acta Radiologica* LI. 449 Since stereoscopy has been successfully adapted to ordinary pantomography.. theoretical and experimental investigations into the possibility of obtaining equally good stereoscopic effects with the new pantomographic method 'orthoradial pantomography' (or orthopantomography for short), were considered to be justified. **1961** *Oral Surgery* XIV. 947 *(heading)* Pantomography and orthopantomography. **1968** *Brit. Jrnl. Radiol.* XLI. 872/2 They reported that during orthopantomography the exposure at the eccentric axis was 1·5 R and at the skin surface it varied from 0·3 R to 0·9 R.

Hence **orthopan'tomogram**, a radiograph obtained by orthopantomography; **orthopan'tomograph**, an instrument for performing orthopantomography.

1959 Y. V. PAATERO in *Annales Medicinae Internae Fenniae* XLVIII. Suppl. 28. 223 As no 'orthopantomograph' suitable for clinical use was yet available, the accompanying pictures were taken of a dry skull with a hand-rotated miniature apparatus. **1959** —— in *Acta Radiologica* LI. 452 The jaws appear flat in orthopantomograms and not curved as in ordinary pantomograms. **1967** L. M. ENNIS et al. *Dental Roentgenol.* (ed. 6) x. 283 In operation of the Orthopantomograph, the patient remains stationary while the x-ray tubehead circulates from his right side around behind his neck to the left side, while the film rotates about an axis and at the same time, revolves from the left side of the patient's face, around the front and to the right side of the face. **1971** *Brit. Dental Jrnl.* CXXX. 429/2 There are two image layers in the orthopantomograph, one on either side of the rotational centre, the object further from the film presenting reversed images. *Ibid.* 433/2 This delicate spur of bone is not visible on the orthopantomogram.

orthophony, -pinacoid, -al: see ORTHO-.

†**orthopnic**, erroneous form for ORTHOPNOIC; in quots. as *sb.* = an orthopnoic patient.

1610 BARROUGH *Meth. Physick* II. vii. (1639) 81 Those which be properly Asthmatick, or Orthopnicks,.. have no Feaver at all. **1616** T. ADAMS *Soul's Sickness* Wks. 1861 I. 505 Let this orthopnic, for the help of his mind, avoid needless perturbations of the body.

‖**orthopnœa** (ɔːθəʊˈpniːə). *Path.* Also 8 -pnea. [L. (Pliny), a. Gr. ὀρθόπνοια in same sense, f. ὀρθόπνο-ος breathing upright, f. ὀρθό-ς upright + πνοή breathing, breath, πνέ-ειν to breathe.] A form of asthma or dyspnœa in which breathing is possible only in an upright position.

1657 *Physical Dict.*, *Orthopnœa*, a straitness of breath by stopping of the lights, that one cannot breath, but holding his neck upright. **1699** HANS SLOANE in *Phil. Trans.* XXI. 152 She fell into so great an Orthopnœa, that she could not, unless erect, Breathe. **1802** *Med. Jrnl.* VIII. 402 The access of orthopnœa occurred between nine and eleven o'clock at night precisely. **1899** *Allbutt's Syst. Med.* VI. 64 All varieties and degrees of such disorders.. from mere shortness of breath, or somewhat hurried breathing to the most urgent and terrible orthopnœa, or even fatal apnœa.

orthopnoic (ɔːθəʊˈpnəʊɪk), *a.* Also 9 -pnœic. [ad. L. *orthopnoic-us*, a. Gr. ὀρθοπνοικ-ός affected with ὀρθόπνοια.] Affected with orthopnœa; unable to breathe except in an upright position.

1601 HOLLAND *Pliny* II. 370 Others also would.. minister them in manner of a clystre unto those that were Orthopnoicke and Rheumaticke. **1748** tr. *Renatus' Distemp. Horses* 71 From which Thing the Horse becomes orthopnoick. **1859** SEMPLE *Diphtheria* 30 The orthopnœic affection of which he speaks was not really Malignant Angina.

So †**ortho'pnoical** *a.*, †**ortho'pnoity**.

1657 TOMLINSON *Renou's Disp.* 202 To help the Hydroptical.. or Orthopnoical Patients. *Ibid.* 297 The decoction of the root.. cures convulsions, orthopnoity.

†**'orthopny**, bad form for ORTHOPNŒA, perh. intended to repr. F. *orthopnée*.

1828 in WEBSTER.

orthopod (ˈɔːθəʊpɒd). *slang.* [Alteration of ORTHOPAEDIC *a.*] An orthopædic surgeon.

1960 'R. GORDON' *Doctor in Clover* ix. 76 We were interrupted by the surgeon himself, a big, red-faced, jolly Irishman. Most orthopods are, when you come to think of it. **1966** I. JEFFERIES *House-Surgeon* vii. 131 We had two male beds and one female, and the orthopods had two spare beds. **1969** D. FRANCIS *Enquiry* xii. 164, I telephoned to the orthopod who regularly patched me up after falls. **1978** *New Yorker* 13 Mar. 82 The problem now was to persuade the orthopod to go in and remove the screws.

orthoprax (ˈɔːθəʊpræks), *a. nonce-wd.* [f. as next, in imitation of *orthodox*.] Correct in practice; doing right.

1852 LYNCH *Orthodoxy* in *Lett. to Scattered* (1872) 270, I know not how I may best convince you that I am orthodox, .. but.. at least I desire to be orthoprax... To be orthoprax, reader, is to do aright according to the commandment of the everlasting God, as to be orthodox is to think aright.

orthopraxy (ˈɔːθəʊpræksɪ). *rare.* [f. ORTHO- + Gr. πρᾶξις doing, action, performance.]

1. [after *orthodoxy*.] Rightness of action; right-doing, practical righteousness; correct practice. Also **orthopraxis**.

1852 LYNCH *Orthodoxy* in *Lett. to Scattered* (1872) 270, I wish there was more orthopraxy in the world. **1859** *Life Eben Henderson* vi. 382 Let us have orthopraxy as well as orthodoxy. **1873** F. HALL *Mod. Eng.* iii. 86 What, then, constitutes grammatical orthopraxy? **1951** *Jrnl. Theol. Stud.* II. 98 The complete obedience of Jesus must be taken to be a complete vindication of the Law, and therefore the champions of legal orthodoxy (and orthopraxis), such as James and Peter, are the heroes of Jewish Christianity. **1960** J. PARKES *Foundations Judaism & Christianity* vi. 297 We cannot.. imagine an orthopraxy, which made a mizwah of reciting a special blessing over a fruit tree in bloom, attached to a Puritan theology which was quick to threaten Hell-fire for any slight disobedience. *Ibid.*, Historically however, rabbinic orthopraxy was lived with an entirely different background. *Ibid.* 311 There does not appear to have been any single system, nor was any particular method of choice a matter of 'orthopraxis'. **1971** *Clergy Review* LVI. 218 The orthodoxy of faith in the coming universal kingdom must constantly be made true in the ortho-praxy of creative flight forward with the world. **1976** E. MACLAREN *Nature of Belief* vii. 73 No amount of impeccable ortho*doxy* is belief. Belief is ortho*praxis*, commitment to certain action.

2. The curative treatment of deformities; orthopædic surgery.

1865 BIGG *Orthopraxy* (1869) 11 Orthopraxy is the legitimate culmination of mechanics as applied to therapeutics. **1866** *Sat. Rev.* 422 Why should not 'Orthopraxy' have a representative in the Council of Medical Education?

orthoprism: see ORTHO-.

orthopsychiatry (ɔːθəʊsaɪˈkaɪətrɪ). [f. ORTHO- + PSYCHIATRY.] A branch of psychiatry concerned especially with the prevention of mental or behavioural disorders. Hence **orthopsychi'atric** *a.*, **orthopsy'chiatrist**.

1924 *Survey* (N.Y.) 15 Aug. 536/1 'Straightness of Spirit'—interpreting this title literally—is the goal toward which the recently organized Association of American Orthopsychiatrists will bend their efforts. **1930** *(title)* American journal of orthopsychiatry. A journal of human behavior (American Orthopsychiatric Association). **1956** O. POLLAK *Integrating Sociol. & Psychoanal. Concepts* III. ix. 221 A field as energetic and imbued with the spirit of experimentation in practice as orthopsychiatry. **1971** E. M. BOWER *Orthopsychiatry & Educ.* 17 *(heading)* The challenge to education and orthopsychiatry.

orthopter (ɔːˈθɒptə(r)). [ad. F. *orthoptère*, f. mod.L. *orthoptera*: see next.] **1.** An insect of the order *Orthoptera*.

1882 in OGILVIE. **1935** *Discovery* July 199/1 Another orthopter, *Ephippigera vitium* Latr... lives in the Pacific and west Mediterranean areas, and in some places in Central Europe as a 'Pontic relic'.

†**2.** *Aeronaut.* Also -ptere. [ad. F. *orthoptère* (de Ponton d'Amécourt 1862: see S. Stubelius *Balloon, Flying-Machine, Helicopter* (1960) 90); so called because of the 'straight' (vertical) motion of the wings.] = ORNITHOPTER. *Obs.*

App. misinterpreted at first in Eng. as referring to a clockwork flying model. The word was superseded *c* 1909 by *ornithopter*, and for a time attempts were made (chiefly in dicts. and glossaries) to differentiate the meanings of the two words on etymological grounds. (See S. Stubelius *Balloon, Flying-Machine, Helicopter* (1960) 93–7.)

1868 *Catal. First Exhib. Aeronaut. Soc. Gt. Brit.* 11 *(heading)* Working models. 12 Orthoptere. Viscount de Ponton d'Amecourt,.. Paris. **1873** J. B. PETTIGREW *Animal Locomotion* 217 MM. Nadar, Pontin [*sic*] d'Amécourt, and de la Landelle have constructed clockwork models (*orthopteres*), which.. raise themselves into the air. **1887** tr. *J. Verne's Clipper of Clouds* vii. 65 If the orthopter—striking like the wings of a bird—raised itself by beating the air, the helicopter raised itself by striking the air obliquely with the fins of the screw as it mounted on an inclined plane. **1906** *Sci. Amer.* 18 Aug. 115/3 'Aéronef', or 'appareil d'aviation' (aviation apparatus) means an apparatus heavier than air, of which there are several kinds, such as.. (3) L'Orthoptère (orthopter) or mechanical bird, i.e., an aëronef sustained and propelled by beating wings. **1909** [see ORNITHOPTER]. **1909** *Westm. Gaz.* 23 Mar. 4/2 The Lamplough orthopter is not dependent for its sustentation in the air on rapid motion. **1910** *Flight* II. 58/1 All types of helicopeters [*sic*] and orthopters. **1917** *Jane's All World's Aircraft* A. 10/2 *Orthopter*, an intended-to-fly machine in which the wings are flapped mechanically in a manner which the designer believes would be the right way for a bird to flap its wings if its Creator had known more about aero-dynamics.

‖**Orthoptera** (ɔːˈθɒptərə), *sb. pl. Entom.* [mod.L., neuter pl. of *orthopterus*, f. Gr. ὀρθό-ς straight + πτερόν wing.] An order of Insects, distinguished by more or less coriaceous and usually straight and narrow fore wings, broad longitudinally-folded hind wings, and incomplete metamorphosis; comprising the cockroaches, walking-stick insects, leaf-insects, crickets, grasshoppers, etc.

1826 KIRBY & SP. *Entomol.* xlvii. IV. 371 *Orthoptera*... This Order.. was very judiciously separated.. by De Geer, under the name of *Dermaptera*... Its present name was, I believe, assigned to it by Olivier. **1828** STARK *Elem. Nat. Hist.* II. 237 A comparatively small number, such as some of the larger Coleoptera, Orthoptera, &c. exist from six to nine, twelve, and even fifteen months. **1868** DARWIN in *Life & Lett.* III. 97 Please tell me where I can find any account of the auditory organs in the Orthoptera.

b. Rarely in sing. **orthopteron** = ORTHOPTER 1.

1880 *Proc. Zool. Soc.* 152 The following remarkable Orthopteron was obtained last year.. by Mr. Kingdon.

Hence **orˈthopteral** *a.* = ORTHOPTEROUS; **orˈthopteran** *sb.* = ORTHOPTER; *adj.* = ORTHOPTEROUS; **orˈthopterist**, a student of *Orthoptera*.

1842 BRANDE *Dict. Sci.*, *Orthopterans, Orthoptera*, an order of insects. **1880** *Proc. Zool. Soc.* 152 The experienced Orthopterist Herr Brunner von Wattenwyl. **1900** *Proc. U.S. Nat. Museum* XXIII. 393 The Orthopteran genus *Trimerotropis*. **1956** *Nature* 10 Mar. 490/1 This is a preliminary report of an investigation in progress dealing with cytogenetics of orthopteran insects of the southern hemisphere.

orthopteroid (ɔːˈθɒptərɔɪd), *a.* and *sb. Ent.* [f. ORTHOPTERA *sb. pl.* (P. A. Latreille in C. S. Sonnini *Buffon's Hist. Nat. Crustacés & Insectes* (1802) III. 267) + -OID.] **A.** *adj.* Belonging or pertaining to a group of insect orders closely related to the Orthoptera. **B.** *sb.* An insect included in this group.

1887 A. HEILPRIN *Geogr. & Geol. Distribution Animals* 146 The discovery..of an apparent orthopteroid (Palæoblattina) in the most nearly equivalent deposits of Calvados, France. **1889** NICHOLSON & LYDEKKER *Man. Palæont.* (ed. 3) I. 593 The Orthopteroid section of the *Palæodictyoptera* includes a group of forms representing the modern Cockroaches. **1910** *Encycl. Brit.* XIII. 432/1 Orthopteroid wing-neuration. **1942** E. O. ESSIG *College Entomol.* ii. 15 Frons—a single sclerite between and below the branches of the epicranial suture; carries the single frontal ocellus of orthopteroid insects. **1973** W. S. ROMOSER *Sci. of Entomol.* xi. 323 Like the paleopterous forms, orthopteroid insects are hemimetabolous.

orthopteˈrology. *rare*$^{-0}$. [f. ORTHOPTERA + -O-LOGY.] That branch of entomology which deals with the *Orthoptera*. So **orˌthopteroˈlogical** *a.*, belonging to orthopterology; **orthopteˈrologist**, one versed in orthopterology.

orthopterous (ɔːˈθəʊptərəs), *a.* [f. ORTHOPTERA + -OUS.] Belonging to the order *Orthoptera*.

1826 KIRBY & SP. *Entomol.* xxviii. III. 41, I know no orthopterous insect that can be called extremely minute. **1859** *Sat. Rev.* 19 Nov. 612/1 The fantastical varieties of orthopterous insects which simulate inanimate nature in the forests of Ceylon. **1895** D. SHARP in *Cambr. Nat. Hist.* V. viii. 198 Three millimetres is the least length known for an Orthopterous insect. **1920** W. J. LUCAS *Monogr. Brit. Orthoptera* p. v, One or two new ones [*sc.* species] may fairly be looked for, when those naturalists who investigate our orthopterous fauna have become more numerous. **1965** D. R. RAGGE *Grasshoppers, Crickets & Cockroaches Brit. Isles* 2 The various types of Orthopterous insect have little in common.

orthoptic (ɔːˈθɒptɪk), *a.* and *sb.* [f. ORTH(O- 'straight' + Gr. ὀπτικ-ός of or pertaining to sight.]

A. *adj.* **1.** *Fire-arms.* Designating an 'orthoptic' (see B 1).

1882 *Pall Mall G.* 15 July 8/2 These competitors were using the orthoptic eye-glasses about which there has recently been so much discussion.

2. *Math.* ***orthoptic locus***: the locus of intersection of tangents to any curve at right angles to each other.

1882 in *Athenæum* 17 June 769/1 'Theory of Orthoptic Loci', by Rev. Dr. Taylor. **1886** C. TAYLOR *Order of Orthoptic Loci* in *Messenger of Math.* XVI. 1 The locus.. may be called its Orthoptic Locus, since at every point thereof the curve subtends or is seen under a right angle.

3. Employing the principles of orthoptics; of or pertaining to orthoptics.

1886 C. M. CULVER tr. *Landolt's Refraction & Accomm. of Eye* v. 407 We may hope to effect a cure of the strabismus by means of orthoptic treatment, with the aid of stereoscopic exercise. **1892** *Syd. Soc. Lex.*, *Orthoptic training*, a mode of correcting monocular vision produced by strabismus, or other defect, by ocular exercises. **1907** J. H. PARSONS *Dis. Eye* xxviii. 559 If there is any evidence of some degree of binocular vision it may be advisable to attempt to cultivate this by orthoptic treatment. **1932** *Brit. Med. Jrnl.* 14 May 918/2 The Royal Westminster Ophthalmic Hospital established an orthoptic department..in January, 1930. **1968** KATZIN & WILSON *Strabismus in Childhood* viii. 65 In most patients with crossed eyes orthoptic exercises play a prominent role in treatment.

B. *sb.* **1.** An opaque disk perforated with three small holes, through one of which the rifleman looks in taking aim.

1881 *Standard* 11 July 3/5 Some disgust has been created amongst the Snider men by a regulation which is to come into force this year prohibiting the use of the 'orthoptic'. **1882** *Pall Mall G.* 15 July 8/2 The advantage derived from the use of the orthoptics is that the eyesight is concentrated, and the sights on a rifle or gun are defined with great clearness. **1890** *Daily News* 27 Jan. 2/5 The use of orthoptics will be forbidden in all competitions in which uniform is ordered to be worn.

2. orthoptics (const. as *sing.*). The treatment (esp. by means of eye exercises) of defects in the action of the eye muscles, esp. those causing defective binocular vision.

1934 *Brit. Jrnl. Ophthalm.* XVIII. 429 The first examination in Orthoptics to be held in London will take place on July 3rd and 4th, at the Royal Westminster Ophthalmic Hospital. **1957** *New Scientist* 9 May 38/2 Many opticians nowadays have specialised in orthoptics.. and it is now included in the training of all ophthalmic students. **1957** A. HUXLEY *Let.* 12 Jan. (1969) 815 Optometrists.. are steadily adopting more and more the Batesian procedures into their system of 'orthoptics'. **1963** [see *orthoptically* below].

Hence **orˈthoptically** *adv.*, by means of or with regard to orthoptics. Also **orˈthoptist**, one who practises orthoptics.

1937 LYLE & JACKSON *Pract. Orthoptics in Treatment of Squint* i. 3 The orthoptist must remember that most squinting children who are old enough to have experienced the taunts of their schoolfellows suffer considerably from self-consciousness and inferiority. **1945** *Brit. Jrnl. Ophthalm.* XXIX. 420 (*heading*) An analysis of one hundred cases of strabismus treated orthoptically. **1963** *Arch. Ophthalm.* LXX. 117/1, 177 cases of accommodative strabismus..had been discharged as orthoptically satisfactory after treatment with glasses or miotics alone, or in combination with orthoptics and surgery. **1969** H. A. KNOLL in R. Kingslake *Appl. Optics* V. x. 282 The orthoptist is trained to diagnose and treat by nonmedical means binocular muscle anomalies. **1972** *Daily Tel.* (Colour Suppl.) 28 Apr. 10/1 On the staff at Ryegate.. are a physiotherapist, an occupational therapist, an orthoptist (a therapist for the eyes), [etc.].

orthopyramid: see ORTHO-.

orthorhombic (ɔːθəʊˈrɒmbɪk), *a. Cryst.* [f. ORTHO- 'right' + RHOMBIC.] Applied to that system of crystalline forms in which the three axes are mutually at right angles and unequal; also called *rectangular*, *prismatic*, *trimetric*, or *orthosymmetric*.

1868 DANA *Min.* Introd. (ed. 5) 25. **1878** GURNEY *Crystallogr.* 37 There may be three planes of symmetry at right angles. Such crystals belong to the Orthorhombic System. **1880** CLEMINSHAW *Wurtz' Atom. Th.* 56 The orthorhombic sulphates of magnesia, zinc, and nickel.

orthoroentgenography (ˌɔːθəʊrɒntgəˈnɒgrəfɪ, *etc.*). *Med.* [f. ORTHO- + *roentgenography* s.v. ROENTGEN-.] A technique for producing radiographs showing the exact sizes of organs or bones by using a narrow beam of X rays perpendicular to the plate or film.

There are other pronuncs. of this word and its derivs. analogous to those of ROENTGENOGRAPHY, -GRAM, etc.

1946 W. T. GREEN et al. in *Jrnl. Bone & Joint Surg.* XLIV. 60 In a study of growth by the Harvard Infantile Paralysis Commission, it was found necessary to develop a method of measuring the lower extremities which would meet the following requirements... The method to be described has been designated 'orthoroentgenography'. **1972** M. O. TACHDJIAN *Pediatric Orthopedics* II. vii. 1486/2 The advantages of orthoroentgenography are that the true length of each bone can be measured, because magnification due to divergence of rays is eliminated by directing only perpendicular rays at the ends of the long bones.

Hence **orthoˈroentgenogram**, a radiograph produced by orthoroentgenography; **ˌorthoroentgenoˈgraphic** *a.*, (done by means) of orthoroentgenography.

1946 *Jrnl. Bone & Joint Surg.* XLIV. 63 The true length of each bone can be measured directly from orthoroentgenograms without computation. *Ibid.* 65 Orthoroentgenographic measurement of a dissected adult femur, 45·7 centimeters long, gave a length of 45·5 centimeters. **1951** L. A. W. KEMP *Students' Radiol. Math.* v. 62 In the second orthoroentgenographic technique, a narrow slit..in a sheet of metal opaque to X-rays, is arranged to be vertically below the source S, so that at any instant there is only a narrow line of X-rays.. across the patient, the plane containing the rays being vertical. **1972** M. O. TACHDJIAN *Pediatric Orthopedics* II. vii. 1486/1 The technique [*sc.* teleoroentgenography] is not satisfactory for serial mensurations and bone detail is much less than that seen on spot orthoroentgenograms.

orthoscope (ˈɔːθəskəʊp). [f. ORTHO- + Gr. -σκοπος viewing: see -SCOPE.] **a.** An instrument for examining the interior of the eye, in which the refraction of the cornea is corrected by a body of water held against it. **b.** An instrument for drawing projections of the skull.

1892 *Syd. Soc. Lex.*

orthoscopic (ɔːθəʊˈskɒpɪk), *a.* [f. as prec. + -IC.] Having or producing correct vision; free from, or constructed to correct, optical distortion; *spec.* of binocular vision: without the reversal of convexity and concavity produced by pseudoscopic instruments.

1853 *Q. Jrnl. Microsc. Sci.* I. 305 To produce orthoscopic binocular vision, simple, not erecting eye-pieces, are required. **1875** H. WALTON *Dis. Eye* 616, I beg to refer the reader to my remarks on orthoscopic spectacles. **1881** *Jrnl. R. Microsc. Soc.* I. 204 Orthoscopic vision is always obtained, when the right half of the right pupil and the left half of the left pupil only are employed—pseudoscopic vision in the opposite case. **1892** *Syd. Soc. Lex.*, *Orthoscopic vision*, the appearance of an object which is viewed through a lens or lenses when its surface represents a plane without any curve, spherical aberration being entirely corrected. **1937** *Jrnl. Optical Soc. Amer.* XXVII. 333/1 The imagery should be as nearly orthoscopic as possible.

orthose (ˈɔːθəʊs). *Min.* [Named 1801 by Haüy, f. Gr. ὀρθό-ς right + -OSE.] = ORTHOCLASE.

1814 ALLAN *Min. Nomencl.* 18 Common feldspar.. Orthose. **1868** DANA *Min.* (ed. 5) 352.

orthosis (ɔːˈθəʊsɪs). *Med.* Pl. -oses. [f. Gr. ὄρθωσις making straight (f. ὀρθοῦν to set straight: see -OSIS.)] An artificial external device, as a brace or splint, which may be powered or unpowered and which prevents or assists relative movement in the limbs or the spine.

1958 H. A. RUSK *Rehabilitation Med.* ix. 196 Above all it is necessary for doctor, orthotist, and therapist to be fully aware of the tremendous physical and emotional impact of the orthosis on the total rehabilitation of the patient. **1966** *3rd Ann. Rocky Mountain Bioengin. Symposium* 79/1 The Rancho Electric Arm is the outgrowth of seven years of experimental work in upper extremity external power orthoses. **1970** J. KJØLBYE in G. Murdoch *Prosthetic & Orthotic Pract.* xi. 459 Orthoses used in conjunction with physiotherapy are of greatest use in the prevention of deformity by protecting the weaker group of muscles from the overactivity of their antagonists.

So **orˈthotic** *a.*, serving as an orthosis; of or employing an orthosis or orthoses; **orˈthotics**, the application of orthoses; **orˈthotist**, one who practises orthotics.

1951 *Jrnl. of OALMA* May 34/1 Skilled technicians now called Certified Orthotists or Prosthetists. **1955** *Artificial Limbs* May 99/1 On March 12 and 13, a two-day session dealing with prosthetic and orthotic devices brought together at the Statler Hotel in Los Angeles a record attendance of prosthetists, orthotists, and orthopedic surgeons. **1957** *Ibid.* Spring 116/1 Approximately 60 percent of the class time in orthotics was used for actual laboratory practice. **1968** *Math. Biosciences* III. 156 Essential problems in prosthetics, orthotics, remote handling, and robot design have a common theoretical background. **1970** R. D. MUCKART in G. Murdoch *Prosthetic & Orthotic Pract.* xi. 481 The orthotist would thus be able to devote his time more profitably to the solution of the splintage problems of the severely disabled patient. **1975** *Observer* 8 June 1/7 A critical report of the orthotic industry..is now circulating among orthopaedic surgeons. **1976** *Alyn & Deeside Observer* 10 Dec. 22/3 (Advt.), The post also offers experience in Plaster Work and Orthotics.

orthospermous (ɔːθəʊˈspɜːməs), *a. Bot.* [f. ORTHO- 'straight' + Gr. -σπερμος having seeds, f. σπέρμα seed.] Having straight seeds or fruits, as certain Umbelliferæ; also said of the seeds.

1859 DARWIN *Orig. Spec.* v. (1872) 116 In the Umbelliferæ.. the seeds being sometimes orthospermous in the exterior flowers and cœlospermous in the central flowers. *Ibid.* vii. (1873) 173 In certain Umbelliferæ the exterior seeds, according to Tausch, are orthospermous.

orthostade (ˈɔːθəʊsteɪd). *rare*$^{-0}$. [ad. Gr. ὀρθοστάδιον, f. ὀρθό-ς ORTHO- 'upright' + στάδιος standing.] A long loose tunic which hung down in straight folds, worn by the ancient Greeks.

1864 in WEBSTER.

orthostat (ˈɔːθəʊstæt). *Archæol.* Also **-state** (-steɪt). [ad. Gr. ὀρθοστάτ-ης upright shaft, pillar, building stone laid with the longest edge vertical.] An upright stone or slab, either forming part of a building or set in the ground as a monument.

[**1909** A. MARQUAND *Greek Archit.* ii. 67 Walls of temples and other buildings were usually provided with both base and crown. The orthostatai were set off from the vertical face of the wall.., and, even when the entire wall was covered with stucco, formed a more or less visible base.] **1926** D. G. HOGARTH *Kings of Hittites* ii. 26 (*caption*) Orthostats of south gateway. **1933** *Antiquity* VII. 222 The orthostates rest against pairs of jambs kept apart by sills rising to about half the height of the chambers. **1950** G. E. DANIEL *Prehist. Chamber Tombs Eng. & Wales* iii. 34 Megaliths used as orthostats, i.e. set in the ground and standing upright. **1950** H. L. LORIMER *Homer & Monuments* 419 The actual remains of Geometric temples would lead us to expect a few courses of undressed stones (possibly with an outer facing of orthostats) supporting a wall of crude brick. **1970** *Encycl. Brit.* XVIII. 454/1 The practice of setting a series of stone slabs, called orthostates, at the bottom of a wall below the mud-brick upper parts became common in the Assyrian period and was seen again in Hittite architecture. **1972** Y. YADIN *Hazor* II. vii. 72 The most important of these is a small orthostat of a lion... The lion is clearly an entrance-jamb orthostat. **1974** F. EMERY *Oxfordshire Landscape* i. 36 They, or their close followers the Beaker people, also built circles of standing stones.. and orthostats.

orthostatic (ɔːθəʊˈstætɪk), *a.* [f. ORTHO- + STATIC *a.*; in sense 1 coined as F. *orthostatique* (J. Teissier 1899, in *Semaine Medicale* 425/1).]
1. *Med.* Caused by, or resulting from, an upright posture; manifested or occurring while a person is standing up.
1902 *Med. Ann.* XX. 90 The condition..variously called intermittent or cyclical albuminuria, is perhaps best defined by the term orthostatic albuminuria, for..position is the factor which determines the appearance and disappearance of the albumin. **1927** *Physiol. Rev.* VII. 466 Disturbed vascular conditions, such as orthostatic albuminuria. **1961** *Lancet* 26 Aug. 475/1 The unusual disorder known as orthostatic hypotension of unknown origin. **1971** *New Scientist* 29 July 249/1 The cosmonauts of Soyuz 9 suffered from severe orthostatic hypotension and for several days were unable to assume the erect posture unaided.
2. *Archæol.* Set on end; constructed of stones or slabs set on end.
1912 T. E. Peet *Rough Stone Monuments* p. iv, The first and most important principle, that on which the whole of the megalithic construction may be said to be based, is the use of the orthostatic block, i.e. the block set up on its edge. *Ibid.*, The orthostatic slabs were often deeply sunk into the ground where this consisted of earth or soft rock. **1926** D. G. Hogarth *Kings of Hittites* ii. 29 Ground-courses of orthostatic slabs. **1941** *Proc. Prehist. Soc.* VII. 1 The use of large stones for orthostatic walling. **1950** G. E. Daniel *Prehist. Chamber Tombs Eng. & Wales* iii. 34 In almost all the chambers with orthostatic walls there is also intercalary walling to fill up the spaces.
Hence **orthoˈstatically** *adv.*
1950 *Chambers's Encycl.* IX. 234/1 The burial chamber or chamber tomb, a vault or chamber walled with megaliths set orthostatically side by side.

ˌorthostereoˈscopic, *a.* [f. ORTHO- + STEREOSCOPIC *a.*] Showing solid objects with their true proportions and perspective, *spec.* without the reversal of convexity and concavity produced in pseudoscopic instruments.
1892 *Jrnl. Quekett Microsc. Club* V. 46 If orthostereoscopic vision is required the transposition must be corrected. **1937** *Jrnl. Optical Soc. Amer.* XXVII. 339/2 In the x-ray clinic, orthostereoscopic radiographs help to reduce error in diagnoses. **1941** R. M. Allen *Photomicrogr.* v. 236 It is not essential, especially for higher-power work with single objectives, that true orthostereoscopic effects be obtained. **1966** H. Asher tr. *Valyus's Stereoscopy* ii. 94 Observation of these conditions ensures that an orthostereoscopic image is produced, i.e. one which shows a correct proportion in depth and undistorted perspective, and allows the visual fusion of the two stereograms into a single spatial percept.
Hence **orthoˈstereoscope**, a binocular microscope giving orthostereoscopic images; **ˌorthostereoˈscopically** *adv.*, in an ortho-stereoscopic manner; **ˌorthostereˈoscopy**, the production of orthostereoscopic images.
1892 *Jrnl. Quekett Microsc. Club* V. 52 If the two prisms were joined into one, it would..make a very efficient orthostereoscope. **1928** B. J. Leggett *Theory & Pract. Radiol.* III. ix. 430 This process of ortho-stereoscopy has important practical bearings. **1937** *Jrnl. Optical Soc. Amer.* XXVII. 333/2 A Greenough type microscope, if the magnification is not too high, may be built to operate orthostereoscopically for related combinations of objective and eyepiece pairs. *Ibid.* 339/2 Accuracy in the making of contour maps by aerial stereophotography depends upon the complete achievement of orthostereoscopy. **1966** H. Asher tr. *Valyus's Stereoscopy* ix. 380 Only when all these conditions are observed will the primary image system 'see' the object orthostereoscopically. *Ibid.* 409 To reproduce a natural relief the conditions of orthostereoscopy must be observed.

orthostichous (ɔːˈθɒstɪkəs), *a. Bot.* [f. ORTHO- 'straight, upright' + Gr. στίχ-ος row, rank, line + -OUS.] Characterized by orthostichies.
1880 Gray *Struct. Bot.*, *Orthostichous*, straight-ranked.

orthostichy (ɔːˈθɒstɪkɪ). *Bot.* [f. as prec. + -Y.] A vertical row or rank; an arrangement of lateral members (e.g. leaves) inserted on an axis or stem one directly above another.
1875 Bennett & Dyer tr. *Sachs' Bot.* 167 If members are so arranged at different heights on an axis that their median planes coincide, they form a straight row or Orthostichy; generally there are two, three, or more orthostichies on an axial structure. **1884** Bower & Scott *De Bary's Phaner.* 567 Species..with five or more marked prominences,..each of these being opposite to one of the orthostichies of leaves.

orthostyle: see ORTHO-.

orthosymmetric (ˌɔːθəʊsɪˈmɛtrɪk), *a.* [f. ORTHO- + SYMMETRIC.]
1. *Math.* ***orthosymmetric determinant***: a symmetric determinant in which all the constituents in the secondary diagonal, and likewise all those in each of the oblique rows parallel to it, are equal.
Example of an orthosymmetric determinant: $\begin{vmatrix} a & b & c \\ b & c & d \\ c & d & e \end{vmatrix}$
2. *Cryst.* Symmetric about two, or three, axes at right angles to each other; *spec.* = ORTHORHOMBIC.
1895 Story-Maskelyne *Crystallogr.* §421 The Ortho-symmetric or Ortho-rhombic system represents the most general case of a crystallographic plane-system referred to rectangular axes; [that] in which the parameters are all different, and the three axes are axes of orthosymmetry.

So **orthosyˈmmetrical** *a.* = prec. 2; **orthosyˈmmetrically** *adv.*; **orthoˈsymmetry**.
1880 Story-Maskelyne in *Nature* XXI. 204/1 Not being a crystal of any of the orthosymmetrical systems. **1895** —— *Crystallogr.* §79 A rhomb is orthosymmetrical to its diagonals, as a rectangle is to diameters parallel to its sides. *Ibid.*, A face of a crystal or any other plane surface or figure ..symmetrical to two lines perpendicular to each other.. will be said to be orthosymmetrically divided by these lines. **1878** Gurney *Crystallogr.* 37 Orthogonal symmetry or orthosymmetry.

‖**orthotes** (ˈɔːθəʊtiːz). [a. Gr. ὀρθότης correctness, rightness, f. ὀρθός right.] Correctness, propriety.
1610 Holland *Camden's Brit.* I. 139 There is among all nations that one Orthoites [*ed.* 1637 orthotes] of names which Plato speaketh of. **1620** T. Granger *Div. Logike* 164 What is the notation, interpretation, origination, true reason, Orthotes, Logos, Etymon, Etymologie of this name?

orthotomic (ɔːθəʊˈtɒmɪk), *a. Math.* [f. Gr. ὀρθο- right + -τόμος cutting (cf. ὀρθότομ-ος equally cut) + -IC.] Intersecting at right angles.
1857 Cayley in *Q. Jrnl. Math.* I. 242 The circle cutting at right angles the three given circles, or, as it may be called, the orthotomic circle. **1863** R. Townsend *Mod. Geom.* I. 17 Any..two figures intersecting at right angles, are said..to be orthotomic.

orthotomous (ɔːˈθɒtəməs), *a. Min.* [f. as prec. + -OUS.] = ORTHOCLASTIC.
1864 Webster cites Dana.

orthotone (ˈɔːθəʊtəʊn), *a.* (*sb.*) *Pros.* [ad. Gr. ὀρθότον-ος having its right or proper accent, f. ὀρθό-ς (ORTHO-) + τόνος tone, accent.] Having its own accent as an independent word; accented; *spec.* said of a word ordinarily unaccented (as an enclitic or proclitic) when it retains or takes an independent accent. **b.** *sb.* An orthotone word.
1882 in Ogilvie (Annandale). **1890** D. B. Monro in *Trans. Oxf. Philol. Soc.* 7 Mar. 22 Enclitics in Homer nearly always follow the first orthotone word of the sentence.
Hence **ˈorthotone** *v. trans.*, to accent (a word ordinarily unaccented).
(In mod. Dicts.)

orthotonic (ɔːθəʊˈtɒnɪk), *a.*[1] *Pros.* [f. as prec. + -IC: cf. TONIC.] = prec.
1885 *Amer. Jrnl. Philol.* VI. 218 In all other positions the verb is orthotonic, *i.e.* the accent falls on the verb if there is only one prefix.

orthoˈtonic, *a.*[2] *Path.* [f. as next + -IC: cf. *tonic.*] Affected with orthotonos.
1748 tr. *Renatus' Distemp. Horses* 315 An Horse is said to be Orthotonic who is stiff all over his Body.

‖**orthotonos** (ɔːˈθɒtənɒs). *Path.* Also -us. [f. ORTHO- 'straight' + Gr. τόνος stretch, strain, sinew.] Spasm in which the body is stretched out straight; a form of tetanus.
1878 tr. *von Ziemssen's Cycl. Med.* XIV. 318 Then they also distinguished an *orthotonos*, when the body was stretched out straight. **1892** *Syd. Soc. Lex.*, *Orthotonus*. **1892** W. Osler *Princ. Med.* (1901) 104 When the muscles of the back are also involved, there is orthotonos, which is more common than opisthotonos.

orthotriæne (ˈɔːθəʊtraɪˌiːn). [f. ORTHO- 'right' + Gr. τρίαινα trident.] A triæne or tridentate sponge spicule, whose three prongs or cladi project at right angles from the shaft; a simple spicule of the rhabdus type, with three secondary rays at one end, at right angles with the shaft.
1887 Sollas in *Encycl. Brit.* XXII. 417/1 The arms make different angles with the shaft;..when extended at right angles an *orthotriæne*.

orthotropal (ɔːˈθɒtrəpəl), *a. Bot.* [f. as ORTHOTROP-OUS + -AL[1].] = ORTHOTROPOUS.
1832 Lindley *Introd. Bot.* 415 *Orthotropal*,..straight, and having the same direction as the body to which it belongs. **1882** *Standard* 9 Oct. 5/3 Orthotropal ovules, and loculicidal dehiscence were the commonplaces of his conversation.

orthotropic (ɔːθəʊˈtrɒpɪk), *a. Bot.* [f. as ORTHOTROP-OUS + -IC.] **1.** Growing vertically upwards or downwards, as a root or stem.
1886 Vines *Physiol. Plants* xvii. 425 Sachs has observed that the young primary shoot of *Tropæolum majus* is at first orthotropic. *Ibid.*, The primary shoot of the seedling [of ivy] is..at first orthotropic, and radial.
2. Having three mutually perpendicular planes of elastic symmetry at each point.
1943 *Q. Appl. Math.* I. 128 Another important special case is that of an orthotropic elliptic plate bent by a linear load, for which the solution is new. **1963** P. Fern tr. *Lekhnitskii's Theory Elasticity of Anisotropic Elastic Body* i. 21 Delta-wood and plywood can be considered as homogeneous and orthotropic in the first approximation. **1971** P. J. Dowling in K. C. Rockey et al. *Devel. in Bridge Design & Constr.* 557 After the war the orthotropic deck bridge was developed and this form of bridge has now become a common form of construction..where saving in weight or depth of construction are important parameters. **1975** Cusens & Pama *Bridge Deck Anal.* i. 18 For long-span steel bridges, the deck is frequently a plate with longitudinal stiffeners (stringers). This form of construction is known to steel designers as an orthotropic plate.

orthotropism (ɔːˈθɒtrəpɪz(ə)m). *Bot.* [f. as next + -ISM.] The condition of being orthotropic; tendency to grow in a vertical direction, upwards or downwards.
1885 Vines in *Encycl. Brit.* XIX. 61/1 Orthotropism is then mainly due to negative geotropism.

orthotropous (ɔːˈθɒtrəpəs), *a. Bot.* [f. mod.L. *orthotrop-us*, a. Gr. type *ὀρθότροπ-ος, f. ὀρθο- straight + -τροπ-ος turning, turned + -OUS. Cf. mod.F. *orthotrope.*] **a.** Of an ovule: Having the nucleus straight, i.e. not inverted, so that the micropyle is at the end opposite the base: = ATROPOUS. **b.** Of an embryo: Having the radicle directed towards the hilum: = HOMOTROPOUS.
1830 Lindley *Nat. Syst. Bot.* 236 The embryo is certainly orthotropous in *Streptocarpus Rexii*. **1880** Gray *Struct. Bot.* vi. §8. 278 Orthotropous, or straight ovule, is the simplest but least common species, being that in which the chalaza is at the evident base, and the orifice at the opposite extremity, the whole ovule straight and..symmetrical. Atropous..is a later and etymologically much better name.

orthotropy (ɔːˈθɒtrəpɪ). *Bot.* [f. Gr. type *ὀρθοτροπία, f. *ὀρθότροπος: see prec.]
1. The condition of being orthotropous.
1848 Lindley *Introd. Bot.* (ed. 3) II. 41 From the frequent examination of the passage from orthotropy to anotropy in ovules I am convinced that the umbilical cord is never soldered to the ovulary leaf.
2. The condition of being orthotropic.
1966 F. J. Plantema *Sandwich Construction* v. 118 Numerical results have been computed only for a few typical cases of orthotropy corresponding to corrugated-core sandwich plates and sandwich plates having standard glass-fabric laminate faces. **1974** R. Szilard *Theory & Anal. Plates* iii. 375 If we assume that the principal directions of orthotropy coincide with the *X* and *Y* co-ordinate axes, it becomes evident that four elastic constants..are required for the description of the orthotropic stress-strain relationships.

orthotypous: see ORTHO-.

orthrawin, orthwart: see OVER-.

ortiard, obs. variant of ORCHARD.

orticant (ˈɔːtɪkənt), *a.* (*sb.*) [ad. It. *orticante* stinging, URTICANT *a.*] Irritating to the skin. Hence as *sb.*, an orticant agent.
1939 L. W. Marrison tr. *Sartori's War Gases* xiv. 217 The introduction of one or more sulphur atoms..between the chloroethyl groups..confers orticant properties. **1944** R. W. Moncrieff *Chem. Senses* vi. 140 In addition to the lachrymatories..there are the skin irritants or 'orticants'. *Ibid.* 141 Sym-dichloroacetone..has an 'orticant' action on the skin as well as being lachrymatory. **1965** *Economist* 27 Mar. 1361/3 Orticants are related to these [*sc.* vesicants like mustard gas] and cause itching. **1970** *Daily Tel.* (Colour Suppl.) 20 Feb. 19 Harassing agents..come in a profusion of varieties. There are..lachrymators..; orticants, which irritate the skin, and vomiting gases.

†**ˈortive**, *a. Obs.* [ad. L. *ortīv-us* pertaining to rising, f. *ortus* rising, rise. So F. *ortive* (1558 in Hatz.-Darm., 1762 in *Dict. Acad.*).]
1. *Astron.* Rising; pertaining to the rising of a heavenly body.
1635 Gellibrand *Variation Magn. Needle* 5 It may likewise be performed by the Amplitude Ortive or Occiduall of the Sunne. **1669** Sturmy *Mariners Mag.* VII. 45 The Suns Azimuth when he riseth, commonly called Ortiue Latitude. **1727–38** Chambers s.v., Ortive or eastern amplitude, is an arch of the horizon intercepted between the point where a star rises, and the east point of the horizon, where the horizon and equator intersect.
2. *Arith.* ***numeration ortive***: that part of arithmetic which deals with multiplication, division, involution, and evolution; as arising or derived from *numeration original*, i.e. numeration (in the mod. sense), addition, and subtraction.
1674 Jeake *Arith.* I. I. iii. (1701) 13 Numeration Ortive, ariseth from the former Species of Numeration Original, and consisteth in two things, *Reduction*, and *Figuration*.

ortment, obs. corrupt form of ORPIMENT.

ortografy(e, -phie, obs. ff. ORTHOGRAPHY.

ortolan (ˈɔːtələn). Also 6–8 **ortolane**, 7 **ortulan**, **hortulan(e**, 8 **ortelan**. [In sense 1, a. obs. F. *hortolan*, *ortolan* gardener (15th c. in Godef.), ad. L. *hortulān-us*, f. *hortul-us*, dim. of *hortus* garden; in sense 2, a. later F. *ortolan* (Cotgr. 1611 *hortolan*), a. Prov. *ortolan* or It. *ortolano* gardener, because this bird frequents gardens: cf. also L. *hortulānus* adj., of or belonging to the garden.]
†**1.** A gardener. *Obs. rare.*
1526 *St. Papers Hen. VIII*, VI. 534, I yielde my sylffe entyerly to the wyll of the moost notable ortolane.
2. A small bird, a species of bunting (*Emberiza hortulana*), found in most European countries, as well as in northern Africa and western Asia, and highly esteemed for its delicate flavour; the garden-bunting. Also called ***ortolan bunting***.
1656 Cowley *Verses & Ess., Horace, Epod.* ii. (1669) 108 Nor Ortolans, nor Godwits, nor the rest Of costly names that glorify a Feast. **1682** Wheler *Journ. Greece* I. 67 As fat

as Hortulans in France and Italie. c **1714** POPE *Lett.* (1735) I. 144, I love no Meat but Ortolans, and no Women but you. **1766** GOLDSM. *Ess., writ. by Ordinary of Newgate*, He.. would eat an ortolan for dinner though he begged the guinea that bought it. **1837** M. DONOVAN *Dom. Econ.* II. 145 The Ortolan is a small singing bird..common in France, Italy, and other parts of Europe. It is the epicure's prime morceau. **1895** LD. ROSEBERY in *Daily News* 3 July 7/4 The choicest morsel that you can put before an epicure, and that is an ortolan inside a quail.

1834 MUDIE *Brit. Birds* (1841) II. 33 The ortolan bunting. **1843** YARRELL *Hist. Brit. Birds* I. 457 The Ortolan Bunting is only a summer visiter to the middle and northern countries of Europe.

b. Applied in America and the West Indies to two other birds somewhat resembling the above, and esteemed as table delicacies, viz. the bobolink or rice-bird (*Dolichonyx oryzivorus*), and the soree or sora rail (*Porzana carolina*).

1666 J. DAVIES *Hist. Caribby Isls.* 89 There are also Black-birds, Feldivars, Thrushes, and Hortolans, in a manner like those of the same name among us. **1793** B. EDWARDS *West Ind.* iv. 99 *note*, The most delicious bird in the West Indies is the Ortolan or October-bird. It is the *Emberiza oryzivora* of Linnæus, or rice-bird of South Carolina.

Ortolani's sign (ˈɔːtəlɑːnɪ). *Med.* [named after Marino *Ortolani*, Italian who described it (*La Lussazione congenita dell' Anca* 1948).] A click which can be obtained from and is diagnostic of congenital dislocation of the hip in the newborn.

1965 RAINS & CAPPER *Bailey & Love's Short Pract. Surg.* (ed. 13) xvii. 346 The Ortolani test takes precedence over radiography. **1974** A. HENRY in R. M. Kirk et al. *Surgery* xv. 322 Diagnosis of the unstable or 'dislocatable' hip should be made in the newborn, and all midwives and doctors who participate in the care of the newborn child should be familiar with the examination of the baby's hip—Ortolani's sign.

† **ˈortrow**, *sb. Obs.* Forms: 3 **ortruwe, -trowe, -trewe, -trou**, 5 **-trow**. [A subst. use of next: cf. OE. *tréow, trýw* truth, faith.] Distrust, diffidence; suspicion.

c **1200** *Trin. Coll. Hom.* 43 Wanrede wecheð on mannes heorte ortruwe þe deuð him on helle. *Ibid.* 73 Ortrowe of agene mihte letteð þe mannes shrifte. **1297** R. GLOUC. (Rolls) 7021 Me þincþ þat in ortrou þou art more To me of þi broþer deþ. c **1425** *Eng. Conq. Irel.* 128 Men hadden grete ortrow vpon hym, that he..wold make hym self kynge I-crouned of the lond.

† **ˈortrow**, *a. Obs.* [OE. *ortríewe, -trýwe, tréowe*, f. OR- privative, 'without' + *tréowe, trýwe*, true, faithful, trustworthy.] **a.** (In OE.) Despairing. **b.** Distrustful, unbelieving.

c **893** K. ÆLFRED *Oros.* IV. i. §7 Hie æt nihstan wæron ortriewe [*MS. C.* ortreowe] hwæþer him æniʒ moneaca cuman scolde. c **1020** WULFSTAN *Hom.* xv. (Napier) 91 We to ortreowe [*v.rr.* ortrywe, -truwe] syndan godes mihta. c **1200** ORMIN 11589 Forr þatt he warrþ orrtrowwe off Crist þurrh niþfull modiȝnesse.

† **orˈtrow**, *v. Obs.* [OE. *ortrúwian, -trýwan* to despair of, f. OR- + *trúwian* to trust, believe.]

1. a. *trans.* To despair of; to distrust. **b.** *intr.* To despair; to be distrustful.

c **1000** ÆLFRIC *On O. Test.* (Gr.) 17 He ortruwode his drihtnys mildheortnysse. c **1175** *Lamb. Hom.* 113 He ne scal nohwer ortrowian bi godes fultum. c **1200** *Trin. Coll. Hom.* 75 þe man þe ortroweð godes mildhertnesse, he is idemd to eche wowe on helle.

2. *trans.* To suspect, have a suspicion of.

a **1225** *Ancr. R.* 382 ȝif eni mon ei swuch þing ortroweð bi him. **1297** R. GLOUC. (Rolls) 2381 Napeles wel me it ortrowede & ne leuede noȝt is glose. **1382** WYCLIF *Judg.* viii. 11 Gedeon..smoot the tentis of the enemyes that weren siker, and no thing of aduersyte ortroweden.

† **ˈortrowth.** *Obs.* [f. prec. vb. + -TH¹: cf. *tréowþ, trýwþ* truth, faith, trust.] Distrust.

c **1200** ORMIN 3145 He wass þa brohht ut off all Orrtrowwþe & orraþnesse.

‖ **ortstein** (ˈɔːtʃtaɪn). *Soil Sci.* [G.] A hard-pan, esp. one in the B horizon of a podzol that is cemented with iron and organic matter.

1906 E. W. HILGARD *Soils* x. 184 The latter class of hardpans is especially conspicuous in the case of swampy ground and damp forests, where 'moorbedpan' and reddish 'ortstein' are characteristic. **1932** G. W. ROBINSON *Soils* iii. 57 The most widely spread type of pan is that formed by deposition of hydrated ferric oxide, the so-called iron pan or 'ortstein'. **1972** C. B. HUNT *Geol. Soils* x. 234 Some hardpans are formed by accumulations of organic matter.. as in the well cemented, lower layers (ortstein) of a Ground Water Podzol Soil.

ortyard, ortyerd, obs. variants of ORCHARD.

Ortygian (ɔːˈtɪdʒɪən). [f. L. *Ortygi-us* (f. Gr. Ὀρτυγία (ὄρτυξ a quail) Quail-island) + -AN.]

1. Of or pertaining to Ortygia, the ancient name of the island of Delos, held to be the birthplace of Apollo and Artemis.

1640 J. GOWER tr. *Ovid's Fasti* v. 120 These prayers make Mercury in heaven to smile, Remembring his Ortygian cheat yerwhile. **1729** G. ADAMS tr. *Sophocles' Tragedies* II. 180 And his [Apollo's] Ortygian Sister like-wise.. Fire-bearing Diana. **1866** J. B. ROSE tr. *Ovid's Metamorphoses* I. 27 A votress of the power Ortygian. **1956** E. POUND tr. *Sophocles' Women of Trachis* 12 Sylvan Artemis, torch-lit Artemis With thy Ortygian girls.

2. Of or pertaining to Ortygia, an island which forms part of the city of Syracuse in Sicily. *rare.*

1820 SHELLEY *Arethusa* in *Posthumous Poems* (1824) 160 And at night they sleep In the rocking deep Beneath the Ortygian shore.

† **ˈorval.** *Obs. Herb.* [Cf. F. *orvale* (14th c. in Hatz.-Darm.), a name given in France to species of Salvia, esp. *S. Clarea* Clary, and *S. pratensis* Meadow Clary (Littré). The connexion between the two senses does not appear.]

a. = ORPINE; **b.** The herb Clary.

14.. *Stockholm Med. MS.* 173 (see *Anglia* XXI. 442) Orpyn or Oruale (crassula maior). **1597** GERARDE *Herbal* App., Oruall is Orpin. **1658** PHILLIPS, *Orval*, a certain herb otherwise called Clary or Clear-eye.

Orvietan (ɔːvɪˈiːtən). *Obs.* exc. *Hist.* [ad. F. *orviétan* (1642 in Hatz.-Darm.) or It. *orvietano*, f. *Orvieto*, the inventor being a native of Orvieto in Italy.] A composition formerly held to be an antidote against poisons; 'Venice Treacle'. Hence *gen.* and *fig.* An antidote.

1676 *Phil. Trans.* XI. 760 The Orvietan and ptisane of Lupins do considerable good to the persons distempered. **1696** PHILLIPS (ed. 5), *Orvietan*, an Alexipharmick Electuary, invented by a Mountebank, who was called Orvietanus. **1702** S. PARKER tr. *Cicero's De Finibus* I. 44 Our Natural Philosophy is our Orvitan against the Fears of Death. **1737** BRACKEN *Farriery Impr.* (1756) I. 310, I knew some Gentlemen who esteem'd the Thing..as a grand Orvietan or Counter-Poison. **1821** SCOTT *Kenilw.* xiii, With these drugs will I..compound the true orvietan. *Note*, Orvietan, or Venice treacle, as it was sometimes called, was understood to be a sovereign remedy against poison.

Orvieto (ɔːvɪˈeɪtəʊ). [Named from *Orvieto*, a city of central Italy: see prec.] **a.** A white wine made near the city of Orvieto. Also *attrib.*

[**1673** J. RAY *Observations Journey Low-Countries* 363 Heer [*sc.* in Rome] is great variety of Wines..as Greco, Lagrime of Naples..Orvietano.] **1846** DICKENS *Pictures from Italy* 159 Such wine in flasks, as the Orvieto. **1849** THACKERAY *Pendennis* I. xxxv. 344 We had some Orvieto wine for dinner. **1860** HAWTHORNE *Marb. Faun* xxv. (1883) 259 The finest Orvieto..is vulgar in comparison. **1926** P. M. SHAND *Bk. Wine* viii. 225 Umbria is chiefly noted for its white wines, of which the most famous name is Orvieto. **1940** M. HEALY *Stay me with Flagons* 70 Orvieto, now sweet, now dry, offers varied charms. **1967** A. LICHINE *Encycl. Wines* 535 Orvieto is white, and one of Italy's most consistently delightful wines, some of it semi-sweet, some of it dry... The market for Orvieto *amabile* or *abboccato*..has fallen off... Sweet Orvieto has a particular charm and special delicacy... Dry Orvieto is usually considerably higher in alcohol. **1974** N. MARSH *Black as he's Painted* ii. 39 Bottles of dry Orvieto..and other Italian wines.

b. Used *attrib.* to designate a type of majolica ware manufactured there.

1925 B. RACKHAM tr. *E. Hannover's Pott. & Porc.* I. III. ii. 96 It requires a practised eye to distinguish between a genuine and a spurious Orvieto jug. **1959** G. SAVAGE *Antique Collector's Handbk.* 70 The earliest *maiolica* was a series of wares painted in green and manganese purple at Orvieto and elsewhere, and most are loosely called 'Orvieto ware'. **1960** R. G. HAGGAR *Conc. Encycl. Cont. Pott. & Porc.* 338/2 *Orvieto*, a distinctive class of early Italian maiolica painted in coppergreen and manganese-purple with decorations and shapes of a distinctly 'Gothic' type. **1973** *Times* 3 Nov. 2/2 A Parke Bernet expert called in to look over what was there found the Medici bowl in a cupboard under a broken Orvieto dish.

Orwellian (ɔːˈwɛlɪən), *a.* [f. the name of 'George *Orwell*', the nom-de-plume of the English writer Eric Blair (1903–50) + -IAN.] Characteristic or suggestive of the writings of 'George Orwell', esp. in his satirical novel *1984* which portrays a form of totalitarian state seen by him as arising naturally out of the political circumstances of his time. Hence as *sb.*, an admirer of the ideas of Orwell.

So **Orˈwellianism, ˈOrwellism.**

1950 M. MCCARTHY *On Contrary* (1962) 187 A leap into the Orwellian future. **1952** *Time* 1 Sept. 19/2 Under the new rules, the Politburo and the Orgburo will be merged and the two ugly Orwellian names replaced by the stern old Latin 'Presidium'. **1958** *Times* 20 Feb. 11/3 In Orwellian language, 'imperious'. **1959** N. MAILER *Advts. for Myself* (1961) 309 Virtually perfect Orwellian ambivalences—(War is Peace, Love is Hate, Ignorance is Knowledge). **1961** [see HUXLEYAN, HUXLEIAN *a.* b]. **1963** *Observer* 3 Nov. 33/1 There is an Orwellian grimness about the naming of the Abolition of Passes Act in South Africa, which ensured that an African had to carry 27 papers combined into one booklet. **1967** *Listener* 2 Nov. 583/2 It is Orwellianism transferred to the world of the commercial, in which machines work beautifully, everybody is on a kind of holiday and wears a blazer and a redcoat number, the daily flavour of the ice-cream is announced on the morning radio, [etc.]. **1970** *Guardian* 30 Nov. 11/2 His election night insistence that the blood on his face was nothing less than the blush of victory can now be seen as a triumph of public relations.., an interesting example of the progress of Orwellism in national politics. **1971** *Ibid.* 14 Jan. 7/1 McLuhanites and Orwellians are likely to block our view of their masters' arguments. **1972** *Ibid.* 17 Feb. 14/5 The Orwellian Newspeak style. **1974** *Daily Tel.* (Colour Suppl.) 20 Sept. 27/4 One sees a future Robin Day as an Orwellian Official Moderator of the Ministry of Received Truth. **1976** *Time* 5 Apr. 22/2 In foreign affairs, says Moynihan, there is something almost Orwellian about the transformation of the word liberal to mean the opposite of what it meant a decade or so ago.

ory (ˈɔərɪ), *a.*¹ Also 7 **orie**, 7–9 **orey**. [f. ORE² + -Y.] Of the nature of, containing, or resembling ore; metallic.

1549 *Privy Council Acts* II. 349/1 Trowes of ory powder, ij dousen. **1628** H. BURTON *Israel's Fast* 32 Out of whose Oarie Bowels the King of England may dig richer Mettals. **1756** *Gentl. Mag.* XXVI. 430 Nor does its orey substance at all penetrate the ground. **1871** R. ELLIS *Catullus* xxix. 19 The spoil from out Iberia, known to Tagus' amber ory stream.

ory, *a.*²: see ORE 5.

-ory¹, formerly **-orie**, a suffix forming sbs., originating in ONorm.Fr. and AFr. *-orie* = Central Fr. *-oire*, as in *glorie, gloire*, which became the form for the adaptation of L. words in *-ōria*, and subseq. of those in *-ōrium*, as *victoire, offertoire, oratoire, purgatoire*; these also took in Eng. the form *-orie*, later *-ory*, which thus came to be the normal Eng. repr. of L. *-ōria, -ōrium*, F. *-oire*. The most numerous of these are adaptations of L. neuter sbs. in *-ōrium*, from adjs. in *-ōrius* (see -ORY²), or formations of the same type. Usually, these denote a place or instrument used in some process, as *crematory, directory, dormitory, factory, laboratory, lavatory, observatory, oratory, purgatory, refectory, repository, stillatory, sudatory*; but occasionally they have other senses, as *auditory, promontory, territory*. In some learned or technical words the L. form in -ORIUM is retained; thus *auditorium* is differentiated from *auditory, crematorium* is more frequent than *crematory*. In a few words *-ory* is the suffix *-y* added to an agent-noun in *-or*, e.g. *orator-y* (the art of the orator), *rector-y* (the seat of a rector).

-ory², formerly **-orie**, a suffix forming adjs. (whence also sbs.), originating in ONF. *-ori, -orie*, and repr. (sometimes through OF. *-oir, -oire*) L. *-ōri-us, -a, -um*, itself a compound suffix consisting of the adj. formative *-i-us* added to derivative sbs. in *-or* (cf. *sorōr* sister, *sorōr-i-us* sisterly), chiefly agent-nouns in *-tor, -sor* (see -OR), but sometimes app. from the cognate ppl. stem in *-t-, -s-*; e.g. *accūsātōr-i-us, suāsōr-i-us, dēcrētōr-i-us*. As an agent-n. in *-or* is possible from every L. vb., an adj. in L. *-ōri-us*, Eng. *-ory* is also always possible, and is often in Eng. use when no corresponding L. adj. is recorded, and even when no agent-n. occurs; thus, we have *compulsory, dispensatory, illusory, persuasory*, without the agent-nouns *compulsor*, etc., and *amatory, hortatory, perfunctory, predatory*, where the L. verb is not even represented in English. Instead of *-ory*, the Eng. adj. has often the extended form -ORIAL, less frequently -ORIOUS.

oryal, oryble, obs. ff. ORIEL, HORRIBLE.

orycterope (ɒˈrɪktərəʊp). *Zool.* [a. F. *oryctérope*, ad. mod.L. *Orycteropus* (*-pod-*), f. Gr. ὀρυκτήρ digger + πούς, ποδ- foot. Now usually in L. form.] A mammal of genus *Orycteropus*: = AARDVARK.

1836–9 TODD *Cycl. Anat.* II. 54/2 In the..Orycterope it [the liver] consists of three lobes. **1840** tr. *Cuvier's Anim. Kingd.* 125 The orycteropes have long been confounded with the ant-eaters... There is but one species known,..the orycterope of the Cape. [Two species are now known.]

So **orycteropodoid** (ɒrɪktəˈrɒpəʊdɔɪd) *a.* [see -OID], resembling the genus *Orycteropus*.

1890 *Cent. Dict.* cites OWEN.

† **oryctics.** *Obs. rare*⁻¹. [ad. Gr. ὀρυκτικ-ός pertaining to digging or mining: see -IC 2.] = ORYCTOLOGY.

1888 R. Y. TYRRELL in *Fortn. Rev.* Jan. 57 He added that his friend is about to sell his books and buy a spade, with a view to graduating with honours in Oryctics.

orycto-, comb. form of Gr. ὀρυκτός dug up (cf. τὰ ὀρυκτά things dug up), used in modern compounds (mod.L., Eng., Fr., Ger., etc.), with the sense of 'fossil' or 'mineral': see below.

† **oryctoˈgnostic**, *a. Obs.* [f. ORYCTOGNOSY, after Gr. γνωστικ-ός in its relation to γνῶσις knowledge.] Pertaining or relating to 'oryctognosy'; mineralogical.

1796 KIRWAN *Elem. Min.* (ed. 2) I. Pref. 13 The second part contains the systematic or oryctognostic collection. **1804** A. JAMESON *Mineralogy* I. Introd. 23 The Wernerian oryctognostic system is framed in conformity with the strictest rules of classification. **1853** TH. ROSS *Humboldt's Trav.* III. xxxii. 401 The amygdaloid of Ortiz approaches, by its oryctognostic characters, to the former of those formations.

So † **oryctoˈgnostical** *a.* = prec.; † **oryctoˈgnostically** *adv.*

1852 TH. ROSS *Humboldt's Trav.* Introd. 10 The simple fossils which compose the mass of mountains, and of which the names and character are the object of oryctognostical knowledge. **1805–17** R. JAMESON *Char. Min.* (ed. 3) 57 One [colour] is, oryctognostically considered, pure or unmixed with any other, and is called the characteristic colour.

†**oryc'tognosy.** *Obs.* [a. F. *oryctognosie* (Littré), f. ORYCTO- + Gr. *γνῶσις* knowledge.] The knowledge of minerals; mineralogy.

1804 *Edin. Rev.* V. 66 Mineralogy might be advantageously substituted for 'Oryctognosie'. **1811** PINKERTON *Petral.* I. Introd. 32 Werner..in his lectures on Oryctognosy, or the general knowledge of minerals. **1852** TH. ROSS *Humboldt's Trav.* I. ii. 89 Confounding descriptive mineralogy (oryctognosy) with geognosy.

†**oryc'tography.** *Obs.* [ad. mod.L. *oryctographia* (Baier, 1708): see ORYCTO- and -GRAPHY. Cf. F. *oryctographie* (1771 in Dict. Trévoux).] The description of 'fossils' or minerals; descriptive mineralogy. So †**orycto'graphic, -ical** *adjs.*, pertaining to 'oryctography'.

1753 CHAMBERS *Cycl. Supp.*, *Oryctography*, is that part of natural history wherein fossils are described. **1811** PINKERTON *Petral.* I. 95 Ferber, in his oryctography of Derbyshire, mentions iron-stone. **1857** MAYNE *Expos. Lex.*, *Oryctographicus*,..oryctographical.

orycto'logical, *a.* [f. as next + -ICAL: cf. F. *oryctologique.*] Pertaining or relating to oryctology; mineralogical or palæontological.

1804 J. PARKINSON *Organic Rem.* I. 22 The oryctological history of..Germany. **1846** J. BAXTER *Libr. Pract. Agric.* (ed. 4) I. 340 A geological, mineral, and oryctological account of this sand district having been given.

oryc'tologist. [f. as next + -IST.] One versed in oryctology; a mineralogist or palæontologist.

1799 DE SERRA in *Phil. Trans.* LXXXIX. 151 Impressions or remains of plants..by more ancient and less enlightened oryctologists, supposed to belong to plants actually growing in temperate and cold climates. **1842** H. MILLER *O.R. Sandst.* xiv. (ed. 2) 301 With which [substances] the oryctologist has still to acquaint himself.

oryc'tology. Now *rare.* [mod. f. (F. *oryctologie*, 1755 in Hatz.-Darm.): see ORYCTO- and -LOGY.] The science of 'fossils' or things dug out of the earth, either (*a*) inorganic or (*b*) organic; **a.** the science which deals with the nature and composition of rocks and minerals, mineralogy; **b.** that department of geology which deals with fossil organic remains, palæontology.

1753 CHAMBERS *Cycl. Supp.*, *Oryctology*, is the part of physics which treats of fossils..Under this head comes the doctrine of salts, sulphurs, stones, gems and metals. **1804** J. PARKINSON *Organic Rem.* I. 21 To enumerate all the writers on oryctology of this period would be unnecessary. **1842** H. MILLER *O.R. Sandst.* vii. (ed. 2) 147 There was almost nothing known at the period of the oryctology of the older rocks. **1846** DANA *Zooph.* (1848) 537, I know of no copy of the Oryctology of Moscow in this country.

†**o,ryctozo'ology.** *Obs. rare*$^{-0}$. [mod. f. ORYCTO- + ZOOLOGY.] That department of geology which deals with fossil animal remains. So †**o,ryctozoo'logical** *a.*

1857 MAYNE *Expos. Lex.*, *Oryctozoologia*,..oryctozoölogy. A work was published under this title by Eichwald in 1821. *Oryctozoologicus*,..oryctozoölogical.

†**oryelle,** obs. variant of ORL *sb.*, alder.

c **1440** *Promp. Parv.* 369/2 Oryelle tre, supra in aldyr tre.

orygine ('ɒrɪdʒaɪn), *a. Zool.* [f. L. *oryg-*, stem of *oryx* (see ORYX) + -INE¹.] Resembling an antelope of the genus *Oryx*, esp. belonging to an African group including the addax, gemsbuck, roan, and sable antelopes, which share certain characteristics with the oryx, such as long horns, tufted tails, and large, square teeth.

1898 *Proc. Zool. Soc.* 352 The Addax, I think, is on the whole more an orygine type than a hippotragine. **1947** J. STEVENSON-HAMILTON *Wild Life S. Afr.* xi. 75 (*heading*) The orygine antelopes.

oryloge, orynal(e, obs. ff. HOROLOGE, URINAL.

oryx ('ɒrɪks). Also 4–7 orix, (4–6 origen, 7 *pl.* origes). [a. L. *oryx* (acc. *orygem*), a. Gr. *ὄρυξ*, *ὀρυγ-* (1) a pickaxe, (2) a kind of antelope or gazelle, so called from its pointed horns.]

a. The name in ancient Greek and Latin for an antelope of northern Africa, perh. *Oryx leucoryx* or *O. beisa*. In the LXX and Vulgate used to render Heb. *thō* (1611 wild ox, wild bull, *R.V.* antelope); hence occurring in Wyclif, etc. but erroneously identified with some small hibernating animal. **b.** In *mod. Zool.*, a genus of African antelopes, of large size, with long straight (or slightly curved) pointed horns in both sexes; an antelope of this genus. The South African species is *O. capensis*, the gemsbok.

1382 WYCLIF *Deut.* xiv. 5 This is the beest that ȝe owen to eete; oxe, and sheep, and she geet,..phigarg, origen. —— *Isa.* li. 20 The vnclene beste..that is clepid orix [**1388** the beeste orix]. **1398** TREVISA *Barth. De P.R.* XVIII. lxxix. (MS. Bodl.) lf. 280 b/2 Orix hatte Tho in Ebrewe and is acounted in þe lawe amonge vnclene bestes,..is a beste liche to a water mows. **1535** COVERDALE *Deut.* xiv. 5 These are the Beestes which ye shal eate: Oxen, Shepe, Goates, Hert, Roo, Bugle, wylde goate, Vnicorne, Origen and camelion. **1601** HOLLAND *Pliny* I. 231 Of this kind be the Origes, the only beasts, as some thinke,..that..haue their haire growing contrariwise and turning toward the head. **1778** BP. LOWTH *Isaiah* Prel. Diss. (ed. 12) 37 Like an oryx (a large fierce wild beast) in the toils. **1827** tr. *Cuvier's Anim. Kingd.* IV. 187 The Caffrarian oryx is an animal of remarkable beauty and vigour. **1876** E. E. FREWER tr. *Verne's Adv. 3 Eng. & 3 Russ. in S. Afr.* xvi. 123 A herd of about twenty of the species of antelope known as the *oryx.*

oryzenin (ɒ'raɪzənɪn). *Biochem.* [f. L. *orȳz-a* (Gr. *ὄρυζα*) rice + *-enin*, prob. after GLUTENIN.] A glutelin that is the chief protein in rice.

1908 ROSENHEIM & KAJIURA in *Jrnl. Physiol.* XXXVI. p. lv, These three proteins appear to be the only ones present in rice and we propose to call them respectively: Rice-globulin, Rice-albumin, and Oryzenin. **1926** *Jrnl. College of Agric. Hokkaido Imperial Univ.* XVI. 76 The differences between the common and the glutinous rice oryzenins are marked by their physico-chemical properties. **1952** *Chem. Abstr.* XLVI. 2747 As tested by fermenting each constituent of rice by *Aspergillus oryzae*, the odor of sake was found to be due mainly to the oryzenin. **1972** B. O. JULIANO in D. F. HOUSTON *Rice* ii. 41 Glutelin or oryzenin is the major protein fraction of brown and milled rice.

oryzivorous (ɒrɪ'zɪvərəs), *a.* [f. mod.L. *oryzivor-us* (f. *oryza*, Gr. *ὄρυζα* rice + *-vorus* devouring) + -OUS.] Rice-eating, feeding upon rice.

1857 in MAYNE *Expos. Lex.*

‖**os¹** (ɒs). *Anat.* [L. *os*, pl. *ossa.*] The Latin word for bone, commonly used in Anatomy in the mod.L. names of particular bones. Such are: *os calcis*, the heel-bone; *os coxæ*, the hip- or haunch-bone; *os hyoides, hyoideum*, or *hypsiloides*, the HYOID or U-shaped bone of the tongue; *os innominatum*, the INNOMINATE or hip-bone; *os orbiculare*, the ORBICULAR bone; *os pubis* = PUBIS; *os sacrum* = SACRUM; etc.

1548–77 VICARY *Anat.* ix. (1888) 75 These bones be..broade towardes the Hanches, and before they ioyne and make *Os pectinis.* **1611** COTGR. s.v. *Os*, *Os de la hanche*, the third part of *Os Ilium.* **1741** MONRO *Anat. Bones* (ed. 3) 192 *Os sacrum* is so called from being offered as a dainty Bit in Sacrifice. **1749** FIELDING *T. Jones* VII. xiii, The *os* or bone very plainly appeared through the aperture. **1754–64** SMELLIE *Midwif.* I. 74 Each *os Innominatum* is in infants composed of three different bones, under the appellation of *os Ilium, Ischium*, and *Pubis.* **1842** E. WILSON *Anat. Vade M.* (ed. 2) 84 The Os Calcis may be known by its large size and oblong figure. *Ibid.* 58 The Os Hyoides..gives support to the tongue.

‖**os²** (ɒs). *Anat.* [L. *ōs*, pl. *ōra.*] The Latin word for mouth, used in anatomy in naming the mouths or entrances of certain passages; esp. in *os uteri* the mouth or orifice of the uterus; *os uteri externum*, also *os tincæ*, the lower or outer orifice of the utero-cervical canal; *os uteri internum*, the upper and inner end of the same.

1737 *Med. Essays* (Edinb.) III. xix. 318, I examined her Condition, and found that the *Os Tincæ* had..not yielded. **1754–64** SMELLIE *Midwif.* I. 193 If the *os uteri* remains close shut. **1872** F. G. THOMAS *Dis. Women* (ed. 3) 35 The changes which the os undergoes during pregnancy.

os, obs. variant of AS, US; see also OSAR.

os ace, an illiterate pl. of *O ace* for *O-yes*, OYEZ.

‖**osaekomi waza** (oːsaekoːmi waza). *Judo.* Also **osae waza.** [Jap., lit. 'art of holding', f. *osae* to press upon or against + *komi* to be packed up + *waza* art.] (See quot. 1932.)

1932 E. J. HARRISON *Art of Ju-Jitsu* v. 64 '*Osaekomi-waza*', otherwise methods of holding down one's opponent on the mats for a longer or shorter interval. *Ibid.* 65 The first trick of *osaekomi-waza*..is the so-called Locking of the Upper Four Quarters. **1941** M. FELDENKRAIS *Judo* 173 Immobilizing or holding down (osae-waza). **1956** K. TOMIKI *Judo* iii. 90 Practice in *katame-waza* (art of grappling) had better be based on that in *osae-waza* (art of holding, or hold-down). **1962** LEBELL & COUGHRAN *Handbk. Judo* vi. 103 (*heading*) Osaekomiwaza—hold on there! Hold down techniques. **1970** A. P. HARRINGTON *Judo Guide* i. 31 Methods of holding the opponent with his back largely on the ground with one or both arms under restrictive control are known as Hold-downs (Osaekomi-waza).

Osage ('əʊseɪdʒ), *sb.* and *a.* [ad. Osage self-designation *wazhazhe.*] **A.** *sb.* A member of a Siouan Indian people coming originally from the Osage river valley, Missouri. Also, their language. **B.** *adj.* Of or pertaining to this people.

1698 tr. *Hennepin's New Discovery* I. 141 Several Savages of the Nations of the Osages, Cikaga, and Akansa, came to see us. **1722** D. COXE *Descr. Carolana* 16 The Yellow [River] is called the River of the Massorites, from a great Nation inhabiting in many Towns near its juncture with the River of the Osages. **1804** [see FIX *v.* 14 b]. **1832** [see HEAP *sb.* 4 d]. **1835** W. IRVING *Tour on Prairies* i. 7 He spoke a Babylonish jargon of mingled French-English, and Osage. **1906** *Indian Affairs: Laws & Treaties* (U.S.) (1913) III. 253 All lands belonging to the Osage tribe of Indians..shall be divided among the members of said tribe. **1931** C. TURNER tr. *von Schmidt-Pauli's We Indians* xiii. 132 The long-drawn-out and piercing war-cry of the Osages. **1933** L. BLOOMFIELD *Language* iv. 72 The Siouan family includes..Dakota,..Omaha, Osage, [etc.]. **1945** J. J. MATHEWS *Talking to Moon* 87 She..said in Osage to the chief, 'I want to tell my son about the way we did things.' **1973** A. H. WHITEFORD *N. Amer. Indian Arts* 90 Oto and Osage also wove hat and neck bands of horsehair. **1974** *Encycl. Brit. Micropædia* VII. 602/3 The discovery of oil on the Osage reservation in the late 19th century..made the Osage a uniquely prosperous people.

osage, obs. variant of USAGE.

Osage orange. [f. OSAGE *sb.* and *a.* + ORANGE *sb.*¹] = MACLURA, a tree native to Arkansas and neighbouring regions formerly occupied by the Osage people; also, the fruit of this tree. Also *attrib.*

1817 J. BRADBURY *Trav. Amer.* 160 *note*, It bleeds an acrid milky juice when wounded, and is called by the hunters the Osage orange. **1838** H. W. ELLSWORTH *Valley Upper Wabash* v. 52 These fences, whose tops are covered with a luxuriant growth of the wild locust hawthorn, or Osage Orange. **1846** D. J. BROWNE *Trees Amer.* 465 The Osage Orange-tree. **1857** *Trans. Illinois Agric. Soc.* II. 23 The practicability of successfully cultivating the Osage Orange plant into a protective hedge. **1859** MARCY *Prairie Trav.* i. 26 Wheels made of the bois d'arc, or Osage-orange wood, are the best for the plains, as they shrink but little. **1890** *Blackw. Mag.* Jan. 60 We had three miles of osage orange hedges. **1891** *Harper's Mag.* Sept. 579/2 There was a hedge of Osage Orange on one side of the yard. **1940** E. FERGUSSON *Our Southwest* ix. 157 Mrs. Hayden found a stately adobe house with water piped in, an osage orange hedge around an orchard. **1970** *New Yorker* 28 Feb. 41/2 When we were little ..we could bowl the Osage oranges down. **1974** A. DILLARD *Pilgrim at Tinker Creek* vi. 100 Beneath the overarching limbs of tulip, walnut, and Osage orange, I see the creek pour down.

Osagyefo (oːsa'gjefɔ). [Fante.] Redeemer: a name given to Kwame Nkrumah (1909–72), first prime minister of Ghana (1952–60), president of the Republic (1960–66).

1961 *Guardian* 29 Sept. 10/1 The Osagyefo (or Redeemer, as he is called by his press). **1964** *Economist* 14 Mar. 983/3 The Osagyefo offered a careful welcome. **1965** *Ibid.* 24 Apr. 389/1 Everyone's suspicions of the Osagyefo (it means redeemer) were discussed. **1975** H. R. ISAACS in H. M. Patel et al. *Say not the Struggle Nought Availeth* 265 He found it impossible to follow Nkrumah on the way to becoming the Osagyefo, the Messiah, the Savior of the People.

osan, osanna, obs. ff. HOSANNA.

osar ('əʊsɑː(r)). *Geol.* [ad. Sw. *åsar*, pl. of *ås* ridge (of a roof or hill), a 'rigg' or long hill ridge of uniform height. In Eng. use sometimes *os*, pl. *osar*, but usually *osar* as sing., with pl. *osars.*] A term for certain narrow ridges or mounds of gravel which occur in glaciated regions, the actual origin of which has not been precisely explained.

They are essentially the same as the *kames* of Scotland and the *eskars* of Ireland; but they are often much elongated, some examples in Sweden being more than a hundred miles in length. Some American geologists restrict the term to these very elongated and special forms.

1854 H. MILLER *Sch. & Schm.* xix. (1857) 429 There is a wonderful group of what are now termed *osars*, in the immediate neighbourhood of Inverness... As all, or almost all, the shells of the boulder clay are of species that still live, we may infer that the mysterious *osars* were formed not very long ere the introduction [of man] upon our planet. **1889** F. G. WRIGHT *Ice Age N. Amer.* 479 Osars and kames, whose conditions of formation were exceptional.

osay, variant of OSEY, *Obs.*, a sweet wine.

osazone ('əʊsəzəʊn). *Chem.* [f. the suffix *-osazone*, ad. G. *-osazon* (E. Fischer 1884, in *Ber. d. Deut. Chem. Ges.* XVII. 580): see -OSE², AZO-, and -ONE.] Any of the yellow crystalline solids whose molecules contain two adjacent hydrazone groups, which are obtained by treating compounds containing the groups $-CO \cdot CHOH-$ or $-CO \cdot CO-$ with phenylhydrazine and are used for characterizing sugars.

1888 *Jrnl. Chem. Soc.* LIV. 1267 The osazones of all saccharoses dissolve in cold, fuming hydrochloric acid with a dark-red coloration. **1938** M. L. WOLFROM in H. Gilman *Org. Chem.* II. xvi. 1404 The three fundamental procedures used by Fischer..in his great feat of elucidating the configuration of the sugars were osazone formation, oxidation to *meso* acids.., and the methods for building up or degrading the members of the sugar series. **1972** J. W. SUTTIE *Introd. Biochem.* iii. 28 Sugars which differ in configuration only at carbons 1 or 2, such as glucose, mannose, and fructose, will give the same osazone.

Osborne ('ɒzbɔən). The name of a former royal residence on the Isle of Wight used *attrib.* and *absol.* to designate a type of sweetish plain biscuit.

Said by the manufacturers (private communication 14 March 1977) to have been first made in 1860. It was originally intended to name them after Queen Victoria, but she asked that the biscuit should be named after her favourite home—Osborne—on the Isle of Wight.

1876 *Official Guide Cunard Steamship Co.* 158 (Advt.), Huntley & Palmers..List of Biscuits..Osborne Biscuits. **1888** *Mrs. Beeton's Bk. Househ. Managem.* ii. 31/2 Biscuits ..Osborne..1*s.* 6*d.* per tin. **1911** A. BENNETT *Hilda Lessways* VI. vi. 402, I should like another biscuit. But I don't want the Osbornes—the others. **1926** W. DE LA MARE *Connoisseur* 49 My stranger in the tea shop had been refreshing himself with Osborne biscuits. **1938** S. BECKETT *Murphy* v. 96 The biscuits..were the same as always, a Ginger, an Osborne, a Digestive, a Petit Beurre. **1960** R. COLLIER *House called Memory* ii. 28 My mother's first memory..was of sitting on the steps..and being given some Osborne biscuits. **1972** D. Bloodworth *Any Number can Play* x. 77 The gibbon..grabbed three Osborne biscuits from a tin on the low, marble table.

osbornite (ˈɒzbɔənaɪt). *Min.* [f. the name of George *Osborn-e* (see quot. 1870) + -ITE[1].] Titanium nitride, TiN, found as small yellow octahedra in oldhamite in the meteorite which fell at Bustee, India.

1870 N. S. Maskelyne in *Phil. Trans. R. Soc.* CLX. 198 This microscopic mineral I wish to name Osbornite in honour of Mr. Osborne, and in order to commemorate the important service that gentleman rendered to science in preserving and transmitting to London in its entirety the stone which his zeal saved at the time of its fall, and in recording all he could collect about the circumstances associated with that fall. **1941** *Mineral. Mag.* XXVI. 36 The minute octahedra of osbornite are easily visible with a lens in the meteorite itself. **1962** B. Mason *Meteorites* x. 156 The only nitrogen mineral recorded from meteorites is osbornite, TiN, a rare accessory known only from Bustee (an enstatite achondrite).

osburow, obs. corrupt f. OSNABURG (linen).

Oscan (ˈɒskən), *a.* and *sb.* Also 6–8 **Oscian**. [f. L. *Osc-us* (pl. *Osci*) Oscan + -AN.]

A. *adj.* **a.** Of or pertaining to the Osci (also called Opsci, Opici), a pre-Sabellian people centred on Campania in southern Italy. **b.** Of or pertaining to the Italic language called Oscan (see sense b of the sb.).

1598 R. Grenewey tr. *Tacitus' Annals* IV. 95 The Oscian play, a light sport pleasing the peoples humor. **1600** Holland tr. *Livy's Romane Hist.* x. 365 Such as were well seene in the Osciane toung. **1649** J. Ogilby tr. *Virgil's Aeneid* VII. 24 Saticulus with them And Oscian bands. **1728** T. Gordon tr. *Tacitus' Annals* IV, in *Works* I. 164 The Oscan Farce, formerly only the contemptible delight of the vulgar. **1731** J. Trapp tr. *Virgil's Aeneid* VII, in *Works* III. 92 And the Oscian Band. **1797** G. Baker tr. *Livy's Hist. Rome* II. x. 356 He..sent persons, who understood the Oscan language. **1845** [see Umbrian *a.* 1]. **1948** D. Diringer *Alphabet* II. ix. 503 The Oscan script..was an offshoot of the Etruscan alphabet in its southern Campano-Etruscan sub-species. **1958** E. Pulgram *Tongues of Italy* xvii. 229, I do not believe in the existence of Umbrian, Oscan, and Latinian types of dialects outside of Italy. **1958** E. Badian *Foreign Clientelae* ix. 195 Of other patrons of Marius we know of the Herennii,..themselves of Oscan origin. **1969** E. T. Salmon *Roman Colonization* v. 88 Atella and Calatia, also joined Hannibal, as did a number of the Oscan and Greek allies of Rome in southern Italy. **1974** *Encycl. Brit. Macropædia* XIV. 789/2 The Oscan village of Pompeii..soon came under the influence of the cultured Greeks..across the bay.

B. *sb.* **a.** A member of the Osci. **b.** A name given to the Italic dialects of central and southern Italy, used by the Sabellian peoples who displaced or absorbed the Osci. See Osco-Umbrian *a.* and *sb.*

1753 C. Pitt tr. *Virgil's Aeneid* VII, in *Works* III. 355 The rough Saticulan and Oscan stood. **1813** J. C. Eustace *Tour through Italy* II. x. 258 Oscan was not unknown even in the age of Cicero and Augustus. **1835** [see Ligurian *sb.*]. **1882** [see Umbrian *sb.* 2]. **1897** R. S. Conway *Italic Dial.* II. 472 In some few cases in Oscan the final -*s* of the Nom. and Gen. is still wanting. **1934** S. Robertson *Devel. Mod. Eng.* (1936) ii. 21 Of the latter [*sc.* non-Latin Italic dialects], the Oscan and the Umbrian..are to be distinguished. **1939** [see Marsian *sb.* and *a.*]. **1948** D. Diringer *Alphabet* II. ix. 501 The Oscans..or Osci, in Greek, Oskoi or Opikoi, from Opsci or Opici..were Italic tribes who inhabited southern Italy in the second half of the first millennium B.C. **1969** H. V. Morton *Traveller in S. Italy* vii. 272 We encountered a workman, still apparently speaking Oscan. **1969** E. T. Salmon *Roman Colonization* ii. 44 In 354, Rome signed an alliance with the Samnites, an Oscan-speaking people of the south. *Ibid.* ix. 149 Sulla's colonies in the north and south had helped to bring the use of Etruscan and Oscan to an end. **1974** *Encycl. Brit. Macropædia* XIV. 789/2 It seems certain that Pompeii, Herculaneum, and Stabiae were first settled by the Oscans. **1976** *Archivum Linguisticum* VII. 62 Latin shares a number of lexical items with Oscan.

Oscar[1] (ˈɒskə(r)). *Austral.* and *N.Z.* Also with lower-case initial. [Rhyming slang on *Oscar Asche* (an Australian actor, 1871–1936).] Cash, money.

1919 W. H. Downing *Digger Dial.* 36 *Oscar*, money. **1931** W. Hatfield *Sheepmates* xix. 161 Sit in, some o' yous that aint flyblown—.., an' their IOU's is good, if there's no real Oscar about the joint. **1942** L. Mann *Go-Getter* ii. 16 Get the oscar off Tom soon's I see him. He's honest. **1945** E. G. Webber *Johnny Enzed in Middle East* 20 'Well, me lending you my balance to get you out of the cart,' said the bloke, 'and them sending me the oscar so that you can pay it back.' **1949** *Newsweek* 31 Oct. 60/2 He would have been glad to buy me a pail of suds if he'd had any Oscar. **1959** D. Niland *Big Smoke* i. 21 If you'd been fighting all those blokes in the ring you'd have more oscar in your kick now than the Prime Minister himself. **1969** [see dinkum B. *adj.*].

Oscar[2]. [Said to be an arbitrary use of the Christian name of *Oscar* Pierce, 20th-c. American wheat and fruit grower (see below).] One of the statuettes awarded by the Academy of Motion Picture Arts and Sciences, Hollywood, U.S.A., for excellence in film acting, directing, etc. These awards have been made annually since 1928. So ***Oscar-winner***, ***-winning***.

A former secretary of the Academy of Motion Picture Arts and Sciences is said to have remarked in 1931 that the statuette reminded her of her 'Uncle Oscar', namely Oscar Pierce.

1936 *Time* 16 Mar. 56/2 Neither Director Ford nor Screenwriter Nichols appeared to claim their prizes—small gold statuettes which Hollywood calls 'Oscars'. **1949** [see Emmy]. **1958** *Punch* 25 June 838/3 A quiet scene, with the camera in close-up, every word counting, and the actors playing for an Oscar. **1962** *Times* 30 Oct. 16/1 The Oscar-winning Fellini pictures. **1968** B. Foster *Changing Eng. Lang.* i. 45 The Oscar statuette is..gold-plated. **1974** *Times* 1 Mar. 13/4 Luis Buñuel's eminence as..1973 Oscar-winner. **1975** C. Nesbitt *Little Love & Good Company* xix. 246 If I were to start thanking the Lunts for all the gifts.. that I have received from them I should sound like an Oscar-winning starlet. **1976** *Southern Even. Echo* (Southampton) 6 Nov. (Advt. Suppl.) 5/1 Ed Begley (he got an Oscar) as a vicious town boss whose daughter (Shirley Knight) gets ruined by Newman.

b. In *transf.* use applied to any award for an outstanding performance or achievement.

1941 *Time* 2 June 82/2 That these trials..did not keep Producer Gabriel Pascal from turning out a polished and distinguished product is a transcendent Oscar in the one-time cavalryman's lap. **1947** *Sun* (Baltimore) 1 July 7/6 René Clair's 'Silence Est D'Or' (Silence Is Golden) won the grand prize of Brussels' world film competition today and was awarded the Belgian 'Oscar', a small statuette of Brussels' patron saint, St. Michael. **1949** *Natural Hist.* Nov. 417/3 If there are any 'Oscars' to be awarded in the world of animal acting, the vote of many naturalists will..go to the hognose snake. **1954** *Economist* 29 May 739/2 The first British 'Oscar' for a company report, represented by a pair of silver wall sconces, has been given to Thomas W. Ward. **1959** *Times Lit. Suppl.* 13 Nov. 662/3 Once a year it publishes an annual which is in effect a kind of collection of Oscars for design in these fields. **1963** *Guardian* 8 Feb. 8/2 An ensemble for spring..which won an export Oscar last year. **1971** *Daily Tel.* 18 Dec. 10 A local artist is being commissioned to make an 'Oscar' which will be presented annually to the publishing house which..has made the most distinctive contribution to literature. **1973** J. Wainwright *Pride of Pigs* 215 An Oscar-winning performance, lad. **1978** *Guardian* 27 Feb. 16/5 QPR had been given their first goal when an Oscar-winning dive in the penalty area by Shanks brought an unbelievable penalty decision from the referee.

oscheal (ˈɒskɪəl), *a.* [f. Gr. ὄσχε-ον (see next) + -AL[1].] Of or relating to the scrotum.

oscheo- (ɒskiːəʊ), before a vowel **osche-**, combining form of Gr. ὄσχεον scrotum; in medical and surgical terms, as **ˈoscheocele** [Gr. κήλη tumour], tumour of the scrotum, scrotal hernia. **ˈoscheolith** [Gr. λίθος stone], a stony concretion formed in the scrotum (Mayne *Expos. Lex.* 1857). **ˈoscheoplasty** [Gr. πλαστός moulded], plastic operation for the restoration of the scrotum (*Syd. Soc. Lex.*); hence **oscheoˈplastic** *a.* (Dunglison *Med. Lex.* 1842).

1727–41 Chambers *Cycl.*, *Oscheocele*, in medicine, a kind of hernia, wherein the intestines or omentum descend into the scrotum. **1878** T. Bryant *Pract. Surg.* I. 674 When the oblique or direct [hernia] has passed into the scrotum it is called a 'scrotal hernia' or 'oscheocele'.

oscillance (ˈɒsɪləns). [f. L. *oscillānt-em*, pr. pple. of *oscillāre*: see OSCILLANT and -ANCE.] An oscillation; a swinging to and fro.

1852 Bailey *Festus* (ed. 5) xxviii. 466 My heart's poles now are fixed like earth's in Heaven,..and all ceased Their torrid oscillances [*ed.* 4, 1848, oscillancies].

ˈoscillancy. [f. as prec.: see -ANCY.] = prec.

1727 Bailey vol. II, *Oscillancy*, a swinging to and fro, a see-sawing. **1848** [see prec., quot. 1852].

ˈoscillant, *a.* [ad. L. *oscillānt-em*, pr. pple. of *oscillāre*: see next.] Oscillating, that oscillates.

1857 Mayne *Expos. Lex.*, *Oscillans*,..anthers attached.. by a very small point situated towards the middle of their length, so as to be sustained as in equilibrium: oscillant.

oscillate (ˈɒsɪleɪt), *v.* [f. L. *oscillāt-*, ppl. stem of *oscillāre* to swing: see -ATE[3].]

1. a. *intr.* To swing backwards and forwards, like a pendulum; to vibrate; to move to and fro between two points.

1726 Stone *Math. Dict.* s.v. *Oscillation*, If a single Pendulum be suspended between two Semi-Cycloids..so that the String as it oscillates, folds about them, all the Oscillations, however unequal, will be Isochronal in a Non-resisting Medium. **1756** Burke *Subl. & B.* IV. xii, Move any body, as a pendulum, in one way, and it will continue to oscillate in an arch of the same circle, until the known causes make it rest. **1802** Playfair *Illustr. Hutton. Th.* 438 There is a certain mean condition, about which our system perpetually oscillates. **1840** Carlyle *Heroes* iv. (1872) 127 You look at the waves oscillating hither, thither on the beach. **1869** Phillips *Vesuv.* iv. 110 The magnetic needles oscillated both vertically and horizontally.

b. *loosely.* To move or travel to and fro.

1865 Dickens *Mut. Fr.* III. iv, Miss Lavinia, oscillating between the kitchen and the opposite room, prepared the dining-table in the latter chamber. **1891** N. Gould *Double Event* 316 He spends his time oscillating between Australia and England and vice-versâ.

c. *Electronics.* Of a circuit or device: to cause oscillations in an electric current flowing in it.

1917 R. D. Bangay *Elem. Princ. Wireless Telegr.* I. 84 The methods employed for causing an aerial to oscillate, and thus radiate electric waves, fall under two headings. **1928** *Times* 23 Mar. 20/1 If too much retroaction is employed the circuit resistance may become negative, when the whole system will begin to oscillate. **1948** A. L. Albert *Radio Fund.* x. 370 If some of the output signal voltage is fed back into the control-grid in the proper manner, a vacuum tube will oscillate. **1971** L. T. Agger *Introd. Electr.* xxiv. 432 A circuit containing inductance and capacitance will oscillate at its own natural frequency, provided it is left undisturbed after the oscillation has been started.

d. Of a radio or (*transf.*) its user: to transmit radio waves owing to faulty operation.

1921 *Wireless World* 29 Oct. 481/1 For a set to 'react' or 'oscillate' it is necessary that the main inductance and the reaction coil should be so connected that the direction of windings bear a certain relation to one another. **1926** *Westm. Gaz.* 3 Feb. 3/1 Listeners-in who oscillate may find themselves deprived of their licences. **1933** 'R. Stranger' *Elem. Wireless* xxxvi. 181 A good way of telling when a receiver is oscillating is to have a milliammeter connected in the anode circuit of the detector... Without the milliammeter you may oscillate and not even know it. **1943** C. L. Boltz *Basic Radio* xiv. 222 An interesting effect is observable if the tuning condenser is used when the receiver is oscillating.

2. *fig.* To fluctuate between two opinions, principles, purposes, etc., each of which is held in succession; to vary between two limits which are reached alternately.

a **1797** Burke *Powers Juries Prosec. Libels* Wks. 1877 VI. 161 If they will oscillate backward and forward between power and popularity. **1820** Hazlitt *Lect. Dram. Lit.* 340 The language oscillates between bombast and bathos. **1860** Hartwig *Sea & Wond.* i. 13 The temperature of the surface-water oscillates..between 82° and 85°. **1875** Jowett *Plato* III. 23 Human nature oscillates between good and evil.

3. *trans.* To cause to swing or vibrate to and fro.

1766 Blackburne *Confess.* iii. 56 The Remonstrants, who oscillate the question backwards and forwards till no mortal can find out what they mean. **1858** Greener *Gunnery* 129 Lancaster's oval shell, oscillated in its flight, took a flight so extraordinary. **1883** *Phil. Trans. R. Soc.* CLXXIII. 663 The ring (with wire circuit open) was oscillated backwards and forwards. **1905** Preece & Sivewright *Telegraphy* (new ed.) 462 The spark gap which oscillates the energy.

4. *intr. Math.* To increase and decrease alternately as successive terms are taken (in the case of a series) or as the variable tends to infinity (in the case of a function).

1898 Harkness & Morley *Introd. Theory Analytic Functions* viii. 102 In the series $(1-1)+(1-1)+(1-1)+\ldots$, each term is 0 and the limit is 0, but the series $1-1+1-1+\ldots$ oscillates. **1940** C. A. Stewart *Adv. Calculus* i. 7 $n^2 \cos n\pi$, $n + (-1)^n n^3$ oscillate infinitely. **1973** D. G. Ball *Introd. Real Anal.* iii. 43 A sequence which has no limit at all is said to oscillate.

ˈoscillating, *ppl. a.* [f. prec. + -ING[2].]

1. a. Swinging or moving to and fro, vibrating.

1743 Emerson *Fluxions* 294 If the oscillating Body is not a Globe. **1835** Kirby *Hab. & Inst. Anim.* I. iv. 146 These oscillating plants owe their existence to different species of animalcules. **1899** *Allbutt's Syst. Med.* VI. 681 When the patient's eyes are closed, he may walk in an uncertain oscillating fashion.

b. *spec.* Applied to machines or parts of them characterized by the oscillatory motion of some part or parts, which in other cases are fixed.

Such are *oscillating cylinder*, a cylinder in a steam-engine mounted on trunnions and oscillating through a small arc, so that the piston-rod can follow the movements of the crank; *oscillating engine*, one having an oscillating cylinder; etc.

1821 *Specif. Manby's Patent* No. 4558. 4 A longitudinal section of the oscillating engine. **1870** *Public Opin.* 16 July 81 The turning gear consists of a small supplemental oscillating cylinder. **1875** Knight *Dict. Mech.* 1580/1 Oscillating steam-engines frequently have oscillating valves working in their trunnions. **1882** *Rep. to Ho. Repr. Prec. Met. U.S.* 21 A Huntington oscillating mill is used, crushing about 7 tons of ore per day.

2. *Math.* Of a series or function (see OSCILLATE *v.* 4).

1898 Harkness & Morley *Introd. Theory Analytic Functions* viii. 102 Most English text-books regard oscillating series as not divergent. **1973** D. G. Ball *Introd. Real Anal.* iii. 59 Consider the sequence $2\frac{1}{2}, -1\frac{1}{3}, 2\frac{1}{4}, -1\frac{1}{5}, 2\frac{1}{6}, -1\frac{1}{7}, 2\frac{1}{16}, -1\frac{1}{17},\ldots$ This sequence is bounded and oscillating.

3. *Electronics.* Of an electric current or the like: undergoing rapid periodic reversals in direction. Of a circuit or device: characterized by such a current (cf. OSCILLATE *v.* 1 c).

Oscillating as used of a current implies a much higher frequency than *alternating* and also a different origin (see OSCILLATOR 2 a).

1906 A. E. Kennelly *Wireless Telegr.* viii. 94 (*heading*) Energy of electric oscillations, or oscillating currents, set up in a vertical receiver. **1920** E. W. Stone *Elem. Radiotelegr.* xi. 44 If two oscillating circuits containing inductance and capacity be..coupled together, they act very differently than when they are allowed to oscillate by themselves. **1948** A. L. Albert *Radio Fund.* x. 386 Variations in the plate output circuit will not be reflected back into the control-grid oscillating circuit. **1974** 'I. Drummond' *Power of Bug* xi. 166 The tiny transmitter..emitted a high, oscillating signal on ultra short wave.

oscillation (ɒsɪˈleɪʃən). [ad. L. *oscillātiōn-em*, n. of action from *oscillā-re* to swing. Cf. Fr. *oscillation* (1701 in Hatz.-Darm.).]

1. a. The action of oscillating; swinging to and fro like that of a pendulum; a periodic movement to and fro, or up and down.

angular oscillation, gyration. ***axis of oscillation***: see AXIS 6. ***centre of oscillation***: see CENTRE 16.

1658 Phillips, *Oscillation*, a hanging or tottering motion, a swinging upon a rope whose ends are tyed to several beams. **1713** B. Taylor in *Phil. Trans.* Abr. VI. 7 (heading) Of Finding the Centre of Oscillation. **1726** [see OSCILLATE

1]. **1822** IMISON *Sc. & Art* I. 80 Observing the oscillations of a lamp which was hung from the ceiling. **1831** BREWSTER *Newton* (1855) I. xiii. 362 The tides are the consequence of the perpetual oscillation of the waters of the ocean. **1865** LIVINGSTONE *Zambesi* xxv. 535 Evidences of the oscillations of land and sea. **1871** B. STEWART *Heat* §77 The rate..of a watch depends upon the time of oscillation of its balance-wheel.

b. In *Acoustics*, sometimes = vibration; sometimes = BEAT *sb.*[1] 8. *rare.*

2. a. *fig.* A swaying to and fro between two states, opinions, principles, purposes, etc.; alternating variation, fluctuation, wavering.

1798 MALTHUS *Popul.* (1817) I. 27 The same retrograde and progressive movements, with respect to happiness.. This sort of oscillation will not probably be obvious to common view. **1809–10** COLERIDGE *Friend* (1865) 216 This oscillation of political opinion. **1876** ROGERS *Pol. Econ.* iii. (ed. 3) 29 There are always oscillations in price. **1884** BOWER & SCOTT *De Bary's Phaner.* 42 Oscillations and transitions between the related types are by no means rare.

b. *Psychol.* Fluctuation of attention or mental efficiency.

1895 *Amer. Jrnl. Psychol.* VII. 84 *Schwankungen der Aufsmerksamkeit*, oscillations *or* fluctuations of the attention. **1927** C. S. SPEARMAN *Abilities of Man* xix. 319 We may now conveniently turn to a phenomenon which may be described as oscillation of cognitive efficiency, and which probably has an intimate connection with..fatigue. *Ibid.* 326 Here in oscillation, then, we have come upon a new single and universal factor, a third in addition to *g* and perseveration. **1943** C. L. HULL *Princ. Behavior* xvii. 306 One may reasonably conjecture that it was produced by some factor in the experimental situation other than the primitive oscillation tendency. **1950** P. E. VERNON *Struct. Human Abilities* viii. 89 An Oscillation factor in rate of fluctuation of reversible perspective figures.

3. *Electronics.* A rapid alternation in the direction of flow of a current; the state of a circuit in which this is occurring; also, a rapidly varying electromagnetic field produced by such a current.

1853 tr. H. Helmholtz in *Sci. Mem. Trans. Foreign Acad.* (*Nat. Philos.*) 143 It is easy to explain this law if we assume that the discharge of a battery is not a simple motion of the electricity in one direction, but a backward and forward motion between the coatings, in oscillations which become continually smaller until the entire *vis viva* is destroyed by the sum of the resistances. **1885** *Electrician* 18 Dec. 106/1 It shows that if the resistance be reduced to nothing, whilst the coefficient of self-induction of the circuit is finite..the oscillations continue for ever undiminished in strength. **1911** *Encycl. Brit.* XXVI. 532/2 The transmitting antenna wire is alternately charged to a high potential and discharged with the production of high frequency oscillations in it. **1932** E. V. APPLETON *Thermionic Vacuum Tubes* 102 Since the applied anode potential is negative no anode current flows unless oscillations are present. **1951** A. SHEINGOLD *Fund. Radio Communication* xii. 254 The desirable operational properties of an oscillator may include the property of being self-starting, the ability to maintain continuous oscillation, [etc.]. **1959** R. L. SHRADER *Electronic Communication* xii. 307 If it is desired to prevent a radio circuit from going into oscillation, it may be necessary to introduce degeneration in it, or neutralize it. **1975** BARRON & JOYCE *Electricity* xv. 450 The electrical oscillations of a capacitor-inductor loop can be used to transmit oscillations of radio frequency.

4. *Math.* **a.** The difference between the greatest and the least values of a function in any given interval.

1893 HARKNESS & MORLEY *Treat. Theory of Functions* ii. 49 If $f(x)$ be a discontinuous function of x, which is always finite between a and b, its values within an interval δ will have an upper and a lower limit. The difference between these upper and lower limits is named the oscillation of the function. **1937** MICHELL & BELZ *Elem. Math. Analysis* I. i. 73 If the focal bounds are unequal, the sequence is said to be divergent and to have a finite oscillation. *Ibid.* 91 The functions sin x, (sin x)/x. The former function has a finite oscillation -1 to $+1$ at $x = +\infty$. **1973** G. KLAMBAUER *Real Analysis* iii. 75 The oscillation is a monotone mapping in the sense that if $\mathcal{J}_1$ and $\mathcal{J}_2$ are bounded open intervals and $\mathcal{J}_1 \subset \mathcal{J}_2$, then $\omega(f; \mathcal{J}_1) \leqslant \omega(f; \mathcal{J}_2)$.

b. Variation consisting of alternate increase and decrease (cf. OSCILLATE *v.* 4).

1908 T. J. I'A. BROMWICH *Introd. Theory Infinite Series* ii. 22 If all the terms..of the series are positive, the sequence ..steadily increases; and so..the series Σa_n must be either convergent or divergent; that is, oscillation is impossible. **1968** FOX & MAYERS *Computing Methods for Scientists & Engineers* vii. 129 A characteristic of a good approximation is a type of oscillation property, effectively produced by the presence of $n + 2$ alternating maxima and minima of the error.

5. *attrib.*, as †*oscillation circuit* (now called *oscillator circuit*), *detector*, †*valve*; **oscillation constant** (see quot. 1940); †**oscillation transformer** = JIGGER *sb.*[1] 5 p.

1906 A. F. COLLINS *Man. Wireless Telegr.* ii. 32 The resistance of an oscillation circuit is practically negligible. **1923** —— *Everybody's Wireless Bk.* xii. 198 The resistance of an oscillation circuit, whether it is a closed circuit or the aerial, must be made as low as possible in order to let the high frequency currents oscillate in it freely. **1908** C. C. F. MONCKTON *Radio-Telegr.* ii. 36 For different circuits, as long as the oscillation constants are the same the natural periods of vibration are the same. **1940** *Chambers's Techn. Dict.* 601/1 *Oscillation constant*, the square root of the product of the inductance (in henries) and the capacitance (in farads) of a resonant circuit. **1908** J. A. FLEMING *Elem. Man. Radiotelegr.* ix. 324 It is necessary to employ in the receiving circuit an oscillation detector which is..not merely affected by oscillations, but affected to some extent proportionately to their amplitude. **1906** Oscillation transformer [see JIGGER *sb.*[1] 5 p]. **1923** A. F. COLLINS *Everybody's Wireless Bk.* viii. 130 There are two distinct types of tuning coils used for continuous wave sending sets, and these are (1) the helix, or close-coupled coil, and (2) the oscillation transformer, or loose-coupled coil. The former gives much better results. **1906** *Proc. Physical Soc.* XX. 177 (*heading*) The construction and use of oscillation valves for rectifying high-frequency electric currents. **1908** J. A. FLEMING *Elem. Man. Radiotelegr.* vi. 205 A very simple but effective form of oscillation valve was invented by the author in 1904.

oscillative (ˈɒsɪleɪtɪv), *a.* [f. L. *oscillāt-*, ppl. stem of *oscillāre* to OSCILLATE + -IVE.] Characterized by oscillating, oscillatory.

1859 I. TAYLOR *Logic in Theol.* 281 This oscillative antagonism between incompatible paradoxes.

Hence **ˈoscillatively** *adv.*, by means of oscillation (physically, in opinion, etc.).

1891 E. A. ABBOTT *Philomythus* ix. 220 Bringing your reader to a predetermined conclusion oscillatively.

oscillator (ˈɒsɪleɪtə(r)). [agent-n. in L. form from L. *oscillāre* to OSCILLATE.]

1. One who oscillates in action or thought.

1835 DE QUINCEY *Tory's Acc. Toryism*, etc. Wks. 1853–5 XV. 207 All others are temporisers, waiters upon occasion and opportunity, compromisers, oscillators.

2. a. An apparatus for generating oscillatory electric currents by non-mechanical means.

1889 *Electrician* 9 Aug. 359/1 A practical application is to the theory of a Hertzian oscillator. **1898** *Newspaper*, Mr. Tesla..claims that he can produce, by means of an instrument called the electrical oscillator, a vibratory force capable of causing brilliant lights to burst forth without material connection with an electrical instrument. **1907**, **1908** [see HERTZIAN *a.*]. **1933** *Geogr. Jrnl.* LXXXII. 327 In the shoal range the sound producer is a Type 399 oscillator mounted inside the ship. **1951** A. SHEINGOLD *Fund. Radio Communication* xii. 263 Special oscillators, viz., the klystron and the magnetron, have been designed for operation in the very-high-frequency range. **1962** A. NISBETT *Technique Sound Studio* xii. 202 An oscillator is a valid 'concrete' sound source. **1970** B. ZEINES *Electronic Communication Syst.* viii. 327 Essentially, a feedback oscillator is an amplifier deriving its input signal from its own output. **1977** N. FREELING *Gadget* v. 222 The oscillator is a multi-vibrator affair using a couple of integrated circuit chips.

b. A person who causes or allows a radio to transmit radio waves (cf. OSCILLATE *v.* 1 d).

1927 *Daily Tel.* 1 Mar. 6 Cases where engineers..have succeeded in tracking down oscillators. **1927** *Glasgow Herald* 20 Sept. 8/2 The running-to-earth of offending oscillators.

3. Something that moves to and fro.

1911 *Sci. Abstr.* A. XIV. 402 In the theory referred to [of 1901] the emission of the elements of energy is assumed to be excited by the continuous steady absorption of energy from the radiation incident upon one of the assumed oscillators. This the author [*sc.* Planck] now replaces by the assumption that the emission and absorption are entirely independent. **1936** P. M. MORSE *Vibration & Sound* ii. 27 Every driven oscillator is mass controlled in the frequency range well above its natural frequency ν_0, is resistance controlled near ν_0.., and is stiffness controlled for frequencies much smaller than ν_0. **1970** G. K. WOODGATE *Elem. Atomic Struct.* iii. 45 In trying to make a model of a one-electron atom out of three classical oscillators (one for each direction of polarization) we do not take account of the fact that the atom can emit many frequencies..whereas the classical oscillators emit only one frequency. **1973** *Country Life* 19 July 151/2 The best oscillators have a device which enables the degree of oscillation to be varied from a wide to a narrow throw.

4. *attrib.*, as **oscillator circuit**.

1931 MOYER & WOSTREL *Radio Handbk.* VII. 390 (*heading*) Typical oscillator circuits. **1970** B. ZEINES *Electronic Communications Syst.* viii. 326 Oscillator circuits are commonly used in communication systems.

‖**Oscillatoria** (ɒsɪləˈtɔərɪə). *Bot.* [mod.L., fem. of **oscillātōrius*: see next and -ORY.] A genus of confervoid Algæ, typifying the N.O. *Oscillatoriaceæ*, growing in dense slimy tufts, in running or stagnant water, and exhibiting an oscillatory or wavy motion. Also called *Oscillaria.*

1861 MISS PRATT *Flower. Pl.* II. 55 The Oscillatorias..are weeds of our fresh or salt water,..whose thread-like forms twist about like worms.

Hence **oscillatoriˈaceous** *a.*, belonging to the Natural Order *Oscillatoriaceæ*: see above.

1881 *Nature* XXIII. 494 Various oscillatoriaceous forms and diatoms.

oscillatory (ˈɒsɪlətərɪ, əˈsɪlət(ə)rɪ), *a.* [f. L. type **oscillātōri-us*, f. *oscillāre*, *oscillāt-* to OSCILLATE: see -ORY.] **1.** Characterized by swinging or moving to and fro like a pendulum.

1738 GRAY *Let.* in *Poems* (1775) 35 My motions at present ..are much like those of a pendulum or (Dr. Longically speaking) oscillatory. I swing from Chapel or Hall home, and from home to Chapel or Hall. **1756** BURKE *Subl. & B.* IV. xxiii, A gentle oscillatory motion, a rising and falling. **1833** HERSCHEL *Astron.* xi. 367 The perihelia describe considerable angles by an oscillatory motion to and fro. **1879** PROCTOR *Pleas. Ways Sc.* ii. 29 Like other movements tending to restore equilibrium, the atmospheric motions are oscillatory.

2. *Electronics.* Of a current: = OSCILLATING *ppl. a.* 3. Of a circuit or device: capable of sustaining oscillations (OSCILLATION 3).

1853 *Phil. Mag.* V. 399 It is probable that many remarkable phenomena which have been observed in connexion with electrical discharges are due to the oscillatory character which we have found to be possessed when the condition..$C < 4A/k^2$ is fulfilled. **1878** *Jrnl. Soc. Telegr. Engin.* VII. 319 The discharge is oscillatory if R is less than 40,000 ohms, and continuous if it is greater than that amount. **1905** *Electrician* Feb. 614/1 The effect on the rate of radiation, of varying the length of that portion of the air wire included in the coupled oscillatory circuit. **1948** SLURZBERG & OSTERHELD *Essent. Radio* x. 449 The essential parts of a vacuum-tube oscillator are (1) the oscillatory or tank circuit,..(2) a vacuum-tube amplifier, (3) a feedback circuit. **1971** L. T. AGGER *Introd. Electr.* 442 Calculate the natural frequency of an oscillatory circuit in which the inductance is 0·1 H and the capacitance is 10 μF. **1973** J. YARWOOD *Electr. & Magnetism* xi. 428 The oscillatory current obtained by the discharge of a capacitor through an inductance decays in amplitude with a logarithmic decrement of $RT/2L$.

3. *Math.* = OSCILLATING *ppl. a.* 2.

1908 T. J. I'A. BROMWICH *Introd. Theory Infinite Series* i. 16 Since an oscillatory sequence always contains at least two convergent sub-sequences (those giving the extreme limits), ..an oscillatory series can always be made to converge by grouping the terms in brackets. **1968** H. M. LIEBERSTEIN *Course in Numerical Anal.* (1969) vii. 126 The error term is oscillatory and unbounded... In computation with small h one will see for small n very good answers being produced, but eventually as n..becomes larger, a 'flowering' will take place as the oscillatory error term takes over.

oscillogram (əˈsɪləgræm). [f. as prec.: see -GRAM.] A record obtained by means of an oscillograph.

1903 *Jrnl. Inst. Electr. Engin.* XXXII. 43 (*heading*) A study of the phenomenon of resonance in electric circuits by the aid of oscillograms. **1917** G. D. SHEPARDSON *Telephone Apparatus* iii. 32 As illustrative of the original oscillograms Fig. 7 shows the record of the sound *d* in *day*. **1938** *Amer. Speech* XIII. 69/1 Simultaneous oscillograms of accented vowels taken from above and below the vocal cords reveal no measurable difference in time for the beginning of the voice vibrations. **1950** *Ann. Reg. 1949* 428 There had been brought back..more than 400 oscillograms from explosions in depths between 300 and 3,500 fathoms. **1976** *Word 1971* XXVII. 57 No matter how phonemically obvious certain vocalized continua may appear to be, the differing articulations producing these phonemic samenesses will not produce phonetically same oscillograms or sound spectrograms, the only reliable measuring artifacts in such assessments. **1976** *Gramophone* Mar. 1530/3 The accompanying oscillograms (Fig. 4) show the distortion at 40Hz for power levels of 1 and 5 watts.

oscillograph (əˈsɪləgrɑːf, -æ-), *sb.* [f. L. *oscillāre* to swing + -O + -GRAPH.] **1.** An instrument for detecting and measuring the motion of a ship or of the sea.

1874 E. BERTIN *Notes on Waves & Rolling* 118 We may.. hope for favourable results from the employment of the oscillograph with two pendulums which Mr. Froude has invented; the French Admiralty has caused a similar instrument to be constructed. **1896** *Trans. Inst. Naval Archit.* XXXVII. 322 The graphic tracing of the movements of the sea with the help of the 'oscillograph' was undertaken. **1904** C. H. PEABODY *Naval Archit.* 344 Investigations of the rolling of ships in quiet water and among waves have been made..by aid of instruments known as oscillographs which have slow and quick pendulums, and registering devices.

2. [ad. F. *oscillographe* (A. Blondel 1893, in *Compt. Rend.* CXVI. 502).] Any instrument for displaying as a continuous curve the form of a varying voltage (e.g. that associated with an oscillatory or alternating current, or one derived from a bodily or non-electrical phenomenon); properly restricted to recording instruments, but freq. also used (esp. formerly) to denote the cathode-ray oscilloscope even without the camera needed for recording the display.

1893 A. BLONDEL in *Electrician* 17 Mar. 571/1 The object of this communication is to describe some new galvanometric apparatus or oscillographs allowing one to determine by direct observation..the periodic curves of alternating currents. **1910** G. W. PIERCE *Princ. Wireless Telegr.* xviii. 181 The necessary sensitiveness..was finally obtained with a Braun's cathode tube oscillograph. **1913** *Electrician* 7 Nov. 172/1 For many purposes, particularly in the teaching of alternating currents to elementary students and in the elucidation of certain problems in the higher branches of alternating-current engineering, the kathode-ray oscillograph is convenient and practical. **1925** *Lit. Digest* 11 July 25/1 The stethoscope makes the heart-beat audible, and the oscillograph gives graphic presentation of its action. **1927**, etc. [see OSCILLOSCOPE d]. **1932** *News Chron.* 23 Sept. 10/6 In one of the wooden huts at Slough I watched lightning flashes from thousands of miles away being recorded on the glass face of an oscillograph some 9in. in diameter. **1933** E. W. GOLDING *Electr. Measurements* xv. 526 In some forms of cathode-ray oscillograph special provision is made for photographing the wave-form under observation. **1968** M. WOODHOUSE *Rock Baby* ix. 93 The single hooded eye of an oscillograph peered from the shadows. **1974** *Sci. Amer.* Mar. 94/3 In the electromechanical oscillograph..a tiny mirror is attached to the moving coil of a galvanometer, which oscillates in sympathy with the applied voltage.

3. = OSCILLOGRAM.

1936 *Discovery* June 197/2 Some excellent oscillographs are shown..of damped and undamped waves. **1957** *Electronics* 1 May 163/2 The same tube inserted in a tapered S-band waveguide circuit produces an oscillograph as shown in Fig. 1B. **1957** *New Biol.* XXIII. 35 Plate 11.. shows some oscillographs (records made with the oscilloscope) of the songs of two species of insects. **1975** *Nature* 5 June 514/3 The photographic and line illustrations are adequate, but the oscillographs and sonograms have reproduced poorly.

oscillograph (əˈsɪləgrɑːf, -æ-), *v.* [f. prec. sb.] *trans.* To record or display by means of an oscillograph.

1910 G. W. PIERCE *Princ. Wireless Telegr.* xviii. 182 The drum must be driven synchronously with the alternating current which is being oscillographed. **1926** *Physical Rev.* XXVIII. 554 The signal is detected, amplified, and oscillographed.

oscillographic (ɒˌsɪləʊˈgræfɪk), *a.* [f. OSCILLOGRAPH *sb.* + -IC.] Of, pertaining to, or employing an oscillograph.

1908 J. ERSKINE-MURRAY tr. *Ruhmer's Wireless Teleph.* II. xiii. 145 Two oscillographic records from a singing arc. **1934** *Amer. Speech* XIV. 311/2 From an oscillographic investigation the author concludes that loudness depends on frequency. **1957** MANVELL & HUNTLEY *Technique Film Music* iii. 171 Soon afterwards Scholpo and Rimsky-Korsakoff began the oscillographic analysis of natural sounds. **1972** C. N. HERRICK *Instruments & Measurements for Electronics* xv. 356 (*heading*) Oscillographic camera equipment.

Hence oˌscilloˈgraphically *adv.*, by means of or as an oscillograph. Also **osciˈllography**, the use of oscillographs.

1925 *Jrnl. Inst. Electr. Engin.* LXIII. 1091/1 After Braun (1897) had produced the first two-dimensional electron-jet instrument.., Zenneck (1899) proceeded to work it oscillographically. **1931** *Proc. Physical Soc.* XLIII. 502 (*heading*) A time base for the cathode-ray oscillography of irregularly recurring phenomena. **1938** *Physical Rev.* LIV. 34/2 Average heights of oscillographically recorded pulses. **1964** *Times Rev. Industry* Apr. 5/3 (Advt.), The workshop.. will feature demonstrations of industrial and scientific applications of instant photography including: Photomicrography, Oscillography, [etc.]. **1974** *Nature* 8 Nov. 122/1 Each utterance was analysed oscillographically.

oscillometer (ɒsɪˈlɒmɪtə(r)). [f. as prec. + -METER.] **1.** A gyroscopic form of oscillograph (sense 1).

1899 *Sci. Amer.* 29 July 71/2 An interesting gyroscopic device termed the 'oscillometer', has been put on the market by a Milanese firm.

2. *Med.* [ad. F. *oscillomètre* (V. Pachon 1909, in *Compt. Rend. hebd. des Séances et Mém. de la Soc. de Biol.* 735).] An instrument for indicating or recording the magnitude and rhythm of the pulse.

1910 *Brit. Med. Jrnl.* 3 Dec. 1765/2 With the oscillometer ..the disappearance or reappearance of the pulse is indicated by the needle. **1934** C. J. WIGGERS *Physiol. Health & Dis.* (1935) xl. 606 Some blood pressure instruments are equipped with a form of oscillometer by means of which the magnitude of the pressure fluctuations created within the bag can be read or recorded. **1974** PASSMORE & ROBSON *Compan. Med. Stud.* III. I. xvii. 3/2 The oscillometer measures the amplitude of pulsation at different levels of the limb and provides an index of pulsatile blood flow.

Hence **oˈscillometric** *a.*; **osciˈllometry**, the use of an oscillometer.

1933 *Amer. Heart Jrnl.* VIII. 398 Oscillometric studies carried out on 214 patients revealed that the maximal oscillometric phase..did not occur at the point of disappearance of the systolic tone. **1934** WEBSTER, Oscillometry. **1961** *Neurology* XI. 25/2 Carotid oscillometry is easy to manage and is harmless as blood pressure determination. **1974** J. D. MAYNARD in R. M. Kirk et al. *Surgery* xi. 234 Oscillometry, skin temperature measurements, and plethysmography at present are only research investigations. **1974** J. R. MARSHALL in Lichtiger & Moya *Introd. Pract. Anesthesia* ix. 93 The oscillometric method of measuring blood pressure requires a wide cuff containing two narrow inflatable bags.

oscilloscope (ɔːˈsɪləskəʊp). [f. as prec. + -SCOPE.] †**a.** (See quot.) *Obs.* exc. as in d.

1909 WEBSTER, *Oscilloscope*, an instrument for showing visually the changes in a varying current; an oscillograph.

†**b.** (See quots.) *Obs.*

1915 R. KNOX *Radiogr.* I. 53 The best method of detecting reverse current is by the use of an oscilloscope tube... Two aluminium wires, separated by a small gap, are enclosed in an oblong glass tube, and the wire connected with the negative pole becomes, when the current passes, surrounded by a violet fluorescence, but if each wire is alternately negative and positive both wires become fluorescent and the length of the fluorescent band indicates the intensity of the current. **1926** *Gloss. Terms Electr. Engin.* (Brit. Engin. Stand. Assoc.) 206 *Oscilloscope*, an auxiliary discharge tube in which the length of the negative glow affords an indication of the amount of current passing.

†**c.** An apparatus in which the principle of the stroboscope is employed to render visible irregularities in the motion of rapidly rotating or oscillating machinery. *Obs.*

1922 *Glasgow Herald* 10 Oct. 6 The Elverson oscilloscope ..is an apparatus for slowing down to the eye..any high-speed machinery. **1924** A. J. H. ELVERSON in *Jrnl. Sci. Instrum.* I. 116 The 'Elverson Oscilloscope' is an opto-mechanical device which has been designed to facilitate the examination of the behaviour of high speed movements *under working conditions.* This is effected by presenting, in rapid succession, accurate pictures of the movement at predetermined intervals of angular displacement in such a way that, owing to persistence of vision, the eye of an observer sees a true representation of the movement at a speed which is a fraction of the true speed. **1927** *Trans. Amer. Inst. Electr. Engin.* May 550/1 There was a device produced in England a few years ago by a Mr. Elverson, designed for visualizing the movements of rapidly oscillating mechanisms. It is purely mechanical and optical in its nature and is now generally known as the Elverson oscilloscope.

d. More fully *cathode-ray oscilloscope.* An electronic instrument in which a moving spot on the screen of a cathode-ray tube represents by its position the relationship between two variables, usu. a steady or varying signal voltage (vertically) and time (horizontally), and which is capable of displaying a periodic variation in voltage as a stationary trace.

1927 BEDELL & REICH in *Trans. Amer. Inst. Electr. Engin.* May 546 These limitations..may be removed and the field of usefulness of the cathode-ray oscillograph so widened that it becomes practically a new instrument. As the instrument developed for this purpose..is primarily intended for visual observation, we have given it the name 'oscilloscope'. Permanent record may be obtained..by a photograph in the usual way. On the other hand, an *oscillograph* of the Blondel or Duddell type, both in name and in fact, is primarily for graphical record. **1936** KARAPETOFF & DENNISON *Electr. Lab. Exper.* xix. 451 The need exists for an oscillograph possessing negligible inertia. Such an instrument is the cathode-ray oscillograph, or oscilloscope. **1953** A. C. CLARKE *Prelude to Space* xxiii. 121 Clifton seemed to be hypnotised by a cathode-ray oscilloscope, the screen of which was filled with fantastic geometrical figures, continually shifting. **1967** G. F. FIENNES *I tried to run a Railway* viii. 99 One weekend the oscilloscope at one depot, Liara, found seven axles flawed. **1972** C. N. HERRICK *Instruments & Measurements for Electronics* xv. 350 A conventional oscilloscope can be converted into an oscillograph by mounting a camera in front of its crt screen. **1976** *Word 1971* XXVII. 522 A small computer generated displays of letter-like elements on an oscilloscope screen.

Hence oˌscilloˈscopic *a.*, oˌscilloˈscopically *adv.*

1949 *Jrnl. Appl. Physics* XX. 1105/1 In all of the oscilloscopic records at 200 volts there are 10 examples of the ends of transient opens. **1961** *Trans. Symposium Electrode Processes 1959* 186 All measurements were made oscilloscopically. **1962** *Trans. Faraday Soc.* LVIII. 389 The potential changes were generally recorded oscilloscopically. **1965** *Math. in Biol. & Med.* (Med. Res. Council) IV. 136 Few, if any, systematic studies have been made to assess an experimenter's information-handling capacity as applied to his ability to view oscilloscopic traces or examine film records.

oscine (ˈɒsɪn), *a.* [f. L. *oscen, oscin-* (see next), the end of the word being app. taken as = -INE[1].] Of or pertaining to the *Oscines*; oscinine.

1883 *Nation* (N.Y.) 29 Mar. 281/2 *Boot*..is used to denote the continuous front sheath of the tarsus of most oscine or singing birds, like the robin. **1885** *Librar. Mag.* (U.S.) Aug. 97 Those liquid bird-phrases that..have been the same since first an oscine throat was filled with music.

‖**oscines** (ˈɒsɪniːz), *sb. pl.* [a. L. *oscinēs*, pl. of *oscen, oscin-*, f. *ob* (OB-) + *can-ĕre* to sing.]

1. *Rom. Antiq.* The birds from whose notes or voices auguries were taken, e.g. the raven, owl, etc.

1621 BRATHWAIT *Nat. Embassie* (1877) 52 The Augur hauing left behind him his Oscines or Prophesing birds. **1656** BLOUNT *Glossogr.*, *Oscines* are these kind of birds, by whose chirping, feeding, noise or voyces the Augures foretold things to come; as the Crow, Pie, Chough.

2. *Ornith.* In some systems of classification, the name of an order or extensive group of birds, the 'Song-birds', containing those families of the *Insessores* or Passerine Birds which possess true song-muscles, attached to the extremities of the bronchial semi-rings and forming a complicated and effective musical apparatus.

Introduced into Ornithology in 1812 by Blasius Merrem, as one of two divisions of the *Hymenopodes*; also used by Keyserling and Blasius 1839–40, Müller 1845–6 (*Oscines* or *Polymyodi*), Cabanis 1847, Sundevall 1872–4, Gadow 1893, and other recent naturalists.

1885 NEWTON in *Encycl. Brit.* XVIII. 28/2 The *Oscines* or true *Passeres*..a group in which the vocal organs..attain the greatest perfection. **1896** —— *Dict. Birds* Introd. 115 Thus we reach the true Oscines, the last and highest group of Birds, and one which..it is very hard to subdivide. *Ibid.* s.v. *Syrinx* 940 Most of the Oscines seem to possess five or seven pairs of syringeal muscles.

Hence **ˈoscinine** (-aɪn), †**oˈscinian** *adjs.*, belonging to the *Oscines*.

1896 NEWTON *Dict. Birds* Introd. 66 In all these species he found the vocal organs to differ essentially in structure from those of other Birds of the Old World, which we now call Passerine, or, to be still more precise, Oscinine [**1885** in *Encycl. Brit.* XVIII. 27/2 Oscinian]. *Ibid.* 95 The other families forming Sundevall's *Scutelliplantares* are not Oscinine [*Encycl. Brit.* 41 Oscinian], nor all even Passerine.

oscitance (ˈɒsɪtəns). [f. as OSCITANT: see -ANCE.] Yawning; failure to be alert, inattention.

1636 FITZ-GEFFRAY *Holy Transp.* (1881) 177 A bosom benefice, A true peculiar, that will not dispense With the least oscitance, my Conscience. **1647** HAMMOND *Power of Keys* iv. 92 The negligence or oscitance of these Grammarians.

oscitancy (ˈɒsɪtənsɪ). [f. as prec.: see -ANCY.]

1. Drowsiness, such as is manifested by yawning; dullness, indolence; negligence, inattention.

1619 W. SCLATER *Exp. 1 Thess.* 168 Tendring their presence in the congregation to fill vp the number, but with such Oscitancie [*printed* Oscitaurie], and gaping drowzinesse, that they regard not what is spoken. *a* **1620** J. DYKE *Sel. Serm.* (1640) 34 An oscitancy of spirit. **1658** W. BURTON *Itin. Anton.* 62, I judge it rather the Historians oscitancie, and supine negligence. **1784** COWPER *Task* II. 774 Her, whose winking eye, And slumb'ring oscitancy mars the brood. **1900** F. HALL in *Nation* (N.Y.) 15 Feb. 127/2 That they all went astray owing to a coincidence of oscitancy is clearly beyond belief.

b. (With *pl.*) An instance or example of this.

1677 R. CARY *Palæol. Chron.* II. II. i. 210 Bishop Usher roundly censures this as an Oscitancy in him. **1782** *Gentl. Mag.* LII. 574 The oscitancies of Mr. Wharton..do certainly deserve reprehension.

2. Yawning; gaping with sleepiness; oscitance.

1717 *Entertainer* No. 2. 11 In the case of Oscitancy, when one Person has extended or dilated his Jaws, he has set the whole Company into the same Posture. **1822–34** *Good's Study Med.* (ed. 4) III. 332 The particular kind of pandiculation..being called, oscitancy, yawning, or gaping.

oscitant (ˈɒsɪtənt), *a.* Now *rare* or *Obs.* [ad. L. *oscitānt-em*, pr. pple. of *oscitāre* to gape, yawn: see OSCITATE and -ANT. Cf. F. *oscitant* (1812 in Hatz.-Darm.).] Gaping from drowsiness, yawning; hence, drowsy, dull, indolent, negligent.

1625 J. KING *David's Strait* 18 They thinke it too long a taske for so short a life,..they growe oscitant, and will peruse none. **1647** *Word for Army* in *Harl. Misc.* (1745) V. 572 An oscitant and untrussed Kind of Deportment in all Men towards publick Affairs. **1690** BOYLE *Chr. Virtuoso* I. 16 Perfunctory looks of Oscitant or Unskilful Beholders. **1809** COLERIDGE *Lett., to T. Poole* (1895) 551 Southey, who has been my corrector, has been strangely oscitant, or..has not understood the sentences.

Hence **ˈoscitantly** *adv.*, drowsily, indolently.

1653 H. MORE *Conject. Cabbal.* (1713) p. iii, Which those drowsie Nodders over the Letter of the Scripture have very oscitantly collected. **1698** FRYER *E. India & P.* 331 These busy Tutors of Mankind, who upbraid the slothful and oscitantly idle.

†**ˈoscitate**, *v. Obs. rare.* [f. ppl. stem of L. *oscitāre* to open (as a mouth), also *-ārī* to gape, yawn, f. *ōs* mouth + *citāre* to move, actuate.] *intr.* To yawn or gape from drowsiness.

1623 COCKERAM, *Oscitate*, to yawne, to gape for want of sleepe. **1755** JOHNSON, *To Yawn*, to gape; to oscitate.

oscitation (ɒsɪˈteɪʃən). [ad. L. *oscitātiōn-em*, n. of action f. *oscitāre*: see prec.]

1. The action of yawning or gaping from drowsiness. Also *fig.*

1547 BOORDE *Brev. Health* cclxii. 88 b, Ossitacio is the latin worde... In englyshe it is named ossitacion, yeanyng, or gapynge. **1615** CROOKE *Body of Man* 289 As it happeneth in oscitations or yawnings when wee hold our breath long. **1787** *Minor* III. iv. 168 The Ladies, after much oscitation, declared they did not understand. **1817** PETTIGREW *Mem. Dr. Lettsom* III. 284 The paroxysm came on at six o'clock in the evening with great oscitation.

2. The condition or fact of being drowsy, listless, inattentive, or negligent; an instance of inattention or negligence.

1656 BLOUNT *Glossogr.*, *Oscitation*,..negligence or idleness. **1697** BENTLEY *Epist. Euripides* Wks. 1836 II. 209 'Tis a mere oscitation of our Scholiast, and of Suidas, that gaped after him. **1741–70** MRS. CARTER, etc. *Lett.* (1808) 45 These transient fits of oscitation, and inactivity, are perhaps no more than a necessary relaxation to the mind. **1869** A. W. HADDAN *Apost. Success.* (1883) 158 The natural oscitation on the part of individuals in the matter of rigorous adherence to admitted principle.

oscnode (ˈɒsknəʊd). *Geom.* [f. OSC(ULATE + NODE.] A node of a plane curve where the two branches have a contact of a higher order.

1852 CAYLEY *Wks.* II. 28 The oscnode is a double point which is a point of osculation on one of the branches through it. **1873** SALMON *Higher Plane Curves* 207 Three nodes may coincide as consecutive points of a curve of finite curvature giving rise not to a triple point but to the singularity called an oscnode, this is in fact an osculation or three-pointic contact of two branches of the curve.

Oscotian (ɒˈskəʊʃən), *sb.* [f. *Oscot(t)* + -IAN.] A member or former member of the Roman Catholic college and seminary called St. Mary's at Oscott, near Birmingham. Also as *adj.*

The date of the original foundation, at Old Oscott, was 1794, and the college was transferred to New Oscott in 1838.

1828 (*title*) The Oscotian or Literary Gazette of St. Mary's..edited by the students of Oscott College. **1828** *Oscotian* I. 45, I met a body of youngsters escorted by a gowned superior: these I concluded to be Oscotians. **1853** J. MORRIS in J. H. Pollen *Life J. Morris* (1896) iv. 88 An Oscotian, thoughtful, gentlemanly, having a turn for philosophy. **1860** F. C. HUSENBETH *Life Mgr. Weedall* iii. 43 Every Oscotian knows the favourite Oscott game of 'Bandy'. **1908** *Catholic Times* 22 May 8/2 No man was ever more of an Oscotian than he. **1956** *Oscotian* 83 Oscott has now acquired a tape-recorder... The 'sounds off' have not yet managed to convice any Oscotian that he is a budding Peter Ustinov. **1968** *Ibid.* 42 Allowing for the time it takes Oscotian cricketers to warm up—..we managed about ten days sporadic cricket.

Osco-Umbrian (ˈɒskəʊˈʌmbrɪən), *a.* and *sb.* Also **Oscan-Umbrian.** [f. L. *Osc-us* OSCAN *a.* and *sb.* + -O + UMBRIAN *sb.* and *a.*] **A.** *adj.* Of or pertaining to a group of Italic languages including Oscan and Umbrian and related dialects. **B.** *sb.* This language-group. Also, a member of the peoples who spoke languages of this group.

1894 J. RHYS in *Trans. Philol. Soc. 1891–4* 117 The Romans used *qu* just as the ancient Irish did..for the Osco-Umbrian dialects replaced *qu* by *p*. *Ibid.* 119 The Siculo-

Latin race had already settled down when the Osco-Umbrians arrived. **1895** C. D. BUCK (*title*) The Oscan-Umbrian verb-system. *Ibid.* 135 The plural and passive forms have developed independently and on different lines in Oscan-Umbrian and in Latin. **1897** R. S. CONWAY *Italic Dial.* II. 469 (*heading*) Accidence of the Osco-Umbrian dialects. **1904** C. D. BUCK *Gram. Oscan & Umbrian* p. iv, This grammar is called a Grammar of Oscan and Umbrian, not of the Oscan-Umbrian dialects, for it does not pretend to treat systematically the minor dialects included under the name Oscan-Umbrian. **1939** [see *Latino-Faliscan* s.v. LATINO-]. **1948** D. DIRINGER *Alphabet* II. ix. 501 'Italic' is mainly used..to indicate the Osco-Umbrian sub-branch of the Italic branch of the Indo-European family. **1958** E. PULGRAM *Tongues of Italy* xvii. 228 Beeler..explains the agreements of Latin with Oscan-Umbrian by their existing in close vicinity over several..centuries. *Ibid.* xviii. 232 The chronologies suggested for all these invasions are hopelessly ..irreconcilable, going as low as..2300 B.C. for the Osco-Umbrians. **1971** *Archivum Linguisticum* II. 99 The *sē*-stem is..an imperfect subjunctive in Latin as well as in Osco-Umbrian. *Ibid.* 100 The complex system of Latin and Osco-Umbrian subjunctives..is also an innovation of the Italic group. **1974** A. WATSON *Legal Transplants* iv. 26 It is not absolutely certain that *poena* is a direct borrowing from Greek: it is possible, though unlikely, that it was borrowed at second hand, first passing through some intermediate language like Osco-Umbrian. **1976** *Archivum Linguisticum* VII. 60 Comparison of the above types with their Oscan-Umbrian counterparts reveals separate historical origins.

oscula, pl. of OSCULUM.

'osculable, *a. nonce-wd.* [f. L. *osculārī* to kiss + -BLE.] Capable of being kissed.

1893 *Westm. Gaz.* 6 Dec. 2/1 The tangible, nay, osculable, Pope may yet..oust the invisible Mahatma.

osculant ('ɒskjuːlənt), *a.* [ad. L. *osculānt-em*, pr. pple. of *osculārī* to kiss.]

1. Kissing. *rare.*

In mod. Dicts.

2. Situated between and connecting two things; intermediate; *spec.* in *Nat. Hist.* applied to two species, genera, or families, that are united by some common characters, and to an intermediate species, genus, or group, which unites in itself the characters of two groups.

[**1819** W. S. MACLEAY *Horæ Entomologicæ* 37 These genera I propose to call *osculantia*, from their occurring as it were at the point where the circles touch one another.] **1826** KIRBY & SP. *Entomol.* IV. 234 The internal sense..is osculant between intellect and sense. *Ibid.* 382 They may form an osculant group, partly winged and partly apterous. **1873** G. HENSLOW *Th. Evolut.* i. 7 Forms..intermediate to other forms hitherto well distinct—'osculant' or intercalary forms as they are called.

oscular ('ɒskjʊlə(r)), *a.* [f. L. type *osculāris* (used in mod.L.), f. *osculum* little mouth, pretty mouth, kiss: see -AR.]

1. Of or belonging to the mouth or to kissing. ***oscular muscle*** (*musculus oscularis*), the *orbicularis oris* or sphincter muscle of the lips, the kissing muscle.

1828 *Blackw. Mag.* XXIV. 870 Neither let indignation curl that oscular lip of thine. **1870** W. K. WIGRAM *12 Wonderf. Tales* (1883) 196 Who smiled upon all—though she kept a far sweeter Constriction of oscular muscle for Peter. **1891** S. MOSTYN *Curatica* 100 They had..lavished such endearments upon Ethel, both verbal and oscular.

2. *Zool.* Of or pertaining to the osculum of a tape-worm, or of a sponge.

1881 P. M. DUNCAN in *Jrnl. Linn. Soc.* XV. 320 The oscular processes are short, unequal, differently directed. **1887** SOLLAS in *Encycl. Brit.* XXII. 420/1 In this sponge.. the function of the oscular sphincters can be readily demonstrated.

3. *Math.* Pertaining to a higher order of contact than the first (cf. OSCULATE 4).

oscular line, a singularity of a surface, consisting of a straight line which lies upon the surface throughout its whole length, and everywhere in the same tangent-plane; the section of the surface by this plane containing this line three times.

1869 CAYLEY *Wks.* VI. 334 The tangent plane containing the..oscular line may be termed..an oscular tangent plane.

†**osculary.** *Obs. rare.* [f. L. *oscul-um* kiss + -ARY.] Something to be kissed: see OSCULATORY *sb.*

1537 LATIMER *Serm. bef. Convoc.* Djb, Some brought forth..Manuaries for handlers of reliques,..some oscularies for Kyssers.

osculate ('ɒskjʊlət), *a.* [f. L. *oscul-um* + -ATE².] Furnished with oscula: see OSCULUM 3.

1857 MAYNE *Expos. Lex.*, *Osculatus*, having well marked little mouths or suckers, as the *Tænia osculata*: osculate.

osculate ('ɒskjʊleɪt), *v.* [f. ppl. stem of L. *osculārī* to kiss, f. *osculum* little mouth, kiss.]

1. *trans.* To kiss, salute with contact of the lips; *intr.* to kiss each other. *rare.*

1656 BLOUNT *Glossogr.*, *Osculate*, to kiss, to love heartily, to imbrace. **1873** *St. Paul's Mag.* Mar. 259 Professedly prudish..they..mutter, nod, osculate.

2. *trans.* To bring into close contact or union.

1671 GREW *Anat. Plants* ii. §16 The two main Branches of the Lobes both meeting, and being osculated together, are thus dispos'd into one round and tubular Trunk.

3. *intr.* To come into close contact or union; to have close contact with each other, to come together. In *Nat. Hist.* To have contact through an intermediate species or genus (cf. OSCULANT).

1737 BRACKEN *Farriery Impr.* (1757) II. 281 You may.. cause..the Blood-Vessels to osculate, or join together, so that the Wound may be closed in its whole Length. **1849** F. W. NEWMAN *Soul* VI. 209 Though in their higher development the Sciences osculate, yet (to the human mind) their bases are quite independent. **1858** FROUDE *Hist. Eng.* xxiii. IV. 478 Osculating in separate points with the deeper impulses of the age. **1866** *Sat. Rev.* 21 Apr. 479/2 To show how these countries crossed, osculated, and reacted upon each other.

4. *Math. trans.* To have contact of a higher order with, esp. the highest contact possible for two loci; to have three or more coincident points in common with; *intr.* (for *refl.*) to osculate each other: as two curves, two surfaces, or a surface and a curve.

1727-41 CHAMBERS *Cycl.* s.v. *Osculum*, A circle described on the point *C*, as a centre,..with the radius of the evolute *MC*, is said to osculate, kiss, the curve described by evolution, in *M*; which point *M* is called by the inventor Huygens, the osculum of the curve. **1841** J. R. YOUNG *Math. Dissert.* ii. 52 Two surfaces osculate at a point when they have a common indicatrix there. **1885** LEUDESDORF *Cremona's Proj. Geom.* 189 Three of the four points of intersection of the conics lie indefinitely near to one another, and may be said to coincide in the point *A*; and the conics are said to osculate at the point *A*. **1896** LONEY *Coord. Geom.* (ed. 2) §428 Contact of the third order is..all that two conics can have, and then they are said to osculate one another... In general one curve osculates another when it has the highest possible order of contact with the second curve.

Hence **'osculating** *ppl. a.*, usually in sense 4, as ***osculating circle, curve, plane, sphere.***

1816 tr. *Lacroix's Diff. & Int. Calculus* 108 This circle, called the *osculating circle*, will be the limit of all the others. **1841** J. R. YOUNG *Math. Dissert.* ii. 64 The surface in the direction of that line will lie more closely to the osculating sphere. **1865** *Pall Mall G.* 25 May 1 Lord Granville..is, as it were, to use a mathematical metaphor, an osculating plane to all the different shades of aristocratic and cultivated liberalism. **1879** THOMSON & TAIT *Nat. Phil.* I. I. §8 The plane of the curvature on each side of any point of a tortuous curve..the *Osculating Plane* of the curve at that point.

osculation (ɒskjuː'leɪʃən). [ad. L. *osculātiōn-em*, n. of action from *osculārī* to kiss, OSCULATE. So F. *osculation* (15th c. in Hatz.-Darm.).]

1. The action of kissing, a kiss.

1658 PHILLIPS, *Osculation*, a kissing or imbracing. **1715** tr. *Pancirollus' Rerum Mem.* I. IV. iv. 164 This Ceremony of Osculation was esteem'd such an Honour. **1855** THACKERAY *Newcomes* I. xxiii. 220 If osculation is a mark of love, surely Mrs. Mack is the best of mothers. **1858** —— *Virgin.* (1879) I. 375 And here, I suppose, follow osculations between the sisters. **1865** *Sat. Rev.* 23 Dec. 779/1 Promiscuous osculation is the last thing he dreams of.

2. Close contact: **a.** in general sense. **b.** *Anat.* The mutual contact of bloodvessels. **c.** *Geom.* Contact of a higher order; the fact of touching at three or more coincident points: see OSCULATE *v.* 4.

1669 W. SIMPSON *Hydrol. Chym.* 130 The osculations of the vessels of the womb. **1671** GREW *Anat. Plants* ii. §15 These Osculations of the Lignous Body, and so the interception of the Insertions of the Cortical, are not to be observ'd by the traverse cut of the Root. **1798** FRERE & CANNING *Loves of Triangles* I. 10 in *Anti-Jacobin*, No Circles join in osculation sweet! **1816** tr. *Lacroix's Diff. & Int. Calculus* 116 Called the contact of osculation. **1838** *Proc. Amer. Phil. Soc.* I. 37 Formation of ring or instant of osculation of limbs. **1860** FARRAR *Orig. Lang.* ix. 202 Are there any points of osculation between the languages of these three great distinct families?

osculatory ('ɒskjʊlətərɪ), *sb.* [ad. med.L. *osculātōri-um* tablet to be kissed during Mass, f. ppl. stem of *osculārī* to kiss: see OSCULATE *v.* and -ORY¹.] A painted, stamped, or carved representation of Christ or the Virgin, formerly kissed by the priest and people during Mass.

1763 BURN *Eccl. Law* I. 265 The parishioners shall find at their own charge..a vessel for the blessed water, an osculatory, a candlestick for the taper at Easter. *Ibid.* II. 130 The osculatory was a tablet or board, with the picture of Christ, or the blessed virgin, or some other of the saints, which after the consecration of the elements in the eucharist, the priest first kissed himself, and then delivered it to the people for the same purpose. **1882-3** SCHAFF *Encycl. Relig. Knowl.* II. 1207.

osculatory ('ɒskjʊlətərɪ), *a.* [ad. L. type **osculātōri-us* (see prec.), f. ppl. stem of *osculārī* to kiss: see -ORY².]

1. Of, belonging to, or characterized by kissing.

1849 THACKERAY *Pendennis* xxiv, The two ladies went through the osculatory ceremony. **1881** LD. DUNRAVEN in *19th Cent.* No. 38. 639 It must be an osculatory process more useful than agreeable.

2. *Math.* Osculating; of or belonging to osculation or the osculating circle.

1753 CHAMBERS *Cycl. Supp.* App. s.v. *Curvature*, Called the circle of curvature..also called, especially by foreign mathematicians, the osculatory circle. **1795** HUTTON *Math. Dict.* s.v., In a circle, all the Osculatory radii are equal, being the common radius of the circle. *Ibid.*, *Osculatory Point*, the Osculation, or point of contact between a curve and its Osculatory circle.

osculatrix (ɒskjuː'leɪtrɪks). [mod.L., fem. of **osculātor*, agent-n. from *osculārī* to kiss, OSCULATE.] (See quot.)

1864 in WEBSTER. **1866** BRANDE & COX *Dict. Sci.* etc., *Developable Osculatrix*, the developable surface generated by the tangents of a non-plane curve. Every tangent plane of the surface is an osculating plane of the curve.

oscule ('ɒskjuːl). [ad. L. *osculum*, dim. of *ōs* mouth.] A small mouth or mouth-like aperture or pore; *spec.* = OSCULUM 3.

false oscule or *osculum*, a pseudostome of a sponge.

1835-6 TODD *Cycl. Anat.* I. 42 By injecting milk into its gastric cavity [of *Rhizostoma*], the canals in its arms, and their oscules can be rendered visible. **1846** DANA *Zooph.* (1848) 645 In other species the polyps are wholly retractile, and leave only a small polyp-pore or oscule, marking their position. **1887** SOLLAS in *Encycl. Brit.* XXII. 416/1 While in some sponges the original oscule is lost, in others secondary independent openings, deceptively like oscules, are added.

oscu'liferous, *a.* [f. L. *oscul-um* + -FEROUS.] Bearing or furnished with oscules or oscula.

In recent Dicts.

oscul-inflexion (ˌɒskjuːlɪn'flɛkʃən). *Geom.* [f. *oscul(ation* + *inflexion.*] ***point of oscul-inflexion***: a point of inflexion on one branch of a curve, at which it osculates another branch.

1873 WILLIAMSON *Diff. Calculus* (ed. 2) xvii. §245 The origin in this case is a double cusp, and is also a point of inflexion on one branch. Such a point is called a point of oscul-inflexion by Cramer.

‖**osculum** ('ɒskjʊləm). Plural **-a**. [L. dim. of *ōs* mouth.]

1. A kiss. ***osculum pacis***, the kiss of peace.

1612 DAVIES *Why Ireland*, etc. (1787) 35 The Earl gave unto each of them *osculum pacis*. **1706** PHILLIPS, *Osculum*, a little Mouth; also a Kiss. **1727-41** CHAMBERS *Cycl.* s.v., Anciently it was a custom in the church, that in the celebration of mass..the people kissed each other, which was called *osculum pacis*.

†**2.** *Math.* = Point of osculation. *Obs.*

1727-41 [see OSCULATE *v.* 4].

3. *Zool.* **a.** A mouth or principal exhalant aperture or 'flue' of a sponge: see quot. 1887. **b.** Sometimes applied to the pit-like suckers on the head of a tape-worm by which it attaches itself.

1727-41 CHAMBERS *Cycl.*, *Oscula*, in anatomy, a term used for the orifices, or openings of the lesser vessels. **1844** J. G. WILKINSON tr. *Swedenborg's Anim. Kingd.* II. 2 The oscula or orifices of the excretory ducts are very conspicuous on this membrane. **1877** HUXLEY *Anat. Inv. Anim.* iii. 114 The working of the flagella of the endodermic cells causes the water contained in the gastric cavity to flow out of the osculum. **1887** SOLLAS in *Encycl. Brit.* XXII. 412/2 [A simple sponge] is a hollow vase-like sac closed at the lower end, by which it is attached, opening above by a comparatively large aperture, the *osculum* or vent, and at the sides by numerous smaller apertures or pores which perforate the walls.

oscurantist, variant of OBSCURANTIST, after It. *oscurantista*.

a **1850** MARG. FULLER *At Home & Abr.* (1860) 279 The influence of the Oscurantist foe has shown itself more and more plainly in Rome.

oscuriis (= *osturis*): see OSTOUR.

ose, obs. form of OOZE.

-ose¹, a suffix representing Latin *-ōsus*, forming adjs. from substantives, with the meaning 'full of', 'abounding in'; e.g. *ann-ōsus* full of years, *clām-ōsus* screaming, *cōpi-ōsus* rich, *pecūni-ōsus* moneyed, *religi-ōsus* scrupulous. As a living suffix *-ōsus* came down to OF. as *-os*, *-us*, later *-eus*, *-eux*, AF. and Eng. *-ous* (ME. also *-ows*), which survives with pronunciation (-əs). But from the 15th c. onward there was a tendency to alter *-ous* words to *-ose* after L., as seen in such forms as *ambitiose*, *gloriose*, *malitiose*, *pompose*, *virtuose*, *zelose*. None of these displaced the earlier forms in *-ous*; but a few words formed directly from L. from the 15th c. onward have taken their place in the language, as *bellicose*, *globose* (15th c.), *jocose*, *morose*, *verbose* (17th c.), *otiose* (18th c.), *grandiose*, *pilose* (19th c.). In a few cases *-ous* and *-ose* forms are both in use, e.g. *acerous*, *acerose*, *acinous*, *acinose*, those in *-ose* being more technical. Originally these words have the stress on the suffix, *jo'cose*, *mo'rose*, but this is not always maintained in more recent usage, esp. in words of more than two syllables. Nouns of state from these adjs., as from those in *-ous*, end in *-osity*: *globosity*, *verbosity*.

-ose², *Chem.*, a suffix originating in the ending of the word *glucose*, and employed in forming the names of the related carbo-hydrates, *saccharose* and *cellulose*, with the isomers of these three, as *dextrose*, *lævulose*, *dambose*, *galactose*, *mannitose*; *lactose*, *maltose*, *melezitose*, *melitose*, *mycose*, *synanthrose*, *trehalose*; *amylose*, etc. Now extended to carbohydrates which are not isomers of glucose, saccharose, or cellulose, as *arabinose*, *rhamnose*, *ribose*, *xylose*, etc., and to classes of sugars, as *aldose*, *furanose*, *hexose*, *pentose*, *pyranose*, etc.

These formations are due to the French chemists, and the earlier of them appeared first as Fr. words. *Glucose* was so named by the committee of the *Académie des Sciences* (Thénard, Gay Lussac, Biot, Dumas), who reported 16 July 1838 upon the mémoire of Peligot: 'il résulte que le sucre de raisin, celui d'amidon, celui de diabète, et celui de miel.. constituent un seul corps, que nous proposons d'appeler *glucose*. (*Note*. γλευκος [mispr. -χος], moût, vin doux.)' *Comptes Rendus* VII. 106 (1838). *Glucose* was thus merely a frenchified representation of the Gr. word γλευκος 'must, sweet wine, sweetness', with *u* for ευ and *-ose* for -ος. (Littré's assumption that the term was derived from γλυκύς sweet, in accordance with which he essayed to alter it to *glycose*, was thus historically erroneous.) The name *cellulose* was given by Brongniart, Pelouze, and Dumas, in reporting upon the mémoire of Payen, 14 Jan. 1839: 'En effet, il y a dans les bois le tissu primitif, isomère avec l'amidon, que nous appellerons *cellulose*, et de plus une matière qui en remplit les cellules, et qui constitue la matière ligneuse véritable.' *C.R.* VIII. 51 (1839). *Cellulose* was thus formed on *cellule*, but there is no evidence that its inventors thought of a L. adj. **cellulōsus*; and app. the ending *-ose* was given simply to match *glucose*. It appears from other statements that the actual author of *glucose*, and presumably also of *cellulose*, was Dumas, the *rapporteur* of the committees. The ending *-ose* was soon extended; contractions of *lævo-glucose* (Berthelot) and *dextro-glucose* (Kekulé) gave *lævulose* and *dextrose*, and the forms *lactose*, *melitose*, etc. followed.

-ose[3], a suffix corresponding to -OSIS, used to form the names of fungal diseases of plants, as ERINOSE.

osed, oset, var. OSSET, *Obs.*, kind of cloth.

osel(l, obs. form of OUZEL.

osen-breges, -brig, obs. var. OSNABURG, kind of linen.

†**osey.** *Obs.* Forms: 4 **osey(e**, 4, 6 **osay**, 5 **ozey**, 5–7 **ossey(e**. [= OF. *Aussay*:—L. *Al(i)satius* Alsace.] A sweet French wine, *vin d'Aussay*, wine of Alsace.

[**1362** LANGL. *P. Pl.* A. Prol. 107 Good wyn of Gaskoyne, And wyn of Oseye [*v.r.* osay; B. Prol. 228 white wyn of Oseye].] ?*a* **1400** *Morte Arth.* 202 Osay and algarde, and oþer ynewe, Rynisch wyne and Rochelle, richere was never. **1436** *Pol. Poems* (Rolls) II. 163 Here londe hathe oyle, wyne, osey, wex, and greyne. **1542** BOORDE *Dyetary* x. (1870) 255 Also these hote wynes, as..basterde, tyre, osay. **1615** MARKHAM *Eng. Housewife* (1683) 115 To make the same drink like Ossey.

Osgood-Schlatter (ˈɒzgʊd ˈʃlætə(r)). *Med.* The names of Robert Bayley *Osgood* (1873–1956), U.S. surgeon, and Carl *Schlatter* (1864–1934), Swiss surgeon, used *attrib.* and in the possessive to denote a disease described independently by them in 1903, viz. epiphysitis of the tibial tubercle.

[**1909** *Edin. Med. Jrnl.* II. 249 The name of Schlatter's Disease has been given to this lesion since it was described by that surgeon in 1903, though Müller had published an account of it in 1887.] **1912** *Amer. Jrnl. Orthopedic Surg.* IX. 317 Some have suggested Osgood-Schlatter disease, but it is my own opinion that the condition was recognized..many years previous to the work of these two gentlemen. **1921** *Ann. Surg.* LXXIII. 77 This condition is usually referred to as Osgood-Schlatter's Disease, but should really be classed as an injury and not a true disease. **1932** W. MERCER *Orthopædic Surg.* ix. 32 The true Osgood-Schlatter disease shows..characteristic bony changes which stamp it as a definite disease entity. **1961** R. D. BAKER *Essent. Path.* xxi. 559 Names of men designate the disease in its various locations. For example, Osgood-Schlatter's disease is idiopathic aseptic necrosis of the tibial tubercle.

‖**oshibori** (ˈɔːʃɪbɔːrɪ). [Jap., f. *o-* deferential prefix + *shibori* that which has been wrung out.] A towel which has been wrung out, usually in hot, but sometimes in cold, water; used in Japan to wash the hands and face before a meal. Also *oshibori towel*, etc.

1959 R. KIRKBRIDE *Tamiko* vii. 47 They..wiped their hands upon first the hot and then the cold oshibori brought to them in bamboo baskets. **1963** *New Yorker* 22 June 14 A fragrant o-shibori hot towel to refresh you. **1970** *Guardian* 12 Dec. 6/6 The little thoughtfulness of the oshibori hot towel to begin a meal. **1974** *New Yorker* 22 Apr. 131 (Advt.), Hot *oshibori* towels. Or, how to freshen up without getting up.

Osi'andrian. [f. personal name *Osiander* (see def.) + -IAN.] One of the section of German Protestants in the 16th c. who adopted the opinion of Andreas Hosemann (latinized *Osiander*, 1498–1552), that the Atonement of Christ was wrought by the power of His divine and not of His human nature. (Also *attrib.*) Also **Osi'andrist**.

1582 G. MARTIN *Discov.* in Fulke *Def.* (Parker Soc.) 59 Bucer and the Osiandrians and Sacramentaries against Luther for false translations. **1585–7** T. ROGERS *39 Art.* (1607) 115 An error of the..Osiandrians. **1727–41** CHAMBERS *Cycl.* s.v., Semi Osiandrians were such among the Osiandrians, as held the opinion of Luther and Calvin with regard to this life; and that of Osiander, with regard to the other. **1882–3** SCHAFF *Encycl. Relig. Knowl.* III. 2235 He immediately entered into the Osiandrian controversy. **1725** tr. *Dupin's Eccl. Hist. 17th C.* VII. v. 287 The Lutherans..desired the Duke of Saxony to assemble a Synod against the Sacramentarians, the Adiaphorists, the Synergists, and the Osiandrists. It was assembled at Jena in 1560. **1857** PUSEY *Real Presence* i. (1869) 80 The Roman Collocutors..required the Lutherans to 'declare their dissent from the..Osiandrists and others external to the Confession of Augsburg'.

†**osiarde.** *Obs. rare.* [Related to OSIER.]

1530 PALSGR. 250/1 *Osiarde*, a place where wyllowes growe, *sausoye*.

†**o side**, obs. variant of ASIDE.

c **1400** MAUNDEV. (Roxb.) xxv. 115 Þai draw þam o syde.

-oside (əʊsaɪd), *suffix. Chem.* [f. -OSE[2] + -IDE, after GLUCOSIDE, GLYCOSIDE.] Used to form the names of glycosides and classes of glycosides, as *furanoside*, *ganglioside*, *glucuronoside*, *pyranoside*, etc.

osie, obs. form of OOZY.

osier (ˈəʊʒ(ɪ)ə(r), ˈəʊzɪə(r)), *sb.* (*a.*) Forms: 4 **oyser**, 5 **osere**, **osyar**, **osyer(e**, **osyȝer**, **ozyer**, 6 **oszer**, 6–7 **osiar(e**, **oysier**, **oziar**, 6– **ozier**, **osier**. *β. dial.* 6 **asheer**, **ausher**, 7 **awshyor**. [a. F. *osier* (13th c. in Littré); app. related to 9th c. L. *ausāria*, *osāria* 'willow-bed' (in *Polyptique* of Irminon), of which the Fr. repr. would be *osière*.]

1. A species of willow (*Salix viminalis*), the tough pliant branches of which are especially used in basket-work; also applied to other species used for the same purpose, notably the golden, purple, and violet willow; one of the shoots of a willow.

13.. *K. Alis.* 6186 Heo buth y-mad of oysers, Y fynde, And y-bounde al with tren rynde. **1426** LYDG. *De Guil. Pilgr.* 22019 The smale osyers, here and ȝonder, To-brake thanne, and wente asonder. **1427** in Amherst *Gardening in Eng.* (1895) 14 [For faggots..Astill and] ozyerys. **1486** *Nottingham Rec.* III. 241 For a lode of osyars. **1574** R. SCOT *Hop Gard.* (1578) 40 Euery yeare after you must cut them.. as you see an Osiers head cut. **1642** FULLER *Holy & Prof. St.* III. xix. 204 Who will make a staff of an osier? **1660** BLOOME *Archit.* C b, That Basket of Osiares. **1718** LADY M. W. MONTAGU *Let. to Mrs. Thistlethwayte* 25 Sept., We began to ascend Mount Cenis..carried in little seats of twisted osiers, fixed upon poles upon men's shoulders. **1832** LYTTON *Eugene A.* I. i, A brook, fringed with ozier and dwarf and fantastic pollards. **1886** RUSKIN *Præterita* I. 276 The poplars and osiers of the marshy level.

β. **1572** *Nottingham Rec.* IV. 144 The aushers by Wylford Pastore. **1624** *Ibid.* 390 The cvtting vp of the awshyors.

2. *attrib.* or *adj.* Of, belonging to, or made of osiers; covered with osiers.

1578 LYTE *Dodoens* v. lxiv. 629 The stalkes..wil twist and winde lyke Ozier withie. **1653** WALTON *Angler* xi. 211 If the Sun's excessive heat Makes our bodies swelter, To an Osier hedge we get For a friendly shelter. **1725** POPE *Odyss.* IX. 507 These, three and three, with osier bands we ty'd. *c* **1750** SHENSTONE *Elegies* viii. 18 On list'ning Cherwell's osier banks reclin'd. **1794** MRS. RADCLIFFE *Myst. Udolpho* i, With a small osier basket to receive plants. *a* **1839** PRAED *Poems* (1864) II. 51 His beaming lance and osier shield.

†**b.** *fig.* Osier-like, pliable, pliant. *Obs.*

a **1661** FULLER *Worthies* (1840) II. 571 Topical and osier accidents, liable to be bent on either side.

3. *Comb.*, as **osier-tree**, **-willow**; **osier-bordered**, **-fringed**, **-woven** adjs.; **osier-ait**, **-isle**, a small islet in a river overgrown with osiers; **osier-bed**, **-holt**, a place where osiers are grown for basket-making; **osier-odoured** *a.*, smelling of osiers; **osier-peeler**, a machine for stripping the bark from willow-wands; **osier-wattled**, wattled or interwoven with osiers.

1767 G. WHITE *Selborne* 4 Nov., They roosted every night in the *osier-beds. **1725** POPE *Odyss.* XIV. 533 We made the *osier-fringed bank our bed. **1785** MARTYN *Rousseau's Bot.* xxix. (1794) 454 Several species are commonly cultivated in *Osier-holts. **1728–46** THOMSON *Spring* 780 The stately-sailing swan..Bears forward fierce, and guards his *osier-isle. **1862** G. MEREDITH *Mod. Love* ad fin., We saw the swallows gathering in the sky, And in the osier-isle we heard their noise. *a* **1881** ROSSETTI *House of Life* xii, An *osier-odoured stream. **1549** *Compl. Scot.* vi. 57 The oliue, the popil, & the *oszer tree. *a* **1693** URQUHART *Rabelais* III. xlv. 365 An *Osier Watled Wicker-Bottle. **1872** YEATS *Techn. Hist. Comm.* 85 Beds of *osier-willow for the purpose of basket-making. **1777** WARTON *Odes, Compl. Cherwell* i, All pensive from her *osier-woven bow'r Cherwell arose.

osiered (ˈəʊʒ(ɪ)əd, ˈəʊzɪəd), *a.* [f. prec. + -ED[2].] **a.** Furnished, covered, or adorned with osiers. †**b.** Of or of the nature of osier. *Obs.* **c.** Twisted or plaited like osiers.

1523 FITZHERB. *Husb.* §130 There be four maner of wethyes..whyte wethy, blacke whethy, reede wethy, and osyerde wethy. *Ibid.*, Osyerde wethy wyll grow best in water & moyst grounde. **1749** COLLINS *Pop. Superst. Highl.* 136 While I lie welt'ring on the ozier'd shore. **1819** KEATS *Lamia* II. 217 Garlands..In baskets of bright osier'd gold were brought. **1893** MCCARTHY *Red Diamonds* II. 20 Pictures of osiered reaches.

'osiery. [f. as prec. + -Y: see -ERY[1].] Osiers in the mass; articles made of osiers; 'a place where osiers are grown' (Webster, 1864).

1837 *New Monthly Mag.* L. 408 Green osiery encased his legs. **1868** HOLME LEE *B. Godfrey* iv. 19 They met the.. basket-woman, carrying some of her lighter osiery.

osill, obs. form of OUZEL.

Osirian (əʊˈsaɪərɪən), *a.* [f. proper name *Osiris* (see def.) + -IAN.] Of or pertaining to Osiris, the Egyptian deity personifying the power of good and the sunlight. So **O'siride**, **Osi'ridean** *adjs.*; **O'sirism**, the cult or ritual associated with Osiris.

Osiride or *Osiridean column* or *pillar*, in Egyptian architecture, a square pier having in front of it a standing figure of Osiris.

1849 [W. M. W. CALL] *Reverberations* II. 105, I see Osirian Egypt stand, Sunward I see her lift her hand. **1862** FAIRHOLT *Up Nile* 285 The portico beside it is remarkable for its Osiride pillars. **1887** *Ch. Q. Rev.* XXIII. 280 The vast Osiride figures that were once attached to its pillars were destroyed. **1897** *Edin. Rev.* Oct. 469 Osiride pillars. **1906** W. M. F. PETRIE *Relig. Anc. Egypt* v. 38 The earliest phase of Osirism that we can identify is in portions of the Book of the Dead. **1968** *New Larousse Encycl. Mythol.* (new ed.) 19/1 Isis, in the Osirian myth, represents the rich plains of Egypt. **1971** E. IVERSEN in J. R. Harris *Legacy of Egypt* (ed. 2) vii. 183 Annius of Viterbo..used Diodorus' version of the myth as a background to his curious efforts to establish a heroic genealogy for his papal patron Alexander VI Borgia, identifying the bull of the papal coat of arms with the Osirian Apis, and making the Pope a descendant of the god himself. **1972** P. M. FRASER *Ptolemaic Alexandria* I. v. 256 This identification [of Sarapis with the powers of the Underworld], which also proceeds from the Osirian character of Sarapis, is not attested by dedications.

Osirify (əʊˈsaɪərɪfaɪ), *v.* [f. the name *Osiris* (see OSIRIAN *a.*): see -FY.] *trans.* To identify (a man or god) with Osiris. Hence **O,sirifi'cation**, identification with Osiris.

1890 *Cent. Dict.*, Osirify. **1906** W. M. F. PETRIE *Relig. Anc. Egypt* iv. 23 The most renowned was the *Hapi* or Apis bull of Memphis..who was Osirified and became the Osir-hapi. **1912** *Encycl. Relig. & Ethics* V. 238/1 In the earliest royal monuments the dance of men in the festival of Osirification of the King is represented.

-osis, *suffix*, representing Gr. -ωσις, originating in the addition of the general suffix -σις, forming verbal nouns of action or condition, to derivative vbs. in -ό-ω from adj. and sb. stems or combining forms in ο-: e.g. ἀμαύρωσις darkening, obscuration of sight, amaurosis, f. ἀμαυρό-ω to darken, f. ἀμαυρός dark; μεταμόρφωσις transformation, f. μεταμορφό-ω, f. μετά + μορφή form. Many such words also were formed directly from the sbs. or adjs. themselves, or their compounds, without the intervention of a vb. in -όω, e.g. ἀνθράκωσις malignant ulcer, anthracosis, f. ἄνθραξ, ἀνθρακο- coal, carbuncle, ἐξόστωσις outgrowth of bone, exostosis, f. ἐξ out + ὀστέο-ν bone.

Many of these Greek terms have been adopted in Latin ancient or modern, whence they have passed into English use, e.g. *anastomosis*, *apotheosis*, *metamorphosis*, rhetorical terms, as *anadiplosis*, *miosis*, and esp. medical terms, as *amaurosis*, *anchylosis*, *cyphosis*, *exostosis*, *sclerosis*, *thrombosis*, etc. On the analogy of these last, others have been freely formed in mod.L., Eng., and other modern langs., from Greek elements, as *chlorosis*, *cyanosis*, *ichthyosis*, *trichinosis*; less frequently from Latin, as *pediculosis*, *tuberculosis*. The stress is etymologically -'ōsis; but popular use has shifted it in *meta'morphosis*; so *ana'morphosis*. The Ger. form of the ending is also *-osis*, the French is *-ose*.

osite ('ɒsaɪt). [irreg. for **ossite*, f. L. *os*, *oss-* bone + -ITE[1].] A deposit, found on the island of Sombrero in the West Indies, consisting largely of the bones of turtles and other marine vertebrates; also called *Sombrero guano*.

1859–65 PAGE *Handbk. Geol.*, *Osite*, a technical term proposed by Dr. Leidy of Philadelphia for the so-called Sombrero Guano. **1876** —— *Adv. Text-bk. Geol.* xx. 430 The osite or Sombrero guano which constitutes the whole of the West India island of that name.

-osity, *comp. suff.* of sbs. = F. *-osité*, L. *-ōsitātem*: see -OSE[1], -OUS, and -ITY.

osken, north. dial. form of OX-GANG, q.v.

†**o'sleped**, var. of *asleped*, ASLEPT *Obs.*, overcome with sleep.

13.. *Guy Warw.* (A.) 4649 What of wakeing, & of fasting, & eke þat oþer treueyling Osleped swiþe sore ich was.

oslet, obs. f. OSSELET, a little bone.

oslin ('ɒzlɪn). *Sc.* [Derivation obscure; perh. of Fr. origin.] Name of a variety of apple, reputed to have been long cultivated in Scotland.

[**1802** W. FORSYTH *Treat. Fruit-Trees* 64 Orzelon Pippin, a small early yellow Apple.] **1817** NEILL *Brit. Hortic.* 209 The Oslin pippin is sometimes called the Original, and sometimes the Arbroath pippin; by Forsyth it is named Orzelon... The Oslin has been for time immemorial cultivated at St. Andrew's and Arbroath. **1861** C. INNES *Sk. Early Sc. Hist.* iii. 464 Only seven sorts of apples, among which is not found the Oslin, the earliest of all, and the favourite of after generations at Kilravock.

Oslo ('ɒzləʊ). The name of the capital of Norway, used *attrib.* in phr. ***Oslo breakfast***: a type of meal for children planned to supply nutritional deficiencies in their diets and introduced into Norwegian schools by Dr. Carl Schiotz. So ***Oslo meal***, etc.

1937 *Bull. Health Organisation* (League of Nations) VI. 197 Certain schools [in Norway] introduced the 'Oslo breakfast', whilst other schools continued the older practice of giving a hot lunch. The quality of this hot meal was less good than that of the 'Oslo breakfast', which consists of protective foods (milk, Kneipp rusks and Kneipp bread, cheese, butter, orange, apple or raw carrot). **1938** *Rep. School Medical Officer (London County Council)* 47 Considerable attention has of late been directed to the method of giving school meals to necessitous school children and others in the schools of Norway and other northern countries. This method is generally referred to as 'the Oslo breakfast'... It has attracted the attention of dieticians in other countries.. and suggestions have been made that it should be introduced into London schools in substitution for the present provision of hot mid-day meals. *Ibid.* 49 It may be held that the Oslo meal would have the same effect if given at midday as if given first thing in the morning. **1949** D. MACARDLE *Children of Europe* vii. 123 The Oslo breakfast was planned by Professor Schiotz to give the child calories ..vitamins..and to..strengthen their jaws by chewing. It consists of..pasteurized milk, two biscuits made of wholemeal wheaten flour,..margarine..cheese made of goat's milk,..rye bread.., a raw carrot.., or half a banana ..orange or..apple. **1952** J. J. MOREL *Progressive Catering* I. ii. 34 An Oslo breakfast, or a health dinner as it is known in England. **1958** R. STOW *To Islands* i. 19 Feed him on.. free milk and Oslo lunches. **1962** *Guardian* 26 Oct. 5/2 'The Oslo breakfast'..consisted of..milk, half an orange, wholemeal bread, and goat's milk cheese.

Osmanli (ɒsˈmænlɪ), *a.* and *sb.* Also 9 -lie, -ly, -lee. [a. Turkish *osmānli* adj. 'of or belonging to Osmān' (the Turkish pronunciation of the Arabic personal name *ʿOthmān*): see OTTOMAN. *Osmānli* is the native word for which *Ottoman* is the usual Eng. expression.]

A. *adj.* Of or belonging to the family or dynasty of Othman or Osman I; of or pertaining to the tribe or branch of the Turks who became under Osman and his dynasty the ruling race of the Turkish empire; = OTTOMAN.

1843 *Penny Cycl.* XXV. 406/1 Osmanli, or Turkish, commonly called so. **1874** ANDERSON *Missions Amer. Bd.* IV. xxxi. 174 Less firmly wedded to the Moslem faith than the remaining million of Osmanly Turks. **1888** *Encycl. Brit.* XXXIII. 658/1 (*Turks*) We are wont to restrict the name [Turks] to the Osmanli Turks, though they themselves refuse to be called Turks.

B. *sb.* A Turk of the family or tribe of Osman; a Turkish subject of the Sultan; an OTTOMAN.

1813 BYRON *Giaour* xxviii. *note*, The turban, pillar, and inscriptive verse, decorate the tombs of the Osmanlies. **1844** ELIOT WARBURTON *Crescent & Cross* vii. (1859) 56 The Turks, or Osmanlis, are of small number, but high consideration in Egypt. **1859** *Blackw. Mag.* Apr. 461/2 And so I take leave of the Osmanli, wishing them..every felicity except that of my company.

osmanthus (ɒzˈmænθəs). [mod.L. (J. de Loureiro *Flora Cochinchinensis* (1790) 28), f. Gr. ὀσμή scent + ἄνθος flower.] An evergreen shrub of the genus so called, belonging to the family Oleaceæ, usually native to eastern Asia or North America, and bearing clusters of small white or cream, usually fragrant, flowers.

1877 *Gardeners' Chron.* 24 Feb. 239/2 (*heading*) Note on Osmanthus. **1912** *Curtis's Bot. Mag.* CXXXVIII. 8459 The *Osmanthus* which is here figured is one of the most pleasing of new evergreen shrubs. **1976** *Country Life* 26 Feb. 478/1, I am advocating..lighter, altogether less domineering shrubs like..phormiums, variegated osmanthus, [etc.].

osmate (ˈɒzmeɪt). *Chem.* [f. OSM(IUM + -ATE¹.] A salt or ester of osmic acid (H_2OsO_4) in which osmium has an oxidation state of 6, and in the case of alkali metals having the formula $M_2[OsO_2(OH)_4]$ and obtainable by the action of a reducing agent such as alcohol on an alkaline solution of osmium tetroxide.

1852 G. FOWNES *Man. Elem. Chem.* (ed. 4) II. 368 Osmate of potassa is produced when the metal is fused with nitre. **1868** J. P. COOKE *First Princ. Chem. Philos.* (1870) xix. 420 Osmic anhydride..is unknown, but potassic osmate..can easily be obtained. **1909** L. KAHLENBERG *Outl. Chem.* xxxi. 525 The chlorides $OsCl_2$, Os_2Cl_6, and $OsCl_4$ are known, as are also osmates like $K_2OsO_4.2H_2O$. **1950** N. V. SIDGWICK *Chem. Elements* II. 1501 The tetroxide reacts with potassium or caesium hydroxide in methyl alcohol to give the tetramethyl osmate $(MO)_2Os^{vi}(O{\cdot}CH_3)_4$. **1973** S. E. LIVINGSTONE in J. C. Bailar et al. *Comprehensive Inorg. Chem.* III. xliii. 1230 Potassium osmate, originally formulated as $K_2OsO_4{\cdot}2H_2O$, has the octahedral structure $K_2[OsO_2(OH)_4]$.

osmatic (ɒsˈmætɪk), *a.* [ad. F. *osmatique* (P. Broca 1878, in *Revue d'Anthropologie* VII. 397), f. Gr. ὀσμή smell + -ATIC.] Having well-developed olfactory organs and a good sense of smell; cf. MACROSMATIC *a.*, MICROSMATIC *a.* So **ˈosmatism**, the degree of development of the olfactory organs.

1890 W. TURNER in *Jrnl. Anat. & Physiol.* XXV. 106 He [*sc.* Broca] has classified the Mammalia, in relation to the magnitude of their olfactory apparatus, into two groups: osmatic mammals, which possess a well-developed rhinencephalon with a keen sense of smell, and anosmatic mammals, in which the rhinencephalon and olfactory sense are either feeble or not developed at all. **1903** *Amer. Anthropologist* V. 638 The related doctrines that the olfactory organs are large in osmatic, small or absent in anosmatic animals. **1903** *Trans. Linn. Soc.* (*Zool.*) VIII. 369 The size of the hippocampal formation does not seem to vary directly..with the degree of osmatism.

osmazome (ˈɒsməzəʊm, ˈɒz-). *Chem.* [a. F. *osmazôme* (1812 in Hatz.-Darm.), irreg. f. Gr. ὀσμή scent + ζωμός soup, sauce.] The name given by Thénard to that part of the aqueous extract of meat which is soluble in alcohol and contains those constituents of the flesh which determine its taste and smell.

1819 J. G. CHILDREN *Chem. Anal.* 307 Osmazome is obtained from muscle; it has a brownish yellow colour, and the flavour and smell of broth... According to Dr. Thomson, it is very doubtful if osmazome be any thing but fibrin, slightly altered by solution in water. **1859** LEWES *Phys. Com. Life* I. ii. 152 It is this osmazome, developed during the process of cooking, which gives their characteristic flavours to beef, mutton, goat-flesh, and birds, etc.

Hence **osmazoˈmatic, osmaˈzomatous** *adjs.* [improp. for **osmaˈzomic*, **osmaˈzomous*, as if from ζῶμα, ζωματ- that which is girded], of the nature of osmazome, connected with or pertaining to the flavouring of meat.

1835-6 TODD *Cycl. Anat.* I. 61/1 Osmazomatous.. principles employed in the nutrition of the several tissues. **1851** *Fraser's Mag.* XLIV. 202 On what osmazomatic principle this cruelty is justifiable we are not informed.

‖**osmeterium** (ɒsmɪˈtɪərɪəm, ɒz-). *Entom.* Pl. -ia. Also osma-. [mod.L., f. Gr. ὀσμά-εσθαι to smell + -τήριον formative suffix, signifying 'instrument', 'organ', 'thing used': cf. κοιμητήριον cemetery.] An organ or apparatus adapted to emit a smell or odour; *spec.* a forked process borne by some caterpillars on the segment immediately behind the head, from which they can emit a disgusting odour.

1816 KIRBY & SP. *Entomol.* (1818) II. xxi. 244 Some are furnished with a kind of scent-vessels which I shall call *osmateria.*

osmiamic (ɒsmɪˈæmɪk, ɒz-), *a.* *Chem.* [f. OSMI-UM + AMIC.] In ***osmiamic acid***: A dibasic acid, $H_2Os_2N_2O_5$, an acid amide of osmium. Its salts are **ˈosmiamates**.

1873 WATTS *Fownes' Chem.* (ed. 11) I. 442 Osmiamic Acid ..The potassium salt of this bibasic acid..is produced by the action of ammonia on a hot solution of osmium tetroxide in excess of potash. *Ibid.*, The osmiamates of the alkali-metals..are soluble in water.

osmiate (ˈɒsmɪət, ˈɒz-). *Chem.* [f. OSMI-UM + -ATE¹.] A salt of osmic acid. **a.** = PEROSMATE. Now *Obs.*

The passage in ed. 8 (1895) of *C. Bloxam's Chem.* corresponding to quot. 1890 occurs s.v. PEROSMATE.

1844 *Phil. Mag.* XXIV. 394 A solution of osmiate of potash. **1849** D. CAMPBELL *Inorg. Chem.* 259 Osmic acid.. forms a class of salts known as osmiates: their solutions are decomposed by boiling, osmic acid being evolved. **1852** [see OSMITE]. **1854** J. SCOFFERN in *Orr's Circ. Sc.*, *Chem.* 514 The fused mass..contains osmiate and iridiate of potash. **1854** *Chem. Gaz.* 1 July 242 The air..which is still saturated with vapour of osmic acid, passes into a solution of potash, and finally to the aspirator; the osmiate of potash thus produced is treated with a few drops of alcohol, and collected in the form of crystallized osmite of potash. **1890** THOMSON & BLOXAM *C. Bloxam's Chem.* (ed. 7) 428 By dissolving osmic anhydride in potash and adding alcohol, the latter is oxidised at the expense of the potassium osmiate, and rose-coloured octahedral crystals of potassium osmite ($K_2OsO_4.2Aq$) are obtained.

b. = OSMATE.

1905 GOOCH & WALKER *Outl. Inorg. Chem.* II. xviii. 490 By fusing osmium compounds with potassium hydroxide and potassium nitrate, potassium osmiate, K_2OsO_4, is formed. **1962** P. J. & B. DURRANT *Introd. Adv. Inorg. Chem.* xxiv. 1033 All three elements in the Group, iron, ruthenium, and osmium, are present in the oxidation state VI in the ferrates, the ruthenates, and the osmiates; the general formula is K_2MO_4.

osmic (ˈɒsmɪk, ˈɒz-), *a.*¹ *Chem.* [f. OSMI-UM + -IC.] Containing osmium: applied to compounds in which osmium is quadrivalent, as ***osmic chloride*** $OsCl_4$, ***osmic oxide*** OsO_2; ***osmic acid***, (*a*) a name given to *osmium tetroxide* OsO_4; (*b*) the acid H_2OsO_4, known chiefly in the form of its salts (osmates).

1842 T. GRAHAM *Elem. Chem.* 692 Osmic acid, OsO_4, or the volatile oxide of osmium is best obtained by the combustion of osmium in a glass tube through which a stream of oxygen gas is passed [etc.]. **1873** WATTS *Fownes' Chem.* (ed. 11) I. 440 Osmic chloride, $OsCl_4$, is the red compound obtained by igniting osmium in chlorine gas. **1877** W. THOMSON *Voy. Challenger* I. i. 17 A very weak solution of osmic acid is of great value for killing and hardening small gelatinous animals for microscopic preparations. **1879** ROSCOE & SCHORLEMMER *Treat. Chem.* II. II. 458 In addition to these the salts of osmic acid, H_2OsO_4, are known, but neither the acid nor the corresponding oxide, OsO_3, have been prepared. **1936** J. W. MELLOR *Comprehensive Treat. Inorg. & Theoret. Chem.* XV. lxxii. 705 H. Moraht and C. Wischin obtained a black substance by the action of heat on a mixture of potassium osmate and nitric acid... [They] found that when dried over phosphorus pentoxide, in vacuo, its composition corresponds with the hydrate, $OsO_3.H_2O$, or osmic acid, H_2OsO_4. O. Ruff and K. Bornemann could not confirm the analysis. **1950** N. V. SIDGWICK *Chem. Elements* II. 1499 Hexavalent osmium... There are two binary compounds.. and a considerable number of complex salts, all of which are in some sense derivatives of osmic acid H_2OsO_4.

osmic (ˈɒzmɪk), *a.*² [f. Gr. ὀσμή smell, odour + -IC.] Of or pertaining to odours or the sense of smell. Hence **ˈosmically** *adv.* Cf. OSMICS *sb. pl.*

1938 G. M. DYSON in *Chem. & Industry* XVI. 647/1 When the mucus linings are inflamed and covered with thickened mucus..the ability to smell will be considerably diminished..by reason of the osmic sensory processes being cut off from access to the air. *Ibid.* 648/1 Certain chemical groups and configurations..lead to the development of intra-molecular frequencies capable of affecting the osmic sensory processes. These are referred to, subsequently, as the osmic frequencies. **1964** *Ann. N.Y. Acad. Sci.* CXVI. 557 If this can be confirmed, it will help to define a lower limit to the range of 'osmic frequencies'. **1966** *Nature* 5 Feb. 551/1 The osmic properties that have been identified are the non-specific ones. They do not correlate with particular odours such as those of rose..or peppermint. The fact is that the osmically specific properties of odorous substances have still not been securely identified.

osmicate (ˈɒzmɪkeɪt), *v.* *Biol.* [f. OSMIC *a.*¹ + -ATE³.] *trans.* To stain or treat with osmic acid (osmium tetroxide). So **ˈosmicated** *ppl. a.*

1914 STEDMAN *Med. Dict.* (ed. 3) 658/1 *Osmicate*, to stain with osmic acid. **1943** *Proc. Nat. Acad. Sci.* XXIX. 228 The classical Golgi apparatus of the fixed and osmicated cell. **1971** *Nature* 2 Apr. 334/2 Random pieces of grossly normal thyroid tissue..were diced.., fixed in 1·5% glutaraldehyde ..post-osmicated, dehydrated and embedded in 'Araldite 502'. *Ibid.* 17 Sept. 199/1 Teased preparations of osmicated nerves from paralysed rabbits revealed focal, segmental myelin loss characteristic of EAN.

Also **osmiˈcation**, treatment with osmic acid.

1899 *Jrnl. Morphol.* XV. Suppl. 73 A curious effect of osmication was noted in some peripherally lying cells..in a preparation of *Spelerpes ruber*, which had been fixed in Flemming's chromo-aceto-osmic mixture. **1928** *Biol. Rev.* III. 337 Nassonow..has made a..study of *Paramecium* and some other protozoa by methods of fixation (osmication) and by study *in vivo*. **1934** L. W. SHARP *Introd. Cytol.* (ed. 3) iv. 69 After osmication or silver impregnation they may appear like hollow structures with a blackened periphery. **1972** B. M. WAGNER in I. Mandl *Collagenase* II. 68 Fixation in glutaraldehyde in the presence of 3% basic fuchsin, followed by osmication, resulted in increased stainability of collagen with phospho-tungstic acid (PTA).

osmics (ˈɒzmɪks), *sb. pl.* (const. as *sing.*). [f. Gr. ὀσμή smell, odour: see -IC 2.] The branch of science concerned with odours and the sense of smell.

1922 J. H. KENNETH *Osmics* 3 Osmics..is a convenient term to connote that area of the field of science which is concerned with smell... Briefly, osmics is the science of the stimuli, organs, and the sense of smell. **1965** *Cold Spring Harbor Symp. Quant. Biol.* XXX. 635/1 It must surely be conceded that the science of osmics has come of age with the recognition of its modulating psychophysical principle as being related to the sizes and shapes of volatile molecules.

osmio-, comb. form of OSMIUM, in names of chemical compounds in which osmium and another element enter into combination with a third, as ***osmio-chloride, osmio-cyanide***. Also used in other words, as OSMIOPHILIC *a.*

1862 MILLER *Elem. Chem.* (ed. 2) III. 692 Osmio-cyanides and Ruthenio-cyanides may..be obtained, corresponding in composition to the ferrocyanides. **1877** WATTS *Fownes' Chem.* (ed. 12) I. 531 Sodium osmiochloride, $OsCl_4.2NaCl$, prepared by heating a mixture of osmium sulphide and sodium chloride in a current of chlorine.

osmiophilic (ɒzmɪəʊˈfɪlɪk), *a.* *Biol.* [f. OSMIO- + -PHILIC.] Having an affinity for, or staining readily with, osmium tetroxide.

1927 *Biol. Bull.* LIII. 182, I am..of the opinion that these fatty granules of Guilliermond..have nothing to do with the osmiophilic platelets here described. **1942** *Nature* 10 Jan. 52/1 Granules..which at some stages produce osmiophilic substances. **1971** *Ibid.* 25 June 535/1 In OsO_4-fixed ultrathin sections of the costo-chondral junctions of 1 month old guinea-pigs, Bonucci has found osmiophilic bodies with mean diameters of 500–2,500 Å.

osmious (ˈɒsmɪəs, ˈɒz-), *a.* *Chem.* [f. OSMI-UM + -OUS.] Containing osmium: applied to compounds in which osmium is divalent, as ***osmious chloride*** $OsCl_2$. (Formerly to the *trichloride*, etc.)

1849 D. CAMPBELL *Inorg. Chem.* 258 Osmious acid, OsO_3. This acid has never been isolated, but it exists in a class of salts. **1868** WATTS *Dict. Chem.* IV. 242 Dichloride of Osmium or Osmious Chloride, $OsCl_2$..Trichloride or Osmioso-osmic Chloride, $OsCl_3$.

osmiˈridium. Orig., another name of the alloy commonly called IRIDOSMINE. Now usu. distinguished from *iridosmine* (see quots. 1968, 1973). [For references to G. *osmiridium* (1828, 1831), *osm-iridium* (1824), and *osmium-iridium* (1821) see *Mineral. Mag.* (1963) XXXIII. 716.]

1880 *Libr. Univ. Knowl.* (U.S.) XII. 845 A native alloy of iridium, osmium, and ruthenium. This is called scaly osmiridium ['a gray, scaly, metallic substance', remaining 'when crude platinum is dissolved in nitro-muriatic acid']. **1938** *Mineral. Abstr.* VII. 162 Osmiridium (nevyanskite) from Bolshaya Victorievka mine, Kusuetsky Alatau, West Siberia..gave Os 40·3, Ir 41·6, Ru 4·2, Pt 1·1, Au 1·8, Fe 8·5. **1963** [see NEVYANSKITE]. **1966** PHILLIPS & WILLIAMS *Inorg. Chem.* II. xxxiv. 609 The platinum metals occur native in the alloy osmiridium. **1968** I. KOSTOV *Mineral.* II. i. 90 Iridosmine (Ir, Os) with Os > 35%, and osmiridium (Os, Ir) with Os < 35%; hexagonal... Occurs as small triangular or hexagonal plates. **1973** *Canad. Mineralogist* XII. 105/1 Iridosmine occurs with osmiridium in two grains (samples 10120, gr. 2 and M12339, gr. 1). *Ibid.* 110 An excellent historical review on the nomenclature of natural Os-Ir alloys was made by Hey (1963)... He suggested that the most suitable nomenclature..be the following: For the *cubic* alloys: *osmiridium* with Os<32 at. %. For the *hexagonal* alloys: *iridosmine* with 32<Os<80 at. %. Native *osmium* for Os>80 at. %... Our proposals for alloys in the Os-Ir-Ru system are that:..e) *Iridosmine* of Hey (1963) be redefined as *hexagonal* (Os, Ir) alloys with no single other element >10 at. % of total, and where Os<80 at. % of (Os + Ir)... f) *Osmiridium* of Hey (1963) be redefined as *cubic* (Ir, Os) alloys with no single other element >10 at. % of total, and where Ir<80 at. % of (Ir + Os).

osmite ('ɒsmaɪt, 'ɒz-). *Chem.* [ad. F. *osmite* (E. Frémy 1844, in *Jrnl. de Pharm. et de Chim.* V. 189), f. OSMI-UM + -ITE^{1}.] A salt of osmious acid. = OSMATE. Now *Obs.*

1844 *Phil. Mag.* XXIV. 394 The liquor..deposits a crystalline powder of osmite of potash. **1849** D. CAMPBELL *Inorg. Chem.* 255 This solution of osmiate of potash when heated with alcohol deposits crystals of osmite of potash (the alcohol deprives osmic acid of oxygen). **1852** tr. *Regnault's Elem. Chem.* II. III. 352 Osmite of potassa is obtained by pouring a few drops of alcohol into a solution of osmiate of potassa. *Ibid.*, No osmite of ammonia is known. **1854** J. SCOFFERN in *Orr's Circ. Sc., Chem.* 514 Osmite of potash may be obtained. **1891** W. RAMSAY *Syst. Inorg. Chem.* xxix. 483 Potassium osmite, $K_2OsO_4.2H_2O$, is prepared by dissolving the tetroxide in potassium hydroxide, and adding alcohol.

osmium ('ɒsmɪəm, 'ɒz-). [f. Gr. ὀσμή odour (see quot. 1804) + -IUM.] **a.** One of the metals of the platinum group, generally found, associated with platinum, in the alloy iridosmine or osmiridium. Chem. symbol Os; atomic wt. 199·6 (Frémy).

1804 TENNANT in *Phil. Trans.* XCIV. 416 A pungent and peculiar smell... This smell..arises from the extrication of a very volatile metallic oxide; and, as this smell is one of its most distinguishing characters, I should on that account incline to call the metal *Osmium.* **1805** *Ibid.* XCV. 317 Metals that were found by Mr. Tennant in the black powder which is extricated by solution from the grains of platina, and which he has called Iridium and Osmium. **1853** W. GREGORY *Inorg. Chem.* (ed. 3) 260 Osmium..is chiefly remarkable for forming with oxygen a volatile acid, which has a pungent smell, like that of chlorine, and is very poisonous. **1892** *Spectator* 19 Mar. 396 Aluminium cannot be obtained without osmium also.

b. Special comb.: **osmium lamp**, a filament lamp in which the filament is made of osmium; **osmium tetroxide**, OsO_4, a poisonous, pale yellow solid that has a distinctive pungent and harmful vapour and is used in solution as a biological stain, esp. for lipids, and a fixative; also called *osmic acid.*

1907 *Westm. Gaz.* 16 Feb. 14/2 The osmium lamp..was expensive to start with, and could be used only in the pendent position. **1952** H. HEWITT *Mod. Lighting Technique* iv. 34 Whilst further developments such as the Nernst lamp, the osmium lamp and the tantalum lamp were all of technical interest, it was not until the adoption of the tungsten filament by Coolidge in 1909 that there was any considerable advance towards more efficient electric lamps. **1876** *Encycl. Brit.* V. 537/2 Osmium tetroxide is reduced at red heat. **1920** *Jrnl. R. Microsc. Soc.* 133 The Golgi apparatus has the following reactions:..2. Black in Kopsch's or Mann-Kopsch's osmium tetroxide methods. **1954** H. W. DEANE in R. O. Greep *Histol.* iii. 43 Many lipid substances will also blacken with osmic acid (osmium tetroxide). In most instances..this blackening apparently depends on the fact that unsaturated fatty acids reduce the colorless osmic acid to black osmium dioxide. However, many nonfatty protoplasmic constituents..may also be blackened with osmic acid. **1968** J. MARCH *Adv. Org. Chem.* xv. 616 There are many reagents which add two OH groups to a double bond. OsO_4 and alkaline $KMnO_4$ give cis addition, from the less hindered side of the double bond. Osmium tetroxide adds rather slowly, but almost quantitatively. **1974** *Nature* 18 Jan. 145/1 White Leghorn chicken embryos..were fixed in glutaraldehyde and osmium tetroxide.

† **'osmiuret.** *Chem. Obs.* [see -URET.] A compound of osmium with another element.

1854 J. SCOFFERN in *Orr's Circ. Sc., Chem.* 514, 100 parts of osmiuret of iridium are..incorporated.

osmo-^{1}, repr. Greek ὀσμο-, combining form of ὀσμή smell, odour, in scientific and technical terms: as **os'mology**, the study of smells, a treatise on odours. **os'mometer**^{1}, an instrument for measuring the acuteness of the sense of smell (*Syd. Soc. Lex.*). **os'mometry**^{1}, measurement of odours or of the acuteness of the sense of smell (Mayne); hence **osmo'metric** *a.*^{1} (Mayne). **osmono'sology** [Gr. νόσος disease], history of the diseases of the sense of smell (Mayne). Also used to repr. OSMIUM (cf. OSMIO-), as in **osmo'philic** *a.*^{1} = OSMIOPHILIC *a.*

1857 MAYNE *Expos. Lex., Osmology.* **1889** *Univ. Rev.* Mar. 364 Literature is much more than osmology, and the world contains something beyond and above its social sewers. **1899** *Q. Rev.* July 90 A treatise..on 'monumental physiology, archaeological symbolism, mystical osmology', for the author sees hidden meanings in smells. **1961** in WEBSTER, Osmophilic. **1961** *Lancet* 16 Sept. 656/1 The appearance of osmophilic densities in the zones of lamellar discontinuity at the nodes of Ranvier. **1972** *Jrnl. Electron Microsc.* XXI. 85/1 In order to check the nature of the osmophilic granules..in enlarged axons, the distribution, origin and properties in the area postrema were studied in a morphological comparison..with neuro-secretory granules in the hypothalamus.

osmo-^{2}, repr. Gr. ὠσμό-ς push, thrust, impulse, used as comb. form of OSMOSE in a few scientific terms. **'osmogene** (cf. GAZOGENE, -GEN), an apparatus for carrying out the process of osmosis. **os'mometer**^{2}, an instrument for exhibiting the force of osmotic action, also, an instrument for the measurement of osmotic pressures. **os'mometry**^{2}, measurement of osmotic force; hence **osmo'metric** *a.*^{2}, **osmo'metrically** *adv.* **osmo'philic** *a.*^{2} *Biol.* [ad. G. *osmophil* (A. A. von Richter 1912, in *Mycolog. Centralbl.* I. 74)], tolerating or thriving in a medium which exerts a high osmotic pressure; so **'osmophile**, an osmophilic organism. **'osmoreceptor** *Biol.*, any sensory organ which reacts to changes in osmotic pressure (concentration) in the body fluids.

1854 GRAHAM in *Phil. Trans.* CXLIV. 181 The quantity of salt diffused from the osmometer in the water-jar during the experiment was also observed. **1855** MILLER *Elem. Chem.* I. 72 This instrument generally used by this gentleman [Prof. Graham] in his experiments, and called by him the osmometer. **1885** GOODALE *Physiol. Bot.* (1892) 224 An osmometer..consists of a small reservoir furnished with a membrane bottom, and a graduated tube at its upper part. **1903** M. H. FISCHER tr. *Cohen's Physical Chem.* ix. 139 Pfeffer measured the osmotic pressure of sugar solutions of various concentrations with a mercury manometer, and obtained with such an osmometer the following results. **1974** TOMBS & PEACOCKE *Osmotic Pressure Biol. Macromolecules* iii. 86 Claesson and Jacobsson..have made an osmometer with a very precise optical method for determining the difference in height of two menisci. **1976** *Nature* 12 Aug. 578/1 The total osmolality of the fluid was obtained with a Clifton nanolitre osmometer. **1913** *Chem. Abstr.* IV. 298 In a series of expts. in an 'osmometric vessel' ..the following mol. wts. are obtained by balancing the pressure of the salt against a sugar soln. on the other side of the membrane. **1964** J. ELIASSAF tr. *Rafikov's Determination Molecular Weights* vi. 169 The osmometric measurement of molecular weight is based on the fact that the osmotic pressure..is proportional to the number..of gram-molecules of dissolved material in a definite volume of solution. **1943** *Jrnl. Physical Chem.* XLVII. 69 The molecular weight of a carefully fractionated sample determined osmometrically checks the value obtained for the same polymer by means of the ultracentrifuge. **1964** J. ELIASSAF tr. *Rafikov's Determination Molecular Weights* vi. 223 It was found that for molecular weights of less than 75,000 a difference begins to appear between the molecular weight determined osmometrically and the molecular weight computed by the Mark-Houwink equation. **1913** *Chem. Abstr.* VII. 297 (*heading*) Osmometry of saline solutions and the theory of Arrhenius. **1973** *Nature* 27 Apr. p. xv (Advt.), It also shows how osmometry, ultracentrifugation, light scattering,..and gel filtration are used to analyze polydisperse systems. **1961** P. L. CARPENTER *Microbiol.* xiii. 201/1 Microorganisms that have become adapted to high osmotic pressure are called osmophiles. **1969** L. DO CARMO-SOUSA in Rose & Harrison *Yeasts* I. iii. 88 She also suggested the possibility of finding obligate osmophiles..in Antarctic soils which have a high content of soluble salts. **1920** F. W. TANNER tr. *A. Guilliermond's Yeasts* iv. 120 The maximum concentration for spore formation in a yeast depends upon the species. For an osmophilic species like *Zygosaccharomyces Mandshuricus* the concentration is high. **1960** L. E. HAWKER et al. *Introd. Biol. Micro-Organisms* xvi. 380 Sugar concentrations of 50 to 70 per cent effectively prevent the growth of most micro-organisms... A few osmophilic yeasts and bacteria may grow slowly. **1972** *Sci. Amer.* Apr. 95/2 Because of the high osmotic pressure of honey, they are yeasts of the type called osmophilic, meaning that they live or thrive in a medium that has a high osmotic pressure. **1946** E. B. VERNEY in *Lancet* 30 Nov. 782/1 The osmoreceptors, wherever they may be, do not accommodate during short-period exposure to a rise in the osmotic pressure of the carotid plasma produced by NaCl. **1947** —— in *Proc. R. Soc.* B. CXXXV. 68 It becomes justified, therefore, to introduce the term 'osmoreceptors' as descriptive of the autonomic receptive elements with which the neurohypophysis is functionally linked, and through whose activation the pituitary anti-diuretic substance is released. **1970** A. J. VANDER et al. *Human Physiol.* xii. 354/2 Receptors must exist which are sensitive to extracellular osmolarity. These osmoreceptors are located in the hypothalamus. **1973** *Nature* 14 Dec. 383/1 The osmoreceptors which control the salt glands in marine birds are located in or near the heart.

osmoceptor ('ɒzməʊsɛptɔː(r)). *Physiol.* [a. G. *osmoceptor* (L. Ruzicka 1920, in *Chem.-Zeitung* XLIV. 94/2), f. Gr. ὀσμο- OSMO-^{1} + G. *re)ceptor* (now *rezeptor*) RECEPTOR.] A sensory receptor for the sense of smell.

1944 R. W. MONCRIEFF *Chem. Senses* xii. 314 (*table*) Author... Ruzicka... Date... 1920... General class... Chemical... Salient features... Osmophore and osmoceptor. **1952** PIRENNE & ABBOTT tr. *H. Piéron's Sensations* II. v. 105 Such a correspondence between osmoceptors and osmophores may be important in the explanation of the qualitative differentiation between smells. **1968** W. MCCARTNEY *Olfaction & Odours* 159 If a substance reacts with the primary but not with the secondary osmoceptors, odourlessness (fatigue) follows saturation of the primary osmoceptors.

osmol ('ɒzmɒl). Also **osmole** (-məʊl). [Blend of OSMOTIC *a.* and MOLE *sb.*^{7}] A thousand milliosmols.

1942 J. L. GAMBLE *Chem. Anat., Physiol. & Path. Extracellular Fluid* (ed. 4) Notes to chart 17-B, 0·64 osmoles per liter. Solute concentration. **1956** A. C. GUYTON *Textbk. Med. Physiol.* xxvi. 302/2 If each molecule ionizes into two ions each of which is osmotically active, then 1 mol of solute equals 2 osmols. **1964** L. MARTIN *Clin. Endocrinol.* (ed. 4) i. 51 In *normal* subjects they found that the initial serum osmolality was 285 ± 4·4 m-osmoles/kg. of water. **1971** W. S. BECK *Human Design* vii. 207/2 The numerical unit in which osmotic pressure is expressed is the osmol. We speak of osmols or milliosmols per liter.

osmolal (ɒz'məʊləl), *a.* [Blend of OSMOTIC *a.* and MOLAL *a.*] Of the concentration of a solution: expressed as an osmolality.

1939 [see *milliosmol* s.v. MILLI-]. **1971** W. S. BECK *Human Design* x. 348/2 The osmotic concentration measured by freezing point depression is properly termed an *osmolal* concentration—milliosmols of solute per kilogram of solvent —in contrast to an osmolar concentration—milliosmols of solute per liter of solution. The two values differ only slightly in ordinary dilute solutions, however.

Hence **osmo'lality**, the number of osmotically effective dissolved particles per unit quantity of a solution, esp. when expressed as (milli)osmols per kilogramme of solvent. Cf. OSMOLARITY.

1959 *Q. Jrnl. Med.* LII. 237 The blood was centrifuged, and the plasma osmolality (m-osmoles per kg.) estimated from the freezing-point depression. **1963** *Jrnl. Amer. Med. Assoc.* 31 Aug. 699/1 Normal subjects are characterized by an initial serum osmolality between 273 and 293 milliosmoles (mOsm) per kilogram. **1968** PASSMORE & ROBSON *Compan. Med. Stud.* I. v. 29/1 Sweat..is essentially a weak solution of sodium chloride. The osmolality lies between 100 and 200 mOsm/l. **1972** [see *milliosmole* s.v. MILLI-]. **1974** *Nature* 12 Apr. 605/1 Controls of the osmotic pressure of the solutions of inorganic ions..showed that their osmolalities were practically independent of temperature. **1976** *Lancet* 25 Dec. 1414/1 A man of 61 was admitted to the neurology unit in stupor, which proved to be hyponatræmic (serum osmolality 236 mosmol/kg).

osmolar (ɒz'məʊlə(r)), *a.* [Blend of OSMOTIC *a.* and MOLAR *a.*^{3}] Of the concentration of a solution: expressed as an osmolarity.

1942 J. L. GAMBLE *Chem. Anat., Physiol. & Path. Extracellular Fluid* (ed. 4) Notes to chart 17-B, Multiplying osmolar concentration by cubic centimeters of urine produces a measurement of total solutes as milliosmoles. **1944** *Proc. Amer. Philos. Soc.* LXXXVIII. 152/1 If we divide degrees of freezing point depression by 1·86 we obtain osmolar concentration. Multiplying osmolar concentration by cubic centimeters of urine, defines the total output of solutes as milliosmoles. **1963** *Jrnl. Amer. Med. Assoc.* 31 Aug. 700/2 The serum osmolar concentration of 25 normal subjects..was 285 ± 4·4.. milliosmoles (mOsm) per kilogram of water. **1971** [see OSMOLAL *a.*].

Hence **osmo'larity**, the number of osmotically effective dissolved particles per unit quantity of a solution, esp. when expressed as (milli)osmols per litre of solution. Cf. OSMOLALITY.

1953 *Lancet* 12 Sept. 540/2 An assumed plasma osmolarity of 310 milliosmols per litre. **1962** J. H. KINOSHITA et al. in A. Pirie *Lens Metabolism Rel. Cataract* 406 The final glucose concentration..was 5 μmoles/ml. The total osmolarity was calculated as 307 μosmoles/ml. **1965** *New Scientist* 24 June 868/1 The most important functions of the kidney are to keep constant the volume, osmolarity and composition of the fluid which surrounds the cells of the body. **1973** *Jrnl. Biol. Chem.* CCXLVIII. 4172/1 Solutions of low osmolarity.

osmond, obs. form of OSMUND^{1}.

osmophore ('ɒzməʊfɔə(r)). [f. OSMO-^{1} + -PHORE; in sense 1 a back-formation from OSMOPHORIC *a.*] **1.** A chemical group whose presence in the molecules of a substance causes it to have a smell.

1919 *Perfumery & Essent. Oil Rec.* 21 May 105/1 Both Rupe and Majewski and Cohn point out that one osmophore can often replace another without distinctly changing the odour. **1944** R. W. MONCRIEFF *Chem. Senses* ix. 185 The ether group is only a weak osmophore and is easily overpowered by other features of the molecule. **1963** W. SUMMER *Methods Air Deodorization* i. 66 One and the same osmophore appearing with different molecules usually causes different odours.

2. [ad. It. *osmoforo* (G. Arcangeli 1883, in *Nuovo Giornale Bot. Ital.* XV. 75).] A scent gland found in the flowers of certain plants belonging to the families Orchidaceæ, Araceæ, Aristolochiaceæ, and Asclepiadaceæ.

1966 S. VOGEL in *Proc. 5th World Orchid Conf.* 254/1 We could find such glands, called osmophores, in many different orchidaceous groups... A genuine scent organ or osmophore..may be defined as a glandular, multicellular and clearly differentiated tissue within the floral region, which is well exposed to the atmosphere. **1967** *New Scientist* 22 June 725/2 Several orchids and a few other flowers have..developed glands (osmophores) producing scent substances (terpenes) in liquid form. **1974** C. L. WITHNER et al. in C. L. Withner *Orchids* vi. 305 The scent tissue is ultimately organized into scent glands, or osmophores.

So **osmo'phoric** *a.* [ad. G. *osmophor* (Rupe & Majewski 1900, in *Ber. d. Deut. Chem. Ges.* XXXIII. 3402)], of, pertaining to, or being an osmophore (in either sense).

1901 *Jrnl. Chem. Soc.* LXXX. I. 103 (*heading*) Osmophoric groups. **1922** G. H. PARKER *Smell, Taste, & Allied Senses* iii. 79 Osmophoric groups are such as the hydroxyl, aldehyde, keton, ester, nitro, and nitril groups. None of these..is associated with a particular odor, but any one may be the occasion of odor, if it occupies an appropriate place on a benzene ring. **1968** W. MCCARTNEY *Olfaction & Odours* 133 These investigations suggest that the quality of the odour of a compound depends largely on the steric structure and is modified .. by the presence of osmophoric groups. **1974** C. L. Withner et al. in C. L. Withner *Orchids: Sci. Stud.* vi. 305 The richness of the osmophoric cells in reserve materials relates to their production of fragrant terpene oils.

osmoregulation (ˌɒzməʊrɛgjʊˈleɪʃən). *Physiol.* [a. G. *osmoregulation* (used, prob. for the first time, by R. Höber 1906, in *Physik. Chem. der Zelle und der Gewebe* (ed. 2) ii. 31): see OSMO-^{2} and REGULATION.] The maintenance of a more or less constant osmotic pressure in the body fluids of an organism.

1931 *Q. Cumulative Index Med.* IX. 870/2 (*heading*), Disturbances of osmoregulation in experimental uremia. **1932** *Sci. Rep. Tôhoku Imperial Univ.* VII. 229 (*heading*) On the osmoregulation of the blood of several marine and fresh water molluscs. **1964** *Oceanogr. & Marine Biol.* II. 306 Osmo-regulation is known in all bony fishes. **1971** *Nature* 16 Apr. 469/2 The role of the amphibian urinary bladder in osmoregulation is well documented.

Hence **osmo'regulate** *v. intr.*, to maintain the osmotic pressure of the body fluids at a constant level; **osmo'regulating** *vbl. sb.*; **osmo'regulator**, an organ or part of the body concerned in osmoregulation; an organism capable of osmoregulation; **ˌosmoregu'latory** *a.* [ad. G. *osmoregulatorisch* (Höber *loc. cit.*)], of, pertaining to, or effecting osmoregulation.

1911 Stedman *Med. Dict.* 616/2 *Osmoregulatory*, influencing the degree and rapidity of osmosis. **1927** *Biol. Abstr.* I. 238/2 Parellel experiments with sucrose instead of urea showed that the more rapid recovery from plasmolysis in etherized solutions was due to more rapid penetration of urea, not to any osmoregulatory or ether stimulus to the production of new cell solutes. **1935** *Biol. Rev.* X. 357 The excretory organs of numerous fresh-water animals act as osmoregulators. **1958** *Jrnl. Exper. Biol.* XXXV. 234 The very great osmo-regulating ability of *Artemia* has been described. *Ibid.* 241 Animals whose branchial epithelium has been damaged by a brief exposure to saturated $KMnO_4$ solution have lost the ability to osmo-regulate. **1959** Southwood & Leston *Land & Water Bugs Brit. Isles* xiv. 395 Its osmo-regulatory mechanism enables the bug to live in waters with from 5 to about 18 parts per thousand of salt in solution. **1960** *Biol. Abstr.* XXXV. 2729/2 The degree of activity of their osmoregulating mechanisms. **1963** R. P. Dales *Annelids* v. 109 In view of the lack of evidence that the nephridia do more than act as drains as far as nitrogenous wastes are concerned, we can but incline to the view that they are primarily osmoregulators. **1964** *Oceanogr. & Marine Biol.* II. 307 Holeurysaline osmo-regulators can regulate in salinities ranging from that of pure fresh water to that of full strength sea water or higher. **1969** *New Scientist* 30 Jan. 243/1 Herring embryos could osmoregulate even before chloride cells had developed. **1970** *Nature* 24 Oct. 378/1 A primary osmoregulatory function of prolactin is the reduction of extrarenal sodium outflux.

osmose (ˈɒsməʊs, ˈɒz-), *sb.* [The common element of the words *endosmose* and *exosmose*, taken (by Graham, 1854) as a generalized term: cf. Gr. ὠσμός thrust, push.] The tendency of fluids separated by porous septa to pass through these and mix with each other; the action of this passage and intermixture; diffusion through a porous septum or membrane.

1854 Graham in *Phil. Trans.* CXLIV. 181 With the same proportion (1 per cent.) of different substances, the osmose varied from 0 to 80 degrees... The fall may be spoken of as negative osmose, to distinguish it from the rise or positive osmose. **1855** Miller *Elem. Chem.* I. 73 When the liquid rises in the osmometer, Professor Graham distinguishes it as positive osmose. **1867** J. Hogg *Microsc.* II. i. 257 An incessant mutual interchange of materials is going on between the fluid contents and matter external to the cell, by a process termed *osmose* or diffusion. **1875** Bennett & Dyer tr. *Sachs' Bot.* 605 The current of water in the woody substance which replaces the loss occasioned in the leaves by transpiration is not caused by osmose.

Hence **os'mose** *v. intr.*, to pass by osmose.

1884 J. C. Cutter *Comprehensive Physiol.* viii. 153 Watery solutions usually osmose readily.

osmosis (ɒsˈməʊsɪs, ɒz-). [Latinized form of OSMOSE, after *endosmosis* and *exosmosis*, conformed to sbs. in -OSIS in Eng. use.]

1. = OSMOSE. (This, rather than *osmose*, is now the usual term.)

1867 J. Hogg *Microsc.* I. iii. 206 The great desideratum of a transparent injecting fluid is, that it shall not by the action of osmosis, dye the tissue meant to be injected. **1876** Foster *Phys.* I. iv. (1879) 122 Permeable .. in the sense of allowing fluids to pass through them by osmosis.

2. *fig.* Any process by which something is acquired by absorption.

1900 *Nation* (N.Y.) 18 Oct. 303/3 The subtile interchange —a sort of moral osmosis—which goes on between the higher conquering race and the lower conquered race. **1930** E. Pound *XXX Cantos* xxix. 137 Languor has cried unto languor about the marshmallow-roast (Let us speak of the osmosis of persons). **1968** *Times Lit. Suppl.* 26 Sept. 1079/1 A director born (like Godard) in 1930 is in a position to know, by a sort of unconscious osmosis, more than a director born in 1898 (like René Clair) can hope to learn, however conscientiously he may try. **1970** *Author* LXXXI. 113 It is not a question how much you teach them but how much they learn, perhaps largely by osmosis. **1977** P. D. James *Death of Expert Witness* III. 128 News percolated through a village community by a process of verbal osmosis.

osmotic (ɒsˈmɒtɪk, ɒz-), *a.* [f. OSMOSE or OSMOSIS, in imitation of adjs. in -OTIC, from Gr. words in -OSIS.] **1.** Of, pertaining to, or caused by osmosis; ***osmotic pressure***, the excess pressure that must be applied to a solution to prevent the entry into it of pure solvent when they are separated by a semipermeable membrane, or the excess pressure that develops in the solution when osmosis is allowed to occur in such circumstances; ***osmotic shock***, rupture of a cell following a sudden drop in the osmotic pressure of the surrounding liquid, owing to the inflow of liquid that occurs.

1854 Graham in *Phil. Trans.* CXLIV. 177 On Osmotic Force. The expression 'Osmotic Force' .. has reference to the endosmose and exosmose of Dutrochet. *Ibid.* 181 Substances of small osmotic power. **1862** H. Spencer *First Princ.* I. iv. §23 (1875) 72 The absorption of nutrient fluids through the coats of the intestines, is an instance of osmotic action. **1876** Bartholow *Mat. Med.* (1879) 3 An acid fluid on one side of the osmotic membrane, and an alkaline fluid on the other, are conditions most favorable to osmosis. **1888** *Jrnl. Chem. Soc.* LIV. 778 (*heading*) Osmotic pressure in the analogy between solutions and gases. **1950** T. F. Anderson in *Jrnl. Appl. Physics* XXI. 70/1 The similar viruses, T2, T4, and T6 which appear in the electron microscope to have membranes surrounding the internal structures of the heads can be disintegrated by what might be termed 'osmotic shock'... Presumably, the virus heads swell when the osmotic pressure is suddenly reduced, and actually burst if the reduction is sufficiently large and sudden. **1970** Ambrose & Easty *Cell Biol.* ii. 83 A solution containing one gramme-molecule of non-ionizable solute in 22·4 litres exerts an osmotic pressure of 1 atmosphere at 0°C. The use of a delicate manometer by Adair and Adair enabled them to determine the molecular weight of proteins by comparing their osmotic properties with those of known solutes. **1973** D. A. Anderson *Introd. Microbiol.* x. 110/1 The cells of many bacteria .. are likely to burst when placed in distilled water. This method (osmotic shock) is often used to release components from inside the cell for biochemical analysis. **1973** R. Krueger et al. *Introd. Microbiol.* v. 201/2 The cytoplasmic water contains a tremendous variety of small organic and inorganic molecules and numerous ions and soluble enzymes... Gram-positive bacteria have an osmotic pressure of 22 atm (atmospheres).

2. In *fig.* senses. Cf. OSMOSIS 2.

1952 W. D. Jacobs *William Barnes* i. 10 There is also the strong and numberless clan which utilizes all the latinic iridescence at its command .. to rejoice that the language had such osmotic good fortune. **1965** *Economist* 24 Apr. 451/2 In the osmotic way these things happen, virtually all of them [*sc.* workers] were absorbed by other local industries. **1975** B. Garfield *Hopscotch* xxii. 236 The joy she took from flying .. in some profound osmotic way .. had communicated itself to him.

os'motically, *adv.* [f. prec.: see -ICALLY.] By osmotic action; by the process of osmosis. Also *fig.*

1882 A. S. Wilson in *Gard. Chron.* XVII. 671 That it may find its way osmotically through the cell-walls of the roots. **1885** Tait *Properties Matter* 262 There need be no surprise that a liquid such as the sap in plants, should be osmotically raised to great heights against gravity. **1974** *Times Lit. Suppl.* 20 Dec. 1437/5 A reminder of how much royal legend is osmotically absorbed by even the most reluctant reader of royal biography. **1976** *Times* 20 Jan. 11/6 The chic of the actresses was absorbed, osmotically, into his ranges [of clothes].

osmund^1 (ˈɒzmənd). Forms: 3–7 **osemond**, 5–8 **osmond**, (5–6 **-monde**), 5– **osmund**, (5–6 **-munde**, 7 **osmound**, 9 **oosement**). [From Sw. or LG.: cf. OSw. (1340) *osmunder*, in comp. *osmunds-(osmunds-iærn* osmund iron), Sw. *osmund*; also Da. (1402) *osmund*, mod.Icel. *ásmundr* (both from Sw.); MLG. *osemunt* (Schiller & Lübben), Westph. dial. *ôsemund* (Woeste).

The actual origin is obscure; the name has been in use in Sweden from early times, and also goes back to an early date in Westphalia; no certain etymology is known either in Sw. or LG. The Eng. form from 1400 appears to be from Sw., but the earlier examples have the MLG. form (which, however, might be due to Hanseatic traders). In 1281 it is referred to as *ferrum Normannicum*, Northmen's iron. Iron and copper were brought to England by Gotlanders *a* 1300. Sense 2 is prob. a distinct word.]

1. A superior quality of iron formerly imported from the Baltic regions, in very small bars or rods, for the manufacture of arrow-heads, fish-hooks, bell-gear, etc. Used as a material-name; also, with pl. *osmunds*, a bar or rod of this. **b.** Also, more fully, ***osmund iron, osmund bar***.

As to the early production of osmund iron in Sweden (from bog-iron ore) see R. Åkerman in *Jrnl. Iron & Steel Inst.* (1898) No. 2; also Kinman *Bergverkslexicon* II. 233, Hildebrand *Sveriges Medeltid* I. 225, 732, Falkman *Om mått och vigt* I. 412, and many other Swedish works. For its appearance in Eng. documents, see E. Peacock in *Proc. Soc. Antiquaries* 22 Jan. 1880, also Rogers *Agric. & Prices* I. 470, etc. (Numerous entries from 1280 to 1510.) The osmunds were imported put up in sheaves, packed in barrels, 12 (or 13) of which made a last.

1280 in Rogers *Agric. & Prices* II. 457/2 (cites from Ersham, Norfolk) [1 garb Osemond 1/2]. **1376** *Rolls Parlt.* II. 328/1 Un last de Osmond. **1408** in Rogers III. 347/1 (cites from Windsor) [Osemond 4 garb at /8]. **1400–12** *Compotus* in C. Frost *Hist. Notices of Hull* App. 18 Dr Willo. Bird pro ij last' dī landirn', ix bund' fruoldirn', ix bar' osmond. **1428** *Surtees Misc.* (1888) 1 Makers and utterers of fals osmundes... He cuttyd aboute xxvj peces of fals Inglysh iryn .. and made þam in shappe of osmundes. *Ibid.* 2 And þay war made to blend with gude osmundes. *a* **1450** *Fysshynge w. Angle* (1883) 6 Ye schall make youre hokes of steyle & of osmonde. **1465** *Mann. & Househ. Exp.* (Roxb.) 301 My mastyr paid for iij. sheffe Osmond .. ffor to make arow hedes, ij.*s.* *a* **1490** Botoner *Itin.* (Nasmith 1778) 315 Polelond .. ibi est coper, osmond, gold, sylver. [Sweden] .. ibi est cuprum, osmond, in magna fertilitate. **1540** *Act 32 Hen. VIII*, c. 14 Item for euery last of osmondes accomptyng .xiii. barrels for a last .viii.*s.* **1598** Hakluyt *Voy.* I. 167 Halfe a last of osmundes. **1753** Maitland *Hist. Edin.* III. 248 For every cwt of Osmond brought into Leith 8 pennies. **1880** E. Peacock in *Proc. Soc. Antiq.* 22 Jan. 257 Osmunds were clearly .. the very best iron, .. probably used only for the finest purposes, such as arrow heads, fish hooks, .. and the works of clocks.

b. [**1488** *Act 3 Hen. VII*, c. 9 §1 Other Stuff as Lynen Cloth .. osmonde Iren Flax and Wax.] **1594** *Compt. Buik Dav. Wedderburne* (S.H.S.) 132 To wair 8 gudlenis on pes or osmond iron. **1823** *Mechanic's Mag.* No. 5. 71 Comparative strength of Metals .. Bar [Iron] 8·492, Oosement bar 8·142, Cable 7·752. **1898** R. Åkerman in *Jrnl. Iron & Steel Inst.* No. 2. 9 In certain very remote parts of the country osmund iron, though in rather small quantity, was still produced from bog ore up to the end of the last century.

c. *attrib.* ***osmund bar, o. iron*** (see b); **osmund furnace**, a small primitive sort of furnace for reducing bog-iron ore, formerly used in Sweden, Finland, etc.; **osmund piece**, an osmund bar.

1864 J. Percy *Metallurgy* 619 Descriptions of other processes, such as the Sulu process, the Osemund process .. will be found in various treatises. *Ibid.* 320, I shall distinguish it by the name of the Osmund furnace, from the Swedish word *osmund*, which was applied to the bloom produced in this kind of furnace. **1898** R. Åkerman in *Jrnl. Iron & Steel Inst.* II. No. 2. 7 In the Middle Ages and down to the 16th century, these osmund pieces were very commonly used as currency in the absence of the more precious metals. **1902** B. H. Brough in *Let.* 16 Apr., Osmund furnaces were in operation in Jemtland in 1830, and in Finland even later.

2. ***osmund stone***: see quots.

1613 M. Ridley *Magn. Bodies* 3 This stone is called the Magnet .. we call it the Load-stone... And it is well termed the Osmound Stone, because he is as it were *Os Mundi*, the bone of the world. **1806** Forsyth *Beauties Scotl.* III. 10 In the parishes of Eaglesham, Kilbarchan, and others, there has been found what is called the osmund stone... It is generally so soft, when lately quarried, that it may be cut with a chisel... It is used for ovens, furnaces, etc.

osmund^2 (ˈɒsmənd, ɒz-). Also 6 **osmende**, **-monde**. [In med.L. *osmunda*, F. *osmonde* (12th c. in Hatz.-Darm.), AF. *osmunde*: of unknown origin.]

†**1.** A name formerly given to various ferns. *Obs.*

(Quot. *c* 1265 may be in sense 2. The Male Fern, *Lastrea Filix-mas*, was formerly called Osmund Royal.)

[*c* **1265** *Voc. Names Pl.* in Wr.-Wülcker 556/43 *Osmunda*, i. osmunde, i. bonwurt.] *c* **1450** *M.E. Med. Bk.* (Heinrich) 192 Tak wermot, .. weybrode, the rote of osmund [etc.]. **1548** Elyot, *Dryopteris*, is an herbe, which groweth on old oken trees .. lyke to ferne: .. Some call it Osmende royall. **1578** Lyte *Dodoens* III. lx. 401 The Male Ferne .. Of Mattheolus and Ruellius it is called Osmunde Royall. *Ibid.* lxiii. 405 Considering the propertie of this herbe [*Dryopteris*, white and black] in taking away heare, as also for a difference from the other Oke Fernes and Osmundes, we do thinke good to name this herbe .. Osmunde Baldepate or Pylde Osmunde... The blacke .. may be very wel called in our tongue, Small Osmunde, or Petie Ferne. **1579** Langham *Gard. Health* (1633) 230 The root of male Fearne, called Osmund roial. **1611** Cotgr., *Feuchiere des chesnes*, Oake-fearne, pettie fearne, mosse-fearne, pild Osmund.

2. Now, the 'Flowering Fern', *Osmunda regalis* Linn., having large bipinnate fronds with terminal panicles of sporangia; also (since 1600) called ***osmund royal, royal fern, king fern***; formerly ***Osmund the waterman, St. Christopher's herb***. **b.** Also as the Eng. form of the name of the genus (of which six species are known).

1578 Lyte *Dodoens* III. lxi. 402 We may cal it .. Osmonde the Waterman, Waterferne, and Saint Christophers herbe. **1611** Cotgr., *Feuchiere aquatique*, Water Fearne, Osmund, Osmund royall, Osmund the Waterman, S. Christophers hearbe. **1658** Sir T. Browne *Gard. Cyrus* iii. 154 In the root of Osmund or Water fern every eye may discern the form of a Half Moon. **1711** *Phil. Trans.* XXVII. 350 A particular sort of creeping Osmund or Flowring Fern. **1851** S. Judd *Margaret* II. i. (1871) 162 Clusters of tall osmunds, straight as an arrow. **1880** Dawkins *Early Man* vi. 125 In the marshes there were alders, osmund royal, and marsh trefoil.

osmunda (ɒzˈmʌndə). [med.L. (see OSMUND^2), adopted as a generic name by J. Petiver in *Musei Petiveriani centuria VI & VII* (1699) 53.] A fern of the genus so called, esp. the royal fern, *Osmunda regalis*.

1789 E. Darwin *Bot. Garden* II. 11 The fair Osmunda seeks the silent dell. **1818** [see *cinnamon fern*]. **1858** J. A. Symonds *Let.* 6 June (1967) I. 144 Is the Osmunda yet in flower? **1865** M. Eyre *Lady's Walks S. of France* xxv. 272 The *Osmunda* grew at the other end of the lake. **1894** W. Brockbank in W. Robinson *Wild Garden* (ed. 4) xiii. 143 The brooklet was .. fringed with marsh plants .. together with Osmundas, Hart's-tongues, and other Ferns. **1974** R. Grounds *Ferns* v. 57 This method [*sc.* container-growing] is ideal if one wants to use a strong-growing osmunda, for example, as a specimen plant.

2. In full, ***osmunda fibre***. A fibre generally made from the roots of *Osmunda cinnamomea* or *O. claytoniana*, used as a potting medium for orchids.

1910 *Gardeners' Chron.* 5 Nov. 329/3 He [*sc.* H. G. Alexander] decided that Osmunda fibre was the best material procurable. **1932** *Bull. Amer. Orchid Soc.* Dec. 87/2 Osmunda fibre taken from swampy land should not be used. **1942** LAURIE & RIES *Floriculture* xix. 460 Osmunda peat makes the best medium for this group [of epiphytic orchids]. **1942** C. L. WITHNER *Orchids: Sci. Survey* viii. 349 Its [*sc.* tree fern's] water-retention and drying capacities are very similar to osmunda. **1951** *Dict. Gardening* (*R. Hort. Soc.*) III. 1440/2 Osmunda is at present the best material for general use [in potting orchids] but in fact several other fibres are in use to eke out and modify Osmunda fibre. **1959** *Listener* 17 Dec. 1094/3 A piece of osmunda fibre, or wire netting filled with moss and fastened round a cane, can be driven into the pot and kept moist with spraying. **1966** T. B. MORRIS *Orchids with Murder* i. 7 The pleasantly familiar smell of damp loam and sphagnum and osmunda fibre. **1974** C. L. WITHNER *Orchids: Sci. Stud.* iii. 154 Osmunda fiber plus water provided adequate fertility for orchids.

osmundaceous (ɒsmən'deɪʃəs, ɒz-), *a. Bot.* [f. mod.L. *Osmundāceæ*: see OSMUND² and -ACEOUS.] Of or belonging to the *Osmundaceæ*, one of the principal subdivisions of the Nat. Ord. *Polypodiaceæ*, the type of which is the genus *Osmunda*.

1857 in MAYNE *Expos. Lex.* **1890** *Athenæum* 29 Nov. 743/1 While not going so far as to refer these carboniferous sporangia..to any distinct genus, he [Prof. Bower] thought the osmundaceous affinity was unmistakable.

osmundine ('ɒzməndiːn). *N. Amer.* [f. OSMUNDA + -INE⁴.] = OSMUNDA 2.

1932 *Bull. Amer. Orchid Soc.* Sept. 52/2 The best compost to use for growing Cattleyas should consist of good fibrous brown fern root, osmundine as it is called. **1934** R. STOUT *Fer-de-Lance* vii. 101 Supplies—pots, sand, sphagnum.. osmundine.

Osnaburg. Also with lower-case initial. Forms: 6 **Osenbreges, Ossenbrydge, Ostenbriges, Ozenbridg(e, (Osburow),** 7 **Osenbrigs,** 8 **Oz-, Osnabrigs, -brug, Ozenbrigs;** 7 **Ossenburgs,** 8 **Osnaburgh,** 8–9 **Osnaburg.** [Named from Osnabrück (in later Eng. corruptly *Osnaburg*), a town and district in North Germany, noted for its manufacture of linen.] A kind of coarse linen originally made in Osnabrück.

1545 *Rates of Customs* cj, Osenbreges the roule *xl.* **1554–5** in Willis & Clark *Cambridge* (1886) III. 363, ix yeardes of Ossenbrydge for a towell to the hye tabyll, iiij*s.* vj*d.* **1597** *Wills & Inv. N.C.* (Surtees 1860) 282, xxi yds of osburow 31*s.* 6*d.* **1669** NARBOROUGH *Jrnl.* in *Acc. Sev. Late Voy.* (1694) I. 2 Cloth, Osenbrigs, Tobacco. **1732** *Pennsylv. Col. Rec.* (1853) III. 430 That to each there be given a couple of Shirts, a Jackett and two pair of trowsers of Oznabrigs. **1733** P. LINDSAY *Interest Scot.* 117 Osnaburgs and other low pric'd foreign goods of that kind..ought likewise to be subjected to a duty. **1757** WASHINGTON *Lett.* Writ. 1889 I. 490, I..beg the favor of you to choose me about 250 yds. osnabrigs. **1791** NEWTE *Tour Eng. & Scot.* 205 A great deal of coarse linen cloth, called Osnaburghs, is made here for exportation. **1799** J. ROBERTSON *Agric. Perth* 381 In some of the villages of the Carse of Gowrie, the inhabitants manufacture osnaburgs. **1827** ROBERTS *Voy. Centr. Amer.* 36 In exchange we gave them ravenduck, osnaburg, checks, blue-baftas and other manufactured goods. **1917** J. HERGESHEIMER *Three Black Pennys* (1918) 38 Tobacco and shoes, ozenbrigs and molasses and rum. **1938** M. K. RAWLINGS *Yearling* xi. 110 Beyond the utensils were the dress goods; calico and Osnaburg, denim and shoddy, domestic and homespun. **1949** *Caribbean Q.* I. I. 12 Every October cloth was issued, at the rate of seven yards of osnaburgs. **1959** POTTER & CORBMAN *Fiber to Fabric* (ed. 3) ix. 153 When made of waste mixed with low-grade cotton it is known as part-waste osnaburg.

b. *attrib.*, made of Osnaburg linen.

1681 *Rec. Court. of New Castle on Delaware* (1904) 493 Twoo Remnants of Osnabriggs Linnen. **1758** in *Essex Inst. Hist. Coll.* (1874) XII. 145 Others very much soaked in their Osombrige Tents. **1774** in *Maryland Hist. Mag.* (1911) VI. 41 John Johnson..had on..a pair of leather breeches and osnabrig trousers. **1813** J. TAYLOR *Arator* 137 A regular supply of a winter's coat,..two oznaburg shirts, a good hat and blanket. **1841** *Southern Lit. Messenger* VII. 775/2 Our slaves in the South-West are annually supplied with two cotton Oznaburg shirts. **1863** 'E. KIRKE' *My Southern Friends* vii. 99 The thin Osnaburg gown.

oso-berry ('əʊsəʊˌbɛrɪ). [? Amer. Ind.] The blue-black drupe of *Nuttallia cerasiformis*, a shrub or small tree of western North America. Also the shrub, bearing racemes of greenish-white flowers.

1884 MILLER *Plant-n.* 223 *Nuttallia cerasiformis*, Oso-berry tree, of California.

osocome, erron. f. NOSOCOME, hospital.

osone ('əʊsəʊn). *Chem.* [ad. G. *oson* (E. Fischer 1889, in *Ber. d. Deut. Chem. Ges.* XXII. 87), f. *-ose* -OSE² + *-on* -ONE.] Any compound containing two adjacent carbonyl groups, obtained by hydrolysing an osazone.

1889 [see *glucosone* s.v. GLUCO-]. **1938** PRESCOTT & RIDGE *Org. Chem.* xx. 353 The osone, which may be isolated as the lead compound, is reduced with zinc dust and acetic acid to a ketose. **1957** J. W. GREEN in W. Pigman *Carbohydrates* vi. 334 The osones exist only as amorphous or sirupy materials.

-osophy, the latter part of *philosophy*, *theosophy*, and the like (see -SOPHY), as a nonce-word.

1897 *Chicago Advance* 28 Oct. 574/2 That man would be hard to please who could not find..some variety of doxy, or osophy, or ism, which would come within hailing distance of his theory of life and destiny.

†'**osor.** *Obs. rare*⁻¹. [a. L. *ōsor*, agent-n. from *ōdisse*, *os-* to hate.] A hater.

1600 W. WATSON *Decacordon* (1602) 238 Princes are alwaies iealous, and many times haue iust cause, and euer more then any other priuate person to be so: for the greater honors the greater, mo, and grieuoser osors.

‖**O-soto-gari** (ɔːsoːtogaːri). Also **Osotogari, o-**. [Jap., f. *o* grand + *soto* outside + *gari* f. *kari* to mow, to reap.] The name of a throw in Judo.

1941 M. FELDENKRAIS *Judo* 45 Pull the opponent's sleeve and attack by the first leg throw (*O-Soto-Gari*). **1956** E. J. HARRISON tr. *H. Aida's Kodokan Judo* iii. 58 Should you anticipate your opponent's attempted Osotogari then just at the moment when he is contemplating the reaping action with his right leg swiftly pull him near you to counter. **1963** P. BUTLER *Judo Complete* iii. 59 The *osotogari* is my own favourite throw and many variations are possible upon the basic method. **1970** A. P. HARRINGTON *Judo Guide to Black Belt* i. 28 Now..try the O-soto-gari against your opponent.

osperaye, obs. form of OSPREY.

‖**osphradium** (ɒs'freɪdɪəm). *Zool.* [mod.L., a. Gr. ὀσφράδιον strong scent, dim. of ὄσφρα smell.] The olfactory organ of some molluscs, consisting of a collection of elongated sense-cells over each gill. Hence **os'phradial** *a.*, of or pertaining to the osphradium.

1883 E. R. LANKESTER in *Encycl. Brit.* XVI. 636/1 Near the base of the stem of each ctenidium is..Spengel's olfactory organ, which tests the respiratory fluid... We propose to call it the *osphradium*. *Ibid.* 645 A simple pair of osphradial patches. **1895** *Edin. Rev.* Oct. 368 Osphradium.

osphresiology (ɒsfriːsɪ'ɒlədʒɪ). [f. Gr. ὄσφρησι-ς smelling, smell + -λογια, -LOGY.] The scientific study of the sense of smell; a treatise on smelling and odours. Hence **osphresio'logic** *a.*, of or pertaining to osphresiology.

1842 DUNGLISON *Med. Lex.*, *Osphresiology*. **1887** *Amer. Jrnl. Psychol.* I. 500 Other osphresiologic anomalies.

osphy-, osphyo-, repr. Gr. ὀσφυ(ο-, comb. form of ὀσφύς loin, forming pathological terms, as ‖**osphy'algia** [Gr. ἄλγος pain], lumbago; hence **osphy'algic** *a.* (Mayne, 1857). ‖**osphyar'thritis** [ARTHRITIS], gout in the loins (Dunglison *Med. Lex.* 1853). '**osphyocele** [Gr. κήλη tumour], lumbar hernia. ‖ˌ**osphyomye'litis**, inflammation of the spinal cord in the lumbar region (Mayne).

ospreng, obs. form of OFFSPRING.

osprey ('ɒspreɪ). Forms: 5–7 **ospray(e,** 7 **aspray, osperaye, ospraie, -eie,** 6– **osprey.** [First found in 15th c.; app. repr. L. *ossifraga*, lit. 'bone-breaker', in Pliny the name of a bird of prey, through an earlier **osphraye* = OF. **osfraie*, whence later F. *orfraie* or *offraie* (Belon, 1555). But the connecting ME. and OF. forms have not been found, and it is remarkable that the word is of so late appearance in both langs.

Pliny's *ossifraga* is identified by modern ornithologists with the Lammergeyer, but it was rendered by Du Ponet in F. *orfraye*, and by Holland '*orfraie* or *ospreie*', and the transference of the name from the Lammergeyer to the Fish-hawk must have occurred at an early date, if *osprey* actually represents *ossifraga*. See OSSIFRAGE.]

1. A large diurnal bird of prey, *Pandion* (*Falco* Linn.) *Haliaëtus*, frequenting rocky sea-shores and borders of lakes, and preying upon fish; also called sea-eagle, fishing-eagle, fish-hawk.

c **1460** J. RUSSELL *Bk. Nurture* 402 Every goos, teele, Mallard, Ospray, & also swanne. *a* **1529** SKELTON *P. Sparowe* 462 The roke, with the ospraye That putteth fysshes to a fraye. **1601** HOLLAND *Pliny* I. 272 These Orfraies or Ospreies are not thought to be a seuerall kind of Egles by themselues, but to be mungrels, and ingendred of diuers sorts. **1607** SHAKS. *Cor.* IV. vii. 34, I think hee'l be to Rome As is the Aspray to the Fish. **1637** HEYWOOD *Dialogues* Wks. 1874 VI. 315 The wary Ospray whilst the fishes play Above the wave, stoopes downe to cease her prey. **1773** G. WHITE *Selborne* 9 Nov. 97 The osprey was shot about a year ago at Frinsham-pond. **1843** YARRELL *Hist. Birds* I. 21 The genus *Pandion* was instituted for the Osprey by M. Savigny. **1895** *Outing* (U.S.) XXVII. 60/2 A splendid osprey circled in the sunlight on the look-out for breakfast.

2. A milliner's name for an egret plume worn as an ornament on a lady's hat or bonnet; sometimes, like *aigrette*, extended to an artificial plume or other ornament used for the same purpose. (It has been thought that this erroneous use arose from associating *osprey* with *spray*.)

1885 *Pall Mall G.* 29 Jan. 3/2 Fine crême Dunstable straw bonnets, trimmed with crême velvet, and crême aigrettes with crême and gold osprey. **1887** *Daily News* 28 Sept. 5/4 A slender spiral feather of the most fragile and delicate appearance... This ornament is called an osprey. **1892** *Ibid.* 1 Mar. 5/4 These [aigret] feathers are white... They are often dyed by milliners to various tints, and have by them for some reason been named 'osprey'. **1893** *Lady* 17 Aug. 178 Velvet bows holding some upright spray, such as oats, jet aigrettes, osprey, or wheat-ears. *Ibid.*, Jet osprey or fancy wings cost from 1*s.* 6½*d.* **1898** *Globe* 19 Jan. 3/2 'Ospreys' (or sprays) is..the milliners' and dressmakers' term, ignorantly and commonly used, for the plumes of the egret or white heron.

ospring(e, -yng(e, etc., obs. ff. OFFSPRING.

†**ospringe,** obs. var. (or error for) OSPREY.

1530 PALSGR. 250/1 *Ospringe*, a byrde.

†**ospytalle,** obs. form of HOSPITAL.

c **1440** *Promp. Parv.* 372/1 Ospytalle, *hospitale.* **14..** *Nominale* in Wr.-Wülcker 719/16 A nospytalle.

oss, mod. dial. form of OSSE.

ossature ('ɒsətjʊə(r)). [a. Fr. *ossature* skeleton, f. L. *os*, *oss-* bone + *-ature*, from ppl. and adj. stems in *-at-*, as *curvat-ure*, *ornat-ure*.]

1. The arrangement and disposition of the bones of the skeleton. *rare.*

1885 *Truth* 28 May 851/2 Frenchmen cannot bear to see her because her ossature is so mannish. **1892** *Syd. Soc. Lex.*

2. *Arch.* The skeleton or framework that supports any structure, as the metal or timber beams of a roof, or the metal frame of a glass window.

1879 SIR G. SCOTT *Lect. Archit.* I. 64 The vaults govern the ossature of the monument. *Ibid.* 70, I then treated only the mechanical framework of the style—its mere ossature, to use M. Viollet le Duc's expression.

osse, oss (ɒs), *v.* Now *dial.* [Found in w. midl. dialect in 14th c., and still common from the Welsh Border to Cumbria and Northampton; much affected by Ph. Holland in his versions of Latin authors, to render *ōminārī* and its synonyms, as is OSSE *sb.* to render *ōmen*. The latter has not been found in previous writers, though Holland (who, as Head Master of Coventry Free School, had opportunity of knowing the facts) refers to both sb. and vb. as old words well known in the North. (See OSSE *sb.* quot. 1600.) According to the known evidence, the sb. appears to be derived from the vb., but the origin of both is involved in obscurity.

Holland was confirmed in his use of these words by believing them to be derived from Gr. ὄσσα 'ominous voice or sound, prophecy, premonition', the coincidence of which and its vb. ὄσσ-εσθαι 'to presage, foretoken, forebode' with *osse* sb. and vb. is certainly very remarkable; yet it is impossible that an English vb. in popular use in the 14th c. could be derived from Greek without many intermediate links, of which in this case none are found. The verb is also used in mod. colloquial Welsh as *osio* 'to give token of, show promise of', but in the opinion of Prof. Rhŷs and Dr. Silvan Evans, this is merely a recent adoption from the adjacent English dialects. (Ray's conjecture of identity with F. *oser* 'to dare' (founded on a modern dialect use), is phonetically and historically futile.)]

†**1.** *trans.* (with *obj. cl.*) ? To signify, indicate, make known, show. *Obs.*

13.. *E.E. Allit. P.* C. 213 He [Jonah] ossed hym by vnnynges þat þay vnder-nomen, þat he watz flowen fro þe face of frelych dryȝtyn.

†**2.** *esp.* To give oracular or prophetic indications; to presage, betoken, or signify as an omen; to prognosticate, forebode, augur, prophesy; to wish auspiciously, wish good luck. Also *absol.* or *intr.* *Obs.*

a **1400–50** *Alexander* 2263 Þus answars þam þaire ald gode & osses on þis wyse. *Ibid.* 2307 Quat, & has þou [Priestess of Diana] ossed to Alexander þis ayndain wirdes? *a* **1545** [EDGEWORTH, temp. Hen. VIII, uses to *oss* for to *prophesy*. Halliw.]. **1600** HOLLAND *Livy* V. xviii. 192 In this Election.. yee osse and presage happely against the yeare ensuing, concord and unitie. **1606** —— *Sueton.* 205 He [Nero] heard withall, an out-crie and showt..of the Souldiours ossing all mischiefe at him & all good unto Galba. *Ibid.* Annot. 18 b, *Nonis, quasi, non is*, which literally osseth as much as, *you go not*.

†**b.** With reverse const. *Obs.*

(If not a mispr. in quot. for 'to osse unto the cittie'.)

1600 HOLLAND *Livy* III. lxi. 129 Vnwilling I am..to boden such miseries and to osse the cittie unto those calamities.

c. Hence (in *mod. dial.*), To point or direct auspiciously, to commend or recommend (a person *to* something advantageous).

1885 T. HALLAM *Four Dialect Words* 60 (Shropsh.), I ossed 'er to a place. **1885–7** T. DARLINGTON *Folk-sp. S. Chesh.* 28 I'll oss yo' to a good heifer.

3. *dial.* To give augury or indication of what one is going to do or be, to bode or promise well or ill, shape well or ill for something; hence, to show signs or give indication of being about (to do), to make a show of (doing), to offer (to do); to make an attempt, to try, essay, venture, dare; to set about, prepare, be about (to do something).

1674–91 RAY *N.C. Wds.*, *Osse*, to offer to do, to aim at, or intend to do; 'Ossing comes to bossing'; Prov. Chesh. 'I did not osse to meddle with it', i.e. 'I did not dare, etc.'; *fortè ab audeo, ausus.* *c* **1746** COLLIER (Tim Bobbin) *Lanc. Dial.* Wks. (1862) 57, I..leet oth' owd Mon ith' Fowd, ossing t' get o Titback. **1790** MRS. WHEELER *Westmld. Dial.* III. 85 Soa yee see Ise ossin towart Hauskeepin. **1828** *Craven Gloss.* (ed. 2), *Osse*, to attempt, to offer. **1854** MRS. GASKELL *North & S.* xxviii, If I did see a friend who ossed to treat me, I never knew hoo lay a-dying here. **1879** MISS JACKSON *Shropsh. Word-bk.* 312 That wench dunna seem to oss very well..'er 's as lazy as Ludlam's dog that laid 'im down to bark. *Ibid.* 313, I think the chap knows his work, 'e osses pretty well.

Hence '**ossing** *vbl. sb.*, presaging; presage.

a **1400–50** *Alexander* 732 Haue a gud eȝe, Les[t] on þine ane here-efterward þine ossyngis liȝt. *Ibid.* 868 For it awe him noȝt sa openly slike ossing to make. **1600** Holland *Livy* 202 This the Gaules supposing to be a fortunate ossing of their successe.

osse, oss, *sb. Obs.* or *dial.* [See prec.]

†**1.** A word of omen, a presage; an ominous or auspicious word; an auspicious greeting, a wishing of good luck. *Obs.*

Almost peculiar to Phil. Holland, who uses it continually for L. *omen*; in Speed prob. from Holland's Camden.

1600 Holland *Livy* 3 We rather should begin with good osses and luckie forespeakings [*bonis ominibus*]. *Ibid.* xli. xviii. 1107 *note*, Valerius Maximus..calleth this Omen of his (which I commonly interprete (Osse) *fortuitum vocis jactum*... For want of a proper tearme to expresse the Latine (Omen) all translators hitherto, French, Italian, and English, have been put to their shifts, and helpe themselves with (Presage)... Whereas that other word (Osse) is very significant, and in analogie æquivalent to (Omen). I mervell much therefore, why it is thought either strange and new (seeing it is English, used no doubt commonly in times past, and at this day currant in the North-parts, where the people haply are more observant of such presages) rather than many other forraine words, brought into our language, and raunged with the English: or why it should be condemned as absonant and not pleasing to the eare, more than ὄσσα in Greek.. from whence, who seeth not (*Osse* and *Ossing* both) are derived. **1601** —— *Pliny* Expl. Words Art, *Osses*, be words cast forth at vnawares, presaging somewhat. **1603** —— *Plutarch's Mor.* 1293 They take all their words which they passe in play and sport, as osses and presages. **1606** —— *Sueton.* 204 Portents..of prodigies and of Osses [*Ominum*]. **1609** —— *Amm. Marcell.* xix. x. 136 But the gods in heaven forfend the Osse. **1610** —— *Camden's Brit.* i. 139 All the osse and presage of good luck. **1611** Speed *Hist. Gt. Brit.* vii. iv. §5. 206 Virgil also maketh the Horse to be a luckie Osse or foretokened successe in Battle.

2. An essay or attempt (at doing something). *Mod. W. Yorksh. dial.* He made an oss at it.

ossean (ˈɒsɪən), *a.* and *sb.* [f. L. *osse-us* bony + -an.] **A.** *adj.* Bony, osseous, as a teleost fish. In mod. Dicts.

B. *sb.* A fish of the order *Teleostei*, having its skeleton well ossified; an osseous fish.

1835 Kirby *Hab. & Inst. Anim.* II. xxi. 388 Osseans in which the skeleton is bony and formed of bony fibres.

osseid (ˈɒsiːɪd). *Chem. rare.* [f. L. *osse-us* bony, after *proteid*.] A name including ossein and the related albuminoids.

1884 *Health Exhib. Catal.* 4 The nitrogenous principles are subdivided into albumen, fibrine and caseine by some physiologists: connected with these, but having a lower value, are the osseids, such as gelatine.

ossein (ˈɒsiːɪn). *Chem.* Also **osseine**. [f. L. *osse-us* bony + -in[1].] Bone-cartilage; the organic gelatinous principle in true bony tissue; the embryonic tissue which develops into bone by the deposit of mineral salts.

1857 Miller *Elem. Chem.* III. 665 The quantity of nitrogen [16·9 per cent.] given in Fremy's analysis of ossein. **1891** *Athenæum* 25 July 131 The restriction of the term albuminoids to ossein, gelatin, chondrin, and the like, not true proteids, will, we hope, be followed.

osselet (ˈɒsəlɪt, ˈɒslɛt). Also 8 **oslet, osslet.** [a. F. *osselet* a little bone (12th c. in Hatz.-Darm.), f. L. *os, oss-* bone: see -let.]

1. A little bone, an ossicle; one of the small bones of the carpus or tarsus.

1686 A. Snape *Anat. Horse* v. xi. 219 The Seven Osselets or little Bones that make the Knee. *Ibid.* xvi. 233 The Leg-bone and Ranges of Osselets which make that part we call the Hock. **1816** Singer *Hist. Cards* 318 Athenæus..says, that the 'games of dice and osselets were in use at the time Troy was besieged by the Greeks'.

2. *Farriery.* (See quot.)

c **1720** W. Gibson *Farrier's Guide* ii. lxxviii. (1738) 234 Oslets are little hard substances that arise among the small bones of the knee. **1737** Bracken *Farriery Impr.* (1756) I. 323 Splents, Osslets, Spavins, and Ring-bones.

3. The cuttle-bone, pen, or calamary of some cephalopods.

1849 Dana *Geol.* App. i. (1850) 708 The osselet in some Cephalopoda. **1862** —— *Elem. Geol.* 455 View reduced of the complete osselet of a Belemnite.

ossements (ˈɒsmənts), *sb. pl. rare.* [a. F. *ossements* bones, ad. med.L. *ossamenta* (13th c. Du Cange), f. *os, oss-* bone: see -ment.] The bones of the dead; bones from which the flesh has been stripped.

1841 I. Taylor *Anc. Chr.* (1842) II. vii. 263 It [blood] had been poured upon these ossements, which were afterwards covered with earth.

Ossene (ˈɒsiːn). Also **Ossæan, Ossen.** [ad. late L. *Ossēni*, a. Gr. Ὀσσηνοί (Epiphanius): see quot. 1863.] A member of an ancient heretical sect, living to the east of the Dead Sea, who adopted from the Essenes a debased form of Christianity.

[**1580** Fulke *Dang. Rocke* xviii. (Parker Soc.) 390 The old heresies, in which the Papists consent with ancient heretics ..the Ossens and Marcosians in their Reliques, and strange tongue in prayers.] **1863** Westcott in Smith *Dict. Bible* s.v. *Essene*, The strange account which Epiphanius gives of the Osseni..appears to point to some combination of Essene and pseudo-Christian doctrines. **1880** G. Salmon in Smith *Dict. Chr. Biog.* s.v. *Elkesai*, His accounts of the Jewish Sect which he calls Ossenes (Haer. 19).

osseo-fibrous (ˌɒsiːəʊˈfaɪbrəs), *a.* [f. *osseo-*, comb. form of L. *osse-us* osseous + *fibrous*.] Consisting of osseous combined with or passing into fibrous tissue.

1845 Todd & Bowman *Phys. Anat.* I. 128 Tendons, such as those of the flexor or extensor muscles of the fingers and toes, as they lie in their osseo-fibrous sheaths in the hand or foot. **1846** Brittan tr. *Malgaigne's Man. Oper. Surg.* 240 An osseo-fibrous vault, formed by the acromion and coracoid process and the ligament that unites them.

osseous (ˈɒsiːəs), *a.* [f. L. *osse-us* bony (f. *os* bone) + -ous. Cf. F. *osseux* (1689 in Hatz.-Darm.).]

1. Of, consisting of, or of the nature of bone; bony; ossified.

1707 J. Drake *Anthrop. Nova* II. ii. viii. 465 The Coats of the Vessels..soonest become Osseous, as they are frequently found. **1760** J. Lee *Introd. Bot.* i. vii. (1765) 15 An osseous Epidermis..commonly called the Shell. **1843** Carlyle *Past & Pr.* ii. ii, Alas, how like an old osseous fragment. **1872** Nicholson *Palæont.* 308 As regards their true osseous system or endo-skeleton, Fishes vary very widely. **1881** Mivart *Cat* 19 Bone, or osseous tissue, is a substance, two-thirds of which..consists of mineral matter.

2. Having a bony skeleton, teleostean.

1828 Stark *Elem. Nat. Hist.* I. 374 The two great divisions [of Fishes], founded on the character of their bones, as being Cartilaginous or Osseous, are natural and well marked. **1873** Mivart *Elem. Anat.* ii. 59 In osseous Fishes the end of the tail is turned up.

3. Abounding in fossil bones, ossiferous.

1823 Buckland *Reliq. Diluv.* 150 The femur of a bear from the osseous breccia of Pisa. **1876** Page *Adv. Text-bk. Geol.* xix. 383 Osseous breccia appears singularly connected with the coasts of the Mediterranean.

4. *fig.* Hard or firm as bone.

1682 Sir T. Browne *Chr. Mor.* iii. §4 The osseous and solid part of Goodness, which gives Stability and Rectitude to all the rest. **1860** Farrar *Orig. Lang.* vi. 130 The osseous fixtures in the flesh garment of Language.

Hence ˈ**osseously** *adv.*, as regards bone.

1877 *Encycl. Brit.* VII. 258/2 The elbow is osseously strong, but this strength..varies with the position of the arm.

†ˈ**osset.** *Obs.* Forms: 5 **osed**, 6 **oset**, (*Sc.* **ousett**), **osset(t).** [Of unascertained origin. It has been conjectured to be a dial. pronunciation of *worsted*, but investigation does not favour this.] Some kind of woven material, app. of wool. Also *attrib.* **osset loom**, a loom for weaving osset.

1482 in *Eng. Gilds* (1870) 321 Receyved of Edmond Colchet vj. yerdes of blew osed to make hym a gowne. **1543** *Will of R. Parsons of Chew* 26 Feb. (MS.), An oset lome other-wysse calyd a narowe lome. **1554** *Will of W. Parkyns* (Somerset Ho.), All my ossett cloaths. **1578** in Wadley *Bristol Wills* (1886) 228 One osset loome.

‖**osseter** (əʊˈsɛtə(r)). *Zool.* [a. Russ. *osétr* = Serb. *jesetra*, Pol. *jesiotr*, Lith. *asetras, ershketras* sturgeon.] A species of sturgeon, *Acipenser Güldenstädtii*.

1887 *Chamb. Jrnl.* IV. 630/2 The sturgeon..and its kindred the great sturgeon or beluga.., the sewruga.., the osseter (A. Guldenstadtii), and the small sturgeon or sterlet.

Ossetian (ɒˈsiːʃən), *sb.* and *a.* Also **Ossetan** (-ˈiːtən), **Osset(e)** (ˈɒsɛt, -iːt), **Ossetic** (ɒˈsɛtɪk). [f. Russ. *osetín*, f. Georgian *os, oset'i* Ossetia (place-name) + -ian.] **A.** *sb.* **a.** A member of a people of the Central Caucasus, inhabiting North Ossetia (the North Ossetian Autonomous Soviet Socialist Republic) and South Ossetia (an Autonomous Oblast of the Georgian Soviet Socialist Republic). **b.** The language of this people, one of the Eastern Iranian group.

1814 [see Chechen]. **1841** [see Median *sb.*[2] 2]. **1869** C. Engel *Examples of Art Workmanship* 4 The Ossetes, or Ossetines, are an Indo-Germanic race dwelling in Central Caucasus. They call themselves Irôn; Oseti is the name given to them by the Georgians and other neighbouring nations. **1888** J. Wright tr. *Brugmann's Elem. Compar. Gram. Indo-Gmc. Lang.* I. 5 Ossetian (spoken in the neighbourhood of the Caucasus). **1902** [see Ingush]. **1913** [see Alan[2]]. **1925** P. Radin tr. *Vendryès's Language* ii. 38 This phenomenon [*sc.* sound-shifting] is found in other languages besides the Germanic: in Armenian, for example, and in Ossetic. **1933** C. D. Buck *Compar. Gram. Greek & Latin* 8 Modern Iranian is represented by..the isolated Ossetan in the Caucasus. **1933** L. Bloomfield *Language* iv. 62 An isolated offshoot [of Iranian], far to the west is Ossete, in the Caucasus, spoken by some 225,000 persons. **1933** *N. & Q.* CLXIV. 192/1 Ossetian is a modern Iranian vernacular, spoken by the Ossetes, a tribe in central Caucasus. **1944** G. A. Nebolsine tr. *Vernadsky's Hist. Russia* (rev. ed.) i. 16 The Caucasian Alans were called *As* or *Os*—a name which their descendants, the Ossetians, still bear. **1959** B. Geiger et al. *Peoples & Lang. Caucasus* 47 Ossetian has the status of a literary language. **1964** R. H. Robins *Gen. Linguistics* viii. 328 Georgian, Armenian, and Ossetic, languages spoken in contiguous regions, but belonging to different families, Armenian and Ossetic being I-E languages, and Georgian one of the members of the Caucasian family. **1965** G. Y. Shevelov *Prehist. of Slavic* 615 Ossetian, the language which to a certain degree continues the Ir[anian] dialects north of the Black Sea, is known only in its modern form. **1970** D. A. Rustow in *Cambr. Hist. Islam* I. iv. vi. 691 The neighbouring Circassians, Chechens and Ossetians proved almost equally tenacious. **1971** L. Zgusta et al *Man. Lexicogr.* vii. 300 The glosses would probably be given in Ossetic, the dictionary being determined for the Ossetes.

B. *adj.* Of or pertaining to this people or their language.

1877 A. H. Keane tr. *Hovelacque's Sci. of Lang.* v. 207 The Ossetian declension is fuller than the Persian. **1910** *Encycl. Brit.* V. 552/2 The Mamison Pass, over which runs the Ossetic military road (made passable for vehicles in 1889).. lies at an altitude of 9270 ft. **1932** *Times Lit. Suppl.* 2 June 398/4 Joseph..Jugashvili (otherwise Koba, otherwise Stalin) was the son of a Georgian father and an Ossetian mother. **1953** R. G. Kent *Old Persian* (ed. 2) 7 The Ossetic dialects, in the general region of the Caucasus; derived from the Scythian of Southern Russia. **1962** D. M. Lang *Mod. Hist. Georgia* i. 9 The Ossetian Military Road runs northward from Kutaisi towards the Mamison Pass. *Ibid.* iii. 49 The Ossete mountaineers and the villagers of Mtiuleti were forced to toil without payment. **1974** *Country Life* 24 Jan. 146/4 An Ossete folk-ballad, adapted by the poet Kosta Khetagurov (the Caucasian equivalent of Robert Burns), begins: The fox has been whetting her teeth for the badger.

†ˈ**ossey,** *a. Obs. rare.* [f. L. *osse-us* bony + -y.] Bony, osseous.

1578 Banister *Hist. Man* i. 24 The ossey substaunce of the ribbes is not euery where alike.

osseye, variant of osey *Obs.*, wine of Alsace.

‖**ossia** (ɒˈsiːə, ˈɒsjə), *conj.* [It., f. *o sia*, or maybe.] In musical directions: or rather, or alternatively.

1876 Stainer & Barrett *Dict. Mus. Terms* 340/2 *Ossia*.., or else, as *ossia più facile*, or else in this more easy way. **1959** *Collins Music Encycl.* 476/2 *Ossia*, 'or'. Used to indicate an alternative, usually simplified, to a passage in a composition.

Ossianesque (ɒʃ(ɪ)əˈnɛsk, ɒsɪəˈnɛsk), *a.* and *sb.* [f. *Ossian* (see next) + -esque.]

A. *adj.* Imitating or suggesting the style of the poems attributed to Ossian.

1889 *Athenæum* 21 Sept. 382/2 The subject being treated with an Ossianesque turgidity of phrase.

B. *sb.* Ossianesque style or manner.

1874 L. Stephen *Hours in Library* III. 359 At its worst it ..degenerates towards a rather unpleasant Ossianesque.

Ossianic (ɒʃɪ-, ɒsɪˈænɪk), *a.* [f. *Ossian*, Macpherson's anglicized form of *Oisin* (ɔʃɪn), name of a legendary Gaelic bard, whose poems Macpherson claimed to have collected and translated as published by him in 1760–63.] Of or pertaining to the legendary Ossian or to the poems ascribed to him; of the style or character of the rhythmic prose of Macpherson's rendering of these poems, which has a peculiar Celtic glamour and charm, but is marred by bombast and rant; hence, magniloquent, bombastic.

1808 *Edin. Rev.* Jan., His Ossianic poetry. **1828** Scott *Jrnl.* II. 122 Ballantyne blames the Ossianic monotony of my principal characters. **1881** *Athenæum* 28 May 715/3 Those who wish to find what traces of the so-called Ossianic legends still linger in Alban.

So ˈ**Ossianism**, the sphere or realm of Ossianic legend and poetry; ˈ**Ossianize** *v.*, to do into the form of Macpherson's English version of 'Ossian'.

1862 *Macm. Mag.* Sept. 430 It is a comfort for the tourist when he comes upon some one spot where he can see the old Gael walking out of Ossianism into the light of record. Such a spot is Dunstaffnage. **1814** Southey in *Q. Rev.* XII. 85 The Ossianized Iliad could do no injury to our literature.

ossicle (ˈɒsɪk(ə)l). [ad. L. *ossiculum*, dim. of *os, ossi-* bone.]

1. A small bone; a small piece of bony substance.

Applied in anatomy to the bones of the middle ear in the tympanic cavity (*auditory ossicles, o. of audition*); also to those of the carpus and tarsus (*carpal* and *tarsal ossicles*), and to the numerous minute bones which strengthen the sclerotic coat of the eye in birds and some reptiles.

1578 Banister *Hist. Man* i. 25 As touchyng the Ossicle, or little bone conteined within the hart. **1599** A. M. tr. *Gabelhouer's Bk. Physicke* 18/2 Take out..of each foote the middlemost ossicle, or Clawe. **1689** Moyle *Sea Chyrurg.* ii. iv. 37 When..I had laid it open, and taken out the splintred ossicles. **1709** Blair in *Phil. Trans.* XXVII. 125 The Ossicles, viz. the Malleolus..Incus..Stapes..are of a proportional bigness. **1835–6** Todd *Cycl. Anat.* I. 308/2 The..tympanic ossicle is moved by one muscle. **1877** Coues & Allen *N. Amer. Rod.* 582 There are eight true tarsal bones, besides a supplementary ossicle.

2. A small plate, joint, etc. of chitinous or calcareous substance in the animal framework.

a. One of the plates or skeletal elements of a starfish or other echinoderm, as the ***ambulacral*** and ***adambulacral ossicles***, the ossicles that support the spines, etc. **b.** One of the joints of the stem or branches of a crinoid or encrinite. **c.** One of the small hard parts of the gastric skeleton of crustacea, as the ***cardiac ossicle*** or plate, ***pterocardiac o.***, etc.

1852 E. Forbes *Echinodermata of Brit. Tertiaries* 2 Vent.. surrounded by a membrane covered more or less with irregular ossicles. **1857** Mayne *Expos. Lex.* 839/1 Having the..nature..of ossicles, as the articulated pieces of which are composed the columns of animals pertaining to the Crinoides. **1892** J. A. Thomson *Outl. Zool.* 204 [In starfishes] the rafter-like plates are called ambulacral ossicles. *Ibid.*, The dorsal surface bears a network of little ossicles, and many of these bear spines. *Ibid.* 238

(Crustacea) The [cardiac] mill is very complex; .. there are supporting 'ossicles' on the walls with external muscles attached to them.

o'ssicular, *a.* [f. as prec. + -AR[1].] Pertaining to, consisting of, or of the nature of ossicles.

1857 in MAYNE *Expos. Lex.* **1889** *Amer. Naturalist* XXIII. 637 The hyomandibular.. breaks up into two or more pieces, as an ossicular chain.

o'ssiculate, *a. rare.* [f. L. type **ossiculāt-us*, f. *ossiculum*: see -ATE[2].] = OSSEOUS 2.

1857 MAYNE *Expos. Lex.*, *Ossiculatus*, applied by Willbrand to an Order of fishes, comprehending those that are provided with a true skeleton; ossiculate.

ossiculated (ɒ'sɪkjʊleɪtɪd), *a. rare.* [f. as prec. + -ED.] Furnished with or made of ossicles.

1752 SIR J. HILL *Hist. Anim.* 201 Of those, which have the rays of the fins bony, some have the branchiæ ossiculated, and others have none of these ossicles about them.

'ossicule. [ad. L. *ossiculum*.] = OSSICLE.

1886 in *Cassell's Encycl. Dict.*

ossiculectomy (ɒˌsɪkjʊ'lɛktəmɪ). *Surg.* [f. L. *ossicul-um*, dim. of *os*, *ossi-* bone + -ECTOMY.] Excision of the auditory ossicles.

1900 *Lancet* 10 Mar. 702/2 An uncomplicated otorrhoea which has resisted all forms of treatment for six months is certainly a case for ossiculectomy. **1959** G. E. SHAMBAUGH *Surg. Ear* xix. 515 (*heading*) Partial ossiculectomy.

‖**o'ssiculum.** Pl. -a. [L., dim. of *os* bone.] A little bone; an ossicle; †the stone of a fruit.

1706 PHILLIPS, *Ossiculum*, a little Bone: Among Herbalists, the stone of a plum, Cherry or suchlike Fruit. **1753** CHAMBERS *Cycl. Supp.*, *Ossicula auditoria*,.. four little bones contained in the cavity of the tympanum. **1874** ROOSA *Dis. Ear* (1876) 20 There is no record of the ossicula auditus until the 15th century. **1877** HUXLEY *Anat. Inv. Anim.* ix. 555 On the antambulacral wall,.. the ossicula are elongated rods of very unequal lengths, united together.

ossiferous (ɒ'sɪfərəs), *a.* [f. L. *os*, *ossi-* bone + -FEROUS.] Containing or yielding bones; said of caves and deposits in which bones have been found.

1823 BUCKLAND *Reliq. Diluv.* 162 Ossiferous caves and fissures. **1833** LYELL *Princ. Geol.* III. 143 In several parts of Australia, ossiferous breccias have lately been discovered in limestone caverns. **1877** DAWSON *Orig. World* xiv. 310 In one of the Belgian caves, there are six beds of ossiferous mud.

'ossifiant, *a. rare.* [f. OSSIFY *v.* + -ANT.] Ossifying; *fig.* becoming hard and rigid.

1862 RUSKIN *Unto this Last* 4 Assuming, not that the human being has no skeleton, but that it is all skeleton, it founds an ossifiant theory of progress on this negation of a soul.

ossific (ɒ'sɪfɪk), *a.* [f. L. *os*, *ossi-* bone + -FIC.] Bone-forming; becoming or making bone; ossifying. ***ossific centre***, a centre of ossification.

1676 WISEMAN *Chirurg. Treat.* II. vii. 184 You may.. dry the Bone, and dispose it by virtue of its ossifick faculty to thrust out a Callus. **1713** CHESELDEN *Anat.* I. i. (1726) 8 The ossific matter not flowing far enough to complete a bone. **1804** ABERNETHY *Surg. Obs.* 103 Without any manifest cause existing to excite such ossific inflammation. **1881** MIVART *Cat* 334 The ordinary ossific centres found in other vertebræ.

†**'ossificated**, *a. Obs.* [f. L. type **ossificāt-*: see next and -ATE[2].] = OSSIFIED.

1727 BAILEY vol. II, *Ossificated*, turned or become Bone, hardened from a softer cartilaginous Substance into one of a firmer Texture. **1765** *Treat. Dom. Pigeons* 43 The bonewen is an ossificated tumor, arising upon the joints as before.

ossification (ɒsɪfɪ'keɪʃən). [n. of action from OSSIFY. So in Fr. (1709 in Hatz.-Darm.).]

1. The formation of bone; the process of becoming or changing into bone; the condition of being ossified.

centre of ossification, the initial point from which this process starts, the point at which cartilage or connective tissue begins to ossify.

1697 R. BAKER (*title*) Cursus Osteologicus: Being a Compleat Doctrine of the Bones.. Shewing their Nature.. manner of Ossification, Nourishment [etc.]. **1733** BELCHIER in *Phil. Trans.* XXXVIII. 196 The gradual Increase of the Bones is described, even from the first Stages of Ossification, to that of an Adult. **1830** R. KNOX *Béclard's Anat.* 203 Ossification of the arteries is most commonly the lot of old age. **1831** —— *Cloquet's Anat.* 45 This bone.. presents three centres of ossification, one for its middle part, and two for the lateral regions. **1855** HOLDEN *Hum. Osteol.* (1878) 24 The bone called the 'sacrum' has as many as 33 centres before its ossification is complete.

2. *concr.* The result of the process, a bony formation or concretion; bone as a formation.

1705 W. COWPER in *Phil. Trans.* XXIV. 1970 The Trunks of the Arteries of the Leg.. were Obstructed by Petrifactions or Ossifications. **1807** M. BAILLIE *Morb. Anat.* (ed 7) 259 It would appear that ossifications are sometimes to be found in this cartilage. **1822** LAMB *Elia* Ser. I. *Chimney-Sweepers*, From the mouth of a true sweep a display.. of those white and shining ossifications, strikes me as.. an allowable piece of foppery.

3. *fig.* The process of becoming hard or callous.

1889 *Spectator* 13 Apr., A misery, not relieved.. by.. ossification of the feelings.

ossificatory ('ɒsɪfɪˌkeɪtərɪ), *a. rare.* [f. L. type **ossificāt-* (in *ossification*) + -ORY.] Of the nature of, or tending to, ossification.

1870 ROLLESTON *Anim. Life* 20 Not as yet closed up by ossificatory ingrowth.

ossified ('ɒsɪfaɪd), *ppl. a.* [f. OSSIFY + -ED[1].] Made or converted into bone; hardened like bone; rendered osseous. Also *fig.*

1798 T. HINDERWELL *Hist. Scarborough* III. ii. 277 This skin was not in an ossified state. **1834** MCMURTRIE *Cuvier's Anim. Kingd.* 53 The first has three ossified phalanges in the middle finger of the wing. **1901** *Yale Fun* 55/2 'Did you hear about the row over in Peabody Museum?' 'What was the trouble?' 'A lot of the exhibits got ossified.' **1922** S. LEWIS *Babbitt* xxix. 337 Oh, but wasn't T. D. stewed! Say, he was simply ossified! **1934** WEBSTER s.v., *Ossified*..2. Figuratively, fixed; hardened; set in a conventional form; ultraconservative. *a* **1953** E. O'NEILL *Long Day's Journey* (1956) IV. 156 What's the matter with the Old Man tonight? Must be ossified to forget he left this out. **1961** in WEBSTER s.v., Bitterly criticized the organization for being ossified. **1976** *Times* 5 Nov. 14/8 That lack of any spirit of initiative .. that is normally the hallmark.. of ossified totalitarianisms.

ossifier ('ɒsɪfaɪə(r)). [f. OSSIFY *v.* + -ER[1].] One who or that which ossifies.

1840 HOOD *Up Rhine* 318 But Power is a frightful ossifier.

ossiform ('ɒsɪfɔːm), *a. rare.* [f. L. type **ossiform-is*, f. *os*, *ossi-* bone: see -FORM.] Of the form of bone; resembling bone; bone-like.

1847-9 TODD *Cycl. Anat.* IV. 126/1 The origin of ossiform particles.. in the brain.

†**o'ssifragant**, *a. Obs. rare*[-0]. [erron. f. L. *ossifragus* bone-breaking + -ANT[1].]

1656 BLOUNT *Glossogr.*, *Ossifragant*, that breaketh bones.

ossifrage ('ɒsɪfrədʒ). [ad. L. *ossifrag-us*, *-a*, name of a bird of prey, the 'bone-breaker', from *ossifragus* bone-breaking, f. *os*, *ossi-* bone + *frag-*, root of *frangĕre* to break. Cf. It. *ossifraga*.

The *ossifraga* of Pliny is identified by modern naturalists with the Lammergeyer, which swallows and digests bones, and is said to let them fall from a great height upon rocks and stones so as to break them. But the name appears to have been early transferred in France and England to the Fish-hawk, to which, in its assumed modern forms *orfraie*, *osprey*, it is now applied. *Ossifrage* has subsequently been taken directly from the L. form, either simply to render the L., or to name the bird held to be meant by Pliny, but has sometimes been used merely as a synonym of OSPREY. (In modern Ornithology, *Ossifraga* has been awkwardly taken by Bonaparte as generic name of the Giant Fulmar, a bird of the petrel family.) See also OSPREY.]

1. As a rendering of L. *ossifraga*, or as a name for the Lammergeyer or Geir Eagle, or of some kindred species identified with the bird called by the Romans *ossifraga*.

1601 HOLLAND *Pliny* x. iii. 272 Some reckon yet another kind of Ægle, which they call Barbatæ; and the Tuscanes, Ossifrage. **1611** BIBLE *Lev.* xi. 13 The Eagle, and the Ossifrage [*R.V.* gier eagle], and the Ospray [COVERD. the Aegle, the Goshauke, the Cormoraunte; WYCLIF an egle, and a griffyn, and a merlyoun; PURVEY an egle, and a grippe, aliete; *Vulg.* aquilam et gryphem, et haliæetum]. **1646** SIR T. BROWNE *Pseud. Ep.* 130 When the Septuagint makes use of this word [γρύψ].. Tremellius and our Translation hath rendred it the Ossifrage, which is one kinde of Eagle. **1656** BLOUNT *Glossogr.*, *Ossifrage*, a kind of Eagle, having so strong a beak, that therewith she breaks bones, and is therefore called a bone-breaker. **1688** R. HOLME *Armoury* II. 256/1 The Ossifrage, or Dispised Eagle.. is of greater Body, yet of different colour, from the Eagle. **1871** WHYTE MELVILLE *Sarchedon* III. xi. 150 Such kin they seemed to their conquerors as the dog to the wolf, the ossifrage to the eagle.

2. Identified with the OSPREY or fish-hawk.

1658 PHILLIPS, *Ossifrage*, a kind of Eagle which breaketh bones with her beak, the same as Osprey. **1678** RAY *Willughby's Ornith.* 59 For the Haliæetus or Sea-Eagle we will present the Reader with the Ossifrage of Aldrovandus.. a fierce and generous bird, preying upon Fish, and frequenting not only Pools and Rivers, but also the Sea. **1871** BROWNING *Balaust.* 123 Crook'd claw o' the creature, cormorant, Or ossifrage, that.. hangs Afloat i' the foam.

o'ssifragous, *a. rare*[-0]. [f. L. *ossifrag-us* (see prec.) + -OUS.] Bone-breaking.

1721 BAILEY, *Ossifrangent*, *Ossifragous*, bone-breaking. Hence in ASH, WORCESTER, WEBSTER, etc.

†**ossi'frangent**, *a. rare*[-0]. [f. L. *os* bone + *frangentem*, breaking.] = prec. q.v.

ossify ('ɒsɪfaɪ), *v.* [f. L. *os*, *ossi-* bone + -FY: cf. F. *ossifier* (1709 in Hatz.-Darm.).]

1. *intr.* To become or turn into bone; to change from soft tissue into bone.

1713 CHESELDEN *Anat.* I. i. (1726) 5 Flat bones.. begin to ossify in a middle point. **1741** A. MONRO *Anat. Bones* (ed. 3) 32 They become more solid,.. and at last ossify. **1872** MIVART *Anat.* 63 The walls of the two concave vertebral articular cups may ossify.

b. *fig.* To become hardened and callous; to become rigid and fixed as regards progress.

1858 FROUDE *Hist. Eng.* III. xv. 297 The natural instinct of veneration had ossified into idolatry. **1891** *Ch. Times* 2 Jan. 9/1 It is said in academic circles of a very successful Fellow who rises too rapidly to high place, that he ossifies.

2. *trans.* To convert into bone; to harden, to make like bone. (Chiefly in *passive*.)

1721 *Phil. Trans.* Abr. V. 341 *heading*, The Arteries Ossified. **1800** *Med. Jrnl.* IV. 227 The coronary arteries.. were ossified. **1849** MURCHISON *Siluria* xii. 303 The skeletons of these animals were all well ossified.

b. *fig.* To harden; to render callous, rigid, unprogressive, or inoperative.

1831 *Fraser's Mag.* III. 7 Their withers are wrung, their feelings are ossified. **1860** FARRAR *Orig. Lang.* v. 114 Our phrases, often repeated, ossify the very organs of intelligence. **1877** R. H. HUTTON *Ess.* (ed. 2) I. 10 Long-continued doubt.. must in the end ossify the higher parts of the mind.

Hence **'ossifying** *vbl. sb.* and *ppl. a.*

1713 CHESELDEN *Anat.* I. i. (1726) 6 By the continual addition of this ossifying matter, the bones increase. **1741** A. MONRO *Anat. Bones* (ed. 3) 32 The ossifying of Bones. **1799** HATCHETT in *Phil. Trans.* LXXXIX. 325 The ossifying substance, which is principally phosphate of lime, is dissolved. **1898** L. STEPHEN *Stud. of a Biogr.* II. iii. 78 His nature had resisted the ossifying process which makes most of us commonplace.. in later life.

ossitacion, obs. form of OSCITATION.

ossivorous (ɒ'sɪvərəs), *a.* [f. L. *os*, *ossi-* bone + *-vor-us* devouring + -OUS.] Bone-devouring, feeding upon bones; in *Path.* bone-destroying.

1676 GREW *Musæum*, *Anat. Stomach & Guts* v. 20 A Dog, and other Ossivorous Quadrupeds. **1842** DUNGLISON *Med. Lex.*, *Ossivorous*.. A species of tumour, mentioned by Ruysch, which destroys the bone. **1857** in MAYNE *Expos. Lex.*

osslet, obs. form of OSSELET.

‖**osso bucco** (ˌosso 'bukko). Also **ossobuco**. [It., lit. 'marrowbone'.] Shin of veal stewed in wine with vegetables.

1935 M. MORPHY *Recipes of All Nations* 144 *L'osso buco* (veal stew). This is one of the most famous Italian dishes. **1961** *Guardian* 21 Apr. 8/7 *Florentine Veal Stew* is reminiscent of the Osso Bucco most of us approve of. **1961** A. WILSON *Old Men at Zoo* ii. 97 She.. had arranged with Grazia my favourite meal—ossobuco, a light red chianti, zabaglione. **1963** E. HUMPHREYS *Gift* II. i. 209, I ordered *osso bucco* and half a litre of Chianti. **1966** *Daily Tel.* 9 Nov. 13/4 There is a super snack bar.. where you can fortify yourself with Osso Bucco, Beef Stroganoff or roast lamb. **1974** *Times* 2 Nov. 11/5 Prepared beef olives and osso bucco.

ossous ('ɒsəs), *a. rare.* [ad. rare L. *ossōs-us*.] Bony, osseous.

1831 T. HOPE *Ess. Origin Man* II. 357 A single ossous tube... The gelatine of each hardens into an ossous plate.

†**'osspringer.** *Obs. rare*[-1]. [Expanded from OSPREY: cf. OSPRING.] = OSPREY or OSSIFRAGE. (In the passage quoted there is no Gr. equivalent.)

c **1611** CHAPMAN *Iliad* XVIII. 557 Like t' the hawk surnam'd the osspringer,.. Stoop'd from the steep Olympian hill.

‖**ossuarium.** *Pl.* -a. [Late Latin.] = next.

1765 H. WALPOLE *Let. to Montagu* 26 May, I will not place an ossuarium in my garden for my cat, before her bones are ready to be placed in it. **1857** BIRCH *Anc. Pottery* (1858) I. 293 A remarkable vase.. found.. in a tomb near the Piraeus, resembles in shape the glass ossuaria of the Romans.

ossuary ('ɒsjuːərɪ). [ad. late L. *ossuārium*, irreg. f. *os*, *ossi-* bone; ? after *mortuārium* mortuary. Cf. mod.F. *ossuaire* (1835 in *Dict. Acad.*).]

A receptacle for the bones of the dead; a bone-vault, charnel-house; a bone-urn.

1658 SIR T. BROWNE *Hydriot.* 25 The earth had confounded the ashes of these Ossuaries. **1678** PHILLIPS (ed. 4), *Ossuary*, a Charnel-house or place where Dead-mens bones are kept. **1832** G. DOWNES *Lett. Cont. Countries* I. 155 The church and castle occupy the same elevated site. Annexed to the former is a well-filled ossuary, or bone-house. **1865** LUBBOCK *Preh. Times* v. (1878) 139 These chambered long barrows may have served as ossuaries. **1896** *Times* 19 Mar. 3/6 Conveyed to an ossuary specially constructed in the new cemetery. **1899** BARING-GOULD *Bk. of West* I. x. 167 The dolmen.. was the family or tribal ossuary.

b. *transf.* A bone-cave, or deposit formed largely of bones, belonging to late geological times.

1861 SIR F. PALGRAVE *Norm. & Eng.* III. 329 Bringing the ossuary of the Kirkdale Cave within the period even of the last population of the wolds. **1862** R. H. PATTERSON *Ess. Hist. & Art* 116 The caves and ossuaries of Franconia and Upper Saxony.

c. *fig.* That in which relics of the dead past are preserved.

1872 O. W. HOLMES *Poet Breakf.-t.* vi. 198, I love to go to his ossuary of dead transactions, as I would visit the catacombs of Rome or Paris.

d. *attrib.* or as *adj.* Of or for the deposit of the bones of the dead.

1857 WIGLEY *St. Charles Borromeo's Instr. Eccl. Build.* xxvii. §5 This ossuary place or charnel house. **1859** JEPHSON *Brittany* iv. 40 Charnel-houses or ossuary chapels.

ost, oste, obs. ff. OAST, HOST *sb.* ([1-4]), HOST *v.*

ostage, obs. form of HOSTAGE.

‖**o'stalgia, o'stalgy.** *Path.* [f. Gr. ὀστέον bone + ἄλγος pain.] Neuralgic pain in a bone.

1853 DUNGLISON *Med. Lex.*, Ostalgia. **1857** MAYNE *Expos. Lex.*, *Ostalgia*.. ostalgy.

ostatki (ɒ'stætkɪ), var. ASTATKI.
1913 V. B. LEWES *Oil Fuel* 71 The oil remaining in the retort, called 'Ostatki' in the Russian distilleries and 'Residuum' in America, is used for fuel.

†**oste**, *v. Obs. rare.* In 5 ostey. [a. OF. *oster*, F. *ôter*.] *trans.* To put or take out, to remove.
c **1450** LONELICH *Grail* xxviii. 357 ȝit him be-hoveth to ben Osteyed [Fr. *ostes*] In the Manere as here Is seide.

osteal ('ɒstiːəl), *a.* [f. Gr. ὀστέ-ον bone + -AL[1].] Of or pertaining to bone; *spec.* of the quality of sound produced by the percussion of bone.
1877 ROBERTS *Handbk. Med.* (ed. 3) II. 11 The percussion note may become somewhat osteal in quality. **1882** OWEN in *Longm. Mag.* I. 66 Differences, osteal or dental. **1893** S. GEE *Auscult. & Percuss.* iii. (ed. 4) 63 The highest pitched tones are called Osteal because they are yielded by the hard solid tissues, cartilage and bone. **1898** *Allbutt's Syst. Med.* V. 605 Osteal and Periosteal Cachexia.

ostectomy (ɒ'stɛktəmɪ). *Surg.* Also †**osteectomy** (ɒstɪ'ɛktəmɪ). [f. OST(EO- or OSTE(O- + -ECTOMY.] (See quots.)
1894 GOULD *Dict. Med.* 946/1 *Osteectomy*, excision of a portion of bony tissue. **1900** DORLAND *Med. Dict.* 465/2 *Ostectomy, osteectomy*, the excision of a bone. **1969** *Gloss. Terms Dentistry (B.S.I.)* 36 *Ostectomy*, the division of a bone at two points with removal of the intervening portion of bone. This procedure is, in effect, similar to a resection.. but the term 'ostectomy' is reserved for operations designed to correct some structural deformity of a congenital, developmental, or acquired nature whereas 'resection' applies to the removal of diseased bone. **1977** *Proc. R. Soc. Med.* LXX. 432/1 Bell & Dann (1973) found no changes in the surgically repositioned bone and only small changes in incisor overbite and overjet in 25 patients following anterior maxillary ostectomies and lower labial segmental procedures.

osteid ('ɒstiːɪd). *Path., Anat.* [f. Gr. ὀστέ-ον bone + -ID[2].] An abnormal bony or calcareous deposit in a tissue, tumour, etc.; also, a bony growth in the pulp-cavity of a tooth.
1892 in *Syd. Soc. Lex.*

osteill, obs. form of HOSTEL.

osteine, -in ('ɒstiːɪn). *Anat.* [ad. Gr. ὀστέϊν-ος made or formed of bone.] The substance of bone, bony tissue, bone as a tissue.
1854 OWEN *Skel. & Teeth* in *Circ. Sc., Organ. Nat.* I. 161 When those salts consist chiefly of phosphate of lime, the tissues called 'osteine', or bone, and 'dentine', or tooth, are constituted, between which the chief distinction lies in the mode of arrangement of the earthy particles. **1872** L. P. MEREDITH *Teeth* (1878) 10 Beside these, are found albumen, fibrine, osteine, globuline, carbonate of lime, fluoride of calcium,.. and other proximate principles.

osteitis (ɒstiː'aɪtɪs). *Path.* Also **ostitis**. [f. Gr. ὀστέ-ον bone + -ITIS.] Inflammation in the substance of a bone.
1839–47 TODD *Cycl. Anat.* III. 64/1 Acute arthritis of the knee may be combined with acute osteitis of the bones. **1899** *Allbutt's Syst. Med.* VI. 551 The microscopic appearances are those of rarefactive osteitis.
Hence **osteitic** (-'ɪtɪk) *a.*, of or pertaining to osteitis.
In recent Dicts.

ostel, obs. form of HOSTEL.

osteler(e, -ore, obs. ff. OSTLER.

ostelment, var. HUSTLEMENT *Obs.*

ostend (ɒ'stɛnd), *v.* Now *rare.* [ad. L. *ostendĕre* to stretch out before one's face, expose to view, f. *ob-, obs-* (OB- 1) + *tendĕre* to stretch. *Ostendĕre* had ppl. stem either *ostens-* or *ostent-*; hence *ostensible, ostension, ostention, ostent.*] *trans.* To show, reveal; to manifest, exhibit.
c **1450** *Mirour Saluacioun* 3486 Dwellyng fourty dayes after oft sith he hym ostendit. *Ibid.* 4144 For vs his Cicatrices he ostendid. **1489** *Sc. Acts Jas. IV* (1814) 222/1 [To] ostend and schew quhat richt þai haid to þe taking of the samyn. **1590** J. PROCTOR in C. S. *Right Relig.* A ij b, To ostend the good will.. I alwaies bare toward your worship. **1613** HEYWOOD *Silver Age* v. Wks. 1874 III. 163 The mortals Ostend their gratitude to vs the Gods. **1897** H. G. WELLS *Plattner Story* (ed. 2) 11 He concealed rather than ostended this curious confirmatory circumstance.
[The sense 'to appear prominently, to show itself' given in Davies and copied by later dicts., founded on a quot. from Bp. Hall, has no existence; the word is *offended*.]
Hence **o'stended** *ppl. a.*, displayed, manifested.
1608 ARMIN *Nest Ninn.* (1880) 45, I am.. made bould in your ostended curtesies.

ostensibility (ɒstɛnsɪ'bɪlɪtɪ). [f. OSTENSIBLE + -ITY.] The quality of being ostensible; †conspicuousness, ostentation (*obs.*).
1775 S. J. PRATT *Liberal Opin.* xxvii. (1783) I. 181 People of low education, and little mind, were always capable of a silly ostensibility, that sooner or later brought them into disgrace. **1795** *Hist.* in *Ann. Reg.* 117 He studiously avoided ostensibility, and left to others the danger, as well as the honour, of acting an open and explicit part.

ostensible (ɒ'stɛnsɪb(ə)l), *a.* (*sb.*) [a. F. *ostensible* (1740 in *Dict. Acad.*), ad. L. type **ostensibil-is* (med.L. in *Laws Hen. I.* c. 80 §11), f. *ostens-*, ppl. stem of *ostendĕre*: see OSTEND.]
†**1.** That may be shown, exhibited, or presented to view, hence, presentable; also, made or prepared to be shown. *Obs.*
1762–71 H. WALPOLE *Vertue's Anecd. Paint.* (1786) II. 140 [Rubens] was called to Paris by Mary de' Medici, and painted the ostensible history of her life in the Luxemburgh. **1783** LD. TEMPLE *Let.* 2 Apr. in Dk. Buckhm. *Crt. Geo. III* (1853) I. 226, I wish you to write me an ostensible letter.. upon the conduct of the Portuguese. **1798** BAY *Amer. Law Rep.* (1809) I. 92 B. was the only ostensible person in the country, P. having gone off, and C.'s estate not being sufficient to make good the loss. *a* **1805** A. CARLYLE *Autobiog.* i. (1860) 31 He took great pains to make them (especially the first, for the second was hardly ostensible) appear among his best scholars. **1828** BENTHAM *Wks.* (1843) X. 591 You should.. send me two letters—one confidential, another ostensible.
†**2.** That presents itself to view or shows itself off; open to public view; conspicuous, ostentatious. *Obs.*
1782 in *Ld. Macartney's Life* &c. (1807) I. 144 Were we to adopt the ostensible and artificial language of that prudence which [etc.]. **1803** MRQ. WELLESLEY *Let. to A. Wellesley* 26 June in Owen *Desp.* (1877) 302 The most direct and even ostensible interposition of the British authority. **1809** MALKIN *Gil Blas* x. ii. ¶12 He has been in an ostensible situation.. and his father ought to be buried with all the forms of state. **1828** LD. GRENVILLE *Sink. Fund* 29 Which.. can exhibit to us only the outward and ostensible workings of this complicated mechanism.
3. Declared, avowed, professed; exhibited or put forth as actual and genuine: often implicitly or explicitly opposed to 'actual', 'real', and so = merely professed, pretended.
1771 *Junius Lett.* liv. 289 The best of princes is not displeased with the abuse which he sees thrown upon his ostensible Ministers. **1786** BURKE *W. Hastings* Wks. 1842 II. 119 A party of British and other troops, with the nabob in the ostensible, and the British resident in the real, command. **1837** HT. MARTINEAU *Soc. Amer.* III. 269 There will be less that is ostensible and more that is genuine, as they grow older. **1848** C. BRONTE *J. Eyre* x. (1873) 85 My ostensible errand on this occasion was to get measured for a pair of shoes. **1874** GREEN *Short Hist.* vii. §4. 381 Her ostensible demand was for English aid in her restoration to the throne.
B. as *sb.* in *pl.* Ostensible matters.
1861 J. PYCROFT *Agony Point* xxiii. (1862) 231 When all these positive essentials and ostensibles were so respectably witnessed.

ostensibly (ɒ'stɛnsɪblɪ), *adv.* [f. prec. + -LY[2].] In an ostensible manner; avowedly, declaredly, professedly: distinguished from, and often implicitly or explicitly opposed to 'actually', 'really', and so = under mere profession or pretence.
1765 H. WALPOLE *Vertue's Anecd. Paint.* II. ii. 60 He was even employed in the treaty of marriage, though ostensibly acting only in the character of a painter. **1837** SYD. SMITH *Wks.* (1867) II. 249 He put his trust really where he put his trust ostensibly. **1871** H. AINSWORTH *Tower Hill* II. i, The neglected Queen was sent to Richmond, ostensibly for change of air, but really that she might be out of the way. **1874** L. STEPHEN *Hours in Library* (1892) I. iv. 154 The characters which ostensibly play the chief part.
†**b.** Conspicuously, ostentatiously. *Obs.*
1855 HT. MARTINEAU *Autobiog.* I. 272 Madame de Stael was exhibited as ostensibly at the British Gallery as any of the pictures on the walls.

ostension (ɒ'stɛnʃən). Also 5 -cion, 6 -tion. [a. F. *ostension* (13th c.), ad. L. *ostens-, ostentiōn-em*, n. of action from *ostend-ĕre*: see OSTEND.]
1. †**a.** The action of showing; exhibition, display; manifestation. *Obs.*
1474 CAXTON *Chesse* IV. ii. 147 For the solace of hym and ostencion of loue. **1489** *Sc. Acts Jas. IV* (1814) 222/1 The saidis personis.. has bene ofttymes Callit for þe ostensioune and schewing of þare Richtis. **1542** *Sc. Acts Mary* (1814) 411/2 All vþeris lordis.. hes maid faith and sworne.. be þe ostentioune of þeir rycht handis. *a* **1625** BOYS *Wks.* (1630) 678–9 Ostension,.. 1. in respect of the solemn inauguration of their Apostleship, on the Feast of Pentecost.. 2. Ostention in regard of the execution of their office. **1650** *W. Sclater's Exp. Rom. iv* Ep. Ded., Not to make use of for ostension and ostentation. **1733** W. CRAWFORD *Infidelity* (1836) 116 Divine punishments.. are for the ostention of his justice. **1789** T. TAYLOR *Proclus* II. 24 The former [Q.E.F.] announcing the production of something, but this [Q.E.D.] the ostension and invention of a thing required.
b. *Logic.* = *ostensive definition* (see next).
1950 W. V. QUINE in *Jrnl. Philos.* XLVII. 629 The ostensions which introduce a general term differ from those which introduce a singular term. **1960** —— *Word & Object* 115 Our explorer learns each of the names by ostension on the part of the natives. **1963** J. LYONS *Structural Semantics* iv. 54, I accept that ostension plays a necessary part in the normal process of learning a language. **1968** —— *Introd. Theoret. Linguistics* ix. 409 The difficulty of explaining the meaning of any word without using others to limit and make more explicit the 'scope' of 'ostension'.
2. *Eccl.* The action of holding forth the Eucharistic elements to the sight of the people.
1607 *Schol. Disc. agst. Antichr.* I. i. 31 Some Churches retaine the eleuation still, not for adoration like the Papists, but for ostension to the people. **1692** BP. PATRICK *Answ. Touchstone* 34 At the ostension of the Bread of the Eucharist, and the Cup of Blessing. **1867** C. WALKER *Ritual Reason Why* 127 The rite was called the 'elevation' or lifting up, viewed under the first aspect; the 'ostension,' or showing, viewed under the second.

Hence †**o'stensional**, *a. Obs.* [L. *ostentiōnālis*.]
1656 BLOUNT *Glossogr.*, *Ostensional*, a Souldier attending the Prince in publique Shews.

ostensive (ɒ'stɛnsɪv), *a.* [ad. late L. *ostensīv-us* ('syllogismus ostensivus' Boeth. *Aristot. Anal.*), f. *ostens-* (see OSTENSIBLE): see -IVE; in F. *ostensif, -ive* (14th c. in Hatz.-Darm.).]
1. a. Manifestly or directly demonstrative; *spec.* in *Logic*, Setting forth a general principle manifestly including the proposition to be proved.
ostensive reduction, reduction by the direct processes of conversion, permutation, and transposition, as opposed to indirect reduction, e.g. *per impossibile*.
1605 BACON *Adv. Learn.* II. xiv. §3 The Proposition.. reduced to the Principle.. they terme a Probation Ostensiue. **1614** JACKSON *Creed* III. ix. §1 It hath beene manifested.. by ostensiue proofe from Scriptures. **1697** tr. *Burgersdicius his Logic* II. ix. 42 Reduction is either ostensive or else by way of impossible. **1711** *Brit. Apollo* IV. No. 8. 1/2 We cannot give an Ostensive Demonstration of this. **1836** SIR W. HAMILTON *Discuss.* (1852) 305 The two species of Mathematics—the Geometric or Ostensive, and the Algebraic or Symbolical. **1870** JEVONS *Elem. Logic* xvii. 150 The simpler process of direct or as it is often called ostensive reduction.
b. Professedly demonstrative; specious.
1844 *Blackw. Mag.* LV. 238 No proof.. can be so showy and ostensive to a stranger, as that which is supplied by this vindictive pamphlet.
2. a. 'Showing, betokening' (J.); declarative.
1755 in JOHNSON. **1877** E. CAIRD *Philos. Kant* II. xix. 661 The ideas of reason are heuristic, not ostensive, they enable us to ask a question, not to give the answer.
b. *ostensive definition* (Philos.), the explanation of a word by pointing at or otherwise indicating, or by presenting, one or more objects to which it applies.
1921 W. E. JOHNSON *Logic* I. vi. 94 We may now introduce the technical term 'ostensive' which will suggest as its opposite the familiar term 'intensive'... Imposing a name in the act of indicating, presenting or introducing the object to which the name is to apply,.. this it is that constitutes ostensive definition. **1940** A. J. AYER *Found. Empirical Knowl.* ii. 88 This is effected by the method of ostensive definition. **1950** R. ROBINSON *Definition* ii. 15 'Ostensive definition' is the name of a method, the method that makes use of pointing or physical introduction. **1953** I. M. COPI *Introd. Logic* iv. 108 An ostensive definition refers to the examples by means of pointing or some other gesture. **1960** K. AMIS *New Maps of Hell* (1961) i. 21 One might under adverse conditions learn a human language, by ostensive definition and the like. **1968** J. LYONS *Introd. Theoret. Linguistics* ix. 409 Ostensive definition, of itself, is never sufficient.
3. = OSTENSIBLE *a.* 3.
1782 MISS BURNEY *Cecilia* IX. xi, I have always observed, that where one scheme answers two purposes, the ostensive is never the purpose most at heart. **1815** *Zeluca* II. 251 She was aware of a motive to the visit, in addition to the ostensive one. **1830** W. PHILLIPS *Mt. Sinai* III. 413 Else, wherefore thus, No cause ostensive.. Desert the people?
Hence **o'stensively** *adv.* [cf. late L. 'per impossibile, et ostensive', Boeth.], in an ostensive manner; (*a*) demonstratively, directly; (*b*) avowedly, professedly, ostensibly; (*c*) by pointing, gesture, or presentation; **o'stensiveness**, the state or quality of being ostensive.
a **1774** LLOYD *Fam. Ep. to Friend* Poems (1790) 275 Affecting cynical grimace.. In rags and tatters, strole the street; Ostensively exceeding wise. **1782** *Hist. Eur.* in *Ann. Reg.* 240*/2 The enemy rested all their hopes now, at least ostensively, on the defeat of Lord Howe's fleet. **1847** DE QUINCEY *Protestantism* Wks. 1858 VIII. 108 A postulate of the human reason,.. not proved ostensively, but indirectly proved as being.. presupposed in other necessities. **1921** W. E. JOHNSON *Logic* I. vi. 94 A simple adjective-name—such as red—cannot be defined analytically but only ostensively. **1933** *Mind* LXII. 190 (*heading*) Tests for ostensiveness. **1948** B. RUSSELL *Human Knowl.* 83 Most children learn the word 'dog' ostensively. **1953** W. V. QUINE *From Logical Point of View* iv. 78 Once a fund of ostensively acquired terms is at hand there is no difficulty in explaining additional terms discursively. **1971** T. F. MITCHELL in *Archivum Linguisticum* II. 40 Ostensive meaning. 'Specification' as a category of linguistic experience may encompass such varied grammatical classes as articles, ordinal numerals, and deictics... It is perhaps particularly to the area of deixis that 'ostensiveness' belongs.

ostensoir, -orio, -orium: see OSTENSORY.

†**ostensor**. *Obs. rare.* = next.
1804 *Captive of Valence* II. 52 He [Joseph II] has forbidden the use of the ostensor to give the benedictions of the holy sacrament, except in particular churches.

ostensory (ɒ'stɛnsərɪ). Also in Fr., It., L. forms in -oir, -orio, -orium. [ad. med.L. *ostensōri-um*, f. *ostens-*, ppl. stem of *ostendĕre*: see OSTEND and -ORY[1].] A receptacle in which to display the Host to the congregation; a monstrance.
1722 J. RICHARDSON *Statues, etc. Italy* 205 The Eucharistical Presence.. is express'd by the Host in the Golden *Ostensorio* on the Altar. **1760–72** tr. *Juan & Ulloa's Voy.* (ed. 3) II. 39 The sacred vessels, the chalices, ostensoriums.. in the richness of which there is a sort of emulation between the several churches. **1833** *Catholic Mag.* July 506 His splendid ostensoir, or remonstrance, supported by angels, which cost 200 florins. **1834** BECKFORD *Italy* II. 49 The light of innumerable tapers blazing on the diamonds of the ostensory. **1839** *New Monthly Mag.* LV. 551 The priest turned round with the glittering ostensory in

his hand. **1861** C. P. Hodgson *Resid. Nagasaki* vi. 143 The lighted tapers on the altar, the chaplet, the aureole, the ostensoir,..the incense, the prayer for the dead, are facts to be noted [in Japanese worship]. **1888** *Harper's Mag.* Feb. 371/2 The priest..walked under the canopy, and held the *ostensorium* up in an imposing manner as high as his head.

ostent (ɒˈstɛnt), *sb.*[1] Now *rare.* [ad. L. *ostent-um* (pl. *-a*) something shown, a prodigy, sb. use of neuter pa. pple. of *ostend-ĕre*: see OSTEND. Rarely in L. form.] A sign, portent, wonder, prodigy.

1563–87 Foxe *A. & M.* (1684) II. 94 Which miraculous ostent, passing the ordinary course of natural causes..was sent of God. **1598** Chapman *Marlowe's Hero & Leander* IV. Argt., Ostents that threaten her estate. *c* **1611** —— *Iliad* II. 280 Wise Jove is he hath shown This strange ostent to us. **1663** J. Spencer *Prodigies* (1665) 185 When he was a Boy in the Low-Countries, some *Ostenta* of like condition were shewn him about the beginning of the Belgick Wars. **1741** T. Francklin tr. *Cicero's Nat. Gods* II. 83 From whence they are called Ostents, Signs, Portents, Prodigies. **1812** W. Tennant *Anster F.* IV. lxi, A globe of fire (miraculous ostent). **1898** T. Hardy *Wessex Poems* 9 The Night waxed wan, As though with an awed sense of such ostent.

ostent (ɒˈstɛnt), *sb.*[2] Now *rare.* [ad. L. *ostentu-s* a showing, displaying, show, display, parade, f. ppl. stem of *ostend-ĕre*: see OSTEND.]

1. The act of showing; manifestation, indication; show, display, appearance.

1596 Shaks. *Merch. V.* II. ii. 205 Vse all the obseruance of ciuillitie Like one well studied in a sad ostent To please his Grandam. *Ibid.* viii. 44 Imploy your chiefest thoughts To courtship, and such faire ostents of loue As shall conueniently become you there. **1646** G. Daniel *Poems* Wks. 1878 I. 59 Dost aright discerne Twixt vertue and ostent. **1657** W. Morice *Coena quasi Κοινή* Diat. v. 245 Those Reasons..whereof they make ostent with so many plausible amplifications. **1784** Cowper *Task* VI. 487 Atheist in ostent, Vicious in act, in temper savage-fierce. **1818** Jas. Mill *Brit. India* II. v. v. 547 In name and ostent, the sovereignty of the Nabob..was not to be infringed. **1861** Patmore in *Macm. Mag.* V. 26 Nature's infinite ostent Of lovely flowers in wood and mead.

2. Vainglorious display, ostentation.

1598 Barckley *Felic. Man* (1631) 183 All such whom glory swels with proud ostent. **1609** Heywood *Brit. Troy* VIII. v, Thou proud Achilles with thy great ostent. **1639** G. Daniel *Ecclus.* v. 1 Trust not in Riches, with a vaine Ostent Of Fullnes. **1895** W. Watson *Father of Forest* 13 Goodly the ostents are to thee And pomps of time.

b. with *pl.* An embodiment of ostentation.

1638 Brideoake in *Jonsonus Virbius*, [Such] may have The vain ostents of pride upon their grave. **1652** Benlowes *Theoph.* XII. xcii, Ambitious obelisks, ostents of Pride.

† **ostent**, *v.* *Obs.* [ad. F. *ostente-r* (16th c. in Godef.), ad. L. *ostentā-re* to show off, freq. of *ostendĕre*: see OSTEND.] = OSTENTATE *v.*

1531 Elyot *Gov.* II. xiv, Semblably ther be some, that by dissimulation can ostent or shewe a high grauitie. **1583** Stubbes *Anat. Abus.* I. (1879) 30 The pride of the mouthe..consisteth..in ostenting and braggyng of some singular vertue..in himselfe or some other of his kinred. **1615** T. Adams *Eng. Sickness* Wks. 1861 I. 415 Malice not only discovers, but ostenteth her devilish effects. **1633** —— *Exp. 2 Peter* i. 7 There is nothing more easy than to ostent the love of God.

† **o'stentate**, *ppl. a.* *Obs. rare*$^{-1}$. [ad. L. *ostentāt-us*, pa. pple. of *ostentāre*: see next.] Boasted, vaingloriously displayed.

1615 T. Adams *Blacke Devill* 53 Like the speckled innocency of the Papists in their ostentate charity.

ostentate (ˈɒstənteɪt), *v.* Now *rare* (? only *U.S.*). [f. L. *ostentāt-*, ppl. stem of *ostentāre*, freq. of *ostend-ĕre*: see OSTEND.]

1. *trans.* To make a show of, show off, display ostentatiously or boastfully.

c **1540** *Surr. Northampton Priory* in Prance *Addit. Narr. Pop. Plot* 36 Christs Holy Evangely, which..wee did ostentate and openly devant to keepe most exactly. **1622** *Fotherby's Atheom.* Pref. 20. **1676** *Doctrine of Devils* 181 He was not for extravagant Rambles, as most Criticks are; Vaingloriously to ostentate their great Reading, and Subtile Conjectures, upon small, or no occasions. **1702** C. Mather *Magn. Chr.* VII. v. (1852) 546 This proud Thraso would in his preaching ostentate skill in Latin, and in Greek. **1886** *American* XII. 264 The viburnums ostentate their cymes of fruit. **1889** *Ibid.* 21 Dec. 192/1 San Marco..ostentates upon the upper portion of its façade all the florid detail of the Venetian manner.

† **b.** *intr.* for *refl.* To boast. *Obs.*

1670 G. H. *Hist. Cardinals* III. III. 323 Let not him that is Head of a Faction, ostentate too much.

† **2.** To show, display. *Obs.*

1630 Lord *Banians & Persees* 37 Not ostentating himselfe to publike view, but living recluse.

ostentation (ɒstənˈteɪʃən). [a. F. *ostentation*, OF. *-acion* (1366 in Hatz.-Darm.), ad. L. *ostentātiōn-em*, n. of action from *ostentāre*: see prec.]

† **1.** The presaging of future events; a presage; a portent, prodigy. *Obs. rare.*

1436 *Pol. Poems* (Rolls) II. 190 Many a day Men have be ferde of here rebellioun By grete tokenes and ostentacioun. **1607** Topsell *Four-f. Beasts* (1658) 263 There have been predictions or ostentations of things to come, taken from a Wolf, a Fox, a Serpent, and a Horse, which were called *Auspicia Pedestria*.

2. The action of showing or displaying; a show, exhibition, display (*of* something). In quot. 1865 = DEMONSTRATION 6 (military). *Obs.* or *arch.*

1534 More *Comf. agst. Trib.* II. Wks. 1191/1 Al theyr wonderful workes draw to no fruteful end, but to a fruitelesse ostentacion and shew. **1587** Fleming *Contn. Holinshed* III. 1557/2 With such other false ostentations of immanitie. **1599** Shaks. *Much Ado* IV. i. 207 Publish it, that she is dead indeed: Maintaine a mourning ostentation. **1606** —— *Ant. & Cl.* III. vi. 52 But you are come A Market-maid to Rome, and haue preuented The ostentation of our loue; which left vnshewne, Is often left vnlou'd. **1608** Topsell *Serpents* (1658) 594 When..they make ostentation hereof in the Market, or publique Stage, they suffer them to bite their own flesh. *a* **1716** South *Serm.* (1744) X. vii. 221 For ostentation of strength and valour, at their publick sights and shows. **1865** Carlyle *Fredk. Gt.* XIX. iv. (1872) VIII. 153 Finck to ride-out reconnoitering..and to make motions and ostentations.

† **b.** Mere show, appearance, apparition; false show, pretence. *Obs.*

1607 Topsell *Four-f. Beasts* (1658) 354 In truth there was no such thing, and all was but a fantastical ostentation. **1649** Milton *Eikon.* ii. 21 He..who thinks by such weak policies and ostentations to gaine beliefe and absolution.

† **c.** A spectacular show or exhibition. *Obs.*

1588 Shaks. *L.L.L.* v. i. 118 The King would haue mee present the Princesse..with some delightfull ostentation, or show, or pageant, or anticke, or fire-worke.

3. Display intended to attract notice or admiration; pretentious parade, vainglorious 'showing off'.

c **1450** tr. *De Imitatione* III. lix. 139 Grace also techiþ to..eschue veyne plesaunce & ostentacion. **1555** Eden *Decades* To Rdr. (Arb.) 49 The fonde and barbarous ostentation of superfluous riches. **1625** K. Long tr. *Barclay's Argenis* II. xvii. 117 Under colour of seeking to learne wisdome, but indeed to make ostentation of his owne. **1661** *Papers on Alter. Prayer-bk.* 22 The ostentation of his good works, is not the work of a good Christian. **1764** Goldsm. *Trav.* 273 Hence ostentation here, with tawdry art, Pants for the vulgar praise which fools impart. **1874** Green *Short Hist.* viii. §3. 483 The frivolous ostentation of Buckingham..gave point to the fierce attack.

ostentatious (ɒstənˈteɪʃəs), *a.* [f. OSTENTATION: see -IOUS. Has displaced the earlier *ostentative*, *ostentatory*, *ostentive*, *ostentous*.]

1. Characterized or marked by ostentation:

a. Of actions, personal qualities, etc.: Performed, exercised, or set forth in a way calculated to attract attention or admiration; boastful.

[**1656** Blount *Glossogr.*, *Ostentatitious* [? *mispr.*], set out for shew or vain-glory.] **1701** *Biog.* in *Stanley's Hist. Philos.* 9 This Philosophy has..charmed a World of People by its Proud and Ostentatious Principles. **1716** Addison *Freeholder* No. 39 ¶5 His Religion was sincere, not ostentatious. **1782** Miss Burney *Cecilia* II. ii, A display of importance so ostentatious made Cecilia already half repent her visit. **1825** Macaulay *Ess., Milton* (1887) 16 To imitate the ostentatious generosity of those ancient knights. **1849** —— *Hist. Eng.* vii. II. 187 Lewis, with that ostentatious contempt of public law which was characteristic of him, occupied Orange..and confiscated the revenues. **1874** Helps *Soc. Press.* xiv. 190 Sir John had taken up his place in a corner of the room, in an attitude of ostentatious humility.

b. Of a person.

In quot. 1673 app. Making a false show, pretentious.

1658 [implied in OSTENTATIOUSNESS]. **1673** Dryden *Marr. à la Mode* IV. v, As ostentatious priests, when souls they woo, Promise their heaven to all, but grant to few. **1700** Dryden *Fables* Ded. (1721) 4 Lest I offend your modesty, which is so far from being ostentatious of the good you do that it blushes even to have it known. **1791** Boswell *Life Johnson* Advt., Were I to detail the books which I have consulted..I should probably be thought ridiculously ostentatious. **1818–60** Whately *Comm.-pl. Bk.* (1864) 150 A woman who is really beautiful and is always making a show of herself..would be justly censured as ostentatious. **1865** Livingstone *Zambesi* xxv. 521 They are not, like the Mohammedans, ostentatious in their prayers. **1884** A. Paul *Hist. Reform.* iv. 71 Active and ostentatious partisans of the French revolutionary movement.

2. Fitted by appearance, position, or the like to attract attention; conspicuous, showy. *Obs.* (or blending with 1 a).

1713 Steele *Guard.* No. 6 ¶5 Coach or troop horses, of which that county produces the most strong and ostentatious. **1790** Pennant *London* (1813) 618 That honorable memorial..should..be placed in the most ostentatious situation. **1883** Froude *Short Stud.* IV. v. 356 This pair..are the chief figures in the most ostentatious monument in the..chapel.

osten'tatiously, *adv.* [f. prec. + -LY[2].] In an ostentatious manner; in a way calculated to attract notice; with boastful parade or display.

1703 J. Savage *Lett. Antients* xiv. 74 You do nothing ostentatiously. **1781** Gibbon *Decl. & F.* (1869) II. xxxvi. 332 The wealth of two empires was ostentatiously displayed. **1850** Lyell *2nd Visit U.S.* II. 83 The prejudices of a white aristocracy, ostentatiously boastful of its love of equality. **1897** Mary Kingsley *W. Africa* 57 When you go outside Clarence you come across the Bubi ostentatiously unclothed —I say ostentatiously for the benefit of ethnologists.

osten'tatiousness. [f. as prec. + -NESS.] The quality or condition of being ostentatious.

1658 Earl Monm. tr. *Paruta's Wars Cyprus* 124 To lose their lives without any advantage, would be rather a sign of foolish ostentatiousnesse, than of true worth. **1782** *Char.* in *Ann. Reg.* 52/1 They learn..to despise ostentatiousness, as being sinful. **1882** L. Stephen *Swift* v. 103 It would be a great mistake to infer that this ostentatiousness of authority concealed real servility.

† **o'stentative**, *a.* *Obs.* [f. L. *ostentāt-* (see OSTENTATE *v.*) + -IVE.] **a.** = OSTENTATIOUS 1 a; **b.** = OSTENSIBLE.

1600 W. Watson *Decacordon* (1602) 73 An ostentatiue sleeght and vaineglorious deuice. **1601** —— *Import. Consid.* (1831) 18 An outward ostentative shew of advancing the Secular Priests. **1638** *Div. & Pol. Observ.* To Rdr. 3 Out of such a vaine glory as ostentative persons affect. **1653** H. More *Antid. Ath.* I. ii. §4. 12 The arguments..I do not bestow that ostentative term of demonstration upon them. **1685** *Gracian's Courtier's Orac.* 251 There are ostentative Nations, and the Spanish with the first. **1689** tr. *Buchanan's De Jure Regni apud Scotos* 34 By the odiousness of one ill deed they loose all the thanks of their Ostentative bounty.

Hence † **o'stentatively** *adv.* = OSTENTATIOUSLY.

1668 H. More *Div. Dial.* III. xxxii. (1713) 266 We do not wantonly and ostentatively produce those Keys, but at a dead lift, when no other method will satisfie him.

† **osten'tator.** *Obs.* [a. L. *ostentātor*, agent-n. from *ostentāre* (OSTENTATE); cf. F. *ostentateur*, 1535.] An ostentatious person; a bragger, boaster.

1611 Cotgr., *Ostentateur*, an ostentator, boaster, bragger, vaunter. **1639** W. Sclater *Worthy Commun.* 38 And yet who such ἀλάζονες, and Thrasonicall ostentatours of antiquity as these? **1642** T. Morton *Presentm. Schismatic* 3 When this ostentator shall look behind him and see..what number of Disciples he draweth behind him.

† **o'stentatory**, *a.* *Obs.* *rare*$^{-1}$. [ad. L. *ostentātōri-us*, f. *ostentātor*: see -ORY. In OF. *ostentatoire* (16th c. in Godef.).] = OSTENTATIOUS.

1657 G. Starkey *Helmont's Vind.* To Rdr., 'Tis no unlikely but some captious Antagonist may censure my Aphorisms as ostentatory.

† **osten'tatrix.** *Obs.* *rare*$^{-0}$. [a. L. *ostentātrix*, fem. of *ostentātor*: see -TRIX. Cf. F. *ostentatrice* (Montaigne, 1580).] An ostentatious woman.

1611 Cotgr., *Ostentatrice*, an ostentatrix, braggardesse, boasting woman.

† **o'stentful**, *a.* *Obs.* [f. OSTENT *sb.*[1] + -FUL.] Full of omen; portentous, ominous.

1608 Chapman *Byron's Trag.* Plays 1873 II. 281 All then together are indeed ostentfull. **1615** —— *Odyss.* xv. 214 If this ostentful thing (This eagle, and this goose) touch us, or you.

† **o'stential**, *a.* *Obs.* *rare*$^{-1}$. [irreg. f. OSTENT *sb.*[2], or L. *ostent-* ppl. stem + -IAL. ? for *ostentual*.] ? Externally shown or apparent.

1609 Tourneur *Fun. Poeme Sir F. Vere* 562 The breath of his divulg'd pretence, Suited with fit ostentiall instruments.

† **osten'tiferous**, *a.* *Obs.* *rare*$^{-0}$. [f. L. *ostentifer* portentous, f. *ostent-um* OSTENT *sb.*[1]: see -FEROUS.]

1656 Blount *Glossogr.*, *Ostentiferous*, that which brings monsters or strange sights.

† **o'stentive**, *a.* *Obs.* [f. L. *ostent-*, ppl. stem: see OSTEND and -IVE.] = OSTENTATIOUS.

1599 Nashe *Lenten Stuffe* 22 The red herring..empals our sage senatours..in princely scarlet as pompous ostentyue as the Vintiquater or Lady Troynouant. **1614** Stirling *Doomsday* iii, That pompous bird which still in triumph bears Rolled in a circle his ostentive taile. **1670** J. Law in *Lauderdale Papers* (Camden) III. App. 234 The Bishop..desired Mr Gilbert Burnett to reply, which he did in an ostentive manner. **1730** *Ld. Mar's Legacy to Son* (1897) 186 The..affected and ostentive way of the Church of Rome.

† **o'stentous**, *a.* *Obs.* [f. OSTENT *sb.*[2] + -OUS: cf. *portentous*. The etymol. form would be **ostentuous*, in late L. *ostentuōsus* (Onomast. Lat. Gr.), f. *ostentu-s*.] = OSTENTATIOUS.

1624 T. Scott *Belg. Sould.* 8 A fourth spareth not the ostentous braverie of Princes, and excesse of apparrell. *c* **1645** Howell *Lett.* I. v. xxix. (1726) 224 Upon the highest Mountain 'mongst the Alps, he [Louis XIII] left this ostentous Inscription upon a great Marble Pillar. **1687** *New Atlantis* I. 377 Ostentous Pomp the simple mind doth please.

Hence † **o'stentously** *adv.*, ostentatiously.

1665 J. Webb *Stone-Heng* (1725) 174 Then enters Olaus Wormius boldly with great Stones; and to him Doctor Charleton ostentously with mighty Stones.

osteo- (ˈɒstɪəʊ), before a vowel also **oste-**, combining form of Gr. ὀστέο-ν bone, entering into many derivatives, chiefly anatomical: see the more important words in their alphabetical places.

osteo-'aneurysm, pulsating tumour of a bone. **osteoar'thritic** *a.*, of, pertaining to, or affected by osteoarthritis. ‖ **osteoar'thritis** [Gr. ἀρθρῖτις gout], degeneration of the joints of the body, which occurs to a greater or lesser extent from the third decade of life, is manifested as pain, discomfort, and stiffness in the joints, and results from progressive deterioration of articular cartilage until finally bone is rubbing directly against bone. ˌ**osteoar'thropathy** [*arthropathy* s.v. ARTHRO-], any disease which affects both the bones and the joints; *spec.* a syndrome (pulmonary osteoarthropathy) marked by broadening and thickening of the fingers, painful swollen joints, and enlarged distal ends of long bones, and seen chiefly as a complication of various chest diseases; hence **ˌosteoarthroˈpathic** *a.* **osteoarˈthrosis** [-OSIS] = *osteoarthritis*; hence **osteoarˈthrotic** *a.* **ˈosteoblast** [Gr. βλαστός bud, germ], Gegenbaur's term for granular corpuscles found in all developing bone as the active agents of osseous growth; hence **osteoˈblastic** *a.*, of, pertaining to, or having the character of osteoblasts. **osteocaˈchexy** [Gr. καχεξία ill condition], defective constitution or structure of the bones (Mayne *Expos. Lex.* 1857); so **osteocaˈchectic** *a.* **osteocartiˈlaginous** *a.*, of or consisting of bone and cartilage. ‖**osteochonˈdritis** [Gr. χόνδρος cartilage], inflammation of cartilage extending to the bone (*Syd. Soc. Lex.*). ‖**osteochonˈdroma** [Gr. χόνδρος cartilage], osteoid tissue containing cartilage which may calcify and ossify. **osteoˈchondrophyte** [Gr. φυτόν growth], an osseous cartilaginous tumour. ‖**osteˈoclasis** [Gr. κλάσις fracture], fracture of a bone to correct a deformity; dissolution or destruction of bone tissue. **ˈosteoclast** [Ger. *osteoklast*, f. Gr. κλαστός broken], (*a*) Kölliker's term for the many-nucleated colossal cells, found in growing bone, and concerned with the absorption of osseous tissue in the formation of the medullary spaces in cartilage; (*b*) a surgical instrument for effecting osteoclasis. **osteoˈclastic** *a.*, of or belonging to osteoclasis. ‖**osteoˈcomma** [Gr. κόμμα a piece], a bone-segment, as a vertebra. **ˈosteocope**, also ‖**osteˈocopus** [Gr. ὀστεοκόπος, f. κόπος striking, toil, fatigue], violent wearing pain in the bones, esp. of syphilitic origin; syphilitic rheumatism; hence **osteoˈcopic** *a.*, relating to osteocope. **ˈosteocyte** [-CYTE], an osteoblast that has ceased its bone-forming activity and is enclosed within a lacuna in the bone matrix. **osteoˈdentine** [DENTINE], Owen's term for ossified connective tissue in the pulp-cavity of a tooth, esp. in the teeth of some cetaceans and fishes. **osteoˈdermal**, **osteoˈdermatous**, **osteoˈdermous** *adjs.* [Gr. δέρμα skin], having a partly ossified skin; having osseous plates or spicules deposited in the skin, as in the sturgeon. **ˌosteoˌdontokeˈratic** *a.* *Anthrop.* [ODONTO- + KERAT(O- + -IC], (of a culture) based on the use of bone, tooth, and horn implements. ‖**osteoˈdynia**, also **-ˈodyny** [Gr. ὀδύνη pain], chronic persistent pain in bones (Mayne). **osteoˈgangrene**, gangrene in a bone. **ˈosteogen** [Gr. ὀστεογενής produced by bone, τὸ ὀστεογενές the marrow], a soft transparent substance in growing bone which undergoes ossification by the deposit of lime salts. **osteoˈlathyrism** *Med.* [LATHYRISM], an experimental skeletal disease of animals produced by the ingestion of seeds of some plants of the genus *Lathyrus* or certain chemicals. **ˈosteolite** [Gr. λίθος stone], compact earthy calcium phosphate, similar to bone-phosphate, resembling lithographic stone. **ˈosteolith** = OSTEOCOLLA. †**osteoˈlithical** *a.*, consisting of petrified or fossil bones. **osteˈolysis** [-LYSIS], the pathological destruction or disappearance of bone tissue; so **osteoˈlytic** *a.*, causing or characterized by osteolysis. ‖**osteomaˈlacia**, **-maˈlakia** [Gr. μαλακία softness], softening of bones due to the gradual disappearance of earthy salts; also called *malacosteon*; hence **osteomaˈlacial**, **osteomaˈlacic** *adjs.*, pertaining to or affected with osteomalacia; softened or half-destroyed as regards bony structure. **osteomaˈlactic** *a.* [Gr. μαλακτικός emollient], having the effect of softening bone (Mayne). **ˈosteomere** [Gr. μέρος part] = *osteocomma*. ‖**osteomyeˈlitis** [Gr. μυελός marrow], inflammation of the marrow of a bone. **osteo-oˈdontome**: see quot. and ODONTOME. ‖**osteoperioˈstitis**, inflammation of the periosteum extending to the bone. **ˈosteophage** [Gr. φαγεῖν to eat] = *osteoclast* (*a*). ‖**osteˈophagus** [after *sarcophagus*], a box or chest of bones: see quot. ‖**osteophleˈbitis** [Gr. φλέψ, φλεβ- vein], inflammation of the veins of a bone (*Syd. Soc. Lex.*). **ˈosteoplast**, a modified *osteoblast* (*Syd. Soc. Lex.*). **osteopteˈrygious** *a.* [Gr. πτερύγιον fin], having bony fins; of or belonging to the *Osteopterygii*, an order of fishes in Macleay's classification. ‖**osteoscleˈrosis** [Gr. σκλήρωσις induration], hardening of a bone. **osteoˈstomatous**, **osteˈostomous** *adjs.* [Gr. στόμα mouth], having a bony mouth or osseous jaws. **osteosyndesmoˈlogical** *a.* [SYNDESMOLOGY], pertaining to the anatomy of bones and ligaments. ‖**Osteoˈzoa**, *pl.* of **Osteoˈzoon** [Gr. ζῷον animal], Blainville's term for *Vertebrata*; hence **Osteoˈzoan** *a.*, vertebrate (Harris *Dict. Med. Term.* 1867). ‖**Osteozoˈaria** [Gr. ζῳάριον, dimin. of ζῷον animal], Milne-Edwards's term for *Vertebrata*.

1902 *Amer. Jrnl. Med. Sci.* CXXIV. 808 The frequency with which *osteo-arthitic changes are found in Paget's disease has not received the attention which they invite. **1962** *Lancet* 8 Dec. 1233/1 Mr. Philip Newman and Mr. Harry Piggott described a ten-year follow-up of osteo-arthritic knees. **1878** HOLDEN *Hum. Osteol.* (ed. 5) 18 Occasionally seen as the result of chronic *osteo-arthritis. **1879** *St. George's Hosp. Rep.* IX. 260 Case of osteo-arthritis of the hip. **1972** HOLLANDER & MCCARTY *Arthritis* (ed. 8) lv. 1009 Osteoarthritis is a non-inflammatory disorder of movable joints characterized by deterioration and abrasion of articular cartilage, and also by formation of new bone at the joint surfaces. **1903** *Med. Rec.* (N.Y.) 21 Feb. 312/1 Walter Berent reports a case which shows the intimate relations which exist between nerve lesions and *osteoarthropathic changes. **1972** HOLLANDER & MCCARTY *Arthritis* (ed. 8) lxxiv. 1369/1 The data failed to demonstrate any factor in the blood of the donor (osteoarthropathic) dog that would produce peripheral vascular effects. **1893** *Brit. Med. Jrnl.* 3 June 1155/2 (*heading*) Three cases of 'hypertrophic pulmonary *osteo-arthropathy', with remarks. **1901** *Encycl. Medica* IX. 4 In leprosy osteo-arthropathies have been described by Heiberg which have many of the characteristics of the osteo-arthropathies of tabes. **1958** *Jrnl. Bone & Joint Surg.* XL. B. 538 (*heading*) Familial osteoarthropathy of the fingers. **1974** J. D. MAYNARD in R. M. Kirk et al. *Surgery* x. 216 Polyneuritis and pulmonary osteoarthropathy..are sinister clinical findings. **1932** W. BOYD *Text-bk. Path.* xxxii. 898 *Osteoarthrosis.—This is commonly called osteoarthritis, but as the condition is essentially degenerative with no suggestion of inflammation it would appear preferable to speak of osteoarthrosis. **1970** *New Scientist* 4 June 487/1 One, rheumatoid arthritis, is an inflammatory condition of unknown cause, starting in the synovial lining... The second, osteoarthrosis, is essentially a disorder of cartilage. **1974** PASSMORE & ROBSON *Compan. Med. Stud.* III. I. xxv. 37/1 Osteo-arthrosis (osteoarthritis) is a common disease of diathrodial joints in both men and animals. **1964** W. S. C. COPEMAN *Textbk. Rhematic Dis.* (ed. 3) xiii. 276 Restriction of the use of a joint may protect it from developing *osteo-arthrotic changes. **1974** PASSMORE & ROBSON *Compan. Med. Stud.* III. I. xxv. 37/1 There are biochemical differences between senescent and osteo-arthrotic cartilage. **1875** SIR W. TURNER in *Encycl. Brit.* I. 855/1 [Bone] is due to a development of new corpuscles, which Gegenbaur has named *osteo-blasts. *Ibid.*, Colossal, many-nucleated cells ..derived from the *osteo-blastic cells in the medulla. **1884** MACKENZIE *Dis. Throat & Nose* II. 480 An *osteo-cartilaginous plate extended..across to the under edge of the lower turbinated body. **1873** T. H. GREEN *Introd. Pathol.* 136 *Osteo-chondroma, which in structure more closely resembles bone than cartilage. **1847–9** TODD *Cycl. Anat.* IV. 135/2 Cruveilhier's *osteochondrophyte is a production of this class. **1872** *Monthly Microsc. Jrnl.* July 134 He [Kölliker] designates them '*osteoclasts' (or osteophages). **1875** SIR W. TURNER in *Encycl. Brit.* I. 856/2 The product of the formation of osseous tissue by the agency of the osteo-blasts, and of its absorption or destruction by the action of the osteo-klasts. **1706** PHILLIPS, **Osteocopi*, Pains in the Bones. **1861** BUMSTEAD *Ven. Dis.* (1879) 685 *Osteocopic pains, and nodes especially, often disappear in an almost marvellous manner. **1897** *Allbutt's Syst. Med.* II. 497 The osteocopic and myalgic pains are agonising at times. **1943** *Q. Jrnl. Exper. Physiol.* XXXII. 9 Superficially placed *osteocytes. **1965** M. C. HALL. *Locomotor Syst.: Funct. Histol.* vi. 87 Once it has formed the matrix around itself this cell, the osteoblast, becomes an inhabitant of its own secretions. Its function changes from a bone forming cell to a bone maintaining cell and it is then known as an osteocyte. **1849–52** TODD *Cycl. Anat.* IV. 867/2 There is also..a small central tract of *osteo-dentine in old teeth. **1854** OWEN *Skel. & Teeth* in *Circ. Sc., Organ. Nat.* I. 265 The transition from dentine to vaso-dentine, and from this to osteo-dentine, is gradual, and the resemblance of osteo-dentine to true bone is very close. **1878** T. BRYANT *Pract. Surg.* I. 561 Radicular odontomes generally consist of osteo-dentine more or less covered-in by a layer of dentine. **1881** OWEN in *Nature* XXIII. 402 A reptilian *osteodermal character in the mammalian class. **1857** MAYNE *Expos. Lex.*, *Osteodermatous. **1957** R. A. DART in *Transvaal Mus. Mem.* No. 10. 1 The purpose of this paper..is to show that ..the essential culture of *Australo-pithecus prometheus* was *osteodontokeratic... This long name indicating literally 'bone-tooth-horn' may appear unduly ponderous. **1963** J. W. KITCHING (*title*) Bone, tooth & horn tools of palaeolithic man: an account of the osteodontokeratic discoveries in Pin Hole Cave, Derbyshire. **1967** *New Scientist* 27 Apr. 202/1 This has been published by Dr Dart under the jaw-cracking title of the osteodontokeratic (literally bone, tooth and horn) culture of the Australopithecines. **1957** H. SELYE in *Revue Canad. de Biol.* XVI. 1 An apparently quite unrelated skeletal disease, '*osteolathyrism', can be induced experimentally in laboratory animals by feeding them the seeds of other types of Lathyrus plants, especially *L. odoratus*. The active principle of the latter is aminopropionitrile. **1971** *Sci. Amer.* June 51/1 One form of this disease, called osteolathyrism, can be produced experimentally in animals by administering aminonitriles and related compounds. In osteolathyrism the inhibition of cross-links in elastin and collagen brings about structural abnormalities in the connective tissues, particularly those of blood vessels and bone. **1875** BENNETT & DYER tr. *Sachs' Bot.* 625 Polished plates of marble, dolomite, or *osteolite (calcium phosphate) are covered with sand to the depth of a few inches, and seeds are then sown in the sand. **1857** MAYNE *Expos. Lex.*, **Osteolith*, another name for the Osteocolla or glue-bone stone. **1794** *Phil. Trans.* LXXXIV. 405 This *osteolithical stratum extends every way far beneath the limestone rock. [**1859** S. WILKS *Lect. Path. Anat.* I. 34 There is a third form of cancer,..to which Lobstein has given the name of osteolyosis, or cancerous erosion.] **1875** —— & MOXON *Ibid.* (ed. 2) 63 These formations appear to be of the same nature as those called *osteolysis by Lobstein. **1926** *Surg., Gynecol. & Obstetr.* XLIII. 308/2 There is regression of bone (osteolysis). **1969** B. S. EPSTEIN *Spine* (ed. 3) ix. 692/2 As a result of the infiltration of the marrow with Gaucher's cells minimal, moderate or extensive osteolysis may occur. **1875** WILKS & MOXON *Lect. Path. Anat.* (ed. 2) 63 (*heading*) *Osteolytic cancer. **1935** *Jrnl. Bone & Joint Surg.* XXXIII. 840 (*caption*) Osteolytic osteogenic sarcoma in the femur of a child. **1974** PASSMORE & ROBSON *Compan. Med. Stud.* III. I. xxvi. 31/1 Giant cell tumour (osteoclastoma)... Commonly a thin shell of bone covers the lesion, which is osteolytic. **1822–34** *Good's Study Med.* (ed. 4) IV. 249 The genus softening of bones, he proposes to call **Osteo-malakia*, and he divides it into two species. **1845–6** tr. *Simon's Anim. Chem.* II. 406 An analysis..of the bones of a man..who died from osteomalacia. **1876** tr. *Wagner's Gen. Path.* 328 In *osteomalacial bones. **1854** JONES & SIEV. *Pathol. Anat.* (1874) 831 *Osteomyelitis..inflammation of the red osseous Medulla and of the pulp contained in the Cancelli of spongy bone. **1898** *Allbutt's Syst. Med.* V. 777 Associated particularly with injuries and diseases of bones, such as osteomyelitis. **1870** tr. *Stricker's Hum. Histol.* xv. 470 We find in the dentine of the teeth..masses with bone lacunæ, termed Odontomes by Virchow, and *osteo-odontomes by Hohl. **1892** *Syd. Soc. Lex.*, *Osteoperiostitis. **1896** *Allbutt's Syst. Med.* I. 840 The frequent occurrence of osteitis, osteoperiostitis, or abscess of bone which so often follow in the wake of the disease. **1872** *Osteophage [see *osteoclast*]. **1895** *Edin. Rev.* Jan. 210 Among the boxes of bones found in the caves of the Mount of Olives,..brought from elsewhere, for interment near the expected site of the Last Judgement,..one *osteophagus bears the name of 'Judah' in Hebrew, with a square cross marked below. **1839–47** TODD *Cycl. Anat.* III. 1005/2 The *osteopterygious Fishes exhibit powers of reproduction equally extraordinary. **1857** MAYNE *Expos. Lex.*, **Osteo-sclerosis*. **1901** *Brit. Med. Jrnl.* 29 June 1604 The bones [in general paralysis of the insane] generally show a high degree of osteo-sclerosis. **1857** MAYNE *Expos. Lex.*, *Osteostomatus*, applied by Duméril to a Family of osseous, holobranchious fishes, comprehending those having jaws naturally osseous, *osteostomatous. **1891** *Cent. Dict.*, **Osteostomous*. **1881** *Catal. Trustees Univ. Pennsylv.* 72 The *osteo-syndesmological laboratory is under the supervision of the Professor of Anatomy.

osteoclastoma (ˌɒstiːɒklæˈstəʊmə). *Path.* Pl. **-omas**, **-omata**. [f. *osteoclast* s.v. OSTEO- + -OMA.] A giant-cell tumour of bone characterized by the presence of numerous osteoclast-like cells; orig. applied to a variety of mostly benign tumours, but now restricted to a type that is often malignant.

1926 *Jrnl. Path. & Bacteriol.* XXIX. 399 (*heading*) A case of osteoclastoma (myeloid sarcoma, benign giant-cell tumour) with pulmonary metastasis. **1931** *Brit. Jrnl. Surg.* XIX. 242 Generalized osteitis fibrosa with multiple osteoclastomata. **1948** [see MYELOMA]. **1961** *Lancet* 30 Sept. 751/2 Osteoclastomas respond well to irradiation. **1974** PASSMORE & ROBSON *Compan. Med. Stud.* III. I. xxvi. 31/1 Giant cell tumour (osteoclastoma)... The nature of the cells is not definitely known, but the possibility that the giant cells are osteoclasts has led to the alternative name, osteoclastoma.

‖**osteocolla** (ˌɒstiːəʊˈkɒlə). [mod.L. (1565 Gesner), f. OSTEO- + Gr. κόλλα glue.] A deposit of carbonate of lime forming an incrustation on the roots and stems of plants: found in sandy ground, esp. in some parts of Germany. Also called *glue-bone*: see quot. 1663.

1661 LOVELL *Hist. An. & Min.* II. 93 Ostiocolla..is glutinative. **1663** BOYLE *Usef. Exp. Nat. Philos.* II. xix. 289 It doth so wonderfully cement together the parts of broken and well-set bones, that it deserves the name it commonly hath in the shops of *osteocolla*. **1799** KIRWAN *Geol. Ess.* iv. 142 One of the roots of a pine tree..converted into the calcareous petrifaction called Osteocolla. **1816** CLEAVELAND *Min.* (1822) 176. **1879** RUTLEY *Stud. Rocks* xiv. 302 The variety of tufa named osteocolla consists of calcareous deposits around twigs and mosses.

osteoderm (ˈɒstiːəʊdɜːm). *Zool.* [Back-formation from *osteodermal* adj. s.v. OSTEO-.] A bony plate in the skin, esp. in reptiles.

1898 H. GADOW *Classification of Vertebrata* 27 Body scaly without osteoderms. **1902** *Proc. Zool. Soc.* I. 208 Exquisite examples of true dermal bones are those ossifications 'within the skin' which in Amphibia and Reptiles are now generally called osteoderms. **1969** A. BELLAIRS *Life of Reptiles* II. vii. 319 Many reptiles have an armour of bony scutes or osteoderms in the dermal layers of the skin.

osteodystrophy (ɒstiːəʊˈdɪstrəfɪ). *Med.* Also as mod.L. **-dystrophia**. [f. (in Ger.) as mod.L. *osteodystrophia* (J. von Mikulicz 1905, in *Verhandl. d. Ges. deutsch. Naturforscher und Ärzte* LXXVI. II. Med. Abt. 108), f. OSTEO- + *dystrophia* s.v. DYS-: see -Y[3].] Any of several disorders affecting the whole skeleton in which there is defective bone development owing to a badly balanced diet or faulty metabolism; *spec.* one in which there is increased resorption of bone and its replacement by fibrous and poorly mineralized tissue, producing skeletal pain and brittle bones, which are often enlarged and deformed in the young; it occurs in animals, esp. horses, as a result of too high a ratio of dietary phosphorus to calcium (*osteodystrophia fibrosa* [coined in Ger. by T. Stenholm in *Pathologisch-anat. Studien über die Osteodystrophia Fibrosa*

(1924) 90]), and in man in association with chronic renal insufficiency and hyperparathyroidism (***renal osteodystrophy***).

1930 *Jrnl. Exper. Med.* LII. 669 (*heading*) Experimental fibrous osteodystrophy (ostitis fibrosa) in hyperparathyroid dogs. *Ibid.* 690 The hypostotic-porotic form of osteodystrophia fibrosa. **1932** W. Boyd *Text-bk. Path.* xxxi. 883 Among these..osteitis fibrosa, osteitis deformans, osteomalacia, rickets,..hereditary chondrodysplasia, and marble bones may be mentioned. As they are disorders of the growth of bone they may be considered together under the heading of the osteodystrophies. **1953** *Jrnl. Path. & Bacteriol.* LXV. 302 In severe renal osteodystrophy the local upheaval in bone formation may result in the development of lesions resembling either osteopetrosis or Paget's disease. **1963** Jubb & Kennedy *Path. Domestic Animals* I. i. 8/1 The classical osteodystrophies are rickets, osteomalacia, and osteodystrophia fibrosa. *Ibid.* 25/1 (*heading*) The osteodystrophy of fluorine poisoning. **1966** Wright & Symmers *Systemic Path.* II. xxxvii. 1384/2 Renal osteodystrophy is..one of the commonest metabolic diseases of bone. The bone changes consist of fibrous replacement of bone..together with rickets or osteomalacia. **1970** A. R. Jennings *Animal Path.* xii. 233 Equine osteodystrophia fibrosa arises if horses are fed on a diet containing large quantities of bran which is rich in phosphorus. The same situation is sometimes seen in pigs... In dogs, however, the prime cause is renal insufficiency with secondary hyperparathyroidism. **1974** Passmore & Robson *Compan. Med. Stud.* III. I. xxii. 10/2 The clinical features of renal osteodystrophy are most marked in children, in whom there is growth retardation.

So ˌ**osteody'strophic** *a.*

1925 *Physiol. Abstr.* IX. 529 Osteodystrophic factors in different animals. **1960** *Proc. Zool. Soc.* CXXXIV. 307 Osteo-dystrophic conditions have been recognized in New World monkeys for many years.

osteofibrosis (ˌɒstiːəʊfaɪ'brəʊsɪs). *Vet. Sci.* [f. OSTEO- + FIBROSIS; perh. ad. F. *ostéofibrose* (Achard & Thiers 1925, in *Gaz. des Hôpitaux civils et militaires* XCVIII. 917/1).] Osteodystrophia fibrosa of animals.

1936 *Vet. Rec.* XLVIII. 1400/1 The third osteodystrophic disease in animals is one which has only come to be recognised within recent years. It is osteodystrophia fibrosa, also known as osteofibrosis. Although by no means uncommon.., it has most often been described as osteomalacia or osteoporosis, conditions which we now know to have a different pathology. **1961** J. O. L. King *Vet. Dietetics* viii. 99 Osteofibrosis is a bone disease, commonly known as bran or millers' disease, which is found in horses fed on rations which are very low in calcium, especially when there is an excess of phosphorus.

Hence ˌ**osteofi'brotic** *a.*

1938 J. R. Greig et al. *Hutyra's Special Path. & Therapeutics* (ed. 4) III. 224 Osteofibrotic pigs with thickening of the cranial bones (snuffles).

osteogenesis (ˌɒstɪəʊ'dʒɛnɪsɪs). [f. OSTEO- + Gr. γένεσις GENESIS.]

a. The genesis, origination, or formation of bone.

1830 R. Knox *Béclard's Anat.* 260 The formation of the bones, ossification, or osteogenesis is a phenomenon which has much occupied the attention of observers. **1842** E. Wilson *Anat. Vade M.* (ed. 2) 5 This..constitutes the gelatinous state of osteo-genesis. **1882** *Nature* XXV. 476 An exceptional form of osteogenesis, viz. metaplastic ossification, or direct transformation of cartilage into bone. **1950** A. W. Ham *Histol.* xvi. 192/2 The formation of bone is usually spoken of as ossification or osteogenesis. **1963** Jubb & Kennedy *Path. Domestic Animals* I. i. 9/2 Alkaline phosphatase..is very active in osteogenesis.

b. osteogenesis imperfecta [mod.L. (W. Vrolik *Tabulæ Illustrandam Embryogenesin Hominis et Mammalium* (1849) tab. 91)], an inherited disease characterized by extreme weakness of the bones, which break frequently even before birth.

1903 *Amer. Jrnl. Med. Sci.* CXXV. 762 The disease called by Vrolik and by Stilling osteogenesis imperfecta, which previously in all probability was classed under fœtal rickets, is a definite, intrauterine process, the chief characteristics of which are great brittleness and softness of the bones, numerous fractures, and resulting deformities, due to as yet obscure disturbances of myelogenic and periosteal bone formation. **1923** *Brit. Jrnl. Surg.* XI. 737 Osteogenesis imperfecta is the name given to a disease which is characterized by a congenital defect in the evolution of the osteoblast, and recognized clinically by defective ossification of the cranium and a multiplicity of fractures resulting from trivial causes. **1974** Passmore & Robson *Compan. Med. Stud.* III. II. xlv. 47/1 Osteogenesis imperfecta congenita is easily distinguished from achondroplasia but unnaturally short limbs, the result of prenatal fractures, create a superficial resemblance.

So **osteoge'netic**, **osteo'genic**, **oste'ogenous** (*rare*) *adjs.*, of or pertaining to osteogenesis; bone-forming; **oste'ogeny**, osteogenesis.

osteogenetic cells, the same as osteoblasts. ***osteogenetic*** or ***osteogenic layer***, the inner layer of the periosteum, concerned in the production of osseous tissue, consisting of loosely-meshed white fibres (***osteogenic fibres***) including osteoblasts. ***osteogenic*** or ***osteogenous substance, tissue***, that which composes the osteogenic fibres. (*Syd. Soc. Lex.*)

1736 R. Nesbitt (*title*) Human Osteogeny explained in two lectures read before the surgeons of London in 1731. **1741** Monro *Anat. Bones* (ed. 3) 39 The Knowledge of this Part of the Osteogeny..I think necessary. **1847–9** Todd *Cycl. Anat.* IV. 647/2 Osteogenie is constant to the laws of serial order. **1857** Mayne *Expos. Lex.*, *Osteogeneticus*,.. bone-generating; of or belonging to Osteogenesis,.. osteogenetic. **1867** *Quain's Elem. Anat.* (ed. 7) I. p. cv, This soft transparent matter, which becomes ossified, may..be distinguished by the name of 'osteogenic substance', as proposed by H. Müller, or simply of 'osteogen'. **1874** A. E. J. Barker tr. *Frey's Histol. & Histochem. of Man* 258 It is easy to recognise here..the similarity of the osteogenetic process to that in other parts of the system. **1905** J. S. Ferguson *Normal Histol.* xi. 177 The osteogenous tissue of this layer, containing osteoblasts, osteoclasts, and developing blood vessels, grows into the cartilage. **1931** M. Sinclair *Fractures* xv. 180 Certain forms of ununited fractures may be stimulated towards union by the presence of actual osteogenetic tissue in a bone graft. **1947** *Radiology* XLIX. 310/2 Similar osteo-genic sarcomas were described in persons poisoned with radium for eight to ten years. **1951** S. Gilder tr. *Lacroix's Organization Bones* xv. 204 Autoplastic grafts of marrow are osteogenic in adult animals as well as in young animals. **1975** *Nature* 29 May 373/3 It was felt that statistical analysis could be based only on that bone tumour type for which solid prognostic data exist, agreed by all to be classical osteogenic sarcoma.

oste'ography. [See OSTEO- and -GRAPHY.] Description of the bones; descriptive osteology.

[**1728** Cheselden (*title*) Osteographia, or, the Anatomy of the Bones.] **1735** J. Douglas *Animadv. Cheselden's Osteographia* 1 The chief end of Osteography, as I take it, is to enable practitioners to cure the diseases to which the bones are liable. **1799** Hooper *Med. Dict.*, *Osteography*, the description of the bones. **1842** in Dunglison *Med. Lex.*

Hence **oste'ographer**, a descriptive osteologist.

1882 in Ogilvie (Annandale).

osteoid ('ɒstɪɔɪd), *a.* and *sb.* [f. OSTE(O- + -OID: cf. Gr. ὀστοειδής and ὀστεώδης bone-like, bony.]

A. *adj.* Resembling bone; of the appearance or structure of bone; bony, osseous; *spec.* consisting of or being the uncalcified amorphous matrix that is the organic constituent of bone.

osteoid osteoma, a characteristic kind of benign tumour of bone, small and usu. painful.

1840 C. West tr. *Müller's Nature of Cancer* I. II. i. 136 The osteoid tumor of the bones..is a growth composed entirely of osseous substance. **1859** *Proc. R. Soc.* IX. 662 It seems to follow that the peculiar distribution of real osseous tissue and of the 'osteoid' structure, as the osseous tissue without [bone-]corpuscles may be called, has a deeper signification. **1859** S. Wilks *Lect. Path. Anat.* I. 31 There is encephaloid and scirrhous cancer of bone,..if the latter is wholly ossified, we have osteoid cancer. **1870** Rolleston *Anim. Life* 46 In their bony or osteoid tissue fish resemble the Amphibia. **1875** Wilks & Moxon *Lect. Path. Anat.* (ed. 2) 54 The microscope shows a structure which can best be compared to those plates of osteoid cartilage which are so common on the spinal pia mater after middle life, *i.e.* it closely resembles bone which has been decalcified by acids. **1899** *Allbutt's Syst. Med.* VI. 9 Normally in molluscs, osteoid fish, and reptiles, only two cusps form. **1916** E. H. Kettle *Path. Tumours* II. 96 A tumour may form osteoid tissue consisting of trabeculæ, almost typical in every respect except that there is no deposition of calcium salts in the matrix. **1935** H. L. Jaffe in *Arch. Surg.* XXXI. 724 One feels forced to conclude that one is dealing here with a benign bone neoplasm the distinctiveness of which has not hitherto been recognized and which I am designating 'osteoid-osteoma'. **1950** A. W. Ham *Histol.* xvi. 190/2 Under normal conditions..newly formed bone exists in an uncalcified or osteoid state for only a transitory period. **1966** Wright & Symmers *Systemic Path.* I. xxxvii. 1400 An osteoid osteoma takes the form of a rounded mass of gritty, reddish-grey tissue... Histologically.., the lesion consists of vascular osteoblastic tissue, containing much osteoid matrix and some calcified bone. **1969** W. A. Beresford *Lect. Notes Histol.* vii. 49 The osteoid seam is a very poorly mineralized zone of matrix, 1–3 μ wide, seen with light microscopy between the true bone and the active osteoblasts.

B. *sb.* †**a.** A kind of malignant tumour composed of osteoid tissue. [The original sense, after G. *osteoid* sb. (J. Müller *Ueber den feinern Bau und die Formen der krankhaften Geschwülste* (1838) 44).] *Obs.*

1847–9 R. B. Todd *Cycl. Anat. & Physiol.* IV. I. 135/2 Osteoid.—Under the names of osteoid or ossifying fungous tumour, Müller describes a growth..composed of a greyish white, vascular, nodulated substance, of the consistence of fibro-cartilage. **1854** W. E. Swaine tr. *Rokitansky's Man. Path. Anat.* I. ix. 181 This series [of new-growths].. separates into the osteoid, and into the bony concretion. *Ibid.* 185 Müller's osteoid is a bone-formation which enters redundantly into the parenchyma of cancer.

b. Osteoid tissue, uncalcified bone. Also *attrib.*

1934 *Vet. Jrnl.* XC. 157 They were not considered to be genuinely rachitic, because the pathognomic osteoid formation was absent, or the amount of osteoid was not considered sufficient. **1943** *Bull. Johns Hopkins Hosp.* LXXII. 236 Osteoid in the normal adult individual is usually absent or very scanty. **1963** Jubb & Kennedy *Path. Domestic Animals* I. i. 9/2 Osteoid consists of fibrillar protein (collagen) in a non-fibrillar medium which is probably largely of mucopolysaccharides. **1972** H. L. Jaffe *Metabolic Dis. Bones* xv. 387 It is the presence of abundant osteoid that characterizes the histologic picture of both rickets and osteomalacia. **1972** *Science* 2 June 1032/3 Light microscopic observations indicated no obvious differences between treated and control cultures with respect to proliferation of boneforming cells or degree of osteoid formation.

oste'ologer. [f. as OSTEOLOGY + -ER[1].] = OSTEOLOGIST.

1666 J. Smith *Old Age* (ed. 2) 176 Osteologers have very well observed, that the parts appertaining to the bones..are either the Adnate, or the Enate parts.

osteologic (ˌɒstiːəʊ'lɒdʒɪk), *a.* [f. as OSTEOLOGY + -IC: see -LOGIC.] = next.

1828 Webster, *Osteologic*, pertaining to a description of the bones. (Also in later Dicts.)

osteo'logical, *a.* [f. as prec. + -AL[1].]

1. Pertaining to, dealing with, or relating to osteology, or the scientific study of bones.

1777 Camper in *Phil. Trans.* LXIX. 148 Galen's osteological performances upon this subject. **1863** Lyell *Antiq. Man* iv. (ed. 3) 66 Engrossed by his osteological inquiries. **1881** Owen *Sect. Addr. Brit. Assoc.* in *Nature* XXIV. 421 For the storage of such specimens, and especially the osteological ones.

2. Of or pertaining to the objects of osteology, i.e. to bones, their structure, arrangement in the skeleton, etc.; coming within the sphere or ken of osteology.

1794 Blumenbach in *Phil. Trans.* LXXXIV. 190 The osteological properties which I have had opportunities to observe in the skulls of mummies. **1854** Owen *Skel. & Teeth* in *Circ. Sc., Organ. Nat.* I. 257 In the osteological structure of man, the vertebrate archetype is furthest departed from. **1875** *Lyell's Princ. Geol.* II. III. xlvii. 567 Fossil skeletons..agreeing..in osteological character with some of the existing races of man.

Hence **osteo'logically** *adv.*

1819 Lawrence *Lect.* (cited in Webster, 1828). **1891** *Proc. Zool. Soc.* 196 It will at once be seen that, osteologically, *Starnœnas* is quite different from any of our other pigeons. **1946** F. E. Zeuner *Dating Past* vii. 206 This form is osteologically quite distinct from *Lynx pardina* Temminck.

oste'ologist. [f. as OSTEOLOGY + -IST.] One who studies or is skilled in osteology.

1731 in Bailey vol. II. **1874** Lyell *Elem. Geol.* x. (ed. 2) 140 A single bone taken from any part of the skeleton may enable a skilful osteologist to distinguish the genus, and sometimes the species to which it belonged.

osteology (ɒstɪ'ɒlədʒɪ). Also 7 **ostiologie, -y.** [ad. mod.L. *osteologia* (1573 Jasolinus), f. Gr. ὀστεο- bone, OSTEO- + -λογια, -LOGY. Cf. F. *ostéologie* (1628 in Hatz.-Darm.).]

1. The science which treats of bones; that branch of anatomy which deals with the structure, genesis, and disposition of bones.

1670 Pettus *Fodinæ Reg.* Introd. 2 If any one would write of the Nature of Ostiologie. **1709** Steele *Tatler* No. 62 ¶ 17 Well known for his Acuteness in Dissection of dead Bodies, and his great Skill in Osteology. **1858** Buckle *Civiliz.* (1869) II. iv. 195 The founders of comparative osteology.

b. A treatise on the bones.

1713 Cheselden *Anat.* Pref. (1726) 4 If I had not been so much engaged about an Osteology, in which every plate is twenty one inches long. **1861** Craik *Hist. Eng. Lit.* II. 168 The eldest Alexander Monro, the author of the Osteology, first published in 1726.

2. *transf.* The objects of this science; the bony structure or system of bones of an animal.

1833 Lyell *Princ. Geol.* III. 4 By a comparison of the osteology of the existing vertebrated animals with the remains found entombed in ancient strata. **1837–9** Hallam *Hist. Lit.* I. I. ix. §13. 468 Vesalius seems not to have known the osteology of the ear. **1881** Huxley *Addr. Brit. Assoc.* in *Nature* XXIV. 454 To obtain a full knowledge of the osteology and of the dentition of these two forms. *fig.* **1856** Dove *Logic Chr. Faith* II. §2. 114 The pantheistic scheme could go no farther than the bare outline of the osteology of the universe.

b. *loosely.* A bony framework or skeleton.

1854 Badham *Halieut.* 235 Here in strange jumble lie.. the several osteologies of inoffensive gurnards, perch, mackerel,..commingled with those of the implacable shark and fierce colossal skate.

‖**osteoma** (ɒstɪ'əʊmə). *Path.* Pl. **-ata.** [mod.L. f. OSTEO- + Gr. -ωμα, as in *carcinoma*, etc.] A tumour composed of osseous tissue.

1847–9 Todd *Cycl. Anat.* IV. 135/1 By osteoma we understand a growth composed of bone. **1873** T. H. Green *Introd. Pathol.* 139 Osteomata or osseous tumours.

osteomancy ('ɒstɪəʊˌmænsɪ). Also 7 **-manty.** [f. OSTEO- + -MANCY.] Divination from bones.

1612 Selden *Illustr. Drayton's Poly-olb.* v. 85 When I haue more skill in Osteomantie, I will tell you. **1831** Burton *Soup* 129 Works on..ostiomancy, Palmistry, oneiromancy and Divination.

osteometry (ɒstɪ'ɒmɪtrɪ). [f. OSTEO- + -METRY.] The measurement of bones; that part of zoömetry (or *esp.* anthropometry) which has to do with the proportions of the different bones.

1878 Bartley tr. *Topinard's Anthrop.* ii. 81 Osteometry.. is a study which has a special reference to the measurement of the facial angle and the direction of the occipital foramen.

Hence **osteo'metrical** *a.*, of or pertaining to osteometry.

In recent Dicts.

osteon ('ɒstɪɒn). *Histology.* Also **osteone.** [a. G. *osteon* (W. Biedermann 1914, in H. Winterstein *Handb. d. vergleich. Physiol.* III. I. 1150), f. Gr. ὀστέον bone.] = *Haversian system.*

1928 Moore & Key tr. *Leriche & Policard's Normal & Path. Physiol. Bone* i. 24 Recently, several histologists have tried to make the Haversian systems the structural units of bone, and have given them the name of osteons. This neologism is useless. **1958** *Jrnl. Bone & Joint Surg.* XL. A. 419 Haversian systems or osteons course primarily longitudinally in the long bones. **1968** Passmore & Robson

Compan. Med. Stud. I. xvi. 12/1 The osteones branch and interweave one with another. **1971** *Nature* 30 July 335/1 The osteons were orientated along the length of the femur, and tangentially to the surface of the frontal bone of the skull.

osteopathy (ɒstɪˈɒpəθɪ). [f. OSTEO- + Gr. πάθος feeling, suffering; in sense 2, after *homœopathy*, *allopathy*, etc.: see -PATHY.]

1. Disease or affection of the bones.

1857 MAYNE *Expos. Lex.*, *Osteopathia*, term for an affection of the bones, osteopathy. **1899** *Allbutt's Syst. Med.* VI. 547 During this period the osteopathies failed to attract the universal attention..so rapidly given to the arthropathies.

2. A theory of disease and method of cure founded on the assumption that deformation of some part of the skeleton and consequent interference with the adjacent nerves and blood-vessels are the cause of most diseases. Hence **osteopath** (ˈɒstɪəʊpæθ), one who practises osteopathy; **osteoˈpathic** *a.*; **osteoˈpathically** *adv.*; **osteˈopathist**, a believer in or practiser of osteopathy.

1897 *Columbus* (Ohio) *Disp.* 26 Mar., The [Iowa] house to-day passed the..medical practice act..driving out osteopaths, faith healers, massage doctors and all others professing to heal, unless they pass examination the same as physicians. **1899** *Brit. Med. Jrnl.* 11 Mar. 616 Dr. A. T. Still ..was, in 1889, delivered of a new system, the name of which was called 'osteopathy'... The following [are] extracts from official publications of the sect..'The osteopath..treats the patient through loose clothing..He does not rub or pat, but manipulates osteopathically'. *Ibid.*, From the point of view of the 'osteopathic' practitioner. *Ibid.* 15 July 168 The method of treatment..used by all osteopathists.

osteopetrosis (ɒstiːəʊpɛˈtrəʊsɪs). *Path.* [f. OSTEO- + L. *petra*, Gr. πέτρα rock + -OSIS.] A rare hereditary disease in man in which there is excessive formation of dense trabecular bone with resulting brittleness; also, any similar disease of animals.

1926 R. G. KARSHNER in *Amer. Jrnl. Roentgenol.* XVI. 405/1 Osteopetrosis is an hereditary disease. *Ibid.* 405/2 The term osteopetrosis (stony bones) is chosen because in one word it describes the primary pathological condition, bone petrifaction. **1947**, etc. [see *marble bone* s.v. MARBLE *sb.* 9]. **1948** *Jrnl. Exper. Med.* LXXXVIII. 579 (*heading*) Hereditary osteopetrosis of the rabbit. **1974** PASSMORE & ROBSON *Compan. Med. Stud.* III. I. xxvi 20/2 (*caption*) In osteopetrosis the bone texture is uniformly dense and no medullary cavity is present.

Hence **osteopeˈtrotic** *a.*

1951 *Jrnl. Bone & Joint Surg.* XXXIII. A. 937 The transverse lines in the metaphyses of osteopetrotic bones are fractures in various stages of healing. **1965** *Ibid.* XLVII. A. 1365 (*heading*) Avian osteopetrotic bone.

osteophone (ˈɒstiːəʊfəʊn). [f. OSTEO- + Gr. φωνή sound, after *telephone*, etc.] An instrument for the transmission of sound-waves through the teeth and the cranial bones to the auditory nerve, for the use of the deaf; = AUDIPHONE.

1892 in *Syd. Soc. Lex.*

osteophyte (ˈɒstiːəʊfaɪt). [f. OSTEO- + Gr. φυτόν a growth.] An osseous outgrowth, a bony excrescence. Hence **osteophytic** (-ˈfɪtɪk), *a.*, of, pertaining to, or of the nature of an osteophyte.

1846 G. E. DAY tr. *Simon's Anim. Chem.* II. 409 In the osteophyte incrustation there were contained: Phosphate of lime, Carbonate of lime [etc.]. **1873** T. H. GREEN *Introd. Pathol.* 140 The osteomata are divisible into two classes, according to their seat—the homologous osteomata or exostoses, and the heterologous osteomata or osteophytes. **1877** BURNETT *Ear* 95 Osteophytes are regularly found in the tympanum of many of the mammals. **1897** *Allbutt's Syst. Med.* IV. 692 Osteophytic periostitis may lead to the most extraordinary overgrowths of the bone itself. **1898** J. HUTCHINSON in *Arch. Surg.* IX. 355 Osteophytic growths on the limbs.

osteoplasty (ˈɒstiːəʊˌplæstɪ). [f. OSTEO- + Gr. πλαστ-ός moulded: see -PLASTY.] The transplantation of a piece of bone with its periosteum to fill up a gap. Hence **osteoˈplastic** *a.*, of, pertaining to, or of the nature of osteoplasty.

1861 *N. Syd. Soc. Year-bk. Med.* 281 Langenbeck.—Contributions to Osteoplasty. **1863** *Ibid.* 289 On osteoplastic resections of the lower jaw. **1892** in *Syd. Soc. Lex.* **1899** *Allbutt's Syst. Med.* VI. 553 Signs of osteoplastic periostitis. *Ibid.* 735 Krause forms an osteoplastic flap.

‖**osteoporosis** (ˌɒstiːəʊpɒˈrəʊsɪs). *Path.* [f. OSTEO- + Gr. πόρ-ος passage, pore + -OSIS.] Morbid absorption of bony substance, so that a bone becomes abnormally porous or spongy.

1846 G. E. DAY tr. *Simon's Anim. Chem.* II. 410 A specimen of osteoporosis growing on the cranium of an aged person. **1854** JONES & SIEV. *Pathol. Anat.* (1874) 841 In osteoporosis the affected bone presents an increase of size. **1896** MACALISTER & CATTELL tr. *Ziegler's Path. Anat.* I. 143 If the compact osseous tissue becomes porous from the widening of the Haversian canals, the condition is termed *osteoporosis*.

Hence **osteopoˈrotic** *a.*, relating to osteoporosis (*Syd. Soc. Lex.*).

1910 *Brit. Jrnl. Dental Sci.* LIII. 482 The bone itself presenting a sclerosed rather than an osteoporotic condition. **1970** *Sci. Jrnl.* Aug. 72/3 All individuals, whether normal or osteoporotic, therefore lose a small amount of bone mineral at night which is made up during the day.

‖**ˌosteosarˈcoma.** *Path.* [f. OSTEO- + SARCOMA.]

1. Sarcoma in the bone; 'term for a disease of the bone in which a fleshy, medullary, or cartilaginous mass grows within it' (Mayne, 1857).

1807–26 S. COOPER *First Lines Surg.* (ed. 5) 391 Osteo-sarcoma, and some inveterate fungous diseases of the lower jaw-bone..might be safely taken away, by amputating a more or less considerable portion of that bone. **1835–6** TODD *Cycl. Anat.* I. 461/1 The osteo-sarcoma is propagated by the continuity of some cancerous affection. **1876** *Clin. Soc. Trans.* IX. 77 Suffering from..osteo-sarcoma of the femur.

2. A sarcoma which undergoes osseous transformation.

1878 T. BRYANT *Pract. Surg.* I. 136 Sarcomata or even carcinomata may directly ossify, and so we get osteo-sarcoma and osteo-carcinoma. **1892** *Syd. Soc. Lex.*, *Osteosarcoma*, same as osteoid sarcoma.

Hence **ˌosteosarˈcomatous** *a.*

1835–6 TODD *Cycl. Anat.* I. 461/1 Osteo-sarcomatous tumours..generally consisting of this firm material.

osteotome (ˈɒstiːəʊtəʊm). *Surg.* [f. as next + Gr. -τομος that cuts.] Any instrument for cutting or dividing bone. So **osteˈotomist** (see quot. 1844).

1844 DUNGLISON *Dict. Med.*, *Osteotomist*..An instrument ..for cutting the bones of the fœtal cranium, when..necessary. **1857** MAYNE *Expos. Lex.*, *Osteotomus*, an instrument for cutting through bones; a kind of chain-saw: an osteotome. **1892** *Syd. Soc. Lex.*, *Osteotome*,..a chain saw for the division of a bone. Also, any bone saw. *O.*, *MacEwen's*..an instrument of the chisel kind.

osteotomy (ɒstiːˈɒtəmɪ). [f. OSTEO- + Gr. -τομία cutting.] **a.** *Anat.* Dissection of the bones. **b.** *Surg.* The cutting of a bone in order to correct a deformity, etc.

1844 DUNGLISON *Dict. Med.*, *Osteotomy*..The part of practical anatomy whose object is the dissection of bones. **1862** *N. Syd. Soc. Year-bk. Med.* 272 Deformity of the Leg, consequent on badly-united Fracture of both bones, cured by Osteotomy. **1876** *Clin. Soc. Trans.* IX. 162 Mr. Maunder's 'On Subcutaneous Osteotomy'.

‖**osteria** (əʊstəˈriːa). Also 7 **hosteria.** [It. *osteria* (in Florio *hosteria*) inn, f. *oste*:—L. *hospite-m* HOST *sb.*²: cf. HOSTRY.] An inn or hostelry, in Italy or a country where Italian is spoken.

1605 B. JONSON *Volpone* II. vi, Ha' not I Known him a common Rogue, come fidling in To th' Osteria. **1625** FLETCHER *Fair Maid of Inn* II. ii, Thy Master that lodges here in my Hosteria. **1766** SMOLLETT *Trav.* 313 He would take me to an excellent osteria where I should be entertained and lodged like a Prince. **1887** T. G. JACKSON *Dalmatia* II. 187 Our lodging..was a palace compared to the osteria where we dined, or rather fed.

Osterizer (ˈɒstəraɪzə(r)). Also with lower-case initial. [f. the name *Oster* (see quot. 1949) + -IZE + -ER¹.] The proprietary name of a type of electric food mixer.

1949 *Official Gaz.* (U.S. Patent Office) 5 Apr. 39 John Oster Manufacturing Company..Osterizer. For electric food mixers. **1967** E. B. NICKERSON *Kayaks to Arctic* xv. 142 Back in the days before osterizers, when celluloid was virtually the only plastic known. **1977** *Rolling Stone* 30 June 73/2 Her kitchen is very white—walls, doors, floors, white appliances, Braun coffee grinder and Osterizer, white salt and pepper shakers, [etc.].

ostery(e, ostesse, obs. ff. HOSTRY, HOSTESS *sb.*

ostey: see OSTE *v.*

†**ostey**, var. of HOSTEY *v. Obs.*, to make war. Hence †**osteying** *vbl. sb.*, warlike expedition; †**osteyour, ostoyour** [OF. *ostoiour*], soldier.

1412–20 LYDG. *Chron. Troy* II. xviii, Replenyshed of all that may auayle The osteyng, and to souldiours. *c* **1450** LONELICH *Grail* xlv. 472 Here Osteyowrs they maden forth gon. *Ibid.* 558 Anon his Ostoyours he bad That his pavylouns Alle pyht they were.

osteyl, obs. form of HOSTEL.

osthexy (ɒsˈθɛksɪ). [ad. mod.L. *osthexia*, f. Gr. ὀστ- from ὀστέον bone + ἕξις habit.] 'Ossific diathesis, or a disposition to the formation or deposition of bony substance' (Mayne *Expos. Lex.*). Hence **osˈthectic** *a.*, connected with osthexy.

1822–34 *Good's Study Med.* (ed. 4) IV. 255 That tendency to the..production of a morbid superabundance of calcareous earth in Osthexia and Lithia. *Ibid.* 300 In treating of vascular osthexy. *Ibid.* I. 449 Where the formation of calcarious matter appears to depend upon an osthectic diathesis, or a constitution prone to generate lime.

Ostiak, var. OSTYAK.

ostial (ˈɒstɪəl), *a. Anat.* [f. OSTI(UM + -AL.] Of, pertaining to, or having an ostium or ostia; of the nature of an ostium (in an insect's heart).

1900 MIALL & HAMMOND *Struct. & Life Hist. Harlequin Fly* 76 All the valves found in the heart of any Chironomus, whether cellular, ostial, or aortic, appear to be derived from the semicircular muscle-cells. **1910** *Practitioner* Jan. 51 The ostial end of the tube dilates to allow of the passage of the mole. **1969** R. F. CHAPMAN *Insects* xxxii. 662 (*caption*) Incurrent ostial valves in the larva of *Chaoborus* at different phases of the heartbeat. **1969** *Jrnl. Thoracic & Cardiovasc. Surg.* LVII. 792/2 At autopsy all showed varying degrees of coronary ostial sclerosis with stenosis.

†**ˈostiar.** *Sc. Obs.* [See -AR².] = OSTIARY I.

1588 A. KING tr. *Canisius' Catech.* 109 Gif ony man deseruis to be ane Bishope, lat him first be secundlie ostiar, lecteur.

ostiary (ˈɒstɪərɪ), *sb.* and *a.* [ad. L. *ostiāri-us* adj., of or pertaining to a door, sb. doorkeeper, f. *osti-um* door, entrance, river-mouth.]

A. *sb.* **1.** *Eccl.* A doorkeeper, esp. of a church; the lowest of the minor orders in the R.C. Church. Also in L. form **ostiarius.**

1432–50 tr. *Higden* (Rolls) V. 97 Gayus the pope..ordeyndede diverse degres of ordres in þe churche, as hostiary, reder, benette, accolette, and oþer. **1647** N. BACON *Disc. Govt. Eng.* I. x, Lastly [come] Ostiaries; which used to ring the bells, and open and shut the Church-doors. **1720** STRYPE *Stow's Surv.* (1754) I. I. xxiv. 165/1 The Library..had at first a Library keeper and an under library keeper, and an Ostiary. **1839** YEOWELL *Anc. Brit. Ch.* App. v. (1847) 182 If any clerk, from an ostiary to a priest, appear without his tunic. **1899** *Westm. Gaz.* 22 Nov. 1/3 As Ostiarius of the Lower House of Convocation..he knew every dignified clergyman in the Southern Province.

†**2.** The mouth of a river; = OSTIUM. *Obs.*

1646 SIR T. BROWNE *Pseud. Ep.* VI. viii. 312 The River of Nilus hath seven ostiaries. **1650** FULLER *Pisgah* IV. v. 82 Some onely counted the grand and solemn ostiaries of Nilus. **1682** SIR T. BROWNE *Chr. Mor.* III. §4 For we are carried into the dark Lake, like the Ægyptian River into the Sea, by seven principal Ostiaries.

B. *adj.* That has charge of the door. *rare.*

1866 BLACKMORE *Cradock Nowell* xlviii. (1883) 320 He pushed the ostiary footman back.

ostiate (ˈɒstɪeɪt), *a. rare.* [f. OSTI(UM + -ATE².] = OSTIAL *a.*

1897 *Natural Sci.* Apr. 266 The parapodial jaws and the ostiate heart cannot be supposed to have been *both* developed independently in each group of arthropods.

ostil, -er, -ary, obs. ff. HOSTEL, -ER, -RY.

‖**ostinato** (ostiˈnato), *a.* and *sb. Mus.* [It., obstinate, persistent.] **A.** *adj.* Recurring, frequently repeated. **B.** *sb.* Pl. **ostinati, ostinatos.** A musical figure which recurs unchanged and at the same pitch. Also *transf.* Cf. *basso ostinato* s.v. BASSO.

1876 STAINER & BARRETT *Dict. Mus. Terms* 340/2 *Ostinato* (*It.*) *Lit.* obstinate, used in the sense of 'frequently repeated', as *basso ostinato*, a ground-bass. **1928** *Daily Express* 27 Aug. 3/2 It is clear that there are three principal themes, the *ostinato* on page three obtruding itself against a version of the second theme. **1934** C. LAMBERT *Music Ho!* II. 126 We find the juxtaposition of short lyrical phrases..with ostinatos of extreme and deliberate bareness. **1946** G. ABRAHAM in A. L. Bacharach *Brit. Music* iii. 62 Neuritis..had exaggerated his [*sc.* Holst's] mannerism of *ostinato* bass-figures through the ease with which they could be indicated by repeat-signs. **1947** A. EINSTEIN *Mus. Romantic Era* xi. 143 The combination of *doloroso* and *agitato*, of *cantabile* and rhythmic *ostinati*, is typical. **1959** R. FULLER *Ruined Boys* II. ix. 131 He became aware of the noises of summer —of insects, larks, leaves—that provide the normally unidentified *ostinato* that nevertheless enriches the obvious themes of colour, sun and cloud. **1971** *Times Lit. Suppl.* 1 Oct. 1180/2 In *Erwartung*..the Way becomes an ostinato figure that marks the beginning of Schoenbergian serialism. **1973** E.-J. BAHR *Nice Neighbourhood* ix. 98 The kids were performing an ostinato of whining. **1974** *Early Music* II. 227 A series of fanfare-like ostinati alternating between the lower two voices. **1975** *Country Life* 2 Oct. 846/1 Mime's forge is equipped with a..mechanical hammer which superimposes its own *ostinato* on Wagner's music. **1976** *Gramophone* May 1766/3 The only place which sounds like a slip-up to me comes three bars before fig. 139, in the 'Action rituelle', where the tam-tam suddenly sticks out of the percussion ostinato of which it forms a part.

†**osting**, obs. f. HOSTING, raising of a host, raid; encampment.

c **1470** HENRY *Wallace* VIII. 1238 How plessis yow our ostyng for to se? **1621** *An. 10 Hen. VII* in Bolton *Stat. Irel.* 65 Whensoever they shall..ride to any jorney or osting.

ostiole (ˈɒstɪəʊl). Also irreg. **osteole**; and in L. form. [ad. L. *ostiolum* little door, dim. of *ostium* door.] A small orifice or opening; **a.** (*Bot.*) the orifice or opening in the conceptacles and perithecia of certain algæ and fungi, through which the spores are discharged; also, openings of the stomata or breathing pores; **b.** (*Entom.*) the orifice of the 'stink-gland' in the thorax of heteropterous insects (*rare*).

1835 LINDLEY *Introd. Bot.* (ed. 2) 234 *Ostiolum*, is the orifice of the perithecium of Sphæria. **1857** MAYNE *Expos. Lex.*, *Ostiolum*, a little door; an ostiole. **1870** BENTLEY *Man. Bot.* (ed. 2) 376 The spermagonium..has one or more cavities, with a small orifice at the top termed the ostiole or pore. **1874** COOKE *Fungi* 61 Opening by a pore or ostiolum at the apex. **1890** [see below].

Hence **ˈostiolar** *a.*, of or pertaining to an ostiole; **ˈostiolate** *a.*, having an ostiole or ostioles.

1857 MAYNE *Expos. Lex.*, *Ostiolatus*, having ostioles or little openings: ostiolate. **1880** GRAY *Struct. Bot.* (ed. 6) 423/1. **1890** *Cent. Dict.* s.v., The ostiolar canal or the channel connected with the ostioles of bugs.

ostir, ostis, obs. form of OYSTER *sb.*, HOSTESS *sb.*

o'stitis, variant of OSTEITIS.

‖**ostium** ('ɒstɪəm). Pl. **ostia**. [L. *ostium* door, entrance, mouth of a river.]

†**1.** The mouth of a river. *Obs.*

1665 SIR T. HERBERT *Trav.* (1677) 89 The great and noble River Ganges in two Ostiums falls under 23 deg. **1695** WOODWARD *Nat. Hist. Earth* I. 43 Mud being reposed.. near the Ostia of those Rivers.

2. *Anat.* Applied to various orifices and openings of vessels in the animal body, e.g. those of the ventricles and pulmonary arteries, the Fallopian and Eustachian tubes, the urethra, etc. Also, a slit-like valve in an insect's heart. Also in combs. with mod.L. adjs.

1828 J. QUAIN *Elem. Anat.* viii. 537 The fimbriated border presents a fissure or opening, (ostium abdominale) into which the impregnated ovum is received at the moment of its liberation from the ovarium, and thence conveyed along the tube, which opens into the uterus by another aperture, (ostium uterinum). **1874** J. HINTON tr. *von Tröltsch's Surg. Dis. Ear* v. 36 The tympanic opening of the [Eustachian] tube (ostium tympanicum) lies directly opposite the irregularly shaped entrances to the mastoid cells. **1877** HUXLEY *Anat. Inv. Anim.* vii. 434 The margins of the ostia may be simple or may be produced inwards into folds which play the part of valves. **1878** BELL tr. *Gegenbaur's Comp. Anat.* 51 It is only when valves appear at the ostia of the cardiac tube, that the direction of the flow is defined. **1898** *Allbutt's Syst. Med.* V. 703 Close to the ostium [of the cardiac pulmonary valves]. **1909** BAILEY & MILLER *Text-bk. Embryol.* x. 232 The valves between the atrium and ventricle .. develop for the most part from the walls of the triangular atrio-ventricular opening (ostium atrio-ventriculare). **1925** A. D. IMMS *Gen. Textbk. Entomol.* 123 The blood enters the heart through lateral inlets or ostia, a pair of which is situated at each constriction between adjacent chambers. **1951** C. K. WEICHERT *Anat. Chordates* viii. 321 The ovum then passes through the ostium tubae into the Fallopian tube. **1962** W. H. HOLLINSHEAD *Textbk. Anat.* xix. 581/1 The atrium opens into the right ventricle by way of the right atrioventricular ostium. **1969** R. F. CHAPMAN *Insects* xxxii. 661 The anterior and posterior lips of each ostium are reflexed into the heart so that they form a valve permitting the flow of blood into the heart.., but preventing its outward passage. *Ibid.* 663 There are unpaired excurrent ostia in the heart of Plecoptera and Embioptera.

ostle, obs. form of HOSTEL *sb.*[1]

ostler ('ɒslə(r)). Forms: (4–9 see HOSTELER); 5 osteler, -eller, -iler, -elere, -elore, 6– ostler, (7 oastler). [A phonetic spelling of HOSTELER, HOSTLER, representing the historical pronunciation with *h* mute. In earlier times it was frequent also in the sense 'keeper of a hostelry' (see HOSTELER 2); but since 16th c. has been restricted generally to the following sense, in which it is also (now less frequently) spelt HOSTLER, q.v. In the 1st Fol. of Shaks. *ostler* appears six times, *hostler* once, but the latter was more frequent in 18th c.]

A man who attends to horses at an inn; a stableman, a groom.

[*c* **1386** *Chaucer's Pars. T.* ℙ366, 15th c. *v.rr.* ostelers, ostilers: see HOSTLER.] *c* **1449** PECOCK *Repr.* v. vii. 521 Stabiling,.. beddis, seruicis of the ostiler. **1467** *Mann. & Househ. Exp.* (Roxb.) 417 My mastyr paid to the osteler of the Tabard.. vij.s. viij.d. **1486** *Bk. St. Albans* F vj b, A Laughtre of Ostelores. **1596** SHAKS. *1 Hen. IV*, II. i. 105 Bid the Ostler bring the Gelding out of the stable. **1630** WADSWORTH *Pilgr.* vi. 57 [He] supplyed the place of an Oastler in pulling of my bootes. **1784** JOHNSON in *Boswell* 15 May, If Burke should go into a stable.. the ostler would say, 'We have had an extraordinary man here'. **1860** R. SULLIVAN *Spelling Book Superseded* (ed. 66), Ostler, Hostler, the man who takes care of horses at a.. hotel or inn. **1861** GEO. ELIOT *Silas M.* ix. 63 Let him turn ostler, and keep himself.

b. *attrib.*, as **ostler-boy**. (**ostler ale** = HOSTEL *ale*; **ostler-wife** = HOSTELER-*wife*.)

1715 RAMSAY *Christ's Kirk Gr.* II. xi, The ostler wife brought ben good ale. **1861** C. INNES *Sk. Early Scotch Hist.* iii. 376 The chief drink of the castle, where ale was distinguished as ostler ale, household ale, and best ale. **1864** *Times* 22 Nov., The cabin-boy might become the leader of armies, and the ostler-boy sit in the Senate Chamber.

c. *Comb.*, as **ostler-wise** *adv.*, after the manner of an ostler.

1846 MRS. GORE *Eng. Char.* (1852) 117 While rubbing down ostler-wise his master's counter.

Hence **'ostlering** *vbl. sb.*, the occupation or exercise of the calling of an ostler.

1857 BORROW *Romany Rye* (1858) I. 344 At the end of perhaps forty years ostlering.

ostleress ('ɒslərɪs). [f. prec. + -ESS.] A woman or girl who acts as ostler.

1639 FULLER *Holy War* I. iv. (1647) 5 Jews and Pagans slander her to have been 'stabularia', an ostleresse or a she stable groom. **1847** TENNYSON *Princ.* I. 223 A plump-arm'd Ostleress.

ostlerie, -rye, obs. forms of HOSTELRY.

ostman, obs. form of HOASTMAN.

Ostmark ('ɒstmɑːk). [G., f. *Ost* east + *mark* MARK *sb.*[2] 2 c.] The name sometimes given in western countries to the currency of the German Democratic Republic, usu. to distinguish it from the West German Mark.

1948 *Times* 9 July 5/6 In the Soviet sector [of Berlin],.. only the *Ostmark*, the temporary currency of the Soviet zone, circulates legally. *Ibid.*, There was no intention that the *Deutschemark* [*sic*] should rival the *Ostmark* as a currency in the western sectors. [**1950** *Britannica Bk. of Year* 300/2 According to a report of the Deutsche Notenbank the note circulation in Eastern Germany was estimated in Feb. 1949 at Deutsche Mark (Ost) 4,112 million.] **1959** *Times* 18 Feb. 14/4 West German demand for Ostmarks is relatively weak. *Ibid.* 14/5 The 'real' value of the Ostmark is about ·50 west mark. **1972** R. W. LAST tr. *Freund's From Cold War to Ostpolitik* 28 The commandants of the western sectors declared that the Soviet orders relating to the introduction of the Ostmark into Greater Berlin were null and void.

Ostmen ('əʊstmən), *sb. pl. Hist.* Also 7 Oost-, Oust-. [a. ON. *Austmenn*, pl. of *Austmaðr*, men of the East; latinized *Ostmanni.*] The name given in Ireland and Iceland to invaders or settlers from Denmark and Norway; *esp.* the Northmen or 'Danes' in Ireland and their descendants settled in some towns on the East coast of that country.

[*a* **1222** GIRALDUS *Topogr. Hiberniae* III. xliii, Dicti sunt autem Ostmanni lingua ipsorum, corrupto quodam Saxonico, quasi Orientales homines.] *c* **1425** *Eng. Conq. Irel.* 82 He.. slogh four knyghtes that weren ouer ham, & four hundret ostmen. **1612** DAVIES *Why Ireland*, etc. (1787) 80 A charter.. granted by Henry the Second, to certain Oostmen, or Easterlings, who were inhabitants of Waterford, long before Henry the Second attempted the conquest of Ireland. **1807** SIR R. C. HOARE *Tour Irel.* 251 The Ostmen took their revenge by setting fire to the abbey. **1842** S. C. HALL *Ireland* II. 347 Numberless proofs occur of these being the work of the Ostmen.

Hence **Ost'mannic** *a.*, pertaining to the Ostmen.

1843 S. C. HALL *Ireland* III. 194 Asserting that they were of Ostmanic construction.

†**o'stomachy.** *Obs. rare*⁻⁰. [ad. Gr. ὀστομαχία a game played with fourteen pieces of bone, f. ὀστέον bone + μάχη combat.]

1656 BLOUNT *Glossogr.*, *Ostomachie*, a playing or fighting with bones. **1658** in PHILLIPS.

ostomy ('ɒstəmɪ). orig. *U.S.* [f. COL)OSTOMY and similar words.] An operation such as colostomy or ileostomy that involves making a permanent artificial opening in the body.

1957 *Ileostomy Q.* July 62/2 (Advt.), 'Ostomy' Skin Cream... United Surgical Supply Co. **1961** *Ibid.* Summer 65/2 Mr. Reynolds.. doesn't look on his 'ostomy' as a handicap or hindrance to work or play. **1963** (*title of periodical*) Ostomy quarterly. **1964** *Hospitals* XXXVIII. 88 At present 35 ostomy clubs.. in this country [*sc.* the U.S.A.] provide a means for persons with ileostomy, colostomy, ureterostomy, and ileal bladder to meet together and learn more about the management of their condition. *Ibid.* 90 Diet need not be a major problem to those with an ostomy. **1975** *Globe & Mail* (Toronto) 22 Aug. 25/8 There are three main types of ostomy: urostomy or urinary diversion, mostly due to cancer or birth defects; ileostomy or diversion of the small intestine due mostly to ulcerative colitis and Crohn's disease; and colostomy or diversion of the large intestine, due mostly to cancer and birth defects.

Hence **'ostomate** [cf. -ATE[1]], a person who has had an ostomy.

1966 *Ostomy Q.* Spring 15/2 What can be more rewarding than the feeling you have after visiting a new ostomate and knowing you have helped them? **1973** *Daily Colonist* (Victoria, B.C.) 2 Mar. 17/7 The ostomate faces a life of carrying the plastic bag outside the body. **1975** *Globe & Mail* (Toronto) 22 Aug. 25/8 Whether or not you are one of the 100,000 or more ostomates in Canada you should be interested in the current convention of the United Ostomy Association going on in Toronto. **1977** *Telegraph* (Brisbane) 2 Aug. 2/1 Ostomates are people who have had operations to by-pass bowel or urinary tracts, and who have to wear bags attached to their body to collect their body wastes.

†**ostour.** *Obs.* Also corruptly 4 ostrey, oscuriis for *osturis* (*pl.*). [a. OF. *ostur*, *-our* (in 11th c. *hostur*, Roland, mod.F. *autour*):—pop. L. *austōrium*, from *austur*, altered from *astur* (Firmicus, *c* 340), lit. an Asturian (hawk or bird), a goshawk. Also in med.L. *asturco*, *asturcus*, *austurco*, *-turcus*, *-turcius* (Du Cange), whence *austurcarius* OSTREGER.] A goshawk.

[**1363** *Rolls of Parlt.* II. 282/2 Laneret, Austour, ou autre Faucoun.] **13..** *Guy Warw.* (Caius) 176 Mikell he kouthe of haukes and houndes, Of Ostours, of Faukons of grete moundes [*A.* Of estriche faucouns of gret mounde]. *Ibid.* 3154 Ostreyes [*A.* Oscuriis] and faukons, girfaukes also.

ostoyour, variant of OSTEYOUR *Obs.*

Ostpolitik ('ɒstpɒlɪˌtiːk). [G., f. *Ost* east + *Politik* policy.] German policy towards Eastern Europe, associated mainly with the Federal Republic of Germany's cultivation of good relations with the Communist block during the 1960s, but applied also, by extension, to the policies of other western countries regarding the East as a whole.

1961 T. PRITTIE *Germany Divided* vi. 155 They will scarcely overlook Hitler's statement,.. 'The goal of *Ostpolitik* is to open up an area of settlement for one hundred million Germans.' **1967** *Economist* 6 May 558/3 Herr Kiesinger.. promised that the government would not pursue its Ostpolitik 'behind the backs of the expellees'. **1968** *Ann. Reg. 1967* 253 Immediately the East German Government, supported by Moscow, took steps to hamper further progress by Bonn's *Ostpolitik*. **1970** *Atlantic Monthly* July 26 In the west, the big change was Willy Brandt's narrow victory in the West German elections last October, and the formation of a new Bonn coalition government dominated by the Social Democrats, prepared to abandon the rigidities of the Adenauer foreign policy of the last twenty years and embark on an entirely new and dynamic course of Ostpolitik. **1971** *Times Lit. Suppl.* 15 Oct. 1246/2 The politicians of Bonn are rather unhappy at the widespread use of the term 'Ostpolitik' by their Western allies. In the history of twentieth-century Germany, this term has signified a whole range of activities, from Hindenburg's humiliation of Russia at Brest-Litovsk to the East-West balancing act of Rapallo, and back to the domination of the East by Schacht's financial diplomacy and Hitler's armies. **1971** *New Yorker* 23 Oct. 156 Nixon as a risk-taker is something of a surprise... But his *Ostpolitik* is daring. It is a repudiation of his entire past. **1972** R. W. LAST tr. *Freund's From Cold War to Ostpolitik* 75 Brandt knows better than anyone else that Berlin is the real test of the new Ostpolitik.

ostracean (ɒ'streɪʃiːən), *a.* and *sb.* [f. mod.L. *Ostracea* or *-eæ*, pl., the family of Bivalve Mollusca containing the Oyster (f. Gr. ὀστράκε-ος earthen, testaceous, f. ὄστρακον earthen vessel, tile, shell of mussel, oyster, etc.) + -AN.]

a. *adj.* Belonging to the *Ostracea* or oyster family, ostraceous. **b.** *sb.* A member of the *Ostracea*, an oyster.

1840 *Penny Cycl.* XVII. 111/1 *Oysters*, or *Ostraceans*, a family of monomyarian conchifers.

ostraceous (ɒ'streɪʃəs), *a.* [f. mod.L. *Ostracea* (see prec.) + -OUS.] Of or pertaining to the *Ostracea*; of the nature of an oyster.

1822–34 *Good's Study Med.* (ed. 4) I. 177 Species of scallops and other coarse ostraceous worms. **1882** *Pall Mall G.* 13 Feb., Our own native.. though absolutely the smallest among the sons of the primitive ostraceous ancestors, is still round and plump and well flavoured.

ostracine ('ɒstrəsɪn), *a. rare*⁻⁰. [f. Gr. ὄστρακον (see above) + -INE[2]: cf. Gr. ὀστράκιν-ος earthen, testaceous.] = OSTRACEAN *a.*

1890 in *Cent. Dict.*

‖**Ostracion** (ɒ'streɪsɪɒn). *Ichth.* [a. mod.L. *ostracion*, a. Gr. ὀστράκιον, dim. of ὄστρακον hard shell.] A genus of fishes notable for the hard encasement of their bodies, consisting of juxtaposed hexagonal plates; a trunk-fish or coffer-fish.

1658 SIR T. BROWNE *Gard. Cyrus* iii. 147 To omit the ruder Figures of the ostracion. **1752** SIR J. HILL *Hist. Anim.* 284 The body of the Ostracion is of an odd figure. **1861** HULME tr. *Moquin-Tandon* II. IV. ii. 244 Adanson saw negroes die after severe vomiting and convulsions from eating of the Ostracions or Trunk Fishes.

o'straciont, *a.* (*sb.*) *Ichth.* [erron. f. OSTRACION, after words in *-odont* from sbs. in *-odon.*] Of or pertaining to the genus Ostracion. **b.** *sb.* A member of the family *Ostraciontidæ*, of which *Ostracion* is the typical genus.

In Dicts.

ostracism ('ɒstrəsɪz(ə)m). [ad. mod.L. *ostracism-us*, a. Gr. ὀστρακισμός, f. ὀστρακίζειν to OSTRACIZE: see -ISM.]

1. A method of temporary banishment practised in Athens and other cities of ancient Greece, by which a citizen whose power or influence was considered dangerous to the state was sent into exile for ten (later for five) years; so called because it was effected by voting with potsherds or tiles, on which the name of the person whom it was proposed to banish was written; hence, Temporary banishment or expatriation in general.

[**1579–80** NORTH *Plutarch* (1676) 109 This manner of banishment for a time, called *Ostracismon*, was no punishment for any fault committed, but a.. taking away of the envy of the people.] **1588** GREENE *Perimedes* 6 As sure a repulse to exile melancholie, as the *Ostracisme* was to the noble of Athens. **1697** POTTER *Antiq. Greece* I. xxv. I. 125 The Archons number'd all the Tyles in gross, for if there were fewer than six-thousand, the Ostracism was void. **1785** REID *Intell. Powers* v. iv. 400 It is easy to see why an attainder in the English Language and ostracism in the Greek language have not names answering to them in other languages. **1821** BYRON *Two Foscari* II. i, Had I as many sons As I have years, I would have given them all.. to ostracism, Exile, or chains. **1847** GROTE *Greece* II. xxxi. IV. 200 By the ostracism a citizen was banished without special accusation, trial or defence.

2. *fig.* Banishment by general consent; exclusion from society, favour, or common privileges.

16.. DONNE *To C'tess of Bedford*, '*To have written then*' 22 Virtue in courtiers hearts Suffers an ostracism and departs. **1693** J. MARSH *To Congreve on 'Old Bachelor'*, To pass an ostracism on poetry. **1827** HARE *Guesses* Ser. I. (1873) 26 A sort of ostracism is continually going on against the best, both of men and measures. **1870** M. D. CONWAY *Earthw. Pilgr.* ix. 120 The social ostracism of a heretic. **1891** H. CROSBY *Conform. to World* 28 Even if social ostracism be the consequence.

ostracite ('ɒstrəsaɪt). (Formerly in L. form.) [ad. L. *ostracītēs*, a stone mentioned by Pliny, a. Gr. ὀστρακίτης earthen, testaceous, f. ὄστρακον shell: see OSTRACEAN.] A fossil shell of a species or genus allied to the oyster.

[**1601** HOLLAND *Pliny* II. 629 As for Ostracites, it took the name of an Oystre shell, which it doth represent.] **1653** CULPEPPER *Pharm. Londin.* 54 Ostrocites, a drachm of it taken in pouder provokes the terms. **1677** PLOT *Oxfordsh.* 113 On Cowley-common we find nothing but Ostracites. **1753** CHAMBERS *Cycl. Suppl.*, *Ostracites*, in natural history, a name given by authors to the fossile oisters, common in many parts of England. **1852** TH. ROSS *Humboldt's Trav.* I. vi. 204 In the greatest part [of the beds] the cardites, the turbinites, the ostracites..are found.

‖**ostracitis** (ɒstrə'saɪtɪs). [a. L. *ostracītis* (Pliny), a. Gr. ὀστρακῖτις cadmia, calamine, f. ὄστρακον: see prec.] A kind of calamine adhering to furnaces in which copper is melted.

1706 PHILLIPS, *Ostracitis*, a sort of Crust that sticks to Furnaces, where Brass-Oar is melted. **1892** *Syd. Soc. Lex.*, *Ostracitis*, an earth of cadmium, from its resemblance to the surface of a shell.

ostracize ('ɒstrəsaɪz), *v.* [ad. Gr. ὀστρακίζειν, f. ὄστρακον earthen vessel, tile, potsherd: see -IZE.]

1. *trans.* (*Gr. Hist.*) To banish by voting with potsherds: see OSTRACISM 1.

1850 GROTE *Greece* II. lxvii. VIII. 478 Damon was.. rendered so unpopular at Athens,..that he was ostracised. **1866** FELTON *Anc. & Mod. Gr.* II. I. vi. 109 Two Athenian statesmen, Nicias and Alcibiades, united to ostracize Hyperbolus, a lamp-maker,..and by ostracizing him they ostracized ostracism itself.

2. *fig.* To banish or expel as by ostracism; to exclude from society, favour, or common privileges.

1649 MARVELL *Death Ld. Hastings* 26 Therefore the Democratick Stars did rise, And all that Worth from hence did Ostracize. **1803** *Edin. Rev.* II. 142 Conjurors who.. endeavour to ostracise this submarine invader. **1853** BRIGHT *Sp. Peace* 13 Oct. (1876) 460 Your newspapers..denounced and ostracised hundreds of good men. **1890** MERCIER *Sanity & Insanity* xiii. 343 Ostracised from society because of the drunken and violent habits of his wife.

Hence '**ostracized** *ppl. a.*, '**ostracizing** *vbl. sb.* and *ppl. a.*; also '**ostracizable** *a.*, capable of being ostracized; '**ostracizer**, one who ostracizes.

1847 GROTE *Greece* II. xxxi. IV. 210 Kleisthenês did not permit the process of ostracising to be opened against any one citizen exclusively. **1849** *Ibid.* xli. V. 174 The ostracised Aristeidês arrived at Salamis. **1854** *Blackw. Mag.* LXXV. 255 He wrote his own name on the ostracising shell. **1862** *All Year Round* Christm. No. 35 He..covertly threw handfuls of grain to the ostracised cockerels. **1876** T. HARDY *Ethelberta* II. 3 A mover in circles from which the greatest ostraciser of all is servitude. **1891** *Pall Mall G.* 11 Sept. 7/3 Our ostracizable Electors.

ostraco-, before a vowel **ostrac-**, combining form of Gr. ὄστρακον hard shell.

Hence **ostra'cology** [see -LOGY], conchology (Mayne); so ˌ**ostraco'logical** *a.* '**ostracoˌphore** [Gr. -φορος bearing], a member of the *Ostracophori*, a Palæozoic sub-class of fishes (Funk); so **ostra'cophorous** *a.* '**ostracoˌpod**, a member of the *Ostracopoda*, an order of entomostracous crustacea; so **ostra'copodous** *a.*, belonging to the *Ostracopoda* (Mayne). **ostra'costean** [Gr. ὀστέον bone] *a.*, pertaining to the *Ostracostei*, a group of extinct placoganoid fishes; *sb.* a fish belonging to this group; so **ostra'costeous** *a.* '**ostracoˌthere** [Gr. θήρ animal], an ostracode crustacean.

1876 tr. *Beneden's Anim. Parasites* 17 Since the molluscs live only on vegetable substances, while the Ostracotheres feed entirely on animal matter.

ostracod ('ɒstrəkɒd), *a.* and *sb.* Also **ostracode** (-kəʊd) and with capital initial. [a. mod.L. *Ostracoda* and Fr. *ostracode* (P. A. Latreille *Genera Crustaceorum et Insectorum* (1806) I. 17), formerly *Ostrachoda*, *ostrachode* (P. A. Latreille in C. S. Sonnini *Buffon's Hist. Nat. Crustacés & Insectes* (1802) II. 361), f. Gr. ὀστρακώδης testaceous: see -ODE[1].] **a.** *adj.* Belonging to the *Ostracoda* or *Ostracopoda*, an order of entomostracous crustaceans. **b.** *sb.* A member of the *Ostracoda*.

1865 *Athenæum* No. 1983. 571/2 The little modest ostracods and phyllopods. **1870** NICHOLSON *Man. Zool.* I. 196 Small Ostracode Crustacea..as fossils..extend from the Lower Silurian period up to the present day. **1888** ROLLESTON & JACKSON *Anim. Life* 534 The eye is moveable ..in the Ostracode *Cypridinidæ*. **1902** *Edin. Rev.* Jan. 194 They found..a living ostracode. **1935** TWENHOFEL & SHROCK *Invertebr. Paleontol.* x. 436 Ostracods are small, bivalved Crustacea which are found inhabiting all waters but are most abundant in marine habitats. **1953** *Ibid.* (ed. 2) xiii. 548 Ostracodes are minute, lentil-shaped crustaceans having a bivalve carapace that completely encloses the indistinctly segmented body. **1956** [see MYSID]. **1957** *New Biol.* XXIV. 70 Some of the ostracods..possess haemoglobin. **1965** B. E. FREEMAN tr. *Vandel's Biospeleol.* ix. 112 Hypogeous ostracods are known from Europe, North America and Japan. **1969** BENNISON & WRIGHT *Geol. Hist. Brit. Isles* viii. 164 Ostracod shales were laid down contemporaneously in deeper waters in the Torquay area. **1974** A. DILLARD *Pilgrim at Tinker Creek* viii. 132 An ostracod, a common fresh-water crustacean of the sort I crunch on by the thousands every time I set foot in Tinker Creek. **1974** *Smithsonian Contrib. Earth Sci.* No. 13. 22/1 Constituents were counted and grouped in the following classes: terrigenous (mica and other, including quartz), bioclastic remains (pelagic forams, benthonic forams, pteropods, and other), plant fragments, and other (including ostracode valves, sponge spicules, unidentifiable fragments, etc.).

So **ostra'codal, ostra'codous** *adjs.*

1887 H. H. HOWORTH *Mammoth & Flood* 372 The ostracodal fauna..in the seas of Australia and the Malay Peninsula.

ostracoderm ('ɒstrəkəʊdɜːm), *sb.* and *a.* [a. mod.L. sub-class name *Ostracodermi* (E. D. Cope 1889, in *Amer. Naturalist* XXIII. 852), f. Gr. ὀστρακόδερμος hard-shelled.] **A.** *sb.* A small, primitive, fossil fish belonging to the group formerly designated the sub-class Ostracodermi. **B.** *adj.* Of or pertaining to this group of fossils. So ˌ**ostraco'dermal** *a.*, ˌ**ostraco'dermous** *a.* (Mayne *Expos. Lex.* 1857), ˌ**ostraco'dermatous** *a.* (*Syd. Soc. Lex.*).

1891 A. S. WOODWARD *Catal. Fossil Fishes in Brit. Mus.* (*Nat. Hist.*) II. p. xvii, The Arachnid theory is based upon a complete misapprehension of the most fundamental points in Ostracoderm skeletal anatomy. **1898** A. S. WOODWARD *Vertebr. Palæont.* 5 The simplest Ostracoderms (Heterostraci) occur in the Upper Silurian and Lower Devonian, and exhibit no bone-cells in any part of their dermal armour. **1933** A. S. ROMER *Vertebr. Paleont.* ii. 24 Almost all are covered with various types of armor, a feature to which the name 'ostracoderms' ('shell-skinned') is due. **1935** *Amer. Jrnl. Sci.* CCXXIX. 323 (*title*) The ostracoderm genus *Dartmuthia* Patten. **1968** A. S. ROMER *Procession of Life* viii. 148 By that time [*sc.* early Devonian] higher fish types descended from the ostracoderm stock were already evolving. **1969** BENNISON & WRIGHT *Geol. Hist. Brit. Isles* viii. 182 The jawless Ostracoderms with dorsal shield and granular armour..had made their appearance in the Upper Ludlow Beds.

ostracoid ('ɒstrəkɔɪd), *a.* and *sb.* [f. Gr. type *ὀστρακοειδής = ὀστρακώδης OSTRACOD: see -OID and -ODE[1].] (See quots.)

1857 MAYNE *Expos. Lex.*, *Ostracoides*, resembling or of the nature of a shell: ostracoid. **1862** DANA *Elem. Geol.* 193 The earliest of the bivalve Crustaceans—very small species having the body enclosed in a bivalve shell somewhat like a clamshell, whence the name Ostracoid.

† '**ostracy**, obs. erron. form for OSTRACISM.

1579–80 NORTH *Plutarch* (1676) 456 The Ostracy devised was for men of noble fame.

ostrage, obs. form of OSTRICH.

ostrakon ('ɒstrəkɒn). Also **ostracon**. Pl. **ostraka, -ca**. [ad. Gr. ὄστρακον potsherd.] A sherd of pottery or (more rarely) limestone used in antiquity as a surface for writing or inscribing, often, at Athens and in other Greek cities, to cast a vote (see OSTRACISM 1), or as a common writing material. Used (freq. in *pl.*) of archæological finds of this kind in the Middle East.

1883 *Proc. Soc. Biblical Archaeol.* V. 84 The British Museum has lately acquired..a considerable number of ostraka or potsherds discovered at Elephantine, Thebes, and other places. *Ibid.* 119 Two ostraka or slices of limestone formed for the purpose, inscribed with hieratic inscriptions. **1900** *Athenæum* 23 June 783/1 The study of Greek ostraca is a comparatively new one. **1921** G. A. F. KNIGHT *Nile & Jordan* 251 The name Bata has been recovered in a hieratic ostrakon. **1934** *Discovery* Apr. 90/2 The smaller finds include..actual *ostraca* from the voting of 483 B.C. when 'Aristides the Just' was banished. **1952** G. SARTON *Hist. Sci.* I. iv. 114 Two late mathematical papyri, ..as well as Coptic ostraca from Wādī Sarga (near Asyūt).. contain unmistakable examples of Egyptian computation. **1960** [see FIND *sb.* 4]. **1968** V. EHRENBERG *From Solon to Socrates* Notes 414 The number of ostraca found by archaeologists gives little evidence as to the actual results of the voting. **1972** *Times* 18 May (Egypt Suppl.) p. iv/4 During the excavation of the temple terrace, many fragments of stone stelae and *ostraca* (inscriptions on potsherds) were found bearing dedications to Isis. **1978** *N.Y. Times Bk. Rev.* 21 May 39/1 Demotic is known today from papyri and ostraca—broken bits of pot that have been scribbled on.

ostray, obs. form of ASTRAY, *adv.* and *a.*

ostre, var. HOSTRY *Obs.*; obs. f. OYSTER *sb.*

ostreaceous (ɒstriː'eɪʃəs), *a.* [f. L. type *ostreāce-us*, f. *ostrea* oyster: see -ACEOUS.] Of the nature of the oyster or its shell; resembling, or proper to, an oyster; oyster-like; ostraceous.

1678 CUDWORTH *Intell. Syst.* I. v. 790 That outer vestment, of the Terrestial Body (styled in Plato τὸ ὀστρεῶδες, the crustaceous or ostreaceous Body). **1833** *New Monthly Mag.* XXXVIII. 223 His very life and being may be said to have been, in a great degree, ostreaceous.

ostreaculture: see OSTREICULTURE.

ostreal ('ɒstrɪəl), *a. rare.* [f. L. *ostrea* oyster + -AL[1].] Of or pertaining to oysters.

1847 *Illustr. Lond. News* 7 Aug. 93/1 The days when poor Britain enjoyed but an ostreal fame. **1884** *Daily News* 25 July, The ostreal resources of the New World.

'**ostrean**, *a. rare.* [f. as prec. + -AN.] = prec.

1838 *New Monthly Mag.* LIII. 546 Forms of ostrean happiness. *Ibid.* 553 By the sudden opening and closing of their valves..the ostrean tribes possess the means of locomotion.

ostreger, ostringer ('ɒstrɪdʒə(r), 'ɒstrɪndʒə(r)). Forms: 5 ostregier, 5–9 -eger, 6 -iger, 7 -idger; 7–8 ostringer, (6 oistrynger). See also AUSTRINGER. [ME. *ostregier, ostreger*, corruption of OF. *ostruchier, austruchier* (F. *autrucier, autoursier*):—late L. *austurcārius*, f. *austurcus* (:—L. *Asturicus* Austurian, from Asturia in Spain), also *austorius, ostorius*, whence OF. *ostour, hostur*, now *autour* goshawk: cf. OSTOUR. For *ostringer*, cf. *messenger, passenger, porringer, wharfinger*.] A keeper of goshawks.

? *a* **1400** *MS. Sloane* 2721 in Harting *Introd. Perf. Bk. Sparhawkes* (1886) p. ix, The skoole for a young ostringer or ffaulkener. **1486** *Bk. St. Albans* Bvb, Thay be calde Ostregeris that kepe Goshawkys or Tercellis. **1575** TURBERV. *Faulconrie* 63 The falconers and ostregers have to these two sorts added a thirde kinde. **1614** MARKHAM *Cheap Husb.* (1623) 155 All Ostringers doe esteeme plumage..to be the best casting a short-winged Hawke can take. **1670** BLOUNT *Law Dict.*, *Austurcus*, a Goshawk; whence we usually call a Faulkoner, who keeps that kinde of Hawks, an *Ostringer*. **1867** OUIDA *C. Castlemaine* (1879) 11 Fulke Ravensworth brought her the bird from the ostreger's wrist.

ostrei-, ostreo- (also erron. **ostrea-, ostra-, ostro-**), combining forms of L. *ostrea, ostreum*, and Gr. ὄστρεον oyster. Hence: '**ostreiform** *a.* [-FORM], having the form of an oyster or of oysters. '**ostreophage** (-feɪdʒ), **ostreophagist** (-'ɒfədʒɪst) [Gr. -φάγος eating], one who, or that which, eats or feeds upon oysters; so **ostre'ophagous** *a.*, eating or feeding on oysters.

1840 *Penny Cycl.* XVII. 361/2 It exists also in the *Ostreiform *Gryphææ*. **1895** *Edin. Rev.* Oct. 369 The Londoner's diet might be thought to be much more largely ostreiform. **1883** *Daily Tel.* 29 Dec. 5/3 The notorious *ostreophage..were he to look in at a few of the West-end oyster shops. **1841** *Fraser's Mag.* XXIII. 463 Astonishing the natives, like Dando the *ostreophagist. **1857** MAYNE *Expos. Lex.*, *Ostreophagous. **1882** *Daily News* 17 Feb. 5/3 A great advantage to the ostreophagous part of our population.

ostreiculture ('ɒstriːɪˌkʌltjʊə(r)). Also erron. **ostr(e)a-, ostreo-, ostri-**. [f. L. *ostrei-*, comb. form of *ostrea* oyster + CULTURE.] The artificial breeding of oysters for the market; oyster-culture.

1861 HULME tr. *Moquin-Tandon* II. III. 169 Ostreaculture. The artificial production of Oysters has become an important branch of industry. **1862** *Illustr. Lond. News* 11 Jan. 50/3 The operations of ostréoculture.

Hence **ostrei'cultural** *a.*; **ostrei'culturist**, one who makes it his business to breed oysters.

1882 *Daily Tel.* 18 Aug. 4/8 The sensation which has been caused in the ostricultural world in consequence of the introduction into our waters of Portuguese mollusca. **1866** *Athenæum* No. 2032. 435/3 A valuable hint for ostreoculturists. **1882** *American* V. 88 The theory of hybridation advocated by some ostreiculturists. **1891** W. K. BROOKS *Oyster* 58 M. Tripota, one of the veteran ostraculturists.

ostreo-: see OSTREI-.

'**ostreoid**, *a. rare*[−0]. [f. L. *ostrea* oyster: see -OID.] Oyster-like. (Mayne, 1857.)

ostreperous, obs. f. OBSTREPEROUS.

ostrey: see OSTOUR; also obs. f. HOSTRY.

ostrich[1] ('ɒstrɪtʃ). Forms: α. 3 ostrice, 4 -icche, 4–5 -iche, 4–6 -ydge, 4–7 -ige, (4 -ig), 5 -ych(e, -ycche, -ygge, (host-), 6 ostrage, (hostryge), 6–8 ostridge, 4– ostrich; 5 oystryche, 6 -eche, -ige, oistrich(e; 7 oestrich, -idge. β. 6 austrich, astridge, 7 austridge, -uch. γ. 5–7 estriche, 5 -yche, 6 -itch, -yge, 6–7 -idge, -ige, 7 -edge, -age, (6 eestryche, 7 eastrich). [ME. *ostrice, -iche*, a. OF. *ostruce, -uche*, mod.F. *autruche* = Sp. *avestruz*, Pg. *abestruz*:—pop.L. *avis strūthio, avistrūthio*, from *avis* bird + late L. *strūthio*, ad. Gr. στρουθίων ostrich (Greg. Naz.), f. στρουθός sparrow, ostrich; the simple L. *strūthio* gave ME. STRUCION: cf. Pr. *estrus*, It. *struzzo*.

In classical Gr. the bird was called commonly ὁ μέγας στρουθός, or simply στρουθός; also στρουθοκάμηλος, whence the cl.L. *strūthiocamēlus* STRUTHIOCAMEL.]

1. a. A very large ratite bird, *Struthio camelus*, the only species of the genus *Struthio* and the family *Struthionidæ*, inhabiting the sandy plains of Africa and Arabia; it is the largest of existing birds.

The habits and peculiarities of the bird, real and fabulous, have afforded much scope for proverb and allusion; such are its indiscriminate voracity and its liking for hard substances, which it swallows to assist the gizzard in its functions; its supposed want of regard for its young, its eggs being partly hatched by the heat of the sun, which has led to the belief that it deserts its nest; and the practice attributed to it of thrusting its head into the sand or a bush when being overtaken by pursuers, through incapacity to distinguish between seeing and being seen.

α. a1225 *Ancr. R.* 132 þe steorc [*v.r.* ostrice] uor his muchele flesche makeð a semblaunt uorte vleon, & beateð þe hwingen. 1382 Wyclif *Lam.* iv. 3 Cruel, as an ostrich [1388 ostrig] in desert. 1388 —— *Job* xxxix. 13 The fethere of an ostriche [1382 strucioun]. 1481 Caxton *Myrrour* ii. xvi. 101 The hostryche by his nature eteth well yron. 1555 Eden *Decades* 317 Theyr fiete and legges are lyke the legs and fiete of the foule cauled the oystreche. 1584 Cogan *Haven Health* ix. (1636) 33 Rusticks, who have stomacks like Ostriges, that can digest hard yron. 1615 G. Sandys *Trav.* ii. 139 Swift horses..of sufficient speed to overtake an Ostridge. 1719 Young *Paraphr. Job* Wks. 1757 I. 211 Who in the stupid Ostrich has subdu'd A parent's care, and fond inquietude? 1794 G. Adams *Nat. & Exp. Philos.* III. xxviii. 162 A cock, a stork, an ostridge..walk directly forwards without waddling. 1857 Livingstone *Trav.* vii. 155 The food of the ostrich consists of pods and seeds of different kinds of leguminous plants.

β. 1580 Lyly *Euphues* (Arb.) 341 It fareth with me..as with the Austrich [*ed.* 1582 Ostridge], who pricketh none but hir selfe, which causeth hir to runne when she would rest. 1594 *1st Pt. Contention* (1843) 63 Ile make thee eate yron like an Astridge, and swallow my sword like a great pinne. 1623 *Someth. Written by Occas. Accid. Blacke Friers* 14 Like the Austridge, who hiding her little head, supposeth her great body obscured. 1663 Gerbier *Counsel* 23 Yet ought the Clark of the Work to be discreet in the distributing them [nails] to some Carpenters, whose pockets partake much of the Austruches stomacks.

γ. 1460 *Will of Tame* (Somerset Ho.), Ciphum cum esterige-feders. 1467 *Mann. & Househ. Exp.* (Roxb.) 403 My mastyr paid for an estryche federe..*v.s.* a1529 Skelton *P. Sparowe* 478 The estryge, that wyll eate An horshowe so great. 1589 *Pappe w. Hatchet* B ij b, Twil digest a Cathedral Church as easilie, as an Estritch a two penie naile. 1646 *To Mr. Hall on his Detractors* in *J. Hall's Poems*, Such plumed Estrages. 1649 Lovelace *Poems* 53 Eastrich! Thou featherd Foole, and easie prey, That larger sailes to thy broad Vessell needst. 1703 Dampier *Voy.* (1729) III. 397 We saw a great many of these Estridges.

b. Applied to the rhea of South America, a ratite bird resembling the ostrich in appearance and habits; more fully ***American ostrich***.

1813 Sir E. Home *Lect. Comp. Anat.* (1814) I. 295 In the cassowaries, and American ostrich, the stones..which those birds swallow must, from their weight, force their way into the gizzard. 1839 Darwin *Narr. Voy. Adv. & Beagle* III. 105 The ostrich..although so fleet in its pace,..falls a prey..to the Indian or Gaucho armed with the bolas. 1845 —— *Voy. Nat.* i. (1852) 43 We saw many Ostriches (*Struthio rhea*).

c. Short for 'ostrich skin'.

1939 R. Stout *Some Buried Caesar* xiii. 161 The brown ostrich card-case, gold-tooled. 1973 J. Drummond *Bang! Bang! You're Dead!* iii. 6 She walked from the room, carrying the jewel-case and a matching ostrich purse.

2. a. *attrib.* Of or pertaining to an ostrich or ostriches; ostrich-like: esp. in reference to the alleged habits of the ostrich; see above.

1598 J. Marston *Pigmalion* Sat. i. 34 Fie that his Ostridge stomack should digest His Ostridge feather. 1603 Dekker *Wonderfull Yeare* D ij b, So hungry is the Estridge disease, that it will deuoure euen Iron. 1635 Quarles *Embl.* iv. i. (1718) 190 When th' ostrich wings of my desires shall be So dull, they cannot mount the least degree. 1658 Wall *Comm. Times* 63 Estridge Consciences, that can digest Iron but not straw. 1681 T. Flatman *Heraclitus Ridens* No. 40 (1713) II. 9 What a kind of Ostrich Faith they must have, who can believe, that the Evidence..should so palpably betray themselves. 1808 Moore *Sceptic* 56 Whole nations, fooled by falsehood, fear, or pride, Their ostrich-heads in self-illusion hide. 1844 E. B. Browning *Let.* 11 Jan. (1954) 212 But the squeamishness of this Age,..this Ostrich age.. which exposes its own eggs, and then hides its head in the sand,..is really to me quite monstrous. 1856 Olmsted *Slave States* 167 The ostrich-habit of burying their heads in the ground before anything they don't like. 1877 Black *Green Past.* xxx. (1878) 237 [They had] hidden themselves in their berths in order to get a sort of ostrich-safety. 1891 *Pall Mall G.* 12 Sept. 1/2 The facts..are too damning to leave much room for an ostrich policy. 1952 Dylan Thomas *Let.* 6 Nov. (1966) 380 These ostrich griefs were always with me. 1976 *Listener* 6 May 585/2 The typical ostrich-Briton of today.

b. *Comb.*, as ***ostrich-breeding***, ***-egg***, ***-skin***; ***ostrich-eyed***, ***-like*** adjs.; † **ostrich-camel**, an old name of the ostrich (after L. *struthiocamēlus*); **ostrich-egg cup**, a decorated cup made from an ostrich-egg; **ostrich-farm**, a farm on which ostriches are reared for the sake of their plumes; **ostrich-farming**, the rearing of ostriches; **ostrich-fern**, the fern *Onoclea struthiopteris* (*S. germanica*); **ostrich-tip**, the tip of an ostrich-feather. Also OSTRICH-FEATHER, -PLUME.

1875 *S. Africa* 220 Nearly twenty years ago, *ostrich-breeding was successfully tried in Algeria. 1607 Topsell *Four-f. Beasts* (1658) 80 His feet like an *Ostrige-Camels. 1653 H. Cogan *Divel. Sic.* 104 Creatures of a mixt nature.. whereof some are called Austridge-camels, being derived from a camel and an austridg. 1599 Hakluyt *Voy.* II. i. 153 In the mids [of the chapel]..is a canopie as it were of a bed, with a great sort of *Estridge egges hanging at it. 1613 M. Ridley *Magn. Bodies* 67 Tipping of cuppes with silver, that be of Ostridge-egges. 1638 Sir T. Herbert *Trav.* (ed. 2) 16 Oestrich egge-shells. 1937 *Burlington Mag.* Apr. p. xxiv/2 The Leipzig **Ostrich Egg Cup* called thus because of the egg being decorated with the figures of birds. 1960 H. Hayward *Antique Coll.* 205/2 *Ostrich egg cup*, sometime supposed to be the eggs of griffins or phoenixes, ostrich eggs were often mounted as cups (and occasionally made into flasks) in the 16th cent. and later. Many surviving specimens are German. 1876 C. M. Yonge *Three Brides* II. i. 10 He has been acting as manager on an *ostrich farm. 1885 A. Newton in *Encycl. Brit.* (ed. 9) XVIII. 63/2 The great mercantile value of Ostrich-feathers..led to the formation in the Cape Colony..of numerous 'Ostrich-farms'. 1926 *Daily Colonist* (Victoria, B.C.) 18 July 21/5 The White and Gold Room at Buckingham Palace, in which ladies sit in rows before passing into the Throne Room to curtsy to Their Majesties, is irreverently referred to on court-nights by junior members of the household as 'the ostrich farm'. 1927 Chesterton *Coll. Poems* 180 Old Noah he had an ostrich farm and fowls on the largest scale. 1974 *Encycl. Brit. Micropædia* VII. 618/1 This demand [for plumes] led to the establishment of ostrich farms in South Africa, the southern U.S., Australia, and elsewhere. 1875 *S. Africa* 223 *Ostrich farmers, in domesticating the bird, have apparently a regard to moral training. *Ibid.* 220 It is difficult to say who was the first to begin *ostrich-farming at the Cape. 1902 *Chambers's Jrnl.* Jan. 53/2 His unconscious host, ..prosed on concerning himself chiefly with..the future of ostrich-farming. 1957 *Encycl. Brit.* XVI. 959/2 Ostrich farming is carried on in Cape Colony, Egypt, Algeria, the French Riviera, Southern U.S. and elsewhere. 1882 *Garden* 16 Sept. 258/3 The hardy Ferns are a grand feature, particularly the large groups of the *Ostrich Fern. 1634 S. R. *Noble Soldier* iv. i. in Bullen *O. Pl.* I. 307 *Estridge-like, To digest Iron and Steele. 1881 *Macm. Mag.* XLIV. 294/2 It is ostrich-like, it is suicidal, to ignore the fact of its disappearance. 1895 *Pop. Sci. Monthly* Apr. 761 Among the existing ostrichlike types we have the Apteryx. 1944 *Sci. Jrnl. R. Coll. Sci.* XIV. 64 Profound influences are continually at work causing changes in the general constitution of man, and no amount of ostrich-like behaviour will prevent their action. 1966 *Guardian* 30 July 3/5 Britian is more ostrichlike in its approach to the problem than America. 1976 *Times* 5 Apr. 3/2 It would be an ostrich-like attitude on the part of the executive if this chance was turned down. 1926–7 *Army & Navy Stores Catal.* 84/3 *Ostrich skin Cigar Case..each 8/6. 1971 P. Driscoll *White Lie Assignment* ii. 17 Transferring the cigarettes.. into an ostrich-skin case. 1976 J. McClure *Rogue Eagle* xiii. 222 He was loading his pipe from an ostrich-skin pouch. 1888 *Lady* 25 Oct. 378/2 A..very fashionable hat..with ribbon loops and *ostrich tips.

Hence **'ostrichism**, the policy of hiding the head like an ostrich; also in allusive and extended use.

1834 *Tait's Mag.* I. 59/1 The Marquis adopted the celebrated system of ostrichism, and hid his head. 1944 J. S. Huxley *On Living in Revolution* 3 The fact that a world war existed and the ostrichism of our reactions to it were most obvious in the case of Spain. 1945 R. Hargreaves *Enemy at Gate* 285 A departure into Maginot Line ostrichism which had ended..in the rigid chain of defence works being 'turned'. 1958 *New Statesman* 1 Mar. 260/2 Geoffrey Dawson's calculated ostrichism towards the Fascist dictators..during the Thirties. 1960 *Spectator* 15 July 106 A new wave of ostrichism in regard to defence is sweeping the country.

†**'ostrich²**, a corruption of ESTRICHE, eastern kingdom or country (q.v.). **ostrich board** = ESTRICHE *board*; **ostrich wool**, a kind of wool formerly imported from Eastern countries.

1449 *Will of W. Bruges* in *Wardr. Acc. Edw. IV* (1830) Gloss., I ordeyn that the ij chapelles..be closed wyth ostrich boarde, and clere storied. 1480 *Wardr. Acc. Edw. IV* (1830) 131 Cupborde of ostriche borde j. [1720 Strype *Stow's Surv.* (1754) II. v. xv. 326/2 The Estridge Wools, that is, the Wools imported from the East Countries, a coarser Sort, amounted not to two hundred Weight.] 1812 J. Smyth *Pract. of Customs* (1821) 311 Ostrich, or Estridge Wool is used as a substitute for Beaver in the manufacture of Hats. It is usually imported from Germany, the Levant, Italy, and other parts of the Mediterranean.

'ostrich-,feather. Also 5–7 **estrich-**.

1. A feather of an ostrich, *esp.* one of the long curly quill-feathers of the wings or tail used as a personal ornament or for decorative purposes. Also *fig.*

1460–7 [see OSTRICH 1 γ]. 1473 Warkw. *Chron.* 14 He.. wered ane estryche feder. ?c1475 *Sqr. lowe Degre* 226 Oystryche fethers of dyvers hewe. a1529 Skelton *Bowge of Court* 366 An eestryche fedder of a capons tayle He set.. vpon his hat alofte. 1629 L. Owen *Spec. Jesuit.* 61 Hauing brought with him a present of Parots and Estrich-feathers. a1771 Gray in *Corr.* (1843) 213 No one who had less than £100 a year..was to wear satin, damask, ostrich feathers. 1868–82 Cussans *Handbk. Heraldry* (ed. 3) ix. 134 The *Ostrich-feathers* of Edward, Prince of Wales, and the *Red* and *White Roses*..are examples of Badges familiar to every student of English History. 1932 D. Gascoyne *Roman Balcony* 12 The ostrich feathers Of the waves That flap against the shore. 1957 M. B. Picken *Fashion Dict.* 238/2 *Ostrich feathers*, wing and tail feathers from an ostrich. Often several feathers are carefully glued together as one to give abundant appearance. Dyed in all colors and beautifully curled. 1977 *Listener* 15 Dec. 794/1 Before I graduated to ostrich feathers..I had absorbed..[a] vital principle: that diplomatic privilege exists mainly not to be made use of.

Comb. 1530 Palsgr. 250/1 Ostrydge fether sellar. 1813 *Examiner* 11 Jan. 22/1 S. Butler,..ostrich-feather-manufacturer. 1884 *List of Subscribers* (London & Globe Telephone Co.) Henry, C. S. & Co...Ostrich Feather Merchants, 12, Jewin Crescent. 1908 *Westm. Gaz.* 27 June 13/1 This suit was worn with a hat and ostrich-feather ruffle of a very charming soft grey tone. 1966 J. Laver *Victoriana* 131 Towards the end of the [19th] century large ostrich feather fans became fashionable.

†**2.** ? A marking or brand on a horse, resembling a feather of an ostrich. *Obs.*

1672 *Lond. Gaz.* No. 657/4 A Bay Mare about six years old,..with an Estrich Feather on the near side, and a black List down the Buttock. 1685 *Ibid.* No. 2524/4 A bright Bay Horse with..three Estery Feathers, one at his breast, and one at each side of his Neck.

ostrich-plume. [See PLUME.]

1. An ostrich-feather, or a bunch of two or three feathers.

[1436 in *Exch. Rolls Scotl.* IV. 679 In ornamento plumarum de hostriche.] 1637 Heywood *Dial.* xix. (1874) VI. 263 In my light chariot..deckt with Estrich plumes. c1820 S. Rogers *Italy, Brides of Venice* 29 A fan, that gently waved, of ostrich-plumes. 1865 J. H. Ingraham *Pillar of Fire* (1872) 321 White horses..richly caparisoned, and with ostrich-plumes nodding on their heads.

2. a. The plumularian hydroid *Aglaophenia struthionides*. **b.** *attrib.* Applied to a variety of Chrysanthemum.

1891 *Daily News* 19 Oct. 3/5 A curious variety of chrysanthemum... American growers have described it as the ostrich plume variety. 1893 *Westm. Gaz.* 16 Oct. 7/1 Ostrich-plume chrysanthemum, which does not often come to perfection in this climate.

Hence **ostrich-plumed** *a.*, decked with ostrich-plumes.

Mod. Newspr. Large white ostrich-plumed hats.

ostridge, -ige, ostridger, -iger, obs. ff. OSTRICH, OSTREGER.

†**ostridge-keeper.** *Obs.* A keeper of goshawks, an OSTREGER.

1653 Urquhart *Rabelais* i. lv, Before them stood the falconrie, managed by Ostridge-keepers and Falconers.

ostrie, ostringer: see HOSTRY, OSTREGER.

†**o'striferous,** *a.* *Obs.* [f. L. *ostrifer* (? for **ostreifer*, f. *ostrea* oyster): see -FEROUS.]

1656 Blount *Glossogr.*, *Ostriferous*, that beareth, or brings forth Oisters.

ostrobogulous (ɒstrəʊ'bɒgjʊləs). *slang.* [Etym. obscure; see quot. 1973.] A word associated with the writer Victor B. Neuburg (1883–1940), used with various shades of meaning to describe the bizarre, unusual, or interesting (see quots.). Hence **ostro'bogulatory** *a.*; **ostrobogu'lation, ostrobogu'losity,** *sbs.*

1951 A. Calder-Marshall *Magic of My Youth* i. 31 'Ostrobogulous' was Vickybird's favourite word. It stood for anything from the bawdy to the slightly off-colour. Any *double entendre* that might otherwise have escaped his audience was prefaced by, 'if you will pardon the ostrobogulosity.' 1952 A. Graves *Ostrobogulous Pigs* 7 Once upon a time there were..five ostrobogulous skipperty flipperty filthy grubby muddy little pigs. *Ibid.* 10, I can no longer endure this ostrobogulatory behaviour. *Ibid.* 11 'I can no longer endure the odorous and objectionable ostrobogulations of those creatures,' said Angelina Boghurst-Fisher. 1963 *Sunday Times* 29 Dec. 19/2 (*heading*), An ostrobogulous year for the toy men. *Ibid.* 19/6 Minnie King works full time for Ostrobogulous—which is a word, they say, used by children and means 'mischievous but gorgeous'. 1965 J. O. Fuller *Magical Dilemma V. Neuburg* i. iv. 58 Some of the entries were not printed because they were ostrobogulous. This was a wonderful word of Vicky's. It was used in the place of indecent or pornographic, and had the advantage..that it implied no moral attitude. *Ibid.* 59 He would speak of an ostrobogulous tale. .. He took Morton's opinion as ostrobogulosity. 1968 *Times Lit. Suppl.* 24 Oct. 1196/3 There has been no developing tradition of the ribald, raw and ostrobogulous (to use the word Victor Neuburg applied to this work) merely because there have been no similar collections. 1972 *Ibid.* 30 June 757/4 His career, fabulous, prestigious, sordid, sinister, and in the word of Victor Neuburg ostrobogulous. 1973 *Ibid.* 27 July 871/2 It was sick, dirty, or more precisely, 'ostrobogulous', which according to Victor Neuburg.. meant etymologically full of (Latin, *ulus*) rich (Greek, *ostro*) dirt (schoolboy, *bog*).

‖**ostrog** (ɒ'strɒg). [Russ. *ostróg* stockade, blockhouse, f. *o* = *ob* about + *sterech'* to guard.] A house or village in Siberia, surrounded by a palisade or wall, and serving as a fort or prison.

1764 *Char.* in *Ann. Reg.* 5/2 Under the name of Ostrog, is understood every habitation consisting of one or more huts, all surrounded by an earthen wall or palisado... The Camchatcans live in these huts all the winter. 1790 *Cook's Voy.* VI. 2191 The principal merchants..reside either at Bolcheretsk, or the Nishnei ostrog. 1799 W. Tooke *View Russian Emp.* I. 356. 1833 R. Pinkerton *Russia* 215 From the ostrog we proceeded to the town hospital.

Ostrogoth ('ɒstrəʊgɒθ). [f. late L. *Ostrogothi* pl., f. OHG., OS. *ōstar* eastward, in the east:—OTeut. **aust(a)r*: see GOTH.] **a.** An East Goth; a name given to the division of the Teutonic race of the Goths which towards the end of the 5th c. conquered Italy, and in 493, under Theodoric, established a kingdom which continued till 555.

1605 J. Sylvester tr. *Du Bartas's Devine Weekes* 456 Normans, Allains, Ostrogothes. 1647–8 Cotterell *Davila's Hist. Fr.* (1678) 3 Famous incursions of the Ostrogoths. 1841 W. Spalding *Italy & It. Isl.* II. 54 Four dynasties which successively ruled that country,—Odoacer's, the East-Goths or Ostrogoths, the Lombards, and the Franks.

b. (See quot.)

a1859 Whewell *Germ. Archit.* Pref., Some traced the pointed arch to the countries of the East; and these persons were, by their brother antiquaries, playfully termed Ostrogoths.

c. as *adj.* = OSTROGOTHIC *a.*

1920 H. G. Wells *Outl. Hist.* 350/1 The adventurous wanderings that ended at last in the Ostrogoth Kingdom in Italy. 1954 Arnold-Baker & Dent *Everyman's Dict. Dates* 275/1 Theodoric..became a figure of Germanic legend, and founded an Ostrogoth kingdom in Italy *c.* 500.

Hence **Ostro'gothian, Ostro'gothic** *adjs.*

1684 H. More *Answer* 42 The fourth [trumpet] is..under the seventh Head, viz. The Ostrogothian Kings. 1815 *Sporting Mag.* XLVI. 56 This coarse, dark, ostrogothic piece of mosaic-painting.

ostry, -ye, obs. variants of HOSTRY.

ostrycch, erron. for OSTOUR, goshawk, from association of OSTREGER with *ostridge*, OSTRICH: cf. OSTRIDGE-KEEPER.

c **1400** MAUNDEV. (1839) xxii. 238 Bryddes, as Ostrycches [F. *oustours*], Gerfacouns, Sparehaukes.

Ostwald (ˈɒstwəld). The name of Wilhelm *Ostwald* (1853–1932), Russian chemist, used *attrib.* and in the possessive to denote apparatus invented and principles enunciated by him, as **Ostwald('s) dilution law**, the law that for dilute solutions of a binary electrolyte the square of the degree of dissociation of the solute, multiplied by its concentration, and divided by one minus the degree of dissociation, is a constant for the solute; **Ostwald pycnometer**, a pycnometer in the form of a bulb joined at the top to a horizontal capillary tube and at the bottom to a U-tube bearing a graduation at the level of the capillary; **Ostwald('s) viscometer**, an instrument in which the viscosity of a liquid is determined by the time taken for a measured volume to pass through a capillary bore in a U-tube.

[**1899** J. WALKER *Introd. Physical Chem.* xxi. 227 Certain empirical relations have.. been found connecting the degree of dissociation and the dilution, and these have a form similar to that of Ostwald's dilution formula.] **1902** H. C. JONES *Elem. Physical Chem.* vii. 354 (*heading*) Testing the Ostwald dilution law. **1930** C. W. DAVIES *Conductivity of Solutions* i. 12 Ostwald's dilution law breaks down completely when it is applied to solutions of the common salts. **1973** A. W. ADAMSON *Textbk. Physical Chem.* xii. 538 Weak electrolytes obey the Ostwald dilution law well, and their behavior is thus determined primarily by a dissociation equilibrium. **1910** A. EWELL *Text-bk. Physical Chem.* 25 An Ostwald pyknometer is very convenient as a weighing pipette. **1962** PERRY & KOENIG in A. Pirie *Lens Metabolism Rel. Cataract* 306 For viscosity measurements, Ostwald viscometers were used to measure flow rates at 25°C. Densities were measured with Ostwald pycnometers. **1924** *Abstr. Bacteriol.* VIII. 2 Direct inoculation of the sterilized gelatin culture media in Ostwald's viscometer was tried for a period of 3 months. **1967** MARGERISON & EAST *Introd. Polymer Chem.* ii. 103 The usual method employed to measure the solution and solvent viscosities utilizes an Ostwald viscometer.

Ostyak (ˈɒstɪ,æk). Also **Ostiac, Ostiack, Ostiak,** etc. [Russ. *ostyák.*] **a.** (A member of) a Finno-Ugric people, also called *Khantý*, living in the Ob River basin in Western Siberia. **b.** The language of this people, belonging to the OB-UGRIAN group. Also *attrib.* or as *adj.*

1722 tr. *Muller's Manners & Customs of Ostiaks* in tr. *F. C. Weber's Present State of Russia* II. 56 The Ostiacks and Samoieds often venture over those high Rocks into the Country, where they kill Elks and Rain-Deer. **1757** J. DYER *Fleece* IV. 143 Land of the lazy Ostiacs, thin dispers'd. **1841** *Penny Cycl.* XXI. 467/1 South of the Samoyedes are the Ostiaks, who occupy both banks of the river Obi. **1859** G. W. DASENT *Pop. Tales from Norse* p. lxvii, The Ostjaks, a tribe akin to the Lapps. **1870** J. LUBBOCK *Origin of Civilisation* iii. 96 The Ostiaks regard it as a crime to marry a woman of the same family or even of the same name. **1880** A. H. SAYCE *Introd. Sci. of Lang.* II. viii. 204 It is difficult .. to distinguish the Ostiak forms .. from the persons of the Sanskrit verb. **1889** T. DUKA *Essay Ugor Lang.* 32 Klaproth .. makes mention of five Finn dialects, but describes .. the Ostjak around the river Ob, and the Magyar. **1911** J. G. FRAZER *Golden Bough: Magic Art* (ed. 3) II. ix. 11 The Ostyaks and Woguls, two peoples of the Finnish-Ugrian stock in Siberia. **1933**, etc. [see OB-UGRIAN]. **1938** *N. & Q.* 23 Apr. 291/1 The Ostyaks of the Tobolsk region have a spirit of death whom they call *xeina.* **1944** [see NENETS]. **1959** *Chambers's Encycl.* XI. 432/2 The Uralics, so termed by Bunak, are perhaps best represented by the western Siberian Voguls and Khuntu or Ostyaks, between the Urals and the Ob basin, in reality a single people who call themselves 'Mansi'. **1966** T. BURROW *Sanskrit Lang.* (ed. 2) 23 Vogul and Ostyak are now found to the East of the Urals, but are considered to have moved there from the West. **1971** [see MORDVIN]. **1972** W. B. LOCKWOOD *Panorama Indo-European Lang.* 152 East of the Zyryene-speaking area, in Siberia, lie Ostyak and Vogul which with Hungarian form the Ugric division of Uralic. **1974** T. P. WHITNEY tr. *Solzhenitsyn's Gulag Archipel.* I. I. i. 6 From Karger they took his archive of the Yenisei Ostyaks. **1975** G. F. CUSHING tr. *Hajdu's Finno-Ugrian Lang. & Peoples* iii. 123 Anthropologically the Voguls and Ostyaks .. are classed by anthropologists as Europo-Sibirid or Uralic.

ostylle, obs. form of HOSTEL.

ostyre, obs. variant of OYSTER *sb.*

‖**osu** (ˈɒsuː). *W. Afr.* [Igbo.] An outcast, an 'untouchable'.

1958 C. ACHEBE *Things fall Apart* xviii. 140 These outcasts, or *osu*, seeing that the new religion welcomed twins and such abominations, thought that it was possible that they would also be received. **1960** —— *No Longer at Ease* vii. 71 'I am an *osu*,' she wept... 'So you see we cannot get married,' she said, quite firmly, almost gaily—a terrible kind of gaiety. *Ibid.* 75 Obi knew better than anyone else that his family would violently oppose the idea of marrying an *osu*. *Ibid.* xiv. 133 Our fathers in their darkness and ignorance called an innocent man an *osu*, a thing given to idols, and thereafter he became an outcast, and his children, and his children's children for ever. *Ibid.* 134 Obi repeated his points again. What made an *osu* different from other men and women? Nothing but the ignorance of their forefathers. **1960** *Spectator* 21 Oct. 616 He falls in love with Clara, an *osu* or 'untouchable'. **1973** *Black World* June 39/2 This.. explains the violent objection of the clansmen to Obi marrying an *osu* (a cult-slave; for this reason ostracized from the normal life of the village).

osul, osyll, obs. ff. OUZEL.

Oswego (ɒzˈwiːgəʊ). [The name of a river and a town in the northern part of the state of New York.] **1. a.** = *Oswego bass.*

1857 [see LUNGE *sb.*[3]].

b. A proprietary name for a type of cornflour.

1881 J. T. GILL *Compl. Bread, Cake & Cracker Baker* I. v. 75 Maizena .. is maize deprived of all its albuminoid or flesh-forming constituents .. and is, therefore, simply pure starch... Corn flour and Oswego are only other names for the same substance. **1907** *Official Gaz.* (U.S. Patent Office) 29 Jan. 1758/2 National Starch Co., Jersey City, N.J. and Oswego, N.Y. Filed Dec. 17, 1906. Used ten years. Oswego. Particular description of goods.—Corn-starch. **1911** *Encycl. Brit.* XVII. 449/1 When deprived of the gluten it [*sc.* maize] constitutes oswego, maizena or corn flour.

c. = *Oswego biscuit.*

c **1900** in A. Davis *Package & Print* (1967) (*frontispiece*) Peek, Frean & Co. Biscuits. Oswego. **1907** *Yesterday's Shopping* (1969) 8 Biscuits .. Oswego ..

2. *attrib.* **Oswego bass** = *large-mouth* (*bass*) s.v. LARGE *a.* 15 a; **Oswego biscuit, cake**, a biscuit or cake made with **Oswego flour** (= sense 1 b); **Oswego tea**, a herbaceous perennial plant, *Monarda didyma*, belonging to the family Labiatæ and native to eastern North America; its leaves were formerly used to make a medicinal tea.

1758 C. REA *Jrnl.* 20 July in *Essex Inst. Hist. Coll.* (1881) XVIII. 112 The Lake affords plenty of a Fish call'd Oswego Bass. **1840** J. F. COOPER *Pathfinder* I. ix. 130 Even the Major himself.. will sometimes swear that an oat-meal cake is better fare than the Oswego bass. **1884** [see *large-mouth* (*bass*)]. **1965** A. J. MCCLANE *Standard Fishing Encycl.* 473/1 The largemouth bass is regionally known as green bass, green trout, Oswego bass, and black bass. **1936** CHESTERTON *Autobiogr.* 324 Do let me offer you an oswego biscuit. **1963** C. MACKENZIE *My Life & Times* II. 94 However well Huntley and Palmer may have made Oswego and Osborne biscuits .. they could not reproduce the authentic flavour of real Petit Beurres. **1907** M. I. RIVERS *Tips for Tea* vii. 50 Oswego cakes... Cream the butter and sugar together until they are white; add the eggs one at a time, and stir in lightly the oswego. **1949** A. R. DANIEL *Baker's Dict.* Oswego flour. A particular type of flour obtained from maize, but not just pure cornflour. **1752** P. MILLER *Gardeners Dict.* (ed. 6) s.v. *Monarda*, The inhabitants drink an infusion of this Herb as Tea, and call it Ozweega Tea. **1759** —— (ed. 7) s.v. *Monarda*, It [*sc.* Monarda with Flowers collected in Heads] is commonly called Oswego Tea, by which title it was brought to England. **1760** [see TEA *sb.* 6]. **1789** [see MONARDA]. **1850** S. F. COOPER *Rural Hours* 117 Humming-birds .. are partial to the bee larkspur also, with the wild bergamot or Oswego tea. **1947** *Nat. Geogr. Mag.* July 62/1 Among the many useful plants they found .. were two of this same Mint Family, Oswego Tea (*Monarda didyma*), and Wild Bergamot (*Monarda fistulosa*). **1954** C. HYLANDER *Macmillan Wild Flower Bk.* 344 Oswego Tea, also known as Bee-balm, has a natural range from New York to Michigan ..; it is frequently cultivated as an ornamental. **1970** B. MILES *Bluebells & Bittersweet* vii. 113/3 *M*[*onarda*] *didyma* (Oswego-tea) is usually red, raising round heads of lipped flowers 4 feet in midsummer.

osyer, obs. f. OSIER.

‖**Osyris** (ˈɒsɪrɪs). *Bot.* [mod.L., a. Gr. ὄσυρις, a plant identified variously with *Osyris alba*, *Linaria vulgaris*, etc.] A genus of shrubs (N.O. *Santalaceæ*), of which the European species *O. alba* is a broom-like plant with narrow dry leaves, small perigynous flowers, and roundish drupes.

1562 TURNER *Herbal* II. 73 The brothe of Osyris dronken is good agaynst ye iaundes or guel sought.

osyt, obs. form of *used*: see USE *v.*

oszer, oszil, obs. forms of OSIER, OUZEL.

-ot, *suffix*[1], repr. F. *-ot*, orig. dim., but the diminutive force is often lost, as in *ballot*, *chariot*, *galliot*, *loriot*, *parrot*, etc. It is not a living suffix in Eng.

-ot, *suffix*[2], repr. F. *-ote*, L. *-ōta*, Gr. -ώτης, expressing nativity, as Ἠπειρώτης Epirot, native of Epirus, in which use it is often represented by -OTE. It occurs also in a few other sbs. of Gr. origin, as *helot*, *idiot*, *patriot*, *zealot*.

otacoustic (əʊtəˈkuːstɪk, -əˈkaʊstɪk), *a.* and *sb. rare.* [f. Gr. οὖς, ὠτ- ear + ἀκουστικ-ός ACOUSTIC: cf. Gr. ὠτακουστής: see OTACUST.]

A. *adj.* Used to assist the sense of hearing.

1775 in ASH. **1828** WEBSTER s.v., Otacoustic instrument.

B. *sb.* An instrument to assist hearing, as an ear-trumpet.

a **1643** LD. FALKLAND, etc. *Infallibility* (1646) 79 Matters of fact, which we see or heare not with our own eyes or eares, but as with perspectives and otacoustickes. **1701** GREW *Cosm. Sacra* I. v. §6 A Hare, which is very quick of hearing .. is supplied with a Bony Tube; which as a natural Otacoustick is so directed backward as to receive the smallest and most distant Sound that comes behind her.

So **otaˈcoustical** *a.*

1802 in *Spir. Pub. Jrnls.* VI. 348 With a few of my otacoustical drops [I] have so entirely recovered him.

‖**otaˈcousticon.** [mod.Lat., f. as prec.] = prec. B.

1615 TOMKIS *Albumazar* I. iii, O let me see this wond'rous instrument. *Ron.* Sir, this is cal'd an *Otacousticon.* **1621** BURTON *Anat. Mel.* II. ii. IV. (1676) 179/1 Otocousticons some speak of to intend hearing, as the other do sight. **1668** PEPYS *Diary* 2 Apr., I did try the use of the Otacousti[c]on, which was only a great glass bottle broke at the bottom, putting the neck to my eare; and there I did plainly hear the dashing of the oares of the boats in the Thames. **1715** tr. *Pancirollus' Rerum Mem.* II. App. 443 Several Kinds of Otacousticons, or Instruments to improve the Sense of Hearing.

†**ˈotacust.** *Obs.* [ad. late L. *ōtacūstēs*, a. Gr. ὠτακουστής listener, spy, f. οὖς, ὠτ- ear + ἀκουστής listener.] A listener, an eavesdropper; a spy.

1632 HOLLAND *Cyrupædia* 118 Who .. should as Otacusts (or priuy Escourts) listen and advertise him of all occurrents. *a* **1693** URQUHART *Rabelais* III. Prol., Something .. which the Persians of old esteemed more of in all their Otacusts.

Otaheitean (əʊtəˈhiːtɪən), *a.* and *sb. Obs.* Also **Otahitean, Otaheite, Otaheitan.** [f. *Otaheite* early name of the Pacific island of Tahiti.]

= TAHITIAN *a.* and *sb.*

Cf. OTAHEITE APPLE.

1773 W. WALES *Jrnl.* 31 Aug. in Cook *Jrnls.* (1961) II. 796 With regard to the Personal Beauties of the Otahitean Ladies, I believe it would be most prudent to remain entirely silent. **1792** W. BLIGH *Voy. to South Sea* vi. 81 Among people so free from ostentation as the Otaheiteans .. the strictness with which the punctilios of rank are observed, is surprising. *Ibid.* xii. 147 In a small vocabulary, that I made .. only four words, out of twenty-four, differed from the Otaheite. **1793** F. BURNEY *Jrnl.* 3 May (1972) II. 104, I saw nothing of this *Tio*:—I accept your otaheité epithet, & like it much. **1799** *Sporting Mag.* XIV. 203/1 Our Otaheitean girl, who was tolerably fair, and had a comely person. **1817** T. COGAN *Ethical Questions* v. 233 The good-natured Otaheite *feels* it to be an obligation of hospitality, to present his wife or daughter to a stranger. **1819** SHELLEY *Let.* 3 Nov. (1964) II. 140 A North American Indian, or an Otaheitan. **1851** *Illustr. Catal. Gt. Exhib.* IV. 980/1 All the above-mentioned sugars are the produce of the Otaheite or Tahiti cane. **1861** R. BENTLEY *Man. Bot.* 674 The starch known as Tacca starch, Tahiti Arrow-root, or Otaheite Salep.

Otaˈheite apple. [Named after *Otaheite*, or *Tahiti*, one of the Society Islands in Polynesia.] The fruit of *Spondias dulcis*, a native of Java, the Moluccas, and the Society Islands; it is of a golden yellow colour, the rind having a taste like turpentine, and the pulp the flavour of pine-apple.

1858 HOGG *Veg. Kingd.* 247. **1887** *Standard* 16 Sept. 5/3 The carambola and the Otaheite apple.

otake, obs. corrupt f. OUT-TAKE, except.

otalgia (əʊˈtældʒɪə). Also **oˈtalgy.** [a. Gr. ὠταλγία ear-ache, f. οὖς, ὠτ- ear + ἄλγος pain.] Ear-ache; neuralgic pain in the ear.

1657 *Physical Dict.*, Otalgia, pain in the ears. **1727–41** CHAMBERS *Cycl.* s.v., The otalgia usually arises from an inflammation. **1836** SMART, Otalgy. **1874** ROOSA *Dis. Ear* (ed. 2) 511 The subject of otalgia belongs, strictly speaking, to the middle ear.

Hence **oˈtalgic** *a.*, of or pertaining to ear-ache; *sb.* a remedial agent for ear-ache.

1737 BRACKEN *Farriery Impr.* (1757) II. 263 Opiates are Ophthalmics, as well as Odontalgics, Otalgics, &c. **1842** DUNGLISON *Med. Lex.*, Otalgic [adj.].

otamy, obs. corrupt form of ATOMY.

otary (ˈəʊtərɪ). [ad. mod.L. *ōtaria*, f. Gr. οὖς, ὠτ- ear: cf. Gr. ὠταρός large-eared.] An eared seal; a member of the *Otariidæ*, a family of pinnipeds having small but perceptible external ears, which includes the fur seals and sea-lions.

1847 in WEBSTER. **1880** J. A. ALLEN *N. Amer. Pinnipeds* 225 The largest species of the Otaries .. are Hair Seals, while the smallest .. are Fur Seals.

Hence **oˈtarian, ˈotarine** *adjs.*, of or pertaining to otaries or eared seals; **oˈtariid**, a member of the family *Otariidæ* (see above); **oˈtarioid** *a.*, resembling or akin to the otaries in form or structure.

1880 J. A. ALLEN *N. Amer. Pinnipeds* 2 The walruses are really little more than thick, clumsy, obese forms of the Otarian type, with the canines enormously developed... The walruses are merely elephantine Otariids.

†**otas**, obs. f. *octaves*: see OCTAVE 1 a.

c **1450** *St. Cuthbert* (Surtees) 7862 Sakird in saint Iohn otas.

otavite (əʊˈtɑːvaɪt). *Min.* [ad. G. *otavit* (O. Schneider 1906, in *Centralbl. f. Mineral., Geol. und Paläont.* 389), f. *Otavi*, name of a town in northern South West Africa: see -ITE[1].] Naturally occurring cadmium carbonate, $CdCO_3$, occurring as crusts of minute rhombohedral crystals usu. white or greyish white in colour.

1906 *Jrnl. Chem. Soc.* XC. II. 620 A new mineral which is named otavite, after the locality. **1943** *Mineral. Abstr.* VIII.

366 Otavite, previously described as a basic carbonate of cadmium from Tsumeb, South-West Africa, forms thin crusts of minute rhombohedra often in parallel growth on smithsonite. X-ray powder photographs agree with Zachariasen's (1928) determination for artificial $CdCO_3$. **1967** *Soviet Physics: Crystallogr.* XII. 417 Artificial otavite, $CdCo_3$, crystals were obtained, which were activated by Co^{+2} so that EPR spectra of the magnetic Co^{+2} ion were observed at varying orientations of the external magnetic field at 4·2°K.

ote, ote-mele, -meel, obs. ff. OAT, OATMEAL.

ote, obs. corrupt form of *hote*, HIGHT *v.*[1]

ote, obs. corruption of *wot* from WIT *v.*, to know, esp. in phrase ***God ote!*** God wot!

-ote, *suffix*, another form of -OT[2], repr. ultimately Gr. *-ώτης*, indicating nativity, and forming the names of inhabitants of places in or near Greece; e.g. *Candiote* (*-ot*), from Candia, *Cypriote* (*-ot*), from Cyprus, *Sciote*, *Suliote*, etc.

otem: see TOTEM.

otemoste, obs. var. UTMOST.

oten, corrupt f. *hoten*, pa. pple. of HIGHT *v.*[1]; obs. f. OATEN.

†**otenchyte.** *Obs.* [ad. L. *ōtenchyta*, ad. Gr. *ὠτεγχύτης*, f. *ὠτ-* ear + *ἐγχύτης*, f. *ἐγχέ-ειν* to pour in. In mod.F. *otenchyte*.] An instrument for injecting liquid into the ears.

1601 HOLLAND *Pliny* II. 369 To infuse the said liquour warme into the eare by a pipe or instrument called an Otenchyte. *Ibid.*, Expl. Words of Art, *Otenchyte*, an instrument, deuised for to infuse or poure some medicinable liquor into the eares.

oter(e, oth, othe, obs. ff. OTTER, OATH.

‖**othæmatoma** (əʊθiːməˈtəʊmə). [mod.L., f. Gr. *οὖς, ὠτ-* ear + HÆMATOMA.] Hæmatoma or vascular tumour of the ear.

1874 ROOSA *Dis. Ear* (ed. 2) 107 Othæmatoma, hæmatoma auris, or vascular tumor of the auricle. **1877** BURNETT *Ear* 247 Othæmatoma, or blood-tumor of the ear, is characterized by congestion and heat in the auricle.

Hence **othæmaˈtomatous** *a.*

1878 T. BRYANT *Pract. Surg.* I. 388 The othæmatomatous requires special mention.

otham, othem: see ODAM *Obs.*, son-in-law.

othe, oþe, ME. f. *on the*: see O *prep.*[1] b.

othenk, var. OFTHINK *Obs.*, to repent.

Hence †**oˈthenking,** *vbl. sb.*, sorrow, regret, repentance.

1382 WYCLIF *Judg.* xxi. 15 And al Yrael greetli sorowide, and dide othenkynge vpon the slauȝter. —— *Jer.* xviii. 10 Othinking Y shal do [1388 Y schal do penaunce] up on the good that Y spac, that Y shulde do to it.

otheoscope (ˈəʊθiːəʊskəʊp). [f. Gr. *ὠθεῖν* to push + *-σκοπος* observing, -SCOPE.] A modification of the radiometer, devised by Sir W. Crookes, in which the black or driving surface is stationary, while the cooling surface is movable.

1877 CROOKES in *Proc. Roy. Soc.* No. 180.

other (ˈʌðə(r)), *adj. pron.* (*sb.*) Forms: 1 **óðer, óþer,** 2–5 **oþer,** *inflected* **oþre,** 4– **other.** Also 3 *Orm.* **oþerr,** 3–4 **oþur, -eir, -air, -ier, -ir, -ere, -ure,** (5 **-yr, -ire**), 4 **oiþer, ooþer,** 4–5 **othur, -yr, -ere, -ar,** 4–6 **othir, oother, -ir,** 5 **othre,** 5–7 **oyer** (= *oþer*), 6 **wother;** *Sc.* 4 **uthyre, wthir(e, -yre, wyther, ouþer,** 4–6 **uthir,** 4–7 **uther, -ere,** 6 **vyer, -ir** (= *uþer, -ir*), 7 **wther,** 8– **ither.** Also 3 *Orm.* **oderr,** 4–6 **oder, -ir, -ur, -yr,** 5 **woder, -ur,** 6 *Sc.* **uder, -ir,** 6– *north.* **udder.** [Com. Teut.: OE. *óþer, óðer* = OFris. *ôther* (*oder, ander*), OS. *ôðar, âðar, andar*, (MLG., MDu., LG., Du. *ander*), OHG. *ander* (MHG., Ger. *ander*), ON. *annar-*, Goth. *anþar* = Skr. *ántara-s*, Lith. *àntras*, and prob. L. *alter*:—OAryan **anteros*; a word formed with the usual comparative suffix of adjs., in Skr. *-tara-s*, Gr. *-τερο-ς*, L. *-ter*, Eng. *-ther*, in *whether*, etc. The same root appears in Skr. *an-yá-s* other, different: cf. L. *al-ius, al-ter*.]

A. *adj.*

†**1. a.** One of the two, the one (of two); L. *alter*. *Obs.*

(This is an OTeut. sense of the word, found also with OS. *ôðar* and ON. *annar-*. The suggestion that in this sense OE. *óðer* was a form of *áwðer, áðer*, ME. OUTHER, 'either', 'one or other', is erroneous: there is no ground for assuming that OE. had any *óðer* except that which was identical with Goth. *anþar*, ON. *annar-*.)

*c*893 K. ÆLFRED *Oros.* III. vii. §3 Him..wearþ oþer eaȝe mid anre flan ut ascoten. *Ibid.* IV. i. §6 Þær wearð Pirrus wund on oþran earme. *a*900 *O.E. Martyrol.* 26 June 106 An stræl..hine ȝewundode on his oðer ȝewenge. **1590** SPENSER *F.Q.* II. iv. 4 Her other leg was lame. **1596** *Ibid.* v. xii. 36 A distaffe in her other hand she had.

(The quots. from Spenser are evidently archaic, and it is possible that in them *other* means 'left' like Germ. *ander*.)

†**b.** ***other..other***: the one..the other (L. *alter..alter*..); one..another (L. *alius..alius*..). Only in OE.

*c*897 K. ÆLFRED *Gregory's Past.* xl. 291 Oðer hira wæs haten Timotheus, oðer Titus. *a*900 *Laws of Ælfred* Introd. c. 43 Ne dem þu oðerne dom þam weleȝan, oðerne þam eorman, ne oðerne þam liofran, and oðerne þam laðran ne dem þu. *c*900 tr. *Bæda's Hist.* II. x. (1890) 136 Cume þurh oþre duru in, ðurh oþre ut ȝewite.

2. a. That one of two which remains after one is taken, defined, or specified; the remaining (person, thing, or group) of two; later, also, of three or more. Usually prec. by *the* or an equivalent demonstrative or possessive word (e.g. his other foot, the man's other name or names); but in OE. *óþer* alone could have this sense.

on the other hand: see HAND *sb.* 32 i.

*c*893 K. ÆLFRED *Oros.* Contents IV. vii, Hu Gallie wunnon on Romane, & Pene on oþre healfe. *Ibid.* IV. vi. §2 Se oðer consul ȝehierde Diulius. *c*900 *Ags. Ps.* (Th.) xlix. 21 Betwuh þe and þinre modor suna oðrum. *c*1175 *Lamb. Hom.* 43 He wes an biscop on eoðre liue. *a*1300 *Cursor M.* 10679 (Cott.) On oþer side he was dredand To bring a custom neu on hand. *a*1425 *Ibid.* 3309 (Trin.) Þis oþere mon myȝte not blin To biholde þis fair maydin. **1462** *Coventry Constitutions* in Ellacombe *Bells of Ch.* ix. (1872) 469 Ye todur dekyn [shall have] ye wodur alffe. *a*1584 MONTGOMERIE *Cherrie & Slae* 44 The turtle, on the vther syde, Na plesure had to play. **1605** SHAKS. *Lear* IV. ii. 81 But (O poore Glouster) Lost he his other eye? **1615** SIR W. MURE *Misc. Poems* xiv. 2 His corps doth heir duell, Bot qr be his oyer halfe no man can tell. **1711** ADDISON *Spect.* No. 56 ¶2 To the great Repository of Souls, or, as we call it here, to the other World. **1724** DE FOE *Mem. Cavalier* I. 48, I was on the other Side the Elbe. **1855** MACAULAY *Hist. Eng.* xii. III. 204 The other member for the county of Dublin was Colonel Patrick Sarsfield.

b. ***every other***, every second, every alternate.

1480 CAXTON *Chron. Eng.* cxlv. 124 For whiche raunsoune to be payed eche other chalyce of englond was molte and made in to moneye. **1588** GREENE *Perimedes* 21 Spending euery other day in such sporte. **1607** TOPSELL *Four-f. Beasts* (1658) 309 Every other day cleanse both the wounds and rols. **1712–13** SWIFT *Let. to Mrs. Dingley* 25 Jan., We now resolve to..have a committee every other week. **1877** MRS. OLIPHANT *Makers Flor.* Introd. 13 Every other year there was a revolution.

c. ***the other half***: (*a*) the other half of the world; people of a different class or those enjoying a different (usu. more affluent) way of life, *spec.* in phr. ***how the other half live***(*s*); (*b*) orig. *Naval slang*: a second drink; a drink bought in return for another.

(*a*) [**1532** RABELAIS *Pantagruel* (1547) II. xxxi. 206 La moitié du monde ne sçayt comment l'aultre vit. **1607** J. HALL *Holy Observations* xvii. 26 One halfe of the world knowes not how the other liues.] **1640** G. HERBERT *Outlandish Proverbs* No. 907, in *Witts Recreations* sig. D7v Halfe the world knowes not how the other halfe lies [*sic*]. **1830** MARRYAT *King's Own* I. x. 141 It is an old proverb that 'one half the world do not know *how* the other half live.' Add to it, nor *where* they live. **1890** J. A. RIIS *How Other Half Lives* 1 Long ago it was said that 'one half of the world does not know how the other half lives'. *Ibid.* 3 The sufferings and sins of the 'other half'..are but..a just punishment upon the community that gave it no other choice. **1945** N. L. MCCLUNG *Stream runs Fast* xiii. 106 We were only amateurs but we did find out a few things about how the 'other half' lived. **1965** E. O'BRIEN *Aug. is Wicked Month* xiii. 141 'Why not, see how the other half live...' she said. .. They would have the pool and servants to wait on them. **1968** J. SANGSTER *Touchfeather* xiii. 140 He said if I was ever in Los Angeles to look him up. Glad I did. Talk about how the other half lives! **1970** 'D. SHANNON' *Unexpected Death* (1971) ix. 141 'My God,' said Higgins. 'How the other half lives.' **1975** *Times* 15 Jan. 15/4 In the interests of national unity, may I support your plea to the other half (and if they do not know they are in it, that is half the trouble) to accept that the shocking conditions of the London comprehensives as reported by you are really good for their children, and for society.

(*b*) **1922** W. S. MAUGHAM *On Chinese Screen* lii. 211 No sooner was your glass empty than he was prompt with the China phrase: 'Ready for the other half?' **1931** C. LITHGOW *Simple Sailor* xv. 184 You won't have the other half? Sure? **1936** 'G. ORWELL' *Keep Aspidistra Flying* v. 117 Drink up! .. It's time we had the other half of that. **1965** R. JEFFRIES *Dead against Lawyers* vii. 69 You'll have the other half, Inspector? Two whiskies under the belt are better than one. **1966** A. PRIOR *Operators* ii. 16 'The other half please, George.' 'Yessir, Mr. Barclay.'.. The barman turned to him. **1975** E. BERCKMAN *Indecent Exposure* viii. 101 'Have to be shoving off now, sorry—.' 'The other half,' Dennison objected. 'What were you drinking, whisky—?'

d. ***the other side***: (*a*) the world to come, the world beyond the grave, esp. as inhabited by the spirits of the dead; (*b*) *Austral.* and *N.Z. slang* (see quots.); (*c*) an opponent or an opposing side; one regarded as such.

(*a*) **1684** BUNYAN *Pilgrim's Progress* II. 220 So he passed over, and the Trumpets sounded for him on the other side. **1819** [see SIDE *sb.*[1] 12 a *fig.*]. **1926** A. CONAN DOYLE *Hist. Spiritualism* I. viii. 187 The sharp detail which we receive from the Other Side is incompatible with any vague grandiose idea of the sort. **1941** AUDEN *New Year Let.* 38 It is Utopian to be dead, For only on the Other Side Are Absolutes all satisfied. **1945** A. HUXLEY *Time must have Stop* vi. 66 Are they still obese on the other side? I'd like to ask next time you have a séance. **1960** M. SPARK *Bachelors* ii. 22 When Patrick's under the control I shouldn't think he could help saying what comes to him from the other side. **1973** *Listener* 8 Mar. 306/2 Max [Aitken]..is devoted to the memory of his father [*sc.* Beaverbrook] and..allows his father to edit the paper from the Other Side. **1974** 'D. SHANNON' *Crime File* xii. 185 They went to Katie May Blaine's funeral... 'You don't want to worry,' she told Mrs. Blaine simply. 'She's being looked after, the other side.'

(*b*) **1855** W. HOWITT *Land, Labour & Gold* ii. 362 Scenery precisely like hundreds of miles which I have seen 'on the other side', as they call Victoria, and as the Victorians call Van Diemen's Land. **1884** A. COX *Recollections* 125, I ax your pardon, zur, but were you ever at the Yan Yean works over the other side? *a*1948 L. G. D. ACLAND *Early Canterbury Runs* (1951) 389 *Other side*,..Australia. **1963** X. HERBERT *Disturbing Element* 2 My parents..were what were called T'othersiders, meaning people who had come to West Australia from the other side of the continent.

(*c*) **1916** 'TAFFRAIL' *Pincher Martin* xiv. 259 Their expeditions to that region known as 'the other side', for the express purpose of discomforting the Hun. **1939** 'N. BLAKE' *Smiler with Knife* iii. 57 They've youth and independence and courage. They're England. And you know what the other side says—'Woman is for the recreation of the warrior'. **1966** I. ASIMOV *Fantastic Voyage* i. 19 I've met him several times at scientific conferences on the other side. **1967** B. NORMAN *Matter of Mandrake* xxv. 211 There was a change of plan... The Other Side was becoming too worried. **1972** *Sat. Rev. Society* (U.S.) Dec. 33/2 The way is far more open..to similar wars of 'agression' or 'national liberation' or whatever the Vietnam War has been. The 'other side' can now engage in such activities with the understanding that the United States will be very reluctant to intervene. **1976** B. FREEMANTLE *November Man* iv. 45 Hugo will know it was an attempt on his life... If he runs to the other side, everything is going to be easy for us.

e. ***the other place***: one place regarded from the point of view of or with reference to another place; *euphem.*, Hell (as opp. Heaven). Also in depreciatory senses; *spec.* Oxford as regarded in Cambridge (and vice versa).

1841 F. A. KEMBLE *Let.* 29 Dec. in *Rec. Later Life* (1882) II. 156, I conclude that letters will occasionally come *to* heaven, and always be written in—the other place. **1874** 'MARK TWAIN' *Gilded Age* xi. 108 Washington was alternately in paradise or the other place just as it happened that Louise was gracious to him or seemingly indifferent. **1880** TROLLOPE *Duke's Children* I. xx. 245 Shall I go to heaven for doing that?.. Or mayn't I rather go to the other place? **1920** 'O. DOUGLAS' *Penny Plain* i. 13, I wouldn't much care to go to heaven myself, for all my friends are in ..the Other Place. **1944** A. THIRKELL *Headmistress* ix. 204 Sir Hosea Weaver..a Cambridge man..had..taken the highest kind of degree that the other place can give in Political Economy. **1958** *Listener* 14 Aug. 232/1 Cambridge has always tried to be more typical and less exotic than the other place. **1967** V. GIELGUD *Conduct of Member* ii. 15 There were Oxford men who persisted in speaking of Cambridge as 'the other place'. **1970** *Guardian* 22 Apr. 24/2 In the *other place*, it had been the rule to have sponsors since 1868 and Stormont had the same rule. **1972** 'M. INNES' *Open House* xi. 101 There being neither youth or age, sir, in the 'eavenly mansions—no, nor in the other place either. **1973** *Deb. Senate S. Afr.* 17 May 2807, I am thinking..of the important task of industrial decentralization about which so much has been said in this House and in the Other Place. **1973** 'M. YORKE' *Grave Matters* v. ii. 84, I don't know Oxford at all well... I know the other place better. Isn't that what you call it? **1974** *Oxford Times* 5 July 1/4 (*heading*) By punt to the other place. **1976** *Gramophone* Oct. 552/2 In the old days, 'the other place' never seemed to me to compete at all, but it is very different now with several excellent offerings from Magdalen under Bernard Rose.

f. ***the other thing*** (colloq.): the contrary, opposite, or reverse; something quite different. *euphem.* sexual activity; the penis. Phr. ***to do the other thing***: to do as one pleases (usu. as an expression of contemptuous dismissal).

1846 *Swell's Night Guide* 89 The wealthy voluptuary cannot choose but be gratified, as far as feasting, drinking, and the other thing goes. **1848** TROLLOPE *Kellys & O'Kellys* I. vii. 172 They'd ax him to come and see his sister married, and av' he didn't like it, he might do the other thing. **1885** C. M. YONGE *Nuttie's Father* II. xix. 224 It's the sort of thing that one only laughs at because otherwise one would have to do the other thing! **1913** A. BENNETT *Regent* I. vi. 165 You mean you won't!.. Well, you can do the other thing! **1922** JOYCE *Ulysses* 359 Besides there was absolution so long as you didn't do the other thing before being married. **1923** E. P. MATHERS tr. *Mardrus's Bk. of Thousand Nights & One Night* VII. 55 His heart is hard, his other thing is soft. **1929** J. VAN DRUTEN *Young Woodley* xii. 241 'You don't believe me?' 'I do not.'.. 'Then you must do the other thing.' **1953** H. CLEVELY *Public Enemy* xxii. 165, I couldn't have a better home.., and anybody who doesn't like it can do the other thing. **1977** 'D. CORY' *Bennett* iv. 127 The C.D.I. wouldn't like it, no. But, then, he could always do the other thing.

g. ***the other man*** (and varr.): a man with whom a woman already in an amatory relationship forms a new attachment; a lover. Similarly ***the other woman***: a woman with whom a man forms a new attachment in such circumstances; a mistress.

Quot. 1867 may not have the overtones of the other examples.

1855 BROWNING *Men & Women* 88 Why must I..Put any kiss of pardon on thy brow? Why need the other women know so much? **1867** TROLLOPE *Last Chron. Barset* I. xxxviii. 331 A woman, when she is jealous, is apt to attribute to the other woman with whom her jealousy is concerned, both weakness and timidity. **1886** KIPLING *The Other Man* in *Plain Tales from Hills* (1888) 80 They married her when she..had given all her poor little heart to another man... We will call him the Other Man. **1909** F. BARCLAY *Rosary* xxiii. 242 The 'other man' is always a problem. **1912** T. DREISER *Financier* xxxvii. 418 Curiously, the other woman did not seem so vastly important—that is, who she was. **1920** *Ladies' Home Jrnl.* Apr. 36 The cast includes Thomas Meighan as the husband, Gloria Swanson as the wife he changed, and Bebe Daniels as the other woman. **1927** E. GLYN *'It'* xiv. 137 What if being in the corner should make Ava go for help to the *other man*? **1935** *Mademoiselle* Aug. 3/2 Mr. Montgomery is the erring husband and Mr. Tone the 'other man'. **1946** G. MILLAR *Horned Pigeon* xxi. 360

She told me that her engagement had been broken, in fact her fiancé..was already married to 'the other woman'. **1953** K. Tennant *Joyful Condemned* xxxix. 391 'Who's the other guy?' 'There isn't any other guy.' **1966** 'S. Ransome' *Hidden Hour* ii. 20 She had been here before. With the 'other man'? **1973** G. Moffat *Deviant Death* i. 15, I had to sit in the corner and keep quiet. I knew how the other woman feels at the posh family funeral of her lover. **1975** *Daily Mirror* 29 Apr. 9/5 They married in 1967 after Miss Smith was named as the 'other woman' by Mr. Stephens' first wife.

h. ***the other end***: the person (or his location) with whom one is communicating by telephone.

1941 B. Schulberg *What makes Sammy Run?* vi. 121 Julian managed to get Sammy on the other end of a telephone. **1974** R. B. Parker *Godwulf Manuscript* iii. 17 The phone rang... The girl's voice at the other end was thick and very slow. **1978** T. Allbeury *Lantern Network* xi. 160 The fruity voice on the other end of the line.

3. †**a.** That follows the first; second (of two or more). *Obs.* (exc. as in b).

*c*900 tr. *Bæda's Hist.* i. xvi. [xxvii.] (1890) 64 þætte..feower dælas beon scyle, an ærest biscope..oðer dæl Godes þeowum, þridda þearfum. *c*1000 Ælfric *Gen.* ii. 13 Ðære oðre ea nama ys Gion. *c*1000 *Sax. Leechd.* I. 214 ȝenim þysse ylcan wyrte croppas, ærest þry, æt oþrum sæle fif. *c*1175 *Lamb. Hom.* 11 Þe oðer heste wes Ne haue þu þines drihtenes nome in nane aða. *c*1250 *Gen. & Ex.* 3642 On ðat oðer twentide dai, of ðe oðe[r] moned. *c*1400 tr. *Secreta Secret., Gov. Lordsh.* 72 Costome ys þe oþer kynde.

b. ***the other day***: †(*a*) orig. The second day, the following or next day. †(*b*) The preceding day, yesterday. (*c*) Now, a day or two ago; a short time ago, recently. So ***the other night, week***, etc. Cf. F. *l'autre jour*.

(*a*) **1154** *O.E. Chron.* an. 1135 Ð[at] oþer dei þa he lai an slep in scip. *c*1300 *Havelok* 1755 Hauelok..and his wif..wel do wayten al þe nith, Til þe oþer day. *c*1435 *Torr. Portugal* 1190 Tille they at myd-mete was, On the other day at none. *a*1440 *Sir Eglam.* 1005, V. and thretty knyghtys he madd, Be that odur day abowte none. **1585** T. Washington tr. *Nicholay's Voy.* i. xiii. 14 b, The other night following, we came to an anker in another roade.

(*b*) **13..** *Cursor M.* 5672 (Gött.) Wil þu me sla as þu did an, þis oder day [*Cott.* þis endir dai]? **1664** Pepys *Diary* 11 Feb., Mr. Falconer came..and brought her a present—a silver state-cup and cover. 12 Feb., Changed Mr. Falconer's state-cup, that he did give us the other day, for a fair tankard.

(*c*) **1421** Hoccleve *Complaint* 309 This othar day a lamentacion Of a wofull man in a boke I sye. *c*1440 *Jacob's Well* 112 The oþer day, J told ȝou a parcell of þe wose in sleuthe. **1596** Shaks. *1 Hen. IV* iii. iii. 112 The other Night I fell asleepe heere behind the Arras. *Ibid.* 152 He..sayde this other day, You ought him a thousand pound. **1711** Steele *Spect.* No. 38 ¶9 A short Letter I writ the other Day to a very witty Man. **1792** *Gentl. Mag.* 17/2 In company with a few friends, the other night. **1824** Medwin *Convers. Byron* (1832) I. 201 The Hartz mountain-scene, that Shelley versified the other day. **1885** *Manch. Even. News* 6 July 2/2 They played a match the other day against a local club.

†**c.** ***other half*** (*lit.* second half): One and a half (G. *anderthalb*). See half *a.* 2. *Obs.*

*c*900 tr. *Bæda's Hist.* iv. xxvi[i]. (1890) 360 Se ilca Eadric oðer healf ȝear þæt rice hæfde. **1297** R. Glouc. (Rolls) 939 Oþer half ȝer we abbeþ now iwend..In þe grete se of occean. *a*1300 *Cursor M.* 16600 Half feirth of eln was þe length, And oþer half þe brede. *c*1330 *Florice & Bl.* (1857) 216 Other half hondred of riche King. *c*1420 *Pallad. on Husb.* i. 687 A strike, or other half a stryke Of barly mele. *c*1430 *Two Cookery-bks.* 25 Take oþer half pound of Flower of Rys, .iij. pound of Almaundys, half an vnce of hony.

4. With plural sb. (in OE. and early ME. *óþre*) = the remaining, the rest of the; L. *cæteri*.

*c*893 K. Ælfred *Oros.* Contents v. iii, Hu Craccus se consul wonn wið þa oðre consulas. *c*1050 *Byrhtferth's Handboc* in *Anglia* (1885) VIII. 304 Þis ylce understand be þam oðrum daȝum. **1154** *O.E. Chron.* an. 1132 And te oþre rice men þe þer wæron. **1388** Wyclif *John* xxi. 8 Symount Petre..girte hym with a coote..and wente in to the see. But the othere disciplis camen bi boot. **1526** Tindale *Gal.* ii. 13 And the wother Iewes dissembled lyke wyse. **1592** Shaks. *Ven. & Ad.* 400 When his glutton eye so full hath fed, His other agents aim at like delight. **1667** Milton *P.L.* i. 194 Satan..With Head up-lift above the wave,..With other Parts besides Prone on the Flood. **1861** Ellicott *Life Our Lord* viii. (1865) 375 The other two have taught us by their very silence, in the first place, to view that last event of the Gospel-history in its true light. **1869** J. Eadie *Galatians* 146 He received his commission..from the same source as did the other Apostles.

5. Existing besides, or distinct from, that already mentioned or implied; not this, not the same, different in identity; further, additional.

†**a.** with singular sb. = another; L. *alius, alter*.

*c*900 tr. *Bæda's Hist.* Pref. ii. (1890) 4 Oððe on þysse bec oððe on oðre. *Ibid.* 6 Ʒif he hwæt ymbe ðis on oðre wisan ȝemete. **971** *Blickl. Hom.* 219 Eft ȝelamp oþer wundor. *c*1175 *Lamb. Hom.* 3 Mid his apostles and ec mid oðere floc manna. *Ibid.* 9 A hu scolde oðermonnes goddede comen him to gode? *Ibid.* 13 Ne wilne þu oðres monnes wif ne nanes þinges þe oðre mon aȝe. *c*1200 *Trin. Coll. Hom.* 89 Alse he doð on oðre stede on his speche.

b. with sing. sb. qualified by *an, any, some, no*, or preceded by a negative expressed or implied.

an other has been normally written since *c* 1600 (often also in earlier times) as one word, another (q.v.). In ME. also divided *a nother*: so *na nother* = none other, no other.

*c*888 K. Ælfred *Boeth.* v. §1 Nan oþer man. **971** *Blickl. Hom.* 113 Sum..þæt hine swyþor lufode þonne æniȝ oþor man. *c*1000 Ælfric *Hom.* I. 364 Helias..oððe sum oðer witeȝa. *c*1200 *Vices & Virtues* 47 And ec sum oðer saule hit wile helpen. *c*1250 *Owl & Night.* 583 An oþer þing of þe ich mene. *a*1300 *Cursor M.* 10663 Oþair husband mai i haf nane. *c*1375 *Sc. Leg. Saints* xviii. (*Egipciane*) 618 Athyre enchesone fand I nocht. *c*1386 Chaucer *Prol.* 461 Housbondes at chirche dore she hadde fyue Withouten oother compaignye in youthe. *c*1400 *Rom. Rose* 6033 Ladyes..Ne sekith never othir vicaire. **1560** Whitehorne *Arte Warre* (1573) 48 Other thing there is not that can withholde it. **1611** Bible *1 Cor.* xv. 37 It may chance of wheat, or of some other graine. **1697** Dampier *Voy.* (1729) I. 88 As if they had no other place in the World to live in. **1732** Pope *Ess. Man* i. 56 One single [movement] can its end produce; Yet serves to second too some other use. **1795** *Gentl. Mag.* 545/1 To prefer to every other spot the places of our birth and education. **1845** M. Pattison *Ess.* (1889) I. 1 Such history,..more than any other branch of literature, varies with the age that produces it. **1857** Buckle *Civiliz.* I. xii. 668 A boldness unknown in any other part of Europe.

c. with pl. sb., or quantitative sing. (In OE. and early ME. *óþ(e)re*.)

*c*888 K. Ælfred *Boeth.* vi, Be þære sunnan & eac be oðrum tunglum. **971** *Blickl. Hom.* 145 Petrus and..oþre Cristes þeȝnas. *c*1000 *Ags. Gosp.* Matt. xii. 45 He him to ȝenymþ seofun oðre gastas. *c*1175 *Lamb. Hom.* 125 He tahte heom þis swulche toforan oðran þingan. *c*1290 *S. Eng. Leg.* I. 16/510 And with oþur melodies al-so. **1362** Langl. *P. Pl.* A. Prol. 101 Masons, Minours And mony oþer craftes. **1387** Trevisa *Higden* (Rolls) I. 7 Among oþere..faire florischers and hiȝteres of wordes. **1457** *Nottingham Rec.* II. 365 For mendyng of a bowt and oder labors. **1483** *Vulgaria abs Terentio* 29, I left all odyr thynges or put a bakk. *a*1548 Hall *Chron., Hen. VIII* 16 b, Gonnes, Bowes, Arrowes, and all other artilery. **1640–1** *Kirkcudbr. W.-C. Min.-bk.* (1855) 63 Naither by thair example nor by thair dilligence in uther things. **1711** Steele *Spect.* No. 49 ¶6 When they are in other Company they speak and act after him. **1725** Ramsay *Gent. Sheph.* iv. ii, To London court, or ither far aff parts. **1832** Tennyson *Lady of Shalott* ii. i, Little other care hath she. **1850** Gladstone *Glean.* II. 74 We have other evidence..how deeply he had drunk..at classic fountains. **1886** Sir N. Lindley in *Law Rep.* 32 Chanc. Div. 28 The same observations are true of all other contracts similarly circumstanced.

d. Archaic and obsolete constructions.

†***other all, other many*** (*obs.*): = all other, many other. †***other mo, other more*** (*obs.*): = other(s) besides. ***other such*** (*arch.*): now generally ***such other(s)***. ***other six***, etc. (*arch.* or *dial.*), ambiguous: = the (or an) other six, or six other(s), etc. ***other the king's enemies*** (*arch.*), ambiguous: = others, (who are) the king's enemies, or other enemies of the king.

*c*893 K. Ælfred *Oros.* i. iv. §1 Hi æfter ðæm wæron on þan mæstan hungre oðre syfan ȝear. *Ibid.* iv. x. §2 Eft wearþ oþer swelc ren. *c*900 tr. *Bæda's Hist.* i. xiii. [xxiii.] (1890) 54 He sende Augustinum and oðre moniȝe munecas. *c*1020 *Rule St. Benet* (Logeman) 40 Oðre sijx sealmas. **13..** *Guy Warw.* (A.) 408 Bi þe be warned oþer mo. *Ibid.* 1149 Þou art me leuest of oþer alle. *c*1489 Caxton *Blanch.* 121 The kynge of Fryse, & other his prysoners. **1512** *Act 4 Hen. VIII*, c. 20 *Preamble*, Archbold with other xl out-lawes. **1526** Tindale *Matt.* xv. 30 Havinge with them halt, blinde, domne, maymed, and other many. **1542** *Act 33 Hen. VIII*, c. 27 Amonges other their peculier actes. *a*1555 Philpot *Exam. & Writ.* (Parker Soc.) 416 Luther and other more of us. *a*1568 Ascham *Scholem.* ii. (Arb.) 110 A great deale of the Ciuill lawe, and other many notable bookes. **1603** Knolles *Hist. Turks* (1621) 246 In their roomes placed other his owne creatures. **1611** Bible *Gen.* viii. 10 He stayed yet other seven days. *a*1648 Ld. Herbert *Hen. VIII* (1683) 531 To joyn with Cardinal Pool and other the Kings Enemies. **1799** J. Robertson *Agric. Perth* 564 A retreat for St Bridget and other nine virgins. **1864** Burton *Scot Abr.* I. i. 18 With other the great men of Scotland. **1871** Ruskin *Fors Clav.* x. 13 There are, indeed, other such in the world.

e. In this sense, *other* may be construed with *than* (†formerly also *but*). Cf. 6.

1679 Pepys *Let to Dk. York* 6 May, Without any alteration..other than what is consequential to [etc.]. **1794** Paley *Evid.* (1825) II. 143 It does not appear that any books, other than our present Scriptures were thus publicly read. **1866** Rogers *Agric. & Prices* II. 273 Gratuities other than money are inconsiderable. **1896** *Law Times* C. 410/1 The acts or defaults of any person other than himself and those claiming under him.

f. ***other ranks***: in the armed forces, non-commissioned officers and ordinary soldiers, seamen, etc. Occas. in *sing.*, a member of the other ranks. Also *transf.* and (in form *other-rank*) *attrib.* Cf. rank *sb.*[1] 5 b.

1925 Fraser & Gibbons *Soldier & Sailor Words* 216 *Other ranks*, the usual official designation for N.C.O.'s and privates in orders, etc., as distinguished from Commissioned Officers. **1926** F. M. Ford *Man could stand Up* ii. ii. 106 There were all these inscrutable beings; the Other Ranks, a brownish mass, spreading underground, like clay strata in the gravel. **1929** T. E. Lawrence *Let.* 18 Apr. (1938) 652 M. B. is an amateur of the R.A.F., like me: but he doesn't know the other ranks in it, and won't like their dirt and brutality. **1931** —— *Let.* 20 Aug. (1938) 733 A book written by an 'other rank' would not mention the officers. **1946** *R.A.F. Jrnl.* May 150 The Sussex Square Club and Hostel..has been opened for male other ranks. **1959** *Encounter* July 85/1 Before the war the young officer really believed that the social circumstances of his upbringing and birth entitled him to give orders to 'other ranks'; and the 'other ranks' were on the whole quite satisfied. **1960** J. MacLaren-Ross *Until Day she Dies* vi. 94 There was a mob of other ranks sitting around on their kitbags. **1960** A. Waugh *Foxglove Saga* vi. 107 The other ranks of the Pigs were mostly recruited from the criminal and the stupid. **1965** G. McInnes *Road to Gundagai* ii. 26 The promenade deck was abruptly curtailed by a wooden grille..with the sign 'Other Ranks Only. No Entry. Military Police.' **1966** *Times* 9 July 9/6 The Army have given the expression 'other ranks' its marching orders. Commands have been told the term 'soldier' is preferred. **1968** R. West *Sk. Vietnam* ii. 46 Many marine other-ranks have college degrees. **1971** S. Hill *Strange Meeting* iii. 169, B Company has lost 2 officers and 3 wounded, and about 30 of other ranks. **1973** *Listener* 5 July 22/1 They, like their other-rank colleagues, knew well enough what it was all about. **1974** K. Royce *Trap Spider* i. 8 'Good man,' he said, as if he'd invited an 'other rank' to the officers' mess for a special treat. **1976** *Daily Tel.* 20 July 4/3 The withdrawal of British regular units from Oman will not affect..the secondment of British officers and other ranks of all three services to the Sultan's forces.

6. Different (in kind or quality). Const. *than* (*from*, †*but*). (See also another 4.)

[OE. expressed 'different' by *óþer..óþer*: e.g. *c*897 K. Ælfred *Gregory's Past. C.* ii. 28 Ðonne hi on oðre wisan libbað on oðre hi lærað = When they live in one way in another (way) they teach.]

*a*1250 *Owl & Night.* 544 'Nay, nay', sede þe nihtegale, 'þu schalt ihere æn oþer tale'. **1375** Barbour *Bruce* i. 392 Bot quha in battaill mycht him se, All othir contenance had he. **1387** Trevisa *Higden* (Rolls) I. 67 Ouþer vnderstondynge bihoueþ of þe ryueres of Paradys, þan auctours writeþ. **1570** Buchanan *Ane Admonit.* Wks. (1892) 26 Yai meane na vyer theng bot ye deid of ye King. **1579** J. Field tr. *Calvin's Serm.* Ded., What should good men looke for other of these blind Balamites, but such condemnation? **1600** Shaks. *A.Y.L.* v. iv. 199, I am for other, then for dancing meazures. **1615** N. R. tr. *Camden's Hist. Eliz.* ii. an. 12. 108 In case any thing other than well should befall the Infant King. **1643** Trapp *Comm. Gen.* xxxiii. 4 Latomus of Lorain wrote, that there was no other a faith in Abraham, then in Cicero. **1673** Ph. Henry *Diaries & Lett.* (1882) 261 A person quite of other principles from her former husband. **1779** Burke *Lett., to R. Shackleton* Corr. 1844 II. 275, I do not know how I could wish him to be,..other than what he is. **1803** Coleridge in Kegan Paul *W. Godwin* (1876) II. 95 It could not be other than pleasant to me. **1808** Scott *Marm.* ii. vi, Far other scene her thoughts recall. **1877** M. Arnold *Last Ess.* 171 Quite other matters from the fundamental matter of the primitive gospel. **1879** F. Harrison *Choice Bks.* (1886) 51 This Italian poetry is in a world far other from ours of to-day.

†**7.** *Other* was formerly used to characterize things as of a different kind from those previously mentioned: e.g. ***other sinful men*** = other men, who are sinful. *Obs.*

This would now be implied by its omission; in modern use the insertion of *other* implies the opposite, viz. that the second class includes the first.

*c*1380 Wyclif *Wks.* (1880) 201 Þerfore, as ihu crist is more worþi than oþere synful men [etc.]. *c*1449 Pecock *Repr.* ii. x. 199 Both preestis and othere lay men. **1481** Caxton *Godfrey* x. 33 Charyottes, horses, camels, beuffes, kyen, & other smale beestys. **1530** Rastell *Bk. Purgat.* ii. v, The lyfe of man is more laborous..than the lyfe of any other brute beste. **1600** Holland *Livy* xxxvii. xxiii. 957 There were 32 quadrireme Gallies and 4 other triremes besides. **1605** Shaks. *Macb.* iv. iii. 90 All these [vices] are portable, With other Graces weigh'd. **1699** Bentley *Phal.* 506 It was immortal Vellum..that could last..in spite of all damp and moisture, that moulders other mortal skins.

B. *absol., pron.*, or *sb.*

†**1.** **a.** One of the two, the one; L. *alter*. Often followed by a genitive pl. (Cf. A. 1.) *Obs.*

*c*893 K. Ælfred *Oros.* iii. xi. §4 Þær wearð Leostenas, oðer heora ladteowa, mid anre flan ofscoten. *Ibid.* iv. x. §5 Þara consula oþres sunu, Scipia wæs haten. *Ibid.* vi. iii. §3 Þa funde mon..twa cista..and on oþerre wæs an ȝewrit. *Ibid.* vi. xxx. §3 Þa ȝesette Galerius ii cyningas under him; oþer wæs haten Seuerus. *a*900 tr. *Bæda's Hist.* v. xiv. [xiii.] (1890) 438 Ða teah heora oðer forð fæȝre boc. **971** *Blickl. Hom.* 169 Se þe hæbbe twa tunecan, selle oðre ðam ðe nane næbbe. *c*1000 *Leg. Holy Rood* 101 ȝif æniȝ man wolde heora oðrum fylstan, ðæt man hine sona ȝefenge. *c*1200 *Trin. Coll. Hom.* 95 Two þeroffe ben swiche þat no man ne mai underfo him seluen to hele bute he haue here oðer on him. **13..** *Cursor M.* 21949 Ooþer [*v.rr.* auþer, ouþer, oon] o þam we most forga, For mai na man haf heuens twa.

b. In OE. *oðer* was used anticipatively to introduce the two members of an alternative; thus, *oðer* (*þara* or *tweȝra*), *oððe..oððe..*, i.e. the one, (of these, or of the two) either..or... (Cf. outher *a.* and *pron.* 1 b for similar use of OE. *áwðer, áðer*.)

*c*888 K. Ælfred *Boeth.* xi. §1 For þam oþer tweȝa, oððe hie næfre..becumað, oððe hi..næfre..ðurhwuniað. *c*893 —— *Oros.* i. x. §1 Him sædon þæt hie oðer dyden, oðþe ham comen oððe hie him woldon oðerra wera ceosan. *c*1000 *Eccl. Inst.* in Thorpe *Laws* II. 412 Wite he þæt oðer ðara, oððe he sceal ðæs hades þolian, oððe hit ȝebetan.

c. ***other..other*** = the one..the other. *Obs.*

*c*897 K. Ælfred *Gregory's Past. C.* xvii. 107 Ðæt..se oðer beo aræred from ðæm oðrum. **971** *Blickl. Hom.* 171 Oþer..is se æresta apostol, oþer se nehsta. *c*1000 Ælfric *Gen.* xl. 2 Ðara oðer bewiste his byrlas, oðer his bæcestran [L. *alter..alter*]. *c*1305 *Life St. Edmund the King* 9 in *E.E.P.* (1862) 87 Hubba was þoþer ihote: & þoþer het Hyngar.

2. **a.** ***the other***: The remaining one of two; later, also of three or more. (Cf. A. 2.)

In this sense esp. contrasted with (*the*) *one*: see one 18.

*c*893 K. Ælfred *Oros.* i. i. §1 Sume men sæȝden þæt þær nære buton tweȝen dælas: Asia, & þæt oþer Europe. *c*900 tr. *Bæda's Hist.* Pref. i. (1890) 2 ȝif se oðer nolde, hu wurð he elles ȝelæred? *c*1000 Ælfric *Gen.* xxix. 27 Hafa þas ane wucan to ȝemæccan, and ic ȝife þe þa oðre. *a*1225 *Ancr. R.* 404 Al so as on neil driueð ut þen oðerne. **1297** R. Glouc. (Rolls) 7017 Þat þe on broþer..in nede helpeþ þere þat oþer. *a*1425 *Cursor M.* 1578 (Trin.) Þe broþer toke þe oþeres wif. *c*1450 *Boke of Curtasye* 814 in *Babees Bk.*, Þe vssher ledes þat on hed ryȝt, Þo aumener þo oþer away shalle dyȝt. *a*1548 Hall *Chron., Hen. VII* 15 When bothe the armyes were approchyng to the other. **1697** Dryden *Virg. Georg.* iv. 143 One Monarch wears an honest open Face,..That other looks like Nature in Disgrace. **1812** J. Wilson *Isle of Palms* ii. 506 The inward flow Of faith..Each from the other hears. **1818** Cruise *Digest* (ed. 2) II. 36 This will excuse the performance of that, and also of the other.

†**b.** Instead of 'the other' the simple *other* was formerly used after *each, either, neither, whether* (rarely after *one, none*). *Obs.*

Hence the extant ***each other***, and the obs. ***either other***, as in *they help each other*, i.e. each [helps] the other: see each 5, either A. 2 d. For 'each other' Sc. also used ***each others***, i.e. each the others, one another (of a number).

*c*893 K. Ælfred *Oros.* i. i. §23, & swa ælc æfter oðrum. *Ibid.* ii. iii. §2 Heora þær æȝðer oðerne ofsloȝ. *Ibid.* iii. i. §4 þæt naðer ne mehte on oþrum siȝe ȝeræcan. *a* **1123** *O.E. Chron.* an. 1101 Loc, hweðer þæra ȝebroðra oðerne ofer bide. **1297** R. GLOUC. (Rolls) 3332 And hor eiþer in oþer armes mid grete ioye hom nom. *a* **1330** *Otuel* 456 And either hugh on other faste. *c* **1375** *Sc. Leg. Saints* xxvii. (*Machor*) 1079 þane can athir wthire kis. *c* **1386** CHAUCER *Knt.'s T.* 274 To me þat am thy cosyn and thy brother Ysworn ful depe and ech of vs til oother. *c* **1400** *Three Kings Cologne* 57 Noon of hem neuer tofore had seye oþer, ne noon of hem knewe oþirs persone ne knewe of oþirs comyng. *a* **1450** *Le Morte Arth.* 2013 Er outher of vs haue other slayne. *c* **1450** *St. Cuthbert* (Surtees) 7107 þai myght unnethis an [= one] othir se. **1523** LD. BERNERS *Froiss.* I. lxi. 83 They wer so nere togyder, that ech of them vnderstode others langage. **1552** LYNDESAY *Monarche* 4023 Atheris deand in vtheris armis. *a* **1649** DRUMM. OF HAWTH. *Hist. Jas. V* Wks. (1711) 97 They mutually entertained and feasted each others at Christmas. **1657** SPARROW *Bk. Com. Prayer* 68 Priest and people interchangeably pray each for other.

†**c.** The simple *other* was formerly used in the sense 'each preceding one (in turn)'. ***thrice after other***, thrice in succession. *Obs.* or *dial.* (*Sc.*)

1297 R. GLOUC. (Rolls) 5032 Ac þo vel he in siknesse and sorwe vpen oþer. **1558** KENNEDY *Compend. Tract.* in *Wodrow Misc.* (1844) 170 Our Salveour thryse efter uther commendit his floke to St. Peter. **1603** SHAKS. *Meas. for M.* IV. iv. 2 Euery Letter he hath writ, hath disuouch'd other. **1660** SHARROCK *Vegetables* 17 The nature of young tulip roots is to runne down deeper into the ground, every year more then other. *a* **1694** TILLOTSON *Serm.* cx. (1742) VI. 1793 Controversy, which I am less fond of every day than other.

†**3.** That which follows the first, the second. (Cf. A. 3.) *Obs.*

c **888** K. ÆLFRED *Boeth.* xxxiii. §5 An þæra is eorðe, oðer wæter, ðridde lyft, feorþe fyr. *c* **900** tr. *Bæda's Hist.* I. xviii. [xxxiv.] (1890) 92 Her endað seo æreste boc and onginneð seo oðer. *c* **1000** *Ags. Gosp.* Matt. xxii. 26 Se forma .. se oðer ealswa and se þrydda, oþ ðone seofoþan. *c* **1175** *Lamb. Hom.* 37 Alra erest þu scalt gan to scrifte .. þe oðer is do þine almesse .. þat þridde is þet þu scalt bi-wepen þine sunne. *Ibid.* 133 An is monnes istreon, þet oðer is godes word. **1340** *Ayenb.* 17 þe uerste boȝ of prede is ontreuþe, þe oþer onworþhede, þe þridde ouerweninge.

4. *pl.* The remaining ones, the rest; L. *cæteri.*

†*a.* In form *other*, OE., ME. *oþ(e)re. Obs.*

971 *Blickl. Hom.* 223 Wæs heora sum reðra .. ðonne þa oþre. *c* **1000** *Ags. Gosp.* Matt. xxvii. 49 Ða oðre cwædon. *a* **1225** *Leg. Kath.* 1374 þa ȝeide þus þat an, & elnede þe oðre. **1340** *Ayenb.* 237 Hi clenzeþ and halȝeþ þe oþre. *c* **1477** CAXTON *Jason* 8 b, The other deffended them with alle their puissaunce. **1526** TINDALE *Rev.* xx. 5 The wother off the deed men lyved not agayne. **1590** SHAKS. *Mids. N.* IV. ii. 71 Awaking when the other doe. **1658** *Whole Duty Man* I. §9 The best groundwork whereon to build both the other. **1662** STILLINGFL. *Orig. Sacr.* III. ii. §17 That Space wherein the other were, is made empty. **1768** G. WHITE *Selborne* xix. 55 That it is a size larger than the two other.

β. In form *others.* (The regular mod. form.)

1542 UDALL *Erasm. Apoph.* 67 b, When the others .. addressed theim selfes to returne. **1611** BIBLE *Ezek.* ix. 5 To the others he said in mine hearing. —— *Dan.* vii. 19 The fourth beast .. was diuerse from al the others. [*Elsewhere* the other.] **1719** DE FOE *Crusoe* I. xviii, The cave where the others lay. **1860** ELLICOTT *Life Our Lord* viii. (1865) 374 The two others direct our thoughts more to Judea.

5. Absolute use of A. 5, the sb. being expressed in the context: **a.** *sing.* One besides. (*a*) Without qualifying word; now only in ***some .. or other***, ***one .. or other***. (*b*) With *an*, *one*, *any*, *no* (*none*), *some*.

an other is now written ANOTHER, q.v.: cf. A. 5 b.

c **1325** *Poem Times Edw. II* (Percy) lxxv, That dured ȝer & other. **1480** CAXTON *Chron. Eng.* ccx. 193 The barons sent to hym o time and other. **1607** TOPSELL *Four-f. Beasts* (1658) 493 To one idols tuition and protection or other. **1625** MILTON *Death Fair Inf.* 55 Or any other of that heav'nly brood. **1635** J. HAYWARD tr. *Biondi's Banish'd Virg.* 203 My Mother .. was by some one or other counselled to send [etc.]. **1712** ADDISON *Spect.* No. 446 ⁋4 Some time or other we may be at leisure. **1801** JANE AUSTEN *Lett.* (1884) I. 263 Hardly a day passes in which we do not have some visitor or other. **1877** SPURGEON *Serm.* XXIII. 55 God will bring His people out of the trouble some way or other. *Mod.* This wool is too dark; have you any other? Use ——'s Soap once, and you will use no other.

b. *plural.* Other things or persons of the kind mentioned. *a.* In form *other* (ME. orig. *oþ(e)re*). Now *arch.*; chiefly in ***other of***.

a **1100** *Gerefa* in *Anglia* (1886) IX. 259 On maneȝum landum tilð bið redre ðonne on oðrum. **1297** R. GLOUC. (Rolls) 29 Yles þer beþ mani on .. Ac þer beþ at uore alle oþere þre. *a* **1300** *Cursor M.* 9293 Sum Iuus said til oþer þan Qua herd euer sli spece o man. **1484** CAXTON *Curiall* 1 Whiche repute thonoures .. to be thynges more blessyd & happy than other. **1637** *Sc. Prayer Bk.* 10 That they .. should be abused as other have been. **1713** BERKELEY *Guard.* No. 3 ⁋1 A body of men whom of all other a good man would be most careful not to violate.

1657 W. RAND tr. *Gassendi's Life Peiresc* I. 154 Other of his friends and rare men. **1691** tr. *Emilianne's Observ. Journ. Naples* 228 Elias and other of the Prophets. **1798** CHARLOTTE SMITH *Yng. Philos.* II. 155 Some other of the servants and dependants. **1826** R. H. FROUDE *Rem.* (1838) I. 152 These writings, and all other of the same class. **1844** J. H. NEWMAN *Lett.* (1891) II. 432, I know two other of his works. **1880** F. G. LEE *Ch. under Eliz.* I. 244 Like other of the Protestant prelates.

β. In form *others.* (The regular mod. form.)

1557 NORTH *Gueuara's Diall Pr.* 141 That thy thoughtes were others than they seemed. **1603** HOLLAND *Plutarch's Mor.* 1307 Of tame beasts .. the most grosse and indocible of all others, namely an asse. **1609** —— *Amm. Marcell.* 337 These matters abovesaid, and others the like. **1651** GATAKER *P. Martyr* in *Fuller's Abel Rediv.* (1867) I. 244 He preached at Rome, Venice .. and in others the cities of Italy. **1827** HALLAM *Const. Hist.* (1842) I. 41 Loans from the citizens of London and others of her subjects. **1868** MILMAN *St. Paul's* 344 In others of his sermons. **1877** MORLEY *Crit. Misc.* Ser. II. 340–1 In Birmingham, the very place, of all others, where it is most likely to be of real service.

** *pronoun.*

6. a. *sing.* = Another person; some one else; any one else. † (*a*) without qualifying word (now expressed by ANOTHER). *Obs.* (*b*) Qualified by *any, some, no* (*none*), *one, an.*

(*a*) *a* **900** *Laws of Ælfred* Introd. c. 19 ȝif hwa oðrum his eaȝe oðdo. *c* **900** tr. *Bæda's Hist.* IV. xxvii[i]. (1890) 362 þonne mæssepreost oðþe oðer in tun com. *c* **1000** *Ags. Gosp.* Matt. vii. 3 Eart þu þe to cumenne eart, oððe we oþres sceolon abidan? *c* **1175** *Lamb. Hom.* 19 þet he ne misdude wið oðerne. *c* **1200** *Trin. Coll. Hom.* 43 Oðer hadde þe gult and ure hlouerd ihesu crist hit acorede. *a* **1300** *Cursor M.* 1974 Ifel agh naman do til oþer For ilkan agh be oþier broiþer. *Ibid.* 21927 Thoru warnissing of oþers wrake. *c* **1440** *Jacob's Well* 180 It was oþerys defaute, & noȝt myn. **1596** DANETT tr. *Comines* (1614) 342 Other than him they haue none ouer them. **1611** BIBLE *1 Cor.* xi. 21 Euery one taketh before other, his owne supper.

(*b*) *c* **1375** *Cursor M.* 14306 (Fairf.) He wepped sorer þan any oþer. *c* **1450** *Merlin* i. 19 Shall eny other do her duresse? **1611** SIR W. MURE *Misc. Poems* i. 76 3it woldst thou teach ane oyer. **1657** W. RAND tr. *Gassendi's Life Peiresc* I. 191 The work should be dedicated to the King, or to some other, who would thankfully accept it. **1811** *Ora & Juliet* III. 208 It is plain .. she likes some other. **1828** PUSEY *Hist. Enquiry* I. 126 *note*, Morgan put together with greater minuteness than any other the historical critical difficulties. **1881** W. H. MALLOCK *Rom. 19th Cent.* II. 205 It was none other than [etc.].

b. *plural.* Other persons. *a.* In form *other* (OE. *oðre*). *arch.*

c **900** tr. *Bæda's Hist.* I. xv. [xxvi.] (1890) 62 Se cyning eac swylce betuh oþre ongon lustfullian. **971** *Blickl. Hom.* 143 Mid hire syndan Godes apostolas and oþre. *c* **1250** *Gen. & Ex.* 3633 Oðere of ðat kin, Sette he hem for to seruen ðor-in. **1297** R. GLOUC. (Rolls) 222, & silui ascaynes sone & oþere þat þer were. *c* **1375** *Sc. Leg. Saints* v. (*Johannes*) 12 God gaf hym wittinge Atoure athire of prewe thinge. *c* **1380** WYCLIF *Wks.* (1880) 19 3if þei .. maken oþere more sikyrly to hopen þus. *c* **1460** FORTESCUE *Abs. & Lim. Mon.* vi. (1885) 122 Lordes, knyghtes, & sqviers, & oþer. **1526** TINDALE *John* vii. 12 Wother sayde naye, but he deceaveth the people. *Ibid.* 41 Wother sayde: This is Christ. **1581** LAMBARDE *Eiren.* II. ii. (1588) 102 Other there were of a contrary opinion. **1607** R. WILKINSON *Merchant Royall* Ep. Ded., I have pleased some and displeased other. *a* **1641** BP. MOUNTAGU *Acts & Mon.* (1642) 22 The Heathen .. (a name comprising all other but themselves). **1870** FREEMAN in W. R. W. Stephens *Life* (1895) II. 38 You and such other as I may catch.

β. In form *others.* (poss. pl. *others'*, formerly *others.*) (The regular mod. form.)

c **1375** *Sc. Leg. Saints* i. (*Petrus*) 29 With oþeris alse in þe se Rouande. *c* **1380** WYCLIF *Sel. Wks.* II. 339 To oþirs is ȝovun .. discrecioun to knowe spiritis. **1535** STEWART *Cron. Scot.* I. 602 Mony nobillis of the Pechtis .. and sindrie otheris mo. **1557** N. T. (Genev.) *Luke* xx. 16 He .. wil let out his vineyard to others [*previous vv.* other, *Rheims and* **1611** others]. *c* **1560** A. SCOTT *Poems* (S.T.S.) xiv. 14 In lykwayis dois hir beuty .. Transcend all vþiris. **1595** SHAKS. *John* IV. ii. 164, I met Lord Bigot and Lord Salisburie .. And others more. *a* **1599** SPENSER *F.Q.* VII. vii. 53 Where were ye borne? Some say in Crete by name, Others in Thebes, and others other-where. **1611** BIBLE *Matt.* xxvii. 42 He saued others [*prev. vv.* other]; himselfe he cannot saue. **1711** STEELE *Spect.* No. 118 ⁋1 This Woman, says he, is of all others the most unintelligible. **1732** BERKELEY *Alciphr.* I. §9 Others indeed may talk. **1753** *Inscription carved on No. 23 High Street, Hawick*, All was Others. All will be Others. **1789** BURNS *Let. to Blacklock* vii, Not but I hae a richer share Than mony ithers. **1894** H. DRUMMOND *Ascent Man* 38 Without the Struggle for the life of Others, obviously there would have been no Others.

7. = Another thing; something else, anything else; ***no(n) other***, nothing else. *Obs.* or *arch.*

c **888** K. ÆLFRED *Boeth.* v. §3 Nat ic nauht oþres. *c* **900** tr. *Bæda's Eccl. Hist.* III. viii. [xi.] (1890) 184 And betweoh oðer spræcon heo be Oswalde. *c* **1000** in Cockayne *Narrat. Angl. Conscr.* (1861) 7 Seo wyrd oft oncyrreþ and on oðer hworfeþ. *a* **1300** *Sarmun* viii. in *E.E.P.* (1862) 2 Whar-of is þe gentil man of eni oþer þan of þis. *a* **1300** *Cursor M.* 4147 (Cott.) Quen ruben sagh þair was nanoþer Bot [etc.]. ? **1370** *Robt. Cicyle* 55 When hyt wolde non odur be. **1483** CAXTON *G. de la Tour* C viij b, All be he of his parente his affynyte or other. **1561** T. HOBY tr. *Castiglione's Courtyer* III. (1577) Q iv b, [He] Neuer thinketh vpon other but to please hir. **1685** R. BURTON *Eng. Emp. Amer.* iv. 83 The Indians .. thinking no other but I had saved the Indian's life. **1690** LOCKE *Govt.* I. iv. §40 'Tis impossible .. to find any other but the setting of Mankind above the other Kinds of Creatures. **1755** *Man* No. 49. 2 This is no other than insulting a person. **1846** TRENCH *Mirac.* xxxii. (1862) 449 Peter was not likely to strike with other than a right good will. **1895** *Westm. Gaz.* 25 July 4/2 He thought he could not do other than send the two prisoners for trial.

8. In reciprocal sense: = Each other, one another. In later use only *Sc.*

Scotch writers also formerly used the plural *others.*

c **1380** WYCLIF *Sel. Wks.* III. 340 Alle dedes and werkes of þe Trinite mai not be departid from oþir. **1582–8** *Hist. Jas. VI* (1804) 294 How they might shift thir three from utheriss seuerally. **1620** *Frier Rush* (1828) 30, I would have caused you to slaye other. **1632** W. LITHGOW *Trav.* III. 85 Figges, Orenges, Lemmons, .. growing all through other. **1637** RUTHERFORD *Lett.* (1862) I. 209 Oh if we were clasped in others arms! **1640–1** *Kirkcudbr. War-Comm. Min.-bk.* (1855) 35 He .. saw thame striking at uthers with thair swordes. **1653** BINNING *Serm.* (1845) 456 You may see here sin and judgement mixed in thorough other in their complaint. **1725** RAMSAY *Gent. Sheph.* III. iii, Let's steal frae ither now and meet the morn. **1786** BURNS *Twa Dogs* 37 Nae doubt but they were fain o' ither. **1809** CAMPBELL *Gertrude* II. vi, We know not other—oceans are between.

9. as *sb. Philos.* That which (in relation to something already mentioned) constitutes the other part of the universe of being, and is thus the counterpart or double of the former; e.g. the *non-ego* is the 'other' of the *ego*, Creation of the Creator, etc.

1863 E. V. NEALE *Anal. Th. & Nat.* 205 It is the essential character of thought to set itself over against itself, as the 'other' of itself, which yet is itself. All our thoughts .. are a something set over against our thinking being by its own action; different from itself and yet one with itself. **1876** FAIRBAIRN *Strauss* II. in *Contemp. Rev.* June 136 He has eternally to cause the other of himself, Nature, to proceed from himself.

10. as *sb.* Sexual activity; sexual intercourse. Also occas., homosexual practices. *slang.*

1922 JOYCE *Ulysses* 358 They would be just good friends like a big brother and sister without all that other. *Ibid.* 429 Bit light in the head. Monthly or effect of the other. **1928** D. H. LAWRENCE *Lady Chatterley* xiv. 241 She loved me to talk to her and kiss her... But the other, she just didn't want. **1936** J. CURTIS *Gilt Kid* 135 'Doing half I was.' 'What for? The other?' 'Yes.' The pansy simpered. *Ibid.*, He gets a stretch for screwing and another stretch on top of that for the other. **1969** F. NORMAN *Banana Boy* 127, I .. usually managed to get Mary behind a haystack for a 'bit of the other'. **1974** *Spectator* 22 June 764/2 I've got to be noticed by any guy who's on the prowl away from home and looking for a bit of the other.

C. Peculiar written combinations and divisions of *an other*, *none other*, *the other*, in A. and B.

a. In ME. writing, *an other*, now *another*, was often divided as **a nother**. Similarly, *non* (*nan*) *other*, now *no* (*none*) *other* was written **no (na) nother**. In ME. and early mod.Eng. *the other* was often written **thother**. These forms are now obs.

a **1300** *Cursor M.* 1942 Suilk a noiþer wengance. *c* **1330** R. BRUNNE *Chron.* (1810) 31 Or fynd a noþer man. *c* **1380** WYCLIF *Wks.* (1880) 19 3if þat o part holdiþ wiþ o pope and þe toþer wiþ o noþere pope. **1426** AUDELAY *Poems* 14 Hit nedus no noder to do. **1428** *Surtees Misc.* (1888) 10 Ne na nother suyte make. **1526** TINDALE *Col.* iii. 13 If eny man have a quarrell to a nother. **1534** JOYE *Subvers. More's False Found.* 7 No nother then this foundacion. **1557** *Brasenose Coll. Munim.* 22. 10 In a nother chamber.

a **1200** *Moral Ode* 166 Ach þoþre habbeþ scome and grome. **1414–15** *Plumpton Corr.* p. cxx, Sir Robert Plompton, .. knight, .. on thother partie. **1581** J. BELL *Haddon's Answ. Osor.* 508 b, Thone of the body, thother of the soule. **1616** CHAMPNEY *Voc. Bps.* 281 Both thone and thother.

b. In Early ME., *þet oþer*:—OE. *þæt óþer*, neuter of *se óþer*, the other, was (app. first in northern, north midl. and east midl. dialects) extended to all genders, and at length analysed as *þe toþer*, the *tother*. See TOTHER. Cf. also TO *adj.*, TONE *pron.*

By some writers *the tone*, *the tother*, were altered by way of correction to *that one*, *that other*.

D. *Comb.*

1. Parasynthetic (from the adj.): as ***other-coloured*** (of a different colour), ***-dimensional*** (of or from another dimension), ***-fashioned*** (of another fashion), ***-featured***, ***-languaged***, ***-minded*** (hence ***other-mindedness***), ***-mouthed***, †***-prized*** (of a different price or amount), ***-sided*** (opp. to *one-sided*; hence ***other-sidedness***).

1551 RECORDE *Pathw. Knowl.* I. Defin., An other fashioned line .. named a twine or twist line. **1593–4** SYLVESTER *Profit Imprisonm.* 24 And whoso list, be mute, if otherminded. **1615** CHAPMAN *Odyss.* I. 282 Of purpose to maintain Course through the dark seas t'other-languag'd men. **1656** H. PHILLIPS *Purch. Patt.* (1676) 38 The true value of any other prized yearly income. **1704** N. N. tr. *Boccalini's Advts. fr. Parnass.* I. 199 If she had a Gallant with other colour'd Hair. **1705** J. PETIVER in *Phil. Trans.* XXV. 1959 This rare Shell, .. being the only one amongst near half a score of the other-Mouth'd. **1887** *Pall Mall G.* 23 June 1/1 The one-sided prosperity and the other-sided misery. **1895** *Athenæum* 13 July 61/3 A one-sidedness must perhaps be complemented by an equal and opposite other-sidedness. **1926** *Public Opinion* 30 Apr. 436/3 The habit of .. other-mindedness. **1940** J. BETJEMAN *Old Lights for New Chancels* 50 Coffee and Ulysses, Tennyson, Joyce, Alpha-minded and other dimensional, Freud or Calvary? Take your choice. **1961** *John o'London's* 25 May 592/2 His humour is so naturally other-dimensional.

2. Objective (from the pron.) as ***other-centred*** (centred in others); ***other-directed*** Sociol. (applied to persons whose behaviour and goals are directed by standards they feel acceptable to others, esp. some kind of peer group; cf. *inner-directed* (INNER *a.* (*sb.*[2]) 1 n), *tradition-directed*; hence as *sb.*; also ***other-directedness***, ***-direction***); † ***other-peering*** (peering or looking at the other); ***other-regard*** (regard for others); ***other-regarding*** (regarding others, altruistic; opp. to *self-regarding*); ***other-regardingness***.

1925 *Inner Life* (Ser. 2) 219 Love of the large room is characteristic of souls that are other-centred. **1950** D. RIESMAN et al. *Lonely Crowd* i. 9 The society of incipient population decline develops in its typical members a social character whose conformity is insured by their tendency to be sensitized to the expectations and preferences of others. These I shall term other-directed people. *Ibid.* 20 It is also my impression that the conditions I believe responsible for other-direction are affecting increasing numbers of people in the metropolitan centers of the advanced industrial countries. *Ibid.* 23 What is common to all other-directeds is that their contemporaries are the source of direction for the individual. **1953** *Brit. Jrnl. Psychol.* XLIV. 187 From having been in the nineteenth century inner-directed .. most

Americans have now become 'other-directed', taking standards and guidance mainly from their contemporaries at each stage in their lives. **1957** V. PACKARD *Hidden Persuaders* xvi. 168 The increasing desire of Americans to make a good impression on their peer group, as a part of the trend to other-directedness. **1959**, etc. [see INNER *a.* (*sb.*[2]) 1 n]. **1966** D. JENKINS *Educated Society* i. 27 Dangers..of excessive 'other-directedness' and the production of 'organization men'. **1973** *Listener* 17 May 635/1 [J. S.] Mill's fears were those of post-war American sociologists like David Riesman, who saw American society as full of 'other-directed' men. **1975** R. H. RIMMER *Premar Experiments* (1976) i. 48 The deep joy and satisfaction he discovers in other-directedness and his love for people-involvement. **1615** G. SANDYS *Trav.* (1637) 26 By reason of the other-peering mountaines. **1938** *Times Lit. Suppl.* 8 Oct. 635/2 When we come..to the consideration of the two major types of Sentiment, Self-regard and Other-regard (or Love), we are on firmer ground. **1879** H. SPENCER *Data of Ethics* iii. §8. 23 The promptings of the other-regarding desires. **1923** J. S. HUXLEY *Ess. Biologist* vii. 273 The instincts that are self-regarding and those that are other-regarding. **1947** *Mind* LVI. 277 If the common good is our principle, we should expect a preference to be given to other-regarding ends over self-regarding ones. **1952** V. GOLLANCZ *My Dear Timothy* xx. 274 At the bottom of it..was an element of something other-regarding. A sense of public service should have taken its place. **1969** *Listener* 6 Feb. 164/1 And protest in our society seems to be of these two kinds also—self-regarding and other-regarding—in rather comparable proportions. **1894** *United Presb. Mag.* XI. 310 That all morality is summed up in altruism—other-regardingness or love. **1958** *Times Lit. Suppl.* 31 Jan. 54/5 Reason, objectivity, tolerance, charity, other-regardingness—these are not natural gifts of men.

other ('ʌðə(r)), *adv.*[1] [Adverbial use of prec., sometimes due to ellipsis.] = OTHERWISE B. 1.

c **1205** LAY. 27898 Al oðer hit itidde. **1628** GAULE *Pract. The.* (1629) 412 Who will care to liue other, then according to this present and euill Life? **1880** SCHOULER *Hist. U.S.* I. 241 Girt round the waist too carelessly to conceal other than temptingly those charms. **1883** *Law Times* 20 Oct. 407/2 It is impossible to refer to them..other than very cursorily.

†**other**, *conj.* and *adv.*[2] *Obs.* Forms: 2–5 **oþer**, 2–6 other, 4–5 **oþere**, othire, othir, -yr(e, 4–6 uther; 6 oder, -ur. *β.* 4 **oiþer**, oither. [The OE. word for 'or' (F. *ou*, L. *aut*, and *sive* or *vel*, G. *oder*) was *oððe*, earlier *oððа* (also *eðða*) = Goth. *aiþþau*, OS. *eþþo*, *oððo*, OHG. *eddo*, *edo*, later *odo*, MHG. *ode*, *oder*, Ger. *oder*. The alternative 'either..or' was expressed by *oððe..oððe*. This form was superseded *c* 1130 by *oðer* (first in O.E. Chron., anno 1127; last example of *oððe*, in a sentence in which *oðer* also occurs, 1131). The MS. of the OE. transl. of *Περὶ διδάξεων* (1200–1225) has regularly *oððer* for OE. *oððe*.

Though the date of the first appearance of this conj. is so narrowly defined, its actual source remains a debated question. It has been held to be identical with the adj. pron. OTHER (see prec.), and (more frequently) with the adj. pron. OUTHER, OE. *áhwæðer*, *áwðer*, *áðer*. Both these pronominal words were indeed in OE. used anticipatively, to introduce the alternative *oððe..oððe..*(see OTHER *adj. pron.* B. 1 b, OUTHER *adj. pron.* 1 b); but there is no trace in OE. of *áwðer* (*áðer*) or *óðer* taking the place of the first member of the alternative *oððe..oððe..*, much less of both members, and least of all of the simple conj. *oððe*. On the contrary, the simple conj. remained invariably *oððe*, and the alternative (so far as the evidence shows) *oððe..oððe..*, down to the abrupt substitution of *oþer c* 1130. It is true that in the 14th c., in northern, north-midl., and e.-midl. Eng., *awþer*, *ouþer*, began to take the place of *oþer* as first member of the alternative *oþer..oþer..*, or *oþer..or..*(the second remaining as *or*, less usually *oþer*), just as later still (in Wyclif and Chaucer) *either* became the midland form of the first member; but these were changes several centuries later than the substitution of *oþer* for *oððe c* 1130, with which they have no historical connexion. It seems more probable that the *oðer* or *oþer* of 1130 was a modification of *oððe* itself, due to some association with words in *-er*; *oððe* being a stressless word was probably reduced in pronunciation to *oðe* (cf. OE. *nalæs* from *nalles*, *sithen* (1140) from *siððan*, etc.). Thus we are reminded of the parallelism of development between HG. *eddo*, *edo*, *odo*, *ode*, *oder*, and OE. *eðða*, *oðða*, *oððe*, (**oðe*), *oðer* or *oþer*, and are led to suspect, for the *r* of German *oder* and of ME. *oþer*, the same or a similar explanation. The form *oððer* used by the early 13th c. scribe of *Περὶ διδάξεων* may either be his accommodation of the *oððe* of his original to the *oðer* of his own day, or an actual intermediate form. It does not seem possible to fix the quantity of the *o* in ME. *oþer*, even from Ormin's spelling; but, if derived from *oððe*, **oðe*, it was presumably short. Ormin's reduced form *oþþr* and *orr* (see OR *conj.*), and the later *or*, had, of course, short *o*, from which the (ɔː) of mod. emphatic *or* is regularly developed.

α. Preliminary illustration of OE. *oððe*:

735 BÆDA *Death-song*, Huaet his gastae godaes aeththa yflaes aefter deoth daege doemid uueorthae. *Riddles* xliv. 17 Hu se cuma hatte eðþa se esne. *c* **825** *Kentish Chart.* (O.E.T. 444) Mittan fulne hunizes oððа tuegen wines. *c* **825** *Vesp. Ps.* viii. 5 Hwet is mon..oððe sunu monnes. *a* **900** *O.E. Chron.* an. 893 Hundtwelftizes mila lang oþþe lengra. **1086–90** *Ibid.* an. 1086 Swa hwa swa sloge heort oððe hinde. **1128–31** *Ibid.* an. 1128 Wær it tweolf monð oððe mare.

1200–25 *Transcript of OE. treatise Περὶ διδάξεων* in *Sax. Leechd.* III. 100 Gnid on win oððer on wearme wætere. *Ibid.* 108 Nim þanne eced oððer win..and nim ele..oððer spic, ʒif man ele nabbe.

β. Illustration of OE. *oððe..oððe..*:

a **900** tr. *Bæda's Hist.* I. i. (1890) 28 Oðþa [*v.r.* oððe] mid freondscipe oðþa [*v.r.* oðþe] mid ʒefeohte. *a* **900** *Ags. Psalms* (Thorpe) xxx. *heading*, Awðer oþþe on mode, oþþe on lichaman. *a* **900** *O.E. Chron.* an. 894 þa scipu eall oðþe tobræcon oþþe forbærndon oþþe to Lundenbyriʒ brohton oþþe to Hrofesceastre. **901** *Ibid.*, [He] sæde þæt he wolde oðer, oððe þær libban oððe þær licgan. **1085–90** *Ibid.* an. 1085 Oððe mid rihte oððe elles. **1100–20** *Ibid.* an. 1100 Ealle he hi oððe wið feo ʒesealde oððe on his aʒenre hand heold.]

A. *conj.* The earlier form of OR *conj.*[2]

a. As simple conj.

1127–31 *O.E. Chron.* (Laud MS.) an. 1127 Þær mihte wel ben abuton twenti oðer þritti horn blaweres. *Ibid.* an. 1131 Swa þæt on þa tun þa wæs tenn ploȝes oðer twelfe gangende ne be læf þær noht an, & se man þa heafde twa hundred oðþe ðre hundred swin ne be leaf him noht an. **1137–54** *Ibid.* an. 1137 Me henged bi the þumbes, other bi the hefed. *Ibid.*, Twa oþer thre men hadden onoh to bæron onne. *Ibid.*, Gif twa men oþer iii coman ridend to an tun. *c* **1175** *Lamb. Hom.* 17 Ec ʒif þu agultest oðer sunegest. *c* **1200** *Trin. Coll. Hom.* 157 Alse þe man doð þe ʒifeð his almes fader oðer moder, suster oðer broðer oðer oðre swo sibbe þat he aghte mid rihte to helpen to feden. *c* **1200** ORMIN 6255, & ʒiff þatt iss þatt aniȝ mann þe shendeþþ oþerr werdeþþ. *Ibid.* 14034, & twafald oþerr þrefald mett þa fétless alle token. *c* **1250** *Gen. & Ex.* 1940 Slo we him noȝt, Oðer sinne may be wroȝt. **1258** *Eng. Proclam. Hen. III* (1868) 19 þurȝ þan to foren iseide rædesmen, oþer þurȝ þe moare dæl of heom alswo. **13..** *E.E. Allit. P.* A. 141 By-ȝonde þe broke by slente oþer slade. **1393** LANGL. *P. Pl.* C. VIII. 108 A blynde man for a bordiour oþer a bedreden womman. **1437** *Rolls of Parlt.* IV. 510/2 In the Kynges Benche, othir in any other place. **1474** *Waterf. Arch.* in *10th Rep. Hist. MSS. Comm.* App. v. 311 No childe, that is to say, son othre doghtre. **1525** TINDALE *Prol. N.T.*, Who ys so blynde.., other so despyghtfull. **1574** *Galway Arch.* in *10th Rep. Hist. MSS. Comm.* App. v. 424 In striffe other variaunces betwixt partye and partye.

β. **13..** *Cursor M.* 11305 (Cott.) Sco suld..offer turtuls douues tua, Oiþer [*Gött.* or; *a* 1425 *Trin.* ouþer; *Laud* othir] o douues duble brid.

b. Preceded by *other*: see B. 1 a.

c. Preceded by *whether*.

c **1350** *Will. Palerne* 3130 Wheþer þow be a god gost.. oiþer any foule fend. *c* **1380** *Sir Ferumb.* 5717 Whather he wolde oþer no. **14..** *Cursor M.* 10779 (Laud) Whethir he wold othir [*Trin.* ouþer] nay. **1526** TINDALE *Luke* vi. 9 Whether is it laufull on the sabath dayes..to saue life oder for to destroye hyt? —— *1 Pet.* ii. 14 Whether it be vnto the kynge..other vnto ruelars.

B. *adv.* **1.** Placed before two (or more) words, phrases, or clauses connected by *other* or *or*, so that *other..other..*, and (later) *other..or..* was equivalent to OE. *oððe..oððe..*, and to mod. Eng. *either..or..*: see EITHER B. 3.

a. In the connexion ***other..other...***

c **1175** *Lamb. Hom.* 37 Oðer þu most hersumian crist, oðer þam deofle. *a* **1200** *Moral Ode* 131 Oþer raþer oðer later milce he scal imeten. **1200–25** (date of MS.) *Περὶ διδάξεων* in *Sax. Leechd.* III. 116 Seo untrumnys cymþ of þrim þingum, oþþer of cyle, oþþer of miclum hæte..oþþer of lytte æte and drince, oþþer of miclum wernesse. *c* **1205** LAY. 8266 Þat þu him sculle oðer don, Oðer slæn oðer a-hon. *a* **1225** *Ancr. R.* 180 Heo is euer oðer of þing wiðuten, oðer of þing wiðinnen. **1297** R. GLOUC. (Rolls) 402 Oþer he smot of þen arm, oþer hand oþer heued. *Ibid.* 6246 Oþer hii mote þanne acordi, oþer fiȝte hom sulue tuo. **1340** *Ayenb.* 25 Oþer ine þe wordle oþer ine religion, oþer clerk oþer lewed. **1545** RAYNOLD *Byrth Mankynde* 35 Other because she accumpanieth not with man, other els for sum other infirmite. **1551** RECORDE *Pathw. Knowl.* Ep. to King, If they mean other your maiesties seruice, other their own wisdome. **1588** A. KING tr. *Canisius' Catech.* 141 Quhen we ar other maintenars..of euill doars, other defends or preaches ony peruers or wickit doctrine.

b. In the connexion ***other..or...***

13.. *Cursor M.* 3855 (Cott.) Þat I suld oþer [*Gött.* ethir] here his saand, Or lat þe folk vte o mi land. *c* **1394** *P. Pl. Crede* 676 Oþer wiþ word or wiþ werke. *c* **1489** CAXTON *Sonnes of Aymon* ix. 213 Brynge theym to me other deed or quycke. **1548** CRANMER *Catech.* 100 b, Other they bryng nothyng to passe..or..theyr losse is greater then theyr gaynes. **1562** TURNER *Baths* Ded., Other in Italy or Germany. *a* **1584** MONTGOMERIE *Cherrie & Slae* 735 Vther few or nane, I trow.

β. *c* **1330** R. BRUNNE *Chron.* (1810) 2 Oiþer bihoues vs defend it, or ʒelde vp our right. **13..** *Cursor M.* 14859 Oiþer for to dei or liue. *c* **1400** *Apol. Loll.* 29 Þat is foly to aferme in þis case oiþer ʒie or nay.

2. Following an alternative clause with *or*: = EITHER B. 5. *rare.*

a **1400–50** *Alexander* 3 Sum farand þing..[that befell] Or [= ere] þai were fourmed on fold, or þaire fadirs oþer.

3. = Whether. *rare.*

1523 LD. BERNERS *Froiss.* I. x. 10 They wist nat in what parte of Inglande they were in: other in the power of theyr frendis, or in the power of theyr ennemies. *Ibid.* I. 145 He wyst nat what way he wolde drawe, other into Normandy, Brebayne, or Gascoyne.

†**oðere**, in early ME. for *o ðere* 'on the'.

a **1240** *Ureisun* 88 in *Cott. Hom.* 195 I-sched oðere rode.

†'**othergate**, *adv. Obs.* [f. OTHER *a.* + GATE *sb.*[2] 9.] Otherwise; = next, A.

c **1350** *Will. Palerne* 3761 Schal no gom under god oþer gate it make. **1390** GOWER *Conf.* II. 95 Whanne it falleth othergate.

othergates ('ʌðəgeɪts), *adv.* and *a. Obs.* exc. *dial.* [f. as prec., with advb. genitive *-es.*]

A. *adv.* In another way, otherwise, differently.

a **1300** *Cursor M.* 1588 (Cott.) Bot god had oþer-gates mint [so *Fairf.*; *Gött.*, *Trin.* oþer wise]. *a* **1340** HAMPOLE *Psalter* cxxxiv. 11 Hit wenys of athing oþergates þen it is. **1362** LANGL. *P. Pl.* A. x. 204 Þat oþer-gates ben I-geten for gadelynges ben holden. *c* **1460** *Towneley Myst.* ii. 121 Other gatis it had beyn seyn. **1528** LYNDESAY *Dreme* 206 Thay dispone that geir all vther gaittis. **1601** SHAKS. *Twel. N.* v. i. 198 If he had not beene in drinke, hee would haue tickel'd you other gates then he did. **1825** BROCKETT *N.C. Gloss.*, *Othergaits*, *othergets*, otherwise, different. **1860** WARTER *Sea-board* II. 28 My ways have been othergates when I was younger, than they ought to have been.

†**B.** *adj.* Of another fashion or kind, different. Frequent in 17th c.

c **1589** *Theses Martinianae* 22 With whome hee might have other gates welcome. **1612** DAY *Festivals* vi. (1615) 136 It was an other-gates Kingdome hee sought after. **1669** WOODHEAD *St. Teresa* II. xxiv. 151 These are Othergates Children than those, you desire.

otherguess ('ʌðəgɛs), *a.* Now only *colloq.* [A phonetic reduction of *othergets* from prec., spelt after *guess.*] Of another kind or sort; = prec. B.

1632 J. HAYWARD tr. *Biondi's Eromena* 55 To place you elsewhere in an other-ghesse shape. **1661** BOYLE *Style of Script.* 125, I have an other-guesse Acquiescence in his Decisions. **1748** SMOLLETT *Rod. Rand.* xxxii, If your kinsman, Lieutenant Bowling, had been here, we should have had other-guess work. **1785** H. WALPOLE *Lett.*, *to C'tess Ossory* 16 Jan., We had other guess winters in my time. **1826** SCOTT *Woodst.* xxii, The riding-suit..hath set him off in other-guess fashion. **1897** *Pall Mall Mag.* June 231 It was otherguess work with Bellamy.

†**otherguise** ('ʌðəgaɪz), *a. Obs.* [Corruption of prec. by folk-etymology, after *guise.*] = prec.

1653 BOGAN *Mirth Chr. Life* 367 Thy soule must have otherguise food, if ever it think to grow. **1688** BUNYAN *Dying Sayings* Wks. 50 The trial we have before God is of otherguise importance. **1727–41** CHAMBERS *Cycl.* s.v. *Book*, To support the same through a volume in folio requires otherguise funds. **1755** SMOLLETT *Quix.* II. III. xiii. (1783) IV. 61 Otherguise cats must scratch my beard, and not such a pitiful muckworm as he.

Also †'**other-guised** *a. Obs.* [An attempt to improve upon prec.]

1768–74 TUCKER *Lt. Nat.* (1834) I. 29 Our perceptions may arise from other guised objects than these whereto we attribute them. *Ibid.* 324 He would make an other-guised calculation than our common gamesters.

otherism ('ʌðərɪz(ə)m). *nonce-wd.* [f. OTHER *a.* or *pron.* + -ISM.] Devotion to the interests of others; altruism.

1883 ARTHUR *Fernley Lect.* 148 Your good feeling towards them is only 'otherism' or 'altruism', not brotherly love. **1894** H. DRUMMOND *Ascent Man* 281 From Self-ism to Other-ism is the supreme transition of history.

'**otherkin, -kins**, *a. Obs.* exc. *dial.* [In 13th c. a genitive phr. *oþerkünnes*, *oþres künnes*, = OE. **óþres cynnes* of another kind: see KIN *sb.*[2] 6 b.] Of another kind; other, different.

a **1200** *Moral Ode* 359 Ne scal þer ben bred ne win ne oþer cunnes este. *c* **1300** *Vox & Wolf* 146 in Hazl. *E.P.P.* I. 62 Her is mete, her is drinke, Her is blisse withouten swinke; Her nis hounger neuer mo, Ne non other kunnes wo. *Ibid.* 224 *ibid.* 65 In euche otheres kunnes quede. **13..** *Cursor M.* 404 Vte-ouer al oþerkin thing. [*a* **1648** LD. HERBERT *Hen. VIII* (1683) 543 Because of his nephews minority, and other kind reasons.] **1855** ROBINSON *Whitby Gloss.* s.v., He has gone an otherkins geeat.

†**otherlike**, *a. Obs.* The two words *other like* = 'other similar', 'the like', formerly sometimes written connectedly as one word.

[**1565–72** COOPER *Thesaurus*, *Vermiculor*..to make checker worke or other lyke [**1620** THOMAS *Lat. Dict.* otherlike] with small pieces colored.] **1603** KNOLLES *Hist. Turks* (1638) 332 In his own Seraglio at Hadrianople, and..in other-like places. **1636** E. DACRES tr. *Machiavel's Disc. Livy* I. viii. 47 Upon these and otherlike occasions. **1670** CAPT. J. SMITH *Eng. Improv. Reviv'd* 78 Trees..oppressed by bushes or other trees growing too near them or otherlike.

†'**otherliker**, *adv.* (*compar.*) *Obs.* Forms: 1 **oðerlícor**, 3 -luker, 4 -laker, -loker. [OE. *oðerlícor* = OS. *oðarlîk-ora*, f. OTHER + *-líce*, -LY[2] + *-or*, -ER[3]: cf. L. *aliter.*] In another manner, otherwise.

c **961** *Rule St. Benet* (Schröer) liv. 87 Se þe oðerlicor ʒedyrstlæce underhniʒe þære reʒulican þreale. *a* **1200** *Moral Ode* 151 Al he walde and oðer luker don oðerluker þenchen. *c* **1200** *Trin. Coll. Hom.* 97 Ac he kidde oðerluker his mihte. **1340** *Ayenb.* 94 To zuiche lyue me comþ oþer be grace oþer be uirtue and naȝt oþerlaker. *a* **1400** *Old Usages of Winchester* in *Eng. Gilds* (1870) 355 ʒif he oþer-loker doþ, be in þe kynges mercy.

otherliness ('ʌðəlɪnɪs). *rare.* [f. OTHER *a.* + -NESS; cf. -LY[1].] The quality of being different or apart in some way.

1949 KOESTLER *Promise & Fulfilment* II. i. 194 That eery odour of otherliness, of vagrancy and jugglery which surrounds Mr. Abramowitz. **1967** E. GRIERSON *Crime of one's Own* x. 86 It was another fault of the romantic spirit to imagine that..agents..[had] some special quality of 'otherliness', whereas their very profession must demand the opposite. **1976** A. KOESTLER in D. Villiers *Next Year in Jerusalem* 101 Do I really consider myself a member of a chosen race...If not, what right have I to go on..inflicting on my children the stigma of otherliness?

otherness ('ʌðənɪs). [f. OTHER *a.* + -NESS.] The quality of being other; difference, diversity.

1587 GOLDING *De Mornay* vi. (1617) 84 There must needs be alwaies both a selfesamenesse and also an anothernesse.. the selfesameness in the Essence or being;..and the othernesse is in the In beings or Persons. **1625** GILL *Sacr. Philos.* I. 83 Absolute perfection..without othernesse or change. **1885** J. MARTINEAU *Types Eth. Th.* I. 29 Negation ..not absolute, but only relative, simply affirming otherness of being. **1893** SIDGWICK *Process Argt.* 143 The relation of sequence involves the relation of 'otherness'.

b. *transf.* The fact of being other; something that is other (than the thing mentioned, or than the thinking subject).

1821 COLERIDGE in *Blackw. Mag.* X. 249 *Outness* is but the feeling of *otherness* (alterity), rendered intuitive, or alterity visually represented. **1868** BUSHNELL *Serm. Liv. Subj.* 120 He is now conscious not of himself only, but of a certain otherness moving in him. **1888** R. POTTER *Relat. Ethics to Relig.* 76 That otherness which He calls into existence is independent of all phenomena. **1892** W. S. LILLY *Gt. Enigma* 141, I am directly conscious of it as an otherness; a non-self.

other-self. *Metaph.* Self other than the subject self; objective personality.

1899 C. F. D'ARCY *Idealism & Theol.* vi. 224 He [Hegel] uses it to overcome the opposition of self and other-self. But other-self, in its true character, eludes the grasp of self.

'other,selfish, *a. nonce-wd.* Relating to other 'selves' or persons; altruistic.

1877 EDITH SIMCOX *Nat. Law* v. 221 The division of human motives into selfish and otherselfish ones.

†**otherside.** *Obs.* The two words *other side* formerly improperly written as one.

a **1548** HALL *Chron., Hen. IV* 29 The duke of Orleance on the otherside beyng highly set up in pride. **1568** GRAFTON *Chron.* II. 251, I have such trust in you..and on the otherside I have such trust in the king.

other some, †**othersome,** *a.* and *pron.* Now *arch.* or *dial.* [The two words OTHER *a.* and SOME *pron.* or *a.*, formerly often improperly written as one. Usually as correlative to *some.*]

adj. Some other; *pron.* Some others.

c **1250** *Gen. & Ex.* 686 After ðis cam swilc oðer sum. **13..** *Cursor M.* 6491 þaa fraward folk..Said þat moyses was slain,.. And oþer sum said þat he Was liuand. **1551** TURNER *Herbal* I. K iij b, In sum placies Cicuta is much stronger then in other sum. **1582** N. T. (Rhem.) *Matt.* xiii. 5 Othersome also fell vpon rockie places. *Ibid.* 8 Othersome fell vpon good ground. **1593** STUBBES *Motive Gd. Wks.* 80 In othersome places I have seene the Churches strawed over either with hay grasse, strawe, sedges. **1611** BIBLE *Acts* xvii. 18 Some said, What will this babbler say? Other some, He seemeth to bee a setter foorth of strange gods. **1651** C. CARTWRIGHT *Cert. Relig.* I. 42 Some think that the English translation..in some places takes away, in other places addes, and other-some places changes the meaning. **1770** C. JENNER *Placid Man* II. v. v. 126 It makes some folks prouder than othersome. **1854** MRS. OLIPHANT *Magd. Hepburn* III. 105 These might be rude missionaries, in some cases, but in other some, they were the highest of heart, and noblest of spirit. **1875** PARISH *Sussex Dial.* s.v., Sometimes my old gal's better than what she be othersome.

†**b.** *esp.* in phr. **othersome time(s** (also *othersometime(s*: cf. *sometime(s)*: At some other times, at other times. So ***othersome whiles.*** *Obs.*

1575 BANISTER *Chirurg.* III. (1585) 448 They are engendred otherwhiles, of..common matter, and othersometime, of some..peculier matter. **1606** G. W[OODCOCKE] *Hist. Ivstine* IV. 21 Some-whiles flashes of fyre, other some-whiles againe..dangerous vapors. **1616** SURFL. & MARKH. *Country Farme* 687 Othersome times.. hee goeth from one thicket to another. **1647** H. MORE *Song of Soul* Notes 165/1 Sometimes it signifieth the soul, othersometime, the naturall spirits. **1671** H. M. tr. *Erasm. Colloq.* 485 Sometimes water, and othersome-times fire.

†**other-times, othertimes,** *adv. phr. Obs.* [The two words OTHER *a.* and *times*, formerly often united: cf. *sometimes.*] At other times.

c **1440** *Promp. Parv.* 376/1 Oþyr tyme, *alias.* **1502** *Ord. Crysten Men* (W. de W. 1506) I. vii. 72 Ypocrytes that men wende other tymes to haue ben true faythfull and good people. **1603** FLORIO *Montaigne* II. xii. (1632) 288 Sometimes reason, othertimes the World. **1625** BP. HALL *Holy Observ.* Wks. 145 The spirit is oftentimes tried by the speech: but other-times the speech must be examined by the spirit. **1705** *Lond. Gaz.* No. 4130/4 Anthony Fensom, a Ropemaker, othertimes a Labourer.

otherwards ('ʌðəwədz), *adv. nonce-wd.* [f. OTHER *a.* + -WARDS.] In another direction.

1858 CARLYLE *Fredk. Gt.* VIII. iii. II. 308 King looks towards the Prince of Baireuth..Queen looks far otherwards.

otherways ('ʌðəweɪz), *adv. Obs.* exc. *dial.* Forms: 2–3 **-weies, -weis,** 3 **-weiis, -weise,** 4 **-weys,** 4–9 **-ways.** Also 4–7 **-waies, -wais,** 5–7 **-wayes,** *Sc.* **-wayis.** [f. OTHER *a.* + *ways*, adverbial genitive of WAY *sb.*] In another way, manner, case, etc.: = OTHERWISE.

c **1175** *Lamb. Hom.* 31 Ilke monne þe he haueð er istolen oðer oðer weis wa idon. *c* **1205** LAY. 18760 Oðere weies þu most agunnen. *c* **1320** *Cast. L.* 623 Another that otherweys were. *c* **1330** R. BRUNNE *Chron.* (1810) 175 How þam felle oþer wais so many woes & hard. **1470–85** MALORY *Arthur* I. xvi, Lordes ye must other wayes than ye do. **1535** CRANMER *Let. to Cromwell* in *Misc. Writ.* (Parker Soc.) II. 315 None otherways but as it shall seem to you just so to do. **1656** H. PHILLIPS *Purch. Patt.* (1676) 16 Those who have any employment for their money otherways. **1720** GAY *Poems* (1745) I. 255, I could not sure do otherways than well. **1808** CURWEN *Econ. Feeding Stock* 38 Other-ways, how should we account for [the fact]?

†**'otherwhat,** *pron. Obs.* [f. OTHER *a.* + WHAT; cf. *somewhat.*] Some other thing; something else.

a **1225** *Ancr. R.* 96 Uor he..spekeð þeonne of oðerwhat. *c* **1305** *St. Lucy* 137 in *E.E.P.* (1862) 105 Oþer what we mote do.

otherwhence ('ʌðəhwɛns), *adv. rare.* [f. OTHER *a.* + WHENCE.] From elsewhere.

1575–85 ABP. SANDYS *Serm.* (Parker Soc.) 285 It cometh otherwhence. **1883** W. LEAF tr. *Iliad* IX. 380 All that now is his, and all that may come to him otherwhence.

otherwhere ('ʌðəhwɛə(r)), *adv.* Forms: see OTHER *a.* and WHERE. Also hyphened, or as two words. [f. OTHER *a.* + WHERE: cf. *somewhere.* Very common in 16–17th c., rare or obs. in 18th, revived in 19th.] In another place; somewhere else; elsewhere.

a **1541** WYATT *Deserted Lover* 8 With words to win The hearts of them which otherwhere doth grow. **1559** MORWYNG *Evonym.* 19 The reason is declared otherwher. *c* **1630** MILTON *Passion* 25 His godlike acts, and his temptations fierce, And former sufferings other where are found. *a* **1677** BARROW *Serm.* Wks. 1716 II. 61 Otherwhere in this Epistle. **1706** LUTTRELL *Brief Rel.* (1857) VI. 5 On board..ships that lie at Portsmouth..and on those otherwhere. **1820** KEATS *Eve St. Agnes* vii, But she saw not: her heart was otherwhere. **1854** HAWTHORNE *Eng. Note-bks.* II. 387 At Charing Cross, and otherwhere about London. **1894** J. R. ILLINGWORTH *Pers. Hum. & Div.* vii. (1895) 186 Analogous with the workings of the human spirit otherwhere.

b. To another place.

c **1375** *Sc. Leg. Saints* xxiii. (*VII Sleperis*) 92 For þat he was far to fare Of þe cyte vthyre-quhare. *c* **1610** *Women Saints* 92 To leaue that place and to goe other-where. **1638** BAKER tr. *Balzac's Lett.* (1654) II. 28 Since your honour calls you otherwere. **1870** MORRIS *Earthly Par.* I. II. 510 It seemed that time had passed on otherwhere Nor laid a finger on this hidden place.

c. quasi-*sb.*, esp. with *some, any*, etc. (better written separately; ***some other where*** = some other place).

c **1300** *Cursor M.* 23906, þat..I sal tel of sum oþer quar [*v.r.* sum elles quar]. **1526** TINDALE *Luke* xiii. 33 It cannot be that a prophet perisshe eny other where save att Ierusalem. **1597** HOOKER *Eccl. Pol.* v. xxx. §4 Any thing done any other-where. **1635** SWAN *Spec. M.* (1670) 36 Else it rained from some otherwhere. *a* **1845** HOOD *Poems* (1846) II. 69 [To] forbear their privacy and seek some other where. **1889** *Voice* (N.Y.) 28 Nov., They are destined for otherwhere than the plowed field with the grave at the end of it.

otherwheres ('ʌðəhwɛəz), *adv. rare.* [f. as prec. with advb. genitive *-s.*] = prec.

1563 *Homilies* II. *Cert. Places Holy Script* I. (1859) 369 Can this be found or gotten otherwheres? **1641** HINDE *J. Bruen* xxxii. 101 In his owne family, and other wheres also. *a* **1864** HAWTHORNE *Amer. Note-bks.* (1879) II. 44 Other-wheres the shadow was deep. **1867** JEAN INGELOW *Songs Voices Birds, Cuckoo* 122 As if some right-joyous elf, While about his own affairs, Whistled softly otherwheres.

otherwhile ('ʌðəhwaɪl), *adv.* Now *rare* or *dial.* Forms: see OTHER *a.* and WHILE. Also as two words, or hyphened. [f. OTHER *a.* + WHILE *sb.*]

1. At one time or other; at times; sometimes, now and then, occasionally. ***otherwhile.. otherwhile***, at one time..at another time (in OE. *hwíle..hwíle*). *Obs.* exc. *dial.*

c **1175** *Lamb. Hom.* 23 Noþeles oðerhwile þu sunegest mid summe of þisse limen. *c* **1200** *Trin. Coll. Hom.* 147 Oðer-wile wanne hie seȝen men wanred þolien. **1340** *Ayenb.* 40 Oþerhuyl of þe on: oþerhuil of þe oþren, oþerhuyl of on and of oþre. **1382** WYCLIF *Ecclus.* xiii. 21 As a wlf shal comune to a lomb otherwhile [1388 sum tyme]. **1432–50** tr. *Higden* (Rolls) I. 71 Tigris and Euphrates, whiche be other while separate and oþerwhile commixte. **1509** HAWES *Past. Pleas.* xx. (Percy Soc.) 98 Besechyng you..Yet other whyle to thynke upon me. **1607** BP. HALL *Art Div. Medit.* xxiii. 117 Otherwhile and ofter thy back is turned unto him through negligence. **1875** PARISH *Sussex Dial.* s.v., I has a horn of beer otherwhile, but never nothing to do me no hurt.

†**b.** as *adj.* Occurring now and then, occasional.

1589 NASHE *Pref. Greene's Menaphon* (Arb.) 16 The other-while vacations of our grauer Nobilitie.

†**c.** quasi-*sb.* in ***every otherwhile*** (properly three words, *every other while*, like *every other minute*), every now and then, at frequent intervals. *Obs.*

1542 UDALL *Erasm. Apoph.* 160 A thyng litle to the benefite of a commen weale, euery other whyle to chaunge the Capitaines. **1617** HIERON *Wks.* (1619–20) II. 315 Euery other-while there commeth newes of some of the gallants of the times. **1736** PEGGE *Kenticisms* (E.D.S.) s.v., 'Every otherwhile a little', i.e. a little now and then.

2. At another time, or at other times. Chiefly as correlative to *sometime* or an equivalent. *arch.*

In the first two quots. the sense is doubtful: it may be 1.

1401 *Pol. Poems* (Rolls) II. 101 Daw, thou herdist me not grucche that ȝe went two togedir; ffor otherwhile ȝe gon three. *c* **1460** FORTESCUE *Abs. & Lim. Mon.* vii. (1885) 124 Oþer while he shall sende his procuratours and messengers to the counselles generalles. **1586** W. WEBBE *Eng. Poetrie* Ded. (Arb.) 14 Alexander..leaned sometime too hard, other-whyle too soft, as neuer hauing beene apprentice to the Arte. **1628** GAULE *Pract. The.* (1629) 92 One while, her holy life bids him not suspect her dishonest; other while, his owne weakenesse and ignorance bids him not be perswaded. **1720** *Connect. Col. Rec.* (1872) VI. 184 A certain man, who was sometime taken for Nathaniel Wilson, other-while for John Clements. **1855** M. ARNOLD *Balder* Poems 1877 I. 152 But the gods went not now, as otherwhile, Into the tilt-yard. **1869** FREEMAN in Stephens *Life* (1895) I. 434 Other while I have never ventured to utter a word.

otherwhiles ('ʌðəhwaɪlz), *adv.* Now *rare* or *dial.* Forms: see OTHER *a.* and WHILES. Also as two words, or hyphened. [f. as prec. with advb. genitive *-s*, in later times often felt as plural.]

†**1.** = prec. 1. *Obs.*

a **1225** *Ancr. R.* 50 Lates þet summe oðer hwules, weilawei! unkundeliche makieð. *Ibid.* 180 þeos fondunges cumeð oðerhules of God, & oðerhules of mon. *c* **1420** *Pallad. on Husb.* VIII. 65 The ky may otherwhiles be withdrawe. **1576** A. FLEMING tr. *Caius' Eng. Dogs* in Arb. *Garner* III. 234 To hunt two divers beasts, as the foxe other-whiles, and other-whiles the hare. **1601** HOLLAND *Pliny* II. 537 Double diligence and ouermuch curiositie both hurt other-whiles. **1671** H. M. tr. *Erasm. Colloq.* 156 She did nothing but weep, and otherwhiles also threw her self upon the ground. **1787** GROSE *Prov. Gloss., Otherwhiles*, sometimes.

2. = prec. 2.

c **1460** FORTESCUE *Abs. & Lim. Mon.* vii. (1885) 125 The kynge shall often tymes sende his comissioners..to represse and punysh riatours and risers; ffor wich cause he shall odre whiles ride in his owne person. **1526** *Pilgr. Perf.* (W. de W. 1531) 269 Somtyme with swete mylke of deuocion or otherwhyles amonge with..swetnes of grace. **1540–1** ELYOT *Image Gov.* 8 Sometyme aboundaunt, otherwyles shorte and compendious. **1683** CHALKHILL *Thealma & Cl.* 100 Tones, Sometimes of Joy, and otherwhiles of Mones. **1719** DE FOE *Crusoe* I. xiii, Other whiles I fancied they were all gone. **1897** *Dublin Rev.* Oct. 394 Sometimes the points are definitive, otherwhiles the writer leaves himself liberty for a different arrangement.

†**b.** ***some otherwhiles*** (properly three words, *some other whiles*), at some other times. *Obs.*

1671 H. M. tr. *Erasm. Colloq.* 294 Sometimes into the stomach..some otherwhiles into the neck.

'other,whither, *adv. rare.* [f. OTHER *a.* + WHITHER.] To another place; 'elsewhither'.

1575 BANISTER *Chirurg.* I. (1585) 124 If the humor yet be flowing draw it otherwhither by blood letting.

otherwise ('ʌðəwaɪz), *sb. phr., adv., a.* Forms: see OTHER *a.* and WISE *sb.* [Orig. a phrase of three words: OE. *on oðre wísan*, in other manner, in late OE. also *oðre wisan*, ME. *oþre wise*, at length written *otherwise*: cf. *in any wise, anywise, crosswise*, etc.: see WISE *sb.*]

A. *sb. phr.* Phrase with *wise*, manner, way, as distinct sb., e.g. ***in other wise***, OE. *on oðre wisan..on oðre*, in one way..in another; ***no otherwise***, OE. *on náne oðre wisan*, ME. *non oþer wise*, 16th c. *none other-wise*, in no other way. *arch.*

c **888** K. ÆLFRED *Boeth.* xxxix. §10 We ongitað hwilum man on oðre wisan, on oðre hine God onȝit. *c* **900** tr. *Bæda's Hist.* III. xii. [xiv.] 194 Ac hit feorr on oðre wisan wæs. *c* **1050** *Ags. Gloss.* in Wr.-Wülcker 341/26 *Aliter*, on æniȝe oðre wisan. *a* **1200** *Fragm. Ælfric's Gram.* I On oþre wisen. *a* **1300** *Cursor M.* 3887 þat mai be nanoþer wis. *Ibid.* 17528 For-soth it es nan oiþer wise. *c* **1460** FORTESCUE *Abs. & Lim. Mon.* iii. (1885) 114 Thai mowe in non oþer wyse leve. **1535** JOYE *Apol. Tindale* (Arb.) 50 For I take yt no nother wyse. **1540** HYRDE tr. *Vives' Instr. Chr. Wom.* (1592) O vj, Shee ought to love him none other-wise than her selfe. **1597** MORLEY *Introd. Mus.* 6 Could you sing it no other wise? **1790** BURKE *Fr. Rev.* 60 To be led any otherwise than blindly. *a* **1873** MILL *Ess. Relig.* (1874) 211 The fact of death will make no sudden break in our spiritual life, nor influence our character any otherwise than as any important change in our mode of existence may always be expected to modify it.

b. (*pl.*) = other ways. *nonce-use.*

1869 BROWNING *Ring & Bk.* XI. 1455 Some one of the hundred otherwises.

c. Phr. ***or*** (occas. ***and***) ***otherwise***, following a noun, adjective, adverb, or verb, to signify a corresponding word of opposite or different meaning.

1886 *Rep. Brit. Assoc. Adv. Sci.* *1885* 872 The index number..is I or 100, according to the use or otherwise of the decimal point. **1892** [see *playing week* s.v. PLAYING *vbl. sb.* 2]. **1895** *Pall Mall Mag.* Jan. 35 The most amusing feature of the case was the conflict of professional evidence as to the merits, or otherwise, of Mr. Whistler's paintings. **1910** *Practitioner* Jan. 84 The question of operability or otherwise is a matter in which surgeons differ considerably. **1911** E. C. WORDEN *Nitrocellulose Industry* II. xiv. 697 These enamels may be closely imitated..by taking a given pattern, enlarging it pantographically or otherwise, [etc.]. **1922** C. MACKENZIE *Altar Steps* vii. 56 Mrs. Lidderdale's dread.. was that her son would acquire a West country burr, and it was considered more prudent, economically and otherwise, to let him go on learning with his grandfather and herself. **1966** *Listener* 22 Sept. 427/2, I do not question the eruption at Santorin,..but the supposed connection of the underwater survey with the historicity or otherwise of the Atlantis myth. **1972** W. A. PANTIN *Oxf. Life* iv. 52 Professor Southern gave us some stimulating reflections about the aims, development, and achievements (or otherwise) of the Honour School of Modern History. **1972** *Times Lit. Suppl.* 13 Oct. 1233/1 The circumstances of the publication of the Penguin Books version of D. H. Lawrence's *Lady Chatterley's Lover* in November 1960 led to much public discussion of the desirability or otherwise of printing these long-banned sexual words. **1973** *Oxford Times* 30 Nov. 10, 12,000 Cowley workers enjoyed (or otherwise) an enforced holiday because of a strike by plant attendants at the car assembly factory.

B. *adv.* †**α. other wise;** *β.* **otherwise.**

1. In another way, or in other ways; in a different manner, or by other means; differently. Constr. *than* (†*but*).

α. [*971 Blickl. Hom.* 177 þe læs þe oðre wisan æniȝ mæn leoȝe.] *c* **1315** SHOREHAM 42 And ȝyf he hyt othere wyse fangeth, He taketh bote the sygne. **13..** *Cursor M.* 1588 (Gött.) Bot god al oþer wise [so *Trin.*; *Cott., Fairf.* oþer gates] had mint. **1482** *Monk of Evesham* 79 He studyd..by a colour of symulacyon odyr wise then he schulde to troble hem. **1535** COVERDALE *1 Macc.* ii. 4 Iudas, other wyse called Machabeus.

β. *c* **1330** R. BRUNNE *Chron.* (1810) 208 Of som he grantise his wille for to do, & som said oþerwise, þat it suld not be so. *c* **1386** *Chaucer's Sqr.'s T.* 526 God woot and he þat ootherwise noght [4 *MSS.* oþer wise]. **1511** in W. H. Turner *Select. Rec. Oxford* 7 George Pykeryng otherwyse Smythe. **1606** HOLLAND *Sueton.* 98 Yet can I not be perswaded other-wise, but to thinke, that [etc.]. **1712**

BUDGELL *Spect.* No. 404 ¶3 Applying his Talents otherwise than Nature designed. **1864** PUSEY *Lect. Daniel* (1876) 553 God saw otherwise.

†**b.** ***otherwise..otherwise***: in one way..in another way. *Obs. rare.*

1645 MILTON *Tetrach.* Wks. (1847) 198/1 (Matt. xix. 4–5) On which place Paræus notes..that Christ is wont otherwise to answer hypocrites, otherwise those that are docible.

2. In another case; in other circumstances; if the case be not so; if not; else.

1390 GOWER *Conf.* II. 74 For otherwise she scholde have failed, If that he had noght travailed. *a* **1425** *Cursor M.* 23505 (Trin.) Oþerwise is not synne forȝyuen But to bete hit whil we may lyuen. **1552** *Bk. Com. Prayer* Communion, Otherwyse the receiuing of the holy Communion, doth nothyng els but encrease your damnacion. **1611** BIBLE *Matt.* vi. 1 Take heed that ye doe not your almes before men,.. otherwise yee haue no reward of your father which is in heauen. **1790** *Cook's Voy.* V. 1685 Enabled them to perform a journey of three or four leagues, which, otherwise, they must have perished before they could have accomplished. **1846** TRENCH *Mirac.* xxxii. (1862) 448 We learn, what perhaps otherwise we might have guessed. *Mod.* I went at once; otherwise I should have missed him.

3. In other respects; with regard to other points.

1594 HOOKER *Eccl. Pol.* I. xvi. §6 The best men otherwise are not alwayes the best in regard of societie. **1647** JER. TAYLOR *Lib. Proph.* Wks. 1836 II. 371 By the report of persons otherwise pious and prudent. **1796** MORSE *Amer. Geog.* I. 24 Having otherwise no reason to suspect them. **1857** BUCKLE *Civiliz.* I. ii. 45, I will give one instance of this from an otherwise sensible writer.

†**4.** On the other hand. *Obs. rare.*

1551 T. WILSON *Logike* (1580) 2 b, A skilfull artificer maie sone put the vain Sophister to silence.. Whereas otherwise an argumente made by the rules of Logike can not bee auoided. **1673** *Vain Insolency of Rome* 35 And otherwise the people could observe him advanced..a cubit above the earth.

C. Adjectival uses.

1. Predicatively, approaching an adj.: In another state or condition; differently conditioned or existing; not so; different; other.

c **1400** *Chaucer's Melib.* ¶99 (Harl. MS.) Whan þe þing semeþ oþerwise [*Gg.* 4. 27 othir wyse, *Petw.* oþer wise, *Lansd.* oþerewise; *Ellesm.* etc. ootherweyes, etc.] þan it was biforn. *a* **1533** LD. BERNERS *Huon* lxx. 238, I byleue the mater be other wyse than he hath sayd. *c* **1680** HICKERINGILL *Hist. Whiggism* I. Wks. 1716 I. 20 Scholars are like other Men, some are wise, and some are otherwise. **1736** MANDEVILLE *World Unmasked* 380 The matter is quite other-wise. **1844** LD. MACAULAY *Speeches* 320 Can an Established Church which has no hold on..the people be otherwise than useless? **1879** M. ARNOLD *Mixed Ess.* 192 Only one or two sentences I could wish otherwise.

2. as *adj.* That would otherwise be...; that would otherwise exist.

1600 W. WATSON *Decacordon* (1602) 51 At the table aboue all others their otherwise equals. **1892** D. A. CLARKE in A. E. Lee *Hist. Columb.* (Ohio) II. 650 Stone crosses..give a decided relief to their otherwise dullness.

D. *Comb.*, as ***otherwise-minded*** adj.; hence ***otherwise-mindedness***.

[**1611** BIBLE *Phil.* iii. 15 If in any thing ye be otherwise minded.] **1865** LOWELL *New Eng. Two Cent. Ago* Pr. Wks. 1890 II. 23 One of the jarring atoms in a chaos of otherwise-mindedness. **1889** —— *Walton* Latest Lit. Ess. (1891) 72 Many-membered periods which in unskilful hands become otherwise-minded as a herd of swine.

Hence **'otherwiseness** (*nonce-wd.*), condition or quality of being otherwise.

1890 J. H. STIRLING *Gifford Lect.* vi. 103 The other, as the difference, the otherwiseness, is just as it is named.

other world, 'other-world, *sb.* and *a.* Also otherworld. [See OTHER *a.* 2.]

1. A world other than this: **a.** The world to come, the world beyond the grave. **b.** The spirit-land of many non-Christian peoples. **c.** The world of idealism, poetry, or romance; also more *gen.*, a range of experiences conceived in imagination or fantasy as lying outside the world as normally known.

c **1200, 1611** [see WORLD *sb.* 1 d]. **1612** W. STRACHEY *Trav. Virginia* (1849) I. iv. 60 The liuetenant..with his dagger, sent him to accompanye his master in the other world. **1679** [see GUARANTEE *sb.* 1]. **1762** STERNE *Tr. Shandy* V. xlii. 141 Baldus..entered upon the law so late in life, that every body imagined he intended to be an advocate in the other world. **1804** M. WILMOT *Let.* 29 June in *Russ. Jrnls.* (1934) I. 107 What think you..the place is like?..to let you at once into the secrets of Other Worlds, know that Kattova is very like a wooden village. **1880** G. M. HOPKINS *Let.* 22 Dec. in Hopkins & Dixon *Corr.* (1935) 37 The other-world of imagination. **1887** G. B. SHAW *Short Stories, Scraps & Shavings* in *Works* (1932) VI. 101 With gho—with people from—with ladies and gentlemen from the other world. **1888** MRS. H. WARD *R. Elsmere* vii. 89 The most determined sacrificing of 'this warm kind world'..to a cold other-world with its torturing inadmissible claims. **1895** A. NUTT *Voy. Bran* 213 Manannan, lord of the Happy Otherworld. **1898** F. B. JEVONS in *Class. Rev.* Feb. 48/1 He sought to show that a belief in the Happy Otherworld was found amongst the Celts and the Greeks. **1920** D. H. LAWRENCE *Women in Love* iv. 46 The whole otherworld, wet and remote, he had to himself. **1953** A. HUXLEY *Let.* 21 June (1969) 678 His [*sc.* the schizophrenic's] commonest experiences are of an Other World, not heavenly but infernal and purgatorial. **1960** S. PLATH *Colossus* 39 These..sheets.. Speak in sign language of a lost otherworld, A world we lose by merely waking up. **1968** T. WOLFE *Electric Kool-Aid Acid Test* v. 60 The whole *other world* that LSD opened your mind to. **1975** *Times Lit. Suppl.* 25 Apr. 445/3 Mr McCarthy sets his saga of Servier County in the strange otherworld of a Tennessee winter.

2. *attrib.* Pertaining or relating to the other world; unearthly; heavenly.

1884 TENNYSON *Becket* Prol., That sweet other-world smile. **1884** J. PARKER *Larger Ministry* 51 The Christian minister is not a chatterer of other-world phrases. **1892** J. S. STUART-GLENNIE in *Proc. Internat. Folk-Lore Congr. 1891* 225 Myths which..I would name..the Sacerdotal. By these I mean especially all the Otherworld Myths. **1917** [see IMMRAM]. **1957** G. ASHE *King Arthur's Avalon* i. 28 A Lake Villagers' burial ground on Ynyswitrin, with a resulting Ghosts' High Noon presided over by other-world deities.

Hence **'other,worldish** *a.*, **'other,worldism** (*nonce-wds.*).

1894 *Q. Rev.* Jan. 245 An other-worldish and rather somnolent party. **1894** *Constance Naden's Poet. Wks.* Introd. 14 Religious exercises of Prayer, Praise, and Spiritualism (other-worldism) generally.

otherworldliness (ˌʌðəˈwɜːldlɪnɪs). [f. the phrase *other world*, after *worldliness*.]

1. Devotion to the other world, or to the interests of a future life; *esp.* the disposition to consider the future state and neglect the affairs of the present; a spirit of worldliness as applied to the future life; morbid, ascetic, or selfish spirituality.

a **1834** S. T. COLERIDGE *Lett. & Recoll.* (1836) I. 98–9 As there is a worldliness or the too-much of this Life, so there is another-worldliness, or rather other-worldliness, equally hateful and selfish with this worldliness. **1847** LEWES *Hist. Philos.* (1867) II. 5. **1855** H. SPENCER *Princ. Psychol.* (1872) II. VIII. vii. 601 Other-worldliness..is a feeling in which the representation of divine approval goes along with a representation of future happiness to be secured by that approval. **1882** FISKE in *Harper's Mag.* Dec. 117/1 The error of mediæval anchorites and mystics in setting an exaggerated value upon otherworldliness.

2. The quality attributed to an ideal world apart from the actual.

1876 LOWELL *Among my Bks.* Ser. II. 172 Full of life and light and the other-worldliness of poetry. **1898** *Fortn. Rev.* LXIV. 291 Burne-Jones..one defines him with true apprehension as the Painter of Otherworldliness.

otherworldly (ˈʌðəˌwɜːldlɪ), *a.* [f. as prec., after *worldly*.]

1. Of or pertaining to a world other than that in which we actually live.

1879 F. J. FURNIVALL *R. Brunne's Chron. Wace* 784/2 Divining, knowledge of other-worldly matters. **1955** A. HUXLEY *Let.* 10 Jan. (1969) 720, I took mescalin yesterday, for the second time... The experience had a human content, which the earlier, solitary experience, with its Other Worldly quality..did not possess. **1957** G. ASHE *King Arthur's Avalon* iii. 107 The poem entangles Arthur in a network of other-worldly themes, a network which takes in Glastonbury and the quest for a miraculous vessel. **1972** *Where* Oct. 275/3 Other..readers..may find the results almost as other-worldly as might a non-literate home in the East End.

2. Of, pertaining to, or devoted to the world of mind or imagination.

1873 PATER *Renaissance* viii. 204 It is easy with the other-worldly gifts to be a *schöne Seele*. **1890** *Cincinnati Chr. Advocate* 5 Feb. 10/3 No one who has ever raised his eyes from his present narrow horizon..will ever sneer at a philosopher as 'otherworldly'.

3. Of or pertaining to the world to come; devoted to the concerns of the world to come; disposed to consider the affairs or interests of a future life to the neglect of those of the present. Also *absol.* as *sb.*

1880 *Sat. Rev.* 6 Nov. 585/1 The series is..a sort of other-worldly imitation of the series of worldly biographies and criticisms edited by Mr. John Morley. **1886** *Athenæum* 9 Oct. 463/2 Among worldly and other-worldly matrons, maids, and men. **1890** *Chicago Advance* 27 Mar., The early Church had to prove that its concerns were not altogether other-worldly. **1920** E. I. WATKIN in C. Hess *God & Supernatural* 141 Nor have these souls merely desired sufferings as the unavoidable price of an other-worldly reward. **1932** C. P. CURRAN in F. J. Sheed *Irish Way* 134 The other-worldly man must put on the man of affairs, the monk-bishop become a politician. **1950** 'G. ORWELL' *Shooting Elephant* 106 The other-worldly, anti-humanist tendency of his [*sc.* Gandhi's] doctrines. **1961** NEW ENG. BIBLE *Luke* xvi. 8 For the worldly are more astute than the other-worldly in dealing with their own kind.

other-worldness (ˌʌðəˈwɜːldnɪs). [f. OTHER WORLD *sb.* and *a.* + -NESS.] = OTHERWORLDLINESS.

1915 J. LONDON *Jacket* i. 1 These child glimpses are of other-worldness, of other-lifeness, of things that you had never seen in this particular world of your particular life. **1956** I. BROMIGE *Enchanted Garden* II. ii. 87 It was an expressive face. In repose, it had an appealing wistfulness, an other-worldness. **1961** P. DOUGHERTY *Mother Mary Potter* iii. 35 In the Portsea-Southsea district..Mary's persevering and unobtrusive other-worldness was inevitably discussed.

†**'othing.** *Obs.* [See O *numeral adj.*, and cf. *nothing*.] One thing.

1573 TUSSER *Husb.* (1878) 184 Ill huswiferie othing or other must craue.

'Othman, *a.* and *sb.* = OTTOMAN *a.* and *sb.*[1]

1813 BYRON *Giaour* xxxi, Yet seems he not of Othman race. **1816** —— *Siege of Cor.* xxix, And now the Othmans gain the gate. **1864** NEALE *Seaton. Poems* 15 Prepare thee for the Othman yoke!

othoȝte, pa. t. of OFTHINK *Obs.*, to repent.

othom: see ODAM *Obs.*, son-in-law.

†**othonne.** *Obs.* [ad. L. *othonna* (Pliny), a. Gr. ὄθοννα; now used as a generic name.] The African or Barbary Ragwort, *Othonna cheirifolia.*

1601 HOLLAND *Pliny* II. 286 Othonne groweth plenteously in Scythia, like vnto Rocket.

othre, othur, othyr, obs. ff. OTHER.

†**'othyl.** *Chem. Obs.* [contr. of *ox-ethyl* = *ethyl oxide*.] A name proposed by Williamson for the oxidized radical of the di-carbon series, C_2H_3O, commonly called ACETYL.

1857 MILLER *Elem. Chem.* III. 311 *note.* **1866–77** WATTS *Dict. Chem.* I. 132 Williamson called the radicle 'othyl'; but on account of the difficulty of forming analogous names for analogous radicles, the name has been generally abandoned for the term acetyl.

otiant (ˈəʊʃɪənt), *a. rare.* [ad. L. *ōtiānt-em*, pr. pple. of *ōtiā-rī* to be at leisure, f. *ōtium* leisure.] At leisure, doing nothing, indolent, at ease.

1878 *N. Amer. Rev.* CXXVI. 483 They who..relegate the Supreme to the otiant ease of Epicurus.

†**oti'ation.** *Obs. rare.* [n. of action from L. *ōtiārī*: see prec.] The condition of being at leisure or doing nothing; a taking one's ease.

1589 PUTTENHAM *Eng. Poesie* III. xxv. (Arb.) 307 To seeme idle when they be earnestly occupied..and do busily negotiat by coulor of otiation. **1620** BP. J. KING *Serm. 26 Mar.* 9 Some shew of indisposition and otiation in God, as if he were gone to rest, and minded vs not.

otiatric (əʊtɪˈætrɪk), *a.* [f. Gr. οὖς, ὠτ- ear + ἰατρικός belonging to healing, medical.] Relating to the medical treatment of the ear.

1861 tr. *Czermak's Pract. Use Laryngoscope* iii. 32 (N. Syd. Soc.) The patient's affection, which could be realised very well by means of the data of the ordinary otiatric method.

Hence **oti'atrics** *sb.*, 'term for the consideration of the nature and principles of the medical treatment of the ear' (Mayne *Expos. Lex.* 1857); **oti'atry**, 'the art of healing the diseases of the ear' (*Syd. Soc. Lex.* 1892).

otic (ˈəʊtɪk, ˈɒtɪk), *a. Anat., Path.* [ad. Gr. ὠτικός, f. οὖς, ὠτ- ear.] Of, belonging to, or relating to the ear; auricular.

otic ganglion, a small oval flattened swelling on the inferior maxillary nerve, which communicates with the auriculo-temporal nerve, and with the branch of the facial nerve which enters the tympanum (*chorda tympani*).

1657 TOMLINSON *Renou's Disp.* 10 Otick [medicaments] to the ears. **1836–9** TODD *Cycl. Anat.* II. 292/1 The ganglion discovered by Arnold, and by him denominated Otic or auricular. **1853** tr. *Romberg's Man. Nerv. Dis.* I. I. xi. 121 (N. Syd. Soc.) We must distinguish otic neuralgia from acoustic hyperæsthesia. **1874** ROOSA *Dis. Ear* 204 The otic ganglion.

-otic (ˈɒtɪk), compound suffix, repr. Gr. -ωτικός, f. sbs. in -ωτ-ης, or adjs. in -ωτ-ος, from vbs. in -όω + -ικ-ός, -IC. Nouns of action from these vbs. are formed in -ωσις; hence, adjs. in -OTIC go in sense with sbs. in -OSIS, -OSE, as *amaurotic*, of, pertaining to, or affected with *amaurosis*; so *chlorotic*, *cyanotic*, *endosmotic*, *exostotic*, *hypnotic*, *narcotic*, *neurotic*, *osmotic*, *sclerotic*, etc. Some words in *-otic* are otherwise derived, as *erotic*, *exotic*, *demotic* (Gr. δημοτικός), or are formed by analogy, as *chaotic*.

otidid (ˈəʊtɪdɪd), *a. Zool.* [f. L. *ōtis*, *ōtid-em* bustard + -ID[3].] Belonging to the *Otididæ* or bustard family of birds. So **o'tidiform** *a.*, resembling a bustard; **'otidine** *a.* = *otidid.*

In mod. Dicts.

‖**o'tidium.** [mod.L., f. Greek type *ὠτίδιον, dim. of οὖς, ὠτός ear; cf. *ommatidium*.] The form of the auditory organ present in the Mollusca. Hence **o'tidial** *a.*, of or pertaining to an otidium.

1890 in *Cent. Dict.*

otiose (ˈəʊʃɪˌəʊs, ˈəʊtɪ-), *a.* [ad. L. *ōtiōsus* at leisure, unemployed, f. *ōtium* leisure. Cf. F. *oiseux*, OF. *ocieux*, *ocios*, Sp. *ocioso*, It. *otioso*.]

1. At leisure or at rest; unemployed, idle; inactive, indolent, lazy.

1850 *Tait's Mag.* XVII. 732/2 A malcontent by necessity, because otiose and resourceless. **1865** *Sat. Rev.* 7 Jan. 24 Our policy in Turkey has now dwindled into an otiose support of the Government. **1885** F. HARRISON *Choice Bks.* (1886) 198 An otiose God..surveying unmoved 'this dusty fuliginous chaos'.

2. That is unattended by action; having no practical result; unfruitful, sterile; nugatory, futile.

1794 PALEY *Evid.* I. II. i. (1827) 354 Such stories..as require, on the part of the hearer, nothing more than an otiose assent. **1844** W. G. WARD *Ideal Chr. Ch.* (ed. 2) 93 We must learn to dismiss all otiose and unfruitful contemplation of external models. **1853** HARDWICK *Chr. Ch. Mid. Age*

(1861) 292 Reposing with a vague and otiose belief on the traditionary doctrines as they had been logically systematized by John of Damascus. **1875** W. JACKSON *Doctr. Retribution* 49 The 'why' of moral duty is not an otiose but a fruitful principle.

b. Having no practical function; idle, superfluous, useless.

1866 *Sat. Rev.* 14 July 54/2 The number of otiose lines and sprawling irrelevant points which swell the piece out. **1878** GLADSTONE *Prim. Homer* xiii. 146, I doubt the opinion sometimes held, that there abound in Homer idle or 'otiose' epithets. **1880** SAYCE in *Nature* XXI. 406 An alphabet which..possesses otiose and needless letters.

'oti,osely, *adv.* [f. prec. + -LY[2].] In an otiose manner; idly; without any practical end.

1886 LOWELL *Progr. World* Latest Lit. Ess. (1891) 178 As has been somewhat otiosely discussed. **1896** HAMMOND *Church or Chapel?* 187 An article of faith..held, not otiosely, but after it has been threshed out again and again.

'oti,oseness. [f. as prec. + -NESS.] The quality of being otiose, or having no practical function.

1867 *Macm. Mag.* Apr. 523/1 They complain of otioseness of letters in some words, of inadequacy in others.

otiosity (əʊʃɪ'ɒsɪtɪ). Forms: 5–6 oci-, ocy-, osyte, -ite, -itee, -itie, 6– otiosity. [a. OF. *ociosité, occiosité* (15th c. in Godef.), f. OF. *occiose*, ad. L. *ōtiōsus* at leisure, f. *ōtium*.]

1. The condition or state of being otiose, unemployed, or idle; ease, leisure, idleness.

1483 CAXTON *Cato* C ij b, By ouerlonge reste and ociosyte been gendred or goten..thre grete synnes..auaryce, lecherye, and ouer moche talkynge. **1532–3** *Act 24 Hen. VIII*, c. 4 The people..liue nowe in idlenesse and ociositee. **1560** ROLLAND *Crt. Venus* Prol. 237 Thocht the corps ly in ociositie. **1848** THACKERAY *Van. Fair* lx, A life of dignified otiosity such as became a person of his eminence. **1866** SHIRLEY BROOKS *Sooner or Later* i, The happy otiosity enjoyed by the million.

2. Indolence; want of action, enterprise, or attention; negligence, carelessness, perfunctoriness.

1632 LITHGOW *Trav.* v. 172 A Towne..of small importance, in regard of..trafficke..: Want of Strangers being one let, and vitious otiosity the other stop.

† **'otious,** *a. Obs. rare.* Also ocious. [ad. L. *ōtiōsus* OTIOSE, or its OF. repr. *ocios, -eus, -eux.*] Leisurely; idle; at ease.

1614 SYLVESTER *Bethulia's Rescue* v. 121 Private men (whose otious care Scarce passe the threshold of their own door dare). **1656** BLOUNT *Glossogr.*, *Ocious*, idle, careless, restful, at ease.

‖ **otitis** (əʊ'taɪtɪs). *Path.* [mod.L., f. Gr. οὖς, ὠτ- ear + -ITIS.] **a.** Inflammation of the ear.

1799 HOOPER *Med. Dict.*, *Otitis*, inflammation of the internal ear. **1822–34** *Good's Study Med.* (ed. 4) III. 197 Inflammations, especially cephalitis and otitis. **1844** DUFTON *Deafness* 51 The causes which produce internal otitis are many of them of the same character, but more severe than those which excite external otitis.

b. In mod.L. collocations: ***otitis externa*** [tr. F. *otite externe* (J. M. G. Itard *Traité des Maladies de l'Oreille* (1821) I. i. 164)], inflammation of the external ear; ***otitis interna*** [tr. F. *otite interne* (loc. cit. 170)], inflammation of the inner ear (†or the middle ear); = LABYRINTHITIS; ***otitis media***, inflammation of the middle ear.

1864 D. B. ST. J. ROOSA tr. *von Tröltsch's Dis. Ear* vi. 60 By Otitis interna I understand the purulent catarrh of the middle ear, or cavity of the tympanum. *Ibid.*, Otitis externa, or diffuse inflammation. **1874** J. HINTON tr. *von Tröltsch's Surg. Dis. Ear* viii. 56 (*heading*) Acute suppurative catarrh of the middle ear, or acute otitis media. **1883** J. P. CASSELLS tr. *Politzer's Text-bk. Dis. Ear* 711 (*heading*) Inflammation of the labyrinth (otitis interna). **1959** *Woman* 16 May 31/1 She has all the signs of a really bad acute otitis media—or infection of the middle ear. **1974** PASSMORE & ROBSON *Compan. Med. Stud.* III. II. xxxii. 5/1 If there is no time to soften the wax in this way, a proprietary wax solvent may be used, but these are more likely to cause otitis externa than the simpler substances. **1976** M. MACHLIN *Pipeline* iii. 36 Diseases that could be easily treated, such as chronic *otitis media*,..were let to run their courses for lack of doctors.

Hence **o'titic** *a.*, connected with otitis.

1822–34 *Good's Study Med.* (ed. 4) II. 105 This is mostly the effect of cold, and is in fact an otitic catarrh.

‖ **otium** ('əʊʃɪəm). The Latin word for 'leisure, freedom from business, ease', in occasional English use; esp. in the phrase ***otium cum dignitate***, leisure with dignity, dignified leisure or ease.

1729 LD. BOLINGBROKE *Let. to Swift* 19 Nov. in *Pope's Wks.* 1751 IX. 110 *Otium cum dignitate* is to be had with 500*l.* a year as well as with 5000. **1815** CHALMERS *Let.* in *Life* (1851) II. 21 A life of intellectual leisure, with the *otium* of literary pursuits. **1820** SCOTT *Monast.* Introd., Intending there to lead my future life in the *otium cum dignitate* of half-pay and annuity. **1849** THACKERAY *Pendennis* lxviii, Mr. Morgan was enjoying his *otium* in a dignified manner, surveying the evening fog, and smoking a cigar.

otmer, obs. form of OUTMORE.

otmest, ottemeste, obs. forms of UTMOST.

oto-, before a vowel ot-, a. Gr. ὠτο-, combining form of οὖς, ὠτ- ear, an element of medical and other scientific words, the more important of which appear in their alphabetical places.

otoca'tarrh, catarrh of the ear (Mayne *Expos. Lex.* 1857). **oto'conia** [F. *otoconie* (Breschet); Gr. κονία or κόνις dust], term for the white pulverulent dust found in the membranous labyrinth of the inner ear, the aggregation of which forms an otolith. (Sometimes treated as if pl. of *otoconium*; also in Eng. form **otokonies.**) Hence **oto'conial** *a.*; **o'toconite** = OTOLITH. **'otocrane** [Gr. κρανίον the skull], the auditory capsule, the portion of the petrous bone which encloses the organ of hearing; hence **oto'cranial, oto'cranic** *adjs.* **'otocyst** [F. *otocyste* (Lacaze Duthies), f. Gr. κύστις bladder], term for the auditory vesicle or organ of hearing in some of the Invertebrata; hence **oto'cystic** *a.*, of or connected with an otocyst. ‖ **oto'dynia** [Gr. ὀδύνη pain], ear-ache; hence **oto'dynic** *a.* (Mayne). **o'tography** [-GRAPHY], description of the ear (Dunglison *Med. Lex.* 1842); hence **oto'graphical** *a.* **otomor'phology,** the morphology of the ear. ‖ **otomy'cosis** [MYCOSIS, Gr. μύκης fungus], the presence of parasitic fungi in the external auditory meatus. **o'topathy** [Gr. πάθος suffering], disease of the ear (Dunglison 1853); hence **oto'pathic** *a.* **'otophone** [Gr. φωνή sound], an ear-trumpet, an apparatus for the conveying of sound to the deaf; also = OTOSCOPE 1. **'otoplasty** [Gr. πλάσσειν to mould], plastic surgery of the ear; hence **oto'plastic** *a.* (Mayne). ‖ **,otopy'osis** [Gr. πύωσις formation of pus], suppuration in the ear. ‖ **oto'rrhœa** [Gr. ῥοία a flow], purulent discharge from the ear; hence **oto'rrhœal, oto'rrhoic** *adjs.*, relating to otorrhœa. ‖ **oto'salpinx** [Gr. σάλπιγξ war-trumpet], the Eustachian tube. **o'tosteal** [Gr. ὀστέον bone] *a.*, relating to the auditory ossicle; *sb.*, applied by Owen to the homologues of the bones of the inner ear, in fishes, etc. **o'totomy** [-TOMY], dissection of the ear (Dunglison, 1843). **oto'toxic** *a.*, having a toxic effect on the ear or its nerve supply; so **,ototo'xicity,** the property of being ototoxic.

1855 HOLDEN *Hum. Osteol.* (1878) 278 The two masses are the '*otoconia' or 'otoliths'. **1881** MIVART *Cat* 301 Two sacs connected by a narrow bent tube and containing within them small crystals of carbonate of lime, called otoliths, or otoconia. **1842** E. WILSON *Anat. Vade M.* (ed. 2) 472 The membranous labyrinth..contains two small calcareous masses called *otoconites. **1854** OWEN *Skel. & Teeth* in *Circ. Sc., Organ. Nat.* I. 171 The organ of hearing,..the surrounding vertebral elements being modified to form the cavity for its reception, which is called '*otocrane'. **1872** MIVART *Elem. Anat.* 138. **1857** MAYNE *Expos. Lex.*, **Otocranial*, of or belonging to the otocrane. **1877** HUXLEY *Anat. Inv. Anim.* iv. 189 In some there is a sac filled with calcareous matter (*otocyst?) attached to the ganglion. **1878** BELL *Gegenbaur's Comp. Anat.* 533 The primitive otocyst is the foundation of a complicated cavitary system. **1880** E. RAY LANKESTER in *Nature* XXII. 147 The presence of velar *otocystic canals constitutes the chief peculiarity of the genus Craspedacusta. **1836–9** TODD *Cycl. Anat.* II. 567/2 *Otokonies..found in the sacculus vestibuli of the ears of Cephalopods. **1900** MISS ELLIS *Human Ear* 42 As otology is a medical term for the science of the ear, we should prefer to use the new word (suggested by Dr. R. Garnett) *otomorphology, the science of the shape of the ear. **1877** BURNETT *Ear* 284 *Otomycosis is said to be much more frequently met among the poorer classes. **1839** D. J. MORIARTY *Husband Hunter* II. 109 Perceiving the *otophone properly fixed. **1888** *Amer. Ann. Deaf* Jan. 85 Examination of 15 deaf persons in the Pennsylvania Inst. by means of Maloney's Otophone. **1818–20** THOMPSON tr. *Cullen's Nosologia* 302 Local Diseases..Of the Secretions and Excretions..*Otorrhœa. **1878** T. BRYANT *Pract. Surg.* I. 89 Deafness is not unfrequent, the hearing failing without any external disease, such as otorrhœa. **1877** tr. *von Ziemssen's Cycl. Med.* XII. 808 *Otorrhœal abscess of the brain. **1857** MAYNE *Expos. Lex.*, **Otorrhoic*. **1854** OWEN *Skel. & Teeth* in *Circ. Sc., Organ. Nat.* I. 177 A body as hard as shell, like half a split almond..it is the '*otosteal'.. or proper ear-bone. **1868** —— *Anat. Vertebr.* III. 246 The otosteals conduct vibrations from the tympanic membrane to the vestibular one. **1951** *Trans. 10th Conf. Chemotherapy of Tuberculosis* 224 The growing list of tuberculostatic antibiotics which have an *ototoxic action..suggests that still other substances derived from Streptomyces may be expected to show a similar toxicity. **1967** BUSCH & LANE *Chemotherapy* v. 86/2 The ototoxic effect is exerted primarily on the cochlear division of the 8th nerve. **1974** *Arch. Path.* XCVI. 304/1 Methyl mercury is a unique ototoxic agent. **1951** *Trans. 10th Conf. Chemotherapy of Tuberculosis* 224 (*heading*) *Ototoxicity of hydroxystreptomycin. **1975** *Nature* 3 Jan. 45/1 Kanamycin ototoxicity yields such cochlear lesions that histological and audiometric measures are well correlated.

otoba butter, o. fat. The almost colourless oil expressed from the seeds of *Myristica Otoba*, a species of nutmeg-tree (*Syd. Soc. Lex.*).

† **otok,** ME. pa. t. of *otake*, OFTAKE *v.*

c **1330** *Arth. & Merl.* 9359 Arthour otok him with drawe sword.

otolaryngology (,əʊtəʊlærɪŋ'gɒlədʒɪ). *Med.* [f. OTO- + *laryngology* s.v. LARYNGO-.] The branch of medicine concerned with the ear and the larynx; also often used to include the nose (avoiding the cumbersome OTORHINOLARYNGOLOGY).

1897 *Jrnl. Laryngol., Rhinol., & Otol.* XII. 554 (*heading*) Holocaine [*printed* holoraine] in oto-laryngology. **1945** *Electronic Engin.* XVII. 555 A book which embodies the experience of twenty five years of research and teaching..in otolaryngology. **1955** *Sci. News Let.* 13 Aug. 109/1 The cat's hearing span was measured by Drs. William D. Neff and Joseph E. Hind of the University of Chicago's Laboratories of Physiological Psychology and Otolaryngology. **1973** PAPARELLA & SHUMRICK *Otolaryngology* I. p. ix/1 We, the editors, felt both honored and challenged when the Saunders Company invited us to prepare a new and definitive reference source in otolaryngology. The new book was to replace the classic Jackson work, *Diseases of the Nose, Throat and Ear.* **1975** FELTON & FOWLER *Best, Worst & Most Unusual* 250 Dr. Eugene M. Batza of Cleveland Clinic's Department of Otolarynology, examined a five-member rock combo and found that all of them suffered from..laryngitis.

Hence **,otolaryngo'logic** (chiefly *U.S.*), **-'logical** *adjs.*, of or pertaining to otolaryngology, or to the ear, (nose) and throat; **,otolaryn'gologist,** one who specializes in otolaryngology.

1898 (*title*) Transactions of the Ophthalmologic Division of the Western Ophthalmological and Oto-Laryngological Association. **1898** *Laryngoscope* May 311 One of the most practical factors of the organization was the division into two sections, one the ophthalmologic, the other the otolaryngologic. **1911** *Jrnl. Laryngol., Rhinol., & Otol.* XXVI. 661 The moral responsibility..rests upon oto-laryngologists as teachers. **1961** *Lancet* 30 Sept. 782/1 A meeting of the North of England Otolaryngological Society is to be held on Saturday, Oct. 7. **1964** D. A. DOLOWITZ *Basic Otolaryngol.* p. vii, These gains have lengthened the otolaryngologic resident training period to four years after internship. **1973** *Sci. Amer.* Sept. 92/1 Gynecologists, urologists, ophthalmologists, otolaryngologists and others each operate on their respective organs and tissues. **1974** *Encycl. Brit. Macropædia* XVII. 822/2 Otolaryngologic surgery is performed in the area of the ear, nose, and throat. *Ibid.*, Benign and malignant tumours of the upper air passages..are currently dealt with by the otolaryngological surgeons.

otolite ('əʊtəlaɪt). [f. OTO- + -LITE.] = next.

1846 OWEN *Lect. Comp. Anat.* I. 211 The large size of the organ of hearing, and especially that of the hard otolites, also relate to the medium through which the sonorous vibrations are propagated to the fish. **1855** H. SPENCER *Princ. Psychol.* (1872) I. I. ii. 38 Those atmospheric waves which..are conveyed to the minute otolites and rods of the inner ear, to be by them impressed on the auditory nerves.

otolith ('əʊtəlɪθ). *Anat.* and *Physiol.* [mod. f. OTO- + Gr. λίθος stone.] An ear-stone; one of the calcareous bodies, often in the shape of rhombic crystals, found in the inner ear of vertebrates and some invertebrates; in fishes often of great size, in the higher vertebrates small particles.

1835–6 TODD *Cycl. Anat.* I. 554/1 An acoustic vestibule, containing..a calcareous body or otolithe. **1883** H. GRAY *Anat.* (ed. 10) 618 The otoliths are two small rounded bodies, consisting of a mass of minute crystalline grains of carbonate of lime, held together in a mesh of delicate fibrous tissue, and contained in the wall of the utricle and saccule, opposite the distribution of the nerves. **1900** SCHÄFER *Physiol.* II. 1205 Lee is of opinion that the otoliths and maculæ form the organ for statical equilibrium.

¶ **b.** By confusion, applied to the otic bones or ossicles of the inner ear in some animals.

Hence **oto'lithic, oto'litic** *adjs.*, of the nature of or pertaining to an otolith; containing otoliths.

1855 T. R. JONES *Anim. Kingd.* (ed. 2) 110 (*Acalephæ*) The otolitic vesicle, which, from analogy..is considered as an organ of hearing. **1875** HUXLEY in *Encycl. Brit.* I. 132/1 A sensory organ, having the characters of an otolithic sac, is seated upon the ganglion. **1900** SCHÄFER *Physiol.* II. 1167 The most primitive form of internal ear is undoubtedly a sac containing fluid in which an otolithic mass is immersed, and having on the wall hair-like processes related to the terminations of a nerve.

otologist (əʊ'tɒlədʒɪst). [f. as next + -IST.] One versed in otology; an ear-specialist.

1874 ROOSA *Dis. Ear* (ed. 2) 47 The high character of the work that has been done by American otologists. **1876** BARTHOLOW *Mat. Med.* (1879) 549 Glycerine is used by otologists to soften cerumen.

otology (əʊ'tɒlədʒɪ). [f. Gr. οὖς, ὠτ- ear + -LOGY.] That branch of science which treats of the ear, its anatomy, functions, and diseases; a treatise on the ear.

1842 DUNGLISON *Med. Lex.*, *Otology*..The part of anatomy which treats of the ear. **1874** ROOSA *Dis. Ear* (ed. 2) 17 Formerly known as aural medicine and surgery, but.. better designated by the term Otology. **1880** (*title*) American Journal of Otology, a quarterly journal of physiological acoustics. **1899** *Westm. Gaz.* 9 Aug. 2/3 The University of Edinburgh has made otology one of the qualifying subjects for her medical degrees.

Hence **oto'logical** *a.*, of or pertaining to otology.

1895 *N.B. Daily Mail* 27 Sept. 5 International Otological Congress in Florence. *Mod.* Otological Society of the United Kingdom.

Otomi (əʊtə'miː). Pl. Otomi, Otomies. [Sp., f. Nahuatl *Otomí*.] A (member of an) Indian people inhabiting parts of central Mexico; also the language of the Otomi. Also *attrib.* or as *adj.*

1787 C. CULLEN tr. *Clavigero's Hist. Mexico* I. II. 105 The Mazahuas were once a part of the nation of the Otomies, as the languages of both nations are but different dialects of the same tongue. **1845** [see HUASTEC]. **1877** L. H. MORGAN *Anc. Society* II. vii. 194 The confederacy was confronted by hostile.. tribes.. the Mechoacans on the west, the Otomies on the northwest. **1883** *Encycl. Brit.* XVI. 207/1 The languages of the Nahua nations.. show no connexion of origin with the language of the Otomi tribes. **1891** D. G. BRINTON *Amer. Race* 338 The Otomi presents so many sounds unfamiliar to the European ear that the attempt to represent it by our alphabets can be only remotely accurate. **1948** D. DIRINGER *Alphabet* vii. 124 They [*sc.* Chichimeca] .. are considered by some experts as of Otomi origin. **1954** *Bible Translator* V. 61 Otomi people suffer from considerable cultural insecurity. **1964** *Language* XL. 81 A great variety of person-tense-aspect prefixes are available to the speaker of Otomi. **1972** *Ibid.* XLVIII. 847, 6b is given by Hockett for.. Otomi nasal vowels. **1972** [see MIXTEC].

‖**Otomys** (ˈəʊtəmɪs). *Zool.* [f. OTO- + Gr. μῦς mouse.] A genus of rodents of the family *Muridæ*, having large hairy ears.

1834 MᶜMURTRIE *Cuvier's Anim. Kingd.* 86 The Otomys are nearly allied to the Field Rats. *Ibid.* (The Cape Otomys.) Size of a rat; fur marked with black and fawn-coloured rings.

otorhinolaryngology (ˌəʊtəʊˌraɪnəʊlærɪŋˈgɒlədʒɪ). *Med.* [f. OTO- + RHINO- + *laryngology* s.v. LARYNGO-.] The branch of medicine concerned with the ear, nose, and throat. Cf. OTOLARYNGOLOGY, E.N.T. s.v. E III.

1900 DORLAND *Med. Dict.* 468/1 Otorhinolaryngology. **1902** *Nature* 2 Oct. 554/1 The congress will be divided into the following sections:—.. oto-rhino-laryngology, [etc.]. **1962** *Lancet* 27 Jan. 195/2 No special techniques need to be learnt, as in neuro-surgery, urology, or otorhinolaryngology. **1968** W. MCCARTNEY *Olfaction & Odours* 235 Author of 'Essai d'Olfactique Physiologique' (1919) and of many papers on oto-rhino-laryngology.

Hence **ˌoto,rhinola,ryngoˈlogical** *a.*; **ˌoto-ˌrhinolarynˈgologist**, one who specializes in oto-rhinolaryngology.

1938 W. H. C. ROMANIS in Rolleston & Moncrieff *Mod. Anæsthetic Pract.* x. 185 Local anæsthesia.. its use in ophthalmic or oto-rhinolaryngological operations. **1948** *Brit. Dental Jrnl.* LXXXV. 223/1 He had.. no history of oto-rhino-laryngological trouble. **1960** *Times* 3 Mar. 5/2 Then there is 'otorhinolaryngologist'. No one would wish to charge large fees if he called himself an ear, nose and throat specialist. **1962** *Listener* 10 May 809/1 Oto-rhinolaryngologists, botanists or X-ray crystallographers.

otosclerosis (əʊtəʊskləˈrəʊsɪs, -sklɪəˈrəʊsɪs). *Path.* [mod.L., ad. G. *otosclerose* (A. Politzer *Lehrb. der Ohrenheilkunde* (ed. 4, 1901) 263): see OTO- and SCLEROSIS.] A disease of the ear in which the normal tissue of the temporal bone is replaced by spongy bone, with the result that movement of the stapes becomes impeded and deafness ensues. Hence **otoscleˈrotic** *a.*, of, pertaining to, or affected by otosclerosis; also as *sb.*, one who suffers from otosclerosis.

1901 *Arch. Otology* XXX. 279 Otosclerosis, so frequent, distressing, and little amenable to treatment, receives 12 pages. **1904** *Jrnl. Laryngol., Rhinol., & Otol.* XIX. 518 It was especially difficult to differentiate between true otosclerosis and fixation of the stapes following tympanic inflammations. **1933** M. YEARSLEY *Otosclerosis* iii. 7 Körner .. recorded the marriage of two otosclerotics. *Ibid.*, The marriage of an otosclerotic male with his otosclerotic niece resulted in seven otosclerotic children. **1933** *Punch* 20 Dec. 700/1 He.. exhibits Swift with much pathos as the sufferer from the particularly cruel disease which now bears the ugly name of otosclerosis. **1974** I. FRIEDMANN *Path. Ear* v. 247 Otosclerosis is very common in Indians and whites. *Ibid.*, Every tenth adult person has otosclerotic foci within his temporal bone.

otoscope (ˈəʊtəskəʊp). [f. OTO- + Gr. -σκόπος observing, observer.]

1. A modification of the stethoscope for auscultation of sounds in the ear; an auscultation-tube.

1849 J. TOYNBEE *Dis. Ear* in *Med.-Chirurg. Trans.* XXXII. 74 When examining the ear with the otoscope. (*Note.* An elastic tube, about eighteen inches in length, tipped with ivory at both ends, one extremity of which is inserted into the external meatus of the patient, and the other into that of the medical man.) **1853** SIR W. WILDE *Pract. Obs. Aural Surg.* 113.

2. An optical instrument for inspecting the cavity of the ear.

1853 SIR W. WILDE *Pract. Obs. Aural Surg.* 113 Otoscope .. also applied to a form of speculum auris. **1884** M. MACKENZIE *Dis. Throat & Nose* II. 243 Brunton's otoscope .. consists of a metallic tube provided with an eye-piece. Into this tube a funnel opens at right angles, through which the light is made to fall on a perforated reflector, which throws the rays through the distal part of the cylinder into an ordinary ear speculum.

Hence **otoˈscopic** *a.*; **oˈtoscopy**, inspection or clinical examination of the ear; the use of the otoscope.

1876 *Clin. Soc. Trans.* IX. 96 Otoscopic examination revealed nothing abnormal in either ear. **1874** ROOSA *Dis. Ear* (ed. 2) 86 Dr. Rossi in a very recent paper on binocular otoscopy, proposes the use of a microscopic object-glass set at an angle of 70° in a spectacle frame, as a simple and efficient binocular otoscope.

otosis (əʊˈtəʊsɪs). [mod. f. Gr. οὖς, ὠτ- ear + -OSIS.] Mishearing; alteration of words caused by an erroneous apprehension of the sound.

1860 HALDEMAN *Analyt. Orthogr.* xii. 65 Otosis is a change in words, due to misconception of the true sound, influencing consonants of the same quality. **1884** J. A. HARRISON *Negro-Eng.* Introd. in *Anglia*, Negro English is an ear-language altogether,.. built up on what the late Professor Haldeman of Pennsylvania called otosis, an error of ear, a mishearing.

‖**otoˈtoi.** Also otototoi. [a. Gr. ὀτοτοῖ, etc.] A Greek exclamation of pain or grief; = *woe! alas!* Hence **ototoi** *v.*, to cry 'ototoi', to utter a wail.

1877 BROWNING *Agamemnon* 1068 Otototoi, Gods, Earth, Apollon, Apollon! *Ch.* Why didst thou 'ototoi' concerning Loxias? **1883** F. M. CRAWFORD *Mr. Isaacs* 3 The ghosts of the slain sometimes appear.. and gibber a feeble little 'Otototoi' after the manner of the shade of Dareios.

otour, otre, obs. forms of OTTER.

otow, contr. f. Sc. *otouth*, OUTWITH, outside of.

‖**otriad** (atrˈjad, ɒtrˈjæd). [a. Russ. *otryád* a detachment.] In Russia: a detachment, group of soldiers (see also quot. 1916).

1916 *Yorkshire Post* 23 Feb. 4/4 An Englishman who works with a volunteer ambulance or otriad, behind the Russian lines. **1919** H. S. WALPOLE *Secret City* I. xvii. 117 Zinaida Fyodorovna had just come back from her Otriad on the Galician front. **1933** —— *Vanessa* IV. i. 672 The Retreat had begun and with the rest of the Otriad he had been flung into the little town of O——.

Otshi-herero (ˌəʊtʃɪhɛˈrɛərəʊ). Also **Otji-herero, Otyi-.** The name used by the Hereros for their language, generally called HERERO.

1859 H. HALL *Man. S. Afr. Geogr.* xviii. 73 Damara and Orampoland, or the land of the Otjiherero, present a belt of sandy country between the coast and the high inhabited table lands. **1871** J. MACKENZIE *Ten Yrs. North of Orange River* 494 Otyiherero (Damara). **1880** *Encycl. Brit.* XI. 732/2 By their language (Otyiherero) the Herero belong to the great Bantu family. **1910** *Ibid.* XIII. 358/1 They call themselves Ovaherero and their language Otshi-herero. **1919** H. H. JOHNSTON *Compar. Study Bantu & Semi-Bantu Lang.* I. 350 Ꞷci-herer ꞷ.

Ottamite, variant of OTTOMITE *Obs.*

ottar, variant form of ATTAR, OTTO.

‖**ottava** (otˈtava). [It. *ottava* eighth, octave.]

1. *Mus.* An octave; chiefly in the phrases ***ottava alta, ottava bassa,*** indicating that a passage is to be played an octave higher, or lower, than written. (Usually abbrev. *8va.*)

1848 RIMBAULT *First Bk. Piano* 13 To avoid many ledger-lines below the staff, the notes are sometimes written eight degrees higher than their real place in the system, and the words *ottava bassa*, or 8ᵛᵃ *bassa*, placed under them, to shew that they are to be played an octave lower than.. written.

2. ***ottava rima*** (ˈrima). An Italian stanza of eight 11-syllabled lines, riming as *a b a b a b c c*; the English adaptation, as used by Byron, has English heroic lines of ten syllables.

1820 SHELLEY *Lett.* Pr. Wks. 1880 IV. 178, I am translating in *ottava rima* the Hymn to Mercury, of Homer. **1875** LOWELL *Spenser* Pr. Wks. 1890 IV. 328 He found the *ottava rima* too monotonously iterative. **1880** *Macm. Mag.* 51 The three important verse-forms which English poetry owes to Italy, the ottava-rima, the sonnet, and the sestina.

Ottawa (ˈɒtəwə). [a. Canad. F. *Outaouais*, f. Ojibwa tribal name *otāwā*.] A North American Indian people of the Algonquian family first encountered on the shores of Lake Huron; a member of this people. Also *attrib.* or as *adj.*

1687 in *Documents Colonial Hist. New-York* (1853) III. 442 A party of Sinnekes and Onnondages have plundered some French.. and have also taken some Ottawa Indians prisoners. **1754** [see CHIPPEWA]. **1768** J. LEES *Jrnl.* Aug. (1911) 39 On the Miami River, the greatest part of the nation of the Ottawas inhabit, they.. are spread about it.. chiefly on the North side of Lake Huron.. and towards the North West. These, the Pous and Chipewas have almost the same language, and is [*sic*] called the Ottawa-Tongue. **1833** A. JACKSON in *Messages & Papers of Presidents* (1896) III. 38, I transmit.. a treaty concluded between the commissioners on the part of the United States and the united nation of Chippewas, Ottawas, and Potawatamies, at Chicago. **1835** [see KICKAPOO]. **1865** [see ALGONQUIN, -KIN *sb.* and *a*]. **1890** J. G. FRAZER *Golden Bough* II. iii. 113 When men of the Bear clan in the Otawa tribe killed a bear, they made him a feast of his own flesh. **1910** F. W. HODGE *Handbk. Amer. Indians* II. 171/1 There were 197 Ottawa under the Seneca School, Okla. **1962** D. H. HYMES in J. A. Fishman *Readings Sociol. of Lang.* (1968) 129 The Ottawa believed the cries of infants to be meaningful. **1967** D. JENNESS *Indians of Canada* (ed. 7) xviii. 282 The Iroquois turned their arms against the Ottawa and drove them from Georgian bay. Some fled west towards lake Superior; others took refuge with their Potawatomi kinsmen in the United States... Many of these refugees returned to.. the north shore of lake Huron. **1977** *Detroit Free Press* 11 Dec. 16-C/1 'It's a hidden attack by commercial interests on native Americans,' said Mrs. Waunetta Dominic, chairwoman of the Northern Michigan Ottawa Association in Petoskey.

ottemest, obs. variant of UTMOST.

otter (ˈɒtə(r)), *sb.* Forms: 1 otr, otor, (octer), 1–5 oter, 3–5 otur, (5 otere, otre, ot(t)our, ottyre, otyr(e, otir, 6 ottre, 9 *dial.* oater), 5– otter. [Com. Teut.: OE. *otr, ot(t)or, oter* = MDu., Du. *otter*, OHG. *ottar* (MHG., G. *otter*), ON. *otr*:—OTeut. **otró-z*, pre-Teut. **udró-s*: cf. Lith. *udra*, OSlav. *vydra*, Skr. *udrá-s*, 'otter'; radically akin to Gr. ὕδωρ, Skr. *udan*, Eng. *water*; cf. Gr. ὕδρος, ὕδρα water-snake.]

1. a. An aquatic fur-bearing carnivorous mammal (*Lutra vulgaris*, Fam. *Mustelidæ*) feeding chiefly on fish, having fin-like legs, webbed feet, and long horizontally flattened tail, which enable it to swim and turn in the water with remarkable rapidity.

Often taken as the type of an amphibious creature.

a **700** *Epinal Gloss.* 585 (O.E.T.) *Lutrus*, otr [*Erf.* octer, *Corp.* otr]. *c* **1000** in Kemble *Cod. Dipl.* III. 418 Of oteres hole. *c* **1000** *Ælfric's Voc.* in Wr.-Wülcker 118/42 *Lutria*, otor. *c* **1275** *Moral Ode* (Jesus MS.) 358 in *O.E. Misc.* 70 Ne oter ne acquerne. Beuveyr ne sablyne. *c* **1290** *S. Eng. Leg.* I. 237/642 On is hindore fet An Otur þare cam gon. *c* **1440** *Jacob's Well* 118 As þe ottyr sleth fysch, & gaderyth it on hepe in-to his hole. *a* **1450** *Knt. de la Tour* (1868) 22 Late us ete the gret ele, and y wille saie to my husbond that the otour hathe eten hym. **14..** *Nominale* in Wr.-Wülcker 700/16 *Hic lutricius*, a notyre. **1525** LD. BERNERS *Froiss.* II. xcii. [lxxxviii.] 273 Lyke an Otter in the water. **1596** SHAKS. *1 Hen. IV*, III. iii. 143 An Otter, sir Iohn? Why an Otter? *Fal.* Why? She's neither fish nor flesh. *a* **1654** SELDEN *Table-t.* (Arb.) 69 A kind of an Otter, a Knight half-Spiritual, and half-Temporal. **1774** GOLDSM. *Nat. Hist.* II. 319 In the first step of the progression from land to amphibious animals we find the Otter. **1811** in C. A. Johns *Week at Lizard* 64 To John Johns for an oater.. 1s. **1839** E. D. CLARKE *Trav. Russia* 136/1 Great quantities of the furs and skins of the otter, beaver, and fox, are annually brought to market by the traders.

b. Applied to other species of *Lutra*, and allied genera (of which there are several), as the **American otter,** *L. canadensis*; **sea otter,** *L.* (*Enhydris*) *marina*, with black glossy fur, which inhabits the American shores of the North Pacific.

1781 PENNANT *Hist. Quadr.* II. 356 *Mustela lutris*.. Sea Otter. **1842** SIR W. JARDINE in *Nat. Libr., Mammalia* XIII. 254. **1883** *Cassell's Nat. Hist.* II. 201 Like the Seal, the Sea Otter is gregarious.

2. The fur or skin of this animal (of any species).

1429 in *Somerset Wills* (1901) 131 [A gown furred (*togam furratam*) with] oter. **1530** PALSGR. 250/1 Ottre, a furre, *peaux de loutres*. **1653** WALTON *Angler* ii. 41 The gloves of an Otter are the best fortification for your hands against wet weather. **1887** J. ASHBY STERRY *Lazy Minstrel* (1892) 46 You never.. saw such A lithe little learner in otter.

†**3.** A sailor. *Obs. slang.*

c **1700** *Street Robberies Consider'd*, Otter, a sailor.

4. a. A tackle consisting of a float with line and a number of hooks, used in fresh-water fishing. **b.** A kind of fishing gear used in deep-sea trawling; also *attrib.*

1851 H. NEWLAND *Erne* 53 The otter is a thin piece of board, about four feet long and a foot or so broad. **1860** [see OTTER *v.* 2]. **1898** *Daily News* 19 Feb. 2/1 The steam catchers .. are of the most approved type, with special steam winches and 'Otter' fishing gear.

c. A type of paravane, used esp. by merchant vessels. Later, any paravane.

[**1910** *Blackw. Mag.* June 899/1 We might adapt to naval use those poaching expedients, the 'cross-line' and the 'otter'.] **1920** *Nature* 8 Jan. 487/1 The paravane or otter.. proved a very effective weapon against both mines and submarines. **1920** *Rep. Brit. Assoc. Adv. Sci. 1919* 273 The Protector Paravanes, or Otters, carry a form of cutter, but no explosive charge whatever. **1954** BRADFORD & QUILL *Gloss. Sea Terms* 138/2 The mooring of a mine coming in contact with this taut tow-line slides along to the otter where it enters a pair of cutting jaws and is cut adrift.

5. Short for *otter-moth*: see 7.

c **1440** *Floris & Bl.* (Taunt. MS.) 96/772 Or y it ere wyst, An Otter fleyȝ ageynst my brest.

6. Name of a breed of sheep: = ANCON.

1890 C. L. MORGAN *Anim. Life & Intell.* vi. (1891) 226 From this one lamb the *otter*, or *ancon*, breed was raised.

7. *attrib.* and *Comb.*, as ***otter-killer, -skin, -track, -trap***; **otter-board,** (*a*) a fishing-tackle consisting of a board with several hooks attached; (*b*) = DOOR 4 b; **otter-canoe,** a kayak used by sea-otter hunters in Alaska; **otter-dog, -hound,** a dog of a breed used for hunting the otter; **otter-hunt,** †(*a*) the huntsman having charge of otter-hounds; (*b*) the chase of the otter; **otter-hunting** = prec. (*b*); **otter-line** = sense 4 (a), (b); **otter-man,** a fisher who uses an otter-line or otter-board; **otter-mark,** a trace left by an otter; **otter-moth,** the GHOST-MOTH (*Hepialus humuli*); **otter-path,** a continuous track left by otters; †**otter-sheep** *U.S.*, a variety of sheep with short, crooked legs; cf. OTTER *sb.* 6; **otter-shell,** the English name of bivalve shells of the genus *Lutraria*; **otter-shrew,** an aquatic insectivorous quadruped, *Potamogale velox*, of western equatorial Africa, having a weasel-like body; **otter-spear,** a spear used in hunting otters; **otter tail** (see quot. 1932); **otter-trawl,** a trawl fitted with the 'otter' device (sense 4 b); hence **otter-trawling** *sb.*, fishing with the otter-trawl.

1901 *Field* 5 Jan. 19/2 The *otter-board was only employed..upon those lakes where the trout were indifferent to the angler's flies. **1904** *Daily Chron.* 21 Nov. 5/7 He lost his otter-board and had to put a new trawl on next morning. **1936** J. Buchan *Island of Sheep* xiii. 247 Look at the trawl. It's absurd. It has no otter-boards... There's something wrong with this ship. **1971** *Daily Tel.* (Colour Suppl.) 21 May 21/3 The net flops into the water and sinks away sideways. When it is some way out it is followed by the shuddering crash of the two otter-boards, ton-weight doors, that are towed at an angle to keep the net open on the bottom. **1653** Walton *Angler* i. 4 All men that keep *Otter dogs ought to have a Pension from the Commonwealth. **1607** Topsell *Four-f. Beasts* (1658) 446 These otters are hunted with special dogs called *otter-hounds. **1854** J. W. Warter *Last of Old Squires* vi. 59 A messenger was despatched for the otter-hounds, which a friend of the squire's kept some ten miles off. **1485** *Rolls of Parlt.* VI. 356/2 Graunte of the Office of *Otterhunte. **1601** F. Tate *Househ. Ord. Edw. II* (1876) 45 An otterhunt, who shal have in his custody twelve dogges running at the ottre. **1815** Scott *Guy M.* xxvi, An otter-hunt the next day, and a badger-baiting the day after, consumed the time merrily. **1735** Somerville *Chase* iv. Argt., Description of the *Otter Hunting. **1840** R. H. Dana *Bef. Mast* xxvii. 90 The brig Convoy..engaged in otter-hunting among the islands. *a* **1676** Walton *Angler* ii. (Cassell) 45 The want of *otter-killers..will in time prove the destruction of all rivers. **1862** *Blackw. Mag.* Mar. 182 Death stauns owre't wi' *otter-line, Oot liftin' ten by ten. **1901** *Field* 5 Jan. 19/2 The *otterman must chuckle inwardly when he sees a perspiring and jaded angler..with one or two fish in his basket. **1856** Dove *Logic Chr. Faith* v. i. §1. 247 We should understand why the *otter-marks led to the water. **1804** *Med. Jrnl.* XII. 229 Hop yards might be preserved from the honey-dew..and from the *ottermoth, by being covered with stones. **1805** R. W. Dickson *Pract. Agric.* (1807) II. 250 The otter moth.. producing its larvæ upon the roots of the plants. **1864** J. C. Atkinson *Stanton Grange* 189 What might have been termed an *otter-path; not merely the track of his feet here and there. **1809** E. A. Kendall *Trav. Northern Parts U.S.* I. 309 Some of the farmers [in Connecticut] are partial to a remarkable variety of sheep, which they call the *otter-sheep. **1863** H. S. Randall *Pract. Shepherd* (ed. 7) v. 42 A family of them, the Otter Sheep—so termed from their short, crooked, rickety legs. **1873** *Amer. Naturalist* VII. 742 The otter sheep..originated on the farm of Seth Wright, near Charles River, Mass. **1884** *Century Mag.* Feb. 516/1 There were also the Otter sheep, said to have originated on some island on our eastern coast. **1865** J. G. Wood *Common Shells* 45 As is implied by the scientific title, *Lutraria*, the *Otter-shells inhabit the mud, into which they burrow deeply, exactly as do the Gapers. *Ibid.* 46 The commonest species, the Oval Otter-shell. *Ibid.* 47 The Oblong Otter-shell is not so plentiful as its oval relative. **1545** *Rates of Customs* C j b, *Otter skynnes the pece xiid.* **1583** *Ibid.* D v, Otter skinnes the peece ijs. **1725** De Foe *Voy. round World* (1840) 266 A jerkin made of otter-skin. **1849** F. Parkman *Calif. & Oregon Trail* x. 144 The dandy carried a bow and arrows in an otter-skin quiver at his back. **1971** *Country Life* 28 Oct. 1128/3 Red chokers about sun-burned necks, and more than one round hat of otter-skin. **1540** in *Wilts Archæol. Mag.* VIII. 272 [They] did assaulte this deponent with their swerdes and an *otter-speare. **1818** Scott *Rob Roy* v, Nets, fishing-rods, otter-spears, hunting-poles, with many other singular devices and engines for taking or killing game. **1932** Lady Howe in A. C. Smith et al. *Hounds & Dogs* viii. 69 The tail..should be very thick towards the base gradually tapering towards the tip, of medium length, should be practically free from any feathering, but should be clothed thickly all round with the Labrador's short, thick, dense coat, thus giving that peculiar rounded appearance which has been described as the '*otter' tail. **1948** B. Vesey-Fitzgerald *Bk. Dog* 1000 Otter tail: A thick tapering tail similar to that of an otter, much desired in the Labrador Retriever. **1973** P. R. A. Moxon *Gundogs* (ed. 9) iv. 71 The Labrador Retriever..is undoubtedly ideal for water, the sleek water-resisting coat and 'otter' tail seeming almost designed for the job. **1863** Atkinson *Stanton Grange* (1864) 192 One or two points near the presumed *otter-tracks. **1897** R. Munro *Prehist. Probl.* 245 Among the fishing gear ..he includes this *otter-trap. **1899** W. C. McIntosh *Resources of Sea* 93 The new *otter-trawls capture more round than flat fishes. **1936** Russell & Yonge *Seas* (ed. 2) 275 In the case of the otter-trawl two 'otters' or 'doors' are used. To these the sides of the net's mouth are attached, and they are set at such angles that as they are drawn over the sea bottom they diverge farther and farther from the centre of the net's mouth until an equilibrium point is reached and the mouth of the net is stretched agape. **1973** W. Elmer *Terminol. Fishing* ii. 71 In many places the otter trawl has ousted the beam trawl. **1973** *Fisheries Fact Sheet* (Environment Canada Fisheries & Marine Service) No. 1. 2/3 The former two [*sc.* the trawler and dragger]..catch fish by dragging an otter-trawl or similar device. This is a large baglike arrangement of nets which captures fish as the vessel tows it through the water.

'otter, *v.* [f. prec. sb., after *to fish*, etc.]

1. *intr.* To hunt the otter.

1902 *Daily Chron.* 3 July 3/2 He writes of..ottering in St. John's Vale, of the Grasmere rush-bearing.

2. To fish with the 'otter' tackle (see prec. 4 a, b).

1860 G. H. K. in *Vac. Tour.* 165 Certain Philistines have increased the mischief by permitting their gillies to use the otter... If the gilly otters for you, he will for himself. **1890** *Daily News* 29 Sept. 4/8 A loch can be 'ottered', fish can thus be made shy and hard to catch. **1892** *Field* 7 May 681/2 The fish..are..shy, having been well whipped over or ottered for by the local fishermen.

otter, variant form of otto, attar.

otter-down, erroneous for eider-down (an unfamiliar word at the time).

1759 Johnson *Idler* No. 40 ¶4 Now to be sold, for ready money only, some duvets for bed-coverings, of down, beyond comparison superior to what is called otter-down.

'ottered, *ppl. a.* [f. otter *v.* + -ed[1].] That has been fished with otter tackle. So **'otterer; 'ottering** *vbl. sb.*

1901 *Field* 5 Jan. 19/2 An observant gamekeeper..tells me that he knows well the signs of an ottered lake. *Ibid.* 19/3 Very gradually, may be, the otterers will learn that they are ruining many fine waters by their malpractices. **1907** *Westm. Gaz.* 24 Jan. 2/1 Trout..obtained by the unsportsmanlike method of netting or 'ottering'.

otterly, obs. form of utterly.

†'ottimacy, obs. var. optimacy (= It. *ottimazia*).

1594 T. Bedingfield tr. *Machiavelli's Florentine Hist.* (1595) 64 Vnder the word ottimacy, or popularitie, they cloake their euill intent.

otto[1] ('ɒtəʊ). Also 8–9 **otter, ottar.** An altered form of the word more accurately spelt attar, in *otto of roses*, the fragrant essence of roses.

1639 Shirley *The Ball* iv. i, I left your kick With your cousin to buy otto. **1785** Mackenzie *Lounger* No. 12 ¶8 With episodes of dancing girls, and *otter* of roses! **1792** A. Young *Trav. France* 186 Roses are a great article for the famous *otter*, all of which is commonly supposed to come from Bengal. **1813** Moore *Post-bag, Hor., Od.* ii. xi, While Otto of Roses Refreshing all noses Shall sweetly exhale from our whiskers and wigs. **1835** *Blackw. Mag.* XXXVII. 440 Sweet as ottar of roses distilled by the alchymic sun. **1908** *Westm. Gaz.* 30 Mar. 10/3 As a scent otto of violets has become increasingly popular each year. **1919** S. Kaye-Smith *Tamarisk Town* i. ii. 48 There was a drift of faint perfumes: flowers, macassar oil, otto of roses, lavender and peau d'espagne. **1939–40** *Army & Navy Stores Catal.* 431/1 Cold cream, 'Otto of Rose' jar, 1/3.

b. Hence, jocularly, a liquid with a fragrant or characteristic odour.

1849 Thackeray *Pendennis* xlviii, The Captain, before issuing..scented himself with otto of whisky.

Hence **'ottoed** *a.*, perfumed with otto of roses.

1810 *Splendid Follies* I. 177 An ell of ottoed cambric.

'Otto[2]. [Named after the inventor in 1877.] A kind of velocipede: see dicycle. Hence **'Ottoist,** a rider of an 'Otto' dicycle.

1885 *Cycl. Tour. Club Gaz.* Sept. 284 One or more tricyclists who are in the habit of riding with good Ottoists. *Ibid.*, My experience is that the 'Otto' is more easily ridden uphill than the F.S. tricycle. **1887** Bury & Hillier *Cycling* (Badm. Libr.) 369 All Ottos built before 1882 were fitted with block breaks.

Otto[3] ('ɒtəʊ). The name of Nikolaus August *Otto* (1832–1891), German engineer, used *attrib.* to designate (*a*) the four-stroke cycle employed in most petrol and gas engines (cf. four-stroke *a.*), idealized as adiabatic compression followed by heat addition at constant volume, adiabatic expansion, and heat rejection at constant volume; and (*b*) an engine employing this cycle.

The cycle was orig. proposed by A. Beau de Rochas in 1862, but Otto was the first to build an engine employing it (in 1876) after conceiving the idea independently.

1878 *Sci. Amer.* 30 Mar. 195/1 The new Otto horizontal gas engine..closely resembles the ordinary horizontal steam engine. **1885** W. Macgregor *Gas Engines* ii. 81 The original and classic type of the Otto engine has received improvements at the hands of both its German and English manufacturers. **1886** D. Clerk *Gas Engine* vii. 183 The indicator diagrams prove the very efficient nature of the Otto cycle. **1930** *Engineering* 7 Feb. 186/1 Theoretically, the Otto cycle..promised higher efficiencies than the constant-pressure Diesel cycle. **1966** *McGraw-Hill Encycl. Sci. & Technol.* VII. 201/1 For an Otto engine, an increase in either the air temperature or density increases the tendency of the engine to knock. **1975** *Sci. Amer.* Jan. 34/3 According to the DOT-EPA report, the 40 percent improvement by 1980 should be attainable with the present Otto-cycle (four-stroke) gasoline engine, in combination with improved transmissions, reduced weight and aerodynamic drag and improved accessories.

†b. Used *ellipt.* for *Otto engine. Obs.*

1886 D. Clerk *Gas Engine* vi. 106 The Otto is only half single acting. **1903** *Work* XXV. 18/2 Petrol car engines are of the vertical single-acting Otto type, any variations consisting chiefly of horizontal Ottos.

Ottoman ('ɒtəmən), *a.* and *sb.*[1] Also 6–7 **Otho-.** [= F. *Ottoman*, It. *Ottomano*, med.L. *Ottomānus*, med.Gr. Ὀτούμανος; of which the L. and It. pl. *Ottomani* was ad. Arab. *ʿuthmānī* or *ʿothmānī*, adj. from *ʿothmān*, name of the founder of the Turkish dynasty and empire. The forms *Othoman* and *Othman* more closely represent the Arabic; but all want the adj. ending *-i*.

The Turkish pronunciation of *Othmān* is *Osmān*, whence, with the Turkish adj. suffix *-li*, the equivalent Osmanli. In It. use these adjs. were orig. sing. and pl., e.g. 'la paga d'un Osmani al giorno, intrando quattro Osmani', Bratutti *Chronica* (Venice 1649); but *-i* being the plural ending in L. and It., a new sing. arose, in L. *-us*, It. *-o*, whence the forms given above.]

A. *adj.* Of or belonging to the former Turkish dynasty founded by Othman or Osman I. *c* 1300, the branch of the Turks to which he belonged, or the Turkish empire ruled by his descendants; Turkish of the dominions of the Sultan; = Osmanli *a.*

Ottoman Porte, the court or palace of the Sultan; the Turkish government; also called the Porte or Sublime Porte.

1603 Knolles (*title*) The Generall Historie of the Turkes ..to the rising of the Othoman Familie. **1686** *Lond. Gaz.* No. 2112/2 The Ottoman Troops appointed for the guard of the Bridge of Essecke. **1686** *Ibid.* 2116/3 In case they enter into the League against the Ottoman Port. **1718** *Life Robt. Frampton* (1876) 60 Thy freedom enables thee to pass the Ottoman empire. **1835** Thirlwall *Greece* vii. I. 263 The ambition of Othman, the founder of the Ottoman dynasty. **1848** W. H. Kelly tr. *L. Blanc's Hist. Ten Years* II. 198 The watch-word..of Western Europe in 1830, was, the 'integrity of the Ottoman empire must be maintained'. **1899** *Times Gazetteer* 1611/1 Turkey, or Ottoman Empire, a number of countries, races, states, and provs. governed by the Turks, or more correctly the Osmanlis or Ottoman Turks.

B. *sb.* A Turk of the family or tribe of Othman or Osman; a Turkish subject of the Sultan; an Osmanli; a Turk in the political sense.

[**1585** T. Washington tr. *Nicholay's Voy.* ii. xiii. 49 b, The title of great..to this day remaineth vnto the house of the Othomannes. **1599** Hakluyt *Voy.* II. i. 175 As you make account of the fauour of the Grand Signor our lord Sultan Murates Hottoman.] **1605** Bacon *Adv. Learn.* ii. viii. §5 As though he had been of the race of the Ottomans. **1685** Travestin *Siege Newheusel* 32 Gone..to fight the Ottomans. **1735** Swift *Lett., to Pulteney* (1766) II. 273 Of the Roman emperors, how many of them were murdered by their own army;..the same may be said of the Ottomans by their janissaries. **1854** Church *Misc. Writ.* (1891) I. 294 It is too late to change, in general use, the familiar Ottomans for the more accurate Osmans or Osmanli. **1872** Freeman *Gen. Sk. Europ. Hist.* xi. §17 Suleiman was the last of the great line of Sultans who had raised the Ottomans to such power.

Comb. *a* **1684** Leighton *Serm.* Wks. (1868) 444 They do not Ottomanlike, one brother kill another to reign alone.

Hence **†Ottoma'nean** *a. Obs.*, **Otto'manic** (in 7 **Othomanique**) *a.* and *sb.*, Ottoman.

1658 J. Durham *Exp. Revelation* ix. (1680) 385 The Turks (having prevailed over the Saracens) did with them combine in one dominion under the Ottomanean family. **1614** Selden *Titles Hon.* 105 All of that Alian sect are..hated by the Othomaniques. **1853** G. S. Faber *Downfall Turkey* 28 The Four Angels or Ottomanic Sultanies bound for a season in the region of the great river Euphrates.

ottoman ('ɒtəmən), *sb.*[2] [f. prec.: prob. through F. *ottomane* (1812 in Hatz.-Darm.).]

1. A cushioned seat like a sofa, but without back or arms, for sitting or reclining on; or a small article of the same kind used as a low seat or footstool.

1806 Surr *Winter in Lond.* II. 146 Arberry..with most abominable malice, placed her on the Ottoman next to me! **1809** Byron *Let. to Mother* 12 Nov., The apartment was surrounded by scarlet ottomans. **1849** Miss Mulock *Ogilvies* xlvi. (1875) 358 Eleanor..was..about to sit down by the couch on a little ottoman. **1866** Geo. Eliot *F. Holt* i. (1868) 12 The frightened old man seated himself with Nimrod the retriever on an ottoman. **1880** Ouida *Moths* I. 166 This person had her feet on an ottoman.

attrib. **1810** S. Green *Reformist* II. 162 The Pembrokes.. had caused to be placed near the fire an elegant ottoman sofa. **1859** W. Anderson *Disc.* (1860) 290 From her ottoman throne in the drawing-room..[she] gives orders.

2. A kind of fabric of silk, or silk and wool. Also *attrib.*

1883 *Truth* 31 May 747/1 Lady Spencer wore a costume of dark red ottoman silk. *Ibid.* 769/2 Another dress is of black ottoman, the skirt front being covered with blue jet. **1884** *Cassell's Fam. Mag.* Oct. 695/1 The woollen Ottoman ..is of the nature of the old rep. **1887** *Daily News* 11 May 5/8 The front, in white ottoman, was very richly embroidered in pearls upon the silk. **1922** Barker & Midgley *Analysis Woven Fabrics* (ed. 2) xv. 301 *Ottoman cloth*, a dress fabric of a warp-rib structure, usually made from hard, crisp yarns. **1948** G. L. Fraser *Textiles by Britain* Gloss., *Ottoman*, dress material in either silk or rayon with a broken rib face and plain-weave back. It is produced in various sizes of rib. **1951** A. T. C. Robinson *Rayon Fabric Construction* viii. 79 A high-class Ottoman suitable for dressy coats. **1968** Mrs. L. B. Johnson *White House Diary* 9 Apr. (1970) 659, I had worn my yellow ottoman cotton with an easy skirt. **1972** M. L. Joseph *Introductory Textile Sci.* (ed. 2) xxii. 239 Many rib-weave fabrics have heavy yarns inserted as picks. Examples of this construction include poplin, faille, bengaline, and ottoman.

Ottomanism ('ɒtəməniz(ə)m). [f. Ottoman *a.* and *sb.*[1] + -ism.] The culture (or aspects of it) of the Ottoman Turks; Ottoman civilization.

1911 *Q. Rev.* July 261 On behalf of an Ottomanism honestly applied to all the Ottoman nationalities. **1930** *Times Lit. Suppl.* 7 Aug. 635/1 Her leaders had been experimenting with Ottomanism. **1930** [see levantinize *v.*]. **1974** C. E. Dawn (*title*) From Ottomanism to Arabism.

Ottomanize ('ɒtəmənaiz), *v.* [f. Ottoman *a.* and *sb.*[1] + -ize.] To make Ottoman or Turkish. So **,Ottomani'zation,** the fact or process of enforcing Ottoman ideals or Ottomanism; **'Ottomanizing** *ppl. a.*

1865 *Sat. Rev.* 5 Aug. 177 Ottomans or Ottomanized functionaries. **1886** *Fortn. Rev.* No. 239. 564 Not one of them made any permanent progress towards Ottomanizing his dominions. **1895** *Eclectic Mag.* Oct. 564 To Ottomanize European Turkey. **1912** *Chambers's Jrnl.* Dec. 817/2 If the Young Turks..had tried fraternisation instead of persisting in Ottomanisation, Turkey's credit would have risen immediately. **1920** *Glasgow Herald* 17 Mar. 10 The inhabitants were anticipating enforced Ottomanisation when the Italian fleet arrived at Astypalea. *Ibid.* 15 July 4 His liberalism earned him the utter hatred of the ottomanising Committee of Union and Progress. **1936** R. C. K. Ensor *England, 1870–1914* xiii. 436 Turkey..had alienated the liberal Powers by reverting to policies of Ottomanization and massacre. *Ibid.* 463 They were united by the Ottomanizing policy of the Young Turks. **1972** D. DAKIN *Unification of Greece* xii. 178 The new policy was to ottomanise the empire, to abolish the nationalist organisations, and to disarm the warring factions.

† '**Ottomite.** *Obs.* Also **Otta-**. [f. OTTOM(AN + -ITE[1].] = OTTOMAN *sb.*[1]

1604 SHAKS. *Othello* I. iii. 235 This present Warres against the Ottamites. **1818** BYRON *Ch. Har.* IV. xiv, Europe's bulwark 'gainst the Ottomite.

Ottonian (ɒ'təʊnɪən), *a.* [ad. late L. *Ottoniān-us*, f. the name of *Otto* I (cf. NERONIAN *a.*): see -IAN.] **a.** Of or pertaining to the East Frankish dynasty of the Holy Roman Empire founded by Otto I (912–73), which ruled from 962 to 1002. Also (*rare*) as *sb.*, a member of this dynasty. **b.** Pertaining to or characteristic of the art of this period, in part a revival of Carolingian art and extending into the 11th century.

1898 H. FISHER *Medieval Empire* I. iii. 95 The dominion of the Ottonian house was one thing in Saxony and another thing outside the Saxon borders. **1928** E. F. JACOB *Holy Roman Empire* v. 73 Yet the theory of the Empire reached its finest and truest form when the days of the Hohenstaufen were over and it was obvious that the unity of the Ottonian Reich could never be restored. **1936** A. W. CLAPHAM *Romanesque Archit.* viii. 179 The splendours of the Ottonian revival in painting, miniature, ivory, and metal work. **1938** *Times Lit. Suppl.* 12 Nov. 732/2 A group of over seventy Carolingian and Ottonian bindings. **1939** *Archit. Rev.* LXXXVI. 130/3 It is no service to German art to maintain that it is best when purest; its real triumphs are those happy marriages of Teutonic exuberance and Latin elegance which bear their first fruit in Ottonian miniatures. **1943** *Burlington Mag.* Sept. 228/2 The style of the work is 'Ottonian', an early phase of Romanesque. **1951** A. R. LEWIS *Naval Power & Trade Mediterranean, 500–1100* vi. 223 The increase of Byzantine gold coins in Germany, the luxury of the Ottonian court, the influence of Byzantine art motifs in German Romanesque architecture. **1958** *Times Lit. Suppl.* 3 Jan. 4/4 Paintings of the Rheims school in Carolingian times are shown to herald the transcendental outlook of Ottonian miniatures. **1967** *Cambr. Hist. Later Greek & Early Medieval Philos.* 587 After 950 the Ottonian dynasty were capable of re-establishing monarchical power. *Ibid.* 590 Bishop Adalbold of Utrecht . . was a man of many-sided activities in his diocese, his territory and at court, representing a type not infrequent under the Ottonians. **1968** *Eng. Hist. Rev.* LXXXIII. 24 It is impossible even to suggest a figure for the size of Saxon contingents during the decades when the Ottonians acquired their *imperium*. **1970** *Oxf. Compan. Art* 799/2 The Byzantine strand, always present in Ottonian art, was particularly strong in the School of Regensburg. **1976** *Times Lit. Suppl.* 19 Nov. 1463/3 Ottonian art (as this art of the Saxon and Salian dynasties is generally called).

ottrelite ('ɒtrəlaɪt). *Min.* [Named after Ottrez, in Belgium, where found: see -LITE.]

†**1.** An obsolete synonym of DIALLAGE. (So named by Wolff of Spa, 1812.)

2. A hydrous silicate of aluminium, iron, and manganese, found in greyish to black crystalline scales. (So named by Damour, 1842.)

1844 DANA *Min.* 529 Ottrelite . . scratches glass with difficulty. **1879** RUTLEY *Stud. Rocks* x. 132.

† '**ottroye**, *sb. Obs. rare.* [a. OF. *otroi*, *ottroy*, in AF. also *ottroy*, vbl. sb. from *otroyer*: see next.] Yielding, concession.

1480 CAXTON *Ovid's Met.* x. vi, Venus . . shewde hyme [Pygmalion] signes of ottroye & consente.

† '**ottroye**, *v. Obs.* [a. OF. *ot(t)roier* (12th c. in Littré), earlier form of *octroyer*: see OCTROY.] *trans.* To accord, concede, grant; = OCTROY *v.* 1.

c **1477** CAXTON *Jason* 7 And after congie and licence taken and ottroied he retourned into his countrey. **1491** —— *Vitas Patr.* (W. de W. 1495) I. li. 106 b/2 The holy man apperceyued that the tresoure of grace was to hym ottroyed and gyuen. **1512** *Helyas* in Thoms *Prose Rom.* (1828) III. 14 The honour . . with good hert I ottroye and graunt you. **1546** *St. Papers Hen. VIII*, XI. 234, I thoughte that the Kinge his maister shuld do as well to punisshe hym for it, as to ottroye hym the combat.

ottur, **ot(t)yr(e**, **otur**, obs. ff. UTTER, OTTER.

† **o'twin**, *adv. Obs.* In 4 **otwyn**, **o twinne**. [See O *prep.*[1] 1 b.] Variant of ATWIN *Obs.*, asunder.

a **1330** *Otuel* 1202 Er þei wolden o twinne gon. *a* **1340** HAMPOLE *Psalter* xxv. 1 We are fere otwyn in soul.

Otyiherero, var. OTSHI-HERERO.

ou ('əʊuː). [Hawaiian.] A green and yellow bird, *Psittirostra psittacea*, belonging to the sub-family Coerebinæ, or honeycreepers.

1887 L. STEJNEGER in *Proc. U.S. Nat. Mus.* X. 93 The Ou, feeds on bugs and sings on the wing. **1890** *Ibis* II. 194 The constant twittering the Ou almost invariably makes while feeding at once betrays its identity. **1903** [see IEIE]. **1944** G. C. MUNRO *Birds of Hawaii* 123 With its yellow head and bright green body in varying shades on different parts the ou is a beautiful bird. **1970** S. CARLQUIST *Hawaii* xi. 191 The ou eats fruits, seeds, leaves, and caterpillars.

† **ou**, *int. Obs.* = O, OH.

1297 R. GLOUC. (Rolls) 4409 Ou louerd þe deol þat þer was of hom of normandye.

ou, obs. form of OWE *v.*, HOW, YOU.

ou-, the ordinary spelling of *ov-* before *c* 1625, as in *oual*, *ouer*, *ouert*: see all such under the modern spelling OVAL, OVER, OVERT, etc.

‖**ouabaio**, better **wabaio** (wæ'baɪəʊ). The Somāli name (Larajasse *Somali Dict.*, *wa'bayo*) of the plant *Acocanthera Schimperi*, the juice of which is used to poison arrows. Hence **ouabaïn**, better **wabaïn** (wæ'bɑːɪn), the glucoside, $C_{31}H_{48}O_{12}$, obtained from this plant, in action and composition closely resembling strophanthin. (The spelling *oua-* for *wa-* is due to the French discoverer.)

1892 in *Syd. Soc. Lex.* **1893** *Pharmac. Jrnl.* 27 May 965 In the year 1882 some roots, stems, and leaves of the plant said to yield the ouabaio poison of the Somalis were sent from Africa to France by M. Revoil. **1893** SQUIBB *Ephemeris* IV. 45 Ouabaïn is a glucoside obtained by extraction from the root and wood of the Ouabaïo. **1897** *Allbutt's Syst. Med.* III. 229.

ouad, var. OUED.

ouakari, var. WAKARI, S. American monkey.

‖**ouananiche** (ˌwænə'niːʃ). Also written ouinanniche, **wananishe**, WINNINISH, etc. [French spelling of native name in Montagnais dialect of Cree; dim. of *wannan*. (Occurs in a book written by Father Masse, Jesuit missionary 1611–46.) The English phonetic spelling would be *wananeesh*.] A French Canadian name of the fresh-water salmon of the Labrador peninsula (*Salmo saler ouananiche*).

1873 *Forest & Stream* 4 Sept. 53/2 When you have had a surfeit of fresh water salmon *ouinanish*—retrace your steps to Chicoutimi. **1896** E. T. D. CHAMBERS (*title*) The Ouananiche and its Canadian Environment. **1897** *Outing* (U.S.) XXX. 217/1 Lordly salmon, gamy trout and buckjumping ouananiche are fit for any man to play. **1907** J. G. MILLAIS *Newfoundland* i. 2 Newfoundland is a most attractive place, with its thousands of lakes and pools; picturesque streams teeming with salmon, trout, and ouananiche. **1966** *Globe & Mail* (Toronto) 15 Jan. 29/5, I . . tied into my first ouananiche with him on Trout Lake near North Bay. **1969** H. HORWOOD *Newfoundland* xvi. 128 All [*sc.* North Harbour, Rocky, Colinet, and Back Rivers] have exceptional fishing for sea trout, brook trout, or ouananiche.

[**ouarine**, a scribal or typographical error for *ouariue*, i.e. *ouarive* (Claude d'Abbeville, *Mission en Maragnan*, 1614, 252), taken over from Buffon by Goldsmith, and repeated by some later writers. The word intended, *ouarive* (wariv), is the Fr. form of GUARIBA, a South American monkey.]

oubaas ('əʊbɑːs). *S. Afr.* Also **ou baas**, **oud baas**. [Afrikaans, f. *ou(d)* old + BAAS.] Elderly head of a family; elderly man, old gentleman. Also used as a form of address and prefixed to a surname or a Christian name.

1869 T. BAINES *Diary* 2 July (1946) I. 59 They recognised at once and were rather pleased with the likeness of 'Oud Baas', Mr. Hartley. **1914** L. H. BRINKMAN *Breath of Karroo* ii. 24 The master of the house is addressed as 'Ou baas' and a young man, 'Klein baas'. **1942** 'B. KNIGHT' *Sun climbs Slowly* IV. xxx. 286 No, it was not the *Oubaas*, she said, but someone she had not seen before. **1946** V. POHL *Land of Distant Horizons* 50 They were so incredulous that the Hottentot exclaimed indignantly: 'Oubaas, if I have never told the truth, I am telling it now'. **1947** *Forum* (Johannesburg) 19 Apr. 1/1 The problems which faced the Oubaas this week ranged from the spreading boycott of Indian traders in the Transvaal . . to the need for separate trade unions for Africans. **1952** E. H. BURROWS *Overberg Outspan* vi. 161 These were the people who congregated on Sundays with the family to hear the *oubaas* read a chapter of the Bible. **1959** *Cape Times* 14 Feb. 3/4 Joe told him that he and Moyisi had hit the *oubaas* with kieries. *Ibid.* 5 June 13/5, I . . recognized him as *oubaas* De Greef. **1973** *Deb. Senate S. Afr.* 17 May 2807 Old Koos . . said: 'Oubaas, . . I don't know why you should start so late.'

oubit, **oubut**, var. WOUBIT, woolly-bear.

† '**oubliance.** *Obs.* Also **oublyaunce**, **-ence**. [a. OF. *oubliance*, *-ience* (13th c. in Littré), f. *oublier* to forget:—pop. L. *oblītā-re*, f. *oblīt-*, ppl. stem of *oblīviscī* to forget.] Forgetting, oblivion.

c **1477** CAXTON *Jason* 91 b, That ye leue and put her in oubliance. **1484** —— *Chivalry* 84 Ire torneth hym in to forgetynge or oublyaunce. —— *Ryall Bk.* D vj, After neclygence cometh oublyence or forgetyng.

oublie, obs. form of OBLEY.

oublietje, var. OBLIETJIE.

‖**oubliette** (ublijɛt), *sb.* [Fr. *oubliette* (14th c. in Littré), f. *oublier* to forget.] A secret dungeon, access to which was gained only through a trap-door above; often having a secret pit below, into which the prisoner might be precipitated.

1819 SCOTT *Ivanhoe* xlii, The place was utterly dark—the oubliette, as I suppose, of their accursed convent. *a* **1845** HOOD *Knight & Dragon* xxviii, In the dark oubliette Let yon merchant forget That he e'er had a bark richly laden. **1872** SPURGEON *Treas. Dav.* Ps. lxix. 15 Forgotten like one in the oubliettes of the Bastille. **1877** TENNYSON *Harold* II. ii, The deep-down oubliette, Down thirty feet below the smiling day—In blackness.

Hence **oubli'ette** *v. trans.*, to shut up in, or as in, an oubliette.

1884 TENNYSON *Becket* IV. ii, Could you keep her Indungeon'd from one whisper of the wind, Dark even from a side glance of the moon, And oublietted in the centre.

ouch (aʊtʃ), *sb.*[1] Forms: α. 4–5 **nouche**, 5–6 **nowche**, (5 **noych(e**, 6 **knowch**). β. 4–5 **uche**, 4–6 **ouche**, 5–6 **owche**, (5 **oyche**), 6– **ouch**. [ME. and AF. *nouche* = OF. *nouche*, *noche*, *nosche*, *nusche*, in ONF. *noske*, *nosque*:—late L. *nusca*, a. OHG. *nuscka*, *nuscha*, MHG. *nuske*, *nusche* buckle, clasp. App. of Celtic origin: cf. OIr. *nasc* ring, *nasgaim* I knit, tie, Gael. *nasg* seal. The form *ouch* has arisen from the erroneous ME. division of *a nouche* as *an ouche* (cf. *an other*, *a nother*, also *adder*, *newt*).

Scarcely in living use since 1600; but known in the Bible and earlier literature; often vaguely or unintelligently used by later writers, as if = gem, jewel, precious ornament.]

1. A clasp, buckle, fibula, or brooch, for holding together the two sides of a garment; hence, a clasped necklace, bracelet, or the like; also, a buckle or brooch worn as an ornament (the chief meaning in later times). (Such nouches or ouches were often set with precious stones, whence sense 2.)

α. **1382** WYCLIF *1 Macc.* x. 89 And he sente to him a golden lase [*gloss* or nouche], as custome is for to be ȝouen to cosyns of kyngus. *c* **1384** CHAUCER *H. Fame* III. 260 And they were set as thik of nouchis. **1390** GOWER *Conf.* III. 39 The Nouches and the riche ringes. **1439** *E.E. Wills* (1882) 118 (Countess of Warwick), I woll my sone . . haue myn oyche with my grete diamond, and my Noych with my Baleys. **1476** SIR J. PASTON in *P. Lett.* III. 162 The ryche saletts, heulmetts, garters, nowchys gelt, and alle is goone. **1562** *Lanc. Wills* (1857) I. 181 Two knowches of gold for a cap. [**1843** LYTTON *Last Bar.* I. ix, I went yesterday to attend my Lord of Warwick with some nowches and knackeries.]

β. *c* **1375** *Sc. Leg. Saints* xxviii. (*Margaret*) 15 Men bryngis It ['margaret'] of ful fare land, for til enhorne vchis & cronis, . . & set it in bruchis & in ryngis. **1494** *Househ. Ord.* (1790) 120 The Kinge must . . lay it aboute his necke & claspe it before with a riche owche. **1563–87** FOXE *A. & M.* (1684) II. 44 Adorned and decked with most rich and precious Ouches and Brouches. **1581** J. BELL *Haddon's Answ. Osor.* 295 Presentyng unto him this precious Owch to set on his cappe. **1611** FLORIO, *Castóne*, . . a brouch or ouch. **1658** PHILLIPS, An *Ouch*, a collar of Gold . . it is called a brooch. **1720** *Stow's Surv.* (1754) II. v. x. 278/2 Such were Owches, Brooches, Agglets. **1848** LYTTON *Harold* I. i, White was the upper tunic clasped on his shoulder with a broad ouche or brooch.

2. The gold or silver setting of a precious stone.

(Usually, however, a brooch or buckle so regarded.)

1481 CAXTON *Myrr.* I. v. 25 The Cock . . demandeth not after the ouche or gemme, but had leuir haue somme corn to ete. **1531** ELYOT *Gov.* III. xxx, As a precious stone in a ryche ouche. **1551** BIBLE *Exod.* xxviii. 11 After the worcke of a stonegrauer . . shalt y[u] graue the ii. stones . . and shalt make them to be set in ouches of gold. **1652** URQUHART *Jewel* Wks. (1834) 241 An asteristick ouch, wherein were inchased fifteen several diamonds. **1737** WHISTON *Josephus*, *Wars* VII. v. §5 Precious stones . . some set in crowns of gold, and some in other ouches.

†**3.** *transf.* A carbuncle or other tumour or sore on the skin. *Obs.*

1612 CHAPMAN *Widowes T.* in Dodsley *O. Pl.* (1780) VI. 145 Up start as many aches in's bones, as there are ouches in his skin.

†**4.** 'The blow given by a boar's tusk' (J.). *Obs.*

1736 AINSWORTH *Thesaurus*, The ouches a boar maketh, *ictus apri dente factus.*

ouch, *sb.*[2]: see OUCH *int.*[1]

ouch (aʊtʃ), *v.*[1] [f. OUCH *sb.*[1]] *trans.* To set or adorn with, or as with, ouches; to spangle.

1610 GUILLIM *Heraldry* III. i. (1611) 191 He beareth Luna, a mantle of estate, Mars . . ouched or garnished with strings fastened thereunto. **1892** HENLEY *Song of Sword*, etc. Lond. Volunt. i. 59 A lamplit bridge ouching the troubled sky.

ouch, *v.*[2] [Cf. next.] *intr.* To utter an exclamation or sound represented by 'ouch'.

1654 GAYTON *Pleas. Notes* IV. ii. 176 But harke Sancho Pancas Runs Ouching round the mountaine like a ranck-Asse, Braying for's Company. **1898** *Westm. Gaz.* 18 Apr. 2/1 You 'ouch' audibly . . and sit down on the floor to meditate.

ouch (aʊtʃ), *int.*[1] [a. Ger. *autsch*, a cry of pain.] An exclamation expressing pain or annoyance. Also as *sb.*[2]

1838 J. C. NEAL *Charcoal Sk.* 38 'Ouch!' shrieked Dabbs; 'my eye, how it hurts!' **1843** 'R. CARLTON' *New Purchase* I. ii. 9 The tiers becoming all vocal with 'bless my soul's'—'my goodnesses!'—and vulgar 'ouches!' **1886** in *Let. fr. Pennsylvanian Correspondent*, Ouch, that hurts. Ouch, don't strike me. **1918** GALSWORTHY *Five Tales* 235 Freda gurgled: 'Ouch! You *are* a beast!' **1958** R. GODDEN *Greengage Summer* v. 56 'Ouch!' said Joss and looked as if she would be sick again. **1972** D. DELMAN *Sudden Death* (1973) iv. 110 'Ouch,' she said, grinning. 'Ouchie-wowchie. Well, that tears that, doesn't it?'

ouch (aʊx), *int.*[2] A representation of the short bark of a dog.

1899 CROCKETT *Kit Kennedy* 160 'Ouch! Get on', Royal said . . 'don't keep me waiting'.

oucher (ˈaʊtʃə(r)). [f. OUCH *sb.*[1] + -ER[1].] A maker of ouches, buckles, or brooches.
c **1515** *Cocke Lorell's B.* 9 Owchers, skynners, and cutlers.

oucht, obs. form of AUGHT, OUGHT.

Ouchterlony (ɒx-, ɒktərˈləʊnɪ). *Immunol.* The name of O. T. G. *Ouchterlony* (b. 1914), Swedish microbiologist and immunologist, used *attrib.* and in the possessive with reference to a standard precipitin test devised by him, which normally involves placing antigen and antibody in separate wells sunk into a layer of agar on a plate and observing the line of precipitation which develops as the substances meet after diffusing through the agar.
1952 *Methods Med. Res.* V. 368 Ouchterlony's technique deviates from the ideal particularly with respect to points (1) and (2). **1954** *Jrnl. Immunol.* LXXIII. 232/1 We undertook an experimental evaluation of Ouchterlony's test. **1955** *Ibid.* LXXV. 460 (*heading*) Interpretation of the Ouchterlony precipitin test. **1962** LUNTZ & WRIGHT in A. Pirie *Lens Metabolism Rel. Cataract* 319 Serum from each patient was put on Ouchterlony plates and tested against..human lens protein. **1975** *Nature* 21 Aug. 656/1 This antiserum gave a single line on Ouchterlony gel diffusion with MAF.

‖**oud** (uːd). Also ood, oude, ʿūd. [ad. Arab. *ʿūd*, lit. 'wood'.] A form of lute or mandolin played principally in Arab countries.
1738 T. SHAW *Trav. Barbary & Levant* 270 They [*sc.* the Moors] have the *Rebebb*, a Violin of two Strings, which is played upon with a Bow: the A-Oude, a Bass double stringed Lute, bigger than our Viol, which is touched with a Plectrum. **1836** E. W. LANE *Acct. Manners & Customs Mod. Egyptians* II. v. 69 The *'ood* is a species of guitar, which is played with a plectrum. **1870** C. ENGEL *Descr. Catal. Musical Instruments S. Kensington Museum* 8 The *Oud*..was brought by the Moors to Spain, where it is still known as the *laud*. *Ibid.*, The Oud is generally provided with frets made of cords of gut. **1883** *Encycl. Brit.* XV. 70/1 The modern Egyptian 'ʿūd' is the direct descendant of the Arabic lute. **1931** H. G. FARMER *Stud. Oriental Mus. Instruments* (Ser. 1) viii. 92 That the *mizhar* and the *'ūd* were distinct types of lute we know from several authorities. **1950** P. BOWLES in *Penguin New Writing* XXXIX. 10 As he passed over into the unlighted district he heard a few languid notes being strummed on an oud. **1957** H. G. FARMER in *New Oxf. Hist. Music* I. 446 The greatest of all the instruments of Islamic peoples was the *'ūd* or lute. **1960** *New Yorker* 16 July 86 A couple of Near Eastern love songs performed..on the oud, a large Egyptian stringed instrument that resembles a gourd sliced in half and that emits an urgent nasal, tinging sound. **1972** J. WAMBAUGH *Blue Knight* (1973) xiv. 252 He plucked and stroked those *oud* strings with the quill of an eagle feather. It's a lute-like instrument and has no frets like a guitar. **1976** D. MUNROW *Instruments Middle Ages & Renaissance* 25/2 The earliest tuning employed [for the lute] is thought to have been a series of fourths, adopted from the *'ūd* and still used by Arab players today.

†**oudemian**, *a.* *Obs. rare.* [f. Gr. οὐδεμία, fem. of οὐδείς no, none, not any + -AN.] Used humorously for: No, none, non-existent.
a **1586** SIDNEY *Arcadia* III. (1598) 345 To meete as that night at Mantinea, in the Oudemian streete, at Charitas vncles house. **1659** *Lively Char. Pretending Grandees Scot.* 5 He values himself at a great Land estate; which in truth stands all upon invisible stones, in the Oudemian street of Eutopia.

oudeˈnology. *nonce-wd.* [f. Gr. οὐδέν nothing + -OLOGY.] Used humorously for the science of nothing, or of things having no real existence.
1838 *New Monthly Mag.* LIII. 302, I had been studying transcendental philosophy, homœopathic medicine, the unknown tongues, and sundry other of the more abstruse branches of oudenology.

ouder, owder, variants of OUTHER *adj. pron.*

Ouds (aʊdz). = O.U.D.S. (O 5 d).
1914 C. MACKENZIE *Sinister St.* II. iv. 567 Are you running the Ouds as well as The Oxford Looking-Glass? **1967** E. COXHEAD *Thankless Muse* vii. 135 Presently the Ouds producer appropriated her.

‖**oud-stryder** (ˈəʊtˌstreɪdər). *S. Afr.* [Afrikaans, = ex-soldier.] A veteran of the South African War (1899–1902) who fought on the side of the Boer republics. Also *gen.*, an ex-soldier.
1947 *Cape Argus* 29 Mar. 1 More than 1,600 Oudstryders to-day waited to give the Royal Family their own special welcome. **1947** *Cape Times* 31 Mar. 6/5 One of the happiest features of the visit of the Royal Family to Pretoria was the sincere welcome they received from the Oudstryders. **1948** *Ibid.* 21 Sept. 4/3 Calculating the means limit of *oudstryders*. **1954** *Sunday Times* (Johannesburg) 26 Sept. 1 Many oudstryders and ex-servicemen of both World Wars will attend. **1957** *Cape Argus* 12 Apr. 6/8 Legislation..had provided for oudstryders' pensions. **1975** *Eastern Province Herald* (S. Afr.) 13 Oct. 11 The uncompromising Boer oudstryder..told the Queen that he could never forgive the British for fighting against the Boers. The Queen was all sympathy; as a Scot, she said, she understood his feelings perfectly.

oue, var. OFFE, HOVE *v.*[1]

‖**oued** (wɛd). Also ouad. [Fr. rendering of Arabic *wādī* WADI, WADY.] = WADI, WADY.
Usu. used only in contexts relating to those territories in N. Africa which were formerly under French control.
1854 J. R. MORELL *Algeria* vii. 121 The Ouad-Foddah, or river of silver, has its rise in a high rugged mountain. **1874** *Q. Jrnl. Geol. Soc.* XXX. 117 Lignite occurs..at El Kheicha on the banks of the Oued M'Zi, a branch of the L'Aghouat river. **1883** *Encycl. Brit.* XV. 608/1 Mascara, a fortified town of Algeria..occupies two small hills separated by the Oued Toudman. **1920** *Glasgow Herald* 27 Nov. 4 For an hour we followed the course of the oued (or river). **1965** MOUNTJOY & EMBLETON *Africa* iv. 180 A large number of small oueds descend from the mountains and water this immediate piedmont zone.

ouen(e: see OVEN.

ouer, obs. f. OVER: so in ME. and early mod.E. compounds, as *ouerbear*, *ouercast*, *ouercome*, etc.

ouerage, variant of OVERAGE *Obs.*, work.

ouert, ouese, obs. forms of OVERT, EAVES.

ouerwhere, variant of OURWHERE *adv. Obs.*

†**ouerwhile**, *adv. Obs. rare.* In 5 ouerwile. [prob. reduced from *outherwhile*; analogous to OURWHERE, *ouerwhere*.] At one time or another; at times; now and then.
c **1400** *Apol. Loll.* 30 Þerfor non of þe bischopis, enblawen wiþ enuy of þe fendis temptacoun, wraþ, if prestis ouerwile exort or monest þe peple.

ouf(f (aʊf, uːf, ʊf), **oof** (uːf, ʊf), *int.*
1. a. An exclamation expressing a sense of stifling, alarm, or annoyance.
1851 LONGFELLOW *Jrnl.* 9 Feb. in S. Longfellow *Life H. W. Longfellow* (1886) II. 189 There was no violent discussion; so that the Count did not, so often as usual, clasp his round head with both hands and say, 'Ouf!' **1855** BROWNING *Fra Lippo* 50, I could not paint all night—Ouf! I leaned out of window for fresh air. **1876** F. E. TROLLOPE *Charming Fellow* II. xii. 193 'Ouf!' panted Miss Chubb, and began to fan herself. **1913** G. B. SHAW *Let.* 9 July in *B. Shaw & Mrs. Campbell* (1952) 130 You shut the door on me..and said 'Ouf!' when it slammed. **1934** WEBSTER, Oof. **1951** R. SENHOUSE tr. *Colette's Chéri* 33 Back in Paris again—ouf! —I'll pack him off to his precious studies. **1958** L. DURRELL *Balthazar* iv. 237 Ouf! I fled. **1966** L. COHEN *Beautiful Losers* (1970) I. 116 You wanted sock! pow! slam! ugg! oof! yulp! written in the air between you and all the world. **1967** A. LASKI *Seven Other Years* iv. 59 'Ouf!' he said... 'This is not my dance.' **1976** 'R. B. DOMINIC' *Murder out of Commission* iii. 27 'Oof! What a night!' he grunted.
b. As an expression of resignation or relief.
1909 MRS. H. WARD *Daphne* iii. 56 Daphne, with an 'Ouf!' of fatigue, took off her hat. **1921** G. B. SHAW *Back to Methuselah* v. 261 *All.* Ouf! (*A great sigh of relief.*) **1964** V. NABOKOV *Defence* xiii. 220 'Ouf,' sighed Mrs. Luzhin, 'we're finally rid of them.' **1976** N. FREELING *Lake Isle* xiv. 109 'Ouf,' said Sophie, sitting down and kicking her shoes off.
2. A representation of the warning bark of a dog. Cf. WUFF *sb.*
1899 CROCKETT *Kit Kennedy* 161 'Ouff! ouff!' barked Royal behind him.

oufe, obs. f. WOOF.

ougard, obs. f. AWARD.

†**ouge.** *Mining. Obs.* [Derivation unknown: cf. WOUGH.] The hard or compact rock forming the sides of a metallic vein.
1747 HOOSON *Miner's Dict.* s.v. *Bind*, The more nearer they resemble the Nature of the approaching Ouges, and are easily distinguished by the experienced Miner. *Ibid.* Q iij, The true set of the Vein is when it cuts into the hard Rock, and formes hard and firme Sides or Ouges.

ougglisome, obs. form of UGLISOME *a.*

ough, *int.*, *sb.*
1. An exclamation expressing disgust.
1565 COOPER *Thesaurus, Ahah, suspirantis*..Ough hoe: in sighyng. **1786** MRS. A. M. BENNETT *Juvenile Indiscr.* III. 197 Ough, he despised such Cattle [people].
2. An imitation of certain sounds: see quots.
1894 *Field* 9 July 815/2 Followed by a deep and angry 'ough!' as a tiger broke cover. **1900** *Blackw. Mag.* Oct. 481/2 The 'ough' 'ough' of the field-guns breaks upon the ear.

ough, obs. f. OWE.

oughly(e, obs. f. UGLY *a.*

ought (ɔːt), *sb.*[1] (*pron.*), *adv.*, var. of AUGHT *sb.*[2]

ought, *sb.*[2] [OUGHT *v.* 5 used for the nonce as a noun.] That which is denoted by the verb *ought*; duty, obligation.
1678 CUDWORTH *Intell. Syst.* I. v. 874 The Will of God, is Goodness, Justice, and Wisdom; or Decorousness, Fitness, and Ought it self, Willing. **1865** MOZLEY *Mirac.* iii. 257 Without the sense of 'ought'..there is nothing to bind the individual to those actions. **1874** GEO. ELIOT *Coll. Breakf. P.* in *Jubal*, etc. 260 The will supreme, the individual claim, The social Ought, the lyrist's liberty. **1878** GLADSTONE *Prim. Homer* VI. §30. 87 The two great ideas of the divine will, and of the Ought, or duty, are the principal factors in the government of our human world. **1908** A. BENNETT *Human Machine* 43 You have a special apparatus within you for dealing with a universe where *oughts* are flagrantly disregarded. **1933** W. DE LA MARE *Lord Fish* 269 His master had told him little about his oughts. **1941** *Daily Progress* (Charlottesville, Va.) 3 July 10/7 (Advt.), Oughts for a great vacation. Bathing, boardwalk and 'loaf-life' specials. Mens & Boys Swim Trunks.

ought, *sb.*[3] Vulgar corruption of NOUGHT in sense 'cipher'.
Prob. originating in an erroneous division of 'a nought' as 'an ought'; but by many associated with the figure o of the cipher, which they take as the initial O of *ought*. ***oughts and crosses***, a children's game with a figure containing nine spaces, which are filled up by two players alternately with ciphers and crosses, the object of each being to place three of one kind in a line; = *noughts and crosses*.
1844 DICKENS *Mart. Chuz.* xix, 'Three score and ten', said Chuffey, 'ought and carry seven... Oh! why—why—why—didn't he live to four times ought's an ought, and four times two's an eight, eighty?' **1854** *N. & Q.* Ser. I. IX. 527/1 (Devonshire saying) Oughts are nothings unless they've strokes to them. **1861** SALA *Dutch Pict.* ix. 130 A vile childish scrawl, done over a half smeared-out game of oughts and crosses. **1874** DASENT *Half a Life* 32 Units were taken for oughts, and oughts added to units.

ought (ɔːt), *v.* Forms: α. 1 **áhte**, 2–4 **ahte**, (3 **æhte, ahhte, hahte**), 3–4 **auhte**, (3 **aucte**), 3–5 **aȝt(e, aght(e, aute**, 4 **achte, awȝte, auht, ahut, awt**, 4–5 **auȝt(e, aughte**, 4–6 **acht**, *Sc.* **awcht**, 4–7 **aught**, 5–6 **awght**, 4– *Sc.* **aucht**. β. 3 **ohte**, 3–4 **oȝte**, 3–5 **ouhte, oute**, 4–5 **oghte, ouȝt(e, out**, 4–6 **oughte**, (5 **owghte**, 5–6 **owte**), 4–7 **owght**, (5 **owȝt, oght**), 4– **ought**, (4– *dial.* **owt**, 6– *Sc.* **oucht, ocht**, *s.w. dial.* **oft**). γ. 4 **iȝte, ight(e, iht**, 5 **eght**. [OE. *áhte*, ME. *ôhte*, *oȝte*, *oughte*, pa. t. of *ágan*, ME. *oȝen*, *owen*, mod. OWE *v.* q.v. This partly retains a past sense; but as an auxiliary of predication it has become indefinite as to time: see branch III, and B.]
A. as finite verb; properly pa. t. of OWE.
I. Pa. t. of OWE *v.* in sense 'to have or possess'.
†**1. a.** Possessed, owned. (Cf. OWE *v.* 1.) *Obs.*
α. *a* **1000** *Beowulf* 31 Leof land-fruma longe ahte. *c* **1175** *Lamb. Hom.* 33 Þah..þu ahtest al weorld iwald. *c* **1205** LAY. 25083 Þeos weoren mine ælderen..ahten [*c* **1275** adde] alle þa leoden þa into Rome leien. *c* **1330** R. BRUNNE *Chron.* (1810) 156 Me salle haf wele alle þat þou euer auht. **1375** BARBOUR *Bruce* I. 45 Off Kingis, that aucht that reawte. *c* **1375** *Cursor M.* 4253 (Fairf.) Alle þe gode and catel þat he aȝt. *c* **1440** *Jacob's Well* 203 It schulde haue be restoryd to hem þat awtyn it. **1552** ABP. HAMILTON *Catech.* (1884) 24 The oxe hes knawin the man that aucht him. *a* **1578** LINDESAY (Pitscottie) *Chron. Scot.* (S.T.S.) I. 249 At the beginning of meate..he that aught the house..sould say the grace. *a* **1670** SPALDING *Troub. Chas. I* (1850) I. 205 The poor men that aucht thame followit in.
β. *a* **1225** *Ancr. R.* 390 He..bead for to makien hire cwene of al þet he ouhte. *c* **1350** *Will. Palerne* 3229 Þe king ebrouns it ouȝt þat was hire lord bi fore. *c* **1400** *Destr. Troy* 12404 By leue of the lord, þat the lond oght. *c* **1440** *Gesta Rom.* liv. 235 (Harl. MS.) He that owte the shelde. **1470–85** MALORY *Arthur* VI. xii, The name of this castel is Tyntygayl & a duke oughte it somtyme. **1534** MORE *Comf. agst. Trib.* III. Wks. 1219/2 Who ought your castel (Cosyn) thre thousande yere agoe? **1632** LITHGOW *Trav.* v. 204 The Turke who ought my Mule.
γ. **13..** *Cursor M.* 6719 (Cott.) Þe lord þat þat beist aght Sal þar-for ansuer at his maght [*G.* iht..miht, *Tr.* ight..myȝt].
b. with inversion of sense: Belonged. *Obs.*
1470–85 MALORY *Arthur* VI. v, There came the knyghte to whome the pauelione ought.
II. Pa. t. of OWE *v.* in its existing sense.
†**2. a.** Had to pay, was under obligation to pay or render; owed. (Cf. OWE *v.* 2.) *Obs.* or *dial.*
The full phrase *ahte to ȝeldanne*, 'had to pay' = *debebat*, owed, appears in the Lindisfarne Gospels; but, for the following two centuries and a half, examples are wanting to show the passing of this into the simple *ahte*: see OWE *v.* 2.
α. [*c* **950** *Lindisf. Gosp.* Matt. xviii. 24 Enne seðe ahte to ȝeldanne [*Vulg.* debebat, *Rushw.* sculde, *Ags. G.* sceolde, *Hatt.* scolde] tea ðusendo cræftas. *Ibid.* 28 Enne of efneðeȝnum his seðe ahte to ȝeldenna [*other vv.* as in 24] hundrað scillinga. *Ibid.* Luke vii. 41 An ahte to ȝeldanne [*Vulg.* debebat, *Ags. Gosp.* sceolde] penningas fif hund.] *a* **1300** *Cursor M.* 21422 Pour he was..And til a juu he mikel aght. **1535** STEWART *Cron. Scot.* I. 226 Quhair is the kyndnes thow aucht to Claudius? *a* **1825** FORBY *Voc. E. Anglia* s.v. *Aught*, He aught me ten pounds.
β. *a* **1225** *Ancr. R.* 124 A mon þet leie ine prisune, & ouhte muche raunsun. *Ibid.* 406 Þu ȝulde þet tu ouhtest. **1382** WYCLIF *Luke* vii. 41 Tweye dettours were to sum leenere..oon ouȝte fyue hundrid pens, and an other fyfty. **1470–85** MALORY *Arthur* I. iii, He asked hir by the feith she ouȝt to hym. ? *a* **1500** *Chester Pl.* (Shaks. Soc.) II. 4 Foure dettores some tyme..oughten moneye to a userere. **1570–6** LAMBARDE *Peramb. Kent* (1826) 279 Whether..the Abbat of St. Augustine and his tenants ought suite to the Bishop's Court. **1596** SHAKS. *1 Hen. IV*, III. iii. 152 He..sayde this other day, You ought him a thousand pound. **1677** *Govt. Venice* 145 The Obedience he ought to his Superiours. *c* **1685** *Life A. Martindale* 231 (E.D.D.) Born, he ought him nothing.
b. *absol.* Was in debt (*to*). (Cf. OWE *v.* 2 b.)
1460 CAPGRAVE *Chron.* 167 The Kyng of Aragon..deneyed it [service], and saide he aute not but to the Kyng of Spain. **1483** CAXTON *Gold. Leg.* 277 b/1 The good man..constrayned hym by his othe to swere whether he ought hym or no. **1610** HEALEY *St. Aug. Citie of God* VI. vii. (1620) 234 That the first man she met..should pay her for the sport that Hercules ought her for.
†**3.** *fig.* **a.** Owed, had to repay (an ill turn, shame, etc.). (Cf. OWE *v.* 3.) *Obs.*
c **1385** CHAUCER *L.G.W.* 1609 *Hypsip.*, Fortune hire oughte a foul myschaunce. *c* **1460** *Towneley Myst.* ii. 314 We! na! I aght the a fowll dispyte. **1575** *Gamm. Gurton* I. iii, The devill, or els his dame they ought her sure a shame. **1652** BROME *Damoiselle* III. i. Wks. 1873 I. 416 The Devill sure Ought me a mischiefe, when he enabled that Old Wretch, my Father to beget me. **1694** R. L'ESTRANGE *Fables*

cclxxviii. (1714) 294 The Devil Ought him a Shame, and paid him both Interest and Principal.

b. Hence, Bore, entertained, or cherished (ill or good will, a grudge, a spite, regarded as something yet to be paid or rendered); sometimes nearly = showed, rendered (favour, allegiance, etc.). *Obs.*

α. **1495** *Plumpton Corr.* (Camden) 112 He haught a favor & good lordship to his servant Kilborne.

β. **1465** MARG. PASTON in *P. Lett.* II. 186 He ought you ryght gode wyll. **1494** FABYAN *Chron.* II. xlviii. 31 By his excercysyng of Iustyce yᵉ Brytons ought to hym more fauour than to eyther of his neuewes. *a* **1529** SKELTON *P. Sparowe* 322 So trayterously my byrde to kyll That neuer ought the euyll wyll! **1535** COVERDALE *Ps.* liv. [lv.] 12 One that ought me euell will dyd threaten me. **1559** *Mirr. Mag.*, *Northumbld.* v, Til Fortune ought both him and vs a spite. **1597** BEARD *Theatre God's Judgem.* (1612) 150 He purposed to stab one whom he ought a grudge vnto with his dagger. **1678** MARVELL *Growth Popery* Wks. 1875 IV. 337 He highly inveighed against many gentlemen..that ought him no homage, as persons disaffected.

†**4.** Was indebted or beholden for; owed. (Cf. OWE *v.* 4.) *Obs.*

1594 ? GREENE *Selimus* Wks. 1881–3 XIV. 217 Your Emperour ought his safetie vnto you. **1651** tr. *De-las-Coveras' Don Fenise* 167, I saw I ought my life to this Cavalier. **1658** CLEVELAND *Rustick Rampant* Wks. (1687) 505 To whose Christian Piety he ought the two last Days of his Life.

III. As auxiliary of predication.

5. The general verb to express duty or obligation of any kind; strictly used of moral obligation, but also with various weaker shades of meaning, expressing what is befitting, proper, correct, advisable, or naturally expected. Only in pa. t. (indic. or subj.), which may be either past or present in meaning. (The only current use in standard Eng.)

The subject is properly the person (or thing) bound by the obligation, which latter is expressed by a following infinitive (with, formerly also without, *to*), sometimes omitted by ellipsis. Followed by a passive infinitive, it expresses obligation on the part of some undefined or unexpressed agent, the subject in this case being the person, etc. to whom the obligation is due (e.g. *parents ought to be honoured* = it is a duty to honour parents).

a. In past sense: = Owed it to duty; was (were) bound or under obligation (*to do* something). Usually, now only, in dependent clause, corresponding to a preceding past tense in principal clause: *he said you ought* = he said it was your duty. (Cf. c below.)

α. *c* **1200** ORMIN 19108 Annd tohh swa þehh ne cnew himm nohht þe werelld alls itt ahhte. **1297** R. GLOUC. (Rolls) 4135 Vor he truste to hom mest, as me þincþ he wel aȝte. *c* **1300** *Havelok* 2787 Yif þat she aucte quen to be. **1382** WYCLIF *Isa.* v. 4. *c* **1425** WYNTOUN *Cron.* VIII. ii. 52 Robert þe Brwys, Erle of Karryk Aucht to succeed to þe Kynryke.

β. *c* **1305** *St. Lucy* 4 in *E.E.P.* (1862) 101 Of such a child wel glad heo was: as heo wel ouȝte. **1388** WYCLIF *Isa.* v. 4 What is it that Y ouȝt [1382 awȝte] to do more to my vyner? **1553** GRIMALDE *Cicero's Offices* (*c* 1600) 140 Hee ought, in that case, to recompence him. **1692** E. WALKER *Epictetus' Mor.* (1737) To Mr. Walker 61 Till you..did kindly teach Apollo, what he out to preach. **1712** STEELE *Spect.* No. 268 ¶1 It is not that I think I have been more witty than I ought of late. **1812** BYRON *Waltz* vii, His Sancho thought The knight's fandango friskier than it ought. **1849** MACAULAY *Hist. Eng.* x. II. 592 To convince him that he ought to stay where he was. **1892** *Law Times* XCIII. 414/2 He [the judge] did not think that the defendant ought to be kept in prison any longer.

b. In present sense: = Am (is, are) bound or under obligation; *you ought to do it* = it is your duty to do it; *it ought to be done* = it is right that it should be done, it is a duty (or some one's duty) to do it. (The most frequent use throughout. Formerly expressed by the pres. t., OWE *v.* 5.)

This appears to be orig. the pa. subj. (which in ME. and mod.Eng. has the same form as the indic.) used first in hypothetical or general cases; e.g. Ought one to tell the truth under all circumstances? If it should rain, he ought not to go. If he cannot go to-day, he ought to go to-morrow. Thence, in definite present sense, as Tell me what I ought to do now. The use of the pa. subj. softens the form of the expression; cf. the parallel *you should* for *it is your duty*; also *would you* for *will you*; *might I* for *may I*; *could you* for *can you*.

(*a*) with *to* and infin.

α. *c* **1175** *Lamb. Hom.* 5 Þes we ahte[n] to beon þe edmoddre. *a* **1200** *Moral Ode* 129 Þet achten we to leuen wel. *c* **1230** *Hali Meid.* 35 Þu ahtest wummon þis werc.. ouer alle þing to schunien. **1307** *Elegy Edw. I*, ii, Al Englond ahte forte knowe, Of wham that song is that y synge. **1447** BOKENHAM *Seyntys* (Roxb.) 70 O doughtir Cristyn..wych awtyst to be The lyght of myn eyn. *a* **1609** *Form Baron Courts* i. §11 in Skene *Reg. Maj.* 100 b, The Clerk aucht to inroll them formallie. **1658** *Hatton Corr.* (Camden) 15 Therefore I aught to begg your pardon.

β. *c* **1374** CHAUCER *Troylus* v. 545 O paleys empty and disconsolat..Wel oughtestow to falle and I to dye. **1484** CAXTON *Fables of Æsop* II. i, Whan men haue that which men oughte to haue they ought to be ioyful and glad. **1529** WOLSEY in *Four C. Eng. Lett.* 10 [This] owt to moue petyfull hertys. **1558** KNOX *First Blast* (Arb.) 8 Suche as oght to mainteine the truth and veritie of God. *c* **1590** GREENE *Orpharion* (1599) 57 We oft rightly to think of women, seeing so oft we seeke their favors. **1662** STILLINGFL. *Orig. Sacr.* II. ii. §2 It ought to be looked upon with veneration. **1717** POPE *Eloisa to Abelard* 183, I ought to grieve, but cannot what I ought. **1749** FIELDING *Tom Jones* VII. xiii, When gentlemen admit inferior Parsons into their company, they oft to keep their distance. **1771** *Junius Lett.* xlviii. 252 The precedent ought to be followed. **1818** CRUISE *Digest* (ed. 2) V. 144 An alien..ought not to be permitted to levy a fine. **1880** MRS. PARR *Adam & Eve* xvii. 244 Up when they oft to be abed, and abed when they oft to be up. **1886** LD. ESHER in *Law Rep.* 32 Chanc. Div. 26 There is nothing here to shew that the parties ought not be bound by their contract.

†(*b*) with simple infin. *Obs.* or *arch.*

α. *a* **1200** *Moral Ode* 2 Mi wit ahte bon mare. **1297** R. GLOUC. 9281 Ich þonke ȝou as ich wel aȝte [*v.r.* aute] do. **13..** *Cursor M.* 267 Cursur o werld man aght it call. **1377** LANGL. *P. Pl.* B. II. 28, I auȝte ben herre þan she. *c* **1430** *Pilgr. Lyf Manhode* IV. xxx. (1869) 192 Þe vengeaunce of god ..of whiche alle auhten haue drede. **1578–1600** *Sc. Poems 16th C.* (1801) II. 271 Than acht he be of all puissance denude.

β. *a* **1225** *Ancr. R.* 326 Nie þinges beoð þet ouhten hien touward schrifte. *c* **1386** CHAUCER *Melib.* Prol. 20 A litel thyng..That oghte liken yow. *c* **1449** PECOCK *Repr.* 218 He ouȝte more tent ȝeue to his owne good lyuyng..than he out ȝeue tent to the good lyuyng of eny other persoon. **1589** *Pasquil's Ret.* B, Her Maiestie layeth such a logge vppon their consciences, as they ought not beare. **1601** SHAKS. *Jul. C.* I. i. 3 You ought not walke Vpon a labouring day, without the signe Of your Profession. **1648** MILTON *Tenure Kings* (1650) 14 On the autority of Law the autority of a Prince depends and to the Laws ought submitt. **1751** ELIZA HEYWOOD *Betsy Thoughtless* IV. 141 Ought my friendship to the husband render me insensible of the beauties of the wife? **1815** *Zeluca* III. 318 Do not get habituated to a word you ought never use. **1868** BROWNING *Agamemnon* 796 How ought I address thee, how ought I revere thee?

c. With past sense indicated by the use of a following perf. infin. with *have*: *you ought to have known* = it was your duty to know, you should have known. (The usual modern idiom.)

1551 BIBLE *2 Kings* v. 13 Yf yᵉ prophet had byd the done some great thinge oughtest thou not then to haue done it? **1552** *Bk. Com. Prayer* Gen. Conf., We haue left vndone those thinges whiche we oughte to haue done. **1715** DE FOE *Fam. Instruct.* I. i. (1841) I. 16 Dear child, you ought to have been told who God is before now. **1796** H. HUNTER tr. *St.-Pierre's Stud. Nat.* (1799) III. 379, I ought to have exhibited an example of valour. **1849** MACAULAY *Hist. Eng.* v. I. 659 *note*, Sir John Reresby, who ought to have been well informed, positively affirms that [etc.]. **1864** TENNYSON *Northern Farmer* I. 20, I thowt a said whot a owt to 'a said an' I coomed awaäy. **1895** *Law Times* XCIX. 465/1 Lord Londesborough knew, or ought to have known, that his bill of exchange was intended to circulate.

†**6.** quasi-*impers.*, with dative object. (Cf. OWE *v.* 6.) **a.** In past sense: Behoved, befitted, was due (to). *Obs.*

α. **1297** R. GLOUC. (Rolls) 7348 Watloker it aȝte her. *a* **1300** *Cursor M.* 6014 (Cott.) Ful wel þam aght þair king to blam. *c* **1400** *Destr. Troy* 3980 Onest ouerall, as aght hir astate. *c* **1420** *Sir Amadace* (Camden) lviii, That ladi gente.. did wele that hur aghte to do.

β. *c* **1366** CHAUCER *A, B, C* 119 But oonly þer we diden not as us ouhte Doo. **1470–85** MALORY *Arthur* VI. xii, I haue no thynge done but that me ought for to doo.

b. In present sense: Behoves, befits, is due (to). *Obs.*

α. *c* **1340** *Cursor M.* 12988 (Fairf.) Þe ne haȝt haue na doute. *c* **1380** WYCLIF *Sel. Wks.* III. 84 Us auȝte not to suppose. ? *a* **1400** *Morte Arth.* 1595 Me aughte to honour theme in erthe Over alle oþer thyngez. *c* **1450** *Mirour Saluacioun* 1185 Than aght vs offre to crist golde of dilectionne.

β. *a* **1225** *Ancr. R.* 2 Þis nis nowt ibet ȝet al se wel hit ouhte. *c* **1385** CHAUCER *L.G.W.* 429 Hym oughte now to haue the lesse peyne. **1477** EARL RIVERS (Caxton) *Dictes* 3 b, If a kyng ..leue to do eny of the lytil thynges that hym ought. *c* **1500** *Lancelot* 2995 For well it oucht o prince or o king Til honore and til cherish in al thing O worthi man.

γ. **13..** *Min. P. Vernon MS.* xxxvii. 126, I ouȝte loue Iesu, ful of miȝte, And worschipe him..as me well iȝte. *c* **1450** *Mirour Saluacioun* 3755 The forsaide stedes eght vs to visit.

IV. 7. The pa. pple. *ought* (*aught*) was formerly in literary use, and is still common in dialectal or vulgar use, to form the perfect tense or passive voice of OWE *v.*: **a.** Owed; **b.** Possessed (*mod. Sc.*); **c.** Been obliged (*vulgar Eng.*).

a. *c* **1375** *Sc. Leg. Saints* xxii. (*Laurentius*) 381 Ȝet paynis are aucht þe mony. **1470–85** MALORY *Arthur* IX. xiv, He hath oughte you and vs euer good wille. **1495** in *Calr. Doc. rel. Scotl.* (1888) 327 [Paying] all maills, fermes, and dewties acht and wont. **1535** COVERDALE *2 Macc.* xii. 3 As though they had ought them no euell wyll. **1639** *Conceits, Clinches*, etc. (Halliw.) 46 A gentleman who had ought him money a long time. **1672** MARVELL *Reh. Transp.* I. 4 The Press hath ought him a shame a long time, and is but now beginning to pay off the Debt.

b. *c* **1560** A. SCOTT *Poems* IV. 31 And nevir speir quhais awcht hir. *a* **1800** in Scott *Old Mort.* Introd., I would give half of what I am aught, to know if it is still in existence. (Here perh. belongs the Sc. *Whae's aucht this?* to whom does this belong? But the analysis is not clear.)

c. **1836** HALIBURTON (Sam Slick) *Clockmaker* Introd., It don't seem to me that I had ought to be made a fool on in that book. **1895** ROSEMARY *Chilterns* 172 (E.D.D.) Rose had ought to get married. *Mod. dial.* Did you do that? You hadn't ought (= ought not to have done it).

8. With periphrastic auxiliary *did*, corresponding to uses under sense 5. *dial.*, *colloq.*, and *vulgar*.

1854 C. M. YONGE *Heartsease* II. III. ix. 236, I..told him he didn't ought to go. **1867** R. YOUNG *Rabin Hill's Excursion to Weston-super-Mare* 12 That's jist how things did ought to be. **1876**, **1888** [see OUGHTA, OUGHTER]. **1932** D. L. SAYERS *Have his Carcase* xxvii. 356, I did ought to have spoke up at the time. **1942** 'M. INNES' *Daffodil Affair* I. 17 And I hope that none here will say I did anything I didn't ought. For I only done my duty.

B. as present stem, with inflexions (*oughteth*, *oughted*, *oughting*). *Obs.* or *dial.*

†**1.** To be under obligation (*to do* something); = A. 5, OWE *v.* 5. *Obs.*

c **1449** PECOCK *Repr.*, Summe symple persoones hadden thilk opinioun tho iij seid persoones ouȝtiden to be slayn. **1526** *Pilgr. Perf.* (W. de W. 1531) 10 The more he oughteth to dispose hymselfe to fede of this heuenly meet. **1654** COKAINE *Dianea* II. 123 The cause is common to all, Kings oughting not to suffer Usurpation of States in others lest they find the experience of it in their owne.

2. *Sc.* To have to pay; = OWE *v.* 2.

1552 ABP. HAMILTON *Catech.* (1884) 4 The reuerence that ye aucht to our Lord Jesus Christ. **1588** A. KING tr. *Canisius' Catech.* Cert. Deuot Prayers 32 To the surly, we aught al that we can doe, al that we liue, al that we vnderstand. **1822** SCOTT *Nigel* v, We aught him the siller, and will pay him wi' our convenience.

3. *Sc.* To possess; = OWE *v.* 1, OWN *v.* 1.

a **1800** in Heslop *Prov. Scot.* (1862) 136 Let him haud the bairn that aughts the bairn. **1816** SCOTT *Bl. Dwarf* ix, I am answerable for her to those that aught her. **1826** J. WILSON *Noct. Ambr.* Wks. 1855 I. 266 Without ony illwill to the master that aughts him. **1886** STEVENSON *Kidnapped* 24 There's naebody but you and me that ought the name. **1896** BARRIE *Tommy* 202 The man as ocht Jerusalem greets because the fair Circassian winna take him.

4. *Pres. pple.* Sc. **aughtand, -en, auchtan(d:** **a.** Owing, indebted; **b.** Due: = OWING *ppl a.* 1, 2.

a **1609** *Form Baron Courts* xiii. §3 in Skene *Reg. Maj.* 104 b, He sall sweir..that he is not aughtand to him sic ane summe of debt. **1644** in Row *Hist. Kirk* (Wodrow Soc.) p. xxvii, My wife gat sum peniworthes fra Nans Girson, quhilk shoe was aughten to the box, and after I had mad all my compt, I was auchtand 2*s.* to the box. **1651** D. CALDERWOOD *Hist. Kirk* (1843) II. 426 To pay to the collectors the summes aughtand.

ought, obs. misspelling of ORT; obs. f. OUT.

oughta, oughter (ˈɔːtə). Also orter. A representation of a colloq. or vulgar pronunciation of *ought to* (see OUGHT *v.* 5, 7 c and 8).

1864 HOTTEN *Slang Dict.* 196 Where's the party as 'ad a orter be lookin' arter this 'ere 'oss? **1876** C. M. YONGE *Three Brides* II. i. 7 They ought to be ashamed of themselves, they did oughter. **1886** F. H. BURNETT *Little Lord Fauntleroy* xiii. 243 'Seems like somethin' orter be done,' said Mr. Hobbs. **1888** RIDER HAGGARD *Col. Quaritch* III. v. 79 You are my lawful husband, and I calls on you to cease living as you didn't oughter and to take me back. **1897** KIPLING *Capt. Cour.* iv. 88, I orter ha' warned you. **1901** M. FRANKLIN *My Brilliant Career* iii. 16 You oughter go out more. **1917** E. O'NEILL *Long Voyage Home* in *Smart Set* Oct. 84/2 Orter wear a muzzle, you ort! **1926** F. M. FORD *Man could stand Up* I. ii. 34 'He hadn't ought'er done it!' He hadn't really oughter. **1931** *Amer. Speech* VII. 91 Ater Maud's death he orter do better'n' he use' to. **1935** 'R. WEST' *Harsh Voice* ii. 151 He reckoned I oughta see London and Paris and Rome. **1943** K. TENNANT *Ride on Stranger* iii. 24 She didn't oughter do it. **1945** A. KOBER *Parm Me* 180 No joking, Mac, you oughta take it easy. **1959** N. MAILER *Advts. for Myself* (1961) 54 He could see the other house. It had oughta be away from the town. **1963** [see DADDY-O]. *a* **1966** M. ALLINGHAM *Cargo of Eagles* (1968) v. 73 His regular mate.. wasn't there to 'elp 'im..like wot 'e orter 'ave bin. **1967** E. GRIERSON *Crime of one's Own* ii. 22 'I expect 'e buys 'er things.' 'So 'e oughter.' **1971** D. HEFFRON *Nice Fire & Some Moonpennies* i. 11 Indian huh? Well she oughta go for this then. **1974** W. GARNER *Big enough Wreath* i. 8 You didn't oughter've done that, Mr. Smith. You know the regs. **1976** M. MAGUIRE *Scratchproof* iii. 45 Somebody oughta lock you away.

†**oughten.** *Obs.* Var. form of UGHTEN, OE. *uht*, the time just before daybreak, early morning.

a **1300** *K. Horn* 1415 (MS. Laud 108) He smyten and he fouten þe nyȝt and eke þe ouȝten [*v.rr.* ohtoun, vȝten]. *c* **1400** *Laud Troy Bk.* 9406 Thretti dayes when he hadde foughten With-outen reste bothe euen & oughten.

oughtness (ˈɔːtnɪs). [f. OUGHT 5 + -NESS.] That quality of an action which is expressed by 'ought'; moral obligatoriness.

1879 J. COOK *Lect. Conscience* i, Every motive has two sides—rightness or its opposite, and oughtness or its opposite... Conscience is that which perceives and feels rightness and oughtness in motives. **1888** H. C. BOWEN in *Jrnl. Educ.* 1 Nov. 521/1 To stimulate and direct..this sense of obligation, of 'oughtness'. **1918** [see GOOD *a.* 14 c]. **1931** W. M. URBAN *Fund. Ethics* i. 9 The forms of conduct or behavior which have this character of *oughtness* are then called standards or norms. **1948** A. O'RAHILLY *Moral Princ.* iv. 21 On the occasion of experience we see the oughtness of certain acts, we have an intuitive appreciation of an objective moral order. **1958** R. C. ANGELL *Free Society & Moral Crisis* ii. 16 The peculiar power of our moral lenses is to pick out and see clearly all the elements in society that reveal 'how oughtness is organized'. **1967** D. VON HILDEBRAND *Trojan Horse in City of God* xxv. 190 The victory of truth and value is the fulfillment of an oughtness.

†**'oughtworth.** *Obs.* [The two words *ought*, AUGHT *sb.* and WORTH *a.* written in combination.] Anything worth, worth anything, of any value.

1587 GOLDING *De Mornay* ix. 119 Neither the ground nor the consequence of this argument are oughtworth.

oughwhere, var. OWHERE *Obs.*, anywhere.

†**ougle**, *a.* *Obs.* Also 5 ogel, oggel, 6 owgle. [app. related to *oglie*, *ouglie*, *owgly*, obs. forms of UGLY *a.*; but the form in *-el*, *-le* is difficult to account for.] Ugly, repulsive, frightful.

14.. *Chaucer's Clerk's T.* 617 (Corp. MS.) Þis Oggel [*MS. Lansd.* ogel, *Ellesm.*, etc. vgly, etc.] sergeaunt. **1553** T.

Wilson *Rhet.* 111 He lookes like a Tyger; a man would thinke he would eate one, his countenance is so ougle. **1554** J. Proctor tr. *Vincentius* To Rdr., How owgle and carrion-lean ye are to se.

ouglesome, obs. f. UGGLESOME, horrible.

ouglie, -ly, ougsome, obs. ff. UGLY, UGSOME.

ouh, ouhte, obs. forms of OWE, OUGHT.

Ouidaesque (wiːdəˈɛsk), *a.* [f. *Ouida*, the nom-de-plume of the English novelist Marie Louise de la Ramée (1839–1908) + -ESQUE.] Characteristic or suggestive of the novels of 'Ouida'; marked by extravagance or lack of restraint.

1909 *Westm. Gaz.* 6 Apr. 4/2 It is the case of the 'Ouidaesque' young man with the big cigar of the motor shows over again. **1915** W. J. Locke *Jaffery* xxi. 287 Like the Ouidaesque hero, who could ride a Derby Winner with one hand, and stroke a University Crew to victory with the other. **1929** *Sunday Express* 20 Jan. 9 The 'dark Odyssey of Gilbert Stroud' is almost Ouidaesque. **1930** *Times Lit. Suppl.* 17 Apr. 338/3 A hero of almost Ouidaesque impressiveness. **1971** E. Mavor *Ladies of Llangollen* xii. 201 In Mr Penruddock's final Ouida-esque version, the successful elopement occurs on the night of a grand ball.

Ouija (ˈwiːdʒə). [f. F. *oui* yes + G. *ja* yes.] A proprietary name for a board having the letters of the alphabet and other signs used for obtaining messages and answers in spiritualistic séances and in the practice of telepathy. Also (with lower-case initial) applied generally to spiritualistic spelling devices. Also ***ouija-board***.

1891 *Official Gaz.* (U.S. Patent Office) 3 Feb. 510/2 Toys known as Talking Boards.—Kennard Novelty Company, Baltimore, Md... Used since July 1, 1890. The word 'Ouija'. **1895** *Montgomery Ward Catal.* 236/2 Ouija, or Egyptian Luck Board. **1895** I. M. Rittenhouse *Maud* (1939) 590 Once or twice he had referred to something a Ouija-board in Chicago had said, and how it had spelled my name in full. **1904** *Pop. Sci. Monthly* Jan. 195 The various alphabet-using forms of amateur mediumship, such as table tipping, the 'Ouija-board', and certain other devices for making our muscles leaky. **1909** H. Carrington *Physical Phenom. Spiritualism* 67 The phenomena of table-tipping, of ouija and planchette writing. **1922** O. Lodge *Raymond Revised* 45 By the use of instruments known as 'planchette' and 'ouija', often employed by beginners. **1931** *Times Lit. Suppl.* 24 Dec. 1036/4 When receiving communications Ingeborg..is all the while writing, or moving swiftly with the pointer of the ouija board. **1944** Auden *For Time Being* (1945) 114, I have prohibited the sale of crystals and ouija-boards. **1949** *Official Gaz.* (U.S. Patent Office) 20 Sept. 638/2 William Fuld, Baltimore, Md. Ouija..for Gameboard, utilizing a Planchette and sometimes known as a Talking Board. Claims use since July 1, 1890. **1968** *Trade Marks Jrnl.* 22 May 835/2 *Ouija*... Board games, being parlour games providing answers to questions. Parker Brothers, Inc. (a Corporation organised and existing under the laws of the State of Maine, United States of America), 190, Bridge Street, Salem, State of Massachusetts, United States of America; Manufacturers. **1968** *Daily Tel.* 10 Sept. 20/6 A television advertising campaign to promote Ouijas as games at Christmas. **1973** *Listener* 20 Sept. 386/2 Professor [John] Taylor's schedule of talks to a medium, a ouija-board operator, a scientist and a hard-line theologian. **1974** *Sci. Amer.* Jan. 108/1 Tens of thousands of young people in the U.S. (particularly in California), caught up in the current occult explosion and eager to know more about Eastern mysticism and early Chinese history, are now consulting the *I Ching* as seriously as they consult the Ouija board or the tarot cards.

ouin, ouir, obs. forms of OVEN, OVER.

†**ouir**, *conj. Sc. Obs.* [app. a reduction of OUTHER *conj.*] Either, or.

1535 Stewart *Cron. Scot.* I. 22 Withoutin tarie ouir nycht ouir day, To Spanȝe lande tha tuke the narrest way.

ouir-, in comb.: see OVER-.

ouistiti, var. WISTITI, S. American monkey.

ouk, oulk, Sc. forms of ME. *wouke*, WEEK.

oukaz, var. UKASE.

ouklip (ˈəʊklɪp). *S. Afr.* [Afrikaans, f. Afrikaans, Du. *oud* OLD *a.* + *klip* (see KLIP *sb.*).] A kind of lateritic conglomerate found in southern Africa.

1892 *Graham's Town* (Cape Province) *Jrnl.* 20 Sept. 2 A few months ago it was discovered..that large beds of Ou Klip (honeycomb gravel rock) on the farm were literally saturated with mercury. **1940** *Min. Resources Union S. Afr.* (Dept. of Mines) (ed. 3) IV. 458 There are many types of laterite or 'ouklip' in this country. The harder types of conglomerate ouklip generally form a very good basecourse for bitumen... Some types of soft conglomerate ouklip which contain an appreciable quantity of sandy soil binder generally yield satisfactory sand-clay bases... The pebble type ouklip..consists mostly of fairly hard lateritic pebbles and soil binder. **1950** *Cape Times Week-end Mag.* 8 Apr. 4/7 This was an outcrop of granite and ouklip. **1955** J. H. Wellington *S. Afr.* I. II. x. 289 In the western highlands of Natal, Peutz recognizes a third grassveld type..in which the infertile sandy soils, underlain by 'ouklip' (i.e. pirolitic ironstone) produce a poor type of veld. **1961** M. M. Cole *S. Afr.* iv. 87 The weathering processes..result in the formation of soils comprising an A horizon of some 12 to 24 inches of friable sand..overlaying a B horizon of mottled clayey-sand containing many ferruginous concretions which in the lower part are cemented to form a hardpan called 'ouklip'.

ould (aʊld), a representation of an Ir. pronunciation of OLD *a.*

c **1675** *Purgatorium Hibernicum* (MS. 470, Nat. Libr. Ireland) 100 Singing 'Ould Rose' and 'Tory Rory'. **1803** G. Colman *John Bull* II. ii. 17 I'm as aisy as an ould glove. **1829** G. Griffin *Collegians* I. vii. 153 O, wirra, Eily! this is the black day to your ould father. *c* **1874** D. Boucicault in M. R. Booth *Eng. Plays of 19th Cent.* (1969) II. 174 This cabin where the remains of the 'ould family', two lonely girls, live. **1898** J. D. Brayshaw *Slum Silhouettes* 8 The ould counthry. **1936** 'N. Blake' *Thou Shell of Death* iii. 46 She's a bit of an ould stick, but there's no harm in her. **1970** S. J. Perelman *Baby, it's Cold Inside* 152 From the moment I had first set foot on the Ould Sod I had yearned to pick up a typical sample of the local crafts. **1977** *Time* 12 Dec. 30/1 Overseas Chinese may not want to go back to live in the People's Republic any more than a U.S. enthusiast for Ireland wants to live on the Ould Sod.

oule, obs. f. OWL.

‖**Ouled Nail** (ˈuːlɪd ˈnɑːiːl, -naɪl, -neɪl). [Fr., f. *Ouled Naïl*, ad. Arab., lit. 'sons of Nail'.] A group of Arab peoples of Algeria; *spec.* in North African cities: an Arab professional dancing girl belonging to these peoples.

1881 A. A. Knox *New Playground* xiii. 324 Perhaps the less said the better about the dancing women, who are, if I remember right, called 'oulad naïl'. They inhabit a street apart at Biskra, and come from some distant part of the desert. **1906** M. W. Hilton-Simpson *Algiers & Beyond* iv. 77 One of the most interesting features..is the *cafés maures*, in which the Ouled Naïl girls dance. *Ibid.* 82 The Ouled Naïls will speak to anyone... Their morality will not bear close investigation. **1914** M. D. Stott *Real Algeria* ii. 20 Khadava admitted with the most sweet of cynical smiles that it was only to English and Germans that she confessed to being an Ouled Nail—it was found to be more profitable. **1956** L. Morgan *Flute of Sand* v. 82 'The psychology of an Ouled Naïl dancing girl,' a French administrator had told me, 'is very difficult to understand.' **1973** Wodehouse *Bachelors Anonymous* ix. 122 'Oh dear. Are you hurt?' she wailed, and ran to where Mr Trout was pirouetting like an Ouled Nail dancer with his hand to his mouth. **1975** 'P. Loraine' *Ask Rattlesnake* I. ii. 53 The Ouled Nails, the North African tribe which trains its women to become whores in the dissolute coastal cities.

oulema, var. ULEMA.

oulette, obs. f. OWLET.

ouller, obs. f. ALDER.

oulong, var. OOLONG.

‖**oulter-le-mer.** *Law Fr.* [= OF. *oultre la mer* beyond the sea; misprinted, in Cowell, *ouster-le-mer* (by confounding the black letter *l* and long *s*), and so repeated in subsequent law dictionaries down to Wharton 1883.] The plea or excuse of being beyond the sea.

1607 Cowell *Interpr.*, *Oufter le mer* (*vltra mare*) commeth of the French (*oultre* i. *vltra*) and (*le mer* i. *mare*) and it is a cause of excuse or Essoine, if a man appeare not in Court vpon Summons. **1617** Minsheu, *Oulter le mer.* [**1670** Blount *Law Dict.*, *Ouster le mer.* So 1729– in Jacob, 1848– in Wharton.]

oultrage, -ance, obs. ff. OUTRAGE, -ANCE.

oultre-, in comb., obs. form of OUTRE-.

†ˈ**oultreli**, *adv. Obs. rare.* [ad. OF. *oultrément*, mod.F. *outrément*, excessively, absolutely, f. *outré*, OUTRÉ. Perh. confused or identified with Eng. *outerly*, UTTERLY.] Absolutely, quite.

1390 Gower *Conf.* III. 230 Thei have him oultreli refused.

‖**oultrepreu**, *a. Obs. rare.* [a. F. *oultrepreux* (15th c. in Godef.), f. *oultre*, *outre* beyond, ultra-, + *preux* valiant, brave.] Exceedingly brave.

c **1477** Caxton *Jason* 32 The uaillyaunt and oultrepreu Jason was in this glorie and triumphe.

ouma (ˈəʊmə). *S. Afr.* [Afrikaans = grandmother, f. *ou* old + *ma* mother.] A name used in addressing or referring to one's grandmother or to an elderly woman.

1910 D. Fairbridge *That which hath Been* 42 A coloured person, mevrouw;—'Ou'ma Jannetje' she calls herself. **1929** P. Smith *Little Karoo* (rev. ed.) 181 Was it but three days ago..that Ou-ma had buried her son? **1937** S. Cloete *Turning Wheels* xxvii. 423 'I am sorry, Ouma,' he said, 'to find you like this.' **1952** *Cape Times* 2 Sept. 14/3 Three drunk *skollies* approached her and asked whether *ouma* had no one to take her home. **1953** J. Packer *Apes & Ivory* iii. 28 Sybella Margaretha Krige, known to her friends as 'Isie' until the Second World War when the Springbok soldiers she helped so devotedly christened her 'Ouma' (Grannie). **1971** *Cape Herald* 15 May 2/9 But how does Ouma busy herself besides sweeping?

oumbylle, oumber, oumer, oumpere, obs. forms of HUMBLE, UMBER, UMPIRE.

oun-, an occasional ME. spelling of UN-.

ounce (aʊns), *sb.*[1] Forms: 4–6 unce, (5 vunce, unch, once, owns, ouns, nouns, nowns, nonsse, oyns, 6 ownce, oonce, oince, ounc, ownche), 5– ounce. [a. OF. *unce* (12th c. in Littré), F. *once*:—L. *uncia* twelfth part (of a pound or a foot). The L. word was already adopted in OE. in the form and sense of *ynce* str. m., INCH; in late OE. it also appears as *yndse*, *ynse* wk. fem., ounce; but the existing word is from French.]

1. a. A unit of weight; originally, as still in Troy weight, the twelfth of a pound, but in avoirdupois or ordinary goods weight the sixteenth of the pound.

The Troy ounce consists of 480 grains, and is divided into 20 pennyweights; the avoirdupois ounce contains 437·5 grains, and is divided into 16 drams. ***fluid ounce***, a measure of capacity, containing an avoird. ounce of distilled water at 62° Fahr. (= 28·4 cubic centimetres). In the United States the fluid ounce is the quarter of a gill or 128th part of a gallon (= 29·57 cubic centimetres), containing 456·033 grains of distilled water at its maximum density. It is thus an aliquot part of the pint, quart, and gallon, which the British fluid ounce is not.

[*c* **1000** *Sax. Leechd.* I. 248 ȝenim..anre yndsan [*v.r.* ynsan] ȝewihte.] *c* **1330** R. Brunne *Chron.* (1810) 54 Mykelle brent gold, as sextene vnce amounte. *c* **1386** Chaucer *Can.-Yeom. Prol.* 203 Fyue or sixe Ounces [*v. rr.* vnce(s]..Of siluer. *c* **1420** *Liber Cocorum* (1862) 27 Take persole, peletre an oyns, and grynde. **14..** *Nom.* in Wr.-Wülcker 714/23 *Hec semiuncia*, half a nouns. **1463** *Mann. & Househ. Exp.* (Roxb.) 154 Gold weyyng xix. ownsys and half a ownsce, the prise off every owns xxx.*s.* **1464** *Paston Lett.* II. 154 *marg.*, After xxx.*d.* the unch. **1472** in *Wilts. Archæol. Mag.* (1868) XI. 337 A sacryng belle..weyng x vuncez. **1481** in *Eng. Gilds* (1870) 316 A spone of selver wayyng a nonsse. **1488–9** *Act 4 Hen. VII*, c. 22 The gold..whiche they nowe sell for a pounde weight weyeth not above vij unces. **1526** Wriothesley *Chron.* (1875) I. 15 An ownce sylvir fyne sterlinge at 3*s.* 8*d.* **1552–3** *Inv. Ch. Goods, Staffs.* in *Ann. Lichfield* (1863) IV. 70 Weynge by estymacon viij oonce. **1554** *Galway Arch.* in *10th Rep. Hist. MSS. Comm.* App. v. 415 Every ounc theof..to passe in iiii.*s.* sterling the ounc allways. **1559** *Wills & Inv. N.C.* (Surtees 1835) 183 A crowne an oince fyue score oinces & thre quarters. **1571** *Will* in *Gentl. Mag.* (1861) July 35 Weyng xvi. ownches and a quarter. **1646** Recorde, etc. *Gr. Artes* 322, 20 pence weight maketh an ounce, and 12 ounces do make a pound. **1725** N. Robinson *Th. Physick* 261 If there be any Signs of a Plethora, twelve Ounces of Blood may be taken away. **1833** J. Holland *Manuf. Metal* II. 305 The origin of the present avoirdupois pound of sixteen ounces, equal to 7680 Troy grains, is involved in obscurity.

b. *loosely*: usually, A small quantity.

c **1386** Chaucer *Prol.* 677 By ounces henge hise lokkes þat he hadde. **1588** Shaks. *L.L.L.* III. i. 136 My sweete ounce of mans flesh, my in-conie Iew. *a* **1617** Bayne *On Eph.* i. (1643) 334 Not all at once, but by ounces, as we say. **1719** De Foe *Crusoe* II. ii, They had not an ounce [of bread and flesh] left in the ship. **1839–40** I. Taylor *Anc. Chr.* (1842) II. ii. 100 The table was spread with some ounces of dry bread.

c. *fig.* of imponderable things; esp. in proverbial expressions.

1526 *Pilgr. Perf.* (1531) 42 Better is one vnce of good lyfe, than x pounde of pardon. **1629** *Bk. Merry Riddles* 26 An ounce of state requires a pound of gold. **1644** Milton *Judgm. Bucer*, *To Parlt.*, To debate and sift this matter to the utmost ounce of Learning and Religion. **1670** Ray *Proverbs, Sc. Prov.* 264 An ounce of mothers wit is worth a pound of Clergy. **1870** J. H. Newman *Gram. Assent* II. viii. 295 An ounce of common sense goes farther than many cartloads of logic.

2. Used to render *onza*, the name of a coin of different values in Spain and Sicily.

The value of the old Spanish *doubloon onza* (of gold) was about 16 dollars, i.e. £3 12*s.*; the Sicilian onza (of silver) was equal to about 10*s.* 3½*d.*

1799 Nelson 8 Mar. in Nicolas *Disp.* (1845) III. 286 You will receive seven thousand ounces or 21,000 ducats. *a* **1850** Rossetti *Dante & Circ.* II. (1874) 275 Then how canst thou think to succeed alone Who hast not a thousand ounces of thine own? **1878** H. Gibbs *Ombre* 10 General Castilla.. never liked playing for less than an ounce (£3 12*s.*) a fish.

†**3. a.** A mediæval measure of time, equal to 47 atoms (7½ secs.): see ATOM *sb.* 7. **b.** A measure of length or of surface, equal to 3 inches. **c.** A local Irish measure of surface: see quot. 1780. *Obs.*

1398 Trevisa *Barth. De P.R.* IX. ix. (1495) Y vj b/2 A moment of tyme conteynyth twelue vnces and an vnce seuen and forty attomos. *Ibid.* XIX. cxxix. nn ij/1 Vncia conteyneth thre ynches in mesure. **1780** A. Young *Tour Irel.* II. 90 In the parish of Tooavister, they have a way of taking land by the ounce... An ounce is the sixteenth of a gineve, and is sufficient for a potatoe garden.

4. a. *attrib.* Of the weight of one ounce or (in comb.) so many ounces.

1846 Greener *Sc. Gunnery* 75 We have obtained a velocity with an ounce ball nearly doubling this. **1898** *Daily News* 6 July 7/3 Next comes Canada's proposal..of a charge of 1½*d.* on ounce letters. **1900** *Ibid.* 9 May 5/5 The present four-ounce bread ration is to be further reduced.

b. *Comb.*, as ***ounce-grape*** (*obs.*), ***-measure***, ***-notch***; **ounce force**, a unit of force equal to the weight of a mass of 1 ounce, esp. under standard gravity (cf. GRAM[2] and *gram force*); †**ounce-land**, a division of land in Orkney, which paid to the earl one ounce of silver; **ounce-thread**, a kind of sewing thread.

1601 Holland *Pliny* I. 410 We haue not spoken..of the Ounce-grapes, whereof euery one weighes a good ounce. **1814** Shirref *Agric. Surv. Orkn.* 31 The lands in Orkney had been early divided into ure or ounce lands, and each ounce land into eighteen penny lands, and penny-lands again into four-merk or farthing lands, corresponding to the feu-money paid at the time. **1844** G. Dodd *Textile Manuf.* iv. 140 The making of sewing-thread, known by the names of 'ounce-thread' and 'nun's-thread', was commenced. **1861** L. L. Noble *Icebergs* 248 The loss of a single ton of ice shifts ..it an ounce-notch on the bar of the mighty scale. **1961** *B.S.I. News* Oct. 26/2 A similar distinction is made between

. . ounce (oz) and ounce-force (ozf). **1966** [see *gram force* s.v. GRAM² b].

Hence **'ouncer**, a thing that weighs one or (in comb.) so many ounces, as a ***three-ouncer***. **'ouncy** *a.*, yielding an ounce of gold to a certain measure.

1864 ROGERS *New Rush* II. 52 The ground . . is thickly interspersed with ouncy dust. **1886** *Pall Mall G.* 21 May 4/1 Tumbling brooks teeming with 'three ouncers'.

ounce (aʊns), *sb.*² Forms: 4 unce, 5–7 once, 6 owns, 7 onse, 6– **ounce**. [ad. OF. *once* (13th c. in Littré), *lonce* (*Voy. de Marc Pol*, Godef. *Compl.*); cf. It. *lonza*, Sp. *onza*, *onça*. OF. *l'once* (according to Hatz.-Darm.) represents an earlier *lonce* (the *l* being confounded with the def. article) = It. *lonza*:—pop.L. type **luncia*, for L. *lyncea*, deriv. of *lync-em* LYNX.]

1. A name originally given to the common lynx, afterwards extended to other species, and still sometimes applied in America to the Canada lynx and other species. From 16th c. applied to various other small or moderate-sized feline beasts, vaguely identified.

13.. *K. Alis.* 5228 Bores, beres, and lyouns, . . Vnces grete, and leopardes. *c* **1470** HENRYSON *Mor. Fab.* v. (*Parl. Beasts*) xvi, The wyld once, the buk, the welterand brok. *a* **1586** SIDNEY *Arcadia* III. Wks. 1724 II. 715 The lion heart, the ounce gave active might. **1590** SHAKS. *Mids. N.* II. ii. 30 Be it Ounce, or Catte, or Beare, Pard, or Boare with bristled haire. **1598** B. YONG *Diana* 91 The pillers were supported with Lyons, Ounces and Tygres, . . cut of brasse. **1601** HOLLAND *Pliny* XXVIII. viii. II. 316 The Onces be likewise taken for strange and forrein, and of all foure-footed beasts they haue the quickest eie and see best [*L.* Peregrini sunt et lynces, quæ clarissimi quadrupedum omnium cernunt]. **1607** TOPSELL *Four-f. Beasts* (1658) 380 The wilde beast which among the Germans is named *Luchss* (by making a name from the *Linx* . . the Spaniards do as yet call him by the Latin name *Lince* . . amongst the barbarous writers he is called by the name of an *Ounce* (which I do suppose to be a panther). **1634** W. WOOD *New. Eng. Prosp.* (1865) 25 The Ounce or the wilde Cat, is as big as a mungrell dog. **1648** GAGE *West. Ind.* xii. (1655) 45 (Montezuma's Palace) Great cages . . wherein were kept in some Lions, in other Tygres, in other Ownzes, in other Wolves. **1658** PHILLIPS, *Ounce*, . . also a kind of spotted beast called a Lynx. **1662** STILLINGFL. *Orig. Sacr.* III. iv. §7 Such as differ in size and shape from each other, as the Cat of Europe, and Ownce of India. **1667** MILTON *P.L.* IV. 344 Tygers, Ounces, Pards Gambold before them. **1672** JOSSELYN *New Eng. Rarities* 16 The Ounce or Wild Cat, is about the bigness of two lusty Ram Cats.

2. In current zoological use: A feline beast (*Felis uncia*), inhabiting the lofty mountain ranges of Central and Southern Asia; it resembles the leopard in markings, but is smaller and of lighter ground colour, and has longer and thicker fur; also called *mountain-panther* and *snow-leopard*.

[**1607** TOPSELL *Four-f. Beasts* (1658) 381 Ounces do commonly seem to be called rather Linxes then Panthers; but although some late writers do attribute the name to a Leopard or a lesser Panther, it seemeth notwithstanding corrupt from the Linx.] [**1761** BUFFON *Hist. Naturelle* IX. 152 La seconde espèce est la petite panthère d'Oppian . . que les Voyageurs modernes ont appelé, *Once* du nom corrompu *Lynx* ou *Lunx*.] **1774** GOLDSM. *Nat. Hist.* (1776) III. 255 We will therefore call that animal of the panther kind, which is less than the panther, and with a longer tail, the ounce. . . The Ounce . . is much less than the panther, being not, at most, above three feet and a half long. **1843** SIR W. JARDINE in *Naturalist's Libr.* III. 192 The ounce is first noticed by Buffon.

†**b.** Applied to the Cheetah or Hunting Leopard: this being at first confounded with the Ounce of Buffon. *Obs.*

1694 in *Churchill's Voy.* (1704) IV. 162 Besides Hawks and Dogs, they make use of a sort of Creatures they call *Onses*, about the bigness of a Fox, very swift, their Skins speckled like Tigers, and so Tame, that they carry them behind them on Horse-back. **1706** PHILLIPS, *Ounce*, is also a kind of tame Beast in Persia, mistaken for a lynx. **1801** SOUTHEY *Thalaba* IX. xviii, And couchant on the saddle-bow, With tranquil eyes and talons sheathed, The ounce expects his liberty. **1821** SHELLEY *Prometh. Unb.* I. i. 609 As hooded ounces cling to the driven hind.

3. *attrib.* and *Comb.* †**ounce-stone**, a rendering of Pliny's *lyncurium*, a reputed precious stone, now understood to have been amber.

c **1505** *Mem. Ripon* (Surtees) III. 196 Et de 13*s.* 5*d.* ex mutacione argenti . . pro owns taylles. **1583** *Rates of Customs* D v b, Ounce skinnes the peece *xs.* **1601** HOLLAND *Pliny* II. 609 That the Once stone or Lyncurium is of the same colour that Ambre ardent which resembleth the fire. **1833** HT. MARTINEAU *Charmed Sea* iv. 44 Mouse, ounce, and hare skins may serve us at present as well as sables could do.

ounce, *v. rare.* [f. OUNCE *sb.*¹] *trans.* To mark with the weight in ounces.

1702 *Lond. Gaz.* 3863/4 It is ounced at the bottom 18. oz.

ounctuous, obs. form of UNCTUOUS.

[**ound:** see note under OUNDY *a.*]

ounde, variant of ONDE *sb. Obs.*, spite.

†**ounded,** *ppl. a. Obs.* [ad. F. *ondé, ondée*, OUNDY, with substitution of Eng. ending -ED².] **a.** Waved, wavy. **b.** *Her.* = UNDEE.

c **1374** CHAUCER *Troylus* IV. 708 (736) Here ownded heer þat sonnyssh was of hewe She rente. ? *a* **1400** *Morte Arth.* 765 Bothe his hede and hys hals ware halely alle over Oundyde of azure, enamelde fulle faire. **14..** *MS. Lincoln* A. i. 17 lf. 39 (Halliw.) The tayle was ounded overthwert with a colour reede as rose.

ounder-: see UNDER-.

†**'ounding,** *vbl. sb. Obs.* [f. **ounde* v., repr. F. *onder* to wave, make wavy.] An adorning with undulating lines in imitation of waves.

c **1386** CHAUCER *Pars. T.* ¶343 The cost of embrowdynge the degise endentynge barrynge owndynge [*v. rr.* owndeynge, owndyng] palynge wyndynge or bendynge and semblable wast of clooth in vanitee.

†**'ounds,** *int. Obs.* [For *wounds*, i.e. *God's wounds*: cf. ZOUNDS.] An obsolete oath, used as an exclamation of anger, surprise, etc.

1706 FARQUHAR *Recruit. Officer* II. iii, Off with your hats; 'ounds, off with your hats!

†**'oundy,** *a. Obs.* Also 4–5 **owndy, ownde,** 6 **oundé**. [a. F. *ondé, -ée* (in 14th c. *ondeit* Godef. *Compl.*):—L. *undāt-um*, f. *undāre* to wave, curl, *unda* wave.] Waved, wavy; in *Her.* = UNDEE.

c **1384** CHAUCER *H. Fame* III. 296 Hir heere that ovndye [*v.r.* owndy] was and crips. [**1599** THYNNE *Animadv.* (1875) 36 Her heare was oundye, that is, layed in rooles vppone and downe, lyke waues of water when they are styrred with the winde.] ? *a* **1400** *Morte Arth.* 193 Ownde of azure alle ouer. *a* **1548** HALL *Chron., Hen. VIII* 79 b, The other side clothe of Tissue of silver, and clothe of gold of Tissue entered ounde the one with yᵉ other, the ounde is warke wavyng up and doune, . . and on the other side that was ounde was sette with signes called cifers of fine gold.

[The passage from Hall's *Chron.* is erroneously reprinted in A. Fleming's *Holinshed* (1587) III. 860/1, with *ound* for *ounde*; it is misunderstood by Halliwell and explained as sb. *ounde* 'a kind of lace, a curl'. The imaginary sb. so explained appears in *Cent. Dict.* and Funk's *Standard* in the form *ound.*]

oune, obs. f. OWN *a.*, ON; obs. pa. pple. of OWE.

‖**oung** (aʊŋ), *v.* Also **aung**. [Burmese.] *trans.* In Burma of an elephant: to push, roll, or drag logs from one place to another or down a stream.

1900 M. & B. FERRARS *Burma* v. 118 (*caption*) Pushing the logs off the shoals (aung). **1901** G. H. EVANS *Treatise on Elephants* i. 9 A well-trained tusker always commands a good price; he is so much more useful both in the yards and forests, as with his tusks he can '*oung*' . . , stack timber, assist in getting logs over obstacles, &c. *Ibid.* xvi. 191 It is advisable for some time after such an accident [to the loins] that the animal be loaded lightly; it is also as well not to put him to any heavy work such as *aunging* heavy timber. **1935** R. CAMPBELL *Teak-Wallah* iv. 44 Is there any spectacle, I wonder, that can surpass in magnificence the sight of twenty or thirty elephants, all in the prime of condition, 'ounging' timber down a swollen jungle stream? *Ibid.* xiv. 208 Mounted on a tusker, I spent all day riding up and down the river, superintending the work of the 'ounging' elephants and seeing that they did not allow stacks to form. **1974** *Encycl. Brit. Macropædia* V. 971/2 In India, Sri Lanka . . and Burma, their chief use now is in lumbering—they drag logs through the jungle and push floating logs around bends and off sandbanks ('aunging').

oupa ('əʊpə). *S. Afr.* [Afrikaans = grandfather, f. *ou* old + *pa* father.] A name used in addressing or referring to one's grandfather or to an elderly man.

1920 R. Y. STORMBERG *Mrs. Pieter de Bruyn* 40, I had secret misgivings that the Nooitgedacht sheep wouldn't pass the test, even though Oupa Cloete is nearly stone blind. **1934** 'N. GILES' *Ridge of White Waters* I. xiv. 165 Ou'pa Wessels, although well over seventy, insisted on accompanying the commando. **1939** S. CLOETE *Watch for Dawn* 161 What is it? Tell me, oupa. **1951** P. ABRAHAMS *Wild Conquest* 88 But Oupa Johannes didn't kill us and we didn't kill him. **1953** U. KRIGE *Dream & Desert* i. 13 When his father had told him of Oupa's death, Jannie had been very sad since he had loved Oupa. **1976** J. MCCLURE *Rogue Eagle* xii. 204 Wolraad grinned. . . 'Where's Pa gone, *oupa*?' he asked.

oupe, owpe, app. var. of AWPE, ALP, OLP, bull-finch.

1591 PERCIVALL *Sp. Dict., Fraylezillo*, ave, an oupe. [**1599** MINSHEU, A bird with blacke feathers on the head, like linget, called of some, an Owpe.]

ouph (aʊf). Also 7– **ouphe**, 7 **owf, ouf.** [A variant of AUF, OAF¹; perh. originating in a scribal or typographical error for *auph* or *oaph*, which seems more prob. than that it is a genuine dial. variant. App. first in Shaks. (folio 1623).]

1623 *Shaks.'s Merry W.* IV. iv. 49 Wee'l dresse Like Vrchins, Ouphes, and Fairies, greene and white. *Ibid.* v. v. 61 Strew good lucke (Ouphes) on euery sacred roome. **1678** RYMER *Trag. last Age* 129 He is turn'd amorous Owf. **1694** MOTTEUX *Rabelais* v. Prol. Pantagr. Prognost., Dolts, Block-heads, Ninnyhammers, and silly Oufs. **1882** SWINBURNE *Tristram of Lyonesse* 108 Or how shall I trust more than ouphe or elf Thy truth to me-ward, who beliest thyself?

Hence **'ouphish** *a.*

1896 J. LUMSDEN *Poems* 140 An implike ouphish ditty.

our (aʊə(r)), *pron.* Forms; 1 úre, 2–5 ure, (hure, 3 hore), 3–5 ur, (4 wr); 3–6 oure, (3–4 hour(e), 4–5 owre, 4– our, (5–7 owr, 5 owur, 6 eure, 7 or). [Com. Teutonic: see below.] In OE. used (invariably) as the genitive pl. of the 1st person pronoun, and (with adj. inflexions) as the corresponding possessive pronoun, whether adjectively or absolutely. In mod.Eng. only the possessive pronoun used adjectively, the absolute form being OURS. See the paradigm in I *pron.*

A. *personal pron.* [OE. (*úser, ússer*) *úre* = OFris., OS. *úser*, OHG. *unsar*, ON. *vár*, Goth. *unsara*.] The genitive plural of the first personal pronoun: = Of us. (In OE. also the genitive governed by some adjs. and vbs.) *Obs.* (or blending with the poss. pron. B. 1, in some phrases, as *in our midst* = in the midst of us, *on our behalf*, and with sense of the objective genitive, as *in our despite, in our defence, our dismissal, our accusers, our pursuers*).

Beowulf 1386 Ure æghwylc sceal ende ʒebidan worolde lifes. *a* **900** *Ags. Ps.* (Th.) xi. 9 Ðeah . . heora sy mycle ma þonne ure. *c* **1000** ÆLFRIC *Gen.* iii. 22 Adam can yfel and god, swa swa ure sum. *c* **1000** *Ags. Ps.* (Th.) cxiii. 21 Weorð ðu ure ʒemyndiʒ. *c* **1175** *Lamb. Hom.* 21 þah ure an heofde idon eower alre sunne. *c* **1200** ORMIN 7766 þat ure nan ne þurrfe Ut off þe rihhte weʒʒe gan. *c* **1205** LAY. 16311 Betere beoð ure fifti. *a* **1225** *Leg. Kath.* 803 Hwuch ure is kempe. *c* **1250** *Gen. & Ex.* 2262 Ne wiste ur non gilt ðor-on. *a* **1300** *K. Horn* 815 Ʒef vre on ouercomeþ ʒour þreo. *c* **1380** *Sir Ferumb.* 2629 Our on mot nedes leuen her.

b. esp. when accompanied by the genitive plural of ALL: *our all*, OE. *úre ealra*, ME. *oure aller*, of us all, all our. See ALLER.

c **1000** *Ags. Ps.* (Th.) lxxxvi. 6 Ure ealra bliss eardhæbbendra on anum þe ece standeþ. *c* **1200** *Trin. Coll. Hom.* 213 þat is ure alre wune. *c* **1200** ORMIN 7491 Ure allre land iss Paradis. *a* **1300** *Fall & Passion* 51 in *E.E.P.* (1862) 14 Maid bere heuen king þat is al ure creatoure. *a* **1300** *Cursor M.* 9709 (Cott.) Wit-vten vr al [*Gött.* all vre] comun a-sent. *c* **1385** CHAUCER *Prol.* 823 Vp roos oure hoost and was oure aller cok [*v. rr.* oure alder, our alþer, owre alder].

B. *possessive pron.* [OE. (*úser*) *úre* = OFris. *ûse*, OS., ODu. *unsa* (MDu. *onse*, Du. *onze, ons*), OHG. *unsêr* (MHG., Ger. *unser*), ON. *vár-r*, Goth. *unsar*), arising from inflecting the genitive pl. in A. as an adj., which in some of the langs. caused a contraction of the original form.

OE. *úre* was declined like ordinary adjs. in *-e*, as *gréne*; remains of this, as gen. sing. masc. and neuter *úres*, dat. sing. and pl. *úrum*, later *úren*, acc. sing. m. *úrne*, were still in use in 12–13th c.]

1. a. Of or belonging to us, i.e. to the speakers, or to the speaker and the person or persons whom he speaks for or includes. The possessive adj. corresponding to WE, US; expressing the genitive of possession; also the objective genitive, as *in our defence, our Maker, our persecutors*: see A.

In the first two OE. instances it has the value of the genitive case in A: *to our both* = to both of us; *of our none* = of none of us.

Beowulf 2659 Urum (*dat.*) sceal sweord ond helm byrne ond byrdu-scrud bam ʒemæne. *c* **897** K. ÆLFRED *Gregory's Past.* 211 ʒe habbaþ ʒecyðed ð æt ʒe ures nanes ne siendon. *c* **893** K. ÆLFRED *Oros.* I. i. §1 Ure ieldran ealne þisne ymbhwyrft þises middanʒeardes . . on þreo todældon. *c* **1000** *Ags. Gosp.* Matt. vi. 11 Urne ʒedæʒhwamlican hlaf syle us todæʒ [*c* 1160 *Hatton G.* ure]. *Ibid.* 12 And forʒyf us ure gyltas swa swa we forʒyfað urum gyltendum [*Hatton G.* ure . . ure]. —— Luke i. 71 He alysde us of urum feondum [*Hatton G.* uren feonden]. *a* **1200** *Moral Ode* 195 Vre forme fader gult we abuʒeð alle. *c* **1250** *Gen. & Ex.* 2261 It was in ure seckes don. *c* **1275** LAY. 3656 And Aganippus hour king. *Ibid.* 8545 Hail beo þou hore kinge. *a* **1300** *Cursor M.* 23698 (Edinb.) For wr [*Cott., Gött.* vr, *Fairf.* our, *Trin.* oure] eldern pliht. *c* **1300** *Havelok* 338 Sa[y] we nou forth in hure spelle. *c* **1325** *Spec. Gy Warw.* 506 Holi writ is oure myrour In whom we sen al vre socour. *c* **1330** R. BRUNNE *Chron. Wace* 3480 What do ʒe, Vs to chalange of vur fe? *c* **1375** *Rel. Ant.* I. 38 Oure uchedayes bred ʒeve us to day. *c* **1485** *Digby Myst.* II. 405 The law ys commyttyd to owur aduysment. **1536** CROMWELL in Merriman *Life & Lett.* (1902) II. 13 My lorde Chaunceler and I by owyr letteres . . aduertsyed you therof. **1593** SHAKS. *Rich. II*, II. i. 245 'Gainst us, our lives, our children, and our heirs. **1712** ADDISON *Spect.* No. 421 ¶9 The Perfection of our Sight above our other Senses. **1848** THACKERAY *Van. F.* xl, 'Miss Briggs and I are plunged in grief . . for the death of our Papa.'

b. Of the body of Christians, as ***Our Lord, Our Saviour, Our Lady***, or of humanity, as ***Our Father***.

971 *Blickl. Hom.* 11 Ure Drihten Hælend Crist. *Ibid.* 13 þonne biþ Drihten ure se trumesta staþol. *c* **1000** *Ags. Gosp.* Matt. vi. 9 Fæder ure þu þe eart on heofonum. *a* **1175** *Cott. Hom.* 235 Bodeden ures hlafordes to-cyme. *c* **1175–1832** [see LADY *sb.* 3]. *a* **1225** *Ancr. R.* 66 Ʒe, mine leoue sustren, uoleweð ure lefdi. **1340** *Ayenb.* 6 þet oure lhord him-zelf ous uorbyet. *a* **1548** HALL *Chron., Hen. VII* 15 In yᵉ yere of our redempcion .M.cccc.lxxxviii. **1568** GRAFTON *Chron.* II. 31 The yere of our Lorde M.c. **1650** FULLER *Pisgah* III. x. 433 Handselled with our Saviour's heavenly Sermon. **1850** ROBERTSON *Serm.* Ser. I. xvi, Our Lord affixed a new significance to the word Love. **1853** *Ibid.* Ser. II. xxii, What did our Redeemer mean?

c. In imperial or royal use, instead of *my*. Corresponding to the similar use of WE, q.v.

[*c* **1075** *Laws of William* in Schmid *Gesetze* 354 Willelmus rex Anglorum, dux Normannorum, omnibus hominibus suis, Francis et Anglis, salutem. Statuimus imprimis super omnia, unum Deum per totum regnum nostrum venerari.] **1258** *Eng. Proclam. Hen. III* 4 And we hoaten alle vre treowe in þe treowþe þæt heo vs oʒen. **1467–8** *Rolls of Parlt.* V. 590/1 Edmund Hampden Knyght, oure Rebell. **1568** GRAFTON *Chron.* II. 103 Geven at Laterane the tenth yere of our popedome. **1594** SHAKS. *Rich. III*, I. i. 120 Heauen will take the present at our hands. **1708** *Royal Proclam.* 18 Jan.

in *Lond. Gaz.* No. 4403/2 The Watermen belonging to.. Our most Dear Consort. **1837** *Royal Proclam.*, VICTORIA R. Our Will and Pleasure is, That, [etc.] Given at Our Court at Kensington, the Twenty-first Day of June 1837, in the First Year of Our Reign.

d. In vaguer sense: With whom or which we have to do; whom we have in mind; of whom (or which) we are speaking; of the writer and his readers, or merely of the writer. Hence used by editors and reviewers. Cf. WE.

1612 *Proc. Virginia* 68 in *Capt. Smith's Wks.* (Arb.) 141 If we should each kill our man. **1612** T. TAYLOR *Comm. Titus* i. 6 This sinne.. against which our Apostle leuelleth. **1653** H. MORE *Antid. Ath.* II. ii. (1712) 47 So our profound Atheists and Epicureans.. do not stick to infer. **1780** BECKFORD *Biog. Mem.* 148 Here our artist remained six weeks. **1784** T. SHERIDAN *Swift's Wks.* Pref., Impropriations which run thro' the whole body of the works, not only of our author, but of all other English writers. **1816** SCOTT *Antiq.* xxvi, We must now introduce our reader to the interior of the fisher's cottage. *Mod.* Here we take leave of our author.

e. Used familiarly with a Christian name to denote a relative (esp. a child) or acquaintance of the speaker. Also, with surname, an employee of a company, and, in joc. address to a patient, the diseased or injured part of the body.

1847 A. BRONTË *Agnes Grey* xi. 163, I sent our Bill to beg Maister Hatfield to be so kind as look in on me some day. **1856** DICKENS *Dorrit* (1857) I. xiii. 118 Now, let's see whether there's anything else the matter, and how our ribs are? **1864** —— *Mut. Fr.* (1865) I. II. ix. 246 Sloppy explained ..that the Orphan (of whom he made mention as Our Johnny) had been ailing. **1911** F. H. BURNETT *Secret Garden* xxvii. 298 He..took a golden sovereign from his pocket and gave it to 'our 'Lizabeth Ellen', who was the oldest. **1932** N. ROYDE-SMITH *Incredible Tale* ix. 131, I sent up our Mr. Wilkinson, who has lived in Russia. **1936** 'G. ORWELL' *Diary* 11 Feb. in *Coll. Ess.* (1968) I. 175 The son 'our Joe', just turned 15. **1952** 'W. COOPER' *Struggles of Albert Woods* I. ii. 23 'What do you think of it, our Albert?' his mother cried. **1968** 'J. FRASER' *Evergreen Death* v. 40 'What are you doing out here then, our Arnold?' his sister asked. **1977** G. MARKSTEIN *Chance Awakening* xxii. 70 'He's a swinger,' said Chance. 'Our Mike gets around.'

f. ***our hero***: used familiarly of the hero by the writer of a work of fiction, biography, etc.

1804 J. BISSET *Crit. Ess. Young Roscius* p. x, Our little Hero caught the first theatric spark. **1854** RAWDON BROWN *Let.* 6 May in M. Lutyens *Millais & Ruskins* (1967) 205 He ..said that he had amused him more than anyone since Robinson Crusoe! A greater compliment could certainly not have been paid our hero. **1905** H. A. VACHELL *Hill* v. 110 Much of our hero's time was spent in the company of the Duffer. **1961** *Mind* LXX. 104 And so our hero escapes from his appalling predicament: with one bound, Jack was free. **1975** *Radio Times* 29 May 13/1 Most of the books have a fair amount of physical violence which leaves Our Hero battered almost to pulp.

†**2.** *absolutely*: = OURS. *Obs.*

In OE. and Early ME. the predicative and absolute use had (as in ordinary adjs.) the same form as the attributive. This continued with some southern writers down to the 17th c., although the differentiated form *ures, oures*, OURS, had arisen in the north before 1300, and had become general Eng. by 1500.

c **897** K. ÆLFRED *Gregory's Past.* xlv. 335 Hiera ægen we him sellað nalles ure. *c* **1000** *Ags. Gosp.* Mark xii. 7 þonne bið ure seo yrfeweardnes. *c* **1200** *Trin. Coll. Hom.* 145 þine sunnen þe beð forgiuene. Swo beo us alle ure. **1297** R. GLOUC. (Rolls) 4396 Vre is þe maystrye. *Ibid.* 9368 þe riȝte al oure is. *a* **1300** *Cursor M.* 7465 (Cott.) A man o þair gains an of vr [*Fairf.* oure]. **1340** *Ayenb.* 112 Hit is oure uor he hit ous let. *c* **1374** CHAUCER *Troylus* IV. 511 (539), I wil be ded or she shal bleuen oure. **1425–6** BP. OF WINCHESTER in *Chron. London* 166 Your owne wele and our alle. *c* **1489** CAXTON *Sonnes of Aymon* xxvi. 545 Your fader dyde assaylle our by treyson. **1554–9** *Songs & Ball. Philip & Mary* (1860) 5 Hys ryghtyusnes ys owr, owr inequyte ys hys. **1601** DANIEL *Civ. Wars* VI. lxi, We rule who liue: the dead are none of our. **1641** 'SMECTYMNUUS' *Vind. Answ.* ii. 38 Our is the more ancient Liturgie, and our the more noble Church.

3. Our Father. Used as a name of the 'Lord's Prayer': = PATERNOSTER.

1882 EDNA LYALL *Donovan* xl, Together [they]..said the 'Our Father' and sealed their reconciliation.

4. Our Lady's, esp. in names of plants: see LADY *sb.* 18, LADY'S CUSHION, etc.

†**our**, *conj. Obs.*, app. reduced from OUTHER: see under OR *conj.* A. β

our, obs. or dial. var. OVER *adv.*, *prep.*, *v.*; obs. f. HOUR; var. of OWHERE *Obs.*

our-, obs. var. (chiefly Sc.) of OVER-, in comb., as in *ourfret*, *ourga* (= OVERGO), *ourhand*, etc.

-our, *suffix* (repr. AF. *-our*, OF. *-or*, *-ur*, *-eör*, *-eür*, mod.F. *-eur*), the earlier spelling of the suffix *-or*, regularly used in ME., and still commonly retained (in Great Britain, but not in America) in some of the words of ME. age, or of subsequent formation on the pattern of these; e.g. *colour*, *honour*, *saviour*, *splendour*, *candour*: see -OR suffix.

b. In a few words, the suffix *-our* (= F. *-eur*), indicating state, is added to roots of Teutonic origin, as in *dreadour*, *quenchour*, *raddour*, q.v.

c. *-our* is in some words a corruption or alteration of some other ending, as in *arbour*, *armour*, *behaviour*, *demeanour*, *endeavour*, *harbour*, *haviour*, *neighbour*, *parlour*, q.v.

ourage, variant of OVERAGE *Obs.*, work.

ourali, variant form of WOURALI.

ouralwhere, oure-: see OVERALLWHERE.

ouran for *our-ran*, obs. pa. t. of OVERRUN.

ourane, *Sc.* = *over one*, together: see OVER *prep.*

ourang-outang, -utang, ff. ORANG-OUTANG.

Ouranian (aʊəˈreɪnɪən), *a.* [f. Gr. οὐράνι-ος heavenly + -AN.] Of or pertaining to heaven or the upper regions. (Cf. URANIAN *a.*[1])

1908 G. G. A. MURRAY in R. R. Marett *Anthropol. & Classics* 68 A great proportion of our anthropological material is already to be found in prehistoric Crete..the stones, the beasts, the pillars, and the ouranian birds.

ourano-: see URANO-.

ourari, variant of CURARE, WOURALI.

†**ourbeld**, *pa. pple. Sc. Obs.* [pa. pple. of *ourbeild*, f. *our-*, OVER- + BEILD *v.*] Covered over.

c **1450** HOLLAND *Howlat* 672 Braid burdis and benkis, ourbeld with bancouris of gold.

our-burd, ourcower, our-croce, obs. Sc. ff. OVERBOARD, -COVER, -CROSS.

†**our'dirk**, *v. Sc. Obs.* [f. *our-*, OVER- + *dirk*, DARK *v.*] *trans.* To overdarken, overcloud.

a **1568** in *Dunbar's Poems* (1893) 329 We may nocht in this vale of bale abyd, Ourdirkit with the sable clud nocturn.

ourdraif, -drave, -driff, etc., obs. ff. OVERDRIVE. *v.*

ourdraw, obs. Sc. form of OVERDRAW.

oure, *sb.*: see OVER, OVRE *sb.*[1], shore.

oure, obs. form of HOUR, ORE, OUR, YOUR.

oure, obs. form, chiefly Sc., of OVER; also in combination, as *oure-al*, *ouredreve* (OVERDRIVE), *ourehaile* (OVERHALE), *ourelip*, *oureman*, *ouresayle* (OVERSAIL), etc.

ourebi: see ORIBI.

ourels, = *owher else*: see OWHERE, anywhere.

ouren, oures, obs. forms of OURN, OURS.

ouretyrve, var. OVERTERVE *Obs.*, to overturn.

ourharl, ourhele, ouer-hie, obs. Sc. ff. OVERHARL, -HELE, -HIGH.

ouric, variant of URIC.

ourie (ˈaʊrɪ, ˈuːrɪ), *a. north. dial.*; now only *Sc.* Forms: 4 ouri, 8–9 **ourie, owrie**, 9 **oory**. [Origin obscure: cf. Icel. *úrig* wet, f. *úr* drizzling rain.] Poor in appearance, shabby; dull, dingy; dreary, melancholy, languid.

c **1325** *Metr. Hom.* 88 He changed son his ouri wed, And forth into the halle he yed. **1785** BURNS *A Winter Night* iii, I thought me on the ourie cattle, Or silly sheep, wha bide this brattle O' winter war. *a* **1810** TANNAHILL *Lasses a' leuch* Poems (1846) 145 Maggie was sitting fu' ourie an' blate. **1837** R. NICOLL *Poems* (1843) 82 The winter rain-drap owrie fa's. **1865** MRS. CARLYLE *Lett.* III. 261 That oory, dingy paint and paper.

'ourishness. *nonce-wd.* [f. OUR *pron.* + -ISH[1] + -NESS.] The quality of belonging to or of being connected with ourselves.

1819 COLERIDGE in *Rem.* (1836) II. 151 Yet there is a sort of unhired fidelity, an ourishness about all this that makes it rest pleasant in one's feelings. **1860** K. H. DIGBY *Even. on Thames* I. 320 There is a sort of ourishness, to use a word of Coleridge's, in the way that some people speak of the country or town they live in.

ourlawer, -layer: see OVERLAYER.

ourloft, ourman, ourpast, etc., obs. Sc. ff. ORLOP, OVERMAN, OVERPAST, etc.

ourn (aʊən), *poss. pron. dial.* Also 5 ouren, ourun. [f. OUR *poss. pron.*, as in *hern*, etc., app. by form-association with *my*, *mine*, *thy*, *thine*: see HISN. These *-n* forms are midland and southern.] = OURS.

c **1380** WYCLIF *Sel. Wks.* II. 154 His conversacioun is in hevene, as ouren shulden be. **1382** —— *Gen.* xxvi. 20 (MS. E, *a* 1390) Ourn is the water [*MS. A*, Oure]. *Ibid.* xxxiv. 21 And oure [*MSS. B, D, E, F, H*, ourn] we shulen ȝyue to hem. *c* **1420** —— *Mark* xii. 7 And the eritage schal be oure [*MSS. G, W*, ourun]. *c* **1420** *Chron. Vilod.* 985 To ȝeue us þe lond aȝeyn þat ouren is. **1711** J. GREENWOOD *Eng. Gram.* 105 Hern, Ourn, Yourn, Hisn, for Hers, Ours, Yours, His, is bad English. **1778** FOOTE *Trip to Calais* II. 52 Instead of doing like our'n, they wear their woollen smocks over the rest of their cloaths. **1861** HUGHES *Tom Brown at Oxf.* xxiii, 'Wer' be 'em then?'..'Aal-amang wi' ourn in the limes'. **1861** LOWELL *Biglow P.* Ser. II. i. 169 Ourn's the fust thru-by-daylight train.

†**ourn**, *v. Obs.* [Of obscure origin; known only in the work quoted. Stratmann compares ON. *orna* to get warm, Sw. *orna* to grow musty.]

1. *intr.* ? To rage, be enraged.

c **1400** *Destr. Troy* 6404 Ector for þat od dynt ournyt in hert, Wode for the wap, as a wild lyon.

b. Of uncertain sense.

c **1400** *Destr. Troy* 2203, I, ournand in elde with arghnes in hert. *Ibid.* 2540 If Elinus be argh, & ournes for ferde,.. let other men Aunter, abill þerfore.

2. *trans.* ? To enrage; to rouse.

c **1400** *Destr. Troy* 4857 We haue ournyt hym with angur, ertid hym mykill.

Hence †**ourning** *vbl. sb.*, ? raging, rage.

c **1400** *Destr. Troy* 4767 Yche freke, þat þai found, felly þai slogh, Old men & other, with ournyng, to dethe. *Ibid.* 12711 This Othe, with ournyng, ordant belyue Letturs by a lede þat he leell trist, To Agamynon gay wif.

ourn, -e, = *orn*, obs. pa. t. of RUN *v.*

ourn, ournement, obs. ff. ORN, ORNAMENT.

ouroboros, var. UROBOROS.

ourology, -mancy, -scopy: see UROLOGY, etc.

our-quar(e, -quhare, var. OURWHERE *Obs.*

our-ryn, obs. Sc. form of OVERRUN.

ours (aʊəz), *poss. pron.* Forms: 4 **ures, uris, urs, ors**, 4–6 **ouris**, 4–5 **ourys, owres**, 5–6 **oures, owris**, 5 **ourez**, 7–9 **our's**, 4– **ours**. [In form a double possessive, f. poss. pron. *ur*, *ure*, OUR + *-es* (cf. *hers*, *yours*, *theirs*); of northern origin: cf. the midl. and southern *ouren*, OURN; and see OUR *poss. pron.* 2.]

a. The absolute form of the possessive pronoun OUR, used when no sb. follows, i.e. either absolutely or predicatively: Our one, our ones; that or those belonging to us; *spec.* = our regiment, chiefly in phr. 'of ours'; also in *transf.* and extended uses. (= F. *le nôtre*, *la nôtre*, *les nôtres*, Ger. *der*, *die*, *das unsere*, *unsrige*.) †***ours two, ours all*** = of us two, of us all.

a **1300** *Cursor M.* 11784 (Cott.) Bot for he es godd mighti sene, Vres ar fallen don be-dene. *Ibid.* 27579 (Cott.) þai haf in þaim sum hidd bunte þat better mai þan ors [*v.r.* owres] be. **13..** *Ibid.* 12285 (Gött.) Ȝour sun has vres [*Cott.* urs nu, *Tr.* haþ oures] feld wid strijf. *c* **1386** CHAUCER *Pard. T.* 458 Ffor wel ye woot þat al this gold is oures [*Camb. MS.* ourys]. *c* **1440** *Generydes* 2989 This day was therys, Another shalbe ourez. *c* **1440** *York Myst.* xiii. 219 þat childe was neuere oures two. **1533** GAU *Richt Vay* 45 He and al his is owris. **1656** WALLER *To my Lord Protector* viii, Your highness, not for ours alone, But for the world's Protector shall be known. **1787** W. DYOTT *Diary* Nov. (1907) I. 38 The company at dinner was..Captain Gladstanes, 57th regiment; Captain Dalrymple, 42nd; Hodgson of ours, and myself. **1796** H. HUNTER tr. *St.-Pierre's Stud. Nat.* (1799) I. 190 The second Current..inclosed between the Continent of America and ours. **1823** *Spirit of Public Jrnls. M. DCCC. XXIII* (1825) I What is't attracts the optic pow'rs Of Ensign gay, when fortune show'rs Down prospects of 'a step' in 'ours'? **1847** DICKENS *Dombey* (1848) xxi. 206 Edith Skewton, Sir,.. married (at eighteen) Granger of Ours. **1847** THACKERAY *Van. Fair* (1848) xxvii. 235 Run Simple (Ensign Simple, of Ours, my dear Amelia). **1874** MORLEY *Compromise* (1886) 129 Ours, as has been truly said, is 'a time of loud disputes and weak convictions'. **1877** G. M. HOPKINS *Let.* 6 Jan. (1938) 94 Lancashire..from where a good many of Ours come. **1894** 'MRS. ALEXANDER' *Choice of Evils* II. ii. 47 We have a young fellow..in 'ours', who has just saved the Colonel's life by a lucky shot. **1922** W. CATHER (*title*) One of ours. **1975** *Listener* 25 Dec. 893/3 A short, highly professional story of a competent war time spy of Ours who goes back to the game. **1977** T. HEALD *Just Desserts* i. 10 You know he was one of ours?.. Provided us with information, tip-offs, odds and ends.

b. ***of ours***: see OF 44.

13.. *Cursor M.* 7465 (Gött.) A man of his again a man of ouris [*Cott.* ur], If ours may winne his in stours. **1413** *Pilgr. Sowle* (Caxton 1483) I. xiii. 8 Muche more wold it semen skyle that he be one of ourys. **1526** TINDALE *1 Cor.* i. 2 All them that call on the name of oure lorde Iesus Christ in every place, both of theirs and of oures [WYCLIF, of hem and oure]. **1578** *Chr. Prayers in Priv. Prayers* (1851) 540 This weak and feeble fortress of ours. **1837** CARLYLE *Fr. Rev.* III. I. vi, O shrieking beloved brother blockheads of mankind, let us close those wide mouths of ours. *a* **1903** *Mod.* This garden of ours has been neglected.

†**c.** *rare use.* As the second of two possessives before a substantive, where *our* is the ordinary form.

1564 JEWEL *Apol. Ch. Eng.* Ded., Whiche..youre and ours moste vertuous and learned soueraigne Ladie and Mastres shal see good cause to commende.

†**our-scalit**, *pa. pple. Sc. Obs.* [From vb. **our-* (= over-)*scale*.] Covered over as with scales.

1508 DUNBAR *Goldyn Targe* 26 The purpur hevyn our scailit in silver sloppis.

ourself (aʊəˈsɛlf), *pron.* Forms: see OUR and SELF. [A parallel formation to next, with *self* instead of *selves*, appearing first in 14th c.

It may have arisen out of *our selven*, through *our selve*, *our selfe*, finally with *e* mute, as in the infinitive of vbs. (e.g. *holden*, *holde*, *hold*); but, on the other hand, it may have been a distinct formation, with the uninflected *self* (cf. *myself*, *ourself*, with *my own*, *our own*).]

Emphatic and reflexive pronoun, corresponding to *we*, *us*, originally not differing in sense from OURSELVES; but subsequently differentiated, so as to be used mostly in those cases in which *we* refers to a single person or is not definitely plural; e.g. in royal, divine, or editorial utterance, or when used vaguely in the sense of *one*, *oneself*.

In mod. South Sc. *oursel* is collective, *oursels* is individual; e.g. 'we do everything *oursel*', but 'we'll settle it atween *oursels*'.

I. *Emphatic*. **1.** Standing alone, as subject, as object direct or indirect, or in predicate after *be*, *become*, or the like.

a **1400–50** *Alexander* 3528 Oure-selfe & oure seruage is surely ȝoure awen. **1509** HAWES *Past. Pleas.* XXXI. (Percy Soc.) 150 Now trouth of his right dooth our selfe exhorte. **1567** *Gude & Godlie B.* (S.T.S.) 16 Our natiue sin in Adame to expell And all trespas committit be our sell. **1611** SHAKS. *Cymb.* V. v. 73 Which our selfe haue granted. **1711** SHAFTESB. *Charac.* (1737) I. 37 So puzzl'd..that they knew not..whether there were really in the world any such person as our-self. **1715–20** POPE *Iliad* XVII. 516 Ourself will swiftness to your nerves impart, Ourself with rising spirits swell your heart. **1785** BURNS *Death & Dr. Hornbook* ii, That e'er he nearer comes oursel 'S a muckle pity. **1814** SCOTT *Ld. of Isles* VI. xxxvii, Ourself will grace..The bridal of the Maid of Lorn. **1847** TENNYSON *Princ.* III. 300, 303 Ourself..learnt..This craft of healing. Were you sick, ourself Would tend upon you.

2. In apposition with *we* or (rarely) *us*.

1484 CAXTON *Fables of Æsop* II. ii, For we oure self ben cause of this meschyef. **1601** SHAKS. *Jul. C.* III. i. 8 *Art.* O Cæsar, reade mine first: for mine's a suite That touches Cæsar neerer... *Cæs.* What touches vs our selfe, shall be last seru'd. **1609** DANIEL *Civ. Wars* VIII. lv, We will our selfe take time to heare Your Cause at large.

II. **3.** *Reflexive*: as direct or indirect object.

13.. *Cursor M.* 23791 (Cott.) Qui sell we vr-self [*Edin.*, *Fairf.*, *Trin.* vs; *Gött.* vs-self] vnto þat soru? **13..** *Chron. R. Glouc.* (Rolls) 1076 (MS. B) þat beþ here bi oure self [*so MSS.* β, γ; *MS. A*, vs sulve; *MS.* α, vs sulf] as at þe worldes ende. *c* **1400** *Destr. Troy* 4933 To macche vs with monhede & might of our selfe [cf. *Ibid.* 7860 We are folke full fele.. Assemblit in this Cite oure seluyn to kepe]. *c* **1460** FORTESCUE *Abs. & Lim. Mon.* vi. (1885) 121 We that mey harme owre selff with all thes defautes. *c* **1489** CAXTON *Sonnes of Aymon* iii. 78 Broder,..let vs make redy ourselfe for to yssue out. **1563** *Homilies* II. *Matrimony* (1859) 501 For this folly is ever..grown up with us,..to think highly by ourself, so that none thinketh it meet to give place to another. **1836–9** DICKENS *Sk. Boz, Vauxhall Gard. by Day*, We, from the mere force of habit, found ourself running among the first. **1884** tr. *Lotze's Metaph.* 179 That a complete vacuum could not be represented to the mind, without at least reserving a place in it for ourself.

ourselves (aʊə'sɛlvz), *pron. pl.* Forms: see OUR and SELF. [The original construction was nom. *we selfe*, acc. *ús selfe*, dat. *ús selfum*; whence ME. *us selven*. In 14th c. this was superseded in north. dial. by *ur selven*, midl. *our(e selven* (whence perh., through *oure selve*, *our(e selfe*, the form OURSELF). Before 1500, *our(e selfs*, *our selves*, appeared and became the standard form: cf. *yourselves*, *themselves*, and see SELF.] The emphatic and reflexive pronoun corresponding to *we*, *us*.

I. Emphatic.

1. Standing alone, as subject, as object direct or indirect, or in predicate after *be*, *become*, or the like.

1591 SHAKS. *Two Gent.* IV. i. 76 The Treasure..with our selues, all rest at thy dispose. **1593** —— *Rich. II*, I. i. 16 Our selues will heare Th' accuser, and the accused, freely speake. **1650** BAXTER *Saints' R.* iii. (ed. 8) 108 Ourselves are the greatest snare to ourselves. **1773** *Life N. Frowde* 47 We were not ourselves till some Weeks after their Departure. **1822** HAZLITT *Table-t.* II. xvii. 388 We had as lief not be, as not be ourselves. **1846** GREENER *Sc. Gunnery* 320 Very satisfactory..to the owners of the ships if not to ourselves. *dial.* [**1890** W. A. WALLACE *Only a Sister?* 87 Nobbut one of oursens dressed up like.]

2. In apposition with *we* or (rarely) *us*.

[**13..** *Cursor M.* 21878 (Cott.) If we cuth oght vr-seluen (*Fairf.* our-seluen; *Edin.*, *Gött.* us seluin) knau.] **1526** TINDALE *John* iv. 42 We have herde hym oure selves. **1611** BIBLE *Transl. Pref.* 1 The light..that we haue attained vnto our selues. **1725** RAMSAY *Gent. Sheph.* III. ii, We anes were young oursells. **1736** BUTLER *Anal.* I. i. 28 Appropriated to us ourselves. **1884** MRS. OLIPHANT *Sir Tom* II. x. 153 When we are ourselves poor.

II. **3.** Reflexive. As direct or indirect object.

[*c* **1400** *Chaucer's Wife's Prol.* 812 We fille acorded by vs seluen two (*Camb.*, *Lansd.*, *Harl.* oure seluyn, seluen, our seluen). *c* **1440** *Gesta Rom.* I. xxxvi. 146 (Harl. MS.) Yf we come afor, and accuse oure selvene.] **1495–6** *Plumpton Corr.* 115 We shall endevor ourselfs. **1526** TINDALE *2 Cor.* iii. 5 Nor that we are sufficient off oure selves to thynke eny thynge as it were of oure selves. **1534** ELYOT *Doctrinal of Princes* 6 We..litle do avaunce our selfes to..vertue. **1611** BIBLE *Transl. Pref.* 1 We subject our selues to euery ones censure. **1665** BOYLE *Occas. Refl.* IV. xvii. (1848) 271 If we ..did not as much flatter our selves, and disguise our selves, to our selves, as we flatteringly disguise our selves to others. **1772** PRIESTLEY *Inst. Relig.* (1782) I. 68 We are capable of governing ourselves. **1786** BURNS *To a Louse* viii, To see oursels as others see us! **1860** THACKERAY *Round. Papers, De Juvent.* Wks. 1872 X. 61 At the pastrycook's we may have over-eaten ourselves. *Mod.* We have given ourselves the pleasure of calling on you.

ourset, oursit, ourslide: see OVER-.

‖**oursin** (ursɛ̃). [Fr.] = SEA-URCHIN 1.

1928 R. HALL *Well of Loneliness* xl. 376 Many loved Prunier's..because of its galaxy of sea-monsters. A whole counter there was of incredible creatures— Oursins, black armoured and covered with prickles; Bigorneaux; serpent-like Anguilles Fumées. **1931** *Daily Express* 21 Sept. 3/4 There are..other strange fish known as oursins, literally 'little bears'. **1950** E. DAVID *Bk. Mediterranean Food* 142 *Oursins* (those spiny sea-urchins cut in half from which you scoop out the coral with a piece of bread). **1966** P. V. PRICE *France: Food & Wine Guide* 274 There are also *oursins* (sea-urchins), which look just like prickly chestnuts, and taste rather like a snail that has been taken to the sea. **1972** *Guardian* 1 Jan. 11/4 Men bring nets full of *oursins* to quayside cafés. **1973** D. MILLER *Chinese Jade Affair* xvii. 156 A basket of shell-fish..belons, oursins, moules, crevettes and Marennes.

†**ourspinner**, *v. Sc. Obs.* [f. *our*, OVER + **spinner*, freq. of SPIN *v.*: see -ER[5].] *trans.* To traverse rapidly, 'spin' along over.

1513 DOUGLAS *Æneis* IV. iv. 53 The hirdis of hartis.. Ourspynnerand with swyft cours the plane vaill.

ourstraught, obs. Sc. f. OVERSTRETCHED.

ourstred, Sc. f. pa. t. of OVERSTRIDE.

†**our'strenkle**, *v. Sc. Obs.* [f. *our*, OVER + *strenkle*, STRINKLE, to sprinkle.] *trans.* To sprinkle over, oversprinkle.

c **1450** *Wisdom Solomon* in *Ratis Raving* etc. 12 þe fresch watter..that be the wertew of the hevyn, ourstrenklys the erde. *Ibid.* 24 The rane our-strenklys the erde.

oursyle, variant of OVERSILE *Obs.*, to cover.

†**ourt** = *hourt*, obs. f. HURT. Hence †**ourt majesté** = *hurt majesty*, LESE-MAJESTY.

c **1375** *Sc. Leg. Saints* xxvi. (*Nycholas*) 388 Sayand: 'þai part had al thre of crime of ourt maieste'.

ourta, -tak(e, obs. northern ff. OVERTAKE *v.*

ourthort, -thourth, -thwart, -thwort, obs. Sc. ff. OVERTHWART.

ourthraw, -throw, Sc. ff. OVERTHROW.

ourtirve, -tyrf, -tyrve, Sc. ff. OVERTERVE *Obs.*, overturn.

ourtummylit, Sc. pa. t. of OVERTUMBLE *v.*

ourweill, obs. Sc. form of OVERWELL *v.*

†**ourwhere, ouerwhere**, *adv. Obs.* Forms: 4 our, ouþer-, our-, or-quar(e; awre-, aure-quare, aure quere, 4–5 ouerwhere, owerwhere, -whare, ourwhar(e; 5 owr-qwher, awre where. [A reduction of *outherwhere*, *autherwhere*, f. OUTHER + WHERE, the contraction being the same as in *outher*, *our*, *ather*, *ar*, *either*, *er*, *other*, *or*, *whether*, *wher*. The etymological sense was thus 'either-where', i.e. 'either one where or the other', 'somewhere or other', and thus at length = OWHERE anywhere.

It is possible that *our-* or *ouer-* was later associated with *over*, and so with such combinations as *overall*, *overall-where*, whence perh. sense b; but the northern forms in *awre-*, *aure-*, could be derived only from *awther*.]

Anywhere; = OWHERE.

a **1300** *Cursor M.* 1837 (Cott.) þe heiest fell þat was our-quare [*Fairf.* awre-quare, *Gö tt.* aware, *Tr.* owhore]. *Ibid.* 11795 (Cott.) Was noght a temple or-quar in tun. *Ibid.* 14570 (Gött.) þe freindes þat we haue ouþerquar [*F.* aure-quare, *C.* our-quar, *Tr.* elles where]. *Ibid.* 15184 (Gött.) Sal we ȝuu ani paskes dight ouþerquar [*F.* aure-quere, *C.* our-quar, *Tr.* o where] in land? **1340** HAMPOLE *Pr. Consc.* 4339 Under erthe, or ourwar elles. *Ibid.* 6983 In helle..or ourwhare elles. *c* **1400** MAUNDEV. (Roxb.) vii. 25 þe fairest smaragdes þat er ower whare. **1435** MISYN *Fire of Love* 46 If any slike be lifand owr-qwher in flesch. *c* **1460** *Towneley Myst.* xxvii. 127 Is ther fallen any affray In land awre whare?

b. Everywhere.

c **1330** R. BRUNNE *Chron. Wace* Prol. 107 Alle þat þai wild ouerwhere. *c* **1425** *Found. St. Bartholomew's* (E.E.T.S.) 20 To his seruyce I shall me subdew Ouerwher' calle hym and preche hym my lorde. *c* **1450** *St. Cuthbert* (Surtees) 394 The child looked here and þare, On þe cowe aboute our whare.

-ous, *suffix*, repr. L. *-ōs-us* (*-a*, *-um*), forming adjs., with the sense of 'abounding in, full of, characterized by, of the nature of', e.g. *cōpi-ōs-us* plentiful, copious, *dolōr-ōs-us* full of sorrow, dolorous, *fām-ōs-us* famous, *gener-ōs-us* distinguished by descent, generous, *glōri-ōs-us* full of glory, glorious, *spīn-ōs-us* full of thorns, thorny, spinous, *visc-ōs-us* of the nature of bird-lime, sticky, viscous, etc. Latin stressed long *ō* passed in OFr. into a closer sound, intermediate between *ō* and *ū*, which was variously written *o* or *u*, less commonly *ou*; hence L. adjs. in *-ōsus*, which either came down in popular use, or were adopted at an early date, had in OF. forms in *-os*, or *-us* (*-ous*), e.g. *coveitos*, *-us*, *doleros*, *-us*, *envios*, *-us*, *glorios*, *-us*, *religios*, *-us*. In the 13th c. the vowel-sound had changed to (ø) written *eu*, so that the suffix had now the form *-eus* (*covoiteus*, *dolereus*, *envieus*, *glorieus*, etc.); and this still later was written in the masc. *-eux* (*convoiteux*, *envieux*, *glorieux*, with fem. however in *-euse*), as still in modern F. In Anglo-Fr. and early ME. the forms were the same as in early OF. (*coveitos*, *-us*, *envios*, *-us*, *glorios*, *-us*), but the vowel was soon identified with OE. long *ú*, and like it written after 1300 *ou* (*covetous*, *envious*, *glorious*), the spelling ever since retained, though the sound has passed through (-uːs, -us, -ʊs) to (-ʌs, -əs). This *-ous*, having thus become the form of the suffix in all words from Norman Fr., became the established type for all those of later introduction, whether adaptations of Fr. adjs. in *-eus*, *-eux*, or L. adjs. in *-ōsus* (but see -OSE[1]), or new formations on the analogy of these, from Fr., L., or other elements.

These new formations are numerous in the Romanic languages. In French they have been formed freely, not only from L. sbs. which had no such derivative in ancient L., but also from French words themselves of L. origin, and from mediæval and modern words from divers sources. Many of these new formations have, in earlier or later times, passed (with change of *-eux*, etc., to *-ous*) from French into English. Such is the history, for example, of *advantageous*, *adventurous*, *courageous*, *dangerous*, *gelatinous*, *grievous*, *gummous*, *hazardous*, *hideous*, *joyous*, *lecherous*, *matinous*, *mountainous*, *orguillous*, *pulpous*, *ravenous*, *riotous*, *slanderous*. This process has been continued in Eng. itself, where new adjs. in *-ous* have been formed, not only on Latin, Greek, and Romanic bases, but also on native Eng. words and on some of obscure origin; e.g. *blusterous*, *boisterous*, *burdenous*, *feverous*, *murderous*, *poisonous*, *slumberous*, *thunderous*, *timous*, *troublous*, *wondrous*.

In some words in late or med.L. the ending *-ōsus* was added to an adj., or at least a form in *-ōsus* is found beside the simple adjective, e.g. *decōr-us*, *decorōs-us*, *dubi-us*, *dubiōs-us*, in It. *decoro*, *decoroso*, *dubbio*, *dubbioso*. In the Romanic languages a few new forms of this kind appear; e.g. L. *pi-us*, F. *pi-eux* (as if from **piōs-us*). But in English, this addition of the suffix has been greatly developed, and has become the ordinary mode of anglicizing L. adjs. of many kinds, esp. those in *-eus*, *-ius*, *-uus*, *-er*, *-ris*, *-āx* *-āci*, *-ōx* *-ōci*, *-endus*, *-ulus*, *-vorus*, *-ōrus*, e.g. *aque-ous*, *igne-ous*, *extrane-ous*, *herbace-ous*, *consci-ous*, *obvi-ous*, *vari-ous*, *ardu-ous*, *exigu-ous*, *adulter-ous*, *aurifer-ous*, *armiger-ous*, *alacri-ous*, *hilari-ous*, *illustri-ous*, *capaci-ous*, *feroci-ous*, *stupend-ous*, *garrul-ous*, *omnivor-ous*, *sonor-ous*.

This tendency to represent a L. adj. by an Eng. form in *-ous* may have been strengthened by the fact that the 'dictionary-form' of the L. adj. is the nom. sing. masc., and that this in the majority of adjs. ends in *-us*, the Eng. pronunciation of which is the same as that of the Eng. word in *-ous*, so that the latter to the cursory observer appears to be merely an Eng. spelling of the L. It is evident however that *igne-ous*, for example, answers not only to L. *igne-us*, but to *igne-a*, *igne-um*, etc., and that the *-ous* is an additional element. And in comparing *alacri-ous* with *alacer*, *hilari-ous* with *hilari-s*, *capaci-ous* with *capax*, *capāci-*, the suffixal nature of the *-ous* is manifest.

b. In some words, *-ous* is a corruption of another suffix, e.g. in *righteous*, *wrongous*, *courteous*, *gorgeous*; in others, as *bounteous*, a contraction of an earlier suffix has taken place before *-ous*: see -EOUS.

c. In *Chem.*, adjectives in *-ous*, formed on the names of elements, indicate acids and other compounds containing a larger proportion of the element in question than those expressed by an adj. in *-ic*: e.g. *chlorous* acid, *sulphurous* acid, *cuprous* oxide, *ferrous* salts, etc.: see -IC 1 b.

d. Nouns of quality from adjs. in *-ous* (however derived), are regularly formed in *-ousness*, as *covetousness*, *consciousness*, *gorgeousness*, *righteousness*; those from L. *-ōsus* have sometimes forms in *-osity*, as *curiosity*, *generosity*, *porosity*, *viscosity*; but this termination more frequently accompanies adjs. in -OSE[1].

ous, ouse, obs. forms of US, OOZE.

†**ouse**, obs. form of HOSE: see HOSE *sb.* 3.

1764 *Museum Rusticum* III. lxvii. 304 There should be two branches..to which the leather ouses should be screwed. *Note*, Ouses are pipes of the same nature with the leather pipes used with the fire-engines.

ousel, -elle, -le, obs. forms of OUZEL.

ousen, obs. Sc. f. *oxen*, pl. of OX.

Ouspenskyist (uːˈspɛnskiːɪst). [f. the name of Peter Demianovich *Ouspensky* (1878–1947), Russian philosopher + -IST.] A follower of Ouspensky or his teaching. Also **Ou'spenskian, Ou'spenskyite** *adjs.*

1958 L. DURRELL *Balthazar* ii. 29 Alexandria is a city of sects.. Steinerites.. Ouspenskyists, Adventists. **1968** T. WOLFE *Electric Kool-Aid Acid Test* iv. 54 Alpert soars in Ouspenskian loop-the-loops. **1975** M. BRADBURY *History Man* v. 81 A radical Catholic priest and his Ouspenskyite mistress.

oust (aʊst), *v.* [a. AF. *ouste-r* = OF. *oster*, mod.F. *ôter* to take away, remove, deprive; of uncertain derivation.

(L. *obstāre* to stand in the way of, obstruct, thwart, would give the form *oster* in OF., but does not suit the sense.)]

1. *trans. Law.* To put out of possession, eject, dispossess, disseise; to deprive (any one) *of* a corporeal or incorporeal hereditament. Const. *of.*

[**1292** BRITTON I. xii. §3 Sauntz rien oster.] **1588** FRAUNCE *Lawiers Log.* I. xix. 67 The suspected men may bee ousted by challenge. **1619** DALTON *Country Just.* lxxvii. (1630) 203 The lessor is not ousted nor disseised of his freehold. **1767** BLACKSTONE *Comm.* II. vii. 116 Farmers were ousted of their leases made by tenants in tail. **1847** C. G. ADDISON *Law of Contracts* II. iii. III. (1883) 635 A recovery by one party ousts the other of his right to recover.

b. To exclude, bar, take away (a right, privilege, etc.).

1656 *Burton's Diary* (1828) I. 83 You oust both the master's and his Highness's right. **1769** BLACKSTONE *Comm.* IV. xxii. 298 In such cases bail is ousted or taken away, wherever the offence is of a very enormous nature. **1848** ARNOULD *Mar. Insur.* (1866) II. IV. i. 1029 Their jurisdiction cannot be ousted by any contract of the parties.

2. *transf.* To eject or expel from any place or position, turn out. Const *of, from,* or with double obj.

1668 PEPYS *Diary* 11 Nov., They.. do bring in Mr. Littleton, Sir Thomas's brother, and oust all the rest. **1787** JEFFERSON *Writ.* (1859) II. 294 An intrigue is already begun for ousting him from his place. **1832** SOUTHEY in *Q. Rev.* XLVII. 512 They prayed, that the popish lords and bishops might be forthwith ousted the House of Peers. **1868** FREEMAN *Norm. Conq.* II. ix. 418 It was impossible altogether to oust him from command.

b. To drive (a thing) out of use or fashion.

1865 RAWLINSON *Anc. Mon.* III. vi. 198 The present language.. ousted the former. **1887** T. HARDY *Woodlanders* I. ii. 33 The.. waggons.. were built on those ancient lines whose proportions have been ousted by modern patterns.

Hence **'ousted** *ppl. a.*, **'ousting** *vbl. sb.*

1813 H. & J. SMITH *Horace in Lond.* 36 Oh, ousted elves! companions boon! **1864** *Reader* 9 Apr. 447/1 Prophesying the ousting of the Philistines from the promised land. **1866** LOWELL *Seward-Johnson Reaction* Pr. Wks. 1890 V. 321 It enabled the new proprietors and the ousted ones to live.. together.

ouster[1] (ˈaʊstə(r)). *Law.* [AF. *ouster* vb. inf. (see prec.) used sbst.: see -ER[4].] **a.** Ejection from a freehold or other possession, deprivation of a corporeal or incorporeal hereditament. Also, eviction (from office, etc.) by judicial process or as a result of revolution or political upheaval.

1531 *Dial. on Laws Eng.* II. liv. (1638) 163 An immediate putting out of the plaintife, which in French is called an ouster. **1642** tr. *Perkins' Prof. Bk.* ix. §600 After the ouster, and before his entry. **1721** *St. German's Doctor & Stud.* 337 To save themselves from confessing of an Ouster. **1768** BLACKSTONE *Comm.* III. x. 167 Ouster, or dispossession, is a wrong or injury that carries with it the amotion of possession.

fig. **1888** TRAILL *Will. III* 169 To this virtual 'ouster' of their jurisdiction over the question the Lords very naturally objected.

b. In lay use: dismissal, expulsion; the action of manœuvring out of (a place or position). Now chiefly *U.S.*

1961 P. HOLMES *Sheppard Murder Case* ix. 82 Mr. Y, who had been asked no questions about a possible criminal record, had answered in the negative when asked if he had ever been a witness in any court. If it could be shown that Mr. Y had testified at his 1943 trial this answer could be made the basis for his ouster. **1967** K. GILES *Death in Diamonds* ix. 164 Mary Smith had to leave because of her bad influence on the other girls. She was fifteen when she got the ouster. **1968** *Telegraph* (Brisbane) 3 May 11/1 Mr. Cecil Harmsworth King lost his job as chairman of the International Publishing Corporation in a 'palace revolution' by his own directors. The ouster came three weeks after.. a critical article. **1972** *Newsweek* 10 Jan. 25/3 When the court ouster came, the vets.. marched out, clenched fists raised. **1973** *Listener* 20 Dec. 842/1 It is the hope.. that enough damning evidence would be found to force the ouster of the President overnight—to make him resign. **1974** *Spartanburg* (S. Carolina) *Herald* 22 Apr. A1/2-3 The report.. forced the resignation of Lt. Gen. David Elazar, the military chief of staff, and fueled demands for the ouster of Defense Minister Moshe Dayan. **1975** *N.Y. Times* 12 Sept. 6/1 The Communists appeared eager not to be isolated from power as a result of the recent ouster from the premiership and the High Council of the Revolution of Gen. Vasco Gonçalves, whom they had backed. **1976** *Honolulu Star-Bull.* 21 Dec. A-2/2 Hay said one problem still open in Chile concerns persons missing since Allende's ouster and death. **1977** *Time* 9 May 17/2 He was especially anxious to court the Kremlin in view of the rapid cooling of the U.S.'s interest in Ethiopia following the junta's ouster of the Emperor.

'ouster[2]. [f. OUST *v.* + -ER[1].] One who ousts.

1886 BLACKMORE *Springhaven* x, Ousters and filibusters, in the form of railway companies and communists.

‖**ouster-le-main.** *Feudal Law.* [a. AF. *ouster la main*, in L. *āmovēre manum* to take away or remove the hand.] A livery of land out of the sovereign's hands, on a judgement given for one who has pleaded that the sovereign has no title to hold it; also, a judgement or writ granting such livery. **b.** The delivery of lands out of a guardian's hands on a ward's coming of age.

[**1321-2** *Rolls of Parlt.* I. 404/1 Il prie a nostre Seignur le Roi, q'il voille comaunder au dit Richard de ouster la main des biens avantditz.] **1485** *Ibid.* VI. 280/2 By Petition, Livere, Ouster la mayne, or otherwise. *a* **1558** STAUNFORD *Kings Prerog.* x. (1567) 37 b, Learne whether the kinges interest is suche that after the deathe of the lunatike.. there must be an *Ouster le mayn* sued. *a* **1625** SIR H. FINCH *Law* (1636) 329 An ouster lemain shall be awarded for the partie out of the Chancerie. **1766** BLACKSTONE *Comm.* II. 68 When the male heir arrived to the age of twenty one, or the heir-female to that of sixteen, they might sue out their livery or *ousterlemain.*

[**ouster-le-mer,** an error in the Law Dicts. for OULTER-LE-MER.]

†**oustil.** *Obs.* In 5 oustyll, 6 oustell. [a. OF. *oustil*, F. *outil*, in 12th c. *ustil*:—pop. L. type **usetilium*, app. from **usetile*, altered from L. *ūtensile* UTENSIL (Hatz.-Darm.).] A tool.

c **1477** CAXTON *Jason* 71 The right oustyll that polisshith and enlumyneth us and our rude ingenyes. **1530** PALSGR. 250/1 Oustell a tole to worke with, *oustil.*

oustiti (ˈuːstɪtɪ). [ad. F. *ouistiti* (used in same sense) (see WISTITI).] = OUTSIDER 4.

¶Properly spelt *ouistiti.*

1941 G. HEYER *Envious Casca* x. 178 'Which would lead one to suppose that the murderer found the door locked, and turned the key from the outside.' 'With an *oustiti*,' nodded the Sergeant. **1962** 'D. BETTERIDGE' *Package Holiday Spy Case* ii. 19 An essential item of a burglar's tool kit is.. an *oustiti*. It resembles a long pair of pliers, but.. has two semi-circular metal tongues. Inserted into a keyhole, it will grip firmly a key on the other side, and gentle but powerful wrist-work will turn it in the lock.

Oustmen, obs. form of OSTMEN.

out (aʊt), *adv.* Forms: 1 út, 2–4 ut, (3 hut, hout, 4–5 ouȝt, 4–6 oute, owte, 5–7 ought, owȝt), 4–7 owt, (6 owtt(e), 3– out, (9 *Sc.* and *north. dial.* oot). [Com. Teut.: OE. *út* = OFris., OS. *ût* (MDu. *uut*, MLG. *ût*, Du. *uit*, LG. *ut*), OHG. *ûz* (MHG. *ûz*, Ger. *aus*), ON. *út* (Sw. *ut*, Da. *ud*), Goth. *ût* = Skr. *ud-* verbal prefix 'out'. Orig. only an adv., but in OHG. sometimes, in MHG. oftener, and in Ger., Du., Fris. regularly, a preposition also. In Eng., OUT *prep.* (q.v.) is exceptional, and felt as elliptical; the prepositional sense = L. *ex*, Gr. ἐξ, ἐκ, is regularly expressed by adding *of*, = OE. *út of*, OS. *ût af*, Sw. *ut af*, Da. *ud af.*

OUT OF *prep. phr.*, on account of its syntactic unity, and its importance as a preposition, is in this Dictionary treated as a Main word. *Out* is also followed by FROM, but in *out from* the two words remain notionally distinct, as in *away from, down from, up from*: see FROM *prep.* 1.]

I. Of motion or direction.

* *simply.*

1. a. Expressing motion or direction from within a space, or from a point considered as a centre.

c **888** K. ÆLFRED *Boeth.* xxxv. §5 Ic ne mæȝ ut aredian. *c* **893** —— *Oros.* I. i. §3 Seo ea.. wið eastan ut on þa sæ floweð. *c* **900** tr. *Bæda's Hist.* III. viii. [x.] (1890) 180 þa fluȝon heo forhte ut. *c* **1000** *Sax. Leechd.* II. 222 Ateon ut þa horhestan wætan. **1140-54** *O.E. Chron.* an. 1140 þat me sculde leten ut þe king of prisun for þe eorl. *c* **1205** LAY. 26533 Sone his sweord he ut abræid. *c* **1250** *Gen. & Ex.* 3124 ȝet ic sal pharaon, Or ȝe gon vt, don an wreche on. **13..** *Cursor M.* 993 (Cott.) Out [so *F., Tr.; Gött.* vte] es put sua wreched adam. **1340** *Ayenb.* 150 þes yefþe.. bestrepþ and kest out þe rote and þe zenne of ire. **1375** BARBOUR *Bruce* II. 352 The blud owt at thar byrnys brest. **1382** WYCLIF *Matt.* viii. 12 Forsothe the sonys of the rewme shulen be cast out in to vttremest derknessis. *c* **1400** MAUNDEV. (Roxb.) xxix. 132 So sall þai fynd þe passage oute. **1486** *Bk. St. Albans* A iij, Wringe the waater owte. **1535** COVERDALE *Exod.* x. 6 And he turned him, & wente out from Pharao. **1551** BIBLE *Matt.* viii. 12 The children of the kyngedome shalbe caste oute into vtter darcknes. **1568** GRAFTON *Chron.* I. 185 None so hardy to looke out into the streetes. **1637** SHIRLEY *Gamester* IV, I'll pour it out. **1719** DE FOE *Crusoe* II. ii, I.. ordered a boat out. **1789** *Hist.* in *Ann. Reg.* 18 Conciliatory expressions were.. thrown out towards the close of the speech. **1854** SIR E. B. HAMLEY in A. I. Shand *Life* (1895) I. iv. 74 General Adams' horse struck out and kicked me on the shin. **1871** MORLEY *Crit. Misc.* Ser. I. *Carlyle* (1878) 175 Here was, indeed, not a way out, but a way of erect living within.

b. From within doors, into the open air.

c **1000** *Ags. Gosp.* John xviii. 29 þa eode pilatus ut to him. *c* **1205** LAY. 19763 And ut wenden [*c* 1275 hout eode] bi-nihte. *c* **1350** *Will. Palerne* 3068, & bi a priue posterne passad ouȝt er daie. **1382** WYCLIF *Matt.* xi. 9 But what thing wente ȝe out for to seen? **1776** *Trial of Nundocomar* 23/1 If he had been so ill as not to be able to come out. **1870** E. PEACOCK *Ralf Skirl.* III. 139 [They] asked him to go out with them for a ride. *Mod.* He seldom goes out in this weather.

c. From home or ordinary home life to an expedition, to the field (of fight or the chase). ***to set out***, to start on an expedition or journey: see SET. ***to call one out*** (see CALL *v.* 32 c), ***come out, have one out***, i.e. to a duel.

1597 SHAKS. *2 Hen. IV*, III. ii. 126 There are other men fitter to goe out, then I. **1613** —— *Hen. VIII*, II. ii. 5 When they were ready to set out for London. **1655** STANLEY *Hist. Philos.* III. (1701) 85/2 His Life being wholly spent at home, saving when he went out in Military Service. **1829** HOOD *Eugene Aram* xxxvi, Two stern-faced men set out from Lynn. **1855** SMEDLEY *H. Coverdale* iii, If he feels aggrieved, he can have you out (not that I admire duelling). **1869** TENNYSON *Holy Grail* 719 Those that had gone out upon the Quest. **1870, 1890** [see GO *v.* 87 c].

d. Of a river: From its channel, beyond its banks.

1854 *Jrnl. R. Agric. Soc.* XV. I. 221 A good rain is sure to send the waters out.

e. From among others; from one's company or surroundings.

See also under CHOOSE, HUNT, SEARCH, SEEK *vbs.*

1297 [see CHOOSE *v.* 11]. *c* **1420** *Pallad. on Husb.* II. 276 Ek of the yonge out trie Oon heer, oon theer. *c* **1425** *Eng. Conq. Irel.* 34 þerfor out chese one of two. *c* **1530** tr. *Erasmus' Serm. Ch. Jesus* (1901) 11 The aungels appoynted out to protecte and defende vs. **1581** MULCASTER *Positions* xxxvii. (1887) 149 Choise is a great prince,.. and culs owt the best. **1589** *Acts Privy Council* (1898) XVII. 427 For the bolting out of the truth thereof. *a* **1649** WINTHROP *Hist. New Eng.* (1853) I. 420, I desire to hear.. whether you have inquired out a chamber for me. **1866** TREVELYAN in *Macm. Mag.* Mar. 416 Magistrates would choose out the most active and fierce of the young citizens. *Mod.* I will look out a book for her.

f. From one's own hands or actual occupation; into the hands or occupation of another.

See also under HIRE, LAY, LEND, LET, PUT, etc.

1449- [see LAY *v.*[1] 56 c]. **1526** [see LET *v.*[1] 37 f]. **1560** DAUS tr. *Sleidane's Comm.* 252 b, Howe they had.. geven out their monie for interest. **1589-** [see HIRE *v.* 3]. **1609** DEKKER *Gull's Horne-bk.* (1812) 129 He shall.. put out money upon his return. **1782** MISS BURNEY *Cecilia* IX. x, I mean to put my whole estate out to nurse.

g. From a stock or store into the hands or possession of many; into portions or parts: implying distribution and division. Esp. with *deal, dole, cantle, parcel, portion, serve, share*, and the like.

1535- [see DEAL *v.* 4 b]. **1583-1674** [see CANTLE *v.* 2]. **1652-62** HEYLIN *Cosmogr.* II. (1682) 39 The great Empire of his Father was parcelled out into members. *c* **1680** BEVERIDGE *Serm.* (1729) I. 406 As if the universe was to be parcell'd out among many. **1741-62** [see DOLE *v.* I, 2]. **1840** R. H. DANA *Bef. Mast* xxvii. 91 Our guns were loaded.. cartridges served out, matches lighted. **1849** MACAULAY *Hist. Eng.* vi. II. 137 The design of again confiscating and again portioning out the soil of half the island. **1868** FREEMAN *Norm. Conq.* (1876) II. vii. 52 England was now portioned out among a few Earls.

h. *Out* may be added to a vb. trans. or intr. with the sense of driving, putting, or getting out, with or by means of the action in question, e.g. *to bow, crowd, din, drum, hiss, hoot, ring, smoke* (a person, etc.) *out.* See the verbs.

2. Away from some recognized place; from the land (as the place inhabited by men); from the shore, into the sea or ocean; from one's own country, to the colonies or distant lands; away, to a distance.

a **1123** *O.E. Chron.* an. 1101 Se cyng.. scipa ut on sæ sende. **1672** C. MANNERS in *12th Rep. Hist. MSS. Comm.* App. v. 25 Our Navy puts out again to sea stronger than at first. **1711** STEELE *Spect.* No. 174 ¶5 The Freight and Assurance out and home. **1722** DE FOE *Col. Jack* (1840) 113 Let us take a walk in the fields a little out from the houses. **1850** *Tait's Mag.* XVII. 466/1 An offer.. to go out to Australia. **1878** HUXLEY *Physiogr.* 131 They are carried by the river right out to sea. *Mod.* Missionaries going out to India and China. Troops were sent out from the mother country. He met interesting people on the voyage out.

3. a. So as to project or extend beyond the general surface or limits; as in ***to hang, jut, shoot,*** or ***stick out. to hold out***: see HOLD *v.* 41.

1535 [see HOLD *v.* 41 a]. *a* **1548** HALL *Chron., Hen. VIII* 134 b, So that it bossed out and frounced very stately to behold. **1658** J. JONES *Ovid's Ibis* 67 A sharp clift shuts [= shoots] out like a woman. **1796** *Hist.* in *Ann. Reg.* 77 The French.. held out language promissory of equitable conditions. **1896** *N. & Q.* 8th Ser. IX. 160/1 The room.. built out to serve as a library and residence for Coleridge.

b. Expressing extension or prolongation (in space or time), as in ***to beat, draw, open, stretch out.***

c **1380** WYCLIF *Sel. Wks.* II. 198 Stretche out þin hond. **1483, 1553** [see DRAW *v.* 87 c, d]. **1596-** [see EKE *v.* 3]. **1608** WILLET *Hexapla Exod.* 718 The sabbathes holding out the whole day. **1632** MILTON *L'Allegro* 111 The Lubbar Fend.. stretch'd out all the Chimney's length. **1674** N. FAIRFAX *Bulk & Selv.* 27 The soul may be every where, where the body is stretched out. **1774** GOLDSM. *Nat. Hist* (1776) II. 200 To lengthen out the period of life. **1806** HUTTON *Course Math.* I. 286 When every Side of any Figure is produced out, the Sum of all the Outward Angles thereby made, is equal to Four Right Angles. **1841-93** [see DRAW *v.* 87 c, d].

c. ***from this out***: henceforth, from now on; also ***from here*** (***on***) ***out, from that out.*** *colloq.* (chiefly *U.S.* and *Anglo-Irish*).

1867 F. A. BUCK *Lett.* (1930) 214 Now, I am going to try to be a Jew from this out. **1882** W. D. HOWELLS *Mod.*

Instance in *Century Mag.* Apr. 925/1 I'll take a back seat from this out. **1899** W. B. Yeats *Let.* 28 Nov. (1954) 330, I imagine I am about the only person who belongs to the orderly world she is likely to meet from this out. She seems to be perfectly mad. **1905** H. Corkran *Lucie & I* 36 From this out I will think of you as a young *diablesse.* **1907** J. J. Horgan *Great Catholic Laymen* (ed. 2) i. 37 Napoleon was then at the height of his power. From that out his Empire began to decline. **1922** Joyce *Ulysses* 432 Mrs Marion from this out, my dear man, when you speak to me. **1941** in H. Wentworth *Amer. Dial. Dict.* (1944) 434/1 He has run the race and is fairly entitled to sit on the sidelines from here out. **1942** *Ibid.*, Bob Maslow's at the controls from here on out. **1972** A. Friedman in Cox & Dyson *20th-Cent. Mind.* I. xii. 420 There are symbolic signs everywhere that Charlotte's and Adam's lives from here on out will be lives of protracted emptiness and captive anguish.

** *in pregnant and transferred uses.*

4. a. Expressing removal from its proper place or from its position when *in.* See put *out.*

*c*893 K. Ælfred *Oros.* iv. v. §2 þa sticode him mon þa eaȝan ut. **1382** Wyclif *Jer.* lii. 11 The eȝen of Sedechie he putte out. *c* **1400** [see cut *v.* 57 a]. **1611** [see break *v.* 55 a]. **1613** Purchas *Pilgrimage* 273 [The book] was after by the Iewes altered, putting out and in at their pleasure. **1840** Thackeray *Catherine* xi, Mr. Wood sat near, laughing his sides out. *Mod.* He has had his shoulder put out at football.

b. From a post or office.

1746 H. Walpole *Let. to H. Mann* 14 Feb., The triumphant party are not at all in the humour to be turned out. **1853** Lytton *My Novel* ix. iv, It does not seem to me possible..that you and your party should ever go out. *Mod.* The seat was contested at the last election, and the former member was turned out.

c. In *Cricket*, etc. From being batsman. (See 19 c in II.)

1755 *Game at Cricket* 8 Though..the Player be bowl'd out. **1772** in Waghorn *Cricket Scores* (1899) 85 *note*, Those marked thus * were off their ground; † run out; ‡ catched out; § bowled out. **1806–7** J. Beresford *Miseries Hum. Life* (1826) iii. ix, Bowled out at the first ball. **1836** in 'Bat' *Crick. Mem.* (1850) 100 All attempts to get him out were futile. **1843** *Blackw. Mag.* LIV. 171 They put our men out pretty fast. Hanmer got..run out after a splendid hit.

5. a. From one's normal or equable state of mind, or ordinary course of action; into confusion, perplexity, or disturbance of feeling. See put *out.*

1588 Shaks. *L.L.L.* v. ii. 172 They do not marke me, and that brings me out. **1600** —— *A.Y.L.* iii. ii. 265 You bring me out. **1875** Kinglake *Crimea* (1877) V. i. 266 He..was 'thrown out'. **1887** A. Birrell *Obiter Dicta* Ser. ii. 282 Neither he nor any other sensible man puts himself out about new books.

b. From one's harmonious relations; into unfriendliness or quarrelling. See also fall *out.*

1530 [see fall *v.* 94 e]. **1637** Shirley *Gamester* i, Wine made them fall out. **1822** Hazlitt *Table-t.* II. vii. 148 Friends not unfrequently fall out and never meet again for some idle misunderstanding.

6. a. So as to be no longer alight or burning; into darkness or extinction; as *to do, go,* or *put out.*

c **1400** [see go *v.* 87 d]. *c* **1440** *Gesta Rom.* i. xviii. 64 (Harl. MS.) And doth oute the fire. *a* **1548** Hall *Chron., Hen. VI* 99 b, When the greate fire of this discencion..was..utterly quenched out. **1560** Daus tr. *Sleidane's Comm.* 119 Fyngereth the candell, putteth it out. **1679** *Hist. Jetzer* 12 Putting out a Candle which remain'd..lighted. **1712** Addison *Spect.* No. 265 ¶9 A Candle goes half out in the Light of the Sun. **1840** Marryat *Poor Jack* xxiii, He snuffed it out.

b. From being in existence or activity; from being in currency or in vogue; into extinction; as *to die, give, go, kill out.*

1523– [see give *v.* 62 e]. **1650** W. Brough *Schism* 556 Will you give out for a lesser time of tryal? **1821** *Examiner* 803/2 The charge is now falsified..and decidedly going out. **1871** Smiles *Charac.* i. (1876) 29 The nations that are idle and luxurious..must inevitably die out. **1878** J. R. O'Flanagan *Irish Bar* (1879) 422 Possibly, if Davis had lived longer, the politician might have killed out the poet.

7. a. To the conclusion or finish; to an end, and so either to completion or to exhaustion.

a **1300** *Cursor M.* 14507 (Cott.) Biscops war þai þan a-bute, Ilkan bot his tueluemoth vte [so *G.*; *Tr.* oute, *Laud* owte]. *c* **1400** *Laud Troy Bk.* (E.E.T.S.) 3459 Or this x ȝere go fully out. **1560** Daus tr. *Sleidane's Comm.* 241 The trewes commeth oute at October nexte. **1668** Davenant *Man's the Master* v. i, Perhaps, I may have patience to hear you out. **1722** Quincy *Lex. Physico-Med.* (ed. 2) 2 When a Woman goes not her full time out with Child. **1746** in Waghorn *Cricket Scores* (1899) 37 The match to be played out. **1817** Keats *Sonn. Grasshopper & Cricket*, Tired out with fun. **1886** Sir J. Stirling in *Law Times Rep.* LV. 284/1 The case has not been tried out.

b. With intrans. vb., forming a compound trans. vb., as *to fight it out, talk it out.* Also, *to have it out*, to bring it to a finish or settlement; also with other objects; also, to discuss fully or reveal (a matter); to settle (a dispute or misunderstanding) *with* someone.

1535 Coverdale *Ps.* lv. 23 The bloudthurstie and disceatfull shal not lyue out half their daies. **1586** T. B. *La Primaud. Fr. Acad.* (1589) 383 If in the mean time he feast it out. **1601** Holland *Pliny* xxxiii. xxiv, Fencers trying it out with unrebated swords. **1601** Shaks. *All's Well* v. iii. 66 While shamefull hate sleepes out the afternoone. **1650** Trapp *Comm. Deut.* xxix. 19 As it were to cross God, and to try it out with him. **1764** S. Johnson 22 July in *Philobiblon Soc.* VI. 38 You will hardly be quite at ease till you have talked yourself out. **1811** Jane Austen *Sense & Sens.* II. viii. 129 She had better have her cry out at once and have done with it. **1825** H. Wilson *Mem.* I. 77 O let us have it all out now, and have done with it. **1839** Dickens *Nickleby* xxxi. 305, I shall double-lock myself in with him and have it out before I die. **1847** J. A. Froude *Shadows of Clouds* iv. 52 The result was the advice which best harmonized with the suggestion of his own heart, to go off at once to Morlands, have it all out with Emma, and put his father's letter into Mr. Hardinge's hands. **1859** Trollope *Bertrams* (1867) 21, I shall have the matter out with him now. **1873** Browning *Red Cott. Nt.-cap* 382 Suppose we have it out Here in the fields, decide the question so? **1880** Trollope *Duke's Children* II. xi. 126 Let us have this out, Mabel, before we go. **1884** G. Moore *Mummer's Wife* (1887) 217 Leave her to have her cry out. **1888** Bryce *Amer. Commw.* III. xc. 247 The best thing was to let him talk himself out. **1932** E. Bowen *To North* xxvi. 385 You must have this out with Emmeline, find how she stands with this young man and ..*strongly* discourage the whole affair. **1959** H. Hamilton *Answer in Negative* x. 118, I was trying to decide whether I ought to leave it alone or have it out with him. **1971** *Where* Dec. 361/1 We eventually went to the LEA and saw an assistant education officer who agreed that we should meet the head and the doctor and have the whole thing out.

c. To a full end, completely, quite, outright. See also all out.

c **1300** *Beket* (Percy Soc.) 1956 Here names for here schrewede: ne beoth noȝt forȝute ut. *c* **1470** Henry *Wallace* viii. 931 Xx^ty dais owt the ost remaynit thar. **1598** Barret *Theor. Warres* 110 Such as bee slaine right out. **1610** Shaks. *Temp.* i. ii. 41 Then thou was't not Out three yeeres old. **1675** E. W[ilson] *Spadacr. Dunelm.* Pref. 20 Those that know it full out as well as they must. **1812** in *Examiner* 7 Sept. 564/1 He must go and kill him out.

8. To an issue; to an intelligible or explicit result or solution; as *to find, make, puzzle, work out; to help out; to come, fall, turn out.*

1534 Tindale *Phil.* ii. 12 Worke out youre awne saluacion with feare and tremblynge. **1709** *Tatler* No. 101 ¶7, I must desire my Readers to help me out..in the Correction of these my Essays. **1743** Emerson *Fluxions* 120 If its Value comes out negative it is concave in that Point. **1887** L. Carroll *Game of Logic* i. §2. 25 We will work out one other Syllogism.

9. To the full, complete, or utmost degree; in a way that bespeaks an effort at completeness, effect, or display, as in *to deck, dress, fit, rig out.*

1555 W. Watreman *Fardle Facions* ii. viii. 180 The women are not sette out to allure. **1637** Shirley *Gamester* iii, More..Than well could furnish out two country-weddings. *a* **1649** Winthrop *Hist. New Eng.* (1853) II. 76 The church furnished him out, and provided a pinnace to transport him. **1863** Fr. A. Kemble *Resid. Georgia* 125 In fitting him out for his departure. **1874** Symonds *Italy & Greece, Siena* 66 A procession of priests and acolytes..and little girls dressed out in white.

10. a. From a state of quiescence into a state of activity; from a contained or involved condition into one of accessibility; as *to break* or *burst out, to open out.*

a **1000–** [see break *v.* 55 b]. **1857** Buckle *Civiliz.* I. viii. 518 The war that now broke out lasted seven years. **1865** H. Kingsley *Hillyars & Burtons* xlvi, You broke out on me, and bullied me, assuming I was going to swindle you. **1894** Wolseley *Marlborough* II. 179 A good line of communication was soon opened out. **1895** *Times* 19 Jan. 11/6 The result..prevented China from putting out her full power.

b. Into outward expression or manifestation; into clearness or distinctness; into blossom or leaf.

a **1548** Hall *Chron., Rich. III* 27 b, They layd the dead bodies out upon the bed. **1560** Daus tr. *Sleidane's Comm.* 27 b, The Byshoppes Tyrrannye is there paynted out. **1594** Shaks. *Rich. III*, i. ii. 263 Shine out faire Sunne,..That I may see my Shadow as I passe. **1642–3** Earl of Newcastle *Declaration* in Rushw. *Hist. Coll.* (1721) V. 134 A Course..chalked out to me by themselves. **1852** M. Arnold *The Future* ad fin., The stars come out. **1895** 'Ian Maclaren' *Days of Auld Lang Syne, For Conscience Sake* ii, Each spring the primroses came out below.

11. a. Into utterance of sound; so as to be heard; aloud; as *to call, cry, shout, speak out.*

1382 [see cry *v.* 21]. **1480** Caxton *Chron. Eng.* ccix. 192 Men myght here ther blowyng out with hornes more than a myle. *a* **1533** Ld. Berners *Huon* lxxxiii. 262 Speke out hyer that ye may the better be herde. **1605** Shaks. *Lear* v. iii. 109 Come hither Herald..And read out this. **1697** Dryden *Virg. Georg.* iv. 510 Cyrene..seiz'd with Fear, Cries out, conduct my Son, conduct him here. **1712** Steele *Spect.* No. 266 ¶2 A muttering Voice, as if between Soliloquy and speaking out. **1869** Tennyson *Pelleas & Ettarre* 359 All the old echoes hidden in the wall Rang out like hollow woods at huntingtide. **1887** Hall Caine *Son of Hagar* i. iii, A solitary crow flew across the sky, and cawed out its guttural note.

b. In the way of disclosure; to the knowledge of others or to public knowledge; openly.

13.. *Cursor M.* 27293 (Cott.) Þe preist..noght sceu his sinnes vte [*Fairf.* out]. *a* **1440** *Sir Eglam.* 57 What some ever that ye to me say, Y schalle hyt nevyr owte caste. *c* **1440** *Jacob's Well* 89 He þat schewyth out wyth his mowth..þe malyce of his herte. **1579** Spenser *Sheph. Cal.* Sept. 173 Say it out Diggon. **1637** Shirley *Gamester* v, That, if things come out, we should keep counsel. **1738** Pope *Epil. Sat.* i. 36 Come, come, at all I laugh he laughs, no doubt; The only diff'rence is I dare laugh out. **1872** *Routledge's Ev. Boys Ann.* 614/1 To stand up to him and tell him right out what a fool he was.

12. a. Into public notice, publicity, or publication; into public circulation; from the printing press.

1542 Udall *Erasm. Apoph.* 197 For epitaphies are..not set out till the parties bee deceassed. *a* **1568** Ascham *Scholem.* ii. (Arb.) 140 Not yet set out in Print. **1573–** [see come *v.* 63 l]. **1662** H. More *Philos. Writ.* Pref. p. xi, Before this second volume of Descartes his came out. **1752** A. Murphy *Gray's Inn Jrnl.* No. 1, I cannot issue out my first Performance, without feeling an extraordinary Solicitude for the Event. **1895** *Bookman* Oct. 12/1 Mr. Hare's Autobiography..is apparently not to come out this season.

b. Of a person: Into society; into professional life; into work or service; upon the stage.

1782 [see come *v.* 63 o]. **1806** A. Hunter *Culina* 269 The great object is to 'bring the young lady out',..in other words, to exhibit her as a show. **1849** Ld. Houghton in *Life* (1891) I. x. 433 My sister in town bringing out a young sister-in-law. **1885** J. K. Jerome *On the Stage* 6 Here the question very naturally arose, 'How can I get out?'

13. a. With ellipsis of intr. vb. (*go, come,* etc.); hence functioning as a verb without inflexion. From the 1960s frequently used as a chant (preceded by the name of a politician or by a word signifying something unwanted) by political demonstrators. Also used in written political slogans.

(In imperative use this approaches an interjection: cf. out *int.* See also the inflected out *v.* below.)

[*c* **1175** Wace *Roman de Rou* 8080 Normanz escrient: Deus aïe! La gent Englesche *Ut, ut!* escrie; Co est l'enseigne que jo di, Quant Engleis saillent hors a cri.] *c* **1386** Chaucer *Prioress' T.* 124 Mordre wol out, certeyn it wol nat faille. *c* **1440** *Jacob's Well* 2 Deep wose..in whiche þe soule styketh sumtyme so faste, þat he may noȝt out, but schulde perysshe. **1544** Bale *Oldcastell* in *Harl. Misc.* (Malh.) I. 254 It was concluded amonge them that..processe shulde oute agaynst hym. **1596** Shaks. *Merch. V.* ii. ii. 85 In the end truth will out. **1605** —— *Macb.* v. i. 39 Out, damned spot: out, I say! **1647** Trapp *Comm. Rom.* vii. 17 An ill inmate that will not out, till the house falleth on the head of it. **1764** Foote *Patron* iii. Wks. 1799 I. 356 The whole secret will certainly out. **1869** Freeman *Norm. Conq.* (1875) III. xv. 478 The English..mocked with cries of 'Out, out', every foe who entered or strove to enter. **1884** Tennyson *Becket* i. i, O drunken ribaldry! Out, beast! out, bear!..begone! **1887** W. Westall *Her Two Millions* xxvii, 'Murder will out'. They say so, because they have no idea how often murders don't out. **1968** *Times* 8 July 1/7 More than 100 Pakistani students took over the Pakistan High Commission in Lowndes Square, S.W., last night... Demonstrators lined the balcony chanting and waving placards saying: 'This building is occupied' and 'Ayub out'. **1970** B. Levin *Pendulum Years* xv. 259 The streets of Britain continued [in the 1960s] to echo to cries of 'Americans out of Vietnam!' and the ritual chanting of 'Ho-ho-ho Chi Minh!' **1970** D. Neville-Rolfe *Power without Glory* ii. 244 Even the stone-throwing rioters displayed their own brand of charm when they paraded in front of the Embassy their very home-made banners boldly declaring '*out—perfide albino*'. **1970** (*recorded from oral evidence*) Wilson *out!* **1973** *Times* 21 Nov. 18/4 'Anti-abortion—*out out out*; Free Abortion on Demand —*in in in*,' they chanted. **1976** *New Society* 26 Aug. 435/2 (*heading*) Hashish, out. **1977** *Woman's Own* 26 Mar. 31/3 Then you notice the blackened buildings, boarded up houses and the painted slogans in the housing estates: 'Brits out.' 'Join the IRA.'

b. So *out with* = have out, bring out. (Cf. the similar *away, down, in, off, on, up with*, and see with.) *out with it*: an exhortation to a speaker to admit or assert something over which he is hesitating.

c **1205** Lay. 23931 Arður ut [*c* 1275 up] mid his sweorde. **1548** Udall, etc. *Erasm. Par. Acts* 87 b, They out with theyr swerdes, and cutte the ropes. **1583** Stubbes *Anat. Abus.* ii. (1882) 54 Out with him..let him go to plow and cart. **1591** Shaks. *Two Gent.* iv. iv. 22 Out with the dog (saies one). **1694** Motteux *Rabelais* iv. xxii. (1737) 95 Out with all your Sails. **1709** Prior *Yng. Gentleman in Love* 67 Our Sex will —What? out with it:—Lye. **1820** Scott *Abbot* xix, Rather too prompt to out with poniard. **1860** Thackeray *Round. Papers, Thorn in Cushion* Wks. 1872 X. 36 Out with your cambric, dear ladies, and let us all whimper together. **1924** Galsworthy *Forest* i. i. 11 Out with it, Mr. Farrell. **1974** 'S. Woods' *Done to Death* 35 Come on, Dick, out with it. What do you know about them?

14. With ellipsis of trans. vb. (*put, bring,* etc.).

1819–20 W. Irving *Sketch-bk., John Bull* (1865) 389 Ready at a wink or nod, to out sabre, and flourish it over the orator's head. **1857** C. Gribble in *Merc. Marine Mag.* (1858) V. 3 Out top-gallant-sails and flying jib! **1891** M. O'Rell *Frenchm. in Amer.* 246 The Westerner may out pistol and shoot you if you annoy him.

II. Of position. (A series of senses corresponding to those in I, as indicating the position resulting from the motion there expressed.)

* *simply.*

15. a. Expressing position or situation beyond the bounds of, or not within, a space.

c **1425** Lydg. *Assembly of Gods* 1999 Neuerthelesse my wyt ys so thynne..That hit ys owte where hyt went ynne. **1560** Daus tr. *Sleidane's Comm.* 94 Where the Sea brake in over the walles, that are made to kepe it out. **1598** Shaks. *Merry W.* ii. iii. 47 If I see a sword out, my finger itches to make one. **1599** —— *Much Ado* iii. v. 37 When the age is in, the wit is out. *a* **1770** Jortin *Serm.* (1771) II. iv. 72 Wee shut out so many enemies to our repose. **1843** *Blackw. Mag.* LIV. 7 My sword was already out. **1860** Gen. P. Thompson *Audi Alt.* III. ci. 4 If these things are not said in parliament, they must be said out.

b. Not within doors; not 'in'; in the open air. So *school is out* (chiefly *U.S.*): school is at an end. *out to lunch*: see lunch *sb.*[2] 2 b. See also *day out* (day *sb.* 19), *night out* (night *sb.* 5 a).

c **1440** *Promp. Parv.* 375/1 Owt, or owte..*Extra, foras.* *c* **1450** *St. Cuthbert* (Surtees) 5337 Þe husbande of þat house was oute. **1603** G. Owen *Pembrokeshire* vii. (1891) 56 They feede not their sheepe with haye in winter..but let them gett their livinge out them selfes. **1775** Sheridan *Rivals* i. ii, Did you see Sir Lucius while you was out? **1814** Jane Austen *Lett.* (1884) II. 231 We were out a great part of the morning ..shopping. **1827** W. Taylor *Poems* (ed. 2) 91 In that whimp'ling burn when the school was out. **1843** Mrs. Stowe *Mayflower* 172 But, when 'school was out', James's spirits foamed over as naturally as a tumbler of soda-water. **1858** RAMSAY *Remin.* vi. (ed. 18) 163 The housemaid was not at home, it being her turn for the Sunday 'out'. **1870** [see EVENING *sb.*[1] 3]. **1887** L. CARROLL *Game of Logic* ii. §6. 50, I have been out for a walk. **1911** in *Sc. Nat. Dict.* (1965) VI. *s.v.*, Word went through the toon like lichtenin, for the school wis out. **1925** WODEHOUSE *Carry On, Jeeves!* v. 108, I have already visited some of New York's places of interest on my evening out. **1948** 'J. TEY' *Franchise Affair* ix. 94 'Shouldn't leave your car. Take it with you... It's Saturday.' 'Saturday?' 'School's out.' 'Oh, I see. But there's nothing in it..that's movable.' **1956** B. HOLIDAY *Lady sings Blues* (1973) ii. 17, I finished up the fifth grade, and as soon as school was out Grandpop put one those big tags around my neck, saying who I was and where I was going. **1965** *Times Lit. Suppl.* 22 Apr. 317/1 In a recent road safety cartoon on B.B.C. television, I was surprised to hear the Americanism 'when school is out'. **1974** 'R. TATE' *Birds of Bloodied Feather* vi. 127 'I trust I'm not disturbing you?' 'What's the time?' 'Four.' 'School's out'... 'Come on in'. **1974** *Times* 8 Apr. 14/7 A retired bricklayer..spoke to me in the owlishly conspiratorial tones of one who has been cheered by his evening out.

c. Away from one's place of residence, abroad, on an expedition; esp. in the field (for war or sport); in arms; away from work, on strike; cf. sense 19b. ***out there***, in the war of 1914–18: at the Western Front; in France (*colloq.*).

1605 SHAKS. *Macb.* IV. iii. 183 There ran a Rumour Of many worthy Fellowes, that were out. —— *Lear* I. i. 33 He hath bin out nine yeares, and away he shall againe. **1697** DAMPIER *Voy.* I. 364, I was a week out with him and saw but four Cows, which were so wild, that we did not get one. **1711** BUDGELL *Spect.* No. 116 ¶4 Sir Roger is so keen at this Sport, that he has been out almost every Day since I came down. **1806** SCOTT *Let. to R. Surtees* Fam. Lett. 1894 I. 66 My great-grandfather was out, as the phrase goes..in 1715. **1887** *Manch. Guard.* 26 Feb. 7 People who had been 'camping out' were beginning to return to their homes. **1890** *Spectator* 29 Sept., Most of the miners are 'out', not for wages, but in defence of the grand principle that non-Union men shall not be employed. **1896** *N. & Q.* 8th Ser. IX. 161/1 [He] was an ardent supporter of Prince Charles Edward, but through illness was unable to be out in 1745. **1917** A. G. EMPEY *Over Top* 302 *Out there*, a term used in Blighty which means 'in France'. Conscientious objectors object to going 'out there'. **1920** W. J. LOCKE *House of Baltazar* xii. 150, I want to kick myself for sitting here in luxury when there's so much to be done out there. I had got my platoon—I was acting first lieutenant—like a high-class orchestra. **1929** *Papers Mich. Acad. Sci., Arts & Lett.* X. 312/2 *Out there*, England's equivalent for 'Over there'. **1974** *Times* 27 Feb. 14/3 The miners are still out; world prices are still rising. **1977** 'J. LE CARRÉ' *Hon. Schoolboy* vi. 121 Pound's in the soup again... Electricians out. Railways out.

d. Of the water of a river: Overflowing its banks, flooding the adjacent ground.

1647 COWLEY *Mistress, Welcome* vi, My Dove..I doubt Would ne're return, had not the Flood been out. *a* **1682** SIR T. BROWNE *Misc. Tracts* (1684) 56 If the River had been out, and the Fields under Water. **1702** THORESBY *Diary* (ed. Hunter) I. 397 The waters were yet out, that we rode through Askwith. **1779** *Hist. Eur.* in *Ann. Reg.* 182/2 The freshes were then out, which seemed to render the river in itself a sufficient rampart. **1854** *Jrnl. R. Agric. Soc.* XV. I. 222 The waters of the Cherwell are soon out, and soon off. *Mod.* At Oxford the floods are now rarely out, and years pass without centre-boards being seen on Port Meadow.

e. Sent forth by authority, issued.

1602 *2nd Pt. Return fr. Parnass.* v. iii. 2105 Writts are out for me, to apprehend me. **1754** *Ess. Manning Fleet* 13 When the Warrants are out, the Men abscond. **1855** MACAULAY *Hist. Eng.* xv. III. 588 Warrants had been out against him; and he had been taken into custody.

f. Not in the hands or occupation of the owner; let or leased; in other hands or occupation.

1591 SHAKS. *Two Gent.* v. ii. 29 *Thu.* Considers she my Possessions?.. *Pro.* They are out by Lease. *a* **1704** LOCKE (J.), The land that is out at rack rent. *a* **1735** ARBUTHNOT (J.), Those lands were out upon leases of four years. *Mod.* Obliged to call in the money that he had lying out.

g. Not included or inserted, omitted; as *to leave out*.

a **1470** [see LEAVE *v.*[1] 14 d]. **1683** MOXON *Mech. Exerc., Printing* xxiii, He makes the mark of Insertion where it is Left out, and only Writes (Out) in the Margin. **1887** L. CARROLL *Game of Logic* i. §1. 6 We agree to leave out the word 'Cakes' altogether.

h. Not in the company; apart; separately.

1607 HEYWOOD *Wom. Kild w. Kindn.* Wks. 1892 II. 121 No by my Faith sir, when you are togither I sitte out.

i. ***to be out for***: to have one's interests or energies directed to, to be intent on (something); also ***to be out to*** (do something). Cf. ALL OUT *adv. phr.* 4. orig. *U.S.*

1901 MERWIN & WEBSTER *Calumet 'K'* i. 13 They're mostly out for results up at the office. Let's see the bill for it. **1901** S. E. WHITE *Westerners* xxix. 272 When they are out to have a good time,..they want somebody they can have their sort of fun with. **1907** BEERBOHM in *Sat. Rev.* 13 Apr. 457/1 She is not 'out for' fun. She is an ardent suffragist. **1912** *Humanitarian* Oct. 76, I am sure that no person in this country, save him who is out for personal gain, wishes us to lag behind in this movement. **1913** H. WALPOLE *Fortitude* III. x. 388 She's out for happiness at any cost and you're out for freedom. *Ibid.* IV. iii. 474 He was 'out' to defend his whole life. **1926** A. L. MAYCOCK *Inquisition* v. 116 All the Inquisitors..were out to convert and reconcile, not to condemn. **1956** A. L. ROWSE *Early Churchills* xii. 236 The Dutch vetoed a battle... Marlborough was exceedingly disappointed: he was out for decision. **1959** N. MAILER *Advts. for Myself* (1961) 42 They kept actin' like they was out to get him first.

16. a. Away or at a distance from some recognized place; away from one's own country, abroad, in a colony or distant land; in quot. *c* 900 afar in the outer ocean (supposed to encircle the earth).

c **900** tr. *Bæda's Hist.* I. iii. (1890) 30 Orcadas þa ealond, þa wæron ut on garsecge butan Breotone. *c* **1200** *Trin. Coll. Hom.* 197 Oder kinnes neddre is ut in oðer londe. *a* **1300** *Cursor M.* 20389, I was ferr heþen at a preching Ferr vte in anoþer land. *a* **1400–50** *Alexander* 23 Oute in þe erth of Egipt enhabet vmquile þe wysest wees of the werd as I in writt fynd. *c* **1400** *Destr. Troy* 1707 With his semly sonnes, þat him sate next, Saue Ector,—was oute, as aunter befelle, In a countre by coursse þat of þe coron helde. **1882** OUIDA *Maremma* I. 42 They have taken him, and they will cage him out on Gorgona yonder. *Mod.* Some members of my family are out at the Cape of Good Hope. He has settled out in New Zealand.

b. At sea, away from the land or shore, or from the bank of a lake or river.

a **1400–50** *Alexander* 75 þan was a wardan ware, oute in þe wale stremys, Of all þe nauè. **1659** D. PELL *Impr. of Sea* 530 Ships whilst out are lyable to a thousand ominous contingencies. **1719** DE FOE *Crusoe* I. ii, The tide was out. *Ibid.* II. i, Contrary winds..keep them out. **1834** MEDWIN *Angler in Wales* I. 174 But we are far enough out; opposite the boat-house. **1843** *Fraser's Mag.* XXVIII. 713 The wind turned perversely a-head the third day out. **1888** *Manch. Exam.* 2 July 5/3 A large number of fishermen were out at sea on the day of election.

17. a. Projecting, protruding; *spec.* through a rent in the clothing, as ***out at elbows, heels***, or ***knees***; see ELBOW *sb.* 4 c, HEEL *sb.*[1] 12.

1553 [see HEEL *sb.*[1] 12]. **1588** *Marprel. Epist.* (Arb.) 32 Out at the heeles with all other vserers. **1593** SHAKS. *2 Hen. VI*, III. ii. 169 His eye-balles further out, than when he liued, Staring full gastly, like a strangled man. **1601** —— *Jul. C.* I. i. 19 Yet if you be out Sir, I can mend you. **1603** [see ELBOW *sb.* 4 c]. **1693** C. DRYDEN in *J. Dryden's Juvenal* vii. (1697) 168 Hither coming, out at Heels and Knees. **1896** *Pall Mall Mag.* Sept. 41 A seedy, out-at-toe shoe.

b. Extended from its attachment, unfurled, displayed, as a flag or the like.

1720 *Lond. Gaz.* No. 5849/1 Admiral Byng sent a..Vessel with British Colours out. **1769** FALCONER *Dict. Marine* (1789), *Out*,..the situation of the sails when..set, or extended,..as opposed to *in*; which is..furled.

18. Without; on the outside; externally. (Opposed to IN *adv.* 5 b.) †***out and in*** = outside and inside, thoroughly, altogether.

a **1300** *Cursor M.* 6485 þir er þe comamentes ten..If we þam heild, bath vt and in. ? *a* **1500** *Chester Pl.* i. 275 But save your self, both out and In. **1598** SHAKS. *Merry W.* v. v. 60 Search Windsor Castle (Elues) within, and out. **1803** NELSON 4 June in Nicolas *Disp.* (1845) V. 79 This Island is bold, too, inside or out. *c* **1860** H. STUART *Seaman's Catech.* 24 Reeve it..from out in.

*** *in pregnant and transferred uses.***

19. a. Removed from its own place or position; displaced, dislocated, extracted. ***out of joint***: see JOINT.

a **1225** [see OUTE]. **1399** *Pol. Songs* I. 363 The bothom is ny ouʒt. *c* **1400** *Lanfranc's Cirurg.* 19 In bringyng to her placis ioyntis þat ben oute & in helynge boones þat ben to broken. *c* **1435** *Torr. Portugal* 1035 Thow the fyndes ey were owte. **1497** *Naval Accts. Hen. VII* (1896) 289 Ketylles for pyche with the Botome owte. **1605** SHAKS. *Macb.* III. iv. 79 The times has bene, That when the Braines were out, the man would dye, And there an end. **1611** —— *Wint. T.* v. iii. 77, I feare (sir) my shoulder-blade is out. **1710** STEELE *Tatler* No. 245 ¶2 Her Mouth wide,..Two Teeth out before. *a* **1756** MRS. HAYWOOD *New Present* (1771) 261 Wiping it till the stain is out.

b. Not in office; rejected or removed from a post. Also, out of work, unemployed. Cf. sense 15 c.

1605 SHAKS. *Lear* v. iii. 15 Talke of Court newes..who's in, who's out. **1728** YOUNG *Love Fame* I. 200 'What lords are those saluting with a grin?' One is just out, and one as lately in. **1835** *Court Mag.* VI. 235/1 The gentlemen out curse the gentlemen in, And vehemently swear their promotion's a sin. **1878** T. WOOD in J. Burnett *Useful Toil* (1974) III. 309, I..was regarded as an enthusiast in some places for seeking work when so many were out who were known to the masters. **1885** G. MEREDITH *Diana* xvi, His party was out, and he hoped for higher station on its return to power. **1890** W. BOOTH *In Darkest England* I. iv. 38, I would often be out of work a fortnight to three weeks at a time. Once earned £3 in a week, working day and night, but then had a fortnight out directly after. **1920** J. FERGUSON in *Northern Numbers* 98 She had been 'out' since May, Her 'panto' savings now were well-nigh spent. **1935** N. MITCHISON *We have been Warned* I. 74 He's a riveter. He came..when there was work going at the docks... Now he's out. **1968** J. BINGHAM *I Love, I Kill* viii. 95 When I told him I was 'out', he bought me a pint instead. And he gave me two tickets for the show he was in. **1973** *Listener* 29 Nov. 736/1 A British prime minister discovered as having been implicated in the same kind of depths as Nixon would be out. **1977** *Times* 6 Dec. 6/6 Because my husband's out of work he's not a man to take anything off us... Since the time he has been out they've never gone short of shoes.

c. No longer in the game, or in the active or leading position denoted by *in* (IN *adv.* 6 d); in Cricket, dismissed from the wickets; also said of the side who are not having their 'innings'. Freq. ***not out*** (cf. NOT-OUT *a.*); also *transf.* and *fig.*

1609 R. ARMIN *Hist. Two Maids of More-clacke* D2[v] *Tutch.* What doe you call it when the ball sir hits the stoole? *Filbon.* Why out. **1746** in J. Nyren *Young Cricketer's Tutor* (1833) 111 England, 1st Innings... Newland 18—not out. **1754** J. LOVE *Cricket* 17 Five on the side of the Counties are out for three Notches. **1755** *Game at Cricket* 10 If a Ball is nipp'd up, and he strikes it again wilfully, before it came to the Wicket, it's out. **1801** STRUTT *Sports & Past.* II. iii. §20 (*Trap-ball*) If the scores demanded exceed in number the lengths of the cudgel from the trap to the ball, he loses the whole, and is out. *Ibid.* §22 (*Tip-cat*) His business is to beat the cat over the ring. If he fails in so doing, he is out, and another player takes his place. **1849** *Laws of Cricket* in 'Bat' *Crick. Man.* (1850) 55 The Striker is Out if either of the bails be bowled off, or if a stump be bowled out of the ground. **1857** HUGHES *Tom Brown* II. viii, The Lords' men were out by half-past twelve o'clock for ninety-eight runs. **1881** *Sportsman's Year-Bk.* 137 He..has been in 36 times, and 'not out' four times. **1894** *Daily News* 20 Dec. 3/7 The referee stopped the fight at the close of the first round.. Smith being heavily punished and all but out. **1906** E. DYSON *Fact'ry 'Ands* vi. 62 The..thermometer..registered 103°, not out. **1937** PARTRIDGE *Dict. Slang* 424/2 *Not out* (96), 96 and still alive. **1955** *Times* 11 July 4/2 Waite, when he had made 61 and with the total at 314, was given not out caught behind the wicket off Lock.

d. No longer in prison.

1885 H. CONWAY *Family Affair* xxvii, I suppose he's out now on ticket-of-leave. **1886** BESANT *Childr. Gibeon* II. xxxii, He had presumably received his ticket of leave, and he was out. **1930** E. WALLACE *Lady of Ascot* i. 13 'How long have you been out?'.. 'I don't know what you mean,' he said. 'How long have you been out of gaol?' **1934** D. L. SAYERS *Nine Tailors* 279 Well, as you know, I wasn't out. I was inside again, owing to a regrettable misunderstanding. **1967** M. PROCTOR *Exercise Hoodwink* xiii. 91 He was a hardened criminal... The days 'out' were great days, a life of affluence and excitement. The days 'in' were the price he paid. **1976** 'B. GRAEME' *Snatch* v. 56 It was Reg Abbott who got two [years], wasn't it? Reg should be out by now.

e. Unconscious; *spec.* in *Boxing*, defeated through failing to rise within the ten seconds allowed after being knocked down; so ***out on one's feet***: dazed or barely conscious, although still in a standing position; ***out like a light***: see LIGHT *sb.* 5 f; ***out to it*** (*Austral. slang*): dead drunk; fast asleep.

1898 B. J. ANGLE in W. A. Morgan *'House' on Sport* I. 45 A competitor stopped by a blow on the mark is as much 'out' as though rendered helpless by a hit on the point. **1901** R. FITZSIMMONS *Phys. Cult. & Self-Defense* 159 Time was up. The champion was out. **1918** *War Birds* (1927) 150 She responded..by hitting him playfully over the head with an empty port bottle... It was a terrific crack and he was out for some time. **1941** BAKER *Dict. Austral. Slang* 52 *Out to it*, dead drunk. **1946** K. TENNANT *Lost Haven* (1947) xi. 171 He was properly out to it that night. We made speeches about how sorry we was to see him go. **1947** 'N. SHUTE' *Chequer Board* 3, I..fell down..on the floor, clean out. **1952** M. ALLINGHAM *Tiger in Smoke* xix. 270 You're ill... You may not know it, but you're out on your feet. **1955** E. HILLARY *High Adventure* 175 For God's sake, Charles, keep an eye on John! He's out on his feet but doesn't realise it! **1963** N. MARSH *Dead Water* (1964) ix. 246 When he opened his eyes he thought with astonishment: 'I was out.' **1973** 'H. HOWARD' *Highway to Murder* vii. 85 He was still out cold but he began coming round just before the ambulance got there.

20. †**a.** At fault, at a loss from failure of memory or self-possession; nonplussed, puzzled. *Obs.*

1588 SHAKS. *L.L.L.* v. ii. 152. **1600** —— *A.Y.L.* IV. i. 76 Verie good Orators when they are out, they will spit. **1607** —— *Cor.* v. iii. 41, I haue forgot my part, And I am out. **1621** BURTON *Anat. Mel.* I. ii. III. vi. (1651) 99 Appollonius Rhodius..banished himself..because he was out in reciting his Poems. **1661** PEPYS *Diary* 2 July, [He] was so much out that he was hissed off the stage. **1681** DRYDEN *Spanish Friar* III. ii, I never was out at a mad frolic.

b. Astray from what is right or correct; in the wrong, in error, mistaken.

a **1641** BP. MOUNTAGU *Acts & Mon.* (1642) 328 Concerning Titius, that learned man is out. **1683** WOOD *Life* 18 May (O.H.S.) III. 49 Sir Thomas Gower..spake an English speech, but miserably out in his delivery of it. **1712** ADDISON *Spect.* No. 26 ¶510 He..has been very seldom out in these his Guesses. **1778** MISS BURNEY *Evelina* (1791) II. xxxvii. 245 There, Lovel, you are out. **1809** MALKIN *Gil Blas* III. vii. ¶2, I was a little out in my calculation. **1887** RIDER HAGGARD *She* (1888) 43 If the captain is not out in his reckoning.

c. Short for *out of practice, time, tune*, etc.: see the sbs.

1588 SHAKS. *L.L.L.* IV. i. 135 Wide a'th bow hand, yfaith your hand is out. **1671** *Westminster Drollery* II. 81 Y'are out, says Dick, 'Tis a lye, says Nick, The Fidler playd it false. **1837** MARRYAT *Dog-Fiend* ix, Jemmy..tuned one string.., which was a little out.

d. At variance, no longer friendly. (Cf. 5 b.)

1565–72 COOPER *Thesaurus* s.v. *Alienus, Pro alienato*, alienated: out with vs. **1596** SHAKS. *Merch. V.* III. v. 34 Launcelet and I are out. **1664** PEPYS *Diary* 17 Aug., Mr. Edward Montagu is..now quite out with his father again. **1858** W. ARNOT *Laws fr. Heaven* i. 21 He is out with his former friend and in with his former adversary. **1873** WILL CARLETON *Farm Ballads, Betsey & I are out* i, Things at home are crossways, and Betsey and I are out.

21. Out of pocket; in default; minus (a sum).

1632 MASSINGER *City Madam* II. i, I am out now Six-hundred in the cash. **1636** SANDERSON *Serm.* II. 59 But the thing he stuck at most was the moneys he was out. **1887** G. R. SIMS *Mary Jane's Mem.* xi. 150 She was out the £5 10s. lent to her mistress. **1889** *Boston* (Mass.) *Jrnl.* 7 Feb. 1/2 Alleges..he is $5000 out, owing to the dishonesty of..an employe.

22. a. No longer burning or alight; extinguished.

c **1325** [see OUTE]. *c* **1440** *Promp. Parv.* 375/2 Owt, or qwenchyd, as candylle, or lyghte, *extinctus*. **1500–20** DUNBAR *Poems* xxxii. 46 Quhen licht wes owt and durris wes bard. **1658** SIR T. BROWNE *Hydriot.* Ep. Ded., When the Funeral Pyre was out and the last Valediction over. **1826** DISRAELI *Viv. Grey* II. xi, The fire was out, but his feet were still among the ashes.

b. No longer in vogue or in fashion; not in season, as game, fish, or fruit.

1660 PEPYS *Diary* 7 Oct., To change my long black cloake for a short one (long cloakes being now quite out). **1745** *Norton Reg.* in Sir C. Sharp *Chron. Mirab.* (1841) 62 Marriage comes in on the 13th of January, and at Septuagesimo Sunday it is out again till Low Sunday. **1773** GOLDSM. *Stoops to Conq.* III, Besides, Child, jewels are quite out at present. **1898** *St. James's Gaz.* 12 Jan. 12/2 White gloves, we are pleased to learn, are 'out'. **1936** M. MITCHELL *Gone with Wind* xii. 227 He had seen no pantalets on the streets, so he imagined they were 'out'. **1954** [see IN *adv.* 6 i]. **1959** *Encounter* Dec. 16/1 It is becoming steadily easier for newspaper or television programmes to dictate what is *out*, what is *in*. **1972** *Daily Tel.* 15 Mar. 14 Creativity is 'in', while spelling, punctuation and well-formed handwriting.. are 'out'.

c. Out of the question, impossible, not to be considered; unwanted, unacceptable, prohibited; out of place, irrelevant.

1936 W. STEVENS *Let.* 27 Jan. (1967) 307 Any form of hell raising is simply out. **1938** *Topeka* (Kansas) *Capital* 15 June 10/1 (*headline*) Rail legislation out? **1940** 'M. INNES' *There came both Mist & Snow* ii. 26 The revolver-shooting fad to which I had been so unexpectedly introduced appeared to me childish in itself and oddly 'out' in the sort of house-party characteristic of Belrive. **1945** *Tee Emm* (Air Ministry) V. 33 Unauthorised low-flying should be out, repeat *out*. **1956** I. BROMIGE *Enchanted Garden* II. ii. 91 Fiona left her velvet coat and tulle dress in the back of the car, tied the raincoat tightly round her waist and rolled up the sleeves... Glamour was out that evening. **1973** 'H. HOWARD' *Highway to Murder* i. 16 'Tell your boss to have a quiet word with the law.'.. 'No, that's out.'

23. a. No longer current or lasting; expired, elapsed; finished, exhausted; at an end. Also, having exhausted one's supply of a particular thing; out of stock of a specified article.

a **1300** *Cursor M.* 4695 (Cott.) Quen þe seuen yeirs war vte [*G.* vte; *F., Tr.* oute]. **1535** COVERDALE *Ruth* ii. 23 She gathered vntill the barley haruest and the wheat haruest was out. —— *Jer.* xxxiv. 14 When seuen yeares are out, euery man shal let go fre his bought seruaunte an Hebrue. **1600** ROWLANDS *Let. Humours Blood* vii. 83 But that dates out. **1610** SHAKS. *Temp.* III. ii. 1 When the But is out we will drinke water. **1682** BUNYAN *Holy War* (Cassell) 229 Lent was almost out. **1743** in Waghorn *Cricket Scores* (1899) 31, 23 notches to fetch, to win, when the time was out. **1806–7** J. BERESFORD *Miseries Hum. Life* (1826) x. xl, Being told by your servant.. that the coals are almost out. **1850** *Tait's Mag.* XVII. 184/2 The thirty miles were out at last. **1885** G. ALLEN *Babylon* v, Before the week was out, he had been duly installed. **1885** *List of Subscribers* (United Telephone Co.) p. xv, The hotel cellarman came up... 'Sir,' said he, 'we have had a run upon minerals, and are nearly out.' **1935** J. STEINBECK *Tortilla Flat* iii. 36 Run down and get four bottles of ginger-ale. The hotel is out. **1942** 'A. BRIDGE' *Frontier Passage* xi. 194 You haven't got a gasper, have you? We're out. **1972** J. MCCLURE *Catepillar Cop* iii. 30 Got a smoke? I'm out.

b. Used in radio communication to indicate that the speaker has finished speaking and expects no reply. ***over and out***: see OVER *adv.* 6 b.

1950 'D. DIVINE' *King of Fassarai* xi. 73 He called the signaller. 'Take this down... "No signs occupation. Out."' **1955** E. WAUGH *Officers & Gentlemen* I. ix. 108 He took the instrument. 'Headquarters to D Troop. Where are you? Over... You can't be... Damn. Out.' **1958** 'CASTLE' & 'HAILEY' *Flight into Danger* i. 23 The acknowledgment came on the air. 'Flight 714. This is Winnipeg Control. Roger. Out.' **1966** D. HOLBROOK *Flesh Wounds* 218 'Hallo Roger Baker, Hallo Roger Baker. Able Zebra asks for hornet support. Roger Baker over.' 'Roger Baker O.K. Out.' **1971** J. WAINWRIGHT *Dig Grave* 16 At County Headquarters Wireless Operations Room they used the more powerful, countrywide air waves... 'Purple Fifteen to Control. Understood and out.' **1976** L. DILLS *CB Slanguage Dict.* (rev. ed.) 51 *Out*, through transmitting.

24. a. Come from a concealed or veiled state; come into sight, become visible; manifest, apparent.

1612 *Two Noble Kinsmen* III. iv, I am very cold; and all the stars are out too. **1703** *Lond. Gaz.* No. 3923/4 The old upper Light-House will be blacked over when the Light is out in the new Light-House. **1897** *Allbutt's Syst. Med.* II. 199 The full amount of eruption is out usually within twenty-four hours of the appearance of the first spot. **1899** J. HUTCHINSON in *Arch. Surg.* X. 112 Whilst the secondary phenomena were fully out, he had had a severe illness.

b. Unfolded from the bud, as a leaf or blossom; hence (of the plant), in leaf, in flower.

1573 TUSSER *Husb.* (1878) 75 Leaue wadling about, till arbor be out. *a* **1626** BACON (J.), Leaves are out and perfect in a month. **1813** MACAULAY in *Life & Lett.* (1880) I. i. 42 The trees are all out. **1896** 'IAN MACLAREN' *Kate Carnegie, Pleasaunce* 83 In the spring-time when the primroses are out.

25. Disclosed, made known, no longer a secret.

1713 SWIFT *On Himself*, Walpole and Aislabie.. Inform the commons, that the secret's out. **1768** GOLDSM. *Good.-n. Man* v. Wks. (Globe Ed.) 637/2 Yes, yes, all's out; I now see the whole affair. **1869** W. P. MACKAY *Grace & Truth* iv, The whole truth is out about us.

26. a. Made public; in circulation (as a report or statement); issued from the press, published (as a book, etc.).

1625 B. JONSON *Staple of N.* III. ii, We gossips are bound to believe it, an't be once out, and a-foot. **1850** LD. HOUGHTON in *Life* (1891) I. x. 445 Wordsworth's new poem will be out next week. **1863** BREWER *Eng. Stud.* 355 On March 7, 1576, he writes to say that the New Testament is out.

b. Of a girl or young woman: (*a*) Introduced into society; (*b*) At work or in domestic service.

c **1792** JANE AUSTEN *Minor Wks.* (1954) 151 This mighty affair is now happily over, and my Girls *are out.* **1813** —— *Pride & Prej.* II. vi. 72 Are any of your younger sisters out, Miss Bennet? *Ibid.* 73 The younger ones out before the elder are married! **1814** —— *Mansf. Park* v, Pray, is she out, or is she not? I am puzzled. She dined at the Parsonage, with the rest of you, which seemed like being out; and yet she says so little, that I can hardly suppose she is. **1831** *Society* I. 228, I can tell her, that if my Jemima were out, her chance would be but slender. **1850** MRS. CARLYLE *Lett.* II. 116 No servant but a little girl who had 'never been out before'. **1866** MRS. GASKELL *Wives & Dau.* xxi. (1867) 212 They are not out, you know, till after the Easter ball.

c. Before the world; in existence. Cf. OUTE.

1857 G. LAWRENCE *Guy L.* vi. 47 Constance Brandon and Flora Bellasys—quite the two best things out. **1859** —— *Sword & G.* xvii. 230 Fanny was the worst casuist out. **1861** MAYHEW *Lond. Lab.* III. 106, I think I'm the cleverest juggler out. **1872** B. JERROLD *London* xv. 127 The ginger-beer merchant.. gesticulating and pattering one sultry morning... 'The Best Drink Out!' was his perpetual cry. **1973** *Times* 15 Oct. 22/8 A Triumph is still the best bike out, as a Norton represents a compromise between design criteria and production costs.

III. 27. Besides the prec. senses, *out* is used idiomatically with many verbs; e.g. to BEAR *out*, CLEAN *out*, CLEAR *out*, CROWD *out*, DOLE *out*, DRAW *out*, EKE *out*, FACE *out*, FILL *out*, OPEN *out*, PLAN *out*, POINT *out*, SET *out*, SHUT *out*, SKETCH *out*, SPIN *out*, TREAD *out*, WRITE *out*, etc., which see under the verbs themselves.

IV. *Adverbial Phrases.*

28. out and about. Going out and going about, as after an illness, etc.

1881 MRS. WALFORD *Dick Netherby* i. 8 Till Mr. Netherby was out and about again. **1884** R. BUCHANAN *Foxglove Manor* II. xxvi. 238 Ellen was already out and about.

attrib. **1899** *Westm. Gaz.* 21 Feb. 9/1 The driver is in his out-and-about way a keen critic of Government measures.

29. out and away. By far; beyond all others.

1834 *Tait's Mag.* I. 43/1 Beggary is a business, a profession, out-and-away the most thriving, profitable, secure [etc.]. **1883** STEVENSON *Treasure Isl.* IV. xvii, 'Who's the best shot?'.. 'Mr. Trelawney, out and away'.

30. out and home. a. To a place at a distance, and home again. Also *attrib.*

1698 FRYER *Acc. E. India & P.* 86 They employing yearly Forty Sail of stout Ships to and from all Parts where they trade, out and home. **1899** *Pall Mall G.* 11 Oct. 9/2 This is a world's record for a lady rider over an out-and-home course.

b. *attrib.* Played alternately on their own ground and that of their opponents.

1895 *Daily News* 10 Dec. 5/4 It may be necessary.. to reduce the minimum of eight out-and-home matches at present insisted on by the M.C.C. Committee.

31. out and in. [Cf. IN AND OUT.] **a.** Out of a place and in again; in and out. **b.** Outside and inside, without and within.

a **1300** *XI Pains Hell* 180 in *O.E. Misc.* 152 And creopeþ vt and in ayeyn. *c* **1375** *Cursor M.* 5615 (Fairf.) Ho.. gert to pik hit oute & in þat þorou hit muȝt na water wyn. **1535** COVERDALE *1 Chron.* x. 28 They bare the vessell out and in. **1792** BURNS *Duncan Gray* ii, Duncan sigh'd baith out and in. **1842** TH. MARTIN *My Namesake* in *Fraser's Mag.* Dec., 'Full, sir, out and in', said the cad.

32. out and return. = sense 30 a.

1963 *Times* 31 May 16/2 The lengths of the out-and-return paths to the ionosphere. **1966** A. BATTERSBY *Math. in Managem.* vi. 157 Each unit represents 1,000 tons making an out-and-return journey of 2 miles.

See also OUT AND OUT.

out, *sb.* [The adv. OUT, used sbst. as a name for itself, or elliptically with some sb. understood.]

1. a. Proverbial phr. †*to drink the three outs*: see quots. *Obs.* ***gentleman of the three outs***: see GENTLEMAN 5 c.

1622 S. WARD *Woe to Drunkards* (1627) 20 Stay and drinke the three Outs first that is, Wit out of the head, Money out of the purse, Ale out of the pot. **1624** T. SCOTT *God & King* (1633) 26 To drink the three Outs, to drink by the dozen, by the yard, and by the bushell. **1656** TRAPP *Comm. Gal.* v. 21 A company of odious drunkards having drunk all the three outs.

b. *slang.* (See quots.) So ***three-out***, a glass holding a third of some measure of liquor.

1835 [see GIN *sb.*[2] 2 a]. **1903** *Daily Chron.* 24 June 7/2 'Two Bass's and three outs' is an order which seems to be instantly comprehended by a barmaid who distributes the contents of two bottles among three glasses. **1908** *Ibid.* 6 Feb. 4/7 In a gin palace an 'out' is a dram glass.

2. a. Short for *outside* (in opposition to *inside*). In quot. 1890, Something external.

1717 PRIOR *Alma* II. 37 The gown.. The out, if Indian figures stain, The inside must be rich and plain. **1819** BYRON *Juan* I. clxxxvii, Juan.. liking not the inside, lock'd the out. **1890** J. H. STIRLING *Gifford Lect.* xviii. 351 It [space] lies there motionless, a motionless infinite Out.

b. ***from out to out***: from one extremity to the other; in total external length or breadth.

1692 *Capt. Smith's Seaman's Gram.* II. xiv. 113 The Diameter.. may from *Out* to *Out* be near 20 Inches. **1707** *Lond. Gaz.* No. 4319/3 A Chapel.. 52 Foot wide from Out to Out. **1834–47** J. S. MACAULAY *Field Fortif.* (1851) 185 The width of the shaft in the clear must be equal to that of the gallery from out to out.

3. a. *pl.* The party which is out of office; the opposition; usually opposed to *ins*: see IN *sb.* 1 a.

1764–1884 [see IN *sb.* 1 a]. **1810** *Edin. Rev.* XV. 511 Ins and outs are equally determined to defend corruption. **1885** *Graphic* 28 Feb. 198/2 The vigilance of the 'Outs' affords the most effective of all guarantees for the good behaviour of the 'Ins'.

b. An outside passenger on a coach.

1844 J. T. HEWLETT *Parsons & W.* i, Room for two outs and an in.

c. *pl.* In games: The side who are not playing; in *Cricket*, who are not having their innings (opp. to IN *sb.* 1 b); also, the players, on either side, who are not taking part in the scrimmage at Rugby football.

1823 M. R. MITFORD *Our Village* (1824) I. 209 He.. thinks nothing of contending with both sides, the ins and the outs, secure of out-talking the whole field. **1853** F. GALE *Public School Matches* 13 The 'Outs' are pleased at the steady pace, and the 'Ins' are equally pleased with the steady batting. **1895** *Westm. Gaz.* 7 Nov. 3/2 The feature of the game [Football] was.. the brilliant passing of the 'Varsity outs.

d. *colloq.* An out-patient at a hospital. So ***outs***, the out-patient department.

1933 PARTRIDGE *Slang To-day & Yesterday* III. iii. 192 *Outs*, out-patient department. **1964** G. L. COHEN *What's Wrong with Hospitals?* iv. 76 Distinction between the 'ins' and the 'outs' is inevitably fading.

4. a. An outward movement; a going out. *rare.*

1755 HUXHAM in *Phil. Trans.* XLIX. 372 The tide had made a very extraordinary out (or recess) almost immediately after high water.

b. An excursion, outing. *dial.*

1762 *Gentl. Mag.* 79 A young batchellor would be far from being detrimented by an out of that kind. **1828** *Craven Gloss.* (ed. 2) s.v., Ye've hed a fine out. **1852** DICKENS *Bleak H.* vii, Us London lawyers don't often get an out, and when we do, we like to make the most of it. **1898** *Daily News* 12 May 6/5 To watch the rustic.. thoroughly happy for the time being at his little out.

c. ***out and ins***, more commonly ***ins and outs***: see IN *sb.* 2.

1773 FERGUSSON *Poems* (1785) 109 He's weel vers'd in a' the laws, Kens baith their outs and ins. **1844** CROSS *Disruption* xxxix, We.. canna pretend to understaund a' the oots and ins o' the Kirk question. **1847** *Illustr. Lond. News* 4 Sept. 158/1 A rather handsome, irregular building; full, in familiar phrase, of 'outs and ins'. **1865** J. S. MILL in *Morn. Star* 6 July, He had not considered the outs and ins of the question of marriage with a deceased wife's sister.

d. An attempt, undertaking; the achievement of a particular result; progress, success; usu. in phr. ***to make an out***. *colloq.* and *dial.*

1843 H. Y. WEBB *Diary* 4 May in *Amer. Speech* (1951) XXVI. 183/1 A man.. that made half as many good resolutions as I have or made a worse out in sticking to them. **1845** M. M. NOAH *Gleanings* 148 He slipped the fatal jack of diamonds from the bottom of the pack, and claimed the money then in stake... I at first thought him in jest, and laughed at him for making so bungling an out. **1853** J. G. BALDWIN *Flush Times Alabama* 31, I might have made a pretty good *out* of it, if I had thrown myself upon the merits of my case. **1854** A. E. BAKER *Gloss. Northamptonshire Words* II. 82 'He made a good out of that speculation.' 'He made a poor out of his speech.' **1893** J. SALISBURY *Gloss. Words SE. Worcestershire* 27 'Making a goodish out' or 'a poorish out', are terms applied to any undertaking when successful or the reverse. **1904** W. N. HARBEN *Georgians* xix. 176 Warren got down on his knees then and actually tried to pray; but he made a pore out. **1938** M. K. RAWLINGS *Yearling* xxvi. 347, I often figger I made a sorry out of it, not encouragin' you. **1951** H. E. GILES *Harbin's Ridge* xv. 125 Let the woman of a house get sick, and it just goes to pieces. In the city, now, a man can make out very well... But in the country he makes a poor out of it when the hub of the house comes down.

e. *Baseball.* The act of getting a player out. *U.S.*

1860 in *Amer. Speech* (1947) XXII. 204/1 Three 'outs' and one 'run'. **1886** H. CHADWICK *Art of Pitching & Fielding* 15 Mere speed costs more in wild pitches, and called and passed balls than it yields in outs or strikes. **1973** *N.Y. Herald Tribune Internat.* 15 June 15/4 Evans, whose only out in 17 straight appearances was a sacrifice fly, wiped out a 3-2 Pirate lead with his 14th homer. **1974** *Index-Jrnl.* (Greenwood, S. Carolina) 18 Apr. 10/1 After two outs in the second, winning pitcher Jack Davenport singled and scored when the next three batters walked.

f. A way out, means of escape; and excuse, defence, alibi. *slang* (orig. *U.S.*).

1919 R. LARDNER *Real Dope* iii. 79, I am not one of the kind that are looking for an out and trying to hide behind a desk.. because I am afraid to go into the trenches. **1926** J. BLACK *You can't Win* vi. 69 If a copper grabs you you've got an out. You ain't exactly beggin'. **1934** R. STOUT *Fer-de-Lance* xvii. 287 There are times when I would welcome.. an escape from life's meaner responsibilities—what Mr. Goodwin would call an out. **1953** P. FRANKAU *Winged Horse* I. i. 4 You like thumbing your nose at common sense... And it gives you an Out from me. **1970** G. F. NEWMAN *Sir, You Bastard* 12 He wanted an out, a plausible story that would extricate his head from the chopping block. **1974** *New Yorker* 22 Apr. 130/2 Ardent pro-Europeans on Mr. Wilson's team would stand firm.. against those ministers who will probably be for rejection of any terms and a quick out.

5. a. *Printing.* An omission, or something omitted.

1784 B. FRANKLIN in *Ann. Reg.* (1817) Char. 389 Their forms too are continually pestered by the *outs*, and *doubles*, that are not easy to be corrected. **1864** WEBSTER s.v., *To make an out*, to omit something in setting up copy.

b. A defect, disadvantage, blemish. *colloq.* and *dial.* (chiefly *U.S.*).

1886 E. S. WARD *Burglars in Paradise* 48 Sound as sense! Hadn't an out about him. **1893** K. SANBORN *Truthful Woman in S. California* 69 Are there no 'outs', no defects in this Pasadena? **1917** H. GARLAND *Son of Middle Border* xiii. 129 Even hostling had its 'outs', especially in spring when the horses were shedding their hair. **1955** W. W. DENLINGER *Compl. Boston* 167 A perfection in one part cannot make up for serious 'outs' elsewhere in the whole dog.

6. *pl.* Amounts paid out; rates and taxes. *local.*

1884 SIR T. ACLAND in *Pall Mall G.* 25 Feb. 2/1 The owner generally pays the 'outs'; that is, the tithe, land tax, and rates. **1887** BARING-GOULD *Gaverocks* lii. III. 154 Worth in the gross about twelve hundred a year—that is, when all outs were paid, about eight hundred. *Mod.* (Devonsh.). Rent 5*s.* a week, the landlord paying all outs.

7. Phr. ***at*** (or ***at the, on the***) ***outs***: at variance or enmity (*with* someone or something). *colloq.* and *dial.*

1824 W. CARR *Horæ Momenta Cravenæ* 97 'To be at outs', is to be at variance. **1877** E. PEACOCK *Gloss. Words Manley & Corringham, Lincolnshire* 185/2 They fell at outs last Brigg fair was three year, an' hev nivver hed a good wod for one another sin'. **1884** *Congress. Rec.* 23 Apr. 3326/1 His church and the Unitarians [were] very much at outs. **1915** D. H. LAWRENCE *Rainbow* iv. 90 She was always at outs with authority. **1917** G. B. MCCUTCHEON *Green Fancy* 87 My daughter and I are..what you might say 'on the outs' at present. **1928** A. WAUGH *Nor Many Waters* ii. 84 We were at outs pretty badly about that time. And when you're at outs it doesn't take much to send you off. **1936** M. DE LA ROCHE *Whiteoak Harvest* ix. 113 You could scarcely have done a worse thing. Renny and Alayne are at the outs. **1955** W. GADDIS *Recognitions* III. i. 732 It's all right, don't explain. I'm on the outs with them too. **1973** J. PORTER *It's Murder with Dover* vii. 67 Soon as he [*sc.* a cat] gets at outs with one of the guests the old devil's off upstairs making a convenience of the chap's bed.

out (aʊt), *a.* [OUT *adv.* used attrib. by ellipsis of a pple. (as *lying* or the like), or by taking the predicative use of the adv. (as in 'which side is out?') as adj., and using it *attrib.* (the out side), or by resolution of compounds with *out-* (e.g. out-worker, out worker). Not distinctly separable from OUT- in comb. 1-6, q.v.]

1. That is or lies on the outside or external surface of anything; external, exterior. Now usually expressed by *outer, outside, external*, or written in combination, as *out-edge*, OUTSIDE.

a **1250** *Owl & Night.* 110 He i-seȝ bi one halve His nest i-fuled ut halve. *c* **1400** tr. *Secreta Secret., Gov. Lordsh.* 68 Yf hete be mad more..by hote metys and stalworthe, or for oon oute hete þat maystres and ouercomes. *c* **1450** *St. Cuthbert* (Surtees) 7706 As þai had bene oute enmys. **1590** PAYNE *Descr. Irel.* (1841) 9 Let the out side [of your ditch] be plum upright. **1703** MOXON *Mech. Exerc.* 230 On the out Edge of the Guide. **1887** MISS WHITMORE JONES *Games of Patience* vii. 18 If two or three are..in the four 'out' cards, you are brought to a standstill.

2. a. Outlying, situated on the outer border, or at a distance outside some place in question.

? *a* **1400** *Morte Arth.* 3909 Bade hir..fflee with hir childire ..Aþere in to Irelande, in to thas owte mowntes. **1494** FABYAN *Chron.* VII. 658 Thenne the Kentysshemen..came vnto the out parties of the cytie of London, as Radclyffe, Seynt Katherynes, and other places, and robbyd & spoyled the Flemynges, & all the berehowses. **1523** FITZHERB. *Surv.* 9 The lordes tenauntes haue commen in all suche out groundes with their catell. **1596** SPENSER *State Irel.* Wks. (Globe) 666/2, I greatly dislike the Lord Deputyes seating at Dublin, being the outest corner in the realme, and least needing the awe of his presence. **1688** *Connect. Col. Rec.* (1859) III. 438, I lately wrott you about Watching and Warding in your out townes. **1726** AYLIFFE *Parergon* 162 Judiciel Offices in the out Parts of his Diocess.

b. *out island* (***out isle***), an isle or island lying away from the mainland. Hence ***out islander***. (Often hyphened.)

Applied esp. to the Shetlands, Orkneys, Hebrides, and other smaller isles at a distance from the mainland of Britain; formerly sometimes to the British Isles as a whole, in reference to their situation with regard to the Continent; also (often with capital initials) *spec.* any of the outlying islands of the Bahamas (see quot. 1957).

a **1340** *Ercyldoun's Proph.* in *Rel. Ant.* I. 30 To nyȝt is boren a barn in Kaernervam, That ssal weld the out ydlis ylc an. ? *a* **1400** *Morte Arth.* 30 Orgayle and Orkenay, and alle this owte iles. **1470-85** MALORY *Arthur* VII. xxvii, Soo the crye was made in England walis and scotland, Ireland, Cornewaille, & in alle the oute Iles. *a* **1568** ASCHAM *Toxoph.* To Gentlem. Eng. (Arb.) 16 The out yles lying betwixt Grece and Asia minor. *a* **1578** LINDESAY (Pitscottie) *Chron. Scot.* (S.T.S.) I. 400 Alswell the out Yillis as ferme land. **1586** HOOKER *Girald. Irel.* in *Holinshed* II. 104/1 The earle of Lennox stood in hope, that the lord of the out Isles would aid him. **1599** HAKLUYT *Voy.* II. 168 Cephalonia..is an out Iland in the dominions of Grecia. **1610** HOLLAND *Camden's Brit., Scot.* 54 Purposing to speake of the out-Isles, Orcades, Hebudes, or Hebrides, and of Shetland in their due place. **1875** *Encycl. Brit.* III. 238/1 The inhabitants of the out-islands were reduced to indigence and want. **1897** *Westm. Gaz.* 19 Jan. 2/1 To the more adventurous there lie the out-islands,..little explored. **1957** *Encycl. Brit.* II. 928/1 New Providence.., although not one of the larger islands, is the most important..; the others are known collectively as the Out Islands. **1971** 'D. HALLIDAY' *Dolly & Doctor Bird* i. 6 A former minor Ambassador..living on one of the Bahamian out-islands. **1971** *Bahamas* XXIII. III. 20 Bahamian Out Islanders are among the world's friendliest people. **1973** *Whitaker's Almanack 1974* 775/1 There are a General Post Office in Nassau, 4 branch offices in New Providence and 109 sub-offices in the Out Islands.

3. In cricket, football, etc.: Played *out*, or away from the home ground; played in the outer parts of the field. (Often hyphened.)

1884 *Lillywhite's Cricket Ann.* 63 The result mainly of creditable out cricket. **1896** *Daily News* 2 Mar. 5/1 Surrey and Lancashire..lost only one out match apiece.

†**4.** Prominent, projecting, protruding. *Obs.*

1652 GAULE *Magastrom.* 186 An out breast. *Ibid.*, High or out shoulders.

5. Beyond the usual or normal (size): see OUTSIZE *sb.* and *a.*).

†**6.** To be paid out. *Obs.*

1475 MARG. PASTON in *P. Lett.* III. 126 He seth that be than that the owt chargys be boryn, and the repracion of the myll at Wyntyrton, we ar lyke to have but lytyll mor mony besyd the barly. **1482** *Brasenose Coll. Munim.* M. 10 (Wycombe) To pay all maner of out charges and rentes.

7. Unfashionable; opp. IN *a.* 2.

1966 *Punch* 29 June 946/1 Nowhere have I come across a word of guidance for the 'out' crowd—the vast, non-swinging, switched-off, palateless, utterly without-it lot who dominate the community. **1969** *Daily Tel.* 24 July 17/6 They [*sc.* children] want to eat savoury things most of all; but there are certain 'in' sweet-stuffs and a very great many 'out' ones.

out, *v.* [OE. *útian* = OFris. *ûtia*, OHG. *ûzôn*, MHG. *ûzen* to put out, f. *út*, OUT *adv.* Perh. formed anew in ME., and in later senses closely related to senses 13, 14 of the adv.]

1. a. *trans.* To put out, turn out, drive out, expel, eject, reject, get rid of, discharge, dismiss, oust (*from* a place, office, possession, etc.); to do out or deprive (*of* a possession). Usually with personal obj. Also with double obj. (by omission of *from* or *of*); cf. *dismiss, expel.* Frequent in 17th and 18th c. Cf. also OUTED.

1008 *Laws of Æthelred* v. c. 10 Æniȝ man..ciric-þen ne utiȝe, buton biscopes ȝeþehte. **1440** [see OUTING *vbl. sb.* 2]. **15..** *Tretyse agayne the Pestelens* (MS. Adv. Lib.) (Jam. Suppl.), Ilk ane of thaim [the heart, the liver, and the brain], has his clengyng plas, quhar he may out his superfluities and cleng him. **1598** KITCHIN *Courts Leet* (1675) 261 The Lord by Knights-service..might have outed a Farmer. **1602** FULBECKE *1st Pt. Parall.* 61 By this plea the Court shall bee outed of iurisdiction. *a* **1680** BUTLER *Rem.* (1759) II. 363 When he is once outed of his Ears, he is past his Labour. **1685** H. MORE *Paralip. Prophet.* xxxix. 339 Outing them of all Political Power in Church or State. **1711** HEARNE *Collect.* (O.H.S.) III. 201 The Bp. of Winchester designing to out him. **1776** ADAM SMITH *W.N.* III. ii. (1869) I. 394 They could..be legally outed of their lease. **1823** GALT *Gilhaize* xvi, Outing her ministers from their kirks and manses. **1927** H. A. VACHELL *Dew of Sea* 269 I'll out 'em both, even if it breaks the contract. **1941** E. R. EDDISON *Fish Dinner* vii. 103 Should a been unlorded long since, outed of all his hopes, for's misgovernment. **1942** E. WAUGH *Put Out More Flags* ii. 137 It was just a question of outing those fellows in the government. Sir Joseph had seen many governments outed. .. He'd soon out Hitler if he were alive and a German. **1968** *Daily Mirror* 27 Aug. 7/3 No one throws things away any more. They 'out' them.

b. To put out; extinguish; blot out; abolish. So ***out pipes*** (*Naut.*), to cease smoking pipes; also as *sb.* (see quots.).

1502 *Ord. Crysten Men* (W. de W. 1506) I. iv. 40 Also the water quenched & owteth the thyrst. **1582** STANYHURST *Æneis* I. (Arb.) 41 Thee night with brightnes is owted. **1621** QUARLES *Argalus & P.* (1678) 77 Witness that Taper, whose prophetick snuff Was outed and revived with one puff. **1653** in Picton *L'pool Munic. Rec.* (1883) I. 167 That the same Wryting bee utterly outed made null and voyde. **1899** *Daily News* 30 Jan. 6/4 The water flooded high the stoke-holes, outing the fires. **1900** *Black & White Budget* 1 Sept. 684/1 The times set apart for smoking are generally from noon till about 1.15, when the marine drummer beats a long roll on his drum as a signal to 'Out-pipes'. **1916** 'TAFFRAIL' *Pincher Martin* ii. 25 At one-ten the bugle sounded 'Out pipes', and the decks were cleared up. **1950** *Publ. Amer. Dial. Soc.* XIV. 50 *Out*,..to extinguish, as a lamp, a fire. **1961** F. H. BURGESS *Dict. Sailing* 154 *Out pipes*, the order to stop smoking.

c. *slang.* (orig. pugilistic): To 'knock out' or disable (an opponent); hence, To render insensible, or kill, by a blow; also, to murder.

1896 *Daily News* 15 June 7/1 The slang of the prize ring, where 'outing' a man signifies to render him insensible. **1898** *Pink 'Un & Pelican* 86 (Farmer) Gently, my lad, gently,..yer don't want to knock 'im out yet; give us a little show o' yer quality afore you outs him. **1899** *Daily News* 11 Sept. 7/3 'Come on lads, shall we out him?' Immediately after Nash rushed at the constable and struck him a heavy blow on the back of the head. **1900** G. R. SIMS *In London's Heart* xlviii. 294 He glanced contemptuously at the prostate form of his accomplice. 'Looks like I've outed him,' he said. 'Good job if I have—he'll never blab again.' **1913** E. C. BENTLEY *Trent's Last Case* ii. 27 The body not being robbed looks interesting, but he may have been outed by some wretched tramp. **1915** E. CORRI *30 Yrs. Boxing Ref.* 221 Lewis..promptly hit him a terrific punch on the point. 'Outed' by bluff! **1927** E. WALLACE *Feathered Serpent* xviii. 229 I've heard fellers in Dartmoor say that if ever they got the chance they'd 'out' him.

d. In a ball game, esp. lawn tennis: to send (the ball) outside the court or playing area.

1865 W. S. BANKS *List Provincial Words Wakefield* 3 *Ahted*, put out. 'Ahted t'first ball.' **1927** *Daily Express* 22 June 2/2 Raymond, striving for extra speed, overhit and outed a succession of returns. **1928** *Ibid.* 5 July 11/4 He outed and netted two drives.

e. In cricket: to put or declare (a batsman) out. ? *Obs.*

1899 *Captain* I. 517/1 Never forget that there are other ways of outing a man besides clean bowling him. **1906** *Daily Tel.* 23 Aug. 9/7 Myers went in, but was almost immediately 'outed' under singular circumstances.

†**2.** To set out, expose (for sale, disposal, etc.); to put out, issue. *Obs.*

c **1386** CHAUCER *Wife's Prol.* 521 With daunger oute [*v. rr.* outen, outer, owten] we al oure chaffare Greet prees at Market maketh deere ware. **1637** RUTHERFORD *Lett., to M. Mowat* (1671) 55 A calling..to out Christ, and his wares, to countrey buyers. *a* **1670** SPALDING *Troub. Chas. I* (1851) II. 101 This Farquhar outit his myttie meill upone the honest people of the toun at ane heighe price.

3. To show forth, disclose, exhibit; to speak out, utter, vent. *Obs.* exc. *dial.*

13.. *Eufrosyne* 428 in *Englische Studien* I. 308 God wol not outen hire. **13..** *Minor Poems fr. Vernon MS.* (E.E.T.S.) 530/136 Þi counseil is outet openliche. *c* **1386** CHAUCER *Can. Yeom. Prol. & T.* 281 Who that listeth outen [*v.r.* outyn] his folie, Lat hym come forth and lerne multiplie. *a* **1420** HOCCLEVE *De Reg. Princ.* 1907 Outë thyn art if þou canst craftily. *c* **1422** —— *Jonathas & Fellicula* 43 Til he of wommen oute wordes wikke. **1822** HIBBERT *Descr. Shetland* (1891) 282 (E.D.D.) For outting of your malice. **1838** HOGG *Tales* (1866) 363 (E.D.D.) The fine flavour.. soon outed the secret.

4. *intr.* [From the elliptical use in OUT *adv.* 13, from which this differs in taking inflexions.]

a. To go out, esp. on a pleasure excursion. Also *to out it. colloq.* (Cf. OUTING *vbl. sb.*)

1846 *P. Parley's Ann.* VII. 65 The sun is shining, And nought confining Pedestrians from 'outing'. **1878** STEVENSON *Inland Voy.* 191 We met dozens of pleasure-boats outing it for the afternoon. **1894** DOYLE *Mem. S. Holmes* 33 With that he ups and he outs.

b. *to out with*: To come out with; to fetch or bring out; to utter. *colloq.*

1802 R. & MAR. EDGEWORTH *Irish Bulls* x. 136, I outs with my bread-earner. **1821** CLARE *Vill. Minstr.* I. 34 And Hodge ..Outs with his pence the pleasing song to buy. **1833** *Blackw. Mag.* XXXIII. 693 He outs carelessly with another duodecimo. **1870** SPURGEON *Treas. David* Ps. xli. 6 He is no sooner out of the house than he outs with his lie. **1896** G. B. SHAW *Let.* 11 Feb. (1965) I. 596 There is something fundamentally unfriendly in having a grievance and not outing with it. **1942** W. FAULKNER *Go Down, Moses* 167 The negro he was shooting at outed with a dollar-and-a-half mail-order pistol..only it never went off. **1975** *Bookseller* 17 May 2540/1, I was just getting ready to say that as sometime chief solo-boy at Exeter College, Oxford, I was as good as Ernest Lough, when McCarry outed with: 'My *Hear My Prayer* was *very* sweet.'

c. Of information, news, etc.: to become known. *dial.*

1893-4 R. O. HESLOP *Northumb. Words* II. 515 'It suin *outed*'—became commonly known. **1905** E. PHILLPOTTS *Secret Woman* I. ix. 87 Yet it outed as she'd said 'no' to him.

out, *prep.* [Prepositional use of the adv. instead of the usual OUT OF *prep. phr.*, q.v. Cf. Ger. *aus*, Du. *uit* prep. See also OUTE.]

1. From within, away from: = OUT OF 1.

Not current in Received Standard in the U.K. but common in dial., and in various regions abroad. Several of the examples are U.S., Austral., and N.Z.

c **1250** *Gen. & Ex.* 2311 Quuan he weren ut tune went, Iosep haueð hem after sent. *c* **1385** CHAUCER *L.G.W.* Prol. 197 Whan that the sunne out the south gan weste. **1545** RAYNOLD *Byrth Mankynde* 100 It wyll not conueniently yssue oute that narowe place. **1607** SHAKS. *Cor.* v. ii. 41 When you haue pusht out your gates the very Defender of them. **1710** STEELE *Tatler* No. 206 ¶4 Not endeavour at any Progress out that Tract. **1875** DASENT *Vikings* III. 165 Sigmund Brestir's son..sprang out the waist of their ship. **1889** MARY E. WILKINS *Far away Melody* (1891) 108 Going out the door, he stopped and listened a minute. **1926** A. G. MCADIE *Man & Weather* 19 The ship would make easier weather by proceeding out the western entrance. **1958** *Otago Daily Times* 24 Feb. 5/2 He flew out the side of the cloud to warmer air. **1960** M. SPARK *Bachelors* x. 150 You should of pushed him out the nest long ago. **1961** *Coast to Coast 1959-60* 34 During this time he had tried to throw everything movable out the ward-room window. **1962** *Amer. Speech* XXXVII. 269 To drive with the left arm out the window. **1967** *Southerly* XXVII. 75 She looked out the window..at all the other houses. **1968** K. WEATHERLY *Roo Shooter* 111 Sam was really crook, leaning out the window spewing. **1969** *Listener* 31 July 162/2 Schoenberg kept the 12 notes we ended up with but threw the hierarchy out the window. **1969** *Eugene* (Oregon) *Register-Guard* 3 Dec. 1D/1 'And,' continued Belko, 'that's when our whole plan went out the window.' **1972** D. E. WESTLAKE *Cops & Robbers* (1973) iii. 46 He looked out the windshield. **1973** *Black World* Aug. 55/2 He slid on back out the kitchen door. **1975** *New Yorker* 29 Sept. 43/2 Mrs. Santana and her children contribute to the refuse by throwing their trash and garbage out their windows.

2. Outside, without, beyond the limits of, beyond (*lit.* and *fig.*): = OUT OF *prep. phr.* 8, 9. *Obs.* or *dial.*

c **1350** *Will. Palerne* 1640 Mornyng out mesure to melior he wendes. **1542-3** *Act 34 & 35 Hen. VIII*, c. 18 Any other person..inhabiting out the liberte of the said citie. **1607** SHAKS. *Timon* IV. i. 38 Both within and out that Wall. *a* **1658** CLEVELAND *Content* 65 Shall I then..Live in, and out the World? **1883** HOWELLS *Woman's Reason* (Tauchn. 1884) I. 240 Its history..could not be known out the family.

†**3.** Without, not with (L. *sine*). *Obs. rare.*

c **1430** *Freemasonry* 378 May sclawndren hys felows oute reson. **1578** COOPER *Thesaurus, Sine arbitrio*,..to doe a thing alone out witnesse.

†**4.** Throughout, to the end of. *Obs. rare.*

1692 LOCKE *Educ.* §129 Having whipped his Top lustily, quite out all the time that is set him.

out, *int.* [f. OUT *adv.* (see sense 13).]

1. As an imperative exclamation, with ellipsis of verb: see OUT *adv.* 13.

2. An exclamation expressing lamentation, abhorrence, or indignant reproach; often conjoined with *alas!* or *harrow! arch.* or *dial.*

c **1386** CHAUCER *Miller's T.* 639 Vp stirte hire Alison and Nicholay And criden out and harrow in the strete. *c* **1440** *Promp. Parv.* 375/2 Owte, owt, *at, at*, interjectio. *c* **1485** *Digby Myst.* II. 433 Ho, owȝt, owȝt! alas, thys sodayne chance! **1566** PAINTER *Pal. Pleas.* II. 87 Alas and out alas I crye, that I shall see no more. **1575** R. B. *Appius & V.* in Hazl. *Dodsley* IV. 128 But out, I am wounded. **1591** SHAKS. *Two Gent.* II. vii. 54 Out, out, (Lucetta) that wilbe illfauord. **1674** PLAYFORD *Skill Mus.* I. 70 Venus cryeth for her son, Out alass she is undone. **1816** SCOTT *Antiq.* xx, I see the men ..that are come ower late to part ye; but, out and alack! sune eneugh and ower sune to drag ye to prison.

b. ***out upon*** (*on*), expressing abhorrence or reproach. (Cf. *fie upon.*) *arch.* or *dial.*

1413 *Pilgr. Sowle* (Caxton 1483) I. vii. 6 Lete us cryen a rowe, and oute upon them all. *c* **1430** *Syr Tryam.* 78 'Owt upon the, thefe!' sche seyde. **1560** DAUS tr. *Sleidane's Comm.* 119 b, They crie, Out upon him Heretike, to the fyre with hym. **1616** HAYWARD *Sanct. Troub. Soul* II. i. (1620) 7 Out vpon me wretched soule! full both of vanity, and of ignorance. **1742** RICHARDSON *Pamela* III. 188 Nor the Censures, and many Out-upon-you's of the attentive Ladies. **1838** JAMES *Robber* vi, 'Out upon the fool!' exclaimed the housekeeper. **1878** GEO. ELIOT *Coll. Breakf. P.* 614 Out on them all!

out, obs. form of OUGHT, AUGHT.

out- in *comb.* is used with substantives, with verbs and their derivatives, and with other adverbs.

In OE. *út* adv. was already prefixed (1) to ordinary sbs. in the sense 'that is without', 'out-lying', 'external', as in *útland* a country that is out, a distant or foreign land, *úthere* an army belonging to or coming from without, a foreign army; (2) to verbal sbs. and nouns of action and agent-nouns derived from verbal roots, as *útfær*, *útfaru*, *útfæreld*, *útgang*, going out, exit, departure, *útdrǽf*, expulsion, *útdrǽfere* one who drives out, *útlád* carriage out, exportation, *útryne* running out, excursion, expiry; (3) to elements forming adjs., either related to the sbs. in 1, as *útlęnde*, *útlęndisc*, outlandish, foreign, or derived from vbs. (ppl. adjs.), *útiernende* out-running, purgative. In these 'nominal compounds' the stress was always on the prefix.

With verbs, *út* like other adverbs formed separable collocations or semi-compounds, in which the position of the adv. was shifted according to the construction of the sentence, as in the separable compound verbs of modern German (although in OE. the order was not yet so rigid). Thus, *út* followed the vb. in the imperative, as *gá út! adó út þone béam*, and in the pres. and pa. indicative in the principal sentence, as *he cymþ út*, *he eode út*, *ða fluȝon hí út*. But in the dependent sentence, and in all other moods or parts of the vb., including the infinitive and pples., and all nominal derivatives, the adv. stood immediately in front of the vb.; thus *ðá he út cymþ* when he comes out, *ȝif he út cyme* if he come out, *nú wille we út gán* now will we go out, *út gangendum ðam mónþe* on the month going out. In OE. the adv. was regularly written separate; but in translations from Latin, compound verbs in *ex-* were sometimes rendered by compound vbs. in *út-* in which the adv. was not only joined, but even retained before the vb. in the principal sentence: e.g. Ps. xviii. 5, 'in omnem terram exivit sonus eorum', *Vesp. Ps.* 'in all eorðan *uteode* swoeȝ heara'. The regular position of *út* before the vb. in the inf., gerund, and pples., naturally tended to make the collocation pass into a combination, esp. when these were used as sbs. or adjs.; and this is the cause why *outgoing*, *outgoer*, *outgone* belong in meaning to *go out*, *outstretching*, *outstretched* to *stretch out*, *outgrowing*, *outgrowth* to *grow out*, *outlook*, *outlooker* to *look out*. It is only in later Eng. that such collocations as a *going-out* dress, a *clearing-out* of cupboards, the *bringers-out* of a new play, a well *thought-out* article, have become possible.

As to the verbs themselves, in ME., usage became more lax. On the one hand, the adv. began to be placed after or away from the vb. in the subordinate sentence, the infinitive, etc.; on the other hand the older usage of the inf. in *út gán*, and the like, was often extended to the indicative, so that we find *he out yede*, *the blod out brast*. This was partly due to a general levelling and loss of old syntactical distinctions, so that beside *he sprang out* and *then sprang he out*, it became allowable also to say *he out sprang* and *out sprang he*, in both of which the adv. stands before the vb. These novelties in word order were especially employed by metrical writers as facilitating the exigencies of rhythm and rime, and it is chiefly in metrical compositions that they are found. But they also occur in translations from Latin, as e.g. in the works of Wyclif, in which L. vbs. in *ex-* are constantly rendered by Eng. verbs preceded by *out*. In ME. the elements were still commonly separated in writing; but modern editors have usually hyphened these collocations as compounds.

As a result of these various causes, there are numerous *quasi*-compound vbs. in *out-* in occasional use, chiefly poetical, in precisely the same sense as the ordinary prose form in which the simple verb is followed by the adv., e.g. *out-pour* = *pour out*. Not unfrequently, moreover, where *out* stands before a vb. as a mere metrical or poetical inversion, as in 'A frightful clamour from the wall out broke', 'Out went the townsmen all in starch', the two words, though merely inversions of *broke out*, *went out*, are hyphened as if compounds. The tendency so to treat them is probably strengthened by the existence of *outbreak* (sb.), *outbreaker*, *outbreaking*, *outbroken*, *outcome*, *outcoming*, and the like. But in these latter the position of the adv. is original, and the stress is on *out*, while in *out broke*, *out went*, the stress is on the vb.

On these accounts it is difficult to deal satisfactorily with the hyphened *quasi*-compounds in *out-*. Such as seem of importance, or occur as senses of *out*-verbs having other senses, are given among the Main words (where it is often indicated that they are not true compounds, or are only poetical); others are given in this article, but no attempt has been made to exhaust them. The same is true of vbl. sbs., and ppl. adjs. in *-ing*, ppl. adjs. in *-ed*, *-en*, etc., and agent-nouns in *-er*, which are permanent possibilities from any verb that can be followed by *out*, as in *outgoing*, *outgone*, *outgoer*, from *go out*.

True compound vbs. in *out-* are those in which it imparts the sense of outdoing, surpassing, exceeding, or beating in some action, as in *outlive*, *outbid*, *outnumber*, *outface*, and the various extensions of these contained in C. II. These are of later origin: a very few (e.g. *outlive*, *outproffer* = outbid, *outpass*) appear in the end of the 15th c.; they increase gradually during the 16th c. (*outrun* in Tindale, *outcry*, *outeat*, *outgo*, *outride*, *outrime*, *outrow*, in Palsgr.), and become numerous only *c* 1600, being freely and boldly employed by Shakspere, who is our earliest authority for many of them, including the curious group typified by 'to outfrown frowns', 'to out-Herod Herod'. It is not very clear how this use arose, or to what sense of *out* it is to be referred. But the earlier of these *out*-compounds were in nearly every instance preceded by a form with *over-*. Thus *outlive* (1472) was preceded in same sense by *overlive* (in OE.) = F. *survivre*; *outpass* in 'the Water of Thamys outpassynge his boundys' (1494), was preceded by *overpass* = F. *surpasser*. It would seem therefore that *out-* has here the sense of 'beyond'. It is possible however that in *outlive* there entered in some association with OUT 6 b, 23, as if it were 'to live to see another *out* or at an end'. One who *outbids* another, bids *beyond* his rival until he drives him *out* of the contest. Cf. also the relation of the two notions in 'the ship outrode the storm', and 'the horseman outrode his pursuers', or 'he outrode all competitors in the race'.

I. *Out-* in comb. forming *sbs.*

* in combination with ordinary sbs.

Of these a few existed already in OE., e.g. *útland* outside or outlying land, foreign land, OUTLAND, *útgársecg* the outer ocean (see OCEAN), *útȝemǽre* extreme boundary, *úthealf* external side, outside, *útweald* outlying wood; *úthere* foreign army, *útwícing* foreign pirate or viking. The number of these has in later times been greatly increased. Those of longer standing are written as single words; in the more recent, the two elements are usually hyphened, but they are also sometimes written separately, in which case *out* functions as an adj. = 'external, exterior, outlying, outer': see OUT *a.* As the meaning is the same either way, the separation or hyphening of the two elements is in many cases optional. (Cf. BACK-.)

1. In the sense 'Outlying, situated outside the bounds, or remote from the centre'; also, 'outside the house, out of doors'; as OUTLAND, OUTFIELD, OUTHOUSE, OUT-CHAMBER, OUTPORT; also ***out-appurtenances***, ***-borough***, ***-bridge***, ***-butchery***, ***-chapel***, ***-city***, ***-country***, ***-district***, ***-freedom***, ***-garth***, ***-ground***, ***-hut***, ***-kitchen***, ***-labour***, ***-oven***, ***-rick***, ***-school***, ***-shed***, ***-town***, ***-township***, ***-village***, ***-yard***, etc.

1599 SANDYS *Europæ Spec.* (1632) 138 In Spaine and those *out-appurtenances. **1832** *Act 2 & 3 Will. IV*, c. 64 Sched. O. 16 The boundary of the *out-borough of Hertford. **1670** MARVELL *Corr.* Wks. 1872–5 II. 327 There is.. discourse.. concerning the *out-bridges, as Mighton bridge [etc.]. *c* **1460** in C. Coates *Reading* (1802) 35 Certen Stalls and Shoppes, called the *Out-bochery, otherwise called the Flesh-shambles, in Reding. **1599** SANDYS *Europæ Spec.* (1632) 123 Other.. are said to have.. obteined some *out-Chappel to have their Masse in. **1642** ROGERS *Naaman* 842 The *out-cities of Egypt. **1639** FULLER *Holy War* xviii. (1647) 28 They had pasturage to feed their cattel in in *out-countreys beyond Palestine. **1849** in *Worcester* (Mass.) *City Documents* No. 1, 33 Most of the schools in the *out-Districts, have been conducted.. under the new order. **1858** J. MORGAN *Let.* 9 June in *Richmond-Atkinson Papers* (1960) I. 408 The sale of spirits on the two-gallon system.. I consider to be the chief curse of the out districts. **1798** C. CRUTTWELL *Gazetteer* (1808) s.v. *Stronsa*, It is the common pasture or *out-freedom of all the farms and houses adjacent to it. **1856** KANE *Arct. Expl.* I. xi. 122 Some little *out-huts, or, as I at first thought them, dog-kennels. **1722** DE FOE *Col. Jack* (1840) 70 An *out kitchen of a gentleman's house. **1776** PENNANT *Zool.* I. 78 In Dauphiné.. they [bears] make great havock among the *out-ricks of the poor farmers. **1927** *Scots Observer* 8 Oct. 11/4 Back this summer from six months in the district in charge of *out-schools. **1957** V. W. TURNER *Schism & Continuity in Afr. Society* v. 154 Chikimbu was the problem child of the local Mission out-school. **1895** J. ROBERTS *Diary* 6 This led into someone's *outshed. **1690** *Andros Tracts* II. 216 No suitable Provision was made for our *out-Towns and Frontiers. **1884** *Manch. Exam.* 22 Feb. 5/2 Three of the *out-townships had resolved.. to become corporate members of the municipality. **1667** PRIMATT *City & C. Build.* 93 Either in an *Out-Yard, or in a convenient corner in the Cellar.

2. In the sense 'Living, residing, or engaged outside (a house, hospital, borough, city, country, etc.)', usually as distinguished from those of the same body or class living, residing, etc., within; as OUT-DWELLER, -PATIENT, -PENSIONER, etc.; also ***out-brother*** (of a fraternity), ***-burgess***, ***-citizen***, ***-clerk***, ***-company***, ***-detachment***, ***-nurse***, ***-poor***, ***-porter***, ***-pupil***, ***-ranger***, ***-servant***, ***-sister***, ***-student***, ***-suitor***, etc.; also in sense 'external, foreign', as † ***out-folk***, ***-merchant***, ***-people***.

1599 NASHE *Lenten Stuffe* 3 If they would bestowe vpon him but a slender *outbrothers annuity of mutton & broth. **1479** *Burgh Rec. Aberdeen* (Spalding Club) I. 37 *Oute-burges and inburgessis. **1847** GROTE *Greece* II. xxxvi. (1849) IV. 448 Kleruchs or *out-citizens whom the Athenians had planted.. in the neighbouring territory of Chalkis. **1714** MANDEVILLE *Fab. Bees* (1725) I. 84 The trusty *out-clerk.. sends him in what beer he wants, and takes care not to lose his custom. **1793** SMEATON *Edystone L.* §101 The *out-company not to return home till the in-company is carried out to relieve them. **1815** *Chron.* in *Ann. Reg.* 74 The *out-detachments of the Scotch brigade are called in. **1493** *Charter* in A. Laing *Lindores Abbey* xvii. (1876) 180 Purchessing of *Outfolkis bringing thaim to the burgh. **1847** GROTE *Greece* II. xii. (1849) III. 225 The large number of.. Kleruchs or *out-freemen, whom Athens quartered upon their lands. **1865** MORRIS in Mackail *Life* (1899) I. 171 O my merchants, whence come ye? *Out-merchants from the sea. **1909** *Englishwoman* Apr. 269 If she has a baby, it has to be dragged from bed and carried to some *out-nurse. **1598** BARRET *Theor. Warres* 113 With the like regard ought the *out-people to enter. **1781** GILBERT *Plan Relief Poor* 9 The greatest Caution must be used.. in settling and superintending those *Out-poor. **1902** *Chambers's Jrnl.* Nov. 717/2 'Boots' will select for him that *out-porter who will most briskly wheel his colossal pile of cases. **1927** *Daily Express* 14 July 9/2 Both men were out-porters at Snow Hill Railway Station. **1853** MRS. GASKELL *Ruth* II. vii. 183 I'm a sort of *out-pupil of yours. **1867** *Routledge's Ev. Boy's Ann.* Feb. 71 He is an out-pupil; not in any master's house. **1715** *Lond. Gaz.* No. 5383/4 Thomas Onslow, Esq., to be *Out-Rainger of Windsor Forest. *a* **1745** SWIFT *Direct. Servants*, *Chanber-maid*, Perhaps one of the *out-servants had, through malice,.. flung in the stone. **1609** *MS. Acc. St. John's Hosp., Canterb.*, Rec. of the enterance of a *novt syster vjs viij*d.* **1657** *Ibid.*, This day Margarett Whitmore was admitted an outsister. **1877** G. M. HOPKINS *Let.* 6 Jan. (1938) 93 The eldest, Milicent, is given to Puseyism: she is what is called an out-sister of the Margaret Street Home. **1939** M. PHILIP *Companions of Mary Ward* I. i. 6 Her entrance.. into the Convent of Poor Clares as an out-sister. **1840** BROWNING *Sordello* III. 335 How dared I let expand the force Within me, till some *out-soul.. should direct it? **1501** DOUGLAS *Pal. Hon.* III. lix, *Outstewartis and catouris to ȝone king. **1835** MACAULAY in Trevelyan *Compet. Wallah* (1866) 325 Amount realized from the *out-students of English for the months of May, June, and July. ? *a* **1600** *Forme of Baron Courts* i. §3 in Skene *Reg. Maj.* (1609) 100 Then the Serjand aught to gar call the soytours anes simplie: First the *out soytours of the court. [Cf. IN-SUITOR].

3. In the sense 'Exterior, external, outward' (one or other of which words would now in most cases be substituted); as in OUTSIDE, OUTLINE, OUTBOUNDS; also ***out-array***, ***-band***, ***-blemish***, ***-border***, ***-bough***, ***-branch***, ***-case***, ***-clothing***, ***-edge***, ***-end***, ***-entry***, ***-firmament***, ***-form***, ***-garment***, ***-heaven***, ***-layer***, ***-leaf***, ***-limb***, ***-limit***, ***-list***, ***-porch***, ***-row***, ***-sense***, ***-stair***, ***-terrace***, ***-tree***, ***-verge***.

1647 H. MORE *Song of Soul* I. II. xiii, Next that is Psyche's *out-array. **1621–31** LAUD *Serm.* (1847) 176 The *out-band of the body is the skin. **1601** SIR W. CORNWALLIS *Disc. Seneca* (1631) 82 Parents.. finde a lovelinesse in their [children's] *out-blemishes, and tolerate their inward. **1769** *Ann. Reg.* 229 The horse.. dispersed them to the *out-borders of the field. **1633** BP. HALL *Hard Texts* 309 Some olives left on the *out-boughs after the tree is most shaken. **1675** *Lond. Gaz.* No. 1008/4 A plain round Watch.. the Box and *Out-case of Gold. **1496** *Dives & Paup.* (W. de W.) III. viii. 331/1 The *outclothynge of men of holy chirche. **1759** STERNE *Tr. Shandy* I. xiii, To the very *out-edge and circumference of that circle. **1768** —— *Sent. Journ.* (1778) II. 80 (*Passport*) A couple of sparrows upon the out-edge of his window. **1855** ROBINSON *Whitby Gloss.*, **Out-end*, the vent or outlet of anything; the outshot or projecting end of a building. **1645** RUTHERFORD *Tryal & Tri. Faith* xxi. (1845) 281 The mouth, throat, and *out-entry of hell. **1635** SWAN *Spec. M.* (1670) 31 Neither may it seem strange how the *out-firmament can be able alwaies to uphold them [the super-celestial waters]. **1616** B. JONSON *Epigr.* I. *To Mistress Philip Sidney*, Cupid, who (at first) tooke vaine delight, In mere *out-formes, until he lost his sight. **1634** SIR T. HERBERT *Trav.* 146 Their *out Garment or Vest is commonly of Callico. **1647** H. MORE *Song of Soul* II. iii. III. xv, The fixed sunne.. shining in this *Out-heaven. **1657** R. LIGON *Barbadoes* (1673) 80 The *out-leaves hang down and rot; but still new ones come within. **1650** FULLER *Pisgah* II. ix. 184 The *out-limits and boundaries of this.. Country. *Ibid.* x. §22. 216 The *out-list of Judah fell into the midst of Dans whole cloth. **1641** MILTON *Reform.* II. Wks. (1847) 19/2 Coming to the bishop.. into the salutatory, some *outporch of the church. **1715** LEONI *Palladio's Archit.* (1742) I. 9 The Space.. between the crossing-rows and the *out-rows of Stones. **1647** H. MORE *Song of Soul* III. I. xxix, What grosse impressions the *out-senses bear The phansie represents. **1715** LEONI *Palladio's Archit.* (1742) I. 66 A Gallery, on both sides of which I would have placed two *out-stairs. **1615** G. SANDYS *Trav.* 233 The vpper roomes of most hauing *out-tarrasses. **1627** SPEED *England* v. §3 The *out-verge doth exceed the middle itselfe.

4. In the sense 'Out of office', as ***out-party***.

1817 [see IN *a.*]. **1818** COBBETT *Pol. Reg.* XXXIII. 468–9. *a* **1860** WHATELY *Commpl. Bk.* (1864) 172 An out-party will generally have more zeal and more mutual attachment among its members than an in-party. **1949** *Manch. Guardian Weekly* 11 Aug. 3 The Opposition is an 'out' party in the brawling 18th century sense. **1965** *N.Y. Times* 18 July IV. 8 For a minority out-party, any position except 'me too' almost inevitably is going to become simple opposition. **1976** *Guardian Weekly* 26 Sept. 7/3 Whichever party does not control the White House—the 'out-party'—does not even have a leader.

5. In the sense 'Lying out; not in hand', as † ***out-money***.

1608 MIDDLETON *Trick to Catch Old One* II. ii, Let my out-monies be reckoned and all.

6. In the sense 'Having an outward direction, leading out', as ***out-path***, ***-trail***, OUTWAY. (These come in sense close to the nouns of action in 7.)

1573 T. CARTWRIGHT *Replye to Whitegift* 27 It is our partes to walke in the broade and beaten way, as it were the common caussie of the commaundement, rather then an *outpathe of the example. **1627** W. SCLATER *Exp. 2 Thess.* (1629) 152 ἀπάτη ἀδικίας; The outpath leading to wickednesse. **1897** G. MACDONALD tr. Schiller in *Rampolli* 64 Could I but the outpath follow—Ah, how were my spirit blest! **1900** *Daily News* 12 Feb. 3/4 The *out-trail, the trail that's always new. **1644** [see OUTWAY 1].

** In comb. with nouns of action, agent-nouns, and verbal sbs., cognate with or derived from the simple vb. followed by *out*.

Some examples already in OE.: see above.

7. With nouns of action; as OUTBREAK [cf. *break out*], OUTBURST, OUTCOME, OUTCRY, OUTFARE, OUTGANG, OUTGROWTH, OUTLET, etc.; also ***outchuck***, ***outflare***, ***outflight***, ***outflood***, ***outgleam***, ***outjert***, ***outsally***, ***outspurt***, ***outstress***, ***outswarm***, ***outvoyage***.

1892 *Sat. Rev.* 22 Oct. 486/2 Product of design or *out-chuck of atoms. **1878** BROWNING *Poets Croisic* lxxiv, He must puff the flag To fullest *outflare. _a_ **1652** BROME _Mad Couple_ I. i. Wks. 1873 I. 18 The inconveniences I have met with in those extravagant *outflights. **1859** W. ARTHUR _Duty of Giving Proport. Income_ 53 In one eternal *outflood benefits stream from Him. **1875** D. McLEAN _Gospel in Ps._ 342 *Outgleam of overawing holiness is here. **1598** FLORIO, _Sortita_, an out-rode, an excursion, an *out-salie. **1884** E. E. HALE _Fortunes of Rachel_ xix. 191 They all laughed at this *outspurt of the classics. **1881** G. M. HOPKINS _Sermons & Devotional Writings_ (1959) 197 The first intention then of God outside himself or, as they say, _ad extra_, outwards, the first *outstress of God's power, was Christ; and we must believe that the next was the Blessed Virgin. **1894** _Edin. Rev._ Oct. 407 An enthusiastic belief and an *outswarm of a tribe. **1808** FORSYTH _Beauties Scotl._ V. 200 The statute [prohibits] any vessel from conveying abroad more than a small number of emigrants in any *out-voyage.

8. With agent-nouns; as OUTCOMER [cf. _come out_], OUTDOER, OUTFITTER, OUTGOER, OUTLIVER, OUTLOOKER, OUTPUTTER, OUTSETTER, etc., q.v.

9. With verbal substantives in _-ing_; as OUTBEARING [cf. _bear out_], OUTBRANCHING, OUTBREAKING, OUTCOMING, OUTGOING, etc.; also **_out-bolting_**, †**_-bossing_**, **_-calling_**, **_-flowering_**, **_-gadding_**, **_-gathering_**, **_-glowing_**, **_-hilding_**, **_-shadowing_**, **_-shedding_**, **_-sifting_**, **_-sprouting_**, etc.

1868 BROWNING _Ring & Bk._ XII. 164 Not an abrupt *out-bolting as of yore. _c_ **1449** PECOCK _Repr._ II. ii. 138 He graued in a greet *out-boocing ymagis of cherubyn. **1676** W. ROW _Contn. Blair's Autobiog._ x. (1848) 250 A more general *out-calling of the body of the people. **1895** _Chicago Advance_ 7 Mar. 800/3 The present *outflowering of Scottish literary genius. **1571** GOLDING _Calvin on Ps._ vii. 8 Their wandering and confused *outgaddinges intoo the way. **1876** GEO. ELIOT _Dan. Der._ VIII. lxix, The star-like *out-glowing of some pure fellow-feeling. _c_ **1449** PECOCK _Repr._ I. xvi. 89 Bi greet plenteouse *out hilding of textis writen in the Bible. **1825** COLERIDGE _Aids Refl._ (1848) I. 292 In prophetic murmurs or mute *out-shadowings of mystic ordinances. **1398** TREVISA _Barth. De P.R._ XI. iv. (Tollem. MS.), By *out-schedynge of rayne. **1582** BENTLEY _Mon. Matrones_ II. 4 The verie outshedding of thy most pretious bloud. **1839** 'J. FUME' _Paper on Tobacco_ 119 The comparatively long shreds or *outsiftings. **1897** _Chicago Advance_ 20 May 664/2 The natural *outsprouting of the new life.

II. _Out-_ in comb., forming _adjs._ (Stress on _out._)

10. With participial adjs. in _-ing_ (OE. _-ende_), from pres. pples.; as OUTBREAKING [cf. _break out_], OUTCOMING, OUTFLOWING, OUTGOING, OUTJUTTING, OUTLYING, OUTSTANDING, etc.; also **_outbeaming_**, **_-curving_**, **_-flooding_**, **_-hanging_**, **_-rushing_**, **_-sallying_**, **_-springing_**, etc.

1886 R. L. STEVENSON _Silv. Squatters_ 59 The *out-curving margin of the dump. **1909** R. KANE _Sermon of Sea_ xix. 306 Its eager essence is roused, directed, loosened, and flung forward in the *out-flooding force of a soul's quest, in the torrent-like tide of love. **1850** W. HOWITT _Year-bk. Country_ ix. 313 In the lower, *out-hanging towers are dungeons. **1851** H. MELVILLE _Moby Dick_ I. ii. 13, I at last came to a dim sort of outhanging light not far from the docks. **1972** D. HASTON _In High Places_ iii. 38 A few words of explanation and 1,500 feet of long, out-hanging, body-burning abseils. **1612** DANIEL _First Part Hist. Eng._ III. 177 By his *out-lauishing humour. **1813** SHELLEY _Q. Mab_ IV. 66 The dreadful path Of the *outsallying victors. **1877** J. T. BEER _Prophet of Nineveh_ III. iii. 193 Watch well the gates, that no outsallying bands Fall on our rear.

11. With ppl. adjs. in _-ed_, _-en_, etc. (from pa. pples.); as OUT-BORN, OUT-BOUND, OUT-BOWED, OUTCAST, OUTGONE, OUTGROWN, OUT-SENT, OUT-SHOT, etc.; also **_out-broken_**, **_-called_**, **_-created_**, **_-crushed_**, **_-curled_**, **_-flown_**, **_-flung_**, **_-fought_**, **_-hunted_**, **_-laid_**, **_-mapped_**, **_-pointed_**, **_-pushed_**, **_-shoved_**, etc.

1535 COVERDALE _1 Kings_ vi. 7 It was buylded of whole and *outbroken stones. _c_ **1550** CHEKE _Matt._ xxi. 13 Th'appointed house for his *outcalled people. **1647** H. MORE _Song of Soul_ II. iii. IV. xxvii, This *out-created ray. **1851** W. R. WILLIAMS _Lord's Prayer_ (1854) I. 194 The last wail of the *outcrushed soul. **1893** H. D. TRAILL _Soc. Eng._ I. 327 Conventional *out-curled leaves. _a_ **1684** E. TAYLOR _Behmen's Theos. Phil._ (1691) xxiv. 39 What is of God in those *outflown Powers. **1894** _Outing_ (U.S.) XXIV. 462/1 A man seated at a desk.. his face buried in his *outflung arms. **1940** W. FAULKNER _Hamlet_ III. i. 159 This time his outflung hands touched the farther bank. **1955** V. CRONIN _Wise Man from West_ xiii. 243 They heaved themselves up by hand and foot over outflung eaves of the plateau. **1892** STEVENSON & OSBOURNE _Wrecker_ xii. 189 Our *out-fought enemy [_sc._ a squall] only a blot upon the leeward sea. **1898** _Pall Mall Mag._ Sept. 25 Taking the *out-held hands, he jumped to her side. **1662** J. CHANDLER _Van Helmont's Oriat._ 246 With the blacknesse of their *out-hunted venal blood. **1622** DRAYTON _Poly-olb._ xxvii. 12 Whereas the rocky Pile Of Foudra is at hand, to guard the *out-layd Isle Of Walney. **1898** J. E. JENNINGS _From an Indian Coll._ 28 *Out-mapped plains, stretching to misty ends. **1869** GOULBURN _Purs. Holiness_ x. 92 The *out-pointed finger of human scorn.

12. With a sb. (as obj. of _out_ prep.), forming adjs., meaning 'Out of or outside the thing named'; as OUT-BOARD, OUT-COLLEGE, OUT-DOOR, etc.; also **_out-sea_**, **_-water_**. Also, away from the thing named, as **_out-shore_**.

1885 _Pall Mall G._ 23 Feb. 11/2 One of these will be an under-water tube; .. one out-water tube finds a place in the bow. **1897** BLACKMORE _Dariel_ 11 No mixed Norman blood of outsea cutthroats. **1947** [see KICK-BACK, KICKBACK c]. **1961** _Times_ 2 Aug. 4/1 Meanwhile, the outshore current looked more attractive to three other good starters.

13. Parasynthetic derivatives from phrases in which _out_ mostly means 'projecting, protruding', forming adjs.; as **_out-bellied_**, **_-breasted_**, **_-eyed_**, **_-kneed_**, **_-lipped_**, **_-shouldered_**, etc.

1570 LEVINS _Manip._ 49/41 *Outbelied, _viscerosus. Ibid._ 49/39 *Outeyed, _strabus. Ibid._ 49/38 *Outkneed, _varus. Ibid._ 49/42 *Outlipped, _labiosus._ **1682** _Lond. Gaz._ No. 1722/4 A little *out-shinn'd. **1724** _Auld Rob Morris_ in _Ramsay's Tea-t. Misc._ (1733) I. 63 He's out-shin'd, in-kneed and ringle-ey'd too. **1579** J. JONES _Preserv. Bodie & Soule_ I. xxvi. 50 Crooke-legged, and *out-shouldred.

III. _Out-_ in comb. forming _verbs._ (Stress on the second element.)

* Separable or syntactic combinations.

In ME. properly two words; in mod. use chiefly poetic or metrical forms, being, more or less, _habitual nonce-words_, made up each time from their elements. The adv. had originally a distinct stress, and still has often a secondary stress.

14. With intrans. vbs., in the same sense as the simple vb. followed by _out_; as OUTBEAM, OUTBREAK, OUTBURST, OUTFLOW, OUTGO, etc. (q.v.); also †**_outbuller_**, **_outdie_**, †**_outflee_**, **_outflood_**, **_outissue_**, **_outlean_**, †**_outpeak_**, **_outslide_**, **_outslink_**, **_outvanish_**, **_outwave_**, **_outwheel_**.

1513 DOUGLAS _Æneis_ IV. xii. 41 Thairwith gan hir seruandis behald.. The blud *outbullerand on the nakit swerd. **1382** WYCLIF _Ps._ xxx. 12 Þat seȝen me, *outfloun fro me. **1920** D. H. LAWRENCE _Women in Love_ xxiii. 349 The marvellous fulness of immediate gratification, overwhelming, *out-flooding from the source of the deepest life-force. **1879** H. PHILLIPS _Notes Coins_ 6 Chests, whence serpents are *out-issuing. **1851** MRS. BROWNING _Casa Guidi Wind._ II. 36 Duke Leopold *outleant And took the.. oath. **1900** HARDY _Poems of Past & Present_ (1902) 170 The land's sharp features seemed to be The Century's corpse outleant. **1582** STANYHURST _Æneis_ II. (Arb.) 58 Much lyke the *owtpeaking from weeds of poysoned adder. **1862** WHITTIER _At Port Royal_ 5 At last our grating keels *outslide Our good boats forward swing. **1861** LYTTON & FANE _Tannhäuser_ 9 Then from.. their long familiar homes, ..*outslunk The wantons of Olympus. **1890** _Lippincott's Mag._ May 679 With that knowledge *outvanished in shame all the weakness of his position. **1594** CAREW _Tasso_ (1881) 116 Ioy, which doth from brimfull hart *out-waue. **1886** W. ALEXANDER _St. August. Holiday_ 137 While the midnight Arctic sun *outwheel'd.

15. With transitive vbs., in the same sense as the simple vb. followed by _out_. **a.** With the force of: Out, away; out of existence; out of a socket or place, loose; outward, so as to project; forth; into the open, into manifestation; as OUTBEAR, OUTBLOT, OUTCAST, OUTFLOW, OUTLAY, OUTPOUR, OUTSHUT, etc. (q.v.); also **_outban_**, **_outbar_**, **_outblast_**, **_outbolt_**, **_outbulge_**, **_outbustle_**, **_outchase_**, **_outcount_**, †**_out-crowd_**, **_outcull_**, **_outeye_**, **_outfan_**, **_outferret_**, **_outget_**, **_outheave_**, **_out-hurl_**, **_out-hew_**, **_outlaunch_**, †**_outlength_**, **_outlengthen_**, **_outmark_**, †**_out-open_**, **_outpress_**, †**_outpry_**, **_outquaff_**, **_outshake_**, **_outshape_**, **_outshower_**, **_outsnatch_**, **_outspue_**, **_outspurn_**, **_outsquat_**, †**_out-thring_**, **_outvaunt_**, **_outwaste_**, **_outweed_**, **_outwrench_**. Also some exemplified only in pa. pple.: **_out-beat_**, †**_out-brede_**, †**_out-carve_**, **_outgather_**, †**_out-gnaw_**, **_out-hire_**, **_out-lance_**, **_outreave_**, **_outspill_**.

1885–94 R. BRIDGES _Eros & Psyche_ Feb. xxiii, And Zeus ..*outban'd From heaven whoever should that word miscall. **1590** SPENSER _F.Q._ II. x. 63 Which to *outbarre.. From sea to sea he heapt a mighty mound. **1627** DRAYTON _Agincourt_, etc. 57 There hang his eyes *out beaten with a mall. **1659** GAUDEN _Tears Ch._ IV. xx. 557 That they may blot and *out-bolt, set up and pull down Magistracy. _a_ **1400–50** _Alexander_ 2615 (Ashm.) Now ere þe baners *out bred [_Dubl._ oute brade]. **1810** COLERIDGE in _Lit. Rem._ (1838) III. 339 The fancy *out-bustled the pure intuitive imagination. ? _c_ **1430** LYDG. _St. Giles_ 294 in Horstm. _Altengl. Leg._ (1881) 374 Doorys tweyne By craft *out corve. _c_ **1400** MAUNDEV. (1839) xxv. 257 O gode cristene man.. scholde ouercomen & *out chacen a M. cursede mys beleevynge men. **1509** BARCLAY _Shyp of Folys_ (1570) ¶¶vj, So great a number, Whose folly from them outchaseth Gods grace. _c_ **1315** SHOREHAM _Poems_ (E.E.T.S.) 33/893 For repentaunce ondeþ þe hel, And schreft hyt mot *out croude Al clene. **1594** CAREW _Tasso_ (1881) 99 And mongst you ten *out-cull, as likes him best. **1930** R. C. CAMPBELL _Adamastor_ 87 Victory-vanned, with her feathers *out-fanned, The palm tree alighting my journey delayed. **1957** —— _Coll. Poems_ II. 253 The Spring with rosy spinnaker outfanned Comes curling silver fleeces through the land. **1855** BROWNING _Old Pict. Florence_ xxv, How a captive might be *out-ferreted. **1588** _Misfort. Arthur_ v. ii. in Hazl. _Dodsley_ IV. 338 With duskish dens *out-gnawn in gulfs below. **1850** W. B. ULLATHORNE _Remarks on Proposed Education Bill_ 14 A momentum with which to *outheave from the soul of youth both the principle of authority and the positive doctrines of religion together. **1908** HARDY _Dynasts_ III. III. iii. 104 Till dawn began outheaving this huge day, Pallidly—as if scared by its own bringing. **1596** SPENSER _F.Q._ v. i. 3 When Justice was not for most meed *out-hyred. **1590** —— _Muiopot._ 82 Two deadly weapons fixt he bore, Strongly *outlaunced towards either side. **1594** KYD _Cornelia_ I. i. 31 Guiltles blood by brothers hands *out-lanched. **1842** MRS. BROWNING _Grk. Chr. Poets_ 36 Outlaunch thee, Soul, upon the æther. **1592** GREENE _Groatsw. Wit_, '_Deceiving World, that with alluring toys_', And scornest now to lend thy fading joys T' *outlength my life. **1827** CARLYLE _Germ. Rom._ III. 215 This *outlengthening of his electorial power! **1861** _Macm. Mag._ IV. 131/1 A red coat against green ground would *outmark a soldier to a foe rifleman. _c_ **1440** LYDG. _Nightingale_ Poems (E.E.T.S.) 21/156 Withouten felawe j gan the wyne *outpresse. **1596** FITZ-GEFFRAY _Sir F. Drake_ (1881) 58 That durst not yet her home-bred nest *out-prie. **1647** R. STAPYLTON _Juvenal_ 170 Or then *out-quaffe those cups Laufella takes. _a_ **1340** HAMPOLE _Psalter_ xvii. 32 In the i sall be *outreft [_eripiar_] fra fandynge. **1897** _Outing_ (U.S.) XXIX. 323 Clear their silvery notes *outshaking. The sleigh bells are ringing. **1899** T. HARDY _Poems, Immortality_ 6 And still his soul *outshaped.. Its life in theirs. **1647** H. MORE _Song of Soul_ I. i. lx, And raging raptures do his soul *outsnatch. **1880** W. WATSON _Prince's Quest_ (1892) 73 The hope that filled youth's beaker to the brim The tremulous hand of age had long *outspilled. **1647** H. MORE _Song of Soul_ III. III. xxvi, All drink from hence, That.. poyson do *outspue. **1601** BRETON _Blessed Weeper_ (1879) 11 When my deere Lord sayd not,.. get thee hence, or like a dogge *outspurne mee. **1558** PHAER _Æneid_ VII. U iv, The greatest sort with slinges, their plummet lompes of lead *outsquats. _c_ **1500** _Lancelot_ 65 The byrdis thar mychty voce *out throng. **1509** BARCLAY _Shyp of Folys_ (1570) 139 Of that foole who.. all *outwasteth by immoderate expence. **1590** SPENSER _F.Q._ II. iv. 35 The sparks soone quench, the springing seed *outweed. **1855** SINGLETON _Virgil_ II. 583 He strains t' *outwrench the weapon.

b. With the force of 'completely, thoroughly', 'to a finish'; as OUTASK (q.v.); also **_out-bake_**, **_out-bathe_**, **_out-dry_**, **_out-end_**, **_out- hear_**, **_out-play_**, **_out-tear_**, **_out-tire_**. (Some only in pa. pple.) .

Some of these directly render L. verbs in _ex-_, _e-_.

By Wyclif the _ex-_ of L. vbs. is often rendered more fully by _full out_, e.g. _exultāre_ full out glad, full out joy; _exōrāre_ full out pray, _exquærere_ full out seek, _exardescere_ to wax full out tend. Modern editors have sometimes hyphened _out_ to the vb., making compound vbs. _out-glad_, _out-joy_, etc.

1382 WYCLIF _Isa._ xlviii. 10, I haue *out bake thee, but not as siluer. _c_ **1540** tr. _Pol. Verg. Eng. Hist._ (Camden) I. 209 The salutiferus water.. wherin being *owtebathed he showlde obteyne his purpose. **1382** WYCLIF _Isa._ xlii. 15 Alle the buriounyng of hem I shall *out drien [Vulg. _exiccabo_]. _a_ **1300** _E.E. Psalter_ lxxix. 14 *Out-ended [L. _exterminavit_] it bare of wode swa. **1382** WYCLIF _Isa._ xli. 17, I the Lord shal *out heren hem [Vulg. _exaudiam_]. **1864** SKEAT _Uhland's Poems_ 220 The jest is now *out-played. **1382** WYCLIF _Ps._ lxxvii[i]. 40 Hou ofte sithis thei *out terreden hym in desert [Vulg. _exacerbaverunt_]. **1796** _Plain Sense_ (ed. 2) I. 125 His obstinacy might *out-tire that of his father's. _a_ **1877** SWINBURNE _Lesbia Brandon_ (1952) xvi. 165 Her limbs shuddered now and then.. as if cold or out-tired. **1905** 'Q' _Shining Ferry_ I. vii. 91 And so, out-tired with their long day, .. they came at nightfall.. to the palace of enchantment.

16. Forming transitive verbs with the sense, 'to put or drive out by means of' the action expressed in the simple vb. (cf. _bow out_, _crowd out_, _hiss out_, etc.: see OUT _adv._ 1 h); as **_outawe_**, **_out-elbow_** (_poet._), **_outfeed_**, **_out-gloom_**, **_out-hiss_**, **_outjeer_**, **_outjest_**. All _nonce-wds._

1889 W. S. BLUNT _New Pilgrimage, Sancho Sanchez_, With a solemn grief *outawing the brute laughter of their eyes. **1936** DYLAN THOMAS _Twenty-Five Poems_ 9 Now that my symbols have *outelbowed space. **1890** J. PULSFORD _Loyalty to Christ_ I. 318 It is 'the Bread of God',.. It *outfeeds corruption, disease and death. **1748** *Out-gloom [see OUT-BLUSTER 1]. **1613** BEAUM. & FL. _Captain_ Prol., For ye may When this is hist to ashes, have a play, And here, to *out-hiss this. **1863** COWDEN CLARKE _Shaks. Char._ v. 129 His professing 'friend' *out-jeers him from drowning. **1605** SHAKS. _Lear_ III. i. 16 The Foole, who labours to *out-iest His heart-strooke iniuries.

** Compound verbs in _out-_, with the trans. force of exceeding or going beyond some thing or person in some action. * _Formed on verbs._

17. To pass beyond, exceed (a defined point, a limit in space, time, degree, etc.), by or in the action expressed by the simple vb.; as OUTASK (2), OUTDWELL, OUTFLOURISH, OUTGROW (2), OUTLAST (2), OUTPASS, OUTRUN, etc.; also **_out-feast_**, **_-journey_**, **_-skip_**, **_-sport_**, **_-study_**, **_-task_**, **_-tower_**, etc.

1651–3 JER. TAYLOR _Serm._ I. II. xv. (R.), He.. hath *out-feasted Anthony or Cleopatra's luxury. **1889** _Univ. Rev._ Nov. 437 Whose dreams *out-journey Sirius nor tire. **1603** B. JONSON _Sejanus_ II. ii, Thou lost thyselfe.. when thou thought'st Thou could'st *out-skip my vengeance: or out-stand The power I had to crush thee into ayre. **1604** SHAKS. _Oth._ II. iii. 3 Let's teach our selues that Honourable stop, Not to *out-sport discretion. **1670** EACHARD _Cont. Clergy_ 24 Some also, of very feeble and crasie constitutions in their childhood, have *out-studied their distempers. **1868** _Pall Mall G._ 24 Sept. 9 Sometimes the 'toucadore' is pushed by emulation to *out-task his strength. **1708** _Brit. Apollo_ No. 55. 3/1 Some Arrow.. Mounts.. upwards and *out-tow'rs the sight.

18. To surpass, excel or outdo (a person, etc.) in the action of the simple vb. In this sense _out-_ may be prefixed to almost any intr. vb. of action or state, and to many trans. vbs. used absolutely; so that the number of these compounds is without limit. Examples are: OUTBAWL, OUTBID, OUTBRAG, OUTDO, OUTGO, OUTLIVE, OUTPROFFER, OUTRIDE, OUTRUN, OUTSHINE, etc.; also **_out-achieve_**, **_-bang_**, **_-banter_**, **_-bark_**, **_-bat_**, **_-beg_**, **_-bleat_**, **_-blunder_**, **_-boil_**, **_-bowl_**, **_-box_**, **_-break_**, **_-brew_**, **_-bribe_**, **_-bury_**, **_-caper_**, **_-carol_**, **_-chat_**, **_-chatter_**, **_-chide_**, **_-clamour_**, **_-club_**, **_-comply_**, **_-cook_**, **_-crash_**, **_-craunch_**, **_-crawl_**, **_-crow_**, **_-curl_**, **_-curse_**, **_-darkle_**, **_-din_**, **_-dine_**, **_-diplomatize_**, **_-dissemble_**, **_-dive_**, **_-drudge_**, **_-equivocate_**, **_-fawn_**, **_-feast_**, **_-flaunt_**, **_-gastronomize_**, **_-grin_**, **_-groan_**, **_-grunt_**, **_-hammer_**, **_-hasten_**, **_-hustle_**, **_-lament_**, **_-lighten_**, **_-limn_**, **_-linger_**, **_-mount_**, **_-peal_**, **_-pipe_**, **_-pity_**, **_-plod_**, **_-populate_**, **_-praise_**, **_-preen_**, **_-procrastine_**, **_-prosper_**, **_-quibble_**, **_-quote_**, **_-rap_**, **_-redden_**, **_-rime_**, **_-rove_**, **_-scream_**, **_-shout_**, **_-shriek_**, **_-sigh_**, **_-skate_**, **_-slander_**, **_-snore_**, **_-speculate_**, **_-sprint_**, **_-squall_**,

-squeal, -sting, -strut, -sulk, -swim, -swindle, -testify, -threaten, -throb, -tinkle, -triple, -tyrannize, -usure, -vapour, -vary, -vociferate, -wait, -wake, -waltz, -warble, -whine, -whip, -whirl, -whore, -wile, -wish, etc.

1960 V. PACKARD *Waste Makers* (1961) xxiv. 295 The Russians *outachieved the United States in launching earth satellites. **1970** *Time* 17 Aug. 39 Getting along with parents has never been easy in the U.S. America has almost begged for trouble by expecting children to out-achieve their parents. **1773** J. DUNCOMBE in R. Freeman *Kentish Poets* (1821) II. 364 To see the Surry cricketers *Out-bat them and out-bowl. **1873** *Chicago Tribune* 4 June 1/7 The Mutuals outbatted their opponents. **1970** Outbat [see *outbowl* below]. **1651** DAVENANT *Gondibert* III. v. 13 Where she *outbeg'd the tardy begging Thief. **1645** J. BOND *Job in West* 31 The Lusts of those strangers.. did often *out-boyle ..the scalding waters of the Bath. **1773** *Outbowl [see *outbat* above]. **1823** *Lady's Mag.* July 388/1 There was no doubt that Andrews could, if he chose, out-bowl Samuel Long, and out-bat Tom Coper. **1970** *Sunday Tel.* 20 Dec. 21/7 This weakened M.C.C. side.. have been outbatted, outbowled and outfielded by South Australia. **1862** *Athenæum* 1 Nov. 555 Who could out-walk, out-leap, *out-box, out-fish every competitor. **1944** *Sun* (Baltimore) 15 Jan. 9/3 *Outbreaking her rivals, the light-coated filly opened up a length advantage in the run to the turn. **1955** *Ibid.* 19 May 20/4 Aeschylus outbroke the opposition but could not keep pace. **1743** *Lond. & Country Brew.* IV. (ed. 2) 286 She thought none could *out-brew her. **1783** BLAIR *Rhet.* xxviii. II. 94 If Oppianicus had given money to Stalenus, Cluentius had *outbribed him. *a* **1763** BYROM *Descr. Beau's Head* (R.), For sometimes at a ball The beau show'd his parts, *out-caper'd 'em all. **1652** BROME *City Wit* I. i. Wks. 1873 I. 283 She that will.. *out-chat fifteen Midwives. **1798** in *Spirit Pub. Jrnls.* (1799) II. 259, I *out-chattered the lawyers at Edinburgh. **1871** SWINBURNE *Songs bef. Sunrise* Prelude 108 *Outchide the north wind if it chid. **1839** DICKENS *Let.* 9 Sept. (1965) I. 578 A woman.. who.. far *out-cooked the cook of Petersham! **1970** N. ARMSTRONG et al. *First on Moon* ii. 34 Mike Collins, who had become fond of dishes like coq au vin.., definitely could outcook Lew Hartzell. **1976** *S. Wales Echo* 23 Nov., He proved it last night when he out-cooked five girls to win the South Glamorgan round of the Wales Gas schools cookery competition. **1769** CHESTERF. *Lett.* (1774) IV. 280, I believe I could now *outcrawl a snail. **1599** NASHE *Lenten Stuffe* (1871) 26 Not Salisbury Plain or Newmarket Heath.. may overpeer, or *outcrow her. ? *a* **1600** DONNE *Curse* iv, For if it be a she, Nature before hand hath *out-cursed me. **1839** BAILEY *Festus* xiv. (1852) 200 A hue which *outdarkles The deeps where they shine. **1848** *Fraser's Mag.* XXXVII. 389 We were as much out-gastronomised as *out-diplomatised by the French. **1660** N. INGELO *Bentivolio & Urania* I. (1682) 136 The Plowman strives to *outdrudg his beasts, that he may grow a wealthy Yeoman. **1681** T. FLATMAN *Heraclitus Ridens* No. 29 He has the Head of a Jesuit, and shall out-wit, out-plot, out-swear, *out-equivocate, and out-face the whole Society. *a* **1680** BUTLER *Hud.* (J.), *Outfawn as much and out-comply. **1711** ADDISON *Spect.* No. 173 ¶3 An Ambition.. of *Out-grinning one another. **1810** W. TAYLOR in *Monthly Mag.* XXIX. 51 Features that outgrin Le Brun's Passions. **1961** in WEBSTER, It is one thing to be beaten and quite another to be *out-hustled. **1966** *Daily Progress* (Charlottesville, Va.) 8 June 30/2 We out-hustle them, out-position them, and in all but two games have actually out-rebounded them. **1975** *New Yorker* 7 Apr. 116/2 The other Knicks,.. out-hustling the Lakers, double-teamed them all over the court. **1899** SWINBURNE *Rosamund* III. 45 Thine eyes *outlighten all the stars. **1665** GLANVILL *Scepsis Sci.* xvii. 104 'Twas never an heresie to *out-limn Apelles. **1868** BROWNING *Ring & Bk.* XI. 1588 One will be found *outlingering the rest. **1602** MARSTON *Antonio's Rev.* IV. v, I scorn't that any wretched should survive, *Outmounting me in that superlative. **1826** MISS MITFORD *Village* Ser. II. (1863) 379 *Out-piping the nightingale, in her own month of May. **1879** HOWELLS *L. Aroostook* viii. 84 In every little village there is some girl who knows how to *outpreen all the others. **1842** S. LOVER *Handy Andy* xxv. 218 It was the bully joker.. who.. *outquibbled the agent about the oath of allegiance. **1856** LEVER *Martins of Cro' M.* 203 To out-talk him, *out-quote, and out-anecdote him. **1852** TENNYSON *Ode Dk. Wellington* viii, Glossy purples, which *outredden All voluptuous garden-roses. **1530** PALSGR. 650/1, I *outryme, *je oultre rysme*. *c* **1728** POPE *Let.* Wks. 1751 VIII. 216 They will out-rhyme all Eaton and Westminster. **1851** *Fraser's Mag.* XLIV. 448 Each trying to *outscream, outroar, outbellow and outblaspheme his neighbour. **1832** MOTHERWELL *Poems, Caveat to Wind*, Go, tear each fluttering rag away, *Outshriek the mariner. **1963** *Times* 4 Mar. 3/7 M. Schnelldorfer.. had some bad falls and was *outskated by his fellow Bavarian, the ebullient S. Schönmetzler. **1968** *Globe & Mail* (Toronto) 15 Jan. 19/1 Detroit Red Wings outskated, outhustled and outshot Chicago Black Hawks Saturday night. *a* **1616** BEAUM. & FL. *Scornful Lady* II. ii, He *out-snores the poet. **1938** *Times* 25 July 5/1 Pender had struck two even shrewder blows for his side by *out-sprinting A. Pennington twice. **1963** *Times* 11 Feb. 3/3 Snell was outsprinted in a mile. **1752** YOUNG *Brothers* v. i, Demetrius' sigh *outstings the dart of death. **1855** KINGSLEY *Westw. Ho* (1889) 453 The only way to cure her sulkiness was to *outsulk her. *a* **1845** HOOD *Two Swans* iii, His ruby eye *out-threaten'd Mars. **1851** *Fraser's Mag.* XLIV. 471 Custom *out-tyrannizes absolutism. **1735** POPE *Donne Sat.* II. 38 *Outusure Jews, or Irishmen outswear. **1609** B. JONSON *Sil. Wom.* IV. ii, He'll watch this se'ennight but he'll have you; he'll *outwait a serjeant for you. **1929** D. H. LAWRENCE *Pansies* 95 Still a man can be A meeting place for sun and rain, Wonder outwaiting pain As in a wintry tree. **1957** T. HUGHES *Hawk in Rain* 28 Where the insects couple as they murder each other, Where the fish outwait the water. **1977** J. B. HILTON *Dead-Nettle* i. 9 She had.. succeeded in out-waiting her antagonists. Her patience.. had become too much for their nerves. **1630** B. JONSON *New Inn* I. i, And now I can *outwake the nightingale, Out-watch an usurer, and out-walk him too. **1742** YOUNG *Nt. Th.* I. 216 To see thy wheel Of ceaseless change *outwhirl'd in human life. **1738** POPE *Epil. Sat.* I. 116 Ye Gods! shall Cibber's Son, without rebuke, Swear like a Lord, or Rich *outwhore a Duke. *a* **1657** *Outwish [see OUTGLAD].

b. To get the better of, overpower, defeat, beat, in some reciprocal action or contest; as OUTBALANCE, OUTBRAVE, OUTJOCKEY, OUTMATCH, OUTRIVAL; also ***outbargain, -batter, -blackguard, -bless, -brawl, -cheat, -compete, -complement, -huff, -mate, -strive, -tease***, etc.

1834 MAR. EDGEWORTH *Helen* xix, The two parties.. try to outwit or *outbargain each other. **1813** W. TAYLOR in *Monthly Rev.* LXXII. 523 Oldham could *out-blackguard Pope. **1621–31** LAUD *Sev. Serm.* (1847) 37 The happy commerce that a Prince hath with his people, when they strive to *out-bless one another. **1600** *Look About You* in Hazl. *Dodsley* VII. 405 Wantons' words Quickly can master men, tongues *out-brawl swords! **1890** *Temple Bar Mag.* Mar. 349 Apt to be *out-competed in their own towns by foreigners. **1648** J. BEAUMONT *Psyche* XXIII. clxxxi, He.. gently strove Her Sorrow's Fullness to *out-compliment. **1681** OTWAY *Soldier's Fort.* II. i, I'll try to *out-huff him. *a* **1851** JOANNA BAILLIE (Annandale), Since the pride of your heart so far *outmates its generosity. **1615** CHAPMAN *Odyss.* I. 18 All the rest that austere death *outstrove.. safe anchor'd are. **1898** *Westm. Gaz.* 24 Feb. 2/3 While giant Titans all the rest outstrove With praises of the New Hyperion. **1748** RICHARDSON *Clarissa* (1811) IV. 197 The sex may thank themselves for teaching me to *out-tease them.

c. To overcome or defeat by the action expressed by the simple verb; as ***out-baffle, -blur, -buzz, -cavil, -flout, -scorn, -war***.

1658 W. BURTON *Itin. Anton.* 128 A bold man, that *out baffled the then Proprietor here. **1669** *Addr. hopeful yng. Gentry Eng.* 7 We have no copy left so foul, which too ingeniously transcribing vice do's not every day *out-blur. **1880** TENNYSON *Columbus* 120 The flies at home, that ever swarm about And.. murmur down Truth in the distance —these *outbuzz'd me. **1614** JACKSON *Creed* III. xxv. §1 As if he meant to *outflout the Apostle for prohibiting all besides.. Christ Iesus. **1605** SHAKS. *Lear* III. i. 10 To *out-scorn The to-and-fro-conflicting wind and rain. **1548** UDALL *Erasm. Par. Luke* xxiv. 190b, By these captaines shall he *outwarre & subdue all the uniuersall kyngdomes of yᵉ worlde. **1611** SPEED *Hist. Gt. Brit.* XI. xii. §138. 704 They desire.. not to seeme by sitting still.. to haue beene out-warred, though ouer-warred.

19. To exceed or do more than is expressed by the simple verb: as ***out-Atlas*** to load more than Atlas, ***out-beggar*** to more than beggar; so ***out-calvinize, out-pay, out-please, out-practise, out-ravish, out-realize, out-resent***, etc.

1603 DEKKER *Grissil* (Shaks. Soc.) 21 If you should bear all the wrongs, you would be *out-Atlassed. **1810** SCOTT *Lady of L.* II. xxiii, O! it *out-beggars all I lost! **1830** *Edin. Rev.* L. 336 The absolute decree.. is here far *out-calvinised. **1733** BUDGELL *Bee* IV. 519 Half a Crown *out-pays his Sweats worth. **1618** T. ADAMS *Faith's Encouragem.* Wks. 1862 II. 203 Having a little fed his eye with that, *outpleaseth him with a sapphire. **1648** BOYLE *Seraph. Love* xiii. (1700) 74 Unless we would say, that he *out-practis'd what he taught. *c* **1425** *St. Mary of Oignies* II. x. in *Anglia* VIII. 176/46 While she so *oute-rauisshed was angwysshed wiþ houge desyre. **1806** A. KNOX *Rem.* I. 14 St. Paul *out-realized this far. *a* **1718** PENN *Tracts* Wks. 1726 I. 900 Some People have *out-resented their Wrong so far.

*** Formed on adjectives.*

20. To exceed or surpass in the quality expressed by the adj.; as ***out-active, -black, -game, -grave, -guttural, -infinite, -modern, -subtle, -swift***. See also *out-old, out-royal*, in 23.

a **1661** FULLER *Worthies, London* II. (1662) 191 No wonder if the Younger *out-active those who are more ancient. **1655** —— *Ch. Hist.* III. ii. §1 Seeing his ink *out-black'd with her expression. **1940** *Sun* (Baltimore) 14 June 20/1 The Greentree filly *outgamed Rosetown in a thrilling battle to the wire. **1957** *Ibid.* 1 Feb. 22/1 Careless Miss.. caught Miss Erlen inside the sixteenth pole and then outgamed that filly, thanks to Brooks's superior handling. **1645** FULLER *Good Th. in Bad T.* (1841) 55 Fools.. endeavouring to *out-infinite God's kindness with their cruelty. **1922** *19th Cent.* Apr. 654 The old dog could in truth *out-modern the best of them. **1935** Out-modern [see sense 23 a]. **1619** FLETCHER *M. Thomas* IV. ii, The Devil I think Cannot *out-subtile thee. **1605** SYLVESTER *Du Bartas* II. iii. I. *Vocation* 855 Thou that.. *Out-swifted Arrows, and out-went the Winde. *a* **1618** —— *Spectacles* xxv, Worldly Pleasures, vain Delights, Far out-swift far sudden flights, Waters, Arrowes, and the Windes.

**** Formed on substantives.*

21. On names of qualities, actions, or objects: To exceed in the quality or action, or in reference to the thing, expressed by the sb.; as OUTFOOT, OUTLUNG, OUTLUSTRE, OUTNUMBER, OUTRANGE, etc., q.v.; also ***out-age*** to exceed in age; ***out-bowl, out-tap***, to excel at the bowl or tap, i.e. in drinking; so ***out-anecdote, -Billingsgate, -billow, -bubble, -colour, -compass, -confidence, -course, -cricket, -crown, -duty, -faith, -fame, -feat, -feature, -figure, -flavour, -gambit, -girth, -glory, -gorget, -grain, -horror, -hymn, -impudence, -letter, -light, -lip, -long-word, -luck, -machine, -mantle, -marvel, -metaphor, -million, -miracle, -monster, -name, -nick, -night, -ochre, -passion, -poison, -poll, -pomp, -price, -privilege, -prodigy, -purple, -purse, -rate, -rebound, -rhetoric, -romance, -savour, -scent, -sentence, -skill, -sonnet, -sound, -sphere, -splendour, -stale, -stall, -state, -stature, -storm, -sum, -supersitition, -syllable, -table, -talent, -taste, -throat, -tint, -title, -tone, -tongue, -trap, -tun, -tune, -venom, -vigil, -wealth, -weapon, -woe, -word, -worth***, etc.

1801 SOUTHEY *Lett.* (1856) I. 140, I mean mine [Pyramids] to outlive and *out-age the Egyptian ones! **1681** HICKERINGILL *Char. Sham Plotter* Wks. 1716 I. 219 Dulness and Slander enough to *out-Billingsgate Heraclitus Ridens. **1622** DEKKER & MASSINGER *Virg. Mart.* II. i, When I was a pagan.. I durst out-drink a lord; but your Christian lords *out-bowl me. **1605** BACON *Adv. Learn.* I. i. §3 Lest it should make it swell or *out-compass itself. **1893** *Nat. Observer* 14 Oct. 558/2 A Parsee team to *outcricket an English eleven! **1655** H. VAUGHAN *Silex Scint.* II. *Favour*, O let no star compare with thee! Nor any herb *out-duty me! **1650** FULLER *Pisgah* II. iv. 109 That good Centurion; who though a Gentile *outfaithed Israel itself. **1614** RALEIGH *Hist. World* IV. ii. §21 (1634) 485 Those two great captains, whom Alexander sought by all means to *out-fame. **1929** R. BRIDGES *Testament of Beauty* I. 714 True beauty of manhood *outfeatureth childish charm. **1866** HARDY *Time's Laughingstocks* (1909) 54 Intently busied with a vast array Of epithets that should *outfigure thee. **1962** L. DEIGHTON *Ipcress File* v. 34, I felt tired and *out-gambited. **1648** J. BEAUMONT *Psyche* III. li. (D.), She blushed more than they, and of their own Shame made them all asham'd, to see how far It was outpurpled and *outgrain'd by Her. *a* **1704** T. BROWN *Last Observator* in *Coll. Poems* (1705) 101 And I'll by far *outhymn the fam'd de Foe. **1836–48** B. D. WALSH *Aristoph., Knights* IV. i, Confound it, I shall be *out-impudenced. **1837** MISS MITFORD in L'Estrange *Life* (1870) III. 71, I.. had the glory of *out-long-wording both parties. **1916** H. TITUS *I Conquered* ix. 119 The hind legs straightened, that mighty force bore on his footing—and the stone slipped. The Captain [*sc.* a horse] was *out-lucked. **1928** *Daily Express* 9 July 13/1, I ran into Charles Kingsley there, who.. was just outlucked as [*sic*] Wimbledon. 'I drew Patterson in the third round... What do you think of that for bad luck?' **1942** *Ann. Reg. 1941* 39 General Wavell had to conduct simultaneously a number of campaigns in each of which he was outnumbered and *outmachined. **1784** COWPER *Task* v. 680 With poetic trappings grace thy prose Till it *outmantle all the pride of verse. **1814** CARY *Dante* (Chandos) 304 And every sparkle shivering to new blaze, In number did *outmillion the account. **1955** E. BOWEN *World of Love* iv. 74 See, today, how even Antonia had been *out-monstered. *a* **1611** BEAUM. & FL. *Maid's Trag.* v. iv, Thou hast.. found out one to *out-name thy other faults. **1667** DIGBY *Elvira* IV. in Hazl. *Dodsley* XV. 60, I took my time i' th' nick, but she *outnick'd me. **1596** SHAKS. *Merch. V.* v. i. 23, I would *out-night you did no body come. **1648** J. BEAUMONT *Psyche* XI. cxxiii, A Stink *Outpois'ning all the Bane of Thessaly! **1705** M. HENRY *Wks.* (1835) I. 87 If the honour of temperance were to be carried by the major vote .. the sober would be *out-polled. **1968** *Economist* 11 May 21/1 A list of delegates pledged to support Mr. Kennedy at the Democratic nominating convention in August.. outpolled by a margin of two to one a list pledged to Mr. Humphrey. **1973** *Guardian* 19 Apr. 4/5 In Oakland, California, incumbent Republican John Reading outpolled Black Panther party chairman Bobby Seale by more than 34,000 votes in an eight-man race for Mayor. **1976** *Time* 27 Dec. 8/2 Soares.. had hinted he might resign if his party was heavily out-polled. **1612** J. DAVIES *Muse's Sacrifice* (1878) 44 Their Vertues price, that doth *out-price the Vice, though more it be. **1966** *Out-rebound [see *out-hustle* in sense 18]. **1974** *State* (Columbia, S. Carolina) 8 Mar. 4-B/5 Maryland badly out-rebounded us when they beat us by 11 points at College Park. They are a great board team. **1977** *Detroit Free Press* 11 Dec. 5-D/2 This is the first time we've been outrebounded all year. **1616** *Marine Records E. Ind. Co.* in *Athenæum* No. 3604. 711/3 But was presently *outrhetorick'd by our new commander. **1655** FULLER *Ch. Hist.* VIII. iii. §34 Their real sufferings *out-romanced the fictions of [etc.]. **1632** MASSINGER & FIELD *Fatal Dowry* IV. ii. *song*, Yet this *out-savours wine,—and this, perfume. **1650** FULLER *Pisgah* II. 65 The stench of his hypocrisie *out-sented all the smell of his burnt offerings. *a* **1667** COWLEY *Poet. Rev.* Wks. 1711 III. 46 Where every Tongue's the Clapper of a Mill, And can *out-sound Homer's Gradivus. **1870** E. H. PEMBER *Tragedy of Lesbos* iv. 73 How very far she doth *outstature me. **1647** R. STAPYLTON *Juvenal* 90 *Out-storme a tempest. **1795** SOUTHEY *Joan of Arc* II. 80 The prisoners of that fatal day *out-summ'd Their conquerors! *a* **1661** FULLER *Worthies, Linc.* II. (1662) 54 Women *out-superstition Men. *Ibid., Warwick* III. (1662) 119 This Nation hankered after the Name of Plantagenet, which.. did *out-syllable Tuthar in the Mouths. **1806** *Sporting Mag.* XXVII. 186 To *out-tap his competitor, and drink his neighbours into an opinion of his sobriety. **1765** GOLDSM. *Ess.* vi. Wks. (1881) 302/2 Calvert's butt *outtastes Champagne. **1593** NASHE *Christ's T.* (1613) 50 They *out-throate me, and put mee downe I cannot be heard. **1611** SHAKS. *Cymb.* III. iv. 37 Whose tongue *Out-venomes all the Wormes of Nyle. *a* **1661** FULLER *Worthies, Kent* II. (1662) 67 The tender care of King Charles did *out-vigil their watchfullness. **1659** GAUDEN *Tears Ch.* II. xxxi. 253 When they did so much out-wit and *out-wealth us! **1602** MARSTON *Antonio's Rev.* II. iii, Let none *out-woe me: mine's Hurculean woe. **1613** SHAKS. *Hen. VIII*, I. i. 123 A Beggers booke *Out-worths a Nobles blood.

22. On names of persons, actors, agents: To excel, surpass, or outdo in executing the office, or acting the part characteristic of the person or agent in question; as OUTFOOL, OUTGENERAL, OUTKNAVE, etc.; also ***out-admiral, -captain, -devil, -epicure, -friend, -king, -lord, -paragon, -paramour, -queen, -rebel, -rogue, -tailor, -victor, -woman, -zany***, etc.

1889 H. D. TRAILL *Strafford* ii. 18 He returned, out-generalled and *outadmiralled. **1883** *Contemp. Rev.* Sept. 371 A determination not to let myself be out-stared or *out-devilled by him. **1634** RAINBOW *Labour* (1635) 25 You shall observe them to *out-Epicure the foole in the Gospell. **1615** TOMKIS *Albumazar* II. vii. in Hazl. *Dodsley* XI. 348 She cannot outlove me, nor you *outfriend me. **1749** HILL *Merope* I. iii. 17 Courage, self-sustain'd, *Out-lords Succession's Phlegm—and needs no Ancestors. **1889** *Academy* 8 June 392/3 A hero who *outparagons the Admirable Crichton. **1605** SHAKS. *Lear* III. iv. 94 Wine lou'd I deerely, dice deerly; and in Woman, *out-Paramour'd the Turke. **1839** BAILEY *Festus* xiv. (1852) 182

We still, one hour, our royalty retain, To *out-queen all in kindness and in care. **1864** *Sat. Rev.* 13 Aug. 220/2 Who alone in Europe have the subtlety and craft to *outrogue and outwit them. **1827** *Westm. Rev.* VII. 278 Unless, indeed, some king Brummel..should *out-tailor him in power. **1876** TENNYSON *Q. Mary* III. i, She could not be unmann'd—no, nor *out-woman'd! **1616** B. JONSON *Epigr.* cxxix, Thou dost *out-zany Cokely, Pod; nay, Gue: And thine owne Coriat too.

23. a. In most of the groups 18–22, the compound vb. in *out-* may be cognate with the object, being formed either on the simple verb belonging to the object, or directly on the object itself, usually unchanged, but sometimes with a verbal ending (e.g. *-ize*). The object may be a person or a thing, and the sense is 'to outdo the agent in his own sphere or work', or 'to exceed or surpass the action, quality, or other thing'. Our earliest examples of this are from Shakspere, who has 'out-frowne Fortune's frowne', and 'out-villaind villanie'; it is rare in the 17th c., but greatly used in the 19th, when also those formed on adjs. appear. Thus, formed on vbs., *to out-cook all cookery*, *out-beg a beggar*, *out-blunder former blunders*; *out-compete competition* or *competitors*, *outfish fish*, *out-rival a rival* or *rivalry*. From adjs., *to out-old the old*, *out-royal royalty*. From sbs., *to out-ambush ambushes*, *out-balderdash balderdash*, *out-blarney blarney*, *out-calvinize Calvinism*, *out-faminize famine*, *out-fiction fiction*, *out-horror all horrors*; *out-bishop the bishop*, *out-devil the devil*, *out-fiend fiends*, *out-jingo the Jingo*, *out-modern the moderns*, *outmonster the monstrosities*, *outrainbow the rainbow*, *out-saint the saint*, *out-usure the usurer*. A few examples are added in chronological order to show the development of this usage.

1593 [see OUTPRAY]. **1601** [see OUT-VILLAIN]. **1605** [see OUT-FROWN]. (All in Shakspere.) **1612** J. DAVIES *Muse's Sacrif.* (1878) 63 So hath a Painter licence too, to paint A Saint-like face, till it the Saint out saint. **1647** CLARENDON *Contempl. Ps.* Tracts (1727) 452 We may be weary of rebellion, because other men have out-rebelled us. *a* **1661** FULLER *Worthies* (1811) I. 500 (D.) He out-equivocated their equivocation. **1781** S. PETERS *Hist. Connect.* 71 My answer is, that those Puritans were weak men in Old England, and strong in New England, where they out-pop'd the Pope, out-king'd the King, and out-bishop'd the Bishops. **1809** MALKIN *Gil Blas* VII. ix. ¶4 He must have out-devilled the devil. **1828** *Examiner* 790/2 Here was balderdash out-balderdashed. **1837** LYTTON *E. Maltrav.* (1851) 74 We out-horror horror. **1844** THACKERAY *May Gambols* Wks. 1900 XIII. 439 Mr. Turner..has out-prodigied almost all former prodigies. **1876** L. STEPHEN *Hist. Eng. Th. 18th C.* I. 114 An attempt to out-infidel the infidel. **1877** TENNYSON *Harold* III. i, Thy patriot passion.. Out-passion'd his! **1884** —— *Becket* Prol., A beggar on horseback, with the retinue of three kings behind him, outroyalling royalty. **1885** *Pall Mall G.* 20 June 1/2 When each dame's object in life was to out-chignon the chignon of her neighbour. **1886** *Homilet. Rev.* (U.S.) Jan. 13 They propose to out-old the old, by going back to the early Greek theology. **1892** *Sat. Rev.* 6 Feb. 165/1 Out-criticking the critics. **1892** *Black & White* 1 Oct. 392/2 One of the strangest instances extant of fact out-fictioning fiction. *a* **1918** W. OWEN *Coll. Poems* (1963) 53 The few who rushed in the body to enter hell, And there out-fiending all its fiends and flames With superhuman inhumanities. **1930** E. BLUNDEN in *Time & Tide* 3 Jan. 16 The new painters, with their endeavours to outmonster the monstrosities of uninspired futurists. **1935** *Amer. Speech* X. 192/2 She *out-moderns* the moderns in a frock that is made for *cocktailing*. **1956** 'H. MACDIARMID' *Stony Limits* 33 The range of the tartans outrainbowing the rainbow. **1960** T. HUGHES *Lupercal* 46 Four-legged yet water-gifted, to outfish fish.

b. Hence esp. with proper names of persons, nations, sects, etc., in the sense of 'to outdo the person, etc., in question in his special attribute'. The classical example is Shakspere's OUT-HEROD *Herod*; a few instances are found in the 17th c., esp. in Fuller, and in the 18th c. in Swift; but the vast development of this, as of so many other Shaksperian usages, belongs to the 19th c., in which such expressions have been used almost without limit. Examples are ***out-Achitophel***, ***-Alexander***, ***-Bentley***, ***-Boniface***, ***-Bonner***, ***-Brutus***, ***-Darwin***, ***-Milton***, ***-Mormon***, ***-Nero***, ***-Ottoman***, ***-Quixote***, ***-Sternhold***, ***-Timon***, ***-Toby***, ***-Trollope***, ***-Turk***, ***-Zola***, etc.; and, with verbal ending, ***out-Calvinize***, ***-Germanize***, ***-Gothamize***, ***-Hobbesize***, ***-Pantagruelize***, etc. A few examples follow in chronological order to illustrate the growth of the usage.

1602 [see OUT-HEROD]. **1650** FULLER *Pisgah* I. vii. 21 Hushi the Archite, who out-achitophelled Achitophell in his policy. **1655** —— *Ch. Hist.* VIII. ii. §24 Herein, Morgan Out-Bonnered even Bonner himself. **1676** MARVELL *Mr. Smirke* Wks. 1875 IV. 12 [He might] out-boniface an Humble Moderator. *c* **1729** SWIFT *Verses on Sir R. Blackmore*, Sternhold himself he out-Sternholded. **1737** *Common Sense* I. 309 Even to out-bentley Bentley. **1800** WOLCOTT (P. Pindar) *P.S.* Wks. 1812 IV. 338 In his accoutrements out-Alexandering Alexander. **1826** *Q. Rev.* XXXIII. 317 The following trait even out-tobies Uncle Toby. **1827** LADY GRANVILLE *Lett.* (1894) I. 438 We shall out-Turk the Turks. **1829** BENTHAM *Justice & Cod. Petit.* 141 Gotham itself would find itself here out-Gothamised. **1833** MACAULAY *Ess., H. Walpole* (1887) 281 When he talked misanthropy, he out-Timoned Timon. **1870** LOWELL *Among my Bks.* Ser. I. (1873) 3 He..out-Miltons Milton in artifice of style. **1886** *Referee* 21 Feb. 7/4 If the Provost-Marshall has..out-Neroed Nero. **1887** *Longm. Mag.* Nov. 24, I came across a peculiar people who in many respects out-mormon Mormons. **1887** *Lit. World* (U.S.) 23 July 229/3 Depicted with a realism which out-Zolas Zola.

intr. *a* **1661** FULLER *Worthies, Essex* I. (1662) 334 He hath out-Alciated therein, in some mens judgement.

*** Compound vbs. in *out-* otherwise formed.

†**24.** *Out-* expressing the notion of 'taking out from the condition in which it is', 'undoing', hence = *un-*; as **outhele** to uncover, **outsheath** to unsheath, **outthrive** to cease to thrive.

a **1300** *E.E. Psalter* xxxvi. 14 Swerde out-scheþed sinne doande. *a* **1340** HAMPOLE *Psalter* xxxiv. 3 Outhell þe swerd, & louk agayns þaim þat folus me. *c* **1430** LYDG. *Min. Poems* (Percy Soc.) 28 And than he outthryveth Fro worldly ioye.

†**25.** With *out-* in place of L. *ex-*, *e-*, in words f. L.; as **outcorporate**, **outsturb**, **outvirtuate**.

1382 WYCLIF *Josh.* vii. 25 For thow has disturblid vs; out stourbe [Vulg. *exturbet*] thee the Lord in this day. **1559** MORWYNG *Evonym.* Pref., Arnold calleth *Exvirtuare* to outverteuat, *Excorporare* to outcorporate.

26. Forming vbs. from sbs. with various senses; as, with *out* = out of, **out-gauge**, to throw out of gauge or proportion; **out-heart**, to put out of heart, dishearten; **out-patience**, to put out of patience; **out-spirit**, to put out of spirits, to dispirit; **out-uncle**, to do out of an uncle; so to **out-grandfather**. Also, **out-finger**, to open out the fingers of (the hand); **outfolio**, to drive out with folios (cf. 16); †**out-nose**, to put out the nose of; †**outpeople**, to empty (a country) of people, to carry the people out of. All *nonce-wds.*

1880 G. MEREDITH *Tragic Com.* (1881) 189 The pen fell from her hand *outfingered in loathing. **1847** WELLINGTON in R. C. Winthrop *Remin. For. Trav.* (1894) 16 These huge Parliamentary Reports..will soon *outfolio us out of our houses and homes. **1891** *Pall Mall G.* 7 Dec. 3/1 Mr. Kipling *out-gauged whatever he touched. **1839** BAILEY *Festus* xx. (1852) 321 Mastering all, Save one thing—love, and that *out-hearted him. **1624** QUARLES *Job* Div. Poems (1717) 155 That done, h' enjoys the crown of all his labour, Could he but once *out-nose his right-hand neighbour. **1892** *Harper's Mag.* Feb. 394/2 Thou dost *outpatience me! *c* **1550** CHEKE *Matt.* i. 11 Josias begot Jechoni and his brethern in yᵉ *outpeopling of yᵉ contree to Babylon. **1643** PH. NYE *Serm.* in Kerr *Covenants & Covenanters* (1895) 148 You will be *outspirited and both you and Your cause slighted. **1748** RICHARDSON *Clarissa* (1811) I. xiii. 86 This little syren is in a fair way to *out-uncle, as she has already out-grandfathered us both!

outa (ˈaʊtə), a representation of a colloq. or vulgar pronunciation of OUT OF *prep. phr.* orig. *U.S.* Cf. OUTER, OUTTA.

1893 [see OUTASIGHT *a.*]. **1906** H. GREEN *At Actors' Boarding House* 42 Outa twelve hundred a week yuh kin pay it back an' have ten-fifty left. **1931** E. LINKLATER *Juan in Amer.* III. ii. 215 My act's *different*. Outa the ordinary, see? **1952** B. MALAMUD *Natural* (1963) 93 Yeah..but we're outa the cellar now and who done that—the wind? **1963** [see BEEZER 1]. **1966** 'J. HACKSTON' *Father clears Out* 51 We must've taken close on a 'undred an' fifty thousan' pounds' worth of gold outa that mine. **1970** R. D. ABRAHAMS *Positively Black* iii. 73 The white man's rooster would then just beat the goddamned shit outa that son-a-bitch. **1973** *Black World* July 56/2 They all looked high outa it. **1976** *New Musical Express* 12 Feb. 28/6, I felt like it might sometimes have got a bit outa hand. The rhythm got lost.

out-Achitophel: see OUT- 23 b.

out-ˈact, *v.* [OUT- 18.] *trans.* To surpass in acting or performing; to excel, outdo.

1644 BULWER *Chiron.* A iv, Demosthenes might here his garbe refine, And Cicero out-act his Cateline. **1776** MRS. DELANY *Lett.* Ser. II. II. 211 Garrick says 'She so much outacted him it is time for him to leave the stage'. **1906** *Westm. Gaz.* 2 June 6/3 The best of Hamlets [is sometimes] outacted by the worst of gravediggers. **1975** D. GRAY *Ride on Tiger* viii. 62 She knew she could out-act Anna any day.

out-active, **-admiral**, **-age**, etc.: see OUT-.

outage (ˈaʊtɪdʒ), *sb.* orig. and chiefly *U.S.* [f. OUT *adv.* + -AGE.] A period or state in which (esp. elecrical) apparatus is not operating as a result of disconnection or failure; *spec.* a power cut.

1903 *Electr. World & Engin.* 18 Apr. 653/1 The lamp hours were 54,187; percentage of lamp outage, 6–10; globes broken, 23. **1951** *Engineering* 5 Jan. 28/2 Outages will occur for about 50 per cent. of the flashovers so that trouble due to lightning can be expected once per annum per 500 miles. **1955** *Tweed* (Ontario) *News* 14 Apr. 10/6 Defective lamps will be replaced on Friday of each week. To report outage phone 207 before Friday each week. **1958** J. G. BROWN *Hydro-Electric Engin. Pract.* III. vi. 118 The outage which is to be expected with hydro plant is less than with steam turbo-generators. **1963** K. NEVILLE in D. Knight *100 Yrs. Sci. Fiction* (1969) 73 There's an outage in the Silver Lake Area. The brakes on a bus failed and took out an overhead section. **1974** *Indian Express* 26 Dec. 1/7 An inspection of the pipelines in all the reactors in America had been ordered. .. It had been decided that the first unit would have an outage for refuelling from January 13. **1976** *Washington Post* 19 Apr. A8/3 The outages were caused by overheating of the fuses that sit atop the power lines' poles. **1976** *Cody* (Wyoming) *Enterprise* 23 June 16/7 Mr. Royale has lived in Wapiti Valley since 1921, has had electric power since 1947, and remarked that this was the longest power outage he could remember.

outake, -taken, obs. ff. OUT-TAKE, -TAKEN.

†**ouˈtalian**, *a.* and *sb.* *Obs. nonce-wd.* [f. OUT *adv.*, after *Italian*.] Foreign; a foreigner.

1667 DK. NEWCASTLE & DRYDEN *Sir Martin Mar-all* IV. i, Or else they are no Englishmen, but some of your French Outalian rogues... I'll keep my daughter at home this afternoon and a fig for all these Outalians.

outan, outane, obs. forms of OUT-TAKEN.

out and out, ˈout-and-ˈout, *adv. phr.* (*a.* and *sb.*) [Cf. OUT *adv.* 7 c.] Thoroughly, completely, entirely; downright.

c **1325** *Chron. Eng.* 828 (Ritson) Tho hevede kyng Knout Al this lond out and out. *c* **1374** CHAUCER *Troylus* II. 690 (739) For out and out he is þe worþiest, Saue only Ector. **14** .. *MS. Rawlinson* C. 86 (Halliw.) She was wyckyd oute and oute. **1483** *Cath. Angl.* 264/1 Oute and oute; *vbi* halely. **1600** HOLLAND *Livy* XXXV. xxxii. 907 b, There was such a masse of gold brought, as would buy all the Romanes out and out. **1807** SOUTHEY *Lett.* (1856) II. 14 If I chose to sell it out and out, as the phrase is, I might certainly get £500 for it. **1880** MRS. LYNN LINTON *Rebel of Family* II. xv, She is..the cleverest woman I know, out and out.

B. *adj.* Complete, thorough-going, unqualified, thorough-paced.

1813 *Europ. Mag.* Sept. 266 Huffey White was, in the slang language, what is termed a complete out-and-out man; no species of robbery came amiss to him. **1831** *Edin. Rev.* LIV. 232 We are..not among the out-and-out admirers of the..political opinions of this school. **1868** E. YATES *Rock Ahead* II. iv, They're the out-and-outest young scamps. **1887** T. A. TROLLOPE *What I remember* II. ix. 163 He was an out-and-out avowed Republican.

C. *sb.* (*nonce use*). Something that extends or stretches farther and farther out.

1890 J. H. STIRLING *Gifford Lect.* iv. 69 Nature as the object..is a boundless out and out of objects, a boundless out and out of externalities.

Hence **out-and-out** *v.*, to knock out, exhaust.

1813 *Sporting Mag.* XLI. 100 Two or three buffers were out and outed by the hardness of the ground.

out-and-ˈouter. *colloq.* or *slang.* [f. prec. + -ER¹.] A thorough-going person or thing; a thorough or perfect type of his or its kind; an out-and-out possessor of some quality, or supporter of some cause; a thorough-paced scoundrel; an out-and-out lie; etc.

1812 J. H. VAUX *Flash Dict.*, *Out and outer*, a person of a resolute determined spirit, who pursues his object without regard to danger or difficulty; also an incorrigible depredator..possessed of neither honour nor principle. **1824** T. HOGG *Carnation* 126 Pittman's flower..is..quite an out-and-outer, a *chef d'œuvre* of nature. **1831** *Examiner* 379/2 How can you look me in the face, and tell such an out and outer? **1833** *Fraser's Mag.* VIII. 31 He declared himself to be an out-and-outer for the ballot. **1852** THACKERAY *Shabby Genteel* iii, Gad, she *was* fine then—an out and outer, sir! **1880** MISS BRADDON *Just as I am* xxviii, What do you expect will happen to you if you tell such out and outers as that? **1890** 'R. BOLDREWOOD' *Col. Reformer* (1891) 92 The horse..was..a great beauty—'a regular out-and-outer' was the expression.

outang, short for ORANG-OUTANG.

1869 BLACKMORE *Lorna D.* i. (1879) 4 The wild beasts of the wood, and the hairy outangs.

out-ˈargue, *v.* [OUT- 18 b.] *trans.* To defeat or get the better of in argument.

1748 RICHARDSON *Clarissa* (1811) III. 84 Out-argued, out-talented. **1778** JOHNSON in *Boswell* 3 Apr., Though we cannot out-vote them, we will out-argue them. **1809** SYD. SMITH *Methodism* Wks. 1854 I. 295 Such men..cannot understand when they are out-argued. **1875** JOWETT *Plato* (ed. 2) III. 69 The disputant is out-argued.

outarm (aʊtˈɑːm), *v.* [OUT- 18 a.] *trans.* To exceed in possession or acquisition of weapons of war. Also *refl.*, to provide (oneself) with more arms than a competitor.

1930 H. BELLOC in *G. K.'s Weekly* 25 Jan. 309/1 Those [governments] who have the less money seek for a pledge from those who have the more not to outbuild them and not to outarm themselves against their power competitors. **1950** *N.Y. Times* 31 Dec. 22/1 We shall not only out-arm our foes but 'out-sacrifice' them. **1955** V. CRONIN *Wise Man from West* xiii. 243 Outnumbered and outarmed, he had recourse to a trick. **1966** *Listener* 8 Sept. 355/3 A country..which is accustomed to ..out-arming everybody.

†**outas, outes**, *sb. Obs.* Forms: 3 **uthes, -heis, -hest**, 4 **outheys**, 5 **out(e)hees, outehese**, 5–6 **outas**, 5–7 **outes**, 6 **owtis**, 7 **outis**. [Early ME. *ūthēs*, whence later *outhees*, *-hese*, and (with shortening of unstressed second element) *outes*, *outis*, *outas*; also, in 13th c., *ūthest*. App. representing an OE. **út-hǣs*, f. *út* out + *hǣs* command, bidding, *calling upon (any one) by name (from *hátan* to call by name, call upon), which also had in 13th c. the two forms *hēs*, *hest*: see HEST *sb.*

Common in 13th c. in legal documents in the Latin forms *uthesium*, *huthesium*, *hutesium*, and later *huesium*. These have been sometimes thought to be the source of the ME. word, and to be themselves of OF. origin, derived from *huer*, *huier*, to cry, *hu*, *huee* cry (*hu e cri*, hue and cry), which suits the sense perfectly. But *hutesium* cannot be etymologically accounted for from this source, nor is the word known in any form, Latin or vernacular, outside England. On the other hand, *ūthēsium* as a latinization of ME. *ūthēs* is quite in order. It is very likely, however, that *hutesium* and (still more) *huesium* are Norman Fr. alterations, due to association with *hutz, hu, huée. Utheis, utheys* are also most easily explained as Anglo-Norman formations from *uthesium*. As to the sense, *ūthēs* could hardly mean 'outcry', but might well be the 'calling upon' people to the pursuit of a thief or other ill-doer, which is the sense in the oldest and other of the quots. (Compare the expressions *levare clamorem, levare huthesium, lever le hu.*)]

An outcry, raised against a thief or the like, hue and cry; also, outcry generally, clamour.

1202 in Maitland *Sel. Pleas Crown* No. 25 Ipse exivit et levavit uthes et clamorem unde vicini ejus et villata.. venerunt. —— No. 36 Quod francum plegium Theobaldi Hautein levavit clamorem et huthes super predictum Robertum. **1203** *Ibid.* No. 91 Quod ipse Henricus et servientes sui levaverunt clamorem et... utheis patrie, et insecuti sunt eum. **1207** *Ibid.* No. 101 Ad levandum uthes et sequendum malefactores. *a* **1250** *Owl & Night.* 1683 Schille ich an uthest [*v.r.* utest] up ow grede. *Ibid.* 1698 Ar ich uthest [*v.r.* utheste] uppon ow grede. *c* **1330** R. Brunne *Chron.* (1810) 339 His hede of snyten & born to London brigge fulle hie with outheys. *c* **1386** Chaucer *Knt.'s T.* 1154 Armed compleint out hees [*v.rr.* outehees, outes] and fiers outrage. **1451** *Paston Lett.* I. 186 That an outas and clamour be made upon the Lord Scalez. **1480** Caxton *Chron. Eng.* ccvi. 187 A redy whan ony oute hese or crye were made. **1566** Drant tr. *Horace, Sat.* A iv, At whose scarcehead and covetyce the worlde did outas make. **1568** Grafton *Chron.* II. 63 The Tipstaves.. commyng downe with an outas agaynst him. **1599** Hakluyt *Voy.* I. 284 The rest of the company answere him with this Owtis, Igha, Igha, Igha. **1662** Gurnall *Chr. in Arm.* verse 17. i. vii. §2 (1669) 264/2 You may hear a greater noise and outis of joy in the Thiefs House than the honest Husbandmans.

Hence †'**outas** *v. intr.*, to cry or shout out.

1547 Bale *Later Exam. Anne Askewe* Concl. I iv, Their wyse preachers outasynge the same at Paules crosse.

outas, obs. form of *octaves*: see octave 1.

outasight ('aʊtə'saɪt), *a.* Also **out-a-sight, outasite.** Colloq. contraction of out-of-sight *adj. phr.*

1893 S. Crane *Maggie* xviii. 150 You're the kind of man we like, Pete. You're outa sight! **1896** *Ibid.* (rev. ed.) v. 43 D'way I plunked dat blokie was outa sight. **1968** *Surf International* (Austral.) I. vii. 44 Sydney's got a lot of girls, but Cape Town has an unbelievably high standard, I reckon. We check them out at lunch time—outasight! Too much! **1969** *Observer* 16 Feb. 40/6 Pendennis boogaloos, falls by cats into numbers, and lays down heavy outasight rappings. Translation: Pendennis arranges events, calls on people in the money, and produces a lot of fantastic gossip. **1971** *Oz* May 5, I gave this guy nearly £30 and he rented a room for me in some outasite neighbourhood. *Ibid.* 7 On they trotted. 'Outasite, outasite,' yelled Lee after them. **1973** *Black World* June 63 This Sistuh here sho give some out-a-sight sets.

out-'ask, *v.* [out- 15 b, 17.]

1. *trans.* To 'ask' the banns of marriage of (a couple) in church for the last time. *dial.*

1719 in Perry *Hist. Coll. Amer. Col. Ch.* I. 223 The usual way is for them to publish the Banes and give the person out-asked a certificat of it to the minister. **1767** *Ann. Reg.* 63/2 About seven months ago the parties were out-asked (as it is called) at the above church. **1842** Barham *Ingol. Leg., Blasphemer's Warn.* (1882) 269 The parties had even been 'out-ask'd' in Church. **1889** *Played On* 17 The couple whose banns were 'out-asked', as they call it, this morning.

†**2.** To ask in excess of. *Obs.*

1642 T. Goodwin *Christ set forth* 161 He can never out-aske the merit of this his service.

out-at-'elbow(s. [See elbow 4 c.] Of a dog (see quots.). Used predicatively (usually without hyphens) and *attrib.*

1922 F. T. Barton *How to choose a Dog* 155 The elbows turn outwards from the chest wall, so plainly seen in the Bulldog, but in other dogs to be out at elbows is a serious fault. **1943** H. N. Beilby *Staffordshire Bull Terrier* vii. 34 A dog that is out of condition.. is just as unsound as one which is out-at-elbow due to incorrect placement of the shoulder-blades. **1954** C. L. B. Hubbard *Compl. Dog Breeders' Man.* 225 Out at Elbows. Having the elbow joints noticeably turned away from the body due to faulty front formation. **1975** T. Gray *Beagle* (ed. 3) 196 Out at Elbow. Elbows turned away from the chest, uneven in appearance, loose.

out-Atlas, -awe, etc.: see out-.

out-'babble, *v.* [out- 15, 18.] *trans.* **a.** To babble out, utter babblingly. **b.** To exceed in babble or noisy talk.

1649 Milton *Eikon.* xxiii, Outbabling Creeds and Ave's. **1845** Carlyle *Cromwell* (1871) V. 39 Babel outbabbled.

'out-'back, *adv. a.*, and *sb. Australia.* Also **out back, outback.** [f. out *adv.* + back *adv.*]

A. *adv.* **1.** Out in or to the back settlements or back-country.

1878 'R. Boldrewood' *Ups & Downs* iii. 31 There was not a streak of crimson in the pearly dawnlight, as the whole party.. rode silently along the indistinct trail which led 'out back'. **1890** —— *Col. Reformer* (1891) 308 That gentleman having been all day 'out back'. *Ibid.*, There's been one or two fine thunderstorms out back. **1893** H. Lawson *Coll. Verse* (1967) I. 447 Scenery outback isn't like Illawarra. **1901** M. Franklin *My Brilliant Career* iii. 12 The boys, as they attained manhood, drifted Out Back to shear, drove, or to take up land. *Ibid.* xxxiv. 289 George Melvyn had a large station Out Back. *a* **1903** *Mod. Austral. Newspr.* He decided to go out-back. **1909** *Daily Chron.* 29 Jan. 4/7 Under the title of 'The Church Outback', Dr. G. H. Frodsham, Bishop of Northern Queensland.. has published in an Australian paper a lively account of his experiences in.. his enormous diocese. **1936** I. L. Idriess *Cattle King* i. 2 Fascinating stories.. of the big mobs outback. **1942** C. Barrett *On Wallaby* i. 13 Out Back I have met honest sundowners. **1944** *Living Off Land* iii. 49 Anyone who has been out-back.. will know.. how every waterhole becomes alive with frogs.

2. (As two words.) Outside at the back of a house or other building; in or into the back garden or back yard. *U.S.*

1892 'Mark Twain' *Amer. Claimant* iii. 36 There was a message, now, from out back, and Colonel Sellers went out there in answer to it. **1964** T. Wolfe in *Esquire* Feb. 97 If this wasn't such a high-class joint we would take wiseacres like you out back and beat you into jellied madrilene.

B. *adj.* Of, pertaining to, or characteristic of the Australian interior or back-country.

1900 H. Lawson *Darling River* in *Prose Wks.* (1948) 269 'The Queenslan' rains'.. seem to be held responsible.. for most of the out-back trouble. *a* **1903** *Mod. Austral. Newspr.* At a recent examination held in an out-back district in Australia. **1906** A. B. Paterson (*title*) An outback marriage. **1913** W. K. Harris *Outback in Australia* i. 2 Of course, you get various opinions of Outback hospitality. **1931** *Times Lit. Suppl.* 1 Oct. 738/1 Sydney was the natural centre of outback adventurers. **1957** *Times* 11 May 7/6 In its own way the project is as brave as any bit of outback pioneering for metals or minerals. **1971** *Southerly* XXXI. 27 We've already rejected the proposition that wallabies are too shamingly outback to be possible material for poetry. **1977** A. Wilson *Strange Ride R. Kipling* iii. 157 'Men only' bars are disappearing even in outback Australia.

C. *sb.* **1.** The Australian interior or back-country.

1907 *Gentl. Mag.* July 78 These young dwellers in the Out Back have often no educational opportunities. **1911** in E. M. Clowes *On Wallaby* iv. 115 The Outback can still breed some true mates. **1920** B. Cronin *Timber Wolves* 9 In the seclusion of the outback they are at liberty to revert to grossness unspeakable. *Ibid.* ii. 40 Such men are not uncommon in the outback. **1930** *Times Lit. Suppl.* 10 July 577/2 Its travesty of the essentially peaceable 'out-back' is no worse than the scenario writer would think permissible. **1955** *Times* 6 July 17/3 The Duke of Edinburgh.. cited, and discussed in detail, the scope for aircraft in the outback. **1971** *Sunday Australian* 8 Aug. 17/3 Australia's tourist future lies in the outback. **1977** *Hongkong Standard* 12 Apr. 9/6 It still has not as yet agreed to finance the cost of building a prototype solar-energy collection and storage plant in the Australian outback.

2. *transf.* Applied to other regions or countries with allusion to the Australian interior. Also *fig.*

1959 *Listener* 15 Jan. 140/3 Tramp your way through Wales's 'outback'. **1963** *Times* 20 Apr. 9/7 The recent wave of village school and mosque building in this hitherto neglected outback [in Turkey]. **1972** *Guardian* 3 Apr. 2/5 Senator Humphrey's statement came after a 14-hour swing around the Wisconsin outback. **1975** *Times* 5 Dec. 1/4 Mr. Wilson's statement.. provided a field day for.. skinheads of the parliamentary outback. **1976** J. van de Wetering *Tumbleweed* x. 91 Cunucu, that's the outback, the outback of Curaçao. **1978** *Globe & Mail* (Toronto) 4 Mar. 8/3 A B.C. government plan to use television and radio to bring higher learning to the outback has thrown academia into a tizzy.

Hence '**outbacker**, a native or inhabitant of the out-back; '**outbackery**, the cultivation of attitudes and values characteristic of the out-back.

1913 W. K. Harris *Outback in Australia* i. 3 Another feature in the character of the Outbacker.. is his honesty. **1918** R. H. Knyvett *Over There* iii. 28 In their enthusiasm the people of the capital city practically mobbed these 'outbackers', loading them.. with cigarettes and candy. **1927** *Blackw. Mag.* Oct. 461 A grove of giant Tasmanian tree-ferns,.. the 'old man' fern of outbackers. **1933** *Bulletin* (Sydney) 18 Jan. 11 Paddy Whelan is far from being the first outbacker to do a perish for water. **1966** T. Ronan *Once there was Bagman* 124 The phase of life, now sneered at by our pharisaical, suburban, scholarship-nurtured intelligentsia—'Outbackery', they call it—has its intervals of excellence. **1971** *Southerly* XXXI. 22 We began to dismiss the image of the explorer, the bush-ranger, the whole outbackery. **1971** *Bulletin* (Sydney) 14 Aug. 49 No violence, no sex, no self-conscious outbackery; the only complaint, the book is too short.

out-baffle, -bake, etc.: see out-.

outbalance (aʊt'bæləns), *v.* [out- 18 b.] *trans.* To outweigh, to exceed in weight or effect.

1644 Milton *Judgm. Bucer* To Parlt., The Autority.. of this man consulted with, is able to out-ballance all that the lightnes of a vulgar opposition can bring to counterpoise. **1772** *Town & Country Mag.* 123 Her passions out-balance her reason. **1895** K. Grahame *Golden Age* 189 Did this and other gains really outbalance my losses?

out-band to **out-batter**: see out-.

'out-basket. [f. out *a.*, out- 6 + basket *sb.*] In an office, etc.: a basket or tray for outgoing correspondence or other documents. Cf. out-tray.

Sometimes written as two separate words with *out* regarded adjectivally.

1940 *Amer. Speech* XV. 247 His incoming mail is put in an in-basket and his outgoing mail in an out-basket. **1944** 'N. Shute' *Pastoral* v. 115 He sealed the letter... He tossed it into the OUT basket. **1952** *Chambers's Jrnl.* Aug. 493/2 The phones stood primly, the in and out baskets were in their places, and he was in charge of it all. **1968** Mrs. L. B. Johnson *White House Diary* 20 Aug. (1970) 704 It looks as if the Russians have emptied their out-basket to us. They have answered *all* of the President's correspondence. **1970** [see in-basket].

out-'bawl, *v.* [out- 18.] *trans.* To outdo in bawling; to surpass in shouting.

1648 *Hunting of Fox* 16 Baal's Priests did outbawle Elias. **1770** Langhorne *Plutarch* (1879) I. 567/1, I will outbawl the orators. **1877** *Sunday Mag.* 53 The proprietors each employ a special 'bawler', who mounted on a barrow.. attempts to outbawl his rival.

out-be, *v.* [out- 18.] To be beyond, excel.

1613 B. Jonson *To Earl of Somerset* (ed. Cunningham) III. 465/2 May she.. Outbee that Wife in worth thy friend did make.

outbeam (aʊt'bi:m), *v.* [out- 14, 18.]

1. *intr.* To beam out or forth.

1797 Coleridge in Cottle *Early Recoll.* (1837) I. 252 In every motion, her most innocent soul outbeams so brightly, that [etc.]. **1858** E. H. Sears *Athanasia* ii. iii. 195 His outbeaming Divinity breaks upon them.

2. *trans.* To surpass in beaming; to outshine.

1839 Bailey *Festus* iii. (1854) 25 In.. brightness like yon moon, Mildly outbeaming all the beads of light.

outbear (aʊt'bɛə(r)), *v.* [out- 15, 15 b, 18.]

1. *trans.* To bear forth, carry away. *poetic.*

a **1300** *E.E. Psalter* ix. 26 Out born be his domes fra his face alle. *Ibid.* lxxvii. 52 And he out bare als schepe his folk. **1844** Mrs. Browning *Sonn., Soul's Expression*, This song of soul I struggle to outbear Through portals of the sense.

†**2.** To bear out; to support; to sustain. *Obs.*

1530 Palsgr. 650/1 Who so ever saye the contrary, I wyll outbeare the. **1587** Mascall *Govt. Cattle, Sheepe* (1627) 205 The Winter.. killeth many Sheepe, the which ye did suppose they would haue out-borne the sayd Winter. **1624** Bp. Mountagu *Gagg* 45 *Satis pro imperio*, if you can out-beare it.

3. *Naut.* = outcarry *v.* 2.

1691 Foulkes in *Lond. Gaz.* No. 2640/4 The *Dover* did out-bear her with Sail, by which means her Foretopmast came by the Board. **1865** *Morn. Star* 30 Aug., Even our handsome Edgar was outborne by the black mass of the Solferino, with her keen, scooped-out bow slowly parting the water.

out-'beard, *v.* [out- 18 c.] *trans.* To overcome by bearding or show of defiance.

1611 Speed *Hist. Gt. Brit.* ix. viii. §12. 539 Did he spare to out-beard his Souvraigne himselfe? **1673** *Mem. Madam Charlton* 1 A bold Metheor.. may out-beard the Sun.

'out,bearing, *vbl. sb.* [f. *bear out*: out- 9.]

†**1.** Production, bringing forth. *Obs.*

c **1350** *All Saints* 93 in Horstm. *Altengl. Leg.* (1881) 143 þat was ordand for þis thing, To pay for þe erth out-bering.

†**2.** Projection. *Obs.*

1611 Cotgr., *Coude de la branche*, the elbow or out-bearing of the branch of a Bit.

3. Self-assertion. *Sc.*

1871 W. Alexander *Johnny Gibb* (1873) 269 Wi' a' 'er ootbearin' an' pride.

†**'out,bearing**, *ppl. a. Obs.* [f. as prec.: out- 10.] Self-assertive, arrogant.

1607 Hieron *Wks.* I. 374 This out-bearing humour.. is so strong in the vnregenerate, that euen when they are condemned and are going away to hell, they will yet turne againe, and say, 'When did wee so and so?' **1626** R. Bernard *Isle of Man* (1627) 157, I tooke it for granted that my Gentrie stood in idlenesse.. in.. great wordes, and in some out-bearing gestures, the formes of Gentry.

out-beg, -beggar, etc.: see out-.

outbelch (aʊt'bɛl(t)ʃ), *v.* [out- 15, 18.] *trans.* **a.** To belch out. **b.** To outdo in belching.

1573 Twyne *Æneid* x. Eej b, Flame forth sparkling hie from head Outbelching spouts forth beames. **1602** *2nd Pt. Return fr. Parnass.* i. vi. 495 Hang him whose verse cannot out-belch the wind.

out-'bellow, *v.* [out- 18, 18 c.] *trans.* **a.** To outdo in bellowing; to roar louder than. **b.** To overcome by bellowing or loud noise.

1623 Bp. Hall *Great Imposter* Wks. (1625) 505 Thus Saul will lie-out his sacrilege, until the very beasts out-bleat and out-bellow him. **1807** *Director* II. 331 To the unspeakable annoyance of the actor, whom they perhaps outbellow in some of his finest passages. **1834** *Fraser's Mag.* X. 16 They .. out-bellow bulls. **1876** Swinburne *Erechtheus* 1340 Its clamour outbellows the thunder.

'outbent, *ppl. a.* [out- 11.] **a.** Bent out or outwards. **b.** Bent upon going or getting out.

1601 Daniel *Civ. Wars* vii. xvi, Which had no power to hold-in minds outbent. **1625** Lisle *Du Bartas, Noe* 151 It is concave and convex, which is as much as to say inbent and out-bent. **1882** W. K. Parker in *Trans. Linn. Soc.* II. iii. 167 The base.. is attached to the most outbent part of the trabecula.

out'bid, *v.* [out- 18, 17.]

1. *trans.* To outdo in bidding or offering a price; to offer a higher price than.

1587 Harrison *England* ii. xviii. (1877) i. 300 One of them doo commonlie vse to out bid another. **1622** Malynes *Anc. Law Merch.* 410 So by outbidding the other, oftentimes to raise the wares. **1741** Middleton *Cicero* I. v. 342 He.. bought the house.. by outbidding all who offered for it. **1901** A. Lang in *Blackw. Mag.* Oct. 490/1 The late Mr. Quaritch outbid me for the only copy of Lautier I ever saw.

2. *fig.* **a.** To offer more than; to outdo or surpass in any quality, statement, etc.

1597 Warner *Alb. Eng.* vi. xxxiii, He.. that would not be out-bid For courage. **1642** Rogers *Naaman* 142 Our out-bidding the Lords owne asking, is no marke of our selfe-deniall. **1853** Herschel *Pop. Lect. Sc.* ii. §5. (1873) 52 He was outbid by Anaximander, who said it was twenty-eight times as large as the earth.

†**b.** Of things: To surpass in value. *Obs.*

1642 ROGERS *Naaman* 392 As much as Crownes or Royalls outbid brasse farthings. **1671** J. ALLEN *Dedham Pulpit* 20 From the unspeakable, unconceivable and excellent worth of this peace, it will outbid all other things in the world.

†**3.** To overestimate, overrate. *Obs.*

1688 SHADWELL *Sqr. Alsatia* v. Wks. 1720 IV. 107 You do me too much honour, you much out-bid my value. **1702** ROWE *Amb. Step-Moth.* I. i. 260 You out-bid my Service; And all returns are vile, but words the poorest.

Hence **out'bidding** *vbl. sb.* and *ppl. a.* Also **out'bidder**, 'one that out-bids' (J.).

1632 I. L. *Law's Resol. Wom. Rights* 146 A thousand out-ridings and out-biddings is no forfeiture. **1830** J. W. CROKER in *C. Papers* (1884) II. xv. 86 The..out-bidding spirit of a tyro at the auction for popularity.

out-Billingsgate, -billow, etc.: see OUT-.

outbirth ('aʊtbɜːθ). [f. OUT- 7 + BIRTH *sb.*[1]]

1. That which is brought forth or produced, or which springs from (something); the outward product or progeny.

1663 W. BAYLY *Visit. fr. on High* 27 They are hid perpetually from the out-birth of the wisdom of this World, and revealed onely to the Babes in the inward spiritual ground in Christ Jesus. **1740** LAW *App. to all that Doubt* (1768) 21 Heaven itself is nothing but the first glorious Out-birth,..the beatific Visibility, of the One God in Trinity. **1842** J. STERLING *Ess.*, etc. *Tennyson* (1848) I. 458 All the rest is the direct outbirth and reflection of our own age.

2. The action or fact of bringing forth. *rare.*

1691 E. TAYLOR tr. *Behmen's Theos. Philos.* vii. 8 The Instrument in the outbirth of this spirit is Venus.

'outblaze, *sb.* [OUT- 7.] A blazing forth.

1843 J. MARTINEAU *Chr. Life* (1867) 87 A more vehement outblaze of human crime.

outblaze (aʊt'bleɪz), *v.* [OUT- 14, 18.]

1. *intr.* To blaze forth, burst out with ardour.

a **1711** KEN *Sion* Poet. Wks. 1721 IV. 384 She to the Hight of heav'nly Ardour rais'd, When next the Daughters met, in Hymn outblaz'd. **1870** MORRIS *Earthly Par.* III. IV. 416 Therewith the smouldering fire again outblazed Within him.

2. *trans.* To surpass in blazing, to obscure by a brighter blaze; *fig.* to outshine in brilliancy.

1742 YOUNG *Nt. Th.* IV. 585 His Wrath inflam'd, his Tenderness on Fire, Like soft, smooth Oil, outblazing other Fires. **1755** J. N. SCOTT *Ess. transl. Homer* 28 In Armour, which out-blaz'd the Lamp of Day. **1861** CRAIK *Hist. Eng. Lit.*, *Milton's Poetry*, A tide of gorgeous eloquence..like a river of molten gold; outblazing..everything of the kind in any other poetry. **1876** OUIDA *In Winter City* vi. 144 To buy big diamonds till she could outblaze Lady Dudley.

†**out'bleed**, *v. Obs.* [OUT- 15, 14, 18.]

1. a. *trans.* To pour out or shed in the form of blood. **b.** *intr.* To flow out as blood. *poetic.*

c **1430** LYDG. *Min. Poems* (Percy Soc.) 235 To paye our raunsoum his blood he did sheede; Nat a smal part, but al he did out bleede. **1580** LD. VAUX in Farr *S.P. Eliz.* (1845) II. 302 Thou, that for loue thy life and loue outblead. **1596** DALRYMPLE tr. *Leslie's Hist. Scot.* VIII. 95 Al the blude of his body is lattne outbleid at the samyn.

2. *trans.* To surpass in bleeding. *nonce-use.*

a **1631** DONNE in *Select.* (1840) 133 To find a languishing wretch in a sordid corner..to set Christ Jesus before him, to out-weep him, out-bleed him, out-die him.

outbloom (-'bluːm), *v.* [OUT- 18.] *trans.* To surpass in bloom. Also *fig.*

1746 W. HORSLEY *Fool* (1748) I. 48 Cheeks that out-bloom the Roses. **1817** BYRON *Beppo* lxxxiv, You still may mark her cheek, out-blooming all. **1861** WHYTE MELVILLE *Good for Nothing* II. 48 She will out-bloom her former self in her new prosperity, even as bleak, barren March is out-bloomed by the merry month of June.

out-'blossom, *v.* [OUT- 18.] = prec.

1695 CONGREVE *Love for Love* v. ii, I have seen fifty in a side-box by Candle-light, out-blossom five and twenty. **1884** TENNYSON *Becket* Prol. 16 True, one rose will out-blossom the rest.

out-'blossoming, *vbl. sb.* [OUT- 9.] The act of blossoming out or forth; a flowering; usu. *fig.*

1907 *Daily Chron.* 31 July 4/4 'Sunday out' has become a well-nigh universal out-blossoming. **1924** W. B. SELBIE *Psychol. Relig.* 178 The religious awakening of adolescence ..is..generally an outblossoming of the whole nature into a larger and more wonderful world. **1932** M. JOYNT tr. *Gougaud's Christianity in Celtic Lands* ii. 45 The wonderful out-blossoming of Christianity which distinguished Ireland in the following ages.

out'blot, *v. poet.* [OUT- 15.] *trans.* To blot out.

1549–69 N. in *Sternhold & Hopkins' Ps.* cix. II. i, Theyr name out blotted in the age, That after shall succede. *a* **1600** *Flodden F.* III. (1664) 32 The chief renown eke of your child Your beastish acts should clear out-blot. *c* **1864** J. ADDIS *Elizab. Echoes* (1879) 16 The heavy fog-wreaths rise..Out-blot the wavering distance. **1901** *Academy* 7 Dec. 572/1 Men, whose sin He would outblot, Ye alone receive Him not.

†**'out-blowed**, *ppl. a. Obs. rare*[-1]. [OUT- 11; ? error for *outblown* or *outbowed.*]

1667 DRYDEN *Ind. Emperor* I. ii. (1668) 6 And at their roots grew floating Palaces, Whose out-blow'd [*ed.* 1725 -blowed] bellies cut the yielding Seas.

'outblowing, *vbl. sb.* [OUT- 9.] A blowing out or outwards. Also **'outblowing** *ppl. a.*, that blows out.

1900 *Geogr. Jrnl.* XVI. 406 Blowing towards and in upon the polar regions to make good the drain caused by the surface outblowing south-easterly winds. **1909** *Daily Chron.* 31 May 4/4 An intaking and outblowing of the breath between the teeth. **1928** PEAKE & FLEURE *Steppe & Sown* 14 The borders..had acquired their characteristic loess soil.. through the outblowing of the winds from the ice sheets over the loose detritus.

outblown ('aʊtbləʊn), *ppl. a.* [OUT- 11.] Blown out, inflated; blown abroad.

1851 MELVILLE *Whale* I. xl. 285 The outblown rumours of the white whale did in the end incorporate with themselves all manner of morbid hints.

out-blunder, -blur, etc.: see OUT-.

out'blush, *v.* [OUT- 18.] *trans.* To outdo in blushing, to surpass in rosy colour.

1634 HABINGTON *Castara* II. (Arb.) 93 Perhaps not the chast morne herselfe disclose Againe, t' outblush th' æmulous rose. **1640** A. MELVILLE *Comm.-pl. Bk.* (1899) 52 The bright sone could not outblusche her. **1703** TATE *On Queen's Pict.* vi, The modest Matron..Out-blush'd her own Vermilion Dye. **1800** T. MOORE *Anacreon* lxvi. 28 Not more the rose, the queen of flowers, Outblushes all the glow of bowers.

out'bluster, *v.* [OUT- 16, 18 b, c.]

1. *trans.* To drive or do out of by blustering.

1748 RICHARDSON *Clarissa* (1811) II. 15 Those wives.. can suffer themselves to be out-blustered and out-gloomed of their own wills, instead of being fooled out of them by acts of tenderness and complaisance.

2. To outdo in blustering, to get the better of by bluster.

a **1863** THACKERAY *Round. Papers, Medal Geo. IV* (1869) 358 If ever I steal a teapot, and my women don't stand up for me..outbluster the policeman, and utter any amount of fibs before Mr. Beak, those beings are not what I take them to be. **1878** J. INGLIS *Sport & Work* xiii. 146 A man..in fierce altercation with another, who tries his utmost to outbluster his furious declamation.

outboard ('aʊtbɔəd), *a.*, *adv. Naut.*, exc. in 3. [f. OUT- 12 + BOARD *sb.* Cf. INBOARD.]

A. *adj.* **1. a.** Situated on the outside of a ship.

1823 CRABB *Technol. Dict.*, *Outboard* (*Mar.*), an epithet for whatever is without the ship. *c* **1850** *Rudim. Navig.* (Weale) 135 *Outboard*, on the outside of the ship, as 'the outboard works'. **1875** BEDFORD *Sailor's Pocket Bk.* VII. (ed. 2) 266 The outboard plane may be made of mess tables.

b. Outward from the median line of a ship.

1893 *Westm. Gaz.* 31 May 6/2 An obstruction had lodged in her outboard pipe. **1895** *Century Mag.* Aug. 597/1 Two passageways..connected the bow and stern 10-inch guns, on the outboard side of each being officers' quarters, etc.

2. Of a motor: attached to the outside of a boat, at the stern; also of a motor-boat propelled by such an engine. Also *ellipt.* as *sb.*, such a motor or boat. Hence ***outboard motor-boating, -motoring, -motorist(e)***.

1909 *National Sportsman* Mar. 488/1 (Advt.), Make a motor boat of any boat in 5 minutes..with the Waterman Outboard Motors. **1914** *Yachting Monthly* XVI. 408 The demand for the outboard motor steadily increases. **1926** S. LEWIS *Mantrap* i. 14 When we don't use the out-board motor, they [*sc.* the Indians] do the paddling, not us. **1928** *Daily Express* 21 Apr. 10/3 The racing 'outboard' boat has given us a fascinating pastime. **1928** *Daily Tel.* 10 July 17/5 Miss Joan Spicer..is one of the best-known of 'outboard-motoristes'. **1928** *Daily Mail* 25 July 17/4 The new pastime of outboard motor-boating. **1928** *Ibid.* 7 Aug. 19/6 One of the big appeals of outboard motoring is the ease with which the boat and engine can be handled. **1935** *Discovery* Mar. 77/1 The journey will be made in the semi-decked whale boat which will be fitted with a 'Seagull' outboard engine. *Ibid.* Aug. 225/1 There are four outboards, with a speed of twenty-five knots. **1943** J. W. DAY *Farming Adventure* iii. 41 In peace-time you would find..the creek noisy with outboards. **1959** P. CAPON *Amongst those Missing* 165 It's probably a canoe with an outboard motor. **1972** D. BLOODWORTH *Any Number can Play* xxi. 214 There's a man looking after the outboard I came in. **1973** J. LEASOR *Host of Extras* v. 66 The roar of an outboard engine splintered my dreams. **1974** *State* (Columbia, S. Carolina) 8 Mar. 4-B/1 (Advt.), Meet the 1974 Mercs. The most advanced outboards in boating. **1977** *Daily Tel.* 24 Feb. 19/7 The water was like glass as the Royal barge came in, chased by.. outboards.

3. (See quot. 1956.)

1928 V. W. PAGÉ *Mod. Aircraft* vii. 267 The parasitic resistance..can be greatly reduced by properly stream-lining the engine supports, especially those of the outboard engines as properly housing the engine mounted in the fuselage offers no particular difficulty. **1956** W. A. HEFLIN *U.S. Air Force Dict.* 365/1 *Outboard.* Of aircraft components: Out toward an airfoil tip; away from the fuselage or hull... *Outboard engine*, on an airplane having four or more engines, an engine farthest from the fuselage or hull.

B. *adv.* **a.** In a direction out from the ship's side, or laterally away from the centre of a ship.

1836–48 B. D. WALSH tr. *Aristophanes* 55 *note*, A strap by which the oar was fastened to the rowlock to prevent its slipping out-board. **1848** J. F. COOPER *Capt. Spike* (Flügel) A window which opened in-board, or toward the deck, and not out-board, or toward the sea.

b. Of position: Outside a ship or boat; nearer to the outside than something else.

1869 SIR E. REED *Ship-build.* xv. 279 The length outboard is 8 feet 6 inches, and that inboard about 3 feet. **1875** STONEHENGE *Brit. Sports* 640 The oar or scull..is always a little heavier outboard than inboard. **1882** NARES *Seamanship* (ed. 6) 154 Which end of the shackle is outboard?

out-boil, -bolt, etc.: see OUT-.

out-bond. A term (in Dictionaries) founded on the phrase *out and in bond*, applied to an alternate disposition of the bricks or stones in forming a quoin or jamb.

1842–76 GWILT *Archit.* Gloss., *Out and in Bond*, a Scotch term for alternate header and stretcher in quoins, and in window and door jambs.

¶ The application of *out-bond* to a 'stretcher' on the face of a wall as given in some recent Dicts. is apparently not in use.

'out-book. In Clearing-house business: Short for *out-clearing book*: see OUT-CLEARING.

1884 HOWARTH *Clearing System* iv. 52 The representative of that bank is obliged to go to the desk of the complainant and take with him his 'out-books'. **1897** *Westm. Gaz.* 5 Mar. 3/1 He puts the cheques, &c., in his case and returns to his office, taking with him his out-books.

out-border, -borough, etc.: see OUT-.

†**'outborn**, *a.* (*sb.*) *Obs.* [OUT- 11.] Born out of the country; of foreign birth. **b.** *sb.* A foreigner.

c **1450** *Cov. Myst.* xxx. (Shaks. Soc.) 302 If Ihesus were outborn in the lond of Galylye. **1532** in Strype *Eccl. Mem.* (1822) I. I. xvii. 207 By whom [an Englishman] the Pope's Holiness may be as well answered..as by an out-born man. *c* **1550** SIR J. CHEKE *Matt.* x. 18 *gloss*, We now cal yem strangers and outborns, and outlandisch.

†**'outborrow**, in phrase *inborrow and outborrow* 'surety in and out': see INBORGH 2. *Obs.*

'out-bound, *a.* [OUT- 11.] Outward bound.

1598 BARRET *Theor. Warres* 120 His home bound Indies fleet being safely arriued, and his outbound sent away. **1666** DRYDEN *Ann. Mirab.* cciv, Outbound ships at home their voyage end. **1842** LONGF. *Sp. Stud.* I. iii, The soft wind Wafts to the out-bound mariner the breath Of the beloved land he leaves behind.

out'bound, *v.* [OUT- 18, 17.] *trans.* **a.** To surpass in bounding. **b.** To leap beyond, overleap.

1760–72 H. BROOKE *Fool of Qual.* (1809) III. 24 He could out-run the rein-deer, and outbound the antelope. **1895** *Westm. Gaz.* 15 Oct. 3/1 It is a case of invention running riot and outbounding restraint.

†**'out-,bounds**, *sb. pl. Obs.* [OUT- 3.] Outward bounds; utmost or extreme boundaries or limits.

1596 SPENSER *State Irel.* Wks. (Globe) 616/2 Knockfargus, Belfast, Armagh, and Carlingfoord, which are now the most out-boundes and abandoned places in the English Pale. **1669** WORLIDGE *Syst. Agric.* (1681) 87 The Propagation of Trees in Hedge-rows, and Out-bounds of his Lands. **1690** *Mor. Ess. Pres. Times* v. 83 Incursion on the Out-bounds of his Lordships Priviledge and Authority.

outbow (aʊt'baʊ), *v.* [OUT- 18.] *trans.* To outdo in bowing.

1728 YOUNG *Love Fame* IV. 74 He can outbow the bowing dean.

†**'out-bowed**, *ppl. a. Obs.* [OUT- 11.] Bowed or bent outwards; bellied, bulged.

1627 BP. HALL *Holy Panegyr.* Wks. 475 The convex or out bowed side of a vessell.

So †**'out,bowing** *ppl. a.* [OUT- 10.], bowing, bending, or bulging outwards, outwardly convex.

1657 PURCHAS *Pol. Flying Ins.* I. xv. 93 The sides being out-bowing.

out-'brag, *v.* [OUT- 18.] *trans.* To outdo in bragging; to go beyond in boastful talk.

1565 GOLDING *Ovid's Met.* XIII. (1593) 297 Thou all others maist outbrag. **1676** WYCHERLEY *Pl. Dealer* I. i. Wks. (Rtldg.) 107/2 To out-flatter a dull poet,..outpromise a lover, outrail a wit, and outbrag a sea-captain. **1837** W. IRVING *Capt. Bonneville* (1849) 181 They..tried to outbrag and out-lie each other. **1886** *All Year Round* 4 Sept. 103.

b. *fig.* To exceed in pride of beauty.

1597 SHAKS. *Lover's Compl.* 95 His phenix downe began but to appeare Like vnshorne veluet, on that termlesse skin Whose bare out-brag'd the web it seem'd to were.

†**out-'braid**, *v.*[1] *Obs.* In pa. t. -braid(e, -breyd(e, etc. [f. OUT- 15 + BRAID *v.*[1] Cf. ABRAID *v.*[1] More correctly written as two words.]

a. *trans.* To wrench, snatch, or pull out; to draw (a sword).

13.. *Coer de L.* 4523 Men off armes the swerdes outbreyde. **1390** GOWER *Conf.* I. 306 And he for wraþþe his swerd out-breide [*rime* seide].

b. *intr.* To start, spring, or burst out.

c **1400** *Sege Jerus.* (E.E.T.S.) 47/827 A womman, bounden with a barn, was on þe body hytte..þat þe barn out brayde fram þe body clene.

c. *trans.* To dart out, to throw out, eject.

1600 FAIRFAX *Tasso* x. i, The snake (that on his crest hot fire out braid) Was quite cut off.

†**out'braid**, *v.*[2] *Obs.* [Altered form of ABRAID *v.*[2] = UPBRAID: prob. due to the equivalence of

prec. with ABRAID *v.*[1]] *trans.* To upbraid, reproach. Hence † **out'braiding** *vbl. sb.*

1509 BARCLAY *Shyp of Folys* (1570) 96 They haue no pleasure, but thought, and great disease, Rebuke, outbrayding, and stripes. *Ibid.* 193 His frende he soone outbraydeth of the same. *c* **1510** —— *Mirr. Gd. Manners* (1570) F v, Thou should straungers in no maner despise, Outbrayding nor scorning with deede or wordes fell.

out'branch, *v. rare.* [OUT- 14.] *intr.* To branch out, ramify. *poet.*

1835 BROWNING *Paracelsus* v. 144 The molten ore.. Winds into the stone's heart, outbranches bright In hidden mines. **1868** STEPHENS *Runic Mon.* I. p. v, Sciences, subtilly out-branching up and down and sideways into yet other near by lore-fields.

'outbranching, *vbl. sb.* [OUT- 9.] A branching out, ramification. So **'outbranching** *ppl. a.* [OUT- 10], branching out.

1855 BAILEY *Mystic*, etc. 123 The holy outbranchings of divinity. **1858** W. ARNOT *Laws fr. Heaven* II. xii. 96 There are many outbranching bypaths. **1880** FAIRBAIRN *Stud. Life Christ* v. (1881) 89 No outbranching trees made a cool restful shade.

outbrast, obs. pa. t. of OUTBURST *v.*

outbrave (aʊt'breɪv), *v.* [OUT- 18 b.]

1. *trans.* To face with show of defiance; to stand out against bravely or defiantly.

1589 NASHE *Ded. Greene's Menaphon* (Arb.) 6 Who.. think to outbraue better pens with the swelling bumbast of a bragging blanke verse. **1605** ROWLANDS *Hell's Broke Loose* 36, I haue knowne men die, That haue out-brau'd the Hangman to his face. **1622** MARKHAM *Decades Warre* v. 200 Let him therefore only outbraue danger, not wooe it. **1796** MORSE *Amer. Geog.* II. 20 Instead of guarding against the inclemency of the weather, they outbrave it. **1828** D'ISRAELI *Chas. I*, I. xii. 326 The Duke sat outfacing his accusers, and outbraving their accusations.

2. To outdo or surpass in bravery or daring.

1596 SHAKS. *Merch. V.* II. i. 28, I would.. Out-brave the heart most daring on the earth.. To win the Ladie. **1612** DRAYTON *Poly-olb.* v. 82 That those proud Airies,.. Outbrave not this our kind in mettle. **1814** BYRON *Lara* II. xiv, Outnumber'd, not outbraved, they still oppose Despair to daring, and a front to foes.

b. To outdo or excel in beauty, finery, or splendour of array; cf. BRAVERY 3.

1589 GREENE *Menaphon* (Arb.) 60 Cupide dismounted from his mothers lappe.. to outbraue the Thessalian dames in their beautie. **1597** GERARDE *Herbal* Pref., The Lillies of the field outbraued him. *a* **1661** FULLER *Worthies* (1840) II. 487 Solomon himself is out-braved therewith [a flower]. **1861** DIXON *Pers. Hist. Bacon* vii. §21 The prodigal bride-groom,.. clad in a suit of Genoese velvet, purple from cap to shoe, outbraves them all.

c. To outrival or surpass (in any quality).

1589 WARNER *Alb. Eng.* VI. xxx, My husband though by trade a Smith, for birth out-brau'd of none. **1622** DRAYTON *Poly-olb.* xxii. 48 Liuells, a large Waste, which other plaines out-braues. **1750** CARTE *Hist. Eng.* II. 310 He affected every where.. to out-brave them on all publick occasions.

Hence **out'braved** *ppl. a.*, **out'braving** *vbl. sb.* and *ppl. a.*

1601 CHESTER *Love's Mart.* (Shaks. Soc.) 56 Their out-brauing termes. **1630** I. CRAVEN *God's Tribunall* (1631) 32 The out-brauings of roaring Ephraimites. **1652** J. WRIGHT tr. *Camus' Nat. Paradox* III. 50, I am no Man to suffer such out-braving Language. **1870** MORRIS *Earthly Par.* II. III. 129 Suffice it, that no outbraved death Might end him. **1871** ROSSETTI *Poems, Jenny* 81 From shame and shame's out-braving too, Is rest not sometimes sweet to you?

out-bray, *v.* [OUT- 15, 18.]

†**1.** *trans.* To bray out, ejaculate, utter: see BRAY *v.*[1] 4, and cf. ABRAY *v.* 3 b. (Properly two words.) *Obs.*

1558 G. CAVENDISH *Poems* (1825) II. 39 Hir voyce she out brayd. **1559** *Mirr. Mag.* (1563) Q j, Whose rufull voyce no sooner had out brayed Those wofull wordes. *Ibid.* X ij, Wyth a sygh outbrayed, With woful cheare these woful wurdes he sayd. **1603** FLORIO *Montaigne* II. xii. (1632) 310 For it enraged rave's, and idle talk outbrayes.

2. To outdo or surpass in braying or roaring.

1806–7 J. BERESFORD *Miseries Hum. Life* (1826) IV. vii, A cart containing a million of iron bars which you must out-bray.

out'brazen, *v.* [f. OUT- 15 b, 18 + BRAZEN *v.*]

1. To brazen out; to face out or maintain defiantly or impudently.

1681 T. FLATMAN *Heraclitus Ridens* No. 29 (1713) I. 190 To out-brazen the Belief of a Conspiracy.. to seize the King. **1755** YOUNG *Centaur* Ded. 15 High-bred, unbridled colts.. with a blaze in their foreheads, to outbrazen my rebukes.

2. To outdo or surpass in unabashedness.

1702 T. BROWN *Lett. fr. Dead* Wks. 1760 II. 216 The expertest devils.. turn pale.. to see their impudence out-brazen'd by a club of mortal puritans. **1710** *Managers' Pro & Con* 39 Did he not.. out-brazen Sacheverell himself? **1878** E. JENKINS *Haverholme* 6 Could you not face the world and outbrazen the Devil?

† **'out-breach.** *Obs.* [OUT- 7.] An outbreak.

1609 BP. W. BARLOW *Answ. Nameless Cath.* 352 This last reuolt and contemptuous out-breach so exceedingly disloyall.. to his Gratious Soueraigne.

outbreak ('aʊtbreɪk), *sb.* [OUT- 7.]

1. A breaking out; an eruption; an outburst of feeling or passion, of hostilities, of disease, of volcanic energy, etc.

1602 SHAKS. *Ham.* II. i. 33 The flash and out-breake of a fiery minde. **1818** LADY MORGAN *Autobiog.* 23 It is the spontaneous outbreak of a good and kind heart. **1830** HERSCHEL *Stud. Nat. Philos.* 348 The first out-break of modern science. **1848** KINGSLEY *Saint's Trag.* III. i. 74, I had expected some such passionate outbreak. **1855** MACAULAY *Hist. Eng.* xiv. III. 419 An outbreak of patriotic and religious enthusiasm. **1878** HUXLEY *Physiogr.* 199 In some case volcanic outbreaks take place actually beneath the sea. **1879** *St. George's Hosp. Rep.* IX. 714 Two diphtheritic outbreaks. **1885** *L'pool Daily Post* 11 Apr. 4/7 Since the outbreak of the Crimean War.

2. *Geol.* The emergence of a rock at the surface; the outcrop of a stratum; the eruption of an intrusive igneous rock.

1806 MARTIN in *Phil. Trans.* XCVI. 345 If the whole.. was an even plain, the border or outbreak of each stratum would appear regular and true. **1828** *Craven Gloss.* (ed. 2) s.v., When a vein of coal, &c. appears on the surface, it is called an *out-breck*, the same as a crop-out. **1873** TRISTRAM *Moab* iv. 65 In the neighbourhood of the basaltic outbreaks which frequently disturb the stratification.

3. A breach of the peace; a public display of opposition to established authority; an insurrection.

1849 MACAULAY *Hist. Eng.* viii. II. 440 If the misgovernment of James were suffered to continue, it must produce.. a popular outbreak. **1851** GALLENGA *Italy* 71 Revolutionary outbreaks in Sicily. **1858** BUCKLE *Civiliz.* (1873) II. viii. 593 Outbreaks, no doubt, there have been and will be; but they are bursts of lawlessness rather than of liberty.

outbreak (ˌaʊt'breɪk), *v.* [OUT- 14.] *intr.* To break out. (In OE. and ME. properly two words; now only poetic.)

c **1000** ÆLFRIC *Saints' Lives* xxxi. 866 Swa þæt him forburnon on þam bæce his reaf and he for ðam bryne ut bræcan ne mihte. **1297** R. GLOUC. (Rolls) 6567 Baldeliche he spac & sturneliche to þis water, þo it alles out brac. *c* **1400** *Ywaine & Gaw.* 3243 Now es the lioun out broken. *c* **1450** LONELICH *Grail* xxvi. 112 And longe it was Er.. Ony word Eiþer myhte Owt Breke. **1604** HIERON *Wks.* I. 574 And now and then outbrake the light. **1870** MORRIS *Earthly Par.* I. I. 95 A frightful clamour from the wall outbroke.

b. To burst into flower.

1870 MORRIS *Earthly Par.* II. III. 193 Round Venus' feet Outbroke the changing spring-flowers sweet.

'out-breaker[1]. [OUT- 8.] One who makes or joins in an outbreak.

a **1670** SPALDING *Troub. Chas. I* (1850) I. 8 But the principall outbrakeris and malefactouris wes spairit.

'outˌbreaker[2]. [f. OUT- 3 + BREAKER *sb.*[1] 5.] A breaker at a distance from the shore.

1801 SOUTHEY *Thalaba* XII. viii, The dash Of the outbreakers deaden'd.

'outˌbreaking, *vbl. sb.* [OUT- 9.] A breaking or bursting out: see *break out* in BREAK *v.* 55.

c **1425** *Foundat. St. Bartholomew's* (E.E.T.S.) 15 Whate fastidious outbrekyngys hadde temptid hym. **1432–50** tr. *Higden* (Rolls) V. 187 Valentinianus Augustus.. deide in a manere outbrekynge of his veynes. **1638** SIR T. HERBERT *Trav.* (ed. 2) 41 He.. is (by the fresh out breaking of her beauty) captivated. **1721** E. ERSKINE *Wks.* (1871) I. 104 They are free of gross outbreakings, being no common drunkards, swearers or Sabbathbreakers. **1838** THIRLWALL *Greece* xx. III. 135 The place of its first outbreaking.. indicates that the contagion came from abroad.

'outˌbreaking, *ppl. a.* [OUT- 10.] That breaks or bursts out: see prec.

1601 DANIEL *Civ. Wars* VII. i, Disordinate Authoritie.. durst not to proceed With an outbreaking course. **1826** E. IRVING *Babylon* II. VII. 176 Denoted by the outbreaking sore. **1837** CARLYLE *Fr. Rev.* I. IV. i, Immeasurable, manifold; as the sound of outbreaking waters.

† **out-'breast,** *v. Obs.* [OUT- 18 b.] *trans.* To surpass in vocal achievement; to excel in singing.

1612 *Two Noble K.* v. vi, Two emulous Philomels.. now one the higher, Anon the other, then again the first, And by and by out-breasted, that the sense Could not judge between 'em.

outbreathe (aʊt'briːð), *v.* [OUT- 14, 15.]

1. *trans.* To breathe out; †to expire; to exhale; to emit as breath. Now *poet.*

1559 *Mirr. Mag.* Induct. (1563) R ij, Outbrething nought but discord euery where. **1572** J. JONES *Bathes Buckstone* 9 Not easely to be outbreathed by vapour. **1658** A. FOX *Wurtz' Surg.* I. iv. 17 This young man out-breathed his last within few houres after. **1860** F. W. FABER *Hymn, Eternal Spirit* xii, Thou art an unborn Breath outbreathed On angels and on men. **1866** CONINGTON tr. *Virg. Æneid* VIII. 266 Cacus in his robber-lair Outbreathing smoke and flame.

2. *intr.* or *absol.*

a **1625** FLETCHER *Love's Pilgr.* I. i, No smoak nor steam, out-breathing from the kitchen. *a* **1851** MOIR *Lament of Selim* i, The flowers outbreathe beneath my feet.

So **'outbreathed** (-briːðd), *ppl. a.*[1], breathed out.

a **1596** SPENSER (J.), That sign of last outbreathed life did seem. **1771** MACKENZIE *Man Feel.* xxviii. (1803) 48 Her look had the horrid calmness of out-breathed despair. **1914** R. M. JONES *Spiritual Reformers 16th & 17th Cent.* 177 This entire manifested or out-breathed universe is, he says, the expression of the divine desire for holy sport and play.

outbreathed (aʊt'brɛθt), *ppl. a.*[2] [f. OUT- 26 + BREATH *sb.* + -ED.] Put out of breath.

1597 SHAKS. *2 Hen. IV*, I. i. 108 Rend'ring faint quittance (wearied, and out-breath'd) To Henrie Monmouth. **1760–72** H. BROOKE *Fool of Qual.* (1809) I. 84 Being all out-breathed in turns, they remitted from their toil. **1816** BYRON *Siege of Cor.* xxiv, Outbreathed and worn, Corinth's sons were downward borne.

'outˌbreathing, *vbl. sb.* [OUT- 9.] A breathing out: an exhalation.

1831 LD. HOUGHTON *Mem. Many Scenes, Italian to Italy* (1844) 75 The bland outbreathings of the Midland Sea. **1846** TRENCH *Mirac.* xiii. (1862) 240–1 An actual outstreaming and outbreathing of the fulness of his inner life.

So **'outˌbreathing** *ppl. a.* [OUT- 10], breathing out.

1849 SEARS *Regeneration* II. i. (1859) 71 The outbreathing influence of a living person.

'outbred, *ppl. a.* [OUT- 11.] Bred from parents not closely related.

1903 *Biometrika* II. 171 Waltzing mice must be crossed with in-bred and out-bred pure-bred albinos and in-bred and out-bred cross-bred albinos. **1955** *New Biol.* XVIII. 38 In an outbred population.. things are very different. **1959** C. D. DARLINGTON *Darwin's Place in Hist.* x. 56 All the 'plasticity' (or variability) is due to the inbreeding of outbred plants and animals, or to the outbreeding of inbred plants and animals. **1977** *Times* 14 Apr. 14/4 There were consistent differences [in I.Q.] between the outbred children and the children of first cousins.

outbreed, *v.* [OUT- 14, 18.] **1.** (Stress even or on first syllable.) *trans.* and *intr.* To breed from parents not closely related.

1919 EAST & JONES *Inbreeding & Outbreeding* xi. 214 Whether plants are inbred or outbred is a matter which is left to regulate itself. **1968** *Times* 23 May 17/4 In the wild it is usually an advantage for plants to outbreed—to reproduce by fertilization with other individuals not themselves.

2. (Stress on second syllable.) *trans.* To be quicker or more prolific in breeding than.

1903 in *N.E.D.* s.v. *out-* 18. **1926** BELLOC *Compan. Wells's Outl. Hist.* ii. 24/2 A slightly faster minority of swallows always outlive and outbreed their slower rivals. **1976** K. BONFIGLIOLI *Something Nasty in Woodshed* i. 10 Only the sparrow.. can outbreed magpies by diddling his mate all the year round.

'outbreeder. [OUT- 8 + BREEDER 1.] A plant which is not self-fertile, or an animal in which breeding pairs are not closely related.

1963 E. MAYR *Animal Species & Evolution* xiv. 421 The entire breeding system of outbreeders is so organized as to accumulate and preserve genetic variation. **1963** DAVIS & HEYWOOD *Princ. Angiosperm Taxon.* xiii. 424 In many forest trees which are outbreeders, pollen may disperse for long distances. **1975** S. K. JAIN in Frankel & Hawkes *Crop Genetic Resources* ii. 22 We speak of.. outbreeders, inbreeders, and apomicts.

'outbreeding, *vbl. sb.* [f. OUTBREED *v.*] Breeding from parents not closely related.

1901 *Bull. U.S. Dept. Agric. Div. Veg. Physiol.* XXIX. 38 'In-and-in breeding', 'outbreeding' and other expressions relating to the close or distant relationship of parents have been prominent subjects among animal breeders. **1902** *Encycl. Brit.* XXV. 372/2 The tribes practised far more in-breeding than outbreeding. **1919** EAST & JONES *Inbreeding & Outbreeding* i. 13 Interest in the effects of inbreeding and of outbreeding is not confined to the professional biologist. **1940** *Nature* 30 Mar. 485/2 If we are to regard unisexuality simply as one of a number of outbreeding mechanisms, it is necessary to account for the fact that it is frequently found in some groups.. but rare in others. **1959** C. D. DARLINGTON *Darwin's Place in Hist.* xii. 70 Outbreeding is necessary for the recombination of differences. **1964** E. J. H. CORNER *Life of Plants* xi. 197 Flowers have devices.. to carry pollen from one flower to another, and, preferably, from one plant to another, to secure outbreeding. **1967** *Economist* 16 Dec. 1108/2 There is no evidence.. that dairy stock are suffering from too close breeding through artificial insemination. Too much out-breeding.. would be a more valid criticism. **1975** S. K. JAIN in Frankel & Hawkes *Crop Genetic Resources* ii. 22 Many specific genetic factors are known which regulate the degree of outbreeding.

outbrew to **out-bubble**: see OUT-.

out'bring, *v. rare.* [OUT- 15. In ME. two words; in 17th c. poetic.] *trans.* To bring out: see BRING *v.* 21.

a **1200** *Moral Ode* 183 His frond he ut brochte. *c* **1374** CHAUCER *Troylus* III. 908 (958) She kowde nought a word a-ryght out brynge. **1623** H. AINSWORTH *Ps.* in Farr *S.P. Jas. I* 78 And he outbrings them out of their anguishes.

outbrist, obs. Sc. form of OUTBURST.

[**out-bud** or **outbud,** *v.*, is given in some Dicts. as from Spenser, who has only the two words *out budding* = *budding out*.

1590 SPENSER *F.Q.* I. vii. 17 Whose many heades, out budding ever new, Did breed him endlesse labor to subdew.]

'out-ˌbudding, *vbl. sb.* [OUT- 9.] A budding out; the bursting forth of a bud or buds.

1840 CARLYLE *Heroes* iii. 159 That strange outbudding of our whole English Existence, which we call the Elizabethan Era.

outbuild (-'bɪld), *v.* [OUT- 18, 17, 15.]

1. *trans.* To surpass in building or durability of building; in quot. 1834 *catachr.* to overbuild.

1742 YOUNG *Nt. Th.* VI. 312 Virtue alone out-builds the Pyramids. **1834** MAR. EDGEWORTH *Helen* viii. I. 160 She had left off building castles in the air, but she had outbuilt herself on earth.

2. To build out. *poetic* and *rhet.*
1847 Emerson *Poems* (1857) 15 Or how the fish outbuilt her shell. **1890** J. Pulsford *Loyalty to Christ* I. 318 In Him the hidden affections and power of our Father are outbuilt and expressed.

'out-,building. [out- 1.] A detached building, subordinate and accessory to a main building; an out-house.
1626 Sir R. Boyle in *Lismore Papers* (1886) II. 191 New owtbwyldings of my stables. **1824** Miss Mitford *Village* Ser. I. (1863) 78 The great farm, with its picturesque out-buildings. **1851** Hawthorne *Seven Gables* xiii, A huge load of oak-wood was passing through the gateway, towards the out-buildings in the rear.

out-'bulk, [out- 18.] *trans.* To exceed in bulk.
1652 Benlowes *Theoph.* v. xlix, And, eight score times out-bulks the Earth. **1879** H. N. Hudson *Hamlet* Pref. 4 We find the gloss, I can not say out-weighing, but certainly far out-bulking, the text.

out-buller, etc.: see out- 14.

out-'bully, *v.* [out- 18, 18 c.] *trans.* To get the better of by bullying; to have the best of in bullying.
1708 *Diss. Drunkenness* 15 That he may not be out-bullied by the Oaths of Hackney-Coachmen. **1825–9** Mrs. Sherwood *Lady of Manor* (1860) V. xxxiii. 376, I myself should have ventured to mount any horse in my father's stud, and could out-bully any groom in his stable.

out-'burn, *v.* [out- 14, 18, 17. (In ME. as two words.)]
1. *intr.* To burn out or away, to be consumed.
1597 Shaks. *Pass. Pilgr.* vii, She burn'd out love, as soon as straw out-burneth.
2. *trans.* To exceed in burning, burn longer than.
1742 Young *Nt. Th.* ix. 165 Amazing Period! when each Mountain-Height Out-burns Vesuvius. **1832** Tennyson *Dream Fair Wom.* 146 Lamps which outburn'd Canopus.
So **'out-burning** *vbl. sb.*, burning out, extinction; **out-burnt** *ppl. a.*, burnt out, exhausted.
1382 Wyclif *Isa.* lxiv. 2 As out brennyng [Vulg. *exustio*] of fyr, they shulden vanshe awei. **1837** Carlyle *Fr. Rev.* I. iii. iii, In dull smoke and ashes of out-burnt Sensualities.

outburst ('aʊtbɜːst), *sb.* [out- 7.]
1. a. An act of bursting out; a violent issue; an outbreak, explosion (of feeling, fervour, indignation, etc.); a volcanic eruption.
1657 Trapp *Comm. Job* iii. 3 They repent of their out-bursts. **1855** Bain *Senses & Int.* ii. i. §12 (1864) 96 The first outburst of muscular vigour in a healthy frame. **1860** Geo. Eliot *Mill on Floss* iii. ii, Tom was a little shocked at Maggie's outburst. **1874** L. Stephen *Hours in Library* (1892) I. vii. 259 This narrative is.. not a volcanic outburst to shake the foundations of society.
b. *Astr.* A solar radio emission of great intensity and several minutes' duration which occurs in conjunction with a solar flare.
1947 C. W. Allen in *Monthly Notices R. Astron. Soc.* CVII. 387 Besides steady noise and bursts, one can detect, rather rarely, sudden outbursts of radio noise, which last for a few minutes, fluctuating violently, and then disappear. *Ibid.* 394 It is this correlation between flares and outbursts that shows that an outburst has a particular physical significance. **1955** *Sci. Amer.* June 42/3 The more common type of burst is a brief surge of intensity lasting only a few seconds; we call this a 'radio flash'. During a week of intense activity on the sun, there may be 100 flashes. The second type, far less frequent, is a burst lasting several minutes; this is called an 'outburst'. The outbursts.. come only during a solar flare. **1971** J. S. Hey *Radio Universe* v. 104 Large flares are often accompanied by very intense outbursts of radiation on metre wavelengths lasting between about 5 and 30 min. In a classification of radio bursts according to their characteristic properties, these outbursts have been designated as Type II radio bursts. *Ibid.* 108 The microwave outbursts, often called microwave Type IV, sometimes accompany large flares and are particularly interesting because of their association with solar cosmic rays.
2. The emergence of a rock or stratum at the surface; an outcrop; = outbreak *sb.* 2.
1708 J. C. *Compleat Collier* (1845) 10 There is an Out-burst or an appearance above ground of some vein of Coal. **1822** J. Flint *Lett. Amer.* 60 The strata being horizontal, and the out-burst of the coal about the middle-steep of the hill.
3. *Comb.* **outburst-bank**, the middle part of a sea-embankment.
1852 Wiggins *Embanking* 25 The outburst bank, 5 feet high and 8 feet wide at top, and with a slope of but 1½ to 1, because this part of the bank will have to sustain but a transient stress from the top of the tide. *Ibid.* 123 The tide will not flow more than 10 feet at ordinary springs, in which case the main bank will not be more than 6 feet in height, and the outburst and swash banks 4 feet more.

out'burst, *v. rare.* Forms: see out *adv.* and burst *v.* [out- 14. (In ME. usually two words, now poetic.)] *intr.* To burst out.
13.. *Cursor M.* 1088 (Gött.) A syhing of his hert vte brast. *c* **1400** *Destr. Troy* 8045 That the blode outbrast, & on brest light. *c* **1430** *Freemasonry* 761 Suche worde myȝht ther outberste That myȝht make the sytte yn evel reste. **1568** *Satir. Poems Reform.* ix. 124 Their boiling malice that lay hid In rageing sort outbrast. **1855** Browning *Saul* xiii, Then safely outburst The fan-branches all round.

'out,bursting, *vbl. sb.* [out- 9.] A bursting out or forth. So **'out,bursting** *ppl. a.* [out- 10].
1846 Trench *Hulsean Lect.* Ser. ii. ii. 170 The outbursting of bud and blossom, the signs of the reviving year. **1853** Talfourd *Castilian* ii. ii, Roar, and speak The strong out-bursting of a nation's soul. **1854** J. Bruce *Biog. Samson* v. 124 Floods of outbursting tears. **1880** W. M. Williams in *Gentl. Mag.* Dec. 749 Such outbursting gases.

out-bury, -bustle, etc.: see out-.

'out-,butting, *vbl. sb.* [out- 7: cf. to *butt out.*] *concr.* A part that butts out; a projection.
1730 A. Gordon *Maffei's Amphith.* 267 The small Out-buttings of the Podium.

out'buy, *v.* [out- 18, 15.] *trans.* To outdo or beat in buying; †to buy at a price beyond the value; †to buy out or off, to pay to be rid of (*obs.*).
1608 Chapman *Byron's Consp.* Plays 1873 II. 234 He that winnes Empire with the losse of faith Out-buies it. **1616** Sir T. Roe *Jrnl.* 10 Aug. (1899) 228 They [Dutch] would both out-present, out-bribe, and out-buy vs in all things. **1634** Bp. Hall *Contempl., N.T.* iv. xv, The wand and the sheet are for poor offenders, the great either outface or out-buy their shame.

out-buzz, etc.: see out-.

,out-'by, -bye, *adv.* (*a.*) *Sc.* and *north. dial.* [f. out *adv.* + by *adv.* Cf. in-by(e.] Out a little way; a short distance out; outside the house, abroad, in the open air; to the outside (of a house, mine, farm, etc.).
a **1400–50** *Alexander* 2762 (Ashm.) Þe ledis out of Landace & all þe landis out-by. **1752** D. Stewart in *Scots Mag.* (1753) July 344/2 There were two gentlemen wanting him out-by. **1819** Scott *Br. Lamm.* vii, A' gaes wrang when the Master's out-bye. *Ibid.* xxv, The very pick-maws and solan geese outby yonder at the Bass. **1881** Raymond *Mining Gloss.*, *Outbye* or *Outbyeside*, Newc., nearer to the shaft, and hence further from the forewinning. **1886** Stevenson *Kidnapped* 30 Step out-by to the door a minute.
b. *attrib.* Outside, out-of-doors, as ***out-by work***, field-labour, ***out-by servant, worker*** (on a farm); out-lying, as 'the sheep in the out-by field'; ***out-by farm***, a moorland farm.
1816 Scott *Bl. Dwarf* x, Harry and I hae been to gather what was on the outbye land, and there's scarce a cloot left. **1896** N. Munro *Lost Pibroch* (1902) 104 Our folk lived the clean outby life of shepherds and early risers. **1898** Paton *Castlebraes* 145 (E.D.D.) The outbye agricultural workers.

out-call, -calvinize, etc.: see out-.

'out-camp. Chiefly *N. Amer.* [out- 1.] A camp at some distance from the main camp.
1844 *Knickerbocker* XXIII. 116 The Sioux.. would not fail to attack, according to their custom, the out-camps. **1944** T. Onraet *Sixty Below* ix. 96, I had a little rice and bacon in one of my out-camps. *a* **1951** E. Hill in Murdoch & Drake-Brockman *Austral. Short Stories* (1951) 292 The lone little cavalcade.. passed a deserted out-camp. **1970** *Islander* (Victoria, B.C.) 1 Nov. 12/2 From his main cabin, Sam had four outcamps along his trapline.

out-'cant, *v.* [out- 18.] *trans.* To surpass or excel in the use of cant (see cant *sb.*³).
1658 Osborn *Adv. Son* (1673) 182, I have heard him.. at another time out-Cant a London Chirurgion. **1670** W. Clarke *Nat. Hist. Nitre* 91 If you would with my Lord Bacon out-cant these or other Artists in their own Terms. **1772** *Ann. Reg.* 7 A prince.. who has.. out-canted the most zealous enthusiasts in his appeals to heaven.

out-caper, -carol, etc.: see out-.

'out,carried, *ppl. a.* [out- 11.] Exported.
1878 A. Barlow *Weaving* 17 Sum of the out-carried commodities in value and custom, £294,184. 17. 2.

out'carry, *v.* [f. out- 15 b, 18 + carry *v.*]
†**1.** *trans.* To carry out, accomplish. *Obs.*
1611 *Char. Author* in *Coryat's Crudities*, But he free from all other symptomes of aspiring will easily outcary that.
2. *Naut.* To carry more sail than; hence, to outsail, sail faster than.
1833 M. Scott *Tom Cringle* viii. (1859) 158 His Britannic Majesty's schooner Gleam will from his greater beam and superior length outcarry and forereach on you. **1844** W. H. Maxwell *Sports & Adv. Scotl.* xiii. (1855) 119 If the breeze freshened, the Clorinde outcarried the schooner.

'out-,carrying, *vbl. sb.* [out- 9.] Carrying out: **a.** Exportation. **b.** Accomplishment in practice.
1579 Fenton *Guicciard.* xviii. (1599) 851 He gaue out ordenance, that there should not be transportation nor out-carying of goods. **1884** J. Parker *Apost. Life* III. 39 The out-carrying of a solemn step that involved the entire life.

outcast ('aʊtkɑːst, -æ-), *sb.*¹ [sb. use of outcast *ppl. a.*]
1. A person 'cast out' or rejected; an abject; a castaway; one rejected or cast off by his friends or by society; an exile; a homeless vagabond.
13.. *Evang. Nicod.* 746 in Herrig *Archiv* LIII. 405 Þou out cast of all men, how dar þou negh þis temple nere. **1388** Wyclif *Ps.* lxxxiii[i]. 11, I chees to be an out cast [Vulg. *abjectus*] in the hous of my God. **1526** *Pilgr. Perf.* (W. de W. 1531) 117, I shall than be reputed as an outcast & nothynge set by. **1535** Coverdale *Ps.* xxi[i]. 6, I am a worme and no man: a very scorne of men and the outcast of the people. **1570** Levins *Manip.* 36/12 An outcast, *abiectus*. **1733** Pope *Ep. Cobham* 204 He dies, sad outcast of each church and state. **1832** Ht. Martineau *Homes Abr.* vi. 78 Being thus made outcasts, they acted as outcasts. **1849** Macaulay *Hist. Eng.* iii. I. 363 Quarters peopled by the outcasts of society.
2. That which is thrown out or away, refuse, offal; a plant thrown out from a garden.
1398 Trevisa *Barth. De P.R.* xvii. cxxxv. (Bodl. MS.) lf. 224/2 Hulkes and offal and oute caste of corne. *c* **1440** *Promp. Parv.* 375/1 Owte caste, or refuse, or coralyce of corne,.. *cribalum.* **1796** Withering *Brit. Plants* (ed. 3) II. 309 Found.. in a situation that would allow of its being an out-cast of a garden. **1842** *Jrnl. R. Agric. Soc.* III. ii. 325 A nobleman.. made a large pond in the solid clay, and burnt all the outcast.
†**3.** An inferior sheep culled from the rest of the flock. *Obs.*
1671 *Inv.* in Anderson *Hist. Lea* 25 (N.W. Lincolns. Gloss.) Fifty-two weathers and hogges, outcasts.
†**4.** A projectile. *Obs.*
1674 N. Fairfax *Bulk & Selv.* 120 The rist or spring of all that swiftness that is given to outcasts. *Ibid.* 129 When we give a dartingness to outcasts.
†**5.** A part thrown out or built out from the main body of a building. *Obs.*
1574 *Nottingham Rec.* IV. 157 For a chymney and ij. out castes or purprestures to his house. **1616** Surfl. & Markh. *Country Farme* 87 You shall make round about the Doue-house, on the outside, two out-casts of hewed stone, or round rings of plaister, as broad as three or four chesse of stones.

'outcast, *sb.*² [out- 7.]
†**1.** The act of casting out; expulsion. *Obs.*
1600 W. Watson *Decacordon* (1602) 46 [There is] no danger at all.. to the Church.. by their [the Jesuits'] outcast.
2. The act of throwing out or from one.
1864 *Gd. Words* 599/2 At each out-cast, it [a net] opens at every mesh.
3. A falling out, quarrel. (Cf. cast *v.* 81 f.) *Sc.*
1634 *Tyninghame Sess. Records* in A. L. Ritchie *Ch. St. Baldred* (1880) 238 Thair was ane outcast between George Shortus and George Foster. **1637** Rutherford *Lett., to Jas. Murray* 21 Nov. (1671) 321, I tremble at the remembrance of a new out-cast betwixt him and me. **1818** Scott *Hrt. Midl.* xlvii, Reuben never sleeps weel, nor I neither, when you and he hae had ony bit outcast.
†**4.** An outlet; a vent. *Obs.*
1601 Holland *Pliny* xxxi. iii. II. 409 On either side of such pits.. certaine out-casts, tunnels, or venting holes, to receiue those hurtfull and dangerous vapours.

outcast ('aʊtkɑːst, -æ-), *ppl. a.* [out- 11: see *cast out*, cast *v.* 81.]
1. Of persons: *orig.* Abject, socially despised; in later use, Cast out from home and friends; hence, forsaken, forlorn, homeless and neglected.
c **1374** Chaucer *Boeth.* iii. pr. iv. 57 (Camb. MS.) So mochel the fowlere and the moore owt cast [*abjectior*] þat he is despised of most folk. *c* **1400** *Rule St. Benet* (E.E.T.S.) 76/1034 Mine awne condicions wil I ken, Reproue & oute kast of al women. *c* **1600** Shaks. Sonn. xxix, I all alone beweep my outcast state. **1795–7** Southey *Juvenile & Minor Poems* Poet. Wks. II. 72 Barbarous climes, Where angry England sends her outcast sons. **1828** S. R. Maitland *Let. Rev. C. Simeon* 20 In this state of out-cast misery he lived for more than four years. **1860** Froude *Hist. Eng.* V. 112 The highways and the villages were covered.. with forlorn and outcast families, now reduced to beggary. **1888** *Pall Mall G.* 23 Oct. 1/2 The bitter cry of outcast London.
2. Of things: Rejected, discarded.
c **1560** R. Morice in *Lett. Lit. Men* (Camden) 25 Emongs the outecaste papers I haue founde one fragment of a Bull of Indulgences. **1605** Camden *Rem.* Ded. 2 The rude rubble and out-cast rubbish.. of a greater and more serious worke. **1853** Kane *Grinnell Exp.* xvii. (1856) 129 To convert several outcast eatables to good palatable food.
†**3.** Thrown out as an extension from the main building. *Obs.*
a **1645** Habington *Surv. Worcs.* in *Worcs. Hist. Soc. Proc.* i. 135 In the Churcheyarde On the Southe syde aboue an outcast chappell.

out'cast, *v.* Now *rare.* [out- 15. (In ME. orig. two words: now poetic.)] *trans.* To cast out: see cast *v.* 81. So **out'cast** *pa. pple.*
a **1300** *E.E. Psalter* lxxxiii[i]. 11, I ches out casten for to bin In þe hous of God is min. *a* **1325** *Prose Psalter* cviii[i]. 9 Ben hij outcusten of her woninges. *c* **1374** Chaucer *Troylus* v. 615 Here I dwelle out cast [*v.r.* cast out] from alle Ioye. *a* **1425** *Cursor M.* 18231 (Trin.) Outcast þou art of goddes aungele. **1483** *Cath. Angl.* 264/2 To Oute caste, *abicere*... Oute castyn, *abiectus*. *c* **1580** *Howers Bless. Virg.* 100 Thou .. wilt, as I think, me utterly outcast. *a* **1662** Heylin *Laud* (1668) 156 It being the custom of all those whom the Court casts out, to labour by all means they can to out-cast the Court. **1741** E. Erskine *Serm.* Wks. 1871 III. 17 Their suspending, outcasting and deposing seven men from the holy ministry. **1855** Lynch *Rivulet* xxiv. ii, Fill us with the love, outcasting Murmur, fearfulness, and sleep.

outcaste ('aʊt,kɑːst, -æ-), *sb.* (*a.*) [Cf. out- 12.] One who has lost or is put out of his caste. Also, One of no caste.
1876 *Encycl. Brit.* V. 191 On a forfeiture of caste by either spouse intercourse ceases between the spouses; if the outcaste be a sonless woman, she is accounted dead. **1894** J. T. Wheeler *Short Hist. India* 59 Besides the four castes [of the Hindu people], there is a large population known as Pariahs or outcastes. They are altogether inferior to the Súdras, and were probably the Helots of India when the Súdras were masters. [But see Pariah.]
b. as *adj.* Outside caste; of no caste.
1894 R. Kipling *Jungle Bk.* 37 They have no law. They are outcaste.

ˌout'caste, *v.* [Cf. OUT- 26: see CASTE *sb.* 2, 3.] *trans.* To put (a person) out of his caste; to deprive of caste; to cause to lose caste. Also *refl.*

1867 *Native Opinion* 1 Dec., A man will be outcasted if he observes mourning for one day instead of two, or partakes of boiled rice with his coat on. **1889** *Times* 21 Oct. 5/3 Two members of the Jain community have recently been outcasted by their co-religionists for visiting England. **1894** *Mission. Herald* (Boston) Aug. 329 By this act he not only outcasted his son but also incurred the displeasure of all his caste people. **1915** KIPLING *New Army in Training* 64 What will be the position..of the young man who has deliberately elected to outcaste himself from this all-embracing brotherhood?

Hence ˌ**out'casted** *ppl. a.*, ˌ**out'casting** *vbl. sb.*

1886 *Pall Mall G.* 27 May 11/2 The caste system has been so very much battered about, that outcasting has lost almost all its terrors. **1891** *Daily News* 12 Jan. 5/6 Measures taken with this object would be illusory so long as 'outcasting' was possible.

outcasting ('aʊtˌkɑːstɪŋ, -æ-), *vbl. sb.*[1] [OUT- 9 (from *cast out*).]

1. The action of casting out; ejection, expulsion; vomiting; rendering outcast.

1398 TREVISA *Barth. De P.R.* VIII. xl. (Tollem. MS.), Also by oute castynge and strecchynge, and ouercastynge..of bemis, lyȝt bryngeþ forþe all þinges. *c* **1400** tr. *Secreta Secret., Gov. Lordsh.* 75 Outkastyng wasshis þe body, & clensis þe stomake of roten & euyl humours. **1535** COVERDALE *Acts* xxvii. 18 On the nexte daye they made an outcastinge. **1826** E. IRVING *Babylon* II. VII. 171 The outcasting and desolation of the Jews.

†**2.** That which is thrown away; refuse; offal.

a **1340** HAMPOLE *Psalter* xv[i]. 6 Thof thai seme laith and outkastynge til some..til me thai ere faire and bright. **1382** WYCLIF *1 Cor.* iv. 13 The paringis, or out-castinge, of alle thingis. *c* **1400** *Rule St. Benet* (E.E.T.S.) 14 It es wrmis and na man, And ut-castyng o men. **1616** SURFL. & MARKH. *Country Farme* 386 Worth nothing but to make refuse and outcastings of.

†**3.** An offshoot. *Obs.*

1340 *Ayenb.* 22 Þe vifte outkestinge of þilke stocke is scorn;..þe zixte kestinge out of the ilke boȝe is wyþstondinge.

outcasting, *vbl. sb.*[2]: see OUTCASTE *v.*

'outcastness. [f. OUTCAST *a.* + -NESS.] The state of being an outcast.

1846 HARE *Mission Comf.* (1850) 124 Shame and scorn and outcastness and destitution and disease and death.

out-cavil, etc.: see OUT-.

†**out'cept**, *v. Obs.* [OUT- 25.] = EXCEPT *v.* 1.

1470–85 MALORY *Arthur* x. lxxii, I oute cepte hym of al knyghtes. **1530** PALSGR. 650/1 He is the strongest man that ever I sawe, I outcept none.

†**out'cept**, quasi-*prep.* and *conj. Obs.* Also 6 -cepte, -sep, -sept. [originally pa. pple. of prec.]

A. quasi-*prep.* = EXCEPT *prep.* 1.

c **1400** *Lanfranc's Cyrurg.* 140 Alle þe membris out cept þe lacertis of þe brest. **1502** ARNOLDE *Chron.* (1811) 230 Outcepte euer the goods marchaundises or dette. **1518** *Waterf. Arch.* in *10th Rep. Hist. MSS. Comm.* App. v. 327 Noo lords..shall drynk no maner of man..outesept ther pleasures and willes. **1633** B. JONSON *Tale Tub.* I. ii[i], Of any other countie I' the kingdome. *Pan.* Out-cept Kent, for there they landed All gentlemen.

B. quasi-*conj.* = EXCEPT *conj.* 2.

1528 PAYNEL *Salerne's Regimen* 2 D iij, Outcept thou trust in the figure. **1550–63** MACHYN *Diary* 249 The menyster wold nott, owtsept she wold com at vj in the mornyng. **1621** B. JONSON *Gipsies Metamorph.* Wks. (Rtldg.) 624/1 Outcept I were with child with an owl, as they say, I never saw such luck.

outch, variant of OUCH *int.*[1]

†**'out'chamber.** *Obs.* [OUT- 1.] **a.** A room outside a house, etc. **b.** An outer room, an antechamber.

14.. *Why I can't be a Nun* 267 in *E.E.P.* (1862) 145 In that couent were they nowȝt; But an owte chamber for hem was wrowȝt. *a* **1631** DONNE *Lett.* (1651) 314, I aske your leave, that I may hide myselfe in your outchamber. **1654–66** EARL ORRERY *Parthen.* (1676) 550 He retired himself into an out-Chamber.

†**'outchange.** *Obs. nonce-wd.* [OUT- 6.] ? Outward or foreign exchange.

1695 W. LOWNDES *Ess. Amendm. Silv. Coin* 41 His Chamberlain, and Master and Worker and Warden of all his Exchanges and Outchanges in England and Calis.

out'charm, *v.* [OUT- 18.] *trans.* To surpass in charming; to charm more potently.

1710 NORRIS *Chr. Prudence* v. 235 To outcharm all the pleasures and Relishes of this sensible world. **1827–44** N. P. WILLIS *Poems, Psyche* 15 One silent look of thine, Like stronger magic, will outcharm it all.

out-chase to **out-chide**: see OUT-.

†**'outˌchoosing**, *vbl. sb. Obs.* [OUT- 9.] The action of choosing out, selection; a levy.

1535 COVERDALE *1 Kings* v. 14 Salomon made an outchosynge (of workmen) thorow out all Israel. And yᵉ outchosynge was thirtie thousande men.

out-citizen to **out-clamour**: see OUT-.

'out-city, *a.* [OUT- 12.] Situated outside a city; suburban.

1939 J. STEINBECK *Grapes of Wrath* xiii. 118 Then the buildings grew smaller... The wrecking yards and hot-dog stands, the out-city dance halls. **1963** *Economist* 9 Nov. 571/1 Those [rents] to be paid in out-city areas.

outclass (aʊt'klɑːs, -æ-), *v. Sporting.* [OUT- 26.] *trans.* To beat or surpass (a rival) so completely as to put him virtually out of the same class or to preclude the notion of his being a competitor; to leave 'nowhere' in a race or contest. Also *transf.* (with connotations of CLASS *sb.* 5 b).

1870 *Daily News* 12 May, She [a yacht] was completely outclassed on that occasion, and never stood the slightest chance from start to finish. **1882** *St. James's Gaz.* 4 Apr. 9/1 A fine young fellow: but..beside the bright and merry-looking athlete who opposed him he seemed quite outclassed. **1893** Q. [COUCH] *Delectable Duchy* 83 As a liar, I out-classed every man on board. **1909** *Chambers's Jrnl.* Jan. 61/1 In the process of production..the Americans soon found themselves outclassed. **1911** *Ibid.* Oct. 702/2 It [*sc.* the aeroplane] can even outclass the telegraph upon short journeys. **1955** *Times* 20 June 13/3 The Ferrari team..was quite outclassed and the chief opposition to the German cars came from the Maseratis. **1966** M. WOODHOUSE *Tree Frog* xii. 105 He was practised in these techniques..and..I was outclassed. **1977** R. L. WOOLF *Gains & Losses* i. 35 A bumbling Church of England rector..hopelessly outclassed in argument by three chief Catholic spokesmen.

'out-ˌclearance. *Commerce.* [OUT- 6.] The act of clearing out; the clearance of a ship by the payment of the custom-house dues.

1778 FOOTE *Trip Calais* I. i, [*Seaman says*] You are welcome to anchor here as long as you list: But you will find the duties high at out-clearance.

'out-ˌclearing, *vbl. sb. Banking.* [OUT- 6.] The sending out of bills of exchange and cheques drawn upon other banks to the Clearing-house, in order to their settlement by the banks on which they are drawn; hence, the bills and cheques collectively thus sent out to be cleared: the converse of IN-CLEARING. Also *attrib.* as **'out-clearing book** (short *out-book*), the book in which these are entered. Hence **'out-clearer**, the representative of a bank at the Clearing-house, who manages the out-clearing; also called *out-clerk*.

[**1827** GILBART *Pract. Treat. Banking* (1849) II. 442 All the articles in the Clearing are entered..in a book called the Clearing Book. On the left hand are entered the bills and drafts upon other Bankers. These are called the 'clearing out'.] **1875** JEVONS *Money* (1878) 278 The exchanges are effected by an equal number of messengers simultaneously walking round the desks, delivering the parcels of 'out clearing' and receiving those of 'in clearing', or, as they are called in New York, the Credit and Debit Exchanges. **1882** A. S. MICHIE *Gilbart's Hist. Banking* II. 325 The In-Clearing Book of each clerk ought to agree, of course, with the portions relating to him of the Out-Clearing Books of the other twenty six Clerks. **1897** *Westm. Gaz.* 5 Mar. 3/1 The 'out-clearers' in the morning sort the various cheques received by their bank on the other clearing banks in alphabetical order, and enter them in their 'out-clearing books' under the names of the different banks.

out-'climb, *v.* [OUT- 18, 17.] *trans.* To surpass in climbing; to climb or ascend beyond.

a **1610** B. JONSON *Pr. Henry's Barriers* Wks. (Rtldg.) 477/1 Buildings..that were the pride of time And did the barbarous Memphian heaps outclimb. **1854** OWEN in *Circ. Sc., Organ. Nat.* I. 198 It can outclimb the monkey. **1892** *Temple Bar Mag.* Oct. 269 They have outclimbed the wood, and are standing on the close..grass of the hillside.

out-clothing, -club, etc.: see OUT-.

†**'out-coat.** *Obs.* [OUT- 3.] An overcoat.

1684 *London Gaz.* No. 1991/4 A brown Cloth Out-Coat. **1760–72** H. BROOKE *Fool of Qual.* (1809) I. 68 Coats, out-coats, shirts, waist-coats.

'out-ˌcollege, *a.* [OUT- 12.] Not residing within the buildings of a college: applied chiefly to members of a college who reside or lodge outside.

1861 TREVELYAN *Horace at Athens*, Colder than out-college breakfasts. **1884** R. ORNSBY *Mem. J.R. Hope-Scott* I. 24 To these must be added his 'out-college' friends. **1893** FOWLER *Hist. C.C.C.* (O.H.S.) 224 Another scholar, for having in his room some out-college men without leave,..was sentenced to be kept hard at work in the library..for a month. *Mod.* (Oxford). 'List of Out-college Residents'.

out-colour, etc.: see OUT-.

outcome ('aʊtkʌm), *sb.* [OUT- 7.]

†**1.** The act or fact of coming out. *Obs.*

a **1225** *Ancr. R.* 80 Wiðuten hope of vtcume. **1375** BARBOUR *Bruce* IV. 361 And we sall neir enbuschit be, Quhar we thair out-cummyng [*MS. E.* outecome] may se. *c* **1500** *Lancelot* 592 Two knichtis..waiting his outcome.

b. The time of the year when the days begin to lengthen (Jam.). *Sc.*

1706 *Mare of Collingtoun* in Watson *Coll. Sc. Poems* I. 43, I pray you, Duncan, thole me here, Until the out-cum of the Year. **1715** *Wodrow Corr.* (1843) II. 87 They talk that Mar ..designs to quarter in Perth this season till the outcome of the year.

2. That which comes out of or results from something; visible or practical result, effect, or product. (orig. *Sc.*: app. made Eng. by Carlyle.)

1788 R. GALLOWAY *Poems* 13 And for the outcome o' the story, Just trust it to your ni'bour tory. **1808–18** JAMIESON, *Outcome*, Termination..Increase, product. **1832** CARLYLE *Misc. Boswell's Johnson* (1857) III. 59 We do the man's intellectual endowment great wrong, if we measure it by its mere logical outcome. **1848** KINGSLEY *Saint's Trag.* III. iii. 138 Scan results and outcomes. **1857** RUSKIN *Pol. Econ. Art* Addenda Note 8 Nothing more than the natural growth and outcome from the little dishonesty of the little buyers and sellers. **1865** *Sat. Rev.* 19 Aug. 227/1 He is, as the modern phrase has it, the outcome of these fine fictional theories. **1874** SULLY *Sensat. & Intuit.* 76 Readiness to act [is] the sure outcome and test of belief.

3. An outlet.

1885 W. D. HOWELLS *Silas Lapham* (1891) II. 185 There ain't going to be the out-come for the paint in the foreign markets that we expected. **1894** H. NISBET *Bush Girl's Rom.* 46 There were lots of other outcomes for her heroic efforts without her going to war for the sake of her country.

†**'outcome**, *ppl. a. Obs.* In 1 útancumen, 5 out(e)-comen. [In OE. f. *útan* from without + *cumen*, pa. pple., come.] Come from without, i.e. from another country or place; foreign.

c **893** K. ÆLFRED *Oros.* v. ii. §5 þæt þær nan utancymen mon cuman ne dorste. *a* **1023** WULFSTAN *Hom.* xv. (1883) 91 Ælþeodige men and utancumene swyðe us swencað. *c* **1425** *Eng. Conq. Irel.* 18 For out-comen men that he lade with hym. *Ibid.*, The owt-comen folk þat was thus in-to the land I-come. **1469** *Waterf. Arch.* in *10th Rep. Hist. MSS. Comm.* App. v. 307 No oute commes man nor strangere.

So **'outˌcomer**, †(*a*) a stranger; one coming from outside. *Obs.* (*b*) One coming out from a place.

1607 in *Hist. Wakefield Gram. Sch.* (1892) 70 By any scholler or outcommer. **1880** L. WALLACE *Ben-Hur* 423 'What is going on?' one of the Galileans asked an outcomer.

†**'out-ˌcomeling.** *Obs.* exc. *dial.* [f. OUT- + COMELING, after OUTCOME *ppl. a.*] One who has come from without; a stranger, sojourner, as distinguished from a native, or original resident.

13.. *E.E. Allit. P.* B. 876 An out-comlyng, a carle. **1555** in Strype *Eccl. Mem.* (1721) III. I. xxxiii. 429, I beseech you, as out-comlings and strangers, to abstain [etc.].

'outˌcoming, *vbl. sb.* [OUT- 9.]

†**1.** A coming out, issuing forth; *concr.* a place of issue or emergence. *Obs.*

a **1300** *Cursor M.* 12593 At þe vte-cuming o þe yatte He turnd agayn. **1375** [see OUTCOME *sb.* 1]. **1398** TREVISA *Barth. De P.R.* v. lx. (Bodl. MS.) lf. 30/2 A seneuȝe..is naisch atte þe oute comynge and hard fortheward. *a* **1548** HALL *Chron., Hen. VI* 107 b, In the plain feld..abidyng the outcommyng and battaile of their enemies.

2. Event, issue; a result, a product.

1382 WYCLIF *Gen.* xli. 13 We herden alle thingis that after-ward the outecomyng of the thing proued. **1858** J. MARTINEAU *Stud. Chr.* 306 They are the separate outcomings of a great life-thrill. **1875** E. WHITE *Life in Christ* III. xxii. (1878) 323 No mere outcoming of modern thought.

3. Emanation.

1845 TRENCH *Huls. Lect.* Ser. I. i. 9 Him of whom the Scripture is the outcoming and the Word. **1860** —— *Serm. Westm. Abb.* xi. 115 Our words are the outcoming of our inmost heart.

out-compass to **out-cook**: see OUT-.

†**'out-ˌcorner.** *Obs.* [OUT- 3.] An outlying, remote, or out-of-the-way corner or spot.

1530 PALSGR. 250/2 Outcorner or secrete corner, *reduyt.* **1626** BERNARD *Isle of Man* (1627) 10 Besides many Backe-sides, By-lanes, and Out-corners, there are foure great streets. **1642** FULLER *Holy & Prof. St.* II. ix. 82 Well skilled in some dark out-corners of Divinity.

outcorporate, *v.*: see OUT- 25.

†**out-'cote**, *v.* [f. OUT- 18 + COTE *v.*[1]] *trans.* To surpass.

1589 WARNER *Alb. Eng.* VI. xxx. (1612) 149 She of the Gods and Goddesses before the wanton noted, Was of the Gods and Goddesses for wantonnesse out-coted.

out-count: see OUT-.

out-'countenance, *v. Obs.* exc. in *arch.* use. [OUT- 26.] *trans.* To put out of countenance; to outface.

1586 BRIGHT *Melanch.* xxix. 166 Then is he presently outcountenaunced through the guiltie conceite. **1603** FLORIO *Montaigne* II. ii. (1632) 190, I have seene him when hee was past threescore yeares of age mocke at all our sports, and outcountenance our youthfull pastimes. **1613** J. DAVIES *Muse's Teares* (1878) 14 While high Content, in what-so-euer Chance, Makes the braue Minde the Starres out-countenance. *a* **1945** E. R. EDDISON *Mezentian Gate* (1958) xxxix. 222 In him..burned..that same recklessness and superfluity which, when he..went on..into known instant peril of death at Middlemead, had outcountenanced the great lamp of heaven.

'out-country, *a.* [OUT- 1, 12.] **a.** Associated with or suggestive of the country (as opp. a town). **b.** Situated or coming from a particular country.

1943 *Time* 22 Feb. 53/2 With his clear, healthy, out-country look..baggy, tweedy clothes..Will White had strolled into his office. **1963** [see IN-COUNTRY].

'out-county, *a.* [OUT- 12.] Situated, or coming from, outside a particular county.

1961 *Observer* 26 Mar. 12/6 A..version of this scheme.. was shown..to representatives of the L.C.C.'s expanding 'out-county' towns. **1963** *Times* 16 Feb. 12/3 This is one of the oldest of the 15 'out-county' estates of the L.C.C. and contains altogether 9,584 dwellings. **1972** *Where?* Feb. 62/2 If the neighbouring borough is the only reasonable alternative then they are pretty well duty bound under Section 8 of the 1944 Act to approach that borough for a place, *but Section 8 in no way binds the out-county borough to offer one.* *Ibid.* 63/2 She could opt to go to another college outside the area, so long as she was prepared to pay the higher fees which generally apply to out-county students.

† **'out-course.** *Obs.* [OUT- 7: after Lat. *excursio*, *excursus* running out, invasion.] An excursion; a hostile inroad or incursion.
a **1603** T. CARTWRIGHT *Confut. Rhem. N.T.* (1618) 721 It so crusheth this opinion of the Saints out-courses upon the earth. **1621** MOLLE *Camerar. Liv. Libr.* v. iv. 333 Made out-courses upon the neighbor-countreys.

out-course, *v.*: see OUT-.

'out-,court. [OUT- 3.] An outer court.
1655 H. VAUGHAN *Silex Scint.* I. *Son-dayes* iii, A taste of Heav'n on earth..the out-courts of glory. *a* **1716** SOUTH *Serm.* (1744) VII. xi. 231 Persons who, like Agrippa, were almost Christians, and have been (as it were) in the Skirts and Out-courts of Heaven.

† **out'crack,** *v. Obs.* [OUT- 18.] *trans.* To make a louder crack or noise than; to outbrag.
1592 GREENE *Groat's w. Wit* (1617) 23 Furnish himselfe with more crownes, least hee were outcrackt with new commers. **1602** *2nd Pt. Return fr. Parnass.* I. vi. 498 Hang him whose verse cannot out-belch the wind:..Cannot out-cracke the scarr-crow thunderbolt. **1606** MARSTON *Fawn* IV. F iij b, Heele out cracke a Germaine when hee is drunke.

out-'craft, *v. rare.* [OUT- 21.] *trans.* To surpass in craft or cunning; to outwit.
1879 H. N. HUDSON *Hamlet* 24 Claudius must get up very early, and be very busy when up, to out-craft him.

† **out-'crafty,** *v. Obs. rare*$^{-1}$. [f. OUT- 20 + CRAFTY (if not a misprint for *out-crafted*).] = prec.
1611 SHAKS. *Cymb.* III. iv. 15 That Drug-damn'd Italy, hath out-craftied him, And hee's at some hard point.

out-crash, out-crawl: see OUT-.

† **'outcrease.** *Obs. rare.* [Formed as the opposite of *increase*, after such pairs as *ingrowth*, *outgrowth*.] Outgrowth, outshoot; emigration.
1625 LISLE *Du Bartas, Noe* 96 As for their Colonies and Outcreases into Spaine they are..hardly proved. *Ibid.* 103 The men of Marseil are counted an Outcrease of Asia.

'out-,cricket. [f. OUT- 3 + CRICKET *sb.*²] In cricket: bowling and fielding, as opposed to batting.
1884 *J. Lillywhite's Cricketer's Ann.* 63 Kent's first victory of the season, the result mainly of creditable out cricket. **1904** *Westm. Gaz.* 22 Feb. 3/1 Bad batting lost us the game, for our out-cricket in both innings was up to a very high standard. **1927** M. A. NOBLE *Those 'Ashes'* 206 Larwood's fast bowling was the feature of England's out-cricket. **1963** *Times* 25 Feb. 4/1 Between luncheon and tea, New Zealand's courage made for such splendid out-cricket that Barrington and Cowdrey were compelled to display most of their resources. **1975** *Sunday Tel.* 27 Apr. 32/3 Lancashire's out-cricket was far too positive for their total of 215 for six to be more than a pious dream for Yorkshire, whose innings closed at 137 for seven. **1977** *Guardian* 3 Jan. 11/5 India, who won the toss, were dismissed by some brilliant English outcricket for 155.

'outcrier. Now *rare.* [OUT- 8.] One who cries out. **a.** One who raises an outcry; a brawler.
1535 COVERDALE *Isa.* xlii. 1 He shal not be an outcryer, ner an hie mynded person. **1561** DAUS tr. *Bullinger on Apoc.* (1573) 150 Plagues, disturbers, outcryers, and iniurious agaynst God and hys Saints. **1584** *Leycesters Commonw.* (1641) 30 To stop the mouths of out-criars. **1902** BEERBOHM *Around Theatres* (1924) I. 344 If..any of our outcriers harbour the delusion that a School would inculcate something more than technical tricks [etc.]. **1931** *Tablet* 23 May 673/1 Once more the outcriers have cried out before they are hurt. **1942** BEERBOHM in *Listener* 24 Sept. 389/1 One is taught to believe that the outcriers are entirely altruistic men.
† **b.** One who sells by auction (OUTCRY *sb.* 2).
1577–87 HOLINSHED *Chron.* III. 1207/1 To be cried through the citie by a man with a bell, and then to be sold by the common outcrier appointed for that purpose.

outcrop ('aʊtkrɒp), *sb.* [OUT- 7: cf. *crop out*, CROP *v.* 10.] *Mining* and *Geol.* The cropping out or emergence of a stratum or vein at the surface; the edge of a stratum or vein that thus crops out.
1805 *Edin. Rev.* VI. 244 Most of our coal has been discovered..by exploring their outcrops. **1815** W. SMITH *Mem. Map Strata Eng. & Wales* 7 The edges of the strata, which may all be crossed in the journey from east to west, are called their outcrops. **1878** HUXLEY *Physiogr.* 29 Rain falling upon the ground..is absorbed by the outcrop, or exposed surface, of the sandy stratum. **1882** J. HARDY in *Proc. Berw. Nat. Club.* IX. No. 3. 452 Outcrops of limestone succeed.
b. *transf.*
1851–6 WOODWARD *Mollusca* 213 Flattened prisms of considerable length, arranged..obliquely to the surfaces of the shell, the interior of which is imbricated by their outcrop.
c. *fig.* A coming into outward manifestation.
1864 BREVIOR *Two Worlds* p. vii, I regard these as only its incidents and outward evidences, not its essentials; the mere outcrop on the surface indicating the presence and operation of underlying spiritual forces. **1897** W. C. HAZLITT *Four Gen. Lit. Fam.* I. II. ii. 92 Here we have an outcrop of that splenetic acrimony.

d. *attrib.* in *Mining.*
1895 HATCH & CHALMERS *Gold Mines Rand* 121 Shafts that are partly vertical and partly inclined..among outcrop properties. **1895** *St. James's Gaz.* 16 Nov. 7/1 With regard to the productive capacity of the outcrop companies.

'outcrop, *v.* [f. prec. sb.] *intr.* **a.** *Mining* and *Geol.* To crop out (see CROP *v.* 10) or emerge at the surface, as a stratum or vein.
1848 *Jrnl. R. Agric. Soc.* IX. I. 61 Wherever it outcrops, the soil is distinguished for its fertility. **1895** *Westm. Gaz.* 27 May 8/1 A number of other reefs..traverse the property, either outcropping on or dipping into it.
b. *fig.* To emerge or come out casually.
1856 C. J. ELLICOTT in *Cambr. Ess.* 172 Because a few suspicious words here and there outcrop in the narrative. **1860** MAURY *Phys. Geog. Sea* (Low) xii. §553 Do we not..find outcropping some reason for the question, what have the winds had to do with the phenomena before us?

'outcropper. [f. OUTCROP *sb.* + -ER¹.] One who takes coal from an outcropping seam or vein.
1926 *Glasgow Herald* 7 Oct. 8/3 The outcroppers are doing good business for themselves. *Ibid.* 5 Nov. 7 Prosecutions which revealed extensive damage being committed by coal outcroppers..were brought in the Airdrie J.P. Court yesterday.

'out,cropping, *vbl. sb.* [OUT- 9.] *Mining, Geol.*, etc. The action or fact of cropping out; the part of a stratum that crops out: = OUTCROP *sb.* a.
1872 RAYMOND *Statist. Mines & Mining* 23 A tunnel..cuts the vein..175 feet below the outcroppings. **1882** STEVENSON *New Arab. Nts.* II. i. 6 An outcropping of rock had formed a bastion for the sand.
b. *fig.* Appearance, emergence: = OUTCROP *sb.* c.
1855 MAURY *Phys. Geog. Sea* vi. §383 Here the outcroppings of the relation between magnetism and the circulation of the atmosphere again appear. **1887** *Athenæum* 25 June 830/2 The sudden outcropping of a school of young ..and promising critics.

'out,cropping, *ppl. a.* [OUT- 10.] Cropping out, emerging at the surface of the ground.
1845 *Silliman's Amer. Jrnl.* Apr. 299 Brine springs..issue, at the outcropping edges of the siliceous portion of the mass. **1885** 'C. E. CRADDOCK' *Prophet Gt. Smoky Mount.* viii, Emerging..upon a slope of outcropping ledges, where his horse left no hoof-print.

'outcross, *sb.* [OUT- 6.] A cross with an unrelated breed or race. Also *attrib.*
1890 J. M. TRACY in *Upland Shooting* 398 It may happen that the outcross has been to some extremely prepotent breed. **1900** *Trans. Highl. & Agric. Soc.* 164 [He] rarely sought an outcross for his broadly founded herd. **1918** *Genetics* III. 475 When double-throwing Matthiola is used as egg parent in an outcross to ordinary singles, half the offspring receive a factor for doubleness. **1949** R. B. KELLEY *Sheep Dogs* (ed. 3) iv. 62 It is not necessary to purchase such out-cross dogs. **1971** *Farmer & Stockbreeder* 16 Feb. 49/1 An unplanned out-cross with an unknown wheat took place and this brought much improved fertility. **1975** *Times* 25 Aug. 8/5 Original out-crosses were Northumberland-bred Scottish Blackfaces. **1977** *Horse & Hound* 14 Jan. 15/3 Malacate stands out as a potential outcross for the majority of high-class European mares.

outcross (stress even), *v.* [f. the sb.] *trans.* To cross (an animal or plant) with one not closely related. Also *absol.*
1918 *Genetics* III. 437 Each [beaded fly] was outcrossed separately to a fly from some non-beaded stock. **1931** E. B. FORD *Mendelism & Evolution* ii. 40 If the now highly inbred stock be outcrossed to ordinary wild-type flies, it is found that the extracted recessives..have returned to the original condition. **1949** R. B. KELLEY *Sheep Dogs* (ed. 3) iv. 62 It will be necessary continually to out-cross by introducing dogs unrelated to the favoured animal, so that close-breeding is avoided.

'outcrossing, *vbl. sb.* [f. OUTCROSS *v.*] The crossing of an animal or plant with one not closely related to it.
1950 *Brit. Jrnl. Psychol.* XL. 132 Vigour is restored by out-crossing. **1973** PROCTOR & YEO *Pollination of Flowers* xii. 382 It is seldom easy to establish the amount of out-crossing which takes place under natural conditions. **1973** B. J. WILLIAMS *Evolution & Human Origins* xiv. 249/2 Heterosis can occur as a result of outcrossing, or mating between breeding isolates.

out-crow, -crowd, -crown: see OUT-.

outcry ('aʊtkraɪ), *sb.* [OUT- 7.]
1. The act of crying out; an excited exclamation or shout; loud clamour; noise, uproar.
1382 WYCLIF *Ecclus.* xxxv. 18 The outcry of hir vp on the ledyng doun of hem. **1534** *Act 26 Hen. VIII*, c. 5 §1 Any outcrie, hute, or fresshe suite of or for anie felonie. **1560** DAUS tr. *Sleidane's Comm.* 51 Carying him awaye, he makinge an outcry and calling for helpe. **1603** KNOLLES *Hist. Turks* (1638) 101 Hee returning..with his army, came vpon them..with a most horrible outcry. **1748** *Anson's Voy.* III. vi. 347 There was an outcry of fire on the forecastle. **1810** SCOTT *Lady of L.* II. xvii, With mingled out-cry, shrieks, and blows. **1875** FREEMAN *Norm. Conq.* (ed. 2) III. xii. 208 The charge..seems..to rest on nothing better than the wild outcries of William's enemies at a drunken revel.
2. a. A public sale to the highest bidder; an auction. Now *local* exc. *U.S.*
? *c* **1600** *Distracted Emp.* II. i. in Bullen *Old Pl.* (1884) III. 195 He sells his goods at outcryes—'Who gives most?' **1607** J. NORDEN *Surv. Dial.* I. 9 One wil outbid another, as at an outcry in London. **1708** *Lond. Gaz.* No. 4412/3 On Wednesday..will be held a publick Outcry for Sale of the Inheritance or Fee-simple Estate of the..Barton of Kentaberry. **1723** DE FOE *Col. Jack* (1840) 213, I broke up housekeeping, and sold my furniture by public outcry. **1848** THACKERAY *Van. Fair* xxxviii, [He] sold it at public outcry, at an enormous loss to himself. **1931** *Amer. Speech.* VII. 20 *Public outcry*, an auction sale. **1961** WEBSTER s.v., *Southeastern Reporter.* The executor's duty to sell it at public outcry. **1974** *News & Reporter* (Chester, S. Carolina) 15-A/6 (Advt.), I, the undersigned Special Referee will sell at public outcry to the highest bidder..the following described real estate.
b. The crying of articles in the streets for sale.
1884 *Times* 29 July 11 Yesterday..a milkman was summoned under a local by-law for selling milk by outcry.
† **3.** *Rhet.* Ecphonesis or exclamation. *Obs.*
1587 GOLDING *De Mornay* xxvi. 396 We would haue him to vse..outcries as Cicero, or fine conceits as Seneca doth. **1589** PUTTENHAM *Eng. Poesie* III. xix. (Arb.) 221 The figure of exclamation, I call him the outcrie because it vtters our minde by all such words as do shew any extreme passion.

out'cry, *v.* [OUT- 14, 15, 18.]
† **1. a.** *intr.* To cry out. **b.** *trans.* To cry aloud, exclaim; to proclaim. *Obs.*
1430–40 LYDG. *Bochas* 39 a/2 The world outcryeth of vs tweyn. **1567** *Gude & Godlie B.* (S.T.S.) 183 Thair fals Hypocresie Throw all the warld is now outcryit. **1626** T. AILESBURY *Passion Serm.* 27 Thus Christ, having outcryed his torments, prayed for reliefe. **1654** GAYTON *Pleas. Notes* II. ii. 38 When Sancho out-cri'd, then Don did not out-ride. **1849** THACKERAY *Pendennis* I. xxii. 204 She at once took side with Helen against Doctor Portman, when he outcried at the enormity of Pen's transgressions.
† **2.** To sell by auction. *Obs.*
1676 *Laws of Barbados* 15 Mar. (1699) 126 Be it Enacted ..That such Effects should be out-cryed and sold within those Hours. **1688** *Ibid.* 19 Dec. (1855) 10 Debtors that have their cattle, coppers and stills, and other chattels brought by execution to the open market to be outcried.
3. To outdo in crying; to cry louder than; to 'shout down'.
1530 PALSGR. 650/2 Lette hym crye as loude as he wyll, yet I wyll outcrye hym. **1628** C. POTTER *Consecr. Serm.* 15 Mar. (1629) 72 If wee cannot outcry it, wee must outlive it. **1641** SYMONDS *Serm. bef. Ho. Comm.* D b, Their dead inventions would out-cry us, and condemne us. **1742** YOUNG *Nt. Th.* IX. 2326 Ev'ry Night Let it out-cry the Boy at Philip's Ear. **1851** RUSKIN *Mod. Paint.* II. III. I. xiv. §5 Neither anger, for that overpowers the reason or outcries it.

'out,crying, *vbl. sb.* [OUT- 9.] A crying out; clamour, shouting. So **'out,crying** *ppl. a.*, that cries out, clamorous; calling loudly or vehemently.
1569–70 *Roy. Proclam.* 4 Mar., With clamors and out-cryinges [they] haue accursed the sayde Leonarde Dacres. **1626** BERNARD *Isle of Man* (1627) 187 Touching this impatient and ingratefull out-crying fellow Poverty. **1676** W. ROW *Contn. Blair's Autobiog.* (1848) 548 The disarming of the militia..occasioned much outcrying. **1890** *Daily News* 3 Nov. 6/1 There was more hooting and ribald outcrying. **1890** *Home Missionary* (U.S.) July 121 A great and outcrying need for some..missionaries.

'out-,cue. *Broadcasting.* [OUT- 7.] A cue (CUE *sb.*² 1 c) that indicates when a particular recording or transmission is about to end.
1962 A. NISBETT *Technique Sound Studio* viii. 139 The main things to mark on the script are as follows:..(iv) Duration (or other means of noting in advance when the outcue is coming up). (v) Type of fade out. **1969** S. HYLAND *Top Bloody Secret* i. 81 The BBC's duty director..waited for the Presentation announcer's out-cue. **1972** D. LEES *Zodiac* 119 It was Zodiac's television experience that led him to leave on a good 'out cue'.

out-cull to **out-curse:** see OUT-.

'out-curl. *Curling.* [OUT- 7.] = OUT-TURN.
1903 [see IN-CURL].

'outcurve. [OUT- 7.] **1.** *Baseball.* The bending or curving of a ball outwards (i.e. away from the batter); the course of such a ball; a ball pitched so as to curve in this way.
1881 *N.Y. Herald* 29 July 6/5 Reipslaugher,..not being used to the difficult delivery of Bond, found great difficulty in handling the in-shoots and out-curves. **1886** [see INCURVE *sb.*]. **1897** [see INSHOOT]. **1910** *Encycl. Brit.* III. 459/2 The commonest of these swerving deliveries, and the first invented, is the out-curve, the ball coming straight towards the batsman until almost within reach of his bat, when it suddenly swerves away from him towards the right. if he be right-handed. **1943** *Amer. Speech* XVIII. 106 Various types of curve ball are the sinker.., the in-curve, the out-curve,.. and the screwball.
2. *gen.* An outward curve or prominence.
1902 *Encycl. Brit.* XXVIII. 622/2 It is convenient to employ a specific name for a projection of a coast-line less pronounced than a peninsula, and for an inlet less pronounced than a bay or bight; outcurve and incurve may serve the turn. **1912** GALSWORTHY *Inn of Tranquility* 68 The sharp outcurve of his dark head. **1945** *Sun* (Baltimore) 19 July 7-O/5 This designer bows to the new round-shouldered vogue, but builds hers in an 'outcurve', to avoid the drooping look apparent in many of the new styles.

'outcurved, *a.* [OUT- 11.] Of the bow of a violin or other stringed instrument: having a curve in the direction away from the hair.
1954 *Grove's Dict. Mus.* (ed. 5) I. 855/2 The mechanics of a bow with slight positive curve (away from the hair; out-curved) necessarily differ somewhat from those of an incurved bow. **1970** *Daily Tel.* 5 May 16/2 She had used an archaic 'outcurved' bow to play gamba sonatas by J. S. and W. F. Bach on a modern viola. **1976** *Early Music* Oct. 513/1

The baroque cello..was strong in gut... The lower pitch, combined with the out-curved bow, which was in current use until the end of the 18th century, help maintain the correct style of playing.

†**out'cut**, *v. Obs.* (exc. in *pa. pple.*) [OUT- 15.] *trans.* To cut out: see CUT *v.* 57.

1666 *Third Adv. Painter* 19 How far the Gentleman out-cuts the Lord. *c* **1706** VANBRUGH *Mistake* III. Wks. (Rtldg.) 450/2, I have seen many a pleasant humour amongst ladies, but you outcut 'em all. **1860** HEWETT *Anc. Armour* II. 188 The sollerets are much outcut at the instep.

So **'outcut** *ppl. a.* [OUT- 11], cut out, excised; **'out,cutting** *vbl. sb.*, cutting out, excision.

1860 HEWITT *Anc. Armour* II. 12 (Cent.) The sollerets are remarkable for the large out-cut piece at the instep. **1752** J. LOUTHIAN *Form of Process* (ed. 2) 9 Robes..distinguished by Outcuttings or Mushings.

out'dacious, dial. corruption of AUDACIOUS.

1838 DICKENS *O. Twist* xvii, That out-dacious Oliver. **1840** MRS. F. TROLLOPE *Michael Armstrong* iv. I. 89 They have the outdaciousness to complain that the rents are raised. **1880** TENNYSON *Village Wife* xii, 'E were that outdacious at 'öäm.

out'dance, *v.* [OUT- 18.] *trans.* To surpass or outdo in dancing.

1663 COWLEY *Cutter Coleman St.* v. vi, We'll out-dance the dancing Disease. **1742** FIELDING *J. Andrews* III. vii, The company all offered the dancing-master wagers that the parson outdanced him. **1834** BECKFORD *Italy* II. 334 We outdid all our former outdancings.

out'dare, *v.* [OUT- 18, 18 c.]

1. *trans.* To overcome by daring; to outbrave, defy.

1596 SHAKS. *1 Hen. IV*, v. i. 40 It was my Self, my Brother, and his Sonne, That..boldly did out-dare The danger of the time. **1613** W. BROWNE *Brit. Past.* I. iii, The holly that outdares cold winter's ire. **1677** GILPIN *Demonol.* (1867) 36 That they might contemn and outdare God to His face. *a* **1711** KEN *Edmund* Poet. Wks. 1721 II. 313 All offer'd up ejaculated Prayer, And felt fresh vigour, Danger to outdare.

2. To exceed or surpass in daring, to dare more than.

1607 SHAKS. *Cor.* I. iv. 53 Oh Noble Fellow! Who sensibly out-dares his sencelesse Sword. **1674** *Govt. Tongue* III. §1. (1684) 109 All inferior prophaneness is as much outdared by Atheism, as is religion it self. **1846** TRENCH *Mirac.* xvii. (1862) 283 He will outdo and outdare the other disciples.

Hence **outdared, outdaring** *ppl. adjs.*

1593 SHAKS. *Rich. II*, I. i. 190 Shall I seeme Crest-falne in my fathers sight,..Before this out-dar'd dastard? **1644** VICARS *God in Mount* 204 Our out-daring enemies.

†**'out-date**, *a. Obs. rare.* [OUT- 12.] Without date, dateless, extending beyond all date.

1630 DRUMM. OF HAWTH. *Flowers Sion* 17 And may thou [Easter-day] be so bless'd to out-date times That, when heaven's choir shall blaze in accents loud The many mercies of their Sovereign Good,.. It may be still the burden of their joy.

out'date, *v.* [OUT- 26.] *trans.* To put out of date, make (a thing) out of date or obsolete.

a **1649** DRUMM. OF HAWTH. *Jas. V* Wks. (1711) 110 Imagining to himself an over-sight and preterition, [he] outdateth, by his stay, his protection. *a* **1716** BLACKALL *Wks.* (1723) I. 178 The ceremonial Law..expired and was outdated, when the Things typified and signified thereby were accomplished. **1868** WHITTIER *Among the Hills* 92 As if the Sermon on the Mount had been Outdated like a last year's almanac.

Hence **out'dated** *ppl. a.*, put or become out of date; grown obsolete; antiquated; **out'datedness**.

1616 *Manifest. Abp. Spalato's Motives* App. iii. 6 Out-dated Kalendars of Gallo-Belgicus. **1698** NORRIS *Pract. Disc.* (1707) IV. 13 None of these talk of Religion; that's a stale, out-dated, antiquated, superannuated Subject. **1909** BELLOC *Marie Antoinette* vi. 106 His outworn, out-dated ambition. **1937** 'C. CAUDWELL' *Illusion & Reality* vi. 115 The development of capitalist production remorselessly turns the craftsman into a labourer... Eventually, employed as a factory hand, he may still cherish his outdated skill by making models. **1960** *20th Cent.* Mar. 259 By his lofty and elusive outdatedness, he has outwitted the practically minded, the men of action and the men of defeat. **1967** KARCH & BUBER *Offset Processes* v. 187 Causes of fog: 1. Poor storage of film. 2. Outdated film. **1976** R. LEWIS *Witness my Death* i. 35 For you, it's a matter of protecting a professional reputation, going by an out-dated rulebook drawn up by old men.

out'dazzle, *v.* [OUT- 18.] *trans.* To outdo in dazzling or brilliancy; to outshine. Also *fig.*

1705 TATE *Warriour's Welc.* i, Fury like Theirs..Out-dazled Danger, and made Horror Bright. **1813** COLERIDGE *Lett., to T. Poole* (1895) 611 Elliston, by mere dint of voice and self-conceit, out-dazzled him. **1879** FARRAR *St. Paul* I. 191 It might be imagined that nothing can outdazzle the glare of a Syrian sun at noon.

out-devil to **out-diplomatize**: see OUT-.

out'distance, *v.* [OUT- 18 b.] *trans.* To leave completely behind (in a race; hence, in any competition or career); to outstrip: cf. DISTANCE *v.* 4, 4 d.

1857 TROLLOPE *Barch. Towers* xxxviii. (1858) 320 Why do you let the Slopes..out-distance you? **1869** *Daily News* 22 May, [In the three miles walking match, he] so soon out-distanced his opponents, that they did not think it worth while to compete further with him. **1890** D'OYLE *Notches* 113 At last our pursuers were outdistanced. **1898** T. ADAMSON *Stud. Mind in Christ* vii. 171 They felt themselves out-distanced by His ideas, even when they saw into them.

outdo (aʊt'duː), *v.* [OUT- 15, 18, 18 c.]

†**1.** *trans.* To put out. (In ME. two words: cf. *do out.*) *Obs.*

13.. *Cursor M.* 989 Adam was out don nais and naked, In to þe land quar he was maked. **1603** DRAYTON *Bar. Wars* v. li, Was ta'en in battle and his eyes out-done.

2. To exceed in doing or performance; to excel, surpass, beat; to be superior to.

1607 SHAKS. *Cor.* II. i. 150 He hath in this action out-done his former deeds doubly. **1623** B. JONSON *On Portr. Shaks.* in *Folio*, Wherein the Grauer had a strife With Nature, to out-doo the life. **1713** STEELE *Guard.* No. 170 ¶28 They outdo us so much in cheapness of labour. **1804** WORDSW. '*I wandered lonely as a cloud*' iii, The waves beside them danced; but they Out-did the sparkling waves in glee. **1877** BLACK *Green Past.* xxxiv. (1878) 274 The other two women were not to be outdone.

b. To beat, defeat, overcome; to exhaust.

1677 YARRANTON *Eng. Improv.* title-p., To Out-do the Dutch without Fighting, to Pay Debts without Moneys. **1776** A. R. ROBBINS *Jrnl.* (1850) 24, I feel weak, and find that a little labor, walking and rowing, seems to out-do me. **1869** J. S. BALDWIN *Preh. Nations* iii. (1877) 107 If they were not outdone by the insane chronology.

Hence **out'doing** *vbl. sb.* and *ppl. a.*; **out'doer**, one who outdoes another.

1679 *Phil. Collections* XII. 38 His Observations so wholly new and out-doing, that no..Reader can think he wants anything but Equals. **1727** POPE, etc. *Art Sinking* 121 They continue to out-do even their own out-doings. **1824** MISS MITFORD *Village* Ser. I. (1863) 173 His rival,..an out-doer by profession. **1840** TH. HOOK in *New Monthly Mag.* LX. 11 The pink of perfection far outdid his usual outdoings.

†**'out-,door**, *sb.* [OUT- 3.] An exterior or outer door.

1646 H. LAWRENCE *Comm. Angells* 185 To keepe well and strictly the out-doores, the sences. **1766** ENTICK *London* IV. 342 A sentinel is stationed..at the out door. **1812** *Examiner* 7 Sept. 564/1 She flung the out-door of the house open.

'out-door, 'outdoor, *a.* (*adv.*) [OUT- 12.]

A. *adj.* **1.** That is done, exists, lives, or is used, out of doors, without the house, or in the open air.

1748 RICHARDSON *Clarissa* III. 208 In other words, to employ itself rather in the *out-door* search, than in the *in-door* examination. **1765** T. HUTCHINSON *Hist. Mass.* I. i. 22 Their out-door work. **1820** LUSCOMBE *Observ. Preserv. Health Soldiers* 93 Employed in agricultural pursuits or as out-door manufacturers. **1856** MRS. BROWNING *Aur. Leigh* II. 331 Maturing by the outdoor sun and air. **1865** *Look before you leap* I. 134 She..put on her out-door attire.

2. Relieved or administered outside or apart from residence in a workhouse, a charitable institution, etc.; as ***out-door pauper, pension, relief.***

1833 HT. MARTINEAU *Berkeley the Banker* I. iii. 51 The outdoor paupers had begun the mischief. **1834** *Act 4 & 5 Will. IV*, c. 76 §52 On what conditions, and in what manner, such out-door relief may be afforded. **1876** FAWCETT *Pol. Econ.* IV. v. (ed. 5) p. xxxi, Out-door relief ought to be greatly restricted. **1899** *Daily News* 19 June 7/2 Aged seamen..admitted..to the benefits of an out-door pension.

3. Existing or arising outside Parliament, or among the people themselves.

1884 A. PAUL *Hist. Reform* ii. 16 A just and equal representation was long a popular outdoor cry. *Ibid.* v. 91 This..had revived the outdoor agitation for Reform.

4. Applied to the outward or down stroke of a Cornish pumping engine.

1875 J. H. COLLINS *Metal Mining* 93 The..plunger lifts are worked by the down or out-door stroke; the weight of the rods forcing the water up the column of pumps.

5. Special collocations: ***outdoor department***, that section of a public house that sells liquor for consumption off the premises; also *ellipt.* as *sb.*; ***outdoor girl***, a girl or young woman who likes an open-air life; ***outdoor things***, clothes that are worn out of doors.

1958 *Times* 29 Apr. (Beer in Britain Suppl.) p. ix/6 *Jug-and-Bottle.* For the purchase of drinks for 'consumption off the premises'. Term now obsolescent. *Off-Licence, Off-Sales, Outdoor Departments*: the modern equivalent. **1961** M. JONES *Potbank* i. 6 Every pub has its off-licence department, known as the Outdoor. **1971** R. ROBERTS *Classic Slum* vi. 94 A great deal of beer bought in jugs from the 'Outdoor Department' was drunk at home... Lower-class women..stood crushed together drinking in the 'Outdoor'. **1907** J. WEBSTER *Jerry Junior* xiii. 198 Nannie was a big wholesome outdoor girl of a purely American type. **1947** M. LOWRY *Under Volcano* ix. 275 The Hawaiian Islands gave us this real outdoor girl who is fond of swimming, golf, dancing. **1969** D. THOMAS *Honey Bk. Beauty* 31/2 Outdoor girls who swear by hair spray must be careful in their choice. **1847** E. BRONTË *Wuthering Heights* II. xiv. 280, I snatched my outdoor things..the way was free. **1904** E. NESBIT *Phoenix & Carpet* x. 185 Every one put on its outdoor things..and all was ready. **1927** E. GLYN '*It*' xiv. 136 Ava..put on her outdoor things and left. **1960** B. COBB *Don't lie to Police* xi. 187 You told me Miss Cart was there when you returned. In her outdoor things?

B. *adv.* in *comb.*, as ***outdoor-grown.***

1895 *Daily News* 10 Aug. 5/3 Tomatoes are pouring..into the London markets, the outdoor-grown fruit being ripe.

Hence **'out,doorish** *a.*, having an out-of-doors, open-air appearance or effect; **,out'doorishness, 'out,doorness**, the quality of being out of doors, open-airness.

1777 T. TWINING in *Recreat. & Stud.* (1882) 50 All outdoor-ness and bodily activity, with a fat lump of quiet mind within. **1880** MISS BIRD *Japan* II. 199 The middle and lower classes have an outdoorishness and visibility about them which offer a thousand points of interest. **1891** *Illustr. Lond. News* Xmas No. 3/1 Perfectly lovely..but a little cold and out-doorish. **1896** *Chicago Advance* 10 Dec. 821 The large out-doorness of the gospel is one element of its power.

,out'doors, *adv.* (*sb.*) [OUT *prep.*] **A.** *adv.* Out of doors; in the open air.

1817 S. R. BROWN *Western Gazetteer* 113 The chimney is sure to be placed out doors. **1846** in WORCESTER. **1882** STEVENSON *Fam. Studies Men & Bks.* (1901) 73 Wisdom keeps school outdoors. **1913** G. STRATTON-PORTER *Laddie* xiii. 404 What you learn there [*sc.* at school] doesn't amount to a hill of beans compared with what you can find out for yourself outdoors. **1937** C. MARSTON *Bible comes Alive* vi. 149 At Jericho..the people mostly lived outdoors.

b. Phr. ***all outdoors*** (*U.S. colloq.*), the whole world; everybody; freq. in comparisons alluding to the immensity of the areas out of doors.

[**1825** J. NEAL *Bro. Jonathan* I. 111 Stuffy feller (that bear) as ever you see'd; big as all out o' doors.] **1830** S. SMITH *Life & Writings J. Downing* (1833) 64, I had a letter from him..as long as all out doors. **1844** 'J. SLICK' *High Life N. York* II. xxii. 60 A great strapping woman as tall as all out-doors. **1846** *Quincy* (Illinois) *Whig* 17 Feb. 2/2, I was going to speak of the President's message—Jimmy K's statement to all out-doors, and some parts of Ashey. **1861** LOWELL *Biglow P.* Ser. II. i. 169 Ourn's the fust thru-by-daylight train with all ou' doors for deepot. **1940** W. FAULKNER *Hamlet* III. 213 The hot sun of July falling through the shadeless and even curtainless windows open to all outdoors. **1948** *Chicago Tribune* 28 Mar. 6/3 Its spirit is literally 'as big as all out-doors'.

B. *sb.* = OUT-OF-DOOR, -DOORS *sb. phr.* Freq. in phr. ***the great outdoors***, the 'great open spaces' (see OPEN *a.* 8 a).

1857 N. P. WILLIS *Convalescent* (1859) 121 The 'down party'..were enjoying the river from the uncommon outdoors of Mr. Grinnell's broad prairies. **1932** *Ann. Reg. 1931* II. 47 The 'great outdoors' was represented most elaborately in 'Cimarron', which starred Richard Dix in a fine dramatisation of the opening up of Oklahoma, and 'Trader Horn', a picture of wild life in Africa. **1940** [see CLIFF-HANGER]. **1949** *Skyline Trail* Mar. 14/2 Trail Hikers, like all lovers of the outdoors, are by nature animal lovers as well. **1968** *Globe & Mail* (Toronto) 17 Feb. 44 During the 30 years (good heavens, is it that long?) that I have been writing about the outdoors, changes have been great. **1968** *Listener* 30 May 713/1 The Victorians worked hard to get the great outdoors inside a theatre. **1977** *Times* 23 Apr. 12/7 Ideal for anyone who wants that taste of the great outdoors without straying too far from..civilization.

Hence **out'doorsman**, one who likes outdoor activities; **out'doorsy** *a.*, associated with or characteristic of the outdoors; fond of an outdoor life; hence **out'doorsiness**.

1952 BERG & SAMUELS *Lady on Beach* vi. 184 In my attempts to be a truly outdoorsy woman at all times I had a ludicrous crab-hunting misadventure of my own. **1958** *Globe & Mail* (Toronto) 24 July 8/6 He's kept busy coping with appetites of outdoorsmen. **1960** I. WALLACH *Absence of Cello* (1961) 105 It was hardly an outdoorsy vacation. **1961** *Guardian* 4 Mar. 4/7 These new-style out-doorsmen. **1967** E. B. NICKERSON *Kayaks to Arctic* xii. 112, I..find no personal satisfaction in..showing an obnoxious out-doorsiness in a dozen..ways. **1973** J. GORES *Final Notice* (1974) vii. 43 Larry Ballard, good-looking in a wind blown, outdoorsy way. **1974** *Publishers Weekly* 18 Mar. 42/1 A poor boy who..became a prodigious outdoorsman and mountain climber. **1976** *Ibid.* 11 Oct. 91/2 His interviews read like scenes out of a good outdoorsy novel. **1976** *Parliamentarian* July p. viii, The hazards of translation in the European Parliament have given Mr Michael Stewart an undeserved reputation as an outdoorsman of unusual dexterity. He had spoken of his job as being like 'paddling a canoe shooting rapids', but the German interpreter thought he had said '..shooting rabbits' and translated accordingly. Mr Stewart was promptly wished good hunting by two German Members. **1976** *National Observer* (U.S.) 18 Sept. 1/4 They're the sort of out-doorsy fellows we usually associate with television shows about tagging grizzlies and spying on beavers in Wyoming.

†**'outdraught**[1]. *Obs.* [OUT- 7: after L. *extractum*, OF. *estrait.*] An extract, an abstract.

c **1449** PECOCK *Repr.* v. xi. 541 In the extract or out-drauȝt of the Donet. **1542** *Sc. Acts Mary* (1814) II. 415/2 Þe extracte and outdraucht of all proces of forfaltoure concerning þe erle of anguiss. *c* **1575** *Balfour's Practicks* (1754) 368 The extract or out-draucht of the chekkar rollis.

'outdraught[2]. [OUT- 7.] An outward draught or current of air; the 'back-wash' of a wave.

1857 KINGSLEY *Two Y. Ago* iii, Then followed the returning out-draught, and every limb quivered with the strain. **1859** R. F. BURTON *Centr. Afr.* in *Jrnl. Geog. Soc.* XXIX. 383 The rapidity required to secure a continuous out-draught. **1877** TENNYSON *Harold* II. i. 32 Clinging thus [I] Felt the remorseless outdraught of the deep Haul like a great strong fellow at my legs.

†**out'draw**, *v. Obs.* [OUT- 15.] *trans.* To draw out. (In ME. prop. two words.)

a **1300** *E.E. Psalter* xxi. 10 Þou art whilk þat me out droghe Fra þe wumbe. **1390** GOWER *Conf.* II. 245 Of which he mot the teth outdrawe. **1558** PHAER *Æneid* VI. Rij, A gastly Gripe, that euermore his growing guttes outdrawes. **1658** A. FOX *Wurtz' Surg.* III. xv. 263 The vertue of the Plaister expels and outdraweth all humors.

'outdrawing, *vbl. sb.* [OUT- 9.] Drawing out.

1598 BARRET *Theor. Warres* 91 At the out drawing of the Ensigne.

out'drawn, *ppl. a.* [OUT- 11.] Extended, drawn out.

1905 E. F. BENSON *Image in Sand* i. 8 Bank after bank of out-drawn stops and keyboard coupled to keyboard makes the air thick with tumultuous melody.

out-'dream, *v. rare.* [OUT- 16, 15 b.]

trans. † **a.** To oust or expel by dreams (*obs.*). **b.** To dream to an end. *nonce-use.*

1621 FLETCHER *Isl. Princess* III. i, I am no flatterer, To promise infinitely, and out-dream dangers. **1798** SOTHEBY tr. *Wieland's Oberon* (1826) II. 214 The moanful dream out-dreamt, the trial o'er.

†**'out-dress,** *sb. Obs.* [OUT- 3.] Outer or outward dress.

1637 B. JONSON *Sad Sheph.* II. i, I ha' but dight ye yet in the out-dress And 'parel of Earine.

out'dress, *v.* [OUT- 18.] *trans.* To outdo in dressing oneself; to dress more finely than.

1786 [see OUTSHOW *v.* 2]. **1807** W. IRVING *Salmag.* (1824) 345 Young people of both sexes, who..try to out-dress each other. **1897** *Chicago Advance* 19 Aug. 247/1 A daughter never should seek nor be allowed to 'outdress' her mother.

out'drink, *v.* [OUT- 15 b, 18.] *trans.* **a.** To drink (anything) out or up, drink dry. **b.** To outdo in drinking, drink more than.

1593 DONNE *Sat.* ii. 33 Nor they which use..To out-drinke the sea. **1622** DEKKER & MASSINGER *Virg. Mart.* II. i, I durst out-drink a lord. **1735** POPE *Donne Sat.* II. 37 Who ..Out-cant old Esdras, or outdrink his heir. **1891** *Miss. Herald* (Boston) Dec. 538 He..tried to outdrink the heaviest drinkers.

out'drive, *v.* [OUT- 15, 18.]

†**1.** *trans.* To drive out, expel. (Prop. two words.)

a **1300** *Cursor M.* 1768 (Cott.) Þe springes cum ouer-all utedriue [*Gött.* vte dreue, *Tr.* oute to dref]. **13..** *E.E. Allit. P.* A. 776 Þou con alle þo dere out dryf.

2. a. To drive faster than.

1665 PEPYS *Diary* 5 Sept., He..out-drives any coach, and out-goes any horse.

b. *Golf.* To drive farther than; = OVERDRIVE *v.* 5.

1906 *Daily Chron.* 22 May 9/4 MacFarlane, after being outdriven from the tee, played a perfect approach to within a yard of the hole. **1923** *Weekly Dispatch* 13 May 1 He seemed to set out not to out-drive his opponent..but to steer a straight course. **1952** B. DARWIN *James Braid* ii. 29 James in a state of bliss straightway outdrove all those who but lately had had the audacity to outdrive him.

†**out'dure,** *v. Obs.* [OUT- 17, 18.] *trans.* To exceed in endurance, outlast.

1612 *Two Noble K.* III. vi, I feele my selfe..able once againe To out-dure danger. **1648** HERRICK *Hesper.*, *Pillar of Fame*, Fame's pillar..Out-during marble, brasse or jet.

So †**out'durer,** one that endures or survives.

1822 B. CORNWALL *Poems, Derwent-Water & Skiddaw*, Out-durer of the storms.

†**out'dwell,** *v. Obs.* [OUT- 17.] *trans.* To tarry or stay beyond (a time).

1596 SHAKS. *Merch. V.* II. vi. 3 And it is meruaile he outdwels his houre, For louers euer run before the clocke.

'outdweller. [OUT- 2, 8.] One who dwells outside of or away from (a certain place).

1594 NASHE *Unfort. Trav.* Wks. (Grosart) V. 40 Anie stranger or out-dweller. **1682** SCARLETT *Exchanges* 163 If the Acceptant be an Out-dweller, (i.e. dwells in another place than where the Bill must be paid). **1895** *Atlantic Monthly* Mar. 387 The outdweller from civilization.. produces only for his and their consumption. **1900** W. WATT *Aberdeen & Banff* iv. 90 All 'outdwellers' of the burgh were to be brought in as far as possible for the common defence.

So **'outdwelling** *ppl. a.* [OUT- 10], dwelling outside.

1893 *Atlantic Monthly* Feb. 148/2 Outdwelling men who had something to sell or to trade.

†**'out-,dwelling,** *sb. Obs.* [OUT- 1, 3.] A dwelling situated on the outskirts of a town, etc.

1677 HUBBARD *Indian Wars* (1865) I. 128 Doing some small Mischief upon some Out-dwellings of Springfield.

†**'oute,** *adv. Obs.* Forms: 1–3 úte, 4–5 oute, owte. [OE. *úte* = OS., OFris. *ûta, ûte*, OHG. *ûze*, ON. *úti*, Goth. *ûta* adv., deriv. of *ût* OUT. Cf. Gr. ἔξω from ἐξ.]

1. Of position: Out, outside. = OUT *adv.* 15, 16; also in some derived senses, e.g. = OUT 22, 23.

c **900** tr. *Bæda's Hist.* IV. iii. (1890) 264 Þonne wæs he ute wyrcende. *c* **1000** *Ags. Gosp.* Matt. xxvi. 69 Petrus soðlice sæt ute [*Lindisf.* úta] on þam cofertune. *a* **1100** *Gerefa* in *Anglia* (1886) IX. 260 ȝe inne ȝe ute. *c* **1200** ORMIN 141 All þe follc þær ute stod. *a* **1225** *Ancr. R.* 150 Þeonne is þet lif ute. Þeonne adeadeð þet treou. *a* **1300** *K. Horn* 245 In þe curt and ute, And elles al abute. *c* **1325** *Poem Times Edw. II* (Camden) 120 There hii clateren cumpelin whan þe candel is oute [*rime* doute]. *c* **1386** CHAUCER *Franklin's T.* 367. **1390** GOWER *Conf.* I. 363 These othre tuelue..wente aboute The holi feith to prechen oute.

b. In existence, existing. Cf. OUT *adv.* 26 c.

1377 LANGL. *P. Pl.* B. XII. 145 Þe hexte lettred oute. *Ibid.* 267 Thus he lykneth in his logyk þe leste foule oute. *c* **1400** *Destr. Troy* 2175 To wreke vs of wrathe for any wegh oute. *a* **1400–50** *Alexander* 598 Þis barne..Miȝt wele a-prefe for his a-port to any prince oute. *Ibid.* 2574, I ne am noght gylty of þis by all þe godes owte! *Ibid.* 4574, 5410. **1480** CAXTON *Chron. Eng.* ccxxxii. 250 [To] lede and vse the moost werst and synfullist lyf oute.

2. Of motion or direction. *rare.*

a **900** *O.E. Chron.* an. 894 Ne com se here..eall ute or ðæm setum. *c* **1200** *Trin. Coll. Hom.* 47 Hie ne cam nauwer ute.

¶ In later use, *oute, owte* (*e* mute), occur as spellings of OUT.

oute, obs. form of OUGHT, AUGHT.

out-'eat, *v.* [OUT- 18, 15.]

1. *trans.* To surpass in eating, eat more than.

1530 PALSGR. 650/2 My horse wyll outete such four jades as thyne is. *a* **1613** OVERBURY *Characters, Button-maker of Amsterdam* Wks. (1856) 126 He will be sure to bee a guest, and to out-eat six of the fattest Burgers. **1807** W. H. IRELAND *Mod. Ships Fools* 36 *note*, The reader must allow.. that the natives of other countries may out-eat us.

†**2.** To eat out or away. ? Only in *pa. pple.*

c **1586** C'TESS PEMBROKE *Ps.* LXIX. iv, With thy temples zeale out-eaten. **1610** HOLLAND *Camden's Brit.* I. 185 Poore men are pitifully out-eaten by usurious contracts. **1665** J. WEBB *Stone-Heng* (1725) 12 Some Antique Inscription.. whose Characters..were so corroded, and out-eaten by Time, that..Antiquaries..could not read it.

outed ('aʊtɪd), *ppl. a.* [f. OUT *v.* + -ED[1].] Put out, driven out, ejected; extracted: see OUT *v.* 1. Also *slang*, killed.

c **1500** ROWLL *Cursing* 170 Thir outtit meiris hes lang gane ydill. **1648** MILTON *Tenure Kings* (1650) 54 Gorging themselves on the preferments of thir outed predecessors. **1676** Row *Contn. Blair's Autobiog.* xii. (1848) 418 The outed ministers still lurked in the country. **1754–62** HUME *Hist. Eng.* (1806) V. lxix. 189 A bold measure of arresting the mayor of London, at the suit of Papillon and Dubois, the outed sheriffs. **1854** H. MILLER *Sch. & Schm.* (1858) 94 He was the outed minister of Small Isles. **1895** CROCKETT *Men of Moss Hags* 145 His lady..harboured outed preachers. **1919** W. H. DOWNING *Digger Dialects* 37 *Outed*, killed. *a* **1945** E. R. EDDISON *Mezentian Gate* (1958) ii. 23 Put case I had fallen in with your fine design to match me to yonder outed Prince of Akkama. **1950** PARTRIDGE *Here, There & Everywhere* 73 The English synonyms for death..are less numerous than the French... *Wiped out*, whether of one's person or one's military unit;..*outed*, from boxing.

out-edge: see OUT-; EDGE *sb.* 7 b.

outehees, -hese, early ff. OUTAS, outcry.

'outen, *adv., prep.* (*a.*) *Obs.* (exc. *dial.*) Forms: 1 útan, 2–3 uten, 4–5 owten, 4– outen. [OE. *útan* and *útane* from without = OS. *ûtan*, OHG. *ûzan* and *uzana*, ON. *útan*, Goth. *ûtana*, a deriv. of *út*: cf. Gr. ἔξωθεν from ἐξ. In ME. reduced to *uten, ute*, and so app. confounded with *ute*, OUTE. It is doubtful whether the modern north. dial. *outen* (see E.D.D.), is historically connected with the OE. word.]

A. *adv.* †**1.** From without, from outside. *Obs.*

885 *O.E. Chron.*, Ælfred com utan mid fierde. *a* **1000** *Andreas* 28 Æȝhwylcne ellþeodiȝra ðara ðe ðæt ealand utan sohte.

†**2. a.** Outside, on the outside, without. *Obs.*

c **888** K. ÆLFRED *Boeth.* xxxiv. §10 Ðæt treow biþ uton ȝescyrped..mid þære rinde. *a* **1000** *Cædmon's Gen.* 1322 Innan and utan eorðan lime ȝefæstnod. *c* **1205** LAY. 5699 Fore alle þan cræften þe heo uten [*c* 1275 hii wið houte] cuððen. [**1781** J. HUTTON *Tour to Caves* (ed. 2) Gloss., *Outen*, out of doors.]

b. Away, distant; absent, wanting.

a **1200** *Moral Ode* 367 He is elches godes ful, nis him noþing ȝit uten [*Tr.* nis him no wiht uten]. **13..** *Cursor M.* 22886 (Edinb. MS.) Þe mar man swink him þar aboutin fra sped þe ferre he sal ben outin [*other MSS.* ute, out(e].

B. *prep.* **1.** †**a.** Without, outside, away from. *Obs.*

c **1250** *Gen. & Ex.* 2739 And sette hi[m] ðor vten ðe town.

b. Out of; out from. *dial.* and *colloq.* (chiefly *U.S.* and *Sc.*).

1854 *Laird of Logan* 441, I cud get as gweed a yane onyday out'n a hedge at the road-side. **1867** 'MARK TWAIN' *Celebr. Jumping Frog* 38 He'd yank a sinner outen (Hades), And land him with the blest. **1895** *Horse Rev.* 31 Dec. 1840/3, I hearn Marse Henry cum outen de house lak he did in de days ob old. **1898** R. BLAKEBOROUGH *Wit, Folklore of North Riding* 425 Sha tumm'l'd outen t' winder. **1926** [see FEISTY *a.*]. **1944** C. HIMES *Black on Black* (1973) 197 They done left me outen it altogether. **1945** in *Sc. Nat. Dict.* (1965) VI. 511/1 Ye're aye tryin tae mak an auld wumman ooten me. **1976** T. GIFFORD *Cavanaugh Quest* i. 16, I come outen the elevator and I'm heading through the delivery hallway.

†**2.** Without, besides. *Obs.*

c **1250** *Gen. & Ex.* 653 Vten childre and vten wimmen, wel fowre and xx ðhusent men.

C. *Comb.* and quasi-*adj.*

†**1.** *Comb.* Forming advbs. as OE. *útan landes*, ME. *uten erdes* in a foreign land, abroad. *Obs.*

c **1000** *Ags. Ps.* (Th.) lxiv. [lxv.] 8 Þeoda..þe eard nymaþ utan landes. *c* **1250** *Gen. & Ex.* 956 And uten erdes sorȝe sen.

†**2. a.** quasi-*adj.* (This appears to have originated in combinations, afterwards sometimes separated.) Coming from without, foreign, alien. *Obs.*

c **1250** *Gen. & Ex.* 1741 Laban ferde..fro caram in-to vten stede. *c* **1300** *Havelok* 2153 Wel to yeme, and wel were Ageynes uten laddes here. *Ibid.* 2580 Hise uten laddes here comen, And haues nu þe priorie numen. *a* **1300** *E.E. Psalter* xvii[i]. 46 Outen [Vulg. *alieni*] sones to me lighed þai, Outen sones elded er þai. *Ibid.* cxxxvi[i]. 5 Hou sal we singe sange ..Ofe lauerd in outen land þat isse?

b. Out-of-the-way, side-, by-. *Obs.*

a **1350** *St. Martin* 259 in Horstm. *Altengl. Leg.* (1881) 155 Þai went þam till ane owten strete, For þai wald noght saint Martyn mete.

outen ('aʊtən), *v. U.S. dial.* [perh. f. OUT *adv.* 22 a, 23: see -EN[5].] **1.** To extinguish, put out, erase.

1916 *Dialect Notes* IV. 338 Be sure to outen the light when you go to bed. **1933** M. K. RAWLINGS *South Moon Under* 331 Outen that light. **1937** *Amer. Speech* XII. 205 The average [Pennsylvania German] speaker will employ in speech, and often in writing, all the forms ascribed above to the educated person, and in addition..such forms as 'outen the light', [etc.]. **1950** *Publ. Amer. Dial. Soc.* XIV. 50 *Outen*: *v.t.*, to extinguish, as a fire. To erase, as writing on a slate. **1961** in WEBSTER, You might outen the candles there.

2. To come out with, utter, tell.

1951 L. CRAIG *Singing Hills* viii. 68 Finally Maje said, 'Outen it, fellow. Give out what you know.' *Ibid.* xiii. 126 There are words we want to outen and we can't.

'outen-town, *a.* and *sb. Sc.* [f. OUTEN *adv., prep.* (*a.*) (?) + TOWN *sb.*] **a.** *adj.* Living or lying outside the town. **b.** *sb.* A person living outside the town. Hence **outen-towner**.

1677 in Ure *Hist. Rutherglen* (1793) 69 Ordered that nane of the inhabitants give or sell, to outtentouns, any Muckmiddins, or foulyie. **1887** *Jamieson's Dict.* Suppl. s.v., Lying or living outside the burgh bounds, not belonging to the town; as, *outen-toun* lands, *outten-townes* burgess, *outen-touns* multure. **1882** W. H. DAWSON *Hist. Skipton* (E.D.D.), *Outen-towners*, the rural inhabitants around a town.

out-entry to **out-equivocate:** see OUT-.

outer ('aʊtə(r)), *a.* (*sb.*[1]) Forms: 5–6 outter, (6 outar), 5, 7– outer. [A new comparative formed immediately on OUT, instead of the inherited form UTTER from OE. *úterra, uttra*, which had ceased to show relationship to *out*; cf. *late, latter, later*. Occasional examples of *outer, outter* occur in Chaucer MSS., and the adv. *outerly* was very common in 14–15th c.; but, though found in the Bible of 1611, *outer* was not frequent till the 18th c., *utter* being usual in the sense 'exterior' till late in the 17th c.

The superlatives going with *outer* are OUTMOST and OUTERMOST. Equivalent forms found in late ME. or early mod.Eng. (doublets of corresponding forms mentioned under UTTER) are compar. OUTERMORE, OUTMER, superl. OUTEREST. Like the other comparatives of this kind, *outer* is not followed by *than*; we do not say *outer than*.]

A. *adj.* **1. a.** That is farther out than another (distinguished as *inner*), exterior; farther removed from the centre or inside; hence, comparatively or relatively far out; that is on the outside, outward, external; of or pertaining to the outside.

c **1410–25** *Chaucer's Troylus* III. 664 (615) (Harl. MS.), I wol in þat outter [*Camb. MS. c* 1425 vttir] hous allone Be warden of ȝoure wommen euerychon. **1611** BIBLE *Matt.* viii. 12 But the children of the kingdom shall be cast out into outer darkness [Gr. το ἐξώτερον]. **1677** GREW *Anatomy Fruits* iii. §3 The Foundation or Ground of the Outer and more Bulky Part of the Stone, is the inner Part of the Parenchyma. **1794** MRS. RADCLIFFE *Myst. Udolpho* xxvi, We shall reach the outer court presently. **1851** CARPENTER *Man. Phys.* (ed. 2) 488 The outer one..is commonly known as the serous layer, and the inner as the mucous. **1874** GREEN *Short Hist.* vii. §8. 435 In manners and outer seeming they had sunk into mere natives.

b. *Printing.* In sheet work, designating the forme containing the type pages from which the outer side of the sheet is printed and including the type page for the first page of the printed sheet.

1755 J. SMITH *Printer's Gram.* x. 262 They [*sc.* compositors] lay one extremity thereof against the hind side of the Fifteenth page, if it is an Inner Form; or against the hind side of the Thirteenth page if it is an Outer Form. **1808** C. STOWER *Printer's Gram.* vii. 171 A sheet in Folio. Outer Form. Inner Form. **1841**, etc. [see INNER *a.* (*sb.*[2]) 1 e].

c. *Phonetics.* Denoting an articulation in a part of the mouth nearer the lips than that designated by the term qualified by 'inner'.

1867 [see CLOSURE 5 c]. **1888** [see INNER *a.* (*sb.*[2]) 1 g]. **1972** HARTMANN & STORK *Dict. Lang. & Ling.* 39/2 The outer closure may occur at the lips, the teeth, the alveolar ridge, the palate, velum, pharynx, or glottis or any intermediate point.

2. a. Said of things and conditions external to man's mind and soul, of the objective or physical as opposed to the subjective or psychical world. Cf. INNER 2.

c **1386** CHAUCER *Sec. Nun's T.* 414 (Ellesm. MS.) Ther lakketh no thyng to thyne outter [so *Heng.*; *Harl.* outer; *Cambr.*, etc. vtter] eyen. *c* **1800** K. WHITE *Poems* (1837) 80 To these I 'plained, or turned from outer sight. **1883** A. BARRATT *Phys. Metempiric* 178 Metaphysic seems to leave us in the contradiction that outer objects are made by mind, yet that the processes of mind are in some way derived from outer objects.

b. Phr. ***outer man***, the body (after *inner man*); hence humorously, outward personal appearance, dress (so ***outer woman***). ***outer world***, the material world outside that familiar or known; also, people generally, outside the individual or his immediate circle.

a **1845** HOOD *Lamia* vi. 80 And say the outer woman is utter woman, And not a whit a snake. **1853** LYTTON *My*

Novel I. ii, Regarding the object in dispute not only with the eye of the outer man, but the eye of law and order. **1868** GLADSTONE *Juv. Mundi* viii. (1869) 245 The key to the inquiry is to be found in the Outer world of the Odyssey. **1874** MORLEY *Compromise* (1886) 119 Though themselves invisible to the outer world, they [convictions] may yet operate with magnetic force.. upon other parts of our belief. **1895** A. NUTT *Voy. Bran* I. 278 The under- is as old as the outer-world conception of a land dwelt in by wise, powerful, and immortal beings. **1897** *Westm. Gaz.* 23 Apr. 2/1 A woman must be uncommonly good inside to present such an outer-man to her fellows.

3. *Combinations* (in which the hyphen is optional): ***outer clothing, deck, door, kirk*** (*Sc.*), ***room, vestment***; also, **Outer Circle**, the road running round the perimeter of Regent's Park, London; **outer edge** (in Skating) = *outside edge*: see EDGE *sb.* 7 b; **outer form**, (*a*) (see sense 1 b above); (*b*) *Linguistics* (see quot. 1972); also ***outer speech form***; **Outer House**: see quot. 1872; †**outer line**, boundary line, circumference; **outer multiplication** *Math.*, the formation of an outer product; **outer product** *Math.* [tr. G. *äusseres produkt* (H. Grassmann *Die lineale Ausdehnungslehre* (1844) p. xi)], a vector product (*rare*); more commonly, a related product of two vectors or tensors that yields a tensor of higher rank than either of them; **outer space**, the region beyond the earth's atmosphere or beyond the solar system; ***from outer space***, a colloq. phr. implying outlandishness and frightfulness as of creatures described in some science fiction; **outer suburb**, one of the more remote suburbs of a city or town; so ***outer-suburban*** adj.; **outer ward** of a castle: see WARD *sb.*[2]; **outerwear**, clothing designed to be worn outside other garments; opp. *underwear*.

1829 *Picturesque Guide to Regent's Park* 29 The *outer circle or Ring consists of a fine level drive, planted with trees on each side; within this is another circle or path-way. **1867** H. LARGE *Large's Way about London* 336/2 *Outer Circle, Regent's Park, N.W.*, from the Marble Arch along Oxford st.. through Orchard st, Portman sq, Baker st, Upper Baker st and Clarence gt to the Outer circle. **1938** E. BOWEN *Death of Heart* I. i. 28 Cars slid lights all round the Outer Circle. **1974** *Kelly's Post Office London Directory* 667/4 Regent's Park.. Outer Circle. Hanover Lodge.. Zoological Society's Gardens. **1891** E. KINGLAKE *Australian at H.* 7 The idea.. to elaborate our present under-clothing into *outer-clothing. **1856** KANE *Arct. Expl.* I. xxvii. 355 To strip off the *outer-deck planking of the brig. **1818** SCOTT *Hrt. Midl.* xviii, The distance of his apartment from the *outer door of the house. **1861** J. RUFFINI *Dr. Antonio* xv, To see.. on the outer-door steps, plates full of oranges. **1902** *Murray's Mag.* XXVI. 473/2 The *outer edge is a gliding movement, forward or backward, performed on the outer edge of the runner. **1972** HARTMANN & STORK *Dict. Lang. & Ling.* 113/2 The grammatical and semantic structure of a particular language is unique to that language (*inner form*), however susceptible its sound system (**outer form*) may be to influences from other languages. **1818** SCOTT *Hrt. Midl.* xii, This case of Marsport against Lackland has made an unco din in the *Outer House. **1872** WHARTON *Law Lex.* (ed. 5), *Outer House*, the name given to the great hall of the Parliament House in Edinburgh, in which the Lords Ordinary of the Court of Session sit as single judges to hear causes. The term is used colloquially as expressive of the business done there in contradistinction to the Inner House, the name given to the chambers in which the First and Second Divisions of the Court of Session hold their sittings. **1875** W. MCILWRAITH *Guide Wigtownshire* 54 In the Cathedral and in the *Outer-kirk were various altars. **1530** PALSGR. 250/2 *Outarlyne or parte of a cercle, *circumference*. **1898** A. N. WHITEHEAD *Treat. Universal Algebra* I. iii. 207 Progressive and Regressive Multiplication are called *Outer Multiplication. **1959** M. R. SPIEGEL *Schaum's Outl. Theory & Probl. Vector Analysis* viii. 169 Inner and outer multiplication of tensors is commutative and associative. **1929** H. W. TURNBULL *Theory of Determinants* xi. 183 It involves a determinantal factor ($\alpha\beta\gamma$) which is an *outer product of the symbolic linear sets α, β, γ. **1959** M. R. SPIEGEL *Schaum's Outl. Theory & Probl. Vector Analysis* viii. 169 The product of two tensors is a tensor whose rank is the sum of the ranks of the given tensors. This product which involves ordinary multiplication of the components of the tensor is called the outer product. **1965** J. ABRAM *Tensor Calculus* iii. 27 We could have written eqn. (3.14) as $a^i(b_ic_j - b_jc_i)$ in which the bracket is an anti-symmetric tensor of order two. It is known as the outer product of the two vectors b_i and c_i. Only in three dimensions can the outer product be replaced by the vector product. **1970** BEDFORD & DWIVEDI *Vector Calculus* iv. 168 Since the outer product of two vectors is not commutative, we stress again the fact that the order of the two factors in the outer product is important. **1727** SWIFT *Art Pol. Lying* Wks. 1755 III. I. 121 In their *outer-room there ought always to attend some persons endowed with a great stock of credulity. **1806–7** J. BERESFORD *Miseries Hum. Life* (1826) IV. xx, The outer-room of a public office. **1901** H. G. WELLS *First Men in Moon* iii. 45 After all, to go into *outer space is not so much worse, if at all, than a polar expedition. **1935** *Discovery* Apr. 105/1 In America it was proposed to explore Mars or Venus or even the very realms of outer space. **1958** *Observer* 16 Mar. 1/2 The Soviet Union yesterday put forward a plan for banning the military use of outer space. **1961** WODEHOUSE *Ice in Bedroom* xxiii. 191 Every time I see this little horror from outer space, I want to sock him. **1964** *Ann. Reg. 1963* 31 On 25 July the treaty banning nuclear tests in the atmosphere, in outer space, and under water was initialled. **1972** 'H. CALVIN' *Take Two Popes* xii. 135 If your job says expend somebody, you expend... Do you think I'm an inhuman thing from outer space? **1973** *Times* 4 Dec. 8/4 Pioneer should be able.. to send pictures of Jupiter.. as it goes past it before flying away into outer space. **1901** *Outer speech form [see INNER *a.* 2 b]. **1937** *Outer suburb [see ASPIRIN]. **1974** P. HEYWOOD *Planning & Human Need* vi. 104 The crisis of the ghetto must be met, at least in part, in the outer suburbs. **1937** *Outer-suburban [see CREEPING *ppl. a.* 2 b]. **1964** P. F. ANSON *Bishops at Large* vi. 202 Ethelbert Lodge.. had been both the archiepiscopal curia and outer-suburban country estate of the Landaffs for several years. **1928** *Daily Express* 7 May 4 (Advt.), Seven guineas and three guineas are probably the two most popular prices for *outerwear garments. **1946** *Daily Tel.* 27 Mar. 5/8 From April 1 elastic can be used without restriction in the manufacture of underwear,.. outerwear,.. and miscellaneous articles. **1963** [see LEISURE *sb.* 6 a and c]. **1971** 'E. LATHEN' *Ashes to Ashes* ix. 91 They wore hairy outerwear and came from socially aware suburbs. **1977** *Times* 24 Dec. 17/1 In the six months to October 31, Forminster, which makes ladies' and children's outerwear clothing, turned in a pre-tax profit of £564,000.

B. *elliptically* as *sb.* **1.** In *rifle-shooting*, that part of the target outside the circles surrounding the bull's eye; hence, a shot that strikes this part.

1862 *Macm. Mag.* Mar. 429 Bewildered with talk going on all around them of outers and centres and bull's eyes. **1884** *Times* 23 July (Farmer), Running through the scoring gamut with an outer, a magpie, and a miss.

2. *Electr. Engin.* In a three-wire distribution system, either of the two conductors whose potentials are respectively above and below that of the earth or neutral by equal amounts.

1900 [see NEUTRAL *a.* and *sb.* B. 4]. **1932** R. RAWLINSON in E. Molloy *Pract. Electr. Engin.* V. 1590/2 The potential difference between the outers is still 500 volts, and.. they may therefore be used for power supply, while lighting load may be taken on a circuit between either outer and the mid-wire. **1970** H. FERRY *Electr. Supply* I. ii. 35 The cancellation of the two currents flowing in opposite directions in the middle wire.. enabled the section to be safely reduced to one-half that of the outers.

3. (*a*) *pl.* Outdoor clothing. (*b*) An outer garment or the outer part of a garment.

1904 E. NESBIT *Phoenix & Carpet* vi. 111 'We'd best put on our outers in case—.' 'We might rescue a traveller buried in the snow.' **1971** C. BONINGTON *Annapurna South Face* xi. 129 It needed a distinct effort of will.. to force on frozen boots. I kept the felt inners inside the sleeping-bag, but the outers were too bulky and I used these as a pillow; even so, each morning they were frozen solid. T. FROST in *Ibid.* xviii. 222, I put on my.. proofed nylon outers. **1976** *Horse & Hound* 3 Dec. 18/2 (Advt.), The Husky Riding Waistcoat, with its strong nylon outer, filled with polyester for thermo-insulated warmth, will keep those biting winter winds at bay.

4. *Austral. slang.* The part of a racecourse outside the enclosure; also *transf.* Hence in phr. ***on the outer***: penniless; out of favour, excluded.

1924 *Truth* (Sydney) 27 Apr. 6 *Outer, on the*, to be poor; to be outside. **1926** 'J. DOONE' *Timely Tips for New Australians* Gloss., *Outer*, a slang word denoting a betting ground overlooking a race-course. **1928** A. WRIGHT *Good Recovery* 157 You told me yourself that you were the cause of my being on the outer. **1953** T. A. G. HUNGERFORD *Riverslake* 174 And you're on the outer for sticking up for him? **1963** A. ROSS *Australia 63* iii. 86 Fine drizzle delayed things for half an hour, then shirts were ripped off again in the Outer, the beer cans were set up, and play proceeded. **1970** I. SOUTHALL *Bread & Honey* 54 Warren had always been on the outer, like a stray dog, always getting pushed.

5. An outer container into which one or several objects already enclosed in their own containers are packed for transport or display.

1920 J. STEPHENSON *Princ. & Pract. Commerc. Corr.* II. xii. 129 Size and description of outer. **1950** J. G. DAVIS *Dict. Dairying* 356 Packing of freshly frozen and packaged ice cream into 'outers' containing dozens of units.. considerably slows the rate of hardening. **1955** *Sales Appeal* Jan.–Feb. 37/2 Display outers, cut-outs and showcards. **1967** *Times Rev. Industry* May 83/3 An instrument.. provided with a carrying case was packed in a corrugated outer for transit. **1971** *Guider* Nov. 407 (Advt.), Your Net Profit per [chocolate] bar: 5p. Your Net Profit per outer (18 bars per outer): 90p.

Hence **'outer** *v. nonce-wd.*, to make outer or external.

1890 J. H. STIRLING *Gifford Lect.* vi. 104 The inner must be outered: the outer innered.

outer, *sb.*[2] [f. OUT *v.* + -ER[1].]

†**1.** One who or that which puts out, utters, or gives vent to; *spec.* one who utters or circulates false coin. *Obs.*

1421–2 HOCCLEVE *Dialog* 175 Vengaunce on yow.. ye false moneyours, and on yowre outeris. *c* **1448** —— *Balade Dk. York.* 17 Be thow an owter of my nycetee.

2. *Pugilism.* A knock-out blow.

1898 *Tit Bits* 22 Jan. 309/1 Boxing Instructor (loquitur), Great Scot! that was an 'outer' you gave me.

outer, colloq. var. OUT OF *prep. phr.* Cf. OUTA, OUTTA.

1856 [see GEEWHILLIKINS *int.*]. **1898** J. D. BRAYSHAW *Slum Silhouettes* 221 "Ave a cigar,' an' 'e pulls a 'andful outer 'is skyrocket. **1926** *Opportunity* Mar. 83/2 The devil often assumes an importance entirely unbecoming to one who has been summarily 'kicked outer heaven'. **1954** M. PROCTER *Hell is City* II. iv. 53 If I could get outer 'ere I could be 'ome in less nor an hour.

[**outer** (in Latham, etc.), mispr. for OUSTER.]

†**'outerest**, *a. Obs.* Also 5 owt(t)erest. [A superlative formed on *outer*: cf. *innerest*. The more frequent form was UTTEREST, q.v.] = OUTERMOST, UTTERMOST.

c **1374** CHAUCER *Boeth.* II. met. vi. 55 (Add. MS.) þe sonne.. comyng from his outerest [*Camb. MS.* owtereste] arysyng til he hidde his bemes vndir þe wawes. *Ibid.* IV. pr. vi. 136 þilke þat is outerest [*Camb. MS.* owtterest].. as it is for þest fro þe mydel symplicite of þe poynt.

outerly ('aʊtəlɪ), *adv.* (*a.*) Now *rare.* Forms: 4– outer-, (4–5 outir-, outre-, owter-, owtre-, 5 outtur-, 5–6 outter-); 4–5 -liche, -li, 5–7 -ly. [Another form of UTTERLY, conformed to *out*, *outer*.

It is remarkable that this was very frequent in 14–15th c., when *outer* itself was rare.]

†**1.** In an utter or extreme degree; entirely, absolutely; in an unqualified manner. = UTTERLY *adv.* ***outerly not***, not at all, in nowise. *Obs.*

c **1330** R. BRUNNE *Chron. Wace* (Rolls) 11520 þan telly þe outrely schent. *c* **1360** *Minor Poems fr. Vernon MS.* 530/131 Schewe not þin herte outerliche To þi seruaunt. *c* **1380** WYCLIF *Sel. Wks.* III. 437 Crist is in ilche mannes soule þat loveþ hym owterliche. *c* **1386** CHAUCER *Pars. T.* ¶ 160 The othere goode werkes.. been outrely [*v. rr.* outerly, vtterly] deede as to the lyf perdurable in heuene. **1388** WYCLIF *Deut.* xv. 4 And outerli [L. *omnino*] a nedi man and begger schal not be among ȝou. **1429** *Rolls of Parlt.* IV. 349/1 Ye weiȝt which is clepid aunselle shal outirli be putt awei. *a* **1541** WYATT *Ps.* li. Poems (1810) 394/1 And seeth hymself not outterly depryued From lygth of grace.

2. In an outward direction; towards the outside. Now *dial.*

1681 GREW *Museum* I. 27 In the lower Jaw, two Tusks,.. like those of a Boar, standing outerly, an inch behind the Cutters.

B. *adj.* Of a wind: Blowing from an outward direction: cf. *westerly*. Now *dial.*

a **1642** SIR W. MONSON *Naval Tracts* II. (1704) 260/1 Open Bays, subject to.. outerly Winds. **1896** CROCKETT *Grey Man* 299 (E.D.D.) An outerly wind might drive him to the coast of Ireland.

outermer, -mere: see next.

†**'outermore**, *a. Obs.* Also 4–5 -mere, 7 -mer. [A variant of UTTERMORE, f. *outer* + *-mer*, -MORE: cf. INNERMORE.] Outer; external, outward.

1388 WYCLIF *Ecclus.* xiii. 32 *marg.*, Thou schalt fynde in fewe men the ynnere goodnesse of soule, and of outermere conuersacioun togidere. —— *Ezek.* xlvi. 21 He ledde me out in to the outermere halle. *c* **1400** *Prymer* (1894) 72 Mi soule be fillid [wiþ] innere fatnesse & outermere fatnesse. *a* **1640** JACKSON *Creed* x. xlv. §3 We cannot allot a lower or outermer mansion in heaven itself than that. **1674** N. FAIRFAX *Bulk & Selv.* 117 One atome in the inner rims, would be even to more than one in the outermore.

outermost, *a.* (*adv.*) Also 6 outter-. [f. OUTER *a.* + -MOST (cf. *hindermost, innermost*); a later formation than UTTERMOST, conformed to *out*, *outer*.] Situated farthest out from the inside or centre; most outward; most external; extremest.

1587 GOLDING *De Mornay* xiv. 197 Descending downe to the centre of the world and mounting vp aboue the outtermost circle of it. **1665** BOYLE *Occas. Refl.*, *Disc.* II. i, Those imaginary spaces, that are beyond the outermost part of the outermost Heaven. **1768–74** TUCKER *Lt. Nat.* (1834) I. 114 The angle formed by the two outermost lines. **1864** BOWEN *Logic* vii. 186 Circles of which the outermost and largest indicates the Predicate of the Conclusion.

b. as *adv.* In the most outward position.

1858 HAWTHORNE *Fr. & It. Jrnls.* II. 154 When the material embodiment presents itself outermost.

'outerness. [f. OUTER *a.* + -NESS.] The quality or fact of being outer or exterior.

†**1.** That which possesses this quality; the outer surface, the exterior. *Obs.*

1674 N. FAIRFAX *Bulk & Selv.* 86 Unevennesses.. in its outerness or surface.

2. Occupation with what is external. *rare.*

1863 *Dublin Lect. Eng. Lit.* 10 An infusion of French character, which gave to the English mind a certain amount of French quickness and outerness, and made it more bright and objective.

outes, variant of OUTAS, outcry.

out-eye, -eyed: see OUT-.

†**'outface**, *sb. Obs.* Also 6 vtface. [OUT- 3.] The outer or external face; outside; surface.

1570 DEE *Math. Pref.* D j b, The vtface or Superficies of the earth. **1635** SWAN *Spec. M.* vi. §2 (1643) 186 The outface of the ground could not be obscured. **1727** BRADLEY *Fam. Dict.* s.v. *Building*, That no Door-Frame, or Window-Frame of Wood, in London and Westminster.. shall be set nearer to the Outface of the Wall than four Inches.

out'face, *v.* [OUT- 18 b, c.]

1. *trans.* To outdo or overcome in facing or confronting; to look (a person) out of countenance; to face or stare down; hence, to put out of countenance, put to shame or to silence, generally; esp. by boldness, assurance, impudence, or arrogance.

to outface with a card of ten: see CARD *sb.*[2] 2 a, and cf. FACE *v.* 3 b.

a **1529** SKELTON *Bouge of Court* 315 Firste pycke a quarell and fall out with him then And soo outface hym with a carde of ten. **1540** COVERDALE *Fruitf. Less.* v. Wks. (Parker Soc.) I. 398 To take too much upon us, that with bragging or arrogancy we would out-face the weak. **1584** FENNER *Def. Ministers* (1587) 43 To rayse tumultes, and by number to out-face our Superiours. **1593** SHAKS. *2 Hen. VI*, IV. x. 49 Oppose thy stedfast gazing eyes to mine, See if thou canst out-face me with thy lookes. **1596** —— *Merch. V.* IV. ii. 17 We shal haue old swearing That they did giue the rings away to men; But weele out-face them, and out-sweare them to. **1615** HEYWOOD *Foure Prentises* I. xiv. Wks. 1874 II. 196 Think'st thou, thou canst outface me? proud man, no. **1658** A. FOX *Wurtz' Surg.* v. 363 These impudent wenches would have outfaced me therein. **1756** WESLEY *Wks.* (1872) XIII. 215 They will outface and out-lung you. **1882** J. PARKER *Apost. Life* I. 103 They will outface the two unlearned and ignorant men.

fig. **1649** N. BACON *Disc. Govt. Eng.* I. lxvi. (1739) 140 In this course they continued till they had out-faced shame itself. **1854** RUSKIN *Two Paths* I. §9, I have put this painful question before you, only that we may face it thoroughly, and, as I hope, out-face it. **1898** *Pall Mall G.* 2 Nov. 3/2 It has happened to me to find myself before a common silk that outfaced all the reds of nature.

†**b.** To force *from* by confronting. *Obs.*

1596 SHAKS. *1 Hen. IV*, II. iv. 283 Then did we too, set on you foure, and with a word, outfac'd you from your prize.

2. To face boldly or defiantly, to confront fearlessly or impudently; to brave, defy.

1574 tr. *Marlorat's Apocalips* 116 This so great assurednesse whereby a man may be bold to outface the diuell, sinne, death, and hell gates. **1577–87** HOLINSHED *Chron.* III. 1148/2 If you meet your brother in the street, shun him not, but outface him. **1605** SHAKS. *Lear* II. iii. 11 Ile..with presented nakednesse out-face The Windes, and persecutions of the skie. **1679** GOODMAN *Penit. Pardoned* II. iii. (1713) 206 The Pharisee stood upon his own justification, and with a brazen impudence outfaces heaven. **1870** LOWELL *Study Wind.* (1886) 9 They..outface you with an eye that challenges inquiry.

fig. **1827** SOUTHEY in *Q. Rev.* XXXVI. 337 Professors of holiness, and professors of patriotism, when they are thoroughly versed in their trade, can outface infamy.

†**3.** To contradict (any one) to his face; to controvert or deny (a statement, etc.) boldly or impudently; to give the lie to boldly or defiantly.

c **1586** C'TESS PEMBROKE *Ps.* CXXXIX. xi, This cursed brood ..Would with proud lies thy truth outface. **1586** T. B. *La Primaud. Fr. Acad.* I. (1594) 359 For a yea or a naie, they foorthwith thinke that the lie is giuen them, and that they are outfaced. **1643** MILTON *Divorce* viii. Wks. (1851) 43 Which ..if we shall still avouch to be a command, he palpably denying it, this is not to expound S. Paul, but to outface him. **1686** GOAD *Celest. Bodies* I. ix. 28 Who can outface so Ancient and Loud Tradition?

†**b.** To maintain boldly or impudently to the face of (a person), *that*, etc. *Obs.*

1631 LYNDE *Case for Spectacles* (1638) 58 They have out-faced the world in their Preface, that their Translation is so exact and precise. **1654** VILVAIN *Theol. Treat.* Suppl. 240 The Ægyptian Sorcerers..outfaced the King, that they were Serpents which looked like Rods. **1678** DRYDEN *Kind Keeper* IV. i, He made me keep Lent last Year till Whitsontide, and out-fac'd me with Oaths, it was but Easter.

†**4.** To maintain (something false or shameful) with boldness or effrontery; to brazen out. *Obs.*

1581 W. FULKE in *Confer.* II. (1584) Kiij b, I see you would outface the matter. **1649** MILTON *Eikon.* xxi, The Damsell,..at sight of her own letter, was soon blank, and more ingenuous than to stand outfacing. **1679** BEDLOE *Popish Plot* Ep. A ij, I scarce know which is greatest, Their Impudence in committing horrid Villanies, or in out-facing them, when they are done. **1692** R. L'ESTRANGE *Josephus, Wars of Jews* I. xvii. (1733) 593 Why cannot you give over this Way of shuffling and outfacing things, and rather make a frank Confession?

Hence **out'faced** *ppl. a.*; **out'facer**, one who outfaces; **out'facing** *ppl. a.* and *vbl. sb.*

1547–64 BAULDWIN *Mor. Philos.* (Palfr.) 126 Defended from..lyers, from out-facers, shamelesse persons, & theeues. **1602** MARSTON *Antonio's Rev.* I. iii, I..pierc't the starre, With an outfacing eye. **1618** BP. HALL *Contempl., O.T.* XIII. i, Conviction of a denied and outfaced disobedience. **1632** BROME *North. Lass* I. v. Wks. 1873 III. 11, I know he is a Bawd by his out-facing. **1681** T. FLATMAN *Heraclitus Ridens* No. 25 (1713) I. 164 Notwithstanding all their Impudent out-facings of the Matter, I doubt not but a horrid Conspiracy will yet..be made out.

out-faith, etc.: see OUT-.

'outfall. [OUT- 7.]

†**1.** A sally or sortie from a camp or fortified place. (Cf. Du. *uitval*, †*uutval*, Ger. *ausfall*.) See FALL *out* c. *Obs.*

1637 R. MONRO *Exped.* I. 11 The first night, the Major made an out-fall. [**1891** *Cornh. Mag.* Oct. 416 His whole life was spent in raids and outfalls upon the Brabanters.]

2. The act of falling out; a quarrel. (See FALL *out* d.) *Sc.* or *north. dial.*

?**16..** in Pennant *Tour in Scot.* 1769 App. (1776) 330 They rysed a cry, as if it hade been upon some out fall among these people. **1825** BROCKETT *N.C. Gloss., Out-fall*, a quarrel, a misunderstanding.

3. a. The outlet or mouth of a river, drain, sewer, etc., where it falls into the sea, lake, etc.

1629 *Drayner Conf.* (1647) B iv, The out falls of Wisbich and Spalding being daily more and more choaked with sands from the sea. *a* **1634** CHAPMAN *Rev. for Honour* III. ii, Rivers with greedier speed run neere their out-falls, than at their springs. **1783** *Phil. Trans.* LXXIV. 8 It is probable, that.. the river Medway..had once an out-fall to the sea. **1833** TENNYSON *Lady of Shalott*, As when to sailors while they roam, By creeks and outfalls far from home. **1869** E. A. PARKES *Pract. Hygiene* (ed. 3) 343 Good sewers, and a proper outfall.

attrib. **1807** VANCOUVER *Agric. Devon* (1813) 285 Convenient situations for forming outfal-drains. **1894** *Westm. Gaz.* 15 Jan. 1/3 To carry away the sewage to outfall works.

b. *fig.* Outlet, channel of disposal.

1883 MRS. LYNN LINTON *Ione* I. iv. 77 At a time when costly fancies were the legitimate outfalls of his wealth. **1933** *Catholic Bulletin* Mar. 182 In *The Commonweal*, Padraic Colum..now finds a suitable outfall for his anti-Irish spate.

†**'outfalling.** *Sc. Obs.* [OUT- 9.] A falling out; a quarrel.

a **1670** SPALDING *Troub. Chas. I* (1850) I. 223 Priuat menis out-fallingis and broyllis ar questionat as nationall querrellis.

†**'outfang.** *Sc. Obs.* Abbreviation of next.

1549 *Compl. Scot.* xiii. **1828** SCOTT *F.M. Perth* iv. [see INFANG].

†**'outfang,thief.** *Old Eng. Law. Obs.* In 2 **utfangene þeof, utfangentheif**; 3 **utefang-, utfangen-**, 3, 4 **outfangen(e)-, -fange-, -thef.** [Answers to an OE. type *útfangenne þéof* (accusative case) 'out-caught thief'; but the expression appears to have come into use later, to match *infangenne þéof*, INFANGTHIEF, q.v.] A franchise of a lord of a private jurisdiction, more extensive than that of INFANGTHIEF; originally, the lord's right to pursue a thief (at least when the latter was 'his own man') outside his own jurisdiction, bring him back to his own court for trial, and keep his forfeited chattels on conviction. But the right was variously defined or circumscribed in the 13th c., when its meaning seems to have already become conjectural.

The term *infangenne þéof* occurs in several OE. Charters, but of *útfangenne þéof* no trace has been found except in an alleged charter of Egbert dated 828 (Birch *Cartul. Sax.* No. 395), which has the Latin phrase 'cum furis comprehensione intus et foris' the apparent equivalent of an OE. 'mid infangenum þéofe and útfangenum'. But this is extant only in the *Liber Roffensis* (1120–50), and may be spurious, or the phrase may be a 12th c. interpolation. The term is wanting from an Eng.-Fr. Glossary of Law Terms compiled 1122–1150 (Wright *Reliq. Antiq.* I. 33) which contains '*Infangenethef*—larum pris ens nostre tere'. On the other hand, *utfangene þeof* occurs in the forged Charter of Edgar to Glastonbury (Birch, No 1277), which was in existence before William of Malmesbury made the third version of his *Gesta Regum* 1130–40 (in which the charter is given); and it may thus go back to 1100, or even earlier.

The etymological sense 'out-caught-thief', i.e. 'thief apprehended outside' (the jurisdiction), is that assigned to it in the Ripon record of 1228, in which the grant of 'infangethef et outfangethef' was explained as giving the grantee the right to try 'his own thief' *ubicumque captum*, whether within or without his territorial jurisdiction. But Bracton and *Fleta* explain it as the right to try thieves coming *from without*, and apprehended within the lord's jurisdiction; they both expressly deny that it meant a thief *taken outside*, or that such a thief might be brought back into the jurisdiction to be tried. *Fleta* however adds that, after his own thief had been condemned by the outside tribunal, the lord might bring him into his jurisdiction and hang him on his own gallows; and the right to do this appears to be all that Britton knows as 'the franchise of outfangenthef'.

a **1135** *Forged Charter of Edgar to Glastonbury* (dated 971), & habeant socam & sacam...infangeneþeof & utfangene þeof, & flemene ferðe, hamsocne, fridebrice..forstealle, toll & team, ita libere & quiete sicut ego habeo in regno meo. **1189–95** in *Regist. de Wetherhal* (1897) 31 Concedimus insuper eidem Abbaithiæ.. soch et sach et tol et theam et infangentheif et utfangentheif. **1228** *Mem. Ripon* (Surtees) I. 52 Suum latronem ubicumque captus fuerit, infangethef et outfangethef. *Ibid.* 57 Et suum latronem ubicumque captum ad judicandum in curia sua..et infangthef et utefangthef, furcam, prisonam, blodewite [etc.]. *c* **1250** BRACTON III. xxxv. 154 *b*, VTFANGENTHEF vero dicitur latro extraneus, veniens aliunde de terra aliena, et qui captus fuit in terra ipsius qui tales habet libertates. **1290–1300** *Fleta* I. xlvii. 62. **1292** BRITTON II. iii. §13 Qe il eynt la fraunchise de outfangenthef, ceo est a dire, qe eux eynt les juises de lour gentz et de lour tenauntz, ou q'il soint pris hors de lour feez, jugez a pendre, qe il les pusent apres jugement rendu prendre et remener en lour fraunchise et fere les pendre illucs sur lour fourches demeyne. ? *c* **1300** *Rolls of Parlt.* I. 462/2 Ovec retorn de Bref infangenethef, outfangenethef, e quite de tonnue, passage, murage, pontage, pavage. **1535** *Act 27 Hen. VIII*, c. 26 §23 Lordshippes Marchers..shall have within the precincte of their said Lordeshippes.. Wayff Straiff Infanthef Outfanthef Treasoure Troves. *c* **1575** *Balfour's Practicks* (1754) 37 Thair is sum Baronis quha hes privilege and libertie of infang and outfang thift. **1579** RASTELL *Expos. Words* 213 *Outfangthiefe*, that is, that theues or felones of your lande, or fee, out of your land or fee taken with felonie or stealinge, shalbee brought backe to your Court, and there iudged. **1597** SKENE *De Verb. Sign.* s.v. *Infangthefe*, Out-fangthiefe is ane forain thiefe, quha cumis fra an vther mans lande or jurisdiction, and is taken and apprehended within the lands perteinand to him quha is infeft with the like liberty. **1814** SCOTT *Waverley* x. **1839** KEMBLE *Cod. Dipl.* I. Introd. 45. **1895** POLLOCK & MAITLAND *Eng. Law* I. 564 *note*, [In the 13th c.] there was much doubt as to what was meant by *hengwite* and as to the exact limits of the right of *utfangenethef*. In cases of *quo waranto* the king's advocates are fond of puzzling their adversaries by asking them to explain what they mean by these old words.

†**'outfare.** *Obs.* [OE. *útfaru* fem., cf. *útfær* neut., a going out, f. *út* (see OUT- 7) + *faru*, *fær*, going, journey, *faran* to go, travel.] A going out, journey, expedition; an outlet.

c **961** *Rule St. Benet* lxvi. (Schröer, 1885) 127 þæt nan neod ne sy munecum, utan to farenne, forþy þe seo utfaru nan þing ne framað hira saulum. *c* **1000** ÆLFRIC *Hom.* I. 484 Ðæt we symle ðone mæran gylt forfleon þurh utfære ðæs læssan. **13..** *Cursor M.* 7890 þat vri was..At kinges ost, and in vte-far.

out-fast (-'fɑːst, -æ-), *v.* [OUT- 18, 17.] *trans.* To surpass in fasting, fast longer than. †*to outfast oneself*, to fast beyond one's power of endurance.

1645 WITHER *Vox Pacif.* 29 Yet, as if they had Pharoah's kine out-fasted. **1683** TRYON *Way to Health* 334, I have out-fasted my self, or my Stomach is gone. **1855** MILMAN *Lat. Chr.* IV. 196 Sow the good seed as the heretics sow the bad. .. Out-labour, out-fast, out-discipline these false teachers.

out-fawn to **out-feed**: see OUT-.

'out-,fence, *sb.* [OUT- 3.] An outer or bounding fence.

1769 *Aclome Inclos. Act* 13 The out-fences of all the lands ..shall be well and sufficiently made. **1797** T. WRIGHT *Autobiog.* (1864) 41 Without putting down a pit within the stakes of any of the out-fences.

out'fence, *v.* [OUT- 15, 18.] *trans.* **a.** To fence out, divide by fences. **b.** To outdo in fencing, or put (one) out of his fence or guard.

1770 *W. Heslerton Inclos. Act* 14 All the lands..shall be well and sufficiently out-fenced. **1880** G. MEREDITH *Tragic Com.* i. (1892) 5 Veteran tricksters..capable of outfencing her nascent individuality.

out-ferret to **out-fiction**: see OUT-.

outfield, out-field ('aʊtfiːld), *sb.* [OUT- 1.]

1. a. The outlying land of a farm; esp. in Scotland, the outlying land which is either unenclosed and untilled moorland or pasture, or was formerly cropped from time to time without being manured. *outfield and infield system*: see INFIELD.

1637 RUTHERFORD *Lett.* (1862) I. 361, I know that it is not my home nor my Father's house: it is but..the outer close of His house, His outfields and muir-ground. **1812** SIR J. SINCLAIR *Syst. Husb. Scot.* I. 315 His land is..originally all outfield, being mostly covered with whins and heath not many years ago. **1861** SMILES *Engineers* II. 94 The chief part of each farm consisted of 'out-field' or unenclosed land, no better than moorland.

attrib. **1765** A. DICKSON *Treat. Agric.* xv. (ed. 2) 123 This land is what is called out-field land; that is, land not improved, and that has received but little manure. When brought into tillage, three or four crops exhaust it. **1820** SCOTT *Monast.* i. **1823** *Blackw. Mag.* XIV. 189 Ropes.. thrown over all the outfield hay ricks.

b. An outlying field.

1676 *Connect. Col. Rec.* (1852) II. 464 Thirty men to be a Guard while we gather in your harvest from your out-fields. **1733–1856** [see INFIELD]. **1775** ADAIR *Amer. Ind.* 406 The chief part of the Indians begin to plant their out-fields, when the wild fruit is so ripe, as to draw off the birds from picking up the grain.

2. *fig.* The region of thought or fact outside defined limits; an outlying region.

1851 TRENCH *Stud. Words* vi. 174 The enclosure of a certain district..from the great outfield of thought or fact. **1859** —— *On Author. Vers.* 22 Words are enclosures from the great outfield of meaning.

attrib. ? *a* **1850** S. MILLER *Serm.* in *Mem.* iv. (1883) 99 We would 'go forth' in more than human might against the outfield masses festering in our midst.

3. In *Cricket* and *Baseball*: **a.** The outlying part of the field, that part most remote from the batsman. Also *transf.* and *fig.*

1851 W. CLARK in W. Bolland *Cricket Notes* 136 If you are in the out field, and the batsman is on the alert, he will steal a run. **1868** H. CHADWICK *Game of Base Ball* 73 The Irvingtons..placed the substitute in the out-field. **1895** *Daily News* 5 Feb. 3/5 The rest of the wickets fell for catches, most of them in the out-field, and the innings closed for 72. **1896** *Ibid.* 11 Aug. 7/2 The outfield ground was so dead that many hits that would ordinarily have been fours and twos only produced twos and singles. **1948** *Denison* (Texas) *Herald* 2 July 12/3 Have you ever played the outfield? **1971** *Times* 16 Feb. 7/6 The groundsman at the cricket ground here has been mowing the out-field. **1975** *Cricketer* May 19/1 When they batted the opening pair put on 85 in the first 20 overs, a splendid rate on an extremely wet outfield. **1976** *Billings* (Montana) *Gaz.* 16 June 1-C/3 Playing both first base and the outfield, Rudi was regarded as one of the most valuable players in the league every season from 1970–75. **1976** P. HARCOURT *Dance for Diplomats* ii. 15 We taxied around the runways..and came to a stop somewhere in the out-field. **1977** J. LE CARRÉ *Hon. Schoolboy* iii. 58 Martindale..in the Whitehall outfield lived in a state of primaeval innocence about the reality of Smiley's world.

b. = OUT-FIELDER. Also, the out-fielders collectively.

1867 *J. Lillywhite's Cricketers' Compan.* 160 [He is] a fine out-field. **1867** H. CHADWICK *Base Ball Player's Bk. Reference* 138 The Out-Field—The out-fielders are the left[,] centre and right-field positions. **1868** —— *Game of Base Ball* 17 The out-field being neither active in their movements, or sure catchers. **1884** *Lillywhite's Cricket Ann.* 101 J. E. K. S——, a magnificent out-field. **1894** *Westm. Gaz.* 18 Dec. 7/2 He is a good out-field. **1910** *Blackw. Mag.* Jan. 93/2 Tyldesly..ten years ago was one of the finest out-fields imaginable. **1948** *Daily Ardmoreite* (Ardmore, Okla.) 30 Mar. 6/4 If the Boston Braves win.., they will do it without an outfield which is particularly strong defensively. **1956** *People* 13 May 13/3 Cliff is an attractive all-round cricketer and an especially good long-throwing fast-moving outfield.

out-field, *v.* *Cricket* and *Baseball.* **1.** *intr.* [f. the sb.] To field in the out-field. *rare.*

1862 *Baily's Monthly Mag.* Aug. 85 The Surrey people.. selecting..an F. Lee, a Daniel, and an E. B. Rowley to out-field.

2. *trans.* [f. OUT- 18.] To surpass (the opposition) in fielding. Chiefly *pass.*

1875 *Chicago Tribune* 17 Aug. 5/6 The Browns were outbatted and outfielded. **1960** *Times* 19 May 21/2 They had been out-batted, out-bowled, and out-fielded. **1970** [see *outbowl* s.v. OUT- 18 a].

ˌout-ˈfielder. [OUT- 1 + FIELDER.] The player or fielder who stands in the out-field: see OUT-FIELD *sb.* 3.

1868 H. CHADWICK *Game of Base Ball* 73 The Irvingtons ..took an out-fielder from his regular position. **1893** *Columbus* (O.) *Disp.* 17 Nov., A deal with the Pittsburgh club for the purchase of Van Haltren, the outfielder. **1898** *Westm. Gaz.* 18 Feb. 3/1 An out-fielder, running for a catch. **1942** *Sun* (Baltimore) 3 Apr. 18 Estel Crabtree, Cardinal out-fielder, attributed his greatly improved batting in 1941 to constant work with the machine. **1972** *Village Voice* (N.Y.) 1 June 69/2 He'd lyricize an outfielder's grace and then demean baseball as a little boy's game. **1974** *Anderson* (S. Carolina) *Independent* 19 Apr. 4B/3 The A's used Allan Lewis, an outfielder with little hitting ability, as a pinch running specialist the last two World Series.

So **ˌout-ˈfielding** *vbl. sb.*, the action of fielding in the 'out-field'; also *attrib.*; **out-ˈfieldsman** = OUT-FIELDER.

1860 in *Ball Players' Chron.* (1867) 12 Dec. 3/1 The out-fielding was only so-so. **1861** *Times* 25 May 9/4 Notwithstanding the truly fine bowling and general good out-fielding, Mr. Burbidge and Griffith defended their wickets in a masterly manner. **1881** *Daily News* 8 July 2/7 Newton's wicket-keeping, and Cave's out-fielding. **1884** I. BLIGH in *Lillywhite's Cricket Ann.* 4 The out-fielding ground was very rough. **1891** W. G. GRACE *Cricket* 268 A brilliant out-fieldsman is worth his place in any eleven for the work he can do there alone. **1973** B. RICHARDS *On Cricket* x. 98 Outfielding, too, requires concentration.

outˈfight, *v.* [OUT- 15 d, 18 b.]

†**1.** *trans.* To take by assault, subdue, conquer, overcome. [Rendering L. *expugnare.*] *Obs.*

1382 WYCLIF *Josh.* x. 35 And [Joshua] went fro Lachis vnto Eglon, and enuyrounde, and out fauȝt [Vulg. *expugnavit*] it the same day. —— *Ecclus.* iv. 33 And God shal outfiȝten [*expugnabit*], or ouercome for thee, thyn enemys.

2. To fight better than; to beat in a fight.

1643 TRAPP *Comm. Gen.* xlix. 17 He could, if not outfight his enemies, outwit them. **1814** *Sporting Mag.* XLIV. 167 He out-fought his adversary left and right. **1875** MERIVALE *Gen. Hist. Rome* xlv. (1877) 339 The elder general both out-manœuvred and out-fought the younger.

out-fighter. [OUT- 2.] One who fights not at close quarters. So **ˈout-fighting** *ppl. a.*, fighting not at close quarters, skirmishing.

1817 *Sporting Mag.* L. 54 As an out-fighter he completely astonished the ring. **1877** KINGLAKE *Crimea* VI. vi. 317 The ensheathing columns were roughly handled and closed in upon by our out-fighting troops.

ˈout-fighting, *vbl. sb.* [OUT- 2.] Fighting that is not at close quarters.

1848 *Sporting Life* 5 Feb. 297/2 At out-fighting, Bateman was decidedly the quickest and the best. **1905** *Times* 6 Mar. 4/2 It is probable that this outfighting, before the adversaries close, will be fruitful in important lessons relating to the art of naval war.

†**out-ˈfind,** *v. Obs.* [OUT- 15.] *trans.* To find out. (*poetic*, and prop. two words.)

1570 PRESTON *Cambyses* in Hazl. *Dodsley* IV. 229 My heart hath you out-found. **1590** GREENE *Never too late* Isabel's Sonn. in Prison, With piercing insight will the truth outfind. **1626** G. SANDYS *Ovid's Met.* XIV. 303 The fatall mouth of Æsarus out-found.

So †**out-finding** *vbl. sb.*, finding out.

1552 LYNDESAY *Monarche* 6102 Strange wayis Investigabyll,—That is to say past out fynding. **1553** GRIMALDE *Cicero's Offices* I. (1558) 3 That to yᵉ outfinding of dutie there might haue been an entrie.

out-finger to **out-firmament**: see OUT-.

outfit (ˈaʊtfɪt), *sb.* [OUT- 7.]

1. The act of fitting out or furnishing with the requisites for a journey or expedition, or for any purpose; *ellipt.* = expense of fitting out.

1769 FALCONER *Dict. Marine* (1789), *Out-fit*, is generally used to signify the expences of equipping a ship for a sea-voyage; or of arming her for war, or both together. **1792** in *New Eng. Hist. & Gen. Register* (1892) XLVI. 174, I expect we shall be able to import wheat for our flour and bread for our next outfit to advantage. **1828** CHANTREY in Lockhart *Scott* May, If you'll secure the commissions, I'll make the outfit easy. **1868** E. EDWARDS *Ralegh* I. ix. 143 One of the chief adventurers in the outfit of the expedition.

2. a. The articles and equipment required for an expedition, etc. Also, equipment of any kind; a set of articles for a particular purpose.

1787 JEFFERSON *Writ.* (1859) II. 225, I believe there is no instance of any nation sending a minister to reside anywhere without an outfit. **1809** A. HENRY *Trav.* 11 On the 15th of June, [I] again arrived in Montreal, bringing with me my outfits. **1848** ARNOULD *Mar. Insur.* (1866) I. I. ii. 19 *Outfit* is sometimes..the necessary stores and provisions put on board the ship for the use of the crew on the voyage. *Ibid.*, In whaling voyages the word *outfit*..means the fishing stores of the ships. **1867** J. F. MELINE *Two Thousand Miles on Horseback* 74 The saddler who sold me my saddle assured me it was the best outfit he had furnished for some time. Bought a hat, and was told, 'Well, Sir, I call that a good outfit.' **1869** A. K. MCCLURE *3,000 Miles through Rocky Mts.* 211 Everything is an 'outfit', from a train..to a pocket-knife. **1873** E. B. TUTTLE *Boy's Bk. Indians* 45 Friday had a beautiful set of arrows, bow and quiver, which I desired to purchase... Friday would not sell his 'outfit', as it is called, for money. **1924** T. E. LAWRENCE *Home Lett.* (1954) 359 A solo isn't as secure on a wet road as a side-car outfit. **1958** *Amer. Speech* XXXIII. 271 *Outfit*, a man's equipment.

attrib. **1898** *Westm. Gaz.* 19 May 2/2 The 'outfit' allowance of £20..now given to officers joining the Volunteers.

b. *fig.* The mental and moral endowments or acquirements with which any one is furnished.

1865 M. ARNOLD *Ess. Crit.* i. (1875) 46 [The] members have, for their proper outfit, a knowledge of Greek, Roman, and Eastern antiquity. **1872** LIDDON *Elem. Relig.* i. 5 The conviction that religion is..an indispensable part of man's moral and mental outfit.

c. A person's clothes; a set of garments.

1852 MRS. STOWE *Uncle Tom's C.* v. 31 Saying these words, she had tied and buttoned on the child's simple outfit. **1875** *Scribner's Monthly* Dec. 286/1 The comfortable dress for the mother or flannel outfit for the baby, can be sent. **1946** *Chicago Daily News* 10 Aug. 12/3 Elaborate ceremonial outfits are fashioned by the women of the tribe. **1968** J. IRONSIDE *Fashion Alphabet* 104 Accessories..really can change the whole feeling of an outfit and turn a last year's garment into something swinging or chic. **1976** C. BERMANT *Coming Home* I. vii. 105 She did not wear the same outfit two days running.

d. The apparatus used by a drug addict for taking drugs.

[**1935** A. J. POLLOCK *Underworld Speaks* 84/2 *Outfitted*, to get a supply of dope.] **1951** *N.Y. Times* 14 June 22/2 'John' went into a drugstore on upper Park Avenue, asked for an 'outfit', and for 45 cents got an envelope containing a medicinal dropper and a hypodermic needle, such as used by 'mainliners' for heroin injections. **1953** W. BURROUGHS *Junkie* (1972) ix. 86, I asked him to come back to my apartment to take a shot. We went back to my room, and I got out my outfit that hadn't been used in five months. *Ibid.* xii. 121 She keeps outfits in glasses of alcohol so the junkies can fix in the joint and walk out clean. **1960** *Times Lit. Suppl.* 16 Sept. 589/4 Anyone who has snorted or used the outfit and then kicked would find it [*sc.* a book] of absorbing interest.

3. a. A collective term for a travelling party or a party in charge of herds of cattle, etc. *U.S. colloq.*

1867 *Harper's Mag.* July 137/2 Their 'outfit' (in the language of the plains this word signifies the conveyance, its contents, and the team) consisted of a Concord coach [etc.]. **1869** S. BOWLES *Our New West* viii. 163 With a mounted escort of about twenty gallant young miners..we made up a grand 'outfit'. **1879** F. H. ATKINS in *Let. to Editor*, The application of 'out-fit' to transportation has led secondarily to its application to the traveling party themselves. It is quite common in the West to hear, 'Do you belong to this outfit?' or 'Where is this outfit going?' **1890** D'OYLE *Notches* 55 The best fellows in this 'outfit' were Choctaw Bill..and Frank Norris, the 'boss', an ex-Yale student. **1891** C. ROBERTS *Adrift Amer.* 174 He belonged to a horse 'outfit' that was travelling north.

b. A group of people; an organization; a business firm or concern.

1883 'MARK TWAIN' *Life on Mississippi* ii. 31 In that day, all explorers travelled with an outfit of priests. De Soto had twenty-four with him... The expeditions were often out of meat, and scant of clothes, but they always had the furniture and other requisites for the mass. **1925** *Amer. Speech* I. 149/2 The big cattle companies or 'outfits'. **1926** J. BLACK *You can't Win* iv. 37, I was left on the bench with the two drunks... The desk man pointed to us. 'What will I do with this outfit, Hayes?' **1927** [see LAY-OUT 2 c]. **1930** D. L. SAYERS *Strong Poison* iv. 48 You must get me passed in as part of your outfit. **1935** WODEHOUSE *Blandings Castle* xii. 310 'Come and join my little outfit,' he said heartily. 'I've always room for a personal friend.' **1939** F. W. CROFTS *Fatal Venture* xi. 154 He's carrying this entire outfit on his shoulders. Only for Stott your job and mine might go phut. **1943** H. L. MENCKEN *Heathen Days* vii. 89, I was presently playing trios and quartettes with an outfit that devoted four hours of every week to the job. **1951** C. W. MILLS *White Collar* I. ii. 23 The great bulk of businesses are small outfits, which do not last long. **1958** S. ELLIN *Eighth Circle* (1959) II. i. 33 There's a couple of other agencies—Inter-American, Fleischer—pretty good outfits that might do just the job you want. **1962** *Observer* 25 Nov. 12/8 Aldermaston is 'less stuffy than Harwell' and usually beats the other nuclear outfits at rugger. **1975** *New Yorker* 21 Apr. 69/2 Investigators working not only for Retail Credit but for other large consumer-investigation outfits confirm this. **1977** J. WAINWRIGHT *Do Nothin'* v. 67 Some of the modern outfits don't have brass. Just a four-piece sax line-up.

c. *spec. Services' colloq.* A group of servicemen; a regiment, squadron, or the like.

1916 [see *anti-tank* s.v. ANTI-¹ 4 (iii)]. **1922** C. E. MONTAGUE *Disenchantment* ii. 18 A man is wanted for Post Corporal... 'Cushiest job in the 'ole outfit!' **1930** F. A. POTTLE *Stretchers* 28 The bowlegged officer flew into a disciplinary rage and addressed the boy as follows: 'What outfit do you belong to? How long have you been in the army?' **1951** H. HASTINGS *Seagulls over Sorrento* I. i, in J. Trewin *Plays of Year* IV. 52 Incidentally, wot are you doing in an outfit like this? **1959** *Times Lit. Suppl.* 30 Jan. 57/3 The sergeant, though a war hero and the only soldier in a slack outfit, is a psychopathic bully and a pathetically lonely man. **1966** *Inland* (Inland Steel Co., Chicago) Autumn 13/1 Recruits from all over the United States are assigned to the same military outfit. **1978** A. PRICE *'44 Vintage* xix. 220 France in '40, then the Middle East... And finally Yugoslavia as a weapons adviser to a big Partisan outfit.

4. *Canad.* The name given to the fiscal year of the Hudson's Bay Company; hence, a year.

1791 in *Beaver* (1947) Dec. 11/2 The difficiency in the order for the carrot tobacco arises from the great over-plus we have for the ensuing outfit. **1833** J. G. MCTAVISH *Let.* 18 Dec. in G. de T. Glazebrook *Hargrave Corr.* (1938) 124, I had thought, of getting away in one or two outfits. **1841** G. SIMPSON *London Corr.* (1973) 9 The lease..will expire..with the close of Outfit 1841/2. **1874** in *Alberta Hist. Rev.* (1956) Spring 16 The Athabasca accounts for the Outfit were closed and the Packet given over to the care of Mr. Moberly. **1913** I. COWIE *Company of Adventurers* 280 The end of each business year—called 'Outfit'—was May 31, upon which date the inventory of everything belonging to the Company at the fort was taken. **1935** in D. Jenness *Eskimo Admin.* (1964) II. 51 Altogether sixteen deaths occurred during the outfit and only four births that I know of. **1973** W. R. SAMPSON *J. McLoughlin's Business Corr. 1847–48* p. xix, He was to be made a wintering partner with a share in the profits of the concern for Outfit 1814.

5. A person (usu. pejorative). *slang* (chiefly *U.S.*).

1867 J. F. MELINE *Two Thousand Miles on Horseback* 74 To cross the plains, or go to the mountains, every one must get an outfit; and having outfitted, you become yourself an outfit. **1924** C. E. MULFORD *Rustler's Valley* xi. 130 You ain't believin' everythin' *this* outfit tells you, are you? **1925** *Ladies' Home Jrnl.* May 26/2 'But that young outfit will drive me wild,' protested Mrs. Denmeade. **1942** BERREY & VAN DEN BARK *Amer. Thes. Slang* §379/2 *Person*,..outfit.

ˈoutfit, *v.* [f. prec. sb.] **a.** *trans.* To provide with an outfit, to fit out. Also simply, to provide or supply (a person or thing) *with*.

1847 MRS. R. LEE *Afric. Wanderers* ii. (1854) 19 The trouble of outfitting the two boys for a public school. **1872** C. KING *Mountain. Sierra Nev.* v. 94, I..outfitted myself with a pack-horse, two mounted men, and provisions. **1877** RAYMOND *Statist. Mines & Mining* 176 This mill has been planned and outfitted with special reference to economizing labor and securing the greatest possible efficiency. **1924** W. M. RAINE *Troubled Waters* xvi. 167, I outfitted some of the boys with guns. **1928** *T. Eaton & Co. Catal.* Spring & Summer 219/4 Two or three suits like this would outfit him for the Summer. **1935** A. SQUIRE *Sing Sing Doctor* xiv. 205 The condemned man is outfitted with new clothing. **1953** K. TENNANT *Joyful Condemned* xxxix. 381 She was smartly outfitted: white shoes, white hat..and a black-and-white striped dress. **1971** *Sci. Amer.* Aug. 24/1 When the slim merchantman was ready for launching, its owner must have visited a ship chandler to buy the gear needed to outfit the vessel. **1972** P. H. KOCHER *Master of Middle-Earth* (1973) ii. 23 They helped to outfit the dwarf expedition when it was penniless. **1973** 'D. HALLIDAY' *Dolly & Starry Bird* iv. 55 Enough polo necks to outfit the entire British Raj. **1975** *Nature* 10 July 150/3 Such cameras are intrinsically sensitive to the near ultraviolet band, and to be used for ultraviolet viewing need only be outfitted with an ultraviolet-transmitting lens and filter. **1976** *National Observer* (U.S.) 19 June 8/6 And began to practice out of the van that he and several seabee friends had outfitted.

b. *intr.* for *refl.* or *pass.*

1881 *N.Y. Times* 18 Dec. 4/3 To 'outfit' is to fit out for any purpose whatever. 'We outfitted at St. Paul.' **1883** *Century Mag.* XXIX. 194/1 Here I 'outfitted', and..we were in a few days on our way to the Bitter Root Mountains. **1902** S. E. WHITE *Blazed Trail* xxv. 168 It's a good place to outfit from because we can probably get freight rates direct by boat. **1919** H. L. WILSON *Ma Pettengill* iv. 129 He outfitted at the Chicago Store in Tucson, getting the best all-wool ready-made suit in Arizona. **1924** C. E. MULFORD *Rustlers' Valley* x. 115 Yestiddy was pay-day, an' if they don't outfit now, some of 'em won't have no money after to-night. **1976** H. & G. GORDON *Ordeal* xv. 108 A party of four went down the trail... Three males and a female. Ring up the Big Rock Trading Post... Get the trader up and find out if they outfitted there.

So **ˈoutfitted** *ppl. a.*; **ˈoutfitting** *vbl. sb.* and *ppl. a.* (also *ellipt.*) [OUT- 9, 10.].

1840 DICKENS *Old C. Shop* xiv, An outfitting warehouse of the first respectability. **1871** MRS. WHITNEY *Real Folks* xii. (1872) 132 The trimming-up and outfitting place. **1908** *Westm. Gaz.* 24 Apr. 7/4 Until the cold weather and overcoats finally disappear there will be no improvement in outfitting. **1932** D. L. SAYERS *Have his Carcase* xxxi. 409, I went to the men's outfitting and asked for collars. **1964** A. ADBURGHAM *Shops & Shopping* xii. 130 Outfitting was the euphemism employed for both men's and women's underclothes. **1975** *Offshore Progress: Technol. & Costs* (Shell Internat. Petroleum Co.) 5 Several semi-submersibles delivered early in 1975 have hulls 300 ft long, and a total outfitted weight of up to 16,500 tons. **1976** *Cody* (Wyoming) *Enterprise* 23 June 1/1 Many of the complaints about the grizzly bear's critical habitat center around the effect such a definition would have on the outfitting business. A confrontation between outfitting camps and grizzlies within a critical habitat area would result in the relocation of the camp rather than the grizzly. **1977** *Times* 30 Nov. 2/4 The decision by more than 1,600 angry outfitting trades at Swan Hunter's [shipbuilding] yard to continue their overtime ban. **1977** *Time* 19 Dec. 31/1 Outfitted in quilted parkas, they can be seen roaming the snow-covered hills and hollows of Appalachia in search of game to keep down meat bills.

ˈoutfitter. [OUT- 8.] One who fits out, or furnishes an outfit; a dealer in outfits for travelling, athletic sports, or the like.

1846 in WORCESTER citing *Cons. Mag.* **1865** DICKENS *Mut. Fr.* II. i, She keeps the stock-room of a seaman's out-fitter. **1868** E. EDWARDS *Ralegh* I. ix. 146 Ralegh..was..the chief outfitter of the fleet. **1883** *Law Times Rep.* XLIX. 134/1 The business of a tailor and outfitter.

ˈoutflame, *sb.* [OUT- 7.] An outburst of flame, or *fig.* of passion or colour.

1889 DOYLE *Micah Clarke* 185, 'I would not barter it.., said he, with a sudden outflame. **1893** *Harper's Mag.* Apr. 735/2 A little island, with..an outflame of scarlet tupelo and sumac.

outˈflame, *v.* [OUT- 18, 14.] **a.** *trans.* To surpass in blaze or brilliancy. **b.** *intr.* To flame out, burst into blaze or brilliancy. *poet.*

1839 BAILEY *Festus* vi. (1852) 74 The conflagration of her eye, Outflaming even that eye which in my sleep Beams close upon me. **1865** SWINBURNE *Atalanta* 1650, I had..on their tombs Hung crowns, and..seen Their praise outflame their ashes. **1890** *Pall Mall G.* 3 Feb. 2/3 Did tropic lands with flowers and fruit out-flame?

ˈoutflaming, *vbl. sb.* [OUT- 9.] Flaming out, blazing up. So **ˈoutflaming** *ppl. a.*

1836 LANDOR *Minor Prose Pieces, St. Santander* Wks. 1853 II. 464/1 The first outflaming of the passions. **1872** TALMAGE *Serm.* 218 The outflaming glories of the countenances of the saved.

outflank (aʊtˈflæŋk), *v.* [OUT- 18 c, 17 (?).]

1. *trans.* To extend or get beyond the flank of the opposing army; to outmanœuvre by a flanking movement.

1765 *Hist. Eur.* in *Ann. Reg.* 10/1 Greatly to outflank any line of battle into which it was possible for the major to form his few forces. **1838** THIRLWALL *Greece* xxii. III. 213 The enemy's superiority in numbers would enable them to outflank him. **1878** BOSW. SMITH *Carthage* 216 The bridleless Numidian cavalry..outflanking the enemy, and riding round towards their rear, first fell on the retreating infantry.

b. *fig.* To 'get round', get the better of.

1773 *Gentl. Mag.* XLIII. 416 We were outflanked by the law. **1884** CHURCH *Bacon* iv. 82 The devising of questionable legal subtleties..to outflank the defence of some obnoxious prisoner.

2. To lie or extend beyond (the flank). Also *intr.*

1796 *Instr. & Reg. Cavalry* (1813) 81 The regiment breaks into column of divisions, to whichever hand the new position out-flanks the old one. *Ibid.* 83 When the new line out-flanks towards the point of intersection, then the regiment breaking to that hand will have its head nearer to the new line than its rear.

Hence **outˈflanking** *vbl. sb.* and *ppl. a.*

1871 *Standard* 24 Jan., We shall have another outflanking movement. **1893** F. ADAMS *New Egypt* 245 The choice lay.. between a direct front attack and an outflanking movement.

outˈflanker. [-ER[1].] One who outflanks.

1920 *Q. Rev.* Jan. 107 As fast as Joffre created a new Army to prolong his left..so fast did the Germans cover their threatened right and seek to outflank their would-be outflankers.

ˈoutflash, *sb.* [OUT- 7.] The act of flashing out.

1889 SKRINE *Mem. E. Thring* 61 The outflash of his spirit did not die with the moment.

outˈflash, *v.* [OUT- 18, 14.] **a.** *trans.* To surpass in flashing, outshine. **b.** *intr.* To flash out.

1833 BROWNING *Pauline* 59 Do I not..burn to see thy calm, pure truths out-flash The brightest gleams of earth's philosophy. **1848** WEBSTER, *Outflash*, to surpass in flashing. **1866** J. THOMSON *Poems, Philosophy* I. ii, Flowers bloomed for maidens, swords outflashed for boys. **1887** BLACKMORE *Springhaven* I. v. 33 The calm sad face, which in the day of battle could outflash them all. **1939** JOYCE *Finnegans Wake* 210 A pretty box of Pettyfib's Powder for Eileen Aruna to whiten her teeth and outflash Helen Arhone.

So **ˈoutˌflashing** *vbl. sb.* [OUT- 9], flashing out.

1831 CARLYLE *Sart. Res.* III. i, Such first outflashing of man's Freewill, to lighten, more and more into Day. **1882** J. PARKER *Apost. Life* I. 91 The Bible..appals me by the outflashing of sudden lights and unexpected glory.

out-ˈflatter, *v.* [OUT- 18.] *trans.* To outdo in flattery; to over-flatter.

1597 [see OUTLIE *v.*[2]]. **1676** WYCHERLEY *Pl. Dealer* I. i. (1735) 19 Turn'd away by the Chaplains, for out-flattering their probation Sermons for a benefice.

out-flaunt to **out-flight**: see OUT-.

†**outfleme.** *Obs. rare*$^{-1}$. [f. OUT- 8 + FLEME *sb.*[1]] A fugitive from his country, an exile.

13.. *E.E. Allit. P.* A. 1176 Me payed ful ille to be out-fleme, So sodenly of þat fayre regioun.

ˈoutfling, *sb.* [OUT- 7.] The act of flinging out; the giving vent to bad temper or ill nature.

1876 GEO. ELIOT *Dan. Der.* xlii, Deronda..could not help replying to Pash's outfling.

outfling (-ˈflɪŋ), *v.* [OUT- 14, 15.] *trans.* and *intr.* To fling out; fling oneself out. (*poetic.*) Hence **outˈflinging** *vbl. sb.*

1579–80 NORTH *Plutarch* (1676) 166 The crauen Cock,.. which cowardly doth run away, or from the pit out-flings. **1892** *Chicago Advance* 3 Nov., The hand of God outflinging wide The gorgeous banner of the autumn-tide. **1894** A. S. WAY tr. *Euripides' Tragedies* I. 135 What speech in thy frenzy outflingest thou? **1896** *Ibid.* II. 186 Through Hades' hall to thee I call, Day after day my cries outflinging. **1922** JOYCE *Ulysses* 415 Outflings my lord Stephen, giving the cry. **1932** S. GIBBONS *Cold Comfort Farm* v. 73 Judith thrust the words aside with a heavy movement of her hand, like the blind outflinging of a tortured beast. **1950** R. BRADBURY *Martian Chronicles* 86 If art was no more than a frustrated outflinging of desire,..what good was life?

out-flood to **outflout**: see OUT-.

ˈoutˌflourish, *v.* [OUT- 15, 17.] *trans.* **a.** To unsheath and flourish (a weapon). **b.** To outlast in flourishing; to flourish after the cessation of.

1871 BROWNING *Pr. Hohenst.* 1428 There was uprising.. Weapons outflourished in the wind. **1872** HOWELLS *Wedd. Journ.* (1892) 172 The wrecks of slavery..may yet outflourish the remains of the feudal system in the kind of poetry they produce.

ˈoutflow, *sb.* [OUT- 7.]

1. The act or fact of flowing out, efflux.

1869 PHILLIPS *Vesuv.* xi. 315 Now rising into sudden jets, then sinking into a difficult outflow. **1879** *St. George's Hosp. Rep.* IX. 772 An opening which permitted the constant outflow of fluid. *attrib.* **1898** *Allbutt's Syst. Med.* V. 453 Inflow and outflow tubes to the water-jacket.

b. The amount that flows out.

1875 BENNETT & DYER tr. *Sachs' Bot.* 610 In the first thirty-three hours the outflow..amounted to 26·45 cubic cm. **1899** *Allbutt's Syst. Med.* VII. 247 The outflow of blood ..has been seen to increase from two to six times.

2. *fig.* Any outward movement analogous to the flowing of water.

? *a* **1800** *Observer* No. 13 (R.) The influx of foreigners, and the out-flow of natives, which the present peace will occasion. **1862** *Sat. Rev.* XIII. 640/2 The outflow of gold.. is certain to continue and increase. **1869** GOULBURN *Purs. Holiness* x. 91 The outflow of His Divine compassion. **1896** *Edin. Rev.* Jan. 108 A strong outflow of poetical feeling.

outˈflow, *v.* [OUT- 14.] *intr.* To flow out. (*poet.*)

c **1580** SIDNEY *Ps.* XLII. ii, My teares out-flowing. *a* **1711** KEN *Edmund* Poet. Wks. 1721 II. 91 To suck th' Effluviums which he smelt out-flow. **1824** CAMPBELL *Theodric* 533 Shall bitterness outflow from sweetness past? **1909** *Daily Chron.* 3 Mar. 5/7 Then outflowed a stream of facts and figures whose accumulated force swept the critics off their feet.

ˈoutflowing, *vbl. sb.* [OUT- 9.] The action of flowing out, efflux, effluence.

1678 CUDWORTH *Intell. Syst.* I. iv. §32. 516 The Supreme God..together with his outflowing, and all the extent of fecundity. **1884** H. B. MACKEY tr. *St. Francis de Sales' Treat. Love of God* VI. xii. 267 The outflowing of a soul into her God is a true ecstasy. **1894** *Daily News* 30 June 5/4 His family feel the outflowings of universal sympathy. **1932** F. J. SHEED *Irish Way* 332 Work itself was..an outflowing or a special directing of the steady fixedness of the soul in God. **1953** R. C. JOHNSON *Imprisoned Splendour* i. 31 Mystical experiences..are, an out-flowing into awareness of something from a higher level of the self even than the buddhic.

outflowing (ˈaʊtfləʊɪŋ, aʊtˈfləʊɪŋ), *ppl. a.* [OUT- 10.] Flowing out; effluent.

1605 TIMME *Quersit.* III. 162 The out-flowing and breathing forth [parts] are the breathes. **1647** H. MORE *Song of Soul* II. ii. II. x, In her outflowing lines. *a* **1711** KEN *Hymnotheo* Poet. Wks. 1721 III. 355 Thou always art out-flowing Deity. **1870** MORRIS *Earthly Par.* III. IV. 190 The bright outflowing golden hair. **1975** *Sci. Amer.* Mar. 33/3 The compact star in its orbit plows through this outflowing wind and captures only a tiny part of its matter.

out-flown to **out-flung**: see OUT-.

ˈoutflush, *sb.* [OUT- 7.] An outward movement (compared to that of the blood when it flushes the face).

1831 CARLYLE *Sart. Res.* II. ix, An outflush of foolish young Enthusiasm. **1878** GEO. ELIOT *Coll. Breakf. P.* 770 The plant Holds its corolla, purple, delicate, Solely as outflush of that energy.

outˈflush, *v.* [OUT- 17.] *trans.* To surpass in rosiness or warmth of colour.

1885–94 R. BRIDGES *Eros & Psyche* July 23 And now the colour of her pride and joy Outflush'd the hue of Eros.

ˈoutflux. [OUT- 7.] Outflow; place of flowing out; outlet. In mod. use, *spec.* the outward movement of ions through a cell membrane.

1739 MAITLAND *London* I. v, Its outflux from the river Thames. *Ibid.*, The outflux of this watercourse. **1759** B. MARTIN *Nat. Hist. Eng.* I. *Surrey* 140 On the East Side was the Out-flux of C'nut's Trench. **1949** *Physiol. Rev.* XXIX. 132 If the high K concentration in muscle and nerve cells as compared with the K concentration of the surroundings is due to a Donnan equilibrium then the K influx and the K outflux through the cell membranes must be the same. **1974** *Nature* 11 Jan. 96/1 The..rate of sodium outflux (15 min) in turkey erythrocytes was not modified.

ˈoutfly, *sb.* [OUT- 7.] The act of flying out (*fig.*), a swift outburst of passion, etc.

1890 CLARK RUSSELL *Ocean Trag.* II. xvii. 74, I awaited some passionate outfly, but..he held his peace.

outˈfly, *v.* [OUT- 14, 17, 18.]

1. *intr.* To fly out. (*poetic.*)

1599 T. M[OUFET] *Silkwormes* 52 Few griefes from Pandors boxe out-flew But here they finde a medcine. **1667** MILTON *P.L.* I. 663 He spake; and, to confirm his words, out-flew Millions of flaming swords. **1725** POPE *Odyss.* XII. 477 Now outflies The gloomy West [wind], and whistles in the skies. **1894** C. H. COOK *Thames Rights* 39 Now and again outflies from sedgy haunt the wary mallard.

2. *trans.* To outstrip or surpass in flight; to fly beyond or past; *spec.* of aircraft and their pilots: to surpass in terms of skill or speed in flying.

1591 SYLVESTER *Du Bartas* I. v. 582 See how the Fowles are from my fancie fled,.. Their flight out-flies me. *c* **1614** SIR W. MURE *Dido & Æneas* II. 458 He..Owtflyes the eagle and the silver swan. **1667** DRYDEN *Tempest* IV. iv. *a* **1711** KEN *Hymnarium* Poet. Wks. 1721 II. 102 To sacred Poets I apply, Who all scholastick Heights out-fly. **1800** MOORE *Anacreon* xxiv. 18 She gave thee beauty—shaft of eyes, That every shaft of war outflies! **1859** G. MEREDITH *R. Feverel* xix, They have outflown Philosophy. **1908** H. G. WELLS *War in Air* viii. 253 Light as this armament was.., it was sufficient for them to outfight as well as outfly the German monster airships. **1942** *Tee Emm* (Air Ministry) II. 94 It's no good outflying the Hun if you can't shoot him down. **1975** *Listener* 17 July 77/1 It could outfly the Focke Wulf Condor and..that sort of German bomber. **1976** *Globe & Mail* (Toronto) 28 Jan. 29/2 Capt. Stinson..flatly states that the computer can 'out-land a human pilot three to one. I'll admit it can outfly me.'

†**ˈoutflying**, *vbl. sb.* [OUT- 9.] The action of flying out; an outbreak. *Obs.*

1641 SANDERSON *Serm.* (1681) II. 141 They have many out-flyings, wherewith their holy Father is not well pleased. *c* **1641** D. CAWDREY *Three Serm.* 49 The out-flyings of other mens corruptions.

ˈoutˌfold. *rare.* [OUT- 1.] A fold or small field lying away from the farm-house: cf. OUTFIELD, OUT-FIELD *sb.*

1860 G. H. K. in *Vac. Tour.* 128 [see INFOLD *sb.*[2]].

out-folio to **out-form**: see OUT-.

outˈfool, *v.* [OUT- 18, 18 c.] *trans.* To outdo in folly or in fooling; to overcome by fooling.

1638–48 G. DANIEL *Eclog.* II. 40 All our Pride Is to out-foole our Selves! **1762** YOUNG *Resignation* II. xxix, In life's decline..The second child outfools the first, And tempts the lash of truth. **1861** *Sat. Rev.* 7 Dec. 584 The minority which..endeavours to effect its purpose by out-fooling the majority.

outˈfoot, *v.* [OUT- 18, 21.] *trans.* To surpass in footing it; to outpace; to outstrip in dancing, running, or sailing; to outrun.

1737 BRACKEN *Farriery Impr.* (1757) II. 187 The Horse in running..seldom was beaten, provided he was not out-footed (as the Jockeys term it). **1857** MRS. MATHEWS *Tea-t. Talk* I. 154 The vivacious Margravine..excelling and outfooting many a youthful dame. **1894** *Times* 11 June 7/1 She made a disappointing show, the Britannia as a matter of fact fairly outfooting the giantess cutter. **1899** *Daily News* 7 Oct. 5/5 Shamrock had both out-pointed and out-footed her opponent when making to windward.

†**ˈout-ˌfooting.** *Obs. rare*$^{-0}$. = FOOTING 12.

1611 COTGR., *Forject*, a iutting, or leaning out, or ouer; a rellish, or out-footing.

ˈout-ˌfort, *sb.* [OUT- 1, 3.] An outlying fort, an outwork.

1625 in *Crt. & Times Chas. I* (1848) I. 66 They won the out-fort of the town. **1873** BURTON *Hist. Scot.* VI. lxxiii. 358 Some small outforts were easily taken.

out-ˈfort, *v.* [OUT- 21.] *trans.* To outdo in the matter of forts.

1755 *St. Colonies N. Amer.* 37 If..we would secure our American dominions against the French, we must out-fort, as well as out-settle them.

†**ˌoutˈforth**, *adv.* (*a.*) *Obs.* [f. OUT *adv.* + FORTH *adv.*] Out; externally, outwardly.

1382 WYCLIF *Isa.* xliii. 8 Bring outforth the blinde puple. **1387–8** T. USK *Test. Love* II. v. (Skeat) l. 85 There the valance of men is demed in riches outforthe. *Ibid.* x. 145 Wonder I trewly why the mortal folk of this worlde seche these ways outforth. ? *c* **1480** *Ragman Roll* 158 in Hazl. *E.P.P.* (1864) I. 76 Thogh they her malys inwarde keuir and wrye, And outfouryth the fayryst that they kane.

B. *adj.* (ˈ*outforth*). Outward, exterior, external.

1541 R. COPLAND *Guydon's Quest. Chirurg.* C ij b, How many maners of skynnes or lether are there?..Two, one is extrynsyke or outforth, and that is proprely called lether. **1559** *Mirr. Mag.* (1563) C viij, Warres both of outforthe and inward enemyes.

¶ † *with outforth*, erroneous division of *without forth*: see FORTH *adv.* 2 b. Cf. *beneath-forth.*

outfox (aʊtˈfɒks), *v.* [f. OUT- 18 b + FOX *v.* 2 c.] *trans.* To outdo in deception or cunning; to outwit.

1962 K. ORVIS *Damned & Destroyed* xii. 81 He finally out-foxed himself. **1965** C. D. EBY *Siege of Alcázar* (1966) ii. 54 Pozas was no fool. Perhaps he had even out-foxed them. **1965** R. SHECKLEY *Game of X* (1966) xix. 133 We have outfoxed Forster at every turn, and we shall out-fox him now for the final time. **1973** J. JONES *Touch of Danger* lvi. 320, I guess you've got the drop on me... You outfoxed me. **1976** *National Observer* (U.S.) 19 June 6/5 As one Republican National Committee official put it: 'The Ford people have no right to be bitter. They were just out-foxed, outmaneuvered, and out-organized.'

out-freedom, -friend, etc.: see OUT-.

outˈfront, *v.* [Cf. OUT- 18 b.] *trans.* To stand face to face to, confront; to face.

1631 P. FLETCHER *Sicelides* H ij b, If furies should out-front me, I'de out-stare them. **1883** BLACK *Shandon Bells* xxxiii, This newer Inisheen out-fronting the sea was more changed than the older part of the town.

out front, *advb.* and *adj. phr.* Chiefly *U.S.* [f. OUT *adv.* + FRONT *sb.*] At or to the front; in front; *spec.* (*a*) at or to the battle-front; (*b*) *Theatr.*, in front of the stage; in the auditorium; (*c*) *fig.*, in the forefront (of a political or intellectual movement); progressive. Also (with hyphen) *attrib.*

1916 'BOYD CABLE' *Action Front* 200 These average good men who had 'joined up' freely, who had longed for the end of home training and the transfer 'out Front'. **1934** J. M. CAIN *Postman always rings Twice* vi. 57 She went out front with an order, and me and the Greek sat down. **1937** C. HIMES *Black on Black* (1973) 129 This little white lain pulled up out front in a big Lincoln touring a block long. **1962** *Listener* 11 Oct. 570/1 Obsolete accommodation, backstage and out-front. **1963** AUDEN *Dyer's Hand* 186 There is no difference for Falstaff between those on stage and those out front. **1968** T. WOLFE *Electric Kool-Aid Acid Test* iv. 53 A community of intelligent, very open, out-front people—out front was a term everybody was using. **1973** *Black World* Mar. 36 His behind-the-scenes rather than vigorous outfront leadership. **1976** L. ALTHER *Kinflicks* ii. 22 'Have you seen the new fishburger franchise?' Mrs Yancy asked, pointing out the window at a red and silver building with a sign out front featuring in neon a one-legged pirate tangoing with a laughing swordfish. **1977** *New Yorker* 10 Oct. 156/3 Powell himself was said to be deeply bothered by that, and to have realized that he had been too 'out front' on the issue.

out'frown, *v.* [OUT- 23 a, 18 c.] *trans.* To outdo in frowning; to frown down, overbear by frowning.
1605 SHAKS. *Lear* v. iii. 6 My selfe could else out-frowne false Fortunes frowne. **1807** W. H. IRELAND *Mod. Ship Fools* 61 *note*, It is only the base-born churl, like Thomas à Becket, that would out-frown the brow of majesty.

†**'out-,funeral.** *Obs. rare*$^{-1}$. [OUT- 1.] A funeral outside a city; extra-mural interment.
1637 BP. HALL *Serm. at Exeter* 24 Aug. (R.), Much might be said to this purpose [out of matter of wholesomnesse] for the convenience of out-funerals.

out-ga, outgait, obs. ff. OUTGO, OUTGATE.

out'gallop, *v.* [OUT- 18.] *trans.* To outdo in galloping; to gallop faster than.
1603 DEKKER *Wonderfull Yeare* D ij b, They that rode on the lustiest geldings, could not out gallop the Plague. **1852** THACKERAY *Esmond* III. i, A hundred huntsmen..each out-bawling and out-galloping the other.

'outgang. Now *Sc.* or *north. dial.* [OUT- 7; OE. *útgang*; cf. Du. *uitgang*, Ger. *ausgang*.]
1. A going out, departure, exit; the giving up of the occupancy or tenure of property.
c **825** *Vesp. Psalter* xviii. [xix.] 7 From ðæm hean heofene utgong his. *a* **1000** *Life St. Guthlac* ii. (1848) 14 þurh sarlicne utgang þæs manfullan lifes. *a* **1300** *E.E. Psalter* xxx. 23 [xxxi. 22] In out-gang of thoghte mine. *c* **1320** *Cast. Love* 878 þorw þe faste ȝat he con in teo, And at þe out-ȝong he lette faste beo. **1887** *Jamieson's Sc. Dict.* Suppl., *Out-ganging,..Outgang,..* outgoing, removal; the act of giving up possession of burghal property.
2. The way or passage out; an outlet, an exit; a road by which cattle went out to the pasture.
c **950** *Lindisf. Gosp.* Matt. xxii. 9 Geongas forðon to ut-ȝeonge ðære weȝara [*c* **975** *Rushw.* to utgengum weoȝas]. *a* **1300** *E.E. Psalter* cxliii. [cxliv.] 16 þair schepe brodefulle mightsomande In þar outgange. *c* **1450** *Customs of Malton* in *Surtees Misc.* (1888) 58 Fre entre and goyng owte to yᵉ more by a large way, the qwhyche is called yᵉ owtegang. **1513** DOUGLAS *Æneis* (Cr. Gl.), Ane narrow path baith outgang and entre. **1664–5** *Act 16–17 Chas. II*, c. 11 §2 The River of Welland from the Outgang at the East end of East Deeping. **1828** *Craven Gloss.* (ed. 2), *Out-gang*, a road from a place. **1896** T. BLASHILL *Sutton-in-Holderness* 26 An ordinary outgang was a place where the cattle of a village assembled when they were to be driven out together to graze in common.

out-garment, -garth, etc.: see OUT-.

outgas (aʊt'gæs), *v.* [OUT- 26.] **1.** *trans.* **a.** To drive off sorbed gas or vapour from (a solid), esp. by heating in a vacuum.
1921 [implied in OUTGASSED *ppl. a.*]. **1925** *Physical Rev.* XXVI. 658 When the surface layer of gas is removed from a fresh specimen the increase in the photo-electric current is greater than the decrease from the maximum value as the specimen is outgassed. **1953** *Electronic Engin.* XXV. 19 The cathodes were out-gassed by eddy-current heating. **1965** C. M. VAN ATTA *Vacuum Sci. & Engin.* iii. 101 After the gauge tube and elements have been thoroughly outgassed, an opposite effect becomes noticeable.
b. To release (sorbed or dissolved gas or vapour).
1971 I. G. GASS et al. *Understanding Earth* ix. 137/2 Only gradually, as volcanoes continued to outgas volatile products still trapped in the mantle, will a secondary atmosphere and ocean have replaced the primary envelope. **1974** *Nature* 31 May 438/1 If NH_3 is outgassed from the Martian crust it would be photolysed.
2. *intr.* To give off sorbed gas or vapour.
1962 [implied in OUTGASSING *vbl. sb.*]. **1965** C. M. VAN ATTA *Vacuum Sci. & Engin.* ix. 365 Untreated metal samples outgas at the rate of about 10^{-7} torr liter/sec cm^2 after 1 hr of vacuum pumping at room temperature. **1975** *Sci. Amer.* Feb. 110/3 Any polymer surface will outgas (a 'virtual leak' into your clean volume) two orders of magnitude more than steel.
So **out'gassed** *ppl. a.*, **out'gassing** *vbl. sb.*
1921 *Proc. Nat. Acad. Sci.* VII. 115 The coarsely granular sample of the thoroughly outgassed material is weighed and placed in a steel pressure bomb which is then evacuated until all adsorbed gases are removed. **1925** *Physical Rev.* XXVI. 657 His thermionic measurements show that the value of A in the Richardson equation..decreases from $4{\cdot}76 \times 10^{27}$ for the slightly outgassed position to $1{\cdot}7 \times 10^{26}$ for continued outgassing. **1952** *Trans. Faraday Soc.* XLVIII. 739 The vessel F was 'protected' by a series of traps in liquid air, some of which..contained carefully outgassed granulated charcoal. **1962** F. I. ORDWAY et al. *Basic Astronautics* iii. 49 Whatever outgassing that may occur from the surface would expectedly give rise to a more substantial, albeit tenuous, atmosphere. **1971** I. G. GASS et al. *Understanding Earth* ii. 43/2 This so-called 'excess' argon is probably produced by heating and outgassing of ancient, potassium-bearing rocks. **1973** *Nature* 3 Aug. 272/2 The relative abundances of these gases will depend critically on the subsequent history of the outgassed methane. **1973** B. J. WILLIAMS *Evolution & Human Origins* vii. 97/2 If these dates are correct then the evolution of life must have begun, as we would expect, almost immediately after the earth's crust melted and the outgassing of the early atmospheric gases ceased.

'outgate, *sb.* (*adv.*) Also *Sc.* -gait. Now *Sc.* and *north. dial.* [OUT- 7.]
1. The action of going out; outgoing, passage out; exit, egress; debouching.
a **1300** *E.E. Psalter* cxiii. [cxiv.] 1 In oute-gate of Israele Oute of Egipt. *c* **1440** *Promp. Parv.* 375/2 Owte gate, *exitus*. **1455** *Rolls of Parlt.* V. 311/2 Free ingate and outgate to the premisses. **1496**, **1598** [see INGATE 1]. **1615** CROOKE *Body of Man* 766 The outgate of the breath is hindered. **1822** GALT *Sir A. Wylie* I. xxviii. 259 (Jam.) She..maybe a wee that dressy and fond o' outgait. **1865** CARLYLE *Fredk. Gt.* XVIII. ii. (1872) VII. 106 Moldau Valley..making, on its outgate at the northern end of Prag..one big loop.
2. A passage or way out, an outlet; a means of egress; *fig.* a way of escape or deliverance.
1456 SIR G. HAYE *Law Arms* (S.T.S.) 179 Than suld never promess na obligacioun bynd a fals man, na he wald get ane outgate. **1513** DOUGLAS *Æneis* IX. vii. 28 Sone ombeset haue thai The outgatis al. **1596** SPENSER *State Irel.* Wks. (Globe) 665/1 Those paces are soe fitt for trade and trafficke, having most convenient out-gates by diverse rivers to the sea. **1616** SURFL. & MARKH. *Country Farme* 688 If he meet with a hedge, he holdeth along by the side of it, to see if he can find any out-gate. **1659** A. HAY *Diary* (S.H.S. 1900) 194 The Lord provyd ane outgate for his people. **1865** CARLYLE *Fredk. Gt.* XX. ix. (1872) IX. 165 The dragoons were a hundred, and..every outgate was beset.
b. Issue, outcome. *Sc.*
1568 MARY Q. SCOTS in H. Campbell *Love-lett.* App. (1824) 29 To the effect the samin sould be the mair promptlie endit with some happy outgait to my honour and contentment. **1663** BLAIR *Autobiog.* ii. (1848) 32 Wondering what would be the outgate. **1786** A. GIB *Sacr. Contempl.* 318 Others are brought more quickly to an happy outgate.
†**3.** Usually in *pl.* Goods 'going' or carried out of a town or port, exports; also, export dues.
1621–1886 [see INGATE *sb.*[1] 4].
B. *adv.* Outwards; outside, without.
1590, **1611** [see INGATE *sb.*[1] B]. **1898** CROCKETT *Standard Bearer* xxxiv. 301 May they burn back and front, ingate and outgate.

'out-,gate. Outer gate: see OUT- 3.
1648 *Depos. Cast. York* (Surtees) 12 Robert Kay, together with 16 or 18 men..with musketts and swords drawne,..broke open the outgate and fower other doores within the said house. **1664** J. WEBB *Stone-Heng* (1725) 94 The Anditus had both an Out-gate, and an inner Gate.

out-gather, -gauge, etc.: see OUT-.

outgear ('aʊtgɪə(r)). *Sc. rare.* [OUT- 1.] Possessions or substance used in out-door occupation.
1834 H. MILLER *Scenes & Leg.* xxiv. [see INGEAR].

out'general, *v.* [OUT- 22.] **a.** *trans.* To outdo or defeat in generalship; to get the better of as by superior military skill; to outmanœuvre.
1767 S. PATERSON *Another Trav.* I. 202 How we were out-generalled indeed! **1776** J. ADAMS in *Fam. Lett.* (1876) 231 In general, our Generals were outgeneraled on Long Island. **1897** *Century Mag.* Feb. 495 In these movements Lee was entirely outgeneraled.
b. *transf.* and *fig.*
1859 J. S. MILL in *Fraser's Mag.* LX. 767/1 A nation which thinks of nothing but of outwitting and outgeneralling its neighbours. **1910** J. DRISCOLL *Ringcraft* 14 He was the better boxer and the stronger man, but was outgeneralled during two-thirds of the bout. **1940** W. FAULKNER *Hamlet* III. ii. 184 At last he outgeneralled himself with his own strategy:..even his father admitted that there was nothing else about the farm for him to learn. **1973** WODEHOUSE *Bachelors Anonymous* x. 128 However confident he may be that he has outgeneralled a woman, a man likes to have reassurance on the point from a knowledgeable third party. **1976** *Billings* (Montana) *Gaz.* 26 June 1-B/6 Tanner has played better tennis—little Kirmayr out-generalled him time and again—but always in reserve was his 140 m.p.h. cannonball service.

out-get to **out-girth**: see OUT-.

out'give, *v.* [OUT- 18, 14.] **a.** *trans.* To outdo in giving, give more than. **b.** *intr.* To give out, come to an end. (*poetic.*)
1693 C. DRYDEN in *D.'s Juvenal* vii. (1697) 173 The bounteous Play'r out-gave the pinching Lord. **1893** BRIDGES *Shorter P.* v. xi. 31 And two days ere the year outgave We laid him low.

'out,giving, *vbl. sb.* [OUT- 9.] The action or fact of giving out; that which is given out: **a.** *pl.* payments, disbursements; **b.** utterance.
1663 BLAIR *Autobiog.* ii. (1848) 25 All the disbursements and outgivings to traders. **1865** *Morn. Star* 20 Jan., The outgivings of some irresponsible editor. **1881** *Times* 15 Apr. 6/1 This was the burthen of all his outgivings before and after inauguration. **1897** *Educat. Rev.* XIII. 70 To regard that as the last outgiving of political philosophy.

outgiving ('aʊtgɪvɪŋ), *ppl. a.* [OUT- 10.] That gives out; open-hearted, generous. Hence **out'givingness**.
1942 J. LEES-MILNE *Ancestral Voices* (1975) 31 K. as outgiving as ever. **1961** *Spectator* 26 May 763/2 [Brendan] Behan is still..a talker and singer for talking and singing's own sake, spontaneous and out-giving. **1963** *London Mag.* Sept. 11 Her face was round and pleasantly fleshed, her eyes cool and outgiving when she was not anguished or perturbed. **1968** *Listener* 10 Oct. 458/2 She had lost a great deal, I think, of her out-givingness in that way and the novels perhaps reflect this. **1972** *Times* 3 July 16/7 There can rarely have been such an outgiving man who was less of an extrovert.

†**out-'glad**, *v. Obs.* [OUT- 20.] *trans.* To surpass in gladness; to delight more.
a **1657** R. LOVEDAY *Lett.* (1663) 26 You have not a friend hath out-gladded me for your well-being, nor out-wish'd me for the continuance. *Ibid.* 192 Might I hope the happiness to meet you at London, nothing would be able to out-glad me.
¶ An intrans. *outglad* has been erroneously inferred from Wyclif's *full out glad*: cf. OUT- 15 b.

out'glare, *v.* [OUT- 18.] *trans.* To surpass or outdo in glare or dazzling effect; to be more glaring or flagrant than.
1648 HERRICK *Hesper.*, *Welcome to Sack* 11 Whose radiant flame Out-glares the heav'ns Osiris. **1822** SCOTT *Pirate* xxxi, Were all my former sins doubled..such a villany would have outglared and outweighed them all. **1837** *Blackw. Mag.* XLII. 329 [She] lavished her money till she out-glared the poorer ranks of the peerage.

out'glitter, *v.* [OUT- 18.] *trans.* To surpass in glitter or splendour.
1648 J. BEAUMONT *Psyche* II. ccxviii, The gracious splendor of this Queen Sweetly outglitters their best tire of Rays. **1662** COKAINE *Tragedy of Ovid* IV. i, I must Out-glitter all the Femals of the Province, Or I shall want my will. **1884** SUS. H. WARD in *Independent Alm.* (N.Y.) 14 You cannot wish the background to outglitter the picture.

out-gloom, -glory, etc.: see OUT-.

out'glow, *v.* [OUT- 18.] *trans.* To excel in glowing; to overcome by superior glow.
1877 E. R. CONDER *Bas. Faith* ix. 390 Capable of dominating every other passion, of outglowing the fire of youth. **1898** T. HARDY *Wessex Poems* 175 My light in thee would out-glow all in others.

out-gnaw, etc.: see OUT-.

'outgo, *sb.* [OUT- 7.]
1. The fact of going out or that which goes out; *spec.* outlay, expenditure; opposed to *income*.
c **1640** J. SMYTH *Lives Berkeleys* (1883) I. 168 To regulate his out-goes..to order and frugality. **1757** FRANKLIN *Ess.* Wks. 1846 II. 98 The Indies have not made Spain rich, because her outgoes are greater than her incomes. **1860** EMERSON *Cond. Life*, *Wealth* Wks. (Bohn) II. 358 The secret of success lies..in the relation of income to outgo. **1895** SIR W. HARCOURT *Sp.* 22 May, Grow as the income or the intake may, the outgo and the waste are always greater.
2. The action of going out; efflux, outflow.
1858 W. ARNOT *Laws fr. Heaven* II. xvii. 142 [Anger] hurts, in its outgo, all who lie within its reach. **1878** FOSTER *Phys.* I. iv. (ed. 2) 108 In a system of elastic tubes..the out-go being as easy..as the income. **1882–3** SCHAFF *Encycl. Relig. Knowl.* I. 33 The spontaneous outgo of the affections.
3. Outward product; issue, outcome.
1870 W. URWICK tr. *Bleek's Introd. N. Test.* II. 175 Their scorn was the outgo of the same frivolous mind.
4. Outlet, means of egress.
1869 S. BOWLES *Our New West* i. 26 The great Salt Lake of Utah..has no visible outgo, though richly fed from various quarters. **1880** S. S. HELLYER *Plumber & Sanit. Ho.* 15 A square-pipe trap, with a round outgo.

outgo (aʊt'gəʊ), *v.* [OUT- 14, 18, 17.]
†**1.** *intr.* To go out, go forth. *Obs.* except *poetic.*
In OE. and ME. usually two words, exc. when imitating L. *exire*; in later use only where modern usage would allow *out go* in two words as a prosodic inversion of *go out*.
c **825** *Vesp. Psalter* xviii. [xix.] 5 In alle eorðan uteode sweᵹ heara. **971** *Blickl. Hom.* 9 Drihten..of þæm úteode. *c* **1250** *O. Kent. Serm.* in *O.E. Misc.* 33 þet on goodman was þat ferst uut yede bi þe Moreghen for to here werkmen. *c* **1250** *Gen. & Ex.* 3076 Quilc ben ðo ðe sulen vt gon? *a* **1300** *E.E. Psalter* xliii. 10 [xliv. 9] In our mightes, God, noght sal tou out ga. *c* **1385** CHAUCER *L.G.W.* 637 *Cleopatra*, With grysely soun out goth the grete gonne. **1530** PALSGR. 650/2, I outgo, I go out of the waye, *Je foruoye*. **1579** SPENSER *Sheph. Cal.* May 20, I sawe a shole of shepeheardes outgoe. *a* **1635** CORBET *Poems* (1807) 15 Out-went the townsmen all in starch. **1899** P. H. WICKSTEED tr. *Dante's Paradiso* xiii. 161 That living Light which so outgoeth from its Source that it departeth not therefrom. **1905** *Outlook* 4 Nov. 629/1 So you, dear Frank, were last of those To whom a tender thought outgoes.
2. *trans.* To outstrip in going; to go faster than, pass; to outdistance. *arch.*
1530 PALSGR. 650/2 Though thou be goynge an hour afore me, yet I wyll out go the. **1596** SPENSER *F.Q.* V. viii. 4 Yet fled she fast and both them farre outwent. **1649** LOVELACE *Poems* (1864) 93 What terror 'tis t' outgo and be outgon. **1678** BUNYAN *Pilgr.* I. 164 Shall we talk further with him? or out-go him at present? **1742** FIELDING *J. Andrews* II. ii, It generally happens that he on horseback outgoes him on foot. **1778** *Eng. Gazetteer* (ed. 2) s.v. *Workington*, Horses, which, changing often, travel day and night with-out intermission, and, as they say, out-go the post.
3. To go beyond (a point, bounds, etc.); to exceed or surpass; to excel, outstrip, outdo.
1553 T. WILSON *Rhet.* 64 b, Wo be to that realme where might outgoeth right. **1579** SPENSER *Sheph. Cal.* Apr. 16 His wonted songs, wherein he all outwent. **1627** MILTON *Vac. Exerc.* 79 In worth and excellence he shall out-go them. **1799** A. HAMILTON *Lett.* in *Washington's Writ.* (1893) XIV. 178 *note*, I do not think it expedient to outgo our supply of clothing. **1885–94** R. BRIDGES *Eros & Psyche* Sept. xxiii, Such sorrow as outwent The utmost pain of other punishment.
†**4.** To pass, go through, spend (time). *Obs.*
1594 SPENSER *Amoretti* lx, One yeare..The which doth longer unto me appeare, Then al those fourty which my life out-went. *a* **1613** OVERBURY *A Wife*, etc. (1638) 275, I have once in my life out-gone night at Sea.
†**5.** 'To circumvent, to overreach' (J.). *Obs.*

c 1650 Denham *On Journ. Poland* x, Mollesson Thought us to have out-gone With a quaint invention.

'out,goer. [OUT- 8.] One who goes out (in various senses: see GO *v.* 87); esp. one who goes out of a place, office, occupation, or tenancy; a player, at cricket or the like, who is dismissed.

1382 Wyclif *1 Sam.* xxii. 17 The kyng seith to the out-goers [Vulg. *emissariis*] in his nedis. **1816** J. Scott *Vis. Paris* (ed. 5) 25 To take cognizance of incomers and out-goers. **1827** J. W. Croker in *C. Papers* 31 Dec. (1884), The King is exceedingly vexed at the outgoers, and will not take them but on compulsion. **1861** *Jrnl. R. Agric. Soc.* XXII. II. 325 Mutual accommodation between incomer and outgoer. **1883** *Daily Tel.* 15 May 2/7 The outgoer had made 9. **1888** *Daily News* 22 Sept. 5/1 Of yore [at golf] there was but one set of holes, not a double set for out-goers and incomers.

'out,going, *vbl. sb.* [OUT- 9.]

1. The action or fact of going out or forth; exit, departure or removal; issue, effluence, emanation.

c **1300** Michael Kildare *Hymn V.* in *Rel. Ant.* II. 191 Povir was thin in comming, So ssal be thin oute going. **1340** *Ayenb.* 32 To habbe þe pyne of stapes to cliue uor his out-guoinge. **1463** *Bury Wills* (Camden) 22 Liberte of fre owth goyng and in comyng at the gate be the strete syde. **1562** Turner *Herbal* II. 47 Men that go out of the bath and drynke muche wyne after theyr outgoyng. **1649** Blithe *Eng. Improv. Impr.* (1653) 55 For close shutting, and suitable opening, to the incomming of the Tide, or out-going of the Floods. **1753** Smollett *Ct. Fathom* (1784) 43/1 To follow the young lady in all her out-goings. **1825–1868** [see incoming *vbl. sb.* 1]. **1850** H. Bushnell *God in Christ* 122 The worlds created are all outgoings from Himself.

2. a. A passage or way of exit or egress.

1387 Trevisa *Higden* (Rolls) I. 221 Dyuers oute goynges, benches, and seges all aboute. **1535** Coverdale *2 Esdras* iv. 7 Which are the outgoinges of Paradise? **1609** Bible (Douay) *Obad.* i. 14 Neither shalt thou stand in the out-goings to kil them that flee. **1864** G. M. Hopkins *Poems* (1967) 130 The hill Which with its lined and creased flank The outgoings of the vale does block. **1918** D. H. Lawrence *New Poems* 49 Each door, each mystic port Of egress from you I will seal and steep in perfect chrism.. So you shall feel Ensheathed invulnerable with me, with seven Great seals upon your outgoings.

b. †The extremity, the outer limit (*obs.*); the upper termination of an inclined stratum.

1388 Wyclif *Josh.* xviii. 19 The outgoyngis therof ben aȝens the arm of the salteste see. **1535** Coverdale *Josh.* xvii. 18 So shall it be the outgoinge of thy porcion. **1611** Bible *Josh.* xvii. 9 The coast of Manasseh also was on the north side of the river, and the outgoings of it were at the sea. **1727** Berkeley *Lett.* 11 Apr., Wks. 1871 IV. 143 The outgoings or fields about St. Kevin's. **1815** W. Phillips *Outl. Min. & Geol.* (1818) 144 The.. rocks.. occasionally cover the summits of mountains, but more commonly rest on their sides; in which case.. the out-going, or upper termination of each, is lower than that immediately preceding it.

3. (Mostly *pl.*) Money which goes out in the way of expenditure; outlay, expenses, charges.

1622 T. Scott *Belg. Pismire* 65 Where.. the returne doth not countervaile the out-going. **1765** Blackstone *Comm.* I. viii. 332 Other very numerous outgoings, as secret service money, pensions, and other bounties. **1816** F. Vanderstraeten *Improv. Agric.* p. xxiii, The tenant paid for repairs and outgoings. **1885** *Law Times* CXXIX. 58/2 The balance of income over outgoings was only £6 a year.

'out,going, *ppl. a.* [OUT- 10.] **a.** That goes out; issuing, outflowing. **b.** Going out or retiring from office, position, or possession.

1633 W. Struther *True Happines* 120 This is the proper worke of faith in her double perswasion. The one direct, and outgoing to the truth... The other reflecting and turning home to us by the work of our Conscience. **1818** A. Ranken *Hist. France* IV. IV. 321 They should invite the late or out-going rector, or rectors to assist. **1863** Fawcett *Pol. Econ.* II. vii. 240 The outgoing tenant receives a certain sum from the incoming tenant. **1897** *Allbutt's Syst. Med.* VII. 395 From the latter two centres outgoing fibres emerge.

c. Suitable for wearing when one goes out.

1867 Queen Victoria *Let.* 19 Nov. in R. Fulford *Your Dear Letter* (1971) I have just returned from a drive with dear Marie F... I can't judge of the figure in her out-going dress. **1909** 'O. Henry' *Roads of Destiny* x. 162 Take him back.. and fix him up with outgoing clothes. Unlock him at seven in the morning.

d. Extrovert, sociable, open-hearted, friendly.

1950 *Brit. Jrnl. Psychol.* XXII. 107 Out-going primary or secondary need-determined behaviour may be thwarted and aggressiveness may result. **1955** in D. Tidyman *Dummy* (1974) iii. 40 He is a rather attractive, out-going child. **1964** J. Philips *Laughter Trap* (1965) III. iii. 132 She was a warm, outgoing girl. **1966** *Tablet* 22 Oct. 1185/1 The.. poem, whose outgoing, solicitous concern is for the whole of man's relation to the world around him. **1973** C. Bonington *Next Horizon* ix. 138 He appeared outgoing, frank, and immensely enthusiastic. **1978** E. Healey *Lady Unknown* ii. 62 Gregarious and out-going, he brought a brilliance and radiance to every gathering.

Hence **'out,goingness.**

1865 J. Grote *Moral Ideals* (1876) 344 Butler.. recognizes the outgoingness of virtue, and the importance of benevolence or the love of our neighbour [etc.]. **1960** G. Ashe *From Caesar to Arthur* vi. 160 For the moment we may leave him in Ireland, fitly typifying the outgoingness of the British saints. **1967** C. Fremlin *Prisoner's Base* ii. 22 Claudia's gifts.. tolerance—outgoingness—sympathy. **1971** *New Scientist* 1 Apr. 44/2 Bondi's natural eloquence and outgoingness could be usefully harnessed to his new job.

'outgone, *ppl. a.* [OUT- 11.] That has gone out; extinguished; retired.

1647 H. More *Song of Soul* II. i. III. xxii, Sols spright, hid form, fair light and out-gone rayes. **1841** E. Miall in *Nonconf.* I. 376 [This] will give it a vast advantage over the outgone administration.

out-gorget to **out-ground**: see OUT-.

outgrabe (aʊt'greɪb), *v.* A factitious word introduced by 'Lewis Carroll' (see quot. 1855[2]). (In quot. 1903 used for 'outdo', after the style of *out-Herod*, etc.)

Quot. 1855[1] also occurs in the first verse of 'Jabberwocky' in *Through the Looking-Glass* (1871) i. 21.

1855 'L. Carroll' *Rectory Umbrella & Mischmasch* (1932) 139 All mimsy were the borogoves; And the mome raths outgrabe. *Ibid.* 140 *Outgrabe*, past tense of the verb to *outgribe*. (It is connected with the old verb to *grike* or *shrike*, from which are derived 'shriek' and 'creak'.) 'Squeaked.' **1876** —— *Hunting of Snark* v. 50 The Beaver had counted with scrupulous care, Attending to every word: But it fairly lost heart, and outgrabe in despair, When the third repetition occurred. **1903** *Sat. Rev.* 7 Feb. 164/1 Deadmanship! wrote.. Dr. Shrapnel..; and the word is fit to stir the jealous admiration of Carlyle or even Lewis Carroll. Indeed Dr. Shrapnel 'outgrabed' them both.

'out-group. [Cf. OUT *a.* 1.] Those people not necessarily forming a group themselves, who are excluded from or do not belong to a specific in-group; also *attrib.* Hence **out-'grouper**, an individual who does not belong to a specific in-group.

1907 [see IN-GROUP]. **1934** K. Young *Introd. Sociol.* I. i. 13 One is prejudiced against the members of the out-group. **1949** R. K. Merton *Social Theory* II. vii. 186 The systematic condemnation of the out-grouper continues largely irrespective of what he does. **1952** M. McCarthy *Groves of Academe* (1953) vi. 119 Where discrimination exists, protection of the out-group is mandatory. **1967** M. Argyle *Psychol. Interpersonal Behaviour* iv. 71 Two people from different groups are apt to treat each other as 'outsiders', members of the out-group, and to reject one another through their failure to conform to the norms of the in-group. **1970** *Jrnl. Gen. Psychol.* Oct. 259 An error was considered.. outgroup intrusion if a word paired with a dissimilar stimulus was elicited. **1970** C. T. Restrepo in I. L. Horowitz *Masses in Lat. Amer.* xiv. 516 Violence developed the conflict with respect to the out-group and institutionalized it. **1976** *Times Lit. Suppl.* 2 Jan. 2/4 Gypsy legends.. provide a charter for the in-group rather than the out-group reference of their morality.

outgrow (aʊt'grəʊ), *v.* [OUT- 18, 17, 14.]

1. *trans.* To surpass in growth, to grow faster than; to grow taller or bigger than. Also *refl.*

1594 Shaks. *Rich. III*, III. i. 104 You said, that idle Weeds are fast in growth: The Prince, my Brother, hath out-growne me farre. **1655** H. Vaughan *Silex Scint.*, *Isaac's Marriage*, But thou Didst thy swift years in piety outgrow. **1760–72** H. Brooke *Fool of Qual.* (1809) III. 119 His avarice outgrew even the growth of his wealth. **1775** Adair *Amer. Ind.* 408 They often let the weeds out-grow the corn. **1878** Hardy *Ret. Native* I. I. iii. 54 His mother cried for scores of hours when 'a was a boy, for fear he should out-grow himself and go for a soldier.

2. To grow out of, or beyond the limits or capacity of, to become too large for (clothes, etc.).

1691–8 Norris *Pract. Disc.* (1711) III. 113 We outgrow our Pleasures, as we do our Clothes. **1833** Marryat *P. Simple* vi, You have enough.. to last you till you out-grow them. **1860** Geo. Eliot *Mill on Fl.* I. vii, 'I doubt they'll outgrow their strength', she added. **1872** *Routledge's Ev. Boy's Ann.* 613 He had out-grown everything. **1876** Merivale *Rom. Triumv.* viii. 156 The population had far outgrown the accommodation it afforded.

3. *fig.* To grow out of or beyond (habits, opinion, circumstances, etc.); to leave behind in the process of growth or development.

1665 Glanvil *Scepsis Sci.* x. 54 Even our gray heads out-grow not those errors which we have learn't before the Alphabet. **1712** Steele *Spect.* No. 263 ⁋6 By my Care you outgrew them [convulsions]. **1832** Ht. Martineau *Homes Abroad* vi. 78 Botany Bay may in time outgrow the odium attached to its name. **1865** Lightfoot *Galatians* (1874) 30 The weak and beggarly elements which they had outgrown.

4. *intr.* To grow out, spring forth. *rare.*

1861 W. Barnes in *Macm. Mag.* June 127 The plantling is cut off; and instead of it there may outgrow two others.

'out,growing, *vbl. sb.* [OUT- 9.] The action of growing out; *concr.* a sprout; an outgrowth.

1577 B. Googe *Heresbach's Husb.* (1586) 60b, If you plucke away the tayles and the outgrowings when you see them. **1579** Langham *Gard. Health* (1633) 68 Apply it.. to all superfluous outgrowing of flesh. **1587** Golding *De Mornay* xi. 162 Thy nailes and the heares of thy head, which are but outgroings, and not parts of thy bodie.

'out,growing, *ppl. a.* [OUT- 10.] Growing forth; growing outward, protruding.

1625 K. Long tr. *Barclay's Argenis* II. ii. 99 Pruned and trimmed from the out-growing sprigges. **1626** Bacon *Sylva* §752 Some Creaturs have Over-long, or Out-growing Teeth, which we call Fangs, or Tuskes; as Boares.

'outgrown, *ppl. a.* [OUT- 11.] †**a.** That has grown out or into prominence. **b.** That has been grown out of, or left behind in growth.

1549 Cheke *Hurt Sedit.* (1641) 37 Counsellours to such an outgrown mischiefe. **1858** O. W. Holmes *Chambered Nautilus* v, Leaving thine outgrown shell by life's unresting sea. **1896** *Allbutt's Syst. Med.* I. 464 The.. deformities.. originating from out-grown and misfitting boots.

outgrowth ('aʊtgrəʊθ). [OUT- 7.] The process of growing out; that which grows (normally or abnormally) out of or from anything; a growth, an offshoot; an excrescence.

1837 Ht. Martineau *Soc. Amer.* III. 52 Those who dislike the mere mention of the outgrowth of individual property. **1857–8** Sears *Athan.* viii. 66 Death is the removal of an outgrowth after it has accomplished its functions and become a hindrance. **1870** H. Macmillan *Bible Teach.* xii. 233 It is not an external addition, but an internal outgrowth.

b. *fig.* Of things immaterial: A natural product.

1850 Maurice *Mor. & Met. Philos.* (ed. 2) 123 The immediate outgrowths of the Socratic philosophy and discipline. **1860** Smiles *Self-Help* i. 2 Only the outgrowth of our own perverted life. **1857** Maine *Hist. Inst.* vii. 223 Primogeniture is not a natural outgrowth of the family.

'out-guard. [OUT- 1, 3.] A guard placed at a distance outside the main body of an army, an advanced guard, an outpost; also *fig.* and *attrib.*

1623 Bingham *Xenophon* 30 They, after they came to our out-guards, asked for the Coronels. a **1671** Fairfax *Mem.* (1699) 66. **1675** *Lond. Gaz.* 1012/3 The outguards of our left Wing, beat the French outguards, and brought in several Prisoners. **1679** Bedloe *Popish Plot* 26 Law being the best humane out-guard to Religion. **1698** Fryer *Acc. E. India & P.* 153 Which makes the Mouth of the Bay to be reckoned from the Head-lands or Out-guards, some Three Leagues over. **1710** Addison *Whig Exam.* No. 4 ⁋11 Holland is our Bulwark, or as Mr. Waller expresses it, our outgard on the Continent. **1743** *Lond. & Country Brewer* II. (ed. 2) 95 This [Dugdale] Wheat will best grow,.. nor will it be damaged by Blights and Wets, when others are, by Reason of its great Out-guards, its Beards. **1865** Carlyle *Fredk. Gt.* xv. xiii. (1872) VI. 105 The enemy.. had no out-guard there, never expecting us on that side.

outguess (aʊt'gɛs), *v.* [f. OUT- 18 b + GUESS *v.*] *trans.* To outwit (someone) by guessing more cleverly or shrewdly.

1913 *Jrnl. Animal Behaviour* III. 90 It was clearly a case of the chick 'outguessing' the experimenter. **1921** E. O'Neill *Emperor Jones* i. 163, I kin outguess, outrun, outfight, an' outplay de whole lot o' dem all ovah de board. **1936** M. Mitchell *Gone with Wind* I. v. 78 Mammy sighed resignedly, beholding herself outguessed. **1956** 'J. Wyndham' *Seeds of Time* 187, I don't know whether he outguessed me or whether he was just lucky. **1972** P. H. Kocher *Master of Middle-Earth* iii. 44 Her function in the story is to warn them, and herself, to tend to the duty in hand and not rashly to presume that finite minds can outguess the supreme architect who plans the whole. **1975** *Publishers Weekly* 6 Jan. 52/3 Murders and cover-ups follow, with the reader trying to outguess the author all the way.

out-'gun, *v.* [OUT- 21.] *trans.* To surpass in guns; to surpass in gunnery; to outshoot. Also *fig.* Hence **out'gunned** *ppl. a.*

1691 Bethel *Providences of God* (1694) 111 We out-tunn'd them, outgunn'd them, and out-mann'd them. **1887** Blackmore *Springhaven* (ed. 4) II. xiii. 180 To outsail friend Englishman is a great delight, and to outgun him would be still greater. **1942** *R.A.F. Jrnl.* 13 June 12 The wolf—helpless, out-ranged and outgunned so far as the *Devonshire* was concerned. **1945** *Sun* (Baltimore) 17 Mar. 9-0/1 We're just out-tanked and out-gunned, that's all. **1960** *Observer* 28 Aug. 25/6 The Corporation has shown that it can outgun its rival. **1973** *Daily Tel.* 28 Nov. 15 The Battle of the River Plate, in which three outgunned cruisers took on the German pocket battleship Admiral Graf Spee. **1977** *Times* 5 May 1/8 Mr Callaghan, Dr Owen.. and Mr Rees.. could well be outgunned by a majority of ministers.

outgush ('aʊtgʌʃ), *sb.* [OUT- 7.] The act of gushing out; a sudden strong outflow. Also *fig.*

1839 Thackeray *Catherine* iv, With a most piteous scream and outgush of tears. **1871** Browning *Balaustion's Adventure* 170 Frank out-gush of the human gratitude Which saved our ship and me. **1884** J. Hatton in *Harper's Mag.* Feb. 342/2 The outgush of water near the church. **1919** [see La, la].

out'gush, *v. rare.* [OUT- 14.] *intr.* To gush out. (Properly two words.)

c **1614** Sir W. Mure *Dido & Æneas* I. 243 The winds out gushing heavens and earth do fill With hiddeows noyse. a **1730** Eusden *Ovid's Metam.* v. (R.), Till from repeated strokes out-gush'd a flood.

So **'out,gushing** *vbl. sb.* and *ppl. a.* [OUT- 9, 10.]

1839 F. Barham *Adamus Exul.* 20 The voice of our out-gushing love Floats joyously. **1842** Mrs. Browning *Grk. Chr. Poets* 105 Her sonnets of tufted primroses, her lyrical outgushings of May. **1888** Spurgeon in *Voice* (N.Y.), Prayer is the natural outgushing of a soul in communion with Jesus.

†**outh, owth,** *prep.* and *adv. Sc. Obs.* Also 4 wth, 5 outhe. [Origin obscure; perh. f. OE. *uf-*, ME. *uv-*, *ov-* above + *-with*: cf. *oututh* = *outwith* without.]

A. *prep.* Above, over.

1375 Barbour *Bruce* xi. 614 Sic ane stew raiss owth thame then. Of aynding, bath of hors and men. *Ibid.* xvii. 598 Of gret gestis ane sow thai maid, That stalward heling owth it had. c **1375** *Sc. Leg. Saints* ii. (*Paulus*) 673 And owth his hevid sittand þar brandiste a brand þat scharply schar. **1389** in Sir W. Fraser *Wemyss of W.* (1888) II. 23 Landys and possessionnys.. als wele vndyr erd as wth. c **1425** Wyntoun *Cron.* vi. ix. 66 In Ycolmkil lyis he, Owth hym thir wers yhit men may se.

B. *adv.* Above, over. Also *at outh.*

1375 Barbour *Bruce* xviii. 418 Thai that owth war twmmyl donne Stanis apon thame fra the hicht. **1456** Sir G. Haye *Law Arms* (S.T.S.) 36 Sum men wenis to be at outhe and abune that is at undir.

'outhalf, out-half. *Rugby Football.* [f. OUT- + HALF *sb.* 6 d.] = *fly-half* (FLY *sb.*[2] 8). Cf. *outside half* s.v. OUTSIDE *a.* 6.

Fly-half is the more usual term in the U.K.

1961 in WEBSTER. **1973** *Irish Times* 2 Mar. 3/7 At their heels was scrum-half Early.., while Spring is a cool out-half. **1976** *Sunday Tel.* 23 May 39/8 'Oh my,' said Mike Quinn, the outhalf, 'if the New Zealand centres are as quick as that what are their wings like?' **1977** *Belfast Tel.* 27 Jan. 25/8 No sooner had he settled into the side than out-half Keith Gilpin was sidelined.

out-hammer, -hasten, etc.: see OUT-.

outhaul ('aʊthɔːl). *Naut.* [OUT- 7.] 'A rope used for hauling out the tack of a jib lower studding-sail, or the clue of a boom-sail' (Smyth *Sailor's Word-bk.* 1867): opposed to *inhaul.*

1840 R. H. DANA *Bef. Mast* xxxiii. 126 We were nearly an hour setting the sail; carried away the outhaul in doing it. **1891** *Harper's Weekly* 19 Sept. 713/4 The forward man sets and furls the jib by means of outhauls and halyards.

'out,hauler. *Naut.* [OUT- 8.] A rope or line for hauling out: esp. **a.** = prec. **b.** 'A line or rope used to haul a net up to the surface of the water' (*Cent. Dict.*).

1793 SMEATON *Edystone L.* §231 By neglecting to belay the tackle-fall of the out-hawler Guy, the shears came down flat upon the rock in the midst of the men. **1794** *Rigging & Seamanship* I. 170 *Outhauler.* A rope made fast to the tack of the jib, to haul it out by. **1848** J. F. COOPER *Capt. Spike* i. I. 28 To loosen this broad sheet of canvas, and to clap on the out-hauler, to set it.

†out-'have, *v. Sc. Obs.* [OUT- 15.] *trans.* To have out, get or take out.

1458 in *Orig. Par. Scot.* II. II. 431 In buying, sellyng,.. and owthawyng of merchandice. *Ibid.*, Quhar sic gudis is owthad.

out-hear to **out-heaven**: see OUT-.

out-'hector, *v.* [OUT- 18, 18 c.] *trans.* To outdo in hectoring; to overcome by bluster and swagger; to bully, intimidate.

1678 BUTLER *Hud.* III. iii. *Lady's Answer* 374 Because your selves are terrify'ed.. Believe we have as little Wit To be Out hector'd, and Submit. **1683** PETTUS *Fleta Min.* I. Ded., That as you never were out-Hector'd by Affronts or Resistences, so you were never out-done by Civilities. *a* **1854** H. REED *Lect. Brit. Poets* ix. (1857) 311 The great struggle of men seemed to be to out-hector each other.

out-hele, *v.*: see OUT- 24.

†outher, *adj. pron. Obs.* exc. *dial.* Forms: *α.* 1 **áhwæðer, áwðer, áuðer, áðer**; 4–5 *north.* **awþer, auþer,** 5 **auther, -ir,** 4– **ather.** *β.* 3–5 **owþer,** 3 (*Orm.*) **owwþerr,** 4 **ouþer, -ir,** 4–6 **outher, owther** (also 9 *dial.*), 5 **owþir, -ere, owdir,** 5–6 **outhir, owthir,** 6 **owthyr, ouyer** (= **ouþer**), **ouder.** [OE. *áwðer, áuðer, áðer*, contr. from *áhwæðer*, lit. 'whichever of the two', 'either of the two', 'one or other', L. *utercumque, utervis*; f. *á* ever + *hwæðer?* which of the two? L. *uter?* Thence the northern ME. forms. The ME. *owþer, outher*, points to an OE. *óhwæðer, ówðer*, f. *ó* ever: cf. the parallel *óhwǽr* = *áhwǽr*, etc.]

1. One or other (of two); either: = EITHER A. 4.

a. as *pron.* After the OE. period chiefly north. or north-midl.

In quot. *c* 1000 = One or another of all, any one whatsoever.

c **888** K. ÆLFRED *Boeth.* vi, þæt mod.. þær þissa twega yfela auðer ricsað. *c* **893** —— *Oros.* III. ix. §13 Ær heora aðer mehte on oþrum siȝe ȝeræcan. *c* **897** —— *Gregory's Past.* xiv. 86 ȝif he auðer ðissa forlæt. *a* **1000** *Riddles* lxxxv. 22 Ne uncer awðer. *c* **1000** *Ags. Ps.* (Th.) lv. 4 (also cxvii. 6) Nis me eȝe mannes for ahwæðer. *c* **1200** ORMIN 2507 All þatt tatt owwþerr hēre comm Off sellþe & off unnsellþe. *Ibid.* 9352 Ær þann þe Laferrd Jesu Crist Bigann owwþerr to donne. *c* **1230** *Hali Meid.* 35 Aðat owðer of ham twa ear lose oðer. **13..** *Cursor M.* 21949 (Gött.) For ouþer [*Cott.* ooþer, *Fairf.* auþer] of þaim we most for-ga For mai na man haue heuens tua. *c* **1380** WYCLIF *Serm.* Sel. Wks. I. 36 Nouþir is wel servaunt to ouþir. *c* **1400** MAUNDEV. (Roxb.) xxi. 96 Þai er mykill lesse þan owþer of þe oþer. *a* **1450** *Le Morte Arthur* 2013 Nys man in erthe.. Shall.. pees make, Er outher of vs haue other slayne.

b. In OE. used anticipatively to introduce the two (or more) members of an alternative, thus *áwðer* (or *áðer*) *oððe.. oððe..*, i.e. either (of the two, or of these), either.. or... Cf. the similar use of *óðer*, OTHER *adj. pron.* B. 1 b.

In this use *áwðer* often became quite adverbial, i.e. when the alternative members to which it referred were not sbs. It thus resembled the modern *either* in 'either on land or on sea' (exc. in being followed by *oððe*, which itself had the place and force of 'either'). In quot. *c* 1000, *auðer* follows the alternative clause: cf. EITHER B. 5. OTHER *conj.* B. 2.

c **880** *Laws of Ælfred* Introd. 9 Awðer oððe on Ines dæȝe, mines mæȝes, oððe on Offan, Myrcena cyninges, oððe on Æðelbryhtes. *c* **888** K. ÆLFRED *Boeth.* xl. §2 Ælc wyrd is nyt þara þe auðer deð, oððe lærð oððe wyrcð. *Ibid.* xli. §5 Forȝifen.. auþer oððe hrorum neatum oððe unhrorum. *c* **893** —— *Oros.* I. i. §18 Eal þæt his man aþer oððe ettan oððe erian mæȝ. *Ibid.* VI. xxxii. §3 Þa oferhoȝode he him aðer dyde, oþþe wiernde, oþþe tiȝþade. *a* **900** —— *Solil.* (1902) 37 Hwæt wille ic ma cwæðan aðer oððe be mete, oððe be drince, oððe be baðe, oððe be welan, oððe be wyrðscype? *c* **1000** *Boeth. Metr.* xx. 42 Næs æror þe æneȝu ȝesceaft þe auht oððe nauht auðer worhte.

c. as *adj.*

c **893** K. ÆLFRED *Oros.* I. xiv. §2 Heora þeh wurdon feawa to lafe on aðre hand. **1571** *Satir. Poems Reform.* xxvi. 78 Bot puneis all the quhilk ye knaw vnclene Of outher blude, and quyte yame for yair meids.

2. Each (of two): = EITHER A. 2. *north. rare.*

1472 *Presentm. Juries* in *Surtees Misc.* (1888) 24 And outhir drewe blode of othir.

outher ('aʊðə(r), 'ɒðə(r)), *adv.* (*conj.*) Now *dial.* Forms: see prec. [The neuter or uninflected form of OUTHER *pron.*, used advb. to emphasize an alternative, and thence sometimes conjunctively.]

1. An early equivalent of EITHER B. 3.

a. In the connexion ***outher.. or..*** (now *dial.*), ***outher.. other..*** (*obs.*). (Cf. prec. 1 b.)

c **1330** R. BRUNNE *Chron.* (1810) 94 Ouþer in word or dede has þou greued him. **1340** HAMPOLE *Pr. Consc.* 1651 He es outher clomsed or wode. **13..** *Gaw. & Gr. Knt.* 702 Wonde þer bot lyte þat auþer God oþer gome wyth goud hert louied. *c* **1375** *Cursor M.* 14859 (Fairf.) Auþer to deye or to liue. **1390** GOWER *Conf.* I. 332 Owther schal he deie or I Withinne a while. *c* **1420** *Sir Amadace* (Camden) xxxix, Authir to gentilmen or to schrewis. *c* **1449** PECOCK *Repr.* III. xvii. 395 This.. muste outhir be doon bi hem.. or bi othere persoones. *c* **1450** LONELICH *Grail* xli. 290 As thowgh it hadde ben Owther led Oþer ston. **1485** CAXTON *Paris & V.* 4 They love outher you or me. **1513** DOUGLAS *Æneis* IX. v. 171 The chans turnis, ouder to weyll or wo. **1530** PALSGR. Introd. 32 Outher in S.. or in one of these thre letters T, U or V. **1567** *Gude & Godlie B.* (S.T.S.) 142 Than suld we outher do or die. *a* **1584** MONTGOMERIE *Cherrie & Slae* 454 Be tane, And outhir hurt or slane. **1868** ATKINSON *Cleveland Gloss.*, *Owther*, conj. pr. of Either.

†b. In the connexion ***outher.. outher..***: see 2.

2. *conj.* = OR. (Chiefly in ***ouþer.. ouþer.***) *rare.*

a **1400** *Serm.* in *Rel. Ant.* II. 42 In myraclis.. þat Crist dude.. outher in hymself outher in hise seyntis. *a* **1425** *Chaucer's Can. Yeom. T.* 596 (Harl. MS.) I-maad ouþer of chalk ouþer of glas [*Ellesm.* ouþer.. or, *Camb.* oþir.. oþir]. *a* **1425** *Cursor M.* 9662 (Trin.) Wiþouten mercy ouþer [*Laud* oþir] reuthe.

out-Herod (aʊt'hɛrəd), *v.* [OUT- 23 b.] *to out-Herod Herod*: to outdo Herod (represented in the old Mystery Plays as a blustering tyrant) in violence; to be more outrageous than the most outrageous; hence, to outdo in any excess of evil or extravagance. (A casual Shaksperian expression, which has become current in the 19th c.)

1602 SHAKS. *Ham.* III. ii. 16, I could haue such a Fellow whipt for o're-doing Termagant: it out-Herod's Herod. Pray you auoid it. **1800** MAR. EDGEWORTH *Belinda* (1832) I. iii. 57 She out-Heroded Herod upon the occasion. **1819** *Metropolis* I. 172 Out-heroding the French cavaliers in compliment and in extravagance. **1853** KINGSLEY *Misc.* I. 276 As for manner, he [Alexander Smith] does sometimes, in imitating his models, out-Herod Herod.

outhes, -hest, -heys, var. ff. OUTAS *Obs.*

out-hild to **out-hiss**: see OUT-.

outhold (aʊt'həʊld), *v. rare.* [OUT- 15.]

1. *trans.* To hold out, extend; †to withhold, retain (*obs.*); to keep out, ward off. Cf. *hold out* in HOLD *v.* 41.

1512 *Drapers' Ordin.* in Brand *Newcastle* (1789) II. 690 Unto yᵉ tyme that he have fully payed such dewtes as he owthalds of the chans felishyp. **1550** *Reg. Privy Council Scot.* I. 107 All the saidis personis.. be himselff, hes uthalden his hand to the Quenis Grace. **1577–87** HOLINSHED *Chron.* II. 22/2 Mistrusting that the wals.. should not have been of sufficient force to outhold the enimie. **1600** FAIRFAX *Tasso* III. xxxiv, No brest-plate could that cursed tree out-hold.

2. To continue to hold. *rare.*

1884 JOAQUIN MILLER *Jewess* in *Memorie & Rime* 192 The same broad hollow of God's hand That held you ever, outholds still.

Hence **†out'holding** *vbl. sb.*, withholding, retention.

1512 *Drapers' Ordin.* in Brand *Newcastle* (1789) II. 690 Yᵉ fornamed stewards.. shall forfett to the.. Drappers for yᵉ owthaldyng of the said money.. 26*sh.* 8*d.*

out-'holl, *v. East Anglian dial.* [OUT- 15.] *trans.* To scour out a ditch: cf. HOLL *sb.*

1781 *Minutes* in W. Marshall *Norfolk* (1795) II. 76, I am determined henceforward to stem, if possible, the vile practices.. of 'outholling' and 'cutting kid'. **1787** *Ibid.* I. 101 *Out-holling*, that is, scouring out the ditch for manure; without returning any part of the soil to the roots of the hedgewood. *a* **1825** FORBY *Out-holl*, to scour a ditch.

†'outhorn. *Obs.* [Cf. OUT- 7, HORN *sb.* 14.] A horn blown to raise the OUTAS (*uthes*), to summon the lieges to the pursuit of a criminal, or the like, and to give the alarm on various occasions. (In later use only *Sc.* and *north. Eng.*)

c **1210** *Pseudo-Alfred* (in Liebermann *Leges Angl. Lond. coll.* 19) Nullus supersedeat outhorn nec outhest uel burhbotam, uel firdfare nec herebode ore aut cornu. [Cf. **1214** in Maitland *Sel. Pleas Crown* No. 115 Et tunc cornaverunt hutes, et illuc convenerunt burgenses de predicto burgo.] **1432** *Sc. Acts Jas. I* (1814) II. 21 Gif it happynis the schiref to persew fugitouris with þe kingis horne.. and the contre rise nocht.. and folowis nocht the oute horne.. ilk gentil man sal pay to the king vnforgeuin xl.s. *c* **1460** *Towneley Myst.* xxi. 139 Now wols-hede and out-horne on the be tane! **15..** *Adam Bel & Clym of Clough* 345 (Ritson) There was an out horne in Caerlel blowen, And the belles bacward did ryng. **1546** *Reg. Privy Council Scot.* I. 61 Thaim that beis warnit be bels, outhornys, frays, and crys or uthairwise, efter the use of the cuntre.

out-horror, etc.: see OUT-.

†out-'hound, *v. Sc. Obs.* [OUT- 15.] *trans.* To instigate, set on (to some evil deed). So **†'out-hounder,** instigator.

a **1670** SPALDING *Troubl. Chas. I* (1829) 23 That the Gordons were the outhounders of these highlandmen. **1752** *Stewart's Trial* Scots Mag. (1753) May 226/2 That Breck committed the murder.. by the council, command, or direction of this pannel, or as our old laws express it out-hounded by him.

outhouse ('aʊthaʊs). [OUT- 1.] **a.** A house or building, belonging to and adjoining a dwelling-house, and used for some subsidiary purpose; e.g. a stable, barn, wash-house, toolhouse, or the like.

1533 *Test. Ebor.* (Surtees) VI. 39 The outhouse in the entreside. **1567** HARMAN *Caveat* 39 Away from my house, either lye in some of my out houses vntyll the morning. **1648** *Bury Wills* (Camden) 212 All my houshold stuffe.. and vtensills belonginge to my milhouse, stables, barnes, and all the outhouses. *a* **1680** BUTLER *Rem.* (1759) I. 61 Our noblest Piles, and stateliest Rooms Are but Out-houses to our Tombs. **1774** GOLDSM. *Nat. Hist.* (1776) V. 143 Some obscure hole in a farmer's out-house. **1828** BAYLEY in Barnewall & Cresswell *Rep.* VIII. 465 [The building] was not an outhouse, because it was not parcel of a dwelling-house. **1849** MACAULAY *Hist. Eng.* vii. II. 208 The Presbyterians were interdicted from worshipping God anywhere but in private dwellings:.. they were not even to use a barn or an outhouse for religious exercises.

b. A privy. Chiefly *U.S.*

1819 W. SEWALL *Diary* 14 June (1930) 53/1 Near the paddles or wheels which propel the vessel forward are two outhouses, which is a very great convenience. **1832** W. IRVING *Jrnl.* Nov. (1919) III. 185 Old Spanish wooden building, with piazza—out houses—French buildings, with casement. **1912** *Dialect Notes* III. 584 *Out-house*,.. a privy. **1921** H. KEPHART *Camping & Woodcraft* (1928) I. xii. 210 If the well is near a stable or outhouse, or if dish-water is thrown near it, let it alone. **1968** C. HELMERICKS *Down Wild River North* I. xviii. 286 They still clung steadfastly to the old outhouse. **1973** *N.Y. Law Jrnl.* 26 July 16/7 (Advt.), Executive hideaway, L.I. Rustic appointments throughout.. attractive 2 seater outhouse.

c. At a school, a house (see HOUSE *sb.*[1] 4 c) separate from, or subsidiary to, the main or central house.

1900 FARMER *Public School Word-Bk.* 144 *Out-houses* (Charterhouse),—all the boarding houses except Sanderites, Verites, and Gownboys. The names of the eight out-houses are Girdlestonites, Lockites, [etc.]. **1933** L. A. G. STRONG *Sea Wall* 187 A tall, genial boy named Adams, belonging to another of the out-houses.

'outhousing. [f. prec. + -ING[1].] A collection of outhouses: cf. HOUSING *sb.*[1] 2 b.

1630 *Ord. & Direct. conc. Relief of Poor* xi, That no man harbour Rogues in their Barnes or Outhouseings. **1647** *Boston Rec.* (1877) II. 168 Theire Messuage and Farme.. with all the outhouseing, fences, wood, and all other appurtenances. **1701** *Lond. Gaz.* No. 3720/4 There is a good House, Barns, Stabling, Outhousing. **1865** E. WAUGH *Goblin's Grave* 9 Whether either of them belonged to the hall or its out-housing.

out'howl, *v.* [OUT- 18.] *trans.* To outdo in howling; to howl louder than.

1654 GAYTON *Pleas. Notes* IV. xx. 269 They would have out-houled an Irish Woolfe. **1706** E. WARD *Hud. Rediv.* I. VI. 5 Where ev'ry gaping thin-jaw'd Brother Strove zealously t' outhowl the other. **1856** WHITTIER *Panorama* 370 So some poor wretch.. Out-howls the Dervish.

outhumour (aʊt'hjuːmə(r)), *v.* [OUT- 26, 21.] *trans.* **†a.** To put or drive (a person) out of his humour or mood. **b.** To surpass in humour.

1607 WILKINS *Miseries Enforced Marr.* v. in Hazl. *Dodsley* IX. 565. I will out humour you, Fight with you and lose my life. **1883** *American* VI. 219 A passage in which our humorist out-humors himself.

out-hunted to **out-impudence**: see OUT-.

outing ('aʊtɪŋ), *vbl. sb.* [f. OUT *v.* + -ING[1].]

†1. The action of going out or forth; an expedition.

1375 BARBOUR *Bruce* XIX. 620 The Erll sperit at hym tithing How he had farn in his outyng.

2. The action of putting or driving out; expulsion; ousting. Now *rare* or *Obs.*

c **1440** *Promp. Parv.* 375/2 Owtynge, or a-woydaunce, *evacuacio, deliberacio.* **1639** LAUD *Wks.* (1849) II. 348 Salvation need not be feared of any dutiful child, nor outing from the church. **1679** *Connect. Col. Rec.* (1859) III. 273 To pursue the outing of the Rohd Islanders from ye Narrogancett Country. **1692** R. L'ESTRANGE *Josephus, Antiq.* XV. xv. (1733) 446 Doing all that was to be done.. towards the outing of him again, and engrossing the Power to himself.

3. *Cricket.* The position of being kept 'out': see OUT *adv.* 19 c.

1849 *Bell's Life in London* 30 Sept. 6/2, I Zingari averages, 1849. Results with bat and ball... Innings... Runs... Outings... Bowled. **1897** *Daily News* 8 June 8/4 The Philadelphians bore their long outing very well, the fielding being sustained at a fairly good pitch of excellence.

4. a. An airing, excursion, pleasure-trip. orig. *dial.*

1821 CLARE *Vill. Minstr.* I. 42 The long rural string of merry games, That at such outings maketh much ado. **1825** BROCKETT *N.C. Gloss.*, *Outing*, an airing, going from home.

1855 ROBINSON *Whitby Gloss.* s.v., 'A bit of an outing', a short journey or pleasure-trip. **1857** MRS. CARLYLE *Lett.* II. 326 Another week at Sunny Bank will make as much 'outing' as should suffice for this year. **1861** *Sat. Rev.* XII. 432/2 They have had, we repeat, their outing. The word may not be found in Richardson or Webster, or, indeed, anywhere within the pale of lexicon orthodoxy, but we are prepared to justify the use of it notwithstanding. **1886** *Illustr. Lond. News* 8 May 489/3 She could not afford two outings in the year.

b. An appearance in an athletic contest, race, etc.

1943 *Sun* (Baltimore) 22 Apr. 18/1 Benefitting from a previous outing at the meeting, Mrs. Ray Feinberg's Charge, ridden by Danny Scocca, closed fast. **1976** J. SNOW *Cricket Rebel* 29 Any young cricketer brought into the traditional twelve for his first Test outing could expect a back page headline in the national newspapers. **1976** *Evening Times* (Glasgow) 30 Nov., Bula, although only once successful in three outings so far this season, is my confident choice to register a repeat victory at Haydock Park.

5. (See quot.)

1844 *Jrnl. R. Agric. Soc.* V. I. 29 Not to turn over the swarths, but.. to leave them upon what is termed the outing, made at the commencement of the preceding swarth by the mower putting his scythe in a sloping direction downwards.

6. The distance out at sea, etc.

1883 *Cent. Mag.* Dec. 201/2 Beyond this,.. in the farthest outing, hill-crowned islands. **1896** HORNE *Countryside* 10 (E.D.D.) In the outing furious waves fight and plunge.

7. *attrib.* (from 4), as ***outing-dress, -hat, -trip***; **outing flannel** *U.S.*, a type of flannelette; also *attrib.*

1890 *Adt.* (Schairer & Millen, Ann Arbor), 15 pieces new stripe outing flannels, 15 cent quality, now 10 cents. **1897** HOWELLS *Landl. Lion's Head* 11 In the outing dress he wore .. he was always effective. **1897** *Sears, Roebuck Catal.* 258/3 Outing flannel. This flannel is suitable for ladies' wrappers, waists, night robes, childrens' cloaks, also men's and boys' shirts and night shirts. **1899** *Boston Even. Transcr.* 22 Apr. 23/6 A few of these outing hats are.. rather elaborately finished by ribbon loops and aigrettes. **1916** *Daily Colonist* (Victoria, B.C.) 9 July 3/6 (Advt.), New awning stripe outing skirts. *Ibid.* 22 July 2/1 (Advt.), Take a Camera Wherever You Go. What is more delightful than having pictures of outing parties, picnics, scenery, etc.? **1925** T. DREISER *Amer. Tragedy* (1926) I. II. xv. 262 He was pleased by the.. summery appearance he made in an outing shirt and canvas shoes. **1938** M. K. RAWLINGS *Yearling* v. 51 The gray fur was as soft as his mother's outing flannel nightgown. **1967** *Boston Sunday Herald* 14 May II. 17/2 Every summer its members provide rafts and guides for vacationing familes, outing groups, and student expeditions.

out island, out isle: see OUT *a.* 2 b.

out-issue to **out-jest**: see OUT-.

ˈoutjet, *sb.* [OUT- 7.] A part that juts out, a projection.

1730 A. GORDON *Maffei's Amphith.* 206 For counter-ballancing the Out-jet or Projection above. **1834** H. MILLER *Scenes & Leg.* iii. (1857) 26 The outjets and buttresses of an ancient fortress. *Ibid.* xxiv. (1889) 352 A small apartment formed by an outjet of the cottage.

So **ˈoutˌjetting** *vbl. sb.*, a jutting out; a projection; **ˈoutˌjetting** *ppl. a.*, jutting out, projecting; †**ˈoutˌjetty**, projection, protuberance.

1650 BULWER *Anthropomet.* 64 Sense and Memory, which he cannot well exercise, unless he have an out-jetty of the occiput. **1652** URQUHART *Jewel* Wks. (1834) 195 Roofs, platforms, outjettings, and other such like parts. **1730** A. GORDON *Maffei's Amphith.* 245 The out-jetting Window added above the Entries.

out-ˈjet, *v.* *nonce-wd.* [OUT- 21.] *trans.* To surpass in intense blackness (jetty quality).

1822 BEDDOES *Poems, Bride's Trag.* II. iv, And something in the air, out-jetting night,.. Featured its ghastly self upon my soul.

outˈjockey, *v.* [OUT- 18 b, c.] *trans.* To get the better of or overreach by adroitness or trickery.

1714 MACKY *Journ. thro' Eng.* (1724) I. viii. 135 At a Horse-Match.. Everybody strives to outjocky (as the Phrase is) one another. **1720** LADY COWPER *Diary* (1864) 139 Sunderland.. has outjockeyed Walpole. **1809** W. IRVING *Knickerb.* IV. iii. (1861) 119 Our worthy forefathers could scarcely stir abroad without danger of being outjockeyed in horseflesh. **1871** *Daily News* 14 Jan., She had allowed herself to be out-manœuvred and out-jockeyed in statesmanship.

out-journey, etc.: see OUT-.

[**out-joy**, a supposed vb. and sb., due to erroneous analysis of the phr. *full out joy* to exult, exultation, in Wyclif: see OUT- 15 b.]

out-ˈjuggle, *v.* [OUT- 18, 18 b.] *trans.* To outdo in juggling.

1620 BP. HALL *Hon. Mar. Clergie* I. iv. 21 A Reader.. might verily thinke that I could out-lie the Legends, and out-iuggle a Iesuite. *a* **1768** STERNE in *Beauties of S.* (1811) 118 (Jod.) It was to out-juggle a juggling attorney. **1859** G. MEREDITH *Juggling Jerry* i, One that outjuggles all's been spying Long to have me.

outˈjump, *v.* [OUT- 18.] *trans.* To surpass or exceed in jumping.

1639 LD. DIGBY, etc. *Lett. conc. Relig.* (1651) 85 So active as to out-jump him a foot. **1891** MISS DOWIE *Girl in Karp.* 246 The silly suggestiveness of a brain that outjumps one's thoughts. **1897** *Voice* (N.Y.) 18 Mar. 1/5 He could outrun, outbox, outjump, and outswim any boy in Portland.

outˈjut, *v.* [OUT- 14.] *intr.* To jut out, project.

1851 HELPS *Comp. Solit.* ix. (1874) 154 An oratory out-jutting from the line of planks. **1899** E. J. CHAPMAN *Drama Two Lives* 7 Gaunt and grey the rocks out-jut Across the jaggèd rift below.

ˈoutjut, *sb.* [OUT- 7.] A projection, projecting part. So **ˈoutˌjutting** *vbl. sb.*; **ˈoutjutting** *ppl. a.*, jutting out, projecting.

1611 COTGR., *Surpenduë*,.. an out-iutting roome. **1730** A. GORDON *Maffei's Amphith.* 399 The Bench or Out-jutting. **1847** G. B. CHEEVER *Wand. Pilgrim* xxiii. 152 The bare outjutting precipices. **1889** C. E. CRADDOCK (Miss Murfree) *Despot Broomsedge* xxii. 395 On a slight out-jutting of the clay and sticks. **1894** *Rep. Mitchell (Glasgow) Libr.* 1892–4 (1895) 28 It is supposed that, on his way to it, he.. had fallen over the rock, on a sharp outjut.

ˈoutkeeper. [OUT- 8.] An instrument used in land-measuring: see quot.

1875 KNIGHT *Dict. Mech.* 1582/1 *Outkeeper*, a small dial-plate having an index turned by a milled head underneath, used with the surveyor's compass to keep tally in chaining. The dial is figured from 0 to 16, the index being moved one notch for every chain run.

out-ˈkick, *v.* [OUT- 18, 15.] *trans.* **a.** To kick more than. **b.** To 'kick out'; to dismiss. *rare.* So **ˈoutkicking** *vbl. sb.*, kicking out.

1772 J. FLETCHER *Logica Genev.* 108 They will grow so excessively fat as to outkick Jeshurun himself. **1883** BESANT *All in Garden Fair* II. iv. 92 A.. quantity of cuffs.. out-kickings.. and so forth. *Ibid.* x. 238 Those who do as little as they possibly can, so as just not to get out-kicked.

outˈkill, *v.* *rare.* [OUT- 18, 15 b.] *trans.* **a.** To outdo, go beyond in killing. **b.** To finish killing, kill outright.

a **1658** CLEVELAND *Gen. Poems*, etc. (1677) 113, I wonder for how many Lives my Lord Hopton took the Lease of his Body. First Stamford slew him, then Waller outkill'd that half a Barr. **1860** PUSEY *Min. Proph.* 65 This is the second death, which never out-killeth, yet which ever killeth.

out-king to **out-kneed**: see OUT-.

out-ˈknave, *v.* *rare.* [OUT- 22.] *trans.* To outdo in knavery; to get the better of by knavery.

1660 BONDE *Scut. Reg.* 286 It grieved them to see the Independents.. out-knave them. *a* **1704** R. L'ESTRANGE (J.), The world calls it outwitting a man, when he's only out-knaved.

outˈlabour, *v.* [OUT- 18, 17.] *trans.* To outdo, exceed, or go beyond in labour, toil, or endurance.

1651 DAVENANT *Gondibert* II. II. xxv, I have.. Out-suffer'd patience, bred in Captives Breasts;.. Outwatch'd the jealous, and outlabour'd Beasts. **1855** MILMAN *Lat. Chr.* IV. 265 The Poor Men of the Church might out-labour and out-suffer the Poor Men of Lyons. **1875** BROWNING *Herakles* 343 Who outlabours what the Gods appoint Shows energy, but energy gone mad.

†**outˈlade**, *v.* *Obs. rare.* [OUT- 15.] *trans.* To discharge (cf. LADE *v.* 5, 6).

1610 HOLLAND *Camden's Brit.* I. 578 Avon.. in the end out-ladeth his owne streame into Severn.

†**ˈout-ˌlading.** *Obs.* [OUT- 6.] The lading or shipping of goods for exportation.

1622 T. SCOTT *Belg. Pismire* 54 Restraints about the out-lading of Corne and Beere.

outlagare, -arie, -ary, obs. ff. OUTLAWRY.

out-laid, -lament, etc.: see OUT-.

outland (ˈaʊtlənd), *sb.* and *a.* [OUT- 1.]

A. *sb.* **1. a.** A land that is outside, a foreign land.

Now only a poetic archaism.

c **1000** *Ags. Ps.* (Th.) cxlvii. 3 [14] He ðine ʒemæru ʒemiclade, ðu on utlandum ahtest sibbe. ? *a* **1400** *Morte Arthur* 3697 When ledys of owt londys leppyne in waters. **1551** ROBINSON tr. *More's Utop.* II. vi. (1895) 220 To thentente they maye the better knowe the owte landes of euerye syde them. **1870** MORRIS *Earthly Par.* II. III. 126 Many a tale.. he had Concerning outlands good and bad That they had journeyed through. **1876** —— *Sigurd* 315 There was a King of the out-lands, and Atli was his name.

†**b.** in genitive case: Of the outland, foreign.

c **1330** R. BRUNNE *Chron. Wace* (Rolls) 5910 Ffor out-landesmen þat come by se. —— *Chron.* (1810) 39 Tuo out-landes kynges on þis lond hauens hent. **1596** DALRYMPLE tr. *Leslie's Hist. Scot.* I. 53 Quhither thay be richer in out-landis geir, and merchandise.

†**2.** The outlying land of an estate or manor. In OE. and feudal tenure, that portion of the land which the lord did not retain for his own use but granted to tenants. (Opposed to INLAND 1.) *Obs.*

950 in Thorpe *Charters* 502 Wulfeʒe þæt inland and Ælfeʒe þæt utland. **1664** SPELMAN, *Utland.* Saxonic. (id est *terra extera*). Dicebatur *terra servilis*, seu *tenementalis*, quod de procinctu terrarum dominicalium, quæ Inland nuncupatæ sunt, in exteriorem agrum rejiciebantur. **1706** PHILLIPS, *Outland* (among the Saxons), such Land as was let out to any Tenant meerly at the Pleasure of the Lord. **1848** WHARTON *Law Lex.*, *Outland*, land lying beyond the demesnes, and granted out to tenants at the will of the lord, like copyholds.

3. a. *out-lands*: the outlying lands of a province, district, or town, chiefly *Amer. Colonies.* Also *transf.*

1676 *Connect. Col. Rec.* (1852) II. 446 Wee are shut vp in our garisones and dare not goe abroad far to our outlandes, without som strength. **1705** R. BEVERLEY *Hist. Virginia* II. vi. 40 When they [Indians] go a Hunting into the Out-lands, they commonly go out for the whole Season, with their Wives and Families. **1731** *Rhode Island Col. Rec.* (1859) IV. 442 An Act for erecting and incorporating the out-lands of the town of Providence, into three towns. **1931** *Sun* (Baltimore) 21 Oct. 14/6 Were it [*sc.* the weasel] the size of a bear or lion.. the outlands would be unsafe for man unless he carried a gun. **1961** WEBSTER s.v., In the outlands, the Yankees had been strangers. **1970** R. LOWELL *Notebk.* 190 Someone comes here from the outlands, Trinidad.

†**b.** The outer land: the opposite of *inland*. *Obs.*

1698 FRYER *Acc. E. India & P.* 23 Ceilon.. bore from us North by West.. the out-Land low.

4. A foreigner, alien, stranger. [? elliptical use of B. Cf. also OE. *útlenda* foreigner.] Now *Sc.*

c **1330** R. BRUNNE *Chron. Wace* (Rolls) 1326 Outlandes hadden wasted þat lond. *Ibid.* 5811 Outlandeis þat were ffledde, Alle swilk wyþ þeym þey ledde. **1825** JAMIESON, *Outlan*, an alien, as 'She treats him like an outlan'; 'He's used like a mere outlan about the house'. **1887** *Jamieson's Sc. Dict.* Suppl., *Outlander, Outland, Outlan*, an alien, a stranger; an incomer to a burgh or parish; also, one who lives beyond the bounds of a burgh.

B. *adj.* [In origin an attrib. use of the sb. OE. had an adj. *útlęnde*, cf. ON. *útlendr* foreign. ME. also used the genitive case *outlandes*: see A. 1 b.]

1. Of or belonging to another country; foreign, alien. Now *poet.* or *arch.*

c **1425** *Eng. Conq. Irel.* 20 Be ensample of these, al other out-lond men to be adrede such folies to begyn. *c* **1470** HENRY *Wallace* VII. 857 Off outland men lat nane chaip with the liff. **1596** DALRYMPLE tr. *Leslie's Hist. Scot.* I. 85 Externe and outland natiouns. **1651** J. MARIUS *Adv. conc. Bills Exch.* Pref. A iij, A Notary Publick for Outland and Inland affairs. **1754** *Dict. Arts & Sc.* II. 1141 There is not.. any peculiar or proper money to be found in specie, whereon outland exchanges can be grounded. **1805** COLERIDGE *Sibyl. Leaves* II. 225 Vales and glens Native or out-land, lakes and famous hills. **1859** TENNYSON *Vivien* 712 Sir Valence wedded with an outland dame.

2. Outlying; lying without the precincts of an estate, a town, etc.

1791 J. LEARMONT *Poems* 261 May finer verdure busk ilk outland bent. **1887** *Jamieson's Sc. Dict.* Suppl., *Outland, Outlan*, outlying, lying.. out of or beyond the bounds of a burgh; as, 'outland burgesses'. **1900** E. V. B. *Sylvana's Letters* xxi. 179 In chosen peeps of outland country.

†**3.** Situated outside the mass of land (as formerly conceived): opposed to *inland*. *Obs. rare.*

1652 NEEDHAM tr. *Selden's Mare Cl.* 12 By the Sea, wee understand the whole Sea, as well the Main Ocean or Out-land Seas, as those which are within-land as the Mediterranean, Adriatic, Ægean.. and Baltick seas.

outlander (ˈaʊtləndə(r)). [Appears about 1600: perh. of Eng. formation, but prob. suggested by Du. *uitlander* (in Kilian *uutlander*), Ger. *ausländer*, and often virtually representing these words.] **a.** A man of foreign nationality; a foreigner, alien, stranger.

1598 FLORIO *Worlde of Wordes* 265/1 Pellegrino.. a stranger, an alien, an outlander, an outlandish man. **1605** VERSTEGAN *Dec. Intell.* 218 *Eltheodisc-men.* Aliens, outlanders, men borne in other countries. **1608** MIDDLETON *Trick to Catch Old One* v. ii, Chiefly dice, those true outlanders, That shake out beggars, thieves, and panders. **1612** AINSWORTH *Annot. Ps.* xviii. 45 Aliens, outlanders, strangers from the Commonwealth of Israel. **1668** WOOD *Life* 30 Dec. (O.H.S.) II. 148 Franc. Dryer (an outlander, borne at Breme) now a sojournour in Oxon. **1715** M. DAVIES *Athen. Brit.* I. 213 John de Coloribus, who by birth was an Out-lander, and by profession a Black-Fryar. **1848** LYTTON *Harold* III. iii, The outlanders rode through the streets with drawn swords. **1887** RIDER HAGGARD *A. Quatermain* 198 Thou art an outlander and therefore do I speak without shame. **1909** W. TUCKWELL *Pre-Tractarian Oxford* iii. 59 Unfortunate outlanders whose digestion of the dinner and relish of the port wine were spoiled by these animated dialectics, went away complaining that Oriel Common Room *stunk* of Logic. **1930** *Time & Tide* 20 Sept. 1167, I think, if it is not an impertinence for an outlander to make a suggestion, that England does need [etc.]. **1938** *Englische Studien* LXXII. 323 The printed page marks the outlander by the use of italics and preservation of the French accents. **1952** G. WILSON *Julien Ware* 117 But, having admitted this outlander to his home and table, Mr. Craig felt it necessary to talk for his education and profit. **1964** *Listener* 24 Sept. 453/2 Mr [Robert] Kennedy is of course Boston Irish... He lives in Virginia... He saw the beguiling prospect of a Senate seat in New York. This State now echoes.. with the cry of 'carpet-bagger' and 'outlander'. **1976** *Ibid.* 15 July 38/2 He tried to go to New York to the big law firms and they turned him down—he was an outlander from California. **1976** *Verbatim* Sept. 8/a In three essays on the phonology of Georgia place-names, Goff discusses local designations, recording divided usage,.. and clarifying accentuation when needed. Outlanders are given the preferred native pronunciations of *Albany* ('All' benny'), *Aragon* ('Arrow'gun' or 'Arrer'gun'), *Schley* ('Sly'), and *Taliaferro*/*Bolivar* (which make a perfect rhyme in Georgia).

b. In reference to South African politics, a rendering of Du. *uitlander*, as applied, before the war of 1899–1902, to aliens settled or sojourning in the South African Republic.

1892 *Pall Mall G.* 10 Oct. 3/3 At Johannesburg this National Union has been formed, comprising not only 'uitlanders' (outlanders) but Boers. **1896** *Daily Tel.* 1 Feb. 6/7 The racial antagonism between Boers and Outlanders. **1899** *Daily News* 24 Apr. 6/6 At the time of the restoration

to the Boers of their internal independence, 'outlanders' and others enjoyed equal rights.
attrib. **1899** *Westm. Gaz.* 25 Apr. 1/2 If this is so, we may indeed dry our eyes about Outlander grievances. **1899** *Daily News* 1 June 5/1 The Outlander population in the Transvaal.

†'outlanding, *ppl. a. Obs. rare.* Foreign.
1643 PRYNNE *Sov. Power Parlt.* Ded. A iv, An Army of English; Irish, Outlanding Papists.

outlandish (aʊt'lændɪʃ), *a.* [In OE. *útlęndisc*, f. *útland*, OUTLAND 1: see -ISH.]
1. a. Of or belonging to a foreign country; foreign, alien; not native or indigenous. Now *arch.*
c **1000** ÆLFRIC *Lev.* xxiv. 22 Si he landes man, si he utlendisc. *c* **1070** *O.E. Chron.* an. 1052 (MS. C) Hiȝ noldon þæt utlendiscum þeodum wære þes eard. *c* **1330** R. BRUNNE *Chron. Wace* (Rolls) 11127 Outlandische kynges þat of hym held. *c* **1374** CHAUCER *Former Age* 22 No Marchaunt yit ne fette owt-landissh ware. *c* **1425** *Found. St. Bartholomew's* (E.E.T.S.) 4 He supposid that God toke vengeawnce of hym for his synnys a-mongis owte-landisshe peple. **1535** COVERDALE *1 Kings* xi. 1 But kynge Salomon loued many outlandish wemen. **1606** DEKKER *Sev. Sinnes* v. (Arb.) 37 Cages, in which are all the strangest out-landish Birds. **1612** WOODALL *Surg. Mate* Wks. (1653) 364 The outlandish Angelica rootes are very good chewed in the mouth. *c* **1710** CELIA FIENNES *Diary* (1888) 125 Yᵉ mouldings..are of a sweete outlandish wood. **1861** CRAIK *Hist. Eng. Lit.* I. 482 Of all our great poets he [Spenser] is the one whose natural tastes were most opposed to such outlandish innovations upon..his native tongue.
b. *absol.* Foreign (language).
a **1626** BP. ANDREWES *Serm., Holy Ghost* (1661) 467 Now they can speak nothing but outlandish. **1752** FOOTE *Taste* II. i, He has got a black wig on, and speaks outlandish.
†c. ***outlandish man*** (sometimes written as one word), a foreigner. *Obs.*
1505 GALWAY ARCH. in *10th Rep. Hist. MSS. Comm.* App. v. 391 Annye oute landish man or enny of the enhabitantes. *a* **1661** FULLER *Worthies* IV. (1662) 12 Two eminent Out-landishmen. **1711** ADDISON *Spect.* No. 46 ¶4 He did not like the Name of the outlandish Man with the golden Clock in his Stockings. [**1868** FREEMAN *Norm. Conq.* II. ix. 327 To rivet the yoke of outlandish men about their necks.]
2. Foreign-looking, of foreign fashion; unfamiliar, strange; hence, odd, bizarre, uncouth. Also, immoderate, exceeding proper limits. (Partly arising from sense 3.)
1596 BABINGTON *Profit. Exp.* 166 We haue..trafiqued with an outlandish rouer called the deuill. **1628** PRYNNE *Love-lockes* 1 Sundry Antique, Horred and Out-landish shapes. **1749** FIELDING *Tom Jones* IV. x, A young woman..who was drest in one of your outlandish garments. **1820** W. IRVING *Sketch Bk.* I. 72 They were dressed in a quaint outlandish fashion. **1885** E. GARRETT (Mrs. Mayo) *At any Cost* ii. 34 You don't mean to tell me that those outlandish old things are still in actual use? **1955** *Times* 6 June 7/4 One or two [people]..will shatter the monotonous efficiency of the [refreshment drinks] machine with some outlandish demand for a highly individual brew. **1977** *Time* 10 Jan. 46/1 The outlandish cost of armaments—$25 million for an F-15 today, v. $4 million for a Phantom jet in 1970—along with the rising prices of other imports, pushed the inflation rate into the stratosphere.
3. Out-of-the-way, remote; far removed from civilization (now usually in a derogatory sense).
1792 J. BYNG *Torrington Diaries* (1936) III. 53 So in an *outlandish* place I must creep to bed and pray for summer. **1842** DICKENS *Let.* 16 Apr. (1974) III. 202 The inns in these outlandish corners of the world would astonish you by their goodness. **1869** BLACKMORE *Lorna D.* v, He resolved to settle in some outlandish part. **1881** TYLOR *Anthrop.* iv. 118 When outlandish people, such as Laplanders, have been brought to be exhibited in our great cities. **1887** T. HARDY *Woodlanders* I. viii. 151, I get dreadfully nervous sometimes, living in such an outlandish place.
4. Of or pertaining to the Outlanders or Uitlanders of South Africa.
1896 *Daily News* 4 Jan. 4/6 Protecting the independence of the country against being upset by an outlandish vote.
Hence **†out'landisher**, a foreigner. **out-'landishlike** *a.* and *adv.* **out'landishly** *adv.*, in an outlandish, foreign, or strange manner; strangely, oddly, uncouthly. **out'landishness**, the quality of being outlandish.
1593 NASHE *Lenten Stuffe* in *Harl. Misc.* (ed. Park) VI. 149 For ten weeks together this rabble rout of *outlandishers are billetted with her. *a* **1568** ASCHAM *Scholem.* II. (Arb.) 156 Hard composition and crooked framing of his wordes and sentences, as a man would say, English talke placed and framed *outlandish like. *a* **1577** GASCOIGNE *Deuice Masque* Poems 1869 I. 78 And why I goe outlandishe lyke, yet being Englishe borne. **1882** in *Chicago Advance* 21 Sept., They would be seized with some uncontrollable spirit to act *out-landishly. **1889** R. ASHE *Two Kings Uganda* (1890) 216 Two outlandishly dressed white men, who kept their fire on a large board which they ate off. **1611** COTGR., *Peregrinité*, strangenesse, *outlandishnesse, forrainenesse. **1833** M. SCOTT *Tom Cringle* xi. (1859) 235 The outlandishness of the fashion was not offensive.

†out'larged, *ppl. a. Obs.* [OUT- 11; after L. *dilātātus*.] Broadened, increased in width.
1382 WYCLIF *Deut.* xxxii. 15 Fulfattid, fulgresid, outlargid [1388 alargid, *Vulg.* dilatatus, 1611 covered with fatness].

outlarie, -ry, obs. forms of OUTLAWRY.

'outlash, *sb.* [OUT- 7.] The act of lashing out, a sudden quick outward stroke.
1876 GEO. ELIOT *Dan. Der.* iv, The outlash of a murderous thought and the sharp backward stroke of repentance. *Ibid.* xxx, But underneath the silence there was an outlash of hatred and vindictiveness.

†out'lash, *v. Obs.* [OUT- 14.] *intr.* To lash out: **a.** To break out into excess; to be extravagant, exaggerate, = OVERLASH *v.* **b.** To strike out violently.
1611 COTGR., *Bobancer*, to riot, squander, waste, outlash. **1614** SYLVESTER *Bethulia's Rescue* v. 536 Mocmur..with Waighty Waves..out-lashing every-way. Tears, overturns, and undermines, much worse Then when hee freely hath his native Course. **1619** W. WHATELY *God's Husb.* I. (1622) 104 If at any time some proue ranke hypocrites, he takes that as a warrant for his tongue to out-lash against all. **1620** BP. HALL *Hon. Mar. Clergy* III. v, Loe the man which, in a reckoning of 200 yeares, did out-lash but 150! **1650** FULLER *Pisgah* 415 They plead, that malice hath a wide mouth, and loves to outlash in her relations.
Hence **†outlashing** *vbl. sb.*, extravagance, excess.
1611 COTGR., *Desreiglemént*..immoderatenesse, immodestie, lauishnesse, outlashing. *Ibid., Irregularité*..vnrulinesse, disorder, outlashing.

outlast (aʊt'lɑːst, -æ-), *v.* [OUT- 17, 18.] *trans.* To last longer than or beyond; to exceed or surpass in duration; to survive.
1573 TUSSER *Husb.* (1878) 171 One bushell well brewed, outlasteth some twaine. *a* **1661** HOLYDAY *Juvenal* (1678) 236 Let him out-last Nestor's years, and out-vie Nero's riches. **1781** MAD. D'ARBLAY *Diary* 26 June, 'I do not..believe that any grief in the world ever outlasted a twelve-month'. **1893** HUXLEY in *Life* (1900) II. xxi. 367, I find myself outlasting those who started in life along with me.
Hence **out'lasting** *ppl. a.*, that outlasts, surviving.
1887 G. MEREDITH *Ballads & P.* 35 Never shall the wrestling cease Till with our outlasting Foe Roll we to the Godhead's feet.

outlaugh (aʊt'lɑːf, -æ-), *v.* [OUT- 18, 18 c, 14.]
†1. *trans.* To laugh down, deride, ridicule. *Obs.*
1477 NORTON *Ord. Alch.* Proem in Ashm. (1652) 7 And Common workemen will not be out-lafte. **1605** CAMDEN *Rem.* (1637) 362 The same Lucian bringeth in Diogenes laughing and outlaughing King Mausolus for that hee was so pittifully pressed and crushed with an huge heape of stones under his stately monument Mausoleum. *a* **1790** FRANKLIN (Webster, 1864), His apprehensions of being outlaughed will force him to continue in a restless obscurity.
2. To surpass or outdo in laughing.
1672 DRYDEN *Arviragus & Phil.* Prol. 17 Each lady striving to out-laugh the rest; To make it seem they understood the jest. **1908** SWINBURNE *Duke of Gandia* i. 32 Her..Whose eyes outlaugh the splendour of the sea.
3. *intr.* To laugh aloud. (Properly two words.)
1844 MRS. BROWNING *Brown Rosary* III. ix, Then outlaughed the bridegroom, and outlaughed withal Both maidens and youths by the old chapel-wall.

out-launch, etc.: see OUT-.

outlaw ('aʊtlɔː), *sb.* Forms: 1 útlaȝa, 1–4 utlaȝe, 3 útlahe, 3–4, 7 *Sc.* utlaw(e, (4 vte-, wtelau, -law), 4–5 outlagh(e, 4–7 outlawe, 4– outlaw, (4–5 owt(e)law(e, 5 outelawe, out-, owtlay). [Late OE. *útlaȝa*, definite form of *útlaȝ*, *útlah* adj. 'outlawed', used absolutely as sb.; a. ON. *útlagi* sb. from *útlagr* outlawed, banished; f. *út* out, out of + ON. **lagu*, *lög* (pl. of *lag*), OE. *laȝu*, LAW. Cf. these examples of the OE. adj.:—
c **924** *Laws of Edward & Guthrum* c. 6. §6 (Schmid) ȝif he man to deaðe ȝefylle, beo he þonne utlah. *a* **1016** *Laws of Æthelred* I. c. 1 §9 Beo se þeof utlah wið eall folc. *c* **1050** *O.E. Chron.* an. 1048 Ða cwæð man Sweȝen eorl utlah.]
1. a. One put outside the law and deprived of its benefits and protection; one under sentence of OUTLAWRY (q.v.).
c **1000** ÆLFRIC *Gram.* ix. (Z.) 70 *Hic et hæc exlex*, utlaȝa oððe butan æ. *a* **1023** WULFSTAN *Hom.* (1883) 296 He scel beon utlaȝa wið me. *c* **1205** LAY. 1121 Vtlaȝen [*c* **1275** vtlawes] hefden i-ræued þat lond. *a* **1300** *Cursor M.* 7686 (Cott.) Als he war vtelau [*v.rr.* vtelaw, outlagh, outlawe] sua wond he. **1377** LANGL. *P. Pl.* B. XVII. 102 For outlawes in þe wode and vnder banke lotyeth. *c* **1386** CHAUCER *Manciple's T.* 130. **1467** in *Eng. Gilds* (1870) 389 Mansleers ffelons Outlawes ravysshers of wymen. *a* **1548** HALL *Chron., Rich. III* 54 b, A compaigne of traytors, thefes, outlawes and ronneagates of our awne nacion. **1643** MILTON *Divorce* II. iii, Sure sin can have no tenure by law at all but is rather an eternall outlaw. **1718** *Free-thinker* No. 1 ¶5 The Outlaw has, of all Men, the least Pretensions to Liberty. **1821** BYRON *Two Fosc.* III. i, Their sire was a mere hunted outlaw. **1848** WHARTON *Law Lex.* s.v. *Outlawry*, The maxim applicable to outlaws is, 'Let them be answerable to all, and none to them'. Accordingly any person outlawed is *civiliter mortuus*.
b. More vaguely: One banished or proscribed; an exile, a fugitive. (In early use not distinguishable from the main sense.)
a **1225** *Ancr. R.* 54 þerefter of þen ilke weren..hire ueader & hire breðren, se noble princes alse heo weren, vtlawes imakede. *c* **1250** *Gen. & Ex.* 431 Caym fro him fleȝ, Wið wif and haȝte, and wurð ut-laȝe. **14..** *Nom.* in Wr.-Wülcker 694/26 *Hic, hec exul*, a nowtlay. **1530** PALSGR. 250/2 Outlawe, *banny.* **1568** GRAFTON *Chron.* I. 179 Some of the Lordes had sent for Edward the outlawe, sonne of Edmond Ironsyde for to be theyr king. **1596** SHAKS. *1 Hen. IV*, IV. iii. 58 A poore vnminded Out-law, sneaking home. **1788** GIBBON *Decl. & F.* I. (1846) V. 12 The posterity of the outlaw Ismael. **1875** JOWETT *Plato* (ed. 2) V. 341 At last necessity plainly compels him to be an outlaw from his native land.
c. One living in transgression of the law; a lawless person.
1880 J. F. CLARKE *Self-Culture* ix. 200 It is only for the outlaws, the dangerous classes..that we build prisons and establish courts. The law is for the lawless.
d. *fig.* A wild, untamed, or hunted beast.
1599 T. M[OUFET] *Silkwormes* 14 Of lions fierce (or if ought fiercer be, Amongst the heards of woody outlawes fell). **1890** 'R. BOLDREWOOD' *Col. Reformer* (1891) 219 They had mustered their own outlaws [wild lean savage cattle].
†2. a. Outlawry. **b.** Sentence or proclamation of outlawry. *Obs. rare.*
1581 MARBECK *Bk. of Notes* 810 Persecute..with banishment and out-lawe, prison..wrongfull iudgements. **1652** WADSWORTH tr. *Sandoval's Civ. Wars Spain* 115 Hee made publick Acts, Proclamations and Out-laws against the Segovians.
3. *Comb.* Also *attrib.* or quasi-*adj.*, esp. in **outlaw strike**, a withdrawal of labour without the authority of a trade union, an unofficial strike.
16.. *Ballad Robin Hood* in Furniv. *Percy Folio* I. 37 The worthy exploits he acted before Queen Katherine, he being an Out-lawman. **1903** *Wide World Mag.* Mar. 546/2 The whole Western country was scoured for the wildest and most vicious 'outlaw' bronchos that could be found. **1912** C. A. SIRINGO *Cowboy Detective* v. 87, I told him to trot out his outlaw horse. **1920** *Harvey's Weekly* 17 Apr. 5/2 The 'outlaw' railroad strikes..are unjustifiable. **1931** *Economist* 6 June 1215/2 Arbitration would consume a good many months at best, and would probably be followed by 'outlaw' strikes. **1937** *Times* 22 Nov. 21/3 On top of this disappointment came a fresh outbreak of 'outlaw' strikes in the motor industry. **1949** *N.Y. Times Bk. Rev.* 13 Mar. 22/4 His brother Billy was thrown by an outlaw bronco. **1977** *New Yorker* 6 June 90/2, I did bring in fifty of them outlaw steers that way once.

outlaw ('aʊt,lɔː), *v.* [Late OE. (*ȝe*)*útlaȝian*, f. *útlaȝ*, *útlaȝa*, OUTLAW *sb.*[1] Cf. ON. *útlegja* and *útlægja* to banish.]
1. *trans.* To put outside the law; to proscribe; †to exile, banish; to deprive of the benefit and protection of law; to declare an outlaw, to inflict OUTLAWRY upon (a person), in a criminal prosecution or civil action.
10.. *O.E. Chron.* an. 1014 (MS. E) And æfre ælcne Denisce cyning utlaȝede [*MS. C.* utlah] of Englalande ȝecwædon. *Ibid.* an. 1055 Utlaȝode [*MS. C.* ȝeutlaȝode] mann Ælfgar eorl. *c* **1290** *S. Eng. Leg.* I. 404/79 þe furste ȝer þat seint Iohan þus i-outlawed was. *c* **1330** R. BRUNNE *Chron.* (1810) 33 He..was outlawed for a felonie. **1382** WYCLIF *Baruch* iii. 19 Thei ben outlawid [1388 distried] and to helle thei wente doun. **1430–1** *Rolls of Parlt.* IV. 377/2 Unto the tyme the same Owen..was utlawed. **1432–50** tr. *Higden* (Rolls) I. 319 Patmos..þere Seynt Iohan þe Euangeliste was, whan he was outlawed oute of oþ er londes. *c* **1440** *Promp. Parv.* 375/2 Outlawyn, *utlego, extermino.* **1552** HULOET, Outlaw, *exulo, proscribo, relego.* *a* **1577** SIR T. SMITH *Commw. Eng.* II. xiv. (1609) 61 The Clarke of the Exigents is to frame all manner of Processes of *Exigi facias*, which doe issue out of that Court to out-law any man, and to record the outlawrie. **1679–88** *Secr. Serv. Money Chas. & Jas.* (Camden) 109 To be..paid over to several tradesmen, creditors of Mrs. Ellen Gwynne, in satisfaction of their debts, for which the said Ellen stood outlawed £729 2*s.* 3*d.* **1836–48** H. COLERIDGE *North. Worthies* (1852) I. 63 One Blood, outlawed for an attempt to take Dublin Castle,..some months ago seized the crown and sceptre in the Tower. **1875** W. MCILWRAITH *Guide Wigtownshire* 76 McDowall had fallen behind in the payment of certain Crown dues, and was outlawed.
b. *transf.* and *fig.*
c **1380** WYCLIF. *Wks.* (1880) 109 Anticrist wolde quenche & owtlaue holy writt. —— *Sel. Wks.* III. 383 Charite is outelawed amonge hom. *a* **1716** SOUTH *Serm.* (J.), A drunkard is outlawed from all worthy and creditable converse.
2. To deprive of legal force. Now only in U.S.: see quot. 1864.
1647 WARD *Simp. Cobler* 18 He will out-law the Law, quite out of the word and world. *a* **1661** FULLER *Worthies* (1840) II. 490 Perceiving that our English common law was outlawed in those parts. **1864** WEBSTER, *Outlaw* 2 To remove from legal jurisdiction or enforcement, as to *outlaw* a debt or claim.
b. *intr.* for *refl.*
1895 'MARK TWAIN' in *Westm. Gaz.* 9 Sept. 8/1 Honour is a harder master than the law. It cannot compromise for less than an hundred cents on the dollar, and its debts never outlaw.

outlawed ('aʊtlɔːd), *ppl. a.* [f. OUTLAW *v.* + -ED[1].] **a.** Put outside the law, declared an outlaw; proscribed, banished, exiled. Also *absol.* as *sb.*
1483 *Cath. Angl.* 264/1 Outelawyde, *religatus, proscriptus.* **1590** SWINBURNE *Testaments* 58 An outlawed person looseth his goods and benefite of the lawe. **1646** BP. MAXWELL *Burd. Issach.* in *Phenix* (1708) II. 299 The Out-lawed's Estate movable (Chattels we call it) become proper to the King. **1772** *Ann. Reg.* 49/1 A small violation of territorial right, in the pursuit of an outlawed smuggler and murderer. **1862** MISS YONGE *Wars of Wapsburg* (1864) 24 Born and bred to an outlawed life.
b. That has been allowed to run wild. *U.S.*
1907 C. E. MULFORD *Bar-20* xx. 197 Yu has got about as much show catchin' one of them as a tenderfoot has of bustin' an outlawed cayuse.

†'outlawing, *vbl. sb. Obs.* [f. as prec. + -ING[1].] The action of the vb. OUTLAW; outlawry.
1387 TREVISA *Higden* (Rolls) II. 219 Man..fel out of hiȝe in to lowh..out of his owne loude and contray in to outlawynge. **1579–80** NORTH *Plutarch* (1656) 728 The greatest

..difference that fell out between them, was about the outlawing of Cicero.

outlawry ('aʊtlɔːrɪ). Forms: α. [4 utlagarie], (6 utlagery, 7–8 -arie), 5–6 outlagarie, -are, -ary. β. 4–7 utlarie, -ary(e, outlarie, 5 owte-, 7 outlary. γ. 4–7 outlaw(e)rie, 4– outlawry, (5 oute-, owt-, -laury(e, 5–6 outlawery(e, 6 -lawrye, 8 -laury). [Anglicised repr. of AFr. *utlagerie, utlarie*, med. (Anglo-)L. *utlagaria, utlaria* (*Laws of Wm. I*, II. c. 3), f. OE. *útlaga* (also Anglo-L.), *útlah* + Romanic suffix *-aria*, F. *-erie*. Early legal use had forms identical with AFr.; but forms with *outlaw-*, conformed to the contemporary Eng. word also occur from 14th c.]

1. a. The action of putting a person out of the protection of the law, or the legal process by which a person is or was proclaimed or made an outlaw; the condition of one so outlawed. †In early use, often = exile, banishment.

'Outlawry, at first a declaration of war by the commonwealth against an offending member, [gradually] became a regular means of compelling submission to the authority of the courts, as in form it continued to be down to modern times'. 'Before the Conquest, outlawry involved not only forfeiture of goods to the king, but liability to be killed with impunity'. In the 13th c. 'outlawry loses some of its gravity; instead of being a substantive punishment, it becomes mere "criminal process", a means of compelling accused persons to stand their trial'. (Pollock & Maitland, *Hist. Eng. Law* I. 27, 459.) In the 14th c. the process was extended from cases of felony to misdemeanours and civil actions, so as to be a punishment for contempt of court in not appearing to answer an indictment or defend a personal action, or for disobedience to a judgement of the court. Outlawry for debt was frequent down to the 18th c. Along with this extension of the process, its conditions and consequence underwent continuous mitigation; in later times, in civil actions, it was reduced to the fact that the outlawed person was incapacitated from prosecuting an action for his own benefit, though he might still defend himself.

Clandestine Outlawries. In civil proceedings, outlawry has long been obsolete, and was formally abolished by the Civil Procedure Acts Repeal Act of 1879 (42 & 43 Vict. c. 59). While it was in use, great injustice was often done in consequence of the insufficiency of the machinery for giving public notice of the fact that a defendant in a personal action had, as a result of civil process, been made an outlaw. In 1588–9, Act 31 Eliz. c. 3 was passed 'for the auoyding of secret Outlawries in Actions Personall against the Queenes Subiects'. This being subsequently considered insufficient, amending measures were introduced; and one such bill has had the singular fortune to become the formal instrument of asserting the right of Parliament to proceed to business without reference to the immediate cause of summons, by being introduced and read a first time as the first business of every session, before the reading of the King's or Queen's Speech. This precaution goes back to early times, being referred to as an established practice in 1603. Formerly some one bill was used for the purpose on each occasion; but since 1 Dec. 1743, the means uniformly employed has been a Bill 'for the more effectual preventing Clandestine Outlawries in personal actions'; and this is still annually introduced, although the outlawries against which it is directed have long disappeared.

α. [*a* **1250** *Laws of Will. I*, II. c. 3 (Schmid) De omnibus utlariae rebus [*v.r.* utlagariae]... Et si Anglicus appellet Francigenam de utlagaria. **1292** BRITTON I. xiii. §3 Femme neqedent ne peut estre utlagé proprement..mes weyvé, qe vaut utlagerie. **1312** *Rolls of Parlt.* I. 284 Les Utlagaries & les Presentementz de ces faitz.] **1440** *Paston Lett.* I. 41 Be the vertue of qwch outlagare, all maner of chattell to the seide John Lyston apperteynyng, arn acruwyd on to the Kyng. **1540** *Act 32 Hen. VIII*, c. 49 All outlagaries promulged or had vpon or agaynst any person or persons. **1642** tr. *Perkins' Prof. Bk.* i. §27. 12 Attainder of Felony.. by utlagery, by verdict and by confession.

β. [*a* **1250** Utlariae [see α]. **1334** *Rolls of Parlt.* II. 74/2 L'avant dit Outlarie fait en la Counte de Kermerdin.] **1432–50** tr. *Higden* (Rolls) VII. 235 The owtelary of Robert arche-bischop of Cawnterbery. **1447** *Rolls of Parlt.* V. 138/2 That the Exigend and Utlarie, and every of them, be hold for none and voyde. **1530–1** *Act 22 Hen. VIII*, c. 15 Excepted always..all vtlaries of high treasons, and of al maner of felonies. **1601** SHAKS. *Jul. C.* IV. iii. 173 That by proscription, and billes of Outlarie, Octauius, Antony, and Lepidus, Haue put to death, an hundred Senators. **1658** CLEVELAND *Rustick Rampant* Wks. (1687) 451 Every Outlary, or Outlaries, if any against them..are or shall be published. **1671** F. PHILLIPS *Reg. Necess.* 250 They may be sued to an Utlary.

γ. **1382** WYCLIF *Rev.* Prol., He was holdun in outlawerie of Domycian, in the ile of Patmos. **1439** *Rolls of Parlt.* V. 17/2 All Outlaweries uppon hym pronowncd. **1503–4** *Act 19 Hen. VII*, c. 35 §1 Outlaweryes..utterly voyd anyntesed adnulled repelled and of no force. **1601** HOLLAND *Pliny* I. 179 He was noted and thought hardly of for those outlawries of Roman citisens. **1686** *Royal Proclam.* 10 Mar. in *Lond. Gaz.* No. 2120/4 And that this Our Pardon be not allowed to Discharge any Outlawry after Judgment, till Satisfaction or Agreement be made to or with the Party at whose Suit the Utlary was obtained. **1766** BLACKSTONE *Comm.* II. xxxii. 499 Outlaws also, though it be but for debt, are incapable of making a will, so long as the outlawry subsists, for their goods and chattels are forfeited during that time. **1792** BURKE *Let. to R. Burke* Corr. 1844 III. 378 The Castle has another system, and considers the out-lawry..of the great mass of the people as an unalterable maxim in the government of Ireland. **1867** FREEMAN *Norm. Conq.* I. vi. 561 *note*, Godwine, on his outlawry, was allowed five days to leave the country. **1883** *Wharton's Law Lex.* (ed. 7) s.v. *Outlawry*. In criminal proceedings it is but little used, but is formally kept alive by 33 & 34 Vict. c. 23. which act.. expressly provides that nothing therein shall affect the law of forfeiture consequent on outlawry. **1899** *Westm. Gaz.* 9 Feb. 2/3 What is a clandestine outlawry, and why should the Leader of the House of Commons have introduced a Bill for its 'more effectual preventing' as the very first Ministerial measure of the Session? Is there..a single member of the House of Commons..who knows..any details concerning the provisions of the Outlawries Bill?

fig. **1833** L. RITCHIE *Wand. by Loire* 161 Faces on which a long course of violence and crime had stamped the outlawry of nature. **1835** I. TAYLOR *Spir. Despot.* iii. 68 On the same ground of outlawry from common sense and scriptural authority. **1855** MILMAN *Lat. Chr.* IX. viii. (1864) V. 408 This papal manifesto broadly asserted the civil as well as religious outlawry of all heretics. **1924** KELLOR & HATVANY (*title*) Security against war... Vol. II. Arbitration. Disarmament. Outlawry. **1946** *Rep. Internat. Control Atomic Energy* (U.S. Dept. of State) I. 4 We..studied..the factors..involved in an international inspection system supposed to determine whether the activities of individual nations constituted evasions or violations of international outlawry of atomic weapons. **1964** *New Statesman* 1 May 682/2 When Baldwin writes about homosexuals he writes with a Negro's sense of another 'outlawry'.

b. Of a debt or claim: The fact of being outlawed or statute-barred: see OUTLAW *v.* 2. *U.S.*

1890 in *Century Dict.*

2. Disregard or defiance of the law.

1869 RUSKIN *Q. of Air* §141 [They] follow, in so far as they are good, one constant law..and in so far as they are evil, are evil by outlawry. **1873** T. W. HIGGINSON *Oldport Days* x. 249 Civilization is tiresome and enfeebling, unless we occasionally give it the relish of a little outlawry.

†3. Outlaws collectively. *Obs.*

1557 NORTH *Gueuara's Diall Pr.* 74 The exiles and outlawries were called againe. **1894** CROCKETT *Raiders* 98 The hill outlawry could a' catch us or ever we wan twa mile.

outlay ('aʊtleɪ), *sb.* [OUT- 7.]

I. 1. The act or fact of laying out or expending; expenditure (of money upon something).

Orig. a Sc. and dial. word; still considered dialectal by Forby 1825; given in Webster 1828.

1798 *Statist. Acc. Scot., Perthshire* XX. 437 It is one which accumulates yearly in value, without an yearly out-lay of expence. **1816** SCOTT *Antiq.* xiii, Sir Arthur himself made great outlay. **1825** BROCKETT *N.C. Gloss.*, *Outlay*, expenditure. **1825–30** *Forby's Voc. E. Anglia* s.v., I made a great outlay before I brought my farm into profit. (Lowland Scotch, Brockett's Gloss.). **1828** WEBSTER. *Outlay*, a laying out or expending, expenditure. **1832** HT. MARTINEAU *Hill & Valley* iv. 61 Observing what comes of such an out-lay of capital. **1855** MACAULAY *Hist. Eng.* xix. IV. 319 The income of the state still fell short of the outlay by about a million. **1879** ROGERS in *Cassell's Techn. Educ.* IV. 67/2 After the first outlay, the demand of the public finds the means for paying the wages.

II. 2. In various obs. or dial. senses.

†a. ? An outlying thing. *Sc. Obs.* **†b.** A place of lying out; an outlying or out-of-the-way lair: see LAY *sb.*[7] 2. **c.** *Coal-mining.* 'The height to which the top of a winning pit is raised above the surface of the ground: commonly called the *outset*' (Heslop *Northumb. Gloss.*).

1563 WINȜET *Wks.* (1890) II. 61 Quhat is prophane? Quhilk hes na halines, na godlines, strange and plane out-lay fra the inwart chalmer of the Kirk, quhilk is the temple of God. **1611** BEAUM. & FL. *Philaster* II. iv, I know her and her haunts, Her layes, leaps, and out layes. **1881** *Borings* 79 (in Heslop) Outlay from the swarth five feet, metal from the swarth four feet.

outlay (aʊt'leɪ), *v.* [OUT- 15.]

1. *trans.* To lay out; to spread out, expose, display. Now *rare* or *poetic*.

1555 W. WATREMAN *Fardle Facions* II. viii. 181 No heare died, no lockes outelaied, no face painted. **1573** KILLIGREW *Let. to Burghley* 17 May in Tytler *Hist. Scot.* (1864) III. 360, I trust..that after the battery shall be outlaid..the matter will be at a point. **1622** DRAYTON *Poly-olb.* xxvii. 133 Where Pellin's mighty Mosse, and Mertons, on her sides Their boggy breasts out lay. **1820** BYRON *Morg. Mag.* I. xxxiv, Thou thought'st me doubtless for the bier outlaid.

†2. To set forth. *Obs.*

1567 DRANT *Horace, Ep.* II. i. G iv, Their pendaunte lockes encompasde rounde, and verses they outlay [HORACE *Epist.* II. i. 110 Carmina dictant].

3. To lay out (money), expend; make outlay of.

1802 FINDLATER *Agric. Surv. Peebles* 38 The proprietor pays all the outlayed money for materials and wages of workmen. **1814** SCOTT *Wav.* vi, The expenditure which he had outlayed. **1862** CHANNING in Salt *Thoreau* (1890) 258 No labor was too onerous, no material too costly, if outlaid on the right enterprise. **1886** *Sat. Rev.* 19 June 839 Money which might be more profitably outlaid.

outlayer: see OUTLIGGER[1] and OUT-.

†out-'lead, *v. Obs.* [OUT- 15.] *trans.* To lead or bring out. (Properly two words.)

a **1300** *E.E. Psalter* lxvii. 7 [lxviii. 6] Þat oute ledes bonden in wa. **1382** WYCLIF *Ps.* xxx. 5 [xxxi. 4] Thou shalt ful out lede me fro this grene [1388 lede out, Vulg. *educes*]. **1471** RIPLEY *Comp. Alch.* VI. xiii. in Ashm. (1652) 164 Fyrst yt outeledyth, and after bryngyth yt yn.

out-leaf, -lean, etc.: see OUT-.

'outleap, *sb.* [OUT- 7.] An act of leaping or springing out; an escape, sally, or excursion; an outburst. *lit.* and *fig.*

c **1250** *Gloss. Law Terms* in *Rel. Ant.* I. 33 Utleph, *Eschapement de prisum.* **1555** W. WATREMAN *Fardle Facions* I. iv. 48 The people..are called Maures, or Moores, as I thincke of their outleapes and wide rowming. **1631** J. BURGES *Answ. Rejoined* Pref. 28 [His] words are set downe punctually, yea euen his out-leapes and digressions. **1692** LOCKE *Educ.* §97 Youth must have some Liberty, some Outleaps. **1863** GEO. ELIOT *Romola* xxxiv, The outleap of fury in the dagger-thrust. *a* **1878** LEWES *Stud. Psychol.* (1879) 147 An immediate outleap of heroic generosity.

†b. A place to which excursions are made. *Obs.*

a **1652** BROME *New Acad.* II. i, When shall we walk to Totnam?..or take Coach to Kensington Or Padington? or to some one or other O' th' City out-leaps for an afternoon?

out'leap, *v.* [OUT- 17, 18, 14.]

1. *trans.* To leap over or beyond. Also *fig.*

1600 ROWLANDS *Lett. Humours Blood* vi. 78 T'out leape mens heades, and caper ore the table. **1897** *Home Messenger* Nov. 173 A world that outleaps all measurement and outruns all duration.

2. To surpass or excel in leaping.

1629 GAULE *Holy Madn.* 166 A lion will outstand a man.. a stagge out-leap him. **1700** WALLIS in *Collect.* (O.H.S.) I. 318 Who did..out-leap..the next-best leaper..by seven inches. **1854** OWEN *Skel. & Teeth* in *Circ. Sc., Organ. Nat.* I. 198 The serpent has no limbs, yet it can..outleap the jerboa.

3. *intr.* To leap out or forth. (*poet.*)

1850 BLACKIE *Æschylus* I. 49 Outleapt a birth Of strong shield-bearers from the fateful horse. **1874** HOLLAND *Mistr. Manse* xvi. 65 Outleaping from the mesh Of memory's net, like bird or bee.

Hence **out'leaping**, *vbl. sb.* and *ppl. a.*, leaping out.

1878 J. TODHUNTER *Alcestis* (1879) 56 Done so simply, In such a frank outleaping of the soul. **1868** GEO. ELIOT *Sp. Gypsy* v. 359 Escaping subtly in outleaping thought.

out'learn, *v.* [OUT- 15, 18, 17.]

†1. *trans.* To find out, learn from others, elicit.

1596 SPENSER *F.Q.* IV. viii. 22 When as nought according to his mind He could out-learne, he them [etc.].

2. To outstrip in learning.

1632 SHERWOOD, To out-learne his fellowes, *apprendre plus que ses compagnons.* **1727** in BAILEY vol. II. **1890** *Pall Mall G.* 2 Sept. 1/3 We were the pupils then, who outlearnt our masters... Will they, in turn, outlearn us?

3. To get beyond the learning or study of.

18.. EMERSON (Webster, 1890) Men and gods have not outlearned it [love].

outleger, variant of OUTLIGGER[1]. *Obs.*

out-length, -lengthen: see OUT-.

'outler. *Sc.* and *north. dial.* [perh. from *outlier.*] An animal that is not housed during the night or winter; *fig.* a person out of work or out of office. Also *attrib.*

1785 BURNS *Halloween* xxvi, The Deil, or else an outler Quey, Gat up an' gae a croon. **1791** LEARMONT *Poems* 160 At length the Outlers grew sae mad Against ilk Inler purse-proud blade. **1826** GRAHAM *Moorland Dial.* 8 (E.D.D.) Sin last our outler nowt was fother'd.

outlet ('aʊtlɪt), *sb.* [OUT- 7.]

1. a. A place or opening at which anything is let out or escapes, or by which exit is possible; a means of issue; a channel of egress or discharge; a vent; a passage or way out, an exit; *spec.* a shop, a retail store; an institution disposing of the produce of a manufacturer; a market (for goods).

a **1250** *Owl & Night.* 1754 He wuneth at Porteshom, At one tune ine Dorsete Bi thare see in ore ut-lete [= By the sea in an outlet]. **1600** HAKLUYT *Voy.* (1810) III. 482 We were alwaies in good hope to find some out-let into the maine Ocean. **1635** PAGITT *Christianogr.* 35 That great Promontory, whose base lying between the out-lets of the River Indus and Ganges stretcheth [etc.]. **1655** FULLER *Ch. Hist.* II. vi. §43 Like the Caspian Sea, receiving all, and having no Out-let. **1727** H. HERBERT tr. *Fleury's Eccl. Hist.* I. 128 John..was master of the out-lets of the Temple. **1845** BUDD *Dis. Liver* 89 The abscess, if large, may discharge through more outlets than one. **1919** *Brit. Manufacturer* Nov. 28/1 India..is the most important outlet for British goods. **1933** [see CONSUMER 2 c]. **1962** *Daily Tel.* 29 May 12/2 The Six are reluctant to guarantee 'comparable outlets' in advance. **1964** *New Society* 27 Feb. 20/2 The shopper.. has a choice between self-service and counter-service, and.. between the supermarket and smaller self-service... Given this rather bewildering variety of 'outlets' for groceries it is of interest to consider why any housewife should choose one shop rather than another. **1966** *Listener* 17 Mar. 376/1 One may hope that the stimulus given by National Library Week will..lead to a permanent improvement in the outlets for the distribution of reading matter. **1975** *Sci. Amer.* Oct. 122/3 Both the motor and its companion controller are available from W. W. Grainger, Inc., an electrical-supply firm with retail outlets in all major U.S. cities. **1976** *National Observer* (U.S.) 27 Nov. 8/2 Yet Moldafsky and Bird are outlet experts. Each has more than 10 years' experience in outlet shopping, and both have researched and written guide books to outlet stores.

b. *transf.* and *fig.* A way out of a difficulty; a means of escape, relief, or discharge, a 'vent'.

1625 BACON *Ess., Seditions* (Arb.) 411 In such manner, as no Euill shall appeare so peremptory, but that it hath some Out-let of Hope. **1667** FLAVEL *Saint Indeed* (1754) 61 Prayer is the best outlet to fear. **1873** HAMERTON *Intell. L.* XI. v. 427 An energetic nature seeking an outlet for energy. **1916** JOYCE *Portrait of Artist* (1969) ii. 64 The ambition which he felt astir at times in the darkness of his soul sought no outlet. **1928** E. O'NEILL *Strange Interlude* I. ii. 67 She's got to find normal outlets for her craving for sacrifice. **1938** 'G. GRAHAM' *Swiss Sonata* 260 You think Mlle Lemaitre and the average wife are doing the same thing; in different ways each one is seeking an outlet. **1978** E. HEALEY *Lady Unknown* iv. 138 Dickens..needed..an outlet for that driving energy.

†c. *fig.* Issue. *Obs.*

1710 HENRY *On Ps.* lxvi. 12 How glorious the issue was at last..for (1)..The outlet of the trouble is happy.

d. *Anat.* The opening of a cavity of the body formed by the skeleton; used orig. of the pelvis and later of the thorax. Opp. INLET *sb.* 5.

1797 J. BELL *Anat. Bones, Muscles & Joints* I. v. 140 The outlet of the pelvis is the lower circle again, composed by the arch of the pubis and by the sciatic ligaments. **1828, 1906** [see INLET *sb.* 5]. **1960** E. GARDNER et al. *Anat.* xxix. 339/1 The thoracic cavity communicates with the abdomen by the inferior thoracic aperture, or thoracic outlet, which is closed by the diaphragm. **1974** PASSMORE & ROBSON *Compan. Med. Stud.* III. II. xliii. 2/1 There are two areas which present the greatest potential mechanical obstruction to descent to the fetus, the pelvic brim and the effective bony outlet at the level of the ischial spines.

e. = POINT *sb.*[1] A. 19 e.

1892 E. A. MERRILL *Electr. Lighting Specifications* 77 The building shall be wired to —— lamp outlets, —— switch outlets... At each outlet the loose wire shall be neatly coiled and the ends carefully taped. **1917** A. L. COOK *Interior Wiring* III. 213 Wherever there is an outlet, such as a lighting fixture or a switch. **1925** G. A. WILLOUGHBY *House Wiring* i. 68 Some local ordinances require the number of watts to be counted for each type of outlet in various rooms. **1958** M. DICKENS *Man Overboard* iv. 54 There was only one electric outlet from which a multiple plug sent fraying wires in all directions. **1968** PASCHKIS & RYDER *Direct Analog Computers* xxvi. 377 A second board is provided having male plugs fitting the female outlets on the board. **1972** C. L. COOPER in W. King *Black Short Story Anthol.* 221 He set it [*sc.* a tape recorder] down next to an..easy chair, unlatched the top, and plugged the cord into one of the wall outlets.

2. a. A place into which anything is let out; *spec.* a pasture into which cattle are let out. **b.** A field, yard, or other enclosure attached to a house.

1752 J. MACSPARRAN *America Dissected* (1753) 13 They will..raise great Quantities of neat Cattle, as the Climate is benign, and their Outlets or Commonages large. **1793–1813** *Rep. Agric.* 33 in Marshall *Review* (1818) II. 39 (E.D.D.) After the cows have been turned into the outlet. **1884** *Chesh. Gloss., Boozing Field,*..the pasture which is contiguous to the *booses*, where the cows are tied up, and which is retained by an outgoing tenant as an outlet for his cattle.

†**3. a.** The outlying parts, the exterior parts; the environs of a town. **b.** The suburban streets or roads passing into the country. *Obs.*

1583 GOLDING *Calvin on Deut.* lix. 356 We see but the outleets (that is to say) the outermost partes of Godes Woorkes. **1762** GOLDSM. *Cit. W.* lv, A dismal-looking house in the outlets of the town. **1771** MRS. GRIFFITH *Hist. Lady Barton* I. 101, I hear the outlets about Dublin are delightful; you will be unpardonable if you don't visit them all.

4. The action of letting out or discharging; discharge, escape by outflow. *lit.* and *fig.*

1640 BP. REYNOLDS *Passions* xi. 109 Melted away, and wasted by an extreame out-let of Love. **1870** SPURGEON *Treas. Dav.* Ps. xxxix. 2 A flood gathering in force and foaming for outlet.

5. *attrib.* and *Comb.* as (sense 1 a), ***outlet-pipe*** etc.; (sense 1 b) ***outlet mechanism***; (sense 1 d) **outlet box**, a box used to contain connections to wires where they are led out of conduits.

1854 RONALDS & RICHARDSON *Chem. Technol.* I. 159 Hot-air pipes enclosed in an oven on a level with the outlet-pipe. **1898** *Daily News* 25 May 5/1 The fine subway under Shaftesbury-avenue, the outlet grating of which is visible at Piccadilly-circus. **1906** N. HARRISON *Electric Wiring* vi. 133 With all metallic conduits whether flexible or not there are employed junction and outlet boxes. **1949** KOESTLER *Insight & Outlook* v. 69 In the gradually emerging sense of humour, we have a further outlet mechanism. **1971** W. N. ALERICH *Electr. Construction Wiring* v. 92/1 An outlet box or the equivalent must be inserted at every point in the system where access to enclosed wires is necessary.

out'let, *v. Obs.* or *rare.* [OUT- 15.] *trans.* To let out, give egress to, pour forth.

1592 DAVIES *Immort. Soul* XXXII. xxxiv, Like Buckets bottomless, which all out-let. **1627–47** FELTHAM *Resolves* I. vii. (1677) 8 Nor ought that blood to be accounted lost, which is out-letted for a noble Master. **1851** MAYHEW *Lond. Labour* (1861) II. 406/2 The sewage..which is 'outletted' (as I heard a flusherman call it) into the Thames.

'out-ˌlet, *ppl. a.* [OUT- 11.] Let out, allowed to go out.

1601 DANIEL *Civ. Wars* VII. lvii, And, from thence, labour to bring-in againe The out-let will of disobediencie.

'out-ˌletting, *vbl. sb.* [OUT- 9.] The action of letting out or pouring forth. Chiefly *fig.*

1659 A. HAY *Diary* (S.H.S. 1900) 185 She and I withdrew and prayed together, wher the Lord allowed me much out-letting. **1676** ROW *Contn. Blair's Autobiog.* viii. (1848) 113 Gradual outlettings of gospel grace. **1818** *Q. Rev.* XVIII. 537 It had been born in upon his mind, during several great out-lettings of the spirit.

outlicar, -licker, var. OUTLIGGER[1], outrigger.

out'lie, *v.*[1] *rare.* [f. OUT- 14, 17 + LIE *v.*[1]]

1. *intr.* To lie out in the open air; to camp out.

1826 J. F. COOPER *Mohicans* xviii, We are not about to start on a squirrel hunt..but to outlie for days and nights, and to stretch across a wilderness.

2. *intr.* To lie stretched out, to extend.

1876 BROWNING *Pisgah-Sights* I. i, How I see all of it, Life there, outlying.

3. *trans.* To lie beyond or on the outside of.

1873 *Gentl. Mag.* Oct. 383 The forests that outlay the broad lagoons of the river. **1882** BURTON & CAMERON *Gold Coast for Gold* (1883) I. i. 15 Next morning showed us to port the Cone of Maritimo: it outlies Marsala.

out'lie, *v.*[2] [f. OUT- 18 + LIE *v.*[2]] *trans.* To outdo in lying.

1597 DONNE *Sat.* iv. 47 In which he can..outlie either Jovius or Surius, or both together. **1653** GATAKER *Vind. Annot. Jer.* 109 He doth in them out-ly..the Devil himself the Father of lies. **1740** GARRICK *Lying Valet* I. ii, To.. deceive his mistress, outlie her chamber-maid, and yet be paid for thy honesty! **1855** MACAULAY *Hist. Eng.* xviii. IV. 144 He had now, they said, outlied himself.

'outˌlier. [OUT- 8.]

1. a. One who lies (*i.e.* sleeps or lodges) out, i.e. in the open air, or away from a place with which he is connected by business or otherwise.

1676 D'URFEY *Mad. Fickle* II. i. (1677) 11 Out-liers, comers, and goers. **1705** STANHOPE *Paraphr.* III. 201 He dispatches another Message to the Highways and Hedges, to fetch in all the Outlyers. *a* **1742** BENTLEY *Lett.* 59 (R.) The party..sent messengers to all their outliers within twenty miles of Cambridge to come to their election. **1866** *N. & Q.* 19 May 421/1 Outliers are soldiers (generally married men) who, when there is not sufficient barrack accommodation, receive an allowance..and provide themselves with lodgings.

b. One that lies outside the pale, an outsider.

1690 D'URFEY *Collin's Walk* A vij b, Every worthy and true English Protestant of the Establish'd Church (for I have no hopes of the Outlyers). **1826** LAMB *Lett., to Bernard Barton* 147, I do not know how friends will relish it, but we outlyers, honorary friends, like it very well.

c. An animal that lies outside the house, fold, or park; esp. an outlying deer.

a **1658** CLEVELAND *Gen. Poems* etc. (1677) 157 It is but Trifling sport for you to pull down an Out-lyer, unless you leap the Pale and let slip at the Herd. **1892** AINSLIE *Land of Burns* 37 (E.D.D.) It wauken'd burdies frae the bough, An' outlyers frae their lair. **1939** JOYCE *Finnegans Wake* 97 From his holt..the outlier, a white noelan.., led bayers the run. **1976** *Abingdon Herald* 25 Nov. 7/2 Another outlier found near Sparsholt went through Sparsholt Copse, across to the Spinneys again, and back to Westcot. **1977** *Field* 13 Jan. 52/1 Hounds found an outlier at the back of Alexton village and hunted him past the hall.

2. a. 'A stone not taken from a quarry, but lying out in the field in a detached state' (Jam.); a boulder. Also †**outlair.** *Sc.*

1610 *Burgh Rec. Aberdeen* (Spalding Club) II. 300 The keaping stane to be of outlairis, frie wark, and boulted with irne. **1807** J. HALL *Trav. Scot.* II. 333 There is, in the parish of Ordiquhill, a large outlier of lime stone some tons weight, and no lime-rock to be found near it. **1846** WRIGHT *Ess. Mid. Ages* II. xvii. 210 On a black moor called Monstone Edge, is a huge moor-stone or outlier. **1955** A. THOM in *Jrnl. R. Statistical Soc.* A. CXVIII. 275 Many of the circles have one or more outliers, i.e. single upright stones outside the ring. *Ibid.* 283 Why not also include *Little Meg* as an outlier to the circle at *Long Meg and her Daughters*?

b. *Geol.* A portion or mass of a geological formation lying *in situ* at a distance from the main body to which it originally belonged, the intervening part having been removed by denudation.

1833 LYELL *Princ. Geol.* III. Gloss. 76 When a portion of a stratum occurs at some distance detached from the general mass..some practical mineral surveyors call it an outlier, and the term is adopted in geological language. **1854** H. MILLER *Sch. & Schm.* viii. (1857) 160 There lies in the Firth beyond, an outlier of the Lias. **1889** CROLL *Stellar Evolution* 55 Occasional outliers of conglomerate on the Highland side of the fault.

c. *generally.* An outlying portion or member of anything, detached from the main mass, body, or system to which it belongs. Also *attrib.*

1849 RUSKIN *Sev. Lamps* ii. 54 Interrupted..by great mountain outliers, isolated or branching from the central chain. **1854** R. G. LATHAM *Races of Russia* 39 Outlyers from the neighbouring Government of Esthonia. **1881** G. ALLEN *Vignettes fr. Natures, Fall of the Year*, Australia remains an isolated outlier of Asia to the present day. **1885** R. F. BURTON tr. *Arabian Nights' Entertainments* V. 177 They took leave of him and departing to the outliers of the city, flew..to their several abodes. **1926** [see HATTIC *a.*]. **1928** *Library Assoc. Rec.* Dec. 244 The Central Library has wisely recruited several of the larger public libraries..to act as outlier libraries. **1961** T. LANDAU *Encycl. Librarianship* (ed. 2) 259/2 Its 'Outlier' libraries, which lend their specialized books and periodicals on the N.C.L.'s request when other resources fail, now number 281. **1973** *Computers & Humanities* VII. 136 What..differentiates 'La Comtesse d'Escarbagnas', at the top of the diagram, from the remaining plays? What is special about an outlier such as 'Dom Garcie'? **1977** *Jrnl. R. Soc. Arts* CXXV. 269/2 The Library is an 'outlier' library of the British Library.

3. *Fishing.* A set-line, out-line. *U.S.*

†**'outˌliggand.** *Obs.* [dial. form of OUTLYING *ppl. a.*] An outlying portion.

1587 HARRISON *England* I. xiv. in *Holinshed* 73/1 A parcell of Monmouthshire, being an outliggand. *Ibid.* 82/2 Betweene Denbighshire, and the outliggand of Flintshire.

†**outligger**[1], **outlicker.** *Naut. Obs.* Forms: α. 5, 8 outligger, 5 -lygger, owtlegger, 6 outleger, 7–8 -lager, 8 -leager, -layer. β. 6 outlicar, 7–8 -licker, 8 -leaker; 7 -looker. [Prob. a dial. form of *outlier* (cf. LIGGER *sb.*), subsequently corrupted in various ways by those to whom the dial. *lig*, to lie, was unknown. Du. has analogous uses of *uitlegger, -ligger* 'outlier'; but the later date of this prevents it (notwithstanding Dampier's assertion: see sense 2) from being viewed as the source of the Eng. word.

Du. *uitlegger* 'outlier' appears in Kilian, 1599, only in the sense of 'stationary guard-ship lying out in front of a port, etc.' From 1671 (Witsen *Scheeps-bouw* 55 a) it is found in a sense akin to 1 below. The 'outrigger' of the Indian seas (sense 2) is described in Du. works from *c* 1600 without any name; in Valentijn *Oud en Nieuw Oost Indien* I. 2 (1724) it is called *vlerk* (i.e. wing), the name still in common use; but beside it the name *uitlegger* is found in Dutch dictionaries of the 19th c. (Twent *Zeemans Woordenb.* 147 b, 1813, etc.) Thus, so far as yet known, both uses of *uitlegger* are later than the corresponding senses of the Eng. word.]

1. A spar projecting from a vessel to extend some sail, or to make a greater angle for some rope, etc.; *esp.* **a.** A long and stout spar extended from the poop to haul down the mizen-sheet.

α. **1481–90** *Howard Househ. Bks.* (Roxb.) 23 Stuff of the Ienete..Item, a pompe..an out lygger .j. tope mast: a chest with gonne stones. **1485** *Naval Acc. Hen. VII* (1896) 51 Outliggers..j, Bitakles..j, Pumps..ij. **1495** *Ibid.* 156 Owte lyggers for the Sterne of a smale ship. *Ibid.* 272 Owtleggers at Sterne..j. **1558** W. TOWRSON in Hakluyt *Voy.* (1589) 124 By the euill worke of his men the shippe fell aboorde of vs.. and the shippes wailes were broken with her outleger.

β. **1594** N. DOWNTON in Hakluyt *Voy.* (1599) II. II. 200 Whereby the ship fell to the sterne of the out-licar of the Carack, which (being a piece of timber) so wounded her fore-saile, that they sayd they could come no more to fight. **1625** *Nomenclator Navalis* (Harl. MS. 2301), Ye Out-Licker. Is a small peece of timber (some two or three yardes long as they have occasion to vse it) and it is made fast to the top of the Poope and so standes right out asterne. [**1644** MANWAYRING *Sea-man's Dict.* expands this greatly, and says 'The use of this is to hale-downe the Missen'. Hence in PHILLIPS 1674, CHAMBERS *Cycl.* 1727, etc.] **1626** CAPT. SMITH *Accid. Yng. Seamen* 29 Trie her with a crose jacke, bowse it vp with the outlooker.

b. A spar to thrust out the breast-back-stays: = OUTRIGGER 1 c.

1731 CAPT. W. WRIGLESWORTH *MS. Log-bk. of the 'Lyell'* 1 May, This morning got outlickers out in the Tops, and the David out forward for a lower outlicker.

2. A contrivance used with canoes in the Indian and Pacific Oceans to prevent capsizing under a press of sail: = OUTRIGGER 2.

1697 DAMPIER *Voy.* I. 299 Along the belly-side of the Boat, parallel with it at about 6 or 7 foot distance, lies another..being a Log of very light Wood, almost as long as the great Boat,..there are two Bamboas..by the help of which the little Boat is made firm and contiguous to the other. These are generally called by the Dutch, and by the English from them, *Outlagers* [*ed.* 1729 out-layers]. *Ibid.* 492 We had a good substantial Mast, and a mat Sail, and good Outlagers lasht very fast and firm on each side..made of strong poles. **1727** A. HAMILTON *New Acc. E. Ind.* II. xxxviii. 71 Fitted them [Canoaes] with Out-leagers to keep them from over-turning,..but in the Way one of the Boats lost her Out-leager, and drowned all her Crew. **1744** A. DOBBS *Hudson's Bay* 68 To prevent even these Canoes from oversetting, by Outlagers or blown Bladders fixed to their Sides. **1747** W. HORSLEY *Fool* (1748) II. 301 These Vessels are built on one Side upright as a Wall;..on the Wall Side, are laid small Poles, called Out-Liggers by the Sea-men. **1755** AMORY *Mem.* (1766) II. 156 *note*, This kind of boat is four foot broad..the greatest danger is its oversetting, and this may always be prevented..by placing two men on the windward outlayer.

β. **1707** W. FUNNELL *Voy.* viii. 228–9 They had two long Poles put out of one side..at the end of which was a long piece of Plank..of the same shape, and about one fourth of the bigness of the bottom of the Boat. This piece.. altogether; is called the Out-leaker. This is always the Weather-side; and the use of it is to keep the Boat from oversetting.

†**'outˌligger**[2]. *Obs.* [f. OUT- + LIGGER.] In Reaping, One who made bands for the sheaves and laid the corn in them for the binder. So †**outligging** *vbl. sb.* or *ppl. a.*

1641 BEST *Farm. Bks.* (Surtees) 49 An outligger carryeth only one loome to the field, and that is..an outligginge rake, or a gatheringe rake. *Ibid.*, A good outligger is knowne by followinge close vnto him that shee gathereth after, and likewise by makinge of her bandes; for some outliggers twine theire bandes, and others againe make them of pulled corne.

out-lighten to **out-limn**: see OUT-.

outline ('aʊtlaɪn), *sb.* [f. OUT- 3 + LINE *sb.*[2]]

1. a. *pl.* The lines, real or apparent, by which a figure is defined or bounded in the plane of vision; the sum of these lines forming the contour of a figure.

1662 EVELYN *Chalcogr.* I. v. 109 Penning the Contours, and out lines with a more even and acute touch. **1718** GILDON *Art Poetry* I. 227 Who is it that draws the Outlines? Why the Master-Painter, and Journeymen fill them up with Colours, Shades, and Lights. **1753** HOGARTH *Anal. Beauty* 9 The true and full idea of what is call'd the out-lines of a figure. **1855** MACAULAY *Hist. Eng.* xiii. III. 301 Charmed by the bold outlines and rich tints of the hills. **1878** HUXLEY *Physiogr.* xix. 334 Suppose the outlines of the various countries of the world depicted on a globular bladder.

b. *sing.* The contour or outer boundary thus defined.

1828 SCOTT *F.M. Perth* xxiii, He lifted up his eyes, and beheld in the distance the black outline of a gallows. **1860** TYNDALL *Glac.* I. ii. 21 A mountain wall projected its jagged outline against the sky. **1866** G. MACDONALD *Ann. Q. Neighb.* xii. (1878) 243 Neither could see more than the other's outline.

fig. **1876** GEO. ELIOT *Dan. Der.* IV. li. 18 She said, in a low melodious voice, with syllables which had what might be called a foreign but agreeable outline.

2. a. A sketch or drawing in which an object is represented by lines of contour without shading.

1735 H. JACOB *Wks.* 391 Carracio, esteem'd for Contours, or Out-Lines, at Bologna. **1799** G. SMITH *Laboratory* II. 32 If your pattern is only an out-line, it will be the better, as you will finish your piece after it with more ease. **1868** *Free-hand Drawing* (Nimmo) 53 The outlines and finished views of these casts are given separately.

b. ***in outline***, with only the outline drawn, represented, or visible.

1814 SCOTT *Ld. of Isles* v. vii, Carrick shore, Dim seen in outline faintly blue. **1844** LD. HOUGHTON *Mem. of Many Scenes, Death of Day* 164 The hills in clear outline..Stand forth. *Mod.* The figure of a horse drawn in outline. A map of England showing the counties in outline merely.

c. The representation of a word in shorthand.

1850 *Phonography, or, Phonetic Shorthand* 1/2 It [*sc.* Phonography] is..as intelligible as speech itself;..and as used in verbatim reporting, a perfect and intelligible outline. **1886** *Encycl. Brit.* XXI. 839/2 By this method the number of possible readings of an unvocalized outline is greatly reduced. **1898** [see PITMAN]. **1933** D. L. SAYERS *Murder must Advertise* i. 14 He..went on dictating and my hand was so shaky I could hardly make my outlines. **1969** G. CHARLESWORTH *Effective Teaching Techniques in Commercial Subjects* 9 The difficulty of outlines should be very gradually increased and only one point of theory at a time should be so revised. **1973** E. M. ARLETT *So You want to be a Shorthand Typist* ii. 18 The pen races smoothly over the pages, filling them with neat outlines that presently will be read back with practised ease.

d. *Typogr.* A display type-face in which the letters are drawn only in outline, perhaps with added shading. Also *attrib.*

1878 *Specimens of Newspaper, Book & Ornamental Founts* (Sir Charles Reed & Sons), Grotesque Outline... Clarendon Outline... English Black Outline. **1970** W. P. JASPERT et al. *Encycl. Type Faces* (ed. 4) 243 Zephyr... An accentuated outline titling, giving a somewhat three-dimensional effect.

3. a. A rough draught or general sketch in words; a description, giving a general idea of the whole, but leaving details to be filled in. Also, a précis of a proposed article, novel, scenario, etc.

1759 STERNE *Tr. Shandy* I. xxiii, There are others again, who will draw a man's character from no other helps..but merely from his evacuations;—but this often gives a very incorrect outline. **1795** L. MURRAY *Eng. Gram.* Introd. 8 A distinct general view, or outline, of all the essential parts of the study. **1865** R. W. DALE *Jew. Temp.* xix. (1877) 217, I have given a bare outline of the contents of this passage. **1928** E. O'NEILL *Strange Interlude* I. iv. 123 Charlie's coming to bring his suggestions on my outline for Gordon's biography. **1967** H. VAN SILLER *Biltmore Call* 164 You know the way he worked. A short outline first, then the first draft. **1968** D. FRANCIS *Forfeit* i. 9 And when you've thought out how you'd like to present it, send us an outline. **1969** L. HELLMAN *Unfinished Woman* vi. 66 It was..too hard to write a shooting script, or even an outline, about a war I did not know. **1976** D. QUINN *Limbo Connection* xi. 189 It is a good story... I just delivered a few pages of outline to my agent... So let nobody forget, I own the film rights.

b. in *pl.* The main features or leading characteristics of any subject; the general principles.

1710 STEELE *Tatler* No. 182 ¶6 His Drama at present has only the Out-Lines drawn. **1751** HUME *Ess. & Treat.* (1777) II. 249 The faint rudiments, at least, or out-lines, of a general distinction between actions. **1864** PUSEY *Lect. Daniel* (1876) 157 All, who speak of that division, agree in the great outlines.

†**4.** The outer line, the border line. *Obs. rare.*

1695 BLACKMORE *Pr. Arth.* II. 624 The shining Squadrons fly To th' Out-lines, and the Frontiers of the Sky.

5. *Fishing.* A set-line or ledger-line. *U.S.*

6. *attrib.* and *Comb.*, as ***outline-drawing, -map, -sketch***; **outline plan**, a draft or sketch lacking many details; **outline planning permission**, permission sought by or from an authority, for building, demolition, or industrial development; so ***outline planning application***; **outline stitch**, in *Embroidery*, stitch used to indicate an outline; *spec.* = stem stitch.

1859 GULLICK & TIMBS *Paint.* 47 Delicate and finely undulating outline drawing. **1882** J. COLLIER *Primer of Art* 25 When the boundaries of an object are represented apart from its other qualities, the process is called outline drawing. *a* **1904** *Mod.* The use of outline maps in teaching geography. **1972** *Guardian* 5 Aug. 11/2 Westminster City Council are sitting on outline plans to knock down..a tenement of 89 flats. **1968** *Act 16 & 17 Eliz. II.* c. 72 §66 'Outline planning permission' means planning permission granted, in accordance with the provisions of a development order, with the reservation for subsequent approval by the local planning authority or the Minister of matters..not particularised in the application. **1971** *Reader's Digest Family Guide to Law* 100/1 If the householder does not wish to spend a lot of money on detailed plans and drawings, he can submit brief details and ask for approval of the building work in principle. If this outline planning permission is granted, it will justify further expenditure on more detailed plans. **1973** *Guardian* 25 Apr. 8/7 A meeting has been called ..to protest against an outline planning application..for underground mining in the parish. **1865** LUBBOCK *Preh. Times* vii. (1869) 232 The facts already ascertained..supply us with the elements of an outline sketch. **188.** *Weldon's Pract. Needlewk.* II. 7/1 Crewel or Stem Stitch, also called Outline Stitch, is the chief and most-used stitch for crewel work. **189.** *Jrnl. Decorative Needlewk.* Ser. II. No. 12. 4 The Bayeux Outline Stitch consists simply of one laid strand tied down. **1908** M. H. MORGAN *How to Dress Doll* iii. 34 Fill in with the chain or outline stitch and work with the embroidery buttonhole stitch. **1960** B. SNOOK *Eng. Hist. Embroidery* 14 Couching, laid-work and outline stitch are used.

outline (ˈaʊtlaɪn), *v.* [f. prec. sb.]

1. *trans.* To draw or trace the exterior line of; to draw in outline.

c **1790** IMISON *Sch. Art* II. 28 Having outlined the folds, and the other parts of drapery, you may next attempt the shadowing your figure. **1853** RUSKIN *Stones Ven.* II. iii. §28. 46 The ornament is merely outlined upon them with a fine incision. **1886** CORBETT *Fall of Asgard* I. 12 Two fierce dragons were outlined on its haft.

b. To indicate or define the outline of; in *pa. pple.* having the outline sharply defined to the eye.

1817 L. HUNT *Poems, On the Avon,* All things appear Strong outlined in the spacious atmosphere. **1849** ALB. SMITH *Pottleton Leg.* (repr.) 176 The great room was outlined with laurel leaves. **1884** *Harper's Mag.* Jan. 197/1 White marble crosses.., outlined against the blue sky. **1889** *Times* 14 Nov. 5/4 The Imperial yacht is outlined with lights, producing a charming effect. **189.** *Jrnl. Decorative Needlewk.* Ser. II. No. 12. 13 A line of the finest gold thread might outline everything.

c. To trace or ascertain the outline of (an area).

1890 *Nature* 30 Oct. 651 It has not yet been found possible to outline exactly the eastern limit of the sea. **1898** P. MANSON *Trop. Diseases* xxiii. 355 Careful outlining of the upper and lower boundaries [of the area] may discover a limited and dome-like increase in one direction.

2. To describe the broad outlines or main features of; to sketch in general terms.

1855 MOTLEY *Dutch Rep.* Introd. (1858) 40 The early progress of the religious reformation..will be outlined in a separate chapter. **1880** *Daily News* 18 Dec., The scheme outlined in Mr. Bright's speech.

Hence **ˈoutlined** *ppl. a.*; **ˈoutlining** *vbl. sb.* and *ppl. a.*

1798 W. TAYLOR in *Monthly Rev.* XXVI. 249 Accompanied with outlined engravings of their leading works. **1853** KANE *Grinnell Exp.* xxxi. (1856) 273 An outlined ridge of doubtful mountain land. **1883** *Athenæum* 17 Nov. 643/2 The beautiful outlining which characterizes [the] etchings. **1896** *Daily News* 23 Oct. 2/2 Only fragmentary pillars and remnants of outlining walls.. remain.

outlinear (aʊtˈlɪniːə(r)), *a.* [f. OUTLINE *sb.* after LINEAR.] Of the nature of an outline.

1835 *Fraser's Mag.* XII. 66, I have..given this outlinear sketch of my life. **1858** TRENCH *Synon. N.T.* viii. (1876) 27 The substantial as opposed to the shadowy and outlinear.

out-linger to **out-list**: see OUT-.

outlive (aʊtˈlɪv), *v.* [OUT- 18, 17.]

1. *trans.* Of a person: To live longer than (another person); to survive; also, to live longer than (a thing lasts).

1472 *Rolls of Parlt.* VI. 234/2 In cas hereafter it happen you..to outleve our seid Sovereigne Lord. **1560** BIBLE (Genev.) *Judg.* ii. 7 All the daies of the Elders that outlyued Ioshua. **1695** BLACKMORE *Pr. Arth.* IV. 341 Asham'd his Country's Freedom to out-live. **1711** ADDISON *Spect.* No. 72 ¶11 The Senior Member has out-lived the whole Club twice over. **1880** MᶜCARTHY *Own Times* IV. lvii. 253 He had out-lived nearly all his early friends and foes.

b. Of a thing: To endure longer than; to outlast.

c **1600** SHAKS. *Sonn.* lv, Not marble, nor the gilded monuments Of princes, shall outlive this powerful rhyme. **1706** ESTCOURT *Fair Examp.* IV. i. 51 When Guilt outlives the Sence of Shame. **1813** J. THOMSON *Lect. Inflam.* 229 The Taliacotian art does not, however, appear to have long outlived its author in Italy. **1865** LIGHTFOOT *Gal.* (1874) 13 The character of a nation even outlives its language.

2. To live through or beyond (a specified time).

1657 S. PURCHAS *Pol. Flying-Ins.* 39 Not one will out-live October. **1726–31** WALDRON *Isle Man* (1865) 67 He is sure not to out-live three days. **1867** MAX MÜLLER *Chips* (1880) III. 334 The mammoth..did not outlive the age of bronze.

b. To live through or beyond (a certain state or experience); to pass through; to outgrow.

1641 J. JACKSON *True Evang. T.* I. 63 How many have out-lived their piety. **1775** JOHNSON *Let. to Mrs. Thrale* 13 July, They have outlived the age of weakness. **1806** *Naval Chron.* XV. 266 The *Montagu* having..outlived the hurricane. **1887** LOWELL *Democr.* etc. 42 The world has outlived much, and will outlive a great deal more.

†**3.** *intr.* To survive. *Obs.*

1588 SHAKS. *Tit. A.* II. iii. 132 But when ye haue the hony we desire, Let not this Waspe out-liue vs both to sting.

4. *trans.* To excel in (virtuous) living.

1883 MACFADYEN in *Congreg. Year-bk.* 58 Bishop Burnet gave his clergy the..advice that if they wished Dissent to cease, they must out-live, out-labour, out-preach Dissenters.

Hence **outˈlived**, **outˈliving** *ppl. adjs.*; **outˈliver**, a survivor.

1800 LAMB *Lett., to Manning* 55 The prattle of age, and outlived importance. **1580** HOLLYBAND *Treas. Fr. Tong*, *Survivant*, the outliuer. **1615** G. SANDYS *Trav.* 186 The out-liuer becomming a conuert to their religion. **1630** MILTON *Passion* 7 In Wintry solstice like the shortn'd light Soon swallow'd up in dark and long out-living night.

ˈout-ˌliving, *ppl. a. rare.* [OUT- 10.] That lives out; living outside a country, city, college, etc.

1766 W. GORDON *Gen. Counting-ho.* 365 No foreigner or out-living trader.

ˈout-ˌlodging, *sb.* [OUT- 1.] A lodging or domicile situated outside a certain limit.

1642 FULLER *Holy & Prof. St.* II. xiv. 103 As for out-lodgings (..necessary evils..) he rather tolerates then approves them. *Ibid.* xx. 130 He counts it a disgrace..that we..should not know the out-lodgings of the same house.

So **ˈout-ˌlodging** *ppl. a.* [OUT- 10], lodging outside, having one's quarters outside a certain limit.

1647 FULLER *Good Th. in Worse T.* (1841) 118 Out-lodging deer are seldom seen to be so fat as those which keep them-selves within the park.

outlook (ˈaʊtlʊk), *sb.* [OUT- 7.]

1. The act or practice of looking out; a looking forth or abroad, esp. for observation or discovery; vigilant watch. *lit.* and *fig.* ***on the outlook***, on the look-out, on the watch for what may turn up.

1815 SCOTT *Guy M.* iv, What cheer, brother? You seem on the outlook, eh? **1820** —— *Monast.* xxii, The means of ascending it as a place of out-look. **1851** RUSKIN *Stones Ven.* I. xvi. §11 The best windows for outlook are, of course, oriels and bow windows. **1862** SKELTON *Nugæ Crit.* i. 46 Jackdaws..on the out-look for plunder. **1895** *United Service Mag.* July 429 The failure of the Egyptians to keep an adequate outlook at night.

b. Vigilance, watchfulness.

1879 G. MACDONALD *Sir Gibbie* I. xi. 162 They had a sharp expression of outlook and readiness.

2. A place from or by which a view is obtained; a look-out.

1667 WATERHOUSE *Fire Lond.* 97 The innocent eyes, those Casements and out-looks of the tender heart. **1877** TALMAGE *Serm.* 291 He sent his servant to the outlook of the mountain to see if there were any signs of rain. **1878** FOSTER *Phys.* IV. vi. 567 Viewed from the distant outlook.

3. The view or prospect from a place or point.

1828 CARLYLE in Froude *Life* (1882) II. 25 One might have sickened and grown melancholy over such an outlook. **1850** KINGSLEY *Alt. Locke* ii, The dreary outlook of chimney-tops and smoke. **1891** E. PEACOCK *N. Brendon* II. 116 There was a picturesque outlook on all sides.

b. A mental view or survey.

1742 YOUNG *Nt. Th.* VIII. 1152 Above Applause; Which owes to Man's short Out-look all its Charmes. **1886** SYMONDS *Renaiss. It., Cath. React.* (1898) VII. viii. 30 His [Tasso's] outlook over life was melancholy.

c. The prospect for the future.

1832 MACAULAY in Trevelyan *Life* (1876) I. v. 324 My political outlook is very gloomy. **1889** JESSOPP *Coming of Friars* iv. 178 They took a much more sober view of the outlook than the populace did.

4. *attrib.*, as ***outlook box, post, tower, window***.

1851 RUSKIN *Stones Ven.* I. xvi. §11 The earth and the doings upon it being the chief object in outlook windows. **1875** W. MᶜILWRAITH *Guide Wigtownshire* 65 Perhaps Burgh Head was an out-look station of the old sea-rovers. **1897** *Daily News* 24 Dec. 2/5 Both outlook glasses were smashed, and the driver and stoker narrowly escaped injury.

outˈlook, *v.* [OUT- 18c, 17, 15, 14.]

1. *trans.* To overcome or disconcert by looking; to look or stare down; to outstare.

1595 SHAKS. *John* V. ii. 115 To out-looke Conquest, and to winne renowne E'en in the iawes of danger and of death. **1600** HEYWOOD *1st Pt. Edw. IV* Wks. 1874 I. 27 They think they can outlook our truer looks. **1707** NORRIS *Treat. Humility* v. 220, I do not..endeavour to look big and great, or outlook others by a confident assurance.

†**2.** To look beyond. *Obs.*

1655 H. VAUGHAN *Silex Sc., Departed Fr.* v, What mysteries do lie beyond thy dust, Could man outlook that mark!

†**3.** To look out, to select by looking. *poet.*

a **1687** COTTON *Angler's Ballad* i. Poems (1689) 76 Away to the Brook, All your Tackle out look.

†**4.** To outdo in looks or appearance. *Obs.*

1731 MRS. DELANY *Lett., to Mrs. A. Granville* 295 No-body's equipage outlooked our's except my Lord Lieutenant's, but in every respect I must say Mrs. Clayton's outshines her neighbours.

5. *intr.* To look out or forth. *poet.*

1888 R. BUCHANAN *City of Dream* XII. 248, I saw those three wan Shapes Outlooking from the greenness of the woods.

out-looker, variant of OUTLIGGER[1] 1.

ˈout-ˌlooker. *rare.* [OUT- 8.] One who looks out or abroad.

1637 BRETON *Packet Lett.* (1879) 43/2 They may be kinde, but not constant, and Loue loues no out-lookers.

So **ˈoutˌlooking** *vbl. sb.* [OUT- 9], a looking forth or abroad; *ppl. a.* [OUT- 10], that looks out.

1610 MARKHAM *Masterp.* I. ciii. 204 An out-looking eye. **1850** BUSHNELL *God in Christ* i. 22 The outlooking of His intelligence.

†**ˈout-loose.** *Obs. nonce-wd.* [OUT- 7?] A means of escape (from an obligation, duty, etc.).

a **1654** SELDEN *Table-t.* (Arb.) 39 If we once come to leave that out-loose, as to pretend Conscience against Law, who knows what inconvenience may follow? *Ibid.* 78 In the new Oath it runs (whereas I believe in my Conscience, &c. I will assist thus and thus) that (whereas) gives me an Outloose, for if I do not believe so, for ought I know, I swear not at all.

†**ˈoutlope.** *Obs.* Also 7 -loape. [app. ad. Du. *uitloop*, in Kilian *uutloop*, a run out, an excursion.] A run out; a sally, an excursion; = OUTLEAP *sb.*

1603 FLORIO *Montaigne* II. x. (1632) 228 *Excursusque breves tentat*, 'Outlopes sometimes he doth assay, But very short, and as he may'. **1630** J. TAYLOR (Water P.) *Jacke-a-lent* Wks. I. 118/2 It cannot be but that so mighty a Monarch as he, hath his inroades and his outloapes.

†**'out,loper.** *Obs. rare*⁻¹. [app. ad. Du. *uitlooper*, in Kilian *uutlooper* 'excursor'; but cf. INTERLOPER.] One who makes a run out; e.g. on a voyage of adventure.
1583 in Hakluyt *Voy.* (1599) II. I. 173 Touching any outlopers of our [English] nation, which may happen to come thither to traffike, you are not to suffer, but to imprison the chiefe officers, and suffer the rest not to traffike at any time.

out-lord: see OUT- 22.

'out-lot, outlot. *U.S. Obs.* exc. *Hist.* [OUT- 1.] A lot or piece of ground situated outside a town or other area.
1643 *Rec. Colony & Plantation New Haven* (1857) I. 94 Mris Eldreds out lotts. **1774** in *Amer. Archives* (1837) (ser. 4) I. 278 An out lot, of ten acres, contiguous to the town, shall be laid off for such as desire the same at an easy rent. **1779** [see IN-LOT 2]. **1837** W. JENKINS *Ohio Gazetteer* 148 A tract of land on the east side of the town has like-wise been divided into 23 outlots of five acres each. **1886** Z. F. SMITH *Hist. Kentucky* 29 [They gave] to each man a half-acre lot and a ten-acre outlot. **1948** [see IN-LOT 2].

out-loud. The phrase (read) *out loud* sometimes hyphened; esp. *attrib.*
1844 L. HUNT *Imag. & Fancy* Pref. 4 In reading out-loud. **1899** *Spectator* 20 May 718 [The] book..deserves a solemn out-loud reading.

out'love, *v.* [OUT- 18, 21.] *trans.* To outdo or surpass in loving.
1614 TOMKIS *Albumazar* II. vii. in Hazl. *Dodsley* XI. 348 She cannot outlove me, nor you outfriend me. *a* **1711** KEN *Sion* Poet. Wks. 1721 IV. 409 They..to out-love each other co-inclin'd. **1847** EMERSON *Repr. Men, Shaks.* Wks. (1901) 192/1 What lover has he not outloved? What sage has he not outseen?

out'lung, *v.* [OUT- 21.] *trans.* To surpass in lung-power; to outdo in shouting.
1756 WESLEY *Wks.* (1872) XIII. 215 They will outface and outlung you. **1890** *Universal Rev.* Dec. 519 Confident that he can out-lung and out-last his own generation.

out'lustre, *v.* [OUT- 21.] *trans.* To surpass in lustre, to outshine.
1611 SHAKS. *Cymb.* I. iv. 78 As that Diamond of yours outlusters many I haue beheld. **1655** FULLER *Ch. Hist.* III. ii. §43 This Henry of Bloys..outlustred the other as far, as an extraordinary Ambassador doth a Leger of the same Nation. **1809** M. A. BIANCHI *Levity & Sorrow* I. 176.

'outly, *adv. Obs.* exc. *dial.* [f. OUT *adv.* + -LY².]
1. Out and out, utterly, completely.
c **1290** *Beket* 383 in *S. Eng. Leg.* I. 117 Þe furste tyme þat seint thomas ovtliche him with seide, Hit was for þe king aȝen pouere Men dude onriȝtul dede. **13..** *Chron. R. Glouc.* (Rolls) 1513 (MS. B) Al is herte outliche [*MS. A.* onliche, *MS. δ.* outturly] on hire on he caste. *Ibid.* 4920+5 (MS. B) Þe byssop..outlych [*v.rr.* outerliche, onlich] yt wyþ seyde. **1789** ROSS *Helenore* 43 But three haill days were outly come and gaen. **1855** ROBINSON *Whitby Gloss., Outly,* thoroughly, out-and-out.
2. Outwardly, externally.
1591 SYLVESTER *Du Bartas* I. ii. 167 It but the Form disguises In hundred fashions, and the Substances..Inly, or Outly, neither win nor leese. **1876** *Whitby Gloss., Ooterly,* or *Ootly,*..externally.

outlygger: see OUTLIGGER¹ *Obs.*

outlying ('aʊt,laɪɪŋ), *ppl. a.* [OUT- 10.]
1. Lying or situated outside certain limits; hence *fig.* extrinsic, extraneous. Of a beast: That makes its lair outside a park or enclosure.
1663 DRYDEN *Wild Gallant* II. ii, Just in the condition of an out-lying deer, that's beaten from his walk for offering to rut. **1689–90** TEMPLE *Ess., Heroic Virtue* v. Wks. 1720 I. 220 The last Survey I proposed of the Four outlying (or, if the Learned so please to call them, barbarous) Empires, was that of the Arabians. **1705** HICKERINGILL *Priest-cr.* II. iii. 36 If this be the Church of England, all the Laity are out of the Pale of the Church, like out-lying Deer that are out of the Park, and subject to be worryed by every Dog or Devil. **1862** ANSTED *Channel Isl.* I. iii. (ed. 2) 37 These distances do not include the outlying rocks. **18..** M. PATTISON in *Mem.* (1885) 136, I wasted time over outlying classics, which did not form part of the degree list.
2. Lying at a distance from the centre of an area; remote, out-of-the-way; living at a distance from centres of population.
1689–90 TEMPLE *Ess., Heroic Virtue* i. Wks. 1720 I. 196 Some of these out-lying Parts of the World. **1871** TYLOR *Prim. Cult.* I. 41 Instances of civilized men taking to a wild life in outlying districts of the world. **1888** BURGON *Lives 12 Gd. Men* II. xii. 396 The example was taken up by remote outlying parishes.

†**'out,making,** *vbl. sb. Obs.* [OUT- 9.] The 'making out' or discernment of the sense.
1680 G. HICKES *Spirit of Popery* 19 They ought to believe the naked Word, when there was no appearance of its outmaking. **1681** R. FLEMING *Fulfill. Script.* (1801) I. 37 The performance and outmaking of the Scripture. **1728** HELEN ALEXANDER *Autobiog.* in *Covenanters in South* (1856) 349 Then I found the outmaking of that word in Isaiah, I will extend peace to her like a river.

†**'outman,** *sb. Obs.* [OUT- 2.] A dweller without the bounds; an outsider; a member of an out-company, one whose work is outside.
1493 *Charter* in A. Laing *Lindores Abbey & Newburgh* xvii. (1876) 180 We ordane that no outman be maid burges but consent of the said abbot & convent. *c* **1570** *Durham Depos.* (Surtees) 116 Sir Thomas..dyd rebuke this examinate for making any busynes in that parish, being an out man. **1793** SMEATON *Edystone L.* §101 Every out-man to take all opportunities of landing upon the rock to work. **1890** FERGUSON *Hist. Cumbld.* xiii. 217 No outman was to bring flesh to the market unless he also brought the skin.

out'man, *v. rare.* [OUT- 21.]
1. *trans.* To surpass in number of men, to outnumber.
1691 BETHEL *Providences of God* (1694) 111 We out-tunn'd, out-gunn'd, and out-mann'd them.
2. To outdo as a man, to excel in manly qualities.
18.. CARLYLE (Ogilvie 1882), In gigantic ages, finding quite other men to outman and outstrip.

outma'nœuvre, -ver, *v.* [OUT- 18.] *trans.* To outdo in manœuvring; to get the better of by superior strategy.
1799 SIR T. TROUBRIDGE 18 May in Nicolas *Disp. Nelson* (1845) III. 357 *note,* I will out-manœuvre him there and push him hard too. **1833** MARRYAT *P. Simple* xlvi, I mean to fight these fellows under sail, and out-manœuvre them, if I can. **1837** *New Monthly Mag.* L. 204 He contrived to outmanœuvre all her manœuvres.

outmantle to **outmapped**: see OUT-.

'outmarch, *sb.* [OUT- 7.] A march out upon an expedition; an advance.
1847 GROTE *Greece* I. xxxiv. III. 230 The adventures..on the out-march and the home-march. **1849** *Ibid.* II. lxxxvii. XI. 436 To meet Philip in any of his sudden out-marches. **1900** *Daily News* 5 Jan. 5/7 The Canadian Contingent had for the out-march been placed in waggons.

out'march, *v.* [OUT- 18.] *trans.* To outdo or outstrip in marching; to march faster or farther than; to march so as to leave behind.
1647 CLARENDON *Hist. Reb.* II. §40 The Horse had outmarched the Foot. **1753** HANWAY *Trav.* (1762) II. XVI. i. 446 He would upon any emergency out-march his baggage. **1870** *Daily News* 27 Dec., The Germans have hitherto outmarched the French in this war.

out-mark to **out-mate**: see OUT-.

out'master, *v.* [OUT- 18 b.] *trans.* To overcome in a contest for mastery.
1799 H. GURNEY *Cupid & Psyche* VI. 12 E'en in her shroud outmasters [*ed.* 2, o'ermasters] fear. **1860** SMILES *Self-Help* vii. 171 Though your force be less than another's, you equal and outmaster your opponent if you continue it longer and concentrate it more.

out'match, *v.* [OUT- 18 b.] *trans.* To be more than a match for; to prove superior to; to surpass, outdo.
1603 BRETON *Dignitie Man* (1879) 14/2 In labour the Oxe will out-toile him, and in subtiltie the Foxe will out-match him. **1846** EMILY BRONTË *Wuthering Heights* xxi. 183 You'll own that I've out-matched Hindley there. **1885** *Manch. Exam.* 18 Mar. 5/1 Their collective strength enormously outmatches ours.

out-match, at *Cricket,* etc.: see OUT *a.* 3.

out'measure, *v.* [OUT- 18 c, or 21.] *trans.* To exceed in measure or extent.
1646 SIR T. BROWNE *Pseud. Ep.* v. xviii. 260 To attempt perpetuall motions, and engines whose revolutions..might outlast the exemplary mobility, and outmeasure time it selfe. **1806** W. TAYLOR in *Ann. Rev.* IV. 110 Such masses of property, as will outmeasure the estates of Russian nobles. **1837** *New Monthly Mag.* XLIX. 478 There are some days that might outmeasure years.

†**'outmer,** *a. Obs.* Also 5 **-mere.** [Variant of UTMER: cf. *utmest,* UTMOST.] Outer.
c **1400** *Prymer* 9 Mi soule be fillid as wiþ inner fatnesse & outmer fatnes. *a* **1410** *Wyclif's Bible* Matt. viii. 12 But the sones of the rewme schulen be cast out in to vtmer [*v. rr.* vttermere, *MS. Harl.* 5017 (*a* 1410) outmere] derknessis.

out-merchant, -metaphor: see OUT-.

'out-migrant. [OUT- 8.] One who leaves one country or place to settle in another. Cf. INMIGRANT *sb.* and *a.*
1953 *Caribbean Q.* II. IV. 53 This year, the number of out-migrants may outstrip even 1951's record figure. **1971** *Sci. Amer.* July 18/3 The state of New York for the first time had more out-migrants than in-migrants.

'out-migrate, *v.* [OUT- 14.] *intr.* To leave one country or place to make one's home in another. Hence **'outmi,gration.** Cf. INMIGRATION.
1953 *Caribbean Q.* II. IV. 53 This January, twice as many net-out-migrated as in January of 1949, 1950, 1951. *Ibid.*, Out-migration grows like snowballs running down hill. **1970** S. L. BARRACLOUGH in I. L. Horowitz *Masses in Lat. Amer.* iv. 157 Without greater agricultural production and accelerated out-migration, however, incomes resulting from reform would be dissipated by population increase within a generation or so. **1971** [see IN-MIGRATION]. **1975** *N.Y. Times* 17 Nov. 24/3 The problem for cities that are victims of outmigration is that population decline correlates with at least a relative fall in average income. **1976** *Time* 27 Sept. 55/3 Meanwhile, the out-migration of young blacks and whites has been reversed. **1977** *Jrnl. R. Soc. Arts* CXXV. 551/1 High rise flats..proved to be particularly unsuitable for families with young children, with the result that out-migration of such families was accelerated.

out-million to **out-miracle**: see OUT-.

outmode (aʊt'məʊd), *v.* [OUT- 21; cf. F. *démoder.*] *trans.* To put out of fashion. (Chiefly in pa. pple.) So **out-moded** *ppl. a.,* no longer in fashion, out-of-date.
1903 *Academy* 17 Jan. 71/1 Jesse Berridge is a poet, not a poetess, to use a somewhat outmoded word. **1906** R. S. HICHENS *Call of Blood* ii. 15 He was not wholly emancipated from la petite femme tradition, which will never be outmoded in Paris. **1906** *Westm. Gaz.* 26 May 2/3 Even the out-moded globe-trotter will find that his trot must be maddeningly slow. **1915** T. BURKE *Nights in Town* 392 The poor laddie is sadly outmoded, but he doesn't know it. **1926** W. J. LOCKE *Stories Near & Far* 133 The joined fragments showed an old photograph of a young man, in out-moded raiment. **1927** *Daily Express* 24 Sept. 8/4 George Ade has been out-moded by Will Rogers, whose jests die as soon as they are born. **1942** *Amer. Speech* XVII. (Reprints & Monogr. No. 4) 4 The people of this region might also have preserved out-moded features of speech. **1952** R. NEILL *Moon in Scorpio* xi. 96 It's new Penny—and you're outmoding all Whitehall. **1971** *Sci. Amer.* Oct. 27/1 He believes such a union would outmode the present broadcast networks. **1978** E. HEALEY *Lady Unknown* vi. 149 Mrs Livingstone in a queer out-moded bonnet.

out-Mormon: see OUT-.

outmost ('aʊtməʊst, -məst), *a.* Also 4 **-mest.** [In origin, an altered form of *utmest,* UTMOST, assimilated to the positive OUT. Isolated instances of this assimilation appear in ME., but *outmost* was hardly an established form till after 1550. Between 1575 and 1675, it gradually supplanted *utmost* in the literal sense as superlative of *out,* in which it is synonymous with *outermost.*]
1. a. Most outward, most external, situated farthest out; farthest from the inside or centre; outermost. Also *fig.*
13.. *Coer de L.* 2931 That outemeste walle was doun caste. *a* **1390** *Wyclif's Bible* Num. xxii. 39 (MS. Bodl. 959) The cytee, that was in the outmost [*v. rr.* vtmost, vttermoost] coost of his kyngdom. **1565** STAPLETON tr. *Bede's Hist. Ch. Eng.* 140 b, This Nonne was alone..in the outmost places of the monasterie. **1578** BANISTER *Hist. Man* v. 83 The first [coat] which is outmost groweth not stretely to the body of the kidneys. **1607** MARKHAM *Caval.* I. (1617) 28 His outmost teeth of each side haue little black holes in the top of them. **1653** WALTON *Angler* iv. 110 Lay the outmost part of your feather next to your hook. **1707** *Curios. in Husb. & Gard.* 31 The first or outmost Skin is called the Cuticle. **1810** SCOTT *Lady of L.* v. xii, Far past Clan-Alpine's outmost guard. **1866** RUSKIN *Crown Wild Olive* ii. 108 The outmost and superficial spheres of knowledge. **1882** FARRAR *Early Chr.* I. 422 *note,* In the Temple all might enter the outmost court.
b. The sense 'most out', 'farthest out' is often inseparable from that of 'most remote', 'farthest off', utmost, uttermost, extreme.
1561 T. NORTON *Calvin's Inst.* Table Script. Quotat., Even unto the outmost parts of the earth. **1570** LEVINS *Manip.* 176/14 Outmoste, *extremus.* **1577** tr. *Bullinger's Decades* (1592) 10 From the very outmost endes of the worlde. **1887** W. MORRIS tr. *Homer's Odyssey* I. I. 2 The far-dwellers outmost of menfolk. **1927** E. S. RAE *Hansel fae Hame* 1 The hert rugs hame fae outmaist eyens o' earth.
c. *ellipt.* The extremest part, the extremity.
1634 PEACHAM *Gentl. Exerc.* I. xix. 63 Aristotle called it *corporis extremitatem,* the extremitie or outmost of a body. **1887** W. MORRIS tr. *Homer's Odyssey* I. IX. 166 And but little it lacked, but the outmost of the helm it lighted on.
†**2. a.** Final; most complete; = UTMOST *a.* 2, 3. *Obs.*
1447 *Rolls of Parlt.* V. 138/2 Greved, to ther outmost destruction. **1587** T. HUGHES *Misfort. Arthur* III. iii, Loe, here the last and outmost worke for blades.
b. *ellipt.* The utmost point, degree, or limit; esp. in phr. *to the outmost. Obs.*
1671 *True Nonconf.* 506 After you have striven to the outmost. **1685** *Scotch Proclam.* 28 Apr. in *Lond. Gaz.* No. 2032/3 They..shall be punished with the outmost of severity. **1692** SIR W. HOPE *Fencing-Master* 83 To the outmost of my power.

out-mount, etc.: see OUT-.

†**'out-,mouth,** *sb. Obs.* [OUT- 6.] A projecting mouth.
1667 DRYDEN *Maiden Queen* I. ii, A full nether lip, an out-mouth, that makes mine water at it.
Hence †**'out-,mouthed** *a. Obs.*
1698 J. COCKBURN *Bourignianism Detected* i. 3 She was Out-mouthed, having Lips and Teeth somewhat big.

out-mouth (-'maʊð), *v.* [OUT- 18 or 21.] *trans.* To outdo in mouthing, exceed in loudness of sound.
a **1625** BOYS *Wks.* (1630) 606 Though hypocrites out-mouth as it were true Christians, in bragging of their familiarity with God. **1849** J. WILSON *Christopher under Canvass* in *Blackw. Mag.* LXVI. 16 He sometimes out-mouths the big-mouthed thunder at his own bombast.

†**out'move,** *v. Obs.* [OUT- 18, 18 b.]
1. *trans.* To surpass or exceed in moving.
1635 QUARLES *Embl.* II. vi. (1718) 86 She'd lend the favour should out-move The Troy-bane Helen, or the Queen of love. **1761** STERNE *Trist. Shandy* III. xxxix, My father's

ideas ran on as much faster than the translation, as the translation out-moved my uncle Toby's.

2. To defeat by a move, as in chess.

1860 Forster *Gr. Remonstr.* 197 Every move they made was outmoved. 1887 *Witness* (N.Y.) 13 Apr. 5 A game of political chess, with the chances that the Prohibitionists will be outmoved.

†**'outnal(l.** *Obs.* [Origin unascertained. It may be orig. a place-name, but no suitable local name has been found in France or the Low Countries.]

A kind of linen thread: see quot. 1812.

1662 *Book of Rates* in *Statutes at large* (1786) II. 417 Lions or Paris thread, the bail,.. £3; Outnall thread, the dozen pound, £3; sisters thread, the pound, 15s. 1721 C. King *Brit. Merch.* I. 290 (An Account of Goods imported from France 1686)..Onions, Pease, Quails,..Outnall Thred, Ticking, Copperas. 1812 J. Smyth *Pract. Customs* (1821) 257 Outnal is the Flemish and Dutch brown flaxen thread.

out-name to **out-Nero**: see out-.

†**out'neme,** *a.* and *adv. Obs.* Also 3-4 **utenem(e, -nemes, utnemis.** [f. OE. *út*, out *adv.* + **næme*, ablaut deriv. of *niman* to take. The form in *-s* is difficult to account for.] Exceptional, special, extraordinary, immense.

a 1300 *Cursor M.* 22591 (Edinb.) þe tend [sign] outnem, [*C.* utenemes, *G.* vte-tan, *F.* outane, *Tr.* out taken] es for to neuin. *Ibid.* 4827 (Cott.) For þis hunger it es vtenem [*Gött.* vte-neme, *Fairf.* out-neme, *rime* barn-teme]. *Ibid.* 1315 (Gött.) A spring Of a welle þat es vtnemis [*Cott.* vte-nemes], þar fra renis four grete stremis.

outness ('aʊtnɪs). [f. out *adv.* or *a.* + -ness.]

1. The quality, fact, or condition of being out or external, esp. of being external to the percipient or to the mind; externality.

1709 Berkeley *Th. Vision* §46 The ideas of space, outness, and things placed at a distance. 1710 —— *Princ. Hum. Knowl.* §43. 1804-6 Syd. Smith *Mor. Philos.* (1850) 5 When the mass of mankind hear..that what mankind consider as their arms and legs, are not arms and legs, but ideas accompanied with the notion of outness. 1821 Coleridge in *Blackw. Mag.* X. 249 Outness is but the feeling of otherness (alterity), rendered intuitive, or alterity visually represented. 1864 C. M. Ingleby *Introd. Metaph.* I. §12 Any luminous impression on the retina at once excites the perception of outness. It is impossible to say to what point this outness is relative.

2. Utterance, outward expression.

1851 Robertson *Serm.* Ser. II. xi. (1864) 145 As if the heart could not bear its own burden, but must give it outness.

3. Occupation with or interest in what is without.

1861 J. Brown *Horæ Subs.* Ser. II. *Educ. through Senses* 486 Cultivate observation, energy, handicraft, ingenuity, outness in boys so as to give them a pursuit as well as a study.

out-nick, -night, etc.: see out-.

†**out'nim,** *v.* (*prep.*) *Obs.* [out- 15.]

1. *trans. lit.* To take out. (Only as two words, OE. *út niman*, pa. t. *nam út*: see nim *v.*)

2. To except.

(In the quot. the construction is obscure.)

c 1350 *Old Us. Winchester* in *Eng. Gilds* (1870) 353 And þat ne no man out nyme by no manere of fraunchise.

3. The imperative = 'except, leave out' is used prepositionally: cf. except *prep.*

1340 *Ayenb.* 250 Alle þe wyttes of þe bodye, outnime þe lhordssip of riȝte scele.

outnoise (aʊt'nɔɪz), *v.* [out- 21.] *trans.* To outdo in making a noise, to excel in noisiness.

1639 Fuller *Holy War* IV. vii. (1840) 188 If these two orders had not helped to out-noise those supposed heretics. 1676 Shadwell *Libertine* v. Wks. 1720 II. 172, I warrant you, when they cry out, let us out-noise 'em. 1846 K. Digby *Broadst. Hon., Tancredus* II. 5 Horrible yells of debauchery which out-noised the storm.

†**out'nome,** *pple.* (*prep.*) *Obs.* Also 4 **outynome.** The pa. pple. of outnim (in full *outnomen*), used in absolute constr. with a following sb. or clause, so as to be at length viewed as a prep. or conj. adv. = except *pple.*, etc. B. 1, C. 1. Cf. out-take(n.

1340 *Ayenb.* 221 Ine þo stat me ssel loki chastete outynome þe dede of spoushod. *c* 1350 in *Eng. Gilds* 350 In hys hows, oþer in oþer stede; out-nome on to þe meyres hows. *Ibid.* 351 þat non ne shal make burelle werk,.. outnome þat eueriche fullere makye oon by ȝere.

'out-nook. [out- 1.] An outlying corner; an out-of-the-way or remote spot.

1598 Sylvester *Du Bartas* II. ii. *Columnes* 194 It's the midst of the concentrik orbs Whom neuer angle nor out-nook disturbs. 1620-55 I. Jones *Stone-Heng* (1725) 5 [That] they chose such an Out-nook or Corner as Anglesey.

out-nose, etc.: see out-.

out'number, *v.* [out- 21.] *trans.* To exceed in number, to number more than. Hence **out'numbering** *ppl. a.*

1670 Dryden *Conq. Granada* I. i, Unarm'd and much out-number'd we retreat. 1760-72 H. Brooke *Fool of Qual.* (1809) III. 82 They out-numbered us three to one. 1795 Southey *Joan of Arc* v. 423 Frequent and fierce the garrison repell'd Their far out-numbering foes. 1879 Froude *Cæsar* xix. 322 He was besieging an army far outnumbering his own.

†**out'numen,** *ppl. a.* and *adv. Obs.* In 3 ut-. [ME. *út-, outnumen, -nomen*, pa. pple. of *út* or *out nimen* to take out, to except.]

A. *adj.* Exceptional, extraordinary, special; eminent; distinguished.

c 1200 Ormin 163 Forr he schall ben utnumenn mann Inn haliȝ lif & læfe. *Ibid.* 460 Forr þatt ȝho shollde childenn an Utnumenn child to manne. *a* 1225 *Juliana* 7 As he hefde bihalden..hire utnumne, feire & freoliche ȝuheðe.

B. *adv.* Exceptionally, especially.

a 1225 *Ancr. R.* 56 He dude þreo vtnummen heaued sunnen & deadliche. *c* 1230 *Hali Meid.* 19 To singe þat swote song & þat englene dream ut nume murie.

Hence †**ut'numenly** *adv.*, exceptionally, specially.

c 1200 Ormin 12283, & lætenn þatt tu cwemesst Godd Utnumennliȝ wiþþ alle.

out of ('aʊtəv), *prep. phr.* Also 1-4 út of, 4- out o, (7- o'), 4-7 out a; 4-6 oute, owt(e of. [orig., and still in writing, two words, viz. the adv. out followed by the prep. of (in its primary sense = from). In analysis *out of* is precisely on the same level with the obs. *down of, up of*, and the current *forth of, out from, out to, down from*, and other instances of an adv. followed by a prep. which defines its relation to an object. But in OE. as in OS. and the Scandinavian langs. *út of* (OS., ON. *út af*, Sw. *ut af*, Da. *ud af*) became the regular equivalent of L. *ex*, Gr. ἐξ, ἐκ (while Ger. and Du. used the adv. itself as a prep.); *out of* has thus acquired a unity of sense and also of pronunciation, which entitle it to separate treatment, whereby also its own sense-development can be more distinctly exhibited.

The history of *out of* is partly parallel to that of *in to*, with the differences that the latter is now written *into* as one word, and that *out of* is the opposite, not only of *into*, but also of the static *in*. One reason why *out of* has not needed to be written as one word may be that the distinction now made between *into* and *in to* is in the case of *out* expressed by *out of* and *out from*: thus 'they came in to me, into my house', 'he went out from me, out of my house'.]

I. Of motion or direction. (Opp. to *into.*)

1. *lit.* From within (a containing space or thing).

c 893 K. Ælfred *Oros.* vi. xxxviii. §1 Hie aforan ut of þære byriȝ. *c* 900 tr. *Bæda's Hist.* iv. xviii. [xvi.] (1890) 308 þa fluȝon ða cneohtas ut of þæm ealonde. 1154 *O.E. Chron.* an. 1137 Sume fluȝen ut of lande. *c* 1290 *Beket* 343 in *S. Eng. Leg.* I. 116 þe king ovt of Noremandie cam In-to Enguelonde. *a* 1440 *Sir Degrev.* 899, I shall teche the a gyn Out of this castel to wyn. 1450 W. Somner in *Four C. Eng. Lett.* 4 Yn the syght of all his men he was drawyn ought of the grete shippe. 1560 Daus tr. *Sleidane's Comm.* 163 b, [He] plucketh out of his bosome a lether bagge, and takynge out of it certen letters, hasteth out of the doers. 1618 S. Ward *Iethro's Iustice* (1627) 11, I wonder not that Christ..whipt out the chapmen out of the Temple. 1742 H. Walpole *Lett.* I. 156 Every body is going out of town. 1819 Scott *Ivanhoe* xliii, To scourge out of thee this boyish spirit of bravado. 1871 M. Collins *Mrq. & Merch.* I. i. 8 It has..cut an awkward cantle out of my property. 1872 *Punch* 2 Mar. 88/1 He fairly laughed the Bill out of the House.

b. Of direction: From within; so as to point, project, or lead away from.

c 1400- [see come *v.* 64 d]. 1560 Daus tr. *Sleidane's Comm.* 163 b, Lookynge downe out of the stowffe wyndowe [L. *ex hypocausti fenestra*] into the courte. 1601 Holland *Pliny* II. 278 It groweth ordinarily vpon rockes bearing out of the sea. 1874 Farrar *Christ* I. 476 Minarets rising out of their groves of palm and citron. 1885 Rita *Like Dian's Kiss* i. 7 Room after room, one opening out of another.

c. From among (a number), from the group of. †*Arith.* From (in subtraction).

1594 Hooker *Eccl. Pol.* Pref. ii. §1 Officers chosen by the people yearly out of themselves. 1594 Blundevil *Exerc.* I. iii. (1636) 7 Take 7 out of 14 and there remaineth 7. 1761 Hume *Hist. Eng.* (1826) II. xi. App. ii. 116 The Jew engaged to pay one mark out of every seven that he should recover. 1883 *Manch. Exam.* 29 Nov. 5/1 There are three..courses open to us, and out of these we have to make our choice.

2. From within (the space to which action, influence, or presence extends); from within the range of.

a 1300 *Cursor M.* 2073 þou do þe suith out o my sight. *c* 1425 Lydg. *Assembly of Gods* 96 Let hym nat escape out of your daungere. 1535 Coverdale *2 Chron.* vii. 20 This house ..wil I cast awaye out of my presence. 1748 *Anson's Voy.* II. v. 171 They flattered themselves they were got out of his reach. 1813 Wellington in Gurw. *Desp.* (1838) XI. 62 Filing out of sight of the trenches.

3. From (a condition or state, bodily or mental); from one literary form (e.g. prose or verse) or one language (*into* another).

c 1205 Lay. 359 þat he heom wolde leaden..out of þeowe-dome. 1390 Gower *Conf.* I. 47 And I abreide Riht as a man doth out of slep. *c* 1485 *Digby Myst.* I. 197, I put the owt of dought. 1490 Caxton *Eneydos* Colophon, The boke of Eneydos..whiche hathe be translated oute of latyne in to frenshe, And oute of frenshe reduced in to Englysshe by me wylliam Caxton. 1560 Daus tr. *Sleidane's Comm.* 5 Nor exclude out of his favour one that were willyng to amende. 1607 J. Norden *Surv. Dial.* II. 67 To bring him out of conceite with the goodness and validitie thereof. 1849 Macaulay *Hist. Eng.* iv. I. 433 His majesty..was thought by the physicians to be out of danger. 1887 Hall Caine *Coleridge* i. 22 The severe teacher who flogged him out of his infidelity ridiculed him out of false taste in poetry.

b. From (a post or office).

a 1592 Greene *George a Greene* Wks. 1831 II. 195, I shall be turned out of mine office. 1607 Shaks. *Timon* I. ii. 207 Well, would I were Gently put out of Office, before I were forc'd out. *a* 1904 *Mod.* They were worried out of their professorships.

4. From (a possession, property, tenet, etc.): expressing deprivation.

1500-20 Dunbar *Poems* xiii. 33 Sum is put owt of his possessioun. 1560 Daus tr. *Sleidane's Comm.* 280 They were taken all and striped out of their armure. 1604 Shaks. *Oth.* IV. ii. 188, I haue wasted my selfe out of my meanes. 1694 Atterbury *Serm., Prov.* xiv. 6 (1726) I. 198 To be talk'd out of their Pleasures and their Privileges. *a* 1782 Bp. Newton *Dissert.* xxii. Wks. II. 462 Cajoled and flattered out of their estate, out of their reputation, out of their understanding. 1875 [see cheat *v.* 2].

5. From (a source or origin): either implying literal motion, or *fig.* derivation. Also of a horse, etc. in reference to its dam.

c 1475 *Rauf Coilȝear* 16 The winde blew out of the Eist. 1535 Coverdale *Matt.* xii. 37 Out of thy wordes thou shalt be iustified. 1568 Grafton *Chron.* I. 119 Mahomet..came out of a base stock. 1611 Tourneur *Ath. Trag.* IV. iii, If yow argue merely out of nature Doe yow not degenerate from that. 1662 Stillingfl. *Orig. Sacr.* I. iii. §10 He quotes it out of Pliny. 1816 *Sporting Mag.* XLVIII. 185 She..was got by Midnight, out of a small well-bred mare. 1870 J. H. Newman *Gram. Assent* II. x. 451 That availableness arises out of their coincidence, and out of what does that coincidence arise? 1875 Jowett *Plato* (ed. 2) III. 34 He should get money out of the Greeks before he assisted them.

b. From (something) as a cause or motive: As the result or effect of; because or by reason of, on account of.

1561 T. Hoby tr. *Castiglione's Courtyer* I. (1577) E vj, But wee..do binde our selues wyth certaine new lawes out of purpose. 1591 Shaks. *Two Gent.* v. iv. 89 My master charg'd me to deliuer a ring to Madam Siluia: wᶜ (out of my neglect) was neuer done. 1690 *Def. Rights Univ. Oxford* Pref., Not only out of respect to ourselves but out of kindness to the City. 1800 Wellington *Let. to Lieut. Col. Close* in Gurw. *Desp.* (1837) I. 80 As you come only out of compliment to me. 1880 McCarthy *Own Times* III. xxxvii. 138 The crowds go for the most part out of curiosity.

c. From (the material of which a thing is made or constructed); = of 20.

1605 Shaks. *Lear* I. iv. 146 Nothing can be made out of nothing. 1764-7 Lyttelton *Hen. II* (1771) III. iv. 94 A fort ..erected out of the ruins of that most ancient city. 1842 Macaulay *Ess., Machiavelli* (1887) 31 Out of his surname they have coined an epithet for a knave, and out of his Christian name a synonym for the Devil. 1866 Sala *Barbary* 112 The feasibility of twisting a rope out of the sands of the Sahara. *Mod.* She made them out of old cigar-boxes.

†**d.** Arising from (in time or succession); from being (so and so), after being. *Obs.*

1423 Jas. I *Kingis Q.* iv, Discryving first of his prosperitee, And out of that his infelicitee. 1638 Junius *Paint. Ancients* 58 He became a very great philosopher out of a shamefully deboist ruffian.

e. From a base in; using (a place) as a centre of operations.

1960 'E. McBain' *Give Boys Great Big Hand* xii. 146 We were going to run away together... I could always get work out of Miami. 1974 *Publishers Weekly* 24 June 56/2 Working out of Bozeman, Montana, Jack Folsom has enjoyed the help of some 60 'friends'. 1975 *Listener* 27 Nov. 712/2 Marshall McLuhan still works out of a ramshackle office in a converted coach-house on the edge of the University of Toronto. 1975 B. Garfield *Hopscotch* xv. 145 He was the District Director out of Atlanta. 1976 *Times Lit. Suppl.* 25 June 784/4 The miscellaneous radio amateurs and visionaries who worked out of shacks and garages. 1976 *Church Times* 26 Nov. 7/4 Mrs. Briant now works out of Vancouver's Christ Church Cathedral, where she has set up a ministry for shut-ins.

6. With ellipsis of verb *go*, or the like, esp. in imperative uses. *out of* (the house, etc.) ***with***: put, or have out of (the house, etc.). Cf. out *adv.* 13.

c 1400 *Lanfranc's Cirurg.* 195 þat þere mowe noon eir out þerof. 1470-85 Malory *Arthur* vii. xx, He wille neuer oute of this countrey vntyl that he haue me ageyne. 1598 Shaks. *Merry W.* iv. ii. 193 Out of my doore, you Witch, you Ragge ..out, out. 1610 —— *Temp.* I. i. 29 Out of our way I say. 1656 Trapp *Expos. 2 Cor.* x. 5 Out of doors with this Hagar. 1692 R. L'Estrange *Josephus, Antiq.* iv. viii. (1733) 92 It will never out of their Memories. 1886 W. J. Tucker *E. Europe* 71 Out of my carriage, at once, you dog!

7. ***from out of***: see from *prep.* 15 c.

c 1375 *Sc. Leg. Saints* ii. (*Paulus*) 400 Fra owt of grece com mony men To rowme. 1594, 1789 [see from *prep.* 15 c].

II. Of position. (Opp. to *in.*)

8. *lit.* Not within (a space or containing thing), beyond the confines of, outside.

It may express the position resulting from the motion in sense 1, or that of opposition to inward motion, or simple position with respect to a boundary.

c 1350 *Will. Palerne* 1691 Hold ȝou ouȝt of heie gates for happes, i rede. 1583 Hollyband *Campo di Fior* 73 My mother is out of the house. 1595 Shaks. *John* iv. i. 17 So I were out of prison, and kept Sheepe I should be merry as the day is long. 1711 Steele *Spect.* No. 141 ¶2 While I was out of Town, the Actors have flown in the Air. 1802-12 Bentham *Ration. Judic. Evid.* (1827) IV. 604 Out of British ground, it would be difficult to form an idea of the pitch to which the grievance..has been raised in England. 1860 Miss Yonge *Stokesley Secret* ix. (1880) 260 It was the first time that Christabel had seen her out of her beplumed hat.

b. On the outer side of, outside. *rare.*

1777 Sheridan *Sch. Scand.* III. iii, The bough-pots out of the window.

c. At a (specified) distance from, away from (a containing space, as a town, or the like).

1420 H. Stafford in Ellis *Orig. Lett.* Ser. iv. I. 66 The which Abbey ys but a lege ouȝt of Mayn. **1459** *Rolls of Parlt.* V. 369/2 At Newcastell, but vi myle oute of Eggleshall, where the Quene and the Prynce then were. **1625** A. Wheelock in *Ussher's Lett.* (1686) 329 He is but Four Miles dwelling out of Cambridg. **1798** Charlotte Smith *Yng. Philos.* IV. 215 He said that Mr. Brownjohn's villa was a little out of the road. **1863** Mrs. Carlyle *Lett.* III. 154 Ealing, some seven miles out of London.

d. (Taken) from among, (occurring) among or in (a number).

Expressing the result of the motion in 1 c.

1562 in W. H. Turner *Select. Rec. Oxford* 291 Three persons owte of the xiij for the tyme beinge. **1766** Goldsm. *Vic. W.* iii, Out of fourteen thousand pounds we had but four hundred remaining. **1866** Sala *Barbary* 89 To shut up the shops one day out of the seven. **1875** Jowett *Plato* (ed. 2) I. p. xx, When one epistle out of a number is spurious.

e. *out of this world*: see world *sb.*

9. Outside the local range of (some action or faculty); as, ***out of reach, sight, hearing, presence***; ***out of one's head***: out of one's mind or memory (see also head *sb.*[1] 36).

c **1450** tr. *De Imitatione* I. xxiii. 30 Whan man is oute of siȝt, sone he passiþ oute of mynde. *a* **1500** Medwall *Nature* (Brandl) II. 796 So that I may stand out of daunger Of gon shot. **1712** Addison *Spect.* No. 407 ¶2 He is placed quite out of their hearing. *a* **1766** Mrs. F. Sheridan *Sidney Bidulph* IV. 92 Put up on a shelf..to be out of both their reaches. **1814** Jane Austen *Mansf. Park* I. i. 6 She could not get her poor sister and her family out of her head. **1849** Macaulay *Hist. Eng.* v. I. 549 The entrance of the Zuyder Zee was out of their jurisdiction. **1882** *Times* 12 July 5 Our gunboats..were supposed to be out of range. **1901** 'L. Malet' *Hist. R. Calmady* v. x. 469 Obviously it was impossible to go back. He must go on rather—out of sight, out of mind. **1912** F. M. Hueffer *Panel* I. iv. 109 You meant to get her out of your head. **1935** M. de la Roche *Young Renny* iv. 32 Lord, what a waist he has! Do you suppose he can put a solid meal out of sight? **1938** W. de la Mare *Memory* 40 So gaily resigned To out-of-sight being out-of-mind.

10. Outside the limits of (something non-material which has definite bounds), as ***out of the Church, the Christian faith, confession, marriage, wedlock, apprenticeship***, etc.

c **1430** *Hymns Virg.* (1867) 120 Bettyr they were to be oute off lyve. **1456** Sir G. Haye *Law Arms* (S.T.S.) 104 Thame that ar out of the faith of Jhesu Crist. **1495** *Act 11 Hen. VII*, c. 2 §5 Noon apprentice..[shall] pley..at the Tenys..in no wise out of Cristmas. **1561** T. Hoby tr. *Castiglione's Courtyer* III. (1577) P vij, This communication now is out of the purpose that I went about. **1565–72** Cooper *Thesaurus*, *Furto conceptus*,..begotten out of maryage. **1713** Steele *Englishm.* No. 3. 19 The Church of England is intirely out of the Dispute. **1829** Carlyle *Misc.* (1857) II. 75 There is no Time and no Space out of the mind. **1849** Lingard *Hist. Eng.* (1855) VII. App. 277/1 Greenway..declares..that Bates never spoke one word to him on the subject, either in or out of confession.

b. Outside the bounds or sphere of, beyond (some condition of things), as ***out of number, measure, comparison, reason, belief, doubt, question, dispute, the common, the ordinary, the usual***, etc.

a **1425** *Cursor M.* 13166 (Trin.), I aske þe nouþer hous ny londe Ny noon oþere þing out of resoun. **1535** Coverdale *2 Esdras* iii. 7 Of him came..people, & kynreddes out of nombre. **1551** Robinson tr. *More's Utop.* I. (1895) 22 A man doubteles owte of comparison. **1581** J. Bell *Haddon's Answ. Osor.* 136 b, It is out of all controversie that Adam..was endued with wonderfull and absolute freedome of will. **1615** Bedwell tr. *Moham. Imp.* I. §10 That is out of doubt true. **1801** Strutt *Sports & Past.* II. iii. 94 Time out of mind. **1807** Southey *Espriella's Lett.* III. 146 His celestial history is more out of the Common. **1849** Macaulay *Hist. Eng.* vi. II. 109 It was therefore out of the power of the government to silence the defenders of the established religion. **1893** *Law Times* XCV. 29/2 It was expected that the meeting..would be a little out of the ordinary.

c. Not in the proper direction or track of, off the line of; having deviated from. Esp. in phrases expressing deviation or error: cf. out *adv.* 20 b.

1691 W. Nicholls *Answ. Naked Gospel* 57, I am afraid he is a little out of his Chronology again. **1719** De Foe *Crusoe* I. xii, I was perfectly out of my duty. **1806** Surr *Winter in Lond.* I. 190 'Upon my honour', said the captain,..'I am quite out of my cue here!' **1896** T. L. De Vinne *Moxon's Mech. Exerc., Printing* 403 Some characters must purposely be out of drawing.

d. *out of it*: not employed or included in (some action or affair); also, astray from the truth or 'true inwardness' of anything.

1830 M. Edgeworth *Let.* 8 Dec. (1971) 442 Poor Davies Gilbert to whom the place was in every way unsuited is well out of it. I hope he thinks so. **1880** *Punch* 25 Dec. 299/1, I was out of it, jolly clean out of it. **1884** *Pall Mall G.* 18 June 4/1 Indeed, 'C' Troop..has been rather 'out of it' in the matter of field service. **1889** *Spectator* 28 Dec., The ability to quit the centre of affairs, to stand 'out of it' without bitterness or spite. **1904** H. James *Golden Bowl* I. I. xxi. 344 He..moved her by..taking pity..on her just discernible depression... He guessed that she felt herself, as the slang was, out of it. **1916** Galsworthy *Sheaf* i. 15 She is simply too 'out of it' to know anything. **1955** *Times* 13 Aug. 8/7 Feeling not a little out of it, we nevertheless took tea with the ladies of the parish. **1959** *News Chron.* 10 July 3/4 Bungalow dwellers..may well have felt out of it. **1973** R. Lewis *Of Singular Purpose* vii. 157 You're well out of it, Harry. Believe me, you're well out of it.

e. (See quots.)

1963 *Amer. Speech* XXXVIII. 174 Drunk: soused, out of it, stoned, bombed. **1967** Wentworth & Flexner *Dict. Amer. Slang* Add. 698/1 *Out of it*... 3. Not concerned with mundane things, as when under the influence of a drug, obsession, all-consuming idea, etc.; in a state of euphoria. 4. Not 'with it'; stupid; 'square'. **1973** *To our Returned Prisoners of War* (Office of U.S. Secretary of Defense) 8 *Out of it*, to be out of touch with reality when under the influence of a drug, especially hallucinogens. To lack understanding and awareness, especially in a sub-culture. **1973** *Black Panther* 27 Oct. 12/3 James Jenkins..describes several inmates on 'F' block, who were once 'sharp dudes' as being 'completely out of it' following 'therapeutic sedation'.

11. Not in (a physical or mental state or condition); without, free from, or destitute of (a quality, etc.).

1340 *Ayenb.* 150 Þet..makeþ þane man al oute of wytte. *c* **1400** *Lanfranc's Cirurg.* 194 Þe skyn·is out of his propir colour. *c* **1449** Pecock *Repr.* II. x. 207 Thei ben out of eese, whanne thei seen tho deedis..doon. **1470–85** Malory *Arthur* IV. xxiii, Wel nyghe shee was oute of her mynde. **1568** Grafton *Chron.* I. 170 His whole armye was quite disordered and out of aray. **1639** Fuller *Holy War* II. xi. (1647) 58 A froward old woman who was never out of wrangling. **1685** Dryden *Thren. August.* 17 It took us unprepared and out of guard. *a* **1745** Swift *Direct to Servants* Wks. (1869) 568/1 Her mouth is out of taste. **1893** Earl Dunmore *Pamirs* II. 105 Our horses being out of condition. *a* **1904** *Mod.* It was foolish to try it, when he was out of training.

b. Not in (use, employment, service, office, work, etc.); usually with the implication of having been, or being normally, *in* the condition in question. ***out of work, out-of-work***: see work *sb.* 27.

1743 Bulkeley & Cummins *Voy. S. Seas* Pref. 13 When they were out of Pay, they look'd upon themselves as their own Masters. *a* **1774** Goldsm. *Surv. Exp. Philos.* (1776) I. 155 In short these kind of pendulums are now entirely out of use. **1776** *Trial of Nundocomar* 60/1, I was out of employment, and obliged to come here to seek it. **1812** Lady Granville *Lett.* (1894) II. 38 Two governesses out of place. *a* **1904** *Mod.* Many people are now out of work and in want.

12. Having lost, parted with, or been deprived of (something previously or normally possessed); destitute of, without.

1599 Shaks. *Hen. V*, III. vii. 163 These English are shrowdly out of Beefe. **1601** —— *All's Well* I. iii. 42, I am out a friends Madam. **1653** Bogan *Mirth Chr. Life* 271 If they be in poverty..yet shall they not be..cleane out of cash. **1822** W. Irving *Braceb. Hall* (1823) II. 64 He returned not long since, out of money, and out at elbows. *a* **1845** Hood *Our Village* 24 It's ten to one she's out of every thing you ask. **1856** Whyte Melville *Kate Cov.* xiv, He is sadly out of wind before he reaches the first landing. **1858** Geo. Eliot *Scenes Clerical Life* II. 189 Furnishing sugar or vinegar to..families that found themselves unexpectedly 'out of' those indispensable commodities. **1973** 'D. Halliday' *Dolly & Starry Bird* iii. 36, I hadn't a light for his cigar; Charles and I were out of matches.

13. Taken from, extracted from, derived from (spec. in giving the dam of a horse: cf. 5); †made from. In current use, both in the *spec.* sense, and as a *fig.* development of this.

a **1400–50** *Alexander* 86 Segis of many syde oute of sere remys. **1606** Shaks. *Tr. & Cr.* I. i. 15 Hee that will haue a Cake out of the Wheate, must needes tarry the grinding. **1611** —— *Wint. T.* I. ii. 122 They say it is a Coppy out of mine. **1652** Needham tr. *Selden's Mare Cl.* 82 The Customs out of this Sea were very great. **1711** Addison *Spect.* No. 121 ¶5, I shall add to this Instance out of Mr. Locke another out of the learned Dr. More. **1856** Lever *Martins of Cro' M.* 221 She's out of Crescent that ran a very good third for the Oaks. **1881** E. D. Brickwood in *Encycl. Brit.* XII. 184/2 Both grandsons of Eclipse and both out of Herod mares. **1892** A. W. Pinero *Magistrate* I. 24 You nominated yourself for the Matrimonial Stakes. Mr. Farringdon's The Widow, by Bereavement, out of Mourning. **1924** Galsworthy *White Monkey* III. xii. 295 The room seemed to him to have been got by a concert-hall out of a station waiting-room. **1950** 'P. Woodruff' *Island of Chamba* vii. 110 Their [*sc.* Muslims'] thought has the same pedigree as ours: by Greece out of Palestine. **1956** N. Marsh *Off with his Head* (1957) viii. 177 Teutonic Dancer by Subsidise out of Substiteuton. **1968** *Listener* 3 Oct. 452/2 If there were a radio stud-book, it could contain some such entry as ' Any Questions? by After-Dinner Speaker out of Group Therapy'. **1973** 'I. Drummond' *Jaws of Watchdog* xvi. 210 Humblebee was bred..by an imported French champion out of a mare by an Argentine quadruple-crown winner.

14. *Out of* is used phraseologically with many sbs., as balance, breath, conceit, countenance, doubt, employ, fashion, frame, hand, heart, humour, joint, keeping, mind, order, phase, place, pocket, print, register, repair, season, sense, sort(s, square, temper, time, trim, tune, use, voice, wit(s, work, etc.: see under the sbs. themselves. When these expressions are used attributively, they become adjective phrases: see III.

III. out-of- with a *sb.*, used *attrib.* as an adjective phrase. When such a phrase as *out of the way* is used predicatively, as in 'the place lies rather out of the way', the elements are written apart, but when used attrib. as in 'a curious out-of-the-way place', the elements are hyphened and the whole becomes an adjective phrase. The number of these is indefinite. Besides the more frequent, as out-of-date, out-of-door(s, out-of-fashion, out-of-time, out-of-the-way, treated among the main words, mention may be made of ***out-of-awareness*** (also as *sb.*), ***out-of-balance*** (also as *sb.* and *v.*), ***out-of-bounds*** (also as *sb.*), ***out-of-breath, out-of-centre, out-of-condition, out-of-context, out-of-control*** (also *ellipt.*), ***out-of-elbows*** (erron. for *out-at-elbows*), ***out-of-employment, out-of-focus*** (also as *sb.*), ***out-of-form, out-of-hours, out-of-humour, out-of-joint, out-of-key, out-of-livery, out-of-office, out-of-phase, out-of-place, out-of-pocket*** (also as *ellipt.*), ***out-of-reach, out-of-school, out-of-season, out-of-sync, out-of-the-beaten-track, out-of-the-body, out-of-the-common, out-of-the-ordinary, out-of-the-season, out-of-the-world, out-of-tune*** (also as *ellipt.*), ***out-of-use, out-of-wedlock, out-of-work***, (also *sb.*), etc. Sometimes derivatives are formed from these, as ***out-of-breathness, out-of-humourness, out-of-jointness, out-of-the-worldish, out-of-the-worldness, out-of-touchness, out-of-trueness, out-of-tuneness, -tunish***, with catachrestic variants, as ***out-of-fashioned, out-of-humoured***. ***out-of-round***: see round *sb.*; ***out-of-true***: see true *sb.*; ***out-of-truth*** see truth *sb.*

1965 *Canad. Jrnl. Linguistics* Fall 36 When one hears the paralanguage of a speaker, one first, rapidly and *out-of-awareness, establishes the base line of the speaker. **1974** *Florida FL Reporter* XIII. 11/2 Children work on language in an out-of-awareness situation. **1921** W. S. Ibbetson *Motor & Dynamo Control* vi. 194 It would not be correct to balance an *out-of-balance pulley by fixing a counter-weight on the armature core. **1932** R. Rawlinson in E. Molloy *Pract. Electr. Engin.* V. 1590/2 The function of voltage balancing on the two sides is done by a '3-wire balancer set', which is designed with regard to the maximum out of balance current which the supply company considers it necessary to legislate for. **1958** *Listener* 13 Nov. 780/1 Friction..and the slightest out-of-balance of the motor cause the axis of the gyroscope to deviate. **1967** L. Holmes *Odhams New Motor Manual* viii. 189/2 Out-of-balance can be caused by wheel damage or brake drum eccentricity. **1968** Burdett & Ellis *Motor Vehicle Mechanics' Course* II. xii. 284 Any 'out-of-balance' weight on the wheel..may give rise to a tendency to 'throw' the wheel up from the road and back down on to it once in every revolution of the wheel. **1974** Harvey & Bohlman *Stereo F.M. Radio Handbk.* v. 119 In this type of detector..the setting of R_4 is arranged to out-of-balance the signal currents in Q_{19} and Q_{22}. **1857** T. Hughes *Tom Brown's School Days* I. ix. 219 Many of the old wild *out-of-bounds habits stuck to them as firmly as ever. **1895** *Pall Mall G.* 15 Oct. 9/1 That long and perilous hole between the out-of-bounds field on the one side and the broken, rabbit-burrowed ground on the other. **1947** M. Lowry *Let.* 24 July (1967) 150 Into what roughs, out-of-bounds and quagmires we shall get ere the book be finished ..one knows not. **1973** *Guardian* 21 May 22/3 The long sixteenth, a treacherous hole into the wind with an out-of-bounds lurking on left. **1939** G. Greene *19 Stories* (1947) 156 Low *out-of-breath tones. **1900** E. Glyn *Visits of Elizabeth* 98 His snorts of *out-of-breathness could be heard for miles. **1972** C. Fremlin *Appointment with Yesterday* xi. 85 She should have realised that her middle-aged, *out-of-condition body would..rebel. **1977** F. Branston *Up & Coming Man* xiii. 133 A puffy, out-of-condition young man. **1951** *Mind* LX. 91 The unused, *out-of-context sentence specifies no speaker. **1973** R. Ludlum *Matlock Paper* ii. 16 Rumor; out-of-context statements..; constructed evidence. **1961** *Daily Mail* 20 July 9/8 His *out-of-control tractor plunged 20 ft. into the River Nar. **1974** H. L. Foster *Ribbin'* vii. 321 Most workers have strong feelings against intervening physically with a child's out-of-control behavior. **1974** G. Jenkins *Bridge of Magpies* vii. 104 Finally the out-of-control twisting of the boat eased. **1977** *O.D.* No. 3. 9/1 The circumstances of our interview with Schmidt were curious, weird, if not verging on the out-of-control. **1897** *Westm. Gaz.* 20 May 5/3 When one looks at these *out-of-elbow men slouching along. **1890** *Murray's Mag.* Aug. 230 An air of decadence, almost of *out-of-elbowness. **1898** *Westm. Gaz.* 14 Feb. 8/2 *Out-of-employment claims rose from £441..in 1896 to £710 last year. **1891** *Anthony's Photogr. Bull.* IV. 48 Persons who admire *out-of-focus art. **1946** *Nature* 30 Nov. 786/1 Thus any error in magnification due to slight out-of-focus in one camera was compensated by the other. **1962** L. S. Sasieni *Princ. & Pract. Optical Dispensing* xii. 303 From this we see the extent of the out-of-focus region. **1966** D. G. Brandon *Mod. Techniques Metallogr.* 29 The out-of-focus image of the specimen surface. **1967** E. Chambers *Photolitho-Offset* xi. 160 Slight out-of-focus and gentle vibration of the front of the camera during exposure are 'dodges' also used. **1961** *Times* 27 Dec. 4/1 Parfitt..must now have a chance of gaining his first Test cap in place of the *out-of-form M. J. K. Smith. **1977** *South China Morning Post* (Hong Kong) 22 July 18/5 Rick McCosker, Australia's out-of-form opener, boosted his chances of retaining his place for the third cricket Test against England next week with a fighting 77 against Warwickshire yesterday. **1967** *Guardian* 3 Aug. 3/7 A scheme for *out-of-hours deliveries in Greater London. **1977** *Times* 9 Sept. 2/3 An out-of-hours repair service for customers. **1675** Wycherley *Country Wife* II. i, Every raw, peevish, *out-of-humoured, affected..fop. **1803** W. Taylor in Robberds *Mem.* I. 441 Much allowance is due to Burnett's *out-of-humourness. **1899** *Westm. Gaz.* 13 June 4/3 That it is a 'cursed spite' which sets him to remedy the *out-of-joint time. **1962** *Times* 17 Jan. 13/1 The..slightly *out-of-key episode with the travelling salesman. **1976** 'J. Fraser' *Who steals my Name?* vii. 89 A tiny little oddness, one of those strange out-of-key facts a policeman is trained to spot. **1846** *Ecclesiologist* V. 142 *Out-of-livery servants might be admitted. **1961** *Times* 4 Sept. 5/1 His *out-of-office activities as a dosshouse owner. **1973** 'W. Haggard' *Old Masters* i. 11 An out-of-office politician. **1938** L. F. Blume *Transformer Engin.* xiv. 369 It would be of no advantage to introduce a circulating current having an *out-of-phase component. **1968** C. G. Kuper *Introd. Theory Superconductivity* iv. 65 The real part and the imaginary part of the dielectric constant respectively relate the in-phase and out-of-phase parts of the displacement to the electric field. **1974** *Country Life* 26 Dec. 1997/3 A smaller telescope..would still be an out-of-place intrusion on the landscape. **1822** Lamb *Elia* Ser. I. *Roast Pig*, I blamed my ..*out-of-place hypocrisy of goodness. **1885** *Law Times*

Rep. LII. 545/1 The plaintiffs..incurred various *out-of-pocket expenses. **1902** G. B. SHAW *Let.* 22 Oct. (1972) II. 284 Actual out-of-pocket loss. **1971** D. C. HAGUE *Managerial Econ.* iii. 67 It is unlikely that prices will be cut below out-of-pocket costs. **1972** G. DURRELL *Catch me a Colobus* ix. 182, I said that..I would be willing to cover his out-of-pocket expenses if he'd join the expedition to help us with our work. **1973** 'I. DRUMMOND' *Jaws of Watchdog* vii. 92 He was to be paid £15,000 in used notes, for his own pay-off and his out-of-pocket. **1891** M. O'RELL *Frenchm. in Amer.* 318 As one might gaze at some coveted but *out-of-reach fruit. **1867** J. W. HALES in Farrar *Ess. Lib. Educ.* 308 Pupils who enjoyed so few *out-of-school advantages. **1930** *Times Educ. Suppl.* 26 July 329/3 Organizational activities are relegated to out-of-school hours. **1959** *Times* 20 Jan. 9/3 The result is to be seen in those out-of-school activities which may land them in the juvenile courts. **1970** G. E. EVANS *Where Beards wag All* xix. 217 One of Mrs. Jay's out-of-school jobs was keeping pigs. **1900** *Westm. Gaz.* 27 July 5/3 Never..has there been such an *out-of-season demand for domestic fuel. **1944** M. LASKI *Love on Supertax* ii. 12 Lack of..out-of-season fruits. **1955** *Times* 3 May 4/2 Permission has been given by the Rugby Union for the Coventry team to play an out-of-the-season game. **1960** *Farmer & Stockbreeder* 12 Jan. 41 (Advt.), Details of the January out-of-season discounts are now available from your New Holland Dealer. **1966** *Listener* 24 Nov. 783/3 A boy, bored and neglected, at an out-of-season hotel. **1948** *Proc. IRE* XXXVI. 904/1 The effect would be to prolong excessively the *out-of-sync condition whenever a discontinuity occurred in the transmitted sync signal. **1956** M. STEARNS *Story of Jazz* (1957) xxiv. 301 The hectic, 'out-of-sync' short, *The Jazz Dance*, was filmed in one evening. **1967** *Listener* 21 Sept. 380/1, I rather miss the deliciously ludicrous sight of a singer trying to catch up with his own voice, like an out-of-sync film. **1977** *New Yorker* 25 July 19/3 Rumbles of thunder interspersed the lightning flashes in belated, out-of-sync fashion. **1946** G. N. M. TYRRELL *Personality of Man* VII. xxii. 199 These *out-of-the-body cases are of exceptional interest. It is worth pointing out that in two such cases..the percipients describe the process of getting out of their bodies in almost identical terms. **1969** *New Scientist* 3 July 33/2 Old wives tales..such as spontaneous telepathy, out-of-the-body experiences or poltergeists. **1890** HATTON *By Order of Czar* (1891) 91 She ..was a pleasant, cultured, odd, *out-of-the-common hostess. **1931** *Times Lit. Suppl.* 15 Oct. 788/1 A disturbing ..absolutely *out-of-the ordinary life-story. **1974** *Times* 9 Nov. 12/5 Andorra..has caught the imagination of many skiers looking for an out-of-the-ordinary holiday. **1775** MRS. GRANT *Lett. fr. Mount.* (1807) I. xxiv. 188 My *out of the world education. **1874** LISLE CARR *Jud. Gwynne* I. iv. 127 Living in such an out-of-the-world place. **1895** SAINTSBURY *Ess. Eng. Lit.* Ser. II. 103 De Quincey was still more bookish and *out-of-the-worldly. **1876** H. SIDGWICK *Let.* 24 Aug. in A. & E. Sidgwick *Henry Sidgwick* (1906) 323 There is a great charm in this scenery and in the feeling of *out-of-the-world-ness. **1916** D. H. LAWRENCE *Let* 9 Jan. (1932) 306 But come and see us here, because of the sea and the silence and peace and the out-of-the-worldness of it all. **1957** M. STEWART *Thunder on Right* iii. 38 The out-of-the-worldness of the place pressed heavily upon her. **1952** M. LOWRY *Let.* May (1967) 317 The essential..points are too often clouded as a result of the technical *out-of-touchness of the writing. **1960** *Guardian* 21 July 8/4 'Out-of-touchness' has produced a fervent desire for recognition. **1921** *Spectator* 26 Feb. 268/2 When you start your wall there seems by eye very little or nothing wrong with it, but when you have got it up some thirty or forty feet the *out-of-trueness is appalling. **1803** H. WYNNE *Diary* 6 July (1940) III. 83 A beautifull *out of tune Symphony, consisting of hair-dressers, butchers, &c. opened the play. **1917** T. S. ELIOT *Prufrock* 20 The voice returns like the insistent out-of-tune Of a broken violin. **1930** J. DOS PASSOS *42nd Parallel* I. 129 A little out of tune orchestra was playing. **1977** J. WAINWRIGHT *Day of Peppercorn Kill* 125 Somebody was whistling an out-of-tune version of *Sleepy-Time Gal.* **1789** WOLCOTT (P. Pindar) *Ld. B. & Eunuch* Wks. 1792 III. 112 Now came an *out-of-tunish note. **1900** MISS BROUGHTON *Foes in Law* xx. 291 Her tone expresses such utter *out-of-tuneness that he looks at her, startled. **1961** M. BEADLE *These Ruins are Inhabited* (1963) ix. 129 Some Irish girls emigrate briefly to give birth to *out-of-wedlock babies. **1972** *Guardian* 22 July 5/7 A single woman experiencing an out-of-wedlock pregnancy. **1887** *National Rev.* Mar. 63 *Out-of-work and sick allowances. **1888** *Pall Mall G.* 25 Aug. 1/1 To provide employment for the out-o'-works.

'out-of-'date, *adj. phr.* [See OUT OF *prep. phr.* III and DATE *sb.* 27.] That continues to exist beyond its proper date or time; obsolete. Also *absol.*

1628 EARLE *Microcosm., Blunt Man* (Arb.) 55 Hee sweares olde out of date innocent othes. *a* **1684** LEIGHTON *Serm.* Wks. (1868) 528 This was to him out-of-date useless stuff. **1887** *Spectator* 19 Mar. 395/1 There are chapters in this out-of-date book that deserve to be studied. **1928** *Manch. Guardian Weekly* 17 Aug. 132/1 This column..is apt to specialise in the out-of-date. **1938** *Times* 27 Aug. 3/5 There is to the comparatively un-modern and out of date something indefinably comforting in a winning score of 300.

,out-of-'dateness. [f. OUT-OF-DATE *adj. phr.* + -NESS.] The state or condition of being out-of-date; obsoleteness.

1915 E. CARPENTER *Healing of Nations* xvii. 208 Finally.. one realizes the monstrosity and absurdity of the present conflict—its anachronism and out-of-dateness in the existing age of human thought and feeling. **1928** *Sunday Dispatch* 30 Dec. 10/5 Consider the rich opportunity to tell the good man of his stuffiness, his out-of-dateness. **1930** A. HUXLEY *Vulgarity in Lit.* i. 3 It took several centuries to reduce Dante's guide-book to out-of-dateness. **1940** 'G. ORWELL' *Inside Whale* 103 They continue to be read in spite of their obvious out-of-dateness.

'out-of-'door, -'doors, *adj.* and *sb. phr.* Also out o' door(s. [The advb. phrase *out of door(s* (see OUT OF *prep. phr.* III, DOOR 5 a, and A-DOORS) used attrib., or subst.; in the attrib. use the form *out-of-door* is the more common.

The earlier form of the phrase was *out at door(s*, to which, however, the attrib. use appears not to go back.]

A. *adj.* **1.** That is outside the house, in the open air; done or grown in the open air; for use outside the house.

α. **1800** HELENA WELLS *Constantia Neville* (ed. 2) II. 94 Ignorance of the routine of out-of-door business. **1845** *Florist's Jrnl.* 115 If out-of-door varieties are most desirable. **1876** BRISTOWE *Th. & Pract. Med.* (1878) 854 Moderate out-of-door exercise.

β. **1831** *Edin. Rev.* LIV. 308 The reform..arms us against the out-of-doors poacher. **1855** MRS. GASKELL *North & S.* ii, Her out-of-doors life was perfect. Her in-doors life had its drawbacks. **1883** A. THOMAS *Modern Housewife* 67 The question of out-of-doors garments for children.

fig. **1855** LONGF. in *Life* (1891) II. 288 What an expansive, sunny, out-of-door nature Rossini has!

2. *spec.* **a.** Outside the Houses of Parliament; **b.** Carried on or given outside a workhouse, as ***out-of-door relief.***

1802 CANNING in *G. Rose's Diaries* (1860) I. 501 No out-of-doors' measure..will attain the end. **1838** DICKENS *O. Twist* xxiii, Don't you think out-of-door relief a very bad thing? **1897** MORLEY in *Daily News* 4 Oct. 8/2 Out-of-doors or extra Parliamentary speaking. Mr. Pitt..only made one out-of-door speech in all his career, and that was a speech.. of three sentences only.

B. *sb.* (the adj. used ellipt.) The world outside the house; the open air; also *fig.*

1819 KEATS *Let.* 4 Feb. (1958) II. 37 One not ill enough to forget out-of-doors. **1856** WHYTE MELVILLE *Kate Cov.* xi, I'm fond of the beautiful 'out-of-doors', instead of the fireside. **1858** GLENNY *Gard. Every-day Bk.* 87/2 To provide Cucumber plants for out-of-doors. **1895** *Outing* (U.S.) XXVI. 34/2 It was the untamed luxuriance of the out-of-doors that we love. **1970** D. MATHEW *Courtiers of Henry VIII* III. vi. 206 Henry VIII had been a great King of the out-of-doors. **1975** R. V. REDINGER *Geo. Eliot* (1976) vi. 377 The many scenes which take place in the unhampered out-of-doors.

Hence **'out-of-'doorer** *nonce-wd.*, one who is or goes out-of-doors; **,out-of-'doorness** *nonce-wd.*, the state or condition of being out-of-doors.

a **1845** HOOD *To St. Swithin* iv, A dripping Pauper crawls along the way, The only real willing out-of-doorer. **1929** W. DEEPING *Roper's Row* xxiii. 255 Hazzard liked..the play of the wind through his aggressive hair. It gave him a feeling of out-of-doorness and of freedom.

'out-of-'fashion, *adj. phr.* [See OUT OF *prep. phr.* III.] That is no longer in fashion or fashionable.

a **1680** BUTLER *Rem.* (1759) II. 148 How to drink, and how to eat No out-of-fashion Wine or Meat. **1805** LD. MOIRA in Moore *Mem.* (1853) I. 185 One of the out-of-fashion pieces of furniture fit to figure in the steward's room. **1895** *Daily News* 13 May 2/3 Inferior, out-of-fashion goods.

So, in same sense, †**out-of-fashioned** (*catachr.* after *old-fashioned*, etc.).

1673 WYCHERLEY *Gentleman Dancing-Master* II. ii, Bashfulness is the only out-of-fashioned thing that is agreeable. **1739** *Wks. Learned* I. 59 He has not even neglected the most out-of-fashion'd Works of this Kind.

out-office ('aʊt,ɒfɪs). [f. OUT- 1 + OFFICE *sb.* 9.] An outside building forming one of the offices of a mansion, farm-house, etc.; an outhouse.

1624 MASSINGER *Renegado* II. vi, There are so many lobbies, Out-offices, and dispartations, here Behind these Turkish hangings. **1741** RICHARDSON *Pamela* I. 233 While the Cook was sent to the Out-offices to raise the Men. **1890** *Guardian* 29 Oct. 1704/2 Two fine rooms for boys' and girls' school, staircases, out-offices.

out of print, *adj. phr.* [See PRINT *sb.* 7 b.] Of a book: no longer available from the publisher; also used with reference to gramophone records. Also as *sb.*

Written with hyphens when used *attrib.*

1674 [see PRINT *sb.* 7 b]. **1800** LOFFT in R. Bloomfield *Farmer's Boy* (ed. 3) 128 (*Appendix*), I am happy to be stopt here, by so good a cause as the urgency of the Publishers to complete a Third Edition; they informing me that the second is entirely out of print. **1895** [see PRINT *sb.* 7 b]. **1896** *N. & Q.* 25 Apr. *Advt.*, All out-of-print books speedily procured. **1927** R. B. MCKERROW *Introd. Bibliogr.* p. vi, I have..been repeatedly asked to reissue the pamphlet (now out of print). **1938** *New Statesman* 13 Aug. 262/1 There are two admirable lieder records. Karl Schmitt-Walker..sings ..two of the very best of Hugo Wolf's songs..the latter only available in the out-of-print Gerhardt album of Wolf. **1950** *John o' London's Weekly* 7 July 398/3 Every reader has got his own favourites among the out-of-print. **1965** *Amer. N. & Q.* Oct. 24/1 *New Variorum Edition of Shakespeare*—What is the status of in- and out-of-print volumes in the set? **1973** L. SNELLING *Heresy* I. 12 Some out-of-print unknown. .. Why, by the way, is he unknown and out of print? **1975** *Times Lit. Suppl.* 22 Aug. 956/6 (Advt.), Any American books, new or out-of-print. **1977** *Gramophone* Sept. 448/2 (Advt.), We still have secondhand LP and 78 Departments where many unusual and out of print records may be found.

out of series, *adj. phr.* [f. OUT OF *prep. phr.* 8, III + SERIES.] (See quot. 1952.)

Written with hyphens when used *attrib.*

1952 J. CARTER *ABC for Bk. Collectors* 128 Of an edition specifically limited in number, there will usually be printed some extra copies... Such copies are understood not to invalidate the certificate of limitation; and their status is sometimes indicated by the words out of series, instead of a number. **1977** *Q. Jrnl. Library of Congress* July 233/2 The copy acquired by the Library is an out-of-series, unnumbered example on Arches paper.

,out-of-'sight, *adj. phr.* (*sb.*) Also *colloq.* out o' sight, OUTASIGHT *a.* [f. OUT OF *prep. phr.* 9, III + SIGHT *sb.*[1] 10 b.]

A. *adj. phr.* **1.** Outside the range of sight; distant.

1876 GEO. ELIOT *Dan. Der.* II. IV. xxxi. 280 She was really getting somewhat febrile in her excitement... Was it at the novelty simply, or the almost incredible fulfilment about to be given to her girlish dreams of being 'somebody'—walking through her own furlongs of corridor and under her own ceilings of an out-of-sight loftiness.

2. Excellent, incomparable, superior; delightful, exciting, surprising. *slang* (orig. *U.S.*).

1893 [see OUTASIGHT *a.*]. **1896** ADE *Artie* xi. 94 She looked out o' sight! Some of 'em have got their sealskins and their sparklers, but this little girl, with that new make-up and the flowers, beat the best of 'em. **1897** C. W. CHESNUTT *Let.* 24 Sept. in H. M. Chesnutt *Charles Waddell Chesnutt* (1952) x. 81, I saw the Shaw Memorial and the new Public Library Building, which are 'out of sight'. **1902** J. D. CORROTHERS *Black Cat Club* i. 26 'Out o' sight!' yelled a dozen voices as the poem was concluded. **1927** C. SANDBURG *Amer. Songbag* 279 The corn we raise is our delight, The melons, too, are out of sight. **1961** *Down Beat* 5 Jan. 23, I find some of the musicians I've encountered on the road rather ridiculous... It seems everything is 'something else' these days. Or is it 'out of sight'? **1966** *Surfer* VII. IV. 11 The waves are a perfection 10 to 15 feet and straight over. Really up tight and out of sight! **1970** *Times* 6 July 8/5 Whenever possible he liked to make a point of talking to drug users on their own ground... An action that led one girl student to remark 'for an official person he's absolutely out of sight.' **1973** *Ottawa Jrnl.* 14 July 24/2, I met this groovy dude at the bowling alley. He is out of sight.

B. *sb.* One who or that which is unseen. *rare.*

1930 AUDEN *Poems* 18 Better where no one feels, The out-of-sight, buried too deep for shafts.

,out-of-'state, *adj. phr.* [f. OUT OF *prep. phr.* 8, III + STATE *sb.* 31 c.] Originating from outside a state of the United States. Also *ellipt.* as *sb.*, the area outside a particular state. Hence **,out-of-'stater,** a person originating from outside a particular state.

1935 *Amer. Mercury* July 290/2, I was also faced with their prejudice against out-of-town and out-of-state teachers. **1938** *Amer. Speech* XIII. 178 The larger southern part [of Idaho]..since the days of the Oregon trail has received a greater percentage of 'out-of-staters'. **1943** *Sun* (Baltimore) 28 Apr. 28/3 Dealers in a poultry black market on the Eastern Shore, including..live-chicken buyers from out-of-State and Baltimore wholesalers. **1948** *Herald-Press* (St. Joseph, Mich.) 14 Aug. 1/1 Many a speeding out-of-state motorist is of the opinion that the St. Joseph policemen are a lot of meanies. **1964** J. MASTERS *Trial at Monomoy* i. 11 Bunch of crackpots, long-hairs, foreigners, out-of-staters. **1973** *N.Y. Law Jrnl.* 26 July 1/6 The law students interviewed, most of them from out-of-state, made these observations. **1973** D. BARNES *See Woman* (1974) 90 A Buick. It had out-of-state plates on it. **1974** *Columbia* (S. Carolina) *Record* 25 Apr. 18-C/5 Many out-of-staters are showing a lot of interest in purchasing real estate in the Santee-Cooper complex. **1976** *CB Mag.* June 23/1 (Advt.), Special Bonding Service—protects you from being arrested if you ever get caught speeding out-of-state without enough money to pay the fine.

'out-of-the-'way, *adj. phr.* [The advb. phrase *out of the way* (see OUT OF *prep. phr.* III and WAY *sb.*), used *attrib.*]

A. *adj. phr.* **1.** Remote from any great highway or frequented route; remote from any centre of population, unfrequented, secluded.

[**1483** *Cath. Angl.* 264/2 Oute of way, *auius, deuius.*] **1797** MRS. RADCLIFFE *Italian* xii, Nobody would think of building one in such an out-of-the-way place. **1838** DICKENS *O. Twist* xlii, The very out-of-the-wayest house I can set eyes on. **1866** *N. & Q.* 3rd Ser. IX. 437/2 The original nautical tradition is still preserved by out-of-the-way people.

2. Seldom met with, unusual, far-fetched; hence, extraordinary, odd, peculiar, remarkable, *outré.*

1704 N. N. tr. *Boccalini's Advts. fr. Parnass.* II. To Rdr., A short Collection of the Polite out of the way Expressions, which are to be met with in their Half Sheet Specimen. **1712** STEELE *Spect.* No. 296 ¶7 My out-of-the-way Capers, and some original Grimaces. **1782** MAD. D'ARBLAY *Lett.* 15 Oct., I know you love to hear particulars of all out-of-the-way persons. **1808** SCOTT *Autobiog.* in *Lockhart* i, Surprise at the quantity of out-of-the-way knowledge which I displayed. **1886** J. K. JEROME *Idle Thoughts* (1889) 63 To hit upon an especially novel, out-of-the-way subject.

3. Departing from the proper path; devious.

a **1732** T. BOSTON *Crook in Lot* (1805) 11 There is.. nothing more apt to occasion out-of-the-way steps. **1825** BROCKETT *N.C. Gloss., Out o' the way*,..wayward.

Hence **,out-of-the-'wayness.**

1800 COLERIDGE *Unpubl. Lett., to J. P. Estlin* (1884) 81 My own subtleties..lead me into strange..transient out-of-the-waynesses. **1887** RUSKIN *Præterita* II. ii. 61 My father and mother's quiet out-of-the-wayness at first interested, soon pleased, and at last won them. **1899** KIPLING *From Sea to Sea* I. xii. 307 It [*sc.* Kobé, in Japan] lives among hills, but the hills are all scalped, and the general impression is of out-of-the-wayness. **1926** S. T. WARNER *Lolly Willowes* II. 129 There's not such another village in Buckinghamshire for out-of-the-way-ness.

B. as *adv.* Oddly; exceptionally, extraordinarily.

1717 MRS. CENTLIVRE *Bold Stroke for Wife* I. i, The most whimsical, out-of-the-way tempered man I ever heard of. **1901** 'M. FRANKLIN' *My Brilliant Career* x. 80, I really believe that on that night I did not look out of the way ugly. **1928** E. M. FORSTER in *Life to Come* (1972) 105 He was completely sincere when he told the Trevor Donaldsons that he had had an out-of-the-way pleasant weekend. **1939** —— in *Ibid.* 118 If only he wasn't so handsome, so out-of-the-way handsome.

C. as *sb.* A remote spot, an out-of-the-way place.

1971 *Islander* (Victoria, B.C.) 7 Nov. 13/4 Colorful people who lived at these out-of-the-ways on the west..coast.

'out-of-'time, *adj. phr.* [See OUT OF *prep. phr.* III.] Not suitable to the time, unseasonable.

1483 CAXTON *Gold. Leg.* 257 b/2 We wold haue..drowned yow by cause your dissolute & oute of tyme ianglyng. **1909** *Westm. Gaz.* 4 Sept. 13/2 He is so full of admiration for James III.—the 'Old Pretender', in common language—that he casts an out-of-time vote for him.

,out-of-'town, *adj. phr.* (*sb.*) [OUT OF *prep. phr.* 8, III.] **A.** *adj.* Situated, originating from, or occurring outside a town. Also, unsophisticated.

1825 HONE *Every-day Bk.* I. 950 My own out-of-town single-room. **1891** *Boston Daily Globe* 24 Mar. 5/8 Out of town people sending to us for wines. **1903** R. BEDFORD *True Eyes* 198 The two walked down the rise on its out-of-town side. **1930** E. WAUGH *Vile Bodies* x. 174 There were a great number of journalists making the best of an 'out-of-town' job. **1937** M. HILLIS *Orchids on your Budget* iv. 71 When an out-of-town cousin turns up, you undoubtedly entertain her more lavishly. **1957** H. ROOSENBERG *Walls came tumbling Down* ix. 209 She was going..to make some out-of-town phone calls. **1959** *Manch. Guardian* 10 Aug. 3/1 Scotland's 'Theatre in the Hills' is a model for out-of-town theatres. **1971** *Daily Hampshire Gaz.* (Northampton, Mass.) 9 Nov. 1/3 Servicemen based in Northampton led groups of out-of-town based gas men to various sections of the town. **1973** J. MANN *Only Security* vii. 81 I've never seen anything so horrible as one of those out-of-town shopping centres I saw in the Midlands. **1977** *New Yorker* 9 May 35/1 Most of them [*sc.* students] were so nice and out-of-town that they were not completely comfortable with escalators and revolving doors.

B. *sb.* A person originating from outside a particular town. Also **,out-of-'towner**.

a **1911** D. G. PHILLIPS *Susan Lenox* (1917) II. vi. 162 Except for 'out-of-towners', the married men were the chief support of their profession. **1941** *Reader's Digest* May 29/1 Sometimes out-of-towners leave no tip at all. **1958** *Manch. Guardian* 7 June 4/6 The out of towners swarm in and laugh in the wrong places. **1966** 'W. HAGGARD' *Power House* xiii. 136 The driver..[had] mistaken him for an out-of-town and he'd cruise him through Regent's Park and..claim the full fare. **1973** J. DRUMMOND *Bang! Bang! You're Dead!* xxv. 84 Out-of-towners or won't-works agitate at so much the hour, never mind what about. **1976** *New Yorker* 15 Nov. 162/2 It had found that many of the out-of-towners in charge of choosing convention sites..had had to be talked out of changing their plans at the last minute.

out-old, -open, oven: see OUT-.

outouth, obs. Sc. form of OUTWITH.

out-'over, ou'tour, out-'ower, *prep.* and *adv.* Now only *Sc.* Forms: 4-6 out(e ouer, etc. (see OUT and OVER); 4 out-our, owtour, 4-6 outour, 5 outter, 5-6 owttour, ? 8 out-oer, 8-9 out owre, 9 out ower, out-ower, outower. [f. OUT *adv.* + OVER *prep.* Cf. ATOUR.]

A. *prep.* **1. a.** Of motion or direction: *orig.* With the force of both words; also (more weakly) Over, across.

a **1300** *Cursor M.* 19720 (Edin.) In a lepe man lete him dune out ouir [*Cott., Gött.* vte ouer; *Fairf.* out ouer] þe wallis of þe tune. **1375** BARBOUR *Bruce* VIII. 393 He thoucht weill that he vald fair Outour the month [i.e. the Grampians] vith his menȝe. *c* **1475** *Babees Bk.* 148 Oute ouere youre dysshe your heede yee nat hynge. **1560** ROLLAND *Crt. Venus* II. 193 Furth can he fair Out ouir the bent. **1785** BURNS *Halloween* xxvi, An in' the pool Out-owre the lugs she plumpit. *a* **1810** TANNAHILL *My Mary* Poems 127 Down frae the bank out-owre the lea.

b. Of position; Over, above.

13.. *Cursor M.* 11489 Vte ouer þat hus þan stode þe stern. **1513** DOUGLAS *Æneis* v. iii. 65 The remanent of the roweris ..With armis reddy outour thair airis fald. **1785** BURNS *Death & Dr. Hornbook* iv, The rising moon began to glowr The distant Cumnock hills out-owre. **1858** M. PORTEOUS *Souter Johnny* 11 To crack a joke..Out ower a gill.

†**2.** *fig.* **a.** Of degree: Over, above; in a position of superiority to; more than; beyond. *Obs.*

a **1300** *Cursor M.* 19625 (Edin.) It es to þe oute ouir [*Cott., Gött.* vte ouer] miȝte Ogain þi stranger for to fiȝte. **1375** BARBOUR *Bruce* IX. 489 Tharfor had he outour his peris renowne. ? **17..** *Earl Richard's Daughter* xliv. in Child *Ballads* (1892) VIII. cclii. B. 405/1 And there he saw that lady gay, The flower out-oer them a'.

†**b.** In transgression of. *Obs.*

13.. *Cursor M.* 6526 (Cott.) Vt ouer þe forbot [*G.* Again þe forbod] sua þai dide.

B. *adv.* Over; across; outside.

13.. *Cursor M.* 3930 He lai on þe ta side o flum jordan, And send his aght vte-ouer ilkan. **1785** BURNS *Halloween* xix, He..tumbl'd wi' a wintle Out-owre that night. **1818** *Edin. Mag.* Oct. 327 (Jam.) *To stand outower*, to stand completely without the inclosure, house, etc.

outpace (aʊt'peɪs), *v.* [OUT- 14, 18.]

†**1.** *intr.* To pass or go out. *Obs. rare.*

1572 GASCOIGNE *Hearbes, Voy. Holland* Wks. (1587) 167 The number cannot from my mind outpace.

2. *trans.* To outwalk or outrun, to exceed in speed; to outstrip in any race or rivalry.

1611 *Panegyr. Verses* in *Coryat's Crudities*, A worke..that doth all other workes out-pace A furlong at the least. **1798** SOTHEBY tr. *Wieland's Oberon* (1826) I. 61 Yet will thy heart at times thy head outpace. **1877** CLERY *Minor Tactics* ii. 37 The enemy followed at full speed..but were outpaced.

out-'paint, *v.* [OUT- 18.] *trans.* To outdo or surpass in painting, to paint more or better than. (In quot. 1689, to outdo in painting oneself.)

1689 SHADWELL *Bury F.* II. Wks. 1720 IV. 146 You and your daughter are notorious for out-painting all the Christian Jezebels in England. **1826** SYD. SMITH *Wks.* (1859) II. 97/1 Mr. Jackson strives to out-paint Sir Thomas.

out-paragon, -paramour: see OUT- 22.

'out-,parish. [OUT- 1.] **a.** A parish lying outside the walls or municipal boundaries of a city or town, though for some purpose considered to belong to it. **b.** An outlying parish.

1577-87 HOLINSHED *Chron.* III. 1212/1 There died in the citie and out parishes of all diseases one hundred fiftie and two. **1659** *Burton's Diary* (1828) IV. 433 The parish of Margaret's, Westminster, and other the out-parishes, in the counties of Middlesex and Surrey, within the weekly Bills of Mortality. **1722** DE FOE *Plague* (1884) 26 The Infection keept..in the out-Parishes. **1894** C. CREIGHTON *Hist. Epidemics Brit.* II. 85 The Liberties of the City and the out-parishes were covered with aggregates of houses.

'out-,part. *Obs.* [OUT- 1, 3. Also as two words: see OUT *a.* and PART *sb.*] An outer, outlying, or exterior part; *esp.* in *pl.*, The parts of a town lying outside its walls or municipal bounds; suburbs.

c **1470** HENRY *Wallace* IX. 1757 On a out part the Scottis set in that tyd. **1598** CHAPMAN *Iliad* IV. 525 The Fell'ffs or out-parts of a wheele that compasse in the whole. **1722** DE FOE *Plague* (1756) 56 Those Parishes, and Places as were called the Hamlets, and Out-parts. **1780** *Ann. Reg.* 201 The imposition being committed in the outparts.

[**outparter**, a spurious word, originating in a mistake for OUTPUTTER (q.v.), which has been handed down in editions of the Statutes, in the Law Dictionaries, and general Dictionaries.]

out-party: see OUT- 4

outpass (aʊt'pɑːs, -æ-), *v.* [OUT- 17, 18.]

1. *trans.* To pass out of (bounds), beyond (a limit).

1494 FABYAN *Chron.* VII. ccxxv. 252 The water of Thamys ..dyd moch harme by outpassynge his boundys in dyuerse places. **1635** QUARLES *Embl.* IV. I. v, Sometimes my trash disdaining thoughts out-pass The common period of terrene conceit. **1650** EARL MONM. tr. *Senault's Man bec. Guilty* 366 Not to out-passe it's bounds. **1928** J. H. MOZLEY tr. *Statius* I. 47 Mayst thou outpass the limits of old Nestor's age. **1929** R. BRIDGES *Testament of Beauty* IV. 150 That fadeth only as it outpasseth mortal sight.

2. *fig.* To surpass, go beyond (in any quality).

1594 CAREW *Huarte's Exam. Wits* xii. (1596) 183 So great was the knowledge and wisedome which Salomon receiued of God, that he outpassed al the Ancients. **1796** KIRWAN *Elem. Min.* (ed. 2) I. Pref. 8 Germany, in every instance, out-passed even its former exertions. **1856** R. A. VAUGHAN *Mystics* I. VI. i. 149 That the poorest beggar may outpass in wisdom and in blessedness all the Popes of Christendom. **1930** *New Statesman* 28 June 360/1 Parties which have historically played their part..but now find themselves outpassed by newer parties.

†**'out-,passage.** *Obs.* [OUT- 7.] Passage out, the action of passing out; way out.

1398 TREVISA *Barth. De P.R.* XIX. lxxv. (1495) 905 Chese eten after meete..shoueth it to the place of outpassage. **1533** BELLENDEN *Livy* v. (1822) 450 Thay war sa inclusit..that thay micht gett na outepassage. **1536** —— *Cron. Scot.* (1821) II. 243 And stoppit baith the entres and outpassage of this gait.

†**'out,passing,** *vbl. sb. Obs.* [OUT- 9.]

1. The action of passing out or away.

a **1340** HAMPOLE *Psalter* xxx[i]. 28, I sayd in outpassynge of my thoght. **1496** *Sc. Acts Jas. IV* (1814) II. 238/2 Anent the inbringing of bulyeoune,..and of the outpassing thairof of the Realme. **1609** SKENE *Reg. Maj.* 52 b (Stat. Robt. III, c. 2 §5), Before the ischew or outpassing of the ȝeare and day.

2. Evacuation, excretion.

c **1400** tr. *Secreta Secret., Gov. Lordsh.* 67 In outpassynge or wythholdynge of þe wombe.

out-passion to **out-patience:** see OUT-.

'out-,patient. [OUT- 2.] **a.** A patient who receives treatment at a hospital without being an inmate; opposed to *in-patient*: see IN *adv.* 12 a.

1715 NELSON *Addr. Pers. Qual.* 208 Above a hundred Persons under Cure, besides the Out-Patients, who are provided with Physick. **1800** *Med. Jrnl.* III. 488 Out-patients continue to be received every Sunday and Wednesday morning.

attrib. **1879** *St. George's Hosp. Rep.* IX. 59 A fortnight's.. out-patient treatment. **1880** BEALE *Slight Ailm.* 23 In the out-patient department of the hospital.

b. *pl.* The out-patient department of a hospital.

1910 *Practitioner* July 87 After death..she was recognised as the woman who had previously attended at out-patients. **1968** 'L. BLACK' *Outbreak* i. 8 There's a smallpox suspect in the Outpatients at St. Swithin's. **1977** B. PYM *Quartet in Autumn* v. 47 A visit to out-patients at the hospital.

out-pay to **out-peal:** see OUT-.

out-'peep, *v. poet.* [OUT- 14.] *intr.* To peep out. So **'out-,peeping** *vbl. sb.*

1600 FAIRFAX *Tasso* VI. iii, Yet none of vs dares at these gates out-peepe. **1818** KEATS *Endym.* I. 253 Being hidden, laugh at their out-peeping. **1827** HOOD *Hero & L.* xxxiv, Or pearls outpeeping from their silvery shells.

'out-peeping, *ppl. a.* [OUT- 10.] That peeps out.

1908 A. AUSTIN *Sacr. & Prof. Love* 72 And on out-peeping roots the sun-god shoots The shafts of his golden quiver.

out'peer, *v.* [OUT- 18 b.] *trans.* To outmate, outrival, excel.

1611 SHAKS. *Cymb.* III. vi. 86 Great men That had a Court no bigger than this Caue,..Could not out-peere these twaine. **1838** CHALMERS *Wks.* XIII. 260 The man outpeers his companions in intellectual wealth.

†**'out-,penny.** *Obs.* [OUT- 6.] A payment on going out of a tenancy. Cf. IN-PENNY.

? **13..** [see IN-PENNY].

'out-,pension, *sb.* [OUT- 2.] A pension given without the condition of residence in a charitable institution. So **'out-,pension** *v. trans.*, to grant an out-pension to, to pension out.

1711 *Offic. Notice* 21 May in *Lond. Gaz.* No. 4850/3 The Out-Pension of the said Hospital. **1766** CARLISLE in *Phil. Trans.* LVI. 135 He was admitted to the out-pension of Chelsea hospital. **1895** *Westm. Gaz.* 7 Dec. 3/1 Eight of those appointed to the Almshouses have asked to be transferred to the out-pension list. **1893** *Daily News* 25 Nov. 3/3 The old residents are to be turned adrift and out-pensioned.

'out-,pensioner. [OUT- 2.] A non-resident pensioner; opposed to *in-pensioner*.

1706 *Lond. Gaz.* No. 4228/3 Arrears due to the Out-Pensioners..belonging to Chelsea Hospital. **1748** *Anson's Voy.* I. i. 6 The out-pensioners of Chelsea college..consist of soldiers, who from their age, wounds, or other infirmities, are incapable of serving in marching regiments. **1849** MACAULAY *Hist. Eng.* iii. I. 307 It was no part of the plan that there should be outpensioners.

out-people, *v.*: see OUT- 26.

outperform (aʊtpə'fɔːm), *v.* [f. OUT- 18 + PERFORM *v.*] *trans.* To perform better than; to surpass in a specified activity or function.

1960 *Farmer & Stockbreeder* 9 Feb. 92 It has been out-performing other light tractors ever since it was introduced and using less fuel in doing it. **1966** *Economist* 26 Mar. 1239/2 The fund..will be expected to outperform other mutual funds. **1972** *Times* 30 Sept. 9/5 Salzburg's cast, in voice and temperament, outperform their studio rivals. **1973** M. WOODHOUSE *Blue Bone* xii. 122 It out-performs structural steel by a factor of ten times. **1975** *Publishers Weekly* 30 June 22/1 In the sweeping stock market recovery of 1975, book publishing companies—after years in the Wall Street doghouse—have sharply outperformed the general market. **1978** R. V. JONES *Most Secret War* xli. 390 The Mustang could outperform all the standard German day fighters.

'out-,picket. [OUT- 1.] A picket posted at a distance out or in advance; an outpost.

1832 SOUTHEY *Hist. Penins. War* III. 430 Marmont himself..surprised and captured the out picquet of the party. **1859** MOWBRAY THOMSON *Story Cawnpore* iv. 68 But if the intrenched postion was one of peril, that of the outpicket in barrack No. 4 was even more so.

out-pipe to **out-pity:** see OUT-.

†**out-'pitch,** *v. Obs.* [OUT- 21 + PITCH *sb.*, highest point of flight, etc.] *trans.* To rise to a higher pitch than, exceed in pitch; to go beyond.

1627 HAKEWILL *Apol.* (1630) 163 Anna the Prophetesse mentioned by S. Luke seemes to have out pitched an hundred [years]. **1646** BUCK *Rich. III*, II. 57 Who had such an influence upon him in his minoritie, that she out-pitched Lewis Duke of Orleance. **1677** W. HUGHES *Man of Sin* III. iii. 97 So large and fair a mark, as hath not been outpitch'd ..by any one upon the spot.

'out-,place, *sb.* [OUT- 1.] An out-lying, out-of-the-way place.

1530 PALSGR. 250/2 Outplace, a corner out of the way, *destour.* **1555** EDEN *Decades* 336 In the hyghe mountaynes or other superficiall owt places. **1690** *Andros Tracts* II. 50 Some out-places began to Fortify and Garrison their houses. **1838** F. OWEN *Diary* 8 Jan. (1926) 94 Most of the inhabitants were absent at the out places or villages. **1911** *Chambers's Jrnl.* Apr. 221/1 It is this longing..that sends the sportsman into the out-places. **1956** W. R. BIRD *Off-trail in Nova Scotia* vi. 176 But that reminds me of my scrap book. You know we in these out places keep such things.

outplace, *v.* [OUT- 18, 15.] *trans.* **a.** To displace or oust. **b.** (See quot. 1970.)

1928 *Daily Express* 16 Jan. 5/3 Skirts dipping at one side will outplace in many houses the skirt dipping at the back that was so popular during the winter. **1970** *Time* 14 Sept. 83 Instead of simply bouncing a subordinate, the boss can send him to a firm that specializes in helping unwanted executives to find new jobs. The practitioners have even coined a euphemistic description for the process: 'outplacing' executives who have been 'dehired'.

out-'plan, *v.* [OUT- 18.] *trans.* To outdo in planning; to outmatch by more skilful planning.

1797 T. PARK *Sonn.* 82 He out-plans me hollow. **1852** M. ARNOLD *Tristram & Iseult* I. 166 Tristram!—sweet love!—we are betray'd—out-plann'd.

'outplay, *sb.* [OUT- 7, 4.]

1. Display, manifestation.

1872 H. W. BEECHER *Lect. Preach.* v. 97 Fervency, which is only another term for emotional outplay.

2. *Cricket.* That part of the game played by the side that is 'out'.

1884 *Lillywhite's Cricket Ann.* 1 They were handicapped in their out-play by the absence of their best bowler.

out'play, *v.* [OUT- 18.] *trans.* To beat or surpass in playing, to play better than.

1648 J. BEAUMONT *Psyche* I. xxxvi, If I Deign to outplay him in his own sly part. **1896** *Westm. Gaz.* 15 Dec. 10 1 Australian athletes, who have shown that they can out-run, out-row, out-shoot, or out-play the athletes of other lands. **1938** L. BEMELMANS *Life Class* II. iii. 144 The bands always tried to outplay each other, waging a musical warfare. **1972** G. GREEN *Great Moments in Sport: Soccer* ii. 35 England has been outplayed..in a number of ways. **1977** J. WAINWRIGHT *Do Nothin'* v. 67 Krupa on tom-toms and James on the horn..two of the best in the business trying to out-play each other.

out-please to **out-plod**: see OUT-.

out-'plot, *v.* [OUT- 18.] *trans.* To outdo in plotting; to outmanœuvre.

1681 T. FLATMAN *Heraclitus Ridens* No. 29 (1713) I. 187 He has the Head of a Jesuit, and shall out-wit, out-plot, out-swear..the whole Society. **1854** CDL. WISEMAN *Fabiola* 335 You have out-plotted me, and you pity me!

out-'pocketing, *vbl. sb. Biol.* [OUT- 9.] The outward movement of part of a surface so as to form a pocket- or sac-like cavity.

1924 L. B. AREY *Developmental Anat.* i. 8 Circumscribed folds..produce (*a*) evaginations, or out-pocketings, and (*b*) invaginations, or in-pocketings. **1968** *Progress in Brain Res.* XXIX. 55 Portions of the outer nuclear envelope..could project into the cytoplasm and pinch off... Out-pocketings of the outer nuclear envelope are frequently seen in early neuroepithelial cells. **1971** *Nature* 16 Apr. 472/2 The glands arise as an outpocketing of the vagina.

out'point, *v.* [OUT- 15, 18.]

†**1.** *trans.* To point out, indicate. (*poetic.*) *Obs.*

1595 R. BARNFIELD *Cynthia* ii. (Arb.) 47 In yonder Wood. [Which with her finger shee Out-poynting)..Yuanished into some other place.

2. *Yachting.* To outdo in pointing; to sail closer to the wind than.

1883 *Harper's Mag.* Aug. 445/2 The smaller..boat outpointed and outsailed.. her..competitor. **1899** *Daily News* 4 Oct. 3/3 Columbia appeared to be out-pointing Shamrock, but the boats were not very far apart.

3. In various sports and games, esp. boxing: to score more points than; to defeat on points. Also *transf.* and *fig.*

1903 *Westm. Gaz.* 19 Feb. 7/3 In the second [coursing] ties, Priestlaw, notwithstanding his speed, was out-pointed cleverly by Handsome Creole. **1909** *Ibid.* 2 Feb. 12/2 With Aiken unable to settle down [in a billiards match] and failing to make any material use of some nice openings, he continued to be outpointed. **1909** *Ibid.* 20 Feb. 16/3 Driscoll outpointed the American featherweight champion. **1922** *Weekly Dispatch* 12 Nov. 11 In a ten-rounds boxing contest here to-night Bermondsey Billy Wells (England) outpointed Johnny Tillman. **1949** *Sun* (Baltimore) 16 July 9/6 Barfly regularly outpoints and out-foots all who sail against her. **1955** *Times* 12 May 4/3 Eddington, the coloured American, had been outpointed in Ireland. **1959** *Economist* 11 Apr. 159/1 BOAC happens to have been outpointed in the never-ending game of poker that the airlines play with traffic rights for chips. **1970** *Globe & Mail* (Toronto) 28 Sept. 21/3 Scot Ken Buchanan won the world lightweight boxing title Saturday in San Juan, Puerto Rico, when he outpointed champion Ismael Laguna of Panama under a blazing sun. **1976** *Daily Record* (Glasgow) 4 Dec. 30/5 The Baillieston man outpointed Irish champion John McLoughlin after both had been floored in an amazing second round.

†**outpointed**, *ppl. a. Obs.* [OUT- 11.] Protruded.

1575 BANISTER *Chyrurg.* I. (1585) 15 The place..which being most outpointed, is soft and easily pressed in with the finger.

out'poise, *v.* [OUT- 18 b.] *trans.* To outweigh, to overbalance. Hence **out'poising** *ppl. a.*

1630 PRYNNE *Anti-Armin.* 268 The meanest of which.. may alone outpoise them all. **1651** HOWELL *Venice* 199 His outpoising power keeps the inferior Princes in peace. **1656** JEANES *Mixt. Schol. Div.* 8 Love of an immortall soule, that in worth out-poyseth the whole world. **1886** SWINBURNE *Misc.* 150-1 A leaf of the Georgics would outpoise in value the whole of the 'Excursion'.

out-poison to **out-porch**: see OUT-.

'out,port[1]. [OUT- 1, 6.]

1. a. A port outside some defined place, as a city or town; in England, a term including all ports other than that of London.

1642 *Ordin. Parl. conc. Tonnage & Poundage* 13 As well of the City of London as the Out-ports. **1719** W. WOOD *Surv. Trade* 295 By these Companies being established at London, the City of Bristol and other the Out Ports, are excluded from any Advantages by them. **1722** DE FOE *Plague* (1756) 250 While the Plague continued so violent in London, the Out-ports, as they are call'd, enjoyed a very great Trade. **1884** *Manch. Exam.* 16 Oct. 5/3 Reprehensible practices employed both in London and in the outports.

attrib. **1707** *Chamberlayne's St. Gt. Brit., List Govt. Officers* 498 Four Examiners of the Out-Port Books. **1731** *Gentl. Mag.* I. 84 Alexander Gould, Esq...made inspector of the out-port collectors accounts.

b. Chiefly in Labrador and Newfoundland, a small remote fishing village. Also *attrib.* Hence **'outporter**, an inhabitant of an outport.

1820 in C. R. Fay *Life & Labour in Newfoundland* (1956) viii. 138 Almost every fifth fisherman is what is termed a 'Planter', particularly in the outports of the Island. **1904** *Westm. Gaz.* 6 May 10/1 The Newfoundland outporters are hardy, courageous, boldly adventurous, simple-lived. **1907** J. G. MILLAIS *Newfoundland* p. xv, I have tried to enter into the life of the true Newfoundlander—the man of the outports. **1949** [see NEW LIGHT 3 a]. **1964** L. E. F. ENGLISH *Historic Newfoundland* 6 Visit the fishing villages, the so-called outports of the Province of Newfoundland. **1966** A. R. SCAMMELL *My Newfoundland* 17 Environment and circumstance..developed in the young outport lad initiative, and a sense of responsibility. **1973** B. BROADFOOT *Ten Lost Years* xix. 214 Mallory and Derek, pretty fancy names for a couple of outporters, eh? **1974** *Nat. Geographic* Jan. 116 Most islanders cling to the seaside in isolated villages called outports. **1978** *Globe & Mail* (Toronto) 14 Jan. 8/2 Trudeau's Government..killed a subsidy that keeps a useful ferry service going between the mainland and outer islands in the Queen Charlottes and between the Vancouver supply area and the tiny outports of the northern coast.

c. A small port, located to support the commerce of a main port.

1935 J. A. FRASER *Spain & W. Country* x. 108 It was from Seville and its little out-port Sanlucar de Barrameda..that nearly all the early Spanish voyages of discovery went forth. **1952** F. W. MORGAN *Ports & Harbours* 76 In order to prevent a loss of trade the port undertakes the development of an 'outport' nearer the sea, which can attract the larger vessels. **1956** *Sun* (Baltimore) 3 Sept. 4/5 It just wouldn't work to have a New York contract cover each of the outports.

2. A port of embarkation or exportation.

c **1790** B. RUSH *Ess., Progr. Popul. Penn.* (1802) 225 Our state is the great outport of the United States for Europeans. **1870** YEATS *Nat. Hist. Comm.* 89 Corn being a long time in reaching its outport. **1872** *Daily News* 20 Jan., Liverpool is the great outport of England—the place where people go who are about to leave the country.

†**outport**[2]. *Obs.* [Cf. OUT- 25.] Conveyance outward; exportation.

a **1603** *Let. to Jas. VI* in Robertson *Hist. Scot.* VIII. Wks. 1826 II. 188 That your Majesty will be pleased to admit free outport of the native commodities of this kingdom.

out-po'sition, *v.* [f. OUT- 21 + POSITION *sb.*] *trans.* In various sports and games, to secure an advantage over (an opponent) in terms of position; to defeat in a contest for a particular position.

1928 *Sunday Express* 24 June 21 Tilden got to everything with that long, easy stride of his, and Hunter was often outpositioned by shots that he did not expect would be returned. **1960** E. S. & W. J. HIGHAM *High Speed Rugby* xi. 131 The further he progresses, the more necessary it will become to out-position and out-think the opposition. **1966** *Daily Progress* (Charlottesville, Va.) 8 June 30/2 We out-hustle them, out-position them, and in all but two games have actually out-rebounded them.

outpost ('aʊtpəʊst), *sb.* [OUT- 1.] **1. a.** A post at a distance from the body of an army; a detachment placed at a distance from a force, when halted, as a guard against surprise.

1757 WASHINGTON *Lett.* Writ. 1889 I. 478 The uncertain and difficult communication with the out-posts. **1779** FORREST *Voy. N. Guinea* 33 Sometimes a serjeant at an out-post..sends an account of his having discovered on a certain spot, a parcel of spice trees. **1803** LAKE in Owen *Mrq. Wellesley's Desp.* (1878) 394 When we had encamped..our outposts were attacked by a body of the enemy. **1844** *Regul. & Ord. Army* 272 Officers, Soldiers, and Followers of the Camp, are not, on any account, to be suffered to pass the Out-Posts, unless they are on duty, or present a regular permit. **1855** MACAULAY *Hist. Eng.* xiii. III. 375 The outposts of the Cameronians were speedily driven in.

b. *transf.* and *fig.* **1813** EUSTACE *Italy* (1815) I. i. 74 Saltzburg, a subalpine city,..may be considered..as forming one of the outposts of Italy. **1856** STANLEY *Sinai & Pal.* i. (1858) 9 A lower line of hills, which form as it were the outposts of the Sinaitic range itself. **1881** D. G. ROSSETTI *Ballads & Sonnets* 196 Shall my sense pierce love,—the last relay And ultimate outpost of eternity? **1917** E. V. LUCAS (*title*) Outposts of mercy.

c. *attrib.* **1823** MOORE *Fables* 80 The sun, who now began To call in all his out-post rays. **1859** LANG *Wand. India* 394 [He] was tried for being drunk whilst on out-post duty. **1776** *Battle of Brooklyn* II. i. 19 We are the remains of the out post guard. **1870** DE B. R. KEIM *Sheridan's Troopers* 206 This simple means is also resorted to by the troops on outpost duty. **1923** KIPLING *Irish Guards in Great War* I. 226 The blockhouse..was absorbed into our outpost-line. **1946** *R.A.F. Jrnl.* May 175 In Berlin and Hamburg..and on airfields and outpost stations, the R.A.F. has taken root. *Ibid.* 176 Then, these outpost men are busy.

2. A trading settlement situated near a frontier or at a remote place in order to facilitate the commercial contacts of a larger and more centrally situated town or settlement. Also, by extension, any of various other kinds of remote settlements and institutions (see quots.). Also *attrib.*

1802 in E. Coues *New Light on Early Hist. Greater Northwest* (1897) I. 204 [I] made up the assortment of goods for the outposts, equipped the summer men, clerks, etc. **1911** A. K. CHIGNELL (*title*) An outpost in Papua. **1955** W. G. HARDY *Alberta Golden Jubilee Anthol.* 212 In Alberta, after World War I, it set up 'outpost hospitals' for the brides and families of soldier-settlers in the outlying reaches of the province. **1956** H. S. M. KEMP *Northern Trader* 17 The red [thumbtacks] represent the Company's permanent, year-round establishments; the blue ones, the winter posts and outposts. **1961** L. VAN DER POST *Heart of Hunter* I. v. 80 Tsane had once possessed a district commissioner, but had declined into a remote police outpost. **1970** *Islander* (Victoria, B.C.) 22 Feb. 5/3 The post here [*sc.* Cambridge Bay] is what is called an Outpost where goods are landed to be drawn on by other posts that may run short.

3. The furthest territory of an empire, esp. in the phr. ***outpost of Empire*** (i.e. the British Empire), common since the end of the nineteenth century, and now occasionally used in a nostalgic or ironic sense. Also *attrib.*

1912 KIPLING *Songs from Bks.* 94 There he shall blaze a nation's ways with hatchet and with brand, Till on his last-won wilderness an Empire's outposts stand. **1924** E. M. FORSTER *Passage to India* xx. 182 His simple words had reminded them that they were an outpost of Empire. **1924** *Granta* 25 Apr. 361/1 Attock Fort, in the Punjab... An outpost of Empire, where the Cabul and the Indus meet. **1929** J. B. PRIESTLEY *Good Companions* II. vii. 448 May she marry the outpost-of-Empire lad in the Sudan. **1934** DYLAN THOMAS *Let.* 25 Apr. (1966) 111 Then I shall walk back.. covering up a..weakness with a look of fierce & even Outpost-of-the-Empire determination. **1937** 'G. ORWELL' *Road to Wigan Pier* ix. 173 In an 'outpost of Empire' like Burma the class-question appeared at first sight to have been shelved. **1970** R. JOHNSTON *Black Camels* ii. 26 You've sure got an impressive outpost of empire here. **1971** R. ROBERTS *Classic Slum* vi. 81 Some families..had male members.. who had soldiered in the outposts of empire.

Hence **'outpost** *v. trans.*, to place as an outpost.

1864 MASSON in *Reader* 13 Aug., The thoughts that habitually come and go in the mind so privileged and out-posted to meditate and to sing!

outpour ('aʊtpɔə(r)), *sb.* [OUT- 7.]. The act of pouring out; that which pours out, an overflow.

1864 *Reader* 24 Dec. 793/2 On the hypotheses..that the Luta Nzige contributes the outpour of the distant Tanganyika. **1895** F. HARRISON in *Forum* Jan. 550 None but the very greatest can maintain for long one incessant outpour of drollery. **1897** *Daily News* 4 Sept. 2/2 The outpour streams down the face of the rock in a number of beautiful falls.

outpour (aʊt'pɔə(r)), *v.* [OUT- 15, 14.]

1. *trans.* To pour out, send forth in or as in a stream. (Chiefly *poetic.*)

1671 MILTON *P.R.* III. 311 He look't and saw what numbers numberless The City gates out powr'd. *a* **1851** MOIR *Poems, Burden of Sion*, Then..would my sorrowing spirit haste Forth to outpour its flood of misery. **1864** SKEAT *Uhland's Poems* 40 Only in the month of blossoms Nightingales outpour their song.

2. *intr.* To flow out in or as in a stream.

1861 LYTTON & FANE *Tannhäuser* 76 She was not of those whose sternest sorrow Outpours in plaints.

'outpoured, *ppl. a.* [OUT- 11.] Poured out. So **'outpourer**, one who pours out; **'outpouring** *ppl. a.*, pouring out, rushing out in a stream.

1884 BROWNING *Ferishtah, Shah Abbas* 113 Had *outpoured life of mine sufficed To bring him back. **1876** GEO. ELIOT *Dan. Der.* lxix, What *outpourer of his own affairs. **1863** COWDEN CLARKE *Shaks. Char.* viii. 199 She is by nature of the most boisterous spirits, irrepressible, *outpouring. **1895** J. W. POWELL in *Physiogr. Processes* I. 4 Modified..by the great gulfs and the outpouring rivers from the land.

'out,pouring, *vbl. sb.* [OUT- 9.]

1. The action of pouring out.

1757 J. EDWARDS *Orig. Sin* I. ix. (1837) 88 A glorious outpouring of the Spirit of God. **1879** FARRAR *St. Paul* (1883) 539 The toil of his hands in no way impeded the outpouring of his soul.

2. That which is poured out; an effusion; an impetuous or passionate utterance. Chiefly in *pl.*

1827 CARLYLE *Misc.* (1857) I. 336 His passionate outpourings would be more effective were they briefer. **1870** FREEMAN *Norm. Conq.* (ed. 2) I. iv. 184 Among the most ridiculous outpourings of his lying vanity.

†**out'power**, *v. Obs.* [OUT- 21.] *trans.* To exceed in power, to overpower.

1654 GAYTON *Pleas. Notes* IV. i. 169 Out-powr'd, out-worded, shee's at last o'rborne. **1655** FULLER *Ch. Hist.* II. iii. §41 In the Saxon Heptarchy there was generally one who out-powered all the rest. **1762** GOLDSM. *Cit. W.* lxxxiv. II. 97 Myriads of men..out-powering [*some later edd.* over-powering] by numbers all opposition.

out-practise, -praise, etc.: see OUT-.

out'pray, *v.* [OUT- 18, 18 c.]

1. *trans.* To outdo in praying, excel in prayer.

1593 SHAKS. *Rich. II*, V. iii. 109 Our prayers do out-pray his. **1666** DRYDEN *Ann. Mirab.* cclxi, He..Outweeps an hermit, and outprays a saint. **1841-4** EMERSON *Ess.* Ser. II. iv. (1876) 105 He will outpray saints in chapel, outgeneral veterans in the field.

2. To overcome by prayer, pray (something) to an end or out of existence.

a **1853** ROBERTSON *Serm.* Ser. IV. lv. (1863) 415 Outpray, —outpreach,—outlive the calumny.

out'preach, *v.* [OUT- 18, 18 c.]

1. *trans.* To outdo, surpass, or excel in preaching; to preach more or better than.

1643 HAMMOND *Serm. John* xviii. 40 Wks. 1683 IV. 517 Able to outpreach all the Orators you ever heard from the Pulpit. **1742** YOUNG *Nt. Th.* IX. 2325 Till then, be This an Emblem of my Grave: Let it out-preach the Preacher. **1854** S. WILBERFORCE in R. I. Wilberforce *Life* (1881) II. vi. 249 Dissenters outpreach them.

2. To preach to an end, preach out of existence.

1826 Milman *A. Boleyn* (1827) 156 Think you your crimes and murders.. Will not out-preach you from the face of earth? *a* **1853** [see outpray *v.* 2].

out-preen to **out-privilege:** see out-.

†**out-ˈprize,** *v. Obs.* [out- 18, 18 b.] *trans.* To exceed in value; to surpass in one's estimation.

1611 Shaks. *Cymb.* i. iv. 88 She's out-priz'd by a trifle. *a* **1657** R. Loveday *Lett.* (1663) 61, I never had recreation nor business that out-prised the pleasant care I alwayes took to keep our Quills in play. *a* **1851** Joanna Baillie (Ogilvie) In truth thy off'ring far outprizes all.

out-procrastine, -prodigy, etc.: see out-.

†**outˈproffer,** *v. Obs.* [out- 18.] *trans.* To proffer or offer more than, to outbid.

1494 Fabyan *Chron.* vii. ccxxv. 253 The kynge called before hym, the .ii. munkis seuerally, & eyther out proferyd other;.. Than the kynge called [the third] and asked if he wolde geue any more than his bretherne had offered to be abbot.

out-ˈpromise, *v.* [out- 18, 17.] *trans.* To exceed or outdo in promising. *refl.* To promise more than one can do.

1676 Wycherley *Pl. Dealer* i. i. Thou mayst easily come to.. out-promise a Lover. **1681** J. Flavel *Right. Mans Ref.* 207 God never out-promised himself. **1692** *Miracles performed by Money* Ep. Ded., Out-lye a News-writer, out-promise a Cit. **1938** *Sun* (Baltimore) 9 July 6/1 Many more experienced statesmen have thought that they had outpromised the field, only to find themselves sadly in arrears at election time.

out-prosper to **out-pry:** see out-.

†**outˈpublish,** *v. Obs.* (New Engl.) = out-ask *v.* 1.

1719 S. Sewall *Diary* 26 Oct. (1882) III. 232, I.. could not be Married sooner, because I was Out-published on the Thanks-giving-Day, and not before. **1727** *Canton* (Mass.) *Rec.* (1896) 22 The Names.. haue ben out published as the Law directs, By me Joseph Tucker town Clerk.

outpunch (aʊtˈpʌn(t)ʃ), *v.* [f. out- 18 + punch *v.*[1] 3.] *trans.* In boxing, to surpass (an opponent) in punching ability.

1950 F. Mills *Twenty Years* xiii. 168 For the next few rounds.., he was gradually coming back.. and for the seventh, eighth and ninth, I think he outboxed and outpunched me. **1956** —— *Forward the Light-Heavies* ix. 99 Delaney made a bad start in 1927 by being out-punched by Jim Maloney over 10 rounds at the new Garden. **1960** *Times* 26 Apr. 17/3 He was outthought, outboxed and.. outpunched by the Mexican. **1961** *Times* 6 June 5/4 J. Malcolm was outpunched and outpointed.

out-pupil, -purple, -purse: see out-.

outpush (ˈaʊtpʊʃ), *sb.* [out- 7.] Outward push; impetus directed outwardly.

1885 *Homilet. Rev.* Aug. 98 Society.. will feel the outpush and the uplift.

out-ˈpush, *v. nonce-wd.* [out- 17.] *trans.* To exceed or go beyond in pushing.

1848 Dickens *Dombey* xxi, A flushed page.. seemed to have in part out-grown and in part out-pushed his strength.

ˈoutˌpushing, *ppl. a.* [out- 10.] Pushing out, enterprising.

1894 *Chicago Advance* 2 Aug., Some outpushing Chinese and still more enterprising Japanese.

output (ˈaʊtpʊt), *sb.* [out- 7.]

1. a. The act or fact of putting or turning out; production; the quantity or amount produced; the product of any industry or exertion, viewed quantitatively; the result given to the world. (Orig. a technical or local term of iron-works, coal-mines, etc.; app. not in general Dicts. till after 1880.)

1858 Simmonds *Dict. Trade, Out-put,* a term in the iron trade for the make of metal or annual quantity made. **1872** *Daily News* 1 Aug., The output in that district [the steam coal field of Northumberland] would not exceed five million tons per annum. **1877** Raymond *Statist. Mines & Mining* 285 The copper out-put remains substantially as it was last year. **1879** Dowden *Southey* vii. 194 It is the out-put of a large and vigorous mind. **1879** M. Pattison *Milton* xiii. 215 If this were the average output of a popular book, the inference would be that *Paradise Lost* was not such a book. **1892** Stevenson *Across the Plains* 285 Such an income as a clerk will earn with a tenth.. of your nervous output. **1942** *R.A.F. Jrnl.* 30 May 34 Dislocation of other factories depending on the Billancourt output. **1959** C. Singer *Short Hist. Sci. Ideas* iv. 116 This drug book [of Pliny's] is the prototype of the medical output of the next fifteen hundred years. **1965** Seldon & Pennance *Everyman's Dict. Econ.* 315 Output is normally understood to be gross output; but.. the most useful definition.. relates to gross output less the goods and services used in production; this amount is called net output. **1971** *Cabinet Maker & Retail Furnisher* 24 Sept. 524/1 The United Kingdom is the planned market for 80% of the output. **1972** *Value Added Tax: Gen. Guide* (H.M. Customs) 16 The goods and services he [*sc.* the taxable person] supplies are called his outputs and the tax he charges is his output tax. **1976** *Times* 21 May 4/1 *Manpower Paper No. 8*... estimated the output of graduates to 1981.

b. *Physiol.* Applied to the waste material expelled from the body by the lungs, skin, and kidneys, as opposed to the *income* or material taken into the bodily system. (The undigested matter or fæces are not included on either side.)

1883 M. Foster *Physiol.* (1889) ii. v. §521 The output [*edd.* 1877–79 outcome] may be regarded as consisting of (1) the respiratory products of the lungs, skin, and alimentary canal,.. (2) of perspiration, consisting chiefly of water and salts.. and (3) of the urine.

c. Energy produced by a device or system; *spec.* an electrical signal delivered by, or available from, an electronic device.

1884 S. P. Thompson *Dynamo-Electr. Machinery* vii. 113 The result is an extraordinary increase in the 'output', or, as Sir William Thomson terms it, 'activity' (i.e. amount of work done per second) of the machine. **1902, 1933** [see input *sb.* 2 b]. **1956** *B.B.C. Handbk. 1957* 57 The equipment used in studio control cubicles for selecting and mixing the outputs of the various microphones. **1962** A. Nisbett *Technique Sound Studio* i. 17 The output of individual studios is fed in 'live', and linked together by station identification and continuity announcements. **1969** *Times* 7 Mar. 15/1 A television camera scans the object to be viewed, and output from the camera controls whether the pad vibrates. **1975** *Which?* Sept. 258/1 For the same output of heat, one of the gas fires.. might land you with a bill of £26 a year, another with one of only £16. **1976** *Gramophone* June 116/3 Using the Bruel and Kjaer wave analyser to measure separate harmonics, rather than distortion factor including noise, suggested even lower figures: 0.048% at full output, 0.038% at −20dB and 0.074% at −30dB.

d. *Computers.* Data or results produced by a computer; also, the physical medium on which these are represented.

1948 *Math. Tables & Other Aids to Computation* III. 7 The 'output' or result of computation consists of numbers only. It has been proposed.. to build a 'thinking' machine whose output would be orders rather than numbers. **1949** [see input *sb.* 2 d]. **1959** E. M. McCormick *Digital Computer Printer* ix. 133 The output punch could be activated and would punch the output into the card. **1964** F. L. Westwater *Electronic Computers* vi. 105 Quite sophisticated computers use punched cards as a supplementary output. **1967** D. Wilson in Wills & Yearsley *Handbk. Managem. Technol.* iii. 44 Figure 3.1 outlines the basic steps for validating (editing), processing (sorting and calculating, etc.), and recording the output (writing the data on magnetic tape or disk, printing out, etc.). **1971** P. Harvey *Computer Sci.* vii. 102 If a decimal print out is required for visual inspection the binary output must be converted to a form suitable for operating a printer.

e. *Linguistics.* A structure resulting from the application of a lexical, grammatical, or phonological rule. Cf. input *sb.* 2 f.

1961, etc. [see input *sb.* 2 f]. **1968** P. M. Postal *Aspects Phonol. Theory* iii. 34 The phonetic representations are the final output of the entire set of phonological rules. **1970** *Language* XLVI. 261 The use of transformational rules applied to the output of structure-free grammars. **1971** *Archivum Linguisticum* II. 139 We can represent the output of the realization rules in the conventional way, partly by orthographic forms and partly by generalized morpheme-symbols such as *-s*.

2. A place where, or device through which, an output is delivered by a system, esp. an electronic device.

1933, 1946 [see input *sb.* 3]. **1958** *Electronic Engin.* XXX. 1/2 The weakest part of a computer installation is, in general, the input and output which is usually slow compared with the speed of the machine itself. **1962** D. S. Halacy *Computers* iii. 66 (*caption*) A high-speed printer is the output of this computer. **1973** N. H. Crowhurst *Basic Audio Syst.* (1974) ix. 169 The essential ingredients of a feedback loop.. are: an amplifier of some sort and feedback from output to input.

3. The action or process of supplying an output.

1947 [see input *sb.* 4]. **1947** D. R. Hartree *Calculating Machines* 12 Functions of calculating machine components... (iii) Input (reception of data from the outside world). (iv) Output (supply of results to the outside world). (v) Transfer. (vi) Control. **1960** Gregory & Van Horn *Automatic Data-Processing Syst.* ii. 64 Output of results is the fourth stage in the flow of data. **1967** D. Wilson in Wills & Yearsley *Handbk. Managem. Technol.* iii. 46 In the early types of machine, input, computing, and output occurred serially so that large areas of expensive hardware were unused for much of the time. **1970** O. Dopping *Computers & Data Processing* xi. 154 When a computer is used for process control, the input and output is largely effected via.. devices which convert analogue to digital information and vice versa.

4. *attrib.* and *Comb.* **a.** simple attributive, as *output circuit, device, impedance, punch, routine, stage, transformer, tube, unit, valve*; **b.** constituting output, as *output current, power, voltage*.

1920 H. J. Van der Bijl *Thermionic Vacuum Tube* vii. 178 Distortionless amplification is obtained if the amplified current in the output circuit is.. an exact enlarged reproduction of the input current. **1973** N. H. Crowhurst *Basic Audio Syst.* (1974) vi. 118 The input circuit requires a fixed component of voltage or current to insure that the device operates at the correct combination of voltage and current in its output circuit. **1920** H. J. Van der Bijl *Thermionic Vacuum Tube* vii. 168 This would produce distortion since the output current is not an exact reproduction of the input. **1962** Simpson & Richards *Junction Transistors* ix. 219 The shift due to the rise in ambient temperature is thus relatively small and can be tolerated for peak-to-peak output-current swings of about 7mA. **1929** K. Henney *Princ. Radio* xii. 281 Output devices are used to (1) keep d.c. current from the loud speaker winding; (2) Prevent serious loss in plate voltage; [etc.]. **1948, 1968** Output device [see *input device* s.v. input *sb.* 5]. **1930** Moyer & Wostrel *Pract. Radio Construction & Repairing* (ed. 2) iv. 54 The plate resistance.. in the case of audio-frequency amplification may be considered as the output impedance. **1962** J. H. & P. J. Reyner *Radio Communication* x. 409 (*heading*) Effect of feedback on output impedance. **1920** H. J. Van der Bijl *Thermionic Vacuum Tube* vii. 237 If the tube is used to amplify modulated high-frequency oscillations.. it must obviously be capable of giving a much larger out-put power. **1972** *IEEE Trans. Geoscience Electronics* X. 13/1 A CW output power of 1 W with a power efficiency of 70 percent has been achieved. **1959** Output punch [see sense 1 d]. **1962** *Gloss. Terms Automatic Data Processing* (*B.S.I.*) 96 *Automatic tape punch, output punch* [deprecated], a tape punch which automatically transcribes coded electrical signals into rows of holes in a paper tape and moves the tape as necessary. *Ibid.* 43 *Output routine,* a routine which organizes the output process of a computer, e.g. starts the output equipment, presents data to it at suitable intervals of time, and specifies format. **1926** *Wireless World* 1 Sept. 317/2 If, however, we are *not* within five miles of a B.B.C. station, the value of extra low impedance in the output stage is unnecessary. **1962** J. H. & P. J. Reyner *Radio Communication* x. 409 Voltage feedback.. has the effect of reducing the effective internal impedance of the output stage. **1929** K. Henney *Princ. Radio* xii. 281 An output transformer is necessary to provide maximum energy transfer from the tube to the speaker. **1968** L. G. Sands *Easy Way to service Radio Receivers* (1973) ii. 52 Between points 1 and 3 you should get a higher resistance reading... If not, the output transformer may be grounded. **1929** J. H. Morecroft *Elem. Radio Communication* vii. 242 If the speaker is to use 100 milliwatts on the average,.. the output tube should be drawing from its battery at least 10 watts. **1959** M. H. Wrubel *Primer of Programming* i. 9 In some cases the output unit can produce a printed sheet of answers directly; in other cases.. the cards or tapes produced by the computer must be fed into an auxiliary machine. **1940** *Chambers's Techn. Dict.* 603/2 Output valve. **1942** *Electronic Engin.* XIV. 726 The stages in the receiver are covered in sequence from R.F. amplifiers to L.F. output valves. **1937** W. G. Dow *Fund. Engin. Electronics* 267 The useful output voltage.. is the alternating component of the voltage across R_L. **1962** A. Nisbett *Technique Sound Studio* 259 Where a microphone impedance is strongly capacitative.. its output voltage is fed to the grid of a valve.

output, *v.*

I. (*outˈput*) [out- 15.] †**1. a.** *trans.* To put out, expel, eject, dismiss. *Obs.* (In ME. chiefly two words, esp, in pa. pple.)

a **1300** *E.E. Psalter* v. 11 Out put þam þare þai sal be, Laverd, for þai taried þe. *a* **1340** Hampole *Psalter* xxxv[i]. 13 Output þai ere of paradise. *c* **1350** *Winchester Usages* in *Eng. Gilds* 362 Be þe askere out putte for euere. **1563** *Aberd. Reg.* XXV. (Jam.), To imput and outpute the tenentis. **1597** Skene *De Verb. Sign.* s.v. *Ballivus,* Chalmerlanes in-put and out-put be the Comptroller. *a* **1670** Spalding *Troub. Chas. I* (1829) II. 30 Thay first mell with the five cinque portis, inputtis and outputtis governouris at their plesour.

b. To put forth, put outside. *Obs.*

1615 Jackson *Creed* iv. viii. §2 Outputting their neighbour's goods for him to drive, or harbouring such as they could not but know to be boot-hailers.

†**2.** To utter, issue (false coin): see outputter 2, outputting 2. *Sc. Obs.*

1576 in Pitcairn *Crim. Trials* (1833) I. ii. 64 Penneis, falslie cuinȝeit and stampit; quhilkis wer output be him.

†**3.** To provide (soldiers). *Obs.*

1640 [see outputter 3].

II. 4. (*ˈoutput*) [f. output *sb.*] To put out, turn out, produce.

1858 *Geologist* I. 352 It was their business to output coal and not stone. **1886** *Pall Mall G.* 18 Feb. 1/1 The great water power of the Mississippi at Minneapolis enables the millers there to output some 1,200 tons of flour per day. **1946** *Nature* 12 Oct. 504/1 Results are output in the form of punched cards. **1965** K. Nicol *Elem. Programming* vii. 31 A comparable output device is the graphical plotter which can directly output the results of a calculation as curves or points on a paper chart. **1972** P. B. Gove in H. D. Weinbrot *New Aspects Lexicogr.* 153 The *Seventh Collegiate*.. has been completely programmed so that most of the relationships seen by the eye on a printed page can be output by the computer. **1976** *Physics Bull.* July 298/2 The most common device for inputting and outputting information is still the venerable teletype.

†**ˈoutˌputter**[1]. *Obs.* [out- 8.] One who puts out.

1. One who puts or pushes out.

Outpulter and *outeputter* are here applied to the same person. Either of these may be a misprint for the other, or the words may be used as synonyms: cf. pelt, pult, put *vbs.* The passage (which, as printed, is incoherent and corrupt) purports to be from a prophecy of Merlin, in which *outpulter* may have been the orig. word. The precise sense is not determinable.

1480 Caxton *Chron. Eng.* ccxi. n iij, The bere sholde flee with a swan.. thurgh an vnkynde outpulter and that the swan than sholde be slayne with sorwe at Burbrugge. *Ibid.* n iij b, Sir Andrewe of Herkela that is called the vnkynde outeputter.

b. A publisher.

1583 *Reg. Privy Council Scot.* Ser. i. III. 587 Sellaris and outputtaris of thair saidis buikis.

2. One who utters or circulates false coin. *Sc.*

1574 *Sc. Acts Jas. VI* (1814) 93/1 The personis.. salbe persewit and ponissit as wilfull outputtaris and changearis of fals and corrupt money.

3. One who was bound or engaged to provide and fit out men for military service.

1640 in Spalding *Troub. Chas. I* (1850) I. 359 If it sall cum to the knouledge of any persone who hath or sall happin to out reache soldiouris, horss or foot,.. that these out reachit by them are disbandit and fled fra there culloris, the said out putteris of thame salbe oblegit to serche, seik, and aprehend the saidis fugitiues. *Ibid.,* Vtherwaies.. the saidis out putteris salbe oblegit to mak wp there number be out putting of men in there places, sufficientlie providit in armes and vther necessareis vpone the saidis out reacheris there owne expenssis. **1652** Urquhart *Jewel* Wks. (1834) 251 A country gentleman, out-putter of foot or horse.

4. An instigator.

1639 GORDON *Hist. Earls Sutherland* (1813) 317 Sir Robert Gordon.. wes blamed by the Earle of Catteynes for this accidentall slaughter, as ane outputter of the rest to that effect.

5. A term applied to certain maintainers and abettors of thieves or freebooters.

In 9 Hen. V. it appears from the context to be applied to persons in Redesdale who maintained and fitted out thieves for depredations in the adjacent counties: cf. senses 3 and 4. Bp. Jackson seems to have understood and used it of persons who put out their neighbours' cattle or goods into places handy for thieves with whom they were in league: cf. OUTPUT *v.* 1 b, quot. 1615. But the *out-putters* of 1421 were not the neighbours of the persons robbed, but felons living beside the thieves in Tynedale and Redesdale.

1421 *Supplic. Commons Northumbld., Cumbld., & Westmld.* in *Rolls of Parlt.* 9 Hen. V. 143/1 Graund partie des ditz suppliantz sont destruitz par plusurs larons & felons appellez In-takers & Out-putters, demurantz deins les Franchises de Tyndale, Rydesdale, & Hexhamshire... Qar le greindre nombre qi inhabitent deins les ditz Franchises, ou sont tiels malfesours, ou mainteinours d'eulx en lour mauveiste. —— *Act 9 Hen. V*, c. 7 Diverses persones larons et felons appellez Intakers & Outputters demourantz deinz la franchise de Ridesdale, en quele franchise le brief du Roy ne court mye. [i.e. divers persons, thieves, and felons called Intakers and Outputters, dwelling within the Liberty of Redesdale, in which Liberty the King's writ does not run.] *a* 1640 JACKSON *Creed* XI. xl. §8 He is a more cunning thief which can steal without an outputter or receiver, than he which always is enforced to use the help of one or other. 1664 SPELMAN *Gloss.* s.v. *Intakers*, Quos *Outparters* vocant .. recentius *Outputters* nuncupati.

Note. Rastell's Eng. transl. of the Statutes (ed. 1543) reads in the Act of 1421 'felons called yntakers and *outparters*', an obvious misprint, which was however repeated in all editions previous to that of Ruffhead in 1763 (which retains 'outparters' in the text with 'outputters' in the margin). Hence 'outparter' was accepted as a genuine word by Cowell, who in his *Interpreter* further identified the 'outparter' with the thief, with which erroneous explanation the bogus word has duly reappeared in the Law Dictionaries down to Wharton, as well in Phillips, Kersey, Bailey, Ash, Crabbe, Ogilvie's *Imperial Dict.*, *Century Dict.*, and Funk's *Standard Dict.*: it was eschewed by Johnson and Webster. As if one error were not enough, Wharton has also *Outputer*, with an explanation founded upon the latter part of Cowell's article, but making 'man or house' into 'manor-house' (!). This last blunder is taken over from Wharton by Cassell's *Encycl. Dict.*, Ogilvie, and *Century Dict.* (all professing to take it from Cowell). In Hodgson, *Hist. Northumbld.* pt. II. I. 60, the 'outparters' of 1543 appear in a new guise as 'outpartners', erroneously said to be used in the Supplication of 1421, which has *Out-putters*.

1607 COWELL *Interpr.*, *Outeparters, anno 9. H. 5. ca.* 8, seemeth to be a kind of theeues in Ridesdall, that ride abroad at their best advantage, to fetch in such catell or other things, as they could light on without that liberty: some are of opinion that those which in the forenamed statute are termed out-parters, are at this day called out-putters, and are such as set matches for the robbing of any man or house: as by discovering which way he rideth or goeth, or where the house is weakest and fittest to be entred. See *Intakers*. 1658 PHILLIPS, *Outparters*, a sort of theeves about Ridesdale, that ride about to fetch in such cattel or other things as they can light on; [*ed.* 1706 *adds*, and make Matches for the robbing of Men and Houses]. 1823 CRABB *Technol. Dict.*, *Outparters* (Law), a sort of freebooters in Scotland, who used to ride out and seize whatever they could which came in their way. 1848 WHARTON *Law Lex.*, *Outparters*, stealers of cattle. *Ibid.*, *Outputers*, such as set watches for the robbing any manor-house. 1882–90 *Ogilvie's Imperial*, & *Century Dict.*, *Out-parter*. In *old law*, a cattle-stealer. *Out-putter*. In *old law*, One who set watches for the robbing of any manor-house. *Cowell*.

'outputter². [f. OUTPUT *sb.* or *v.* 4.] One who turns out some industrial product; a producer.

1902 *Spectator* 22 Nov. 784/1 The increased proportion of wages to output is being met by a reduction in the necessary number of outputters.

'out,putting, *vbl. sb.* [OUT- 9.]

1. The action of putting out: **a.** Expulsion, ejection; evacuation; **b.** A putting forth, holding out, stretching forth.

1387 TREVISA *Higden* (Rolls) VIII. 95 Þe wrong of her violent out puttynge [L. *violentæ expulsionis injuriam*]. 1398 —— *Barth. De P.R.* XVII. clxxxv. (1495) 726 Wyne excytyth the vertue of outputtynge. 1435 MISYN *Fire of Love* 93 Releve of greif & out-puttynge of wardly hevynes. 1494 *Acta Audit.* (1839) 194 In þe eiectioune & outputting of Johnne guthre.. out of þe tak & maling of þe landis of petpowokis. 1883 J. PARKER *Apost. Life* II. 156 The outputting of a hand should be the finding of an altar. 1888 *Chicago Advance* 9 Feb. 90 The out-puttings of his infinite love.

†**2.** The uttering or issuing of (false) coin. *Sc. Obs.*

1576 in Pitcairn *Crim. Trials* (1833) I. II. 65 Acquit him of all outputting of onye vther fals hardheidis. 1581 *Sc. Acts Jas. VI* (1814) 206/1 Forgeing.. of our souerane lordis money.. And for his treassonable outputting thairof Amongis our souerane lordis liegis.

†**3.** The furnishing or equipping of men. *Sc.*

1640 [see OUTPUTTER 3]. 1640–1 *Kirkcudbr. War-Comm. Min.-bk.* (1855) 37 To compeir befoire the Committie of Estaites.. to answer for thair neglect for not out-putting of the troupe and baggage horss ilk ane of thame for thair awn pairtes.

'out-,quarter. [OUT- 1, 3.]

1. *Milit.* usually in *pl.* A station or quarter (cf. QUARTER *sb.* 15) away from the head-quarters of a regiment (see quot. 1876).

1651 JER. TAYLOR *Serm. Ret. Prayer* Wks. 1831 I. 88 [He] that.. sets up his closet in the out-quarters of an army, and chooses a frontier-garrison to be wise in. *a* 1671 LD. FAIRFAX *Mem.* (1699) 66 Sir John Henderson.. gave the allarm to some of our out-quarters. 1844 *Regul. & Ord. Army* 301 Opposite to the name of each Officer, who is employed at any out-quarter of the Regiment, the Station at which he is detached is to be stated. 1876 VOYLE & STEVENSON *Milit. Dict.* 320/2 Small bodies of troops, when detached away from head-quarters of their regiment, are said to be at out quarters.

2. The outer quarter of a horse's hoof; cf. QUARTER *sb.* 20.

1727 BRADLEY *Fam. Dict.* s.v. *Cut*, Unshoe the Horse, and pare his Out-quarters, as before, if he Cuts behind.

out-'quench, *v. Obs.* exc. *Hist.* [OUT- 15.] *trans.* To put out, extinguish. (Properly two words.) Hence **out-'quencher**, an extinguisher.

1513 DOUGLAS *Æneis* XI. v. 42 Observand weyll the gledis half owt quent. 1596 SPENSER *F.Q.* VI. xi. 16 The candlelight Out quenched leaves no skill nor difference of wight. 1535 COVERDALE *Exod.* xxv. 38 Snoffers and out quenchers of pure golde. 1959 L. GROSS *Housewives' Guide to Antiques* viii. 84 Similar in appearance are the 'douters' or out-quenchers, which were used to extinguish candle flames... these had two discs between which the burning wick was nipped.

out-quibble, etc.: see OUT-.

†**out'quit, -'quite**, *v. Sc. Law. Obs.* [f. OUT- + QUIT *v.*] *trans.* 'To free a subject from adjudication, by full payment of the debt lying on it' (Jam.). Hence †**out'quitting** *vbl. sb.*

1466 *Acta Audit.* (1839) 4 For out quiting of þe saide annuel. 1482 *Ibid.* 104/1 Of þe Redeming & owtquyting of þe landes of sawling be dauid haliburtoun. *c* 1575 *Balfour's Pract.* (1754) 445 Gif ony man's landis be wodset, he may outquite and redeme the samin quhen he pleisis except [etc.].

out-Quixote to **out-quote**: see OUT-.

out'race, *v.* [OUT- 18 b.] To outrun in a race; to outstrip.

1657 W. MORICE *Cœna quasi Κοινή* Def. xxii. 224 In them also who have outraced them, and gone beyond the goale. *a* 1845 HOOD *Desert-Born* 48 But Fancy fond out-raced them all, with bridle loose and free.

outrage ('aʊtreɪdʒ), *sb.* Forms: 3–4 **utrage**, (4 **uterage**), 3– **outrage**; also 4–6 **oultrage**, 4–5 **outtrage**, **owt(e)rage**, 5–6 **outerage**, 6 **owtrag**. [ME. a. OF. *ultrage*, *oltrage* (11th c. in Littré), *oultrage*, *outrage* (12th c.), = Pr. *oltratge*, Cat. *ultratge*, Sp. *ultraje*, It. *oltraggio*:—Com. Rom. type **ultragium* (also med.L.), f. L. *ultrā* beyond + suff. *-agium*, *-aggio*, *-age*: see -AGE. In Eng. often analysed as from OUT and RAGE; a notion which affected the sense-development: cf. sense 2.]

†**1. a.** The passing beyond established or reasonable bounds, want of moderation, intemperance; excess, extravagance, exaggeration: excessive luxury. Rarely with *an* and *pl. Obs.*

1297 R. GLOUC. (Rolls) 8900 Þe king vnderstod þat þe maide ne sede non outrage. 13.. *Cursor M.* 28457 O mete and drink to do vtrage. 1340 HAMPOLE *Pr. Consc.* 1516 Gret outrage we se In pompe and pride and vanité. 1387 TREVISA *Higden* (Rolls) III. 459 We useþ no glotenye oþer outrage of mete and drynke. *c* 1430 *Hymns Virg.* 74/512 He loueþ more mesure þan outrage. 1484 CAXTON *Royal Bk.* F j, By suche excessys and suche oultrages comen and sourden many maladyes and sekenessys. 1590 SPENSER *F.Q.* II. ii. 38 With equall measure she did moderate The strong extremities of their outrage.

b. Excess of boldness; foolhardiness, rashness; presumption. *Obs.*

1375 BARBOUR *Bruce* XIX. 408 For thame thoucht foly and outrage To gang wp to thame. *a* 1548 HALL *Chron., Hen. VI* 114 Of a greate outrage, and more pride and presumpcion, she demaunded, to beare the noble and excellent Armes of Fraunce. 1553 EDEN *Treat. Newe Ind.* (Arb.) 42 Yet do not I commende rashenes or outrage.

†**2. a.** Extravagant, violent, or disorderly action; mad or passionate behaviour, fury; tumult of passion, disorder; violence of language, insolence. Also rarely with *an* and *pl. Obs.* or *arch.*

a 1330 *Otuel* 329 Þauȝ otuwel speke outrage, For he was comen on message King Charles.. [Nolde] soffre him habbe nouȝt bote god. *c* 1375 *Cursor M.* 6986 (Fairf) Qua herde euer of suche outerage? *c* 1386 CHAUCER *Knt.'s T.* 1154 Yet saugh I woodnesse laughynge in his rage Armed compleint out hees and fiers outrage. 1560 DAUS tr. *Sleidane's Comm.* 295 b, In this dissolute outrage, and confusion of things. 1592 KYD *Sp. Trag.* III. xii. 79 What meanes this outrage? Will none of you restraine his fury? 1595 SHAKS. *John* III. iv. 106, I feare some out-rage, and Ile follow her. 1705 J. PHILIPS *Blenheim* (1715) 25 See, with what Outrage from the frosty North, The early Valiant Swede draws forth his Wings In Battailous Array. 1750 JOHNSON *Rambler* No. 75 ⁋7, I bore the diminution of my riches without any outrages of sorrow. 1791 PAINE *Rights of Man* (ed. 4) 47 Mr. Burke, with his usual outrage, abuses the Declaration of the Rights of Man. 1845 MRS. S. C. HALL *Whiteboy* ii. 10 The noise, and opposition, and outrage of the little resolute, but most mechanical, steamer.

b. Violent clamour; outcry. *Obs.*

a 1548 HALL *Chron., Rich. III* 50 They sodeinly put fyer in the lanthornes and make showtes and outrages from toune to toune. 1590 SPENSER *F.Q.* I. xi. 40 Hart cannot thinke what outrage and what cries,.. The hell-bred beast threw forth unto the skies.

3. a. Violence affecting others; violent injury or harm. † *to do outrage*, to exercise violence, to do grievous injury or wrong *to* any one (*obs.*).

c 1290 *S. Eng. Leg.* I. 348/95 Al hire þouȝt was.. to bi-þenche sum outrage þat þis child were i-brouȝt of dawe for-to habbe is heritage. 1297 R. GLOUC. (Rolls) 3646 Þat þe scottes & þe picars dude hym gret outrage. 1390 GOWER *Conf.* I. 345 To.. vengen him of thilke oultrage, Whiche was vnto his father do. *c* 1430 LYDG. *Min. Poems.* (Percy Soc.) 50 A laxatif dide hym so grete outrage. 1490 CAXTON *Eneydos* xxvii. 98 After that I had be auenged of his falsenes and oultrage. 1560 DAUS tr. *Sleidane's Comm.* 286 b, The townes men feared chiefly the outtrage of the souldiours. 1590 SPENSER *F.Q.* II. i. 30 And playnd of grievous outrage, which he red A knight had wrought against a Ladie gent. 1614 RALEIGH *Hist. World* I. (1634) 154 To defend themselves from outrage. 1667 MILTON *P.L.* I. 500 The noyse Of riot ascends.. And injury and outrage. 1781 COWPER *Lett.* 5 Mar., Wherever there is war there is misery and outrage. 1844 H. H. WILSON *Brit. India* I. 271 Guilty of violent and inflammatory proceedings, and of acts of outrage.

b. with *an* and *pl.* A deed of violence committed against any one or against society; a violent injury or wrong; a gross or wanton offence or indignity.

agrarian outrage: see AGRARIAN *a.*

[1306 *Rolls of Parlt.* I. 211/2 Des amendes de trespas & d'outrages soulement faitz a nous.] *c* 1380 *Sir Ferumb.* 1669 Wilt þou þe selue & ous a slo þorw such a fol outtrage? 1529 MORE *Dyaloge* IV. xviii. Wks. 285/2 Great outrages & temporal harmes that suche heretykes haue been alway wont to doe. 1584 *Galway Arch.* in *10th Rep. Hist. MSS. Comm.* App. v. 434 To mentayne the peace.. and suppresse outrages. 1591 SHAKS. *Two Gent.* IV. i. 71 Prouided that you do no outrages On silly women, or poore passengers. 1791 BURKE *Let. to R. Burke* Corr. 1844 III. 226 The Emperor may likewise justly complain of the outrages offered to his sister. 1835 THIRLWALL *Greece* I. v. 151 All the chiefs of Greece.. to avenge this outrage, sailed with a great armament to Troy. 1880 MCCARTHY *Own Times* IV. liv. 154 Outrages began to increase in atrocity, boldness, and numbers.

fig. 1695 WOODWARD *Nat. Hist. Earth* I. (1723) 155 A fresh Collection of this Fire committs the same Outrages as before.

c. *transf.* Said of gross or wanton wrong or injury done to feelings, principles, or the like.

1769 *Junius Lett.* iv. 21 It is possible to condemn measures without a barbarous and criminal outrage against men. 1808 *Med. Jrnl.* XIX. 562 If Mr. B. had not disgraced himself by this unpardonable outrage upon private feelings. 1849 MACAULAY *Hist. Eng.* v. I. 621 To see him and not to spare him was an outrage on humanity and decency.

d. A person of strange or wild appearance, or one who is extravagant in behaviour.

1869 'MARK TWAIN' *Innoc. Abr.* 35 Who is that smooth-faced, animated outrage yonder in the fine clothes? 1884 —— *Huck. Finn* 236 Blamed if he warn't the horriblest-looking outrage I ever see. 1909 'O. HENRY' *Roads of Destiny* 351 This old medical outrage floated down to my shack when I sent for him.

†**4.** A violent effort or exertion of force. *rare.*

1484 CAXTON *Fables of Æsop* II. vii, How in myn yong age I was stronge and lusty, And how I made grete outtrages and effors the whiche [etc.]. 1503 HAWES *Examp. Virt.* vii. 95 He .. bete theym downe by a grete outrage.

5. *Comb.* **outrage-monger**, one who trades in outrages, who employs (agrarian or other) outrages for political ends.

1882 *Daily News*, [To] increase the force to such an extent that intending murderers or outragemongers will not be able to evade them. 1887 *Spectator* 16 Apr. 517/1 We do not suppose that the outragemongers are playing Mr. Parnell's game.

†**outrage**, *a.* (*adv.*) *Obs.* [app. from the sb.: not so used in Fr.] = OUTRAGEOUS.

1. Intemperate, violent, presumptuous.

c 1330 R. BRUNNE *Chron.* (1810) 263 Snowdon gan he hald, als his heritage, & prince þei him cald, þat bastard outrage. *c* 1400 *Rowland & O.* 199 Rowlande sayde: 'Sir, thou art to outrage'. *a* 1450 *Cov. Myst.* vi. 62 (Shaks. Soc.) Of speche bethe not owtrage. *c* 1470 HENRY *Wallace* v. 571 Felloune, owtrage, dispitfull in his deid.

2. Extravagant, wasteful, luxurious.

a 1420 HOCCLEVE *De Reg. Princ.* 499 Pryde hath wel leuer bere an hungry mawe To bedde, than lakke of array outrage. 1450–80 tr. *Secreta Secret.* 8 The Rentis and profetis.. myght not susteyne ne mayntene ther outrage dispenses. 1483 *Cath. Angl.* 264/2 Outerage, *excessiuus, prodigus jn expensis, superfluus*. 1550 CROWLEY *Epigr.* 1064 The idlenes of abbays made them outrage.

3. Excessive, severe: said of climate or weather.

c 1400 MAUNDEV. (Roxb.) xiv. 65 Þare es owtrage calde, by cause it es at þe north syde of þe werld... On þe south syde .. es it.. so hate þat na man may dwell þare for þe owtrage hete. *c* 1440 *Jacob's Well* 155 Sykenes, or pouerte, or outerage wedyr, or fayling of frute.

4. Extraordinary, unusual, out of ordinary course.

13.. *Gaw. & Gr. Knt.* 29 An aunter in erde I attle to schawe,.. an outtrage awenture of Arthurez wonderez. *c* 1430 LYDG. *Min. Poems* (Percy Soc.) 119 Thynges outrage bien founde in every kynde.

B. as *adv.* Excessively, extraordinarily.

c 1400 *Destr. Troy* 3774 Aiax oelius was outrage grete.

outrage ('aʊtreɪdʒ), *v.*¹ [f. OUTRAGE *sb.*: cf. F. *outrager*, †*oultrager* (14–15th c. in Hatz.-Darm.), It. *oltraggiare*, Sp. *ultrajár*. In all the obs. senses, and formerly in 2, stressed on -'*rage*.]

† **1.** *intr.* To go beyond bounds; to go to excess, act extravagantly or without self-restraint; to commit excesses, run riot. *Obs.*

1303 R. BRUNNE *Handl. Synne* 10892 þoȝ þey outrage, ande do folly, He shal nat sle hem wyþ felony. **1387** TREVISA *Higden* (Rolls) III. 187 þere were i-made tweye consuls, þat ȝif þat oon wolde outrage, þe oþer myȝte hym restreyne. *c* **1440** *Promp. Parv.* 375/2 Owtragyn, or doon excesse, *excedo.* **1496** *Dives & Paup.* (W. de W.) IX. vii. 356/1 Couetouse folke.. outrage & seke to be in hygher degre of rychesses & of worshyp than theyr neyghbours ben. *a* **1568** ASCHAM *Scholem.* I. (Arb.) 69 If three or foure great ones in Courte, will nedes outrage in apparell, in huge hose, in monstrous hattes. **1718** *Entertainer* No. 40. 274 He outrages in Riot, and runs up to Seed in the grossest Impieties.

2. *trans.* To do violence to; to subject to outrage; to wrong grossly, treat with gross violence or indignity, injure, insult, violate.

1590 SPENSER *F.Q.* I. vi. 5 Ah heavens! that doe this hideous act behold, And heavenly virgin thus outraged see. **1622** BACON *Hen. VII*, Wks. 1879 I. 745/1 The news.. put divers young bloods into such a fury, as the English ambassadors were not without peril to be outraged. **1663** PEPYS *Diary* 10 May, The Bishop of Galloway was besieged in his house by some women, and had like to have been outraged. **1726** POPE *Odyss.* XVI. 296 If outrag'd, cease that outrage to repel. **1849** MACAULAY *Hist. Eng.* iv. I. 464 In peace he continued to plunder and to outrage them. *Ibid.* x. II. 600 The king stopped, robbed, and outraged by ruffians.
absol. **1884** *Nonconf. & Indep.* 14 Feb. 151/1 Plundering, outraging, and practising every form of oppression.

b. To violate or infringe flagrantly (law, right, authority, morality, any principle).

1725–6 *Pope's Odyss.* (J.), This interview outrages all decency. **1848** W. H. KELLY tr. *L. Blanc's Hist. Ten Y.* II. 74 They were charged.. with.. the offence of outraging public morality and virtue. **1871** FREEMAN *Hist. Ess.* Ser. I. x. 291 [Frederick II] contrived, by the circumstances of his vices, to outrage contemporary sentiment in a way in which his vices alone would not have outraged it.

† **3.** *intr.* To break away, stray: see OUTRAY *v.*[1] 1.

1447 BOKENHAM *Seyntys* (Roxb.) 62 Hir curage.. was goddys to serue From whos seruyce she nolde outrage.

† **4.** *trans.* To drive out by force. *Obs. rare*⁻¹.

14.. LYDG. *Bochas* II. xv. (MS. Bodl. 263) lf. 117/2 To putte their labour in execucioun And to outrage, this is veray trouthe, Fro mannys liff, necligence & slouthe.

† **5.** *intr.* (Influenced by RAGE *v.*) To burst out into rage, to be furious, to rage; to rush out in rage. *Obs.*

1548 CRANMER *Catech.* 23 b, When you shall heare other outragyng with such horrible curses, flye from theym as frome pestilence. **1571** GOLDING *Calvin on Ps.* xxv. 8 Though the wicked outraged ageinst him without cause. **1582** STANYHURST *Æneis* II. (Arb.) 65 So rushing to the streets I posted in anger. But my feete embracing, my pheere me in the entrye reteyned, Too father owtraging thee soon [i.e. the son] shee tendred Iülus. **1606** G. W[OODCOCKE] *Hist. Iustine* IX. 42 Alexander, outraged not against his enemies, but his especiall friends.

† **out'rage,** *v.*[2] *Obs. rare.* [perh. f. OUT- + RAGE *v.* But very prob. arising from erroneous analysis of OUTRAGE *v.*[1]: cf. prec. 5.]

1. *trans.* To rage against.

1584 HUDSON *Du Bartas' Judith* III. in *Sylvester's Wks.* (1621) 718 All this could not the peoples thirst asswage; But thus with murmurs they their Lords out-rage.

2. To surpass in rage or violence. [OUT- 18.]

1742 YOUNG *Nt. Th.* III. 164 Their Will the Tyger suck'd, outrag'd the Storm.

'outraged, *ppl. a.* [f. OUTRAGE *v.*[1] + -ED[1].] Subjected to outrage, gross violence, or indignity; violated.

a **1711** KEN *Div. Love* Wks. (1838) 242 Was ever any Love, O outraged Mercy, like that love thou didst shew in dying for sinners? **1856** KANE *Arct. Expl.* I. xxviii. 366 With the prompt ceremonial which outraged law delights in. **1869** TENNYSON *Holy Grail* 208 An outraged maiden sprang into the hall, Crying on help.

† **'outragely,** *adv. Obs.* [f. OUTRAGE *a.* + -LY[2].] = OUTRAGEOUSLY.

a **1340** HAMPOLE *Psalter* xxiv. [xxv.] 3 Confoundid be all wirkand wicked thyngis: outragely [*v.r.* outerageusly]... þat is, þai doe wickidly.. & outragely [*v.r.* out raiusliche] trauails in vanytes. **1445** *E.E. Wills* (1882) 131 Y wille.. that myn exequies be not outragely done in expenses of vanites. *c* **1470** HENRY *Wallace* XI. 160 Than Wallace said: 'Ye wrang ws owtragely'.

So † **'outrageness** = OUTRAGEOUSNESS.

1483 *Cath. Angl.* 264/2 An Outeragenes, *excessus, superfluitas.*

outrageous (aʊt'reɪdʒəs), *a.* (*adv.*) Forms: 4– outrageous; also 4 ut-, 4–5 oute-, 4–6 owt-, 5–6 oult-; 4 *Sc.* -eouss, 5 -uous, 5–6 -yous, -ios, 5–8 -ious, 6 -eus, -iowse, etc. [a. OF. *outrageus*, AF. *oult-*, F. *-eux*, f. *outrage* OUTRAGE *sb.*[1]: see -OUS.]

1. Exceeding proper limits; excessive, immoderate, extravagant, superfluous; enormous, extraordinary, unusual. In later use coloured by sense 2.

c **1325** *Metr. Hom.* 89 His frendes.. gert him wel eet and drinc, And lef his utrageous swinc. **1340** HAMPOLE *Pr. Consc.* 9440 Outrageous hete and outrageouse calde. *c* **1386** CHAUCER *Pard. T.* 322 Vengeance shal nat parten from his hous That of his othes is to outrageous. **14..** in *Alexander*, etc. (E.E.T.S.) 283 For þe outragez hight of housez. *c* **1416** HOCCLEVE *Bal. Hen. V* 14 The somme.. Is nat excessif ne outrageous. **1447** *Rolls of Parlt.* V. 137/2 Outeragious assemble of pepill. **1484** CAXTON *Chivalry* 77 By ouer outragyous drynkynge and etynge. **1502** ATKINSON tr. *De Imitatione* I. xxi. 170 Remembre the outragious peynes of hell & pourgatory. *c* **1550** R. BIESTON *Bayte Fortune* B ij b, By arrogance oultrageous thy tounge on vanting swerueth. **1555** EDEN *Decades* 67 Beinge pricked forwarde with owtragious hunger. **1585** T. WASHINGTON tr. *Nicholay's Voy.* II. xi. 46 b, We found the streame.. so violent and outragious. **1696** WHISTON *Th. Earth* IV. (1722) 378 [It] would.. afterward descend in violent and outragious Rains. **1818** MISS MITFORD in L'Estrange *Life* (1870) II. ii. 46 The Romans [always seemed to me] the most outrageous, strutting, boasting barbarians on the face of the earth. **1868** BROWNING *Ring & Bk.* XII. 55 Yesterday he had to keep indoors Because of the outrageous rain that fell.

2. Excessive or unrestrained in action; violent, furious; †excessively bold or fierce (*obs.*).

1375 BARBOUR *Bruce* IX. 102 For hys outrageouss manheid, Confortit his men on sic maneir. *c* **1386** CHAUCER *Pars. T.* ¶485 In his outrageous anger and Ire. *c* **1420** *Anturs of Arth.* 421 Thou hase wonnen thaym one werre, with owttrageouse wille. **1484** CAXTON *Fables of Æsop* I. xvi, There was a lyon whiche in his yougthe was fyers and moche outragyous. **1523** LD. BERNERS *Froiss.* I. cxxxvii. 165 He came with a thre thousande of the moost outragyoust people in all that countrey. **1609** ROWLANDS *Whole Crew of Kind Gossips* 30 Sometimes her out-ragious madding fits, Makes me as mad as she, beside my wits. **1658** J. JONES tr. *Ovid's Ibis* 117 So is revenge furiously out-ragious and outragiously furious. **1751** EARL ORRERY *Remarks Swift* (1752) 169 From an outrageous lunatic, he sunk afterwards into a quiet, speechless idiot. **1806** H. SIDDONS *Maid, Wife, & Widow* I. 198 The old man was outrageous: Frederick acted with more policy.

3. Excessive in injuriousness, cruelty, or offensiveness; of the nature of violent or gross injury, wrong, or offence, or of a gross violation of law, humanity, or morality; grossly offensive or abusive.

1456 SIR G. HAYE *Law Arms* (S.T.S.) 174 [If he] do him sum outrageous injure. *Ibid.* 287 And he persevere in his outrageous langage. **1502** *Ord. Crysten Men* II. v. (1506) 95 Whyche thynge is outragyous & presumpcyon detestable ayenst god. **1560** DAUS tr. *Sleidane's Comm.* 274 b, Which outragious crueltie, I doubt not but God wyll ones avenge. **1583** GOLDING *Calvin on Deut.* ii. 65 If a man that hath no need doe rob or fleece his Neighbour of his goodes: therein appeareth so much the lewder and outragiouser naughtinesse. **1642** in Clarendon *Hist. Reb.* v. §66 To punish those horrible, outragious cruelties, which had been committed in the murthering, and spoiling so many of his Subjects. **1852** MRS. STOWE *Uncle Tom's C.* xxxv. 313 The outrageous treatment of poor Tom had roused her still more. **1864** TENNYSON *Aylmer's F.* 286 Pelted with outrageous epithets. **1888** A. K. GREEN *Behind Closed Doors* ii, Whether I am to be made the victim of an outrageous scandal that will affect my whole future career.

† **B.** as *adv.* = next. *Obs.*

1375 BARBOUR *Bruce* IX. 483 He wes outrageouss hardy. **1526** SKELTON *Magnyf.* 2570 To day hote, to morowe outragyous colde.

out'rageously, *adv.* [f. prec. + -LY[2].] In an outrageous manner: **a.** To an immoderate degree, excessively, extravagantly; violently, furiously; **b.** In violation or with shameless disregard of law, morality, or humanity; atrociously, flagrantly.

a **1340** HAMPOLE *Psalter* xxx[i]. 7 þou hatid þe kepand vanytes outrageusly. *Ibid.* Cant. 501 þaim þat lufis þis life outrageusly. **1387** TREVISA *Higden* (Rolls) IV. 205 Julius Cesar.. dede outrageousliche aȝenst þe customs and fredom of Rome. *c* **1400** MAUNDEV. (1839) xxii. 239 He may despende ynow, and outrageously. **1474** CAXTON *Chesse* II. iv. C v b, Which supposid that hit had been his squyer that he entretid so outragyously. **1517** TORKINGTON *Pilgr.* (1884) 59 All nyght it blew owtrageowsly. *c* **1540** tr. *Pol. Verg. Eng. Hist.* (Camden) I. 257 Hee fell to the grownde, crienge owtrageuslie that hee was slaine. **1561** T. NORTON *Calvin's Inst.* I. 27 It is good that this outragiously wicked madnesse be bewraied. **1625** K. LONG tr. *Barclay's Argenis* IV. ii. 239 Nobody durst speake to him thus outragiously fuming. **1713** STEELE *Englishm.* No. 1. 3, I was most outragiously insulted by that Rascal of yours. **1854** DE QUINCY *War* Wks. IV. 283 It gives a colourable air of justice.. to a war which is, in fact, the most outrageously unjust.

out'rageousness. [f. as prec. + -NESS.] The quality of being outrageous: **a.** Excess, extravagance; excessive violence, fury, ferocity; **b.** Flagrant wrongfulness or indignity; enormity, atrociousness, heinousness.

1470–85 MALORY *Arthur* XIV. i, I see wel ye haue grete wylle to be slayne as your fader was thorugh oultrageousnes. **1545** ASCHAM *Toxoph.* To Gentlem. Eng. (Arb.) 17 That the outragiousness of great gamyng shuld not hurte the honestie of shotyng. *a* **1548** HALL *Chron., Hen. VII* 48 b, This aunswere.. could not mittigate or assuage the Scottes angre and outrageousnes. *c* **1594** CAPT. WYATT *R. Dudley's Voy. W. Ind.* (Hakl.) 11 The weather growinge into such a monstrous outragiousnes. **1695** J. EDWARDS *Perfect. Script.* 19 An example of the impudence and outragiousness of lust. **1798** *Hist.* in *Ann. Reg.* 96/2 The violence and outrageousness that had characterised its original champions. **1869** E. S. FFOULKES *Church's Creed or Crown's Creed?* 36 The outrageousness of the whole proceeding.

'outrager. [f. OUTRAGE *v.*[1] + -ER[1].] One who subjects to outrage or gross violence, a violator.

1873 H. SPENCER *Study Sociol.* ix. (1874) 208 An outrager of all laws and social duties. **1892** *Columbus (O.) Disp.* 12 Apr., Assaulters and outragers of children.

'outraging, *ppl. a.* [f. OUTRAGE *v.*[1] + -ING[2].] That outrages or grossly offends; that violates justice, morality, or decency; acting in an outrageous manner; †furious, raging (*obs.*).

1567 DRANT *Horace, Ep.* xix. F viij, For plaie ingenders tremling stryfe and strife outraginge ire. **1612** CHAPMAN *Widdowes T.* III. F ij b, These are the ditches.. in which outraging colts plunge both themselues and their riders. **1642** BRIDGE *Wound. Consc. Cured* i. 9 The outraging licenciousnesse of Kings. **1895** *Daily News* 17 Jan. 6/4 It is gratuitously outraging to his unfortunate readers.

† **outragi'ousitie.** *Obs.* In 4 outragiouste, 5 -gyousyte. [a. AFr. type **outrageousté*, f. *outrageous* + *-te*, -TY: not recorded in OF. (Cf. JOYOUSITIE.)] The quality of being OUTRAGEOUS: **a.** Going beyond usual bounds, abnormality, monstrosity; **b.** Violence.

1340 HAMPOLE *Pr. Consc.* 5010 If any lyms be here unsemely, Thurgh outragiousté of kynd namely, God sal abate þat outrage, thurgh myght, And make þa lyms semely to sight. **1470–85** MALORY *Arthur* III. xv, [He] charged hem neuer to doo outragyousyte nor mordre.

outraie, variant of OUTRAY *v.*[1] *Obs.*

out-'rail, *v.*[1] [OUT- 18.] *trans.* To outdo in railing; to surpass in the use of raillery.

1676 WYCHERLEY *Pl. Dealer* I. i. (1735) 20 Thou mayst easily come to.. out-rail a Wit. *a* **1704** T. BROWN *Sat. on Fr. King* Wks. 1730 I. 59 He'd out-rail Oats, and curse both thee and Boufflers. **1876** L. STEPHEN *Eng. Th. 18th C.* I. 178.

out-'rail, *v.*[2] *nonce-wd.* [f. OUT- 21 + RAIL *sb.*[2] 2 b.] *trans.* To surpass in respect of a railing.

1866 RUSKIN *Crown Wild Olive* p. xii, The publichouse-keeper on the other side of the way presently buys another railing, to out-rail him with.

† **outraious,** *a. Obs.* Also 6 outraous, -rayious. [app. f. OUTRAY *sb.* + -OUS.

In the first quot. repr. *outraius*, i.e. *outrajus* in the F. original, so that the Eng. also may be for *outrajous* = *outrageous*. On the other hand *outraous* in quot. 1523 cannot be so explained.]

= OUTRAGEOUS *a.*, in its various senses.

1303 R. BRUNNE *Handl. Synne* 5492 ȝyf þou haue be so coueytous To mercs men ouer outraious. *c* **1450** LONELICH *Grail* xxxv. 162 And Redyn Al day with gret peyne In An Owtraious Contre Certeyne. **1523** LD. BERNERS *Froiss.* I. xliv. 61 Kyng Phylyppe.. made light therof, and sayd how his nephue was but an outraous fole.

Hence † **outraiously** *adv. Obs.*

1303 R. BRUNNE *Handl. Synne* 2196 ȝyf þou be a lordyng, And outraiusly takyst mennys þyng Yn tyme of werre or tyme of pes. **13..** [see OUTRAGELY, *a* 1340].

† **out'rake**[1]. *Obs.* Also **oute reche, utrack, -rak(e.** [? corrupt. of *outrage*.] Outrage, excess.

13.. *Cursor M.* 4133 (Cott.) If yee do suilk an outrake [*v.rr.* vtrack, outerake] Ful siker may yee be o wrake. *Ibid.* 6295 (Cott.) For ogh [*v.r.* oft] on him þai soght vtrak]*v.rr.* outrake, oute reche, vtrake] Quar-for oft sith þai fand his wrak. *Ibid.* 29075 (Cott.) For þof we fast we agh noght take Noþer o mete ne drink vtrake.

'outrake[2]. *dial.* [f. OUT- 7 + RAKE *sb.*[3]] † **a.** An expedition, a raid. *Obs.* **b.** (See quot. 1825.)

a **1765** *Northumbld. betrayed by Dowglas* xxxii. in Child *Ballads* (1889) III. VI. clxxvi. 413/2 And I haue beene in Lough Leven The most part of these yeeres three: Yett had I neuer noe out-rake. **1802** SIBBALD *Chron. Sc. Poetry* Gloss., *Outrake*, an expedition, an out-ride.. also an extensive open pasture for sheep or cattle. **1825** BROCKETT *N.C. Gloss.*, *Outrake*, a free passage for sheep from inclosed pastures into open grounds, or common lands. **1889** *Shreds & Patches* 26 June (E.D.D.), The records of the Court Baron of Holgate twice mention an outrack. **1976** G. MOFFAT *Short Time to Live* v. 49 This lady at Burblethwaite. .. I saw her walking up the outrake.

† **'outrance.** *Obs.* exc. as. Fr. (utrɑ̃s). Forms: 5–6 oultra(u)nce, 5 out-, owtraunce, 7 outterance, 5– outrance. See also UTTERANCE. [a. OF. *oultrance*, *outrance* (13th c. in Hatz.-Darm.) going beyond bounds, excess, extremity, f. *oultrer*, *outrer* to pass beyond, surpass, conquer, drive out of bounds or to extremity, = Pr. *ultrar*, It. *oltrare* to go beyond, f. L. *ultrā*, It. *oltra*, F. *oltre*, *outre* beyond. In this form the word has been more or less obs. since 17th c., since which time however the Fr. phrase *à outrance*, *à toute outrance* (erroneously *à l'outrance*), to excess, to extremity, has been in occasional use, instead of the Eng. *at* or *to* (*the*) *outrance*. But already *c* 1400 the same vowel-shortening which changed *outer*, *outmost* to *utter*, *utmost*, shortened *outrance* to *uttrance*, subseq. often extended to UTTERANCE, in which form the word is still occasional in literary use.]

a. A degree which goes beyond bounds or beyond measure; excess: only in the phrases ***to* (*unto*) *outrance***, beyond all limits, to the utmost, to extremity, ***at outrance***, at the last extremity; ***to fight to* (*the*)** or ***at outrance***, to fight to the bitter end, to the death (rendering F. *combattre à outrance*, *à toute outrance*, 13th c. in Littré).

1412–20 LYDG. *Chron. Troy* I. ii, Fyrste he must.. Unto oultraunce with these bulles to fyght. **14..** HOCCLEVE *Bal. Virg. & Christ* 48 Lest.. The feend me assaille, & haue at the outrance. *a* **1420** —— *De Reg. Princ.* 3217 Rathir hadde I-putte hym to þe outraunce. *c* **1550** R. BIESTON *Barte*

Fortune A vj, But poore men to punishe vnto the oultrance. **1601** HOLLAND *Pliny* I. 280 As if sword-fencers were brought within the lists to fight at outterance. **1609** —— *Amm. Marcell.* XIX. ii. 125 They were so stiffely set to fight to the outrance. **1755** SMOLLETT *Quix.* II. v. (1783) I. 89 *note*, To fight the owner to extremity or outrance. **1819** SCOTT *Ivanhoe* viii, The combat was understood to be at *outrance*.

‖**b.** The corresponding Fr. phrase (also erron. *à l'outrance*).

1600 TATE in Gutch *Coll. Cur.* I. 8 The manner of fight is ..by Capitulation, or a Toute Outrance. **1837**, **1860** [see À L'OUTRANCE]. **1883** *Standard* 24 Oct. 5/2 (Stanf.) Every duellist *à outrance* binds himself to commit suicide or murder. **1955** *Times* 19 May 10/2 Powerful Mau Mau 'generals'..are in favour of continuing the struggle *à outrance*. **1959** *Listener* 8 Oct. 589/1 The destruction of her fragile world and the war *à outrance* to keep something of it intact.

outrange (aʊt'reɪndʒ), *v.* [OUT- 21, 18, 17.]

1. a. *trans. Gunnery.* To exceed in range, have a longer range than.

1858 GREENER *Gunnery* 85 The best rifles on my principle will out-range by several hundred yards the best 'six-pounder' in her Majesty's service. **1899** *Westm. Gaz.* 2 Nov. 7/2 Our forces were seriously outnumbered, and our guns outranged until the arrival of the Naval Brigade.

b. *transf.* In certain ball games, to have a greater command of the field of play than (an opponent).

1930 *Times* 15 Mar. 6/1 At fullback, Scotland will have.. R. C. Warren, but he may be outranged by J. C. Hubbard.

2. To surpass in extent of time.

1887 *Pall Mall G.* 1 June 5/2 The red deer..can outrange them all in the historic records of his antiquity.

3. a. To range beyond.

1883 *Philad. Telegraph* XL. No. 35. 3 Their brethren who outranged the forest fastnesses and fell into the hands of men.

b. *Naut.* To range past or ahead of, to outsail.

1890 in *Cent. Dict.*

c. *Aeronaut.* Of an aircraft: to have a greater range than (another aircraft).

1942 [see OUT-GUN *v.*].

out'rank, *v.* [OUT- 21.] *trans.* To be superior in rank to, to take precedence of. Hence **out'ranked** *ppl. a.*

1842 *Spirit of Times* (Philad.) 1 Sept. (Th.), It won't be long before he fills the place of some one of the drones and cakes who now outrank him. **1864** in WEBSTER. **1881** P. DU CHAILLU *Land Midnight Sun* II. 150 The Norwegians.. outrank every other nation in Europe in that respect. **1903** *Westm. Gaz.* 26 Aug. 4/1 Barr did not outrank Wringe here as he had done at the start. **1948** K. ANTHONY *Lambs* i. 11 She laid some strange claim to a gentility outranking her husband's. **1973** J. WAINWRIGHT *Pride of Pigs* 179 You haven't a leg to stand on... You don't even out-rank me. **1974** S. GULLIVER *Vulcan Bulletins* 21 The luckless, outranked, beautifully-spoken captain of shooting.

out-'rant, *v.* [OUT- 18 or 21.] *trans.* To exceed in ranting.

1646-8 G. DANIEL *Poems* Wks. 1878 I. 211 High Stories, to out-rant our dull Gazetts. **1681** HICKERINGILL *Char. Sham Plotter* Wks. 1716 I. 219 He has..Prophaneness enough to out-rant a Tory. **1885** *L'pool Post* 27 Mar. 4/6 He attempts to out-rant and..out-slang the *Pall Mall Gazette*.

outraous, obs. form of OUTRAIOUS.

out-rape, -rate, etc.: see OUT-.

†**out-'rase, -raze,** *v. Obs.* [OUT- 16.] *trans.* To pluck or root out, to destroy; to erase, efface or rub out. Hence †**out-'rased** *ppl. a.*

1412-20 LYDG. *Chron. Troy* IV. xxxi, Let not his prease thy royall booke defface But in all haste his renowne outrace. **1422** tr. *Secreta Secret., Priv. Priv.* 128 Fryst he makyd his owyn eigh to be out-rasit. *c* **1586** C'TESS PEMBROKE *Ps.* LXXIV. xviii, Nor utterly out-rase From tables of thy grace The flock of thy afflicted ones. **1621** G. SANDYS *Ovid's Met.* VII. (1626) 142 Out-razed by the sterne Diseases rage. **1638** —— *Paraphr. Div. Poems, Job* (1648) 14 No Eye shall his out-raz'd impression view.

outraught, obs. pa. pple. of OUTREACH.

outrave, Sc. past t. of OUTRIVE *v. Obs.*

†**'outray,** *sb. Obs.* Also 5 owtray(e. [f. next.]

1. = OUTRAGE *sb.* in various senses.

14.. *Ser. J. Mandevelle & Souden* 78 in Hazl. *E.P.P.* (1864) I. 157 In most outraye. Sathanase was lowset, and cawsit this syn. *c* **1475** *Rauf Coilȝear* 156 He start vp stoutly agane..For anger of that outray that he had thair tane. **1610** HOLLAND *Camden's Brit.* (1637) 134 With..great cruelty they committed outraies along these shores. *c* **1611** CHAPMAN *Iliad* XXIII. 506 You..know well the outrays that engage All young men's actions.

2. ? An outgoing; a going out of bounds.

c **1624** CHAPMAN *Batrachom.* 80 The cat and night-hawke, who much skathe confer On all the outraies, where for food I erre.

ou'tray, *v.*[1] *Obs.* exc. *dial.* [a. AngloF. *ultreier, outreier* (of which Godef. cites *ultrea* for *ultreia* from *Horn et Rimenhild*):—late L. type **ultricāre*, f. *ultrā* beyond; practically identical in sense with OF. *oultrer, outrer*:—L. **ultrāre*; hence cognate with *outrage*, med.L. *ultrāgium*, and its derivative *outrage* vb., of which *outray* is, in its earlier senses, to a great extent a doublet. But it appears to have been sometimes felt as a compound of OUT- and RAY *sb.* and *v.*, aphetic for ARRAY: cf. quots. 1387, *c* 1611 in sense 1.]

†**1.** *intr.* To go beyond or exceed bounds; to stray; to break away from a certain place or order; to be or get out of array. *Obs.*

13.. *Coer de L.* 2713 Befell that a noble stede Outrayyd fro a paynym. *c* **1374** CHAUCER *Boeth.* III. pr. vi. 61 (Camb. MS.) þat they ne sholden nat owtrayen or forlyuen fro the vertuus of hyr noble kynrede. *c* **1386** —— *Clerk's T.* 587 This warne I yow þat ye nat sodeynly Out of youre self for no wo sholde outreye. **1387** TREVISA *Higden* (Rolls) VII. 243 þe Normans arrayed hem eft, and tornede aȝen uppon þe Englische men þat outrayed [*v.r.* were out of aray], and chased hem in every side. *c* **1611** CHAPMAN *Iliad* v. 793 Your foes, durst not a foote addresse Without their ports..And now they out-ray to your fleete.

2. *intr.* To go beyond the bounds of moderation or propriety; to be extravagant; to go to excess.

c **1440** *York Myst.* xxxiii. 100 Agayne Sir Cesar hym selfe he segges and saies, All þe wightis in this world wirkis in waste, þat takis hym any tribute; þus his teching outrayes. **1624** JACKSON *Christ's Answ.* §14 Reason itself must be regulated..otherwise it will outray farther in its desires than sense. **1625** —— *Creed* v. v. §8 Without whose lists should he tempt them to outray much in notorious dissoluteness. **1878** *Cumberld. Gloss.*, *Oot ray*, to exceed propriety.

3. *trans.* To go beyond, overcome; to vanquish, crush; to surpass, excel. Now *dial.*

c **1420** *Anturs of Arth.* xxiv, The child playes atte the balle, That outray schalle ȝo alle Derfly that daye! *c* **1430** LYDG. *Chichev. & Byc.* in Dodsley *O.P.* XII. 336 Wymmen han made hemself so stronge, For to outraye humylite. **1430** —— *St. Margaret* 343 Thi chast lyf, thy parfyt holynesse Han me venquysshed and outrayed in distresse. *c* **1440** *Generydes* 2426 What knyghte is yender..That in the feld outrayth eurychone? **1523** SKELTON *Crown Laurel* xxiii, The cause why Demosthenes so famously is bruted Onely proceeded, for that he did outray Eschines. *a* **1529** —— *P. Sparowe* 84 Where Cerberus doth barke,..Whom Hercules dyd outraye. **1876** F. K. ROBINSON *Whitby Gloss.*, *Outray*, to outshine; to excel.

†**4.** *intr.* To be outrageous, commit outrages.

1377 *Pol. Poems* (Rolls) I. 217 Ȝif that his enemys ouȝt outrayed, To chasteis hem wolde he not lete. *c* **1450** LONELICH *Grail* xlvi. 41 Anon kyng Mordrayns gan to Owtraye, And Al the Contre gan for to Afraye And brend bothe Castel and town.

†**5.** *trans.* To outrage, to treat outrageously; to injure, insult, abuse. *Obs.*

c **1400** *Melayne* 12 And saide þaire gaumes weren alle gone Owttrayede with hethen thede. *c* **1475** *Rauf Coilȝear* 374 Ȝone man that thow outrayd Is not sa simpill as he said. **1530** PALSGR. 651/1, I outray a persone (Lydgate), I do some outrage or extreme hurt to hym. *Je oultrage*.

†**6.** To put out (of bounds), turn out, expel. *Obs.*

1415 HOCCLEVE *To Sir J. Oldcastle* 279 In your fals errour shul yee been outrayed And been enhabited with Sathanas. **1430-40** LYDG. *Bochas* III. xxii. *heading*, Evagoras King of Cipre was by Artaxerxes outrayed and putte from his kingdom. *c* **1470** HARDING *Chron.* CCIX. xi, They two warryed..Vpon the duke of Burgoyne, and hym outrayed, That he went into Burgoyne all formayed.

Hence †**ou'trayer,** one who abuses or insults; †**ou'traying** *vbl. sb. Obs.*

1375 BARBOUR *Bruce* XVIII. 182 Bot gif the mair misaduenture Befell thame, it suld richt hard thing Be till leid thame till outraying. **1600** W. WATSON *Decacordon* (1602) 215 Howsoeuer some surly syres, or mincing outraiers doce scorne and scoffe at them behinde their backes.

out'ray, *v.*[2] *rare.* [f. OUT- 14, 21 + RAY *v.*, *sb.*]

a. *intr.* To flash out as a ray; to radiate, emanate. **b.** *trans.* To surpass in radiance.

1647 H. MORE *Poems* 144 Mans soul from Gods own life outray'd. **1652** BENLOWES *Theoph.* I. viii, Thou outray'st all diamonds of the skies. **1895** LD. DE TABLEY *Poems* Ser. II. 1 An aureole outrayed upon her brow.

outrayious, variant of OUTRAIOUS. *Obs.*

out-raze, variant of OUT-RASE, *v. Obs.*

outre, obs. variant of UTTER *v.*

‖**outré** (utre), *a.* (*sb.*) [F. *outré*, pa. pple. of *outrer* to go beyond limits, to push to excess.]

A. *adj.* Beyond the bounds of what is usual or considered correct and proper; unusual, eccentric, out-of-the-way; exaggerated.

1722 RICHARDSON *Statues Italy* 191 The Sword comes above a Yard through her Body; the Expression is something Savage, and *Outré*. **1742** FIELDING *J. Andrews* Pref., A judicious eye instantly rejects anything *outré*. **1791** MRS. RADCLIFFE *Rom. Forest* vii, In these solitary woods it is quite *outre*. **1816** SINGER *Hist. Cards* 66 Some of them are extravagant and *outré*. *a* **1859** DE QUINCEY *Conversation* Wks. 1860 XIV. 169 He will talk upon *outré* subjects. **1883** C. M. YONGE *Stray Pearls* I. iv. 42 Madame de Port Royal ..is..suspected of being outrée in her devotion. **1934** C. LAMBERT *Music Ho!* v. 304 He will adopt a more eclectic and less outré manner. **1961** J. MCCABE *Mr. Laurel & Mr. Hardy* (1962) vii. 139 Physical humour was becoming outré. **1975** L. FARAGO *Aftermath* xix. 320 The prosecution of criminal Nazis is coming to be widely regarded as a kind of séance in which the spirits of another era are conjured up by some *outré* hocus-pocus. **1975** *Times* 20 Sept. 6/2 Poirot.. was the Englishman's notion of the comic foreigner, *outré* as everybody knew foreigners to be.

†**B.** as *sb.* That which is extravagant or fantastic. *Obs.*

1759 GOLDSM. *Pol. Learn.* x, To exhibit the ridiculous *outré* of a harlequin under the sanction of that venerable name. **1760-72** H. BROOKE *Fool of Qual.* (1809) II. 53 A sumptuous *outré* of terms, and new cut of phrase.

outreach ('aʊtriːtʃ), *sb.* [OUT- 7.] The act of reaching out. Also, the extent or length of reaching out; *spec.* the fact or extent of an organization's involvement in the community. Also *attrib.*

1870 WHITTIER *To L.M. Child* 30 No proof beyond this yearning, This outreach of our hearts, we need. **1884** PHILLIPS BROOKS *New Starts in Life* v. 80 What a different thing this life and this outreach toward man becomes. **1941** F. MATTHIESSEN *Amer. Renaissance* III. ii. 114 That has caught Browne's ability to take the familiar and to give it an unexpected outreach. **1950** *Theology* LIII. 417 The spiritual outreach of the body politic. **1965** R. B. ORAM *Cargo Handling* i. 15 The management should have, ready for hire, cranes that may provide an outreach of 38 metres, as are to be found in Rotterdam. **1967** *Times* 27 Jan. 17/1 (*caption*) Each lantern is attached to 12ft. long outreach brackets on..tapered steel columns. **1967** *Gleaner* (Jamaica) 12 Nov. 9 Means and methods of furthering the outreach of the Jamaican church. **1972** *Evening Telegram* (St. Johns, Newfoundland) 24 June 35/5 Real preaching instead of the kind that people grow fat on; real outreach concern, whether it's over the back fence or overseas. **1974** *Times Lit. Suppl.* 18 Jan. 50/3 That was how he came to think of the Church, in its 'out-reach' into the complex social whole. **1977** M. WILES in J. Hick *Myth of God Incarnate* viii. 162 In his attitudes towards other men his life was a parable of the loving outreach of God to the world. **1978** *Amer. Libraries* IX. 67 As assistant deputy director of Buffalo and Erie County (N.Y.) Public Library, William Miles..oversees such special services as library outreach for community centers.

outreach (aʊt'riːtʃ), *v.*[1] [OUT- 17, 18 c, 14, 15.]

1. *trans.* To exceed in reach, to reach or extend beyond; to exceed, surpass.

a **1568** ASCHAM *Scholem.* I. (Arb.) 21, I found the site so good..but the making so costlie, outreaching my habilitie. **1646** SIR T. BROWNE *Pseud. Ep.* 385 This..may seeme to outreach that fact, and to exceed the regular distinctions of murder. **1681-6** J. SCOTT *Chr. Life* (1747) III. 173 It puzzles my Conceit, and out-reaches my Wonder. **1879** PHILLIPS BROOKS *Influence of Jesus* ii. 131 He..did a larger work which has far outreached the Jewish people.

†**2.** To overreach; to deceive, cheat; to outwit.

1579-80 NORTH *Plutarch* (1676) 163 Fabius..was outreached and deceived by Hannibals fine stratagem of his Oxen. **1634** FORD *P. Warbeck* IV. iv, The man Of cunning is out-reach'd; we must be safe. **1643** HERLE *Answ. Ferne* 47 The Doctor hath outreached him.

3. *intr.* To reach too far; to go beyond bounds.

1651 N. BACON *Disc. Govt. Eng.* II. vi. (1739) 28 A Prince that knew how to set a full value upon Church-men,..and, it may be, did somewhat outreach in that course.

4. *trans.* and *intr.* To reach out, stretch out, extend. *poet.*

1594 *Sc. Metr. Ps.* CXXXVI. vi, Yea, he the heauy charge Of all the earth did streache, And on the waters large The same he did out reache. **1801** SOUTHEY *Thalaba* VIII. xiii, They stood with earnest eyes, And arms out-reaching, when again The darkness closed around them. **1818** KEATS *Endym.* I. 867 With wings outraught And spreaded tail, a vulture could not glide Past them. **1887** BOWEN *Virgil Æneid* II. 535 Hand outreaching to hold him, and spear uplifted to smite!

So **'out,reaching** *vbl. sb.* and *ppl. a.*

1587 GOLDING *De Mornay* xxxi. 501 And for the out-reaching of abhominations, there shalbe desolation vnto the ende. **1875** H. E. MANNING *Internal Mission of Holy Ghost* xiv. 405 The symmetry and outlines of the Tree of Life, with its outreaching branches. **1897** *Outing* (U.S.) XXX. 359/1 Other craft at anchor, sheltered by the outreaching land. **1902** A. T. MAHAN *Retrospect & Prospect* iv. 111 This outreaching of an imperialistic arm by all the greater nations ..constitutes..the motive to a closer union. **1905** *Daily Chron.* 14 Dec. 3/4 Such entire absence of out-reachings towards 'virility', 'grip', and 'tenseness'. **1972** *Science* 26 May 855/1 Certainly strong, outreaching, and complete fertility-control programs are desirable.

†**out'reach,** *v.*[2] *Obs. rare.* A variant of OUTREIK *v.*, to fit out, equip. Hence †**out'reacher,** an outfitter.

1640 in Spalding *Troub. Chas. I* [see OUTPUTTER 3].

outread (aʊt'riːd), *v.* [OUT- 15 b, 18.]

†**1.** *trans.* To read through or to the end. *rare.*

1659 A. HAY *Diary* (S.H.S. 1901) 141 [I] outred the first book, which caryes on the story till the birth of Christ.

2. To outdo in reading; to read more than.

1815 *Zeluca* III. 260 She would out-read Lydia Languish herself. **1888** F. WARDEN *Witch of Hills* II. xxiii. 209 Ladies out-read us, out-write us.

†**out'reader.** *Obs. rare.* [For **outredder*, f. OUTRED *v.*[1] 2.] One who fits out (a ship).

1622 MALYNES *Anc. Law-Merch.* 444 Against Pirats, their assisters or abettors, Outreaders or Receiuers.

out'reason, *v.* [OUT- 18 c, 18.] *trans.* To overcome by reasoning or argument; to outdo or surpass in reasoning.

1644 J. GOODWIN *Dang. Fighting agst. God* 30 That way which shall be able to out-reason..all other wayes, will at last exalt unitie. **1677** GALE *Crt. Gentiles* II. IV. 117 A carnal mind vainly puffed up out-reasons al good convictions of dutie. **1821** *Examiner* 46/2 They were alike out-voted and out-reasoned. **1891** C. COLE *Cy Ross* 139 He did not attempt to outreason the silly superstition.

out-reave to **out-redden**: see OUT-.

out-'reckon, *v.* [OUT- 18.] †**a.** *trans.* To exceed in reckoning or computation. *Obs.*

1617 FLETCHER *Valentinian* I. i, A power that can preserve us after ashes, And make the names of men out-reckon ages. **1698** TYSON in *Phil. Trans.* XX. 141 But Jul. Cæs. Scaliger ..out-reckons them all.

b. To overestimate. *rare.*

1898 HARDY *Wessex Poems* 154 But though, your powers outreckoning, You hold you dead and dumb.

outrecuidance (utrəkɥidɑ̃s, uːtəˈkwiːdəns). *arch.* Also 5–6 oultre-, -cuyd-, -quyd-, 6 -cuid-, -a(u)nce, 5 **utterquidaunce**, 6 **ultrequed-**, 7 **outercuidance**. [a. F. *outrecuidance* (12–13th c. in Hatz.-Darm.), f. *outrecuider* (12th c.), f. *outre* beyond, to excess + *cuider* to think, plume oneself:—L. *cōgitāre* to think.] Excessive self-esteem; overweening self-confidence or self-conceit; arrogance; conceit, presumption.

1435 in *Wars Eng. in France* (Rolls) II. 584 Grete pride and outrecuidaunce, and setting noo store be none othere mannes frenship. *c* **1495** *Epitaffe* etc. in *Skelton's Wks.* (1843) II. 392 Sore may thou rue thy vtterquidaunce. **1524** *St. Papers Hen. VIII*, IV. 255 She shal remayne in overmoche estymacion and oultrecuidance of her self. **1599** *Broughton's Let.* ii. 10 To such an outrecuidance hath your self-conceit caried you. *a* **1652** BROME *Mad Couple* I. i. Wks. 1873 I. 5 Therein was your outrecuidance. **1819** SCOTT *Ivanhoe* ix, It is full time..that the outrecuidance of these peasants should be restrained. **1888** *Sat. Rev.* 18 Aug. 195/2 Admiral Hornby has rebuked the outrecuidance of Englishmen who seemed to think so.

†**ˈoutred**, *sb. Sc. Obs.* [f. OUT- 7 + RED *sb.*]

1. Clearance from debt or liability; settlement of accounts; finishing of a business.

1491 *Acta Dom. Concil.* (1839) 205/1 As ȝit he has gottine na payment nor outred. **1330** in Pitcairn *Crim. Trials* I. 244* For outred and payment of his faderis dettis. **1695** J. SAGE *Article* Wks. 1844 I. 282 Why else would his Grace have so earnestly required expedition and hasty outred?

2. Outfit, equipment (of a ship, a man).

1491 *Acta Audit.* (1839) 154 þat patrick liel..sal..pay.. for þe outred of his parte of his schip callit þe mare of dunde. **1592** *Sc. Acts Jas. VI* (1814) III. 541/1 Sen the outred of the saidis schippis. **1610** J. MELVILL *Diary* (1842) 710 They tuo wer left to mak outred for thame selffis.

†**outˈred**, *v.*[1] *Sc. Obs.* [f. OUT- 15 + RED *v.*]

1. *trans.* To disentangle; to extricate from difficulties by settlement of liabilities; to clear of encumbrances.

1467 *Sc. Acts Jas. III*, c. 23 (1597) For their payment, and to outred their selfe. **1488** *Acta Dom. Concil.* (1839) 103/2 His executoris has gudis aneuch for þe outredding of his dettis. **1610** J. MELVILL *Diary* (1842) 710 We wantit no credite to outred our selffis out of all expensis. **1670** in H. Miller *Scenes & Leg.* x. (1850) 150 For outredding them of their necessary and most urgent affairs.

2. To fit out (a ship).

1535 *Ld. Treas. Acc. Scot.* in Pitcairn *Crim. Trials* I. 285* To George Wallace, for outredding of the Kingis gracis schip towart Deip. **1592** *Sc. Acts Jas. VI* (1814) 541 Being commandit be his hienes to wictuall and outred the schipis.

out-ˈred, *v.*[2] [f. OUT- 20 + RED *a.* and *sb.*[1]] *trans.* To surpass in redness.

1648 HERRICK *Hesper.*, *Weeping Cherry*, I saw a cherry weep,..Because my Julia's lip..did out-red the same.

out-rede: see ATREDE *v.*

out-ˈreign, *v.* [OUT- 17, 18.] *trans.* To reign to the end of, beyond, or longer than.

1590 SPENSER *F.Q.* II. x. 45 Till they outraigned had their utmost date. **1641** SIR E. DERING *Sp. on Relig.* 20 Nov. xiv. 64 Antichrist hath out-raigned him for 1600 yeares. **1801** W. TAYLOR in *Monthly Mag.* XI. 19 [Rome] governed by twelve Cæsars in succession, of whom the second Augustus, out-reigned the others.

†**outˈreik**, *v. Sc. Obs.* [f. OUT- 15 + REIK *v.*] *trans.* To fit out or equip.

1640–1 *Kirkcudbr. War-Comm. Min. Bk.* (1855) 102 A roll of the number, bothe of horss and foote, which may be outreiked..for the foirsaid recerve. **1694** *Lond. Gaz.* No. 2959/3 The Men to be outreiked for this present Levy.

So †**ˈoutreik** *sb.*, †**ˈoutreiking** *vbl. sb.*, equipment, outfit; †**ˈoutreiker**, one who equips or fits out.

1644 *Sc. Acts Chas. I* (1819) VI. 74/2 That there be a moneths pay advanced for their outreike and furnisheing their horses. **1648** *Ibid.* VI. 317/1 *title*, Act in favours of the outreikers of Horse and Foot in this Levie. **1708** M. BRUCE *Good News* 21 Many..that seemed to be very far behind, get a new Stock, and a new Out-reiking.

ˈout-reˌlief. **a.** = *out-door relief*: see OUTDOOR *a.* 2. Also *fig.*

1892 *Pall Mall G.* 7 Sept. 6/2 You have got an out-relief officer. **1894** *Westm. Gaz.* 31 May 3/1 There are successful out-relief unions as well as successful anti-out-relief unions. **1900** *New Cent. Rev.* VII. 399 Even under the system of out-relief there is some little incentive left. **1973** G. E. AYLMER *State's Servants* ii. 51 Ireland was still regarded as an out-relief centre for the less hopeful and worse-qualified members of the English governing class.

†**b.** *concr.* A person receiving out-door relief. *Obs.*

1904 *Westm. Gaz.* 22 Apr. 3/2 Still worse is the case of the aged 'out-relief', with his 3*s.* a week.

outrely, obs. form of OUTERLY.

outréness (ˈuːtreɪnɪs). [f. OUTRÉ + -NESS.] The quality of being *outré*, unusual, or peculiar.

1832 MOTLEY *Corr.* (1889) I. ii. 19 The University towns [in Germany] are the homes of 'outré-ness'. **1882** HAWTHORNE *Dr. Grimshawe* viii, A certain seemly beauty in him showed strikingly the..outréness of the rest of their lot.

†**ˈout-ˌrent.** *Obs.* [OUT- 6.] Rent paid out; payment of the nature of rent or rent-charge, esp. as deducted from or opposed to income or rent received.

1479 *Bury Wills* (Camden) 51 That the seid Roberd shall beer alle oute rentys and seruices of olde tyme charged vpon the seid maner to the chief lordes of the same fee. **1523** FITZHERB. *Surv.* 31 Than must there be deduct out of the sayd grose somme all maner of out rentes and ordynary charges. **1635** EARL STRAFFORD *Lett. & Disp.* (1739) I. 487 Also that all the other Out-Rents forth of my Estate be orderly paid. **1769** *Aclome Inclos. Act* 15 Persons having any ..Rent, Out-rent, Fee-farm rent. **1794** HUTCHINSON *Hist. Cumbld.* I. 259 *note*, Reserving to the vicar..an out-rent of 6*s.* 8*d.* yearly.

†**ˈoutreˌpass**, *v. Obs.* [a. F. *outrepasser* (12th c. in Hatz.-Darm.), f. *outre* beyond + *passer* to pass.] *trans.* To pass beyond, surpass. Hence †**outrepassed** *ppl. a.*, surpassing. So †**outrepasse** *sb.*, that which surpasses all others.

c **1477** CAXTON *Jason* 20 b, Certaynly my lady ys the oultrepasse of al other ladyes. *Ibid.* 32 The..oultrepassed beaute of the vertuous Myrro. **1645** *City Alarum* 21 Why should a few Accomptants stand up like Hercules Colomnes, which no man dares outrepasse?

outrequydaunce, obs. f. OUTRECUIDANCE.

out-resent to **out-rhyme**: see OUT-.

outride (ˈaʊtraɪd), *sb. rare.* [f. next.]

1. The act of riding out, a ride out; an excursion.

1740 SOMERVILLE *Hobbinol* Ded., Your province is the town; leave me a small outride in the country. **1765** *Percy Reliques* Gloss., *Outrake*, an out-ride; or expedition.

2. The district of an outrider or commercial traveller. *local.*

1884 *Upton-on-Severn Gloss.* **1896** *Warwicksh. Gloss.*

3. In the writings of Gerard Manley Hopkins: (see quots.).

1880 G. M. HOPKINS *Let.* 22 Dec. (1935) 41 By means of the 'outrides' or looped half-feet..I secure a strong effect of double rhythm, of a second movement in the verse besides the primary and essential one. *c* **1883** —— *Poems* (1918) 5 Two licences are natural to Sprung Rhythm. The one is rests, as in music... The other is *hangers* or *outrides*, that is one, two, or three slack syllables added to a foot and not counting in the nominal scanning. **1934** C. DAY LEWIS *Hope for Poetry* ii. 10 What Hopkins called 'outrides', unstressed syllables occasionally placed before the stressed ones at the beginning of the foot. **1973** *Studies Eng. Lit.: Eng. Number* (Tokyo) 24 In certain of the poems written in sprung rhythm..'outrides' appear to be extensively used, and these Hopkins has taken great pains to indicate... Without the help of these signals, there is little chance of the reader being able to distinguish between an 'outriding' and an ordinary foot.

outˈride, *v.* [OUT- 14, 15, 18, 17.]

1. *intr.* and *trans.* To ride out. *Obs.* or *poet.*

1460 *Lybeaus Disc.* 952 Gyffroun hys hors outryt, And was wode out of wyt. **1815** *Chron.* in *Ann. Reg.* 629 The bravest that ever in battle outrade.

2. a. To outdo in riding, to ride better, faster, or farther than; to leave behind or outstrip by riding.

1530 PALSGR. 650/2 Take as swyfte a geldynge as thou canste fynde and I holde the twenty nobles I outryde the. **1597** SHAKS. *2 Hen. IV*, I. i. 36. **1685** DANGERFIELD *Mem.* 3 Feb. 21 We..by much out-rode all the Pursuers for the space of an hour Whip and Spur. **1861** THACKERAY *Four Georges* (1880) 53 What postilion can outride that pale horseman? **1890** 'R. BOLDREWOOD' *Col. Reformer* (1891) 243 He tried ineffectually to outride..the furious animal.

b. *transf.* and *fig.*

1672 DRYDEN *Conq. Granada* II. i. (1725) 40 Like a Tempest that out-rides the Wind. **1791** PAINE *Rights of Man* (ed. 4) 115 Their anxiety now was to outride the news lest they should be stopt.

c. To ride out of or beyond.

1903 J. L. WESTON tr. *Sir Gawain at the Grail Castle* I. 15 In that one night had he outridden Britain and all that country.

3. Of a ship: To ride out, to survive the violence of (a storm).

1647 N. BACON *Disc. Govt. Eng.* I. v. (1739) 11 Who by patience out-rode the storms of foreign force. **1827** HALLAM *Const. Hist.* I. v. (1876) 247 Those perils appear less to us, who know how the vessel outrode them. **1856** R. A. VAUGHAN *Mystics* (1860) I. 202 By what divine art was it that his ark was so skilfully framed as to out-ride those deluges of trouble?

4. *intr.* To ride in advance of or beside a carriage as an outrider. (*Cent. Dict.*)

1964 *Albertan* (Calgary) July 15/6 He's driving two chuckwaggon outfits [and] will probably outride for a couple more.

5. *trans.* To keep cattle from going beyond (a tract of land) by riding along the boundaries of it. *U.S.* (? *Obs.*).

1874 J. G. MCCOY *Hist. Sk. Cattle Trade* 375 He does not herd his cattle but designates certain bounds within which the employees permit the stock to range at will. This manner of holding stock is termed 'out riding' the country.

outrider (ˈaʊtˌraɪdə(r)). [OUT- 8.] One who rides out or forth.

†**1.** An officer of the sheriff's court whose duties included collecting dues, delivering summonses, etc.

1340 *Act 14 Edw. III*, c. 9 Et que per tieux baillifs & hundreders, et lour soutzbaillifs, le Roi & le poeple soient serviz, en oustant pur touz jours toux les outriders & autres qui en divers Countees avant ces hures notoriement ont destruit le poeple. **1406** *Rolls Parl.* III. 598/1 Plusours Visconts..les ditz amerciaments levent par lour Ministres appellez Outryders. *c* **1460** *Towneley Myst.* xx. 26 Bot all fals indytars, Quest mangers and Iurers, And all thise fals out rydars. **1607** COWELL *Interpr.*, *Owtryders*, seeme to be none other but bayliffe errants, employed by the Shyreeues or their fermers, to ride to the fardest places of their counties or hundreds, with the more speede to summon to their county or hundred courts. [So 1706 in PHILLIPS, 1848 in WHARTON.]

2. † **a.** An officer of an abbey or convent, whose duty it was to attend to the external domestic requirements of the community, esp. to look after the manors belonging to it. *Obs.*

c **1375** *Sc. Leg. Saints* xxx. (*Theodera*) 424 þai ordenyt hyr þare out-rydere, þar witale so þe house to by. *c* **1386** CHAUCER *Prol.* 166 A Monk ther was a fair for the maistrie An outridere that louede venerie [cf. *Shipman's T.* 65]. **1393** LANGL. *P. Pl.* C. v. 116 Til..religious out-ryders reclused in here cloistres. **1526** in *Visitat. Norwich* (Camden) 214 (Abbey St. Benet's, Hulme) Dompnus Willelmus Hornyng, oute-rider. **1532** *Ibid.* 279 Dominus Ricardus Norwych, owte-ryder.

b. *spec.* A fellow of New College, Oxford, accompanying the Warden on an official visitation of the estates of the college. Hence **outˈridership**.

1901 RASHDALL & RAIT *New College, Oxf.* 187 The out-ridership..was claimed by two Fellows,..who both wanted to accompany the Warden on progress. *Ibid.* 251 The Warden (or Sub-warden) accompanied by a Fellow known as 'Out-rider'..and the Steward, visit the farms on some part of the College estates. **1952** A. H. SMITH *New College, Oxf.* iii. 47 An out-rider is still appointed each year to go with the warden on his summer progress around the estates.

†**3. a.** A forager of an army. **b.** A highwayman.

1581 SAVILE *Tacitus, Hist.* IV. l. (1591) 207 The cohorts.. recouered all the spoile, saue onely that which certaine outriders had caryed further into the cuntrey. **1598** GRENEWEY *Tacitus, Ann.* IV. vi. (1622) 97 The out-riders and forragers were conducted by certaine chosen Moores. **1600** HEYWOOD *1st Pt. Edw. IV*, III. i. Wks. 1874 I. 43, I feare thou art some outrider that liues by taking of purses here, on Bassets Heath. **1625** K. LONG tr. *Barclay's Argenis* I. i. 4 Some outriders of Lycogenes his campe, which..lay in wait for any passengers.

4. A commercial traveller; a tradesman's travelling agent. *dial.*

1762 *Misc. Ess.* in *Ann. Reg.* 205 When the humble outrider astride his saddle-bags, goes his rounds for fresh orders, to dealers and chapmen in the country. **1785** TRUSLER *Mod. Times* I. 19 An outrider to a tradesman in London. **1814** MARSHALL *Rev.* IV. 220 (E.D.D.) Mr. M. was some years out-rider and clerk to Mr. W. **1901** *N. & Q.* s. 9 VIII. 462/1.

5. A mounted attendant who rides in advance of or beside a carriage; *spec.* an escort mounted on a motor-cycle. Also *fig.*

1530 PALSGR. 250/2 Outryder, *auant courreur.* **1791** MAD. D'ARBLAY *Diary* 2 Aug., We saw a very handsome coach, and four horses, followed by..outriders, stop at the gate. **1801** *Ann. Reg.* 13 She set off for Brighton with four horses and out-riders. **1851** H. MELVILLE *Moby Dick* II. 164 Sharks also are the invariable outriders of all slave ships crossing the Atlantic. **1860** ADELAIDE A. PROCTER *Sailor Boy* iii, Outriders first, in pomp and state, Pranced on their horses through the gate. **1869** BLACKMORE *Lorna D.* vii, There were..light outriders of pithy weed. **1939** *Sun* (Baltimore) 25 Aug. 6/4 A motor-cycle out rider was killed in Vermont while escorting a troop train. **1957** *Economist* 21 Sept. 912/2 The panoply of police cars, blue lights and motorised outriders with which the Chancellor chooses to move about. **1971** *Daily Tel.* 9 Aug. 11/4 We were given the full VIP treatment, including an escort of police motorcycle outriders all the way from Boulogne to Le Touquet. **1975** T. ALLBEURY *Special Collection* xiii. 86 Under his chin were all tell-tale outriders of a dewlap. **1977** *Belfast Tel.* 22 Feb. 5/5 The Belfast councillors were driven through Dublin's streets in a convoy, with Gardai motorcycle outriders halting traffic so the entourage could travel speedily.

6. *U.S.* A mounted herdsman who prevents cattle from straying beyond a certain limit (see also quot. 1872).

1872 *Kansas Magazine* 319/2 Where the grower does not drive his own stock to market, the buying and driving is done by a class of speculators known in Texas as 'outriders'. **1874** J. G. MCCOY *Hist. Sk. Cattle Trade* 348 [The] trail escapes the vigilant eye and Indian cunning and proficiency of the herdsman or outrider. **1907** S. E. WHITE *Arizona Nights* I. vi. 117 We saw..the whole herd and the outriders and the mesas far away. **1939** P. A. ROLLINS *Gone Haywire* 230 Cowboys, patrolling as 'out-riders' and 'line riders', had always to keep an eye on them. **1968** R. F. ADAMS *Western Words* (rev. ed.) 214/2 *Outrider*, a cowboy who rides about the range to keep a sharp lookout for anything that might happen to the detriment of his employer; also called *range rider.*

7. *U.S.* A mounted official who escorts racehorses to the starting post.

1947 *Sun* (Baltimore) 8 Nov. 11/4 Them outriders ought to get extra pay for steeplechases. **1961** ATKINSON & FREEMAN *All the Way!* iv. 50 The outriders in their red hunting coats also accompany the field. Years ago there was only one..but today there are three at several of the major tracks. *Ibid.*, One outrider stands just to the outside in front of the gate, one takes a position outside the gap, three-sixteenths down the track, and the third remains behind the gate. **1968** M. T. Malloy *Racing Today* 42/1 A couple of other horses meanwhile may be running away with their jockeys hanging on for dear life, and with the track's red-coated outriders in hot pursuit.

8. *Canad.* 'In a chuckwagon race,.. one of the four riders who load the wagon, direct the horses during the starting turns, and gallop with the outfit to the finish line' (*Dict. Canad.*).

1955 W. G. Hardy *Alberta Golden Jubilee Anthol.* 169 There are four outriders to each of the four outfits in every heat. When the starting-horn blows, one outrider holds back the team of horses fighting to be on its way. Another throws the stove in the rear of the chuckwagon. The remaining two pitch the flies and poles into the covered wagon. **1958** *Encycl. Canadiana* IX. 393 A new feature introduced in the 1923 [Calgary] stampede was the chuckwagon race... Each wagon is pulled by a four-horse team.. and each has its outriders. **1964** *Albertan* (Calgary) 7 July 1/2 Three crack-ups.. saw all drivers, outriders and horses come out unscathed.

'out,riding, *vbl. sb.* [out- 9.] The action of riding out; *spec.* raiding, marauding. Also, *U.S.*, the work of an outrider (sense 6); a spell of executing this. Also as *ppl. a.*; *spec.* applied to a syllable in the poetry of Gerard Manley Hopkins: see outride *sb.* 3.

1568 Grafton *Chron.* I. 185 When the tyme came of her out ryding none sawe her, but her husband. *a* **1641** Bp. Mountagu *Acts & Mon.* (1642) 287 The Inhabitants of Thrachonitis.. were by him restrained of out-riding, robbing, and spoyling of their neighbours, and their ancient practise. **1812** Scott *Let. to Crabbe* in *Lockhart*, His [Robin Hood's] indistinct ideas concerning the doctrine of *meum* and *tuum* being no great objection to an outriding Borderer. **1877** G. M. Hopkins *Let.* 21 Aug. (1935) 45 There are no outriding feet in the *Deutschland*. An outriding foot is.. a recognized extra-metrical effect; it is and it is not part of the metre.. not being counted... Outriding feet belong to counterpointed verse. *c* **1883** —— *Poems* (1918) 5 These outriding half feet or hangers are marked by a loop underneath. **1907** C. E. Mulford *Bar-20* 6 Skinny Thompson took his turn at outriding one morning after the season's round-up. **1926** D. Branch *Cowboy & his Interpreters* 94 Groups of cowboys rode on inspection trips, 'out-ridings', to locate the scattered groups of cattle, to note the condition of grass and water [etc.]. **1953** W. H. Gardner in G. M. Hopkins *Sel. Poems & Prose* 224 The rhythm is sprung and outriding. **1968** R. F. Adams *Western Words* (rev. ed.) 214/2 *Outriding*, performing the duties of an *outrider*..; also called *range riding*. **1973** [see outride *sb.* 3].

out'rig, *v.* [Back-formation from outrigger 3.] *trans.* To furnish with outriggers.

1883 *Harper's Mag.* Oct. 713/1 It could be outrigged for rowing.

outrigged ('aʊtrɪgd), *ppl. a.* [out- 11; after outrigger *sb.* 3.] Fitted with outriggers.

1861 *Times* 27 Sept., A rowing expedition abroad.. in the first 'outrigged' four which has been upon foreign waters. **1867** *Routledge's Ev. Boy's Ann.* Apr. 202 A pair-oar gig outrigged. **1888** W. B. Woodgate *Boating* 143 Half-outrigged gigs became common. **1900** W. E. Sherwood *Oxford Rowing* 26, 1845 saw the general introduction into Oxford of outrigged boats, an innovation viewed with much alarm by the University authorities.

outrigger ('aʊt,rɪgə(r)). [f. out *adv.* + rig *v.*[1] + -er[1]: but in various senses preceded by outligger, of which it may be in part an alteration.] Something rigged out or projecting.

1. *Naut.* **a.** A strong beam passed through the port-holes of a ship, used to secure the masts and counteract the strain in the act of careening; **b.** A spar to haul out a sheet; **c.** A small spar to thrust out and spread the breast-backstays; **d.** A boom swung out to hang boats clear of a ship; **e.** The cathead of a ship (Knight *Dict. Mech.*); **f.** Any framework rigged up outside the gunwales of a ship.

1769 Falconer *Dict. Marine* (1789), *Out-rigger*, a strong beam of timber, of which there are several fixed on the side of a ship, and projecting from it, in order to secure the masts in the act of careening. *Out-rigger* is also a small boom, occasionally used in the *tops* to thrust out the breast-back-stays to windward, in order to increase their tension, and thereby give additional security to the top-mast. *Ibid.*, *Entennes*, the props, or out-riggers, fixed on the side of a sheer-hulk, to support the sheers. **1858** in *Adm. Hornby's Biog.* vi. (1896) 61, I have fitted two splendid outriggers of the fore- and main-top-gallant-masts, and if I can get some new royals shall do well. **1873** *Q. Rev.* 121 Torpedoes have now been made available for ocean warfare.. being carried into action either on an outrigger stretching ahead of a ship or towed abreast of the ship.

2. A contrivance used in the Indian and Pacific Oceans to steady the native canoe and prevent it from capsizing. Formerly called outligger, q.v.

A common form consists of a boat-shaped block of wood or bamboo, laid parallel to the length of the canoe, and joined to it at each end by long bamboo poles. Sometimes one, sometimes two of these are used.

1748 *Anson's Voy.* iii. v. 341 The frame is intended to ballance the proa, and.. is usually called an outrigger. *Ibid.*, The mast, yard, boom, and outriggers are all made of bamboo. **1777** Miller in *Phil. Trans.* LXVIII. 174 They are about ten feet long, and about a foot broad, and have an outrigger on each side, to prevent their over-setting. **1838** Poe *A. G. Pym* Wks. 1864 IV. 163 Sixty or seventy Rafts, or flatboats with outriggers. **1865** Lubbock *Prehist. Times* xiii. (1869) 429 They use canoes.. fitted with an outrigger.

3. a. An iron bracket, fixed to the side of a rowing boat, bearing a rowlock at its outer edge, so as to increase the leverage of the oar while allowing the boat to be constructed very narrow. **b.** A light boat fitted with such appendages, an outrigged boat; colloq. abbreviated to *rigger*.

According to the Badminton book on Rowing, outriggers were introduced on the Tyne between 1830 and 1840; they were first seen in London, and at Oxford and Cambridge, in 1844–5; an outrigger boat was built for the Cambridge crew for the University Boat-race of 1845, but not used till the next year, when both crews rowed in outriggers (April 3).

1845 *Illustr. Lond. News* 29 Mar. 205/2 New Boat [for Cambridge crew].. She is an outrigger, built on the same principle as the boat brought from Newcastle by the Claspers, and used at the Thames Regatta. **1845** *Vice-Chancellor's Regul. Boats Oxford* 3 Dec., All skiffs or boats constructed for less than four oars of which the rowlocks are projected from the sides by means of outriggers (commonly called Clasper-built boats). **1846** *Times* 4 Apr. 6/5 (Boat race) The winners [Cantabs] rowed in a beautiful outrigger built by the eminent Searles, of Stangate. **1851** *Illustr. Lond. News* 16 Aug. 222/2 A fatal accident, resulting from the use of the 'outrigger' below bridge. **1858** J. Payn *Foster Brothers* xviii. (1859) 322 An innumerable fleet of fairy shallops, delicatest outriggers, wherein to sneeze is to be capsized. **1865** Knight *Pass. Work. Life* III. i. 4 The solitary youth in his outrigger.. training for the contest of a regatta. **1871** F. J. Furnivall *Trial Forewords* 98 *note*, Mr. Beasley of St. John's will recollect our spending the leisure of a Long Vacation at Cambridge—was it 1845?—in building a pair of outriggers.. the first really narrow ones ever built. **1900** W. E. Sherwood *Oxford Rowing* 26 Oriel introduced the first outrigger this year [1844] in their four. *Ibid.* 97 The early outriggers were all clinker-built, and.. were first made with outriggers to fold into the boat, for convenience in packing.

4. a. An addition to a wagon or farm-cart to increase its carrying capacity; a set of harvest-shelvings. *local.*

1794 T. Davis *Agric. Wilts* 69 The waggons.. seldom use any overlays or outriggers, either at the ends or sides.

b. An addition to a trailer to increase its carrying capacity.

1971 M. Tak *Truck Talk* 113 *Outriggers*, the short brackets that extend, if needed, from the sides of a low-boy trailer. **1973** *Amer. Speech 1969* XLIV. 207 *Outrigger*, device used for increasing the width of a trailer.

5. a. *Building* and *Mech.* Applied to various structures placed so as to project from the face of a wall, a frame, etc., e.g. a beam projecting from a wall to support hoisting-tackle; the jib of a crane; a wheel or pulley outside the frame of a machine for the communication of motion, etc.

1835 Ure *Philos. Manuf.* 51 The steam or impelling pulleys, frequently called riggers (outriggers? as they stand out from the side of the machine, like outrigger-sails in a ship) by engineers. **1863** *Q. Rev.* CXIV. 311 Another platform was inserted under the lantern, and tied to the lower platform by a chain inside the tower and straps of iron out-side, and great shores from the outriggers of the lower platform completed the cradle in which the building was supported.

b. *Aeronaut.* A supporting structure that projects outwards from the main part of an aircraft or spacecraft.

1909 *Flight* 27 Mar. 176/2 One of the most characteristic features of the machine is that derived from the appearance of the outrigger framework which carries the biplane elevator in front and the rigid biplane tail behind. **1922** *Encycl. Brit.* XXX. 20/2 In the pusher.. the controlling surfaces are carried on an open frame ('out-riggers') in front, at the rear, or in both positions. **1928** Chatfield & Taylor *Airplane & its Engine* xiii. 235 The tail surfaces of the flying boat are usually carried on the stern of the hull, but sometimes.. they are supported on outriggers, or booms. **1969** *Times* 3 June (Moon Suppl.) p. iii/7 The clusters were mounted on outriggers 90° apart on the ascent stage. **1978** *Aeroplane Monthly* Jan. 6/1 The new W.11 [helicopter] used the same engine and transmission as the original design, but married them to a skeletal fuselage and outriggers with three three-bladed rotors.

6. An extension of the splinter-bar of a carriage, to admit of a second horse being harnessed alongside of that which is in the shafts; hence, An extra horse running outside the shafts.

Outriggers were also used with heavy gun-carriages.

1811 L. Hawkins *C'tess & Gertr.* (1812) III. 273 So I see you drive here with an outrigger! **1844** Mrs. Houston *Yacht Voy. Texas* II. 279 Sometimes a second horse is attached as an outrigger, and has a pretty effect. **1902** E. L. Brandreth *Note*, I used to drive in India (1865) a cart with shafts intended for one horse (the common hill *tonga*), to which I often attached another fastened to an outrigger which consisted of a projecting piece of wood, so that the horses were driven like a pair.

7. *fig.* An outsider, not a regular member; an onhanger.

1852 R. S. Surtees *Sponge's Sp. Tour* (1893) 177 It generally drew the picked men from each, to say nothing of outriggers and chance customers.

8. *attrib.* and *Comb.*, as ***outrigger canoe, -sail, skiff***, etc.; **outrigger hoist**, a hoisting apparatus rigged out from an outer wall: see sense 5.

1835 Outrigger-sail [see sense 5]. **1853** 'C. Bede' (E. Bradley) *Verd. Green* (1857) 18 The former occupied his outrigger skiff. **1862** *Macm. Mag.* Aug. 293 The famous six-oar outrigger boat of Harvard College. **1878** *Sci. Amer.* XXXVIII. 223/1 (*Improved Hoisting Machinery*).. In the outrigger hoist.. the advantages are that two pinion gears are employed, gearing into two large gears. **1892** E. Reeves *Homeward Bound* 131 The other side [of the catamaran] is taken up by an outrigger keel about 7 feet off, attached to the boat by two long-arched, spider-like arms. **1908** E. J. Banfield *Confessions of Beachcomber* ii. i. 238 The grandfathers of the blacks of Hinchinbrook Island.. have been popularly credited with the art of making out-rigger canoes, such as were common a few miles to the north. **1967** J. Severson *Great Surfing* 155 *Outrigger canoe*, a canoe employing the use of an outrigger. **1974** 'M. Allen' *Super Tour* (1975) ix. 322 The [Fijian] natives.. rode in outrigger canoes.

Hence **'out,riggered** *a.*, fitted with an outrigger; **'out,riggerless** *a.*, without an outrigger.

1884 *Q. Rev.* Apr. 326 Sailing boats of the 'catamaran' model, long black boats, outriggered. **1767** Wallis *Circumnav. Globe* vi. (R. Suppl.), One of their sages.. had.. foretold that.. an outriggerless canoe would come to their shores [Otaheite] from a distant land. **1884** *Bib. Soc. Rec.* (N.Y.) Feb., Skilful paddlers propel their outriggerless canoes.

'out,rigging, *vbl. sb.* [out- 9.] That which is rigged out, or with which anything is rigged out; also, outside rigging.

1864 A. Graham *Terrible Wom.* II. 108 The tall masts of a man-of-war, or the more humble outrigging of a brig or collier. **1899** *Westm. Gaz.* 19 Sept. 4/1 The gunboat.. ran so closely alongside the *Diamante* that her guns tore away the steamer's outrigging.

outright (aʊt'raɪt), *adv.* (*a.*) [f. out *adv.* + right.]

1. Of direction in space: Straight out; directly onward; straight ahead. Now *rare.*

13.. *E.E. Allit. P.* A. 1054 A reuer of þe trone þer ran out-ryȝte. **1564** P. Moore *Hope Health* ii. ix. 38 Sothern-woode .. is good for them yt can not breath, but when they hold their necke outright. **1601** Holland *Pliny* I. 167 The same writer maketh mention of one that could see and discerne out-right 135 miles. **1685** *Gracian's Courtiers Orac.* 17 It is easie to shoot a Fowl that flies out-right, but not a Bird which is irregular in its flight. **1719** De Foe *Crusoe* i. viii, I never travell'd in this journey above two Miles outright in a Day, or thereabouts. **1849** Whately *Let.* in *Life* (1866) II. 145 You get a brighter view of a comet, or some other of the heavenly bodies, when you are looking not outright at it, but at some other star near it.

†**b.** Without a break, straight away; 'on end', consecutively, continuously. *Obs.*

1579–80 North *Plutarch* (1676) 464 Nicias.. thus travelling eight days journey out-right together. **1607** Topsell *Four-f. Beasts* (1658) 253 So would they ride them an hundred and fifty miles out right.

†**2.** Of time: Straight, straightway; forthwith, immediately, without delay. *Obs.*

c **1290** *S. Eng. Leg.* I. 457/16 Seint leonard nolde it graunti nouȝht: ake outriȝt it gan for-sake. **1577–87** Holinshed *Chron.* I. 37/2 Such as he found abroad in the countrie he slue out right on euerie side. **1611** Heywood *Gold. Age* iv. Wks. 1874 III. 69 If you but offer't, I shall cry out right. **1714** *Fr. Bk. of Rates* 294 They shall be sent out of the Kingdom outright without delay. (*To slay outright* appears to have passed from this sense to the next.)

3. So that the act is finished at once; altogether, entirely; ***to kill outright***, i.e. so that the victim dies on the spot; ***to sell*** or ***purchase outright***, i.e. so that the thing disposed of becomes at once the full property of the buyer.

1603 Drayton *Bar. Wars* iii. lxxvi, Where slaine out-right, I now the same behold. **1623** Ld. Carew in *Lismore Papers* (1888) Ser. ii. III. 61 Lett me knowe.. whether I should sett it for a yearely rent, or sell it out righte. **1656** H. Phillips *Purch. Patt.* (1676) 19 What may be the value of them to buy them out right? **1772** *Phil. Trans.* LXII. 452 *note*, A man.. was killed outright by one blow of a poker. **1775** Sheridan *Duenna* ii. ii, Touch her lips, and she swoons outright. **1884** *Manch. Exam.* 21 Mar. 5/1 The majority of those who fell were not killed outright by the bullet which sent them to the ground. **1885** *Law Times* LXXVIII. 458/1 The interests might have been disposed of outright.

4. To the full extent, fully out, completely, entirely, quite; without reservation or limitation; openly, without reserve of manner or expression.

13.. *Guy Warw.* (E.E.T.S. 1887) 440 And þei he be þe fende out-riȝt Y schal for þe take þe fiȝt. **1532** More *Confut. Tindale* i. Wks. 483/1 Within a whyle after.. the frere made the foole madde outright. **1593** Shaks. *2 Hen. VI*, i. ii. 41 Nay Elinor, then must I chide outright. *a* **1625** Beaum. & Fl. *Honest Man's Fort.* v. i, I simper'd sometime,.. But never laugh'd outright. *a* **1719** Addison (J.), He neigh'd outright, and all the steed exprest. **1875** Jowett *Plato* (ed. 2) V. 404 Some bold man who.. will say outright what is best for the city. **1895** T. Hardy *Tess* Pref., In planning the stories the idea was that large towns.. should be named outright.

B. *adj.* **1.** Directed or going straight on. *rare.*

1611 Cotgr., *Dressiere*, a straight or outright path, or tract. *Ibid.* s.v. *Balancer*, Without any certain, or outright course in his flight. **1878** Stevenson *Inland Voy.* 192 When the river now.. only glided seaward with an even, outright, but imperceptible speed.

2. Direct; downright; thorough, out-and-out.

1532 More *Confut. Tindale* Wks. 404/2 A mouthe.. playeth sometime ye frere, sometime ye foxe, sometime the foole, & sometime the outeright ribauld. **1851** H. W. Beecher *Lect. Yng. Men* iv. 98 The young are seldom tempted to outright wickedness. **1856** J. W. Kaye *Life Sir J. Malcolm* I. vii. 98 Malcolm did everything in a hearty outright manner.

3. Complete, entire, total.

Mod. Newspaper, He mentioned the probable outright cost of such an undertaking.

Hence †**out'rightly** *adv. Obs.* = A. 3.

1642 J. Eaton *Honey-c. Free Justif.* 14 Adjudged unto him that did outrightly kill a man.

ˈoutright, *v. U.S. Sports slang.* [f. OUTRIGHT *adv.* (*a.*).] *trans.* To give (a baseball player) a free transfer.
1975 *Cleveland* (Ohio) *Plain Dealer* 6 Apr. 9-C/1 It was very difficult when Joe was outrighted to Oklahoma City on Saturday. **1975** *New Yorker* 23 June 46/1 The Pirates had finally released him late in March ('outrighted' him, in baseball parlance).

outˈrightness. [f. OUTRIGHT *adv.* (*a.*) + -NESS.] The quality of being outright in speech or thought; directness, straightforwardness.
1865 MRS. WHITNEY *Gayworthys* xxvi. (1879) 250 It was the outrightness that pleased him, was it? **1881** *Blackw. Mag.* Mar. 369 Simplicity of style, plainness of language, or outrightness of thought.

out-rime, etc.: see OUT-.

ouˌtˈring, *sb.*[1] [OUT- 3.] Outer ring or circumference; in quots. applied *attrib.* to the outer drain and bank of a drainage area.
1763-4 *Act 4 Geo. III*, c. 47 §28 Or in any other of the Outring or Barrier Banks. **1832** *Holderness Drainage Act* §43 All the Outring and Division Drains, Dikes, and Ditches.

†**ouˌtˈring,** *sb.*[2] *Sc.* In *Curling*: = OUTWICK.
1824 MACTAGGART *Gallovid. Encycl.*, *Outring*, a channle-stone term, the reverse of *Inring*. To take an outring is generally allowed to be more difficult than taking an inring.

outˈring, *v.* [OUT- 14, 15, 18.]
1. a. *intr.* To ring out, sound with a clear loud note. **b.** *trans. poet.* (Prop. two words.)
c **1374** CHAUCER *Troylus* III. 1237 And after syker doth here voys out rynge. **1851** MRS. BROWNING *Casa Guidi Wind.* I. 15 Sweet songs which for this Italy outrang From older singers' lips. **1896** *Chicago Advance* 6 Feb. 188/1 We listen for your blending voice Outringing o'er the murderous noise.
b. 1834 *Tait's Mag.* I. 232/1 Where the sweet Sabbath-bell its note outrings.
2. *trans.* To outdo in ringing, to ring louder than.
a **1635** CORBET *Gt. Tom Ch. Ch.* 2 Be dumb, ye infant-chimes,..That ne're out-ring a tinker and his kettle. **1677** W. HUGHES *Man of Sin* III. iii. 92 Such a Twanger as quite outringeth Mr. Cressy's loud, and so admired one! **1868** J. H. NEWMAN *Verses Var. Occas.* 43 Sure, this is a blessing, Outrings the loud tone Of the dull world's caressing.
Hence **outringing** *ppl. a.*, that rings out or sounds with ringing note.
1894 F. S. ELLIS *Reynard Fox* 321 Outringing peals to heaven we fling, For Reynard and our noble King.

outˈrival, *v.* [OUT- 18 b.] *trans.* To outdo as a rival; to surpass or excel in any competition.
1622 MASSINGER & DEKKER *Virg. Mart.* III. ii, The Christian Whose beauty has outrivalled me. **1705** MAIDWELL *Necess. Educ.* Pref. 7 He Had then out rival'd his Neighbour's Praetensions. **1860** MOTLEY *Netherl.* (1868) I. viii. 494 Each seeking to outrival the other in [her] good graces.

†**outˈrive,** *v. Obs.* [OUT- 15, 14.]
1. *trans.* To rive out, to tear out or apart forcibly; to break up (moorland or rough pasture land).
1597-8 BP. HALL *Sat.* IV. i. 11 Should all in rage the curse-beat page out-rive. **1677** *Corshill Baron-Court Bk.* in *Ayr & Wigton Arch. Coll.* IV. 138 For the sowme of sex pond scotis money for outriveing of bent land. **1749** *Fairfax's Tasso* XVI. lxiii. (ed. 4), I will o'ertake him, and out-rive his Heart.
2. *intr.* To tear or burst asunder. *Sc.*
1535 STEWART *Cron. Scot.* (1858) I. 312 Breist plaittis brak and all the ruvis outrave.

†**ˈoutroad.** *Obs.* [OUT- 7.] A riding out, an excursion; *esp.* a warlike excursion or raid; a sally. Also *fig.*
1560 BIBLE (Genev.) *1 Macc.* xv. 41 He set horsemen and garisons, that they might make outrodes by the waies of Iudea. **1609** HOLLAND *Amm. Marcell.* XVIII. ii. 107 All those captives, whome in many out-rodes they had taken and carried away. *a* **1656** HALES *Gold. Rem.* I. (1673) 82 He stood the shock of fifty set Battels, beseide all Seiges and Outrodes. **1865** CARLYLE *Fredk. Gt.* XIX. i. (1872) VIII. 102 Still another assault, or invasive outroad, northward against the Russian Magazines.

ˈoutroar, *sb.* [OUT- 7.] A loud noise or roar, uproar.
1845 *Dublin Rev.* June 314 'God strike you, Satan' was the Reformer's outroar. **1882** in OGILVIE (Annandale). **1886** in *Cassell's Encycl. Dict.* **1891** G. MEREDITH *One of our Conq.* II. ii. 28 As it were, the towering wood-work of the cathedral organ in quake under emission of its multitudinous outroar. **1955** V. CRONIN *Wise Man from West* vii. 139 On the day of a solar eclipse..all the inhabitants of China were assembled by townships, prostrate on the ground, to frighten away with cymbals, drums and an outroar of yelling the monster that would otherwise swallow the sun.

outroar (aʊtˈrɔə(r)), *v.* [OUT- 18, 18 c.] *trans.* To exceed in roaring, to roar louder or more than; to drown the roaring of.
1606 SHAKS. *Ant. & Cl.* III. xiii. 127 O that I were Vpon the hill of Basan, to out-roare The horned Heard. **1649** W. M. *Wandering Jew* (Halliw. 1857) 55 Lions roare, and yet at one time or other are out-roar'd. *a* **1814** *Gonzaga* IV. vi. in *New Brit. Theatre* III. 140 Let..the falling rocks Dash'd on the troubled ocean far outroar The warring elements! **1866** FELTON *Anc. & Mod. Gr.* I. I. vi. 98 A thrust that makes him outroar nine thousand troopers.

outroll (aʊtˈrəʊl), *v.* [OUT- 15.] *trans.* To roll out or forth; to unroll, unfurl, uncoil.
a **1585** MONTGOMERIE *Flyting* 352 Outrowde bee thy tongue, yet tratling all times. **1647** H. MORE *Song of Soul* II. iii. II. xxi, Drove into the Sun, or thence out-rol'd. *Ibid.* III. I. xiv, Thus weak of her own self..that she no'te out-roll Her vitall raies. **1815** SOUTHEY *Roderick* I. 41 And gently did the breezes..Curl their long flags outrolling. **1880** G. MEREDITH *Tragic Com.* (1881) 252 A day that outrolled the whole Alpine hand-in-hand of radiant heaven-climbers.
So **ˈoutroll** *sb.*; **ˈoutˌrolling** *vbl. sb.*
1860 F. W. FABER *Bethlehem* 16 The out-rolling of an uncreated ocean. **1891** G. MEREDITH *One of our Conq.* III. v. 88 Barmby paused on his outroll of the word.

out-romance, etc.: see OUT-.

ˈout-room. [OUT- 1.] An outlying room; an out-building or outhouse. Also *fig.*
1602 B. JONSON *Poetaster* II. i. Wks. (Rtldg.) 111/1 Lay them..in some out-room or corner of the dining-chamber. **1642** FULLER *Holy & Prof. St.* II. vii. 74 If our artist lodgeth her in the out-rooms of his soul for a night or two. **1668** DRYDEN *Mart. Mar-all* III. ii, In an out-room, upon a trunk. **1865** A. D. WHITNEY *Gayworthys* ii. 21 Gersham..ran up and down the out-room staircase. *Ibid.* 28 As she came into the out-room again. **1929** J. SHELTON *Salt-Box House* xii. 88 The floors were..sprinkled with white sea sand, that on the 'out-rooms' being swept lightly in fanciful patterns by brooms. **1971** *Islander* (Victoria, B.C.) 22 Aug. 5/2 He has a basement and an outroom full of bottles waiting to receive attention.

†**ˈoutroop.** *Obs.* Also 7 -rop(e. [a. Du. *uitroep*, in Kilian *wt-roep* an auction-sale, f. *uit* OUT + *roepen* to call.] An auction; = OUTCRY 2.
1598 W. PHILLIPS *Linschoten* (1864) 170 The principall street of the Citie named the Straight street, and is called the Leylon, which is as much to say, as an outroop. **1611** COTGR. s.v. *Baston*, The third (and last) knock of the Cryers staffe in an Outrope. **1618** BOLTON *Florus* (1636) 249 The statelyest free Townes of Italy were sold as at an outrop, who would give most. *a* **1693** URQUHART *Rabelais* III. xliv. 364 It was his ..Custom to sell Laws.., as at an Outroop or Putsale, to him who offered most for them.

†**ˈouˌtrooper, -roper.** *Obs.* [f. prec.: cf. Du. *uitroeper*, in Kilian *wtroeper*.] An auctioneer: at one time the specific title of the Common Crier of the City of London.
1612 (Apr. 30) *Petition to Ld. Mayor, Remembrancia* (City of London) III. 47 His suite unto you is, to grant unto him the office called ye Outroper of the cittie of London. **1638** *1st Charter Chas. I to London* in Luffman *Charters* (1793) 275 We..do erect and create in and through the said City..a certain office, called Outroper or Common Cryer, to and for the selling of houshold stuff, apparel, leases..and other things, of all persons who shall be willing that the said officers shall make sale of the same by public and open claim, commonly called outcry and sale. **1688** *London Gaz.* No. 2404/4 Whereas an Ancient Office (called, the Outropers Office) hath been Established and Used within this City and Liberties thereof..for all Publick Sales of Goods. **1691** *House of Lords MSS.* 1690-1 (1892) 303 The office of Outroper was anciently exercised by the Common Cryer and chiefly for the benefit of Orphans in the sale of goods of citizens deceased.

outroot (aʊtˈruːt), *v.* [f. OUT *adv.* + ROOT: prob. after L. *ērādīcāre*; cf. F. *déraciner*.] *trans.* To pluck out or up by the root, root out, eradicate, exterminate.
1558 J. HALES in Foxe *A. & M.* (1596) 1918/2 Also to your vttermost power endeuour to outroote them. **1624** *Essex's Ghost* in *Harl. Misc.* (Malh.) III. 514 T' out-root the plant, which Christ himselfe hath sown. **1834** LYTTON *Pompeii* III. v, Idolatry has never thoroughly been outrooted. **1865** CARLYLE *Fredk. Gt.* XX. xii. (1872) IX. 226 How..hinder Ferdinand's besieging them, and quite outrooting us there?
So **outˈrooting** *vbl. sb.*, a rooting out.
1562 WINȜET *Cert. Tractates* i. Wks. 1888 I. 11 For the dountramping of ydolatrie, to the outruiting of the quhilk we beseik thy princelie Maiestie. **1831** CARLYLE *Sart. Res.* II. iv, Finding indeed, except the Outrooting of Journalism (*die auszurottende Journalistik*), little to desiderate therein.

out-rove, -row, -royal, etc.: see OUT-.

out-row (aʊtˈrəʊ), *v.* [OUT- 18.] *trans.* To outdo or outstrip in rowing.
1530 PALSGR. 650/2, I wyll outrowe the or thou come to Westminster for xiid. **1823** COL. HAWKER *Diary* (1893) I. 260 Trying to out-row me with a huge black boat.

out-run (ˈaʊtrʌn), *sb.* [OUT- 1, 7.]
1. a. An outlying or distant 'run' for cattle or sheep; outlying pasture land.
1890 'R. BOLDREWOOD' *Col. Reformer* vi. 47 They'd come off a very far out-run. **1895** *Daily News* 3 Apr. 5/4 More attention is being paid to cultivation, to rotation of crops, to reclamation of outruns.
b. *spec.* in Shetland: see quot.
1898 *Shetland News* 3 Dec. (E.D.D.), The 'outrun', or enclosed arable land which surrounds the homestead.
2. Outcome; result.
1800 *Asiat. Ann. Reg., Proc. Parl.* 34/1 A comparison of the revenues and charges of the year 1798-9 as estimated, and according to the actual out-run.
3. The act or fact of running out; *spec.* the outward run of a sheepdog.
1884 *American* VIII. 308 To check the outrun of this. **1938** [see FETCH *sb.*[1] 1]. **1955** [see LIFT *sb.*[2] 5 i]. **1973** *Country Life* 25 Oct. 1292/1 The collie's gathering outrun follows a wide curving natural cast..and ends behind the sheep.
4. [G. *auslauf*]. In *Skiing*: see quots.
1913 F. H. HARRIS *Dartmouth out o' Doors* 101 The 'outrun'—the level stretch at the foot of the hill on which the jumpers check their speed. **1957** *Encycl. Brit.* XX. 749/2 He leans far forward over the points of his skis with arms outstretched, planing his body to increase his distance, lands with a slight give to his knees and speeds onto the outrun. **1963** *Amer. Speech* XXXVIII. 206 *Out run*, in general, the bottom end of a ski run. In ski-jumping, the distance between the take-off and the landing point. **1974** *Encycl. Brit. Macropædia* XVI. 836/2 After the slope levels off, the jumper stops by turning on the outrun.

outrun (aʊtˈrʌn), *v.* [OUT- 14, 18, 17.]
1. *intr.* To run out. †**b.** Of time: To expire.
1340 HAMPOLE *Pr. Consc.* 5297 Þe croun of thornes þat was thrested On his heved fast, þat þe blode out rane. **1387-8** T. USK *Test. Love* III. i. (Skeat) l. 51 Too moche wolde out ren. **1550** *Reg. Privy Council Scot.* I. 108 The xxty dayis..being outrunin. **1617** SIR W. MURE *Misc. Poems* xxi. 71 Long may thy subjects, ere thy glasse outrunne, Enjoy the light of thee, their glorious Sunne. **1819** W. TENNANT *Papistry Storm'd* (1827) 135 (E.D.D.) Hurryin' frae their doors Out-ran in thousands to the Scores.
2. *trans.* To outdo or outstrip in running, to run faster or farther than; to leave behind by superior speed; hence, to escape or elude.
1526 TINDALE *John* xx. 4 They ranne bothe to gether and that other disciple dyd out runne Peter and cam fyrst to the sepulcre. **1599** SHAKS. *Hen. V*, IV. i. 176 If these men haue defeated the Law, and outrunne Natiue punishment. *a* **1649** DRUMM. OF HAWTH. *Poems* Wks. (1711) 36 To pierce the mountain-wolf with feather'd dart;..Out-run the wind-out-running dædale hare. **1711** *Lond. Gaz.* No. 4887/3 We chased them till Ten..they out-running us so very much, that [etc.]. **1858** SEARS *Athan.* II. ii. 188 John outruns the sturdy Peter.
b. *fig.* To outstrip or get ahead of in any course.
1593 SHAKS. *3 Hen. VI*, I. ii. 14 By giuing the House of Lancaster leaue to breathe, It will outrunne you, Father, in the end. *a* **1656** BP. HALL *Rem. Wks.* (1660) 39 Our forward young men out-run their years. **1776** ADAM SMITH *W.N.* (1869) I. I. xi. III. 233 The increase of stock and the improvement of land are two events..of which the one can nowhere much out-run the other. **1849** MACAULAY *Hist. Eng.* viii. II. 347 The zeal of the flocks outran that of the pastors. **1875** JOWETT *Plato* (ed. 2) IV. 232 The power of analysis had outrun the means of knowledge.
3. *fig.* To run beyond a fixed limit or point; to go beyond in action.
1655 FULLER *Ch. Hist.* XI. iii. §14 Those who formerly had outrunne the canons with their additional conformitie. **1665** GLANVILL *Scepsis Sci.* ix. 51 They must needs transcend, and outrun our faculties. *a* **1797** H. WALPOLE *Mem. Geo. II* (1847) III. i. 6 In general, his friends outran his intentions. **1819** SCOTT *Ivanhoe* iii, Silence, maiden; thy tongue outruns thy discretion. **1873** J. A. SYMONDS *Grk. Poets* i. 10 The poet's imagination had probably outrun the fact.
†**4.** To run through; to pass or spend (time); to wear out (clothes, etc.). *Obs.*
1611 SPEED *Hist. Gt. Brit.* VII. ix. 240 Ethelrik..hauing out-run his youth in pernicious obscuritie, attained in his old yeeres to the Gouernment of both the Prouinces. **1687** *London Gaz.* No. 2276/5 The Spahi's having out-run all their Equipage, would not be in a condition of Service.
5. *to outrun the constable*: see CONSTABLE 6.
Hence **outˈrunner**[1], one who outruns.
1885 J. C. JEAFFRESON *Real Shelley* II. 257 The young man..like most other outrunners of the constable, was often without money.

ˈoutˌrunner[2]. [OUT- 8.]
1. One who or that which runs out; *spec.* an attendant who runs in advance of or beside a carriage; a horse which runs in traces outside the shafts; the dog which acts as leader of a team of sledge dogs; *fig.* a forerunner, an avant-courier.
1598 FLORIO, *Scorritore*, an outrunner, a gadder to and fro. **1891** ELIZ. BISLAND *Flying Trip* iii. 76 These outrunners accompany all folk of importance in Japan. **1891** *Pall Mall G.* 19 Mar. 3/1 Further on you hail with an increasing sense of pleasure the outrunners of a forest. **1893** *Voice* (N.Y.) 16 Nov., The outrunners for the Whig organization worked the temperance question for all it would bring them. **1894** *Daily News* 12 Oct. 7/6 They are harnessed in numbers from 3 to 11..with one dog as an outrunner to shew the way. **1897** J. Y. SIMPSON in *Blackw. Mag.* Jan. 12 Supported by an outrunner trotting abreast.
†**2.** An outrunning branch or creek. *Obs.*
1653 W. LAUSON in J. D[ennys] *Secr. Angling* in Arb. *Garner* I. 194 In a shallow river, or in some out-runner of the river.
So **ˈoutˌrunning** *vbl. sb.* [OUT- 9], the running out, †expiry, termination (*obs.*); *ppl. a.* [OUT- 10], that runs out.
1546 *Reg. Privy Council Scot.* I. 39 Twa dayis befor the outrynning of the said xxty dayis. **1597** SKENE *De Verb. Sign.* s.v. *None-enters*, After the ischue and out-running of the saidis three tearmes. **1890** 'R. BOLDREWOOD' *Miner's Right* (1899) 109/2 The wooden wedge, which..arrests and acts as a brake to the outrunning rope. **1894** *Outing* (U.S.) XXIV. 58/2, I found the out-running water perfectly clear.

ˈoutrush, *sb.* [OUT- 7.] A rushing out; a violent outflow.
1872 PROCTOR *Ess. Astron.* xix. 236 Direct evidence of an outrush of matter. **1876** GEO. ELIOT *Dan. Der.* v, A perceptible outrush of imprisoned conversation. **1898** *Century Mag.* Jan. 405/2 The outrush of the air from the lock.

out-ˈrush, *v.* [OUT- 14.] *intr.* To rush out. (Prop. two words.)
1600 FAIRFAX *Tasso* XIII. lxxv, Moist heau'n his windowes open laid, Whence cloudes by heapes out-rush. **1717** GARTH

Ovid's Met. XIV. *Adv. Macareus*, Forthwith out-rush'd a gust.

out'sail, *v.* [OUT- 18, 17.] *trans.* To outdo or surpass in sailing; to sail faster than; *transf.* and *fig.* to outstrip.

a **1616** BEAUM. & FL. *Wit without Money* I. ii, She may spare me her mizen, and her bonnets, strike her main petticoat, and yet out-sail me. **1675** COCKER *Morals* 31 Let none out-sail you in your Occupation. **1748** *Anson's Voy.* II. v. 177 The *Centurion*..outsailed the two prizes. **1883** DIXON KEMP in *Fortn. Rev.* 1 Sept. 323 'Smugglers'..could out-sail the cruisers on any point of sailing.

b. To sail beyond or farther than.

1865 E. BURRITT *Walk Land's End* 245 Drake..outsailed Columbus by two thirds of the earth's circumference.

out-saint to **out-savour**: see OUT-.

† **'outsale.** *Obs. rare.* [OUT- 7.] **a.** A sale to outsiders. **b.** An auction: cf. OUTCRY, OUTROOP.

1331 in *Coucher Bk. Selby* (Yorks. Rec. Soc.) II. 375 Fodiendo turbas ibidem et faciendo outsale ad valentiam xx^{s} per annum. *a* **1670** HACKET *Life Abp. Williams* I. (1692) 206 Did they ever think of that, that make away the Inheritance of God's Holy Tribe in an Out-sale?

out'say, *v.* [OUT- 15, 17.]

† **1.** *trans.* To utter or speak out; to inform upon. (Prop. two words.)

c **1330** R. BRUNNE *Chron.* (1810) 238 Ilk thefe oþer out said. **1422** tr. *Secreta Secret., Priv. Priv.* 206 Moche is the vertue of Prayer, whych out sayd in erthe, worchyth in hevyn.

2. To say more than.

1658 FLATMAN *Commend. Verses Sanderson's Graphice*, He outsays all, who lets you understand, The head is Sanderson's, Faithorne's the hand.

† **'outscape**, *sb. Obs.* [f. OUT- 7 + SCAPE, aphetic f. ESCAPE; cf. also OUT- 25.] **1.** Escape, release from restraint; means of escape.

1555 J. BRADFORD *Lett.* (Parker Soc.) II. 186 He will never leave you, but in the midst of temptation will give you an outscape. **15..** FOXE in Holinshed *Chron.* (1587) III. 1151/2 The miraculous custodie and outscape of this our soueriegne ladie..in the strict time of queene Marie hir sister. **1615** CHAPMAN *Odyss.* IX. 423 It past Our powers to lift aside a log so vast, As barr'd all outscape.

2. *rare.* [SCAPE *sb.*[3]] The outward appearance of a region. Cf. INSCAPE *sb.*

1868 G. M. HOPKINS *Jrnls. & Papers* (1959) 184 In the afternoon we took the train for Paris and passed through a country of pale grey rocky hills of a strong and simple outscape.

† **out'scape**, *v. Obs.* $rare^{-1}$. [See prec.] = ESCAPE *v.*

1562 PHAER *Æneid.* VIII. (1573) Bb iv, He through their slaughter throngs to Rutil realme outskaping sprang.

† **out-'schoven**, *pple. Obs.* [f. OUT- 11 + *shoven*, obs. pa. pple. of SHOVE *v.*] Shoved or pushed out.

a **1400** *Prymer* (1891) 40 As arwes in myȝti mannes honde; so the sones of owtschouen [WYCLIF, the out shaken; Vulg. *filii excussorum*; cf. OUTSHOT].

outscold (-'skəʊld), *v.* [OUT- 18 b.] *trans.* To outdo or get the better of in scolding.

1595 SHAKS. *John* v. ii. 160 There end thy braue,..We grant thou canst out-scold vs. **1764** T. BRYDGES *Homer Travest.* (1797) II. 203 What need he for help to call, Whose clapper can outscold them all? **1870** L'ESTRANGE *Miss Mitford* I. vi. 204 A friend of mine who went into hysterics because she was out-scolded by her husband.

out'score, *v.* [OUT- 18.] *trans.* In various sports and games: to score more than; to surpass in scoring.

1958 *Times* 17 Oct. 20/1 Keenan..then settled down to outscore the Canadian consistently. **1960** E. W. SWANTON *W. Indies Revisited* ii. 24 Nurse..actually out-scored Sobers, who found himself humorously slow-clapped. **1968** *Globe & Mail* (Toronto) 5 Feb. 17/2 In other games yesterday, Brampton Rockets outscored Aurora Tigers 8–7 and league-leading Dixie Beehives edged North York Rangers 3–2. **1968** [see PACE *v.* 5]. **1977** *Daily Mirror* 16 Mar. 30/4, I thought Mo outscored Dagge by at least five punches to one throughout most of the fight.

'outscour. [OUT- 7.] The act of scouring out; the action of water scouring out a channel.

1883 G. K. GILBERT in *Nature* XXVII. 261/2 The natural rate of denudation by means of the outscour of rivers.

So **'outscouring** *vbl. sb.*, that which is scoured out.

1828 WEBSTER (citing BUCKLAND), *Outscourings*, substances washed or scoured out.

† **'out,scourer.** *Obs.* [f. OUT- 8 + SCOURER runner.] A scout; = next.

a **1548** HALL *Chron., Edw. IV* 229 The Englishe outskourers perceivyng by his cote, that he was an officer of armes, gently saluted hym.

† **'outscout**, *sb. Obs.* [OUT- 2.] One sent out as a scout; an advanced scout or look-out. Also, in *Cricket*, An out-fielder.

1708 *London Gaz.* No. 4420/6 The Ships our Out-scouts saw off of Calais, were Privateers. **1745** P. THOMAS *Jrnl. Anson's Voy.* 115 One Man on Horseback, whom they supposed to be a Centinal, or Outscout. **1798** H. TOOKE *Purley* 405 Is an Out-scout at cricket sent to a distance, that he may the better listen to what is passing? **1831** *Lincoln Herald* 8 July 2/3 The public press, and the outscouts of the public press had deluded and deceived the whole country.

† **out'scout**, *v. Obs.* $rare^{-1}$. [OUT- 16.] *trans.* To drive out with scouting or scorn.

1602 MARSTON *Antonio's Rev.* v. iii, Alarum mischief, and with an undanted brow, out scout the grim opposition Of most menacing perill.

out-scream to **out-sea**: see OUT-.

† **out-'scruze, -scruse**, *v. Obs. rare.* [OUT- 15.] *trans.* To press or squeeze out.

1621 G. SANDYS *Ovid's Met.* VII. (1626) 134 She cuts the old mans throte; out-scrus'd His scarce warme blood.

outsearch (-'sɜːtʃ), *v. rare.* [OUT- 15.] *trans.* To search out; to explore.

1510–20 *Everyman* in Hazl. *Dodsley* I. 102 Lord, I will in the world go run over all, And cruelly out-search both great and small. ? **15..** in Strype *Cranmer* (1848) II. App. 599 Christ's sacraments..rather of us to be believed, than by our natural reason to be out-searched. **1860** PUSEY *Min. Proph.* 238 Obadiah 6. How are the things of Esau searched out! lit. How are Esau outsearched.

out'see, *v.* [OUT- 18, 17.]

1. *trans.* To surpass in length or accuracy of sight; to surpass in mental insight.

1605 CHAPMAN *All Fooles* in Dodsley *O.P.* (1780) IV. 185 You that can out-see clear-ey'd jealousy. **1847** [see OUTLOVE]. **1894** H. DRUMMOND *Ascent Man* 138 It is nothing to him [Man] to be distanced..in vision by the eagle: his field-glass out-sees it.

2. To see beyond (a point or limit).

1645 RUTHERFORD *Tryal & Tri. Faith* xiii. (1845) 137 Fancy and nature cannot out-see time, nor see over or beyond death. **1664** POWER *Exp. Philos.* I. 78 Our Posterity may come by Glasses to out-see the Sun, and discover Bodies in the remote Universe. **1837** EMERSON *Misc.* 92 Would we be blind? Do we fear lest we should outsee nature and God?

† **out'seek**, *v. Obs.* [OUT- 15.] *trans.* To seek out, seek for; to search out. (In ME. two words.) So † **'out-seeking** *vbl. sb.*, seeking out.

1297 R. GLOUC. (Rolls) 8956 Poueremen wel ofte in to hire chambre heo drou,..And wess hor vet & clene þe quiture out soȝte. **1382** WYCLIF *Isa.* xxxi. 1 The Lord thei han not out soȝt. —— *Wisd.* xiv. 12 The outseching of maumetis [1388 the sekyng out of idols]. ? *a* **1500** *Chester Pl.* v. 440 + 58 The fayrest wemen he hath outsought.

outseg (aʊt'sɛg), *v. U.S. colloq.* [f. OUT- 18 + SEG, abbrev. of SEGREGATIONIST.] *trans.* To support or advocate a more segregationist policy than (someone else).

1967 *Time* 13 Oct. 19 Governors Spiro Agnew of Maryland and Winthrop Rockefeller of Arkansas won office even though their Democratic opponents 'outsegged' them. **1970** *Manch. Guardian Weekly* 4 Apr. 14 Brewer..acquired a reputation as an effective administrator, and, most important, he has no intention of being 'Out-segged' by Wallace. **1970** M. PEI *Words in Sheep's Clothing* xvii. 166 'Segregation', a word that has given rise to such slang abbreviations as 'seg' and 'to outseg'. (Someone was once described as 'outsegging' Wallace.)

out'sell, *v.* [OUT- 18, 18 b.]

1. *trans.* To sell for more than; to exceed in price when sold; *fig.* to exceed in value.

1611 SHAKS. *Cymb.* II. iv. 102 She stript it from her Arme:..Her pretty Action, did out-sell her guift. *a* **1625** FLETCHER *Noble Gentlem.* II. i. Wks. (Rtldg.) 264/1 His wines Were held the best, and out-sold other men's. **1770–4** A. HUNTER *Georg. Ess.* (1803) IV. 578 One of these little bullocks outsell a coarse Lincolnshire ox.

2. To have or secure a larger sale than.

a **1687** PETTY *Pol. Arith.* (1690) 13 The Hollanders can out-sell the French. **1727** SWIFT *Woman's Mind* 63 She has my commission To add them in the next edition; They may out-sell a better thing. **1961** WEBSTER s.v., Nonfiction..continues to outsell fiction in the bookstores—*Publishers' Weekly*. **1968** *Globe & Mail* (Toronto) 17 Feb. 40 (Advt.), Again in 1967, Islington Plymouth outsold every metro Plymouth dealer. **1976** *National Observer* (U.S.) 10 Apr. 3/1 Washington outsold the Soviet Union, its nearest rival in the arms business, by almost two to one in 1974. **1977** *Times* 29 Dec. 17/1 A fine car found itself being outsold on its home ground by Continental competitors.

† **out'send**, *v. Obs.* exc. in pples. [OUT- 15.] *trans.* To send out or forth; to emit.

a **1300** *E.E. Psalter* ciii. 30 Out send þi gaste and made þai sal bene. *c* **1580** *Howers Blessed Virg.* 105 For then should I be..Now brought into the world, and streight againe outsent. **1647** H. MORE *Song of Soul* II. iii. II. xlii, What? doth the Sun his rayes that he out-sends Smother or choke? **1846** TRENCH *Mirac.* xxxiii. (1862) 456 *note*, St. John nowhere employs ἀπόστολος to distinguish one of the Twelve. He uses it but once (xiii. 16) and then generally, for one outsent.

So **'out,sending** *vbl. sb.*, the action of sending out; that which is sent out or put forth. **'outsent** *ppl. a.*, sent out or forth; emitted, dispatched.

1382 WYCLIF *Song Sol.* iv. 13 Thin outsendingus [1388 Thi sendingis out ben] paradis of poungarnetes, with the fruits of appilis. **1613–18** DANIEL *Coll. Hist. Eng.* (1626) 122 The sea being open vnto him, his out-sendings might bee without view or noting. **1627** PERROT *Tithes* 70 Returning to his coffers an hundred fold for his outsent adventures. **1795** J. FAWCETT *Art of War* 29 Into whose dragon broil, and high-wrought rage..all her out-sent soul Alecto breath'd.

out-sense, -sentence, etc.: see OUT-.

'out-,sentinel. = next.

1728 DE FOE *Mem. Capt. Carleton* (1840) 44 My out-sentinel challenged them, and..they answered, Hispanioli.

'out-,sentry. [OUT- 2.] A sentry placed at a distance in advance; an outpost.

1691 *Proceedings agst. Fr.* in *Select. Harleian Misc.* (1793) 479 Having given orders to the out-centries that were placed towards the fort, to fire, without challenging, at any who should come that way. *a* **1773** LD. CHESTERFIELD in *Deb. Ho. Lords* V. 522 (Jod.) The stage, my lord, and the press are two of our outsentries. **1886** STEVENSON *Kidnapped* 220 We're just to bide here with these, which are his out-sentries, till they can get word to the chief of my arrival.

outset ('aʊtsɛt), *sb.* [OUT- 7.]

1. An enclosure from the outlying moorland, pasture, or common. *Sc.*

1540 *Sc. Acts Jas. V* (1814) 379/1 Of all and sindry þe landis of estir Wischart..wᵗ þe corne mylne multuris & outseitis þarof [L. *multuris et* lie-outsettis *earundem*]. **1600** *Sc. Acts Jas. VI*, c. 2 Towers, Maner-places, Outsets, Yardes, Orchards, Kirks [etc.]. **1641** [see ONSET *sb.* 3]. **1808** in Shirreff *Agric. Shetl. Isl.* (1841) App. 59 By making what we call *outsets* to a certain extent, a good deal of ground might be brought under cultivation, from the commons or hill-pasture. **1884** *Scotsman* 26 July 3/1 *advt.*, Common Pastures, Outsets, Insets..belonging to the said Lands.

2. The action or fact of setting off; ornament, embellishment; also, that which sets off or embellishes. *Sc.*

1596 DALRYMPLE tr. *Leslie's Hist. Scot.* I. 94 Bracelets about their armes, iewalis about thair neck..baith cumlie and decent, and mekle to thair decore and outsett. **1645** RUTHERFORD *Tryal & Tri. Faith* Ded. (1845) 5 Christ is the outset: the master flower, the uncreated garland of Heaven. **1881** THOMSON *Musings* 179 (E.D.D.) Her graceful' form an' modest air Micht be an outset tae a queen.

3. The act or fact of setting out upon a journey, course of action, business, etc.; start, commencement, beginning.

1759 *Ann. Reg.* 6 Placed at their first outset at a very high point of military rank. **1780** BURKE *Sp. Econ. Ref.* Wks. III. 234 This is no pleasant prospect at the outset of a political journey. **1788** REEVE *Exiles* III. 179, I will give five hundred pounds..this will be an outset for you in any way you shall choose. **1795** MASON *Ch. Mus.* ii. 140 These Masters, at least in the outset of their careers, were careful to preserve Air. **1822** W. IRVING *Braceb. Hall* i. 2 A good outset is half the voyage. **1877** BLACK *Green Past* xxiii, Perhaps he had from the outset been induced to enter his own name as the purchaser. **1891** L. KEITH *Halletts* I. xi, She had witnessed the outset from her seat in the window.

† **b.** That with which a venture starts; primary outlay. *Obs.*

1719 W. WOOD *Surv. Trade* 275 Ships which..have brought home Cargoes of Goods amounting to 10, 12, and 15 Times the Value of their Outset.

attrib. **1766** W. GORDON *Gen. Counting-ho.* 268 Ebenezer pays the outset charges at Port Glasgow.

† **4.** *pl.* Outgoings, expenditure. *Obs.*

1762 *Gentl. Mag.* 428 My income greatly exceeds my outsets. **1764** T. HUTCHINSON *Hist. Mass.* (1765) I. 3 Discouraged..by the long continued expence and outset, with-out any return.

5. *Mining.* (See quot. 1888.)

1881 *Borings & Sinkings* in *Northumbld. Gloss.*, From the outset to the soil depth one fathom. **1888** NICHOLSON *Coal Tr. Gl.* (E.D.D.), *Outset*, an artificial elevation of the ground, or an erection of timber or stone, round the mouth of a sinking pit to facilitate the disposal of the debris produced in sinking.

† **out'set**, *v. Obs.* [OUT- 15.]

1. *trans.* To set forth, display, set off, adorn; to maintain with proper splendour. *Sc.*

15.. *Aberd. Reg.* (Jam.), To outsett the honour of this burgh. *a* **1578** LINDESAY (Pitscottie) *Chron. Scot.* (S.T.S.) II. 18, xxx^{m} crouns to be deliuerit to the earle of Lennox allvayis to outsett [*MS. I*, to be spendit to] his honour and fortifiecatioun. **1596** DALRYMPLE tr. *Leslie's Hist. Scot.* I. 68 Mony thingis to decore and outsett.

2. To place as a set-off (*for* something).

1656 *Rhode Isl. Col. Rec.* (1856) I. 339 It is ordered, that five pounds starling due from Mr. Randall Holden for not executing office accordinge to choyce, is outsett for his former service in publique employment.

3. To put out, exclude.

1613 WITHER *Abuses Stript & Whipt* II. ii, I hope 'twill not offend the Court, That I..outset others though men thinke me bold.

† **'out-set**, *ppl. a. Obs. rare.* [OUT- 11.] Placed outside or remote from the centre.

? *a* **1600** TIMME *Silver Watch-Bell* iv. §9 (ed. 10) Then shall be prepared an out-set habitation.

† **'out,setter.** *Obs.* [OUT- 8, 2.]

1. One who sets forth. *Sc.*

15.. in Lindesay (Pitscottie) *Chron. Scot.* (S.T.S.) I. 309 The outsettaris, mainteinaris and worschiper is of the same. *a* **1578** LINDESAY *Ibid.* II. 111 They..brunt thame cruellie ffor preiching of the evangell quho said they war the outsettaris of the samin thamselffis.

2. An outdweller.

1674 N. FAIRFAX *Bulk & Selv.* To Rdr., The same kinreds of men unmingled with Out-setters that were among them then. **1712** H. PRIDEAUX *Direct. Ch.-wardens* (ed. 4) 44 No Out-setter, who occupieth Lands in the Parish, but doth not ..inhabit there, is capable of being chosen Church-warden.

'out,setting, *vbl. sb.* [OUT- 9.]

1. The setting out or starting upon a journey, course of action, undertaking, etc.; a start.

1676 W. ROW *Contn. Blair's Autobiog* ix. (1848) 141 Mr. Livingstone, before their outsetting, often said [etc.]. **1754** RICHARDSON *Grandison* (1781) III. ii. 19 Who might, from such an outsetting, begin the world..with some hope of success. **1824** ANNE GRANT in *Mem.* (1844) III. 62, I shall leave your son to tell of our outsetting. **1827** CARLYLE *Germ. Rom.* I. 292 They used to look at one another, at outsetting, or when cross-ways met, with an air of sadness. **1903** W. B. YEATS *In Seven Woods* 42 It's time to build up Emain that was burned At the outsetting of these wars. **1909** *Tablet* 17 Apr. 606/1 The start was made from Blois a few days later, as strange an outsetting as ever was made by a fighting army.

†**2.** The action of fitting out; provision for a journey, enterprise, etc. *Obs.*

1561 *Rental of Dunkeld* (Clarendon Hist. Soc. 1883) 13 Thay grantit to give hir Grace, for the outsetting of hir Majesties honest effairis, the fourt pair of thair levingis for ane ȝeir allanerlie. *a* **1578** LINDESAY (Pitscottie) *Chron. Scot.* (S.T.S.) II. 241 This taxt was raisit for the out-setting of the ambassadour to Ingland.

3. What is outside the self. *rare.*

1880 G. M. HOPKINS *Sermons & Devotional Writings* (1959) 127 This applies to the universal mind or being too; it will have its inset and its outsetting; only that the out-setting includes all things, with all of which it is in some way ..identified.

'out,setting, *ppl. a.* [OUT- 10.]

†**1.** That lives or lies in the open or outside an enclosure, park, etc.: cf. OUTLYING 1. *Obs.*

1658 GURNALL *Chr. in Arm.* verse 15. xv. §4 (1669) 164/2 The out-setting Deer is observ'd to be lean..because alwayes in fear. **1662** *Ibid.* III. (1669) 318/1 These like the out-setting deer are shot, while they within the Pale are safe.

2. That sets or flows steadily outward.

1763 W. ROBERTS *Nat. Hist. Florida* 19 The course of this outsetting current. **1875** BEDFORD *Sailor's Pocket Bk.* viii. (ed. 2) 293 If there be a strong 'outsetting' tide,..then get on your back and float till help comes.

'out-,settlement. [OUT- 1.] An outlying or remote settlement.

1747 *Boston News-Letter* 16 July 2/1 Hendrick, the Indian who went out..to annoy the French in their Out-Settlements at Canada, with thirty odd Indians. **1761** *Nova Scotia Archives* (1869) 490 The troops..will be scarce sufficient for the protection of the Out Settlements. **1828** P. CUNNINGHAM *N.S. Wales* (ed. 3) II. 310 A felon working out a sentence in a penal gang at one of our out-settlements.

'out,settler. [OUT- 2, 8.] **a.** A settler outside of or in the outlying parts of a district. **b.** An emigrant.

1756 *Boston News-Letter* 15 Apr. 2/1 Their [Indians'] cruel and barbarous outrages on the four Outsettlers of those Parts last Winter. **1852** GROTE *Greece* II. lxxv. VI. 516 During the Peloponnesian War, Ægina had been tenanted by Athenian citizens as outsettlers or kleruchs.

out-shadow, -shake, etc.: see OUT-.

out'shame, *v.* [OUT- 18.] *trans.* To outdo in shamefulness; to put to shame.

a **1661** HOLYDAY *Juvenal* 22 This baggage quite all civil war out-shames. **1798** *Hist.* in *Ann. Reg.* 230 The indecency of those appearances far out-shamed any thing of a similar nature that had ever been exhibited. **1824** T. FERBY *Young Girl* x, Why blast the prospects of thy life; Out-shame thy sex's feelings tender?

out-'sharpen, *v.* [OUT- 15 b, 23 a.] *trans.*

†**a.** To excite thoroughly to sharpness or bitterness (*obs.*). **b.** To exceed in sharpness.

1382 WYCLIF *Jer.* v. 23 To this puple forsothe is maad an herte mystrowende and oute sharpende [L. *exasperans*]. **1865** DICKENS *Mut. Fr.* II. i, She would glance at the visitors ..with a look that out-sharpened all her other sharpness.

out-sheath, -shed, etc.: see OUT-.

outshet, obs. pa. t. of OUTSHUT *v.*

'outshift. Now *dial.* [f. OUT- 3 + *shift*, of uncertain application in this combination.] In *pl.* Outskirts (of a town).

1592 NASHE *P. Penilesse* 22 b, In backe lanes, and the out-shiftes of the Citie. **1594** —— *Terrors of Nt.* E j b, Not in the heart of the Cittie..but in the skirts and out-shifts. *a* **1825** FORBY *Voc. E. Anglia* s.v., He lives somewhere in the outshifts of the town.

out'shine, *v.* [OUT- 18, 14.]

1. *trans.* To excel in shining or brightness; to shine brighter than.

1596 SPENSER *F.Q.* v. ix. 21 And all their tops bright glistering with gold, That seemed to out-shine the dimmed skye. **1667** MILTON *P.L.* I. 86 How changed From him, who in the happy Realms of Light..didst outshine Myriads. **1820** SHELLEY *Vision Sea* 74 Those eyes where the radiance of fear Is outshining the meteors. **1899** SWINBURNE in *19th Cent.* Jan. 90 With stars outshining all their suns to be.

b. *fig.* To surpass in splendour or excellence.

1612 DRAYTON *Poly-olb.* xviii. 287 And he, all him before that cleerely did out-shine. **1712** STEELE *Spect.* No. 268 ¶3 How few are there who do not place their Happiness in out-shining others in Pomp and Show. **1858** HAWTHORNE *Fr. & It. Jrnls.* (1872) I. 64 One magnificence outshone another, and made itself the brightest.

2. *intr.* To shine forth or out. *poet. rare.*

1878 GILDER *Poet & Master* 11 Even the night is mine When Northern Lights outshine.

Hence **out'shining** *vbl. sb.*[1] and *ppl. a.*[1] (in sense 1); **out'shiner**, one who outshines or surpasses.

1754 R. O. CAMBRIDGE *Intruder* 16 No art, no project, no designing, No rivalship and no outshining. **1818** BYRON *Ch. Har.* IV. clviii, This Outshining and o'erwhelming edifice [St. Peter's] Fools our fond gaze. **1864** *Askerdale Park* I. 128 The weak young woman who had been outshone on some occasion at which she had reckoned on being the universal outshiner.

'out-,shining, *vbl. sb.*[2] [OUT- 9.] The action of shining out; the emission of light or brightness.

1678 CUDWORTH *Intell. Syst.* I. iv. §36. 582 The Effulgency or Out-shining of Light and Splendour from the Sun. **1863** J. G. MURPHY *Comm. Gen.* i. 14–19 Whatever remained of hinderance to the outshining of the sun, moon, and stars on the land. **1866** —— *Comm. Exod.* xxviii. 2 Glory is the out-shining of intrinsic excellence.

So **'out-,shining** *ppl. a.*[2], that shines out, effulgent.

1594 SHAKS. *Rich. III*, I. iii. 268 My Sonne,..Whose bright out-shining beames, thy cloudy wrath Hath in eternall darknesse folded vp. **1647** H. MORE *Song of Soul* I. III. xix, Surly Superstition, That clear out-shining Truth cannot abide. **1865** MRS. WHITNEY *Gayworthys* xl. 373 With a purpose in his face, the sailor came..and all through her, this outshining purpose of his quivered and thrilled.

out-shinned: see OUT-.

outshoot ('aʊt-ʃuːt), *sb.* [OUT- 7.]

1. The act or fact of shooting or thrusting out.

1897 *Outing* (U.S.) XXX. 237/1 A smart out-shoot of the hands before commencing the swing forward [in rowing].

2. Something that shoots out or projects; a projection or extension. Also *fig.*

1613 MARKHAM *Eng. Husbandman* I. II. i. (1635) 121 That wall would have upon the inside..Iames or outshoots of stone or brick. **1650** BULWER *Anthropomet.* 11 When the hinder eminence or out-shoote is wanting. **1887** *Amer. Missionary* (N.Y.) May 129 Churches and schools, with all their multitudinous outshoots of work.

3. = OUTFLOW.

1622 SIR R. HAWKINS *Voy. S. Sea* (1847) 107 It hath great rivers of fresh waters, for the out-shoot of them colours the sea in many places.

4. *Baseball.* = OUTCURVE 1.

1887 *Courier-Jrnl.* (Louisville, Kentucky) 5 May 6/3 He has a queer drop and out-shoot on which McQuaid failed to give him strikes. **1903** R. H. BARBOUR *Weatherby's Inning* 230 Then followed an out-shoot and a drop, neither of which did Joe take to. **1911** W. PATTEN *Bk. Baseball* 63/1 The plain horizontal outshoot, by the way, is no more in fashion. **1972** B. SHAW *Pitching* v. 86 Years ago, terms like 'drops', 'downer', 'out-shoot' were used to describe the curve ball.

outshoot (aʊt-'ʃuːt), *v.* [OUT- 18, 17, 15.]

1. *trans.* To surpass in shooting; to shoot farther or better than.

1530 PALSGR. 650/1, I outshote, *je oultretyre.* **1581** SIDNEY *Apol. Poetrie* (Arb.) 51 As if they out shot Robin Hood. **1605** BACON *Adv. Learn.* II. xxiii. 88 b, I doubt not but learned men with meane experience, woulde..outshoote them in their owne bowe. **1730** T. BOSTON *Mem.* xii. 404 Satan was outshot in his own bow and plied another engine. **1900** *Westm. Gaz.* 13 July 6/3 Again we hear of our guns being outranged and outshot.

b. To shoot beyond as a young branch; also *fig.*

1772 HOLWEL in *Phil. Trans.* LXII. 129 The first he grafted is six years old, and has out-shot his parent 2 feet in heighth. **1857** W. SMITH *Thorndale* 424 The individual mind is progressive, and here and there one outshoots the others.

2. To shoot beyond (a mark or limit).

1545 ASCHAM *Toxoph.* I. (Arb.) 19 This thyng maketh them summtyme to outshoote the marke. *a* **1711** NORRIS (J.), Men are resolved never to outshoot their forefathers' mark.

3. To shoot out or forth; to project.

1658 GURNALL *Chr. in Arm.* verse 14. II. iv. (1669) 19/1 They..that are so farr outshot from Natures weak Bow. *a* **1851** MOIR *Evening Tranquillity* ii, The woods outshoot their shadows dim.

'out,shooting, *vbl. sb.* [OUT- 9.] The action of shooting out or projecting; †**a** projection (*obs.*).

1387 TREVISA *Higden* (Rolls) II. 13 Outake þe lengest out schetynge of dyuerse forlondes, wiþ þe whiche Britayne is al aboute eyȝte and fourty siþe seuenty þowsand paas.

So **'out-,shooting** *ppl. a.* [OUT- 10], that shoots out, projects, or protrudes.

1622 W. WHATELY *God's Husb.* II. 104 A good and husbandly Gardener will take away from the Vine all out-shooting and ouer growing things.

'outshot, *sb.* [OUT- 7.]

1. A projection; a portion of a building projected beyond the general line; a projecting upper story or the like; a part built on as an extension. *north.*

1626 in *York Myst.* (1885) Introd. 36 Of the Walkers for an Outeshott, iiij*d.* *c* **1817** HOGG *Tales & Sk.* I. 37 An outshot from the back of the house. **1820** SCOTT *Monast.* xxviii, There was connected with this chamber, and opening into it, a small 'outshot', or projecting part of the building. **1957** E. E. EVANS *Irish Folk Ways* v. 69 In the traditional house of the north-west..a small bed-wing—the outshot or *cailleach*—projects out from one of the side-walls at the chimney end of the kitchen. **1961** M. W. BARLEY *Eng. Farmhouse & Cottage* II. iii. 88 Sometimes the third room is called 'the room below the entry'; in other cases it is a 'backend', like the backhouse in East Anglia. In two cases it is an 'outend', presumably an outshot. **1975** *New Society* 14 Aug. 363/2 The rubble-walled, barrel-roofed, thatched cottage [in rural Ireland] with end chimney and no division, but with a projection or 'outshot' for the bed—a feature of the western and northern fringes.

2. Outlying land; rough untilled ground. *Sc.*

1825 in JAMIESON.

3. Technical uses: **a.** Short for *outshot hemp*: see next 3. (Simmonds *Dict. Trade* 1858.) **b.** White rags of the second grade (*Cent. Dict.* 1890).

1880 J. DUNBAR *Pract. Papermaker* 13 Fines, Seconds, Thirds, Cords both dark and light, Outshots, Prints, and the various qualities of Hemp and Jute Bagging. **1883** R. HALDANE *Workshop Receipts* (Ser. 2) 389/1 Fines consist of fine white cottons; seconds, soiled white cottons;..out-shots, good, strong, and sound rags. **1937** E. J. LABARRE *Dict. Paper* 171/2 *Outshots*, a class of canvas or low white cottons found among rags.

'outshot, *ppl. a.* [OUT- 11.]

1. Shot or thrust out; projected, thrown out.

a **1340** HAMPOLE *Psalter* cxxvi[i]. 5 As armys in hand of myghty swa þe sunnys of outshote [Vulg. *filii excussorum*].

2. That is 'thrown out' or made to project beyond the main line of building, etc.

1820 SCOTT *Monast.* xiv, From the out-shot or projecting window she could perceive that [etc.]. **1836** M. MACKINTOSH *Cottager's Daughter* 52 When that she came to the outshot stane she then fell till her wark.

3. Applied to Russian hemp of the second quality.

1794 *Rigging & Seamanship* 59 Petersburgh out-shot hemp is little inferior to the Petersburgh braak hemp. **1812** J. SMYTH *Pract. of Customs* (1821) 107 Riga hemp is distinguished by the Trade by the names of Rhyne, Outshot, Pass, and Codilla Hemp. That from Petersburgh, consisting of Clean, Outshot, Half-clean, and Codilla.

out-shouldered to **out-shove**: see OUT-.

†**'outshout**, *sb. Obs.* [OUT- 7.] The act of shouting out; a loud shout.

1579–80 NORTH *Plutarch* (1676) 321 Crows fell down.. which by chance flew over the Shew-place at that time that they made the same outshout.

out'shout, *v.* [OUT- 18.] *trans.* To outdo or surpass in shouting; to shout louder than. Also *fig.*

a **1661** HOLYDAY *Juvenal* 120 As if he would implie that she outshouted them. **1889** C. EDWARDES *Sardinia* 190 Trying to outshout his neighbour. **1934** T. N. WILDER *Heaven's my Destination* ix. 165 The hold-up man finally outshouted them: 'Say, shut up, you two! What's the idea? ..I'm not fooling.' **1962** R. P. JHABVALA *Get Ready for Battle* ii. 105 But Mala outshouted them both and..shut the door behind them. **1962** *Spectator* 24 Aug. 272/3 Ronald Fraser..outshouts the rest of the cast. **1971** *Daily Tel.* (Colour Suppl.) 8 Jan. 15/4 It is still too early to say whether the voices calling for a new airways system will outshout those in favour of improving the present set up. **1976** *New Yorker* 15 Nov. 131/1 The story of Demosthenes, who learned to speak clearly by out-shouting the surf through a mouthful of pebbles.

out'shove, *v.* [OUT- 18.] *trans.* To outdo or surpass in shoving; to shove harder than.

1938 D. RUNYON *Furthermore* vii. 142 Then the next thing anybody knows, the Yales outshove the Harvards, and now the game is over. **1960** *Times* 29 Feb. 3/3 Often they outshoved the French pack. **1963** *Times* 11 Mar. 3/5 With the Irish forwards outshoving Wales in the tight and felling all in their path in the loose, Wales were unable to free themselves of anxiety of some sort.

†**'outshow**, *sb. Obs.* [OUT- 7.] Display, exhibition.

1553 GRIMALDE *Cicero's Offices* II. (1558) 90 Deeme themselues able to attein stedfast glorie by false pretence and vaine outshow.

outshow (aʊt-'ʃəʊ), *v.* [OUT- 15, 21.]

1. *trans.* To show forth, exhibit. *poet.*

1558 PHAER *Æneid.* VII. U iij b, Duke Auentine.. Victoriously outshewes his charet faier. *a* **1600** in *England's Helicon* C ij b, He blusht..Ne durst again his fierie face out-show. **1898** T. HARDY *Wessex Poems* 2 Then high handiwork will I make my life-deed, Truth and light outshow.

2. To exceed or outdo in show.

1786 MRS. BENNETT *Juvenile Indiscret.* III. 71 Mrs. Gab's sole ambition was to out-show and out-dress her neighbours.

So **'out,showing** *vbl. sb.* [OUT- 9], indication.

1868 MRS. WHITNEY *P. Strong* xix. (1869) 220 The home that this is the sign and outshowing of.

out-shower, -shriek, etc.: see OUT-.

out'shrill, *v.* [OUT- 18, 14.]

1. *trans.* To outdo or surpass in shrilling; to make a shriller noise than; to exceed in shrillness.

1605 SYLVESTER *Du Bartas* II. iii. III. *Law* 20 For the loud Cornet of my long-breath'd stile Out-shrils yee still. **1644** Z. BOYD *Gard. Zion* in *Zion's Flowers* (1885) App. 10/2 Let not the words of vaine men with their noise, Out shrill the precepts of God's divine voice. **1894** G. MOORE *Esther Waters* xxxii. 260 Like so many challenging cocks, each trying to outshrill the other.

2. *intr.* To shrill out; to sing shrilly. *poet.*

a **1879** J. ADDIS *Elizab. Echoes* 29 Peace, Save when the nightingale outshrilleth.

out'shut, *v.* Pa. t. 5–6 **-schet, -shet, -shyt.** [OUT- 15.] *trans.* To shut out, exclude. *lit.* and *fig.*

c **1430** *Pilgr. Lyf Manhode* II. xxxviii. (1869) 90 The bodi ..of whiche j haue spoken to thee is in alle degrees outshet. **1501** DOUGLAS *Pal. Hon.* III. 498 That garitour tho,..Was clepit Lawtie, keipar of that hald Of hie honour, and thay pepill outschet. *a* **1541** WYATT *Poet. Wks.* (1861) 6 When fortune him outshyt Clean from his reign. *a* **1631** DONNE *Lam. of Jeremy* iii. 8 When I cry out he outshuts my prayer.

ˈoutshut, *ppl. a. poet.* [OUT- 11.] Shut out. So **ˈoutˌshutting** *ppl. a.* [OUT- 10.]

1868 GEO. ELIOT *Sp. Gypsy* IV. 297 Chanting, in wild notes Recurrent like the moan of outshut winds. **1876** MRS. WHITNEY *Sights & Ins.* vi. 58 Where nothing is small or far-away, and nothing—even the glory—close and out-shutting.

ˈoutshut, var. OUTSHOT *sb.* 1.

1624 in S. O. Addy *Gloss. Words Sheffield* (1888) 167 Richard Staniforth 2 out shutts in lease, iiijs. **1637** *Ibid.*, Sisley Bagshaw widow holdeth at will the chiefe dwelling house belonging to Aslopp Farme with the barnes and out shuts one parcell of the demesnes by the yearly rent of £6. 8s. 4d. **1943** H. J. MASSINGHAM *Men of Earth* iii. 26 A limestone village.. with stone-slats to the roofs and even the byres, outshuts and barns. **1945** —— *Wisdom of Fields* v. 94 We were in his outshut, and I sat, half-frozen and half-choked by the fog, watching him [*sc.* a basketer].

outside (aʊtˈsaɪd, ˈaʊtsaɪd), *sb.*, *adv.*, and *prep.* [f. OUT *a.*, OUT- 3 + SIDE *sb.*; cf. INSIDE.

As to the varying stress, see INSIDE.]

A. *sb.*

1. a. That side of anything which is without, or farther from the interior; the external surface.

1505 *Charter relat. to St. George's Chapel, Windsor* in *Rel. Ant.* II. 116 The fanes on the outsides of the quere, and the creasts, corses, beasts above on the outsides of Maister John Shornes Chappell. **1526** TINDALE *Matt.* xxiii. 26 Clense fyrst that which is within the cuppe and the platter, that the outsyde maye also be clene [in *v.* 25 'vtter side']. **1587** GOLDING *De Mornay* vi. 64 The spirit of the Lord houered vpon the outside of the deepe. **1615** G. SANDYS *Trav.* 121 On each foot he hath five fingers, 3 on the outside, and two on the inside. **1657** R. LIGON *Barbadoes* (1673) 61 They have climbed six foot high upon the outside of a wall, come in at a window, down on the inside, .. and away again. **1705** ADDISON *Italy* 13 The Duke of Doria's Palace has the best Outside of any in Genoa. **1809** MALKIN *Gil Blas* I. v. ¶9 He .. showed the goddess of my devotions the outside of the door. **1893** *Bookman* June 79/1 Years of service in the Library had made him familiar with the outsides of books, but very little with their contents.

b. The outer part or parts of anything, as distinguished from the interior.

1598 BARRET *Theor. Warres* 21 The most place of honour is the left and right outsides [of a line of soldiers]. **1655** E. TERRY *Voy. E. Ind.* 282 They usually live in the skirts or out sides of great Cities, or Townes. **1799** tr. *H. Meister's Lett. Eng.* 11 *note*, This absurd custom of riding on the outside of a coach.

c. *Fencing.* (See INSIDE *sb.* 1 b, quot. 1863.)

2. a. The outer surface considered as that which is seen and presented to observation; the external person as distinguished from the mind or spirit; outward aspect or appearance as opposed to inner nature.

1592 DAVIES *Immort. Soul* II. xii. (1714) 30 Sense Outsides knows, the Soul thro' all things sees. **1596** SHAKS. *Merch. V.* I. iii. 104 O what a goodlie outside falsehood hath. **1711** STEELE *Spect.* No. 33 ¶1 She is no other than Nature made her, a very beautiful Outside. **1793** BURKE *Let. to Windham* Corr. 1844 IV. 201 Since I wrote last, the outside of affairs is a good deal mended. **1859** GEO. ELIOT *A. Bede* v, You'll never persuade me that I can't tell what men are by their outsides.

†**b.** Outer garments; clothes. *Obs.*

1614 B. JONSON *Barth. Fair* II. i, I have seen as fine outsides as either of yours, bring lousy linings to the brokers. *a* **1625** FLETCHER *Love's Cure* III. ii, My Lord has sent me outsides, But.. the colours are too sad.

†**c.** Something worn on the outside which conceals the real features; a mask, a visor; an effigy. *Obs.*

a **1656** BP. HALL *Rem. Wks.* (1660) 122, I speak not for those that are meer outsides and visors of Christianity. **1676** HOBBES *Iliad* VIII. 210 Disgrace of Greece, meer outsides, where are now Your Brags?

d. That which is merely external; outward form as opposed to substance; an externality.

1660 tr. *Amyraldus' Treat. conc. Relig.* III. vi. 416 A Religion which seem'd to consist wholly in out-side. **1694** PENN *Rise & Prog. Quakers* i. 16 Christians degenerated a-pace into outsides, as Days and Meats, and divers other Ceremonies. **1742** YOUNG *Nt. Th.* viii. 148 A region of outsides! a land of shadows! **1886** PATER *Imag. Portraits* iii. (1887) 113 A penurious young poet, who.. would have grasped so eagerly.. at the elegant outsides of life.

3. a. The position or locality close to the outer side or surface of anything.

1503 *Plumpton Lett.* 180, I lay at outside ij dayes or I cold have it. **1535** COVERDALE *Ezek.* xl. 5 There was a wall on the outsyde rounde aboute the house. *a* **1578** LINDESAY (Pitscottie) *Chron. Scot.* (S.T.S.) I. 301 [He] chapit him be the ost ane lyttill, and at ane outsyde watchit him. **1611** BIBLE *Judg.* vii. 19 So Gideon and the hundred men.. came vnto the outside of the campe. *a* **1677** *Lovers Quarrel* xlviii. in Child *Ballads* (1886) IV. cix. B. 448/1 Will you walk with me to an out-side, Two or three words to talk with me? **1699** BENTLEY *Phal.* 186 An Altar.. which is yet standing on the out-side of the Town. **1784** R. BAGE *Barham Downs* II. 167 It waits my Lord's appearance on the outside the iron pales. **1844** DICKENS *Mart. Chuz.* xxxvi, Can I open the door from the outside, I wonder?

b. In isolated regions of Northern Canada and Alaska: the world outside these regions, esp. as an area of settlement and civilization.

1827 in *Beaver* (Winnipeg) (1927) Dec. 141 He was to bring in the last letters from outside which we could expect until next spring. **1898** *Yukon Midnight Sun* (Dawson, Yukon Territory) 11 June 5/2 Many of these are men who have just arrived from the outside. **1904** J. LYNCH *Three Yrs. Klondike* 54 On September 22 the last boat left for the 'outside' *viâ* the Lakes and Skagway. **1941** G. DE M. PONCINS *Kabloona* 13 Only the Arctic existed for them; and everything that lay below the Mackenzie River, was to them the remote, the virtually non-existent 'Outside'. **1968** R. M. PATTERSON *Finlay's River* 108 From there the survey party travelled with the horses, passing over the Wolverines in the first snow, headed for Fort St. James and 'the outside'. **1972** *Globe & Mail* (Toronto) 5 Dec. 35/1 He believes the story of Old Crow is valuable because it also shows how little people in The Outside—the rest of Canada in Yukon language—understand of the situation inside the territory.

c. *Austral.* The unsettled areas in the interior or bush.

1888 'R. BOLDREWOOD' *Robbery under Arms* I. vii. 95 Dick Dawson came in from outside, and he said things are shocking bad; all the frontage bare already, and the water drying up. **1949** *Geogr. Mag.* Feb. 371 Rural life offers you such terms as *backblocks*, *outback* and *outside*, meaning remote, inland country. **1959** BAKER *Drum* 132 *Outside*, unsettled districts in the interior or bush.

d. *slang.* The world out of prison; also the world out of the Army, civilian life.

1903 'J. FLYNT' *Rise of R. Clowd* ii. 80 A boy in a Reform School with a 'plant' on the 'outside' takes a high place among his companions. **1919** D. G. ROWSE *Doughboy Dope* 9 A is the Army at that stage of your young life when you were on what the Army calls 'the outside'. **1933** *Amer. Speech* VIII. III. 26/2 'Whitey', who escaped three times from solitary confinement clear to the outside, was an acknowledged eel. **1965** C. D. B. BRYAN *P. S. Wilkinson* 369, I never asked.. what you did on the outside. **1972** C. DRUMMOND *Death at Bar* ii. 56 Kath hasn't been having it so good, what with a couple of worthless sons who haven't the sense to keep on the outside.

e. In Surfing: see quots.

1963 *Surfing Yearbk.* 42/2 *Outside*, surfing area past the breaking surf. **1963** *Pix* 28 Sept. 62/3 *Outside*, the surfing area outside the breaking wave.

4. The outmost limit; the fullest or highest degree or quantity. Chiefly in phr. *at the outside*, at the utmost, farthest, longest, or most. *colloq.*

1707 MORTIMER *Husb.* IV. v. 78 Two hundred Load upon an Acre, which they reckon the out-side of what is to be laid. **1852** *Lit. Gaz.* Jan. 70/2 In a few weeks, at the outside, we may expect to see [etc.]. **1863** FR. A. KEMBLE *Resid. Georgia* 39 This woman is young, I suppose at the outside not thirty. **1885** *Law Times Rep.* LIII. 60/2 A red light.. distant a quarter of a mile at the outside.

5. Anything situated on or forming the outer side, edge, or border: *spec.* (*pl.*), the outermost sheets, more or less damaged, of a ream of paper.

1615 W. LAWSON *Country Housew. Gard.* (1626) 9 Little Orchards, or few trees, being (in a manner) all out-sides, are so blasted and dangered. **1851** MAYHEW *Lond. Labour* I. 267/2 The half-quires.. contain, generally, 10 sheets; if the paper, however, be of superior quality, only 8 sheets. In the paper-warehouses it is known as 'outsides', with no more than 10 sheets to the half-quire. **1858** SIMMONDS *Dict. Trade*, *Outsides*, the exterior sheets of a ream of printing or writing paper; spoiled sheets.

6. a. Short for *outside passenger* on a conveyance.

1789 J. WOODFORDE *Diary* 13 June (1927) III. 114 For the remaining part of our fare paid.. for 1 outside 12/0. *a* **1800** in *Norfolk Fair* (1970) Nov. 31/7 This Coach from Norwich to London by Newmarket every Day Convey 8 Insides.. and 6 Outsides in the most Pleasant And Agreeable Stile. **1804** in *Spirit Pub. Jrnls.* VIII. 324 With the outsides he keeps no measures, insisting upon five per cent. on all their baggage. **1824** MISS MITFORD *Village* Ser. I. (1863) 38 The outsides, and the horses, and the coachman, seemed reduced to a torpid quietness. **1842** SYD. SMITH *Let. Locking in on Railw.* Wks. 1859 II. 322/2 When first mail coaches began to travel twelve miles an hour, the outsides.. were never tied to the roof. **1902** *Chambers's Jrnl.* Nov. 715/1 The 'George' at Grantham is still.. one of the best inns in England, as it was when these two prudent 'outsides' left the Yorkshire coach and 'turned in' there. **1914** 'I. HAY' *Lighter Side School Life* vi. 152 He was called at half-past two.. and by three o'clock was off as an 'outside' upon the Tally-Ho Coach.

b. = OUTSIDER 2.

1898 [see BEHIND *sb.* 2 b]. **1899** *Captain* II. 186/1, I headed out to the right, [and] saw our outside get it. **1906** *Field* 13 Oct. 610/1 Their outsides showed so crude a conception of passing that [etc.]. **1927** *Observer* 21 Aug. 18/3 The team are young and play attractive football, with a clever set of outsides who combine well. **1963** *Times* 23 Feb. 3/1 Although their forwards were playing such a solid game the Westminster outsides were too slow to beat their opposite numbers.

7. In phr. *outside in* (usually with *turn*): So that the outer side becomes the inner; = inside out.

1771 SMOLLETT *Humph. Clinker* 23 Apr., The Circus.. looks like Vespasian's amphitheatre turned outside in. **1825** J. NEAL *Bro. Jonathan* II. 166 Preaching.. as if the great world were to be turned.. inside out, or outside in. **1863** KINGSLEY *Water Bab.* i. 18 He did not know that a keeper is only a poacher turned outside in, and a poacher a keeper turned inside out.

8. Short for *outside paddle-wheel* on a river steamboat.

1876 'MARK TWAIN' *Tom Sawyer* 29 Come ahead on the stabboard! Stop her! Let your outside turn over slow. **1894** —— in *Century Mag.* May 19 Set her back on de outside... Come ahead on de inside.

B. *adj.* **1.** That is on, or belongs to, the outer side, surface, edge, or boundary.

outside callipers, a pair of callipers for measuring the outside diameter of a body; ***outside edge*** (*Skating*): see EDGE *sb.* 7 b; ***outside finish***, requisites for completing the exterior of a wooden building (Webster 1892); ***outside (jaunting) car***: see also JAUNTING-CAR; ***outside passenger***, one who travels on the outside of a conveyance.

1634 SIR T. HERBERT *Trav.* 184 [The] out-side beauty [of the durian is] no way equall to the inside goodnesse and vertues. **1703** MOXON *Mech. Exerc.* 244 Outside and inside Lathing for Plastring. **1733** TULL *Horse-hoeing Husb.* xi. 129 The Outside Rows of Wheat, from which the Earth is Hoed off, before or in the Beginning of Winter. **1748** *Anson's Voy.* II. iv. 158 They found her wales and outside planks extremely defective. *c* **1810** W. HICKEY *Mem.* (1960) 326 One of the stage-coaches, with a number of outside passengers.. frightened our horse. **1815** *Chron.* in *Ann. Reg.* 69 A Sailor, who was an outside passenger. **1824** J. JOHNSON *Typogr.* II. 560 Twenty quires to the ream, of which the two outside quires are called corded or cassie. **1829** [see JAUNTING-CAR]. **1849** W. ALLINGHAM *Diary* 30 June (1907) 49 Our party took leave and mounted a back outside-car in Gloucester Street. **1849** DICKENS *Dav. Copp.* (1850) v. 51 The story of my supposed appetite getting wind among the outside passengers, they were merry upon it. **1854** RONALDS & RICHARDSON *Chem. Technol.* I. 249 The outside walls are built hollow, having an air-vent 3 inches wide. **1867** SMYTH *Sailor's Word-bk.*, *Outside Muster-paper*, a paper with the outer part blank, but the inner portion ruled and headed; supplied.. to form the cover of ships' books. **1874** KNIGHT *Dict. Mech.* 429/2 Inside and outside calipers. **1874** 'G. RAMSAY' *Thomas Grant* i. 23 They drove up on an outside car to the quays. **1887** *Spectator* 25 June 866/1 On his arrival in Dublin, he was profoundly impressed by the Irish outside-car.

2. a. Situated, or having its origin or operation, without; that resides without some place or area; that works out of the house, or out of a workshop or factory.

In some uses indistinguishable from sense 3.

1841 *Penny Cycl.* XIX. 260/1 Some engines have been recently introduced.. in which an attempt is made to combine the advantages of inside and outside bearings. **1858** HAWTHORNE *Fr. & It. Jrnls.* II. 38 Enough to have an outside perception of his degree and kind of merit. **1862** MRS. CARLYLE *Lett.* III. 101 Mine [room] is quiet as the grave from outside noises. **1871** *Routledge's Ev. Boy's Ann.* Dec. 28 Outside-cylinder engines are those in which the cylinders are placed outside the smoke-box. **1900** *Fabian News* X. 28/1 'Outside' work means work done entirely in the home by an 'outside' worker. *a* **1904** *Mod.* Engage an outside porter to wheel your luggage from one station to the other. A window affording no view of the outside world. *a* **1902** S. BUTLER *Way of all Flesh* (1903) lxxx. 366 Days before those in which he had begun to bruise himself against the great outside world. **1926** GALSWORTHY *Silver Spoon* I. iii. 22 Our trade-unionists despise the outside world. They've never seen it. **1947** E. F. RUSSELL in Aldiss & Harrison *Decade 1940s* (1975) 168 He.. looked out through the dome... The outside world slumbered. **1969** *Times* 9 Jan. 4/5 They [*sc.* the Hutterites].. live in almost complete isolation from their neighbours and the outside world. **1976** *Listener* 29 July 104/2 All of us [blacks] will want to see blacks on television. The outside world will be astonished at the talent we have. **1976** *Norwich Mercury* 19 Nov. 2 Mr Sims finished his comments with a reference to the outside world's contact with the school—the wide range of evening classes available, [etc.].

b. *Austral.* Situated without the line of settlement; situated in the bush.

1881 A. C. GRANT *Bush-Life in Queensld.* I. xi. 162 The cattle-buyer, who had a large experience on the out-side country. **1885** MRS. C. PRAED *Head-Station* II. ix. 178 I'm to have charge of one of the outside sheep stations, at what seems to me a liberal salary.

c. *spec.* of a water closet: situated outside the house, building, etc.

1939 M. SPRING RICE *Working-Class Wives* iv. 73 Mrs. P. of Glasgow... Under the drawbacks of her house she says 'Outside lavatory, (used by six families.) Public house at close which is objectionable [etc.].' **1943** *Our Towns* (Women's Group on Public Welfare) iii. 88 The outside closets are generally much less well kept than the inside ones... The majority of houses have outside W.C.'s only. **1959** B. J. FARMER *Murder Next Year* ii. 7 The keys of the house had been left in the outside w.c. **1960** P. HASTINGS *Sandals for my Feet* I. i. 13 I'm tired of.. the smell of damp and that filthy outside loo. **1974** P. HIGHSMITH *Ripley's Game* ii. 11 The little brick structure, formerly an outside toilet, that served as a tool shed.

3. a. Not included in or belonging to the place, establishment, institution, or society in question.

1881 *Daily News* 13 Sept. 5/1 Outside opinion has evidently had its influence on the City Fathers. **1884** *Manch. Exam* 14 May 5/5 The outside public appear disposed to take Mr. C—at his own valuation. **1886** in *Pall Mall G.* 7 Aug. 1/2 In matters relating to its exhibitions the Royal Academy stands on the same footing with regard to 'outside' artists, as the Society of British Artists, the Institutes, and other private societies holding open exhibitions. **1894** *Westm. Gaz.* 23 Apr. 6/1 More destructive to the business of 'outside' brokers than the action of the Stock Exchange in depriving them of the 'tape'.

b. In Northern Canada and Alaska: belonging to or obtained from another part of the world, esp. from the settled or urbanized parts.

1896 C. WHITNEY *On Snow-Shoes to Barren Grounds* 40 Gairdner had annoyed me a great deal, and no doubt we had worried him not a little, breaking in upon the even and lethargic tenor of his monotonous life with our 'out-side' (as the great world is called by the denizens of this lone land) hustling ways. **1904** J. LYNCH *Three Yrs. Klondike* 141 The leader is always a small 'outside' dog, usually of the Scotch collie breed. **1922** H. FOOTNER *Huntress* 189 No bannock and sow-belly; no sir! Real raised outside bread and genuine cow-butter from the mission. **1958** P. BERTON *Klondike Fever* ix. 307 Expense!.. Don't show your ignorance by using that cheap Outside word. **1977** *Globe & Mail* (Toronto) 8 Jan. 11/7 By special arrangement, one outside reporter will attend the dance.

†**4.** That has only an outside, or external appearance, without internal reality or substance; having empty show; superficial. *Obs.*

1643 MILTON *Divorce* I. vi, Where love cannot be, there can be left of wedlock nothing, but the empty husk of an outside matrimony. **1679** PRANCE *Addit. Narr. Pop. Plot* 12

Used by the Professors of that out-side Religion. **1728** POPE *Dunc.* I. 135 The rest [books] on Out-side merit but presume, Or serve..to fill a room.

5. Reaching the utmost limit; utmost, farthest, greatest, extreme.

1857 TROLLOPE *Barchester T.* i. 2 The outside period during which breath could be supported within the body of the dying man. **1893** MUNDELLA in *Daily News* 21 Feb. 3/3, I believe..I have given you the very outside prices that are being paid.

6. Special collocations: **outside broadcast** (see quot. 1941); **outside broadcaster,** (*a*) one who makes or supervises an outside broadcast; (*b*) an outside contributor to broadcasting; **outside broadcasting**, the action of making an outside broadcast; **outside cabin**, a cabin with a window or porthole on the side of the ship; **outside chance**, a very unlikely chance; **outside forward**, in association football and hockey, either of the two players, called the outside left or right (see below), of the forward line; **outside half** = *fly-half* (FLY *sb.*² 8); **outside interest**, an interest not directly or necessarily connected with one's everyday life or interests; **outside job** *slang*, a crime committed in a house, etc., by a person not connected or associated with the household or building concerned; **outside leaf**, an outer leaf on a vegetable, esp. cabbage; **outside left, right**, in association football and hockey, a player playing on the extreme left or right of the forward line; **outside line**, a telephonic connection with an external exchange (cf. LINE *sb.*² 1 e); **outside man** *U.S. slang*, one involved in any of various special roles in a confidence trick or robbery; **outside right** (see *outside left* above).

1927 *B.B.C. Handbk. 1928* 274 *Outside broadcast*, a broadcast item taking place at some point other than the studio. **1937** *Discovery* Nov. 331/1 Outside broadcasts of entertainments and public events can be readily arranged. **1941** *B.B.C. Gloss. Broadcasting Terms* 22 *Outside broadcast* (*abbrev.* O.B.), programme originating elsewhere than in the studio of a broadcasting organization; specifically broadcast description of an event in progress. **1953** *News Chron.* 2 June 3/5 It is a long way from 1937, when B.B.C television mounted its first outside broadcast from Hyde Park Corner on another Coronation day. **1972** I. HAMILTON *Thrill Machine* xv. 63 He had brought the outside broadcast truck. **1971** R. LEWIS *Error of Judgment* i. 10 The technicians were already bundling out of the van, unloading..mysterious television equipment. Outside broadcasters. **1972** P. BLACK *Biggest Aspidistra* III. ii. 164 Gilbert Harding..began on the entertainment side of radio as an outside broadcaster. **1929** *Melody Maker* Apr. 363/2 Outside broadcasting is now not so much worth your while. **1937** *Discovery* Feb. 43/2 Much of the popularity of television will be linked up with the development of outside broadcasting. **1972** P. BLACK *Biggest Aspidistra* I. iii. 27 In the early days the bands played mostly in clubs and hotels, and so were part of outside broadcasting. **1963** Outside cabin [see INSIDE *adj.* a]. **1966** *Guardian* 29 Oct. 5/5 Two-berth outside cabins with private shower and w.c. **1971** 'A. GARVE' *Late Bill Smith* i. 33 The Greek motor vessel *Circe* specially built as a luxury yacht for a limited number of privileged passengers; fully air-conditioned and stabilised; swimming pool and two bars; all outside cabins. **1909** *Daily Chron.* 11 Jan. 4/6 The chance that the right marriage of poetry and music should come is an outside one. **1928** R. A. KNOX *Footsteps at Lock* xiv. 135 By an outside chance you might find it lying about somewhere. **1930** A. P. HERBERT *Water Gipsies* xx. 300 Here she was, risking everything..going all out for an outside chance. **1973** 'D. RUTHERFORD' *Kick Start* viii. 169 He had an outside chance of lifting the moon stones from under Hadim's nose. **1897** *Encycl. Sport* I. 517/1 (*Hockey*) Of the two outside forwards, he on the right has much the easier position in which to play. **1898** J. GOODALL *Assoc. Football* 18, I would not tell the outside forward that it is his duty to centre the ball. **1935** *Encycl. Sports* 289/1 (*Association Football*) The throw-in is usually done by a half-back or by an outside forward. **1949** *Rugby League Football* ('Know the Game' Series) 8 Stand off half back or outside half. **1969** *Programme* (Llanelli *v.* Swansea 1 Apr.) 6 Gwyn Ashby. Maswr. Outside-half. **1971** *Guardian* 22 Feb. 16/5 Dick Cowman..gave a superb exhibition of outside-half play. **1860** J. W. PALMER tr. *Michelet's Love* IV. vii. 235 It is the fault of the labor, the business, the outside interests and the cases with which I have been occupied. **1925** R. HALL *Saturday Life* xxix. 301 Could two deeply-loving and devoted people tolerate outside interests? **1974** R. RENDELL *Face of Trespass* ii. 26 What you need..is some outside interest, something to take you out of yourself. **1925** A. CHRISTIE *Secret of Chimneys* xii. 120 Either he was killed by someone in the house, and that someone unlatched the window after I had gone to make it look like an outside job..or else..I'm lying. **1928** WODEHOUSE *Money for Nothing* v. 104 It's got to look like an outside job. **1931** A. CHRISTIE *Sittaford Mystery* xi. 92 The police are quite certain that this is not what they call an 'outside job'—I mean, it wasn't a burglar. The broken open window was faked. **1972** Outside job [see *inside job* s.v. INSIDE *a.* e]. **1739** E. SMITH *Compl. Housewife* (ed. 9) 37 Take a well-shap'd Cabbage, peel off some of the out-side leaves. **1747** H. GLASSE *Art of Cookery* iv. 57 Take a fine White-heart Cabbage..half boil it..take great Care not to break off any of the the outside Leaves. **1861** MRS. BEETON *Bk. Househ. Managem.* 560 *Boiled cabbage*... Pick off all the dead outside leaves. **1960** *Good Housek. Cookery Bk.* (rev. ed.) 217/1 Wash the chicory and remove the outside leaves. *Ibid.* 218/1 *Leeks*... Remove the coarse outside leaves. **1900** *Football Who's Who* 134 Cassidy, Joseph, Manchester City (outside left). **1905** GIBSON & PICKFORD *Assoc. Football* I. 161 Every one knows Alec Smith. He's the outside left of the Rangers. **1960** B. LIDDELL *My Soccer Story* xvi. 102 To get down to my final choice at outside-left, I vote for Peter McParland, an unorthodox type of winger with a wonderful turn of speed. **1965** *Men's Hockey* ('Know the Game' Series) (rev. ed.) 24/2 The outside right when about to pass to his left will find it more convenient to have the ball a little in front of his left foot. The outside left, however, must make a half turn to the right when passing right [etc.]. **1975** *Liverpool Echo* (Football ed.) 1 Feb. 3/1 There seems to have been some debate as to who was the Liverpool outside left before Billy Liddell. **1944** Outside line [see LINE *sb.*² 1 e]. **1962** E. S. GARDNER *Case of Blonde Bonanza* (1967) x. 117 You can't get an outside line on these phones unless they connect you. **1972** D. BLOODWORTH *Any Number can Play* xx. 203 Ivansong seized the telephone (which..was automatically switched to an outside line). **1926** J. BLACK *You can't Win* ix. 111 He..made his living serving as 'target' or outside man, for the yegg mobs that preyed on country banks. **1937** *N.Y. Times* 22 Dec. 22 *Outside man*, a spy under a cover, but not masquerading as an employe of a plant. **1938** F. D. SHARPE *Sharpe of Flying Squad* xiv. 151 She was acting as look out or 'outside man' for two expert safe breakers. **1947** *Amer. Speech* XXII. 169/1 *Outside-man*, the member of a *shell-mob* who locates promising suckers on the lot, steers them to the game, and assists in the play. **1890** C. W. ALCOCK *Football: Assoc. Game* 48 The outside-right should not be more than eight or ten yards beyond him. **1974** *Sunday Mail* 14 Apr. 39/1 Both goals..were scored by the outside rights.

C. *adv.* (Short for *on* or *to the outside*.)

1. a. Of position: On the outside of certain limits; externally; out in the open air; in the open sea beyond a harbour; not within some body, association, or community that may be in question.

1813 T. D. BROUGHTON *Lett. fr. Mahr. C.* (1892) 55 They could..see every thing that took place outside. **1845** M. PATTISON *Ess.* (1889) I. 17 The body..posted themselves, fully armed, outside, under the portico. **1848** DICKENS *Dombey* iii, It was as blank a house inside as outside. **1865** E. LUCAS in *Essays* Ser. I. 309 While the world outside was being opposed, convinced [etc.]. **1866** WHITTIER *Maids of Attitash* 133 He better sees who stands outside Than they who in procession ride. **1872** MARK TWAIN *Innoc. Abr.* ii. 20 'Outside'..there was a tremendous sea on.

b. In Northern Canada and Alaska: in the settled or urbanized areas outside these regions; abroad.

1898 F. RUSSELL *Explor. Far North* 80 To 'go in', by the way, is to descend the Athabasca; to return to civilization is to 'go outside'. **1923** F. WALDO *Down Mackenzie through Gt. Lone Land* 246, I had thought that life beyond the 65th parallel or so was life beyond the pale; but I was now to learn that the Arctic Circle is the inner circle, and the real outsider is—of course—the one who lives 'Outside'. **1945** R. W. SERVICE *Ploughman of Moon* 321 If I had been Outside it would have taken me five years to save a thousand dollars. **1955** *Whitehorse* (Yukon Territory) *Star* 24 Feb. 2/1 One of the outstanding characteristics of the Yukon is the general indifference to what is going on Outside. **1970** *Islander* (Victoria, B.C.) 1 Nov. 13/3 Sam Otto spent 14 years in the Barren Lands and Northwest Territories, without going outside once.

c. *Austral.* In the interior or bush. *rare.*

1911 C. E. W. BEAN *'Dreadnought' of Darling* xxxv. 317 But, be the 'inside' country never so tame and densely populated, there will always be a huge stretch of country 'outside' which cannot by any known means be closely settled.

d. *slang.* Out of prison; in civilian life.

1919 W. LANG *Sea-Lawyer's Log* ix. 108 You *got* to 'ave some bloody religion in the Navy. Now, wot church did you go to outside? **1937** *Research Stud.* (Washington State Coll., Pullman) V. 19 A boy entering this institution [*sc.* a reformatory] learns more bad habits than he would ever think of learning out side. **1961** PARTRIDGE *Dict. Slang* Suppl. 1210/1, I don't care what you were 'outside'; you're in the Andrew now, so don't forget it, or you'll be in the rattle.

e. In Surfing: see quots.

1962 T. MASTERS *Surfing made Easy* 65 *Outside*, out past the breaking waves, or at the furthest break. **1962** *Austral. Women's Weekly* 24 Oct. (Suppl.) 3/3 *Outside* or *out the back*, a long way out at sea, beyond the first line of breakers.

2. Of motion or direction: To the exterior.

1889 'R. BOLDREWOOD' *Robbery under Arms* xxiv, The men and women were ordered to come outside. *Mod.* Some of the party stepped outside to get a better view of the lightning.

3. outside of, *prep. phr.* (cf. OUT OF *prep. phr.*).

a. Without the walls, limits, or bounds of; not within; exterior to; also, To the exterior of, outward from.

outside of a horse (*colloq.*) on horseback; *to get outside of* (*slang*), (*a*) to swallow (so *to be outside of*); (*b*) *U.S.* to master or understand (Farmer *Americanisms* 1889).

1839–40 I. TAYLOR *Anc. Chr.* (1842) II. vii. 303 The sepulchre lay outside of the ancient city. **1869** *Galaxy* June 831 Don't let's get outside of more'n a bottle apiece, and that plain whiskey. **1878** O. W. HOLMES *Motley* 69 His objects of interest outside of his special work. **1886** [see GET *v.* 45]. **1889** 'R. BOLDREWOOD' *Robbery under Arms* xv, He looked better outside of a horse than on his own legs. **1890** D. ARROWSMITH in *Big Game N. Amer.* 521 My wife said she knew, from his [a racoon's] full stomach and his sneaking look, that he was outside of her pet turkey. **1915** J. WEBSTER *Dear Enemy* 174 He likes to dine outside of the family vault. **1943** G. GREENE *Ministry of Fear* I. ii. 29 Murderers..are very, very seldom..gentlemen. Outside of story-books. **1975** *Nature* 20 Mar. p. xx (Advt.), These books are..distributed outside of the U.S.A. and Canada by Academic Press. **1976** *Gramophone* Nov. 903/2, I was able to spend some time in their CD-4 four-channel disc cutting room—the most important such facility outside of Japan.

b. *colloq.* (orig. *U.S.*) Beyond the number or body of, with the exception of.

1859 A. L. ELWYN *Gloss. Supposed Americanisms* 82 *Outside*, this word is frequently used by writers in newspapers in a sense not known to the language. In a *Ledger* of a late date, there is a phrase..'*outside* of the Secretary of War', for 'no one but that official'. **1889** FARMER *Americanisms* s.v., Outside of the tradesmen there was no one at the meeting. **1890** *Century Mag.* 127/2, I do not often see anybody outside of my servants, being not at all given to visiting. **1913** R. FRY *Let.* 5 Apr. (1972) II. 367 I'm very much interested by what you said about the need of some big belief outside of art. **1968** *Listener* 22 Aug. 234/1 The only power we have is to expel a union for corruption or for following a communist or a fascist policy. Outside of that the unions pretty much take care of their own business. **1972** *New York* 8 May 62/2 Outside of a slightly annoying tendency to call all female customers 'Hon', everything about Mr. Blume inspires confidence.

D. *prep.* (Shortened from *outside of.*)

(*Without-side the door* is used, *c* 1760, by Mrs. F. Sheridan *Sidney Biddulph* II. 298, III. 221.)

1. a. Outside of; on the outer side of; external to. ***outside the ropes*** (*slang*), without knowledge of a matter; in the position of an outsider.

1826 J. H. NEWMAN *Lett.* (1891) I. 140 As I came outside the Southampton coach to Oxford, I felt as if I could have rooted up St. Mary's spire. **1846** *Penny Cycl.* Suppl. II. 670/1 [Engines] in which the cylinders are fixed outside the framing. **1852** GLADSTONE *Glean.* (1879) IV. 151 All countries outside the Roman border. **1861** LEVER *One of Them* lii, Until I came to understand the thing, I was always 'outside the ropes'. **1878** HUXLEY *Physiogr.* 180 The cause of the tides is to be found outside our earth.

b. Beyond the limits of (any domain of action or thought, any subject or matter).

1852 GLADSTONE *Glean.* (1879) IV. 210 Those services, which lie outside the common routine. **1877** L. TOLLEMACHE in *Fortn. Rev.* Dec. 848 Natural forces are in themselves neither moral nor immoral, but outside morality. **1894** J. T. FOWLER *Adamnan* Introd. 67 Any description of them would be outside the purpose of the present work.

c. Beyond, in addition to, besides, except. *dial.*

1868 YATES *Rock Ahead* I. ii, 'Outside them two, and the Squire in his grave..nobody..knows the rights of the story.'

2. Of motion or direction: To the outer side of, to the exterior of, to what lies without or beyond.

1856 KANE *Arct. Expl.* I. xxix. 384 [They] flung themselves outside the skin between us. **1885** *Law Rep.* 29 Chanc. Div. 451 The Court cannot go outside the pleadings in the present action. **1896** *Daily News* 29 Sept. 6/2 'Will you be so kind as to go outside the door and shut it?'

3. *Comb.* **outsideman**, a man who does work outside.

1851 MAYHEW *Lond. Labour* (1861) II. 447/1 The outsideman, whose business it is to attend to the pipe, which reaches from the cesspool..to the gullyhole.

out'sided, *a. rare.* [f. prec. sb. + -ED².] Having (such and such) an outside or surface.

1674 N. FAIRFAX *Bulk & Selv.* 146 There are not two bodies..so smoothly outsided, but that being clapt together, would leave as many leastings of room between them, as those they touch at.

out'sidedness. [f. prec. + -NESS.]

a. The quality of having an outside or surface. **b.** Outsideness, externality.

1854 J. SCOFFERN in *Orr's Circ. Sc., Chem.* II. 224 Dependent on the depth of the basket—on the amount of *outsidedness*, to use an allowable expression, possessed by the apparatus. **1897** *Contemp. Rev.* Oct. 536 A Celt standing outside his social world, would doubtless exaggerate whatever he had happened to carry with him into his outsidedness.

'outside-ˌinside, *a. rare.* [f. OUTSIDE *a.* + INSIDE *a.*] Of or pertaining to both the outside and the inside.

1930 R. GRAVES *Ten Poems More* 11 Neat outside-inside, neat below-above Hermaphrodising love. **1951** M. MCLUHAN *Mech. Bride* (1967) 35/2 It can be picture-framed by a Pond's ad for the 'special outside-inside face treatment'.

†**'outˌsidely,** *adv. Obs. rare*⁻¹. [f. OUTSIDE *a.* + -LY².] Externally.

1803 W. TAYLOR in Robberds *Mem.* I. 457 You say something outsidely rude and insidely civil about its being my choice to edit.

out'sideness. [f. OUTSIDE *a.* + -NESS.] The quality of being outside; externality, externalism.

1647 TRAPP *Comm. Matt.* vi. 16 Their outsideness is an utter abomination. —— *Comm. Rev.* xvii. 4 To note her hypocrisie and outsidenesse, gold without, copper within. **1850** BUSHNELL *God in Christ* 267 Our modern..piety has an air of lightness and outsideness rather as if it were wholly of ourselves, not a life of God in the Soul. **1883** *Fortn. Rev.* 1 Mar. 336 His evident outsideness towards it.

outsider (aʊt'saɪdə(r)). [f. OUTSIDE *sb.* + -ER¹.]

1. a. One who is outside any enclosure, barrier, or boundary, material or figurative; *esp.* one who is outside of or does not belong to a specified company, set, or party, a non-member; hence, one unconnected or unacquainted with a matter, uninitiated into a profession or body having special knowledge, or the like. Also *attrib.*

1800 JANE AUSTEN *Lett.* (1884) I. 245 There was a whist and a casino table, and six outsiders. **1833** FONBLANQUE *Eng. Under 7 Administ.* (1837) II. 354 Those he cannot entertain, the outsiders, ' without a home to cover them'. **1844** in Marsh *Eng. Lang.* (1860) 274 [At the Baltimore convention of 1844,..a prominent member energetically protested against all interference with the business of the meeting by] outsiders. [The word, if not absolutely new, was at least new to most of those who read the proceedings..and it was now for the first time employed in a serious way.] **1847** *Lit. Gaz.* July 499/1 All Irish fights ought to be left, by outsiders who value their own safety, to be fought out by the combatants. **1852** DICKENS *Bleak Ho.* li, He is only an outsider, and is not in the mysteries. *a* **1860** *Lowell Jrnl.* (Bartlett), A large number of outsiders have gone to the free-soil convention at Buffalo. **1886** J. K. JEROME *Idle Thoughts* 31 Outsiders, you know, often see most of the game. **1897** J. MCCARTHY *Gladstone's Life* xxvii. 90/2 The outsider class..quarreled with Mr. Gladstone because he was always giving them a surprise. **1912** T. E. LAWRENCE *Let.* 10 Feb. (1938) 136 About the Jerablus seals:—I can't give you those, only the five outsiders: the Jerablus ones were bought [etc.]. **1935** *Amer. Speech* X. 271/2 *Outsiders*, buyers who ship special kinds of livestock to other markets. **1944** F. BROWN in B. W. Aldiss *Introd. SF* (1964) 69 No one knew who the Outsiders were..or from what far galaxy they came. **1958** *Amer. Speech* XXXIII. 167 (*Australian Cattle Lingo*) *Outsider*,..a stray. **1974** *Nat. Geographic* Jan. 114/2 The fishermen talked shyly in the presence of an outsider from upalong. (An 'outsider' is any off-islander, including even other Canadians.) **1977** *Globe & Mail* (Toronto) 5 July 8/3 So far, he says, the inquiry has been lucky enough to be seen as a unit, not as two Yukoners—one for whites and one for Indians led by an outsider.

b. *Horse-racing.* A horse not included among the 'favourites', and against which in betting long odds are laid; one not 'in the running'; also *fig.*; *transf.*, a person who fails to gain admission to the 'ring'; a person who habitually backs outsiders in a race; ***rank outsider***, (*a*) an outsider at very long odds; (*b*) a person who is considered socially inferior (cf. sense 1 c below).

1836 R. S. SURTEES *Let.* in A. Mathews *Mem. Charles Mathews* (1839) IV. ix. 185 An unfortunate outsider, called Astracan. **1836** *Spirit of Times* 5 Mar. 20/1 The Brother to Maria, the Babel colt, and Taishteer, are a shade worse, owing, no doubt, to the money laid out upon Brother to Nell Gwynne. No change amongst the outsiders. **1845** *Ibid.* 31 May 158 The 'outsiders' won 'smartly' on both races, and the staunch friends of Fashion, who have backed her 'all through', have 'got hunk' and a good deal over. **1855** J. R. PLANCHÉ *New Haymarket Spring Meeting* in *Extravaganzas* (1879) V. 1. 94 Which are the favourites, and which outsiders? **1857** G. A. LAWRENCE *Guy Livingstone* xxv, It was evident he was still the favourite, and that all others were complete 'outsiders'. **1871** R. A. PROCTOR *Light Sci.* (Ser. 1) 288 The success of a rank outsider will be described as 'a misfortune to backers'. **1874** BURNAND *My Time* xxviii. 273 As an outsider from an unknown stable may falsify all prognostications about a Derby favourite. **1890** BARRÈRE & LELAND *Dict. Slang* II. 170 *Rank outsider* (common), a vulgar fellow, a cad. From a racing term applied to a horse outside the rank. **1902** FARMER & HENLEY *Slang* V. 116/1 *Outsider*,..(racing), a person who fails to gain admission to the 'ring' from pecuniary or other causes. **1908** *Magnet* I. 1. 8/2, I ask you if you ever saw such a rank outsider in all your natural?

c. A person who is isolated from or does not 'fit' into conventional society either through choice or on account of some social, intellectual, etc., reason. (Often deprecating.) *spec.* In literary criticism: the archetypal artist or intellectual seen as a person isolated from the rest of society. Also *attrib.*

1907 'I. HAY' *Pip* x. 322 'I didn't think you ought to play [golf] with him,' said Pip coolly. 'He's an utter outsider.' **1908** *Magnet* I. 1. 7/1 'You rotten outsider!' said Bulstrode, in tones of concentrated rage. 'You're not fit to be at a decent school.' **1913** H. KEPHART *Our Southern Highlanders* xiii. 294 A bastard is a woods-colt or an outsider. **1946** S. GILBERT tr. *Camus's L'Étranger* (*title*) The Outsider. **1956** C. WILSON *Outsider* i. 14 Many great artists have none of the characteristics of the Outsider. Shakespeare, Dante, Keats were all apparently normal and socially well-adjusted. **1957** *Times Lit. Suppl.* 25 Oct. 640/1 His [*sc.* C. Wilson's] original contribution was simply the Outsider gimmick. **1958** [see DOWN AND OUT *adj. phr.*]. **1958** J. RAYMOND *England's on Anvil!* 40 Like Proust the Jew, Pope the Roman Catholic son of a linen-draper was an outsider. **1959** *Times Lit. Suppl.* 1 May 261/4 It throws light on two generations of 'outsider' philosophers grappling with their own sudden emergence into the world of letters and art. **1963** *Spectator* 4 Oct. 430/1 *The City of Dreadful Night*..is Outsider poetry. **1966** C. SWEENEY *Scurrying Bush* xiv. 201, I remember an odd fellow when I was in Nigeria. Bit of an outsider, really, but do anything with snakes.

2. In literal sense: One whose position is on the outside of some group or series; an outside man.

1857 HUGHES *Tom Brown* I. v, Here come two of the bulldogs, bursting through the outsiders [of a football scrummage]; in they go, straight to the heart of the scrummage. **1897** P. WARUNG *Tales Old Regime* 84 One day, Phillips was 'outsider' on his chain. That is to say, he was working nearest the shaft in a gallery... West was outsider in the adjacent gallery.

3. An outside jaunting-car.

1900 *Westm. Gaz.* 19 Jan. 10/2 If we are to judge by the figures set out by the Chief Commissioner of the Dublin Police in his latest report, the popularity of the 'outsider' is on the wane. In a single year the number of cars has been reduced by sixty-two.

4. *pl.* A pair of nippers with semi-tubular jaws, which can be inserted into a keyhole from the outside so as to grasp and turn the key.

1875 in KNIGHT *Dict. Mech.* **1896** *Columbus* (Ohio) *Disp.* 15 Jan. 1/8 The burglary must have been well planned. Three of the doors..were opened by means of outsiders.

Hence **out'siderdom**, **out'siderhood**, the condition or state of being an outsider (in sense 1 c, above); **out'siderish** *a.*, of the nature or character of an outsider; so **out'siderishness**; **out'siderism**, the theory or practice of being an outsider; **out'siderliness**, the quality or fact of being an outsider (in sense 1 c); **out'siderly** *a.*, characteristic of an outsider or of outsiderliness.

1956 C. WILSON *Outsider* viii. 216 He had accepted his 'Outsider-ishness', not as a symptom of some strange disease, but as a sign that his healthy soul was being suffocated in a world of trivial, shallow, corrupted fools. **1957** *Times Lit. Suppl.* 25 Oct. 640/4 That the seeds of outsiderliness are found in us all may well account for Mr. Wilson's success. **1958** *Ibid.* 28 Mar. 165/3 A final view of Mr Freund..might be that he is a sort of Colin Wilson without a theory of Outsiderdom, searching for the religious viewpoint that will include the complexities of modern science. **1958** *Listener* 26 June 1070/1 Genuine outsiderhood, as experienced by delinquents, psychotics, alcoholics, unmarried mothers, and a whole host of people who..find themselves the wrong side of the law. *Ibid.* 10 July 63/3 His 'outsiderism' made him enjoy shocking the professional scientists. **1959** *Times Lit. Suppl.* 23 Jan. 44/1 His account of that heredity is wry, humorous, and outsiderish. His Jewish ancestry has its roots in Poland and Slovakia. *Ibid.* 4 Sept. 503/3 The outsiderly novel by Henri Barbusse, *L'Enfer*, which was the starting point of Mr. Wilson's first book. **1960** *Ibid.* 8 Apr. 221/1 Poetic abstraction and 'outsiderish' philosophical terminology. **1961** *Guardian* 23 June 9/6 The jigging of today's young is their alternative to 'outsiderism'. **1961** *John o' London's* 16 Nov. 548/2 The trouble with Outsiderdom as a philosophy is the squalid assortment of fellow-travellers it attracts. **1962** *Times Lit. Suppl.* 21 Sept. 710/2 Accompanying such pieces of outsiderly narcissism is a certain amount of fashionable philosophizing. **1966** *New Statesman* 8 July 61/1 An outsiderly Old Etonian whose rebellion against the ethics of his upbringing has driven him mad.

out-sifting to **out-sigh**: see OUT-.

outsight[1] ('aʊtsaɪt). [OUT- 7. Cf. Ger. *aussicht*, Du. *uitzicht*.]

1. Sight of that which is without; perception of external things; faculty of observation or outlook.

1605 BRETON *Old Man's Lesson* D j, If a Man have not both his Insight and his Outsight, he may pay home for his blindnesse. **1863** E. FITZGERALD *Let.* in *Edin. Rev.* (1894) Oct. 383 Wiser men with keener outsight and insight. **1868** BROWNING *Ring & Bk.* I. 747 A special gift, an art of arts, More insight and more outsight and much more Will to use both of these than boast my mates.

†**2.** Prospect beyond or ahead; outlook. *Obs.*

a **1598** ROLLOCK *Lect. 1. Thess.* iii. (1606) 165 When a man ..will not followe on Gods will, except he see a faire outsight, and get great reasons wherefore he should doe this, or that..The Lord will let him followe his owne will.

†**3.** The act of looking, look. *Obs.*

1681 RYCAUT tr. *Gracian's Critick* 183 She showed a fair face, and outsight to all, but evil actions.

'outsight[2]. *Sc.* and *north. dial. Obs.* or *arch.* [Derivation uncertain: cf. INSIGHT *sb.*[2]] Movable goods or substance out of doors; also *attrib.* as ***outsight plenishing***.

a **1670** SPALDING *Troub. Chas. I* (1851) II. 417 He distroyit the haill rawis of Strathbogie. Cornefeild landis, outsicht, insicht, horss, nolt, scheip. **1773** ERSKINE *Instit.* III. viii. §18 In what is called outsight plenishing or moveables without doors, the heirship may be drawn of horses, cows, oxen; and of all the implements of agriculture, as ploughs, harrows, carts, etc. **1814** SCOTT *Wav.* xv, Their whole goods and gear, corn, cattle, horse, nolt, sheep, outsight and insight plenishing. **1818** —— *Hrt. Midl.* viii, Poindings of outsight and insight plenishing. [**1892** H. AINSLIE *Pilgrim. Land of Burns* 69 (E.D.D.), I saw nae wanworths gaun either in the outsight or insight plenishin'.]

out'sin, *v.* [OUT- 18, 17.]

1. *trans.* To surpass in sinning; to sin more than.

1606 SYLVESTER *Du Bartas* II. iv. I. *Trophies* 1227 The Heav'n-sunk Cities in Asphaltis Fen.. Glad, by thy Sons, to be out-sinned so. **176.** WESLEY *Serm.* lxvi. 29, Wks. 1811 IX. 216 We..The Heathens unbaptiz'd out-sin! **1772** FLETCHER *Logica Genev.* 105 Should I out-sin Manasses himself.

2. To go beyond the limit of in sinning.

1646 H. LAWRENCE *Comm. Angells* 151 In a word, wee cannot out-sin his pardon, or grace, by any thing but unbeliefe. **1677** W. SHERLOCK *Answ. T. Dawson* 17 Some men may out-sin the day of Grace. **1724** R. WELTON *Christ. Faith & Pract.* 209 A man has out-sinned the vertue of his Saviour's sacrifice.

out'sing, *v.* [OUT- 18, 14, 15.]

1. *trans.* To excel in singing. Also *refl.*

1603 BRETON *Dignitie of Man* (1879) 14/2 In sweetnesse the Nightingale [will] outsing him. **1733** SWIFT *On Poetry*, How wrong a taste prevails among us; How much our ancestors out-sung us. **1878** J. TODHUNTER *Alcestis* (1879) 9 Our old Chrysippus, His eyes aglow with an immortal fire, Vows to outsing himself. 'Twill be rare singing.

b. To overcome or get the better of by singing.

1830 MISS MITFORD *Village* Ser. IV. (1863) 222 She would sing over the mashing tub..out-singing Martha's scolding. **1885** *Athenæum* 19 Sept. 378/3 Each appeared to be trying to outsing the other.

2. a. *intr.* To sing out; to burst out into song. **b.** *trans.* To express by singing.

1877 WHITTIER *Witch of Wenham* 226 The meadow-lark outsang. **1886** *Good Words* 308 This joy the birds outsing.

out-sister: see OUT- 2.

out'sit, *v.* [OUT- 17, 18.]

1. *trans.* To sit beyond the time or duration of.

1658 OSBORN *Adv. Son* (1673) 24 That such as begin then, though they out-sit the Sun, will be delivered of the fury.. before the Watch be set. **1692** SOUTH *Serm.* (1697) I. 28 He that prolongs his meals..how quickly does he out-sit his pleasure? **1882** WOODFORD in *Life of Bp. Wilberforce* III. 357 We outsate the twilight, drawing from the rich stores of the old statesman's memory.

2. To sit longer than.

1885 G. MEREDITH *Diana* xxviii, Dacier could allow Mr. Hepburn to outsit him. **1894** *Cornh. Mag.* May 496 Bab outsits all the other guests at tea.

'outsize, *sb.* and *a.* [f. OUT *a.* + SIZE *sb.*[1]]

A. *sb.* **a.** A person or thing larger than the normal or the majority; esp. a ready-made garment larger than the standard sizes. Also *transf.* **b.** Greater size than normal.

1845 *Ainsworth's Mag.* VII. 213 The borrowed child being *ra*-ther an out-size..rendered Cora's carrying him a matter of difficulty. **1883** *Morning Star* (Washington) 31 Oct. 3/6 A stocking of an out size is one with the same foot as another, but wider in the..middle [of the leg]. **1894** *Eng. Illustr. Mag.* Oct. 91 She was 'rather an out size' as they say in the Duchy. **1902** E. NESBIT *Five Children & It* viii. 211 Robert was indeed what a draper would call an 'out-size' in boys. **1924** *Mod. Draper* II. 69 With regard to all ladies' underclothing it is necessary to keep a good assortment of outsizes. **1924** A. CHRISTIE *Man in Brown Suit* xii. 96 'I don't think he'll have any out sizes,' murmured Pagett, measuring my figure with his eye. **1933** CHESTERTON *St. Thomas Aquinas* i. 14 In the present case the outline is rather an outsize. The gown that could contain that colossal friar is not kept in stock. **1957** M. B. PICKEN *Fashion Dict.* 238/2 *Outsize*, size larger than the regular sizes; generally used for sizes larger than 46 bust. Also applied to hosiery having a top larger than average. **1970** V. GIELGUD *Candle-Holders* I. iv. 34 This impression of massive outsize was only exaggerated by the sight of George Eltham standing at the top of the flight of shallow steps which linked the drive with the great front doors.

B. *adj.* Larger than the average, usual, or stock size. Also *transf.* Also **'outsized** *ppl. a.* Hence **out'sizeness**, the fact or quality of being outsize.

1880 *Good Words* 46/1 He was what is sometimes called an 'outsized man'..imposing in appearance. *c* **1890** in *American Mail Order Fashions* (1961) 12 Ladies' outsize plated silk hose. **1895** *Westm. Gaz.* 20 July 2/1 She was a great outsized woman. **1904** H. G. WELLS *Food of Gods* I. ii. 19 He conceived a picture of coops and runs, outsize and still more outsize coops, and runs progressively larger. **1906** *Westm. Gaz.* 5 May 5/1 'An out-sized cat, I call him,' remarked the cook soon after his arrival. **1922** JOYCE *Ulysses* 715 A pair of outsize ladies' drawers of India mull, cut on generous lines. **1928** *Blackw. Mag.* May 709/1 A valley of utter desolation,..with an outsize snow mountain..at either end of it. **1937** AUDEN & MACNEICE *Lett. from Iceland* xii. 173 She wears an amazing woollen helmet with earflaps which combined with her goggles and general outsizeness makes her look like a piece of Archaic Greek sculptuary. **1952** *Manch. Guardian Weekly* 9 Oct. 3/4 The Republicans are undoubtedly united in an outsize bed where there is room for everybody except the few liberals who got the General [*sc.* Eisenhower] his nomination. **1958** *Times* 31 Oct. 3/5 Her voice is of a rich mezzo-soprano quality, not outsize, but certainly amply big enough for most lieder. **1974** A. WILLIAMS *Gentleman Traitor* v. 86 He..dressed in an outsize suit of white slub-silk. **1976** *Publishers Weekly* 26 Apr. 3/3 (Advt.), A massive, out-sized book of more than 800 pages.

out-skill to **out-skip**: see OUT-.

†**'out,skin.** *Obs.* [f. OUT- 3 + SKIN.] Outer or external skin; epidermis. Also *fig.*

1640 SHIRLEY *Coronation* v. i, The barke and outskinne of a common wealth.

'out,skirrer. *Sc. rare.* [f. OUT- 8 + *skirrer*, SCURRIER, a scout.] A scout; = OUTSCOURER.

1831 TYTLER *Lives Scott. Worthies* I. 413 He had acquired by his spies and outskirrers a perfect knowledge of the disposition of the army of Lorn.

outskirt ('aʊtskɜːt), *sb.* [OUT- 3.]

1. The outer border. Now usu. in *pl.*

a. 1596 SPENSER *State Irel.* Wks. (Globe) 668/1 They mighte keepe both the O-Relyes, and also the O-Farrels, and all that out-skirte of Meathe in awe. **1891** HARDY *Tess* I. xix. 245 The outskirt of the garden in which Tess found herself had been left uncultivated for some years. **1943** J. BETJEMAN *Eng. Cities & Small Towns* 14, I am reminded of that moving passage about a provincial suburb in Gissing's story *Fate and the Apothecary* describing, I think it must be, an outskirt of Exeter.

b. 1647 CLARENDON *Hist. Reb.* II. §84 He lay near Newburn in the Out-skirts of Northumberland. **1732** W. FOWNES in *Swift's Lett.* (1766) II. 167 There are many places, in the out-skirts of the city..very proper. **1778** *Phil. Trans.* LXVIII. 136 The parishes..comprehend many central parts..and also contain all the out-skirts. **1832** HT. MARTINEAU *Life in Wilds* viii. 102 On the outskirts of the wood were the dwellings. **1861** GEO. ELIOT *Silas M.* 3 One of those barren parishes lying on the outskirts of civilisation ..inhabited by meagre sheep and thinly-scattered shepherds.

fig. **1821** LAMB *Elia* Ser. I. *Old Benchers I. T.*, The remote edges and outskirts of history. **1829** CARLYLE *Misc.* (1857) II. 78 The wondrous outskirts of Idealism.

2. *attrib.* or quasi-*adj.* Situated on the outskirts.

1835 ISAAC TAYLOR *Spir. Despot.* vi. (1855) 270 Horrid and sanguinary rites prevailed among the less civilized and outskirt nations of the empire. **1841-4** EMERSON *Ess.* Ser. II. vi. (1876) 156 This is but outskirt and far-off reflection and echo of the triumph. *a* **1930** D. H. LAWRENCE *Last Poems* (1932) 46 Corpse-eaters They dwell in the outskirt fringes of nowhere.

Hence **ˈoutskirter**, one who stands or hangs on the outskirts.
1831 COL. HAWKER *Diary* (1893) II. 28 At least 100 more [rooks] were picked up by outskirters and other parties. **1878** STEVENSON *Inland Voy.* (1896) 223 To be even one of the outskirters of art, leaves a fine stamp on a man's countenance.

outˈskirt, *v. rare.* [f. prec. sb.: cf. SKIRT *v.*] *trans.* To skirt. **a.** To form one of the outskirts of, to border. **b.** To pass along the outskirts of.
1818 KEATS *Endym.* I. 250 What time thou wanderest at eventide Through sunny meadows that outskirt the side Of thine enmossed realms. **1870** T. HARDY *Wessex Poems* 41, I did not out-skirt the spot That no spot on earth excels.
Hence **outskirting** *ppl. a.*, bordering, lying on the outskirts.
1845 DARWIN *Voy. Nat.* iii. (1879) 42 The outskirting houses rose out of the plain like isolated beings.

out-slander, etc.: see OUT-.

outˈslang, *v.* [OUT- 21.] *trans.* To outdo in the use of slang.
1848 THACKERAY *Van. Fair* xxxiv, Put him at Iffley Lock, and he could out-slang the boldest bargeman. **1866** FELTON *Anc. & Mod. Gr.* II. I. ix. 156 Dealing in slander and slang until they have outslandered and outslanged the natural masters of these vulgar arts.

outˈsleep, *v.* [OUT- 17, 18, 16.]
1. *trans.* To sleep beyond (a specified time, etc.).
1590 SHAKS. *Mids. N.* v. i. 372, I feare we shall out-sleepe the comming morne, As much as we this night haue ouer-watcht. **1814** CARY *Dante* (Chandos) 310 [A] babe, that had outslept his wont.
2. To sleep longer than (another).
1690 SHADWELL *Am. Bigot* v, Thou wouldst outsleep the seven sleepers.
3. To sleep (a period of time, etc.) out or to an end; to sleep till or beyond the end of.
1784 COWPER *Task* VI. 313 Where on his bed of wool and matted leaves He has outslept the winter. **1862** MRS. MALCOLM tr. *Freytag's Pict. Germ. Life* I. 172 When he had outslept his drunkenness he roused himself. **1871–4** J. THOMSON *City Dreadf. Nt.* XIII. ii, He would outsleep another term of care.

out-slide to **out-slink**: see OUT-.

†**outˈsling**, *v. Obs.* [OUT- 15.] *trans.* To sling out, throw out from or as from a sling.
c **1400** *Rom. Rose* 5987, I shal hym make his pens out-slynge, But they in his gerner sprynge. **1535** STEWART *Cron. Scot.* II. 13 Tha within hes maid defence richt lang, Baith arrowis schot, and greit stonis outslang Attouir the wall. **1647** H. MORE *Song of Soul* II. ii. III. v, 'Tis opinion That makes the .. thundring engine murd'rous balls out-sling.

†**outˈslip**, *v. Obs.* [OUT- 15, 17.]
1. *trans.* To slip away from; to evade, escape.
a **1643** J. SHUTE *Judgem. & Mercy* (1645) 193 Filthy people that outslip the morning prayer. **1693** PRIDEAUX *Lett.* (Camden) 164 Ye officers on horseback rod after him .. but he outslipd them all and got clear away.
2. To let slip by, to miss.
1649 BLITHE *Eng. Improv. Impr.* (1653) To Husband Man, I am confident better sometimes lose the land, than land, seed, and all your labour, as many do that outslip the season.

outsmart (aʊtˈsmɑːt), *v.* [f. OUT- 20 + SMART *a.*] *trans.* To get the better of or overcome by superior craft or ingenuity; to prove too clever for; to outwit. Also *refl.*
1926 H. C. WITWER *Roughly Speaking* iii. 95 Young Farrell seemed to have more than recovered from Ben's terrible right hand blow, for he was now doing what Pete told me was 'outsmarting' Ben. **1948** E. WAUGH *Loved One* 105 'All his stories are about the same thing—American innocence and European experience.' 'Thinks he can outsmart us, does he?' **1954** J. STEINBECK *Sweet Thursday* xxi. 131 It is such fun to outsmart a smart guy. **1957** P. FRANK *Seven Days to Never* 48 It takes a machine to outsmart a machine. **1961** 'B. WELLS' *Day Earth caught Fire* viii. 128 Hell, we're all so bloody clever at outsmarting nature. Anything you can split I can split better. **1974** J. HELLER *Something Happened* 296 'I'm going to sock you one, Daddy,' he squeals in frustration, as he feels himself outsmarted. **1975** J. F. BURKE *Death Trick* (1976) xii. 156 Like all smart crooks, he outsmarted himself. **1977** *R.A.F. News* 8–21 June 4/2 While the authorities dither and disagree on a plan of action, the beast continues his rampage of death, outsmarting every move to trap him.

†**outˈsmell**, *v. Obs.* [OUT- 15, 18.]
1. *trans.* To smell out, discover by smelling.
c **1550** BALE *K. Johan* (Camden) 77 *S.* Naye, that is suche a lye as easely wyll be felte. *D.* Tush, man, amonge fooles it never wyll be out smelte.
2. To surpass in pungency of smell; to smell stronger than; also *fig.*
1603 HARSNET *Pop. Impost.* 71 Verily these doe out-smel the Devil by farre. **1647** *Pol. Ballads* (1860) I. 44 The plot outsmells old Atkins' breeches.

out-ˈsmile, *v.* [OUT- 18c, 18.] *trans.* **a.** To overcome by smiling. **b.** To outdo in smiling.
1830 MISS MITFORD *Village* Ser. IV. (1863) 222 She would .. smile through the washing-week .. out-smiling Martha's frowns. **1894** R. BRIDGES *Shorter Poems* 39 Autumn lingers but to outsmile the May.

out-snatch, -snore, etc.: see OUT-.

outsoar (aʊtˈsɔə(r)), *v.* [OUT- 18.] *trans.* To soar above or beyond; to exceed in height of flight. Chiefly *fig.*
1674 *Govt. Tongue* ix. §13 Let them clog their wings with the remembrance of those who have outsoar'd them .. in true worth. **1741** RICHARDSON *Pamela* II. 286 This amiable Girl .. will out-soar us both, infinitely out-soar us. **1856** MRS. BROWNING *Aur. Leigh* I. 410 By how many feet Mount Chimborazo outsoars Teneriffe. **1892** *Literary World* 5 Feb. 117/1 Attempting to outsoar Milton's eagle wings.

ˈout-sole. [OUT- 3.] The outer sole of a shoe, which comes in contact with the ground.
1884 KNIGHT *Dict. Mech.* Suppl. 649/2 To secure the out-sole to the insole for future sewing or pegging. **1894** *Daily News* 1 May 8/3 One stall where oak outsoles, hemlock half-soles, Virginian oak sides, .. are displayed.

out-sonnet, -sound, etc.: see OUT-.

ˈoutˌspan, *sb.*[1] *S. Africa.* [f. OUTSPAN *v.*[1]] The action of outspanning or unyoking; the time or place of outspanning or encampment.
1822 W. J. BURCHELL *Trav. S. Afr.* I. iv. 92 These *uitspan*, or *outspan places*, are, in fact, the caravanserays of the Cape. **1844** *Colburn's United Service Mag.* May 23 *Outspan*, .. place of rest, where the oxen are unyoked and turned out to graze. **1852** *Blackw. Mag.* LXXI. 294 You take a stroll with your gun during the 'out-span'. **1885** W. GRESWELL in *Macm. Mag.* Feb. 284/2 An extemporised lunch at a well-known outspan, consisting of many veldt dainties. **1899** *Westm. Gaz.* 1 Nov. 4/3 Every town has a public outspan, where cattle can graze and travellers stop for the night.
attrib. **1872** *Routledge's Ev. Boy's Ann.* 339/2 After reaching our outspan ground. **1884** *Chr. World* 21 Feb. 134/3 A walk round about the outspan places was interesting.

ˈoutˌspan, *sb.*[2] [OUT- 7: cf. OUTSPAN *v.*[2]] The extended or outstretched span (of an arch).
1887 BROWNING *Parleyings, B. de Mandeville* x, Earth's centre and sky's outspan, all's informed Equally by sun's efflux.

outspan (ˈaʊtˌspæn), *v.*[1] *South Africa.* [ad. Du. *uitspannen*, f. *uit* adv., out + *spannen* to span, stretch, bend, put horses to.] To unyoke or unhitch oxen from a wagon; to unharness horses; hence, to encamp. **a.** *intr.* **b.** *trans.*
a. **1824** BURCHELL *Trav.* I. 52 They very frequently unyoke, or outspan, as it is called, at Salt River. **1850** R. G. CUMMING *Hunter's Life S. Afr.* (ed. 2) I. 59, I marched right through the town and outspanned about a quarter of a mile beyond it. **1893** SELOUS *Trav. S.E. Africa* 10 We outspanned near a Boer farm.
b. **1866** *Port Eliz. Telegr.* 6 Nov., Found guilty of stealing twenty reims .. from a wagon .. outspanned at the North-end. **1883** J. MACKENZIE *Day-dawn in Dark places* 8 The six waggons, when 'outspanned' for the night, were drawn near to each other.
Hence **ˈoutˌspanned** *ppl. a.*, **-ˌspanning** *vbl. sb.*
1893 *Month* Feb. 197 He was standing by the out-spanned wagon. **1899** *Strand Mag.* Mar. 270/1 [He] pointed .. to the outspanned bullocks. **1894** H. NISBET *Bush Girl's Rom.* p. iii, I do not think we forget these 'out-spannings' while we are driving our cattle in other directions.

outˈspan, *v.*[2] *rare.* [OUT- 14, 17.]
a. *intr.* To stretch out or extend in span, as an arch. **b.** *trans.* To extend beyond the span of.
1882 H. S. HOLLAND *Logic & Life* (1885) 254 The lines of connection .. lose themselves, vanish, outspan our sight. **1884** SKRINE *Under Two Queens* I. 18 When the storm-rack drives leeward, the rainbow outspanneth.

outˈsparkle, *v.* [OUT- 18.] *trans.* To exceed in sparkling; to sparkle more than. Hence **outˈsparkled** *ppl. a.*
1648 J. BEAUMONT *Psyche* I. lxxxiv, When the starry Peacock doth display His train's full Orb, the winged People all .. Let their out-sparkled Plumes sullenly fall. **1655** tr. *Com. Hist. Francion* I. 18 Eyes that out-sparkled his preciousest Stones. **1821** BYRON *Sardan.* II. i. 47 As many glittering spears As will out-sparkle our allies—your planets. **1871** BROWNING *Pr. Hohenst.* 1151 Earthborn jewelry Out-sparkling the insipid firmament Blue above Terni.

outspeak (aʊtˈspiːk), *v.* [OUT- 17, 18, 15, 14.]
†**1.** *trans.* To utter or express more than; to be superior to in meaning or significance. *Obs.*
1603 B. JONSON *Sejanus* I. ii, Why, this indeed is physic! and outspeaks The knowledge of cheap drugs. **1613** SHAKS. *Hen. VIII*, III. ii. 127 His Treasure, .. I finde at such proud Rate, that it out-speakes Possession of a Subject.
2. To outdo or excel in speaking; to speak louder, better, or more forcibly than.
1603 B. JONSON *K. Jas.'s Coronat. Entertainm.* Wks. 530/2 Whose graces do as far outspeak your fame As fame doth silence. **1658** COKAINE *Trappolin* I. ii, Admired Princess, you out-speak me much, But never shall out-love me. **1868** LYNCH *Rivulet* CXXI. ii, What, will the prince outspeak the voice That pierced to Lazarus in his grave?
3. To speak (something) out; to utter, declare.
1635–56 COWLEY *Davideis* II. 177 The Praise you pleas'd (great Prince) on me to spend, Was all out-spoken when you stil'd me Friend. **1850** LYNCH *Theo. Trin.* xii. 231 A love is imaged in the sky, Too great to be outspoken.
4. *intr.* To speak out, utter one's voice.
[**1804** CAMPBELL *Ld. Ullin's Dau.* v, Out spoke the hardy Highland wight, I'll go, my chief, I'm ready.] **1832** LYTTON *Eugene A.* I. ii, And now outspake the Corporal. *a* **1865** AYTOUN *Scheik of Sinai* ii, And thus outspake the Moor.

ˈoutˌspeaker. [OUT- 8.] One that speaks out.
1858 TRENCH *Synon. N.T.* vi. (1876) 20 The προφήτης is the outspeaker.

ˈoutˌspeaking, *vbl. sb.* [OUT- 9.] The action of speaking out or uttering in words, esp. straight out or without reserve; frank or candid utterance.
1845–6 TRENCH *Huls. Lect.* Ser. I. ii. 29 These may be deep out-speakings of the spiritual needs of man. **1865** *Sat. Rev.* 29 July 136/1 Briskness and outspeaking and brevity are virtues which go a long way in buying and selling.
So **ˈoutˌspeaking** *ppl. a.* [OUT- 10], that speaks out, that speaks plainly or candidly.
1844 DICKENS *Mart. Chuz.* xxxvi, You are for ever telling her the same thing yourself in fifty plain, out-speaking ways. **1859** HELPS *Friends in C.* Ser. II. I. 133, I have always been an outspeaking man.

†**outˈspeckle**, *sb. Sc. Obs. rare*[−1]. A spectacle or laughing-stock.
16.. *Jamie Telfer* xxx. in *Bord. Minstrel.*, 'Whae drives thir kye?' gan Willie say, 'To make an outspeckle o' me?'

ˈoutspeech. *rare.* [OUT- 7.] Frank or candid words; plain language or terms; outspeaking.
1919 W. DE MORGAN *Old Madhouse* 439 Outspeech would be the safest course as well as the easiest, with this girl. **1921** —— *Old Man's Youth* xxvii. 267, I was sorry a moment after for my own outspeech.

outˈspeed, *v.* [OUT- 18.] *trans.* To surpass or outstrip in speed; to run faster than.
1704 HEARNE *Duct. Hist.* (1714) I. 324 Twelve Colts they bore him cou'd their Sire out-speed. **1724** R. WELTON *Christ. Faith & Pract.* 150 As swift as he rode he could not outspeed the Divine vengeance. **1802** CAMPBELL *Lochiel's Warning* 27 Lo! the death-shot of foemen outspeeding, he rode Companionless. **1867** J. B. ROSE tr. *Virgil's Æneid* 337 The maiden .. on foot outsped the horse. **1911** *Chambers's Jrnl.* Jan. 57/1 If the black, whirling maelstrom of a cyclone looms up before him, he will make a detour or even outspeed it. **1930** R. CAMPBELL *Adamastor* 31 Bold is he .. And swift —outspeeding as he runs The corposants of Leda's sons. **1962** *Times* 28 Mar. 4/2 He had outspeeded Spinks in the early rounds. **1977** 'O. JACKS' *Autumn Heroes* viii. 112 It became clear that the truck would survive once it outsped the fire line.

outˈspend, *v.* [OUT- 17, 18.]
1. *trans.* To exceed (resources, a limit, etc.) in spending.
1586 WHETSTONE *Eng. Mirror* 152 His ryot in the end outspended both his fortune and credit. **1667** PEPYS *Diary* 20 Feb., He do confess our straits here and everywhere else arise from our outspending our revenue. **1811** W. TAYLOR in Robberds *Mem.* II. 345 We out-spend our means. **1895** *Chamb. Jrnl.* XII. 828/1 She divined that otherwise he would outspend his fortune.
2. To surpass in spending; to spend more than (another).
1840 MRS. F. TROLLOPE *Michael Armstrong* ii, He had already acquired more envy and hatred among his friends and neighbours by [etc.] than by all his successful struggles to outspend them all. **1866** HOWELLS *Venet. Life* xx. 350 King Cole was not a jollier old soul than Illustrissimo of that day; he outspent princes.
3. In *pa. pple.* **outˈspent**, exhausted.
1818 BYRON *Mazeppa* iii, Outspent with this long course, The Cossack prince rubb'd down his horse. **1825** HOGG *Queen Hynde* 62 His steed outspent was clotted o'er His neck with foam.

ˈoutspend, *sb. rare*[−1]. [f. prec.: see OUT- 7.] Expenditure, outlay.
1859 I. TAYLOR *Logic in Theol.* 275 It is a mere outspend of savageness, to no end.

ˈout-spent, *ppl. a.* [OUT- 11.] Exhausted, completely spent.
1652 BENLOWES *Theoph.* VII. xxxvii, Lord fill My out-spent raptures by thy all repairing skill. **1821** SHELLEY *Prometh. Unb.* III. iv. 141 His own [will] Which spurred him, like an outspent horse, to death.

out-sphere to **out-spill**: see OUT-.

outˈspin, *v.* [OUT- 14, 15b, 18.]
†**1.** *intr.* To spout out. *Obs. rare*[−1].
1596 SPENSER *F.Q.* IV. ix. 27 That through the clifts the vermeil bloud out spinne.
2. *trans.* To spin (a thread) to its full length; said *fig.* of the thread of life, etc.
1616 B. JONSON *Epigr.* xlii, Or that his long-yearn'd life Were quite out-spun. **1634** SIR T. HERBERT *Trav.* 127 Till hee had out-spun the yeares of old Methusala. **1844** WHITTIER *Texas* 13 Patience .. with her weary thread outspun Murmurs that her work is done.
3. To outdo or excel in spinning.
1742 YOUNG *Nt. Th.* I. 380 On this perhaps .. we build Our mountain-hopes, spin out eternal schemes As we the Fatal Sisters could outspin.

out-spirit to **out-splendour**: see OUT-.

out-ˈspit, *v.* [OUT- 18.] *trans.* To outdo or surpass in spitting (venom).
1648 J. BEAUMONT *Psyche* XVIII. clxi, Menander .. by That cankering liquor so infected grew That Simon he out-spit in Heresy.

ˈoutˌspitting, *vbl. sb.* [OUT- 9.] The action of spitting out; that which is spat out.
1870 A. B. MITFORD in *Fortn. Rev.* 1 Aug. 143 These outspittings from pious mouths.

ˈoutˈspoken (stress variable), *ppl. a.* orig. *Sc.* [OUT- 11, from *speak out*; the pa. pple. has here a resultant force, as in 'well spoken', 'well read'.]
1. Given to speaking out; free or unreserved in speech; candid, frank; direct in speech.
1808 JAMIESON, *Outspoken*, Given to freedom of speech, not accustomed to conceal one's sentiments, *S.* **1820** *Smugglers* II. iv. 63 I've heard she was a wee out-spoken. **1824** SCOTT *Let. to Joanna Baillie* 9 Feb. in Lockhart, He is not, you know, very outspoken. **1837** CARLYLE *Fr. Rev.* II. I. iv, Camille is wittier than ever, and more outspoken. **1849** DICKENS *Dav. Copp.* xvi, I am perfectly honest and outspoken. **1884** PAE *Eustace* 15 He is very outspoken; but he does not mean to be rude.
b. Of things said: Free from reserve, distinct.
1869 TROLLOPE *He Knew* lviii. (1878) 323 Priscilla's approval of her sister's conduct was clear, outspoken, and satisfactory. **1880** *Fortn. Rev.* Feb. 213 Mr. Gladstone's outspoken observations. **1882–3** SCHAFF *Encycl. Relig. Knowl.* III. 2034 A party with very outspoken reformatory tendencies.
2. Spoken out, uttered, expressed in words.
1882 MISS BRADDON *Mt. Royal* I. i. 33 'All that is to be known of the outside of him', said Jessie, answering the girl's outspoken thought.

ˌoutˈspokenly, *adv.* [f. prec. + -LY².] In an outspoken manner; straightforwardly, candidly.
1855 *Tait's Mag.* XXII. 422 Many women do love as eagerly,.. as outspokenly, as pursuingly—as Caroline Helstone is said to have done. **1869** RUSKIN *Q. of Air* §9 Both of them outspokenly religious, and entirely sincere men.

ˌoutˈspokenness. [f. as prec. + -NESS.] The quality of being outspoken; frankness of speech.
1852 S. G. ROWE *Recoll. of R. R. Wormeley* (1879) 113 The main feature of his character was openness, or, to coin a word, outspokenness. Whatever he thought he spoke right out. **1854** MRS. GASKELL *North & S.* viii, But the very outspokenness marked their innocence of any intention to hurt her delicacy. **1893** A. V. DICEY *Leap in Dark* 194 You cannot from the nature of things combine the advantages of reticence and of outspokenness.

outsport, etc.: see OUT-.

outspread (ˈaʊtsprɛd), *sb.* [OUT- 7.]
1. The action of spreading out; expansion.
1841 CALHOUN *Wks.* III. 604 The rapid and wide outspread after game, pasturage, or choice spots on which to settle down. **1848** R. I. WILBERFORCE *Doct. Incarnation* v. (1852) 96 That mighty outspread of the Fourth Empire.
2. *concr.* An expanse or expansion.
1856 MRS. BROWNING *Aur. Leigh* VII. 291 Pushing wide Rich outspreads of the vineyards and the corn. **1895** A. I. MCCONNOCHIE *Deeside* viii. (ed. 2) 89 Formerly the haugh .. at this point was but a barren out-spread of the Tanner.

ˈoutspread, *ppl. a.* [OUT- 11.] Spread out or abroad; expanded, extended; diffused abroad.
1695 J. EDWARDS *Perfect. Script.* 326 This *expansum* is the .. out-spread firmament. **1743** J. DAVIDSON *Æneid* VII. 181 On the outspread skins. **1858** KINGSLEY *Saint Maura* 19 And plead .. with outspread arms.

outspread (aʊtˈsprɛd), *v.* [OUT- 15, 18.]
1. *trans.* To spread out; to stretch out, expand, extend.
a **1340** HAMPOLE *Psalter* xliii. 22 If we outsprede our hend til alien god. *c* **1400** tr. *Secreta Secret., Gov. Lordsh.* 109 It ys a dispytous Instrument, þat outspredys it in many maners. **1600** FAIRFAX *Tasso* XIII. lxv, Scorching sunne so hot his beames outspreads. **1820** KEATS *Hyperion* I. 287 Their plumes immense Rose, one by one, till all outspreaded were. **1885** H. M. STANLEY *Congo* xxvi. II. 6 That white-collared fish eagle out-spreading his wings for flight.
†**2.** To exceed in expanse. *Obs.*
1650 FULLER *Pisgah* III. ix. 338 Grant the King's Palace outspread the Temple in greatness.
3. *intr.* To spread out, extend itself.
1906 *Westm. Gaz.* 26 June 2/3 Each young branch, out-spreading in the sun, Reflects in shadow on the sod below. **1925** [see ASILE].

ˈoutˌspreading, *vbl. sb.* [OUT- 9.] The action of spreading out.
c **1400** tr. *Secreta Secret., Gov. Lordsh.* 90 þe kynde of þe planetys ressayues þe kynde of out-spredyng of waterys. **1860** PUSEY *Min. Proph.* 112 So wide and universal shall the outspreading be. **1883** A. ROBERTS *O. T. Revision* v. 106 Can any understand the outspreading of the clouds?
So **ˈoutˌspreading** *ppl. a.*, that spreads out.
1818 SCOTT *Hrt. Midloth.* xxi, Then, weel may we take wi' patience our share and portion of this outspreading reproach. **1850** BUSHNELL *God in Christ* 328 An outspreading era of life.

ˈoutspring, *sb.* [OUT- 7.] The act of springing out or forth; the issuing out.
1557 *Primer Sarum* Ps. lxiv, Thou .. multipliest the springes of it with soft showers, it shall englad the out-springes. **1891** FROUDE *Cath. Aragon* Introd. 12 The era of Elizabeth was the outspring of the movement which Henry VIII commenced.

outˈspring, *v.* [OUT- 14, 18.]
1. *intr.* To spring out, issue forth. (In ME. two words; now only poetic.)
1297 R. GLOUC. (Rolls) 9442 Duntes þer were strong inou, þat þet fur out sprong Of þe helmes al aboute. *c* **1386** CHAUCER *Doctor's T.* 111 The fame out sprong on euery syde Bothe of hir beautee and hir bountee wyde. **1500–20** DUNBAR *Poems* xxxiii. 111 The fowlis all at the fedrem dang .. Quhill all the pennis of it ow[t]sprang. **1818** SHELLEY *Rev. Islam* v. vi. 5 From every tent .. Our bands outsprung and seized their arms.
†**b.** To spring by birth. *Obs.*
a **1547** SURREY *Æneid* IV. (1557) E ij, There comen is to Tyrians court Aeneas one outsprong of Troyan blood. **1596** DALRYMPLE tr. *Leslie's Hist. Scot.* I. 110 Flurished, and sum-tyme outsprang frome thir generatiouns .. mony men excellent in the commendatione and gude reporte of leirning & virtue.
2. *trans.* To spring beyond or farther than.
1621 LADY M. WROTH *Urania* 402 A .. second Brother liued, whose ill out-sprung .. the elder.
So **ˈoutˌspringing** *vbl. sb.*
1398 TREVISA *Barth. De P.R.* VIII. xxviii. (1495) 341 Shinynge is outspryngynge and streming out of the substaunce of lyghte.

out-sprout to **out-spurt**: see OUT-.

†**ˈout-spy.** *Obs.* One sent out to spy, a scout.
c **1470** HENRY *Wallace* VII. 802 The out spy thus was lost fra Makfadȝhane.

out-squall to **out-stall**: see OUT-.

outstand (aʊtˈstænd), *v.* [OUT- 15 b, 17, 14.]
I. *trans.* **1.** To stand or hold out against; to resist to the end, to endure successfully. Now *dial.*
1571 GOLDING *Calvin on Ps.* xli. 13 David .. manfully outstood those assaults of temptacions. **1629** GAULE *Holy Madn.* 165 A Lion will outstand a Man. **1695** WOODWARD *Nat. Hist. Earth* I. (1723) 40 Sure never to outstand the first Assault. *c* **1800** K. WHITE *Lett.* Poet. Wks. (1837) 323 Outstand the tide of ages. **1805** EUGENIA DI ACTON *Nuns of Desert* II. 87 Who has experienced and outstood the base designs of him she loved and trusted. **1875** *Sussex Gloss.* s.v., He wanted to have the calf for three pound ten, but I out-stood him upon that.
b. To maintain in opposition; to contradict (a person) obstinately. *dial.*
1658 A. FOX *Wurtz' Surg.* v. 362 Those Nurses .. which were to look to the Children, .. outstand it most that the Child was not hurt. **1883** *Hampsh. Gloss.* s.v., She outstood me wi' that 'ere lie. **1887** *Kent Gloss* s.v., He outstood me that he hadn't seen him.
2. To stand out or stay beyond (in time). *arch.*
1611 SHAKS. *Cymb.* I. vi. 207, I haue out-stood my time. **1705** STANHOPE *Paraphr.* II. 458 If we out-stand the Season of Grace. **1856** EMERSON *Eng. Traits* xvi. (1902) 161.
II. *intr.* Cf. OUTSTANDING *vbl. sb.* and *ppl. a.*
3. To stand out distinctly or prominently.
1755 JOHNSON, *Outstand*, to protuberate from the main body. **1848** CLOUGH *Bothie* vi, Cottages here and there outstanding bare on the mountain. **1900** S. PHILLIPS *Paolo & Francesca* II. 50 The foam is on his lips, The veins outstand.
4. Of a ship: To stand out or away from the land; to sail outwards.
1866 WHITTIER *Dead Ship Harpswell* 13 Many a keel shall seaward turn And many a sail outstand.

ˈoutˌstander. *Sc.* [Agent-n. from prec. (sense 1).] One who stands out in dissent or resistance.
a **1670** SPALDING *Troub. Chas. I.* (1850) I. 153 To bring the Marques .. and all vther outstanderis to cum in and subscrive thair covenant. *Ibid.* (1792) I. 223 He was a papist, and outstander against the good cause. **1900** W. WATT *Aberdeen & Banff* xi. 267 The only important outstanders from the subscription to the promise of canonical obedience.

ˈoutˈstanding, *vbl. sb.* [OUT- 9: cf. OUTSTAND *v.*]
†**1.** A jutting out or projecting; a projection.
1611 COTGR., *Surmontement des ioues*, a chuffie outstanding, or swelling of the cheeks. **1624** WOTTON *Archit.* in *Reliq.* (1651) 245 *Pergoli* ... which are certain ballised out-standings to satisfie curiosity of sight.
2. The action of standing out in opposition. *Sc.*
a **1670** SPALDING *Troub. Chas. I* (1850) I. 231 Banf payit seveirlie for his outstanding. **1900** W. WATT *Aberdeen & Banff* x. 251 For outstanding against the good cause Irvine of Drum and Gordon of Haddo .. were arrested.
3. *pl.* Outstanding amounts; unsettled accounts.
1861 GOSCHEN *For. Exch.* 5 Such as had outstandings abroad which they were entitled to draw in. **1892** *Pall Mall G.* 20 Apr. 5/2 If the Argentine Government were unable to pay up outstandings.

ˈoutˈstanding (stress variable), *ppl. a.* [OUT- 10: cf. OUTSTAND *v.*]
1. That stands out or projects; projecting, prominent, detached.
1611 COTGR. s.v. *Herce*, Full of sharp, strong, and outstanding .. pins. **1870** H. MACMILLAN *Bible Teach.* vii. 148 The gigantic leaf .. furnished .. with outstanding veins of great depth. **1878** HUXLEY *Physiogr.* 168 The outstanding wedge-shaped masses were once connected with this main body. **1896** *Daily News* 9 Apr. 6/5 Those who prefer supple and clinging fabrics to those which are stiff and outstanding.
2. *fig.* Standing out from the rest; prominent, conspicuous, eminent; striking.
1830 HERSCHEL *Stud. Nat. Phil.* II. vi. (1851) 154 A violent outstanding exception. **1860** PUSEY *Min. Proph.* 264 The great outstanding facts, which our Lord has pointed out. **1890** *Blackw. Mag.* CXLVIII. 670/1 The most outstanding speaker in the General Assembly. **1899** *Spectator* 11 Feb. 208 There are many interesting articles .. but there is hardly one of outstanding importance.
3. That stands out in resistance or opposition.
a **1670** SPALDING *Troub. Chas. I* (1792) I. 132 (Jam.) Outstanding ministers.
4. That stands over or continues in existence; that remains undetermined, unsettled, or unpaid. ***outstanding term***: see TERM.
1797 W. TAYLOR in *Monthly Rev.* XXIII. 447 The difference between the outstanding debts and credits. **1833** HERSCHEL *Astron.* xi. 341 Still leaving outstanding and uncompensated a minute portion of the change, which requires a whole revolution of the node to compensate. **1858** J. MARTINEAU *Studies Chr.* 222 A nobleman whom he had dunned for an outstanding debt. **1875** JOWETT *Plato* (ed. 2) V. 77 Among citizens there should be no outstanding quarrels.
5. That sets a course outward.
1775 ADAIR *Amer. Ind.* 216 The outstanding parties for war, address the great spirit every day till they set off.

outˈstandingly, *adv.* [f. OUTSTANDING *ppl. a.* + -LY².] In a notable or outstanding manner; in or to an exceptional degree; remarkably or conspicuously.
1909 *Westm. Gaz.* 18 Jan. 12/2, I don't mean to say that he is an outstandingly good putter. **1922** A. S. M. HUTCHINSON *This Freedom* II. ix. 150 There was outstandingly one such day of absorption in delight .. for Rosalie. **1928** *Observer* 18 Mar. 23/3 Her Wagner songs are outstandingly fine. **1961** R. J. CORSINI et al. *Role-playing in Business* ix. 142 A district manager who had been recently appointed to his position after being outstandingly successful as a store manager, found that in supervising other managers he was having a difficult time.

outˈstare, *v.* [OUT- 18 b.] *trans.* To outdo in staring; to stare longer or harder than; to put out of countenance by staring; to look on (the sun, etc.) without blinking or flinching.
1596 SHAKS. *Merch. V.* II. i. 27 (Qo. 1), I would outstare the sternest eyes that look. **1602** MARSTON *Antonio's Rev.* III. v, I will .. Outstare the terror of thy grimme aspect. **1646** CRASHAW *Delights Muses, On Isaacson's Chronol.*, The eagle's eye, that can Outstare the broad-beam'd day's meridian. **1855** BAILEY *Mystic* 47 He sate and all the stars outstared, Gazing them down, dog, centaur, eagle, bull.

ˈoutstart, *sb.* [OUT- 7.] The act or point of starting out; outset.
1866 DORA GREENWELL *Ess.* 152 In the first outstart of his immortal journey. **1899** BARING-GOULD *Bk. of West* I. v. 75 The whole effect is marred by the one mistake made at the outstart.

outˈstart, *v.* [OUT- 14, 15, 17, 18.]
1. *intr.* To start, spring forth suddenly. (Properly two words.)
1382 WYCLIF *Judith* xiv. 15 And he out sterte with oute to the puple. *c* **1386** CHAUCER *Nun's Pr. T.* 227 The peple out sterte and caste the Cart to grounde. **1855** BROWNING *Heretic's Trag.* ix, Petal on petal, fierce rays unclose; Anther on anther, sharp spikes outstart.
†**b.** *trans.* (or *intr.* with dative). To start out from, escape from. *Obs.*
1412–20 LYDG. *Chron. Troy* I. ii, Pelleus .. kept him close yᵗ nothing him outsterte.
2. *trans.* To spring or go beyond; to take or have the start of, to go ahead of.
1593 *Pass. Morrice* (1876) 80 He cannot see a werck outstart the bounds of modestie. **1625** JACKSON *Creed* v. i. §4 Even when this faith .. shall be converted into perfect sight, everlasting confidence shall not outstart, but rather follow it. **1865** *Pall Mall G.* 16 May 10 Watermen can usually outstart amateurs.
Hence **outˈstarter**, one who starts out in front; a pioneer; **outˈstarting** *vbl. sb.*
1738 in Mrs. Barbauld *Life Richardson* (1804) I. 16 The .. servile pursuit of those tracks which are opened for them by anti-ministerial more popular outstarters. **1794** COLERIDGE *Relig. Musings* I. 94 He from his small particular orbit flies With blest outstarting!

ˈoutstate, out-state, *a. U.S.* [f. OUT- + STATE *sb.* 31 c.] **a.** Of or pertaining to a part of a state away from the largest population centre (see also quot. 1931). **b.** Coming from or living in another state; = OUT-OF-STATE *adj. phr.*
1931 *Amer. Speech* VI. 310 'Out-state' is a compound word not yet recognized by the dictionaries but frequently used by Nebraskans, Iowans, Coloradans, and Wyomingites. University students from these states reported two meanings: out in the state away from the main city, and out in the state away from the speaker's home. **1934** *Sun* (Baltimore) 2 Nov. 2/1 The vote which Mr. Picard would have to pile up there to overcome his opponent's out-State lead. **1961** in WEBSTER, Lost the governorship because the outstate vote went against him. *Ibid.*, A gorge of unusual natural beauty which few out-state visitors see—M. W. Fishwick. **1967** *National Observer* (U.S.) 12 June 5/1 The pattern of an all-too-familiar Western movie, the one about the clever outstate cattle barons displacing the local nesters.

out-state to **out-stature**: see OUT-.

ˈout-ˌstation. [OUT- 1, 3.] **a.** A station at a distance from head-quarters or from the centre of population or business; a subordinate station on the outskirts of a district, etc. Also *attrib.* Esp. in *Austral.* and *N.Z.* use (cf. STATION *sb.* 14).

1844 *Asiatic Jrnl.* June 120 Life in an Indian outstation is, indeed, as simple a one as can well be imagined. *Ibid.* June 127 In outstation life there is..more intercourse between European and native society. **1844** *Port Phillip Patriot* 11 July 1/3 (Morris), There are four out-stations with huts, hurdles..and every convenience. **1859** H. KINGSLEY *G. Hamlyn* xxvii, Sam started off..to visit one of their out-station huts. **1859** F. FULLER *Five Years' Residence N.Z.* viii. 157 Out-stations are started for the shepherds, who watch separate flocks, to live in. **1862** R. HENNING *Let.* 29 Sept. (1966) 107 Another bedroom wherein reside any other members of the 'staff' who happen to be at home—more than half are always at the out-stations. **1870** WENTWORTH *Amos Thorne* III. 26 On an outstation in the Australian bush. **1882** DE WINDT *Equator* 34 The remainder are quartered at the various forts or out-stations along the coast, and in the interior of the country. **1911** C. E. W. BEAN '*Dreadnought' of Darling* xxxv. 311 When the out-station was reached, she rang up. **1944** F. CLUNE *Red Heart* 64 Southwards he trudged, came to the out-station of the Darling Downs. **1947** P. NEWTON *Wayleggo* (1949) 154 Some high country districts are so extensive that it is necessary to have a second homestead situated in some distant part of the property. Such a place is termed an 'out-station'. **1954** G. DURRELL *Three Singles to Adventure* v. 122, I prefer not to remember the ride to the outstation.

b. A subordinate branch of a business or other enterprise. Also *attrib.*

Some examples are not clearly distinguishable from those in sense a.

1872 W. F. BUTLER *Great Lone Land* (ed. 2) xi. 161 About five miles from the mouth of Rainy River there was a small out-station of the Hudson Bay Company kept by a man named Morrisseau. **1962** *Housewife* (Ceylon) Feb. 8 For the benefit of our outstation members, who have borne with us for so long, we will be opening branch Associations in Kandy and Galle very shortly. **1968** D. LAMPE *Last Ditch* xii. 135 Underground broadcasting from fixed stations is untenable. The out-station operators would have been in great danger. **1970** *Guardian* 24 Aug. 14/1 Small outstations dealing with separate processes in the manufacturing cycle have been established in towns up to 20 miles from the city. **1973** *Sunday Advocate-News* (Barbados) 21 Jan. 2/5 He first appeared in uniform on normal patrol work attached to Central Station. He next underwent a short spell of duty at 'out-stations' before returning to the Bridgetown Division office to take up clerical duties. **1975** *Times* 9 June 13/8 (Advt.), National Railway Museum..York..an out-station of the Science Museum London.

'out,stationed, *ppl. a.* [OUT- 11.] Stationed or placed outside, in the open air, etc.

1862 ADM. FITZROY in *Times* 12 Apr., Causes of rain or snow which we can feel by the outstationed instruments.

outstay (aʊt'steɪ), *v.* [OUT- 17, 18.]

1. *trans.* To stay beyond the limit of; to exhaust by staying; to overstay.

1600 SHAKS. *A.Y.L.* I. iii. 90 If you out-stay the time, vpon mine honor..you die. **1635** QUARLES *Embl.* Hieroglyph vi. (1718) 338, I have out-staid my patience. **1692** SOUTHERNE *Wives Excuse* III. i. **1881** H. JAMES *Portr. Lady* li, She had already outstayed her invitation. **1893** FENN *Real Gold* (1894) 31 You are afraid of outstaying your welcome.

2. a. To stay longer than.

1689 SHADWELL *Bury F.* IV, I will out-stay him. **1783** MAD. D'ARBLAY *Diary* 19 June, Mr. Pepys, and I, outstayed the rest near an hour. **1880** MRS. FORRESTER *Roy & V.* II. 181 Mrs. Fitzallan outstayed all the other guests.

b. To surpass in endurance.

1877 *Coursing Calendar Autumn 1876* 5 Laughter made the early points with Lady Don, but the latter fairly outstayed the dog. **1951** *Publ. Amer. Dial. Soc.* XVI. 48 *Outstay*, to be able to equal the speed of one's nearest competitors long enough to defeat them... *Outstay the field: phr.*, of a horse: to take the lead and hold it until the finish.

out'steal, *v.* [OUT- 14, 15.]

1. *intr.* To steal out, slip away furtively. (In ME. two words.)

c **1250** *Gen. & Ex.* 2882 Ðu art min ðral, ðat hidel-like min lond vt-stal. *a* **1510** DOUGLAS *K. Hart* II. 401 Strenth is away, outstolling [= outstolen] lyk ane theif.

2. *trans.* To steal away from (a person) secretly.

1672 O. HEYWOOD *Diaries*, etc. (1883) III. 197 She..charg'd him not to goe but he out-stole her, and went. **1877** BROWNING *Agamemnon* 685 Either some one outstole us or out-prayed us—Some god—no man it was the tiller touching.

out'steam, *v.* [OUT- 18.] *trans.* To excel in steaming; to steam faster than.

1862 *Sat. Rev.* XIV. 187/2 A ship big enough to eat her up, and also..to have outsailed and outsteamed her.

†**out-'stent,** *ppl. a. Sc.* [f. OUT- 11 + STENT stretched.] Outstretched.

1605 MONTGOMERIE *Mindes Mel.* Ps. xix. 2 The firmament And heauens out-stent..Thy handywork and glorious praise proclaim.

'outstep, *sb.* [OUT- 7.] **1.** The act of stepping out; the 'step' in a march. *rare.*

1869 BROWNING *Ring & Bk.* x. 426 Careful lest the common ear Break measure, miss the outstep of life's march.

2. In full *outstep well.* An oil well drilled beyond an area already drilled in order to extend the productive area or ascertain its limits.

1947 *Economist* 5 July 40/1 Some of these wells were considerable outsteps to test the possibilities of outlying areas, thereby extending the limits of the proven producing area to the west and north. **1955** *Bull. Amer. Assoc. Petroleum Geologists* XXXIX. 1353 In the latter part of the year a contract National 80 B rig began drilling a program of outsteps to evaluate the oil find at Alcata-I. **1973** R. E. CHAPMAN *Petroleum Geol.* xii. 256 More problems arise when planning an 'out-step' well, to prove an extension to the accumulation, or to define its limits.

out'step, *v.* [OUT- 17.] *trans.* To step outside of or beyond; to overstep.

1759 GOLDSM. *Enquiry* x. Misc. Wks. (Globe) 441/2 The actor..who by outstepping nature, chooses to exhibit the ridiculous *outré* of a harlequin under the sanction of that venerable name [Shakspere]. **1819** *Metropolis* III. 12 He outstepped the bounds of moderation. **1875** JOWETT *Plato* (ed. 2) I. 119 Here..Socrates and Plato outstep the truth.

So **'out,stepping** *vbl. sb.* [OUT- 9], a stepping out of one's course.

1632 SANDERSON *Serm.* (1681) II. 18 When a man, thus walking with God in the main, hath yet these outsteppings and deviations upon the by.

'out-still. [f. OUT- 3 + STILL *sb.*, a distillery.] In India: A private still licensed by government outside the limits of the areas supplied with liquor from central distilleries. Also *attrib.*

1884 *Pall Mall G.* 30 Aug. 1/2 The so-called outstill system which finds favour with the Bengal Government carries death and ruin into the sober and peaceful homes of frugal industry. **1897** J. A. GRAHAM *Thresh. Three Closed Lands* iii. 41 This is one of the out-stills for whose abolition there was much agitation a few years ago.

out-sting, etc.: see OUT-.

out'stink, *v.* [OUT- 18c, 18.]

1. *trans.* To overpower or drive out by stench.

a **1661** HOLYDAY *Juvenal* 86 African oile..out-stinks, nay drives-away African, or the most rank, serpents.

2. To stink more than, surpass in stench.

c **1620** *Trag. Barnavelt* II. vi. in Bullen *O. Pl.* II. 241 Body a me, How their feare outstincks their garlick! **1656** EARL MONM. tr. *Boccalini, Pol. Touchstone* (1674) 290 Assafœtida that would out-stink a Pole-cat. **1808** SOUTHEY *Lett.* (1856) II. 74 In Borrowdale there is a well which, I dare be sworn, will out-stink Leamington water.

†**'out-,stop.** *Obs. rare.* [OUT- 3.] (app.) An outside guard.

14.. *Fencing* in *Rel. Ant.* I. 308 [see IN-STOP].

out-storm, etc.: see OUT- 21.

out'strain, *v.* [OUT- 15, 18.]

1. *trans.* To strain out; to stretch out tightly.

1591 SPENSER *Virg. Gnat* 280 All his [a serpent's] folds are now in length outstrained. **1801** SOUTHEY *Thalaba* III. xviii, When the door-curtain hangs in heavier folds: When the out-strain'd tent flags loosely.

2. To outdo by straining or strenuous effort.

1648 J. BEAUMONT *Psyche* XV. cxliv, But vivid John..Quickly his Fellow-traveller outstrein'd In Ardor's race.

†**'outstray.** *Obs.* [OUT- 7.] The act of straying from the right way; aberration.

1643 TRAPP *Comm. Gen.* xxii. 3 The mother and nurse of all our distempers and outstrayes. **1647** —— *Comm., Mell. Theol.* 683 He sends for us by his Spirit in our out-straies, and looks us up again.

†**'out-,straying,** *vbl. sb. Obs.* = prec.

1619 W. WHATELEY *God's Husb.* I. 105 The wickednesse, and out-strayings, and finall reuolts of some. *a* **1639** —— *Protot.* (1640) 152 If he finde us in our outstrayings, and give us both direction and will to come into the right way againe.

out'stream, *v. poetic.* [OUT- 14.] *intr.* To stream out.

1600 FAIRFAX *Tasso* VI. xxxiv, Wide was the wound, the blood outstreamed fast. **1878** WHITTIER *To W. F. Bartlett* 31 When..the white light of Christ outstreams From the red disk of Mars.

So **'out,streaming** *vbl. sb.* and *ppl. a.*

1846 TRENCH *Mirac.* xiii. (1862) 240 An actual outstreaming and outbreathing of the fulness of his inner life. **1886** *Athenæum* 20 Feb. 266/3 Rapid out-streamings of matter from the head [of a comet]. **1895** *Thinker* VII. 354 The eternal world, whose atmosphere is God's outstreaming glory.

†**out'streat,** *v. Obs. rare.* [f. OUT- 14 + STREAT *v.*] *intr.* To exude; to distil or flow out.

a **1631** DONNE *Progr. Soule* 344 They did not eat His flesh, nor suck those oyls which thence outstreat. [**1879** BROWNING *Ned Bratts* 180, I strike the rock, outstreats the life-stream at my rod! (Refers to Donne in note.)]

†**'out-,street.** *Obs.* [OUT- 1, 3.] A street outside the walls or in the outskirts of a town.

1704 HEARNE *Duct. Hist.* (1714) I. 438 With..lodging in those out-streets for the Riders of the said Horse. **1722** DE FOE *Plague* (1756) 216 When the People came into the Streets from the Country..they would see the Out-streets empty. **1755** in JOHNSON.

'outstretch, *sb.* [OUT- 7.]

1. The act or fact of stretching out.

1863 MRS. WHITNEY *Faith Gartney* xi. (ed. 18) 94 Brought her thoughts home again from their far outstretch. **1871** BROWNING *Balaust.* 2486 Its outstretch of beneficence Shall have a speedy ending on the earth.

2. An outstretched tract; extension, extent.

1864 *Gd. Words* 12/1 This south-western outstretch of England. **1918** A. SYMONS *Cities & Sea-Coasts* iii. 312 Grass, or any soil, was but a rare interval between a broken and distracted outstretch of grey rock.

3. The distance to which anything stretches out.

1888 O. CRAWFURD *Sylvia Arden* 308 A passage..little broader than the outstretch of my two arms.

out'stretch, *v.* [OUT- 15, 15b, 17, 18.]

1. *trans.* To stretch out or forth. (Chiefly *poetic.*)

? *a* **1366** CHAUCER *Rom. Rose* 1515 And doun on knees he gan to falle, And forth his heed and nekke out straughte To drinken of that welle a draughte. **1591** SPENSER *Muiopot.* 87 So did this flie outstretch his fearefull hornes. *c* **1614** SIR W. MURE *Dido & Æneas* III. 236 Ships..With wings owt-streatch't, all vnder equall saile. **1823** BYRON *Island* IV. ix, Abelard..his arms outstretch'd. **1877** BROWNING *Agamemnon* 1108 Hand after hand she outstretches.

2. To extend in area or content; to expand.

1647 H. MORE *Song of Soul* II. App. xlv, Wherefore this wide and wast Vacuity, Which endlesse is outstretched thorough all. **1687** *Sc. Metr. Ps.* cxxxvi. 6 Who did outstretch This Earth so great and wide. *a* **1758** RAMSAY *Fox turned Preacher* 48 [He] preach'd, And with loud cant his lungs out-stretch'd. **1840** DICKENS *Barn. Rudge* iii, The great city, which lay outstretched before him.

3. To stretch to its limit, to strain.

1607 SHAKS. *Timon* V. iii. 3 Tymon is dead, who hath out-stretcht his span. **1645** MILTON *Tetrach.* Wks. 1738 I. 251 Outstretching the most rigorous nerves of Law and Rigour.

4. To stretch beyond (a limit, etc.).

1597 BEARD *Theatre God's Judgem.* (1612) 277 So farre did his impudencie outstretch the bond of reason. **1839** BAILEY *Festus* i. (1852) 6 My mercy doth outstretch the universe. **1869** J. EADIE *Comm. Gal.* 194 The divine and illimitable will always outstretch its [dogma's] precision and logic.

†**5.** To outstrip in a race. *Obs.*

a **1642** SIR W. MONSON *Naval Tracts* II. (1704) 270/1 Grey-hounds strove to..outstretch one another in a Course. **1703** COLLIER *Ess. Mor. Subj.* II. (1709) 94 They..out-stretch the Speed of Gunpowder, and Distance Light and Lightning.

'outstretched (-strɛtʃt), *ppl. a.* [OUT- 11.]

1. Stretched out in length or breadth; held forth; extended. Said esp. of the arms.

1535 COVERDALE *Jer.* xxi. 5, I my selff will fight agaynst you, with an outstretched honde. *Ibid.* xxvii. 5 With my greate power & outstretched arme. *a* **1625** FLETCHER *Double Marriage* IV. i, We that have..Laught at the out-stretch'd arm of tyranny. **1725** POPE *Odyss.* XII. 298 They call, and aid with out-stretch'd arms implore. **1891** T. HARDY *Tess* (1900) 142/2 He knelt down beside her outstretched form, and put his lips upon hers.

2. Stretched in area or compass; distended.

1603 SHAKS. *Meas. for M.* II. iv. 153 With an out-stretcht throate Ile tell the world aloud What man thou art.

Hence †**out'stretchedness,** extension.

1674 N. FAIRFAX *Bulk & Selv.* 42 For as Gods Eternity is not endless longsomness, so neither is his Immensity unbounded outstretchedness. *Ibid.* 34, 105.

'out,stretcher. [OUT- 8.] One who or that which stretches out; an extensor. So **'out,stretching** *vbl. sb.* and *ppl. a.* [OUT- 9, 10], stretching out, extending, extension.

1480 CAXTON *Descr. Brit.* 44 The contre which is now named scotland is an outstretchyng of the north partie of britayn. **1600** J. PORY tr. *Leo's Africa* Introd. 41 A cape very well knowen in regard of the eminency and outstretching thereof. **1654** GATAKER *Disc. Apol.* 52 A haughtie, bold, out-stretching, and selfe-confiding spirit. **1854** OWEN *Skel. & Teeth* in *Circ. Sc., Organ. Nat.* I. 227 In the bat the fingers are lengthened, attenuated, and made outstretchers and supporters of a pair of wings. **1866** J. G. MURPHY *Comm. Ex.* xiv. 30 On the outstretching of Moses's hand.

out'stride, *v.* [OUT- 18.] *trans.* To surpass in striding, to excel in length of stride; also *fig.*

1610 B. JONSON *Pr. Henry's Barriers* Wks. (Rtldg.) 577/2 With arcs triumphal for their actions done, Out-striding the Colossus of the Sun. **1621** BP. H. KING *Serm.* 25 Nov. 57 That which outstrides the largest fable in Ouid, the Golden Legend. **1798** JANE AUSTEN *Let.* 17 Nov. (1952) 27 Though she does not gain strength very rapidly, my expectations are humble enough not to outstride her improvements. **1898** *Westm. Gaz.* 31 May 5/2 He [a horse] was apparently beaten rather for speed than for stamina, or possibly outstridden by his gigantic rival. **1972** *Times* 11 Sept. 3/1 The department outstrides those of many universities in equipment and reputation.

out'strike, *v.* [OUT- 18, 15.]

1. *trans.* To excel in striking; to deal swifter or heavier blows than.

1606 SHAKS. *Ant. & Cl.* IV. vi. 36 A swifter meane Shall out strike thought, but thought will doo't. **1663** DAVENANT *Siege of R.* II. 50 [A] Few Rhodian Knights, making their several stands, Out-strike Assemblies of our many Hands.

†**2.** To strike out (letters or words). *poetic. Obs.*

1598 DRAYTON *Heroical Ep., Matilda to K. John* Poems (1637) 188 This sentence serves, and that my hand out strikes; That pleaseth well, and this as much mislikes. **1604** HIERON *Wks.* I. 565 That which one..author likes, The same another cleane out-strikes.

outstrip (aʊt'strɪp), *v.*[1] [f. OUT- 18, 18c, 17 + STRIP *v.*[2], to run or advance swiftly, to speed, scud, 'whip'.]

1. *trans.* To pass in running or any kind of swift motion; to outrun, leave behind in a race; to escape from by running. Also *fig.* with direct imagery of a race.

1580 LYLY *Euphues* (Arb.) 419 When I runne as Hippomanes did with Atlanta, who was last in the course, but first at the crowne: So that I gesse that woemen are eyther easie to be out stripped [*ed.* 1582 tripped], or willing. **1594** SHAKS. *Rich. III*, IV. i. 42 Thy Mothers Name is ominous to Children, If thou wilt out-strip Death, goe crosse the Seas, And liue with Richmond. **1603** DEKKER *Grissil* (Shaks. Soc.) 4 The deer Outstrips the active hound. **1748** *Anson's Voy.* III. iii. 328 Mr. Gordon.. being fresh and in breath, easily outstripped the.. man, and got before him to the Commodore. **1860** TYNDALL *Glac.* II. xxvii. 382 If a plastic substance.. flow down a sloping Canal, the lateral portions.. will be outstripped by the Central ones.

2. *transf.* and *fig.* To excel, surpass, get ahead of, or leave behind, in any kind of competition, or in any respect in which things may be compared.

1592 NASHE *P. Penilesse* D ij b, He so far outstript him in vilanious words.. that the name of sport could not perswade him patience. **1607** NORDEN *Surv. Dial.* I. 9 They striue one to outstrip another in giuing most. **1665** BUNYAN *Holy Citie* (1669) 91 They out-stript all the Prophets that ever went before them. *a* **1797** H. WALPOLE *Mem. Geo. II* (1847) II. ix. 301 Fox, not to be outstripped in homage to Argyle, justified the measure. **1834** PRINGLE *Afr. Sk.* xi. 342 Promising ere long to rival, if not to outstrip the present capital.

†**b.** To exceed as a quality. *Obs.*

1610 B. JONSON *Alch.* v. Epil., If I have outstript An old man's gravity, or strict canon, think What a young wife and a good brain may do. **1632** LITHGOW *Trav.* III. 123 The Riuer Simois: whose breadth all the way hath not outstripd the fields aboue two miles.

†**3.** To pass beyond, leave behind (a place). *Obs.*

1632 LITHGOW *Trav.* VIII. 345 Scarcely had we out-stripd Rhyneberg.. a Dutch mile.

outstrip (aʊt'strɪp), *v.*[2] [f. OUT- 18 + STRIP *v.*[1]] *trans.* To surpass in stripping; to wear less clothing than. (With punning reference to OUTSTRIP *v.*[1])

1887 *Daily News* 29 Dec. 5/3 'Yes,' replied his cynical friend, after a glance at the young lady, 'I admit that she out-strips them all.' **1897** W. C. HAZLITT *Four Generations Lit. Family* II. 155 The abridged petticoats of the ladies proceeded to an intolerable pitch; and many tried, as Byron said, to outstrip one another. **1938** H. M. ALEXANDER *Strip Tease* 19 'Then it was competition that was responsible for the peeling.' 'Yeah.' Garns laughs. 'They tried to outstrip each other.'

out-strive, etc.: see OUT- 18b.

'outstroke. [OUT- 7.]

1. A stroke directed outwards.

1874 KNIGHT *Dict. Mech.* 627/1 On the completion of the stroke, the steam is allowed to pass freely from one side of the piston to the other, producing an equilibrium of effect during the out-stroke.

2. *Mining.* The act of striking out: see quot. 1893–4. Also *attrib.* in ***outstroke-rent***.

1851 GREENWELL *Coal-trade Terms Northumb. & Durh.* 42 *Outstroke rent*, for the privilege of breaking the barrier, and working and conveying underground the coal from an adjoining royalty. **1857–8** *Act 21 & 22 Vict.* c. 44 §20 By way of out-stroke or other underground communication. **1893–4** *Northumbld. Gloss.* s.v., Instroke is the passing out of a working royalty into another royalty. Outstroke is the act as regarded by the lessor of the entered royalty.

out-strut to **out-subtle**: see OUT-.

outsucken ('aʊtˌsʌk(ə)n), *a. Sc. Law.* [f. OUT- 12 + SUCKEN.] Outside the sucken; free from restriction to a particular mill for the grinding of corn; not subject to astriction. The opposite of *insucken*.

1773 ERSKINE *Instit.* (ed. 2) II. ix. §20. 314 The duties payable by those who come voluntarily to the mill are called outsucken or out-town multures. **1896** J. SKELTON *Summ. & Wint. Balmawhapple* I. 172 The sma' sequels o' the outsucken multures.

out-'suffer, *v.* [OUT- 18.] *trans.* To surpass in suffering.

1651, 1855 [see OUT-LABOUR].

out-suitor to **out-superstition**: see OUT-.

out'swagger, *v.* [OUT- 18.] *trans.* To surpass in swaggering.

1607 *Lingua* v. vii. in Hazl. *Dodsley* IX. 439 Ay, wilt see me outswagger him? **1630** B. JONSON *New Inn* IV. ii, They out-swagger all the wapentake. **1884** L. OLIPHANT *Haifa* (1887) 203 They [Orientals] must never be allowed to out-swagger you.

out-swarm, etc.: see OUT- 7.

outswear (-'swɛə(r)), *v.* [OUT- 18, 18c.] *trans.* To outdo or surpass in swearing; to overcome or bear down with swearing.

1588 SHAKS. *L.L.L.* I. ii. 67 Me thinkes I should out-sweare Cupid. **1596** —— *Merch. V.* IV. ii. 17 Weele out-face them, and out-sweare them to. **1690** SHADWELL *Am. Bigot* II, I will out-swear the deepest gamester in Madrid. **1816** *Sporting Mag.* XLVIII. 217 Always allowable, as long as it can be concealed or out-sworn.

out-sweat (-'swɛt), *v. Obs. rare.* [OUT- 16.] *trans.* To work out by sweat or toil.

a **1625** BEAUM. & FL. *Wit without M.* I. i, Out upon't! Caveat emptor! Let the fool out-sweat it, That thinks he has got a catch on't.

out'sweep, *v.* [OUT- 14, 18b.]

1. *intr.* To sweep out, move out with a sweep.

1867 G. MACDONALD *Poems, Three Horses* xviii, If a man withstand, outsweeps my brand: I slay him on the spot.

2. *trans.* To sweep beyond.

1887 G. L. TAYLOR *Centen. Poem* 13 Apr. in *Libr. Mag.* (U.S.) Jan. (1888) 403 Our Davies' three-legged nothing's integration Outsweeps sublimest winged imagination.

'outˌsweeping, *vbl. sb.* [OUT- 9; cf. *sweep out.*] The action of sweeping out; *concr.* that which is swept out, refuse.

1535 COVERDALE *1 Cor.* iv. 13 The very outswepinges of ye worlde, yee the of scowringe of all men.

out'sweeten, *v.* [OUT- 18.] *trans.* To surpass in sweetening or in sweetness.

1611 SHAKS. *Cymb.* IV. ii. 224 No, nor The leafe of Eglantine.. Out-sweetned not thy breath. **1867** TENNYSON *Let.* in *Life* (1897) II. ii. 47 The sweets of office outsweetened by the sweets of out of office.

out'swell, *v.* [OUT- 18, 17, 14, 15.]

1. *trans.* To exceed in swelling or inflation; to swell out more than.

1606 SHAKS. *Tr. & Cr.* IV. v. 9 Blow villaine, till thy sphered Bias cheeke Out-swell the collicke of puft Aquilon. **1809** W. IRVING *Knickerb.* VI. i. (1849) 312 Striving to outstrut and outswell each other like a couple of belligerent turkey cocks.

2. To swell beyond (a point or limit).

1658 HEWYT *Repent. & Convers.* 185 The waters.. out-swelling and breaking down their banks, have overflown both our Church and State. **1659** FULLER *App. Inj. Innoc.* II. 69 But this outswelleth the proportion of my booke. **1695** WOODWARD *Nat. Hist. Earth* III. i. (1723) 141 So filling the Rivers as to make them out-swell their Banks.

3. To swell out, inflate.

1800 HURDIS *Fav. Village* 122 Shudd'ring he sits, in horrent coat outswoln.

So **'outˌswelling** *ppl. a.* [OUT- 10], swelling out.

1678 CUDWORTH *Intell. Syst.* I. v. 826 Body being bulkie or out-swelling extension.

out-swift, etc.: see OUT-.

out'swim, *v.* [OUT- 18.] *trans.* To surpass or excel in swimming, swim faster or farther than.

1603 BRETON *Dignitie of Man* (1879) 14/2 In swiftnesse the Hare will outrunne him, and the Dolphin outswim him. *a* **1618** SYLVESTER *Mayden's Blush* 595 Some on swift Horse-backe to outswim the winde. **1897** *Daily News* 17 June 5/4 The bird [penguin] can outswim the fish with the greatest ease.

out-swindle to **out-tailor**: see OUT-.

outswinger ('aʊtˌswɪŋə(r)). [f. OUT- 7 + SWING *v.*[1]] **1.** *Cricket.* A ball bowled with a swerve or swing from the leg to the off in its flight; also, the bowler of such a ball. So **'outswing**, the swerve or swing imparted to such a ball. Also **'outˌswinging** *ppl. a.*

1920 E. R. WILSON in P. F. Warner *Cricket* 67 Mr. E. W. Clark bowled 'out-swingers'. **1925** *Country Life* 18 July 93/2 To make a ball swerve in the air from the leg stump into the slips (the out-swinger, it is called). **1953** MILLER & WHITINGTON *Cricket Typhoon* 144 It was perfectly controlled late out-swing. **1955** A. ROSS *Australia 55* 211 He drove the out-swinging ball. **1958** P. RICHARDSON *Tackle Cricket this Way* iii. 50 Trueman, also, is primarily an outswinger. **1963** A. ROSS *Australia 63* iii. 82 Barrington, reaching out, played an out-swinger beautifully wide of mid-off. **1968** N. CARDUS in J. Arlott *Cricket: Great Bowlers* 21 He told me that he obtained his out-swing by spin. **1975** *Cricketer* May 9/1 His lifting out-swing is more difficult and his pace changes more skilful.

2. (*Assoc.*) *Football.* A pass, usu. across the mouth of the goal, in which the flight of the ball curves away from the centre of the goal.

1959 *Times* 19 Mar. 18/3 Riley lost his man and sent over an out-swinger. **1961** F. C. AVIS *Sportsman's Gloss.* 37/1 *Outswinger*, a centre pass, particularly from a corner kick, that moves in its flight to goal in a slight arc away from the centre of the goal.

outta ('aʊtə), colloq. contraction of OUT OF *prep. phr.* orig. and chiefly *U.S.* Cf. OUTA.

1937 C. HIMES *Black on Black* (1973) 142 You keep outta dis, yellow niggah. **1958** KEITH & BERGMAN (*song-title*) Outta my mind. *Ibid.*, And I came out-ta my spin, That dizzy spin I was in, Don't ask me, 'Where have I been?' Been out-ta my mind! **1967** *Boston Sunday Herald* 14 May (Comic Section), Outta the way, Barrey boy. **1971** B. BRANDON (*title*) Outta sight, Luther. **1973** *Black World* Jan. 65/1 Tears was dripping down the Grand Worthy Matron's face, making a mess outta all her powder and rouge. **1977** *Ripped & Torn* VI. 2/2 Is this a last ditch attempt by me to make some money outta this thing?

†**out-'take**, *v. Obs.* Forms: see OUT *adv.* and TAKE *v.*; also *contr.* 4–6 **outake**, (5 **owtake**, **otake**), *pa. pple.* **outaken**, **outane**, etc. [f. OUT- 15 + TAKE *v.*; orig. rendering L. *ēripere*, *excipere*.]

1. *trans.* To take out (*lit.*); to extract, draw forth; to deliver, set free.

a **1300** *E.E. Psalter* vi. 5 Torn, Laverd, and my saule out-take [L. *eripe*]. *Ibid.* cxxiii. 7 Our saule als sparw es of land Outane [L. *erepta*] fra snare of huntand. *c* **1450** *Merlin* vi. 100 Neuer noon.. ne shall it not oute take. **1596** DALRYMPLE tr. *Leslie's Hist. Scot.* I. 47 Excepte.. it schortlie had beine outtakne, incontinent the coue it had fillit full.

2. To take out from the reckoning; to exclude from a class or category; to specify as left out; to except.

a **1300** *Cursor M.* 764 (Cott.) Of al þe tres [we ette] bot of an, þe midward tre is vs outtan [*v.rr.* out tane; vte tane; out taken]. *c* **1380** WYCLIF *Sel. Wks.* III. 516 Seynte Poul þat putteþ alle men in subjeccioun to kyngis, outtakeþ nevere on. *c* **1450** tr. *De Imitatione* III. xlii. 113, I outake no þinge, but in all þinges I wol finde þe made bare. **1464** *Rolls of Parlt.* V. 534/2 That they be except, forprised, and outtaken of this Acte. **1567** *Gude & Godlie B.* (S.T.S.) 147, I out tak nane greit nor small.

Hence **out-'taking**, †**ou(t)'takand** *pr. pple.*, quasi-*prep.* = EXCEPTING A. 1, 2.

c **1375** *Sc. Leg. Saints* xi. (*Symon & Judas*) 119 þai suld al de owtakand nane. *Ibid.* xxxiii. (*George*) 57 Man ore best, outakand nane. **1839** BAILEY *Festus* xix. (1848) 211 Out-taking those who have eyes trained to see.

†**out-'take**, *pple.*, *prep.* (*conj. adv.*) *Obs.* Forms: see prec. [Originally a southern form of OUT-TAKEN *pa. pple.*, q.v., passing, like it, imperceptibly from a pple. to a prep. and a conj. adv.

But as *out-take* was not a northern form of the pa. pple. (which was there *out-taken* and *out-tan(e)*, its participial nature would not be apparent to northern writers, and these probably took it for the imperative of the vb.: see b below.]

a. as pple.: Excepted, being excepted.

1387 TREVISA *Higden* (Rolls) I. 337 Out take men [*Caxton* reserued men; *Higd.* exceptis hominibus] alle bestes beeþ smallere þere. *Ibid.* V. 369 All Italy outake Rome [*MS. Harl.* Rome excepte; *Higd.* excepta Roma]. *c* **1420** *Chron. Vilod.* st. 619 þe organys of þe lemys ouȝt take. *c* **1420** *Pallad. on Husb.* I. 723 Al maner puls is good, the ficche outake. *c* **1422** HOCCLEVE *Jereslaus's Wife* 628 Neuere so shal ther man do to me.. outake oonly he.

b. app. as imperative: Except.

c **1330** R. BRUNNE *Chron.* (1810) 332 In alle Breteyn was nouht.. A fest so noble wrouht.. Out tak Carleon. **1513** DOUGLAS *Æneis* v. xii. 61 Wes all the navy, out tak four schippis lost [L. *quatuor amissis*].

c. Where the participial or imperative notion is merged in a preposition: Except; with the exception of; save, but; = EXCEPT *prep.* 1.

(For the α instances, in which the elements are written separate, the prepositional analysis is doubtful.)

α. *c* **1375** *Cursor M.* 652 (Fairf.) Of trees and frute.. al sal be þyne oute take [*other MSS.* bot, but] ane. **1398** TREVISA *Barth. De P.R.* v. ii. (Tollem. MS.), þat hauen all þe body of a man out take þe heed [L. *præter caput*]. *c* **1440** *Gesta Rom.* xxxvi. 141 (Add. MS.) The Stewarde.. put of alle his clothes, oute take his sherte.

β. ? *a* **1366** CHAUCER *Rom. Rose* 948 For al was golde, men myght it see, Outake the fetheres and the tree. **1387** TREVISA *Higden* (Rolls) II. 139 Hely haþ vnder hym Cantebriggeschire outake Merslond [*Harl. tr.* Merlonde excepte; *Higd.* præter Merlond]. **1444** *Rolls of Parlt.* V. 111/2 He vilanisly toke of all.. her clothis of her body, otake her smokke. **1496** *Dives & Paup.* (W. de W.) I. xxiii. 59/1 Euery planete is more than all the erthe outake the mone & mercury. **1520** M. NISBET *New Test. in Scots* Mark xi. 14 He fand nathing outtak leeues [WYCLIF[2] out takun leeues; *Vulg.* præter folia]. **1612** T. JAMES *Corrupt. Scripture* III. 11 No citie.. out-take Euey, that dwelled in mount Gabaon.

d. As conj. adv., preceding *that* (= EXCEPT *conj.* 1) or a preposition.

1387 TREVISA *Higden* (Rolls) III. 423 Out take þat [*Higd.* nisi quod] he is þe worse þeef þat steleþ most. *Ibid.* IV. 39 In every place out take in þe Psawter [*Higd.* præter quam in psalterio]. **1433** *Rolls of Parlt.* IV. 452/1 Outake alweys, yat al clothes, called Streites.. have licence of sale and deliveraunce [etc.].

out-take ('aʊtteɪk), *sb.* [f. OUT- 7 + TAKE *sb.*] A length of film or tape rejected in editing.

1960 O. SKILBECK *ABC of Film & TV* 92 *Out takes*, takes rejected in the cutting room. **1970** *Guardian* 27 Jan. 1/3 Unused film, what in the industry are called 'the out-takes'. **1972** I. HAMILTON *Thrill Machine* xxxii. 147, I got the original neg. all the out-takes, and seven prints.. and the film was out of circulation. **1974** T. CHASTAIN *Pandora's Box* (1975) xv. 149 We're going to show you.. all the film we shot yesterday.. including the out-takes—that is, the stuff we won't be using on the air after we've finished editing. **1977** *Zigzag* Mar. 29/3 Both the album's opener, Gene's 'Home Run King', and the traditional 'In The Pines' could have easily been outtakes from either D & C album. **1977** *Time* 24 Oct. 54/3 *Looking for Mr. Goodbar* has narrative lapses, jerky editing and confusing fantasy sequences that look like Ken Russell outtakes.

†**out-'taken**, *pa. pple.*, *prep.*, *conj. adv. Obs.* Forms: see OUT-TAKE *v.* [pa. pple. of OUT-TAKE *v.*

Orig. used in concord with a sb. or pron. in the absolute case (= Latin ablative absolute), e.g. *exceptā suā mātre*, ME. 'his moder out-taken', 'out-taken his moder'. Both these orders were in use, but the latter was the prevailing one; and the position and effect of the pple. being thus equivalent to those of a preposition, it became at length identified with the prepositions: cf. the equivalent EXCEPT. Like other prepositions also (e.g. *before, for, till*), it was used to connect a subordinate to a principal sentence, orig. with *that*, subseq. alone, and thus became a conjunctive adv. or subordinating conjunction.]

A. *pa. pple.* (in concord with, and following, a noun in absol. case) = (Being) excepted. Cf. EXCEPT *v.* 1 b.

c **1375** *Sc. Leg. Saints* ii. (*Paulus*) 940 Owtwart thingis neuir-þe-les Owtane, þat wes þe besynes þat he had. *Ibid.* xxxiii. (*George*) 93 Man na [= nor] wif outane nane. **1409** in *Exch. Rolls Scotl.* IV. ccix, His allegiance acht till.. the King anerly outane. **1429–30** *Papers of Coldingham Priory* (Surtees) 104 The warand wod and venyson all way oute taken. **1530** PALSGR. 320/2 Outtaken, excepté.

B. *prep.* (In the α instances, in which the elements are written separate, perh. still felt as a pple.)

1. = OUT-TAKE C, EXCEPT *prep.* 1.
α. **13..** *Cursor M.* 5411 (Cott.) Vte tan [*v.rr.* out tane, vte take; *a* 1425 outake] þe landes of þat lede. *a* **1340** HAMPOLE *Psalter* xxi. 18 þai partid his clathes..out takyn his kirtil. **1362** LANGL. *P. Pl.* A. x. 169 Alle schulen dye..Out taken Eihte soules. *c* **1400** MAUNDEV. (Roxb.) i. 4 He has lost all, oute taken Greece. *c* **1450** *St. Cuthbert* (Surtees) 4330 Oute tane Elfride, þai destruyde All' þe kynges lynage.
β. *c* **1375** *Sc. Leg. Saints* xxi. (*Clement*) 491 þare was nane þat hyme saw..Ovtane petyre. **1387** TREVISA *Higden* (Rolls) I. 261 Wel nyȝ all manere metal..outakyn tyn [*Harl. tr.* tynne excepte, *Caxt.* reserued tyn, *Higd.* excepto stanno]. **1388** WYCLIF *Mark* xii. 32 Ther is noon other, outakun [1382 out taken] hym [Vulg. *præter eum*]. *a* **1400** *Burgh Laws* ix. (*Sc. Stat.* I.), Outtane salt [*præter sal*] and heryng. **1501** DOUGLAS *Pal. Hon.* III. ii, With all the rout, outtane my nimphe and I. **1816** SCOTT *Old Mort.* xlii, Ane o' the maist cruel oppressors..(out-taken Sergeant Bothwell). **1816** —— *Antiq.* xxiv, I question if there's ony body in the country can tell the tale but mysell—aye out-taken the laird though.

2. Leaving out of account; except as regards; besides in addition to; = EXCEPT *prep.* 2.
1340–70 *Alex. & Dind.* 153 For, out-taken viij wokus of al þe twelf monþe..Dredful dragonus drawen hem þiddire. *c* **1375** *Sc. Leg. Saints* xi. (*Symon & Judas*) 389, lxx thowsande cristyne..Ovtane princis, kynge, and quene, Wyffis, and barnys alsa bedene. *c* **1400** MAUNDEV. (Roxb.) vii. 26 Men may go in, oute taken þe tyme þat þe bawme growes. *c* **1440** *York Myst.* xxiv. 147 Owtane goddis will allone.

C. *conj. adv.*

1. Introducing a subordinate clause (with or without *that*): = EXCEPT *conj.* 1.
c **1375** *Sc. Leg. Saints* ix. (*Jacobus*) 21 He wane nan of þa, Ovtane þat vith gret pyne He purchasit discipulis nyne. *Ibid.* xl. (*Ninian*) 1444 Bath his schank and his kne Ware als haile..As þai..befor wes, Owtane þare wes les of flesche. **1375** BARBOUR *Bruce* VI. 407 He wes arayit at poynt clenly, Outakyn that his hede wes bair. **1496** *Dives & Paup.* (W. de W.) v. xv. 216/2, I haue take them all to you..out taken that ye shall not ete flesshe with the blood.

2. Introducing a hypothetical clause: in quot. with *if* (= except if, unless): = EXCEPT *conj.* 2.
1389 in *Eng. Gilds* (1870) 35 Out taken ȝef he be a theffe proued.

3. Preceding a phrase formed of a preposition and its object: = EXCEPT *conj.* 3.
a **1350** *St. Thomas* 20 in Horstm. *Altengl. Leg.* (1881) 20 Send me to folk of ilk a kynde Outaken vnto folk of Ynde. *c* **1375** *Cursor M.* 5388 (Fairf.) For hungre dyed mony an, Out takin in egipte and chanaan. *c* **1400** MAUNDEV. (Roxb.) xxvi. 121 Plentee of all maner of bestes, oute taken of swyne.

†**out-'taking,** *vbl. sb. Obs.* [f. OUT-TAKE *v.* + -ING[1].] The action of the verb OUT-TAKE; taking out, deliverance; exception.
1483 *Cath. Angl.* 264/2 An Outetakynge, *excepcio.* **1530** PALSGR. 250/1 Outtakyng, *exception.* *c* **1610** SIR J. MELVIL *Mem.* (1683) 90 Warned..by divers who were upon the Council of her out-taking.

†**out-'takingly,** *adv. Obs.* [f. *out-taking* pr. pple. (or error for *out-taken* pa. pple.) of OUT-TAKE *v.*] By way of exception; exceptionally.
1549 CHALONER *Erasm. on Folly* Hjb, Few are accustomed to erre so outtakyngly. **1566** DRANT *Horace, Sat.* x. Evb, But nowe and then outtakyngly, he wyll be overseene.

out-talent to **out-tease:** see OUT-.

out-talk (aʊt'tɔːk), *v.* [OUT- 18, 18b.] *trans.* To outdo, go beyond, excel, or overcome in talking.
1596 SHAKS. *Tam. Shr.* I. ii. 248 What, this Gentleman will out-talke vs all. **1672** PETTY *Pol. Anat.* 363 The priests ..can often out-talk in Latin those who dispute with them. **1772** *Ann. Reg.* 7 A prince, who..has out-talked the most rigid republicans in his discourses upon liberty. **1863** W. PHILLIPS *Speeches* vi. 115 We are weak here,—out-talked, out-voted.

out-tane: see OUT-TAKEN.

out-'tell, *v.* [OUT- 18, 15, 15b.]

†**1.** *trans.* To tell or count beyond; to exceed the reckoning of. *Obs.*
1613 BEAUM. & FL. *Coxcomb* I. vi, I have out-told the clock For haste; he is not here.

2. To tell out or forth, declare.
1818 KEATS *Endym.* I. 392 Thus all out-told Their fond imaginations.

b. To tell or reckon to the end or completely.
1868 J. H. NEWMAN *Verses Var. Occas.* 215 And of our crimes the tale complete,..Outtold by our full numbers sweet.

outter, outterance: see OUTER, OUTRANCE.

†**'out-'term,** *sb. Obs. rare*[−1]. [OUT- 3.] Outward figure; external or bodily form; mere exterior. (Cf. TERM *sb.*)
1601 B. JONSON *Poetaster* v. i, Not to bear cold forms, nor men's out-terms, Without the inward fires and lives of men.

†**out-'term,** *v. Obs. rare.* [OUT- 25: after L. *ex-termināre.*] *trans.* To exterminate.
a **1340** HAMPOLE *Psalter* xxxvi. 9 þai sall be out termyd. *Ibid.* lxxix. 14 þe bare of þe wod outtermyd it.

out-terrace, -testify, etc.: see OUT-.

out-'think, *v.* [OUT- 15b, 18, 17.]

†**1.** *trans.* To think out, contrive or devise by thinking. *Obs.*
1382 WYCLIF *Wisd.* xv. 4 Forsothe not in to errour inladde vs the oute thenking of the euele craft of men [*Vulg.* hominum malæ artis excogitatio].

2. To excel or go beyond in thinking; to pass or advance out of (a condition, etc.) by thinking.
1704 NORRIS *Ideal World* II. ii. 94 They will not only think, but out-think us. **1857** W. SMITH *Thorndale* 602, I have outlived this state of mind; I have out-thought it. **1877** E. R. CONDER *Bas. Faith* iv. 142 We cannot outthink the bounds of thought. **1934** *Sun* (Baltimore) 10 Jan. 1/1 The farmers..out-thought the railway officials. They telephoned back to Burlington and appraised the pickets there of the train's approach. **1941** STEINBECK & RICKETTS *Sea of Cortez* xvi. 161 The mule..knows he can out-think a horse and he is pretty sure he can out-think a human. **1954** D. DODGE *Lights of Skaro* ii. 50 They could outrun us, outfight us, or overwhelm us, but they couldn't out-think us. **1962** L. DEIGHTON *Ipcress File* xiii. 78 What chance did I stand..they were both out-thinking me at every move. **1972** 'H. CALVIN' *Take Two Popes* vi. 48 His quarry had out-thought him, and fled into the unexpected area on the other side of the road.

†**out-thrappe,** app. var. of OUTROOP. *Obs.*
1578 T. N. tr. *Conq. W. India* 365 This newe Iudge.. commaunded all his goodes to be sold by out-thrappe, for a greate deal lesse then his goodes were woorth.

out-threaten to **out-throb:** see OUT-.

†**'outthrift.** *Obs.* [Cf. OUT- 12.] One without thrift; an unthrift.
1534 in W. H. Turner *Select. Rec. Oxford* 128 The punishment of outthrifts and offenders.

out-'through, *prep.* and *adv. Sc.* [f. OUT *adv.* + THROUGH *prep.*, q.v. for Forms.]

A. *prep.* Right through, quite through, from end to end (or side to side) of; through the whole of, throughout.
1456 *Sc. Acts Jas. II* (1597) §59 To the intent, that the Demyes, that ar keiped in hande, haue course and come out-throw the Realme. **1547** *Reg. Privy Council Scot.* I. 71 To haif course and passage commonlie outthrouch this realme. *c* **1560** A. SCOTT *Poems* (S.T.S.) xiii. 21 That crewell dert outthrow my hart wald boir. **1699–1825** [see INTHROUGH *prep.*]. **1724** RAMSAY *Vision* ii, Boreas branglit out-through the cluds. **1825** JAMIESON s.v., 'He gaed out-trough the bear-lan''. *Clydes.*

B. *adv.* Right through; throughout; thoroughly.
c **1250** *Gen. & Ex.* 2688 Moyses bi-sette al ðat burȝ, Oc it was riche & strong ut-ðhurȝ. *c* **1375** *Sc. Leg. Saints* x. (*Mathou*) 436 A felone..come be-hynd hyme at þe bake, And owt-throw with a swerd hym strake. **1682** PEDEN *Lord's Trumpet* 9 The blood of the saints hath run in throw and out throw. **1768** ROSS *Helenore* Invoc. 4 I'm out-throw as clung.

'out-throw, 'outthrow, *sb.* [OUT- 7.]

1. The act of throwing out; ejection, emission; output; outburst of energy; matter ejected.
1855 M. PATTISON in *Oxford Ess.* 273 It would be of no use to appeal to the rise and fall of the scholastic philosophy... For this reason, we pass over the wonderful purely philosophical out-throw of the thirteenth century. **1869** PHILLIPS *Vesuv.* viii. 228 We see in it a local outthrow of stony, ashy, and perhaps muddy materials. **1892** *Cornh. Mag.* Oct. 415 Its outthrow of mud and stones.

2. A throwing or being thrown out of line.
1855 *Cornwall* 113 The more obtuse the angle, the more considerable is the out-throw.

out-throw, outthrow (aʊt'θrəʊ), *v.* [OUT- 15, 17, 18.]

†**1.** *trans.* To throw out, cast out. *Obs.* (Properly two words.)
a **1300** *E.E. Psalter* lxxii. 18 þou out þrew þam when up-hoven ware þai. **1413** *Pilgr. Sowle* IV. xx. (Caxton 1483) 65 On the wylle I oute throwe my salt teres. **1596** SPENSER *F.Q.* IV. ii. 1 Firebrand of hell..from thence out throwen, Into this world to worke confusion. *a* **1711** KEN *Hymns Evang.* Poet. Wks. 1721 I. 119 Foul Invida with Gall she had outthrown.

2. To throw beyond (a point); to surpass (a person) in the length of a throw.
1613 *Uncasing of Machiav.* 18 Out-throw it [the jack at bowls] not, lest thou lose the cast. **1638** MAYNE *Lucian* (1664) 201 Striving who shall hurle farthest, and outthrow the rest. **1676** HOBBES *Iliad* (1677) 358 And with the spears I Polydore out-threw.

†**b.** *fig.* To exaggerate. *Obs.*
a **1680** BUTLER *Rem.* (1759) I. 12 T'out-throw, and stretch, and to enlarge Shall now no more be laid t'our Charge.

'out-ˌthrowing, *vbl. sb.* [OUT- 9.] Throwing out. So **'out-thrown** *ppl. a.* [OUT- 11], thrown out, cast out.
1889 C. EDWARDES *Sardinia* 163 Needless out-throwing of heels. **1891** *Pall Mall G.* 23 Dec. 7/3 The end of Leather-lane was completely blocked with the out-thrown goods. **1927** *Month* May 398 The sides of the outthrown head-land are too steep to be rushed. **1978** *Nature* 26 Jan. 318/2 The 'grid', however, may result principally from the overlapping of outthrown debris produced by the giant basin forming collisions.

'out-thrust, *sb.* [OUT- 7.] The act or fact of thrusting or forcibly pushing outward; an outward thrust or thrusting pressure in any structure. Also *transf.* and *fig.*
1842 *Mech. Mag.* Jan. 2 A bridge..so perfectly equilibrated, as to rest perpendicularly on its piers without any out-thrust whatever. **1855** ROBINSON *Whitby Gloss.*, *Out-thrust*, a push forward or out at the door. A projection from a building. **1950** J. JENKS *From Ground Up* xxi. 215 It was social and economic self-reliance at home that made possible an out-thrust of such vigour, that we became for a time not only the workshop of the world, but its merchant, carrier, and banker as well. **1955** J. R. R. TOLKIEN *Return of King* 162 An out-thrust of the eastward hills. **1973** *Baptist Federation of Canada Prayer Calendar* 16 Aug., Pray that the out-thrust of the Gospel by individual Christians will be unobstructed by timidity, busyness and fear.

'out-thrust, *ppl. a.* [OUT- 11.] Thrust out or forth, extended, projected.
1870 *Pall Mall G.* 2 Nov. 11 The boy-Love seeking to bar the entry with his arm and strong outthrust wings. **1882** W. M. WILLIAMS *Science* xxiii. 164 The out-thrust glaciers, the overflow down the valleys.

out-'thrust, *v.* [OUT- 15.] *trans.* To thrust out. So **'out-thruster.** [OUT- 8.] One who thrusts out.
1387–8 T. USK *Test. Love* II. ix. (Skeat) l. 86 It closeth hertes so togider, that rancour is outthresten. **1563–87** FOXE *A. & M.* (1596) 1421/2 Phasher was..the chiefe hereticke taker,..the outthruster of true godlinesse. **1855** ROBINSON *Whitby Gloss.*, *Out-thrusten*.., turned out of doors; projected or thrown forward. **1875** BROWNING *Aristoph. Apol.* 4522 Outthrusting eyes—their very roots—like blood! **1887** W. MORRIS tr. *Homer's Odyssey* I. x. 89 Sheer out-thrusting nesses each other hold in face. **1892** G. MEREDITH *Poems*: *Empty Purse* 40 From him are the brutal and vain, The vile, the excessive, out-thrust. **1907** *Daily Mail* 7 Dec. 6/4 He sat his horse as if he were a part of it, the reins dangling carelessly, his feet out-thrust in the huge Moorish stirrups. **1963** C. D. SIMAK *They walked like Men* iii. 17 He lay back in the chair, with..his long legs outthrust into the shadow underneath the radio console.

out-'thunder, *v.* [OUT- 18, 15.]

1. *trans.* To surpass in thundering; to make a more thundering noise than; to outnoise, outroar.
1616 T. ADAMS *Three Divine Sisters* Wks. 1862 II. 277 Though he out-thunder heaven with blasphemies. **1624** MASSINGER *Renegado* III. iii, There's no tongue A subject owes that shall out-thunder mine. **1846** PROWETT *Prometheus Bound* 41 A clang out-thundering the thunder-peal.

2. To thunder out, utter in a voice of thunder.
1710 *Pol. Ballads* (1860) II. 89 The Commons out-thunder New votes to guard the pulpit.

out-Timon to **out-Toby:** see OUT-.

out-'toil, *v.* [OUT- 15b, 18.]

1. *trans.* To exhaust or weary out with toil.
1603 HOLLAND *Plutarch's Mor.* 506 Because he would thereby vexe, out-toile consume and waste his poore subjects. **1610** —— *Camden's Brit.* II. 130 His souldiers out-toyled with travailing. **1676** OTWAY *Don Carlos* III. (1736) 42 Since my griefs cowards are, and dare not kill, I'll try to vanquish and out-toil the Ill.

2. To surpass in toiling or labouring.
1603 BRETON *Dignitie of Man* (1879) 14/2 In labour the Oxe will out-toile him. **1806** H. SIDDONS *Maid, Wife, & Widow* I. 196 He hired himself to a carpenter, and out-toiled all his competitors.

†**'out-ˌtoll.** *Sc. Obs.* [OUT- 6.] A payment made to the bailie upon giving up possession of burghal property.
1872 C. INNES *Sc. Legal Antiq.* 91 [see INTOLL].

out-tongue (aʊt'tʌŋ), *v.* [OUT- 21.] *trans.* To excel with the tongue; to exceed in power of tongue.
1604 SHAKS. *Oth.* I. ii. 19 Let him do his spight; My Seruices..Shall out-tongue his Complaints. **1607** MIDDLETON *Your Five Gallants* v. i, What, shall we suffer a changeable forepart to out-tongue us? **1844** *Fraser's Mag.* 465, 30,000 preachers that out-tongued her Mamelucks in eloquence.

out-top, outtop (aʊt'tɒp), *v.* [OUT- 18b.] *trans.* To rise above, surmount; = OVERTOP.
1674 JOSSELYN *Voy. New Eng.* 161 To the Northwest is a high mountain that out-tops all, with its three rising little hills. **1777** G. FORSTER *Voy. round World* II. 170 Innumerable coco-palms out-topped the woods. **1877** MACLEAR *St. Mark* iv. (1879) 55 The thorns gradually out-topped it.
fig. **1624** LD.-KEEPER WILLIAMS *Let.* 24 May in *Cabala* (1654) 94 The Treasurers..began then to out-top me, and appeared..likely enough..in time to do as much to your Grace. **1764** *Mem. G. Psalmanazar* 73 He doubted not but to see me outtop all the rest in less than a year or two. **1860** TEMPLE in *Ess. & Rev.* 12 The idea of monotheism out-tops all other ideas in dignity and worth.

out-tower, -town, etc.: see OUT-.

out-'trade, *v.* [OUT- 18b.] *trans.* To surpass or outdo in trading.
1677 YARRANTON *Eng. Improv.* Ep. to Rdr., The English Merchants complaining how the Dutch out-trade them, and that they are not able to live. **1690** CHILD *Disc. Trade* (1694) 237 They may out-trade us and undersel us. **1807** *Edin. Rev.* X. 352 The Americans will certainly out-trade the East India Company.

†**'out-ˌtrader.** *Obs. rare*[−1]. (?) One who fits out by way of trade or traffic: cf. OUTPUTTER.
1660 *Virginia Stat.* (1823) I. 538 Against pyrats, their assistors or abettors, out-traidors or receptors.

outtrage, obs. form of OUTRAGE.

out-trail to **out-triple**: see OUT-.

out-'travel, *v.* [OUT- 17, 18.] *trans.* To travel farther than or beyond the bounds of; to exceed in extent or swiftness of travelling.
a **1619** FOTHERBY *Atheom.* I. iv. §3 (1622) 22 No Traueller could euer out-trauell religion. **1633** BENLOWES *Pref. Poem* in *P. Fletcher's Purple Isl.*, Out-travell wise Ulysses (if you can). **1782** MISS BURNEY *Cecilia* x. ii, She then besought him to go instantly, that he might out-travel the ill news, to his mother. **1828** MISS MITFORD *Village* Ser. III. (1863) 131, I ..had..forsaken all track, and out-travelled all landmarks.

out-tray ('aʊttreɪ). [f. OUT- 3 + TRAY *sb.*²] In an office, etc.: a tray for outgoing and completed correspondence and other papers. Cf. IN-TRAY, OUT-BASKET.
Sometimes written as two separate words with *out* regarded adjectivally.
1943 [see IN-TRAY]. **1943** G. GREENE *Ministry of Fear* I. ii. 25 There were two trays on his desk marked In and Out, but the Out tray was empty. **1947** L. HASTINGS *Dragons are Extra* ix. 198 Invariably they were removed to the 'out' tray, probably with the tongs. **1959** *Punch* 30 Sept. 249/1, I looked around at the dusty chaos and saw how orderly it all could be..files here, records there, in-trays, out-trays. **1969** J. ARGENTI *Managem. Techniques* 247 Put this piece of paper in the Out-tray. **1976** DEAKIN & WILLIS *Johnny go Home* vi. 90 His desk is adorned with..wire In and Out trays.

out-'trick, *v.* [OUT 18, 21.] *trans.* To outdo in or by trickery.
1678 MRS. BEHN *Sir P. Fancy* II. i, I shall go near to out-trick your Ladyship, for all your politick learning. **1838** LYTTON *Alice* III. v, The weaker party was endeavouring to out-trick the stronger. **1855** MILMAN *Lat. Chr.* XIV. ii. (1864) IX. 68 His very tricks are often out-tricked.

out-'trot, *v.* [OUT- 18.] *trans.* To excel in trotting; to exceed in speed. Also *fig.*
1562 J. HEYWOOD *Prov. & Epigr.* (1867) 140 Gallop yonge wyues, shall tholde trot, out trot you? **1713** STEELE *Guardian* No. 6 ⁋5 Not to mend their pace into a gallop, when they are out-trotted by a rival. **1837** THACKERAY *Carlyle's Fr. Rev.* Wks. 1900 XIII. 249 Mr. Bulwer.., on his Athenian hobby, had quite out-trotted stately Mr. Gibbon.

out-'trump, *v.* [OUT- 18.] *trans.* To surpass or outdo in trumping (at cards). In quots. *fig.*
1809 W. IRVING *Knickerb.* v. iii. (1861) 159 The consternation of the wise men at the Manhattoes when they learnt how their commissioner had been out-trumped by the Yankees. **1886** W. GRAHAM *Social Prob.* 48 The landlords and capitalists, out-trumping each other in the political game.

†**out-'try**, *v. Obs.* [OUT- 15.]
1. *trans.* To choose out.
c **1420** *Pallad. on Husb.* I. 514 And for vche yok of exon in thi plough, Eighte foote in brede, & goodly lenght outtrie. *Ibid.* XII. 257 Ffresh, ripe, & grete of hem to sette outrie.
2. To sift out.
c **1550** R. BIESTON *Bayte Fortune* B iij b, That euer thou wast founden or fro the erth out tried.

†**out-'tuft**, ? *pa. pple. Obs.* [OUT- 11.] ? Pulled out in tufts or frills; puffed out.
1603 J. DAVIES *Microcosm., Extasie* (1878) 90/2 Yee might betweene the Buttons see, Her smocke out-tuft to show her levitee.

out-tun to **out-Turk**: see OUT-.

'out-turn. [OUT- 7, from *turn out.*] **1. a.** The quantity turned out or yielded; produce, output; spec. *Econ.*, an amount or result attained, as distinct from an estimate.
1800 *Asiat. Ann. Reg., Proc. Parl.* 35/1 The prospects of the year 1799–1800 will be found to vary but little in the aggregate from the actual out-turn of the preceding year. **1863** GLADSTONE *Sp. Ho. Comm.* 16 Apr., I estimated..the probable outturn of the revenue at 70,190,000*l.* **1880** C. R. MARKHAM *Peruv. Bark* 423 The outlay, as regards labour, .. is the same whether the out-turn is large or small. **1928** R. S. TROUP *Silvicultural Syst.* ix. 115 Both [the farmer and the gardener] take such measures as they can to improve the quality and increase the outturn of their field or garden crops. **1930** *Economist* 5 July 19/2 The wheat harvest has begun in the south-west... The out-turn promises to be about as large as last year. **1932** *Times* 29 Sept. 15/3 The Budget had been balanced on paper, but it remained to be seen what the actual result would be at the end of the financial year. The outturn proved the soundness of the balancing. **1957** *Times* 18 Nov. (Ann. Financial & Commerc. Rev.) p. xxxii/1 Barring frosts or other calamities, the out-turn delivered to the market can be reduced only by the action of growers or of some intermediary agency in withholding stocks. **1963** *Guardian* 15 Mar. 3/2 The figures for the outturn of defence expenditure in 1961–62 are provisional. **1972** *Accountant* 21 Sept. 350/1 Some indication of the out-turn for the current year. **1976** *Daily Tel.* 3 Apr. 17 There is little point in the Government producing White Papers on public expenditure since the outturn has been so consistently different from official projections.
b. *gen.* A result, outcome.
1881 W. PAUL *Past & Present of Aberdeenshire* 19 Rahab, spoken of in the Bible, made a bad beginning, but she had a fine out-turn,—she had a fine out-turn, she married Salmon. **1961** *Atom* Feb. 12/2 Any statement on the future cost of power involves a complicated judgment of the out-turn of many factors.
2. *Curling.* A turning motion given to a stone which causes it to curve to the left.
1890 J. KERR *Hist. Curling* 411 No curler is..entitled to be reckoned a graduate of arts in curling until he has mastered the knowledge of the *in-turn* and the *out-turn*. **1900** —— in A. E. T. Watson *Young Sportsman* 200 The in-turn is made when the curl is to be toward the right, the out-turn when it is to the left. **1969** R. WELSH *Beginner's Guide Curling* xi. 82 The..'in-turn' and 'out-turn', are activated in different ways.

'out-turned, *ppl. a.* [OUT- 11.] Turned out or outwards.
1894 BARING-GOULD *Kitty Alone* II. 143 The contents of his out-turned pocket.

†**out-'twine**, *v. Obs.* [OUT- 15, 24.] *trans.* **a.** To twist out. **b.** To untwine or untwist.
a **1400** CHAUCER *To Rosemounde* 11 Your seemly voys that ye so smal out-twyne. ? **1600** FAIRFAX (Webster 1864), He stopped And from the wound the reed outtwined.

out-tyrannize to **out-usure**: see OUT-.

out'value, *v.* [OUT- 21.] *trans.* To surpass in value.
1613–16 W. BROWNE *Brit. Past.* II. v. 177 His little boat.. fraught with what the world beside Could not out-value. **1634** SIR T. HERBERT *Trav.* 97 His attire was very ordinary, his Tulipant, could not out-value fortie shillings. **1846** LANDOR *Exam. Shaks.* Wks. II. 291 In ancienter days a few pages of good poetry outvalued a whole ell of the finest Genoa. **1871** H. B. FORMAN *Living Poets* 194 One stanza.. outvalues twenty volumes of mosaics.

out-vanish to **out-victor**: see OUT-.

†**out-vent.** *Obs. rare.* [f. OUT- 7 + VENT *sb.*, sale.] Public sale: = OUTCRY 2.
1542 UDALL *Erasm. Apoph.* 310 Thynges are saied proprely, in latine, *proscribi*, which are at another preisyng sette to out vent or sale.

outvie (aʊt'vaɪ), *v.* [OUT- 18 b.] *trans.* To outdo or excel in a competition, rivalry, or emulation; to vie with and excel.
1594 O. B. *Quest. Profit. Concern.* 2 b, Who set enuious patterns to outvie and vndoe one the other. **1640** HABINGTON *Edw. IV* 156 Twelve persons..out-vying each other in the curiosity and riches of their apparell. **1718** *Freethinker* No. 3 ⁋4 [It] made the Emerald out-vie the Verdure of the Field. **1887** ANNA FORBES *Insulinde* 28 Attitudes outvying the achievements of a *danseuse*.
Hence **out'vying** *vbl. sb.* and *ppl. a.*; **outvier** (aʊt'vaɪə(r)), one who or that which outvies.
1652 J. WRIGHT tr. *Camus' Nat. Paradox* x. 243 My Friendship can admit of no out-vier. **1757** JOS. HARRIS *Coins* 9 Men,..in their outvying, will undersell one another. **1854** J. S. C. ABBOTT *Napoleon* (1855) I. xvi. 280 These gorgeous saloons..were now adorned with outvying splendor.

out-vigil to **out-village**: see OUT-.

out-'villain, *v.* [OUT- 22.] *trans.* To exceed or surpass in villainy.
1601 SHAKS. *All's Well* IV. iii. 305 He hath out-villain'd villanie so farre, that the raritie redeemes him. *a* **1814** *Gonzaga* v. v. in *New Brit. Theatre* III. 161 Villany Will ever be outvillain'd, when it trusts To aught but its own dagger's point.

out-virtuate to **out-vociferate**: see OUT-.

out'voice, *v.* [OUT- 21.] *trans.* To surpass in loudness of voice; to make a louder noise than.
1599 SHAKS. *Hen. V*, v. Prol. 10 Men, Wiues, and Boyes, Whose shouts & claps out-voyce the deep-mouth'd Sea. **1681** GLANVILL *Sadducismus* Pref., They are sure to be out-voiced by the rout of ignorant contemners. **1856** R. A. VAUGHAN *Mystics* (1860) I. VI. viii. 268 He..outvoiced their angry cries with loud rebukes of their cowardice.

out'vote, *v.* [OUT- 18.] *trans.* To outnumber in voting; to defeat by a majority of votes.
1647 H. MORE *Poems* Pref., The sense of the soul will be changed, being outvoted as it were by the overswaying number of terrene particles. **1661** MORGAN *Sph. Gentry* III. ix. 107 A contest between the women and the men, wherein the females did out-vote the males, and carried it for Minerva against Neptune. **1778** [see OUT-ARGUE]. **1861** MAY *Const. Hist.* (1863) I. vii. 480 In 1852, Lord Derby's ministry were out-voted on their proposal for doubling the house tax.

'out-vote, *sb. rare.* [OUT- 2.] The vote of an out-voter; such votes collectively.
1790 E. SHERIDAN *Let.* June in T. Moore *Mem. Life R. B. Sheridan* (1825) 465, I suppose you have sent for the out-votes; but, if they are not good, what a terrible expense will that be! **1945** G. B. GRUNDY *55 Yrs. at Oxf.* 121 Rosebery was defeated on the out-vote.

'out-ˌvoter. [OUT- 2.] In the system for parliamentary elections in the United Kingdom: One who has a vote in a constituency in which he does not reside; a non-resident voter qualified by holding property. Also *transf.*
1855 MACAULAY *Hist. Eng.* xix. IV. 345 He must go through all the miseries of a canvass,..must hire conveyances for outvoters [etc.]. **1894** *Daily Tel.* 3 Apr. 5/7 There is a large proportion of 'outvoters', many of whom journeyed from the Midlands. **1931** *Birmingham Post* 24 Oct. 8/1 (*headline*) Aeroplane to bring up out-voters. **1965** W. R. WARD *Victorian Oxford* v. 96 Out-voters were told that a scheme designed by the heads to keep dissenters out on respectable grounds was a plan to let them in. **1967** *Economist* 6 May 575/1 Some distinguish between freeman electors and ten-pound householders, and between resident voters and out-voters.

outwait to **outwaltz**: see OUT-.

'outwale. *Obs.* exc. *dial.* [f. OUT- 7 + WALE *sb.*, choice.] That which is selected to be taken out or removed; refuse, dregs; one who is cast out, an outcast.
14.. *Siege Jerus.* (E.E.T.S.) 140 Semeliche twelue, Pore men & noȝt prute, aposteles wer hoten, þat of catifs he ches, ..þe out-wale of þ is worlde. *c* **1480** HENRYSON *Test. Cres.* 129 Now am I maid an unworthy outwaill. **1582** STANYHURST *Æneis* IV. (Arb.) 120 Poore caytief, desolat owtwayle. **1825** BROCKETT *N.C. Gloss., Outwale*, refuse. *a* **1835** HOGG *Tales* (1866) 362 (E.D.D.) The out-wale, wallie, tragle kind o' wooers.

†**'outwalk**, *sb. Obs.* [OUT- 6 or 7.] ? A promenade.
1698 FRYER *Acc. E. India & P.* 100 Chap. ii. Shews the Tombs, Outwalks, Ceremonies, and Austerities of the Gentiles, with the Ships and River about Surat.

outwalk (aʊt'wɔːk), *v.* [OUT- 18, 17.] *trans.* To outdo or outstrip in walking; to walk faster, farther, or better than; to walk beyond.
1626 B. JONSON *Fortunate Isles* Wks. (Rtldg.) 648/1 Have I..outwatch'd, Yea, and outwalked any ghost alive. **1720** POPE *Lett.* (1735) I. 271 But indeed I fear she would out-walk him. **1846** MRS. BROWNING in *Lett. R. Browning* (1899) II. 201 She is old now. Yet she can outwalk my sisters. **1856** OLMSTED *Slave States* 325, I..walked on. For a time I could occasionally hear the cry,..gradually I outwalked the sound.

'out-wall (-wɔːl). [OUT- 3.] The outer wall of any building or enclosure.
1535 COVERDALE *Ezek.* xli. 11 The thicknesse of the out-wall was v cubites rounde aboute. **1624** WOTTON *Archit.* in *Reliq.* (1672) 57 Various colours on the out-walls of Buildings have alwayes in them more Delight then Dignity. **1793** SMEATON *Edystone L.* §114 The out-wall was in a remarkably leaning condition.
b. *fig.* The clothing; the body, as enclosing the soul. Used by Edmund Blunden in the sense 'outward appearance'.
1605 SHAKS. *Lear* III. i. 45 For confirmation that I am much more Then my out-wall; open this Purse, and take What it containes. **1631** R. H. *Arr. Whole Creature* x. §2. 86 The Windes of afflictions beat upon the outwals of his flesh. **1933** E. BLUNDEN *Charles Lamb* v. 131 He [*sc.* Wordsworth] does express the *altitudo* of Lamb's personality and influence far more thoughtfully than a host of subsequent writers to whom Lamb's outwall with its Punch and Judy shows and all the fun of the fair has been the principal thing to report. **1937** —— in *Essays & Stud.* XXII. 60 Acquaintances who did not always separate the man from his outwall. *Ibid.*, The candour and keenness of the first period, when the outwall had not yet become necessary.

†**out'wander**, *v.* [OUT- 14.] *intr.* To wander out or away. Hence **out'wandering** *vbl. sb.*, a wandering out or outwards (in quot. *fig.*).
13.. *Cursor M.* 22620 þat þou vtewandre us suffers sua. **1880** H. COLLINS *Heaven Opened* II. xiv. 215 God does not mind the out-wanderings of our vagabond imaginations. **1922** JOYCE *Ulysses* 379 On her stow he ere was living with dear wife and lovesome daughter that then over land and seafloor nine years had long outwandered.

outwandered, *ppl. a.* [After G. *ausgewandert.*] That has wandered; migrated, emigrated.
1876 *Trans. Clinical Soc.* IX. 92 If thus out-wandered, the white blood-cells are to all intents and purposes lymph-cells. **1887** *Blackw. Mag.* May 643 Are not the Hungarians themselves an outwandered Asiatic race?

outwar, -warble, etc.: see OUT-.

outward ('aʊtwəd), *a.* (*sb.*¹) Forms: 1 útan-, úte-, útweard, 2–5 **utward**; 4–5 oute-, 4–6 **outwarde**, 4–5 *Sc.* owt(e)wart, -ward(e, 5– **outward**, (5 **utteward**, 6 **uttwarde**, **vtward**, *Sc.* **wtuert**). [OE. *útan-*, *úte-*, *útweard*, f. *útan*, *úte*, *út* (see OUTEN, OUTE, OUT *adv.*) + *-weard*, -WARD: cf. MHG. *ûzwert*, Ger. *auswärtig* external, foreign, MLG. *ûtward*.]
1. That is turned or lies towards the region or space outside the boundary of any enclosure or the surface of anything; that is without or on the outer side; out, outer, external, exterior. *Obs.* or *arch.*
a **900** *O.E. Chron.* an. 893 (Parker MS.) Hi tuȝon up hiora scipu of þone weald iiii. mila fram þæm muþan ute weardum. *c* **1000** ÆLFRIC *Voc.* in Wr.-Wülcker 160/9 *Femur* utanweard þeoh. **1530** PALSGR. 250/2 Outwarde parte of any thynge, *superfice*. **1535** COVERDALE *Ezek.* xliv. 1 Yᵉ outwarde dore of the Sanctuary. **1555** EDEN *Decades* 42 That..beaste ..bearing her whelpes abowte with her in an outwarde bellye. **1605** BACON *Adv. Learn.* II. vii. §7. 30 Contraction of pores is incident to the outwardest parts. **1660** BARROW *Euclid* I. xvi, The outward angle will be greater than either of the inward and opposite angles. **1709** STEELE & ADDISON *Tatler* No. 103 ⁋12, I heard a Noise in my outward Room. **1853** STOCQUELER *Mil. Encycl.* 206/2 In wheeling time 120 paces..the outward file stepping thirty-three inches.
b. Directed or proceeding towards the outside; pertaining to what is so directed.
[*Beowulf* (Z.) 761 Fingras burston, eoten wæs utweard.] **1700** DRYDEN *Sigism. & Guisc.* 61 The fire will force its outward way. **1884** *G.W.R. Time Tables* July 86 The first or Outward Halves of Return Tickets. **1898** Outward postages

[see INWARD *a.* 7]. **1899** *Allbutt's Syst. Med.* VII. 282 Some downward and outward displacement of the left eye.

†**c.** Known outside, generally known, public.
1430-40 LYDG. *Bochas* III. v. (1554) 77b, The death of Mergus outwarde was not Nor plainly published in that region.

†**d.** Done outside, out-of-door. *Obs.*
1621 BURTON *Anat. Mel.* II. ii. IV. (1651) 269 The most pleasant of all outward pastimes.

2. Of or pertaining to the outer surface of the body and its clothing; also to the body itself as opposed to the mind, soul, or spirit, and to bodily as opposed to mental faculties; external, bodily.
*a***1225** *Ancr. R.* 100 þeo ancre þet schulde beon his [Christ's] leofmon, & secheð þauh utward ȝelunge & froure, mid eie oðer mid tunge. **14..** *Why I can't be a Nun* 356 in *E.E.P.* (1862) 147 As by owtewarde aray in semyng Beth so wyth-in my ladyes dere. **1509** HAWES *Past. Pleas.* xxiv. (Percy Soc.) 108 The eyen, the eres, and also the nose, The mouth, and handes, inwarde wyttes are none; But outwarde offyces. *Ibid.*, These outwarde gates to have the knowledginge,.. the inwarde wyttes to have decernynge. **1526** TINDALE *Gal.* vi. 12 With uttwarde aperaunce to please carnally. **1548-9** (Mar.) *Bk. Com. Prayer, Communion* Collects, The wordes whiche we haue hearde this day with our outwarde eares. **1603** SHAKS. *Meas. for M.* III. ii. 286 Oh, what may Man within him hide, Though Angel on the outward side? **1713** YOUNG *Force Relig.* I. (1757) 50 When charms of mind With elegance of outward form are join'd. **1867** MAURICE *Patriarchs & Lawg.* viii. (1877) 159 The vision was not to the outward eye.

b. Said of medical applications or treatment applied externally; = EXTERNAL *a.* 1 c.
1612 WOODALL *Surg. Mate* Pref., Wks. (1653) 6 Some.. would.. confine the Surgeon onely to outward medicine, and outward healing. **1710** ADDISON *Tatler* No. 221 ¶5 By inward Medicines or outward Applications. *Mod.* (Label on Liniment.) 'For outward application only.'

c. ***outward man*** (*Theol.*), the body as opposed to the soul or spirit; *humorously*, outward guise, clothing.
1526 TINDALE *2 Cor.* iv. 16 But though oure vttward [WYCLIF 1388 vtter] man perisshe, yet the inwarde man is renewed daye by daye. *a***1555** LATIMER *Let. to Sir E. Baynton* in Foxe *A. & M.* (1583) 1747/2 Eyther my Lord of London wil iudge myn outward man onely.. or els he will be my God, and iudge mine inwarde manne. **1664** [see INWARD *a.* 2]. **1678** BUTLER *Hud.* III. iii. 94 Till he began To scruple at Ralph's Outward Man. **1848** DICKENS *Dombey* iv, The only change ever known in his outward man, was from a complete suit of coffee-colour.. to [etc.].

†**3.** External to the country; foreign. *Obs.*
1467-8 *Rolls of Parlt.* V. 623/1 Called uppon.. by outward Prynces, as the Duke of Burgoyn. **1470** *Paston Lett.* II. 409 Our auncient ennemyes of Fraunce and our outward rebells and traitors. **1503-4** *Act 19 Hen. VII*, c. 4 Preamb., Honour & Victorie hathe ben goten ageyne utwarde enymyes. *a***1548** HALL *Chron., Edw. IV* 237 Affaires of outwarde warres. **1675** tr. *Camden's Hist. Eliz.*, These Perils.. would be either inward or outward. Outward, either from the Bishop of Rome.. or from the French King.

†**b.** Lying outside some sphere of work, duty, or interest; external. *Obs.*
*c***1375** *Sc. Leg. Saints* ii. (*Paulus*) 939 Owtwart thingis.. Owtane, þat wes þe besynes þat he had of all þe kirk. **1535** COVERDALE *Neh.* xi. 16 The chefe of the Leuites, in the outwarde busynes of yᵉ house of God. **1611** BIBLE *1 Chron.* xxvi. 29 Chenaniah and his sonnes were for the outward busines ouer Israel, for officers and Iudges.

4. Applied to actions, looks, and other externally visible manifestations, as opposed to internal feelings, spiritual or mental states or processes, etc.; of or pertaining to outer form as opposed to inner substance; formal.
1526 *Pilgr. Perf.* (W. de W. 1531) 122 In all yᵉ outwarde workes that man oughteth to do for his Saluacyon. **1533** GAU *Richt Vay* 19 God lukis nocht the wtuert richtusnes quhilk mony keipis and dois wtuertlie in the sicht of men. **1604** *Bk. Com. Prayer, Catechism, Q.* What meanest thou by this word Sacrament? *A.* I mean an outward and visible sign of an inward and spiritual grace. **1667** MILTON *P.L.* XII. 534 The rest.. Will deem in outward Rites and specious formes Religion satisfi'd. *a***1703** BURKITT *On N.T.* Mark ii. 28 The good of man is to be preferred before the outward keeping of the sabbath. **1813** SCOTT *Rokeby* I. ii, While her poor victim's outward throes Bear witness to his mental woes. **1856** FROUDE *Hist. Eng.* I. ii. 96 The church, to outward appearance, stood more securely than ever. **1871** FREEMAN *Norm. Conq.* IV. xvii. 54 It was the master-piece of William's policy of outward legality. **1871** MORLEY *Voltaire* (1886) 8 To reduce the faith to a vague futility, and its outward ordering to a piece of ingeniously reticulated pretence.

5. Applied to things in the external or material world, as opposed to those in the mind or thought.
1573-80 BARET *Alv.* O 212 By means of our bodie, images come from outward things into our mind. **1803-6** WORDSW. *Ode Intim. Immort.* ix, Those obstinate questionings Of sense and outward things. **1875** JOWETT *Plato* (ed. 2) IV. 273 We cannot think of outward objects of sense or of outward sensations without space. **1881** BESANT & RICE *Chapl. of Fleet* I. 3 When we are in great grief and sorrow, outward things seem to affect us more than in ordinary times.

b. Applied to things that are external to one's own personality, character, or efforts, or that concern one's relations with other persons and external circumstances; extrinsic. Rarely in relation to a thing (quot. 1756).
1607-12 BACON *Ess., Fortune* (Arb.) 374 Outward Accidentes conduce much to a Mans fortune; favour; oportune death of others; occasion fitting vertue. **1685** SOUTH *Serm., Will for Deed* (1715) 385 Suppose we now, a Man be bound Hand and Foot by some outward Violence. **1709** BERKELEY *Th. Vision* Ded., The outward advantages of fortune. **1756** C. LUCAS *Ess. Waters* I. 39 The different heat or cold of water is owing to outward accidents. **1869** J. MARTINEAU *Ess.* II. 72 The law must define men's outward rights and relations. **1875** JOWETT *Plato* (ed. 2) I. 116 Man, who in his outward conditions is more helpless than the other animals.

†**c.** Outside, superficial. *Obs.*
1658 SIR T. BROWNE *Hydriot., Answ. Dugdale's Quære* (1736) 51 Upon a single View and outward Observation, they may be the Monuments of any of these three Nations.

6. †**a.** Unspiritual, secular. *Obs.* **b.** Dissipated, wild or irregular in conduct. *dial.*
1674 OWEN *Holy Spirit* (1693) 130 After a while they have fallen into an outward state of things, wherein, as they suppose, they shall have no Advantage by [spiritual gifts]. **1875** MISS POWLEY *Echoes Cumbld.* 149 (E.D.D.) In wild outwart days I spent time. **1893** SNOWDEN *Tales Yorks. Wolds* 95 He had led a very outward life—that is to say, he had been a drunkard and a reputed wife-beater.

B. *sb.* (ellipt. or absol. use of the adj.)
†**1.** An outer part (of anything). *Obs.*
*c***1470** HENRY *Wallace* IX. 1076 Thre hundreth in place About hym stud.. Defendand him,.. Quhill all the owtwart off the feild was tynt. *Ibid.* x. 718 Off the outward thre thousand thair thai slew. **1545** RAYNOLD *Byrth Mankynde* Prol. Biv, An absolut & perfeict knowledge, of all the inwardes & outwardes of mans and womans body.

2. Outward appearance; the outside, exterior.
1606 SHAKS. *Tr. & Cr.* III. ii. 169 Out-liuing beauties outward, with a minde That doth renew swifter than blood decaies. **1611** —— *Cymb.* I. i. 23 So faire an Outward, and such stuffe Within. **1644** H. VAUGHAN *Serm.* 19 The specious outwards of a whited Sepulchre. **1844** J. PAYNE *Tales fr. Arabic* I. 106 O vizier.. make thine inward like unto thine outward. **1885-94** R. BRIDGES *Eros & Psyche* Mar. iii, Yet in their prime they bore the palm away; Outwards of loveliness.

3. in *pl.* Outward things, circumstances, or conditions; externals.
1627-77 FELTHAM *Resolves* I. xxxviii. 63 Nature.. makes us all equal: we are differenc'd but by accident and outwards. *a***1655** VINES *Lord's Supp.* (1677) 78 Of the outwards of this ordinance of the supper. **1721** WODROW *Hist. Suff. Ch. Scotl.* (1829) II. 295 They wanted not their discouragements as to outwards.

4. That which is outside the mind; the external or material world.
1832 TENNYSON *Eleanore* i, There is nothing here, Which, from the outward to the inward brought, Moulded thy baby thought. **1849** SEARS *Regeneration* I. iii. (1859) 31 As man sinks lower and lower into the outward he loses the power of spiritual sight and intuition. **1878** GEO. ELIOT *Coll. Breakf. P.* 521 Since human consciousness awaking owned An outward.

C. *Comb.* †**'outward‚shine** [perh. two words], outward show or appearance (*obs.*).
1549 E. ALLEN tr. *Paraph. Leo Jude Rev.* 4 No hipocrisye nor outwardeshyne of godnes.. is of any value before god.

outward ('aʊtwəd), *adv.* Forms: see the adj. [OE. *útan-, úte-, út-weard*: cf. OHG. *úzwert*.]
1. a. Of position or situation: On the outside; without.
*c***950** *Lindisf. Gosp.* Matt. xxiii. 25 ȝie clænsas þæt utaword is cælces. —— Luke xi. 39 þæt utteweard is calices & disces ȝie clænsað. *c***1375** *Sc. Leg. Saints* xl. (*Ninian*) 1139 In my mouth þe heft þou set þe blad of a knyfe. **1398** TREVISA *Barth. De P.R.* XVII. i. (1495) 592 A tree hath somwhat that longeth therto outwarde: as the rynde. **1471** RIPLEY *Comp. Alch.* VI. ix. in Ashm. *Theatr. Chem. Brit.* (1652) 163 The Mater ys alterate, Both inward and outward substancyally. **1534** TINDALE *Matt.* xxiii. 28 Whited tombes which appere beautyfull outwarde. **1719** DE FOE *Crusoe* II. xv, Sheepskins, with the wool outward.

b. Of motion or direction: From the inside to or towards the outside of a space or thing.
*c***1290** *Becket* 2167 in *S. Eng. Leg.* I. 168 Heom þouȝte euere ase heo eoden outward.. þat þe eorþe openede onder heom. **1393** LANGL. *P. Pl.* C. x. 85 Boþe a-fyngrede and a-furst to turne þe fayre out-warde. *c***1475** *Rauf Coilȝear* 608 As he went outwart bayne, He met ane Porter swayne. **1497** *Nav. Acc. Hen. VII* (1896) 149 They myght have their costes outeward & homeward. **1562** [see OUTWARDLY 1 b]. **1601** SHAKS. *Twel. N.* III. i. 14 How quickely the wrong side may be turn'd outward. **1859** TENNYSON *Guinevere* 105 Lancelot.. rushing outward lionlike Leapt on him. **1879** HARLAN *Eyesight* vi. 88 One eye is turned outward by the opposing muscle, forming an external squint.

†**2.** Outside (of a specified or understood place); out of one's house; out of one's country, abroad.
1387 TREVISA *Higden* (Rolls) III. 469 ȝe.. werreþ outward aȝenst men. **1413** *Pilgr. Sowle* IV. xxxiii. (Caxton 1483) 82 That by them his counceylle be nought shewed ne publysshed outward. **1428** in *Surtees Misc.* (1888) 9 For other occupacions that he had to doo utteward. *c***1450** *St. Cuthbert* (Surtees) 1612 Bathe outeward and als at hame. **1673** PENN *The Chr. a Quaker* iii, Men's Minds.. being Outward and Abroad, God was pleased to meet them.. in some External Manifestations.

†**3. a.** On, or with reference to, the outside of the body, as opposed to its internal parts; externally.
1523 FITZHERB. *Husb.* §108 The stryng halte is an yl disease.. and doth not appere outwarde. *c***1532** DU WES *Introd. Fr.* in Palsgr. 901 Membres longyng to mannes body aswell inwarde as out warde. **1542-3** *Act 34 & 35 Hen. VIII*, c. 8 *title*, An Acte that persones being no comen Surgeons maie mynistre medicines owtwarde.

†**b.** On the visible outside of the body or person, esp. as opposed to the inner nature or character; in the body as opposed to the mind or spirit; in outward appearance as opposed to inner reality; outwardly, externally; publicly. *Obs.*
*c***1386** CHAUCER *Pars. T.* ¶861 A woman to haue a fair array outward and in hir self foul inward. *c***1400** *Rom. Rose* 5755 Outward shewing holynesse Though they be fulle of cursidnesse. **1483** CAXTON *Gold. Leg.* 327b/2 That he myght haue alle the rewle aboute the kynge as wel secretely as outward. **1526** TINDALE *2 Cor.* vii. 5 Outwarde was fightynge, in warde was feare. **1534** WHITINTON *Tullyes Offices* I. (1540) 21 Which semeth rather to ryse of pride outwarde shewed than of lyberal wyl. **1603** SHAKS. *Meas. for M.* III. i. 89 This outward sainted Deputie.. is yet a diuell. **1673** PENN *The Chr. a Quaker* xvi, As Abraham outward and natural was the great Father of the Jews.

c. From the soul or mind into external actions or conditions.
1805 FOSTER *Ess.* I. vii. 87 He will endeavour to trace himself outward, from his mind into his actions. **1849** SEARS *Regeneration* I. vii. (1859) 56 Superabundant life unfolding from within outward.

4. *Comb.*, as ***outward-bent, -looking, -parting, -set, -steeled, -turning*** adjs. Also OUTWARD-BOUND.
1597 MIDDLETON *Wisd. of Solomon* IV. xv, With outward-fac'd eye and eyed face. **1890** W. JAMES *Princ. Psychol.* I. x. 296 Our considering the spiritual self at all is a reflective process, is the result of our abandoning the outward-looking point of view. **1927** A. HUXLEY *Proper Stud.* 52 How repulsive, how incomprehensible I find the philosophy which is the rationalization of these people's outward-looking passion for their fellows! **1975** *Times* 5 Apr. 3/3 Teachers try to capture the interests of these pupils with vocationally oriented, out-ward-looking courses. **1836** GLADSTONE *Communion Hymn* (in *Good Words* July 1898), As Thy temple's portals close Behind the outward-parting throng. **1871** PALGRAVE *Lyr. Poems* 119 Free from outward-set control. **1888** G. M. HOPKINS *Poems* (1918) 69 The heroic breast not outward-steeled. **1930** *Times Lit. Suppl.* 30 Oct. 888/4 As in a maze, the outward-turning paths lead back to the centre. **1976** *Listener* 12 Aug. 176/3 This bodily prosperity, this outward-turning energy.

out-ward ('aʊt‚wɔːd), *sb.*² [OUT- 1.]
1. An outlying ward; a ward outside the original bounds of a borough.
1871 *Windsor & Eton Expr.* 4 Nov., In the Out-Ward the election has terminated in the only way that could have been anticipated.
2. A ward of a hospital detached from the main building, or having a separate outer door.
1890 in *Cent. Dict.*

†**out-'ward,** *v. Obs. rare.* [OUT- 15.] *trans.* To ward off, keep out.
1596 SPENSER *F.Q.* V. i. 10 Ne any armour could his dint out-ward.

'outward-'bound, *a.* (*sb.*) [f. OUTWARD *adv.* + BOUND *ppl. a.*¹] **1. a.** Directing the course outward, esp. going from a home port to a foreign one: of a ship, vehicle, or person; *transf.* of a voyage. Also *absol.* as *sb.*
1602 [see HOMEWARD-BOUND]. **1668** CLARENDON *Vind.* Tracts (1727) 7 Six or seven merchant ships, whereof some were outward-bound with merchandize. **1702** *Lond. Gaz.* No. 3811/2 Our outward-bound Brasil Fleet will sail in few days. **1755** MAGENS *Insurances* II. 238 If an Accident happen to Ship or Cargo on the outwardbound Voyage. **1777** P. THICKNESSE *Year's Journey* II. xlvi. 110 My entertainment at this house, *outward-bound*, was half a second-hand roasted turkey. **1832** *Chambers's Edin. Jrnl.* I. 86/3 He would find himself on the top of one of the outward-bound coaches of the metropolis. **1838** W. ELLIS *Madagascar* iii. (1858) 63 Sighted by outward-bound ships to India. **1887** *Pall Mall G.* 6 July 5/1 There is no precaution taken against outward-bounds meeting homeward-bounds?
b. *fig.* Departing this life, dying.
1809 MALKIN *Gil Blas* II. v. ¶6 The mistress joined the outward-bound colony of my patients. **1890** HALL CAINE *Bondman* x, He's really past help. He's outward bound, poor chap.
c. *fig.* Bent on wandering or straying.
1742 YOUNG *Nt. Th.* v. 149 Thought outward-bound.. flies off In fume and dissipation. **1860** WARTER *Sea-board* II. 128 An outward-bound youth, and difficult to handle by reason of his carelessness.
2. (With capital initials.) The name of a sea school founded by Kurt Hahn at Aberdovey in 1941, on the basis of which an Outward Bound Trust was formed in 1946 with the aim of establishing further residential schools for the training of boys and girls in mountaineering as well as naval and other outdoor activities. Also *transf.* Hence **Outward-Bound course, scheme, school,** etc. (see quots.).
1943 *Times* 28 June 2/4 Dr G. M. Trevelyan.. at Aberdovey on Saturday gave the name of Garibaldi to a sea-going ketch presented by the partners of Alfred Holt and Co., shipowners, to the Outward Bound Sea School. **1947** *Times* 23 Sept. 2/5 To-day the experiment begun in war-time is firmly established as a permanent undertaking operated by the Outward Bound Trust. **1950** *Times Educ. Suppl.* 16 June 474/1 Variety is the spice of the Outward Bound life. **1957** K. HAHN in D. James *Outward Bound* 10 In July 1941.. Lawrence Holt, the shipowner.. secured the financial support of his firm, the Blue Funnel Line, for the foundation of the first Short-Term School at Aberdovey. The name Outward Bound Sea School was his invention. **1958** *Listener* 12 June 976/1 Sir Richard Livingstone and 'Outward Bound' enthusiasts both saw in the training of character a panacea for a world adrift. **1961** VISCT. MONTGOMERY *Path to Leadership* xi. 173 In my opinion the best character training given to boys in Britain is that

provided by the Outward Bound Trust, through their sea and mountain schools... Outward Bound can take only some 4,000 boys a year. **1965** M. MORSE *Unattached* v. 159 He had been sent on the Outward Bound course by his firm. **1973** C. BONINGTON *Next Horizon* xiv. 213 Sebastian in the mist, looking like a bedraggled outward-bound schoolboy in the mists of Wales or the Lakes. **1977** P. THEROUX *Consul's File* 42 He was the local magistrate. An Outward Bound type..dead keen to go camping.

'outward-'bounder. **1.** An outward-bound vessel. *colloq.*

1851 H. MELVILLE *Moby Dick* II. xi. 72 The long absent ship, the outward-bounder, perhaps, has letters on board. **1884** CLARK RUSSELL *Jack's Courtship* xix, An outward-bounder she was from the vane above the truck [etc.]. **1888** *Daily News* 27 June 5/5 Outward-bounders to the Colonies, East Indies, China, Japan, and the Java Seas never go within three hundred miles of Cape L'Agulhas.

2. (With capital initials.) A pupil at an 'Outward Bound' school; an advocate of such schools and their methods.

1961 *Sunday Times* 19 Feb. 34/2 Knowing how to tie reef-knots,..with all the other indispensable appurtenances of the Outward Bounder. *Ibid.* 26 Feb. 39/3 We 'intelligent' talkers have to thank the 'Outward Bounders' for the liberty and freedom to be so.

outwardly ('aʊtwədlɪ), *adv.* (*a.*) [f. OUTWARD *a.* + -LY².]

1. On the outside or outer surface; externally.

c **1480** HENRYSON *Test. Cres.* 509 The idole of ane thing in cace may be Sa deip imprintit in the fantasy, That it deludis the wittis outwardly. *a* **1547** SURREY *Descr. Fickle Affect. Love* 20 When in my face the painted thoughtes would outwardly apere. **1634** SIR T. HERBERT *Trav.* 209 The tree is outwardly couered with barque. **1660** BARROW *Euclid* III. xii, If two circles touch one the other outwardly. **1671** SALMON *Syn. Med.* III. xxii. 422 Penyroyal,..outwardly it is good against cold affections of the Nerves and Joynts. **1796** MORSE *Amer. Geog.* I. 206 Nothing appears outwardly but its hands and feet. **1866** J. G. MURPHY *Comm. Ex.* xxiv. 10 The spectators..only describe the outwardly visible glory.

b. Towards or in the direction of the outside; in an outward direction.

1562 J. HEYWOOD *Prov. & Epigr.* (1867) 204 My wife doth euer tread hir shooe a wry. Inward, or outward? nay, all outwardly. **1597** HOOKER *Eccl. Pol.* v. lvi. §5 Outwardlie issuing from that one onely glorious deitie. **1822–34** *Good's Study Med.* (ed. 4) I. 63 Before the end of another month the ulceration stretched outwardly under the upper lip.

2. In outward manifestation or appearance; in external action or observance: often as contrasted with inward spirit or character.

1509 HAWES *Past. Pleas.* xix. (Percy Soc.) 92 He wyped our chekes our sorowe to cloke, Outwardly fayning us to be glad and mery. *a* **1533** [see OUTWARD *a.* 4]. *a* **1548** HALL *Chron., Hen. V* 64 b, Outwardly reioysyng what soever inwardly thei thought. **1605** SHAKS. *Macb.* I. iii. 54 Are ye fantasticall, or that indeed Which outwardly ye shew? **1724** SWIFT *Drapier's Lett.* Wks. 1755 V. II. 97 But since my betters are of a different opinion..I shall outwardly submit. **1883** FROUDE *Short Stud.* IV. II. iv. 207 The country was outwardly quiet, but there were ominous undertones of disaffection.

B. *ellipt.* or *attrib.* as *adj.* = OUTWARD *a.*

a **1642** SIR W. MONSON *Naval Tracts* v. (1704) 457/2 No Road..with an outwardly Wind, is able..to give him conveniency of..Landing. **1656** SANDERSON *Serm.* (1689) 264 God giveth to no man all the desire of his heart in these outwardly things.

†**'outwardmost,** *a. Obs.* [f. OUTWARD *a.*: see -MOST.] Most outward, outermost.

1598 R. HAYDOCKE tr. *Lomazzo* I. 116 When you would make a lanke, slender, and swift horse, you shall draw him upon the outward-most line. **1654–66** EARL ORRERY *Parthen.* (1676) 691 Behind the outwardmost divisions..I placed some of our best Archers. **1685** BOYLE *Effects of Mot.* v. 56 The outwardmost were of (what they call) Chagrine, and the innermost of Gold. **1707** SLOANE *Jamaica* I. 260 The outwardmost calicular leaves inclosing the flowers.

'outwardness. [f. OUTWARD *a.* + -NESS.]

1. The quality or condition of being outward; externality, outward existence; objectivity.

1580 HOLLYBAND *Treas. Fr. Tong, Extérieureté*, outwardnesse. **1678** CUDWORTH *Intell. Syst.* I. v. 829 Magnitude or Extension as such is meer outside or outwardness, it hath nothing within. **1825** COLERIDGE *Aids Refl.* (1848) I. 19 These..give an outwardness and sensation of reality to the shapings of the dream. **1856** R. A. VAUGHAN *Mystics* (1860) II. VIII. vi. 68 Whatsoever I could bring into outwardness that I wrote down.

2. Occupation with, concernment or belief in outward things; esp. as opposed to that which is introspective or arises from within.

?*c* **1835** J. STERLING in Courtney *Mill* (1889) 73 He has been gradually delivered from this outwardness..individual reform must be the groundwork of social progress. **1840** CARLYLE *Heroes* iii. (1872) 87 He dwells in vague outwardness, fallacy and trivial hearsay. **1840** *Blackw. Mag.* XLVIII. 270 The outwardness, or materiality of Vecelli. **1891** *Wesley. Meth. Mag.* Jan. 68 Owing..to his native volatility and *outwardness*, he did not come to the crisis of his spiritual history until 5 years after leaving school.

outwards ('aʊtwədz), *adv.* (*a.*) [OE. *útweardes*, f. *útweard* OUTWARD *adj.*, with advb. genitive *-es*. Cf. OHG. *ûzwertes* (Ger. *auswärts*), MDu. *útwaerts*, Du. *uitwaards*.]

1. In an outward direction; towards that which is outside or without.

c **897** K. ÆLFRED *Gregory's Past.* xi. 70 Suæ bið sio costung ærest on ðæm mode, & ðonne færeð utweardes to ðære hyde. *a* **1225** *Ancr. R.* 92 Euer so þe wittes beoð more ispreinde utwardes, se heo lesse wendet inwardes. **1517** TORKINGTON *Pilgr.* (1884) 68 We..spendyd owtwardes be twyne Venyce and Jaffe on Moneth and ij Dayes. **1583** [see INWARDS *adv.* 1 b]. **1677** MOXON *Mech. Exerc.* (1703) 205 Do not direct the cutting Corner of the Chissel inwards, but rather outwards. **1712** STEELE *Spect.* No. 485 ¶3 A new night gown, either side to be worn outwards. **1828** P. CUNNINGHAM *N.S. Wales* (ed. 3) II. 155 To embark his capital outwards in a mercantile speculation. **1846** BRITTAN tr. *Malgaigne's Man. Oper. Surg.* 203 To cut a semicircular flap from within outwards.

†**2.** In an outward position; outwardly, outside; externally. *Obs. rare.*

1436 *Pol. Poems* (Rolls) II. 158 To werre oughtwardes and youre regne to recovere. *c* **1530** TINDALE *Pathway Holy Scripture* Wks. (Parker Soc. 1848) 14 Yet are we full of the natural poison,..and cannot but sin outwards,..if occasion be given.

B. *attrib.* (as *adj.*) For outward goods.

1878 F. S. WILLIAMS *Midl. Railw.* 638 We pass on..to the 'Outwards' department of the great goods shed. This 'Outwards' platform..runs the length of the shed.

'outwash. *Geol.* [OUT- 7.] Material (chiefly sand and gravel, or further away silt and clay) carried out from a glacier by melt-water and deposited beyond the terminal moraine. Freq. *attrib.*

1894 T. C. CHAMBERLIN in *Jrnl. Geol.* II. 533 There were, however, tracts of assorted material formed by waters outflowing from the ice where no definite terminal ridging took place. Such forms may be designated *outwash* aprons in distinction from *overwash* aprons. **1905** *Ibid.* XIII. 245 One of the pronounced features of the outwash is the pitted-plain development. **1908** *Amer. Jrnl. Sci.* CLXXV. 108 The river terraces of outwash gravel. **1934** *Antiquity* VIII. 306 The retreat of the ice and the formation of the outwash plain in front of the moraine. **1947** AUDEN *Age of Anxiety* v. 116 And you, bright Prince,..O stiffly stand, a staid monadnock, On her peneplain; placidly graze On her outwash apron, her own steed. **1957** [see OVERWASH *sb.*]. **1963** D. W. & E. E. HUMPHRIES tr. *Termier's Erosion & Sedimentation* vii. 163 During the recession of the Quaternary ice sheets, detrital accumulations were left behind, either in the form of outwash fans deposited at the snouts of glaciers by subglacial streams..., or as fluvio-glacial ridges often filling in lakes (eskers). **1971** R. F. FLINT *Glacial & Quaternary Geol.* vii. 187 In the downstream direction, outwash is diluted by an ever-increasing proportion of nonglacial alluvium derived through tributary streams that did not originate in glaciers. **1972** J. G. CRUICKSHANK *Soil Geogr.* ii. 59 Outwash alluvium is usually similar in texture, but may include some fine debris where the melt water has spread over a large area.

out-waste: see OUT- 15.

outwatch ('aʊt,wɒtʃ), *sb.*¹ *rare.* [OUT- 7.] The act of reconnoitering or watching the enemy.

1853 LYTTON *My Novel* IX. iii, He occasionally sallied forth upon a kind of outwatch or reconnoitring expedition.

outwatch (aʊt'wɒtʃ), *v.* [OUT- 18, 17.] *trans.* To outdo in watching, watch longer than; to watch (an object) till it disappears; to watch through and beyond (a period of time).

1626 [see OUTWALK]. **1632** MILTON *Penseroso* 85 Or let my Lamp at midnight hour, Be seen in som high lonely Towr, Where I may oft out-watch the Bear. **1728** YOUNG *Love Fame* vii. 175 His eye..inur'd to wake, And outwatch every star, for Brunswick's sake. **1833** HERSCHEL *Astron.* ii. 44 To outwatch a long winter's night. **1872** O. W. HOLMES *Poet Breakf.-t.* iv. 17 The old man of West Cambridge, who outwatched the rest so long after they had gone to sleep in their own churchyards.

Hence **out'watch** *sb.*², the act of outwatching.

1865 SWINBURNE *Poems, St. Dorothy* 58 Nor with outwatch of many travaillings Come to be eased of the least pain he hath.

out-water, -wave: see OUT- 12, 14.

†**outwaxing,** *vbl. sb. Obs. rare.* [OUT- 9; after L. *ex-crēmentum, ex-crēscentia,* f. *ex-crēscĕre* to grow or wax out; cf. Ger. *auswuchs*, Du. *uitwas.*]

a. Excrement. **b.** An excrescence, outgrowth.

1541 R. COPLAND *Galyen's Terapeutyke* 2 E iij, That all the body muste be emptyed and purged of all his outwaxynges. **1562** TURNER *Herbal* II. 31 Laser..healeth..outwaxynges or to growinges in the fleshe.

†**'outway,** *sb. Obs.* [OUT- 6.]

1. A way or passage leading out, an outlet.

1571 GOLDING *Calvin on Ps.* x. 9 Like as theeves beset yᵉ outwayes of villages. **1633** P. FLETCHER *Purple Isl.* IV. xxvii, In divers streets and out wayes multipli'd. **1644** VICARS *God in Mount* 147 To make good all the out-waies.

2. A by-way lying off the main route.

1566 ADLINGTON *Apuleius* 9 In greate feare, I rode through many outwaies and deserte places. **1597** BEARD *Theatre God's Judgem.* (1612) 492 He betooke him to flight, and hid himselfe in an outway amongst thornes and bushes.

†**'out-way,** *a. Obs. rare.* [OUT- 12.] = OUT-OF-THE-WAY. *out-way going*, going out of the way, deviation.

1387–8 T. USK *Test. Love* I. viii. (Skeat) I. 15 As the sorowe and anguisshe was greet in tyme of thyne out-waye goinge. **1615** CHAPMAN *Odyss.* IX. 166 We..still with sad hearts sail'd by out-way shores.

out-wealth, -weapon, etc.: see OUT-.

outwear (aʊt'wɛə(r)), *v.* [OUT- 15, 15 b, 18.]

1. *trans.* To wear out, wear away; to wear down to nothing, or to an end; to consume by wearing.

a **1541** WYATT *Poet. Wks.* (1861) 17 Though..Change hath outworn the favour that I had. **1596** SPENSER *F.Q.* IV. ii. 33 Wicked Time that..doth..workes of noblest wits to nought outweare. **1665** J. WEBB *Stone-Heng* (1725) 82 The Characters..were..wholly outworn by Time. **1711** *Let. to Sacheverell* 13 Subjects are insulted, and their Patience outworn. **1851** MRS. BROWNING *Casa Guidi Windows* I. 76 The..clay From whence the Medicean stamp's outworn.

b. To exhaust in strength or endurance: chiefly in pa. pple. ***outworn*** = worn out, exhausted.

1610 HOLLAND *Camden's Brit.* I. 690 He being outworne with travell and labour, died in peace. **1654** G. GODDARD in *Introd. to Burton's Diary* (1828) I. 20 As if he had served so long that he had been outworn. **1828** WORDSW. *Wishing-gate* viii, Some, by ceaseless pains outworn, Here crave an easier lot. **1887** BOWEN *Virg. Æneid* III. 78 The crews outworn by the sea.

†**c.** *intr.* To become worn out or exhausted.

1614 C. BROOKE *Ghost Rich. III* Poems (1872) 86 Life (sencible of pleasure) now feeles paine, Earth must to earth; as Nature's course outweares.

2. *trans.* To wear out, spend, pass (time).

1590 SPENSER *F.Q.* III. xii. 29 All that day she outwore in wandering And gazing on that Chambers ornament. **1603** DEKKER *Grissil* (Shaks. Soc.) 15 You and your son,..Shall live to outwear time in happiness. **1725** POPE *Odyss.* v. 601 Here by the stream, if I the night out-wear. **1821** KEATS *Isabella* iii, And with sick longing all the night outwear To hear her morning-step upon the stair.

b. To do away with or get over (something) by process of time; to outlive, outgrow.

1592 *Nobody & Someb.* in Simpson *Sch. Shaks.* (1878) I. 347 It joyes me that you haue outworne your pride. **1642** FULLER *Holy & Prof. St.* II. xxii. 144 The merits of Posterity have outworn the disgraces of their Ancestours. **1698** FRYER *Acc. E. India & P.* 349 As soon as he hath outworn his Dose, he with most greedy haste returns to his Vomit before he comes to himself. **1830** TENNYSON *Sonnet* Poems 122 Could I outwear my present state of woe With one brief winter. **1900** *Westm. Gaz.* 1 Aug. 2/1 He..may outwear those unattractive qualities of character.

†**3.** To hollow out or excavate (marks) by wearing away a surface. *Obs.*

1600 FAIRFAX *Tasso* XX. cxxii, Her palfraies feete signes in the grasse outware.

4. To wear longer than, to outlast in wear.

1579 SPENSER *Sheph. Cal.* Dec., Epil. 2 Loe I haue made a Calender for euery yeare, That steele in strength, and time in durance, shall outweare. **1684** T. BURNET *Th. Earth* I. 180 Stone and iron would scarce out-wear them. **1893** KATH. L. BATES *Eng. Relig. Drama* 88 Like teaspoons that have outworn their set.

outweary (aʊt'wɪərɪ), *v.* Chiefly *poet.* [OUT- 15 b.] *trans.* To weary out; to tire or fatigue utterly, to exhaust in endurance.

1609 HOLLAND *Amm. Marcell.* 75 Outwearied at last with so much painefull toile. **1683** A. D. *Art Converse* 9 Others do out-weary your patience. *a* **1732** T. BOSTON *Crook in Lot* (1805) 145 Unbelievers may soon be outwearied, and give it over for altogether. **1861** M. ARNOLD *South. Nt.* in *Victoria Regia* 181 Some youthful Troubadour,..Who here outwearied sank and sang A dying strain.

Hence **out'wearied** *ppl. a.*

1853 RUSKIN *Stones Ven.* II. iii. §1. 27 The decay of the city of Venice is..like that of an outwearied and aged human frame. **1885–94** R. BRIDGES *Eros & Psyche* Jan. xix, Thou wilt o'ertake a lame outwearied ass.

out'weave, *v.* [OUT- 15 b, 15.] *trans.* **a.** To weave to an end or completion. **b.** To weave from within outwards.

a **1649** DRUMM. OF HAWTH. *Poems* Wks. (1711) 36/1 May never hours the web of day out-weave; May never night rise from her sable cave. **1890** J. PULSFORD *Loyalty to Christ* I. 11 All the trees of the wood throb with new life, and out-weave their lovely attire.

out-weed: see OUT- 15.

outweep (aʊt'wiːp), *v.* [OUT- 16, 18.]

1. *trans.* To weep out, to expel or emit by weeping. *poetic.*

1597 LYLY *Wom. in Moone* IV. i, Sighing my breath, out-weeping my heart bloud. *a* **1649** DRUMM. OF HAWTH. *Poems* Wks. (1711) 25/1 These eyes,..Their trait'rous black before Thee here out-weep. **1821** SHELLEY *Adonais* x, With no stain She faded, like a cloud which had outwept its rain.

2. To outdo or surpass in weeping.

a **1631** DONNE in *Select.* (1840) 133 To set Christ Jesus before him, to out-sigh him, out-weep him. **1632** MASSINGER & FIELD *Fatal Dowry* II. ii, You have outwept a woman, noble Charalois. **1767** W. L. LEWIS *Statius' Thebaid* vi. 44 The childless Mother raves, And far out-weeps her Lord. **1865** SWINBURNE *Atalanta* 1866 Lo mine eyes That outweep heaven at rainiest.

outweigh (aʊt'weɪ), *v.* [OUT- 18, 18 b.]

1. *trans.* To exceed in weight; *fig.* to be too heavy or onerous for.

1597 SHAKS. *2 Hen. IV*, I. iii. 45 Then must we rate the cost of the Erection, Which if we finde out-weighes Ability, What do we then, but draw a-new the Modell In fewer offices? **1646** SIR T. BROWNE *Pseud. Ep.* 382 The taile of an African weather outweigheth the body of a good Calfe,..according unto Leo Africanus. **1728** PEMBERTON *Newton's Philos.* 76 The weight..will outweigh it, and draw the beam of the lever down. **1875** JOWETT *Plato* (ed. 2) I. 171 Weigh them, and then say which outweighs the other.

2. To exceed in value, importance, or influence.

1632 HEYWOOD *2nd Pt. Iron Age* I. i. Wks. 1874 III. 361 Hate will out-way my loue. *a* **1703** BURKITT *On N.T.* Acts xxiii. 11 The presence of God with his suffering servants outweighs all their discouragements. **1835** THIRLWALL *Greece* I. viii. 297 This variation..cannot be allowed to outweigh the concurrent testimony. **1866** G. MACDONALD *Ann. Q. Neighb.* xxxiii. 582 With you, position outweighs honesty.

outwell (aʊtˈwɛl), *v.* [OUT- 15, 14.]

†**1.** *trans.* To pour forth. *Obs.*

1590 SPENSER *F.Q.* I. i. 21 His fattie waves doe fertile slime outwell. **1591** —— *Virg. Gnat* 502 When..Simois and Xanthus blood outwelde.

2. *intr.* To well out, to gush or flow forth.

1600 FAIRFAX *Tasso* IX. lxxxvi, Midst his wrath, his manly teares outwell. **1748** THOMSON *Cast. Indol.* II. 320 From virtue's fount the purest joys outwell. **1830** TENNYSON *Claribel* 18 The slumbrous wave outwelleth.

Hence **out'welling** *vbl. sb.* and *ppl. a.*

1821 LAMB *Elia* Ser. I. *Quaker's Meeting*, Sitting..in deepest peace, which some out-welling tears would rather confirm than disturb. **1878** DOWDEN *Stud. Lit.* 158 A fresh, quick outwelling of thought. **1882** *Pop. Sci. Monthly* XX. 358 Fissures formed during the outwelling of igneous materials from below.

out-wend to **outwhore**: see OUT-.

out West (aʊt ˈwɛst), *sb.* and *adv. phr.* [f. OUT *adv.* 2, 16 + WEST *adv.* 2c.] **A.** *sb.* Orig., the territory to the west of the early American settlements; by extension, the distant West of the U.S. as regarded by inhabitants of the East (cf. WEST *sb.* 3b). Also *attrib.* **B.** *adv. phr.* In or to this region. Also *transf.* in or to the western parts of Canada or Australia.

1835 C. F. HOFFMAN *Winter in West* II. 119 Old Kaintuck ..whips all 'Out-West' in prettiness. **1848** R. W. GRISWOLD *Passages from Corr.* (1898) 243 The 'out West Editor' would inform her..as to who he is. *Ibid.* 244 Why is it your new volume is not out West? **1857** *Lawrence* (Kansas) *Republican* 4 June 2 Any one who has spent any time in farming 'out west', will see that this is a mistake. **1887** C. B. GEORGE *40 Yrs. on Rail* 62 New York State was considered 'out West' then. **1890** S. M. ST. MAUR *Impressions Tenderfoot* xiii. 173 All ponies and dogs 'out West' seem shy of women. **1898** P. L. FORD *Tattle-Tales of Cupid* 205 As they say out West, it's come to stay and grow up with the country. **1944** *Living off Land* iv. 81 The country out-west is full of dead men's bones. **1952** *Manch. Guardian Weekly* 17 July 15 He worked as a section hand out west on the Union Pacific railroad. **1961** *Maclean's Mag.* 29 July 36/1 I've worked freights that have carried more passengers than the passenger runs did, especially out west in the Depression.

outwick (ˈaʊtˌwɪk), *sb. Sc. Curling.* [f. OUT- 7 + WICK *v.* (?)] A shot that cannons off the outside of another stone so as to impel it nearer the tee; practised when a well-guarded adversary's stone is *in*, and an 'inwick' cannot be taken.

1805 MCINDOE *Poems* 56 (E.D.D.) Mony a nice out-weik's been ta'en.

out'wick, *v. Sc. Curling.* [f. OUT- 14 + WICK *v.*] *intr.* To take or make an outwick; to strike the outside of another stone so as to send it within either circle.

1831 *Blackw. Mag.* XXX. 970 Out-wicking, is to strike the outer angle of a stone, so as thereby to put it into the spot. Though a much more difficult operation, it can sometimes be practised with effect when in-wicking cannot. *fig.* *c* **1896** A. BENVIE *Raid of Pictonello* ii. in *R. Caledon. Curling Club Ann.* (1897–8) p. clxviii, Alas, his wits Are wandered, and his tongue makes sport of words Outwicking from the sense, the mind elsewhere.

out-wile, *v.*: see OUT- 18.

†**out-'win,** *v. Obs.* [OUT- 14, 15. (Two words in ME.)] **1.** *intr.* To get out.

1340 HAMPOLE *Pr. Consc.* 4462 A qwene..þat haldes þam in, Thurgh strengthe, þat þai may noght out wyn.

2. *trans.* To get (something) out.

c **1400** *Alexius* (Laud 463) 450 þat writ he drow & ȝerne tey, He ne myght it out winne. *c* **1400** *Melayne* 1582 Be that tyme he myghte nowe wele a worde owt wyn.

3. To get out of. *rare.*

1596 SPENSER *F.Q.* IV. i. 20 It is a darksome delve farre under ground, With thornes and barren brakes environd round, That none the same may easily out-win.

†**out-wind** (ˈaʊtˌwɪnd), *sb. Obs.* [OUT- 1.] A wind from the offing; a wind blowing inshore.

1676 C. JEAFFRESON *Lett.* in *Yng. Sqr. 17th C.* (1878) I. 173 [Near Funchal there is] a rock, a small distance from the land, between which and the shoar, the Porteguise ships ride in out-windes. *a* **1703** H. WINSTANLEY in Smiles *Engineers* (1861) II. 17 The sea would be so raging about these rocks, caused by outwinds and the running of the ground seas coming from the main ocean. **1754** T. GARDNER *Hist. Acc. Dunwich* 214 Choaked by most boisterous Outwinds.

†**outwind** (-ˈwaɪnd), *v.*[1] *Obs.* [OUT- 14, 15, 24.]

1. *intr.* To wind off or become unwound. In quot. *fig.*

a **1562** G. CAVENDISH *Metr. Visions, Weston* Poems 1825 II. 30 Which caused my welthe full soon to outwynd.

2. *trans.* To unwind; to disentangle, extricate.

1596 SPENSER *F.Q.* v. iii. 9 They have him enclosed so behind, As by no meanes he can himselfe outwind. **1647** H. MORE *Song of Soul* I. II. lxxi, When shalt thou once outwind Thy self from this sad yoke?

outwind (aʊtˈwɪnd), *v.*[2] [f. OUT- 26 + WIND *sb.*] *trans.* To put out of wind or breath.

1708 OCKLEY *Saracens* (1848) 121 Your enemies are two to one; and there is no breaking them but by out-winding them. **1721** DUDLEY in *Phil. Trans.* XXXI. 167 A Moose soon outwinds a Deer. *c* **1825** CHOYCE *Log Jack Tar* (1891) 94 Several more men..soon came up with two more of our number, who were out-winded.

†**'out-ˌwing,** *sb. Sc. Obs.* [OUT- 3.] A wing (of an army); = L. *āla.*

1536 BELLENDEN *Cron. Scot.* (1821) I. 268 At last the out-wingis of Romanis, be multitude of pepil, ouirset thair ennimes fornens thaim. **1596** LODGE *Marg. Amer.* 8 Embattailed in due order, the pikemen in a Macedonian phalanx, the horsemen in their outwings.

outwing (aʊtˈwɪŋ), *v.* [OUT- 21.]

1. *trans.* To exceed in swiftness of wing, to surpass in flight; to fly beyond.

1717 GARTH *Ovid's Metam.* XIV. *Picus & Canens* 42 His courser springs O'er hills and lawns, and ev'n a wish out-wings. **1747** *Gentl. Mag.* 538 Fame flies before, Out-wings the wind! **1898** *Advance* (Chicago) 6 Jan. 23/1 Mr. Morse's robins must have despaired of their effort to out-wing the limit of snow.

2. *Mil.* Of an army: To extend with its wings beyond (the enemy's); to outflank.

1648 CROMWELL *Let.* 20 Aug. in *Carlyle*, Colonel Dean's and Colonel Pride's [regiments] outwinging the Enemy, could not come to so much share of the action. **1755** *Mem. Capt. P. Drake* II. ii. 28 Both the Enemy's Lines out wing'd ours considerably. **1876** BANCROFT *Hist. U.S.* III. xii. 189 His right came in contact with the enemy's left, outwinged it, and attacked it in front and flank.

outwinter (ˈaʊtwɪntə(r)), *v.* Also **out-winter.** [OUT- 15.] *trans.* To keep (animals) in the open during the winter. So **'outwintered** *ppl. a.*, **'outwintering** *vbl. sb.* Cf. IN-WINTER *v.*

1959 *Times* 2 Nov. 21/1 Our first decision was to have our own acclimatized breeding outwintered cattle. **1960** *Farmer & Stockbreeder* 8 Mar. 109/3 Gimmer hoggs that are outwintered well in North-East Cheshire have yielded fleeces up to 11 lb. *Ibid.* 15 Mar. 81/3 An average of 35s for outwintering. **1965** COOPER & THOMAS *Profitable Sheep Farming* viii. 75 Grazing obtained by out-wintered ewes in a more normal season is not appreciable.

out-'winterer. [OUT- 8; from *winter out.*] A beast that winters out.

1770–4 A. HUNTER *Georg. Ess.* (1803) IV. 351 *Out-winterers*, as they are called, or cattle kept out all winter.

out-wish, *v.*: see OUT- 18.

†**'outˌwit,** *sb. Obs.* [OUT- 3.] The faculty of observation or perception; an external sense.

1377 LANGL. *P. Pl.* B. XIII. 289 A lyer in soule; With Inwit and with outwitt ymagenen and studye, As best for his body be. *c* **1380** WYCLIF *Wks.* (1880) 291 Sum good iugement is of mennes out-wittis, as þei iugen whiche mete is good & whiche mete is yuel, and sum men iugement is of mennes witt wiþinne, as men iugen how þei schal do, by lawe of consience.

outwit (aʊtˈwɪt), *v.* [OUT- 21.]

1. *trans.* To excel in wit; to surpass in wisdom or knowledge. *arch.*

1659 GAUDEN *Tears Ch.* II. xxxi. 253 What arts did Church-men in former times use, when they did so much out-wit and out-wealth us. **1694** HOWE *Princ. Oracles God* xvii, A thing whereon the wisdom of the Creator hath infinitely outwitted us, and gone beyond us. **1847** EMERSON *Poems* (1857) 138 Thou..Shalt outsee seers, and outwit sages.

2. To overreach or get the better of by superior craft or ingenuity; to prove too clever for.

1652 KIRKMAN *Clerio & Lozia* 114 Her Uncle was out-witted. **1705** HICKERINGILL *Priest-cr.* III. Wks. 1716 III. 164 Rebekkah that club'd with her beloved Son Jacob..to cheat or, rather (as the Quakers word it) to Outwit his own Father and Brother. **1846** TRENCH *Mirac.* v. (1862) 178 There reveals itself here the very essence and truest character of evil, which evermore outwits and defeats itself. **1857** BUCKLE *Civiliz.* I. iv. 197 Every commercial treaty was an attempt made by one nation to outwit another.

Hence **out'witted** *ppl. a.*; **out'witting** *vbl. sb.* and *ppl. a.*; also **out'wittal** (*nonce-wd.*), the fact of outwitting; **out'witter,** one who outwits.

1705 HICKERINGILL *Priest-cr.* II. viii. 78 Their Cheating, ..Outwitting, and Over-reaching, in Shops and Exchange. **1775** LANGHORNE *Country Justice* II. 20 The worship'd Calves of their outwitting Knaves. **1862** MAURICE *Mor. & Met. Philos.* IV. iv. §2. 96 If he can outwit the great outwitter. **1865** TYLOR *Early Hist. Man.* i. 11 The outwitted beast. **1875** *Contemp. Rev.* XXV. 750 The tricks of Sir Robert..and their outwittal by Matilda. **1891** *Athenæum* 9 May 599/3 This perpetual outwitting of examiners.

outwith (ˈaʊtwɪθ), *prep.* and *adv.* Chiefly *north.* and *Sc.* Forms: α. 3 (*Orm.*) utenn wiþþ, utwiþþ; 3 utewiđ, 4 utewit, -wid, utwit, -wyth; oute-, out-wiþ, 4–5 utwith, 4– outwith (6 owt-, oute-). β. *Sc.* 4 ututh, 4–5 owtouth, outhouth, otouth, otow, 4–6 utouth. [f. OUT *adv.* + WITH *prep.*: cf. INWITH, and WITHOUT (in which the same elements are transposed).]

A. *prep.* **1.** Without; outside of. **a.** Of position.

c **1200** ORMIN 13116 Ȝho wat þatt utwiþþ Crisstenndom Niss nohht tatt Crist maȝȝ cwemenn. *a* **1300** *Cursor M.* 20922 (Cott.) Vt-wit [*Gött.* vtewid, *Edin.* outwiþ, *Fairf.* wiþ-out, *Trin.* wiþoute] þe toun apon þe est side. *Ibid.* 588 (Cott.) Vtewit [*Fairf.* Oute-wiþ] paradis [was adam] wroght. *a* **1400** *Burgh Laws* vii. (*Sc. Stat.* I.) Ututh þe burgh. *c* **1420** *Pallad. on Husb.* I. 317 Enlarge it half a foote Out-with the wough. **1536** BELLENDEN *Cron. Scot.* (1821) I. 87 Takin utouth thair munitions. **1591** BRUCE *Eleven Serm.* Dva, Iesus Christ..out-with whome there is nather comfort nor consolatioun. **1640** *Bk. War Comm. Covenanters* 133 The awners quhairof are outwith the kingdome. **1875** *Proc. Soc. Antiq. Scot.* X. 286 It is only probable that *outwith* this row there had been an outer course of piles. **1885** *Law Rep.* 10 App. Cas. 457 Any Court or tribunal outwith Scotland. **1927** W. D. SIMPSON *Historical St. Columba* 17 Of the four peoples..who struggled for mastery in what is now Scotland, the Angles alone were entirely outwith the pale of Christianity. **1947** H. FARMER *Hist. Music Scotl.* 216 In music, there was but one name, John Abell (d. 1724), and he gained his fame *outwith* Scotland, to use the appropriate Scots word. **1970** 'E. FERRARS' *Seven Sleepers* iv. 46 I'm moving into a small bungalow outwith the town. **1972** G. HENDERSON *Early Medieval* vi. 232 Outwith history painting the image of the crucified Christ, as an evocation of the Passion and redemption, was slow to make itself felt. **1975** C. N. MANLOVE *Mod. Fantasy* iv. 99 What he came to demand was 'rational' friendship, the bond of a common interest in something outwith the self. **1978** *Dumfries & Galloway Standard* 21 Oct. 1/8 Attempts might be made.. to promote the greater use of existing static caravan sites outwith the July/August period.

b. Of motion: Out of, out from.

1375 BARBOUR *Bruce* VIII. 90 He, but swerd, his vayis raid Weill otow [*MS. E.* otowth] thame. *Ibid.* 448 Richt as thai wald to lanrik fair, Otow [*MS. E.* owtouth] quhar the enbuschement var. *c* **1375** *Sc. Leg. Saints* l. (*Katerine*) 1104 þe tyrand gert hir furth be had outhouth þe ȝeittis of þe cite. **1553–4** *Reg. Privy Council Scot.* I. 155 Thai sall nocht evaid nor eschaip owtwith this burcht of Edinburch. **1705** in *Aberdeen Jrnl. N. & Q.* (1909) II. 309/1 It shall be leisum to them..to take themselves outwith the family. **1958** *Times* 5 Dec. 8/7 Their value may also extend outwith the narrow sphere of medicine.

†**2.** Of time: Beyond. *Obs.*

13.. *Cursor M.* 10346 (Cott.) Bath þam bar tua wimmen geld þat vte-wit [*other texts* out of] birth o barn was teld. **1479** *Act. Dom. Conc.* 36/2 Gif ony personis..before or eftir, vtwith þe said iiij yeris [etc.].

B. *adv.* **1.** Of position: Without; on the outside; outwardly.

c **1200** ORMIN 4778 All þiss wass utenn wiþþ unnhal þurrh swiþe unnride unnhæle. *c* **1230** *Hali Meid.* 39 Hit ne faređ nawt swa as [ha] weneđ þat iseođ utewiđ. **13..** *E.E. Allit. P.* A. 968 Vt-wyth to se þat clene cloystor, þou may, bot in-wyth not a fote. *c* **1400** *Destr. Troy* 12201 This Vlixes, þat vtwith aunterit hym neuer. *c* **1520** M. NISBET *N.T. in Scots* Mark iii. 32 Thi modere & thi brethire out-with seekis thee. **1582–8** *Hist. James VI* (1804) 147 That thair interpryse should nather be devulgat in the toune nor outewith.

2. Of direction: Out.

1375 BARBOUR *Bruce* II. 299 Till thaim wtouth send thai sone, And bad thaim herbery thaim that nycht. **1768** ROSS *Helenore* II. 78 Colin her father, who had outwith gane. **1871** W. ALEXANDER *Johnny Gibb* xli. (1873) 233 The two being.. only 'freens fae the teeth ootwuth'.

out-woe, out-woman: see OUT- 21, 22.

'outˌwood. [OUT- 1, 3.] **a.** A wood lying outside a park or demesne. **b.** The outer border of a wood or forest.

1449 *Lett. Marg. Anjou & Bp. Beckington* (Camden) 98, x oks of tymbre, to be taken in yo[r] outwods of Kenelworth. **1485** *Rolls of Parlt.* VI. 359/1 The Graunte of Kepyng of the Parke called the Moote Parc, with the Oute Wodes of Crambourne, within the Forest of Wyndesore. **1523** FITZHERB. *Surv.* 4 The thirde maner of commen pasture is in y[e] lordes out wodes that lye commen to his tenauntes, as commen mores or hethes, the whiche were neuer errable landes. **1883** STEVENSON *Black Arrow* (1888) 52 The two lads..hurried through the remainder of the outwood.

out-word, *v.*: see OUT- 21.

outwork (ˈaʊtwɜːk), *sb.* [OUT- 1, 3.]

1. Any part of the fortifications of a place lying outside the parapet; any detached or advanced work forming part of the defence of a place; an outer defence or outfort.

1639 MASSINGER *Unnat. Combat* v. ii, Our outworks are surprized, the sentinel slain. **1642** CHAS. I *Message to Both Houses* 11 July, Out-works to defend the Town. **1748** *Anson's Voy.* II. vi. 190 This fort..had neither ditch nor outwork. **1766** ENTICK *London* IV. 327 The tower is light, supported by outworks at the angles. **1855** MACAULAY *Hist. Eng.* xvi. III. 679 Cork was vigorously attacked. Outwork after outwork was rapidly carried.

b. *transf.* and *fig.*

c **1615** BACON *Advice to Sir G. Villiers* v. §7 Wks. 1872 VI. 44 The care of our out-work, the Navy Royal and shipping of the kingdom, which are the walls thereof. **1622** DONNE *Lett.* (1651) 134 All our moralities are but our outworks, our Christianity is our citadel. **1872** LIDDON *Elem. Relig.* ii. 65 Belief in creation is a necessary outwork of any true theism whatever.

†**2.** An extra dish served as a relish; an *hors-d'œuvre. Obs.*

1693 EVELYN *De la Quint. Compl. Gard.* I. III. 69 A pretty Basket well fill'd with the choice eating Fruits of the Season, ..which in the Courts of Kings and Princes, is called the *Hors-d'oeuvre*, or the Out-work. **1727** BRADLEY *Fam. Dict.* s.v. *Anchovy*, You may..serve it up to Table for an Out-work, with Orange and fry'd Parsley.

3. Work upon the outside or exterior of anything.

1691 *Lond. Gaz.* No. 2655/4 A Golden Sword drawn with some Outworks upon the Head and Shell. **1716–17** in Willis & Clark *Cambridge* (1886) II. 223 For the workmen in fitting up the six chambers their out work, in his new Addition to his Refronting the Coll. wth freestone.

4. (*out-work.*) Work done outside, i.e. out of doors, out of the house, out of the shop or factory, etc.; in *Cricket* = OUT-FIELDING.

1793 SMEATON *Edystone L.* Contents 10 Commencement of the Outwork of the ensuing Season. **1813** R. KERR *Agric. Surv. Berw.* xv. 420 What is called out-work, as helping to fill muck carts, spreading the muck, setting and hoeing potatoes [etc.]. **1899** *Westm. Gaz.* 3 June 7/1 He cordially joined in I——'s pæan over the out-work of the 'Varsity. 'The fielding of the Oxonians has been grand.'

outwork (aʊtˈwɜːk), *v.* [OUT- 15, 15 b, 21, 18.] **1.** *trans.* †**a.** To bring out as a result of work, to produce (*obs.*); **b.** To work out to a conclusion; to complete. (*poetic.*)

c **1250** *Gen. & Ex.* 4144 Ydolatrie..ofte ut wroȝte hem sorȝes dref. **1590** SPENSER *F.Q.* II. vii. 65 For now three dayes of men were full outwrought, Since he this hardy enterprize began. **1901** T. HARDY *Mute Opinion* 14, I saw, in web unbroken, Its history outwrought.

†**2.** To excel in work or workmanship. *Obs.*

1599 NASHE *Lenten Stuffe* Wks. (Grosart) V. 253, I do not thinke but all the Smiths in London, Norwich, or Yorke.. would enuy him, if they could not outworke him. **1606** SHAKS. *Ant. & Cl.* II. ii. 206 She did lye In her Pauillion.. O're-picturing that Venus, where we see The fancie outwork Nature. **1782** HAN. MORE *Belshazzar* II. Dramas 175 Thou hast out-wrought the pattern he bequeath'd thee, And quite outgone example.

3. To surpass or outdo in working; to work more strenuously or faster than.

1611 B. JONSON *Catiline* III. iii, But, in your violent acts, The fall of torrents and the noise of tempests,..Be all outwrought by your transcendant furies. **1647** TRAPP *Comm. Rev.* xii. 12 He makes all haste he can to outwork the children of light. **1880** A. H. HUTH *Buckle* II. 171 Captain Cook found that his sailors could outwork the islanders.

'out-ˌworker. [OUT- 2.] One who works outside, i.e. out of doors, out of the house, out of the shop or factory for which he works.

1813 R. KERR *Agric. Surv. Berw.* xv. 420 Their occupiers [were] bound to shear at the ordinary wages, and to supply certain outworkers when wanted. **1856** KANE *Arct. Expl.* II. ix. 95 Then the few tired outworkers were regaled by the groans and tossings of the sick. **1894** *Daily News* 24 Mar. 3/4 The lists of out workers which are now required to be kept by the manufacturers of all kinds of wearing apparel, cabinet and furniture making [etc.].

'outˌworking, *vbl. sb.* [OUT- 9.] **1.** The action or process of working out; practical operation.

1863 J. G. MURPHY *Comm. Gen.* v. 1, 2 The generations, evolutions, or outworkings of the skies and the land. **1880** T. C. MURRAY *Origin Ps.* ix. 286 The outworking of this applied force in the physical phenomena of life. **1881** W. M. THOMSON *Land & Bk.* 2 The long ongoing and outworkings of the Mosaic Economy. **1958** *Church Times* 5 Dec. 1/3 If the outworking of *apartheid* policies meant such cruelty and callousness, then even the Slightest Smell of a *Compulsory apartheid* must be removed from our Churches. **1961** B. R. WILSON *Sects & Society* III. xiv. 288 Christadelphians do take a keen interest in political events, as out-workings of biblical prophecy. **1976** M. WILES *What is Theology?* iv. 108 Philosophical assumptions implicit in these [Freudian] ideas and their practical outworking in therapy.

2. [See OUTWORK *sb.* and *a.*] The work of an out-worker.

1970 G. GREER *Female Eunuch* 131 As an alternative to nursing or outworking, waitressing..is not conspicuously preferable. **1974** *Daily Tel.* 12 Jan. 2/6 There are..areas of the country where 'out-working' has been traditional, as with lace at Nottingham.

'outˌworld, out-world, *sb.* [OUT- 3.] The external or outside world; the world external to a person's mind, sphere of action, etc.; an outlying or outer world.

1647 H. MORE *Resolution* 60 And long acquaintance with the light Of this Outworld. **1840** BROWNING *Sordello* I. 755 Forth glided—not alone Each painted warrior, every girl of stone,—..But the entire out-world. **1899** BARING-GOULD *Vicar Morwenstow* vii. 193, I hope to hear from you what is going on in the out-world.

'out-world, *a.* [OUT- 12.] Out-of-the-world.

1884 MAY CROMMELIN *Brown-Eyes* iii. 28 Sometimes.. came a foreigner or two from far lands,..attracted, by hearing at Amsterdam of this strange out-world spot.

†**out'worldish,** *a. Obs. rare.* [Cf. *outlandish.*] Fairfax's word for: Extramundane.

1674 FAIRFAX *Bulk & Selv.* 58 If outworldish boak be yielded at all, it must needs be yielded infinite to boot. **1880** G. MACDONALD *Bk. Strife* 73 A strange auroral bliss, an Arctic awe, A new, outworldish joy awoke intense.

outworn, out-worn (aʊtˈwɔːn, *attrib.* ˈaʊtwɔːn), *ppl. a.* [OUT- 11, from *wear out.*]

1. Worn out, as clothes; wasted, consumed, or obliterated by wear or by the action of time; hence *fig.* of beliefs, customs, institutions, etc., that have ceased to be useful; obsolete, out of date.

1565 JEWEL *Def. Apol.* (1611) 362 To seek to procure vs enuie only with stale and outworne Lies. **1624** SANDERSON *Serm.* I. 226 In old marbles and coins and out-worn inscriptions. **1806** WORDSW. *Sonn.*, '*The world is too much*' 10 I'd rather be A Pagan suckled in a creed outworn. **1822** SHELLEY *Hellas* 1063 The earth doth like a snake renew Her winter weeds outworn. **1897** CREIGHTON *Hist. Papacy* VI. VI. i. 15 The out-worn ideals of feudalism.

2. Of living beings, their faculties, etc.: Exhausted as to physical vigour or vitality; spent.

1597 HOWSON *Serm.* 24 Dec. 31 A spent and outworne life. **1671** MILTON *Samson* 580 Better at home lie bed-rid,.. Inglorious, unemployed, with age outworn. **1817** BYRON *Lament Tasso* viii, The Powers of Evil can..prevail Against the outworn creature they assail. **1884** J. PARKER *Apost. Life* III. 273 We pray for the..sated and outworn man.

out-worth, *v.*: see OUT- 21.

outwrangle (aʊtˈræŋg(ə)l), *v.* [OUT- 18.] *trans.* To outdo or surpass in wrangling, quarrelsome disputing, or altercation.

1589 *Pappe w. Hatchet* (1844) 15 Thinkst thou..as none can outwrangle thee? **1618** ROWLANDS *Sacr. Mem.* 5 You Coniurers..That boast you can the fiends of hell outwrangle. *a* **1659** OSBORN *Observ. Turks* (1673) 292 If Law did not out-wrangle Nature.

out-wrench, *v.*: see OUT- 15.

†**out'wrest,** *v. Obs.* [OUT- 15.] *trans.* To draw out or extract as with a forcible twist; to extort; to extract by superior force.

1590 SPENSER *F.Q.* II. iv. 23 My engreeved mind could find no rest, Till that the truth thereof I did out wrest. *a* **1631** DONNE *Bait* Poems (1650) 38 Let coarse bold hands, from slimy nest The bedded fish in banks out-wrest.

out'wrestle, *v.* [OUT- 14, 18 b.]

†**1.** *intr.* To escape by wrestling, to struggle free.

1562 PHAER *Æneid* IX. C c iij, Loke how the tempest storm, whan winds outwrastling blowes at south.

2. *trans.* To overcome in wrestling; to grapple or strive successfully with; to wrestle better than.

1559 *Mirr. Mag.* (1563) A a ij, Where other vnlyke in workyng or skyll, Outwrestle the world, and wyeld it at wyll. **1657** S. PURCHAS *Pol. Flying-Ins.* 99 If they [bees] outwrastle all these difficulties, yet they will scarce swarm that year. **1854** R. OWEN in *Circ. Sci.* (*c* 1865) II. 62/1 It can outwrestle the athlete.

out'wring, *v.* [OUT- 16.] *trans.* To force out (liquid) by or as by wringing.

c **1385** CHAUCER *L.G.W.* 2527 *Phillis*, Youre teres falsly out wronge. **1562** PHAER *Æneid* IX. C c iij, Whan god from skies..His watry showres outwrings.

So **out-'wrung** *ppl. a.*, outstretched and wrung.

1850 MRS. BROWNING *Isobel's Child* x, I am not used..to prayer With shaken lips and hands out-wrung.

outwrite (aʊtˈraɪt), *v.* [OUT- 18, 17, 15 b.]

1. *trans.* To surpass or excel in writing; to write better than.

1643 T. COLEMAN *Serm.* in Kerr *Covenants & Cov.* (1895) 180 You outwrite your copy. **1671** SHADWELL *Humorist* Epil. 30 He would with ease all Poets else out-write. **1711** STEELE *Spect.* No. 96 ¶4 My half-Education and Love of idle Books, made me outwrite all that made Love to her by way of Epistle. **1888** [see OUTREAD 2].

2. To get over or beyond by writing.

1837 DISRAELI *Venetia* IV. viii, These wild opinions of his, ..He will outwrite them. **1852** MISS MITFORD in L'Estrange *Friendships Miss M.* (1882) II. x. 168 It was a miserable feeling. At last I out-wrote it.

3. *refl.* To write oneself out, exhaust one's powers of writing. *rare.*

1883 *Manch. Exam.* 22 Nov. 5/5 The music..has all Offenbach's charm of tone and melody. He has clearly not out-written himself yet.

'outˌwriting, *vbl. sb.* [OUT- 9.] The action of writing out or at length.

1871 HAWTHORNE *Sept. Felton* (1879) 184 This was the full expression and outwriting of that crabbed little mystery.

outwrought, pa. t. and pple. of OUTWORK *v.*

†**out'wry,** *v. Obs. rare*$^{-1}$. [app. f. OUT- 24 + WRY *v.*[1] to cover: cf. BEWRY.] *trans.* To discover.

13.. *K. Alis.* 6483 Now haþ he in Egipte y-seyȝe, Al þat any mon can outwryȝe [*Bodley MS.* bywreye].

outy (ˈaʊtɪ). *colloq.* [f. OUT *adv.* + -Y[6].] The act of letting a dog or other pet out of the house, or taking it for a walk; 'walkies'. Freq. in *pl.*

1949 C. H. B. KITCHIN *Cornish Fox* xi. 167 He was Mrs. Ropford's dog, and Mrs. Steele was giving him his evening 'outy'. **1962** N. MARSH *Hand in Glove* vii. 230, I was going to bed and he asked for outies. **1967** B. WHITAKER *Chained Crocodile* iii. 37, I must see to Skipper first, 'e wants outies rather bad.

out-yard: see OUT- 1.

out'yell, *v. rare.* [OUT- 14, 18.]

†**1.** *intr.* To yell out, utter a yell. *Obs.*

1573 TWYNE *Æneid* X. D d iv b, Tryton..blew with whelkid shell Whose wrinckly wreathed flue, did fearful shril in seas outyell.

2. *trans.* To outdo in yelling; to yell louder than.

1825 HOGG *Queen Hynde* 395 Dire echoes that outyell The grovelling, bellowing sounds of hell. **1866** BLACKMORE *Cradock N.* xxxviii, Every engine outyelling its rival.

†**out'yet,** *v. Obs.* [f. OUT- 15 + YET (*yhet, ȝet*) *v.*] *trans.* To pour out, diffuse, shed. Hence †**out'yetting** *vbl. sb.*

1340 HAMPOLE *Pr. Consc.* 7119 In helle,..out-yhetted salle be, Ma teres þan dropes er in þe se. *c* **1340** —— *Prose Tr.* 1 Oyle owt-ȝettide es thi name. *c* **1375** *Sc. Leg. Saints* xxxiii. (*George*) 805 Thru þe outȝetyng of hyre blude.

outyield (aʊtˈjiːld), *v.* [f. OUT- 18 + YIELD *v.* 8.] *trans.* To surpass in terms of yield; to produce more than.

1927 *Daily Tel.* 15 Nov. 12/1 The Danish swede crop outyields ours by about six tons per acre. **1957** *Times* 2 July (Agric. Suppl.) p. i/1 Wheat after sugar beet will almost invariably outyield wheat taken after a one-year mixed ley.

out-zany, out-Zola: see OUT- 22, 23 b.

ouu-, obs. spelling of *ouv-, ov-, ow-*, as in *ouuen, ouuerage, ouurage, ouuerture*, obs. ff. OVEN, OVERAGE, OVERTURE.

ouvala, var. UVALA.

ouvarovite, var. UVAROVITE.

ouver, ouvert, ouverture, obs. ff. OVER, OVERT, OVERTURE.

‖**ouvert** (uvɛr). *Ballet.* [Fr., = open.] (See quots.)

1914 *Techn. Encycl. Theory & Pract. Art of Dancing* 110 *Ouvert*,..any movement in which the legs are open sideways to right or left. **1952** KERSLEY & SINCLAIR *Dict. Ballet Terms* 72 *Ouvert(e)*,..a position of the feet in which the feet do not touch. **1968** J. WINEARLS *Mod. Dance* (ed. 2) iv. 103 The name given to all opening and closing movements of this type is Ouvert.

‖**ouvreuse** (uvrœz). [Fr.] In France, a woman who 'opens' theatre boxes; an usherette in a French theatre or cinema.

1892 G. B. SHAW *Let.* 21 Apr. (1965) I. 338 It took the united strength of my three companions, the *ouvreuse*, the acting manager, the fireman, and a commissionaire to hold me down and restrain me from hurling an opera glass at her head. **1944** H. CROOME *You've gone Astray* i. 11 A disgruntled old *ouvreuse* in a Paris theatre. **1968** *Guardian* 27 Apr. 9/8 An ouvreuse in a theatre or cinema. **1972** *Ibid.* 5 Feb. 3/8 An inescapable one franc for the cloak-room and another for the *ouvreuse*.

‖**ouvrier** (uvrije). [Fr.] A workman. Also *fem.* **ouvrière**, a working woman.

1848 J. ARNOLD *Let.* 28 Mar. in J. Bertram *N.Z. Lett. T. Arnold* (1966) 36 France has been absorbed into the great cities, the cities into Paris, Paris into the middle and lower classes—these into the 'ouvriers', the Ouvriers into the clubs. *a* **1855** C. BRONTË *Professor* (1857) II. xxiv. 205 You, a scion of Seacombe, have proved your disdain of social distinctions by taking up with an *ouvrière*. **1857** C. M. YONGE *Dynevor Terr.* I. xx. 334 She..had seen him.. preceded by a brave and faithful *ouvrier*. **1904** A. BENNETT *Great Man* xxiv. 267, I come from the *ouvriers*,..the working peoples. **1972** R. COBB *Reactions to French Rev.* iv. 142 All that the *ouvrière* might know of the Revolution was that it appeared to be..oppressive and interfering. **1975** —— *Paris & its Provinces* v. 199 An extended family group ..Marie-Anne Deloutre, *tricoteuse*; Ludovine Deloutre, *ouvrière*; and Constance Deloutre, *ouvrière*.

Hence **ouvrierism, -isme, ouvrierist** (see quots.).

1969 G. STEDMAN JONES in Cockburn & Blackburn *Student Power* 29 Such ouvrierism—the belief that the traditional working class has a monopoly of socialist potential—is a mystification. **1974** J. WHITE tr. *Poulantzas's Fascism & Dictatorship* IV. i. 166 The fascist and national socialist *leaders* are extremely cautious in the use of this double-edged weapon, the 'ouvrierist' use of corporatist themes. **1976** F. ZWEIG *New Acquisitive Society* II. x. 134 Ouvrierism implies that the worker can never be the wrongdoer, he can be wronged but he can-not wrong others. **1977** *Foreign Affairs* LV. 805 There has been little of the *ouvrièrisme* in this party that has marked the French.

ouwarovite, ouwarowite, varr. UVAROVITE.

ouwe, ouwer, obs. forms of OWE, YOUR.

ouwhar, ouwher(e, var. OWHERE *Obs.*

ouyr, ouyrley, obs. forms of OVER, OVERLAY.

ouze, obs. form of OOZE.

ouzel, ousel (ˈuːz(ə)l). Forms: α. 1 ósle, 4 osul, (hosel), 4–5 osel, (5 owsille, osill, -ulle, -ylle), 6 osell, -yll, osȝil, oozel, owsell, -yl, ousil, -syl, -zell, 6–7 ousell, 6–8 owsel, 7 ou-, owsle, 7–8 ouzle, 6–ousel, 8– ouzel, (9 *dial.* uzzle, ussel). β. 4 (?) wesel, 6–7 woosell. [OE. ósle wk. fem.:—*ǫmsla = OHG. *amsala* (MHG., Ger. *amsel*); ulterior etymology unknown. The form *wesel* in Trevisa is prob. an error for *wosel*.]

1. A name of certain birds of the genus *Turdus*.

a. An old name of the blackbird or merle (*T. merula*). This is app. the original application of the name (although sense b may have been included); it is now mainly a literary archaism, but appears to be in local use in the qualified form **black-** or **garden-ouzel**. Also *attrib.* in *ouzel-cock*.

a **700** *Epinal Gloss.* (O.E.T.) 665 *Merula*, oslae. *a* **725** *Corpus Gl.* ibid. 1306 Osle. *c* **1000** *Ags. Voc.* in Wr.-Wülcker 260/26 *Merula*, osle. *c* **1325** *Gloss W. de Bibbesw.* in Wright *Voc.* 164 *En braunche seet la merle*, an hosel-brit. **1387** TREVISA *Higden* (Rolls) I. 187 þe wesels [L. *merulæ*, CAXT. ousels] be blak among vs; þere [Arcadia] þey beeþ white. *Ibid.* 237 In towne, as it longes, þe osul twytereþ mery songes. *c* **1450** *Bk. Hawkyng* in *Rel. Ant.* I. 296 Owsilless, and þresches. and other smale briddes. **1533** ELYOT *Cast. Helthe* (1541) 20b, Blacke byrdes or ousyls, amonge wylde fowle hath the chiefe prayse. **1590** SHAKS. *Mids. N.* III. i. 128 The Woosell cocke, so blacke of hew, With Orenge-tawny bill. **1594** R. BARNFIELD *Affect. Sheph.* II. x, Gins and wyles, the Oozels to beguile. **1746** W. THOMPSON *Hymn to May* xxvii, The ouzle sweetly shrill. **1842** TENNYSON *Gardener's Dau.* 93 The mellow ouzel fluted in the elm. **1843** JAMES *Forest Days* x, It is difficult there to know a carrion crow from an ousel. **1875** *Lanc. Gloss.*, *Black-ousel*, the blackbird.

b. Applied to the allied species *T. torquatus*, usually distinguished as **ring-ouzel**; also known locally as *crag-*, *moor-*, *mountain-*, *rock-*, *tor-ouzel*.

The earlier quots. under sense a may have included this: in the following it is distinguished from the *merle* or otherwise identified.

c **1450** HOLLAND *Howlat* 713 The Maviss and the Merle syngis, Osillis and Stirlingis. **1549** *Compl. Scot.* vi. 39 The maueis maid myrtht, for to mok the merle..the lyntquhit sang cuntirpoint quhen the osȝil ȝelpit. **1601** HOLLAND *Pliny* x. xxiv. 284 Ousles, Throstles, Blackbirds, and Stares,.. depart aside from us, but goe not farre. *a* **1705** RAY *Synops. Meth. Avium* (1713) 65, *Merula torquata*, The Ring-Ouzel or Amzel. **1768** G. WHITE *Selborne* xx. 57 The ousel is larger than a blackbird, and feeds on haws. **1885** SWAINSON *Prov. Names Birds* 8 Ring ouzel..so called from the white gorget on the bird's breast.

†**c.** *transf.* Applied to a person (prob. of dark hair or complexion). *Obs.*

1597 SHAKS. *2 Hen. IV*, III. ii. 9 *Shal.* And how doth.. your fairest Daughter, and mine, my God-Daughter Ellen? *Sil.* Alas, a blacke Ouzell. **1628** FORD *Lover's Mel.* II. i, *Rhe.* .. What new ouzle's this? *Tham...* This stranger, an Athenian, named Parthenophill.

2. Applied with distinctive adjuncts to other birds, popularly associated with the prec.

a. brook ouzel, the Water Rail (*Rallus aquaticus*).

1611 COTGR., *Mere des cailles*, a Rayle; or, a brooke-Owsell. **1678** RAY *Willughby's Ornith.* 314 The Water-Rail called by some the Bilcock or Brook-Owzel. **1885** SWAINSON *Prov. Names Birds* 176.

b. rose-coloured ouzel, the Rose-coloured Pastor or Starling, *Pastor* (*Turdus* Linn.) *roseus*.

1766 PENNANT *Zool.* (1768) II. 489 The rose colored ouzel. **1832** JOHNSTON in *Proc. Berw. Nat. Club* I. No. 1. 4 It was mentioned that a male bird of the rose-coloured ouzel (*Pastor roseus*) had been shot at West Ord.

c. water ouzel, the DIPPER (*Cinclus aquaticus*); also the American Dipper (*C. mexicanus*).

1622 DRAYTON *Poly-olb.* xxv. (1748) 366 The water-woosell next all over black as jet. **1793** G. WHITE *Selborne* II. vii. (1875) 156 The water-ousel is said to haunt the mouth of the Lewes river. **1849** KINGSLEY *N. Devon* Misc. II. 243 The startled water-ousel, with his white breast, flitted a few yards. **1874** ALLEN in Coues *Birds N.W.* 12 The American Ouzel (*Cinclus mexicanus*) is doubtless a frequent inhabitant of nearly all the mountain-streams of Colorado.

ouzo (ˈuːzəʊ). Also ouso. [mod.Gr. οὖζο.] A Greek spirituous drink flavoured with aniseed; a glass of this.

The etymology of the Greek name οὖζο is disputed. A popular etymology derives it from the Italian designation *uso Massalia* 'for the (commercial) use of Marseilles' stamped on packages of selected silkworm cocoons exported in the 19th century via Volos from the Thessalian town of Tyrnavos. The designation came to stand for 'superior quality', which the spirit distilled as *ouzo* was thought to possess: see A. Tzartzanos in *Indogermanische Forschungen* (1932) LII. 217–20.

1898 H. N. BRAILSFORD *Broom of War-God* 4 The Prefect had placed a chair beside him and had pledged his in *ouso*. **1935** *Chem. Abstr.* 880 (*heading*) Method for controlling the purity of alcohol used in the preparation of 'ouzo'... The beverage known as 'ouzo' in Greece has an alc. content of 35–45%. **1957** L. DURRELL *Bitter Lemons* 25 The excellent *ouzo* and his general affability transformed the journey. **1957** F. KING *Man on Rock* ii. 61, I devoured a whole tin of American bully-beef, washed down with ouzo. **1965** O. MANNING *Friends & Heroes* xx. 202 Alan had a bottle of ouzo on his table and he started filling the glasses. **1973** D. LANG *Freaks* 8 Stavros downed another ouzo. **1975** *Daily Colonist* (Victoria, B.C.) 18 May 4/6 Constantine, late of Greece, could..take to peddling ouzo.

ova, plural of OVUM.

ovablastic (əʊvəˈblæstɪk), *a. rare*⁻¹. [f. L. *ova*, pl. of OVUM egg + Gr. βλαστικ-ός springing forth.] Making eggs burst open (in the womb).

1922 JOYCE *Ulysses* 397 Mr Dixon..took on to ask Mr Mulligan himself whether his incipient ventripotence.. betokened an ovablastic gestation in the prostatic utricle.

Ovaherero (ˌəʊvəhɛˈrɪərəʊ) = HERERO; also a tribe of the Hereros.

1855 F. N. KOLBE in W. Holden *Hist. Natal* 436 Damaraland is inhabited by a nation divided into two principal tribes, the Ovaherero and Ovampantera. **1856** C. J. ANDERSSON *Lake Ngami* iv. 52 The Damaras are divided into two large tribes, the Ovaherero and the *Ovapantiereu*. **1880** *Encycl. Brit.* XI. 731/2, 110,000 are Herero (80,000 Ova Herero and 30,000 Ova-mbanderu). **1884** A. LANG *Custom & Myth* 20 The Ovahereroes in South Africa.. appease with a black sheep the spirits of the departed. **1910** *Encycl. Brit.* XIII. 358/1 Herero or Ovaherero.

oval (ˈəʊvəl), *a.*[1] and *sb.*[1] Also 6 ovalle, 6–7 -all, 7 -ale. [prob. ad. mod.L. *ōvāl-is*, *-e*, f. *ōvum* egg. (The ancient L. word was *ōvāt-us*.) Hatz.-Darm. cite F. *oval* adj. from Rabelais 1546.]

A. *adj.* **1.** Having the form of an egg; egg-shaped; approximately egg-shaped, ellipsoidal.

1577 DEE *Relat. Spir.* I. (1659) 398 She standeth as in a hollow shell, or Oval figure concave. **1599** T. M[OUFET] *Silkwormes* 18 [They] spinne silke..Leauing their oual bottoms there behind. **1693** J. EDWARDS *Author. O. & N. Test.* 264 It was from the oval or round figure of the world that they represented it by an egg. **1796** H. HUNTER tr. *St. Pierre's Stud. Nat.* (1799) I. 531 Suspending..sometimes the oval date, and sometimes the rounded cocoa-nut. **1866** *Treas. Bot.* 292 Of the cultivated varieties [of the Citron] some are oval, others round... The Lemon..fruit oval or ovate.

2. Having the outline of an egg as projected on a surface; having more or less the form or outline of an elongated circle or ellipse; elliptical.

Oval Office, the office of the President of the United States in the White House. *oval window*, the *fenestra ovalis* of the ear: see WINDOW.

1610 B. JONSON *Alch.* II. ii, Mine oval room Fill'd with such pictures as Tiberius took From Elephantis. **1634** SIR T. HERBERT *Trav.* 95 The Caspian Sea is..in forme Ouall. **1716** LADY M. W. MONTAGU *Let. to C'tess Mar* 14 Sept., At proper distances were placed three oval pictures. **1802** PALEY *Nat. Theol.* i. §1 Does one man in a million know how oval frames are turned? **1834** MRS. SOMERVILLE *Connex. Phys. Sc.* ii. (1849) 6 The planets describe ellipses or oval paths around the sun. [**1962** *N.Y. Times Mag.* 8 Apr. 38 (*caption*) New look—The oval office in the White House's west wing reflects increasingly the interests and personality of the man who spends upwards of seven hours of his long working day in it.] **1965** L. P. JONES *First Bk. White House* 30 In 1909, seven years after the President's offices had been moved into the West Wing, the President's Oval Office was added. **1966** P. B. FAY *Pleasure of his Company* xxiv. 259 One Saturday morning in the Oval Office I asked the President, 'Is there any truth to the rumor that you intend to dump Lyndon in '64?' **1972** W. MCGIVERN *Caprifoil* viii. 133 This is the first time I've ever interrupted the President. .. Mary Donovan..walked to the door that connected her office to the Oval Office. **1973** *Times* 18 June 1/6 Mr Krogh told him that the order for the break-in came 'from the Oval Office'. **1973** *Time* 13 Aug. 20/1 The President rarely appears in testimony. The word comes from 'the Oval Office'. **1974** *Times* 9 Aug. 8/5 The President of the United States will address the nation on radio and television from his Oval Office. **1977** *Time* 17 Jan. 16/1 With Carter in the Oval Office, the Democrats chose in Byrd a man well equipped to push the Administration's programs.

3. Of or pertaining to an egg. *rare.*

1646 SIR T. BROWNE *Pseud. Ep.* III. vii. 121 Their ovall conceptions, or egges within their bodies. **1716** M. DAVIES *Athen. Brit.* III. *Diss. Physick* 5 Generation by and in Oval Conceptions. **1884** *Morning Herald* (Reading, Pennsylv.) 14 Apr., Never before probably was there so much done in the way of oval confectionery.

4. In specific names of tools, etc.:

oval chuck = elliptic chuck: see quot. 1842; **oval compass**, a compass for describing ovals; **oval file**, a file whose cross-section is elliptical or oval; used sometimes as a gulleting file (Knight *Dict. Mech.*); **oval lathe**, a lathe for turning ovals.

1779 *Specif. Taylor's Patent* No. 1232. 2 The turning of potts is performed by an oval lathe made for that purpose. **1842** FRANCIS *Dict. Arts*, *Oval Chuck*, an appendage to a lathe, of such a nature that the work attached to it and cut by the tool in the usual manner becomes of an oval form.

5. *Comb.* (in senses 1 and 2). **a.** parasynthetic, as *oval-arched* (having an oval arch), *oval-berried*, *-bodied*, *-bored*, *-faced*, *-figured*, *-headed*, *-leaved*, *-shaped*, etc.; **b.** with another adj., expressing an intermediate or blended form, as *oval-lanceolate*, *-truncate*, etc. Also *oval-wise* adv. and adj.

1884 HARRIS in *Littell's Living Age* (U.S.) CLXI. 91 A magnificent *oval-arched gateway. **1752** SIR J. HILL *Hist. Anim.* 181 The greenish, *oval-bodied Cochlea. **1858** GREENER *Gunnery* 115 The gun has since been made two inches larger in the bore, and even *oval-bored. **1886** RUSKIN *Praeterita* I. 326 A graceful *oval-faced blonde of fifteen. **1976** J. DRUMMOND *Funeral Urn* xxi. 109 They.. looked alike, oval-faced, straight-nosed, small-mouthed. **1698** KEILL *Exam. Th. Earth* (1734) 51 The Theorist's *Oval-figured earth not being sufficient for such an effect. **1752** SIR J. HILL *Hist. Anim.* 113 The great *oval-headed Testudo. **1751** —— *Hist. Plants* 292 The *oval-leaved Rhamnus. **1835–6** TODD *Cycl. Anat.* I. 765/1 The first of the..masses is *oval-shaped. **1856** W. L. LINDSAY *Brit. Lichens* 160 The spermo-gones are oval or *oval-truncate. **1689** *Lond. Gaz.* No. 2483/4 One John Allen,..*Oval-Visaged,..run away from his Master. **1611** SPEED *Theat. Gt. Brit.* xxxiii. (1614) 65/1 For forme long and *ovall-wise doubling in length twice her bredth. **1625** LISLE *Du Bartas* 73 A young wood's whizzing boughs that..oual-wise bewal'd the flowre embossed field.

B. *sb.*

1. a. A plane figure resembling the longitudinal section of an egg; a closed curve having the chief axis considerably longer than the one at right angles to it, and the curvature greatest at each end; strictly, with one end more pointed than the other, as in most eggs, though popularly applied also to a regular ellipse; in *mod. Geom.* applied to any closed curve (other than a circle or ellipse), esp. one without a node or cusp.

carpenter's oval, a figure formed of two pairs of unequal circular arcs joined alternately where their tangents coincide, so as to form a continuous closed curve, approaching an ellipse. *Cartesian oval*, or *oval of Descartes*: see quots. 1842, 1877; for *Cassinian*, *conjugate oval*, see these words.

1570 DEE *Math. Pref.* A iv b, A Perfect Square, Triangle, Circle, Ouale..and such other Geometricall figures. **1615** G. SANDYS *Trav.* 31 The principall part thereof riseth in an ouall surrounded with pillars admirable for their proportion. **1672** COLLINS in Rigaud *Corr. Sci. Men* (1841) I. 201 Possibly they might not at London know one of the best ways of making a carpenter's oval to any ratio of diameters. **1795** HUTTON *Math. Dict.* s.v., *Oval* denotes also certain roundish figures, of various..shapes, among curve lines of the higher kinds. **1842** BRANDE *Dict. Sci.* etc. s.v., The Ovals of Descartes are a species of geometrical curves... They may be defined as the locus of the vertex of a triangle on a given base, one of whose sides has a given ratio to the sum or difference of a given line and the other side. *c* **1865** LD. BROUGHAM in *Circ. Sci.* I. *Introd. Disc.* 12 The planets move in ovals, from gravity. **1877** B. WILLIAMSON *Int. Calc.* (ed. 2) viii. §166 The Oval of Descartes..consists of two ovals, one lying inside the other. *Ibid.*, The arc of a Cartesian Oval.

b. An egg-shaped or ellipsoidal body.

1898 P. MANSON *Trop. Diseases* i. 25 The gradual evolution of the flagellated body from crescent through oval and sphere can with patience be easily followed.

2. a. Applied to various things having an oval or (usually) elliptical outline; e.g. an oval picture frame, an oval window; the CARTOUCHE in which royal names are phonetically represented in Egyptian hieroglyphics; an enclosure or piece of ground, water, etc., of elliptical shape.

Kennington Oval, in athletics 'the Oval', an open space at Kennington in South London (opened in 1846), where cricket-matches, etc., are played.

1654 GAYTON *Pleas. Notes* IV. viii. 226 About his breast hung her Picture, set in a rich Ovall. **1677–8** in Willis & Clark *Cambridge* (1886) III. 23 A new ouall to give light to the starecase. **1703** MOXON *Mech. Exerc.* 93 The Oval is fitted stiff upon the Staff, that it may be set nearer or farther from the Tooth. **1755** *Monitor* No. 9 I. 71 It is a fine political picture in miniature:..in an oval of an inch square. **1857** CHAMBERS *Inform. for People* 686/1 The Surrey Club at the Kennington Oval..keep cricket going throughout the season. **1877** A. B. EDWARDS *Up Nile* vii. 183 The royal oval in which the name of Cleopatra (Klaupatra) is spelt with its vowel sounds in full. **1910** *Blackw. Mag.* Jan. 89/1 On the Oval, Surrey..had snatched a victory by five runs. **1927** *Daily Express* 26 Mar. 9/2 The Prince of Wales..will..open a games oval. **1928** M. ARLEN *Lily Christine* (1929) iii. 42 Her father..liked nothing so much as spending long afternoons at Lords' or the Oval. **1973** *Sun-Herald* (Sydney) 26 Aug. 15/4 Police were searching late tonight for two girls, who disappeared from the crowded Adelaide Oval while attending a football match with parents and friends. **1977** C. STORR *Tales Psychiatrist's Couch* 118 I'll be back to take her off to the Oval... She's a cricket fan.

†**b.** *Arch.* An ornament in the shape of an egg, often carved upon an echinus or ovolo: see OVUM; also the OVOLO itself. *Obs.*

1706 PHILLIPS (ed. Kersey) s.v. *Echinus*, This Ornament is now made use of in Cornices of the Ionick, Corinthian, and Composit Orders, being Carved with Anchors, Darts, and Ovals or Eggs. *Ibid.* s.v. *Oval*, In Architecture Oval or Ovolo is the same as Echinus.

†**c.** One of the seven balls (*ova*) used in the ancient Roman circus to indicate the number of rounds run in a race. *Obs.*

1600 HOLLAND *Livy* XLI. xxvii. 1114 The Ovales to marke and skore up the number of courses.

†**ˈoval**, *a.*[2] and *sb.*[2] *Obs. rare.* [ad. L. *ovāl-is* belonging to an ovation.]

A. *adj.* (See quot. 1656.)

1430 LYDG. *Bochas* IV. i. (1494) n v, The crowne also which called was Ouall Toke first name of ioye and gladnesse. **1656** BLOUNT *Gl.*, *Oval*, belonging to the triumph called Ovation. **1658** SIR T. BROWNE *Gard. Cyrus* ii, The Triumphal, Oval, and Civicall Crowns of Laurel, Oake, and Myrtle.

B. *sb.* An oval crown (L. *corōna ovālis*), i.e. that conferred in an ovation: see OVATOR.

1614 SYLVESTER *Parl. Vertues Royall* 768 Yet hundred Laurels never widow-curst, And hundred Ovals, which no skin hath burst; Prove I haue often Conquer'd without Thee.

oval (ˈəʊvəl), *v.* [f. OVAL *a.*[1] and *sb.*[1]] **a.** *trans.* To make oval, to give an oval shape to. **b.** *intr.* To move in oval-shaped curves. Hence **ˈovalling** *ppl. a.*

1665 HOOKE *Micrographia* 218 The more the limb is flatted or ovalled, the more red does the body appear. **1874** M. CLARKE *His Natural Life* II. viii. 121 The rings were too strong to be 'ovalled', or he would have been free long ago. *Ibid.*, 'To oval', is a term in use among convicts, and means to so bend the round ring of the ankle fetter that the *heel* can be drawn up through it. **1922** JOYCE *Ulysses* 444 The odour of the sicksweet weed floats towards him in slow round ovalling wreaths. **1969** 'R. STARK' *Blackbird* iv. 26 Grofield's plane ovaled between massed gray clouds and the grubby sprawl of New York City.

ovalbumen, -in (əʊvælˈbjuːmən, -ɪn). *Chem.* [f. L. *ovi albumen* (Pliny), white of egg.] The albumen or white of egg; egg albumen. In mod. use written **ovalbumin** and applied to the albumin that is the principal protein of egg-white.

1835–6 TODD *Cycl. Anat.* I. 89/2 Coagulated ovalbumen, when long boiled in water, becomes bulky and falls into pieces. **1857** MILLER *Elem. Chem.* III. 652 The reactions of albumen from the white of the hen's egg (ovalbumen), therefore, differ in some respects from those afforded by albumen contained in the serum of blood (seralbumen). **1892** *Syd. Soc. Lex.* s.v., Ovalbumin is not precipitated by ether. **1905** C. E. SIMON *Text-bk. Physiol. Chem.* (ed. 2) xxi. 457 According to Gautier and some of the older observers, white of egg (albumen) contains a number of different albumins, which in part seem to belong to the true albumins and in part to the globulins. They have been designated as α-, β-, and γ-ovalbumin, and α- and β- ovoglobulin. **1934** W. R. FEARON *Introd. Biochem.* vi. 86 Ovalbumin makes up the greater part (10–13 per cent.) of egg-white. **1959** [see OVOGLOBULIN]. **1970** R. W. MCGILVERY *Biochem.* viii. 150 The principal protein of egg whites, ovalbumin, is especially susceptible to denaturation in this way.

ova'lescent, *a.* [f. OVAL *a.*[1] + -ESCENT.] Approaching an oval form: approximately oval.

1890 in *Cent. Dict.*

ovali-, comb. form of mod.L. *ōvāli-s* oval, as in ***ovali-globose*** adj.

1775 J. JENKINSON *Brit. Pl.* Gloss., *Ovali-globose*, a globose leaf partly oval.

o'valiform, *a.* [f. mod.L. *ōvāli-s* OVAL *a.*[1] + -FORM.] = OVAL *a.*[1] 1.

1826 KIRBY & SP. *Entomol.* IV. 264 *Ovaliform*, whose longitudinal section is oval, and transverse circular.

'ovalish, *a.* *rare*[−1]. [-ISH[1].] Somewhat oval.

1690 *Lond. Gaz.* No. 2578/4 A Rose Diamond of an Ovallish shape.

ovality (əʊ'vælɪtɪ). [f. OVAL *a.*[1] and *sb.*[1] + -ITY.] = OVALNESS.

1937 *Times* 13 Apr. p. xv/1 Some idea of the precision to which this one operation alone is worked can be appreciated from the fact that the tolerance of error allowed is only one ten-thousandth part of an inch combined taper and ovality. **1947** *Times* 30 Sept. 3/2 The gauge is used to check the internal diameter of the bore in the body of the injector, and reveals any ovality, taper, barrel-shape, or bell-mouth inaccuracies. **1962** *Gloss. Terms Glass Industry* (*B.S.I.*) 42 *Ovality*, deviation of a glass article from a circular towards an elliptical cross section. **1976** *Drive* Nov.–Dec. 61/2 A rake-adjustable steering column and slight steering wheel ovality.

ovally ('əʊvəlɪ), *adv.* [-LY[2].] In an oval manner or form.

1664 POWER *Exp. Philos.* I. 5 The Common Fly..her eyes are most remarkable, being exceeding large, ovally protuberant. **1882** VINES *Sachs' Bot.* 336 Delicate papillæ which become spherically or ovally dilated at their free ends.

ovalness ('əʊvəlnɪs). [-NESS.] The quality of being oval.

1727 BAILEY vol. II, *Ovalness*, the being in the Form of an Egg. **1882** LEDGER *Sun* 118 Of different degrees of ovalness. **1892** *Leisure Hour* Oct. 851/1 The 'eccentricity' or ovalness of Mars's orbit.

'ovaloid, *a.* [-OID.] Resembling an oval; imperfectly oval.

1890 in *Cent. Dict.*

Ovaltine ('əʊvəltiːn). Also with small initial. [Prob. a fanciful extension of OVAL *a.*[1] 3.] The proprietary name of a powder composed principally of malt extract, milk, and eggs; a drink made from this.

1906 *Trade Marks Jrnl.* 13 June 820 Ovaltine... Alimentary products..Albert Wander,..Berne, Switzerland; manufacturer of alimentary products. **1907** *Yesterday's Shopping* (1969) 516/2 Ovaltine—tin, 1/4½. **1912** R. BROOKE *Let.* 26 Jan. (1968) 354 These things go on round, ..Mrs Digby on India, and Mrs Fox at Bridge, and Ovaltine. **1930** J. CANNAN *No Walls of Jasper* 64 The parlourmaid..set down a cup of Ovaltine on the corner of the writing table. **1937** J. BETJEMAN *Continual Dew* 22 He gives his Ovaltine a stir And nibbles at a 'petit beurre'. **1940** F. STARK *Winter in Arabia* xv. 290 Qasim woke me with hot ovaltine at one-thirty. **1960** S. PLATH *Colossus* 58 You fed My brother and me cookies and ovaltine. **1969** *Trade Marks Jrnl.* 19 Feb. 306/2 Ovaltine... Food preparations (not medicated) in powder or tablet form composed principally of malt, milk and eggs, the malt predominating; and rusks. A. Wander, Limited,..London,..manufacturing chemists. *Ibid.* 29 Oct. 1802/2 Ovaltine... Preparations of milk, malt and eggs, flavoured with cocoa, the malt predominating, for use in making food beverages; biscuits (other than biscuits for animals), cakes, rusks, chocolate and non-medicated confectionery. A. Wander, Limited,..London,.. manufacturing chemists. **1973** 'P. LORAINE' *Voices in Empty Room* II. iv. 115 Lulu Jenkins..lay slumped up on the pillows of her large bed, sipping Ovaltine.

Ovambo (ɒ'væmbəʊ), *sb.* and *a.* Also **Ambo, Avamba, Ovampo.** [f. Bantu *ova-* pl. prefix + *ambo* man of leisure.] **A.** *sb.* **a.** A member of a Bantu people living in the northern part of South-West Africa; this people collectively. **b.** The language of the Ovambos. **B.** *adj.* Of or pertaining to the Ovambos.

1853 F. GALTON *Narr. Explorer Trop. S. Afr.* vi. 179 The Ovampo were twenty-four in number with a tall enterprising-looking young man as captain. **1856** C. J. ANDERSSON *Lake Ngami* xiv. 163 At a considerable distance to the north, there lived a nation called Ovambo. **1864** T. BAINES *Explor. S.-W. Afr.* ii. 40 The Damaras..could not even make an assegai, but bought their weapons of the Ovampo. **1884** *Encycl. Brit.* XVII. 318/2 Many..of the Bantu-speaking southern races..[including] Ovambos of the south-west coast..are also variously affected by foreign elements. **1897** J. BRYCE *Impressions S. Afr.* v. 42 On the higher grounds and generally in the far northern parts [of German South West Africa], where the Ovampo tribe dwell, grass is abundant. **1902** *Encycl. Brit.* XXXII. 736/2 The Ovambo or Ambo, in the northern part of the protectorate, are agriculturists. **1909** *Daily Chron.* 28 July 4/4 Three and a-half days' work with a mere handful of Ovambo 'boys'. **1911** J. G. FRAZER *Golden Bough: Magic Art* (ed. 3) I. iii. 63 The Ovambo of South-western Africa believe that some people have the power of bewitching an absent person by gazing into a vessel full of water till his image appears to them in the water. **1953** L. G. GREEN *Lords of Last Frontier* ii. 18 Battels deserted and lived for sixteen months among the Ovambos. *Ibid.* xvi. 235 Finnish missionaries learn Ovambo before they leave Finland. **1959** *Chambers's Encycl.* X. 277/2 The Ovambo people are the largest community of South-west Africa. **1967** *Courier-Mail* (Brisbane) 20 Apr. 18/6 It was interesting to find the tall, slim, gentle houseboy employed by my host and hostess was an Ovambo. **1973** *Daily Tel.* 21 Nov. 4/6 They were familiar with Ovambo tribal customs. **1974** *Encycl. Brit. Micropædia* I. 295/3 Ambo, also known as Ovambo or Avamba, people located in the dry glassland country of northern South West Africa and southern Angola... They speak a language of the Bantu group. **1974** *Times* 14 Oct. 7/2 Oshakati, the Ovambo capital near the Angolan border.

†'ovant, *a.* *Obs.* [ad. L. *ovāns*, *ovānt-em*, pr. pple. of *ovāre* to have an ovation.] Celebrating an ovation; triumphing in or as in an ovation; of the nature of an ovation.

1598 GRENEWEY *Tacitus' Ann.* III. ii. (1622) 65 That for.. exploits done the sommer past, hee should enter the citie, ouant, or with a small triumph. **1600** HOLLAND *Livy* IV. xliii. 166 A Generall was said to enter Ovant into the citie, when ordinarily without his armie following him, he went on foot, or rode on horsebacke only, and the people in their Acclamations for joy, redoubled Ohe, or Oho. **1631** W. SALTONSTALL *Pict. Loquent.* E xij b, [In a horse-race] the forerunner is receiv'd ovant, with great acclamations of joy. **1652** BENLOWES *Theoph.* VI. v. 82 These ovant souls, Knights of Saint Vincent are For high atchievements gain'd. **1658** BURTON *Itin. Anton.* 161 Whatsoever stuff or provisions Suetonius Paullinus..might design for a triumphal, or an ovant shew at Rome.

o'varial, *a.* *rare.* [f. OVARI-UM + -AL[1].] = OVARIAN.

1822–34 *Good's Study Med.* (ed. 4) IV. 324 *note*, An ovarial dropsy. **1888** ROLLESTON & JACKSON *Anim. Life* 297 Development of ovarial tubes in Insecta.

‖ovari'algia. *Path.* Also **ovaralgia.** [f. OVARIUM + *-algia*, f. Gr. ἄλγος pain.] Ovarian neuralgia.

1857 in MAYNE *Expos. Lex.* **1878** tr. *von Ziemssen's Cycl. Med.* XIV. 502 This phenomenon (which has been designated ovaralgia..) is one of frequent occurrence in the hysterical.

Hence **ovari'algic** *a.*, pertaining to or affected with ovarialgia (*Syd. Soc. Lex.* 1892).

ovarian (əʊ'vɛərɪən), *a.* [f. OVARI-UM + -AN; in mod.F. *ovarien.*] Of, pertaining to, or of the nature of an ovary or ovaries. **a.** *Anat.* and *Zool.*

ovarian vesicle, (*a*) a Graafian follicle (*Syd. Soc. Lex.* 1892); (*b*) = GONOPHORE 2.

1840 E. WILSON *Anat. Vade M.* (1842) 350 The Ovarian veins communicate with the uterine sinuses. **1872** THOMAS *Dis. Women* 623 Ancient literature is singularly barren upon the subject of ovarian diseases. **1877** HUXLEY *Anat. Inv. Anim.* iv. 185 In some..the embryos are developed in the ovarian sacs, or in the cavity of the body.

b. *Bot.*

1857 HENFREY *Elem. Bot.* 122 In true compound pistils the union does not always extend to the summit of the ovarian region.

ovari'ectomy. *Surg.* [f. as prec. + Gr. ἐκτομή excision.] Excision of an ovary; oophorectomy.

1889 *Lancet* 27 Apr. 854/2 Professor d'Antona gave a list of thirty-two successful ovariectomies. **1932** S. ZUCKERMAN *Social Life Monkeys* v. 77 If the ovaries of any mature mammal are experimentally removed (the operation of ovariectomy), all cyclic activity in the accessory reproductive organs ceases. **1958** *Sci. News* XLVII. 85 Removal of the ovary (ovariectomy) from a young hen results in the growth of cock-like spurs, a large comb, and male plumage. **1969** J. H. GREEN *Basic Clin. Physiol.* xviii. 104/2 Once the placenta has developed, the corpus luteum of pregnancy in the ovary is no longer essential for the maintenance of pregnancy and an ovariectomy (oophorectomy) could be carried out.

Hence **ovari'ectomize** *v. trans.*, to deprive of one or both ovaries; **ovari'ectomized** *ppl. a.*

1924 *Physiol. Abstr.* IX. 33 In two ovariectomised hens.. a testis was found. **1928** *Proc. Soc. Exper. Biol. & Med.* XXV. 490 Guinea pigs..on the fourth day after œstrum were ovariectomized. **1958** *Sci. News* XLVII. 85 The antlers of young stags do not develop after castration, and ovariectomized female deer may produce horns. **1974** *Nature* 5 Apr. 525/1 All rats were ovariectomised and thyroidectomised on day 1 of the experiment.

ovario- (əʊ'vɛərɪəʊ), combining form of OVARI-UM, combined with adjs. to express the participation of the ovary with some other part, as ***ovario-abdominal, -lumbar, -tubal***; also with sbs. in sense 'ovarian', as ***ovario-insanity***.

1872 PEASLEE *Ovar. Tumours* 18 Delicate muscular fibres ..which he calls the ovario-lumbar ligament. **1874** BUCKNILL & TUKE *Psych. Med.* (ed. 3) 346 Utero- or ovario-Insanity.

o'variole. [ad. L. type **ōvāriol-um*, dim. of mod.L. *ōvārium*: see below.] A small ovary; one of the tubular glands of the compound ovary of some insects.

1877 HUXLEY *Anat. Inv. Anim.* vii. 417 The finely tapering anterior ends of the ovarioles of each side are continued forwards by delicate cellular prolongations. **1925** A. D. IMMS *Gen. Textbk. Entomol.* 147 Each organ [*sc.* ovary] is composed of a variable number of separate egg-tubes or ovarioles which open into the oviduct. **1965** B. E. FREEMAN tr. *Vandel's Biospeleol.* xxii. 364 The female of *Aphaenops*..has a single ovariole on each side of the body. **1976** *Nature* 17 June 614/2 Cells which display the highest levels are those which have been assumed to be the most active and specialised, such as..the trophocytes of insect ovarioles.

ovariotomy (əʊˌvɛərɪ'ɒtəmɪ). *Surg.* [f. OVARI-UM + Gr. -τομία cutting, f. -τομ-ος cutting, cut. In mod.F. *ovariotomie* (1878 in *Dict. Acad.*).] The operation of cutting into an ovary to remove an ovarian tumour; also, oophorectomy.

1844 *Lond. & Edin. Monthly Jrnl. Med. Sci.* IV. 58 Her case..is believed only by the few who have lately come into the field as the champions of Ovariotomy. **1852** J. MILLER *Pract. Surg.* xxvii. (ed. 2) 342 As yet, they [certain methods of cure] have mostly proved even more fatal than ovariotomy. **1863** *N. Syd. Soc. Year-Bk. Med.* 393 This instrument is devised for the purpose of more readily separating the adhesions encountered in ovariotomy operations. **1891** *Lancet* 3 Oct. 761 Ovariotomy, which was so condemned fifty years ago, is now daily performed with but comparatively little risk to the patient.

So **o'variotome**, an instrument for cutting out an ovarian tumour; **ovario'tomics**, the theory or practice of ovariotomy; **ovari'otomist**, one who practises ovariotomy; **ovari'otomize** *v. trans.* = OVARIECTOMIZE *v.*; **ovari'otomized** *ppl. a.*

1872 PEASLEE *Ovar. Tumours* 34 The incision made by the ovariotomist. **1882** *Brit. Med. Jrnl.* 28 Jan. 184 At last listerism was applied to ovariotomics. **1916** *Biol. Bull.* XXX. 293 The ovariotomized duck may or may not undergo a change in plumage, corresponding to that of the male. **1927** *Jrnl. Physiol.* LXII. 312 Does a lactating ovariotomised mouse require more œstrin to produce œstrous symptoms than a non-suckling ovariotomised mouse? To answer this question a number of mice were ovariotomised soon after parturition. **1964** *Biol. Abstr.* XLV. 7553/1 Ovariotomized rats..were starved for 20–22 hours.

o'various, *a.* *rare.* [f. OV-UM: see -ARIOUS.] Of, pertaining to, or of the nature of eggs.

1730–46 THOMSON *Autumn* 875 Here the plain harmless native..to the rocks Dire-clinging, gathers his ovarious food. **1830** *Blackw. Mag.* XXVIII. 114 The ovarious state of their [birds'] future offspring.

'ovarism. *Biol.* [a. F. *ovarisme.*] = OVISM. So **ovarist** = OVIST.

1842 DUNGLISON *Med. Lex.*, *Ovarist.* **1892** *Syd. Soc. Lex.*, *Ovarism.*

‖ovaritis (əʊvə'raɪtɪs). *Path.* [f. OVARI-UM + -ITIS.] Inflammation of the ovary.

1857 in MAYNE *Expos. Lex.* **1860** TANNER *Pregnancy* ii. 58 Sub-acute ovaritis. **1889** DUNCAN *Lect. Dis. Wom.* xxvii. (ed. 4) 217 Ovaritis is a disease eminently liable to relapses.

‖ovarium (əʊ'vɛərɪəm). Pl. -ia. [mod.L. (16–17th c.) f. *ōvum* egg: see -ARIUM. L. had *ōvārius* egg-keeper; Du Cange cites *ōvāria* fem., the ovary of a bird, from 13th c.]

1. *Anat.* and *Zool.* = OVARY 1.

1692 tr. *Blancard's Phys. Dict.* 153/1. **1730** *Hist. Litteraria* I. 33 The Eggs made two clusters like the Ovaria of Birds. **1797** M. BAILLIE *Morb. Anat.* (1807) 401 Conveying the ovum from the ovarium to the uterus.

2. *Bot.* = OVARY 2.

[**1750** LINNÆUS *Philos. Botan.* § 146.] **1760** J. LEE *Introd. Bot.* Gloss., *Ovarium*, the Germen. **1830** LINDLEY *Nat. Syst. Bot.* Introd. 30 An ovarium either consists of one or several connected pericarpial leaves..arranged around a common axis, or of several combined into a single body. **1862** DARWIN *Fertil. Orchids* iv. 131 In all Orchids the labellum..assumes its usual position as the lower lip, by the twisting of the ovarium.

ovary ('əʊvərɪ), *sb.* [ad. mod.L. *ōvāri-um*: see prec. In F. *ovaire* masc. (1690 Furetière).]

1. *Anat.* and *Zool.* The female organ of reproduction in animals, in which ova or eggs are produced.

1658 SIR T. BROWNE *Pseud. Ep.* III. xxviii. (ed. 3) 225 The ovary or part where the white involveth it, is in the second region of the matrix. **1677** H. SAMPSON in *Phil. Trans.* XII. 1001 The right Testicle or Ovary was but small. **1774** GOLDSM. *Nat. Hist.* (1776) VII. 42 The organs of generation ..consist in each muscle of two ovaries, which are the female part of its furniture. **1840** E. WILSON *Anat. Vade M.* (1842) 559 The Ovaries are two oblong flattened and oval bodies of a whitish colour, situated in the posterior layer of peritoneum of the broad ligaments. **1878** HUXLEY *Physiogr.* xiv. 226 The female bird possesses an organ termed the ovary, in which nucleated cells, the primitive ova, which correspond with the embryo cells of the plant, are developed.

2. *Bot.* The organ in which the ovules of an angiospermous plant are produced, being the lowest part of the pistil in the flower, consisting of one or more carpels, which ultimately becomes the fruit or seed-vessel; the germen.

When separate from the calyx, it is termed a ***superior ovary***; when adherent to the calyx, an ***inferior ovary***.

1744 J. WILSON *Synops. Brit. Pl., Bot. Dict., Ovary*, is the rudiment of fruit. **1785** MARTYN *Rousseau's Bot.* i. 25 The Pistil.. is divided into.. the swollen base with three blunted angles, called the Germ or Ovary,.. the Style,.. the Stigma. **1835** LINDLEY *Introd. Bot.* (1848) I. 363. **1872** OLIVER *Elem. Bot.* I. iii. 23 The ovary contains a minute seed-bud, the ovule.

3. *fig.*

1849 SEARS *Regenerat.* I. v. (1859) 42 There is a sensuous nature which includes the ovaries of the worst of vices.

† **'ovary**, *a. Obs.* [Erroneous for L. *ovālis*, OVAL *a.*²] Of or pertaining to an ovation.

a **1682** SIR T. BROWNE *Tracts* ii. (1683) 91 Their honorary Crowns triumphal, ovary, civical, obsidional, had little of Flowers in them.

ovate ('ɒvət), *sb.* [f. an assumed Latin plural *Ovātēs*, representing *Οὐατεῖς*, *vātēs*, soothsayers, prophets, mentioned by Strabo, along with *Δρυΐδαι* 'Druids', and *Βάρδοι* 'Bards', as a third order in the Gaulish hierarchy. Cf. EUHAGES.]

A term used as the English equivalent of Welsh *ofydd*, now applied to an Eisteddfodic graduate of a third order, beside 'bard' and 'druid'; the name and its application being artificially affiliated to those of the Gaulish *Οὐατεῖς* mentioned by Strabo.

Note. *Οὐατεῖς* was Strabo's Greek transliteration of the Proto-celtic **vāteis* (Stokes), pl. of **vātis* (or **wātis*) 'soothsayer, prophet' = L. *vātis*, OIr. *faith*, mod.Ir. and Gael. *faidh*. *Ofydd* occurs in Middle Welsh as a second element in some compounds, where it appears to have the sense of 'lord' (app. for *ddofydd*, mutated form of *dofydd*). It is also the Welsh form, in 14th c. bards, of the proper name *Ovid*. It has no connexion, etymological or historical, with *οὐατεῖς*. The imaginary connexion appears first in Henry Rowlands in 1723. From him it was taken up by Edward Williams (Iolo Morgannwg) and W. Owen (Pughe) who introduced *ovate* as the English equivalent, 1792–4.

1723 H. ROWLANDS *Mona Antiqua* 65 Different Classes and Fraternities, which, as Strabo (lib. iv) reckons, were three, that is *Δρυΐδαι, Drudau* or *Drudion*; *Οὐατεῖς, Offwyr* or *Offyddion*; and *Βαρδοὶ Beirdd*. Ammianus Marcellinus (lib. xv) gives the same reckoning.. 'inchoata per Bardos, Euvates, & Druidas', *i.e.*.. begun and set by *Bards, Euvates*, and Druids. —— *Ibid.* Of these, says Strabo, the *Bardi* were Singers; the *Ouvates*, Priests and Physiologers; and the *Druids* to Physiology added Ethicks and Moral Learning. *Ibid.* 251 Their *Ovates*, so call'd by Strabo and Ammianus Marcellinus,.. must express some Name they had at that Time on one of their Orders, sounding like *Ovydd* or *Offydd*. **1792** W. OWEN (PUGHE) *Eleg. Llywarc Hen*, Introd. xlii, *Bardd, Ovydd, a Derwydd* = Bard, Ovate, and Druid. **1794** E. WILLIAMS *Poems* II. 230 There are three orders of the Primitive Bards.—The *Ruling Bard*, or Primitive Bard positive..: the *Ovate* (or *Euvate*..) whose avocation it is to act on the principles of inventive genius: and the *Druid* [etc.]. **1834** PLANCHÉ *Brit. Costume* 11 The Priesthood.. was divided into three orders. The Druids, the Bards, and the Ovates... The Ovate or Ovydd, professing astronomy, medicine, &c., wore green, the symbol of learning. **1877** RHYS *Lect. Welsh Philol.* vi. 314 *Ofydd*.. is defined to be an Eisteddfodic graduate who is neither bard nor druid, and translated into ovate.

ovate ('əʊvət), *a.* Chiefly *Nat. Hist.* [ad. L. *ōvāt-us* egg-shaped, f. *ōv-um* egg: see -ATE² 2.]

1. Egg-shaped. **a.** In reference to a solid body.

1775 J. JENKINSON *Brit. Pl.* 113 The fruit is a hard, ovate, fleshy berry. **1807** J. E. SMITH *Phys. Bot.* 114 Root.. growing with an ovate juicy bulb on the top of a dry wall. **1816** W. SMITH *Strata Ident.* 8 Ovate Echini.. may be found anywhere on the surface of Upper Chalk. **1874** COOKE *Fungi* 62 Pear-shaped or ovate asci.

b. In reference to a superficial figure.

1760 J. LEE *Introd. Bot.* I. xiv. (1765) 36 *Ovate*, Egg-shaped. *Note, Ovate* is used to express an elliptical Figure, when it is broader at one End than the other; and.. *Oval* for the same Figure, when the Ends are alike. **1825** *Greenhouse Comp.* I. 65 Long ovate leaves. **1828** STARK *Elem. Nat. Hist.* I. 337 Legs short, covered with ovate scales. **1880** GRAY *Struct. Bot.* iii. §4 (ed. 6) 95 *Ovate*, when the outline of leaf-blades is like a section of a hen's-egg lengthwise.

c. *absol.* as *sb. Archæol.*, an implement having an oval blade.

1946 F. E. ZEUNER *Dating Past* ix. 283 It is clear, however, that by the end of this interglacial the Acheulian had acquired all its characteristic attributes, like ovates and the S-twist. **1956** A. L. ARMSTRONG in D. L. Linton *Sheffield* 91 Three more hand-axes, all ovates of middle Acheulean type and refined technique, are recorded from our area. **1959** J. D. CLARK *Prehist. Southern Afr.* vi. 157 The same assemblage of wood-working tools occurs—small, nearly parallel-sided picks, small flat ovates, miniature 'tea cosies', [etc.].

2. In combination with another adj., indicating a modification of the form denoted by the latter, inclining to ovate: as ***ovate-acuminate***, ***-conical***, ***-cordate***, ***-cuneate***, ***-deltoid***, ***-elliptic***, ***-lanceolate***, ***-oblong***, ***-rotundate***, ***-serrated***, ***-triangular***, etc.

1819 *Pantologia, Ovate-lanceolate leaf*, between these two forms, but inclining to the latter. *Ibid., Ovate-subulate capsule*, between ovate and awl-shaped, but most tending to the latter. *Ibid., Ovate-oblong.* **1845** LINDLEY *Sch. Bot.* v. (1858) 67 Lower leaflets ovate-cuneate. **1847** W. E. STEELE *Field Bot.* 199 Fruit ovate-acuminate, as long as the lanceolate scales. **1870** HOOKER *Stud. Flora* 268 Leaves.. sessile, ovate-rotundate or oblong.

Hence **'ovately** *adv.*, in an ovate way, with an ovate form; = ovate-, ovato-.

1865 *Reader* No. 145. 408/3 Ovately dolichocephalic.

'ovate, *v.*¹ *rare.* [f. OVATE *a.*: see -ATE³.] *trans.* To render ovate.

1878 *Fraser's Mag.* XVII. 128 A sphere flattened by gravity and other resistance, and ovated by the forward movement.

o'vate, *v.*² *journalistic.* [repr. L. *ovā-re* to exult, rejoice, celebrate an ovation; but prob. immed. from *ovation*: cf. *orate*.] *trans.* To give a popular ovation to; to greet with public applause.

1864 SALA in *Daily Tel.* 24 May, As to the manner in which Garibaldi might be 'ovated' here [America]. **1870** [see OVATOR]. **1890** *Sat. Rev.* 3 May 521/1 Mr. Stanley returned to England, and was 'ovated' at Dover.

† **o'vated**, *a. Obs.* [-ED¹.] = OVATE *a.*

1752 SIR J. HILL *Hist. Anim.* 566 The head is large, and of a kind of ovated figure, large and broad at the temples, and smaller to the mouth. *c* **1755** GARDEN in *Phil. Trans.* LI. 930 The leaves are ovated.

† **o'vatic**, *a. Obs. rare*⁻⁰. [irreg. f. L. *ōv-um*.]

1623 COCKERAM, *Ouatike season*, the time when Hens lay.

ovation (əʊ'veɪʃən), *sb.*¹ [ad. L. *ovātiōn-em*, lit. rejoicing, n. of action f. *ovāre*, to exult, rejoice.]

1. *Rom. Hist.* A lesser triumph characterized by less imposing ceremonies than the triumph proper, and granted to a commander for achievements considered insufficient to entitle him to the distinction of the latter. Also, allusively.

1533 BELLENDEN *Livy* IV. (1822) 367 The triumphe wes denyit to him; yit becaus he put away the schame and dishonoure that fell afore be necligence of Sempronius, he gat the loving of ovacioun. **1579–80** NORTH *Plutarch* (1676) 265 At the second Triumph called the Ovation, he onely sacrificed a Mutton, which the Romans call in their tongue *Ovem*, and therefore it was called Ovation. **1682** SIR T. BROWNE *Chr. Mor.* I. §2 Rest not in an Ovation, but a Triumph over thy Passions. **1770** LANGHORNE *Plutarch* (1879) I. 348/1 When a general, without fighting, gained his point by treaty and the force of persuasion, the law decreed him this honour, called ovation, which had.. more of the appearance of a festival than of war. **1841** BREWSTER *Mart. Sc.* III. iv. (1856) 112 His was the unpretending ovation of success, not the ostentatious triumph of ambition. **1842** ARNOLD *Hist. Rome* (1846) III. xlvi. 322 He entered Rome with the ceremony of an ovation, walking on foot according to the rule, instead of being drawn in a chariot in kingly state, as in the proper triumph.

† **2.** Exultation. *Obs.*

1649 LOVELACE *Poems* 122 When his fair Murdresse shall not gain one groan, And He expire ev'n in Ovation. **1659** HAMMOND *On Ps.* xc. Paraphr. 453 We may have some matter of ovation and rejoycing. **1710** T. FULLER *Pharm. Extemp.* 117 It operates primarily.. upon the Stomach.. raising up the Spirits into a kind of Ovation. **1818** MILMAN *Samor* 306 And bounds in wild ovation down the vale.

3. *transf.* An enthusiastic reception by an assembly or concourse of people with spontaneous acclamations and expressions of popularity; a burst of enthusiastic applause.

1831 SOUTHEY in *Q. Rev.* XLIV. 299 Gale Jones the veteran seditionist, whom Sir Francis Burdett so unkindly disappointed of an ovation in the year 1812. **1847** *Illustr. Lond. News* 10 July 27/1 The ovations to the artists.. were highly complimentary. **1860** FROUDE *Hist. Eng.* VI. 87 He [Pole] still clung to his conviction that.. he had but himself to set his foot upon the shore to be received with an ovation. **1885** *Durham Univ. Jrnl.* 27 June 132 Dr. Stainer received the ovation that was his due.

Hence **o'vation** *v. colloq.*, *trans.* to give an enthusiastic reception to; **o'vational** *a.*, of or pertaining to an (ancient Roman) ovation; resembling or in the nature of an ovation; **o'vationary** *a.*, of the nature of an ovation.

1894 *Punch* 26 May 245/1 Druriolanus, watching the proceedings from a stall,.. was of course recognised, and ovationed. **1868** MILMAN *St. Paul's* xviii. 474 Before their ovational pomps. **1893** J. H. TURNER *Hist. Brighouse* 241 Charles.. received an ovationary welcome as king. **1928** *Music & Lett.* July 235 The ovational ecstasy is not essentially connected with the musical impression.

† **o'vation**, *sb.*² *Obs. rare*⁻⁰. [f. L. *ōvum* egg.]

1656 BLOUNT *Glossogr., Ovation*, the season when hens lay eggs, or a laying of eggs.

ovato- (əʊ'veɪtəʊ), combining advb. form of L. *ōvāt-us* OVATE, used in same sense as 'ovately', 'ovate-', as ***ovato-acuminate***, ***-conical***, ***-cordate***, ***-deltoid***, ***-ellipsoidal***, ***-globose***, ***-lanceolate***, ***-oblong***, ***-orbicular***, ***-pyriform***, ***-quadrangular***, ***-rotundate***, ***-triangular***, etc.

1752 SIR J. HILL *Hist. Anim.* 284 The body of the Ostracion is of an odd figure.. it is oval, or ovato-oblong; or, finally, ovato-quadrangular, or approaching to conic. **1785** MARTYN *Rousseau's Bot.* xxvi. (1794) 400 The leaves are ovato-cordate or egg-shaped. **1838** BABINGTON in *Proc. Berw. Nat. Club* I. No. 6. 177 Leaves ovato-triangular, unequally sinuato-dentate. **1852** DANA *Crust.* I. 95 Horns ovato-lanceolate, acute, entire. **1882** *Nature* XXV. 572 Ovato-acuminate implements, scrapers, flakes and nuclei.

o'vator. [agent-n. in L. form from *ovāre*: see OVATE *v.*²] † **a.** *Rom. Hist.* One who receives an ovation (*obs.*). **b.** *colloq.* One who takes part in a spontaneous enthusiastic welcome.

1661 MORGAN *Sph. Gentry* III. iv. 35 The Triumpher had a Lawrel crown, the Ovator one of Fir, being different in their pomp. **1870** *Even. Standard* 22 Oct., The probable termination of the scene by a grand pyrotechnic display, in which ovators and ovated would alike be grilled alive on the rails of the flaming station.

ovelty, variant form of OWELTY, equality.

† **'ovemest**, *a. superl. Obs.* Forms: α. 1–3 ufemest, 3 uuemest, -mast, 5 umast, 6 umest, owmest. β. 3–4 ovemest, 4–5 ovemast, omast, omest, omyst. [OE. *ufemest*, superl. of *ufera*, *-re*, comp. (also *yfera*, *yf(e)mest*), OVER *a.*; f. root *uf-* in adv. *ufan* above, from above, *ufe-weard*, uplying, top-, = Goth. *uf* 'beneath', in comb. 'from beneath', 'up-'. For the later change to *ove-*, cf. OVER *a.*] Highest, upmost, uppermost, topmost.

α. *c* **1000** ÆLFRIC *Hom.* II. 76 On midne dæʒ bið seo sunne on ðam ufemestum ryne stiʒende. *c* **1200** *Trin. Coll. Hom.* 219 þe huuemeste bou of þe treuwe springed of the neþemeste rote... Alse þe uuemeste bou is sib þe neþemeste rote. *a* **1225** *Ancr. R.* 328 Heo.. doð an alre vuemeste [*v.r.* uuemaste] on viterokes al to torene. *c* **1425** WYNTOUN *Cron.* VIII. xxxi. 48 Endlang the wode war wayis twa; The Erle in the umast lay off tha. **1535** LYNDESAY *Sat.* 3900 Thay salbe.. denudit, Baith of cors present, cow, and umest claith.

β. *c* **1290** *St. Michael* 414 in *S. Eng. Leg.* I. 311 þe Ouemeste is þe riȝtte heouene. **13..** *Minor Poems fr. Vernon MS.* xxxviii. 815 And seþþen þe ouemaste Bayle Bi-tokneþ hire holy sposayle. *c* **1430** *Art Nombryng* 3 Write the nombre wherto the addicioun shalle be made in the omest ordre by his differences, so that the first of the lower ordre be vndre the first of the omyst ordre, and so of others. *c* **1470** HENRY *Wallace* VI. 458 Atour a bray the omast [*v.r.* vpmest] pot gert fall, Brak on the ground.

oven ('ʌv(ə)n), *sb.* Forms: α. 1–2 ofn, 1–3 ofen, (hofen), 3–6 ouen, 3– oven, (4 ouin, 4–5 oue, ouene, houen, 5 ovuen, oven(n)e, ovon, owen, 5–6 ovyn(e, owyn, 6 oueen). β. *Sc.* 4–6 oyne, (hoyne), 6 une, 8–9 oon. [Com. Teut.: OE. *ofn*, *ofen* = OLG. **ov(e)n* (MLG., MDu., Du. *oven*), OHG. *ovan* (MLG. *oven*, Ger. *ofen*), ON. *ofn*, *ogn* (Sw. *ugn*, ONorw. *ogn*, Da. *ovn*), Goth. *auhn-s* :—OTeut. **ohno-*:—pre-Teut. **uqno-*; cf. Gr. *ἰπνός* oven, furnace, also Skr. *ukhá-s* cooking-pot, orig. perh. 'something hollowed out'. *Heof(o)ne* in Lindisf. G. must be a scribal error; Sc. *oyn*, *oon* (pronounced øn, YN), is like *aboon* from *aboven*.]

† **1.** A furnace. *Obs.*

a **900** *O.E. Martyrol.* 3 May 70 þa het he sendan hi ealle þry on byrnendne ofn. *c* **950** *Lindisf. Gosp.* Matt. vi. 30 Gers *uel* heʒ londes þæt todæʒ is & tomorʒen in heofone [*Rushw.* in ofne] bið ʒesended. *Ibid.* xiii. 42 And sendas hia *uel* ða in ofn fyres. *c* **1200** *Vices & Virtues* (1888) 73 Al swo is þe pott ðe is idon on ðe barnende ofne. *a* **1300** *Cursor M.* 2926 Als it war a brinand ouen [*v.r.* ouin]. **13..** *Minor Poems fr. Vernon MS.* xxix. 93 In to the houene the child he caste. *c* **1375** *Sc. Leg. Saints* xxxi. (*Eugenia*) 860 [Men] put hyr in ane oyne brinande. *c* **1450** *Mirour Saluacioun* 3055 The aungels sent in to the oven to confort the childre. **1535** COVERDALE *Song 3 Childr.* 22 The kynges seruauntes.. ceassed not to make the ouen hote with wylde fyre, drye strawe, pitch & fagottes. **1642** J. EATON *Honey-c. Free Justif.* 128 The three Children of Israel cast into the hot fierie Oven. **1722** SEWEL *Hist. Quakers* (1795) I. 52 The day of the Lord is coming that shall burn as an oven.

fig. and *transf.* *a* **900** tr. *Bæda's Hist.* IV. xi. [ix.] (1890) 288 þætte eal þæt se ofn þære singalan costnunge asude. **1590** SPENSER *F.Q.* I. xi. 26 [The Dragon] from his wide devouring ouen sent A flake of fire.

2. a. A chamber or receptacle of brick, stonework, or iron, for baking bread and cooking food, by continuous heat radiated from the walls, roof, or floor. Variously distinguished as ***baker's***, ***brick***, ***domestic***, ***out-*** (= outside) ***oven***; and, with modern mechanical appliances, as ***continuous***, ***reel***, ***revolving***, ***rotary***, ***travelling oven***.

Dutch oven, (*a*) a large pot heated by surrounding it with fuel, and placing hot coals on the lid; (*b*) a cooking utensil made of sheet-metal, placed in front of a grate and heated by radiation and by reflection from the back of the chamber. † ***Egyptian oven***, a large earthenware vessel sunk in the ground, and heated from the inside by fuel which is withdrawn before introducing the articles to be baked.

c **1000** ÆLFRIC *Exod.* viii. 3 Hi.. gaþ.. on þine ofnas. *c* **1200** ORMIN 993 Bulltedd bræd þat bakenn wass inn ofne. *c* **1375** *Sc. Leg. Saints* xxii. (*Laurentius*) 589 He saw.. In his awne hoyne.. A laf quhyt as snaw. **1432–50** tr. *Higden* (Rolls) I. 405 Whete that is baken in an oue. **1477** *Tintinhull Churchw. Acc.* (Som. Rec. Soc.) 193 It. for the owyn.. viij. **1486** *Bk. St. Albans* B viij, A whyte looff.. sumwat colder then it commyth owt of the oouen. **1513** *Ld. Treas. Acc. Scot.* IV. 488 To the baxtaris of the greit schip for clay to make an une in the greit schip. *c* **1532** DU WES *Introd. Fr.* in Palsgr. 916 To put in the ouuen, *enfourner*. **1555** EDEN *Decades* 197 Rosted or stewed in an ouen. **1583** *Leg. Bp. St. Androis* 305 Had careit hame heather to the oyne, Cutted off in the cruik of the moone. **1627** tr. *Bacon's Life & Death* (1650) 47 Bread.. which is baked in an oven thorowly heated. **1766** WESLEY *Jrnl.* 17 July, I preached.. in a house as warm as an oven. **1769** MRS. RAFFALD *Eng. Housekpr.* (1778) 129 Put them in a Dutch oven to brown. **1824** SCOTT *St. Ronan's* ii, I will make better confections than ever cam out of his oon. **1838** T. THOMSON *Chem. Org. Bodies* 1030 The mean heat of a baker's oven, as ascertained by M. Tillet, is 448°. **1849** DICKENS *Dav. Copp.* xxiv, I'll toast you some bacon in a bachelor's Dutch-oven that I have got here.

fig. **1593** NASHE *Christ's T.* Wks. (Grosart) IV. 186 Damme vp the Ouen of your vttrance, make not such a bigge sound with your empty vessels.

b. In various proverbial sayings.

a **1250** *Owl & Night.* 292 þat me ne chide wiþ þe gidie Ne wiþ þan ofne me ne ʒeonie. **1546** J. HEYWOOD *Prov.* (1867) 69 No man will an other in the ouen seeke, Except that him selfe haue beene there before. **1577** [see GAPE *v.* 1]. **1596** NASHE *Saffron W.* 151 Of the Good-wife..finding her daughter in the ouen, where she would neuer haue sought her, if she had not been there first her selfe. *a* **1677** BARROW *Serm.* III. 394 To gape against an oven, to blow against the wind, to kick against the pricks. [So Du. *tegen een ovengapen.*] **1856** READE *Never too late* xiv, It is no use now I've been and gone into the same oven like a fool.

c. *transf.* A small oven-like tomb built at ground level.

1851 E. S. WORTLEY *Trav. U.S.* I. xxi. 237 The graves are also elevated. The dead are buried in sepulchral houses, which are termed here 'ovens'. **1879** *Cassell's Techn. Educ.* IV. 267/2 Owing to the damp nature of the ground..there are no graves in the cemeteries, the coffins with the dead being deposited in tombs or 'ovens' erected above the soil. **1921** *Chambers's Jrnl.* Aug. 511/1 There was no system in the arrangement of the 'ovens'.

d. A cremation chamber; *spec.* one of the chambers used by the Germans during the war of 1939–45 for the cremation of Jewish corpses.

1945 [see *gas oven*]. **1962** M. PROCTER *Body to Spare* xxi. 158 The two incinerators, invariably called ovens by local undertakers. **1964** L. DEIGHTON *Funeral in Berlin* xxiii. 129 He couldn't eat his lunch for the stink of the cremation ovens. **1967** C. POTOK *Chosen* xiii. 228 Where else [but Palestine] could the remnant of Jewry that had escaped Hitler's ovens go? **1976** L. SANDERS *Hamlet Warning* (1977) ix. 75 This beats those Nazi ovens.

e. *fig.* A woman's womb; chiefly in colloq. phr. ***to have something in the oven*** (and variants), to be pregnant. See also BUN *sb.*[2] 1 a, PUDDING *sb.* 5 c.

1962 'B. GRAEME' *Undetective* ii. 19 Good lord! You mean there's something in the oven? **1967** H. W. SUTHERLAND *Magnie* ii. 24 She knew definitely she had one in the oven. **1976** 'D. FLETCHER' *Accomplices* v. 143 She's in the club, you know. Got one in the oven, eh?

3. A chamber, fixed or portable, for the heating or drying of substances in chemical, metallurgical, or manufacturing processes; a small furnace, kiln, etc. Often with defining or descriptive addition, as ***air-***, ***anchor-***, ***annealing-***, ***bee-hive-***, ***coke-***, ***drying-***, ***heating-***, ***porcelain-***, ***proving-***, ***tile-oven***, etc.

1753 CHAMBERS *Cycl. Supp.*, *Oven*, or Assaying Oven, in metallurgy, is the particular sort of furnace, used by the assayers in their operations on metals. **1823** P. NICHOLSON *Pract. Build.* 360 An inclosed closet, with an iron grating, for the tin to stand on, called the Proving Oven. **1881** *Porcelain Works, Worcester* 26 A china oven..is built of fire bricks. **1884** F. J. BRITTEN *Watch & Clockm.* 65 The 'oven' is a box made of sheet copper or iron, generally with a water-jacket to the bottom, the exterior of which is heated by a gas jet.

4. *attrib.* and *Comb.*, as ***oven-bat***, ***-blast***, ***-fork***, ***-house***, ***-keeper***, ***-maker***, ***-mouth***, ***-rake***, ***-stirrer***, ***-sweeper***, etc.; ***oven-baked*** (***-baken***), ***-dry***, ***-hot***, ***-like***, ***-ready***, ***-shaped*** adjs.; ***oven-wise*** adv. and adj. Also **oven-bottom(ed)** *a.*, designating cake or bread baked at the bottom of the oven; **oven-bread**, **-cake**, bread or cake baked in an oven; **oven-cloth**, a heat resistant cloth used for handling dishes in an oven; **oven-coke**, coke obtained by heating coal in a closed retort; **oven-cook** *v.*, to cook in an oven; **oven-glass**, glass ware suitable for use in an oven; **oven glove**, an oven cloth made in the form of a glove; **oven-man**, a man who attends to an oven; **oven mit(t)** = *oven glove* above; **oven-mouth**, the mouth or entrance of an oven; *fig.* a wide or gaping mouth; **oven-peel**, a baker's peel; **ovenproof** [PROOF *a.* (*adv.*) 1 b], suitable for use in an oven; **oven's-nest**, the nest of the great titmouse, also = OVEN-BIRD (Swainson); **oven-stone**, a stone which closes the mouth of an oven; stone used for building ovens; **oven timer** (see quot. 1961); **oven-to-table** *a.*, designating ovenware designed also for use at the table for serving; **ovenware**, dishes that can be used for cooking in an oven; **oven wood**, wood for heating an oven. Also OVEN-BIRD, -BUILDER.

c **1000** ÆLFRIC *Voc.* in Wr.-Wülcker 127/27 *Formentum*, *ofenbacen hlaf. **1682** DRYDEN *Dk. of Guise* III. i, You *Oven-Bats, you Things so far from Souls, Like Dogs, you're out of Providence's Reach. **1849** AYTOUN *Poems, Scheik of Sinai* iv, The dark defile is blazing Like a heated *oven-blast. **1956** G. MANN *Good Food from Old England* 185 A piece of dough was always reserved for Leather Cake, or *Oven Bottom Cake. The name Oven Bottom Cake naturally came from the fact that the cake was baked on the bottom of the oven where the heat was. **1957** J. KIRKUP *Only Child* ix. 121 We..ate warm, freshly-baked 'oven-bottom cake'. **1959** *Times* 9 Mar. (Britain's Food Suppl.) p. xii/5 Many..in the over-40 age group..look back with nostalgia to the crusty oven-bottomed bread of their youth. **1967** 'S. WOODS' *And shame Devil* 74 [She] did her own baking and ate oven-bottom cake and treacle every day for tea. **1600** J. PORY tr. *Leo's Africa* II. 45 Neither shall you finde many in Hea which eate *ouen-bread. **1772** GRAVES *Spir. Quix.* VII. ii, He might have offered us a bit of his *oven-cake. **1821** COMBE *Dr. Syntax, Wife* III. 1020 And he did such a breakfast make On new bak'd loaf and oven-cake. *c* **1909** D. H. LAWRENCE *Collier's Friday Night* (1934) ii. 38 *Ernest* (rising and going to the oven, picking up the *oven-cloth from the hearth). **1957** J. KIRKUP *Only Child* ii. 44 Whenever she opened the oven door she used an 'oven-cloth'. **1969** D. CLARK *Death after Evensong* v. 133 Maria carried in a pizza... She slid it off the glove oven-cloth. **1977** *Limerick's Catal.* Spring 5 Oven cloth... To protect the hands. Mitten type. Each 68 p. **1854** RONALDS & RICHARDSON *Chem. Technol.* (ed. 2) I. 117 Coke, which is much more porous and less dense than *oven-coke. **1953** *Britannica Bk. of Year* 639/1 Compounds like *oven-cook (verb)..also occurred. **1974** *Times* 7 Mar. 13/7 If your frying pan is on the small side, there's no reason why you should not oven-cook the chicken halves. **1966** A. W. LEWIS *Gloss. Woodworking Terms* 63 **Oven dry*, wood which has been baked in an oven at 100°C (212°F), until it ceases to lose weight, i.e. until all the moisture has been removed. **1971** *Gloss. Soil Sci. Terms* (Soil Sci. Soc. Amer.) 12/1 *Oven-dry soil*, soil which has been dried at 105C until it reaches constant weight. **1611** COTGR., *Fourgon*, an *Ouen-forke.. wherewith fuell is both put into an Ouen, and stirred when it is (on fire) in it. **1939–40** *Army & Navy Stores Catal.* p. xlviii/1 *Oven Glass, Phoenix. **1961** *Guardian* 12 June 6/7 Phoenix oven glass..[is] one of the reliable heat-proof glasses. **1965** *Sun* 3 Nov. 40/4 *Oven gloves help to cheer up a kitchen on a dull morning. **1968** 'E. PETERS' *Grass Widow's Tale* vi. 84 Her nursery towelling oven gloves. **1976** *Oadby & Wigston Advertiser* 26 Nov. 9/2 Oven gloves..make very welcome gifts. **1922** BLUNDEN *Shepherd* 30 The night drooped *oven-hot. **1962** [see JAFFA]. **1976** E. WARD *Hanged Man* xx. 118 Parma ham and oven-hot bread. *c* **1425** *Voc.* in Wr.-Wülcker 670/22 *Hoc furnium*, *ovenhouse. **1886** B. HARTE *Snowbound* 26 *Oven-like cañons in the long flanks of the mountains. **1483** *Cath. Angl.* 263/1 An *Owen maker or keper, *clibanarius.* **1832** G. R. PORTER *Porcelain & Gl.* 63 The *oven-man places trial pieces in different parts of the oven. **1969** *Guardian* 10 Feb. 9/4 Trendy gifts like *oven mits. **1973** 'D. HALLIDAY' *Dolly & Starry Bird* ii. 21 He put both hands around the handle like oven mitts. **1593** HARVEY *Pierce's Super.* Wks. (Grosart) II. 231 To stoppe thy *Ouen-mouth with a lidde of Butter. *a* **1845** HOOD *To Grimaldi* ix, Thy oven-mouth, that swallow'd pies. **1660** HEXHAM *Dutch Dict.*, *Een School, ofte Oven-pael*, an *Oven-peele to set-in bread. **1877** B. R. MAJOR *Discov. Pr. Henry* ii. 17 Brites d'Almeida, the baker's wife, slew with her oven-peel no less than seven Castilian soldiers. **1939–40** *Army & Navy Stores Catal.* 714 *Phoenix* is the latest *oven proof glass-ware. **1957** *Housewife* Sept. 89/2 Scandinavian saucepan in oven-proof pottery. **1961** *Harper's Bazaar* Feb. 29/2 Two casserole dishes..are flame-proof and oven-proof. **1974** *Country Life* 5 Dec. 1735/3 Ramekins..in ovenproof pottery. *c* **1000** ÆLFRIC *Voc.* in Wr.-Wülcker 106/39 *Rotabulum*, myxforce, *uel* *ofenraca. **1580** HOLLYBAND *Treas. Fr. Tong*, *Vn fourgon*, a makon, an Ouen rake. **1960** A. E. BENDER *Dict. Nutrition* 90/2 **Oven ready*, term applied to poultry that have been plucked, neck, legs and entrails removed,..and finally sealed into heat-shrinkable Cryo-vac wrapping—ready for oven without any further handling. **1960** *Farmer & Stockbreeder* 23 Feb. 64/3 A new firm..has been formed with the aim of becoming one of the largest producers of oven-ready turkeys and ducklings in the country. **1962** [see *fish finger* s.v. FISH *sb.*[1] 7]. **1973** *Times* 16 Nov. 4 Wholesale prices of oven-ready turkey and chicken have fallen slightly in the past week. **1865** KINGSLEY *Herew.* I. ii. 85 Within the old *oven-shaped Pict's house. *a* **1825** FORBY *Voc. E. Anglia*, **Oven's nest*, the nest of that very pretty bird [the oven-bird]. It is otherwise..called a *pudding-poke's* nest. **1611** COTGR., *Fourgonneur*, an Ouen-tender, or *Ouen-stirrer. **1602** *How Man may Chuse good Wife* III. iii. in Hazl. *Dodsley* IX. 54 Bid the cook take down the *oven-stone, [lest] the pies be burned. **1838** *Murray's Hand-bk. N. Germ.* 271 The cave-like excavations of Bell, whence oven-stone (*pierre au four*) is obtained. **1580** HOLLYBAND *Treas. Fr. Tong*, *Escouillon*, an *Ouen sweeper. **1961** *Which?* Oct. 250/1 One cooker..had an automatic **oven timer*. This, like the ringers had a clockwork mechanism, which turned the oven on and off after a pre-set time. **1977** *Transatlantic Rev.* LX. 87 Then he [mimes] a man shaving and showering in a flurry of interruptions: the phone, the doorbell, the oven timer. **1977** *Jrnl. R. Soc. Arts* CXXV. 215/2 A wide range of ceramic items from the early beginnings to the latest *oven-to-table ware. **1979** *House & Garden* Mar. 78/3 (Advt.), Oval casserole from versatile range of oven-to-table ware. **1926–7** *Army & Navy Stores Catal.* 785 Pyrex transparent 'glass' *oven ware. **1933** *Archit. Rev.* LXXIV. 26 (*caption*) Some very well shaped Vitreosel quartz ovenware. **1959** *Listener* 5 Feb. 267/1 Bake fillets of cod or haddock in an ovenware dish. **1973** *Guardian* 23 May 9/5 Prestige's second eleven price range, Skyline, for their ovenware passes on many of the blessings of their first team's design. **1715** LEONI *Palladio's Archit.* (1742) I. 60 Their Arches round or *oven-wise. *Ibid.* 63 The great Rooms are arch'd with a *Fascia*, the square ones Oven-wise. **1794** COWPER *Needless Alarm* 12 Oaks..that had once a head But now wear crests of *oven-wood instead.

oven ('ʌv(ə)n), *v.* [f. prec.]

†**1.** *trans.* To bake in an oven. *Obs.* or *dial.*

1685 *Lintoun Green* (1817) 65 (E.D.D.) The first I bought ..Was o'ened and buttered weell. **1688** R. HOLME *Armoury* III. 293/2 A Jannock..is Ovened very soft.

2. To shut up as in an oven.

1596 NASHE *Saffron Walden* Wks. (Grosart) III. 203 One angle or corner..to hide him in..& brickil & ouen vp his stinking breath. **1864** *Gd. Words* 100/1 The earth's own temperature, not now radiated into the celestial spaces, is shut in—it is ovened, or muffled up.

Hence **ovened** ('ʌv(ə)nd), *ppl. a.*, *dial.* dried up, shrivelled, sickly. (Halliwell.)

1866 J. E. BROGDEN *Prov. Words Lincolnsh.* (E.D.D.), The eddish is very ovend.

'oven-bird. A name given to various birds which build a domed or oven-shaped nest.

a. Applied by ornithologists generally to the genus *Furnarius* of the neotropical Family *Dendrocolaptidæ*, esp. *F. rufus.* **b.** Locally applied to (*a*) the Willow Wren, in Norfolk also ***oven-tit*** and ***ground-oven***; (*b*) the Long-tailed or Bottle Titmouse, also ***oven-builder*** and ***bush-oven***; (*c*) the American Golden-crowned Thrush (*Seiurus auricapillus*).

a **1825** FORBY *Voc. E. Anglia*, *Oven-bird*, the long-tailed titmouse... The allusion is to the nest. **1848** *Zoologist* VI. 2186 Sylvia Trochilus is the 'oven-bird', so called..from the shape of its nest. **1867** WOOD *Illust. Nat. Hist.* II. 259 The oven-birds derive their name from the peculiar form of their nest. **1882–5** W. H. D. ADAMS *Bird World* 455 In the neighbourhood of the South American rivers is found the oven-bird, one of the Certhiidæ, or creepers. **1892** W. H. HUDSON *Nat. La Plata* 63, I could not endure to see the havoc they were making amongst the ovenbirds (*Furnarius rufus*). **1893** *Advance* (Chicago) 18 May, The oven-bird or accentor, announcing his presence with his startling song.

oven-builder, a local name of the Long-tailed Titmouse: see prec. b.

ovenchyma (əʊ'vɛŋkɪmə). *Bot.* [f. L. *ov-um* egg + Gr. ἔγχυμα infusion.] Plant tissue consisting of oval cells, oval cellular tissue.

1866 in *Treas. Bot.*

ovenette (ʌv(ə)'nɛt). [f. OVEN *sb.* 2 + -ETTE.] A small or subsidiary oven.

1919 [see KITCHENETTE]. **1976** *Southern Even. Echo* (Southampton) 11 Nov. 7/2 (Advt.), Eye-level grill-rotisserie-ovenett [*sic*], plus roomy autotimed warming drawer.

†**ovenon, -an**, *adv.* and *prep.* *Obs.* Forms: 1–3 ufenan, -on, 3 uuen-, ouenan, -on, 4 ovenon. [f. OE. *ufan* adv. from above, above + *an*, *on*, ON. Cf. ANOVEN (where the same elements are reversed) and ANOVENON.]

A. *adv.* From above.

c **1000** *Ags. Gosp.* John iii. 31 Se ðe ufenan com se is ofer ealle. *a* **1023** WULFSTAN *Hom.* xvi. (Napier) 97 He deð, þæt fyr cymð ufene [*MS. Corpus* ufenon]. **11..** *O.E. Chron.* an. 1052 (MS. C), Ṡeo landfyrd com ufenon and trymedon hiʒ be þam strande.

B. *prep.* Over and above; upon, down upon.

a **1000** *Be Domes Dæʒe* 144 Ufenan eall þis. *c* **1205** LAY. 18090 He smat hine uuenen [*c* **1275** ouenon] þat hæued. *a* **1300** *K. Horn* 1485 (Harl. MS.) Ouen o þe sherte hue gurden huem wiþ suerde.

over ('əʊvə(r)), *adv.* Forms: α. 1–3 ofer, (1 ofor, 3 *Orm.* oferr, offr), 2–7 ouer, 3– over, (4 ouur, ouver, owver, 4–5 ouir, -yr, -ere, -ire, 4–6 ovir, -yr). β. *north. Eng.* and *Sc.* 4– ower, (4–5 owur, owyr, 4–6 our, oure, 6– owre). γ. *contr.* 4 or, (6 ore, 7–8 o're), 6– o'er. The contracted form *o'er* (ɔə(r)) is now poetic and rhetorical. [Com. Teut.: OE. *ofer* adv. and prep. = OFris. *over*, OS. *obar*, (MDu., MLG., Du., LG. *over*), OMG. *obar* (MG. *ober*), OHG. *ubar* prep., *ubiri* adv. (MHG. *über*, Ger. *über*, *ober*), ON. *yfer* adv. and prep. (Sw. *öfver*, Da. *over*), Goth. *ufar* prep. and adv. prefix, = Gr. ὑπέρ, Skr. *upari* adv. and prep., locative form of *upara* adj. 'over, higher, more advanced, later', comparative formation from *upa*, in Teut. *ufa-*, *uf-*, whence the adverbial *ufan* (see OVENON, ANOVEN), and *be-ufan*, *bufan*, with the compound *a-bufan*, ABOVE. *Over* was thus in origin an old comparative of the element *ufa*, *ove*, in *ab-ove*. Besides its uses as a separate word, *over-* is in all the Teut. langs. an important adverbial prefix: see OVER-.]

I. With sense Above, and related notions.

1. a. Above, on high.

The first quot. shows the adv. becoming prepositional: 'be to us the brightness over', i.e. be the brightness over us.

c **1000** *Ags. Ps.* (Th.) lxxxix. 19 Wese us beorhtnes ofer bliðan Drihtnes ures. *a* **1300** *Cursor M.* 21639 Ouer and vnder, right and left, In þis compas godd all has left. **1819** BYRON *Juan* I. cliii, Search them under, over.

†**b.** Above on a page; on a previous page.

1456 SIR G. HAYE *Law Arms* (S.T.S.) 33 We have our sene how the kirk and the cristyn faith has bene.

c. After *hang*, *project*, *jut*, *lean*, and the like (in reference to the space beneath: see OVER *prep.* 1); hence *ellipt.* projecting, leaning, or bent forward and downward (quot. 1887).

1546 LANGLEY *Pol. Verg. De Invent.* III. x. 77 a, The plomline whereby the Euenes of the Squares bee tried whether they batter or hang ouer. **1780–1836** J. MAYNE *Siller Gun* in Chambers *Pop. Scot. Poems* (1862) 132 Beneath yon cliff, high beetling ower, Is chaste Diana's Maiden-Bower. **1869** FITZWYGRAM *Horses & Stables* (1901) IX. lx. §901 Horses, which stand over at the knees, generally do so from effect of severe and constant work. **1880** C. B. BERRY *Other Side* 244 The ship is so beamy that she don't heel over much. **1887** MRS. RIDDELL *Nun's Curse* I. iv. 66 The knight's knees were a little 'over', after the fashion of a horse that has been hard driven. *a* **1904** *Mod.* Don't lean over too far, or you'll fall over.

2. a. Above so as to cover the surface, or so as to affect the whole surface: with such verbs as *brush*, *cover*, *clothe*, *daub*, *dust*, *furrow*, *paint*, *plaster*, *powder*, *rub*, *scribble*, *strew*, *stud*, *sweep*, *varnish*. See also ALL OVER 1.

c **1400** MAUNDEV. (Roxb.) viii. 29 A faire kirk all ouer whyte blaunched. *a* **1440** *Sir Degrev.* 1470 The floure was.. overe keveryd with a pal. **1567** *Gude & Godlie Ball.* (S.T.S.) 50 And war the warld..Cled ouer with gold. *a* **1611** BEAUM. & FL. *Maid's Trag.* I. i. She..will..make her maids Pluck 'em [flowers], and strew her over like a corse. **1667** MILTON *P.L.* VIII. 83 Gird the Sphear With Centric and Eccentric scribl'd o're. **1701** ROWE *Amb. Step-moth.* I. i, Thy function too will varnish o're our Arts. **1871** R. ELLIS *Catullus* lxiv. 293 Whereto the porch wox green, with soft leaves canopied over. **1891** *Leeds Mercury* 27 Apr. 4/7 The.. sleeves studded thickly over with tiny silver sequins.

b. *to be* (someone) *all over*: to be very characteristic of (that person); to be exactly what one might expect of (someone specified). Also *transf.*

1721 R. PALMER *Let.* 31 Aug. in M. M. Verney *Verney Lett.* (1930) II. xxiv. 90 [Mr. Churchill is] Vulponi all over. **1799** C. LAMB *Let.* 20 Mar. (1935) I. 153 The last stanza hath nothing striking in it, if I except the two concluding lines, which are Burns all over. **1821** SCOTT *Pirate* II. v. 114, I see where you would be—this is Sebastian and Dorax all over. **1852** [see ALL OVER *advb. phr.* 1 a]. **1863** J. S. MILL *Let.* 22 Nov. (1910) I. 310 This is Spencer all over; he throws himself with a certain deliberate impetuosity into the last new theory. **1898** J. D. BRAYSHAW *Slum Silhouettes* 14 Ah! gal, that's married life all over—fight and agree, fight and agree! **1906** GALSWORTHY *Man of Property* II. xii. 257 That's Phil all over—he was always like that. **1913** A. BENNETT *Regent* II. viii. 249 He's his father all over, that lad is! **1945** H. CLOSS *High are Mountains* 56 It was old Longshanks all over to send one off on some futile errand. **1973** A. HOLDEN *Girl on Beach* 37, I could have killed Dick when he.. said he'd asked these two men to dinner, but that's Dick all over of course, just expects me to cope.

II. With sense To or on the other side.

3. Indicating a motion or course that passes or crosses above something, usually rising on one side and descending on the other; as *to climb, jump, run, flow, boil over, to look over, shoot over, throw* something *over*; sometimes (*b*) esp. with the sense of passing above and beyond, instead of reaching or hitting, and so *fig.* of going beyond, exaggeration.

c **893** K. ÆLFRED *Oros.* v. xii. §8 He eode to ðære burȝe wealle, and fleah ut ofer. *a* **1225** *Ancr. R.* 266 Nule he nout, he seið, wenden ouer, auh wule sitten ful ueste. *c* **1440** *Promp. Parv.* 43/1 Boilyn ouyr, as pottys on the fire. **1560** BIBLE (Genev.) *Ps.* xxiii. 5 My cup runneth ouer. **1641** FRENCH *Distill.* ii. (1651) 50 Distill them.. and there will come over a water of no small vertue. **1724** DE FOE *Mem. Cavalier* (1840) 99 The king.. lays over his bridge. **1841** MARRYAT *Poacher* i, If we were to toss him.. over the bridge .. Shall we over with him? *a* **1904** *Mod.* Climb over into the garden. Jump over and escape. There is a high wall to prevent people seeing over into the grounds.

(*b*) **1599** SHAKS. *Hen. V*, III. vii. 133 You haue shot ouer. **1626** R. HARRIS *Hezekiah's Recov.* 4 The Orator spake not over, when hee intimated that Ingratitude was a kinde of Unjustice. **1681** DRYDEN *Sp. Friar* I. i, They're all corrupted with the Gold of Barbary To carry over, and not hurt the Moor. **1796** in Nicolas *Disp. Nelson* (1846) VII. p. xxxiii, Many shot went over, but none struck us.

4. a. Hence used of the latter part of the motion or course described in 3, corresponding to the position in 1 c = over the edge or brink and down, forward and down, as in *to fall, jump, throw* oneself, *push* any one *over* (cf. *over a precipice*, OVER *prep.* 12). Also, **b.** of a similar movement from the erect position, without reference to any brink, as in *to fall, tumble, topple, knock* a person, a vase, etc. *over*; and **c.** in *to bend, double, fold, turn, roll* a thing *over*, in which the upper surface is turned forward (or laterally) and downward, so as to become the under, i.e. is turned upside down. ***to roll*** or ***turn over and over***, i.e. so that each part of the surface in succession rolls forward and downward, and is alternately up and down.

a. *c* **1400** *Laud Troy Bk.* 5743 Ther hors fel doun and thei ȝede ouer, Bothe were besy up to couer. **1814** SCOTT *Ld. of Isles* III. xv, For from the mountain hoar.. Loose crags had toppled o'er. *a* **1904** *Mod.* Do not go too near the edge of the precipice; you might fall over. It is on the very brink; a very slight push would send it over.

b. **1649** G. DANIEL *Trinarch., Hen. IV*, ccciii, One single Gunne, tumbles the whole towne ore. **1660** H. MORE *Myst. Godl.* VIII. xvii. 441 The leaking vessel of this mortal Body .. ready to sink or topple over. **1694–1826** Fall over [see FALL *v.* 96]. **1814–93** Knock over [see KNOCK *v.* 15]. **1853** KANE *Grinnell Exp.* xxiv. (1856) 196 When these [ice-piles] attain their utmost height,.. they topple over.

c. *a* **1548** HALL *Chron., Rich. III* 29 b, He tourned over the leffe, and began an order of a new life. **1662** GLANVILL *Lux Orient.* Pref. (1682) 10 If they turn o're Libraries. **1674** R. GODFREY *Inj. & Ab. Physic* 6 We.. who have tumbled over so many Volumes. **1710** ADDISON *Tatler* No. 243 ¶3 He turned himself over hastily in his Bed. **1726** SWIFT *Gulliver* II. v, Expecting every moment to.. fall.. and come tumbling over and over from the ridge to the eaves. **1807** *Med. Jrnl.* XVII. 176 *note*, Very few.. have thought it worth their while to tumble over the dirty pages of this publication. **1840** LARDNER *Geom.* xxii. 309 If the curve VP were folded over on VP', the point P would fall upon P'. *a* **1904** *Mod.* Turn him over on his face.

5. a. From side to side of an interjacent surface or space: in early use esp. said of crossing the surface of the sea or other water (closely akin to 3), a street, a common, or other defined tract; in later use often said merely of traversing the space or distance between two places, and so adding some notion of completeness to *go, come, run, take*, etc.; e.g. 'Take this over to my friend's house'.

c **893** K. ÆLFRED *Oros.* II. v. §6 An fiscere.. uneaþe hiene ænne ofer brohte. *c* **1175** *Lamb. Hom.* 141 Sunnedei smat Moyses þe rede see, and þe se to-eode and þet iraelisce folc wende ouer. *c* **1330** R. BRUNNE *Chron.* (1810) 59 Whan þe erle was exiled, his sonnes tille Irland ouer. *a* **1400–50** *Alexander* 1028 In-to þe coste of Calodone he comes him ouer first. **1567** MAPLET *Gr. Forest* 97 To sende ouer Owles to Athens. **1591** SHAKS. *1 Hen. VI*, v. iii. 167 Ile ouer then to England with this newes. **1676–7** MARVELL *Corr.* Wks. 1872–5 II. 523 Whose opinion was, that he ought to be sent for over. **1869** *Contemp. Rev.* XI. 65 The Duke.. had asked him over. **1894** A. ROBERTSON *Nuggets*, etc. 156 My mother will send over every day to inquire how Miss McLean is. **1895** *Scottish Antiquary* X. 81 He.. darted for the ford, and got over before they came up to him.

b. Of measurement: Across from side to side; in outside measurement.

1585–6 EARL LEYCESTER *Corr.* (Camden) 477 The breadthe therof, in the narrowest place, is a mylle over. **1624** J. PORY in Capt. Smith *Virginia* IV. 142 The land is not two daies iourny ouer in the broadest place. **1660** F. BROOKE tr. *Le Blanc's Trav.* 279 On the West they had deserts of fifteen dayes over. **1663** GERBIER *Counsel* 69 If the Ballisters be two inches over, it is two shillings a doozen. **1719** DE FOE *Crusoe* I. xii, The cave.. might be about twelve feet over. **1872** *Routledge's Ev. Boy's Ann.* 10/1 A small sixty sized [flower] pot, which is about three inches over.

c. *Cricket.* The umpire's call for the players to pass to the opposite places in the field, on a change of the bowling to the other end of the wicket, after a certain number of balls (4, 5, or 6) have been bowled from the one end. (Hence OVER *sb.*[2] 4.)

17.. *Laws of Cricket* in Grace *Cricket* (1891) 15 When ye 4 Balls are bowled he [the umpire] is to call over. **1849** *Laws of Cricket* in 'Bat' *Cricketer's Man.* (1850) 59 After the delivery of four balls the umpire must call 'Over'.

6. a. From one person, side, party, opinion, etc., to another: expressing transference or transition; esp. in *deliver, hand, bring, make, take over, go, come, pass over*. ***give over***: see GIVE *v.* 63. (See also GET *v.* 74 e.)

1585 T. WASHINGTON tr. *Nicholay's Voy.* I. ii. 2 b, Forgetting.. that whiche duty & fidelity commanded him, [he] went ouer to the king of Spayne. **1593** SHAKS. *2 Hen. VI*, I. i. 60 [The Duchies of Anjou and Maine] shall be released and deliuered ouer to the King her Father. **1595** —— *John* III. i. 127 And dost thou now fall ouer to my foes? **1608** WILLET *Hexapla Exod.* 461 So might the seruant be sold ouer. **1766** GOLDSM. *Vic. W.* ii, The profits of my living,.. I made over to the orphans and widows of the clergy of our diocese. **1776** *Trial of Nundocomar* 104/2 The balance.. is brought over into this [account]. **1894** *Temple Bar Mag.* CI. 62, I made over.. every farthing of the fortune. *Mod.* Part of the auxiliary forces went over to the enemy.

b. Used in radio communication to indicate that the speaker has finished speaking and intends his communicator to reply. ***over and out***: used to indicate that the communication is at an end. Cf. OUT *adv.* 23 b. Also *transf.*, esp. in ***over to you***: it is your turn (to speak, act, etc.).

1926 J. L. PRITCHARD *Bk. Aeroplane* viii. 144 'Hullo, Croydon,.. now passing Biggin Hill. Over!'.. The final word 'Over' tells the Croydon operator that the pilot is switching his transmitting apparatus over to receiving so that he can hear what Croydon has to say. **1940** 'GUN BUSTER' *Return via Dunkirk* II. iv. 117 X calling Robert Eddy... I can hear you.... remain on receive... over to you over. **1955, 1966** [see OUT *adv.* 23 b]. **1967** 'R. FOLEY' *Fear of Stranger* (1968) x. 105 Over to you, pal, Kay thought in amusement. **1969** *Guardian* 22 July 11/1 Thank you Peter, thank you Paul, to name but two. Over, like, and out. **1972** N. MARSH *Tied up in Tinsel* v. 123 'Well, ta for the tip anyway. Over and out.' Alleyn hung up. **1973** G. MITCHELL *Murder of Busy Lizzie* xv. 175 'But, for the moment, we are concerning ourselves with the Lovelaine family, I thought.' 'Sorry! Over to you, then.' **1974** P. WRIGHT *Lang. Brit. Industry* xiv. 135 It [*sc.* language repetition] occurs particularly where.. actions and accompanying words amount to a drill, as in the radio operator's *Over and out.* **1976** L. DILLS *CB Slanguage Dict.* (rev. ed.) 51 *Over*, through transmitting but listening.

7. a. On the other side of something intervening, e.g. a sea, river, street; hence, merely, on the other side of some space, at some distance.

c **1330** R. BRUNNE *Chron.* (1810) 219 Whan Edward was ouere graciously and wele, He hoped haf recouere at Wigemore castele. **1513** DOUGLAS *Æneis* I. i. 22 The mouth of lang Tibir our forgane. **1823** LOCKHART *Span. Ball., Song of Galley* vi, It is a narrow strait, I see the blue hills over. **1845** BROWNING *How they brought the Good News* vii, Over by Dalhem a dome-spire sprang white. *a* **1904** *Mod.* He has been over in America for some time.

b. ***over against*** (*prep. phr.*): opposite to. So ***over-anenst*** dial., † ***overynentes*** obs.

c **1400** MAUNDEV. (Roxb.) xi. 46 Ouerynentes þe forsaid well, es ane ymage of stane. **1517** TORKINGTON *Pilgr.* (1884) 19 Over a gens the forseyd yle of Cirigo. **1526** TINDALE *Mark* xiii. 3 As he sate on mounte olivete over agenst the temple. **1632** LITHGOW *Trav.* IV. 139 Perah is ouer against Constantinople. **1710** STEELE *Tatler* No. 261 ¶1 The Wheat-Sheaf over-against Tom's Coffee-house. **1855** ROBINSON *Whitby Gloss.*, *Ower-anent*, over-against, opposite. **1864** PUSEY *Lect. Daniel* viii. 475 It exhibits the vain tumults of men, and, over-against them, the calm supremacy of God.

III. With the notion of exceeding in quantity, etc.

8. Above or beyond the quantity named or in question. **a.** Remaining or left beyond what is taken. **b.** Present beyond the quantity in question; in excess, in addition, more. ***over or under***, † ***over or short***: more or less.

a **900** tr. *Bæda's Eccl. Hist.* I. xvi. [xxvii.] (1890) 66 Eall ðæt ofer bið to lafe is to syllane, swa swa Crist lærde *Quod superest date eleemosynam*: ðæt ofer si and to lafe sellaþ ælmessan. *c* **1050** *Byrhtferth's Handboc* in *Anglia* (1885) VIII. 303 ȝyf þær byð an ofer. *a* **1340** HAMPOLE *Psalter* Cant. 495 Eftere his seknes & grauntynge of life fyften ȝere ouyr. **1393** *Test. Ebor.* (Surtees) I. 184 If there be oght over. **1412–20** LYDG. *Chron. Troy* 80 b, An hundred men of armes them beforne, And twenty over. **1596** DANETT tr. *Comines* (1614) 330 At the selfe same time within two moneths ouer or vnder. **1603** SIR C. HEYDON *Jud. Astrol.* v. 147 To come neare to it ouer or short is commendable. **1613** SHAKS. *Hen. VIII*, IV. ii. 151 That they may haue their wages,.. And something ouer to remember me by. **1657** W. RAND tr. *Gassendi's Life Peiresc* I. 130 A certain rare Aloes tree, which .. shot up 32 feet high.. and near half a foot over. **1777** MACBRIDE in *Phil. Trans.* LXVIII. 129 A score of pounds over or under making no.. difference in the strength. **1854** DICKENS *Hard T.* I. ii, The principle that two and two are four, and nothing over. **1856** *Titan Mag.* Dec. 499/1 Twelve will go once in fourteen, and leave two over.

9. a. Remaining or left unpaid, unsettled, or uncompleted after the time of settlement; remaining for the time being; left till a later time or occasion; esp. with *remain, lie, stand, hold, leave.*

1647 [see HOLD *v.* 42 a]. **1848** CRAIG, *To lie over*, to remain unpaid, after the time when payment is due. **1852** [see HOLD *v.* 42 b]. **1862** TROLLOPE *Orley F.* I. xix. 144 The matter was allowed to stand over till after Christmas. **1884** *Mil. Engineering* (ed. 3) I. II. 51 The front ditch.. may be left over, in the absence of strong enough working parties.

b. Until a later time or period; till the next season; overnight.

1861 *Trans. Illinois Agric. Soc.* IV. 317 Old bugs live over, and produce eggs the following season. **1884** J. HAY *Bread-Winners* xi. 172, I am so glad you resolved to stay over. **1899** A. NICHOLAS *Idyl of Wabash* 53 We don't want to winter them steers over. **1953** N. GORDIMER *Lying Days* II. xx. 168, I was going to sleep over at the house of an old friend of my mother's. **1968** J. SANGSTER *Touch-feather* xiv. 149 'You're staying over.'.. 'But I haven't brought any clothes.' **1973** 'D. SHANNON' *No Holiday for Crime* (1974) vi. 91 He.. put a second shirt and a razor in a briefcase in case he had to stay over.

† **10. a.** Beyond or in addition to what has been said; more than that, moreover, besides; further.

c **1380** WYCLIF *Sel. Wks.* III. 163 Bot se we owver how þis synne is partid in þo Chirche. **1382** —— *1 Macc.* ix. 55 Nether he miȝte spek overe [1388 more] a word. *c* **1430** *Pilgr. Lyf Manhode* I. cxi. (1869) 58 And ouer j sey þee,.. who so hath [etc.]. **1509** *Act 1 Hen. VIII*, c. 3 And ouer, that it be ordeined [etc.].

b. So † ***over and besides***; also OVER AND ABOVE.

1583 STOCKER *Civ. Warres Lowe C.* III. 101 a, Ouer and besides, they fortified them selues sundry dayes with many Fortes, or trenches. **1594** R. ASHLEY tr. *Loys le Roy* 75 b, They had 200000 men.. and ouer and besids iij hundred thousand harnesse of prouision. **1622** MABBE tr. *Aleman's Guzman d'Alf.* I. 127 And you must over and besides, allow her her wine into the bargaine.

11. Beyond what is normal or proper; too much; excessively; too. Cf. OVER AND ABOVE B. 2.

Modifying adjs. and advbs., and now usually hyphened or combined, as *over-anxious, overmuch*: see OVER- 28, 30. In Sc. and north. Eng. dial. (*ower, owre*) the regular word for 'too', and always written separate, as ***ower muckle***.

a **1225** *Ancr. R.* 86 Nis hit nout nu,.. so ouer vuel ase me hit makeð. *c* **1330** R. BRUNNE *Chron.* (1810) 36 Bot it was ouer litelle, in alle maner way. **13..** *Cursor M.* 26251 (Cott.) þi plight es owur vgli. **1456** SIR G. HAYE *Law Arms* (S.T.S.) 36 Na man suld.. be our blythe, na.. be our disconfourt or aferde. **1470–85** MALORY *Arthur* x. lxxxv, That one repenteth.. for he is ouer good a knyghte to dye suche a shameful dethe. **1475** *Paston Lett.* III. 122, I thynke it wolde be to yow ovyr erksom a labor. *a* **1568** ASCHAM *Scholem.* I. (Arb.) 57 It is ouer greate a ieopardie. **1625** BACON *Ess., Delays* (Arb.) 525 To teach dangers to come on, by ouer early Buckling towards them. **1627** E. F. *Hist. Edw. II* (1680) 12 Some few days pass, which seem'd o're long. **1766** FORDYCE *Serm. Yng. Wom.* (1767) I. vii. 297 You are over hasty in your apprehension. **1786** BURNS *Twa Dogs* 140 Still it's owre true that ye hae said, Sic game is now owre aften play'd. **1804** WORDSW. *Kitten & Falling Leaves* 38–9 Over happy to be proud, Over wealthy in the treasure Of her own exceeding pleasure! **1868** ATKINSON *Cleveland Gloss.* s.v., He is ower fond for owght. **1874** BLACKIE *Self-Cult.* 22 Be not over anxious about mere style. **1875** JOWETT *Plato* (ed. 2) I. 93 Do you understand now what I mean? Not over well.

IV. Of duration, repetition, completion, ending.

12. a. Through its whole extent; to the end; from beginning to end: esp. with *read, repeat, say, tell, reckon, count*; with *talk* and *think*, this passes into the notion of detailed consideration.

1399 LANGL. *Rich. Redeles* Prol. 55 If it happe to ȝowre honde beholde þe book onys,.. And if ȝe sauere sum dell, se it forth ouere. **1560** DAUS tr. *Sleidane's Comm.* 102 He toke great displeasure to reade over the whole discourse. *Ibid.* 231 Let the poorer sorte oftymes saye over theyr Pater noster. *c* **1680** *Doubting Virgin* in *Roxb. Ball.* IV. 344 Stay and hear 't o're, before you go. **1782** MISS BURNEY *Cecilia* IX. x, Cecilia.. took the letter, and ran it over. **1871** R. ELLIS *Catullus* lxi. 215 (203) He shall tell them, ineffable, Multitudinous, over. **1875** JOWETT *Plato* (ed. 2) III. 605 We talked the matter over. **1884** G. ALLEN *Philistia* III. 166 Let's talk it over and think it over. **1892** *Law Times* XCII. 146/1 The indorsement was read over to her.

b. For temporal phrases of the type 'all the year over', which partly belong here, see OVER *prep.* 17 b.

13. Expressing repetition.

a. orig. ***over again***, or with numeral adv., as ***twice or thrice over***.

c **1550** *Jyl of Brentford's Test.* (Ballad Soc.) 41 Pray doe it over again! **1596** SHAKS. *Merch. V.* III. ii. 309 You shall haue gold To pay the petty debt twenty times ouer. **1682** SIR T. BROWNE *Chr. Mor.* III. §25 Men would not live it over again. **1766** GOLDSM. *Vic. W.* xiv, He read it twice over. **1875** JOWETT *Plato* (ed. 2) I. 218 This is the old, old song over again. **1884** SIR W. B. BRETT in *Law Times Rep.* 10 May

315/2 To be verbose and tautologous, and to say the same thing twice over.

b. *over* in the sense 'over again'.

1588 SHAKS. *L.L.L.* I. i. 33, I can but say their protestation ouer. **1592** —— *Rom. & Jul.* I. ii. 7 But saying ore what I haue said before. **1601** —— *Twel. N.* v. i. 276 All those sayings, will I ouer sweare. **1611** —— *Cymb.* I. vi. 165 And shall make your Lord, That which he is, new o're. **1704** SWIFT *T. Tub* Apol., He had however a blotted Copy.. which he intended to have written over with many Alterations. **1872** H. W. BEECHER *Lect. Preaching* II. 39 Perhaps he may be able to make himself over. **1889** *Scribner's Mag.* Aug. 217/2 Old iron rails..are worked over at the rolling mills into crowbars and shovels [etc.].

c. ***over and over, over and over again***, repeatedly, many times over.

1598 SHAKS. *Merry W.* III. iii. 18, I ha told them ouer and ouer, they lacke no direction. **1637** GILLESPIE *Eng. Pop. Cerem.* IV. i. 1 Vpon this string they harpe over and over again. **1647** R. STAPYLTON *Juvenal* 215 Let rich men do it, ore and ore agen. **1707** HEARNE *Collect.* 21 May (O.H.S.) II. 14 Nothing..but what has been observ'd over and over. *a* **1860** J. A. ALEXANDER *Gospel Jesus Chr.* iii. (1861) 44 He has over and over refused to accept God's invitation. **1869** FREEMAN *Norm. Conq.* III. xii. 188 The name..appears over and over again.

14. Past, gone by, finished, done with, at an end. Phr. ***over (and done) with***: completed, finished; dispensed with.

[*c* **1330** R. BRUNNE *Chron.* (1810) 282 A prophecie sais he salle die, & whan he is ouere, After þat day Scotland may haf gode recouere.] **1611** BIBLE *Song Sol.* ii. 11 For loe, the winter is past, the raine is ouer [COVERD. awaie, *Geneva* changed], and gone. **1624** QUARLES *Div. Poems, Job* x. 105 O that thy Hand would hide me close..till all thy Wrath were over! **1625** BACON *Ess., Anger* (Arb.) 565 To looke backe vpon Anger, when the Fitt is throughly ouer. **1697** DRYDEN *Virg. Georg.* III. 345 Nor when the War is over, is it Peace. **1719** DE FOE *Crusoe* I. xv, His astonishment was a little over. **1802** MAR. EDGEWORTH *Moral T.* (1816) I. i. 5 The ceremony of dinner is over. **1865** BARING-GOULD *Hymn*, Now the day is over, Night is drawing nigh. **1875** STUBBS *C.H.* II. xiv. 149 The struggle was not yet over. **1938** R. D. FINLAYSON *Brown Man's Burden* 53 The others..were glad when they were free to go, for..the salutations were over and done with. **1970** AUDEN in *New Yorker* 21 Feb. 118/1, I have one slight criticism..which I will get over with at once. **1977** S. WOODS *Thief or Two* 136, I thought, if I was going to do it, I'd get it over with.

15. In addition to the prec. senses, *over* is used idiomatically with many verbs, as GIVE, PASS, PUT, THROW, WALK, etc. See these verbs.

over (ˈəʊvə(r)), *prep.* Forms: see prec. [The same as OVER *adv.* with object.

OE. *ofer* was const. with dative or accusative, the former orig. in the sense of position, the latter in that of motion to. There are however several uses of *ofer* in which these distinctions are not clear, which app. led to looseness in the use of the cases generally, so that in many senses either case was used with no apparent difference of sense, the preponderance being in favour of the accusative.]

I. In sense *above*.

1. a. Above, higher up than. Said either of position or of motion within the space above; also, after ***hang, project, jut, lean***, etc., in relation to anything beneath.

c **888** K. ÆLFRED *Boeth.* xl. §4 Hi wuniaþ nu ofer ðæm tunglum. *c* **893** —— *Oros.* I. iii. §1 Ðær wæs standende wæter ofer þam lande. *c* **1000** *Sax. Leechd.* II. 38 Bræd þonne þæt heafod hider & ȝeond ofer þæt fyr. *a* **1225** *Ancr. R.* 400 Ich holde her hetel sweord ouer þin heaued. *c* **1420** LYDG. *Assembly of Gods* 1608 Ouer her heede houyd a culuer ..whyte. *c* **1425** *Cursor M.* 11489 (Trin.) Ouer þe hous stood þe stern. *a* **1548** HALL *Chron., Hen. VI* 116 b, [They] received hym with a Canapie of blewe velvet,..and bare the same over hym, through the toune. *c* **1590** [see LEAN *v.* 4]. **1676** HOBBES *Iliad* II. 394 The Entrails o're the fire they broiled. **1736** BERKELEY *Discourse* Wks. III. 424 Having his house burnt over his head. **1805** WORDSW. *Prelude* VIII. 95 Mountains over all, embracing all. **1821** KEATS *Isabella* xxiii, He leant..o'er the balustrade. **1864** DASENT *Jest & Earnest* (1873) I. 42 Flitting about like a petrel over those stormy isles. *a* **1904** *Mod.* The upper story projects over the street.

b. In various *fig.* uses.

c **888** K. ÆLFRED *Boeth.* xli. §5 (MS. B.) Ne þæt ne secð þæt him ofer is. *c* **897** —— *Gregory's Past. C.* xvii. 108 Eower eȝe and broȝa sie ofer ealle eorðan nietenu. *a* **900** *Ags. Ps.* (Th.) xxxii. 18 Sy, Drihten, þin mildheortnes ofer us. *c* **1000** ÆLFRIC *Num.* xvi. 46 Godes yrre is ofer hiȝ. **1549** LATIMER *3rd Serm. bef. Edw. VI* (Arb.) 95 He loketh hye ouer the poore. **1593** SHAKS. *Rich. II*, II. i. 258 Reproach and dissolution hangeth ouer him. **1849** MACAULAY *Hist. Eng.* i. I. 72 A grave doubt hung over the legitimacy both of Mary and of Elizabeth. **1887** *Times* (weekly ed.) 1 July 2/1 The best part proved to be a little over the heads of his audience.

c. *over* (one's) ***signature, name***, etc.: with one's signature, etc. subscribed to what is written.

1805 in *Spirit of Public Jrnls.* (1806) 96 A writer over the signature of Zanga, is another buckram expression. **1826** *New Harmony* (Indiana) *Gaz.* 22 Mar. 207/2 A writer over the signature of 'A Farmer'..states that he has been completely successful..in saving his wheat [from weevils]. **1857** *N. & Q.* 2nd Ser. IV. 87 He says, over his own signature: 'If in passing the comet [etc.]'. **1875** STEDMAN *Victorian Poets* 261 Who relieved his eager spirit by incessant poetizing over the pseudonym of 'Spartacus'. **1934** H. G. WELLS *Exper. Autobiogr.* II. viii. 626 Bennett.. wrote much of the little weekly paper, *Woman*, he was editing..over the signature..of 'Aunt Ellen'. **1946** *Sunshine Mag.* Apr. (front cover), New preface over the author's own signature.

†**2.** To a position above. OE. (w. *acc.* or *dat.*).

a **900** *Ags. Ps.* (Th.) xxiii. 2 He ȝesette þa eorþan ofer þære sæ. *c* **1000** ÆLFRIC *Gram.* xlvii. (Z.) 274 Se þe astah ofer heofenas.

3. *Idiomatic use.* In (or into) a position in which water, or the like, rises above one's shoes, boots, ears, head, etc. Also *fig.* See also OVER SHOE.

1503 HAWES *Examp. Virt.* x. 7 He must nedys into this water fall Ouer the heed and be drowned with all. **1530–1867** Over head and ears [see HEAD *sb.*[1] 39 b]. *a* **1553–** Over the ears [see EAR *sb.*[1] 1 c]. *a* **1555** PHILPOT *Exam. & Writ.* (Parker Soc.) 227 Now I am over the shoes: God send me well out! **1589** R. HARVEY *Pl. Perc.* (1590) 8 Another.. puls him ouer the pumpes into the same puddle. **1591** SHAKS. *Two Gent.* I. i. 24–5 He [Leander] was more then ouer-shooes in loue. *Val.* 'Tis true; for you are ouer-bootes in loue. **1677** GILPIN *Demonol.* (1867) 80 To go on and enjoy the fulness of that delight which we have already stolen privately: over shoes, over boots. **1768** WESLEY *Jrnl.* 23 Sept. (1827) III. 336 My horse got into a ditch over his back in water. **1834** D. MACMILLAN in Hughes *Mem.* (1883) 66, I am always over head and ears with one trouble or another.

4. The spatial sense 'above' passes into other notions: the literal notion is **a.** combined with that of purpose or occupation, as in *over the fire, a bowl, a glass*; **b.** sunk in that of having something under treatment, observation, or consideration, as in *to watch*, or *talk over, make merry over*.

c **897** K. ÆLFRED *Gregory's Past. C.* l. 391 Mid hu micelre ȝiefe ofer him wacað se Scippend & se Stihtere ealra ȝesceafta. *Ibid.* lii. 411 Mara ȝefea wyrð on heofonum ..ðonne ofer niȝon & hundniȝontiȝ ryhtwisra. *a* **900** tr. *Bæda's Hist.* I. vii. (1890) 40 þæt he ofer him deadum ȝefeȝe. *c* **1000** *Ags. Gosp.* Luke xix. 41 He weop ofer hiȝ. *c* **1000** ÆLFRIC *Hom.* I. 36 þæt he symle wacol sy ofer Godes eowode. *c* **1200** *Trin. Coll. Hom.* 31 þe herdes..wakeden ouer here oref. **1483** CAXTON *G. de la Tour* F v b, That none may haue enuye ouer hym. **1579** FULKE *Refut. Rastel* 735 The Lords praier..was not said ouer the sacrament. **1592** SHAKS. *Rom. & Jul.* III. v. 175 Vtter your grauitie ore a Gossips bowles. **1593** —— *Lucr.* 421 As the grim lion fawneth o'er his prey. **1600** —— *A.Y.L.* I. ii. 139 The poore old man..making such pittiful dole ouer them. **1657–83** EVELYN *Hist. Relig.* (1850) I. 137 The Almighty's especial vigilance is over the greater societies of men,..yea, and over whole nature. **1711** STEELE *Spect.* No. 52 ¶6 When you did me the Honour to be so merry over my Paper. **1791** *Gentl. Mag.* 20/2 Those hours..which others consume..over the bottle. **1811** LADY GRANVILLE *Lett.* (1894) I. 29 If you had seen us..sitting over the fire with Mr. Hughes. **1847** HELPS *Friends in C.* (1851) I. 3 Over this he had wasted two days. **1865** MRS. CARLYLE *Lett.* III. 286 We sit down to breakfast, and talk over it till eleven. **1874** FARRAR *Christ* I. 408 Let us pause a moment longer over this wonderful narrative. **1875** JOWETT *Plato* III. 389 Apt to yawn and go to sleep over any intellectual toil.

†**c.** With reference to, regarding, concerning, about (a subject of discourse, thought, feeling, etc.).

c **1000** ÆLFRIC *Gen.* xvii. 20 Ofer Ysmahel eacswilce ic ȝehirde þe. *c* **1340** HAMPOLE *Prose Tr.* 36 Thow may.. thynke ouer thi synnes before donne. **1535** COVERDALE *Lev.* xi. 46 This is the lawe ouer yᵉ beestes and foules. —— *1 Chron.* xx. 2 He sent messaungers to comforte him ouer his father.

II. In sense *on, upon.*

5. On the upper or outer surface of; upon: sometimes implying the notion of supported or resting upon, sometimes (now more frequently) that of covering the surface.

In *Her.* said of a charge placed upon others so as partly to cover them (distinguished from *above* = on a higher part of the shield). Usually ***over all***.

c **880** *Laws of Ælfred* c. 36 (Schmid) ðif mon hafað spere ofer eaxle. *c* **950** *Lindisf. Gosp.* Matt. xxi. 5 Sittende ofer [*Rushw.* on, *Ags. G.* uppan] asal. **971** *Blickl. Hom.* 71 Sittende ofor eoselan folan. *Ibid.* 79 Her ne bið forlæten stan ofor stan. *c* **1435** *Torr. Portugal* 2100 Ffader, than have thou this ryng, I ffound it over this swete thing. **1592** SHAKS. *Ven. & Ad.* 31 Over one arm the lusty coursers rein. **1766** PORNY *Heraldry* v. (1787) 156 The twelfth is Azure, a Chief Gules over-all a Lion rampant double queued Or. **1870** TROLLOPE *Phineas Finn* 39 Sitting with his hat low down over his eyes.

6. a. To a position on the surface or top of, or so as to cover; upon (with verbs of motion).

c **897** K. ÆLFRED *Gregory's Past. C.* xlix. 383 Ðæt mon his sweord doo ofer his hype. *a* **900** tr. *Bæda's Hist.* II. ii. (1890) 100 Nimað ȝe min ȝeoc ofer eow. **971** *Blickl. Hom.* 93 þonne hie cweþaþ to þæm dunum:..Feallaþ ofor us. *c* **1000** *Ags. Gosp.* Matt. xi. 24 Se hys hus ofer stan ȝetimbrode. *c* **1470** HENRY *Wallace* I. 241 A soudly courche our hed and nek leit fall. **1560** DAUS tr. *Sleidane's Comm.* 353 They had all put over their harnesse white shirtes. **1652** C. B. STAPYLTON *Herodian* XIV. 114 This hit the Alexandrians o're the Thumbs. **1704** CIBBER *Careless Husb.* v. ii, Throw my Night-Gown over me. **1861** *Temple Bar Mag.* I. 307 Let us draw a veil over this dismal spectacle.

b. *fig.* Upon, down upon, as an influence.

a **900** tr. *Bæda's Hist.* I. xi. [xiv.] 50 ðestihtad wæs þæt yfell wræc come ofer ða wiþcorenan. *Ibid.* IV. xxv[i]. 354 On ðinum daȝum ðis wite ofer ðas burȝ ne cymeð. *c* **1000** ÆLFRIC *Hom.* I. 182 Ða tacna þe he worhte ofer ða untruman men. *c* **1175** *Lamb. Hom.* 93 Ðe halie gast com ofer þa apostlas mid furene tungen. **1588** SHAKS. *L.L.L.* v. ii. 278 Lord Longauill said I came ore his hart. **1834** MACKAY *Tubal Cain* iii, But a sudden change came o'er his heart.

†**c.** Up to the top of, up to. (OE.)

c **897** K. ÆLFRED *Gregory's Past. C.* xiv. 80 Asteȝ ofer heanne munt. *c* **1000** ÆLFRIC *Gram.* xlvii. (Z.) 274 Ofer healice dune astih ðu.

7. a. (Position) on all parts of the surface of; everywhere on; here and there upon. Often strengthened by *all*, now esp. ***all over***. (See also ALL OVER *advb. phr.* 1 c).

c **893** K. ÆLFRED *Oros.* II. vi. §3 Ofer eall Romana rice seo eorþe wæs cwaciende & berstende. *Ibid.* VI. vii, þa wearð eft sibb ofer ealne Romana anwald. *c* **1175** *Lamb. Hom.* 3 þa wes hit cuð ouer al þe burh. *c* **1430** *Syr Tryam.* 349 Ovyr alle the wode they hur soght, But..fonde hur noght. **1456** SIR G. HAYE *Law Arms* (S.T.S.) 2 [He] is lufit and redoubtit our all the warld. **1624** CAPT. SMITH *Virginia* III. 58 They..sell it all ouer the country. **1722** DE FOE *Plague* (Rtldg.) 10 The People..began to be allarm'd all over the Town. **1796** JANE AUSTEN *Pride & Prej.* II. xxv, The expression of heartfelt delight, diffused over his face. **1841** ELPHINSTONE *Hist. Ind.* I. 13 Rice is more or less raised all over India. **1895** *Scot. Antiq.* X. 79 Around the firesides of the cottages, which were studded over the moor.

b. (Motion) from place to place on the surface of; to and fro upon; all about; throughout. Often ***all over***.

a **900** tr. *Bæda's Hist.* II. xii. (1890) 128 Moniȝra ȝeara tida ofer ealle Breotone ic flyma wæs. *c* **1000** ÆLFRIC *Exod.* viii. 5 Alæd upp þa froxas ofer eall Egipta land. **1568** GRAFTON *Chron.* I. 156 In the Wynter he used to ryde over the lande. **1600** SHAKS. *A.Y.L.* I. iii. 134 Heele goe along ore the wide world with me. **1735** SOMERVILLE *Chase* III. 110 The hunter crew wide straggling o'er the plain! **1843** RUSKIN *Mod. Paint.* I. II. ii. §6. 406 We may range over Europe, from shore to shore. *a* **1904** *Mod.* They travel all over the country.

c. Through every part of, all through. (Sometimes including the notion of examination or consideration: cf. 4.)

1647–8 COTTERELL *Davila's Hist. Fr.* (1678) 29 They might purposely be carefully looked over. **1773** JOHNSON *Lett.* Wks. 1825 I. 321 A wild notion, which extends over marriage more than over any other transaction. **1830** MOORE *Mem.* (1854) VI. 108 Took Miss Macdonald to see over new Athenæum. **1892** MRS. OLIPHANT *Marr. of Elinor* III. xxxiv. 20 She would have liked to go over all his notes about his case.

d. In the above senses (esp. a and b) often placed after its object, esp. when this is qualified by *all* or the like. (Cf. *through.*)

a **1400–50** *Alexander* 18 þat aȝte euyn as his awyn all the werd ouire. *c* **1590** MARLOWE *Faust.* iv. 53, I should be called kill-devil all the parish over. **1657** SPARROW *Bk. Com. Prayer* (1661) 164 *Christ is risen*, the usual Morning salutation this day, all the Church over. **1675** *Lond. Gaz.* No. 1039/3 This inundation is almost general Holland over. **1795** BURNS *For a' That* v, That man to man, the warld o'er, Shall brothers be for a' that. **1832** HT. MARTINEAU *Life in Wilds* ii. 23 A test which holds good all the world over. **1916** T. MACDONAGH *Lit. in Ireland* 120 The characteristic qualities of the ancient Irish lyrics are those of good lyric poetry the world over. **1930** *Publishers' Weekly* 23 Aug. 675/2 There are many more like me, the country over, really anxious to feed their fanaticism. **1971** *Guardian* 14 Jan. 11/8 Policemen love one another the world over.

For the corresponding use in reference to time, 'as in all the year over', in which *over* may be explained adverbially, see 17 b. Even in the local use, in 'all the world over' and the like, it is difficult to separate the preposition from the adverb: cf. 'you may search London over (= London from end to end) before you find another like it'.

e. *Math.* (Defined or expressed) in terms of (the elements of); *esp.* having coefficients or co-ordinates in, or having elements with coefficients or co-ordinates in.

1932 *Trans. Amer. Math. Soc.* XXXIV. 171 (*heading*) Theory of cyclic algebras over an algebraic number field. **1938** A. A. ALBERT *Mod. Higher Algebra* ii. 40 The most interesting and important linear sets for our purposes are those of finite order n over a field $\mathcal{F}$... Their elements may be thought of as points in an n-dimensional space with coordinates in $\mathcal{F}$. **1965** J. J. ROTMAN *Theory of Groups* vi. 103 A number $\alpha \epsilon C$ is algebraic over F in case $F(\alpha)$ is a finite-dimensional vector space over F (otherwise α is transcendental over F). **1972** A. G. HOWSON *Handbk. Terms Algebra & Analysis* xi. 55 The polynomials form a subring ..called the ring of polynomials over K.

III. Above in authority, degree, amount, etc.

8. Above in authority, rule, or power; with sbs., as ***king, lord over; jurisdiction, rule, triumph, victory over***; adjs., ***victorious over***; vbs., ***to reign, rule, triumph, appoint*** or ***set*** any one ***over***.

c **893** K. ÆLFRED *Oros.* I. ii. §3 Hio ȝesette ofer eall hyre rice þæt nan forbyrd nære [etc.]. *Ibid.* III. i. §5 For þæm lytlan siȝe þe hie þa ofer hie hæfdon. *a* **900** tr. *Bæda's Hist.* II. v. (1890) 108 Se hæfde rice ofer ealle Breotone. *Ibid.* v. xi. [x.] 416 þætte hio onsende to ðæm aldormen þe ofer hine wæs. *a* **900** *Ags. Ps.* (Th.) xvii. 48 þa hælo þæs cynges ðe ðu ȝesettest ofer folcum. **971** *Blickl. Hom.* 35 Gif he nære soþ God ofer ealle ȝesceafte. *c* **1000** *Ags. Gosp.* Luke xix. 19 Beo þu ofer fif ceastra. *c* **1200** ORMIN 590 Alls iff itt wære laferrdflocc Offr alle þoþre flockess. *c* **1320** *Cast. Love* 1110 Nou ouer þe nabbe I no mihte. **1422** tr. *Secreta Secret., Priv. Priv.* 210 Show thy Victori ouer hym. **1558** KNOX *First Blast* (Arb.) 37, I will not, that a woman haue authoritie, charge or power ouer man. **1611** BIBLE *Ps.* xii. 4 Who is Lord ouer vs? **1678** WANLEY *Wond. Lit. World* v. ii. §83. 472/2 Over this Emperour the Christians were Victorious in ..the Battel of Lepanto. **1709** STEELE & ADDISON *Tatler* No. 147 ¶3 Venus, the Deity who presides over Love. **1796** JANE AUSTEN *Pride & Prej.* I. xxiv, Oh that my dear Mother had more command over herself. **1849** MACAULAY *Hist. Eng.* i. I. 2 Ireland, cursed by the domination of race over race, and of religion over religion. **1896** *Law Times Rep.* LXXIII. 690/1 This court has no jurisdiction over the property in America.

9. a. Above or beyond in degree, quality, or action; in preference to; more than.

c **893** K. ÆLFRED *Oros.* I. iv. §1 Ioseph, se þe ȝingst wæs ..& eac gleawra ofer hi ealle. *c* **897** —— *Gregory's Past. C.* xviii. 132 Ðæt gold þe is swæ deorwierðe ofer eal oðer ondweorc. *a* **900** —— *Solil.* i. (1902) 11 þe anne ic lufiȝe ofer ealle oðre þing. *Ibid.* 43 Hine ic lufiȝe ofer eallum oðrum þing. **971** *Blickl. Hom.* 11 Lufian we urne Drihten..ofer ealle oþru þing. *Ibid.* 13 Heo wæs seo eadȝeste ofer eall wifa cynn. *a* **1000** *Ps.* I. (Cotton) 75 (Gr.) Ofer snawe self scinende. *c* **1175** *Lamb. Hom.* 39 þet þu luuie þine drihten ofer þin wif, and ofer child, and ofer alle eorðliche þing. *a* **1300** *E.E. Psalter* cxviii. 103 Over hony to mi mouth ere þai. **1340** *Ayenb.* 170 He ne þoleþ þet no vyend ous uondy ouer oure miȝte. *c* **1375** *Sc. Leg. Saints* xvi. (*Magdalena*) 472 þane wes I fule or þe lafe. **1388** Wyclif *2 Cor.* i. 8 For ouer maner we weren greued ouer myȝt [*supra virtutem*]. **1398** Trevisa *Barth. De P.R.* vii. lv. (1495) 269 Ouer all thynge the dyete shal be temperate. **1526** *Pilgr. Perf.* (W. de W. 1531) 8 b, He neuer suffreth man or woman to be tempted, ouer that they may resyste. **1590** Shaks. *Mids. N.* i. i. 226 How happy some ore othersome can be? **1650** Trapp *Comm. Deut.* xvi. 10 So good-cheap is Gods service to us, over what it was to them. **1749** Collins *Ode Superst. Highlands* 155 But, Oh! o'er all, forget not Kilda's race. **1796** Jane Austen *Pride & Prej.* II. xxiv, I cannot help giving him the preference even over Wickham. **1802** Jefferson *Autobiog. & Writ.* (Ford's ed.) VIII. 133 Virginia is greatly over her due proportion of appointments in the general government. **1855** Macaulay *Hist. Eng.* xiv. III. 413 The preference given to him over English captains.

†**b.** *Conjunctively* (by ellipsis). Above or beyond what.... *Obs.*

1450 *Paston Lett.* I. 127 The world is changed gretely over it was. **1627** Sanderson *Serm.* (1681) I. 274 Natural conscience.. will boggle now and then at a very small matter in comparison over it will do at some other times. **1644** Milton *Areop.* (Arb.) 55 What advantage is it to be a man over it is to be a boy at school?

†**10. a.** In addition to, further than; besides, beyond. ***over this, overthat***, moreover, = L. *præterea*.

c **880** *Laws of Ælfred* Introd. c. 32 (Schmid) Se þe godgeldum onsæcge ofer God anne, swelte se deaðe. *c* **888** K. Ælfred *Boeth.* xxiii. (MS. B), Ðu ne wilnast nanes oðres þinges ofer þa. *c* **1000** *Ags. Gosp.* Mark vii. 12 And ofer þæt ȝe ne lætað hine ænig þing don his fæder oððe meder. *a* **1350** *Cursor M.* 311 (Gött.) And ouyr þat him seluen wroght All thinges quen þat þai war noght. *c* **1380** Wyclif *Sel. Wks.* III. 356 It were for to wite over þis, how popis ȝyven þes beneficis. **1413** *Pilgr. Sowle* iv. viii. (Caxton 1483) 61 Nought only they owen this restitucion but also they owen ouer this for to payen hym amendys. **1509** in Willis & Clark *Cambridge* (1886) I. 477 And ouerthat the saide Provost and scolers covenaunteth and bindeth theym and their successours. **1577–87** Holinshed *Chron.* II. 43/2 Over his exact knowledge in the common lawes, he was a good orator. **1592** West *1st Pt. Symbol.* § 103 C, And ouer this the said H. M. for him.. doth couenant.. that he [etc.]. **1760–72** H. Brooke *Fool of Qual.* (1809) II. 114 [He] has plunged you a thousand pounds in debt, over the large sums that we carried with us.

b. So †***over and besides***, †***over and beyond***. (See also over and above A. 3.)

c **1449** Pecock *Repr.* 280 Ouer and biȝonde alle þe xlviij. citees wiþ her seid suburbis. *Ibid.* 281. **1533** Cranmer *Let.* in *Misc. Writ.* (Parker Soc.) II. 260 Over and besides the xvi[li] with iiii[li] more. **1607** R. C[arew] tr. *Estienne's World of Wonders* 44 Ouer and besides those which they kept at home. **1659** H. L'Estrange *Alliance Div. Off.* 25 Over and besides the Canonical Scriptures.

11. In excess of, above, more than (a stated amount or number).

[*c* **1330** *Arth. & Merl.* 6648 To a castel.. Thennes ouer thre mile.] **1405** in *Roy. & Hist. Lett. Hen. IV* (Rolls) I. 158, I have nought ylafte with me over two men. **1519** Sir T. Boleyn in Ellis *Orig. Lett.* Ser. i. I. 147 His realme was to hym six millions yerely, and over that, in value. **1640** Fuller *Joseph's Coat* (1867) 179 Had Naaman washed.. under or over seven times, would so small a matter have broken any squares? **1660** Sharrock *Vegetables* 18 By that means you shall gain a year in the growing, over that you should doe if you sowed it the next spring. **1858** Kingsley *Prose Idylls* 92 Besides several [fishes] over a pound [in weight]. **1868** M. Arnold *Sch. & Univ. Cont.* 99 His diploma.. has cost him a little over £50. **1896** *Law Times Rep.* LXXIII. 615/1 A distance of over 700 yards.

IV. Across (above, or on a surface).

12. a. Indicating motion that passes above (something) on the way to the other side. Sometimes expressing only the latter part of this, as in *falling* or *jumping over a precipice*, i.e. over the edge or brim and down.

c **888** K. Ælfred *Boeth.* xxxvi. § 3 (MS. B) þæt ic mæg fliogan ofer þone hean hrof þæs heofones. *c* **897** —— *Gregory's Past. C.* xiii. 76 Ðylæs he ofer ðone ðerscold.. stæppe. *a* **900** *Ags. Ps.* (Th.) xvii. 28 Ic utgang ofer minre burȝe weall. *c* **1205** Lay. 9420 Ouer þene wal heo clumben. **1399** Langl. *Rich. Redeles* iv. 82 þey had be þrowe ouere þe borde backewarde ichonne. **1567** *Ps.* lxxix. in *Gude & Godlie B.* (S.T.S.) 118 Watter, [that] fast rinnis ouer ane lin. **1568** Grafton *Chron.* I. 152 He lept ouer the table and plucked that theefe by the heare of the head to the ground. **1621** Sanderson *Serm.* I. 188 Like an unruly colt, that will over hedge and ditch. **1794** *Rigging & Seamanship* 247* *By the Board.* Over the ship's side. **1824** Scott *Redgauntlet* Let. v, Our guest made a motion with his glass, so as to pass it over the water-decanter.., and added, 'Over the water'. **1827–35** Willis *Lord Ivon & Dau.* 133 A winter, and a spring, Went over me. **1843** *Fraser's Mag.* XXVIII. 230 The sun is peering over the roofs. **1852** Dickens *Bleak Ho.* xviii, She turned.. and spoke to him over her shoulder again. **1896** *N. & Q.* 8th Ser. IX. 160/1 The room looking over Nightingale Lane.

b. ***over the wicket***: see bowl *v.*[1] 4 b.

13. From side to side of a surface or space; across, to the other side of (a sea, river, boundary, etc.); from end to end of (a line), along; by means of (a telephone, radio communication, or the like); = on *prep.* 1 d.

c **893** K. Ælfred *Oros.* ii. iv. § 10 þa Cirus for ofer þæt londȝemære, ofer þa ea þe hatte Araxis. **898** *O.E. Chron.* an. 896 (Parker MS.) þa forleton hie hie, and eodon ofer land. *c* **1000** *Ags. Gosp.* Mark v. 1 Ða comen hi ofer þære sæs muðan on þæt rice. **1154** *O.E. Chron.* an. 1135 (Laud MS.) On þis ȝeare for se king Henri ouer sæ. *c* **1375** *Cursor M.* 6957 (Fairf.) Quen [Iosue] passed ouere þe flume iordan. *c* **1400** Maundev. (Roxb.) viii. 32 Men gase ower a grete valay till anoþer grete mount. *c* **1440** *Promp. Parv.* 372/2 Ovyr, *ultra, trans.* **1697** Dryden *Virg. Georg.* iii. 315 Thus o'er th' Elean Plains, thy well-breath'd Horse Impels the flying Carr. **1775** S. J. Pratt *Liberal Opin.* cxxix. (1783) IV. 167 Gim me my daughter, I say, or I'll send you over the herring-pond, take my word for 't. **1894** *Times* (weekly ed.) 9 Feb. 113/2 A free pass over this company's lines of railways. **1899** *Pall Mall Mag.* Mar. 326 A report has come over the wire that [etc.]. **1928** Blunden *Overtones of War* iv. 43 Persons who, speaking over the field telephones, gave away any information at all.. would be court-martialled. **1929** *Radio Times* 8 Nov. 387 'Pickwick', and other such novels, should be read serially over the microphone. *Ibid.*, Over the wireless a reading can be listened to without.. irrelevant disturbances. **1946** *Ibid.* 8 Feb. 3/3 His boys and girls who had been heard over All-India Radio. **1966** *Listener* 17 Nov. 725/1 He is asking you over the telephone, so you cannot point or use gestures. **1969** *N.Y. Rev. Books* 2 Jan. 5/1 In his Security Gap speech over CBS on October 25, Nixon said one of his major aims would be to 'correct its (the Pentagon's) over-centralization'.

†**14.** *fig.* In transgression or violation of; in contravention of, contrary to. *Obs.*

c **893** K. Ælfred *Oros.* vi. xxxv. § 2 On þæm daȝum ȝecuron Brettanie Maximianus hem to casere ofer his willan. *a* **900** tr. *Bæda's Hist.* ii. xvi. [xx.] (1890) 148 Se æfter fæce from him unrihtlice ofsleȝen wæs ofer aðas and treowe. **971** *Blickl. Hom.* 91 þa þing þe we ær ofor his bebod ȝedydon. **10..** *O.E. Chron.* an. 1015 Ðenam þæt wif ofer þes cynges willan. *c* **1380** Wyclif *Sel. Wks.* III. 392 þei bynden hom ouver þo comaundementis of God. **1502** *Ord. Crysten Men* (1506) ii. i. 86 We may offende our neyghbour in desyryng his goodes ouer reason & ayenst Iustice.

15. a. On the other side of; across (of position).

c **893** K. Ælfred *Oros.* i. i. § 12 Be norþam him ofer þa westenne is Cwenland. *Ibid.* § 23 Se ðridda [lið] norðwest.. onȝean Scotland ofer ðone sæs earm. *a* **900** tr. *Bæda's Hist.* i. xi. [xiv.] (1890) 50 þæt hi Seaxna þeode ofer þam sælicum dælum him on fultum ȝecyȝdon. *c* **1440** *York Myst.* xxxiv. 65, I haue bene garre make þis crosse,.. Of þat laye ouere þe lake. ? *a* **1500** *Peblis to the Play* v, When they were ower the wald. **1517** Torkington *Pilgr.* (1884) 64 Ovyr the watyr on the other syd,.. ys the yle of Cecyll. **1769** Gray in *Corr. w. Nicholls* (1843) 92, I have a bed over the way offered me at three half-crowns a night. **1820** Keats *St. Agnes* xxxix, For o'er the southern moors I have a home for thee. **1855** Macaulay *Hist. Eng.* xxi. (1871) II. 556 The less warlike members of the [Jacobite] party [in 1696] could at least take off bumpers to the King over the water. **1898** *Tit-Bits* 3 Sept. 446/3 At a wedding over the herring-pond. *a* **1904** *Mod.* Our neighbours over the way.

b. Having recovered from (an illness, disease, or the like). Cf. get *v.* 46 b.

1929 'S.N.D.' *Sir W. Howard, Visct. Stafford* iii. 29 He was in England, just over an illness, and straitened for lack of money in the autumn of 1646. **1942** D. Powell *Time to be Born* (1943) vi. 139 You're over it, aren't you, Vicky? That's wonderful. **1964** L. Deighton *Funeral in Berlin* xviii. 109 Finally there is not being in love and liking that —you are over it then—cured. **1975** J. Grady *Shadow of Condor* (1976) i. 18 My wife just got over the flu.. she's over it now. **1977** P. Smalley *Trove* ii. 78 He had guessed about the alcoholism as soon as Daley said he had been in hospital... He probably was over it, but you never knew for sure.

V. Of time.

16. Beyond in time; after. *Obs.* exc. *dial.*

a **900** *O.E. Chron.* an. 878 Her hiene bestæl se here on midne winter ofer tuelftan niht to Cippanhamme. *a* **900** tr. *Bæda's Hist.* v. vi. (1890) 402 Ðæt is an tid ofer midne dæȝ. **971** *Blickl. Hom.* 93 þy feorþan dæȝe ofor undern. *c* **1000** Ælfric *Gen.* iii. 8 He eode on neorxena wange ofer middæȝ. **1101–23** *O.E. Chron.* an. 1101 And se eorl syððan oððet ofer Sce. Michaeles mæsse her on lande wunode. **13..** *Coer de L.* 5949 Ovyr this ilke dayes thre Myself schal thy bane be. *a* **1350** *Cursor M.* 15944 (Gött.) Bi þis was time of night passid ouer midnight and mare. *c* **1380** Wyclif *Wks.* (1880) 57 ȝif þe salt be fonnyd it is not worthi ower þis. *c* **1400** *Destr. Troy* 265 þat no tarying shuld tyde ouer a tyme set. **1535** Coverdale *2 Chron.* x. 5 Come to me agayne ouer thre dayes. *a* **1904** *Mod.* (Mid-Essex groom to master) 'Sir, we shall want some hay over a few days.'

17. a. During, all through. (In mod. use transf. from space.)

855 *O.E. Chron.*, Her hæþne men ærest on Sceapiȝe ofer winter sætun. *c* **893** K. Ælfred *Oros.* iv. x. § 10 Siþþan he hi sloȝ ofer ealne þone dæȝ fleonde. *c* **1000** *Sax. Leechd.* III. 270 þa seofon steorran þe.. ofer ealne winter scinað.. Ofer ealne sumor hi ȝað on nihtlicre tide under þissere eorðan. *c* **1000** *Ags. Treat. Astron.* in Wright *Treat. Science* 16 He went adune and hwilon up ofer dæȝ and ofer niht. **1886** *Act 49 & 50 Vict.* c. 44 § 13 The repayment.. should be spread over a series of years. **1895** *Law Times Rep.* LXXII. 817/1 The case is governed by a line of authorities extending over a century.

b. The OE. use, in quot. 893, is sometimes expressed in ME. and mod.Eng. by *over* following the time phrase; as in *all the year over, the whole day over*. Cf. the corresponding local use in sense 7 d. In the temporal use, *over*, being appended to a phrase which is itself an adverbial adjunct, may with equal propriety be viewed as an advb.: cf. 'he works in the field all day', with 'he sings at his work all day over', i.e. all day from beginning to end.

c **1400** Maundev. (Roxb.) xv. 71 He gert his men wake all þe nyght ouer [*MS. Cott. Titus* C. xvi, wake all nyghte]. *c* **1475** *Rauf Coilȝear* 330 Ane thousand, and ma, of fensabill men War wanderand all the nicht ouir. *Mod.* I remained the whole day over near the spot. Some persons bathe in the Serpentine daily all the year over.

†**18.** During or in course of the (eve or night) preceding; on the preceding (evening or night). *Obs.* except in overnight.

1399 Langl. *Rich. Redeles* iv. 55 Some had ysoupid with Symond ouere euen. *c* **1420** *Liber Cocorum* (1862) 51 Fyrst sly þy capon over þo nyȝght, Plump hym in water wher he is dyȝt. *c* **1430** *Two Cookery-bks.* 20 Take fowre pounde of Almaundys, & ley in Water ouer eue, an blanche hem. *c* **1500** *Lichfield Gild Ord.* (E.E.T.S.) 15 The days next folloyng that they haue monyshion by the bell-man ouer Evyn. **1528** Tindale *Obed. Chr. Man* Wks. (Parker Soc.) I. 182 Other-wise are we disposed.. over even, and otherwise in the morning: yea, sometimes altered six times in an hour.

19. Till the end of; for a period that includes.

1806–7 J. Beresford *Miseries Hum. Life* (1826) vii. lxii, To stay over the farce after a play. **1817** *Parl. Deb.* 213 It was agreed that the House should adjourn over to-morrow, it being Her Majesty's Birthday. **1845** E. Noel *Richter's Flower Pieces* 79 If we only live over to-day. **1858** Mrs. Carlyle *Lett.* II. 346 In case you should stay over Wednesday.

†**over, ovre**, *sb.*[1] *Obs.* [Com. W. Ger.: OE. *ofer* = OFris. *overa, overe* (mod. Fris. *over*, EFris. *över, öfer*), MLG. *over*, MDu., Du. *oever*, MHG. *uover*, Ger. *ufer*; ulterior relations obscure: see Kluge.] A border or margin; *spec.* of the sea or a river: the shore, the bank.

Beowulf (Z.) 1371 Ær he feorh seleð aldor on ofre. *c* **1000** Ælfric *Gen.* xli. 3 And hi [seofon oxan] eodon be ðære ea ofrun. *c* **1000** *Sax. Leechd.* II. 108 Smire mid þa ofras þær hit readiȝe. *c* **1205** Lay. 8584 He ferde ut of Doure bi þe sæ oure [*c* **1275** ofre]. *c* **1300** *Havelok* 321 And dede leden hire to doure, þat standeth on þe seis oure. *c* **1330** R. Brunne *Chron. Wace* (Rolls) 4336 Cassibola[n] was redy at Douere & renged his men by þe ouere.

'**over**, *sb.*[2] [Absolute use of over *adv.*]

1. (*nonce-use* f. over *adv.* 11.) That which is excessive; an excess, extreme.

a **1584** Montgomerie *Cherrie & Slae* 435 All ouirs are repuit to be vyce; Ore hich, ore law, ore rasch, ore nyce [etc.]. *a* **1904** *Mod. Sc.* A' owres is ill (i.e. All excesses are evil).

2. a. An amount in excess, or remaining over; an extra.

1882 *Pall Mall G.* 10 Oct. 3 It does not appear in the accounts, nor does 'overs'. **1886** *Rep. of Sec. of Treasury* (U.S.) 180 (Cent.) In counting the remittances of banknotes received for redemption during the year, there was found $25,528 in overs, being amounts in excess of the amounts claimed, and $8,246 in shorts, being amounts less than the amounts claimed.

b. *pl. Printing.* Copies printed in excess of the number ordered, to allow for wastage.

1888 C. T. Jacobi *Printers' Vocab.* 92 *Overs*, the 'plus' copies beyond a certain number. **1901** D. Cockerell *Bookbinding* i. ii. 36 The printers usually keep a number of 'overs' in order to make good such imperfections. **1946** J. A. Eisler in H. Whetton *Pract. Printing & Binding* xxvii. 328/2 Finding the net amount of paper entailed in the production of a job (exclusive of overs) should present few difficulties to the man familiar with ordinary paper usage. **1961** T. Landau *Encycl. Librarianship* (ed. 2) 269/2 Overs. The number of sound copies over after the printing of the net number of copies ordered.

3. An act of going over or across something; a leap over a fence, etc. in hunting.

1883 *Pall Mall G.* 30 July 5/1 The downfall of the front rank at an over.

4. *Cricket.* (f. over *adv.* 5 c.) The number of balls (four, five, or six) bowled from either end of the wicket before a change is made to the other end; the portion of the game comprising a single turn of bowling from one end. Since 1900, an 'over' has normally consisted of 6 balls, except in Australia, and recently occas. elsewhere, where it is 8. Also *attrib.* Cf. maiden *a.* 4 b

1833 *New Sporting Mag.* V. 325 The Anglesea are in the field, And Floyer bowls the over. **1850** 'Bat' *Crick. Man.* 48 Some clubs make it a rule to mark the number of 'overs' that each bowler gives, at the foot of the scoring papers. **1859** *All Year Round* No. 13. 305 He caught two of the town off my first 'over'. **1899** *Westm. Gaz.* 18 Nov. 2/3 The first alteration proposed—the substitution of six balls for five in an over. **1921** Ld. Harris *Few Short Runs* xi. 284 Under such circumstances how we welcome the umpire's 'Last over, gentlemen.' **1955** *Times* 9 May 15/1 When one says that only one hook was aimed at Tayfield in 37 overs the reader will get some idea of the fullness of his length. Before each over he stands over his stumps and performs a kind of ritual. **1960** E. W. Swanton *W. Indies Revisited* 282 The over-rate during the First Test was higher than in any subsequent one. **1974** B. Johnston *It's been a lot of Fun* xvi. 116 'Stick to the play, Percy, and keep that sort of chat for between the overs,' said the producer. **1977** *Times* 18 Jan. 9/8 The fact that the ball had to be replaced three times,.. and that the sightscreens are not easily shifted, all helped to bring down the Indian over rate.. to just under 11 to the hour.

5. *Mil.* (chiefly *pl.*). A bullet, shell, or other missile that passes beyond its target. *colloq.*

1915 W. H. L. Watson *Adventures Despatch Rider* v. 66 He believes the Uhlans were North Irish Horse and the bullets 'overs'. **1928** Blunden *Undertones of War* iv. 43 A familiar place far enough from the Brickstack which we held to receive the 'overs'. **1944** A. Jacob *Traveller's War* 238 Men on the fringe of the battle area.. receive the 'overs' and keep ducking flat as they hear the hissing approach of tank ammo, that has missed its mark. **1969** I. Kemp *Brit. G.I. in Vietnam* vi. 140, I.. laid them behind a tree..; they should be moderately safe there from 'overs'.

over ('əʊvə(r)), *a.* Forms: α. 1 ufera, -e, 2–3 ufere, 3 vuere (= uvere) (*mod. dial.* uvver). β. 3–5 ouere, 4–7 ouer, 5– over. [OE. had *ufer(r)a, -e, yfer(r)a, -e* adj., the former of which survived in early ME. *ufere, uvere* (written *vuere, uuere*), for which in writing *over(e* was substituted bef. 1300. (Cf. OHG. *obaro*, MHG. *obere*, Ger. *ober*, which represents an OTeut. **ubaro-*, while the OE. forms repr. the types **ubarōzo-*, **ubirōzo-*.)

Dialectally, the form *uvver* ('ʌvə(r)) is still widely current for the adjective (see E.D.D.); so that the ME. spelling *over(e* (as in the later Layamon text for the earlier *uvere*) may originally have been only graphical, *ov* (*ou*) for *uv* (*uu*, *vu*), as in *above*, *dove*, *love*, etc. But in ME. the adj. fell together in use with OVER- *adv.* in comb., from which indeed it cannot always be separated, many important examples being written either way; thus, the OE. *ufera lippa*, in mod. dial. *uvverlip*, occurs in Chaucer MSS. as *over(e lippe* and *overlippe*. This would naturally tend to level the pronunciation of *over* from *ufera* with that of *over-* from OE. *ofer-*, a result prob. completed in Standard Eng. during the ME. period. And this identification led further to the adjectival use of the adverbial prefix in other senses: e.g. 3, 4.

Although originally itself a comparative form, *over* having no positive of its own has been in some respects treated as positive, and has been compared with OVERER, OVEREST (so OHG. *obarôro*, *obarôst*, mod.Ger. *oberer*, *oberst*), and OVERMORE, OVERMOST, only the last of which is now in (occasional) use. See these.]

1. The upper, the higher in position.

Only attrib., prec. by *the* or an equiv., and used of one of two things, the other being *the nether*, *lower*, or *under*. Now obs. or dial. exc. as preserved in comb., and in place-names of villages, farms, fields, etc.

α. *c* **897** K. ÆLFRED *Gregory's Past. C.* iii. 32 Ðone wisdom ðara uferrena gasta. *a* **900** tr. *Bæda's Hist.* v. ii, On ðam uferan dæle ðæs heafdes. *a* **1225** *Ancr. R.* 332 Þe two grindstones: þe neðere þet lið stille. þe vuere ston bitocneð hope. *c* **1275** *XI Pains of Hell* 98 in *O.E. Misc.* 150 Summe ..stondeþ vp to heore kneon And summe to heore myd-þeyh And summe to heore vuere breyh. **1788** [see OVERLIP]. **1879** MISS JACKSON *Shropsh. Word-bk.* s.v., 'Who lives i' the uvver 'ouse now?'

β. *a* **1300** *Sat. People Kildare* iv. in *E.E.P.* (1862) 153 Hit is at þe ouir end crokid as a gaffe. *a* **1300** *Cursor M.* 539-40 Þe ouer fir gis man his sight, þat ouer air of hering might. **1387** TREVISA *Higden* (Rolls) I. 125 Þe ouer Galilea and þe neþer Galilea. **1398** —— *Barth. De P.R.* IV. vii. (1495) 90 In the nether partes of the body blode is blacker than in the ouer partes. *c* **1450** *Bk. Curtasye* 36 in *Babees Bk.* 300 Pare þy brede and kerue in two, Tho ouer crust þo nether fro. **15..** *Sir A. Barton* xxv. in *Surtees Misc.* (1888) 71 He shoott throughe his over decke. **1526** R. WHYTFORD *Martiloge* (1893) 161 Theyr ouer tethe knocked out. **1551** ROBINSON tr. *More's Utop.* II. v. (1895) 163 The ouer ende of the halle. **1596** DALRYMPLE tr. *Leslie's Hist. Scot.* I. 14 In vuir Clydisdale and in nethir Clidisdale. **1610** BARROUGH *Meth. Physick* I. xxxi. (1639) 51 With your left hand lift up the over eyelid. **1715** PENNECUIK *Descr. Tweeddale*, etc. 13 Here stands.. Rommano Grange, Over and Nether.

b. Placed so as, or serving, to cover something else; upper, outer.

Now usually written in comb., as *over-garment*, *overcoat*; see OVER- 8 c and the Main words.

c **1000** *Sax. Leechd.* II. 224 þæt uferre hrif. *c* **1050** *Suppl. Ælfric's Voc.* in Wr.-Wülcker 188/15 *Ependeton*, cop, *uel* hoppada, *uel* ufrescrud. *c* **1386** [see OVERSLOP]. **1535** COVERDALE *Exod.* xxviii. 25 The two shulders of the ouer body cote. **1598** *Knaresborough Wills* (Surtees) I. 216 One paire of over britches. **1601** HOLLAND *Pliny* I. 518 The ouer rind or barke would be taken away. **1889** *John Bull* 2 Mar. 150/1 A skirt of black satin with over drapery of guipure lace.

2. *fig.* Higher in power, authority, or station; upper, superior.

In existing words usually written in comb., as *over-superior*, *overlord*; see OVER- 2 and the Main words.

c **1205** LAY. 1520 Wheðer ich maȝe þe ufere [*c* **1275** ouere] hond habben of þan kinge. *Ibid.* 1289 Ah Brutus hefde þa ouere hond. **1297** R. GLOUC. (Rolls) 5152 Þe king of west sex adde euere þe ouere hond. *c* **1485** *Digby Myst.* (1882) v. 300 Se that the nether parte of reason In no wyse ther-to lende, than the ouer parte shall haue fre domynacion. **1570** *Satir. Poems Reform.* xxiii. 90 His Kirk sall haue the ouer hand. **1780** *Voy. to Japan* in *Phil. Trans.* LXX. App. 2 These Over Banjoses may be compared to the Mandarins of China... They inspect every thing. **1874** *Act 37 & 38 Vict.* c. 94 §7 No consolidation.. shall.. extend the rights or interests of any over superior.

3. That is in excess or in addition; remaining beyond the normal amount; surplus, extra. (See OVER *adv.* 8, OVER- 19.)

1494 *Act 11 Hen. VII*, c. 13 The half-deal of the over Price of her, being above vi.*s.* viii.*d.* to be to the King. **1832** HT. MARTINEAU *Homes Abroad* v. 74, I am soon to begin building you a house at over hours. **1896** *Daily News* 21 Nov. 3/3 He knew nothing about the practice.. whether over or spoiled copies were given to the employés.

4. That is in excess of what is right or proper; too great, excessive.

Now mostly written in comb., as *over-hastiness*, *over-care*: see OVER- 29 and the Main words.

1561 DAUS tr. *Bullinger on Apoc.* (1573) 69 b, Through our owne ouer curiousnesse in searchyng and siftyng Gods workes. **1596** DALRYMPLE tr. *Leslie's Hist. Scot.* I. 105 Thair ouir haistines, and ouer bent to reuenge. **1710** E. WARD *Brit. Hud.* 38 To.. cool him after two Hours sweating, With over Pains, and over Prating. **1758** S. HAYWARD *Serm.* xvi. 469 Occasioned by an over thirst for government. **1801** tr. *Gabrielli's Myst. Husb.* IV. 45 Had my over precautions rendered you.. miserable. **1849** RUSKIN *Sev. Lamps* ii. §1. 29 Without over care as to which is largest or blackest.

†**5.** Later, after. (In form *ufera*, *uvere*.) *Obs.*

c **893** K. ÆLFRED *Oros.* IV. v. §2 Þy læs hit monn uferan doȝore wræcce. *c* **1000** *Sax. Leechd.* III. 438 Eallum þæm þe þa stowe on uferum tidum ȝeseoð. *c* **1205** LAY. 27794 Þat he mihte an uuere daȝe[n] [*c* 1275 þar after] ȝelpen uor þere dede(n).

ˈ**over**, *v.* Also *north.* and *Sc.* **our**, **ower**, **owre**. [f. OVER *adv.* Cf. L. *superāre*.]

†**1.** *trans.* To make higher (in amount); to raise, increase. In quot. 1602 *absol.* To go to a higher figure (by so much). *Obs.*

1546 *Supplic. of Poore Commons* (E.E.T.S.) 80 Oueryng both fynes & rentes, beyond all reason and conscience. **1550** CROWLEY *Epigr.* 1206 To leauye greate fines, or to ouer the rent. **1602** CAREW *Cornwall* 37 b, They will rather take bargaines, at these excessiue fines, then a tolerable improved rent, being in no sort willing to ouer a penny.

2. To leap or jump over; to clear.

1837 DICKENS *Pickw.* xxix, Playing at leap-frog with the tombstones:.. 'overing' the highest among them, one after the other, with the most marvellous dexterity. **1882** *Society* 28 Oct. 19/1 You never made mud pies, or played at tipcat, or 'overed' a post.

†**3.** To get the better of, to master. *Sc. Obs.*

1456 SIR G. HAYE *Law Arms* (S.T.S.) 228 A seke man that may nocht our himself in syk a rage and malady. *Ibid.* 271 Gif ony of thame may our his falow, be ony habilitee or strenthe, or suteltee.

4. *ellipt.* To get over; to pass over. *dial.*

1825 JAMIESON s.v., 'He never over'd the loss of that bairn'. **1825** BROCKETT *N.C. Gloss.* s.v., I'm sadly afraid she'll never over it. **1847** A. BRONTË *Agnes Grey* xi. 163, I was sore distressed Miss Grey—thank God it's owered now. *Ibid.* xii. 185 You'll *both* stay while this shower gets owered. **1855** ROBINSON *Whitby Gloss.* s.v., 'It ower'd a bit', it ceased a little,—the rain. [See E.D.D.] **1933** L. A. G. STRONG *Sea Wall* II. xiv. 219 He done an operation on a woman and she never overed it. **1936** 'N. BLAKE' *Thou Shell of Death* xiii. 231 Master Dermot was killed in France, the year of the Easter Rising. His da never overed it. **1949** *Amer. Speech* XXIV. 111 *Over*, to recover from, as a disease or an injury.

over- is used with adverbial, prepositional, and adjectival force, in combination with sbs.; with adverbial and prepositional force in comb. with verbs; with adverbial force in combination with adjs., advbs., and prepositions. Its combinations are therefore exceedingly numerous, and, from the wide range of its meaning, very diverse in character. The following are the chief classes; but many words have senses falling under two, three, or more of these, and there are individual words in which the original sense of the prefix is so modified that it is difficult to assign them to any class. In some of its uses, moreover, *over* is a movable element, which can be prefixed at will to almost any verb or adjective of suitable sense, as freely as an adjective can be placed before a substantive or an adverb before an adjective. Although usually hyphened or even written as one word, such combinations are hardly dictionary facts; they are really syntactic combinations which make the use and construction of *over* in the particular position more clear and obvious. In some of these combinations, however, there is a closer unification of sense, and others have a long history which it is desirable to show. All important combinations of *over-*, therefore, including such as occur in more than one sense, and all such as seem to require explanation, are treated as Main words in their alphabetical places; of the unimportant or obvious ones, examples are here given under the classes to which they belong, with a few illustrations; but no attempt is made to enumerate all that have been used, much less all that are possible.

Ofer- (like *ufar-* in Gothic, *ubar-* and *ober-* in OHG., *obar* in OS., *über* in Ger., *over* in Du., *yfer-*, *ofr-*, *of-* in ON.) was already in OE. used in comb. with vbs., as *oferclimban*, *ofercuman*, *oferdón*, *oferdrincan*, *oferlibban*; with sbs., as *ofercaldorman*, *oferbrú*, *ofersegl*, *oferslop*, *oferwrit*, *oferlufu*, *oferbiternes*; with adjs., as *ofergylden*, *ofermǽte*, *ofermódig*, *oferbliðe*, *oferfull*, *ofermicel*; also in advbs. formed from adjs., and in derivatives of phrases, as *ofersǽlic*, *ofersǽwisc* from *ofer sǽ*. Many of the OE. compounds are still in use, but the more part failed to live into ME., and the great majority of existing *over-* combinations are of later formation, chiefly since *c* 1550.

For the original stress of verbal and nominal compounds respectively, and later modifications, see OUT-. As *over* is of two syllables, there is necessarily a subordinate stress on *o*, even in verbal compounds, where the main stress is on the root syllable. This rises in sense 27 to a distinct secondary stress, distinguishing e.g. ˌ*over-*ˈ*bend* 'bend too much' from *over*ˈ*bend* 'bend over'. In verse, the unstressed *over-* is often reduced to *o'er-*, a single stressless syllable, as *o'er-*ˈ*bend*, *o'er*ˈ*shadow*; but *over-* with main or secondary stress is not properly reduced to *o'er-* unless the position allows the stress to be retained, as in ˌ*o'er-e'namoured*, ˌ*o'er-in'curious*, ˌ*o'er-a'ssumption*, ˌ*o'er-re'pletion*. See senses 27–30.

I. *over-* in spatial and temporal senses, and in uses directly related to these.

1. a. With verbs, or with sbs. forming vbs., in the sense 'over in space, on high, above the top or surface of', as OVERBROOD, -CANOPY, -DROP, -HANG, -SOAR, etc. Also (*b*) in sense of 'rising above, overtopping', as OVER-RISE, -TOP, -TOWER; and (*c*) with the sense of position implying other notions of which it is a condition or element, as OVEREYE, OVERLOOK, OVERJOY, OVERWEEP, which see.

The compound verb is equivalent sometimes to the simple vb. with *over* adv., as in OVERLAY, to lay (something) over; or, more frequently, to the simple vb. (usually intr.) with *over* prep., as in OVERHANG, to hang over (something), OVERLIE, to lie over or above (something); but in many cases, as OVERARCH, it is difficult or impossible to distinguish these.

Examples: ***over'billow***, ***-'branch***, ***-cap***, ***-cluster***, ***-crown***, ***-dangle***, ***-dome***, ***-droop***, ***-frown***, ***-glint***, ***-helm***, ***-hover***, ***-leer***, ***-pentise***, ***-plumb***, ***-spire***, ***-stoop***, ***-surge***, ***-tip***, ***-turret***, ***-vista***, ***-wave***, etc.

1814 COLERIDGE *Lett., to J. Murray* (1895) 626 Any more peccant thing of Froth, Noise, and Impermanence, that may have *overbillowed it on the restless sea of curiosity. **1850** MRS. BROWNING *Island* xv, With trees that *overbranch The sea. **1839** *Fraser's Mag.* XX. 44 The moon, rising with unclouded refulgence, *overcapped the crest of eternal forests. **1871** B. TAYLOR *Faust* (1875) I. iii. 60 Lo! in a shower Grapes that *o'ercluster Gush into must. **18..** G. MEREDITH *Poems*, *Lark Ascending*, Like water-dimples down a tide Where ripple ripple *overcurls. **1869** BROWNING *Ring & Bk.* XI. 1814 Like bubble that *o'erdomes a fly. **1881** H. JAMES *Portr. Lady* xxiii, High-walled lanes, into which.. blossoming orchards *overdrooped and flung a perfume. **1861** M. ARNOLD *Southern Night*, There, where Gibraltar's cannon'd steep *O'erfrowns the wave. **1805** W. TAYLOR in *Ann. Rev.* III. 544 Like the star which *over-hovered the manger at Bethlehem. **1850** MRS. BROWNING *Wine of Cyprus* ii, Cyclops' mouth might plunge aright in, While his one eye *over-leered. **1631** BRATHWAIT *Whimzies*, *Gamester* 42 A broad-brim'd hat *o'erpentising his discontented looke. **1888** STEVENSON *Black Arrow* 189 A piece of ruinous cliff.. almost *overplumbed the deck. **1844** MRS. BROWNING *Crowned & Buried* iii, Altars *overstooped By meek-eyed Christs. **1610** WILLET *Hexapla Daniel* 94 Set in a plaine, where no hils were, that it might not be *ouertipped by them. **1810** W. TAYLOR in *Monthly Mag.* XXIX. 418 Shall .. No golden cloud of praise *O'erwave his way?

b. Some verbal compounds occur chiefly or only in the pples. or gerund: cf. c. Such are ***over-banded***, ***-being***, ***-placed***, ***-shrined***, etc.

a **1653** G. DANIEL *Idyll* iii. 89 The Lust of Tyrants (*over-banded still By hooded Law) carnalls the world at Will. **1382** WYCLIF *1 Kings* vi. 18 And with cedre al the hows with ynforth was clothid, hauynge.. grauyngis *ouerbeynge [1388 apperynge aboue, L. *eminentes*]. *a* **1618** SYLVESTER *Mysterie of Myst.*, *Father* 8 Over All things, not *over-plac't. **1895** J. W. POWELL *Physiogr. Processes* in *Nat. Geog. Monogr.* I. i. 14 The overplaced materials brought down by the floods. **1559** *Mirr. Mag.* (1563) Aa viij, Standynge on a ladder, *ouershryned wyth the Tyborne, a meete trone for all suche.. Trayters.

c. So in ppl. adjs. and vbl. sbs., as OVERHANGING, -SHADED, ***over-awning***, ***-beetling***, ***-bellying***, ***-boding***, ***-curling***, ***-greeting***, ***-jutting***, ***-pending***, ***-shelving***, ***-swinging***, etc. (These may be formed to any extent.)

1801 SOUTHEY *Thalaba* XII. xiii, Above the depth four *over-awning wings.. Bore up a little car. **1854** H. MILLER *Sch. & Schm.* iv. (1857) 78 A small stream came pattering.. from the *over-beetling precipice above. **1895** REYNOLDS in *Expositor* Nov. 336 The strange and *overboding sense of man's life after death. **1895** J. MUIR in *Century Mag.* June 238/2 [Snow] in massive *overcurling cornices. **1799** H. GURNEY *Cupid & Psyche* xiv. 31 From that *o'erjutting crag. **1812** ANNE PLUMPTRE tr. *Lichtenstein's Trav.* I. 132 It presents the appearance of a high sunken *overshelving wall. **1859** DICKENS *T. Two Cities* vi, Under the *over-swinging lamps.

d. with sbs., in sense 'situated above' or 'higher'; also, 'the upper' of two (or more) things: = OVER *a.* 1: as OVERBRIDGE, -BROW, -CHEEK, -WORLD; so ***overcord***, ***-deyhouse***, ***-half***, ***-park***, ***-pool***.

1513-14 *Durham Acc. Rolls* (Surtees) 663, j long Roppe for the kyln, iiij*s.*, et j *overcorde, ij*d.* **1421-2** *Ibid.* 303 Pro cariacione feni ad le *Overdeyhous, iiij*s.* *c* **1450** *Mirour Saluacioun* 1463 On the *overhalf the Arche the watere no ferthere ranne. **1533** in Weaver *Wells Wills* (1890) 205 Keper of his *overparke. **1535** COVERDALE *Isa.* xxxvi. 2 By the condite of the ouerpole.

e. In transferred senses of 'higher, upper', e.g. in pitch, as OVERBLOW *v.*, OVERSOUND, OVERTONE.

2. a. With the sense 'above in power, authority, rank, station'. In verbs, as OVERGOVERN, -LEAD, -LORD, -MASTER, -RULE, -SWAY, etc. q.v.; so ***over-command***, ***-order***, etc.

a **1600** HOOKER *Eccl. Pol.* VIII. ii. §3 There is no higher nor greater that can in those causes *over-command them. **1839** BAILEY *Festus* (1852) 521 May He who *over-orders all, Speed thee upon thy quest!

b. So in sbs. and adjs., derived from or related to vbs., as OVERRULE, -RULER, -RULING, -SEER, -SWAY, etc.; also in other sbs., in sense of 'higher, superior', as OVER-KING, OVERLORD, etc.; so ***over-chanter***, ***-chief***, ***-dignity***, ***-god***, ***-plot***, ***-shepherd***.

1535 *Goodly Primer* Ps. xxii. (*title*), It is the song of David, committed to the *overchaunter. **1853** J. STEVENSON tr. *Beda's Eccl. Hist.* 505 If they should come into the presence of their *over-chief. **1607** DAY *Trav. Eng. Bro.* (1881) 49 Though my humillitie (I vow by heauen) Doth not affect that *ouerdignitie. **1847** EMERSON *Poems* (1857) 122 Speaks not of self that mystic tone, But of the *Overgods alone. **1882-3** SCHAFF *Encycl. Relig. Knowl.* III. 1933 The lawful *overshepherd [Ger. *oberhirt*] of the Protestants living in his see [Paderborn].

3. With the sense of inclination to one side so as to lean over the space beneath. In vbs., as OVERBEND, -BIAS, -LEAN, -SAIL², -WEIGH, q.v.

Also in derived sbs. and adjs., as OVERBIAS, OVERLEANING, etc.

4. With the sense of passing across over head, and so 'away, off'. In verbs, as OVERBLOW, -CARRY, -DRIVE, -GIVE, -GO, -PASS, etc., q.v. So in derived sbs. and adjs.

5. a. With the sense of surmounting, passing over the top, or over the brim or edge. In verbs, as OVERCLIMB, -BOIL, -BRIM, -FLOW (q.v.), ***overbubble, -burst, -well***, etc. Sometimes (*b*) implying 'passing over without hitting, missing', as OVERLEAP, -LOOK, -SHOOT. Also (*c*) *fig.* of surmounting or getting over an obstacle, an illness, a calamity, or the like, as OVERCOME. **b.** Also in derived and related sbs. and adjs., as OVERFLOW, -FLOWING, -SIGHT, ***overbubbling, oversplash***, etc.

1896 *Godey's Mag.* Feb. 158/1 They showed such an *over-bubbling of good-nature. **1856** MRS. H. O. CONANT *Eng. Bible Transl.* i. (1881) 3 Outraged humanity has *overburst the bounds of discreet submission. **1888** SPURGEON *Serm.* in *Voice* (N.Y.) 31 May, A sort of *over-splash of the great fountain of mercy. **1869** BLACKMORE *Lorna D.* xix, The water *overwelled the edge.

6. With the sense of motion forward and down, and hence of overturning, inversion. In verbs, as OVERBALANCE, -BEAR, -BEAT, -BLOW, -CAST, -SET, -THROW, -TURN, etc. So in derived sbs. and adjs., as OVERBEARING, -FALL, -SET, -TURN, etc.

7. With the sense 'down upon from above'. In verbs, as OVERCOME, -FALL, -GANG, -GO, -LEAP, -LOOK, -SEE, etc., q.v.

8. a. With the sense 'upon the surface generally, all over, so as to prevail or abound over, cover, hide'. Also with the sense 'upon the surface so as to cover in part', as in OVERPAINT *sb.*, OVERPRINT *v.* II. In verbs, as OVERCLOUD, to cloud (a thing) over, cover over with cloud, OVERCLOTHE, -COVER, -GLAZE, -GROW, -HEAP, q.v. So ***overbalm, -bepatch, -black, -blind, -cheer, -curtain, -dark, -darken, -dash, -drench, -dust, -encrust, -file, -fling, -flower, -froth, -fruit, -gall, -gird, -gloss, -hurl, -husk, -ink, -lace, -letter, -moss, †-noint, -prick, -rust, -scatter, -scent, -scourge, -scratch, -screen, -scribble, -sculpture, -seal, -shower, -silver, -spangle, -spatter, -stamp, -stud, -web, -wheal, -wipe, -wound***, etc.

a **1851** MOIR *Child's Burial* v, That 'the joy of grief' (as Ossian sings) *o'erbalm'd the very air. *a* **1657** LOVELACE *Poems* (1864) 164 Me thought she look'd all *ore-bepatch'd with stars. **1613–18** DANIEL *Coll. Hist. Eng.* (1626) 6 [Gildas] *ouer-blacks them [the Britons] with such vgly deformities. **1613** F. ROBARTS *Rev. Gosp.* 78 If self-loue and couetousnesse did not *ouerblind and entangle the men of this age. **1555–8** PHAER *Æneid* I. B iv b, His mother..with a roset youth his eies and countnaunce *overcheared. **1577** *Test. 12 Patriarchs* (1706) 52 If you be *overdarkned with wickedness. **1589** GREENE *Orpharion* Wks. (Grosart) XII. 70 Linaments, wherevpon this native colour was *ouerdasht. **1590** —— *Orl. Fur.* Wks. (Rtldg.) 111/1, I stand amaz'd deep *over-drench'd with joy. **1606** SHAKS. *Tr. & Cr.* III. iii. 179 And giue to dust, that is a little guilt, More laud then guilt *oredusted. **1632** LITHGOW *Trav.* x, The Hals..most exquisitly *ouer-filed, and indented with Mosaicall worke. **1876** BROWNING *Nat. Magic* i, Embowered With—who knows what verdure, *o'erfruited, *o'erflowered? **1606** SHAKS. *Tr. & Cr.* v. iii. 54 Their eyes *ore-galled, with recourse of teares. **1641** MILTON *Ch. Govt.* vi. (1851) 125 When the gentle west winds shall open the fruitfull bosome of the earth thus *over-girded by your imprisonment. **1673** HICKERINGILL *Gregory Father Greybeard* 145 This realm was..*overhurl'd with the new modern orthodox. **1824** BEDDOES *Let.* Dec. in *Poems* p. xxxvi, Lost to German and all humane learning, *o'erhusked with sweet dozing sloth. **1855** BROWNING *Cleon* 2 The sprinkled isles, Lily on lily, that *o'erlace the sea. **1827** POLLOK *Course T.* VII. (1860) 187 *O'erletter'd by the hand Of oft frequenting pilgrims. **1610** G. FLETCHER *Christ's Tri.* I. xx, Our ships so *over-moss't, and brands so deadly blown. *c* **1550** LLOYD *Treas. Health* (1585) X ij, *Over noynt the burned place therewith, for it healeth wonderfullye. **1535** LATIMER *Serm. 21st Sund. Trinity* Wks. I. 28 How hath this truth *over-rusted with the pope's rust? **1655** FULLER *Ch. Hist.* VII. i. §1 *Over-sented with the fragrant ointment of this Prince's memory. **1906** HARDY *Dynasts* II. I. ii. 17 Draw down the curtain, then, and *overscreen This too-protracted verbal fencing-scene. **1535** COVERDALE *2 Esdras* vi. 20 Whan the worlde..shalbe *ouersealed, then wyl I do these tokens. **1608** SHAKS. *Per.* IV. iv. 26 Pericles..With sighs shot through, and biggest tears *o'er-shower'd, Leaves Tarsus. *a* **1628** F. GREVIL *Sidney* (1652) 176, I beheld this grave subject..*over-spangled with lightnesse. **1935** *Burlington Mag.* June 288/1 *Over-stamping on Sheffield-made candlesticks the London date-letter 1775–6. **1963** *Times* 23 May 9/6 She would inquire about what they were suffering from 'and they would tell me nerves, flu, bronchitis, or gastritis and so on, and I just wrote out the certificate and signed "T. G. Boyle", and overstamped'. **1977** *Belfast Tel.* 22 Feb. 3/1 Your book will be overstamped to include an extra £1 a week for your first child from 4th April, 1977, and posted back to you. **1532** MORE *Confut. Barnes* VIII. Wks. 797/2 These synnes onely whiche are with the pencell of daily prayer *ouerwyped.

b. So with ppl. adjs. and vbl. sbs., as OVERGROWN, -GROWTH, -LAYER, -LYING, etc.; so ***overnoting, -wooded*** adjs.; ***overscribble***, sb.

1567 DRANT *Horace* B ij, Correcting and perfyting them with *ouernotyng hand. **1890** E. JOHNSON *Rise Christendom* 39 We may distinguish in this great palimpsest the old Roman Scripture from the monkish *over-scribble. **1797** COLERIDGE *Lime-tree Bower* 10 The roaring dell, *o'er-wooded, narrow, deep.

c. With sbs. in the sense 'overlying, covering, worn over or above', 'upper or outer' (cf. OVER *a.* 1 b); as in OVERBODY, -CLOTH, -COAT, -DRESS, -GLAZE, -SHOE, etc.; so ***over-bodice, -bolster, -boot, -cape, -cloak, -collar, -cover, -gaiter, -gown, -jacket, -jumper, -mitt, -shirt, -sock, -stocking, -trousers***, etc.; also attrib. or adj., as OVERCUP.

1897 *Westm. Gaz.* 15 July 3/2 A design demanding some skill in the arrangement of its *overbodice. **1917** D. H. LAWRENCE *Phoenix II* (1968) 64 A single bed, opened for the night, the white *over-bolster piled back. **1939–40** *Army & Navy Stores Catal.* 607/2 Motoring *Overboots, in Brown Sheepskin. **1959** *Times* 2 Oct. 14/6 Her..macintosh, rain hood, and over-boots testified to a careful preparation for the realities of the English climate. **1971** C. BONINGTON *Annapurna South Face* xiii. 143 Mick got ready for the next pitch, removing crampons and overboots in readiness for what was obviously going to be a hard piece of free rock climbing. **1893** *Amer. Missionary* Oct. 325 Many of the people wear cotton *over-cloaks. **1915** F. M. FORD *Good Soldier* IV. ii. 224 Fishing-rods in green baize *over-covers. **1963** *Times* 23 Feb. 11/3 Plentiful over-cover induced the deer to stay. *a* **1904** *Mod. U.S. Advt.*, These leggings are a sort of *overgaiter made of waterproof material. **1908** 'O. HENRY' *Voice of City* 233 It was Rosalie, in..gray walking suit, and tan oxfords with lavender overgaiters. **1470–85** *Over-garment [see OVER-GARMENT]. **1895** *Daily News* 5 Feb. 6/6 The elaborate *over-jacket of the Louis XV period. **1975** *Times* 7 Oct. 11/4 *Over-jumper with wide sleeves.. and a square neck. **1971** *Overmit [see LINER[1] 3]. **1971** C. BONINGTON *Annapurna South Face* 298, Gloves with waterproof over-mitts are standard. **1805** LEWIS & CLARK *Orig. Jrnls. Expedition* (1905) II. 159 The weather being warm I had left my leather *over shirt and had woarn only a yellow flannin one. **1869** *Routledge's Ev. Boy's Ann.* 347 He wore a bright scarlet over-shirt. **1974** *Country Life* 2 May 1096/2 The man wears a cotton..striped overshirt, denim shorts and pull-on hat. **1911** WEBSTER, *Over-sock. **1929** *Footwear Organiser* Jan. 31 (*heading*) The Oversock vogue spreads throughout the country. **1971** 'D. HALLIDAY' *Dolly & Doctor Bird* iii. 29 For golf, I have always worn.. oversocks with good shoes. **1892** KIPLING *Lett. of Travel* (1920) 6 The driver with red mittens on his hands, felt *overstockings that come up to his knees, and, perhaps, a silvery-gray coon-skin coat on his back, walks beside me. **1852** *Harper's Mag.* Apr. 707/1 My duck *over-trousers.. were beginning to be rather tender in certain places. **1968** *Daily Tel.* 28 Sept. 9/4 Come rain or snow the lot would be covered by over-trousers or over-skirts and waterproof jackets. **1976** *Good Motoring* Nov. 24/1 Coats, jackets and overtrousers.

9. With the sense of motion over a surface generally, so as to cover in whole or part; also of motion to and fro upon or all over; as in OVERBLOW, -BREDE, -GANG, -GLIDE, -RIDE, -RUN, -SWEEP, etc. So ***overbreak, -browse, -circulate, -range, -riot, -rush, -scour, -skim, -slur, -trail, -twist, -whisper***, etc. Also with derived sbs. and adjs., as OVERTHRUST.

1850 BROWNING *Easter Day* xvii, A final belch of fire ..*Overbroke all heaven. **1850** MRS. BROWNING *Soul's Travelling* viii, Banks too steep To be *o'erbrowzèd by the sheep. **1632** LITHGOW *Trav.* v. 229 That Orient maiesty arising to *ouercirculate the earth. **1840** BROWNING *Sordello* I. 216 Too sure to *over-riot and confound..each brilliant islet with itself. *c* **1590** GREENE *Fr. Bacon* xv. 4 To scud and *ouer-scour the earth in poast. **1811** SHELLEY in Hogg *Life* (1858) I. 383 Without..employing any kind of declamation, *overslurring, or sophistry. **1833** TENNYSON *Lady of Shalott* Poems 10 The little isle is..*overtrailed With roses. **1806** J. GRAHAME *Birds Scot.* 40 Ivy close, that *over-twisting binds.

10. a. With the sense 'across, from side to side, to the other side (L. *trans*)'; as OVERBRING, -CARVE, -CROSS, -DRAW, etc. So ***over-festoon, -link, -send, -split***, etc.

1840 BROWNING *Sordello* I. 662 Thus thrall reached thrall: He *o'erfestooning every interval. **1599** HAKLUYT *Voy.* II. II. 77 A bridge made of many barges, *ouerlinked al together with two mightie cheines. **1382** WYCLIF *Judg.* iii. 28 The foordis of Jordan that *ouersenden [Vulg. *transmittunt*] in to Moab. **1593** *Tell-Troth's N.Y. Gift* 29 Loyalty recovereth a world of *oversplit infirmities.

b. So in derived sbs. and adjs., as OVERCUT *sb.*, etc.

11. a. With the sense of bringing or gaining over to a party, opinion, etc. In verbs, as OVERBRIBE, -INTREAT (*-entreat*), -PERSUADE, q.v. So ***over-force, -influence, -pray, -tempt***.

1603 DRAYTON *Bar. Wars* VI. lxii, Phœbus (she said) was *over-forc'd by art. **1762** *Life Sprat* in *Biogr. Dict.* X. 486 He owns himself to have been *over-influenced to it by the powers above. **1610** G. FLETCHER *Christ's Vict.* I. xxvii, The judge might partiall be, and *over-prayed. **1643** MILTON *Divorce* I. xiv, Lest the soul of a Christian..should be *over-tempted and cast away. **1749** FIELDING *Tom Jones* XVIII. ii, A small breach of friendship which he had been over-tempted to commit.

b. So with derived sbs. and adjs., as OVER-PERSUASION, and other sbs. as †OVER-MONEY.

12. With the sense of 'across a boundary'; hence, of transgression; as in OVERGANG, -GO, -LASH, etc. Also in derivatives, as OVERLASHING.

13. a. With the sense 'beyond a point or limit, farther than'; in vbs., as OVERFLY, -GO, -GROW, -REACH, ***over-clasp***, etc. Also in derivatives, as OVERGOING.

1775 ADAIR *Amer. Ind.* 310 The hunter..makes off to a sappling, which the bear by over-clasping cannot climb.

b. Prefixed to a plural number (or occas. a singular number used *attrib.*) to denote persons who are older than that particular age.

1940 GRAVES & HODGE *Long Week-End* xvii. 303 The *Evening News*..throwing open its columns to the over-forties. **1959** *Manch. Guardian* 19 Aug. 3/6 Sir Compton Mackenzie and Miss Ruby Miller, for the over-70s, sparring with youthful zest. **1960** *Guardian* 13 Apr. 6/6 There seems to be no place for the over-fifties. **1960** C. WATSON *Bump in Night* ii. 25 We shall want to take a closer look..without being trampled to death by the Over-Sixty clubs. **1972** M. J. BOSSE *Incident at Naha* 47 They had their hair done in an over-thirty style. **1973** M. AMIS *Rachel Papers* 22 The over-twenties, I grant you, must see it [*sc.* sex] largely as a matter of obligation, too: but obligation to the partner, not to oneself, like us. **1975** B. MEYRICK *Behind Light* xiv. 183 After the boys' competitions, where I came in second in the over-twelves, came..community hymn singing. **1977** *New Wave* No. 7. 8 The only night spots, right, are an over-25's place and Mecca.

14. With the sense as in OVERTAKE, q.v. So in OVERCATCH, -GET, -HALE, -HAUL, -HENT, -HIE, -NIM.

15. With the sense as in OVERHEAR, q.v. So in OVERLISTEN, OVERSEE 4.

16. With the sense 'all through' (something extended), 'through the extent of', 'from beginning to end'; in vbs., as OVERLOOK, -NAME, -PASS, -READ, -VIEW, etc.

17. With the senses 'through', 'to the end of' in time; 'to an end or issue', 'to extinction' (= OUT- 15 b); in vbs., as OVERPASS, -RUN, -SEY; so ***overdream, -dure, -last, -waste***.

1818 MILMAN *Samor* 171 As though they had *o'erdream'd The churlish winter. **1633** J. DONE *Hist. Septuagint* 197 But this story of Aristeus hath *overdured those flames. **1885–94** R. BRIDGES *Eros & Psyche* Jan. x, She begs but what shall well *o'erlast a day. **1603** DRAYTON *Bar. Wars* VI. lxxiii, None regarded to maintaine the light, Which being *over-wasted, was gone out.

18. With the sense 'beyond' in time, 'too long', 'too late'; in vbs., as OVERBIDE, -KEEP, -LIVE, -STAY, etc.; so ***overtarry***. In sbs. in the sense 'surviving', as OVER-BELIEF; so ***over-structure***.

1843 LYTTON *Last Bar.* IV. iv, I have overtarried, my lord.

19. With the sense 'remaining over' or 'in addition or excess', 'surplus', 'extra'; as in vb. OVERLEAVE; in sbs. as OVERDEAL, OVERTIME; so ***over-hours, -matter, -wages***.

1832 *Over hours [see OVER *a.* 3]. **1887** ROGERS in *Contemp. Rev.* May 686, I was astonished at discovering where the worst cases of over-hours were. **1887** *Pall Mall G.* 5 Feb. 5/2 It contains seven pages of '*over-matter' put in type for 'Fors' but never before published. **1928** *Daily Express* 7 Feb. 3/6 Early buyers of lingerie had all the advantages, for most of the real bargains..belonged to ranges that..were 'overmatter' that had to be cast out of stock. **1967** *Economist* 2 Dec. p. iii/2 This one book is only a bit of overmatter from all his earlier over-writings. **1972** *Observer* 12 Mar. 16/8 Large quantities of titanium overmatter..were just thrown into the dustbin. **1977** *Oxf. Diocesan Mag.* Oct. 4/1 The carry-forward of over-matter means that no issue can be planned as 'an island, entire of itself'. **1856** OLMSTED *Slave States* 103 All that they choose to do more than this they are paid for..; and invariably this *over-wages is used by the slave for himself... Nearly all gained by overwork $5 a month.

20. With the notion of repetition, 'over again'; in vbs., as OVERACT, -HEAR, -READ, -SAY; in sbs., as OVERCOME, -WORD. So ***overqueath*** OE. *ofercweðan*, to say over again, repeat; ***over-fought*** ppl. adj.

971 *Blickl. Hom.* 15 We hit sceolan eft ofercweþan. **1902** *Westm. Gaz.* 3 Dec. 4/2 There is something of an over-fought battle, and a slaying of the slain.

21. With the sense of overcoming, putting down, or getting the better of, by the action or thing expressed; in vbs., as OVERAWE, -BRAVE, -DARE, -FACE, q.v.; so ***overbray, -choke, -cow, -daze, -deave, -drowse, -fright, -lume, -noise, -stifle, -war, -wrestle***. So in verbal derivatives, as ***overcowed***, etc.

It is possible that *overburden, overcark, overload, overweigh*, and the like, belong originally here, rather than to 27.

1876 BLACKIE *Songs Relig. & Life* 202 To *overbray The voice of grave authority. **1603** FLORIO *Montaigne* I. xxx. (1632) 102 We have altogether *overchoked her [Nature]. **1834** PRINGLE *Afr. Sk.* x. 312 *note*, One feels oneself fairly '*overcowed', and dare not even aspire to be heard. **1632** QUARLES *Div. Fancies* II. xxxii. (1660) 64 She smiles, she wonders, being *overdaz'd With his bright beams, stands silent, stands amaz'd. **1817** WORDSW. *Vernal Ode* iv, To lie and listen—till *o'er-drowsèd sense Sinks, hardly conscious of the influence. **1711** SHAFTESB. *Charac.* (1737) I. 88 This ..cou'd never have been acted by other than mean spirits, such as had been held in awe, and *over-frighted by the magi. **1794** J. WILLIAMS *Shrove Tuesday* 3 When..lesser planets Phœbus had *o'erlumed. *a* **1667** COWLEY *Greatness* in *Verses & Ess.* (1687) 126 No Mirth or Musick *over-noise your Fears. **1666** W. BOGHURST *Loimographia* 25 *Overstifling and weakening people with too much sweating. **1589** WARNER *Alb. Eng.* v. xxv. Q ij b, The chiefe and grauest of the Peeres, did *ouer-warred flye Into the Woods. **1590** SPENSER *F.Q.* I. vii. 24 When life recover'd had the raine, And *over-wrestled his strong enimy.

II. *over-* in the sense of 'over or beyond' in degree or quality; hence, of surpassing, excelling, exceeding, excess.

22. a. With the notion of doing some action over or beyond another agent, of going beyond, surpassing, or excelling in the action denoted by the simple vb. In verbs, as OVERBID 2, OVERLEAP 4, OVERRUN 9; so ***overamble, -bandy, -bark, -blaze, -cackle, -chant, -cry, -perk, -ring, -ruff, -scream, -smite, -squeak, -stare.*** etc.

1582 STANYHURST *Æneis* I. (Arb.) 28 Herpalicee, sweeft queene, steeds strong *ouerambling. **1592** NASHE *P. Pennilesse* D ij b, He so far outstript him in vilanious words, and *ouerbandied him in bitter tearmes. **1652** SCLATER *Civ. Magistracy* (1653) 2 The sparkling of the one, *overblazed the duskishnesse of the other. **1562** *Ouercakill [see OVERCROW]. **1628** SHIRLEY *Witty Fair One* I. ii, An hundred nightingales Shall fall down dead.. For grief to be *o'er-chanted. **1571** GOLDING *Calvin on Ps.* xlviii. 3 That that gorgeousnesse or that loftines *overperk not Gods power. **1604** T. M. *Ant & Nightingale* C iv, He walkt the chamber with such a pestilent Gingle, that his Spurs *ouersqueakt the Lawyer. **1596** SHAKS. *Merch. V.* II. i. 27, I would *ore-stare the sternest eies that looke: Out-braue the heart most daring on the earth.

b. In verbs formed on sbs., with the sense of surpassing in, or in the rôle of, as ***over-'bulk, -'multitude***; esp. in nonce-phrases, as ***overgospel the gospel, over-Macpherson Macpherson, over-puppy***, etc. Cf. OUT- 21, 23.

1606 SHAKS. *Tr. & Cr.* I. iii. 320 The seeded Pride.. must or now be cropt, Or shedding breed a Nursery of like euil To ouer-bulke vs all. **1634** MILTON *Comus* 731 The herds would over-multitude their Lords. **1647** WARD *Simp. Cobler* 17 He will outlaw the Law,..over-Gospell the Gospell. **1735** SHERIDAN in *Swift's Lett.* (1768) IV. 124 My two puppies have..overpuppied their puppyships. **1826** SOUTHEY *Lett.* (1856) IV. 17 This is over-Macphersoning Macpherson.

23. In reflexive vbs., with the sense of surpassing oneself, i.e. one's former or ordinary achievements, one's capacity, strength, etc.; often with the sense of exhausting oneself by the action; sometimes merely of doing to excess or too much, as in 27: as OVERBLOOM itself, OVERDRINK, -EAT, -SLEEP oneself; so ***over-bowl, over-plot, over-polk***, etc. Cf. also sense 27 a.

1844 *W. Lillywhite's Illustr. Hand-bk. Cricket* 18 Do not *over bowl yourself by random bowling. **1886** *Daily News* 6 Sept. 3/4 He will over-bowl himself if he is not very careful. **1962** *Punch* 1 Aug. 152/3 A Cowdrey who would certainly not overbowl himself. **1748** RICHARDSON *Clarissa* (1811) IV. 57, I have *over-plotted myself. **1853** MISS YONGE *Heir of Redcl.* xii, She has *over-polked herself in London, and is sent here for quiet and country air.

24. a. In sense 'more than': with verbs, as OVERBALANCE, -FILL, -MATCH, -MATE, etc.; so ***over-conquer, -empty, -equal, -fit, -overcome, -parallel, -satisfy.***

1602 CAREW *Cornwall* 64 b, The women would be verie loth to come behinde the fashion, in new-fanglednes.. if not in costlynes,..which perhaps might *ouer-empty their husbands purses. **1716** M. DAVIES *Athen. Brit.* II. 186 Bona is *over-equall'd by Bishops Kidder and Ken. **1726-31** WALDRON *Isle of Man* (1865) 72 Shoes..of such a monstrous length and bigness, that they would infinitely have *over-fitted the feet of the giants set up in Guild-hall. **1647** TRAPP *Comm. Rom.* viii. 37 We do *over-overcome, because through faith in Christ we overcome before we fight. **1620** FORD *Linea V.* (Shaks. Soc.) 68 Nor shall [it] euer [be] *ouer-paralleled by any age succeeding. **1609** BP. HALL *No Peace w. Rome* §12 Who can abide that any mortall man should *ouer-satisfie God for his sinnes?

b. So in derivatives; also in other adjs., as OVER-DUE, OVERFULL, ***overcomplete, over-womanly.***

1868 G. STEPHENS *Runic Mon.* I. 280 The alphabet thus inscribed being occasionally incomplete or *overcomplete. **1682** DRYDEN *Duke of Guise* I. iii, Such an habitual *over-womanly goodness.

25. With the sense 'exceedingly, beyond measure, lavishly'. In verbs, often rendering L. *super-*, as OVERABOUND, -FLOURISH, -GLAD, -GRIEVE, -HIGH, -HOPE, -JOY, etc. In adjs., as OVERDEAR, ***over-excelling, over-glorious.*** Now *obs.* or *arch.*, the sense having usually passed into 27.

a **1656** BP. HALL *Invis. World* III. i, Those *over-excelling glories of the good Angels. **1633** FORD *'Tis Pity* v. v, How *over-glorious art thou in thy wounds, Triumphing over infamy and hate!

26. With the sense 'to a greater extent, or at a greater rate, than is usual, natural, or intended; too far'. In verbs, as OVERACT, -BID, -BUY, -CARRY, -COUNT, -ENTER, -ESTEEM, -ESTIMATE, -HOLD, -LAUNCH, -LET, -PAY, -PRIZE, -RATE, -SELL, etc. In adjs., as OVERAWFUL, etc.

** With the sense 'in or to excess, too much, too'. Now a leading sense of *over-* in combination with verbs, adjectives, substantives, and adverbs.

In mod. Eng. very common with a negative (esp. in adjs. and their derivatives), as in *not over-brave, not over-obliging, 'he was not over-pleased with the result'*; in which *not over-* is said by litotes for 'not quite enough', 'somewhat deficiently': *not over-wise* = rather wanting in wisdom.

This sense was approached in Gothic by the adj. *ufarfulls* 'full to overflowing', and the vb. *ufarwahsian* 'to grow exceedingly' (repr. Gr. ὑπεραυξάνειν); it was frequent in ON., expressed by *ofr-, of-*, before adjs., nouns of quality and action, rarer with vbs.; occasional in OHG. (*ubarezzan, ubartrinchan, -trenkan, ubarfullî*: cf. MHG. *ubervol*). In OE. it occurs in many adjs., a few vbs., and numerous derivative or other sbs. In OE. and the cognate langs., *over* was in true combination; its generalized use in mod. Eng. renders it much more a distinct element, often merely in syntactical combination, so that, except in a few words of old standing, it is usually hyphened to the word which it qualifies.

In verbs, there is a distinct secondary stress on *over-* which may, in case of antithesis or emphasis, become the main stress. Adjectives, substantives, and adverbs have normally even stress: *'over-'apt, 'over-ab'stemious, 'over-'worry, 'over-'often*; either stress being liable to be subordinated, according to the construction and emphasis. Thus, *an 'over-ˌapt scholar, we think him 'over-'apt; we want culture, not 'over-ˌculture.* In this sense, *over-* is rarely contracted in verse to *o'er-*, and properly only where the stress can be retained, as in *ˌo'er-e'namoured.*

27. a. With verbs (or with sbs. or adjs. forming verbs). A few occur in OE., e.g. *oferdón, -drencan, -drincan, -fyllan, -sieman, -sprecan* (some of which however only approach this sense, or can be otherwise explained). ME. added to these, *a* 1300, OVERCARK, -CHARGE (F. *surcharger*); *a* 1400 OVERHEAT, -LADE, -PRAISE, -RUN, *over-dread, -sup*; *a* 1500 OVERDRIVE. In the 16th century they began to abound, as OVERBLOW, -BOIL, -BURDEN, -BUSY, -CLOY, -CRAM, -DARE, -EAT, -FEAR, -GORGE, -LABOUR, -LOAD, -LOVE, -PLEASE, -REACH, -ROAST, -WOO, ***over-bake, -black, -cull, -dull, -itch.*** By 1600 It had become allowable to prefix *over-* to any vb. whose sense admitted of it, so that we find, besides those entered as Main words:

a 1700 ***over-afflict, -argue, -cherish, -chill, -cleave, -commend, -confute, -creed, -doze, -engage, -expect, -fancy, -feel, -fix, -gird, -grace, -grasp, -honour, -know, -linger, -loath, -magnify, -marl, -meddle, -mix, -moisten, -multiply, -nourish, -oblige, -pamper, -preface, -promise, -prove, -reward, -sauce, -sot, -store, -thick, -till, -vilify, -worship***, etc.

a 1800 ***over-agonize, -boast, -digest, -gratify, -nurse, -pepper, -plot, -possess, -relax***, etc.

a 1900 ***over-accentuate, -blame, -book, -borrow, -bowl, -breed, -cultivate, -damn, -dance, -decorate, -doctrinize, -edit, -educate, -egg, -emphasize, -enjoy, -enrich, -exaggerate, -express, -fag, -fatten, -feast, -fee, -flatten, -flog, -gamble, -generalize, -gun, -hate, -horse, -humanize, -inflate, -influence, -insure, -job, -kick, -land, -mill, -objectify, -organize, -pack, -peacock, -pet, -plum, -puff, -quarter, -race, -rapturize, -represent, -scare, -scrub, -slander, -staff, -teach, -worry***, etc.

20th-c. ***over-bowl, -commit, -complicate, -condense, -control, -cook, -deflate, -dramatize, -elaborate, -ink, -interpret, -invest, -order, -rank, -regulate, -rev*** (trans. and intr.), ***-secrete, -stress.***

1885 A. BRERETON *Dramatic Notes* 31 She slightly *over-accentuated certain passages. **1977** *Gramophone* Jan. 1160/1 If anything the conductor over-accentuates at the expense of broader phrasing. **1645** BP. HALL *Remedy Discontents* 69 He that *over-afflicts his body, kills a Subject. **1598** *Epulario* L ij, But let them not bee *ouerbaked. **1593** NASHE *Christs T.* Wks. (Grosart) IV. 91 Shuld I *ouer-blacke mine Incke, perplexe pale Paper.. with the sadde tedious recitall? **1896** NEWTON *Dict. Birds* Introd. 35 We must not *over-blame those who caused it. **1962** *Times* 15 May 4/2 It must be a temptation for his captain to *overbowl him. **1976** J. SNOW *Cricket Rebel* 41 In his first full championship season in 1974 Andy [Roberts] was overbowled consistently throughout the summer while Hampshire tried to retain the county title. **1657-83** EVELYN *Hist. Relig.* (1850) I. 231 Endeavour that we do not *over-cherish their emotions and solicitudes. **1664** —— *Kal. Hort.* Jan. in *Sylva* etc. (1729) 191 Such seeds are in peril of being..*over-chill'd and frozen. **1616** SURFL. & MARKH. *Country Farme* 352 Take heed, not to *ouer-cleaue the stocks of your trees. **1964** Y. MALKIEL in *Archivum Linguisticum* XVI. 15 W. J. Entwistle may have *over-committed himself. **1973** *Guardian* 11 Apr. 8/7 A few [families] were found to have overcommitted themselves with hire purchase. **1966** A. BATTERSBY *Math. in Managem.* v. 130 One can easily *over-complicate a model, and the manager and mathematician must collaborate closely to decide not only what is relevant, but what is significant. **1976** H. TRACY *Death in Reserve* xiv. 113 You're over-complicating the whole thing. **1933** *Mind* XLII. 391 The actual statement of the theory is, in view of its importance, somewhat *over-condensed, and ought perhaps to have been expanded. **1962** A. NISBETT *Technique Sound Studio* xiii. 232 Pace is not achieved by over-condensing vital information. **1941** *Sun* (Baltimore) 28 June 1/5 He simply *overcontrolled the ship. **1904** *Daily Chron.* 30 May 8/3 So you can *over-cook even a sauce. **1963** R. CARRIER *Great Dishes of World* xiii. 225 Be careful not to overcook *pasta.* **1975** I. DALY in D. Marcus *Best Irish Short Stories* (1977) II. 32, I want the steak medium-rare... All you Irish overcook meat. **1977** *Harpers & Queen* Sept. 28/1 The salmon was overcooked. **1605** SYLVESTER *Du Bartas, Sonn. late Peace* xxxvi, One *ouer-Creeds, another Creeds too-short. **1593** NASHE *Four Lett. Conf.* Wks. (Grosart) II. 251, I do not *overcull my owne workes. **1809** HAN. MORE *Cœlebs* I. xxi. 318 Such a fear of *over-cultivating learning, that [etc.]. **1962** *Daily Tel.* 15 June 14/2 The reported trends are signs..that the economy has been *over-deflated and that confidence in future expansion needs fostering. **1974** *Times* 28 Feb. 19/2 A Labour Government would be tempted to overdeflate in the Budget in order to make itself more attractive to foreign lenders. **1955** S. SPENDER *Making of Poem* iv. 63 Perhaps I *over-dramatize the affair. **1976** M. BUTTERWORTH *Remains to be Seen* vii. 111 The flat.. he now saw as a fortress... He hoped he was over-dramatizing his situation. **1303** R. BRUNNE *Handl. Synne* 5166 Holde þe evene hem betwene Nat *over-drede ne overwene. **1597** J. PAYNE *Royal Exch.* 31 The multitude of there worcks *over dulleth and burdeneth. **1905** *Daily Chron.* 2 Sept. 3/1 Mr. Phillpotts has resisted the temptation..to *over-elaborate his descriptions of natural scenery. **1933** W. E. ORCHARD *From Faith to Faith* ix. 206 These [dogmas] were over-elaborated during the early controversies, and have only obscured His personal power by theories about Him. **1905** *Outlook* 7 Oct. 485/1 He *over-emphasises when he suggests that Hungary is a solid State and Austria but a bundle of provinces. **1926** J. S. HUXLEY *Ess. Pop. Sci.* 153 This..we must discount unless we are to over-emphasize the antinomy between the microcosm and the macrocosm. **1968** H. HARRIS *Nucleus & Cytoplasm* i. 12 It cannot be over-emphasized that actinomycin D is an extremely toxic compound. *a* **1680** CHARNOCK *Attrib. God* (1834) II. 127 He never *over-engageth himself above his ability. **1852** MILL *Pol. Econ.* (ed. 3) I. II. ii. 276 Wealth which could no longer be employed in *over-enriching a few. **1883** 'MARK TWAIN' *Life on Mississippi* 399 Terms which did not *over-express the admiration with which the people viewed him. **1959** N. MAILER *Advts. for Myself* (1961) 17, I am not suited for this sort of confrontation despite..a bloody season of overexpressed personal opinions as a newspaper columnist. **1635** BP. PETERBORO' in *Buccleuch MSS.* I. 275 Your Lordship..might well judge me otherwise, if I should *over-fancy that way. **1611** BEAUM. & FL. *King & No King* I. i, You think to *ouer-grace me with The marriage of your sister. **1755** *Man* No. 10. 4 The drunkard, who seeks his pleasure in drink, *over-gratifies his appetite. **1805** NELSON 2 Jan. in Nicolas *Disp.* (1846) VI. 313 The Ventura..is *over-gunned. **1813** WELLINGTON in Gurw. *Desp.* X. 77 Great care must be taken..not to *overhorse any [regiments]. Too many horses are worse than too few. **1927** *Observer* 12 June 9 The literary man..is apt to *over-ink his pictures of contemporary morals. **1939** T. S. ELIOT *Family Reunion* II. i. 77 You *overinterpret. I am sure that your mother always loved him; There was never the slightest suspicion of scandal. **1963** *Times* 9 May 16/4 She.. sometimes fell into the opposite trap of overinterpreting detail. **1975** *Nature* 18 Dec. 562/3 There is a danger, however, that such a negative result could be over-interpreted as suggesting that recombinant experiments are inherently safe. **1934** WEBSTER, *Overinvest. **1958** *New Statesman* 25 Jan. 94/3 The trouble about Poland today..is that we are rather like a furniture manufacturer who has plenty of table legs but no table tops. We have over-invested in legs and now we want more capital for the tops. **1599** SANDYS *Europæ Spec.* (1632) 93 So huge a multitude of.. works as in this over-ranke age mens finger *over-itching have produced. **1639** FULLER *Holy War* III. xiv. (1647) 133 Neither ignorant of his greatnesse, nor *over-knowing it. **1642** FULLER *Holy & Prof. St.* IV. i 242 He loves not to *over-linger any in an afflicting hope, but speedily dispatcheth the fears or desires of his expecting clients. **1895** W. B. YEATS *Poems* 23 He has over-lingered his welcome. **1646** SIR T. BROWNE *Pseud. Ep.* 28 The Chymistes ..*overmagnifying their preparations. *a* **1700** CREECH (J.), Little pleasure *overmixt with woe. **1626** BACON *Sylva* §422 It will *over-Moisten the Roots, so as the Wormes will eate them. *a* **1656** BP. HALL *Rem. Wks.* (1660) 13 Our Romanists exceed..both in *over-multiplying and over-magnifying of it. **1658** OSBORN *Adv. Son* Wks. (1673) 80 If it be dangerous to *over-oblige a King, it is mortal in relation to a Free-State. **1950** *Times* 20 Feb. 7/7 It was not surprising that, when steel was most scarce, the distribution scheme worked least well: firms *over-ordered and accumulated stocks and there was nothing to encourage them to use as little steel as possible. **1977** D. BENNETT *Jigsaw Man* v. 106 'You aren't liking your good grub.' 'I think I over-ordered.' **1633** BP. HALL *Occas. Medit.* (1851) 123 Who would *over-pamper a body, for the worms? **1720** R. MEAD *Plague* Pref., Wks. (1762) 233 Wrong notions..may sometimes *over-possess their minds. **1912** A. LANG *Shakespeare, Bacon & Great Unknown* iv. 81 Mr. Collins, 'a violent Stratfordian', *overproved his case. **1929** R. GRAVES *Poems* 31 Now is a sheet of paper, A not blank expectation,.. A being, over-proved, A report of happiness. **1958** *New Statesman* 23 Aug. 222/3 In answering poll-questionnaires..'we tend to *over-rank ourselves'. **1972** *Korea Times* 17 Nov. 2/3, I am no longer willing to remain patient with the parade of overranked non-entities whose actions reflect their own ignorance. **1938** *Sun* (Baltimore) 16 Apr. 8 Mr. Roosevelt is equally muddled in his general attitude toward trade and industry. For five years he has *overregulated trade and industry. **1973** *Sci. Amer.* Sept. 165/1 Some observers believe that the pharmaceutical industry is now overregulated and that bureaucratic interference with the industry has reached such a level that the American public is being denied certain drugs available overseas. *a* **1754** —— *Fevers* ii. ibid. 482 That very warmth..becoming prejudicial, by *over-relaxing the fibres. **1935** C. G. BURGE *Compl. Bk. Aviation* 87/1 The control stick is pushed forward to give the diving position and the throttle eased slightly back to avoid *over-revving the engine. **1978** *Daily Tel.* 26 July 3/2 Mr Wheatcroft adjusted the accelerator, but ..he noticed that the coach seemed to be 'over-revving', as though the driver was not using the brakes to slow it down. **1682** WHELER *Journ. Greece* 312 We had like to have *over-sawc'd it [the Supper] with wine. **1927** HALDANE & HUXLEY *Animal Biol.* viii. 164 If the pituitary begins to *over-secrete before the epiphyses have been joined by bone to the shafts, the patient becomes a giant. *a* **1643** J. SHUTE *Judgem. & Mercy* (1645) 119 Men have so *oversotted themselves, that ..they have turned the courses of men. **1916** T. MACDONAGH *Lit. in Ireland* 66 An Irish reader would be content to pronounce the words as they come,..not *overstressing 'in' and 'up'. **1933** *Mind* XLII. 238 It is also admitted that children have to be taught cleanliness (which parents often over-stress from snobbishness!). **1970** *Daily Tel.* 26 Sept. 9/7 It would however be wrong to overstress the importance of colour in lithography. **1977** *Bitumen* (Shell Internat. Petroleum Co.) 7 Knowledge of such properties has made it possible to design roads and airfield runways on sound engineering principles, ensuring that no part is over-stressed even under the heaviest loads. **1393** LANGL. *P. Pl.* C. VII. 429 Ich gloton..*ouer-sopede at my soper. **1601** HOLLAND *Pliny* I. 555 Nothing is lesse profitable, and expedient, than to labor a ground exceeding much, and to *ouer-til it. **1651** BAXTER *Inf. Bapt.* 345, I quickly found too many over-valuing it, and some *overvilifying it. **18..** in *Macm. Mag.* (1880) XLI. 225 Overworked, *over-worried, Over-Croker'd, over-Murray'd. **1635** *Over-worship [see OVERPRAISE].

b. This use is often found with pa. pples., when the other parts of the verb occur with *over-* rarely or not at all: as in ***over-agitated, -answered, -assessed, -bitten, -blessed, -bred, -browned, -brushed, -chafed, -characterized, -chased, -chidden, -coached, -concentrated, -concerned, -corned, -culled, -cumbered, -delighted, -disciplined, -discounted, -dunged, -exacted, -exalted, -explained, -fagged, -famed, -fawned, -furnished, -goaded, -handicapped, -harassed, -helped, -hurried, -imported, -instructed, -involved, -iodized, -listed, -mortgaged, -mucked, -pained, -pointed, -polished, -preoccupied, -protracted, -provoked, -ravished, -recovered, -rehearsed, -represented, -restored, -retched, -rigged, -sated, -saturated, -scented, -seasoned, -seeded, -settled, -smitten, -soaked, -stalled, -stent, -stored, -stowed, -sweated, -technicized, -thronged, -tippled, -tutored, -vexed, -withered,*** etc.

1649 BP. HALL *Cases Consc.* III. vii. 290 What is fit to be determined in a business so *over-agitated. **1851** RUSKIN *Stones Ven.* I. App. viii. 364 They [plates]..are *over-bitten, they are hastily drawn. *c* **1804** WORDSWORTH *Vaudracour & Julia* in *Misc. Poems* (1820) I. 283 His spirit sank, Surcharged, within him,—*overblest to move Beneath a sun that wakes a weary world. **1918** *Nation* (N.Y.) 7 Feb. 130/1 Not by any means a leader even in a body that has not of late been overblessed with outstanding personages. **1977** D. CLARK *Gimmel Flask* iii. 58 Green wasn't over-blessed with good manners. **1659** GAUDEN *Tears Church* Pref. 14 *Over-bred, and too much Gentlemen. **1806** A. HUNTER *Culina* (ed. 3) 117 Take care that it be not *overbrowned. **1561** HOLLYBUSH *Hom. Apoth.* 21 It is good for the stomake that is *ouerchafed. **1959** *Times* 9 Nov. 6/1 To begin with they [*sc.* the figures] are heavily *over-characterized (by the dangerous means of self-description). **1616** SURFL. & MARKH. *Country Farme* 666 Nature will not be *ouer-chased. **1957** K. G. WITTFOGEL *Oriental Despotism* 24 On-the-spot rains create additional dangers when they are *overconcentrated. **1934** WEBSTER *s.v.* Over- 6, *Overconcerned. **1941** *Mind* L. 2 You are under-concerned about the cases which don't trouble you at the moment, and over-concerned about the one that is striking you at the moment. **1976** P. HILL *Hunters* vi. 67 Was he then weak.. over-concerned with what others thought of him. **1565** JEWEL *Def. Apol.* (1611) 620 To be too careful, and *ouercombred about the iudgements of mortal Men. *a* **1600** HOOKER *Serm. Pride* i. Wks. 1888 III. 598 The fearful estate of iniquity *over-exalted. **1642** FULLER *Holy & Prof. St.* v. xviii. §14 The city..was instantly conquered, whose strength was much *over-famed. **1602** BRETON *Mother's Blessing* xliii, And neuer be with flatterers *ouerfawnd. **1703** COLLIER *Ess.* II. 158, I dont think myself *over-furnished. **1841–4** EMERSON *Ess.* Ser. II. vi. (1876) 142, I am *overinstructed for my return. **1965** M. MORSE *Unattached* iii. 90 Even the most..skilled of workers can..become *over-involved with the..situation at hand. **1878** ABNEY *Photogr.* (1881) 62 The solution is '*over-iodized'; that is, it is super-saturated with silver iodide. **1665** *Conn. Col. Rec.* (1852) II. 23 Mr. Edward Palmes appeales to this Court.. for being *ouerlisted by James Rogers and Cary Latham. **1868** *Dublin Univ. Mag.*, The travelling histrionics commemorated, or rather *over-over-coloured by Crabbe. **1589** GREENE *Menaphon* (Arb.) 25 When thou art *over-pained with passions. **1725** BLACKWALL *Sacr. Class.* I. I. ii. §5. 85 A judicious ear would be offended with a style *over-polish'd. **1975** *Times Lit. Suppl.* 13 June 669/1 Historians.. had been *overpreoccupied with what was done to the slaves and had slighted what slaves had done for themselves. **1633** BP. HALL *Occas. Medit.* (1851) 149 It grieves him, to be *over-provoked to our punishment. **1962** *Which?* (Car Suppl.) Jan. 11/2 Where there is a minus figure, it means that the braking system had *over-recovered and needed less pressure than usual; this may make control difficult. **1967** D. GOCH in Wills & Yearsley *Handbk. Managem. Technol.* 147 Fixed over-heads, being relatively unaffected by fluctuations in the number of units produced during the period, will be either under- or over-recovered to the extent that output varies from that which was assumed to be normal when the standards were set. **1976** *Gramophone* May 1732/1 Most concerts are under-rehearsed and rely too much on the inspiration of the moment, or are *over-rehearsed and so dead. **1900** *Daily News* 17 Oct. 4/5 In Wales the Liberals are *over-represented. In the predominant partner the Tories are over-represented. **1965** J. HAJNAL in Glass & Eversley *Population in Hist.* vi. 121 The deaths of young women are very probably over-represented. **1974** *Howard Jrnl.* XIV. 39 ESN schools, where West Indian youths are significantly over-represented, mainly because they have been wrongly placed there. **1627** CAPT. SMITH *Seaman's Gram.* v. 18 Shee is *ouer-rigged. **1819** SHELLEY *Cyclops* 507 I'm..With the young feast *over-sated. **1621** FLETCHER *Pilgrim* IV. ii, Had I been *over-season'd with base anger, And suited all occasions to my mischiefs. **1615** W. LAWSON *Country Housew. Gard.* (1626) 22 One could not thriue for the throng of his neighbours..like a Corne-field *ouer-seeded, or a towne ouer-peopled. *a* **1639** W. WHATELEY *Prototypes* II. xxvi. (1640) 82 Be not *over-setled in a purpose about things of this nature. **1628** GAULE *Pract. The.* (1629) 153 That we are either vnacquainted, or *ouerstalled with it. **1786** *Har'st Rig* in Chambers *Pop. Hum. Scot. P.* (1862) 46 Frae this they tell, as how the rent O' sic a room was *overstent. *a* **1677** HALE *Prim. Orig. Man.* II. ix. 208 The Ocean it self would have been long since *over-stored with Fish. **1953** *Mind* LXII. 424 It is a joy to go back to the beginnings of a subject which has since become *over-technicised. **1610** HOLLAND *Camden's Brit.* 493 Richard the last Abbot..being *ouer-tipled as it were with wealth. **1691** NORRIS *Pract. Disc.* Pref. 6 They suffer in their Morals by being *over-tutour'd, as some men do in their Health by being over-physick'd.

28. a. With adjectives, simple or derivative.

These appear already in OE. and the cognate langs. In OE. nearly 30 examples are recorded, including *oferbliðe, oferceald, ofereald, oferfætt, oferfull, ofergrædig, oferhéah, oferhlúd, ofermicel, oferranc; oferæte, -etol, ofersprecol, oferglenged, ofermódig, ofermódlic*, etc. In OE. these were treated as true compounds. In ME. *over* was often written separately, and its use began to be extended beyond the words handed down from OE. Since *c* 1500, the tendency has been to treat *over* as a movable element which can be prefixed at will to any adj.; and in Sc. and north. Eng. dialects, where *ower, owre* is the regular equivalent of Standard Eng. *too*, it is always written as a separate word. In literary English it is usually hyphened, exc. in a small number of combinations of ancient standing and frequent use, which are usually written as single words: e.g. OVERFOND, OVERFULL, OVERMUCH, etc. But even in literary Eng., *over* is sometimes treated as a separate word, and the consciousness that it is such is seen in the colloquial strengthened form ***over and above***, 'not over and above particular'.

The more important of these are treated as Main words: see OVERACTIVE, -BITTER, -BOLD, -BUSY, etc. Other examples are: Of OE. age *overblithe*.

a 1400 ***over-sour, -steadfast, -wroth.***

a 1500 ***over-blind, -covetous, -dainty, -delicious, -felon, -foul, -good, -huge, -mighty.***

a 1600 ***over-apt, -base, -battle, -capable, -captious, -charitable, -childish, -corrupt, -deep, -extreme, -faint, -faithful, -fierce, -foolish, -frail, -gamesome, -general, -gentle, -greasy, -gross, -haught, -heinous, -idle, -insolent, -lightheaded, -lofty, -meek, -merry, -ordinary, -painful, -passionate, -pert, -piteous, -plausible, -plentiful, -politic, -potent, -presumptuous, -prolix, -prone, -rife, -rude, -russet, -sapless, -severe, -slack, -small, -soft, -stale, -stately, -timorous, -true, -vehement, -young,*** etc.

a 1700 ***over-abstemious, -apprehensive, -barren, -big, -bookish, -bounteous, -careless, -circumspect, -copious, -courteous, -coy, -distant, -exquisite, -factious, -fellowly, -frequent, -fruitful, -godly, -grateful, -guilty, -haughty, -heady, -hollow, -homely, -honest, -inclinable, -just, -lascivious, -lawyerlike, -laxative, -lewd, -licentious, -lively, -logical, -loose, -malapert, -mean, -merciful, -mild, -moist, -nimble, -obedient, -obese, -obsequious, -open, -orthodox, -oscitant, -peremptory, -pervicacious, -plain, -plenteous, -polemical, -ponderous, -popular, -positive, -precise, -pregnant, -public, -puissant, -ready, -resolute, -rough, -sad, -saucy, -scrutinous, -serious, -servile, -sick, -silent, -simple, -slavish, -slight, -slope, -solemn, -spacious, -steady, -stiff, -sublime, -superstitious, -sure, -terrible, -thrifty, -tight, -uberous, -unsuitable, -valiant, -venturous, -voluble, -wanton, -wary, -wayward, -wily, -woody,*** and others.

a 1800 ***over-bashful, -diligent, -elegant, -famous, -jealous, -judicious, -learned, -luxuriant, -neat, -new, -notable, -pensive, -provident, -rational, -righteous, -sanguine, -tame, -tart, -tense, -thick, -vigorous,*** and many others.

a 1900 ***over-clean, -complimentary, -conscientious, -conscious, -controversial, -fastidious, -genial, -incurious, -ingenious, -mellow, -particular, -patient, -prompt, -quiet, -rapid, -squeamish, -studious,*** and others without limit.

20th-c. ***over-articulate, -concise, -dependent, -elaborate, -fast, -friendly, -fussy, -insistent, -keen, -obvious, -optimistic, -pessimistic, -picturesque, -plump, -prolific, -sensational, -shy, -susceptible,*** etc.

1699 BENTLEY *Phal.* 240 Mr. Selden was not *over accurate in copying the Inscription. **1598** DRAYTON *Heroic Ep.* (1637) 332 By each temptation *over apt to slide. **1975** *Christmas Greeting* (Rhodes House, Oxford) 6 When dons behave badly, they behave very badly: it is partly the fault of being *over-articulate, though early rearing probably has something to do with it too. **1548** UDALL, etc. *Erasm. Par.* Pref. 5 All temporall..rewardes were incomparably *ouer basse. **1597** HOOKER *Eccles. Pol.* v. iii. §4 In the Church of God sometimes it commeth to passe, as in *ouer battle grounds, the fertile disposition whereof is good. *c* **1412** HOCCLEVE *De Reg. Princ.* 861 þey þat nat konne lerned be ne taght By swiche ensaumples..Me þinkeþ, certes, *ouer blynde been. *c* **897** K. ÆLFRED *Gregory's Past. C.* lxi. 455 Oft ða *oferbliðan weorðað ʒedrefde for unʒemetlicre onetunga. **1711** J. GREENWOOD *Eng. Gram.* 196 Over-blith or (merry). **1633** FORD *'Tis Pity* II. vi, You must forsake This *over-bookish humour. **1594** HOOKER *Eccl. Pol.* Pref. iii. §10 Men credulous and *ouer-capable of such pleasing errors. *c* **1806** D. WORDSWORTH *Jrnl.* (1941) I. 327 Two beds, with not *over-clean bedclothes. **1818** 'A. BURTON' *Adventures J. Newcome* I. 32 The Bed-cloaths, when by daylight seen, They did not fancy over-clean. **1867** MILL *Exam. Hamilton's Philos.* (ed. 3) p. vii, Some of the writers are..even *over-complimentary. **1940** W. STEVENS *Let.* 30 Aug. (1967) 374 The trouble here is that the lines are *over-concise. **1965** *Language* XLI. 142 In his desire to be complete..and informative, Kukenheim is over-concise. **1851** H. MELVILLE *Moby Dick* I. i. 5 Whenever I begin to.. be *over conscious of my lungs. **1862** H. SIDGWICK *Let.* 28 Jan. in A. & E. M. Sidgwick *Henry Sidgwick* (1906) 74 It seems smashing, but he loses by being *over-controversial. **1649** MILTON *Eikon.* Wks. 1738 I. 442 In an argument *over-copious rather than barren. **1481** CAXTON *Reynard* (Arb.) 95 *Ouer couetous was neuer good. *c* **1440** *Jacob's Well* 144 þe iiij. fote brede of wose in þis glotony is, for to ete *ouyr-deynte metys. **1598** SYLVESTER *Du Bartas* II. i. I. *Eden* 404 When the pencill of Cares *over-deep Our day-bred thoughts depainteth in our sleep. **1975** *New Yorker* 21 Apr. 127/2 We fought the war for them and made them *overdependent on air support. **1711** SHAFTESB. *Charact.* (1737) III. 30 The very reading of treatises..of melancholy has been apt to generate that passion in the *over-diligent and attentive reader. **1931** A. ESDAILE *Student's Man. Bibliogr.* vi. 198 Incised bindings..also became *over-elaborate, especially in Germany. **1634** MILTON *Comus* 359 Peace, brother, be not *over-exquisite To cast the fashion of uncertain evils. *a* **1591** H. SMITH *Wks.* (1867) II. 486 Hence, *over-faint, or over-full; Too-pined, or too-plentiful. **1934** WEBSTER, *Overfast. **1949** R. BLESH *Shining Trumpets* ii. 41 Overfast tempos did not appear in Afro-American music until very recently. **1819** SHELLEY *Cenci* Pref., An *over-fastidious and learned choice of words. **1626** DONNE *Serm.* lxxviii. 691 That is by not being *over-fellowly with God, not over homely with places and acts of Religion. **1483** CAXTON *Gold. Leg.* 136/1 *Ouer felon and cruelle tyraunt hast thou noo shame. *a* **1600** *Praise of Measure Keeping* (R.), Nor overmeke nor *overferce he was. **1482** *Monk of Evesham* (Arb.) 77 The whyche dede specialy yn a byshoppe, was *ouerfowle and abhomynable. *a* **1625** FLETCHER *Fair Maid Inn* I. i, You are Observ'd..to be *over-frequent In giving or receiving visits. **1939** R. CAMPBELL *Flowering Rifle* VI. 142 In their own tanks they have to be locked up As in a box an *over-friendly pup. **1962** E. GODFREY *Retail Selling & Organization* xii. 131 Personal comments and an over-friendly manner also amount to discourtesy. **1974** N. FREELING *Dressing of Diamond* 135 Richard asked..whether I'd perhaps let myself get over-friendly with Colette. **1668** DRYDEN *Ess. Dram. Poesie* (R.), The labour of rhyme bounds and circumscribes an *over-fruitful fancy. **1962** *Times* 16 Feb. 15/2 The ballet-boyish treatment of the pirate chorus is new, and inclined to look *over-fussy. **1560** DAUS tr. *Sleidane's Comm.* 194 He hym selfe hath bene *ouer-gentle to hym. **1754** H. WALPOLE *Lett.* (1846) III. 80 You are *over-good to me..in..telling me. **1587** GOLDING *De Mornay* xi. 150 A manifest guyle, or at leastwise an *ouergrosse ignorance. **1432–50** tr. *Higden* (Rolls) VI. 381 For *over-huge familiarite betwene hir and the bischop Vercellense. **1871** R. ELLIS *Catullus* lxxviii. 5 An *o'er-incurious husband. **1858** BAGEHOT *Coll. Works* (1965) II. 70 It would be *over-ingenious to argue..that he had no peculiar interest in young ladies in general. **1977** A. WILSON *Strange Ride R. Kipling* iv. 208 The over-ingenious method of Kipling's narration. **1915** D. H. LAWRENCE *Let.* 26 Feb. (1962) I. 323, I wish you'd tell me when I am foolish and *overinsistent. **1977** *N.Y. Rev. Bks.* 13 Oct. 35/2 The slightly overinsistent Ciceronianisms here draw attention to themselves. **1934** WEBSTER *s.v.* Over- 6, *Overkeen. **1959** I. & P. OPIE *Lore & Lang. Schoolch.* x. 181 The word 'sap'.. at Eton is primarily used to castigate someone who is over-keen on his work. **1977** J. BINGHAM *Marriage Bureau Murders* x. 130 A girl in trouble with an over-keen lover. **1592** G. HARVEY *Four Lett.* Wks. (Grosart) I. 200 The Grecians generallie were *ouer-lightheaded. **1641** MILTON *Animadv.* iii, They have..thought him, if not an *over-logical, yet a well-meaning man. **1920** W. R. INGE *Truth & Falsehood in Relig.* 19 Exclusive intellectualism in religion.. commits us to an over-logical scheme. **1966** *Eng. Stud.* XLVII. 299 Occasionally Williams seems to make Shakespeare over-logical. **1832** TENNYSON *Loto-seaters* 78 The full-juiced apple, waxing *over-mellow. **1930** WYNDHAM LEWIS *Let.* 30 July (1963) 190 Joyce is like an over-mellow hot-house pear. **1596** SHAKS. *Tam. Shr.* Induct. i. 137 Haply my presence May well abate the *ouer-merrie spleene. *c* **1460** FORTESCUE *Abs. & Lim. Mon.* ix. *heading*, Perellis that mey come to the Kyng by *ouer myghtye subgettes. **1887** W. MORRIS tr. *Homer's Odyssey* I. x. 188 There was one Elpenor, the youngest;..In war not over-mighty. **1920** G. ROBINSON *David Urquhart* 11 The ephemeral predominance of an over-mighty subject. **1950** *Catholic Times* 17 Feb. 6/3 Some will perceive first the dangers of the Overmighty State. **1966** *Economist* 15 Jan. 170/3 Officialdom is also angry with the overmighty bishops for taking a political initiative without consulting the government. **1978** *Jrnl. R. Soc. Arts* CXXVI. 212/2 Monopolistic bodies have a tendency to become over-mighty. **1626** *Over-moist [see OVER-DRY *a.*]. **1885** W. B. YEATS in *Dublin Univ. Rev.* June 111/2 Cease! no more! Thou hast an *over-nimble tongue. **1925** I. A. RICHARDS *Princ. Lit. Crit.* xxxv. 287 If to some readers parts of it appear unnecessary—either *irrelevant*, in the one case; or **over-obvious* in the other—I have nothing to add. **1951** KOESTLER *Age of Longing* II. iv. 243 Not to mention such over-obvious facts as the disparity in the number of divisions. **1953** *Encounter* July 48/1 If *The Tempest* is over-pessimistic and manichean, *The Magic Flute* is *over-optimistic and pelagian. **1976** *Broadcast* 29 Mar. 4/1 Over-optimistic predictions of BBC income in the coming year. **1861** DICKENS *Gt. Expect.* xvii, I am not *over-particular. **1599** SANDYS *Europæ Spec.* (1632) 130 The dreames..of some *over-passionate desires. **1881** 'MARK TWAIN' *Prince & Pauper* 137, I like not much bandying of words, being not *overpatient in my nature. **1624** DONNE *Serm.* ii. 16 Be not overvehement *Overperemptory. **1934** WEBSTER, *Overpessimistic. **1953** Over-pessimistic [see *over-optimistic* above]. **1938** L. MACNEICE *Mod. Poetry* 10 His [*sc.* Housman's] hanged man, his soldiers, are *over-picturesque. **1592** NASHE *Four Lett.* Wks. (Grosart) I. 193 Whilest I am be-moaning his *ouer-pitteous decay. **1561** DAUS tr. *Bullinger on Apoc.* (1573) 111 b, Exceedingly *ouerplentifull was this darnell throughout the vniuersall church. **1932** W. FAULKNER *Light in August* xiii. 300 Hightower leans there..in the August heat, oblivious of the odor in which he lives—..that odor of *overplump desiccation and stale linen as though a precursor of the tomb. **1599** SANDYS *Europæ Spec.* (1632) 102 This *over-politick and too wise Order. **1644** MILTON *Education* §1 An unfit and *over-ponderous argument. **1684** T. BURNET *Th. Earth* II. To Rdr., The greatest fault..is to be *over-positive and dogmatical. **1594** Hooker *Eccl. Pol.* I. x. §14 The priuate intents of men *ouer-potent in the Commonwelth. **1923** D. H. Lawrence *Birds, Beasts & Flowers* 179 Those *over-prolific white mice. **1597** *Ibid.* v. xlvi. §3 Rash, sinister, and suspitious verdits, whereunto they are *ouer-prone. **1976** N. Freeling *Lake Isle* viii. 51 His ma.. was overprone, maybe, to well-meant advice about bringing up the children and such. **1828** *Lights & Shades* II. 184 An old *over-provident housekeeper. **1848** Mill *Pol. Econ.* I. II. xi. 413 Where a labouring class.. refrain from *over-rapid multiplication, the cause.. has always hitherto been, either actual legal restraint, or a custom of some sort [etc.]. **1964** *Ann. Reg. 1963* 263 Credit also became tighter, and full employment created the conditions for an over-rapid rise in wages and salaries. **1628** O. Feltham *Resolves* (ed. 3) xcvii. 283 And yet there are, that are *over-ready in the wayes of pleasing, and labour. **1782** Miss Burney *Cecilia* ix. vi, We are all over-ready.. to blame others. **1859** Bagehot *Coll. Works* (1965) II. 114 We may seem to make unusual criticisms, and to be over-ready with depreciation or objection. **1906** *Westm. Gaz.* 24 Mar. 2/3 They may be gazing on the.. over-ready-to-burst chestnut-buds. **1791** 'G. Gambado' *Ann. Horsem.* ix. (1809) 105, I suspected my Divine was none of the *over-righteous. **1633** Ford *Broken H.* II. i, She is so *over-sad. **1959** *Times* 3 Sept. 13/2 He is sometimes *oversensational and has tried to stuff too much into one book. **1668** H. More *Div. Dial.* v. xvii. (1713) 464 To unbewilder some *over-serious Souls. **1586** T. B. *La Primaud. Fr. Acad.* I. (1594) 559 It falleth out so, that an *over-severe magistrate becommeth odious. **1939** L. MacNeice *Autumn Jrnl.* xi. 46 *Over-shy at times, morose, defeatist. *a* **1600** Hooker *Eccl. Pol.* VI. v. §7 Men are commonly *overslack to perform this duty. **1616** Hieron *Wks.* I. 586 *Ouer-slight, too loose, and superficiall. **1581** Campion in *Confer.* I. (1584) Fivb, The print was *ouer small. **1393** Langl. *P. Pl.* C. xvi. 49 Here sauce was *ouere soure and vnsauerliche grounde. *a* **1300** *Cursor M.* 27999 If þou.. loked wit *ouur stedfast sight. **1671** Milton *P.R.* II. 142 Perswasion *over-sure. **1934** Webster, *Oversusceptible. **1966** *Eng. Stud.* XLVII. 286 The connection.. is made by the over-susceptible sensibility of Emily. **1589** Nashe *Pref. Greene's Menaphon* (Arb.) 14 Their *ouertimerous cowardise. **1597** Hooker *Eccl. Pol.* v. lxv. §16 We have by *over-true experience been taught how often.. the light even of common understanding faileth. **1627** Drayton *Miseries Q. Margaret* Wks. 1753 II. 400 The Lord Lisle his *over-valiant son. *a* **1637** B. Jonson tr. *Horace Art of Poetrie* 358 And nere the hall reherse Their youthfull tricks in *over-wanton verse. **1614** Raleigh *Hist. World* v. ii. §3 The one being so *over-wary, and the other so hasty. **1390** Gower *Conf.* I. 298, I am therfore So *overwroth in al my thoght.

b. with pres. pples., forming ppl. adjs.; as over-abounding, etc.; also, ***over-bragging***, ***-boasting***, ***-dazzling***, ***-demanding***, ***-depressing***, ***-exciting***, ***-itching***, ***-laughing***, ***-nipping***, ***-pressing***, ***-refining***, ***-soothing***, ***-sparing***, ***-staring***, etc. (Can be formed at will.)

1576 Turberv. *Venerie* 93 Those *ouerbragging bluddes Amusde your mynde. **1707** Norris *Treat. Humility* ii. 20 The *over-dazzling glory of their own perfections. **1949** M. Mead *Male & Female* iii. 74 Too much emphasis upon the assertive demanding aspects of the mouth may build a female picture that is over-active, *over-demanding, and threatening. *a* **1600** Hooker *Serm. Pride* Wks. 1888 III. 610 Shake off that *over-depressing heaviness. *c* **1400** *Rule St. Benet* (E.E.T.S.) 14/31 Bidis þat ye ne sal noght be *ouir-laȝand. **1586** J. Hooker *Hist. Irel.* in *Holinshed* II. 104/2 Albeit their wether were bitter and *ouernipping. **1893** *Harper's Mag.* Aug. 335/1 The finding.. such a palpable motive as revenge against an *overpressing and clamorous creditor tipped the balance. **1940** Dylan Thomas *Portrait of Artist as Young Dog* 122 And I never felt more a part of the remote and overpressing world, or more full of love and arrogance and pity and humility. **1855** Bagehot *Coll. Works* (1965) I. 322 The sceptical, *over-refining Toryism of Hume and Montaigne. **1598** J. Dickenson *Greene in Conc.* (1878) 131 Valeria, whose *ouersoothing humor made her interprete flatterie for truth. **1603** Knolles *Hist. Turks* (1638) 338 He was thought *ouersparing vnto himselfe, as well in his apparel as in his diet. *a* **1568** Ascham *Scholem.* (Arb.) 54 Either a slouinglie busking, or an *ouer-staring frounced hed. **1647** Clarendon *Contempl. Ps.* Tracts (1727) 455 Like over-skilful musicians, who by an *over-warbling desire to make the voice not intelligible, are without that vociferation which he expects.

c. with pa. pples. in *-ed*, *-en*, etc., forming ppl. adjs., as overacted, -civilized, -crowded, -done, -grown, etc. So ***over-apprehended***, ***-arranged***, ***-blessed***, ***(-blest)***, ***-contented***, ***-controlled***, ***-cooked***, ***-cultivated***, ***-cultured***, ***-dignified***, ***-distempered***, ***-dubbed***, ***-educated***, ***-emotionalized***, ***-emptied***, ***-enamoured***, ***-enlarged***, ***-expanded***, ***-formed***, ***-franchised***, ***-handled***, ***-inflated***, ***-inked***, ***-interested***, ***-jaded***, ***-mechanized***, ***-nourished***, ***-offended***, ***-oiled***, ***-packed***, ***-padded***, ***-pampered***, ***-perfumed***, ***-polished***, ***-qualified***, ***-ravished***, ***-reserved***, ***-restrained***, ***-schematized***, ***-sensitized*** (also as sb.), ***-sophisticated***, ***-speculated***, ***-spiritualized***, ***-structured***, ***-stuffed***, ***-sugared***, ***-swilled***, ***-tamed***, ***-tossed***, ***-twisted***, ***-vitrified***, ***-womanized***, ***-wrested***, etc. (Unlimited in number.)

1663 Boyle *Usef. Exp. Nat. Philos.* II. App. 347 By the *over-apprehended unpleasantness of the smell. **1924** R. H. Mottram *Spanish Farm* 148 She was after all only saying the same thing in French, when a frail, fair, *over-arranged lady kept her waiting in the glove department of the Bon Marché. **1956** G. Coulter in M. T. Williams *Art of Jazz* (1960) 167 Most of these bad performances take place in an over-arranged, be-violined setting. **1977** *New Musical Express* 12 Feb. 10/5 We hated over-arranged stage acts and gimmicks constructed just to go with one particular piece of music. **1964** M. Argyle *Psychol. & Social Probl.* ix. 123 Anxiety neurosis is an extreme case of the *over-controlled personality resulting from a strict upbringing. **1968** J. S. & B. M. Bruner in *Internat. Jrnl. Psychol.* III. 239 In early human growth, the initially well-organized systems seem to be predominantly of the automatic or 'overcontrolled' type, as with breathing, swallowing, and initial sucking. **1868** W. James *Let.* 5 Apr. in R. B. Perry *Tht. & Char. W. James* (1935) I. 268 The cool acceptance by the bloody old heathens of everything that happened around them [etc.].. would all make their society perfectly hateful to these *overcultivated and vaguely sick complainers. **1970** S. L. Barraclough in I. L. Horowitz *Masses in Lat. Amer.* iv. 138 Erosion of overcultivated hillsides is prevalent. **1643** Milton *Divorce* Ded., Wks. (1847) 122 To put a garrison upon his neck of empty and *over-dignified precepts. **1650** B. *Discolliminium* 50 Our late *over-dubb'd Justices of Peace, and under-bred Committee-men. **1938** R. G. Collingwood *Princ. Art* iii. 52 Plato.. thinks that the new art of the decadence is the art of an over-excited, *over-emotionalized world. **1586** A. Day *Eng. Secretary* II. (1625) 22 To shroud their lauish and *ouer-emptied expence, by whatsoeuer kinde of lucre. **1742** Young *Nt. Th.* v. 992 Some, *o'er-enamour'd of their Bags, run mad. **1594** Hooker *Eccl. Pol.* I. xi. §6 With pressed and heaped and euen *ouer-inlarged measure. **1965** H. J. Habbakuk in Glass & Eversley *Population in Hist.* vii. 157 These epidemics.. cannot have been a Malthusian punishment inflicted on an *overexpanded population. **1647** Ward *Simp. Cobler* 51 *Over-franchised people are devills with smooth snaffles in their mouthes. **1592** Shaks. *Ven. & Ad.* 770 You will fall againe, Into your idle *ouer-handled theame. **1934** E. Pound *Eleven New Cantos* xxxiii. 14 The meeting decided we were *over-inflated. **1964** W. G. Smith *Allergy & Tissue Metabolism* i. 3 The post mortem picture shows over-inflated lungs. *a* **1974** R. Crossman *Diaries* (1975) I. 585 The economy was over-inflated now, we needed to take some of the heat out and to drive a little of the employment out of it. **1978** *New York* 3 Apr. 71/2 His reputation is overshadowed.. by that of Sir Edward Elgar, on whose inflated scores a grossly overinflated revival is now being perpetrated. **1967** Karch & Buber *Offset Processes* viii. 281 A heavy flow of ink will cause *over-inked copy resulting in scum. *a* **1744** Pope *Let. Mrs. Blount* in Ayre *Mem.* (1754) II. 56 Methinks, it shews an *over-interested Affection to be sad, because she has left us to better her Condition. **1615** Brathwait *Strappado* (1878) 49 May you liue, Till you haue nought to take, nor none to giue, For your *ore-iaded pleasure. **1960** *Farmer & Stockbreeder* 1 Mar. 135 (Advt.), If you haven't got a Lundell today, you're *overmechanised. **1977** *Listener* 20 Oct. 517/2 It provides.. a record.. of what happens when a lumpish, over-mechanised and wrongly-trained army.. meets a lightweight but adept Asian guerilla force in its own country. **1931** H. Read *Meaning of Art* II. 94 'Barock' with its dark and loaded sound implying well the heavy, swollen, *over-nourished forms that must be urged into movement to make their impression. **1712** Steele *Spect.* No. 266 ¶1 Will. Honeycomb calls these *over-offended Ladies, the Outragiously Virtuous. **1957** E. Pound tr. *Rimbaud* 13 A woman's head with brown *over-oiled hair. **1938** L. MacNeice *Mod. Poetry* i. 4 Reaction from this poetry, which they felt to be priggish or pontifical or merely dull and *overpadded. **1583** Golding *Calvin on Deut.* iii. 17 They play the *ouer-pampered Iades which fall to kicking against their maisters. **1857** Bagehot *Coll. Works* (1965) II. 28 An *over-perfumed softness pervades the poetry of society. **1938** H. Nicholson *Let.* 22 Apr. (1966) 337 An ex-diplomatist with those *overpolished manners, that *boulevard extérieur* elegance, which always faintly annoys me. **1957** Manvell & Huntley *Film Music* iv. 180 The lighting cameraman may be concerned with a range of problems, from the over-polished console of an electric organ to the number of arcs required to illuminate the Royal Albert Hall. **1968** *N.Y. Times* 3 Feb. 19/5 It is often hard to get the message across to personnel men 'who make points hiring *over qualified people for less than they're worth'. **1969** *Time* 28 Mar. 41 Applications are flooding colleges across the country. The problem is how to cull the lucky few from the over-qualified many. **1977** *Times* 19 Aug. 6/3 The unemployed PhD.., the over qualified school-leaver, have already brought home.. the consequences of.. rising unemployment and rising qualifications. **1594** Nashe *Terrors of Nt.* Wks. (Grosart) III. 268 Too much sodaine content and *ouer-rauished delight. **1688** Ld. Delamer *Wks.* (1694) 21 You ought not to be *over-reserved to any.. Company. **1597** Hooker *Eccl. Pol.* v. xlviii. §11 An *ouer-restrained consideration of prayer. **1962** U. Weinreich in Householder & Saporta *Probl. Lexicogr.* 35 *Over-schematized though it may be, ad hoc intralinguistic considerations suggest [etc.]. **1965** *Language* XLI. 504 Rigid, overschematized synchronic analysis. **1926** E. Hemingway *Sun also Rises* xiv. 154, I read the Turgenieff.. in the *oversensitized state of my mind after much too much brandy. **1965** *Punch* 17 Mar. 397/2 This double disability may at first sight seem hard on the over-sensitised. **1975** *New Yorker* 26 May 18/2 *Blow-up*.. An over-sensitized and wildly misaccented account of the mod, mad world of London, 1966. **1918** *Oversophisticated [see *film fan* s.v. film *sb.* 7c]. **1971** *Guardian Weekly* 10 Apr. 14/4 An overdeveloped oversophisticated country. **1971** D. Potter *Brit. Eliz. Stamps* xv. 163 Prices began to rise on all sides. Only the *overspeculated commemoratives failed to make progress. **1951** S. Spender *World within World* iii. 118 With him I escaped to some extent from the *over-spiritualized, puritan, competitive atmosphere in which I had been brought up. **1959** N. Mailer *Advts. for Myself* (1961) 18, I find to my perhaps *over-structured horror that I rather enjoy the high-pressured rubber of bridge. **1971** *Nature* 27 Aug. 591/1 The organization that has resulted from all the wrangles and compromises is over-structured. **1906** *Westm. Gaz.* 15 Aug. 4/2 No better corrective of their *over-sugared literature, with its artistic embellishment, could be suggested than Mary Wollstonecraft's unflattering plain-dealing. **1968** *Daily Tel.* 17 Dec. 13/7 Much of this [Amontillado] sold here tends to be rather flat and over-sugared. **1789** Mrs. Piozzi *Journ. France* I. 186 Like *over-swilled voters at an election. **1782** Wedgwood in *Phil. Trans.* LXXII. 306 At some times an unvitrified mass, and at others an *over-vitrified scoria. **1860** O. W. Holmes *Elsie V.* vii. (1891) 105 This *over-womanized woman might well have bewitched him. **1606** Shaks. *Tr. & Cr.* I. iii. 157 Such to be pittied, and *ore-rested seeming He acts thy Greatnesse in.

d. with adjs. in *-ed* from sbs. (= provided with too much, or too many, of what is denoted by the sb.); as ***over-ambitioned***, ***-banked***, ***-brained***, ***-commentaried***, ***-garrisoned***, ***-hopped*** (ale), ***-leisured***, ***-melodied***, ***-mettled***, ***-muscled***, ***-officered***, ***-provendered***, ***-renneted*** (cheese), ***-sorrowed***, ***-timbered***, ***-tongued***, ***-weaponed***, etc. (Can be formed at will.)

1661 Boyle *Style of Script.* 175 Out of a Criminal fondnesse of the *over-ambition'd Title of a Wit. **1930** *Times* 27 Mar. 21/2 The Port of Karachi.. is considerably *over-banked. **1966** *Economist* 18 June p. xxxiii/1 It has reduced its branches in Scotland, which is more overbanked than England. **1650** B. *Discolliminium* 17 *Over-brain'd Burrow-headed Men, restlesse in studying new things. **1888** Froude *Eng. in W. Indies* 357 If she [England] decides that her hands are too full, that she is *over-empired and cannot attend to them. **1572** J. Jones *Bathes Buckstone* 10 Meane Ale, neyther to new, nor to stale, not *ouerhopped. **1640** Bp. Hall *Chr. Moder.* (ed. Ward) 30/2 An *overleisured Italian hath made a long discourse, how a man may walk all day through the streets of Rome in the shade. **1760–72** H. Brooke *Fool of Qual.* (1809) IV. 136 The fractured harness of an *over-mettled horse. **1956** H. Gold *Man who was not with It* (1965) ix. 74 His weary *overmuscled body. **1977** *Gay News* 7–20 Apr. 23/1 No, I don't like that, over-muscled... I do like people who keep their bodies in shape though. **1641** Milton *Prel. Episc.* 27 Reducing into order their usurping and *over-provendered episcopants. **1643** —— *Divorce* Pref. (1851) 18 The much wrong'd and *over-sorrow'd state of matrimony. **1674** Petty *Disc. Dupl. Proportion* 46 If the Ship of 50 Tuns were not *over-timbered. **1596** Nashe *Saffron Walden* Wks. (Grosart) III. 134 Wherein he.. so farre outstrips *ouer-tunged Beldam Roome. **1593** —— *Four Lett. Confut.* ibid. II. 214 His inuention is *ouerweapond.

29. With substantives.

(Of these OE. shows examples under b, c, d; e.g. *oferǽt*, *oferdrync*, *ofersprǽc*; *oferbiternes*, *oferetolnes*, *oferséocnes*; *ofercræft*, *oferield*, *oferlufu*, *oferméod*, *oferȳð*.)

a. Verbal sbs. in *-ing*, from vbs. in *over-* (27), or formed independently by prefixing *over-* to sbs., as overabounding, -crowding, -doing, -feeding; ***over-aggravating***, ***-belling***, ***-boasting***, ***-caring***, ***-cleaning***, ***-cockering***, ***-deeming***, ***-descanting***, ***-drugging***, ***-farming***, ***-fasting***, ***-judging***, ***-liking***, ***-meddling***, ***-packaging***, ***-packing***, ***-padding***, ***-pinching***, ***-planning***, ***-ploughing***, ***-pruning***, ***-revving***, ***-soiling***, ***-striving***, etc. (Unlimited in number.)

a **1639** W. Whateley *Prototypes* II. xxiv. (1640) 12 An *over-aggravating of faults to make ourselves seem no children. **1575** Turberv. *Faulconrie* 245 The *overbelling of a falcon puts hir to a greater payne and trouble than needes. **1630** *Conceits, Clinches* (1860) 40 A cobler newly underlayd Here for his *overboasting. **1938** Belloc *Sonnets & Verse* 39 Believe in none and die of *over-caring. **1583** Golding *Calvin on Deut.* xl. 238 Learne that this *ouercockering is wicked. **1612** T. Taylor *Comm. Titus* ii. 6 These ouerweenings and *ouerdeemings of youth. **1655** Fuller *Ch. Hist.* VII. i. §32 *Over-descanting with wit, had not become the plain song, and simplicity of an holy style. **1868** A. B. Garrod *Materia Medica* (ed. 3) 375 Much discredit has been thrown upon the whole subject of the medicinal treatment of disease by the practice of indiscriminate prescribing and *over-drugging. **1946** *Nature* 23 Nov. 733/1 In his keen observation, in his reflexion and deductions, and in his dislike of over-drugging, More had all the endowments of a wise physician. **1943** J. S. Huxley *TVA* vi. 33 *Over-farming was not the only exploitation. **1626** Bacon *Sylva* §831 *Over-fasting doth (many times) cause the Appetite to cease. **1640** Bp. Reynolds *Passions* xxvii, The overflowing of their fears seems to have been grounded on the *overjudging of an adverse power. **1597** J. Payne *Royal Exch.* 6 To increase your.. longinge vpwards, and to decrease all *over-lyking here beneathe. **1861** Mill *Repr. Govt.* iv. 82 A government.. required to hold its hands from *over-meddling.. is not to the taste of such a people. **1972** *Computers & Humanities* VII. 81 Rarely has the sociology of knowledge provided such an obvious example of technology shaping the formulation of research conception as in the *over-packaging of most social science statistical analysis. **1967** Karch & Buber *Offset Processes* vii. 262 Repeat until satisfactory, but avoid *overpacking. **1962** *Economist* 8 Sept. 925/1 Wasteful *overpadding of junior executive posts. *a* **1591** H. Smith *Wks.* (1866) I. 30 Her *overpinching at last causeth her good housewifery to be evil spoken of. **1974** T. P. Whitney tr. *Solzhenitsyn's Gulag Archipel.* I. I. x. 393 To defend *quality*.. amid the general uproar about *quantity*, planning, and *overplanning. **1977** *Times* 16 Feb. 15/5 The country has suffered from intensive over-planning. **1976** F. Greenland *Misericordia Drop* I. v. 39 After some predictable *over-revving with the clutch out, they were off. **1959** *Times* 12 Jan. 11/3 It is advisable to avoid *over-soiling and consequent hard rubbing.

b. Nouns of action or condition, formed from vbs., or from sbs. belonging to vbs., or on the type of such. These have often the same form as the vb. or a modification of it, as overcharge, overissue, over-speech; or such endings as *-ion*, *-ment*, *-ure*, *-nce*, *-age*, *-ice*, as over-action, -excitement, -payment, -exposure, -abundance, -confidence, etc. So ***over-abuse***, ***-blame***, ***-broil***, ***-claim***, ***-concern***, ***-control***, ***-demand***, ***-discharge***, ***-drain***, ***-exercise***, ***-ornament***, ***-recovery***, ***-self-esteem***, ***-stress***, ***-worry***; ***over-accentuation***, ***-accumulation***, ***-addiction***, ***-aspiration***, ***-assumption***, ***-attention***, ***-classification***, ***-consumption***, ***-decoration***, ***-devotion***, ***-distension***, ***-dramatization***, ***-exaltation***, ***-expansion***, ***-expression***, ***-extension***, ***-flexion***, ***-imitation***, ***-importation***, ***-inflation***,

-interpretation, -lactation, -laudation, -legislation, -moralization, -multiplication, -nutrition, -organization, -ornamentation, -provision, -regulation, -repletion, -representation, -secretion, -sophistication, -speculation, -tension; over-attachment, -commitment, -enrichment, -involvement, -treatment; over-expenditure, -rapture; over-insistence, -influence, -reliance; over-drainage; over-service, etc. (Unlimited in number.)

1907 R. Fry *Let.* 11 Jan. (1972) I. 280, I find even in Dürer's portrait of himself here a certain *over-accentuation, a self-consciousness. **1867** M. Arnold *Celtic Lit.* 177 Her *over-addiction to the Ilissus. **1928** I. C. Ward *Phonetics of Eng.* xiii. 115 In order to cure *over-aspiration, it is necessary to tell the pupil to make the contact firm and the release vigorous. **1964** Crystal & Quirk *Syst. Prosodic & Paralinguistic Features Eng.* iii. 38 Voice qualities... Over-aspiration (excessive pressure being released as compared with normal articulation) particularly noticeable on vowels, and on those consonants where there is normally little aspiration. **1871** R. Ellis *Catullus* xxix. 6 Shall he in *o'er-assumption, o'er-repletion, he Sedately saunter every dainty court along? **1833** J. H. Newman *Arians* I. i. (1876) 21 An *over-attachment to the forms. **1874** Tennyson *Merlin & Vivien* in *Wks.* VI. 12 Of overpraise and *overblame We choose the last. **1597** Middleton *Wisd. Solomon* ix. 18 The one doth keep his mean in *overbroil. **1880** Muirhead *Gaius* IV. §53 There is *over-claim in respect of amount. **1955** *Bull. Atomic Sci.* Apr. 127/3 In other defense activities it is undoubtedly true that *overclassification is the rule. **1961** *Lancet* 26 Aug. 497/1 He was.. a little bit impatient with the fussy over-classification that was coming into vogue in his specialty. **1964** Y. Malkiel in *Archivum Linguisticum* XVI. 14 Undercommitment versus *overcommitment. **1865** M. Arnold *Ess. Crit.* Pref. (1875) 13, I thought this *over-concern a little unworthy. **1934** Webster, *Overconsumption. **1974** *Daily Colonist* (Victoria, B.C.) 15 Nov. 1/6 The Norwegian delegation is pushing a conference resolution stating that overconsumption impairs the health of the affluent. **1941** O. E. Patton *Aircraft Instruments* vii. 114 A follow-up mechanism is a necessary part of an automatic control, in order to prevent *overcontrol, which gives rise to oscillations, or hunting, of the aircraft. **1957** J. S. Bruner in *Psychological Rev.* Mar. 144/2 George Klein's work.. suggests that, in general, people who are not able to shift categorization under gradually changing conditions of stimulation tend also to show what he describes as 'overcontrol' on other cognitive and motivational tasks. **1813** J. Thomson *Lect. Inflam.* 45 The pain.. depends partly on the *over-distention of the vessels and fibres. **1758** *Herald* No. 24 (1758) II. 144 Weakened by an incautious *over-drain of the vital moisture. **1973** *Sociometry* XXXVI. 135 A false fire-alarm went off precisely as the stimulus-subject in a severe condition was screaming from the electrical shock, providing an extremely amusing *overdramatization of an already impactful event. **1976** R. Hill *Another Death in Venice* I. i. 21 Out there was a young *mafioso*... No, that was an absurd over-dramatization. **1860** Forster *Gr. Remonstr.* 76 The supposed enrichment of the country by the *over-enrichment of himself. **1935** *Planning* III. LIII. 5 The legacy of war-time *over-expansion, often in uneconomic locations, and of post-war over-capitalisation is a second [factor]. **1964** E. H. Powell in I. L. Horowitz *New Sociol.* xx. 332 The drive for profit produced a disastrous fluctuation of the business cycle, with periods of over-expansion and prosperity followed by bleak times of contraction and business failure. **1899** W. James *Talks to Teachers* viii. 75 This ceaseless over-tension, over-motion, and *over-expression are working on us grievous national harm. **1908** *Edin. Rev.* July 71 That greatest snare of Faber's unquestionable eloquence: over-expression. **1655** Fuller *Ch. Hist.* IX. iii. §38 Tell me whether the Ape did not well deserve a whip for his *over-imitation therein. **1837** Emerson *Misc.* (1855) 78 Genius is always sufficiently the enemy of genius by *over-influence. **1966** 'H. MacDiarmid' *Company I've Kept* iii. 85 The Scottish public has been.. debauched and distorted by English over-influence. **1934** Webster, *Over-insistence. **1953** K. Reisz *Technique Film Editing* ii. 114 An over-insistence on one aspect of the theme.. may.. divert the spectator's attention from the main theme. **1965** W. S. Allen *Vox Latina* Appendix B. 109 His [Erasmus'] conclusions appear to arise partly out of an *over-interpretation of Marius Victorinus. **1968** F. G. Lounsbury in J. A. Fishman *Readings Sociol. of Lang.* 53 The above.. is possibly also an overinterpretation of the facts. **1964** P. Worsley in I. L. Horowitz *New Sociol.* 385 Their problem would not be separateness.. but *over-involvement. **1976** *Times* 20 May 18/7 [Jerry] Brown.. has reportedly made himself a pain in the neck by over-involvement in detail and incapacity to delegate. **1836–48** B. D. Walsh *Aristoph.* 78 *note*, Every nation has been addicted, more or less, to *over-legislation. **1933** A. N. Whitehead *Adventures of Ideas* xii. 201 The forgetfulness of this doctrine leads to an *over-moralization in the view of the nature of things. **1931** J. S. Huxley *What dare I Think?* i. 28 Can he [*sc.* the biologist], by studying the pest in its original home, discover what are the other species that normally act as checks on its *over-multiplication? **1899** *Overnutrition [see *undernutrition* s.v. under-[1] 10b]. **1936** *Discovery* Apr. 98/2 While diseases associated with under-nutrition (tuberculosis, etc.) are steadily decreasing here, those associated with good nutrition—not to say over-nutrition—(diabetes, etc.) are on the increase. **1971** *New Scientist* 25 Feb. 407/1 Enormous problems of malnutrition and overnutrition remain unsolved and untackled. **1976** *Sci. Amer.* Sept. 40/2 Malnutrition may come about in one of four ways. A person.. may be taking in too many calories or consuming an excess of one component or more of a reasonable diet; this condition is overnutrition. **1946** *Nature* 21 Sept. 392/2 There was no disposition on the part of the delegates to encourage the *over-organisation of such interchange or movement of scientific workers. **1968** C. A. Doxiadis *Betw. Dystopia & Utopia* 18 In 1959, Aldous Huxley.. explains what disasters we should expect because of over-population, over-organization, and brain-washing. **1933** R. Tuve *Seasons & Months* iv. 188 Poets had come to take delight in *over-ornamentation. **1685** Evelyn *Mrs. Godolphin* 143 O with what.. *over rapture did I hear her pronounce it. **1967** D. Goch in Wills & Yearsley *Handbk. Managem. Technol.* 148 At an output level of 510,000 there is an *over-recovery of 10,000 × 1s. 0d. = £500. **1897** W. P. Ker *Epic & Rom.* 235 That touch of *over-reflexion and self-consciousness. **1875** *Encycl. Brit.* II. 575/1 Appointments.. were made under the purchase system... Every regimental commission had a fixed regulation price.. in addition to which an *over-regulation price, which sometimes even exceeded the regulation price, had sprung up. **1950** A. L. Rowse *England of Elizabeth* iv. 113 The natural energy, inventiveness, enterprise of the people, that was.. not discouraged, thwarted and stifled by over-regulation. **1976** *National Observer* (U.S.) 4 Dec. 10/2 What is really wrong with government overregulation is not that business people find it burdensome and costly, but that its principal victim is the consumer. **1833** J. S. Mill in *Monthly Repos.* VII. 663 *Over-reliance on our own judgment is one thing, over-reliance on the judgment of the world when in unison with our own, is another. **1961** L. F. Brosnahan *Sounds of Language* iii. 50 An apparent over-reliance on the spelling as a means of identification of dental fricatives. **1948** Martin & Hynes *Clin. Endocrinol.* i. 20 Acromegaly... A disease due to *over-secretion of the hormones of the acidophil cells of the pars anterior in adult life. **1934** C. Lambert *Music Ho!* I. 44 That modern craving—essentially a product of *over-sophistication—for the dark and instinctive that we find in D. H. Lawrence. **1857** J. S. Mill in *Coll. Wks.* (1967) V. 502 To prevent the Bank, at times when there is a tendency to *overspeculation, from encouraging that tendency. **1866** *Ch. Times* 19 May, Over-speculation has been checked. **1940** *Times* 27 Feb. 14/4 The Spanish Council of Ministers has approved the reopening of the stock exchanges at Madrid, Barcelona, and Bilbao on March 1... The reopening is subject to various restrictions aimed at curbing over-speculation. **1965** G. J. Williams *Econ. Geol. N.Z.* iii. 23/1 A period of depression resulted from over-speculation. **1923** J. S. Huxley *Ess. Biologist* I. 55 Whatever *overstress and maladjustment the complexity of modern civilization has brought with it, [etc.]. **1971** *Daily Tel.* 26 July 11/1 The effect of overstress is cumulative, causing structural weaknesses over a period of time. **1899** *Over-tension [see *over-expression* above].

c. Nouns of quality or state, formed from adjectives, or from sbs. belonging to adjs., or on the type of these. The endings are such as *-ness, -ity, -ty, -nce, -ncy, -acy, -tude, -ism, -ry, -ure, -th*, as in over-bitterness, -credulity, -anxiety, -indulgency, -length, -height. Other examples are *over-acuteness, -cheapness, -consciousness, -coyness, -diffuseness, -exactness, -expressiveness, -keenness, -learnedness, -lusciousness, -preciseness, -promptness, -proneness, -quietness, -readiness, -righteousness, -seriousness, -squeamishness, -truthfulness, -venturesomeness; over-ability, -capacity, -complexity, -facility, -fertility, -intensity, -loyalty, -security, -severity, -simplicity, -susceptibility, -variety; over-diligence, -dominance, -luxuriance, -negligence; over-brilliancy, -complacency, -elegancy, -frequency; over-accuracy; over-gratitude, -magnitude, -plenitude; over-individualism, -optimism, -realism, -scepticism, -sentimentalism; over-bravery, -knavery; over-moisture; over-strength, -wealth*, etc. (Unlimited in number.)

1934 Webster, *Overcapacity. **1960** *New Left Rev.* May–June 20/1 Under-capacity use of the railways.. and over-capacity use of the roads. **1971** *New Scientist* 8 Apr. 96/1 Industry is currently suffering from some over-capacity following the cutback in the aerospace effort. **1726–31** Waldron *Descr. Isle of Man* (1865) 40 The *over-cheapness renders them frequent. **1911** J. Ward *Realm of Ends* xv. 337 *Only* to differentiate this '*Over-consciousness' from all such consciousness as we can conceive is the term 'the Unconscious'.. applied to it. **1745** Ayre *Mem. Pope* II. 170 Daphne,.. she can no longer bear with this *Over-coyness of Sylvia to a Lover. **1870** Lowell *Among my Bks.* Ser. I. (1873) 184 The bias of the former is toward over-intensity, of the latter toward *over-diffuseness. **1639** Fuller *Holy War* IV. vii. (1840) 189 A great error, and.. a neglect in *over-diligence. **1960** *Farmer & Stockbreeder* 1 Mar. 65/1 From a geneticist's point of view in-breeding deterioration is explained by a decrease in those combinations showing *overdominance. **1976** *Nature* 15 July 227/2 Population geneticists have never agreed on the extent to which over-dominance of fitness—that is, the situation in which the fitness of the heterozygote exceeds the fitness of both homozygotes—is responsible for the maintenance of genetic variability in populations. **1642** Fuller *Holy & Prof. St.* IV. xv. 316 The affected *over-elegancy of such as prayed for her by the title of defendresse of the faith. *a* **1866** J. Grote *Treat. Moral Ideals* (1876) 169 In danger of erring on the side of.. *over-exactness. **1976** *Gramophone* Apr. 1598/3, I found a trace of *over-expressiveness in such movements as the second of the *Norwegian Melodies* and the Sarabande from the *Holberg Suite*. **1727** Bradley *Fam. Dict.* s.v. *Burning of Land*, To abate the *Over-fertility caused by the Fire there. **1583** Golding *Calvin on Deut.* cxi. 683 Ye pride or *ouerheaddinesse of ye deceiuers. **1604** Hieron *Wks.* I. 505 Religion, which.. the world is pleased to call *ouer-holinesse. **1640** Fuller *Joseph's Coat* (1867) 118 Out of an *over-imitativeness of holy precedents. **1858** Bagehot *Coll. Works* (1965) II. 101 We endure the *over-intensity.. of the surrounding misery. **1899** W. James *Talks to Teachers* viii. 74 Our faces, all contracted as they are with the habitual American over-intensity and anxiety of expression. **1978** *N.Y. Rev. Bks.* 23 Feb. 30/1 TB was understood, like insanity, to be a kind of one-sidedness: a failure of will or an overintensity. **1677** Baxter *Let.* in *Answ. Dodwell* 118 The Lord forgive the Presbyterians their *over-keenness against Sects. *c* **1611** Chapman *Iliad* XIII. Comm. 30 A man may wonder at these learned Critics *overlearnedness. **1860** Froude *Hist. Eng.* xxx. VI. 47 Her chief embarrassment.. was from the *over-loyalty of her subjects. **1898** G. Saintsbury *Short Hist. Eng. Lit.* x. i. 671 A certain *over-lusciousness traceable in his [*sc.* Keat's] earlier work. **1626** Bacon *Sylva* §693 The *over-moisture of the brain doth thicken the spirits visual. **1963** *Times* 25 Apr. 12/7 If the facts are as stated this is the biggest step towards the controlled release of the energy obtainable from the fusion of heavy hydrogen nuclei since the phase of early *overoptimism represented in Britain by Zeta (Zero Energy Thermonuclear Apparatus). **1976** B. Freemantle *November Man* ii. 14 Dennison had an aptitude for over-optimism. *a* **1677** Hale *Prim. Orig. Man.* 215 A Natural Consequence of the *over-plenitude and redundancy of the Number of Men in the World. **1622** Malynes *Anc. Law-Merch.* 329 The *ouer-precisenes therin may breed a great inconuenience to the Common-wealth. **1643** Sir T. Browne *Chr. Mor.* I. §33 To strenuous minds there is an inquietude in *over-quietness. **1711** Shaftesb. *Charac.* (1737) III. 262 An *over-regularity is next to a deformity. **1658** Osborn *Q. Eliz.* Pref., An *over-remissness or excess in Sanctity or Profaneness. **1882** Miss Braddon *Mt. Royal* II. x. 239 She did not know how much selfishness.. was at the bottom of her *over-righteousness. **1741** Richardson *Pamela* I. 222 His *Over-security and Openness, have ruin'd us both! **1697** Collier *Ess. Mor. Subj.* I. (1703) 184 The *over-smoothness of an argument is apt to abate the force. **1768–74** Tucker *Lt. Nat.* (1834) I. 176 An *over squeamishness and nicety of taste, which renders the imagination too delicate. **1684** Burnet *Th. Earth* II. 47 Disproportion and *over-sufficiency is one sort of false measures. **1596** *Prayer by Queen* in *Liturg. Serv. Q. Eliz.* (1847) 666 That no neglect of foes, nor *over-surety of harm. **1843** J. S. Mill *Let.* 21 Oct. in *Coll. Wks.* (1963) XIII. 600, I cannot charge myself with any *oversusceptibility in the matter. *a* **1661** Holyday *Juvena.* 260 They will serve ye up, in an *over-variety, the dainty birds called the fig-eaters.

d. Various sbs. denoting action, condition, state, quality, or anything subject to degree (often in sense, if not in form, agreeing with those in b or c): as over-care, -caution, etc.; so *over-ambition, -culture, -custom, -democracy, -dogmatism, -effort, -elaboration, -emphasis, -faith, -force, -majority, -opinion, -plenty, -precision, -religion, -saliva, -sorrow, -weal*, etc.

1929 A. N. Whitehead *Process & Reality* p. xi, Speculative philosophy and *overambition. **1973** *Times* 18 Oct. 15/3 His career was blighted by over-ambition. **1830** Wordsworth in Chr. Wordsw. *Mem.* II. 221 Free from.. that *overculture, which reminds one.. of the double daisies of the garden, compared with their modest and sensitive kindred of the fields. **1626** Bacon *Sylva* §300 Another Cause of Satiety, is an *Over-Custome. **1901** *Chambers's Encycl.* VII. 141/2 A frequent *over-elaboration of style and strainedness of wit that fatigues rather than exhilarates. **1940** *Mind* XLIX. 69 Many readers may feel that there is a danger in mathematical over-elaboration. **1974** tr. *Wertheim's Evolution & Revolution* i. 72 Phonetic spelling could not be realized in Egypt precisely because of the over-elaboration of the cumbersome hieroglyphic system. **1897** *Chicago Advance* 17 June 785/2 An itching desire for *over-emphasis. **1912** J. S. Huxley *Individual in Animal Kingdom* i. 24 By an over-emphasis of the species-individuality of which we are the parts, it is often said that our bodies are only 'cradles for our germ cells'. **1935** *Planning* III. XLIX. 1 Many of these arguments.. are based on a more or less crude over-emphasis of certain aspects at the expense of the whole. **1949** M. Mead *Male & Female* x. 215 Human children.. will make well-balanced but individual selections [of food], compensating one day for an over-emphasis of the day before. **1841–4** Emerson *Ess.* Ser. II. vi. (1876) 152 The *overfaith of each man in the importance of what he has to do or say. *a* **1700** Dryden *Meleager & Atalanta* 112 His [Jason's] javelin seemed to take, But failed with *over-force, and whizzed above his [the boar's] back. **1628** Earle *Microcosm., Scepticke* (Arb.) 67 His *ouer-opinion of both spoyls all. **1377** Langl. *P. Pl.* B. XIV. 73 *Ouer-plente maketh pruyde amonges pore & riche. **1926** Fowler *Mod. Eng. Usage* 684/1 That is the logical arrangement, which.. is free from any taint of *over-precision. **1952** C. P. Blacker *Eugenics* 112 It is difficult.. to steer a course that shall keep clear of the mudflats of platitude on the one hand, and not come to grief against the rocks of over-precision on the other. **1795** *Jemima* I. 87 The.. opinion, that *over religion, as we called it, shut the door of the heart. **1871** R. Ellis *Catullus* xxiii. 16 Thee sweat frets not, an *o'er-saliva frets not. **1885** *Border Lances* 23 Beware lest in thine *oversorrow thou lose the true profit thereof. *a* **1300** *Cursor M.* 2901 Mani man, for *ouer-wele, þam-self can noþer faand ne feil.

30. With adverbs, simple or derived from adjs.: as overmuch, over-boldly, over-daringly, over-soon. (A few examples occur in OE., as *oferswiðe, ofermódlíce*.) So *over-fast, -nigh, -often; over-casually, -cheaply, -cheerily, -closely, -deeply, -diligently, -honestly, -merrily, -wantonly*, and many others.

c **1450** tr. *De Imitatione* III. xix. 86 He stondiþ *ouer-casuely & like to falle. **1947** Dylan Thomas *Let.* 20 May (1966) 307 Did you receive the postcard, *overcheerily scribbled with messages? **1909** *Westm. Gaz.* 15 Apr. 12/2 The loving parent does well not to examine *overclosely into the reasons for this regret. **1606** Bryskett *Civ. Life* 53 Hauing regard not to vse them either *ouer-curstly, or ouer-fondly. **1690** Locke *Essay Hum. Und.* III. vii. 228 This part of Grammar has been, perhaps, as much neglected, as some others *over-diligently cultivated. *c* **1440** *York M.* xx. 19 To go *ouere fast we haue be-gonne. **1586** T. B. *La Primaud. Fr. Acad.* I. (1594) 676 When he saw the Hebrewes increase over-fast amongst his subjects. **1612** Brinsley *Lud. Lit.* 254, I feare indeede.. that this is *ouer-generally neglected. **1697** Dryden tr. *Virgil, Aeneis* Ded. civ, He.. left them there not *over-honestly together. **1807** Coleridge *Lett., to R. Southey* (1895) 523, I did not *overhugely admire the 'Lay of the Last Minstrel'. *c* **1530** *Crt. Loue* 406 See that thou sing not *ouermerely. *a* **1500** *Sir Beues* 3304 (Pynson) For he.. cam a lytel *ouer-nye. **1594** Hooker *Eccl. Pol.* IV.

vii. §4 Tertullian *ouer-often through discontentment carpeth iniuriously at them. **1603** B. JONSON *Sejanus* II. iv, Which..may By the over-often, and unseasoned use Turn to your loss. **1976** R. BARNARD *Little Local Murder* iii. 38 His sports jackets did not go over-often to the dry cleaner's. **1571** GOLDING *Calvin on Ps.* lii. 2 Doeg..behaved himself *overstoutly. **1601** HOLLAND *Pliny* I. 219 Toying and dallying *ouerwantonly with the king her husband.

III. Combinations consisting of OVER *prep.* (in any of its senses) with object. These naturally form advbs. and adjs.; exceptionally they give rise to sbs. and vbs. As advbs. they are often written as two words, as *over all* or *overall*, *over board* or *overboard*.

31. Forming adverbs: as OVERALL, OVERBOARD, OVERCROSS, OVERHAND, OVERHEAD, OVERLAND, OVERNIGHT, OVERSEAS, etc.; so ***overchannel, overfields, overhip, overleg, overpage, overshipboard***, etc.

1885 G. MEREDITH *Diana of Crossways* I. i. 13 Critic ears not present at the conversation catch an echo of maxims and aphorisms *overchannel. **1585** FETHERSTONE tr. *Calvin on Acts* xiii. 50 They do coldly and as it were *ouerfields play with God. **1785** BURNS *Scotch Drink* xi, The brawnie, banie, ploughman chiel, Brings hand *owrehip, wi' sturdy wheel, The strong forehammer. **1858** HAWTHORNE *Fr. & It. Jrnls.* II. 132 Men and horses, wading not *overleg. **1870** D. G. ROSSETTI *Let.* 29 July (1965) II. 893, I send another correction *overpage. **1932** R. A. CRAM in *Newsletter Mediaeval Acad. Amer.* 15 Nov. 3 Over page is a list of a few books recently issued by these publishers. **1970** *Daily Tel.* 5 Sept. 15 Money-go-round is continued overpage. **1600** ABP. ABBOT *Exp. Jonah* 156 That they had..inducements inough to throw him *overship-boarde.

32. Forming adjs.: as OVER-AGE, OVERCROSS, OVERGROUND, OVERHEAD, OVERHILL, OVER-KNEE, OVERLAND, OVERSEA, etc.; so ***over-centre, over-deck, -life-size, -ocean, -shoulder, over-winter***.

1975 *Sunday Times* 23 Feb. 17/4 McDonnell Douglas designed a rear-cargo door with four electrically-driven '*over-centre latches'. They were to close over spools in the aircraft body and pull the door shut against its seal. **1883** WALSH *Irish Fisheries* 16 (Fish. Exhib. Publ.) Superior speed, extensive *over-deck room, and the removal of the engines and boilers. **1937** *Burlington Mag.* Mar. 133/2 The little terra-cottas are to the finished, often *over-life-size, sculptures what the drawings are to the big pictures of the same period. *Ibid.*, A finely executed sketch for the over life-size bronze statue of *Innocent X*. **1955** S. SPENDER *Making of Poem* 40 Over-life-size people seen through the eyes of his childhood. **1967** E. SHORT *Embroidery & Fabric Collage* iii. 64 A round rug could be worked with one giant over-life-size sunflower as its basis. **1906** *Daily Chron.* 22 Feb. 3/2 Mr. Raleigh is at some pains to show how those *over-ocean discoveries and adventures acted on the poetry and imagination of their own times. **1946** R. A. MCFARLAND *Human Factors Air Transport Design* x. 420 In the early stages of overocean flying, an extra station for the navigator has received little criticism. *Ibid.* 410 (*caption*) The flight deck of the B-314 flying boat. The photograph shows a typical layout of stations for multiple flight crews employed in long-range overocean flying. **1957** *Economist* 21 Dec. 1021/2 On the flight deck other qualified Clipper pilots (at least four are on every overocean flight) relieve him. **1955** W. GADDIS *Recognitions* II. viii. 674 Some of the guests were leaving, with *over-shoulder looks of last-minute anticipation. **1959** *Daily Tel.* 22 July 7/1 Air attack 'over-shoulder' bombing... There was a spectacular demonstration of 'over-the-shoulder' bombing, when projectiles..climb thousands of feet before plunging into the sea while the delivery aircraft flies off at top speed. **1900** CHENEY in *Eng. Hist. Rev.* XV. 38 Doing all the ploughing in the autumn for *over-winter crops.

33. Forming sbs.: as OVER-ALL, OVERALL, OVER-DOOR, OVER-MANTEL, etc.

34. Forming vbs.: as OVERBANK, OVERHAND.

over-ability: see OVER- 29.

ˌover-aˈbound, *v.* [OVER- 25, 27, 22, 8.]

1. *intr.* To abound more, be more plentiful: rendering L. *superabundāre*. *arch.* or *Obs.*

1382 WYCLIF *1 Tim.* i. 14 Sothli the grace of oure Lord ouer habounde [Vulg. *superabundavit*, **1388** ouer aboundide, 1526 TINDALE was more aboundaunt]. **1577** *St. Aug. Manual* (Longman) 68 Whereas sinne hath abounded, there hath grace overabounded. **1604** T. WRIGHT *Passions* v. §4. 237 As Saint Paul witnesseth..where sinne abounded, grace over-abounded [*Vulg.* Rom. v. 20 *superabundavit gratia*].

2. To abound too much *with* or *in* something; also, of things, to be too abundant or plentiful.

1597 HOOKER *Eccl. Pol.* v. lxxii. §16 As the World ouer-aboundeth with malice. **1620** FORD *Linea V.* (1843) 66 Hee is a physitian..by purging such as ouerabound. *a* **1744** POPE *Lett.* (J.), The learned, never overabounding in transitory coin, should not be discontented. **1877** MORLEY *Crit. Misc.* Ser. II. 9 Diderot, in every page of his work,..abounds and overabounds in those details.

†**3.** *trans.* To surpass in abundance. *Obs.*

1590 A. CONHAM *To Reader* in *Babington's Exp. Commandm.*, The haruest ouer-abounded his labour, and exceeded his hope.

†**4.** *nonce-use.* To abound all over. *Obs.*

1612 R. SHELDON *Serm. St. Martin's* 28 O damnable custome ouerflowing Italy! O wretched practise ouer-abounding Spaine!

Hence **ˌoveraˈbounding** *vbl. sb.* and *ppl. a.*

1608 WILLET *Hexapla Exod.* 492 He calleth it *super-effluentem iustitiam*, ouerabounding iustice. **1683** J. HOWE *Let. to Lady Russell* in H. Rogers *Life* (1863) 203 That there is sin in an over-abounding sorrow. **1726** LEONI *Alberti's Archit.* II. 101/1 Those overabounding channels of water were..stopt. **1757** MRS. GRIFFITH *Lett. Henry & Frances* (1767) II. 178 The overabounding of his civility.

over-abstemious: see OVER- 28.

ˌover-aˈbundance. [OVER- 25, 29 c.] Too great abundance; superabundance, excess.

1382 WYCLIF *Ezek.* xviii. 17 [If he] shal not take vsure and ouere-aboundance [Vulg. *superabundantiam*]. *c* **1400** tr. *Secreta Secret., Gov. Lordsh.* 53 Man awe gretly eschewe ouerdoynge and ouerabundance of despensz. **1615** HIERON *Wks.* I. 608 Lest I should..dul you by the ouer aboundance of that matter, by which my desire is to quicken you. **1760–72** H. BROOKE *Fool of Qual.* (1809) III. 125 You..blessed me with an over-abundance of blessings. **1971** *Nature* 19 Feb. 548/1 The large overabundances of Li, Be and B are probably due to spallation.

So **ˌoveraˈbundant** *a.*, too abundant, excessive; **ˌoveraˈbundantly** *adv.*, superabundantly.

1503 *Kalendar of Sheph.* D vij, To be ower abondant wyth owt necessyte. **1862** GOULBURN *Pers. Relig.* 159 No one ever sought to please our Heavenly Master without succeeding and being over-abundantly recompensed. **1887** HISSEY *Holiday on Road* 190 The Palace, the Grand, the Railway Hotel..with overabundant show and overlittle comfort. **1964** *Ann. Reg. 1963* 249 And though wine, wheat, and beef production were well below the previous year's exceptionally high figures, milk, fruit and vegetables were over-abundant. **1971** *Nature* 19 Feb. 548/1 The element F is undetected in several energy ranges, but may be over-abundant in the 50–200 meV/nucleon range.

over-abuse to **over-accuracy**: see OVER- 29.

over-aˈchiever. *Psychol.* [f. OVER- 22 + ACHIEVER.] One who achieves more, as a result of environmental or personality factors, than tests based only on intelligence predict; someone who achieves more than is expected.

1953 *Jrnl. Abnormal Psychol.* XLVIII. 533/1 Ambitious students regularly achieve beyond their predicted 'aptitude' by dint of hard work; such 'overachievers' will not usually fail. *Ibid.* 534/2 Overachievers among public school boys who are most frequently and fiercely driven by ambition. **1964** M. ARGYLE *Psychol. & Social Probl.* ii. 26 There is evidence that people who produce a lot of achievement imagery tend to be over-achievers at school work. **1973** *Times* 17 Nov. 12/2 Mr Kirstein turned out to be one of nature's over-achievers. He founded a great American school of ballet. **1975** *Listener* 13 Mar. 331/2, I would never have been an over-achiever if it hadn't been for that unhappy love-affair with my mother. **1976** *Kingston* (Ontario) *Whig-Standard* 10 Jan. 6/3 It is even more boring than all those grabbers about the man of the year, the women of the year, and grannies, do-gooders, athletes, tots, and other over achievers of the year.

So **over-aˈchieve** *v. trans.* and *intr.*; **over-aˈchievement; overaˈchieving** *vbl. sb.* and *ppl. a.*

1953 *Jrnl. Abnormal Psychol.* XLVIII. 533/2 Academic overachieving and underachieving were measured by the difference between a man's Predictive Rank List..and his attained Rank List. *Ibid.* 536/1 Academically acceptable groups who are over- and underachieving. **1961** J. S. BRUNER in *Harvard Educ. Rev.* XXXI. 26 Our tests on such children show them to be lower in analytic ability than those who are not conspicuous in overachievement. **1967** *Economist* 2 Sept. 788/2 Mr Funston has..over-achieved his goal of selling America on the delights of investing. **1968** *N.Y. Times* 2 May 58 This succinct yet passionate ballet overachieves its immediate purpose by choreographically summing up the Dumas story with a series of brilliantly visualized cinematic-style vignettes. **1971** *Time* 15 Feb. 33 When the 'morning after' rolls around, many an overachieving boozer prays for a hangover cure. **1972** *Accountant* 6 Apr. 444/1 Where budgetary control is employed..the sales variance analyses would explain the reasons for over- or under-achievement. **1973** *Jrnl. Genetic Psychol.* CXXIII. 252 Overachieving high school males tend to rely less on RV. **1976** *Woman's Day* (N.Y.) Nov. 54/2 David continued to 'overachieve' all through high school, college and a distinguished law school.

overact (ˌəʊvərˈækt), *v.* [OVER- 26, 27, 20, 22, 21, 13.]

1. *intr.* To act in excess of what is proper, requisite, right, or lawful; to go too far in action.

1611 B. JONSON *Catiline* II. iii, You over-act, when you should under-do. **1671** MARVELL *Corr.* Wks. 1872–5 II. 383 Indemnity..for those who have bin punished by the former law as for them who have overacted in the execution of it. **1885** MABEL COLLINS *Prettiest Woman* ii, She is a grand creature, but she over-acts.

2. *trans.* To act or render (a part) with exaggerated or unnecessary action or emphasis; to overdo in action.

1631 MASSINGER *Beleeve as you list* v. i, You disgrace your courtship In overacting it, my lord. **1660** WOOD *Life* (O.H.S.) I. 370 So zealous a worshipper towards the east in his College chappell, that, overacting it, he became ridiculous. **1760** LLOYD *Actor* in *Ann. Reg.* 218 Of all the evils which the Stage molest, I hate your fool who overacts his jest. **1849** MACAULAY *Hist. Eng.* x. II. 659 Afraid of not sustaining well a part which was uncongenial to her feelings, she had overacted it.

†**b.** To act (a part) over and over again. *Obs.*

1653 J. HALL *Paradoxes* 44 Hee that killed himselfe, out of a wearinesse of overacting the same things.

†**3.** To go beyond or surpass in acting; to outdo.

1643 *Plain English* 6 Wise as they take themselves, [they] may be over-acted in their own designs. **1647** *Case Kingd.* 5 To supplant the Bishops..and over-act them at their owne game. **1657–61** HEYLIN *Hist. Ref.* 43 Candidianus, a Count Imperial..over-acted any thing that Cromwel did.

†**4.** To actuate or influence too powerfully; to overcome. *Obs.*

1663 J. SPENCER *Prodigies* (1665) 287 The true fears thereof would be ready to fly away (like the Spirits of over-heated liquors) if overacted by such strong and continued jealousies of heaven. **1669** W. SIMPSON *Hydrol. Chym.* 149 The one by its greater proportion, over-acts or overcomes the other. **1677** GILPIN *Demonol.* (1867) 238 By overacting their fears, or astonishing their minds.

5. To act beyond or in excess of. *nonce-use.*

1858 BUSHNELL *Serm. New Life* xii. (1869) 169 As he once overacted his will in self-conduct, so now he is underacting it in quietism.

Hence **ˌoveˈracted** *ppl. a.*, overdone.

1665 J. SPENCER *Vulg. Proph.* 90 To become ridiculous by an over-acted imitation. **1777** ROBERTSON *Hist. Amer.* (1783) I. 214 Over-acted demonstrations of regard.

ˌover-ˈaction. [OVER- 29 b.] Excessive or exaggerated action.

1741 MONRO *Anat.* (ed. 3) 173 A spasmodic Overaction of the Muscles. *a* **1862** BUCKLE *Civiliz.* (1873) III. ii. 48 Overaction on one side produces reaction on the other. **1899** *Allbutt's Syst. Med.* VII. 579 Auditory over-action or hyperæsthesia occasionally occurs in hysteria.

ˈover-ˈactive, *a.* [OVER- 28.] Excessively active, too much given to action. So **ˈover-ˈactiveness, ˈover-acˈtivity,** excessive activity.

1647 JER. TAYLOR *Lib. Proph.* xvi. 215 His opinion may accidentally disturbe the publick peace through the over-activenesse of the person. **1854** J. S. C. ABBOTT *Napoleon* (1855) I. xxvii. 436 The over-active, precipitate dispatch of others. **1865** MANNING in *Ess. Relig. & Lit.* Ser. I. (1865) 37 Like the mental over-activity of men dying of consumption.

over-acute to **over-afflict**: see OVER-.

ˌover-aˈffect, *v.*[1] [f. OVER- 27 + AFFECT *v.*[1]] *trans.* To affect or care for unduly, to have too great regard for.

1628 BP. HALL *To Bp. of Salisbury* Wks. 1837 IX. 410 God so love me, as I do the tranquillity and happiness of his Church, yet can I not so overaffect it that I would sacrifice one dram of truth to it. **1641** MILTON *Ch. Govt.* I. (1851) 13 Those that over-affect Antiquity.

ˌover-aˈffect, *v.*[2] [f. OVER- 27 + AFFECT *v.*[2]] *trans.* To affect or influence too much.

1645 BP. HALL *Remedy Discontents* xxi. 127 How can he be over-affected with triviall profits, or pleasures, who is taken up with the God of all comfort?

over against: see OVER *adv.* 7 b.

†**ˈoverage,** *sb.*[1] *Obs.* Forms: 5 ouur- (= ouvr-), ouuer-, oeuur-, 6 our-, ouerage, 7 overage, (ourage). [a. AF. *overage* (Gower), F. *ouvrage*, f. *ouvr-er*:—L. *operāre* to work: see -AGE.]

1. Work, workmanship; achievement.

1490 CAXTON *Eneydos* i. 14 The yate was made of soo hye and excellente ouurage, that it passed alle other. *a* **1529** SKELTON *How Dk. Albany*, etc. 418 A prince to play the page It is a rechelesse rage, And a lunatyke ouerage. **1656** BLOUNT *Glossogr.*, *Ourage*, a work; also work or labor.

2. A piece of workmanship; a work.

1474 CAXTON *Chesse* III. i, Than hit behoueth to deuyse the oeuurages and the offices of the werkemen. **1481** —— *Godeffroy* (1893) 237 They of the toun brake all theyr ouurages. *a* **1533** LD. BERNERS *Huon* cx. 380 The .ii. leuys of the gate were coueryd with fyne gold intermedelyd with other rych ouer-agis. **1648** J. RAYMOND *Il Mercurio Italico* 87 Stupendous Pillars.., besides other diversity of Overages.

overage (ˈəʊvərɪdʒ), *sb.*[2] [f. OVER *a.* 3 + -AGE.] A surplus, an excess; an additional amount; *spec.* an actual amount (of goods, money, etc.) greater than that estimated.

1945 MENCKEN *Amer. Lang.* Suppl. I. 366 *Overage* (a bank term: the opposite of a *shortage*). **1949** *Richmond* (Virginia) *Times-Dispatch* 30 Aug. 2/2 The warehouse-men agreed to the..sales plan with an 'overage schedule' which is intended to assure Danville the sale each day of 8,800 baskets of tobacco. **1957** *Britannica Bk. of Year* 512/1 *Overage*, costs in excess of estimated or contracted price. **1965** *Economist* 11 Dec. 1235/1 Those export earnings..have not been offset by earlier unforeseen *increases* in export proceeds, inelegantly christened 'overages'. **1968** *Punch* 27 Mar. 447/1 A barman who doesn't show a regular ten per cent 'overage' in favour of his employers will be dismissed because he either gives the customers too much (or too little ice) or he fiddles on his own behalf beyond the customary limits tolerated by the management. **1971** *Daily Colonist* (Victoria, B.C.) 26 Nov. 39/2 His normal welfare allowance would be only \$95 a month. However..the man was eligible for overages, which would make his total monthly allowance \$120.50. **1973** *Times* 10 May 25/5 A good average for overages is about 6 per cent on monthly sales, minus the minimum rent. In other words, if a store does \$50,000 of business in a month and pays a minimum rent of \$1,000 a month it has to pay an additional \$2,000 in overages. **1975** *Budget* (Sugarcreek, Ohio) 20 Mar. 8/2 Every shortage, or overage, has to be accounted for.

ˈover-ˈage (stress var.), *adj. phr.* [OVER *prep.* 11, and AGE *sb.* 4; see OVER- 32.] That is over a certain age or limit of age.

1886 C. SCOTT *Sheep-Farming* 174 Rather keep a good over-age ewe than a bad young one. **1893** *Academy* 11 Mar. 221/3 He was elected to an exhibition at Merton College, Oxford, being over age for a scholarship.

over-aged (ˌəʊvərˈeɪdʒɪd, -ˈeɪdʒd), *a.* [OVER- 26, 28.] **1. a.** Over a certain limit of age; too old. **b.** Out of date, antiquated.

1483 CAXTON *G. de la Tour* G viij, A quene of Cypre which was ouer aged so that she myght haue no children. *c* **1489** —— *Blanchardyn* xxi. 69 How well he ys ouerraged, take no hede and care not therfore. **1623** LISLE *Ælfric on O. & N. Test.* Pref., It is far from a fault, to know these over-aged and outworne dialects, especially of our own tongue.

1668 G. C. in H. More *Div. Dial.* Pref. (1713) 25 Laugh'd at..by an over-aged Sarah. **1884** H. Gersoni tr. *Turgenieff's Diary Superfluous Man* 24 Mar. (N.Y.) 78 His wife was somewhat like an over-aged chicken.

2. *Metallurgy.* Subjected to over-ageing.

1953 *Jrnl. Inst. Metals* LXXXII. 265/2 The normal-purity alloys gave ductile fractures when tested in the overaged condition. **1967** A. H. Cottrell *Introd. Metallurgy* xxi. 405 After plastic working, the over-aged structure gives the stronger alloy.

over-ˈageing, *vbl. sb. Metallurgy.* Also over-aging. [over- 29 a.] Prolonged artificial ageing of metal so that its hardness begins to decrease.

1954 *Gloss. Terms Iron & Steel (B.S.I.)* 21 Overageing. **1955** *Jrnl. Inst. Metals* LXXXIII. 529/1 This work provides direct evidence for the supposition that over-ageing during fatigue has a controlling influence on the fatigue strength of precipitation-hardening aluminium alloys. **1970** *Materials & Technol.* III. i. 32 This 'over-aging' effect is due to the increased diffusion giving rise to precipitation and agglomeration into more massive particles.

over-agitated to **over-agonize**: see over-.

overall (ˈəʊvərɔːl), *sb.* [over- 33: lit. 'over everything'.]

1. An external covering; an outer garment such as a cloak, ulster, or waterproof; a tunic, blouse, or the like worn over the other clothing as a protection against wet, dirt, etc.

1815 Simond *Tour Gt. Brit.* II. 286 My companions, dressed in the costume of the place, a flannel over-all. **1831** Carlyle *Sart. Res.* I. i, The vestural Tissue..which Man's Soul wears as its outmost wrappage and overall. **1888** J. Payn *Myst. Mirbridge* xxii, Protected from the pouring rain by water-proof and overall. **1895** *Strand Mag.* Oct. 395/1 Outside stockings are worn, also a canvas overall to protect the dress.

attrib. **1883** *Act 46 & 47 Vict.* c. 53 Sched. 5 An overall suit with head covering. **1884** E. Ingersoll in *Harper's Mag.* Aug. 402/2 A manufactory for canvas 'overall' clothing.

2. *spec.* in *pl.* **a.** Trousers of strong material, worn, with a similar shirt, as an outer garment by travellers, explorers, soldiers, cowboys, etc.: app. orig. *U.S.* **b.** Trousers worn by cavalry soldiers, riders, etc. as an outer garment, esp. as a protection of the ordinary dress in riding; hence, a cavalryman's trousers. Also, close-fitting trousers worn as a part of army uniform. Also *overall trousers.* **c.** Long leather or waterproof leggings reaching to the thigh. **d.** Loose-fitting trousers of canvas, etc., worn by workmen and others over the ordinary ones to protect them from stains, dirt, wet, etc. Now often made with a bib and strap top, and sometimes worn by themselves or with a shirt and not over trousers.

1782 in Bancroft *Hist. U.S.* (1876) VI. lvii. 462 Our men are almost naked for want of overalls and shirts. **1797** F. Baily *Jrnl. Tour N. Amer.* (1856) 332 We had each of us furnished himself with a proper dress for travelling the wilderness: it consisted of a pair of coarse brown overhauls, and a shirt of the same materials. **1807** Sir R. Wilson *Jrnl.* 17 July in *Life* (1862) II. viii. 322 He looked at the king's over-alls, which were fastened down the leg with numerous buttons and made to fit very close. **1811** Wellington in Gurw. *Desp.* VII. 478 All the regiments of cavalry should be supplied with cloth overalls by the Colonels. **1816** Scott *Bl. Dwarf* i, Having a hat covered with wax-cloth,..boots, and dreadnought overalls. **1828** Webster, *Overalls*, a kind of trowsers. **1848** Alb. Smith *Chr. Tadpole* xlv, Christopher, in a common velveteen shooting jacket and overalls. **1860** *All the Year Round* No. 64. 331 The Wellington boot at present worn by our dragoons under their trousers—or 'over-alls', as cavalry men call them. **1863** A. Blomfield *Mem. Bp. Blomfield* I. ii. 38 He used to ride to the petty sessions..equipped in yellow overalls to protect him from the mud. **1897** *Sears, Roebuck Catal.* 178/2 Painters' white drill overalls, made with apron and shoulder straps. **1900** *Dress Regulations Officers of Army* 76 Units may decide to wear either white waistcoat, kamarband instead of waistcoat, white mess dress with kamarband, or white jacket with kamarband and cloth overalls or trousers. **1926–7** *Army & Navy Stores Catal.* 748/1 Bib and brace overall. Blue and Brown Dungaree. Price, 8/6. **1938** J. Cary *Castle Corner* 152 Some sticky substance on the General's chair had glued him to his seat. His overalls were ruined. **1942** E. Waugh *Put out More Flags* iii. 177 He looked very elegant and old-fashioned in his blue patrol jacket and tight overall trousers. **1949** 'G. Orwell' *Nineteen Eighty-Four* I. 6 A smallish, frail figure, the meagreness of his body merely emphasized by the blue overalls which were the uniform of the Party. **1960** A. Waugh *Foxglove Saga* xii. 223 Martin had donned the Pig's Full Dress Mess Kit..and in its smart red monkey-jacket, narrow blue overalls with a broad red stripe..he really did look most striking. **1967** *National Observer* (U.S.) 3 July 12/3 France entered the war and started uniforming the American troops: Blue regimental coats, waistcoats, breeches or overalls, and black cocked hats. **1969** R. T. Wilcox *Dict. Costume* (1970) 253/2 *Overalls*, loose-fitting overtrousers with a front bib held by a strap around the neck.

Hence ˈ**overalled** *a.*, wearing overalls.

1908 *Smart Set* June 94/1 The familiar spectacle of half-grown boys and overalled and unshaven men. **1916** C. H. Stagg *High Speed* i. 2 He saw an overalled boy jump into the air and crack his heels together. **1928** *Sunday Express* 12 Feb. 9 Plainly there was something seriously amiss with the engine... The overalled mechanic gave an impatient stamp of his foot. **1972** *Guardian* 23 Oct. 11/1 White-overalled, stethoscoped Napoleons. **1974** N. Freeling *Dressing of Diamond* 53 Two overalled characters..on the garbage-collection round.

ˌ**ove'rall, over-all**, *adv.* [over- 31.]

1. †**a.** Everywhere; in every direction. *Obs.*

c **1000** Ælfric *Saints' Lives* (1885) I. 514 þæt mann us toniht ofer eall sohte. *c* **1200** *Trin. Coll. Hom.* 163 þat lond ..bicam waste, and was roted oueral and swo bicam wildernesse. *a* **1225** *Ancr. R.* 50 Pine is oueral þurh creoiz idon to understonden. *a* **1300** *Cursor M.* 12610 Ioseph and maria turnd a-gain To seke him..Ouer all a-bute. **1382** Wyclif *Wisd.* ii. 9 Ouer al lefe wee signes of gladnesse. *c* **1440** *Promp. Parv.* 372/2 Ovyral, *ubique, utrobique.* **1525** Ld. Berners *Froiss.* II. 681 The marchauntes of Gennes.. are knowen over all. **1596** Dalrymple tr. *Leslie's Hist. Scot.* I. 86 In thir lattir dayes..the Inglise toung is leirned ower all.

†**b.** In every part; all over, all through. *Obs.*

a **1225** *Ancr. R.* 42 þeo ureisuns þet ich nabbe bute imerked beoð iwriten oueral, bute one þe laste. ? *a* **1366** Chaucer *Rom. Rose* 1580 The place overalle, Bothe foule and tree, and leves grene, And alle the yerde in it is seene. *a* **1440** *Sir Degrev.* 1470 The floure [= floor] was paned over-al With a clere crystal. **1590** Spenser *F.Q.* I. xi. 9 And over all with brasen scales was armed, Like plated cote of steele.

c. Taking all aspects into consideration; generally.

1958 *Spectator* 6 June 753/2 Overall, the profits from trading for the year..were somewhat less than in 1956. **1959** *Wall St. Jrnl.* 30 June 2/3 'Over-all our line is up,' J. D. Bassett, Jr., of Bassett Furniture Industries,..said. **1967** *Autocar* 5 Oct. 50/3 In the up to 1,300 cc race, John Fitzpatrick..was mopping up the opposition to win the up to 1,000 cc class easily and also came fourth overall. **1974** *Cape Times* 1 Aug. 1/6 The United Party was thought to have the edge overall through having a commanding lead in the postal and special votes. **1975** *Physics Bull.* Aug. 365/3 Overall, an excellent and stimulating book. **1976** *Church Times* 16 July 6/5 'Sylvia's Lovers' is the most tantalising of Mrs. Gaskell's books: a failure over-all, maybe, but embodying some exceptionally brilliant scenes. **1976** *Oxford Mail* 6 Mar. 1 All these figures are up. So is crime overall. **1976** *Nature* 25 Mar. 376/3 There are some strange omissions too, in what is overall a very comprehensive text. **1976** *Gramophone* Mar. 1525/2 The latter was virtually flat overall.

†**2.** Beyond everything; pre-eminently; especially. *Obs.*

c **1175** *Lamb. Hom.* 57 þet is and wes and efre scal beon iblecced ofer al. *a* **1300** *Cursor M.* 10356 Maria sal þou do hir call Fild wit godds grace ouer-all. *c* **1400** *Destr. Troy* 2965 Kepe hom from company and comonyng of folke, And over all there onesty attell to saue. **1483** Caxton *G. de la Tour* A j b, Many tymes they wolde haue oueral deduyte. **1687** *Sc. Metr. Ps.* xvi, I set the Lord still in my sight And trust him over all.

ˈ**over-**ˈ**all** (stress var.), *adj. phr.* Now usu. written **overall** (stressed ˈ*overall*) and treated as a fully developed adj. [The phrase *over all* (over *prep.* 13) used *attrib.*] Including everything between the extreme points. Also with wider meaning: Considered over the whole range of components, features, or aspects.

[**1876** *S. Kens. Mus. Catal.* §2159 The length of the 'Leinster' is 350 feet over all.] **1894** *Westm. Gaz.* 11 May 4/3 A fine steel cruiser, with an 'over-all' length of 335 ft. **1904** R. M. Walmsley *Mod. Pract. Electr.* IV. iv. 984 (*caption*) Overall dimensions of tramcar motors. **1927** R. T. Nicholson *Austin Seven Bk.* iii. 6 Overall length, 9 ft. 2 ins. Overall width, 3 ft. 10 ins. **1930** *Daily Express* 6 Sept. 3 The New B P has 'high overall volatility'. All of it evaporates quickly. **1940** *Economist* 20 July 83/1 The recent fall in the over-all rate of net interest..has been due..to higher taxation on all investment income. **1941** *B.B.C. Gloss. Broadcasting Terms* 22 *Over-all merit*, technical rating of a radio channel, expressed in numerals ranging from nought to five to represent the combined effect on reception of signal strength, fading, interference, depth of modulation, and distortion. **1956** A. L. Rowse *Early Churchills* viii. 139 We must add an appreciation of the importance of sea-power in the conduct of over-all military operations. **1958** *Oxf. Univ. Gaz.* 7 Mar. 679/2 Approximately equal in its overall area to the Weldon Room it differs from the latter in design in that it is not a single room covering the entire space available, but has been subdivided into three. **1958** *Engineering* 11 Apr. 455/2 The estimated overall efficiency of the rectifier is 94·2 per cent. **1967** M. Argyle *Psychol. Interpersonal Behaviour* x. 195 In some studies there has been an overall decline in effectiveness, possibly due to unskilled trainers. **1972** P. Olyslager *Handbk. Ford Cortina Mk. III* 3 The overall length is the same as on the Mk II Cortina. **1974** *Country Life* 26 Dec. 2019/1 It is the overall balance of trade that is important. **1976** *Daily Tel.* 30 June 4/6 They had taken a 'significant step forward in cooperation' aimed at seeing that the current overall recovery..does not touch off a new round of inflation.

†ˌ**over-all'where**, *adv. Sc. Obs.* [Cf. overall and allwhere.] Everywhere.

c **1375** *Sc. Leg. Saints* xviii. (*Egipciane*) 379 þe takine of þe croice scho lad One hyr body ouralquhare. **1563** Winȝet *Wks.* (1890) II. 6 That is, quhilk ouer-alquhar, quhilk at al tymes..hes bene beleuit. **1570** *St. Andrews Kirk-Sess. Reg.* (1889) 345 Content to remain wytht hym oure-alquhair.

overamble: see over- 22.

overance: see owerance, dominion, superiority.

over and above, *phr.* [The two words, *over* and *above*, used pleonastically for emphasis.]

A. as *prep.* **1.** Above in rank, in a superior position to; = over *prep.* 8. *rare.*

c **1449** Pecock *Repr.* 418 Ech preest is ouer and aboue a deken..and ech deken is ouer and aboue a lay persoon. **1765** Blackstone *Comm.* I. vii. 239 That special pre-eminence, which the king hath, over and above all other persons.

2. In addition to, besides; = over *prep.* 10.

1521 *St. Papers Hen. VIII*, I. 23 The Kynge, over and above thys, signifieth unto Your Grace oon of hys owne secrete devisis. **1585** T. Washington tr. *Nicholay's Voy.* I. vii. 7 Ouer and aboue al that it had cost him. **1654** Bramhall *Just Vind.* vi. (1661) 123 Over and above all the former grounds which the Romanists themselves do in some sort acknowledg. **1766** Blackstone *Comm.* II. vi. 86 Both were..subject (over and above all other renders) to the oath of fealty. **1885** *Manch. Exam.* 5 June 5/3 There ought..to have been an army over and above these garrisons, ready to be moved..to a threatened point.

3. More than: = over *prep.* 11. *rare.*

1568 Grafton *Chron.* II. 135 There be (saith Fabian),.. or at those dayes were, over and above .xl. thousand knightes fees.

B. as *adv.*

1. In addition, besides; = over *adv.* 8, 10.

1588 Parke tr. *Mendoza's Hist. China* 391 They had so great affection vnto them, that ouer and aboue they sent them good charity. **1681** R. L'Estrange *Tully's Offices* 120 Not that I would serve a good man ever the less, for being Rich over and above. **1723** Dk. Wharton *True Briton* No. 25 I. 217 Alexander not only forgave the Affront..but gave the poor Fellow his Freedom over and above. **1849** F. W. Newman *The Soul* iv. 175 When that other, who is the sole teacher, is, over and above, younger than many who are to be taught.

2. (Qualifying an adj.) Overmuch, too much, too; = over *adv.* 11, over- 28. *Obs.* exc. *dial.*

1749 Fielding *Tom Jones* iii. vi, Mrs. Blifil..was not over and above pleased with the Behaviour of her Husband. **1809** Malkin *Gil Blas* x. ii. ¶3 Your mother..is not over and above hale and hearty herself. **1824** Mrs. Cameron *Marten & Scholars* v. 31 May be Dainty won't let his mule go, he is so over and above particular.

b. *attrib.* or as *adj.* Overmuch, too great, excessive; = over *a.* 4, over- 29. *rare.*

1865 Leslie & Taylor *Sir J. Reynolds* II. vii. 257 His over-and-above attention to his fame.

ˈ**over-and-**ˈ**under**, *a.* [over *adv.* 1.] Designating a kind of shotgun in which the barrels are mounted not side by side as is usual but one above the other. Also *ellipt.* as *sb.*

1930 G. Burrard *In Gunroom* 30, I have ordered a pair of Over and Under guns as I prefer the grip on this type of gun. **1961** C. Willock *Death in Covert* iv. 89 Under his arm he carried a beautiful Churchill over-and-under gun. **1968** *Globe & Mail* (Toronto) 17 Feb. 44 Most of the over-and-unders have only one trigger, to be pulled once for each shot, the fastest two shots in the sport. **1973** *Country Life* 28 July 268/2 Over and under shotguns. **1973** D. Lees *Rape of Quiet Town* vii. 118 He was carrying an over-and-under that must have set him back the thick end of a thousand quid, and, behind that much gun, even plus-fours..couldn't make him look silly. **1976** *Field* 30 Dec. 1272 (Advt.), These superb over-and-unders meet the growing demand from the modern sportsman for a genuine dual purpose gun, combining the advantage of the over-and-under for clay shooting with balance and handling qualities of the game gun.

†**over-**ˈ**ane**, *adv. Sc. Obs.* Also 6 ourane. [f. over *prep.* + *ane* one.] On one and the same footing; in common; together.

1513 Douglas *Æneis* vi. x. 104 Certane duelling nane In this countre haue we, bot al our ane [*ed.* **1553** ouer ane] Walkis and lugis in thir schene wod schawis. *Ibid.* x. vii. 89 Than schame and dolour, mydlit baith ourane.

ˈ**over-**ˈ**anxious**, *a.* [over- 28.] Excessively or unduly anxious, too anxious.

1741 Richardson *Pamela* II. 182 That over-anxious Sollicitude which appears in the charmingest Face in the World. *c* **1820** S. Rogers *Italy* (1839) 205 Almost all men are over-anxious. **1874** [see over *adv.* 11].

So ˈ**over-an**ˈ**xiety** *sb.*, ˈ**over-**ˈ**anxiously** *adv.*

1775 Ash, *Over-anxiously.* **1826** J. S. Mill in *Parl. Hist. & Rev. 1826* 658/1 The discredit into which the small notes had fallen through their over-anxiety to get rid of them in a hurry. **1829** —— *Autobiogr.* (1924) 302 They did not consider it very dignified to evince an over-anxiety to stand forth in defence of themselves on slight occasions. **1955** *Times* 13 July 3/4 The issue hung in the balance for the last two hours and both sides made mistakes through over-anxiety. **1976** J. Wainwright *Who goes Next?* 145 He'd have to watch his step..not to make a hash of things, because of over-anxiety.

over-apt, etc.: see over- 27.

overarch (əʊvərˈɑːtʃ), *sb.* [over- 1, or f. next.] An arching over, an arch overhead.

1884 J. Tait *Mind in Matter* (1892) 91 There is..the ordinary over-arch of blue sky or gray cloud. **1889** F. M. Peard *Paul's Sister* I. ix. 236 He..knew the warm red of the banks; the over-arch of the trees.

overarch (əʊvərˈɑːtʃ), *v.* [over- 1.]

1. *trans.* To arch over, to bend over in or like an arch, to form an arch over.

1667 Milton *P.L.* I. 304 In Vallombrosa, where th' Etrurian shades High overarch't imbowr. *Ibid.* ix. 1107 A Pillard shade High overarch't, and echoing Walks between. **1784** Cowper *Task* vi. 71 Under oaks and elms, Whose outspread branches overarch the glade. **1878** Spurgeon *Treas. Dav.* Ps. cviii. 4 As the heavens over-arch the whole earth.

2. *intr.* See overarching *ppl. a.*

So **over'arching** *vbl. sb.*, an arching over.

1893 E. L. Wakeman in *Columbus* (Ohio) *Disp.* 20 Apr., High overarchings of ancient ash trees.

over'arching, *ppl. a.* [f. prec. + -ING².] Arching over; forming an arch overhead; bending over as an arch. Also *fig.*

1720 GAY *Dione* III. ii, Hast thou yet found the over-arching bower, Which guards Parthenia from the sultry hour? **1725** POPE *Odyss.* IX. 216 A fence of marble from the rock, Brown with o'er-arching pine, and spreading oak. **1845** HIRST *Poems* 32 From the valley dark and deep To the over-arching sky. **1913** [see *lamp-shine* s.v. LAMP *sb.*¹ 4 a]. **1926** J. S. HUXLEY *Ess. Pop. Sci.* 192 The great biological invention, the amnion, came into existence—an overarching membrane grown by the embryo for its own protection. **1929** V. WOOLF *Granite & Rainbow* (1958) 98 Some over-arching conception, something which we may call 'a reading of life.' **1938** E. BEVAN *Symbolism & Belief* iii. 62 The wholly separate world he sees overhead.. gives, as nothing else can give, the vision of overarching immensity. **1972** *Listener* 9 Mar. 301/3 There is a hunger for sociological theory—but there is no over-arching Newtonian scheme.. by which the differences can be resolved. **1976** *Brit. Jrnl. Sociol.* XXVII. 348 The 'world economy'.. is a *world*-system like the world-empire—but which has no overarching political structure.

overargue: see OVER- 27.

'over,arm, *a.* **1.** *Cricket.* = OVERHAND *a.* Also as *adv.*

1864 *Realm* 13 July, We have long been discussing at our cricket meetings the lawfulness of overarm bowling. **1897** K. S. RANJITSINHJI *Jubilee Bk. Cricket* iii. 85 All bowling—fast, medium, or slow—may be delivered either over-arm, round-arm, or under-arm. *Ibid.* 92 Over-arm bowling.. is the kind most generally adopted now. **1907** *Westm. Gaz.* 22 Aug. 20/1 The earliest over-arm bowlers were very fast, and ..when Brighton Browne and Mynn were in rapid mood, nine of the ten fieldsmen were placed behind the wicket. **1934** W. J. LEWIS *Lang. Cricket* 30 *Over-arm* or *over-hand bowling*, that in which the hand is raised above the level of the shoulder in delivery, the ball being delivered with a downward swing of the arm. **1970** R. BOWEN *Cricket* viii. 127 The Demon bowler, F. R. Spofforth, who is generally credited with introducing true over-arm bowling to England. **1975** *Oxf. Compan. Sports & Games* 195/1 Virtually all bowling nowadays is over-arm. *Ibid.* 200/2 Over-arm—as distinct from the lower bowling actions (under-arm and round-arm)—had a profound effect upon the character of the game.

2. *Swimming.* Applied to a stroke in which one or both arms are lifted out of the water before being advanced; also of a swimmer, that employs an over-arm stroke.

1887 *Encycl. Brit.* XXII. 770/1 Harry Gardener.. used the overhand or overarm stroke. **1893** SINCLAIR & HENRY *Swimming* iii. 79 The old-fashioned over-arm swimmer lay on the water, with his shoulder blades at right angles to the surface. **1908** [see BACK-STROKE c]. **1912** F. SACHS *Compl. Swimmer* 133 Until the last few years a swimmer who desired to race, first endeavoured to master the over-arm side stroke. **1933** [see BACK-STROKE c]. **1968** W. ANDERSON *Teaching Physically Handicapped to Swim* iii. 37 In the prone position he can cultivate a side stroke and an alternative over-arm stroke with bi-lateral breathing. **1975** *Oxf. Compan. Sports & Games* 1015/1 From breast-stroke came side stroke, then English overarm, or side overarm stroke.

3. *Lawn tennis.* Of a style of service, in which the racket is swung above the shoulder to hit the ball.

1929 W. E. COLLINSON *Spoken Eng.* 90 Last time some of your overarm serves were unplayable. **1978** J. SYMONS *Blackheath Poisonings* II. 111 I'm better than George, because.. his horizontal service.. can never really compare with an overarm service in strength.

'over,arm, *sb.* [OVER- 1 d.] An overhanging arm, esp. that which extends over the work-table of a milling machine.

[**1903** W. H. VAN DERVOORT *Mod. Machine Shop Tools* xxiii. 321 Suitable ties are now furnished with most makes of milling machines connecting the outer end of the over-hanging arm with the knee.] **1922** H. D. BURGHARDT *Machine Tool Operation* II. viii. 169 Braces for tying the overarm, outer arbor support and knee together. **1964** S. CRAWFORD *Basic Engin. Processes* vi. 148 The overarm is accurately located on the top face of the column, providing support and correct alignment for the cutter arbor. **1976** *Gramophone* Oct. 695/1 The British-made Collaro B610.. is a record changer for up to six records, or its overarm can be removed and a stub spindle can be substituted for single record use.

,over-ar'ticulate, *v.* [OVER- 27.] *trans.* To articulate or pronounce too carefully. Hence **,over-ar'ticulated** *ppl. a.*; **,over-articu'lation.**

1921 H. E. PALMER *Princ. Lang. Study* 72 The teacher may have considered it his duty to over-articulate his words. **1935** A. L. JAMES *Broadcast Word* iii. 103 Is he pedantic? (i.e. over-articulating sounds); is he clerical? **1935** G. K. ZIPF *Psycho-Biol. of Language* (1936) 217 It [*sc.* the speech of the obsessed speaker] offends the auditor because it is over-articulated in meaning. *Ibid.* 218 The normal stream of speech steers between the Scylla of over-articulation and the Charybdis of under-articulation. **1975** *Time Out* 9 May 13/2 To overarticulate is a mistake because making a film is an attempt to express the unconscious.

over-assess to **over-attention**: see OVER-.

†over-Atlas, *v. Obs. nonce-wd.* [See ATLAS *v.*] *trans.* To load or burden more than Atlas; to overburden; = *out-Atlas* (OUT- 19).

1593 NASHE *Christs T.* Wks. (Grosart) IV. 176, I will not bee so vnweaponed-ieopardous, to ouer-throwe both thy cause and my credite at once, by ouer-Atlasing myne inuention.

'over-award. [OVER- 19.] In Australia, used *attrib.* to designate a sum paid by an employer in addition to an agreed minimum wage or salary award.

1950 A. W. FOSTER in Copland & Barback *Conflict of Expansion & Stability* (1957) ix. 677 The Court.. has no power to fix maximum rates nor to impose any sanction upon an employer who pays over award rates. **1963** G. PALMER *Guide Austral. Econ. Statistics* v. 101 The wages referred to.. are simply the minimum wages as prescribed in specific awards. They do not include overtime, over-award payments, bonuses, etc. **1965** *Economist* 14 Aug. 583/1 Australian arbitration awards are minima only and a major problem of the post war period has been the growth of 'over-award' payments (i.e. wage drift). **1969** *West Australian* 5 July 2/2 A sub-contractor on the S.E.C. power house site.. could increase his contract price to cover an award rise of $5 a week. However, his contract would not allow him to pass on over-award rises.

overawe (əʊvər'ɔː), *v.* [OVER- 21.] *trans.* To restrain, control, or repress by awe; to keep in awe by superior influence.

1579 SPENSER *Sheph. Cal.* Feb. 142 The Oake.. with shame and greefe adawed, That of a weede he was ouerawed [*ed.* 1597 ouercrawed]. **1591** SHAKS. *1 Hen. VI*, I. i. 36. **1683** *Brit. Spec.* Pref. 8 Acknowledged by all our Ancient Parliaments, that were neither over-awed by Force, nor seduced by Faction. **1754–62** HUME *Hist. Eng.* (1806) V. lxx. 273 That he might.. overawe the mutinous people. *a* **1832** MACKINTOSH *Rev. of 1688*, Wks. 1846 II. 23 The jury were at length over-awed into a verdict of 'guilty'.

Hence **overawed** (-'ɔːd) *ppl. a.*; **ove'rawing** *vbl. sb.* and *ppl. a.*

1593 *Tell-Troth's N. Y. Gift* 37 They say that overawing makes fooles. **1625** BP. MOUNTAGU *App. Cæsar* II. ii. 125 Councils have no such over-awing power. **1805** FOSTER *Ess.* I. iv. 57 Over-awed timidity. **1899** J. STALKER *Christol. of Jesus* ii. 83 *note*, The effect is overawing in a high degree.

†over'awful, *a. Obs.* [OVER- 26.] Excessively reverential, too full of awe.

1641 MILTON *Animadv.* iv. Wks. (1847) 64/1 To free ingenuous minds from an overawful esteem of those more ancient than trusty fathers.

over-awning, over-baked: see OVER- 1 c, 27.

overbalance (əʊvə'bæləns), *sb.* [f. next.]

1. Excess of weight, value, or amount; preponderance.

1659 HARRINGTON *Lawgiving* I. i. Wks. (1700) 387 The overbalance of Land, three to one or therabouts, in one Man against the whole People, creates Absolute Monarchy. **1659–60** PEPYS *Diary* 14 Jan., I.. heard exceeding good argument against Mr. Harrington's assertion, that overbalance of propriety [i.e. property] was the foundation of government. **1736** BUTLER *Anal.* I. vii. 127 An Overbalance of Good will, in the End, be found produced. **1853** DE QUINCEY *Autobiog. Sk.* Wks. I. 339 Amongst all the celebrated letter-writers of the past or present times, a large overbalance happens to have been men.

†b. *Commerce. spec.* Excess in the value of the exports over the imports of a country. *Obs.*

1641 *Decay Trade* 1 The profit or losse which is made by the over or underbalance of our Forraigne Trade. **1691** LOCKE *Lower. Interest* Wks. 1727 II. 71 An Over-balance of Trade, is when the Quantity of Commodities which we send to any Country do more than pay for those we bring from thence. **1721** C. KING *Brit. Merch.* II. 6 The French Trade exhausted our Treasure... By bringing in upon us a great Over-ballance of the Manufactures of that Country; and by taking from us the Ballance in Money.

c. *in overbalance*: as a preponderating element or consideration.

1724 SWIFT *Drapier's Lett.* II. vii. Wks. 1761 III. 127 Putting our interest in overbalance with the ruin of the country.

2. Something that turns the scale, outweighs, or overbalances.

1658–9 *Burton's Diary* (1828) III. 217, I am not willing, nor free to trust him with your militia. I speak plain. The army will be an overbalance.

overbalance (əʊvə'bæləns), *v.* [OVER- 24, 6.]

1. *trans.* To do more than balance; to outweigh.

1608 SYLVESTER *Du Bartas* II. iv. III. *Schism* 117 My little finger over-balanceth My Father's loynes. **1690** CHILD *Disc. Trade* (ed. 4) 169 When the Exports over-ballance the Imports. **1726** SHELVOCKE *Voy. round World* 432, I had vexation enough to over-ballance the satisfaction of that. **1855** *Cornwall* 221 The expenses overbalanced the profit.

†b. To prove more influential than. *Obs.*

a **1670** SPALDING *Troub. Chas. I* (1851) II. 96 In end he over-ballanced the erll, do what he could, and wan his poynt.

c. *absol.* To preponderate, to have greater power or influence.

1658–9 *Burton's Diary* (1828) IV. 40 When they had great estates they did overbalance. **1736** PULTENEY in *Swift's Lett.* (1766) II. 245 Learning and good sense he hath.. if the love of riches and power do not overbalance.

†2. To bias by superior weight or numbers.

1647 CLARENDON *Hist. Reb.* I. §184 The number of them [Bishops] was thought too great, so that they Over-ballanced many Debates.

3. To destroy the balance or equilibrium of; to capsize; *refl.* and *intr.* To lose one's balance.

1834 LYTTON *Pompeii* III. ii, Permit me to move opposite to thee, or our light boat will be overbalanced. **1861** *Times* 25 June 9 A man alone in a boat.. reaching out.. overbalanced, and fell into the water, and was drowned. **1881** J. F. KEANE *Journ. Medinah* i. 16 You may over-balance and bring down the whole concern. **1884** PAE *Eustace* 9 He overbalanced himself, and the next moment, he, too, was in the river.

Hence **over'balancing** *vbl. sb.* and *ppl. a.*

a **1586** SIDNEY *Arcadia* (1622) 463 But when they did set it to the beame.. they could not but yeeld in their hearts, there was no ouerballancing. **1648** *Eikon Bas.* i, By the weight of Reason I should counterpoize the over-ballancings of any factions. **1719** W. WOOD *Surv. Trade* 85 Unless the Goods we import from an over-balancing Country be Re-exported. **1805** FOSTER *Ess.* I. iii. 32 A gigantic and overbalancing strength.

,over'ballast, *v.* Also 7 -ballise. [OVER- 27.] *trans.* To overload (a ship) with ballast; to overload.

1601 SIR W. CORNWALLIS *Ess.* II. xl. (1631) 171 A shippe over-ballasted in the middest of the ocean. **1607** WALKINGTON *Opt. Glass* 58 If wee doe not overballise our stomachs with superfluity. **1895** *Westm. Gaz.* 31 Dec. 5/1 The other charges.. apart from the allegation of overballasting.

over-balm to **overbanded**: see OVER-.

'overbank, *a. Artillery.* [f. OVER *prep.* + BANK *sb.*] Applied to a kind of gun-carriage for muzzle-loading guns, so constructed as to allow of the gun's being fired over the parapet.

1879 *Man. Artillery Exerc.* 8 The adoption of overbank carriages, jointed rammers, &c., for our siege guns. **1884** *Mil. Engineering* I. II. 54 The guns of the siege train being adapted for overbank fire, embrasures are not required.

over'bank, *v. Watch and Clock-making.* [OVER- 27, 34.]

1. *intr.* See quot. and cf. BANK *v.*¹ 4.

1884 F. J. BRITTEN *Watch & Clockm.* 132 There is no fear of overbanking, which is often observed after careless winding. *Ibid.* 181 When.. the ruby pin pushes past the lever from the outside of it, the escapement is said to overbank. A chronometer escapement is said to overbank when from the same cause the escape wheel is unlocked a second time.

2. *Aeronaut.* **a.** *trans.* To bank (an aircraft) too much when making a turn; also with the turn as obj.

1915 *Tech. Rep. Advisory Comm. Aeronaut. 1914–15* 307 If a turn be overbanked it will bring into play a lateral component of gravity which produces sideslip. **1919** W. G. ASTON *Aeronaut. made Easy* xvii. 160 If on the turn the machine is overbanked, it will side-slip inwards. **1936** *Discovery* Mar. 72/2 It is essential that the machine is not overbanked on a turn, since there are no ailerons to correct this.

b. *intr.* Of an aircraft: to bank too much. Also said of the pilot.

1929 F. A. SWOFFER *Learning to Fly* iv. 38 (*heading*) Why an aeroplane overbanks. **1932** D. GARNETT *Rabbit in Air* I. 17, I overbanked and didn't use enough rudder. **1952** A. Y. BRAMBLE *Air-plane Flight* xii. 181 During the turn.. there is a greater tendency to overbank in a climb than in level flight.

Hence **over'banking** *vbl. sb.*

1915 *Tech. Rep. Advisory Comm. Aeronaut. 1914–15* 307 (*heading*) Objections to extreme overbanking. **1921** *Sci. Amer.* 15 Oct. 275/3 The side-slip—a lateral movement of a plane caused by overbanking or by underbanking—is measured.

'overbank, *sb. Aeronaut.* [OVER- 29.] The action of overbanking (OVERBANK *v.* 2).

1919 A. W. JUDGE *Handbk. Mod. Aeronaut.* xiii. 676 Inward slip.. results from an overbank, which causes the machine to turn inwards, and slip down sideways. **1955** M. ROYCE *Studies for Student Pilots* II. 94 The inner main-plane now experiences the greater A[ngle of] A[ttack] and the increment of lift it obtains tends to neutralize the over-bank tendency.

†over-'bar, *v. Obs.* [OVER- 8] *trans.* To cover with bars or a barrier.

1589 GREENE *Tullies Loue* Wks. (Grosart) VII. 214 But Loue.. had ouerbard hir heart with such former fancies. **1600** NASHE *Summer's Will* Wks. (Grosart) VI. 150 He [Winter] over-bars the christall streames with yce.

overbarish. Error for OVER-LAVISH *a.*

1579 G. HARVEY *Letter-bk.* (Camden) 59 Behoulde what millions of thankes I recounte unto you, and behoulde how highely I esteeme of youre good Mastershipps overbarish and excessive curtesy, first in publishing abroade in prynte to the use or rather abuse of others.

over-bark. [f. OVER- 8 c + BARK *sb.*¹ 1.] Used *attrib.* to designate measurements of logs taken before the bark has been removed.

1953 H. L. EDLIN *Forester's Handbk.* xiv. 214 As a rule, logs are measured.. while they still have their bark on. This is over-bark measure, and is of course greater than the volume of actual timber. **1967** SCOTT & PALMER *Hiley's Woodland Managem.* (ed. 2) ix. 131 (*caption*) Percentage of bark in the over-bark volume.

over-bark, *v.* to **over-battle**: see OVER-.

overbear (əʊvə'bɛə(r)), *v.* [OVER- 4, 6, 22.]

†1. *trans.* To carry over, transfer, remove; to put away. (In Wyclif rendering L. *transferre*). *Obs.*

1382 WYCLIF *Deut.* xxvii. 17 Cursid that ouerberith the teermes of his neiȝbore. —— *2 Sam.* xii. 13 The Lord hath overborn thi synne, thou shalt not die. —— *Isa.* xxxiii. 20 A plenteous cite, a tabernacle that shal not moun ben ouerborn [1388 borun ouer].

2. a. To bear over or down by weight or physical force; to thrust, push, or drive over; to overthrow; to overwhelm, break or crush down.

1535 COVERDALE *Ezek.* xxvii. 26 But ye easte wynde shal ouerbeare the in to the myddest off the sea. **1559** *Mirr. Mag., Rich. Dk. York* (1563) G vij b, See how force oft ouerbereth ryght. **1608** SYLVESTER *Du Bartas* II. iv. IV. *Decay* 600 Whose numbrous Arms..Have over-born as many as with-stood. **1719** *Freethinker* No. 121 ¶2 The Mounds of their ancient Discipline, over-born by the Inundation of foreign Luxuries. **1859** TENNYSON *Lancelot & Elaine* 484 As a wild wave..overbears the bark, And him that helms it, so they overbore Sir Lancelot and his charger.

b. *fig.* To overcome, put down, or repress, as by power, authority, or influence; to overpower, oppress; to exercise an oppressive influence upon.

1565 T. STAPLETON *Fortr. Faith* 69 The vsurpers haue ouerboren the right inheritours. **1590** MARLOWE *Edw. II*, III. ii, The barons ouerbear me with their pride. **1599** SHAKS. *Much Ado* II. iii. 157 The extasie hath so much ouerborne her, that my daughter is sometime afeard she will doe a desperate out-rage to her selfe. **1676** GLANVILL *Seasonable Reflect.* 180 The friends of Truth and Reason.. are liable to be still over-born, and out-nois'd by the Tumult. **1705** HEARNE *Collect.* 17 Nov. (O.H.S.) I. 82 This was overbore so y^t it came not to ye Question. **1861** TRENCH *Comm. Ep. Seven Ch. in Asia* (ed. 2) 26 What we may call the mystical or symbolic interest overbears and predominates over the actual. **1864** D. G. MITCHELL *Wet Days at Edgewood* 116 They overbear one with the grand air they carry.

3. To surpass in weight, importance, cogency, etc.; to outweigh.

1712 ADDISON *Spect.* No. 412 ¶1 The Horror or Lothsomness of an Object may over-bear the Pleasure which results from its Greatness, Novelty, or Beauty. **1884** *American* VIII. 347 The interest of the subject is so great that it might overbear even more serious deficiencies.

4. *intr.* To produce too much fruit, thereby affecting the quality of it.

1863 *Horticulturalist* XVIII. 295/2 You can now point out every tree that was allowed to overbear. **1872** *Rep. Vermont Bd. Agric.* I. 118 The Bartlett and Louise Bonne de Jersey commence bearing young, and are inclined to over bear. **1901** *U.S. Dept. Agric. Yearbk. 1900* 387 It is a great mistake to allow pear trees to overbear.

overbearance (-'bɛərəns). [f. prec. + -ANCE: cf. *abearance, forbearance.*]

†**1.** The action of bearing or weighing down; preponderance. *Obs.*

1639 LD. DIGBY, etc. *Lett. conc. Relig.* (1651) 121 A confession of the ballances being so equally poysed in this affaire..that the overbearances of either scale is hardly perceptible.

2. Overbearing behaviour; imperiousness.

1760–72 H. BROOKE *Fool of Qual.* (1859) I. ix. 216 Will this benevolent and lowly man retain the same front of haughtiness, the same brow of overbearance? **1863** J. SHERMAN in *Mem.* 152 The overbearance of one ruling spirit made it pretty plain that I must either sacrifice my own opinion of right and wrong, or be ever at war. **1884** *Law Times* 20 Sept. 347/1 A judge who has not either of these checks may acquire an inveterate habit of overbearance.

over'bearer. *rare.* [f. as prec. + -ER^1.] One who or that which overbears.

a **1618** SYLVESTER *Mem. Mortalitie* II. xl, Self-swelling Knowledge, wit's own Overbearer, Proves Ignorance, and finds it nothing knowes.

over'bearing, *vbl. sb.* [f. as prec. + -ING^1.]

1. The action of the vb. OVERBEAR: a bearing or thrusting over by force; overpowering, forcible subversion.

1596 *Acts Privy Counc.* XXVI. 106 If we should accept your wordes of overbearinge to have bene done or suffered by us. **1661** GLANVILL *Van. Dogm.* xxiii. 227 The Judgement..if it be led by the over-bearings of passion.. the practice will be as irregular, as the conceptions erroneous. **1691** T. H[ALE] *Acc. New Invent.* p. lxii, The over-bearing of their Course..by a Northwest Wind.

2. Imperious or dictatorial action; an arrogant exercise of superior power.

1729 BUTLER *Serm.* Wks. 1874 II. 165 Wrath and fury and overbearing upon these occasions proceed..from men's feeling only on their own side. **1849–53** ROCK *Ch. of Fathers* III. x. 423 The English people's spokesman against the feudal overbearings..of the Anglo-Norman dynasty. **1890** *Spectator* 9 Aug., The man of whose overbearing and coarseness history and tradition tell us that they must have known enough.

overbearing (əʊvə'bɛərɪŋ), *ppl. a.* [f. as prec. + -ING^2.]

†**1.** Bearing or weighing down; overpowering, overwhelming, oppressing. *Obs.*

a **1677** HALE *Prim. Orig. Man.* I. i. 38 By conviction of some Truths, and this may be..by a strong and over-bearing presenting of them to the Understanding. **1736** BUTLER *Anal.* II. vi. 313 Evidence acknowledged real, if it be not overbearing. **1806** BERESFORD *Proclam. Buenos Ayres* in *Lond. Gaz.* No. 15956 He will then make such Reductions in the overbearing Duties as may seem most conducive to the Interest of the Country. **1822–34** *Good's Study Med.* (ed. 4) I. 630 That they could force the system to yield to its powers by the overbearing arms of weight and measure.

†**b.** Overruling, preponderating. *Obs.*

a **1708** BEVERIDGE *Priv. Th.* I. (1730) 9 Tis natural for all Men to have an overbearing Opinion and Esteem for that particular Religion they are born and bred up in.

2. Disposed to repress or overrule others; imperious, domineering, bullying, masterful.

1732 BERKELEY *Alciphr.* VI. §32, I see a bigot wherever I see a man overbearing and positive without knowing why. **1841** ELPHINSTONE *Hist. Ind.* II. 255 His temper was harsh and severe, his manners haughty and overbearing. **1880** MCCARTHY *Own Times* IV. lxiii. 414 He was an effective and somewhat overbearing speaker.

over'bearingly, *adv.* [f. prec. + -LY^2.] In an overbearing manner; domineeringly.

1824 *New Monthly Mag.* XII. 427 The most overbearingly despotic. **1888** BURGON *Lives 12 Gd. Men* I. iii. 347 [He] behaved himself somewhat overbearingly at dinner.

over'bearingness. [f. as prec. + -NESS.] The quality or character of being overbearing.

a **1797** H. WALPOLE *Mem. Geo. II* (1847) II. 358 [He was] no match for the art of the one, or the overbearingness of the other. **1824** *Examiner* 66/1 The overbearingness of his temper. **1860** MILL *Repr. Govt.* (1861) 328 Filled with the scornful overbearingness of the conquering nation.

over'beat, *v. rare.* [OVER- 6.] *trans.* To beat down; to put down, overthrow, overpower.

1618 BOLTON *Florus* IV. iv. (1636) 296 Antonius..lastly, enterprised a warre for over-beating the yong noble gentleman. *a* **1652** BROME *City Wit* III. iv, Or has not my Mother overbeaten you, Father? **1881** *Daily News* 22 Aug. 5/7 He soon warmed up and was able to not only overbeat hostility, but to command general and enthusiastic applause.

over-beaten, *ppl. a.* [OVER- 9.] Beaten down by treading over.

1896 *Westm. Gaz.* 11 May 2/3 The men are likely to be a little off the over-beaten track.

over'beating, *vbl. sb.* [OVER- 20, 29 a.]

†**1.** The action of beating over, or dwelling with iteration upon (a subject). *Obs.*

1628 in Rushw. *Hist. Coll.* (1659) I. 521 We must take heed of too much repetition, and over-beating of Grievances.

2. Excessive beating (of the heart).

1819 BYRON *Venice* i, The overbeating of the heart, And flow of too much happiness.

overbeetling, -being: see OVER-.

overbelief. [OVER- 1 e, 18, 29 c.] **a.** A belief which determines other beliefs. **b.** A belief surviving from the past. **c.** Belief in more than is warranted by the evidence or in what cannot be verified; also, such belief beyond that which is customary among adherents of a particular faith or sect.

1897 W. JAMES *Will to Believe* p. xiii, The most interesting and valuable things about a man are his ideals and over-beliefs. **1900** J. MORLEY *Oliver Cromwell* I. iii. 51 Faith in the literal construction of the word was pushed to an excess ..resembling a true superstition or over-belief. **1901** W. W. PEYTON in *Contemp. Rev.* Dec. 838 Some of them are over-beliefs, preserving the traditions of their great past. **1920** 'W. S. PALMER' *Christianity & Christ* 153 We have these 'over-beliefs'; and we even count men poor who are without them. **1930** *Times Lit. Suppl.* 27 Nov. 1011/1 All is well, or will be well, when the new over-beliefs dominate. **1961** M. LASKI *Ecstasy* xxviii. 295 Whatever may be the ultimate source of these beliefs, which I shall call primary overbeliefs, it is generally accepted that their expression must at least partially be a temporal, local and natural matter. **1971** E. CARPENTER *Cantuar* VI. iv. 340 He [*sc.* Archbishop Tait] was sensitive to the contemporary agnosticism of such as Tennyson, and was convinced that this could not be combated by insisting on the 'over-belief' characteristic of the protagonists of the Oxford Movement. **1973** M. PAFFARD *Inglorious Wordsworths* II. xii. 162 Their overbeliefs—their own assumptions or conclusions about the significance (if any) of the experiences they described.

overbelling, -bellying: see OVER-.

over'bend, *v.* [OVER- 3, 1, 27.]

1. a. *trans.* To bend (something) over or to one side. **b.** To bend over (something). **c.** *intr.* To bend or stoop over.

1617 HIERON *Wks.* II. 359 Like some bulrush that is ouer-bent with the strength and violence of a storme. **1845** HIRST *Poems* 168 Like Endymion, over-bent By dazzling Dian. **1856** WHITTIER *Ranger* 71 Overbending, till she's blending With the flaxen skein she's tending..Sits she. *c* **1886** G. M. HOPKINS *Poems* (1967) 97 Her earliest stars, earlstars, stárs principal, overbend us.

2. *trans.* To bend too much or to excess.

1624 DONNE *Devot.* 290 Vpon misplacing, or ouer-bending our naturall faculties. *a* **1656** BP. HALL *Christian* §3 Meet relaxations to a mind over-bent. **1897** E. L. TAUNTON *Eng. Monks St. Benedict* I. 86 The bow cannot be kept over-bent.

'overbend, *sb.* [OVER- 5 b.] The curved stretch of pipe above the point of inflexion in the S-shaped length of pipeline being lowered on to the sea bed from a barge. Cf. SAGBEND.

1969 *Preprints 1st Ann. Offshore Technol. Conf.* II. 38/1 As the lay barge proceeds into deep water the articulated stinger curves downward and the suspended pipe span acquires a distinct S-shaped curve. The upper part of this curve, called the over-bend, is supported by the stinger. **1976** *Offshore Platforms & Pipelining* 130/1 The overbend is supported by rollers on the barge and stinger.

over-bepatch: see OVER- 8.

overberg ('əʊvəbɜːg), *a. S. Africa.* [f. OVER *prep.* + Du. *berg* mountain, hill.] Over a mountain or mountains; that passes over the mountains.

1879 ATCHERLEY *Boërland* 61 The sale of rum to over-berg travellers. **1900** *Blackw. Mag.* Mar. 324/2 A railway which derives the bulk of its revenue from the overberg trade.

†**over-'bias,** *v. Obs.* [OVER- 3 or 6.] *trans.* To bias to one side. Hence **over-'biasing** *ppl. a.*

1659 GAUDEN *Tears of Ch.* II. x. 180, I find some men of worth..over-awed by the vulgar, or over-biassed by their own private interests. **1711** SHAFTESB. *Charac.* (1737) II. 161 This over-byassing inclination towards rest; this slothful, soft, or effeminate temper, averse to labour and imployment.

overbid (əʊvə'bɪd), *v.* [OVER- 26, 22.]

†**1.** *intr.* To bid more than the value, to bid too high. *Obs.*

a **1616** BEAUM. & FL. *Scornful Lady* II. iii, Take it, h'as overbidden by the sun: bind him to his bargain quickly.

2. a. *trans.* To go beyond (a person) in bidding; to outbid.

1645 RUTHERFORD *Tryal & Tri. Faith* (1845) 99 None could over-bid him in his market for souls. **1850** GROTE *Greece* II. lxvii, The poor citizens were overbid, and could not get places. **1882** *Athenæum* 15 July 71 The English could always overbid the Russians in bribing Afghans.

b. To bid or offer more than the value of (a thing); to overpay.

1646 EVANCE *Noble Ord.* 13 The benefits..outvye, and overbid all the..service of the Creature. **1681** DRYDEN *Spanish Friar* II. i. 20 A Tear! You have o'erbid all my past Sufferings, And all my future too! **1793** in Vesey, jr. *Rep.* (1801) II. 55 The sum overbid is larger..amounting to one-fourth part of the original price.

c. *trans.* and *intr.* In *Bridge* = OVERCALL *v.* Also *fig.*

1908 R. F. FOSTER *Auction Bridge* 51 If the hand is overbid, the suit named may be a guide as to the advisability of changing to no-trumps. **1908** [see BID *sb.* 2]. **1917** E. BERGHOLT *Royal Auction Bridge* 87 It is imperative to overbid with Two Clubs, as a warning—colloquially known as a 'rescue'. **1918** R. F. FOSTER *On Auction* (1919) 169 Overbidding a suit just because there are four honours in it is quite unnecessary. **1923** *Daily Mail* 6 Oct. 6/4 The partner of the under-bidder..cannot make any further bid unless the opponents double or over-bid. **1936** A. HUXLEY *Eyeless in Gaza* iv. 35 'Poor child!' his father said to himself; and then, overbidding as it were, 'Poor motherless child!' he added deliberately. **1947** S. HARRIS *Fund. Princ. Contract Bridge* I. i. 17 If one of the adversaries did overbid him, North would almost certainly make a sacrifice bid of four Spades. **1952** I. MACLEOD *Bridge* vii. 82 Be chary of overbidding a suit bid with one No Trump. **1952** PHILLIPS & REESE *Bridge with Mr. Playbetter* xxviii. 118 Mrs. Portly raised to Two Spades; an aggressive player, at the score, might have risked a shut-out bid of Three Spades, but Mrs. Portly knew better than to overbid when playing with Hurry. **1973** *Bridge Mag.* Feb. 123/2 Let us not forget that partner might have overbid slightly in this position. **1974** *Times* 15 June 9/1 They scrape up a bid whenever they can, convinced that by overbidding him they make the declarer work harder for his contract. **1975** *Times* 5 Dec. 14/6 Some European leaders, in overbidding the Brussels game, had seriously misled the public.

Hence **'overbidder,** one who makes an overbid (see next); **'overbidding** *vbl. sb.*, the action of one who overbids.

1912 F. IRWIN *Fine Pts. Auction Bridge* 85 There is no fault as common in Auction as overbidding. **1929** M. C. WORK *Compl. Contract Bridge* iii. 15 This artificial system is apt to cause overbidding. **1936** E. CULBERTSON *Contract Bridge Complete* II. xxix. 345 When the overbidder is vulnerable, the extent of the overbid should be less than two tricks. **1964** *Official Encycl. Bridge* 404/1 The overbidder must not be allowed to think that he is playing with an underbidder, or worse will follow. **1974** *Country Life* 17 Jan. 98/1 It is rewarding to study hands..and see what caused a poor result... Here is the tragedy of *Over-bidding.*

'overbid, *sb. Bridge.* [f. the vb.] A bid that is higher than is justified by one's cards; also = OVERCALL *sb.*

1917 [see *flag-flying* s.v. FLAG *sb.*^{4} 7]. **1947** S. HARRIS *Fund. Princ. Contract Bridge* I. i. 15 If one of the adversaries then makes an overbid of Diamonds or Clubs,.. North can then bid his Spades. **1952** I. MACLEOD *Bridge* iv. 46 When I use the term 'bid suit' that means a suit bid as a genuine suit —it does not include cue-bids or over-bids in the opponent's suit. **1967** P. ANDERTON *Play Bridge* v. 40 The number of points lost when you go down on the overbid should represent a considerable saving on what you would lose if the opponents obtained game and rubber. **1969** *Bridge Mag.* Oct. 219/2 North made a slight overbid of three hearts, but ensured the right strain. **1972** *Ibid.* June 386/2 He bid three clubs. Scared of..the overbid of three spades or the underbid of two spades.

†**over'bide,** *v. Obs.* [OVER- 18.] *trans.* To remain over or after; to outlast, outlive, survive.

1050 in Thorpe *Charters* (1865) 583 ðif ic hire ouerbide ..ȝif he me ouerbide. *a* **1300** *Cursor M.* 22687 Þe men þat þat dai sal ouerbide, Under a fell þai sal þam hide. **13..** *Seuyn Sag.* (W.) 1731 He hadde i-wedded two jolif wives; He liuede and bothe hem overbod. *c* **1386** CHAUCER *Wife's T.* 404 Grace touerbyde hem þat we wedde.

b. *intr.* To remain over the time, to tarry.

13.. *Cursor M.* 3008 (Cott.) O birth sco moght not ouer-bide. *Ibid.* 26627 (Cott.) Þi scrift agh noght at ouer bide.

over-big, over-billow: see OVER-.

'overbite. *Dentistry.* [OVER- 8(?).] The overlapping of the lower teeth, esp. the incisors, by the corresponding upper teeth; now usu.

confined to overlap in a vertical direction. Cf. OVERJET.

1887 W. G. A. BONWILL in W. F. Litch *Amer. Syst. Dentistry* II. 487 It will be found in 95 per cent. of cases that the upper teeth project over the lower, and that the depth of overbite varies as the depth of the cusps of the bicuspids are deep or shallow. **1924** T. GOODHUGH *Art of Prosthetic Dentistry* x. 246 The least amount of overbite occurs with the wisdom teeth, and the greatest amount at the incisors. **1947** E. HYAMS *William Medium* vii. 137 An immensely long upper lip rising from a prominent over-bite and barely covering a number of long, yellow horse-teeth. **1971** R. M. & F. M. KEESING *New Perspectives in Cultural Anthropol.* 55 The 'overbite' in the mouths of most of today's readers is apparently an adaptation in the maturation process to eating soft foods.

over-bitten: see OVER- 27 b.

'over-'bitter, *a.* [OVER- 28.] Too bitter. So **'over-'bitterly** *adv.*; **'over-'bitterness**, excessive bitterness.

c **1000** *Ags. Ps.* (Spelm.) xiii. 6 *Amaritudine*, oferbyternysse. **1340** HAMPOLE *Pr. Consc.* 3474 When þou spekes over bitterly Til any man with noyse or cry. *a* **1586** SIDNEY *Arcadia* (1622) 45 Musidorus had ouer-bitterly glaunced against the reputation of womankind. **1600** R. PERSONS in *Publ. Catholic Rec. Soc.* (1906) II. 120 But the rest for that it was longe and over bitter against some particular men, I thought good to leave it out. **1626** in Rushw. *Hist. Coll.* (1659) I. 360 His overbitterness in the Aggravation upon the whole Charge. **1927** H. CRANE *Lett.* (1965) 283 A good dig at certain people, but I think the sarcasm is over-bitter. **1943** *Pope & People* (Catholic Truth Soc.) ix. 171 There is now commonly much dispute, and sometimes over-bitter dispute, on this topic.

overblack to **overblaze**: see OVER-.

over'bleach, *v.* [OVER- 27.] *trans.* To bleach excessively so that the material bleached deteriorates. Hence **over'bleached** *ppl. a.*, **over'bleaching** *vbl. sb.*

1921 S. H. HIGGINS *Bleaching* xiii. 111 The 'copper value' standardised by Schwalbe is the most definite measure available for the diagnosis of chemical modification in celluloses, particularly by overbleaching. *Ibid.*, The copper value of strongly overbleached cottons may rise as high as 16. **1946** L. E. WISE *Wood Chem.* vi. 150 In pulp manufacture, overbleaching gives a paper with lowered strength, due to oxycellulose formation. **1950** B. E. HARTSUCH *Introd. Textile Chem.* vii. 188 If the specific viscosity of the cotton is greater than 1, the cloth has been overbleached. **1963** A. J. HALL *Textile Sci.* ii. 25 Overbleached cotton containing oxycellulose resists dyeing with direct cotton dyes, so that if this overbleaching is not even, the bleached yarn or fabric is liable to dye unevenly. **1972** L. PALLADINO *Princ. & Pract. Hairdressing* xi. 153/1 Overbleached hair when wet is almost like chewing gum.

over-blessed to **overblithe**: see OVER-.

overbloom ('əʊvəbluːm), *sb.* [OVER- 8 b.] A bloom covering the surface.

1883 SYMONDS *Ital. Byways* iv. 67 Chivalry..was fast decaying in a gorgeous overbloom of luxury.

over'bloom, *v.* [OVER- 23.] *refl.* To bloom or flower beyond its strength.

1849 *Florist's Jrnl.* 198 Calceolarias.—Do not let them overbloom themselves to the destruction of the plants.

'over-blouse. [OVER- 8 c.] A blouse worn over another outer garment.

1921 *Daily Colonist* (Victoria, B.C.) 2 Apr. 20/1 (Advt.), A new style Over-Blouse of Silk Crepe de Chine, in shades of white, flesh, navy and black, effectively embroidered with silk floss in contrasting shades. **1923** *Daily Mail* 13 Feb. 15 In usefulness no similar garment can compete with the over-blouse. **1960** *Times* 20 Jan. 8/4 Suits were generally accompanied by sleeveless silk overblouses. **1963** *New Yorker* 23 Nov. 189 Our double-knit 2-piece dress with slender skirt and scalloped overblouse. **1974** *Country Life* 28 Feb. 456/3 Full overblouse with..a matching full-length skirt.

overblow (əʊvə'bləʊ), *v.*[1] [f. OVER- 4, 6, 9, 27, 26 + BLOW *v.*[1]]

1. *trans.* To blow (a thing) over the top of anything, over one's head, etc.; to blow off or away.

1387 TREVISA *Higden* (Rolls) VI. 95 But al þe creem and fatnesse of þat mylke..schulde be overblowe and i-take awey. **1471** RIPLEY *Comp. Alch.* Rec. iv. in Ashm. *Theatr. Chem. Brit.* (1652) 187 Than clouds of darknes be overblowyn & all aperyth faire. **1601** B. JONSON *Forest, Epode* 36 This doth from the cloud of Error grow, Which thus we ouer-blow. **1659** FULLER *App. Inj. Innoc.* (1840) 363 The best way to over-blow this fear is, to confute the five arguments. **1718** WATTS *Ps.* LVII. i, Hide me beneath thy spreading wings, Till the dark cloud is over-blown.

2. *intr.* Of a storm: To blow over, to pass away overhead; to abate in violence; hence *fig.* of danger, anger, passion, etc.: To pass away, to be past. (Perf. tenses often with *be*.)

c **1385** CHAUCER *L.G.W.* 1287 *Dido*, The hote ernest is al ouerblowe. **1390** GOWER *Conf.* II. 396 The colde wyndes overblowe, And stille be the scharpe schoures. **1503** HAWES *Examp. Virt.* v. 8 Sythens that your wyldnes is ouerblowen. **1575** CHURCHYARD *Chippes* (1817) 193 But all those blasts, in fine did ouerbloe. **1690** DRYDEN *Don Sebastian* v. i, The tempest is o'erblown, the skies are clear. **1829** CARLYLE *Misc.* (1857) II. 11 There lies land-locked till the hurricane is overblown.

3. *trans.* To blow (a thing) over, to overthrow or upset by blowing; to blow down.

1562 J. HEYWOOD *Prov. & Epigr.* (1867) 163 This winde will ouer blow vs first I trow. **1585** LUPTON *Thous. Notable Th.* (1675) 2 A certain Poet did wear leaden soles under his shoos, lest the wind should overblow him. **1608** HIERON *Def. Ministers' Reasons Refus. Subscr.* II. 171 Which neither ..the windes nor waves of his answeres will overflow or over-blow. **1631** R. H. *Arraignm. Whole Creature* xii. §4. 128 To overthrow, and overblow her strongest Bulwarkes.

4. *trans.* To blow over the surface of; to cover by blowing over (as sand or snow does).

c **1420** *Pallad. on Husb.* I. 808 So shal ereither werk ben ouerblowe With coold or hoot vndir the signys twelue. *c* **1630** RISDON *Surv. Devon* §328 (1810) 338 The Sand.. hath overblown many hundred acres of land. **1794** HUTCHINSON *Hist. Cumberld.* I. 258 *note*, Sheep..when overblown and buried in snow by a storm. **1830** TENNYSON *Ode to Memory* v, A sand-built ridge..Overblown with murmurs harsh. **1872** WHITTIER *Penn. Pilgrim* 514 The music the wind drew..from leaves it overblew.

†**5.** *intr. Naut.* Of the wind: To blow with excessive violence; to blow too hard for top-sails to be carried. *Obs.*

1599 HAKLUYT *Voy.* II. 185 To get out the ship..was vnpossible, for the winde was contrary and ouerblowed. **1622** R. HAWKINS *Voy. S. Sea* (1847) 20 If the wind had not over-blowne, and that to follow them I was forced to shut all my lower ports, the ship I undertooke..had never endured to come to the port. **1627** CAPT. SMITH *Seaman's Gram.* x. 46 It ouer blowes when we can beare no top-sailes. **1726** SWIFT *Gulliver* II. i, Finding it was like to overblow, we took in our sprit-sail. **1823** in CRABB *Technol. Dict.*

6. *trans. Music.* To blow or play (a pipe or wind-instrument) with such force as to produce a harmonic or overtone instead of the fundamental note. Also *refl.* (of the pipe or instrument) and *intr.* for *refl.*

1852 SEIDEL *Organ* 79 The pipe will over-blow itself, that is it will sound an octave higher. **1880** E. J. HOPKINS in Grove *Dict. Mus.* II. 575/1 An organ thus supplied with wind could not be *over-blown.* **1938** *Oxf. Compan. Mus.* 228/1 The cornet is horrible when overblown. **1946** MEZZROW & WOLFE *Really Blues* (1957) 363 They have to overblow their instruments, fighting to be heard. **1956** M. STEARNS *Story of Jazz* (1957) xvii. 214 Benny Goodman reacted differently: 'This is the first time..that I've ever heard a tenor sax played the way it should be and not overblown.' **1976** *Early Music* Oct. 511/1 Then Jacob Denner (1732) developed an instrument, which, by means of a key, overblew into the higher register, at an interval of an octave plus a tritone (the modern clarinet overblows at an interval of a twelfth).

7. *Metallurgy.* To subject (a charge) to an excessive length of blast. Cf. OVERBLOWN *ppl. a.*[1] 3.

1869 *Chem. News* 9 Apr. 170/2 If a charge is 'over-blown' —that is, if it be subjected to the action of the air for too long a period,..the steel will be found to be defective in proportion to its unskilful treatment. **1932** E. GREGSON *Metall.* ii. 32 Great experience is necessary at this point, since if the metal is 'over-blown' for only 15 seconds, steels containing a large proportion of iron oxide are obtained. **1951** G. R. BASHFORTH *Manuf. Iron & Steel* II. ii. 26 Frequently a heat that has been overblown may be dirty.

over'blow, *v.*[2] *rare.* [f. OVER- 8 + BLOW *v.*[2]] *trans.* To cover with blossom.

1856 MRS. BROWNING *Aur. Leigh* VII. 58 He overblows an ugly grave With violets which blossom in the spring.

overblow ('əʊvəbləʊ), *sb. Metallurgy.* [f. OVERBLOW *v.*[1]] A period or instance of overblowing.

1879 *Jrnl. Iron & Steel Inst.* 158 One minute overblow and the phosphorus came down to ·75 per cent. **1946** *Ibid.* CLII. 12P This rather long overblow only caused a reduction of about 0·03% in the blown-metal carbon content.

over'blowing, *vbl. sb.* [f. OVERBLOW *v.*[1] + -ING[1].] **1.** *Metallurgy.* Subjection to an excessive length of blast.

1879 *Jrnl. Iron & Steel Inst.* 121 The removal of phosphorus was assisted by slight over-blowing. **1890** W. M. WILLIAMS *Chem. Iron & Steel Making* xvi. 301 An experimentally overblown sample..in spite of overblowing, produced a high quality of mild steel after the addition of spiegeleisen. **1932** E. GREGORY *Metall.* ii. 35 Over-blowing results in the production of over-oxidised and 'wild' metal. **1949** *Jrnl. Metals* Dec. 27/2 One of the most important features of end-point control is the elimination of overblowing.

2. *Mus.* In the playing of a pipe or wind instrument: production of a harmonic or overtone instead of the fundamental note through extra force of air.

1879 *Organ Voicing & Tuning* 17 *Overblowing, or speaking the octave.* Causes:—(*a*), languid too low; (*b*), excessive wind-hole. **1898** STAINER & BARRETT *Dict. Mus. Terms* (ed. 2) s.v. *Harmonic stops*, They will take a very strong pressure of wind without overblowing. **1938** *Oxf. Compan. Mus.* 59/1 Other wood-wind instruments..obtain their second octave by overblowing. **1954** *Grove's Dict. Mus.* (ed. 5) VI. 468/2 Overblowing greatly increases the natural compass of wind instruments. **1977** *Times* 13 Apr. 11/1 Michel Portal, a splendid clarinettist, was playing ill-toned microtones and strident chords (faked by overblowing in a manner now common in new music). **1977** *Early Music* July 351/1 A minute hole in the crook, especially on lower shawms, aids overblowing into the second octave.

overblown, *ppl. a.*[1] [From OVERBLOW *v.*[1]]

1. Blown over; that has passed away.

1596 SHAKS. *Tam. Shr.* v. ii. 3 To smile at scapes and perils ouerblowne. **1601** WEEVER *Mirr. Mart.* E vij, The Clergie's mallice (not o're-blowne) will haue me.

2. Inflated, swollen to excess (with vanity, etc.).

1864 KINGSLEY *Rom. & Teut.* iii. (1875) 83 Overblown with self-conceit. **1929** R. BRIDGES *Testament of Beauty* III. 55 The empty mind may float lightly in the full moonshine of o'erblown affluence. **1971** *New Yorker* 30 Oct. 25/2 This overblown, frolicsome Western [film].

3. *Metallurgy.* In the Bessemer steel process: Injured or burnt by continuance of the blast after all the carbon has been removed from the metal.

1879 *Jrnl. Iron & Steel Inst.* 156 The paper admitted that ferrous oxide was employed in the process, and he should wish to ask..how much of it was produced by oxidation in an overblown charge. **1946** *Ibid.* CLII. 9P A later shut-off results in overblown metal. **1951** G. R. BASHFORTH *Manuf. Iron & Steel* II. ii. 21 It is claimed that this application has reduced the likelihood of over-blown heats and considerably improved the control of quality. **1958** A. D. MERRIMAN *Dict. Metallurgy* 222/2 If the blast is allowed to continue after this, oxidation of part of the iron occurs and the charge is then overblown.

'over'blown, *ppl. a.*[2] [f. OVER- 28 c + BLOWN *ppl. a.*[2]] Too much blown, more than full blown.

1616 B. JONSON *Epigr.* xcvii, His rosy ties and garters so o'erblown. *a* **1625** BEAUM. & FL. *Knt. Malta* v. i, Thus over-blown, and seeded, I am rather Fit to adorn his chimney than his bed. **1821** SHELLEY *Adonais* xxxiii, His head was bound with pansies over-blown. **1844** E. B. BROWNING *Poems* II. 121 From those over-blown faint roses, Not a leaf appeareth shed. **1916** JOYCE *Portrait of Artist* v. 260 The great overblown scarlet flowers of the tattered wallpaper. **1933** *Jrnl. R. Hort. Soc.* LVIII. 232 No useful purpose is served by leaving the flowers until they are in the overblown condition. **1960** P. GALLICO *Mrs. Harris goes to N.Y.* 178 Tired greens, dispirited cabbages and overblown sprouts. **1976** 'J. Ross' *I know what it's like to Die* v. 39 A creamy, overblown peach blonde.

overboard (əʊvə'bɔəd, 'əʊvə-), *adv.* [f. OVER *prep.* 12 + BOARD *sb.*, q.v. for Forms. Usually treated as two words to *c* 1600; hyphened to *c* 1800; as one word from late in 18th c.]

1. a. Of motion: Over the side of a ship or boat, out of or from the ship into the water.

c **1000** ÆLFRIC *Hom.* I. 246 Hi ða wurpon heora waru ofor bord. **13..** *E.E. Allit. P.* C. 157 Þer watz busy ouer borde bale to kest. *c* **1386** CHAUCER *Man of Law's T.* 824 The theef fil ouer bord al sodeynly. ? *a* **1400** *Morte Arth.* 3703 Alle þe kene mene of kampe, knyghtes and oþer, Killyd are colde dede, and castyne over burdez! **1495** *Naval Acc. Hen. VII* (1896) 278 Rotteyn And for their ffeblenes cast ouer Borde. **1572** GASCOIGNE *Hearbes, Voy. Holland* Wks. (1587) 168 Whych cast the best fraight ouer-boord away. **1610** SHAKS. *Temp.* II. ii. 126, I escap'd vpon a But of Sacke, which the Saylors heaued o're-boord. **1623** BP. HALL *Best Bargaine* Wks. (1625) 520 At last turned ouer-boord into a sea of Desperation. **1745** P. THOMAS *Jrnl. Anson's Voy.* 17 The *Pearl*..had thrown about 14 Ton of Water over board. **1762** FALCONER *Shipwreck* II. 266 In such extremes, no moment should be lost But over-board, the cumb'rous cannon tost. **1869** FREEMAN *Norm. Conq.* III. xii. 98 He fell overboard and was drowned.

b. Beyond the side of the ship, outside the ship.

1823 J. BADCOCK *Dom. Amusem.* 80 He rigged out a spar, one end of which projected overboard.

2. *fig.* **a.** esp. in phr. *to throw overboard*, to cast aside, discard, reject, renounce. **b.** excessively, beyond one's means; chiefly in phr. *to go overboard*, to behave immoderately; to go too far; to display excessive enthusiasm.

1641 J. JACKSON *True Evang. T.* III. 193 That Religion which is more turbulent, seditious, and stormy, let it be throwne over-board to lighten the ship of the Church. **1679** *Establ. Test* 9 They threw over-board all their Loyalty. **1831** LAMB *Elia* Ser. II. *To Shade of Elliston*, The judge's ermine; the coxcomb's wig; the snuff box *à la Foppington* —all must overboard. **1931** D. RUNYON in *Collier's* 26 Sept. 8/2 We go over-board today. We are washed out. We owe every book-maker.., and now we are out trying to raise some scratch to pay off. *Ibid.* 9/4 We do not have anything to bet on these races, or any way of betting on them, because we are overboard with every bookmaker we know. **1945** [see BUST *v.*[2] f]. **1951** J. P. MARQUAND *Melville Goodwin* (1952) viii. 113 Did you ever hear about General Goodwin going overboard over an American girl in Paris..? **1953** 'S. RANSOME' *Hear no Evil* (1954) xv. 140 The man went overboard in a big way morally—he made himself a thief, deserted his family. **1960** *N.Z. Listener* 30 Sept. 11/1, I cannot admire 'abstract' interpretations any more than I can go overboard about sculpture rigged up out of bicycle parts. **1968** *Wall St. Jrnl.* 28 Feb. 16/2 It is easy to go overboard on the new techniques, for all their virtues. **1971** *Jrnl. Gen. Psychol.* Jan. 153 Many psychologists..have gone overboard in hypothetical and speculative associations of this sort. **1978** *Times* 9 Jan. 8/6 Lord Allen..has been convinced of the importance of money..without going overboard in defence of it.

3. = ABOVE-BOARD; plainly and openly.

1834 H. O'BRIEN *Round Towers Irel.* 327 To speak over-board, the lapses..were to him ethically unavoidable.

Hence **over'board** *v.* (*nonce-wd.*), to throw overboard.

1585-6 EARL LEYCESTER *Corr.* (Camden) 312, I will rather be overthrowne by her majesties doings then overborded by their churles and tinkers.

overboast to **over-boding**: see OVER-.

'over,body, *sb.* [f. OVER- 8 c + BODY *sb.* 6.] An upper or outer bodice.

1573 *Richmond. Wills* (Surtees) 235, I give vnto ye wyfe of Robart my soon my browne kyrtle with ye chamlet overbodye. **1615** in *N. Riding Rec.* (1884) II. 98 Two men presented for stealing a woman's overbody value 8*d.* **1845** E. H. NOEL *Richter's Flower Pieces* II. xix. 241 The first and last army whose uniform was a kind of fine over-body.

So †**overbody coat** *Obs.*, an ephod.

1535 COVERDALE *Exod.* xxv. 7 Onix stones and set stones for the ouerbody cote and for the Brestlappe. —— *1 Sam.* ii. 18 The childe was gyrded with an ouer body cote of lynnen.

†**'over'body**, *v. nonce-wd.* [f. OVER- 27 + BODY *sb.* or *v.*] *trans.* To give too much body to, make excessively material.

1641 MILTON *Ch. Govt.* I. (1851) 2 Till the Soule by this meanes of over-bodying her selfe, given up justly to fleshly delights, bated her wing apace downeward.

overboil (əʊvəˈbɔɪl), *v.* [OVER- 5, 27.]

1. *intr.* To boil over; to boil so as to overflow the pot, etc. Chiefly *fig.*

1611 SPEED *Hist. Gt. Brit.* IX. xx. (1623) 972 Which made her spirits ouer-boyle with impatience. **1816** BYRON *Ch. Har.* III. lxix, To keep the mind Deep in its fountain, lest it overboil. **1868** BROWNING *Ring & Bk.* VI. 1119 No word, lest Crispi overboil and burst.

†**b.** *trans.* To cause to boil over. *Obs.*

1687 MONTAGUE & PRIOR *Hind & P. Transv.* 12 Till Pride of Empire, Lust, and hot Desire Did over-boile him, like too great a Fire.

2. *trans.* (ˌ*over-'boil.*) To boil too much.

1584 COGAN *Haven Health* (1636) 131 Fine meats in hot stomacks, be, as it were, over-boiled, when the grosser are but duely concocted. *a* **1643** W. CARTWRIGHT *Ordinary* I. iii, They are A little over-boyl'd or so.

'overboil, *sb. rare.* [f. the vb.] phr. *on the overboil*: in an overboiling condition, a state of ebullience.

1883 RUSKIN *Let.* 30 Oct. in *Igdrasil* (1890) June 218 And my brains always on the overboil, if I don't mind.

ˌover'boiling, *vbl. sb.* [f. OVERBOIL *v.* + -ING[1].] A boiling over; an ebullition.

a **1774** HARTE *Vision of Death* Poems (1810) 371/1 Or wild o'er-boiling of ungovern'd health. **1861** W. S. PERRY *Hist. Ch. Eng.* I. iii. 126 This may perhaps have been a little over-boiling of spite.

So **overboiling** *ppl. a.*, boiling over; *fig.* excessively ardent or fervent.

1594 NASHE *Terrors of Night* Wks. (Grosart) III. 257 With anie ouerboyling humour which sourseth hiest in our stomackes. **1670** DRYDEN *1st Pt. Conq. of Granada* Ded., A hero.. of an excessive and over-boiling courage. **1682** —— *Dk. Guise* v. iii, Do these o'erboiling answers suit the Guise? **1726** LEONI *Alberti's Archit.* III. 19/2 A proof of the over-boyling genius of the Painter. *a* **1814** *Spaniards* I. ii. in *New Brit. Theatre* III. 209 Restrain Thy over-boiling wrath.

'over-'bold, *a.* [OVER- 28.] Too bold, unwarrantably or unduly bold; presumptuous.

c **1530** *Crt. of Love* 360 That I and alle Should ever drede to be too overbold Her to displese. **1605** SHAKS. *Macb.* III. v. 3 (Beldams) as you are, Sawcy, and ouer-bold, how did you dare To Trade and Trafficke with Macbeth? *a* **1791** WESLEY *Husb. & Wives* vi. §4 Wks. 1811 IX. 84 Why should a woman be so over bold as to call her husband, *Tom, Ned, Dick?* **1883** STEVENSON *Treas. Isl.* v. xxii, I was going to do a foolish, over-bold act.

'over-'boldly, *adv.* [OVER- 30.] In an over-bold manner, with too much boldness.

1547 *Homilies* I. *Falling from God* II. (1859) 89 They do overboldly presume of God's mercy and live dissolutely. **1684** *Scanderbeg Rediv.* iv. 60 [They] Killed two Gentlemen upon the place, who spake over-boldly against their Choice. **1860** TRENCH *Serm. Westm. Abb.* vii. 73 It is not over-boldly said.

'over-'boldness. [OVER- 29 c.] Excessive boldness, presumption, audacity.

1583 GOLDING *Calvin on Deut.* xlix. 292 God also would put me to shame for mine ouerboldnesse. *a* **1668** DAVENANT *Epil.* Wks. (1673) 301 An over-boldness, rais'd from too much fear. **1846** TRENCH *Mirac.* xvii. (1862) 284 What of carnal overboldness there was in it.

overbook (əʊvəˈbʊk), *v.* [f. OVER- 27 + BOOK *v.*] *trans.* To make more bookings for (a theatre, hotel, aircraft, etc.) than there are places or seats available; to book an excessive number of (customers, passengers, etc.). Also *intr.* Hence **overbooked** *ppl. a.*; **over'booking** *vbl. sb.*

1903 *Daily Chron.* 10 Nov. 9/1 The booking clerks had by some oversight overbooked the theatre. **1964** G. L. COHEN *What's Wrong with Hospitals?* v. 104 A Ministry report on waiting time [at hospital clinics] pointed to the same causes of delay: over-booking and arbitrary appointment intervals. **1967** N. BUXTON *Travel '67* 674 The traveller is told.. that the flight has been over-booked and that he must wait for the next plane. *Ibid.* 675 Over-booking may sometimes happen even in the most competently run organization. **1971** *Guardian* 28 July 7/8 An approach to end overbooking at some Spanish holiday hotels will begin in Madrid. **1972** J. POTTER *Going West* 77 All airlines overbooked by fourteen per cent as a matter of policy. **1973** *Daily Tel.* 5 Sept. 6/7 If we did not overbook our flights the jumbos would be flying with a mass of empty seats. *Ibid.*, We overbooked 31 passengers on a flight to Canada today. **1975** *Times* 24 June 19/5 Over-booking—the practice of selling seats twice over, followed by almost every airline in the world. **1976** *Times* 26 Jan. 19/4 The over-booked passenger, despite his protests, finds himself 'bumped' off the flight. **1978** *TV Times* 28 Jan. 65 (Advt.) Want a really carefree holiday this year? Like to stay overnight where and when you like, and not bother about over-booked hotels?

over-bookish: see OVER-.

overborne (-ˈbɔən), *ppl. a.* [pa. pple. of OVERBEAR *v.*] Borne down by superior force or pressure; oppressed: see OVERBEAR *v.*

1611 SPEED *Hist. Gt. Brit.* VII. vii. 222 And euer bare as hard an hand ouer the ouerborne Britains. **1762** J. WOOLMAN *Wks.* (1840) 225 An overborne discontented reaper. **1901** G. B. SHAW *Devil's Disciple* I. 19 Uncle Titus, overborne, resumes his seat on the sofa. **1961** in WEBSTER *s.v.*, Art, industry, and commerce, so long crushed and overborne. **1977** *Navy News* Sept. 7/1, I seem to remember reading in Navy News a while ago that the Navy was so overborne with cooks that some could expect to be drafted to non-cooking billets.

overbought, *ppl. a.* [f. OVERBUY *v.*] (See quot. 1957.)

1957 CLARK & GOTTFRIED *University Dict. Business & Finance* 252/2 *Overbought.* 1. The condition of having purchased more than is needed to meet requirements. However, as used, the condition does not necessarily result from excessive buying, but may be the result of shrinking needs or resale volume. 2. In securities trade usage, a condition in which the demand for securities at existing prices has been filled, so that prices tend to drop. **1961** *Spectator* 26 May 774 When a market becomes.. overbought, prices are extra sensitive to bad news. **1962** E. GODFREY *Retail Selling & Organization* xx. 199 If a buyer is overbought, he is informed of this fact immediately by stock control office. **1968** *Economist* 16 Mar. 86/2 One of the Americans' hopes would be that, after an initial soaring, the free market price of gold could come down again; partly because hoarders and speculators are now so over-bought. **1974** S. MARCUS *Minding Store* iv. 61 They.. would never pass a desirable garment, however over-bought they might be.

over'bound, *v.*[1] *rare.* [cf. BOUND *v.*[3] = ABOUND.] *intr.* To superabound; = OVER-ABOUND *v.* Hence **over'bounding** *vbl. sb.* and *ppl. a.*

1587 GOLDING *De Mornay* xiv. 223 An ouerbounding of some melancholike humour. **1956** T. DRIBERG *Guy Burgess* iii. 45 Churchill seemed a little pleased. 'My eloquence!' he said. 'Ah, yes, that.. Herr Beans can rely on in full and indeed.. some would say, in overbounding measure.'

over'bound, *v.*[2] *rare.* [f. OVER- 5 + BOUND *v.*[2]] *trans.* To bound or leap over.

1813 SHELLEY *Q. Mab* II. 94 All-prevailing wisdom.. o'er-bounds Those obstacles, of which an earthly soul Fears to attempt the conquest.

†**over-bound**, *adv. Obs. rare*[−1]. [OVER- 10.] Bound over or across (the sea).

1669 N. MORTON *New Eng. Mem.* 124 (Cent.) They went .. away, the greater ship towing the lesser at her stern all the way over-bound.

over-bounteous, etc.: see OVER- 28.

over-bow (-ˈbaʊ), *v.* [OVER- 27, 1.]

1. *trans.* (ˌ*over-'bow.*) To bend in excess.

1639 FULLER *Holy War* III. xx. (1647) 142 The best way to straighten what is crooked is to over-bow it.

2. (*over'bow*) To arch over.

1878 DOWDEN *Studies in Literat.* 271 These poems are.. overbowed with the firmament of adult thought.

'over-bowed (-ˈbəʊd), *a.* [f. OVER- 28 + BOWED *ppl. a.*[2]] (See quot.) So **over-'bow** *v.*[2] *refl.*, to adopt too strong a bow.

1875 *Encycl. Brit.* II. 378/2 An archer is said to be over-bowed when the power of his bow is above his command. **1939** P. H. GORDON *New Archery* 72 Beginners should be most careful not to overbow themselves. **1976** *St. Louis* (Missouri) *Globe-Democrat* 17 Sept. 5 B A bow with a draw weight of 40 pounds or more is adequate for the taking of many deer. Many beginners 'overbow' themselves and sacrifice accuracy for unnecessary power.

over'bower, *v.* [OVER- 1.] *trans.* To form a bower over; to overarch.

1807 SOUTHEY *Espriella's Lett.* II. 220 A part [of a road] which was almost completely overbowered. **1823** —— *Hist. Penins. War* II. 440 Long and wide avenues were over-bowered with elms.

over-bowl to **overbranch**: see OVER-.

'over-'brave, *a.* [OVER- 28.] Too brave; very brave (in negative constructions); †excessively splendid or showy (*obs.*).

a **1653** GOUGE *Comm. Heb.* xi. 37 (1655) 230 This sheweth the vanity of over-brave and costly apparell. *Mod.* It wasn't over-brave of him to attack such a little boy.

†**over-'brave**, *v. Obs.* [OVER- 21.] *trans.* To play the 'brave' over; to treat with bravado.

1624 FORD *Sun's Darling* I. i, Knaves over-brave wise men, while wise men stand with cap and knee to fools. **1631** BRATHWAIT *Whimzies, Gamester* 38 Hee so over-braves and abuseth the poor dice.

overbray to **over-break**: see OVER- 21, 9.

over-'breathe, *v.* [f. OVER- 22, 8, 26.]

†**1.** *trans.* To put out of breath. *Obs.*

1589 WARNER *Alb. Eng.*, *Æneidos* 165 Least (perhaps) I ouer-breathe thy tickled Conceite with more selfe-liking than is expedient. *a* **1783** H. BROOKE *Fox-Chase* Poems (1810) 438/2 O'er-breath'd we come where, 'twixt impending hills, Ran the joint current of two gurgling rills.

2. *intr.* To breathe over.

1802 [Implied in *overbreathing* below].

3. *intr. Physiol.* = HYPERVENTILATE *v.* a.

1928 F. W. BRODERICK *Dental Med.* xi. 221, I.. advise the parent to see that the child is sitting or lying down at the time they are over-breathing. **1961** *Lancet* 5 Aug. 304/2 All divers should therefore be instructed not to overbreathe before diving.

Hence **overbreathing** *vbl. sb.*

1802 W. TAYLOR in Robberds *Mem.* I. 419 Young acolytes were sweetening with incense the warm over-breathings of thronging devotion. **1920** *Jrnl. Biol. Chem.* XLIII. 9 A continuation.. of overbreathing and blowing off of CO_2 results in a compensatory disappearance of alkali from the blood. **1954** W. MAYER-GROSS et al. *Clin. Psychiatry* iv. 131 A prolonged period of over-breathing, causing alkalinity of the blood. **1968** *Brit. Med. Bull.* XXIV. 202/1 On overbreathing there are a few bilateral episodes of delta activity, maximal posteriorly.

over-bred, overbreed: see OVER- 27 b, 27.

†**over'brede**, *v. Obs.* [OE. *oferbrǽdan*, f. *ofer-* OVER- 8 + *brǽdan*, BREDE, to spread out.] *trans.* To overspread, cover all over.

c **897** K. ÆLFRED *Gregory's Past. C.* xlv. 336 Swæ se fiicbeam ofersceadoð ðæt land.. ac ðæt land bið eall unnyt swæ he hit oferbræt. *c* **1205** LAY. 19045 Wes þat kinewurðe bed Al mid palle ouer bræd [*c* 1275 ouer sprad]. *c* **1400** *Sege Jerus.* (E.E.T.S.) 600 So was þe bent ouer brad, blody by-runne With ded bodies aboute.

†**over-'bribe**, *v. Obs.* [OVER- 11, 20.] *trans.* To gain over by bribery; to bribe over again.

1618 BOLTON *Florus* (1636) 162 Iugurtha so over-bribed his Army also, that.. he got the Victory. **1748** RICHARDSON *Clarissa* (1811) III. 116 He who would be bribed to undertake a base thing by one, would be over-bribed to retort the baseness.

over'bridge, *v.* [f. OVER- 5 + BRIDGE *v.*[1]] *trans.* To make a bridge over; to bridge over.

c **1000** ÆLFRIC *Hom.* II. 304 Þa het Maxentius mid micclum swicdome oferbricgian ða ea, eal mid scipum. **1805** WORDSW. *Prelude* v. 348 These mighty workmen.. Who, with a broad highway have overbridged The froward chaos of futurity. **1874** F. H. LAING in *Ess. Relig. & Lit.* Ser. III. 246 An infinite gulf, which can never be overbridged.

'over-ˌbridge, *sb.* [OVER- 1 d.] A bridge over a railway, as distinct from a subway or a road over which the railway crosses. Also, a bridge across a road. Also as *adj.*, travelling or placed across bridges.

1876 [see UNDER-BRIDGE]. **1878** F. S. WILLIAMS *Midl. Railw.* 174 There were many of the overbridges that would need to be rebuilt. **1898** *Engineering Mag.* XVI. 77 The access would be by a subway, and, if in cutting, by an over-bridge. **1905** *Daily Chron.* 3 Feb. 6/6 Who.. were the people who objected to the over-bridge trams? *Ibid.* 1 June 4/3 The Select Committee on the over-bridge tramways. **1959** *Manch. Guardian* 11 Aug. 6/5 More pedestrian overbridges and underpasses. **1962** *Engineering* 14 Dec. 775 The works will include.. four overbridges. **1973** *Inverness Courier* 31 July 6/5 Because of the single track and few overbridges, this would be a relatively cheap route to electrify.

'over-'bright, *a.* [OVER- 28.] Excessively bright; too bright.

1587 GOLDING *De Mornay* xiv. 209 We forbid them to beholde the thinges that are ouerbright. **1830** TENNYSON *Isabel* I Eyes not down-dropt nor over bright. **1861** MISS BRADDON *Lady Lisle* xxiv, I don't see that you're any of you such an over-bright lot.

over'brim, *v.* [OVER- 5.]

1. *intr.* To overflow at the brim; to brim over. (Said of the liquid or the vessel.) Mostly *fig.*

1607 BARKSTED *Mirrha* (1876) 57 And ere night you will.. orebrim with your teares. **1817** SCOTT *Harold* III. viii, When 'gins that rage to over-brim. **1826** —— *Woodst.* xxix, If the pitcher shall overbrim with water. **1880** WEBB *Goethe's Faust* III. viii. 172 Whene'er he drained its measure, His eyes would overbrim.

2. *trans.* To flow over the brim of.

1818 KEATS *Endymion* I. 137 Each having a white wicker, overbrimm'd With April's tender younglings. **1871** BROWNING *Pr. Hohenst.* 563 The liquor that o'erbrims the cup.

Hence **over'brimmed** *ppl. a.*, **over'brimming** *vbl. sb.* and *ppl. a.*

1830 TENNYSON *Confess. Sensit. Mind* 113 That grace Would drop from his o'erbrimming love, As manna on my wilderness. **1839** BAILEY *Festus* (1852) 58 Through his misty, o'erbrimmed eye. **1858** HAWTHORNE *Fr. & It. Jrnls.* II. 197 The overbrimming of the town in generations subsequent.

'overˌbrimmed, *a.* [OVER- 3.] Having a brim that projects or hangs over.

1814 SCOTT *Wav.* xxxv, He.. touched solemnly, but slightly, his huge and overbrimmed blue bonnet.

†**over'bring**, *v. Obs. rare.* [OVER- 10.] *trans.* To bring over or across. (Prop. two words.)

a **1300** *Cursor M.* 6959 Til he þe folk had ouerbroght [*v.r.* ouer broȝt] In-to þe land þat þai soght. **1615** CHAPMAN *Odyss.* XVI. 633 What in my way chanced I may over-bring.

over-broil: see OVER- 29 b.

over'brood, *v.* [OVER- 1.] *trans.* To brood or hover over.

1818 MILMAN *Samor* 115 To rise.. and o'er-brood The dim and desert beacon of revenge. **1865** WHITTIER *Eternal Goodness* 25 Ye see the curse which overbroods A world of pain and loss.

†**'overˌbrow**, *sb. Obs.* [OVER- 1 d.] Eyebrow.

c **1000** *Sax. Leechd.* III. 188 Mæden [hæfð] tacn on ofer-brawe swiþran. **1555** EDEN *Decades* 287 A foule of darke coloure.. with redde ouerbrowes. **1561** HOLLYBUSH *Hom.*

Apoth. 2 Good to use, specially for ouerbrowes and eye liddes.

over'brow, *v.* [OVER- 1.] *trans.* To overhang like a brow. Hence **over'browing** *ppl. a.*

1742 COLLINS *Ode Poet. Char.* 58 Strange shades o'erbrow the vallies deep. **1814** SOUTHEY *Roderick* XIV. 58 Beneath the overbrowing battlements. **1824** LONGF. *Woods in Winter* i, The hill That overbrows the lonely vale.

overbrowned to **overbubble**: see OVER-.

overbuild (əʊvəˈbɪld, ˌəʊvə-), *v.* Pa. t. and pple. overbuilt. [OVER- 1, 8, 27.]

1. *trans.* To build over or upon; to cover or surmount with a building or structure. Chiefly *fig.*

1649 G. DANIEL *Trinarch., Hen. IV*, ccxci, When Iustice, by Ambition over-built, Is fronted with new Turretts. **1784** COWPER *Task* III. 193 Sage, erudite, profound, Terribly arch'd, and aquiline his nose, And overbuilt with most impending brows. **1857** WILLMOTT *Pleas. Lit.* xi. 47 Some men overbuild their nature with books.

2. To build too much or to excess. Also *fig.*

1642 FULLER *Holy & Prof. St.* III. vii. 168 Who by overbuilding their houses have dilapidated their lands. **1713** C'TESS WINCHELSEA *Misc. Poems* 124 'Twas not to save the Charge: That in this over-building Age, My House was not more large. **1909** *Daily Chron.* 17 July 3/2 This is an enjoyable book... It has faults of plot—it is over-built—and of character-drawing [etc.]. **1946** *Sun* (Baltimore) 4 June 11/7 France also has some merit in his charge of 'overbuilding' players. **1946** 'R. WEST' *Train of Powder* (1955) 9 The German tendency to overbuild which has done much to get them into.. recurring financial troubles. **1977** *Time* 8 Aug. 43/1 As a result of the slowdown in the growth of petroleum consumption and some reckless overbuilding by shipyards in the early 1970s, the tanker business is in the worst depression in memory.

3. To build too much upon; to erect more buildings than are required upon (an area). Also *fig.*

1601 HOLLAND *Pliny* I. 554 Prouided alwaies, that a mans land be not ouer-built. **1864** WEBSTER, *Overbuilt*, built too much; having too many buildings; as an overbuilt part of a town. **1865** W. WHITE *Eastern England* II. xxi. 283 To me.. its especial charm is that it is not overbuilt or cockneyfied. **1870** A. T. DE VERE *May Carols* (ed. 2) 12 That, wholly overbuilt by grace, Nature might vanish, like some isle In great towers lost. **1893** A. JESSOPP *Studies by Recluse* (ed. 2) iii. 97 It was one of the many religious houses that started in a very ambitious way, and early overbuilt themselves. **1895** *Chicago Advance* 21 Nov. 737/1 A city which has been overbuilt, which has 'superfluous' houses and flats by the block and mile. **1939** *Sun* (Baltimore) 11 Apr. 3/3 'It seems a paradox,' he added, 'that in order to revive building operations and furnish employment for a class of workmen it must be carried on in places already overbuilt and becomes the real cause of the idleness of this class of workers.' **1961** *Wall St. Jrnl.* 24 Mar. 1/1 'I don't think the lower interest rates are going to have the slightest effect on housing demand,' says Henry Bubb, president of Capitol Federal Savings & Loan Association of Topeka, 'We're just over-built.' **1977** *Sat. Rev.* (U.S.) 17 Sept. 54/2 Is little New Orleans overbuilt? Perhaps not. By early summer the Hilton had already booked one million room-nights.

overbulk: see OVER- 22.

over-'bull, *v.* [f. OVER- 27 + BULL *v.*[1] 2.] *trans.* To raise the price of (stocks, etc.) excessively. Hence **over-'bulled** *ppl. a.*; **over-'bullishness.**

1905 *Daily Report* 14 Oct. 2/4 Readings were heavy, having apparently been over-bulled. **1938** *New Statesman* 16 July 132/1 Happily Wall Street has gone through a corrective period and over-bullishness has given way to more restrained optimism. **1965** *Economist* 23 Oct. 436/1 The market ignores the sad fate of so many American wonder electronic stocks: over-bulled, then crashing at the first set-back.

'over-bump, *v.* [f. OVER- 14 + BUMP *v.*[1] 3.] In bumping-races, to catch and bump (a boat ahead of a pair of other boats that have withdrawn after a bump), thus going up three places. So **'over-bump** *sb.*

1905 *Daily Chron.* 2 Mar. 7/3 One boat (Corpus) overbumped Selwyn and ascended three places. **1920** 'TWO OF 'EM' *Guide Cambr. Univ. Life* 10 If three or more boats bump simultaneously the rear boat goes to the front of those boats, and is said to have made an 'over-bump'. **1930** *Magdalene Boat Club 1828–1928* v. 19 The year 1868 is notable as providing the only occasion upon which the first boat ever made an overbump. **1963** *Times* 31 May 5/3 Merton II also attempted a big task in going for an overbump on Queen's II and it was only by one foot that they failed to make it.

'over'burden, *sb.* Also †-burthen. [OVER- 29 d, 1 d.]

1. Excessive burden; excess of burden.

1579–80 NORTH *Plutarch* (1657) 42 The vitall spirits not being.. kept downe, or spreade abroad by the quantity or over-burden thereof [meat], do enlarge themselves. *a* **1618** SYLVESTER *Job Triumphant* IV. 440 Who hath dispos'd the upper Spouts and Gutters, Whereby the Aire his overburthen utters? **1893** *Daily News* 8 Feb. 5/1 The overburden of work in the House of Commons makes the effort to get real business done a mere struggle and scramble.

2. *Mining*, etc. **a.** The overlying clay, rock, or other matter which has to be removed in quarrying or mining, in order to get at the deposit worked.

1855 J. R. LEIFCHILD *Cornwall Mines* 25 The quantity of 'overburthen', or waste, removed, has been upwards of 200,000 tons. **1894** *Times* 27 Feb. 10/3 The overburden is a reddish clay soil of an average depth of 10 ft.

b. The material lying over any particular point underground, esp. over a tunnel or pipeline; also, the pressure due to the weight of this material.

1948 TERZAGHI & PECK *Soil Mech. in Engin. Pract.* ii. 68 With respect to the present overburden, the clay on the right-hand side is a precompressed soft clay, and that on the left-hand side is a normally loaded soft clay. **1968** G. N. SMITH *Elem. Soil. Mech.* iv. 88 The overburden pressure at a point in a soil mass is simply the weight of the material above it. The effective overburden is the pressure from this material less the pore water pressure. **1970** *Daily Tel.* 27 June 2/5 The pipeline was laid in December 1967.. but the unexpectedly heavy scouring action of the bottom waves in the shallow North Sea soon removed the two foot overburden.

c. Loose, unconsolidated material lying above bedrock.

1955 *Proc. Colorado Sci. Soc.* XVI. 102/1 *Overburden*,.. a term used by geologists and engineers in several different senses. By some it is used to designate material of any nature, consolidated or unconsolidated, that overlies a deposit of useful materials, ores, or coal, especially those deposits that are mined from the surface by open cuts. As employed by others *overburden* designates only loose soil, sand, gravel, etc., that lies above the bedrock. The term should not be used without specific definition. **1969** *Civil Engineering* (U.S.) June 43/2 A more detailed soil investigation of the upper 50 ft or so of the overburden.. showed that the allowable bearing capacity was only about 200 to 300 psf, much too low for the proposed bridge foundations.

ˌover'burden, -'burthen, *v.* [OVER- 27.] *trans.* To put too great a burden or weight upon; to burden too much; to overload, overcharge.

1532 MORE *Confut. Tindale* Wks. 824/1, I neither wil for so plain a matter ouerburdein the reader in this boke, with the.. rehersyng of euerye place. *a* **1584** MONTGOMERIE *Cherrie & Slae* 1041 The waik anes that oreburdenit bein. **1725** POPE *Odyss.* XI. 379 The earth o'erburthen'd groan'd beneath their weight. **1726** LEONI *Alberti's Archit.* I. 56/1 To avoid over-burthening the Arch. **1881** RAYMOND *Mining Gloss.*, *Overburden*,.. to charge in a furnace too much ore and flux in proportion to the amount of fuel. **1885** *Spectator* 25 July 976/2 Mr. Leland does not overburthen his.. myths and legends with comment.

Hence **ˌover'burdened, -'burthened** *ppl. a.*; **ˌover'burdening, -'burthening** *vbl. sb.* and *ppl. a.*; whence **ˌover'burdeningly** *adv.*

1713 C'TESS WINCHELSEA *Misc. Poems* 240 The Miser.. fears the *over-burthened Floor. **1871–4** J. THOMSON *City Dreadf. Nt.* IX. ii, The hugeness of an overburthened wain. **1580** HOLLYBAND *Treas. Fr. Tong* s.v. *Affaissement*, A shrinking vnder a great burthen, an *ouerburthening. **1851** R. NESBIT in J. M. Mitchell *Mem.* xii. (1858) 303 Mr. James Mitchell's *overburdening duties. **1865** MRS. WHITNEY *Gayworthys* xxiii, Not officiously or *overburdeningly; there were kindnesses accepted, even asked for, in return.

'over-'burdensome, -'burthensome, *a.* [OVER- 28.] Excessively burdensome.

1614 RALEIGH *Hist. World* IV. iii. §11. 230 Eumenes did not onely thinke all carriages to be ouer-burdensome, but the number of his men to be more troublesome than auaileable. **1820** SCOTT *Monast.* Introd., The shopkeeper.. his custom was by no means over-burdensome. **1883** W. MORRIS in Mackail *Life* (1899) II. 99 All men may live at peace, and free from over-burdensome anxiety.

over'burn, *v.* [OVER- 21, 27.]

†**1.** *trans.* To burn down; to overthrow by fire.

1616 T. ADAMS *Forest of Thorns* Wks. 1862 II. 471 A strong engine set to the walls of purgatory, to overturn them, and overburn them with the fire of hell.

2. (ˌ*over-'burn*) To burn too much or to excess.

1707 MORTIMER *Husb.* (1721) I. 82 In burning of the Turf, you must take care not to over-burn it.. for the over-burning of it to white Ashes, wastes the nitrous Salt. *c* **1865** LETHEBY in *Circ. Sc.* I. 129/1 The supply of.. air is too great, and the gas is overburnt.

So **'over'burning** *vbl. sb.*; **'over'burning** *ppl. a.*, excessively burning or ardent (whence **'over'burningly** *adv.*, over-ardently); **'over-'burnt** *ppl. a.*

1707 *Over-burning [see sense 2]. **1849** JOHNSTON *Exp. Agric.* 260 By over-burning, clays lose their fertilising virtues. **1586** T. B. *La Primaud. Fr. Acad.* (1589) 449 When a man seeketh after any of them with an *overburning desire. **1303** R. BRUNNE *Handl. Synne* 7203 And ouþer spyces haþ glotonye, To ete þe mete *ouer brennyngl ye. **1834** *Brit. Husb.* I. 305 Lime.. if burnt with too violent a fire.. will not slake, and becomes useless, or what is termed *over-burnt, and, in some places, dead-lime. **1837** J. T. SMITH tr. *Vicat's Mortars* 115 A dark red, or purplish colour, similar to that of an over-burnt brick.

overburst: see OVER- 5 b.

overbusy (ˈəʊvəˈbɪzɪ), *a.* [OVER- 28.] Excessively busy; too much occupied; *esp.* that busies himself too much or is obtrusively officious.

1340 HAMPOLE *Pr. Consc.* 1095, I hald þat man noght witty, þat about þe world is over bysy. **1612** WOODALL *Surg. Mate* Wks. (1653) 5, I wish young Artists not to be over-busie in.. raising the fractured Cranium. *a* **1641** BP. MOUNTAGU *Acts & Mon.* (1642) 264 She should doe well, not to be over-busie in matters that concerned her not. **1770** LANGHORNE *Plutarch* (1879) II. 764/1 A troublesome and overbusy man.

So **'over'busily** *adv.*, too busily.

c **1440** *Jacob's Well* 142 þis wose of glotonye is v. fote brede, þat is, ouyrtymely, outeragely, ouerhastely, ouyrdeyntuously, & ouerbesyly. **1668** *Lond. Gaz.* No. 281/4 The French.. at Madagascar, having.. overbusily engaged themselves.., in a war between the Neighbouring Princes.

ˌover'busy, *v.* [OVER- 27.] *trans.* To busy too much; to engage or occupy too assiduously. Hence **ˌover'busied** *ppl. a.*

1586 FERNE *Blaz. Gentrie* 142 Had not our Cuttor ouerbusied himself. **1644** MILTON *Jdgm. Bucer* 159 Bucer is more large than to be read by overbusied men. **1863** MRS. WHITNEY *Faith Gartney* xxxvi. 330 The errand-boys in the shops were overbusied and uncertain.

over'buy, *v.* [OVER- 26, 23, 4, 11.]

1. † **a.** *trans.* To buy at too high a price; to pay too much for. *Obs.*

c **1430** *Pilgr. Lyf Manhode* IV. ix. (1869) 180 If men made of you saale, mihte no man livinge ouerbigge yow, ne loue yow to michel. **1530** PALSGR. 647/2, I overbye, I bye a thynge above the price it is worthe. **1639** FULLER *Holy War* IV. xxxiii. (1840) 239 Conceiving so convenient a purchase could not be over-bought. **1662** PETTY *Taxes* 21 The farmer for haste is forced to under-sell his corn, and the King.. is forced to overbuy his provisions. **1700** DRYDEN *Ep. to J. Driden* 138 And he, when want requires, is truly wise, Who slights not foreign aid, nor over-buys.

b. To buy goods at a (wholesale) price beyond the means of (a competitor).

1886 HARDY *Mayor Casterbr.* II. iii. 36 We'll under-sell him, and over-buy him, and so snuff him out.

2. *refl.* and *intr.* To buy beyond one's means, or to too great an extent. Also, of a wholesaler or retailer: to buy goods, materials, etc., in excess of those needed; to accumulate surplus stock. See also OVERBOUGHT *ppl. a.*

1745 *De Foe's Eng. Tradesman* vi. (1841) I. 37 If the tradesman overbuys himself, the payments perhaps come due too soon for him, the goods not being sold. **1938** *Sun* (Baltimore) 26 Feb. 18/8 The high level of delinquencies in Maryland results from several conditions—business recession, unemployment, 'overbuying'. **1950** *Times* 11 Mar. 9/7 Last year the Government overbought imported frozen fish and now fresh fish was being sold at a very low price. **1966** J. M. SHEWAN in *Proc. Internat. Symp. Food Irrad.* (Internat. Atomic Energy Agency) 496 Merchants, both wholesalers and retailers, frequently 'over-buy', particularly when supplies are plentiful and prices cheap.

†**3.** To buy off; to procure the release of (any one) by payment. *Obs.*

15.. *Priests of Peblis* in Pinkerton *Scot. Poems Repr.* I. 12 The theif ful weill he wil himself overby; Quhen the leill man into the lack wil ly.

†**4.** To buy over to one's side. *Obs.*

1709 MRS. MANLEY *Secret Mem.* (1736) III. 169 The Emperor had no Money.. to bestow upon Theodecta, by which they might have over-bought the Empress.

'over-by, *adv. Sc.* and *north. dial.* Also **ower-**, **owre-by.** [f. OVER *adv.* 7, 5 + BY *adv.*] Over or across the way; at or to a place at a short distance across; at or to the house or place opposite.

1768 ROSS *Helenore* 76 (Jam.) Quo' she unto the sheal, step ye o'erby. **1816** SCOTT *Bl. Dwarf* vi, Some canny boys waiting for me down amang the shaws, owerby. **1825** BROCKETT *N.C. Gloss.*, *Ower-by*, over the way. **1896** MUNRO *Lost Pibroch* 279 (E.D.D.) They told me at the ferry overby. *a* **1904** *Mod. Sc.* Our neighbours ower-by have lent us a hand.

overcackle *v.*: see OVER- 22.

overcall (əʊvəˈkɔːl), *v. Bridge.* [OVER- 22, 26.]

a. *trans.* and *intr.* To make a bid higher than (a previous bid or another player).

1908 R. F. FOSTER *Auction Bridge* 54 Neither should he bid a number of tricks which is more than necessary to overcall the previous declaration. **1916** F. IRWIN *Compl. Auction Player* 66 There is also a perfectly good suit with which to over-call. **1917** E. BERGHOLT *Royal Auction Bridge* 85 Here Y... is justified in over-calling with One Spade. **1918** R. F. FOSTER *On Auction* (1919) 183 The partner may be called upon to assist.. when the second hand overcalls the dealer. **1929** M. C. WORK *Compl. Contract Bridge* ii. 9 He may overcall a No Trump with a suit-bid, or overcall a suit-bid with another suit or No Trump. **1974** *Country Life* 17 Jan. 98 To overcall One Club with One Spade on a modest hand is worthwhile.

b. To bid more on (one's hand) than it is worth. Also *fig.*

1927 A. H. POLLEN in 'Neon' *Gt. Delusion* p. xvi, The bright young conjurers of Kingsway have been overcalling their hands. **1930** *Time & Tide* 11 Apr. 463 His partner had been overcalling. **1934** L. H. DAWSON *Hoyle's Games Modernized* 31 Sometimes a forced bid is also a forcing bid, in that the intention is to make the opponents over call.

overcall (ˈəʊvəkɔːl), *sb. Bridge.* [f. the vb.] A bid which is higher than a previous bid (see also quot. 1959). Cf. OVERBID *sb.*

1916 F. IRWIN *Compl. Auction Player* 65 To bid against your partner, when no one else has bid, is to use the overcall. **1917** E. BERGHOLT *Royal Auction Bridge* 85 Third hand should not carry on the contest further, unless he has some additional reason which his first overcall was not sufficient to proclaim. **1959** REESE & DORMER *Bridge Player's Dict.* 159 An overcall is a bid made after an opponent has opened the bidding. **1973** *Country Life* 10 May 1331/1, I had to take West's One Spade overcall into account. He was likely to have both missing Kings.

over'canopy, *v.* [OVER- 1.] *trans.* To form a canopy over; to extend over or cover as or with a canopy.

1590 SHAKS. *Mids. N.* II. i. 251 Quite ouer-cannoped with luscious woodbine, With sweet muske roses, and with

Eglantine. **1623** COCKERAM, *Ouercanopie*, to couer. **1742** GRAY *On Spring* ii, Where'er the rude and moss-grown beech O'er-canopies the glade. **1870** BRYANT *Iliad* XIII. 28 On the summit of th' Olympian mount He sat o'ercanopied by golden clouds.

overcap, -capable, -cape: see OVER-.

ˌover-ˈcapitalize, *v.* [OVER- 27.] *trans.* To fix or estimate the capital of (a joint-stock company, etc.) at too high an amount; to give or ascribe too great a capital value to (an industrial undertaking, etc.), esp. when forming it into a joint-stock concern.

1890 *Pall Mall G.* 22 Feb. 1/2 Was the business over-capitalized or was it not? **1897** *Review of Rev.* 55 The prevalent habit of overcapitalizing such corporations.

Hence **ˌover'capitalized** *ppl. a.*, **ˌovercapitali'zation**.

1882 *Rep. to Ho. Repr. Prec. Met. U.S.* 437 The over-capitalization of wholly undeveloped and but imperfectly opened mines. **1898** *Daily News* 9 June 3/2 His over-capitalised companies began to decline.

over-captious, etc.: see OVER- 28.

'over-'care, *sb.* [OVER- 29 d.] Too much care, undue or excessive care.

1599 SANDYS *Europæ Spec.* (1632) 206 The world having extinguished the care of the publike good, by an over-care of their private. **1693** DRYDEN tr. *Persius' Satires* II. 81 The very over-care, And nauseous pomp, wou'd hinder half the Pray'r. **1751** ELIZA HEYWOOD *Betsy Thoughtless* III. 7 It was only his over-care to please her. **1833** C. LAMB *Last Essays* 103 Sunday itself—that unfortunate failure of a holyday.. with my sense of its fugitiveness, and over-care to get the greatest quantity of pleasure out of it—is melted down into a week day. **1937** V. MCNABB *God's Way of Mercy* xii. 103 There is no over-care about tomorrow; just a love of God.

'over-'careful, *a.* [OVER- 28.] Too careful, excessively careful. Hence **'over'carefully** *adv.*, **'over'carefulness**.

a **1591** H. SMITH *Serm.* (1592) 988 If we bee carefull, wee are ouer carefull. **1597** SHAKS. *2 Hen. IV*, IV. v. 68 The foolish ouer-carefull Fathers. **1648** *Petit. Eastern Ass.* 31 We are not overcarefull, whether we live, or whether we die. **1842** MANNING *Serm.* (1848) I. 359 Over-careful about money, or fretful in a low estate. **1852** THACKERAY *Esmond* III. ii. **1865** DICKENS *Mut. Fr.* I. II. xiv. 296 'The sister,' said Bradley, separating his words over-carefully, and speaking as if he were repeating them from a book, 'suffers under no reproach.' **1870** —— *Edwin Drood* ii. 9 Life, for *you*, is a plum with the natural bloom on; it hasn't been over-carefully wiped off for *you*. **1881** *Chicago Advance* 18 May 312 Without over-carefulness as to the future. **1939** JOYCE *Finnegans Wake* 122 Three *basia* or shorter and smaller *oscula* have been overcarefully scraped away.

over-careless, etc.: see OVER- 28.

'over-'caring, *a.* [OVER- 28 b.] Caring too much; excessively anxious.

1766 CHALKLEY *Wks.* 442 He would have us without an incumbered and over-caring Mind.

†**'overcark**, *sb.* *Obs.* [OVER- 29.] An overcharge; an extra load or burden.

a **1300** *Cursor M.* 9843 Ouercark o kind had þe tan, And kind was to þe toþer wan.

†**over'cark**, *v.* *Obs.* [OVER- 27.]

1. *trans.* To overcharge, overweight.

a **1300** *Cursor M.* 9834 Man mai find a barn ouercarked sua wit kind, þat [has] thre fete and handes thre.

2. To burden with excessive charges; to oppress.

1393 LANGL. *P. Pl.* C. IV. 472 Shal noþer kyng ne knyȝt, constable ne meyre Ouer-cark þe comune.

So †**'over-'carkful**, **'over-'carking** *adjs.*, troubling oneself too much, over-anxious.

c **1449** PECOCK *Repr.* III. xv. 377 Ouer thouȝtful and ouer carkful and ouermyche louyng toward them. **1655** FULLER *Ch. Hist.* VIII. iii. §23 Disswaded..from being solicitously over-carking for the future.

overcarry (-'kærı), *v.* Now *rare.* [OVER- 10, 13, 26.]

1. † **a.** *trans.* To carry over or across; to convey to the other side; to transport. *Obs.*

1382 WYCLIF *Wisd.* x. 18 He ouercariede them [1388 bar hem ouer] thurȝ ful myche water. **1513** DOUGLAS *Æneis* VI. xi. 30 How mony seis ourcareit in thi barge.

b. To carry or convey beyond the proper point.

1897 [implied in OVERCARRIED *ppl. a.*]. *a* **1904** *Mod.* (Railway Guard) 'Are you the gentleman that was over-carried to Louth this evening?' **1972** M. MEAD *Blackberry Winter* xi. 148 The National Research Council had insisted on mailing my checks to me, and the next boat overcarried the mail. This meant that for six weeks I had no money.

2. To carry (action or proceedings) too far, overdo; to do more than carry.

1606 BIRNIE *Kirk-Buriall* vi. B iv, According to the forked foly vsed in buriall, which either is contemned, or else ouercaried in pomp. **1823** CHALMERS *Pauperism* Wks. 1839 XVI. 236 The point has not only been carried; but greatly over-carried.

†**3.** *fig.* To carry (a person) beyond the bounds of moderation, or into error, etc.; to carry away.

1579 FENTON *Guicciard.* (1618) 280 Publike respects fell not so strongly into consideration, but that they were ouer-carried with priuate interests. **1648** BP. HALL *Select Thoughts* §89 Their appetite over-carries them to a misconceit of a particular good.

absol. **1617** HIERON *Wks.* II. 275 Zeale, not guided by knowledge, may soone ouer-carry.

Hence **overcarried** *ppl. a.*

1897 MARY KINGSLEY *W. Africa* 193 We stop to pick up cargo, or discharge over-carried cargo. **1903** KIPLING *Five Nations* 25 The galloping breakers stride, And their over-carried spray is a sea—a sea on the landward side.

†**over'carve**, *v.* *Obs.* In 4 **-kerve**. [OVER- 10.] *trans.* To cut across, intersect.

c **1391** CHAUCER *Astrol.* I. §21 This zodiak..ouer-kerueth the equinoxial; and he ouer-kerueth hym again in euene parties.

overcast ('əʊvəkɑːst, -kæst), *sb.* [f. OVERCAST *v.* or *ppl. a.*]

1. A person or thing that is cast away, 'thrown over', or rejected; an outcast. *Obs.* exc. *dial.*

1569 GOLDING *Heminges Post.* Ded. 3 All Estates, from the Magistrate to the poore afflicted overcast among men. **1868** SALMON *Gowodean* 70 (E.D.D.) Gipsy ow'rcast.. found stickin' in the fen.

2. Something cast or spread over; a covering, coating; a cloud covering the sky or part of it, as in dull or threatening weather (also *fig.*); *spec.* in *Aeronautics*, cloud-cover which restricts visibility and necessitates reliance on instruments for navigation.

1686 GOAD *Celest. Bodies* I. iii. 10 [If not a Fog] something cognate to it, a little Frost perhaps, or thin Overcast. **1798** MITCHELL tr. *Karsten's Min. of Leskean Mus.* 284 Red Scaly Iron Ore as a very thin overcast. **1809** MALKIN *Gil Blas* v. i. ⁋25 The lowering overcast of his swarthy aspect. **1895** *Daily News* 27 June 3/1 The dangerous formation of clouds that fringed the overcast of steel blue. **1938** [see *contact flying* s.v. CONTACT *sb.* 6]. **1942** *Tee Emm* (Air Ministry) II. 69 In the past you scraped above the undergrowth, now, through the overcast. **1946** *Happy Landings* (Air Ministry) July 5/1 The aircraft..was seen emerging from the overcast. **1946** R. A. MCFARLAND *Human Factors Air Transport Design* ix. 396 The flight was progressing normally at an altitude of 10,000 ft until it entered a rapidly forming thunderstorm. Shortly thereafter, parts of the plane began to fall from the overcast. **1967** S. BLANC *Rose Window* (1968) xix. 183 It was only mid-morning and a high overcast that obscured the sun had not yet burned away. **1972** B. F. CONNERS *Don't embarrass Bureau* (1973) I. 6 He felt the sun starting to burn through the overcast as he climbed the ladder.

†**3.** A reckoning or calculation above the true amount. *Obs.*

1771 *Connect. Col. Rec.* (1885) XIII. 482 There was an overcast made by the listers upon the grand levy of the year 1761, of the sum of £427 0 0. **1772** *Ibid.* XIII. 579 Abatements for over-cast of the list..shall be made.

4. *Mining.* A bridge which carries one subterranean air-passage over another.

1867 *Morning Star* 12 Jan., We went up the board-gate to the overcast or archway supporting a roadway above, and we found that standing, but an overcast further on near the ending was blown down.

5. *Needlework.* = OVERCASTING 4, overcast work.

c **1840** LADY WILTON *Art of Needlework* xx. 317 There is back stitch—overcast—and seam stitch. **1867** C. AUSTEN *My Aunt Jane Austen* (1952) 7 She was a great adept at overcast and satin stitch—the peculiar delight of that day. **1891** *Weldon's Pract. Needlewk.* VI. No. 68. 12/1 When working the overcast be careful to make each stitch as nearly as can be the same in size.

6. *Comb.* **overcast-staff** (see quot.); **overcast-stitch** (see OVERCAST *v.* 7).

1769 FALCONER *Dict. Marine* (1789), *Over-cast-staff*, a scale, or measure, employed by shipwrights to determine the difference between the curves of those timbers which are placed near the greatest breadth, and those which are situated near the extremities of the keel, where the floor rises and grows narrower.

overcast (əʊvə'kɑːst, -kæst), *v.* Forms: see OVER and CAST. [OVER- 6, etc.: see below.]

1. a. *trans.* To overthrow, overturn, cast down, upset (*lit.* and *fig.*). *Obs.* exc. *dial.* [OVER- 6.]

a **1225** *Ancr. R.* 275 Þet nis..nout monlich, auh is wummonlich, eð to ouerkesten. *a* **1300** *Cursor M.* 14733 [Iesus] þair bordes ouerkest, þair penis spilt. *c* **1440** *Boctus* (Laud MS. 559 lf. 10 b), His travaylle thus was ouer caste. **1548** UDALL *Erasm. Par.* Pref. 5 b, Honey is waloweish and ouercasteth the stomake, if it be plenteously taken by it selfe alone. **1710** SWIFT *On Lit. House by Churchyard* 6 Once on a time a western blast, At least twelve inches over-cast. **1873** MURDOCH *Doric Lyre* 7 (E.D.D.) Theekit stacks the bangster blast Had shaken as 'twad them owrecast.

†**b.** To turn over. *Obs.*

c **1430** *Two Cookery-bks.* 49 Opyn hem a-bowte þe myddel; and ouer-cast þe openyng vppon þe lede [= lid]. **1570** *Satir. Poems Reform.* xx. 46 Auld bukis quha will ouer cast.

2. To cast or throw (something) over or above something else. Now *rare.* [OVER- 1, 8.]

c **1330** R. BRUNNE *Chron.* (1810) 70 To bank ouer þe sond, plankes þei ouer kast. **1470–85** MALORY *Arthur* VI. xvi, A Faucon..flewe vnto the elme to take her perche, the lunys ouer cast aboute a bough. *c* **1580** SIDNEY *Ps.* XVI. iv, Night with his black wing Sleepy Darknes doth orecast. **1742** POPE *Dunc.* IV. 289 Thro' School and College, thy kind cloud o'ercast, Safe and unseen the young Æneas past. **188.** R. G. H[ILL] *Voices in Solitude* 12 Thou..on my brightest days dost overcast A pleasing melancholy.

3. To cover, overspread, overlay (*with* something). Now *rare* in general sense. [OVER- 8.]

1390 GOWER *Conf.* I. 325 Thei ne mihte his hand ascape, That he his fyr on hem ne caste:..her herte he overcaste To folwe thilke lore. *c* **1440** *Promp. Parv.* 372/2 Ovyr caste, or ovyr hyllyd, *pretectus, contectus.* **1497** *Churchw. Acc. St. Mary Hill, Lond.* (Nichols 1797) 94 A lode of lome to ovircast the floore. **1577** HANMER *Anc. Eccl. Hist.* (1619) 427 There is a loft overcast with the like rouffe. **1608** SYLVESTER *Du Bartas* II. iv. III. *Schism* 1045 Her head..With dust and ashes is all over-cast. **1706** PHILLIPS (ed. Kersey), *To Over-cast*,..to case or line a Wall with Stone, etc. **1807** J. BARLOW *Columb.* I. 21 He saw the Atlantic heaven with light o'ercast.

4. a. *spec.* To cover or overspread with clouds, or with something that darkens or dulls the surface. Most frequently in *pa. pple.*; usually of the weather.

c **1290** *Beket* 1379 in *S. Eng. Leg.* I. 146 Ouer-cast heo is with þis cloudene. *c* **1305** *St. Edmund* 354 in *E.E.P.* (1862) 80 þe grislikeste weder þat miȝte beo..ouercaste al þan toun. **1530** PALSGR. 648/1 Se howe soone the sonne is overcaste for all the fayre mornyng. **1559** W. CUNNINGHAM *Cosmogr. Glasse* 110 The skie is ouer cast with cloudes. **1635–56** COWLEY *Davideis* II. 684 But Prophets angry Blood o'er-cast his Day. **1722** DE FOE *Plague* (Rtldg.) 270 A dark Cloud..overcasts the Air. **1846** GROTE *Greece* (1862) II. xi. 349 The fair sky was immediately overcast.

b. *fig.* To overshadow, render gloomy, darken.

c **1386** CHAUCER *Knt.'s T.* 678 Right so kan geery Venus over caste The hertes of hir folk. **1571** GOLDING *Calvin on Ps.* xi. 5 When sorowfull confusion of thinges overcasteth them with darknesse. **1614** RALEIGH *Hist. World* III. (1634) 51 Xerxes..prayed Artabanus not to over-cast those joyes.. with sad remembrances. **1725** POPE *Odyss.* XVIII. 181 Stung to the soul, o'ercast with holy dread. **1850** W. R. WILLIAMS *Relig. Prog.* (1854) 210 It is his loss of this [holiness] that overcasts the eternal world and makes the expected vision of God one of terror.

5. *intr.* To become overspread with clouds; to become dark or gloomy. ? *Obs.* exc. *dial.*

c **1400** *Destr. Troy* 13157 All the calme ouercast into kene stormes, Full wodely the windes wackont aboue. **1511** GUYLFORDE *Pilgr.* (Camden) 67 The wether bygan to ouer-caste with rayne, wynde, thondre. **1655** GURNALL *Chr. in Arm.* I. 342 What day shines so fair, that over-casts not before night? **1725** DE FOE *Voy. round World* (1840) 333 In the evening it overcast and grew cloudy. **1900** *Norfolk Dial.* (E.D.D.), It's overcasting for rain.

†**6.** *trans.* To transform. *Obs.* [OVER- 10.]

1387 TREVISA *Higden* (Rolls) I. 225 Þere was at Rome a bole of bras in þe schap of Iupiter ouercast and schape.

7. *Needlework.* To throw rough stitches over a raw edge or edges of cloth to prevent unravelling; to sew over and over; also, to strengthen or adorn such an edge by buttonhole- or blanket-stitch; in *Embroidery*, to cover overlaid threads or outlines by smooth and close oversewn stitches; in *Bookbinding* (see quot. 1956). [OVER- 5.]

1706 PHILLIPS (ed. Kersey), *To Over-cast*,..to whip a Seam, as Taylors do. **1819** *Metropolis* II. 116 Whilst a tailor, and in the act of over-casting a button-hole. **1879** ATCHERLEY *Boërland* 258 The vein [is] closed by passing a pin transversely through the cut edges, and overcasting it with a hair plucked from the beast's tail. **1880** J. W. ZAEHNSDORF *Art of Bookbinding* iii. 13 Each section is then overcast or oversewn along its whole length. **1891** *Weldon's Pract. Needlewk.* VI. No. 69. 8/2 Run a thread of cotton in darning stitch upon the line of tracing.., and overcast this in tiny close stitches of even size. **1893** *Ibid.* VIII. 90. 9/2 A narrow margin..is filled with threads darned tolerably thickly.., and these threads are afterwards overcast, or sewn smoothly over. **1901** [see OVERCAST *ppl. a.* 3]. **1951** L. TOWN *Bookbinding by Hand* xx. 244 At this point the book must be marked up for sewing, as this cannot be done after the sections have been overcast. **1956** *Bookman's Conc. Dict.* 209/1 *Overcast*, to sew leaves, especially single leaves, in bookbinding, with a long hem-stitch style of sewing; also known as Whip Stitch. **1963** B. C. MIDDLETON *Hist. Eng. Craft Bookbinding Technique* iii. 25 The usual method.. involves overcasting separately a series of groups of leaves.

8. To sum up in excess of the correct amount; to over-estimate. ? *Obs.* [OVER- 26.]

1622 BACON *Hen. VII* 17 The King, in his accompt of peace, and calmes, did much ouer-cast his fortunes. **1765** J. INGERSOLL *Lett. Stamp-Act* (1766) 49 'Tis most likely we rather under than overcast the probable Amount of it.

9. To throw off (illness or misfortune); to get over. *Sc.* [fig. from OVER- 5.]

1820 SCOTT *Monast.* xiv, See that..the red stag does not gaul you as he did Diccon Thorburn, who never overcast the wound that he took from a buck's horn. *a* **1904** *Mod. Sc.* She hes gotten what she'll never owercast.

10. *Bowls.* (? *intr.*) To cast beyond the jack. (Also *pass.* in same sense.) ? *Obs.* [OVER- 13.]

1611 COTGR. s.v. *Passé*, *Ie suis passé*, I am gone, or ouer-cast, I haue throwne ouer, at Bowles, etc. **1681** W. ROBERTSON *Phraseol. Gen.* (1693) 964, I am overcast at bowls; *ultra metam jeci.* **1706** PHILLIPS (ed. Kersey), *To Over-cast*,..to throw beyond the Jack in Bowling.

'over'cast (stress var.), *ppl. a.* [Pa. pple. of prec.]

1. Cast away, overthrown, etc.: see the verb.

1569 [see OVERCAST *sb.* 1]. **1688** R. HOLME *Armoury* III. 243/1 A Spaniel..licking of the overcast Cream from the Churn-side. **1839** I. TAYLOR *Anc. Chr.* I. ii. 221 Invited.. to accept the overcast Christianity of Chrysostom.

2. Of the weather: Clouded over, dull, gloomy.

1625 BACON *Ess., Gardens* (Arb.) 564 For the Morning, and the Euening, or Ouer-cast Dayes. **1835** W. IRVING *Tour Prairies* 284 It was a raw overcast night.

3. *Needlework.* Sewn or embroidered by overcasting; ***overcast stitch***, the stitch by which overcasting is done. Also in *Bookbinding* and *Lace-making*. (See OVERCAST *v.* 7.)

1865 F. B. PALLISER *Hist. Lace* xiii. 181 It is only 'bride ordinaire';..very different from the clear 'over-cast' hexagon of the last century. **1891** *Weldon's Pract. Needlewk.* VI. No. 68. 12/1 Overcast outline. Overcast stitch is a favourite outline for fine work. *Ibid.* No. 69. 10/2 The outline is embroidered in smooth overcast stitch. **1901** D. COCKERELL *Bookbinding* v. 81 To 'overcast' the first and last sections..fails in the object aimed at by merely transferring the strain to the back of the overcast sections.

4. That is in excess of the correct amount.

1892 *Daily News* 17 Dec. 7/4, I generally kept the over-cast money for a few days and then gave some of it to Mr. H.

over'casting, *vbl. sb.* [f. OVERCAST *v.* + -ING[1].] The action of the verb OVERCAST.

1. a. The action of casting over or upon, or of covering or coating with something; *spec.* the coating of brick or stone work with plaster.

1483 *Cath. Angl.* 263/1 Ouercastyng, *obduccio, obductus.* **1599** in Willis & Clark *Cambridge* (1886) II. 478 For the overcasting of..the stone wall. *Ibid.* 486 For the over-casting of the greate Tower 10 dayes xxs. **1601** HOLLAND *Pliny* I. 314 Some are busie in building, others in plaistering and ouercasting.

†**b.** Used to render L. *intersectio*, intersection (= throwing over or across). *Obs.*

1398 TREVISA *Barth. De P.R.* VIII. xl. (Tollem. MS), By oute castynge, and strecchynge and ouercastynge..of bemis, ly3t bryngeþ forþe all þinges.

†**2.** The action of overthrowing or casting down; upsetting. *Obs.*

1497 *Naval Acc. Hen. VII* (1896) 129 Poudre..brent in the botom of the Tour of Aiton for the spedy ouercasting of the same. **1552** ELYOT *Dict., Malachia*..the longyng of women with childe, and ouercastynge of theyr stomacke, if thei haue not that they longe for.

3. A covering with or as with clouds; an over shadowing, darkening (*lit.* and *fig.*).

1598 FLORIO, *Nebbia*, a cloude, an ouercasting of the skie. **1610** BARROUGH *Meth. Physick* VIII. (1639) 446 Qualming and overcasting of the heart. **1875** BEDFORD *Sailor's Pocket Bk.* iv. (ed. 2) 86 An overcasting of murky vapour.

4. *Needlework* and *Bookbinding.* (See OVERCAST *v.* 7.)

1885 BRIETZCKE & ROOPER *Plain Needlewk.* I. 20 Over-casting is used to prevent raw edges of materials from getting unravelled. **1885** W. J. E. CRANE *Bookbinding for Amateurs* vi. 54 There is another way of overcasting more used in London. **1893** *Weldon's Pract. Needlewk.* VIII. No. 90. 9/2 The outline of this pretty leaf is defined in raised overcasting. **1894** *Ibid.* IX. No. 106. 6/2 It is the custom to put an overcasting of buttonhole stitch round the edge of blankets to ensure against unravelling..and also to add to its good appearance. **1901** D. COCKERELL *Bookbinding* 316 Overcasting, over-sewing the back edges of single leaves or weak sections. **1931** A. ESDAILE *Student's Man. Bibliogr.* vi. 182 Overcasting, a more respectable form of stabbing, by which the folds are sewn together beyond, and enclosing, the ordinary sewing.

over'casting, *ppl. a.* [f. as prec. + -ING[2].] That overcasts: see the verb.

1837 WARE *Lett. fr. Palmyra* xvi. (1860) 409 No over-casting shadows which at all disturb your peace. **1901** D. COCKERELL *Bookbinding* ii. 51 The custom with binders is to overcast the backs of the leaves in sections, and to sew through the overcasting thread. **1964** *McCall's Sewing* 134/2 A row of machine-stitching close to the raw edge serves as a guide for keeping overcasting stitches even.

over-casual, etc.: see OVER- 28.

over'catch, *v. Obs.* exc. *dial.* [OVER- 14.]

1. *trans.* To overtake, 'catch up'.

1570 LEVINS *Manip.* 38/21 To ouercatche, *assequi.* **1596** SPENSER *F.Q.* IV. vii. 31 She sent an arrow forth with mighty draught, That in the very dore him overcaught. **18..** LAHEE *Owd Yem* (Lancash. Dial.) 9 (E.D.D.) It ud o tak'n a hunter to o'ercatch him.

†**2.** *fig.* To 'catch', ensnare, deceive, outwit. *Obs.*

1577 WHETSTONE *Life of Gascoigne*, Hypocrisie a man may over catch. **1622** BRETON *Strange Newes* (1879) 13/1 For feare the Ducke with some odde craft, the Goose might ouercatch.

'over-'caution. [OVER- 29 d.] Too great caution, excessive caution.

1775 MRS. DELANY in *Life & Corr.* Ser. II. II. 108 My over-caution..prevented my doing just what you wanted. **1886** *American* XII. 189 A strange commentary on their habitual overcaution.

'over-'cautious, *a.* [OVER- 28.] More cautious than is needful, too cautious.

1706 PHILLIPS, *Over-cautious*, too wary, too heedful. **1712** ADDISON *Spect.* No. 295 ¶7 It is observed of over-cautious Generals, that they never engage in a Battle without securing a Retreat. **1836–41** BRANDE *Chem.* (ed. 5) 55 An over-cautious modesty which marked all his proceedings.

Hence **over-cautiously** *adv.*; **over-cautiousness**.

1847 WEBSTER, *Overcautiously.* **1895** *Funk, Overcautiousness.*

,over-centrali'zation. [OVER- 29 b.] Excessive centralization of administrative functions, leading to inefficiency. So **over'centralized** *a.*

1882 E. W. HAMILTON *Diary* 20 June (1972) I. 290 He spoke strongly of the dreadful 'administrative chaos' and over-centralisation which existed in Dublin Castle. **1896** L. T. HOBHOUSE *Theory of Knowl.* 276 The over-centralisation of the imperial government. **1944** J. S. HUXLEY *On Living in Revolution* xi. 118 An overcentralized administration is always characterized by the fact that its field officers tend to become messengers and office boys. **1949** I. DEUTSCHER *Stalin* vii. 241 Stalin obviously erred in the direction of over-centralization. **1962** *Punch* 7 Feb. 261/3 Jellicoe..had to fight with a machine encrusted with over-centralisation. **1971** *Time* 29 Mar. 36/3 Now the country [*sc.* Poland] is tense but quiet, as [Edward] Gierek attempts to consolidate his position and cope with an appalling economic mess caused by years of overconcentration on heavy industry, overcentralization and postponement of reforms. **1977** *Times* 7 Nov. 14/6 The [Soviet] economy is still an overcentralized shambles.

†**,over-'cess,** *v. Obs.* [OVER- 27.] To rate, or assess too highly. Hence †**,over-'cessing** *vbl. sb.*

1611 COTGR., *Surtaux*, an ouer-cessing, ouer-rating ..*Surtaxé*, ouer-cessed,..surcharged.

over-chafed: see OVER- 27 b.

†**over'change,** *v. Obs.* [OVER- 10.] *trans.* To change into something else, or into another condition; to transmute. Hence †**over-'changing** *vbl. sb.*, transmutation.

c **1375** *Sc. Leg. Saints* xxxiii. (*George*) 772 Bot gyf sume cristine mane had þe Ourchangit þis [= thus] for to lef me. **1382** WYCLIF *Jas.* i. 17 The fadir of li3tis anentis whom is not ouerchaunginge [Vulg. *transmutatio*]. **1387–8** T. USK *Test. Love* III. ii. (Skeat) l. 49 As mater by due ouerchaunginges foloweth his perfection.

over-channel to **-chanter**: see OVER-.

overcharge ('əʊvətʃɑːdʒ), *sb.* [OVER- 29 b.] An excessive charge; the fact of overcharging.

1. An excessive charge or load; an excessive supply, an excess, a surplus.

a **1611** BEAUM. & FL. *Maid's Trag.* v. ii, A thing out of the overcharge of nature; Sent..to disperse a plague Upon weak catching women. **1803** JEFFERSON *Autobiog. & Writ.* (1830) IV. 9 These circumstances have..produced an over-charge in the class of competitors for learned occupation. **1864** WEBSTER, *Overcharge*,..3 An excessive charge, as of a gun. *Mod.* The bursting of the gun was due to an overcharge.

2. A pecuniary charge in excess of the right or just amount; the act of demanding too much in payment, or the sum demanded in excess of the proper amount; an exorbitant charge.

1662–3 PEPYS *Diary* 19 Feb., Drawing out copies of the overcharge of the Navy. **1668** *Ormonde MSS.* in *10th Rep. Hist. MSS. Comm.* App. v. 81 A respit until your petitioner be eased in the overcharge. **1765** *Act 5 Geo. III*, c. 49 §5 Action..for repetition of any overcharge. **1861** HUGHES *Tom Brown at Oxf.* xxviii, The landlord..looking as if he had never made an overcharge in his life.

attrib. **1866** RUSKIN in Spielmann *Life* (1900) 50, I shouldn't mind placing the over-charge sum at her bankers.

overcharge (,əʊvə'tʃɑːdʒ), *v.* [OVER- 27; cf. F. *surcharger.*] To charge in excess.

1. *trans.* To load, fill, furnish, or supply to excess (*with* something); to overload, overburden; to fill too full; to overstock.

1398 TREVISA *Barth. De P.R.* XIV. lv. (1495) F iij/2 Ofte by grete heuynesse of the erthe those pylars in mynes ben ouer-chargyd and fall. *a* **1425** *Cursor M.* 9834 (Trin.) Men may fynde a childe ouer charged so with kynde þat [haþ] feet or hondes þre. **1531** *Dial. on Laws Eng.* II. li. (1638) 157 If he throw them [goods] out for feare that they should over-charge the Ship. **1569** *Towneley Nowell MS.* (Grosart 1877) 384 A poor man ouerchardged with children. **1681** E. MURPHY *State Ireland* §30 The said Cormucke having..over-charged one of his Pistols. **1771** CAVENDISH in *Phil. Trans.* LXI. 586 If the body contains more than this quantity of electric fluid, I call it overcharged. **1836** HOR. SMITH *Tin Trump.* I. 9 If the wielder of the weapon..overcharge his piece, he must not be surprised if it explode.

b. To place, lay on, or apply in excess. *rare.*

1849 RUSKIN *Sev. Lamps* i. §15. 25 Ornament cannot be overcharged if it be good, and is always overcharged when it is bad.

c. *fig.* To make, or represent as, greater than the reality; to magnify too much, overdraw, exaggerate, overdo.

1711 ADDISON *Spect.* No. 86 ¶6 A little overcharging the likeness. **1782** MISS BURNEY *Cecilia* IX. v, In both the assertions there was some foundation of truth, however..basely over-charged. **1822–34** *Good's Study Med.* (ed. 4) I. 331 This account may be rather overcharged, from the ardent mind of its intelligent inventor.

†**2.** To lay an excessive burden (of trouble, care, responsibility, etc.) upon; to press hard, oppress, distress, overtax; to overbear by superior force.

a **1375** *Joseph Arim.* 552 He nedde bote fourti men..And þei were weri of-fou3ten and feor ouer-charged, Of þe peple afurst and þe pres after. **1444** *Rolls of Parlt.* V. 107/2 Longe tyme hath ben oppressed and overcharged, by Sheryffs. **1549–62** STERNHOLD & H. *Ps.* xxxi. 8 Thou hast not left me in their hand, that would me overcharge. **1604** EDMONDS *Observ. Cæsar's Comm.* 97 Our men being ouer-charged on all sides with the losse of sixe and fortie Centurions, were beaten downe from the place. **1711** *Light to Blind* in *10th Rep. Hist. MSS. Comm.* App. v. 165 After fighting a while he was overcharged with numbers.

†**b.** To accuse too much or extravagantly. *Obs.*

1626 DONNE *Serm.* iv. (1640) 36 Neither doth any one thing so overcharge God with contradictions, as the Transubstantiation of the Roman Church. **1636** MASSINGER *Gt. Dk. Flor.* IV. ii, Treason! 'tis a word My innocence understands not... I must be bold To tell you, sir,..'tis tyranny to o'ercharge An honest man.

3. *spec.* To overburden (a person) with expense, exactions, etc.; to put to too great expense; now, To charge (any one) too much as a price or payment.

1303 R. BRUNNE *Handl. Synne* 6848 He seyde he wulde hym ouercharge, To wete wheþer seynt Ihoun were large. **1401** *Pol. Poems* (Rolls) II. 30 What charitie is this, to overcharge the people by mightie begging, under colour of preaching? **1586** T. B. *La Primaud. Fr. Acad.* I. (1594) 675 They were over-charged with exactions. *c* **1613** ROWLANDS *Paire Spy-Knaves* 23 Madam, you ouercharge me with expence. **1712** PRIDEAUX *Direct. Ch.-wardens* (ed. 4) 57 If any be overcharged, or others undercharged, the Ordinary will condemn the Wrong done. *Mod.* No one likes to be overcharged for what he buys.

b. To charge (so much) as a price or payment, in excess of the amount that is justly due.

1667 *Ormonde MSS.* in *10th Rep. Hist. MSS. Comm.* App. v. 39 We require..their Deputy..to suspend so much as the petitioner alleages to be over-charged accordingly. **1733–4** BERKELEY *Let. to Prior* 23 Feb. in Fraser *Life* vi. (1871) 215 The 20 pounds overcharged for the widows. *Mod.* The Company have overcharged fifteen shillings on the carriage of the goods.

Hence **,over'charged** *ppl. a.*, overloaded, exaggerated, overburdened, oppressed, etc.; **,over'charging** *vbl. sb.*, overloading, imposition of too high a price, etc.; also **,over'charger**, one who overcharges or makes an overcharge.

1593 SHAKS. *2 Hen. VI*, III. ii. 331 These dread curses..like an *ouer-charged Gun, recoile, And turnes the force of them vpon thy selfe. **1766** GOLDSM. *Vic. W.* xviii, Those overcharged characters, which abound in the works you mention. **1822** LAMB *Elia* Ser. II. *Confess. Drunkard*, Persons..may recoil from this as from an overcharged picture. **1611** COTGR., *Oppresseur*, an oppressor; *ouer-charger, ouerlayer; extreame dealer. **1529** MORE *Dyaloge* III. xiii. Wks. 229/2 As though sainct Poule had leuer that the priest had twenty [wives] saue for *ouerchargyng. **1612** BRINSLEY *Lud. Lit.* ii. (1627) 12 Not any way overloaded or discouraged, nor yet indangered by the overcharging of their wits and memories.

†**'over-'chargeable,** *a. Obs.* [OVER- 28.] Too burdensome or troublesome; too costly.

1513–14 *Act 5 Hen. VIII*, c. 7 Preamble, Compelled to..buy..Ledder..with overchargeable price. **1539** TAVERNER *Gard. Wysedome* II. 25 To greuouse and ouerchargeable to the commons. *a* **1639** W. WHATELEY *Prototypes* I. xi. (1640) 141 Decent, not flaring not over-chargeable garments.

So †**'over'chargeful** *a. Obs.* = prec.; †**'over'chargement** = OVERCHARGE *sb.*

1451 *Rolls of Parlt.* V. 218/1 Overchargefull and noyus unto youre people. **1686** *Chardin's Coron. Solyman* 94 They pleaded that they were not obliged to that over-chargement.

over-charitable to **-chased**: see OVER-.

†**'over,chaving.** *Obs.* [f. OVER- 19 + *chaving*, f. CHAVE *v.*; cf. *cavings* s.v. CAVE *v.*[4]] Refuse of threshed corn; 'cavings'.

1607 MARKHAM *Caval.* I. (1617) 6 Maungers, in which you may cast the ouerchawings of Wheate, Barley, or other white corne. **1614** —— *Cheap Husb.* VII. xviii. (1623) 149 A little Barley, or other ouer-chauing of corne.

over-cheaply, -cheapness: see OVER-.

'overcheck, *a.* (*sb.*[1]) [OVER- 5.] In ***overcheck rein***, a rein passing over a horse's head between the ears, so as to pull upward upon the bit; ***overcheck bridle***, a driving bridle having an overcheck rein.

1875 in KNIGHT *Dict. Mech.*

'overcheck, *sb.*[2] [OVER- 8.] On cloth: a check pattern superimposed on a pattern of smaller check.

1906 *Daily Chron.* 25 Apr. 8/5 There will be a few very neat stripes,..while the finely-traced overchecks will be much in evidence. **1923** [see GLENURQUHART, GLEN URQUHART]. **1959** [see HOUNDSTOOTH]. **1967** N. FREELING *Strike Out* 27 The suit was..mohair in a large complicated overcheck of fuchsia, havana and off-white. **1974** *Daily Tel.* 6 Mar. 15 Tweedy, sporty men should be in their element as checks..get bigger, plaids get bolder and over-checks more aggressive.

So **over'checked** *ppl. a.*

1925 *Eaton's News Weekly* 2 May 10 A fine brown and blue tweed, overchecked in rust. **1960** *Harper's Bazaar* Aug. 56/2 Predominantly bright red, it [*sc.* a coat] is over-checked in yellow and black. **1969** *Times* 30 Sept. 14/5 (Advt.), Stunning dresscoat in bold overchecked..wool. **1970** *Vogue* May 21/2 A willow green tweed jacket..over-checked in brown and navy.

†**'overcheek.** *Obs. rare.* [f. OVER- 1 d + CHEEK *sb.* 9.] The lintel of a door.

a **1420** *Wyclif's Bible* Exod. xii. 7 (MS. Norwich Libr.) Lyntels [*gloss* ether hi3er threschfoldis, *v.r.* either ouercheckis].

overcheer to **-choke**: see OVER-.

over-'chosen, *a. Sociology.* [OVER- 28 c.] Denoting those who, in a sociometric group study, are chosen by others well above the average number of times; the 'stars' of a sociometric group; also *ellipt.* as *sb.* Cf. UNDER-CHOSEN *a.*

1943 H. H. JENNINGS *Leadership & Isolation* iv. 66 The test of whether or not this is true might be made by examining the choice behavior of the 'over-chosen' as compared with the 'under-chosen'. *Ibid.* 68 In Group A_{11} in which 16 percent are over-chosen..the number by whom they are chosen extends from 16 to 24 individuals, while the under-chosen who comprise 17 percent..are chosen by from zero to 3 individuals. **1956** J. KLEIN *Study of Groups* 91 The fact that certain people are over-chosen or under-chosen implies that members share certain standards which the over-chosen exemplify and the under-chosen fall short of. **1958** W. J. H. SPROTT *Human Groups* ix. 150 On work and living—with choice..there was considerable overlap among what she calls the 'over-chosens'.

overcirculate to **-circumspect**: see OVER-.

'over-'civil, *a.* [OVER- 27.] Too civil, showing excessive civility. (Usually *ironical*, with negative expressed or implied.)

1680 H. MORE *Apocal. Apoc.* Pref. 19 You may think me not over-civil. **1741** RICHARDSON *Pamela* (1824) I. 188, I know my sister's passionate temper too well, to believe she could be over-civil to you. **1855** MRS. GATTY *Parables fr. Nat.* Ser. I. (1869) 69 You are not over-civil with all your learning.

So **'over-ci'vility**, excessive civility.

1766 GOLDSM. *Vic. W.* xxi, I dont believe she has got any money, by her over-civility.

'over-'civilized, *a.* [OVER- 28 c.] Too highly civilized.

1822 SHELLEY *Ess. & Lett.* (1852) II. 282 The arts and conveniences of that over-civilised country. **1881** *Atlantic Monthly* XLVIII. 515 The uncivilized and the over-civilized are brothers.

†over'clad, *v. Obs. rare.* [f. OVER- 8 + CLAD *v.*] = OVERCLOTHE *v.*

1591 LODGE *Hist. Robt. Dk. Normandy* (Hunt. Cl.) 31 The vale of heauinesse ouercladdeth me.

overclad, -cled, pa. t. and pple. of OVERCLOTHE.

over-claim: see OVER- 29.

over-'clamour, *v.* [OVER- 21.] *trans.* To overcome, subdue, or reduce by clamour.

1713 C'TESS WINCHELSEA *Misc. Poems* 240 Contention with its angry Brawls By Storms o'er-clamoured, shrinks and falls. **1853** DE QUINCEY *Autobiog. Sk.* Wks. I. 139 She allowed herself to be over-clamoured by Mr. Lee..into a capital prosecution of the brothers.

overclasp to **overcleave**: see OVER-.

overclimb (-'klaɪm), *v.* [OVER- 5.] *trans.* To climb over; to get over by climbing, surmount.

c **893** K. ÆLFRED *Oros.* III. ix. §14 Alexander..hrædlice þone weall self oferclom. *a* **1547** SURREY *Æneid* II. (1557) B j b, This fatall gin thus ouerclambe our walles, Stuft with armd men. **1607** *Lingua* I. v, The..childhood of the cheerful morn Is almost grown a youth, and overclimbs Yonder gilt eastern hills. **1882** 'OUIDA' *Bimbi* v. 149 A loggia ..all overclimbed by hardy rose-trees.

overcloak: see OVER- 8 c.

over-'clog, *v.* [OVER- 25, 27.] *trans.* To clog to excess.

1660 BOYLE *New Exp. Phys. Mech.* xli. 332 The Air was over-clogg'd by the steams of their Bodies. **1768–74** TUCKER *Lt. Nat.* (1834) I. 72 The palate being over-clogged, no longer receives the flavour in the same manner.

over-close ('əʊvə'kləʊs), *a.* and *adv.* [f. OVER- 28 + CLOSE *a.* and *adv.*] Too close. So **'over'closeness**.

1812 SIR J. SINCLAIR *Syst. Husb. Scot.* I. 380 Evils arising from over-closeness of texture. **1851** MRS. BROWNING *Casa Guidi Wind.* I. 777 Best unbar the doors Which Peter's heirs keep locked so overclose.

†overclose (-'kləʊz), *v. Obs.* [f. OVER- 8 + CLOSE *v.*] *trans.* To cover over or shut in so as to hide; to cover up.

1393 LANGL. *P. Pl.* C. XXI. 140 Þe cause of þis eclipse þat ouer-closeþ [*MS. I* (*c* 1400) ouercloþeth] now þe sonne. *c* **1430** LYDG. *Min. Poems* (Percy Soc.) 24 The night doth folowe,..Whan Western wawis his stremys overclose.

over'closure. *Dentistry.* [OVER- 29.] A condition in which the lower jaw is raised more than normal in relation to the upper jaw when put into the rest position.

1934 *Ann. Otol., Rhinol. & Laryngol.* XLIII. 7 (*caption*) Broken lines spheno-mandibular ligaments and pterygoid muscles further relaxed by marked overclosure of edentulous mouth. **1948** *Brit. Dental Jrnl.* LXXXV. 225/1 Men with severe recently acquired malocclusion (extreme voluntary overclosure after removal of their full dentures). **1975** H. THOMSON *Occlusion* iv. 51 A vertical extension of mandibular displacement where the IOD [*sc.* interocclusal distance] is in excess of 4 mm. is referred to as mandibular overclosure.

'over-cloth. [OVER- 8 c.] A cloth placed over or upon something; *spec.* in *Paper-making* (U.S.), 'The blanket or endless apron which conveys the paper to the press-rolls in a straw-paper machine', called in Great Britain *blanket-felt*.

1888 *Sci. Amer.* 11 Aug. 81/1 It is highly requisite that the paper be well pressed and dried on the cylinders of the press and that the 'overcloth' be neither too dry nor too damp.

overclothe (-'kləʊð), *v.* Pa. t. and pple. **-clothed, -clad** (Sc. **-cled**). [OVER- 8.] *trans.* To clothe over; to cover over as with clothing.

c **1400** [see OVERCLOSE *v.*, quot. 1393]. **1582** N. T. (Rhem.) *2 Cor.* v. 2 For in this also do we grone, desirous to be ouerclothed with our habitation that is from heauen. **1585** JAMES I *Ess. Poesie* (Arb.) 15 Fra tyme they see The earth and all with stormes of snow owercled. **1632** LITHGOW *Trav.* III. 87 Mount Ida is..ouer-clad euen to the toppe with Cypre trees. **1724** RAMSAY *Health* 368 Fertile plains.. O'erclad with corn.

'over,clothes (-kləʊðz), *sb. pl.* [OVER- 8 c.] 'Upper' or outer garments.

1856 KANE *Arct. Expl.* I. xxix. 382 Under our wet over-clothes.

overclothing. [OVER- 8 c.] **a.** (*'over,clothing*). 'Upper' or outer garments collectively. **b.** (*,over'clothing*). The putting on or wearing of too much clothing.

1425 in Entick *London* (1766) IV. 354 That the over-cloathing..be dark and brown of colour. **1882** *Society* 21 Oct. 24/2 The evils of tight lacing, tight shoeing, or over-clothing.

overcloud (-'klaʊd), *v.* [OVER- 8.]

1. *trans.* To cloud over; to overspread or cover with a cloud or clouds, or with something that dims or conceals like a cloud.

1592 KYD *Sp. Trag.* II. iv, To ouer-cloud the brightnes of the Sunne. **1697** DRYDEN *Æneid* XI. 1193 A gathering mist o'erclouds her cheerful eyes. **1794** SULLIVAN *View Nat.* II. 403 The dull, heavy, terreous parts, which overclouded the expansum. **1869** PHILLIPS *Vesuv.* ii. 27 This dust was so abundant that..it overclouded the sun.

2. *fig.* To cast a shadow over, render gloomy; to make obscure or indistinct to perception, or deprive of clearness of perception; to obscure.

1593 NASHE *Christs T.* Wks. (Grosart) IV. 115 Yea, the Chiefetaines of them, were ouer-clowded in conceite. **1660** tr. *Amyraldus' Treat. conc. Relig.* III. viii. 482 The Speculations of our Scholasticks..will overcloud our Religion. **1781** COWPER *Conversation* 339 Yet still, o'erclouded with a constant frown, He does not swallow, but he gulps it down. **1842** MANNING *Serm.* ii. (1848) I. 23 The passing thoughts of evil which overcloud his soul.

3. *intr.* To become overclouded; to cloud over.

1862 *Macm. Mag.* July 217 He had not been long in office till this fair scene began to overcloud.

Hence **over'clouded** *ppl. a.*, **over'clouding** *vbl. sb.* and *ppl. a.*

1603 FLORIO *Montaigne* II. xii. (1624) 320 In earthly, ignorant, and overclouded man. *a* **1845** HOOD *Captain's Cow* xix, At last with overclouding skies A breeze again began to rise. **1880** G. MEREDITH *Tragic Com.* (1881) 82 It came to an overclouding and then a panic.

overcloy (-'klɔɪ), *v.* [OVER- 25, 27.] *trans.* To cloy excessively; to surfeit, satiate.

1576 FLEMING *Panopl. Epist.* 383 A certaine sycophant, and false varlot..ouercloyeth me with many and continuall troubles. **1599** H. BUTTES *Dyets drie Dinner* H ij, I feare mee, I have overcloy'd you with rootes. **1695** BLACKMORE *Pr. Arth.* IV. 248 O'ercloy'd with Carnage, and opprest with Blood. **1839** BAILEY *Festus* (1872) 121 With worldly weal o'ercloyed.

Hence **over'cloyed, over'cloying** *ppl. adjs.*

1594 SHAKS. *Rich. III*, v. iii. 318 Base Lackey Pezants, Whom their o're-cloyed Country vomits forth To desperate Aduentures. **1594** J. DICKENSON *Arisbas* (1878) 62 To winne him with ouer-cloying kindnesse.

overcluster, *v.*: see OVER- 1.

overcoat ('əʊvəkəʊt). [OVER- 8 c.] A large coat worn over the ordinary clothing, esp. in cold weather; a great-coat, top-coat. Also *attrib.*

1802 *Monthly Mag.* XIV. 325/1 [He] presented to the king of Spain a very light and thin over-coat, which rain could not penetrate. **1807** *Salmagundi* 31 Dec. 395 Observing it to be dressed in a man's hat, a cloth over-coat, and spatterdashes, I framed my apology accordingly. **1848** CRAIG, *Overcoat*, a greatcoat or topcoat. **1852** MRS. STOWE *Uncle Tom's C.* xxxv, Saddles, bridles, several sorts of harness, riding-whips, overcoats, and various articles of clothing. **1857** P. CARTWRIGHT *Autobiogr.* 201 My pistol..was in my overcoat pocket. **1887** LOWELL *Democr.* 16 The only argument available with an east wind is to put on an overcoat. **1958** M. KELLY *Christmas Egg* I. 9 He put his hands in his overcoat pockets. **1976** *Publishers' Weekly* 19 Apr. 80/1 The neighborhood gossips about a most unlikely overcoat flasher.

b. *transf.* and *fig. spec.* (*slang*) with ref. to means of disposing of a body; ***wooden overcoat***, a coffin.

1860 MAYNE REID *Odd People* 136 Not contented with being tatooed, these also *paint* their bodies, by way of 'overcoat'. *c* **1864** E. DICKINSON *Poems* (1955) II. 705 The Spirit turns away Just laying off for evidence An Overcoat of Clay. **1894** *Daily News* 17 Jan. 3/1 The Russian bears have magnificent overcoats. **1903** FARMER & HENLEY *Slang* VII. 362/2 *Wooden-overcoat* (or *-surtout*),..a coffin. **1909** *Dialect Notes* III. 389 *Wooden-overcoat*, coffin. **1940** H. W. THOMPSON *Body, Boots & Britches* xix. 486 Your wooden overcoat won't have any pockets. **1942** [see MEASURE *v.* 2 c]. **1969** *Times* 15 Nov. p. vi/7 Felco secateurs are exceedingly popular... Their model..has one handle with a plastic 'overcoat' which rotates as you squeeze the handles together. **1971** *Guardian* 12 Aug. 11/2 The paratroops were edgy and the one who let me through the barricade reckoned I would come out in a wooden overcoat. **1972** K. BONFIGLIOLI *Don't Point that Thing at Me* xvii. 147 He.. had to get us to ground of his own choosing before he could fit us for cement overcoats. **1974** *Times* 14 Dec. 1/7 The Foreign Office..asked Miami police searching for Mr John Stonehouse, the missing British MP..for a special report of ..a Mafia style 'concrete overcoat' known to have contained a body.

Hence **'overcoated** *a.*, wearing an overcoat; **'overcoating**, material for overcoats.

1886 *Tinsley's Mag.* July 49 It was the 29th May..and still ..discreet men were over-coated. *c* **1900** in *American Mail Order Fashions* (1961) 25 The fabric is a regular overcoating Vicuna... A firm but soft finished overcoating in one of the new shades. **1948** *Hansard Commons* 16 Mar. Written Answers 224 We have stipulated that half of the Italian supplies should be in men's suitings and overcoatings. **1967** *Times Rev. Industry* Apr. 53/3 J. and J. Crombie is to make 96,000 yards of overcoating, worth more than £250,000, for the Soviet Union.

'overcoatless, *a.* [f. OVERCOAT + -LESS.] Not having, or not wearing, an overcoat.

1908 L. A. HARKER *His First Leave* vi. 60 An old gentleman, overcoatless, umbrellaless. **1929** J. B. PRIESTLEY *Good Companions* II. v. 389 Her hatless and overcoatless companion. **1936** E. SITWELL *Victoria of Eng.* xii. 149 So, overcoatless, since his threadbare overcoat was in pawn, he went out into the rainy streets.

'over-coil. [OVER- 8 c.] (See quots.)

1884 F. J. BRITTEN *Watch & Clockm.* 16 Rules for the form of curve best suited for overcoils. *Ibid.* 181 [An] Overcoil..[is] the last coil of a Bréguet spring which is bent over the body of the spring.

'over-'cold, *sb.* [OVER- 29.] Excessive cold.

c **1420** *Pallad. on Husb.* XI. 54 Ffor ouer cold do dowues donge at eue Aboute her roote. **1626** BACON *Sylva* §411 The Earth doth..save it from over-heat and over-cold.

'over-'cold, *a.* [OE. *oferceald*: see OVER- 28.] Too cold, excessively cold (*lit.* and *fig.*).

a **1000** *Runic Poem* xi, Is byð oferceald, ungemetum slidor. **1608** BP. HALL *Char. Vertues & V.* II. *Enuious* 169 Whom hee dares not openly to backbite, nor wound with a direct censure, he strikes smoothly with an ouer-cold praise. **1652–62** HEYLIN *Cosmogr.* Introd. (1674) 19/2 The two over-cold, or Frigid Zones. **1726** LEONI *Alberti's Archit.* I. 7/1 Sometimes too hot and sometimes over cold. **1823** BYRON *Juan* VI. xv, Over-warm Or over-cold annihilates the charm.

,over'colour (-kʌlə(r)), *v.* [OVER- 27.] *trans.* To colour too highly (usually *fig.*); to represent too strongly or in an exaggerated way. So **,over-'colouring** *vbl. sb.*

1823 SCOTT *Romance* (1874) 81 To overcolour the importance and respectability of the minstrel tribe. **1843** PRESCOTT *Mexico* (1850) I. 325 It was this, too, which..led him into gross exaggeration and over-colouring in his statements. **1858** J. B. NORTON *Topics* 16 He has no motive for over-colouring or distorting facts.

over'comable, -comeable, *a.* [f. OVERCOME *v.* + -ABLE.] Capable of being overcome; that can be conquered or surmounted.

1483 *Cath. Angl.* 263/2 Ouercomabylle, *expug[n]abilis.* **1549** LATIMER *7th Serm. bef. Edw. VI* (Arb.) 192 Christ dyd suffer..to sygnifye to vs, that death is ouercomable. *a* **1586** SIDNEY *Arcadia* III. (1622) 331 That they were mortall, &.. both ouercomeable by death. **1880** BURTON *Reign Q. Anne* I. i. 56 It overcomes all overcomable opposition.

'overcome, *sb. Sc.* Also 6– our-, ower-, 8– o'er-. [OVER- 19, 20, 7, 5, 10 b.]

†1. That which is left over; a surplus, excess. *Obs.*

15.. *Aberdeen Reg.* (Jam.), The ourcome of thre pesis of clayth. **1725** RAMSAY *Gentle Sheph.* I. i, He that has just enough can soundly sleep; The o'ercome only fashes fowk to keep. **1881** STRATHESK *Blinkbonny* (1891) 36 (E.D.D.) To share o' the o'ercome when a' thing was paid.

2. A phrase that comes over and over again; the burden of song or discourse; a hackneyed phrase.

? *a* **1800** *Jacobite Relics* Ser. II. (1821) 192 And aye the o'ercome o' his sang Was 'Waes me for Prince Charlie!' **1814** *Saxon & Gael* I. 109 The grace o' a grey bunnock is the baking o't. That was aye her o'ercome. **1893** STEVENSON *Catriona* xvii. 190 'We'll ding the Campbells yet', that was still his overcome.

3. Something that overwhelms or prostrates a person; a sudden attack or shock.

1821 GALT *Ann. Parish* xviii. 174 Mrs. Balwhidder thought that I had met with an o'ercome, and was very uneasy.

4. Outcome, issue.

1822 GALT *Sir A. Wylie* l, Heaven only knows what will be the o'ercome o' this visitation.

5. A crossing, a voyage across.

1880 JAMIESON, 'We had a wild ourcome fae America.'

overcome (əʊvə'kʌm), *v.* Forms: see OVER and COME *v.* [OE. *ofercuman*, f. *ofer*, OVER- + *cuman*, COME: in MLG., MDu., Du. *overkomen*, OHG. *ubarqueman*, MHG. *überkomen*, Ger. *überkommen*, Da. *overkomme*, Sw. *öfverkomma*.]

†1. *trans.* To come upon, get at, reach, overtake. *Obs.* (Only OE.) [OVER- 7.]

c **725** *Corpus Gloss.* (O.E.T.) 1420 *Obtinuit*, ofercuom. *a* **900** tr. *Bæda's Hist.* IV. i. (1890) 252 Se Wigheard & lytestne alle his ȝeferan..þy ofercumendan wole fordilȝade wæron & forðȝeleorde. *a* **900** *Judith* 235 (Gr.) Nanne ne sparedon þæs herefolces..þe hie ofercuman mihton. *c* **1050** *Cott. Cleopatra Gloss.* in Wr.-Wülcker 459/8 *Obtinuit*, ofercom.

2. a. *trans.* To overpower, prevail over, overwhelm, conquer, defeat, get the better of in any contest or struggle. Since 17th c. chiefly with non-material object. [OVER- 2, 21.]

Beowulf (Z.) 1274 He þone feond ofer-cwom. *c* **893** K. ÆLFRED *Oros.* II. iv. §3 Þonne hie hwelc folc mid ȝefeohte ofercumen hæfdon. *c* **1000** *Sax. Leechd.* III. 170 Ofercymeþ he ælle his feond. *c* **1175** *Lamb. Hom.* 155 Mid þis wepne wes dauid iscrud þa he goliam þe fond ouer-com. *c* **1200** ORMIN 6275 Forr þu mihht cwemenn swa þin Godd & oferr-cumenn deofell. *a* **1300** *Cursor M.* 16338 Wit na word ouercum him he mai. **1382** WYCLIF *John* xvi. 33 Triste ȝe,

I haue ouercome [1388 ouercomun] the world. **1456** SIR G. HAYE *Law Arms* (S.T.S.) 110 [To] ourcum malice with vertu of pacience. **1573** G. HARVEY *Letter-bk.* (Camden) 3 Miht had alreddi overcumd riht. **1579** LODGE *Repl. Gosson's Sch. Abuse* (Hunt. Cl.) 12 Pindarus colledg is not fit for spoil of Alexander ouercome. *c* **1648–50** BRATHWAIT *Barnabees Jrnl.* IV. xxvii, But their purpose I o'ercommed. **1651** HOBBES *Leviath.* Concl. 391 He..that is slain, is Overcome, but not Conquered. *a* **1703** BURKITT *On N.T.* Mark xiv. 72 His fears overcame his faith. **1825** J. NICHOLSON *Operat. Mechanic* 82 The quotient will be the resistance overcome at the circumference of the wheel. **1875** MANNING *Mission H. Ghost* x. 268 Unless we have fortitude to overcome these temptations, they will overcome us.

†**b.** To be victor in, gain, win (a battle). *Obs.*

c **1205** LAY. 31684 And ȝif Oswy..þat feht maȝen ouercumen we him sculleð to luken. *c* **1330** R. BRUNNE *Chron.* (1810) 6 Tuenty grete batailes Ine ouerkam. **1574** HELLOWES *Gueuara's Fam. Ep.* 1 On the day they had ouercome any battaile. **1585** T. WASHINGTON tr. *Nicholay's Voy.* III. iii. 73 [They] haue gotten & ouercome diuers battels.

c. *absol.* or *intr.* To be victorious, gain the victory, conquer.

a **1325** *Prose Psalter* l[i]. 5 Þa-tou be made ryȝt-ful in þy wordes, and þatou ouercum whan þou art iuged. **1382** WYCLIF *Rev.* iii. 21, I shal ȝiue to him that shal ouercome, for to sitte with me in my troone, as and I ouercam, and sat with my fadir in his troone. **1489** CAXTON *Faytes of A.* III. iii. 171 They of the chyrche ought not to reuenge hem but ought to ouercome by suffraunce. **1561** DAUS tr. *Bullinger on Apoc.* (1573) 74 A Lion of the tribe of Iuda hath ouercommed. **1652** F. OSBORNE *Plea Free State comp. w. Monarchy* 4 Making that arbitrary and at the will of the Vanquished, which is imposed without exception, on all that Overcame. **1842** TENNYSON *Godiva* 10 But she Did more, and underwent, and overcame.

d. Phr. *we shall overcome*, used as a slogan by minority groups, with allusion to the text of a Negro Gospel song.

[**1901** C. A. TINDLEY in Miles & Clifton *New Songs of Gospel* No. 27 (*title*) I'll overcome some day.] **1948** *People's Songs* Sept. 8 We will overcome, We will overcome, We will overcome some day. Oh Down in my heart, I do believe, We'll overcome some day. **1961** *Jet* 14 Dec. 53 That the Freedom Riders left their imprint on the prison was evident from the songs and slogans they scribbled on the walls. A favorite was the crusaders' theme *We Shall Overcome.* **1963** *N.Y. Times* 23 July 21/1 The theme song of the integration movement, 'We Shall Overcome', has had its own history of integration, passing from Negro singers to white and back again to Negro. **1968** 'EBON' *Revolution* 15 'We shall overcome' And black Truth bombs Explode In the back, Alleys, Of Newark's Asshole. **1973** *Black World* Sept. 8/1 The Christian strains of 'We shall Overcome' gave way to the more Garrisonian 'We Shall be heard!' as the Sixties progressed.

3. a. Of some physical or mental force or influence: To overpower, overwhelm; to exhaust, render helpless; to affect or influence excessively with emotion. Chiefly in *pass.*; const. *with*, rarely *by*. In *pa. pple.* sometimes (euphemistically) = overcome by liquor, intoxicated. [OVER- 2, 21.]

c **1050** *Cott. Cleopatra Gloss.* in Wr.-Wülcker 374/1 *Consternati*, ofercymene. *Ibid.* 458/24 *Obstipuit*, forhtode, ofercymen wæs. **1297** R. GLOUC. (Rolls) 6290 He ne dorste ys feblesse telle Edmond, vor fere Laste, ȝyf he vnderȝete, þat he were so ouercome, þat he nolde fine ar he adde is lif him binome. *c* **1386** CHAUCER *Miller's Prol.* 27 Thou art a fool, thy wit is ouercome. *c* **1430** *Life St. Kath.* (1884) 33 A merueylous lyght wherof þe holy virgyn was nyȝe ouer-come wyth wonder and merueylynge. *c* **1450** *Mirour Saluacioun* 2897 She was so feynt and ouercomen for sorowe. **1530** PALSGR. 648/1 I ranne so faste that I was almoste overcome with ronnyng. **1590** SPENSER *F.Q.* II. i. 23 And now exceeding griefe him overcame. **1658** A. FOX *Wurtz' Surg.* II. i. 48 A strong Medicine is to powerfull for a weak body, and overcomes his nature. **1756** TOLDERVY *Hist. 2 Orphans* IV. 30 In a very short time this female was (what good women term) overcome. **1844** DICKENS *Mart. Chuz.* xxx, The architect was too much overcome to speak. **1849** MACAULAY *Hist. Eng.* I. iv. 500 One of the proscribed Covenanters, overcome by sickness, had found shelter in the house of a respectable widow. **1882** DE WINDT *Equator* 116 'Schnapps'..had..been too much for them, and ere dinner was over they were all—to use a mild expression—overcome.

†**b.** To obtain or have sway over (the mind or conduct); to dominate, possess. *Obs. rare.*

1377 LANGL. *P. Pl.* B. XIII. 11 How þis coueitise ouercome clerkes and prestes. **1568** GRAFTON *Chron.* I. 61 He was so overcome with wrath and cruelnesse, that commonly he was the death of any that angred him. **1607** SHAKS. *Cor.* IV. vi. 31 A worthy Officer i' th' Warre, but Insolent, O'recome with Pride.

†**c.** *fig.* (with a thing also as obj.). To be too much for; to exhaust or surpass the capacity of; to overload, overflow. *Obs.*

1697 DRYDEN *Virg. Georg.* II. 748 Till..A Crop so plenteous, as the Land to load, O'ercome the crowded Barns. **1708** J. PHILIPS *Cyder* I. 34 Th' unfallow'd Glebe Yearly o'ercomes the Granaries with Store Of Golden Wheat.

4. To 'get over'; to surmount (a difficulty or obstacle); to recover from (a blow, disaster, etc.). [OVER- 5.]

c **1205** LAY. 1934 Þa hæfde þa Troinisce men Ouer-comen [*c* **1275** ouercome] heora teonen þa weoren heo bliðe. **1648** *Hamilton Papers* (Camden) 244, I found that all the considerable difficultie I wold meet with wold be in point of the Divine worship, and I was threatned to purpos that that was not to be overcome. **1725** DE FOE *Voy. round World* (1840) 255 The more difficult..it was..the more it would please me to attempt and overcome it. **1846** GREENER *Sc. Gunnery* 261 We have studied long and hard to overcome those objections. **1860** TYNDALL *Glac.* I. x. 66 Enormous difficulties may be overcome when they are attacked in earnest. **1884** D. GRANT *Lays North* 22 (E.D.D.), I do believe 'twis full a raith Ere we overcam' the blow.

5. To go beyond, exceed, surpass, excel, outstrip (in quality, measure, etc.). *arch.* [OVER- 13.]

c **1220** *Bestiary* 749 Ut of his ðrote cumeð a smel..ðat ouer-cumeð haliweie wið swetnesse. **1340–70** *Alex. & Dind.* 583 But oure kinde konninge ȝou ouur-comeþ nouþe In alle dedus þat ȝe don. **1387** TREVISA *Higden* (Rolls) VII. 149 His body overcome ȝe heiȝt of þe wal. *c* **1610** *Women Saints* 197 To goe forward and to ouercome precedent vertuous actions with better. **1643** BURROUGHES *Exp. Hosea* ii. (1652) 176 The idols they had..did even overcome the Egyptian idols in number. **1859** TENNYSON *Elaine* 448 But there is many a youth Now crescent, who will come to all I am And overcome it.

†**6.** To get over, get through or to the end of; to master, accomplish. *Obs.* [OVER- 17.]

a **1225** *Ancr. R.* 116 Nu beoð, Crist haue þonc, þe two dolen ouercumen. Go we nu, mid Godes helpe, up oðe þridde. *Ibid.* 198 Þeo þet nimeð more an hond þen heo mei ouer-cumen. **1573** TUSSER *Husb.* li. (1878) 118 If meadow be forward, be mowing of some; but mowe as the makers may well ouercome. **1598** W. PHILLIPS *Linschoten* in Arb. *Garner* III. 434 With great misery and labour, they ouer-came their voyage. **1652** DOR. OSBORNE *Lett. to Sir W. Temple* (1888) 32, I am extremely glad..to find that you have overcome your long journey. **1697** DRYDEN *Virg. Georg.* III. 538 Thus, under heavy Arms, the Youth of Rome Their long laborious Marches overcome.

7. To come or pass over, traverse (a road, space, etc.). Now *rare.* [OVER- 10.]

c **1250** *Gen. & Ex.* 1633 Longe weie he siðen ouer-cam. *c* **1540** tr. *Pol. Verg. Eng. Hist.* I. (Camden No. 36) 42 After thei hadd overcomme the Alpes. **1697** DRYDEN *Virg. Past.* IX. 82 Already we have half our way o'ercome. **1835** A. B. LONGSTREET *Georgia Scenes* 7, I had over-come about half the space which separated it from me. **1875** W. MORRIS tr. *Virgil's Aeneids* XII. 907 And e'en the hero-gathered stone.. O'ercame not all the space betwixt.

8. a. To come or spread over; to overrun; to cover. Now *rare.* [OVER- 9.]

c **1386** CHAUCER *Knt.'s T.* 1942 Vp to his brest was come The coold of deeth that hadde hym ouercome. *c* **1475** *Lament Mary Magd.* 129 With blood ouercome were bothe his iyen. **1588** SHAKS. *Tit. A.* II. iii. 95 The Trees..Ore-come with Mosse, and balefull Misselto. **1607** NORDEN *Surv. Dial.* v. 240, I haue a peece of land, ouercome with a kind of weed that is full of prickles. **1855** BROWNING *Grammar. Fun.* 18 All the peaks soar, but one the rest excels; Clouds overcome it.

†**b.** To come over suddenly, take by surprise. *Obs.*

1605 SHAKS. *Macb.* III. iv. 111 Can such things be, And ouercome vs like a Summers Clowd, Without our speciall wonder?

†**9.** *intr.* To come about (in the course of time); to happen, befall; to supervene. *Obs.* [? OVER- 14.]

c **1374** CHAUCER *Troylus* IV. 1041 (1069) Thinges alle and some That whylom ben byfalle and ouer-come. **1382** WYCLIF *Prov.* xxvii. 1 Vnknowende what the dai to ouercome [Vulg. *superventura*] bringe forth.

10. *intr.* To 'come to', 'come round', recover from a swoon. Now *dial.* [? OVER- 17.]

1375 BARBOUR *Bruce* XVIII. 134 Schir philip of his desynaiss Ourcome, and persauit he wass Tane. *c* **1430** *Syr Gener.* (Roxb.) 8399 A swoun she fel as she stoode;.. Clarionas at last ouercam And of hir ring grete hede she nam. ? *a* **1550** *Freiris of Berwik* 575 in *Dunbar's Poems* 304 Fra the wind wes blawin twyiss in his face, Than he ourcome within a lytill space. **1714** THOMSON *Cloud of Witnesses* (1871) 420 (E.D.D.), I fell into a sound; and when overcame again, they were standing about, looking on me. **1768** ROSS *Helenore* 20 When she o'ercame, the tear fell in her eye.

Hence **over'come** († **overcomen, overcomed**) *ppl. a.*, conquered, vanquished: also used *absol.*

1470–85 MALORY *Arthur* IX. xi, An ouercomen knyghte I yelde me vnto you. **1530** PALSGR. 320/1 Overcome, *espris..mat.* **1549** CHEKE *Hurt Sedit.* (1641) 63 The overcommed cannot fly, the overcommer cannot spoile. **1585** T. WASHINGTON tr. *Nicholay's Voy.* I. xxi. 26 b, Two great figures of the ouercome. **1607** TOPSELL *Four-f. Beasts* (1658) 49 The poor over-comed beast, with shame retireth from the herd.

over'comer. [f. prec. + -ER[1].]

1. One who overcomes; a conqueror, vanquisher.

c **1340** HAMPOLE *Prose Tr.* 30 Þan sall þou be..ouerganger and ouercommere of all synnes. *c* **1450** tr. *De Imitatione* II. iii. 43 He þat can wel suffre, shal finde most pes; he is an ouercomer of himself. *a* **1548** HALL *Chron. Rich. III* 55 Other stode stil and loked on, entendynge to take parte w[t] the victors and overcommers. **1687** J. RENWICK *Serm.* xxviii. (1776) 339 The Saints are overcomers and they have palms in their hands. **1861** TRENCH *7 Ch. Asia* 48 Christ sets himself forth here as the overcomer of death natural.

2. An appellation assumed by a religious sect which was started in U.S. in 1881 and founded a colony at Jerusalem in Palestine.

The name is derived from their interpretation of the promises made to 'him that overcometh' in Rev. ii, iii.

1882–3 in *Schaff's Encycl. Relig. Knowl.* III. 1889 Developments of the same kind [as Millerites and other pre-millennialists] may be instanced in the so-called 'Overcomers' of America.

over'coming, *vbl. sb.* [f. as prec. + -ING[1].] The action of the vb. OVERCOME; a conquering, overpowering, overmastering.

a **1300** *Cursor M.* 25175 Thoru ouer cuming o þat faand. **1398** TREVISA *Barth. De P.R.* IX. xxxi. (MS. Bodl.) 99 b/1 Ouercomynge of deþe and openynge of Paradise. **1585** T. WASHINGTON tr. *Nicholay's Voy.* IV. iii. 115 b, The armie of Darius, at the ouercomming of Grecia, were armed after this manner. **1859** J. BROWN *Rab & F.*, Eyes..full of suffering, but also full of the overcoming of it.

over'coming, *ppl. a.* [f. as prec. + -ING[2].] That overcomes; overwhelming, overpowering.

1704 NORRIS *Ideal World* II. v. 303 We..shall wish to shade our eyes from thy too powerful and overcoming light. *a* **1716** SOUTH *Serm.* (1717) IV. 68 Crushed to Death under Heaps of Gold, stifled with an overcoming Plenty. **1824** MISS FERRIER *Inher.* lxix, My Cloak would be quite overcoming.

Hence **over'comingly** *adv.*, in an overcoming manner; presumptuously; oppressively.

1653 H. MORE *Conject. Cabbal.* iii. 73 That they should so boldly and overcomingly dictate to him such things as are not fit. **1840** *Tait's Mag.* VII. 195 Smelling over-comingly of musk.

over-command to **over-commentaried**: see OVER-.

'over'common, *a.* [OVER- 28.] Too common, excessively common. So **'over-'commonness,** too great frequency.

1480 CAXTON *Ovid's Met.* XIV. iv, The entre [to helle] is ouercomune.., but fewe of them that goon theder fynde the retourne. **1594** HOOKER *Eccl. Pol.* II. vi. §4 Objecting that with vs Arguments taken from authoritie negatiuely are ouer-common. **1604** HIERON *Wks.* I. 537 They say the ouer-commonnesse of preaching will breed contempt of preaching. **1690** DRYDEN *Amphitryon* Ep. Ded., Vertues not over-common amongst English Men.

ˌover-'compensate, *v.* Also as one word. [OVER- 24.] *trans.* and *intr.* To compensate excessively for (something); spec. in *Psychol.*, to exhibit over-compensation (see next). Hence **ˌover-'compensated** *ppl. a.*; **ˌover-compen'satory** *a.*

1768–74 TUCKER *Lt. Nat.* (1834) II. 678 A damage.. which will be over-compensated by its produce to the party sustaining it. **1917** *Psychol. Bull.* XIV. 207 By psychological investigation and analysis, one may disclose the psychic phase of these compensatory and over-compensatory processes. **1934** H. C. WARREN *Dict. Psychol.* 190/1 *Overcompensate*, to make more than the necessary amount of allowance or adjustment. **1937** 'M. INNES' *Hamlet, Revenge!* II. viii. 194 One builds on the over-compensated Oedipus—Dad Advises Sonny-boy. **1947** *Partisan Rev.* XIV. 476 As a result he..over-compensates by consciously immersing himself in parochial attitudes shared by the folk. **1949** M. MEAD *Male & Female* iv. 88 Their sons again grow up similarly focussed on women, similarly in need of over-compensatory ceremonial to rescue them. **1958** 'E. CRISPIN' *Best SF Three* 11 As to human intellect, science fiction has emphasised its inadequacy over and over again. The *genre* 'overcompensates', no doubt, in showing the man animal so often defeated, or all but defeated, by the Other Thing, and this over-compensation is the origin of the accusations of pessimism that are so often levelled against it. **1962** SIMPSON & RICHARDS *Physical Princ. Junction Transistors* xii. 280 In case (b) (perfect compensation), the dashed curve coincides with the extrapolated linear sections of the transfer characteristics, and in the overcompensated case (c) it lies between the two linear sections. **1968** L. DURRELL *Tunc* i. 17 We sparred gracefully in the fashion of well-educated Englishmen overcompensating. **1973** 'D. HALLIDAY' *Dolly & Starry Bird* xxiii. 277 Innes..will shortly give you a brandy because he is overcompensating. He thought you were guilty and is now ashamed. **1973** C. MULLARD *Black Brit.* II. iv. 44 In others [*sc.* classrooms] the teachers overcompensated and patronized their new pupils.

ˌover-compen'sation. Also as one word. [OVER- 29 b. Cf. G. *überkompensation.*] A term used in psychological analysis by A. Adler to denote the exaggerated striving for power, etc., that can activate someone suffering from a severe sense of inferiority; an exaggerated response of making allowance or amends for something; more than equitable compensation.

1917 *Psychol. Bull.* XIV. 207 Adler thought he had discovered 'a remarkable relationship between somatic inferiority and somatic psychic over-compensation'. **1917** GLUECK & LIND tr. *Adler's Neurotic Constitution* (1921) I. i. 4 This fetal character..furnishes the increased possibility for compensation and over-compensation. **1932** *Brit. Jrnl. Psychol.* Apr. 347 Occasionally, over-compensation for this error [in colour memory] seems to be taking place. **1941** J. S. HUXLEY *Uniqueness of Man* xi. 228 Bias of this type has the additional danger that those who make an effort to discount it may readily swing into over-compensation—a bias of opposite sign. **1955** T. H. PEAR *Eng. Social Differences* vi. 138 Theories of compensation and over-compensation for inferiority-complexes. **1969** V. H. VROOM in Lindzey & Aronson *Handbk. Social Psychol.* (ed. 2) V. 220 The evidence reported concerning overcompensation and undercompensation pertains to its short-term effects on performance. **1977** D. CLARK *Gimmel Flask* vi. 106 Her over-compensation in over-spending may be due to her disappointment.

over-complacency to **over-complimentary**: see OVER-.

ˌover'compound, *a. Electr. Engin.* [f. OVER- 24 b + COMPOUND *a.*] = next.

1931 G. C. BLALOCK *Princ. Electr. Engin.* ix. 95 The overcompound generator is adapted to more remote loads, since its rising characteristic will compensate for linedrop. **1972** I. L. KOSOW *Electr. Machinery & Transformers* iii. 99 Most commercial compound dc dynamos..are normally supplied by the manufacturer as overcompound machines.

ˌovercomˈpounded, *ppl. a. Electr. Engin.* [f. OVER- 24 b + COMPOUND *v.* + -ED[1].] Of a dynamo: compounded in such a way that the voltage increases with load.

1892 S. P. THOMPSON *Dynamo-Electr. Machinery* (ed. 4) xi. 295 For such work as supplying current to an electric tramway, an over-compounded dynamo with laminated field-magnets is the best generator. **1927** A. E. CLAYTON *Performance & Design D.C. Machines* viii. 181 With an over-compounded machine the value of the current in the shunt winding actually increases with increasing load. **1971** L. T. AGGER *Introd. Electr.* xvi. 299 If..the load has to be supplied over a considerable distance, the rising characteristic of the over-compounded generator..may be desirable.

So **overˈcompounding** *vbl. sb.*; also (as a back-formation) **overˈcompound** *v. trans.*

1892 S. P. THOMPSON *Dynamo-Electr. Machinery* (ed. 4) xi. 295 The same process suits for over-compounding, the excitation at full load being raised until the volts at terminals rise to the higher number of volts that will allow for the drop in the leads. **1914** A. GRAY *Princ. & Pract. Electr. Engin.* xiii. 75 For railway service the generators are overcompounded so as to maintain the trolley voltage at some distance from the power house. **1937** H. E. STAFFORD *Troubles of Electr. Equipment* iii. 46 To over-compound a generator not provided with diverters, the only permanent way is to increase the strength of the series and interpole fields. **1966** J. MEISEL *Princ. Electromechanical-Energy Conversion* ix. 394 Making $G_{af}\omega_o$' greater than *Ra* + *Rs*, or overcompounding the machine, gives an increasing output voltage with increasing load current. *Ibid.*, By a slight overcompounding the droop can be taken into account and the output voltage at no load..can be made equal to the output voltage at full-load current.

over-concentrated to **over-condense**: see OVER-.

ˈover-ˈconfidence. [OVER- 29 b.] Too great confidence, excess of confidence.

1700 LOCKE *Hum. Und.* IV. xiv. (ed. 3) 394 To check our over-confidence and presumption, we might by every day's Experience be made sensible of our short-sightedness. **1862** MISS MULOCK *Mistress & Maid* xxiv, In the over-confidence of her recovery some slight neglect had occurred.

ˈover-ˈconfident, *a.* [OVER- 28.] Too confident, having excess of confidence.

1617 HIERON *Wks.* (1619–20) II. 321 Not being aware of the euill of that ouer-confident humour which was in him. *a* **1677** HALE *Prim. Orig. Man.* III. i. 250 Aristotle himself seems not to be over-confident of this Opinion. **1836** W. IRVING *Astoria* I. 67 Mr. Astor was not over-confident of the stability and firm faith of these mercurial beings.

So **ˈover-ˈconfidently** *adv.*

1847 in WEBSTER.

over-conquer to **over-consciousness**: see OVER-.

ˌoverconˈsolidated, *ppl. a.* [OVER- 24 b.] Of soil or clay: consolidated to a greater degree than could have been produced by the present pressure of overburden.

1936 *Proc. Internat. Conf. Soil Mech. & Foundation Engin.* III. 52 Tests with strongly overconsolidated soils. **1957** BISHOP & HENKEL *Measurement of Soil Properties in Triaxial Test* 115 A series of tests on an over-consolidated clay. **1969** C. R. SCOTT *Introd. Soil Mech. & Foundations* vi. 139 Dense sands and over-consolidated clays increase in volume when sheared, if they are free to do so.

So **ˌoverconsoliˈdation.**

Quot. 1960 represents a simple non-technical use.

1936 *Proc. Internat. Conf. Soil Mech. & Foundation Engin.* III. 51 In order to investigate the influence of the voids ratio on the shearing resistance, the test specimens were reconsolidated in three different ways, so that they at the start of the shearing test would be in a state of either natural consolidation, simple overconsolidation, or cyclic overconsolidation. **1960** *Farmer & Stockbreeder* 1 Mar. 94/3 There is no danger of over-consolidation with tractors in the silo. **1969** LAMBE & WHITMAN *Soil Mech.* xxix. 452/2 The natural water content considered in relation to the liquid and plastic limits gives some idea of the degree of overconsolidation.

over-consumption to **overcooked**: see OVER-.

ˌover-ˈcool, *v.* [OVER- 27.] *trans.* To make too cool, to cool below the proper temperature, to chill. So **ˌover-ˈcooled** *ppl. a.*

1597 SHAKS. *2 Hen. IV*, IV. iii. 98 Thinne Drinke doth so ouer-coole their blood. **1616** SURFL. & MARKH. *Country Farme* 137 The ouer-cooled Horse is cured by giuing him to drinke Swines bloud all hot with Wine. **1700** FLOYER *Cold Baths* I. ii. 42 Heat helps the Parts over-cooled.

†**overˈcope,** *v. Obs. rare.* [f. OVER- ? 23 + COPE *v.*[2]] *intr.* To exceed one's power of coping.

1628 JACKSON *Creed* VI. I. xii. §5 Whilst the chief ringleader of this rebellious rout sought to satisfy this infinity of his desire..his capacities did overcope.

over-copious to **overcorned**: see OVER-.

ˌover-coˈrrect, *v.* [OVER- 24.] **1.** *Optics. trans.* To correct (a lens) so that there is an aberration opposite to that of the uncorrected lens; *spec.* to correct for chromatic aberration to such an extent that red light is focused beyond violet light. Opposed to *under-correct.* So **ˌover-coˈrrected** *ppl. a.*

1829 H. CODDINGTON *Treat. Reflexion & Refraction of Light* vi. 253 If a concave flint glass lens..be too powerful for a convex crown glass one when placed in contact, so as to over-correct the colour, as it is said, the achromatism may be made more perfect by separating them a little. **1867** J. HOGG *Micros.* I. ii. 47 The effect..of projecting the blue image beyond the red..is called over-correcting the object-glass. **1884** *Science* III. 487/2 An over-corrected object-glass may be adjusted to any desired extent, while one that is under-corrected can only be used in the state in which it left the maker's hands. *Ibid.*, If we suppose a person to be blind to the extreme blue and the violet rays only of the spectrum, to him an over-corrected object-glass would be perfect. **1885** T. LONGMORE *Illustr. Optical Manual* (ed. 3) ii. 43 It should be ascertained if the M[yopia] has not been over-corrected by the lenses supplied, and the eyes brought into a condition of H[ypermetropia]. **1975** M. RUBEN *Contact Lens Pract.* ii. 19/2 In hypermetropia..one eye (the non-dominant) can..be overcorrected by as much as 1·5 D so as to give the best binocular acuity for distance.

2. *trans.* and *intr.* To make an excessive correction to or in (something); to correct (someone) too frequently.

1956 *Publ. Amer. Dial. Soc.* XXVI. 45 But he may still have trouble remembering which sound belongs in which words, and in his anxiety he will overcorrect and hear *sung* for *sun* or *some.* **1966** J. DERRICK *Teaching Eng. to Immigrants* iii. 117 In this, as in all questions of pronunciation teaching, the greatest care and tact is necessary, so that the nervous pupil, from being over-corrected, does not become more nervous and inhibited. **1966** *Publ. Amer. Dial. Soc.* *1964* XLII. 5 To overcorrect a slide, causing rear of car to waggle like a fishtail. **1966** *Rep. Com. Inquiry Univ. Oxf.* II. 325 This calculation almost certainly over-corrects for any error. **1967** J. RATHBONE *Diamonds Bid* iv. 39 The car..slewed towards the right. I over-corrected and the on-side fender hit a low wall. **1974** L. DEIGHTON *Spy Story* xx. 215 The machine tottered into the air, swinging as the nervous pilot over-corrected. **1976** *Columbus* (Montana) *News* 10 June 4/3 The driver overcorrected, causing the vehicle to go into a skid, overturning in the median after crossing the road.

over-coˈrrection. [OVER- 29 b.] An excessive correction; a correction which results in error in the opposite direction; *spec.* (*a*) *Optics*, correction of a lens to such a degree as to produce the opposite aberration; (*b*) *Linguistics* = HYPERCORRECTION.

1885 T. LONGMORE *Illustr. Optical Manual* (ed. 3) ii. 43 If there be no over-correction, but the concave lenses ordered are found to be only equivalent to the excess of refraction, or, in other words, to the degree of M[yopia] which they have been calculated to neutralise, [etc.]. **1947** E. H. STURTEVANT *Introd. Linguistic Sci.* viii. 80 Sometimes..he has caught himself creating such forms as [dju·, tju·] for *do* and *two.* Such 'over-corrections' have been observed very often in many languages. **1957** F. & R. LOCKRIDGE *Practise to Deceive* (1959) x. 137 That was prejudice, to be corrected. But, then, there was the danger of over-correction. **1961** F. G. CASSIDY *Jamaica Talk* iii. 46 All too easily this attempt leads to what is called 'over-correction', for he puts sounds into places where they do not belong in Standard. **1966** A. BATTERSBY *Math. in Managem.* vii. 185 Fifteen weeks after the sales increased, the rate of production at the factory had surged up to an increase of 45%; forty weeks later it had swung back in an over-correction. **1975** M. RUBEN *Contact Lens Pract.* ii. 19/1 In hypermetropia associated with convergence,..overcorrection with a contact lens can be just as effective as spectacle lenses.

ˈover-ˈcostly, *a.* [OVER- 28.] Too costly, that costs too much; too expensive.

[**1395** PURVEY *Remonstr.* (1851) 95 If freris bilde ouir costlew housis.] **1603** FLORIO *Montaigne* II. xii. (1632) 309 If it be over-costly to be found. **1642** FULLER *Holy & Prof. St.* III. xiv. 188 Overcostly tombes are only baits for Sacriledge.

overcount (-ˈkaʊnt), *v.* [OVER- 22, 26.]

1. *trans.* To exceed in number, outnumber.

1606 SHAKS. *Ant. & Cl.* II. vi. 26 At land thou know'st How much we do o're-count thee. **1838** *Penny Cycl.* 2nd Suppl. 360/2 Compared with the population of these cities ..the whole of them little over-counting London alone [etc.].

2. To count or reckon in excess of the reality; to overestimate.

1593–4 SYLVESTER *Profit Imprisonm.* 350 Nor hurt they any one, but him that over-counts them. **1897** *Review of Rev.* Nov. 547 It is not overcounting to say that millions are convinced.

overcourt to **overcoyness**: see OVER-.

overcover (əʊvəˈkʌvə(r)), *v.* [OVER- 8.] *trans.* To cover over; to cover up completely, bury.

1382 WYCLIF *Judith* v. 9 Whan hungir hadde ouercouered al the lond, thei wenten doun into Egipt. *c* **1450** LONELICH *Grail* lvi. 433 As sone as vnder the ȝate was he gon, On hym there fyl a gret kernel of ston, And Ouercovered hym bothe tope and to. **1500–20** DUNBAR *Poems* xii. 15 Welth, warldly gloir, and riche array Ar all bot thornis..Ourcowerd with flouris. **1540** HYRDE tr. *Vives' Instr. Chr. Wom.* (1592) F iij, Why then dust thou overcover it with dirt and mire? **1691–2** WOOD *Fasti Oxon.* II. (R.), The bags were old and overcovered with dust as if they had lain there 40 years. *a* **1814** *Prophetess* II. iii. in *New Brit. Theatre* I. 195 Turret, dome, and spire Are all o'ercover'd with the human swarm.

ˌover-ˈcram, *v.* [OVER- 27.] *trans.* To cram or stuff to excess or too much, esp. with food, and *fig.* with information. Hence **ˌover-ˈcrammed** *ppl. a.* So **ˈover-ˈcram** *sb.*: cf. CRAM *sb.* 4.

1599 A. M. tr. *Gabelhouer's Bk. Physicke* 28/2 Take a good Capone, which hath binne choackede, & overcrammed. **1683** TRYON *Way to Health* 316 Many there are, that be not content to Over-cram Nature with too great a Quantity of Food, but they will needs drown her too, with a deluge of Drink. **1828** S. R. MAITLAND *Let. to C. Simeon* 30 The miserable, inadequate, and now over-crammed tenement. **1895** ANNA M. STODDART *J. S. Blackie* II. 89 Pedantry hallowed by the dry-rot of ages, or jubilant over-cram, its mushroom product.

overcraw, obs. form of OVERCROW.

†**ˈover-crease.** *Obs.* [f. OVER- + CREASE *sb.*[1]] An overgrowth, increase causing overflow.

1625 LISLE *Du Bartas, Noe* 121 Some great man of authority or cunning Pilot..led the over-creases of some people thither.

ˈover-creˈdulity. [OVER- 29 c.] Too great credulity; the quality of being over-credulous.

1688 *Pulpit-Sayings* 22 An over-credulity in matters of Piety and Devotion. **1827** SCOTT *Let.* 14 Sept. in *Lockhart* lxxiv, If I have been quilty of over-credulity in attaching more weight to General Gourgaud's evidence than it deserves.

ˈover-ˈcredulous, *a.* [OVER- 28.] Too credulous, too ready to believe.

1605 SHAKS. *Macb.* IV. iii. 120 Modest Wisedome pluckes me From ouer-credulous hast. **1651** WITTIE tr. *Primrose's Pop. Err.* To Rdr. 2 Cheating the over-credulous people both of their Money and Health. **1688** *Pulpit-Sayings* 22 In such things as these it is the Papists are condemn'd for over-credulous. **1936** L. MACNEICE tr. *Aeschylus' Agamemnon* 29 The over-credulous passion of woman expands In swift conflagration.

overcreed, etc.: see OVER- 27.

overˈcreep, *v.* [OVER- 9.] *trans.* To creep over.

1640 SIR J. CULPEPER in Rushw. *Hist. Coll.* III. (1692) I. 33 A Nest of Wasps, or Swarm of Vermin, which have overcrept the Land. **1810** CRABBE *Borough* i, Faint lazy waves o'ercreep the ridgy sand. **1854** WHITTIER *Fruit-gift* 17 Its parent vine..O'ercrept the wall.

†**ˈover-ˈcritic.** *Obs.* [OVER- 29 d.] One who is critical to excess; a hypercritic.

a **1661** FULLER *Worthies, Devon* (1662) 269 Let no over-critick causlesly cavill at this Coat.

So **ˈover-ˈcritical** *a.* [OVER- 28], too critical, hypercritical; **ˈover-ˈcriticism,** the practice of being over-critical, hypercriticism.

1851 MRS. GASKELL *Let.* 1 Sept. (1966) 161 She..is inclined to be *over*-critical & fastidious with everybody & everything. **1859** HELPS *Friends in C.* Ser. II. II. v. 102 The habit of over-criticism, a hindrance to pleasantness. **1893** *Chicago Advance* 31 Aug., Hampered by..an over-critical spirit. **1946** *Nature* 28 Sept. 457/1 The points of inflexion of various thermodynamical functions in the overcritical region. **1976** J. WILSON *Let's Pretend* v. 57 Lately she'd been over-critical of Margaret, finding her exasperating instead of endearing.

overcroft (ˈəʊvəkrɒft). [f. OVER- 8 c + CROFT *sb.*[2]] In early church architecture, a series of small rooms below the roof (see quot. 1925).

1925 P. POWER *Early Christian Ireland* ii. 22 On the inside the little building is roofed, or ceiled, by a barrel vault, between which and the outer stone roof there is an overcroft, or series of very small rooms, lighted by opes in the gable. **1964** B. WHELPTON *Unknown Ireland* xi. 149 The thirteenth-century Church of St. Doulough with its steep stone roof and overcroft.

ˌover-ˈcrop, *v.* [f. OVER- 1, 27 + CROP *v.* or *sb.*]

I. †**1.** *trans.* To rise above, overtop. *Obs.*

1567 MAPLET *Gr. Forest* 38 The old Prouerbe is herein verified: the ill weede ouercroppeth the good corne.

†**2.** To crop or lop the head of (a plant). *Obs.*

fig. **1583** GOLDING *Calvin on Deut.* cviii. 667 That..all our affections be subdued to him and that our lust be ouercropped when they would carie vs here and there.

II. 3. To crop (land) to excess, to exhaust by continuous cropping. Also *transf.*

1789 *Trans. Soc. Arts* VII. 43 In over-cropping the land. **1850** JAMES *Old Oak Chest* I. 283 The eternal cultivation of the mind is like overcropping a field. **1881** W. BENCE JONES in *Macm. Mag.* XLIV. 128 The bad tenant has taken the value out by over-cropping and little manure. **1946** *Nature* 2 Nov. 606/2 Sometimes his [*sc.* man's] responsibility is brought home to him by physical disaster,..as in the effects of deforestation, over-cropping or over-grazing. **1960** *Farmer & Stockbreeder* 9 Feb. 97/1 Many instances of 'soil sickness'..in the past would have been put down to thin or hungry soil, overcropping or bad drainage. **1974** *Times* 25 Apr. 12/6 He worries..about the over-cropping of the sea.

b. *refl.* See quot. (*U.S. local.*)

1860 BARTLETT *Dict. Amer.* s.v., A planter or farmer is said to overcrop himself when he plants or 'seeds' more ground than he can attend to.

So **ˈover-ˌcrop** *sb.*, an excessive or too large crop.

1878 *Lumberman's Gaz.* 26 Jan., The fears entertained.. that there would be a ruinous over-crop of logs..harvested this winter may be dismissed.

†**over-ˈcross,** *adv.*, *prep.*, *a. Obs.* [f. OVER *prep.* + CROSS: cf. *on cross, across,* CROSS *sb.* 22.]

A. *adv.* Crossing over something or each other; across, crosswise.

c **1450** HOLLAND *Howlat* 345 Syne twa keyis our croce, of siluer so cleir In a feild of asure flammit on fold. **1601** HOLLAND *Pliny* I. 74 The compasse of this arme of the sea is 80 miles, the cut ouer-crosse 20 miles.

B. *prep.* Across, over, from side to side of.

1611 COTGR., *Chaine de drap*, the woofe of cloth; the thread which in weauing runs overcrosse it. **1657** THORNLEY tr. *Longus' Daphnis & Chloe* 16 Laying over-crosse the Chasm, long, dry, and rotten sticks.

C. *adj.* (ˈ*overcross*). Lying or placed across; extending from one side to the other; transverse.

1634 BRERETON *Trav.* (Chetham) 3 Birch twigs, or bushes, which they hang upon overcross poles, into the cisterns.

over'cross, *v. rare.* [OVER- 10.] *trans.* To pass or lie across; to cross. *lit.* and *fig.*

1567 MAPLET *Gr. Forest* 13 That other black Lead.. groweth next by siluer, and ouercrosseth his vaines with it. *Ibid.* 70 Vnlesse he..escapeth..by often turning and ouercrossing the way. *c* **1592** *Greenes Vision* G.'s Wks. (Grosart) XII. 244 If my constant thoughts be ouercrost. **1870** MISS BROUGHTON *Red as a Rose* (1878) 288 Wet nettles and faded bents overlie, overcross each cold hillock.

overcrow (əʊv'əkrəʊ), *v.* Also 6 -craw. [OVER- 2, 21.] *trans.* To crow or exult over; to triumph over; to overpower.

1562 J. HEYWOOD *Prov. & Epigr.* (1867) 110 Whan euer thou wouldest seeme, to ouer crow mee, Than will I surely ouer cakill thee. **1590** SPENSER *F.Q.* I. ix. 50 Then gan the villein him to overcraw. **1597** [see OVERAWE quot. 1579]. **1602** SHAKS. *Ham.* v. ii. 364 The potent poyson quite ore-crowes my spirit. **1616** SURFL. & MARKH. *Country Farme* 85 The Cocks also doe beat one another for the Hennes..and he that ouercommeth, ouer-croweth the other which is ouercome. **1642** ROGERS *Naaman* 329 Shall I endure such a base fellow to overcrow me? **1818** SCOTT *Rob Roy* xvii, I sunk it and my head at once, fairly *overcrowed*, as Spenser would have termed it. **1843** BORROW *Bible in Spain* li. 293/2 The coasts are exceedingly high and bold, especially that of Spain, which seems to overcrow the Moorish. **1889** 'R. BOLDREWOOD' *Robbery under Arms* viii, There wasn't another man living that could overcrow me.

overcrowd (ˌəʊvə'kraʊd), *v.* [OVER- 27.]

1. *trans.* To crowd to excess; to overfill with or as with a crowd.

1766 SMOLLETT *Trav.* II. xxxi. 122 It does not, on the whole, appear over-crouded with ornaments. **1848** W. H. KELLY tr. *L. Blanc's Hist. Ten Y.* I. 603 To prevent the hospitals being overcrowded. **1883** 'ANNIE THOMAS' *Mod. Housewife* 86 Be sure you don't overcrowd your rooms... There is nothing more disagreeable to my mind than a crush.

2. *intr.* To crowd together to excess, or in too great a number.

1899 *Daily News* 24 Jan. 3/3 These people overcrowd into the already overcrowded smaller properties that lie around. *Ibid.* 7 Apr. 4/7 The Council's practice of turning out of the municipal dwellings all families who overcrowd.

Hence **ˌover'crowded** *ppl. a.*, crowded too much; **over'crowdedness**; **ˌover'crowding** *vbl. sb.* and *ppl. a.*

1836 J. S. MILL in *London & Westm. Rev.* Apr. 18 In every overcrowded department there will arise a tendency among individuals..to unite their labours or their capitals. **1848** —— *Pol. Econ.* I. II. xiv. 472 A sufficient degree of overcrowding may depress the wages of women to a much lower minimum than those of men. **1861** BERESF. HOPE *Eng. Cathedr. 19th C.* 204 The risk with chairs is that of overcrowding. **1862** *Macm. Mag.* Nov. 62 The overcrowded ranks of greedy aspirants. **1865** J. SIMON in E. R. Pike *Human Doc. Victorian Golden Age* (1967) vi. 292 Where 'overcrowding' exists in its sanitary sense, almost always it exists even more perniciously in certain moral senses. **1888** MRS. H. WARD *R. Elsmere* VII. xlix, Her restless and over-crowded mind. **1894** *Westm. Gaz.* 11 Sept. 4/3 The pilgrims, who attended in overcrowding numbers. **1902** *Daily Chron.* 29 Sept. 3/3 It is here that the over-crowdedness of his pages comes most into evidence. **1911** G. B. SHAW *Doctor's Dilemma* p. lxxxiv, He is struggling for life in an overcrowded profession. **1932** J. S. HUXLEY *Probl. Relative Growth* vii. 207 With overcrowding and less favourable food conditions 'degeneration' set in. **1950** T. S. ELIOT *Cocktail Party* II. 126 But they can't *all* stay there! I mean, it would make the place so over-crowded. **1955** M. GILBERT *Sky High* ii. 22 Every time we meet he's got a fresh reason for it. Overcrowding, parking offences, congestion of pavements. **1960** *Encounter* Mar. 56/1 The spiritual effects of over-crowdedness. **1976** *Language* LII. 30 The unit in relation to which over-crowding must be described is the syntactic configuration, and not just the simplex S. **1976** H. NIELSEN *Brink of Murder* ix. 81 Small businessmen, seeking relief from overcrowded cities..gravitated seaward to create new forms of overcrowding. **1977** *Listener* 17 Mar. 339/1 A cell which..would beggar description in terms of coldness, smallness, over-crowdedness.

overcrown, overcry, etc.: see OVER- 1, 22.

over'crust, *v.* [OVER- 8.] *trans.* To cover over with a crust or layer. Chiefly in pa. pple. **over'crusted**. Hence **over'crusting** *vbl. sb.*

1603 FLORIO *Montaigne* II. xxxvii. (1632) 434 Keeping our bodies all over-crusted, and our pores stopt with grease and filth. **1670–98** LASSELS *Voy. Italy* I. 62 The church of S. Ambrosio..is neatly overcrusted with marble. *Ibid.* 104 The roof is to be vaulted all over with an overcrusting of Lapis Lazuli. **1848** CLOUGH *Amours de Voy.* I. 111 Here, overcrusting with slime, perverting, defacing, debasing, Michael Angelo's dome.

over-culled to **-cultivate**: see OVER-.

'over-'cunning, *sb.* [OVER- 29 d.] Excess of cunning; too great knowingness.

1603 FLORIO *Montaigne* III. i. (1632) 446 Truely they make my cunning overcunning. **1616** *Rich Cabinet* 80 Knauery is an ouercunning of wit and craft, which hath twenty tricks to cozen others. **1640** HABINGTON *Edw. IV* 31 This I believe an overcunning in conjecture.

So **'over-'cunning** *a.*, too cunning; **ˌover-'cunning** *v. trans.* (*nonce-wd.*), to manage too cunningly.

a **1634** MARSTON (Webster), Unadvisedly overcunning in misunderstanding me. **1801** EARL MALMESBURY *Diaries & Corr.* IV. 5 Loughborough and Auckland appear to have over-cunning'd the business.

'overcup, *a.* [OVER- 8 c.] Applied to oaks in which the acorn is covered by the cup, as in two N. American species, *Quercus macrocarpa*, also called Bur or Mossy-cup Oak, and *Q. lyrata*, the Swamp Post-oak or Water White Oak.

1795 *Jrnl. of A. Michaux* 15 June, Quercus glandulibus magnis, capsula includentibus, nommé Overcup White Oak. **1817** J. BRADBURY *Trav. Amer.* 288 Of the oak only, there are fourteen or fifteen species, of which the over cup (*Quercus macrocarpa*) affords the best timber. **1865** *Michaux's N. Amer. Sylva* I. 40 *Quercus lyrata*..is called the Swamp Post Oak, Overcup Oak, and Water White Oak ..the acorn is covered by the cup. The name 'Overcup Oak' is most common in South Carolina.

'overcure, *sb.* [OVER- 29.] The process or result of overcuring; overvulcanization.

1915 *Jrnl. Soc. Chem. Industry* 15 Oct. 990/1 The load at breaking point was found to increase with the time of cure to a certain point and then to collapse, the rubber becoming very brittle at an overcure. **1952** J. DELMONTE *Plastics Molding* ix. 265 Translucent urea molded parts are the first to show the effects of overcure—by dullness or chalkiness in finished products. **1964** [see OVERCURING *vbl. sb.*].

overcure (stress variable), *v.* [OVER- 27.]

a. *trans.* To cure (plastic or rubber) for longer than the optimal period; to overvulcanize. Also *absol.* **b.** *intr.* To undergo overcuring.

1916 *Jrnl. Soc. Chem. Industry* 31 Aug. 872/1 It is.. common in the case of many goods for manufacturers when vulcanising to undercure rather than overcure the rubber so as to avoid the danger of over-vulcanising and consequent deterioration. **1949** B. L. DAVIES *Technol. Plastics* xxi. 405 The whole board is cured in the usual manner in the press, care being taken not to overcure. **1952** J. DELMONTE *Plastics Molding* viii. 211 Before the advent of thorough internal heating by high frequency, thick-molded parts would overcure on outside surfaces before the interior reached molding temperature. **1972** *Materials & Technol.* V. xiv. 523 The outside of a thick rubber article has to be cured longer than the optimum curing time (overcured) in order to ensure an optimum cure within the article.

So **'overcured** *ppl. a.*; **over'curing** *vbl. sb.*

1912 *Jrnl. Soc. Chem. Industry* 16 Dec. 1100/1 It is important to note that (3) was almost fully cured at 35 lb. and over-cured at 45 lb. *Ibid.* 1101/2 Beyond this point it was probable that a decrease merely indicated overcuring. **1952** J. DELMONTE *Plastics Molding* ix. 265 An overcured plastics part is even more difficult to recognize than an undercured piece, primarily because most plastics are not critical in their time of cure. **1964** A. E. JUVE in Alliger & Sjothun *Vulcanization of Elastomers* ii. 30 Vulcanization occurs in three stages; (1) an induction period, (2) a curing or cross-linking stage, and (3) a reversion or over-cure stage. .. Some systems..have little or no tendency toward reversion or increased tightness of cure as the result of overcuring.

overcure, obs. form of OVERCOVER.

'over-'curious, *a.* [OVER- 28.] Excessively curious; †**a.** Too careful, fastidious, or particular (*obs.*); **b.** Too inquisitive.

1561 DAUS tr. *Bullinger on Apoc.* (1573) 76 Who dares be ouercurious hereafter in searching out the workes and iudgementes of hym, whom [etc.]. **1579** G. HARVEY *Letter-bk.* (Camden) 63 The commendation of an eloquente and orator-like stile by overcurious and statelye enditinge. **1684** T. BURNET *Th. Earth* II. Pref., To whom therefore such disquisitions seem needless, or over-curious, let them rest here. **1773** BURKE *Corr.* (1844) I. 425, I would not have that care degenerate into an effeminate and over-curious attention. **1885** *Harper's Mag.* Dec. 86/2 May I ask, without seeming overcurious..has it any regular haunt?

Hence **'over-'curiously** *adv.*, in an over-curious manner; † too particularly or carefully (*obs.*); too inquisitively; **'over-'curiousness**.

1561 DAUS tr. *Bullinger on Apoc.* (1573) 154 But when this wo shal be..is knowen to the father alone, and therfore must not be searched of vs ouercuriously. *Ibid.* 69 b, Ouer curiousnesse [see OVER *a.* 4]. **1624** DONNE *Serm.* ii. (1640) 16 Aske not thy selfe overcuriously, when this mystery was accomplished. **1714** MAUNDEVILLE *Fab. Bees* (1733) II. 16 It is an incivility strictly to examine and over-curiously to look into matters.

'overcurrent. *Electr.* [OVER- 29.] A current in excess of that which is normal, safe, or allowed for.

1931 H. W. BROWN *Electr. Equipment* (ed. 2) i. 19 (*heading*) Automatic protection against ground, short circuit, and overcurrent. **1971** MOORE & ELONKA *Electr. Syst. & Equipment for Industry* ii. 31 Direct-acting over-current trips are generally used on low-voltage circuit breakers.

over'curtain, *v. rare.* [OVER- 8.] *trans.* To cover as with a curtain; to shadow, obscure.

1621 BRATHWAIT *Nat. Embassie, Odes* Ded. (1877) 287 To see how sin's orecurtained by night.

over-custom: see OVER- 29.

'overcut, *sb.* [OVER- 5, 1.] †**a.** A cut or direct way over a hill, etc. *Obs.*

1636 *Boston Rec.* (1877) II. 13 All the ground lying betweene the two brookes..and soe to the other end unto shortest over-cut beyond the hill towards the north west.

b. A cutting or incision from above or on the upper surface.

1883 E. INGERSOLL in *Harper's Mag.* Jan. 202/1 A big two-handed saw [was] set at work to make the overcut.

c. *Mining.* A cut at or near roof level in a seam.

1940 *Trans. Inst. Mining Engin.* XCIX. 55 When the undercut is in coal, the importance of effective shovelling may be less, but it must always remain to give freedom of working to the machine, and it is only when an intermediate or overcut is taken that it is unnecessary. **1960** J. SINCLAIR *Winning Coal* vi. 170 When overcuts at a greater height are required..a hydraulic turret machine..is generally most satisfactory.

d. In electrochemical machining, the distance between the outside surface of the cathode and the side of the cut in the part being machined.

1965 *New Scientist* 5 Aug. 336/2 If the voltage is allowed to fluctuate, the size of the overcut will fluctuate, and it becomes impossible to machine parts to close tolerances. **1974** J. A. MCGEOUGH *Princ. Electrochem. Machining* v. 146 The amount of overcut can be diminished by several devices, including insulation along the external side walls of the cathode.

over-cut, *v.* **1.** [OVER- 27.] *trans.* To fell too many trees in (a forest) at once, upsetting the regular supply of trees suitable for cutting.

1906 W. SCHLICH *Man. Forestry* (ed. 3) I. v. 75 Private owners are inclined to favour their own monetary interests to the disadvantage of future generations by overcutting.. their forests. **1913** *Q. Rev.* Oct. 446 In the case of private ownership, there is always a danger of the forests being overcut to obtain quick returns.

2. *Mining.* [OVER- 1.] *trans.* (See quot. 1967.) Also *absol.*

1907 *Trans. Inst. Mining Engin.* XXXI. 387 So far as the machine is concerned, it will overcut as well as undercut. **1947** *Ibid.* CVI. 18 The first seam to be overcut with a machine designed specially for roof-forming was the Cockshead Seam in North Staffordshire. **1967** *Gloss. Mining Terms (B.S.I.)* VIII. 20 *Overcut*, to cut by machine at or near roof level in a seam.

3. [OVER- 27.] *intr.* To cut or produce a groove in a gramophone record with such amplitude as to run into an adjacent groove.

1935 H. C. BRYSON *Gramophone Record* iv. 73 For sounds of constant absolute intensity over the frequency range of 30–250, all the sounds have an equal tendency to over-cut. **1962** W. R. WELLMAN *High Fidelity Home Music Syst.* (ed. 2) viii. 175 When a recording is made, it is possible for the recording stylus to 'overcut', or run into an adjacent groove. **1976** *Gramophone* Sept. 514/3 The audible improvements over the transformer are subtle but very real, totally abolishing my previous reservations about slight sibilance on overcut records with the SL15/Mk. II.

Hence **ˌover'cutting** *ppl. a.* and *vbl. sb.* Also **'overˌcutter**, a machine for overcutting.

1923 *M. & C. Machine Mining* II. 283 (*caption*) A repeat order for overcutting turbine driven universal machines for heading and longwall service. **1928** M. D. WILLIAMS *Pract. Machine Mining* iv. 45 The 'Samson' chain machine when adapted for overcutting is fitted with a jacking device which permits the raising or lowering of the machine in case of variation in the position of the band to be cut. **1928** *Daily Tel.* 9 Oct. 9/7 Wasteful over-cutting, forest fire, fungi, insects, and wind combined are rapidly wiping out Canada's available trees. **1935** H. L. BRYSON *Gramophone Record* iv. 83 If overcutting seems likely to occur, the electrical input of the recorder is cut down to the safety line, i.e., the amplitude is reduced. **1944** J. S. HUXLEY *On Living in Revolution* xi. 117 Over-cutting of the forests resulted in the closing of its [*sc.* Elma's] one big mill. **1946** *Trans. Inst. Mining Engin.* CVI. 20 (*caption*) Overcutting coal-cutter arranged to cut at 7 ft. *Ibid.* 21 An overcutter was required to cut at 4 ft. **1962** W. R. WELLMAN *High Fidelity Home Music Syst.* (ed. 2) viii. 175 Overcutting is prevented, during recording, by limiting the swing of the cutting stylus on low frequencies. **1966** S. D. WOODRUFF *Methods of Working Coal & Metal Mines* III. A. iv. 158 (*caption*) Hydraulic turret overcutter with down-curved jib for roof cutting. *Ibid.* 173 The cutting unit consists of a special long-wall coal cutter which is equipped with two horizontal jibs—one for undercutting and the other for overcutting.

over-dainty to **-dangle:** see OVER-.

over'damped, *a.* [OVER- 24.] Of a physical system: damped to a greater extent than the minimum needed to prevent oscillations. So **over'damp** *v. trans.*

1922 GLAZEBROOK *Dict. Appl. Physics* II. 373/1 The galvanometer system is non-oscillatory and overdamped. **1936** *Jrnl. Sci. Instruments* XIII. 101 Even with a resistance which overdamps the movement the rapidity of indication is said to compare favourably with that obtainable with pivoted instruments of a similar type. **1939** *Amateur Radio Handbk.* v. 79/2 The aerial should damp the network to flat resonance, though if it overdamps it, it may not be possible to draw any power from the anode circuit. **1962** SIMPSON & RICHARDS *Physical Princ. Junction Transistors* xv. 374 If the reverse is true the response will be overdamped and the output voltage will rise exponentially. **1975** *Nature* 10 July 121/1 If large, complex systems have the property that their linear connectivity is low, then they are more likely to be stable, and if stable, are more likely to be over-damped than to oscillate.

ˌover'dare, *v.* [OVER- 27, 22, 21.]

1. *intr.* To be too daring; to dare too much.

1586 WARNER *Alb. Eng.* III. xvi. (1589) 68 And Danger ouer-dares, if it from Iustice disagree. *a* **1592** H. SMITH *Wks.* (1867) II. 483 The young man stalks, the old man stoops, That over-dares, this ever droops. **1599** B. JONSON *Cynthia's Rev.* I. i, We should be said to overdare in speaking to your nimble deitie.

†**2.** *trans.* To surpass in or overcome by daring; to daunt. *Obs.*

1590 MARLOWE *2nd Pt. Tamburl.* III. v, I am come, As Hector did into the Grecian camp, To overdare the pride of Græcia. *c* **1611** CHAPMAN *Iliad* xx. 116 Let not the spirit of Æacides, Be ouer-dar'd; but make him know, the mightiest deities Stand kind to him.

So **'over'daring** *vbl. sb.*, the action of daring too much or being too rash; presumptuous boldness.
1614 R. TAILOR *Hog hath lost Pearl* II. in Dodsley *O. Pl.* (1780) VI. 405 That pride cost them the loss of a limb or two, by over-daring. **1630** B. JONSON *New Inn* IV. iii, Over-daring is as great a vice As over-fearing. **1656** EARL MONM. tr. *Boccalini's Advts. fr. Parnass.* I. lxxviii. (1674) 106 To quell the over-daring of those Courtiers.

'over-'daring, *ppl. a.* [OVER- 28 b.] Too daring; unduly or imprudently bold; foolhardy.
1590 MARLOWE *Edw. II*, I. iv, Meet you for this? proud over-daring peers? **1656** EARL MONM. tr. *Boccalini's Advts. fr. Parnass.* I. lii. (1674) 67 By the over-daring boldness of dissemblers. **1879** DOWDEN *Southey* ii. 37 A mild reproof on over-daring speculation.
Hence **'over-'daringly** *adv.*
1652 GAULE *Magastrom.* 129 Yea, have not their astrologicall falsehoods too often prevailed both to instigate over-daringly?

over'dark, *adv.* [OVER- 31.] Till after dark; in the dark. (Better as two words: cf. *over night.*)
18.. *N. Brit. Rev.* (Ogilvie), Whitefield would wander through Christ-Church meadows overdark.

overdark, -darken, *v.*: see OVER- 8.

†**over'dated,** *a. Obs.* [OVER- 18.] Of which the date is past; antiquated; out of date.
a **1641** BP. MOUNTAGU *Acts & Mon.* iv. (1642) 251 But the man..had forgotten those out-worn and over-dated courtesies of Antipater. **1641** MILTON *Reform.* I. (1851) 1 The gospel..winnow'd, and sifted, from the chaffe of overdated Ceremonies. **1649** —— *Eikon.* xi, Had he also redeem'd his over-dated minority from a Pupillage under Bishops. [**1850** J. BROWN *Disc. our Lord* (1852) I. vii. 415 Where is 'over-dated Judaism' and its magnificent temple?]

'overday, *a.* [OVER- 32]. Designating a herring that is not freshly caught. Also *absol.*
1883 WALSH *Irish Fisheries* 14 (Fish. Exhib. Publ.) Making the fish (what is called) 'over day', or stale fish. **1889** *Tit-Bits* 17 Aug. 298 About 24 hours after capture the herring is liable to the pouring out of extravasation of blood about his gills and fins, which..bruised appearance is quaintly called in the fish trade *over-day tarts.* **1927** *Sunday Express* 23 Oct. 5/1 Some of the herrings caught to-day are what is known as 'overdays'. A herring becomes an 'overday' if not sold within twelve hours of leaving the water, and its price drops precipitately. **1958** *New Statesman* 23 Aug. 218/1 'Overdays' herring, not completely fresh, can still make oil and meal, though 'sludge' needs fresh fish.

over-daze to **overdazzling**: see OVER-.

†**'overdeal,** *sb. Obs.* [f. OVER- 19 + DEAL *sb.*] A part left over or in excess; surplus, overplus.
1600 HOLLAND *Livy* XL. xxxvi. 1083 The over-deale of twelve thousand footmen of Latines, and sixe hundred horse-men. **1610** —— *Camden's Brit.* I. 818 Concerning Berwicke haue heere now for an Ouerdeale, these verses of Maister I. Ionston.

,over-'deal, *v.* [OVER- 27.] *intr.* To deal too much.
1789 WOLCOTT (P. Pindar) *Subj. for Painters* Wks. 1812 II. 126, I come not to impute to thee the crime Of over-dealing in the true Sublime.

'over-'dear, *a.* [OVER- 25, 27.] Excessively or exceedingly dear (in various senses); too costly.
[**1297** R. GLOUC. (Rolls) 8008 Þer ne ssolde no mete ne drinke, bote it were ouer dere, Come wiþinne is wombe, ne cloþ ouer is suere.] **1483** CAXTON *Gold. Leg.* 117/1 O my overderest sones that were the sustenance and staf of myn old age. **1619** T. MILLES tr. *Mexia's Treas. Anc. & Mod. Times* II. 965/2 Which (to my greefe) I finde now by ouer-deare experience. **1655** FULLER *Ch. Hist.* VIII. ii. §34 Queen Mary..not over-dear to her own husband. **1895** *Forum* (N.Y.) Nov. 280 Even success..may be bought at a price over-dear to pay.
as adv. [*c* **1500** DUNBAR *Poems* xxxiv. 49 'ȝett', quod the Deuill, 'thou sellis our deir'].
Hence **'over-'dearness.**
1680 J. COLLINS *Plea Irish Cattle* 6 His Majesty loseth much..by the Over-dearness of Provisions for his Navy.

over-deaved: see OVER- 27 b.

,over'deck, *v.* [OVER- 8, 27.]
†**1.** *trans.* To 'deck' or cover over. *Obs.*
1509 BARCLAY *Shyp of Folys* (1570) 63 If that he her suspect, With a hood shall he unwares be overdeckt. **1599** A. M. tr. *Gabelhouer's Bk. Physicke* 114/2 He causeth the sayede Image to be overdeckede with an Oxehyde.
2. To deck or adorn to excess.
1712 STEELE *Spect.* No. 282 ¶6 Out Clerk..has this Christmas so over-deckt the Church with Greens, that he has quite spoilt my Prospect. **1866** *Cornh. Mag.* Nov. 633 Their heads and necks are overdecked with jewels, feathers, and flowers.
Hence †**over'decking** *vbl. sb.* (see quot.).
1605 VERSTEGAN *Dec. Intell.* iii. (1628) 61 The ouerdecking or couering of beere came to be called berham and afterward barme. **1658** PHILLIPS, *Barm*, yest, the flourring, or over-decking of Beer.

over-deck, *a.*: see OVER- 32.

†**'overdeed,** *sb.* (*a.*) In 3–4 -dede. [OVER- 29 d. Cf. Du. *overdaad* excess, MHG. *übertât* transgression.] **A.** *sb.* Overdoing; excess, intemperance.
c **1200** *Trin. Coll. Hom.* 55 On two wise on drinke, untimeliche and on ouerdede, and on swiche drinkeres cumeð godes curs. **1340** *Ayenb.* 55 Me ssel euremo habbe drede, þet me ne mys-nyme be ouer-dede.
B. *adj.* Excessive, intemperate.
12.. in *O.E. Misc.* 193 Inne mete and inne drinke ic habbe ibeo ouerdede.

over-deeming, -deep, etc.: see OVER-.

over'deepen, *v. Geol.* [OVER- 22; *overdeepening* is tr. G. *übertiefung* (A. Penck 1899, in *Verhandl. des 7en Internat. Geographen-Kongr.* (1901) II. 232).] *trans.* To deepen further, to make even deeper. So **over-'deepened** *ppl. a.*, **-'deepening** *vbl. sb.*
1900 *Proc. Boston Soc. Nat. Hist.* XXIX. 308 Penck has suggested that glaciated valleys of the Alpine kind should be called 'overdeepened'. **1902** *Q. Jrnl. Geol. Soc.* LVIII. 703 The hanging valleys in the lower part of the Val Ticino are attributed to the overdeepening of the main valley by ice. **1905** *Jrnl. Geol.* XIII. 392 As soon as a shallow wind-blown hollow is formed, that part of the integrated drainage system which leads to the hollow will supply waste to it whenever rain falls there;..the coarser waste will accumulate, and thus the tendency of the winds to overdeepen local hollows will be..counteracted. **1913** *Bull Geol. Soc. Amer.* XXIV. 214 Similarly, a valley glacier, while actively overdeepening its trough, might develop a more or less abrupt step in the trough floor. **1968** R. W. FAIRBRIDGE *Encycl. Geomorphol.* 327/1 Regardless of whether the overdeepening of the river mouth is primarily due to eustatic rise of sea level or tectonic subsidence, it is said to be a drowned valley. *Ibid.* 743/2 The rock floors of overdeepened troughs remain bare in parts. *Ibid.*, Overdeepening is responsible for the production of numerous lakes, some of very large size. **1970** C. A. LEWIS *Glaciations Wales* ii. 25 The major through-valleys of Snowdonia were overdeepened and straightened at this time by lowering of the watersheds by ice moving radially outwards from a centre near Llyn Tegid.

'over-'delicacy. [OVER- 29 c.] Too great delicacy.
1751 SMOLLETT *Per. Pic.* (1779) IV. xcv. 162 An over-delicacy in this respect..I shall look upon as a disapprobation of my own conduct. **1768–74** TUCKER *Lt. Nat.* (1834) I. 42 A fantastic air, and an over-delicacy of expression.

'over-'delicate, *a.* [OVER- 28.] Too delicate; excessively delicate.
1630 *R. Johnson's Kingd. & Commw.* 183 Hee was over-delicate in his dyet. **1640** BP. HALL *Chr. Moder.* I. vii. 62 We should not be wanton, and over-delicate in our contentments. **1828** P. CUNNINGHAM *N. S. Wales* (ed. 3) II. 36 They are not over-delicate in their food at any time.

over-delicious to **-descanting:** see OVER-.

overde'sign, *v.* [OVER- 26.] *trans.* To design to a standard of reliability or safety higher than the usual or minimum standard.
1964 M. GOWING *Britain & Atomic Energy, 1939–1945* x. 278 The team in fact decided to 'over-design' the pile. **1969** *Word Study* Apr. 4/2 Rocket boosters must contain.. hundreds of redundant systems to preclude failure and to provide reliability; they are overdesigned, well beyond what is necessary for normal function. The same over-design appears in much of the prose. **1970** *Nature* 18 July 218/2 Once a tower has been shown to live up to its specification, the designer likes to see by how much he has over-designed it, and about fifty per cent of the towers are eventually tested to destruction.
Hence as *sb.*, the action of overdesigning; an instance of this.
1969 [see above]. **1972** *Lebende Sprachen* XVII. 134/2 Greater reliability, without penalties caused by over-design, are expected to be achieved through use of a simulator.

'over-de'sire. [OVER- 29 d.] Excessive desire.
a **1635** NAUNTON *Fragm. Reg.* (Arb.) 54 Carried and transported with an over-desire and thirstinesse after fame. **1795** *Jemima* I. 196 By her over desire to spare my wife's fatigue. **1838–9** HALLAM *Hist. Lit.* III. III. viii. 413 *note*, It seems..to have been this over-desire to prove his theory orthodox, which incensed the church against it.

'over-de'sirous, *a.* [OVER- 28.] Excessively desirous; †exceedingly desirable (*obs.*).
1483 CAXTON *Gold. Leg.* 132 b/2 What ioye..that they haue in the ouerdesirous syght of our lord. **1647** TRAPP *Marrow Gd. Auth.* in *Comm. Ep.* 604 Over-desirous of those dainties.

,overdetermi'nation. [f. next.] The existence of more than one cause or contributory factor; *spec.* in *Psychol.*, the expression in one symptom of two or more needs or desires.
1917 C. R. PAYNE tr. *Pfister's Psychoanal. Method* 143 We have often had opportunity..to show these over-determinations. **1925** A. & J. STRACHEY tr. *Freud's Analysis of Case of Hysteria* in *Coll. Papers* III. 73 In the world of reality..a complication of motives, an accumulation and conjunction of mental activities—in a word, over-determination—is the rule. **1940** *Mind* XLIX. 370 A doubt such as 'I can never really know what another person is feeling' may arise from more than one of these sources. This over-determination of sceptical symptoms complicates their cure. **1955** J. STRACHEY tr. *Freud's Infantile Neurosis* in *Compl. Psychol. Wks.* XVII. 56 The contradiction is easily resolved if we regard it as a case of overdetermination. **1967** *Philos.* XLII. 374 There is a special kind of plurality, namely overdetermination. **1970** B. BREWSTER tr. *Althusser & Balibar's Reading Capital* (1975) 315 The overdetermination of a contradiction is the reflection in it of its conditions of existence within the complex whole, that is, of the other contradictions in the complex whole, in other words its uneven development. **1973** S. HEATH in *Screen* Spring/Summer 111 Underground cinema..has attempted to break through..the particular ideological overdetermination of the camera. **1975** *New Left Rev.* Nov.–Dec. 14 The ideological over-determination is itself a forced response, and what forces it is a material dilemma.

overde'termine, *v.* [OVER- 24.] *trans.* To determine, account for, or cause in more than one way, or with more conditions than are necessary. So **overde'termined** *ppl. a.*, having more determining factors than the minimum necessary; having more than one cause; *spec.* in *Psychol.*, giving expression to more than one need or desire; **overde'termining** *vbl. sb.*
1879 *Encycl. Brit.* X. 377/2 The definitions which have not been mentioned are all 'nominal definitions', that is to say, they fix a name for the thing described. Many of them overdetermine a figure. **1917** C. R. PAYNE tr. *Pfister's Psychoanal. Method* 143 The neurotic symptom has several determining factors, at least two. Therefore, it is called over-determined. **1924** C. M. BAINES tr. *Freud's Ætiology of Hysteria* in *Coll. Papers* I. x. 213 The idea chosen as the basis of a symptom will be one which various factors combine to arouse and which is stirred up from several directions simultaneously;—a state of affairs I have elsewhere tried to formulate by saying that hysterical symptoms are over-determined. **1950** *Mind* LIX. 199 My large-scale map of the small area occupied by θ will show that its display of Q is over-determined. **1959** I. POOL in Saporta & Bastian *Psycholinguistics* (1961) 308/1 The third of the overdetermining influences in the development of contingency analysis was structural linguistics. **1969** G. STEDMAN JONES in Cockburn & Blackburn *Student Power* 30 Mass student insurgency is *par excellence* an 'overdetermined' phenomenon. **1974** J. WHITE tr. *Poulantzas's Fascism & Dictatorship* I. iii. 40 The economic process is overdetermined by the class struggle, which has primacy.

,over-de'velop, *v.* [OVER- 27.] *trans.* To develop too greatly or to excess; *spec.* in *Photogr.*: see DEVELOP *v.* 5 b.
1869 *Eng. Mech.* 19 Nov. 238/3 He would be likely to over-develope it. **1884** *Century Mag.* XXVII. 945 A principle as good as this may be over-developed.
Hence **,over-de'veloped** *ppl. a.*; **,over-de'velopment,** too great development; *spec.* in *Photogr.* development continued too long or with too strong a developer (q.v.).
1842 MANNING *Serm.* (1848) I. 157 Over-development of peculiarities in the individual character. **1861** *Photogr. News Alm.* in *Circ. Sc.* (*c* 1865) I. 160/2 There is great danger of over-development, as some photographers are not content until the sky is..black. **1974** *Environmental Conservation* I. 17/2 The kind of agricultural system that now predominates in the over-developed countries. **1974** B. PEARCE tr. *Amin's Accumulation on World Scale* I. ii. 157 In the overdeveloped economies,..the tendency to (relative) underconsumption weighs heavily upon investment. *Ibid.* II. iv. 507 A favourable trade balance has beneficial effects only if saving tends to be superabundant, in a context of overdevelopment. **1976** *Survey* Summer–Autumn 156 The recognition of the planet's economic unity springs from a justifiable alarm at overdevelopment. **1977** G. FISHER *Villain of Piece* ii. 14 Majorca's over-developed coastline.

over-deyhouse to **-digest:** see OVER-.

,over-differenti'ation. *Philol.* [OVER- 29 b.] The unnecessary differentiation of elements in a phonemic, graphemic, or grammatical system, or in its analysis. So **,over-diffe'rentiated** *a.* Cf. DIFFERENTIATION 1 b.
1933 L. BLOOMFIELD *Language* 223 Some irregular paradigms are *over-differentiated.* Thus, corresponding to a single form of an ordinary paradigm like *play* (*to play, I play, we play*), the paradigm of *be* has three forms (*to be, I am, we are*). *Ibid.* 269 Among the substantives are some pronoun-forms which, by over-differentiation, do not serve as actors: *me, us, him,* [etc.]. **1955** H. A. GLEASON *Introd. Descriptive Linguistics* xvii. 174 Over-differentiation can be discovered and corrected from the record alone by rigorous procedures. **1962** *Canadian Jrnl. Linguistics* VII. 105 The choice of an under- as against an over-differentiated graphemic system must be made by comparing the practical difficulties of each in relation to reading and writing. **1965** *Language* XLI. 67 This grammar is characterized by functional overdifferentiation... I mean the distinguishing of constructions that are functionally identical. **1965** *Amer. Speech* XL. 108 Overdifferentiation of phonemes involves the imposition of phonemic distinctions from English into the phonemic system of Texas German, where they are not required.

†**over'dight,** *v. Obs.* [OVER- 1, 8.] To cover overhead; to clothe or deck all over. (In *pa. pple.*)
1590 SPENSER *F.Q.* II. vii. 53 A silver seat, With a thick Arber goodly over-dight. **1596** *Ibid.* IV. viii. 34 Soone as day discovered heavens face To sinfull men with darknes overdight. **1607** *Barley-Breake* (1877) 30 And pittied as a Deare amongst an heard, When he with soyle hath al him ouer-dight.

,over-dis'charge, *v.* [OVER- 27.] *trans.* To discharge too greatly: *spec.* in *Electr.*, to discharge an accumulator or storage-battery beyond a certain limit, an operation injurious to the battery. So **'over-dis'charge** *sb.*, the act of over-discharging or fact of being over-discharged.

1893 SIR D. SALOMONS *Managemt. Accumulators* 133 The causes may..be traced..more generally to the cells having been habitually over-discharged, or left standing for a long period with little charge in them. **1890** *Cent. Dict., Over-discharge*, sb. *Mod.* The sulphating of the plates was due to over-discharge. Frequent over-discharges had caused the plates to buckle.

over-disciplined to **-distant**: see OVER-.

over-dispersion (,əʊvədɪˈspɜːʃən). *Ecology.* [f. OVER- 29 b + DISPERSION.] A greater unevenness in the distribution of individuals than would be the case if the existence and position of each were independent of the rest, so that there is an increased proportion of the area with a large or small concentration of individuals. Hence **,over-diˈspersed** *a.*, distributed in this manner.

1936 *Jrnl. Ecol.* XXIV. 234 If in a set of counts of numbers of individuals per sample area the relative variance is greater than unity, this indicates that the dispersion is greater than would be expected on the assumption of random (Poisson) distribution... [This] first condition, over-dispersion, implies that individuals are scattered less evenly than would be expected. *Ibid.* 250 Over-dispersion shows itself in an excess of quadrats containing no 'individuals' or a large number of 'individuals', there being a corresponding deficit in central classes. **1946** *Ecology* XXVII. 329/2 The writer [*sc.* L. C. Cole] prefers the terms 'contagious' and 'negatively contagious' to 'overdispersion' and 'underdispersion' both of which have suffered reversals of meaning in the hands of different authors. **1948** *Bot. Rev.* XIV. 226 The study of over-dispersion is of major importance in statistical ecology. *Ibid.*, Over-dispersion is the rule rather than the exception among animals. *Ibid.* 227 Cole applied this technique to the analysis of various over-dispersed populations. **1957** P. GREIG-SMITH *Quantitative Plant Ecol.* iii. 56 The former has been termed overdispersed (referring to the distribution curve obtained) and the latter underdispersed. Unfortunately these terms have sometimes been used in the reverse sense (referring to the pattern of individuals on the ground)..and are better avoided. **1964** V. J. CHAPMAN *Coastal Vegetation* ii. 24 The plants are over-dispersed or aggregated into clumps.

overdo (,əʊvəˈduː, əʊvəˈduː), *v.* Forms: see DO. [OE. *oferdón* = OHG. *ubartuan*, MHG. *übertuon*, f. *ofer-*, OVER- (26, 27; 21, 22, 24, 17) + DO *v.*]

1. *trans.* To do to excess or too much; to carry to excess; to overact; to exaggerate.

c **1000** ÆLFRIC *Hom.* II. 532 Þonne sceal his steor beon mid lufe ʒemeteʒod, na mid wælhreawnysse oferdon. *a* **1225** *Ancr. R.* 286 Euerich þing me mei, þauh, ouerdon. Best is euer imete. **1393** LANGL. *P. Pl.* C. XIV. 191 Thei ouer-don hit day and nyght. **1602** SHAKS. *Ham.* III. ii. 22 Any thing so ouer-done, is from the purpose of Playing. **1638** CHILLINGW. *Relig. Prot.* I. vi. §73. 381 Often what he took in hand, he did not doe it but over doe it. *a* **1770** JORTIN *Serm.* (1771) I. v. 87 A disposition and behaviour which may be overdone as well as underdone. **1871** FREEMAN *Hist. Ess.* Ser. I. iv. 106 With the zeal of a new convert he overdid matters.

2. *intr.* or *absol.* To do too much; to go to excess; to exceed the proper limit.

1387 TREVISA *Higden* (Rolls) VII. 317 But he passede and over dede in gadringe of money. **1539** TAVERNER *Erasm. Prov.* (1552) 21 Some can not do but they overdo. **1657** W. RAND tr. *Gassendi's Life Peiresc* I. 12 Wherein I conceive he overdid. *a* **1711** GREW (J.), Nature so intent upon finishing her work, much oftner over-does than under-does. **1890** *Univ. Rev.* 15 June 214 He overdoes in both the burnt-sienna glow of the 'Venetian' hair and the unctuosity of the body-colour.

3. *trans.* To treat or affect in some way to excess; to carry too far.

1623 *State Papers, Col.* 182 [Lilly was dismissed] because he would sometimes be overdone in drink. **1847** L. HUNT *Men, Women, & B.* I. xiii. 217 Don't you see that it overdoes your argument? **1875** GREEN *Lett.* (1901) 403, I wish he didn't overdo his case.

4. To cook (food) too much. (Most frequently in pa. pple. *overdone.*)

1683 TRYON *Way to Health* 111 That it [roast flesh] be neither over nor under-done, but of the two, it is better that it be under-done. **1842** GRESLEY *B. Leslie* (1843) 254 Aristotle tells of a baker, who asked his employer whether he liked his meat overdone or underdone.

5. To overtax the strength of; to fatigue, exhaust, overcome. Also in phr. ***to overdo it***, to do too much for one's health; to overtax one's strength.

1817 M. WHALLEY *Let.* 23 Apr. in J. Constable *Corr.* (1962) I. 164, I trust however that your Darling is better than when you wrote, & was not overdone with company yesterday. **1822** LD. KENYON in *Life A. Bell* (1844) III. 283 Dr. Russell..was quite overdone with his labours. **1853** J. RUSKIN *Let.* 18 Aug. in M. Lutyens *Millais & Ruskins* (1967) 85 He overdid it last winter and now evidently stands in need of rest. **1858** BP. S. WILBERFORCE in R. G. Wilberforce *Life* (1881) II. xi. 385 At night ran down too fast, and overdid myself. **1866** GEO. ELIOT *Let.* 5 June (1956) IV. 267, I..have been a new creature ever since, though a little over-done with visits from friends and attention (miserabile dictu!) to petticoats etc. **1897** W. H. THORNTON *Remin. W.-Co. Clergyman* vii. 233, I have never overdone a horse in all my life. **1901** M. FRANKLIN *My Brilliant Career* v. 31 We were too overdone to make more than one-worded utterances, so waited silently in the blazing sun, closing our eyes against the dust. **1920** N. COWARD *I'll leave it to You* II. 24 You work terribly hard. I only hope you won't overdo it. **1924** A. HUXLEY *Let.* 3 Dec. (1969) 237 We must be careful not to make him overdo it, unless we want him laid up. **1973** N. MEYER *Target Practice* (1975) xv. 185, I worked at being normal. Perhaps I overdid it.

6. To surpass or exceed in performance; to outdo, excel. *arch.*

a **1625** FLETCHER *Double Marriage* IV. iii, Are you she, That over-did all ages with your honour? **1658** CLEVELAND *Rustic Rampant* Wks. (1687) 392 One who could overdo all Men in Dissembling. **1859** TENNYSON *Elaine* 468 Wrathful that a stranger knight Should do and almost overdo the deeds Of Lancelot.

7. *intr.* To do more than suffice; cf. DO *v.* 20.

1710 PRIDEAUX *Orig. Tithes* i. 7 In large Towns..this provision of a Tenth part will not do; and in other places..it will over-do.

¶ **8.** Rendering L. *transigĕre*: To pass, spend (time). *Obs.*

1382 WYCLIF *Ecclus.* xxxviii. 28 Eche smythe..the whyche the nyȝt as the day ouerdoth [1388 that passith the niȝt as the dai].

Hence **ˈover-do** (the vb. stem taken as) *adj.* (*nonce-use*); **overdoer** (-ˈduːə(r)), one who overdoes.

1681 BAXTER *Answ. Dodwell* 150 It is an easie Matter for Overdoers to add but a clause or two more to their Oaths and Subscriptions. **1748** RICHARDSON *Clarissa* (1811) II. 6 Your overdoers generally give the offence they endeavour to avoid. *Ibid.* VIII. 362 A good deal of blunder of the over-do and under-do kind.

over-doctrinize, over-dogmatism, etc.: see OVER-.

ˈoverdog. [OVER- 2 b.] A superior dog; usu. *fig.*, a dominant or victorious person. (Opp. UNDERDOG; cf. *top dog* s.v. TOP *sb.*[1] 34.) Hence **ˈoverdoggery.**

1908 *Westm. Gaz.* 17 Oct. 5/1 But the smart terrier was an Overdog, And knew a trick worth two of that. **1938** *Richmond* (Virginia) *Times-Dispatch* 6 Apr. 8/4 It's contrary to all instinct, yet, as one looks over the world today, one has to feel sorry for the overdogs. **1957** T. GUNN *Sense of Movement* 30, I praise the overdogs from Alexander To those who would not play with Stephen Spender. **1962** T. ZINKIN *Caste Today* 40 When the underdog begins to feel that he is as good as his neighbour, the result depends largely upon whether the overdog has stopped believing in his own over-doggery. **1966** *New Statesman* 28 Oct. 638/3 Underdogs abandoned by or abandoning inadequate male overdogs..revisit old haunts, look up old lovers, drift unsatisfactorily through a hostile world. **1970** R. LOWELL *Notebk.* 204 Dear Mary, with her usual motherly Solicitude for the lost overdog.

,overˈdoing, *vbl. sb.* [f. OVERDO + -ING[1].] The action of the verb OVERDO; doing to excess.

1340 *Ayenb.* 260 Sobrete lokeþ mesure ine mete and ine drinke, þet me ne maki ouerdoinge. *c* **1400** tr. *Secreta Secret., Gov. Lordsh.* 53 Man awe gretly eschewe ouer-doynge and ouerabundance of despensz. **1643** NETHERSOLE *Proj. for Peace* (1648) 22 In amendment of..our failings, and over-doings. **1891** *Athenæum* 2 May 563/1 The short-comings—or rather the overdoing—of the author are only too apparent.

ˈoverˈdoing, *ppl. a.* [f. as prec. + -ING[2].] That overdoes or does too much.

1612 CHAPMAN *Widowes T.* IV. i, This strain of mourning..like an overdoing actor, affects grossly. **1614** B. JONSON *Bart. Fair* I. i, You grow so insolent with it, and overdoing, John. **1756** W. DODD *Fasting* (ed. 2) 9 The very extraordinary and over-doing hypocrites. **1858** BUSHNELL *Serm. New Life* xxii. (1869) 318 The one thing needful, quite passed by in her overdoing carefulness.

overdome, *v.*: see OVER- 1.

overdone (ˈəʊvəˈdʌn: stress var.), *ppl. a.* (*adv.*, *sb.*) [Pa. pple. of OVERDO *v.*]

A. *ppl. a.* Done too much (in various senses of OVERDO *v.*); carried to excess; exaggerated; overcooked; exhausted; overcome.

c **1000** ÆLFRIC *Saints' Lives* I. 20 *Omnia nimia nocent*, þæt is ealle ofer-done þing dæriað. *c* **1175** *Lamb. Hom.* 101 Þet is on englisc alle ofer done þing deriað. *c* **1430** *How Wise Man tauȝt Sonne* 87 in *Babees Bk.* 50 For ouer-doon þing vnskilfully Makiþ grijf to growe whanne it is no nede. **1774** MAD. D'ARBLAY *Early Diary* 18 Oct., With an over done civility. **1781** J. WOODFORDE *Diary* 24 Sept. (1924) I. 322 It was a shabby dinner and overdone. **1853** DICKENS *Child's Hist. Eng.* II. xvi. 25 All the sandy prospect lay beneath the blazing sun burnt up like a great overdone biscuit. **1870** FREEMAN *Norm. Conq.* (ed. 2) I. App. 698 The studied obscurity and overdone piety of the special panegyrist. **1964** L. DEIGHTON *Funeral in Berlin* xx. 117 A finger like a Lyons sausage—slightly overdone. **1975** B. WOOD *Killing Gift* (1976) II. iv. 75 The waiter..brought two plates of the overdone roast beef. **1977** P. G. WINSLOW *Witch Hill Murder* I. 20 She was not fond of overdone hamburger.

†**B.** *adv.* Excessively. *Obs.*

13.. *Minor Poems fr. Vernon MS.* (E.E.T.S.) 609/631 Þe ouerdon gredi mon Beggeþ ofte his bred. *c* **1440** *Jacob's Well* 106 Sumtyme þou art to ouerdone mery, & sumtyme to ouyr-done sory & to ouyr-done hevy. **1496** *Dives & Paup.* (W. de W.) VII. xxviii. 320/2 Moche of our nacyon is gylty in theft, & ouerdone moche blent with false couetyse.

†**C.** *sb.* in phrase ***at overdone***, at an excessive rate, to excess. *Obs.*

c **1200** ORMIN 2575 Swa þatt nan þing att oferrdon Ne keppte ȝho to follȝhenn. *Ibid.* 4592 All þatt iss att oferrdon Itt drifeþþ fra þin herrte.

Hence †**overˈdonely** *adv.*, excessively.

c **1440** *Jacob's Well* 137 Ȝif þou ȝyve þi stodye to ouyrdonly to temperall occupacyoun, for lucre.

ˈover-,door, *sb.* and *a.* [OVER- 33, 32.]

A. *sb.* A piece of ornamental woodwork, etc., placed over a door.

1873 C. SCHREIBER *Jrnl.* 25 Oct. (1911) I. 236 Went on to Dirksen's, bought an over-door, also Watteau, for Ivor. **1884** *Health Exhib. Catal.* 89/2 Mantels, doors, overdoors, screens, and various articles of furniture, &c. ornamented with Lincrusta. **1899** *Pall Mall Mag.* Apr. 461 The State Ante-room, with its over-doors and over-mantels by Gibbons. **1967** A. EELES *Canaletto* 9/2 Smith also commissioned a group of 'over-doors', obviously intended to be part of a decorative scheme.

B. *adj.* Placed over a door.

a **1904** *Mod.* An over-door light.

†**ˈoverdorne.** *Obs. rare*[−1]. [f. OVER- 1 d + *dorne* DURN.] The lintel of a door.

c **1325** *Gloss. W. de Bibbesw.* in Wright *Voc.* 170 [see DURN].

overˈdosage. [OVER- 29 b.] The administering or taking of too large a dose (of medicine, drugs, etc.).

1922 *Encycl. Brit.* XXX. 137/2 To find a method of preventing these chloroform deaths, by enquiring into the conditions of overdosage. **1929** *Irish Jrnl. Med. Sci.* Apr. 183 Such symptoms were obviously due to overdosage. **1964** L. MARTIN *Clin. Endocrinol.* (ed. 4) i. 12 The excessive secretion of, or therapeutic overdosage with ACTH produces the clinical picture of Cushing's syndrome. **1976** *Times* 11 Mar. 2/3 The recommendations on aspirin and similar pain killers reflect growing concern about over-dosage.

overdose (ˈəʊvədəʊs), *sb.* [OVER- 29 a.] An excessive dose, too large a dose.

1700 LOCKE *Essay Hum. Und.* (ed. 4) II. xxxiii. 223 Had this happen'd to him, by an overdose of Honey, when a Child, all the same Effects would have followed. **1762** FREWEN in *Phil. Trans.* LII. 454 One..who had taken an over-dose of opium, and died of it. **1858** W. ARNOT *Laws fr. Heaven* II. xxiv. 197 We shall not be spoilt by over-doses of loving kindness. **1916** [see COBBER *sb.*[2]]. **1931** H. CRANE *Let.* 22 June (1965) 375, I have to leave most of this to your judgment of the potency and malfeasance of an overdose of tequila. **1952** M. LASKI *Village* ix. 147 An overdose of Miss Beltram produced the inevitable effect..you couldn't help taking the other point of view. *a* **1953** E. O'NEILL *Long Day's Journey* (1956) III. 105, I hope, sometime, without meaning it, I will take an overdose. **1965** *New Statesman* 7 May 729/3 Rosetti's..wife died after only two years of marriage, of an overdose of drugs. **1971** *Black Scholar* June 53/2 There are brothers..who have been singled out for overdoses of the atrocities that we are being subjected to. **1973** *Times* 16 July 14/7 Others were either seeking immediate emotional release or were trying to produce a dramatic effect on friends or relatives—and in both such cases an overdose achieved the desired result.

,overˈdose, *v.* [OVER- 27.]

1. *trans.* To administer (medicine, etc.) in too large a dose.

1727 SOMERVILLE *Martial Epigr.* 47 in *Occ. Poems* 128 A merry Bottle to engender Wit, Not over-dosed, but *Quantum sufficit.* **1777** WRIGHT in *Phil. Trans.* LXVII. 511 Fatal accidents have happened..from over-dosing the medicine.

2. To dose (a person, etc.) to excess; to give too large a dose to; also *transf.* of the admixture of an ingredient, the issuing of stock, etc.

1758 REID tr. *Macquer's Chem.* I. 228 As apt to take fire as common Sulphur, if it were not over-dosed with the Acid. **1822–34** *Good's Study Med.* (ed. 4) I. 151 If we over-dose the patient at first, we add to the disease. **1893** *Daily News* 13 Feb. 2/6 Neither Paris nor London has been overdosed with new issues of foreign stocks for years past.

3. *intr.* To take an overdose of drugs. Hence **ˈoverdosing** *vbl. sb.*

1973 R. LUDLUM *Matlock Paper* xxx. 261 The doctor told me that he'd prescribe heavier 'medication' but warned me not to overdose. **1974** G. MCDONALD *Fletch* (1976) xvii. 100 She was dead... He guessed she had overdosed. **1977** *Times* 19 Jan. 14/2 Heroin smoking..throws overdosing figures into doubt. **1977** WOOD & GEASLAND *Twins* 21 You don't take a full bottle of an anticonvulsant if you mean to overdose on Seconal.

overdoze, *v.*: see OVER- 27.

over-drafe, -drave, obs. pa. t. OVER-DRIVE.

ˈover,draft (-drɑːft, -æ-). [OVER- 27.]

1. *Banking.* The action of overdrawing an account; a draft on a bank in excess of the sum standing to the drawer's credit; the amount by which a draft exceeds the balance against which it is drawn.

1878 JEVONS *Prim. Pol. Econ.* xiii. 114 A banker naturally takes care not to allow overdrafts, unless he has great confidence in his customer, or has received a guarantee of repayment. **1891** *Pall Mall G.* 22 Aug. 6/2 The company has a banking overdraft of £135,000.

2. An excessive draft of men, esp. for military purposes, also *fig.*

1902 *Westm. Gaz.* 5 Feb. 3/2 So it went on, until the country was exhausted by these overdrafts.

over-drain: see OVER- 29 b.

ˈover,draught, -,draft (-drɑːft, -æ-). [OVER- 1.] A draught passing over or admitted from above a fire, furnace, kiln, etc. *attrib.* in ***overdraft kiln***, a form of brick- or tile-kiln in which the heated products of combustion are made to pass down through the contents of the kiln before escaping by the chimney flue or flues.

1884 DAVIS *Manuf. Bricks*, etc. vi. 278 The circular, domed 'over-draft' kilns are largely used for burning fire-bricks and terra-cotta products. *Ibid.* vii. 323 The principal gain in the circular overdraft kilns is, the impartial and equitable distribution of heat.

'overdraw, *sb.* [f. next.]

1. An act of overdrawing; an excessive draft or demand.

1873 H. SPENCER *Stud. Sociol.* viii. (1874) 197 There is such an overdraw on the energies of the industrial population [of France] that a large share of heavy labour is thrown on the women.

2. (In full *overdraw check.*) = OVERCHECK rein. *U.S.*

1902 A. D. MCFAUL *Ike Glidden* xvi. 122 He was prancin' ..until he got him hitched inter this new bitin' gear an' overdraw. **1905** *Springfield* (Mass.) *Weekly Republ.* 8 Sept. 5 Much has been accomplished to abolish the pernicious practice of docking horses, but it is just as important that the abuse of the overdraw check should be corrected.

overdraw (əʊvə'drɔː, ˌəʊvə'drɔː), *v.* Forms: see DRAW *v.* [OVER- 10, 4, 11, 27.]

I. †**1. a.** *trans.* To draw over or across. (Separable comb.) *Obs.*

1375 BARBOUR *Bruce* xv. 286 In-till a litill spass, Thar flot all weill our drawyn wass. *c* **1400** *Sowdone Bab.* 2183 Cheynes he didde ouer drawe That noo man passe myght.

b. To draw off into another vessel. *Obs.*

1703 *Art & Myst. Vintners* 34 Overdraw the Hogshead of Wine some five or six Gallons. *Ibid.* 56 If the Claret be not sound and good, overdraw it 3 or 4 gallons, then replenish the Vessel with as much good Wine Red.

†**2.** *intr.* To draw or move over or across; to pass over or away. *Obs.*

c **1400** *Destr. Troy* 673 Sone the day ouerdroghe & the derke entrid. *Ibid.* 7630 When the derke ouerdrogh, & þe dym voidet, The stourme wex still, stablit the course. *a* **1415** LYDG. *Temple of Glas* 610 Alas! when shal þis tempest ouerdrawe, To clere þe skies of myn aduersite.

†**3.** *trans.* To draw over or induce to some course: see DRAW *v.* 26, 28. *Obs.*

1603 FLORIO *Montaigne* I. xlvii. (1632) 155 A higher power forsooth us over-drawes, And mortall states guides with immortall lawes.

II. 4. *Banking.* To draw money in excess of the amount which stands to one's credit, or is at one's disposal. *Const.* To overdraw *one's account* (*allowance*, *salary*, etc.); formerly, *one's banker*; also *absol.*, to make an overdraft.

1734 BERKELEY *Let. to Prior* 30 Apr., Wks. 1871 IV. 227, I hope Skipton's first payment hath been made,..otherwise I have overdrawn. *c* **1766** COWPER *Let. to J. Hill* Wks. 1837 XV. 11, I am sorry my finances are not only exhausted, but over-drawn. **1798** *Geraldina* I. 195 He was my banker,.. and used to give me a lecture whenever I overdrew him. **1848** THACKERAY *Van. Fair* xliv, How the bankers and agents were overdrawn. **1878** JEVONS *Prim. Pol. Econ.* xiii. 113 One of the simplest ways of lending money is to allow customers to overdraw their accounts. **1890** 'R. BOLDREWOOD' *Col. Reformer* (1891) 263 Don't overdraw.. more than you can help.

5. To draw too far; to strain.

1889 *Electrical Rev.* XXV. 574/2 Mr. A. has..overdrawn the bow in endeavouring to make out [etc.].

6. To exaggerate or overdo in drawing, depicting, or describing.

a **1817** JANE AUSTEN *Northanger Abbey* (1818) II. vii. 140 Characters, which Mr Allen had been used to call unnatural and overdrawn. **1844** E. E. NAPIER *Wild Sports Europe*, etc. I. 204 Are not all these yarns about India rather overdrawn? **1850** F. W. NEWMAN *Phases Faith* 210 Many biographies overdraw the virtue of their subject. **1912** *Chambers's Jrnl.* June 359/1 Perhaps it will be said that the above statements are over-drawn.

7. *intr.* In card-games: to exceed the maximum permissible score by drawing too many cards. Also *refl.*

c **1805** JANE AUSTEN *Watsons* in J. E. Austen Leigh *Mem. J. Austen* (1871) 358 Vingt-un is the game at Osborne Castle... Lord Osborne enjoys it famously... I wish you could see him over-draw himself on both his own cards. *c* **1863** T. TAYLOR in M. R. Booth *Eng. Plays of 19th Cent.* (1969) II. 150 (*Draws card.*) Thirty-four—overdrawn—confound it! Now let's see your hand. **1950** *Hoyle's Games Modernized* (ed. 20) 158 Many players habitually stand at fifteen, and if the dealer is a reckless player, with a tendency to overdraw, it may be good policy to stand upon an even smaller figure.

Hence **over'drawer**, one who overdraws a bank account, or has an overdraft; **ˌover-'drawing** *vbl. sb.*; **'over'drawn** (stress var.) *ppl. a.*, that has been overdrawn; *spec.* (of tea) infused too long.

1413 *Pilgr. Sowle* (Caxton) I. iv. (1859) 5 Smertely was my syght derkyd by ouer drawynge of a grete corteyne. **1463** *Mann. & Househ. Exp.* (Roxb.) 235 Payd for pesynge off bowys and ovyrdrawynge off bowis. **1846** MRS. GORE *Sk. Eng. Char.* (1852) 134 On the first overdrawing of his account. **1847** A. BRONTË *Agnes Grey* xii. 189 Other thoughts assisted to..impart a relish to the cup of cold, overdrawn tea. **1866** CRUMP *Banking* iii. 76 With overdrawn accounts only the sum required is drawn, and on that alone interest is charged. **1883** SCHAFF *Hist. Church* I. iv. 268 The dramatic account of James by Hegesippus is an over-drawn picture. **1906** W. DE MORGAN *Joseph Vance* xxxvii. 378 Among the overdrawers, C. Vance & Co. was a conspicuous instance, figuring for a good round sum among the Debtors. **1969** V. C. CLINTON-BADDELEY *Only Matter of Time* 94 Cigarettes and cups of overdrawn tea.

over-dread, -dream: see OVER-.

†**over'dredge**, *v.*[1] *Obs.* [f. OVER- 8 + DREDGE *v.*[2]] *trans.* To sprinkle powder over.

1594 NASHE *Terrors of Nt.* Wks. (Grosart) III. 226 Vpon a haire they [spirits] will sit like a nit, and ouer-dredge a bald pate like a white scurffe.

over-dredge (ˌəʊvə'drɛdʒ), *v.*[2] [f. OVER- 27 + DREDGE *v.*[1]] *trans.* To dredge (for oysters, etc.) too much, so as to deplete the beds or waters. Hence **ˌover-'dredging** *vbl. sb.*

1862 ANSTED *Channel Isl.* IV. xxii. (ed. 2) 509 M. Costa.. has repeopled a number [of oyster beds]..exhausted by over-dredging. **1882** *Standard* 18 Feb. 5/2 The beds were over-dredged, undersized oysters were brought to market.

overdreep, obs. variant of OVERDRIP *v.*

'over-dress, *sb.* [OVER- 8c, 29d.]

1. a. An outer dress; a dress worn over another.

1812 SIR R. WILSON *Priv. Diary* I. 247, I hurt myself..by falling on a pocket pistol which I carry in my over-dress. **1975** *Country Life* 6 Feb. 346/1 The chemise has now become universally known as the overdress..because..we have been pulling it over sweaters and shirts. **1976** *Ibid.* 19 Feb. 442 The beautiful, bright-green suede overdress by Jean Muir.

b. The outer part of a gown made to appear as if one dress were worn over another, showing in parts the underdress; the two parts being of different material or colour.

1881 *Truth* 31 Mar. 446/1 The second [dress] is of dark-blue Genoa velvet, with Pompadour overdress of palest blue. **1891** *Ibid.* 10 Dec. 1240/2 A superb dinner-gown,.. The under-dress..has a front of white satin,..The over-dress is in velvet of..dahlia red.

2. (*'over-'dress*). Excessive display in dress.

1824 *Body & Soul* (ed. 4) I. 60 An absurd aim at preposterous over-dress.

ˌover'dress, *v.* [OVER- 27.]

1. *trans.* To dress to excess; to dress with too much display and ornament. Also *intr.* for *refl.*

1706 WALSH in *Pope's Lett.* (1735) I. 58, I have seen many Women over-dress'd, and several look better in a careless Night-gown, with their hair about their ears. **1731** POPE *Ep. Burlington* 52 Treat the Goddess like a modest fair, Nor over-dress, nor leave her wholly bare. **1880** *Daily Tel.* 4 Nov., Servants waste their wages.., they overdress and squander. **1883** *American* VII. 169 They don't overdress themselves.

2. To embellish too elaborately.

1866 *Sat. Rev.* 7 Apr. 421/1 Theocritus..never overdoes his subject or overdresses his language. **1947** *Sat. Rev. Lit.* (U.S.) 1 Mar. 23/2 There are times, too, when Mr. Miller overdresses the phrasing of his dialogue.

3. To dress or cook (food) too much.

1775 ADAIR *Amer. Ind.* 412 In order to destroy the blood, ..they over-dress every kind of animal food they use. **1802** BEDDOES *Hygëia* IV. 31 To overdress the meat till it is unfit to be eaten.

Hence **ˌover'dressed** *ppl. a.*; **ˌover'dressiness**; **ˌover-'dressing** *vbl. sb.*

1820 M. EDGEWORTH *Let.* 10 Aug. in C. Colvin *M. Edgeworth in France & Switz.* (1979) 209 Enter 3 English ladies overdressed in silks blonde and flowers! **1836** DICKENS *Sunday under Three Heads* i. 2 There is a great deal of very unnecessary cant about the over-dressing of the common people. **1874** J. BROWN *Let.* 4 Sept. (1907) 240 We saw the Duke with his eagle's feather, the Duchess in purple and lace, petite and overdressed. **1891** O. WILDE *Pict. Dorian Gray* i. 9 After I had been in the room about ten minutes, talking to huge overdressed dowagers and tedious Academicians, I suddenly became conscious that some one was looking at me. **1927** *Daily Express* 26 Aug. 1 What would look indecent in a London hotel becomes overdressiness here. **1932** W. W. JACOBS *Night-Watchman* iv. 680 Nothing looks worse than an over-dressed woman. **1939** JOYCE *Finnegans Wake* 441 What's overdressed if underclothed? **1962** J. D. MACDONALD *Girl* ix. 113, I got maybe forty [girls] stripped entire... Compared to them sixty broads, I was *over-dressed*. **1975** J. F. BURKE *Death Trick* (1976) ix. 132 An overdressed old mama.

†**over-'dreve**, *v. Obs. rare.* [In form from OVER- 8 + DREVE *v.*, but the sense appears to be connected rather with DRIVE *v.*] *trans.* To stud as with nails driven in over the whole surface.

c **1400** *Rowland & O.* 1205 Alle his armours was ouer dreuede With stones of grete renoun.

ˌover-'drink, *v.* [OE. *oferdrincan* = OHG. *ubartrinchan*, MHG. *übertrinken*, Du. (*zich*) *overdrinken*; f. *ofer-*, OVER- 27 + *drincan* to DRINK. The 16th c. use may be a new formation: cf. OVEREAT *v.*] *intr.* and *refl.* To drink too much, drink to excess or to intoxication.

c **897** K. ÆLFRED *Gregory's Past. C.* xlix. 381 Swa hwa swa oðerne drencð, he wirð self oferdruncen. *c* **1000** *Eccl. Inst.* c. 40 in Thorpe *Laws* II. 438 Ne oferdrincað ȝe eow wines. **1577** *Test. 12 Patriarchs* (1706) 69 Ashamed to over-drink himself. **1598** SYLVESTER *Du Bartas* II. ii. I. *Ark* 541 Noah.. One-day..making merry drinking, over-drunk. **1626** BACON *Sylva* §462 Cucumbers..doe extremely affect Moisture; And over-drinke themselves. **1730** BURDON *Pocket Farrier* (1735) 21 If he..is hot, he will over-drink himself. **1865** MILL in *Even. Star* 10 July, It did not say that they were to over-eat and over-drink themselves. **1904** 'J. O. HOBBES' *Vineyard* iv. 55 They over-eat and over-drink, and they try to forget what they really want. **1932** KIPLING *Limits & Renewals* 79, I steadily overdrank for a fortnight out of pure hunger. **1952** H. WAUGH *Last seen Wearing* (1953) 53 She..says he's a show-off and over-drinks. **1967** N. FREELING *Strike Out* 29 Typical Bavarian, overate, overdrank, no exercise. **1976** *Times* 20 Oct. 14/3 Many of us over-eat, over-drink, and over-smoke.

So **'overdrink** *sb.*, drinking to excess, drunkenness; **ˌover-'drinking** *vbl. sb.*

[*c* **897** K. ÆLFRED *Gregory's Past. C.* xviii. 129 Behealdað eow ðæt ȝe ne ȝehefeȝien eowre heortan mid oferæte & oferdrynce.] *c* **1175** *Lamb. Hom.* 153 Hwenne þe muð.. suneȝeð on muchele ete and on ouer drinke. *a* **1902** S. BUTLER *Way of all Flesh* (1903) vi. 23 Even his excellent constitution was not proof against..over-feeding and what we should now consider overdrinking. **1906** *Westm. Gaz.* 19 Sept. 2/3 The Bishop of Oxford, in the protest..against the over-drinking of healths, appears to think that little was done in the way of similar protest between the far-off days of King Ahasuerus..and those of Queen Victoria. **1907** *Ibid.* 29 Oct. 12/1 The publicans are held responsible for the over-drinking of their customers. **1928** J. J. WALSH *Catholic Church & Healing* vi. 66 Bartholomew was aware, moreover, that insanity may come from overeating as well as from the overdrinking of strong wine. **1951** T. STERLING *House without Door* vii. 89 Her hands..had that luminous, slightly puffy look which comes from overdrinking. **1974** E. BRAWLEY *Rap* (1975) 4 And her mother..had followed him two years later of love and overdrink. **1977** *Times* 7 Sept. 7/6 A first line of recovery from over-drink.

†**over'drip**, *v. Obs.* Also 6 -dreep(e. [f. OVER- 1 + DRIP *v.*: cf. OVERDROP *v.*] *trans.* To drip over; to overhang, overshadow; also *fig.*

1587 GOLDING *De Mornay* xi. 157 When thou seest it [the Sea] ouerdreepe the earth, and threaten it with drowning. **1592** NASHE *P. Penilesse* I ij, The aspiring nettles with their shadie tops shall no longer ouer-dreep the best hearbs, or keep them from..the sunne. **1601** SIR W. CORNWALLIS *Ess.* II. lii. (1631) 332 These.. plants, that grow in the shadow, ..since greatnesse cannot so overdrip them. *a* **1659** BP. BROWNRIG *Serm.* (1674) I. ii. 25 They may sometimes over-drip us, but they are a shelter to us. **1897** F. THOMPSON *New Poems* 176 Shake the lilies till their scent Over-drip their rims. **1898** A. S. WAY tr. *Tragedies of Euripides* III. 198 'The altar, overdripped with Hellene blood?'..'Blood-russet are its rims in any wise.'

overdrive (see below), *v.* [OE. *oferdrífan* = MHG. *übertrîben*, Du. *overdrijven*, f. *ofer-* OVER- 4, 5, 17, 10, 27 + *drífan* to DRIVE.]

†**1.** *trans.* (*over'drive*). To drive away, dispel; to overthrow. *Obs.*

a **950** *Durham Ritual* (Surtees) 38 God ðv ðe ðiostro gidvoles wordes ðines lehte oferdrifest [L. *depellis*]. *c* **1000** ÆLFRIC *Saints' Lives* (1885) I. 232 Oðþæt se eadiȝa petrus þone arleasan ofer-draf. **1375** BARBOUR *Bruce* IV. 661 Bot feill anoyis thoill ȝhe sall,..Bot ȝhe sall thame ourdriff ilkane. **1573** *Satir. Poems Reform.* xxxix. 22 And, as I dout not, wil ourdryue thir dangeris.

†**2.** *trans.* To cause (time) to pass; to bring to an end; to pass; spend. *Sc. Obs.*

1375 BARBOUR *Bruce* XIX. 481 Qwhen thai [that] day ourdrivyn had. **1528** LYNDESAY *Dream* 32 More pleasandlie the tyme for tyll ouerdryue. *a* **1550** *Freiris of Berwik* 417 in *Dunbar's Poems* 299 On this wyiss the lang nicht thay ourdraif. *a* **1600** MONTGOMERIE *Misc. Poems* xxxix. 26 Sair weeping, but sleeping, The nichts I ouerdryve.

b. *intr.* Of time: To pass away, elapse. Of a person: To let the time pass; to delay. *Obs.*

1375 BARBOUR *Bruce* V. 3 Quhen vyntir tyde Vith his blastis..Wes ourdriffin. *a* **1400-50** *Alexander* 1505 Sone þe dyrke ouer-drafe & þe day springez. *c* **1450** *St. Cuthbert* (Surtees) 5253 þus þai our draue som what lange. **1513** DOUGLAS *Æneis* XIII. ix. 51 The lang..nycht Gan schape full fast to mak schort and ourdryve. **1533** BELLENDEN *Livy* V. (1822) 437 The time wes lang oure drevin but ony inclinacioun of victorie to athir side.

†**3.** *trans.* To drive over. *Obs. rare.*

c **1420** *Sir Amadace* (Camden) xlviii, Stithe stormes me ore-drofe.

4. (ˌəʊvə'draɪv). To drive too hard; to drive or work to exhaustion; to overwork. Also *fig.*

a **1450** MYRC 1813 When þat he ys so ouer-dryue[n] þat he may no lengur lyue[n]. **1551** BIBLE *Gen.* xxxiii. 13 Ewes and kyne with yong..which yf men shoulde ouerdryue but euen one daye, the hole flocke woulde die. **1677** GILPIN *Demonol.* (1867) 341 Satan is gradual in his temptations..and is very careful he do not over-drive men. **1703** COLLIER *Ess. Mor. Subj.* II. (1709) 176 They don't over-drive their Business. **1884** *Expositor* Jan. 26 He..ruins his analogy by overdriving it.

5. *Golf.* To drive farther than (an opponent); to outdrive.

1900 *Gentl. Mag.* Feb. 126 If the opponent is a longer driver one is spared the temptation..of pressing to avoid being overdriven.

Hence **ˌover'driving** *vbl. sb.*

1837 DE QUINCEY *Revolt of Tartars* in *Blackw. Mag.* July 101/2 The cattle suffered greatly from over-driving. **1909** *Chambers's Jrnl.* Mar. 203/1 The electrical equipment is provided with suitable automatic devices to prevent over-driving. **1972** *Science* 16 June 1236/2 Control of the intensity is necessary to prevent overdriving by strong signals.

'overdrive, *sb.* [OVER- 26.] **1. a.** In a motor vehicle, a speed-increasing gear which may be brought into operation in addition to the ordinary (reducing) gears, so providing a gear higher than direct drive (the usual top gear), and in some cases correspondingly raising other gears, and thereby enabling engine speed to be reduced for a given road speed.

1929 *Trans. Soc. Automotive Engineers* XXIV. 335/1 The functioning of a transmission with either an over-drive or an underdrive through a double-internal-gear set in combination with a suitable clutch is exactly equivalent to that of a two-speed axle. **1932** ELLIOTT & CONSOLIVER *Gasoline Automobile* (ed. 4) xviii. 479 As a general thing, the high gear [on heavy trucks and buses] is a direct drive, although in some cases the high gear ratio is an overdrive, that is, the engine crankshaft turns at a slower speed than the propeller shaft. **1938** *Times* 23 Aug. 8/5 The overdrive is engaged by merely pushing in a lever just below the instrument board. **1958** *Times* 1 Oct. 8/3 To this can be added at extra cost a Laycock de Normanville overdrive operating on second and top gear. **1959** [see *gear ratio* s.v. GEAR *sb.* IV]. **1959** C. CAMPBELL *Sports Car* (ed. 2) ix. 174 Some designers prefer to use the overdrive on top gear only, giving in effect a 5-speed gear-box. Others prefer to make it operative on both top and third, so that overdrive third gear is an intermediate step between direct third and direct top. **1970** *Motoring Which?* July 83/1 The 3-litre was comfortable up to about 95 mph (helped by its overdrive on 3rd and top). **1973** J. WAINWRIGHT *Devil you Don't* 5 It was a great car—a Jag. Mark II—well capable of three-figure speeds at the flick of the overdrive switch.

b. *fig.*

1962 L. DEIGHTON *Ipcress File* i. 18 Dalby's voice trailed off as he slipped his mind into over-drive. **1967** *Times* 28 Oct. 20/2 Always the narrative is in smooth overdrive, even when it whisks you in successive paragraphs through Haiti ..or the Preseli. **1969** *Times* 13 Dec. p. iv/7 The Websters knew everyone... Here, too, are Lilian Baylis and Sybil Thorndike, in overdrive as ever. **1970** G. GREER *Female Eunuch* 44 If women find that the clitoris has become the only site of their pleasure instead of acting as a kind of sexual overdrive in a more general response, they will find themselves dominated by the performance ethic. **1977** *Rolling Stone* 30 June 101/1 He shifts into overdrive on the first track, a fiery and propulsive Clarke composition entitled 'The Heat of the Battle', and never looks back for the whole album.

2. *Science Fiction.* = HYPERDRIVE.

1953 [see INTERSTELLAR *a.*].

overdriven (ˈəʊvəˈdrɪv(ə)n: stress var.), *ppl. a.* Also 8 -drove. [Pa. pple. of OVERDRIVE *v.*]

1. That is driven too hard.

1767 *Ann. Reg.* 96 An over-drove ox, entering the Guildhall, threw the whole Court into consternation. **1849** MACAULAY *Hist. Eng.* x. II. 601 The sufferings..of an overdriven post-horse. **1884** ANNIE S. SWAN *Dorothea Kirke* iii. 30 The wandering of an over-driven brain.

b. *fig.* Used to excess, hackneyed.

1888 W. MINTO in *Encycl. Brit.* XXIV. 670/2 The banishment of a few overdriven phrases and figures of speech from poetic diction.

2. Driven or made to project beyond the general line.

1830 *Edin. Encycl.* IV. 503 An overdriven Keystone, or Console, as it is termed, is one of the most usual ornaments of the Archivolt.

overdroop: see OVER-.

†**overˈdrop**, *v. Obs.* [OVER- 1.] *trans.* To drop over or upon; to overhang, overshadow.

1608 DOD & CLEAVER *Expos. Prov.* xi–xii. 135 Their toppes aloft, and braunches broad, and thereby ouerdroppe all that is under them. **1677** in *Cleveland's Gen. Poems* Ep. Ded. A iv, How enviously our late Mushrom-wits look up at him because he overdroppeth them.

†**overˈdrown**, *v. Obs.* [OVER- 8.] *trans.* To flood with water; to submerge, inundate; to drench or wet excessively. Hence †**overˈdrowned** *ppl. a.*, †**overˈdrowning** *vbl. sb.*

c **1400** tr. *Secreta Secret., Gov. Lordsh.* 59 Yn rayns fallys thondres & leuenynges, & ouer-drownynges þurgh flodes. **1579** FENTON *Guicciard.* (1618) 255 Subiect to raines, which, by reason of the lownesse of the place, do so ouerdrowne it. **1615** BROWNE *Brit. Past.* II. i. 7 Casting round her ouer-drowned eyes. **1633** FORD *Love's Sacr.* II. iv, Those eyes, Which lately were so overdrown'd in tears.

over-drowse, -drugging: see OVER-.

ˈ**over-ˈdry**, *a.* [OVER- 28.] Too dry. So ˈ**over-ˈdryness**, excessive dryness.

1591 SYLVESTER *Du Bartas* I. ii. 396 The better so, with a moist cold, to temper Th' one's over-drinesse, th' other's hot distemper. **1616** SURFL. & MARKH. *Country Farme* 500 That brings it [hay] to a rottennesse or ouer-drinesse, which is verie ill for milke. **1626** BACON *Sylva* §706 Either by an over-dry heat, or an over-moist heat. **1879** *Encycl. Brit.* X. 753/2 In extremely frosty weather..they acquire so little moisture that then a difficulty arises from their over-dryness. **1891** W. SCHLICH *Man. Forestry* II. 32 *Dry Mould* ..is formed by the decomposition of certain lichens on over-dry soil. **1959** A. H. NISSAN *Textile Engin. Processes* xi. 293 It is then necessary to bring up the water content of the overdry parts by re-moistening them to a uniform and acceptable value. **1962** J. T. MARSH *Self-Smoothing Fabrics* xiii. 199 If the fabric is not sufficiently dry, then the subsequent mechanical operation is adversely affected; if the fabric is over-dry, then the durability of the finish, but not the initial effect, is adversely affected.

ˌ**over-ˈdry**, *v.* [OVER- 27.] **a.** *intr.* To become too dry, dry up. **b.** *trans.* To dry too much, make too dry. Hence **over-ˈdrying** *vbl. sb.*

1495 *Trevisa's Barth. De P.R.* XVII. clxxx. (W. de W.) V vij/2 In grauely londs..the vyne ouerdryeth [*Bodl. MS.* fordrieþ] and faylleth. **1621** BURTON *Anat. Mel.* I. ii. I. i. (1676) 43/1 Buttered meats, condite, powdred, and over-dryed. **1867** K. H. DIGBY *Day on Muses' Hill* 146 The subsoil may be overdried. **1888** *Encycl. Brit.* XXIV. 657/1 Over-drying of wool has to be specially guarded against. *Ibid.* 657/2 Unless the wool is spread with great evenness.. at points where the hot air escapes freely it may be much over-dried. **1959** A. H. NISSAN *Textile Engin. Processes* xi. 293 It has already been demonstrated that overdrying the material before it is allowed to leave the drier consumes disproportionately longer time than drying it to the water content required in use. *Ibid.*, Unless there is close control, manual or automatic, on the uniformity of the final moisture content of the material in all directions, it is necessary to overdry the material so that its wettest part is within drying specification. **1962** J. T. MARSH *Self-Smoothing Fabrics* iii. 24 For many years the effect of drying has been recognised by the practical dyer in a qualitative manner, and there has been much warning as to the dangers of 'over-drying'. **1966** A. W. LEWIS *Gloss. Woodworking Terms* 14 *Check*,..also called 'honeycombing'; due to over-drying too rapidly in the kiln.

overˈdub, *v.* [f. OVER- 8 + DUB *v.*[5]] *intr.* and *trans.* To impose (additional sounds) on to an existing recording. So **overˈdubbing** *vbl. sb.*

1962 *John o' London's* 16 Aug. 162/4 His particular interest lies in multi-taping, or 'overdubbing'. **1969** *Rolling Stone* 28 June 19/1 On rhythm dates I only do bass, drums, guitar, overdub the guitar, overdub whatever,..and then Al overdubs the strings, the horns, or whatever. **1970** *Times* 18 July 7 Apparently Crosby, Stills and Nash went back to the studios to overdub their vocals on 'Suite: Judy Blue Eyes', but the rest are left as orginally played. **1971** *Times* 5 Jan. 9 She also prefers to use her own voice, overdubbed several times, as a backing choir. **1973** *Sci. Amer.* Apr. 2/2 (Advt.), Overdubbing has become a familiar term to every knowledgeable musician... To overdub properly, the artist recording on the second track has to listen to the material recorded on the first track while performing in perfect synchronization to it. **1977** *New Yorker* 8 Aug. 66/3 The singing actors..then overdubbed the lyrics.

Hence ˈ**overdub** *sb.*, an act or instance of imposing additional sounds on to an existing recording.

1976 in *6,000 Words* 146 The last big album it took them eight months of overdubs to produce. *Ibid.*, Vocal overdubs. **1976** *Gramophone* Aug. 353/2 By means of numerous synchronized re-recordings or 'overdubs', a typical pop recording is now built up over a period of days or weeks. **1977** MCKNIGHT & TOBLER *Bob Marley* vi. 83 Wayne Perkins..is supposed to have added some overdubs.

overdue (ˈəʊvəˈdjuː: stress var.), *a.* [OVER- 24 b.] More than due; past the time when due. **a.** Of a bill, debt, etc.: Remaining unpaid after the assigned date. **b.** Of a ship, train, etc.: That has not appeared, or arrived, at the time fixed.

1845 STEPHEN *Comm. Laws Eng.* (1874) II. 97 Overdue bonds for the payment of money. **1858** SIMMONDS *Dict. Trade*, *Overdue*,..as an unpaid account or bill of exchange; a vessel, train, etc. past time. **1884** *Weekly Notes* 17 May 124/1 Mortgage debentures of the company, the interest on which was overdue. **1899** *Daily News* 2 Mar. 9/1 It is of vast importance, when an overdue ship is reported to be safe, that those concerned should know it. *a* **1904** *Mod.* The train is already half an hour overdue.

c. Of a library book: that has been retained by the borrower or reader longer than the period allowed; ***overdue notice***, a notification sent to a reader requesting the return of an overdue book. Hence as *sb.*, an overdue book.

1890 T. GREENWOOD *Public Libraries* xxiii. 376 With this, as with other indicators,..books are shown in or out instantaneously,..and overdue books can be detected with little trouble. *Ibid.* 378 The borrowers' cards if arranged in a series of dated compartments, can be made to show the overdues. **1903** J. D. BROWN *Man. Library Economy* xxix. 384 Overdue books could easily be detected by a register of this kind, on simply scanning the column of returns, filled up by the librarian. *Ibid.* 387 This personal form of ledger ..makes the detection of overdues difficult. **1938** L. M. HARROD *Librarians' Gloss.* 109 *Overdue notice*, a request to a reader asking for the return of books which have been kept out beyond the time allowed. **1965** SMITH & BAXTER *College Library Administration* vii. 133 Whether the incidence of seriously overdue books is significantly reduced by charging fines is a matter for conjecture. **1966** E. V. CORBETT *Introd. Librarianship* (ed. 2) I. xviii. 205 (*heading*) Fines and over-dues. *Ibid.* 206 Other libraries may find that it is more economical to send out the first overdue notice not earlier than two months after the date due for return. **1970** *Times* 19 Nov. 15/6 He smiled only when he had returned them, like library books both overdue and unread, to the safety of the house. **1978** T. ALLBEURY *Lantern Network* xiii. 199 A library reminder for two overdue books.

d. Of a woman: not having had a menstrual period at the expected time. *colloq.*

1970 M. TRIPP *Man without Friends* iii. 28 She placed her hand on mine, tenderly, 'I'm not overdue,' she said. **1972** F. WARNER *Maquettes* 16 He doesn't even know I'm overdue. And he hasn't had it for a week. **1976** D. FRANCIS *In Frame* viii. 115 She's feeling sick... I don't want a kid yet. She isn't overdue or anything.

over-dull, -dure, -dust: see OVER-.

overˈdye, *v.* [OVER- 8.] *trans.* To dye (something already dyed) with a second dye. Hence **overˈdyeing** *vbl. sb.*

1946 HORSFALL & LAWRIE *Dyeing of Textile Fibres* (ed. 2) iv. 71 The question of overdyeing particularly concerns the production of shirtings or dress materials which are woven from grey unmercerised cotton, together with grey cotton dyed with fast-to-bleaching dyestuffs, and either undyed or dyed immunised cotton. These goods are piece bleached and overdyed with dyestuffs fast to light and washing in such a manner that the immunised and dyed cotton effects are unaffected. **1952** *Dyeing of Nylon Textiles* (I.C.I.) xi. 124 A two-bath process is necessary, the Vat dyestuff first being applied and oxidized and the union material then being over-dyed with the acid dyestuff.

†ˈ**over-dyed**, *ppl. a. Obs.* [OVER- 8.] Dyed over with a second colour.

1611 SHAKS. *Wint. T.* I. ii. 132 But were they false As o're-dy'd Blacks, as Wind, as Waters.

ˈ**over-ˈeager**, *a.* [OVER- 28.] Too eager, excessively eager or keen.

1575 TURBERV. *Faulconrie* 333 [She] feedeth so greedily upon it by reason she was kept overeager and sharp. **1684** J. GOODMAN *Wint. Ev. Conf.* I. (1705) 20 Extravagance in the more modest and private, but over-eager pursuits of these Recreations [games of chance]. **1865** DICKENS *Mut. Fr.* II. xii, Over-eager for the cause of justice.

Hence ˈ**over-ˈeagerly** *adv.*, ˈ**over-ˈeagerness**.

a **1600** HOOKER *Eccl. Pol.* VII. xvii. §4 Of such nature, that to himself no man might over-eagerly challenge them, without blushing. **1670** MILTON *Hist. Eng.* v. Wks. (1847) 532 Pursuing them overeagerly into York. *a* **1720** SHEFFIELD (Dk. Buckhm.) *Wks.* (1753) II. 100 Such an over-eagerness, ..instead of hurting me, only exposes themselves. **1885** *Spectator* 25 July 963/2 Over-eagerness for office had compelled them to sacrifice all their respectable principles.

ˈ**over-ˈearly**, *adv.* and *a.* [OVER- 30, 28.] Too early; premature; prematurely.

[*c* **1400** *Rule St. Benet* (E.E.T.S.) 11 þe barne þat is done fra his modir milke ouir-arlike.] **1605** BACON *Adv. Learn.* I. v. §4 Another Errour..is the ouer-early and peremptorie reduction of Knowledge into Arts and Methodes. **1856** MRS. BROWNING *Aur. Leigh* I. 56 Children learn by such Love's holy earnest in a pretty play And get not over-early solemnised. **1871** C. KINGSLEY *At Last* II. x. 49 This over-early marriage among the Coolies is a very serious evil. **1922** M. E. CHRISTIE *Henry VI* iv. 119 The young Henry..now found the responsibilities of government over-early thrust upon him.

ˈ**over-ˈearnest**, *a.* [OVER- 28.] Too earnest. So ˈ**over-ˈearnestly** *adv.*, ˈ**over-ˈearnestness**.

[**1581** PETTIE tr. *Guazzo's Civ. Conv.* I. (1586) 6 It is not good..to occupie your minde ouer earnestlie.] *a* **1586** SIDNEY *Arcadia* (1622) 285 His men following ouer-earnestly. **1601** SHAKS. *Jul. C.* IV. iii. 122 Yes Cassius,.. When you are ouer-earnest with your Brutus, Hee'l thinke your Mother chides, and leaue you so. **1774** BURKE *Amer. Tax.* Wks. II. 392 Some mischief happened..from this over-earnest zeal. **1864** WEBSTER, *Overearnestness*.

ˈ**over-ˈeasy**, *a.* [OVER- 28.] Too easy. So ˈ**over-ˈeasily** *adv.*, ˈ**over-ˈeasiness**.

1597 HOOKER *Eccl. Pol.* v. xxix. §2 S. Ierome, whose custome is not to pardon ouer-easily his Aduersaries. **1626** DONNE *Serm.* iv. 33 Him that is over-easie to be scandalized. **1843** J. H. NEWMAN *Miracles* 340 The historian had no leaning towards over-easiness of belief. **1977** A. WILSON *Strange Ride R. Kipling* iii. 153 Trix's view of Violet Garrard has been..over-easily accepted.

†ˈ**overeat**, *sb. Obs.* [OE. *oferǽt* masc., f. **oferetan*: cf. OS. *ovarât*, OHG. *ubarâz*.] The action, or an act, of overeating; a surfeit.

c **897** K. ÆLFRED *Gregory's Past. C.* xviii. 129 Behealdað eow ðæt ȝe ne ȝehefeȝien eowre heortan mid oferæte & oferdrynce. *c* **1200** *Trin. Coll. Hom.* 63 Wiðtiȝing of est-metes, and oueretes, and untimliche etes.

overeat (ˌəʊvərˈiːt), *v.* [OVER- 27, 22, 8. (An OE. **oferetan* = OHG. *ubarezzan*, MHG. *überezzen*, is not recorded.)]

1. *intr.* and *refl.* To eat too much, eat to excess, surfeit oneself with eating.

1599 T. M[OUFET] *Silkwormes* 43 Yet hath your fruit this blotte, to ouer-eate, And glutton-like to vomit vp their meate. **1678** MRS. BEHN *Sir P. Fancy* IV. iii, Nay, Sir, he hath overeaten himself at breakfast. **1848** THACKERAY *Van. Fair* xiv, She has only overeaten herself—that is all. **1879** [see MOST *a.* II. 5 e]. **1888** NYE & RILEY *Railway Guide* 8 My appetite is four sizes too large for a man of my height and every little while I over-eat. **1904** [see OVER-DRINK *v.*]. **1944** L. P. HARTLEY *Shrimp & Anemone* iii. 33 You must see that he doesn't..over-eat himself. **1946** M. C. SELF *Horseman's Encycl.* 291 A horse that from illness or some other cause is not being exercised will overeat. **1967** [see OVER-DRINK *v.*]. **1972** D. S. MCLAREN *Nutrition & its Disorders* viii. 158 The view, commonly held, that all obese people overeat has not been substantiated by several surveys.

†**2.** *trans.* To eat more than (another): in quot., by his cattle. *Obs.* (Cf. EAT *v.* 6 b.)

1523 FITZHERB. *Husb.* §123 Than shall not the ryche man ouer-eate the poore man with his cattell.

†**3.** To eat or nibble all over or on all sides.

fig. **1606** SHAKS. *Tr. & Cr.* v. ii. 160 The fragments, scraps, the bits, and greazie reliques, Of her ore-eaten faith are bound to Diomed.

Hence **overˈeaten** *ppl. a.* (see 3); ˌ**overˈeating** *vbl. sb.*

1828 MISS MITFORD *Village* Ser. III. (1863) 105 She..sent me cakes with cautions against over-eating, and needle-cases with admonitions to use them. **1892** *Spectator* 19 Mar. 403 The greedy dog, which continually falls ill from over-eating.

over-edit: see OVER-.

over-ˈeducate, *v.* [OVER- 27.] *trans.* To educate to excess or for too long. So **over-ˈeducated** *ppl. a.*; ˌ**over-ˈeducatedness**.

1845 J. S. MILL in *Edin. Rev.* LXXXI. 510 The fears of the patrons and managers lest the poor should be 'over-educated'. **1899** W. JAMES *Talks to Teachers* 257 To be imprisoned or shipwrecked or forced into the army would permanently show the good of life to many an over-educated pessimist. **1922** N. COWARD *Coll. Sketches & Lyrics* (1931) 24 I've over-educated myself in all the things I shouldn't have known about at all. **1935** D. L. SAYERS *Gaudy Night* xvii. 364 How many women care..about anybody's intellectual integrity? Only over-educated women like us. **1970** *Time* 19 Oct. 66 Critics contend that..new students are being 'over-educated' for non-existent jobs. **1970** *Worship* Oct. 491, I distinctly recall how self-conscious I felt of my over-educatedness the moment I sat down with him. **1977** *N.Y. Rev. Bks.* 14 Apr. 43/1 (Advt.), Seattle

Professional Man, 36, newly settled, witty, travelled, over-educated, gentle, 5'9", seeks attractive woman counterpart.

over-egg, *v.* [OVER- 27 a.] *fig.*, in phr. ***to over-egg the pudding***, to argue a point with disproportionate force; to exaggerate.

1892 *Review of Reviews* Jan. 8/2 It is possible to over-egg your pudding and M. Stambuloff is doing it. **1961** *Daily Tel.* 9 Feb. 24/3 Mr Foot seems to have been ill served by his seconder, Mr Will Griffiths.., who is reported to have made the mistake of 'over-egging the pudding'. **1976** *Times* 2 Nov. 4/5 Mr Page, though remaining confident, wonders whether some of the recent [election] forecasts may have over-egged his pudding.

over-elaborate to **over-emphasize**: see OVER-.

over-em'ployment. [OVER- 29 b.] A situation in which vacancies for jobs, esp. skilled jobs, exceed the number of unemployed, producing a labour shortage; a state of insufficient unemployment.

1944 *Times* 9 Nov. 5/3 Sir William Beveridge believes that ..'Full employment'..'should mean a floating balance of not more than about three per cent unemployed'... The dangers of inflation implicit in an attempt to secure 'over-employment' are real enough in any full employment policy. **1958** *Times* 11 June 11/5 The contraction of demand has been felt in the United States in the form of unemployment, and in Great Britain in a relaxation of the state of over-employment.

over-emptied to **over-encrust**: see OVER-.

† **'over-'end, overend.** *Obs.* [OVER *a.* + END *sb.*, written as one word; see OVER- 1 d.] The upper end, the top.

[*a* **1300** See OVER *a.* 1 β. *c* **1440** *Jacob's Well* 214 Syttynge on þe ouer ende of a laddere.] **1448** in Willis & Clark *Cambridge* (1886) II. 8 At the netherend squar vij inch and at the overend vi inches. **1551** [see OVER *a.* 1 β]. **1725** in S. O. Addy *Hall of Waltheof* (1893) 155 A place..called Campo Lane, being the overend of the said croft.

over-engage: see OVER-.

,over-engi'neer, *v.* [OVER- 26, 27.] *trans.* To engineer to a standard higher than is technically necessary, or to an extent greater than is technically desirable. Hence **over-engi'neering** *vbl. sb.*

1964 M. GOWING *Britain & Atomic Energy 1939–1945* ix. 259 Certain units were very much 'over-engineered' which in itself led to complications. **1967** *Gramophone* Dec. 317/1 Walter gives the warmest reading, though..the recording is certainly over-engineered. **1971** *Flying* Apr. 89/2 (Advt.), The brakes have been purposely over-engineered by twenty percent. **1977** *Gramophone* June 113/2 Some over-engineering seemed to have taken place, however, at the expense of complete fidelity.

,over-'english, *v. Obs. rare*$^{-1}$. [OVER- 27.] *trans.* To overdo in English; to exaggerate in description. (Cf. Shaks. *Merry W.* I. iii. 52.)

1599 B. JONSON *Ev. Man out of Hum.* (Dram. Pers., Puntarvolo), A vain-glorious knight, over-englishing his travels.

over-enjoy to **over-enrichment**: see OVER-.

,over-'enter, *v.* [OVER- 26 or 27.] *trans.* To enter (an item in an account) in excess of the proper amount. So **,over-'entry**, an excess entry.

1769 BURKE *Pres. St. Nat.* Wks. II. 74 Every thing which the author can cut off with any appearance of reason for the over-entry of British goods. **1812** J. SMYTH *Pract. Customs* (1821) 337 The over entry must be obtained in the following manner: On the back of the Warrant, at the bottom, must be certified the quantity of the goods over entered, thus: Upon examination, we find the merchant has over entered sixty-seven pounds of thrown Silk. *Ibid.*, *note*, Explanation of the London mode of making out Over Entry Certificates.

over-en'thusiasm. [OVER- 29 d.] An excess of enthusiasm. So **,over-enthusi'astic** *a.*

1927 *Melody Maker* Aug. 781/2 Some of my readers.. have said that I am over-enthusiastic about Harry Richman. **1962** A. NISBETT *Technique Sound Studio* viii. 148 Over-enthusiasm has..resulted in the operator flicking the disc completely free from the turntable and skimming it across the room! **1962** A. BATTERSBY *Guide to Stock Control* viii. 77 There is also the over-enthusiastic salesman who offers to provide non-standard varieties of his company's products. **1970** *Nature* 24 Oct. 303/1 An over-enthusiasm for classifying projects of very marginal secrecy may have hampered progress. **1976** M. DRABBLE *Genius of T. Hardy* 166 The dog that destroys Gabriel Oak's sheep is over-enthusiastic, not malicious.

overeorninde, -ernne, obs. ff. OVERRUNNING, -RUN.

† **'overer**, *a.* and *sb.*[1] *Obs.* [Comparative of OVER *a.*: cf. OHG. *oberôro*, MHG. *oberer*, and Eng. INNERER.]

A. *adj.* Upper; higher in position.

1388 WYCLIF *Job* xxxviii. 30 The ouer [*v.r.* ouerer] part of occian. *c* **1430** *Art Nombryng* (E.E.T.S.) 12 That the last of the lower nombre may not be with-draw of the last of the ouerer nombre for it is lasse than the lower.

B. *sb.* (the adj. used elliptically).

1. The upper part or region.

a **1340** HAMPOLE *Psalter* Prol. 3 An instrument..of ten cordis, and gifes þe soun fra þe ouerer, thurgh touchynge of hend. *Ibid.* ciii. 3 þou þat hilis wiþ watirs þe ouerer of it [L. *superiora eius*]. *Ibid.* 14 Wetand hilles of his ouyrere [L. *de superioribus suis*].

2. The upper of two things.

c **1430** *Art Nombryng* (E.E.T.S.) 10 In the place of the ouerer sette a-side, write a digit that is a part of the componede. *Ibid.* 16 Suche a digit founde and withdraw fro his ouerer.

3. A person higher in station, a superior.

c **1449** PECOCK *Repr.* Prol. 1 Correccioun..longith oonli to the ouerer anentis his netherer, and not to the netherer anentis his ouerer. *Ibid.* 299 Forwhi in two maners ouerers mowen holde and vse her ouerte vpon her vndirlingis.

overer ('əʊvərə(r)), *sb.*[2] *local.* [f. OVER *adv.* + -ER.] See quot.

1892 E. B. JAMES *Lett. I. of Wight* (1896) II. 347 The local and familiar word 'overers', by which the people of the Isle of Wight designate such of the inhabitants as are not born natives. **1892** *Edin. Rev.* July 237 The list of 'overers' whose connection with it has enriched its fame, is longer and more brilliant.

over-e'ruption. *Dentistry.* [OVER- 29.] Excessive extension of a tooth in the direction of the opposing teeth.

1961 H. R. B. FENN et al. *Clin. Dental Prosthetics* (ed. 2) xxiii. 628 Consideration must be given..to the extraction of the offending tooth..if the over-eruption is gross. **1975** H. THOMSON *Occlusion* viii. 130 Over-eruption of unopposed teeth..can be prevented by the muscle forces of tongue or cheek.

So **over-e'rupt** *v. intr.*, to undergo or exhibit over-eruption; **over-e'rupted** *ppl. a.*

1961 H. R. B. FENN et al. *Clin. Dental Prosthetics* (ed. 2) xxiii. 628 (*heading*) Over-erupted teeth. **1963** C. R. CROWELL et al. *Inlays, Crowns & Bridges* vii. 79 This wear may proceed to such an extent that the opposing teeth gradually overerupt. **1974** E. M. BARNETT *Pediatric Occlusal Therapy* vi. 161/1 The twin-wire arch is set so that the anterior wires lie slightly apical to where they should lie if the teeth were not overerupted.

† **'overest**, *a.*, *sb.*, *adv. Obs.* [Superlative of OVER *adj.* and *adv.*: cf. OHG. *obarôst*, MHG. *oberest*, Ger. *oberst*; also the Eng. *utterest*.]

A. *adj.* **1.** Highest in position, uppermost; outermost, covering all the rest.

1382 WYCLIF *Exod.* xxxix. 21 And thei maden..a hode in the ouerest [1388 hiȝere, Vulg. *superiori*] parti aȝens the myddel. *c* **1386** CHAUCER *Prol.* 290 Ful thredbare was his ouereste courtepy. **1481** CAXTON *Godeffroy* cv. 161 The oueste part of hym fyl to the ground and that other parte abode styll syttyng on the hors. **1483** —— *Gold. Leg.* 81 b/1 Anon she wente in to ouerest parte of her hows.

2. *fig.* Highest in station, quality, etc.

1481 CAXTON *Reynard* (Arb.) 68 Who that wylle taste of the ouerest wysehede..he muste faste and make hym redy ayenst the hye festes. **1567** *Gude & Godlie B.* (S.T.S.) 43 They straif quha suld be ouerest. [**1894** F. S. ELLIS *Reynard* 214 For they who overest wisdom love, Must fast against the festals high.]

B. *sb.* **1.** The uppermost part or region.

a **1300** *E.E. Psalter* ciii. 3 þat hiles with watres overestes [L. *superiora*] his. **14..** *Stockh. Med. MS.* I. 137 in *Anglia* XVIII. 298 Scome of þe ouerest twye or thrye, And þanne late it stonde kole & drye.

2. A person supreme over others; a ruler.

1474 CAXTON *Chesse* III. ii. (1883) 88 As sone as the masse is doon he deliuerith hit to his ouerest or procuratour. **1483** —— *Gold. Leg.* 376 b/1 By the commaundemente of his oueryst and requeste of the kynge he was sente in to.. Englond.

C. *adv.* In the highest or uppermost place; over all, so as to cover all the rest.

a **1450** *Le Morte Arth.* 846 An Appille ouereste lay on lofte, There the poyson was in dighte. *a* **1450** *Cov. Myst.* (Shaks. Soc.) 307 (*Stage Direct.*) Thei xal don on Ihesus clothis, and overest a whyte clothe.

,over-e'steem, *v.* [OVER- 27.] *trans.* To esteem too highly, or beyond the true worth; to think too highly of.

a **1639** W. WHATELEY *Prototypes* I. xix. (1640) 239 Pride is a vice..in this, that it causeth a man to over-esteeme himselfe. **1745** J. MASON *Self Knowl.* II. x. (1853) 158 He does not overesteem them for those little accidental Advantages in which they excel him.

,over-'estimate, *v.* [OVER- 27.] *trans.* To estimate too highly; to reckon or value at too high a rate.

1823 J. S. MILL in *Bermondsey Bk.* (1929) VI. 16, I may be told..that I over-estimate the effect of these motives on bad men. **1825** —— in *Westm. Rev.* Apr. 297 The habitual propensity of mankind to over-estimate advantages which they do not possess. **1840** R. H. DANA *Bef. Mast* xxiii. 73 Like most self-taught men he over-estimated the value of an education. **1858** LD. ST. LEONARDS *Handy-bk. Prop. Law* xx. 155 A man over-estimating the value of his property, or not allowing for its depreciation.

So **'over-'estimate** *sb.*, too high an estimate; **'over-esti'mation**, the action of over-estimating.

1809 HAN. MORE *Cœlebs* I. xix. 275 An over-estimation of character..is an infirmity from which even worthy men are not exempt. **1846** WORCESTER, *Overestimate*, too high an estimation. *Norton.* **1854** C. M. YONGE *Heartsease* I. II. xv. 357 A very good child, but spoilt..by John's over-estimate of her. **1856** LEVER *Martins of Cro' M.* 124. **1895** *Geogr. Jrnl.* VI. 184 The liability..to an over-estimate of density [of population]. **1899** *Westm. Gaz.* 15 Feb. 8/1 The loss through systematic over-estimates..will probably amount to £200,000. **1977** *Listener* 17 Mar. 327/1 The real membership of the Labour Party..is now 445,000..and.. even this figure is probably an overestimate.

over-exact to **over-excelling**: see OVER-.

,over-ex'cite, *v.* [OVER- 27.] *trans.* To excite too much.

1825 J. NEAL *Bro. Jonathan* I. 25 If he were over excited. **1865** *Pall Mall G.* 4 Aug. 3/1 The whole principle of the cure is to excite, and not over-excite, the organic activities.

So **'over-ex'cited, 'over-ex'citing** *ppl. adjs.*; also **'over-excita'bility; 'over-ex'citable** *a.*; **'over-ex'citement.**

1822 M. EDGEWORTH *Let.* 7 Jan. (1971) 313, I shall so arrange and *limit* our goings out..that Fannys health shall not suffer by over excitement. **1836** SIR H. TAYLOR *Statesman* xi. 78 One who should feel himself to be over-exciteable in the transaction of business. **1847** WEBSTER, *Overexcitement.* **1849** H. MAYO *Pop. Superstit.* v. 81 France appears to be..a product of over-excitability, which time blunts. **1856** LEVER *Martins of Cro' M.* 376 The mere wanderings of an overexcited mind. **1884** J. SULLY *Outlines of Psychol.* xi. 466 All transition from states of over-excitement to modes of quiet activity is agreeable.

over-exercise: see OVER- 29 b.

,over-e'xert, *v.* [OVER- 27.] *trans.* To exert too much; usually *refl.* to exert oneself beyond one's strength, to put forth too much effort. So **'over-e'xertion**, excessive exertion.

1837 *Lett. fr. Madras* (1843) 66 He fell a victim to over-exertion of mind and body. **1848** DICKENS *Dombey* ii, 'Don't you over-exert yourself, Loo', said Chick. **1882** MISS BRADDON *Mt. Royal* II. iii. 46 Be sure that she doesn't over-exert herself.

over-expenditure, etc.: see OVER-.

over-ex'ploit, *v.* [OVER- 27.] *trans.* To exploit excessively. So **,over-exploi'tation; over-ex'ploited** *ppl. a.*

1922 W. SCHLICH *Man. Forestry* (ed. 4) I. 273 The more accessible areas of the merchantable forests have been considerably over-exploited in the past. **1952** G. SARTON *Hist. Sci.* I. xi. 296 The mines were overexploited in the fifth century. By the middle of the following century only old workings were open. **1957** MANVELL & HUNTLEY *Film Music* iv. 191 Like all good ideas, they tend to be over-exploited to their own detriment. **1961** *Carolina Q.* Spring 18 It seems that only in today's Southern fiction does Tobacco Road..continue to live—but only as a weary, overexploited phantom. *Ibid.* 21 This legend..well deserves a rest after the overexploitation of the past century. **1963** *Times* 6 Feb. 8/7 U. P. Gerasimov and E. K. Fedorov, commenting on over-exploitation of fisheries, alleged that trawlers..'are ploughing the seas near African and Asian shores in search of fish'. **1964** V. J. CHAPMAN *Coastal Vegetation* vi. 137 The question has been asked whether such dunes are the result of man's negligence or over-exploitation. **1970** *New Scientist* 3 Dec. 374/1 Improved international cooperation should limit overexploitation of important [fish] stocks. **1977** *Sci. Amer.* May 26/1 The floods of 1969 in Tunisia replenished all the reservoirs that up to then had been described as overexploited.

,over-ex'pose, *v.* [OVER- 27.] *trans.* To expose too much; *spec.* in *Photogr.* to expose (a sensitized plate) to the light for too long a time, so as to produce a faulty negative. Also *absol.* So **'over-ex'posed** *ppl. a.*

1869 *Eng. Mech.* 3 Dec. 281/3 By judicious management of the developer, an over-exposed and under-exposed plate can be made to work equally well. **1890** *Anthony's Photogr. Bull.* III. 287 The best negatives are not those taken the quickest; sooner over expose, than under expose. **1894** B. POTTER *Jrnl.* 12 Sept. (1966) 338 Went to Berwick again with papa who had over-exposed on Monday. We got out at Tweedmouth and he photographed from the same side at first and afterwards amongst the boats. **1925** B. BEETHAM in E. F. Norton *Fight for Everest, 1924* 325 We were all inclined to under-expose in tropical Sikkim and to over-expose in arctic Tibet. **1937** AUDEN & MACNEICE *Lett. from Iceland* iv. 45 In Iceland, even if you are using a meter, there is a tendency to over-expose. *a* **1963** S. PLATH *Ariel* (1965), 46, I could draw no breath, Dead and motionless, Over-exposed, like an X-ray. **1971** *Radio Times* 23 Sept. 62 They hope that by not being over-exposed they'll be able to last longer, keep their standard higher. **1976** *Gramophone* Dec. 978/2 Nobody could say that this much maligned instrument [*sc.* the saxophone] is over-exposed now that it has faded from the pop scene.

Hence **'over-ex'posure** *sb.*; *spec.* an excessive number of public appearances by an entertainer, actor, or the like.

1873 *Routledge's Yng. Gentl. Mag.* Sept. 615 My portraits will suffer from over-exposure. **1889** *Atlantic Monthly* Nov. 586 Passion cannot possibly hold out. It gets chilled by over-exposure. **1947** *Radiology* XLIX. 364/2 Is the peripheral blood picture as reliable an indicator of over-exposure as radiologists have considered it to be? **1969** *Guardian* 15 July 18/4 The company's general manager said that 'over-exposure' of records inhibited sales. **1971** *Ibid.* 6 Feb. 6/6 Future plans? A repeat of the 'Basil Brush Show' on the BBC, but careful avoidance of overexposure. **1974** *Times* 1 Feb. 19/6 We are all for exposure [on television], but we are against over-exposure. As anyone knows who handles films and photographs, you get unwanted results from over-exposure. **1974** *Physics Bull.* May 179/1 CO is not cumulative either in man or the environment but although moderate overexposure seems to cause no permanent damage to health, concern has been expressed about possible effects on the foetus following exposure of the pregnant mother. **1978** *Times* 5 Jan. 5/5 Perhaps renaissance is only the flip-side of over exposure.

over-express to **over-extreme**: see OVER-.

over-ex'tend, *v.* [OVER- 27.] *trans.* **a.** To extend or reach further than (something). *rare.* **b.** To extend (a thing) too far. **c.** To take on (oneself) or impose on (another) an excessive burden of work, commitments, etc.; to attempt more than is practicable. Hence **over-ex'tended** *ppl. a.*; **over-ex'tension.**

1937 R. ERSKINE *Stout Adventure M. Stewart* iii. 62 A culture and a civilization,..which, reckoned in the gross, outweighed and over-extended by a deal feudal, that is to say, English culture, manners and customs. **1938** *Sun* (Baltimore) 6 May 3/5 We are no longer over-extended in new construction or in capital equipment. **1962** L. DAVIDSON *Rose of Tibet* ii. 46 The arrangement was for a car to pick him up..but when..no car appeared, he realized he must have overextended Mr. Mukherjee, and took a bus instead. **1963** C. R. COWELL et al. *Inlays, Crowns & Bridges* iii. 25 The air-turbine instrument is usually less unpleasant for the patient, but there is risk of overextension. *Ibid.* vi. 64 If a temporary crown is overextended cervically the gingivae may be forced back. **1966** *Economist* 5 Mar. 898/2 Mr McNamara has defended himself vigorously, calling it 'absolutely false to say that we are over-extended.' **1968** *Blues Unlimited* Dec. 12 He never overextended himself and impressed with his command of the idiom. **1970** F. C. WEFFORT in I. L. Horowitz *Masses in Lat. Amer.* xi. 386 The sociological analysis..often considers what is merely possible, thus overextending the limits which the Brazilian historical situation allows for in the way of planned social change. **1973** *Daily Tel.* 7 Feb. 16 They have over-extended themselves in the purchase of jumbo jets and do not wish to make further capital commitments at this time. **1976** *National Observer* (U.S.) 3 July 9/4 In much the same way ..it's easy to overextend yourself on vacations by scheduling too much sight-seeing and other activity.

†**over-'eye**, *v. Obs.* [OVER- 1 (*c*).] *trans.* To cast one's eye over, have an eye to; to watch, observe; to look after, watch over, take care of.

1588 SHAKS. *L.L.L.* IV. iii. 80 Here sit I in the skie, And wretched fooles secrets heedfully ore-eye. **1638** FORD *Fancies* v. i, 'Twere better live a yeoman, And live with men, than over-eye your horses, Whilst I myself am ridden like a jade. **1681** RYCAUT tr. *Gracian's Critick* 64 A Woman,..who diligently over-eyed, and watched her Charge.

†**'over,face**, *sb. Obs.* [OVER- 1 d.] Upper face, surface.

c **1400** *Apol. Loll.* 91 Wene we not þe gospel to be in wordis of writingis, but in wit; not in ouer face, but in þe merowe. **1561** T. NORTON *Calvin's Inst.* IV. xx. 169 The liuing creatures that are on the ouerface of the earth.

over'face, *v.* [OVER- 21, 8.]

1. a. *trans.* To look out of countenance, to abash or overcome, *esp.* by boldness or effrontery; = OUTFACE *v.* 1; in recent use also, to alarm or intimidate (a person, animal, etc.) by presenting too great a task or obstacle. Hence **over'faced** *ppl. a.*

c **1535** R. LAYTON *Let. to Cromwell* in *West's Antiq. Furness* (1805) 144 Nor then we cannot be our fayssede, nor suffer any maner injurie. *a* **1587** FOXE *A. & M.* (1847) VII. XI. 149 The lord chancellor earnestly looked upon him, to have, belike, over-faced him. **1607** MARKHAM *Caval.* II. (1617) 206 If you make a strange horse stand before him, as it were to ouer-face him. **1831** EVERETT *Blacksmith* (1834) 99 (E.D.D.) The parson, poor young man! was overfaced with us, and could not preach. **1926** A. BENNETT *Lord Raingo* I. xliv. 196 There she stood, over-faced and dumb and apologetic in her plain brown dress. *Ibid.* lvii. 254 He scorned them, but in their collectivity they still over-faced him. **1944** *R.A.F. Jrnl.* Aug. 261 You cannot imagine any situation which would over-face them. **1950** W. A. RILEY in C. R. Acton *Dog Ann. 1951* 94 Personally, I think it is a great mistake to over-face them [*sc.* dachshunds], they are so game and will 'have a go', but they are not killers. **1958** *Times* 13 Dec. 9/4 Undoubtedly one of the most important points to remember is not to 'overface' the pony or its enthusiastic rider. **1971** R. ROBERTS *Classic Slum* vi. 94 Lower-class women, bold enough to enter a pub but too 'overfaced' to sit, ..stood crushed together drinking in the 'Outdoor'. *Ibid.* vii. 109 Social intimidation..confused and 'overfaced' the simple. **1976** *Horse & Hound* 10 Dec. 69/3 (Advt.), This horse has been brought on slowly, never being overfaced.

†**b.** To brazen out, to carry off with a bold face; = OUTFACE 4. *Obs.*

1600 ABP. ABBOT *Exp. Jonah* 530 Boldly to over-face that, which justly may be reproved.

†**2.** To cover the face or surface of. *Obs.*

1632 LITHGOW *Trav.* x. 498 The delectable planure of Murray.., ouerfaced with a generous Octauian Gentrye.

over-facility, -fag, -faith: see OVER- 27–29.

overfall ('əʊvəfɔːl), *sb.* [OVER- 5, 6.]

1. *Naut.* A turbulent surface of water with short breaking waves, caused by a strong current or tide setting over a submarine ridge or shoal, or by the meeting of contrary currents. Also *transf.* and *fig.*

1542 UDALL *Erasm. Apoph.* 119b, A daungerous goulfe, makyng sore ouerfalles by reason of the meetyng of soondry streames in one pointe. **1599** HAKLUYT *Voy.* II. II. 36 Certaine Currants, which did set to the West Southwestward so fast as if it had bene the ouerfall of a sand, making a great noyse like vnto a streame or tide-gate when the water is shoale. **1633** T. JAMES *Voy.* 40 We..came amongst many strange races, and ouer-falles. **1726** SHELVOCKE *Voy. round World* 386 The frightful riplings and over-falls of the water. **1748** *Anson's Voy.* III. ii. 315 This tide runs at first with a vast head and overfall of water. **1774** M. MACKENZIE *Maritime Surv.* Plate IV, Overfalls; or rough, breaking Seas. **1867** J. MACGREGOR *Voy. Alone* (1868) 75 All over the British Channel there are patches of sand, shingle, or rock..even without any wind they cause the tide-stream to rush over them in great eddies and confused bubbling waves... These places are called..in some charts *overfalls.* **1947** A. C. DOUGLAS *Gliding & Advanced Soaring* i. 32 The cloud currents, the heat turbulence, high winds and mountain overfalls, which the aeroplane pilot finds so unpleasant or even dangerous, are regarded by the sail-plane pilot as friends, not as enemies. **1961** B. FERGUSSON *Watery Maze* iv. 89 Radiating in every direction from C.O.H.Q. were heavy overfalls, as they are called in seaman's parlance, or troubled waters, in landsmen's, needing more than a modicum of oil. **1970** *Motor Boat & Yachting* 16 Oct. 35/1 We didn't bother to avoid an area marked on the large scale chart with those squiggly lines that denote dangerous overfalls. **1975** J. R. L. ANDERSON *Death in North Sea* viii. 139 There were two main tidal streams... They might run up to about two knots, with a somewhat faster rate by some overfalls off Spurn Head.

2. A sudden drop in the sea-bottom, as at the edge of a submarine terrace or ledge.

1798 S. WILCOCKE in *Naval Chron.* (1799) II. 61 It is broken ground, and overfalls of about half a fathom, every cast of the lead. **1804** A. DUNCAN *Mariner's Chron.* I. 300, I heard that he had very great overfalls, from twenty seven to thirteen fathoms at one cast, when he was standing in the bay towards the village of Felix. **1817** *Chron.* in *Ann. Reg.* 562/2 The channel..is perfectly clear of shoals, but the overfalls are sudden from 15 to 21 and 12 to 7 fathoms. **1859** R. F. BURTON *Centr. Afr.* in *Jrnl. Geog. Soc.* XXIX. 236 The shingly shore shelves rapidly, without steps or overfalls, into blue water.

3. A waterfall in a river, a cataract or rapid.

1596 RALEIGH *Discov. Gviana* 67 Marched ouer land to view the strange ouerfals of the riuer of Caroli, which rored so farre of... There appeared some ten or twelve ouerfals in sight, every one as high ouer the other as a Church tower. **1600** J. PORY tr. *Leo's Africa* Introd. 44 It is reported that Nilus doth the like at his Cataracts or ouerfals. **1613** *Voy. Guiana* in *Harl. Misc.* (Malh.) III. 195, I travelled up the river of Wiapoco, to view the overfalls. **1811** D. BUCHAN in K. Winter *Shananditti* (1975) ii. 24 This day's distance is estimated at eleven miles allowing seven from the island.. up to the overfall. **1921** H. GUTHRIE-SMITH *Tutira* i. 5 A meandering serpentine creek..which..breaks into a series of overfalls.

4. A structure to allow the overflow of water from a canal or a lock on a river, when the water reaches a certain level. (Also used to keep the water up to the required level.)

1791 W. JESSOP *Rep. River Witham* 15 Culverts and Overfalls, £90. **1805** Z. ALLNUTT *Navig. Thames* 22 The new constructed open Weir at Windsor,..it will be perceived how trifling..stop or pen, it can possibly make when the moveable Gates, Overfalls, and Rimers are taken away. **1829** SOUTHEY *Inscript. Caled. Canal* 2 in *Anniversary* 196 [Thou hast seen] the rivulet Admitted by its intake peaceably, Forthwith by gentle overfall discharged. **1846** KANE tr. *Rühlman on Turbines* 23 In the watercourse,..is to be built up a partition of boards, or, as it is termed, an overfall. **1881** TAUNT *Thames Map* 13/2 The village [Streatley], with the weirs and overfalls in the foreground.

5. *Comb.*, as **overfall-mill**, a mill worked by an overshot wheel; **overfall-weir**, a weir which water passes over.

1615 G. SANDYS *Trav.* 127 So plentifull a streame, as able to turn an ouerfall mill. **1861** SMILES *Engineers* II. 467 A little above it was an ancient overfall weir.

overfall (əʊvə'fɔːl), *v.* [OE. *oferfeallan* = MHG. *übervallen*, Ger. *überfallen*; MDu., Du. *overvallen* to attack, surprise: see OVER- 7, 6.]

1. *trans.* To fall upon or over.

c **1200** ORMIN 4799, & tær fell dun þatt hus þurrh wind, & oferrfell hemm alle. *a* **1425** *Cursor M.* 16661 (Trin.) þe hilles shul þei bidde ouerfalle vs. **1895** A. NUTT *Voy. Bran* 190 A thick mist overfell them.

b. To fall upon, attack, assail.

971 *Blickl. Hom.* 203 Hie..oferfeollan þa ðe þa..yrmþo ʒenæson. **1382** WYCLIF *Lev.* xx. 27 With stonus men shulen overfalle hem. **1837** CARLYLE *Fr. Rev.* I. III. viii. 144 Silence: which some liken to that of the Roman Senate overfallen by Brennus.

2. *intr.* To fall over.

[*a* **1300** *E.E. Psalter* lvii[i]. 9 Over fel þe fire sa bright (1382 WYCLIF, fyr fel ouer).] **1530** TINDALE *Pract. Prelates* Wks. (Parker Soc.) II. 251 It cannot be chosen but that many shall overfall. **1844** MRS. BROWNING *Duchess May* xcv, Horse and riders overfell.

Hence **over'falling** *vbl. sb.*, a falling over.

18.. J. WILSON *Trees* in *Blackw. Mag.*, The shape being indistinct in its regular..over-fallings, and over-foldings, and over-hangings, of light and shade.

over-famed: see OVER- 27 b.

'over-fa'miliar, *a.* [OVER- 28.] Too familiar. So **'over-famili'arity**, too much familiarity; **'over-fa'miliarly** *adv.*, too familiarly.

1491 CAXTON *Vitas Patr.* (W. de W. 1495) I. clviii. 164 a/2 Pardonne..yf I ouerfamylyerly do declare my pouertee unto you. **1529** MORE *Dyaloge* I. Wks. 127/1 The pore man ..had founde ye priest ouer famyliar with his wife. **1601** B. JONSON *Poetaster* III. i, His over-familiar playing face. **1631** MASSINGER *Emp. East* v. i, His confirm'd suspicion,..That you have been over-familiar with her. **1676** TOWERSON *Decalogue* 74 The extreme in excess, which is an over-familiarity with our Maker. **1862** C. J. VAUGHAN *Bk. & Life, Triple Vail* 12 The ignorance of over-familiarity must be grappled with even like that of non-acquaintance. **1936** R. W. CHAPMAN *S.P.E. Tract* XLVII. 237 'Your wife' may be over familiar, if I do not know Jones very well. **1955** H. KUTTNER in Aldiss & Harrison *Decade 1950s* (1976) 173 He saw the reflection of the over-familiar scene. **1976** B. BALL *Keegan: One-Way Deal* 16 Holmyard frowned. Ross was over-familiar. There was a time and a place for such things.

over-famous to **over-fancy:** see OVER-.

'over-'far, *adv.* [OVER- 30. In ME. and mod. dial. written as two words.] Too far; to too great a distance, extent, or degree.

[*a* **1300** *Cursor M.* 4894 Ar þai ouer far be on þeir fare. *c* **1400** *Destr. Troy* 6123 And ouer fer on þi fose fare by þi seluyn! *c* **1450** *St. Cuthbert* (Surtees) 454 We won our farr fra þe wode.] **1523** LD. BERNERS *Froiss.* I. ccxxxii. 322 They durst nat aduenture ouerfarr. **1597** HOOKER *Eccl. Pol.* v. ix. §2 Such rules are not safe to be trusted ouer-farre. **1634** W. TIRWHYT tr. *Balzac's Lett.* 154, I fear lest my zeal should over-far transport me. **1720** STRYPE *Stow's Surv.* (1754) I. I. xxx. 323/2 That the poor might not go over-far to Church. [*Mod. Sc.* Dinna gange owre ferr.]

†**over'fare**, *v. Obs.* [OE. *oferfaran* = OHG. *ubarfaran*, MG. *übervarn*, Ger. *überfahren*, MDu., Du. *overvaren*: see OVER- 9, 10.]

1. *intr.* To pass over, across, or through.

c **1000** *Ags. Ps.* (Spelm.) x. 1 Oferfare on munt swa swa spearwa. *c* **1250** *Gen. & Ex.* 2487 To flum iurdon..he ben cumen, And ouer pharan til ebron. **13..** *Guy Warw.* (A.) 1241 Anoþer ȝer þow miȝt ouer fare.

2. *trans.* To pass over, to cross, traverse.

a **1000** *Cædmon's Gen.* 1801 (Gr.) Hi..forð oferforan folcmæro land. *a* **1023** WULFSTAN *Hom.* (Napier) 210 Moyses oferfor þa readan sæ. *a* **1250** *Owl & Night.* 387 An over-vareth fele theode. *a* **1300** *E.E. Psalter* cxxiii[i]. 5 Over-faren had our saule swift-lik Watre þat was un-tholand-lik.

over-fast, -fastidious, etc.: see OVER-.

'over-'fat, *a.* [OE. *oferfæt*: see OVER- 28.] Too fat. *lit.* and *fig.*

c **1050** *Suppl. Ælfric's Voc.* in Wr.-Wülcker 172/10 *Obesus*, oferfæt. *a* **1568** ASCHAM *Scholem.* II. (Arb.) 112 As certaine wise men do, that be ouer fat and fleshie. **1609** C. BUTLER *Fem. Mon.* v. (1623) K iij, If they be ouer-fat, or want a Ruler, undoubtedly they will not prosper. **1897** *Allbutt's Syst. Med.* IV. 614 The over-fat are certainly a bad class.

'over-fa'tigue, *sb.* [OVER- 29.] Too great fatigue; excessive fatigue.

1727 BRADLEY *Fam. Dict.* s.v. *Bee*, Many of them die thro' their Over-fatigue and Labour. **1768–74** TUCKER *Lt. Nat.* (1834) II. 617 Some over-fatigue, or cold, or external accident. **1899** *Allbutt's Syst. Med.* VII. 257 In states of over-fatigue..the arterial blood is..run at high pressure.

,over-fa'tigue, *v.* [OVER- 27.] *trans.* To fatigue too much, to overtire. Hence **'over-fa'tigued** *ppl. a.*

1741 WATTS *Improv. Mind* I. xiv. §12 Do not over-fatigue the spirits. **1838** LYTTON *Alice* I. vii, You are pale, you have over-fatigued yourself. **1897** *Allbutt's Syst. Med.* IV. 494 The tremor..which may be observed in over-fatigued muscles.

overfault ('əʊvəfɔːlt). *Geol.* [OVER- 3 + FAULT *sb.* 9.] A term applied to a fault of which the inclination or *hade* is in the opposite direction to what it is in a normal or ordinary fault, that is, towards the upthrow side (hence also called *inverted* or *reverse* fault).

The result is that the dislocated strata, instead of slipping down the fault-plane (as in a normal fault), have been pushed or slidden up and over the fault-plane: see OVERTHRUST.

1883 LAPWORTH in *Geol. Mag.* X. Aug. 342 The various stages of rock deformation under lateral pressure (folds, overfolds, overfaults, and overthrusts). —— *in Letter to Editor*, An overfault is sometimes produced by the development of an overfold until it has a plane of dislocation or 'thrust-plane' in lieu of its middle limb.

,over-'favour, *v.* [OVER- 27.] *trans.* To favour, like, or take to (a thing) too much.

1610 HOLLAND *Camden's Brit.* I. 315 King Henrie the third, ouer-favouring forrainers, granted the Honor de Aquila..to Petre Earle of Savoy. **1867** OUIDA *C. Castlemaine* (1879) 9 She did not over-favour her exile in the western counties.

'over-'favourable, *a.* [OVER- 28.] Too favourable. So **over-'favourably** *adv.*

1538 STARKEY *England* I. iv. 140 Seyng they are ouer-fauerabyl therin. **1617** HIERON *Wks.* II. 164 Fearing..that he should deale somewhat ouer-fauourably with himselfe. **1877** RAYMOND *Statist. Mines & Mining* 4 The conditions of such a test are usually overfavorable to the process.

†**'over-'fear**, *sb. Obs.* [OVER- 29.] Too great fear; excess of fear.

1639 FULLER *Holy War* v. xii. (1647) 251 In such over-fear they were no less injurious to themselves than to the western Pilgrimes.

†**,over-'fear**, *v. Obs.* [OVER- 27.] *intr.* To fear too much. So **,over-'fearing** *vbl. sb.*

a **1591** [see OVER-LOVE]. **1630** B. JONSON *New Inn* IV. iii, Over-daring is as great a vice As over-fearing.

over'fearful, *a.* [OVER- 28.] Too fearful. So **over'fearfully** *adv.*; **over'fearfulness.**

a **1626** W. SCLATER *Serm. Exper.* (1638) 32 Over-fearfulnesse, dismaying to approach unto the Throne of Grace. *a* **1639** W. WHATELEY *Prototypes* II. xxvi. (1640) 82 Take heed of being so fond and over-fearefull of your children.

'over-'fed (stress var.), *ppl. a.* [OVER- 28 c.] Fed too much, fed to excess.

1579–80 NORTH *Plutarch* (1676) 42 These gross, corpulent, and ouer-fed bodies do encounter Nature. **1608** SHAKS. *Per.* III. Prol. 3 Snores..Made louder by the o'er-fed breast Of this most pompous marriage-feast. **1825** J. Neal *Bro. Jonathan* I. 100 Like an over-fed infant. **1899** *Allbutt's Syst. Med.* VIII. 557 The worst instances of psoriasis are found in the overfed.

ˈover-ˈfeeble, *a.* [over- 28.] Too feeble.
c **1449** Pecock *Repr.* 147 Thilk proces is ouerfeble forto weerne ymagis to be had & vsid.

†**over-ˈfeeble**, *v.* *Obs. rare*⁻¹. [over- 21.] *trans.* To overcome with weakness; to enfeeble.
1398 Trevisa *Barth. De P.R.* v. xxviii. (1495) 138 The hondes ben drye in men that ben..ouerfebled with aege, traueylle and dysease.

ˌ**over-ˈfeed**, *v.* [over- 27.]
1. *trans.* To feed too much, or to excess.
1609 J. Davies in Farr *S.P. Jas. I* (1848) 183 The London lanes.. Did vomit out their undigested dead,.. For all these lanes with folke are overfed. **1616** Surfl. & Markh. *Country Farme* 105 The Husbandman is of opinion, that you cannot ouer-feed or make your Swine too fat. **1714** Mandeville *Fab. Bees* (1725) I. 349 If he keeps but one [horse], and overfeeds it to shew his wealth, he is a fool for his pains. **1896** *Allbutt's Syst. Med.* I. 399 It is a common error to over-feed and over-stimulate in this condition.
2. *intr.* (for *refl.*) To feed to excess, take too much food.
1774 Goldsm. *Nat. Hist.* V. 113 When they [vultures] have over-fed, they are then utterly helpless. **1856** Kane *Arct. Expl.* I. xxix. 399, I have seen pups only two months old risk an indigestion by overfeeding on their twin brethren.
Hence **ˈover-ˈfeeding** *vbl. sb.* and *ppl. a.*
1621 H. Wotton *Let.* 26 Nov. in L. P. Smith *Life & Lett. Sir H. Wotton* (1907) II. 219 As may excuse the English, whom otherwise they think an overfeeding nation. **1836** F. Mahony *Rel. Father Prout, Apol. Lent* (1859) 19 Gibbon.. notices this vile propensity to overfeeding. **1881** Michell in *Macm. Mag.* XLV. 41 You must hit off exactly the golden mean between overfeeding and underfeeding. **1902** G. B. Shaw *Let.* 18 Nov. (1972) II. 289 Who is Doctor Buzzi? Is it starvation cure, or overfeeding cure, or water cure, or faith healing, or what?

overfeel to **over-festoon**: see over-.

ˈover-ˈfew, *a.* Now *dial.* [over- 28.] Too few.
[**1470–85** Malory *Arthur* v. x, Ouer fewe to fyght with soo many.] **1538** Starkey *England* ii. ii. 191 Of them [i.e. ministers of the law] are ouer-many, though ther be among them ouer-few gud. *a* **1687** H. More in Norris *Theory Love* (1688) 181 Else they would be in the state of sincerity, which over-few..are. [*Mod. Sc.* Owre few o' the richt sort.]

over-fields to **overfile**: see over-.

overˈfill, *v.* [OE. *oferfyllan*, f. *ofer-*, over- 24 + *fyllan* to fill: cf. MHG. *überfüllen.*]
1. *trans.* To do more than fill; to fill to overflowing.
c **1230** *Hali Meid.* 19 He earneð him ouerfullet ful & ouer-eorninde met of heuenliche mede. **1495** *Trevisa's Barth. De P.R.* vi. xx. (W. de W.) 207 The stomak is ouerfilled, and is stretchid abrode. **1575–85** Abp. Sandys *Serm.* (1841) 9 They who are over-filled with works of supererogation. *a* **1700** Dryden (J.), The tears she shed, Seem'd..to discharge her head, O'er fill'd before. **1869** Phillips *Vesuv.* iii. 56 On the 13th the lava overfilled the great fissure. **1908** B. Stoughton *Metall. Iron & Steel* viii. 200 With open passes, the collars cannot be made to quite touch..and the pressure may squeeze some metal between them, forming a 'fin' along the side of the piece. This is known as 'overfilling the pass'. **1953** D. J. O. Brandt *Manuf. Iron & Steel* xxxii. 239 When the first portion of the rod enters the stands, there is no tension and the passes are overfilled but if there is tension when all the stands are rolling this will cause underfilling which will go on until the back end of the rod leaves the first stands, and the tension is relaxed, then overfilling will take place again. **1968** R. N. Parkins *Mech. Treatm. Metals* iii. 135 The method adopted in this latter work was to determine the filling characteristic of a pass sequence, since this may be used to determine whether a given ingoing bar will under- or over-fill the pass.
2. *intr.* To become full to overflowing.
1615 Chapman *Odyss.* xiii. 358 Water'd with floods, that ever over-fill With heaven's continual showers. **1676** Hobbes *Iliad* (1677) 63 Suddenly the river overfills, Supply'd by Jove with mighty showers of rain. **1684** T. Burnet *Th. Earth* ii. 77.
Hence **ˈoverˈfilled** *ppl. a.*, **overˈfilling** *vbl. sb.*
1606 Sylvester *Du Bartas* ii. iv. ii. *Magnificence* 867 Th' over-burdned Tables bend with weight Of their Ambrosiall over-filled fraight. **1900** *Daily News* 6 July 3/3 Overfilled, undermanned hospital, without medical necessities. **1953** [see sense 1 above]. **1968** R. N. Parkins *Mech. Treatm. Metals* ii. 78 Overfilling will cause the excess metal to spread into the roll joints..giving fins.

ˈoverfill, *sb.* *Metallurgy.* [f. the vb.] A projection on rolled metal due to the metal being too large for the aperture through which it was forced in rolling, so that the excess spread between the junction of the rolls; also, a bar or the like that is too large for the rolling it is to undergo.
1924 F. W. Dencer *Detailing & fabricating Struct. Steel* xxvii. 355 Material with overfills is not necessarily defective. **1929** *Rolling Mill Jrnl.* Jan. 16/1 If a bar when passing through a pass does not fill the groove, it is spoken of as an underfill. If it more than fills the groove and squeezes out at the sides, it is spoken of as an overfill and the material squeezing out at the sides is known as a fin or a flash. **1957** *Making, Shaping & Treating of Steel* (U.S. Steel) (ed. 7) xxx. 556/2 Overfills are broad and less sharp than fins. As a rule, overfills occur more frequently than fins and in many cases are associated on the same bar with underfills. **1964** N. Weinstein tr. *Polukhin's Rolling Mill Pract.* xvii. 286 Fills and overfills obtained in rolling section steel are illustrated.

overˈfilm, *v.* [over- 8.] *trans.* To cover with a film, to put a film over.
1593 Nashe *Christ's T.* (1613) 57 Their eies were ouer-filmed or blinded. **1854–6** Patmore *Angel in Ho.* ii. x. *Last Nt. at H.* 38 Fear O'erfilms her apprehensive eye.

ˈover-ˈfine, *a.* [over- 28.] Too fine; superfine; over-refined.
1577 tr. *Bullinger's Decades* (1592) 243 Pure flowre for ouerfine breade. **1668** H. More *Div. Dial.* iv. xx. (1713) 339 This fetch of yours is over-fine and witty. **1707** Norris *Treat. Humility* vi. 273 Aiming at hard words, or an over-fine pronunciation of such as are common. **1862** *Athenæum* 8 Nov. 588 The phrases 'Our Feathered Families', and 'Birds of Song' are, we submit, affected and over-fine.
Hence **ˈover-ˈfineness.**
1859 Tennyson *Vivien* 645 (794) In the mouths of base interpreters, From over-fineness not intelligible.. Is thy white blamelessness accounted blame!

ˌ**over-ˈfire**, *v.* [over- 27.] *trans.* To fire or heat too much. (Used in Ceramics.)
1626 Bacon *Sylva* §327 Gold might be made but the Alchymists over-fired the Work. **1875** *Ure's Dict. Arts* III. 628 The risks in the oven of being 'over-fired', by which it [porcelain] would be melted into a mass, and of being 'short-fired', by which its surface would be imperfect. **1885** Lock *Workshop Receipts* Ser. iii. 207/1 Great attention is required in this operation to prevent the enamel from being over-fired.

ˌ**over-ˈfish**, *v.* [over- 27.] *trans.* To fish (a stream, etc.) too much; to fish to depletion. Now used esp. in reference to marine fishing grounds and the types of fish or shellfish caught there. Hence ˌ**over-ˈfishing** *vbl. sb.*
1867 *Q. Rev.* Apr. 328 If any trawling-ground should be overfished. **1871** *Echo* 15 Dec., Some..asserting that the falling off was due to overfishing. **1902** *Daily Chron.* 27 Feb. 3/6 A species which might speedily be over-fished, to the lasting detriment of the industry. **1925** J. T. Jenkins *Fishes Brit. Isles* 137 All this statistical information has an important bearing on the vexed question of over-fishing [of cod]. **1941** *Sun* (Baltimore) 29 Nov. 6/3 Next year we won't have any oysters, and then, no doubt, we will be told that we overfished the beds this year. **1946** *Nature* 10 Aug. 189/2 Russell and Graham, discussing the overfishing problem, have recently emphasized that sea fisheries under present conditions have reached, if not over-reached, the limits of profitable yield. **1958** *New Statesman* 23 Aug. 218/1 Everybody who knows anything about fish..is anxious about over-fishing. **1973** *Daily Colonist* (Victoria, B.C.) 21 June 3/3 Industry spokesmen..have been pressing for action by Ottawa to halt alleged overfishing by foreign fleets. **1975** *Nature* 24 Jan. 290/3 Some [species], notably the European hake..have been heavily overfished.

overfit (ˈəʊvəfɪt), *a.* *Physical Geogr.* [f. over- 28, after *misfit.*] Pertaining to or designating a stream which, if its average flow in the past was at present-day levels, would be expected to have eroded a larger valley than it has done.
1913 *Ann. Assoc. Amer. Geogr.* III. 18 Conversely, the capturing branch, AB, and its river, BD, below the entrance of the capturing branch, being increased in volume, should exhibit for a time an overfit relation to their valley curves, in the sense of actively enlarging them. **1954** W. D. Thornbury *Princ. Geomorphol.* vi. 156 It is difficult to cite examples of overfit rivers, or streams with floodplains too small for the size of the stream. Hence there may well be a question whether overfit streams exist. The reason..may be that a stream cannot long remain overfit, for an increase in volume will be accompanied by increased erosive power and rapid adjustment of valley size. **1968** R. W. Fairbridge *Encycl. Geomorphol.* 706/2 Davis..also recognizes overfit streams.

overfit *v.* to **overflag**: see over-.

†**overˈflame**, *v.*¹ *Obs.* [over- 5, 25.] *intr.* To flame over, or beyond measure.
1634 *Documents against Prynne* (Camden) 22 This man's zeale hath soe overflamed, that there is not by him any recreacion att all lefte for Christians.

†**overˈflame**, *v.*² *Obs. rare*⁻¹. [Derivation obscure.] (app.) To smear or plaster over.
c **1420** *Pallad. on Husb.* i. 1139 Make hit lyk a salue, and ouerflame [L. *alline*] Vche hole and chene.

†**ˈover-flap.** *Obs.* [over- 6.] A pasty or turn-over.
1692 Tryon *Good House-w.* xi. 87 The best fashion to make these Pyes in, is that of Pasties, which in some countries they call Overflaps.

†**overˈflee**, *v.* *Obs.* [OE. *oferfléon* to flee over, also for **oferfléoȝan* to fly over: see overfly, and cf. flee, fly *v.*]
1. a. *intr.* To flee over; to escape. **b.** *trans.* To escape from, flee.
Beowulf 2525 Nelle ic beorȝes weard ofer fleon fotes trem. *c* **1330** *Owayn Miles* 46 The child that was y-born to night Er the soule be hider y-dight The pain schal ouer fle. **1382** Wyclif *2 Kings* xxv. 11 The thorȝ fleers, that ouerflowen [1388 hadden fled ouer] to the kyng of Babiloyn.
2. [In sense of fly *v.*] To fly over.
c **1000** Ælfric *Gram.* xlvii. (Z.) 276 *Superuolo*, ic oferfleo. **1382** Wyclif *Wisd.* v. 11 As a brid that ouerfleth [1388 flieth ouer] in the eir.
3. = overfly *v.* 3, q.v.

overˈfleece, *v.* *poet.* [over- 8.] *trans.* To cover with or as with a fleece or fleeces.
1717 Fenton *Odyss.* xi. Poems 102 Iolcos, whose irriguous Vales His grazing Folds o'er-fleec'd. **1725** Pope *Odyss.* xix. 280 Short woolly curls o'erfleeced his bending head.

†**overˈfleet**, *v.* *Obs.* [f. over- 5, 9 + fleet *v.*¹, OE. *fléotan*: cf. OHG. *ubarfliozan*, MHG. *überfliezen*, Ger. *überfliessen*, MDu. *over-vlieten.*]
1. To flow over, overflow. **a.** *intr.* **b.** *trans.*
a. *c* **1250** *Gen. & Ex.* 586 Fiftene elne it ouer-flet, Ouer ilk dune, and ouer ilc hil. *c* **1320** *Cast. Love* 849 þorw whom þe grace þat ouer-fleot Socoureþ al þe world ȝut. *a* **1586** Montgomerie *Misc. Poems* l. 46 Waill, and wit of womanheid, That sa with vertew dois ouerfleit.
b. **1513** Douglas *Æneis* ix. i. 78 Vmquhile the fertill fluide, Nylus, Ourfletand all the feildis, bank and bus.
2. *trans.* To cover with floating things. *rare.*
1513 Douglas *Æneis* x. v. 135 And saw the navy cum and mekill ost, Semand the sey of schippis all our flet.

overflexion, -fling, etc.: see over-.

overflight (ˈəʊvəflaɪt). [f. over- 4 + flight *sb.*¹] The flight of an aircraft over specified territory without landing. Formerly also used of birds. Also *transf.*
1598 Florio *Worlde of Wordes* 383/1 *Soruólo*, an ouerflight, a surflight. **1883** J. S. Stallybrass tr. *Grimm's Teutonic Mythol.* III. xxxv. 1133 Our early ages appear also to have seen a meaning in the *overflight* of certain birds. **1958** *Times* 8 Aug. 7/2 United States aircraft have now been given permission to fly over, but it was not clear yesterday whether British aircraft had permission. The question of overflights has been given much prominence. **1960** *N.Y. Times* 12 June 6E/2 The U-2 reconnaissance 'overflights' provided, by aerial photography and tape recording of Soviet radio and radar emissions, the most important intelligence gathered by the C.I.A. **1966** T. Pynchon *Crying of Lot 49* ii. 37 The can [of hair spray] hit the floor, something broke,.. propelling the can swiftly about the bathroom. She looked up,..her field of vision cut across by wild, flashing overflights of the can, whose pressure seemed inexhaustible. **1970** C. Duerden *Noise Abatement* v. 88 Overflights are the problem. Once they are experienced, the reaction of the general public will be the deciding factor and supersonic flights may be prohibited over this country. **1970** *New Scientist* 1 Oct. 37/2 A single supersonic overflight cracked 95 per cent of the eggs of the terns breeding on the Dry Tortugas in Florida. **1973** *Sci. Amer.* Feb. 17/3 When Francis Gary Powers was shot down in May, 1960, the U-2 overflights ended, except for certain minor incursions. **1976** *Daily Tel.* 21 Jan. 2/6 It was bewildering that Britain and France, builders of the plane [*sc.* Concorde], did not allow supersonic overflights.

†**ˈoverfloat**, *sb.* *Obs.* Also -flote. [over- 5 b.] = overflow *sb.*
1619 J. Dyke *Counterpoyson* 42 Men..hauing enough, should lay vp no more, but make the ouerfloate of their cup seruiceable to the maintenance of Gods worship. **1652–62** Heylin *Cosmogr.* i. (1682) 267 Occasioned by the divided streams of Nen and Ouse, with the over-flotes of other Rivers.

over-ˈfloat, *v.* Also -flote. [over- 9, 1. In sense 1 perh. for *overfleet*, through confusion with its pa. pple. *overfloten.*]
†**1.** *trans.* To overflow: = overfleet *v.* 1 b.
1601 Holland *Pliny* II. 405 The water..giueth a stonie coat or crust to all the earth that it either ouerfloteth or runneth by. **1610** —— *Camden's Brit.* i. 690 Doue that often riseth heere and ouerfloteth the fields. **1697** Dryden *Æneid* x. 34 The town is fill'd with slaughter, and o'erfloats, With a red deluge, their increasing moats.
2. To float over. *lit.* and *fig.*
1658 W. Burton *Itin. Anton.* 175 But it o're-floated rides, And still doth keep its constant tides. **1844** Mrs. Browning *Lady Geraldine's Courtship* xxii, Heard..her pure voice o'erfloat the rest. **1878** *Masque Poets* 66 This frail yacht, that like a flower Overfloats the rolling foam.

†**ˈover-ˈfloaty**, *a.* *Obs. rare*⁻¹. [f. over- 28 + floaty *a.*, buoyant.] Too buoyant, as a ship under-ballasted and so unsteady in the water.
1706 Phillips s.v. *Keel*, When a Ship is over-floaty, and rolls too much.

overflood (əʊvəˈflʌd), *v.* [over- 5, 9.] *trans.* To pour over in a flood; to inundate. Hence **overˈflooded** *ppl. a.*, **overˈflooding** *vbl. sb.* and *ppl. a.*
1821 Byron *Sardan.* v. i. 194 The Euphrates..O'erfloods its banks. **1881** E. W. Hamilton *Diary* 3 Nov. (1972) I. 182 The danger for the moment in Ireland seems to be the over-flooding of the Land Court. **1882** H. S. Holland *Logic & Life* (1885) 306 An answer which over-floods our senses with its fulness and compass. **1890** T. W. Allies *Peter's Rock* 341 The Arabians, overflooding Gaul after the conquest of Spain. **1921** W. de la Mare *Veil* 47 Then silence, and o'er-flooding noon. **1955** E. Pound *Classic Anthol.* i. 16 At the over-flooded ford. **1973** *Nature* 21/28 Dec. 450/2 The whole is cut by a dyke swarm which is especially dense at the contact between the layered plutonic rocks and the other components of the formation, and was subsequently overflooded by three different basalt series.

†**overˈfloten**, *ppl. a.* *Obs.* [pa. pple. of overfleet *v.*, in OE. *oferfloten.*] Overflowed, flooded.
c **1400** *Laud Troy Bk.* (E.E.T.S.) 4306 Many a darte was ther cast and schotyn, And many a bodi ouer-floten. **1469** *Plumpton Corr.* 21 The corneland is overflotin with water.

1601 HOLLAND *Pliny* II. 13 Fresh-water Spunges, which commonly are seene vpon ouer-floten medowes.

over'flourish, *v.* [OVER- 25, 8, 27.]

†**1.** *intr.* To flourish exceedingly. *Obs.*

1597 GOLDING *De Mornay* xix. 302 They that worship.. God,..dwelling in Paradise alike ouerflorishing green.

2. *trans.* To cover with blossom or verdure.

1601 SHAKS. *Twel. N.* III. iv. 404 Vertue is beauty, but the beauteous euill Are empty trunkes, ore-flourish'd by the deuill. **1861** LYTTON & FANE *Tannhäuser* 114 A wither'd staff o'erflourish'd with green leaves.

†**3.** To embellish too greatly; to set forth with too much embellishment. *Obs.*

1703 COLLIER *Ess. Mor. Subj.* II. 66 As they are likely to over-flourish their own case, so their flattery is hardest to be discovered. **1716** *Gentl. Instructed* (ed. 6) 279, I cannot think, that the fondest Imagination can over-flourish, or even paint to the Life, the Happiness of those who never check Nature.

overflow ('əʊvəfləʊ), *sb.* [OVER- 9, 5.]

1. The act or fact of overflowing; an inundation, a flood. Also *fig.*

1589 GREENE *Menaphon* (Arb.) 62 Ouerwhelmed with the ouerflowe of a second aduersitie. **1600** J. PORY tr. *Leo's Africa* VIII. 299 The inundation or ouerflow of Nilus. **1610** HOLLAND *Camden's Brit.* I. 130 Some, by overflowes and floods, are growen to be that sea, which at this day they call Zuider-Sea. **1849** MURCHISON *Siluria* iii. 53 The relations are obscured by an..overflow of igneous rocks.

2. a. A flowing over from a vessel which is too full; that which flows over. *lit.* and *fig.*: applied esp. to an excess of attendance or population.

1640 J. STOUGHTON *Def. Divinity* i. 53 From the overflow of this place all parts of the kingdom are full of knowledge. **1823** *Examiner* 89/2 The house, full to overflow. **1825** SOUTHEY in *Q. Rev.* XXXI. 384 Every garden has its tank.. the overflow of one being conducted..to another. **1852** MISS YONGE *Cameos* I. i. 4 The overflow of Teutons came very early thither.

b. *Prosody.* (See quot. 1885.)

1885 E. GOSSE *Fr. Shaks. to Pope* 6 Mr. Austin Dobson has proposed to me the term *overflow* for these verses in which the sense is not concluded at the end of one line or of one couplet, but straggles on,..until it naturally closes;.. equivalent to the *vers enjambé* of the French. *Ibid.* 55 In thirty-two lines [of Waller's 'To the King'] we find but one overflow. **1894** VERITY *Milton's P.L.* Introd. 59 Further it [blank verse] never extended till Marlowe..broke up the fetters of the couplet-form, and by the process of over-flow carried on the rhythm from verse to verse as the sense required.

c. *Telephony.* A situation in which more calls are directed to a group of switches or lines than they are able to handle; a call so directed. Usu. *attrib.*

1924 J. G. MITCHELL *Mech. Manual Switching* i. 27 When the traffic reaches a peak so high as to prevent the prompt dispatch of calls by the operators on duty, those lines which are not receiving service will display a continuous signal on the overflow section. **1934** G. S. BERKELEY *Traffic & Trunking Princ. Automatic Telephony* vii. 146 The overflow meter..records the number of calls lost due to the insufficiency of the plant. *Ibid.* 147 One overflow meter is provided to record the number of overflows occurring on the two levels. **1962** J. RIORDAN *Stochastic Service Syst.* iii. 39 Turn now to the size of over-flow traffic, and write $P_n(t;r)$ for the stationary probability that in an interval of length t, whose initial point is an arbitrarily chosen point, there are n overflow calls from the first r servers. **1972** *Guardian* 19 Feb. 8/6 The BBC..recorded 4,300 overflow calls. **1974** R. N. RENTON *Internat. Telex Service* x. 383/2 Calls failing to find a free outlet in the level will hunt to the 11th bank contact, receive the appropriate service signal and operate the overflow meter. *Ibid.*, Tables of critical overflow are published.

d. *Computers.* The generation of a number having more digits than the capacity of the device holding it; also, the excess digit(s). Freq. *attrib.*

1951 *Proc. IRE* XXXIX. 275/1 *Overflow.* (1) The condition which arises when the result of an arithmetic operation exceeds the capacity of the number representation in a digital computer. (2) The carry digit arising from this condition. **1959** J. JEENEL *Programming for Digital Computers* iv. 187 The instruction..will cause program execution to proceed from 0104 to 0105 regardless of whether the overflow indicator is on or off. **1965** SWALLOW & PRICE *Elem. Computer Programming* xv. 279 The arithmetic operations of addition and subtraction are slightly more complex in the IBM 1401 than in the 141. One difference is in the handling of overflows. *Ibid.* 287 Whenever an overflow bit is carried into the zone of the high-order digit during an ADD or SUBTRACT operation, this indicator is turned on. **1969** P. B. JORDAIN *Condensed Computer Encycl.* 364 The most significant digit(s) are considered to be overflow. **1973** C. W. GEAR *Introd. Computer Sci.* vi. 241 Most systems provide monitor sub-routines that can be called to specify what is to happen in the case of overflow or underflow.

3. Such a quantity as runs over; excess, superfluity, superabundance.

1589 NASHE *Pref. Greene's Menaphon* (Arb.) 6 The ingrafted overflow of some Kilcow conceipt. **1595** SHAKS. *Rich. II*, v. iii. 64 Thy ouerflow of good, conuerts to bad. **1725** BROOME in *Pope's Odyss.* Notes (J.), The expression may be ascribed to an overflow of gratitude. **1817** MISS MITFORD in L'Estrange *Life* (1870) II. i. 5 A prodigious overflow of stupid faces, royal and other.

4. a. Short for *overflow-pipe* or *-drain*, a pipe or drain for carrying off excess of water.

1895 *Daily News* 17 Oct. 2/6 When the rainfall is more than ordinarily heavy, the storm overflows carry off the flow of water with sufficient rapidity to prevent any overflow into houses from the sewers.

b. *Geol.* A natural notch or channel formed by water overflowing from a lake.

1902 *Q. Jrnl. Geol. Soc.* LVIII. 481 When the watershed is very uniform in height, and the ice has at one stage actually surmounted it, then several parallel overflows may be developed out of the gutters which are trenched in the outer slope by water flowing off the ice itself. The overflows ..which cut through the Northern Cleveland watershed above the village of Egton are typical of this arrangement. **1973** R. J. PRICE *Glacial & Fluvioglacial Landforms* v. 128 So long as evidence for the existence of the ice-dammed lakes does not simply consist of the meltwater channels themselves, the interpretation of such meltwater channels as overflows cannot be disputed.

5. *attrib.* and *Comb.*, as ***overflow condition***, ***incontinence***, ***meeting***, ***population***, ***work***; ***overflow-basin***, ***-gauge***, ***-pipe***; **overflow-bug** (*U.S.*), a caraboid beetle, *Platynus maculicollis*, occasionally appearing in vast swarms in southern California; **overflow channel** *Geol.* = sense 4 b above; **overflow table**, a table used to accommodate extra people attending a dinner, meeting, etc.

1869 E. A. PARKES *Pract. Hygiene* (ed. 3) 68 When the overflow-pipe of a cistern opens into the sewers. **1875** KNIGHT *Dict. Mech.*, *Overflow-basin*, one having a pipe to convey away excess of water and prevent it running over the brim. **1880** *Daily News* 4 Feb. 3/1 Hengler's was filled to the brim..and an 'overflow' meeting was immediately organized at the Drill Shed hard by. **1897** *Westm. Gaz.* 15 Mar. 3/3 Their great want was new territory fit for the overflow population to settle in permanently. **1898** *Engineering Mag.* XVI. 107/1 The shallow, widespread overflow-floods which occur in some parts of India can hardly be controlled at all. **1899** *Allbutt's Syst. Med.* VII. 15 If the distended bladder be left unrelieved, the sphincter yields, and the excess of urine comes away, forming the so-called 'overflow incontinence'. **1902** *Q. Jrnl. Geol. Soc.* LVIII. 473 The criteria by which ancient extra-morainic lakes can be recognized are mainly four:—(1) beaches; (2) deltas; (3) floor-deposits; and (4) overflow-channels. **1923** *Radio Times* 28 Sept. 2/1 The voice of a public man has been ..made to operate loud-speakers of overflow meetings. **1969** BENNISON & WRIGHT *Geol. Hist. Brit. Isles* xvi. 356 Associated water-cut channels (called overflow channels) from ice-dammed lakes generally thought to result from water flowing marginally along ice sheets may, in many cases, also be a product of subglacial drainage. **1973** A. BEHREND *Samarai Affair* i. 14 There was a smaller overflow table where the members of the Pilotage Committee..liked to congregate. **1974** *Times* 20 Feb. 1/1 Two eggs were hurled at Mr Wilson as he struggled through a crowd to enter Oxford Town Hall last night to address an overflow meeting of more than 1,000 people. The eggs went wide.

overflow (əʊvə'fləʊ), *v.* *Pa. pple.* 1–7 -flowen, 6–9 -flown, 6– flowed: see FLOW *v.* [OE. *oferflówan* = MLG. *overvlôjen*, MDu., Du. *overvloeien*: see OVER- 9, 5.]

I. *trans.* **1. a.** To flow over; to overspread or cover with water or other liquid; to flood, inundate. Said of water; in quot. 1741 causatively of a person.

c **893** K. ÆLFRED *Oros.* I. iii. § 1 Seo ea ælce ʒeare þæt land middeweard oferfleow mid fotes þicce flode. *c* **1250** *Gen. & Ex.* 556 Ðo wex a flod ðis werlde wid-hin, and ouer-flowʒed men & deres kin. *c* **1400** MAUNDEV. (Roxb.) xvi. 72 It es like as it schuld ouerflowe all þe land. **1477** J. PASTON in *P. Lett.* III. 175 The causey..is so over flowyn that ther is no man that may on ethe passe it. *c* **1585** in Willis & Clark *Cambridge* (1886) II. 411 Trinitie Colledge greene..is in the winter time overflowne with water. **1600** J. PORY tr. *Leo's Africa* VII. 290 At the inundation of Niger all the fields of this region are ouerflowed. **1673** RAY *Journ. Low C.*, *Rome* 385 Ravenna..lies indeed very low, yet I believe nowadays is never overflown. **1741** *Compl. Fam. Piece* II. iii. 524 Over-flow Meadows, and drain your Corn-fields by cutting Water-furrows. **1863** BATES *Nat. Amazon* ix. (1864) 263 The beaches..during most months of the year are partly over-flown by the river. **1886** HALL CAINE *Son of Hagar* II. xv, The river had overflowed the meadows.

†**b.** To flow over or across. *Obs.*

c **1400** *Destr. Troy* 10660 Myche watur he weppit of his wale ene, Ouer-flowet his face, fell on his brest.

2. *transf.* and *fig.* **a.** To pass or spread over like a flood, so as to pervade, fill, cover, submerge, overwhelm, etc.

1533 MORE *Apol.* 266 The fayth of Cryste shall never be overflowen with heresyes. *c* **1611** CHAPMAN *Iliad* v. 708 With which his spirit flew, And darkness over-flew his eyes. **1635–56** COWLEY *Davideis* I. 350 A Place o'erflown with hallowed Light. **1712** POPE *Messiah* 103 One tide of glory, one unclouded blaze O'erflow thy courts. **1749–51** LAVINGTON *Enthus. Meth. & Papists* (1820) 382, I was overflowed with joy. **1830** TENNYSON *Madeline* iii, The flush of anger'd shame O'erflows thy calmer glances. **1899** R. KIPLING *Stalky, Little Prep.* 171 So they overflowed his house, smoked his cigars, and drank his health.

†**b.** in *pa. pple.* Overcome with excess of liquor; drunk. *Obs.*

1607 MIDDLETON *Phoenix* IV. ii, I was overflown when I spoke it, I could ne'er ha' said it else. **1642** R. CARPENTER *Experience* I. vii. 21 A cloud settles in his [the drunkard's] eyes, and the whole body being overflowne, they seeme to float in the flood.

3. a. To flow over (the brim, banks, or sides). Also *fig.*

a **1548** HALL *Chron.*, *Hen. VII* 36 Thinking that the vessel of oyle..would overflowe the brymmes. **1592** SHAKS. *Ven. & Ad.* 92 Rain..Perforce will force it [a river] overflow the bank. **1697** DRYDEN *Virg. Georg.* I. 394 The Dregs that overflow the Brims. **1709** *Tatler* No. 43 ¶12 The Loire having overflowed its Banks, hath laid the Country under Water for 300 Miles together. **1890** *Forum* (N.Y.) VIII. VI. 700 The fiery lava of passion overflowing the appointed bounds. **1916** G. B. SHAW *Androcles & Lion* p. cviii, The causes which have produced this sudden clearing of the air include the transformation of many modern States, notably ..the tight little Island of Britain, into empires which overflow the frontiers of all the Churches. **1973** R. J. WILLIAMS in D. J. Wiseman *Peoples of Old Testament Times* iv. 80 Fed by the yearly rains in the Abyssinian highlands, the river [*sc.* the Nile] rose steadily and overflowed its banks.

b. To cause to overflow; to fill (a vessel) so full that it runs over. Also *fig.*

a **1667** JER. TAYLOR (J.), Sure that some excellent fortune would relieve..thee so as to overflow all thy hopes. **1868** F. WILLIAMS *Lives Eng. Card.* I. 137 This outrage overflowed the cup of bitterness that had been presented to the Pope. **1894** R. BRIDGES *Shorter Poems* 42 Again shall pleasure overflow Thy cup with sweetness.

†**4.** To overflow with, pour out. *Obs. rare.*

1598 SHAKS. *Merry W.* II. ii. 157 Such brooks are welcome to mee, that ore'flowes such liquor. **1598** B. JONSON *Ev. Man in Hum.* III. i, I..take pen, and paper presently, and ouerflow you halfe a score, or a dozen of sonnets, at a sitting.

II. *intr.* **5. a.** To flow over the sides or brim by reason of fullness.

c **1000** *Ags. Gosp.* Luke vi. 38 Ofer-flowende hiʒ syllaþ on eowerne bearm. **1382** WYCLIF *Luke* vi. 38 A good mesure, and wel fillid, and shakun to gidere, and ouerflowynge. *c* **1400** tr. *Higden* Harl. Contin. (Rolls) VII. 505 This ȝere twey dayes tofore Octobre the see overflowide and passide the clyves and dreynt many men and tounes. **1560** DAUS tr. *Sleidane's Comm.* 94 This tyme at Rome the Ryver of Tiber overflowed exceadingly. *a* **1682** SIR T. BROWNE *Tracts* 56 Not when the river had overflown. **1838** LARDNER *Hand-bk. Nat. Phil.*, *Hydrost.* etc. 47 At the top..there is a small reservoir to receive the mercury, which overflows by expansion.

†**b.** *transf.* and *fig.* To get beyond bounds, to become excessive or inordinate. *Obs.*

c **1200** ORMIN 10721, & tiss meocnesse iss oferrmett Swa þatt itt oferrfloweþþ. *a* **1547** SURREY *Æneid* IV. (1557) F iij b, Loue doth rise and rage againe, And ouerflowes with swellyng stormes of wrath. **1628** tr. *Mathieu's Powerfull Favorite* 146 Hee would not correct the luxury, nor the dissolutenesse which were ouerflowne, by reason of the dis-esteeming of the Sumptuary Lawes.

c. To remove from one part to another owing to want of room or other pressure. (In quot. 1858 jocularly of a single person.)

1858 HAWTHORNE *Fr. & It. Jrnls.* I. 295 When I like, I can overflow into the summer-house or an arbor. **1865** LIGHTFOOT *Comm. Gal.* (1874) 10 The Jewish colonists must in course of time have overflowed into a neighbouring country. **1899** *Allbutt's Syst. Med.* VI. 46 The painful commotion may extend or overflow to higher or lower centres. *a* **1904** *Mod.* The crowd overflowed into the adjoining gardens.

6. a. Said of the containing vessel or the like: To be so full that the contents run over the brim.

c **1400** tr. *Secreta Secret.*, *Gov. Lordsh.* 73 Wellys ouer-fluen, moistures styen vp to þe croppys of trees. **1588** SHAKS. *Tit. A.* III. i. 222 When heauen doth weepe, doth not the earth oreflow? **1606** HEYWOOD *2nd Pt. If you know not me* Wks. 1874 I. 297 Come, let our full-crown'd cups oreflow with wine. **1712–14** POPE *Rape Lock* v. 85 Sudden, with starting tears each eye o'erflows. **1884** tr. *Lotze's Metaph.* 324 Like the last drop which makes a cup overflow.

b. *transf.* and *fig.* To be filled beyond containing, to be exceedingly full, to superabound.

1601 SHAKS. *All's Well* II. iv. 47 To make the comming houre oreflow with ioy. **1703** MAUNDRELL *Let. to Sir C. Hedges* in *Journ. Jerus.* (1732) Pref., We are apt to overflow in speaking of it. **1871** B. TAYLOR *Faust* (1875) I. xxv. 215 The square below And the streets overflow.

Hence **over'flowable** *a.*, capable of being overflowed; **over'flowed** *ppl. a.*; **over'flower** *sb.*, one who or that which overflows.

1668 T. SMITH *Voy. Constantinople* in *Misc. Cur.* (1708) III. 12 The land..of Ægypt, lying very low, and easily overflowable. **1822–34** *Good's Study Med.* (ed. 4) I. 645 The overflowed swamps at its feet. **1848** BUCKLEY *Iliad* 392 The plain was all filled with the overflowed water. **1899** W. JAMES in *Talks to Teachers on Psychol.* 215 The final over-flowers of our measure.

overflower (-'flaʊə(r)), *v.* [OVER- 23, 8.] *trans.* **a.** To deplete by flowering too much. **b.** To cover with flowers.

1850 *Beck's Florist* Sept. 213 They are shy growers, and apt to overflower their strength. **1884** MAY CROMMELIN *Brown-Eyes* i, The pond was all over-flowered with water-lilies.

'over'flowing (stress var.), *vbl. sb.* [f. OVERFLOW *v.* + -ING[1].]

1. The action of the verb OVERFLOW; an overspreading or covering with water; an inundation.

1530 PALSGR. 250/1 Overflowyng with water, *inundation.* **1629** *Drayner Conf.* (1647) B, In Meddowes, over-flowings will doe good. **1846** GROTE *Greece* (1862) II. xx. 481 The overflowings of the Nile.

fig. **1540** BIBLE *Ps.* xviii. 3 The ouerflowinges [1611 floods] of vngodlynesse made me afrayed.

2. The action of flowing over because the containing vessel is too full; also, that which flows over; hence, excess, superfluity, superabundance. Esp. in phr. (***full*** or ***to fill***) ***to overflowing***: more than full, so as to overflow.

1573–80 BARET *Alv.* O 174 An ouerflowing, a superfluous abunding. **1615** LATHAM *Falconry* (1633) 103 The ouerflowing of the gall, a disease that most Hawkes are subiect vnto. **1778** [W. MARSHALL] *Minutes Agric.* 28 Aug. an. 1776, Some over-flowings of clover, I ordered to be made into a square cock for the cart-horses. **1857** C. BRONTE *Professor* i, I anticipated no overflowings of fraternal tenderness. **1879** R. A. STERNDALE *Afghan Knife* II. vii. 69 In the meantime fugitives kept pouring into the house, which was full to overflowing. **1898** SKEEL & BREARLEY *King Washington* (1899) xii. 75 The boys..were filled to overflowing with the excitement of the hour. **1920** H. M. PIM *Short Hist. Celtic Philos.* v. 62 They might have produced a Tartarus, and filled it to overflowing. **1961** *Washington Post* 1 June A24 The jails were filled to overflowing with political prisoners who had incurred his displeasure.

ˈoverˈflowing (stress var.), *ppl. a.* [-ING².] That overflows: in the senses of the verb; flowing over the brim; superabounding, exuberant, etc.

c **1020** *Rule St. Benet* lxi. (Logeman) 102 ȝif bið ȝemet oferflowende oððe leahterfull. *c* **1450** tr. *De Imitatione* III. lxiii. 148 Fulfilled wiþ so gret loue of þe godhede & so ouerflowing ioy. **1611** BIBLE *Jer.* xlvii. 2 Waters rise up out of the north, and shall be an overflowing flood. *a* **1614** DONNE *Βιαθανατος* (1644) 188 To expresse the abundant and overflowing charitie of our Saviour. **1876** BANCROFT *Hist. U.S.* II. xxiv. 118 Benevolence gushed prodigally from his ever overflowing heart.

Hence **overˈflowingly** *adv.*; **overˈflowingness** (in ME. = luxury, extravagance).

c **1175** *Lamb. Hom.* 115 ȝif heo edmodnesse habbeð and ouerflowendnesse forletað. **1648** BOYLE *Seraph. Love* xiv, The goods, which he so overflowingly abounds with. **1854** *Tait's Mag.* XXI. 333 Wilson was brimfully, nay, overflowingly, imbued with the poetic element. **1883** G. MEREDITH *Let.* 30 Oct. (1970) II. 718, I have been hearing from Will of your radiant overflowingness.

ˈoverˈflown, *ppl. a. arch.* or *dial.* [The original pa. pple. of OVERFLOW *v.*] = OVERFLOWED *ppl. a.*

1579 W. WILKINSON *Confut. Fam. Love, Heret. affirm.* bj b, Whosoeuer feadeth of the ouerflowne word..eateth truely the flesh of Christ. **1653** R. G. tr. *Bacon's Hist. Winds* 96 Vapours out of the Sea and Rivers, and over-flowne Marishes. **1707–12** MORTIMER *Husb.* (1721) I. 217 Foul Flood, as overflown Hay, Grass rotted by the long standing of Water on it in wet Summers. **1818** SOUTHEY in *Q. Rev.* XIX. 6 Crossing an overflown stream on the way to Boulogne.

ˈover-ˈfluent, *a.* [OVER- 28.] Too fluent. So **ˈover-ˈfluency**, too great fluency.

a **1672** ANNE BRADSTREET *Poems* (1875) 3, I do grudge the muses did not part 'Twixt him and me that overfluent store. **1901** *Daily Chron.* 8 Nov. 4/3 Doubtless the circumstances of Buchanan's life had something, much, to do with this over-fluency.

ˌoverˈflush, *v.* [OVER- 27, 8.] *trans.* **a.** To flush too much. **b.** To flush over, cover with a flush. *rare.* So **ˈoverˈflushed** *ppl. a.*; also **ˈoverflush** *sb.*, superfluity; **ˈoverˈflush** *a.*, too flush.

1581 MULCASTER *Positions* xliii. (1887) 268 Such an ouerflush of bookes growes chargeable to the printer. *a* **1652** J. SMITH *Sel. Disc.* iv. 78 A jolly fit of his over-flushed and fiery fancy. **1712** ADDISON *Spect.* No. 265 ¶9 A Face which is overflushed appears to advantage in the deepest Scarlet. *a* **1825** FORBY *Voc. E. Anglia, Over-flush*, superfluity. **1835** BROWNING *Paracelsus* III. 840 To overflush those blemishes with all The glow of general goodness they disturb. **1860** THACKERAY *Lovel the Wid.* iv, You don't look as if you were overflush of money.

overˈflutter, *v.* [OVER- 1.] *trans.* To flutter over.

a **1631** DONNE *Progr. Soul* xx, Already this hot cock in bush and tree, In field and tent o'rflutters his next hen. **1869** BROWNING *Ring & Bk.* XI. 371 Would benignant Gospel interpose, O'erflutter us with healing in her wings.

†**ˈoverflux.** *Obs.* [OVER- 5.] = OVERFLOW *sb.*

1633 FORD *'Tis Pity* III. ii, May be, 'tis but the maids-sickness, an over-flux of youth. **1660** T. M. *Hist. Independ.* IV. 103 The overflux of such a sudden, yet joyful change.

overfly (əʊvəˈflaɪ), *v.* [f. OVER- 4, etc. + FLY *v.*¹: cf. MHG. *übervliegen*, Ger. *überfliegen*, Du. *overvliegen*. For this, OE. and ME. had *oferflēon*, *ouerfle*: see OVERFLEE.]

1. a. *trans.* To fly over, to cross or pass over by flying. [OVER- 4.]

1558 PHAER *Æneid* IV. Kj b, Non otherwise Mercurius..Did shear the winds, and ouerflew the shores of Lybi sands. **1693** DRYDEN *Persius' Sat.* iv. (1697) 459 A sailing Kite Can scarce o'erfly 'em in a Day and Night. **1725** POPE *Odyss.* III. 412 A length of Ocean and unbounded sky, Which scarce the Sea-fowl in a year o'er-fly. **1885** J. MARTINEAU *Types Eth. Th.* I. 18 Overflying it with a dangerous transcendental wing.

†**b.** *fig.* To pass over, omit, skip. *Obs.*

1592 G. HARVEY *Four Lett.* Wks. (Grosart) I. 179 Some like accidents of dislike for breuity I ouerfly: young bloud is hot.

c. To fly beyond. [OVER- 12.]

1876 J. MARTINEAU *Ess.* (1891) IV. 263 We cannot overfly our own zone.

d. Of an aircraft or its passengers: to fly over (a specified point, area, etc.). Also *absol.* Hence **ˈoverflying** *vbl. sb.* and *ppl. a.*

1944 L. L. SELL *Eng.-Spanish Techn. Dict.* 861 Over-fly the field, to. **1946** *Happy Landings* (Air Ministry) July 7/1 Istres was planned as our first stop, but a 'mistral' put that airfield out of action and we had to overfly to Elmas (Sardinia). **1948** *Shell Aviation News* No. 120. 8/3 Following winds enabled us to overfly Marseilles, which we had intended as our first stop. **1957** *Times* 19 Sept. 8 A proposal by South Africa that she should be granted certain over-flying rights in the High Commission Territories has been accepted in principle by the British Government. **1958** 'N. SHUTE' *Rainbow & Rose* vi. 228 With the greater range of these aircraft we could overfly Canton and go direct to Fiji. **1965** *Listener* 2 Sept. 338/1 Any society will have..its quota of nuclear installations where overflying is prohibited. **1966** *New Scientist* 22 Dec. 669/2 The aircraft overflown by the supersonic liners, will 'take a fine old walloping'. **1973** *Daily Tel.* 17 Mar. 7/1 Mr Josefsson has been fighting for years to get rid of the Nato base at Keflavik, a vital link in tracking overflying Russian aircraft. **1973** 'A. HALL' *Tango Briefing* ii. 22 Did you get official overflying permission?.. Did you get official permission from the Algerian government to overfly their territory? **1977** *R.A.F. News* 5–18 Jan. 2/4 By remarkable coincidence, the golf course was overflown by two Phantom aircraft on a local low-level route.

2. To surpass in flight; to fly higher, faster, or farther than; to outsoar. [OVER- 22.]

1592 SHAKS. *Ven. & Ad.* 324 Out-stripping crows that strive to over-fly them. **1595** MARKHAM *Sir R. Grinvile* cxxxii, Thine honour, former honours ouer-flyes. **1825** COLERIDGE *Aids Refl.* (1848) I. 148 Were I to ask for angel's wings to overfly my own human nature. **1870** LOWELL *Study Wind., Pope* (1886) 337 Gray, whose 'Progress of Poetry'..overflies all other English lyrics like an eagle. **1954** D. A. BANNERMAN *Birds Brit. Isles* III. 278 It is of interest to note that the northern birds in general arrive somewhat earlier in the south of the Iberian Peninsula and so 'over-fly' their relatives from more southerly breeding places.

†**3.** To fly (a hawk) too much. *Obs.* [OVER- 27.]

[**1575** TURBERV. *Faulconrie* 155 The higher fleeing that a hawke is, the more neede..to regarde that you ouerflee hir not.] **1616** SURFL. & MARKH. *Country Farme* 714 His owner can seldome ouer-flye him, no, though he flye him sixe or seuen flights in a morning.

4. To exceed (the maximum flying-time allowed by regulations).

1966 *Daily Tel.* 1 Nov. 12/3 One or two of the pilots had 'overflown' their regulation number of hours and had to present themselves for 'medicals'.

overfold (ˈəʊvəfəʊld), *sb. Geol.* [f. OVER- 3, 6 + FOLD *sb.*, after Ger. *überfaltung* (Brögger *Silurische Etagen*).] A fold of strata in which the axes of the component anticline and syncline have both been tilted or pushed over beyond the vertical, so that the strata involved in the middle third of the fold are turned upside down. (Also *inclined*, *overturned*, *inverted*, or *reflexed fold*.)

1883 LAPWORTH in *Geol. Mag.* X. May 199 A sigmaplex or sigmoidal fold (Overfold of Brögger). *Ibid.* Aug. 340 In overfolds of vast extent the arch limb being nearer the surface is more rigid, the trough limb, being buried under more than double the burden, is more ductile. *Ibid.* 342 [see OVERFAULT]. **1896** VAN HISE *N. Amer. Pre-Cambrian Geol.* (U.S. Geol. Surv.) 674 It has been long recognized that thrust faults are often related to overfolds... The overfolds may be broken along the reversed limbs, and the arch limbs be thrust over the trough limbs.

overfold (əʊvəˈfəʊld), *v.* [OVER- 8, 3, 6.]

1. *trans.* To fold over, or so as to cover.

a **1400–50** *Alexander* 5463 Quen it was hewyn at his hest with heggis ouire-folden, þan entirs in of his erles. *c* **1420** *Pallad. on Husb.* I. 523 A stondyng most be maad and ouer-folde And couered wel with shingil, tile, or broom. *a* **1814** *Prophetess* II. ii. in *New Brit. Theatre* I. 192 Peace, whose cheering plough o'erfolds the bloody track Of his [the God of War's] throne-shaking chariots.

2. *Geol.* Of folded strata: (In *passive*) To be pushed over beyond the vertical, so as to overhang or overlie the strata on the other side of the axis: see OVERFOLD *sb.*

1883 LAPWORTH in *Geol. Mag.* X. Aug. 343 The causes and results of overfolding of rocks under tangential thrust. **1896** VAN HISE *N. Amer. Pre-Cambrian Geol.* (U.S. Geol. Surv.) 604 A fold is overturned or overfolded when the axial plane is inclined and the limbs have equal or unequal dips in the same direction at corresponding points.

ˈover-ˈfond, *a.* [OVER- 28.] Too fond.

1. Too silly or foolish. *Obs.* exc. *dial.*

c **1585** *Fair Em* III. 1123 Causing your grief, by overfond affecting a man so trothless. **1599** JAS. I. *Βασιλ. Δωρον* III. 2 b, As for the Chesse, I think it ouer fonde, because it is ouerwise & Philosophick a folly. [**1868** see OVER *adv.* 11.]

2. Too affectionate; having too great an affection or liking for a person or thing (const. *of*).

1611 SHAKS. *Wint. T.* v. ii. 126 Ouer-fond of the Shepheards Daughter. **1774** FOOTE *Cozeners* III. Wks. 1799 II. 180, I never was over-fond of my bed. **1876** MISS BRADDON *J. Haggard's Dau.* I. 41 What have I to live for.. that I should be overfond of life?

Hence **ˈover-ˈfondly** *adv.*; **ˈover-ˈfondness**.

1614 RALEIGH *Hist. World* IV. vii. §4 (1634) 538 To exasperate their furious choler, by uncourtious words or usage as Ceraunus had overfondly done. **1690** LOCKE *Hum. Und.* IV. x. §7 Out of Over-fondness of that darling Invention. **1842** MANNING *Serm.* xxii. (1848) I. 326 What they over-fondly doated on, we have coldly forgotten. **1876** L. STEPHEN *Eng. Thought 18th Cent.* II. 54 Overfondness for ourselves, like over-fondness for children may defeat its own object.

ˌover-ˈfondle, *v.* [OVER- 27.] *trans.* To fondle too much.

1714 MANDEVILLE *Fab. Bees* (1725) I. 143 Infants that are froward, and by being over-fondled made humoursome.

over-foolish to **over-force**: see OVER-.

†**overforth**, *adv. Obs. rare.* [f. OVER *adv.* + FORTH.] Very far forth, forward, or onward.

a **1225** *Ancr. R.* 288 Hwon þe delit iðe luste is igon so oueruorð þet ter nis non wiðsigginge, ȝif þer were eise uorto fulfullen þe dede.

ˈoverˈforward, *a.* [OVER- 28.] Too forward.

1631 GOUGE *God's Arrows* III. lviii. 291 Such as are over-forward to warre. **1749** FIELDING *Tom Jones* IV. x, Better to see a Daughter over-modest, than over forward.

So **ˈoverˈforwardly** *adv.*; **ˈoverˈforwardness**.

1593 *Pass. Morrice* (1876) 75 Her overforwardnes seemed to overlay her lovers affection. **1669** *Lond. Gaz.* No. 403/4 Who..has over-forwardly advanced the Negotiation. **1742** RICHARDSON *Pamela* III. 298 What shall I do, if I have incurred Mr. B.'s Anger by my Over-forwardness?

overfought to **-franchised**: see OVER-.

ˌoverˈfraught, *ppl. a.* [OVER- 27, 28.] Too heavily freighted or laden.

1589 NASHE *Pref. Greene's Menaphon* (Arb.) 11 Their ouer-fraught Studies, with trifling Compendiaries maie testifie. **1634** MILTON *Comus* 732 The Sea o'refraught would swell. **1827** POLLOK *Course T.* I. 16 The muse that.. raves through gaudy tale, Not overfraught with sense.

ˈoverˈfree, *a.* [OVER- 28.] Too free. So **ˈoverˈfreedom**, excessive or too great freedom; **ˈoverˈfreely** *adv.*, too freely.

1639 FULLER *Holy War* III. xiv. (1840) 139 His valour was not over-free, but would well answer the spur when need required. **1648** BOYLE *Seraph. Love* iv, We may easily play the prodigals in parting (over-freely) with our gifts. **1672** DRYDEN *Maiden Q.* II. i. Wks. 1808 II. 413 That frown assures me I have offended, by my over-freedom. **1742** RICHARDSON *Pamela* IV. 13 An over-free or negligent Behaviour in a Lady.

ˌoverˈfreight (-ˈfreɪt), *v.* [OVER- 27.] *trans.* To overload.

1530 PALSGR. 648/1, I overfreyt a shyppe, *je surcharge.* **1602** CAREW *Cornwall* 108 A boat ouerfraighted with people ..was, by the extreme weather, sunk. **1711** SHAFTESB. *Charac.* (1737) III. 300 They themselves are over-freighted with this merchandize of thought.

So **ˈoverfreight** *sb.*, an overload.

1850 BROWNING *Christmas Eve* xiv, The while ascends.. Step by step, deliberate, Because of his cranium's over-freight..The hawk-nosed high-cheek-boned Professor. **1883** *Pall Mall G.* 27 Sept. 11/2 He..had for above thirty years to fight without result against an overfreight of 50 lb. of fat.

over-frequency, -frequent: see OVER- 28, 29.

†**overˈfret**, *ppl. a. Obs.* [f. OVER- 8 + *fret*, pa. pple. of FRET *v.*²] Covered with embroidered work; overspread with rich ornament.

a **1440** *Sir Degrev.* 626 Sche come in a vyolet With whyȝthe perl overfret. **1535** STEWART *Cron. Scot.* III. 232 And all the feild with fynest gold ouirfret. **1560** ROLLAND *Crt. Venus* I. 95 With Emeraudis so michtelie ouirfret.

overˈfret, *v.* [f. OVER- 21, 23 + FRET *v.*¹] *trans.* To wear down with fretting; *refl.* to fret beyond one's power of endurance.

1563 *Myrr. for Mag., Buckingham* xl, Yet was his hart wyth wretched cares orefret. **1851** HELPS *Comp. Solit.* x. (1874) 182 Do not overfret yourself.

†**overˈfrieze**, *v. Obs.* [f. OVER- 8 + FRIEZE *v.*²] *trans.* To embroider over with gold.

a **1548** HALL *Chron.* (1809) 519 On their heddes were bonnettes opened at the iiij quarters overfrysed with flat gold of Damaske.

overfright to **over-frolic**: see OVER-.

ˈoverfront, *sb.* [OVER- 8 c.] A piece which hangs over the front of a cloak, and covers the arm instead of a sleeve.

1889 *Daily News* 23 July 7/2 The travelling mantle..is provided with over-fronts which fall straight from the shoulders, and protect the arms without embarrassing their movements. **1891** *Ibid.* 19 Sept. 2/1 The sleeves being formed by the over-fronts, which fall over the arms.

†**overˈfront**, *v. Obs.* [OVER- 22, 24.] *trans.* **a.** To extend in front beyond (another army). **b.** To stand over against the front of, confront.

1623 BINGHAM *Xenophon* 75 That the out-most companies may over-front, and be without the points of the enemies wings. **1643** MILTON *Divorce* To Parl. Eng., When things indifferent shall be set to over-front us, under the banners of sin.

over-froth, overfrown: see OVER- 8, 1.

overˈfrozen, *ppl. a.* [OVER- 8, 10.] Frozen over the whole surface, or from side to side.

1494 FABYAN *Chron.* VII. ccxxxiii. 267 The ryuer of Thamys was so strongly ouer frorne, yᵗ horse & carte passed ouer vpon yᵉ ice. **1599** HAKLUYT *Voy.* II. II. 78 *margin*, At Cacan Riuers ouerfrosen in China. **1654** TRAPP *Comm. Job* xxxviii. 30 Yea, some seas are over-frozen..in the Northern part of the world.

overfruit, -fruitful: see OVER- 8, 28.

ˌoverfulˈfil, *v.* Also (*U.S.*) overfulfill. [OVER- 24.] †**1.** *trans.* To fill more than full, fill too full. *Obs.*

1398 TREVISA *Barth. De P.R.* VI. xx. (Bodl. MS.) lf. 42/2 In suche doinge..þe stomake is ouere fulfilde and istreiȝte to swiþe. **1538** STARKEY *England* I. iii. 76 Thys body ys replenyschyd and ouerfulfyllyd wyth many yl humorys.

2. To achieve more than the mere fulfilment of (a plan, goal, etc.); to reach (a target) before the expected time. So **ˌoverfulˈfilment**, (*U.S.*) **-fulfillment**.

1950 *Sun* (Baltimore) 2 June 14/7 When the Russian whalers returned to their home port of Odessa on the Black Sea they had overfulfilled their production plan by 29·9 per cent. *Ibid.* 7 Aug. 10/2 If present rates [of Soviet production] are continued to December 31, a massive overfulfillment of the 1950 goals will result. **1952** KOESTLER *Arrow in Blue* 70 To omit a single one [*sc.* slogan]—say 'the strengthening of the production-offensive for the over-fulfilment of the light metal industry's revised counter-plan'..would have laid the lecturer open to the accusation [etc.]. **1964** K. G. LOCKYER *Introd. Critical Path Analysis* vii. 61 Bars to the *left* of the observation line represent under-fulfillment, whilst those to the *right* represent over-fulfillment. **1966** J. PORTER *Sour Cream* iv. 51 Even the waitresses had something to take their minds off their feet and the difficulties of over-fulfilling the latest five-year-plan. *Ibid.* v. 68 The current ten-year plan was going to be over-fulfilled. **1971** *New Society* 25 Mar. 475/2 Factories have undertaken commitments to overfulfil production targets in honour of the congress. **1975** *Nature* 16 Oct. 527/2 Soviet planners see agriculture as being essentially one more branch of industrial production, amenable to the same system of fulfilment and overfulfilment of plans. **1976** *Chinese Law & Govt.* IX. 101 We should fulfill or overfulfill the Fourth Five-Year Plan in 1975.

'over'full, *a.* [OE. *oferfull* = OHG. *ubarfol*, intoxicated, Goth. *ufarfulls*: see OVER- 24, 28.] Excessively full, too full.

a **1000** *Lamb. Ps.* lxxvii. 65 (Bosw.) *Crapulatus* (glossed) oferfull. *a* **1225** *Ancr. R.* 160 þeos þreo maner men habbeð ine heouene mid ouer fulle mede. **1590** SHAKS. *Mids. N.* I. i. 113 But being ouer-full of selfe-affaires, My minde did lose it. **1825** J. NEAL *Bro. Jonathan* III. 317 His heart was overfull. **1897** *Allbutt's Syst. Med.* III. 560 The stomach dilates and becomes over-full.

Hence ˌ**over'fullness.**

1612 WOODALL *Surg. Mate* Wks. (1653) 199 Repletion or overfulnesse, as well as too much fasting is to be avoided. **1884** M. D. CONWAY in *Manch. Exam.* 2 July 5/4 His great heart burst with its overfullness of emotion and energy.

'overfur. [OVER- 8.] The outer layer of an animal's fur.

1913 [see *guard hair* s.v. GUARD *sb.* 18.] **1968** J. IRONSIDE *Fashion Alphabet* 153 *Top fur.* This refers to the guard hairs or overfur; it is stiffer, coarser and usually darker than the underfur.

†**'overfyll,** *sb. Obs.* [OE. *oferfyll*, *-fyllo* = OHG. *ubarfullî* intoxication, Ger. *überfülle*, Goth. *ufarfullei*, f. *ubarfulls* + abstr. suffix *-ei*, *-î*, *-e*:—*în*.] Overfullness, esp. in reference to eating or drinking; surfeit, repletion.

c **888** K. ÆLFRED *Boeth.* xxxi. §1 Seo oferfyll simle fet unþeawas. *c* **1000** *Sax. Leechd.* II. 178 Wið manegum adlum ..ðe þe cumað of oferfyllo. *a* **1250** *Owl & Night.* 354 Over-fulle maketh wlatie.

overga, etc., obs. forms of OVERGO, etc.

over-gaiter to **-gamesome:** see OVER-.

over'gang, *v.* Now *Sc.* and *north. dial.* [OE. *ofergangan* = OHG. *ubargangan*, Goth. *ufargaggan*: see OVER- in various senses.]

1. *trans.* To tread over, trample upon, conquer, overpower, get the better of. [OVER- 1, 21.]

a **1000** *Riddles* xli. 10 (Gr.) Mec..slæp ofergongeð. *a* **1000** *Cædmon's Exod.* 561 (Gr.) þæt ge feonda gehwone forð ofergangað. *c* **1200** ORMIN 10228 To werenn hemm wiþþ wiþerrþeod þatt wollde hemm oferrganngenn. *a* **1300** *Cursor M.* 5505 (Cott.) Ioseph kin ouer-ganges all, þat to our eldres was a thrall. **1567** *Gude & Godlie B.* (S.T.S.) 141 Allace! ȝour grace hes done greit wrang, To suffer tyrannis in sic sort, Daylie ȝour liegis till ouergang. **1715** PENNECUIK *Many's Truth's Trav.* in *Poems* 94 For fear that Truth should clean ou'rgang them. **1795** BURNS *Old Song, 'O ay my wife'*, If ye gie a woman a' her will, Guid faith, she'll soon o'ergang ye.

†**2.** To go over, cross, overstep; to transgress; = OVERGO *v.* 2, 2 b. (*OE.* and *ME.*) [OVER- 12.]

a **1000** *Boeth. Metr.* xx. 71 Heora ænig oðres ne dorste mearce ofergangan. *c* **1000** *Ags. Ps.* (Spelm.) xvii. 31 Ic ofergange weall. *a* **1275** *Prov. Ælfred* 444 in *O.E. Misc.* 129 þanne sal þi child þi forbod ouer-gangin.

3. To go over; to overrun, overspread. [OVER- 9.]

a **1300** *Cursor M.* 22132 (Cott.) Ouer all þar crist was wont to ga, [Anticrist] þaim sal ouer-gang alsua. **1570** *Satir. Poems Reform.* xvi. 86, I thinke the holkis ouergangis ȝour ene. **1596** DALRYMPLE tr. *Leslie's Hist. Scot.* I. 122 Quha.. lattis gude ground..ouirgang wᵗ weidis. **1766** PITCAIRN *Assembly* 13 (E.D.D.) That place is all overgrown with briers and thorns, and they'll soon o'ergang Scotland too. **1828** *Craven Gloss.* (ed. 2), *Ower-gang*, to over-run.

4. To go beyond, exceed. [OVER- 13.]

1737 RAMSAY *Prov.* (1750) 95 The pains o'ergangs the profit. **1822** GALT *Provost* xxxv, The outlay I thought as likely to o'ergang the profit.

Hence †**over'ganger,** (*a*) one who overcomes, a conqueror; (*b*) an overseer, superintendent (*Sc.*).

c **1340** HAMPOLE *Prose Tr.* 29 By Jacob in Haly Writt es vndirstande ane ouerganger of synnes. *Ibid.* 30 Ouer-ganger and ouercommere of all synnes.

'over-ˌgarment. [OVER- 8 c.] A garment worn over the others, an outer garment.

1470–85 MALORY *Arthur* ix. i, His ouer garment sat ouerthwartly. **1882–3** SCHAFF *Encycl. Relig. Knowl.* I. 500 The over-garment..which was thrown around the person. **1884** BROWNING *Ferishtah, Two Camels* 17 Thou hast already donned Thy sheepskin over-garment.

over-garrisoned: see OVER- 28 d.

†**'overgart,** *sb. Obs.* [app. f. OVER- + the radical part seen also in ANGARD, *-gart*, OGART, *ongart*, app. from ONorse, but the ultimate derivation is uncertain.] Arrogance, presumption, pride.

c **1200** ORMIN 8163 Acc þær wass mikell oferrgarrt & modiȝnesse shæwedd. *Ibid.* 15770 Fra werelldshipess oferrgarrt. *a* **1225** *St. Marher.* 16 Hwen a meiden ure muchele ouer-gart þus afalleð. *Ibid.* 10 His muchele ouergat. [Cf. *Cursor M.* 478, where *ouengart* in Cott. may be error for *ouergart* or for *ongart*; F. has *awgart*, G. & Tr. *pride*. In l. 7318 Cott. has *ougard* (? *ongard*), F. *awgarde*, G. & Tr. *enuy*.]

†**'overgart,** *a.* and *adv. Obs.* [Cf. prec.]

A. *adj.* Immoderate, excessive, presumptuous.

c **1325** *Poem Times Edw. II* 391 in *Pol. Songs* (Camden) 341 For tho God seih that the world was so over gart, He sente a derthe on earthe, and made hit ful smart.

B. *adv.* Immoderately, excessively.

c **1320** *Cast. Love* 993 þat al he bi-comeþ ouergart proud, And mis-doþ his neiȝebors boþe stille and loud. *c* **1350** *Will. Palerne* 1069 þe douȝti duk of saxoyne drow to þat londe Wiþ ouer gart gret ost godmen of armes. **13..** in *Rel. Ant.* II. 226 Ich am overgard agast, and quake al in my speche.

'overgate, *sb.* Also 8 **-gait.** [f. OVER- 5 b + GATE *sb.*[2]] **a.** A way over a wall, stream, etc. *north. dial.* **b.** *Mining.* An overhead air-passage.

1796 W. MARSHALL *Yorksh.* (ed. 2) Gloss. (E.D.S.), *Ower-gait*, (accented on the first syllable), [a] stile-place, or imperfect gap, in a hedge. Also a 'stepping-place' across a brook. **1851** in GREENWELL *Coal-trade Terms Northumb. & Durh.* **1855** ROBINSON *Whitby Gloss.*, *Ower-gate*, a stepping-style in a field. **1894** *Northumbld. Gloss.*, *Over-gate*, an air-way overhead in a pit, where one air-course is carried by a bridge over another.

†**'overgate,** *adv. Obs. rare.* [f. OVER *prep.* 9 + GATE *sb.*[2] 9 b.] In the way of excess, excessively.

a **1450** MYRC 1307 Hast þow I-coueted ouer gate Worldes worschype or any a-state?

over'gaze, *v. rare.* [OVER- 23, 5.]

1. *refl.* and *pass.* To dazzle oneself with gazing.

1600 BRETON *Melanchol. Hum.* (1879) 13/2 Oh that..his eyes [were] not ouergazed In Minervas excellences.

2. To gaze over, overlook.

1816 BYRON *Ch. Har.* III. xci, His altar the high places and the peak Of earth's o'ergazing mountains. **1879** A. T. DE VERE *Legends Saxon Saints* 41 Meadow banks, Not yet o'ergazed by Windsor's crested steep Or Reading's tower.

over-general: see OVER-.

over-'generalize, *v.* [OVER- 27.] *intr.* To draw general conclusions from inadequate data; to argue more widely than is justified by the available evidence, by circumstances, etc. Also *trans.*, to draw an over-general conclusion from (data, circumstances, etc.). Hence ˌ**over-generali'zation; over-'generalized** *ppl. a.*

1904 in N.E.D. s.v. *Over-* 27 a. **1937** *Mind* XLVI. 243 He over-generalises. For example, he claims that implicit is superior to explicit comparison. **1947** J. G. WEIGHTMAN *On Language & Writing* 87 In trying to think with precision we oscillate between two extremes, over-generalization and over-particularization. **1956** *Nature* 10 Mar. 478/2 The properties of larval blow-fly carbohydrases do not completely exemplify Weidenhagen's hypothesis of bond specificity, the over-generalized nature of which has been criticized more recently. **1957** K. A. WITTFOGEL *Oriental Despotism* 370 Overgeneralizing the experience of a rapidly changing Western world, they naively postulated a simple, unilinear, and progressive course of societal growth. **1970** S. L. BARRACLOUGH in I. L. Horowitz *Masses in Lat. Amer.* iv. 97 To avoid falling into the more obvious errors of overgeneralization about Latin America as a whole. **1971** *Sci. Amer.* Aug. 75/3 Although Sherrington was careful not to overgeneralize from his findings, less circumspect workers soon adopted the extreme position that most animal behavior consists of reflexes. **1975** R. V. REDINGER *Geo. Eliot* (1976) v. 245 Slanted and overgeneralized as are many of its discussions, this book fulfilled a real need.

over-genial, -gentle: see OVER-.

overget (əʊvə'gɛt), *v.* [OVER- 14, 5.]

1. *trans.* To overtake. Now only *dial.*

c **1330** R. BRUNNE *Chron. Wace* (Rolls) 12708 ȝif þy felawes þe ouer gete, Sey, 'þe messegers wente here forþ god spede'. *c* **1450** *Merlin* 276 Thei slough and maymed alle that thei myght ouer-gete. **1530** PALSGR. 648/2, I made suche dylygence that at the laste I overgate hym. **1591** HARINGTON *Orl. Fur.* XXIX. lxiv, Orlando still doth her pursue so fast That needs he must ov'rget her at the last. **1787** GROSE *Provinc. Gloss.* s.v., He is but a little before; you will soon over-get him. **1825** BROCKETT, *Overget*, to overtake.

2. To get over, surmount, recover from the effects of (an illness, shock, etc.). (A midland dial. sense, which has passed into literary use.)

1803 SOUTHEY *Lett.* (1856) I. 230 Edith cannot sleep, and till she overgets this, she cannot be better. **1862** MRS. H. WOOD *Mrs. Hallib.* II. 60 She had overgot the temporary indications of illness. **1886** *Charity Organis. Rev.* Feb. 75 The difficulties to be overgot are great.

3. 'To get the better of; to overreach, to outwit.'

1886 in *Cassell's Encycl. Dict.*

4. To prevail upon; to take possession of (a person).

1904 *Tradesman's Price-list* (Herbert Morris & Bastert) 11 Similarity of appearance so far overgets a customer as to induce him to pass us. **1928** *Sunday Dispatch* 16 Sept. 2/3 The thought to marry Fanny overgot the man, and he set out to see if it could be done. **1953** D. D. C. P. MOULD *Rock of Truth* xi. 193 When I had been a Catholic some time and perhaps begun to grasp some idea of what God was really like, then the fear of hell did overget me.

overgild (əʊvə'gɪld), *v.* [f. OVER- 8 + GILD *v.* (q.v. for Forms).] *trans.* To gild over, cover with gilding; *fig.* to tinge with a golden colour. Chiefly in *pa. pple.*

c **1200** ORMIN 2612 Butt iff itt beo þurrh þildess gold All full wel oferrgildedd. *c* **1290** *S. Eng. Leg.* I. 96/159 An ymage, briȝt and schene Ouer-guld and quoynte i-nov. **1387** TREVISA *Higden* (Rolls) V. 445 A combe of yvorie somdel overgilt. **1420** in *E.E. Wills* (1882) 46 Also a spyce dısshe of seluer, & ouerguld. **1508** DUNBAR *Golden Targe* 27 The purpur hevyn our scailit in silvir sloppis Ourgilt the treis, branchis, lef[is] and barkis. **1592** NASHE *P. Penilesse* (ed. 2) 27 All cunning drifts ouerguylded with outward holinesse. **1612** W. PARKES *Curtaine Dr.* (1876) 22 Those golden words that so ouerguild such bitter pilles. **1821** BYRON *Foscari* III. i. 65 The full sun, When gorgeously o'ergilding any towers. **1861** TRENCH *Comm. Ep. to 7 Ch.* 149 Royal sceptres are not usually of iron, but of wood overgilded.

Hence **over'gilding** *vbl. sb.*, **over'gilt** *ppl. a.*

?*a* **1366** CHAUCER *Rom. Rose* 873 In an overgilt samet Cladde she was. **1477** *Rolls of Parlt.* VI. 184/2 The thyng in which any such overgildyng shal be.

†**over'gilted,** *pa. pple. Obs.* = *overgilt*, pa. pple.

c **1400** MAUNDEV. (Roxb.) i. 4 Ane ymage of Justinyane þe emperour, wele ouergilted. **1480** CAXTON *Chron. Eng.* VII. (1520) 136 b, Two basyns of sylver and overgylted.

overgird: see OVER- 8.

over'give, *v. Obs.* exc. *dial.* [f. OVER- (in various senses) + GIVE *v.* In sense 2 corresp. to OE. *ofgifan*.]

†**1.** *trans.* To give over, to expend. *Obs. rare.* (rendering L. *superimpendĕre*.)

1382 WYCLIF *2 Cor.* xii. 15 Forsoth I moost wilfully schal ȝyue, and I my silf schal be ouerȝouun for ȝoure soulis.

†**2.** To give over or up, hand over, surrender.

1444 *Reg. Magni Sig.* (1882) 63/2 Wit yhe us..till have renounsit ouregevin quyt clemyt..all richt..in or to all landis [etc.]. **1591** SPENSER *M. Hubberd* 249, I am a Souldiere,..And now, constrain'd that trade to overgive, I driven am to seeke some meanes to live. **1682** in *Scott. Antiq.* (1901) July 8, I..demitt and overgive my place of dean of facultie in the said wniversaty.

†**3.** *intr.* To give over, desist, cease. *Obs.*

1592 WARNER *Alb. Eng.* VII. xxxvi. (1612) 175 The Hound at Losse doth ouer-giue. **1591** SYLVESTER *Du Bartas* I. iii. 804 And never over-give Till they both dying give Man leave to live.

b. *intr.* To give way as frost, to thaw. *dial.*

a **1825** in FORBY *Voc. E. Anglia.*

4. *trans.* To give in addition.

1622 BP. HALL *Contempl. O.T.* XVII. *Solomon's Choice*, So doth God loue a good choyce, and hee recompences it with ouer-giuing.

Hence †**over'giving** *vbl. sb.*, handing over, surrender. *Obs.*

1546 *Reg. Privy Council Scot.* I. 66 At the ourgeving of the said Castell it wes convenit that [etc.]. **1571** in Spottiswood *Hist. Ch. Scot.* v. (1677) 254 The said pretended Dimission, Renunciation and Overgiving of the Crown by the Queen.

'over-'glad, *a.* [OVER- 25, 28.] Excessively glad; too glad.

1390 GOWER *Conf.* I. 133 Anon he wext of his corage So overglad, that [etc.]. **1845** DISRAELI *Sybil* IV. v, I am not surprised at your opinion,..I should not be over-glad to meet you in a fray. **1870** MORRIS *Earthly Par.* III. IV. 186 To make more mirth, For folk already overglad.

†**over-'glad,** *v. Obs. rare.* [OVER- 25.] *trans.* To gladden exceedingly.

1631 CAPT. SMITH *Advts. Planters* 2 If it over-glad me to see Industry..make use of my aged endevours.

†**over'glance,** *v. Obs.* [OVER- 16.] *trans.* To glance over, cast the eye over.

1588 SHAKS. *L.L.L.* IV. ii. 135, I will ouerglance the superscript. **1599** —— *Hen. V*, v. ii. 78, I haue but with a curselarie eye O're-glanc't the Articles. **1883** *Century Mag.* XXV. 859 The eye that overglances the..sunny leagues of surrounding distance.

overglase, obs. form of OVERGLAZE *v.*

'over-ˌglass, *sb.* [OVER- 1.] A glass or mirror placed over a mantelpiece.

1898 *Tit-Bits* 26 Mar. 490/2 A chimney-piece and over-glass.

over'glass, *v. rare.* [OVER- 8.] *trans.* To cover over as with glass.

1883–4 MRS. WHITNEY in *Chicago Advance* 10 Jan., The brook..overglassed With icy sheathing.

'overglaze, *sb. Ceramics.* [OVER- 8.] A second glaze applied to a piece of pottery, e.g. when the first glaze has been painted on. Also in *Painting*.

1880 *Harper's Mag.* Nov. 904/1 The work most familiar to us as taught in America during the last three or four years has all been on the over-glaze. **1884** *American* VII. 217 Enthusiastic amateurs have grappled with the pottery question, and the mysteries of 'overglaze' and 'underglaze' have engrossed [etc.]. **1947** J. C. RICH *Materials & Methods Sculpture* ii. 49 Overglazes can be applied in several ways, the most frequent of which are direct painting with a soft brush, and fine spraying. **1948** F. A. STAPLES *Water-Color Painting* x. 116 Now that the first tone..is dry, the second, an overglaze, is painted. **1974** SAVAGE & NEWMAN *Illustr. Dict. Ceramics* 208 Over-glaze..is by means of colours termed enamels.

ˈoverglaze, *a.* [OVER- 8.] **a.** Of painting: On or connected with a glazed surface. **b.** Suitable or used for painting on glazed surfaces.

1879 J. C. L. SPARKES *Handbk. Pract. Pottery Painting* 28 Oil mediums may be used for over-glaze and for under-glaze work. *Ibid.* 31 In painting on china, earthenware and all 'over-glaze' ware with enamel colours the procedure is as follows. **1881** *Harper's Mag.* May 835/1 It was..the most extensive and satisfactory exhibit of amateur overglaze decoration made up to that time. **1883** *Ibid.* July 259/1 The overglaze painting of tea-cups. **1936** *Burlington Mag.* Oct. 145/2 Figural designs in polychrome over-glaze painting. **1970** *Ashmolean Mus. Rep. Visitors 1969* 46 Ginger jar with underglaze blue landscape decoration and later added dragons and flowers in overglaze colours. **1973** *Country Life* 7 June 1591/3 By the early 1770s..the head colourman, Constantine Smith, had invented a dark, semi-matt, overglaze blue enamel of exceptional brilliance.

overˈglaze, *v.* Also 6 -glase. [OVER- 8.] *trans.* To glaze over, to cover with a glaze or polish; hence, †to coat or plate with a thin covering of something better, to veneer (*obs.*). Hence ˌ**overˈglazing** *vbl. sb.*

1592 GREENE *Upst. Courtier* F iij, The Sadler, he stuffes his pannels with straw or hay, and ouer glaseth them with haire. *Ibid.* F iij b, You sell him a swoorde or rapier newe ouerglased, and sweare the blade came either from Turkie or Toledo. **1947** J. C. RICH *Materials & Methods Sculpture* ii. 49 Overglazing is a process in which color or overglazes are applied over glazes for decorative effects; they require an additional exposure to heat. *a* **1977** *Harrison Mayer Ltd. Catal.* 18/2 Over-glazing. This usually occurs on very porous or easy fired ware. Over-glazing can frequently lead to stuck ware and can cause underglaze colours to run.

overˈglide, *v. poet.* [OVER- 9.] *trans.* To glide over, pass over gently or smoothly.

a **1541** WYATT *Ps.* xxxii, That sonne..whose glaunsing light the cords dyd ouer-glyde. **1598** SYLVESTER *Du Bartas* II. i. III. *Furies* 761 We plainly call the *Fever*, *Fever*, The *Dropsie*, *dropsie*: over-gliding never, With guile-full flourish of a fained phraze, The cruell Languors that our bodies craze. **1844** MRS. BROWNING *Drama of Exile* Poems 1850 I. 12 Ideal sweetnesses shall overglide you.

overglint: see OVER-.

overˈgloom, *v.* [OVER- 8.] *trans.* To cover with gloom, to overshadow; to cast a gloom over, to sadden.

1795 COLERIDGE *To Author Poems publ. Bristol* 20 The cloud-climbed rock..That like some giant king o'erglooms the hill. **1812** —— *Lett., to Mrs. Coleridge* (1895) 580 Nothing intervenes to overgloom my mind. **1883** L. MORRIS *Songs Unsung, St. Christopher* 154 A dark road stole to it O'er-gloomed by cypress, and no boat was there Nor ferry.

ˈover-ˈgloominess. [OVER- 29.] Excessive or too great gloominess.

1742 RICHARDSON *Pamela* III. 264, I said that this Over-gloominess was not Religion.

over-glorious, -gloss: see OVER-.

overˈglut, *v.* [f. OVER- 25, 27 + GLUT *v.*[1]] *trans.* To glut to excess. Hence **overˈglutted** *ppl. a.*

1589 PUTTENHAM *Eng. Poesie* I. iv. (Arb.) 24 By that occasion the eare is ouerglutted with it. **1600** BRETON *Melancholike Hum.* (1879) 9 While epicures are over-glut, I ly and starue for foode. **1660** SHARROCK *Vegetables* 108 Some caution is to be had that by too much water you do not chill or over-glut the ground. **1792** FENNEL *Proceedings at Paris* 390 Blood, rubbed from the murderers' over-glutted hands. *a* **1814** *Sulieman* I. v. in *New Brit. Theatre* II. 18 The sword O'erglutted with the blood of Hassem's friends.

overgo (əʊvəˈgəʊ), *v.* Forms: see OVER *adv.* and GO *v. Pa. t.* α. 1 oferéode, 4 -3ede, -3ide, -yod(e, *Sc.* 6 -3eid, 8 -yeed; β. 4– overwent. [OE. *ofergán* = OLG. **obargân* (MDu. *overgaen*, Du. *overgaan*), OHG. *ubargân* (MHG. *übergân*, *-gên*, Ger. *übergehen*): see OVER- in various senses.]

I. Transitive senses.

†**1.** To come upon suddenly; to overtake; to catch, apprehend, detect. *Obs.* [OVER- 7, 14.]

a **1000** *Andreas* 821 (Gr.) Hine..slæp ofereode. *c* **1000** ÆLFRIC *Hom.* (Th.) I. 86 Wæter-seocnyss hine ofereode. *a* **1300** *Cursor M.* 4721 (Cott.) Qualm has beistes al ouergan. **13..** *Guy Warw.* (A.) 3277 3if he þe may ouer-go, He wil þe bren oþer slo. *a* **1425** *Cursor M.* 13700 (Trin.) A wif þat wiþ horedome was ouergon. **1581** MARBECK *Bk. of Notes* 346 This bird [the ostrich]..cannot mount vp to flie aloft, but flickereth in such wise as he cannot be ouergone.

2. a. To pass over (a wall, river, boundary, or line); to surmount; to cross. *Obs.* exc. *dial.* [OVER- 5, 12.]

c **825** *Vesp. Psalter* xvii. 30 [xviii. 29] In gode minum ic ofergaa wall. *c* **1000** ÆLFRIC *Hom.* (Th.) II. 200 Ærðan ðe hi þa Readan sæ ofereodon. *c* **1000** *Sax. Leechd.* III. 252 On langiendum dagum he ofer gæþ ðone suðran sunnstede. *c* **1250** *Gen. & Ex.* 3490 God bad hem ðat merke ouer-gon. **1382** WYCLIF *Deut.* xxvii. 3 Jordan ouergoon. **1609** DANIEL *Civ. Wars* IV. i, The bounds once ouer-gone, that hold men in, They neuer stay. **1657** W. RAND tr. *Gassendi's Life Peiresc* II. 50 When Druentia, or Rhodanus over-went their banks. **1789** ROSS *Helenore* 31 Ere I bridle drew, O'eryeed a' bounds afore I ever knew.

†**b.** *fig.* To pass (a moral limit), to transgress. Phr. ***to overgo the balance*** (see quot. 1539); ***to overgo one's bed***, to break wedlock. *Obs.*

c **950** *Lindisf. Gosp.* Matt. xv. 2 Forhuon ðegnas ðinne hia ofergæs..setnesa ðara ældra. **1382** WYCLIF *Ecclus.* xxiii. 25 Eche man that ouergoth his bed [*Vulg.* transgreditur lectum]. **1539** TAVERNER *Erasm. Prov.* (1545) 141 Ouergo not the beame or balaunce. That is to say, do nothynge besyde ryght and equitie.

†**3.** To go or rise higher than, or over the top of; to surmount. *Obs.* [OVER- 1.]

1382 WYCLIF *Ps.* xxxvii[i]. 5 For my wickidnesses ouer3iden [1388 ben goon ouer] myn hed. **1613–16** W. BROWNE *Brit. Past.* II. v. 692 Springs..swelled forth and overwent the top. *a* **1619** FOTHERBY *Atheom.* I. ix. §3 As much as loftiest Cedars show, The lowest Shrubs doe ouergoe.

4. *fig.* To go beyond, exceed, excel. [OVER- 13.]

c **1230** *Hali Meid.* 23 Maidenhad wið hundred fald ouer geað baðe. *c* **1375** *Sc. Leg. Saints* xxxvi. (*Baptista*) 179 For he oure-gais prophetis al & patriarkis þat we cal. **1471** RIPLEY *Comp. Alch.* Rec. viii. in Ashm. *Theatr. Chem. Brit.* (1652) 188 Pekoks fethers in color gay, the Raynbow whych shall overgoe. *a* **1586** SIDNEY *Arcadia* III. Wks. 1724 II. 509 Abhorring to make the punishment overgo the offence. **1601** HOLLAND *Pliny* II. 499 Euthycrates his third sonne ouerwent his brethren. *a* **1718** PENN *Tracts* Wks. 1726 I. 617 English Custom has very much overgone English Law in this Business of Oaths. **1825** JEFFERSON *Autobiog.* App., Wks. 1859 I. 113 He so far overwent the timid hesitations of his colleagues. **1825** HOGG *Queen Hynde* 151 Threatening their force to overgo. **1917** *Ampleforth Jrnl.* Jan. 127 He resolves to emulate, perhaps even to overgo, the 'Orlando Furioso'. **1923** W. RENWICK *Spenser Selections* p. ix, Ronsard's *Franciade*..*Orlando Furioso*. Spenser would overgo both.

5. a. To overcome, overpower, get the better of; to oppress, overwhelm. Now *dial.* [OVER- 21]

c **1205** LAY. 7712 Whær is þe ilke mon þat me ne mæi mid mede ouer-gan? *c* **1400** *Rom. Rose* 6821 The stronge the feble overgoth. *c* **1430** *How Good Wife taught Dau.* 97 in *Babees Bk.*, For with 3iftis men may wommen ouer goon. **1535** COVERDALE *Hab.* i. 3 Tyranny and violence are before me, power ouergoeth right. **1596** SPENSER *F.Q.* v. ii. 7 With his powre he all doth overgo, And makes them subject to his mighty wrong. *a* **1611** BEAUM. & FL. *Maid's Trag.* III. ii, I am so o'ergone with injuries Unheard-of. **1924** [see FEATHER *sb.* 1 b].

†**b.** To 'get over', overreach, cheat. *Obs.*

c **1205** LAY. 15183 For nis nauer nan mon þat me ne mai mid swikedome ouergan. **1382** WYCLIF *1 Thess.* iv. 6 That no man ouergo [so **1582** Rhem.] nether disseyue his brother in cause, or nede. **1587** TURBERV. *Trag. T.* (1837) 139 The simple minde will soone be overgone.

†**6.** To go or spread over so as to cover. *Obs.* [OVER- 8, 9.]

c **1000** *Sax. Leechd.* III. 272 Lyft is lichamlic 3esceaft swyðe þynne, seo ofer gæð ealne middaneard. **1390** GOWER *Conf.* II. 183 A large cloude hem overwente. *c* **1450** tr. *De Imitatione* III. xlii. 113 Derknesses shul not ouergo þe. *c* **1595** J. DICKENSON *Sheph. Compl.* (1878) 8 As when a blacke thicke Meteore doth ore-goe Heau'ns light. *a* **1634** CHAPMAN (T.), Rather, that the earth shall overgo Some one at least.

7. To overrun, overflow, pass or spread over in a hostile or injurious way. Now *dial.* [OVER- 9.]

c **1000** *O.E. Chron.* an. 993 (Parker MS.) [Unlaf] for..to Sandwic, and swa ðanon to 3ipeswic, and þæt eall ofereode. *a* **1122** *Ibid.* an. 1070 (Laud MS.) þæt land folc..wændon þæt he sceolde þet land ofer gan. *a* **1300** *Cursor M.* 10524 Ioseph þe gode..wel witstode þe hunger þat egypte ouer-yod. *Ibid.* 11820 þe scab ouer-gas [*Trin.* ouergoþ] his bodi all. **1546** in W. H. Turner *Select. Rec. Oxford* 186 So that the water may not overgo and destroye the grounde. **1607** NORDEN *Surv. Dial.* v. 233 It is..good pasture, but so ouergone with Thistles, as we can by no meanes destroy them. **1675** R. BURTHOGGE *Causa Dei* 95 Persons overgone with Wickedness and Vice. **1808–18** JAMIESON, *To ourgae.* I. To overrun. 'He's ourgane with the scrubbie'. **1814** NICHOLSON *Poet. Wks.* (1897) 95 (E.D.D.) If no o'ergane wi' information, At least quite free frae affectation.

8. a. To go or pass over the surface or extent of; to travel through, traverse. [OVER- 9, 16.]

13.. *Guy Warw.* (A.) 1777 Mani lond he hadde ouergo, To seche his lord wiþ sorwe & wo. **1387** TREVISA *Higden* (Rolls) VII. 83 þis Ive..ouer3ede þe spaces of many landes. *a* **1425** *Cursor M.* 22132 (Trin.) Ouer al þere crist was wont to go He [Anticrist] shal ouer gone hem also. **1513** DOUGLAS *Æneis* VI. xiii. 99 Nevir..Hercules..Sa meikle space of erd or land our3eid. **1588** SHAKS. *L.L.L.* v. ii. 196 How manie wearie steps, Of many wearie miles you haue ore-gone. **1850** BROWNING *Easter Day* xiv, I overwent Much the same ground of reasoning. **1854** MISS BAKER *Northampt. Gloss.* s.v., It is often said, when a person wishes to inspect a house or church, 'I should like to over-go it'.

†**b.** To tread over: = OVERGANG *v.* 1. *Obs.*

c **1470** HENRY *Wallace* VI. 725 Stampyt in moss, and with rud hors ourgayne.

†**9.** To pass, live through, spend (time); also, of time, to pass over (a person). *Obs.* [OVER- 17, 4.]

a **1300** *Cursor M.* 2640 Abram had þan Sex and fourscor yeir ouergan. **1588** FRAUNCE *Lawiers Log.* Ded., There bee almost seaven yeares now overgone mee since first I began to be a medler with these Logicall meditations.

†**10.** To go faster than, leave behind in going, outstrip, overtake. *Obs.* [OVER- 22.]

1530 PALSGR. 648/2 He is so lyght a man that he wyll sone overgo me. *c* **1611** CHAPMAN *Iliad* x. 298 If it chance, that we be overgone By his more swiftness, urge him still to run upon our fleet. **1635** QUARLES *Embl.* v. xi. (1718) 290 At length by flight, I over-went the pack.

†**11.** To pass over, pass by, let alone, omit. *Obs.* [OVER- 5 (*b*).]

1609 DANIEL *Civ. Wars* VIII. lxxvii, But, I must ouergoe these passages; And hasten on my way. **1622** WITHER *Mistr. Philar.* Wks. (1633) 623 Her faire eyes doe checke me now, That I seem'd to passe them so, And their praises over-goe.

II. Intransitive senses.

12. To go or pass by; to pass over or away; to pass (in time). Now *dial.* [OVER- 4.]

c **893** K. ÆLFRED *Oros.* v. ii. §5 Hie witon þeah þæt þæt ilce yfel ofereode butan 3eblote. *c* **897** —— *Gregory's Past. C.* lix. 447 Hu hrædlice se eorðlica hlisa ofergæð. *a* **1250** *Owl & Night.* 952 þe nihtegale hi understod, An over-gan lette hire mod. *c* **1330** R. BRUNNE *Chron.* (1810) 220 þe erle ansuerd nouht, he lete þat word ouer go. *c* **1374** CHAUCER *Troylus* I. 790 (846) That as here Ioyes moten ouer gone [*v.r.* ouergon] So mote hire sorwes passen euerychone. *c* **1430** *Hymns Virg.* (1867) 51 Ful myche ioie haddist þou tho;..But ri3t soone it was ouer-goo. *c* **1580** *Howers of Bless. Virg.* 98 The yeeres of men, which so soone overgoe. **1623** BINGHAM *Xenophon* 64 They gladly remembred their trauel ouer-gone. **1871** W. ALEXANDER *Johnny Gibb* xliii, The time's lang owregane.

†**13.** *fig.* To pass on to another part of a narrative, etc. (sometimes with implication of omission). *Obs.* [OVER- 4, 5 (*b*).]

c **1250** *Gen. & Ex.* 1903 Hear haued moyses ouer-gon, Ðor-fore he wended eft agon. **1430–40** LYDG. *Bochas* I. ii. (1554) 4 Mine autor lightly overgoeth, Maketh of ye age no special remembraunce.

†**14.** To go or pass over (to another place); to cross. *Obs.* [OVER- 10.]

c **1330** R. BRUNNE *Chron.* (1810) 69 Edward is dede, allas! messengers ouerwent To William.

Hence ˌ**overˈgoing** *vbl. sb.*, a going over; a transgression; a crossing; the point of going over, the brink; **overˈgone** *ppl. a.*, gone out of use, obsolete; gone beyond bounds, far gone.

1382 WYCLIF *Lam.* iii. 19 Recorde of porenesse and of myn ouergoing. **1581** PETTIE tr. *Guazzo's Civ. Conv.* III. (1586) 127 b, He is so overgone in fatherlie affection towardes them,..he cannot abide to see them trauaile and labour as he hath done. **1612** W. SCLATER *Christians Str.* 9 What availes it..whether..by overgoing, or vndergoing; we be deprived of salvation? **1634** RUTHERFORD *Lett.* (1862) I. 126 A man who was at the very overgoing of the brae and mountain; but God held a grip of him. **1654** GATAKER *Disc. Apol.* 85 To be scandalized with these overgone, or overgrown expressions. **1903** J. K. JEROME *Tea-Table Talk* v. 95, I was very severe upon both the shortcomings and the overgoings of man.

overgod to **over-good**: see OVER-.

ˌ**overˈgorge** (-gɔːdʒ), *v.* [OVER- 27.] *trans.* To gorge to excess, to cram with too much food, to glut. Hence ˌ**overˈgorged** *ppl. a.*

1575 TURBERV. *Faulconrie* 285, I warne all falconers to beware howe they overgorge their hawkes. **1641** EARL MONM. tr. *Biondi's Civil Warres* v. 96 Like unto Rivers overgorged with raine, which when flood of water cease returne to their former channell. **1784** COWPER *Task* I. 737 Thieves at home must hang, but he that puts Into his overgorg'd and bloated purse The wealth of Indian provinces, escapes. **1814** BYRON *Lara* II. vii, Such as long power and overgorged success Concentrates into all that's merciless.

overgospel: see OVER- 22 b.

over-govern (-ˈgʌvən), *v.* [OVER- 2, 27.]

†**1.** *trans.* To rule over. *Obs.*

1470–85 MALORY *Arthur* I. vi, It was grete shame vnto them all..to be ouer gouernyd with a boye of no hyghe blood borne.

2. To govern too much; to subject to too much government interference.

1863 LOWTH *Wand. W. France* 205 He overgoverns his people, and so he makes them discontented. **1938** *Sun* (Baltimore) 16 Apr. 8 For five years he [*sc.* F. D. Roosevelt] has overgoverned. It was not enough to have specific reform of specific evils, say, stock market practices. **1976** *Daily Record* (Glasgow) 29 Nov. 14/2 Another sign of distrust is shown by the fact that nine out of ten replies believe that Scotland is in danger of being over-governed.

So **over-ˈgoverned** *ppl. a.*; **over-ˈgoverning** *vbl. sb.*; **over-ˈgovernment,** (*a*) excessive government, too much government interference; (*b*) higher government or control.

1847 J. S. MILL *Lett.* (1910) I. 131 The habitual over-governing by which power and importance are too exclusively concentrated upon the Government and its functionaries. **1848** —— *Pol. Econ.* II. v. xi. 529 The inferior capacity for political life which has hitherto characterized the over-governed countries of the Continent. **1861** —— *Repr. Govt.* iv. 83 The more popular the institutions,..the more monstrous the overgovernment exercised by all over each, and by the executive over all. **1861** M. ARNOLD *Pop. Educ. France* 11, I believe, as every Englishman believes, that over-government is pernicious and dangerous. **1894** *Rep. Unif. London* in *Westm. Gaz.* 29 Sept. 5/1 Besides the over-government of the future Corporation, there must be subsidiary bodies to discharge local highway, sanitary, and other duties. **1976** *Times* 13 May 4/2 Scotland is over-governed, over-taxed and over-subsidized. **1976** *Scotsman* 15 Dec. 12/3 The Tories may have added to 'over government' by their reform of local government.

overgown, over-grace: see OVER-.

overˈgrain, *v.* [OVER- 8.] *trans.* To grain over (a surface that has already been grained), so as to put on additional lights and shades. Hence **overˈgraining** *vbl. sb.*; **overˈgrainer,** one who or that which overgrains; an overgraining brush.

1873 SPON *Workshop Receipts* Ser. I. 420/1 *Overgraining.* —This operation is performed in the same manner both upon work which has been oil grained or spirit grained. In overgraining, water-colours are used. *Ibid.* 420/2 There are several descriptions of overgraining brushes in use... The knots and figures must be lightly touched up with the overgrainer, and the whole gone over quickly with a badger softening brush. The overgraining dries quickly, and the varnish may be then applied.

†**over'grassed,** *pa. pple. Obs.* In 6 -grast. [OVER- 8.] Covered or overgrown with grass.
1579 SPENSER *Sheph. Cal.* Sept. 130 For they bene like foule wagmoires ouergrast.

over-grateful to **over-gratitude**: see OVER-.

overgrazed ('əʊvəˌgreɪzd), *ppl. a.* [OVER- 27.] Of grassland: made susceptible to erosion by the destruction of vegetation through excessive grazing. Also *fig.*
1929 WEAVER & CLEMENTS *Plant Ecol.* vii. 142 The latter [*sc.* dominant species] are handicapped..in over-grazed mixed prairie. **1949** *Pacific Discovery* July–Aug. 2/1 In the South I have seen cattle tracks in overgrazed land become gullies ten feet deep. **1972** 'G. NORTH' *Sgt. Cluff rings True* i. 10 Thin, patchy grass, overgrazed, badly in need of lime. **1977** *Times Lit. Suppl.* 1 Apr. 402/2 He [*sc.* Christopher Isherwood] may cover ground..that no doubt will be covered until there is not a blade of grass left on it when the PhD herd have moved on from the overgrazed 1920s.

over'grazing, *vbl. sb.* [OVER- 29 a.] Damage to vegetation, esp. grassland, by excessive grazing.
1935 *Discovery* Aug. 232/2 Overgrazing has removed most of the nutritious native grasses. **1943** J. S. HUXLEY *TVA* vi. 33 The method of row cropping allowed the top-soil to be washed away. Overgrazing followed, and now the land is completely useless. **1946** *Nature* 2 Nov. 606/2 There is also the risk of over-grazing, especially where the natural vegetation consists rather of shrubs and bushes than of turf. **1956** *Ibid.* 3 Mar. 417/1 Failure of natural regeneration in juniper forests in Somaliland is now attributed to microclimatic changes following over-grazing. **1964** E. J. H. CORNER *Life of Plants* xv. 268 We can form no idea of the destructive power..of over-grazing where trees, for lack of rain, are disappearing. **1971** *Country Life* 12 Aug. 390/2 Examination of the intensively grazed patches showed no overgrazing such as occurs when hill sheep become concentrated on heather. **1976** *Conservation News* Sept./Oct. 4/1 Over-grazing..has led to the whole vast area becoming degraded.

'over-'great, *a.* [OVER- 28.] Too great, excessive.
[*c* **1386** CHAUCER *Can. Yeom. Prol. & T.* 95 Ffor whan a man hath ouer greet a wit fful oft hym happeth to mysusen it.] **1489** CAXTON *Faytes of A.* I. xii. 32 In an ouergrete quantite is confusion. **1583** *Proclam. Privy Council* 14 Jan., Inconueniences happening by the ouergreat libertie of late vsed in riding poste. **1774** FOOTE *Cozeners* II. Wks. 1799 II. 179, I am at no time an over-great eater. **1870** EMERSON *Soc. & Solit.* xi. 237 In good hours we do not find Shakspeare or Homer over-great,—only to have been translators of the happy present.

So **'over-'greatly** *adv.*, too greatly, excessively; **'over-'greatness**, excessive greatness.
[**1433** *Rolls of Parlt.* IV. 425/2 Over gretly empoveryssched, or elles..over gretly charged.] **1579** FENTON *Guicciard.* (1618) 75 They feared the ouergreatnesse of the vantgard, and that they were more neare to the maine army. **1599** SANDYS *Europæ Spec.* (1632) 142 Two..horse-leeches which neuer lin sucking it, will never suffer it to swell over-greatly in treasure. **1675** tr. *Camden's Hist. Eliz.* III. (1688) 415 By reason of the Over-greatness and Sluggishness of the Spanish Ships.

'over-'greed. [OVER- 29.] Excessive greed.
1880 DIXON *Windsor* IV. xii. 115 That over-greed had been his great mistake in life.

'over-'greedy, *a.* [OE. *ofergrǽdiȝ*: see OVER- 28.] Too greedy, excessively greedy.
a **1023** WULFSTAN *Hom.* xiii. (Napier) 81 Men..beoð ofergrædiȝe woruldȝestreona. **1535** COVERDALE *Prov.* xxiii. 3 Be not ouer gredy of his meate, for meate begyleth and disceaueth. **1597** SHAKS. *2 Hen. IV*, I. iii. 88 Their ouergreedy loue hath surfetted. **1642** MILTON *Apol. Smect.* Introd., Wks. (1851) 261 While he is so overgreedy to fix a name of ill sound upon another. **1741** WATTS *Improvem. Mind* I. xvii. Wks. 1813 VIII. 123 An over-greedy grasp does not retain the largest handful. **1887** RUSKIN *Præterita* II. v. 176 Some meat for the over-greedy foreigners.

So **'over-'greedily** *adv.*, too greedily.
c **1450** tr. *De Imitatione* III. vii. 72 þou failest in þinges taken, and ouergredely sekist consolacion. **1584** COGAN *Haven Health* (1636) 215 To eat overgreedily..is hurtfull, and hindereth concoction. **1668** *Lond. Gaz.* No. 246/2 Their infected Goods..being over-greedily seised on by some persons, twelve of them..died of the Contagion.

†**over'green,** *v. Obs. rare.* [OVER- 8.] *trans.* To cover with green, clothe with verdure; hence *fig.*, to cover so as to conceal a defect, embellish.
c **1600** SHAKS. *Sonn.* cxii, For what care I..So you oregreene my bad, my good alow?

ˌover-'grieve, *v.* [OVER- 25, 27.] **a.** *trans.* To grieve or afflict excessively. **b.** *intr.* To grieve too much, to feel excessive grief.
1603 KNOLLES *Hist. Turks* (1621) 1176 The citizens overgrieved with the insolent outrages of these men of war. **1631** BP. WEBBE *Quietn.* (1657) 32 Not to overjoy our grief, nor over-grieve our joyes. **1648** T. HILL *Spring of Grace* 11 We are apt to overgrieve or undergrieve at crosses.

Hence **ˌover-'grieved** *ppl. a.*; **ˌover-'grieving** *vbl. sb.* and *ppl. a.*
1601 *Downf. Earl Huntington* I. iii. in Hazl. *Dodsley* VIII. 113 Bridle this over-grieving passion, Or else dissemble it to comfort her. **1618** WITHER *Motto, Nec Habeo* Wks. (1633) 525, I have not their base cruelty, who can Insult upon an over-grieved man. *a* **1684** T. LYE in *Treas. Dav.* Ps. lxii. 8 Now is a time, not for overgrieving, murmuring.

'over-'grievous, *a.* [OVER- 27.] Too grievous.
1480 CAXTON *Ovid's Met.* XII. xx, Let Menelaus tak another wyf; ffor this is overgrevous for to conquere.

over-gross, etc.: see OVER- 28.

'overˌground (-graʊnd), *sb.* [OVER- 1.] †**1.** An upper or higher ground. *Obs.*
1600 ABP. ABBOT *Exp. Jonah* 569 Looking downe upon the city from some hill-side or overground.

2. (See quots: in most modern senses used in deliberate antithesis to *underground.*)
1931 *N. & Q.* 11 Apr. 267/2 There has been for some long time past a line of motor-omnibuses running from Hadley Woods and Barnet to Victoria Station on the sides of which ..is the word 'Overground'. **1966** *Evening Standard* 24 Feb. 16/2 The overground is an aerial railway with completely automatic operation. *Ibid.*, Buses would run through the suburbs to the edge of the city's centre... Passengers would change on to one or other of the over-grounds, a series of independent, six-mile rail loops. **1969** *Gandalf's Garden* VI. 11/1 *Overground*, like the Underground, from which it grew, it exists in the spirits of those who are living it, in the act of seeking a deeper understanding of life, in the expression of an aspirational lifestyle working in harmony with natural and mystical laws.

'overground, *a.* [OVER- 32.] **a.** Situated over or above ground, raised above the ground; opposed to *underground.*
1879 SIR G. G. SCOTT *Lect. Archit.* I. 182 The chapel is.. elevated on an overground crypt. **1894** *Westm. Gaz.* 19 Nov. 2/1 An underground railway is preferable..its construction ..is far less expensive than would be an overground line. **1897** *Naturalist* 23 Overground stolons rooting at the nodes.

b. *fig.* Overt; unconcealed; publicly acknowledged. Opp. UNDERGROUND *a.* 4.
1943 *Ann. Reg. 1942* 244 'Overground' resistance to the Germans was as strong as ever. **1961** *Times* 14 Jan. 7/7 But wherever they went the journalists were approached by 'overground' sympathizers with the independence fighters. **1970** *New York* 16 Nov. 50/2 They have been..whipped around in the over- and underground press. **1971** *Times* 15 Jan. 12/8 Now even overground publishers are jumping on the revolutionary bandwagon. **1971** *Guardian* 27 Sept. 14/6 Overground media generally treat sex, drugs, and violence in a misguided matronly tone.

ˌover'ground, *adv.* [OVER- 31.] Above the ground; into the open; opp. *underground.*
1930 *Sat. Even. Post* 22 Mar. 15/2 There was a rumbling as of a subway train heard over-ground. **1944** F. CLUNE *Red Heart* 6 After descending a few feet underground to have a look at the lode, I felt a desire to fly a few thousand overground to get a different angle of view. **1951** E. D. M. *St. Philomena the Wonder-Worker* (ed. 6) i. 16 The Christians could not safely perform the burial services in the presence of their heathen enemies over ground. **1963** *Times* 22 Apr. 11/1 Thought has been given to procedures by which rebels would 'come overground' and give up their weapons. **1968** *Economist* 3 Feb. 15/2 This seemed likely to mean that commercial gaming would continue underground in the pre-1960 manner..; but instead gaming popped overground into open places. **1973** *Times Lit. Suppl.* 23 Nov. 1455/4 Douglas Hayes has had an underground reputation... It is time for that reputation to appear overground.

overgrow (əʊvə'grəʊ), *v.* [OVER- 8, etc.]
1. *trans.* To grow over, to cover with growth; to overrun, overspread. (Now chiefly in *pa. pple.*)
13.. *Gaw. & Gr. Knt.* 2190 þis oritore is vgly, with erbez ouer-growen. *c* **1440** *Partonope* 4338 Wyth here hys vysage was ouergrow. **1535** COVERDALE *Hos.* ix. 6 The nettles shall ouergrowe their pleasaunt goodes. **1599** T. M[OUFET] *Silkwormes* 33 Hence leprosie the Cuckoes ouergrew. *a* **1661** FULLER *Worthies, York* (1662) 228 He was..kept so long in Prison, Manicled by the wrests, till the Flesh had overgrown his Irons. **1725** BRADLEY *Fam. Dict.* s.v. *Pruning*, The best time to prune Trees is in February..that so the Tree may easily overgrow the Knot. **1855** KINGSLEY *Heroes, Theseus* I. 196 He found a great flat stone, all overgrown with ivy.

b. *transf.* and *fig.*: sometimes with the notion of 'overcome, overburden'.
1471 RIPLEY *Comp. Alch.* VII. ii. in Ashm. *Theatr. Chem. Brit.* (1652) 169 That watry humors not overgrow the blood. **1565** T. STAPLETON *Fortr. Faith* 84 b, Heresy can not continew and owergrow the true church. **1643** TRAPP *Comm. Gen.* xxiii. 2 Here Jacob forgat himself, when so overgrown with grief for his Joseph. **1701** CIBBER *Love makes Man* I. 5 To Buy and sell my stock to the best Advantage, and Cure my Cattle when they are over-grown with Labour. **1861** GEO. ELIOT *Silas M.* i, Their imagination..is all overgrown by recollections that are a perpetual pasture to fear.

†**c.** *intr.* To be or become grown over. *Obs.*
a **1643** J. SHUTE *Judgem. & Mercy* (1645) 102 The Field unplowed overgrowes with weeds.

2. *trans.* To grow over so as to choke; to grow more vigorously than. Also *fig.* [OVER- 21, 22.]
1523 FITZHERB. *Husb.* §146 [The garden] must be weded, or els the wede wyll ouergrowe the herbes. **1605** CAMDEN *Rem.* 13 But the Britishe overgrewe the Latine. **1623** T. SCOT *Highw. God* 60 The tares ouergrow the wheat. **1896** F. B. JEVONS *Introd. Hist. Relig.* viii. 89 It overgrows healthy social tendencies and kills them.

3. *intr.* To grow too large; 'to grow beyond the fit or natural size' (J.); to increase unduly. (Perfect tenses often with *be.*) [OVER- 26.]
1490 CAXTON *Eneydos* xxxviii. 129 Siluya had norisshed a herte [= hart] tyll that he was ouergrowen and grete. **1581** MARBECK *Bk. of Notes* 326 She liueth long: but at the length hir beake ouergroweth, so as she cannot receiue meate, but onelie is faine to sucke in the bloud of it. **1619** W. SCLATER *Exp. 1 Thess.* (1630) 58 Before Atheisme quite ouergrowes. **1659** WOOD *Life* (O.H.S.) I. 282 One..Kinaston, a merchant,..with a long beard and haire over-grown, was at the Miter-Inn; and faigning himself a Patriarch. **1709** ADDISON *Tatler* No. 100 ¶3 Many others, who were overgrown in Wealth and Possessions. **1842** MANNING *Serm.* viii. (1848) I. 108 To him the world is overgrown, and all its cares are swollen to an unnatural greatness.

†**b.** To grow too much or too luxuriantly. *Obs.*
1523 FITZHERB. *Husb.* §124 The wedes yf they ouer grow wyll kyll the settes. **1541** R. COPLAND *Galyen's Terapeutyke* 2 Fiij, They that are purged as it behoueth..in them the flesshe ouergroweth nat.

4. *trans.* To grow over, above, or beyond; to grow too big or tall for; to outgrow (clothes, etc.). ***to overgrow oneself***, to grow beyond one's strength, proper size, etc. [OVER- 13, 23.]
c **1536** SIR A. WINDSOR in M. A. E. Wood *Lett. R. & Illust. Ladies* II. 217 She hath overgrown all that ever she hath. **1712** MORTIMER *Husb.* II. 231 If the [hop] Binds be very strong, and much over-grow the Poles, some advise to strike off their Heads with a long Switch. **1833** HT. MARTINEAU *Tale of Tyne* iii. 63, I think government should, while giving privileges, take care that they do not overgrow just bounds. **1868** MRS. WHITNEY *P. Strong* ix, We don't outgrow, but only overgrow, many things. **1872** *Routledge's Ev. Boy's Ann.* 102/1 The plant apparently overgrows itself.

†**b.** *fig.* To grow beyond, surpass, or exceed in some quality. *Obs.*
1399 LANGL. *Rich. Redeles* III. 344 This was a wondir world..þat gromes ouere-grewe so many grette maistris. **1578** *Chr. Prayers* in *Priv. Prayers* (1851) 465 So she may over-grow in reigning the reign of her father. **1655** FULLER *Ch. Hist.* III. vi. §37 No wonder then, if easily they did overgrow others in wealth.

Hence **over'growing** *vbl. sb.* and *ppl. a.*
1541 R. COPLAND *Galyen's Terapeutyke* 2 Fij, In the moste parte of them come none ouergrowynge nor superfluyte of flesshe. **1612** WOODALL *Surg. Mate* Wks. (1653) 213 For the overgrowings of the gums in the Scurvy. **1677** G. MOUNTAGU in *Buccleuch MSS.* (Hist. MSS. Comm.) I. 326 Right measures..against this powerful and overgrowing interest of France. **1795–1814** WORDSW. *Excursion* I. 930 That secret spirit of humanity Which, 'mid her plants, and weeds, and flowers, And silent overgrowings, still survived.

'over'grown (stress varies), *ppl. a.* [pa. pple. of OVERGROW *v.*]
1. Grown over (with vegetation, weeds, etc.). Also *fig.*
1634 RAINBOW *Labour* (1635) 40 To draine and scoure this fenny and viciously over-growne..ground. **1804–20** W. BLAKE *Jerusalem* iv, in *Compl. Writings* (1972) 732 Of blood thro' all my nervous limbs; soon overgrown in roots I shall be closed from thy sight. **1907** R. BROOKE *Let.* Dec. in E. Marsh *Rupert Brooke* (1918) 26, I have already..got some faith in the real, sometimes overgrown, goodness of all men. **1938** E. AMBLER *Cause for Alarm* xvi. 273 There's an old disused road... It's overgrown by trees now. **1975** A. DILLARD *Pilgrim at Tinker Creek* xii. 213 The forested cliffs ..gave way to overgrown terraces.

2. That has grown too much; too big, abnormally large, of excessive size.
1398 TREVISA *Barth. De P.R.* III. xix. (1495) 66 The vertu of smellynge is lette somtyme by stoppynge by ouergrowe flessh. **1603** SHAKS. *Meas. for M.* I. iii. 22 Like an ore-growne Lyon in a Caue That goes not out to prey. **1627** CAPT. SMITH *Seaman's Gram.* x. 47 An ouer-growne Sea [is] when the surges and billowes goe highest. **1711** ADDISON *Spect.* No. 65 ¶4 He calls the Orange-Woman, who..is inclined to grow Fat, An Over-grown Jade. **1807** *Med. Jrnl.* XVII. 193 Travelling from the one end to the other of this overgrown metropolis. **1888** MISS BRADDON *Fatal Three* I. i, She is a great overgrown girl.

Hence †**ˌover'grownly** *adv.*, in an overgrown degree, excessively. *Obs.*
1668 *World's Mistake Cromwell* in *Select. fr. Harl. Misc.* (1793) 395 Their king..overgrownly great and rich himself.

'overgrowth. [OVER- 29, 8.]
1. Excessive or too rapid growth, growth beyond the normal amount; also, the result of this, over-luxuriance or abundance.
1602 SHAKS. *Ham.* I. iv. 27 So, oft it chances in particular men,..By the o'ergrowth of some complexion. **1667** MILTON *P.L.* XII. 166 A sequent King, who seeks To stop thir overgrowth, as inmate guests Too numerous. **1862** MERIVALE *Rom. Emp.* (1865) V. xl. 43 The Forum and other public places were deliberately thinned of their overgrowths of sculpture. **1885** *Law Times* LXXIX. 187/2 To trim the roadside hedges and prevent their overgrowth.

2. A growth over or upon something; an accretion.
1879 *Jrnl. Chem. Soc.* XXXVI. 769 Those substances only should be considered as isomorphous which are capable of forming mixed crystals or which are capable of forming 'overgrowths' (*Ueberwachsen*), *i.e.*, when a crystal of the one is suspended in a solution of the other, the crystal increases in size, owing to the deposition on it of the substance in solution. **1883** H. DRUMMOND *Nat. Law in Spir. W.* Pref. (ed. 2) 19 The monstrous overgrowths which conceal the real lines of truth. **1893** LIDDON, etc. *Life Pusey* I. xvi. 361 To separate original Christianity..from the overgrowth of later ages. **1896** G. B. SHAW *Let.* 14 Jan. (1965) I. 586 Those auburn tresses..concealed a grey—nay, a *white* —undergrowth, which is now an overgrowth. **1940** GLASSTONE *Text-bk. Physical Chem.* (1941) v. 342 Many instances of the production of overgrowths, e.g.,..alums, monoclinic double sulfates, etc., are known. **1971** I. G. GASS et al. *Understanding Earth* xiii. 170/2 Silica can be deposited as overgrowths around detrital quartz grains.

overguilty, overgun, etc.: see OVER-.

overhair (ˈəʊvəhɛə(r)). [OVER- 8.] In fur-bearing quadrupeds, the long straight hair that grows over or beyond the fur.

1879 M. M. BACKUS in *Encycl. Brit.* IX. 836/2 Certain animals..have a covering upon the skin called fur, lying alongside of another and longer covering, called the over-hair. **1880** *Libr. Univ. Knowl.* (N.Y.) I. 353 [Furs] differ widely in elegance of texture, delicacy of shade, and fineness of overhair.

†**overˈhale,** *v. Obs.* [f. OVER- 8, etc. + HALE *v.*[1]]

1. *trans.* To draw over something as a covering.

1579 SPENSER *Sheph. Cal.* Jan. 75 The frosty Night Her mantle black through heaven gan ouerhaile [*gloss*, drawe ouer]. *a* **1641** BP. MOUNTAGU *Acts & Mon.* ii. (1642) 117 He was as a guide by night, so bee the starres of heaven, in overhailed darknesse.

b. To cover, as with something drawn or laid over; const. *with*.

c **1470** HENRYSON *Mor. Fab.* III. (*Cock & Fox*) xxviii, Now, worthie folk, suppois this be a fabill, And ouerheillit with typis figurall. *a* **1510** DOUGLAS *K. Hart* I. xii, That dois thame quhile ourhaill with snaw and sleit.

2. To pull or drag across. [OVER- 10.]

1581 J. BELL *Hadden's Answ. Osor.* 452 b, So doe they also ..with their owne cable overhale themselves into an unrecoverable gulfe.

3. To turn over or revolve in the mind. [OVER- 6.]

1423 JAS. I *Kingis Q.* x, All myn auenture I gan oure-hayle. *Ibid.* clviii, Straucht furth the range I held a way, oure-hailing in my mynd From quhens I come.

4. To overtake. Cf. OVERHAUL *v.* 3. [OVER- 14.]

1536 BELLENDEN *Cron. Scot.* Proheme Cosmogr. 318 For he that nold aganis his lustis striue..Eildis richt fast, and deth him sone ouir hailis.

5. To pass over, disregard, overlook. [OVER- 5.]

1571 *Satir. Poems Reform.* xxvi. 65 And gif ȝe dreid yat sum will aithis ouirhaill, And will not keip nor ȝit obserue thair bands. *c* **1600** MONTGOMERIE *Cherrie & Slae* 848 Thair be mae sences than the sicht; Quhilk ȝe owre-hale for haste.

6. To harry, harass, molest, oppress. See HALE *v.*[1] 2 b. [OVER- 9.]

a **1575** *Diurn. Occurr.* (1833) 217 Albeit the said quene of Ingland wald owirhaill for ane tyme ane pair of this cuntrie. *a* **1578** LINDESAY (Pitscottie) *Chron. Scot.* XXI. ii. (S.T.S.) I. 284 The realme was ewill gydit and ower haillit [*MS. I.* ovirharllit] be my lord of Angus and his men. **1611** SPEED *Hist. Gt. Brit.* IX. iii. §20. 444 So that his ouer-haled subjects fled daily out of the Realme.

7. To overpower, overmaster. [OVER- 21.]

1581 RICH *Farewell* (Shaks. Soc.) 3 Though harebrained youth overhaled me for a tyme. *Ibid.* 203 That our fathers.. should bee so overhaled with the furie of their fonde and unbrideled affections. **1596** HARINGTON *Ulysses upon Ajax* (1814) 54 Either passion devoureth him, ambition overhaleth him. **1612** DRAYTON *Poly-olb.* iii. 40 Hounds.. That cold doth sildome fret, nor heat doth overhaile.

8. *Naut.* = OVERHAUL *v.* 1.

1692 *Capt. Smith's Seaman's Gram.* xvi. 78 *To over Hale*, is when a Rope is haled too stiff, to hale it the contrary way, thereby to make it more slack.

9. *Naut.*, etc. To examine thoroughly: = OVERHAUL *v.* 2.

1748 *Anson's Voy.* I. v. 42 Our next employment was.. overhaling our rigging. *Ibid.* II. ii. 134 Our best hands were sent..to overhale and fix her rigging. **1806–7** J. BERESFORD *Miseries Hum. Life* xiv. Introd., I want as..much of your ear as you please, while I overhale my tablets of Misery here.

Hence †ˈ**overhale** *sb. Obs.* = OVERHAUL *sb.*

1748 *Anson's Voy.* II. ii. 133 We deferred the general over-hale, in hopes of the daily arrival of the *Gloucester*.

over-half, upper half: see OVER- 1 d.

†ˈ**over-ˌhand, over hand,** *sb. Obs.* [Properly two words, OVER *a.* and HAND *sb.* Cf. MHG. *über-, oberhant*, Ger. *ober-, überhand.*] The 'upper hand'; mastery, victory, superiority. (Usually obj. to *get, have*, or the like.)

c **1200** ORMIN 5458 To winnenn oferrhannd off uss. *c* **1205** LAY. 2482 Guendoleine hæfde þa vfere hond [*c* **1275** ouere hond]. *a* **1300** *Cursor M.* 2508 (Cott.) Fra þai had geten þe ouer hand [*Gött.* ouerhand]. *c* **1470** HARDING *Chron.* CXVII. iv, Eyther of them tryste the ouerhande to gette. **1524** WOLSEY *Let. to Pace* in Strype *Eccl. Mem.* I. App. xii. 25 If he may have an overhande in Italy. **1535** COVERDALE *Hos.* iv. 2 Theft and aduoutry haue gotten the ouerhande. **1602** WARNER *Alb. Eng., Epit.* 368 [They] had sundrie ouerhands of the Northumbrian Danes. **1828** *Craven Gloss.* (ed. 2) s.v., 'To have the over-hand', to obtain the mastery.

overhand, *adv.* and *a.* [f. OVER *prep.* and *adv.* + HAND *sb.*]

A. *adv.* (ˌoverˈhand). †**1.** Over, upside down.

1579–80 NORTH *Plutarch* (1676) 171 A man that aspired to be King, and would subvert and turn all overhand.

†**2.** Out of hand, aside. *Obs.*

1816 J. WILSON *City of Plague* II. iii. 146 The poor Or niggardly, I put them overhand In a somewhat careless way.

3. a. With the hand over or above the object which it grasps; with the knuckles upwards in holding or throwing something; in *Cricket* and *Baseball* (with reference to bowling or pitching), with the hand raised above the shoulder: see B. 2.

1861 DICKENS *Gt. Expect.* xxii. The spoon is not generally used over-hand, but under. **1865** —— *Mut. Fr.* I. vi, He now clutched his knife overhand and struck downward with it.

b. *Archery.* (See quots.)

1875 *Encycl. Brit.* II. 378/2 Shooting over-hand is to shoot at the mark over the bow-hand. **1939** P. H. GORDON *New Archery* 404 *Overhand*, of shooting, same as ..*Forehand.*

4. *Mining.* From below upwards (in reference to the working or 'stoping' of a vein).

5. *Needlework.* In *to sew overhand* = OVERSEW.

B. *adj.* ˈ*overhand*). **1.** Characterized by bringing the hand from above downwards.

1656 EARL. MONM. tr. *Boccalini's Advts. fr. Parnass.* I. xxxvii, Men..of generous hearts, did usually write injuries received from mean men, in Sand; but over-hand blows given by men of power, in Characters never to be blotted out. **1888** KIPLING *Barrack-Room Ballads* (1892) 122 The overhand stabbing-cut silenced the yell.

2. a. *Cricket* and *Baseball.* Of bowling or pitching: Done with the hand raised above the shoulder: see BOWL *v.*[1] 4.

1828 in W. Denison *Cricket: Sk. Players* (1846) 44 It is the over-hand delivery to which I principally object,..it has all the qualities of a throw, except the force. **1870** BLAINE *Encycl. Rur. Sports* I. III. §454 The overhand bowling would appear likely to admit of dangerous abuse. **1901** A. LANG in *Blackw. Mag.* Oct. 490/2 England added the third stump, the straight bat, overhand bowling and other essentials. **1975** *New Yorker* 17 Nov. 154/2 The Oakland scouting report on him warned he had six pitches..all of which he could serve up from the sidearm, three-quarters, or overhand sectors, and points in between.

b. *Swimming.* Applied to a variety of the side-stroke in the performance of which one hand is raised above the water and carried forward. Also *ellipt.* as *sb.*

c **1881** 'CAPT. CRAWLEY' *Swimming* 38 There are two styles of Side Swimming, severally known as the side-stroke and the over-hand. **1886** J. FINNEY *Hints on Swimming* 5 Taking into consideration the high rate of speed attainable by its means, the overhand stroke, when exhibited by a first-class swimmer, far exceeds any other style. **1905** 'NATATOR' *Swimming* 13 Overhand stroke. To change from the ordinary side stroke to the Overhand is simple. When the upper arm has finished its stroke, advance it *above* water, beyond the head, where it again enters, with the palm of the hand facing out. **1931** J. BUCHAN *Blanket of Dark* xiv. 260 Peter's long arms in an overhand stroke devoured the waters.

c. *Lawn Tennis.* Of a stroke: made with the racket above the arm or shoulder.

1889 H. W. W. WILBERFORCE *Lawn Tennis* 30 The form of service almost universally used is the overhand service. **1900** A. E. T. WATSON *Young Sportsman* 379 For the ordinary overhand service the ball should be thrown up in line with the right ear and slightly backwards. **1911** *Encycl. Brit.* XVI. 301/2 High overhand service, by which alone any great pace can be obtained, was first perfected by the brothers Renshaw between 1880 and 1890. **1978** J. SYMONS *Blackheath Poisonings* II. 105 For..ladies an overhand service was a great waste of strength.

3. *Mining.* Of the working of a vein: Performed from below upwards.

4. *overhand knot*: a simple knot made by passing the end of a rope, string, etc., over the standing part and through the loop or bight so formed.

1840 R. H. DANA *Bef. Mast* xxxv. 134 Riggers' seizings and overhand knots in place of nice seamanlike work. **1841** —— *Seaman's Man.* (1863) 36 An Overhand Knot. Pass the end of a rope over the standing part, and through the bight.

overhand, *v. Needlework.* [f. phr. *to sew overhand* (prec. A. 5).] To oversew, sew over and over. So **overhanding** *vbl. sb.*

1871 BURROUGHS *Wake-Robin, Bird's Nests* (1884) 163 The mouth [of the Baltimore oriole's nest] is hemmed or over-handed with horse-hair. **1897** MARY SLEIGHT in *Chicago Advance* 8 Apr. 452/2 All little maids in our grandmother's day..[learned] the art of hemming and 'overhanding', stitching and felling. **1908** M. H. MORGAN *How to dress Doll* ii. 20 Overhanding is the real sewing of the seam...simply sewing over-and-over, close to the edge, with very small stitches. *Ibid.* v. 51 Overhand the neck and armholes with lace. **1964** *McCall's Sewing* ii. 31/1 *Overhanding*, a straight stitch used to hold finished edges together when a strong, flat, invisible seam is needed, as in table linen, undergarments, sewing on lace or patching.

ˈ**over-ˈhanded,** *a.* [OVER- 28 d, OVER *adv.* 1.]

1. Supplied with too many 'hands' or workers.

1765 *Museum Rusticum* IV. i. 5 Those children..are now set out to trades..by which means most trades are over-handed. **1886** *Pall Mall G.* 27 Aug. 11/2 'The trade is over-handed', the men cry.

2. (ˈ*over-ˌhanded*). **a.** With the hand over the object grasped; in quot. as adv. = OVERHAND *adv.* 3.

1840 BLAINE *Encycl. Rur. Sports* §454 Bowled by an over-handed twist. **1852** DICKENS *Bleak Ho.* xxvi, The person.. tosses the money into the air, catches it over-handed, and retires.

b. *overhanded knot* = *overhand knot* (OVERHAND *a.* 4).

1883 *Man. Seamanship for Boys' Training Ships R. Navy* (Admiralty) (1886) 91 *Q.* How do you make a reef-knot..? *A.* ..First make an over-handed knot round the foot of the sail, [etc.].

over-handicapped, -handled: see OVER-.

ˈ**overˌhang,** *sb.* [f. next. Cf. MHG. *überhanc.*]

a. The fact of overhanging, or the extent to which something overhangs; a projection, a jutting out. Also *concr.* an overhanging or projecting part; the projection of the upper parts of a ship, fore and aft, beyond the water line.

1864 *Daily Tel.* 19 Nov., There was just time for the lieutenant to lower the torpedo from its spar and pull the trigger, exploding it right beneath the over-hang of the Albemarle. **1883** *Standard* 3 Aug. 5/6 The amphibious reptiles are prevented from escaping by the overhang of the rim of the basin. **1892** *Field* 19 Nov. 793/1 She [a yacht] has a considerable overhang of bow. Such overhang..is only of advantage in rough water sailing. **1908** H. G. WELLS *War in Air* v. 158 The overhang of the gas-chambers intervened. **1919** T. K. HOLMES *Man from Tall Timber* ix. 101 The two women..lived alone on Paradise Knoll, just under the overhang of its crown. **1924** J. BUCHAN *Three Hostages* xxi. 306 The corrie face..seemed nothing but slabs and rotten rocks, while the few chimneys had ugly overhangs. **1940** W. FAULKNER *Hamlet* I. i. 19 Once more Varner looked down into the cold impenetrable agate eyes beneath the writhen over-hang of brows. **1957** *Brit. Commonwealth Forestry Terminol.* II. 89 *Hang*, the forward lean given to the blades in a vertical frame saw so that the teeth engage with the wood in succession and not simultaneously (the *lead-in*). Syn. *Overhang. Ibid.* 127 *Overhang*, the forward slope given to the front of a stack of converted timber for protection against weathering. **1960** *Times* 22 Oct. 9/4 One lone perch will take up residence in a deep undercut or an overhang of bushes in much the same manner as a big trout. **1973** C. BONINGTON *Next Horizon* v. 81 The rock juts steeply above, in a series of bristling overhangs, cut by a broken crack. **1975** *New Yorker* 21 Apr. 34/2 She retreated only after high winds began to shred the plastic overhang that had been keeping the stage dry.

b. *Electr. Engin.* The part of an armature winding which projects beyond the armature core.

1915 M. WALKER *Specification & Design Dynamo-Electr. Machinery* vii. 172 (*caption*) Dimensions of the over-hang of concentric coils. **1936** SAY & PINK *Performance & Design A.C. Machines* x. 193 The problem of the estimation of eddy current losses in overhang conductors is very difficult.

c. *Aeronaut.* (*a*) (The length of) the part of a wing beyond its outermost point of support; (*b*) in a biplane or multiplane, (the length of) the part of a wing that extends beyond the tip of an adjacent wing.

1915 *Flight* 9 Apr. 248/2 In plan form the main planes, of which the upper one has a slight overhang, have a pronounced taper towards the tips. **1919** PIPPARD & PRITCHARD *Aeroplane Struct.* iv. 17 The position of the top plane extending beyond the outermost interplane strut is called the extension plane or the overhang. **1928** V. W. PAGE *Mod. Aircraft* v. 180 A typical training biplane which has both a pronounced forward stagger and an overhang as well. **1933** W. MUNRO *Marine Aircraft Design* vi. 91 In older types of biplanes the upper wing used to be built with a much longer span and overhang than the lower wing. **1953** J. H. STEVENS *Shape of Aeroplane* i. 29 The weight of the overhang when on the ground was taken by wires attached to kingposts protruding from the top plane above the outer pair of interplane struts. *Ibid.*, It was common practice on early aeroplanes to make the upper wing of larger span than the lower. This extra length was called the overhang. **1977** *Aeroplane Monthly* May 274/2 The B.E.2e was.. distinguished by the large overhang of the upper wing extensions.

d. In a turntable unit, the distance between the stylus point and the centre of the turntable when the pickup arm is placed so that these two points and the pivot of the pickup are in line and the turntable centre is between the other two points.

1937 *Radio Engin.* Mar. 17/1 The curves in Fig. 3 have been calculated to show the initial tracking angle which occurs with a conventional pickup arm as a function of the radius R of the playing circle, the length of the arm L, and the overhang D, which is the distance between the center of the turntable and the needle point when the needle point is in line with the centers of the base and turntable. **1945** *Electronics* Mar. 111/2 If the needle point overhang *D* is 13/16 inch..the tracking angle varies from 32 deg at 6 inches through 27 deg at 3·3 inches back to 32 deg at the 2-inch radius. **1953** G. A. BRIGGS *Sound Reproduction* (ed. 3) xxvi. 330 The calculations for best offset angle and overhang.. were made on the basis of zero tracking error at the inside groove of a standard 12″ record. **1958** S. KELLY in E. Molloy *High Fidelity Sound Reproduction* viii. 139 With a 7½ in. arm, this [*sc.* minimum distortion] requires an offset angle of 24½° and an overhang of 0·56 in. **1976** *Gramophone* Feb. 1406/1 The headshell has..a slot screw fitting to permit accurate setting of the effective pivot-to-stylus distance (overhang).

e. *Econ.* An excess of (estimated) expenditure over available or budgeted funds.

1953 *Sun* (Baltimore) 13 May 4/2 Humphrey pointed out that no revenue has been provided to cover the $81,000,000,000 'overhang' of appropriations which will be outstanding at the close of this fiscal year. **1954** *Britannica Bk. of Year* 638/1 Economic policy produced *Overhang*, an appropriation in excess of actual funds. **1974** *Financial Times* 19 July 22/8 The dollar overhang has disappeared, the Middle East war has ended. **1976** *Washington Post* 13 Mar. A19/3 That [*sc.* a big increase in the outflow of U.S. capital] meant a sizeable addition to the existing 'overhang' of dollars, amounting to nearly $200 billion held outside of the United States.

f. In sound recording and reproduction, the (usu. undesired) continued oscillation of a system after the cessation of the signal causing it; *spec.* that of a loudspeaker, esp. in the bass when the cone is insufficiently damped near its resonant frequency. Cf. HANG-OVER, HANGOVER 3, quots. 1961, 1967.

1971 J. EARL *How to choose Pickups & Loudspeakers* v. 126 When the cone oscillates at resonance it vibrates quite violently unless well damped. This can cause 'over-hang' effects at the bass end. **1975** G. J. KING *Audio Handbk.* ii. 34 A very low R_s in parallel with the loudspeaker inhibits overshoot and rings on transient type signal, and this is particularly desirable at the loudspeaker's bass resonance frequency where, without such damping, the cone can oscillate vigorously when triggered by a transient, an effect which is responsible for 'over-hang' and 'boomy' bass. **1976** *Gramophone* Dec. 1028/3 The sound has warmth and resonance (the long overhang of the King's acoustic is expertly handled without the slightest muddying of the textures). **1977** *Ibid.* May 1774/3 Square wave response of all the cartridges showed virtually no overhang and an adequate rise time with little ringing.

overhang (əʊvəˈhæŋ), *v.* Pa. t. and pple. **overhung.** [OVER- 1, 3, 8. Cf. Du. *overhangen*, Ger. *überhangen*.]

1. *trans.* To hang over (something); to be suspended above; to project or jut out above. (Also said hyperbolically of a steep slope or hill, etc., in relation to what is at the foot of it.)

1599 SHAKS. *Hen. V*, III. i. 13 As fearefully, as doth a galled Rock O're-hang and iutty his confounded Base. **1628** SIR W. MURE *Doomesday* 426 Caught vp, when on immortall wings, To aire this stage which ouerhings. **1725** POPE *Odyss.* XIV. 4 With cliffs and nodding forests over-hung. **1805** WORDSW. *Waggoner* I. 165 Sky, hill, and dale, one dismal room..overhung with gloom. **1875** JOWETT *Plato* (ed. 2) III. 327 Ascend the hill which overhangs the city.

b. *fig.* To be as if about to fall upon; to impend over; to threaten.

1653 *Nissena* 96 What mischiefe might overhang him and Nissena. **1890** *Spectator* 17 May, As if life were always overhung by a possibility almost as depressing as a known liability to madness.

2. *intr.* To hang over; to project beyond the base; to jut out above.

1667 MILTON *P.L.* IV. 547 The rest was craggie cliff, that overhung Still as it rose, impossible to climbe. **1703** T. N. *City & C. Purchaser* 29 When it leans towards you, they say it over-hangs. **1887** HISSEY *Holiday on Road* 174 The sea keeps eating the cliffs away here. Do you notice yonder how they overhang?

3. *trans.* To cover or adorn with hangings.

1831 CARLYLE *Sart. Res.* I. iv, Neither is any Drawing-room a Temple, were it never so begilt and overhung.

4. To support from above; see OVERHUNG 3.

Hence **overˈhanging** *vbl. sb.*, the action of the verb, also *concr.* something that overhangs; *ppl. a.*, that overhangs.

1548–67 THOMAS *Ital. Dict.*, *Pendice*, the ouerhangynge or holowe of a rocke. **1602** SHAKS. *Ham.* II. ii. 312 Look you, this braue ore-hanging, this Maiesticall Roofe, fretted with golden fire. **1778** [W. MARSHALL] *Minutes Agric.* 13 Oct. 1776, He trimmed-back the over-hangings of the outside furrow of a field of wheat. **1860** TYNDALL *Glac.* I. ix. 63, I descended, and found my friend beneath an over-hanging rock.

ˈover-ˈhappy, *a.* [OVER- 25, 28.] Happy beyond measure; too happy.

1577 *St. Aug. Manual* (Longman) 24 But overhappy shuld I be, might I once atteine to sing a song myself. **1602** SHAKS. *Ham.* II. ii. 232 Happy, in that we are not ouer-happy. **1742** RICHARDSON *Pamela* III. 119 What Pleasure can those over-happy People taste, who never knew that of Hunger or Thirst? [**1804** see OVER *adv.* 11.]

over-harassed, etc.: see OVER- 27 b.

ˈover-ˈhard, *a.* and *adv.* [OVER- 28, 30.]

A. *adj.* Too hard; excessively hard.

1538 STARKEY *England* II. iii. 197 How be hyt, thys semyth ouer-hard to punnysch the chyld for the fatherys offence. **1587** GOLDING *De Mornay* Ep. Ded. 1 A right great enterprise, and (in the judgement of most men) over-hard. **1851** TRENCH *Stud. Words* v. 149 Ben Jonson is overhard on 'neologists'. **1854** WHITTIER *Voices* 25 Thy task may well seem over-hard.

B. *adv.* Too hard.

1677 GILPIN *Demonol.* (1867) 46 He will not urge it over-hard. **1826** SCOTT *Woodst.* xxii, That the party had been over-hard travelled.

So ˌ**over-ˈharden** *v.*; ˌ**over-ˈhardly** *adv.*; **ˈover-ˈhardness.**

[*a* **1568** ASCHAM *Scholem.* I. (Arb.) 39 Not stamering, or ouer hardlie drawing forth wordes.] **1582** T. WATSON *Centurie of Loue* xxxvi. *heading*, He blameth her ouerhardnes of heart, and the froward constellation of his owne natiuitie. **1610** HOLLAND *Camden's Brit.* (1637) 6 Not onely too farre fetched, but also over-hardly streined. *a* **1691** BOYLE (J.), It was brittle like over-hardened steel.

ˈover-ˈhardy, *a.* [OVER- 28.] Too hardy; overbold. So **ˈover-ˈhardiness.**

[*c* **1330** R. BRUNNE *Chron.* (1810) 23 Bot Alfride his broþer ȝede to þe bataile, He was ouer hardy, þe Danes he gan assaile. **1393** LANGL. *P. Pl.* C. IV. 300 Ich halde hym ouer hardy oþer elles nouht trewe.] **1589** *Rare Tri. Love & Fortune* II. in Hazl. *Dodsley* VI. 162 Hid under cloak of over-hardy love. *a* **1592** GREENE *Selimus* 823 To resist them, were over-hardiness. **1623** MILTON *Ps.* cxxxvi. 70 And large-lim'd Og he did subdue, With all his over hardy crew.

†**overˈharl,** *v.* *Sc. Obs.* [f. OVER- 9 + HARL *v.*[1]]

1. *trans.* To harass; to oppress; to handle roughly.

1535 STEWART *Cron. Scot.* II. 20 Tane wes the toun that tyme and all ouirharld. **1570** *Satir. Poems Reform.* xiii. 27 Sum time be tratouris ar Innocentis ouerharld. *a* **1578** [see OVERHALE 6]. **1581** SIR J. MELVIL *Diary* (1829) 88 Thair bread winner, thair honour, thair estimation, all was gean, giff Aristotle sould be sa owirharled in the heiring of thair schollars.

2. 'To handle, treat of, relate' (Jam.).

a **1500** *Colkelbie Sow* I. 429 (Bannatyne MS.) Thay war in the est warld, As is heir breuely ourharld.

†**overˈharry,** *v.* *Obs.* [OVER- 9, 25.]

1. *intr.* or *absol.* To pass over with devastation.

1600 R. C. *Fumée's Hist. Hungary* 22 Though the enemies should ouerharrie from Mohacz vnto Poson.

2. *trans.* To harry or worry beyond measure.

1579–80 NORTH *Plutarch* (1895) II. 74 His army was continually turmoyled and overharried. **1665** J. WEBB *Stone-Heng* (1725) 167 The English over-harried with the former long Troubles..submitted willingly to his Power.

ˌ**over-ˈharsh,** *a.* [OVER- 28.] Too harsh. So **ˈover-ˈharshly** *adv.*; **ˈover-ˈharshness.**

a **1639** WHATELEY *Prototypes* I. xi. (1640) 144 Good people are apt to be overharsh to them that wrong them. *Ibid.* xx. 203 Overharshnesse towards others for faults which we finde in them. **1668** H. MORE *Div. Dial.* II. xvi. (1713) 136 That they be not over-harshly censorious. **1867** TROLLOPE *Claverings* xxxv, He took..a delight in being thus over-harsh in his harshness to her.

ˈover-ˈhaste, *sb.* [OVER- 29 b.] Too great haste, excessive haste.

c **1374** CHAUCER *Troylus* I. 972 But if drerines Or over-hast our bothe labour shend. **1626** BACON *Sylva* §525 We would not have [readers]..account it strange or thinke that it is an over-haste. **1860** TYNDALL *Glac.* I. xii. 89, I escaped with a wounded hand, caused by over-haste.

So ˌ**over-ˈhaste** *v.*; ˌ**over-ˈhasten** *v.*

1390 GOWER *Conf.* I. 335 Yit sit it wel that thou eschuie That thou the Court noght overhaste. **1608** TOPSELL *Serpents* To Rdr., If I had not been overhastened in the businesse. **1896** *Daily News* 10 Jan. 5/7 Not to overhasten matters.

ˈover-ˈhasty, *a.* [OVER- 28.] Too hasty; rash, precipitate.

[*c* **1400** tr. *Secreta Secret., Gov. Lordsh.* 111 Be noght ouer hasty yn þi werkys.] **1571** GOLDING *Calvin on Ps.* xxxvii. 28 Least any man should bee overhastie and swift in judgment. **1602** SHAKS. *Ham.* II. ii. 57 Our o're-hasty Marriage. **1615** CROOKE *Body of Man* 254 The safest way is not to be ouer-hasty to burie women..for some haue beene knowne so long after their supposed deaths to reuiue. **1864** BOWEN *Logic* ix. 288 The Fallacy of over-hasty generalization is very frequent.

So **ˈover-ˈhastily** *adv.*; **ˈover-ˈhastiness.**

c **1440** *Jacob's Well* 144 Whan þou etyst ouer-hastely, as it were an hownd. **1571** GOLDING *Calvin on Ps.* lv. 23 The vyce of over-hastynesse cannot otherwyse bee corrected. **1577–87** HOLINSHED *Chron., Hist. Eng.* VIII. xi. *heading*, Manie of the Normans pursuing the Englishe ouerhastilie procure their owne death. **1844** STANLEY *Arnold* (1858) I. iii. 147 The defect of occasional over-hastiness. **1862** ANSTED *Channel Isl.* 522 When he over-hastily condemns it.

over-haught, -haughty: see OVER- 28.

overhaul (əʊvəˈhɔːl), *v.* [OVER- 5, 14.]

1. *Naut. trans.* To slacken (a rope) by pulling in the opposite direction to that in which it is drawn in hoisting; to release and separate the blocks of (a tackle) in this way.

1626 CAPT. SMITH *Accid. Yng. Seamen* 28 Hawle off your ley sheats, overhawle the ley bowlin, ease your mayne brases. **1793** SMEATON *Edystone L.* §158 Having so many times to stop, overhawl, and flit,..the work could not go on very speedily. **1867** SMYTH *Sailor's Word-bk.* s.v., A tackle when released is overhauled. To get a fresh purchase, ropes are overhauled. To reach an object, or take off strain, weather-braces are overhauled. **1882** NARES *Seamanship* (ed. 6) 61 Overhaul the bights down.

2. *Naut.* and *general.* To pull asunder for the purpose of examining in detail; to investigate or examine thoroughly (e.g. with a view to repairs, etc.). Cf. HAUL *v.* 1 b.

1705 J. LOGAN in *Pa. Hist. Soc. Mem.* X. 63 To appoint any person to overhaul these papers and accounts. **1743** BULKELEY & CUMMINS *Voy. S. Seas* 4 The People were generally employ'd in over-hauling the Rigging. *Ibid.* 89 To-day I over-haul'd the Powder, and told the Lieutenant that I had twenty-three half Barrels in Store. **1800** JEFFERSON *Writ.* (1859) IV. 324 We have..decided in Senate on the motion for overhauling the editor of the Aurora. **1830** DE QUINCEY in *Blackw. Mag.* XXVIII. 673 His own expressions of 'overhaul', for *investigate*, and 'attackable', are in the lowest style of colloquial slang. **1884** MRS. C. PRAED *Zéro* xiii, The drains..are being overhauled.

3. To overtake, come up with; to gain upon. See OVERHALE *v.* 4.

1793 SMEATON *Edystone L.* §266 The tide had overhauled us, and driven us to the eastward of our proper mooring-place. **1836** MARRYAT *Midsh. Easy* xix, We shall fall in with plenty of boats and vessels if we coast it up to Palermo, and they may overhaul us. **1867** SMYTH *Sailor's Word-bk.* s.v., A ship overhauls another in chase when she evidently gains upon her. **1886** *Pall Mall G.* 27 Sept. 10/2 The empty carriages were..overhauled by a down fast goods train, which ran with great violence into the excursion train. **1933** D. L. SAYERS *Hangman's Holiday* 187 He..drove on, overhauling the police car. **1955** *Times* 12 May 4/3 (*heading*) American boxers overhauled. **1976** *Horse & Hound* 3 Dec. 53/2 Their pilot..circling left-handed..doubled back to Loscar Common Plantation again and was overhauled in some kale after a good 35 min.

Hence **overˈhauler; overˈhauling** *vbl. sb.*

1769 FALCONER *Dict. Marine* (1789), *Overhauling.* **1809** MALKIN *Gil Blas* VII. xv. (Rtldg.) ¶11 The most aggravating circumstance..was the overhauling of his accounts. **1860** TOMLINSON *Useful Arts, Textile Fabr., Paper* 12 The rags undergo another careful examination by women called over-lookers, or over-haulers. **1893** *Chicago Advance* 21 Dec., The wholesale overhauling and threatened turning upside down of existing tariff conditions.

overhaul (ˈəʊvəhɔːl), *sb.* [f. prec.] The action, or an act, of overhauling; a thorough examination or scrutiny, esp. with a view to repairs.

1826 CAPT. B. HALL *Voy. Loo-Choo* I. i. 28 In the course of this overhaul, to which I most willingly submitted, they lighted on a pocket compass. **1891** *Labour Commission Gloss.*, *Overhaul*, the survey made by the Board of Trade inspector or other Government Official when a ship is about to undergo repairs.

†**ˈover-ˈhaving,** *ppl. a.* *Obs.* [f. OVER- 28 + HAVING *ppl. a.*] Having or inclined to have too much; greedy, avaricious.

a **1600** HOOKER *Eccl. Pol.* VII. xxiii. §5 No cause there was, why that which the clergy had should in any man's eye seem too much, unless God himself were thought to be of an over-having disposition.

overhead (see below), *adv.*, *sb.*, *a.* Forms: see OVER and HEAD *sb.*[1] [The phrase *over head* written as one word: see OVER- 31, 32, 33.]

A. *adv.* (əʊvəˈhɛd).

1. a. Above one's head; on high, aloft; up in the air or sky, *esp.* in or near the zenith; on the floor or story above. (See also HEAD *sb.*[1] 37 a.)

1532 in W. H. Turner *Select. Rec. Oxford* 109 Tymber owerhedde, as rafters and lathes. **1667** MILTON *P.L.* I. 784 Over head the Moon Sits Arbitress, and neerer to the Earth Wheels her pale course. **1769** FALCONER *Dict. Marine* (1789) Y y iv, It is..hung over-head in the..cabin. **1884** W. C. SMITH *Kildrostan* II. i. 49 Like the merle That sees a gled o'erhead.

b. So that the water or other surrounding substance is over one's head; so as to be completely submerged or immersed; also *fig.* (See OVER *prep.* 3; HEAD *sb.*[1] 37 b, 39 b.)

1653 [see HEAD *sb.*[1] 37 b]. **1706** *Refl. upon Ridicule* 110 Her Husband was over-head in Debt. **1782** PRIESTLEY *Corrupt. Chr.* II. VII. 69 They thought] it indecent to plunge persons over-head in water. **1816** J. WILSON *City of Plague* II. v. 20 This standing overhead within a grave Hath made me colder than an icicle.

2. †**a.** In each case, one with another, together. *Obs.* (Cf. Ger. *überhaupt.*) *esp.* **b.** Taken together, or one with another; reckoned per head. *Sc.*

c **1000** ÆLFRIC *Hom.* I. 30 þæt ælc man ofer heafod sceolde cennan his ȝebyrde. *c* **1400** MAUNDEV. (Roxb.) xxv. 119 Sum tyme it fallez,..þat þe..childer wendez togyder in a company, and þaire men menged owerheued [*MS. Cott. Titus* her folk ben all medled in fere]. **1504–6** *Ld. Treas. Acc. Scot.* III. 89, xxvj elne carsay blew, rede, quhit and ȝallow; ..ilk elne iiijs. viijd. our hede. **1547** in W. Hunter *Biggar & Ho. Fleming* xxiv. (1862) 312, xxxij score viij sheep, price of the piece overheid. **1799** J. ROBERTSON *Agric. Perth* 516 The rent, over-head..was under 1s. 6d. per acre. **1824** SCOTT *St. Ronan's* i, Just a Scots pint overhead..and no man ever saw them the waur o't.

†**3.** Headlong, precipitately. *Obs.*

a **1578** LINDESAY (Pitscottie) *Chron. Scot.* (S. T. S.) I. 77 Quhat mischeif befallis them that runes owerheid to ony porpois witht out regaird or foirsight to god or man.

B. *sb.* (ˈəʊvəhɛd; sense 2 also əʊvəˈhɛd).

†**1.** Old term of Fence: app. A blow over the head. *Obs.*

13.. *K. Alis.* (Laud MS.) 7385 Wel hij fiȝtten on þe pleyn Wiþ tresgat, wiþ reremeyn Wiþ ouerheued & wiþ stook Aiþer on oþere þe swerd so shook.

2. That which is above; the firmament.

1865 G. M. HOPKINS *Poems* (1967) 151 The grass was red And long, the trees were colour'd, but the o'er-head, Milky and dark, with an attuning stress Controll'd them to a grey-green temperateness. **1911** *Chambers's Jrnl.* Jan. 79/1 It forms a handy guide, philosopher, and friend to the vast unfathomable overhead. **1959** E. COLLIER *Three against Wilderness* i. 8 Live sparks rocketed up into the smoky overhead.

3. (Freq. *pl.*) Ellipt. for *overhead charges, expenses*, etc.

1914 *Automobile Topics* XXXIV. 31/2 One of the numerous fallacies of business..is the argument that the small organization is in a position to serve the customer to better advantage for the reason that its 'over-heads' are small. **1915** *Lit. Digest* 21 Aug. 360/1 (Advt.), Her typewriter is standing idle and adding to 'overhead'. **1922** *Public Opinion* 29 Dec. 629/2 We are able to reduce over-heads through the employment of far more automatic machinery. **1930** J. B. PRIESTLEY *Angel Pavement* i. 36 The first thing, the very first thing, we've got to do is to reduce the overheads in this business. **1954** *Encounter* Dec. 79/1 The two million families..are the enemies of the workers in the modern sectors of the French economy. Their overhead is more than the traffic will bear, and the worker feels, if he does not understand, this. **1972** *Accountant* 17 Aug. 215/1 Work in progress to be stated at cost including overhead. **1972** *Computer Jrnl.* XV. 199/1 A possible objection to the use of streams might be that the overheads associated with their structure make them excessively inefficient. **1974** *Terminol. Managem. & Financial Accountancy* (Inst. Cost and Managem. Accountants) 19 *Overhead*, the total cost of indirect materials, wages and expenses.

4. *Lawn Tennis.* An overhead stroke.

1969 *New Yorker* 14 June 46/3 His overhead is hit with his whole arm—no mere flick of the wrist. **1972** D. DELMAN *Sudden Death* vi. 145 I'll hit lobs to you so you can work the kinks out of your overhead. **1977** *Transatlantic Rev.* LX. 108 He slashes, he wheels, he whaps an easy overhead into the net.

C. *adj.* (ˈəʊvəhɛd).

1. a. Placed or situated overhead, or at some distance above the ground. (In mechanics also applied to driving mechanism placed above the object driven, or to a machine having such mechanism.)

1874 *Trans. Amer. Inst. Mining Eng.* II. 68 The bell and hopper are suspended from an overhead railroad track. **1875** KNIGHT *Dict. Mech.*, *Overhead-gear*, driving-gear above the object driven.. *Overhead Steam-engine*, an engine in which the cylinder is above the crank, the thrust motion being downward. **1884** *Law Times Rep.* LI. 160/2 A telephone company were the owners of certain overhead wires. **1895** *Funk's Stand. Dict.*, *Overhead check*, same as *Overcheck*. **1898** *Westm. Gaz.* 26 Feb. 6/3 Efforts are being made to introduce overhead wire electric tramways into London and the suburbs. **1917** 'CONTACT' *Airman's Outings* 36, I awoke to the roar of engines, followed by an overhead drone as a party of bombers circled round until they were ready to start. **1921** *Times Lit. Suppl.* 8 Sept. 574/3 Stress is laid on the complete clearance of overhead cover [from teak plantations]. **1949** P. LATHAM in Aldiss & Harrison *Decade 1940s* (1975) 204 Stoddard turned off the overhead light. **1959** *Chambers's Encycl.* V. 97/2 With A.C. systems difficulties may arise due to the inductance of overhead lines and the capacitance of underground cables. **1976** *Billings* (Montana) *Gaz.* 16 June 10-C/4 (Advt.), Comm. Warehouse Space 300, 400, 600 and 1000 sq. ft., paved, lighted, security fence, overhead door, cold storage.

b. ***overhead cam-shaft***, a cam-shaft mounted above the cylinder block of an internal-combustion engine; ***overhead valve***, a valve in an internal-combustion engine which has its seat in the top of the combustion chamber, in the surface opposite the piston.

1912 R. W. A. BREWER *Motor Car Construction* iii. 42 One of the principal objections to overhead valves in the past was the difficulty of driving an overhead camshaft... With the introduction of silent chain drives for camshafts these difficulties no longer exist. **1921** A. W. JUDGE *Automobile & Aircraft Engines* viii. 316 Another reason for the better volumetric efficiency of the overhead valve lies in the fact that in the case of the side-by-side valves the charge has to pass over a larger combustion chamber area before it arrives in the cylinder. **1958** *Times* 1 July 6/6 Instead of having a side valve engine of 1,265 c.c., the new model has the overhead valve 1,390 c.c. engine. **1966** *McGraw-Hill Encycl. Sci. & Technol.* XIV. 263/2 In overhead valve engines, the cam shaft may be mounted on the cylinder head near the valves. **1974** *Country Life* 21 Nov. 1579/1 The engine with its twin overhead cam-shafts is buzzy at high revs.

2. Applicable to one with another; 'all-round'; general, average: see A. 2.

1891 *Law Times* XCII. 188/2 To give a fair overhead sample of the wheat. **1892** *Pall Mall G.* 3 Aug. 3/3 An overhead charge of so much per ton [for parcels] leaving Euston.

3. *Lawn Tennis.* Of a stroke: made with the racket above one's head.

1904 J. P. PARET et al. *Lawn Tennis* 345 *Overhead*, with the racket above the head. **1919** C. HIERONS *Lawn Tennis* xiv. 61 In overhead volleying there is far too much pat ball. **1925** K. MCKANE *Lawn Tennis* vi. 98 The most important of all overhead strokes—the service. **1951** HARMAN & MONROE *Use your Head in Tennis* v. 45 For the overhead slice serve, take hold of your racket handle in the eastern grip.

4. Of costs or expenses: incurred in the production of a batch of articles apart from the prime cost of each (cf. ONCOST), or in the upkeep of plant and premises.

1909 J. L. NICHOLSON *Factory Organization & Costs* i. 7 The distribution of manufacturing expenses, sometimes called overhead charges, and in other instances, indirect expense or burden. **1911** F. E. WEBNER *Factory Costs* xvii. 212 Under such a system most of the usual overhead expenses become direct. **1922** *Westm. Gaz.* 8 Dec. 6/2 The overhead cost of every factory that is gas-lighted will go up. **1930** A. H. CHURCH *Overhead Expense* I. i. 1 Overhead expense in manufacturing is defined usually as consisting of the so-called 'fixed' charges (such as rent, interest, depreciation, insurance, taxes, etc.) plus all that large class of expenditure on labor and materials which cannot be charged definitely to any given job or lot of product. **1958** J. F. MAGEE *Production Planning & Inventory Control* iii. 26 Under absorption costing, the value includes not only direct costs but also allocated overhead charges (usually only factory overhead). **1970** *Encycl. Brit.* XVI. 1167/2 Overhead costs are various business expenses that cannot be readily identified with specific products or services produced or sold. **1974** *Terminol. Managem. & Financial Accountancy* (Inst. Cost and Managem. Accountants) 42 *Overhead distribution sheet*, a columnar form used for the purpose of distribution of overhead expenditure over cost centres, and for the apportionment of the accumulated expenses of service cost centres over others.

over-heady: see OVER- 28.

†**over'heal**, *v. Obs.* [f. OVER- 8 + HEAL *v.*[1]] *trans.* To heal (a wound or sore) over the surface. Hence †**over'healer** *Obs.*, one who or that which heals superficially.

1550 DK. SOMERSET in *Coverdale's Spir. Perle* Pref. (1588) A iv b, All Medicines of the soule.. not hauing that clenser with them, be but overhealers. **1560** A. L. tr. *Calvin's Foure Serm. Songe Ezech.* Epist., Which so overheale the wound that it festreth and breaketh out afresh. **1601** HOLLAND *Pliny* II. 265 When any wound or sore is ouer healed.

overheap (əʊvə'hiːp), *v.* [OVER- 25, 8. Cf. Ger. *überhäufen*.]

1. *trans.* To heap up or accumulate to excess.

c **1450** tr. *De Imitatione* III. xxxv. 103 To restore all þinges, not only holy, but also abundantly & ouerhepid. **1830** PUSEY *Hist. Enquiry* II. 433 Its dicta classica (overheaped as they are) were published by Reineccius.

2. To overlay with a heap or large quantity; to load, charge, or fill to excess by or as by heaping.

1549 COVERDALE, etc. *Erasm. Par. Titus* 3 Yᵉ knowledge of trueth which among yᵉ Ethnikes was ouer heaped with the inuencions of mans wysedom. **1610** HOLLAND *Camden's Brit.* I. 522 Ouer-heaped with honourable benefits. **1831** CARLYLE *Sart.* I. viii, Overheaped with shreds and tatters.

overhear (əʊvə'hɪə(r)), *v.* [OE. *oferhíeran*: see OVER- ? 5, 16, 15, 20.

In OE. *oferhíeran* appears as (1) = hear (simply), (2) = not listen, disregard, disobey; the latter sense is found also with MHG. *überhœren* and MDu. *overhôren*; Kilian has '*ouer-hooren* audire' (hear), mod.Du. *overhooren* hear, hear one his lessons, mod.G. *überhören* miss hearing, fail to hear or catch; also, hear (a lesson) through. Mod.Eng. *over hear* was app. a new combination in 16th c., meaning perhaps 'hear *over* or *beyond* the intended reach of the voice; or, *in excess of* the usual degree': see quot. 1579–80 in sense 3.]

†**1.** *trans.* Not to hearken to; to disregard, disobey. (OE.)

c **893** K. ÆLFRED *Oros.* III. x. §3 Swa he ær.. þara goda biscepum oferhirde. *Ibid.* IV. xii. §2 Hie.. þurh his lare oferhierdon þæm godum.

†**2.** To hear; to hear through. *Obs.*

c **893** K. ÆLFRED *Oros.* I. xii. §4 And eac þæt se æþeling æʒðer hæfde, ʒe his pleʒan ʒe his ʒewill, þonne he þara manna tintrego oferhierde. *a* **1300** *Cursor M.* 11332 (Cott.) For gladnes he gaf a cri þat all ouerherd þat stode him bi [*Gött.* ouer herde; *Tr.*, *L.*, herde]. *c* **1325** *Childhood of Jesus* 443 His Maister schal beo Zacharie, þat him schal techen of clergie; Al ore lawe he hauez ouer herd, Of him he may beo wel i lered. *c* **1400** *Destr. Troy* 11004 Pantasilia the pride of Pirrus ouer herd.

3. To hear (speech or utterance) that is not intended to reach one's ears; to hear (a speaker) without his intention or knowledge. Also *absol.*

1549 LATIMER *4th Serm. bef. Edw. VI.* (Arb.) 117 He [Ld. Seymour before his execution] turnes me to the leuetenauntes seruaunte, and sayeth 'Byd my seruaunte spede the thynge that he wottes of'. Wel, the worde was ouer heard. **1579–80** NORTH *Plutarch* (1676) 658 Cato over-heard them, for indeed his hearing was very quick. **1588** SHAKS. *L.L.L.* IV. iii. 130, I should blush.. To be ore-heard. **1660** F. BROOKE tr. *Le Blanc's Trav.* 312, I fell into lamentations, till my Brother-in-law over-heard me. **1706** SWIFT *Baucis & Philemon* in *Poems* (1958) I. 92 The Strangers overheard, and said [etc.]. **1712** STEELE *Spect.* No. 422 ⁋2 He whispered a Friend the other Day, so as to be overheard by a young Officer. **1858** FROUDE *Hist. Eng.* III. xv. 310 The English government had agents in Rome whose business was to overhear conversations. **1913** *Cassell's Mag.* June 2/1 Glancing over his shoulder to make certain that the nurse hadn't overheard. **1922** JOYCE *Ulysses* 114 Mr Bloom, chapfallen, drew behind a few paces so as not to overhear. **1929** E. O'NEILL *Dynamo* III. i. 132 He lowers his voice carefully as if he didn't want the dynamo to overhear. **1976** M. MILLAR *Ask for me Tomorrow* (1977) ii. 19, I couldn't talk to you freely this morning because I didn't want.. that witch in his office to over-hear.

4. *nonce-use.* To hear told over, or over again.

1588 SHAKS. *L.L.L.* V. ii. 95, I stole into a neighbour thicket by, And ouer-heard, what you shall ouer-heare.

Hence **over'heard** *ppl. a.*, **over'hearing** *vbl. sb.*; also **over'hearer**, one who overhears.

1652 LOVEDAY tr. *Calprenede's Cassandra* II. 88 To avoid overhearers in a matter of that secrecy. **1832** MISS MITFORD *Village* Ser. v. (1863) 503 This is the third time.. that I have appeared in the very equivocal character of an over-hearer. **1883** *Daily News* 25 Sept. 2/2 The overhearing [in telephones].. is due to the fact that the electric current passing over one wire induces a similar current in its neighbour in a reverse direction.

overheat ('əʊvəhiːt), *sb.* [OVER- 29.] Too great heat, excessive heat; overheated condition.

1599 T. M[OUFET] *Silkwormes* 59 Colde sometimes kills them, sometimes ouer-heate. **1626** [see OVER-COLD *sb.*]. **1885** *Pall Mall G.* 11 Mar. 9/1 The cause of the fire is attributed to 'overheat of gas stove'.

b. *fig.* Excessive ardour, fervour, vehemence, etc. (cf. HEAT *sb.* 11).

c **1640** J. SMYTH *Lives Berkeleys* (1883) I. 379 The overheat and boldnes of whose ill-guided manhood. **1756** MRS. F. BROOKE *Old Maid* No. 10. 72 An over-heat of temper. **1870** J. H. FRISWELL *Mod. Men of Lett.* iv. 85 This author has an overheat and vigorous fertility in his invention.

overheat (ˌəʊvə'hiːt), *v.* [OVER- 27; cf. Ger. *überheizen*.] **1. a.** *trans.* To heat too much, heat to excess, make too hot.

1398 TREVISA *Barth. De P.R.* VII. lxiv. (1495) 281 The leprouse pacyent shall beware of meetes.. that ouerheetyth the blood. **1580** SIDNEY *Ps.* XXII. ix, Whose hart,.. like wax oreheated, Doth melt away. **1657** *North's Plutarch, Add. Lives* (1676) 76 Fearing lest he should endanger his life by overheating himself. **1785** MRS. ASTLEY *Let.* in *Mrs. Delany's Corr.* Ser. II. III. 408 You will be discreet, and not over-heat yourself in dancing. **1866** MRS. CARLYLE *Lett.* III. 333 Furnaces overheated in casting Landseer's 'great lion'.

b. *fig.* To excite to excessive warmth of feeling, etc.

a **1667** COWLEY *Ode Ld. Broghill's Verses* v, When it were dangerous for me To be o'er-heat with praise! **1682** N. O. *Boileau's Lutrin* I. 133 So storm'd the Prelate, with his Dream o're-heated.

2. *intr.* To become too hot.

1902 C. S. ROLLS in A. C. Harmsworth et al. *Motors & Motor-driving* 172 How to tell when a Motor is Overheating. **1908** *Westm. Gaz.* 27 Oct. 4/1 The engine overheated twice, .. but this was when the car was taken out without any water in the radiator. **1950** *Sci. News* XV. 81 It may be found that the rocket overheats in spite of this cooling. **1971** *Sci. Amer.* Aug. 108/3 The compressors developed the required low pressure but overheated after several hours of continuous use. **1974** *Country Life* 21 Mar. 654/3 The mill overspeed, the stones overheated, and the mill caught fire.

3. (Usu. as *pa. pple.*, as *ppl. a.*, or as *gerund.*) Of a national economy: to bring about a condition of marked inflation by placing excessive pressure on resources during a period of expansion in demand.

1956 *Ann. Reg. 1955* 227 Heavy industry had.. been 'over-heated', but there was no strain on producers of consumer goods, and retail prices in this field had hardly risen. **1962** *Daily Tel.* 16 July 10/2 Most people would accept that an economy must not become 'overheated'. **1962** *Economist* 1 Sept. 800/2 Its [*sc.* Japan's] balance of payments crises and periods of 'overheating'. **1965** *Ibid.* 16 Oct. 269/1 The money and securities markets in New York have allowed themselves in the past month a nice frenzy of fear about the economy's 'overheating'. **1971** *Observer* 14 Mar. 8/4 It was argued in the 1960s that a faster rate of growth produced so-called 'overheating'—the situation in which demand exceeds resources, whether of labour or plant. **1973** *Times* 16 May 27/3 The danger of an over-heated economy was 'reasonably small'. **1974** *Times* 23 Mar. 13/2 The second layer of trouble was the progressive overheating of the economy last year. *Ibid.* 9 Oct. 5/2 Successive governments ..had overheated the economy by increasing public spending and boosting demand, consequently pushing up inflation. **1976** F. ZWEIG *New Acquisitive Society* II. ii. 94 No labour legislation can replace.. general economic policy based on the discipline of the market system and avoidance of over-heating of the economy.

Hence **over'heated** *ppl. a.*; **over'heating** *vbl. sb.* (cf. also sense 3).

1612 WOODALL *Surg. Mate* Wks. (1653) 188 An overheating or boyling in the blood by reason of the hot humors. **1660** INGELO *Bentiv. & Ur.* II. (1682) 115 To give the over-heated Earth leave to cool it self. **1872** LIDDON *Elem. Relig.* v. 183 Like children, with overheated imaginations. **1875** KNIGHT *Dict. Mech.*, *Overheating pipe*, a pipe through which steam is caused to pass in order to be superheated. **1961** *Family Handyman* Oct., Too light a feed .. causes overheating of the tool and burning of the cutting edge. **1969** *Gloss. for Landscape Work* (*B.S.I.*) v. 13 *Overheating*, an undesirable spontaneous temperature rise, due to the action of bacteria during the decomposition of vegetable matter. **1973** J. LEASOR *Host of Extras* i. 13 Early models.. beset by unlucky snags like over-heating, and gears that jumped out on the over-run. **1977** M. SOKOLINSKY tr. *R. Merle's Virility Factor* xvi. 314 The rumors had appeared spontaneously among the blacks due to the overheating caused by the tense period.

overheave (əʊvə'hiːv), *v.* [OE. had *oferhębban* (only in sense 'to pass over'); cf. OHG. *ubarhepfan*, *-heven* to pass over, leave out, refl. to exalt oneself, Goth. (refl.) *ufarhafjan* to exalt oneself; f. OVER- ? 5 + HEAVE *v.* The mod. sense 4 (OVER- 21) has no connexion with the earlier senses.]

†**1.** *trans.* To pass over, neglect, omit. *Obs.*

c **893** K. ÆLFRED *Oros.* I. viii. §4 Ic wat ʒeare, þæt ic his sceal her fela oferhebban [*prætereire*]. *c* **924** *Laws of Edward* c. 8 (11) (Schmid) Gif hit hwa oferhebbe, bete swa we ær cwædon. **13..** *Body & Soul* 61 in *Map's Poems* (Camden) 341 The pore eoden al besyde For ever hem thou over-haf. *c* **1330** R. BRUNNE *Chron.* (1810) 245 Rightfulle dome he gaf on foles for þer misdede, No man be ouerhaf, bot alle þorgh lawe ȝede. *Ibid.* 296 Oure Kyng Sir Edward ouer litille he gaf, Tille his barons was hard, ouerhipped þam ouerhaf.

†**2.** (?) To overcome, conquer. *Obs.*

1303 R. BRUNNE *Handl. Synne* 6911 A sykenes hym ouer haf. *c* **1330** —— *Chron. Wace* (Rolls) 13754 So harde strokes þe Bretons gaf, þe Romayns route al ouer-haf.

†**3.** To lift or raise above something else; to exalt. *Obs.* [OVER 1 (*b*).]

a **1300** *E.E. Psalter* lxxi[i]. 16 Over-hoven sal be Over Yban his fruyte.

4. *refl.* To overstrain oneself in heaving or lifting.

1808 *Med. Jrnl.* XIX. 502 A Hernia.. which was.. increased.. by overheaving himself, in carrying water.

'over-'heavy, *a.* [OVER- 28.] Too heavy; of excessive weight. So **'over-'heaviness**.

[**1508** DUNBAR *Tua Mariit W.* 165 [It] wes berdin our hevy. **1533** MORE *Debell. Salem* Wks. 993 If they be not ouer heauy they may beare theim home, and those that be to heauy.. tye ropes to theyr tailes and draw them home.] **1611** SPEED *Hist. Gt. Brit.* VII. xxv. §1. 308 King Ethelred.. set his seeming ouer-heauy Crowne vpon his Nephew Kenreds head. **1622** MALYNES *Anc. Law-Merch.* 417 The reformation of the ouerheauinesse of our pound weight Troy in the Tower. **1657** [see OVER-HOT].

overheghere, -heȝere: see OVER-HIGH.

'over-'height, *sb. rare.* [OVER- 29.] Excessive height. Also †**'over-'height** *v. Obs.* [OVER- 22 b], *trans.* to surpass in height, *fig.* to excel; ˌ**over-'heighten** *v.* [OVER- 22, 27], †(*a*) = prec. (*obs.*); (*b*) to heighten too much.

1611 SPEED *Hist. Gt. Brit.* VII. xi. (1623) 263 The greatnesse of his Port, that much in her eyes ouer-heighted her husbands. *c* **1611** CHAPMAN *Iliad* II. 411 So Agamemnon Jove that day made overheighten clear That heaven-bright army. **1664** POWER *Exp. Philos.* I. 63 Subterraneous Damps do sometimes.. grow to that over-height of fermentation, that they fire of themselves. *Mod.* Such expressions do not merely heighten the effect, they over-heighten it.

over-heinous: see OVER- 28.

†**over'held**, *v.* [f. OVER- 3, 6 + HELD *v.*]

1. *intr.* To bend, slope, incline, or fall over.

a **1400–50** *Alexander* 726 Full hiȝe þingis ouer-heldis to held oþer-quile [*Dubl. MS.* The hyest thyng raþest heldes oþer while].

2. *trans.* To pour over or across.

1382 WYCLIF *Jer.* xlviii. 11 He restede in drestis, ne is ouerheld [1388 sched out] fro vessel in to vessel.

overheld, pa. t. and pple. of OVERHOLD.

†over'hele, *v. Obs.* Also *Sc.* -heild. [OE. *oferhelian* to cover over, conceal, f. *ofer-*, OVER- 8 + HELE *v.*, HEILD *v.*] *trans.* To cover over. Hence **†over'heling** *vbl. sb.*

a **1050** *Liber Scintill.* xliii. (1889) 144 Reaf..na to fægernysse ac for nedbehefe oferhelincge. *c* **1200** *Trin. Coll. Hom.* 73 Min shamfastnesse..ouer-heleð min bend ofte. *c* **1470** HENRYSON *Mor. Fab.* III. (*Cock & Fox*) xxviii, Ane fabill,..ouerheillit with typis figurall. **1513** DOUGLAS *Æneis* I. iv. 17 Ane wode abuife ourheildis with his rank bewis.

overhelm, -helped, etc.: see OVER-.

†over'hent, *v. Obs.* [f. OVER- 14 + HENT *v.*] *trans.* To lay hold upon; to overtake.

c **1330** R. BRUNNE *Chron. Wace* (Rolls) 9115 (Petyt MS.) When al were slayn þey mot ouerhent, To Wynchestre sire Vter went. **1590** SPENSER *F.Q.* II. x. 18 But she so fast pursewd, that him she tooke..Als his faire Leman flying through a brooke She overhent. **1596** *Ibid.* v. x. 36 The hindmost in the gate he overhent. **1714** *Orig. Canto Spencer* xxv, When Phœbus..clears the Sky with Vapours overhent.

†'over,her, -herre. *Obs.* [f. OVER- 2 b + HER *sb.*, lord.] Superior lord, overlord.

c **1230** *Hali Meid.* 29 Hare ouerherren witið ham.

overhie (əʊvə'haɪ), *v.* ? *Obs.* [f. OVER- 22 (14), 4 + HIE *v.*[1] to haste. (OE. had *oferhīʒian* in sense 'overreach'.)]

1. *trans.* To overtake by hastening after. *Sc.*

1375 BARBOUR *Bruce* III. 737 Bot the kingis folk that..war Deliuer off fute, thaim gan our-hy. *c* **1420** *Avow. Arthur* xix, He prekut oute prestely, And aure-hiet him radly. **1535** STEWART *Cron. Scot.* (1858) I. 145 Quhome tha ouir-hyit into ony place, Tha dang thame doun as dourlie as tha docht. **1634-5** MARY SPENCER *Evidence* in *Cal. State Papers*, She would run along after it to overtake it, and did overye it sometimes. **1652** URQUHART *Jewel* Wks. (1834) 182 Which of us should overhye the other in celerity. **1749** CROOKSHANK *Hist.* I. 395 (Jam.) At last one of the best mounted overhighed the postilion. **1834** HOGG in *Fraser's Mag.* IX. 276 Angus..with his long strides began to overhie Campbell.

b. To leave behind by hastening on. *rare.*

a **1621** FLETCHER *Wild-goose Chase* I. i, Within this eight hours I took leave of him, And over-hied him, having some slight business That forced me out o' th' way.

2. *intr.* To pass over swiftly (as time). *rare.*

1582 STANYHURST *Æneis* III. 86 Nor yeet was mydnight overhyed, when that Palinurus, From bed nimbleye fleeth.

,over-'high, *a.* and *adv.* [OE. *oferhéah*: see OVER- 25, 28. Cf. MHG., Ger. *überhoch.*] Exceedingly high; too high (*lit.* and *fig.*).

A. *adj.*

a **1000** *Runic Poem* 26 (Gr.) Æsc byþ oferheah, eldum dyre. *c* **1200** ORMIN 12061, & tatt wass oferrheh & all Unnfæle modiȝnesse. **1508** DUNBAR *Flyting* 188 And oft beswakkit with ane ourhie tyd. **1587** GOLDING *De Mornay* xxxiv. 541 To esteeme more the bookes that are darke by reason of their ouerhigh stile. **1642** LD. MOUNTAGU in *Buccleuch MSS.* (Hist. MSS. Comm.) I. 300 Things may be carried with an over-high hand. **1897** *Daily News* 31 Dec. 8/3 Before the sun was overhigh in the heavens.

B. *adv.*

1597 HOOKER *Eccl. Pol.* v. lxxvi. §5 Men ouer-high exalted either in honor, or in power. **1627** DRAYTON *Miseries Q. Margt.* 70 Their Ambition looking ouerhie.

So **†over'higher (-heȝere)** *a.*, used to render L. *superior*; **over-'highly** *adv.*

1382 WYCLIF *Job* xxxi. 21 What I saȝ me in the ȝate overheȝere. **1614** RALEIGH *Hist. World* 596 Neither of these two Authors is ouer-highly commended of trustinesse.

†over'high, *v. Obs.* [OVER- 27, 25: cf. MHG. *überhoehen.*] *trans.* **a.** To lift or raise too high. **b.** To exalt supremely (tr. L. *superexaltāre* Vulg.)

c **1340** HAMPOLE *Prose Tr.* (1866) 8 Þat sche be noghte lyghtly ouer-heghede in the ayre of wynde. *c* **1380** WYCLIF *Sel. Wks.* III. 62 (*Benedicite*) Herie ȝe and overe-hiȝe ȝe him in al tyme..þat þing overhiȝiþ anoþir þing þat seiþ it passiþ alle oþere creaturis: and so overhiȝinge, propirly is lovynge proprid to God. *Ibid.* 66, etc.

over-hill, *a.* and *adv.* [OVER- 32, 31.]

A. *adj.* *'over-hill.* **a.** Situated or dwelling beyond a hill or hills. **b.** The route of which is across the hills. **B.** *adv.* *over-'hill.* Over the hill.

1765 H. TIMBERLAKE *Mem.* Title-p., Illustrated with an Accurate Map of their Over-hill Settlement. **1895** J. WINSOR *Misssiss. Basin* 183 To prepare the way for a revival of this over-hill trade. **1901** *Dundee Advert.* 7 June 4 This ridge divides the underhill and the overhill men. Overhill, to the south, they raise corn and sheep; underhill, to the north, they are graziers and dairy folk.

†over'hill, *v. Obs.* [f. OVER- 8 + HILL *v.*[1]] *trans.* To cover over, cover up; = OVERHELE *v.*

a **1300** *E.E. Psalter* xliii. 16 Schenschipe of mi face over-hild me ai. *c* **1440** *Anc. Cookery* in *Househ. Ord.* (1790) 460 Overhille the flesshe with the syrippe. **1553** BALE *Gardiner's De vera Obed.* G vj b, He..thinketh he lyeth closely in couert, as though his sides were overhilled. **1608** B. JONSON *Masque Beauty*, Thy haire, thy beard..ore-hil'd with snow.

†over'hip, *v. Obs.* [f. OVER- 5 + HIP *v.*[1] Cf. MHG. *überhüpfen.*] *trans.* To hop over; always *fig.* to pass over, pass by, omit, miss, 'skip'.

c **1330** R. BRUNNE *Chron. Wace* (Rolls) 64 For Mayster Wace þe Latyn alle rymes, Þat Pers ouerhippis many tymes. *c* **1440** *Promp. Parv.* 372/2 Ovyr hyppyn, or ouer skyppyn, ..*omitto.* **1513** DOUGLAS *Æneis* I. Prol. 154 The thre first bukis he hes ourhippit quyte. **1600** HOLLAND *Livy* v. xiv. 189 Excellent men..whom to passe by and ouerhip, they thought the people would have bene ashamed. **1608** T. HUTTON *2nd Pt. Def. Ministers' Reas. Ref. Subscr.* 65 When they come to the genealogies in S. Matthew & S. Luke, over-hipp the places, pretending they are a ranck of hard words.

b. *absol.* or *intr.*

c **1300** in *Langtoft's Chron.* in *Pol. Songs* (Camden) 303 For he haves overhippede, hise tipet is typpede, hise tabard es tome. **1377** LANGL. *P. Pl.* B. xv. 379 Wher-fore I am afered of folke of holikirke, Lest þei ouerhuppen as other don in offices & in houres. **1483** CAXTON *Quatuor Serm.* (Roxb.) 21 They must also in the quere red and synge wyth ..deuocion of soule, not ouerhippyng ne momblyng.

overhip, *adv.*: see OVER- 31.

,over-'hit, *v.* [OVER- 27, 13.] *trans.* **a.** To 'hit' or affect unduly (with adversity, etc.). **b.** To hit beyond the mark aimed at; to go beyond instead of exactly hitting.

1816 *Sporting Mag.* XLVIII. 173 The Captain..being over-hit with bets, rushed into the presence of his Creator. **1868** BROWNING *Agamemnon* 796 How ought I revere thee, —nor yet overhitting Nor yet underbending the grace that is fitting? **1919** C. HIERONS *Lawn Tennis* xiii. 57 The beginner should take care that he does not over-hit the ball.

overhohe, variant of OVERHOW, *Obs.*

†over'hold, *v. Obs. rare.* [OE. had *oferhealdan* to hold over, delay to do, neglect; but the 17th c. senses were new formations.]

1. *trans.* To over-estimate; to hold at too high a rate. [OVER- 27.]

1606 SHAKS. *Tr. & Cr.* II. iii. 142 If he ouerhold his price so much, Weele none of him.

2. To hold back, withhold, restrain. (Cf. OFHOLD.)

1627 SANDERSON *Serm.* I. 258 It was God that over-held him from doing it.

over-hollow to **over-honour**: see OVER-.

†'overhope, *sb. Obs.* [OVER- 29.] Too great hope or confidence; presumption.

c **1330** R. BRUNNE *Chron. Wace* (Rolls) 6289 (Petyt MS.) Bot his ouerhope [*v.r.* ouerwenyng] gan faille. *a* **1400** *Relig. Pieces fr. Thornton MS.* (1867) 10 Ne we sall noghte com so ferre in-to ouerhope for to trayste so mekill in Goddes gudnes þat we sall hope to haue þat blysse with-owttene gude dedys. *c* **1440** *Jacob's Well* 85 Oon is presumpcyoun, þat is, ouyr-hope.

†over'hope, *v. Obs.* [OVER- 25.] To hope exceedingly: rendering L. *supersperāre.*

a **1300** *E.E. Psalter* cxviii. 43 For in þi domes over-hoped I ai. **1382** WYCLIF *Ibid.*, For in thi domes I ouer hopide. *a* **1669** TRAPP in Spurgeon *Treas. Dav.* Ps. cxix. 74 The Vulgate rendereth it *supersperavi*, I have over-hoped.

over-hopped: see OVER- 28 d.

'over-'hot, *a.* [OVER- 25, 28.] Excessively hot; too hot.

c **1386** CHAUCER *Can. Yeom. Prol. & T.* 402 Another seyde the fir was ouer hoot [*v.r.* ouerhoot]. **1575** TURBERV. *Faulconrie* 295 Make it in manner redde whote in the fire, but yet not overwhote: (for yron is very violent if it be too much het). **1652-62** HEYLIN *Cosmogr.* Introd. (1674) 19/2 The over-hot, or Torrid Zone, is betwixt the two Tropicks. **1657** *Divine Lover* 166 Cloths..ouer heauy, & ouerhott for the summer. *Mod.* The greenhouse is over-hot.

overhours: see OVER- 19.

overhouse ('əʊvəhaʊs), *a.* [f. OVER *prep.*, OVER- 32 + HOUSE *sb.*] Passing over and supported by the roofs of houses (instead of posts): said of telegraph or telephone wires.

1859 *Town Talk* 26 Mar. 566/2 The completion of the overhouse line of telegraph uniting her Majesty's Printing Office, Fleet Street, and the..House of Lords. **1876** PREECE & SIVEWRIGHT *Telegraphy* 226 In large towns, where it becomes impossible to plant poles for the support of the wires, overhouse telegraphs are had recourse to.

over-housed (,əʊvə'haʊzd), *ppl. a.* [f. OVER- 28 d + HOUSED *ppl. a.*[1]] Having house accommodation in excess of one's requirements or means. Hence (as a back-formation) **over-house** *v. refl.*, to have house accommodation in excess of one's requirements or means.

1863 W. M. THACKERAY *Let.* 23 Sept. in J. Brown *Lett.* (1907) 332 If I don't mistake there was a man who lived at Abbotsford [*sc.* Sir W. Scott] overhoused himself. **1887** *Spectator* 5 Mar. 318/2 A doctor is always over-housed from professional necessities. **1887** JESSOPP *Arcady* i. 15 The rural clergy..too many of them find themselves quite overhoused. **1921** *Spectator* 26 Feb. 261/1 Young people marrying on little and determined not to 'overhouse' themselves. **1963** *Guardian* 8 Mar. 4/4 Many of the chronic invalids were overhoused in that they were not able to make full use of their accommodation. **1970** *Times* 14 Mar. 3 In 1965 they found themselves over-housed and decided to sublet the fourth floor.

†over'hove, *v. Obs.* [f. OVER- 1 + HOVE *v.*[1]] *trans.* To hover or float over or above.

1362 LANGL. *P. Pl.* A. III. 201 Þat is þe Riccheste reame þat Reyn ouer houeþ! **1377** *Ibid.* B. XVIII. 169 What þis liȝte bymeneth, þat ouer-houeth helle þus. *c* **1420** *Pallad. on Husb.* I. 974 Whenne other seen derke cloudis ouerhowue.

overhoven, obs. pa. pple. of OVERHEAVE.

overhover, *v.*: see OVER- 1.

†over'how, *v. Obs.* [OE. *oferhoȝian*, f. *ofer-*, OVER- 7 + *hoȝian*, HOW *v.*[1] to think, consider: cf. OHG. *ubarhugen*, Goth. *ufarhugjan* to despise.] *trans.* To despise, disdain.

c **888** K. ÆLFRED *Boeth.* vii. §2 Oferhoȝa hi and adrif hi fram ðe. **971** *Blickl. Hom.* 49 Se þe Godes bebod ofer-hoȝaþ. *a* **1250** *Prov. Ælfred* 445 in *O.E. Misc.* 128 Þanne deþ hit sone þat þe biþ vnyqueme Ofer-howeþ þin ibod. *a* **1250** *Owl & Night.* 1406 An over-hoheþ þanne lasse.

over-humanize: see OVER- 27.

overhung (stress variable), *ppl. a.* [pa. pple. of OVERHANG *v.*]

1. a. Placed so as to project or jut out above.

1708 *Lond. Gaz.* No. 4400/4 Taken out of the Stable... a bay Nag.., his fore Teeth a little over-hung.

b. = OVERHANGING *ppl. a.*

1923 H. G. WELLS *Men like Gods* II. iii. 206 The gully was ..difficult, he thought, to ascend, but quite practicable downward. It was completely overhung.

2. Having something (as a cloud, darkness, etc.) hanging over it.

1845 *P. Parley's Ann.* VI. 280 The dark overhung streets.

3. Suspended or supported from above.

1887 D. A. LOW *Machine Draw.* (1892) 43 A wrought-iron overhung crank. **1890** *Cent. Dict.* s.v. *Door, Overhung door*, a door supported from above, as in some forms of sliding barn- and car-doors. **1928** C. F. S. GAMBLE *Story N. Sea Air Station* 8 Somewhat similar to a Blériot monoplane, except for..the 'overhung' system of mounting the engine.

4. [OVER- 18.] That has been hung too long (see HANG *v.* 1 b).

1895 *Punch* 11 May 222/3 An over-hung hare.

5. = *hung-over* (HUNG *ppl. a.* 4).

1964 I. FLEMING *You only live Twice* v. 60 He was considerably overhung. The hard blue eyes were veined with blood. **1974** *Times* 4 Apr. 20/6 A young man hurried in at about 10, looking overslept and overhung. **1977** K. BENTON *Red Hen Conspiracy* xiv. 115 Juan arrived..looking rather overhung.

over-'hunt, *v.* [OVER- 27.] *trans.* To hunt (an animal) to such an extent that an excessive number is killed; to hunt (a country) too much or to depletion. Also *fig.*

1862 *Q. Rev.* III. 229 That enthusiastic temper which leads men to overhunt a beaten enemy. **1936** *Discovery* Sept. 293/1 From time to time the moose is over-hunted in some districts, but after a few years' protection they come back again. **1968** C. HELMERICKS *Down Wild River North* II. xxiv. 385 The whole North has been overtrapped and overhunted.

over-hurl to **-importation**: see OVER-.

,overhy'dration. *Med.* [OVER- 29 b.] An excessive amount of water in the body or a part of it.

1943 *Jrnl. Clin. Investigation* XXII. 471 (*heading*) The relationship of dehydration and overhydration of the blood plasma to collapse in the management of artificial fever therapy. **1956** *Circulation* XIV. 1029/1 The physiologic and clinical consequences of an absolute excess of water consist of cellular overhydration, pulmonary edema..and convulsions. **1974** PASSMORE & ROBSON *Compan. Med. Stud.* III. II. xlix. 6/2 While the physiological defences against the naturally occurring hazard of dehydration are extremely effective, those against the iatrogenic hazard of overhydration are much less efficient.

So **,overhy'drated** *ppl. a.*

1943 *Jrnl. Clin. Investigation* XXII. 482/1 Although definitely overhydrated..the patient did not become edematous. **1974** PASSMORE & ROBSON *Compan. Med. Stud.* III. II. xlix. 7/2 Patients with acute renal failure or oliguria may readily become overhydrated since water can be lost only by extrarenal routes.

,overin'clusion. *Psychol.* [OVER- 29 b.] The indiscriminate inclusion of irrelevant responses to a stimulus, observed in some cases of severe mental illness. Hence **,overin'clusive** *a.*

1939 *Jrnl. Mental Sci.* LXXXV. 1019 The inability to select and to restrict, and to eliminate the less closely related elements from the conceptual structure, means that the psychological boundaries are functionally insufficient. The result of this situation is *over-inclusion.* **1942** HANFMANN & KASANIN *Conceptual Thinking in Schizophrenia* vii. 95 Some of the examples that Cameron brings as illustrating overinclusion can be also seen as examples of extreme primitivisation of thinking. **1951** CAMERON & MAGARET *Behavior Pathol.* xv. 457 The concept of overinclusion was first developed operationally, in connection with the sorting of behavior of schizophrenic patients. But its use since then has been expanded to cover a wide range of behavioral disorganization, both normal and abnormal. *Ibid.* 458 Excitement of any kind can lead to overinclusive behavior. **1974** *Psychiatric Q.* XLVIII. 109 (*title*) Investigation of factors related to stimulus overinclusion.

†over-increase. *Obs.* [OVER- 5, 19.] A surplus, an overplus.

1579-80 NORTH *Plutarch* (1676) 27 He..made Colony of it (as a place to send the over-increase of Rome unto). **1600** HOLLAND *Livy* XXXII. i. 809 To cause all the treasure taken out of the temple of Proserpina, to bee restored thither againe, with an ouer-encrease to make satisfaction.

,over-in'dulge, *v.* [OVER- 27.] *trans.* To indulge too much or to excess. Also *intr.* for *refl.* So **'over-in'dulged** *ppl. a.*

1741 RICHARDSON *Pamela* (1824) I. 228, I shall..teaze him like any over-indulged wife. **1759** SARAH FIELDING *C'tess of Dellwyn* II. 29 Their own over-indulged Imaginations. **1862** LYTTON *Str. Story* II. 175 The character..over-indulges its own early habit of estranged contemplation. **1898** *Voice* (N.Y.) 24 Feb. 4/2 To tempt and induce young men to over-indulge in strong drink.

ˈover-inˈdulgence. [OVER- 29.] Excessive indulgence. So †**over-inˈdulgency**; also **over-inˈdulgent** *a.*, too indulgent; indulging too much (*in* something).

a **1631** DONNE *Serm.* li. 516 Sleepe not lazily in an over-indulgency to these affections. **1754** RICHARDSON *Grandison* II. xxxvi. 354 The Lady having, by her early over-indulgence, ruined the morals of her child. **1853** MOODIE *Life Clearings* 13 They may spoil your children by over-indulgence. **1870** J. ORTON *Andes & Amazons* II. xlv. (1876) 618 Over-indulgence in stimulating food is a fruitful source of disease. **1879** *St. George's Hosp. Rep.* IX. 90 The former of these patients was over-indulgent in tea.

over-inflation to **-influence**: see OVER-.

ˌover-inˈform, *v.* [OVER- 27.] *trans.* To inform, actuate, or animate to excess. So **over-inˈformed** *ppl. a.*

1681 DRYDEN *Abs. & Achit.* I. 158 A fiery soul, which.. o'er-informed the tenement of clay. **1779–81** JOHNSON *L.P.*, *Congreve* Wks. III. 159 Wit so exuberant, that it o'er-informs its tenement. **1870** LOWELL *Among my Bks.* Ser. I. (1873) 184 Shakespeare's temptation is..to make a passion over-inform its tenement of words. **1899** *Daily News* 5 July 9/3 A rest..for over-strained nerves, over-worked brains, and over-informed minds.

ˌoverinˈhibited, *a. Psychol.* [OVER- 28 c.] Applied to a person whose reactions, esp. in a social context, are abnormally inhibited. So **ˌoverinhiˈbition**, the state or fact of being overinhibited.

1899 W. JAMES *Talks to Teachers* xv. 179 Certain melancholiacs furnish the extreme example of the over-inhibited type. **1942** PARTRIDGE *Usage & Abusage* (1947) 353/2 Thanks to the Freudians, we have..heard almost too much about the over-inhibited person. **1946** HEWITT & JENKINS *Fund. Patterns Maladjustment* 31 The..syndrome pattern of overinhibited behavior is of unquestionable familiarity to clinicians and mental hygienists. **1970** *Jrnl. Gen. Psychol.* LXXXII. 162 The apparent over-inhibition by schizophrenic Ss.

over-ink to **-insolent**: see OVER-.

†**over-inˈspection.** *Obs.* [OVER- 1.] Overlooking.

1655 FULLER *Hist. Camb.* vi. §14. 94 The Students when writing private letters, were used to cover them with their other hand to prevent over-inspection.

ˌover-inˈsurance. [OVER- 29 b.] Insurance (of goods, property, etc.) in excess of their real value.

1755 N. MAGENS *Ess. Insurances* I. 92 The Law of Spain ..ordains, 'That the Insurers who signed last in Date should return the Premium, in case of an Over-Insurance.' **1802** S. MARSHALL *Treat. Insurance* I. I. iv. 118 In the case of an over-insurance..the first underwriters on the policy were formerly holden to be answerable, to the extent of the loss, and the subsequent ones discharged. **1880** *Encycl. Brit.* XIII. 185/1 When the value proved under an open policy falls short of the sum originally insured, the difference..is technically termed an over-insurance. **1965** 'W. HAGGARD' *Hard Sell* xii. 136 Suspicion, the over-insurance of risks which were seldom worth the premium. **1970** M. GREENER *Penguin Dict. Commerce* 232 *Over-insurance*. Property is over-insured if insured for more than it is worth. **1977** *Times* 5 May 4/3 If cover were provided for a longer period an element of over-insurance would lead to unnecessarily high subscription rates.

ˌover-inˈsure, *v.* [OVER- 27.] *trans.* To insure for more than the real value; to insure excessively. (Chiefly as pa. pple.)

1904 in *N.E.D.* s.v. *Over-* 27 a. **1910** *Times* 28 June 6/1 An old vessel, trading at a loss, over-insured. **1922** *Blackw. Mag.* Sept. 318/2 Ship and cargo are over-insured about ten times, I suppose! **1970** [see OVER-INSURANCE]. **1976** D. FRANCIS *In Frame* iv. 68 If it was over-insured it was to allow for inflation.

ˌover-inteˈllectual, *a.* [OVER- 28 a.] Excessively intellectual; concerned too much with reason or mental processes.

1854 BAGEHOT *Coll. Works* (1965) I. 219 It had no feverish excitement, nor over-intellectual introspection. **1944** J. S. HUXLEY *On Living in Revol.* xv. 184 Over-intellectual and over-specialized.

So **ˌover-intellectualiˈzation**; **ˌover-inteˈllectualize** *v. trans.*; **ˌover-inteˈllectualized** *ppl. a.*

1924 P. C. BUCK *Scope of Music* 72 Preaching the over-intellectualization of their art until the red blood has gone out of it. **1929** A. N. WHITEHEAD *Process & Reality* 263 The interest in logic, dominating overintellectualized philosophers, has obscured the main function of propositions. **1933** —— *Adventures of Ideas* iii. 53 Even here we must not over-intellectualize the various types of human experience. **1975** R. L. SIMON *Wild Turkey* (1976) xii. 86 The sauna of some over-intellectualized exhibitionists. **1975** *Verbatim* Sept. 7/1 Over-intellectualization is rampant: if the Old Believers in Russia avoided the use of the future tense, the only effect would have been to create a new future of some kind, to refer to tomorrow's planting of potatoes, with the old future relegated to taboo—no deep change in speech habits would have resulted. **1977** *Early Music* July 308/2 We must avoid the temptation to over-intellectualize the artists' procedure.

over-intensity to **over-interpretation**: see OVER-.

†**over-inˈtreat,** *v. Obs.* [OVER- 11, 10.] *trans.* **a.** To prevail upon by entreaties (*to do* something); to over-persuade. **b.** To persuade to come over.

a **1639** W. WHATELEY *Prototypes* II. xxvi. (1640) 81 Either over-intreated, or by threatenings overborne, to doe some evill thing at a superiours motion. **1658** *Whole Duty Man* viii. §19 They have at the first been over-intreated to take a cup, after that another. *a* **1661** FULLER *Worthies*, *Bedfordshire* (1662) 117 John Coles Esquire of Somerset-shire over-intreated him into the western parts.

over-invest to **over-iodized**: see OVER-.

over-issue (ˈəʊvərˈɪʃ(j)uː, -ˈɪsjuː), *sb.* [OVER- 29.] An issue in excess: see next.

1803 *Edin. Rev.* III. 252 A general depreciation of the currency, by a universal over-issue of notes. **1861** GOSCHEN *For. Exch.* 63 When, through the over-issue of paper money, a general rise of prices ensues, the price of gold, as measured by paper money, rises with the rest. **1886** *Law Times* LXXX. 280/2 The personal liability of the five directors upon an over-issue of debenture stock.

ˌover-ˈissue, *v.* [OVER- 27.] *trans.* To issue in excess; e.g. to issue legal tender notes, stocks, shares, or debentures of a joint-stock company, beyond the amount authorized by law or by the articles of association; to issue any notes in excess of the issuer's ability to pay them on demand. Also to print or 'issue' postage-stamps beyond the needs of the postal service.

1837 CALHOUN *Wks.* III. 64 The banks had over-issued, it is true, but their over-issues were to the Government. **1879** LUBBOCK *Addr. Pol. & Educ.* ii. 41 The bank directors ought not to over-issue notes.

over-itch to **over-jaded**: see OVER-.

ˈoverjet. *Dentistry.* [OVER- 13 (?).] The extent to which the upper teeth, esp. the incisors, project forward in a horizontal direction beyond the corresponding lower teeth. Cf. OVERBITE.

1930 I. G. NICHOLS *Prosthetic Dentistry* vi. 149 A greater overjet or projection forward of the maxillary teeth is required in cases of deep overbite than in cases of shallow overbite. **1940** M. G. SWENSON *Compl. Dentures* xxvi. 445 The incisal guidance is governed mostly by the operator's choice of the desired inclination. This inclination may be changed by the amount of overbite (vertical overbite) and overjet (horizontal overbite). **1962** BLAKE & TROTT *Periodontology* xv. 155 In patients with abnormal overbite or overjet an habitual rest position may be established which assists the patient to form an efficient lip seal. **1977** *Proc. R. Soc. Med.* LXX. 432/1 Bell & Dann (1973) found..only small changes in incisor overbite and overjet in 25 patients following anterior maxillary ostectomies.

ˈover-ˈjoy, *sb.* [OVER- 29.] Excess of joy, too great joy. So **ˈover-ˈjoyful** *a.*, too joyful; **ˈover-ˈjoyous** *a.*, too joyous.

[**1593** SHAKS. *2 Hen. VI*, I. i. 31 Termes, such as my wit affoords, And ouer ioy of heart doth minister.] *a* **1631** DONNE *Lett.* (1651) 299 The over-joy of that recovered mee. **1711** J. GREENWOOD *Eng. Gram.* 196 Overjoyfull. **1791** MAD. D'ARBLAY *Diary* Aug., Tears shed..all for over-joy. **1856** MRS. BROWNING *Aur. Leigh* I. 47 Born To make my father sadder, and myself Not overjoyous. **1870** SPURGEON *Treas. Dav.* Ps. xxxii. 11 One who died at the foot of the scaffold of overjoy at the receipt of his monarch's pardon.

overjoy (əʊvəˈdʒɔɪ), *v.* [OVER- 1 (*c*), 25, 27, 21.]

†**1.** To rejoice over (rendering L. *supergaudēre*).

1382 WYCLIF *Ps.* xxxiv. [xxxv.] 19 Ouerioȝe not to me that enemyen to me wickeli [*Vulg.* Non supergaudeant mihi].

2. *trans.* To fill with extreme joy; to transport with joy or gladness. (Now chiefly in *pa. pple.*)

1571 GOLDING *Calvin on Ps.* xxiii. 1 Prosperitie maketh many so drunken, that they..overjoy themselves. **1678** SHADWELL *Timon* II. Wks. 1720 II. 320 You over-joy me with your presence! **1768–74** TUCKER *Lt. Nat.* (1834) II. 527 I..should be overjoyed to lend him a helping hand. **1844** DICKENS *Mart. Chuz.* xii, I..have been perfectly charmed and overjoyed to-day, to find you just the same as ever.

b. *intr.* To rejoice too much.

1720 BOSTON *Fourf. State* (1797) 208 We are apt to overjoy.

†**3.** To overcome or overwhelm with joy. *Obs.*

1631 BP. WEBBE *Quietn.* (1657) 32 We shall..be so far master over our passions as not to overjoy our grief, nor overgrieve our joyes.

Hence **overˈjoyed** *ppl. a.*, whence **overˈjoyedness**.

1634 B. JONSON *Love's Welc. Bolsover*, The overjoyed master of the house. **1647** W. BROWNE *Polex.* v. 4 His overjoyedenesse, his transports, and extasies, at the sight of that beauty. **1720** DE FOE *Capt. Singleton* xiii. (1840) 223 The poor overjoyed men were in haste to go back.

over-judging, -judicious: see OVER-.

overˈjump, *v.* [OVER- 5, 26, 23.]

I. *trans.* and *intr.* To jump over; *fig.* to pass over; to transcend.

1608 SYLVESTER *Du Bartas* II. iv. IV. *Decay* 798 A stiff-throw'n Bowl, which running down a Hill, Meets in the way some stub,..but instantly it hops, It over-jumps. *a* **1634** MARSTON (Webster 1864), We can not so lightly overjump his death. **1877** BLACKIE *Wise Men* 233 If there be gods, or if there be not, overjumps my ken.

2. *trans.* To jump too far over. **b.** *refl.* To jump too far for one's strength.

1861 WHYTE MELVILLE *Mkt. Harb.* 72 She [a mare] was prone to overjump herself when she didn't run through them [fences]. **1894** *Daily News* 11 Dec. 2/6 If he has a fault it is a tendency to overjump his fences.

over-just, -jutting, etc.: see OVER-.

ˌover-ˈkeep, *v.* [OVER- 27, 18.] *trans.* **a.** To keep or observe too strictly. **b.** To keep too long. Hence **ˈover-ˈkept** *ppl. a.*

1608 BP. HALL *Pharisaism* Wks. (1627) 410 God would haue a Sabbath kept: they ouer-keepe it. **1679** O. HEYWOOD *Diaries* (1881) II. 265 It [flesh] was good for nothing being over-kept. **1816** *Sporting Mag.* XLVIII. 258 If birds are overkept their legs will be dry. **1837** LOCKHART *Scott* xli, An over-kept haunch of venison.

ˈoverˈkill (stress var.), *v.* orig. *U.S.* [OVER- 27.] *trans.* and *intr.* To kill or destroy to a greater extent than is necessary. Also *fig.*

1946 *Sun* (Baltimore) 17 Jan. 4/5 It pointed all, or a great majority, of the guns at a single object. This method resulted in missing most of the in-coming attackers and of over-killing those which could be hit. **1958** *Lincoln* (Nebraska) *Evening Jrnl.* 8 Aug. 4/4 The argument that you do not need the power to 'overkill', if you already have H-bombs [etc.]. **1965** *New Statesman* 30 Apr. 690/3 His magnanimity towards those who ordained that Dresden should be overkilled. **1967** *Economist* 23 Dec. 1227/3 Mr Humphrey's oratory..overkilled the McCarthy ridicule of what the Senator assails as an immoral and, equally unforgiveably, an irrational war. **1968** *Punch* 27 Nov. 751 We maintained armed forces to defend a non-existent Empire and spent uselessly and prodigally in a vain attempt to keep abreast of the titans in capacity to kill and overkill. **1971** B. CALLISON *Plague of Sailors* iv. 157 When you intend to decimate a whole nation, why get puritanical about over-killing a few dozen more?

ˈoverkill, *sb.* orig. *U.S.* [OVER- 29.] **a.** The capacity, esp. of nuclear weapons, to kill and effect destruction in excess of strategic requirements. Also *attrib.*

1958 *Time* 17 Mar. 25/2 A word coming more and more into Pentagon usage is 'overkill'—a blunt but descriptive term implying a power to destroy a military target not once but many times more than necessary. **1959** *Times* 18 May 7/2 The Chiefs of Staff of the Navy and the Army..told Congress..that this 'over-kill' capacity is unnecessary. **1962** *Economist* 30 June 1307/1 It is military nonsense for Britain and France to produce nuclear weapons, when the United States has an 'overkill' of those weapons coming out of both its ears. **1965** H. KAHN *On Escalation* 280 Overkill by a factor of ten or more, so that even the blind..would understand the situation. **1968** W. ASH *Ride Paper Tiger* xii. 191 There's no point in plastering a target which has already been demolished. Anyone carrying the weapons you do has to be a bit careful about the problem of overkill. **1971** *Guardian* 27 Sept. 13/3 The nuclear club reached the point of H-bomb overkill. **1976** J. COX *On Warpath* 7/1 A mere pin-head of a man-made poison could kill everyone alive today. Military strategists talk of 'Doomsday' and 'Overkill'.

b. *transf.* and *fig.*

1965 *New Scientist* 24 June 841/1 There is only a limited number of whales in the sea and the delegates must decide between an irrational short-term overkill or long-term conservation. **1967** *New Yorker* 1 Apr. 94 Its producer..is a misguided champion of cinematic overkill: twice as large is twice as good, twice as loud is twice as convincing. **1968** *Guardian* 20 Mar. 10/1 Just how much Mr Jenkins ought to cut consumption is arguable. The world monetary crisis provides a strong psychological reason for going for 'overkill'. **1970** *Globe & Mail* (Toronto) 26 Sept. 7/5 The.. social and economic consequences..ascribed to 'advertising overkill'. **1973** *Times Lit. Suppl.* 21 Dec. 1555/3 It is astonishing, in these days of critical overkill, that Peter Wolfe's little book is the only one yet written on Rebecca West. **1975** *Listener* 3 July 22/3, I have only the smallest objection to the [Wimbledon] coverage, apart from the serious danger of overkill (three hours daily on BBC 1, over six on BBC 2). **1976** *Times* 30 Jan. 17/2 What point is there in producing things if over-kill taxation means that nobody will buy them?

ˈover-ˈkind, *a.* [OVER- 25, 28.] Excessively kind, too kind. So **ˈover-ˈkindly** *adv.*; **ˈover-ˈkindness**, excessive kindness, too great kindness.

1476 SIR J. PASTON in *P. Lett.* III. 153 They leyhe to me onkyndenesse ffor ovyrkyndenesse. **1599** SHAKS. *Much Ado* V. i. 302. **1601** SIR W. CORNWALLIS *Disc. Seneca* (1631) 61 How subject the people are to take over kindly, upon the actions performed for their good by great men. **1611** SHAKS. *Wint. T.* I. i. 23 Sicilia cannot shew himselfe ouer-kind to Bohemia. **1824** MISS MITFORD *Village* Ser. I. (1863) 9, I love them, 'not wisely, but too well', and kill them with over-kindness. **1899** CROCKETT *Kit Kennedy* 38 To such, Miss Keturah was often over-kind.

ˈover-king, ˈoverking. *Hist.* [OVER- 2 b.] A superior king; a king who is the superior of other rulers having the title of king.

c **1200** ORMIN 6906 Onnȝæn hiss aȝhenn oferrking Itt birrde himm wel abiggenn. *a* **1300** *Cursor M.* 11194 To mak knaulage wit sum-thing Til sir august, þair ouer-king. **1851** SIR F. PALGRAVE *Norm. & Eng.* I. 516 His brother Gorm quarrelled with their King or 'Over-king'. **1874** GREEN *Short Hist.* vii. §8. 433 The King of Connaught, who was recognized as overking of the island by the rest of the tribes. **1885** FREEMAN *Ælfred* in *Dict. Nat. Biog.* I. 160/2 The over-king at Winchester [Ælfred] understood the position of the over-king at Mykênê [Agamemnôn] so much better [etc.].

over-knavery, etc.: see OVER-.

ˈover-knee, *a.* [OVER- 32.] Reaching above the knee.

1858 CARLYLE *Fredk. Gt.* I. i, High over-knee military boots. **1880** *Plain Hints Needlework* 28 There are ten distinct parts in a full-sized over-knee stocking. **1895** *Century Mag.* Aug. 573/2 Ample over-knee boots.

ˌover-ˈknow, *v.* [OVER- 27.] *trans.* To know or recognize too much.

1639 FULLER *Holy War* III. xiv. (1840) 140 His humility was admirable; as being neither ignorant of his greatness, nor over-knowing it.

So **ˈover-ˈknowing** *ppl. a.*, too knowing.

a **1656** BP. HALL *Gt. Imposter* (R.) The heart of man is wholly set upon cozenage; the understanding over-knowing, mis-knowing, dissembling.

ˈover-ˈlabour, *sb.* [OVER- 29.]

†**1.** *Rhet.* Excessive elaboration in literary style, loading with too much detail (rendering Gr. περιεργία; cf. L. *curiositas*).

1589 PUTTENHAM *Eng. Poesie* III. xxii. (Arb.) 265 The Greekes call it *Periergia*, we call it ouer-labor, iumpe with the originall.

2. Excessive labour or toil.

1814 *Sporting Mag.* 147 The weariness of over-labour.

over-labour (-ˈleɪbə(r)), *v.* [See below.]

1. *trans.* To overwork; to overcome, fatigue, or harass with excessive labour; to overburden. [OVER- 21 (?), 23, 27.]

1530 PALSGR. 648/2, I overlabour, *je me surlaboure*,.. he overlaboured hym selfe yesterday. **1598** GRENEWEY *Tacitus, Germanie* iii. (1622) 262 It is a rare matter to beat their slaues, or ouer-labour or emprison them. **1671** MILTON *Samson* 1327 With shackles tir'd, And over-labour'd at thir publick Mill. *a* **1718** PENN *Maxims* Wks. 1726 I. 848 If any Point over-labours thy Mind, divert and relieve it, by some other Subject. **1803** J. KENNY *Society* 11 Those careful thoughts that oft O'er labour Reason to untimely ruin. **1842** MANNING *Serm.* xiv. (1848) I. 205 Those who cannot wait on God daily, because they are so over-laboured in doing the nothingnesses of society.

2. To labour excessively at, take too great pains with; to elaborate to excess. [OVER- 27.]

1588 GREENE *Perimedes* 29 Nature in them seemeth to be ouerlaboured with arte. **1797** BURKE *Regic. Peace* iii. Wks. VIII. 304 Over-labouring a point of this kind, has the direct contrary effect from what we wish. **1823** *Examiner* 673/2 Earl Grey does not.. over-labour a part of a subject.

†**3.** To surpass in labour. *Obs.* [OVER- 22.]

1607 MARKHAM *Caval.* I. (1617) 67 The good stond horse will euer beate and ouerlabour the good Gelding.

†**4.** ? To belabour. *Obs.* [OVER- 8 (?).]

1632 LITHGOW *Trav.* VIII. 373 These Sauages.. ouer-laboured vs with Bastinadoes.

Hence **over-ˈlaboured** *ppl. a.*, **-ˈlabouring** *vbl. sb.*

1604 EDMONDS *Observ. Cæsar's Comm.* 123 The wearied and ouerlaboured were seconded by fresh supplies. **1626** BERNARD *Isle of Man* (1627) 174 Covetousnesse.. causeth niggardly house-keeping, and over-labouring of servants. **1734** WATTS *Reliq. Juv.* lxxv. (1789) 263 My midnight lamp, and my o'er-labour'd head. **1842** MANNING *Serm.* xiv. (1848) I. 205 The poor working man wrings a scant livelihood out of an over-laboured week.

overlace: see OVER- 8.

overˈlade, *v.* [f. OVER- + LADE *v.* In sense 2 = OHG. *ubarhladan*, Ger. *überladen*.]

†**1.** *trans.* To lade or draw water out of. *Obs.*

a **1225** *Ancr. R.* 368 Pot þet walleð swuðe, nule he beon ouerladen, oðer kold water iworpen þerinne and brondes wiðdrawene?

2. *trans.* To load with too heavy a burden, to overload; to overburden. [OVER- 21, 27.]

(Chiefly in pa. pple. *overladen*, in ME. *-lade*, in 16–17th. c. also *-laded*.)

c **1385** CHAUCER *L.G.W.* 621 *Cleopatras*, Men may ouer-lade a schip or barge. ? *a* **1412** LYDG. *Two Merchants* 610 And yiff a tre with frut be ovirlade.. Both braunche and bough wol enclyne and fade. **1531** TINDALE *Exp. 1 John* (1537) 27 The byshoppes.. solde theyr penaunce to the riche, and ouerladed the poore. **1587** FLEMING *Contn. Holinshed* III. 1969/1 One of the kings ships.. was drowned in the middest of the haven, by reason that she was overladen with ordinance. *a* **1618** RALEIGH *Rem.* (1664) 44 Their fleece taken from them lest it overlade them, and grow too heavy. **1856** MRS. BROWNING *Aur. Leigh* II. 806 Since friend Betwixt us two, forsooth, must be a word So heavily overladen.

Hence **overˈladen** *ppl. a.*; **overˈlading** *vbl. sb.*

1494 FABYAN *Chron.* VII. ccxxxi. 263 He was vnweldly by reason of ouer ladynge of flesshe. **1654** GAYTON *Pleas. Notes* VI. vi–vii. 209 Will you like an overladen Tree, be propt up with a fork? **1811** *Two Rep. Thames Navig.* 28 To prevent the overlading of barges. **1866** RUSKIN *Crown Wild Olive* iv. (1898) 195 Help up the overladen horses.

overlaid, *ppl. a.*: see under OVERLAY *v.*

†**ˈoverlaik.** *Obs.* Also -layke, -lake. [f. OVER *adv.* + -LAIK.] The fact or quality of being over; superiority.

a **1400–50** *Alexander* 1861 To olle ay on his vndireling for ouer-laike [*v.r.* ouerlayke] a quyle. *Ibid.* 3101 þinke þat allanely of god þis ouirlaike [*v.r.* ouerlake] þou haues.

overlair, obs. form of OVERLAYER.

ˈoverˌland, *sb. local.* Land held by a particular tenure in the west of England: see quots.

1769 *Eng. Displayed* 44/2 The tenures are copyhold-lands, over-lands, and reve-lands. Over-lands are subject to fines, but not to heriots, suits and service. **1801** *Enclosure Commissioners of Cheddar Moor* (E.D.D.), By Overlands or Overland Tenements are to be understood all lands whether open or inclosed, which do not, nor at any time heretofore did belong to auster, or ancient tenements, and for which no right of common in the moors or on the hill have been allowed. **1885** T. S. HOLMES *Hist. Wookey* II. 53 Overland .. I rather think that under that head was included such villein holdings as fell into the hands of the lord by way of escheat from time to time. These.. would after a time be regranted to other villeins. **1886** ELWORTHY *W. Somerset Word-bk.*, *Overland*,.. land having no farm-house upon it. .. Any piece of land let without farm buildings is called 'a overland'. **1894** *Tablet* 16 June 942 Lord Bute.. inherited certain ancient feudal overlands in Glamorganshire.

attrib. **1796** W. MARSHALL *W. Eng.* I. Gloss. (E.D.S.), *Overland farm*,.. a parcel of land, without a house to it. **1817** *Trewman's Exeter Flying-post* 7 Aug. 4 To be let.. an Overland Tenement.

ˌoverˈland, over land, *adv.* [Properly two words, OVER *prep.* and LAND *sb.*[1]: often hyphened or written as one.] Over or across land; by land (as opposed to 'by sea'). †In Langland: 'over the country'.

[**1362** LANGL. *P. Pl.* A. v. 258 þat *Penitencia* his pike schulde polissche newe, And lepe with him ouerlond al his lyf tyme. **1393** *Ibid.* C. x. 159 Lolleres lyuyng in sleuthe and ouer londe [*v.r.* ouerlond] strykers.] **1589** HORSEY *Trav.* (Hakl. Soc.) App. 317 None of the Companies servauntes shuld be suffered to goe overland with letters. **1611** SHAKS. *Cymb.* III. v. 8, I desire.. A Conduct ouer Land, to Milford-Hauen. **1664** PEPYS *Diary* 29 Oct., That De Ruyter is come overland home. **1748** *Anson's Voy.* II. iv. 165 The account sent over land by Pizarro. **1786** LD. CORNWALLIS in *Corresp.* 28 Dec. (Y.) The packet that was coming to us overland.. was cut off by the wild Arabs between Aleppo and Bussora. **1792** *Misc.* in *Ann. Reg.* 452 Observations on the Passage from India, commonly called Over Land. *Note.* This expression, though extremely incorrect, is warranted by general use. **1872** YEATS *Techn. Hist. Comm.* 61 The traffic being overland by way of Malacca. **1889** 'R. BOLDREWOOD' *Robbery under Arms* xii, I'll go back overland.

overland (ˈəʊvəlænd), *a.* (*sb.*) [Attrib. use of prec. with change of stress: see OVER- 32.] Proceeding or lying over or across land; performed by land; for or connected with a journey over land. Also *ellipt.* as *sb.*

overland route, a route entirely or partly by land, as opposed to an alternative route by sea; *spec.* (1) the route to India by the Mediterranean, 'which in former days involved usually a land journey from Antioch or thereabouts to the Persian Gulf' (Yule s.v.), but of which in later times the Isthmus of Suez was the only overland part left; (2) in America, any route westward from the Atlantic to the Pacific Ocean across the continent.

1800 *Asiatic Ann. Reg., Acc. Bks.* 51/1 The present establishment for the conveyance of over-land dispatches. **1803** CASTLEREAGH in *Wellesley's Desp.* (1877) 581 You will probably hear from me, by an overland express. **1841** *Niles' Reg.* 6 Feb. 353/2 The news from China and India we have received by the overland mail. **1848** *Alfred in India* 158 Passengers went.. across the desert to Alexandria, and from thence in another steamer... This is called the 'overland route'. **1857** GEN. P. THOMPSON *Audi Alt.* (1858) I. xxi. 75 [In 1822] I travelled.. in Arab vessels, by what was nevertheless called the Overland route, from Bombay to Alexandria. **1861** W. FAIRBAIRN *Addr. Brit. Assoc.*, That country [India] may be reached by the overland route in less than a month. **1861** B. I. HAYES *Let.* 11 Feb. in *Pioneer Notes from Diaries* (1929) vii. 253 By the Overland Stage arriving here on the 8th inst., I received your valued favor of the 12th ult. **1862** MRS. J. B. SPEID *Our Last Yrs. in India* iv. 79 Her Majesty's mail! What would England.. say, could they witness the bi-monthly arrival of the overland here! **1901** *Daily Colonist* (Victoria, B.C.) 24 Oct. 1/5 The northbound Southern Pacific overland express.. was held up by robbers .. but the robbers secured little booty. **1977** C. ALLEN *Raj* 20 Before the opening of the canal the fastest means of getting to and from India was by taking the overland route .. from Alexandria to Suez.

overˈland, *v. Australia.* [f. OVERLAND *adv.*]

a. *intr.* To go overland from one colony or part of Australia to another. **b.** *trans.* To drive (stock) overland from one market to another. So **overˈlanding** *vbl. sb.* and *ppl. a.*

1871 M. CLARKE *Old Tales of Young Country* 163 'Overlanding' was a profitable and, withal, romantic occupation. Young men of spirit, wearied of the capital, and prompted by love of gain and adventure, purchased cattle and sheep in New South Wales, and drove them 'overland' to the 'New Orleans' of Colonel Torrens. **1873** RANKEN *Domin. Australia* xiii. (1874) 232 Herds used to be taken from New South Wales to South Australia across.. the deserts of Riverina. That used to be called 'overlanding'. **1885** MRS. C. PRAED *Head Station* (new ed.) 116, I can't imagine you overlanding cattle! **1900** *Daily News* 8 Oct. 3/1 He has gone exploring from South Australia to the Carpentaria, overlanding. **1916** *Chambers's Jrnl.* Nov. 729/1 Men live in the saddle.. when 'over-landing' cattle. **1925** *Ibid.* Dec. 810/1 Overlanding drovers who were opening up new country passed by. **1933** *Bulletin* (Sydney) 16 Aug. 20/2 Overlanding from the N.T. to Queensland. **1941** I. L. IDRIESS *Great Boomerang* xviii. 128 Any of the great overlanding or exploring treks would have been more instructive to remember. **1965** *Sunday Truth* (Brisbane) 17 Oct. 32/4 In 1839 the entire Wills establishment.. overlanded to.. western Victoria. *Ibid.* 32/5 Heading an overlanding expedition of 25 men and women and 10,000 sheep Wills led his party slowly north to a destination in central Queensland. **1975** *Australasian Express* (London) 10 Oct. 24/2 Overlanding is a wonderful way of travelling.

†**ˈoverˌlander**[1]. *Obs.* [app. a. Du. *Overlander* = Ger. *Oberländer*, i.e. a dweller in the *Oberland* or upper country.] A dweller in the uplands of a country, a highlander; *spec.* one dwelling in the higher lands of Germany, as opposed to a Netherlander or Low German.

a **1548** HALL *Chron., Hen. VII* 17 King Maximiliaen assembled a company of Almaynes and Overlanders. **1555** W. WATREMAN *Fardle Facions* I. iv. 38 Two countreies there ware of that name [Ethiope], Ouerlanders, and Netherlanders. **1605** VERSTEGAN *Dec. Intell.* x. (1628) 315 The Germans or ouerlanders.

overˈlander[2]. [f. OVERLAND *v.*] **1. a.** *Australia* and *N.Z.* One who journeyed overland from one colony or capital to another (*obs.* exc. *Hist.*); *spec.* one taking cattle from one colony to another or over a long distance. Also *slang*, a sundowner, a tramp.

1841 G. GREY *Jrnls. Two Expeditions of Discovery* ii. 183 The Overlanders are nearly all men in the pride of youth, whose occupation is to convey large herds of stock from market to market and from colony to colony. **1843** W. PRIDDEN *Australia* 335 (Morris) The class of men called Overlanders must not be omitted. Their occupation is to convey stock from market to market, and from one colony to another. **1848** C. STURT *Centr. Australia* I. 45 Conflicts between the natives and overlanders. **1852** *Lyttleton Times* (N.Z.) 27 Mar., Mr. A. Clifford has succeeded in driving about 1500 ewes from the Wairau district... Two other parties of 'over-landers' are reported to be close on his heels. **1877** M. CLARKE *Sch. Hist. Australia* 60 An expedition was planned with the purpose of reaching Western Port. Thus began the *First Overlanders*. **1889** 'R. BOLDREWOOD' *Robbery under Arms* xii, Puts 'em in mind of Hawdon and Evelyn Sturt in the old overlander days. **1898** MORRIS *Austral. Eng.* 333/1 *Overlander*... (2) A slang name for a *Sundowner*. **1907** A. SEARCY *In Austral. Tropics* 125 If a crowd of over-landers and backblockers happened to be present, things would be made lively. **1933** L. G. D. ACLAND in *Press* (Christchurch, N.Z.) 11 Nov. 15/7 *Overlander*, an Australian word for a man driving sheep or cattle a long distance. It was sometimes used in Canterbury in the early days. **1941** BAKER *Dict. Austral. Slang* 52 *Overlander*, a traveller. (2) One who makes long expeditions from one State to another with stock. (3) A settler from another State. (4) A drover. (5) A sundowner. **1967** *Woman's Day* (Austral.) 27 Feb. 10/3 Now in her early sixties, she still lives her life with all the zest of her overlander days.

b. *N. Amer.* One who moves from one part of the country to another; a migrant. *Obs.* exc. *Hist.*

1857 *Hutching's Mag.* Mar. 398/1 Reader, if you have never been an *over-lander*, I will tell you a little about camp life. **1916** A. C. LAUT *Cariboo Trail* 55 Some of the Overlanders had narrowly escaped a massacre. **1950** B. HUTCHINSON *Fraser* 88 The most remarkable immigrants of all deserve to be remembered—the Overlanders of '62, the men.. who walked to Cariboo across the Rocky Mountains. **1963** *Canad. Geogr. Jrnl.* Oct. 112/3 Among those who heard the call of 'Gold in the Cariboo!' were the Over-landers. **1968** E. RUSSENHOLT *Heart of Continent* III. vii. 116 This summer [*sc.* 1859], three parties of 'Overlanders', some 60 in all, leave from Assiniboia for the Cariboo.

2. In general use: one who travels overland to a country which can also be reached by sea or air; one who travels a long distance overland.

1953 J. PACKER *Apes & Ivory* xxiii. 240 There were many 'overlanders' after the war, when it was impossible to get a sea-passage to Southern Africa. **1960** *Guardian* 22 Nov. 7/5 Everywhere beyond Austria the overlander will attract.. the attentions of the idle bystander. **1974** *Country Life* 26 Dec. 2008/1 The intrepid long-distance overlander of today.

overlap (ˈəʊvəlæp), *sb.* [f. OVERLAP *v.*] **1. a.** An occurrence or instance of overlapping; a partial superposition or coincidence; the part or place at which one edge or thing overlaps another; *spec.* in *Geol.* (see next, 3). Also *transf.* and *fig.*

1813 S. SMITH *Agric. Surv. Galloway* 85 (Jam.) When the stones are small, the dykes should be proportionally narrowed, to make the two sides connect more firmly, and afford more overlaps. **1852** *Jrnl. R. Agric. Soc.* XIII. II. 298 The nails.. are driven through the overlap of both sheets at a time. **1880** DAWKINS *Early Man* i. 4 What we may term the overlap of history [on archæology]. **1931** A. KEITH *Place of Prejudice* 19 Head and heart are never quite separated; there is a large overlap in their fields of action. **1955** *Bull. Atomic Sci.* June 205/3 Perhaps outside help with parts of the investigation should be arranged, with some of the 'second laboratory' type of overlap providing the spur of competition. **1960** *Times* 31 Oct. 4/4 Later Glover scored a good try after Willcox had made the overlap in a set-piece movement. **1962** L. DEIGHTON *Ipcress File* xxiv. 156 That camera went out of action.. but luckily we have overlap on the camera fields. **1970** K. BALL *Fiat 600, 600D Autobook* 164/2 *Overlap*, period during which inlet and exhaust valves are open together. **1970** *Times* 1 Oct. 10/3 Hollins again at the 29th minute.. joined in an overlap with Mulligan. **1974** *Country Life* 3/10 Jan. 25/3 For the Garvan Gallery the William and Mary style runs from 1685 to 1730, Queen Anne from 1715 to 1765, Chippendale from 1750 to 1790 and Federal from 1788 to 1830. The overlaps are perfectly acceptable. **1974** *Times* 19 Dec. 6/8 There is a considerable overlap between the committee's membership and that of the Council for.. Arab-British understanding. **1975** *Times* 11 Jan. 12/4 Allowing for duplications and overlaps.. the CIA.. 'spies on 100,000,000 Americans'. **1976** *Sunday Post* (Glasgow) 26 Dec. 36/2 Better goal-kicking did the trick, since the try count was three-all, but Gala could have popped the result into their Christmas stockings a lot earlier if they had not so persistently kicked away overlaps.

b. In yacht-racing, a position in which a yacht overtaking another is debarred by the rules from passing one side, or in which the yachts concerned cannot turn toward each other without risking a collision.

1898 *Encycl. Sport* II. 585/2 If in rounding any mark in a race, or any obstruction, an inside yacht has an overlap, the outside yacht or yachts must give her sufficient room. **1935** *Encycl. Sports* 760/2 Provided that the overtaking yacht makes her overlap on the side opposite to that on which the overtaken yacht then carries her main boom, the latter may luff as she pleases [etc.]. **1958** *Times* 23 Sept. 14/2 The

American yacht then went smoothly forwards to establish an overlap.

c. *Phonetics.* Concurrence of the concluding sound of one phoneme with the opening of the next, as represented spectrographically; homonymy (as French /sã/, *cent* and *sans*).

1942 *Amer. Speech* XVII. 42 There is no over-lap between the length of this vowel when full grade..and its length when reduced grade. **1964** *Language* XL. 62 It is possible to raise the question of phonemic overlap... This instance of overlapping phonetic values..need not be regarded as a violation of phonemic principles.

d. *Linguistics.* (See quot. 1948).

1948 E. A. Nida in *Language* XXIV. 431 Instances of 'overlap', i.e. forms which are in complementary distribution except at certain points where there is a contrast resulting from fluctuation of forms. **1973** *Archivum Linguisticum* IV. 12 /de/ and /bi/ and /bi/ and /na/ do have areas of overlap.

2. *Geol.* The extension of a stratum beyond or over the edges of younger underlying strata; also, the upper stratum; esp. = onlap (a ***transgressive overlap***); also = offlap (a ***regressive overlap***); less commonly = overstep *sb.* 2.

1846 H. T. De la Beche in *Mem. Geol. Survey Gt. Brit.* I. 24 Proceeding westward..the overlap of the Old Red Sandstone becomes such that from Middleton Hall to the vicinity of Caermarthen, it rests on the lower Silurian rocks, covering up the higher Silurian beds. A. C. Ramsay in *Ibid.* 319 This..shows a tendency to a certain amount of contemporary depression of coast and sea bottom on the south to admit of an overlap during the formation of these deposits. **1857** Jukes *Stud. Man. Geol.* vii. 262 Overlap may take place in a perfectly continuous series, merely proving the fact of a depression of the area contemporaneously with that deposition. **1876** *Q. Jrnl. Geol. Soc.* XXXII. 377 By the term *overlap* no unconformity is here meant, but the concealment of lower beds by the extension, through a progressive subsidence, of those next in time upon the old rocks. **1883** [see overstep *sb.* 2]. **1906** A. W. Grabau in *Bull. Geol. Soc. Amer.* XVII. 569 The types of overlap of sedimentary strata may be classified as follows: A. Irregular or discontinuous overlap. B. Regular continuous or progressive overlap. 1. Marine. *a.* Transgressive. *b.* Regressive. 2. Non-marine. *c.* Fluviatile. **1913**, etc. [see offlap]. **1947** *Bull. Amer. Assoc. Petroleum Geol.* XXXI. 1868 There is much confusion in the uses of the word 'overlap' in geological literature. In recent years it has often been used to describe..: (1) the regular and progressive pinching-out of sediments above unconformities, and (2) the regular truncation of sediments below unconformities. **1962** Read & Watson *Introd. Geol.* xii. 616 Stratigraphical traps are the result of unconformities, lensing, overlap and reflected buried hills. **1972** B. B. Brock *Global Approach to Geol.* xvii. 224 The Lower Division forms remnants of a regressive overlap left by a contracting and retreating inland basin.

3. *Railways.* The distance beyond a signal that must be unoccupied before an engine is allowed to approach it past the previous signal.

1925 Tweedie & Lascelles *Mod. Railway Signalling* x. 145 To work without overlaps it would be necessary to have some system of positive speed control which would bring a train to a stand at a stop signal independently of the driver. **1956** *Railway Mag.* Mar. 351/2 The standard British block telegraph overlap of 440 yd. beyond the home..signal can be modified by special instructions. **1969** H. R. Broadbent *Introd. Railway Braking* i. 6 The overlap beyond the stop signal is therefore a form of margin on the distance between the warning and stop signals to cover for contingencies.

4. *Computers.* The strictly simultaneous performance of two or more operations during the execution of a program.

1963 L. Schultz *Digital Processing* xi. 239 In a machine with a modular memory..the execution of a program might be significantly speeded by locating variables in one module and instructions in another, and by providing an overlap in the time needed for executing one instruction and fetching the next. **1969** P. B. Jordain *Condensed Computer Encycl.* 365 I/O overlap is a great improvement over strictly sequential operations, but it still leaves the electronics waiting for the slower main memory.

5. *attrib.* **overlap fault**, an overthrust fault; **overlap joint**, a joint in which one edge overlaps the other, instead of merely butting against it.

1883 W. S. Gresley *Gloss. Terms Coal Mining* 180 *Overlap fault*, a peculiar kind of fault where a seam is reversed or doubled back over itself. **1886** J. Prestwich *Geol.* I. xv. 257 (*caption*) Great slide or overlap fault in the Radstock coalfield.

overlap (əʊvəˈlæp), *v.* Also 8 -lop. [f. over- 8 + lap *v.*[2] (cf. esp. sense 7, *lap over*). In sense 4 partly at least from lap *v.*[1]]

1. a. *trans.* To lap over; to lie or be situated so as partly to extend over and cover part of (something else); to overlie partially. Also *fig.* To extend over part of the (non-physical) territory, period, etc., occupied by (another thing); to coincide partly with.

1726 A. Munro *Anat. Bones* II. 74 An Infant, one of whose *Ossa parietalia* overloped the other. *Ibid.* (1782) 82 These cells..are overlopped by the maxillary bones. **1813** S. Smith *Agric. Surv. Galloway* 88 (Jam.) It is essential.. that the stones frequently overlap one another. **1872** Nicholson *Palæont.* 323 Ganoids in which the scales are rounded and overlap one another. **1887** Saintsbury *Hist. Elizab. Lit.* v. (1890) 159 Their lives overlapped each other considerably. *a* **1904** *Mod.* The lead overlaps the uppermost row of slates.

b. *absol.* or *intr.*, usually in reciprocal sense.

1799 Kirwan *Geol. Ess.* 285 In the Pyrenees, they sometimes overlap. **1886** Stubbs *Lect. Med. & Mod. Hist.* xiii. 296 Three conjoint systems of jurisprudence.. overlapping. **1911** R. Brooke *Let.* 13 Dec. (1968) 325 Ka appears some days later. James for a weekend... But some (e.g. Ka and Margery) will not overlap; so there'll not be too much of a crowd. **1971** *Nature* 22 Oct. 509/2 The Rothschild inquiry and the Dainton inquiry overlap only at the edges. **1977** K. O'Hara *Ghost of T. Penry* viii. 65 The generations overlapped because the Binns were an enormous family.

c. *trans.* in causal sense.

1846 Greener *Sc. Gunnery* 149 As a brazier would overlap the edge of a tin pipe, for boys to blow peas with.

†**d.** *Fencing.* (*absol.*) ? To cross one's own blade over one's adversary's. *Obs.*

1692 Sir W. Hope *Fencing-Master* 71 When you overlapp, do it with the broad side of your blade, and not with the Edge.

2. To cover and extend beyond (*lit.* and *fig.*).

1802 Paley *Nat. Theol.* xvi. §4. 301 The upper bill of the parrot is so much hooked, and so much overlaps the lower, that [etc.]. **1853** Kane *Grinnell Exp.* xxii. (1856) 175 The plantigrade base of support overlapped by long hair heightens the resemblance. **1875** J. F. Clarke in *N. Amer. Rev.* CXX. 48 A demand which continually overlapped the supply. **1879** Dixon *Windsor* I. xxiv. 246 He perceived the enemy overlapped and covered by his mighty host.

3. *Geol.* Said of a newer formation which extends beyond the area or edge of the older one on which it mainly rests, and thus partly overlies a still older one below that. *trans.* with either of the lower formations as obj. (= sense 1 or 2), or *absol.*

1832 De la Beche *Geol. Man.* 265 The great European sheet of chalk and green sand, produced at the cretaceous epoch..overlapped a great variety of pre-existing rocks from the gneiss of Sweden to the Wealden deposits of south-eastern England inclusive. **1871** Lyell *Elem. Geol.* v. 72 *Overlapping strata.*—Strata are said to overlap, when the upper bed extends beyond the limits of a lower one. **1885** *Ibid.* v. 69 Sediment spread over a region of subsidence has the area of deposit gradually increased, and the newest formed strata will overlap the next below them.

4. To 'lap' or ripple over (see lap *v.*[1] 4, 5).

1863 A. C. Ramsay *Phys. Geog.* xxxiv. (1878) 581 It has been so largely overlapped and worn away by succeeding waves of Celtic invasion. **1872** Browning *Fifine* lxxxi. 24 No lift of ripple to o'erlap Keel, much less, prow.

Hence **overˈlapping** *ppl. a.*

1849 Freeman *Archit.* I. I. i. 37 Overlapping stones cut into the semblance of an arched form. **1869** Gillmore *Reptiles & Birds* i. 7 The surface of the body is..smoothly covered with overlapping scales. **1871** [see 3 above]. **1926–7** *Army & Navy Stores Catal.* 854/3 Golfing requisites.. Harry Varden's own overlapping grip. Each 4/6. **1958** *Jrnl. Social Issues* XIV. I. 39 A major research question in changing attitudes and behavior is involved in this issue of overlapping situations. **1964** *Language* XL. 62 This instance of overlapping phonetic values therefore need not be regarded as a violation of phonemic principles. **1971** *Brit. Med. Bull.* XXVII. 7/1 According to the theory of overlapping population distribution, the population screened is comprised of a diseased and a non-diseased group, both of whom possess the attribute being measured, though with different frequencies at various test levels. **1977** *New Yorker* 10 Oct. 124/2 A certain touring professional golfer barely missed equalling the record for fewest putts in a tournament round by a man using the ordinary overlapping (as opposed to the more popular reverse overlapping) grip. **1978** A. Price *'44 Vintage* ix. 103 The flick-knife was held, for the upwards [blow]..which came in under the overlapping ribs.

overˈlapped, *ppl. a.* [-ed[1].] That overlaps or is overlapped (in various senses).

1839 [see *double coal* s.v. double *a.* A. 6]. **1898** G. Saintsbury *Short Hist. Eng. Lit.* VIII. ii. 498 The constant preference of overlapped or enjambed lines for the strict couplet. **1926** J. Adams *Christian Good of Scotland* viii. 126 To neglect or overlook the nobler ideals of the Church, because of its presently divided and overlapped system, is neither politic nor wise. **1962** A. Nisbett *Technique Sound Studio* 263 *Permanent joint*, cemented joint in three slightly overlapped tape.

overˈlapping, *vbl. sb.* [f. overlap *v.* + -ing[1].] The action or condition expressed by the verb overlap; partial overlying or coincidence. In *Fencing* (quot. 1692): see overlap *v.* 1 d.

1692 Sir W. Hope *Fencing-Master* 71 If he slipp my overlapping, I..make use of Binding. **1802** Paley *Nat. Theol.* xvi. §4. 302 This hook and overlapping of the bill could not be spared, for it forms the very instrument by which the bird climbs. **1851** Turner *Dom. Archit.* I. i. 3 One of the periods where an overlapping of styles must be looked for. **1872** *Spectator* 5 Oct. 1264 The foldings and overlappings of strata in mountainous regions. **1896** [see coalescence 3]. **1935** *Discovery* Sept. 278/1 Room within this waveband..to accommodate several independent high-definition sound and picture channels without overlapping or interference. **1942** *Amer. Speech* XVII. 46 'Coarticulation' and 'overlapping'. **1956** Jakobson & Halle *Fund. of Lang.* ii. 14 The so-called overlapping of phonemes confirms the manifestly relational character of the distinctive features... The same sound [e] in one position implements the diffuse, and in another, the compact term of the same opposition. **1963** B. Fozard *Instrumentation Nucl. Reactors* x. 112 Overlapping, i.e. failure to resolve the pulses, may cause errors of measurement in three main ways.

b. *concr.* A part that overlaps.

1858 G. Macdonald *Phantastes* xxi. 269 His body-armour was somewhat clumsily made,..the overlappings in the lower part had more play than necessary.

overlard (əʊvəˈlɑːd), *v.* [f. over- 8 + lard *v.*] *trans.* To lard over, smear over; to interlard or garnish copiously or to excess.

1820 W. Irving *Sketch Bk.* I. 235 So completely had the bard..been overlarded with panegyric. **1862** T. C. Grattan *Beaten Paths* II. 147 We have not that overlarding with quotations [etc.] which form the staple of ordinary authorship.

ˈover-ˈlarge, *a.* [over- 28.] Too large; of excessive magnitude or extent; excessive.

1532 More *Confut. Tindale* Wks. 373/2 Whoso do interprete his necessitie ouer large, or differre [etc.]. **1561** T. Hoby tr. *Castiglione's Courtyer* I. (1577) Diij, This is ouerlarge a scope of matters. **1647** Diggs *Unlawf. Taking Arms* ii. 47 This immunity is overlarge by our owne confession. **1890** *Spectator* 31 May, A big shop, an over-large estate.

So **ˈover-ˈlargely** *adv.*; **ˈover-ˈlargeness.**

1576 Fleming *Panopl. Epist.* 81 To be parciall of my pen, and to do that I did not ouer largely. **1867** Bushnell *Mor. Uses Dark Th.* 89 He will not let us keep ourselves on hand over-largely. **1725** Cheyne *Health* ii. §1 Viscidity in the Juices, or the over-largeness of their constituent particles.

overˈlash, *v. Obs.* exc. *dial.* [f. over- 12 + lash *v.*[1]] *intr.* To 'lash out' excessively (see lash *v.*[1] 5); to break out into excess (in conduct, or *esp.* in language); to go beyond bounds, be extravagant; to exaggerate. Cf. outlash.

1579 Tomson *Calvin's Serm. Tim.* 143/1 The worde.. signifieth moderation and gravitie, as when men doe not overlashe and give them selves to all wickednesse. *a* **1656** Ussher *Ann.* vi. (1658) 257 Who..thinks,..in this reckoning, he did overlash. **1701** J. Sage *Vind. Cyprianic Age* Wks. 1847 II. 50 The excellent rhetorick they were endowed with made them overlash sometimes in their expression.

b. *trans.* To go beyond, exceed.

1601 Deacon & W. *Answ. to Darel* Ded. 2 That either they, or our selues, should ouer-lash the limits alotted vnto vs.

Hence †**overˈlashing** *vbl. sb.*, extravagance, exaggeration; *ppl. a.*, extravagant, exaggerative (whence †**overˈlashingly** *adv.*).

1579 Gosson *Sch. Abuse* (Arb.) 39 Ouerlashing in apparel is so common a fault, that..very hyerlings..jet under Gentlemens noses in sutes of silke. **1579** Lyly *Euphues* (Arb.) 105 To the intent he might bridle the ouerlashing affections of Philautus. **1612** Brerewood *Lang. & Relig.* viii. 74, I be far from their opinion, which write too over-lashingly, that the Arabian tongue is in use in two third parts of the inhabited world. **1710** tr. *Werenfels's Disc. Logom.* 221 It would be overlashing to say with Seneca, *Nullum intra se manet hodie Vitium.*

overlast *v.*: see over- 17.

ˈover-ˈlate, *a.* and *adv.* [f. over- 28, 30 + late *a.*[1], *adv.*] Excessively late; too late.

A. *adj.* (†Also in sup. *over-latest.*) **B.** *adv.*

a. 1574 tr. *Marlorat's Apocalips* 14 But this ouerlate repentance shall nothing auayle them. **1640** Bp. Hall *Episc.* I. i. 5 Such an act, as can scarce by expiated with floods of overlatest teares. **1649** Milton *Eikon.* Bij, These overlate Apologies and Meditations of the dead King. **1958** T. Stanwell-Fletcher *Clear Lands* 245 The diminishing supply of native animals..despite overlate measures of restocking and conservation.

b. 1340 Hampole *Pr. Consc.* 3455 And comes overlate tyl Goddes servise. **1548** Udall *Erasm. Par. Luke* xxiii. 193 b, Iudas ouerlate repenting him of his facte, honge himselfe. *a* **1641** Bp. Mountagu *Acts & Mon* (1642) 77 Nor can it be said to have been accomplished over late. **1875** W. Morris tr. *Virgil's Aeneids* VII. 597 And over-late the Gods thou shalt adore.

So **ˈover-ˈlately** *adv.*

1556 Olde *Antichrist* 158 This mater is more newe and ouer lately done than to be denyed.

over-laudation, -laughing, etc.: see over-.

overˈlaunch, *v.* [over- 26, 8.]

†**1.** *intr.* To 'launch out' excessively, go to excess, act extravagantly. *Obs.*

1579 Tomson *Calvin's Serm. Tim.* 1007/1 One that ouer-launcheth so farre to withstand God.

2. *trans. Shipbuilding.* (See quots.)

1711 W. Sutherland *Shipbuild. Assist.* 162 Overlaunching; splicing or scarfing one Piece of Timber to another, to make firm Work. *c* **1850** *Rudim. Navig.* (Weale) 135 *To over-launch*, to run the butt of one plank to a certain distance beyond the next butt above or beneath it, in order to make stronger work. *Ibid.* 147 Disposing the butts of the planks, &c. so that they may over-launch each other.

ˈover-ˈlavish, *a.* [over- 28.] Too lavish; excessively profuse or extravagant.

1584 Lodge *Alarum* Ep. Ded., Those who are like by overlavish profusenesse to become meate for their mouths. **1611** Speed *Hist. Gt. Brit.* VIII. 387 The ouer-lauish report thereof. **1898** *Westm. Gaz.* 17 May 8/1 The company did not enjoy an over-lavish appreciation by the investing public.

So **ˈover-ˈlavishly** *adv.*

1593 *Bacchus Bountie* in *Harl. Misc.* (Malh.) II. 272 Licking vp ouerlauishly the small crums that tumbled out of his tunne.

†**ˌoverˈlavish**, *v. Obs.* [over- 27.] *intr.* To be too lavish; to exaggerate.

1607 *Schol. Disc. agst. Antichr.* II. ix. 131 Others censure Prudentius and Ephreem as overlavishing in their speeches about the crosse. **1625** Bp. Mountagu *App. Cæsar* II. iii. 128 To overlavish transcendently in their commendation.

† 'over-ˌlaw, *sb. nonce-wd.* [OVER- 2 b.] A higher or overruling law.

1883 BP. BROWNE in *Guardian* 1457 Well..may we believe the over-law of the Papacy to be the forerunner of the un-law of Antichrist.

† **over'law**, *v. Obs.* [OVER- 21.] *trans.* To overcome by law; to defeat in an action at law.

1562 J. HEYWOOD *Prov. & Epigr.* (1867) 193 Pray hir to let fall thaction at law now, Or els..she will ouerlaw yow.

overlay (əʊvə'leɪ), *v.* Pa. t. and pple. over'laid. Forms: see OVER and LAY *v.*[1] [Not in OE.; but cf. Goth. *ufarlagjan* to lay upon, MHG. *überlegen*, MDu. *oferlegghen*. In several of its senses equivalent to OVERLIE (which during 17–18th c. it entirely displaced): cf. LAY *v.* 43.]

I. To lay over.

1. a. *trans.* To lay or place over, above, or upon something else; to put on the top; to superimpose. *rare.* [OVER- 1, 8.]

1570 LEVINS *Manip.* 197/20 To ouerlay, *superponere.* **1641** MILTON *Ch. Govt.* II. Introd., If..what it wanted of being a load to any part of the body, it did not with a heavy advantage overlay upon the Spirit! **1760** *Ann. Reg.* 136 A guard..forced us into the hold, and overlaid the hatches.

b. To surmount or span *with* something extending over. *rare.* [OVER- 1.]

c **1611** CHAPMAN *Iliad* VI. I v b, The horse-haire plume, with which he was so ouerlaid. **1671** MILTON *P.R.* III. 333 To..overlay With bridges rivers proud.

2. a. To cover the surface of (a thing) *with* something spread over it; to deck all over. [OVER- 8.]

a **1300** *Cursor M.* 13464 þe dales was wit folk ouer-laid. **1482** *Monk of Evesham* (Arb.) 21 As a manne had ouyr leyde hem with mekyl bloode. **1590** SPENSER *F.Q.* I. vii. 34 Phœbus golden face it did attaint, As when a cloud his beames doth ouer-lay. **1647** CRASHAW *Poems* 102 Ere Hebe's hand had overlaid His smooth cheeks with a downy shade. **1780** SIR J. REYNOLDS *Disc.* x. (1876) 17 The defect..of being overlaid with drapery. **1857** RUSKIN *Pol. Econ. Art* 30 You may make king's thrones of it, and overlay temple gates with it.

b. *Printing.* To put an overlay upon (see next, 2); also *absol.* to use an overlay.

1888 C. T. JACOBI *Printer's Vocab.* 93 *Overlay*, to make ready by overlaying—the reverse of underlaying. **1894** *Amer. Dict. Printing & Bookmaking* 413/1 *Overlay*,..to secure proper effects in printing by means of graduated impression between the impressing surface and the sheet, using different thicknesses of paper. **1940** *Chambers's Techn. Dict.* 604/2 *Overlay*.., to adjust the impression surface of a machine by cutting and patching.

† **3. a.** To cover superfluously or excessively, or so as to encumber, smother, or extinguish; *spec.* to overstock (a pasture *with* cattle, etc.). [OVER- 8, 27.]

1523 FITZHERB. *Husb.* §70 Beastes alone..wyll not eate a pasture euen, but leaue many tuftes and hygh grasse in dyuers places, excepte it be ouer layde with cattell. **1538** STARKEY *England* I. iii. 74 A pastur ys ouerlayd wyth catel, when therin be mo then may be conuenyently nuryschyd and fed. **1633** BP. HALL *Medit. & Vows* (1851) 16 Here is a tree overlaid with blossoms. *a* **1733** *Shetland Acts* in *Proc. Soc. Ant. Scot.* (1892) XXVI. 35 That all horses.. oppressing and overlaying the neighbourhood, be instantly removed.

b. To lay in excess; to impose too much of. *rare.* [OVER- 27.]

1836 JAS. GRANT *Rand. Recoll. Ho. Lords* xiii. 270 He was ..ample in his illustrations without overlaying them.

II. To lie over.

4. To lie over (something else): more properly OVERLIE. (Cf. LAY *v.*[1] 43.) [OVER- 8.]

13.. *Cursor M.* 5934 (Cott.) Frosse þat na tung moght tell ..al þe land ouer-laid a-boute. **1793** SMEATON *Edystone L.* §143 *note*, A piece of strong timber overlaying the bows of a vessel. **1806–7** J. BERESFORD *Miseries Hum. Life* (1826) XVII. iv, Overlaying one of your arms till it is cramped, and exposing the other till it is frost-bitten. **1860** TYNDALL *Glac.* I. xvi. 107 Loose shingle and boulders overlaid the mountain.

5. *spec.* **a.** To lie over or upon (a child, etc.) so as to suffocate it; to smother by lying upon; = OVERLIE 2 a.

1557 NORTH *Gueuara's Diall Pr.* 170 When the weomen are heavy a sleepe..they many times overlay the poore infant, and so smother it alive. **1573–80** BARET *Alv.* O 176 Sowes Ouerlaie and squise to death their pigges. **1741** RICHARDSON *Pamela* (1824) I. lxxi. 414 He would hire the nurse to over-lay him. **1863** KINGSLEY *Water Bab.* v, All the little children who are overlaid.

† **b.** To lie with (sexually): = OVERLIE 2 b. *Obs.*

a **1450** *Cov. Myst.* xiv. 138 But if sum man the had ovyr-layd, Thi wombe xulde never be so gret i-wys.

† **6.** *fig.* To extend over, include in its scope, 'cover'. *Obs. rare.*

13.. *Cursor M.* 27096 (Cott.) To min on his ouer-sight þat al wranges has to right, On þiskin sight þat al ouer-lais.

7. To affect like or as with a superincumbent weight (with various implications and shades of meaning). [OVER- 8, 21.] † **a.** To press severely upon, press hard with arms or exactions; to distress; to overwhelm, overpower, crush by force. *Obs.*

13.. *Cursor M.* 27883 (Cott.) He es ouerlaid wit drunkenhede. *Ibid.* 29339 þaa þat pouer men ouer-lais, and herijs þam. *c* **1450** *Merlin* 161 The peple of Pharien were sore ouerleide. **1549** COVERDALE, etc. *Erasm. Par. 2 Cor.* 50 We are on euery syde ouerlayed with aduersitee. **1593** Q. ELIZ. tr. *Boeth.* I. Pr. iv. 12 Me thinkes I see..euery wickedst man overlayeng me with new fraudes of accusation. **1678** MARVELL *Growth Popery* Wks. 1875 IV. 309 They were overlaid by numbers. **1769** *Ann. Reg.* 21 The shattered remains of Prosorowski's army..were continually overlaid and oppressed by the Turkish cavalry.

b. To press upon so as to impede the working or activity of; to overburden, encumber, weigh down; to crush, smother, stifle.

1609 HOLLAND *Amm. Marcell.* D iij b, Diocletian and Maximian being overlaied with businesse, adopted unto them two Cæsars. **1663** CHAS. II in Julia Cartwright *Henrietta of Orleans* (1894) 137, I have been overlayd with businesse. **1744** BERKELEY *Siris* §298 Men in those early days were not overlaid with languages and literature. **1844** LD. BROUGHAM *A. Lunel* III. ix. 266 He neither overlays you with his books nor with his adventures.

8. To conceal or obscure as if by covering up; to render indistinct or imperceptible by addition of something figured as superimposed. [OVER- 8.]

1719 YOUNG *Busiris* Prol., Nor wou'd these scenes in empty words abound Or overlay the sentiment with sound. **1841** HERSCHEL *Ess.* (1857) 535 Sufficient..to overlay and conceal that minute quantity of which astronomers were in search. **1886** SYMONDS *Renaiss. It., Cath. React.* (1898) VII. xii. 198 Though the words were more intelligible, the fugal artifices overlaid their clear enunciation.

9. *Naut.* To cross the cable or anchor of another vessel so as to cause chafing or obstruction. [OVER- 10.]

1796 NELSON in Nicolas *Disp.* (1846) VII. p. xciv, The damage a Swedish Vessel's cable sustained by the Peterel's overlaying her. **1854** G. B. RICHARDSON *Univ. Code* v. (ed. 12) 419 You will overlay my anchor.

Hence **'overˌlaid** (stress var.) *ppl. a.*

1858 GEN. P. THOMPSON *Audi Alt.* II. lxxi. 14 These underground or overlaid classes. **1901** W. W. PEYTON in *Contemp. Rev.* Sept. 445 An overlaid germ which has been saved from death by the healing virtue of the Unknowable.

overlay ('əʊvəleɪ), *sb.* [f. prec.: see OVER- 8.]

1. A cravat, necktie (cf. OVERLAYER, quot. 1635). *Sc.*

1725 RAMSAY *Gentle Sheph.* I. ii, He falds his owrelay down his breast with care. **1816** SCOTT *Antiq.* xxxvi, The Captain says a three-nookit handkercher is the maist fashionable overlay. **1884** C. ROGERS *Soc. Life Scotl.* I. vii. 245 The usual necktie or overlay was a square tweeling of coarse yarn.

2. *Printing.* **a.** A piece of paper cut to the required shape and pasted over the impression-surface of a printing-press in order to make the impression darker in particular places, as in a woodcut.

1824 J. JOHNSON *Typogr.* II. xv. 521 Should any wood cuts be in the form,..if too low, they may be humoured a little by means of an overlay. **1888** WILSON & GREY *Pract. Treat. Mod. Printing Machinery* xxi. 337 The object of an overlay is not to equalise the impression, but to intensify the pressure upon the dark parts or solids, that they may be firm and bright, and to lessen the impression upon the lighter shades, in order to give them that degree of delicacy and cleanliness that would be altogether wanting if the pressure exerted were uniform. **1946** V. S. GANDERTON in H. Whetton *Pract. Printing & Binding* xi. 132/2 In letterpress the gradation in tone of a half-tone plate corresponds to a gradation in resistance to pressure... The object of an interlay or overlay is to balance the variation in resistance by varying the pressure on the different areas. **1970** E. A. D. HUTCHINGS *Survey of Printing Processes* iv. 57 Many of these operations [in make-ready] can be carried out..in the pre-press department, using..register tables..and other precision equipment such as mechanical overlay systems.

b. In offset lithographic printing: (see quot. 1974).

1967 KARCH & BUBER *Offset Processes* 548 *Overlay*, in offset, the transparent..covering on the copy on which directions..are placed in conjunction with the original. **1974** J. CRAIG *Production for Graphic Designer* 172/1 The copy for each additional color is pasted on acetate overlays, each one representing a color. *Ibid.* 190/2 Overlay. Transparent paper or film flap placed over artwork for the purpose of (1) protecting it from dirt or damage, (2) indicating instructions to the platemaker or printer, or (3) showing the breakdown of color in mechanical color separations.

3. a. Something laid as a covering over something else; a covering, a superincumbent layer, etc.; esp. in various special senses (*e.g.* a coverlet, a small cloth laid upon a table-cloth, etc.); also *fig.* Also *attrib.*, as ***overlay mattress***.

1794 [see OVERLAYER quot. 1811]. **1828** *Craven Gloss.* (ed. 2), *O'erlay*, a coverlet or cloak. **1844** *Jrnl. R. Agric. Soc.* V. I. 171 Two or three harrows are kept together by a rider, or overlay, and the horses draw abreast. **1881** MRS. LYNN LINTON *My Love* II. ix. 170 She had determined to brave her memories and suppress them by the overlay of a new association. **1884** *West. Morn. News* 3 Sept. 1/2 Folding spring mattress, wool overlay. **1886** J. BARROWMAN *Gloss. Scotch Mining Terms* 48 *Overlay*, the material above the rock in a quarry. **1893** J. PULSFORD *Loyalty to Christ* II. 307 Christ clothed Himself with the overlay of our flesh, in order to meet us on our own ground. **1926–7** *Army & Navy Stores Catal.* 1076 Overlay mattresses for children's bedsteads and cots. **1930** *Daily Tel.* 9 Apr. 6/3 (Advt.), No bumps, no lumps, no sag in the 'Vi-Spring', the overlay mattress. **1949** H. M. CAUTLEY *Norfolk Churches* 38 Another feature came into perfection, namely the overlay, with its imposed and crocketted hood-moulds on the face of tracery, giving such depth and solidity to the whole, as at Scarning..and Bedingham. **1953** *B.U. Encycl. Handbk.* (Bedding Publications Ltd.) App. 198 Upholstered overlay mattresses with spring or cellular rubber interior. **1962** A. MCINTOSH in Davis & Wrenn *Eng. & Medieval Stud.* 234 Just as we concluded earlier that Thornton transcribed B_1 and M_1 without very much tampering, so must we now conclude that S transcribed M_2 with sufficient fidelity for his own overlay not to have obliterated strong traces of an underlying language. **1968** *Lebende Sprachen* XIII. 104/2 *Overlay*, the action accomplished in the interfacing technique wherein linking events are meshed into a single event. **1972** H. KURATH *Studies Area Linguistics* viii. 124 The replaced language was an overlay (superstratum), as French in England or Frankish in northern France.

b. A transparent sheet bearing additional information, which is laid over a map or diagram.

1938 E. RAISZ *Gen. Cartogr.* xv. 172 Transparent tracing papers are made of straw and cornstalk base and are used in map work for sketching, for copying, and for tissue overlays which indicate various colors and tints. **1952** V. CANNING *House of Seven Flies* viii. 128 He put the overlay on the chart so that the cross..fell on the position of the house. **1964** G. LYALL *Most Dangerous Game* vi. 45, I did the real work using a celluloid overlay with wax-pencil marks. **1973** J. S. KEATES *Cartogr. Design & Production* xx. 200/2 It is more satisfactory to produce the pattern stick-up on a separate overlay, and then combine this with the line image in a separate processing stage. **1974** *Sci. Amer.* May 126/1 The plastic overlay rotates around the pin. The track on the earth's surface over which the satellite passes during any orbit is plotted as a curved line on the overlay.

c. A layer of coloured glass added on top of clear glass in decorative glass-ware; usu. *attrib.* in ***overlay glass***, ***paper-weight***, ***weight***; hence *ellipt.* for *overlay paper-weight*.

1940 E. H. BERGSTROM *Old Glass Paperweights* ii. 12 In an encrusted overlay weight, the color overlays and faceting were apparently followed by a final dip into clear crystal to complete the weight. **1954** E. M. ELVILLE *Paperweights & Other Glass Curiosities* i. 16 Also highly prized by connoisseurs are the overlay paperweights. Overlays were usually made with the millefiori mushroom in a crystal globe ..given..a final casing of a colour such as red, blue or green. **1958** G. B. HUGHES *Eng. Glass for Collector 1660–1860* xx. 220 Those who toured the Continent in the early nineteenth century enthusiastically adorned their dining-tables and dressing rooms on their return with specimens of colourful Bohemian work known as cased or overlay glass. **1967** WODEHOUSE *Company for Henry* iii. 45 A French eighteenth-century paperweight alluded to as follows:.. Clichy double overlay weight. **1968** *Canad. Antiques Collector* Aug. 9/1 We know that Burlington produced many sophisticated types of glass including overlay glass. **1973** J. MACKAY *Glass Paperweights* viii. 54 The majority of these overlay weights are doubles with an inner overlay of white and an outer overlay in shades of red, green or blue.

d. *Med.* A gelling layer spread on top of a layer of cells in culture and containing an indicator of the presence or absence of some cell product.

1954 *Jrnl. Exper. Med.* XCIX. 168 The agar overlay, used to overlay the cultures after infection, consisted of 12 parts of 2·7 per cent agar (*A*), 12 parts of neutral red solution (*B*), 8 parts of fourfold Earle's saline (*C*), and 5 parts of embryo extract (*D*). **1960** *Virology* X. 377 The difference in diameter of plaques grown under agar over-lay with and without viral antibodies serves as a measure of antigenic difference. **1974** *Nature* 20 Dec. 745/2 Virus pools were grown in Vero cells and titrated by plaque assay with a methylcellulose overlay as before.

4. *Dentistry.* A structure intended to improve the occlusal surface of the tooth or teeth over which it fits.

1935 G. M. ANDERSON *Dewey's Pract. Orthodontia* (ed. 5) xxi. 443 To stabilize the canine anchorage, the canine overlays are connected on the lingual surface with a clasp metal wire. **1954** *Brit. Dental Jrnl.* XCVII. 268/1 An upper acrylic bite overlay, sliding the mandible forward at the same time as opening the bite, gave complete relief in three days by preventing the condyles from being forced back in the fossæ. **1973** ANDERSON & STORER *Immediate & Replacement Dentures* (ed. 2) iv. 33 The retentive type of the overlay prosthesis should be considered where the residual ridges are almost non-existent and in cases where for reasons of speech, retching or excessive salivation, a palateless type of upper denture is necessary.

5. In betting, odds which are unjustifiably high. *U.S.*

1944 *Sun* (Baltimore) 21 Sept. 17/4 There is always a section that keeps in keen pursuit of the 'overlay', which means a horse rated, say, at 4 to 1 which closes at 10 to 1 or 12 to 1, well above his 'morning line' price. **1944** D. RUNYON *Runyon à la Carte* (1946) 102 Everybody around is saying The Sky makes a terrible over-lay of the natural price in giving Brandy Bottle a G against his soul. **1955** *Amer. Speech* XXX. 27 The term *overlay* originally described the situation which existed if a bookmaker laid odds which, viewed objectively, were too high. At the present time *overlay* is used to describe odds meeting this test which appear in the pari-mutuel machine. Most often odds are considered an overlay if they are higher than the odds quoted in the so-called *morning line*.

6. *Computers.* The process of transferring a block of instructions or data to internal storage in place of what is already there, esp. in order to utilize a limited high-speed memory for those parts of a program that are in active use; also, a section of program so transferred.

1963 *Automatic Data Processing Gloss.* (U.S. Bureau of Budget) 38/1 *Overlay*, a technique for bringing routines into high-speed storage during processing, so that several routines will occupy the same storage location at different times. **1965** SWALLOW & PRICE *Elem. Computer Programming* xiv. 273 Once the new table is determined for a given run, the original table and the program for calculating the new one can be discarded, so the main program may be loaded over the previous one... This is frequently called an overlay. **1969** P. B. JORDAIN *Condensed Computer Encycl.* 367 When a program and its data are too large for the computer, the program must be divided into segments and so constructed that only the active segments (or overlays) need be in core. **1970** O. DOPPING *Computers & Data Processing* xiv. 219 We can have a special memory area for overlay, or we can let a part of the program normally used—the main program, be overwritten. **1972** J.-L. BAER in A. F. Cardenas et al. *Computer Sci.* v. 170 If subroutines A and B will never call each other, then they can occupy the same positions in memory. If, at run-time, B is called while A is present, an overlay will be performed replacing A by B, and vice versa.

'over,layer. [f. OVERLAY *v.* + -ER[1].] One who or that which overlays or overlies something; †in *Sc.* = prec. 1 (*obs.*).

1611 COTGR., *Oppresseur*, an oppressor; ouercharger, ouer-layer. **1635** BRERETON *Trav.* (Chetham) 188 We call here [in Scotland]..a band an ourlayer. **1725** BRADLEY *Fam. Dict.* s.v. *Washing of Hemp or Flax*, You must..take off the Gravel, Stone, and over-layers of Wood, that keep 'em together in the Water. **1735** *Prompter* 17 Jan. 2/2 What a Providence it is, that these bloody-minded Over-layers happen'd to be so Light in their Pressure. **1811** T. DAVIS *Agric. Wilts.* xxxviii, The waggons..seldom have any overlayers [*ed.* 1794 overlays] or outriggers. **1917** *19th Cent.* Jan. 132 Faith in God and in a hereafter has been accompanied in history by an overlayer of superstition.

over'laying, *vbl. sb.* [f. OVERLAY *v.* + -ING[1].] The action of the verb OVERLAY, in various senses (in early quots. *fig.* oppression); *concr.* that with which something is overlaid, a covering.

c **1380** WYCLIF *Sel. Wks.* II. 212 In þe world shulen ȝe haue over-leiynge [*MS. Douce* 321 over-lyinge; *John* xvi. 33 in the world ȝe schulen haue pressing, *gloss* or ouer-leying]. **1611** BIBLE *Exod.* xxxviii. 17 The overlaying of their chapiters of silver. **1839** T. C. HANSARD *Treat. Printing & Type-Founding* (1841) 117 Anciently, the artist in wood contented himself with producing his lights and shades by cutting his lines..upon a plane, leaving to the printer the task of producing the required effects by a tedious process of overlaying. **1862** R. H. PATTERSON *Ess. Hist. & Art* 135 Marked..by an overlaying rather than by any displacement of the native population. **1890** *Newcastle Daily Chron.* 26 Dec. 3/1 Last week no less than twenty-one London infants under a year old died from suffocation—in other words from 'overlaying'. **1896** T. L. DE VINNE in *Moxon's Mech. Exerc., Printing* 426 The underlaying or overlaying of types..to correct inequalities of impression. **1967** V. STRAUSS *Printing Industry* vii. 428/2 Overlaying serves two purposes: one is to level the impression and the other to provide varying pressure.

†over'lead, *v. Obs.* [OE. *oferlǣdan* to oppress: see OVER- 2; cf. OHG. *ubarleitan* 'transducere'.]

1. *trans.* To overwhelm; to oppress; to domineer or tyrannize over.

971 *Blickl. Hom.* 203 Ða wæs Garganus se munt..mid mycclum broȝan and mid ongryslan eall oferlæded. **1377** LANGL. *P. Pl.* B. III. 314 Shal neither kynge ne knyȝte constable ne Meire Ouer-lede þe comune to don hem pliȝte here treuthe. *c* **1400** *Sowdone Bab.* 2502. **1413** *Pilgr. Sowle* (Caxton 1483) IV. xxxiv. 83 That the poure peple be nought ouerled with tyrannye. *c* **1440** *Promp. Parv.* 373/1 Ovyr ledyn, or oppressyn, *opprimo*.

2. To lead as a superior; to rule, govern.

c **1440** CAPGRAVE *Life St. Kath.* IV. 2060 Thys mayde wil ouere-leede us, sirs, we are caught In oure artes, be we neuere so proude. *Ibid.* v. 975. *c* **1450** *Merlin* 122 For that he may not hem now Iustice and ouerlede. **1720** *Humourist* 92 Shewing how little his best Actions are overled by what ought to be his Standard of Action.

3. To lead over, across, or to another place; *fig.* to lead into some way of acting or thinking; to lead astray, mislead; to 'carry away', impel. [OVER- 10, 11.]

1382 WYCLIF *Isa.* xxiii. 13 In to caitifte thei ouerladden [1388 ledden ouer] the stalwrthe men of it. **1447** BOKENHAM *Seyntys* (Roxb.) 107 Wyth the rage of woodnesse ovyrled. **14..** in *Babees Bk.* (1868) 332 Lette neuer þy wylle þy witt ouer lede. **1636** HEYWOOD *Challenge* II. i, Could opportunity have mov'd, words tempted,..or griefes have o'reled, Beneath my much importance she had falne.

Hence **†over'leading** *vbl. sb.* oppression; also, leading over; also **†over'leader**, an oppressor.

1382 WYCLIF *Wisd.* ii. 14 He is mad to vs in to ouerleding [Vulg. *in traductionem*] of oure thoȝtis. *c* **1440** *Jacob's Well* 86 Because he is pruddere, þe more teraunt, þe more ouerledere, þe more cursyd lyvere. *c* **1440** *Promp. Parv.* 373/1 Ovyrledare (or ovyr settar, infra), *oppressor*. **1496** *Dives & Paup.* (W. de W.) v. vii. 203/2 Mansleers that by extorcyon, raueyne and ouerledynge..robbe men of ther good.

overleaf (,əʊvə'liːf), *adv.* [Properly two words, OVER *prep.* and LEAF *sb.*[1]: see OVER- 31.] On the other side of the leaf (of paper, esp. of a book).

[**1613–39** I. JONES in Leoni *Palladio's Archit.* (1742) II. 49 As I have noted over leaf.] **1843** J. H. NEWMAN *Miracles* 163 *note*, Dr. Robinson, as is said over-leaf, cannot escape a bend. **1893** SIR R. BALL *Story of Sun* 259 The picture overleaf exhibits the mare crisium on the Moon.

attrib. **1829** SOUTHEY in *Corr. w. C. Bowles* (1881) 154 These overleaf lines are the very bad reason why I have been silent so long.

'over-'lean, *a.* [OVER- 28.] Too lean.

1657 M. LAWRENCE in Spurgeon *Treas. Dav.* Ps. cvi. 15 We look on it as an affliction to have an over-lean body.

overlean (əʊvə'liːn), *v.* [f. OVER- 3 + LEAN *v.*[1]] *trans.* To lean over.

1827 HOOD *Hero & Leander* xxii, The drowsy mist..o'erleans the sea. **1875** LANIER *Symphony* 87 Where many boughs the still pool overlean.

So **over'leaning** *vbl. sb.* and *ppl. a.*

1762 DUNN in *Phil. Trans.* LII. 467 All forms and shapes, as sloping, perpendicular, overleaning. **1865** CAMERON *Malayan India* 53 They are two stories high..with heavy overleaning eaves. **1896** D. L. LEONARD *Cent. Congregat. Ohio* 74 The Welsh churches, which had stood quite aloof with over-leaning towards Independency.

overleap (əʊvə'liːp), *v.* [OE. *oferhléapan*; answering in form to MDu. *overlôpen*, Du. *overloopen*, MHG. *überloufen*, Ger. *überlaufen*, 'to run over, overrun, overflow'; OHG. had a deriv. *ubarhlaupnissî* prevarication, transgression.]

1. *trans.* To leap over, across, or to the other side of. [OVER- 5.]

a **900** tr. *Bæda's Hist.* v. vi. (1890) 400 Wæs þæt hit sume sloh on þæm wæȝe mid swiðran ræse oferhleop and oferstælde. **1605** SHAKS. *Macb.* I. iv. 49 That is a step, On which I must fall downe, or else o're-leape, For in my way it lyes. **1667** MILTON *P.L.* IV. 181 Th' arch-fellon..At one slight bound high overleap'd all bound Of Hill or highest Wall. **1860** MOTLEY *Netherl.* (1868) I. i. 5 The ambition of the Spaniard, which has overleaped so many lands and seas.

b. *fig.* with immaterial obj. (usually *bounds*, *limits*, or the like).

1775 DE LOLME *Eng. Const.* I. xii. (1853) 118 Procuring a public advantage by overleaping restraints. **1875** JOWETT *Plato* (ed. 2) V. 247 His ingenuity does indeed far overleap the heads of all your great men.

†c. *intr.* To leap over. *Obs. rare.*

1382 WYCLIF *Ecclus.* xxxviii. 37 [33] In to the chirche thei shul not ouerlepen [*Vulg.* transilient].

2. *trans.* To pass over, pass by, omit, leave out, 'skip'. (Now only as consciously *fig.* from 1.)

c **1000** *Sax. Leechd.* III. 264 Se dæȝ is ȝehaten saltus lunæ, þæt is ðæs monan hlyp, for þan þe he oferhlypð ænne dæȝ. **1303** R. BRUNNE *Handl. Synne* 2916 Y wyl now ouer lepe hyt here. *c* **1425** *Craft Nombrynge* (E.E.T.S.) 25 Ouer lepe alle þese cifers & sett þat neþer 2 þat stondes toward þe ryght side. **1589** PUTTENHAM *Eng. Poesie* II. x. (Arb.) 99 Your rime falleth vpon the first and fourth verse ouerleaping two. **1641** SMECTYMNUUS *Vind. Answ.* i. 5 Whatever objection made by us, he finds too heavy to remove, he over-leaps it. **1846** TRENCH *Mirac.* i. (1862) 109 All the intervening steps of these tardier processes were overleaped.

†b. *intr.* To turn aside from the main discourse; to digress. *Obs. rare.*

1393 LANGLAND *P. Pl.* C. XXI. 360 A lytel ich ouer-lep for lesynges sake.

†3. To leap or spring upon. *Obs. rare.* [OVER- 7.]

1377 LANGL. *P. Pl.* B. Prol. 150 For a cat of a courte cam whan hym lyked, And ouerlepe hem lyȝtlich and lauȝte hem at his wille. *Ibid.* 199 þat cat..þat canȝow ouerlepe.

†4. To leap farther than, surpass in leaping; *fig.* to surpass, excel. *Obs.* [OVER- 22.]

a **1340** HAMPOLE *Psalter* lxi. 1 þe halyman ouerlepand in thoght of heuen all warldis lufers. **1603** FLORIO *Montaigne* I. xx. (1632) 41 Leaping, and straining himselfe to overleape another.

b. *refl.* To leap beyond one's measure or mark, or beyond what one intends; to leap too far.

1605 SHAKS. *Macb.* I. vii. 27 Vaulting Ambition, which ore-leapes it self, And falles on th' other.

So **†'overleap** *sb. Obs.*, a leaping over; omission.

1610 BP. HALL *Apol. Brownists* 34 We like not these bold ouer-leapes of so many Centuries.

over'learn, *v.* [OVER- 27 a.] *trans.* To learn excessively; *spec.* in *Psychol.*, to learn (something) beyond the stage of initially successful performance. Hence **over'learned** *ppl. a.*; **over'learning** *vbl. sb.*

1874 L. TOLLEMACHE in *Fortn. Rev.* Feb. 238 A lesson which..most Englishmen have already overlearnt. **1918** E. C. TOLMAN in *Psychol. Monogr.* XXV. I. 48 The first hypothesis would assume that this longer time corresponded to relatively more just supraliminal and relatively fewer 'over-learned' associations. **1929** R. S. WOODWORTH *Psychol.* (1930) iii. 94 Material that has been 'over-learned', i.e., studied beyond the point where it can barely be recited without error, is forgotten more slowly. **1939** —— *Experimental Psychol.* ii. 30 Nagel went further; he pushed the original learning to the point of great overlearning. **1948** E. R. HILGARD *Theories of Learning* xii. 339 The most evident effect of overlearning is this one upon recall. It provides the explanation for the long retention of overlearned skills like swimming or bicycle riding. **1953** H. SCHUELL *Aphasia Theory* (1974) x. 203 Using some of the highly over-learned automaticisms of speech often produces this result quickly. **1963** W. B. KOLESNIK *Educ. Psychol.* x. 248 She wants him to overlearn the material. **1972** J. L. DILLARD *Black English* vii. 269 The technique consists of intensive practice to the point of overlearning.

overleather ('əʊvə,lɛðə(r)). [f. OVER *a.* + LEATHER. So Ger. *oberleder*, Du. *overleêr*.] The upper leather of a shoe.

1408 *Nottingham Rec.* II. 54 Viginti paria de ovurlethres. *c* **1440** *Promp. Parv.* 373/1 Ovyr lethyr of a schoo (ouer-ledyr *H.*). **1569** *Wills & Inv. N.C.* (Surtees 1835) 307, ij dakers of soles x[s].—vij dakers of ou'lethers, xvj[s]. x[s]. **1596** SHAKS. *Tam. Shr.* Induct. ii. 12 Such shooes as my toes looke through the ouer-leather. **1603–4** *Act 1 Jas. I*, c. 22. §23 Without mixinge or minglinge Overleathers, that is to say, parte of the Overleathers beinge of Neates Leather, & parte of Calves Leather. **1641** J. TRAPPE *Theol. Theol.* 164 To stretch..their greasie overleathers with their teeth.

†over'leave, *v. Obs.* In 4 -leeue, *pa. t.* -lafte. [ONorthumb. *oferlǣfa* = OE. **oferlǣfan*, f. *ofer-* OVER- 19 + LEAVE *v.*[1] 12.] **a.** *trans.* To leave over. **b.** *intr.* To be left over, remain.

c **950** *Lindisf. Gosp.* Luke xi. 41 þætte ofer-hlæfeð *vel* þætte wona is seallað ælmissa. *c* **975** *Rushw. Gosp.* Luke ix. 17 ȝinimen wæs ðætte ofer-læfed wæs him. **1382** WYCLIF *Exod.* viii. 31 There overlafte not oon forsothe. —— *Lev.* xxv. 46 Thurȝ riȝt of erytage ȝe shulen ouerleeuen hem to the after comers.

over-leaven (-'lɛv(ə)n), *v.* [OVER- 27.] *trans.* To leaven too much; to imbue to excess with some modifying element; to cause to rise or swell too much, to 'puff up'.

1602 SHAKS. *Ham.* I. iv. 29 Some habit, that too much o'er-leavens The form of plausive manners. *a* **1644** CHILLINGW. *Serm.* (1664) vii. §48, I beseech you..to free yourselves from the burden and weight of other men's riches, lest they over-leaven and swell you so unmeasurably. **1648** HERRICK *Hesper., To Bk.* (1869) 3 Come thou not neere those men, who are like bread O're-leven'd.

So **†'over-'leaven** *a.*, having an excess of leaven. *Obs. nonce-wd.*

1648 HERRICK *Hesper., To M. Jo. Wicks* (1869) 344 Yet sho'd I chance, my Wicks, to see An over-leven look in thee, To soure the bread, and turn the beer To an exalted vineger.

overleer, -leg, -legislation, etc.: see OVER-.

†over'lend, *v. Obs.* [f. OVER- 12 + LEND *v.*[1]] *trans.* To pass over or beyond.

a **1400–50** *Alexander* 5069 Qua list þis lymit ouir-lende, lene to þe left hand.

'over-'length, *sb.* (*a.*) [OVER- 29.] Too great length. Also as quasi-*adj.*

1829 BENTHAM *Justice & Cod. Petit.* 89 The time allowed, is it too long? If yes, then by the overlength is created so much needless delay. **1902** *Daily Chron.* 17 May 3/3 Over-length means necessarily a surplus of the inessential. **1959** HALAS & MANVELL *Technique Film Animation* xviii. 170 If a film..becomes overlength through the addition of essential sound, it is usually better to consider cutting out a complete sequence. **1962** A. NISBETT *Technique Sound Studio* vii. 117 A programme..turns out to be seriously overlength. **1977** *Times Lit. Suppl.* 29 Apr. 537/1 *Middlemarch*, an over-length novel even by the generous Victorian reckoning.

†'overlet, *sb. Obs. rare.* [f. OVER *adv.* + LET *v.*[1]: cf. *outlet*.] An overhanging or projecting part.

1656 HEYLIN *Surv. France* 19 The houses [are] without juttings or overlets, four stories high.

over-letter to **over-lewd**: see OVER-.

'over-'liberal, *a.* [OVER- 28.] Too liberal. So **†'over-libe'rality**; **'over-'liberally** *adv.*

[**1513** MORE in Grafton *Chron.* (1568) II. 756 In his later dayes with ouer liberall diet, somewhat corpulent.] **1601** HOLLAND *Pliny* XIX. vi. 44 It hurteth the stomach, over-liberally taken. **1621** SANDERSON *Serm.* I. 203, I..would chuse rather by an over-liberal charity to cover a multitude of sins. **1641** MILTON *Animadv.* xiii. Wks. (1847) 71/2 A man would think you had eaten over-liberally of Esau's red porridge. **1824** MISS MITFORD *Village* Ser. I. (1863) 223 To protect her from the effects of her over-liberality.

over'lick, *v. rare.* [OVER- 9.] *trans.* To lick all over, pass or rub the tongue over.

1567 TURBERV. *Epitaphs* &c., Epil., The worst he wild in couert scrole to lurke Untill the Beare were ouerlickt afresh. **1614** COOK *Greene's Tu Quoque* in Dodsley *O. Pl.* VII. 90 Such food As..children, nay sometimes, full-paunched dogs Have overlick't.

overlie (əʊvə'laɪ), *v.* Pa. t. overlay; pa. pple. overlain. Forms: see OVER and LIE *v.*[1] [Early ME. *oferliggen*:—OE. type **oferlicgan*: see OVER- 8. Cf. MHG. *überligen*, Ger. *überliegen*. In use from 12th to 16th c.; in 17–18th displaced by OVERLAY; reintroduced in 19th c., chiefly in geological use.]

1. *trans.* To lie over or upon; in *Geol.* said of a stratum resting directly upon another. Also *fig.*

c **1175** *Lamb. Hom.* 53 Þeos ilke ehte þe þeos þus ouerliggeð. **1387–8** T. USK *Test. Love* III. vii. (Skeat) I. 39 Wel the hoter is the fire, that with ashen it is ouerlein. **1552** HULOET, Ouerlye, *supercubo*.

1813 BAKEWELL *Introd. Geol.* (1815) 362 Beds..which are part of the regular coal formation, and overlie coal. **1851** WHITTIER *To Old Schoolm.* 95 Shapes the dust has long o'erlain. **1885** J. BALL in *Jrnl. Linn. Soc.* XXII. 27 Where the Palæozoic rocks do not appear to be overlain by recent marine deposits.

2. *spec.* **a.** To smother by lying upon. (Cf. OVERLAY *v.* 5 a.)

13.. *Propr. Sanct.* (Vernon MS.) in Herrig's *Archiv* LXXXI. 301/200 þis is aȝeyn þeos wymmen þat ouerliggen heor children. **1382** WYCLIF *1 Kings* iii. 19 The sone of this womman is deed to nyȝt, for slepynge she ouerlaye hym. *a* **1450** MYRC 1769 þe modur þat þe chylde ouer lyth. **1530** PALSGR. 648/1, I overlye, as an oversene noryce dothe her chylde. [**1557–1741** cf. OVERLAY.] **1800** SOUTHEY *Lett.* (1856) I. 126 The mothers and the nurses who over-lie the children. **1856** MRS. BROWNING *Aur. Leigh* IV. 63 The old idiot wretch Screamed feebly, like a baby overlain.

†b. To lie with, have sexual intercourse with (a woman). *Obs.* (Cf. OVERLAY 5 b.)

1422 tr. *Secreta Secret., Priv. Priv.* 160 Oone of ham that was callid absolon..ouer-lay his fadyr Concubynes. **1480** CAXTON *Chron. Eng.* IV. (1520) 35/2 Whan he sawe them so fayre he and his company wolde have overlayne them.

†3. *fig.* To oppress. *Obs.* (Cf. OVERLAY *v.* 7.)

1390 GOWER *Conf.* III. 224 The comun poeple is overlein And hath the kinges senne aboght. **1430–40** LYDG. *Bochas* VIII. xviii. (1558) 12 b, By the romayns he was so ouerlaine.

1530 PALSGR. 648/2, I overlye, as a tyranne or myghty man overlayeth his subjectes.

overlier ('əʊvə'laɪə(r) (stress var.)). [Agent.-n. from OVERLIE *v.*, or *lie over*: see LIE *v.*[1] and -ER[1].]

† **1.** One who lies upon or encumbers; applied to beggars who exacted lodging at farmhouses.

1449 *Sc. Acts Jas. II*, c. 9 (1814) II. 36/1 For þe away putting of sornaris ouerlyaris & masterful beggaris.

2. That which lies over or upon something else. **b.** *spec.* A horizontal timber in a scaffolding; = LEDGER *sb.* 2, LIGGER *sb.* 2. (Cf. OVERLIGGER.)

1614 *MSS. at Stratford-on-Avon* (N.), Item, x. peces of woode callyd overleers, xx.*d.* **1620** MARKHAM *Farew. Husb.* (1625) 91 Then shall you take strong ouerlyers of Wood, and lay them foure-square from one board to another. **1868** G. STEPHENS *Runic Mon.* I. 255, 3 flat stones, the two standing as sides while the third was an overlier.

over'lift, *v.* [Cf. OVER- 23, 26.] **a.** *intr.* To lift a weight too heavy for one's strength. **b.** *trans.* To lift too high, raise beyond the proper point. Hence **'overlift** *sb.*, an act of overlifting; a device whereby the bolt is secured, on one of the tumblers of a lock being overlifted.

1745 *De Foe's Eng. Tradesman* vi. (1841) I. 36 Over-trading is among tradesmen as overlifting is among strong men. **1850** CHUBB *Locks & Keys* 27 If the tumbler was lifted any higher, it caught the bolt anew, and (by what was called 'overlift') detained it as securely, as if the tumbler had not been lifted high enough... If the step was too long, the tumbler would be overlifted, and thereby detain the bolt.

† **over'ligger.** *Obs.* [See LIGGER *sb.*] = OVERLIER 2 b.

1511 *Nottingham Rec.* III. 330, iiij. ouerlyggers for a scaffold. **1616** *Ibid.* IV. 348 For ouer liggers and trasinges for y[e] same bridge.

'over-'light, *sb. rare.* [f. OVER- 29 d + LIGHT *sb.*] Too much light, excess of light; also *fig.* So **'over-'lighted** *pa. pple.*; **'over-'lightsome** *a.* [LIGHTSOME *a.*[2]].

a **1586** SIDNEY *Arcadia* III. (1633) 239 Her chamber was over-lightsome. **1626** BACON *Sylva* § 871 We see that an Over-light maketh the Eyes dazzle. **1847** MEDWIN *Shelley* II. 302 Had full time been allowed for the over-light of his imagination to be tempered by the judgment. **1874** MICKLETHWAITE *Mod. Par. Churches* 184 Most churches are now either over-lighted or under-lighted.

'over-'light, *a.* [f. OVER- 28 + LIGHT *a.*[1]] Too light (in various senses); of too little weight; too frivolous; too easy, etc.; see LIGHT *a.*[1]

[*c* **1400** *Rule St. Benet* (E.E.T.S.) 1064 Not to lagh with ouer lyght chere.] **1538** STARKEY *England* I. iv. 122 Our law ys some what ouer-lyght agayn the accusarys. **1583** PEELE *Commend. Verses* in *T. Watson's Centurie of Loue*, If grauer headdes shall count it ouerlight, To treate of Loue. *a* **1656** USSHER *Ann.* vi. (1658) 331 Giving over-light credit to this report. **1707** *Curios. in Husb. & Gard.* 126 Such Soils are over-light, and very apt to be..parch'd up. **1908** *Daily Chron.* 21 Apr. 4/4 Now and then he was a trifle..over-light in his treatment of opponents.

So **'over-'lightly** *adv.* (in early use chiefly in sense 'too easily').

[**1340** HAMPOLE *Pr. Consc.* 3482 When þou ert over lyghtly wrathe, Or sweres and may noght hald þin athe.] **1422** tr. *Secreta Secret., Priv. Priv.* 222 The x[e]. is ouerlyghtely mevynge of coloure and semblante. **1586** T. B. *La Primaud. Fr. Acad.* I. 434 They overlightly give credit to backbiters. **1843** H. ROGERS *Ess.* (1860) III. 82 To charge us with treating grave subjects over-lightly.

overline (-'laɪn), *v.*[1] [f. OVER- 1 + LINE *sb.*[2], *v.*[2]] *trans.* To draw a line over or above (a piece of writing: opp. to *underline*); also, to insert an interlinear translation or the like above. Hence **over'lined** *ppl. a.*, having a line above it (usu. said of a printed character or number).

1853 ROCK *Ch. of Fathers* III. II. 14 Latin hymns over-lined with an Ango-Saxon translation. **1879** *Proc. Lond. Math. Soc.* X. 21 The terms under-lined and over-lined may both be omitted. **1891** DRIVER *Introd. Lit. O.T.* 75 The reader who will be at the pains to under-line (or, if he uses the Hebrew, to *overline*)..the passages. **1900** *Athenæum* 21 July 84/2 The latest (redactional) changes in the respective documents..are marked by overlining. **1963** *Amer. Jrnl. Physics* XXXI. 339/1 The overlined quantities are suitably taken average values of the specific heats indicated. **1967** A. BATTERSBY *Network Analysis* (ed. 2) xii. 200 An overlined duration, e.g. 12, means that the present method calls for one man, but two men could be put on the job and would do it in half the time.

over'line, *v.*[2] *nonce-wd.* [f. OVER- 8 + LINE *v.*[1]] *trans.* To 'line' on the outside; to cover with a second layer of material.

1853 KANE *Grinnell Exp.* xl. (1856) 365 Rough Guernsey frock, overlined by a red flannel shirt.

† **'overliness.** *Obs.* [f. OVERLY *a.* + -NESS.] The quality of being 'overly'.

1. Superficiality; carelessness.

1653 WATERHOUSE *Apol. Learn.* 221 We lament the Overliness of Preaching..many Ministers imbasing themselves and their Message by trite and impertinent discourses.

2. Contemptuousness, haughtiness.

1610 BP. HALL *Apol. Brownists* ii. 4 Would God ouerlinesse and contempt were not yours. **1633** —— *Hard Texts, N.T.* 37 A proud overlinesse and insolent domineering over your brethren.

'overling. [f. OVER *adv.* + -LING. Cf. *underling.*] One who is over others; a superior.

1340 *Ayenb.* 8 To þam þet habbeþ þe lokingge ous to teche ..ase byeþ þe ouerlinges of holy cherche. ? *a* **1400** *Morte Arth.* 289 Thow aughte to be overlynge over alle oþer kynges. **1917** [see IDLE *a.* 8 a]. **1976** *New Yorker* 22 Nov. 109/2 In Pinter's world, servants and other underlings are always filled with menace; the ominous likelihood is that they will prove to be overlings.

over-linger, -link, etc.: see OVER-.

'over-'lip. Now *dial.* [Orig. two words; in ME. *overe lippe*:—**ufera lippa* (cf. *niðera lippa*), mod. dial. *uvver lip*, but from 1400 often conjoined, or in later use hyphened. Cf. Ger. *oberlippe.*] The upper lip.

c **1325** *Gloss W. de Bibbesw.* in Wright *Voc.* 146 *La bas levere et la levere suseyne*, the overe lippe ant the nethere. *c* **1386** CHAUCER *Prol.* 133 Hire ouer [*Camb.* ouere] lippe [*Harl.* overlippe] wyped she so clene. **1480** CAXTON *Descr. Brit.* 37 Noble fruyt hangyng downe to the ouer lyppe. **1788** W. MARSHALL *E. Yorksh.* II. Gloss. (E.D.S.), *Uvver*, upper; as 'the uvver lip'. **1881** MISS JACKSON *Shropsh. Word-bk.* s.v., 'Er uvver-lip's swelled as big as two.

overlip (əʊvə'lɪp), *v. literary.* [OVER- 1.] *trans.* To overflow the lip or brim of.

1868 G. M. HOPKINS *Jrnls. & Papers* (1959) 181 The Jumeaux and..the Breithorn, both over-lipped with heavy cowls of snow. **1872** S. BUTLER *Erewhon* v. 38 The clouds rolled up to the very summit of the pass, though they did not overlip it.

over'lipping, *ppl. a. Sc.* [f. OVER- 5 + *lipping*, from LIP *v.*[1]] 'Lipping' or brimming over (see LIP *v.*[1] 3 a), overflowing; superfluous.

1836 R. M. M[c]CHEYNE in *Mem.* (1872) 295 The overlipping drops of love. **1871** J. BALLANTINE *Winter Promptings*, Gie your puir neighbours your owrelipping share.

overlisten (-'lɪs(ə)n), *v.* [f. OVER- 15 + LISTEN, after OVERHEAR q.v.] *trans.* To listen so as to overhear; to listen to (a speaker, or what is spoken) without the speaker's knowledge or consent.

1609 ROWLEY *Search for Money* (Percy Soc.) 9 As wee were but asking the question, steps mee from over the way (overlistning us) a news-searcher. **1832** J. WILSON in *Blackw. Mag.* 192 Like an eavesdropper, overlistening our soliloquy.

'over-'little, *a.* and *adv. Obs.* exc. *dial.* [OVER- 28, 30.] Too little.

[*c* **1330** R. BRUNNE *Chron.* (1810) 36 It was ouer litelle, in alle maner way. **1340** HAMPOLE *Pr. Consc.* 1459 Now haf we or litel, now pas we mesur.] *c* **1440** *Promp. Parv.* 373/1 Ovyrlytyl(l)e, *minus, vel nimis modicum.* *a* **1568** ASCHAM *Scholem.* II. (Arb.) 116 If they giue ouer moch to their witte, and ouer litle to their labor and learning.

overlive (əʊvə'lɪv), *v.* [OE. *oferlibban*, f. *ofer-* OVER- 18 + LIVE *v.*; cf. MHG. *überleben*, MDu., Du. *overleven.*]

Now somewhat *rare*: cf. OUTLIVE.

a. *trans.* To live longer than, or after the death of (a person); to live after or beyond (an event, etc.); to survive, outlive; also *fig.* of things. Also, to live beyond (one's income).

830 in Thorpe *Charters* (1865) 465 Wes hit [ðet lond] becueden Osbearte his broðar suna, ȝif he Cyneðryðe oferlifde. *c* **1330** R. BRUNNE *Chron.* (1810) 254 If Blanche ouer lyue Edward, scho salle haf hir lyue Gascoyn afterward. *c* **1450** *Mirour Saluacioun* 3785 Howe lange marie ouer lyved hire sons Ascensionne. **1513** DOUGLAS *Æneis* XI. iv. 49, I, allace, allace! Ourlevit hes my fatis profitable. **1551** BIBLE *Josh.* xxiv. 31 And Israel served the Lorde all the dayes of Iosua, and all the daies of ye elders that ouerliued Ioshua. **1650** R. HOLLINGWORTH *Exerc. Usurped Powers* 19 These oathes binde..to an allegiance over-living his Majesties person. **1749** J. CLELAND *Mem. Woman Pleasure* I. 124 He was the only son of a father, who..rather over-liv'd his income. **1818** CRUISE *Digest* (ed. 2) VI. 297 If his three daughters..should overlive their mother. **1842** TENNYSON *Poems* II. 102 Perish in thy self-contempt! Overlive it—..be happy! wherefore should I care? *a* **1877** SWINBURNE *Lesbia Brandon* (1952) iii. 36 His clear, wary, untameable eyes which had seen many dangers through, had overlived and overcome much trouble. **1881** S. EVANS *Evans's Leicestershire Words* (new ed.) 207 *Overlive*,..to out-live; survive.

b. *intr.* To survive, continue in life.

c **1000** ÆLFRIC *Gram.* ix. §26. (Z.) 51 *Superstes*, laf ōððe oferlybbende. **1422** in *E.E. Wills* (1882) 50, I will þat þe mony..turn to þ[e] use of her susters ouerlyuyng. **1450** *Rolls of Parlt.* V. 208/1 Such of theyme as shal over lyf severally emongs theyme. **1524** *Sir R. Sutton's Will* in Churton *Life* App. 543, I will that these iii that overlyve make a new feoffment. **1667** MILTON *P.L.* x. 773 Why do I overlive, Why am I mockt with death, and length'nd out To deathless pain? **1897** *Saga-Bk. of Viking Club* Jan. 371 These divisions have overlived to the present time.

c. *refl.* To live beyond one's proper date or time of action, live too long. Also, to live too intensely, or too actively. [Cf. OVER- 23.]

1861 M. PATTISON *Ess.* (1889) I. 42 The Hanse had overlived itself. **1921** GALSWORTHY *To Let* II. ii. 126 He had only just relapsed, from having overworked, or overlived, himself again.

Hence **'over'living** (stress var.) *ppl. a.*, surviving; living too long; also as *vbl. sb.* **'over'lived** *ppl. a.*, *nonce-wd.*, made to live too fast or under too high pressure. † **over'liver** *Obs.*, a survivor.

c **1440** *Promp. Parv.* 373/1 Ovyrlevare after a noþer, *superstes.* **1568** GRAFTON *Chron.* II. 375 And if any of them happened to die, the over lyvers should doe the same. **1578** T. PROCTER *Gorg. Gallery* in *Heliconia* I. 172 A sure beleefe did straight invade his overlyving Minde. **1622** BACON *Hen. VII* 191 To continue for both the kings liues, and the ouer-liuer of them, and a yeare after. *a* **1683** OLDHAM *Poet. Wks.* (1686) 101 All the Bill of Maladies, Which Heaven to punish over-living Mortals sends. **1817** SCOTT *Let.* 11 Aug. (1933) IV. 496 The task of maintaining a poor renderd effeminate and vicious by over wages and over-living and necessarily cast loose upon society. **1856** MRS. BROWNING *Aur. Leigh* III. 40 Overtasked and overstrained And overlived in this close London life!

over-lively, etc.: see OVER-.

overload ('əʊvə'ləʊd), *sb.* [OVER- 29.] **a.** An excessive load or burden; too great a load.

1645 RUTHERFORD *Tryal & Tri. Faith* xx. (1845) 270 Can the father see the child sweat, wrestle under an over-load till his back be near broken? **1772** *Phil. Trans.* LXII. 491 Phlogiston, an overload of it may infect air. **1856** MRS. BROWNING *Aur. Leigh* VII. 20 A beaten ass Who, having fallen through overloads [etc.]. **1937** J. ORR tr. *Iordan's Introd. Romance Linguistics* iii. 166 Semantic hypertrophy, or semantic overload, as it has been called. **1938** *Sun* (Baltimore) 11 July 2/6 The cabin behind the cockpit was crowded with..elaborate radio and navigation equipment. The plane weighs 25,000 pounds—an overload of 7,500 pounds. **1969** *Advancement of Sci.* XXVI. 72/1 Much the same applies to officials..who are responsible for the continuity of policy. They frequently live in a state of perpetual overload from which there is no obvious escape. **1974** *Gen. Systems* XIX. 62/2 A confused oldster may easily be maneuvered to sign a contract accepting the machine's uncompensible expensiveness. She thereby converts her overload into culturally-encouraged 'pathways to madness'.

b. *spec.* A current or voltage in excess of that which is normal or allowed for. Freq. *attrib.*, esp. designating devices for protecting against overloads.

a **1904** *N.E.D.*, Overload switch. **1904** *Westm. Gaz.* 1 Dec. 8/1 A representative..was conducted through the mighty power-house... 'This is the biggest thing of its kind running in England. It is designed for 20,000 horse-power; at a pinch it could stand a 50 per cent. overload.' **1908** *Installation News* II. 38 There is always some novel addition to our Conduit System,..in addition to various side issues such as overload cut-outs. **1930** *Engineering* 3 Jan. 32/2 The overload trips are operated through a relay. **1962** A. NISBETT *Technique Sound Studio* 10 Striking a reasonable balance between noise levels, on the one hand, and overload or peak distortion, on the other, may take so much time and effort that the best part of the programme is lost. **1974** *Sci. Amer.* Nov. 34/1 The blackout was traced to the tripping of a circuit breaker in Ontario during a momentary overload. **1975** *Hi-Fi Answers* Feb. 38/1 The disc input has a fixed sensitivity of 2.5mV with an overload margin of 100mV. **1975** G. J. KING *Audio Handbk.* v. 112 A stereo amplifier switched to the mono mode may have an overload value which differs from that in the stereo mode.

overload (ˌəʊvə'ləʊd), *v.* [OVER- 21 (?), 27.]

a. *trans.* To load with too great a burden or cargo, to put an excessive load on, to overburden; to overcharge (a gun). Also *absol.*

1553 T. WILSON *Rhet.* (1580) 79 Thei died in faith, not wearie of this worlde, nor wishyng for death, as ouerloden with sinne. **1612** BRINSLEY *Lud. Lit.* v. (1627) 51 So that the memory be not overloaden. **1669** STURMY *Mariner's Mag.* v. xii. 57 Take care of over-loading your Piece. **1727** SWIFT *Vanbrugh's House* 4 A verse would draw a stone or beam, That now would over-load a team. **1883** P. SCHAFF *Hist. Chr. Ch.* I. I. ix. 65 They overloaded the holy Scriptures with the traditions of the elders. **1962** A. NISBETT *Technique Sound Studio* 254 Frequency modulation... Limiters are not needed to avoid overloading transmitter valves. **1973** *Times* 30 Nov. 6/7 He thought some circuits were overloaded by as much as four kilowatts. **1976** G. A. BROWNE *Slide* (1977) 8 The woman..hoped she wouldn't overload again... Anyway, today she was prepared with eight extra fuses.

b. *intr.* To become overloaded.

1961 *Jrnl. Water Pollution Control Federation* XXXIII. 1280/1 Ice caused the aerator to overload, straining the drive belts. **1977** *Times* 16 July 5/8 The safety devices to stop them [*sc.* power lines] overloading came into action.

Hence **overloaded, -loaden** (stress var.) *ppl. adjs.*; **over'loading** *vbl. sb.* and *ppl. a.*

a **1586** SIDNEY *Arcadia* III. (1622) 372 Made their pillowes weake propps of their overloden heads. **1576** GASCOIGNE *Steel Gl.* (Arb.) 77 Pray you to god, the good be not abusde, With glorious shewe, of ouerloding skill. **1821** LAMB *Elia* Ser. I. *My Relations*, An over-loaded ass is his client for ever. **1889** R. FRY *Let.* 2 Aug. (1972) I. 123 Ashbee..got hold of ..*Atalanta in Calydon*, and read it with such overloading of sentiment as is usual with him. **1896** *Allbutt's Syst. Med.* I. 400 Overloading of the stomach..may cause or aggravate some of these [disorders]. **1907** *Daily Chron.* 3 Oct. 2/2 The rapid increase in the number of companies not being admired by the somewhat overloaded bulls. **1958** *Spectator* 11 July 68/3 It is essential to retain its [*sc.* the Government's] legislative apparatus of control of borrowing. Overloading will never be prevented without it. **1962** A. NISBETT *Technique Sound Studio* iii. 67 There should be no trouble with this except where the output of a close balance on heavy brass is fed through pre-amplifiers of fixed gain; this can result in overloading and consequent distortion. **1962** R. H. SMYTHE *Anat. Dog Breeding* 70 These are the muscles which when well developed cause 'overloading' of the shoulders. *Ibid.* 77 What judges term, 'overloaded shoulders'. **1974** *Times* 9 Jan. 3/3 Surplus, damaged and overloaded goods were sold to people in the trade.

overlock (əʊvəˈlɒk), *v.* [OVER- 1, 24.] *trans.* **a.** To interlock or intertwine above; to cover with intertwined growth. **b.** To turn (the bolt of a lock) beyond the point at which it is locked.

1632 LITHGOW *Trav.* IX. 415, I found the.. Vines ouer locking the trees. **1882** SIR E. BECKETT in *Encycl. Brit.* XIV. 746/2 The way to open it then is to turn the key the other way, as if to overlock the bolt. *Ibid.*, It is set right by overlocking the bolt as before.

c. *trans.* and *intr.* To secure (the edge of cloth) so as to strengthen it and to prevent fraying; also, to oversew (by machine). Usu. as **ˈoverlocking** *vbl. sb.*

1901–2 *T. Eaton & Co. Catal.* Fall & Winter 64/2 Men's fine imported natural wool night robes, made with collar attached,.. overlocked seams, [etc.]. **1909** *Public Ledger* (Philadelphia) 24 June 5/2 Fishnet Lace Curtains, overlocked edge. **1921** *Dict. Occup. Terms* (1927) §376 *Overlocking machinist*,.. stitches round scolloped edge of finished lace curtain with overlocking machine. **1960** *Textile Terms & Definitions* (Textile Inst.) (ed. 4) 106 *Overlocking*, ..effecting the joining of two or more pieces of fabric by means of an double or treble chain stitch... This operation is performed on overseaming machines. **1973** *Guardian* 12 Mar. 9/4 Most of the women work in.. linking, cutting, and overlocking. **1976** *Leicester Trader* 24 Nov. 17/2 (Advt.), Klynton Davis require experienced employees with the following skills: lockstitching, overlocking, welting, [etc.]. **1978** *People's Friend* 13 May 24/2 (Advt.), Every detail is perfect—like the needle overlocking technique that ensures incredible strength at the seams.

overlocker (ˈəʊvəlɒkə(r)). [f. OVERLOCK *v.* c + -ER[1].] (See quot. 1921.)

1921 *Dict. Occup. Terms* (1927) §419 *Overlocker*.., guides cut edges and seams of knitted fabrics under needles of power-driven overlock machine, thereby joining them together.. with an overlock stitch. **1964** *Age* (Melbourne) 15 Aug. 62 (Advt.), Experienced overlockers and plain sewing machine operators and juniors to be trained are required for our making-up rooms. **1975** *Evening Herald* (Dublin) 8 May 12/5 (Advt.), Experienced overlockers, button machine operators and flat machinists. This staff is required for our slacks factory. **1976** *Leicester Mercury* 16 July (Advt.), Leta Knitwear Ltd., outerwear and underwear manufacturers require very urgently overlockers, binders, and designer.

over-lofty, -logical, etc.: see OVER-.

ˈover-ˈlong, *adv.* and *a.* [f. OVER- 30, 28 + LONG *a.*[1], LONG *adv.*] Too long.

A. *adv.* For too long a time.

[*a* **1250** *Owl & Night.* 450 Þe more ich singe, þe more i mai,.. Ac noþeles noht ouer longe.] **1377** LANGL. *P. Pl.* B. xx. 358 He lat hem ligge ouerlonge, and loth is to chaunge hem. **1526** TINDALE *Acts* xxvii. 9 Because.. we had overlonge fasted. **1617** HIERON *Wks.* (1620) II. 230 Not to remayne abroad ouer-long. **1892** STEVENSON & L. OSBOURNE *Wrecker* xi, This characteristic scene, which has delayed me overlong.

B. *adj.* Of too great length or duration, too long.

1377 LANGL. *P. Pl.* B. XI. 216 It is ouerlonge ar logyke any lessoun assoille. **1560** DAUS tr. *Sleidane's Comm.* 23 The decree is ouerlonge, but the summe is this. **1614** RALEIGH *Hist. World* III. (1634) 51 The shortest life doth oftentimes appear unto us over-long. **1887** *Pall Mall G.* 12 Oct. 2/1 The voyage to Lechlade is overlong for a single day.

†over-ˈlong, *prep. Obs.* [f. OVER *prep.* + *long*, aphetic f. ALONG *prep.* Cf. *overthwart*.] Along, over the length of.

1470–85 MALORY *Arthur* X. lx. 515 Sir Tristram behelde the maroners how they sayled ouer longe humber.

overlook (ˈəʊvəlʊk), *sb.* [OVER- 16, 7, 5.]

1. The action or an act of overlooking (see next, 3–6); a glance or survey; inspection or superintendence.

1584 LODGE *Hist. Forbonius & Prisc.* (Shaks. Soc. 1853) 84 Our noble young gentleman, having past over many personages with a slight over looke. **1865** MRS. WHITNEY *Gayworthys* I. 226 This typified properly her social position of overlook and scrutiny.

b. A look down from a height upon the scene below; a place that affords such a view.

1861 L. L. NOBLE *Icebergs* 37 Paths wound among rocky notches and grassy chasms, and led out to dizzy 'over-looks', and 'short-offs'. **1884** *Lit. World* (U.S.) 23 Feb. 51/3 High overlooks upon the smiling valley.

c. Name in Jamaica for the leguminous plant *Canavalia ensiformis*: see quot.

1837 MACFADYEN *Flora of Jamaica* I. 292 They are commonly planted, by the Negroes, along the margin of their provision grounds, from a superstitious notion.. that the Overlook fulfils the part of a watchman, and.. protects the provisions from plunder. **1866** *Treas. Bot.* s.v. *Canavalia.*

2. An act of overlooking (see next, 2); a failure to see or notice something; an oversight.

1887 T. BAYNE in *Athenæum* 9 July 62/3 When his attention is thus called to a manifest overlook. **1897** R. MUNRO *Prehist. Prob.* 264 Simply an overlook on my part.

overlook (əʊvəˈlʊk), *v.* [f. OVER- + LOOK *v.*]

1. *trans.* To look over the top of, so as to see what is beyond. [OVER- 5.]

1559–60 *Cott. Libr. Cal.* B. ix, Use ws as a fote stole to overlooke 30w. **1610** GUILLIM *Heraldry* II. vii. (1660) 85 The walls of townes were but low,.. the walls of Winchester.. were overlooked by Colebrand the Chieftaine of the Danes. **1863** HAWTHORNE *Our Old Home* (1883) I. 215 The wall was just too high to be overlooked.

fig. **1636** RUTHERFORD *Lett.* (1862) I. 160 If great men be kind to you, I pray you overlook them;.. Christ but borroweth their face to smile through them upon His afflicted servant.

b. *fig.* To rise above, overtop.

1567 TURBERV. *Epitaphs* &c., *Time conquereth all Things* 70 b, It makes the Oke to ouerlooke the slender shrubs bylow. **1599** SHAKS. *Hen. V*, III. v. 9 Our Syens.. Spirt vp so suddenly into the Clouds, And ouer-looke their Grafters. **1700** DRYDEN *Iliad* I. 827 The laughing Nectar overlook'd the Lid. **1748** SMOLLETT *Rod. Rand.* iii. (1804) 10 A.. hat, whose crown over-looked the brims about an inch and a half.

2. To look over and beyond and thus not see; to fail to see or observe; to pass over without notice (intentionally or unintentionally); to take no notice of, leave out of consideration, disregard, ignore. (The chief current sense.) [OVER- 5.]

1524 Q. MARGARET *to Hen. VIII* (MS. Cott. Calig. B. I, lf. 216 b) (cf. Mrs. Wood *Lett. Illust. Ladies* I. 326) Wylke wol be grett danger to ye Kyng my sonis parson, and thys tyme be owr lokyd. **1570** *Satir. Poems Reform.* xvi. 9 Our Lordis ar blinde and dois ouerluik it. **1692** BENTLEY *Boyle Lect.* v. 147 He overlooks those gross Absurdities that are so conspicuous in it. **1762** HUME *Hist. Eng.* I. iii. 98 The French.. found it prudent to overlook this insult. **1829** K. DIGBY *Broadst. Hon., Godefridus* I. 240 Agesilaus punished great men for the same faults which he overlooked in their inferiors. **1872** SPURGEON *Treas. Dav.* Ps. lxvi. 7 He oversees all and overlooks none.

†b. *refl.* ? To fail to perceive one's duty; to forget oneself; = OVERSEE *v.* 7. *Obs.*

1723–4 DK. WHARTON *True Briton* No. 65 II. 550 Vex'd that I.. should have overlooked myself so far as to have given any Room [etc.].

3. To look (a thing) over or through; to examine, scrutinize, inspect, 'survey'; to peruse, read through. Now *rare* or *arch.* [OVER- 16.]

c **1369** CHAUCER *Dethe Blaunche* 232 Whan I had redde thys tale wel And ouer loked hyt euerydel. **1546** *Supplic. Poore Commons* (E.E.T.S.) 69 Youre Highnes.. appoynted two of them to ouer loke the translation of the Bible. **1591** SHAKS. *Two Gent.* I. ii. 50 And yet I would I had ore-look'd the Letter. **1674** JEAKE *Arith.* (1696) 249, I have.. transited Decimals.. and shall now.. overlook Logarithmes. **1744–91** WESLEY *Wks.* (1872) VIII. 319 To over-look the accounts of all the Stewards. **1870** BRYANT *Iliad* I. IV. 115 Carefully O'erlooked the wound and cleansed it from the blood.

4. To look down upon; to survey from above, or from a higher position. [OVER- 7.]

a **1425** *Cursor M.* 8211 (Trin.) God þat al haþ to kepe And al ouerlokeþ in his si3t. **1530** PALSGR. 648/1, I overlooke, *je regarde par dessus.* **1667** DRYDEN *Wild Gallant* III. i, Have you no more manners than to overlook a man when he's a writing? **1741–3** WESLEY *Extract of Jrnl.* (1749) 60 At dinner their little table, and chairs were set.. where they could be overlooked. **1852** IDA PFEIFFER *Journ. Iceland* 32, I went on deck and overlooked the boundless waters.

fig. **1631** MAY tr. *Barclay's Mirr. Mindes* I. 284 From hence, hee.. began with a scornefull pride to ouerlooke the wealth of Europe.

b. Of a place: To afford or command a view of.

1632 LITHGOW *Trav.* x. 494 Goatfield Hill.. ouer-looketh our Westerne Continent. **1634** BRERETON *Trav.* (Chetham) 44 To build a chamber, which may command and overlook the river. **1756** C. LUCAS *Ess. Waters* III. 259 The pump room windows overlook the King's Bath. **1895** *Scot. Antiq.* X. 80 The brow of the hill overlooking the Nairn valley.

†5. *fig.* To 'look down upon' as from a higher social or intellectual position; to despise; to treat with contempt, to slight. *Obs.*

1399 LANGL. *Rich. Redeles* II. 35 Thus leuerez ouere-loked 3oure liegis.. busshid with her brestis, and bare adoune the pouere. *c* **1412** HOCCLEVE *De Reg. Princ.* 429 Þogh he iette forth a-mong þe prees, And ouer loke euerey pore wight. **1534** MORE *Comf. agst. Trib.* II. Wks. 1200/1 An whole floud of all vnhappy mischief, arrogant maner.. ouerlooking the poore in woorde and countenance. **1646** H. LAWRENCE *Comm. Angells* 170 To be supercilious, to overlooke men, and little things. **1794** G. ADAMS *Nat. & Exp. Phil.* II. xxi. 420 The success of the present age.. is very apt to elate the minds of men, and make them overlook the ancients.

6. To watch over officially, keep an eye on, look after, superintend, oversee. [OVER- 7.]

1532 HERVET *Xenophon's Househ.* (1768) 20 They that occupy housebandrye.. with ouer lokynge and takynge hede to other mens warkes. **1605** *Play Stucley* in Simpson *Sch. Shaks.* I. 260 And lest they loiter we ourself in person Will overlook them. **1650** EARL MONM. tr. *Senault's Man bec. Guilty* 340 He was overlooking his harvest men.. judging their labour by their sheaves. **1798** WASHINGTON *Writ.* (1893) XIV. 85 For overlooking this farm I would stretch the wages to £45. *c* **1830** MRS. CAMERON *Village Nurse* 2 Mary Read had little else to do than overlook the other servants.

7. To look upon with the 'evil eye'; to bewitch. (The most common word for this in popular use.)

1596 SHAKS. *Merch. V.* III. ii. 15 Beshrow your eyes, They haue ore-lookt me and deuided me. **1598** —— *Merry W.* v. v. 87 Vilde worme, thou wast ore-look'd euen in thy birth. **1697** DAMPIER in *Phil. Trans.* XX. 51 They.. told them, they were Over-look'd by some unlucky Person. **1825** *Sporting Mag.* XVI. 342 'I wish', said the man, 'we may not be overlooked'. **1887** JESSOPP *Arcady* ii. 59 [The] firm belief in being 'overlooked' is very much more common.. than is generally supposed. **1895** ELWORTHY *Evil Eye* i. 11 In England, of all animals the pig is oftenest 'overlooked'.

8. To look or appear more than. *nonce-use.*

1822 BYRON *Let. to J. Murray* 23 Sept., My mind misgives me that it [the bust] is hideously like. If it is, I can not be long for this world, for it overlooks seventy.

Hence **overlooked** (-ˈlʊkt) *ppl. a.* (usually in sense 2); **overˈlooking** *vbl. sb.* and *ppl. a.* (in various senses of the vb.).

1483 *Cath. Angl.* 264/1 An Over lokynge, *horoscopium*, *.i. horarum speculacio.* **1601** SHAKS. *All's Well* I. i. 45 His sole childe my Lord, and bequeathed to my ouer looking. **1674** BOYLE *Excell. Theol.* I. i. 45 Unheeded prophecies, overlooked mysteries, and strange harmonies. **1676** WYCHERLEY *Pl. Dealer* I. i, I wou'd justle a proud, strutting, over-looking Coxcomb, at the head of his Sycophants. **1711** ADDISON *Spect.* No. 169 ¶10 This Part of Good-nature.. which consists in the pardoning and overlooking of Faults. **1856** KANE *Arct. Expl.* II. i. 14, I found an overlooked godsend this morning. **1898** MOULE *Coloss. Stud.* ii. 22 Habituated to the scenery of its.. rushing river and.. overlooking hills.

overlooker (əʊvəˈlʊkə(r)). [f. OVERLOOK *v.* + -ER[1].] One who overlooks.

1. One who surveys, watches, or inspects from a position of vantage; an observer; a spy.

1483 *Cath. Angl.* 264/1 An Over loker, *horuspax*, .. *horoscopus.* **1523** LD. BERNERS *Froiss.* I. ccccciii. 700 Phylip Dartwell, the regarde and ouerloker of Flaunders. **1598** in *Harington's Nugæ Ant.* (ed. Park 1804) I. 242, I know there are overlookers set on you all, so God direct your discretion. **1651** FULLER *Abel Rediv.* (1867) I. 361 He was a careful overlooker and strict observer. **1862** MRS. H. WOOD *Mrs. Hallib.* III. i. (1888) 304 A shaded walk,.. very little fear there of overlookers.

2. One whose business it is to overlook or superintend; a superintendent, overseer.

1387–8 T. USK *Test. Love* I. iii. (Skeat) l. 128 Soche people should haue no maistrie, ne been ourlookers, ouer none of thy seruauntes. **1494** FABYAN *Chron.* VII. 586 The duke of Glouceter, Sir Humfrey, was that daye ouerloker, and stode before the quene bare hedyd. **1576** R. CURTEYS *Two Serm.* E vj, The holy Ghost hath made you *Episcopos*, ouerseers, ouerlookers, and watchmen ouer the flock of Christe. **1798** WASHINGTON *Writ.* (1893) XIV. 86 The present Overlooker of my Carpenters. **1868** ROGERS *Pol. Econ.* ii. (1876) 14 An unnecessary number of overlookers or foremen. **1963** *Times* 25 May 9/7 'But t'brig isn't t'world', a sewing-shop overlooker says over his gill of mild. **1973** *Guardian* 12 Mar. 9/1 She has worked as an overlooker at Mansfield Hosiery for five years. **1974** *Times* 5 Dec. 5/2 A mill in the Preston area [where].. the first Asian overlooker was recently promoted. **1976** T. JEAL *Until Colours Fade* ix. 111 A group of all but naked men, working under an overlooker, raking out white-hot coke.

overloop, -lop, -lope, -loppe, obs. ff. ORLOP *sb.*[1]

over-loose, etc.: see OVER-.

†overlop, *sb. Obs. rare.* [f. OVER- 5 b + LOPE *sb.*[1] (if not a scribal error for *overlep*, OVERLEAP *sb.*).] An act of overleaping, an omission.

c **1325** *Metr. Hom.* 32 And als I red, far gan I drede, For ouerlop moht I mac nan [*Vernon text* Ouer lepe mihti make non].

overˈlop, *v. rare.* [f. OVER- 8 + LOP *v.*[2]] *trans.* To lop or hang loosely over.

1893 R. KIPLING *Many Invent.* 130 His cap overlopped one eye.

overlop, early variant of OVERLAP *v.*

overlord (ˈəʊvəˌlɔːd), *sb.* [OVER- 2 b.] **1. a.** A lord superior; one who is the lord of other lords or rulers; a lord paramount, supreme lord.

c **1200** ORMIN 6903 Biforr þe Romanisshe king þatt wass hiss oferrlaferrd. **13..** *Coer de L.* 4592 Kyng Rychard was her ovyr-lord. *c* **1470** HENRY *Wallace* I. 67 Byschope Robert .. said that 'we deny Ony our lord, bot the gret God abuff'. **1547** *Reg. Privy Council Scot.* I. 78 Siclik of all uthair ourlordis.. baith of vassallis and subvassallis. **1609** SKENE *Reg. Maj.* 17 The ane sall be over-lord, and the other sall be vasall. **1647** DIGGES *Unlawf. Taking Arms* 82 As holding of an over Lord, or Lord paramount, who is the King. **1814** SCOTT *Wav.* liii, The command of his king and overlord. **1844** LD. BROUGHAM *Brit. Const.* xi. (1862) 146 The King, the universal overlord of the realm.

b. *transf.* A person (occas. an animal) in a position of superiority, authority, or power; *spec.* in British politics, a member of the House of Lords given charge of one or more government ministries; hence in the politics of other countries, and in industry.

1932 S. ZUCKERMAN *Social Life Monkeys* xiv. 228 Baboons are not promiscuous. Very few observations have been made of females having sexual relations with males other than their overlords. **1939** JOYCE *Finnegan's Wake* I. 97 To ongoad and unhume the great shipping mogul and underlinen overlord. **1951** *Economist* 8 Dec. 1394/2 Departmental ministers subject to an overlord would, under arrangements of this kind, rarely have direct access to the cabinet. **1953** *Ann. Reg. 1952* 36 The Opposition had long been critical of Mr. Churchill's 'overlords'—super-departmental Ministers screened from cross-examination by their membership of 'another place'. **1954** *Economist* 31 July 355/1 General Perón.. did reduce the nominal number of ministries..; but this was accompanied by the appointment of four.. 'overlords'.. concerned with defence, economic, technical, and political affairs. **1957** *Observer* 13 Oct. 1/4 Instead of appointing a missile overlord, as is being urged, the President has referred the whole problem.. to yet another committee. **1969** *Daily Tel.* 20 Nov. 3/1 Lord Beeching.. is being tipped for the job of 'overlord' to run BOAC and BEA. **1970** *Guardian* 11 May 10/1 The old problem of the Overlord Minister which re-emerged from the Churchillian past after Mr Wilson's last big reshuffle. **1970** *Daily Tel.* 11 Sept. 6/5 Under the reorganisation Vauxhall will become part of a European division of General Motors... Mr L. Ralph Mason.. will become the European 'overlord'. **1977** *Time* 21 Feb. 24/2 In Mexico the destruction of planted fields and the arrests of several overlords,.. have led to fierce internecine battles for control of the business.

2. (With capital initial.) The code-name for the allied invasion of German-occupied Normandy in June 1944.

1943 J. REITH *Diary* 18 Sept. (1975) vi. 310 Meeting.. about a ridiculous Churchill demand for a twenty-five per cent increase in Overlord (invasion of Europe) force. **1947** J. R. DEANE *Strange Alliance* I. ii. 22, I emphasized our commitments to Overlord, the Mediterranean, the Pacific. **1948** C. FALLS *Second World War* xxiv. 219 The title given to the plan for the invasion of the European Continent from the west, Operation Overlord, possessed a special significance. It was the over-riding operation. **1950** W. S. CHURCHILL *Second World War* III. II. xxxiv. 585 It was my earnest desire that the crossing of the Channel and the liberation of France (the operation then called 'Round-up', which was subsequently changed to 'Overlord') should take place in the summer of 1943. **1961** E. WAUGH *Unconditional Surrender* III. ii. 239 'Overlord', that one huge hazardous offensive operation on which, it seemed, the fate of the world depended. **1974** G. MARKSTEIN *Cooler* lxvi. 230 We've been working very hard to sell them the idea that the Pas de Calais is the objective of Overlord.

overlord (əʊvəˈlɔːd), *v.* [OVER- 2.] *trans.* To lord it over, domineer over; to rule as an overlord or superior authority. Hence **over-ˈlorded, overˈlording** *ppl. adjs.*

c **1629** LAYTON *Syons Plea* (ed. 2) 8 Overlording Prelacy, sitting in the Temple of God is Popish Prelacy. **1644** MAXWELL *Prerog. Chr. Kings* 144 When Zedekiah was overlorded by his Nobles, he could neither save himselfe nor his people. **1881** A. ROBERTS *Comp. Rev. V.N.T.* II. iv. 74 His will overlorded.. by an alien might. **1910** GALSWORTHY *Sheaf* (1916) 132 Our dim consciousness of this serene and overlording principle of Equity. **1959** *Catholic Herald* 27 Nov. 5/3 The Ukrainians of Kiev.. resisted the attempts of the Moscow Orthodox Patriarchate to overlord them. **1961** B. VAWTER *Conscience of Israel* vi. 139 A fact that can help account for its economic expansion in a world overlorded by the Great King. **1966** *Economist* 24 Sept. 1234/3 They were feeling too overlorded. **1970** *Daily Tel.* 11 May 16/5 The appointment of a single executive to overlord the Dutch and British ends of the business would represent a major switch. *Ibid.* 16 Oct. 19/5 (*heading*) David Barran to 'overlord' Shell.

ˈoverˌlordship, *sb.* [f. OVERLORD *sb.* + -SHIP.] The position or authority of an overlord.

1867 FREEMAN *Norm. Conq.* I. ii. 60 Eadward's.. overlordship extended over the whole island. **1877** BROCKETT *Cross & Cr.* 318 After the brief over-lordship of Stephan Dushan. **1892** *Daily News* 15 Mar. 5/1 The overlord puts [into the mine].. nothing but his overlordship, his right of fixing the price of his permission to bring every ton of coal to the surface.

†**overˈlordship,** *v. Obs.* [f. OVER- 2 + LORDSHIP *v.*] *trans.* To exercise dominion over.

? *a* **1412** LYDG. *Two Merchants* 340 As yif a man haue deep impressioun, That ovirlordshipith his imagynatif.

ˈover-ˈloud, *a.* and *adv.* [OVER- 28.] Too loud; †exceedingly loud. So **ˈover-ˈloudly** *adv.*

a **1000** *Gloss.* in Wr.-Wülcker 205/25 *Clamosa*, oferhlud. **1470–85** MALORY *Arthur* III. xii, She cryed ouer lowde, helpe me knyghte for crystes sake. **1819** SHELLEY *Mask* xvii, Like a bad prayer not over loud, Whispering—'Thou art Law and God!' **1870** MORRIS *Earthly Par.* III. IV. 379 His armour's clinking seemed An overloud and clean unlooked for sound. **1887** G. MEREDITH *Ballads & P.* 81 Then the warriors, each on each Spied, nor overloudly laughed.

ˈoverloup, owerloup. *Sc.* and north *dial.* Also our-, owre-. [f. OVER- 5 b + LOUP *sb.*, leap.]

1. An overleaping, a leap over a barrier or over bounds; hence, encroachment, transgression.

1776 LD. HAILES *Annals* I. 319 In Scotland, an occasional trespass of cattle on a neighbouring pasture is still termed *ourlop*. **1819** W. TENNANT *Papistry Storm'd* III. (1827) 100 Though I'm a man o' little drink, I wadna been sae doons perjink, But taen an over-loup for sport. **1824** SCOTT *St. Ronan's* iii, How could she hinder twa daft hempie callants from taking a start and an owerloup? **1894** *Northumbld. Gloss.*, *Owerloup*, an overleap.

2. The change of the moon, i.e. new or full moon; the spring tide occurring at that time.

a **1710** A. WRIGHT in Sibbald *Hist. Fife* II. i. (1710) 39 At the Stream, which is at the Change of the Moon, which is call'd the *Overloup*. **1750** *Phil. Trans.* XLVI. 413 In the Spring Tides which happen upon the Change of the Moon, called by the Commonalty, the Overloup.

ˈover-ˈlove, *sb.* [In OE. *oferlufu*: see OVER- 29 b.] Excessive love, too great love.

a **1023** WULFSTAN *Hom.* xxx. (Napier) 149 Swa læne ys seo oferlufu eorðan ȝestreona. **1806** WORDSWORTH in Chr. Wordsw. *Mem.* (1851) II. 168 Subject to fits of over-love and over-joy. **1895** J. M. MATHER *Lancashire Idylls*, Would her over-love be punished by the child's death?

ˌover-ˈlove, *v.* [OVER- 27.] To love too much, love to excess. (*trans.* and *intr.*)

1583–91 H. SMITH *Wks.* (1592) 988 If we loue, we do ouer-loue, if we feare, we doe ouer feare. *a* **1639** W. WHATELEY *Prototypes* II. xxvi. (1640) 81 This is a weaknesse of Parents.. to over-love some child above the rest. **1685** BAXTER *Paraphr. N.T.* Matt. v. 4 The common fruits of overloving some Creature, and distrusting God. **1892** LADY GREVILLE in *Nat. Rev.* May, Don't worry men, and don't over-love them.

So **ˈover-ˈloving** *vbl. sb.* and *ppl. a.*; **ˈover-ˈlover,** one who loves too much.

1561 T. HOBY tr. *Castiglione's Courtyer* III. (1577) Pjb, See for that shee was ouerlouyng she didde yll to hirselfe, to her husband, and to hir chyldren. *a* **1661** FULLER *Worthies* (1840) III. 485 Indeed some souls are over-lovers of liberty. *a* **1668** DAVENANT *Dying Lover* Wks. (1673) 318 Who kindly at his Mistress feet Does die with over-loving.

ˈover-ˈlow, *a.* and *adv.* [OVER- 28, 30.] Too low. So **ˈover-ˈlowness.**

c **1374** CHAUCER *Boeth.* III. metr. ix. 68 (Camb. MS.) Ne þat the heuynysse we drawen nat a-down ouer lowe the erthes. **1496** *Dives & Paup.* (W. de W.) I. xiv. 46/2 By flaterye and ouerlowenesse of the people.. many worshyppes that longeth sometyme to god allone, ben now used in the worshyppynge of synfull man and woman. **1647** WARD *Simp. Cobler* 52 Deifying you so over-much, that you cannot be quiet in your Spirit, till they have pluckt you down as over-low.

overlume, *v.*: see OVER- 21.

ˈover-ˈluscious, *a.* [Over- 28.] Too luscious.

1626 BACON *Sylva* § 624 Because Honey.. will give them a Taste Overlushious. **1681** GLANVILL *Sadducismus* I. (1726) 28 Warm Imagination and overluscious Self-flattery.

ˈover-ˈlusty, *a.* [OVER- 28.] Too lusty: see LUSTY. So **ˈover-ˈlustiness.**

1583 GOLDING *Calvin on Deut.* iii. 13 That fancie of theirs caryeth them into so fond or rather furious ouerlustinesse. **1587** —— *De Mornay* xii. 184 Sometimes also when we bee ouer-lustie, God suffereth vs to fall into some sinne. **1605** SHAKS. *Lear* II. iv. 10 When a man's ouerlustie at legs, then he weares wodden nether-stocks.

overˈlute, *v. rare.* [f. OVER- 8 + LUTE *v.*[2]] *trans.* To lute over; to smear or coat with some adhesive substance.

1527 ANDREW *Brunswyke's Distyll. Waters* Bjb, It is necessary.. to overlute them more than halfe the parte of the glasse with the fornamed lome or claye.

over-luxuriant, etc.: see OVER- 28.

overly (ˈəʊvəlɪ), *a. Obs.* exc. *dial.* [f. OVER *adv.* + -LY[1]. (Cf. ON. *ofrligr* excessive.)]

†**1.** Supreme. *Obs.*

1340 *Ayenb.* 123 Hope [y-ziȝþ ine gode] ouerlyche heȝnesse and ouerliche mageste. Charite ouerliche guodnesse.

†**2.** Superficial; slight, careless, cursory. *Obs.*

c **1425** *St. Mary of Oignies* Prol. in *Anglia* VIII. 134/32 Þerfore I leeue alle þat proheme, excepte þis shorte ouerly touchynge. **1597–8** BP. HALL *Sat.* III. iii. 2 The courteous citizen bade me to his feast, With hollow words, and overly request. *a* **1668** J. ALLEINE in *Life* (1838) v. 51 Have not I neglected or been very overly in the reading of God's holy word? *a* **1769** RICCALTOUN *Galatians* (1772) 258 On an overly view, it may be thought nearly the same sense which way we take it. **1833** *Chambers's Edin. Jrnl.* 27 Apr. 97/1 Some day, your wife mentions to you, quite in what Mrs Pringle called an overly way, that she happened to meet her old friend Mrs Nicholson on the street that day.

3. Supercilious, imperious, overbearing, haughty. Now only *dial.*

1627 BP. HALL *Heauen vpon Earth* §27 Wks. 97 Our answers are coy and ouerly. **1633** —— *Hard Texts, N.T.* 360 In an overly and imperious manner tyrannizing over the Church. **1707** HUMFREY *Justif. Baxter.* 4 The whole.. is so overly, and appears proud, slighting, and does me wrong. **1820** COLERIDGE in *Lit. Rem.* (1839) IV. 140 The somewhat overly and certainly most ungracious resentments of Baxter. **1895** *Gloss. E. Anglia*, *Overly*, arbitrary, tyrannical.

overly (ˈəʊvəlɪ), *adv.* [f. OVER *adv.* + -LY[2]. OE. had *oferlice* excessively: cf. prec.]

1. Above or beyond the proper amount or degree; overmuch, too much, too, excessively; = OVER *adv.* 11.

Apart from *O.E.*, *Sc.* and *U.S.* until the 20th cent., often regarded as an Americanism in the U.K.

10.. WULFSTAN *Hom.* xiii. (Napier) 83 Nu ða yfelan and ða swicelan swa oferlice swyðe brædað on worulde. **1014** *Ibid.* xxxiii. 166 *note*, Hu hi mid heora synnum swa oferlice swyðe god ȝegræmedon. **1827** J. F. COOPER *Prairie* I. ii. 28 To my eye it seems not to be overly peopled. **1830** GALT *Lawrie T.* II. vii. (1849) 63, I thought he was a little overly particular in his questions. **1833** *Fraser's Mag.* VIII. 286 Elina was not overly pleased. **1854** [see DOGAN]. **1860** BARTLETT *Dict. Amer.* 305 'Is old man Boone rich?' 'Why, not overly so.' Western. **1891** *Harper's Mag.* Aug. 346/2 Mr. H. was not of an overly sensitive organization. **1894** CROCKETT *Lilac Sunbonnet* 50 Half an hour of loneliness.. was overly much for her. **1903** KIPLING *Five Nations* 21 Yet, caring so, not overly we care To brace and trim for every foolish blast. **1924** B. G. ELLIOTT *Automobile Repairing* x. 131 An overly rich mixture may be caused by the fuel nozzle valve being open too wide. **1926** J. A. MULLER *Stephen Gardiner* ii. 11 The intense, overly conscientious Thomas Bilney. **1929** M. C. WORK *Compl. Contract Bridge* v. 111 Overly sanguine or 'bad break' slam tries. **1942** *Sun* (Baltimore) 10 Oct. 10/2 A panting, frantic lady.. is.. not overly generous after she has been shouting for a while.. shouting for an invisible porter. **1956** D. KARP *All Honourable Men* 50 She took one with an overly feline movement of her body and looked into his face as she accepted his light. **1963** *Wall St. Jrnl.* 25 Jan., As for the future, however, even the most annoyed American official seems not to be overly alarmed. **1968** *Globe & Mail* (Toronto) 17 Feb. 8/1 The Manitoba Minister of Agriculture is not overly impressed with the horsemen's woes. **1970** *Nature* 17 Jan. 213/1 Scientists are not going to be overly interested in the 'sociology of the sociology of science' if nothing is forthcoming except internal disagreement. **1970** G. F. NEWMAN *Sir, You Bastard* i. 27 Whoever had covered them hadn't been overly careful about the tubes. **1972** *Times Lit. Suppl.* 2 June 624/4 Those overly rationalistic readers who demand to see in her work plentiful evidence of a higher or deeper 'sanity'. **1977** *Dædalus* Summer 157 This is the methodological point lying behind Popper's overly propositional thesis about the eternal falsifiability of scientific truths.

2. †**a.** Superficially, slightly, carelessly. *Obs.*

c **1440** *Promp. Parv.* 373/1 Ovyrly, *superficialiter*. *a* **1564** BECON *Comp. betw. Lord's Supper & Pope's Mass* Prayers, etc. (Parker Soc.) 374 Beholding them as it were by the way, or overly. **1649** BLITHE *Eng. Improv. Impr.* (1653) 52 If that men drain those Lands wherein they are like to have an interest, throughly, and those the Commoners have, more overly. **1710** R. WARD *Life H. More* 143 Other things he look'd upon more overly and sparingly, as he saw Occasion. **1832–53** A. MACLAGAN in *Whistle-Binkie* (Scot. Songs) Ser. II. 117 He o'erly just speer'd for the men, But he cadgily cracket wi' aunty.

b. Incidentally, casually, not intentionally. *Sc.*

1825 JAMIESON, *Overly*,.. by chance. *a* **1904** *Mod. Sc.* (Roxb.) I happened overly to say that I had seen him there.

†**3.** In position over, on the surface. *Obs.*

1567 MAPLET *Gr. Forest* 43 It then ariseth vp againe to the waters top, and so keepeth ouerlie and aboue the waters highest superficie. **1573** TUSSER *Husb.* xxiii. (1878) 64 The strawberies looke to be couered with strawe Laid ouerly trim vpon crotchis and bows.

†**4.** Haughtily, superciliously, slightingly. *Obs.*

1610 BP. HALL *Apol. Brownists* i. 3 They vse to behold such as they oppose too ouerlie, and not without contempt. **1650** BRINSLEY *Antidote* 27 To look overly upon others, despising and contemning them.

†**5.** (?) Moreover: = OVER *adv.* 10.

1599 *Life Sir T. More* in Wordsw. *Eccl. Biog.* (1853) II. 165 And overlie this worde *maliciouslie* is in this statute materiall.

overlying (əʊvəˈlaɪɪŋ), *vbl. sb.* [f. OVERLIE *v.* + -ING[1], or f. OVER- 8 + LYING *vbl. sb.*[1]] The action of the verb OVERLIE.

c **1380** [see OVERLAYING]. **1871** tr. *Schellen's Spectr. Anal.* xlv. 173 Produced by the overlying of the reversed spectra of such substances as are to be found in the earth. **1891** *Daily News* 31 Dec. 5/3 The proportion of deaths from overlying is more than twice as high on Saturday night as on any other night in the week.

ˈoverˈlying (stress var.), *ppl. a.* [f. OVERLIE *v.* + -ING[2], or f. OVER- 8 + LYING *ppl. a.*[1]] That overlies; superincumbent.

1872 LYELL *Princ. Geol.* II. 244 The proximity of large overlying bodies of water. **1878** HUXLEY *Physiogr.* 35 The water having been absorbed by the overlying loose limestones.

over-Macpherson, etc.: see OVER-.

overman (ˈəʊvəmən), *sb.* Chiefly *north.* Forms: see OVER. (Also OVERSMAN.) [OVER- 2 b.]

†**1.** A man having authority or rule over others; a superior, leader, ruler, chief. *Obs.* exc. as in 3.

c **1250** *Gen. & Ex.* 3424 And if he riȝten it ne can, He taune it al his ouer-man. *a* **1300** *Cursor M.* 6968 (Cott.) Ilk kinredd o þe tuelue Had þair ouer man ham selfe. *c* **1375** *Sc. Leg. Saints* xxxii. (*Justin*) 598 Bot sene þu þe kirk is in As oure-man saulis to wyne. **1456** SIR G. HAYE *Law Arms* (S.T.S.) 113 Redy at bidding of his our-men to do his honour and charge of his lord. **1625** in *Cosin's Corr.* (Surtees) I. 61, I shall wholy and totally make you overseer, and overman to, of my book at presse.

2. An arbiter, arbitrator, umpire.

c **1470** HENRY *Wallace* VIII. 1332 Throuch ii clemyt, thar hapnyt gret debait,.. Ȝour king thai ast for to be thair ourman. **1552** *Reg. Privy Council Scot.* I. 127 Hes chosin.. George Commendatour of Dunfermling, odman and ourman in the saidis materis. **1884** *Pall Mall G.* 5 Dec. 2/1 The two having the power to call in the services of an overman.

3. The man who is over a body of workmen; a foreman, overseer; *spec.* in a colliery (see quots.).

1708 J. C. *Compl. Collier* (1845) 36 It is the Over-Man's Business to place the Miners in their Workings. **1789** BRAND *Hist. Newcastle* II. 682 The overman's office is to go through the pit to view the places where the men have wrought, to see that the pit is clear of sulphur, &c. **1805** *Trans. Soc. Arts* XXIII. 33 My over-man being unacquainted with the drill husbandry. **1867** *Colliery Rules* in W. W. Smyth *Coal & Coal-mining* 231 None but the over-man, or similar officer, to be allowed to carry a lamp key.

4. (ˈəʊvəmæn.) [tr. G. *übermensch*.] = SUPERMAN.

1895 tr. *M. Nordau's Degeneration* III. v. 470 The 'bullies' gratefully recognise themselves in Nietzsche's 'overman'. **1900** *Q. Rev.* July 116 In such old religion he discovers no prophecy of the man that is to be; he reaches forward to some 'overman' beyond it. **1908** H. G. WELLS *War in Air* xi. 365 His mind ran to 'improving the race' and producing the Over-Man. **1915** *Lond. Q. Rev.* Jan. 59 Such a process of superabstraction would involve either an overman or a *deus ex machina*. **1928** A. HUXLEY *Point Counter Point* vi. 108 If you were a little less of an overman,.. what good novels you'd write! **1932** [see NIETZSCHEAN *sb.* and *a.*]. **1971** *Black Scholar* June 50/1 The 'magnificent savage', 'the mindless overman', is even dying with the deficiency. **1976** M. & G. GORDON *Ordeal* xi. 69 He would overlook Charlie's shortcomings. An overman had to... Vince had read as much of Nietzsche as necessary to learn about the overmen—the supermen—and the inferiors, the masses.

overman (əʊvəˈmæn), *v.* [OVER- 21, 27.]

1. *trans.* To overcome, overpower. *rare.* [= Du. *overmannen*, Ger. *übermannen*.]

1607 ROWLANDS *Famous Hist.* 28 I'le never dread I shall be over man'd While I have hands to fight, or legs to stand. **1851** H. MELVILLE *Moby Dick* I. xxxvii. 270 My soul is more than matched; she's overmanned—and by a mad-man! **1865** *Reader* No. 144. 366/3 Every foe is overmanned.

2. (ˌ*over-ˈman*). To furnish with too many men.

1636–7 *Let.* in *Crt. & Times Chas. I* (1849) II. 269 All the ships were overmanned which had infection among them. **1774** FRANKLIN *Lett.* Wks. 1887 V. 371 Three ships of the line are fitting out for America, which are to be overmanned. **1899** *Daily News* 12 Sept. 6/4 In my times.. some departments were overmanned and some were undermanned.

Hence (in sense 2) **over-'manning** *vbl. sb.*

1971 *New Scientist* 9 Sept. 553/1 Output has reflected this over-manning. **1975** *Broadcast* 28 July 4/1 The ACTT does not consider overmanning..to be a central issue in the financial problems confronting ITV. **1975** *Times Lit. Suppl.* 12 Sept. 1028/4 During the winter over-manning was enforced—one labourer per fifteen acres. **1975** *Daily Tel.* 19 Sept. 3/3 (*heading*) Sir Keith urges TUC to curb overmanning. **1978** *Jrnl. R. Soc. Arts* CXXVI. 656/1 The overmanning in all the factories that I visited was very considerable.

overmantel ('əʊvəˌmænt(ə)l). [OVER- 33.] A piece of ornamental cabinet-work, often including a mirror, placed over a mantelpiece.

1882 J. HATTON in *Harper's Mag.* Dec. 23/2 The overmantel is ornamented with some trophies of the chase. **1899** *Q. Rev.* Apr. 389 The plain panelling of the walls is relieved by an elaborately carved overmantel.

over'mantle, *v.* [OVER- 8.] *trans.* To cover over like a mantle.

1827 CARLYLE *Misc., German Lit.* I. 50 Flowers and foliage, as of old, are..overmantling its sternest cliffs. **1831** MOIR in *Blackw. Mag.* XXIX. 327 Snow o'ermantles hill.

'over-'many, *a.* [OVER- 28; but usually two words.] Too many.

[**1484** CAXTON *Fables of Æsop* v. iii, Kepe thy self fro ouer many wordes.] **1538** STARKEY *England* II. ii. 191 Of them are ouer-many. **1586** T. B. *La Primaud. Fr. Acad.* I. 409 We know by over-many experiences. **17..** *Song, Tibbie Fowler*, Tibbie Fowler o' the Glen, There's ower-mony wooing at her. [**1894** 'IAN MACLAREN' *Bonnie Brier Bush* VII. i. 243 He's been eatin' over mony berries.]

overmarch (-'mɑːtʃ), *v.* [OVER- 26, 13.]

1. *trans.* To march (soldiers, etc.) too far or too long; to overpower or exhaust with marching.

1660 PHILLIPS in *Baker's Chron.* (1696) 532 The Prince his Horse were so over-marcht, and the Foot so beaten off their Legs by long Marches. **1823** SOUTHEY *Hist. Penins. War* I. 707 His men had been over-marched.

2. To march over or beyond, pass over in marching.

1807 J. BARLOW *Columb.* III. 137 They journey'd forth, o'ermarching far the mound That flank'd the kingdom on its Andean bound.

over'mark, *v.* (Chiefly in *pa. pple.*) [f. OVER- 26, 8, 27a + MARK *sb.* or *v.*]

†**1.** *trans.* ? To furnish with too distant a mark (to aim at). *Obs.*

c **1560** T. LUCY *Let.* in Halliwell *Shaks.* (1887) II. 388 Take hede that Burnell be not over-marked, for he is hable to shute no farr grounde.

2. To mark over, make marks upon the surface of.

1838 *Voice from Font* 3 Drawn and rubbed out, marked and overmarked diagram upon diagram.

3. *Horsemanship.* (See quot. 1875.)

1866 *Lond. Rev.* 28 Apr. 471/1 Sometimes..the noble animal is overmarked, and falls a victim to his own spirit and the stupidity of his owner. **1875** 'STONEHENGE' *Brit. Sports* II. I. v. §7. 442 The overmarked horse is detected by his dull heavy eye. *Ibid.*, Overmarking is the effect produced upon the horse constitutionally, as well as locally upon the legs, by overwork and overfeeding.

4. To award too many marks to (a candidate in an examination, competition, etc.).

1947 C. S. LEWIS *Miracles* xvii. 198 Some examiners tend to overmark any candidate whose opinions and character, as revealed by his work, are revolting to them. **1970** *Times* 5 Mar. 13 One judge admitted that she had overmarked Wood, for no good reason that I could discover other than sympathy for a champion in distress.

over-marl, etc.: see OVER-.

†**over-'marry,** *v. Obs.* [OVER- 23.] *refl.* To marry above one's station or means.

1610 HOLLAND *Camden's Brit.* I. 368 John..repudiated his wife and passes her over, with the Honor of Glocester, to Geffrey Mandevil, for 20,000 markes, who thus ouer-marrying himselfe was greatly impoverished.

over'mask, *v.* [OVER- 8.] *trans.* To cover or conceal as with a mask.

c **1600** *Battle of Balrinnes* in Child *Ballads* (1861) VII. 218 Owermaskit was the moone. **1885–94** R. BRIDGES *Eros & Psyche* June xxv, They with outward smile O'ermask'd their hate, and called her sweet and dear.

overmast (-'mɑːst, -mæst), *v.* [f. OVER- 26 + MAST *sb.*[1]] *trans.* To furnish (a ship) with too high or too heavy a mast or masts. Hence **over'masting** *vbl. sb.*

1627 CAPT. SMITH *Seaman's Gram.* iii. 15 If you ouermast her, either in length or bignesse, she will lie too much downe by a wind. **1697** DRYDEN *Æneid* v. 202 Cloanthus better mann'd, pursu'd him fast, But his o'ermasted gally check'd his haste. **1769** FALCONER *Dict. Marine* (1789). **1902** CONRAD *Youth* 40 She was certainly over-masted. **1906** —— *Mirror of Sea* xi. 58 It was a fine period in ship-building, and also..a period of over-masting. **1930** J. MASEFIELD *Wanderer of Liverpool* 27 Mr. Potter was inclined to think that the *Wanderer* had been over-masted.

overmaster (əʊvə'mɑːstə(r), -mæst-), *v.* [f. OVER- 21 + MASTER *v.*, q.v. for Forms.]

1. *trans.* To make oneself master over; to master completely; to gain the victory over, get the better of, overcome, conquer, overpower. (Chiefly *fig.* with abstract subj. or obj., *e.g.* a feeling, faculty, condition, force, etc.)

1340 *Ayenb.* 15 To viȝte wyþ þe halȝen an his to ouercome and to ouermaistri. *c* **1489** CAXTON *Sonnes of Aymon* xvii. 392 The one cowde not overmayster the other. **1532** MORE *Confut. Tindale* Wks. 696/1 So shall neuer any mannes tale ..ouermaister that inward mocion of God. **1581** SIDNEY *Apol. Poetrie* (Arb.) 40 Where once reason hath so much ouer-mastred passion. **1607** HIERON *Wks.* I. 178 His strength is such as can not be ouer-mastred. **1632** LITHGOW *Trav.* III. 104 He ouer-maisterd a Turkish towne and..put two thousand Turkes to the sword. **1800** COLERIDGE *Christabel* II. xxiii, O'er-mastered by the mighty spell. **1879** M. ARNOLD *Democracy* Mixed Ess. 26 English democracy runs no risk of being overmastered by the State.

†**b.** To surpass, excel, 'beat'. *Obs. rare.*

1627 SPEED *England* xxxviii. §9 It ouer-masters all the other places of this Country for fairenesse.

†**2.** To be master over; to dominate; to hold in one's power or possession. *Obs.*

c **1550** CHEKE *Matt.* xx. 25 Je know y[t] y[e] princes of y[e] heyen do overmaster y[em]. **1595** SHAKS. *John* II. i. 109 Liuing blood doth in these temples beat Which owe the crowne, that thou oremasterest. **1648** GAGE *West Ind.* xviii. (1655) 136 A hill which discovereth all the City, and standeth as overmastring of it.

Hence **over'mastered** *ppl. a.*, **over'mastering** *vbl. sb.* and *ppl. a.*, **over'masteringly** *adv.*

1645 RUTHERFORD *Tryal & Tri. Faith* iii. (1845) 37 There is an overmastering apprehension of Christ's love. **1649** MILTON *Eikon.* xxvi, A weak and over-master'd enemy. **1816** SCOTT *Old Mort.* vi, One in whom some strong o'ermastering principle has overwhelmed all other passions and feelings. **1818** BYRON *Ch. Har.* IV. xvi, The car Of the o'ermaster'd victor stops. **1860** GEO. ELIOT *Mill on Floss* III. 209 He had been tortured by scruples, he had fought fiercely with over-mastering inclination. **1866** DOWDEN in *Contemp. Rev.* II. 539 The blinding gladness of life was overmasteringly strong. **1899** *Daily News* 10 June 7/4 It would result in the immediate overmastering of the old citizens. **1903** *Cambr. Mod. Hist.* II. xviii. 644 He [*sc.* Paul III] was not a zealot, possessed with one overmastering idea. **1915** F. S. OLIVER *Ordeal by Battle* iv. 120 Nietzsche is not concerned to evolve a sovereign and omnipotent state, but a high overmastering type of man. **1942** *R.A.F. Jrnl.* 13 June 2 What a blockade by sea can do..an overmastering force of bombers can most certainly do. **1957** J. S. HUXLEY *Relig. without Revelation* (rev. ed.) v. 110 Some have this in an overmastering degree.

'over-'masterful, *a.* [OVER- 28.] Masterful to excess, too masterful. Hence **'over-'masterfulness.**

1883 A. FORBES in *Fortn. Rev.* 1 Nov. 663 The German strategy was daringly overmasterful. **1899** *Month* Sept. 242 One fault..amongst them at that time was overmasterfulness.

over-'mastery, *sb.* [f. OVERMASTER *v.*]

†**a.** Speriority or ascendancy in a contest. *Obs.*

c **1375** *Cursor M.* 6420 (Fairf.) þe quilest moises helde vp his hende..had goddis folk þe over maistri.

b. Supreme authority, sovereignty.

1901 T. SHAW *Patriotism & Empire* (Young Scots Soc. Publ. No. 1) 4 We are free..to think with a lifting of the heart of the struggle for Scottish independence against the overmastery of England. **1971** J. F. WATHEN *Great Sacrilege* ii. 28 God Himself..would prevent such a thing from happening, either directly or through His ordinary over-mastery of all creatural actions.

So †**over'mastery** *v. Obs.* = OVERMASTER *v.*

1377 LANGL. *P. Pl.* B. IV. 176 Mede ouer-maistrieth lawe, and moche treuthe letteth. **1477** EARL RIVERS (Caxton) *Dictes* 57 If the witte of a man ouermaistrie not his frailte. **1483** CAXTON *G. de la Tour* A vj, To thende that..none euyll temptacions ouermaystrye you not.

overmatch (əʊvə'mætʃ), *sb.* [OVER- 24.]

†**1.** The condition of being overmatched; a contest in which one side is more than a match for the other. *Obs.*

1542 UDALL *Erasm. Apoph.* 311 b, Tenne eagles to seuen is an ouermatche. **1581** SAVILE *Tacitus' Hist.* IV. xii. (1591) 177 Yet were they not, as it happeneth in such ouermatches, spoiled of their riches. **1590** MARLOWE *2nd Pt. Tamburl.* III. v, Thou wouldst with overmatch of person fight.

2. A person or thing that is more than a match for some other. Const. with genitive or *for*.

1589 R. HARVEY *Pl. Perc.* (1860) 4 The greatest quarrellers meet often with their ouer-match. **1667** FLAVEL *Saint Indeed* (1754) 44 Is he not an overmatch for all his enemies? **1747** W. HORSLEY *Fool* (1748) II. 332 The French Privateers alone are quite an Over-match for..the British Navy. **1845** NAPIER *Conq. Scinde* II. v. 229 Having to deal with a man his over-match in policy.

over'match, *v.* [OVER- 24, 2.]

1. *trans.* To do more than match; to be more than a match for; to be too powerful, skilful, or crafty to be overcome by; to defeat by superior strength, skill, or craft; to surpass, excel.

c **1350** *Will. Palerne* 1216 So was he ouer-macched þat þei wiþ fyn force for-barred his strokes And woundede him wikkedly. **1470–85** MALORY *Arthur* x. lix, Be a man neuer soo valyaunt nor soo bygge, yet he may be ouermatched. **1568** Q. ELIZ. *Let.* in H. Campbell *Love Lett. Mary Q. Scots* (1824) App. 56 Ye have not any in loyaltie and faithfulnes can overmatch him. **1588** in *Harl. Misc.* (Malh.) II. 73 Ships of war..whose service was seen this year to have overmatched the great Armadas and castles of Spain and Italy. **1641** J. TRAPPE *Theol. Theol.* 81 A treasury of heavenly comforts, such as no good can match, no evill overmatch. **1725** POPE *Odyss.* II. 280 The valiant few o'er-match an host of foes. **1870** ROCK *Text. Fabr.* I. 206 The combination..of its two colours in such a way that neither overmatches the other.

†**b.** To furnish with what is more than a match.

1567 GOLDING *Ovid's Met.* VIII. 187 He knits A rowe of feathers one by one..overmatching still ech quill with one of longer sort.

2. To give in marriage above one's station. *rare.*

1621 BURTON *Anat. Mel.* III. ii. VI. v. (1651) 579 If a Yeoman have one sole daughter, he must overmatch her, above her birth and calling, to a gentleman forsooth.

Hence **over'matched, over'matching** *ppl. adjs.*; so also †**'over-'matchable** *a.*, too matchable, too comparable; †**over-'matchful** *a.*, that is more than a match, excelling.

1591 SHAKS. *1 Hen. VI*, IV. iv. 11 Our ore-matcht forces. **1593** —— *3 Hen. VI*, I. iv. 21 With bootlesse labour swimme against the Tyde, And spend her strength with ouer-matching Waues. **1607** ROWLANDS *Famous Hist.* 5 We toyl so much in other Nations praise, That we neglect the famousing of our own, Which over-matchful unto them were known. **1611** SPEED *Hist. Gt. Brit.* VI. vii. §8. 66 Putting them in remembrance of their wonted valours, which now was farre ouermatchable vnto a fearefull flock of weak women. **1633** BP. HALL *Medit. & Vows* (1851) 88 None, but thou,..canst relieve his distressed and over-matched soul.

†**over'mate,** *v. Obs.* [OVER- 24.] = prec. 1.

1571 GOLDING *Calvin on Ps.* lvi. 5 Their assaults rushe ageinst God himself, as if they strived to overmate him. **1660** HICKERINGILL *Jamaica* 90 Poor men..that are thus o're-mated.

overmatter, -mean, etc.: see OVER-.

over-measure ('əʊvə'mɛʒ(j)ʊə(r), -ʒə(r)), *sb.* [OVER- 19, 29d.] Measure above what is ordinary or sufficient; excess, surplus.

[**1581** SAVILE *Tacitus* II. xxiv. (1591) 67 An ouer measure if fortune hapned to go on their side. **1607** SHAKS. *Cor.* III. i. 140 Enough, with ouer measure.] **1641** MILTON *Reform.* Wks. 1738 I. 29 Where they..shall clasp inseparable hands with Joy and Bliss, in over-measure for ever. **1710** PALMER *Proverbs* 294 They rarely fail of over-measure in the return of an injury. **1851** TRENCH *Poems* 77 [God] had answered all her prayers With such an overmeasure of his grace.

over-'measure, *v.* [OVER- 26, 10.] *trans.* **a.** To measure or reckon above the proper amount. **b.** To measure across, to traverse.

1625 BACON *Ess., Kingdomes* (Arb.) 471 That neither by Ouer-measuring their Forces, they leese themselues in vaine Enterprises; Nor..by vnderualuing them, they descend to Fearefull and Pusillanimous Counsells. **1877** TENNYSON *Harold* IV. iii. 119 By St. Edmund I over-measure him. **1896** *Chicago Advance* 18 June 905/2 Their gloomy shadow would twice have over-measured our country's expanse.

'over-'measure, *advb. phr.* [Properly two words, OVER *prep.* 11 and MEASURE *sb.*] Above the proper measure or amount; in excess.

1387 TREVISA *Higden* (Rolls) II. 257 [þey] preysede þe dedes hugeliche and ouermesure [*laudibus nimium extulerunt*]. **1483** CAXTON *G. de la Tour* H iij b, Wyn taken ouer mesure troubleth the syght. **1656** H. PHILLIPS *Purch. Patt.* (1676) 164 Allow rather a little over-measure than any thing under. **1705** STANHOPE *Paraphr.* II. 404 If he give more, all that is Over-measure.

over-melodied, -merry, etc.: see OVER-.

'over-'merit, *sb.* [OVER- 29d.] Excessive merit. So **over-'merit** *v. trans.* [OVER- 22], to exceed or surpass in merit.

1622 BACON *Hen. VII* 133 Those Helpes were ouer weighed by diuers things that made against him... First, an Ouer-merit; for conuenient Merit, vnto which Reward may easily reach, doth best with Kings. **1658** BAXTER *Saving Faith* iv. 22 If bulk might go for worth and weight, I had over-merited you in this Controversie.

†**over'mete,** *a.* and *adv. Obs.* [OE. *ofermǽte* adj. excessive, f. *ofer* OVER *adv.* + *mǽte* measured, moderate, ablaut deriv. of *met-an* to measure.]

A. *adj.* Above measure; immoderate, excessive.

c **893** K. ÆLFRED *Oros.* I. vii. §2 God..hyra ofermætan ofermetto ʒenyðerode. *c* **897** —— *Gregory's Past. C.* lxiii. 459 Moyses behelede ða ofermætan biərhto his ondwlitan. *c* **1200** ORMIN 10720, & tiss meocnesse iss oferrmett Swa þatt itt oferfloweþþ. *c* **1200** *Trin. Coll. Hom.* 137 Wiðteo þi lichame fro orguil, and idel and ouer mete wede.

B. *adv.* Immoderately, excessively.

a **1225** *Ancr. R.* 296 So sone so þu euer ivelest þet þin heorte mid luue ualle touward eni monne, ouermete.

†**over'mete,** *v. Obs.* [f. OVER- 4, 10 + METE *v.*, OE. *metan* to measure, traverse, pass over.]

a. *intr.* To pass over, pass by, elapse. **b.** *trans.* To pass over, cross, traverse; = OVERMEASURE *v.* b.

c **1250** *Gen. & Ex.* 1665 Quanne a moneð was ouer-meten. *c* **1375** *Sc. Leg. Saints* xxxi. (*Eugenia*) 461 As I sal prowe it is alsa Be Iugment of yrne hat... And scho on it with fet bare But abaysing it ouremet, Vnhurt or hafand ony lat.

'over-'mickle, *a.* and *adv. Now Sc.* and *north. dial.* [OE. *ofermicel* adj. = ON. *ofrmikill*: see OVER- 28.] Too much, overmuch.

c **893** K. ÆLFRED *Oros.* I. vii. §3 On þære tide wæs sio ofermycelo hæto on ealre woruldе. *c* **961** *Rule St. Benet* xli. (Schr.) 65 Butan hy ouermicel ʒeswinc habben. *a* **1300** *Cursor M.* 13066 (Cott.) Iohn, ouer mikel [*Tr.* to muche] has þou spoken. *c* **1400** *Rule St. Benet* 8 Ne ete our-mikil; Ne drinc ouir-mikil. **1482** *Monk of Evesham* (Arb.) 99 Sche louyd her kynnys folke ouermekyl carnaly. **1483** *Cath. Angl.* 263/1 Ouer mekylle, *nimis.* **1552** ABP. HAMILTON *Catech.* (1884) 48 Thai quhilkis traistis owyr mekle in thair awin wisdome. **1825** BROCKETT *N.C. Gloss., Overmickle, owermickle,* overmuch. *Mod. Sc.* It wad be ower muckle fash.

over-mild, -mill, etc.: see OVER-.

†ˌ**over'mind,** *v. Obs.* [OVER- 27.] *trans.* To mind too much, think too much of, attach too great importance to.

1571 GOLDING *Calvin on Ps.* xxii. 2 Least by overmynding their owne infirmitie theyr hartes should fayle them. **1649** G. DANIEL *Trinarch., Hen. V* ccci, Soe much a Monarch overminds what they By Loans and Subsidies bring in.

† **over'mirth,** *v. Obs. rare*⁻¹. [Cf. OVER *prep.* 4 b.] To make merry over (tr. L. *insultare*).

a **1300** *E.E. Psalter* xxxiv. 19 Noght over-mirthe þai to me for-þi, þat wiþer-þretes me wickeli.

over-mix, etc.: see OVER- 27.

† **'overmod,** *sb. Obs.* [OE. *ofermód* = OHG. *ubarmuot* (MHG. *übermuot,* Ger. *übermuth*), MDu. *overmôd* (Du. *overmoed*): cf. OS. *obarmôdi*; f. *ofer* OVER + *mód* MOOD.] 'High-mindedness', pride, haughtiness.

993 *Battle of Maldon* 89 Ða se eorl ongann for his ofermode alyfan landes to fela laðere þeode. *a* **1000** *Cædmon's Gen.* 272 (Gr.) Feala worda ʒespræc se engel ofermodes. *c* **1175** *Lamb. Hom.* 9 For his ouer-mod, oðer for his prude.

So † **'overmod** *a.* [OE. *ofermód*], proud, haughty; † **over'modi** *a.* [OE. *ofermódiʒ*] = prec.; † **over'modiness** [OE. *ofermódiʒness*].

971 *Blickl. Hom.* 61 þa oformodan men. *c* **1000** *Ags. Gosp.* Mark vii. 22 Sceamleast, yfel ʒesihð, dysinessa, ofermodiʒnessa. *c* **1000** *Sax. Leechd.* III. 191 Mæden tacn on neccan hæfð oððe on þeo, ofermodiʒ, þancfull, þriste on lichaman mid maneʒum werum. *c* **1175** *Lamb. Hom.* 5 Ne beo þu þereuore prud ne..ouer modi. *Ibid.* 19 Prude and ouer-modinesse. *c* **1275** *Sinners Beware* 269 in *O.E. Misc.* 81 And wo is þenne þe ouermode þat er þar-of ne rouhte. *c* **1300** *Regret Maximian* 57 (MS. Digby 86 lf. 135/1) Ich wes to overmod [*rime* blod].

'over-'modest, *a.* [OVER- 28.] Too modest. So **'over-'modestly** *adv.*; **'over-'modesty.**

1614 RALEIGH *Hist. World* v. v. §4. 659 Doubtfull how to order the matter, in such wise as they might neither too rudely..nor yet ouer-modestly..forbeare the occasion of making themselues great. *a* **1656** HALES *Rem., Serm. Luke* xviii. 1. (1673) 143 It is the Courtiers rule, That over modest suitours seldom speed. **1742** RICHARDSON *Pamela* l. IV. 66 Over-modesty borders so nearly on Pride. **1829** LYTTON *Devereux* I. viii, A fine youth, but somewhat shy and over-modest in manner.

ˌ**overmodu'lation.** *Electronics.* [OVER- 29 b.] Amplitude modulation that is so great as to result in unacceptable distortion; *spec.* modulation that causes the amplitude of the carrier to become zero for a significant part of each cycle of the modulating wave.

1927 *Exper. Wireless & Wireless Engin.* IV. 3/1 The strengths of..undesired harmonics relative to the desired fundamental decrease as the modulation ratio *a/a* is decreased. This is the ground for the term 'over-modulation' as a fault at the transmitter. Over-modulation shows, of course, only during the relatively loud passages. **1937** *Wireless World* 2 Dec. 563/1 Over-modulation of broadcast transmitters has been a serious problem. **1962** A. NISBETT *Technique Sound Studio* vii. 132 One of the problems which may arise when tape is re-used is a background 'chatter' from the previous recording. This can be due..to overmodulation of the previous recording. **1968** *Radio Communication Handbk.* (ed. 4) ix. 4/2 In frequency modulation there is no condition equivalent to over-modulation.

So **over'modulate** *v. trans.,* to subject to overmodulation; *intr.,* to cause or suffer overmodulation.

1928 L. S. PALMER *Wireless Princ. & Pract.* xi. 418 As long as the modulator be not overworked, the oscillatory current cannot be over-modulated. **1937** *Wireless World* 2 Dec. 563/1 Automatically graduated compression, or limiting,..makes it almost impossible to overload or over-modulate the transmitter. **1962** A. NISBETT *Technique Sound Studio* ii. 48 Completely dead sound is difficult to balance: the transient peaks tend to over-modulate.

over-moist, -moisture, etc.: see OVER-.

† **over'money,** *v. Obs. nonce-wd.* [OVER- 11 b; after *undermine.*] *trans.* To prevail over with money; to win by means of a bribe.

a **1661** FULLER *Worthies, Lancs.* (1662) 124 Some suspect his Officers trust was undermined (or over-moneyed rather). **1665** D. LLOYD *State Worthies* (1670) 197.

† **'overmore,** *a. Obs.* [f. OVER *adv.* or *a.* + MORE *adj.*; used as a compar. of *over*: cf. INNERMORE, OUTERMORE, etc., and see OVERMOST.] Upper, higher; = OVERER *a.*

1382 WYCLIF *Josh.* xvi. 5 The possessioun of hem aʒens the est..vnto the ouermore [*v.r.* ouere; 1388 hiʒere] Betheron. **1387** TREVISA *Higden* (Rolls) VII. 125 William evermore i-bore awey þe overmore and þe hyʒer hond. *c* **1400** MAUNDEV. (Roxb.) x. 40 Egipte, bathe þe ouermare and þe neþer mare.

†ˌ**over'more,** *adv. Obs.* [f. OVER *adv.* + MORE *adv.*] In addition, furthermore, moreover.

1390 GOWER *Conf.* I. 155 This Maiden..hise charitees Comendeth, and seide overmore My liege lord [etc.]. **1393** LANGL. *P. Pl.* C. IX. 35 And ʒut on poynt..ich praye ʒow ouermore. **1475** *Bk. Noblesse* (Roxb.) 11 And overmore the said King Edwarde first kept under subjeccion bothe Irelond, Walis, and Scotlond. *a* **1547** SURREY *Æneid* II. 813 Yet overmore, against the Trojan power He doth provoke the rest of all the gods.

b. Further, longer.

a **1450** MYRC 159 Tho þat bydeth ouer more, The fader & þe moder mote rewe hyt sore.

c. ? Farther up, farther away.

1375 BARBOUR *Bruce* II. 440 To this word thai assentyt all, And fra thaim walopyt owyr mar [*Hart's ed.* vppermere]. *Ibid.* VI. 632 The twa that saw sa suddanly Thair fallow fall, effrayit var And stert a litill ouirmair.

† **over'morrow,** *adv. Obs.* [Cf. OVER- 18: prob. after Ger. (and MHG.) *übermorgen,* Du. *overmorgen.*] The day after tomorrow. Also *attrib.*

1535 COVERDALE *Tobit* viii. 4 Vp Sara, let vs make oure prayer vnto God to daye, tomorow, and ouermorow. **1577** tr. *Bullinger's Decades* (1592) 280 Thou needest not by thy morrowe and ouer-morrowe delayes to augment his discommoditye.

over-mortgage to **over-moss:** see OVER-.

'overmost, *a.* (*sb.*) *Obs.* exc. *dial.* Also 4 **-mast**(e, **-mest**(e, **-mist.** [f. OVER *adv.* or *a.* + -MOST: cf. OVERMORE. Perh. an alteration of OVEMEST; but *overmest* does not appear so early as the northern *overmast*(*e* = midl. and south. *-most.*] **A.** *adj.* Uppermost, highest; = OVEREST *a.*

a **1300** *Cursor M.* 395 In þe ouermast element of all. *Ibid.* 22232. *a* **1350** *St. Andrew* 168 in Horstm. *Altengl. Leg.* (1881) 6 His ouermast clothes þan of he did. *c* **1380** WYCLIF *Serm.* Sel. Wks. I. 340 In þe overmeste part of þe eir. *c* **1380** —— *Wks.* (1880) 340 An harpe haþe þre partis of hym; þe ouermost in which ben stringis wrastid. **1398** TREVISA *Barth. De P.R.* III. xvi. (Tollem. MS.), In þe ouermist party of a man. *c* **1410** LOVE *Bonavent. Mirr.* xliii. (Gibbs MS.), Whanne he come up to þe ouermoste ende of þat schorte laddere. **1590** RECORDE, etc. *Gr. Artes* (1646) 235 Take the overmost line..as if it were the lowest line. **1649** BLITHE *Eng. Improv. Impr.* (1653) 115 To plant it in the Over-most and Fattest Earth.

B. *absol.* or as *sb.* The uppermost part; = OVEREST *sb.* 1.

a **1300** *E.E. Psalter* ciii[i]. 13 Fra his overmastes [L. *de superioribus*] hilles watrand. **1382** WYCLIF *Isa.* xiii. 5 Fro the ouermost of heuene. **1413** *Pilgr. Sowle* (Caxton) I. iii. (1859) 4 The ouermost of the erthe was moost clere.

overmount (əʊvə'maʊnt), *v.* [OVER- 1, 26.]

1. *trans.* To mount or rise above, transcend.

? **1370** *Robt. Cicyle* 63 For pryde wolde..Ovyr-mownte Goddys dygnyté. **1552** HULOET, Ouermounte, *transcendo.* **1613** SHAKS. *Hen. VIII,* II. iii. 94 With your Theame, I could O're-mount the Larke. **1804** J. GRAHAME *Sabbath* (1839) 5/1 While from yon lowly roof, whose curling smoke O'ermounts the mist, is heard at intervals The voice of psalms.

2. *intr.* To mount too high.

1591 SHAKS. *1 Hen. VI,* IV. vii. 15 And in that Sea of Blood, my Boy did drench His ouer-mounting Spirit. **1592** HARVEY *Four Lett.* Wks. (Grosart) I. 193 How many..youthes, haue in ouermounting, most ruefully dismounted?

overmount ('əʊvəˌmaʊnt), *sb.* [OVER- 8.] A piece of stiff paper or board cut to correspond with the margin of a picture, so as to fit round it when framed and glazed; a mount.

1890 in *Cent. Dict.*

'over-'mounts, *advb. phr.* [Properly two words, OVER *prep.* and *mounts,* pl. of MOUNT *sb.*; after It. *oltramonti.*] Beyond the mountains.

1840 BROWNING *Sordello* III. 476 This lion's-crine From over-mounts—(this yellow hair of mine). **1884** —— *Ferishtah, A Bean-stripe* 239 Though, over-mounts,—to trust the traveller,—Snow, feather-thick, is falling while I feast.

ˌ**over-'mourn,** *v.* [OVER- 27, 23.] To mourn too much; to lament excessively. (*trans.* and *intr.*; in quot. 1607 *refl.* in intr. sense.)

1594 KYD *Cornelia* Argt., Hauing ouer-mourn'd the death of her deere husband. **1607** TOPSELL *Four-f. Beasts* (1658) 237 Lest the Mare over-mourn her self for want of her foal. **1650** BAXTER *Saint's R.* x. (1656) 281 When he dies we mourn and usually overmourn.

overmuch ('əʊvə'mʌtʃ, with shifting stress), *a.* and *adv.* [OVER- 28, 30. Cf. OE. *ofermicel* OVERMICKLE.] Too much.

A. *adj.* Too great in amount; excessive, superabundant.

1297 R. GLOUC. (Rolls) 10788 þou sucst [= seest] þis folc ouer muche þat aʒe þe is, And þin owe ouer lute [= little]. *c* **1450** *Voc.* in Wr.-Wülcker 597/40 *Nimius,* overmyche. **1568** GRAFTON *Chron.* II. 193 He gave himselfe also to over-muche drinking. **1641** PRYNNE *Antip.* 17 The Kings over-much earnestnesse. **1745** *De Foe's Eng. Tradesman* vi. (1841) I. 41 This was the effect of giving overmuch credit. **1814** CARY *Dante, Paradise* XXII. 24 Fearful of o'er-much presuming. *a* **1875** HELPS *Ess., Org. Daily Life* 134 Listened to with overmuch credulity.

b. *absol.* (rarely as *sb.*) Too great an amount; too much; excess; superfluity.

1303 R. BRUNNE *Handl. Synne* 6518 Ouermoche ys abominable & stynk. **1541** R. COPLAND *Galyen's Terapeutyke* 2 B ij, In an other place we shall speke of the ouer moche or lacke of yᵉ partyes. *a* **1568** ASCHAM *Scholem.* (Arb.) 115 That is, by way of Epitome, to cut all ouer much away. **1784** R. BAGE *Barham Downs* I. 166 In short, this over-much of it is the weakness of the mind. **1847** EMERSON *Poems* (1857) 52 The world hath overmuch of pain.

B. *adv.* To too great an extent or degree; excessively.

c **1380** WYCLIF *Sel. Wks.* III. 364 þes newe ordris and þer fautours failen ouer myche in charite. **1490** CAXTON *Eneydos* xxv. 92 Hym thought ouer moche diffycile and to longe a thinge to make the walles. **1560** DAUS tr. *Sleidane's Comm.* 381 b, If they see themselues ouermuche aggravated. **1653** GATAKER *Vind. Annot. Jer.* 3 For one to be over-much seen in geomancie, palmistrie,..or aruspicie. **1788** *Trifler* No. 14. 189 We are commended not to be religious overmuch. **1850** TENNYSON *In Mem.* lxxxv, I woo your love: I count it crime To mourn for any overmuch.

Hence **over'muchness** [cf. OE. *ofermicelnes*], the condition of being overmuch; excess, superabundance.

1636 B. JONSON *Discov.* Wks. (Rtldg.) 758/2 Superlation and over-muchness amplifies. **1660** tr. *Paracelsus' Archidoxis* II. 80 Sulphur..rules over that which is the overmuchness or superfluity of the other two. **1867** DE MORGAN in *Athenæum* 19 Jan. 90 The omitted words, which Mr. Reddie..no doubt took for pleonasm, superfluity, overmuchness.

over-muck, -multitude, etc.: see OVER-.

†ˌ**over'muse,** *v. Obs. rare.* [OVER- 21, 23.]

1. *trans.* To overcome with bewilderment.

c **1400** *Beryn* 3481 But yee shul fele in every veyn þat ye be vndirmyned, And I-brouʒt at ground, & eke ovir-musid.

2. *refl.* To muse too much; to weary or bewilder oneself by excessive meditation.

a **1652** BROME *City Wit* III. iv, Have you not overmus'd, or overthought your selfe?

† **'overname,** *sb. Obs.* [Rendering Sp. *sobrenombre* = F. *surnom.*] An additional name, surname.

1574 HELLOWES *Gueuara's Fam. Ep.* (1584) 4 Nero the Cruell,..Antony the Meeke. The which ouernames the Romanes gaue them. **1577** —— *Gueuara's Chron.* 254 Iulianus would take that ouername of Commodus.

over'name, *v. rare.* [OVER- 16.] *trans.* To name over or in succession.

1596 SHAKS. *Merch. V.* I. ii. 39. I pray thee ouer-name them, and as thou namest them, I will describe them. **1902** J. H. SKRINE *Pastor Agnorum* 31 Twenty faces in three ranks, and, though no face is like another, we could have safely overnamed the varieties before we fronted them.

over-neat to **over-new:** see OVER-.

overner ('əʊvənə(r)). *local.* [? f. OVER *adv.* + -ER¹, after *northerner, southerner,* etc.] In the Isle of Wight, a visitor or immigrant from the mainland; = OVERER *sb.*² Cf. OVERUN *a.* and *sb.*

1886 W. H. LONG *Dict. Isle of Wight Dial.* 46 *Overner,* or *overun feller,* a person whose home is over the water, on the main land; not a native of the Island. West countrymen, who come to work in the Island, are always 'overun fellers'. .. 'I wish it had capsized they there overners, comen across.' **1951** B. VESEY-FITZGERALD in E. Molony *Portraits of Islands* 65 You may still find in the interior men who speak of people from the mainland as 'overners' (foreigners). **1965** L. WILSON *Portrait of Isle of Wight* i. 15 As well as a strong feeling of security it confers on the inhabitants a sense of identity which 'overners', as they call them, people from over the water, do not possess. **1974** *Isle of Wight County Press* 12 Oct. 19/6 Now there's myself (an Overner, surely) shedding a tear for a scene that had to go.

over'net, *v.* [OVER- 8, 27.]

1. *trans.* To spread a net over; to cover with or as with a net.

1837 CARLYLE *Fr. Rev.* II. v. v, Calonnes, Breteuils hover dim, far-flown, overnetting Europe with intrigues. **1881** PALGRAVE *Visions Eng., P'cess Anne* 160 As a bird by the fowlers o'ernetted.

2. To use nets to excess in fishing.

1899 *Westm. Gaz.* 19 May 2/2 Over-netting is chiefly responsible for the unsatisfactory state of many salmon rivers.

'over-'nice, *a.* [OVER- 28.] Too nice; too fastidious, scrupulous, or particular.

c **1315** SHOREHAM *Poems* IV. 313 þys senne [pride] hys ouer-nyce,..þe senne of meste malice Aʒeyns charyte. **1577** tr. *Bullinger's Decades* (1592) 452 Their..ouernice brauerie in gawdy apparell. **1687** SHADWELL *Juvenal* Ded. A ij, These Nymphs though they are so over nice in words, may perhaps, be frank enough in their actions. **1789** JEFFERSON *Autobiog. & Writ.* (1859) II. 559 Not over-nice in the choice of company. **1856** MRS. BROWNING *Aur. Leigh* VIII. 769 Not being overnice to separate What's element from what's convention.

So **'over-'nicely** *adv.*; **'over-'niceness; 'over-'nicety.**

a **1693** LD. DELAMER *Wks.* (1694) 86 The fierceness of the High Church-Men will be abated, and the overniceness of the Dissenters taken off. **1700** CONGREVE *Way of World* I. vi, You don't take your friend to be over-nicely bred? **1748** RICHARDSON *Clarissa* (1811) V. 8 Overniceness may be underniceness. **1754** —— *Grandison* VI. xxvii. 165 A little over-nicety at setting out, will carry them into a road they never intended to amble in. **1897** CROCKETT *Lads' Love* xxv. 258 It was no time for over-nicety in regard to the fifth commandment.

over-nigh: see OVER- 30.

overnight, over night (ˌəʊvəˈnaɪt), *adv. phr.* (*sb.*, *a.*) [f. OVER *prep.* 18 + NIGHT *sb.*]

A. *adv. phr.* **1.** Before the night (as considered in relation to the following day); on the preceding evening; the night before (with implication that the result of the action continues till the following morning).

c **1374** CHAUCER *Troylus* II. 1500 (1549) Deiphebus had hym prayed ouer nyght To be a frend and helpyng to Criseyde. *c* **1440** *Generydes* 2028 They..dressid all ther harnes ouer nyght, That they myght on the morow..be redy to Batell. **1548–9** (Mar.) *Bk. Com. Prayer, Baptism*, The parentes shall geue knowledge ouer nyght or in the mornyng. **1599** SHAKS. *Much Ado* III. iii. 174 Claudio.. swore hee would..before the whole congregation shame her with what he saw o're night. **1612** BRINSLEY *Lud. Lit.* 296 Their exercises which were giuen ouernight. **1711** ADDISON *Spect.* No. 105 ¶1 His Head ached every Morning with reading of Men over-night. **1886** J. K. JEROME *Idle Thoughts* (1896) 124 We had ordered a duck for dinner over night. **1888** BURGON *Lives 12 Gd. Men* II. ix. 227 His fire was laid overnight, and he lighted it himself when he pleased.

2. During the night, through the night (till the following morning).

1535 COVERDALE *Neh.* xiii. 20 Then remayned the chapmen and marchauntes once or twyce ouer nighte without Ierusalem. **1591** SHAKS. *Two Gent.* IV. ii. 133 And so, good rest. *Pro.* As wretches haue ore-night That wait for execution in the morne. **1879** *Scribner's Mag.* XIX. 682/2 If I feel tired..I'll stay overnight. **1894** H. GARDENER *Unoff. Patriot* 49 He preferred to stay overnight with the family.

3. In the course of a single night; hence, rapidly, instantaneously; without any perceptible or significant passage of time.

1939 JOYCE *Finnegans Wake* II. 378 The unnamed non-irishblooder that becomes a Greenislander overnight! **1942** E. WAUGH *Put out More Flags* 246 Alastair's battalion found itself overnight converted from a unit in the early stages of training into first line troops. **1955** H. ROTH *Sleeper* viii. 60 Adults don't change—rarely, at any rate, and not overnight. **1955** 'A. GILBERT' *Is she Dead Too?* ii. 30 She'd been there two years when Alice Poulden died. It all seemed to happen overnight as you might say. **1957** F. & R. LOCKRIDGE *Practise to Deceive* (1959) vi. 90 Lane..was already 'the' polo player. A handicap justifying such phrasing is not acquired over-night. **1963** *Cambr. Rev.* 4 May 400/1 An article which overnight catapulted him to fame. **1966** *Word Study* Dec. 5/2 Overnight the vernacular of space became a popular idiom. **1972** P. GREEN *Shadow of Parthenon* 15 The classics have nearly half a century of revolutionary critical development to catch up on: the thing cannot be achieved overnight. **1972** *Observer* 12 Nov. 36/7 The great original thinker, the noble if flawed human being, the entranced and hallowed poet-sage—all these have virtually been blown away overnight. **1973** [see OUSTER[1]].

B. *sb.* **1.** The preceding evening. (Now chiefly *U.S.*)

1581 MULCASTER *Positions* xxxii. (1887) 117 Before the ouernightes diet be thoroughly digested. **1601** SHAKS. *All's Well* III. iv. 23 If I had giuen you this at ouer-night, She might haue beene ore-tane. **1607** —— *Timon* IV. iii. 227 To cure thy o're-nights surfet. **1705** S. WHATELY in W. S. Perry *Hist. Coll. Amer. Col. Ch.* I. 170 Came to Town the over night before that general meeting. **1824** *Compl. Hist. Murd. Weare* App. 19 He had heard the report of a Gun in the lane on the overnight. **1871** HOWELLS *Wedd. Journ.* (1892) 28 The air,..freshened by the over-night's storm.

2. A stop or halt lasting for one night; also, a person who stops at a place for a single night (see quots.); something that arrived during the night.

1959 *Times Lit. Suppl.* 9 Oct. 573/4 A highly convincing background of aviation and suburbia, dinettes, lounges (domestic, not airport), overnights and rosters. **1964** *Economist* 11 Jan. 114/2 The YHA..had a record number of ..'overnights' (the total number of nights that beds were occupied). **1968** J. LOCK *Lady Policeman* xiii. 117 The gaoler brings the 'overnights' from the cells. **1974** *Guardian* 23 Mar. 14/3 With two overnights in Interlaken..it sounded..soothing enough. **1976** C. WESTON *Rouse Demon* (1977) i. 4 Ten minutes to spare, pounding up the stairs to the Detective Bureau... Time to skim through the overnights before the morning rundown.

C. *attrib.* or *adj.* **1.** Of or belonging to the previous evening; done, happening, etc., overnight.

1824 GALT *Rothelan* I. II. xi. 250 He found no other traces of the Scottish army there, than the broken weapons of the overnight assault. **1859** LANG *Wand. India* 19 The result of the two over-night glasses of brandy. **1870** *Daily News* 25 Nov., The limit of my overnight journey.

2. a. Designating a price or value as at the end of business on a particular day. **b.** Applied to money lent or borrowed, or otherwise made available, from one day to the next.

1909 *Westm. Gaz.* 7 Aug. 12/1 Finishing on the other side very strongly, the overnight prices were well above those ruling in the 'House' at the close of yesterday afternoon. **1928** *Daily Mail* 9 Aug. 18/6 Borrowers occasionally paid up to 4½ per cent. for fresh overnight money. **1930** M. CLARK *Home Trade* xxix. 233 Sometimes the loan is merely one from one day to the next—often termed 'overnight loans'; at other times it is for a short period of say seven days ('weekly loans'). **1973** *Times* 2 Feb. 14/7 New York money men have been known to quake in the knowledge that they have on deposit $1,000m of overnight money—money which can be withdrawn the next morning.

3. Of a person: transient, staying overnight; *fig.*, instantaneously esteemed or popular. Of a thing: achieved or accomplished rapidly.

1934 [see *air hostess* s.v. AIR *sb.*[1] III. 4]. **1960** *News Chron.* 18 Mar. 6/6 He has become an over-night hero to countless people. **1961** *Sunday Express* 7 May 15/5 One really eye-catching picture in a top magazine, and she is an overnight star. **1974** S. SHELDON *Other Side of Midnight* iv. 86 The war, like all wars, had created overnight millionaires. **1974** HAWKEY & BINGHAM *Wild Card* xv. 127 His novel advances in the field of biodegradable materials..had brought him an overnight reputation.

4. Special collocations, as ***overnight bag, case***, a light case or holdall carried by a traveller; ***overnight telegram***, a telegram intended for delivery the following morning.

1925 *New Yorker* 17 Oct. 32/2 This is simply wonderful for travelers, though, as an *overnight bag, it has the disadvantage of having no room in the bag for anything except, perhaps, a French nightie. **1955** 'N. SHUTE' *Requiem for Wren* i. 2 He took the overnight bag from me. **1972** M. CRICHTON *Terminal Man* I. v. 43 She lifted a small blue overnight bag. **1934** WEBSTER, *Overnight case. **1935** *Montgomery Ward Catal.* 582 Wards finest—tray fitted overnight case. **1952** 'J. TEY' *Singing Sands* xiv. 238, I indicated my small overnight case which was lying..on the bunk. **1970** G. F. NEWMAN *Sir, You Bastard* 265 The overnight case belonged to Sneed. **1955** *P.O. Guide* July 309 *Overnight telegrams are accepted between the hours of 8 a.m. and 10 p.m. daily for delivery next day..normally by the first post. **1974** *Ibid.* Nov. 367 An Overnight telegram may be sent between 8 a.m. and 10.30 p.m. for delivery, normally by first post, the following morning... The charge is 40p for 10 words or less and 2p for each extra word.

overˈnight, *v.* [f. the adv. phr.; cf. G. *übernachten*.] *intr.* To pass the night (*at* or *in*); to lodge for the night.

[**1876** GEO. ELIOT *Let.* 2 Sept. (1956) VI. 275 We saw no English or American visitors, except such as 'übernachten' there and pass on.] **1891** M. M. DOWIE *Girl in Karpathians* xiii. 177 He invites us to over-night at his house. Will you go? **1962** *Daily Progress* (Charlottesville, Va.) 2 Nov. 6/6 When a stewardess 'overnights' she spends the night in the city where the flight terminates. **1965** *Harper's Bazaar* Dec. 80/1 Anyone who has over-nighted in pre-Hilton Istanbul. **1971** R. FALKIRK *Chill Factor* v. 47 Her Icelandic philosophy was immensely popular..wherever Icelandair overnighted. **1971** *Advocate-News* (Barbados) 20 Mar. 1/2 At the conclusion of his South American visits the President and party will again over night in Barbados on March 31 and leave for home on April 1. **1972** *Drive* Spring 49/2 With the horses provided you could trek deep into the forest, overnighting in a bivouac. **1976** J. B. HILTON *Gamekeeper's Gallows* xviii. 182 Fletcher over-nighted at Derby.

Hence **overˈnighting** *vbl. sb.* (also *attrib.*).

1948 K. ANTHONY *Lambs* vi. 132 The clambering in and out of stage-coaches, the overnighting in strange taverns. **1966** *Guardian* 19 Mar. 1/3 Overnighting facilities for climbers have been cut off, and visitors generally discouraged. **1969** 'J. MORRIS' *Fever Grass* x. 95 D'you have a spare shirt for this big man here? He didn't plan on overnighting.

ˌoverˈnighter. [f. OVERNIGHT *adv. phr.* + -ER[1].]

a. = *overnight bag* (see OVERNIGHT *a.* 4).

1959 *Sears, Roebuck Catal.* Spring–Summer 865/1 Easier Packing... 18-inch Overniter. **1967** 'S. MARLOWE' *Second Longest Night* vi. 58 Armed with two overnighters and the necessary toilet articles. **1967** K. GILES *Death in Diamonds* iv. 75 One suitcase..and a little overnighter with electric razor and stuff. **1972** M. CRICHTON *Terminal Man* I. v. 45 Benson placed the screwdrivers into the overnighter.

b. A person who stops at a place overnight (cf. OVERNIGHT *sb.* 2).

1961 F. & R. LOCKRIDGE *Murder has its Points* (1962) ix. 96 At the Hotel Dumont there had, at the time in issue, been twenty-three overnighters. **1977** *Daily Tel.* 7 June 1/1 The area approaching St Paul's Cathedral was also becoming filled with overnighters.

†**overˈnim**, *v. Obs.* Pa. pple. overnome. [f. OVER- 14 + NIM *v.* to take. See OVERTAKE. (OE. had *oferniman* in senses 'take by violence, violate, carry off by force.')] *trans.* To overtake.

c **1325** *Poem Times Edw. II* (Percy) i, Hunger & derthe The poor hath overnome. *c* **1430** *Syr Gener.* (Roxb.) 8156 To the Citie or that thei come, Many good knightes wer ouernome.

overnoint to **over-nourish**: see OVER-.

ˈover-note. [OVER- 1 e.] A note heard through or above other sounds; an overtone.

1917 CONRAD *Shadow-Line* 204 He..burst into..a loud laugh... It was a provoking, mocking peal, with a hair-raising, screeching over-note of defiance.

†**ˈover-ˈnumber**, *sb. Obs.* [OVER- 29 d.] An excessive number. So **ˌoverˈnumber** *v. trans.* [OVER- 22], to exceed in number, to outnumber; **ˈover-ˈnumerous** *a.* [OVER- 28], too numerous.

1599 SIR E. WATSON in *Buccleuch MSS.* (Hist. MSS. Comm.) I. 234 The *over number of people. **1681** *Whole Duty Nations* 50 In such a proportion of number..that the principal Duties may not be defeated by the over-number. **1654–66** EARL ORRERY *Parthen.* (1676) 268 Those Divisions ..being infinitely *over-numbered..were totally routed. **1805** SOUTHEY *Madoc* II. xv, In tenfold troops Their foemen overnumbering. **1701** GREW *Cosm. Sacra* IV. viii. §43. 246 These Precepts..are not *overnumerous. **1735** SOMERVILLE *Chase* III. Argt., Censure of an overnumerous pack.

over-nurse to **over-offended**: see OVER-.

†**over-ˈoffice**, *v. Obs. nonce-wd.* [Cf. OVER *prep.* 8, OVER- 2.] *trans.* To lord it over by virtue of one's office; to exercise one's office over.

1602 SHAKS. *Ham.* V. i. 87 It might be the Pate of a Polititian which this Asse o're Offices: one that could circumuent God, might it not?

ˈover-oˈfficious, *a.* [OVER- 28.] Too officious. So **ˈover-oˈfficiousness.**

a **1610** HEALEY *Theophrastus* (1636) 51 Impertinent dilligence, or over-officiousnesse. **1647** H. MORE *Song of Soul* To Rdr. 7/2 Some sportfull or over officious spirit. **1703** COLLIER *Ess. Mor. Subj.* II. (1709) 75 To fortify him in an Errour by an Over-officiousness. **1842** SYD. SMITH *Locking in on Railw.* Wks. 1859 II. 322/2 Nothing..can be more utterly silly..than this over-officious care of the public.

over-often: see OVER- 30.

ˈover-ˈold, *a.* [OVER- 28.] Exceedingly old, too old, antiquated. Hence **ˈover-ˈoldness.**

c **1374** CHAUCER *Boeth.* I. pr. iii. 6 (Camb. MS.) Of which foolk the renon nis neyther ouer old ne vn-solempne. **1561** DAUS tr. *Bullinger on Apoc.* (1573) 78 b, We who..haue departed from the oueroldness of the lawe written, and walke in newnesse of life. **1611** COTGR., *Suragé*, decrepite, ouer-old, growne farre in yeares. **1875** W. MORRIS tr. *Virgil's Aeneids* VIII. 509 My body over-old for deeds begrudged such government. **1883** LD. R. GOWER *My Reminisc.* II. 140 Their children..have a delicate over-old look for their age.

over-open to **over-painful**: see OVER-.

overpaint (-ˈpeɪnt), *v.* [OVER- 8, 27.]

†**1.** *trans.* To paint over, cover with another colour. *Obs.*

1611 SPEED *Hist. Gt. Brit.* IX. xii. §135. 702 To ouer-paint his collusions and deuises for sauing his honour. **1614** RALEIGH *Hist. World* II. xvi. §1 (1634) 394, I shall not need to over-paint that which is garnished with better colours already, than I can lay on.

2. To colour or depict too highly.

a **1750** A. HILL (T.), Him whom no verse overpaints. **1870** J. H. FRISWELL *Mod. Men Lett.* iv. 84 It is doubtful whether he over-paints the truth.

overpaint (ˈəʊvəpeɪnt), *sb.* [OVER- 8 c.] A second or further layer of paint; a paint used for overpainting.

1958 *Times* 1 July 5/4 The overpaint has now been cleaned off, revealing not only the skull which Petty holds but also two other skulls engraved on the page of the book to which the left hand is pointing. **1973** *Canad. Antiques Collector* Jan.–Feb. 17/1 This cupboard, when found, was over-painted; the over-paint was carefully removed to expose the original red on the cupboard proper, and the blue-green on the cornice and decorative mouldings. **1973** F. TAUBES *Painter's Dict.* 168 The evidence or absence of brushstrokes in the underpainting should be considered, for these may interfere with the overpaints.

ˌoverˈpainted, *ppl. a.* [OVER- 8 b.] That has been painted over another painted surface.

1967 J. N. BARRON *Lang. of Painting* 195 The painter plans the underpainting to obtain the variety of effects and optical mixtures he wishes in combination with, or in contrast to, the subsequent overpainted layers of paint. **1973** *Guardian* 16 Mar. 13/5 The National Portrait Gallery is.. showing again..the family portrait of Sir Thomas More... The overpainted nineteenth century brown background has been removed.

overˈpainting, *vbl. sb.* [OVER- 8 b.] The action of the verb OVERPAINT (sense 1); a layer of paint applied over another.

1928 *Daily Express* 20 Dec. 1/3 The explanation of the over-painting is simple. The sitter..decided to have his sheriff's robes painted over the clothes in Holbein's picture. **1935** E. NEUHAUS tr. *Doerner's Materials of Artist* iv. 203 The overpainting must be applied somewhat more liquidly —at least in the first layer—than the underpainting. **1954** M. RICKERT *Painting in Brit.: Middle Ages* i. 23 The overpainting in thick white and yellow pigment. **1958** tr. *K. Herberts's Artists' Techniques* 140 Overpainting must be done with great care, since the lower layers of paint remain effaceable. **1973** *Guardian* 16 Mar. 26/1 Restoration..has removed the overpainting which had made the picture look unnaturally flat.

over-pamper, -park, etc.: see OVER-.

overˈpark, *v. U.S.* [OVER- 27.] *intr.* To park a motor vehicle for longer than the permitted period. So **overˈparked** *ppl. a.*, **overˈparking** *vbl. sb.*

1938 *Daily Progress* (Charlottesville, Va.) 3 Mar. 1/8 The case of Clyde Anable, charged with overparking. **1957** *Times* (Seattle) 12 Sept. 38 The City Council today authorized the Police Department to hire ten 'meter maids', uniformed women who will patrol the streets and write tickets for overparking. **1974** *Keowee Courier* (Walhalla, S. Carolina) 24 Apr. 7/1 Gaillard also reported that the police are now issuing 'courtesy tickets' to people who overpark. These tickets provide only a friendly warning, and no fine, unless a person accumulates two in one day or three within a week. **1976** 'J. ROSS' *I know what it's like to Die* xxviii. 177 His Renault car had..been there all day... It had incurred fines for overparking. **1977** 'L. EGAN' *Blind Search* iv. 53 Officious meter maids checking overparked cars.

†**ˈoverˌpart.** *Obs.* [prop. two words: see OVER *a.* 1.] The upper part.

1398 [see OVER *a.* 1]. **1562** TURNER *Herbal* II. 77 b, It groweth not depe in yᵉ grounde, but in the ouerparte of it. **1562** —— *Baths* 6 It weakeneth the ouerparte and netherparte of the stomack. **1623** COCKERAM I, *Horizon*, a circle diuiding the ouerpart of Heauen from the other halfe.

overparted (ˌəʊvəˈpɑːtɪd), *a.* [f. OVER- 26 + PART *sb.* + -ED[2].] Having too difficult a part, or too many parts, to play. Also *transf.*

In quot. 1975[2] the sense is 'having a voice too strong for the part'.

1588 SHAKS. *L.L.L.* v. ii. 588 He is a maruellous good neighbour insooth, and a verie good Bowler: but for Alisander, alas you see, how 'tis a little ore-parted. **1614** B. JONSON *Barth. Fair* III. iv, How now, Numps! almost tir'd i' your Protectorship? ouerparted? ouerparted? **1896** *Nation* (N.Y.) 16 July 56/2 Viewed in comparison with the magnitude of the results, he is distinctly overparted. **1896** G. B. SHAW *How to become Mus. Critic* (1960) 240 As Siegmund the Unlucky he was quite overparted. *Ibid.* 244 He was overparted in Siegfried. **1959** *Times* 19 Nov. 16/2 Mr. William McAlpine seemed vocally over-parted as Boris. **1966** *New Statesman* 25 Mar. 437/3 Overparted Mr Constantine is persuaded to deliver himself of some grand lines, among which '*Je crois aux données immédiates de la conscience*' is probably as ludicrous as any. **1975** *Bookseller* 26 July 315/1 Seemed rather over-parted as the *Sunday Telegraph* lead reviewer. **1975** *Gramophone* Sept. 505/1 For some, Fischer-Dieskau is considerably over-parted. **1977** *Listener* 5 May 592/2 The baritone and tenor soloists.. rather seized the attention from the sadly overparted soprano.

'over-'partial, *a.* [OVER- 28.] Too partial; unduly partial.

a **1586** SIDNEY *Arcadia* (1622) 109 Shee would,.. clasping with him, come downe together, to be parted by the ouer-partiall beholders. **1668** H. MORE *Div. Dial.* i. § 12 (1713) 23, I cannot but deem you an over-partial Mechanist. *a* **1720** SHEFFIELD (Dk. Buckhm.) *Wks.* (1753) II. 20 The Court was inclined before, not to be overpartial to Prince Rupert. **1895** *Chamb. Jrnl.* XII. 784/1 This person.. was overpartial to whisky.

over-particular: see OVER- 28.

†**'overˌparty**. *Obs.* [See OVER *a.* 1.] = OVERPART; upper part; surface.

1398 TREVISA *Barth. De P.R.* VIII. xxviii. (Tollem. MS.), Also he.. often cloþeþ and reneweþ þe ouerparti of þe erþe with herbes. **1483** CAXTON *Gold. Leg.* 75 b/1 Y^e cyte of Neptalym whiche is in the ouerpartyes of galylee.

overpass (əʊvəˈpɑːs, -pæs), *v.* Now somewhat *rare.* Pa. t. and pple. **overpassed, -past.** [f. OVER- 9, 10, etc. + PASS *v.*]

I. Transitive senses, in which *over-* stands in prepositional relation to the object.

* Literal or physical senses.

1. To pass over, travel over, move across or along.

1297 R. GLOUC. (Rolls) 228 And suþþe he ssulde mani lond over passi and wende. **1495** *Trevisa's Barth. De P.R.* XIII. v. (W. de W.) C v b/1 The ryuer Nilus makyth the londe that he ouerpassyth be full plenteuous of corne and fruyte. **1571** GOLDING *Calvin on Ps.* lxi. 2 He overpassed ye distance that was betwixt him and it. **1891** R. KIPLING *Light that Failed* ii, The stream was falling and.. the next few miles would be no light thing for the whale-boats to overpass.

2. To pass across, to the other side of, or beyond; to cross.

a **1340** HAMPOLE *Psalter* xvii. 32 In my god i sall ouerpasse þe wall. **1422** tr. *Secreta Secret., Priv. Priv.* xii. 141 The ryuers and wateres [the rain] makyth ouer-Passe har boundys. **1599** THYNNE *Animadv.* Ded. (1865) 2 He whiche hathe once ouer passed the frontiers of modestye. **1681** DRYDEN *Spanish Friar* III. 37, I stood on a wide River's bank, Which I must needs o'erpass. **1846** TRENCH *Mirac.* xxiii. (1862) 342 At no time.. does our Lord seem to have overpassed the limits of the Holy Land.

3. To rise above; to extend or project beyond.

a **1425** *Cursor M.* 1838 (Trin.) þe heȝest hille.. þe flood ouer passed seuen elle & more. **1737** BRACKEN *Farriery Impr.* (1756) I. 323 If the upper overpass the under Teeth. **1938** *Times* 16 Aug. 15/4 The stream.. swelled uproariously. It did not anywhere overpass its deeply engraved channel, but raced helter-skelter and bank high to the road and the beach.

4. To pass by; to come up to or alongside of and go beyond. [OVER- 13.]

1530 PALSGR. 649/1, I overpasse, as a man dothe.. a companye that he overtaketh. **1553** EDEN *Treat. Newe Ind.* (Arb.) 38 Saylinge farre beyond this Region, and ouerpassinge manye countreyes.. we came to another nacion.

** Figurative senses corresponding to prec.

5. a. To pass through, get through, get to the end of (a period, or an action, experience, etc.); often including the notion 'to get through or out of successfully or safely, get over, surmount'; more rarely, to pass, spend (time). [OVER- 16, 17.]

a **1300** *Cursor M.* 24280 Þis ilk pine es for me dight,.. Ouer-pas it sal i son. *c* **1375** *Ibid.* 26633 (Fairf.) Ouer-passe þou noȝt þe lentin-tide. *c* **1470** HENRY *Wallace* v. 369 Wallace him herd, quhen he his slepe ourpast. **1577** NORTHBROOKE *Dicing* (1843) 44 Halfe of the year, and more, was ouer-passed.. in loytering and vaine pastimes. **1645** MRQ. WORC. in Dircks *Life* viii. (1865) 125 Having overpassed many rubs and difficulties. **1831** COLERIDGE in *Lit. Rem.* (1838) III. 101 Having now overpassed six-sevenths of the ordinary period allotted to human life. **1876** T. HARDY *Ethelberta* (1890) 161 It became imperative to consider how best to overpass a more general catastrophe.

†**b.** To pass through in one's mind. *Obs.*

1658 J. WEBB *Cleopatra* VIII. I. 10 The faire Princesse sensible at this remembrance could not overpasse it in her spirit without sighs and sobbs.

†**6.** To come over or affect, as an influence, emotion, etc.; in quot. 1679, to overspread. *Obs.*

a **1300** *Cursor M.* 8987 (Cott.) Ouer passed [*Trin.* Ouer-passed him] has þat caitiue kind, And mad king salamon al blind. **1500–20** DUNBAR *Poems* lxxiv. 18 Sic deidlie dwawmes.. Ane hundrithe tymes hes my hairt ouirpast. **1679** KING in G. Hickes *Spirit of Popery* 47 The horrid Prophanity that has overpassed the whole Land.

7. a. To go (or be) beyond in amount, rate, value, excellence, etc.; to extend or lie beyond the range or scope of; to exceed, excel, transcend, surpass.

a **1300** *Cursor M.* 12707 Sent Ion, þe wangelist.. All þe appostells he ouer-past. *c* **1374** CHAUCER *Boeth.* v. pr. vi. 135 (Camb. MS.) The science of him þat ouer passeth al temperel moeuement. **1530** PALSGR. 649/1, I overpasse, I excede in value or in any other thyng. **1622** MALYNES *Anc. Law-Merch.* 111 A Factor is bound to answere the losse which happeneth by ouerpassing or exceeding his Commission. **1835** I. TAYLOR *Spir. Despot.* iii. 103 A generous enthusiasm.. will probably overpass the necessities of the occasion. **1871** DIXON *Tower* IV. vii. 63 He overpassed his sire in comic power.

b. To go beyond the limits or restrictions of, to transgress. [OVER- 12]

c **1399** *Pol. Poems* (Rolls) II. 7 The werre maketh the grete citee lasse, And dothe the lawe his reules overpasse. **1450–80** tr. *Secreta Secret.* 11 He ouyr passith the wey of trouthe, he settith at nought.. goddis lawe. **1597** BEARD *Theatre God's Judgem.* (1612) 527 This neither ought nor can be done.. without ouerpassing the bounds of his limited power. **1905** *Daily Chron.* 24 Oct. 1 The Russian and Austrian agents in Uskub overpass their duties. *a* **1973** J. R. R. TOLKIEN *Silmarillion* (1977) 262 But the design of Manwë was that the Númenóreans should not.. desire to overpass the limits set to their bliss.

8. a. To pass over, leave unnoticed or unmentioned, leave out, omit. Now *rare.* [OVER- 5 b.]

1382 WYCLIF *Gen.* xviii. 4 Lord, if I have foundun grace in thin eyen, overpasse thow not thi servaunt. **1494** FABYAN *Chron.* v. lxxviii. 57 But for the names.. be derke to Englysshe vnderstandynge, therfore I ouerpasse theym, and folowe the Storye. **1559** MORWYNG *Evonym.* 284 Manye other thinges which for brevities sake I overpas. **1601** HOLLAND *Pliny* II. 627 The bloud-stone Hæmatites.. a stone that I must not ouerpasse in silence. **1779–81** JOHNSON *L.P., Dryden* Wks. II. 336 The reason which he gives for printing what was never acted, cannot be overpassed. **1831** SIR W. HAMILTON *Discuss.* (1852) 233 Some lesser errors.. we overpass. **1872** G. M. HOPKINS *Let.* 5 Mar. (1956) 118, I cannot tell how I have overpassed your birthday and only been recalled to it now too late by seeing the date March 3 on a letter.

†**b.** Of a thing: To pass by, leave unaffected, 'escape' (a person). *Obs.*

1535 COVERDALE *Ecclus.* xiv. 14 Let not ye porcion of ye good daie ouerpas the.

II. Intrans. senses, in which *over-* is adverbial.

9. To pass over, pass across or overhead.

a **1340** HAMPOLE *Psalter* x. 1 How say ȝe til my saule, Ouerpasse in til þe hill as a sparow? *c* **1400** *Rom. Rose* 5343 Till whan the shadow is ouerpast. **1797** SOUTHEY *Triumph of Woman* 288 And birds o'erpassing hear, and drop, and die. **1874** F. E. ABBOT *Little Margaret*, When the shadows overpass.

10. a. Of time, actions, experiences, etc.: To pass away, come to an end; to pass, pass by, elapse. Most often in *pa. pple.* = At an end, past, 'over'.

c **1325** *Song Deo Gratias* 54 in *E.E.P.* (1862) 125 And sumtyme plesaunce wol ouerpas. **1494** FABYAN *Chron.* VI. clxxxi. 179 The monkes.. layde it in the church of seynt Anyan tyll the persecucion were ouerpassed. **1514** BARCLAY *Cyt. & Uplondyshm.* (Percy Soc.) p. lxxii, No day overpasseth exempt of busynes. *c* **1592** MARLOWE *Massacre Paris* II. vi, Come, my lords; now that this storm is overpast. **1603** KNOLLES *Hist. Turks* (1621) 54 Afterwards the furie of the people overpassed. **1874** H. R. REYNOLDS *John Bapt.* ii. 91 The strange eclipse of His beams is overpassed. **1895** *Edin. Rev.* July 162 The crisis was virtually overpast.

†**b.** To 'pass', take place, happen. *Obs. rare.*

1530 PALSGR. 382 The partyculer actes & cyrcumstances whiche overpassed in the meane whyle.

†**11.** To exceed, go to excess; to be in excess, be over. *Obs.*

c **1400** tr. *Secreta Secret., Gov. Lordsh.* 67 Who so ouerpassys yn ful or voyd, yn slepynge or wakynge,.. he mowe noght eschewe maladyes. **1530** PALSGR. 649/1, I overpasse, I remayne besydes the juste nombre and quantyte.. *je surabonde*. This somme is nat just yet for this overpasseth.

†**12.** To pass or remain unnoticed, to be let alone or omitted; chiefly in phr. ***to let it overpass*** = to let it pass, take no notice of it (= sense 8).

c **1350** *Will. Palerne* 4113, I leued hire þan lelly and lett it ouer-pase. *c* **1400** *Destr. Troy* 5084 Laghe at it lightly and let it ouer pas. **1525** LD. BERNERS *Froiss.* II. lxxxv. [lxxxi.] 254 Thynke you y^t y^e frensshe kynge wyl suffre y^t matter thus to ouerpas? *a* **1575** *Wyfe lapped Morrelles Skin* 695 in Hazl. *E.P.P.* IV. 208 O, good wife, cease and let this ouerpasse.

Hence **over'passed, -past** *ppl. a.*, that has come to an end, past; **over'passing** *vbl. sb.*, a passing over or across, excess, etc.; **over'passing** *ppl. a.*, surpassing; *poet.* as *adv.* exceedingly, 'passing'.

c **1340** HAMPOLE *Prose Tr.* (1866) 38 To behalde þe vertus and þe ouer-passande grace of þe saule of Ihesu. **1382** WYCLIF *Obad.* i. 19 And transmygracioun, or ouer passynge. **1552** HULOET, Ouerpassynge, *transcursus*. **1582** T. WATSON *Cent. Loue* xcviii. Argt., The present title of his ouerpassed Loue. **1865** MILL *Auguste Comte* 14 He deemed all real knowledge of a commencement inaccessible to us, and the inquiry into it an overpassing of the essential limits of our mental faculties. **1898** S. EVANS *Holy Graal* 107 So overpassing rich was it.

'overpass, *sb.* orig. *U.S.* Also **over-pass.** [OVER- 1 d.] A raised stretch of road or railway line that passes over another road or railway line; = FLY-OVER 1. Also *attrib.*

1929 *Amer. City* Oct. 104/2 In certain cases where the construction of under- or over-passes cannot be avoided.. my system simplifies them to an astonishing extent. **1933** [see *clover-leaf* s.v. CLOVER *sb.* 4]. **1938** *Sun* (Baltimore) 31 Aug. 7/3 Overpasses were built in both communities after years of agitation and numbers of serious crossing accidents. **1952** [see EXPRESSWAY]. **1959** *Daily Tel.* 9 Nov. 1/1 But they refused to allow a car, scooter or even a bicycle to be pushed on these overpass roads. **1964** L. DEIGHTON *Funeral in Berlin* li. 313 Dominating the whole scene is the gleaming stone pillar of the Cenotaph like the freshly-built leg of a new overpass. **1969** *New Scientist* 17 Apr. 105/1 A major earthquake would.. cause the over-passes into the city to collapse. **1973** H. NIELSEN *Severed Key* i. 11 The traffic lanes leading away from the airport were packed. Once over the overpass, Keith made a sharp right turn. **1974** *Anderson* (S. Carolina) *Independent* 23 Apr. 3A/5 A 180-foot overpass over Clinchfield railroad tracks on secondary road 126 in Spartanburg went to Dickerson, Inc., of Monroe N.C., which entered a low bid of $335,360. **1976** *National Observer* (U.S.) 5 June 1/1 As you top an overpass, your eyes are drawn to a red, white, and blue water tower on the horizon.

overpassionate *a.*: see OVER- 28.

overpay (əʊvəˈpeɪ), *v.* [OVER- 26.] To pay too higly, pay more than is due.

1. *trans.* To pay or recompense (a person, a service, etc.) beyond what is due or deserved; to give, or be, a more than sufficient recompense for; *fig.* to do more than compensate; to make up for superabundantly. Also *absol.* or *intr.*

1601 SHAKS. *All's Well* III. vii. 16 Let me buy your friendly helpe thus farre, Which I will ouer-pay, and pay againe When I haue found it. **1611** —— *Cymb.* II. iv. 10 Your very goodnesse, and your company, Ore-payes all I can do. **1702** PEPYS *Let.* 3 Oct., I cannot but think myself already overpaid. **1709** PRIOR *Henry & Emma* 8 And with one Heav'nly Smile o'erpay his Pains. **1855** MACAULAY *Hist. Eng.* xv. III. 539 His services were overpaid with honours and riches. **1859** TENNYSON *Enid* 1069 My lord, you overpay me fifty-fold.

2. *trans.* To pay more than (an amount or price); to pay (money) in excess of what is due.

1664 ATKYNS *Orig. Printing* 15 Sell the Impression for 1600*l.*.. which Impression alone over-payes them all the Moneys they are out of Purse. **1679–88** *Secr. Serv. Money Chas. & Jas.* (Camden) 130 To reimburse him so much money he hath overpaid for fee-farme rents. **1784** COWPER *Task* VI. 860 Thou hast made it thine by purchase,.. And overpaid its value with thy blood.

So **'over-pay** *sb.*; **over-'payment**.

1702 PEPYS *Corr.* Diary, etc. 1879 VI. 249, 14 Nov... I beg their believing me most sensible of this their over-payment. *a* **1816** BENTHAM *Offic. Apt. Maximized, Introd. View* (1830) 21 Supposing, indeed, the over-pay derived from crime—obtained, for example, by false pretences. **1884** *Weekly Notes* 26 Apr. 105/2 Whether there had been an over-payment to the society by one of its members.

over-peacock *v.*: see OVER- 27.

overpeaze, obs. form of OVERPOISE.

over-'pedal, *v.* [OVER- 27.] *intr.* and *trans.* To over-use a piano's sustaining pedal; to play using the sustaining pedal too much. Hence **over-'pedalled** *ppl. a.*, **over-'pedalling** *vbl. sb.*

1961 *Times* 12 Apr. 6/1 He [*sc.* the pianist] was liable to force his tone, over-pedal. **1968** *Daily Tel.* 1 Nov. 21/3 The tempestuous coda to the Ballade, for instance, was smudged through over-pedalling. **1976** *Gramophone* June 69/1 Berman himself often overpedals in an over-resonant studio so that bigger climaxes are just a confused noise. **1976** *Ibid.* Sept. 421/3 The cadenza.. is over-pedalled. **1976** *Daily Tel.* 29 Nov. 11/1 More control of rubato and over-pedalling is needed, but she has all the musical and technical talent to be an important pianist.

overpeer (əʊvəˈpɪə(r)), *v.* [OVER- 7, 1 (*b*). In sense 1 f. PEER *v.* to look; but in 2 app. associated with PEER *sb.* equal, etc., or its derived vb. PEER to equal, rival, vie with: cf. OUTPEER *v.*, of which *overpeer* is in some cases a synonym.]

1. *trans.* To peer over, look over, look across from above, look down on.

1589 GREENE *Menaphon* Wks. (Grosart) VI. 36 A hill that ouer-peered the great Mediterraneum. **1591** SHAKS. *1 Hen. VI*, I. iv. 11 To ouer-peere the Citie, And thence discouer, how with most aduantage They may vex vs with Shot or with Assault. **1596** H. CLAPHAM *Briefe Bible* I. 63 Moses.. mounteth the Mount Nebo: from whence overpeering Iordan, he beholdeth the land of Promise. **1898** *Daily Chron.* 17 Oct. 5/1 The nymph.. fancied that an officer overpeering her garden wall like that must necessarily be on horseback!

†**b.** To 'look down upon', treat with contempt, domineer over. *Obs.*

1583 GOLDING *Calvin on Deut.* xxxv. 209 If we be so high-minded that euerie of vs could finde in his heart to ouer-peere his Neighbour. **1590** MARLOWE *Edw. II*, I. iv, We will not thus be faced and over-peered.

2. To rise or appear above; to tower over; to have a higher position than; to excel, outpeer.

1565 GOLDING *Ovid's Met.* III. (1593) 60 Phœbe was of personage so comely and so tall, That by the middle of her necke she over-peerd them all. **1586** KYD *Wks.* (1901) 339 With thy Roselike, Royal peace (O Prince) all other princes thou must ouer-peere. **1596** SHAKS. *Merch. V.* I. i. 12 Your Argosies, with portly saile, Like Signiors and rich Burgers on the flood, .. Do ouer-peere, the pettie Traffiquers That curtsie to them. **1599** NASHE *Lenten Stuffe* (1871) 26 For a commodious green place, .. not Salisbury Plain or Newmarket Heath .. may overpeer, or outcrow her. **1647** TRAPP *Marrow Gd. Authors* in *Comm. Ep.* 652 Like the Ivy which rising at the foot, will over-peer the highest wall. **1899** J. SMITH *Chr. Charac. as Soc. Power* 123 Generous and unselfish principles overpeer the coarser and more self-regarding impulses.

Hence **over'peering** *vbl. sb.* and *ppl. a.*

1598 J. DICKENSON *Greene in Conc.* (1878) 150 Wind-tossed waues which with a gyring course Circle the Centers-ouer-peering maine. **1611** COTGR., *Sursaille*, .. an ouerpeering, or ouergrowing. **1615** G. SANDYS *Trav.* 188 This valley of Iehosaphat .. to the East of the City, contracted betweene it and the ouer-pearing hils of the opposite Oliuet. **1895** *Q. Rev.* Apr. 349 The penalty of overpeering science.

overpending, -pentise: see OVER- 1.

ˌover-'people, *v.* [OVER- 27.] *trans.* To people too much, overstock with people. (Chiefly in *pa. pple.*) So **ˌover-'peopled** *ppl. a.*

1683 *Apol. Prot. France* Pref. 2 Now that we should be over-peopled, I think there is no danger. **1711** SHAFTESB. *Charac.* (1737) III. 42 Nothing more dangerous than the over-peopling any manufacture. **1821** BYRON *Cain* I. i. 520 The unpeopled earth—and the o'er-peopled Hell. **1830** MISS MITFORD *Village* Ser. IV. (1863) 262 That fair demesne of theirs, which is to say, over-peopled. **1832** HT. MARTINEAU *Weal & Woe* vi. 83 The half-starved multitudes of an over-peopled kingdom.

†over'perch, *v. Obs.* [OVER- 5.] *trans.* To surmount as by perching upon; to fly over.

1592 SHAKS. *Rom. & Jul.* II. ii. 66 (Qo. 2) With loues light wings did I orepearch these walls.

over-peremptory, -perk, etc.: see OVER-.

over-per'suade, *v.* [OVER- 11.] *trans.* To bring over by persuasion, persuade effectually; *esp.* to persuade (a person) to some action or course against his own judgement or inclination.

1624 in CAPT. J. SMITH (K.O.). **1639** FULLER *Holy War* III. xxvi. (1840) 166 They overpersuaded him not to starve an army by feeding his own humours. **1749** FIELDING *Tom Jones* III. ii, Nor had he done it now, had not the younger Sportsman .. over-persuaded him. **1897** HENTY *On Irrawaddy* 350, I had proposed to myself not to marry .. but your sister overpersuaded me.

So **over-per'suasion.**

1741 RICHARDSON *Pamela* II. 158, I drank two Glasses by his Over-persuasion. **1755** MAGENS *Insur.* II. 242 Made Use of in any over-persuasion, or hazardous Inducements. *a* **1817** JANE AUSTEN *Persuasion* (1818) III. vii. 142 It had been the effect of over-persuasion.

†ˌover-'perted, *pa. pple. Obs.* [OVER- 27 b.] Made too pert or saucy.

1614 RALEIGH *Hist. World* II. xxii. §10 (1634) 474 A thing of dangerous consequence; especially when an unable spirit, being over-perted with so high authority, is too passionate in the execution of such an office.

†ˌover-'pester, *v. Obs.* [OVER- 27.] *trans.* To 'pester', i.e. crowd or encumber, excessively.

1599 DANIEL *Musophilus* Wks. (1717) 388 No marvel then, tho' th' over-pester'd State Want Room for Goodness. **1614** RALEIGH *Hist. World* II. (1634) 309 Hiram allowed him Timber, with which Libanus was, and yet is over-pestered. **1675** J. LOVE *Clavis Med.* 42 Let no house be over-pestered with too many Lodgers. **1720** STRYPE *Stow's Surv.* (1754) II. v. xx. 405/1 Their Over-pestering of small rooms with many of them.

'overpick, *a.* [OVER- 1 d.] Said of a loom in which the shuttle-driving arrangement, or picking arm, is placed above the loom.

1884 in KNIGHT *Dict. Mech.* Suppl. 650/2. **1888** R. BEAUMONT *Woollen Manuf.* viii. 229 There are three distinct kinds of picking mechanisms: first, the cam and cone motion; second, the over-pick motion; and third, the under-pick motion. **1894** F. W. FOX *Mech. Weaving* x. 278 When some portion of it projects above the boxes the motion becomes an over-pick.

over-'picture, *v.* [OVER- 26, 8.]

1. *trans.* To represent or picture in excess of the reality; to depict or describe with exaggeration.

1606 SHAKS. *Ant. & Cl.* II. ii. 205 She did lye In her Pauillion, cloth of Gold, of Tissue, O're-picturing that Venus, where we see The fancie out-worke Nature. **1856** OLMSTED *Slave States* 406 The beautiful rural cemetery .. which Willis has .. a little over-pictured.

2. To picture over; to cover with pictures of.

1850 SYD. DOBELL *Roman* vii, The future years .. with the unborn dead o'erpictured.

overpitch (ˌəʊvəˈpɪtʃ), *v.* [OVER- 26. (Chiefly in pa. pple.)]

1. *Cricket. trans.* To pitch (a ball) too far in bowling, so that the batsman can hit it before it touches the ground. Also *absol.*

1851 [see BOWL *v.*[1] 4 b]. **1859** *All Year Round* No. 13. 306 The first ball they bowled me was slow, overpitched, and to leg. **1958** D. BRADMAN *Art of Cricket* 104/1 If one's length is faulty, over-pitch rather than under-pitch that new ball. **1963** *Times* 28 May 4/5 On a perfect pitch, he played each good length ball with care, but those overpitched he punished severely and his 100 included four sixes and 10 fours.

2. *fig.* To pitch too high; to exaggerate.

1886 F. H. DOYLE *Remin.* 193 These praises appeared to me a little overpitched. **1976** N. ROBERTS *Face of France* vi. 69 He is nondescript and correct, she high-coloured and over-pitched. **1977** *Church Times* 28 Jan. 6/4 The tone of much of Kingsley's writing .. now seems overpitched to an almost hysterical degree.

Hence **over'pitched** *ppl. a.*, of a ball: that is pitched too far.

1855 [see BREAK *sb.*[1] 5]. **1897** RANJITSINHJI *Cricket* 170 These on-drives should be kept for rather overpitched balls. **1900** A. E. T. WATSON *Young Sportsman* 147 He has lunged out as far as he can reach, hoping to 'smother' a somewhat over-pitched ball. **1958** D. BRADMAN *Art of Cricket* 101/2 Learn to bowl the yorker if you can but be prepared to get hit for some fours off the overpitched balls in the process.

'over-'pitched (-pɪtʃt), *a.* [OVER- 26.] Of a roof: Having a greater than ordinary pitch; having an excessive slope.

1677 PLOT *Oxfordsh.* 274 Roofs .. whereof some are flat or under-pitched, .. others due proportion'd, or over-pitched.

overplaced, -plain, etc.: see OVER-.

'overplacement. *rare.* Superposition.

1895 J. W. POWELL *Physiographic Processes, Nat. Geogr. Monogr.* I. No. 1. 14 The lowlands have a great overplacement of these rock materials.

ˌover'plant, *v.* [In sense 1, ONorthumb. *oferplontia*, f. *ofer-* OVER- 10 + *plantian* to PLANT. In sense 2 f. OVER- 27 + PLANT *v.*]

†1. *trans.* To transplant. *Obs.*

c **950** *Lindisf. Gosp.* Luke xvii. 6 Ofwytrumia & oferplontia on sæ. **1388** WYCLIF *Luke* xvii. 6 Be thou drawun vp bi the rote, and be ouerplauntid in to the see.

2. To plant too much or to excess.

1770 ARMSTRONG *Misc.* II. 239 Some gardens .. are so smoothly regular, so over-planted. **1887** *Fisheries U.S.* Sect. v. II. 527 The high price of oysters caused overplanting, which led to the impoverishment of the planting-grounds.

†'overplaw. *Obs. rare*⁻⁰. [f. OVER- 5 + PLAW *sb.*] A boiling over.

c **1440** *Promp. Parv.* 373/2 Ovyrplaw, *ebullicio.*

ˌover-'play, *v.* [OVER- 27, 22.]

1. a. *trans.* To play (a part, etc.) to excess; to play too much. So **'over-'played** *ppl. a.*, **'over-'playing** *vbl. sb.*

16.. *Sale Houshold-Stuff* iv. in *3rd Collect. Poems* (1689) 27/1 Here's a Pack of nasty Court Cards, Much foul'd with over-playing. **1819** *Metropolis* I. 183 John offers to box, in a most ridiculous, overplayed manner. **1896** *Peterson's Mag.* Jan. 93/1 He had overplayed his part in a way that was unpardonable.

b. *fig.* To emphasize too much; to attach too great an importance to; *spec.* in phr. ***to overplay one's hand***, to spoil a good case by exaggerating its value (from *Card-playing*).

1930 *Times* 27 Mar. 15/3 Conditions are clearly more favourable to agreement .. provided only that *Nahas Pasha* does not over-play his hand. **1933** *Sun* (Baltimore) 16 Aug. 10/7 American newspaper headline writers .. 'overplay' the news for which they write captions. **1952** *Essays in Crit.* II. 325 He [*sc.* Empson] thinks Tillyard and Dover Wilson .. overplayed their hands in attending too exclusively to the 'official' explanations of Shakespeare's history plays. **1956** A. L. ROWSE *Early Churchills* 269 Here was the one chance of the Allies .. thrown away by overplaying their hand. **1960** I. PEEBLES *Bowler's Turn* 190 Dexter over-played his luck and ran himself out. **1965** *New Statesman* 20 Apr. 673/3 One building society told me that the 'crisis' had been 'very much overplayed' and that there were already signs of the investment situation easing. **1968** *Globe & Mail* (Toronto) 13 Jan. 29/2 The problem has been overplayed, he said. The recent slump doesn't indicate a trend. **1977** F. DURBRIDGE *Passenger* iii. 146 Judy may have over-played her hand and tried to cut herself in on one of Andy's little rackets.

2. To surpass or overcome in playing; to play better than, and so gain the victory over.

1892 *Pall Mall G.* 4 Aug. 5/2 As in the game at Trent Bridge, they steadily overplayed their formidable opponents.

ˌover-'please, *v.* [OVER- 27.] *trans.* To please too much. So **'over-'pleased, 'over-'pleasing** *ppl. adjs.*

1611 SPEED *Theat. Gt. Brit.* (1614) 132/2 An over-pleasing repose, and ever flourishing happinesse. **1626** BACON *Sylva* §835 The Senses love not to be Over-pleased; But to have a Commixture of somewhat that is in it selfe Ingrate. **1664** DRYDEN *Rival Ladies* Ded., That eagerness of Imagination which by over-pleasing fanciful Men, flatters them into the Danger of Writing. **1766** FORDYCE *Serm. Yng. Wom.* (1767) II. x. 130 The insinuation .. will not .. be over-pleasing. **1888** F. A. GASQUET *Hen. VIII & Eng. Monast.* I. 81 He was not overpleased at the difficulties that had been raised.

over-plenty to **-plumb:** see OVER-.

†overplow, *v. Obs. rare.* ? To plough over.

1596 W. SMITH *Chloris* (1877) 19 Content my selfe in silent shade to sit In hope at length my cares to ouerplow.

overplume (-'plu:m), *v. rare.* [OVER- 1, 27.]

a. *trans.* To hang over or surmount as with a plume. **b.** *refl.* To plume oneself to excess.

1854 J. D. BURNS *Vision Prophecy* 97 Orange-groves Overplumed here and there by some tall palms. **1890** *Temple Bar Mag.* Nov. 429 Determined that I should not overplume myself.

†over'plunge, *v. Obs. rare. trans.* To plunge over head and ears, submerge.

1602 ROWLANDS *Greenes Ghost* 43 Least thou in time be .. ouerplunged in a deeper bog.

overplus ('əʊvəplʌs), *sb.* (*adv.*, *a.*) [app. a partial translation of F. *surplus* (12th c. in Hatz.-Darm.), f. *sur* over + F. and L. *plus* more.]

A. *sb.* **a.** That which is over in addition to the main amount, or to what is allotted or needed; an additional or extra quantity; an amount left over, a surplus.

1387 TREVISA *Higden* (Rolls) I. 407 And alle the ouer pluse He kepeþ to his owne vse. **1420** in *E.E. Wills* (1882) 42 The overe-plus of alle thys. **1555** W. WATREMAN *Fardle Facions* I. iii. 36 Hercules passyng the seas .. and bringyng an ouerplus of people thence with hym. **1610** HEALEY *St. Aug. Citie of God* 545 Wee read two hundred yeares and the overplus. **1736** BUTLER *Anal.* II. vi. 299 To balance pleasure and pain .. so as to be able to say on which side the overplus is. **1875** MAINE *Hist. Inst.* 262 The landlord is paid out of the proceeds. The overplus is returned to the tenant.

¶**b.** *catachr.* That which remains in the mind, conclusion. *Obs.*

1536 BOORDE *Let.* in *Introd. Knowl.* (1870) Forewords 58 Vnto the tyme you haue seen them, & knowyng þe ouerplus of my mynd. **1547** —— *Brev. Health* §384 The ouerplus of my mynde in this matter .. I do commyt it to the industry of wyse & expert Phisicions.

c. *loosely.* Excess, superabundance.

1721 M. W. MONTAGU *Let.* May (1966) II. 5, I beleive [I] shall take care another time not to involve my selfe in difficulties by an overplus of Heroic Generosity. **1794** D. O'CONNELL *Let.* 22 Apr. (1972) I. 17, I could spend three months at home in my native air free from all cost; which would compensate for the overplus of travelling charges. *a* **1817** JANE AUSTEN *Two Chapters of Persuasion* (1926) 27 To .. pay for the overplus of Bliss, by Headake & Fatigue. **1850** B. TAYLOR *Eldorado* ii. (1862) 14 An idea of the splendid overplus of vegetable life within the tropics. **1870** LOWELL *Among my Bks.* Ser. I. (1873) 274 The imagination is so much in over-plus, that thinking a thing becomes better than doing it. **1934** E. POUND *Eleven New Cantos* xxxvi. 28 Cometh he to be when the will From overplus Twisteth out of natural measure. **1969** *Worship* XLIII. 394 In origin, the sacred is an overplus of meaning expressed with such power that it overwhelms everyone who perceives it. This overplus is beyond analysis.

B. as *adv.* or predicate: In addition, in excess, besides, over. Now *rare* or *Obs.*

1388 WYCLIF *Luke* xi. 41 Netheles that that is ouerplus, ȝyue ȝe almes, and lo! al thingis ben cleene to ȝou. **1560** WHITEHORNE *Ord. Souldiours* (1573) 5 b, Parting the roote into 3, there remaynethe ouerplus onelye one. **1598** *Archpriest Controv.* (Camden) II. 157 Wee adde this wishe overplus that yow had not made this edicte. **1606** SHAKS. *Ant. & Cl.* IV. vi. 22. **1655** MRQ. WORCESTER *Cent. Inv.* Ded. ii. 9 Whatever should be overplus or needless for the present day.

C. as *adj.* in attrib. relation: Remaining over, additional, extra, surplus.

1640 *Boston Rec.* (1877) II. 51 Sargient Savage his demand to have the overplus land at Hogg Iland. **1726** BERKELEY *Let. to T. Prior* 24 Aug., Wks. 1871 IV. 133 Transmit the third part of the overplus sum to Swift and Company. **1883** W. MORRIS in Mackail *Life* (1899) II. 107 If they can only learn the uselessness of mere overplus money.

overply (ˌəʊvəˈplaɪ), *v.* [OVER- 27.] *trans.* To ply or exercise too much; to exhaust by too much exercise. So **'over'plied** *ppl. a.*

c **1655** MILTON *Sonn. Cyriack Skinner upon his Blindness*, The conscience .. to have lost them overply'd In libertyes defence. **1858** *Nat. Rev.* Oct. 490 Her overplied strength worn down .. by his children and the impossible problems of his house. **1863** KINGLAKE *Crimea* (1877) II. xvi. 270 He overplied the idea of discipline.

overpoise ('əʊvəpɔɪz), *sb.* [f. next.] The act or fact of outweighing; that which outweighs; 'preponderant weight' (J.).

1697 DRYDEN *Virg. Georg.* (1721) Ded. 179 His Judgment was an Overpoize to his Imagination. **1842** MANNING *Serm.* (1848) I. xxiv. 361 In the concerns of this life, the lightest overpoise of probability determines our strongest resolutions. **1856** MRS. BROWNING *Aur. Leigh* VII. 1056 The moths, with that great overpoise of wings.

overpoise (əʊvəˈpɔɪz), *v.* Forms: α. 6–7 overpeise, (6 -peaze, -paise, 7 -peyse). β. 7–8 -poize, (7 -poyse, 8 -poyze), 6– overpoise. [f. OVER- 3, 22, 27 + POISE *v.* (earlier *peise*).]

1. *trans.* To weigh more than, outweigh: mostly *fig.* In quots. 1598, 1652 causatively: To make something outweigh (something else).

α. *c* **1555** HARPSFIELD *Divorce Hen. VIII* (Camden) 218 Nor the man's oath shall overpeise the woman's denial. **1598** J. DICKENSON *Greene in Conc.* (1878) 133 To ouerpeaze the feare of danger with the care of dutie. **1652** H. L'ESTRANGE *Amer. no Jewes* 12 Nor will the weight of his experience .. be overpeised by any.

β. *a* **1600** in *Bodenham's Bel-vedére* 22 False faith is ouerpoisde with weakest weight, The ballance yeelds vnto the lightest feather. **1608** DOD & CLEAVER *Expos. Prov.* ix–x. 17 The gaine .. wil counteruaile and ouerpoise the losse. *a* **1711** KEN *Christophil* Poet. Wks. 1721 I. 438 One minute in my Jesu's Arms Will an Eternity o'repoise Of your false Joys. **1884** BP. THOROLD *Yoke Christ* 5 The joys of matrimony may be overpoised by its cares.

b. *intr.* or *absol.*

1684 T. HOCKIN *God's Decrees* 245 The best deserving, or whose merits overpoize, is chosen. **1717** DESAGULIERS in *Phil. Trans.* XXX. 575 All the while the Plummet was falling, the Water descended rather than rose; and when the Lead was at the bottom, the Water overpois'd.

†**2.** *trans.* To overweight, weigh down, overload (*lit.* and *fig.*). *Obs.*

1581 J. BELL *Haddon's Answ. Osor.* 115 b, There was no mortal creature but was overpaised, and pressed doune with this heavy burden. **1655** MOUFET & BENNET *Health's Improv.* (1746) 378 A full and troubled Body, over-poised with Variety and Plenty of Meats.

†**3.** To overbalance (in quot. *fig.*). *Obs.*

1641 M. FRANK *Serm.* ii. (1672) 534 If your honours puff you up, overpoise you.

ˌover-ˈpole, *v.* [f. OVER- 27 + POLE *v.*[1]] Chiefly in pa. pple. **over-poled.**

1. *trans.* To furnish (hops, or a hop-ground) with too long a pole or poles.

1707 MORTIMER *Husb.* 135 The Hop will soon run itself out of heart if over-poled: more especially be sure not to over-pole them for length the first Year.

2. To pole (copper) too much in refining, so as to remove too much oxide and render it brittle.

1861 etc. [see *overpoled, overpoling* below].

Hence **overˈpoled** *ppl. a.*, **overˈpoling** *vbl. sb.*

1742 W. ELLIS *Mod. Husbandman* Aug. xx. 98 Over-poling [of hops] is worse than Under-poling. **1758** R. BROWN *Compl. Farmer* II. (1760) 113 Neither can you expect a crop [of hops] from an over-poled ground. **1861** J. PERCY *Metallurgy* 274 One of the most characteristic properties of commercial overpoled copper is brittleness. **1890** *Sci. Extracts* 171 The terms, underpoling, overpoling, and tough pitch. *Ibid.*, The removal of this small quantity of oxygen will suffice to render copper overpoled and useless. **1910** *Jrnl. Inst. Metals* IV. 207 In the case of 'overpoled' copper the gases were released in such a quantity as to not only neutralise the effect of shrinkage, but to elevate the surface of the ingot. *Ibid.* 230 'Poling' could be pushed further, before the stage of 'overpoling' was reached, than could be done in the case of pure copper. **1930** *Ibid.* XLIII. 121 Hence a very slight further poling beyond the point *A* will cause a marked increase in the porosity of the ingot; the surface will rise and all the defects of overpoling will appear. **1937** ARCHBUTT & PRYTHERCH *Effect of Impurities in Copper* iii. 34 Overpoled metal is not in a satisfactory condition to withstand rolling and fabrication for two reasons. **1949** J. E. GARSIDE *Process & Physical Metall.* xxii. 378 If poling has been too prolonged the cuprous oxide content is very low. This gives rise to the evolution of considerable quantities of water vapour on solidification and the metal expands in the mould, forming a ridge. Such material, too brittle for many purposes, is termed 'overpoled copper'.

over-polemical to **over-polk**: see OVER-.

†**overˈponderate**, *v. Obs. rare.* To overweigh.

1729 GREENWOOD in *Phil. Trans.* XXXVI. 189 Being then *in Æquilibrio* to so great a Degree of Exactness, that half a Grain would over-ponderate on either Side.

ˌover-ˈpopulate, *v.* [OVER- 27, 22.]

1. *trans.* To overstock with people, over-people. (Chiefly in *pa. pple.*)

1870 EMERSON *Soc. & Solit.* vii. 132 When Europe is over-populated, America and Australia crave to be populated. **1882** in A. R. Wallace *Land National.* (ed. 3) 83 By the clearances one part is depopulated and the other over-populated.

2. To exceed in population.

1868 BUSHNELL *Mor. Uses Dark Th.* vii. 152 The new solidarity in good..will thus overpopulate and virtually live down the more corrupted families.

So **ˈover-popuˈlation**; **ˈover-ˈpopulous** *a.* (whence **ˈover-ˈpopulousness**).

1798 MALTHUS *Popul.* (1817) I. v. 117 Over-populousness would at all times increase the natural propensity of savages to war. **1823** J. S. MILL in *Black Dwarf* XI. 754 Not only the master manufacturer but the landowner also, has an interest in over population. **1826** MALTHUS *Diary* 10 July (1966) 265 Landlord at Kenmore complained of the drought, the fall in the price of cattle, and the overpopulation of the country. **1862** RUSKIN *Unto this Last* 99 There is not yet, nor will yet for ages be, any real over-population in the world. **1959** A. HUXLEY *Let.* 26 Nov. (1969) 880 It may turn out to be hideously tragic when their efforts to modernize the country break down under the combined pressures of inefficiency and over-population. **1971** *Daily Tel.* (Colour Suppl.) 3 Dec. 24/3 Forrester has designed a model of the world system to try to discover the long term effects of pollution and overpopulation. **1977** *Times* 31 May 5/4 Mexico..is exporting its over-population.

over-positive, over-possess: see OVER-.

†**overˈpost**, *v. Obs.* [f. OVER- 9 + POST *v.*] *trans.* To 'post' over; to get over (the ground, or any matter) quickly and easily.

1597 SHAKS. *2 Hen. IV*, I. ii. 171 You may thanke the vnquiet time, for your quiet o're-posting that action.

ˌover-ˈpot, *v.* [f. OVER- 27 + POT *v.*] *trans.* To plant in too large a pot.

1825 *Greenhouse Comp.* I. 170 Caution is necessary to avoid over-potting such kinds as grow in peat soil. **1897** *Garden* 24 July 63/1 Nothing is gained by overpotting the plants.

overpotential (ˈəʊvəpətɛnʃəl). [OVER- 19, 29.] = OVERVOLTAGE 1, 2.

1920 *Jrnl. Amer. Chem. Soc.* XLII. 94 Overpotential varies with the nature of the electrode. **1961** A. C. WHISH in G. F. Tagg *Pract. Electr. Engin.* II. 292 For the overpotential tests the transformer is excited in the normal way on one winding to twice or more than twice the value of its rated voltage. **1974** *Encycl. Brit. Macropædia* VI. 644/1 The overpotential can be considered as logarithmically dependent on the current density.

overpour (-ˈpɔə(r)), *v. rare.* [OVER- 5.] *trans.* To pour over from one receptacle into another, transfer by or as by pouring, transfuse.

1585 LUPTON *Thous. Notable Th.* v. § 84 (1595) 130 It is certain..that daungerous and many effects..are turned, or overpowred into him.

over-power, *sb. rare.* [OVER- 29, 2.]

1. (ˈ*over-*ˈ*power.*) Too great or excessive power.

1625 BACON *Ess., Viciss. Things* (Arb.) 574 When a State growes to an Ouer-power, it is like a great Floud, that will be sure to ouerflow.

2. (ˈ*over-*ˌ*power.*) A superior or supreme power.

1887 H. R. HAWEIS *Light of Ages* vi. 176 No flight or fall of birds could take place without the ken and guidance of the 'Overpower'.

overpower (əʊvəˈpaʊə(r)), *v.* [OVER- 22 b.]

1. *trans.* To overcome with superior power or force (physical or moral); to reduce to submission; to subdue, defeat, vanquish, master.

1593 SHAKS. *Rich. II*, V. i. 31 The Lyon dying..wounds the Earth, if nothing else, with rage To be o're-powr'd. **1639** FULLER *Holy War* IV. x. (1840) 195 The Christians..though overpowered in number, made a great slaughter of their enemies. **1778** MISS BURNEY *Evelina* (1791) II. xxvi. 158 Mrs Selwyn quite overpowered me with the force of her arguments. **1855** MACAULAY *Hist. Eng.* xi. III. 39 Those officers who attempted to restrain the rioters were overpowered and disarmed.

2. To render (a thing, agency, quality, etc., material or immaterial) ineffective or imperceptible, by excess of force or intensity.

1646 SIR T. BROWNE *Pseud. Ep.* 4 Whether the efficacie of the one had not overpowred the penalty of the other, we leave it unto God. **1748** GRAY *Alliance* 65 Can..suns.. O'erpower the fire that animates our frame? **1806** A. HUNTER *Culina* (ed. 3) 187 Strong sauces that overpower the natural flavour of the fish. **1849** MACAULAY *Hist. Eng.* iv. I. 463 All such sympathies were now overpowered by a stronger feeling.

3. To overcome by intensity (as fatigue, emotion, etc.); to be too intense or violent for, 'be too much for'; to crush, overwhelm.

1667 MILTON *P.L.* VIII. 453 My earthly by his Heav'nly overpowerd..sunk down. **1775** SHERIDAN *Duenna* II. i, Lord! Lord! I am afraid I shall be overpowered with her beauty. **1791** MRS. RADCLIFFE *Rom. Forest* i, The violent agitation of mind and fatigue of body, had overpowered her strength. **1832** LYTTON *Eugene A.* II. iv, The shy and secluded student, whom it was his object to dazzle and overpower. **1881** BESANT & RICE *Chapl. of Fleet* I. 91 We might be overpowered with the grandeur of the house.

overˈpowering, *ppl. a.* [f. prec. + -ING[2].] That overpowers; so powerful as to subdue or overcome; irresistible, overwhelming.

1700 DRYDEN *Palamon & Arc.* I. 235 Struck blind with overpowering light he stood. **1884** A. PAUL *Hist. Reform* v. 101 The demand..was too overpowering to be successfully resisted.

Hence **overˈpoweringly** *adv.*, in an overpowering manner or degree; irresistibly, overwhelmingly.

1812 *Examiner* 7 Sept. 571/2 Overpoweringly droll. **1828** MACAULAY in *Life & Lett.* (1880) I. iii. 153 Sleep comes on him overpoweringly. **1886** SYMONDS *Renaiss. It., Cath. React.* (1898) VII. xiii. 218 One of his overpoweringly virulent invectives.

overpowr, obs. f. OVERPOUR, OVERPOWER.

overpraise (ˈəʊvəˈpreɪz), *sb.* [OVER- 29 b.] Excessive praise; praise beyond what is deserved.

1694 DRYDEN *Love Triumphant* I. i, This over-praise You give his worth, in any other mouth, Were villainy to me. **1875** EMERSON *Lett. & Soc. Aims* i. 58 Our overpraise and idealization of famous masters.

overpraise (ˌəʊvəˈpreɪz), *v.* [OVER- 27.] *trans.* To praise excessively; to praise more than one deserves.

1387 TREVISA *Higden* (Rolls) V. 339 It may wel be þat Arthur is ofte overpreysed. **1635** A. STAFFORD *Fem. Glory* (1860) Ep. Ded. 60 As we cannot over-worship the True Deity, so wee cannot over-praise a true Piety. **1733** POPE *Let. to Swift* Wks. 1751 IX. 250, I like much better to be abused and half-starved, than to be so over-praised and over-fed. **1858** J. B. NORTON *Topics* 116 The Company's petition..appears to me to have been singularly over-rated and over-praised.

So **ˈoverˈpraised** *ppl. a.*; **ˈoverˈpraising** *vbl. sb.*

a **1225** *Ancr. R.* 86 He hit heueð to heie up mid ouerpreisunge & herunge. **1667** MILTON *P.L.* IX. 615 Serpent, thy overpraising leaves in doubt The vertue of that Fruit, in thee first prov'd. **1826** SYD. SMITH *Wks.* (1859) II. 106/2 A very great blot in our over-praised criminal code. **1863** J. C. JEAFFRESON *Sir Everard's Dau.* 121 The rather mean and very much over-praised quality, called common-sense.

overpray: see OVER- 11.

overpreach (ˌəʊvəˈpriːtʃ), *v.* [OVER- 1 e, 23.]

1. *trans.* To preach above or beyond.

1659 GAUDEN *Tears Ch.* I. xiv. 117 Many of us so overpreached our peoples capacities, that [etc.].

2. To overdo or exhaust with preaching. (Chiefly *refl.*)

1865 *Pall Mall G.* 6 Oct. 5 Dr. Hook..was not present, having, as it was said, 'overpreached himself'. **1899** *Daily News* 19 May 9/3 Both..had this in common that they would not 'overpreach' themselves—a vice into which apparently all modern preachers..seem to fall.

over-precise, -pregnant, etc.: see OVER-.

ˌoverpreˈscribe, *v.* [OVER- 27.] *trans.* and *intr.* To prescribe an excessive amount of (a drug). Hence **ˌoverpreˈscribing** *vbl. sb.*; **ˌoverpreˈscription**.

1953 *Times* 31 Oct. 4/3 Many doctors admitted that since the introduction of the shilling prescription they often tended to over-prescribe to save the patient coming back for an extra shilling's worth. **1967** N. LUCAS *C.I.D.* x. 138 The over-prescribing of drugs by a small number of doctors. **1968** *New Scientist* 28 Mar. 679/2 There is the agricultural merchant who bends the regulations, there is the veterinary surgeon who over-prescribes, and finally there is the unscrupulous retail pharmacist. **1969** *Observer* 9 Nov. 3/5 Doctors could exercise greater control by restraining themselves from over-prescribing drugs. **1970** *Times* 4 Nov. 6 Dr. Hindmarch blames overprescription by doctors as the main source of illicit amphetamines. **1972** *Science* 26 May 883/2 Yet physicians themselves have a sense that they, as a group, over-prescribe and overuse psychoactive drugs. **1974** M. C. GERALD *Pharmacol.* xi. 205 In a recent survey of 55 physicians in the Boston area, 37 felt that their fellow physicians were overprescribing sedatives.

overpress (ˌəʊvəˈprɛs), *v.* Now somewhat *rare.* [app. orig. a variant of OPPRESS, repr. L. *opprimĕre*; afterwards associated with more literal senses of PRESS *v.*, with various senses of OVER-.]

I. 1. *trans.* To oppress; to burden or afflict with severity or cruelty; to oppress beyond endurance.

1382 WYCLIF *Gen.* xlvii. 13 In al the world breed lackide, and hungur oppresside [*v.r.* ouerpressid] the erthe. **1496** *Dives & Paup.* (W. de W.) VII. xxviii. 318/2 Thou shalt not therfore..ouerpresse hym with usurye. **1525** LD. BERNERS *Froiss.* II. lxxxiii. [lxxix.] 247 He wolde ouerpresse them with taxes and subsydyes. **1644** MILTON *Jdgm. Bucer* Testimonies, P. Martyr, My mind is overpressed with grief. **1744** ELIZA HEYWOOD *Female Spect.* No. 7 (1748) II. 49 Her heart, overpressed beneath a weight of anguish, refused its accustomed motion.

†**2.** To press upon with physical force, so as to overthrow or overwhelm. *Obs.*

1489 CAXTON *Faytes of A.* I. xii. 32 They ouerpresse and ouerstep one ouer that other. **1523** LD. BERNERS *Froiss.* I. ccxxxvii. 338 He was closed in amonge his enemyes, and so sore ouerpressed that he was felled downe to the erthe. **1612** DRAYTON *Poly-olb.* viii. 116 His valiant Britans slaine ..(o'represt with Roman power). **1654–66** EARL ORRERY *Parthen.* (1676) 680 He and all that followed him, over-pressed with multitudes were every one kill'd or taken.

†**3.** To press down with a heavy weight; to overburden, overload. *Obs.*

a **1577** GASCOIGNE *Flowers* Wks. (1587) 169, I sawe the boat was overprest. **1634** BRERETON *Trav.* 5 The ship..was heavy laden with merchants' goods, and more over-pressed with passengers. **1713** SWIFT *Atlas* Wks. 1755 III. II. 74 A pedlar overpress'd Unloads upon a stall to rest.

II. 4. 'To overcome by entreaty; to press or persuade too much'. *rare.*

1818 in TODD (with no quotation).

5. To press or insist upon (a matter) unduly.

1865 M. ARNOLD *Ess. Crit.* x. (1875) 426 The motives of reward and punishment have come..to be strangely over-pressed by many Christian moralists. *Mod.* He sometimes overpresses his point.

6. To put too much pressure on (a person).

1886 C. BROWNE in *Pall Mall G.* 16 Sept. 11/2 To educate a half-starved child at all is to over-press it.

So **ˈoverˌpress** *sb.* = OVER-PRESSURE; **ˈoverˈpressed, -ˈprest** *ppl. a.*, oppressed, overcrowded, etc.; **ˌoverˈpressing** *vbl. sb.*

1523 FITZHERB. *Husb.* § 51 For feare of murtheryng or ouer pressyng of their felowes. *a* **1586** SIDNEY *Arcadia* (1622) 272 Care vpon care..To ouer-pressed breasts, more grieuous waight. **1846** E. FORBES *Let.* in Wilson & Geikie *Mem.* xii. (1861) 394 This weather, and the overpress of work.. impede a fair recovery. **1871** *Daily News* 6 Jan., Horses which had succumbed under overpress of work.

†**overˈpressor**. *Obs. rare.* [f. prec., after *oppressor*.] An oppressor.

1610 HOLLAND *Camden's Brit.* I. 352 Fitz Stephen calleth him *Violentus Cantii incubator*, that is, the violent overpressor of Kent.

ˈover-ˈpressure. [OVER- 29 b, c.] **a.** Excessive pressure; the act of pressing or fact of being pressed too hard (esp. with study or intellectual work); pressure (of a fluid) in excess of that which is normal or allowed for.

1644 VICARS *God in Mount* 147 Being forced at last..by over-pressure of numbers. **1834** HT. MARTINEAU *Moral* II. 37 The over-pressure of the people upon its food. **1899** *Allbutt's Syst. Med.* VII. 470 Overpressure in education has also been alleged as a factor. **1936** B. JONES *Elem. Pract. Aerodynamics* xviii. 290 The pressure gages should be watched closely, especially before take-off. Overpressure indicates a stoppage in the line. **1941** O. E. PATTON *Aircraft Instruments* x. 153 The suction and overpressure tests are given to find out what will happen to the gauge if it is subjected to pressures below atmospheric or exceeding their normal range. **1962** *Trans. Faraday Soc.* LVIII. 194 A quantitative hydrogenation of a solution of the polymer in benzene was attempted using..an over-pressure of hydrogen (*ca.* 700 mm). **1963** *Ann. Med. Internae Fenniae* LII. 212 The idea of employment of over-pressure directed into the human organism may be questioned in principle. **1977** *Sci. Amer.* Mar. 82/1 Just above the vocal folds are the two 'false' vocal folds, which are engaged when someone holds his breath with an over-pressure of air in the lungs. *attrib.* **1884** KNIGHT *Dict. Mech.* Suppl., *Overpressure Valve*, a valve which opens when a predetermined pressure in a boiler has been reached. A *Safety Valve*.

b. *spec.* The difference between the (highest) instantaneous pressure at a point subjected to a shock wave and the ambient atmospheric pressure.

1955 *Communications Pure & Appl. Maths.* VIII. 340 We evaluated the *D* corresponding to the shock over-pressure of 5°. **1961** *Shell Aviation News* No. 278. 9/2 It's quite conceivable that a ground overpressure of only 0·1 lb per square foot may be decidedly unacceptable to the farmer... and 0·04 lb per square foot to those who value peace and quiet. **1967** *Guardian* 5 July 1/8 Overpressures will vary from 1 to 1·5 lb a sq. ft. which is less than the maximum Concord bang. **1975** *Sci. Amer.* July 15/3 Overpressure is proportional to the energy released by a nuclear charge and is inversely proportional to the cube of the distance from the point of explosion.

'over,price, *sb.* ? *Obs.* [OVER- 29 d.] Excess of price; an excessive price.

1622 MALYNES *Anc. Law-Merch.* 247 Omitting to reckon the ouerprices, which were made and gotten by the sale thereof in forraine countries. **1680** OTWAY *Orphan* II. iv, Pride.. will usurp a little, Make us.. Pay over-price. **1702** FARQUHAR *Twin-Rivals* I. ii, My assiduity beforehand was an overprice.

over'price, *v.* [OVER- 22, 27.] *trans.* To price (something) more highly or excessively highly; to price a commodity beyond the means of (someone). Also *absol.* Hence **'over-'priced** *ppl. a.*, having too high prices. Also, of a commodity: priced too highly; **over'pricing** *vbl. sb.*

1605 P. ERONDELLE *French Garden* sig. Kv, Buye for me yonder waistcoate.. for if I cheapen it, they will ouer price it me by the halfe, As for you, they knowe you haue better skill in it. **1881** A. KNOX *New Playgr.* (1883) 56 Over-populated, over-priced Mustapha. **1972** K. BONFIGLIOLI *Don't point that Thing at Me* i. 5 He was the second greatest art-dealer of the century: he poisoned his life trying to over-price Duveen out of the field. **1976** 'Z. STONE' *Modigliani Scandal* I. iii. 29 My view is that you have been over-priced for some time... At present few of your canvases deserve to fetch more than £325. **1977** T. HEALD *Just Desserts* vii. 153 Rubbery prawns with over-priced vinegary Mexican wine. **1977** D. CLARK *Gimmel Flask* iii. 49 The antique world offers tremendous scope for faking,.. underselling, overpricing and so on. **1978** M. KENYON *Deep Pocket* i. 5 The vendors of over-priced ice-cream at Marble Arch.

†**'over-'pride.** *Obs. rare.* [OVER- 29 d.] Excessive pride.

a **1250** *Prov. Ælfred* 286 in *O.E. Misc.* 120 Idelschipe and ouer prute þat lereþ yong wif vuele þewes. **1484** CAXTON *Fables of Auian* xxvi, I knowe wel thy ouer pryde.

'overprint, *sb.* **1.** [OVER- 19.] = OFFPRINT *sb.*

1892 *Ch. Times* 11 Mar. 245/2 The paper sent to you was only an overprint from the 'Archaeologia'. **1898** R. C. CLEPHAN *(title)* Notes on the Defensive Armour of Medieval Times. Overprint from the Archæologia Aeliana, Vol. xx.

2. [OVER- 8 c.] **a.** Overprinted matter, esp. on a postage stamp (see quot. 1913). **b.** The action or result of overprinting.

1876 *Let.* 6 Sept. in J. Easton *De La Rue Hist. Brit. & Foreign Postage Stamps, 1855–1901* (1958) xxiv. 710 We should be furnished with the duties which are to fall in the stamps clearly written or printed, so that we might avoid mistakes in making the overprint. **1899** *Captain* I. 421/2 The correct over-print should have been 'Z.C. de peso'. **1912** KNECHT & FOTHERGILL *Princ. & Pract. Textile Printing* VII. 319 Its darker colour will mask the paler tint of the over-print. **1913** E. B. EVANS *Stamps* (ed. 4) 58 *Overprint*, some addition to the design or inscriptions, printed or written upon a stamp which was already complete and fit for use without any such addition. **1928** *Daily Mail* 7 Aug. 18/4 On three values of this printing some sheets received the overprint upside down. **1938** KNOPF & INGERSON *Struct. Petrology* xiv. 197 Upon this earlier movement there was stamped an oblique overprint of a later deformation, now recorded in the quartz fabric. **1938** E. RAISZ *Gen. Cartography* xvi. 188 Each drawing must have register marks for perfect overprint. **1965** *Jrnl. Neurosurg.* XIII. 346 The pulses received by the scaler may be recorded by statistical overprint with a telegraphic printer. **1971** *Nature* 18 June 463/1 *(caption)* At top, 3 weeks raw data in °F with overprint of best fit cosine ware. **1973** *Daily Tel.* 23 June 25/6 The 10F on 90c exists with inverted overprint and makes about £1,500 in this condition.

,over-'print, *v. Photogr.*

I. [OVER- 26.] **1.** *trans.* To print (a positive) darker than it is intended to be.

1853 *Family Herald* 3 Dec. 510/2 He must over-print, or allow the positive to become very much darker than he intends it to be when finished, as in the.. fixing, it will become much lighter. **1861** *Photogr. News Alm.* in *Circ. Sc.* (*c* 1865) I. 155/2 It is necessary that the prints be considerably over-printed.

2. To print too many copies of (a book, etc.). Also *absol.*

1909 in WEBSTER. **1931** H. G. WELLS *Work, Wealth & Happiness of Mankind* (1932) ix. 353 The belligerent governments withdrew gold from internal circulation and resorted to the printing press to replace it. Each in its own measure overprinted. **1962** *Which?* Sept. 274/2 We always overprint and there are a few copies of this available if you should want it.

II. [OVER- 8.] **3.** *trans.* **a.** To print additional matter on (a surface already bearing print); to mark by a subsequent printing process. Also *transf.*

1863 in J. Easton *De La Rue Hist. Brit. & For. Postage Stamps, 1855–1901* (1958) xii. 263 Printed first from the Sixpenny plate and afterwards overprinted one penny & fourpence. **1876** *Let.* 6 Sept. in *Ibid.* xxiv. 710 As it is impossible to overprint the full sheet at one operation, and at the same time ensure the overprinted matter falling truly in the panels left blank for it, we could only overprint half the sheet at a time. **1899** *Captain* I. 187/1 The current stamps of Great Britain were overprinted with the company's name. **1912** KNECHT & FOTHERGILL *Princ. & Pract. Textile Printing* VII. 319 Dry the goods well and then —(2) Over-print them with either a cover or pad roller in steam Alizarin red or pink. **1912** *Chambers's Jrnl.* Nov. 750/2 In 1903 permission was again granted to firms to overprint the backs of stamps. **1950** *Chambers's Encycl.* II. 788/1 A white spot on a coloured ground will be obtained by first printing the fabric with a paste containing a reserve chemical and then over-printing with a thickened solution of a dye which will be destroyed or its fixation be prevented by the reserve chemical. **1967** *Q. Jrnl. Geol. Soc.* CXXIII. 274 In the north-west corner of Sheet 10/iii at Lepeidere the *A* and *B* domains come together and both are 'overprinted' and partly obliterated by *C* tectonism. **1974** *B.S.I. News* Jan. 14 BSI is prepared to accept bulk orders for copies of any one standard and have the covers overprinted to the purchaser's requirements. **1974** *Nature* 27 Sept. 296/2 Granite was part of a widespread event which overprinted any isotopic record of the early history of the gneisses in the area.

b. To print (additional matter) on a surface already bearing printing; to add by a subsequent printing process. Also *transf.*

1926 C. F. D. MARSHALL *Brit. Post Office* I. vi. 54 On the 1st of January, 1883, the 3d... and 6d... made their appearance in lilac, with the value overprinted in carmine. **1937** *Q. Jrnl. Geol. Soc.* XCIII. 583 There may be complete obliteration of the earlier fabric.., but frequently a second fabric is 'overprinted' on the earlier.. without complete loss of the latter's characteristics. **1938** E. RAISZ *Gen. Cartography* xvii. 199 The French over-printed a network of even kilometer squares upon their maps. **1975** J. B. HARLEY *O.S. Maps* ii. 21 This grid.. was overprinted on War Office editions of Ordnance Survey maps.

So **,over'printed** *ppl. a.*, **,over'printing** *vbl. sb.*

1876 Overprinted [see sense 3 a above]. **1912** KNECHT & FOTHERGILL *Princ. & Pract. Textile Printing* VII. 320 The ground will be plain or 'patterned' according as the roller used in the second- or over-printing was a 'pad' or a cover. **1931** H. G. WELLS *Work, Wealth & Happiness of Mankind* (1932) ix. 353 The overprinting of paper money continued. **1962** *Collier's Encycl.* XVIII. 679/2 *Surcharged and overprinted*, stamps on which a new value or name has been printed; 'surcharge' is used when overprinting involves change in value. **1971** I. G. GASS et al. *Understanding Earth* ii. 51/1 Overprinted age patterns may span the entire interval between two (or more) thermal events. **1975** J. B. HARLEY *O.S. Maps* ix. 143 In addition to the coloured administrative diagrams, 1:100 000 scale base maps printed in grey are available without overprinting.

over-'privileged, *a.* [OVER- 28 d.] Possessing or enjoying too many privileges. Also *absol.*

1934 *Word Study* Mar. 6/2 If this country has an over-privileged class, it is the railroad phoneticians. **1941** *Times Educ. Suppl.* 6 Dec. 581/1 The over-privileged classes.. and in general what is crudely described as the 'old school tie' influence in Government, business, and the professions, see their privileges threatened. **1956** C. W. MILLS *Power Elite* i. 14 The moral conception of the elite, however, is not always merely an ideology of the over-privileged. **1971** P. WORSTHORNE *Socialist Myth* viii. 192 Today.. the majority .. is not only overprivileged politically; it is overprivileged economically. **1973** *Nature* 16 Mar. 210/2 The weak and the poor are under-privileged because we are over-privileged.

overprize (-'praɪz), *v.* [OVER- 26, 22.]

1. *trans.* To prize, esteem, or value too highly; to over-estimate, overrate.

1589 NASHE *Almond for Parrat* 15 You, like Midasses, haue ouerprised his musick. **1663** BP. PATRICK *Parab. Pilgr.* xix. (1668) 191 Overprizing what they have already acquired, they make no further search. **1761** YOUNG *Resignation* I. xlvi, Blind Error.. Bids us for ever Pains deplore, Our Pleasures overprize. **1813** COLERIDGE *Remorse* I. ii, I am much beholden to your high opinion, Which so o'erprizes my light services.

2. To exceed or surpass in value. *Obs.* or *arch.*

1593 B. BARNES *Parthen.* Madrigal xxiii, Those tresses, Whose train.. Apollo's locks did overprize. **1610** SHAKS. *Temp.* I. ii. 92 That, which but by being so retir'd Ore-priz'd all popular rate. **1669** ETHEREDGE *Love in Tub* V. i, These tears.. which for me you shed, O'erprize the blood which I for you have bled.

Hence **over'prizer**, one who overprizes.

1611 SPEED *Hist. Gt. Brit.* VIII. iii. §15. 385 To conuict these his fawning ouer-prizers.

,over-pro'duce, *v.* [OVER- 27.] *trans.* To produce (a commodity) in excess of the demand or of a defined amount.

1894 H. D. LLOYD *Wealth agst. Commw.* 155 If the owner of a well over-produced only the one-hundredth of a barrel, he got a notice to go slower. **1899** *Daily News* 24 Apr. 3/4 Pig iron has been over-produced.. in recent years.

'over-pro'duction. [OVER- 29 b.] Excessive production; production in excess of the demand. Also *attrib.*

1822 COBBETT *Weekly Reg.* 9 Mar. 607 You insist upon over-production. **1863** FAWCETT *Pol. Econ.* III. xiv, Over-production has two meanings; it may either signify that commodities produced cannot be sold at remunerative prices, or it may signify that commodities are produced which are really not wanted. **1934** C. LAMBERT *Music Ho!* IV. 233 The present age is one of overproduction. **1948** G. CROWTHER *Outl. Money* (rev. ed.) v. 151 'Over-production' and a slump result. *Ibid.* 153 The 'over-production' theory, then, like the 'under-consumption' theory, is, in a sense, sometimes right, but for the wrong reasons. **1960** *Farmer & Stockbreeder* 19 Jan. (Suppl.) 50/3 Over-production of Eggs sank prices to rock-bottom in 1959. **1974** M. B. BROWN *Econ. of Imperialism* viii. 199 The general opinion held in Germany in the mid 1880s was that colonies were needed to solve the problem of overproduction. **1974** *Country Life* 26 Dec. 2019/1 In America there has been overproduction resulting in shutdowns. **1975** *New Yorker* 21 Apr. 7/2 She is most effective as a live performer of her own material—projecting a loose, direct, unpretentious, spontaneous style that, unfortunately, is lacking on her records, which suffer from overproduction.

over-prolix, -promise, -prone: see OVER-.

'over-proof, *a.* (*sb.*) [OVER- 32.] That is 'above proof'; containing a larger proportion of alcohol than that contained in proof-spirit: see PROOF. Also *fig.* and *ellipt.* as *sb.* = over-proof spirit.

1807 T. THOMSON *Chem.* II. 390 The strength of spirits stronger than proof, or over-proof as it is termed. **1840** DICKENS *Barn. Rudge* liv, Show us the best—the very best —the over-proof that you keep for your own drinking, Jack! **1906** *Daily Chron.* 11 May 9/2 The appeal to the Government.. asking them to prohibit the importation of over-proof spirits into British territory. **1967** N. MARSH *Death at Dolphin* iv. 94 She really *is*.. the original overproof *femme fatale*. **1973** J. WOOD *North Beat* x. 131 'Try a punch at the brew,' the sergeant suggested. Collins tried a punch. He coughed.. 'What is it—some of the overproof stuff?'

'over-pro'portion, *sb.* [OVER- 29 c.] Excessive proportion; excess *of* one thing in proportion to another.

1666 S. PARKER *Free & Impart. Censure* (1667) 143 By the Over-proportion of one of them [Pleasures against Misery], he may rate the value of himself. **1805** R. W. DICKSON *Pract. Agric.* I. 291 The over-proportions of moisture.

So **,over-pro'portion** *v. trans.*, to make or estimate in excess of the true proportion; **'over-pro'portionate, -pro'portionated, -pro'portioned** *adjs.*, that is above the proper or ordinary proportion, excessive, disproportionate; **'over-pro'portionately** *adv.*, in excessive proportion, out of proportion *to* something. (All *rare* or *Obs.*)

1642 FULLER *Holy & Prof. St.* IV. xiii. 302 He that should have guessed the bignesse of Alexanders souldiers by their shields left in India, would much overproportion their true greatnesse. **1647** H. MORE *Song of Soul* To Rdr. 7/2 Would it not be an overproportionated engine? **1662** —— *Philos. Writ.* Pref. Gen. (1712) 11 Where men have an over-proportioned Zeal for or against such Things in Religion. **1671** GREW *Anat. Plants* i. §20 The Parenchyma.. is so far over-proportionate, as to make at least nine Tenths of the whole Lobe. **1676** H. MORE *Remarks* 165 A greater sign that there is no such Tension.. than that in the Pump should be so over-proportionately tended. **1697** COLLIER *Ess. Mor. Subj.* I. (1709) 231 Misapprehensions conveyed into them by over-proportioned Respect.

,overpro'tection. *Psychol.* [OVER- 29 b.] The condition or act of protecting (someone, esp. a child) to an undue or unhealthy extent.

1930 *Smith Coll. Stud. Social Work* I. 42 Such overprotection would be increased if the child were sickly or handicapped in any way. **1938** D. M. LEVY in *Psychiatry* I. 569/2 We would thus succeed in isolating those personality factors.. that would be.. a result of maternal overprotection. **1949** S. A. STOUFFER et al. *Amer. Soldier* iv. 135 A theory currently of considerable interest in psychiatry seeks to trace some types of neurotic behavior to overprotection by the mother. **1964** M. ARGYLE *Psychol. & Social Probl.* ix. 123 Hysteria and psychosomatic complaints, especially in women, are related to a history of overprotection by the mother. **1970** H. EDELSTON *Foundations & Growth of Character* III. i. 96 Just as maternal deprivation can be harmful in its effects, so can maternal overprotection. **1977** A. WILSON *Strange Ride R. Kipling* vi. 275 Much of her over-protection may have come from her sense of his strain.

So **overpro'tective** *a.*, that protects to an undue or unhealthy extent; **overpro'tectiveness**, the state or condition of being overprotective. Also **overpro'tect** *v. trans.*; **overpro'tected, -pro'tecting** *ppl. adjs.*

1930 *Smith Coll. Stud. Social Work* I. 58 One or both parents over-protective, rejecting, or were overambitious, as the category indicates. **1938** D. M. LEVY in *Psychiatry* I. 569/2 How their personality traits resulting from growth in the medium of the overprotecting mother have shaped their destinies. **1949** M. MEAD *Male & Female* xv. 310 He is often ..over-protective towards his son. **1957** R. B. CATTELL *Personality & Motivation* iv. 135 It is a sociological pattern, varying from family to family of 'Overprotectiveness —vs — Tough Neglect'. **1961** WEBSTER s.v. *Overprotect*, Overprotected children. **1964** M. ARGYLE *Psychol. & Social Probl.* vi. 80 Women are prone to hysteria, especially when they have had a dominating mother who has over-protected them, thus concentrating attention on bodily complaints. *Ibid.* ix. 120 Several investigators reported that schizophrenics have mothers who are over-protecting, but when control groups have been used no such difference is found. **1969** M. D. VERNON *Human Motivation* x. 161 Even over-protectiveness.. tends to create anxiety. **1973** R. LEWIS *Blood Money* v. 60 She hadn't wanted him to talk to her daughter... She was over-protective. **1976** *Times* 1 Sept. 14/1 A warning against over-protecting elderly people. **1977** R. BARNARD *Blood Brotherhood* xiv. 150 Over-protected and over-driven, Philip had drifted through.. life.

'over-'proud, *a.* [Late OE. *ofer-prút*: see OVER- 28.] Too proud; excessively proud.

a **1050** *Liber Scintill.* lviii. (1889) 183 Willa on him sylf oferprut ys. **1340** HAMPOLE *Pr. Consc.* 589 Whar-for I hald a man noght witty þat here es over prowde and ioly. **1592** *Nobody & Someb.* in *Sch. Shaks.* (1878) I. 315 Insulting, over-proude, ambitious woman. **1606** SHAKS. *Tr. & Cr.* II. iii. 132 We thinke him ouer proud, And vnder honest.

over-prove, -provoke, etc.: see OVER-.

†**over'pry,** *v. Obs. rare.* [OVER- 7.] *trans.* To look over pryingly; to examine inquisitively.
1566 DRANT *Horace, Sat.* iv. C b, Not Tygille nor such alecunners my workes do overprye. **1590** GREENE *Never too late* Wks. (Grosart) VIII. 48 When my father like Argos setteth a hundred eies to ouerpry my actions.

'over-'prying, *a.* [OVER- 28 b.] Excessively prying; too inquisitive.
1655 FULLER *Ch. Hist.* IX. ii. §21 It is a bad signe, when suspicious persons are over-preying to know the windows, doors,..and contrivances of their neighbours houses.

over-public, -puissant, etc.: see OVER- 28.

ˌover-'publicize, *v.* [OVER- 27 a.] *trans.* To publicize too much or to excess; to give undue importance to by publicizing. So **ˌover-'publicized** *ppl. a.*
1939 *War Illustr.* 4 Nov. p. ii/1, I regard Lindbergh's pronouncement on the War as a piece of gratuitous impertinence... One of the most grossly over-publicised personalities of our age he expects too much if he thinks his words must carry weight just because he once flew the Atlantic. **1957** L. FEATHER *Bk. of Jazz* (1959) xv. 132 Admittedly the drummer today is over-publicized, over-featured and over-praised in proportion to the role he should play as a member of an ensemble. **1964** E. A. NIDA *Toward Sci. Transl.* xii. 252 It is unfortunate that MT (standard abbreviation for machine translation) has been over-publicized. **1965** 'W. HAGGARD' *Hard Sell* i. 1 Over-publicized world beaters which mysteriously disintegrated.

†**'over-ˌpull.** *Obs.* [OVER- 29 b.] An excessive or too strong pull; excessive extortion.
1615 T. ADAMS *White Devill* 53 To racke the poore with over-puls, al (but Devils) hold monstrous.

'overpunch, *sb. Computers.* [OVER- 1 d.] A hole or hole position in the upper portion of a punched card.
1969 MAISEL & WRIGHT *Introd. Electronic Digital Computers* xiii. 325 If the overpunch is a 12, the number is positive, and if it is an 11 punch, the number is negative. **1970** O. DOPPING *Computers & Data Processing* ii. 44 The two top rows are called zone punches or overpunches. The uppermost row is called 12 or Y, the second from the top, 11 or X. In addition, the uppermost numerical row, the 0 row, is used as a third overpunch. **1973** MURRILL & SMITH *Introd. Computer Sci.* vi. 219 When programs written in programming languages such as Cobol read numerical data, the sign does not normally occupy a separate column. Instead, it is entered as an overpunch in the rightmost digit.
So **'overpunch** *v. trans.*, to represent by means of an overpunch; **'overˌpunching** *vbl. sb.*
1962 *Gloss. Terms Automatic Data Processing* (*B.S.I.*) 90 *Over-punching*, the use of the upper curtate to represent a digit independently of the use of the lower curtate. **1973** MURRILL & SMITH *Introd. Computer Sci.* vi. 220 Figure 6·6 also illustrates the situation when the & symbol is overpunched in the same column as the 3.

'overpunish (-'pʌnɪʃ), *v.* [OVER- 27.] *trans.* To punish to excess or more than one deserves.
a **1639** W. WHATELEY *Prototypes* I. xix. (1640) 224 For his inferiours he is likely tyrannical..and cares not how he overpunisheth them. **1823** DE QUINCEY *Lett. on Educ.* i. Wks. 1860 XIV. 9 The evil is..overpunished by the mortifications which attend any such juvenile acts of presumption.

overpuppy, *v.*: see OVER- 22 b.

ˌover-'purchase, *v.* [OVER- 26.] *trans.* To purchase at too high a price; to buy too dear.
1651 FULLER *Abel Rediv.* (1867) II. 82 Unwilling to over-purchase his safety at the price of a lie. **1703** COLLIER *Ess. Mor. Subj.* II. (1709) 191 He that buys his Satisfaction at the Expence of Duty and Discretion, is sure to over-purchase.
So **ˌover-'purchase** *sb.*
1697 COLLIER *Immor. Stage* (1698) 161 Mirth at the expence of Virtue is an Over-purchase.

over'put, *v. Sc.* and *north. dial.* [OVER- 4.] *trans.* To throw off, 'get over', recover from.
c **1400** *Destr. Troy* 160 His pride well ouerput, past into elde. **1586** *Durham Depos.* (Surtees) 318 The said Luke did aske him..how he did: he answeared, 'Sore sicke, but I hope to God to overputt it'. **1725** RAMSAY *Gent. Sheph.* v. i, Alake! I'll never be mysell again; I'll ne'er o'erput it. **1825–80** JAMIESON, *To ourput*, to recover from, to get the better of; applied to disease or evil.
So †**over'putting** *vbl. sb.* (in *Hunting*), running beyond the proper point, so as to lose the scent.
1590 COCKAINE *Treat. Hunting* B iv b, At euery ouer putting off the hounds, or small stop, euery huntsman.. ought to begin his rechate, and..the hounds will be in full chase agaïne.

over-'quantity. [OVER- 19.] Quantity in excess, surplus amount.
1596 BACON *Max. Com. Law* v. (1636) 26 The overquantity is not forfeited. **1669** WORLIDGE *Syst. Agric.* (1681) 85 Till..the over-quantity of the Soil in the Pit.. oblige him to remove it. **1805** R. W. DICKSON *Pract. Agric.* I. 281 It may exist in such over-quantities..as to prove highly injurious.

over-quarter, -queath: see OVER-.

†**over-'quat,** *v. Obs.* [f. OVER- 27 + QUAT *v.*[1]] *trans.* To oppress with too much food; to overfill, glut.
a **1250** *Owl & Night.* 353 Mid este þu þe miȝt over-quatie. And over-fulle makeþ wlatie.

†**over'quell,** *v. Obs.* [OVER- 21.] *trans.* To quell, crush, overcome, overpower, subdue.
c **1450** *St. Cuthbert* (Surtees) 6301 When he wakend, sone he feld þat a serpent him our qweld; his nek full' sare it grepyd. **1549–62** STERNHOLD & H. *Nunc dimittis*, The Gentiles to illuminate, And Sathan overquell. **1604** EDMONDS *Observ. Cæsars Comm.* 97 Much to be pitied, that vertue should at any time be overquelled with a greater strength. [Cf. '*Ouerquall'd*, Overrun, as with vermin' (Jam.).]

overquelm, -qwert: see OVERWHELM, -THWART.

'over-'quick, *a.* [OVER- 28.] Too quick. So **'over-'quickly** *adv.*, too quickly, too readily.
1538 STARKEY *England* I. iv. 132, I somewhat feare that we admyt ouer-quykly thes fautys in the Church. **1560** DAUS tr. *Sleidane's Comm.* 6 b, He graunteth that he was ouer quicke. **1663** BOYLE *Usef. Exp. Nat. Philos.* II. ii. 166 The fire..must be kept pretty quick, and yet not over-quick, least the oyle boil over. **1859** TENNYSON *Vivien* 724 Overquick art thou To catch a loathly plume fall'n from the wing Of that foul bird of rapine.

over-race, *v.*: see OVER- 27.

†**ˌover-'rack,** *v. Obs.* [f. OVER- 27 + RACK *v.*[3]] *trans.* To rack or strain to excess; to overstrain. Hence †**ˌover-'racked** *ppl. a.*
1589 NASHE *Pref. Greene's Menaphon* (Arb.) 8 So shoulde ..their ouer-rackte Rhethorique, bee the Ironicall recreation of the Reader. **1598** SYLVESTER *Du Bartas* II. i. I. *Eden* 293 A drooping life, and over-rackèd brain. *a* **1625** BEAUM. & FL. *Faithful Friends* III. i, I'm over-racked with expectation Of the event.

over-rack, variant of OVER-RAKE *v.*

overrad(de, obs. pa. t. and pple. of OVERREAD.

overrade, -raid, obs. pa. t. of OVERRIDE.

over-raft, -raght, obs. pa. t. of OVERREACH.

†**over-'raise,** *v. Obs.* [OVER- 1 (*b*).] *trans.* To raise or exalt over or above.
a **1300** *Cursor M.* 2373 (Cott.) Þar sal þi nam ouerraised be.

†**over-'rake,** *v. Naut. Obs.* Also 7 -rack. [f. OVER- 5, 10 + RAKE *v.*[1]] *trans.* To rake or sweep over, or from end to end: said of waves breaking over or of shot traversing a ship.
1599 E. WRIGHT *Voy.* in Arb. *Garner* III. 389 The raging waves..over-raked the waist of the ship. **1624** CAPT. SMITH *Virginia* 56 Such mighty waues ouerracked vs in that small barge. *Ibid.* 128 [The Spaniards] followed with their great Ordnance, that many times ouerracked our ship. **1706** PHILLIPS s.v., The Waves are said to over-rake a Ship, when they break in and wash her from Stem to Stern, or from one end to the other. **1867** in SMYTH *Sailor's Word-bk.*

overrange ('əʊvəreɪndʒ), *sb. Electr.* [OVER- 5, 13.] **a.** A signal larger or condition stronger than an instrument is designed to accept or measure. Freq. *attrib.* **b.** An extension of the nominal range of an instrument.
1941 T. J. RHODES *Industr. Instruments for Measurement & Control* iii. 73 This may result in dangerously high pressures if the instrument is subjected to temperatures much higher than those for which it was designed. Usually these overrange temperatures are accidents which can be avoided. *Ibid.* 74 Where the instrument is subject to periodic overrange..it is necessary to provide a means of overrange protection. **1974** *Nature* 15 Nov. p. ix/2 (Advt.), 4-digit electronic display read-out, with 100% over-range, i.e. up to 19999. **1976** *Physics Bull.* Mar. 131/3 This instrument also has a digital voltmeter output and meter overrange protection.

over-range, *v.*: see OVER- 9.

'over-'rank, *a.* [OE. *oferranc*: see OVER- 28.] Too rank or vigorous in growth; too gross.
a **1023** WULFSTAN *Hom.* vi. (Napier) 46 God..reafjan læteð eowere dohtra heora gyrla and to oferrancra heafodȝewæda. *a* **1568** ASCHAM *Scholem.* (Arb.) 113 If Osorius would leaue of..his ouer rancke rayling against poore Luther. **1609** DRAYTON *Leg. T. Cromwell* cxvii, Things ouer ranck doe neuer kindly beare, As in the corne the fluxure when we see Fill but the straw when it should feed the eare. **1689** SWIFT *Ode to W. Sancroft* v, Our British soil is over rank, and breeds Among the noblest flowers a thousand pois'nous weeds. **1712** MORTIMER *Husb.* II. 228 If your [Hop] Ground..be apt to produce over-rank Binds.
Hence **'over-'rankness.**
1626 BACON *Sylva* §670 Over-Ranknesse of the Corne; Which they use to remedy, by Mowing it after it is come up; Or putting Sheepe into it. **1707** MORTIMER *Husb.* (1721) I. 81 Wheat, about the latter end of October is best [sowed] because of preventing the over-rankness of it.

'over-'rash, *a.* [OVER- 28.] Too rash.
1554 in Holinshed *Chron.* III. 1117/1 Forgiue & forget my ouerrash boldnesse. *a* **1653** GOUGE *Comm. Heb.* xi. 32 Jephthah's vow is on all sides granted to be over-rash.
So **'over-'rashly** *adv.*
a **1653** GOUGE *Comm. Heb.* xi. 35 Not over-rashly to censure them. **1818** SCOTT *Hrt. Midl.* xliv, Marriage..over-rashly coveted by professors, and specially by young ministers.

'over-ˌrate, *sb.* [OVER- 29 d, 19.] **a.** An excessive rate. **b.** An extra rate.
1624 MASSINGER *Parl. Love* v. i, Which might witness for me, At what an over-rate I had made purchase Of her long-wish'd embraces. **1682** J. COLLINS *Salt in Eng.* 94 To which may be added the Overrate and profit in Foreign Countries. **1757** JOS. HARRIS *Coins* II. vii. §25 Silver bullion will get up as much above coin, as this over-rate amounts to.

overrate (ˌəʊvə'reɪt), *v.* [OVER- 26, 27, 22.]
1. *trans.* To rate too highly or above the real value or amount, to over-estimate; to give to (coins) a forced currency as legal tender beyond the intrinsic value.
1611 SHAKS. *Cymb.* I. iv. 41 Sir, you o're-rate my poore kindnesse. **1674** *Essex Papers* (Camden) I. 226 Essex House is now to be sold, & valued at about 7000*l*....it seemeth to me not to be overrated. **1788** J. AIKIN *Eng. Delineated* 248 Its population has been greatly over-rated. **1858** LD. ST. LEONARDS *Handy-Bk. Prop. Law* xx. 155 In disposing of your residue, neither overrate nor underrate its value.
b. To assess too highly for rating purposes.
1884 SIR E. FRY in *Law Rep.* 13 Q. Bench Div. 376 A person who considers that he has been overrated by the quinquennial list.
2. *Rowing.* To row at a faster rate than (an opponent).
1960 *Times* 4 Apr. 14/1 They [*sc.* Oxford] were still overrating Cambridge. **1961** *Times* 10 July 4/6 Lady Margaret made no mistakes in the Ladies' Plate, snatched an early lead, and, always overrating Eton, came home by a length and a third.
So **'over'rated** *ppl. a.*, **'over'rating** *vbl. sb.*, *ppl. a.*
1589 WARNER *Alb. Eng., Prose Add.* (1612) 339 The repentant payment of mine ouer-rated pleasure. **1651** HOBBES *Leviath.* II. xxvii. 154 A foolish over-rating of their own worth. **1790** BEATSON *Nav. & Mil. Mem.* I. 30 In regard to overrated and unjust claims. **1804** ANNA SEWARD *Mem. Darwin* 114 A convalescent,..full..of overrating thankfulness to Miss S. for the offer she had made. **1879** M. ARNOLD *Falkland* Mixed Ess. 208 Horace Walpole pronounces him a much overrated man.

over-rational, -ravished: see OVER-.

over-raucht, -raught: see OVERREACH *v.*

overreach ('əʊvəriːtʃ), *sb.* [f. next.]
1. a. A reaching over some thing or person. **b.** Too great a reach, stretch, or strain; an excessive reach. **c.** Exaggeration.
1556 J. HEYWOOD *Spider & F.* lxx. 116 An ouer-rech aboue the weake wittes cure. **1644–7** CLEVELAND *Char. Lond. Diurn.* Poems (1677) 101 It is like over-reach of Language, when every..Quack must be called a Doctor. **1815** *Sporting Mag.* XLVI. 21 In an over-reach by Harmer a close took place, and Harmer was thrown. **1961** B. FERGUSSON *Watery Maze* xv. 370 In Burma the Japs made their classic over-reach between March and June of 1944, when..they attempted to surround and defeat the British and Indian forces in Manipur. **1977** *Time* 10 Jan. 55/3 Felker's personal grandeur may match his managerial overreach. Since last spring he has asked for: 1) a 25% increase in his 1975 salary of $120,461, 2) the wherewithal to buy a house in Long Island's ducal Hamptons, and 3) company purchase of his super-duplex.
2. In reference to a horse: The act of striking one of the fore feet with the corresponding hind foot; the injury so caused. (Cf. OVERREACH *v.* 4.) Also *attrib.*
1607 TOPSELL *Four-f. Beasts* (1658) 309 If he halt..in the heel, as by over-reach or otherwise, then he will tread most on the toe. *Ibid.* 313 An upper attaint, or over-reach, upon the back sinew of the shanke, somewhat above the joynt. **1735** BURDON *Pocket Farrier* 12 If your Horse is Lame, occasion'd by an over-reach of his Hind-Foot. **1737** BRACKEN *Farriery Impr.* (1757) II. 210 A Horse is said to have got an Over-reach when he has cut his Fore-heel with the Point of his Hind shoe. **1900** *Trans. Highl. & Agric. Soc.* 275 Some writers confine the term 'over-reach'..to that form in which the hind foot over-reaches the fore one to such an extent as that the toe of the hind shoe comes in contact with the heel or the hollow of the heel of the fore-limb. **1932** J. BUCHAN *Gap in Curtain* iv. 193 Verona's mare got an overreach in a bog. **1949** 'J. TEY' *Brat Farrar* xxviii. 250 All the horses were safely back and all well except that Buster had an overreach. **1963** E. H. EDWARDS *Saddlery* xx. 151 A common injury sustained when jumping is caused by an over-reach and, in show jumpers, this often occurs low down on the heel or just above it. A rubber over-reach boot is usually the answer. **1976** *Horse & Hound* 10 Dec. 5/1 You would still have to change your clothes before riding and again when you returned, in order to remove muddy over-reach boots and turn your horse out.
3. An act of overreaching in dealing; the gaining of an advantage by deception. (Cf. next, 6.)
1615 CHAPMAN *Odyss.* XIII. 425 Thou still-wit-varying wretch! Insatiate In over-reaches! **1859** W. CHADWICK *Life De Foe* vi. 323 No possible overreach could..be perpetrated on the other.

overreach (əʊvə'riːtʃ), *v.* Also in *pres. t.* †-reche, -retche, -reke, reik; *pa. t.* and *pple.* -reached; also †-raght, -raucht, -raught, -raft, etc.: see REACH *v.* [OVER- 5, 14, 9, 13, 21, 23, 26.]
1. *trans.* To reach or extend over or beyond; to rise above; to stretch beyond in space or time.
a **1300** *Cursor M.* 1838 (Cott.) Þe heiest fell þat was our-quare þe flod ouer raght [*v.r.* -raȝt] seuen eln and mare. **1596** SPENSER *F.Q.* v. xii. 30 Her hands were foule and durtie,

never washt In all her life, with long nayles over-raught. **1610** MARKHAM *Masterp.* II. clxvii. 478 His vpper teeth will ouerreach, and hang ouer his neather teeth. *a* **1677** HALE *Prim. Orig. Man.* II. iii. 144 That number.. will arise to above 40000 Years, which will over-reach the Creation of Mankind. **1793** BEDDOES *Math. Evid.* 22 The other end will neither over-reach nor fall short of the other end of the lower. **1890** ABP. BENSON in *Life* II. 295 They did realise that there was a knowing and a thinking which far overreached themselves.

2. To reach or get at (a person, etc.) over an intervening space, to get within reach of; to overtake, come up with, attain to. Now *dial.*

a **1300** *Cursor M.* 22375 Þaas oþer all he [anticrist] mai ouer-reke Wit suerd he sal apon þam wreke. *c* **1330** R. BRUNNE *Chron.* (1810) 170 Alle to dede he brouht, þat his Galeie ouer rauht. ? *a* **1400** *Morte Arth.* 1508 Raunsone me resonabillye as I may ouer-reche, Aftyre my renttez in Rome may redyly forthire. **1596** SPENSER *F.Q.* VI. iii. 50 So that at length, after long weary chace,.. He over raught him. **1602** SHAKS. *Ham.* III. i. 17 Certaine Players We ore-wrought on the way. **1748** *Anson's Voy.* III. viii. 379 Mr. Anson overreached the galeon, and lay on her bow. **1874** G. MACDONALD *Malcolm* I. v. 34 The rising tide had overreached and surrounded her. **1885** MUCKLEBACKIT *Rhymes* 235 (E.D.D.), I overreached the couple, just as they were passing through the first gate beyond the village.

†**b.** To overtake, overpower. *Obs.*

c **1400** *Destr. Troy* 13898 Þan he braid to the buerne.. Ouerraght hym full roidly, reft hym his swerd. *c* **1430** *Freemasonry* 114 But he be unbuxom to that craft, Or with falssehed ys over-raft. **1513** DOUGLAS *Æneis* v. vi. 122 War nocht the sam misfortoun me ourraucht Quhilk Salyus betyde? **1586** A. DAY *Eng. Secretary* I. (1625) 59 Ouerreached with the tediousnesse of the enterprise. **1638** DRUMM. OF HAWTH. *Irene* Wks. (1711) 163 So did.. [they] find themselves surprised and over-reach'd with unexpected and inexpressible joys.

†**c.** *intr.* To reach over or across a boundary; to encroach. *Obs.*

1377 LANGL. *P. Pl.* B. XIII. 374 And if I repe, ouer-reche or ȝaf hem red þat repen, To seise to me with her sykel þat I ne sewe neure.

3. *trans.* To extend or spread over (something) so as to cover it. Also *absol.* or *intr.* (OVER- 9.)

? *a* **1400** *Morte Arth.* 921 Þey roode by þat ryver, þat rynnyd so swythe, Þare þe ryndez ouerrechez with realle bowghez. **1565** JEWEL *Reply Harding* (1611) 184 The Empire of Rome, which then ouerreached a great part of the world. **1643** BAKER *Chron.* II. 73 All favours from the King and Queene must passe by him, and the extent of his power over-reacheth all the Councell. **1838** MAURICE *Kingd. Christ* II. 14 This book.. should overreach the feelings, notions and decisions of each particular mind.

4. *intr.* Of a horse or other quadruped: To bring a hind foot against the corresponding fore foot in walking or running; *esp.* to strike and injure the heel of the fore foot with the hind foot. (Cf. OVERREACH *sb.* 2.) **b.** Also, generally, to bring a hind foot in front of or alongside a fore foot.

1523 [see OVERREACHING *vbl. sb.*]. **1589** R. HARVEY *Pl. Perc.* 5 A horse may ouer reach in a true pace. **1601** HOLLAND *Pliny* I. 350 Lions and Camels only.. keep pace in their march, foot by foot, that is to say, they neuer set their left foot before their right, nor ouer-reach with it. **1706** PHILLIPS, *To Over-reach*,.. to hit the Fore-feet with the hinder, as some Horses do. **1737** BRACKEN *Farriery Impr.* (1757) II. 48 They are also apt to over-reach, or hit their Hind-Shoes against their Fore-Shoes.

†**c.** *trans.* (from b.) *Obs.*

1616 SURFL. & MARKH. *Country Farme* 693 The elder Harts in their gate doe neuer ouer-reach the former foot with the hinder.. but it is not so in young Harts, for they in their gate doe ouer-reach and set the hinder foot more forward than the fore-foot, after the manner of the ambling Mule.

5. To reach beyond, to overshoot (a mark, etc.).

1540 COVERDALE *Fruitf. Less.* v. Wks. (Parker Soc.) I. 414 Whereas there be some men which overreach and go beyond this mark. **1877** BARING-GOULD *Myst. Suffering* 79 The infant will grasp at the moon and overreach an apple.

6. To gain an advantage over, get the better of, outdo: **a.** in early use, in a neutral sense; **b.** now always in a bad sense: to circumvent, outwit, cheat in dealing.

a. 1577 HANMER *Anc. Eccl. Hist.* (1619) 240 How he overreached their sleights and subtle combats. *c* **1590** GREENE *Fr. Bacon* x. 82 Think'st thou with wealth to overreach me? **1623** BINGHAM *Xenophon* 46 It behoueth vs.. to be no more ouerreached by them. **1702** PENN in *Pa. Hist. Soc. Mem.* IX. 172 Watch him, out-wit him, and honestly over-reach him.

b. 1596 SPENSER *F.Q.* IV. ii. 10 For that false spright,.. Was so expert in every subtile slight, That it could overreach the wisest earthly wight. **1611** BIBLE *1 Thess.* iv. 6 That no man goe beyond and defraud his brother. *Marg.*, Or, oppresse, or, ouerreach. **1727** DE FOE *Syst. Magic* I. iv. (1840) 118 An evidence how shrewdly the Devil overreached mankind. **1754** FIELDING *Jonathan Wild* II. ii, He never made any bargain without over-reaching (or, in the vulgar phrase, cheating) the person with whom he dealt. **1848** MILL *Pol. Econ.* I. vii. §5 (1876) 68 There is in all rich communities, a predatory population, who live by pillaging or over-reaching other people.

7. *refl.* To reach, stretch, strain oneself, or advance beyond one's strength, beyond one's aim, etc.

a **1568** ASCHAM *Scholem.* II. (Arb.) 99 Some men of our time,.. haue so ouer reached them selues, in making trew difference in the poyntes afore rehearsed. **1607** BEAUM. & FL. *Woman-Hater* IV. ii, Prove it again, sir; it may be your sense was set too high, and so over-wrought itself. **1689** WOOD *Life* 16 July (O.H.S.) III. 306 A terrible fit of the crampe above the ancle.. occasion'd.. by over-retching my self. **1886** QUALTROUGH *Boat Sailer's Man.* 138 A common error when working to windward in a race for the purpose of rounding a weather mark-boat, is for a boat to overreach herself.

b. *refl.* and *intr.* with admixture of sense 6.

1589 WARNER *Alb. Eng.* v. xxii. 99 The Parasite doth ouerreach, And beares away the game. **1727** GAY *Fables* I. xxvii. 10 But all men over-reach in trade. **1847** JAMES *J. Marston Hall* x, The first thing that excited suspicion in my mind that I had overreached myself. **1855** MACAULAY *Hist. Eng.* xv. III. 566 Their cupidity overreached itself. **1859** THACKERAY *Virgin.* xii, 'Tis known that American folks have become perfectly artless and simple in later times, and never grasp, and never overreach, and are never selfish now.

†**8.** *trans.* ? To turn over and examine; to overhaul. *Obs.*

c **1400** *Destr. Troy* Prol. 69 The whiche bokes barely bothe as þai were, A Romayn ouerraght & right hom hym-seluyn, That Cornelius was cald. **1513** DOUGLAS *Æneis* VI. ix. 136 Ane hiddeous grip [*vultur*] with busteous bowland beik His maw [*jecur*] immortale doith pik and ourreik.

9. *intr.* To reach too far (*lit.* and *fig.*); †to go beyond limits, go to excess; to exaggerate (*obs.*).

a **1568** ASCHAM *Scholem.* II. (Arb.) 116 They will sonest ouer reach in taulke, and fardest cum behinde in writing. **1600** HOLLAND *Livy* X. xxx. 374 But some have overreached a little, & written, that the enemies were 40330 foot, and 46000 horse strong. **1619** WILLET *Hexapla Daniel* 311 The first account commeth short.. so the other ouerreacheth aboue 60 yeares. **1638** CHILLINGW. *Relig. Prot.* I. vii. §35. 408 You overreach in saying they cannot. **1896** *Daily News* 6 Aug. 7/3 A small boy.. overreached and fell from an ornamental bridge into the stream.

†**b.** *trans.* To exaggerate, overrate. *Obs.*

1610 BP. HALL *Apol. Brownists* §55 That this Leprosie infects all persons and things is shamefully ouer-reacht. **1822** PETERKIN *Notes* 160 (E.D.D.) His Lordship's rents are over-reatched in the last valuation.

c. *trans.* To stretch out (an arm, etc.) too far.

1890 *Lancet* 1 Feb. 241/1 She 'over-reached' her right arm and felt pain in the shoulder.

over'reacher. [f. prec. + -ER[1].] One who or that which overreaches. †**a.** One who exaggerates; hence (in Puttenham) = HYPERBOLE. **b.** One who gets the better of another by craft or fraud. **c.** A horse that overreaches (see prec. 4).

1589 PUTTENHAM *Eng. Poesie* III. xviii. (Arb.) 202 The figure which the Greeks call *Hiperbole*, the Latines *Dementiens* or the lying figure. I for his immoderate excesse cal him the ouer reacher. **1589** R. HARVEY *Pl. Perc.* (1590) 11 Is there no penaltie to represse such lauish ouer reachers as offer legends of lies to the presse? **1611** COTGR., *Surpreneur*,.. ouerreacher, cheater, cousener, craftie dealer. **1879** FARRAR *St. Paul* II. 67 Nor thieves, nor over-reachers, nor drunkards,.. shall inherit the kingdom of God.

ove'rreaching, *vbl. sb.* [f. as prec. + -ING[1].] The action of OVERREACH *v.* in its various senses.

1523 FITZHERB. *Husb.* §113 Atteynt is a sorance, that commeth of an ouer rechynge. **1573** TUSSER *Husb.* Ep. to W. Paget ii. 11 At first for over reaching, And lack of taking hid. **1607** MARKHAM *Caval.* II. (1617) 83 Over-reaching is a fault incident to young horses, weake horses and euill trotting horses. **1768–74** TUCKER *Lt. Nat.* (1834) II. 321 Quarrels, thefts, over-reachings, amours, and partialities among them. **1802** [see DICKER *v.*]. **1933** H. BELLOC *William the Conqueror* 55 At that moment appeared the go-between who settled the whole affair, earning thereby the permanent gratitude and protection of Godwin and his sons. But it was an overreaching. They had better have kept away from such an ally! **1971** *New York Law Jrnl.* 23 Nov. 18/5 The 1955 amendment.. was adopted.. to protect such tenants from overreaching by landlords who authorized commercial and business leases upon tenants. **1977** A. WILSON *Strange Ride R. Kipling* iv. 202 His apprehensions of disaster brought on by overreaching and vainglory.

attrib. **1875** KNIGHT *Dict. Mech.*, *Over-reaching device*,.. an attachment to the leg or foot of a horse to prevent the catching of the toe of the hind foot upon the heel of the fore foot.

over'reaching, *ppl. a.* [f. as prec. + -ING[2].] That overreaches; reaching or extending over; cheating; †exaggerating (*obs.*).

1579 FULKE *Heskins's Parl.* 340 He must note an hyperbole or ouerreaching speach in this sentence. **1603** SIR R. WILBRAHAM *Jrnl.* (1902) 59 By reason of her great reading and over-reaching experience. **1782** MISS BURNEY *Cecilia* IX. i, The character of Briggs,.. rapacious, and overreaching. **1890** L. C. D'OYLE *Notches* 159 Not a breath.. swayed the over-reaching pines upon the silent cliffs.

So **over'reachingly** *adv.*, **over'reachingness.**

1571 GOLDING *Calvin on Ps.* xxxv. 9 Although hee speake overreachingly. **1611** COTGR., *Cauteleusement*,.. cunningly, .. craftily, deceitfully, ouerreachingly.

over-react (ˌəʊvəriː'ækt), *v.* [OVER- 27.] *intr.* To respond with excessive force or emotion to a given situation. Hence ˌ**over-re'acting** *vbl. sb.*; ˌ**over-re'action.**

1961 L. MUMFORD *City in Hist.* i. 26 At the same time, the male over-reacted against the feminine side of his own nature. **1962** *Times* 21 Aug. 5/6 The more emotional.. person tended to over-react to stress. **1965** *Economist* 13 Nov. 705/3 Some critics do think that the United States is in danger of getting its priorities wrong, by over-reacting to the threat of China and under-reacting to the possibilities of easing the Soviet dominance of east-central Europe. **1967** C. COCKBURN *I Claud* xxxiv. 424 This 'over-reaction' to what were.. reasonable queries and doubts, was psychologically very revealing. **1968** *Listener* 26 Sept. 410/1 This was the first escalation, triggered off when the militants goaded the authorities into over-reacting, closing the faculties and calling in the police. **1971** J. OSBORNE *West of Suez* I. 22, I just hope he.. gets some innocent pleasure out of it, which he's entitled to without censorious philistines like me over-reacting. **1973** E.-J. BAHR *Nice Neighbourhood* x. 106 Jack cried despairingly. He always over-reacted. **1973** *Times* 16 Nov. 7/2 A number of Government members believed that the espionage charges levelled against the editors constituted an over-reaction to the articles published in the magazine. **1974** M. C. GERALD *Pharmacol.* i. 12 Whether this was an over-reaction to questionable laboratory results or a sound scientific decision destined to rescue mankind remains to be seen at a future, less emotionally charged time. **1976** *Times Lit. Suppl.* 22 Oct. 1324/4 The hostility to the medium which he encountered in the early days led Strand (like some other major photographers) to over-react, to overcompensate by being rather too serious, too ponderous, too unbending.

over-read (-'riːd), *v.* [OE. *oferrǣdan*: see OVER- 16, 20, 22, 23.]

1. *trans.* To read over, read through. ? *Obs.*

c **1000** ÆLFRIC *Hom.* (Th.) I. 166 Oðþæt we ðone traht mid Godes fylste oferrædan magon. —— *Gram.* xxviii. (Z.) 176 *Perlego* ic oferræde. *c* **1375** *St. Augustin* 1192 in Horstm. *Altengl. Leg.* (1878) 81 No mon miht'.. His bokes alle ouer-rede. **1390** GOWER *Conf.* I. 191 Sche tok the lettres whiche he hadde, Fro point to point and overradde. **1509** BARCLAY *Shyp of Folys* (1570) ¶¶j, Let euery man beholde and ouerrede this Booke. **1601** SHAKS. *Jul. C.* III. i. 4 Trebonius doth desire you to ore-read (At your best leysure) this his humble suite. **1648** HERRICK *Hesper.*, *Dep. Gd. Dæmon*, Nothing now but lonely sit, And over-read what I have writ.

2. To read over again, re-read.

c **1489** CAXTON *Blanchardyn* xxxvi. 135 All ynough she red and ouered the sayd letters. **1636** EARL OF CORK in *Lismore Papers* (1888) Ser. II. III. 255 He told me, he had read, and overread them, and weighed euery word in them. **1925** W. DE LA MARE *Two Tales* 14 He was merely over-reading what he had read.

†**3.** To exceed or outdo in reading. *Obs. rare.*

1651 SHIRLEY *To Edmund Prestwich*, When you.. speak your own free muse, My admiration over-reads my eye.

4. *refl.* and *intr.* To read too much, to injure oneself with too much reading.

1805 H. K. WHITE *Let. to Neville White* 16 Dec., I have over-read myself and I find it absolutely necessary to take some relaxation. **1884** G. ALLEN *Philistia* I. 129 To let him run the chance of over-reading himself.

So '**over-'read** (-rɛd) *ppl. a.*, that has read too much; †**ove'rreader**, one who peruses.

c **1449** PECOCK *Repr.* I. xx. 130 Of tho bokis the ouerreder and attentijf studier. **1545** RAYNOLD *Byrth Mankynde* Prol. Bj, The vtilite & proffet whiche maye ensue, to the dyligent and attentyfe ouerreader therof. **1889** *Academy* 4 May 305/1 For him, as for few in this overread age, literature meant the time-tested masterpieces. **1895** R. LE GALLIENNE in *Westm. Gaz.* 22 Oct. 2/1 An age that is over-read and over-fed.

over-realism: see OVER- 29 c.

over-reave (əʊvə'riːv), *v.* [Etym. uncertain; perhaps f. OVER- 16 + a confusion of REEVE *v.*[1] and WEAVE *v.*[1]] *trans.* A term used of the metre of his poetry by G. M. Hopkins, to denote scansion continued for a complete stanza, as distinct from that confined to individual lines (see quots.). So **over-'reaving** *vbl. sb.*

1879 G. M. HOPKINS *Lett. to R. Bridges* (1935) 86 These little graces help the 'over-reaving' of the verse at which I so much aim, make it flow in one long strain to the end of the stanza and so forth. **1880** —— *Let.* 22 Dec. in Hopkins & Dixon *Corr.* (1935) 40 In lyric verse I like sprung rhythm also to be *over-rove*, that is the scanning to run on from line to line to the end of the stanza. **1881** —— *Lett. to R. Bridges* (1935) 120 In my lyrics in sprung rhythm I am strict in overreaving the lines when the measure has four feet, so that if one line has a heavy ending the next must have a sprung head. **1973** *Studies in Eng. Lit.: Eng. Number* (Tokyo) 25 'Over-reaving', or the scanning of verse without break from line to line, is a structural necessity following upon the method of scansion Hopkins proposes for sprung rhythm.

ˌ**over-'reckon,** *v.* [OVER- 27, 22.]

1. *trans.* To reckon, calculate, or estimate in excess; to overestimate. Also *absol.*

a **1646** J. GREGORY *Terrestr. Globe* Posthuma (1650) 290 Here the proportion of 60 miles to a Degree will over-reckon the Distance almost by the half. **1691** tr. *Emilianne's Observ. Journ. Naples* 102, I found my share to be overreckon'd, and that the Hostess had a mind to make up the Expense of her Charity.. out of my Purse. **1704** HEARNE *Duct. Hist.* I. 3 In allowing six Hours every Year, he over-reckon'd eleven Minutes. **1833–5** LANE *Mod. Egypt.* (1849) II. xv. 301 O God, if he were a doer of good, over-reckon his good deeds.

†**2.** To overcharge in a reckoning. *Obs.*

1615 T. ADAMS *Blacke Devill* 74 Thus the great Parasite.. now takes him in the lurch and over-reckons him. **1634** BRERETON *Trav.* (Chetham) 134 The knave tapster over-reckoned us in drink. *a* **1680** BUTLER *Rem.* (1759) II. 274 He over-reckons the Parish in his Accompts.

†**3.** To exceed in a reckoning or amount. *rare.*

a **1635** CORBETT *Iter Bor.* 120 William is hee, Who, though he never saw three score and three, Ore-reckons us in age.

over-record, *v.* [OVER- 27.] *trans.* **a.** To record using too large a signal, so that distortion occurs. **b.** To make too many recordings of (a work or performer). So **over-re'corded** *ppl. a.*, **over-re'cording** *vbl. sb.*

1961 E. N. BRADLEY *Records & Gramophone Equipment* i. 23 Inter-groove modulation is caused by over-recording, or by too small a spacing between grooves. **1976** *Gramophone* Sept. 432/2 The comparatively little-recorded *Hamlet*.. is linked with the vastly over-recorded *Serenade* for strings. **1977** *Ibid.* Mar. 1467/1 They might well buy the disc for Sabicas, who is not over-recorded these days. **1977** *Rolling Stone* 24 Mar. 79/3 The expanded 'louds' would cause overrecording or tape saturation.

†**over-'red**, *v. Obs.* [OVER- 8.] *trans.* To cover over with red, redden over.
1605 SHAKS. *Macb.* v. iii. 14 Go pricke thy Face, and ouer-red thy feare Thou Lilly-liuer'd Boy. [**1826** SCOTT *Woodst.* xxxi, Fill too, a cup to thyself, to over-red thy fear, as mad Will has it.]

†**over-'rede**, *v. Obs. rare.* [OVER- 22.] *trans.* To surpass or outdo in counsel.
c **1450** *Chaucer's Troylus* II. 1456 (1428) (MS. Harl. 3943) Men may þe olde ouer-renne & nat ouer-rede [*most MSS.* at-renne, at-rede].

ˌ**over-refine** (-rɪ'faɪn), *v.* [OVER- 27.] *trans.* To refine too much or with excess of subtlety; in quots. *absol.* to make over-fine distinctions.
1832 LYTTON *Eugene A.* III. iii, Perhaps I over-refine. **1845** P. M. LATHAM *Lect. Clin. Med.* xii. I. 239, I am not over-refining in this matter.
So ˌ**over-re'fined** *ppl. a.*, too refined (whence ˌ**over-re'finedly** *adv.*); ˌ**over-re'finement**, excessive or too subtle refinement; ˌ**over-re'fining** *vbl. sb.*, the action of refining too much.
1711 SHAFTESB. *Charac.* (1737) II. 185 For some intricate or over-refin'd speculation. *Ibid.* III. 261 Over-refinement of art and policy.. naturally incident to the experienc'd and thorow politician. **1830** PUSEY *Hist. Enq.* II. 304 A certain necessity.. of speaking over-refinedly on all subjects. **1876** BLACKIE *Lang. Sc. Highl.* i. 65 Over-refinements, and therefore corruptions and degradations, of the Latin language.

over-regulate, -reliance, etc.: see OVER-.

over-reik, -reke, obs. forms of OVERREACH *v.*

'over-ˌrent, *sb.* [OVER- 19, 29 d.] A higher or extra rent.
1546 *Yorks. Chantry Surv.* (Surtees) 341 For a rent, called over rent, x[d]. **1754** in Picton *L'pool Rec.* (1886) II. 166 Persons who.. after they quitt sitting in them.. do take upon them to sett the said seats for an over-rent to themselves.

ˌ**over-'rent**, *v.* [OVER- 27.] *trans.* To rent (land, etc.) too highly; to charge (a tenant) too high a rent. Hence **'over-'rented** *ppl. a.*
1589 WARNER *Alb. Eng.* v. xxii. 99 The Lords and Landed ouer-rent,.. The Parasite doth ouer-reach. **1622** MABBE tr. *Aleman's Guzman d'Alf.* II. 293 We were ready (being thus over-rented) to perish for want of food. **1770** MASSIE *Reas. agst. Tax on Malt* 4 Unless he hath over-rented his Land. **1846** MCCULLOCH *Acc. Brit. Empire* (1854) I. 393 The occupier of any over-rented patch.. never fails to get a considerable sum for the 'tenant's right'. **1886** *Manch. Exam.* 18 Jan. 5/6 The farmers.. are overrented to an extent quite incompatible with the reduced profits of farming.

over-repletion to **over-reward**: see OVER-.

'over-'rich, *a.* [OVER- 28.] Too rich. Hence **'over-'richness**.
1583 GOLDING *Calvin on Deut.* xlvii. 282 We see howe euen Salomon was afraide to bee ouerriche. **1622** MALYNES *Anc. Law-Merch.* 417 The ouerrichnesse of our sterling standard of moneys. **1855** BROWNING *Bp. Blougram's Apol.* 332 An uniform I wear though over-rich.

†ˌ**over-'rich**, *v. Obs. rare.* [OVER- 27.] *trans.* To enrich too much.
1616 SURFL. & MARKH. *Country Farme* 155 Should you let it rest, and bestow meanure vpon it.. you would so much ouer-rich it, that it would either mildewe and spoyle your Graine, or else choake and slay it with.. Weeds.

override (əʊvə'raɪd), *v.* [OE. *oferrídan* to ride across: see OVER- 5, 9, 22, 14, 27.]
1. a. *trans.* To ride over or across; to cross by riding. *lit.* or *fig.*
a **900** tr. *Bæda's Hist.* III. xii. [xiv.] (1890) 196 Geaf he & sealde þæt betste hors.. ðæt he hwæðre on þæm meahte fordas oferridan, þonne he to hwelcere ea cwome. **1801** SOUTHEY *Thalaba* XI. xl, Now is the ebb, and till the ocean flow We cannot over-ride the rocks. **1825** LONGF. *Spirit of Poetry* 9 When the fast ushering star of morning comes O'er-riding the gray hills with golden scarf.
b. To ride all over (a country), esp. with an armed force, so as to harry, crush opposition, etc.
c **1350** *Will. Palerne* 4147, I wol þat reaume ouer-ride & rediliche destrue. **1375** BARBOUR *Bruce* v. 471 Þai durst nocht ȝeit tak on hand Till our-ride þe land planly. **1470-85** MALORY *Arthur* v. x, He hath ben rebelle vnto Rome and ouer ryden many of theyr londes. *c* **1500** *Three Kings' Sons* 144 They counseiled the kynge to tary not, but to ouir-ride his reaume.
2. To ride over or upon (the fallen); to overthrow and trample down by riding.
c **1330** R. BRUNNE *Chron.* (1810) 18 Bituex vndernon & noen was þe feld alle wonnen, For alle þat wild abide were ouer riden & ronnen. *c* **1386** CHAUCER *Knt.'s T.* 1164 The Cartere ouer ryden with his Carte Vnder the wheel ful lowe he lay adoun. **1470-85** MALORY *Arthur* IX. xxxiii, Thenne foote hote syr Palomydes cam vpon sir Tristram as he was vpon foot to haue ouer ryden hym. *a* **1557** *Diurn. Occurr.* (1833) 45 The lord Gray with the bairdit horss.. ordaynit to have ourriden the wangaird of the Scottis. *a* **1845** HOOD *Desert-Born* xii, 'Twas my unhappy fortune once to over-ride a youth!
3. *fig.* **a.** To 'trample under foot', set oneself forcibly above (an ordinance, right, etc.); to set aside arrogantly, set at nought, supersede; to assume or have authority superior to, to prevail in authority over.
to override one's commission: to go beyond one's commission, exceed the power granted under the commission, discharge one's office in a high-handed and arbitrary manner.
1827 HALLAM *Const. Hist.* (1876) I. vi. 349 The unconstitutional and usurped authority of the star-chamber over-rode every personal right. *a* **1850** CALHOUN *Wks.* (1874) III. 589 The Constitution must override the deeds of cession, whenever they come in conflict. **1857** GEN. P. THOMPSON *Audi Alt.* I. xxi. 76 Such difficulties.. occur only where men are not wise, or where the wise are over-ridden. **1874** H. R. REYNOLDS *John Bapt.* v. §1. 296 Some of the methods used to over-ride or solve this obvious difficulty. **1888** BRYCE *Amer. Commw.* I. xxviii. 434 *note*, These provisions are overridden by the fifteenth constitutional amendment.
b. To prevail or dominate over.
1867 F. FRANCIS *Angling* i. 29 Owing to these causes, they [dace] soon considerably outnumber and override the trout. **1932** *Amer. Jrnl. Physiol.* C. 116 There is a significant difference between the amounts of theelin needed to blot out the normal progestational picture as compared to the amount it takes to over-ride a rabbit unit of injected corporin.
c. To cause the operation of (an automatic device) to be suspended, esp. in favour of manual control.
1946 [implied in *overriding* ppl. adj. below]. **1949** *Gloss. Aeronaut. Terms* (*B.S.I.*) II. 11 *Boost control override*, a device to override the boost control so that a pressure higher than the normal controlled pressure can be obtained. **1967** *Instrumentation Technol.* Aug. 38/1 (*caption*) Differential pressure across column overrides temperature control. **1971** *Daily Tel.* 20 Oct. 2/2 It has four forward gears and reverse controlled by a speed-sensing governor which can be overridden by the driver using a gear lever. **1975** *Nature* 20 Mar. 193/1 An interactive computer display system using manual intervention where necessary to override automatic procedures has proved adequate.
†**4.** To pass beyond or come up to by riding faster; to overtake by or in riding; to outride. *Obs.*
1441 *Plumpton Corr.* (Camden) p. lvi, The souldiers.. thought to have overridden and slayne this said forty persons. **1558** PHAER *Æneid.* IV. I iij b, Askanius.. somtyme these, and sometyme those, w[t] swift course ouerrydes. **1597** SHAKS. *2 Hen. IV*, I. i. 30 My Lord, I ouer-rod him on the way. **1642** *Lanc. Tracts* (Chetham) 64 We over-rode our Foote being carried with a fervent desire to overtake the enemie.
5. To ride (a horse) too much, to exhaust by excessive riding.
1600 [see OVERRIDDEN below]. *c* **1621** in Hore *Hist. Newmarket* (1885) I. 355 These gentlemen's horses.. being over-rid, past their strength and breath. **1773** JOHNSON *Note on Shaks. Hen. V*, III. v, It is common to give horses over-ridden or feverish.. a mash. **1890** 'R. BOLDREWOOD' *Col. Reformer* (1891) 273 He discovered that there was no other stage available without over-riding Osmund.
6. To extend or pass over; to slip or lie over, to be superimposed on; *Surg.* to overlap, as when a bone is fractured and one piece slips over the other.
1852 WIGGINS *Embanking* 236 The tendency of these land-slips to override any such footing. **1882** GEIKIE *Text Bk. Geol.* VI. v. (1885) 892 A northern ice-sheet which overrode Canada. *Ibid.* 898 As the ice-sheet had overridden the land. **1886** WILLIS & CLARK *Cambridge* II. 218 The parlour.. retains its ancient ceiling of molded beams over-riding the instrusive partitions.
Hence **over'ridden** *ppl. a.*, that has been ridden too hard, exhausted by excessive riding; **over'riding** *vbl. sb.* and *ppl. a.*: see the vb.; *spec.* ***overriding commission***, an extra or additional commission. Also ˌ**over'ridingly** *adv.*
1600 HEYWOOD *1 Edw. IV*, Wks. 1874 I. 27 Like a troop of rank overidden jades. **1830** H. N. COLERIDGE *Grk. Poets* (1834) 186 The supremacy of the Jupiter of the Iliad does not seem openly incumbered by any overriding fate. **1876** FOX BOURNE *Locke* I. vi. 276 Its avowed overriding of the decisions of parliament. **1883** LAPWORTH in *Geol. Mag.* Aug. 338 The advancing movement of the over-riding and under-thrust masses. **1892** *Syd. Soc. Lex.*, *Overriding*,.. the displacement of the fractured ends of a bone, consisting in one lying over or upon the other. **1894** DOYLE *Mem. S. Holmes* 61 You are to have an over-riding commission of 1 per cent. on all business done by your agents. **1906** *Westm. Gaz.* 15 Feb. 11/1 As a rule, the terms of commission, both underwriting and 'over-riding', are very literal. **1930** W. S. CHURCHILL *My Early Life* xiii. 184, I had not heard a word in Cairo of how Sir Herbert Kitchener had received the over-riding by the War Office of his wishes upon my appointment. **1930** A. PALMER *Company Secretarial Pract.* 47 Companies frequently pay 'overriding' commission also. This is a commission paid to persons for procuring other persons who are willing to underwrite blocks of shares. **1946** R. A. MCFARLAND *Human Factors Air Transport Design* x. 148 Many pilots feel.. that in the event of an emergency they must have immediate access to engine instruments. Overriding throttle controls for the pilot may be advisable. **1956** A. H. COMPTON *Atomic Quest* II. 126 If Oppenheimer has an 'Achilles' heel, it is his overriding loyalty to his friends. **1957** J. S. HUXLEY *Relig. without Revelation* (rev. ed.) ix. 232 If the full development of human individuals and the fulfilment of human possibilities is the over-riding aim of our evolution, then any over-population which brings malnutrition and misery, or which erodes the world's material resources.., is evil. **1968** *Lebende Sprachen* XIII. 5/1 All diverse organizations must be harnessed together into a single team directed towards the single overriding objective. **1969** W. K. ROOTS *Fund. Temperature Control* v. 118 An inexpensive overriding command system provides both the 'night shut down' and 'vacant-room shut down', features that can significantly reduce the heating cost of public buildings. **1973** A. QUINTON *Nature of Things* 378 He cannot.. maintain that morality is overridingly authoritative in this sense.

'override, *sb.* [f. prec. vb.] The action or process of suspending an automatic function; a device for performing this. Freq. *attrib.*
1946 *Aircraft Engin.* XVIII. 112/1 A manual over-ride for landing operation would be necessary. **1949** [see OVERRIDE *v.* 3 c]. **1952** A. Y. BRAMBLE *Air-Plane Flight* x. 154 There is an 'over-ride' control introduced, by which the automatic limitation of boost can be exceeded at the will of the pilot in particular circumstances. **1957** *Practical Wireless* XXXIII. 697/1 The only connections yet to be made are those coupling up the override switch to the appropriate part in the circuit. **1963** *Amat. Photographer* 7 Aug. 43/1 (Advt.), Fully automatic [camera] with manual over-ride. **1968** *Instrumentation Technol.* Aug. 53/1 Overrides can be designed to provide gradual, rather than abrupt, corrective action and they can function in both directions so that manual reset is not required. **1974** 'A. HAIG' *Peruvian Printout* 39 He pressed the override switch and the computer came instantly to life. **1976** *Offshore Platforms & Pipelining* 203/1 Mechanical overrides are provided should any of the automatic equipment fail.

overrider ('əʊvəˌraɪdə(r)). Also **over-rider**. [f. OVER- 8 c + RIDER 12.] One of a pair of projecting pieces attached to the bumper of a car, affording added protection to the bodywork.
1937 *Times* 18 Oct. 20/3 The bumpers have over-riders. **1959** *Times* 6 Jan. 12/1 The overriders on bumpers must not have dangerous protuberances. **1963** J. T. STORY *Something for Nothing* iii. 83 The Jaguar with its big over-riders had suffered not at all. **1963** [see *mud flap* s.v. MUD *sb.*[1] 5]. **1974** 'A. HAIG' *Peruvian Printout* 123 The bastard was ramming her back bumper. Thank God she had over-riders fitted. **1975** J. PIDGEON *Flame* ii. 32 The charging Chevy's [*sc.* Chevrolet's] chrome overriders gored the big red and white arrow that pointed diagonally across the carriageway and tossed it high over the roof.

over-rife, -rigged, etc.: see OVER-.

ˌ**over-'right**, *adv.* and *prep.* Now *dial.* [f. OVER *adv.* and *prep.* + RIGHT *adv.*] Over against, right opposite (to).
1565 COOPER *Thesaurus*, *Aduersum*, *E regione.* Plin., Ouerright agaynst. **1798** J. JEFFERSON *Let. to Jonathan Boucher* 19 Mar. (MS.), [Hampshire words] *Over-right* for *over-against*. **1826** MISS MITFORD *Village* Ser. II. (1863) 328 He lived exactly over-right our house. **1886** ELWORTHY *W. Somerset Word-bk.* s.v., You turns into a gate over-right a blacksmith's shop.

'over-rigid (-'rɪdʒɪd), *a.* [OVER- 28.] Too rigid. So **'over-ri'gidity**, excessive rigidity.
c **1630** H. R. *Mythomystes* 28 In the meane between the whining Heraclite, and ouer-rigid Democritus. **1866** *Ch. Times* 2 June, Over-rigid formalism in Divine worship. **1884** W. F. CRAFTS *Sabbath for Man* (1894) 620 That the desecration of Sunday is a reaction from Puritan over-rigidity.

'over-'rigorous, *a.* [OVER- 28.] Too rigorous. So **'over-'rigorously** *adv.*
1583 GOLDING *Calvin on Deut.* cxliv. 888 Hee will punishe them which haue vexed vs, and dealte ouerrigorously with vs. **1597** HOOKER *Eccl. Pol.* v. lx. §1 Wee thereupon inferre a necessitie ouer-rigorous and extreme. **1835** J. H. NEWMAN *Par. Serm.* (1837) I. xx. 302 An over-rigorous bond upon Christian liberty.

over-ring, -riot, etc.: see OVER-.

'over-'ripe, *a.* [OVER- 28.] Too ripe. Also *fig.*
1671 MILTON *P.R.* III. 31 Thy years are ripe, and over-ripe. **1760-72** H. BROOKE *Fool of Qual.* (1809) III. 8 [She] began to decline, and.. dropped, like over-ripe fruit. **1862** MISS MULOCK *Mistress & Maid* xxiv, She refuses to drop into his mouth like an over-ripe peach from a garden wall.
Hence **'over-'ripeness**.
1824 MISS MITFORD *Village* Ser. I. (1863) 51 They are so full too, we lose half of them from over-ripeness. **1876** G. MEREDITH *Beauch. Career* III. x. 183 Immense wealth and native obtuseness combine to disfigure us with the aspect of over-ripeness, not to say monstrosity. **1904** [see *hypermaturity* s.v. HYPER- IV.]. **1976** *Listener* 12 Aug. 172/1 Henry James appraised Warwickshire.... He felt a ripeness, he hints at an over-ripeness.

ˌ**over-'ripen**, *v.* [OVER- 27.] To ripen too much. So **'over-'ripened** *ppl. a.*, ripened to excess, too ripe.
1593 SHAKS. *2 Hen. VI*, I. ii. 1 Why droopes my Lord like ouer-ripen'd Corn, Hanging the head at Ceres plenteous load?

over-'rise, *v.* Now *rare.* [OVER- 1 (*b*).] *trans.* To rise over or above (a certain point).
a **1350** *Cursor M.* 1838 (Gött.) þe heiest montayn þat was aware [= awhare] þe flod ouer ras [*Cott.* ouer raght, *Trin.* ouer passed] seuen elne and mare. **1862** MRS. CROSLAND *Mrs. Blake* II. 223 A sort of fixed high-water mark of their capabilities, which.. they will never 'over-rise'.

'over-'risen, *ppl. a.* [OVER- 28 c.] That has risen or is raised too much or too high.
1647 WARD *Simp. Cobler* 49 Over-risen Kings, have been the next evills to the world, unto falne Angels. **1867** SMYTH *Sailor's Word-bk.*, *Over-risen*, when a ship is too high out of the water for her length and breadth, so as to make a trouble of lee-lurches and weather-rolls.

ˌ**over-'roast**, *v.* [OVER- 27.] *trans.* To roast too much. Hence ˌ**over-'roasted** *ppl. a.*, ˌ**over-'roasting** *vbl. sb.*
1528 TINDALE *Obed. Chr. Man* 130 Yf the podech be burned.. or the meate ouer rosted, we saye, the bysshope hath put his fote in the potte. **1596** SHAKS. *Tam. Shr.* IV. i.

178 Better.. Then feede it with such ouer-rosted flesh. **1712** ADDISON *Spect.* No. 482 ¶4 The over-roasting of a Dish of Wild-Fowl. **1822** LAMB *Elia* Ser. I. *Roast Pig*, The crisp, tawny, well-watched, not over-roasted crackling.

over'roll, *v.* [OVER- 6, 8, 1, 4.] *trans.* **a.** To roll (something) over, to push over. **b.** To cover up with a roll or by rolling; to envelop. **c.** To revolve over or above (something).
1513 DOUGLAS *Æneis* XIII. v. 50 With quhou gret fard our-rollyt and doun cast So hastely bene thir fatis, behald! *a* **1548** HALL *Chron., Hen. VIII* 80 Theyr hosen of riche gold satten called Aureate satten, ouerrouled to yᵉ kne with Skarlet. **1865** *Macm. Mag.* July 275 Seeing the stars.. overroll me. **1892** *Harper's Mag.* 396 His honey tongue.. overrolls the bitter of his words As..honey deadens nauseous drugs.
Hence **over-rolling** *vbl. sb.*, rolling over.
1883 LAPWORTH in *Geol. Mag.* Aug. 340 An overfold with gradual development of a middle limb, which has originated in the over-rolling of the beds at the apices of the curves.

over'roof, *v.* [OVER- 8.] *trans.* To roof over, cover as with a roof. So **over'roofing** *ppl. a.*
a **1828** D. WORDSWORTH *Jrnl.* (1941) II. 272 The track.. was..over-roofed, like an outside staircase of a Castle. **1855** BAILEY *Spir. Legend* in *Mystic*, etc. (ed. 2) 91 Walls, O'er-roofed with sparkling spires and pendent stars. **1875** BROWNING *Aristoph. Apol.* 3642 These domes that overroof, This long-used couch, I come to. **1877** —— *Agam.* 378 Thou who didst fling on Troia's every tower The o'erroofing snare.

ove'rrooted, *ppl. a.* [OVER- 28c, 8b.] †**a.** Too deeply rooted (*obs.*). **b.** Covered over with roots (*poet.*).
1587 GOLDING *De Mornay* xxii. (1617) 365 Notwithstanding that ouerrooted custome haue like a waterstreame carried folk away. **1855** BROWNING *Love among Ruins* iv, The single little turret that remains On the plains, By the caper overrooted, by the gourd Overscored.

over-rought, obs. pa. t. of OVERREACH *v.*

over-rude, -ruff, etc.: see OVER-.

over-'ruff, *v.* [OVER- 22.] *trans.* To over-trump. Also *absol.* and (with stress on first syllable) as *sb.*, an act or instance of over-ruffing.
1813 *Hoyle's Games of Whist & Quadrille* 50 *Ruff*, and *over-ruff*, to trump a suit led, second or third hand. *c* **1890** *Up to Date Games of Cards* 37 Ruff means to trump a suit second or third hand, when you are rid of that suit: *over-ruff* means to trump above. **1906** *Westm. Gaz.* 13 Oct. 14/1 Had A held neither of these cards he would have surely led a diamond.., instead of putting his partner to an over-ruff in the spade. **1926** M. C. WORK *Auction Bridge Complete* II. ii. 331 He should lead trumps before taking the ruff and so avoid any chance of an over-ruff... Dummy's ruff of the losing Club might be over-ruffed. **1974** *Oxford Times* 12 July 10/8 North can ruff in whenever he likes, but dummy overruffs and plays a diamond. **1975** *Times* 16 Aug. 7/4 East was end-played, whether or not he over-ruffed. **1976** *Country Life* 26 Feb. 498/1 When you see the chance of an easy overruff, don't be in too much of a hurry to take it.

'over-ˌrule, *sb.* [OVER- 2b.] Superior rule; the rule of a higher or supreme power.
1893 J. PULSFORD *Loyalty to Christ* II. 341 The only possible way in which men can rid their souls of Christ is by persistently refusing His over-rule. **1891** CAINE in *Pall Mall G.* 8 Jan. 3/1 It is not British over-rule that is becoming intolerable to Educated India, but Brahman over-rule.

overrule (əʊvə'ruːl), *v.* [OVER- 2.]
†**1.** *trans.* To rule over, have authority over. *Obs.*
1581 MARBECK *Bk. of Notes* 839 It is so necessary a thing, that one onely man, ouer rule the whole Church. **1582** N. T. (Rhem.) *Matt.* xx. 25 You know that the princes of the Gentiles ouerrule them. **1640** BP. HALL *Episc.* II. xvii. 180 Those Presbyters must have an head, that head is to over-rule the body.
2. To govern, control, or modify the rule of (a person, a law, etc.) by superior power or authority.
1576 GASCOIGNE *Steele Gl.* (Arb.) 57 Realmes and townes ..Where mighty power, doth ouer rule the right. **1596** in *Buccleuch MSS.* (Hist. MSS. Comm.) I. 229 To overrule them in their prices, so as the same be not sold at any dearer rates. **1606** BRYSKETT *Civ. Life* 85 Yet did he not onely not seeke to ouer-rule the law, but became a law to himselfe. **1702** *Eng. Theophrast.* 194 There is a secret order and concatenation of things directed and overruled by Providence. **1860** HOOK *Lives Abps.* I. ii. 43 Shaping all things to his own wise ends, and overruling the actions of men.
3. To prevail over (a person) so as to change or set aside his opinion. Also *absol.*
1591 SHAKS. *1 Hen. VI*, II. ii. 50 When a World of men Could not preuayle with all their Oratorie, Yet hath a Womans kindnesse ouer-rul'd. **1594** GIBSON in *Lett. Lit. Men* (Camden) 222 If a good reward could over-rule the doctor. **1622** F. ANNESLEY in *Fortescue P.* (Camden) 184, I was overruled by most voyces to subscribe therunto, eaven against my will. **1719** DE FOE *Crusoe* II. i. (1840) 22, I over-ruled him in that part. **1853** C. BRONTE *Villette* xx, I found myself led and influenced by another's will, unpersuaded, quietly overruled.
4. Of a thing: To prevail over, overcome.
a **1586** SIDNEY (J.), Which humour perceiving to over-rule me, I strave against it. **1662** R. MATHEW *Unl. Alch.* §31. 27 How speedily and effectually this Pill in few hours doth over-rule the disease, and in a little time doth cure them. **1748** HARTLEY *Observ. Man* I. i. 78 The violent Vibrations soon over-rule the natural Vibrations. **1877** OWEN in *Wellesley's Desp.* p. xlvii, The general causes that overrule personal aims.
5. To rule against, set aside, as by higher authority; *spec.* in *Law*: **a.** To set aside or reject the authority of (a previous action or decision) as a precedent; to annul, pronounce invalid. **b.** To rule against, reject (an argument, plea, etc.); to disallow (an action).
1593 NASHE *Christ's T.* 67 Sutes in Lawe ouer-ruled by Letters from aboue. **1611** BIBLE *Transl. Pref.* 6 Therefore he [Clement VIII] ouerruleth and frustrateth the grant of Pius the fourth. **1660** *Trial Regic.* 52 This Plea, which you have spoken of, it ought to be over-ruled, and not to stand good. **1855** MACAULAY *Hist. Eng.* xvi. III. 629 Schomberg.. when his opinion was overruled, retired to his tent in no very good humour. **1875** STUBBS *Const. Hist.* III. xviii. 140 *note*, The chancellor overruled the objections.
c. To rule against (a person), to disallow or set aside the arguments or pleas of.
1660 R. COKE *Power & Subj.* 208, I myself have seen Chief Justice Littleton overrule the Ordinary..after the Ordinaries Deputy had pronounced *legit ut clericus*, and give sentence of death upon him for his *non legit.* **1667** POOLE *Dial. betw. Protest. & Papist* (1735) 109 You will needs overrule the Apostle. **1849** MACAULAY *Hist. Eng.* vi. II. 19 Sir John Ernley..insisted that the delay should not exceed forty-eight hours: but he was overruled.
Hence **over'ruled** *ppl. a.*; **over'ruling** *vbl. sb.* and *ppl. a.*; **over'rulingly** *adv.* (Webster 1847).
1586 B. YOUNG *Guazzo's Civ. Conv.* IV. 208b, We are not inueagled with those ouerrulinge passions, as youthes are. **1615** BACON *Let. Jas. I* 12 Feb., If you take my lord Coke.. your Majesty shall put an overruling nature into an over-ruling place. **1622** —— *Hen. VII* 135 It was a plaine and direct ouer-ruling of the king's title. **1806** SURR *Winter in Lond.* (ed. 3) I. 154 Both have been decreed by an over-ruling Providence. **1842** MANNING *Serm.* xxvi. (1848) I. 402 There shall be strange overrulings of our blind judgments. **1898** *Westm. Gaz.* 17 Oct. 3/2 Mr. R. C. Lehmann..is part author of a 'Digest of Overruled Cases'.

over'ruler. **a.** One who overrules, controls, or directs. †**b.** (*'overˌruler*) One who has rule over the laws or ordinary rulers (*obs.*).
1581 SIDNEY *Apol. Poetrie* (Arb.) 30 Then loe, did proofe the ouer ruler of opinions, make manifest, that all these are but seruing Sciences. **1647** WARD *Simp. Cobler* 23 States are unstated. Rulers growne Over-rulers. **1695** J. EDWARDS *Perfect. Script.* 358 The wise Over-ruler of the world. **1874** HELPS *Soc. Press.* xxv. (1875) 400 He that hath a fellow-ruler, hath an over-ruler.

†**over-'ruly**, *a.* ? That tends to overrule.
1657 S. PURCHAS *Pol. Flying-Ins.* II. 311 Contributaries to the commands of over-ruling and over-ruly lusts.

overrun ('əʊvərʌn), *sb.* [OVER- 22, 5.]
†**1.** Excess or superiority in running. *Obs.*
a **1225** *Ancr. R.* 398 Asaeles swiftschipe, þet strof wið heortes ouervrn.
2. a. Amount carried over as balance or surplus.
1899 *Daily News* 10 May 2/7 This is inclusive of over-run previous to 30th April.
b. An excess of expenditure over that estimated or budgeted for.
1956 *Wall St. Jrnl.* 10 Oct. 12/3 Some of our government officials get carried away with the thought of spending $156 million plus the over-run beyond the estimate. **1960** *Times* 21 Nov. (Canada Suppl.) p. xiii/2 Among these were cases of capital overruns and operating returns poorer than expected. **1973** *Nature* 23 Mar. 224/3 If there are cost overruns on the first two missions, the third may be scrapped. **1974** *Times* 26 Oct. 15/1 Britain's own advanced gas cooled reactor programme is hopelessly compromised by massive cost overruns brought about by..constructional delays. **1976** *Sci. Amer.* July 122/1 The total cost had been $8 million, an overrun of some 40 percent. **1978** *Daily Tel.* 13 Apr. 21 This sum..is just under half what remains in the contingency reserve for overruns on public expenditure.
c. An excess of production.
1958 T. LANDAU *Encycl. Librarianship* 230/2 *Overrun*, copies surplus to the number ordered. **1962** J. N. WINBURNE *Dict. Agric.* 539/2 *Overrun*,..the excess amount of lumber actually sawed from logs over the estimated volume or log scale, usually expressed as a percentage of log scale. **1970** *Toronto Daily Star* 24 Sept. 27/1 (Advt.), Our huge purchase includes many carloads of the top lines of merchandise, plus close-outs, over-runs, sample bales.
3. *Print.* An instance of overrunning: see next 11.
1898 J. SOUTHWARD *Mod. Printing* I. xxxiv. 210 When there is a long over-run, the matter should be placed upon a small galley, which should be turned, so that the last line rests against its head. **1902** T. L. DE VINNE *Pract. Typogr.: Correct Composition* (ed. 2) xvi. 309 Every paragraph containing an alteration that compels one or more overruns should be re-read. **1935** B. PERRY *And gladly Teach* vii. 169 When the forms were made up, there was an over-run of three lines. **1977** *New Yorker* 26 Sept. 64/3 The *Times*..ran a front-page story, with a four-column overrun on a rear page.
4. The proportional increase in bulk that occurs when butter fat is made into butter or an ice-cream mix is made into ice-cream.
1906 H. SNYDER *Dairy Chem.* vii. 71 During the process of butter making, the slight loss of fat in the skim milk and buttermilk is more than compensated for by the added water, casein, and salt in the butter. The additional butter made from a pound of butter fat is called the overrun. **1922** MOJONNIER & TROY *Techn. Control Dairy Products* xv. 443 Insufficient overrun greatly increases the cost of the ice cream, and yields a product that is immediately detected by its heavy and soggy appearance. **1958** *Sunday Times* 22 June 23/6 Overrun is the aeration or amount any given mix [for ice-cream] will swell in volume when subjected to the freezing process. **1972** *New York* 15 May 4/1 (Advt.), The best coffee ice cream in New York... Sixteen per cent butterfat, 50 per cent overrun; one pint weighs 12¾ ounces.
5. Motion of a vehicle at a speed greater than that being imparted by the engine; freq. in phr. ***on the overrun.*** Also *attrib.*, designating a system of braking in a towed vehicle (see quot. 1967).
1928 *Observer* 8 Jan. 21/4 The engine runs smoothly and quietly throughout most of its range. There is a certain drumming noise, rather difficult to define and trace, on the over-run, but it is comparatively trifling. **1959** *Motor Manual* (ed. 36) v. 141 This..is at a maximum when the engine is on the over-run. *Ibid.* xiii. 273 When the car brakes are applied, or the car slows down against a closed throttle, the caravan tends to overrun, thus causing the bar to move back against the spring, push back the operating lever and thus apply the caravan brakes. This is known as the 'over-run' method. **1962** *Which? Car Suppl.* Oct. 131/2 The washers..would only operate properly when the engine was on the overrun, i.e. when the foot was taken off the accelerator. **1967** *Gloss. Caravan Terms (B.S.I.)* 2 *Overrun braking*, a system of braking in which the caravan brakes are automatically operated by the momentum of the caravan when the towing vehicle is braked. Normally this is achieved by mounting the coupling head on a shaft moving on the drawbar and restrained by a compression spring or a damper. **1969** J. G. GILES *Gears & Transmissions* i. 23 On down gradients heavy vehicles will drive the engine... On these over-run conditions, the transmission torques are reversed. **1977** *Good Motoring* May 3/1 A trailer with over-run brakes can weigh more than the kerb weight of the car, providing a limit of 40 mph is observed.

overrun (əʊvə'rʌn), *v.* Forms: see OVER and RUN *v.* [OVER- 4, 5, 9, 10, 16, 17, 22, 13, 23, 27.]
I. To run over (something).
†**1. a.** *trans.* To run over or across (a line or surface); to cross or traverse by running; to pass over quickly. *Obs.*
c **1000** *Sax. Leechd.* III. 240 He [se mona] næfð þære sunnan leoht þa hwile þe he þære sceade ord oferyrnð. **13..** *Guy Warw.* (A.) 6730 He ouer-ernnes dounes & cuntre þe brod lond, and þe valays. **1597** A. M. tr. *Guillemeau's Fr. Chirurg.* 9/1 The prevet or searchinge iron..should not prætermit & ouerrunne a smalle dilaceratione, without perceavinge and staying therat. *a* **1649** DRUMM. *Poems* 5 In vain, love's pilgrim, mountains, dales, and plains I over-run.
b. To flow over, overflow.
c **1470** *Gol. & Gaw.* 855 The blude of thair bodeis..As roise ragit on rise, Our ran thair riche vedis. **1596** SHAKS. *Tam. Shr.* Ind. ii. 67 Til the teares that she hath shed for thee, Like enuious flouds ore-run her louely face. **1684–90** BURNET *Th. Earth* (J.), A general flood of waters would necessarily over-run the whole earth. **1791** NEWTE *Tour Eng. & Scot.* 160 The Spey occasionally overruns a tract of ground of about fifteen hundred acres. **1856** KANE *Arct. Expl.* II. xxvii. 272 One torrent..overran the icefoot from two to five feet in depth.
†**2.** To run through or go over (a book, etc.) in reading, (a subject) in writing, speech, or thought; to pass in rapid review, glance through rapidly, pass over lightly (sometimes implying omission).
c **1000** ÆLFRIC *Hom.* (Th.) I. 104 Nu wille we eft oferyrnan þa ylcan godspellican endebyrdnysse. *Ibid.* I. 202 We wyllað scortlice oferyrnan ða diȝelystan word. *a* **1300** *Cursor M.* 268 (Cott.) Cursur o werld man aght it call, For almast it ouer-rennes all. **1538** STARKEY *England* I. iii. 71 To put me also in remembrance of such fautys..wych you schal perauenture see me ouerrun and, by neclygence, let pas. **1577** VAUTROUILLIER *Luther on Ep. Gal.* 255 Of this commaundement I haue largely entreated in an other place, and therefore I will now but lightly ouerrunne it. **1656** STANLEY *Hist. Philos.* v. (1701) 223/1 Having first over-run in our Thoughts that our Senses are all entire, and that we behold this waking, not in a dream.
†**3. a.** To run over destructively, to overwhelm (as waves); to run over (as a horse or vehicle), run down, trample down, crush. *Obs.*
c **1000** ÆLFRIC *Hom.* (Th.) II. 194 Moyses ða astrehte his hand onȝean ðære sæ, and heo oferarn Pharao. *c* **1330** [see OVERRIDE *v.* 2]. **1546** BALE *Eng. Votaries* II. (1550) N iv, Peters little ship..was very like..to be ouer rowne and drowned. **1596** SPENSER *State Irel.* Wks. (Globe) 645/1 Pasture, that nowe is all trampled and over-runne. **1606** SHAKS. *Tr. & Cr.* III. iii. 163 Like a gallant Horse falne in first ranke, Lye there for pauement..neere Ore-run and trampled on. **1667** *Lond. Gaz.* No. 197/1 Yesterday a Hoy laden with Bay-salt..was unfortunately over-ran by another ship, and lost.
absol. **1596** SPENSER *F.Q.* IV. viii. 32 Despisd and troden downe of all that over-ran.
†**b.** *fig.* To overwhelm, overpower, crush. *Obs.*
a **900** tr. *Bæda's Hist.* v. ix. (1890) 410 Mid þy..ic mine limo on beddstowe strehte & me liht slep oferorn, þa æteaude me min ȝiu maȝister. *c* **1460** FORTESCUE *Abs. & Lim. Mon.* iii. (1885) 115 Ellis all his enymes myght ouerrenne hym. **1586** J. HOOKER *Hist. Irel.* in Holinshed II. 27/1 That hauing his aid he might ouer-run his owne father, and shorten his old yeares. *c* **1654** WALLER *Panegyric Ld. Protr.* xlv, Tell of towns stormed, of armies overrun. **1667** PEPYS *Diary* 31 Oct., It troubles me that we must come to contend with these great persons, which will over-run us.
4. To ride or rove over (a country) as a hostile force and so to harry and destroy; †to harass (a people) by such ravages, to spoil (a city, etc.).
1395 PURVEY *Remonstr.* (1851) 62 Thei myghten lightli ovirrenne us cristene, as bi mannis power. *c* **1420** *Anturs of Arth.* 263 (Thornton MS.) How salle we fare,.. That riche rewmes ouer rynnes agaynes the ryghte? *Ibid.* 280 ȝete salle þe riche Romaynes with ȝow bene ouer-ronnene. **1456** SIR G. HAYE *Law Arms* (S.T.S.) 160 [They] may for occasioun of the weris..ourryn the landis..and tak the pure labouraris prisounaris. **1551** ROBINSON tr. *More's Utop.* I. (1895) 49

Cityes..haue bene ouerrunned. 1631 GOUGE *God's Arrows* iii. §95. 363 The Northerne parts were over-run and harried by the Scots. 1756 MRS. F. BROOKE *Old Maid* No. 31. 256 It must be confessed..for fame he [Alexander] over-run whole nations unprovoked. 1841 W. SPALDING *Italy & It. Isl.* III. III. v. 52 The invaders, pouring from the highlands, over-ran Lombardy.

5. Of vermin, weeds, etc.: To spread and swarm injuriously over; also, of ivy or other vegetation: To grow or spread over rapidly, to cover. Chiefly in *pa. pple.*, and const. *with*.

1669 STURMY *Mariner's Mag.* b, Briars and Thorns my Grave shall over-run. 1709 STEELE *Tatler* No. 11 ¶5 That Swarm of Lawyers, Attorneys, Serjeants, and Bailiffs, with which the Nation is over-run. 1791 MRS. RADCLIFFE *Rom. Forest* i, It was sometimes overrun by luxuriant vegetation. 1820 W. IRVING *Sketch Bk.* I. 20, I saw the mouldering ruin of an abbey overrun with ivy. 1887 *Pall Mall G.* 14 Dec. 14/1 To sleep in a small cell overrun with mice.

6. In various *fig.* and *transf.* senses (from 4 and 5): To spread over injuriously, infest, infect widely, etc. Now chiefly in *pa. pple.*, const. *with*.

1538 STARKEY *England* II. i. 165 So many affectys and vycyouse desyrys,..that (except man wyth cure, dylygence and labur, resy[s]te to the same) they ouer-run reson. *a* 1547 SURREY *Æneid* II. 152 The chilling cold did over-runne their bones. 1586 T. B. *La Primaud. Fr. Acad.* (1589) 43 Vice alwaies watcheth to over-run us so soone as we let ourselves loose unto idlenes. 1699 BENTLEY *Phal.* 405 The Latin Names of Offices, and Terms of Law, &c. over-run the old Greek Language. 1711 ADDISON *Spect.* No. 128 ¶10 The Wife is over-run with Affectation. 1806–7 J. BERESFORD *Miseries Hum. Life* (1826) VI. Conclusion, I have..been over-run with cards of invitation without number. 1809 MALKIN *Gil Blas* XI. ii. (Rtldg.) 396 Overrun with impatience to inquire what the king had been talking about. 1907 A. T. RITCHIE *Let.* 4 July (1924) xii. 273 It [*sc.* Norway] is like Switzerland, but softer and bigger and not over-run. 1914 G. B. SHAW *Misalliance* p. li, We are over-run with Popes.

7. *intr.* To run over, to overflow (said of a liquid or the containing vessel); to be superabundant or excessive.

c 1230, 1870 [see OVERRUNNING *ppl. a.* 1]. *c* 1430 *Two Cookery-bks.* 36 Þan hang þe croddys..in a fayre cloþe, and lat it ouer-renne. *a* 1710 E. SMITH (J.), Though you have left me, Yet still my soul o'erruns with fondness towards you.

†**8.** *intr.* Of time: To run to an end, run out.

c 1375 *Sc. Leg. Saints* xviii. (*Egipciane*) 1136 Quhen be-gonnyn was þe fastine, þe ȝere our-[r]unnyne, & cummyne was þe fyrst sonday. 1526 *Pilgr. Perf.* (W. de W. 1531) 267 b, Whan the vij yeres were ouerronne & past.

II. To surpass in running, to run beyond, etc.

9. a. *trans.* To run faster than, outdo in running, = OUTRUN; hence, to overtake or leave behind by or in running; also *fig.* to surpass. Now chiefly *Mech.*; *spec.* to rotate faster than.

a 1400 *Sir Perc.* 342 The moste mere he thare see Smertly over-rynnes he. *c* 1450 [see OVER-REDE]. *c* 1510 *Gesta Rom.*, *Addit. Stories* (1879) 429 No man sholde haue her to wyfe, but suche as myght ouer renne her, and take her by strength of foot. *a* 1586 SIDNEY *Arcadia* II. (1598) 124 Pyrocles.. seemed so to ouerrun his age in growth, strength [etc.]. *a* 1618 RALEIGH in Gutch *Coll. Cur.* I. 79 The sun over-runneth the moon in light. 1653 BAXTER *Meth. Peace Consc.* 25 Suffering their zeal to over-run their Christian wisdom and meekness. 1857 DUFFERIN *Lett. High Lat.* (ed. 3) 150 It would seem..a pity to neglect such an opportunity of overrunning the time that has been lost. 1932 J. A. MOYER *Gasoline Automobiles* (ed. 4) viii. 382 The free-wheeling unit or overrunning clutch *G* is given this name because in this arrangement the driven member may overrun the driving member. 1955 W. H. CROUSE *Automotive Transmissions* v. 123 The inner race drives, the outer race is driven. Also, the outer race can overrun, or turn faster than, the inner race. 1959 *Motor Manual* (ed. 36) xiii. 274 As the caravan over-runs the car, the shaft moves backwards against the spring and operates the brake-actuating lever. 1966 *McGraw-Hill Encycl. Sci. & Technol.* IX. 455/2 The second function [of an over-drive] is to permit the output shaft to overrun the transmission shaft.

b. To escape from by running faster than, to run away from; hence, ***to overrun one's creditors, the*** CONSTABLE, q.v.; also *fig.* to run away from (duty, etc.); to desert, leave undone or unfinished. Now only *dial.*

1583 STUBBES *Anat. Abus.* II. (1882) 96 These fugitiues, that ouerrun their flocks in time of infection. 1602 F. HERING *Anatomyes* A iij, Euery Bankerupt who hath ouer-runne his Creditors. 1737 WHISTON *Josephus, Antiq.* v. i. §26 Impossible it is to over-run his power or the punishment he will bring on men thereby. 1847 HALLIWELL, *Over-run*, to leave unfinished. *West.* 1859 GEO. ELIOT *A. Bede* iv, I shall overrun these doings before long. 1884 *Cheshire Gloss.*, *O'er-run*,..to go without permission;..'He's o'er-run his work'.

10. a. To run farther than or beyond (a certain point, a limit, etc.); *fig.* to exceed. ***to overrun the scent***: see quot. 1886.

1633 BP. HALL *Hard Texts, N.T.* 44 Ye will rather over-run the precept of God. *c* 1640 J. SMYTH *Lives Berkeleys* (1883) II. 284 Having, in his first fower years after his marriage, much over ranne his purse. 1703 DE FOE *Reas. agst. War France* Misc. 183 Away they go with it, like Hounds on a full Cry, till they over-run it, and then they are at a Halt. 1859 WHITTIER *For Autumn Festival* 27 The bounty overruns our due. 1867 *Ball Players' Chron.* 14 Nov. 4/3 He fell over Murtha, who was in his way, and overran his base. 1884 *Cheshire Gloss.*, *O'er-run one's country*,..to run away from creditors, or to escape being imprisoned, or called to account for any misbehaviour. 1886 ELWORTHY *W. Somerset Word-bk.* s.v., The hounds are said to over-run the scent, when they continue running past a point where the hare or fox turned off, and thus have lost the scent. 1889 E. DOWSON *Let.* 24 Mar. (1967) 54 This appears to be an *extra* special [letter]: it is overrunning [*sic*] all limits. 1895 *Funk's Standard Dict.*, *Overrun*. In baseball, to continue in a straight course beyond (a base); allowed at first base. 1948 *News-Palladium* (Bluton Harbor, Mich.) 14 Aug. 6/3 Hazel, going down to second, overran the base as Joe Mack rifled the ball to McCoy. 1973 *Guardian* 1 Sept. 3 When he whispered to her she had overrun the schedule. 1974 M. S. EHRICH *Reincarnation of Peter Proud* xiv. 117 Daley stopped the Movieola... 'I overran it a little..I'll reverse the film.' 1977 *Times* 7 Feb. 7/2 In the opening three minutes Macdonald put Ross clean through, only for the wing half to overrun the ball after dribbling past the goalkeeper.

b. ***to overrun oneself***: to run beyond one's mark, or beyond one's strength; to run too far; to exhaust or injure oneself with running. Also *fig.*

1633 SHERLEY in *Bradford's Plymouth Plant.* (1898) 368 By Mr. Allertons faire propositions and large promises, I have over rune my selfe. 1810 *Naval Chron.* XXIV. 439 He over-ran himself, and fell into the area. 1883 *Manch. Guardian* 22 Oct. 5/6 Probably both men have a little overrun themselves, and may never be at their best again.

c. To extend or project so as to overlie.

c 1850 *Rudim. Navig.* (Weale) 147 The butts may overrun each other, in order to make a good shift.

d. *intr.* To extend beyond the due or desired length, or beyond any prescribed or desired limit; *spec.* in *Broadcasting*, to exceed the allotted time.

1864 in WEBSTER. 1959 *Sunday Express* 30 Aug. 17/3 Last time Borge overran by 15 minutes—and was kept on the air. 1962 A. NISBETT *Technique Sound Studio* i. 17 The announcer on duty in the continuity studio..must intervene if any contribution under-runs, over-runs, breaks down in the middle, or completely fails to materialize. 1962 *Rep. Comm. Broadcasting 1960* 95 in *Parl. Papers 1961–2* (Cmnd. 1753) IX. 259 The BBC bulletin is free to over-run when the service requires it. 1974 *Listener* 14 Feb. 209/1 Arthur Henderson, leader of the Labour rump, lost his head half-way through, thinking he was going to over-run, and ended in a gabble.

11. *Printing.* (*trans.* or *absol.*) To carry over words or lines of type into another line or page to provide for the addition of new matter or the removal of matter already composed; to cause to run over.

1683 MOXON *Mech. Exerc.*, *Printing* xxii. ¶8 If there be a long word or more left out, he cannot expect to Get that in into that Line, wherefore he must now Over-run; that is, he must put so much of the fore-part of the Line into the Line above it, or so much of the hinder part of the Line into the next Line under it, as will make room for what is Left out. *Ibid.*, If he Left out much, he must Over-run many Lines, either backwards or forwards, or both, till he come to a Break. 1896 T. L. DE VINNE in *Moxon's Mech. Exerc.*, *Printing* 424 The practice of overrunning matter in the form. 1900 SOUTHWARD *Pract. Print.* I. 225 A very simple insertion may cause a whole page to be overrun, if the type is large.

III. 12. To run (something) excessively; *spec.* (see quot. 1899).

1899 W. P. MAYCOCK *Electr. Wiring* i. 48 If ordinary lamps..marked for 100 volts..be put on a circuit at, say, 105 volts, the light given will be increased by about 25 per cent., and the watts absorbed per candle-power diminished. This is called over-running lamps, and their life will..be short. 1926 T. T. BAKER *Wireless Pict.* v. 67 It has been found convenient to use a 4·5 volt lamp over-run by a 6, 8, or even 10-volt battery. *Ibid.* 68 When a lamp is over-run it ..becomes highly incandescent instantaneously. 1938 G. H. SEWELL *Amateur Film-Making* iii. 35 The Photoflood is essentially a tungsten lamp of normal type which is 'overrun' by having a much higher pressure (voltage) of current passed through it than is normal for domestic burning. 1962 *Which?* Oct. 297/1 It is possible that many people over-run their [water-softening] units—that is, they are not aware of the moment when the water starts running hard, and go on using the hard water for a time.

over'runner. [f. OVERRUN *v.* + -ER[1].] One who or that which overruns (in senses of the vb.).

a 1350 *Cursor M.* 270 (Gött.) Here endis the prolouge of þis boke þat es cald ouerrener of þe werld. *a* 1657 LOVELACE *Poems* (1659) 83 Vandall ore-runners, Goths in Literature, Ploughmen that would Parnassus new manure. 1742 FIELDING *J. Andrews* III. vi, Ringwood the best hound..no babbler, no over-runner, respected by the whole pack. 1898 G. MEREDITH *Odes Fr. Hist.* 44 Gallia's over-runner, Rome's inveterate foe.

b. The shrew-mouse. *dial.*

1883 *Hampshire Gloss.*, *Our-runner*, for *Over-runner*,..a shrew-mouse; which is supposed to portend ill-luck if it runs over a person's foot.

over'running, *vbl. sb.* [-ING[1].] The action of the vb. OVERRUN in its various senses.

1555 J. PROCTOR *Hist. Wyat's Rebell.* in Arb. *Garner* VIII. 75 To defend the Realm from our overrunning by Strangers. 1627 SPEED *England* xix. §4 The Danes also in their ouerrunnings, sought to stay themselues in this Shire. 1867 SMYTH *Sailor's Word-bk.*, *Over-running*,..Applied to ice, when the young ice overlaps and is driven over. 1882 SOUTHWARD *Pract. Print.* (1884) 148 This kind of correction is called 'railroading' or overrunning. 1884 G. B. SHAW *Let.* 29 Aug. (1965) I. 95 The proofs..ought not to be paged, as the insertion of additional slips would cause over-running. 1908 *Westm. Gaz.* 3 Apr. 12/1 Over-running in the cricket-field had..brought the doctors..several youthful cases of a rather severe type. 1970 J. SEYMOUR *Compan. Guide E. Anglia* ix. 166 The fishermen haul the shanks by hand using the technique known as 'overrunning'—or letting the boat drive down over the shank carried by the swift tide.

over'running, *ppl. a.* [f. as prec. + -ING[2].]

1. That overruns; overflowing.

c 1230 *Hali Meid.* 19 He earneð him ouerfullet ful and ouereorninde met of heuenliche mede. 1611 BIBLE *Nahum* i. 8 With an over-running flood he will make an utter end of the place thereof. 1870 SWINBURNE *Ess. & Stud.* (1875) 90 The passion of overrunning pleasure.

2. ***overrunning clutch***: a clutch in which the normally driven member is able to rotate faster than the normally driving member.

1921 J. A. MOYER *Gasoline Automobiles* vii. 172 The engine is prevented from driving the [starting] motor by the use of an over-running clutch, which slips when the engine tends to drive the motor. 1930 [see FREE WHEEL, FREE-WHEEL]. 1966 *McGraw-Hill Encycl. Sci. & Technol.* III. 224/1 The driven shaft can run faster than the driving shaft with an overrunning clutch. This action permits freewheeling as the driving shaft slows down or another source of power is applied.

Hence †**over'runningly** *adv.*: see OVERRUN *v.* 2.

1561 T. NORTON *Calvin's Inst.* I. xiii. 43 Such thinges..he doth either leaue wholly vnspoken, or but lightly, and as it were ouerrunningly touch them.

overrush, -rust, -sad, etc.: see OVER-.

oversaid, *ppl. a.* [OVER- 1; cf. *abovesaid.*] Mentioned previously; abovesaid.

1840 E. E. NAPIER *Scenes & Sp. For. Lands* I. ix. 268 Still could we boast of..our leg of mutton, our oversaid ten or twelve couple of the finest snipe.

over'sail, *v.*[1] [f. OVER- 5, 10, 6 + SAIL *v.*[1]]

1. *trans.* To sail over or across; to cross in a sailing vessel. (In OE. *intr.*)

c 1000 *Ags. Gosp.* Matt. xiv. 34 And þa hiȝ ofer-seȝelodon [*c* 1160 *Hatt. Gosp.* ofer-seiȝledon] hi comon on þæt land Genesareth. 1375 BARBOUR *Bruce* III. 686 Till our-saile thaim [stremys] in-to schipfair. 1491 CAXTON *Vitas Patr.* (W. de W. 1495) II. 251 b/1 We shall oversaylle the peryllous and myserable see of this worlde. 1864 SKEAT *Uhland's Poems* 164 Together [they] had o'ersailed the tossing sea.

†**2.** To run down or sink (a vessel) by sailing over it. *Obs.*

1449 *Paston Lett.* I. 85 But [= unless] he wyll streke don the sayle, that I wyld over sayle ham by the grace of God. 1480 CAXTON *Chron. Eng.* ccxxxii. 250 A stronge vessel of hir [the Danes] nauye that was ouersailed by the englysshmen and was perisshed and dreynt. 1601 SIR W. CORNWALLIS *Ess.* II. (1631) 53 Like a barke oversayled he turnes himselfe under water, and sinkes.

3. To sail beyond.

1851 H. MELVILLE *Moby Dick* III. xlix. 295 I've over-sailed him [*sc.* Moby Dick]... Aye, he's chasing *me* now; not I *him.*

†**over'sail,** *v.*[2] *Obs. rare.* [f. OVER- 7 + SAIL *v.*[2], aphetic f. ASSAIL. Cf. OF. *sursaillir* to leap upon.] *trans.* To overthrow.

c 1425 *Eng. Conq. Irel.* 16 On euery side smytynge vp the host, as they wolden in wode raas ferly ouersaill hame [L. *tanquam in impetu furoris sui cuncta devorantium*].

over'sail, *v.*[3] *dial.* [app. f. OVER- 1, 3 + F. *saillir* to project, be salient: cf. OF. *sursaillir* to project over. The form *oversailyie* in sense 1 answers phonetically to the Fr., but the sense seems to connect it rather with CEIL *v.*]

1. *trans.* To roof or ceil over (an open passage between houses).

1673 FOUNTAINHALL in M. P. Brown *Suppl. Decis.* (1826) III. 16 Robert Lermont..obtained..an act giving him liberty to oversailyie the close, having both sides thereof, and cast a transe over it for communicating with both his houses.

2. a. *intr.* To project beyond the base, as when a stone or brick is laid so as to project beyond or overhang that on which it rests.

1828 *Craven Gloss.* (ed. 2), *Ower-sail*, to overhang, to project beyond the base. 1960 N. SCARFE *Suffolk* 97/2 Columbine Hall..is an ancient moated manor house of beauty, standing straight out of the moat, its upper storey oversailing. 1978 A. & G. RITCHIE *Anc. Monuments Orkney* 31 The lower parts of the walls are vertical, but the upper courses oversail slightly as they rise.

b. *trans.* To lay (stones, bricks, etc.) so that each projects over that on which it rests.

1897 *Archæol. Æliana* XIX. II. 177 A pointed doorway.. formed by oversailing the horizontal ashlar courses.

c. To project beyond or overhang (a base).

1912 C. E. POWER *Eng. Mediaeval Archit.* II. 483 In the Decorated period the triple roll base..begins to rise in height, often oversailing the plinth with flat under-side. 1931 *Antiquity* V. 48 The successive courses of the inner wall begin to oversail one another. 1938 *Proc. Prehistoric Soc.* IV. 199 The lowest layer was laid horizontally and each succeeding course was laid at an angle, each stone oversailing the other.

So **over'sailing** *ppl. a.*

1833 J. C. LOUDON *Encycl. Cottage, Farm & Villa Archit.* 227 These walls..should have what is called a Welsh cornice (two or three oversailing (protruding) courses of brickwork). 1880 R. BLACKMORE *Mary Anerley* I. xvii. 278 Strong sunshine glared upon the over-saling [*sic*] tiles, and white buckled walls, and cracky lintels. 1954 N. PEVSNER *Essex* 291 It has very heavy timbers and brackets to carry an oversailing upper storey. 1972 J. FLEMING et al. *Penguin Dict. Archit.* (ed. 2) 209/2 *Oversailing courses*, a series of stone or brick courses, each one projecting beyond the one below it. 1976 *National Trust Newsletter* Autumn 12/1 A striking black and white timbered building with high oversailing gables.

'oversail, *sb. techn.* [f. OVERSAIL *v.*[3]] The projection of anything over its base; overhang.

1688 R. HOLME *Armoury* III. 101/1 *Over seile*, is when one part of a Cornish stands further out than another. Some term it a Project, or Projecting. 1778 *Encycl. Brit.* (ed. 2) I. 618/1, *a* represents the oversail of the step. 1828 *Craven*

Gloss. (ed. 2), *Ower-sail*, projection. 'Let them slaates hev plenty of ower-sail'.

'over,sale. [OVER- 29 d.] Speculative sale for future delivery to a greater amount than can be supplied; *pl.* sales beyond the available supply.

1889 *Daily News* 11 Dec. 2/2 This artificial price was probably due to large oversales by 'bears', and the advance may have been brought about by the struggle to secure warrants to cover these sales. **1899** *Ibid.* 10 May 2/5 This alarmed the 'bears', who rushed in to cover their oversales.

'over-'salt, *a.* [OVER- 28.] Too salt.

1584 COGAN *Haven Health* (1636) 25 It must be temperately salted; for..bread over-salt is a drier. **1885** *Harper's Mag.* LXX. 221 These [oysters] we thought were oversalt.

,over'salt, *v.* [OVER- 27.] *trans.* To salt to excess, make too salt. So **,over'salted** *ppl. a.*, too much salted, too salt.

1575 TURBERV. *Faulconrie* 297 Put thereto Larde that is neither restie, nor ouersalted. *a* **1610** HEALEY *Theophrastus* (1636) 56 Hee..so oversalts them that they cannot be eaten. **1816** JANE AUSTEN *Emma* II. iii. 41 They must not oversalt the leg. **1837** M. DONOVAN *Dom. Econ.* II. 237 The common method of freshening oversalted meat. **1939** S. SPENDER tr. *Toller's Pastor Hall* I. 14 Julie, tell cook not to oversalt the roast.

over-sanguine: see OVER-.

over'saturated, *ppl. a.* [OVER- 24 b.] Supersaturated; chiefly in *Petrol.*, applied to a rock or magma in which there is free silica (or some other specified oxide). Hence **,oversatu'ration**, the property of being oversaturated.

1913 S. J. SHAND in *Geol. Mag.* Decade V. X. 510 Any rock which contains free quartz or tridymite of magmatic origin will be termed oversaturated. *Ibid.* 513 The connexion between mineral and chemical composition need not be obscured thereby, but rather the reverse, especially if ..the relative degrees of oversaturation or undersaturation were introduced..in the classification. **1946** *Nature* 19 Oct. 549/1 We would rather expect such condensations to show no more rotation than the water droplets in a fog formed from oversaturated vapour. **1947** E. E. WAHLSTROM *Igneous Minerals & Rocks* ix. 253 Rocks may be oversaturated, saturated, or undersaturated with respect to alumina or other oxides as well as with respect to silica. *Ibid.*, Free silica, which indicates oversaturation, is not present in rocks containing undersaturated minerals such as leucite and nephelite. **1974** A. D. EDGAR in H. Sørensen *Alkaline Rocks* v. i. 357/1 The genesis of oversaturated alkaline rocks. **1974** W. C. LUTH in *Ibid.* VI. vi. 506/2 Since the liquid is always silica oversaturated the crystalline assemblage must be silica undersaturated when a liquid is present.

oversauce, etc.: see OVER-.

,over'say, *v. rare.* [OVER- 27, 20.] †**a.** *intr.* To say too much. *Obs.* †**b.** *trans.* To say over, repeat (Ogilvie, citing Ford, 17th c.) *Obs.*

1655 SANDERSON *Serm.* (1681) II. Pref. 10 How hard a thing it is..to do or say all that is needful in a weighty business, and not in some thing or other to over-say, or overdo. **1874** [see UNSWEAR *v.*].

c. To exaggerate, overstate.

1900 *Scribner's Mag.* Sept. 368/2 This is oversaying it, of course, but the truth is in what I say. **1933** *G.K.'s Weekly* 21 Sept. 41/2, I assure you that if what I say runs towards superlatives it does not oversay what I still think and feel.

Hence **over'saying** *vbl. sb.*

1916 T. MACDONAGH *Lit. in Ireland* 46 Latin dispenses with the redundancies, the over-sayings, compressing a phrase into a verb.

†**over'scape,** *v. Obs.* [f. OVER- 5 + SCAPE *v.*, aphetic f. ESCAPE.] *trans.* **a.** To escape from. **b.** To escape the notice of. **c.** To pass over or fail to notice; to overlook.

1390 GOWER *Conf.* I. 117 As thing which thou miht overscape. *Ibid.* 296 Him mai som liht word overscape, And yit ne meneth he no Cheste. **1534** WHITINTON *Tullyes Offices* (1540) 4 To defyne what is offyce, whyche to be over-scaped of Danecus, I mervayle. **1581** J. BELL *Haddon's Answ. Osor.* 416 b, An Exposition of this place hath over-scaped so many sharpe sighted Doctours of Divinitie.

Hence †**'overscape** *sb.*, omission, oversight.

1581 J. BELL *Haddon's Answ. Osor.* 328, I began to be.. in some doubt: whether this were an overscape of your penne, or the oversight of Theobald your printer.

over-scare, -scepticism, etc.: see OVER-.

†**over'schippen,** *v. Obs.* [a. Du. *overschepen* to load into another ship.] *trans.* To transfer (goods) from one ship to another; to trans-ship.

1759 *Ann. Reg.* 71 The Dutch West-India ships..took in their cargoes in the manner called *overschippen*. *Ibid.*, St. Eustatia has but one road where the ships have no other way to take in their cargo but that of *overschippen*, that is, to take the goods out of the French boats to put them on board the Dutch vessels.

†**over'scorch,** *v. Obs. rare*$^{-1}$. [OVER- 8: cf. SCORCH *v.*^{2}] *trans.* To hew over, to rough-hew.

1382 WYCLIF *1 Kings* v. 18 The gret stoonus..the masouns of Salomon, and the masouns of Yrum han overscorchide [*v.r.* slascht, 1388 hewiden, Vulg. *dolaverunt*].

over'score, *v.* [OVER- 8, 27.] *trans.* **a.** To score over; to cover with scores, cuts, or deleting lines. **b.** To obliterate by scoring across. Also *fig.*

1849 POE *Assignation* Wks. 1856 I. 379 It had been originally written *London*, and afterwards carefully overscored—not, however, so effectually as to conceal the word from a scrutinizing eye. **1855** BROWNING *Love among Ruins* iv, The single little turret..By the caper overrooted, by the gourd Overscored. **1875** H. JAMES *R. Hudson* vi. 210 The soft atmospheric hum was overscored with distincter sounds. **1901** E. F. BENSON *Luck of Vails* III. xii. 115 The gentle hum of the warm afternoon came languidly in. Suddenly a fuller note began to overscore these noises in gradual crescendo. *Ibid.* xx. 233 The boon of the doctor's arrival quite overscored that sinister impression he had formed of him.

c. To score (music) with excessively elaborate orchestration. Also *absol.*

1947 N. CARDUS *Autobiogr.* III. 263 There is a fine sensibility moving darkly in the symphonies of Arnold Bax, but he tends to let his texture become congested; he overscores. **1947** C. GRAY *Contingencies* i. 37 The characteristic vice of overscoring is significant [in music of the Edwardian era]. **1977** *Gramophone* Feb. 1249/1 It is all too easy to dismiss his post-war orchestral works as garrulous, repetitive and over-scored.

overscour: see OVER-.

over'scrawl, *v.* [OVER- 8.] *trans.* To scrawl over or on. Hence **over'scrawled** *ppl. a.*

1871 BROWNING *Prince Hohenstiel-Schwangau* 28 Why keep each fool's bequeathment, scratch and blur Which overscrawl and underscore the piece? **1879** G. MEREDITH *Egoist* II. xi. 220 A yet more instructive passage than the over-scrawled Seventieth, or French Section.

over-scrub, etc.: see OVER-.

'over-'scruple. [OVER- 29 b.] Excess of scruple; the being too scrupulous.

1894 FROUDE *Life & Lett. Erasmus* 41 You may even displease God by over-scruple.

'over-'scrupulous, *a.* [OVER- 28.] Too scrupulous, excessively scrupulous.

1597 HOOKER *Eccl. Pol.* v. xxix. §4 Their ouer-scrupulous dislike of so meane a thing as a Vestment. *a* **1711** KEN *Man. of Prayers* Wks. (1838) 382 Be not over-scrupulous, to make yourself guilty of more sins than you really are. **1836** H. ROGERS *J. Howe* iv. (1863) 113 Without supposing the recusants to be..over-scrupulous fools. **1908** *Westm. Gaz.* 17 Aug. 2/1 Mr. Bryan's over-scrupulous attitude towards advertisements. **1952** E. GRIERSON *Reputation for Song* xxi. 173 She was..a giver, if he'd ever seen one, and not over-scrupulous in conscience or other things.

So **'over-scrupu'losity, -'scrupulousness.**

1741 RICHARDSON *Pamela* II. 160 Try to subdue this Over-scrupulousness and unseasonable Timidity. **1856** *Q. Rev.* Sept. 505 The man cannot be taxed with an over-scrupulosity.

oversculpture *v.*: see OVER- 8.

over'scurf, *v.* [OVER- 8.] *trans.* To cover over with or as with scurf.

1881 SWINBURNE *Mary Stuart* II. ii, O'erscurfed with poisonous lies. **1887** —— *Locrine* II. ii, Such tongues as fraud or treasonous hate o'erscurfs With leprous lust.

†**over'scutched,** *ppl. a. Obs.*

Taken by Nares as = 'whipped, probably at the cart's tail', f. SCUTCH *v.*, and by some equated with Ray's 'Overswitch housewife, i.e. a whore; a ludicrous word' (N.C. Wds.); Malone, 'perhaps with more propriety' (Schmidt), suggests 'worn in the service', in which sense it is used by Scott.

1597 SHAKS. *2 Hen. IV*, III. ii. 340 (Qo., 1598) A came ouer in the rereward of the fashion, and sung those tunes to the ouer-schutcht huswiues, that he heard the Car-men whistle. **1813** SCOTT *Trierm.* III. Introd. v, For Harp's an over-scutched phrase, Worn out by bards of modern days. **1827** —— *Two Drovers* Introd.

oversea, *a.* and *adv.* [f. OVER *prep.* + SEA. (OE. had *ofersǽwisc* transmarine, foreign.) Cf. OVERSEAS *adv.* (*sb.*) and *a.*]

A. *adj.* (*'oversea*). **1.** Of or pertaining to movement or transport over the sea; transmarine.

1552 HULOET, Oversea, *transmarinus*, as well in goynge as commynge. **1570** BUCHANAN *Chamæleon* Wks. (1892) 46 The oursey trafficque of mariage growing cauld. **1710** *Lond. Gaz.* No. 4674/1 An Act..for taking off the Oversea Duty on Coals exported in British Bottoms. **1812** G. CHALMERS *Dom. Econ. Gt. Brit.* 416 The..amount of the Irish over-sea trade. **1894** C. N. ROBINSON *Brit. Fleet* 6 The Navy..for oversea attack is plainly essential.

†**2.** Imported from beyond the sea; of foreign make; made abroad; foreign. *Obs.*

1509 *Test. Ebor.* (Surtees) V. 5 To Sir Thomas Pilley my wedding ringe and a overse bed. **1552** *Inventories* (Surtees) 14 One crosse of leade of oversee work. **1600** *Acc.-Bk. W. Wray* in *Antiquary* XXXII. 279 Item, one over sea coveringe, xvs. *a* **1651** CALDERWOOD *Hist. Kirk* (Wodrow Soc.) III. 369 His new opinions, and over-sea dreams touching discipline and policie of the Kirk.

3. Situated beyond the sea; connected or having to do with countries beyond the sea; foreign.

1645 RUTHERFORD *Tryal & Tri. Faith* (1845) 6 The wife of youth, that..expects he [her husband] shall return to her from over-sea lands. **1881** GLADSTONE *Sp. at Knowsley* 27 Oct., The questions of what I may call over-sea policy in Europe, Asia, and America. **1893** *Times* 6 July 11/1 They were..betrayed by their oversea accents. **1931** *Times* 17 Feb. 9/1 The competition of our rivals in the home and oversea markets. **1953** [see DOMINION *sb.* 2 b]. **1955** P. TOWNSEND *China Phoenix* 9 He was Fukienese by birth, from a province of China from which came many oversea Chinese. **1959** *Times* 30 July 6/6 (*heading*) Council formed for oversea research. **1969** *IEEE Trans. Antennas & Propagation* XVII. 254/1 In ship-to-ship detectability studies it is important to have a method of estimating oversea radar range distribution.

B. *adv.* (*'over 'sea*). Across or beyond the sea; on the other side of the sea; abroad.

[*a* **1450** tr. *Higden, Contin.*, Rolls VIII. 485 All oþer castells and towres over see longynge to the crowne of Ynglonde.] **1616** SIR G. HAY *Let.* in J. Russell *Haigs* vii. (1881) 146 If he be not found there [at Court], it is likely that he pretended Court, and meant over-sea. **1641** MILTON *Reform.* II. (1851) 50 And what though all this go not oversea? 'twere better it did. **1760–72** H. BROOKE *Fool of Qual.* (1809) IV. 2 By the help of canvas wings..[he] proposes to fly over-sea from Dover to Calais. **1895** *Daily Chron.* 16 Jan. 3/3 Now living oversea in a quiet farmstead. **1903** W. B. YEATS *In Seven Woods* 15 And you are more high of heart than she For all her wanderings over-sea. **1955** *Times* 9 May 11/2 Private investment oversea. **1974** *Black World* Jan. 55/2 He have to go leave that Ford car when he go oversea from Fort Benning, and it stay in our front yard.

overseal, *v.*: see OVER- 8.

'overseam, *sb. Needlework.* [OVER- 5.] A seam in which two edges are sewn together by oversewing or overcasting. So **over'seam** *v.*

In some mod. Dicts.

†**'over,search,** *sb. Obs. rare.* [OVER- 9.] A thorough search.

1490 CAXTON *Eneydos* xiii. 47 But what ouerserche [Fr. *recherche*] nedeth more to be enquered.

over'search, *v.* [OVER- 9, 16.] *trans.* To search all over or through, examine thoroughly.

1532 MORE *Confut. Tindale* Wks. 423/2 When I had ouersearched all my booke and ransaked vp the verie bottom of my brest. **1590** GREENE *Orl. Fur.* Wks. (Rtldg.) 89/2 The matchless beauty of Angelica,..Forc'd me to cross and cut th' Atlantic seas, To oversearch the fearful ocean.

over'seas, *adv.* (*sb.*) [f. OVER *prep.* + *seas* (app.) sb. pl. (cf. 'the narrow seas', 'the four seas'); though the *-s* may have originated as advb. genitive: cf. *half-seas-over*.]

a. = OVERSEA *adv.*

1583 STUBBES *Anat. Abus.* II. (1882) 22 These [goods] they transport ouer seas, whereby they gaine infinit summes of mony. **1631** WEEVER *Anc. Fun. Mon.* 253 He fled ouer Seas into Denmarke. **1842** TENNYSON *Walking to Mail* 18 He.. sick of home went overseas for change. **1886** *Longman's Mag.* Mar. 552 Our brethren of the pen over-seas.

b. quasi-*sb.* Foreign parts; abroad.

1919 *Empire Rev.*, Munition workers who have come from overseas. **1926** A. BENNETT *Lord Raingo* I. lix. 264 Every traveller from overseas was knocked silly by the spectacle. *Ibid.*, Britons whose secret conceit, compared to the ingenuous self-complacency of overseas, was as Mount Everest to Snowdon. **1966** *Listener* 8 Sept. 335/1 In the years before the war our financial income from over-seas provided finance to pay for more than a third of our imports.

over'seas, *a.* [f. the adv.] = OVERSEA *a.*; *overseas Chinese*, a native of China residing in another country.

Overseas is now more frequently used than *oversea*.

1892 KIPLING *Lett. of Travel* (1920) 47 Some day a man will bethink himself and write a book..called 'The Book of The Overseas Club'. **1905** *Daily Chron.* 29 Mar. 3/2 The political liberties of these islands were..deeply endangered by the overseas dominion..of Spain. **1908** *Westm. Gaz.* 26 June 9/3 The magnitude of the overseas possessions which we had to defend. **1912** *Chambers's Jrnl.* Nov. 754/1 In athletic prowess we are now far inferior to those overseas descendants of our race. **1918** P. S. ALLEN *Let.* 9 June (1939) 146 At Merton we are hoping to have some 'overseas' undergraduates next term. **1920** *Act 10 & 11 Geo. V* c. 29 (*title*) An Act to authorise the granting of credits and the undertaking of insurances for the purpose of re-establishing overseas trade. **1933** A. THIRKELL *High Rising* xi. 195 She'll be able to vamp the overseas students and have a splendid time. **1942** 'G. ORWELL' *Diary* 21 June in *Coll. Ess.* (1968) II. 433 The BBC simply isn't listened to overseas, a fact known to everyone concerned with overseas broadcasting. **1947** *Sun* (Baltimore) 22 Aug. 6/4 'Overseas' Chinese will participate in the elections not only as voters but as candidates as well. **1961** S. CHANDRASEKHAR *Communist China Today* viii. 155, I learned that Communist China was anxious to attract the savings of the overseas Chinese who would like to return to their homeland. **1966** [see HOME *a.* 3 b]. **1968** D. TORR *Treason Line* 16 He was tall for an Overseas Chinese. **1970** V. CANNING *Great Affair* xii. 205 That..was in the overseas edition of *The Times*. **1972** J. BALL *Five Pieces Jade* viii. 96, I consider myself a Chinese-American, in other words an American citizen of Chinese descent. So do almost all of us. But to the Chinese in China —Taiwan or the mainland—either way, we are overseas Chinese. **1974** *Guardian* 27 Mar. 1/1 Tax to be charged on 90 per cent of overseas earnings whether remitted to UK or not. **1975** *Encounter* Feb. 43/2 My wife, phoning Chicago from London, asked, 'Is this the overseas operator?' A pitying male voice replied, 'This is *one* of them, madam.' **1977** 'J. LE CARRÉ' *Hon. Schoolboy* iv. 81 It was an overseas Chinese outfit.

over-seasoned, -secure, etc.: see OVER-.

oversee (əʊvəˈsiː), *v.* Forms: see OVER and SEE. [OE. *oferséon* = OS. *obarsehan* (MDu. *oversien*, Du. *overzien*), OHG. *ubarsehan* (MHG., Ger. *übersehen*), f. *ofer-* OVER- + SEE *v.* Cf. OVERLOOK.]

I. 1. *trans.* To look down upon, look at from (or as from) a higher position, overlook; to survey; to keep watch over; to watch. [OVER- 7.]

c **888** K. ÆLFRED *Boeth.* iv, Eala min Drihten, þu þe ealle ȝesceafta ofersihst. *a* **1200** *Moral Ode* 75 Houene and horþe he ouer sich. *a* **1250** *Owl & Night.* 30 The niȝtingale hi i-seȝ,

And hi bi-hold and over-seȝ. **1603** H. Crosse *Vertues Commw.* (1878) 31 Such men..are duly watcht, and attentiuely ouer-seene. *a* **1628** F. Grevil *Sidney* xvi. (1652) 202 Even hee who oversaw the rest, might have his owne greatnesse overseen. **1796** Burke *Let. Noble Ld.* Wks. VIII. 49 As long as this awful structure shall oversee and guard the subjected land.

2. To look over, look through, look into the various parts of; to inspect, examine; to peruse, esp. by way of revision for the printing-press. *Obs.* or *arch.* [over- 16.]

1362 Langl. *P. Pl.* A. vii. 106 Perkyn lette þe plouȝ stonde, While þat he ouer-seȝe him-self ho þat best wrouhte. **1377** *Ibid.* B. x. 328 That þis worth soth, seke ȝe þat oft ouer-se þe bible. *c* **1420** Lydg. *Assembly Gods* 772 [He] prayed hym hertyly hit to ouerse. **1490** Caxton *Eneydos* Prol. 1, I wrote a leef or tweyne, whyche I ouersawe agayn to corecte it. **1528** in *Vicary's Anat.* (1888) App. xiv. 249 [Committee] appoynted to pervse and oversee suche Bookes of Actes & ordynaunces as heretofore were given. **1588** *Marprel. Epist.* (Arb.) 4 John Cant. ouersawe euery proofe. **1655** Fuller *Ch. Hist.* iii. ii. v. §14. 62 The Legate..fearing to be poisoned, appointed his Brother to over-see all food for his own eating. [**1895** F. S. Ellis in *Daily News* 2 Nov. 6/5, I used the word 'overseen' in preference to 'edited',..because it indicates exactly all I had a right to claim.]

†**b.** To examine mentally, consider. *Obs.*

c **1477** Caxton *Jason* 111 So alle thing well ouerseen hit is better to the that thou retorne.

3. To see to officially, as one holding a position over those who do the work; to supervise, superintend; to see after, look after, attend to the doing or working of. (Cf. overlook *v.* 6.)

c **1449** Pecock *Repr.* 416 And aboue..alle Patriarkis is oon Pope forto ouerse and reule and amende the Governauncis of Patriarkis. **1485** in *10th Rep. Hist. MSS. Comm.* App. v. 320 To rule and oversee the crafte undre the Maire. **1495** *Act 11 Hen. VII*, c. 22 §6 Any persone assigned to comptroll and oversee theym in their werking. **1596** H. Clapham *Briefe Bible* i. 67 Othoniel was chosen Iudge, who oversawe them for 40 yeares. **1611** Bible *1 Chron.* ix. 29. **1665** *Surv. Aff. Netherl.* 25 The four Bishops..were unable to oversee effectually the 17 large Provinces of Belgium. **1735** Swift *Ep. Corr.* Wks. 1841 II. 745 Can I oversee my workmen and a school too? *a* **1864** N. Hawthorne *Little Daffydowndilly* Tales 1871 II. 155 He..is overseeing the carpenters.

†**b.** With obj. clause (or obj. and compl.): To see, see to it (that something be done). *Obs.*

1470–85 Malory *Arthur* xviii. xx, Hit wyl be your worshyp that ye ouer see that she be entered worshypfully. **1569** in W. H. Turner *Select. Rec. Oxford* 327 The Baillies ..shall..oversee that every man shall kepe his stynt of beastes. **1697** *View Penal Laws* 202 Power to search all Oyls ..and to oversee that the same be not mixed.

c. *absol.* To superintend, act as overseer.

a **1548** Hall *Chron.* Introd. 8b, Being an euil sheperd or herdeman before time, dyd not plie, kepe and diligently ouerse. **1647** N. Bacon *Disc. Govt. Eng.* i. v. (1739) 13 The Bishop of Caerleon upon Uske, who is to oversee under God over us. **1798** W. Hutton *Autobiog.* 34 But I, who had no land near, no team to assist, or servants that could oversee, was obliged to hire all the work.

4. To see against the intention or without the knowledge of the person seen; to catch sight of; to have a sight of. (Cf. overhear 3.)

1742 Fielding *J. Andrews* iii. ii, Fanny, not suspicious of being overseen by Adams, gave a loose to her passion. **1862** Wraxall *Hugo's Misérables* i. li. (1877) 24 A moment after he blew out his light, for..he fancied he might be overseen.

†**5.** To look at with the 'evil eye', bewitch: = overlook *v.* 7. *Obs. rare.*

1641 W. Hooke *New Eng. Tears* 7 When any are bewitched, it is a phrase of speech among many to say, they are over-seene, *i.e.* lookt upon with a malicious eye.

II. 6. To fail or omit to see or notice (through inattention, or intentionally); to neglect, pass over, disregard; = overlook *v.* 2. *Obs.* exc. *dial.*

a **1023** Wulfstan *Hom.* l. (Napier) 270 Ðencan þa nu ..þæt hiȝ god oferseoð. **1500–20** Dunbar *Poems* lxiii. 77 And gar me mony falt ouerse, That now is brayd befoir myn E. **1535** Coverdale *Bible* Prol., Thynke yᵗ..it is happlye ouer-sene of yᵉ interpreters. **1613** Jackson *Creed* ii. i. §2. 239 Many things he cannot see, and many things he may over-see. **1700** Congreve *Way of World* ii. iii, 'Twas for my ease to oversee and wilfully neglect the gross advances made him by my wife. **1774** Pennant *Tour Scot. in 1772*, 200 Adding numbers of remarks over-seen by him.

7. *refl.* To fail to perceive what is befitting or right for one to do, or what is the truth or fact of a matter; to forget oneself, act unbecomingly; to fall into error, make a mistake, err, blunder, act imprudently. Also *intr.* (quots. 1615, 1639: cf. overseen 1.) *Obs.* exc. *dial.*

1377 Langl. *P. Pl.* B. v. 378, I, glotoun..gylti me ȝelde, For I haue..ouer-seye me at my sopere, and some tyme at nones. **1529** More *Dyaloge* iv. Wks. 255/1 Luther..dothe so madly ouersee himselfe, that he discloseth vnware certayne folies of him selfe. **1615** Jackson *Creed* iv. iii. v. §2 Who notwithstanding mightily oversee in prognosticating of a joyful harvest by this gladsome or forward spring. **1639** Mayne *City Match* iv. iii, *Aur.* Sir, please you, partake Of a slight banquet? ..*Plot*..Be sure you do not oversee. *a* **1677** Barrow *Serm.* (1810) II. 564 Immoderate selfishness so blindeth us, that we oversee and forget ourselves.

III. 8. *nonce-use.* To see too strongly or vividly. [over- 27.]

a **1600** Hooker *Serm. Habak.* ii. 4 Wks. 1888 III. 607 It then maketh them cease to be proud, when it causeth them to see their error in overseeing the thing they were proud of. **1856** Kane *Arct. Expl.* II. iii. 47 We had so grovelled in darkness that we oversaw the light.

Hence **over'seeing** *vbl. sb.* and *ppl. a.* (in various senses: see above).

1513 in *10th Rep. Hist. MSS. Comm.* App. v. 395 That no honie be brought to town but it be good and merchantable, by overseinge of such as shalbe..chossen by the Maior. **1651** Jer. Taylor *Clerus Dom.* 48 In the overseeing providence of thy rich mercies. **1799** Wordsw. '*Three years she grew*' ii, The girl..Shall feel an overseeing power To kindle or restrain. **1890** 'R. Boldrewood' *Col. Reformer* (1891) 68, I have jobs of overseeing now and then.

over-seeded: see over- 27b.

†**over'seek, -seche,** *v. Obs.* [over- 9. (OE. had *ofersécan* in sense 'exact too much'.)] *trans.* To search through.

c **1425** *Eng. Conq. Irel.* 138 Me may rede & ouerseche the boke of kynges, þe prophetes.

†**over'seeming,** *sb. Obs. rare.* Used to render Gr. ἐπιφάνεια outward appearance.

1398 Trevisa *Barth. De P.R.* xix. viii. (Bodl. MS.) lf. 293/2 Pictagoraci..cleped coloure ephipania, þat is ouersemynge þat is vttemoste partie of a clere bodie þat is termynyd.

†**over'seeming,** *a. Obs.* Appearing above, supereminent (rendering L. *superēminens*); seeming to be over or higher.

1382 Wyclif *Eph.* i. 19 Which is the ouersemynge [1388 excellent, *Vulg.* supereminens] greetnesse of his vertu into vs that han bileuyd. *a* **1635** Naunton *Fragm. Reg.* (Arb.) 30 A room in the Queens favour, which eclipsed the others over-seeming greatnesse.

overseen (əʊvəˈsiːn), *ppl. a.* Forms: 4 **ouerseie,** 4–6 **-seyn(e,** 5–6 **-sayne, -sene,** 5–7 **-seene,** 5– **-seen,** (6 **-sayne, -sean**). [Pa. pple. of oversee. In part with active meaning: cf. *mistaken.*]

1. That has 'overseen himself' (see oversee 7); betrayed into a fault or blunder; deceived, deluded, mistaken, in error; acting imprudently, hasty, rash (in an action). Now *arch.* or *dial.*

1390 Gower *Conf.* III. 373 It were a thing unresonable, A man to be so overseie. Forthi tak hiede of that I seie. **1491** Caxton *Vitas Patr.* (W. de W. 1495) iii. iii. 318b/1 They that wyll saye that he was an heretyke ben fooles & ouerseen. **1519** *Interlude Four Elements* in Hazl. *Dodsley* I. 33 Methink you far oversayne. **1535** Coverdale *Prov.* xxiv. 10 Yf thou be ouersene & negligent in tyme of nede, then is thy strength but small. **1608** Willet *Hexapla Exod.* 151 How Rupertus was so much ouerseene to alleage a text no where extant. **1786** Nelson *Let.* June in Nicolas *Disp.* (1845) I. 177 However Mr. Adye might have been overseen in his Opinion as to the right of Seizure. **1872** *St. James' Mag.* May 164 She..had been so overseen as to encourage the young man's visits.

b. *overseen with* (or *in*) *drink*, also simply *overseen*: Drunk, intoxicated. *Obs.* exc. *dial.*

c **1475** *How Good Wife taught Dau.* 164 in *Q. Eliz. Acad.* 49 Syte not to longe vppe at euene, For drede with ale þou be ouer-sene. **1532** Elyot *Let.* in *Gov.* (1883) Life 78 Men callyth him overseene, that is drunke, whan he neither knowith what he doeth, nor what he owght to doo. **1628** Earle *Microcosm., Colledge Butler* (Arb.) 37 Hee is a very sober man considering his manifold temptations of drinke, ..and if hee be ouer-seene, tis within his owne liberties, and no man ought to take exceptions. **1678** *Robin Hood* in Thoms *Prose Rom.* (1858) II. 122, I cannot well tell whether he was overseen with wine or rage.

†**2.** That has looked into or studied a subject (cf. oversee 2); versed, skilled, 'well seen' *in* some department of knowledge. (Cf. *well-read.*)

1533 More *Answ. Poysoned Bk.* Wks. 1094/1 The man is a wyse man and wel ouer sene in arguing. **1550** Bale *Apol.* 51 Ye are a great wise prelate & wel oversean in matters. **1610** Guillim *Heraldry* ii. vi. (1660) 68 They would be thought to be well overseen in Heraldry.

†**3.** Overlooked, unnoticed: see oversee 6. *Obs.*

1608 Bp. Hall *Char. Virtues & V., Honest Man*, He bewraies the fault of what he sells, and restores the ouerseene gaine of a false reckoning.

overseer (ˈəʊvəsɪə(r)), *sb.* [f. oversee + -er¹.]

1. a. One who oversees or superintends, a supervisor; *esp.* one whose business it is to superintend a piece of work, or a body of workmen; a superintendent (of workmen, slaves, convicts, etc.).

1523 Fitzherb. *Surv.* 34 The name of a surueyour is a frenche name, and is as moche to say in Englysshe as an ouerseer. **1530** Tindale *Answ. More* Wks. (1573) 252/1 Those ouersears which we now call Byshops after the Greke word, were alway bidyng in one place to gouerne the congregation there. **1644** Vicars *God in Mount* 206 Overseers of the Out-workes of the City. **1709** Steele *Tatler* No. 144. ¶4 The Overseers of the Highway and Constables. **1766** W. Stork *Acc. East Florida* 62 The overseer, and other white servants, will..be hired much cheaper in a plentiful and good climate, than in a scarce and sickly one. **1845** S. Austin *Ranke's Hist. Ref.* III. 423 There was a disturbance in Göttingen, because the overseers of the commune were at first hostile. **1882** Ouida *Maremma* I. 24 Saturnino to be.. set to work with an axe or a spade in dockyard or on highway, and cowed with the whip of the overseer. *a* **1904** *Mod. Advt.*, To Printers.—Working Overseer wanted in a country news and jobbing office. Must be a good disciplinarian, sober and capable.

†**b.** A person (formerly) appointed by a testator to supervise or assist the executor or executors of the will. *Obs.*

1395 in *E.E. Wills* (1882) 11 My seketour, William Kyllet of Essex,..John Cosyn of London, ouerseer, þat my wylle be fulfylyd in þe worschip of god. **14..** *Prov.* in *Rel. Ant.* I. 314 Too secutors and an overseere make thre theves. **1532** Elyot *Let.* in *Gov.* (1883) Life 77 The Busshop..is in the case that overseers of testamentes be in England, for he shall have leve to looke so that he meddle not. **1612** J. More in *Buccleuch MSS.* (Hist. MSS. Comm.) I. 124 The great pains he hath taken..to strengthen his will with so powerful overseers, and to make so cunning executors. **1666–7** P. Henry *Diaries & Lett.* 21 Jan., For mourning clothes for myself, my wife, my son John, and Cosin Martha Warter, as was thought fit by the overseers of the will—£12. 6. 8.

c. (In full, *overseer of the poor.*) A parish officer (appointed annually) to perform various administrative duties mainly connected with the relief of the poor.

The office was created by Act 43 Eliz. c. 2, and the duties were defined to include causing able-bodied paupers to work, giving relief to the disabled poor, putting poor children to work, apprenticing them, etc., and raising by rate the necessary funds for these purposes; the chief duties latterly were to assess, collect, and distribute the 'Poor Rate' (the actual relief of the poor in most cases belonging to the 'guardians of the poor': see guardian 1 b), to make out the lists of voters for parliament and for municipal and other councils, jury lists, etc. The office belonged to England and Wales, and was gratuitous, but, where the duties required it, paid or *assistant overseers* were appointed. Officers having the same name, whose duties were restricted to the administration of relief to the poor, existed in some of the United States of America.

1601 *Act 43 Eliz.* c. 2 §1 Be it enacted..That the Church-wardens of euery Parish, and foure, three, or two substantiall householders..to be nominated yearely in Easter weeke..shall be called Ouerseers of the Poore of the same Parish. **1625** Massinger *New Way* i. i, The poor income..hath made me..Thought worthy to be scavenger, and in time May rise to be overseër of the poor. **1690** Child *Disc. Trade* (ed. 4) 97 All constables, churchwardens, overseers, or other officers in all parishes. **1712** Prideaux *Direct. Ch.-wardens* (ed. 4) 23 The Churchwardens were anciently the sole Over-seers of the Poor. **1866** Geo. Eliot *F. Holt* Introd., The inhabitants..were in much less awe of the parson than of the overseer.

d. *U.S.* A member of a board of officials which manages the affairs of a college, esp. Harvard College, Massachusetts.

1643 *New Englands First Fruits* 13 Over the Colledge are twelve Overseers chosen by the generall Court. **1812** in *Proc. Mass. Hist. Soc.* (1890) 2nd Ser. V. 176 [Harvard Commencement] The Corporation and Overseers arrived at 20 minutes past ten. **1832** W. D. Williamson *Hist. State Maine* II. 563 Its government was committed to a board of 13 Trustees, including the President, and a supervisory body of 45 Overseers. **1900** *Dialect Notes* ii. 47 *Overseers, board of*, a special governing board of Harvard, chosen by the alumni from their own number. **1946** *Sat. Rev. Lit.* (U.S.) 14 Sept. 5 Then he too retired, but was promptly elected to a seat on the Board of Harvard Overseers. **1973** *Amer. Universities & Colleges* (ed. 11) 729/1 *Harvard University... Governing Board.* President and Fellows of Harvard College: self-perpetuating board of 7 members; life terms. Many board actions subject to consent of Board of Overseers, which is composed of 30 members elected by alumni for 6-year terms.

e. A Friend (friend *sb.* 7) chosen for the pastoral supervision of the congregation to which he belongs.

1785 *Bk. of Discipline New England Yearly Meeting Soc. of Friends* 39 That each monthly meeting choose two or more sober and judicious men friends, and two or more women friends, to be overseers in each preparative-meeting, which overseers are to render account of their service to the monthly meeting at least once a quarter, and to be annually appointed or re-chosen. **1832** W. D. Williamson *Hist. State Maine* II. 699 Each society [of Quakers] has at least four Overseers, two males and two females. **1921** R. M. Jones *Later Periods Quakerism* I. iv. 131 These Overseers.. were in the course of time charged with responsibility for the moral life of the membership. *Ibid.* 132 Like the Elders, they had no absolute rules to guide them, but there slowly accumulated..a body of Advices and Queries which furnished the Overseers with a pretty clear line of procedure. **1963** A. Heron *Towards Quaker View of Sex* i. 7 Particularly does this apply to elders and overseers in the Society of Friends. **1974** G. Hubbard *Quaker by Convincement* iv. iii. 209 The responsibilities of Overseers are to encourage attendance at Meetings for Worship and for business, to exercise a care over younger members and children and those in need of assistance, [etc.].

†**2.** One who looks down upon or at anything; a beholder, onlooker, spectator. *Obs.*

1551 Robinson tr. *More's Utop.* ii. ix. (1895) 279 Hauing a trust and affiaunce in such ouerseers [the dead, called just above 'beholders' and 'witnesses']. **1562** Turner *Baths* Pref., If that I write not so perfitly of it, as sum perfit idle overseers would that I shuld have done. *a* **1656** Bp. Hall *Rem. Wks.* (1660) 252 Study..to be approved of so glorious witnesses and overseeres.

†**3.** One who 'oversees' a book for the purpose of criticism or revision; variously = critic, censor, reviser, editor. *Obs.*

1597 Hooker *Eccl. Pol.* v. xxxi. §3 There are in the world certayne voluntarie ouer-seers of all Bookes, whose censure in this respect would fall as sharpe on us. **1624** Bedell *Lett.* vii. 116 In the Margent,..the ouerseers of Plantines edition, set this note. **1642** Rogers *Naaman* To Rdr., That I may be the overseer of mine owne Bookes. **1685** Wood *Life* 27 Feb. (O.H.S.) III. 133 Half the verses that were made for the said book were cast aside by the overseers, Dr. Aldrich and Jane.

Hence **'over,seer** *v. trans.*, to act as overseer over; **'over,seering** *vbl. sb.*, acting as overseer; **'overseerism,** the system of overseers.

1709 Thoresby *Diary* II. 50 Both days entirely spent with labourers directing and overseering the sows [= 'sews', drains] to drain water. **1870** *Athenæum* 3 Dec. 721 A dark and melancholy wild, where..Absenteeism, Overseerism, all sorts of other 'isms' gather griffin-like around the porches of the proud..land-proprietors. **1892** *Daily News* 25 Jan.

5/4 The forest is, at present, overseered and cared for by the ..deputy surveyor, with three assistants [etc.]. **1893** F. F. Moore *I Forbid Banns* (1899) 72, I did a little in the overseering line.

'overseership. [f. prec. + -ship.] The office or position of an overseer.

1647 N. Bacon *Disc. Govt. Eng.* i. xlix. (1739) 85 Leaving to the King only an overseership. **1813** *Examiner* 8 Feb. 91/2, I was..appointed Overseer of the parish; and..six months before my overseership terminated, I received another paper. *Mod. Advt.*, To master Printers.—Overseership or Clickership required by good practical Printer.

†over'seethe, *v. Obs.* [over- 5.] *trans.* and *intr.* To boil over.

1633 P. Fletcher *Pisc. Ecl.* iii. vi, Your stately seas (perhaps with love's fire) glow, And overseeth their banks with springing tide. **1656** Trapp *Comm. 3 John* 10 It is a metaphor taken from over-seething pots.

overseil: see oversile.

'over-self. [over- 2 b.] The finer, stronger, or more assertive part of one's nature (see also quot. 1960).

1888 E. Clodd *Story of Creation* xi. 223 The terrible mass of wrong-doing can only be lessened and finally removed by suppression of the over-self. **1908** *Daily Chron.* 30 Apr. 3/1 It is the Shakespeare that projected his over-self into two score of masterpieces of poetry and drama that is Shakespeare for us. **1960** J. Hewitt *Yoga* 7 The Yogi believes that there is a universal Overself with whom he can make contact and identify himself in moments of higher consciousness. *Ibid.* xi. 155 To the Yogi Samadhi is the merging of the individual Soul or Self with the universal Soul or Overself.

over'sell, ˌover-'sell, *v.* [over- 26, 27.]

1. †**a.** *trans.* To sell at more than the real value. *Obs.*

1580 Hollyband *Treas. Fr. Tong, Survendre*, to ouer-sell. **1697** Dryden *Æneid* ix. 265 The thing call'd life, with ease I can disclaim, And think it over-sold to purchase fame. **1768** *Woman of Honor* III. 247 If he waits to do it, for his asking him, he oversells the benefit.

b. To make excessive or unrealistic claims for (goods advertised or offered for sale, etc.); to give (someone) an exaggerated idea of the value or worth of something. Also *absol.*, *transf.* and *fig.*

1928 *Publishers' Weekly* 10 Nov. 1978/2 We remember—how perfectly!—the names and the publishers of books on which we were oversold last season, and had, subsequently, to send the way of all deadwood. **1957** *Technology* July 174/1 The word 'syndicate' and the syndicate method in management training has been over-sold for some time. **1960** *20th Cent.* Sept. 234 Mr. Wesker's enemies dismiss him as a mere brand-name oversold by the theatrical Left. **1970** A. Toffler *Future Shock* (1974) xx. 463 It would be foolish to oversell the ability of science, as yet, to forecast complex events accurately. **1971** P. Dickinson *Sleep & his Brother* iii. 56 'Why does he want to see me?' 'Aha! I fear I may have oversold you. We are his hobby, and he is not a patient man.' **1971** *Nature* 19 Nov. 118/3 The current disenchantment with science arises because science was oversold in the postwar years. **1973** E. Lemarchand *Let or Hindrance* xi. 132 Chap oversells himself..but he knows his way round in business. **1977** R. E. Harrington *Quintain* iv. 34 'They believe they're safe.' Diamond..knew he was over-selling to Felix, and he damned himself for it.

†**2.** To fetch a higher price than. *Obs. rare.*

1618 Fletcher *Chances* ii. i, A distressed Lady..whose beauty Would over-sell all Italy.

3. *Speculation.* To sell more of (a stock, etc.) than one can deliver, or than is in existence. Also *refl.*

1879 Webster Suppl., *Oversell*,..(Stock Exchange), to sell beyond one's means of delivery. **1881** *Daily News* 14 Sept. 4/6 He secured nearly 500,000 bales, or, in fact, considerably more cotton than was actually in existence, the market thus being what is termed 'oversold'. **1891** *Pall Mall G.* 14 Sept. 6/2 The state of affairs..is due to..cultivators having oversold the paddy crop. **1897** *Daily News* 26 Feb. 8/7 For mohairs there is a good many inquiries, some merchants having apparently over-sold themselves.

Hence **over'selling** *vbl. sb.*; **over'sold** *ppl. a.*

1583 Babington *Commandm.* viii. (1637) 71 It condemneth all over-selling: I meane knowne and wilful ouerselling of any thing. **1879–90** Webster s.v. *Oversell*, *Oversold market*, a market in which stocks have been sold 'short' to such an extent that..it is difficult to obtain them for delivery. **1934** *Sun* (Baltimore) 5 Apr. 27/1 Word of this amendment..caught the wheat market in apparently an oversold condition. **1968** L. Sellers *Doing it in Style* 206 If a reporter writes a story too hard it may get into the paper unqueried and result in trouble. If he oversells in advance he will only infuriate the executives... Overselling is the way to trouble. **1971** *Daily Tel.* 28 Oct. 19/4 The market is in a heavily oversold condition.

oversell ('əʊvəsɛl), *sb.* [f. the vb.] Excessive or ambitious claims for, or promotion of, goods offered for sale; also *transf.* and *fig.*

1969 *Computers & Humanities* IV. 53 No doubt we are partly the victims of oversell by our IBM salesmen and computer directors, who promised us the computer would do things it is quite unsuited for. **1970** G. Greer *Female Eunuch* 13 Perhaps the sexual sell was oversell. **1974** 'G. Black' *Golden Cockatrice* i. 17 It was another case of oversell, like that soap powder campaign..which drove irritated women to buy the brands which didn't promise..a ten per cent whiter wash.

†over'seme, *v. Obs.* [OE. *ofersíeman*, f. *ofer-*, over- + *síeman*, seme *v.*, to load.] *trans.* To overload, oppress.

c **961** Æthelwold *Rule St. Benet* lxiv. (1885), þæt..þa unstrangan ofersymede heora þeowdom ne forfleon. *a* **1050** *Liber Scintill.* x. (1889) 50 ȝif æfter þam metta oferfylle oððe ofermicelnysse sawl byð ofersymed. *c* **1200** *Trin. Coll. Hom.* 65 þanne unbinde we þe burden þe he hadde us mide ouersemd.

oversend, *v.*: see over- 10.

'over-'sensible, *a.* [over- 28.] Too sensible; †too sensitive. So **'over-'sensibly** *adv.*, too sensibly; †in an over-sensitive manner.

1579 G. Harvey *Letter-bk.* (Camden) 66 Doist thou not oversensibely perceive that the markett goith far otherwise in Inglande? **1601** Holland *Pliny* xxiii. ii. 156 It hardeneth the throat and the mouth of the stomack which is over-sensible. **1748** Richardson *Clarissa* (1811) III. viii. 63 A mother over-notable; a daughter over-sensible; and their Hickman, who is—over-neither. **1823** Lamb *Elia* (1860) 93 His nation in general have not over-sensible countenances.

'over-'sensitive, *a.* [over- 28.] Too sensitive. So **'over-'sensitiveness; over-sensi'tivity.**

1846 Mrs. Gore *Eng. Char.* (1852) 101 A mere 'cook' would never have..lost his place in the royal kitchen from over-sensitiveness. **1857** Hughes *Tom Brown* Pref. (1871) 8 Excitement to nerves that are over-sensitive. **1953** K. Reisz *Technique Film Editing* iii. xv. 266 He becomes over-sensitive to his surroundings and suspicious of casual passers-by. **1965** House & Storey *Lett. of Dickens* I. 146 Seymour..seems to have suffered from over-sensitivity. **1977** H. Innes *Big Footprints* ii. ii. 137 The over-sensitivity of a boy who has lost his natural parents. **1978** E. Healey *Lady Unknown* i. 43 An over-sensitive skin that broke out in a rash when she was under strain.

over-sentimental to **-service:** see over-.

'overset, *sb.* [f. overset *v.*]

The act or fact of oversetting, in various senses of the vb.: †**a.** Overthrow, defeat. *Obs.* **b.** Overturn, upsetting, upset. †**c.** Putting off, postponement. *Obs.* †**d.** Overload, excess. *Obs.* **e.** *Printing.* Matter set up in excess of space.

1456 *Sc. Acts Jas. II* (1814) 45/2 Quhen ony gret ourset is lik to cum on the bordouraris þai think þe Inland men sulde be redy in þar supple. **1456** Sir G. Haye *Law Arms* (S.T.S.) 238 He wald nocht pay, bot geve him delayis and oursettis. *c* **1470** Henry *Wallace* viii. 1628 [The king of France] knew rycht weill schortly to wndyrstand The gret supprys and ourset off Ingland. *a* **1715** Burnet *Own Time* (1823) I. ii. 321 With this overset of wealth and pomp..they..became lazy and negligent. **1727** *Philip Quarll* 239, I..was over-set with the same Sea, under the flat bottom'd Boat, where you found me. That was a happy Overset for thee. **1789** Twining in *Select. Papers T. Family* (1887) 193, I suppose you have heard from my brother of my downfall?.. A thundering overset—such as might have been felt, I conceive, at the Antipodes. **1864** Webster, *Overset*,..An upsetting; ruin; overturn. **1895** *Funk's Stand. Dict.*, *Overset* ..*Print.* Excess of composition. **1896** *MS. Let. from printer*, We had some overset from Feb. number.

overset (əʊvə'sɛt), *v.* [over- 7, etc. An OE. **ofersęttan* is not cited: cf. however OHG. *ubarsezzan*, MHG. *übersetzen*, to set (any one) over (e.g. a river), to set (with), to overburden, oppress; some of which senses also occur in ME.]

†**1.** *trans.* To oppress; to press hard. *Obs.*

c **1200** *Trin. Coll. Hom.* 51 And þat lond folc hem ouersette mid felefelde pine. **1398** Trevisa *Barth. De P.R.* vi. xix. (Tollem. MS.), Also ryȝtful lordshipe ouersetteþ not [*non opprimit*] his subiectis by tyraundes. **1422** tr. *Secreta Secret., Priv. Priv.* 182 This Prynce Dermot, Seynge hym-Selfe..hugely ouersette with enemys..flow ouer the See into Normandy. **1549** *Compl. Scot.* xv. 127, I am sa violently ouerset be them. **1572** Bossewell *Armorie* ii. 59 b, The harte..whan hee is overset with houndes.

†**2.** To overcome, overpower by force or violence, overthrow, overwhelm, discomfit. *Obs.*

c **1375** *Sc. Leg. Saints* xxix. (*Placidas*) 772 A lyone..oure-set in his mouth hynt me. *c* **1440** *Promp. Parv.* 373/2 Ovyr settyn, or ovyr comyn, *supero, vinco.* **1470–85** Malory *Arthur* xx. xii, To wayte vpon sir launcelot for to ouersette hym and to slee hym. **1568** Grafton *Chron.* I. 116 Ethelfride king of Northumberlande overset the Britons at the Citie of Chester, and forced them to flee. **1618** Bolton *Florus* (1636) 51 Decius..over set in the bosome of the Valley, tooke upon his own head..all the wrath of the Gods. *transf.* *c* **1420** *Pallad. on Husb.* i. 144 Yet yf that wynd Vulturnus ouersette A vyne in heete.

†**b.** *fig.* To overcome (the mind, feelings, etc.).

1390 Gower *Conf.* II. 218 Thus he, whom gold hath overset, Was trapped in his oghne net. **1423** Jas. I *Kingis Q.* lxxiii, Ourset so sorow had bothe hert and mynd. **1567** *Gude & Godlie B.* (S.T.S.) 27 Quhen sadnes hes ouerset my hart. **1698** Norris *Pract. Disc.* IV. 99 A Man whose Mind is fill'd and overset with these great Ideas.

3. To cause to fall over; to upset, overturn, capsize; to turn upside down. Now *rare.* [over- 6.]

1592 Shaks. *Rom. & Jul.* iii. v. 137 The Barke thy body is..the windes thy sighes, Who..will ouer set Thy tempest tossed body. **1669** Pepys *Diary* 8 Mar., The King and the Duke of York went by three in the morning, and had the misfortune to be overset;..the King all dirty, but no hurt. **1719** De Foe *Crusoe* i. v. (1840) 83, I overset my raft. **1755** J. Shebbeare *Lydia* (1769) II. 110 Rushing forward, [he] overset the table, the bottles and glasses accompanying him in the fall. **1782** Miss Burney *Cecilia* viii. v, The postilion, in turning too suddenly..overset the carriage. **1842** M. Russell *Polynesia* vi. (1849) 223 Their small vessel being overset, hope itself nearly deserted them.

b. *intr.* To turn or fall over, capsize; to be overturned, upset. Now *rare.*

1641 Earl Monm. tr. *Biondi's Civil Warres* i. 4 He was like a ship which not fit to beare so great sayle, oversets. **1707** *Lond. Gaz.* No. 4305/3 The Hastings..Struck on the Sands, and..over-set. **1793** Smeaton *Edystone L.* §318 So violent a storm of wind, that he thought the house would overset. **1879** Stevenson *Trav. Cevennes* 11 It will assuredly topple and tend to overset.

4. *fig.* **a.** *trans.* To upset or subvert the order or condition of (an institution, state, or the like); to cause to fall into confusion. Now *rare.*

1679 Crowne *Amb. Statesman* i. 8 I'le make 'em glad to give me Sea-room enough, or I'le oreset the Kingdom. **1719** De Foe *Crusoe* i. xix, The sudden Surprize of Joy had over-set Nature, and I had dy'd upon the Spot. **1782** Crevecœur *Lett.* 79 Their ancient conquest has been a great detriment to them by over-setting their landed property. **1831** Carlyle *Sart. Res.* ii. v, A certain Calypso-Island..as it were falsifies and oversets his whole reckoning.

b. To overturn the normal mental or physical condition of (a person); to overcome mentally or physically; to discompose, disorder, 'upset' (the stomach, etc.).

1583 *Leg. Bp. St. Androis* 1061 His contagious stomack Was sa owersett with Burdeous drummake. **1703** Collier *Ess. Mor. Subj.* ii. 195 A glorious appearance from the other world has often over-set the best men. **1824** Miss Ferrier *Inher.* ix, The smell of Lord R.'s boots and shoes was enough to overset her. **1861** Tennyson *Let.* in *Life* (1897) I. xxii. 476 France, I believe, overset me, and more especially the foul ways and unhappy diet of..Auvergne. **1870** Dickens *E. Drood* xiii, The news is sure to overset him.

c. *intr.* To lose one's balance or ordered condition; to be upset, fall into disorder.

1749 Lavington *Enthus. Meth. & Papists* ii. (1754) Pref. 16 You was in Danger of oversetting from a Torrent of Popularity and Contempt. **1792** Gouv. Morris in Sparks *Life & Writ.* (1832) II. 244 The late constitution of this country has overset. **1830** Tennyson *Talking Oak* 257 While kingdoms overset, Or lapse from hand to hand.

†**5.** *trans.* To set (a surface, a garment, etc.) over *with* (jewels, ornaments). *Obs.* [over- 8.]

14.. *Tundale* (Wagner) 1879 The whylke wer alle over sette and dight With besandes of gold and silver bright. **1755** J. Shebbeare *Lydia* (1769) I. 107 As bright as ivory overset with sapphires.

†**6.** *trans.* and *intr.* To put off, postpone. *Obs.*

1422 tr. *Secreta Secret., Priv. Priv.* 162 That a prynce Sholde execute the dynte of Swerde in his enemy..not ouer-settynge the houre of fortune. **1500–20** Dunbar *Poems* xc. 62 The synfull man that all the ȝeir our settis, Fra Pasche to Pasche, rycht mony a thing forȝettis.

†**7.** *trans.* To lay *upon* as an impost or burden, to impose. *Obs.* [over- 7.]

c **1500** *Melusine* 301 The trybut that thou hast ouersette vpon the peuple of my lord.

†**8. a.** To overcharge, assess excessively. **b.** To overload. *Obs.* [over- 21, 27.]

1532 Tindale *Exp. Matt.* v–vii. Wks. (Parker Soc.) II. 71 The usurers and publicans..bought in great the emperor's tribute, and, to make their most advantage, did overset the people. *c* **1645** Howell *Lett.* iv. x. 12 Coming (for more frugality) in the common Boat, which was oreset with Merchandize, and other passengers, in a thick Fog the Vessell turn'd ore, and so many perished.

†**9. a.** To pass or get over. **b.** To set or settle over. *Obs.* [over- 5, 1.]

1536 Bellenden *Cron. Scot.* (1821) I. 151 Na litil honour apperis to us quhilkis hes ouirset sa mony strait montanis, woddis, fludis, and dangerus firthis of this region. **1649** Howell *Pre-em. Parl.* 4 This fatal black Cloud, which now oresets this poor Island.

10. To get over (an illness, etc.), recover from. *dial.* [over- 5.]

1535 Stewart *Cron. Scot.* II. 48 This Planctius..Throw sair seiknes that tyme..Set him so soir that he micht nocht ouirset, To God and nature quhill he payit his det. **1866** Brogden *Provinc. Words Linc.* (E.D.D.), He has overset his last ailment. **1877** *N. W. Linc. Gloss.* **1886** *S. W. Linc. Gloss.* s.v., I shall have to have some medicine before I overset it. It upset me, and she never seemed to overset it.

†**11.** In various uncertain senses, now *Obs.*

c **1470** Harding *Chron.* cxlv. i, At Lancastre, yᵉ yere of Christ then writen, A thousand whole twoo C. and fourty mo, And one therto, in Flores as is wryten, And in the yere next after then ouersetten. *a* **1547** Surrey *Æneid* iv. 152 And whiles they raunge to overset the groves. **1622** Malynes *Anc. Law-Merch.* 89 He that dealeth in barter must be very circumspect, and the money giuen in barter cannot be ouerset. **1729** Capt. W. Wriglesworth *MS. Log-bk. of the 'Lyell'* 13 Dec., At 1 afternoon overset the Sheat Cable in the Hold, then Veered away.

12. (ˌ*over-'set*) To set up (type) in excess.

1897 W. T. Stead in *Review of Rev.* Jan. 75/1, I have arrived at a chronic state of over-setting. On the last day of the month a piteous scene of..slaughter takes place.

Hence **'overset** *ppl. a.*; **over'setting** *ppl. a.* (in quot. 1456 = off-putting, dilatory); also **over'setter**, one who oversets, †an oppressor.

c **1440** *Promp. Parv.* 373/1 Ovyrledare (or ovyr settar), *oppressor.* **1456** Sir G. Haye *Law Arms* (S.T.S.) 243 And he be lathe, and our settand, and favourable in punycioun of mysdoaris. **1665** Boyle *Occas. Refl.* iv. xi. (1848) 230 One of those easily over-set Boats.

over'setting, *vbl. sb.* [f. prec. + -ing¹.] The action of the vb. overset; upsetting; †oppression; †off-putting.

1398 Trevisa *Barth. De P.R.* ii. xii. (1495) b vj b/2 Thise angellis..ben free of alle manere oppressynge and oueręsettynge. *c* **1440** *Promp. Parv.* 373/2 Ovyr settynge, or ovyr syttynge of dede or tyme, *omissio.* **1499** *Ibid.* (ed. Pynson), Ouersettinge, *oppressio.* **1626** CAPT. SMITH *Virginia* I. 15 Vpon the oversetting of their boat. **1869** MRS. WHITNEY *Hitherto* ix, Augusta Hare told me something.. which nearly completed my mental oversetting.

over-severe, -severity, etc.: see OVER-.

oversew (ˈəʊvəˌsəʊ), *v.* [OVER- 5.] *trans.* To sew overhand; to sew together two pieces of stuff, by laying them face to face with the edges coinciding, and passing the needle through both always in the same direction, so that the thread between the stitches lies over the edges. Sometimes called *overhand*, *overseam*, or *overcast*: see these words. In *Embroidery*, = OVERCAST *v.* 7. Also *transf.* Hence **ˈoverˌsewing** *vbl. sb.*, **ˈoverˌsewn** *ppl. a.*

1864 in WEBSTER. **1882** CAULFEILD & SAWARD *Dict. Needlework*, *Over-sewing*, a method of Plain-sewing, otherwise known as Seaming, or Top-sewing, and executed somewhat after the manner of Over-casting. But the great difference between Over-sewing and Over-casting is that the former is closely and finely executed for the uniting of two selvedges or folds of material, and the latter is very loosely done, and only for the purpose of keeping raw edges from ravelling-out... In olden times this stitch was known by the name of Overhand. **1903** *Tregaskis' Catal.* Jan. 11/1 Six Handkerchiefs, hemstitched, very small cobweb border and oversewn ornament in the corners. **1938** L. M. HARROD *Librarians' Gloss.* 109 *Oversewing*, the act or process of sewing over and over the leaves of a book. **1969** R. MAINGOT *Abdominal Operations* (ed. 5) I. xxv. 428/2 The duodenal stump is next oversewn, securely closed, and inverted with sutures of fine silk.

over-sexed (əʊvəˈsɛkst), *a.* [OVER- 28 d.] Having sexual propensities or qualities in an excessive degree; inordinately desirous of sexual gratification. Also *fig.* Hence **over-ˈsexedness.**

1898 C. P. STETSON *Women & Econ.* iii. 43 The male.. is a far more normal animal than the female of his species,—far less over-sexed. *Ibid.* 44 The secretion of milk is a maternal function,—a sex function. The cow is over-sexed. **1901** G. B. SHAW *Three Plays for Puritans* p. xi, I did not find that matters were improved by the lady pretending to be 'a woman with a past', violently over-sexed. **1908** A. NOYES *William Morris* 98 A creature so gluttonously over-sexed and selfishly serpentine as Gudrun. **1923** C. MACKENZIE *Parson's Progress* viii. 95 Nobody questions the ethical value of Christianity except a few oversexed egomaniacs. **1923** *Daily Mail* 5 Feb. 5 His.. terra-cotta-coloured nudes.. are repulsive and over-sexed. **1937** G. FRANKAU *More of Us* x. 112 Fearful lest one more line of such o'er-sexed stuff Leave us no energy to do our next stuff. **1941** AUDEN *New Year Let.* III. 54 Hearing how circumstance has vexed A broker who is over-sexed. **1953** *Encounter* Nov. 31/1 Y. is the political equivalent of a *nymphomaniac*... This kind of neurosis.. flourishes chiefly in the climate of the Left—for, generally speaking, the Left is politically over-sexed. *Ibid.* 31/2 The unfulfilled urge 'to belong' may lead to 'political oversexedness', expressing itself in blind, self-sacrificing devotion to some unholy cause. **1973** 'D. HALLIDAY' *Dolly & Starry Bird* xv. 229 You've laid your oversexed little claws on my girl. **1977** 'H. CARMICHAEL' *Grave for Two* ix. 111 To put it mildly she was inclined to be over-sexed.

†**overˈsey,** *v. Obs. rare.* (Better **oversie.**) [f. OVER- 4, 17 + ME. *siȝen*, OE. *sīgan*, to pass, as time: see SIE *v.*] *intr.* To pass by, elapse.

13.. *E.E. Allit. P.* B. 1686 þus he countes hym a kow, þat watz a kyng ryche, Quyle seuen syþez were ouer-seyed someres I trawe.

oversey, obs. f. OVERSEA; obs. infl. OVERSEE.

overshade (əʊvəˈʃeɪd), *v.* [OVER- 8.]

1. *trans.* = OVERSHADOW *v.* 2.

c **1000** *Ags. Gosp.* Luke i. 35 þæs heahstan miht þe ofer sceadað [*c* **1160** *Hatton G.* ofer-scædeð; *Vulg.* obumbrabit]. **1594** GREENE & LODGE *Looking-Gl.* Wks. (Grosart) XIV. 113 The hand of mercy ouershead her [the Church's] head.

2. To cast a shade over; to render gloomy or dark; to overshadow, shade. Also *absol.*

1588 SHAKS. *Tit. A.* II. iii. 273 The Elder tree Which ouershades the mouth of that same pit. **1667** MILTON *P.L.* v. 376 Lead on then where thy Bowre Oreshades. **1670** DRYDEN *Tyrannic Love* I. i, The monster of the wood; O'ershading all which under him would grow. **1727** DESAGULIERS in *Phil. Trans.* XXXV. 323 Plants which are overshaded.. cannot so well imbibe Air. **1812** WORDSW. *Song for Spinning Wheel* 5 Dewy night o'ershades the ground.

fig. **1593** SHAKS. *3 Hen. VI*, II. vi. 62 Darke cloudy death oreshades his beames of life. **1823** LAMB *Elia* Ser. II. *Old China*, A passing sentiment seemed to overshade the brows of my companion.

Hence **overˈshading** *ppl. a.*

1601 CHESTER *Love's Mart.*, *Dial.* lxi, Pleasant ouershading bowers.

overshadow (əʊvəˈʃædəʊ), *v.* [OE. *ofersceadwian*: see OVER- 8. So MHG. *überschatewen*, MDu. *overschaduwen*, Goth. *ufarskadwjan*, all rendering L. *obumbrāre* in N.T.]

1. *trans.* To cast a shadow over; to cover or obscure with shadow or darkness, overcloud; to overshade, shade over.

c **1000** *Ags. Gosp.* Mark ix. 7 Seo lyft hi ofer-sceadewude. —— Luke ix. 34 Ða wearð ȝenip & ofer-sceadude hiȝ [*c* 1160 *Hatton*, ofer-scadede]. *c* **1050** *Suppl. Ælfric's Voc.* in Wr.-Wülcker 178/44 *Obumbro*, ic ofersceadewiȝe. **1388** WYCLIF *Luke* ix. 34 A cloude was maad, and ouerschadewide hem. **1535** COVERDALE *Baruch* v. 8 The woddes & all pleasaunt trees shal ouershadowe Israel. **1600** J. PORY tr. *Leo's Africa* IX. 345 The moone being ouershadowed with clouds. **1791** BOSWELL *Johnson* 2 Aug. an. 1763, A long narrow paved court in the neighbourhood, overshadowed by some trees. **1883** S. C. HALL *Retrosp.* II. 143 The dark cloud thus early cast on her life continued to overshadow it for many years.

fig. **1574** tr. *Marlorat's Apocalips* 5 Wrapped in mysticall figures, and ouershadowed with images. **1856** FROUDE *Hist. Eng.* II. vii. 141 Those misfortunes which were soon to overshadow her. **1864** PUSEY *Lect. Daniel* v. 255 One prophecy of woe overshadowed all the later years of David.

2. To cover or overspread with some influence, as with a shadow; to shelter, protect.

c **825** *Vesp. Psalter* cxxxix. 8 Dryhten meȝen haelu minre ofersceadwa heafud min in deȝe ȝefehtes. **1388** WYCLIF *Luke* i. 35 The Hooly Goost schal come fro aboue in to thee, and the vertu of the Hiȝeste schal ouerschadewe thee. **1578** *Chr. Prayers* in *Priv. Prayers* (1851) 502 Overshadow me in the day of battle. **1662** STILLINGFL. *Orig. Sacr.* II. v. §2 It may seem that when the Divine Spirit did overshadow the understanding of the Prophets, yet it offered no violence to their faculties. **1859** SINGLETON *Virgil* II. 433 The queen's high name O'ershadows him.

3. To tower over so as to cast its shadow over; hence, to rise above, 'cast into the shade', diminish the apparent eminence or importance of. [OVER- 1.]

1581 LAMBARDE *Eiren.* III. i. (1588) 327 The authoritie of the undershirife, is ouershadowed by the Shirifes presence. **1601** DENT *Pathw. Heaven* 244 Faith and infidilitie.. striue to ouer-master and ouer-shadow one another. **1611** SPEED *Theat. Gt. Brit.* iv. (1614) 7/2 All their monuments.. overshadowed by the height of Beckett's tomb. **1624** CAPT. SMITH *Virginia* II. 24 A low pleasant valley overshaddowed in many places with high rocky mountaines. **1870** DICKENS *E. Drood* xi, No neighbouring architecture of lofty proportions had arisen to overshadow Staple Inn. *a* **1862** BUCKLE *Civiliz.* (1873) III. i. 42 It was natural that the Crown, completely overshadowed by the great barons, should turn for aid to the Church.

4. To shade or darken too much. [OVER- 27.]

1642 FULLER *Holy & Prof. St.* IV. xx. 348 If Authours in painting his deeds do not overshadow them, to make them blacker than they were.

Hence **overˈshadowed** *ppl. a.*; also **ˈoverˌshadow** *sb. rare*; **overˈshadower.**

1618 BACON *Let. to King* 2 Jan. in *Cabala* (1654) 9 No oppressors of the people, no overshadowers of the Crown. **1849** C. BRONTË *Shirley* ii. 22 The period.. was an overshadowed one in British history. **1875** MCLEAN *Gosp. in Psalms* 330 Round about it, not a literal overshadow of mountains. **1878** MOZLEY *Ess.* I. *Carlyle's Cromwell* 262 A man.. who always would be his rival and overshadower.

overˈshadowing, *vbl. sb.* [f. prec. + -ING[1].] The action of the vb. OVERSHADOW.

1388 WYCLIF *Jas.* i. 17 The fadir of liȝtis, anentis whom is noon other chaungyng, ne ouerschadewyng of reward. **1665** J. SPENCER *Vulg. Proph.* Pref., That the Minds of Holy Men should conceive (like the Virgin Mary) by the sole overshadowings of the Holy Ghost. **1860** PUSEY *Min. Proph.* 326 The visible kingdom of God.. underwent an almost total eclipse by the overshadowing of earthly power.

overˈshadowing, *ppl. a.* [-ING[2].] That overshadows. Hence **overˈshadowingly** *adv.*, in an overshadowing manner.

1667 MILTON *P.L.* VII. 165 My overshadowing Spirit and might with thee I send along. **1801** SOUTHEY *Thalaba* VII. xviii, Large as the hairy Cassowar Was that o'ershadowing Bird. **1824** LANDOR *Imag. Conv.*, *Southey & Porson* Wks. 1853 I. 81/2 Which rarely happens to literary men overshadowingly great. **1856** STANLEY *Sinai & Pal.* viii. (1858) 319 Those mysterious hills, which close every eastern view with their overshadowing height.

†**overˈshadowy,** *a. Obs.* [f. OVERSHADOW + -Y.] Having the quality of overshadowing.

1601 HOLLAND *Pliny* I. 474 The Fig tree, which hath her Figs aboue the leaf, because it is so large and ouershadowie.

†**overˈshake,** *v. Obs.* [OVER- 4, 27.]

1. *trans.* To shake off or away; to dispel.

c **1330** R. BRUNNE *Chron.* (1810) 224 þe Juerie misferd, þer tresorie ouerschaken. *c* **1412** HOCCLEVE *De Reg. Princ.* 1655 Whan hir luste is ouershake, And þere-with wole hir loues heteasswage. **1530** PALSGR. 649/2, I overshake, *je secous.*

b. *intr.* To become shaken off, pass away, abate.

1412–20 LYDG. *Chron. Troy* III. xiii. (1513) H vj b/2 Wherfore I rede to let ouershake All heuynesse. *a* **1415** —— *Temple of Glas* 614 Alas when wil þis turment ouershake [*v.r.* overslake]?

2. *trans.* To shake overmuch. [OVER- 27.]

1634 W. TIRWHYT tr. *Balzac's Lett.* 40 The Pope, a body over-shaken, and trembling with age.

ˈover-ˈsharp, *a.* [OVER- 28.] Too sharp, excessively sharp. Hence **ˈover-ˈsharpness.**

1477 NORTON *Ord. Alch.* v. in Ashm. *Theatr. Chem. Brit.* (1652) 73 Abhominable sower, Over-sharpe, too bitter. **1586** T. B. *La Primaud. Fr. Acad.* (1589) 503, I would not that fathers should be over-sharpe and hard to their children. **1795** SEWARD *Anecdotes* III. 38 They.. were not over-sharp in discovering the intrigues and artifices. **1858** BAGEHOT *Coll. Works* (1965) II. 84 'Over-sharpness' in the student is the most unpromising symptom of the logical jurist. **1896** T. L. DE VINNE in *Moxon's Mech. Exerc.*, *Printing* 404 The superior beauty of over-sharp hair-lines. **1955** J. L. AUSTIN *How to do Things with Words.* (1962) vii. 90 Alice-in-Wonderland over-sharpness. **1970** *Nature* 19 Dec. 1218/1 The quality of suprathreshold vision in the fovea results from a balance between optical unsharpness.. and neural 'oversharpness' (lateral inhibition).

ˈover-shave. *U.S.* A shave or drawing-knife used by coopers for shaping the backs of barrel-staves.

1875 in KNIGHT *Dict. Mech.*

overshelving, -shepherd: see OVER- 1, 2.

overshine (-ˈʃaɪn), *v.* [OE. *oferscīnan*: see OVER- 7, 8. So OHG. *ubarskînan*, MHG. *überschînen*, Du. *overschijnen.*]

1. *trans.* To shine over or upon, to illumine.

971 *Blickl. Hom.* 129 Næs na þæt an þæt þæt leoht þa dune ane oferscineþ.. ac eac swylce.. þa burh. *c* **1000** *Ags. Gosp.* Matt. xvii. 5 Beorht-wolcn hiȝ ofer-scean. **1593** SHAKS. *3 Hen. VI*, II. i. 38 That wee.. Should notwithstanding ioyne our Lights together, And ouer-shine the Earth, as this the World. *a* **1711** KEN *Sion* Poet. Wks. 1721 IV. 400 It kindled in Me heavn'ly Flame, I felt it gently over-shine my Breast. **1832** *Fraser's Mag.* VI. 392 A ruddy sun was overshining his face.

2. To surpass in shining, to outshine; chiefly *fig.*, to surpass or excel in some quality. [OVER- 22.]

1588 SHAKS. *Tit. A.* I. i. 317 (Qo.) That.. Dost ouershine the gallant'st Dames of Rome. *c* **1590** GREENE *Fr. Bacon* i. 139 And ouer-shine the troupe of all the maides. **1643** TRAPP *Comm. Gen.* xxxvii. 11 Others precellencies, whereby we are over-shined. **1827** CARLYLE *Germ. Rom.* III. 86 She would so gladly.. have.. overshone many a female dignitary.

Hence **overˈshining** *vbl. sb.*

1587 GOLDING *De Mornay* iii. 30 Like as the Moone shineth not, but by the ouershining of the Sunne vpon her.

over-shipboard to **over-shirt**: see OVER-.

ˈovershoe (-ʃuː), *sb.* [OVER- 8 c; cf. Du. *overschoe*, Ger. *überschuh.*] A shoe of india-rubber, felt, or other material, worn over the ordinary shoe as a protection from wet, dirt, cold, etc.

1851 MELVILLE *Whale* viii. 42 Hat, coat, and overshoes were one by one removed. **1862** *Catal. Internat. Exhib.* II. xxvii. 55 The Kensington Golosh, or solid leather overshoe. **1882** *Century Mag.* XXIV. 842/2 The peasants are bundles done up in fur caps, coats, and overshoes.

over-shoe, over-shoes (ˌəʊvəˈʃuːz), *adv. phr.* [orig. two words: see OVER *prep.* 3.] Of water, mud, etc.: So deep as to cover the shoes, shoe-deep; hence, ***to be, go, run over-shoes***, e.g. in water, or *fig.* in any course or enterprise.

1579 GOSSON *Sch. Abuse* (Arb.) 75, I beseech them to looke to their footing, that run overshooes in al these vanities. **1590** SHAKS. *Com. Err.* III. ii. 106 A man may goe ouer-shooes in the grime of it. **1778** ISRAEL ANGELL *Diary* (1897) 31 It cleared off in the night with Snow about over Shoe. **1891** T. HARDY *Tess* (1900) 55/1 The result of the rain had been to flood the lane over-shoe. [See other examples, *a* 1555–1677, s.v. OVER *prep.* 3.]

overshoot (əʊvəˈʃuːt), *v.* [OVER- 13, 4, 5, 7, 22, 23, 27. Cf. MHG. *überschiezen*, Ger. *überschieszen*, Du. *overschieten.*]

I. 1. a. *trans.* To shoot, dart, run, or pass beyond (a point, limit, stage, etc.).

c **1369** CHAUCER *Dethe Blaunche* 383 The houndes had ouershette hym alle And were vpon a defaulte y-falle. **1592** SHAKS. *Ven. & Ad.* 680 The purblind hare,.. to ouer-shut his troubles, How he outruns the wind, and with what care, He crankes and crosses with a thousand doubles. **1755** J. SHEBBEARE *Lydia* (1769) II. 94 Dogs, who running fleeter, over-shoot their game. **1822–34** *Good's Study Med.* (ed. 4) II, The first stage of inflammation.. must have been overshot in the violence of the action. **1885** *Law Times* LXXX. 135/2 In consequence of the train overshooting the platform.

†**b.** *Naut.* To sail past (a port, etc.). *Obs.*

c **1565** *Sir J. Hawkins's 2nd Voy. to W. Ind.* in Arb. *Garner* V. 113 A Spaniard, who told him how far off he was from Rio de la Hacha: which, because he would not over-shoot, he anchored that night again. **1599** HAKLUYT *Voy.* II. i. 106 Wee were short 80 miles of the place, whereas we thought we had beene overshot by east fiftie miles. **1711** *Lond. Gaz.* No. 4912/2 This Vessel.. hath over-shot her Port. **1803** *Naval Chron.* IX. 160 She overshot her port in the night.

†**c.** To pass over (a period of time); to allow (time) to pass by. *Obs.*

a **1584** MONTGOMERIE *Cherrie & Slae* 556 Persawis thou nocht quhat precious tyme Thy slewthing dois ouirschute? **1610** WILLET *Hexapla Dan.* 312 The first beginning right, ouershoote the 70 weeks. *a* **1617** BAYNE *Lect.* (1634) 206 If wee have overshot time wherein wee might have saved some twenty pound matter, what a griefe is it to be so overshot?

d. *trans.* and *intr.* To fly beyond (a designated landing-point) while attempting to land an aircraft. Also *transf.*

1920 *Flight* XII. 368 (*caption*) Pilot heads.. for aerodrome, knowing for certain he will overshoot. **1928** *Lit. Digest* 12 May 73/1 To 'put her on hot' is to land fast, usually resulting in 'overshooting' the field. **1932** D. GARNETT *Rabbit in Air* I. 35 In my first attempt I thought I had overshot for some reason when I had undershot hopelessly. **1958** 'CASTLE' & 'HAILEY' *Flight into Danger* vi. 79, I can't guarantee at all that this plane will get down on the field. She's just as likely to pan down short or overshoot. **1973** C. BONINGTON *Next Horizon* xviii. 248 We over-shot the runway once. **1974** P. ERDMAN *Silver Bears* iii. 54 The MG suddenly swung off the road... Doc was caught by surprise and overshot. Slowly he backed up.

2. a. To shoot a missile, etc., over or above (the mark or thing aimed at) and so to miss; to shoot beyond; also, of the missile: To pass over or beyond (the mark).

In quot. *a* 1400–50 the sense is uncertain: perh. = *if thou over-shoot* (*the*) *shot*.

[*a* **1400–50** *Alexander* 1767* (Dubl. MS.) Yf þou shote ouer sheet þou shendes þi flayne.] *a* **1548** HALL *Chron.*, *Hen. VII* 18 b, Their enemyes discharged their ordinaunce..and ouer-shot them. **1555** EDEN *Decades* 108 So to ouershute them that none myght be hurt therby. *a* **1674** CLARENDON *Hist. Reb.* IX. §39 [They] discharged their Cannon at them, but over-shot them. **1897** *Chicago Advance* 9 Sept. 327/3 This charge goes wide from the mark. It hits some, but it over-shoots the body.

b. *fig.* esp. in ***overshoot the mark***, to go or venture too far, or farther than is intended or is proper.

1588 FRAUNCE *Lawiers Log.* Ded., See how farre I have overshot my marke. **1670** MILTON *Hist. Eng.* Wks. 1738 II. 5 In this, Diana overshot her Oracle. **1702** *Eng. Theophrast.* 303 The greatest fault of a penetrating wit is not coming short of the mark but overshooting it. **1835** BROWNING *Paracelsus* v. 135 Your cunning has o'ershot its aim. **1871** FREEMAN *Hist. Ess.* Ser. I. vii. (1875) 196 We have somewhat overshot our mark in order to complete the history of the English dominion in France.

c. *absol.* (*lit.* and *fig.*)

1625 MARKHAM *Souldiers Accid.* 9 The hindmost must.. shoot their fellowes before through the heads, or els will overshoot. **1733** POPE *Ess. Man* III. 89 But honest Instinct comes a volunteer, Sure never to o'er-shoot, but just to hit. **1897** *Outing* (U.S.) XXX. 330/1 If I happened to overshoot I was bound to bag a heifer.

3. a. ***to overshoot oneself***: to shoot over or beyond one's mark; to go farther than one intends in any course; to overreach oneself, miss one's mark by going too far; to exaggerate; to fall into error.

1530 PALSGR. 649/2, I never wyste wyseman overshote hymselfe thus sore. **1538** CROMWELL in Merriman *Life & Lett.* (1902) II. 165. **1611** BIBLE *Transl. Pref.* 11 He was the first in a maner, that put his hand to write Commentaries.. and therefore no marueile, if he ouershot himselfe many times. **1678** NORRIS *Coll. Misc.* (1699) 84 So th' eager Hawk makes sure of's prize, Strikes with full might, but overshoots himself and dyes. **1748** RICHARDSON *Clarissa* (1785) IV. 214 And there she stopt; having almost overshot herself; as I designed she should. **1831** CARLYLE *Sart. Res.* III. x. (*ad fin.*), His irony has overshot itself; we see through it, and perhaps through him.

†**b.** *fig.* ***to be overshot***: to have overshot oneself, to be wide of the mark; to be mistaken, deceived, or in error. *Obs.*

1535 CROMWELL in Merriman *Life & Lett.* (1902) II. 44 Ye ar farre ouershotte. **1584** R. SCOT *Discov. Witchcr.* XIV. v. (1886) 306 Even wise and learned men hereby are shamefullie overshot. **1599** SHAKS. *Hen. V*, III. vii. 134 'Tis not the first time you were ouer-shot. **1656** JEANES *Fuln. Christ* 20 Then are they much overshot and deeply to be blamed, who..harden their hearts against Gods..calling.

†**4.** *fig.* To shoot too hard, utter (a word) too violently, throw out or allow to escape unguardedly.

1549 COVERDALE, etc. *Erasm. Par. 2 John* 53 As whan by occasion we ouershote a worde agaynste oure frende, whiche we are sory for by and by that it ouer shot us. **1621** BURTON *Anat. Mel.* II. iii. III. (1651) 325 A word overshot, a blow in choler, a game at tables..may make us equal in an instant.

5. To push or drive beyond the proper limit.

1668 CULPEPPER & COLE *Barthol. Anat.* II. vii. 109 Least in the Contractions of the Heart, the Valves being forced beyond their pitch and overshot, should be unable to retain the Blood. **1795** HERSCHEL in *Phil. Trans.* LXXXV. 392 This method will even throw back the figure upon the dial, if it should have been overshot a little.

6. To shoot or dart over or above.

a **1774** HARTE (T.), High rais'd on fortune's hill, new Alpes he spies, O'ershoots the valley which beneath him lies. **1784** COWPER *Task* I. 496 While yet the beams Of day-spring overshoot his humble nest. **1887** G. MEREDITH *Ballads & P.* 114 She, with the plunging lightnings overshot.

†**7.** *intr.* To shoot or rush down from above. *Obs.*

c **1400** *Destr. Troy* 7620 A thondir with a thicke Rayn.. Ouershotyng with shoures thurgh þere shene tenttes.

†**8.** *trans.* To surpass in shooting. *Obs.*

a **1628** F. GREVIL *Sidney* (1652) 85 [Sir Philip] over-shoots his father in-law in his own bow. **1673** O. HEYWOOD *Diaries*, etc. (1882) I. 357 Who knows but god may overshoot the devil in his oun bow.

9. *refl.* To exhaust oneself with too much shooting.

1883 COL. HOWARD in *Times* 26 July 7/6, I think, perhaps, there was a little conspiracy..to offer us so much practice that we should overshoot ourselves.

10. *trans.* To shoot too much over (a moor, etc.) so as to deplete it of game. [OVER- 27.]

1884 *Manch. Exam.* 1 Aug. 5/3 Disease, together with overshooting by greedy lessees, had played such havoc with the moors.

Hence **over'shooting** *vbl. sb.* and *ppl. a.*

a **1586** SIDNEY *Arcadia* v. (1622) 452 To require you, not to haue an ouershooting expectation of mee. **1795** HERSCHEL in *Phil. Trans.* LXXXV. 392 The point of the angle sinking down between the two teeth..prevents their overshooting. **1897** *Daily News* 4 Sept. 6/5 The cause of the accident was the overshooting of the points, owing to the driver not pulling up in time.

overshoot ('əʊvəʃuːt), *sb.* [f. the vb.] The action or result of OVERSHOOT *v.*; *spec.* in *Electronics* (see quot. 1971).

1944 *Flight* 1 June 584/1 Uncorrected over-shoot generally means a write-off. **1945** *Electronic Industries* Sept. 214 *Overshoot*, an excessive potential attained by a portion of the main body of a pulse. **1947** R. LEE *Electronic Transformers & Circuits* ix. 249 Added to this is a slight oscillation overshoot. **1956** AMOS & BIRKINSHAW *Television Engin.* II. i. 25 The consequent disturbance of the phase relationships frequently causes the phenomenon of overshoot illustrated in Fig. 11. This is an effect which can be compared with that of inertia in mechanical systems and causes the voltage, after executing the transient, to exceed momentarily the final steady value. **1963** R. P. DALES *Annelids* viii. 156 They have found that with posterior pieces there is often an 'overshoot', the new thoracic region having more segments than it should. **1969** J. J. SPARKES *Transistor Switching* iv. 113 Overshoot or undershoot of the output waveforms will result. **1970** *New Scientist* 17 Dec. 515/2 He sees the market economy as a system with high gain and strong feedback, possessing self-regulation, but troubled by overshoots. **1971** *Gloss. Electrotechnical, Power Terms* (*B.S.I.*) III. i. 37 *Overshoot*, transient exaggeration of the magnitude of the leading or trailing edge of a steep-sided signal. **1977** *Gramophone* Oct. 744/3 The square wave showed one sharp overshoot and was then well damped.

'over-'short, *a.* [OVER- 28.] Too short. †**b.** as *adv.* Very abruptly. So **'over-'shortly** *adv.*, too shortly, too briefly.

13.. *Cursor M.* 12399 þe knaue þat þis timber fett Heild noght graithli his mett, Bot ouer scort [*v.r.* schort] he broght a tre. **1538** STARKEY *England* II. i. 162 Wherfore me thynke you passe them ouer-schortly. **1587** GOLDING *De Mornay* xx. 318 Here they stoppe ouershort eueryChone of them. **1704** SWIFT *T. Tub* Wks. 1760 I. 91. **1899** A. BALFOUR *To Arms* i. 8 A steed some two sizes overshort for his long legs.

,over-'shorten, *v.* [OVER- 27.] *trans.* To shorten too much.

1642 FULLER *Holy & Prof. St.* IV. xxi. 353 To maintain his just Prerogative, that as it be not outstretched, so it may not be overshortned.

overshot ('əʊvəʃɒt), *a.* (*sb.*) [In origin the same as OVERSHOT *ppl. a.*, with change of stress.]

A. *adj.* **1.** Driven by water shot over from above.

overshot wheel, a water-wheel turned by the force of water falling upon or near the top of the wheel into buckets placed round the circumference. ***overshot mill***, a mill to which the power is supplied by an overshot wheel.

c **1535** *Surv. Yorksh. Monast.* in *Yorksh. Archæol. Jrnl.* (1886) IX. 209 Item there is a litle ouershot mylne goynge w[t] a litle water. *Ibid.* 328 Item the ouershot water mylne hardby the gate. **1673** E. BROWN *Trav. Germ.* (1677) 164 An Overshot-wheel in the Earth, which moves the Pumps to pump out the Water. *c* **1710** CELIA FIENNES *Diary* (1888) 227 They have only the mills w[ch] are overshott. **1805** R. W. DICKSON *Pract. Agric.* I. Plate xiv, An overshot water-wheel fourteen feet diameter. **1880** [see HIGH *a.* 4 c]. **1904** KIPLING *Traffics & Discov.* 389 Mechanically, an overshot wheel with this head of water is about as efficient as a turbine. **1914** *Chambers's Jrnl.* Mar. 205/1 The sewage passes over a wheel of overshot or undershot type. **1968** J. ARNOLD *Shell Book of Country Crafts* xii. 175 The overshot wheel was used where there was a higher fall of water and was intended to turn by the *weight* of the descending water against the buckets or floats. **1978** J. B. HILTON *Some run Crooked* iii. 22 The Powder Mill..was a mid-nineteenth-century ruin..an overshot water-wheel, now crippled over a leaking weir.

2. Supplied or 'fed' from above: see quot.

1884 KNIGHT *Dict. Mech.* Suppl., *Over-shot Separator* (*Agric.*), one in which the sheaf grain is fed into the threshing machine above the cylinder.

B. *sb.* The stream of water which drives an overshot wheel.

1759 SMEATON in *Phil. Trans.* LI. 138 An overshot, whose height is equal to the difference of level, between the point where it strikes the wheel and the level of the tail-water.

over'shot, *ppl. a.* [pa. pple. of OVERSHOOT *v.*]

1. Shot or forced over or across a surface, etc.

1797 HOLCROFT *Stolberg's Trav.* (ed. 2) III. lxxxiii. 328 This earthquake gave birth to lawsuits..between the proprietors of the overshooting and the possessors of the overshot earth.

2. Carried too far or to excess; exaggerated.

1774 MAD. D'ARBLAY *Early Diary* (1889) I. 324 He presented his plate to me, which, when I declined, he had not the over-shot politeness to offer all round.

3. Intoxicated. *slang.*

1605 MARSTON, etc. *Eastward Ho* IV. i. Death! Colonel, I knew you were overshot. **1931** T. R. G. LYELL *Slang* 668 There are innumerable synonyms applicable to different degrees of intoxication. Those most in general use are ..*muddled, overcome, overshot*, [etc.]. **1942** BERREY & VAN DEN BARK *Amer. Thes. Slang* §106/7 Drunk,..*overshot.*

4. Said of a partially dislocated fetlock joint, in which the upper bone is driven over or in front of the lower bones.

1881 *Times* 18 Jan. 12/1 The horse was suffering from an overshot fetlock joint, which was incurable. **1897** *Daily News* 26 Mar. 7/2 The fetlocks were only overshot.

5. Having the upper jaw projecting beyond the lower.

1885 in C. Scott *Sheep-farming* (1886) 196 The skull of the collie should be quite flat and rather broad, with..mouth the least bit overshot.

6. Of the leaves of *Jungermanniæ*: see quots.

1884 K. E. GOEBEL in *Encycl. Brit.* XVII. 67/2 Overshot leaves..are those in which the anterior margin, turned towards the vegetative point of the stem, stands higher than the posterior one, and thus the anterior margin of each leaf overlaps the posterior margin of the leaf which stands before it. *Ibid.*, If the growth of the upper side preponderates, then we have the overshot, in the opposite case the undershot mode of covering.

7. Of a pattern or weave: that is characterized by uninterrupted lines of weft where the yarn has been made to pass over two or more warp threads before re-entering the fabric.

1952 H. J. BROWN *Hand Weaving* vi. 102 Any design that can be arranged on a formation of squares may be reproduced in overshot weaving... Many of the fine old American colonial coverlets that have been handed down as heirlooms were made in overshot design. **1965** E. TUNIS *Colonial Craftsmen* iv. 102 Such were the 'overshot' coverlets in wide variety which are prized examples of old weaving. **1970** E. REGENSTEINER *Art of Weaving* v. 77/1 In the weaver's language, patterns produced by this system are called 'overshot', because when the harnesses are raised, the weft threads skip or 'float' over the groups of warp threads.

over'shroud, *v. Pa. pple.* 6 **-schroud.** [OVER- 8.] *trans.* To cover over as with a shroud.

1513 DOUGLAS *Æneis* XI. xi. 139 Persand the ayr wyth body all ourschroud And dekkyt in a watry sabill cloud. **1592** BRETON *C'tess of Pembroke's Loue* (1879) 23/1 What shadowes here doe ouershroude the eie? **1916** A. S. WAY tr. *Virgil's Aeneid* I. III. 113 A night of rain overshrouds The sky.

†**'overshut,** *sb. Obs. rare.* [for *overshoot.*] That which shoots over or overhangs.

1630 *R. Johnson's Kingd. & Commw.* 120 The residue [of Lundy Isle] is inclosed with high and horrible overshuts of Rocks.

overshut, obs. form of OVERSHOOT *v.*

over-sick, etc.: see OVER- 28.

†**'over-,side,** *sb. Obs.* [f. OVER *a.* + SIDE *sb.*: properly two words.] Upper or superior side.

1398 TREVISA *Barth. De P.R.* XIII. i. (Add. MS. 27944) Water..resteth neuere of meuyng til the ouere syde therof be euyn. **1479** *Searchers' Verdicts* in *Surtees Misc.* (1888) 20 The saide grounde conteyneth..at the ovirsyde in breede, ..vj yerdes ane ynche lakk, ande at the neþere syde v yerdes, halfe yerde and halfe quarter. *c* **1530** LD. BERNERS *Arth. Lyt. Bryt.* cix. (1814) 520 Than King Alexander rode on the ouer side of King Emendus, and the Duke of Britaine on the other side. **1691** tr. *Emilianne's Journ. Naples* 263 The one of them having rudely thrust the Fryer to the over-side of the Street, the other laid hold upon the Basket.

overside, *adv.* and *a.* [Short for *over the side*: cf. OVERBOARD.]

A. *adv.* (əʊvə'saɪd). Over the side of a ship (into the sea, or into a lighter or boat).

1889 *Engineer* 13 Sept. 232 The bulk of the cargo..is discharged overside into lighters. **1896** *Daily News* 19 Oct. 4/6 The proposed agreement as to unloading 'overside' in the Port of London.

B. *adj.* ('əʊvəsaɪd). Effected over the side of a ship; unloading or unloaded over the side into lighters; discharging over the side.

1884 *Law Times Rep.* 12 Jan. 580/1 The consignee demanded overside delivery into lighters. **1895** *Daily Tel.* 15 Feb. 3/1 No overside work is being carried on in the docks. **1899** *Westm. Gaz.* 23 Nov. 11/1 When the Dock Company obtained their charter, the right for barges to overside delivery of goods was specially reserved.

oversight ('əʊvəsaɪt), *sb.* [OVER- 7, 5.] The action of overseeing or overlooking.

1. a. Supervision, superintendence, inspection; charge, care, management, control.

13.. *Cursor M.* 27094 (Cott.) To min on his ouer-sight þat al wranges has to right. **1413** *Pilgr. Sowle* (Caxton 1483) IV. xxxiv. 83 The shyrreue sholde haue the pryncipall ouersight for to see and knowe that eueriche doo his deuoyre. **1526** *Pilgr. Perf.* (W. de W. 1531) 108 To haue the ouersyght & instrucyon of nouyces. **1647** N. BACON *Disc. Govt. Eng.* I. xii. (1739) 23 The smallest Precinct was that of the Parish, the oversight whereof was the Presbyters work. **1722** SEWEL *Hist. Quakers* (1795) I. Pref. 23, I have been fain to trust the oversight and correction of my work to others. **1887** ABP. BENSON in *Times* 23 Mar. 11/5 The episcopal oversight of the clergy and congregations..in Palestine. **1931** H. J. ROSE tr. *W. Schmidt's Orig. & Growth Relig.* xvi. 275 The Supreme Being, thus exercising oversight on the doings of men, is likewise able to reward..and punish. *Ibid.* 277 His oversight of what men do and leave undone in the moral sphere. **1935** F. H. HAYWARD *Alfred the Great* xii. 81 There was no centralised mint and probably little centralised oversight. **1971** *Nature* 4 June 292/1 The need to continue investigations on a broad front to keep an ecological oversight of the biogeodynamics of each metal. **1977** *Time* 21 Feb. 38/1 Congressional oversight has proliferated.

†**b.** An examination, review, survey. *Obs.*

1550 HOOPER (*title*) An ouersighte and deliberacion vppon the holy prophet Ionas.

c. A survey, view. *rare.*

1889 F. E. GRETTON *Memory's Harkback* 291 You have a closer and more direct oversight of the home, or Herefordshire, view.

2. a. The fact of passing over without seeing; omission or failure to see or notice, inadvertence.

1477 *Rolls of Parlt.* VI. 176/1 Youre seid suppliant, of grete oversight of him self and simplenesse, did and committed ayenst youre Highnes grete tresons and offences. **1549** COVERDALE, etc. *Erasm. Par. Tit.* 2 Suche faultes as were therin eyther by the printers neglygence or myne ouersyght. **1676** TEMPLE *Let. to Ambassadors France* Wks. 1731 II. 406 It is all rather owing to Oversight, than to any ill Intention. **1868** E. EDWARDS *Ralegh* I. xxv. 600 A similar piece of oversight had befallen one of the captains. **1927** *Public Opinion* 8 Apr. 329/2 The generous-hearted demand that we accord to China the recognition due to a modern nation is sometimes made in oversight of the fundamental elements in the problem. **1959** J. L. AUSTIN *Sense & Sensibilia* (1962) ii. 13 These are the quite common cases of misreadings, mishearings, Freudian oversights, &c. **1976**

Washington Post 19 Apr. A4/5 The back-room view in the White House is that there should be a single oversight committee on Capitol Hill to answer the clamor for corrective action.

b. An instance of this; a mistake of inadvertence. Also, a person who is passed over.
1531 *Dial. on Laws Eng.* II. xlii. (1638) 135 He shall answer as well for an untruth in any such clerk as for an oversight. **1666** PEPYS *Diary* 31 Jan., There being several horrible oversights to the prejudice of the King. **1748** *Anson's Voy.* Introd. 6 In so complicated a work, some oversights must have been committed. **1865** LIGHTFOOT *Gal.* (1874) 121 It [the omission] may have been an oversight. **1955** T. H. PEAR *Eng. Social Differences* 241 When one studies the failures among those who were selected for grammar schools and the oversights among those who were not selected, not a few mistakes.. might have been avoided had the child's social environment been taken into account.

Hence †**'oversight** *v. intr.*, to commit an oversight (*obs. nonce-wd.*); **over'sighted** *ppl. a.*, overlooked.
1613 F. ROBARTS *Rev. of Gosp.* 143 (To Rdr.) The Printer hath faulted a little; it may be the author ouersighted more. **1857** J. HYDE *Mormonism* (ed. 2) ix. 215 There is one oversighted contradiction that stares us in the face.

†**over'sile**, *v. Obs.* Chiefly *Sc.* Also 6 **-syle**. [f. OVER- 8, 1 (*b*) + *sile*, *syle*, obs. forms of CEIL *v.*]
1. *trans.* To cover over; to conceal, hide.
a **1510** DOUGLAS *K. Hart* II. xxxix, My solace sall I sleylie thus oursyle [*rimes* begyle, quhyle]. **1535** STEWART *Cron. Scot.* I. 359 Wodis wyld, And ron and roche with mony rammall ouirsyld. **1584** HUDSON *Du Bartas' Judith* I. in *Sylvester's Wks.* (1621) 695 Ere I my malice cloke or oversile.
2. To obscure or dim the physical or mental sight; hence, to blind mentally, delude, beguile.
c **1560** A. SCOTT *Poems* (S.T.S.) iii. 40 Be the wy that all the warld wrocht, Maist witt hes hie that moniest owrsylis. *a* **1584** MONTGOMERIE *Cherrie & Slae* 418 Fuil-haist ay almaist ay Ouirsylis the sicht of sum. **1632** LITHGOW *Trav.* I. 34 Sathan, thou Prince of darknesse, hast so ouer-sylled the dimmed eies of their wretched soules.
3. ? To overtop, exceed, surpass.
1584 HUDSON *Du Bartas' Judith* I. in *Sylvester's Wks.* (1621) 691 The height and beauty did surpass, And overseilde the famous work of Pharie, Ephesus Temple.

Hence †**over'siling** *vbl. sb.*, overarching, arched roof; *ppl. a.*, overarching, covered in.
1632 LITHGOW *Trav.* VI. 267 The ouersilings loaden with Mosaick worke. *Ibid.* x. 440 Faire Arbors, spacious ouersiling walkes, and incorporate Trees of interchanging growths.

oversilent, -silver, -simple: see OVER-.

ˌoversimplifi'cation. [OVER- 29 b.] The action or process of simplifying to excess; the result of this; a simplistic style or procedure.
1930 R. A. FISHER *Genetical Theory Nat. Selection* 42 It is a patent oversimplification to assert that the environment determines the numbers of each sort of organism that it will support. **1934** *Discovery* Dec. 339/2 The danger of over-simplification of exceedingly complex problems. **1958** 'P. BRYANT' *Two Hours to Doom* 91 'Since the war a dozen countries have gone Communist.'.. 'I realise that. But I think it's an over-simplification of the issue.' **1968** M. S. LIVINGSTON *Particle Physics* p. vi, The author accepts responsibility for any shortcomings or over-simplifications in these descriptions. **1975** *Listener* 4 Dec. 734/3 When the cars are there, they sell... This, of course, is an over-simplification.

over'simplify, *v.* [OVER- 27.] *trans.* To render excessively or delusively simple; to explain in simplistic terms. Also *absol.* Hence **over'simplified** *ppl. a.*; **over'simplifying** *vbl. sb.* and *ppl. a.* Also **over'simplifier**, one who oversimplifies.
1934 WEBSTER, Oversimplify. **1936** *Mind* XLV. 222 Preformation.. errs by over-simplifying the problem. **1940** *Amer. Speech* XV. 67 The old fallacy of the over-simplifiers, searching for 'the' cause where there usually is a complex of causes, has also bedeviled philology. **1942** *Scrutiny* X. IV. 360 The difference cannot be explained simply by saying that the comic parts of *Chuzzlewit* are good and the 'serious' or 'sentimental' parts bad, because that is an over-simplifying of the case. **1946** *Sun* (Baltimore) 11 Mar. 10/3 (*heading*) It is easy to oversimplify about the Russians. **1946** J. S. HUXLEY *Unesco* ii. 47 In somewhat over-simplified terms. **1953** D. F. POCOCK tr. *Durkheim's Sociol. & Philos.* iii. 74 This.. would be preferable in our schools to the over-simplified.. explanations with which we too often deceive the curiosity of youth. **1963** *Times* 21 Jan. 9/2 These two stubborn, oversimplifying old men. **1965** C. WALSH in J. Gibb *Light on C. S. Lewis* 114 He berated Lewis as an oversimplifier. **1975** R. BROWNING *Emperor Julian* i. 27 An oversimplified summary of results must suffice. **1976** *Listener* 28 Oct. 550/1 Magnus Pyke.. has been accused.. of 'popularising' his subject, of oversimplifying.

†**over'sit**, *v. Obs.* [OE. *ofersittan*: see OVER- 1, 4, 2. Cf. MHG., Ger. *übersitzen*, Du. *overzitten*.]
1. *trans.* To sit over or upon; to occupy, possess.
c **825** *Vesp. Psalter* lviii. 4 Forðon sehðe ofersetun [*L.* occupaverunt] sawle mine. *c* **888** K. ÆLFRED *Boeth.* xviii. §1 þone mæstan hæfð sæ oferseten. *c* **1205** LAY. 8035 For auere to ure liue we maȝen ouer-sitten þis lond.
2. To refrain, abstain, or desist from; to omit.
Beowulf (Z.) 684 Ac wit on niht sculon secge ofer-sittan. *Ibid.* 2528 þæt ic wið þone guð-flogan gylp ofer-sitte. *c* **1000** ÆLFRIC *Gram.* xlvii. (Z.) 276 *Supersideo*, ic ofersitte. **1303** R. BRUNNE *Handl. Synne* 10284 ȝyf þou forgete or ouer-syttes Tyme of housel þat þou weyl wytes. *c* **1440** *Promp. Parv.* 373/2 Ovyr settynge or ovyr syttynge of dede or tyme, *omissio*. **1456** SIR G. HAYE *Law Arms* (S.T.S.) 132, I may nocht tak it agayne.. gif I oursytt ony quhile.
3. *trans.* To sit over or above, preside over.
1587 GOLDING *De Mornay* iii. 31 His power and prouidence oursitting them from aboue.

'overˌsize, *sb.* [OVER- 29 d.] **1.** A size in excess of the proper or ordinary size.
1849 W. A. SCOTT in *Nat. Preacher* Mar., A statue placed in an elevated niche, that must be cut somewhat roughly and of a proportioned oversize to produce the proper effect. **1920** E. SITWELL *Wooden Pegasus* 88 Neutralize The overtint and oversize. **1920** *New Yorker* 12 Sept. 90/1 (Advt.), This most unusual watch,.. shown here in its actual over-size.
2. That which is above a certain size.
1902 *Encycl. Brit.* XXXI. 374/1 It then goes to a screen with eleven holes to the linear inch, and yields a granular undersize and oversize. **1905** *Electrochem. Industry* Mar. 124/2 The oversize, which contains no slime whatever, is delivered directly to four Wilfley concentrating tables.

'oversize, *a.* [f. the sb.] = OUTSIZE *a.*
1909 *Cent. Dict.* Suppl., *Oversize*.., of excessive size; specifically, noting material which is too large to pass through the meshes of a given screen or size. **1924** *T. Eaton & Co. Catal.* Spring & Summer 292/2 Oversize cord tires need special cord size inner tubes. **1936** W. FAULKNER *Absalom! Absalom!* vi. 195 A new oversize overall jumper coat. **1960** I. CROSS *Backward Sex* i. 12 That bald head, like an over-size tennis ball, the worse for much wear. **1973** *Publishers Weekly* 25 June 16 (Advt.), A magnificently illustrated, oversize book. 10″ × 11⅞″. **1976** *Billings* (Montana) *Gaz.* 1 July 2-D/5 (Advt.), Nearly new three bedroom split entry home featuring large bedrooms, a fully equipped oversize kitchen with lots of cabinets.

ˌover'size, *v.*[1] [OVER- 22 b, 26.]
1. *trans.* To exceed in size. **2.** To increase (something) beyond the usual size; to make too large.
1615 G. SANDYS *Travels* I. 3 [People] bred in a mountanous countrey, who are generally obserued to oversize those that dwell on low leuels. *Ibid.* 63 Little copped caps.. he the greatest that weareth the greatest, the Mufties excepted, which ouer-sizes the Emperours. **1648** *Regall Apol.* 41 They have.. brought in a Garrison of strangers, and laid aside or over-sized the ordinary Guard. **1688** in Harwood *Lichfield* (1806) 70 His error in oversizing the eight bells he has cast. **1879** 'MARK TWAIN' *Lett. to Publishers* (1967) 114, I say $1100 instead of $1042 to cover little possible mistakes in over-sizing the plates. **1904** — in *Harper's Weekly* 2 Jan. 19/1 The whole of that is intelligible to me.. except.. [one] remark... That one oversizes my hand. Gimme five cards. **1930** *Flight* 25 Apr. (Suppl.) 460*e*/1 With various wheel forms, the effect of oversizing tyres and the use of smooth or safety treads. **1957** R. LISTER *Decorative Wrought Ironwork* 230 *Oversizing*. Iron oxidizes while being worked, and it is therefore sometimes necessary to work it slightly larger than its intended final size, or oversize it, in order to counteract any loss by this.

over'size, *v.*[2] [f. OVER- 8, 27 + SIZE *v.*[2]]
†**1.** *trans.* To size over, cover over with size. *Obs.*
1602 SHAKS. *Ham.* II. ii. 484 And thus o're-sized with coagulate gore.
2. (ˌ*over-'size*) To size too much.
1878 ABNEY *Photogr.* (1881) 167 A great point is the selection of the paper. It will be found advantageous to use rather a porous kind, not over-sized.

Hence ˌ**over-'sizing** *vbl. sb.*, excessive sizing.
1884 *Manch. Exam.* 5 Sept. 4/6 Resolutions were.. passed against the over-sizing of cotton yarns. **1900** *Daily News* 10 Aug. 2/1 The defect in the cloth was due to over-sizing.

'over'sized (stress shifting), *ppl. a.* [f. OVERSIZE *sb.* + -ED[2].] Over or above the normal size, abnormally large.
1853 KANE *Grinnell Exp.* xxxi. (1856) 274 Can read ordinary over-sized print. **1869** COLERIDGE *Mem. Keble* II. 310 The parish was a country one, not over-sized. **1885** E. D. GERARD *Waters Hercules* xiii, An undersized man or an oversized boy.

overskim: see OVER- 9.

†**over'skip**, *v. Obs.* [OVER- 5, 13.]
1. *trans.* To skip or jump lightly over.
1558 PHAER *Æneid* VI. Rj, Whan first that fatall horse our contrey walls did ouerskippe. **1594** HOOKER *Eccl. Pol.* Pref. iii. §2 Neither seeke yee to ouer-skip the fold.
2. *fig.* To 'skip over', pass over without notice, omit, pretermit.
c **1369** CHAUCER *Dethe Blaunche* 1208 Many a worde I ouer skipte In my tale. **1432-50** tr. *Higden* (Rolls) V. 65 Marcus Aurelius Antonius.. oversckippede not eny kynde of lecchery. **1526** *Pilgr. Perf.* (W. de W. 1531) 179 Ouerskyppyng many wordes y[t] pleased hym not. **1602** *Narcissus* (1893) 404 How can I overskippe To speake of love to such a cherrye lippe? **1605** SHAKS. *Lear* III. vi. 113. **1675** *Art Contentm.* I. xv. (1684) 180 Not.. confin'd to some few particular persons, and wholly overskipping the rest. *absol.* **1607** ROWLANDS *Famous Hist.* 55 Tell me.. In reading rashly, if I over-skip.
3. To overleap; to go beyond in skipping. *rare.*
1628 GAULE *Pract. The.* (1629) 89 We would faine ouerskip euen Nature in her seruerall passages.

Hence †**over'skipper**, one who overskips or omits; †**over'skipping** *vbl. sb.*, omission. *Obs.*
1377 LANGL. *P. Pl.* B. XI. 302 In þe sauter seyth dauyd to ouerskippers. *c* **1440** *Jacob's Well* 108 In syncopyng, in ouyr-skyppyng, in omyttyng. **1582** T. WATSON *Centurie of Loue* lxxx. Poems (Arb.) 116 Transilition or ouer skipping of number by rule and order, as from 1 to 3, 5, 7, and 9.

'overskirt. [OVER- 8 c.] An outer skirt; a second skirt, worn over the skirt of a dress.
1870 *Harper's Bazaar* 22 Oct. 675 Over-skirts are elaborate, and show great variety in design. **1873** *Young Englishwoman* Mar. 131/2 An over-skirt of tulle looped up with a scarf sash. **1883** *Philad. Press* 7 June 4 Underskirt concealed, or very nearly concealed, by a light overskirt. **1884** M. E. WILKINS in *Harper's Mag.* Oct. 788/1 There was a green under-skirt, and a brown over-skirt.

over-slack: see OVER-.

†**'overslaht.** *Obs.* [OVER- 1: cf. OE. *sleaht* = *sleȝe* stroke: cf. OVERSLAY.] = OVERSLAY.
c **1175** *Lamb. Hom.* 87 þet heo sculden.. merki mid þan blode hore duren and hore ouersleaht. *Ibid.* 127 Mid his blode we sculen.. þa postles and þet ouerslaht of ure huse.. bisprengan.

†**over'slake**, *v. Obs.* [f. OVER- 4 + SLAKE *v.*] *intr.* To slacken off, become allayed or quenched.
c **1400** *Laud Troy Bk.* 3112 Iff thow haue cause suche dole to make, Lete it passe and ouer-slake! *a* **1415** [see OVERSHAKE 1 b].

over-slander: see OVER-.

overslaugh ('əʊvəslɔː), *sb.* Also 8 **-slagh, -slaw**. [ad. Du. *overslag*, f. *overslaan* (see next); or (in sense 1) from the Eng. vb.]
1. *Mil.* The passing over of one's ordinary turn of duty in consideration of being required for a duty which takes precedence of it.
1772 SIMES *Milit. Guide* Dict. s.v., The three blanks [in a form of Roster] shew where the *overslaghs* take effect. **1777** — *Milit. Course* 25 The Nature of a Table for Overslaghs. *c* **1785** J. WILLIAMSON *Elem. Milit. Arrangemt.* II. Notes 51 In a roster, therefore, of eight columns, the smaller corps will be allowed two overslaughs. (This *overslaugh* is a Dutch expression signifying to leap, or skip over.) **1802** in JAMES *Milit. Dict.* **1859** *Musketry Instr. Army* 8. **1868** *Regul. & Ord. Army* ¶837 When an Officer's tour of duty comes along with other duties, he is detailed for that duty which has the precedence, and he is to receive an overslaugh for any other duties. **1901** *King's Regulations* ¶243 When an officer is on duty, he will receive an 'overslaugh' for all other duties which may come to his turn.
fig. **1857** GEN. P. THOMPSON *Audi Alt.* (1858) I. xiii. 45 In something of this kind it is, that the Working Classes should look for what soldiers call their 'overslaugh', or compensation for extra duty done.
2. *U.S.* A bar or sand-bank which impedes the navigation of a river; *spec.* that on the Hudson River below Albany.
1776 C. CARROLL *Jrnl. Miss. Canada* in B. Mayer *Mem.* (1845) 42 Having passed the overslaw, had a distinct view of Albany. **1796** MORSE *Amer. Geog.* I. 479 Ship navigation to Albany is interrupted by a number of islands, 6 or 8 miles below the city, called the Overslaugh. **1860** BARTLETT *Dict. Amer.*, *Overslaugh*. A bar, in the marine language of the Dutch. The overslaugh in the Hudson river, near Albany, on which steamboats and other vessels often run aground, is, I believe, the only locality to which this term is now applied among us.

overslaugh ('əʊvəslɔː), *v.* [ad. Du. *overslaan* to pass over, omit, pass by, f. *over-* OVER- 5 + *slaan* to strike; Ger. *überschlagen*.]
1. *trans.* To pass over, skip, omit. **a.** *Mil.* To pass over, skip, or remit the ordinary turn of duty of an officer, a company, etc., in consideration of his (or its) being detailed on that day for a duty which takes precedence.
The officer does the higher duty, and skips his turn for the lower, which is taken by him whose turn comes next.
1768 SIMES *Milit. Dict.* [not in ed. 1, 1766] *Overslagh*, originally derived form the Dutch language, signifies to *skip over*. For instance, suppose four battalions [etc.].. If, in the Buffs, the second Captain is doing duty of Deputy-adjutant-general, and the fourth and seventh Captain in the King's are acting, one as Aid-de-Camp, the other as Brigade-major, the common duty of these three Captains must be overslaghed; that is, equally divided among the other captains. A sketch of the table formed for this purpose may .. help still further to explain the term *overslagh*. **1777** — *Milit. Course* 128 Captain C... having leave of absence is overslaghed. **1779** in CAPT. G. SMITH *Milit. Dict.* **1802** in JAMES *Milit. Dict.*
b. *U.S.* To pass over in favour of another, as in nomination to an office; also, generally, to pass over, omit consideration of, ignore.
1846 in *N. York Com. Adv.* 21 Oct. (Bartlett), It was found that public opinion would not be reconciled to overslaughing Taylor, and he was nominated. **1848** *N. York Courier & Enq.* Oct. (ibid.), The attempt to overslaugh officers entitled to rank in the highest grade in the service, is about to be repeated in a somewhat different way in a lower grade. **1881** *Contemp. Rev.* Mar. 434 The other [province] is so small that it is tempted to pursue an obstructive course.. to prevent its being overslaughed altogether.
2. To stop the course or progress of, to bar, obstruct, hinder. [Cf. OVERSLAUGH *sb.* 2.]
1864 WEBSTER, *Overslaugh*... To hinder or stop, as by an overslaugh or unexpected impediment; as, to *overslaugh* a bill in a legislative body, that is, to hinder or stop its passage by some opposition. **1865** *Morning Star* 15 Mar., The Gulf States or their representatives in Congress,.. killed the bill or overslaughed it for the time by voting against it. **1872** W. MATHEWS *Getting on in World* 89 (Cent.) Society is everywhere overslaughed with institutions.

†**'overslay.** *Obs.* [OE. *oferslege*, f. *ofer-* OVER- 1 d + *sleȝe* stroke, blow, (in comb.) beam, bar:

cf. ON. *slá* beam, cross-bar.] The lintel of a door.

c **1000** ÆLFRIC *Gram.* ix. §12 *Limen*, ofersleȝe oððe þerexwold. *c* **1000** ÆLFRIC *Exod.* xii. 23 þonne he ȝesihþ þæt blod on þam ofersleȝe. *c* **1250** *Gen. & Ex.* 3155 Ðe dure tren and ðe uerslaȝen, wið ysope ðe blod ben draȝen. *c* **1425** *Voc.* in Wr.-Wülcker 668/5 *Hoc superliminare*, ouverslay. *c* **1440** *Promp. Parv.* 374/1 Ovyrslay of a doore, *superliminare.*

oversleep (əʊvəˈsliːp), *v.* [OVER- 18, 23.]

1. To sleep too long; to sleep beyond the time at which one ought to awake. **a.** *intr.*

1398 TREVISA *Barth. De P.R.* XVII. lv. (1495) 636 Meue thy body leest that thou ouerslepe. **1602** WARNER *Alb. Eng.* XII. lxxiv. (1612) 306 His man fain'd feare to ouer-sleepe, and would not downe him lay. **1881** MRS. H. HUNT *Childr. Jerus.* 158, I will not let you over-sleep, be sure.

b. *refl.* In same sense.

c **1430** *Syr Gener.* (Roxb.) 2646 That she her self not ouerslept. **1571** GOLDING *Calvin on Ps.* xvii. 15 Although he never overslept himself, yet..after long forweryìng, he lay as it were in a slomber. **1719** DE FOE *Crusoe* II. iii. (1840) 51 They were weary, and overslept themselves. **1893** LELAND *Mem.* I. 218 Which sight I missed by over-sleeping myself.

2. *trans.* To sleep beyond (a particular time).

1526 *Pilgr. Perf.* (W. de W. 1531) 133 b, To be ware, that we ouerslepe not our tyme. **1828** WEBSTER s.v., To oversleep the usual hour of rising.

overˈsleeping, *vbl. sb.* [-ING[1].] The action of the verb OVERSLEEP.

1908 *Westm. Gaz.* 31 Oct. 3/2 What with your smashings, and your over-sleepings, and burning the dinner on Sunday, and all. **1912** R. BROOKE *Let.* 25 Feb. in E. Marsh *Rupert Brooke* (1918) iv. 70 My cure consists in perpetual overeating and oversleeping. **1977** J. AIKEN *Last Movement* vii. 136 Over-sleeping is as bad as over-eating.

oversleeve (ˈəʊvəsliːv). [OVER- 8 c.] An outer sleeve covering the ordinary sleeve.

1857 MRS. MALCOLM tr. *Freytag's Debit & Credit* (1858) 21 The Gentleman..pulled off his grey oversleeve, folded it carefully, and locked it up with a parcel of papers in his desk. **1888** *Daily News* 1 May 5/7 The sleeves are made entirely of white cloth, with an oversleeve of ottoman falling partly over the top of the arms, but not hiding the gold embroidery.

overslide (əʊvəˈslaɪd), *v.* [OVER- 4, 5.]

†**1.** *intr.* To slide or slip away (in *fig.* sense); to pass by, pass unnoticed. Usually with *let. Obs.*

c **1350** *Will. Palerne* 3519 þe þroli þouȝt þat him meued þer-of þat ilk time Sone he let ouer-slide. *c* **1420** LYDG. *Story of Thebes* II. in *Chaucer's Wks.* (1561) 363 b/1 For lacke of tyme, I lat ouer slide. *c* **1560** A. SCOTT *Poems* (S.T.S.) xxi. 41, I slip, and lattis all ourslyd Aganis the feld of the.

†**2.** *trans.* To pass lightly over, let alone, leave unnoticed (= *to let overslide* in 1). *Obs.*

c **1470** HENRY *Wallace* IV. 415 This matir now herfor I will ourslyde. **1570** B. GOOGE *Pop. Kingd.* III. 43 The rest I ouerslide.

3. *trans.* (*lit.*) To slide, slip, or glide over (a place or thing). Also *intr.* or *absol.*

1513 DOUGLAS *Æneis* v. xi. 31 Of thir salt fludis sa braid ane way Remanis ȝit for till ourslyd and saill. **1648** HERRICK *Hesp., Ring presented to Julia* iii. (1869) 67 And be, too, such a yoke, As not too wide, To over-slide; Or be so strait to choak. **1855** WHITTIER *Dream* 15 The goodly company.. One by one the brink o'erslid.

over-slight, etc.: see OVER-.

overslip (əʊvəˈslɪp), *v.* Now *rare.*

1. *trans.* To slip or pass by (*fig.*), pass over without notice; to let slip, let pass; to fail or neglect to notice, mention, use, or take advantage of; to leave out, omit, miss. Common in 16th and 17th c.; now *rare* or *Obs.* [OVER- 4, 5.]

a **1425** *Cursor M.* 12900 (Trin.) But miȝte he neuer ouer slip þat him self seide of warship. **1513** DOUGLAS *Æneis* x. xiii. 81 Forsuyth, I sall nocht ourslyp in this steyd Thy hard myschance, Lawsus, and fatale deyd. **1535** COVERDALE *Esther* ix. 28 The dayes of Purim, which are not to be ouerslipte amonge the Iewes. **1599** THYNNE *Animadv.* (1875) 62, I must speake of one woorde in the same, deservinge correctione, whiche I see you ouerslipped. **1672** *Essex Papers* (Camden) 20 That y[e] Advantages of y[e] Crowne by this Regulation bee not overslipt. **1759** BROWN *Compl. Farmer* 98 A little before Michaelmas, or, if you have overslipt that time, then about the end of February. **1860** MOTLEY *Netherl.* (1868) I. vii. 446, I had overslipt the good occasion then in danger.

†**b.** *intr.* or *absol.* To act inadvertently, make a slip. Also *refl.* in same sense. *Obs.*

1600 W. WATSON *Decacordon* (1602) 148 Ouerslipping himselfe at vnawares in his words. **1609** ROWLANDS *Knaue of Clubbes* 28 But see how wise ingenious men, Do often ouerslip! **1641** MILTON *Animadv.* (1851) 214 The easines of erring, or overslipping in such a boundlesse and vast search.

†**2.** *intr.* To slip or pass by; to pass unnoticed or unused; of time, to elapse (usually implying the missing of an opportunity). *Obs.* [OVER- 4.]

1470–85 MALORY *Arthur* VIII. xiv, For sire Segwarydes durste not haue ado with sir Tristram..therfore he lete it ouer slyp. **1513** [see OVERSLIPPING *ppl. a.* below]. **1603** KNOLLES *Hist. Turks* (1621) 1002 Being very desirous not to let such an opportunitie to overslip. **1607** in *Hist. Wakefield Gram. Sch.* (1892) 65 If (upon time overslipped) the election ..shall be in the Maister and Fellowes of Emanuel Colledge.

†**3.** *trans.* To slip away from, escape (a person); usually *fig.*, to escape the notice of, pass unnoticed or unused by, be missed by. *Obs.*

1574 WHITGIFT *Def. Answ.* i. Wks. 1851 I. 178, I think it hath but overslipped you, and that upon better advice you will reform it. **1593** SHAKS. *Lucr.* 1576 Which all this time hath overslipp'd her thought. **1630** WADSWORTH *Pilgr.* viii. 82, I would not let any occasion ouerslip me. **1688** HOOLE *Sch.-Colloquies* 394, I had rather write it my self lest any thing should perhaps overslip me.

4. To slip past or beyond (*lit.*); to pass beyond, esp. secretly or covertly. [OVER- 13.]

c **1595** CAPT. WYATT *R. Dudley's Voy. W. Ind.* (Hakl. Soc.) 19 It was thearefore concluded secretlie..that in the night they shoulde overslip them [the islands]. **1616** SURFL. & MARKH. *Country Farme* 687 Hiding himselfe therein, and letting the dogges by that means to ouerslip him, as not being able to find the sent of him. **1628** DIGBY *Voy. Medit.* (1868) 26 And shortened saile, least before morning I might ouerslippe them. **1660** INGELO *Bentiv. & Ur.* II. (1682) 8 That is not my house said [he] you have over-slipt it a League.

†**5.** To slip beyond or outside of (*fig.*); to transgress through inadvertence. *Obs.*

1534 WHITINTON *Tullyes Offices* I. (1540) 13 Many causes are wont to be..of ouerslyppynge of mannes offyce and dutie. **1590** GREENE *Orl. Fur.* Wks. (Rtldg.) 92/1 Lest..My choler overslip the law of arms. *a* **1592** —— *Poems* 120 She [Nature] over-slipped her cunning and her skill, And aimed too fair, but drew beyond the mark.

6. *intr.* ? To slip or slide beyond the proper point in stepping: said of a horse. ? *Obs.*

1706 *Lond. Gaz.* No. 4212/4 When he trots out he overslips, and is shod short before for it.

Hence **overˈslipped** *ppl. a.*, **overˈslipping** *vbl. sb.* and *ppl. a.*

1513 DOUGLAS *Æneis* XIII. ix. 50 The lang declinand and ourslippand nycht Gan schape full fast to mak schort and ourdryve. **1582** STANYHURST *Æneis* Ded. (Arb.) 7 Thee ouerslipping of yt were in effect thee chocking of thee poet his discourse. **1616** R. C. *Times' Whistle*, etc. *Ad Lectorem* (E.E.T.S.) 111, I had noe competencie of time..to correct any easily overslipped errour.

†**ˈoverslip,** *sb. Obs.* [f. prec. *v.*] An act of 'overslipping' or inadvertence; a slip.

1593 *Pass. Morrice* (1876) 82, I let not them passe in whom I discouer not many ouer-slippes. **1650** T. B[AYLEY] *Worcester's Apoph.* 94 After that he had seen him express so much of sorrow for that over-slip.

†**ˈoverslop.** *Obs.* [OE. *oferslop* (in ON. *yfirsloppr*), f. OVER- 8 c + SLOP a smock.] A loose upper garment; a cassock or gown; a stole or surplice.

c **950** *Lindisf. Gosp.* Luke xx. 46 [*Ambulare in stolis*] geonga in stolum *vel* on oferslopum. *c* **1000** *Sax. Leechd.* III. 200 Oferslop hwit habban blisse ȝetacnað, oferslop bleofah habban ærende fullic ȝetacnað. *c* **1386** CHAUCER *Can. Yeom. Prol. & T.* 80 (Ellesm.) His overslope [*Petw.* ouersclope, *other MSS.* ouer(e sloppe] nys nat worth a myte..It is al baudy and to-tore also.

over-slope: see OVER-.

ˈover-ˈslow, *a.* [OVER- 27.] Too slow, unduly slow. So **over-ˈslowness.**

1571 GOLDING *Calvin on Ps.* xxxvii. 11 The understanding of the flesh thinketh him to bee then overslow. **1896** MRS. CAFFYN *Quaker Grandmother* 140 The consciences of the two appear to have been especially created for their present fluctuating state of being. For hers was as over-slow, as his was over-sure. **1902** *Westm. Gaz.* 29 May 3/1 The weak spot will come from the over-slowness and air of calculation.

†**overˈslow,** *v. Obs. rare.* [Cf. OVER- 21.] *trans.* To make slow, slacken down, retard.

a **1660** HAMMOND *Serm. Ezek.* xvi. 30 Wks. 1684 IV. 563 To perswade our selves, that there is no means on earth.. able to trash, or overslow this furious driver.

ˈoverslung, *a.* [OVER- 1 c.] Supported above the main part, or some particular part, of an apparatus.

1960 SHEPHERD & WITHERS *Mech. Cutting & Loading of Coal* v. 78 A number of low-type cutters provide for a range of appropriate adjustable positions between the underslung and overslung position of the reversible turret. **1971** B. SCHARF *Engin. & its Lang.* xvi. 228 Overhead travelling cranes consist of (1) a load girder with a roller mounted carriage at each end running on top (overslung gantry type), or along the bottom flanges of gantry rails (underslung gantry type); (2) a trolley..; and (3) a hoist. **1971** J. M. PAXTON *Man. Civil Engin. Plant* (ed. 2) I. 190/2 Both rear axles are driven via double reduction hubs with an overslung worm and wheel from a 12-speed gearbox, giving 12 forward and 3 reverse speeds.

overslur to **over-small:** see OVER-.

oversman (ˈəʊvəzmən). *Sc.* and *north. dial.* [A variant of OVERMAN, prob. after words formed on a genitive, such as *daysman, townsman*, etc.]

1. A man having authority, or holding an official position, over others; = OVERMAN 1.

1596 DALRYMPLE tr. *Leslie's Hist. Scot.* I. 127 In euerie prouince ar owrismen quhome of ane ald titil we cal Schirreffis. [**1894** HEWAT *Little Scot. World* 84 The earliest provosts or ouirsmen of Prestwick.]

2. An arbiter, umpire; = OVERMAN 2.

1540 *Decreet Arbitral* in *5th Rep. Hist. MSS. Comm.* 609/1 Robert Abbot of Kinloss, oversman chosen by the said parties. **1593** in Row *Hist. Kirk* (1842) 153 Each shall choose so many out of his awin Presbyterie with an oversman. **1874** *Act 37 & 38 Vict.* c. 94 §35 A decree of division of commonty..pronounced..by arbiters or by an oversman.

3. A foreman in a colliery; = OVERMAN 3.

1863 *Mining Rep. W. Scot.*, Enforced by the occasional visit of the underground oversman, particularly in long-wall working.

†**overˈsmite,** *v. Obs.* [OVER- 13.] *trans.* To exceed or go beyond in smiting.

a **1450** *Fysshynge w. Angle* (1883) 18 Se þat ȝe neuer ouer smyt þe strynght of ȝowr lyne for brekyng.

overˈsmoke, *v.* [OVER- 8, 23, 27.]

1. *trans.* To cover over with smoke or the like.

1855 BROWNING *Up at Villa* v, The hills over-smoked behind by the faint grey olive-trees.

2. *intr.* and *refl.* To smoke too much.

1890 *Cornh. Mag.* Oct. 417, I work as hard as I can and oversmoke myself and am happy. **1895** *Westm. Gaz.* 26 Oct. 3/1 [He] may have drunk too much tea..or oversmoked.

overˈsnow, *v. poetic.* [OVER- 8.] *trans.* To whiten over with or as with snow.

c **1600** SHAKS. *Sonn.* v, Sap check'd with frost and lusty leaves quite gone, Beauty o'ersnow'd, and bareness every where. **1697** DRYDEN *Æneid* v. 553 Ere age unstrung my nerves, or time o'ersnow'd my head.

overˈsoar, *v.* [OVER- 1, 5.] *trans.* To soar above, fly over the summit of.

1591 SYLVESTER *Du Bartas* I. vii. 623 As the wise Wildegeese, when they over-soar Cilician Mounts. **1821** SHELLEY *Epipsych.* 16 It oversoared this low and worldly shade. **1839** BAILEY *Festus* (1848) xxi. 268 My mind o'ersoars The stars.

†**over-sob,** *v. Obs. rare.* [f. OVER- 26 + SOB *v.*] *trans.* To charge with excess of moisture.

1664 EVELYN *Sylva* (1776) 41 That you cast no seeds into the earth whilst it either actually rains, or that it be over-sobb'd, till moderately dry.

over-soft: see OVER-.

oversold: see OVERSELL *v.*

over-solemn, etc.: see OVER-.

ˈover-soˈlicitous, *a.* [OVER- 28.] Excessively or unduly solicitous. So **ˈover-soˈlicitude.**

1664–5 PEPYS *Diary* 28 Feb., My being over-solicitous and jealous and froward and ready to reproach her do make her worse. **1711** SHAFTESB. *Charac.* (1737) II. 58 The over-sollicitous regard to private good. **1768–74** TUCKER *Lt. Nat.* (1834) II. 507 An over-solicitude retards the speed and misguides the judgement.

ˈover-ˈsoon, *adv.* (*a.*) [OVER- 30: cf. OVER *adv.* 11.] **A.** *adv.* Too soon; †too quickly or readily (*obs.*).

1340 HAMPOLE *Pr. Consc.* 3907 Penance..done Parchaunce over reklesly and over sone. *c* **1440** *Jacob's Well* 153 As whann a man sweryth ouersone,..& whanne he hath don, he repentyth hym. *a* **1586** SIDNEY (J.), The lad may prove well enough, if he oversoon think not too well of himself. **1634** W. TIRWHYT tr. *Balzac's Lett.* (vol. I.) 97 Having over-soone desired them. **1878** HARDY *Ret. Native* II. II. vi. 10, I told him 'twas barely decent to come so oversoon; but words be wind.

†**B.** *adj.* Too early; too ready or quick. *Obs.*

a **1586** SIDNEY *Arcadia* IV. (1622) 415 Lamenting..such as the turtle-like loue is wont to make for the euer ouersoone losse of her onely loued make.

†**ˈoverˈsore,** *adv. Obs.* [f. OVER- 30 + SORE *adv.*] Too 'sore'; too severely or violently.

1297 R. GLOUC. (1724) 280 (MS. B) þys Edwyne was þus kyng þre ȝer, and somdel more, And þat lond vor ys deþe ne wep noȝt ouersore [*v.r.* no þing sore]. *c* **1460** FORTESCUE *Abs. & Lim. Mon.* x. (1885) 133 It is not good a kynge to ouer sore charge his peple. *a* **1568** ASCHAM *Scholem.* (Arb.) 34 Thies sciences, as they sharpen mens wittes ouer moch, so they change mens maners ouer sore.

over-sorrow to **-sot:** see OVER-.

ˈover-soul, *sb.* [OVER- 2.] Emerson's name for the Deity regarded philosophically as the supreme spirit which animates the universe; used by later writers in the same or an analogous sense. Also, = SUPERMAN.

1841–4 EMERSON *Ess., Over-soul* 270–1 That great nature in which we rest as the earth lies in the soft arms of the atmosphere; that Unity, that Over-soul within which each man's particular being is contained and made one with all other. **1856** R. A. VAUGHAN *Mystics* (1860) II. 19 With the American [Emerson], every elevated thought merges man for a time in the Oversoul. **1887** H. R. HAWEIS *Lt. of Ages* I. i. 4 The Divine Spirit, the Great Oversoul has always been in contact with the human spirit. **1908** [see BEYOND *adv.* and *prep.* D].

ˈover-soul, *v.* [f. the sb.] *trans.* In passive, to be ruled or dominated in respect of the soul. Hence **over-ˈsouling** *vbl. sb.*

1916 'A. E.' *National Being* ii. 13 None of our modern States create in us such an impression of being spiritually oversouled by an ideal as the great States of the ancient world. **1925** D. H. LAWRENCE *Refl. Death Porcupine* 168 A primrose has its own peculiar primrosy identity, and all the oversouling in the world won't melt it into a Williamish oneness.

overˈsound, *v. Mus.* [OVER- 1 e.] (See quot.)

1852 SEIDEL *Organ* 43 If the wind be too strong, the pipes oversound (or produce the higher octave of the tone they ought to sound).

over-sour: see OVER-.

oversow (əʊvəˈsəʊ), *v.* [In OE. *ofersáwan*, f. *ofer-*, OVER- + SOW *v.*; cf. OS. *obarsâian*, OHG. *ubarsâen*, all repr. late L. *superseminâre* (Vulg.).]

1. *trans.* To sow (seed) over other seed, or a crop, previously sown. [OVER- 1, 8.]

c **975** *Rushw. Gosp.* Matt. xiii. 25 Cuom feond his and ofer-seow weod [*superseminauit zizania*] in midle þæs hwætes. **1565** W. ALLEN in Fulke *Confut. Purg.* (1577) 409 It was long after ouersowen. **1582** N.T. (Rhem.) *Matt.* xiii. 25 His enemy came and oversowed cockle among the wheate. **1610** BOYS *Wks.* (1629) 182 In Heaven Lucifer over-sowed Pride. .. In Paradise Satan over-sowed disobedience. **1887** T. W. ALLIES *Throne Fisherman* 487 Enemies, who while men sleep, oversow tares upon that good seed.

2. To sow (ground) *with* seed in addition to some already sown. [OVER- 8, 20.]

c **1000** *Ags. Gosp.* Matt. xiii. 25 þa com his feonda sum and ofer-seow hit mid coccele on middan þam hwæte. **1616** T. ADAMS *Soul's Sickness* Wks. 1861 I. 480 Whilst he sleeps, the enemy over-sows the field of his heart with tares. **1882** G. F. PENTECOST *Out of Egypt* viii. 195 The Devil .. came by night and oversowed the field with tares.

3. To scatter seed over, to sow *with* seed. Also *fig.* in *pa. pple.*: Strewn over *with* something, bestrewn, besprinkled, spotted (F. *parsemé*). [OVER- 8.]

a **1618** SYLVESTER *Panaretus* 125 An Azure Scarf, all over-sow'n With Crowned Swords. **1648–60** HEXHAM, *Een Overzaeyt, ofte Gortigh vercken*, an Oversowne or a Mealzed Hogge. **1891** G. F. X. GRIFFITH tr. *Fouard's Christ* I. 303 He likened it to a land which, being once oversown, 'produces its fruit of itself'.

4. To sow too much of (seed); to sow too much seed upon (land). [OVER- 27.]

1890 *Cent. Dict.* s.v., To oversow one's wheat.

overspan (əʊvəˈspæn), *v.* [OVER- 10, 22.]

1. *trans.* To extend above and across (something else) from side to side, as a bridge or the like; to span; in quot. 1513, to cross over.

1513 DOUGLAS *Æneis* III. iii. 19 Wnder thy gard to schip we ws addres Ourspannand [*permensi*] mony swelland seis salt. **1854** OWEN in *Circ. Sc.* (*c* 1865) II. 87/2 They overspan and protect .. the .. blood-vessels. **1884** *Expositor* Feb. 100 The heavenly arch that overspans the earth.

†**2.** To exceed in width of span. (In quot. *fig.*)

1649 G. DANIEL *Trinarch., Rich. II*, cccxvi, Mighty Cæsar: Hee who overspan'd All Souldiers in his conduct.

†**3.** To span (a space) with an arch or crossing structure, to 'throw' (an arch, bridge, etc.) over a space. Also *absol.*, in *spec.* use: see quot. *Obs.*

1703 T.N. *City & C. Purchaser* 49 Before it is closed up at the top, it is almost filled with Wood.., and then they over-span the Arch. *Ibid.* 109 The Place to receive the Fuel .. being over-span'd like an Arch. *Ibid.*, Instead of Arching, they *truss-over*, or *over-span*, as they phrase it, *i.e.* they lay the end of one Brick about half way over the end of another, and so, till both sides meet within half a Bricks length, and then a bonding Brick at the top finishes the Arch. *c* **1817** FUSELI in *Lect. Paint.* xi. (1848) 541 Michelangelo, .. by the perpetual use of a convex line, over-spanned the forms.

over-spangle: see OVER-.

ˌover-ˈsparred (-ˈspɑːd), *a.* [f. OVER- 28 d + SPAR *sb.* + -ED².] Of a ship: Having too many or too heavy spars (masts, yards, etc.), so as to be top-heavy. Hence *fig.* (*Naut. slang*), unsteady.

1871 *Echo* 18 Jan., They say that our ships draw too much water, are over-sparred. **1890** CLARK RUSSELL *Ocean Trag.* I. i. 8 He could have carried a whole bottle .. without exhibiting himself as in the least degree oversparred.

over-spatter, etc.: see OVER-.

overspeak (ˌəʊvəˈspiːk), *v.* Now *rare.* [OVER- 27, 22.]

1. †**a.** *trans.* To speak of, or proclaim, too strongly; to overstate, exaggerate. *Obs.*

1628 BP. HALL *Old Relig.* (1686) Ded., If fame do not over-speak you there are not many soils that yield either so frequent flocks or better fed. **1681** R. FLEMING *Fulfill. Scripture* (1801) II. ii. 16 A truth which none can overspeak, Yea where no possible hyperbole can ever be.

b. *intr.* To speak too strongly; to speak extravagantly, exaggerate. Also *refl.* in same sense.

a **1656** HALES *Gold. Rem.* (1673) 229 [He] extremely over-worded, and over-spake himself in his expression of it. *a* **1661** FULLER *Worthies, Hants.* (1662) 5 Seing ill usage .. may make a Sober man Overspeak in his passion.

2. *trans.* To surpass or outdo in speaking.

1826 SYD. SMITH *Wks.* (1859) II. 97/1 Mr. Jackson strives to out-paint Sir Thomas; Sir Thomas Lethbridge to over-speak Mr. Canning.

So ˈ**overˈspeaking** *vbl. sb.*, too much speaking; exaggeration; ˈ**overˈspeaking** *ppl. a.*, that speaks too much.

1609 OVERBURY *State of France* (1626) 28 In their Conuersation, the Custome [of] shifting, and ouerspeaking, hath quite ouercome the shame of it. *a* **1610** HEALEY *Theophrastus* (1636) 28 Of Loquacitie or Over-speaking. **1612** BACON *Ess., Judicature* (Arb.) 454 An ouerspeaking Iudge is no well tuned Cymball.

ˌover-specialiˈzation. [OVER- 29 b.] Too much specialization, esp. in education or evolution.

1931 J. S. HUXLEY *What dare I Think?* iv. 144 Over-specialization produces .. individuals with scientific hypertrophy and religious atrophy. **1936** *Discovery* Oct. 328/2 The author emphasises the importance of correlation between laboratory and clinical observation and deplores the over-specialisation which has gradually crept in and checked many valuable conclusions in medical science. **1957** *Technology* Mar. 3/4 The evils of over-specialization at school are never easily wiped out. **1958** *Spectator* 22 Aug. 258/2 Two extant species [of elephant] alone survive from 352 branches. Mr. Carrington suggests that the elephant declined more from this over-specialization than from unscrupulous Romans or Asiatics. **1974** tr. *Wertheim's Evolution & Revolution* i. 75 As soon as the dead end produced by over-specialization is reached, only a forceful .. breakthrough can produce a reversal of the involutionary trends.

ˌover-ˈspecialize, *v.* [OVER- 27.] *intr.* To specialize too much (in a particular endeavour). So **ˌover-ˈspecialized** *ppl. a.*

1926 J. S. HUXLEY *Ess. Pop. Sci.* p. vi, Science herself is over-specialised. **1930** G. R. DE BEER *Embryol. & Evolution* xiii. 95 If a race has become excessively over-specialized, even the younger stages of the ontogenies of its individuals may have lost their plasticity. **1944** J. S. HUXLEY *On Living in Revolution* xv. 184 To overwork and over-specialize. **1953** N. TINBERGEN *Herring Gull's World* ii. 5 They [*sc.* gulls] are not over-specialised gliding fliers like the shearwaters. **1960** *Farmer & Stockbreeder* 16 Feb. (Suppl.) 8/2 The emphasis must be changed from the over-specialized Wiltshire baconer.

ˌover-ˈspecify, *v.* [OVER- 27.] *trans.* To specify too narrowly; to limit excessively in scope; to specify in excessive detail. So **ˌoverspeˈcific** *a.*; **ˌoverspecifiˈcation.**

1957 R. K. MERTON *Social Theory* (rev. ed.) x. 389 The practical problem had been overspecified in its initial formulation. *Ibid.*, This overspecification for a time diverted our attention from salient alternatives of investigation. **1962** U. WEINREICH in Householder & Saporta *Probl. Lexicogr.* 32 A definition like *triangle* 'a figure that has three sides and three angles, the sum of which is 180°' is avoided as overspecific, since *triangle* is sufficiently defined by the number of sides. **1965** *Language* XLI. 234 Using it .. might risk being overspecific in this instance, but this is preferable to a less unified system of description in which several concepts are used with less general application. **1968** M. S. LIVINGSTON *Particle Physics* ix. 167 The relationships between isotopic spin, multiplicity of charge states, .. and baryon number for hadrons are overspecified. **1975** N. CHOMSKY *Logical Struct. Linguistic Theory* vii. 200 It is at once clear that the grammar 26 provides an overspecification since the following simpler grammar corresponds to 26.

over-speculate: see OVER-.

ˈ**over-speech.** [OVER- 29 b.] Loquacity; indiscretion.

1865 SWINBURNE *Atalanta* 1200 Keep ye on earth Your lips from over-speech. **1920** E. POUND *Umbra* 115 Arnaut loves, and ne'er will fret Love with o'er-speech. **1922** E. R. EDDISON *Worm Ouroboros* iv. 48 'Keep thou thy lips from overspeech,' said the King. 'These be mysteries whereon but to think may snatch thee into peril.'

ˈ**overspeed,** *sb.* [OVER- 29 b.] (An instance of) overspeeding.

1914 H. PENDER *Amer. Handbk. Electr. Engineers* 1315 Over-Speeds.—All types of rotating machines shall be so constructed that they will safely withstand an over-speed of 25 per cent. **1926** J. KIRSOPP *Use of Power in Colliery Working* ii. 156 The entire device prevents overspeed of any description. **1950** *Sun* (Baltimore) 12 Apr. 32/1 The plane, flying at a speed of 135 miles per hour, developed 'a structural failure due to overspeed'. **1969** *Power System Protection* (Electr. Council) II. ix. 250 The governing system which requires an actual overspeed to produce a response and take corrective action.

overˈspeed, *v.* [OVER- 27.] *intr.* To drive or operate faster than is permitted or allowed for. So **overˈspeeding** *ppl. a.* and *vbl. sb.*

1906 *Westm. Gaz.* 24 Apr. 4/2 The police had been .. engaged elsewhere to look out for over-speeding drivers. **1913** *Collier's* 11 Jan. II. 50/2 There were but three convictions for overspeeding. **1950** W. W. LEWIS *Protection Transmission Syst. against Lightning* xi. 367 It is believed that generator overspeeding and loss of load as single factors without solid faults will seldom give rise to dangerous overvoltages. **1971** M. TAK *Truck Talk* 114 *Overspeed*, to run an engine at an excessive number of revolutions per minute for the gear being used. **1972** *Lebende Sprachen* XVII. 134/2 A turbine undergoing tests at Calder Hall 'B' atomic power-station in Cumberland overspeeded last night and exploded. **1974** [see OVERHEAT *v.* 2].

overspend (ˌəʊvəˈspɛnd), *v.* [OVER- 17, 13, 26, 23.]

1. a. *trans.* To 'spend' or use till no longer fit for service; to exhaust, wear out. Usually in *pa. pple.* **overspent**: Completely 'spent', worn out; exhausted with fatigue, tired out. *arch.*

a **1618** RALEIGH *Royal Navy* 27 They make their Ocum .. of old seere and weather-beaten ropes, when they are over-spent and growne .. rotten. **1636** DEKKER *Wonder of Kingd.* Wks. 1873 IV. 239 Now I see th'art too farre gone, this lady hath overspent thee. **1697** DRYDEN *Virg. Past.* II. 10 Harvest Hinds o'erspent with Toil and Heat. **1877** L. MORRIS *Epic Hades* II. 110 Where ofttimes overspent I lay upon the grass.

b. In reference to the force of a storm, life, time: (in *pa. pple.*) Spent, at an end.

1826 E. IRVING *Babylon* II. VI. 100 Till this last storm of the terrible ones being overspent [etc.]. **1839** BAILEY *Festus* (1848) 6/2 When this vain life o'erspent Earth may some purer beings' presence bear. **1951** L. MACNEICE tr. *Goethe's Faust* 39 He backs away, gives way, the day is overspent.

2. a. To spend more than (a specified amount); to exceed in expenditure.

1667 PEPYS *Diary* 10 Apr., It is plain that we do overspend our revenue. **1895** *Daily News* 26 Apr. 2/4 At present they were over-spending their income of 60,000*l.* by 9,000*l.* a year.

b. To spend in excess or beyond what is necessary.

1857 GEN. P. THOMPSON *Audi Alt.* I. xxiv. 89 The principal argument .. that what one man over-spends, some other must gain;—in short the old argument in favour of luxury.

c. *refl.* and *intr.* To spend beyond one's means.

1890 *Spectator* 7 June, Although Italy has not overspent herself like France. **1946** L. P. HARTLEY *Sixth Heaven* v. 107, I doubt if it's even wise to offer to pay half... You mustn't overspend yourself. **1953** E. SIMON *Past Masters* III. 159 From the outset [you] overspent... The money has all gone on inessentials. **1959** M. SUMMERTON *Small Wilderness* xiii. 159 Money? Overspent yourselves in this place?

Hence **overˈspending** *vbl. sb.* (in sense 2 of the vb.); **overˈspent** (†**overspended**) *ppl. a.*

a **1586** SIDNEY *Arcadia* (1622) 241 Such whom any discontentment made hungrie of change, or an ouer-spended want, made want a ciuill warre. **1760–72** H. BROOKE *Fool of Qual.* (1809) I. 66 Slowly leading their over-spent horses. **1932** *Ann. Reg. 1931* 300 The country [*sc.* the U.S.A.] regrets the over-spending of the past few years. **1963** *Times* 9 Jan. 9/2 They cover underspending less comprehensively than overspending, and without knowledge of both it is impossible to make an accurate interim assessment of trends in Government expenditure. **1976** *Times* 20 Oct. 14/3 The borrowing requirement (a euphemism for government overspending).

ˈ**overspill,** *sb.* [OVER- 5.] **a.** That which is spilt over or overflows; usually *fig.*, esp. of surplus population leaving a country. Now usu. the movement of surplus population from a city to a less heavily populated area of the same country; this surplus population or the housing or new area occupied by it. Also *transf.*

1884 *Pall Mall G.* 8 Nov. 12/1 A colony capable of receiving the overspill of her population, or of furnishing her with all tropical produce. **1892** BARING-GOULD *Trag. Caesars* I. 206 In the middle ages the overspill of the men became mercenaries to foreign courts. **1899** *Edin. Rev.* Oct. 289 This stream is an overspill from the main river. **1930** *Times* 22 Apr. 6/7 On the south lie the famous South Downs, within range of the overspill from the seaside towns. **1940** J. BUCHAN *Memory Hold-the-Door* vi. 145 Emigration undertaken as a reasoned policy .. and not as a mere overspill of population. **1944** *Daily Tel.* 12 July 4/4 When one member objected to Mr. Morrison's use in connection with population of the word 'overspill', the Minister admitted that it was ugly, though convenient. **1946** *Nature* 13 July 39/1 Public interest has been stimulated equally by the controversies over the proposals for dealing with Manchester's overspill in a new town at Mobberley, or the even larger overspill problem of Liverpool. **1947** *Daily Mail* 22 May 1/1 We are apt to be too much concerned with the new satellites and 'overspills'. We should first reconstruct the other cities. **1955** *Times* 12 May 15/2 Since 1951 Socialist power there has been improved by an overspill of families of men and women who work in the factories and machine shops of Swindon. **1958** *Times* 3 Oct. 14/5 Although an overspill has been necessary to accommodate them all comfortably .. most of the paintings look very handsome. **1959** *Economist* 3 July 42/1 Diversification may thus proceed from an overspill of strength in one department or another. **1965** A. GARNER *Elidor* xv. 111 'That's what you must expect when you have overspill in a decent area,' said Mrs. Watson. 'They shouldn't be allowed to build out in the country. People aren't going to change when they move from the city.' **1972** F. WARNER *Lying Figures* II. 15 Epigyne is lit by the overspill from the two spots. **1972** *Times* 21 Dec. 4/4 *Overspill*, the planned movement of people who do not want to go to towns that do not want to have them. **1976** 'D. HALLIDAY' *Dolly & Nanny Bird* xvi. 212 The next wave .. struck us .. and the two men huddled on the floor of the cockpit received the first overspill .. from the lee side.

b. *attrib.*

1945 *Ann. Reg. 1944* 63 The Bill for the purchase of so-called 'overspill' areas where those who were crowded out could be accommodated. **1946** [see sense a above]. **1952** *Economist* 21 June 799/2 No less than 28 of these [district councils] are intended under the plan to absorb 'overspill' population coming from Wolverhampton, Walsall, .. and other congested towns... Over a quarter of the new houses .. would form part of 'overspill' schemes. **1958** *Spectator* 30 May 710/1 Recent 'overspill' housing policies. **1966** *New Statesman* 28 Jan. 140/2 Nor are we likely to get any transitional or 'overspill' benefit because of the restrictive provisos. **1972** *Guardian* 8 Sept. 6/5 Official overspill schemes and the movement to the suburbs .. account for only half the population drift: the rest are leaving the country. **1975** COX & BOYSON *Black Paper 1975* 30/1 The school is built on the edge of a city overspill estate. *Ibid.* 31/2 There will be difficulties in any overspill area where people are moved away from family and familiar surroundings. **1976** T. STOPPARD *Dirty Linen* 9 An overspill meeting room for House of Commons business in the tower of Big Ben.

overˈspill, *v.* [OVER- 5.] *trans.* To spill over the edge of the containing vessel. Also, to cause (something) to spill over; *spec.* to remove (surplus population) from a city. Also *intr.*, to spill over; to overflow. Hence **overˈspilling** *ppl. a.*

1855 BAILEY *Mystic* 7 Ere earth Like the libation of a crowned bowl, O'erspilled the depths of the unknown abyss. **1887** G. L. TAYLOR *Centennial Poem* 13 Apr., Her Newton, born a quart cup not o'erspilling. **1958** *Times Rev. Industry* Feb. 24/1 Some 70,000 people are to be 'overspilled' from Glasgow City .. into the new towns of East Kilbride and Cumbernauld. **1961** *Times Lit. Suppl.* 27 Jan. 51/2 We overspill our savings .. onto the backward nations. **1962** *Times* 7 Mar. 11/4 The process of being over-spilled in a familiar country-side .. is bound to be at least slightly deterrent to the true Cockney. **1963** *Listener* 21 Mar. 516/1

The need to re-house ever more overspilling Londoners. **1970** G. F. NEWMAN *Sir, You Bastard* vii. 196 The eighteen prisoners who finally stood charged over-spilled the dock at the committal proceedings. **1972** *Accountant* 28 Sept. 392/2 It is an illusion..for internal auditors to think that, by overspilling into management functions and systems design, they will enhance the status..of their profession. **1977** *Daily Tel.* 14 Feb. 6/7, 30,000 homes were bulldozed inside 10 years and the occupants 'overspilled' beyond the city boundaries in the new or expanded towns of Runcorn, Skelmersdale, [etc.].

over'spin, *v. rare.* [OVER- 18.] †**1.** *trans.* To spin out, protract too much. *Obs.*

1643 CARTWRIGHT *On Death Sir B. Grenvill* 34 Things were prepar'd, debated, and then done, Not rashly broke, or vainly overspun.

2. To confuse (an opponent) with overspin (see next).

1940 G. MARX *Let.* 5 Sept. (1967) 25 He's a left-hander and slashes and cuts and overspins his opponent dizzy.

'overspin, *sb.* [OVER- 6.] In *Cricket* and other ball games: a rotating motion imparted to a ball in which the upper part turns in the direction of flight, or is struck with upward inclination. Also (in full *overspin ball*), such a delivery. Now usu. called *topspin*. So **'over,spinner**, a ball delivered with overspin.

1904 F. C. HOLLAND *Cricket* 54 The over spin gives to the ball the same over-and-over motion that is seen in a ball that has been topped at golf or billiards. **1908** A. W. MYERS *Compl. Lawn Tennis Player* 109 A strong forward or over-spin is thus imparted to the ball. **1925** *Country Life* 18 July 93/1 The over-spin ball is the logical outcome of the googlie, inasmuch as..the hand turns over more than in the leg-break, but not so much as in the googlie. **1927** M. A. NOBLE *Those 'Ashes'* 178 Hendren was bowled by a faster overspin, which he mistook for a leg break. **1930** C. V. GRIMMETT *Getting Wickets* iii. 57 It would..have what is called 'overspin', and, after striking the pitch, gather pace as the spin took effect. *Ibid.* 60 An overspinner will be produced if the back of the hand is outwards, and the hand pointing horizontally to the demonstrator's left. **1961** F. C. AVIS *Sportsman's Gloss.* 130/1 *Overspin*, a forward rotating movement of the ball in flight, causing an acceleration off the pitch. *Ibid.* 259/1 (Lawn Tennis), *Overspin*, top spin imparted to the ball, to give power and unexpected movement off the court. **1970** H. TAYLOR *Golf Dict.* 150 *Overspin*, a word sometimes used for topspin.

overspire to **oversplit**: see OVER-.

'overspray. [OVER- 19.] Sprayed liquid that does not adhere to the object or area being sprayed.

1948 L. W. LAMMIMAN in W. von Fischer *Paint & Varnish Technol.* xxvi. 453 Arcing the gun on a surface causes overspray to bounce obliquely off the surface. **1955** EDWARDS & WRAY *Aluminium Paint & Powder* (ed. 3) iv. 95 The amount of paint sprayed is greatly reduced as most of the overspray is eliminated. **1972** *Materials & Technol.* V. xi. 371 Spraying is normally carried out in spraybooths.. and overspray is removed by an efficient exhaust system. **1977** *Hot Car* Oct. 50/4 For a single pin stripe you must of course mask either side of the tapes to stop overspray going on to the base colour.

overspread (əʊvə'sprɛd), *v.* [OE. *ofersprǣdan*, f. *ofer-*, OVER- 8, 9; in MHG. *überspreiten.*]

1. *trans.* To spread (something) over or upon something else; to diffuse over a place or region.

c **961** *Rule St. Benet* liii. (Schröer 1885) 84 Beon þær symble bedd ʒenihtsumlice ofersprædde. *c* **1375** *Cursor M.* 5486 (Fairf.) Þe ospring þat of Ioseph bred was mykil in lande ouerspred. **1567** *Gude & Godlie B.* (S.T.S.) 173 This nycht I call Idolatrie, The clude ouerspred, Hypocresie.

2. To spread something over (something else); to cover *with* something spread upon the surface.

c **1386** CHAUCER *Knt.'s T.* 2013 After this, Theseus hath ysent After a beere, and it al ouer spradde With clooth of gold. **1608** SHAKS. *Per.* I. ii. 24 With hostile forces he'll o'erspread the land. **1860** HAWTHORNE *Marb. Faun* (1878) II. ix. 104 Dealers had..overspread them with scanty awnings. **1879** BROWNING *Ivàn Ivànovitch* 222.

b. in *passive* with *with* (the subject being left indeterminate).

c **1275** LAY. 19045 Was þat kineworþe bed Al mid palle ouer sprad. *c* **1375** *Sc. Leg. Saints* vii. (*Jacobus minor*) 813 Al þe feld, þat wes our-sprad With fare quhyte dew a-bout þat sted. **1563** *Mirr. Mag., Buckingham* vi, Northampton fyeld with armed men orespred. **1647** MAY *Hist. Parl.* III. iii. 55 The whole Kingdome..was now overspread with a generall Warre. **1748** *Anson's Voy.* II. xii. 261 High mountains overspread with trees. **1870** BRYANT *Iliad* I. II. 70 Pyrasus Sacred to Ceres and o'erspread with flowers.

3. Of a thing: To spread or extend over (something else); to diffuse itself over; to cover completely. *lit.* and *fig.*

c **1205** LAY. 14188 Swa muchel lond..Swa wule anes bule hude ælches weies ouer-spræden. **1297** R. GLOUC. (Rolls) 7803 He wende him in to france, & þe contreie ouer spradde, & robbede & destruede. *c* **1330** *Assump. Virg.* 864 (B.M. MS.) A lyʒt cloude..ouer-sprad hem euery man. **1426** LYDG. *De Guil. Pilgr.* 14555 My mantel overspredeth al. **1594** T. B. *La Primaud. Fr. Acad.* II. 9 Being heires of that corruption that hath ouerspread the whole nature of man. **1697** DRYDEN *Virg. Georg.* II. 254 Here wild Olive-shoots o'erspread the Ground. **1748** SMOLLETT *Rod. Rand.* xvii. (1804) 99 You Scotchmen have overspread us..as the locusts did Egypt. **1863** GEO. ELIOT *Romola* vi, A pink flush over-spread her face.

absol. **1651** C. CARTWRIGHT *Cert. Relig.* To Rdr., Surely, if Popery overspread againe, barbarism and illiterateness is a most likely means to effect it.

Hence **over'spreading** *vbl. sb.*, the action of spreading over; *ppl. a.* that spreads over. Also **'overspread** *sb.*, the fact of spreading over; *concr.* that which is spread over.

1563 MAN *Musculus' Commonpl.* 16b, The beginning of sinne, and the ouerspreading of it abrode. **1610** WILLET *Hexapla Dan.* 64 In the bedchamber there was an ouerspreading vine made of gold. **1627** SANDERSON *Serm.* I. 265 Those general truths, which by the mercy of God were preserved amid the foulest overspreadings of popery. **1826** R. HALL *Wks.* VI. 34 The overspreading of thick darkness. **1866** *Reader* 31 Mar. 331 The main contour of surface..was acquired prior to the overspread of the glacial series.

over'spring, *v.* [OVER- 1, 5: cf. OHG. *ubarspringan*, MHG. & Ger. *überspringen.*] *trans.* To spring or leap over; *fig.* to surmount.

c **1386** CHAUCER *Frankl. T.* 332 That fyue fadme at the leeste it ouersprynge The hyeste Rokke. **1801** W. TAYLOR in *Monthly Mag.* XII. 583 An Arabian wildness of fancy,.. which seldom shakes off the costume, or oversprings the range of Arabian idea. **1847** EMERSON *Poems, Hafiz* Wks. (Bohn) I. 479 Bring wine, that I overspring Both worlds at a single leap.

over'sprinkle, *v.* [OVER- 8.] *trans.* To sprinkle over, besprinkle.

1563 *Homilies* II. *Rebellion* VI. (1859) 593 So is there no country..which..hath not been oversprinkled with the blood of subjects. *c* **1576** GASCOIGNE *Devyll's Will*, Item I geve to the Butchers new freshe blood to ouersprinkle their stale mete that it may seme..newly kylled. *a* **1849** POE *Bells* Poems (1859) 73 The stars that oversprinkle All the heavens.

over-'sprung, *ppl. a.* [OVER- 27 b.] Fitted with too many or too flexible springs.

1923 *Daily Mail* 12 July 12 The saddle for my weight was over-sprung, and over pot-holes was inclined to bounce on to the frame. **1937** *Daily Herald* 16 Apr. 18/2, I have no very high opinion of the rather flashy high-powered over-sprung American car. **1962** L. DEIGHTON *Ipcress File* xxi. 146, I.. pulled the big oversprung Lincoln Continental on to the road.

†**over'spurn** *v. Obs. rare.* [OVER- 6.] *trans.* To kick over, overturn with the foot.

c **1495** *Epitaffe* etc. in *Skelton's Wks.* (1843) II. 392 Caused to surrendre Lyfe vp to Deth that al ouerspurneth.

oversquare (stress variable), *a.* [OVER- 28.] Of an internal-combustion engine or its cylinders: having a bore greater than the stroke.

1959 *Times* 23 Sept. 5/4 The new engine is 'over-square' and has a cubic capacity of 6¼ litres. **1966** *Economist* 9 July p. xxv/1, If exaggerated, the over-square cylinder tends to have a wafer-thin combustion chamber with limited compression turbulence, and to suffer from indifferent combustion at low operating speeds. **1967** *Ibid.* 8 July p. xxix/1, Hauliers also fear wear on the fast (up to 3,300 rpm) V-engines: these are often oversquare, with neat chunky cylinders. **1971** *Motor* 16 June 26/1 The new 1971 cc engine in the 504 is a four-cylinder in-line oversquare unit.

oversqueak, -squeamish: see OVER-.

†**over'stad,** *pa. pple. Obs.* [f. OVER- 21 + *stad*, later STED, placed: cf. BESTED *pa. pple.* sense 4.] Overset, overwhelmed.

c **1330** R. BRUNNE *Chron. Wace* (Rolls) 12770 Anoþer strok he scholde haue had, But wiþ þe Romayns þey were ouerstad.

overstaff: see OVER-.

over-'stain, *v.* [OVER- 8, 27.]

1. *trans.* To cover with a stain or stains.

1595 SHAKS. *John* III. i. 236 Our hands..besmear'd and ouer-staind With slaughters pencill.

2. *Biol.* To stain (tissue) excessively, usu. in order that certain parts may be differentiated by selective removal of some of the stain; also *absol.*

1885 C. O. WHITMAN *Methods of Research in Microsc. Anat.* ii. 39 If by any chance the sections are over-stained, the superfluous color may be extracted by a brief sojourn in very dilute ammonia. *Ibid.* 48 Diffuse staining may generally be avoided by first overstaining and then withdrawing the color to any desired extent by means of alcohol. **1935** KINGSBURY & JOHANNSEN *Histol. Technique* 38 In regressive staining the tissue is over-stained and the excess of stain removed by the application of a differentiator. *Ibid.* 40 The rule is to over-stain and watch the differentiation carefully with the microscope. **1971** A. LAMELA *Introd. Med. Lab. Methods* xxiii. 238 The tissue is over-stained and then decolorized until the correct depth of color is obtained.

Hence **over-'staining** *vbl. sb.*

1885 C. O. WHITMAN *Methods of Research in Microsc. Anat.* ii. 42 Minot's picric-acid carmine..gives a stronger differential coloring than Ranvier's picro-carmine; but over-staining must be most carefully avoided. **1929** C. E. MCCLUNG *Handbk. Microsc. Technique* i. 23 Regressive stains..are allowed to act until overstaining is accomplished, after which the desired degree of differentiation is brought about by removal of the excess coloration.

over-stalled: see OVER-.

over'stand, *v.* [OVER- 1, 17: cf. MHG. *überstân*, Ger. *überstehen.*]

1. *trans.* To stand over; to stand beside.

c **1330** *Amis & Amil.* 1986 Y bad him fain Forsake the lazer in the wain, That he so ouerstode [cf. 1970 ouer him stode a naked swain]. **1888** G. M. HOPKINS *Poems* (1967) 198 Fairyland; silkbeech, scrolled ash, packed sycamore, wild wychelm, hornbeam fretty overstood By. **1938** *Venerabile* Oct. 61 The lofty roof o'erstands the graceful shrine.

†**2.** To stand, endure, or stay to the end of; to get through; to outstay, overstay. *Obs.*

1600 ABP. ABBOT *Exp. Jonah* 168 If they can over-stand that journey and escape well from danger. **1666** BUNYAN *Grace Ab.* ¶66 How, if you have overstood the time of mercy? **1784** J. POTTER *Virtuous Villagers* I. 51 She was too nice and particular..and so overstood her market.

3. To pass over; to cross.

1949 *Sun* (Baltimore) 27 Aug. 8/8 But Colie outguessed him, for while Reckord was watching the Jersey boat, he overstood the mark. Colie whipped about and Scanty was second before the Baltimore sailor realized what had happened. **1976** *Yachts & Yachting* 20 Aug. 372/1 Colin Evans overstood the line, thus losing the much-disputed 3rd place to Geoff Tindale.

4. *to be overstanding for honours*: in the University of Oxford, to be incapable of obtaining honours in an examination because of the lapse of more than the permitted number of terms (normally twelve) since matriculation.

The phrase 'disqualified for Honours by standing' is preferred in the O.U. *Examination Decrees and Regulations.*

1933 V. BRITTAIN *Testament of Youth* III. x. 476 They had undertaken, since I was so excessively 'over-standing' for Honours, a special procedure on my behalf. **1965** N. COGHILL in J. Gibb *Light on C. S. Lewis* 52 Had we taken two [years] we would have been overstanding for Honours.

†**over'start,** *v. Obs. rare.* [OVER- 5.] *trans.* To overleap, miss, 'skip', omit.

c **1420** LYDG. *Assembly of Gods* 1593 Som of the felyshyp that I there say, In all thys whyle, haue I ouerstert.

overstate (,əʊvə'steɪt), *v.* [f. OVER- 27, 26 + STATE *sb.* and *v.*]

†**1.** *to over-state it*: to assume too great 'state' or stateliness; to play the grandee to excess. *Obs.*

1639 FULLER *Holy War* IV. xix. (1647) 202 Or else that they should over-state it, turn Tyrants, and only exchange their slavery by becoming vassals to their own passions.

2. *trans.* To state too strongly; to exceed the limits of fact in stating; to exaggerate.

1803 W. TAYLOR in *Ann. Rev.* I. 397/2 If Sir Francis Burdett has overstated the misgovernment of a prison, appropriated for the seditious, he [etc.]. **1837** SYD. SMITH *Let. Archd. Singleton* Wks. 1859 II. 279/2, I hate to overstate my case. **1873** SYMONDS *Grk. Poets* x. 324 To say that the Greeks had no conceits, is perhaps overstated.

overstatement ('əʊvə,steɪtmənt). [OVER- 29 b.] The action, or an act, of overstating; statement which exceeds the limits of fact; exaggeration.

1803 W. TAYLOR in *Ann. Rev.* I. 397/2 It does not appear that his account was an overstatement at the time. **1848** MILL *Pol. Econ.* I. 168 This..is one of those over-statements of a true principle, often met with in Adam Smith. **1874** GLADSTONE in *Contemp. Rev.* Oct. 673 In commenting on over-statement I do not seek to understate.

overstay (əʊvə'steɪ), *v.* [OVER- 18.] *trans.* To stay over or beyond (in time).

1646 BP. HALL *Satan's Fiery Darts quenched* I. vi, Now that he onely over-stayes the time of our misgrounded expectation. **1668** *Ormonde MSS.* in *10th Rep. Hist. MSS. Comm.* App. v. 71 Overstayed leave [of absence], caused by illness. **1858** MRS. CARLYLE *Lett.* II. 369 Fear of over-staying one's welcome. **1862** B. TAYLOR *Home & Abroad* Ser. II. II. x. 194 We had already overstayed by a fortnight the time which we had allotted to our visit.

overstayed (,əʊvə'steɪd), *a. Naut.* [OVER- 28.] Too heavily stayed; having the stays too rigid.

1880 *Times* 25 Dec. 7/4 Ship's efficiency not what my recollection of such a ship should be; masts overstayed.

'overstayer. *N.Z. colloq.* [f. OVERSTAY *v.* + -ER[1].] A Polynesian or other immigrant who stays beyond the time permitted by a work permit.

1977 *N.Z. Herald* 5 Jan. 1-4/4 While expressing sympathy for the plight of overstayers, the Maori leader said the laws of the nation had to apply to everyone, regardless of race. **1977** *N.Z. Woman's Weekly* 10 Jan. 38/4 We have heard so much lately about the overstayers and while agreeing wholeheartedly that the law must be held in regard and obeyed, I have been wondering if we realize just how much we depend on some of these Island people. **1978** *Guardian Weekly* 22 Jan. 9/2 In October, 1975, the Auckland police suddenly cracked down on 'overstayers'—those Pacific Islanders who had stayed beyond the length of their work permits.

†**over'stays,** *adv. phr. Obs.* [f. OVER *prep.* + STAY *sb.*: cf. OVER- 31.] Over to the other tack: in quots. *fig.*

1637 GILLESPIE *Eng. Pop. Cerem.* II. iii. 17 Are their mindes so aliened from us? and must we be altogither drawne overstayes to them? *Ibid.* vii. 27 When they had both spoken and disputed against them; what drew them overstayes to contend for them?

over-steadfast, -steady: see OVER-.

over'steepened, *ppl. a. Physical Geogr.* [OVER- 22.] Steepened further; *esp.* (of a valley) having a greater steepness than running water would have caused owing to the predominantly downward erosive action of a glacier. So **over'steepening** *vbl. sb.*

1900 W. M. DAVIS in *Proc. Boston Soc. Nat. Hist.* XXIX. 308 In the same way, the waterfalls from the hanging valleys, the showering waste that forms the falls, and the landslides from the basal cliffs, all show that the banks of the glacial channel—the lower walls of the existing valleys—are too steep; and they may be therefore called 'oversteepened'. **1922** *Bull. U.S. Geol. Survey* No. 730. 13 In the Black Canyon..the broad floor of the valley and the steep cliffs that rise precipitously 2,000 feet at its side suggest oversteepening of the walls by ice. **1942** O. D. von Engeln *Geomorphol.* xix. 462 That side of a valley reach against which the glacier current impinges is regularly oversteepened. **1964** *Amer. Jrnl. Sci.* CCLXII. 783 Over the bar itself the steepened profile increases velocity and tends to erode the obstruction. This enhancement of erosion in the over-steepened reach and deposition in the flat area will..tend to eliminate the original bar. **1970** R. J. Small *Study of Landforms* iv. 131 Each stream profile displays several apparent knick-points or oversteepened sections coincident with the gorges.

'oversteer, *sb.* [over- 29 b.] A tendency in a motor vehicle to increase the sharpness of the turn when made to deviate from the straight.

1936 *Proc. Inst. Automobile Engin.* XXX. 759 This proportion of the total roll couple carried by the front and rear tyres is found to have a very marked effect on steering, and has to be proportioned by trial to avoid excessive effects in the direction either of 'oversteer' or 'understeer'. **1957** *Which?* Autumn 25/2 Slight oversteer is noticeable if the boot is well loaded, but this is easily compensated by a slight increase of pressure on the rear tyres. **1972** *Sci. Amer.* Aug. 20/2 In a vehicle with oversteer the driver must turn the steering wheel away from the center of the turn as speed increases. **1977** *Hot Car* Oct. 23/2 The average driver can handle understeer more safely than oversteer.

over'steer, *v.* [over- 27.] *intr.* To exhibit oversteer. So **over'steering** *vbl. sb.* and *ppl. a.*

1936 *Proc. Inst. Automobile Engin.* XXX. 730 Parallel-motion rear springing would give excessive over-steering because of the slip angle of the rear tyres. *Ibid.*, Almost every car over-steers to a certain extent. **1948** R. Dean-Averns *Automobile Chassis Design* ii. 49 An oversteering vehicle when negotiating a bend above the certain critical speed of the vehicle for straight running will tend to run into its turn. **1959** *Motor Manual* (ed. 36) v. 147 When the slip angle is greater at the rear, the car oversteers (i.e. turns more sharply than the driver intends). **1962** *Times* 10 Apr. 6/5 Does this Volkswagen oversteer? **1962** *Which? Car Suppl.* Oct. 117/2 The car changed from having a strong understeering characteristic to the opposite oversteering one—that is, the rear wheels tended to turn the car more than the driver wanted. **1971** C. Williams *Car Conversions* ii. 29 An oversteering car..does not slow down appreciably when the steering correction is applied. **1972** S. Abbey *Bk. of Marina* xii. 110 If the rear tyre pressures are too low, the car will 'oversteer'.

overstezing: see oversty *v. Obs.*

over'step, *sb.* [f. the vb.] **1.** An act of overstepping or passing beyond a limit.

1822–34 *Good's Study Med.* (ed. 4) III. 64 This apparent overstep, be it what it may, in the march of insanity beyond that of the population of the country, is a real retrogression.

2. *Geol.* In an unconformity, the structural relationship between the lowest stratum of the upper series and the truncated ends of the underlying strata when, as is often the case, these have a different dip from the upper series (chiefly *British*).

1883 A. J. J. Browne in *Geol. Mag.* Decade II. X. 336 Both cases involve an unconformity, and..the difference between them is really this: in overlap the basement member of the upper series has a limited extension, while in overstep the basement bed has a continuous extension... The unconformity between the two series will generally be much greater in the case of overlap than in the case of overstep, for in the latter the beds all dip in the same direction, and the existence of an unconformity is usually only made patent by the fact of overstep. **1937** *Q. Jrnl. Geol. Soc.* XCIII. 120 In the two marginal parts of the Wealden trough..there is a definite overstep, due to the fact that while the freshwater Wealden beds were being deposited in the central subsiding area the margins of the trough were being gently uptilted. **1948** *Bull. Amer. Assoc. Petroleum Geologists* XXXII. 2297 The word *overstep*..in more than 60 years of existence..has not succeeded in gaining any recognition among American geologists and very little in England. **1969** Bennison & Wright *Geol. Hist. Brit. Isles* i. 10 In the case of any angular unconformity the lowest bed of a series of strata is seen to rest on beds of differing ages. Such a phenomenon is known as overstep, and the post-unconformity bed is said to overstep onto successively older beds.

over'step, *v.* [OE. *ofersteppan*, f. *ofer-* over- 5, 12; = OHG. *ubarstephen*, Du. *overstappen*.]

1. *trans.* To step over or across; to pass beyond or to the other side of (a boundary or thing material or immaterial). Also *intr.* ***to overstep the mark***: see mark *sb.*[1] 12 e; also *ellipt.*

a **1000** *Lamb. Ps.* xvii. 30 (Bosw.) Ic ofersteppe weall [*transgrediar murum*]. **1489** Caxton *Faytes of A.* i. xii. 32 They ouerpresse and ouerstep one ouer that other. **1592** Greene *Philomela* Wks. (Grosart) XI. 126, I will ouerstippe the conceit of mine own folly. **1871** R. Ellis *Catullus* lxxxviii. 7 Infamy none o'ersteps, nor ventures any beyond it. **1875** Bryce *Holy Rom. Emp.* xx. (ed. 5) 363 France..by the annexation of Piedmont, had overstepped the Alps. **1931** W. Faulkner *Sanctuary* xvi. 118, I made a fire in the stove. I guess I over-stepped.

2. *Geol.* Of the upper strata of an unconformity: to extend over (underlying strata) in such a way as to form an overstep. Also *intr.* with *on to*. Chiefly *British*.

1883 J. G. Goodchild in *Geol. Mag.* Decade II. X. 227, I have found it convenient..to speak of this stratigraphical relation of unconformable beds to the various rocks immediately beneath as Overstepping. For example, I should say that the Roman Fell Beds in the neighbourhood of Melmerby overlap the Upper Old Red, while the Carboniferous formation..oversteps the older rocks there. **1937** *Q. Jrnl. Geol. Soc.* XCIII. 107 Some of the older records..seem to suggest that the Gault in East Sussex oversteps the Folkestone Sands within a short distance of their outcrop. **1938** A. K. Wells *Outl. Hist. Geol.* ii. 12 In the diagram section the Cambrian rocks overstep the Pre-Cambrian, and higher divisions overlap lower ones. **1969** [see overstep *sb.* 2]. **1972** *Gloss. Geol.* (Amer. Geol. Inst.) 507/1 An unconformable stratum that truncates the upturned edges of the underlying older rocks is said to 'overstep' each of them in turn (except where the stratum and the underlying beds have the same strike).

So **over'stepping** *vbl. sb.*, *spec.* in *Cricket*, the action of bowling with either foot illegally positioned in relation to the creases.

1869 Mill *Subj. Women* i. 32 An overstepping of the proper bounds of authority. **1959** *Oxford Mail* 2 Feb. 8/7 Rorke..lost a lot of his fearsomeness after being rightly no-balled because of his long drag, called over-stepping in Australia. **1976** J. Snow *Cricket Rebel* 98 Rowan reports remarks I am alleged to have made..after I had been no-balled for overstepping.

overstien, -stihen: see oversty *v. Obs.*

over-stiff, -stifle, etc.: see over-.

,over-'stimulate, *v.* [over- 27.] *trans.* To stimulate too much or excessively; to over-excite. (Chiefly in *pa. pple.*) Also *absol.* So **'over-'stimulated** *ppl. a.*; **'over-stimu'lation.**

1798 Edgeworth *Pract. Educ.* (1822) I. 331 It is the debility of an over-stimulated temper. **1835–6** Todd *Cycl. Anat.* I. 678 Over-stimulation..of the minute vessels of the lungs by the dark blood. **1865** Dickens *Mut. Fr.* ii. xii, Over-stimulated by them feelings which rouses a man up. **1928** A. B. Callow *Food & Health* 24 Condiments..have the effect of stimulating gastric secretion, but..they tend to over-stimulate.

†over'stink, *v. Obs.* [over- 22, 21.] *trans.* To stink more than; to drown the stench of.

1610 Shaks. *Temp.* iv. i. 184, I left them I' th' filthy mantled poole,.. There dancing vp to th' chins, that the fowle Lake Ore-stunck their feet.

overstock ('əʊvəstɒk), *sb.* [over- 8 c, 29 d.]

†1. *pl.* Knee-breeches; cf. *nether-stocks. Obs.*

1565 *Richmond Wills* (Surtees) 177 Item to Samuall Pullayne a pare of black overstocks, cutt in longe paynes. **1573–80** Baret *Alv.* B 1160 Breeches, or mens ouerstockes.

2. A superabundant stock or store; a supply in excess of demand or requirement.

1710 Steele *Tatler* No. 195 ¶ 5 This over-stock of Beauty, for which there are so few Bidders, calls for an immediate Supply of Lovers and Husbands. **1757** *Herald* No. 12 (1758) I. 196 This drain of an overstock of corn can be no other than that of exportation to foreign countries. **1885** Howells *Silas Lapham* (1891) I. 158 There's an overstock in everything, and we've got..to shut down. **1976** *Author* Summer 51 The remainder merchants, who prefer to be called overstock dealers. *Ibid.*, A firm called B.S.C. Remainders—founded 12 years ago as an overstock wholesaler. **1976** *Billings* (Montana) *Gaz.* 18 June 4-B (Advt.), Powell's furniture outlets buy factory overstock.

overstock (,əʊvə'stɒk), *v.* [over- 27.] *trans.* To stock to excess; to supply with more than is required; to fill too full, overcharge, glut.

1649 Blithe *Eng. Improv. Impr.* (1653) Ded., Every man laies on at random, and as many as they can get, and so Overstock the same. **1676** Towerson *Decalogue* 536 Some of those fish, wherewith I find his ponds to be overstockt. **1788** Jefferson *Writ.* (1859) II. 539 In consequence of the English treaty, their oils flowed in, and overstocked the market. **1842** in Bischoff *Woollen Manuf.* II. 382 Every judicious farmer will be careful not to over-stock his land.

Hence **,over'stocked** *ppl. a.*, **-'stocking** *vbl. sb.*

1719 W. Wood *Surv. Trade* 298 The overstocking of a Country with goods may lessen the gain of particular Merchants. **1844** Mill *Ess. Pol. Econ.* ii. 71 An overstocked state of the market is always temporary. **1865** *Sat. Rev.* 5 Aug. 161/1 The treatment which fish bestow on each other in an overstocked pond.

over-stoop: see over-.

'overstorey. [over- 1 d.] = over-wood.

1959 *Ecology* XL. 478 The survival and average total height growth of loblolly pine seedlings in Arkansas were best under overstory openings of 43 feet in diameter and larger. **1962** A. Fry *Ranch on Cariboo* xv. 155 A rolling country where the cattle browsed under an overstorey of open timber. **1976** *Nature* 22 Jan. 207/2 It [*sc.* the cocoa crop] is thus in intimate contact with an overstorey of forest trees and an understorey of ground vegetation.

over-'storied, *pa. pple.* [over- 8.] Covered with stories or historical paintings.

1855 Browning *Cleon* 53 The Pœcile, o'er-storied its whole length..with painting, is mine too.

†'over,story. *Arch. Obs.* [f. over *a.* + story.] An upper story; *spec.* a clerestory.

a **1490** Botoner *Itin.* (Nasmith, 1778) 78 Item in le ovyrhistorie sunt 10 fenestræ. *Ibid.* 82 Et quælibet fenestra in le ovyrstorye continet 5 panellas glaseatas.

overstowed, etc.: see over-.

overstrain ('əʊvəstreɪn), *sb.* [over- 29 b.] Excessive strain; the act of overstraining or fact of being overstrained; *spec.* the condition of having been strained beyond the yield point.

1754 Richardson *Grandison* (1812) VI. 144 (D.) It was such an overstrain of generosity from him that it might well overset him. **1854** H. Miller *Sch. & Schm.* (1858) 5 Such was his state of exhaustion, in consequence of the previous overstrain on every nerve and muscle. **1878** Holbrook *Hyg. Brain* 101 How is the merchant to avoid mental overstrain? **1895** [see fatigue *sb.* 1 d]. **1931** H. J. Tapsell *Creep of Metals* iii. 32 The raising of the yield point at air temperature of mild steel was even more marked if the stress producing the overstrain were continued for a time. **1941** H. Gilkey et al. *Materials Testing* 132 The general nature of cold-working, of whatever sort, is simply overstrain.

overstrain (,əʊvə'streɪn), *v.*

†1. *trans.* To strain, stretch, or extend (something) over or across. *Obs. rare.* [over- 10.]

1575 Laneham *Let.* (1871) 51 Which, with a wire net.. eeuen and tight, waz al ouerstrained.

†2. To go beyond in straining or exertion; to surpass in effort. *Obs. rare.* [over- 22.]

1590 Greene *N. too late* (1600) 18, I haue..sought to ouer-match thy father in pollicie, as he ouerstraines vs in iealousie.

3. To strain too much, subject to excessive strain; to stretch or exert (an organ or faculty) more than it will bear. [over- 27.] **a.** *lit.* or in physical sense; *spec.* to strain (a substance) beyond the yield point.

1589 R. Harvey *Pl. Perc.* (1590) 2 Neuer will I ouerstraine my strength. **1640** Bp. Hall *Chr. Moder.* (ed. Ward) 28/2 He so overstrained his lungs, in calling upon his troops, that he presently died. **1745** *De Foe's Eng. Tradesman* vi. (1841) I. 36 At last..[they] overstrain their sinews..and are cripples ever after. **1873** Hamerton *Intell. Life* i. vii. (1875) 40 You must not sacrifice your eyesight by overstraining it. **1899** J. A. Ewing *Strength of Materials* iii. 40 This operation was carried far enough to overstrain the piece a second time, and curve *D* then shows that a very imperfectly elastic condition has reappeared. **1931** H. J. Tapsell *Creep of Metals* iii. 33 The effect of a period of rest on iron and steel overstrained at air temperature is to produce a recovery of elasticity and an increase in hardness. **1962** R. E. Smallman *Mod. Physical Metall.* vii. 242 If a specimen which has been overstrained to remove the yield point is allowed to rest.., the yield point returns as shown.

b. *fig.*

1633 Bp. Hall *Occas. Medit.* (1851) 148 His justice will not let his mercy be overstrained. **1782** Miss Burney *Cecilia* vii. v, Those scruples..she herself thought might be overstrained. **1863** J. G. Nichols *Herald & Geneal.* I. 497 This argument is greatly overstrained.

c. *absol.* or *intr.*

1703 Collier *Ess. Mor. Subj.* ii. (1709) 76 To endeavour not to Please is Ill-nature; altogether to Neglect it, Folly; and to Over-strain for it, Vanity and Design. *a* **1742** Oldmixon in *Southey's Comm.-pl. Bk.* IV. 261/1 Writers of comedy are very apt to overdo and overstrain, in complacency to the judgment of their audience.

Hence **,over'strained** *ppl. a.* (whence **,over'strainedness**); **,over'straining** *vbl. sb.* and *ppl. a.*

1599 Thynne *Animadv.* (1875) 57 Yt maye, after a harde and ouerstreyned sorte, beare somme sence. **1671** F. Phillips *Reg. Necess.* 417 An overstraining conjecture which is not here endeavoured to be asserted. **1695** Dryden *Observ. Du Fresnoy's Art of Painting* § 54 With overstraining and earnestness of finishing their pieces, they often did them more harm than good. **1839** Bailey *Festus* (1852) 74 That eye which..Beams close upon me till it bursts from sheer O'erstrainedness of sight. **1859** Tennyson *Vivien* 372 As some wild turn of anger, or a mood Of overstrain'd affection. **1895** *Proc. R. Soc.* LVIII. 131 The tendency to creeping is found..to be much reduced in consequence of the hardening and recovery of elasticity which the overstrained material undergoes. **1900** *Phil. Trans. R. Soc.* A. CXCIII. 15 Curve No. 2 illustrates the semi-plastic condition of the material immediately after the removal of the overstraining load. **1931** H. J. Tapsell *Creep of Metals* iii. 32 An overstrained material does not resemble its former state: it is physically a new material. **1962** R. E. Smallman *Mod. Physical Metall.* vii. 242 The absence of a yield point at the beginning of plastic flow is characteristic of a specimen in an overstrained condition. **1962** P. G. Forrest *Fatigue of Metals* vi. 191 The beneficial effect of tensile overstraining on the fatigue strength of a notched bar. **1971** *Afr. Wildlife* XXV. 51/1 During the past few years an increasing number of wild animal species has been found to be prone to the development of a disease complex for which the new name, overstraining disease, is suggested. *Ibid.*, It is characterized by muscular degeneration, paralysis especially of the hind limbs and the passage of dark red-brown urine. The course is variable and affected horses may die from acute heart failure or the accumulation of toxic amounts of excretory products, resulting from kidney damage. Overstraining disease in game..may result from various capturing techniques. **1974** *Nature* 22 Feb. 577/1 Capture myopathy (so-called overstraining disease) in wild animals has gained increasing prominence.

'over-'strait, *a.* [f. over- 28 + strait *a.*]

†a. Too strict or severe. *Obs.* **b.** Too narrow.

1538 Starkey *England* ii. iii. 197 Dethe ys ouer-strayte punnyschment for al such theft pryuely commyttyd. **1561** T. Hoby tr. *Castiglione's Courtyer* iii. (1577) P vij b, Kepte vnder with ouerstreight looking to, or beaten of their husbandes or fathers. **1645** Bp. Hall *Remedy Discontents* 91 For the enlarging of their over-strait lodgings, hard at work.

So **'over-'straitly** *adv.*; **'over-'straitness.** Also **,over-'straiten** *v.*

1571 Golding *Calvin on Ps.* xvii. 1 Some take the woorde overstreightly. **1580** Hollyband *Treas. Fr. Tong, Severité*, crueltie, ouerstraightnesse. **1679** Puller *Moder. Ch. Eng.* (1843) 160 The fourth Commandment doth not bind Christians over-streightly. **1735** *Phil. Trans.* XXXIX. 58

To prevent the Juice, that re-unites the Wound..from overstreightening the Canal.

overstream (əʊvə'striːm), *v.* [OVER- 9.] *trans.* To stream over or across; to flow over in a stream. Hence **over'streaming** *ppl. a.*

1616 HAYWARD *Sanct. Troub. Soul* I. v. (1620) 74 When an vniuersall floud of fire shall ouer-streame the whole world. **1860** PUSEY *Min. Proph.* 478 The fulness of the over-streaming Love of God. **1864** TENNYSON *Islet* 20 Overstream'd and silvery-streak'd With many a rivulet high against the Sun.

over-strength: see OVER- 29.

over'stretch, *v.* [OVER- 27, 10; in sense 2 = MHG. *überstrecken.*]

1. *trans.* To stretch too much, or beyond the proper length, amount, or degree. *lit.* and *fig.*

overstreit in quot. 1330 appears to be for *overstreiht* (= overstretched); but may possibly be = *overstrait.*

c **1330** R. BRUNNE *Chron. Wace* (Rolls) 13270 How þeir hap was ner ouer-streit, And how Vtred was þer socour. **1388** WYCLIF *2 Cor.* x. 14 For we ouerstretchen [*superextendimus*] not forth vs, as not stretchinge to ȝou. **1552** *Act 5 & 6 Edw. VI*, c. 6 §1 Clothiers..practise Falshood..by over-stretching them upon the Tenter. **1590** MARLOWE *Edw. II*, II. ii. 158 The murmuring Commons, overstretched, break. **1735** BRACKEN in Burdon *Pocket Farrier* 26 *note*, The Muscles of the Shoulder being overstretched or relaxed. **1868** MILMAN *St. Paul's* 269 This supremacy, however it may have been overstretched by Elizabeth herself.

2. a. To stretch (something) over or across. **b.** To stretch or extend across (something).

1423 JAS. I. *Kingis Q.* clxiv, And on the quhele was lytill void space, Wele nere oure-straught fro lawe vnto hye. **1883** *Century Mag.* XXVI. 821 That line of arches which over-stretches London.

So **'overstretch** *sb.*; **'over'stretched** (-'strɛtʃt) *ppl. a.*; **'over'stretching** *vbl. sb.*

1631 SANDERSON *Serm.* (1681) II. 9 The preeminence of a good name thus far just, beware ye make not unjust by over-stretching. **1676** WISEMAN *Chirurg. Treat.* I. xxi. 111 The Tumour was..gangrened by reason of the overstretching of the Skin. **1760–72** H. BROOKE *Fool of Qual.* (1809) II. 101 The already over-stretched thread of his age and infirmities. **1769** *De Foe's Tour Gt. Brit.* I. 257 The prodigious Compass of this great Arch..appears like an Over-stretch, or an Extreme. **1806** H. K. WHITE *Let. to Maddock* 17 Feb., A very slight over-stretch of the mind in the daytime. **1861** W. S. PERRY *Hist. Ch. Eng.* I. xiv. 519 One of the suicidal counsels of an overstretched and impossible conformity. **1964** *Listener* 3 Sept. 335/2 Her overstretch was made fatal by this by-passing strategy. **1974** *Daily Tel.* 7 Feb. 2/6 Reasons for this are said to be the considerable 'overstretch' in the Navy's resources caused by shortage of ships and manpower.

overstrew (-'struː, -'strəʊ), *v.* Forms: see STREW. [OVER- 8: cf. MHG. *überströuwen*, G. *überstreuen*, Du. *overstrooijen.*]

1. *trans.* To strew or sprinkle (something) over something else.

1570 LEVINS *Manip.* 181/6 To Ouerstrowe, *supersternere.* **1798** G. MITCHELL tr. *Karsten's Min. Leskean Museum* 294 Iron Ore, with overstrewed Crystals of Copper Pyrites.

2. To strew or sprinkle something over (something else); to oversprinkle *with.* (Chiefly in *pa. pple.*)

1578 LYTE *Dodoens* V. i. 545 The leaues be..as if they were ouerstrowen with meale or flower. **1592** SHAKS. *Ven. & Ad.* 1143 The top o'erstraw'd With sweets. *a* **1661** FULLER *Worthies* I. (1662) 20 Were the Subject we treat of over-strewed with Ashes, (like the floor of Bells Temple). **1708** J. PHILIPS *Cyder* I. 27 The clammy Surface all o'er-strown with Tribes Of greedy Insects. **1868** LOCKYER *Guillemin's Heavens* (ed. 3) 400 Brilliant spirals, overstrewn with a multitude of stars.

'over-'strict, *a.* [OVER- 28.] Too strict.

1607–12 BACON *Ess., Counsel* (Arb.) 320 Where there hath bene, either an overgreatnesse in one [Counsellor], or an over-strict Combinacion in diuerse. **1862** GOULBURN *Pers. Relig.* 147 The fear of being accounted over-strict, methodistical, puritanical or what not.

So **'over-'strictly** *adv.*; **'over-'strictness.**

a **1653** GOUGE *Comm. Heb.* i. 6 (1655) 50 A faithfull Interpreter stands not overstrictly upon the letter. *Ibid.* xii. 25. 366 Misconceit of the over-strictness of the Gospel, terming it 'cords', 'bonds'. **1818–60** WHATELY *Commpl. Bk.* (1864) 179 Over-strictness may have led to a rebellious reaction.

overstride (-'straɪd), *v.* [OVER- 5, 10, 13, 22, 26; cf. MLG. *overstrîden.*]

1. To stride over or across. **a.** *trans.* To pass or move across (something) by striding.

c **1200** *Trin. Coll. Hom.* 111 Here he cumeð stridende fro dune to dune, and ouer strit þe cnolles. **1576** TURBERV. *Venerie* 68 You must looke..amongest the fearnes and small twigges the whiche he hath overstridden. **1590** SPENSER *F.Q.* III. vi. 31. **1861** *All Year Round* V. 14 A man o'er-strides the tomb, and drops beneath.

b. To stretch the legs across; to stand or sit with one leg on each side of; to bestride.

1508 DUNBAR *Flyting* 209 Strait Gibbonis air, that nevir ourstred ane horse. **1591** SPENSER *Ruines of Time* 541 From the one he could to th' other coast Stretch his strong thighes, and th' Ocean overstride. **1855** BROWNING *Bp. Blougram's Apol.* 393 You see one lad o'erstride a chimney-stack. **1875** JOWETT *Plato* III. 107 The Great Protector..overstrides others, and stands like a colossus in the chariot of State.

†**c.** *intr.* To pass or cross over. *Obs.*

a **1400–50** *Alexander* 5477 Ouire-stride þar any strange man,..þai droȝe þam doun in-to þe depe.

2. *trans.* To stride or extend beyond; *fig.* to go beyond, surpass.

1637 GILLESPIE *Eng. Pop. Cerem.* II. vii. 28 Now our Opposites doe farre overmatch us and overstride us in contention. **1641** BEST *Farm. Bks.* (Surtees) 50 Such a seeds-man doth overstride his cast, and thereupon cometh the lande to bee hopper-galde. **1925** *Glasgow Herald* 5 Nov. 11/2 In conception and in achievement it [*sc.* The British Empire Exhibition] overstrode the confines of mere commercial partisanship.

3. *intr.* To take longer strides than is natural.

1899 HILLIER in *Westm. Gaz.* 5 Jan. 9/1 For the first couple of miles I thought he was 'over-striding', but I soon found that the stride was his natural one.

over'strike, *v.* [OVER- 7, 23.]

†**1. a.** *trans.* ? To bring down a stroke upon; **b.** *refl.* to strike too far. *Obs.*

1375 BARBOUR *Bruce* V. 630 Vith þe ax he him ourstrak. *a* **1586** SIDNEY *Arcadia* III. (1590) 317b, The forsaken Knight ouer-strake himself so, as almost he came downe with his owne strength. **1596** SPENSER *F.Q.* V. xi. 13 For as he in his rage him overstrooke, He, ere he could his weapon backe repaire, His side all bare and naked overtooke.

2. *Pianoforte-making* (in **overstriking** *vbl. sb.* or *ppl. a.*). See quot.

1880 HIPKINS in Grove *Dict. Mus.* II. 646/2 [Pape] repeated the old idea..of an overstriking action—that is, the hammers descending upon the strings. *Ibid.* 712/1 Both overstriking and understriking apparatus had occurred to Marius.

3. [tr. F. *surfrapper*: see OVER- 8.] *trans.* To strike (a coin) with a new die, imposing a second design on the original; to strike (a new design) on a coin. Hence **'overstrike** *sb.*, an overstruck coin; **over'struck** *ppl. a.*

[**1884** *Encycl. Brit.* XVII. 630/2 A coin is said to be *surfrappé* when it has been struck on an older coin, of which the types are not altogether obliterated.] **1905** *Numismatic Chron.* V. 110 Supposing a sufficient number of overstruck pennies of the same type are available. *Ibid.*, A well-known instance of overstriking coins in modern times occurred in 1804, when..two million Spanish dollars..were overstruck with new dies in the Boulton presses at Soho, and issued as British currency. **1911** *Encycl. Brit.* XIX. 871/1 A coin is said to be 'over-struck' or 're-struck' when it has been struck on an older coin, of which the types are not altogether obliterated. **1914** *Brit. Mus. Return* 114 in *Parl. Papers* LXXI. 193 Another [penny] of the same reign showing the ninth type..overstruck on the seventh. **1932** *Proc. Brit. Acad.* XVIII. 212 Sextantes, with mint-marks C and MA, of the same class as certain early denarii, are commonly found in Sardinia overstruck on Sardinian bronze. We cannot assign such overstrikes to any date earlier than 237 B.C. **1936** *Proc. Prehist. Soc.* II. 144 The Whaddon Chase type coins have been heavily overstruck. **1955** C. SELTMAN *Greek Coins* (ed. 2) 24 The coiners in a particular mint saved themselves the trouble of preparing metal blanks, and employed instead the actual coins of some other city, heating them first in the furnace and then striking them between their own punch- and anvil-dies... Such coins, technically known as overstruck coins, [etc.]. **1970** *Ashmolean Mus. Rep. Visitors 1969* 33 Fifth century overstrikes at Rhegium and Messana.

over'string, *v.* *Pianoforte-making.* [OVER- 1, 10.] *trans.* To arrange the strings of (a piano) in two (or three) sets crossing over one another obliquely. So **over'stringing** *vbl. sb.*

1880 HIPKINS in Grove *Dict. Mus.* II. 720/2 The invention of overstringing has had more than one claimant. **1896** —— *Pianoforte* 21 In overstrung grand pianos..the bars and scale are so adjusted as to overstring the bass at an angle which opens out in a double curve fan shape from the hammer striking-place down to the hitch-pins. *Ibid.* 22 Overstringing (sometimes double overstringing) prevails in the larger upright instruments of America and Germany.

'overstroke. [OVER- 6.] An overarm stroke in swimming.

1902 *Encycl. Brit.* XXV. 696/4 Over-stroke. **1934** E. POUND *Eleven New Cantos* xxxix. 44 Came Mara swimming with light hand lifted in overstroke. **1948** —— *Pisan Cantos* (1949) lxxvi. 44 No overstroke No dolphin faster in moving Nor the flying azure of the wing'd fish under Zongli.

'over-'strong, *a.* [OVER- 28.] Too strong, excessively strong (in various senses: see STRONG).

a **1225** *Ancr. R.* 294 Ne þerf hit nout beon so ouerstrong ase his [salue] was. **1477** NORTON *Ord. Alch.* v. in Ashm. *Theatr. Chem. Brit.* (1652) 73 Or Venamous, stinking, or over-stronge. **1671** MILTON *Samson* 1590 O lastly over-strong against thy self! **1897** *Pop. Sci. Monthly* Nov. 74 This is not an overstrong statement.

So **'over-'strongly** *adv.*

1711 SHAFTESB. *Charac.* (1737) III. 370 Shou'd this effort be over-strongly express'd..the figure wou'd seem to speak.

overstructure: see OVER- 18.

'over'strung (stress shifting), *pa. pple.* and *ppl. a.* [OVER- 28c; and pa. pple. of OVERSTRING *v.*]

1. Too highly strung; intensely strained.

1810 SCOTT *Lady of L.* III. vi, With fired brain and nerves o'erstrung. **1892** ZANGWILL *Bow Mystery* 114 The overstrung nerves of the onlookers.

2. Of a piano: Having the strings arranged in two (or three) sets crossing obliquely over one another.

1880 HIPKINS in Grove *Dict. Mus.* II. 720/2 [In] 1835.. Theobald Boehm..contrived an overstrung square, and an overstrung cottage piano. **1894** *Westm. Gaz.* 15 Mar. 3/3 In '59 the overstrung scale in which the strings are disposed in fan-like form was invented.

overstud: see OVER-.

,over'study (-'stʌdɪ), *v.* [OVER- 27, 23.] *trans.*, *refl.*, and *intr.* To study too much.

1641 MILTON *Ch. Govt.* Concl., Wks. (1847) 53/1 Fondly over-studied in useless controversies. *a* **1652** BROME *City Wit* III. iv, Alas, he has overstudied himself! **1871** FRASER *Life Berkeley* vii. 229 He had overstudied, we may suppose.

So **'over'study** *sb.*, excessive study.

1855 *Westm. Rev.* July 101 It is proved that students ruin their health by over-study. **1861** H. SPENCER *Educ.* i. 15 Eyes spoiled for life by over-study.

,over'stuffed, *ppl. a.* [OVER- 8b, 27b, 28c.]

1. Of furniture: completely covered with a thick layer of stuffing.

1904 [cited in *N.E.D.* s.v. OVER- 27b]. **1925** T. DREISER *Amer. Trag.* (1926) I. II. xxi. 302 An old, faded and somewhat decrepit overstuffed chair. **1928** S. LEWIS *Man who knew Coolidge* i. 46 You sit at home in the ole over-stuffed chair. **1930** U. PARROTT *Strangers may Kiss* 28 The two armchairs were guaranteed by the landlady to be overstuffed. **1931** *Times* 16 Mar. 22/6 (Advt.), Overstuffed Chesterfield suites in tapestry. **1962** M. DUCKWORTH in C. K. Stead *N.Z. Short Stories* (1966) 362 He passed a..man seated on an overstuffed couch. **1973** W. M. DUNCAN *Big Timer* x. 66 There were three over-stuffed armchairs.

2. *fig.* Inflated, exaggerated; obese, fat.

1936 L. C. DOUGLAS *White Banners* xi. 233 Hannah's fears that an overstuffed optimism might involve them all in a financial disaster were gradually allayed. **1946** E. LINKLATER *Private Angelo* xviii. 230 Some great overstuffed history of the world's calamities. **1972** *Daily Tel.* 15 Jan. 9/2 The vulgar antics of the overstuffed striptease dancers.

†**over'sty**, *v.* *Obs.* [OE. *oferstígan*, f. *ofer-* OVER- 1 (*b*) + *stígan* to mount, ascend: = OHG. *ubarstîgan*, Goth. *ufarsteigan.*] *trans.* To rise or mount over or above (*lit.* and *fig.*); to surmount; to transcend, surpass, excel. Hence †**over'stying** *vbl. sb.* (in quot. = passing over or across).

c **893** K. ÆLFRED *Oros.* IV. vi. §4 He..on anre dieȝelre stowe þone munt oferstaȝ. *a* **900** tr. *Bæda's Eccl. Hist.* II. ix. [xii.] (1890) 130 Ealle þine yldran..þu in meahte and in rice feor oferstiȝest. *a* **1175** *Cott. Hom.* 225 þat flod wex þa and ..hit ofer-stah ælle duna. *c* **1250** *Will & Wit* I in *O.E. Misc.* 192 Hwenne so wil wit ofer-stieð, þenne is wil and wit for-lore. **1382** WYCLIF *Isa.* xvi. 2 In the ouersteȝyng [1388 passyng ouer] of Arnon.

,over-sub'scribe, *v.* [OVER- 27.] *trans.* To subscribe for (a loan, shares, etc.) in excess of the amount required.

1891 *Daily News* 5 Nov. 2/2 Both Preference and Ordinary shares..being largely oversubscribed. **1894** *Westm. Gaz.* 22 Sept. 3/3 The fourth and cheap edition.. was much over-subscribed before publication.

So **'over-sub'scription.**

1896 *Current Hist.* (Buffalo N.Y.) I. 131 The large over-subscription to the loan was a surprise to the country.

'over-'subtle, *a.* [OVER- 28.] Too subtle, excessively subtle. So **'over-'subtlety.**

c **1489** CAXTON *Sonnes of Aymon* vii. 171 He weneth well hymselfe to be over subtyll. **1728** T. COOK *Hesiod, Wks. & Days* I. 77 Son of Iapetus, o'er subtle, go, And glory in thy artful Theft below. **1833** J. H. NEWMAN *Arians* IV. ii. (1876) 297 Resisting..the orthodox doctrine from over-subtlety, timidity, pride, restlessness, or other weakness of mind. **1870** LOWELL *Among my Bks.* Ser. I. (1873) 205 If they have been sometimes over-subtile, they..had the merit of first looking at his works as wholes.

†**'over-,sum**, *sb.* *Obs.* [OVER- 19.] A sum over and above a defined amount; a surplus.

1587 HARRISON *England* I. xviii. (1878) III. 137 The bishop there had yearelie three or foure tunne at the least giuen him *Nomine decimæ*, beside whatsoeuer ouer-summe of the liquor did accrue to him by leases and other excheats.

,over-'sum, *v.* [OVER- 27.] *trans.* To estimate too highly, overrate.

1627–47 FELTHAM *Resolves* I. xxii. 79 To let them goe without sorrowing or over-summing them. **1929** R. BRIDGES *Testament of Beauty* IV. 108 The imperativ obligation cannot be over-summ'd.

over-superstitious: see OVER-.

'over-su'pply, *sb.* [OVER- 29b.] An excessive supply; a supply in excess of the demand or requirement. Also *attrib.*

1833 HT. MARTINEAU *Cinnamon & Pearls* vi. 102 A compensation for the loss occasioned by an over-supply. **1848** MILL *Pol. Econ.* II. xv. §4 (1876) 250 Either from over-supply or from some slackening in the demand for his commodity. **1932** *New Yorker* 14 May 42/2 You will write things..that will get the public interested in that oversupply of pongee somebody is trying to unload. **1964** *Times Rev. Industry* Apr. 3/2 Until the oversupply position improves, there will not be enough work for Britain's shipyards. **1971** *New Scientist* 2 Sept. 510/2 Even in these days of apparent oversupply of scientists it is clear there are never enough really creative minds on the genius level to go around. **1975** *Physics Bull.* Nov. 477/1 In Britain, despite the oversupply of staff and the shortage of money, every department is well equipped. **1977** *Living with Tanker Surplus* (Shell Internat. Petroleum Co.) 2 An impressive amount of new capacity will continue to add to the over-supply.

So **,over-su'pply** *v. trans.*, to supply in excess.

1865 M. EYRE *Lady's Walks S. of France* ii. 18 The markets at Bordeaux and Pau and Tarbes were *over*-supplied with fruit, butter, poultry, and eggs. **1878** JEVONS *Prim. Pol. Econ.* ii. 20 Nothing must be over-supplied, that is manufactured in such large quantities that it would have been better to spend the labour in manufacturing other things. **1890** 'R. BOLDREWOOD' *Col. Reformer* (1891) 221 We are not over supplied with resources..as yet. **1960** *Farmer & Stockbreeder* 15 Mar. 74/3 The market becomes over-supplied.

over-sure, susceptible, etc.: see OVER-.

†**over'swallow,** *v. Obs.* [OVER- 6.] *trans.* To swallow down.

1486 *Bk. St. Albans* C viij, Cut it and depart it as the hawke may ouerswolow it.

overswarm (-'swɔːm), *v.*

1. *intr.* and *refl.* To swarm to excess; to assemble in or grow to too great a swarm or crowd. [OVER- 27, 23.]

1587 GOLDING *De Mornay* viii. (1617) 113 As folke ouerswarmed in a place. **1679** M. RUSDEN *Further Disc. Bees* 25 That is the cause that Bees so often overswarm themselves.

2. *trans.* To swarm over (a place or region); to spread over or cover with a swarm or multitude. Also *absol.* or *intr.* (quot. 1875). [OVER- 9.]

1632 LITHGOW *Trav.* x. 443 These Flockes of Studientes ..ouer-swarme the whole land with rogueries, robberies, and begging. **1851** H. MELVILLE *Whale* xiv. 70 Let the English overswarm all India. **1875** BROWNING *Aristoph. Apol.* 26 When wave broke and overswarmed, and, sucked To bounds back, multitudinously ceased.

3. To swarm beyond or in excess of. [OVER- 13.]

1897 MARY KINGSLEY *W. Africa* 678 If you destroy the things that prey on them, they are liable to overswarm the food-producing power of their locality.

So **over'swarming** *vbl. sb.* (from sense 2).

1598 GRENEWEY *Tacitus' Ann.* I. Proeme (1622) 1 Untill they were by the ouerswarming of flatterers utterly discouraged. **1894** *Edin. Rev.* Oct. 400 The successive overswarming of Bulgarians, Magyars, Seljukian Turks.

†**'overswarth,** *sb. Obs.* ? The surface sward.

1649 BLITHE *Eng. Improv. Impr.* (1652) 144 The Mud of old standing pooles and ditches, the shovelling of Streets, and Yards, and Highwaies, the Overswarths of Common Lanes..is very good [for the land].

overswarth (-'swɔːθ), *v.* [f. OVER- 8 + *swarth*, var. of SWART *a.*] *trans.* To darken over, cover with blackness.

1822 W. TAYLOR in *Monthly Mag.* LIII. 403 When towering clouds o'erswarth the sky.

oversway ('əʊvəsweɪ), *sb. rare.* [OVER- 2.] Sway or command over any one, ascendancy; superior sway or command; overlordship.

1702 DE FOE *Mere Reform.* 453 Where it gets a little oversway It hurries all our Honesty away. **1902** W. WATSON in *Westm. Gaz.* 13 June 9/2 Kingdom in kingdom, sway in oversway, Dominion fold in fold.

oversway (əʊvə'sweɪ), *v.* Now *rare.* [OVER- 2, 22, 21, 11, 3, 6.]

†**1.** *trans.* To exercise sway over, rule over, govern; *esp.* to exercise power or dominion over one who or that which itself rules or ought to rule; to domineer over, overrule, overmaster, overpower. *Obs.*

1577–87 HOLINSHED *Chron.* (1807–8) II. 299 The perplexed state of princes, chieflie when they are overswaied with forren and prophane power. *a* **1600** HOOKER *Eccl. Pol.* VII. viii. §5 A number of captains, all of equal power, without some higher to oversway them. **1649** MILTON *Eikon.* ix, The parliament should oversway the King and not he the parliament. **1680** FILMER *Patriarcha* ii. §6 (Rtldg.) 29 Three parts of five..have power to oversway the liberty of their opposites.

†**b.** To surpass in commanding quality; to prevail over by superior authority. *Obs.*

1601 BP. W. BARLOW *Defence* 188 Not ouer-swaying the scriptures by authoritie and nomber. **1602** SHAKS. *Ham.* v. i. 251 Her death was doubtfull, And but that great Command, o're-swaies the order, She should in ground vnsanctified haue lodg'd, Till the last Trumpet. *a* **1619** FOTHERBY *Atheom.* I. ii. §3 (1622) 13 This Authority..ouerswayeth both all their reasons and authorities together. **1878** *N. Amer. Rev.* CXXVII. 171 To oversway all other authority.

absol. **1594** HOOKER *Eccl. Pol.* I. vii. §7 As oft as the preiudice of sensible experience doth ouersway. **1648** MILTON *Tenure Kings* Wks. 1738 I. 319 Had not their distrust in a good Cause, and the fast and loose of our prevaricating Divines oversway'd.

†**c.** In reference to physical qualities: To overpower by superior strength or intensity. *Obs.*

1605 TIMME *Quersit.* I. xiii. 54 The sulphur..doth exceed in qualitie the other two beginnings, and doth ouersway them. **1658** tr. *Porta's Nat. Magic* xx. 396 Hot-waters of salt-waters..have a lightness that oversways the weight of the salt.

†**2.** To lead, influence, or persuade into some course of action; to prevail upon. *Obs.*

1581 SIDNEY *Apol. Poetrie* (Arb.) 69 Ouer-swaying the memory from the purpose whereto they were applyed. **1601** SHAKS. *Jul. C.* II. i. 203 If he be so resolu'd, I can ore-sway him. **1619** VISCT. DONCASTER *Let.* in *Eng. & Germ.* (Camden) 136 The reasons which overswayed me to adventure on the transgression. *c* **1710** SWIFT *Change in Queen's Ministry* Wks. 1841 I. 280/1 His ungovernable temper had over-swayed him to fail in his respects to her majesty's person.

3. *trans.* and *intr.* To sway over; to cause to swing, lean, or incline to one side, or so as to be overturned; to swing or incline thus.

1622 F. MARKHAM *Bk. War* I. iv. §4. 15 If honor suffer or hang in the ballance, ready to bee ouerswaied with the poyze of iniurie. **1664** J. WEBB *Stone-Heng* (1725) 15 Such ponderous Masses be subject to overswaying. **1741** H. BROOKE *Constantia* Poems (1810) 397/2 By his bulk of cumb'rous poise o'ersway'd, Full on his helm receiv'd th' adverse blade.

Hence **over'swayed** *ppl. a.*, **over'swaying** *vbl. sb.* and *ppl. a.*

1601 SIR W. CORNWALLIS *Disc. Seneca* (1631) 11 When any affection of the minde..usurps an over-swaying authority. **1611** SPEED *Hist. Gt. Brit.* IX. ix. §105. 626 Permitting the depredation of himselfe and his whole Kingdome by Papall ouer-swayings. **1613** BEAUM. & FL. *Coxcomb* v. i, Such an overswayed sex is yours. **1705** in W. S. Perry *Hist. Coll. Amer. Col. Ch.* I. 150 Now deliver'd from that Mighty overswaying Power.

over-sweated, etc.: see OVER-.

oversweep (-'swiːp), *v.* [OVER- 9, 12.] *trans.* To sweep over or across (a surface, boundary, etc.); to pass over with a sweeping motion.

1611 SPEED *Theat. Gt. Brit.* (1614) 123/1 The Sun to dissolve them and the windes to over-sweepe them. **1820** BYRON *Mar. Fal.* I. ii. 147 To see your anger, like our Adrian waves, O'ersweep all bounds.

'over-'sweet, *a.* [OVER- 28.] Too sweet. So **,over-'sweeten** *v.*; **'over-'sweetness.**

1584 COGAN *Haven Health* (1636) 25 Bread over sweet is a stopper, and bread over-salt is a drier. **1759** SARAH FIELDING *C'tess of Dellwyn* I. 287 Whomsoever Oversweetness disgusted. **1901** *Westm. Gaz.* 8 Jan. 2/1 For a generation which has discarded sugar, are they not over-sweetened? **1935** [see ICKY, IKKY *a.* and *sb.*]. **1951** S. SPENDER *World within World* v. 267 At the end of a lecture on the effect of gases.., I hid for half an hour in a telephone box, overwhelmed by the vision of human beings asphyxiating one another in poisonous over-sweet scents. **1976** *Times* 20 Oct. 14/7 The 2½-lb Christmas puddings.. taste fine, if a bit over-sweet.

over'swell, *v.* [OVER- 25, 27, 5, 13.]

1. *trans.* or *intr.* To swell unduly, or to excess. (Chiefly in *pa. pple.* **overswollen.**)

1586 A. DAY *Eng. Secretary* II. (1625) 49 Ouer-swolne with your humours. *a* **1619** FOTHERBY *Atheom.* I. vi. §4 (1622) 48 Monstrously ouerswolne with pride and vanity. *c* **1745** H. BROOKE *Last Sp. John Good* in *Coll. Pieces* (1778) II. 101 Hence the Earth..grew animated..and, through its emptiness, it became overswoln and overweening.

2. a. *trans.* Of a body of water, etc.: To swell so as to overflow or cover.

1595 SHAKS. *John* II. i. 337 The currant..Whose passage ..Shall leaue his natiue channell, and ore-swell..euen thy confining shores. **1633** BP. HALL *Hard Texts* Amos v. 8. 554 Who causeth the waters of the sea to over-swell their bankes. **1846** POE *J. W. Francis* Wks. 1864 III. 40 A natural..flow of talk always overswelling its boundaries.

b. *absol.* or *intr.*

1599 SHAKS. *Hen. V*, II. i. 97 Let floods ore-swell, and fiends for food howle on. **1640** BP. REYNOLDS *Passions* xxx. 320 The Latter resisting the natural course of the streame.. makes it..to overswell on all sides.

Hence **over'swelling** *vbl. sb.* and *ppl. a.*; **over'swollen** *ppl. a.*

1594 NASHE *Terrors of Night* Wks. (Grosart) III. 268 The ouerswelling superabundance of ioy and greefe. **1652** J. WRIGHT tr. *Camus' Nat. Paradox* IX. 189 The burthen of her overswollen Heart. **1695** J. EDWARDS *Perfect. Script.* 563 Ὑπέρογκα..may better be rendred over-swelling.

'over-'swift, *a.* [OVER- 25, 28.] Too swift or rapid; excessively swift.

c **1374** CHAUCER *Boeth.* IV. metr. v. 103 (Camb. MS.) Whi þat Boetes the sterre vnfoldith his ouerswifte arysynges. **1638** tr. *Bacon's Life & Death* 221 A good strong Motion; But not over swift.

over-swilled, etc.; see OVER-.

over'swim, *v.* [OE. *oferswimman* = MHG. *überswimmen*: see OVER- 1, 8, 9.] *trans.* To swim or float over, across, or upon. Hence **over'swimmer; over'swimming** *vbl. sb.*

a **1000** *Beowulf* 2367 Oferswam ða sioleða bigong sunu Ecgðeowes. *c* **1374** CHAUCER *Boeth.* v. metr. v. 132 (Camb. MS.) Oother beestis..betyn the wyndes, and ouerswymmyn the spaces of the longe eyr, by moyst fleeynge. **1621** S. WARD *Life of Faith* 81 The Oile that euer ouerswims the greatest quantitie of water you can poure vpon it. **1633** P. FLETCHER *Purple Isl.* II. xlv, The first from over-swimming takes his name. *Note*, Epiploon (or overswimmer) descends below the navill, and ascends above the highest entrails, of skinny substance all interlaced with fat. *a* **1834** COLERIDGE *Picture* 133 Dimness o'erswum with lustre.

'overswing. 1. [OVER- 29 b.] An excessive swing.

1921 *Studies* Sept. 385 The overswing of a pendulum slipping from benevolent despotism of the priest into confiscation of church property. **1926** *Amer. Speech* I. 632 *Overswing*, a common fault [in golf]. **1971** I. G. GASS et al. *Understanding Earth* x. 142/2 We can speculate that such an overswing would eventually correct itself.

2. [OVER- 6.] In gymnastics, a movement in which the body swings or turns over.

1955 *Simple Gymnastics* ('Know the Game' Series) 22 *Overswing vault*—Take off both feet and spring high above the apparatus. Drop into the angle position with bent arms and head well back beyond the far edge of the apparatus. Keep the legs down while the hips fall forward. Then extend the hips and push hard with the hands. **1964** G. C. KUNZLE *Parallel Bars* ii. 63 You can also do this overswing off one bar outwards. **1965** *Trampolining* ('Know the Game' Series) 43/2 A simple dismount is to walk to the end of the bed, drop into a knee bounce, place the hands on the end rail and perform an overswing on to the feet, in the same way as you would do an overswing over a box horse.

†**over'swithe,** *adv. Obs.* In 3 **ouerswuðe** (*ü*). [OE. *oferswiðe*, f. *ofer-* OVER- 30 + *swiðe* very much, exceedingly.] Too greatly, too much; exceedingly, excessively; very greatly.

a **1100** *O.E. Chron.* an. 1086 Se cyng & þa heafod men lufedon swiðe and ofer swiðe ȝitsunge on golde and on seolfre. *a* **1225** *Ancr. R.* 408 So ouerswuðe he lueð luue þet he makeð hire his efning. *a* **1250** *Owl & Night.* 1518 Overswiþe þu hi herest.

†**over'swive,** *v. Obs.* In 2–3 **-swifen.** [f. OVER- 2 + SWIVE, OE. *swifan* to move, ON. *svífa* to rove, turn, sweep.] *trans.* To overcome, overpower.

c **1200** ORMIN 1848 þatt Godess Sune shollde wel þe deofell oferrswifenn. *Ibid.* 1884.

†**'overt,** *sb. Obs. rare.* [a. OF. *overt* opening, sb. use of *overt* pa. pple. and adj.: see next.]

1. An opening, aperture.

1340 HAMPOLE *Pr. Consc.* 627 What comes fra þe What thurgh mouthe, what thurgh nese,..And thurgh other overtes of his body.

2. ? An opening, introduction.

c **1440** CAPGRAVE *Life St. Kath.* III. 1302 þe song þat þei sungen..Was þis same: *Sponsus amat sponsam*; þe ouert þertoo: *Saluator uisitat illam.*

3. The open. *in overt* = OF. *à l'ouvert* openly.

1599 T. M[OUFET] *Silkwormes* 50 Let mountaine mice abroad in ouert lie.

overt ('əʊvət, now usu. əʊ'vɜːt), *a.* Also 4 **overte,** 7–8 **ouvert.** [a. OF. *overt*, 13th c. *ouvert*, pa. pple.: see next.]

†**1.** Open, not closed; uncovered. *Obs.*

c **1384** CHAUCER *H. Fame* II. 210 The aire therto ys so overte..That euery sovne mot to hyt pace. *a* **1440** *Sir Degrev.* 632 All of pall work fyn,..Anerlud with ermyn, And overt for pryde. **1460** *Lybeaus Disc.* 126 Hys surcote was overt. **1552** HULOET s.v. *Abrod*, That whyche is abrode, ouert, or without coueryng.

b. *Her.* (See quot.)

1828–40 BERRY *Encycl. Herald.* I. Dict., *Overt*, or *Overture*, terms applicable to the wings of birds, &c. when spread open..as if taking flight... It is, likewise, applied to inanimate things, as a *purse overt*, meaning an open purse.

2. Open to view or knowledge; patent, evident, apparent, plain, manifest; performed or carried out openly or publicly, unconcealed, not secret.

13.. *E.E. Allit. P.* A. 592 In sauter is sayd a verce ouerte þat spekez a poynt determynable. **1594** CAREW *Tasso* (1881) 96 She faines..Not see the mind whose words it ouert made. **1600** HOLLAND *Livy* II. xiv. 53 Any open and ouvert sale of the kings goods. **1628** T. SPENCER *Logick* 49 Parts..more overt, and better knowne. **1705** STANHOPE *Paraphr.* I. 87 The General Judgment shall extend, not only to Mens Overt, but even their most secret Acts. [**1813** BYRON in Moore *Life* (1875) 347 His vanity is *ouverte*, like Erskine's, and yet not offending.] **1874** STUBBS *Const. Hist.* II. xvii. 511 The overt struggles of the fourteenth century.

b. *overt act* (*Law*): an outward act, such as can be clearly proved to have been done, from which criminal intent is inferred.

[**1351–2** *Act 25 Edw. III*, Stat. v. c. 2 De ceo provablement soit atteint de overt faite [Rastell 1527, 1542 'open dede'] par gentz de lour condicion.] **1533** MORE *Debell. Salem* Wks. (1557) 959/1 Than be such wordes yet no treason, without some maner of ouert & open actual dede therwith. *a* **1631** DONNE *Serm.* xi. 107 *Fides visa*, Faith which by an ouvert act was declared and made evident. **1660** *Trial Regic.* 36 'Tis the Thought of the Heart, which makes the Treason: the Overt-Act is but the Evidence of it. **1769** BLACKSTONE *Comm.* IV. ii. 21 In all temporal jurisdictions an overt act, or some open evidence of an intended crime, is necessary.. before the man is liable to punishment. **1855** MACAULAY *Hist. Eng.* xx. IV. 419 One argument..was that, as the art of printing had been unknown in the reign of Edward the Third, printing could not be an overt act of treason under a statute of that reign.

3. *letters overt* = letters PATENT (q.v.); *market overt*, open MARKET; *pound overt*, open or public POUND: see these words.

[**1321–2** *Rolls of Parlt.* I. 413/2 Com les lettres overtes l'Evesqe de Salesbuyrs lour tesmoigne.] **1717** *Blount's Law Dict.*, *Letters Patent*... They are sometimes called also Letters Overt.

†**overt,** *pa. pple. Obs.* [a. OF. *overt*, pa. pple. of *ovrir*, F. *ouvrir* to open.] Opened, laid open.

? *a* **1412** LYDG. *Two Merchants* 519 To hym Fortune hir falsnesse hath overt..For he is fallen and plonget in povert.

overtake (,əʊvə'teɪk), *v.* [Early ME. f. OVER- 14 + TAKE *v.*, q.v. for Forms.

Overtake is the earliest exemplified of a small group of synonymous vbs., including *overnim, overhent, overget, overcatch*, in all of which the second element means *take* or *catch*; the original application being apparently to the running down and catching of a fugitive or beast of chase: cf. the synonymous 'catch up'. The sense of *over-* is not so clear. *A priori* we might explain it as 'to *take* by *over*-running, or by getting *over* the intervening space', and compare *overreach* = reach *over* or across a space. But it is doubtful whether this was the original notion. Beside these *-take* verbs, a fig. sense of *overtake* (viz. 4 below) was expressed before 1000 by *overgang* and *overgo*; but in these *over-* can be explained in the sense 'down upon' (OVER- 7), so that their orig. sense would be 'descend' or 'fall upon'. The sense of 'overtake' was expressed later also by *overhie, overrun, overhale, overhaul*; but these prob. imitated *overgo* or *overtake*. In Early ME. *overtake* and *overgo* had the parallel forms OFTAKE, OFGO, which seem to have been the strictly southern equivalents (*oftake* being actually exemplified earlier than *overtake*): the relation between *of-* and *over-*here, as well as in OFTHINK, OVERTHINK, has not been clearly determined.]

1. a. *trans.* To come up with (a person or thing going or running in front of one and in the same direction); to come up to in pursuit; to 'catch up'. Now esp. of a motorist: to drive a vehicle past (another vehicle travelling in the same direction). Also *absol.*, and with the vehicle as subj.

†*well overtaken*, a traveller's greeting to one he has overtaken: cf. *well met*. *Obs.*

a **1225** *Ancr. R.* 244 Þe veond.. wearð ibunden [hete]ueste mid te holie monnes beoden, þet of-token [*MS. T.* ouer-token] him ase heo clumben upward touward te heouene. c **1250** *Gen. & Ex.* 1756, vij. niȝt forð-ȝeden.. Or laban iacob ouer-toc. *Ibid.* 2313 Iosep haueð hem after sent. Ðis sonde hem ouertakeð raðe. **1297** R. GLOUC. (1724) 64 He ouer [*v.r.* of] tok hym at an hauene & sloȝ hym ryȝt þere. **13..** *E.E. Allit. P.* C. 127 Bot, I trow, ful tyd, ouer-tan þat he were. **13..** *Cursor M.* 3925 (Cott.) Laban it mist, ouertok and soght. c **1375** *Sc. Leg. Saints* xliii. (*Cecile*) 76 In a rew, callit 'via apia', Syndry poure men þu sal ourta. c **1386** CHAUCER *Friar's T.* 86 (Harl. MS.) Sir, quod þis sompnour, heyl and wel ouertake. c **1400** MAUNDEV. (Roxb.) xxii. 100 Þai will owertake wylde bestes and sla þam. **1415** SIR T. GREY in *43rd Deputy Kpr.'s Rep.* 584 Þer cum Luce and awrtoke me and bade gode morow And said I was wil awrtaken. **1583** STUBBES *Anat. Abus.* II. (1882) 1 God blesse you my friend, and well ouertaken. **1596** SHAKS. *Merch. V.* IV. ii. 5 Faire sir, you are well ore-tane. **1601** SIR W. CORNWALLIS *Ess.* II. li. (1631) 327 They have the start that are borne great, but hee that overtakes hath the honour. **1653** WALTON *Angler* i, You are wel overtaken Sir; a good morning to you; I have stretch'd my legs up Totnam Hil to overtake you. **1738** WESLEY *Wks.* (1872) I. 89 We were overtook by an elderly gentleman. a **1771** GRAY *Dante* 39 His helpless offspring soon O'erta'en beheld. **1888** ANNIE S. SWAN *Doris Cheyne* viii. 134 She would walk along the Keswick Road.. until the coach should overtake her. **1936** J. PRIOLEAU *Motorist's Compan.* xxix. 418 The commoner examples of dangerous driving are.. cutting-in and overtaking another car travelling at any but an obviously lower speed [etc.]. **1938** M. CAMPBELL *Key to Motoring* ix. 107 One of the greatest dangers of fog-driving lies in overtaking or in passing stationary vehicles. **1959** [see CHEESED *a.*] **1959** E. H. CLEMENTS *High Tension* vi. 100 'The journey back was worth it... West overtook me.'.. 'Where did he overtake you?' 'Rannoch.' **1973** R. HILL *Ruling Passion* II. iv. 114 A slow lorry suddenly appeared ahead... He swung out sharply to overtake. **1976** *Southern Even. Echo* (Southampton) 12 Nov. 5/2 Marshall was riding a motorcycle on dual carriageway.. when a car in front pulled out to overtake.

b. *fig.* To come up with in any course of action; *esp.* to get through or accomplish (a task) when pressed for time or hindered by other business, etc.; to work off within the time. In quots. c 1330, 1375 with *inf.*

c **1330** R. BRUNNE *Chron.* (1810) 133 [Þei] Ouertok it to ȝeme, & saued þat cite. **1375** BARBOUR *Bruce* VIII. 190 Gif he mycht nocht weill our-ta To met thame at the first. **1402** HOCCLEVE *Let. of Cupid* 146 Reson yt [the tongue] seweth so slowly and softe, that it him neuer ouer-take may. **1575–85** ABP. SANDYS *Serm.* (1841) 292, I must here make an end, for the time hath overtaken me. **1602** FULBECKE *Pandectes* Ded. 1 To ouer-take euerie thing which they vndertake. **1752** J. LOUTHIAN *Form of Process* (ed. 2) 237 Staitened in point of Time, so that they could not overtake the whole Trials. **1856** MAXWELL *Let.* in *Life* ix. (1882) 255, I have two or three stiff bits of work to get through this term here, and I hope to overtake them. **1893** STEVENSON *Catriona* ii. 16 It's a job you could doubtless overtake with the other.

†**c.** To take in hand, proceed to deal with, 'tackle'.

1581 J. BELL *Haddon's Answ. Osor.* 247 This Objection must be overtaken after this maner. **1585** ABP. SANDYS *Serm.* Ep. to Rdr., To meet with and overtake all practices and inconveniences.

†**2. a.** To get at, reach, get hold of; to reach with a blow. *Obs.*

c **1300** *Havelok* 1816 The fifte that he ouertok, Gaf he a ful sor dint ok. **1375** BARBOUR *Bruce* II. 381 He all till-hewyt that he our-tuk. **1456** SIR G. HAYE *Law Arms* (S.T.S.) 205 To tak ony man of that contree.. that he may ourta. c **1532** DU WES *Introd. Fr.* in *Palsgr.* 938 To hitte or ouertake, *attaindre*. **1673** *Wedderburn's Voc.* 28 (Jam.) *Percussit me pugno*, he overtook me with his steecked nieff. **1680** *Life Edw. II* in *Harl. Misc.* I. 87 The bruit of this novelty, like a Welch hubbub, had quickly overtaken the willing ears of the displeased Commons.

†**b.** *intr.* To get as far as, reach. *Obs. rare.*

a **1225** *Juliana* 56 Hit as hit turnde ne ouer teoc nowðer abuuen ne bineoðen to þer eorðe.

†**c.** *absol.* or *intr.* Of fire: To 'catch', take hold. *Obs.*

a **1300** *Cursor M.* 6759 (Cott.) If fire be kyndeld and ouer-tak Thoru feld, or corn, or mou, or stak.

†**3.** To 'take', 'catch', surprise, or detect in a fault or offence; to convict. *Obs.*

a **1300** *Cursor M.* 8644 (Cott.) Parfai! þou lighes, wik womman, And þar-wit sal þou be ouer-tan. *Ibid.* 19416 (Edin.) In worde moȝt tai him neuir ouirtac. **1375** BARBOUR *Bruce* XIX. 55 Thir thre planly, War with ane assis thar ourtane. c **1400** *Rule St. Benet* (E.E.T.S.) 1232 If sche ȝit be ouer-tayn,.. Sche salbe cursid for þat same þing. **1551–2** *Reg. Privy Council Scot.* I. 123 Thaim.. at.. beis ourtane and convict.

4. Of some adverse agency or influence, as a storm, night, disease, death, misfortune, punishment (rarely, as in quot. c 1630, of something good or favourable): To come upon unexpectedly, suddenly, or violently; to seize, catch, surprise, involve.

c **1375** *Cursor M.* 4721 (Fairf.) Qualme has bestes alle ouertane [*other MSS.* ouergan]. c **1420** *Pallad. on Husb.* I. 51 The stomak als of aier is ouertake. **1500–20** DUNBAR *Poems* lxxiii. 14 And the deith ourtak the in trespas. c **1560** A. SCOTT *Poems* (S.T.S.) ii. 192 Nycht had thame ourtane. **1606** SHAKS. *Ant. & Cl.* III. x. 11 Yon ribaudred Nagge of Egypt, (Whom Leprosie o're-take). **1611** BIBLE *1 Thess.* v. 4 That that day should ouertake you as a thiefe. c **1630** MILTON *Time* 13 And Joy shall overtake us as a flood. **1794** SULLIVAN *View Nat.* II. 58 So unfortunate as to be overtaken by a thunder storm. **1878** BOSW. SMITH *Carthage* 222 The magnitude of the disaster which had overtaken him.

†**5.** To apprehend mentally; to comprehend, understand. *Obs.*

a **1300** *Cursor M.* 575 (Cott.) Godd.. Wit nankyn creature mai be vnderfanged ne ouertan, And he ouertakes þam ilkan. *Ibid.* 10787 Had he ani-wais ouertaine A child be born of a maiden.

†**6.** To take up or occupy the whole of (a space); to extend over, cover. *Sc. Obs.*

1375 BARBOUR *Bruce* XI. 125 Men that mekill host mycht se Our-tak the landis so largely. *Ibid.* XII. 439 That folk our-tuk ane mekill feld On breid.

7. To overcome the will, senses, or feelings of; to win over, captivate, ensnare, 'take'; to overpower with excess of emotion. *Obs.* or *dial.*

c **1375** *Cursor M.* 24824 (Fairf.) Þa þat he had na giftis tille Wiþ hotis faire he ouer-toke þaire wil. **1422** tr. *Secreta Secret., Priv. Priv.* xxxvi. 192 A fole in flesly thyngis is ouer-taken. **1535** COVERDALE *Gal.* vi. 1 Yf eny man be ouertaken of a faute. a **1586** SIDNEY *Arcadia* II. (1590) 107 If her beauties haue so ouertaken you, it becomes a true Loue to haue your harte more set vpon her good then your owne. **1620** J. PYPER tr. *Hist. Astrea* I. x. 335 Your Neece is so ouertaken with Celadon, as I know not if Galathee be more. **1666** PEPYS *Diary* 6 June, We were all so overtaken with this good news, that the Duke ran with it to the King. **1822** GALT *Provost* xxxvi, At first I was confounded and overtaken, and could not speak.

†**8.** To overcome the judgement of; to deceive, 'take in'; in *pa. pple.* deceived, mistaken, in error.

1581 W. CHARKE in *Confer.* IV. (1584) A a iv, Here you are manifestly ouertaken: for they are worde for worde in the 9. Chapter. **1584** R. SCOT *Discov. Witchcr.* VII. iv. (1886) 107 The preestes were so cunning as they also overtooke almost all the godlie and learned men. **1623** BINGHAM *Xenophon* 40 The other sought to circumuent him, as being easie to be ouertaken. **1702** S. PARKER tr. *Cicero's De Finibus* IV. 261 'Tis certain, you were strangely overtaken, in supposing that [etc.].

9. To overcome or overpower with drink, intoxicate, make drunk. (Chiefly in *passive.*) Now *dial.*

1587 HARRISON *England* II. vi. (1877) I. 152 [These] are soonest overtaken when they come to such bankets. **1602** SHAKS. *Ham.* II. i. 58 There was he gaming, there o'retooke in's Rouse. **1659** WOOD *Life* (O.H.S.) I. 298 They would.. tiple and smoake till they were overtaken with the creature. **1712** STEELE *Spect.* No. 450 ¶6, I do not remember I was ever overtaken in Drink. **1770** FOOTE *Lame Lover* III. Wks. 1799 II. 91 To be sure the knight is overtaken a little; very near drunk. **1869** KENNEDY *Evenings Duffrey* 282 (E.D.D.) Better luck, sir, next time you let yourself be overtaken.

10. *Bridge. intr.* To take with a higher card a trick already taken by one's partner. Also *trans.*, to play a higher card than (the card played by one's partner).

1904 J. B. ELWELL *Advanced Bridge* 164 With no re-entry in a hand, overtaking is often the only means of making a suit. **1939** N. DE V. HART *Bridge Players' Bedside Bk.* xviii. 73 Declarer ducked in dummy, but Herr von Bludhorn overtook. *Ibid.* xxxviii. 118 Declarer played out the King, Knave, and Ten of Trumps, overtaking the Ten with dummy's Queen. **1959** REESE & DORMER *Bridge Players' Dict.* 161 South.. leads the jack of spades and, depending on which suit West unguards, overtakes or not with dummy's queen of spades. **1974** *Country Life* 17 Jan. 98/3 East should have overtaken the Spade King and switched to Diamonds.

Hence **over'taking** *vbl. sb.* and *ppl. a.*; also **over'takable** *a.*, that can be overtaken; **over'taker**, one who or that which overtakes.

1591 PERCIVALL *Sp. Dict.*, *Alcance*, ouertaking, obteining, pursuing, reaching. **1599** MINSHEU *Sp. Dict.*, *Alcançador*.. an ouertaker. **1798** COLERIDGE *Anc. Mar.* I. xi, He struck with his o'ertaking wings. **1838** CHALMERS *Wks.* XII. 213 One assigned and overtakeable district. **1880** R. G. MARSDEN *Treat. Law Collisions at Sea* vi. 187 Article 20 is express as to the duty of an overtaking sailing-ship to keep out of the way. **1885** MRS. LYNN LINTON *Christ. Kirkland* II. viii. 259 He is looked on as a fossilized kind of Conservative by his successors and overtakers. **1897** W. E. NORRIS *Clarissa Furiosa* xxxvii. 328 No more.. than a spent fox can escape the overtaking hounds. **1928** R. TOWNSEND *Motoring made Easy* v. 74 No attempt should be made at overtaking on a curve in the road or at a corner. **1960** [see CUTTING *vbl. sb.* 9 c]. **1961** F. H. BURGESS *Dict. Sailing* 155 *Overtaking light*, a fixed white light, screened so as to be visible 12 points, i.e. from right astern to 2 points abaft the beam each side, and from two miles away; carried by all ships under way. **1966** [see *fast lane* s.v. FAST *a.* 11]. **1970** *Motoring Which?* July 116/1 Five mirrors specifically designed for door-mounting (often called 'overtaking mirrors'). **1975** J. CLEARY *Safe House* ii. 100 He saw the beam of the overtaking vehicle's headlamps.

over-talk (-'tɔːk), *v.* [OVER- 27, 23, 11.] **a.** *intr.* and *refl.* To talk too much. **b.** *trans.* To gain over or overcome with talking, to talk over.

1635 A. STAFFORD *Fem. Glory* (1860) 94 If in this rude speech of mine I have over-talked my selfe, or under-spoken thee, impute it to my declining and doting yeares. **1859** TENNYSON *Vivien* 963 For Merlin, overtalk'd and overworn, Had yielded, told her all the charm, and slept. **1903** E. M. FORSTER in *Temple Bar* Dec. 682 They shook him and tried to overtalk him, but he still went on.

So **'over-'talk**, *sb.*; **'over-'talkative** *a.*; **'over-'talkativeness**; **,over-'talker**; **'over-'talking** *vbl. sb.* [OVER- 28, 29.]

1649 MILTON *Eikon.* viii. (1851) 393 By his overtalking of it, [he] seems to doubt either his own conscience, or the hardness of other mens belief. **1670** BROOKS *Wks.* (1867) VI. 302 There are many over-talkers; and they are such who spend a hundred words when ten will serve the turn. **1685** BAXTER *Paraphr. N.T.* 1 Tim. ii. 11 Let them use silence.. and not be over-talkative. **1876** MISS YONGE *Womankind* xxviii. 247 Everybody agrees as to the evils of over-talkativeness. *Ibid.*, Perhaps it is only those who had rather hold their tongues who are safe from over-talk.

over-tame, -tarry, -tart: see OVER-.

,over'task, *v.* [OVER- 27.] *trans.* To task too severely; to impose too heavy a task upon. Hence **,over'tasked** *ppl. a.*

1628 BP. HALL *Serm. at Westminster* 5 Apr., Wks. (1634) III. 309 Many a good Husband over-taskes himselfe, and undertakes more, then his eye can over-looke. a **1711** KEN *Direct. for Prayer* Wks. (1838) 341 If you should overtask them, religion should seem to them rather a burden than a blessing. **1869** 'MARK TWAIN' *Innoc. Abr.* 289 Relief for overtasked eyes and brain from study and sightseeing. **1875** STUBBS *Const. Hist.* III. xviii. 129 Work which had overtasked the greatest kings. **1895** A. I. SHAND *Life Gen. Sir E. B. Hamley* I. iv. 93 The sufferings of the starved and overtasked horses.

,over'tax, *v.* [OVER- 27.] *trans.* To tax too greatly or heavily; to exact or demand too much of; *esp.* to overburden or oppress with taxes; to impose taxes upon beyond what is equitable.

1650 [see OVERTAXED below]. **1774** GOLDSM. *Nat. Hist.* VIII. 87 Their abilities may be over-taxed. **1835** TALFOURD *Ion* IV. ii, Hast thou beheld him overtax his strength? **1835** LYTTON *Rienzi* IV. ii, I know that poor men won't be overtaxed. **1842** TENNYSON *Godiva* 9 We.. have loved the people well, And loathed to see them overtaxed.

Hence **,over'taxed** *ppl. a.*, **,over'taxing** *vbl. sb.*; so also **,overtax'ation**.

1650 B. *Discolliminium* 48 They.. grow too heavy for my over-tax'd leggs. **1823** J. S. MILL in *Black Dwarf* XI. 749 Over-taxation cannot lower wages. a **1859** MACAULAY *Hist. Eng.* xxiv. V. 181 The most ravenous of all the plunderers of the poor overtaxed nation. **1877** TENNYSON *Harold* I. i. 6 Nay, there be murmurs for thy brother breaks us With over-taxing. **1881** *Education* Feb. 26/2 Anything.. which avoids the overtaxation of the memory with useless matter. **1897** *Daily News* 20 Jan. 8/7 A question to Ministers concerning the overtaxation of Scotland.

†**'overte, -tee.** *Obs. rare.* [f. OVER *a.* + *-té*, -TY, after words from Fr. such as *poverty*.] The condition of being over or above another; superiority.

c **1449** PECOCK *Repr.* III. iv. 299 Preestis ouȝten not haue ouerte among hem silf.. neither eny preest ouȝte haue ouerte upon eny lay persoon. *Ibid.* 426 Sithen it is now bifore proued that preesthode and bischophode.. ben ouertees to hem for which thei ben had and usid.

over-teach, etc.: see OVER- 27.

'over-'tedious, *a.* [OVER- 28.] Too tedious.

1591 SHAKS. *1 Hen. VI*, III. iii. 43 Speake on, but be not ouer-tedious. **1668** in *H. More's Div. Dial.* Pref. (1713) 15, I have too long detained thee by an over-tedious Preface.

,over'teem, *v.* [OVER- 26, 21.] **a.** *intr.* To teem or breed excessively, be excessively productive; also *fig.* **b.** *trans.* To wear out or exhaust by excessive breeding or production. Hence **,over'teemed**, **,over'teeming** *ppl. adjs.*

1602 SHAKS. *Ham.* II. ii. 531 For a Robe About her lanke and all ore-teamed Loines, A blanket. **1818** KEATS *Endym.* I. 575 Such a dream, That never tongue, although it overteem With mellow utterance, like a cavern spring, Could figure out. **1818** SHELLEY *Let. T.L.P.* 22 Dec., Ess. etc. 1852 II. 142 The overteeming vegetation. **1828** MACAULAY *Misc. Writ.* (1860) I. 255 His mind is a soil which is never overteemed. **1877** BARING-GOULD *Myst. Suffering* 32 If productiveness were conceivable without death to check the increase, the world would overteem.

over'tell, *v.* [OVER- 26, 16.]

1. *trans.* To tell (count, or narrate) in excess of the fact; to exaggerate in reckoning or narration.

1511 in W. H. Turner *Select. Rec. Oxford* 3 Thomas Foster dyd overtell hymselfe in the gȝyld hall xx[ti] voyces. **1755** AMORY *Mem.* (1766) II. 98 There may be some things overtold,.. that would bear mitigation.

†**2.** To count over. *Obs.*

c **1610** ROWLANDS *Terrible Battell* 11 We came vnto a Marchant in this towne That mighty bags of money ouer-tels.

over-tempt, -tension, etc.: see OVER-.

'over-'tender, *a.* [OVER- 28.] Too tender; excessively or unduly tender. So **'over-'tenderly** *adv.*; **'over-'tenderness**.

a **1631** DONNE *Serm.* ix. 95 By abusing an over-tendernesse which may be in thy conscience then. **1685** BAXTER *Paraphr. N.T.* Matt. xxvi. 67–68 Why should we look for better, and be over-tender of our Flesh or Reputation? **1795** ANNE SEWARD *Anecdotes* (1796) IV. 8 A child, who by the carelessness or overtenderness of his parent was brought up to no trade or profession. **1836** KEBLE *Serm.* (1848) 177 Do not shrink thus overtenderly from the thought of losing me. **1889** SKRINE *Mem. Thring* 137 A moral sensitiveness which made him over-tender.

†'**over-tenth.** *Obs.* [OVER- 19.] An increased or additional tenth or tithe.

c **1550** CROWLEY *Inform.* Wks. (1872) 171 The Cleargie of the Citie of London haue..optayned by Parliament authoritie to ouertenthes euen after the exemple of the landlordes and leasemongers.

†**over-'terve,** *v. Sc. Obs.* Also -tarve, -tirwe, -tyrve, -tyrfe, -tyrwe. [f. OVER- 6 + TERVE *v.*, to turn round, roll.] *trans.* To overturn, overthrow, upset.

(Often misread *overterne*, and mistaken for *overturn.*)

c **1330** R. BRUNNE *Chron. Wace* (Rolls) 4627 Þe mastes faste to-gidere burte, & somme ouer terued [*pr.* -terned], & lay on syde. *c* **1375** *Sc. Leg. Saints* xvii. (*Martha*) 33 As fysche wald he dwel in þe flud & our tyrwit batis þat rowyt þare. *c* **1375** BARBOUR *Troy-bk.* II. 908 The Cite..brent Ande oure-tyrvede of fundement. *c* **1425** *Cursor M.* 18266 (Laud) With the kyng of blisse hast þou werrid And so thy-self ovyr-tarvid. *c* **1440** LYDG. *Nightingale* (E.E.T.S.) 208 Elles all oder..In that gret flood were dreynt and ouer-terved. *c* **1470** HARDING *Chron.* xx. ii, They durst no thing ouer terue Againe his lawe nor peace, but theim conserue. *a* **1500** *Ratis Raving* I. 1608 Our tyrfand kindly cours ilk day.

over-the-board, *a.* [OVER *prep.* 12.] Of chess competition: with the participants actually present, as opp. to correspondence play; with opponents facing each other across the chess-board.

1932 E. LASKER *Manual of Chess* IV. 228/2 His talent for over-the-board play was not considerable. **1954** H. GOLOMBEK *World Chess Championship 1954* 54 He has retired from over-the-board play and has devoted himself to writing about and teaching the game. **1974** C. H. O'D. ALEXANDER *On Chess* III. ix. 214 For various reasons—no chess club in the locality, lack of time, finding over-the-board play too much nervous strain—a number of people don't play it.

over-the-counter, *adv.* (*a.*). [OVER *prep.* 12.] **a.** See COUNTER *sb.*[3] 4. **b.** orig. *N. Amer.* With reference to the selling of stocks and shares: as a direct transaction, (business concluded) outside the system of a recognized stock exchange. **c.** Hence of purchase and selling generally: (transacted) directly between seller and buyer; openly, legitimately. (Cf. *under the counter* s.v. COUNTER *sb.*[3] 4 b.) **d.** Of pharmaceutical products: obtainable without a doctor's prescription. Also *transf.* and as *adj. phr.*

1875, 1889 [see COUNTER *sb.*[3] 4]. **1921** *Mag. of Wall St.* 10 Dec. 179/2 There is another field which readers have expressed the desire to see us cover. That is the great field comprising unlisted securities, which are dealt in over-the-counter... In response to this demand, we are inaugurating, beginning with this issue, a new department to appear under the caption, 'Over-the-Counter'. *Ibid.*, It will be our effort to confine our analysis of over-the-counter stocks to as brief a space as possible. **1925** A. M. SAKOLSKI *Princ. Investment* x. 108 'Over-the-counter' transactions (i.e., those which occur privately, whether consummated directly by negotiation between buyer and seller or through dealers and brokers) generally, in the absence of special agreements, follow the common practices of the exchanges. **1929** WILLIS & BOGEN *Investment Banking* iii. 50 This market is referred to as the unlisted or over-the-counter market, because business is transacted..'over the counter' of the individual broker or dealer, rather than at..an exchange. **1934** *Sun* (Baltimore) 27 Apr. 2/3 The committee has heard evidence of extensive manipulation in certain New York bank stocks after their withdrawal from the New York Stock Exchange and while they were being sold 'over the counter'. **1936** WODEHOUSE *Laughing Gas* xv. 165 'You think this tooth could be sold?' 'Over the counter, sir, over the counter.' **1944** *Amer. N. & Q.* July 64/1 A North Carolinian illustration of this futile neologistic tendency found in high places is 'over-the-counter salesperson', for the simple ..*clerk.* **1957** CLARK & GOTTFRIED *University Dict. Business & Finance* 253/2 The securities are traded on a face-to-face, or over-the-counter basis. In the actual operation of over-the-counter trading, a trader who specializes in a particular security arranges for all transactions, either by bringing buyers and sellers together, or by buying and selling the security for his own account. **1958** *Spectator* 11 July 58/3 The over-the-counter service of spit-roasted chicken is a development in the catering trade. *Ibid.* 60/1 The over-the-counter charge for the spit-roasted bird is 12s. 6d. **1959** *Economist* 21 Feb. 722/1 'Over the counter' dealings in TI. **1963** *Times* 23 Apr. 20/3 Sales of bottles to take home ('Off-Sales') have increased very considerably, and there has been a reduction of sales by the glass—'Over the counter'—with a consequent reduction in profit. **1965** [see *OTC* s.v. O 5 d]. **1965** *McGraw-Hill Dict. Mod. Econ.* 367 In addition to common and preferred stocks, almost all U.S. government securities and municipal and corporate bonds are traded over the counter. **1968** *Globe & Mail* (Toronto) 17 Feb. B2/1 An over-the-counter speculative issue that rose from 25 cents a share to $4.50 in the past six months. **1969** *Times* 5 May (Suppl.) p. iv/4 The National Association of Securities Dealers, the self-regulatory organization for the over-the-counter market, is moving to create a national clearance operation for unlisted stocks. **1969** *Guardian* 25 July 6/6 If 'over the counter' pregnancy testing is to come to Britain, the tests should be carried out by the pharmacist. **1972** *Times* 16 May (Wall Street Suppl.) p. iv/7 For 25 years he was a broker and then from 1964 to 1967 headed the National Association of Securities Dealers which regulates over-the-counter deals. **1974** M. C. GERALD *Pharmacol.* ii. 20 Nonprescription (over-the-counter, OTC) sleep-facilitating products..have capitalized on the drowsiness induced by methapyrilene. **1974** *Guardian* 22 Mar. 11/5 The retailers wanted to simplify the collection of air fuel surcharges on package holidays by including the sum on the over-the-counter invoice presented to the customer. **1977** *Addictive Dis.* III. 275 Almost all the conditions and diseases that over-the-counter drugs of the past century were purported to relieve are still prevalent today. **1986** *Daily Tel.* 16 Apr. 17/1 This [third tier market] will cover the current over-the-counter shares traded off the stock market which will have prices listed on the Stock Exchange's electronic screens.

over the moon: see MOON *sb.*[1] 3 b.

over-the-road, *a.* [OVER *prep.* 13.] Of, pertaining to, or used in long-distance road transportation.

1945 *Sun* (Baltimore) 24 Oct. 14-0/8 Approximately 1500 members of Local 557, Freight Drivers and Helpers.. yesterday went on strike which threatens to halt about 50 per cent of trucking operations in the city and practically all over-the-road, inter-city hauling into and out of Baltimore. **1967** *Jane's Surface Skimmer Systems 1967–68* 63 Movement of shipment in cages installed on air-in-floor pallets eliminates rehandling between city pick-up trailers, terminal site, over-the-road trailers, second city terminal site and final delivery unit. **1969** *Jane's Freight Containers 1968–69* 407/3 Both the 20 ft and 40 ft units are designed to be used as over-the-road trailers. **1971** M. TAK *Truck Talk* 114 *Over-the-road driver*, a driver who hauls goods long distances. **1977** *Time* 13 June 36/2 Last week's decision ended a long and hard-fought case against..a trucking company based in Lubbock, Texas, which the Government accused of discriminating against blacks and Hispanics in deciding who would get over-the-road driving jobs.

over-thick, -thicken, etc.: see OVER-.

over'think, *v. Obs.* in I; now *rare* in II.

†**I.** = OE. *ofþyncan.*

†**1.** *intr.* To seem not good; to displease, vex, cause regret or repentance; = OFTHINK; cf. also FORTHINK. Chiefly *impers.* with dative of person.

c **1200** ORMIN 8920 Ta þeȝȝ misstenn þeȝȝre child, & itt hem offerrþuhhte. *Ibid.* 19596 Iohan Bapptisste wisste itt wel & itt himm oferrþuhhte. *c* **1330** R. BRUNNE *Chron. Wace* (Rolls) 2350 Hure ouer-þoughte mykel more þe wraþthe of hure fader þe kyng. *a* **1350** *Cursor M.* 2732 (Gött.) If schoe did it, hir ouerthoght [*other MSS.* for thoght]. **1387–8** T. USK *Test. Love* I. ii. (Skeat) l. 69, I se well (and that me ouerthinketh) that wit in thee faileth.

†**b.** *trans.* To regret, repent. *Obs.*

c **1430** *Syr Gener.* (Roxb.) 1721 Nou it is to late to ouer-think, As I haue brew, so most I drink. *c* **1440** CAPGRAVE *Life St. Kath.* v. 951 Thei shul it ouerethynke If it be proued thei ȝoue hir mete or drynke. *c* **1440** *Gesta Rom.* xviii. 332 (Camb. MS.) One of hem seyde, 'herith my counceill, & ye shull not ouerþink it' [*Addit. MS.* forthynke].

II. From senses of OVER-, 1 (*c*), 26, 27, 23.

2. To think over, to consider. *Obs.* or *arch.*

c **1477** CAXTON *Jason* 13 b, Whan I haue ouerthought these saide thinges I answere yow. *c* **1489** —— *Sonnes of Aymon* xix. 418 Yf ye overthynke wel al, ye shall fynde that [etc.].

†**3.** To think too highly of, over-estimate. *Obs.*

a **1618** SYLVESTER *Job Triumphant* IV. 147 What man, like Job, himselfe so over-thinks? **1645** RUTHERFORD *Tryal & Tri. Faith* xxvi. (1845) 398 You may over-think and over-praise Paradise.

4. *refl.* To exhaust oneself with too much thinking.

a **1652** BROME *City Wit* III. iv, Have you not overmus'd or overthought your selfe?

So **over-'thinking** *vbl. sb.*, too much thinking.

1711 SHAFTESB. *Charac.* (1737) III. 300 It was never their over-thinking which oppress'd them.

†**over'thought,** *ppl. a. Obs. rare.* [pa. pple. of OVERTHINK *v.*] Grieved, vexed.

c **1250** *Gen. & Ex.* 2219 Oc alle he weren ouer ðoȝt, And hauen it so to iacob broȝt.

overthought ('əʊvəθɔːt), *sb.* **a.** [OVER- 29 b.] Excessive thought, too much thinking. So **'over'thoughted** *a.*, filled with excess of thought, over-weighed with thinking.

1839 BAILEY *Festus* ii. (1852) 17 This strange phantom comes from overthought. **1877** RUSKIN *Let. to Faunthorpe* i. (1895) 5, I..being in every way overworked and overthoughted. **1892** E. P. BARROW *Regni Evangel.* iii. 73 Because overthought for the morrow is deprecated, is forethought, therefore, discouraged?

b. [OVER- 2 b.] Conscious thought; an explicit concept; = OVERSOUL.

1883 G. M. HOPKINS *Let.* 14 Jan. (1938) 105 Two strains of thought..the overthought that which everybody, editors, see..which might for instance be abridged or paraphrased ..the other, the underthought, conveyed chiefly in the choice of metaphors etc used and often only half realised by the poet himself. **1884** W. JAMES in R. B. Perry *Tht. & Char. W. James* (1935) I. 583 Those who must answer this question negatively are forced to the notion of an Over-thought behind the phenomenal real.

over-'thoughtful, *a.* [OVER- 28.] Too thoughtful, too full of thought, too anxious.

c **1449** PECOCK *Repr.* III. xv. 377 Ouer thouȝtful and ouer carkful and ouermyche louyng toward hem. **1678** NORRIS *Coll. Misc.* (1699) 93. **1741** RICHARDSON *Pamela* II. 156 Only the foolish Weakness of an over-thoughtful Mind.

†**over'thrall,** *v. Sc. Obs.* [OVER- 21.] *trans.* To enthrall, take captive.

1536 BELLENDEN *Cron. Scot.* (1821) I. Proheme Cosmogr. 10 Thoucht thay may no wais me ouirthrall.

†**'over'threshold.** *Obs.* [OVER- 1 d.] A door-lintel.

1382 WYCLIF *Exod.* xii. 22 Sprengith of it the ouerthreswold [1388 lyntel], and either post.

over-thrifty, -thronged: see OVER-.

overthrow ('əʊvəθrəʊ), *sb.*

I. [f. OVERTHROW *v.*]

1. a. An act of overthrowing; the fact of being overthrown; defeat, discomfiture; deposition from power; subversion, destruction, ruin.

1513 MORE in Grafton *Chron.* (1568) II. 758 Sundry victoryes had he, and sometyme ouerthrowes. *c* **1560** A. SCOTT *Poems* (S.T.S.) xxi. 31 This is not þe first ourthraw That thow hes done to me. **1593** SHAKS. *Rich. II*, v. vi. 16 Two of the dangerous consorted Traitors, That sought at Oxford, thy dire ouerthrow. **1669** GALE *Crt. Gentiles* I. III. xi. 115 Their often recoveries from so many Overthrows and Captivities. **1774** *Chesterfield's Lett.* I. xx. 87 Camillus.. came upon the Gauls in the rear..and gave them a total overthrow. **1853** J. H. NEWMAN *Hist. Sk.* (1876) I. [II.] I. ii. 91 Mere material power was not adequate to the overthrow of the Saracenic sovereignty.

†**b.** Phr. ***to give the overthrow***, to defeat, overthrow; ***to have the overthrow***, to be defeated.

1553 EDEN *Treat. Newe Ind.* (Arb.) 16 In this fight the Elephant had the ouerthrowe. **1564** HAWARD *Eutropius* VII. 61 When these three capytaines were gone forthe againste Antonius they gave him thouverthrow. **1591** SHAKS. *1 Hen. VI*, III. ii. 106 We are like to haue the ouerthrow againe. **1601** —— *Jul. C.* v. ii. 5 And sodaine push giues them the ouerthrow.

†**c.** That which overthrows or brings down.

1581 MULCASTER *Positions* vi. (1887) 44 These foure ouerthrowes of our bodies and health, olde age, waste, aire, and violence. **1607–12** BACON *Ess., Empire* (Arb.) 298 Vespasian asked him what was Neroes ouerthrowe.

d. The state of being overthrown.

1903 *Daily Chron.* 12 Sept. 5/1 Half a dozen great trees were torn up by the roots, and lay in disorderly overthrow ready for the saws. **1906** F. THOMPSON *Ode Eng. Martyrs* in *Wks.* (1913) II. 136 Till she shall know This lesson in her overthrow: Hardest servitude has he That's jailed in arrogant liberty.

2. *Geol.* An overturning or inversion of strata.

1891 DK. ARGYLL in *19th Cent.* Jan. 19 The overthrows and the overthrusts, the sinkings and the underthrusts, which have inverted the order of original formation.

3. Anything thrown overboard. *nonce-use.*

1885–94 R. BRIDGES *Eros & Psyche* Nov. xxiv, Like twin sharks that in a fair ship's wake Swim constant..and hasty ravin make Of overthrow or offal.

II. [f. OVER- 13.]

4. In *Cricket*: A return of the ball by a fielder in which it is not caught or stopped near the wicket, giving the batsman opportunity of making further runs. In *Baseball*: A throwing of the ball over or beyond the player to whom it is thrown.

1748 in H. T. Waghorn *Dawn of Cricket* (1906) 21 To play or pay, bye balls, and overthrows to count. **1749** in Waghorn *Cricket-Scores* (1899) 43 Five of Addington Club challenge any five in England for 50 guineas, to play bye-balls and overthrows. **1849** *Laws of Cricket* in 'Bat' *Crick. Man.* (1850) 60 Neither byes nor overthrows shall be allowed. **1856** *Spirit of Times* 8 Nov. 165/1 Gessner [made]..three homes in succession, one of them being helped by an overthrow. **1891** W. G. GRACE *Cricket* 258 He must back up the wicket-keeper to save overthrows. **1949** *Telephone-Reg.* (McMinnville, Oregon) 4 Aug. 1/2 There is no sliding and a player cannot run on overthrows. **1955** *Times* 13 July 3/4 The Middlesex fielding was uncertain and Warwickshire were helped by indiscriminate throwing, which led to many over-throws.

5. *Archit.* A panel of decorated wrought-iron work forming the architrave of a gateway or arch.

1911 J. S. GARDNER *English Ironwork 17th & 18th Centuries* 26 The base of the overthrow took the form of a latticed girder, or two bars braced together by scrolls. **1932** *Times Lit. Suppl.* 10 Nov. 835/2 Making artistic ironwork —gates simple or elaborate, with or without 'overthrows'. **1957** R. LISTER *Decorative Wrought Ironwork Gt. Brit.* iii. 89 The overthrow, a composition built up from sixteen simple scrolls, reaches up symmetrically in the centre of the stretcher..terminating into a large disc bearing a garter and shield, and crested by a coronet. **1971** *Illustr. London News* Oct. 54/1 A good quality 18th century Italian Istrian marble wellhead with wrought iron overthrow. **1975** *Oxf. Compan. Decorative Arts* 481/2 The overthrows of the gates, swollen to gigantic size, plainly prefigure the Rococo.

overthrow (əʊvə'θrəʊ), *v.* [f. OVER- 6, 27 + THROW *v.*, q.v. for Forms. Takes the place of OVERCAST, as that did of OVERWARP, OE. *oferweorþan.*]

1. a. *trans.* To throw (a person or thing) over upon its side or upper surface; to upset, overturn; to knock (a structure) down and so demolish it.

c **1330** *Owayn Miles* 23 So bitter and so cold it blewe That alle the soules it ouer threwe That lay in purgatory. **1362** LANGL. *P. Pl.* A. IX. 31 Þe wynt wolde with þe water þe Bot ouer-þrowe. *c* **1400** *Sowdone Bab.* 388 Every man Shulde withe Pikeys or with bille The Wallis over throwe. **1484** CAXTON *Fables of Æsop* v. xii, The wulf ouerthrewe the dogge vpsodoune to the ground. *a* **1533** LD. BERNERS *Huon* lxxxi. 242 He ouerthrewe cuppes and dysshes vpon the table. **1535** COVERDALE *Jonah* iii. 4 There are yet xl. dayes, and then shal Niniue be ouerthrowen. **1627** CAPT. SMITH *Seaman's Gram.* xi. 54 To ouerset or ouerthrow a ship, is by bearing too much saile you bring her Keele vpwards, or on shore ouerthrow her by grounding her, so that she falls vpon one side. *a* **1704** T. BROWN *On Dk. Ormond's Recov.* Wks. 1730 I. 49 Your sacred seats by cruel rage o'erthrown. **1875** JOWETT *Plato* (ed. 2) I. 159 One who is already prostrate cannot be overthrown.

†**b.** To turn (a wheel) upside down. *Obs.*

1390 GOWER *Conf.* I. 8 After the tornynge of the whiel, Which blinde fortune overthroweth.

2. *fig.* To cast down from a position of prosperity or power; to defeat, overcome, vanquish; to ruin, destroy, or reduce to impotence.

*c***1374** CHAUCER *Boeth.* II. metr. i. 22 (Camb. MS.) A whiht is seyn weleful And ouerthrowe [by Fortune] in an houre. *c***1449** PECOCK *Repr.* 208 Alle the repugners ben openli ouerthrowe. **1470–85** MALORY *Arthur* I. xvii, Yonder xj kynges at this tyme wyll not be ouerthrowen. *a***1548** HALL *Chron., Edw. IV* 204 b, Hys partye was ouerthrowen and vanquyshed. **1602** WARNER *Alb. Eng.* IX. lii. 233 For peace we warre, a peruerse warre that doth our selues ore-throe. **1712–14** POPE *Rape Lock* III. 61 Mighty Pam, that Kings and Queens o'erthrew. **1894** *Times* (weekly ed.) 19 Jan. 57/1 He ..was overthrown with Thiers seven days afterwards.

3. a. To overturn (any established or existing condition or order of things, a device, theory, plan, etc.); to subvert, ruin, bring to nought, demolish.

*c***1374** CHAUCER *Troylus* IV. 357 (385) Who wolde haue wend þat yn so lytel a þrowe Fortune oure Ioye wolde han ouer-þrowe. *a***1548** HALL *Chron., Rich. III* 49 b, Suche thinges as were..to be set forward, were nowe dasshed and ouerthrowen to the grounde. **1591** SHAKS. *1 Hen. VI,* I. iii. 65 Here's Gloster,..That seekes to ouerthrow Religion. **1611** BIBLE *2 Tim.* ii. 18 Who..ouerthrow the faith of some. **1798** MALTHUS *Popul.* (1817) II. 75 This overthrows at once the supposition of any thing like uniformity in the proportion of births. **1868** LIGHTFOOT *Phil.* (1873) 94 He determined to overthrow the worship of the one true God.

b. To bring down or put an end by force to (an institution, a government).

*a***1578** LINDESAY (Pitscottie) *Chron. Scot.* (S.T.S.) I. 27 His authoritie sould be contempnit and the commonweill.. ovirthrawin. **1585** T. WASHINGTON tr. *Nicholay's Voy.* III. iii. 74 This Oriental empire..shall one day be cleane ouer-throwen. **1727** DE FOE *Syst. Magic* I. ii, The Persians.. over-threw their empire. **1847** MRS. A. KERR *Servia* 422 Thus was overthrown a government raised up by the force of events.

4. †**a.** To cast down or upset in mental or bodily state (*obs.*). **b.** To overturn or destroy the normal sound condition of (the mind).

*c***1374** CHAUCER *Boeth.* I. pr. iv. 13 (Camb. MS.), I se þat goode men beth ouerthrowen for drede of my peril. **1562** TURNER *Baths* 1 They [brimstone baths] undo and ouer-throwe the stomacke. **1602** SHAKS. *Ham.* III. i. 158 O what a Noble minde is heere o're-throwne! **1621** BURTON *Anat. Mel.* II. ii. VI. iii. (1651) 306 They..contract filthy diseases, ..overthrow their bodies. **1816** J. WILSON *City of Plague* III. i. 321 O misery! His mind is overthrown.

†**5.** *intr.* To fall over or down, tumble; to throw oneself or be thrown down. *Obs.*

13.. *Sir Beues* (A.) 2850 Tweies a ros and tweies a fel, þe þredde tim ouer-þrew in þe wel; þar inne a lai vp riȝt. **1387** TREVISA *Higden* (Rolls) IV. 269 Whan Crist entrede into Egipt, þe mawmettes overþrewe and fil doun. *c***1450** *Merlin* 53 His palfrey stombled on his knees, and he ouer-threw, and brakke hys neke. **1509** HAWES *Past. Pleas.* xl. (Percy Soc.) 44 Warre ones begon, it is hard to know Who shall abyde and who shall overthrowe. **1546** J. HEYWOOD *Prov.* (1867) 29 The best cart maie ouerthrowe.

6. *trans.* To throw farther than is necessary or desired; to throw too far; *spec.* in *Cricket,* to throw (the ball) beyond or wide of the wicket, so as to concede overthrows.

1833 *Field Bk.* 141/1 The batters may take the advantage of running when a ball has been over-thrown. **1862** *Chambers's Encycl.* III. 320/1 Misconception of this [distance] may lead to overthrowing the ball, or throwing it short. **1875** *Baily's Mag.* Apr. 403 A ball..overthrown, on the ground where he learnt his cricket, means the loss of four, five, or even six or seven runs.

Hence **over'throwable** *a.*, capable of being overthrown.

1653 BOYLE *Let. to Mallet* 23 Sept., Wks. 1772 I. Life 53 Which..I found, though hardly overthrowable in equity, yet to be questionable in strictness of law.

overthrowal (əʊvəˈθrəʊəl). [f. OVERTHROW *v.* + -AL II.] The act of overthrowing; subversion, defeat.

1916 W. J. LOCKE *Wonderful Year* xxiii. 333 Thus came the overthrowal of all Corinna's scheme of values. **1920** —— *House of Baltazar* xxi. 257 The ultimate object of this gathering was the overthrowal of the Government. **1941** 'R. WEST' *Black Lamb* II. 196 The upsetting of kings and the overthrowal of empires. **1949** *Tablet* 3 Sept. 147/1 The overthrowal of the Second Reich of the Hohenzollerns. **1968** *Progressive* Nov. 10/3 Spiro Agnew..had coined at least two new words by early October: 'overthrowal' and 'uprisal'.

over'thrower. [f. OVERTHROW *v.* + -ER[1].] One who overthrows.

*a***1548** HALL *Chron., Edw. IV* 205 He was the ouerthrower and confounder of the house of Lancastre. **1650** S. CLARKE *Eccl. Hist.* I. (1654) 8 This is that Doctor of Asia, the Overthrower of our Gods. **1772** *Hist. Eur.* in *Ann. Reg.* 99/2 The overthrower of Bolingbroke. **1836** LYTTON *Athens* (1837) II. 332 Plato rightly considers Ephialtes the true overthrower of the Areopagus.

over'throwing, *vbl. sb.* [f. OVERTHROW *v.* + -ING[1].] The action of the vb. OVERTHROW; a throwing down; overturning, destruction, ruin.

*c***1374** CHAUCER *Boeth.* II. metr. iv. 31 (Camb. MS.) Al thowgh the wynde trowblynge the see thondre with ouerthrowynges. **1535** COVERDALE *Ecclus.* xiii. 13 Thou walkest in parell of thy ouerthrowinge. **1675** tr. *Camden's Hist. Eliz.* I. (1688) 127 The overthrowing of the Duke. **1850** TENNYSON *In Mem.* cxiii, With overthrowings, and with cries, And undulations to and fro.

over'throwing, *ppl. a.* [f. OVERTHROW *v.* + -ING[2].] That overthrows. †**a.** Headstrong, headlong, prone (*obs.*). **b.** Overwhelming, overturning, upsetting.

a. *c***1374** CHAUCER *Boeth.* II. metr. vii. 47 (Camb. MS.) Who so þat with ouerthrowynge thowght oonly seketh glorye of fame. *Ibid.* IV. pr. vi. 109 The nature of som man is so ouerthrowenge to yuel.

b. *c***1374** CHAUCER *Boeth.* I. metr. ii. 3 (Camb. MS.) The thowt of man dreynt in ouerthrowynge depnesse. *Ibid.* III. metr. xii. 84 Tho ne was nat the heued of yxion I-tormented by the ouerthrowinge wheel. **1592** G. HARVEY *New Letter* Wks. (Grosart) I. 261 Take away that overthrowing or weakening property from Truce: and Truce may be a diuine Scammony. **1839** BAILEY *Festus* i. (1852) 8 The overruling, overthrowing power.

'over'thrown (shifting stress), *ppl. a.* and *sb.* [pa. pple. of OVERTHROW *v.*]

A. *ppl. adj.* **1.** Thrown over on its side, face, or upper surface; upset; overcome; vanquished, demolished.

1579–80 NORTH *Plutarch* (1676) 35 Some easie medicine, to purge an overthrown body. **1667** MILTON *P.L.* VI. 856 The overthrown he rais'd. **1814** SOUTHEY in *Q. Rev.* XII. 189 The ruins of overthrown edifices. **1877** *N.W. Linc. Gloss., Farwelted,* overthrown; said of sheep.

†**2.** Thrown too strongly. *Obs.* [OVER- 28 c.]

1642 FULLER *Holy & Prof. St.* I. ii. 29 A rubbe to an overthrown bowl proves an help by hindering it.

†**B.** *sb.* A supine (in grammar). *Obs. rare.*

*c***1532** DU WES *Introd. Fr.* in *Palsgr.* 935 The overthrowen or supins which ben called *reuerses.*

overthrust (ˈəʊvəθrʌst), *sb. Geol.* [OVER- 1, 9.] The thrust of the strata or series of rocks on one side of a fault over those on the other side, esp. of lower over higher strata, as in an OVERFAULT or faulted OVERFOLD; a reverse fault; (used more particularly in reference to the distance through which the mass of dislocated strata has been thrust or moved forward over the thrust-plane). In mod. use (also ***overthrust fault***), a reverse fault in which the fault plane makes a relatively small angle with the horizontal. Also *attrib.*

1883 [see OVERFAULT]. **1885** C. CALLAWAY in *Daily News* 8 Jan. 3/5 The extraordinary overthrust of old rocks on to newer strata in Sutherlandshire. **1888** *Q. Jrnl. Geol. Soc.* 385 Confirming Nicol's conclusions..that the line of junction of the unaltered Palaeozoic rocks is a line of fault and overthrust. **1890** BOYD DAWKINS in *Nature* 31 July 320 The coal-measures are folded, broken and traversed by great 'overthrust' faults. **1892** LAPWORTH *Pres. Address Brit. Ass. Edin.,* The overthrust plane or overfault, where the septal region of contrary motion in the fold becomes reduced to, or is represented by, a plane of contrary motion. **1894** *Jrnl. R. Agric. Soc.* June 390 Eastbourne, where on the foreshore the Cretaceous strata are repeated by faults and overthrusts. **1903** A. GEIKIE *Text-bk. Geol.* (ed. 4) I. 690, 1. Normal Faults... 2. Reversed Faults or Overthrusts. **1944** A. HOLMES *Princ. Physical Geol.* vi. 80 Reverse or Thrust Faults... When the resulting fracture is inclined at an angle between 45° and the horizontal..the corresponding fault is described as an overthrust. **1957** *Bull. Geol. Soc. Amer.* LXVIII. 168/1 The Medicine Lodge overthrust, a low-angle fault with a displacement of many miles. **1969** *Ibid.* LXXX. 953 Overthrust fault surfaces are actually undulatory rather than plane.

So **over'thrust** *v.*; hence **'overthrust** *ppl. a.*, **over'thrusting** *vbl. sb.*

1883 LAPWORTH in *Geol. Mag.* Aug. 339 In many cases this overthrusting effect is due to the relief of downward pressure caused by the erosion of the brow of the arch. **1900** [see CRUST *sb.* 13 b]. **1901** *Nature* 3 Jan. 234/1 Huge masses of country have been overfolded, fractured, and overthrust, the older being pushed over the newer. **1942** M. P. BILLINGS *Structural Geol.* x. 184 The thrusts dip north, and the overthrust sheets have traveled northward relative to the underlying formations. **1956** W. J. ARKELL *Jurassic Geol. World* ix. 225 The Jurassic and Cretaceous systems were strongly folded and overthrust in the post-Oligocene, pre-Miocene orogeny. **1968** [see FORELAND 5].

overthwart (əʊvəˈθwɔːt), *adv.* and *prep.* Now *Obs.* or *rare* exc. *dial.* Also 4 ouerthuert, 4–5 -thwert(e, -þwert(e, -twert, 4–6 *Sc.* ourthwort, 5 ouereþwart, ouerþewert, ouertwart, -twarde, overhwarte, orthward, (auerthwert, -thward, aurthwart, -thewert, awrthwert, awterwart), 5–6 ouerthward(e, -thart(e, *Sc.* ourthort, -thourth, ouerthort, ouirthort, 6 ortwharte, orewharte, 6–7 (9 *dial.*) overwhart(e, 8–9 *dial.* overwart, overquart. [ME. f. OVER *adv.* + *þwert* adv., a. ON. *þvert* neuter of *þverr* = OE. *þweorh* cross, transverse: see THWART *adv.*]

A. *adv.*

1. Over from side to side, or so as to cross something; across, athwart; crosswise, transversely.

*c***1300** *Havelok* 2822 And demden him to binden faste Vpon an asse..Andelong, nouht ouerthwert. **1375** BARBOUR *Bruce* VIII. 172 Thre dykis ourthwort he schar Fra bath the mossis to the vay. *c***1400** MAUNDEV. ii. 10 The pece [of the Cross] that wente overthwart. *c***1489** CAXTON *Sons of Aymon* ix. 238 They..layed hym vpon a lityll horse overhwarte like as a sacke of corne. **1513** DOUGLAS *Æneis* V. vi. 84 But kest hym evin ourthortour Salyus way. **1600** HOLLAND *Livy* I. xiii. 10 Then the Sabine dames,..hauing thrust themselues violently overthwart betweene them, began to part these bloodie armies. **1692** tr. *Sallust* 168 The Yoke was two Spears fixed in the Ground, and a third fastened overthwart from one to the other, like a Gallows. **1764** *Museum Rusticum* III. lxxiv. 321 Third ploughing, ribbling it overwart. *a***1825** FORBY *Voc. E. Anglia* s.v., To plough overwhart is to plough at right angles to the former furrows.

b. ***overthwart and endlong***: crosswise and lengthwise, in breadth and length, transversely and longitudinally; hence *fig.* wholly, completely.

1340 HAMPOLE *Pr. Consc.* 8582 Þe devels sal, ay, on þam gang To and fra, over-thewrt and endlang. **1417** *Surtees Misc.* (1888) 13 All the alde stuffe of lede that lay thare before, endelang and overthwart. *c***1460** *Towneley Myst.* xii. 48 He saue you and me, ouerthwart and endlang.

†**2.** *fig.* Adversely; wrongly, amiss, perversely; angrily, 'crossly'. *Obs.*

13.. *Cursor M.* 12084 (Cott.) A maister..Wit ioseph wordes spak ourthuert [*Fairf.* ouer-thwert]. *c***1330** R. BRUNNE *Chron. Wace* 2318 Þat word tok he yuel til herte, He vnderstod hit al ouerþwerte. *c***1430** *Syr Gener.* (Roxb.) 2104 And answerd the king ful ouertwert. **1535** *Goodly Primer, Exp. Ps. li.* (v. 18) With the wicked shalt thou play overthwart. **1556** J. HEYWOOD *Spider & F.* xxxiii. 19 Run thei right: run thei ouertharte, Out wyll I powre them.

†**3.** Over against something else, opposite. *rare.*

1596 SPENSER *F.Q.* IV. x. 51 And her before was seated overthwart Soft Silence, and submisse Obedience.

†**4.** Here and there, all about. *Sc. Obs.*

1596 DALRYMPLE tr. *Leslie's Hist. Scot.* IV. 211 S. Palladie Bischope, and vthires..ouirthort [L. *sparsim*] in his kingdome, he promouet thame to steddings and feildes.

B. *prep.* **1.** From side to side of; so as to cross; across, athwart.

*c***1380** *Sir Ferumb.* 3721 Ys body was tornd ouer-thwart þe way. *c***1391** CHAUCER *Astrol.* I. §5 Ouer-thwart this for-seide longe lyne, ther crosseth hym a-nother lyne. *c***1470** HENRY *Wallace* IV. 234 A loklate bar was drawyn our-thourth the dur. **1551** ROBINSON tr. *More's Utop.* II. (1895) 163 That table standeth ouer wharte the ouer ende of the halle. **1610** BARROUGH *Meth. Physick* I. xxxi. (1639) 51 Cause him to sit overthwart a stoole in riding fashion. **1663** GERBIER *Counsel* 43 Lay Bridges overtwhart the Joyses. **1736** BAILEY *Househ. Dict.* 116 Cut it into collars overthwart both the sides. **1892** MORRIS *Yorksh. Folk-talk* s.v., He ran owerquart t' clooas.

†**2.** Over against, opposite. *Obs.*

1588 PARKE tr. *Mendoza's Hist. China* 353 They..twentie leagues overthwart the port. *a***1592** GREENE *Alphonsus* I. Wks. (Rtldg.) 228/2 Dost thou know the man That doth so closely overthwart us stand? **1630** WADSWORTH *Pilgr.* iii. 15 Disputing..in two pewes one ouerthwart the other.

3. On the opposite side of; across, beyond.

1784 COWPER *Task* I. 169 Far beyond, and overthwart the stream..The sloping land recedes into the clouds. **1854** MISS BAKER *Northampt. Gloss.* s.v., He lives o'erwart the way.

overthwart (ˈəʊvəθwɔːt), *a.* and *sb. Obs.* exc. *dial.* Forms: see prec.; also 5 **authwart, awthwert, ouerqwert.** [f. prec.]

A. *adj.* **1.** Placed or lying crosswise, or across something else; transverse, cross-.

13.. *E.E. Allit. P.* B. 1384, & þiker þrowen vmbe þour with ouer-þwert palle. *c***1400** MAUNDEV. (Roxb.) ii. 6 Þai made þe ouerthwert pece of palme. *c***1540** tr. *Pol. Verg. Eng. Hist.* (Camden) I. 72 Suetonius..camm throughe an overthwarte waye to London as to a place of safetie. **1545** RAYNOLD *Byrth Mankynde* 7 Nominatyd the ouerthwart muskles, in latin: *musculi transuersi.* **1623** T. SCOT *Highw. God* 8 Two crosse or ouerthwart wayes. **1796** MORSE *Amer. Geog.* II. 112 The transomes, or over-thwart stones [at Stone-henge], are quite plain.

†**b.** Crossing the right line; oblique, slanting; wry, skew: cf. OVERTHWARTLY 3. *Obs.*

1594 BLUNDEVIL *Exerc.* IV. Introd. (1636) 435 There is another great stooping and overthwart Circle, called the Ecliptique line.

†**c.** *fig.* Indirect: cf. OVERTHWARTLY 4. *Obs.*

1545 ASCHAM *Toxoph.* (Arb.) 88 You wyl haue some ouer-twhart reason to drawe forthe more communication withall. **1656** EARL MONM. tr. *Boccalini, Pol. Touchstone* (1674) 283 [They] take impious and overthwart revenge of even those that would not be secure.

†**2.** Situated or residing across or on the opposite side of something intervening; opposite. *Obs.*

1555 EDEN *Decades* 264 The soonne leaueth those regions, and goth by the contrarye or ouerthwarte circle towarde the south in wynter. **1692** DRYDEN *Cleomenes* V. ii, We whisper, for fear our o'erthwart neighbours should hear us cry, Liberty.

3. *fig.* Inclined to cross or oppose; perverse, froward, contrarious; contentious, captious, contradictious, quarrelsome, testy, 'cross'; adverse, contrary, hostile, unfriendly, unfavourable.

*c***1325** *Poem Times Edw. II.* (Percy Soc.) lxxviii, When God Almyȝty seth The work is overthwart. **1382** WYCLIF *2 Tim.* iii. 4 Traitours, proterue, or ouerthwert, bollun with proude thouȝtis. *c***1400** *Destr. Troy* 1960 He onswaret hym angerly with Awthwert wordis. *c***1530** tr. *Erasmus' Serm. Ch. Jesus* (1901) 20 A..kynde of chyldren, which is cleane ouertwart. **1595** DANIEL *Civ. Wars* I. xxvi, Of a Spirit averse and over-thwart. **1647** CLARENDON *Hist. Reb.* I. (1702) I. 64 That overthwart [*ed.* 1888 §174 thwartover] humour was enough discover'd to rule in the breasts of many. **1868** ATKINSON *Cleveland Gloss., Overquart, Overthwart,*.. perverse, contrary, contradictory or contentious.

†**B.** *sb.* [Absolute use of adj.] *Obs.*

1. A transverse or cross direction. In phrases ***at an overthwart, to overthwart***: in a transverse direction, crosswise, across.

1470–85 MALORY *Arthur* VII. viii, At the last at an ouerthwart Beaumayns with his hors strake the grene knyghtes hors vpon the syde. *Ibid.* xvii, The reed knyghte..

at an ouerthwart smote hym within the hand. **1562** TURNER *Herbal* II. 86b, Phu..hath litle rootes growyng to ouerthwart.

b. A transverse passage, a by-way, a crossing; a transverse line.

1580 *Will* in *Gentl. Mag.* Sept. (1861) 258, I leave my eldest sonn..also the newe overthwarte in the cittie of Corcke, and all the lands east of it to the Queenes walls. *a* **1631** DONNE *Poems, Anat. World* 256 To finde out..Such diuers downe-right lines, such ouerthwarts, As disproportion that pure forme.

c. Opposite point.

1674 N. FAIRFAX *Bulk & Selv.* 92 It cannot be meted by a streight line drawn from it to its overthwart.

2. An adverse experience; a 'cross', a rebuff.

a **1547** SURREY *Praise of mean Estate* 12 A hart well stayd, in ouerthwartes depe Hopeth amendes. **1587** GOLDING *De Mornay* xxvi. 406 The ouerthwartes that Abraham indured for Sara his wife in Aegypt. **1609** F. GREVIL *Alaham* III. iii, I feare the cariage: it hath many parts, And Hazards courses may finde ouerthwarts.

b. Contradiction; a rebuff; a repartee.

c **1555** ABP. PARKER *Ps.* xxxiv. 86 Keepe ye hys tong from ouerthwart. **1595** COPLEY *Wits, Fits, & F.* 147 For these wittie ouerthwarts the Gent. entertain'd the boy into his seruice.

overthwart (əʊvə'θwɔːt), *v.* Now *rare.* Also 5 -twert, 5–7 -whart, 6 -twhart, 8 -wart. [f. prec. adv. or adj.]

1. a. *trans.* To pass or lie athwart or across; to traverse, cross.

1426 LYDG. *De Guil. Pilgr.* 12072 At wyketys or wyndowys..Ouerthwertyd with no latys. *c* **1430** —— *Reas. & Sens.* (E.E.T.S.) 4786, I Gan to crosse dovne and dale And ouer twerten hille and vale. **1545** RAYNOLD *Byrth Mankynde* 18 The one embrasynge, compassyng and ouerthwarting thother. **1552** *Inv. Ch. Goods* (Surtees, No. 97) 31 Two tunacles of whyt bustian..overthuarde withe read vorsted. **1632** LITHGOW *Trav.* x. 504 Each Tide ouerthwarting another with repugnant courses. **1832** TENNYSON *Œnone* 137 Her clear and barèd limbs O'erthwarted with the brazen-headed spear Upon her pearly shoulder leaning cold.

b. To lie across, or place something across, so as to stop the way; to obstruct.

1654 tr. *Martini's Conq. China* 135 These places might have been easily defended if they had but.. overthawrted the ways by any incumbrances. **1719** D'URFEY *Pills* (1872) VI. 89 If the Seas should overthwart him, He would swim to the shore.

c. To plough across.

1764 *Museum Rusticum* III. lxxiv. 320 Ploughing up the tare land,.. Overwarting another clean earth.

2. *fig.* **a.** To act in opposition to; to cross, oppose; to hinder, thwart. Also *absol.*

a **1529** SKELTON *Ware Hauke* 230 He sayde, for a crokid intent The wordes were paruerted: And this he ouerthwarted. **1611** SPEED *Hist. Gt. Brit.* VII. xviii. §11. 292 They..endeuored to ouerthwart and gainsay whatsoeuer he proposed. *a* **1640** W. FENNER *Sacrifice Faithfull* ii. (1648) 62 Sinne may be said to be civilized, when it is overwharted by a higher principle. **1937** *John o' London's* 5 Feb. 761/2 My parents were for ever overthwarting me, both on 'em. Always to school I had to go till I was twelve, and to church I had to go regular as clockwork.

†**b.** To render 'overthwart'; to pervert. *rare.*

1430–40 LYDG. *Bochas* II. xxvii. (1554) 62b, A wuluishe thyrst to shede mannes blood, Whych ouerwharted..His royal corage, into tyrannye.

Hence **over'thwarting** *vbl. sb.* and *ppl. a.*

1552 HULOET, Ouerthwartynge, *peruicatia, pravitas. Ibid.*, Ouerthwartynge knaue, *perperus.* **1616** *Rich Cabinet* Z vj, All quarrelling, wrangling, and ouerthwarting must be auoided. **1632** LITHGOW *Trav.* IX. 421 Their..heads are.. couered with ouerthwarting strokes of crooked shables. **1942** W. ROSE *Good Neighbours* iii. 20 A field was first evenly ploughed all over, after which cross ploughing—called *overa-thurting*—often followed, severing the furrows and leaving the soil thoroughly exposed to the air.

†**over'thwarter.** *Obs.* [f. prec. + -ER¹.] One who 'overthwarts'; an adversary, opponent.

a **1450** *Knt. de la Tour* (1868) 53 Usureres, bariters, overthwarteres and lyers. **1596** NASHE *Saffron Walden* 96 M. Wathe his ouer-wharter (betwixt whom and him there was such deadly emulation).

†**over'thwartly,** *adv. Obs.* [f. OVERTHWART *a.* + -LY².] In an 'overthwart' manner.

1. In a direction across; transversely.

c **1440** *Promp. Parv.* 374/1 Ovyrthwer(t)ly (*MS. K.* ouerqwertly), *transverse.* **1597** A. M. tr. *Guillemeau's Fr. Chirurg.* 16b/1 Both the endes of the threde wherwith the Iugulare Vayne is ouerthwartely tyede. **1652** WHARTON tr. *Rothman's Chiromancy* Wks. (1683) 553 Many Lines in the uppermost Joynt, and they proceeding overthwartly.

2. At diagonally opposite points.

1621 AINSWORTH *Annot. Pentat.* Lev. i. 5 Upon the two corners of the Altar overthwartly, on the northeast horne, and on the southwest horne.

3. Obliquely; askew, awry.

1470–85 MALORY *Arthur* IX. i, His ouer garment sat ouerthwartly. **1591** HARINGTON *Orl. Fur.* XXII. lxvi, The stroke fell overthwartly so, That quite beside Rogeros shield it slipt. **1597** BEARD *Theatre God's Judgem.* (1612) 67 Euen when the quenchlesse torch, the worlds great eye, Aduanc't his rayes orethwartly from the skie.

4. *fig.* In oblique terms; indirectly.

1571 GOLDING *Calvin on Ps.* ii. 10 When he biddeth them to be lerned, he overthwartly taunteth their fond trust in their owne wisdome. **1579–80** NORTH *Plutarch* (1676) 993 The boy of Lacedæmon set out to accuse Plutarch overthwartly with a lie.

5. Adversely, perversely, frowardly; contrariwise; 'crossly'.

1387–8 T. USK *Test. Love* III. vii. l. 155 (Skeat) Pray her ..that for no mishappe, thy grace overthwartly tourne. *a* **1450** *Knt. de la Tour* xix. 28 She shulde not ansuere hym ouerthwartly atte euery worde. *a* **1568** ASCHAM *Scholem.* (Arb.) 35 Wrought as it should, not ouerwhartlie, and against the wood, by the scholemaster. **1603** KNOLLES *Hist. Turks* (1621) 1063 Seest thou not how overthwartly..they ..have dealt with thee and thy father?

†**over'thwartness.** *Obs.* [f. as prec. + -NESS.] The quality or character of being 'overthwart'; perversity, frowardness; contrariness.

c **1400** *Apol. Loll.* 107 Wat ouerþwartnes is þis to wil not obey to þe lesson? **1533** *St. Papers Hen. VIII*, II. 170 A perpetuall discourage to others, that doo use overthwartnes and contrariositie. *c* **1643** LD. HERBERT *Life* (1886) 81 My younger sister, indeed, might have been married to a far greater fortune, had not the overthwartness of some neighbours interrupted it.

†**over'thwartwise,** *adv. Obs.* [f. as prec. + -WISE.] In an 'overthwart' direction; crosswise, athwart. So †**over'thwartways** *adv. Obs.*

1594 PLAT *Jewell-ho.* III. 24 Fasten this bar ouerthwartwise in the middle point of the ouen mouth. **1656** RIDGLEY *Pract. Physic* 44 If the Artery be cut long, or over-thwartwaies.

over-tight, -till: see OVER-.

over'tilt, *v.* [OVER- 6.] *trans.* To tilt over, upset, overthrow.

1377 LANGL. *P. Pl.* B. xx. 134 He..ouertilte [C. ouertulte] al his treuthe with 'take þis vp amendement'. *c* **1430** *Pol. Rel. & L. Poems* 197 As a traitour þou schalt be ouer tilt. **1905** *Westm. Gaz.* 1 Feb. 2/3 Our house tottereth To ruin; because this people with the breath Of pity would overtilt it.

over-timbered: see OVER-.

overtime ('əʊvətaɪm), *sb.*, *adv.* [OVER- 19.]

A. *sb.* **a.** Time during which one works over and above the regular hours; extra time. Also, payment for work performed in excess of normal hours. Also *attrib.* ***overtime ban,*** industrial action in which the working of overtime is suspended.

[**1536** *Hampton Court Accts.*, Carpenters workyng their owre tymes and drynkyng tymes uppon thffonte in thchappell.] **1846** *Swell's Night Guide* 42 There are instances of the awful enemy lodging itself here, through some private tailing in overtime. **1858** SIMMONDS *Dict. Trade, Over-time, Over-work,* extra labour done beyond the regular fixed hours of business. **1861** *Times* 23 July, The grievance seems reduced to the single point of overtime, as it is allowed on both sides, that..10 hours is to be the standard. **1861** *Sat. Rev.* 20 July 60 The loss of the overtime bonus. **1870** ROGERS *Hist. Gleanings* Ser. II. 132 Piecework or overtime labour. **1911** *Daily Colonist* (Victoria, B.C.) 26 Apr. 14/5 A conference is to be held..with regard to the demand being made by the seamen for overtime pay. **1916** 'BOYD CABLE' *Doing their Bit* iv. 63 Their haggling over 8*d.* or 8½*d.* an hour pay, or Saturday half-holidays, or double overtime for Sunday. **1928** F. B. YOUNG *My Brother Jonathan* III. iii. 446 Joe Matthews..'picking up' six pounds a week, to say nothing of overtime, in Higgins's shell factory. **1952** *Times* 1 Dec. 2/5 (*heading*) Miners' overtime ban ended. **1968** *R. Comm. Trade Unions & Employers' Associations Res. Papers* No. 9, 82 The negotiations broke down during 1964 and the unions imposed an overtime ban and a work to rule. **1972** *Times* 15 May 17/3 Workers at another Ferranti factory are due to impose the restrictions —an overtime ban, work to rule and boycott of piecework —from today. **1973** C. D. GARRATT *Masterpieces in Steam* 128 My visit to Brynlliw was during the overtime ban prior to the miners' strike. **1973** *Times* 4 Dec. 3/6 The miners' overtime ban yesterday went into its fourth week.

b. In sporting contests: extra time added in the event of a draw. *N. Amer.*

1921 *Daily Colonist* (Victoria B.C.) 15 Mar. 11/1 Overtime game goes in favor of Towers. The Towers Club ..defeated the Senators..by 8 goals to 7, the game having to go into overtime to decide the match. **1946** *Richmond* (Virginia) *Times-Dispatch* 20 Mar. 17/3 His keen floor generalship..built up to a terrific climax—his 55-foot shot in the last two seconds that tied the score at 74–74 and led to the Ram's 82–79 overtime triumph. **1961** J. S. SALAK *Dict. Amer. Sports* 315 *Overtime,* continuance of play after the regulation time for a contest has expired when the score is tied. **1970** *Washington Post* 30 Sept. D 1/7 The Senators.. lost two overtime games to the Baltimore Orioles. **1974** *State* (Columbia, S. Carolina) 3 Mar. 2-D/5 Freshman Walter Davis banked in a 35-foot jump shot at the end of regulation time to cap an incredible North Carolina comeback Saturday as the fourth-ranked Tar Heels nipped arch rival Duke, 96–92 in overtime.

B. *adv.* During extra time; over hours. Also *fig.*

1873 HAMERTON *Intell. Life* I. ii. (1876) 6 She worked over-time. **1894** *Brit. Jrnl. Photogr.* XLI. 5 Sixty hands.. working overtime. **1938** E. AMBLER *Cause for Alarm* xvi. 262 In that moment my brain worked overtime. **1953** A. HUXLEY *Let.* 25 Sept. (1969) 685 They are pork manufacturers, with a farm where five thousand sows work overtime eating the garbage of the city of Long Beach and producing fifty thousand piglets per annum. **1971** *Nature* 26 Nov. 179/1 Washington's science policy machinery has been working overtime on plans that could significantly alter relationships between science and government. **1974** G. BUTLER *Coffin for Canary* i. 9 My tongue had worked overtime at the week-end..talking with my sister.

ˌ**over-'time,** *v. Photogr.* [OVER- 27.] *trans.* To time too long; to give too long a time to an exposure or other process.

1889 *Anthony's Photogr. Bull.* II. 211 Should a negative be overtimed and developed flat. **1896** *Kodak News* Sept. 36/1 As much difference..as there is between an overtimed and an undertimed negative.

†'**over'timely,** *adv.* and *a. Obs.*

A. *adv.* Too early, before the proper time, prematurely; untimely, unseasonably. [OVER- 30.]

1303 R. BRUNNE *Handl. Synne* 6613 Ȝyf þou any day shuldest fast, And þou ouertymely þy mete aske. *c* **1374** CHAUCER *Boeth.* I. metr. i. 1 (Camb. MS.) Heeres hoore arn schad ouertymeliche vpon myn heued. *c* **1440** *Jacob's Well* 142 þe ferst fote brede of wose in glotonye is, to ete or drynke ouertymely, ouersone or ouyrlate. **1532** HERVET *Xenophon's Househ.* (1768) 77 Suffreth his workemen to l(e)ue their worke and go theyr way ouer tymely. **1655** MOUFET & BENNET *Health's Impr.* (1746) 343 Nourishment, which else being too liquid would turn to Crudities by passing overtimely into the Guts.

B. *adj.* Too early, premature, untimely. [OVER- 28.]

1548 UDALL, etc. *Erasm. Par. Mark* 40b, Lamentably bewaylyng her ouertymely deathe. **1577–87** HOLINSHED *Chron.* I. 25/1 The vaine youthfull fantasie and ouertimelie death of thy fathers and thy brethren.

'**over-ˌtimer.** [f. OVERTIME *sb.* + -ER¹.] One who works overtime.

1926 S. BALDWIN *On England* 99 The just and the unjust, the half-timers, the whole-timers and the over-timers.

overtimorous: see OVER-.

over'tip, *v.* [f. OVER- 27 + TIP *v.*⁴] *trans.* To give an excessive gratuity to (one who has been of service). Also *absol.* Hence ˌ**over-'tipping** *vbl. sb.*

1926 E. HEMINGWAY *Fiesta* (1927) III. xix. 269 The waiter seemed a little offended..so I overtipped him. **1928** A. HUXLEY *Point Counter Point* xxi. 388 The fare was three-and-six. Philip gave the driver two half-crowns... He made a habit of over-tipping. **1938** L. MACNEICE *Earth Compels* 38 And there are the men who appear to be men of sense,.. For fear of opinion over-tipping in bars, For fear of thought studying stupefaction. **1941** *Penguin New Writing* VIII. 62 The guests in the guest-house, they were charmed with him too. They over-tipped him. **1965** *New Statesman* 7 May 729/3 If we had reason to believe that he once overtipped a cab-driver, it would be recorded here. **1976** E. WARD *Hanged Man* xvii. 98 He stopped the taxi..paid and overtipped. *Ibid.* xxxiii. 214 A taxi-driver collected the message for him. Anonymity is worth over-tipping.

overtippled: see OVER-.

overtire (ˌəʊvə'taɪə(r)), *v.* [OVER- 21, 27.] *trans.* To tire out, exhaust with fatigue; to tire excessively. Hence ˌ**over'tired** *ppl. a.*, 'tired out,' excessively tired; ˌ**over'tiring** *vbl. sb.* and *ppl. a.*

1557–8 PHAER *Æneid* VI. Sj, Though he with dart the wyndyfooted hinde did ouertyer. **1599** HAKLUYT *Voy.* I. 613 Marching with al possible speede on foote, notwithstanding ..the ouertiring tedious deepe sands. **1634** W. TIRWHYT tr. *Balzac's Lett.* 117 Such rest, as wearinesse and weakness affordeth to over-tired bodies. **1641** BP. HALL *Serm.* Ps. lx. 2. Wks. 1837 V. 442 Which..must be, for fear of your overtiring, the last of our discourse. **1671** MILTON *Samson* 1632. **1870** *Routledge's Ev. Boy's Ann.* June 330 You'll overtire yourself. **1897** MARY KINGSLEY *W. Africa* 689 When you have got very chilled or over-tired, take an extra five grains with a little wine or spirit at any time.

†ˌ**over-'title,** *v. Obs.* [OVER- 26.] *trans.* To give too high a title to; to style or denominate by too high a name.

1620 BP. HALL *Hon. Mar. Clergy* III. §3 The Bishop of Rome is stiled Supreme Head and Gouernour of the Whole Church..When he that so humbly ouer-titles the person resists the Doctrine. **1639** FULLER *Holy War* v. xii. (1840) 264 Diverting the pilgrims, and over-titling his own quarrels to be God's cause.

overtly ('əʊvətlɪ), *adv.* [f. OVERT *a.* + -LY².] In an overt manner.

1. Openly, manifestly, without concealment or secrecy; in quot. 1614, Outwardly, publicly.

c **1325** *Metr. Hom.* 137 Us au to thinc na ferlye Thoh Godd it warnes ouertlye. **1579** J. STUBBES *Gaping Gulf* D v, The king could not, for bewraying that counsail, declare his wyll ouertly. **1614** RALEIGH *Hist. World* Pref. Cjb, For whatsoeuer hee ouertly pretended, Hee held in secret a contrary councell with the Secretarie. **1703** YOUNG *Serm.* II. 389 Good men are never overtly despised, but that they are first calumniated. **1859** *Times* 2 Sept. 1st Leader §1 A position with which no European Power could overtly quarrel.

†**2.** So as to be or lie open. *Obs.*

1601 HOLLAND *Pliny* I. 525 The plot wherin you mean to haue Chestnuts grow must be ouvertly broken vp aloft, from between Nouember and Februarie.

'**overtness.** [f. as prec. + -NESS.] Openness, want of reserve or concealment.

1887 T. HARDY *Woodlanders* III. xiii. 258 My success with you..has not been great enough to justify such overtness.

'**over-'toil,** *sb.* [OVER- 29.] Excessive toil.

1872 TALMAGE *Serm.* 198 These died of overtoil in the Lowell carpet factories.

overtoil (əʊvə'tɔɪl), *v.* [OVER- 21.] *trans.* To wear out or exhaust by excessive toil; to overwork, fatigue. Hence **over'toiled** *ppl. a.*, **over'toiling** *vbl. sb.*

1577 NORTHBROOKE *Dicing* (1843) 52 Wearied nature's ouertoyled bodies. **1607** MARKHAM *Caval.* III. (1617) 59 Seeke to ouertoile him, and make him glad to giue ouer striuing to get the leading. **1612** BRINSLEY *Lud. Lit.* v. (1627) 51 To prevent the overtoyling and terrifying of Schollers with it. **1727** BRADLEY *Fam. Dict.* s.v. *Girdle Wheel*, Ladies that love not to overtoil themselves. **1847-8** H. MILLER *First Impr.* xviii. 325 An overtoiled young man in delicate health. **1859** TENNYSON *Enid* 1225 Overtoil'd By that day's travel.

† **over-'toise**, *v. nonce-wd.* [f. OVER- 10 + TOISE *sb.*] *trans.* To measure out in toises.

1840 BROWNING *Sordello* II. 828 Implements it sedulous employs To undertake, lay down, mete out, o'ertoise Sordello.

overtone ('əʊvətəʊn), *sb. Acoustics* and *Mus.* [ad. Ger. *oberton*, used by Helmholtz as a contraction for *oberpartialton*, upper partial tone: cf. OVER- 1 e.] **1.** An upper partial tone; a harmonic: see HARMONIC B. 2. Also, an analogous component of any non-acoustic oscillation, having a frequency that is an integral multiple of the fundamental frequency.

1867 TYNDALL *Sound* iii. 117 The Germans embrace all such sounds under the general term *Obertöne*. I think it will be an advantage if we, in England, adopt the term overtones as the equivalent. **1879** G. PRESCOTT *Sp. Telephone* 7 Helmholtz succeeded in demonstrating that the different qualities of sounds depend altogether upon the number and intensity of the overtones which accompany the primary tones of those sounds. **1880** in Grove *Dict. Mus.* II. 618/2 The word Overtones is rejected by the English translator of Helmholtz's work as not agreeing with English idiom. **1922** A. D. UDDEN tr. *Bohr's Theory of Spectra* III. ii. 83 This apparent difficulty is explained by the occurrence in the motion of the hydrogen atom..of harmonic components corresponding to values of *r*, which are different from 1; or using a terminology well known from acoustics, there appear overtones in the motion of the hydrogen atom. **1937** JENKINS & WHITE *Fund. Physical Optics* xii. 283 If the charged oscillator is bound by a force which does not obey Hooke's law,..it will be capable of re-radiating not only the impressed frequency, but also various combinations of this frequency with the fundamental and overtone frequencies of the oscillator. **1973** *Physics Bull.* July 421/2 The first overtone spectrum of HBr near 4·95 μm has been obtained in this way.

2. *fig.* (Freq. in *pl.*) Applied to literature, esp. poetry: what is suggested or implied by the sound or meaning of the words. More generally, a connotation or subtle implication in thought, language, or action.

1890 W. JAMES *Princ. Psychol.* I. ix. 258 Let us use the words psychic overtone, suffusion, or fringe, to designate the influence of a faint brain-process upon our thought. *Ibid.* 281 The total idea..is the overtone, halo, or fringe of the word, as spoken in that sentence. **1904** J. G. HUNEKER (*title*) Overtones, a book of temperaments. **1911** BRERETON & ROTHWELL tr. *Bergon's Laughter* ii. 96 There would be nothing amusing in the saying, 'It serves you right, George Dandin', were it not for the comic overtones that take up and re-echo it. **1922** H. CRANE *Let.* 2 Apr. (1965) 83 The very effective literary device of under-accentuation in just the right place to produce 'overtones' of overwhelming effect. **1940** *Mind* XLIX. 209 Stripped of these mental overtones, his definition is quite close to the etymological meaning of the word *infinite*. **1952** *Jrnl. Theol. Stud.* III. 64 Once Israel had again fallen under the 'yoke of the heathen', the festival of dedication would have reminded the Jews of the exploits of Judas and could easily have taken on nationalistic overtones. **1957** *Economist* 21 Sept. 953/1 Seven per cent would have been a stronger gesture of resolve, if it had not been left so late as to suggest some overtones of desperation. **1965** *Listener* 25 Nov. 869/1 There are overtones of Aldous Huxley and Norman Douglas, and echoes of Firbank. **1976** 'D. HALLIDAY' *Dolly & Nanny Bird* xix. 258 The kidnapping and holding to ransom of an American child, in order to raise money for the self-styled Croatian Liberation Army. A simple crime with political overtones which the militia would work out for themselves.

overtone (ˌəʊvə'təʊn), *v.* [OVER- 22, 27.]

1. *trans.* To drown (a tone) with a stronger one.

1862 MASSON in *Macm. Mag.* 323 A prayer, the general solemnity of which so overtones the discords from common belief which the expert ear may nevertheless detect in it.

2. *Photogr.* To 'tone' too much, give too deep a tone to.

1868 [see TONE *v.* 5]. **1889** *Anthony's Photogr. Bull.* II. 333 Overtoning is a common fault which gives a gray photograph, and causes it to lose its brilliancy.

3. To give an overtone or implication to. *rare.*

1871 G. MEREDITH *H. Richmond* II. xvii. 269 She threw a kindly-comical look, not overtoned, at the miniature ships on the mantelpiece, and the picture of Joseph leading Mary with her babe on the ass.

† **'over-tongue.** *Obs.* [A literal repr. of Gr. ἐπιγλωττίς.] The epiglottis.

1615 H. CROOKE *Body of Man* 766 Galen is of opinion that the motion of the Epyglottis or ouer-tongue is in a man not voluntary but naturall.

over-tongued: see OVER- 28 d.

ˌover'top, *adv. rare.* [f. OVER *prep.* + TOP *sb.*: cf. OVER- 31.] Over the top, overhead.

1776 W. NIMMO *Stirlingsh.* (1880) I. xxi. 392 Trees, magnificent in foliage and limb, meet overtop. **1921** 'J. O'BRIEN' *Around Boree Log* (1937) 82 And every creek a banker ran, And dams filled overtop.

overtop (əʊvə'tɒp), *v.* [OVER- 1, 3.]

1. *trans.* To rise over or above the top of; to surpass in height, surmount, tower above, top.

1593-4 J. DAVIES in *Sylvester's Wks.* (1880) II. 67 Lo here a Monument admir'd of all..O'r-topping Envie's clouds. **1622** R. HAWKINS *Voy. S. Sea* (1847) 128 The crabbed mountaines which overtopped it. **1784** COWPER *Task* I. 558, I see a column of slow-rising smoke O'ertop the lofty wood. **1855** MACAULAY *Hist. Eng.* xviii. IV. 173 He..showed his brazen forehead, overtopped by a wig worth fifty guineas, in the ante-chambers. **1884** CHILD *Eng. & Sc. Pop. Ball.* II. xxx. 279/1 Charles overtopping Hugo by fifteen inches.

2. *fig.* **a.** To rise above in power or authority; to be superior to; to override.

1561 T. N[ORTON] *Calvin's Inst.* IV. xi. (1634) 602 *marg.*, The time when the Pope began first to overtop the Emperour. **1649** MILTON *Eikon.* xxviii, If Kings presume to overtopp the Law by which they raigne for the public good. **1859** GROTE *Greece* II. lxxxiv. XI. 199 That intense antipathy against a despot who overtops and overrides the laws.

b. To rise above or go beyond in degree or quality; to excel, surpass.

1581 MULCASTER *Positions* xliii. (1887) 272 So the height of their argument ouertop not their power. *a* **1680** CHARNOCK *Attrib. God* (1834) II. 297 None can overtop him in goodness. **1747** CARTE *Hist. Eng.* I. 176 This prince much over-topping the other Scotch chieftains in power. **1876** LOWELL *Among my Bks.* Ser. II. 276 In them the man somehow overtops the author.

† **3.** To render top-heavy. *Obs.* [OVER- 3.]

1643 [ANGIER] *Lanc. Vall. Achor* 2 If the height of the Sail did not overtop the Ship.

Hence **over'topped** *ppl. a.*, *spec.* of a small tree: growing beneath the canopy formed by larger trees and receiving no direct light; **over'topping** *vbl. sb.* and *ppl. a.*

1610 SHAKS. *Temp.* I. ii. 81 Who t'aduance, and who To trash for ouer-topping. **1611** SPEED *Hist. Gt. Brit.* VII. xliv. §14. 360 The Saxons, whose ouer-topped Monarchy, and weake walles now wanted props to hold vp the weight. **1675** BROOKS *Gold. Key* Wks. 1867 V. 203 Look that ye love the Lord Jesus Christ with a superlative love, with an over-topping love. **1897** D. H. MADDEN *Diary Silence* 38 The overtopping hound is not necessarily a bawler, or even a babbler. **1903** W. B. YEATS *In Seven Woods* 39 And he, The one over-topping man that's in the world, Keeps far away. **1917** *Jrnl. Forestry* XV. 74 The crown classes usually distinguished are: Dominant... Co-dominant... Intermediate... Overtopped. Trees with crowns entirely below the general forest canopy and receiving no direct light. **1948** *Ibid.* XLVI. 833/2 Seedlings overtopped but with considerable side light survive and grow just about as well as seedlings in small openings. **1959** *Times* 2 Nov. 21/1 Undertopping in no case exceeded 5 lb. to the hundredweight and overtopping with three machines did not exceed 3·4 lb. **1976** M. GREEN *Children of Sun* vi. 234 America's overtopping of England—England's overshadowing and diminution. **1976** G. W. SHARPE et al. *Introd. Forestry* (ed. 4) ix. 187 Suppressed. Pertaining to trees with small crowns that are entirely below the level of the canopy receiving no direct light from above or from the sides. Also called overtopped.

overtopple (-'tɒp(ə)l), *v.* [OVER- 6, 3.]

1. *trans.* To cause to topple over; to overthrow (something in unstable equilibrium).

1543 BECON *N. Y. Gift* Wks. (1843) 335 This one text..is able to subvert, overtopple, and throw down all the building. **1864** 'ANNIE THOMAS' *Denis Donne* III. 355 Joy o'ertoppled all his prudence.

2. *intr.* To topple over; to overhang as if on the point of toppling over.

1839 CLOUGH *Early Poems* ii. 3 And vanity o'ertoppling fell. **1855** BAILEY *Mystic* 70 Higher than lark can soar, or falcon fly..Lamalmon's pass, O'ertoppling.

Hence **over'toppling** *vbl. sb.* and *ppl. a.*

1860 T. MARTIN *Horace* 218 Black Eurus, snap each rope and oar With the o'ertoppling surge! **1876** MISS YONGE *Womankind* xxviii. 242 The already overtoppling mass of froth of feminine silliness.

ˌover'torture, *v.* [OVER- 25, 27.] *trans.* To overcome with torture; to torture beyond endurance. Hence **ˌover'tortured** *ppl. a.*

c **1590** MARLOWE *Faust.* Wks. (Rtldg.) 133/2 This ever-burning chair Is for o'er-tortur'd souls to rest them in. **1818** BYRON *Mazeppa* xiii, O'ertortured by that ghastly ride, I felt the blackness come and go. **1896** BLACK *Briseis* xx, To gain some quiet for his overtortured spirit.

over'tower, *v.* [OVER- 1 (*b*).] *trans.* To tower over or above, to overtop.

1831 JANE PORTER *Sir E. Seaward's Narr.* I. 58 The high rock which overtowered our vessel. **1850** *Pique* (1875) 184 Money was the grand desideratum which enabled people to overtower their fellows. **1928** E. BLOM *Limitations of Music* 18 As an artist..he [*sc.* Mozart] overtowers every other figure in musical history. **1954** N. PEVSNER *Essex* 385 The church is..cut off by the railway from the village and now overtowered by a modern factory.

So **over'towering** *ppl. a.*

1639 FULLER *Holy War* II. xxx. (1840) 89 To abate their overtowering conceits of him. **1685** COTTON tr. *Montaigne* (1877) I. 71 The proud and overtowering heights of our lofty buildings. **1872** A. J. GORDON *In Christ* vi. (1888) 130 Under the shadow of some overtowering greatness.

over'trace, *v.* Also 5 -trase. [OVER- 8, 10.] *trans.* **a.** To trace over; to cover or mark with tracery or tracings. **b.** To trace one's way over, pursue the track over.

a **1440** *Sir Degrev.* 636 With topyes and trechoure Overtrasyd that tyde. **1573** TWYNE *Æneid* x. Ffij b, Tarience none he makes, but bridges hie doth ouertrace. **1826** MILMAN *A. Boleyn* 108 The..walls Are all o'ertraced by dying hands.

overtrade (-'treɪd), *v. Comm.* [OVER- 26, 23.] *intr.* and *refl.* To trade in excess of one's capital, beyond one's means of payment, or beyond the requirements of the market. **b.** *trans.* To do trade beyond (one's capital, stock, etc.).

a **1734** NORTH *Lives* (1826) I. 427 A famous builder that overtraded his stock about £1000 per ann. **1745** *De Foe's Eng. Tradesman* vi. (1841) I. 36 For a young tradesman to over-trade himself, is like a young swimmer going out of his depth. **1805** W. TAYLOR in *Ann. Rev.* III. 299 Glasgow.. had overtraded, and was visited with diffusive failure. **1894** *Forum* (N.Y.) Nov. 384 There may be doubt whether particular firms have not been overtrading.

So **ˌover'trader**, one who trades too much; **ˌover'trading** *vbl. sb.*, †(*a*) a surpassing in trading, getting the balance of trade (*obs.*); (*b*) trading in excess of one's capital or the needs of the market.

1622 BACON *Hen. VII* 60 Whereby the Kingdomes stocke of Treasure may be sure to be kept from being diminished, by any ouer-trading of the Forrainer. **1776** ADAM SMITH *W.N.* IV. i. (1869) II. 15 This occasioned..a general overtrading in all the ports of Great Britain. **1846** MCCULLOCH *Acc. Brit. Empire* (1854) II. 41 That these or any other measures..would wholly prevent unsafe speculation and over-trading. **1846** WORCESTER, *Overtrader*, ..one who trades too much. *Baker.*

overtrail *v.*: see OVER- 9.

ˌover-'train (-'treɪn), *v.* [OVER- 27.] *trans.* **a.** To train or cultivate the powers of (a person, etc.) too much, to injure by excessive training. **b.** To train (a creeping plant) too much or too high. Hence **ˌover-'training** *vbl. sb.*

1872 H. W. BEECHER *Lect. Preaching* viii. 157 You may over-train a man, so that he is carried beyond his highest power. **1881** *Daily News* 2 June 5 It was very doubtful if Iroquois could 'stay', and he was besides 'overtrained'. **1883** J. Y. STRATTON *Hops & Hop-pickers* 19 Several beautiful and delicate varieties [of the hop] are easily overtrained if sixteen, or in some localities fourteen, feet are exceeded. *a* **1904** *Mod.* The decrease in weight suggests over-training. **1910** *Blackw. Mag.* Jan. 135/1, I was as hard as nails..; but was over-trained, and after a time did the walking, and even the shooting, with some loss of the keenness with which I began it. **1971** *Nature* 10 Sept. 126/2 Here rats are overtrained (by means of foot shock) to avoid entering a black box. **1976** A. GREY *Bulgarian Exclusive* v. 35 They're over-training the Olympic squad.

over'trample, *v.* [OVER- 1, 9.] *trans.* To trample over or upon, tread down; also *fig.* So **over'trampled** *ppl. a.*, **over'trampling** *vbl. sb.*

1589 COOPER *Admon.* 250 That the beastes of the fielde may ouer trample vs. **1593** NASHE *Christs T.* Wks. (Grosart) IV. 93 The irruptive ouer-trampling of the Romans. **1610** HOLLAND *Camden's Brit.* I. 792 Under foote they over-trample it, as if it had bin standing corn ready for harvest. **1744** A. HILL *Let.* 24 July, Wks. 1753 II. 305 Overtrampling all propriety. *a* **1845** HOOD *Monkey Martyr* i, He could not read Of niggers whipt, or over-trampled weavers.

over-'trap, *v.* [OVER- 27.] *trans.* To trap (a region) too much in such a way as to deplete the fauna. So **over-'trapped** *ppl. a.*

1964 P. WORSLEY in I. L. Horowitz *New Sociol.* 381 Over-trapped areas around the settlements. **1968** [see OVER-HUNT *v.*].

† **'over-'travail**, *sb.* [OVER- 29.] Overwork.

1496 *Dives & Paup.* (W. de W.) x. v. 377 Let not your horse..be to feble for mysfare & ouertrauayle.

† **ˌover'travail**, *v. Obs.* Also -eil(e, -eyl(e, -el(l. [OVER- 27.] *trans.* To work too much, oppress or harass with toil; to overwork.

c **1340** HAMPOLE *Prose Tr.* 17 He..ouertrauells by ymagynacions his wittes. **1382** WYCLIF *Exod.* i. 11 He bifore putte to hem maystris of werkis, that thei shulden ouertraueylen hem with birthens. **1563** GOLDING *Cæsar* VII. (1565) 203 b, Ouertrauelling oure men wyth continuall toyle.

'over-'travel, *sb.* [OVER- 29.] **a.** Excessive travel, too much travelling.

1856 KANE *Arct. Expl.* I. xxviii. 365 If the rest of my team had not been worn down by over-travel.

b. Movement of part of a machine beyond the desired point; an allowance made for such travel. Freq. *attrib.*

1923 R. GRIERSON *Electr. Lift Equipment* xiii. 87 Over-travel spaces at both the top and the bottom of the shaft are essential, as the brake is subject to wear. **1939** R. S. PHILLIPS *Electr. Lifts* xii. 177 The top overtravel is defined as the distance provided for the car floor to travel above the level of the top terminal landing before the car is stopped by the ultimate limit switch. **1962** E. G. DAVIES in G. A. T. Burdett *Automatic Control Handbk.* iii. 21 Series limit switches..are generally employed as emergency over-travel switches not called upon to operate except after the failure of the normal stopping or reversing pilot limit switch. **1977** *Economist* 3 Sept. 50/3 (Advt.), Overflow valves. Overtravel switches. Oxide magnets.

So **ˌover-'travel** *v.* [OVER- 23], (*a*) *refl.* to travel or journey beyond one's power of endurance; (*b*) (see quot. 1909).

1654 in F. L. Hawks *Hist. N. Carolina* (1858) II. 19 The interpreter, with over-travelling himself, fell sick. **1909** *Cent. Dict.* Suppl., *Overtravel...* In *mech.*, to travel farther than is necessary to do a certain act or perform a definite function. **1955** *Archit. Rev.* CXVII. 143/4 At top and bottom of the well there are Limit Switches which automatically cut off the lift motor in the event of the car overtravelling in either direction.

over-ˈtrawl, *v.* [OVER- 27.] *trans.* To trawl (a fishing-ground) too much or to depletion. So **over-ˈtrawling** *vbl. sb.*

1913 *Q. Rev.* Apr. 444 In 1892 the Trawlers' Society.. again protested against over-trawling.

overˈtread, *v.* [OE. *ofertredan*: cf. MHG. *übertreten*, Du. *overtreden*: see OVER- 1, 9, 13.] *trans.* **a.** To tread over, trample under foot; *fig.* to crush, oppress, subdue. **b.** To step beyond.

a **1000** *Gloss. to Prudentius* 9 a (Bosw.), Se ȝeleafa ofertret ðæt deofolgyld. *c* **1200** ORMIN 12493 Þærþurrh þe Laferrd oferrcomm & oferrtradd te deofell. **1422** tr. *Secreta Secret., Priv. Priv.* 168 Traiane his Sonne rode an hors vndauntdid, that ouer-trade a weddowes Sone in the strete. **1576** GASCOIGNE *Steele Gl.* (Arb.) 49 When wrong triumphes and right is overtrodde. *c* **1620** *How Good* in Farr *S.P. Jas. I* (1848) 99 Yet must we not this circle overtread.

Hence **ˈovertread** *sb.*, **ˈoverˈtreading** *vbl. sb.*, the act or action of treading over; ***overtread(ing) plough***, the foot-plough used in primitive husbandry; **overˈtrodden** *ppl. a.*, trodden down.

a **1586** SIDNEY *Arcadia* III. Wks. 1724 II. 625 The footsteps of my over-trodden virtue lie still as bitter accusations unto me. *a* **1843** SOUTHEY *Comm.-pl. Bk.* III. 748 The land before his time having been tilled only with a mattock and overtread plough. **1893** A. C. FRYER *Llantwit Major* 26 To cultivate their ground with the mattock and over-treading plough.

†overˈtreat, *v. Obs.* [OVER- 11.] *trans.* To prevail upon by entreaty; = OVER-INTREAT.

a **1547** SURREY *Æneid* IV. 563 Why lettes he not my wordes sinke in his eares So harde to overtreate? **1593** *Printer's Postscr.* in *Harvey's Pierce's Super.* Wks. (Grosart) II. 341, I was finally entreated, or rather ouertreated, to giue them also their welcome in Print.

over-treatment: see OVER- 29 b.

ˈovertrick. *Bridge.* Also with hyphen. [OVER- 19.] A trick taken in excess of the number contracted for. Also *attrib.*

1921 F. IRWIN *Compl. Auction Player* 15 Each over-trick is worth twice its value below the line. **1927** *Observer* 5 June 19/2 All over-trick bonuses gained by a vulnerable side.. count double. **1929** M. C. WORK *Compl. Contract Bridge* i. 2 A trick-score of 20 or 30 plus two over-tricks each worth 50. **1947** S. HARRIS *Fund. Princ. Contract Bridge* 88 This play may cost West an overtrick. **1966** *Listener* 16 June 891/3 One overtrick is a small premium with which to insure a hazardous contract. **1973** *Times* 10 Feb. 12/8 If he had kept three spades, declarer would have made an overtrick by putting him on play with a club or a heart.

overˈtrim, ˌover-ˈtrim, *v.* [OVER- 6, 27.]

†1. *trans.* To overbalance (a boat). *Obs.*

1591 HARINGTON *Orl. Fur.* XXXIX. lxxxii, But on another bark while they take hold, They now full fraught, and fearing overtrimming, With cruell sword..Cut of their hands.

2. To trim (a dress, etc.) too much, or with excess of trimming. Hence **ˈover-ˈtrimmed** *ppl. a.*, **ˈover-ˈtrimming** *vbl. sb.*

1816 JANE AUSTEN *Emma* II. xvii. 328, I have the greatest dislike to the idea of being overtrimmed. **1893** GEORGIANA HILL *Hist. Eng. Dress* II. 229 A tendency to over-trim. **1895** *Daily News* 2 Aug. 6/6 Over-trimmed bodices with absolutely plain skirts. **1897** *Ibid.* 17 Apr. 6/6 The over-trimming..of the early Victorian era.

†overˈtrip, *v. Obs.* [OVER- 5, 10.] *trans.* To trip or skip over; to pass lightly over.

a **1583** GRINDAL *Fruitf. Dial.* Wks. (1843) 49 As touching St. Augustine, he not only overtrippeth it, as no wonder, but by plain and express words testifieth that there is no marvel in it. **1596** SHAKS. *Merch. V.* v. i. 7 In such a night Did Thisbie fearefully ore-trip the dewe.

ˌover-ˈtrouble (-ˈtrʌb(ə)l), *v.* [OVER- 27.] *trans.* To trouble excessively. So **ˈover-ˈtroubled** *ppl. a.*, excessively troubled.

1582 T. WATSON *Centurie of Loue* xxxviii. *heading*, Howe fondly his friendes ouertrouble him, by questioninge with him touching his loue. **1646** BP. HALL *Balm Gil.* 172 Why art thou over-troubled to see the great Physitian of the world take this course with sinfull mankind?

ˈoverˌtrow, *sb.* [See next.]

†1. Over-trust, over-confidence. (*O.E.*)

a **941** *Laws Æthelstan* VI. c. 8. §7 (Schmid) Menn ne reccean, hu heora yrfe fare, for þam ofertruan on þam friðe.

†2. Distrust, suspicion. (*M.E.*)

c **1350** *Will. Palerne* 1402 He ne durst openly for ouertrowe of gile.

3. (See quot.) *nonce-use.* [OVER- 29.]

1891 ATKINSON *Moorland Par.* 69 What I would willingly call overtrow or believing overmuch, not superstition.

†ˌoverˈtrow, *v.*[1] *Obs.* [OVER- ? 4, 27.]

1. *trans.* To mistrust, distrust.

c **1175** *Lamb. Hom.* 21 Leofe broðre ne ouertrowiȝe cristes milce..al swa monimon seið and weneð, Hu mei ic efre ibete.

2. *intr.* To trust overmuch, be too confident.

1422 tr. *Secreta Secret., Priv. Priv.* 169 Thow arte a fole dotdrat [= dottard] and ouer-trowes.

Hence **†ˌoverˈtrowing** *vbl. sb.*, over-confidence; *ppl. a.*, over-confident; **†ˈover-ˈtrowship, †ˈoverˈtrowth**, over-confidence.

1422 tr. *Secreta Secret., Priv. Priv.* 187 Who-so suche losengeris belewyth othyr trowyth, they shal falle in Pride and ouertrouth. *c* **1425** *Eng. Conq. Irel.* lix. 142 Euery wysman vnderstond hym by Roboam, Salomones sone, how mych harme falleth of pryde & ouertrowshype. *c* **1430** *Pilgr. Lyf Manhode* II. v. (1869), Serteyn,..the disturblaunce cometh of thin ouertrowinge [*oultrecuidance*].

†overˈtrow, *v.*[2] *Obs.* [app. an erroneous expansion of ORTROW *v.*, due to the frequent reduction of original *over-* to *o'er-*, *ore-*, *or-*.] *trans.* (with obj. cl.). To suspect; to believe, suppose.

c **1305** *St. Kenelm* 292 in *E.E.P.* (1862) 55 Þe contrai men ..þat vnder-ȝete þat cas Ouertrowede [*c* 1290 *Laud MS.* ortreweden] wel whar hit lay. **1382** WYCLIF *1 Kings* xxii. 32 Thei ouertroweden [1388 suposiden, *Vulg.* suspicati sunt] that he hadde ben kyng of Irael.

Hence **†overˈtrowable** *a.*, to be suspected, suspect; **†overˈtrowing** *ppl. a.*, suspecting.

[**1382** WYCLIF *Ecclus.* xxv. 9 Nyne vnouertrowable thingus [*Vulg.* novem insuspicabilia] of the herte I magnefiede.] **1388** —— *1 Cor.* iv. 4, Y am no thing ouer trowynge to my silf [*Vulg.* nihil..mihi conscius sum].

over-true: see OVER-.

ˌoverˈtrump (-ˈtrʌmp), *v.* [OVER- 22.] *trans.* To trump with a higher card than that with which an opponent has already trumped; also *absol.* and *fig.* Hence **overˈtrumping** *vbl. sb.*

1746 HOYLE *Whist* (ed. 6) 27 Do not over-trump him. **1862** 'CAVENDISH' *Whist* (1879) 109 If you refuse to overtrump..your partner should conclude either that [etc.]. **1885** *Manch. Exam.* 17 Feb. 5/3 There is a widespread opinion that he has over-trumped the Protectionists.

ˈoverˌtrust, *sb.* [OVER- 29.] Excessive trust; over-confidence, presumption.

a **1225** *Ancr. R.* 332 Þeos two unðeawes, untrust and ouertrust, beoð þes deofles tristren. *c* **1425** *Eng. Conq. Irel.* vii. 22 We haue for vs..ayeyn har boldenesse and ouer-truste, mekenesse and maner. **1852** TENNYSON *Ode Death Dk. Wellington* vii. 20 But wink no more in slothful overtrust.

ˌoverˈtrust, *v.* [OVER- 27.]

1. *intr.* To trust or confide too much; to be over-confident.

a **1225** *Ancr. R.* 332 Dred wiðuten hope makeð mon untrusten: and hope wiðute dred makeð ouertrusten. **1553** GRIMALDE *Cicero's Offices* I. (1558) 40 Unbridled with prosperitie and ouertrusting to themselues. **1667** MILTON *P.L.* IX. 1183 Thus it shall befall Him who to worth in Women overtrusting Lets her Will rule.

2. *trans.* To trust (a person or thing) too much.

1649 BP. HALL *Cases Consc.* III. ix. (1650) 249 Some there are that doe so over-trust their leaders eyes, that they care not to see with their own.

†ˈover-ˈtrusty, *a. Obs.* [OVER- 28.] Over-confident, presumptuous.

a **1225** *Ancr. R.* 334 Alre uormest he cleopeð þe ouertrusti, unbileued.

†ˈovertruth. *Obs. rare.* [OVER- 24.] A statement in excess of the truth.

1638 CHILLINGW. *Relig. Prot.* I. vi. §23 Who know how great over-truths men usually write to one another in letters.

over-truthful, etc.: see OVER-.

overˈtumble, *v.* [OVER- 6, 5.]

†1. *intr.* To tumble or fall over; to capsize. *Obs.*

1375 BARBOUR *Bruce* XVI. 643 In sum bargis sa feill can ga, For thair fais thame chasit swa, That thai ourtummyllit, and the men..all drownit then. *a* **1649** DRUMM. OF HAWTH. *Poems* Wks. (1711) 33 The ocean in mountains..over-tumbling tumbling over rocks, Casts various rain-bows.

2. *trans.* To cause to fall over; to upset, overthrow. Now only *poetic.*

1600 ABP. ABBOT *Exp. Jonah* 404 Yet the breath of one mortall man..doth overtumble all. **1639** DRUMM. OF HAWTH. *Speech* Wks. (1711) 218 The whole frame built on it is ready to be over-tumbled. **1875** BROWNING *Aristoph. Apol.* 4536 That..I, with my bent steel, may o'ertumble town!

†3. *trans.* To tumble or fall over (something).

c **1630** RISDON *Surv. Devon* §225 (1810) 238 Ock, Which, for more haste, o'ertumbleth many a rock.

†overˈturcased, *ppl. a. Obs.* [OVER- 8.] = 'Over-turquoised', covered with turquoises.

1647 WARD *Simp. Cobler* 27 But now our Roses are turned to Flore de lices,..our City-Dames, to an indenominable Quæmalry of overturcas'd things.

overture (ˈəʊvətj(ʊ)ə(r)), *sb.* Also 5–8 **ouverture.** [a. OF. *overture*, mod.F. *ouverture* opening, f. *ouvert* open, OVERT.]

†1. An opening, aperture, orifice, hole. *Obs.*

13.. *E.E. Allit. P.* A. 218 Vche a hemme, At honde, at sydez, at ouerture. **1422** tr. *Secreta Secret., Priv. Priv.* 239 Thay men wyche..haue throgh al the body the ouertures large, that clerkys callyth Pores. *a* **1548** HALL *Chron., Hen. V* 56 b, Diuers ouertures and holes were made vnder the foundacion by the pyoners. **1611** COTGR., *Escoutilles*,..th' ouertures, or trap doores, whereat things are let downe into the hold. **1714–21** POPE *Let. to Dk. Buckhm.* Wks. 1737 VI. 27 The Kitchin [at Stanton Harcourt]..being one vast Vault to the Top of the House; where one overture serves to let out the smoak and let in the light. **1727** SWIFT *Country Post* Wks. 1755 III. I. 176 To possess themselves of the two overtures of the said fort. **1749** MRS. R. GOADBY *Carew* (1750) 105 The false Belly, in which the Female [Opossum] carries her Young..In the hinder Part of it is an Overture big enough for a small Hand to pass.

fig. **1603** HOLLAND *Plutarch's Mor.* 49 [This] will make an overture and way unto the minde of a yoong ladde. **1643** MILTON *Soveraigne Salve* 31 Deluges of sinne breake in at this so great an overture of the faith.

†b. An open or exposed place. *Obs. rare*$^{-1}$.

1579 SPENSER *Sheph. Cal.* July 28 The wastefull hylls vnto his threate Is a playne ouerture [*gloss.* an open place].

c. *Her.* The state of being expanded: said of the wings of a bird so represented: see OVERT *a.* 1 b.

†2. The opening up or revelation of a matter; a disclosure, discovery, declaration. *Obs.*

a **1548** HALL *Chron., Hen. VII* 34 The kyng had knowledge of the chief Capitaynes of this tumulte by the ouerture of hys espyes. **1605** SHAKS. *Lear* III. vii. 89 It was he That made the ouerture of thy Treasons to vs. **1654** H. L'ESTRANGE *Chas. I* (1655) 4 Upon the prime overture of his message at the French Court, he found so ready and fluent an inclination in king Lewes.

3. An opening of negotiations with another person or party with a view to some proceeding or settlement; a formal proposal, proposition, or offer; e.g. *an overture of marriage, overtures of peace.*

1433 *Rolls of Parlt.* IV. 425/1 [He] made hem yerinne diverse faire overtures and offris. **1453** *Paston Lett.* I. 261 In case ye make not to me ouverture of justice upon the seyd caas. **1501** in *Lett. Rich. III & Hen. VII* (Rolls) I. 154 The whiche overture..[was] for the renovelling of the said amitie. **1601** SHAKS. *All's Well* IV. iii. 46 *Cap. E.* I heare there is an ouerture of peace. *Capt. G.* Nay, I assure you a peace concluded. **1655** DIGGES *Compl. Ambass.* 101 Any time these five years there have been overtures of marriage made unto him. **1752** FIELDING *Amelia* XI. iii, She was not one of those backward and delicate ladies, who can die rather than make the first overture. **1885** *Law Times Rep.* LII. 648/1 They had had overtures from several persons to purchase..the trust property.

4. a. In the Scottish Parliament or Convention of the Estates: A motion introduced to be made an Act. *Obs.* exc. *Hist.*

1561 *Reg. Privy Council Scot.* 193 It wes thocht gude and expedient be hir Hienis that ane Generall Conventioun suld be appointit the xv day of December instant,..and be the avyise of the hale, ane ressonable overture maid and ordoure takin for..quieting of the hale cuntre. **1641** *Sc. Acts Chas. I* V. 625 Agreed by the whole estates that when an overture is proposed, every estate have 24 hours to advise the same before he be urged to answer thereto. **1707** *Vulpone; or Remarks Proc. Scot. Union* 2 In the first Session of this present Parliament in 1703..the E[arl of Marchmont].. gave in an Overture (as they call it) by way of Act, for Settling the Succession upon the foot of Limitations.

b. In the General Assembly of the Church of Scotland, and in the supreme court of other Presbyterian churches: A formal motion proposing or calling for legislation.

In current use, an overture is a proposal to make a new general law for the Church or to repeal an old one; to declare the law; to enjoin the observance of former enactments; or generally to take any measure falling within the legislative or executive functions of the Assembly. Such a proposal must first be made in an inferior court (presbytery or synod), and, if there adopted, is transmitted by that court as its overture to the supreme court. If adopted by the supreme court as an overture, it is submitted to the various presbyteries for approval by them or a majority of them before it can be passed as an act.

1576 *Recds. of 33rd Gen. Assembly* in *Bk. of Univ. Kirk of Scotl.* (1839) 155 Brethren appointed to make ane overture of the policie and jurisdiction of the Kirk. **1676** W. ROW *Contn. Blair's Autobiog.* ix. (1848) 143 Mr. Livingstone proponed an overture. **1723** *Wodrow Corr.* (1843) III. 52 Some very good overtures, if put in practice, against Popery, were passed, and Synod-books were taken in. **1737** J. CHAMBERLAYNE *St. Gt. Brit.* II. II. iii. 358 Matters of great weight that bind the whole Church [of Scotland] are first brought in by way of overtures, and then debated in the house. **1864** BURTON *Scot Abr.* I. v. 273. **1871** H. MONCRIEFF *Pract. F.C. Scot.* (1877) 65 It is competent for any Presbytery to transmit what is called an Overture, either to the Provincial Synod or to the General Assembly, with the view of inducing the Superior Court to adopt any measure within its legislative or executive functions.

†5. An 'opening' for proceeding to action. *Obs.*

1610 DONNE *Pseudo-martyr* 128 To vnderstand..where any ouerture is giuen for the Popes aduantage. **1617** MORYSON *Itin.* II. 10 They..escaped out of prison, being all prisoners of great moment, whose inlargement gaue apparant ouerture to ensuing rebellion. **1679–1714** BURNET *Hist. Ref.*, He was casting about for new overtures how to compass what he so earnestly desired. **1768** *Woman of Honor* III. 65 If I had seen the least glimpse of an overture of succeeding with the invincible Clara.

†6. An opening, beginning, commencement; *esp.* a formal opening of proceedings; a first indication or hint *of* something. *Obs.*

1595 DANIEL *Civ. Wars* II. xxxiv, If the least imagin'd overture But of conceiv'd revolt men once espie. **1612** DAVIES *Why Ireland* etc. (1747) 78 Let us therefore take a briefe view of the seueral impediments which arose in euery Kings time since the ouerture of the Conquest. **1656** FINETT *For. Ambass.* 154 The next day being that of the overture of parliament. **1658** JER. TAYLOR *Let.* in *12th Rep. Hist. MSS. Comm.* App. v. 5 If ever you have noted or heard of any overtures of unkindnesse betweene them. **1727–41** CHAMBERS *Cycl.* s.v., The overture of the jubilee, is a general procession, etc.

7. a. *Mus.* An orchestral piece, of varying form and dimensions, forming the opening or introduction to an opera, oratorio, or other extended composition; often containing or made up of themes from the body of the work, or otherwise indicating the character of it.

Also applied to a similar piece intended for independent performance; and, rarely, to the introductory piece of a series for a single instrument, as a harpsichord.

1667 DAVENANT & DRYDEN *Tempest* I. i, While the overture is playing, the curtain rises. **1706** PHILLIPS, *Overture*,.. also a Flourish of Musick, before the Scenes are open'd in a Play-house, especially before the beginning of an Opera. **1729** GAY (*title*) The Beggar's Opera.. The third edition: With the Ouverture in Score, the Songs, and the Basses. **1797** *Monthly Mag.* III. 149 The overture, which is in the favourite overture key, D major, is bold and dashing. **1880** H. J. LINCOLN in Grove *Dict. Mus.* II. 618 *Overture*.., *i.e.* Opening. This term was originally applied to the instrumental prelude to an opera, its first important development being due to Lulli, as exemplified in his.. French operas and ballets, dating from 1672 to 1686.

b. *fig.* (Cf. *prelude*.)

1802 WOLCOTT (P. Pindar) *Ld. Belgrave* Wks. 1812 IV. 523 Soon as the Winds begin to sing, Or rather play their overture to thunder. **1847** W. IRVING in *Life & Lett.* (1864) IV. 18 Unless you come up soon, you will miss the overture of the season—the first sweet notes of the year.

c. The opening or introductory part of a poem.

1870 SWINBURNE *Ess. & Stud.* (1875) 269 The.. verses headed 'Tears in Solitude'—exquisite as is the overture, faultless in tone and colour, and worthy of a better sequel. **1881** SAINTSBURY *Dryden* 98 Dryden's overtures are very generally among the happiest parts of his poems.

¶**8.** Erroneous obsolete use, app. due to association with *over*: Overturning, overthrow.

1591 GREENE *Disc. Coosnage* Pref. (1592) 3 No man knoweth.. better which waie to raise a gainefull commodity, and howe the abuses and ouerture of prices might bee redressed. **1593** NASHE *Christ's T.* 27 Consider, howe his threats were after verified in Ierusalems ouerture. **1616** BULLOKAR *Eng. Expos.*, *Ouerture*, an ouerturning, a sudden change. **1633** PRYNNE *Histriomastix* 2 The very fatall plagues, and ouertures of those States and Kingdomes where they are once tollerated.

'overture, *v.* [f. prec. sb.]

1. *trans.* To bring or put forward as an overture or proposal; to offer, propose.

1637–50 [see OVERTURED below]. *a* **1665** J. GOODWIN *Filled w. the Spirit* (1867) 486 He shall not only want one of the greatest arguments and motives to persuade men and women unto ways that are excellent, but also overture such a thing which would be a snare and temptation to fight low. **1880** SID. SMITH in *Daily News* 7 Apr. 3/3 A prominent Tory overtured to a leading Liberal that the party of the latter need not further trouble themselves with precautions against Tory opposition.

2. In the supreme court of a Presbyterian Church: To bring forward as an overture; to introduce as a motion.

1671 *True Nonconf.* 100 It had become you rather, who would be accounted a kindly child of the Church of Scotland, to have overtured a way how the Church Patrimony.. may be recovered from the Harpyes who devoure it. **1715** *Wodrow Corr.* (1843) II. 36 The sub-committee overtured the form of an act anent it. **1726** *Ibid.* III. 241 We overtured that either the act might be repealed or execute. **1898** in *Westm. Gaz.* 3 Mar. 4/3 It is therefore hereby humbly overtured to the Very Reverend the Synod of the Presbyterian Church of England.. to take the premises into consideration.

b. To present or transmit an overture to (a church court); to approach with an overture.

1864 BURTON *Scot Abr.* I. v. 273 A motion is made in a presbytery 'to overture' the General Assembly. **1895** *Westm. Gaz.* 17 June 2/1 The Free Presbytery of Skye 'overtured' the General Assembly to take into its serious consideration 'the views of man's origin propounded by Professor Drummond in his work on the "Ascent of Man".'

3. To introduce with, or as with, a musical overture or prelude; to prelude.

1870 J. HAMILTON *Moses* vii. 122 Needing no thunder nor trumpet to overture His discourse and astonish His audience.

Hence **'overtured** *ppl. a.*, proposed.

1637–50 ROW *Hist. Kirk* (1842) 83 A little more or less nor the overtured summes, according to the abilitie and extent of the rents in the place.

overturn ('əʊvətɜːn), *sb.* [OVER- 6, ? 4, 10.]

1. The act of overturning or fact of being overturned; an upsetting; a revolution.

c **1592** BACON *Conf. Pleasure* (1870) 25 Her intentiue witt in contriuing plotts and ouertournes. **1658** CLEVELAND *Rustic Rampant* Wks. (1687) 392 A Marius.. fitter to remove things, to overturn overturns, than for Peace. **1789** MAD. D'ARBLAY *Diary* 19 Nov., He was still rather lame, from a dreadful overturn in a carriage. **1823** SCOTT *Fam. Lett.* 11 Feb., How we have escaped overturn is to me wonderful. **1868** E. EDWARDS *Ralegh* I. xxvii. 631 The death of young Ralegh drew after it the overturn of the expedition.

2. *Geol.* = OVERFOLD.

1877 LE CONTE *Elem. Geol.* I. (1879) 176 When in strong foldings the strata are pushed over beyond the perpendicular,.. we have what is called an *overturn dip*.

3. The burden or refrain of a song. *Sc.*

1825 JAMIESON, *Overturn of a sang*, that part of it which is repeated, or sung in chorus. **1827** MOTHERWELL *Wee Wee Man* viii, And aye the owreturn o' their tune Was—Our wee wee man has been lang awa!

4. The act of turning over in the course of trade, circulation of books, etc.; turn-over.

1882 ALEXANDER *Ain Folk* 99 (E.D.D.) Lyin i' the bank wi' nae owreturn. **1901** *Academy* 7 Dec. 532/2 The libraries, where fiction is always 70 to 80 per cent. of the total overturn, run up to a circulation of 400,000 volumes of fiction a month in American cities.

5. A turn-over, as of voters or votes from one side to the other.

1894 *Westm. Gaz.* 8 May 5/2 A reduction of the Liberal majority by over a thousand.. It is certainly a tremendous overturn which has been effected.

6. *Limnology.* The mixing or circulation of the water in a thermally stratified lake that usu. occurs once or twice each year as a result of the cooling or warming of the epilimnion.

[**1898** G. C. WHIPPLE in *Amer. Naturalist* XXXII. 27 Soon the surface and bottom layers come to have substantially the same temperature, and vertical currents extend from top to bottom. This is the 'period of spring circulation', or the 'spring overturning'.] **1911** BIRGE & JUDAY in *Bull. Wisconsin Geol. & Nat. Hist. Survey* XXII. p. xi, The stratum of circulating water becomes increasingly thinner until.. the permanent summer conditions are established. Thenceforward, until the overturn, only the water of the epilimnion can have direct contact with the air. **1935** P. S. WELCH *Limnology* iv. 38 During the spring and fall overturns.., when the water is of uniform density from top to bottom, return currents may extend even to the bottom of relatively deep inland lakes. **1972** *Ann. Rep. Freshwater Biol. Assoc.* XL. 42 Before the overturn, the epilimnetic population of both Grasmere and Blelham Tarn went through the whole [nitrate] reduction process. **1974** *Encycl. Brit. Macropædia* X. 607/1 Mixing due to cooling or warming processes that increase the density of surface waters sufficiently to cause them to sink results in what is termed circulation, or overturn, of lake water.

overturn (əʊvə'tɜːn), *v.* [OVER- 6, ? 4, 10.]

†**1.** *intr.* Of a wheel, and *fig.* of time: To turn round, revolve. *Obs.*

a **1225** *Ancr. R.* 356 Heo beoð her hweolinde ase hweoles þet ouerturneð sone, and ne lesteð none hwule. **13..** *E.E. Allit. P.* B. 1192 Þay feȝt & þay fende of, & fylter togeder Til two ȝer ouer-torned. **1387** TREVISA *Higden* (Rolls) VII. 145 Suche a day þe ȝere ouertorned [*anno revoluto*] þey boþe deide. *a* **1450** *Le Morte Arth.* 3186 Hym thowht he satte.. vpon A whele.. The whele over-tornyd ther wyth Alle, And eueryche by A lymme hym caught. **1649** T. FORD *Lusus Fort.* 83 Neither Power nor Riches can scotch the over-turning wheel of fortune.

2. a. *trans.* To turn (anything) over upon its side or face, esp. to throw over with violence; to upset, overset, overthrow; to cause to fall over or down.

13.. *Life Jesu* 857 Þe Muteres Moneye he schedde al, and þe bordes ouer turnde. **1377** LANGL. *P. Pl.* B. XVI. 131 I shal ouertourne þis temple and adown throwe, And in thre dayes after edifye it newe, And make it as moche other more in alle manere poyntes, As euere it was. **1526** *Pilgr. Perf.* (W. de W. 1531) 138 b, Man hath.. subuerted or ouerturned his citees. **1555** EDEN *Decades* 7 They ouer-turned their Canoa with a great violence. **1604** E. G[RIMSTONE] *D'Acosta's Hist. Indies* III. xxvi. 198 Vpon the coast of Chille.. there was so terrible an Earthquake, as it overturned whole mountains. **1687** *Lond. Gaz.* No. 2240/4 A Hackney Coach.. overturned in Fleetstreet. **1774** GOLDSM. *Nat. Hist.* (1776) VI. 207 The whale sometimes overturns the boat with a blow of its tail. **1850** PRESCOTT *Peru* II. 149 Men and horses were overturned in the fury of the assault.

†**b.** To turn over (a lying stone, a leaf of a book, etc.) without throwing down. *Obs.*

c **1330** *Assump. Virg.* 765 (B.M. MS.) Thei ouerturned þat ilke stone, Bodi þei founde þer none. **1390** GOWER *Conf.* III. 67 [He] overtorneth many a bok, And thurgh the craft of Artemage Of wex he forgeth an ymage.

c. *intr.* To turn over, capsize, upset; to fall.

1393 LANGL. *P. Pl.* C. XVIII. 209 For coueytyse of þat croys clerkes of holy churche Schullen ouerturne as templers duden. **1659** LEAK *Waterwks.* 20 The Water.. shall fill the said Vessel and make it to overturn. *Ibid.*, Every minute of an hour the said Vessel may overturn. **1769** FALCONER *Dict. Marine* (1789), *Over-setting*,.. the movement of a ship when she over-turns. **1856** KANE *Arct. Expl.* II. x. 98 The sledge is portable, and adapted.. to overturn with impunity.

3. a. *trans.* To overthrow, subvert, destroy, overwhelm, bring to ruin (a person, institution, principle, etc.).

c **1374** CHAUCER *Boeth.* II. pr. ii. 23 (Camb. MS.) The dedes of fortune þat with a vnwarstroke ouertorneth realmes of grete noblye. **1430–40** LYDG. *Bochas* VIII. xviii. (1558) 12 b, His power short was ouertourned bliue. *a* **1548** HALL *Chron.*, *Hen. VII* 43 b, Assone as Kyng Henry had subdued and ouerturned his adversaries. **1596** SHAKS. *1 Hen. IV*, IV. i. 82 If we.. can make a Head To push against the Kingdome; with his helpe, We shall o're-turne it topsie-turuy downe. **1667** MILTON *P.L.* VI. 463 But pain is perfet miserie.. and excessive, overturnes All patience. **1757** BURKE *Subl. & B.* (ed. 2) Pref., This can never overturn the theory itself. **1802** MAR. EDGEWORTH *Moral T.* (1816) I. xiv. 112 Without overturning all existing institutions. **1859** TENNYSON *Enid* 1678, I schemed and wrought Until I overturn'd him.

b. To reverse (a judicial decision).

1969 *Morning Star* 8 Aug. 1/3 Last month, the US circuit court of appeals in Boston overturned the verdict. **1973** *Observer* 22 July 10/1 The House of Lords unanimously overturned this decision.

†**4.** To 'upset', disorder (stomach, brain, etc.).

1390 GOWER *Conf.* III. 5 So drunke I am, that my wit faileth And al mi brain is overtorned. **1578** LYTE *Dodoens* III. xxviii. 355 It will not ouertturne nor torment the stomacke. **1579** LANGHAM *Gard. Health* (1633) 232 It bringeth headach, and ouerturneth the stomacke. **1601** HOLLAND *Pliny* II. 174 Yet there is a wine of Myrtles.. which wil neuer ouerturn the brain or make one drunk. **1704** SWIFT *T. Tub* ix, A person whose intellectuals were overturned.

†**5.** To turn in the opposite direction. *Obs.*

1387 TREVISA *Higden* (Rolls) I. 83 In som hulles of Ynde beeþ men þat haueþ soles of hir feet ouertorned [*Higd.* adversas plantas habentes]. **1398** —— *Barth. De P.R.* XVIII. c. (1495) 846 Some bulles.. hauynge theyr heere ouertornyd: and growyth towardes theyr eyen.

†**6.** To turn over from one thing or side to another; to turn away; to pervert.

1382 WYCLIF *Ecclus.* IV. 1 Ouerturne thou not thin eȝen fro the pore [1388 turne not ouere; *Vulg.* transvertas]. **1390** GOWER *Conf.* III. 384 [Love] which many an herte hath overtake, And ovyrturnyd as the blynde Fro reson in to lawe of kynde. *a* **1568** ASCHAM *Scholem.* I. (Arb.) 75, I know.. many worthie Ientlemen of England, whom all the Siren songes of Italie.. nor no inchantment of vanitie [could] ouerturne them, from the feare of God, and loue of honestie. **1587** GOLDING *De Mornay* xvi. (1617) 283 Seeing that man is so ouerturned, whereof can he brag.

Hence **over'turned** *ppl. a.*, *spec.* in *Geol.* applied to a fold or the limb of a fold that is tilted beyond the vertical (cf. OVERFOLD *sb.*); **over'turning** *vbl. sb.* and *ppl. a.*; also **over'turnable** *a.*, capable of being overturned.

1387–8 T. USK *Test. Love* I. ix. (Skeat) I. 83 Sothlie none age, none ouertournyng tyme, but hitherto had no tyme ne power, to chaunge the weddyng, ne that knotte to vnbinde. **1393** LANGL. *P. Pl.* C. XIX. 164 Þe ouerturnyng of þe temple bytokned þe resureccion. **1645** MILTON *Colast.* Wks. (1851) 356 The overturning of all human society. **1649** [see sense 1]. **1757** T. BIRCH *Hist. Royal Soc.* IV. 323 A commodious land-carriage.. far more secure than any coach, not being overturnable by any hight, on which the wheels can possibly move. *a* **1758** EDWARDS *Hist. Redempt.* I. vi. (1774) 141 There were three great general overturnings of the world before Christ came. **1809** PINKNEY *France* 38, I fell in with an overturned Chaise. **1861** *Amer. Jrnl. Sci.* LXXXI. 218 Sometimes it may overlie the overturned Utica formation. **1896** [see OVERFOLD *v.* 2]. **1907**, **1970** [see FORELAND 5].

over'turner. [f. prec. + -ER[1].] One who or that which overturns.

1591 PERCIVALL *Sp. Dict.*, *Rebolvedor*, an ouerturner. **1599** SANDYS *Europæ Spec.* (1632) 97 Underminers of government,.. overturners of Christendome. *a* **1716** SOUTH *Serm.* (1727) VI. ii. 54 By.. which these Overturners of all above them have done such mighty Execution. **1820** *Examiner* No. 619. 119/2 The only sure and final overturner of abuses. **1898** BODLEY *France* II. 274 The Overturners of the Monarchy.

overturret to **-tutored**: see OVER-.

overtwart, -twert: see OVERTHWART.

overtwine (-'twaɪn), *v.* [OVER- 8.] *trans.* To twine over or round about, wreathe.

1819 SHELLEY *Let. to Peacock* 23 Mar. in Dowden *Life* II. 262 Masses of the fallen ruin overtwined with the broad leaves of the creeping weeds. **1821** —— *Prometh. Unb.* IV. 272 Like swords of azure fire, or golden spears With tyrant-quelling myrtle overtwined.

overtwist, *v.*: see OVER- 9.

overtype ('əʊvətaɪp), *a. Electr.* [OVER- 1.] Said of a bi-polar dynamo in which the armature is situated above the yoke of the field-magnets.

1892 S. P. THOMPSON *Dynamo-Electric Mach.* 487 The latest and best construction of 2-pole machine is.. of the 'over' type with the armature and shaft at the summit of the field-magnet. **1894** BOTTONE *Elect. Instr.* 206 Overtype drum armature dynamo.

overtyrve, variant of OVERTERVE *v. Obs.*

over-uberous, etc.: see OVER- 28.

overun ('əʊvərən), *a.* and *sb. local.* Also overrun(ner. [f. OVER *adv.* or *a.* + UN[2].] **A.** *adj.* In the Isle of Wight, coming from the mainland; not native to the Island. **B.** *sb.* = OVERNER.

1881 H. & C. R. SMITH *Isle of Wight Words* 48 *Overun*, coming from 'across the water', from the mainland of the county. **1882** [see OVERNER]. **1889** F. COWPER *Captain of Wight* x. 130 There'll have to be some overrunners asked over. *Ibid.* xiv. 176 That's what I call a hardy knight... 'Tis a pity he's an overrun.

over-use ('əʊvə'juːs), *sb.* [OVER- 29 b.] Excessive use, too frequent use.

1862 ANSTED *Channel Isl.* IV. xxii. (ed. 2) 509 The oyster beds are becoming impoverished, partly by over-use. **1880** *Fortn. Rev.* Apr. 488 Invective may be a sharp weapon: but over-use blunts its edge.

over-use (ˌəʊvə'juːz), *v.* [OVER- 27.] *trans.* To use too much; to injure by excessive use.

1677 GALE *Crt. Gentiles* II. IV. 21 When ever we overuse any lower good we abuse it. **1873** M. ARNOLD *Lit. & Dogma* (1876) p. xxiii, Without the use of so many books that he can afford not to over-use and mis-use one. **1897** *Allbutt's Syst. Med.* IV. 824 'Singer's nodules' often seen in singers and actors who have over-used their vocal organs.

'over-'usual, *a.* [OVER- 28.] Too usual, too customary. So **'over-'usually** *adv.*

1605 BACON *Adv. Learn.* II. xix. § 1. 69 In Annotacions and Commentaries.. it is ouer vsual to blaunch the obscure places, and discoarse vpon the playne. **1668** H. MORE *Div. Dial.* IV. xxxvii. (1713) 396 A Softness over-usually accompanied with a Falsness and Perfidiousness to all Truth and Vertue.

over-vail, -vaill, -vale, obs. ff. OVER-VEIL *v.*

†**over-'vain,** *a. Obs.* [OVER- 25.] Superfluously vain or worthless (rendering L. *supervacuus*). So

† **over-'vainly** *adv.*, superfluously, utterly in vain, without cause (rendering L. *supervacue*).
1382 WYCLIF *Wisd.* xi. 16 Summe errende herieden doumbe edderes, and ouer veyne bestes [1388 superflu, *Vulg.* bestias supervacuas]. —— *Ps.* xxiv. [xxv.] 4 Confoundid be alle doende wickid thingus ouer veynly [1388 superfluli, *Vulg.* iniqua agentes supervacue]. *Ibid.* xxxiv. [xxxv.] 7 Ouer veynly [*Vulg.* supervacue] thei acuseden my soule.

'overvalu'ation. [OVER- 29 b.] The action of overvaluing.
1622 MALYNES *Anc. Law-Merch.* 419 To imbase our coynes as they do theirs, and to imitate oueruualuation of gold and siluer as they do. **1661** BOYLE *Style of Script.* 113 When ..the Peoples fondnesse and Overvaluation of them produc'd a Neglect of the Study of the Bible. **1850** GROTE *Greece* II. lvii. VII. 188 That foolish overvaluation of favourable chances so ruinous even to first-rate powers.

over-value ('əʊvə'vælju:), *sb.* [OVER- 19, 29 d.]
† **1.** Excess or surplus of value. *Obs.*
c **1592** BACON *Conf. Pleasure* (1870) 18 The ouervalue, besides a reasonable fine, lefte for the releef [of tenants] and rewarde of seruantes.
2. A value or estimate greater than the worth of a thing; more than the value.
1611 COTGR., *Survaleur*, ouer-value. **1623** DONNE *Serm.* xviii. 175 He doth not pamper them with an overvalue of them, he lets them know their Worst as well as their Best. **1754** FIELDING *Jonathan Wild* I. v, I am not insensible of my obligations to you,.. for the over-value you have set on my small abilities. **1884** *Law Rep.* 26 Ch. Div. 119 [They] induced the directors..to join in the purchase of the Park Company's property at an overvalue. **1890** 'R. BOLDREWOOD' *Col. Reformer* (1891) 97 You'll get over-value for this bit o' paper some day.

overvalue (,əʊvə'vælju:), *v.* [OVER- 26, 22 b.]
1. *trans.* To value (a thing) above its true worth; to value too highly, overestimate.
1597 HOOKER *Eccl. Pol.* v. xxii. §7 By thus ouervaluing their Sermons, they make the price and estimation of Scripture..to fall. **1651** HOBBES *Leviath.* I. x. 44 If he resolve not, he overvalues little things, which is Pusillanimity. **1876** GROTE *Eth. Fragm.* vi. 230 Aristotle never overvalues the advantages of riches.
b. To put too high a money valuation upon.
1641 T. LECHFORD *Note-Bk.* (1885) 432 John Seberry against Walter Merry for £15 w[ch] he over-valued the house he bought of him. **1656** H. PHILLIPS *Purch. Patt.* (1676) 15 The long Lease is much over-valued. **1847** C. G. ADDISON *Contracts* II. iv. §2 (1883) 676 If the policy be enormously overvalued, that will be evidence of fraud. **1885** *Law Times* 7 Feb. 269/1 There was a strong reason why Mr. Thomas should over-value rather than under-value the goods.
† **2.** Of a thing: To surpass in value. *Obs.*
1608 DOD & CLEAVER *Expos. Prov.* xi-xii. 190 A little gold oueruallueth much leade or yron. *a* **1657** R. LOVEDAY *Lett.* (1663) 107 A single remembrance over-values it. *a* **1701** SEDLEY *Tyrant of Crete* I. i, Such a jewel would overvalue all the rest. **1760-72** H. BROOKE *Fool of Qual.* (1809) IV. 105 She gave me a look that overvalued the ransom of a monarch.
Hence ,**over'valued** *ppl. a.*; ,**over'valuing** *vbl. sb.* and *ppl. a.*
1627 HAKEWILL *Apol.* IV. xi. §8. 425 The partiall overvaluing of their manhood by their owne Historians. *a* **1711** KEN *Hymnotheo* Poet. Wks. 1721 III. 123 [He] On his own Deeds sets over-valuing Rates. **1805** M. A. SHEE *Rhymes Art* (1806) 107 To crown th' o'ervalued skill of foreign skies. **1885** *Athenæum* 30 May 690/3 Cases where an overvalued coinage has passed current for a long period of years because of the careful limitation of the quantities issued.

over-variety: see OVER- 29 c.

overvault (əʊvə'vɔ:lt), *v.*[1] Also 7 *Sc.* -voit. [OVER- 1.] *trans.* To vault or arch over. Hence **over'vaulted, over'vaulting** *ppl. adjs.*
a **1610** SIR J. SEMPILL in *Sempill Ballates* (1872) 242 His deere and Loving sweit Ouervoited with the vailles of balme-rebaiting trees. **1801** SOUTHEY *Thalaba* IX. xxvii, Polycarp of old..By the glories of the burning stake O'ervaulted. **1832** TENNYSON *Pal. of Art* 54 That over-vaulted grateful gloom, Thro' which the livelong day my soul did pass. **1866** *Cornh. Mag.* Nov. 547 The snows and overvaulting clouds which crown its mountains shine all day.

overvault (əʊvə'vɔ:lt), *v.*[2] [OVER- 5.] *trans.* To vault or spring over. Also *fig.* Hence **over'vaulting** *ppl. a.*
1879 BAIN *Educ. as Science* viii. 270 An over-vaulting and premature attack on the citadel. **1886** *Homilet. Rev.* Aug. 119 All this comes of the endeavor to overvault deliberation.

over-vehement: see OVER- 28.

over-veil (əʊvə'veɪl), *v.* Also 6 -vayl, 7 -vail, -vale. [OVER- 8.] *trans.* To veil over; to cover, shroud, or obscure with or as with a veil. (Chiefly *poet.*)
1591 SHAKS. *1 Hen. VI*, II. ii. 2 Night is fled, Whose pitchy Mantle ouer-vayl'd the Earth. **1606** BIRNIE *Kirk-Buriall* (1833) 9 That natures obscenities be decently couered and oueruailed with her mothers mouldes. *a* **1639** WOTTON *Ps.* CIV. vi, Thou mak'st the Night to over-vail the Day. *a* **1849** MANGAN *Poems* (1859) 354 The thin wan moon, half over-veiled By clouds.

over'ventilate, *v.* *Physiol.* [OVER- 26.]
a. *trans.* = HYPERVENTILATE *v.* b.
1917 J. S. HALDANE *Organism & Environment* i. 13 The very rapid and shallow breathing of a dog in hot weather does not over-ventilate its lungs. **1931** *Amer. Jrnl. Physiol.* XCVIII. 202 A dog with a low Ca of 6·05..was overventilated..with the corresponding precipitation of violent convulsions. **1963** SPALDING & SMITH *Clin. Pract. & Physiol. Artific. Respiration* iii. 43 A patient who has been overventilated during artificial respiration.
b. *intr.* = HYPERVENTILATE *v.* a.
1927 *Jrnl. Physiol.* LXIV. p. xxiv, Nahun showed that there is a decrease in limb volume when a normal man over-ventilates. **1961** *Ibid.* CLVI. 240 The subject was instructed to overventilate from a 100 l. Douglas bag containing 4% carbon dioxide in air.

,**overventi'lation.** *Physiol.* [OVER- 26.] = HYPERVENTILATION.
1911 *Amer. Jrnl. Physiol.* XXVIII. 387 Over-ventilation of the lungs..is at once suggested as an explanation. **1927** *Jrnl. Physiol.* LXIV. p. xxiv, The vessels of the skin play some part in maintaining the blood-pressure during over-ventilation in man. **1963** SPALDING & SMITH *Clin. Pract. & Physiol. Artific. Respiration* v. 76 Artificial overventilation may alter the response to CO_2 of the mechanism controlling respiration and may induce a volume-dependent type of respiration.

over-venturesome, -vexed: see OVER-.

over-vert, the trees in a forest (as opposed to the undergrowth): see VERT *sb.*[1]

over'view, *v.* [OVER- 7, 16.]
1. *trans.* To view from a superior position, look down upon, survey. Also, of a place: To afford a view over, overlook.
1564 J. RASTELL *Confut. Jewell's Serm.* 20 Euery contrie, Which the glorious light of the Ghospell hath now oueruewed. *c* **1600** *Timon* I. iv, A man of greate accompt, that hath oreveiu'd Soe many countreyes. *a* **1627** MIDDLETON *Sp. Gypsy* III. (1653) Fij, It [the Window] over-views a spacious Garden. **1640** BP. REYNOLDS *Passions* xxiv, A lame man placed upon some high Tower can overview with his eyes more ground than [etc.]. **1864** S. WARNER *Old Helmet* I. xii. 247 Mrs. Powle's fair face would overview a moral desolation more hopeless and more cheerless [etc.].
2. To look (a thing) over or all through; to examine, inspect, peruse.
The use in quot. 1977 is influenced by OVERVIEW *sb.* 2.
1549 CHALONER *Erasm. on Folly* L ij, How they are faine to writhe their wittes in and out..in oueruewyng it againe. **1577** HELLOWES *Gueuara's Chron.* 252 Commodus had ouerviewed and ransackt their store. **1632** SIR S. D'EWES *Autobiog.* (1845) II. 71, I spent the remainder of this month in overviewing and sorting them [coins]. **1935** E. R. EDDISON *Mistress of Mistresses* xi. 197 From the sweep of eagles' wings it becometh us overview the matter, and what's just and allowable of our greatness, choose that. **1977** *Canad. Jrnl. Linguistics 1976* XXI. I. 17 The interplay of physiological-cognitive factors with respect to early speech perception and production has been critically overviewed by Gilbert (1975).
Hence **over'viewing** *vbl. sb.*
1590 Q. ELIZ. in Tolstoy *1st 40 Yrs. Interc. Eng. & Russ.* (1875) 364 We refferre the effect of all thos causes generall to your h[ighnes]s delyberat overvewing againe. **1935** E. R. EDDISON *Mistress of Mistresses* xii. 225, I would have you, as a politic prince.., refer the whole estate you are in to your highness' deliberate overviewing again.

'overview, *sb.* [f. prec.] † **1.** Survey, inspection; supervision; overlooking. *Obs.*
1588 SHAKS. *L.L.L.* IV. iii. 175 Too bitter is thy iest. Are wee betrayed thus to thy ouer-view? **1644** LAUD *Wks.* (1854) IV. 242 The business of leaving the care of these books and the overview of them to my chaplains.
2. orig. *U.S.* A survey, summary, or comprehensive review of facts or ideas; a concise statement or outline of a subject. Hence **'overviewer,** one who formulates an overview.
1934 *Amer. Speech* IX. 318/2 Editors testify that the new noun *overview* is now being worked as hard by educationists as 'purposeful', 'challenge', 'objective', 'motivation', *et al.*, have been in the past. **1944** *Mind* LIII. 276 According to the jacket..the purpose of this book is to present 'an overview of present-day philosophical trends'. **1958** *Times Lit. Suppl.* 28 Mar. 173/4 Her 'overview' of psycho-analytical thought is therefore followed by detailed expositions of the views of the principle dissidents. **1967** *Wall St. Jrnl.* 4 May 4/3 The first step is to take an 'overview' of the problem. **1969** M. CRICHTON *Andromeda Strain* v. 44 A scientist with a conscience, an overview, an appreciation of the significance of events. **1969** M. SCRIVEN in N. R. Hanson *Perception & Discovery* p. vii, There is a..tension between the demands of exact historical scholarship and the more free-ranging interests of the overviewer. **1973** *Nature* 6 July 59/3 The chief drawback of this volume is that it lacks a chapter devoted to a critical overview of the comparative relevance of particular models as they relate to particular experimental ends. **1974** *Florida FL Reporter* XIII. 31/2 With presumably Ms. Hess as overviewer making some critical commentary on which of the arguments were stronger and why. **1975** A. S. MISKIMIN *Renaissance Chaucer* viii. 230 In an overview such as this, many questions will be begged. **1975** *Sci. Amer.* May 119/2 The first 50 pages of overview include a neat account of the logical architecture of possible machines. **1975** *Listener* 31 July 130/2 In its latest policy 'overview', the State Department ponders [etc.].

overvigorous, -vilify: see OVER-.

'over-'violent, *a.* [OVER- 28.] Excessively violent, too violent. So **'over-'violently** *adv.*, too violently.
1594 MARLOWE & NASHE *Dido* IV, The motion was so over-violent. **1614** RALEIGH *Hist. World* II. (1634) 527 To draw all matters over-violently to mine owne computation. **1681** DRYDEN *Abs. & Achit.* 557 So over violent, or over civil, That every man with him was God or Devil. **1826** SCOTT *Woodst.* xxx, We are called to act..neither luke-warmly nor over-violently.

† **over'visor.** *Obs. rare*$^{-1}$. [A partial rendering of L. *supervisor.*] A supervisor.
1653 LD. VAUX tr. *Godeau's St. Paul* A iij b, Great Saint Augustine..who desires severe judges as over-visours of his learned works.

overvista to **overvitrified:** see OVER-.

† **over'void,** *a.* *Obs.* [OVER- 25.] Vain, superfluous (rendering L. *supervacuus*). So † **over'voidness,** vanity (rendering L. *supervacuitas*).
1382 WYCLIF *Wisd.* xiv. 14 The oueruoidenesse [*Vulg.* supervacuitas] forsothe of men these thingis fond in to the roundnesse of erthis. *Ibid.* xv. 9 For thingus ouervoide [1388 superflu, *Vulg.* res supervacuas] he maketh.

'over,voltage. [f. OVER- 19, 20 + VOLTAGE[2], as tr. G. *überspannung* (W. A. Caspari 1899, in *Zeitschr. f. physikal. Chem.* XXX. 91).] **1.** The difference between the electrode potential for a reaction (as the liberation of a gas) in practical, irreversible conditions and the theoretical, reversible value.
1907 WHITNEY & BROWN tr. *Le Blanc's Text-bk. Electro-Chem.* viii. 299 Not only in the case of hydrogen, but also in that of oxygen, an over-voltage which varies with the nature of the electrode..is produced by the separation of the gas. **1922** GLAZEBROOK *Dict. Appl. Physics* II. 60/1 Platinised platinum as a cathode has the lowest overvoltage among the elements commonly available. **1965** PHILLIPS & WILLIAMS *Inorg. Chem.* I. xi. 421 Using a mercury electrode the over-voltage of hydrogen is so great that the sodium is discharged and taken into the mercury as an amalgam.
2. A voltage in excess of that which is normal, safe, or allowed for.
1921 S. Q. HAYES *Switching Equipment for Power Control* v. 157 Relays are built to furnish protection on A.C. or D.C. circuits against overvoltage, no voltage, overload, no load, reverse load and reverse phase. **1963** B. FOZARD *Instrumentation Nucl. Reactors* v. 56 It may sometimes occur that a tube must be used with an insensitive scaling equipment, in which case a high overvoltage may be necessary to give satisfactory operation.

† **over'volve,** *v.* *Sc. Obs. rare*$^{-1}$. In 6 ouer-, oure-, our-. [? f. OVER- + L. *volvĕre* to roll, turn: cf. L. *supervolvĕre.*] ? To turn over or aside.
(But the reading is doubtful: the original may have been 'Onrevolvit (i.e. not turned over) this volume lay ane space'.)
1513 DOUGLAS *Æneis* VII. Prol. 154 For byssines, quhilk occurrit on cace, Ourvoluit [*v. rr.* oure-, ouer-] I this volume, lay ane space: And, thocht I wery was, ne lyst nocht tyre.

† ,**over'vote,** *v.* *Obs.* [OVER- 22.] *trans.* To defeat by a majority of votes; = OUTVOTE.
1641 *Exam. Answ. Reas. Ho. Comm. Votes Bps. Parl.* 65 How easily Bishops may bee over-voted in Parliament. **1664** PEPYS *Diary* 18 Nov., Four all along did act for the Papists, and three only for the Protestants, by which they were overvoted. **168.** in Somers *Tracts* I. 324 Let us suppose now, that all this should be over-voted (for I am sure it can never be answered).

,**overvulcani'zation.** [OVER- 29 b.] Vulcanization for longer than is necessary to achieve the maximum modulus of elasticity.
1900 W. T. BRANNT *India Rubber, Gutta-Percha & Balata* iii. 111 If the articles are allowed to remain too long in the solution, over-vulcanization may take place, that is, the surface of the article becomes hard and brittle. **1967** tr. *W. Hofmann's Vulcanization & Vulcanizing Agents* i. 24 Its symptons [*sc.* those of postvulcanization] are thus very similar to the rising characteristic of tensile stress at a given elongation which is associated with overvulcanization.

over'vulcanize, *v.* [OVER- 27.] *trans.* To subject (rubber) to overvulcanization; to make hard or brittle by vulcanizing. Hence **over'vulcanizing** *vbl. sb.*
1911 P. SCHIDROWITZ *Rubber* xi. 172 Bysow..found that with a total sulphur of from 3·44 per cent. to 8·91 per cent. equilibrium was not produced until the samples were over-vulcanized. **1916** [see OVERCURE *v.*]. **1922** *Encycl. Brit.* XXX. 35/1 In 1916 some resistance to petrol was introduced by using pure para heavily loaded with mineral matter and rather over-vulcanized. **1967** tr. *W. Hofmann's Vulcanization & Vulcanizing Agents* i. 24 When an article is wholly or partly overvulcanized (thick-sectioned articles, for example, are sometimes overvulcanized at the surface), efficient protection against ageing is always necessary.

† **over'wade,** *v.* *Obs.* [OE. *oferwadan*: see OVER- 10, and cf. OHG. *uberwaten* (Notker).] *trans.* To wade across.
c **893** K. ÆLFRED *Oros.* II. iv. §6 Ða ȝebeotode Cirus..þæt hie mehte wifmon be hiere cneowe oferwadan, þær heo ær wæs niȝon mila brad. **1382** WYCLIF *Ezek.* xlvii. 5 Deep waters of the streme of reyn wexiden grete, whiche may not be ouer wad [*Vulg.* transvadari]. **1456** SIR G. HAYE *Law Arms* (S.T.S.) 37 He suld mak that ryver sa lytill that a wyf ..suld nocht wete hir kneis till ourwade it.

† **over'wait,** *v.* *Obs. rare.* [OVER- 1 (*c*).] *trans.* To watch over, supervise.
c **1449** PECOCK *Repr.* IV. v. 449 Aboue manye to gidere of these..hiȝer lordis..be oon other to ouer waite hem.

†**over'wake**, *v. Obs.* [OE. *oferwacian*, f. *ofer-* OVER- 1 (*c*) + *wacian* to wake: cf. mod.Ger. *überwachen*. See also OVER- 22, 23.]

1. *trans.* To keep watch over. (*O.E.*)

c **1000** ÆLFRIC *Saints' Lives* (1885) I. 66 Iulianus wycode wið þa ea eufraten and him oferwacedon syfanfealde weardas [*text* weardes].

2. a. *trans.* To remain awake longer than (another). **b.** *refl.* To keep oneself awake too long.

1590 GREENE *Never too late* (1600) 17 Thus watching thee, he ouerwaketh himselfe. **1609** DEKKER *Raven's Alm.* D iv, If I ouerwake him then he puls me by the haire of the head, and saith I watch to cut his throat when he is asleepe.

over'walk, *v.* [OVER- 9, 10, 23.]

1. *trans.* To walk over, traverse by walking.

1533 MORE *Confut. Barnes* Wks. 770/1 Ye saye shee is some where abrode in the wylde world, whych worlde is a place to wyde.. for a woman to ouerwalke well. **1596** SHAKS. *1 Hen. IV*, I. iii. 192 As full of perill and adueunturous Spirit, As to o'rewalke a Current, roaring loud On the vnstedfast footing of a Speare. **1789** WORDSW. *Evening Walk* 165 Some.. O'erwalk the slender plank from side to side.

2. *refl.* To walk too much or too far; to fatigue oneself with too much walking.

1662 STRYPE *Let.* in Wordsw. *Schol. Acad.* (1877) 292 *note*, Be carefull of y^rselfe and do not over walk yrselfe for y^t is wont to bring y^o upon a sick bedd. **1799** JANE AUSTEN *Lett.* (1884) I. 212 My uncle overwalked himself at first, and can now only travel in a chair. **1826** SCOTT *Diary* 26 Aug. in Lockhart, I rather overwalked myself yesterday.

So **'over-'walking** *vbl. sb.*, walking too much.

1870 DICKENS *Let. R. S. Ralston* 16 May, Violent neuralgic attacks in the foot. That originated in over-walking in deep snow. **1894** *Obit. Rec. Graduates Yale Univ.* 266 By over-walking during vacation, he injured one foot.

'over-walker. *rare.* [-ER[1].] One who walks too much or too far.

1876 R. L. STEVENSON in *Cornhill Mag.* XXXIII. 685 It is here that your over-walker fails of comprehension.

†**over'walt**, *v. Obs.* [f. OVER- 6, 9 + WALT *v.*, to roll: cf. OVERWELT.]

1. *trans.* To roll or turn (a thing) over; to overturn: = OVERWELT *v.* a.

13.. *Gaw. & Gr. Knt.* 314 Now is þe reuel & þe renoun of þe rounde table Ouer-walt wyth a worde of on wyȝes speche. *c* **1400** *Destr. Troy* 8155 Tyll the toun be ouerteruyt, & tumblid to ground;.. And the wallis ouerwalt into þe wete dyches.

2. To roll or flow over; to overflow.

13.. *E.E. Allit. P.* B. 370 þe flod ryses, Ouer-waltez vche a wod and þe wyde feldez.

over'wander, *v. rare. poet.* [OVER- 9.] *trans.* To wander over. So **over'wandered, over'wandering** *ppl. adjs.*

a **1547** SURREY *Æneid* II. 378 After time spent in thouer-wandred flood. **1833** TENNYSON *Œnone* Poems 56 Above, the overwandering ivy and vine.. in many a wild festoon Ran riot. **1886** BURTON *Arab. Nts.* (abr. ed.) I. 8 Let us overwander Allah's earth.

over-wanton, -war: see OVER-.

†**overward**, *adv.* and *prep. Obs.* [In form = OVER *adv.* + -WARD; but app. perverted from OVERTHWART; cf. the variant *overwart.*]

A. *adv.* In a direction over or across a surface, an intervening space, etc.; across, transversely.

c **1290** *S. Eng. Leg.* I. 268/246 He ne miȝte finde no schip, him ouer for-to lede. he sat and weop and bi-heold ouerward. **1393** LANGL. *P. Pl.* C. v. 128 And alle rome-renners.. Bere no suluer ouer see.. Vp forfeture of þe fee he so fynt hym ouerwarde. *c* **1420** *Pallad. on Husb.* III. 139 (Colch. MS.) Overward [*Fitzw. MS.* orthward, *i.e.* o'erthwart] and afterlonge extende a lyne.

B. *prep.* Across, from side to side of, athwart.

1486 *Bk. St. Albans* A viij b, Ther gooth blacke barris ouerwarde the tayle.

'over-'ward, *sb.* [prop. two words: OVER *a.* and WARD *sb.*] The upper ward.

1485 *Rolls of Parlt.* VI. 384/2 The Forster of the Overwarde of our Forest of Inglewoode. **1547** *Reg. Privy Council Scot.* I. 71 And with him the ouir ward of Cliddisdaile. **1773** ERSKINE *Instit.* I. iv. §5. 54 In the shire of Clydesdale, Lanerk is the head borough of the overward,.. Hamilton is the head borough of the nether ward. **1862** J. GRANT *Capt. of Guard* i, David Liberton, sergeant of the overward of the constabulary of Edinburgh, in the time of David II.

'over-'warm, *a.* [OVER- 28.] Too warm. So **'over-'warmth**, too great warmth.

1713 ADDISON *Cato* I. vi, Marcus is over-warm. **1822** BYRON *Juan* VI. xv, A sincere woman's breast,—for over-warm Or over-cold annihilates the charm. *Ibid.* xvi, For over-warmth, if false, is worse than truth.

,over-'warm, *v.* [OVER- 27.] *trans.* To warm too much.

1598 SYLVESTER *Du Bartas* II. i. III. *Furies* 352 Manie and Phrenzie.. th'one drying, th'other over-warming The feeble brain. *a* **1633** AUSTIN *Medit.* (1635) 291 There shall no Sunne nor Weather overwarme him. **1650** TRAPP *Comm. Lev.* x. 1 Over-joied haply of their new emploiment, and over-warmed with wine.

†**over'warp**, *v. Obs.* [OE. *oferweorpan*, f. *ofer-* OVER- 6 + *weorpan* to throw, WARP: cf. OHG. *ubarwerfan*, Ger. *überwerfen* to overthrow, upset. Cf. OVERCAST, OVERTHROW.] *trans.* To overthrow, throw or cast down.

c **897** K. ÆLFRED *Gregory's Past. C.* xxvi. 180 Ðu þe art mid ðy storme.. onwend & oferworpen. *c* **1000** *Sax. Leechd.* I. 384 Nim eorþan, oferweorp mid þinre swiþran handa under þinum swiþran fet. *a* **1225** *Ancr. R.* 142 Uorte holden þet schip, þet uðen ne stormes hit ne ouerworpen. *c* **1330** R. BRUNNE *Chron. Wace* (Rolls) 8197 (Petyt MS.) When þey [the dragons] hadde longe to-gyder smyten.. Wipped wyþ uenges, ouerwarpen & went.

overwart: see OVERTHWART.

over-wary: see OVER-.

'overwash (-wɒʃ), *sb. Geol.* [f. next.] The act or fact of washing over; the material carried by running water from a glacier and deposited over or beyond the marginal moraine. Also *attrib.*, as ***overwash gravel, plain***, etc.

1889 LEVERETT in *Nature* 3 Oct. 558/1 In the newer moraines the terminal loops meet on opposite sides of large interlobate moraines, and correlation is made only after critical study of their connections, over-riding, overwash, etc. **1890** F. W. PUTNAM in *Century Mag.* Mar. 698/2 At least ten times ten centuries have passed away since the implements of stone, fashioned by this early man, were lost and covered by the overwash of the glacial gravels. **1894** [see OUTWASH]. **1909** *Jrnl. Geol.* XVII. 375 Locally overwash plains are conspicuous topographic features. **1957** J. K. CHARLESWORTH *Quaternary Era* I. xxii. 442 Thus outwash may occur with or without moraines; the two types constitute respectively Chamberlin's overwash aprons and outwash plains or aprons.

overwash (-'wɒʃ), *v.* [OVER- 5, 9.] *trans.* To wash or flow over (something); to lave or bathe by flowing over.

1577 HARRISON *England* II. xi. (1877) I. 229 Pirats and robbers by sea are.. hanged on the shore at lowe water marke, where they are left till three tides haue ouerwashed them. **1589** GREENE *Menaphon* (Arb.) 77 Her lips like roses ouerwasht with dew. **1593** SHAKS. *Lucr.* 1225 But durst not ask.. Why her two suns were cloud-eclipsed so, Nor why her fair cheeks over-wash'd with woe. **1837** CARLYLE *Fr. Rev.* III. VII. v, The ship of the State again.. overwashed, near to swamping, with unfruitful brine.

overwaste, etc.: see OVER-.

†**'over-watch**, *sb. Obs.* [OVER- 18, 29, 1 (*c*).]

a. A watching too long or too late, too much watching. **b.** A person who watches over another.

1399 LANGL. *Rich. Redeles* III. 282 And euere shall þou ffynde.. That wisdom and ouere-wacche wonneth ffer asundre. **1494** FABYAN *Chron.* VI. clxx. (1533) 98 b/1 Tyred.. wyth ouer watche and laboure. *a* **1650** *Eger & Grine* 944 in Furniv. *Percy Folio* I. 383 Gray-steele had ouer-waches 2. They went & told their Master anon right.

overwatch (əʊvə'wɒtʃ, ,əʊvə-), *v.* [OVER- 1 (*c*), 17, 21.]

1. *trans.* To watch over, keep watch over.

1618 *Hist. Perkin Warbeck* in *Select. Harl. Misc.* (1793) 66 To attend the arrival of his enemies abroad; yea, peradventure, to overwatch the actions of his freinds at home. **1661** R. L'ESTRANGE *Relapsed Apostate* (1681) 18 It was his Part to overwatch their Appetites. **1784** COWPER *Tiroc.* 262, I blame not those, who with what care they can O'er-watch the num'rous and unruly clan. **1865** SWINBURNE *Atalanta* 1360 Olive and ivy and poplar dedicate And many a well-spring overwatched of these.

†**2.** To watch all through (a night). *Obs.*

1590 SHAKS. *Mids. N.* V. i. 373, I feare we shall out-sleepe the comming morne, As much as we this night haue ouer-watcht. *c* **1590** GREENE *Fr. Bacon* xi. 26 If Argus liv'd, and had his hundred eyes, They could not over-watch Phobetors night.

3. To fatigue or wear out with excessive watching; to weary or exhaust by keeping awake or by want of sleep. Now chiefly in *pa. pple.*

1563 FOXE *A. & M.* 750/2, I answer and saye, that this bishop belike had ouerwatched hym selfe in this matter. For.. he neuer slept til he red it. **1591** UNTON *Corr.* (Roxb.) 235, I crave pardon, beinge overwearyede and overwatched in the trenches. **1607** MARKHAM *Caval.* I. (1617) 77 Some horsmen aduise you.. to keep your horse from sleep, and so by ouerwatching him, to make him tame. **1760–72** H. BROOKE *Fool of Qual.* (1809) II. 100 Overtoiled and overwatched, I fell into a deep sleep. **1821** SCOTT *Kenilw.* xv, Tressilian, fatigued and over-watched, came down to the hall.

Hence **,over'watched** *ppl. a.*, wearied with too much watching; **,over-'watching** *vbl. sb.*, too much watching; too long vigil. Also **over-'watcher**, one who watches over.

1568 GRAFTON *Chron.* I. 138 His knightes and Souldiours were tyred, and weried with ouer watching and labour. **1582** T. WATSON *Centurie of Loue* lxxix, The belly neither cares for meate nor drinke, Nor ouerwatched eyes desire to winke. *a* **1656** BP. HALL *Christian* iii, His [the Christian's] Recreations.. are.. like unto a sweet nap after an overwatching. **1822** SCOTT *Pirate* iv, She was up early, and down late, and seemed, to her overwatched and overtasked maidens, to be as 'wakerife' as the cat herself. **1846** ELIZ. B. BARRETT in *Lett. R. Browning & E. B. B.* (1899) II. 426 Perhaps you will go home through it—but I shall not see—I cannot watch, being afraid of the over-watchers.

over-'water, *v.* [OVER- 25, 27, 8: cf. Du. *overwaeteren* to inundate (Kilian).]

†**1.** *trans.* To water thoroughly. Also *fig. Obs.*

1645 RUTHERFORD *Tryal & Tri. Faith* Ded. (1845) 11 A sea, and boundless river of visible, living, and breathing grace,.. to over-water men and angels. *a* **1682** SIR T. BROWNE *Tracts* 165 The river gave the fruitfulness unto this valley by over-watring that low Region.

2. To water too much. (Chiefly in *pa. pple.*)

1828 MISS MITFORD *Village* Ser. III. (1863) 51 Myrtles over-watered, and geraniums, trained as never geraniums were trained before. **1879** BEERBOHM *Patagonia* vii. 117 They proceeded to taste the liquor, in order to see whether it had been overwatered. **1898** *Westm. Gaz.* 15 Jan. 2/3 The extent to which the streets of London are over-watered is known only to cyclists.

3. To cover with water. *rare.*

1890 L. LEWIS *Proving of Gennad* 47 Brave sights, now over-watered, quenched and stilled.

,over-'water, *a.* [OVER- 32.] **a.** Performed or proceeding across water (in quot. 1900 = 'foreign'). **b.** Situated on or located over water.

1900 W. C. MURRAY *Week's Rambling with 'Bra Quamin'* 11 De talkin' tree is a ober water duppy tree. **1933** *Sun* (Baltimore) 7 Dec. 1/7 It was the longest over-water flight of their aerial survey tour. **1942** *R.A.F. Jrnl.* 16 May 16 It has a long range.. which renders it suitable for over-water operation from shore bases. **1946** *Sun* (Baltimore) 30 July 8/2 If geophysical reports are favorable, over-water rigs will be erected later for drilling tests. **1960** *Washington Post* 20 Mar. B8/4 Air Guard spokesmen emphasized that missions.. are routed over nonpopulated areas to an over-water course to the Buck Target Range in North Carolina. **1967** *Jane's Surface Skimmer Systems 1967–68* 2/1 Research and development programmes are dedicated in the main to the task of speeding up over-water transport. **1976** B. LECOMBER *Dead Weight* II. vii. 82 All aero-engines immediately go into auto-rough whenever you think about them on the over-water flight.

'over-'watery, *a.* [OVER- 28.] Too watery; containing too much water.

1626 BACON *Sylva* §509 They are all overwatry.

overwave, *v.*: see OVER- 1.

†**over-'wax**, *v. Obs.* [OE. *oferweaxan*, f. *ofer-* OVER- 8 + *weaxan* to grow, WAX: = OHG. *uberwahsen*, Ger. *überwachsen*. See also OVER- 25, 27.]

1. *trans.* To overgrow, grow over. (*O.E.*)

971 *Blickl. Hom.* 159 Cweþende þæt his sæd oferweoxe ealle þas woruld. *c* **1000** ÆLFRIC *Hom.* I. 508 þæs muntes cnoll wiðutan is sticmælum mid wuda oferwexen.

2. *intr.* **a.** To wax or grow exceedingly. **b.** To grow too large, to overgrow.

1382 WYCLIF *2 Thess.* i. 3 Ȝoure feith ouerwexith [*Vulg.* supercrescit]. **1413** *Pilgr. Sowle* I. xx. (Egerton MS. 615), And if thi conscience had be more streite, this taile ne schuld haue be so ouerwaxen. *c* **1450** *R. Gloucester's Chron.* (1724) 482/1 *note* (MS. Coll. Arms) In a too of his foot the naile groweth ouer to the flesshe, and in harme to the foot hugeliche ouerwexethe.

†**'over-way.** *Obs.* [OVER- 1 d.]

1. (prop. two words). The upper or higher way. *Sc.*

c **1575** *Hist. James VI* (1804) 171 He gaue command to thrie hundrethe horsmen to pas ye ouerway, and to cum in.. be a priuey furde.

2. = OVERSLAY. (? an error.)

1674 N. FAIRFAX *Bulk & Selv.* Ep. Ded., Castles in the Air, whose Groundsils are laid with Whims, their Overwayes with Dreams, and rooft with Cream of thinking. **1692** in *Athenæum* (1895) 20 Apr. 505/3 A timber-beam called ye Overway of ye house which on yt side that is towards ye street is adorned with ancient carved worke and beareth this date 1372.

'over-'weak, *a.* [OVER- 28.] Too weak.

1565 JEWEL *Repl. Harding* (1611) 2 That yee haue hitherto shewed vs,.. is ouerweake, and will not serue. **1651** C. CARTWRIGHT *Cert. Relig.* I. 137 This reason is over-weak. **1840** DICKENS *Barn. Rudge* xix, Warm brandy-and-water not over-weak.

,over-'weaken, *v.* [OVER- 27.] *trans.* To weaken too much, make too weak.

1747 tr. *Astruc's Fevers* 308 Bleeding, when it is moderate.. and not so plentiful as to over-weaken him. **1880** *District Order*, Pretoria 16 Dec., Never to endanger the safety of their posts through over-weakening their garrison.

overweal, -wealth, etc.: see OVER-.

overwean, obs. form of OVERWEEN.

overwear (əʊvə'wɛə(r)), *v.* [OVER- 21, 17.]

1. To wear out or exhaust (with toil, etc.). Chiefly in *pa. pple.*

1578 *Chr. Prayers* in *Priv. Prayers* (1851) 470 We have endured much punishment, being overworn with so many wars. *c* **1600** SHAKS. *Sonn.* lxiii. **1655** *Theophania* 152 Being overworn with sorrow, she ended this life before I had attained to the thirteenth year of my age. **1801** SOUTHEY *Thalaba* IV. xxv, At his feet the gasping beast Lies, over-worn with want. **1879** H. SPENCER *Data of Ethics* x. §64. 178 Limbs over-worn by prolonged exertion, cannot without aching perform acts which would at other times cause no appreciable feeling.

2. To wear out (clothes, etc.), wear threadbare.

1630 J. TAYLOR (Water P.) *Water Cormorant* Wks. III. 6/1 And yearely they vpon their backes oreweare, That which oft fed fiue hundred with good cheare. **1671** MILTON *Samson* 123 In slavish habit, ill-fitted weeds O're worn and soild. **1819** SHELLEY *Cenci* III. i. 208 That you put off, as garments overworn, Forbearance, and respect, remorse, and fear.

3. To wear (something) away or to an end; to outwear.

1581 [see OVERWORN 2]. **1605** VERSTEGAN *Verses* in *Dec. Intell.*, Time ouerweares what earst his licence wrought.

1636 SANDERSON *Serm.* II. 55 A man, that, having gotten some sore bruise in his youth, and by the help of surgery and the strength of youth overworn it, may yet carry a grudging of it in his bones or joynts.

4. To cease to wear as having outgrown.

1887 J. BASCOM *Sociology* vi. 142 (Funk) A corrupt political party..may have lost or overworn its principles.

'over-,wear, *sb. U.S.* [OVER- 8 c.] The action or fact of wearing over other clothes; garments so worn, outer clothing. (Opposed to *underwear.*)

1890 in *Cent. Dict.*

overweary (əʊvə'wɪərɪ), *v.* [OVER- 21, 27.] *trans.* To overcome with weariness; to weary to excess.

1576 TURBERV. *Venerie* 72 Recomfort their members which are sore overwearied. **1612** BRINSLEY *Lud. Lit.* 269 When the master is compelled to diuide his pains both amongst little and great, he may much ouer-wearie himselfe. **1821** SHELLEY *Prometh. Unb.* IV. 271 Like to a child o'erwearied with sweet toil. **1875** *Dental Cosmos* XVII. 513 Rather than over-weary the patient,..one sitting may be given to the preparation of the cavities.

Hence **over'wearied, over'wearying** *ppl. adjs.* So **over-'weary** *a.*, overcome with weariness; excessively weary, too weary to hold out.

1591 *Murther of Ld. Brough*, Overwerying plaints abreviate the libertie of speach. **1677** GILPIN *Demonol.* (1867) 332 Satan so molested Job..that, as an overwearied man, he cries out he had no quiet. **1794** SOUTHEY *Poems Slave Trade* Sonn. iii, Beneath thy hard command O'erwearied nature sinks. **1851** C. L. SMITH tr. *Tasso* VI. cx, Give rest to her o'erweary mind. **1888** STEVENSON *Black Arrow* 83 Half starved and over-weary as they were, they lay without moving.

†**over'weathered**, *ppl. a. Obs. rare*⁻¹. In quot. ouer-wither'd. [OVER- 21.] Worn or damaged by exposure to the weather.

1596 SHAKS. *Merch. V.* II. vi. 18 How like a prodigall doth she returne With ouer-wither'd ribs and ragged sailes, Leane, rent, and begger'd by the strumpet winde?

over'weave, *v. poet.* [OVER- 1, 8.] *trans.* To weave over the top or surface. (In *pa. pple.*)

1818 KEATS *Endymion* I. 431 An arbour, overwove By many a summer's silent fingering. **1869** BLACKMORE *Lorna D.* vii, I found it strongly over-woven.

†**overween, -wene**, *sb. Obs. rare.* [f. OVER- 29 b + ME. *wene*, OE. *wén* thought, opinion. Cf. OHG. *uberwân, -wânî* arrogance, pride.] Overweening, presumption.

c **1220** *Bestiary* 335 Giuernesse and wising, Pride and ouerwene; Swilc atter i-mene.

overween (əʊvə'wiːn), *v.* Now chiefly in *ppl. a.* OVERWEENING. [OVER- 26, 27.]

1. *intr.* To have too high expectations, or too high an opinion of oneself; to be conceited, arrogant, presumptuous, or too self-confident; to presume.

1303 R. BRUNNE *Handl. Synne* 5164 Nat ouerdrede ne ouerwene. *c* **1532** DU WES *Introd. Fr.* in *Palsgr.* 955 To over wene, *surcuider.* **1593** SHAKS. *3 Hen. VI*, III. ii. 144 My Eyes too quicke, my Heart o're-weenes too much. **1597** —— *2 Hen. IV*, IV. i. 149 Mowbray, you ouer-weene to take it so. **1642** MILTON *Apol. Smect.* Wks. 1738 I. 127 Is there cause why these Men should overwean, and be so queasy of the rude Multitude, lest their deep worth should be undervalu'd for want of fit Umpires? **1702** *Eng. Theophrast.* 192 We all of us naturally overwean in our own favour. **1866** J. B. ROSE tr. *Ovid's Fasti* 156 Happiest of mothers Niobe had been Had happiness not caused her to o'erween.

†**2.** To think too highly, have an exaggerated or conceited opinion (*of*). *Obs.*

1555 [see OVERWEENING *vbl. sb.* 2]. **1605** CAMDEN *Rem.* 94 Whatsoever some of their posteritie doe overweene of the antiquitie of their names. **1621** BURTON *Anat. Mel.*, Some are too partial, as friends to overween, others come with a prejudice to carp, vilify, detract, and scoff.

†**3.** *trans.* (and *refl.* = 1). To think too highly of, over-esteem, hold an exaggerated opinion of (usually oneself, or something of one's own).

1588 FRAUNCE *Lawiers Log.* II. ix. 101 b, The disputers.. must [not] overweene themselves, or bee obstinate and singuler in conceipt. **1621** S. WARD *Happiness of Practice* (1627) Ep. Ded., It was a pride in Montanus to ouerweene his Pepuza and Tymium, two pelting Parishes in Phrygia, and to call them Hierusalem. **1674** N. FAIRFAX *Bulk & Selv.* 10 To make it likely..that the doctrine of atoms is not wound up in those darknesses that some mens understandings have may-hap over-weened.

†**4.** To cause to overween (sense 1); to render presumptuous or arrogant. *Obs.* (See also next.)

1590 GREENE *Mourn. Garm.* Ded. (1616) 1 While wantonnesse..ouer-weaned the Niniuites, their sur-coates of bisse were all polished with gold. **1620** FORD *Linea V.* (Shaks. Soc.) 66 Injuries can no more discourage him, than applause can ouer-weene him.

†**over'weened**, *ppl. a. Obs.* [f. prec. + -ED.] Conceited; overweening; presumptuous, arrogant.

1600 W. WATSON *Decacordon* (1602) 8 Their owne ouerweend conceit. **1622** T. STOUGHTON *Chr. Sacrif.* viii. 107 Many..are so ouer-weened and puft vp with a conceit of their owne knowledge. **1646** BUCK *Rich. III*, I. 15 Presuming upon the strength of it [his castle] and the peoples affection, but over-weaned in his opinion and hope.

over'weener. ? *Obs.* [f. as prec. + -ER¹.] One who overweens; a conceited, presumptuous, or arrogant person.

1340 *Ayenb.* 21 Þe proude and þe ouerwenere weneþ more by worþ, oþer more conne: more þanne enie oþre. **1588** KYD *Househ. Phil.* Wks. (1901) 269 Substance..in the manurance and handling of an ignorant, or ouerweener, dooth not only decrease but perisheth. **1625** BP. HALL *No peace w. Rome* §9 What insolent over-weeners of their owne workes are these Papists, which proclaime the actions which proceed from themselves, worthy of..heaven. **1647** TRAPP *Comm. Matt.* xxi. 31 These over-weeners of themselves.

over'weening, *vbl. sb.* Now *rare.* [-ING¹.] The action of the verb OVERWEEN.

1. Too great expectation, or opinion as to oneself; excessive self-importance; presumption, arrogance, self-conceit.

c **1330** R. BRUNNE *Chron.* (1810) 97 Als Anselme þe strif gan pes of þe duke & þe kyng, Com Roberd de Beleyse, þorgh his ouerwenyng, & passed hider ouer þe se. **1340** *Ayenb.* 17 Þe uerste boȝ of prede: is ontreuþe... Þe bridde: ouerweninge. Þet we clepeþ presumcion. **1484** CAXTON *Fables of Æsop* II. xv, The Jaye..by his oultrecuydaunce or ouerwenynge wold haue gone and conuersed among the pecoks. **1592** DAVIES *Immort. Soul* XXXIV. viii. (1714) 131 Take heed of Over-weening, and compare Thy Peacock's Feet with thy gay Peacock's Train. **1671** MILTON *P.R.* I. 147 He [Satan] might have learnt Less over-weening, since he fail'd in Job. **1742** RICHARDSON *Pamela* IV. 8 Half the Misunderstandings among marry'd People are owing to.. mere Words, and little captious Follies, to Over-weenings, or unguarded Petulances.

2. A thinking too highly *of* something; excessive esteem, over-estimation.

1555 J. PROCTOR *Hist. Wyat's Reb.* in Arb. *Garner* VIII. 72 Such overweening had they of themselves. **1614** RALEIGH *Hist. World* III. (1634) 111 Who..failed at the last through too much over-weening of his owne wisedome. **1720** WELTON *Suffer. Son of God* II. xvii. 467 By a too great overweening of their own perverse Will. **1808** COLERIDGE *Lett., to F. Jeffrey* (1895) 536 An honest gentleman..having overhurried the business through overweening of my simplicity and carelessness. **1827** J. FEARN in Barker *Parriana* (1828) I. 557 *note*, Any overweening of my own strength to fly alone.

over'weening, *ppl. a.* [f. as prec. + -ING².]

1. Of a person: That thinks, expects, or has an opinion, beyond what is reasonable or just; overconfident or sanguine in one's own opinion; conceited, arrogant, presumptuous, self-opinionated.

1340 *Ayenb.* 169 Mochel is he fol and ouerweninde, þet wyþ-oute ouercominge abit to habbe þe coroune. *c* **1489** CAXTON *Blanchardyn* xlviii. 186 Olde vnfamouse myschaunt, how arte thou soo folyshe and so ouerwenynge as for to wene to haue her. **1591** SHAKS. *Two Gent.* III. i. 157 Goe base Intruder, ouer-weening Slaue, Bestow thy fawning smiles on equall mates. **1605** *Play Stucley* in *Sch. Shaks.* I. 238 But generally I censure th' English thus—Hardy but rash, witty but overweaning. **1690** LOCKE *Hum. Und.* IV. xix. §7 The Conceits of a warm'd or over-weening Brain. **1703** ROWE *Ulyss.* I. i, O'erweening, Insolent, Unmanner'd Slave. **1873** M. ARNOLD *Lit. & Dogma* (1876) 185 Its professors are nevertheless bold, overweening, and even abusive, in maintaining their criticism against all questioners.

fig. **1599** *Broughton's Lett.* iv. 14 Your..attendant..doth play her part, with a cup of overweening liquour, hauing.. intoxicated your..braine.

2. Of opinion, estimate, pretension, desire, etc.: Conceited; excessive, exaggerated, too high.

c **1489** CAXTON *Blanchardyn* xxii. 72 Grete foly it is to youre doughters to haue such an ouerwenyng [Fr. *oultrecuidant*] wylle. **1595** DANIEL *Civ. Wars* III. xxxvi, Whose mind not wonne With th'over-weening thought of hot excesse. **1604** E. G[RIMSTONE] *D'Acosta's Hist. Indies* VII. xiv. 535 The vanquished..with many teares craved pardon of their overweening follie. **1640** BP. HALL *Episc.* III. viii. 260 To be led by the nose, with..an over-weening opinion of some persons, whom you thinke you have cause to honour. **1712** BUDGELL *Spect.* No. 307 ¶14 The overweening Fondness of a Parent. **1729** FRANKLIN *Ess.* Wks. 1840 II. 43 An overweening desire of sudden wealth. **1850** PRESCOTT *Peru* II. 355 Pizarro..cannot be charged with manifesting any overweening solicitude for the propagation of the Faith. **1879** M. ARNOLD *Democracy* in *Mixed Ess.* 15 Her airs of superiority and her overweening pretensions.

Hence **over'weeningly** *adv.*; **-'weeningness.**

1611 COTGR., *Oultrecuidamment*, ouer-weeningly, presumptuously, arrogantly. **1621** BP. MOUNTAGU *Diatribæ* 28 By turning our fingers home vpon our selues..make our selues for ouer-weeningnesse, the ordinary by-word of other mens tongues. **1634** C. DOWNING *State Eccles. Kingd.* 27 The Florentine is so overweaningly wise. **1877** MORLEY *Crit. Misc.* Ser. II. 390 It is over-weeningness and self-confident will that are the chief notes of Macaulay's style. **1882** *Society* 30 Dec. 18/2 You are sometimes described as over-weeningly self-sufficient.

over'weep, *v. poet.* [OVER- 20, 1 (*c*).]

1. *trans.* To weep over again.

1598 ROWLANDS *Betraying Christ* 29 Weepe Christs deniall, worst of all thy crimes, And ouerweepe each teare tenne thousand times.

2. To weep over (something), shed tears over.

1844 MRS. BROWNING *Catarina to Camoens* xvi, Feeling, while you overweep it, Not alone in your despair. **1853** —— *Sleep* iii, A little dust to overweep.

overweigh (əʊvə'weɪ), *v.* Forms: see OVER and WEIGH. [OVER- 22, 21, 26; cf. OHG. *ubarwegan*, MHG. *überwegen*, Du. *overwegen.*]

1. *trans.* To exceed in weight (physical or moral); to be heavier or weightier than; to preponderate over, overbalance, outweigh.

a **1225** *Ancr. R.* 386 Þeo þet mest luuieð, þeo schullen beon mest iblisced, nout þeo þet ledeð herdest lif, uor luue ouerweið hit. **1549** COVERDALE, etc. *Erasm. Par. Rom.* 12 In all pointes Christes goodnes ouerwaigheth the offence of Adam. **1603** SHAKS. *Meas. for M.* II. iv. 170 Say what you can; my false ore-weighs your true. *c* **1620** A. HUME *Brit. Tongue* (1865) 9 This auctoritie wald over-weegh our reason. **1672** SHADWELL *Miser* I, One kind look from you will over-weigh a thousand such small services. **1818** MRS. SHELLEY *Frankenst.* viii. (1865) 106 If their testimony shall not over-weigh my supposed guilt, I must be condemned.

2. To overcome with or as with weight; to weigh down, overburden, oppress.

1577 VAUTROUILLIER *Luther on Ep. Gal.* 78 Blessed is he.. which can say, when sinne ouerwayeth him, and the lawe accuseth him: what is this to me? **1641** R. BAKER *Chron.* (1660) 56 One Raynerus,..crossing the Seas with his Wife ..so with his iniquity overweighed the ship, that in the midst of the stream, it was not able to stir. **1760–72** H. BROOKE *Fool of Qual.* (1809) IV. 105 The grief of her heart over-weighed her spirits. **1849** M. ARNOLD *Strayed Reveller*, Who is he That he sits, overweighed By fumes of wine and sleep, So late, in thy portico?

3. *intr.* To weigh more than something else, to preponderate; to be over weight, weigh too much.

1862 F. HALL *Hindu Philos. Syst.* 47 Intellect, when darkness overweighs in it, is torpid. **1887** *Chicago Advance* 29 Sept. 613 If a letter overweigh, we are fined one shilling and eleven pence.

Hence **over'weighing** *ppl. a.*; **over'weighingly** *adv.*

1586 MARLOWE *1st Pt. Tamburl.* V. i, The means the overweighing Heavens Have kept to qualify these hot extremes. **1595** *Polimanteia* (1881) 23 If..I ouerweyingly valew you at too high a rate. **1896** W. BLACK *Briseis* xvii, This overweighing war of the elements that distracted his attention.

overweight ('əʊvə,weɪt), *sb.*¹ [OVER- 19, 29 c: cf. MLG. *overwicht*, Du. *overwicht*, Da. *overvægt.*]

1. Something over or beyond the exact or proper weight; extra weight; excess of weight.

1552 HULOET, Ouerweyght, *superpondium.* **1639** HORN & ROB. *Gate Lang. Unl.* lxxv. §768 If any thing be put to, above the over-weight, allowance or remedy; it is a vantage, a surplusage cast in over and besides. *a* **1661** FULLER *Worthies* I. (1662) 64 They are cast in, as *Superpondium*, or Overweight, our work being ended before. **1886** J. BARROWMAN *Gloss. Scotch Mining Terms* 48 *Overweight*, excess weight of disposals over outputs. **1888** W. E. NICHOLSON *Gloss. Terms Coal Trade Northumb. & Durham* 62 *Overweight*, the difference between the standard weight and the average weight for a fortnight when over the standard.

2. Greater weight (than that of something else); preponderance; preponderating weight, power, influence, or importance.

1626 BACON *Sylva* §773 Sinking into water is but an over-weight of the body put into the water in respect of the water. *Ibid.* §798 If you take so much the more silver as will countervail the over-weight of the lead. **1683** DRYDEN *Life Plutarch* 107 Cicero and the Elder Cato, were far from having the overweight against Demosthenes and Aristides. **1805** W. TAYLOR in *Ann. Rev.* III. 68 [He] had greatly the overweight of popularity.

3. a. Too great weight; an excessive weight or burden; also *fig.*

a **1577** GASCOIGNE *Workes, Hearbes* (1587) 183 A peece which shot so wel, so gently and so streight, It neither bruised with recule, nor wroong with ouerweight. **1770** *Chron.* in *Ann. Reg.* 113/2 A scaffold..broke down with the over-weight of the spectators. **1891** H. HALIBURTON *Ochil Idylls* 136 With overweight of care on my mind.

b. Applied to a person: obesity, excess of weight.

1917 *Med. Times* (N.Y.) Aug. 217/2 (*heading*) Reduction cures for overweight. **1918** J. BROADHURST *Home & Community Hygiene* xviii. 298 (*heading*) The relation of overweight to death rates. **1923** J. W. BARTON *That Body of Yours* 102 There are two kinds of overweight. First..the kind you inherit. You have always been a little overweight. Then there is the kind that is acquired at the age of 27 to 37. **1925** MRS. BELLOC LOWNDES *Diary* 10 Jan. (1971) 102 Lord Northcliffe was..distressed at what he regarded as my overweight. He told me that he and his wife weighed each other constantly. **1951** I. B. ALLEN *Youth after Forty* vi. 53 Raw fruits do not induce overweight. **1973** M. SENECHAL *Guarding your Family's Health* iv. 56/1 One of the commonest of all health problems revealed by a checkup is overweight. **1975** *Times* 20 Dec. 12/5 She needs to lose weight..an overweight caused by a careless diet.

†**4.** An alleged name of avoirdupois weight. *Obs.*

1656 H. PHILLIPS *Purch. Patt.* (1676) 210 There are two sorts of weights used by us in England, the one is called Troy-weight, the other is called Avoir-du-poiz, or overweight.

5. *Pros.* An instance of overweighting (see quot.).

1940 J. R. R. TOLKIEN in Clark Hall & Wrenn *Beowulf & Finnesburg Fragment* p. xxxi, An example with double overweight would be *wéllmàde wárgeàr.*

overweight (,əʊvə'weɪt), *a.* (*sb.*²) [OVER *prep.* + WEIGHT *sb.*; see OVER- 32.]

Above, or in excess of, the proper or ordinary weight; too heavy. *spec.* of a person: too heavy for one's height and build; obese. Also *fig.* **a.** As predicate, or following the sb.

1638 BAKER tr. *Balzac's Lett.* (vol. II.) A b, The Authors Gold is so much over weight. **1670** COTTON *Espernon* II. VIII. 415 His Majesty would yet make her overweight, by giving her himself two hundred thousand Crowns in Dowry. **1852** MRS. CARLYLE *Lett.* II. 203, I wonder if my letter will be over-weight. **1856** KANE *Arct. Expl.* I. ix. 97 We found.. that a very few pounds overweight broke us down. **1899** G. R. SHEPHERD in *Med. Examiner* 212/1 Are people who are overweight likely to live longer than those who are.. underweight? **1925** C. E. TURNER *Personal & Community Health* ii. 52 The tendency to become overweight is no doubt constitutional. **1941** F. SILVER *Foods & Nutrition* iv. 117 A child.. is considered overweight if he is 20 per cent above the average for his age and height. **1951** I. B. ALLEN *Youth after Forty* vi. 50 'She is an obese person' sounds right down [*sic*] unattractive—but if she is pounds overweight, that's just what she is.

b. *attrib.* as *adj.* ('əʊvəweɪt).

1639 FULLER *Holy War* II. xlii. (1647) 101 He displaced Guy, because he found him of no over-weight worth. **1888** *Pall Mall G.* 22 June 6/1, I was charged for a few pounds of overweight luggage. **1958** *Which?* Autumn 20/1 Overweight people can reduce their weight by reducing their food intake. **1976** 'L. BLACK' *Healthy Way to Die* ii. 12 How often must he have heard every possible comic remark about overweight women!

c. *absol.* or as *sb.* (stress variable).

1899 G. R. SHEPHERD in *Med. Examiner* July 211/2 From our mortality records the overweights are clearly less desirable than the underweights. **1910** A. BRYCE *Laws of Life & Health* vii. 247 No 'over-weight' dies of old age or senility. **1935** H. ROBERTS *Everyman in Health & Sickness* II. iv. 152 Insurance companies find that 'overweights' are bad lives. **1974** *Times* 4 Jan. 5/3 The overweight have become America's largest, least protected minority group.

ˌover'weight (-'weɪt), *v.* [OVER- 27.]

† **1.** *trans.* To give or attach too much weight to, exaggerate the importance of. *Obs.*

1603 FLORIO *Montaigne* II. viii. 220 We also overweight such vaine future conjectures, which infant-spirits give us.

2. To weight too heavily; to impose an excessive weight or burden upon; to overburden, overload. *lit.* and *fig.* (Chiefly in *pa. pple.*)

1819 SYD. SMITH *Wks.* (1850) 253 *note*, There should be two or three colonial secretaries instead of one; the office is dreadfully overweighted. **1879** F. G. LEE *Ch. under Q. Eliz.* I. p. liv, The author.. has thought it wise to avoid over-weighting.. an 'Historical Sketch' with too many of such quotations. **1897** *Daily News* 22 Feb. 8/6 Their boat was overweighted with household produce... It is supposed the craft foundered.

3. *Pros.* To stress as in overweighting.

1940 J. R. R. TOLKIEN in Clark Hall & Wrenn *Beowulf & Finnesburg Fragment* p. xxxi, The second dip of B, C and the dip of D, E may not be overweighted.

Hence **ˌover'weighted** *ppl. a.*; **-'weightedness.**

c **1860** FABER *Old Labourer* iv, To take to God their overweighted hearts. **1878** *N. Amer. Rev.* CXXVII. 189 An overcharged and overweighted people. **1895** *Dublin Rev.* Apr. 308 The historic overweightedness, to which the Jews were succumbing. **1927** BOWLEY & STAMP *Nat. Income 1924* 23 When we pass from the accidental grouping in the returns, overweighted by banks, to the whole numbers according to the census, the averages are brought up again to the medians. **1948** *Mod. Philology* XLVI. 86 Besides these.. light or weak verses there are, of course, many which are extra-heavy, 'overweighted', and many which seem overlong. **1949** *Penguin Music Mag.* Feb. 85 Such a combination provides a monotonous tone colour and the bass seems turgid and overweighted.

over'weightage. [f. prec. vb. or sb. + -AGE.] Amount of overweight, or a charge for this.

1841 *Blackw. Mag.* L. 333 How much have they not to pay for carriage, porterage, overweightage, custom-house officerage?

ˌover'weighting, *vbl. sb.* [-ING[1].] The act or fact of giving or having too much weight; overloading, overload (see also quot. 1940).

1905 *Westm. Gaz.* 1 Sept. 2/3 The frightful overweighting of the postman because of the flood of pictorial postcards. **1914** R. M. JONES *Spiritual Reformers 16th & 17th Cent.* xv. 289 Their gravest difficulty being an overweighting of learning which they sometimes failed to fuse with their spiritual vision. **1940** J. R. R. TOLKIEN in Clark Hall & Wrenn *Beowulf & Finnesburg Fragment* p. xxxi, Overweighting and extension.. are a means of including certain common but slightly excessive patterns in the metre; also of adding weight to the line where required, and of packing much significant word-material into a small space. .. It consists in replacing the dip by a long (subordinate) stress.

'over-'weighty, *a.* [OVER- 28: cf. Du. *overwichtig.*] Too weighty or heavy; of excessive weight.

1627 HAKEWILL *Apol.* III. i. §7. 156 The pressing of Nature with over-weighty burdens.

'over-'well, *adv.* [f. OVER- 30 + WELL *adv.*] Too well.

c **1375** *Sc. Leg. Saints* xl. (*Ninian*) 1335 þat is oure-weile kyd one me. **1422** tr. *Secreta Secret., Priv. Priv.* 199 Whan he was in his goodnes, ouerwel atte ayse. **1587** GOLDING *De Mornay* xvi. 268 To thinke ouerwell of our selues. **1709** STRYPE *Ann. Ref.* I. lii. 522 A proclamation.. which was not overwell regarded in most parts of the realm. *a* **1803** S. ADAMS in Bancroft *Hist. U.S.* (1876) V. xx. 566 Not.. over-well pleased with what is called the Fabian war in America.

overwell, *v.*: see OVER- 5 b.

over'welt, *v. Sc.* and *north. dial.* [f. OVER- 6 + WELT *v.*, to turn: cf. OVERWALT.] **a.** *trans.* To overturn, upset; in *pass.* said *spec.* of a sheep when fallen on its back so as to be unable to rise: cf. AWALT, FAR-WELTED. **b.** *intr.* To tumble over. Hence **'overwelt** *sb. dial.* (see quot. 1788).

1513 DOUGLAS *Æneis* VIII. xii. 37 Ourweltit wyth the bensell of the ayris, Fast fra the forstammis the flude swouchis and raris. *Ibid.* x. vii. 105 Ourweltis Retheus in ded thrawis atanis, And with hys helys smayt the Rutilian planis. **1788** W. MARSHALL *Yorksh.* Gloss. (E.D.S.) s.v., A sheep which gets laid upon its back in a hollow is said to be in an owerwelt. **1828** *Craven Gloss.* (ed. 2.), *Ower-welted,* overturned. **1876** *Gloss. Mid-Yorks.* s.v., A cart is *welted*, or upturned, in order to discharge its load; but it is *overwelted* when entirely overturned for repairs, or by an act of mischief.

† **over'welter,** *v. Obs. rare.* In 6 *Sc.* **-walter.** [OVER- 9.] *trans.* To roll over and over.

1513 DOUGLAS *Æneis* VII. Prol. 18 The rageand storm ourwalterand wally seis.

† **over'wend,** *v. Obs.* Pa. t. and pple. **-went.** [OVER- 8, 9, 13.]

1. *intr.* To go over, pass over. *rare.*

c **1250** *Gen. & Ex.* 2285 Him ouer wente his herte on-on; Kinde luue gan him ouer gon.

2. *trans.* **a.** To pass over, go over, traverse, cross. **b.** To pass beyond, exceed. **c.** *pa. pple.* **overwent,** overgone, covered; overwhelmed.

c **1330** R. BRUNNE *Chron. Wace* (Rolls) 7800 Bot þei dide nought his comandement; þe dedes conseyl ys sone ouer went. *c* **1350** *Will. Palerne* 2140, & loke þat hirde-men wel kepe þe komune passage & eche brugge þer a-boute þat burnes overwende. **1390** GOWER *Conf.* I. 317 Whan I my wittes overwende, Min hertes contek hath non ende. **14..** *Tundale's Vis.* 1908 With all oder ryches hit was over went. **1579** SPENSER *Sheph. Cal.* Mar. 2 Why sytten we soe, As weren ouerwent [*gloss.* ouergone] with woe, Upon so fayre a morow? *a* **1649** DRUMM. OF HAWTH. *Poems* Wks. (1711) 30/2 As a pilgrim,.. When he some craggy hills hath over-went.

overwene, obs. form of OVERWEEN.

'over-'wet, *a.* [OVER- 28.] Too wet. So **'over-'wet** *sb.*, **'over-'wetness,** too great wetness, excess of moisture. Also **ˌover-'wet** *v. trans.*, to wet too much.

1626 BACON *Sylva* §669 Another ill accident is, over-wet at sowing time. **1703** T. N. *City & C. Purchaser* 205 When you slack the Lime, you must.. not over-wet it. **1725** BRADLEY *Fam. Dict.* s.v. *Sycomore*, They are also propagated by Roots and Layers in moist Ground, not over-wet or stiff. **1812** SIR J. SINCLAIR *Syst. Husb. Scot.* I. 380 Over-closeness of texture, producing over-wetness and infertility.

overwhart: see OVERTHWART.

overwheal: see OVER- 8.

over-'wheel, *v.* [OVER- 6, 26.]

† **1.** *trans.* To overturn, turn upside down. *Obs.*

1599 T. M[OUFET] *Silkwormes* 59 Yea.. whisprings soft of men or falling floud, Doth so their harts and senses ouer-wheele That often headlong from the boord they reel.

2. *Mil.* (*intr.* and *trans.*) To wheel too far, or beyond the proper point.

1832 *Regul. Instr. Cavalry* III. 98 They are to allow their Troops rather to over-wheel on approaching the Line. *Ibid.* 99 They will thus be somewhat over-wheeled.

So **'over-wheel** *sb.* (*Mil.*).

1796 *Instr. & Reg. Cavalry* (1813) 14 The leader must take care to time his words, Halt! Dress! the instant before the wheel is completed, otherwise an overwheel or reining back will be the consequence.

over'whelm, *sb. rare.* [f. next.] The act of overwhelming, or fact of being overwhelmed.

1742 YOUNG *Nt. Th.* IX. 685 In such an overwhelm Of wonderful, on man's astonish'd sight, Rushes Omnipotence. **1863** MRS. WHITNEY *Faith Gartney* xxxiv. (1869) 318 The first overwhelm of astonishment.

overwhelm (əʊvə'hwɛlm), *v.* Also 5 **-qwelm,** 6 **-quelm,** 6–7 *Sc.* **-quhelm.** [f. OVER- 6, 8 + WHELM *v.* to roll.]

1. *trans.* To overturn, overthrow, upset; to turn upside down. *Obs.* exc. *dial.*

c **1330** R. BRUNNE *Chron.* (1810) 190 He smote him in þe helm, bakward he bare his stroupe. þe body he did ouer-whelm, his hede touched þe croupe. **1513** DOUGLAS *Æneis* VII. Prol. 18 Quhen brym blastis of the northyne art Our-quhelmit had Neptunus in his cart. *a* **1547** SURREY *Æneid* IV. 585 Like to the aged.. oke The which.. the Northerne windes.. Betwixt them strive to overwhelme with blastes. **1600** J. PORY tr. *Leo's Africa* IX. 344 Barkes and botes.. sayling downe the riuer of Niger are greatly endangered by this sea-horse, for oftentimes he ouerwhelmeth and sinketh them. **1796** MORSE *Amer. Geog.* I. 85 The earthquake.. overwhelmed a chain of mountains of free stone more than 300 miles long.

† **b.** To turn (a wheel) round, cause to revolve.

? *a* **1400** *Morte Arth.* 3262 A-bowte cho whirllide a whele with hir whitte hondez, Over-whelme alle qwayntely þe whele as cho scholde.

† **c.** To throw (something) over in a heap *upon* something else; to turn or wind (something) about something else. *Obs.*

1634 HEYWOOD *Maidenhead well lost* II. Wks. 1874 IV. 120 Thou hast ouerwhelm'd vpon my aged head Mountaines of griefe. **1684** PAPIN in Birch *Hist. Roy. Soc.* (1757) IV. 288 Then I overwhelm a broader pipe about the first.

† **d.** *intr.* To turn over, revolve; to roll or tumble over. *Obs.*

1387–8 [see OVERWHELMING *vbl. sb.*]. *c* **1400** *Rom. Rose* 3775 The see may never be so stil, That with a litel winde it nil Overwhelme and turne also. *a* **1400–50** *Alexander* 560 All flames þe flode as it fire were,.. And þane ouer-qwelmys in a qwirre and qwatis euer e-like.

2. *trans.* To cover (anything) as with something turned over and cast upon it; to bury or drown beneath a superincumbent mass; to submerge completely (usually implying ruin or destruction).

c **1450** *St. Cuthbert* (Surtees) 4964 þe erthe sall' þaim ouer whelme. **1573–80** BARET *Alv.* O 201 To Ouerwhelme: to couer cleane ouer and ouer with earth, or with other things, to hide in the ground. **1613** PURCHAS *Pilgrimage* (1614) 116 Adrian.. dedicated another Temple to Iupiter, that former being ouer-whelmed with earth. **1756** LUCAS *Ess. Waters* I. 32 Large tracts.. are every winter over-whelmed with an inundation. **1878** HUXLEY *Physiogr.* 192 Pompeii was overwhelmed by a vast accumulation of dust and ashes.

† **b.** To overhang so as to cover more or less. *Obs.*

1592 SHAKS. *Ven. & Ad.* 183 His louring brows o'erwhelming his fair sight, Like misty vapours when they blot the sky. **1599** —— *Hen. V,* III. i. 11 Then lend the Eye a terrible aspect:.. let the Brow o'rewhelme it, As fearefully, as doth a galled Rocke O're-hang and iutty his confounded Base.

3. *fig.* **a.** To overcome or overpower as regards one's action or circumstances; to bring to ruin or destruction; to crush.

1529 MORE *Dyaloge* I. Wks. 157/2 Certayne conclusions of the lawe of nature, whiche (their reason ouer whelmed with sensualyte) hadde than forgotten. **1573–80** BARET *Alv.* O 201 To be ouerwhelmed with businesse, or to haue more to do than he can turne himselfe to. **1692** tr. *Sallust* 29 We Starve at home, abroad our debts ore-whelm us. **1751** JOHNSON *Rambler* No. 153 ¶10 Neither my modesty nor prudence were overwhelmed by affluence. **1843** PRESCOTT *Mexico* (1850) I. II. iii. 217 Such an event must overwhelm him in irretrievable ruin.

b. To overcome completely in mind or feeling; to overpower utterly with some emotion.

1535 COVERDALE *Ps.* liv. 4 An horrible drede hath ouerwhelmed me. **1721** DE FOE *Moll Flanders* (1840) 309, I was overwhelmed with the sense of my condition. **1872** W. BLACK *Adv. Phaeton* xxxi. 410 Here a shout of laughter overwhelmed the young man.

c. To treat with an excess of something (figured as 'heaped' upon one); to 'deluge' *with.*

1806 SURR *Winter in Lond.* (ed. 3) I. 255 He found him.. surrounded by the whole party.. who were overwhelming him with praises. **1819** LADY MORGAN *Autobiog.* (1859) 309 The Baron Bonstetten overwhelms us with hospitality and kindness. **1853** KINGSLEY *Hypatia* xvi, He began overwhelming the old man with enquiries about himself, Pambo, and each and all of the inhabitants.

overwhelmed (-'hwɛlmd, *poet.* -'hwɛlmɪd), *ppl. a.* [f. prec. + -ED[1].] Overturned (*obs.*), submerged, overpowered, etc.: see the verb. Hence **over'whelmedness.**

c **1440** *Promp. Parv.* 374/1 Ovyr qwelmyd, or ouer hyllyde, *obvolutus.* **1616** J. LANE *Cont. Sqr.'s T.* (1888) 169 *note*, Whose teeres.. weare his seaes.. in which o'rewhelmd experience [etc.]. **1860** PUSEY *Min. Proph.* 253 No image so well expresses the overwhelmedness under affliction or temptation.

over'whelmer. [f. as prec. + -ER[1].] One who or that which overwhelms.

1513 DOUGLAS *Æneis* XII. ix. 108 Fers Achilles.. That was ourquhelmar of king Pryamus ring [= kingdom]. **1807** ANNA SEWARD *Lett.* (1811) VI. 357 It is not in the power of that universal overwhelmer [time] to push him from my memory.

over'whelming, *vbl. sb.* [f. as prec. + -ING[1].] The action of the verb OVERWHELM; †turning over, revolution (*obs.*); submersion, over-powering, etc.

1387–8 T. USK *Test. Love* III. iv. (Skeat) I. 145 The course of the planettes, and overwhelminges of the sonne in dayes and nightes. **1645** MILTON *Tetrach.* (1851) 195 The overwhelming of his afflicted servants. **1883** *Athenæum* 4 Aug. 134/3 A story of a sharp fight for existence and an ultimate overwhelming.

over'whelming, *ppl. a.* [f. as prec. + -ING[2].]

1. That overwhelms, overthrows, overturns, or submerges utterly; so powerful as to overcome utterly by strength of numbers, influence, etc.

1667 [implied in OVERWHELMINGLY below]. **1742** YOUNG *Nt. Th.* III. 219 O'erwhelming Turrets threaten ere they fall. **1818** LADY MORGAN *Autobiog.* (1859) 217 The concourse of people of all nations that assemble here, on a Wednesday evening, is overwhelming. **1845** DARWIN *Voy. Nat.* xiv. (1879) 303 The island itself.. showed the overwhelming power of the earthquake. **1855** MACAULAY *Hist. Eng.* xv. III. 536 Two Tories were returned by an overwhelming majority. **1887** *Spectator* 8 Oct. 1337 The temptation to close the Canal against our troopships may be overwhelming.

† **2.** Overhanging. *Obs.*

1592 SHAKS. *Rom. & Jul.* v. i. 39 An Appothecarie.. In tattred weeds, with ouerwhelming browes.

† **3.** ? Overpowered with emotion. *Obs.*

(? For *overwhelmed* or *overflowing.*)

1571 DK. NORFOLK in *14th Rep. Hist. MSS. Comm.* App. IV. 574 Prayinge..with an ouerwhelminge harte and watered cheekes.

Hence **over'whelmingly** *adv.*, in an overwhelming or overpowering manner; **over'whelmingness.**

1667 *Decay Chr. Piety* (1671) 142 Light and trivial;.. indeed in respect of the acquest, but overwhelmingly ponderous in regard of the.. pernicious consequents. *a* **1834** COLERIDGE *Lit. Rem.* II. 174 You see in him..the overwhelmingness of circumstances, for a time surmounting his sense of duty. **1881** *Blackw. Mag.* May 570/2 Its force, its overwhelmingness, and its harshness, found a more congenial place in the colder regions. **1885** *Manch. Exam.* 13 Jan. 5/3 The probabilities in their favour are overwhelmingly great.

over'whelmment. [f. OVERWHELM *v.* + -MENT.]

= OVERWHELMEDNESS; OVERWHELMINGNESS.

1866 W. M. THOMAS tr. *Hugo's Toilers of Sea* II. VII. i. 90 There is a degree of overwhelmment which abstracts the mind entirely from its fellowship with man. **1960** *Angling Times* 9 Sept. 6/2 Our river may cause love at first sight, a sudden instantaneous overwhelmment with its manifest beauty.

†**over'whelve,** *v. Obs.* [f. OVER- 6 + WHELVE *v.* to roll.]

1. *trans.* To overturn; to cause to roll or tumble, as waves. (Cf. OVERWHELM *v.* 1.)

c **1374** CHAUCER *Boeth.* II. metr. iii. 39 (Add. MS.) þe horrible wynde aquilon moeueþ boylyng tempestes and ouer whelweþ [*v.rr.* wheluetħ, weluetħ, -weluetħ] þe see. *c* **1420** *Pallad. on Husb.* I. 781 In the somer do thy cure Vppon Septemtrioun to ouerwhelue Hit vpsodoun.

2. *fig.* To overthrow, bring to ruin. (Cf. OVERWHELM *v.* 3.)

c **1420** *Pallad. on Husb.* I. 161 (Colch. MS.) For harme and stryffe of that upon thi self May ryse, ye and perchaunce the over whelve [*Fitzw. MS.* ouer thee whelue]. *a* **1618** SYLVESTER *Tobacco Battered* 128 A Burthen able..to sink The hugest Carrak; yea, those hallowed Twelve, Spain's great Apostles, even to over-whelve.

†**over'whirl,** *v. Obs.* [OVER- 6.] *trans.* To whirl or hurl over.

1577–87 HOLINSHED *Chron.* II. 26/2 Their ship was dasht ..against the rocks, and all the passengers over-whirled in the sea. **1591** SYLVESTER *Du Bartas* I. iii. 1094 His wandering Vessell, reeling to and fro, On th' irefull Ocean.. With sudden Tempest is not over-whurl'd.

overwhisper: see OVER- 9.

†**over'wield,** *v. Obs.* Also 6 **-weld.** [OVER- 2.] *trans.* To gain the mastery over, overcome, subdue. So †**over'wielding** *vbl. sb.*

1592 WYRLEY *Armorie, Ld. Chandos* 106 No fretting time shall yet decay my name, Thou strengthles art bright glory to oreweild. **1597** BEARD *Theatre God's Judgem.* (1612) 266 The pacifying of Spaine, and the ouerwelding of the commotions that were therein.

†**'over-,willed,** *a. Obs.* [OVER- 28 d.] Having an excessively strong will; imperious.

1650 B. *Discolliminium* 17 Over-will'd Men, who..will spurgall all possibilities to the Bones.

'over-'willing, *a.* [OVER- 28.] Exceedingly willing, too willing. So **'over-'willingly** *adv.*

a **1600** HOOKER *Eccl. Pol.* VII. xvi. §6 Their malicious accusations he over-willingly hearkened unto. **1701** CIBBER *Love makes Man* V. ii, *Lou.* Nay, if you are so over-willing. *Car.* Speak, and I obey you. **1861** L. L. NOBLE *Icebergs* 205 We whiled away, not overwillingly, the best part of two hours.

over'win, *v. Obs.* exc. *dial.* [OE. *oferwinnan*, f. *ofer-* OVER- 2 + WIN: cf. OHG. *ubarwinnan*, MDu. and Du. *overwinnen* to conquer.]

1. *trans.* To overcome, conquer, vanquish.

c **893** K. ÆLFRED *Oros.* I. ii. §1 He Ninus Soroastrem Bactriana cyning..oferwann & ofsloh. *c* **1000** ÆLFRIC *Hom.* II. 544 Se ðe his mod gewylt is betera ðonne se ðe burh oferwinð. *a* **1300** *E.E. Psalter* cviii. [cix.] 3 Vm-gafe þai me witerli, And ouerwonnen me selwilli. *c* **1440** *York Myst.* xxxii. 104 What! wenys þat woode warlowe ouerewyn vs þus lightly? **1535** COVERDALE *2 Esdras* xi. 40 And the fourth came, and ouerwanne all the beastes that were past. *a* **1568** —— *Ghostly Ps. & Spir. Songs* Wks. (Parker Soc.) II. 563 There was no man that coulde overwynne The power of death, nor his myght. **1876** *Whitby Gloss.* s.v., 'Will he owerwin, think you?' gain his point in the matter.

†**2.** To gain (one) over; to persuade. [OVER- 11.]

1654 WHITLOCK *Zootomia* 324 Seconding it with an overwinning them to Pacification.

Hence †**over'winner,** conqueror, overcomer.

1535 COVERDALE *1 Sam.* xv. 29 The ouerwynner in Israel also shal not lye.

over-wind, (,əʊvə'waɪnd), *v.* [OVER- 26.] *trans.* To wind too tight, as in tuning a musical instrument; to wind (a watch, or other mechanism) beyond the stop or point at which it is fully wound up; to wind too far; in *Mining*, to wind (the rope or chain bearing the cage) above its proper place so that the cage is drawn over the drum.

1682 DRYDEN *Dk. of Guise* III. i, Love to his tune my jarring heart would bring, But reason over-winds and cracks the string. **1717** *Entertainer* No. 19. 128 Like a Watch over-wound he strains his Voice. **1816** L. HUNT *Rimini* III. 529 His wearied pulse felt over-wound. **1883** GRESLEY *Gloss. Coal Mining, Overwind*, to draw a cage or bowk up into the headstocks.

Hence **,over-'wound** (-'waʊnd), *erron.* **,over-'winded** *ppl. a.*; **,over'winding** *vbl. sb.*, also attrib. ***overwinding check*** (see quot. 1884). Also **'over,winder,** (*a*) *attrib.* = *overwinding* above; (*b*) a device which guards against overwinding.

1858 MORRIS *Geffray Teste-Noire* Poems 145 So piercing sharp That joy is, that it marcheth nigh to sorrow, For ever, like an overwinded harp. **1884** KNIGHT *Dict. Mech.* Suppl., *Over-winding Check*, a device to cast loose a cage from the hoist when a certain height is attained, to avoid accident by carrying the cage over the drum. *Ibid.*, In the overwinder check at the Justice mine on the Comstock..the cage moves a lever and half the steam is shut off at the engine. **1896** *Westm. Gaz.* 20 Feb. 5/1 Eight miners have been killed through the overwinding of a cage at the West Leigh Colliery Lancashire. **1912** MCCULLOCH & FUTERS *Winding Engines* xv. 328 On overwinders working in pits in which double or treble decking takes place, a 'fourth attachment' is added. **1935** G. POOLE *Haulage & Winding* xiii. 309 If..the cage is exceeding the predetermined speed at a particular point, the speed hook engages with the winged nut moving on the screw, and the overwinder comes into action. **1958** I. C. F. STATHAM *Coal Mining Pract.* II. iv. 343 The Whitmore overwinder is shown in Fig. 59, from which it may be seen that there is a separate swinging overspeed arm and travelling nut for each cage or skip.

'overwind (-waɪnd), *sb. Mining.* [OVER- 29.] An instance of overwinding.

1892 *Trans. Fed. Inst. Mining Engin.* I. 58 With 'The Visor' applied to prevent a fast overwind, the arrangement in headgear to prevent the engines being started the wrong way, and good detaching hooks, disastrous overwinding seems an impossibility. **1929** H. COTTON *Electr. applied to Mining* x. 531 In the case of an overwind the pressure cylinder of the brake engine is opened to exhaust. **1958** I. C. F. STATHAM *Coal Mining Pract.* II. iv. 347 To protect against the aggravation of an overwind by starting the engine in the wrong direction, the overwind switches are connected through directional contacts in the master controller for the motor. **1973** *Daily Tel.* 31 July 1 An 'overwind' could have caused the descending cage, which works on the same winding system, to run out of control.

over'wing, *v.* [OVER- 22, 12.]

†**1.** *trans.* To extend the wing of an army beyond that of (the adversary), to outflank. *Obs.*

1623 BINGHAM *Xenophon* 19 He wound and turned his battell to the left hand, to the intent to ouerwing and encompasse in his aduersaries. **1654–66** EARL ORRERY *Parthen.* (1676) 691 The Enemy did much over-wing us. **1670** MILTON *Hist. Eng.* II. Wks. (1851) 60 Suetonius,..had chos'n a place narrow, and not to be overwing'd, on his rear a Wood.

2. To pass on the wing, fly over. (*poet.*)

1818 KEATS *Endymion* II. 816 My happy love will overwing all bounds!

over-'winter, *v.* [OVER- 17, 34. In OE.; with which however the mod. use has no historical connexion, but is app. after Norw. and Da. *overvintra*, Sw. *öfvervintra*; so Du. *overwinteren* (Kilian), Ger. *überwintern* to winter, L. *hiemāre*.]

†**1.** *intr.* To get over or through the winter. (*OE.*)

a **1000** ÆLFRIC *Colloquy* in Wright *Voc.* 9 Nan eower nele oferwintran [*hiemare*] buton minon cræfte.

2. In mod. use: To pass the winter, to winter (in high latitudes).

1895 tr. *Let. from Nansen* (17 July 1893) in *Daily News* 10 July 6/4 In that case we shall have to over-winter somewhere on the North Asian coast. **1900** *Westm. Gaz.* 10 Sept. 6/3 Southern Cross Fjord is..another place where an ice-vessel might over-winter with a scientific party.

3. To live through the winter: said esp. of insects and fungi.

1933 *Jrnl. R. Hort. Soc.* LVIII. 227 The larvae [of apple sawfly] overwinter in cocoons in the soil. **1946** *Nature* 28 Sept. 454/2 The most probable causes of the disease [*sc.* tomato stem and fruit rot] are spores in propagating soil and spores which have overwintered in cracks of old cases. **1953** D. A. BANNERMAN *Birds Brit. Isles* I. 138 Either the Greenland or Hornemann's redpoll 'over-winters' in north-east Greenland. **1959** *New Biol.* XIX. 60 Temperate species [of midge] must normally overwinter as larvae. **1960** *Times* 9 July 9/2 Black spot overwinters on pieces of rose foliage. **1967** *Times* 23 Nov. 4/8 Two species of ticks and four of fleas ..overwinter on the island [*sc.* Macquarie Island]. **1972** SWAN & PAPP *Common Insects N. Amer.* xxii. 589 *Culex* mosquitoes overwinter as fertilized females. **1977** J. L. HARPER *Population Biol. Plants* xiii. 431 The butterfly lays its eggs in batches of 20–400 on the leaves of *Aster*, the larvae feed gregariously until the third instar when they disperse, over-winter and then start feeding again as solitary feeders.

4. *trans.* To keep (animals or plants) alive through the winter.

1945 *Scythe* Mar. 10 Primitive farming with low yields and no fodder crops on which to over-winter more than a minimum of domestic cattle. **1961** *Listener* 7 Dec. 992/3 The Chabaud and Nice types [of carnation] raised from August sowings would be safer if over-wintered in frames or under cloches. **1970** *Jrnl. R. Hort. Soc.* XCV. 358 The glaucous-leaved *Eucalyptus globulus*, sown in the previous July or August and overwintered under glass. **1976** *Evening Chron.* (Newcastle) 26 Nov., In this case the plants can be potted up into fairly large pots and over-wintered in a cold frame until they can be planted out when the better weather comes along.

Hence **over'wintered** *ppl. a.*, **over'wintering** *vbl. sb.* and *ppl. a.*

1901 *U.S. Dept. Agric. Yearbk. 1900* 90 The overwintering crop. **1916** J. P. LOTSY *Evolution by Means of Hybridization* vii. 90 This experiment is yet in progress with the overwintered F_1 plants. **1923** *Glasgow Herald* 17 July 7 Preparations [are to be] made for a probable overwintering there next year. **1925** *Jrnl. Agric. Res.* XXXI. 1 (*title*) Further studies on the overwintering and dissemination of cucurbit mosaic. **1936** *Amer. Bee Jrnl.* LXXVI. 452 (*title*) Influence of pollen reserves on the surviving population of over-wintered colonies. **1958** *New Biol.* XXVI. 33 A lateral bud grows out from the corm [of the bulbous buttercup] in the autumn and gives rise to an over-wintering rosette of foliage leaves. **1963** *Field Archaeol.* (Ordnance Survey) (ed. 4) 120 Overwintering sites may not have had very strong defences since they made use of natural obstacles and did not look far beyond the needs of a season. **1967** *Oceanogr. & Marine Biol.* V. 417 The spawning and over-wintering concentrations of Bank herring. **1971** *Farmer & Stockbreeder* 23 Feb. 45 (Advt.), Dose your overwintered cattle with 'Helmatac' now, and remove the winter worm burden. **1973** *Times* 18 June 16/2 The overwintered wild oat can produce at least twice as much seed to cause future trouble as those that start their lives in the spring. **1974** A. DILLARD *Pilgrim at Tinker Creek* viii. 135 Look at an overwintering ball of buzzing bees.

over-winter, *a.*: see OVER- 32.

over-wipe, *v.*: see OVER- 8.

'over-'wise (-waɪz), *a.* [OVER- 28: cf. MHG. *überwīse.*] Too wise, exceedingly or affectedly wise. ***not over-wise***, rather deficient in wisdom.

[**1535** COVERDALE *Eccl.* vii. 16 Be thou nether to rightuous ner ouer wyse.] **1588** A. KING tr. *Canisius' Catech.* 54 Gif we be nocht ouerwyse in our awin conceit. *a* **1611** BEAUM. & FL. *Philaster* IV. iii, Fear it not, their overwise heads will think it but a trick. **1711** ADDISON *Spect.* No. 170 ¶11 Who are so wonderfully subtle and over-wise in their Conceptions. **1864** TENNYSON *Grandmother* 3 And Willy's wife has written: she never was over-wise, Never the wife for Willy: he wouldn't take my advice.

Hence **'over-'wisely** *adv.*, too wisely; **'over-'wiseness, 'over-'wisdom,** the condition, fact, or affectation of being overwise.

1596 RALEIGH *Farewell* viii, Tell Wisdome she entangles Herself in ouer-wiseness. **1842** MANNING *Serm.* xxiv. (1848) I. 357 They that slight the prophecies of Christ, and they that over-wisely expound them, alike fall into the same snare. **1845** J. H. NEWMAN *Ess. Developm.* 87 Both sacred and profane writers witness that overwisdom is folly. **1865** KINGSLEY *Herew.* vii, Behaving, alas for her! not over wisely or well.

†**over'wit,** *v. Obs.* [OVER- 21.] *trans.* To overreach or get the better of by craft or acuteness; to outwit.

1647 CLARENDON *Hist. Reb.* IV. §48 Some..disdaining to be overwitted by them [the Scots]..resolved to do the same things with them. **1671** BAXTER *Power of Mag. & Church P.* I. 8 The Popes Agents are commonly bred up in Learning, and so are made able to over-wit the Laity. *a* **1745** SWIFT *Answ. Paulus* 60 Yet well they merit to be pitied, By clients always overwitted.

†**,over-'witted,** *a. Obs. rare.* [OVER- 28 d.] Over-furnished with wit or sense; too acute.

a **1716** BLACKALL *Wks.* (1723) I. 333 This poor Man may (if he is not over-witted) be apt to think that surely this blustering Hector is not one of the Sons of Adam.

over-womanized: see OVER- 28.

'over-wood. [OVER- 1 d.] The layer of vegetation formed by the tallest trees in a forest. Cf. OVERSTOREY.

1889 W. SCHLICH *Man. Forestry* I. iii. 202 In fertile low lands Oak appears as overwood and underwood. **1928** R. S. TROUP *Silvicultural Syst.* iv. 39 Silviculture may require the overwood to be retained for seeding purposes or for the protection of the young crop. **1969** *Gloss. Landscape Work (B.S.I.)* v. 34 *Overwood.* 1. Large free-growing trees growing above coppice. 2. The upper layer of a two-storeyed forest.

'overword, *sb.* Chiefly *Sc.* Also **owerword.** [OVER- 20.] A word or phrase repeated again and again; *esp.* the burden or refrain of a song. (Cf. OVERCOME *sb.* 2.)

1500–20 DUNBAR *Poems* lviii. 4 Ay is the ouir-word of the geist, Giff thame the pelffe to pairt amang thame. **1585** JAMES I *Ess. Poesie* (Arb.) 69 Gif ȝe lyke to put ane ouer-word till ony of thame, as making the last lyne of the first verse to be the last lyne of euerie vther verse in that ballat. **1724** RAMSAY *Tea-t. Misc.* (1733) II. 120 Ay the o'erword of the fray Was ever, alake my auld goodman. **1786** BURNS *Lines Written at Loudon Manse* 7 And aye the o'erword o' the spring, Was Irvine's bairns are bonie a'. **1870** MORRIS *Earthly Par.* II. III. 126 Muttering as o'erword to the tune, East of the Sun, West of the Moon. **1895** CROCKETT *Men of Moss Hags* xiii. 96 This was a favourite overword of my mother's that suffering was the Christian's golden garment.

†**,over-'word,** *v. Obs. nonce-wd.* [OVER- 23.] *refl.* To express oneself too wordily.

a **1656** HALES *Gold. Rem.* (1673) 22 Describing a small fly, [he] extremely over-worded, and over-spake himself in his expression of it; as if he had spoken of the Nemean Lion.

overwork (see below), *sb.* [OE. *oferweorc*, f. *ofer-*, OVER- 1: cf. Du. *overwerk* in sense 2.]

I. ('əʊvəwɜːk). † **1.** A work placed or raised over something, a superstructure; *spec.* in OE. a sepulchral monument. *Obs.* [OVER- 1.]

[*c* **1000** ÆLFRIC *Hom.* II. 404 Wa eow hiwerum, ȝe sind ȝelice ȝemettum ofer-ȝeweorcum.] *c* **1000** *Aldhelm Gloss.* (Napier) 3501 Sarcofagi, i. tumba, [gloss] oferweorces.

c **1200** Ormin 1035, & tær oferr þatt arrke wass An oferrwerrc wel timmbredd, þatt wass Propitiatoriumm O Latin spæche nemmnedd. *Ibid.* 1046, & tær uppo þatt oferrwerrc þeȝȝ haffdenn liccness metedd Off Cherubyn.

2. Extra work, work beyond the regular or stipulated amount. [over- 19.]

1858 Simmonds *Dict. Trade, Over-time, Over-work*, extra labour done beyond the regular fixed hours of business. **1883** *St. James's Gaz.* 23 Sept. (Cassell), The injustice and mischief of the exaction of overwork.

II. (ˈəʊvəˈwɜːk). **3.** Excessive work, work beyond one's capacity or strength. [over- 29 b.]

1818 J. W. Croker in *C. Papers* (1884) 8 Dec., My complaint is an uneasiness in the head..from overwork. **1860** Mrs. Carlyle *Lett.* III. 36 A sleepless, excited condition through prolonged over-work. **1874** Ruskin *Hortus Inclusus* (1887) 12, I am a little oppressed just now with overwork.

overwork (əʊvəˈwɜːk, ˌəʊvə-), *v.* Pa. t. and pple. **-wrought, -worked.** [OE. *oferwiercan*, f. over- 8: cf. Du. *overwerken.* See also below.]

I. 1. *trans.* To work all over, to figure or decorate the surface of. (Only in *pa. pple.*) [over- 8.]

a **1000** *Sal. & Sat.* (Kemble) 150 Sy fram oðrum to ðam midle mid ðy gulliscan seolfre oferworht. **1579** Dee *Diary* (Camden) 6 My dream of being naked, and my skyn all overwrought with worke like some kind of tuft mockado, with crosses blew and red. **1658** Sir T. Browne *Hydriot.* 18 Long brass plates overwrought like the handles of neat implements. **1711** Pope *Temp. Fame* 120 Of Gothic structure was the Northern side, O'erwrought with ornaments of barb'rous pride. **1836** S. Rogers *Inscript. in Crimea* 4 This cistern of white stone, Arched, and o'erwrought with many a sacred verse.

†**2.** To work upon successfully; to influence, gain over to a certain course. *Obs.* [over- 11.]

1593 Nashe *Christ's T.* Ded. 2 The cunning courtship of faire words, can neuer ouer-worke mee to cast away honor on anie. **1634** Sanderson *Serm.* II. 292 In that, he is overwrought by craft; in this, over-born by might. **1661** *Sir H. Vane's Politics* 14 These I over-wrought, won, and made mine own.

II. 3. a. *trans.* To cause to work too hard; to impose too much work on; to work (a man, horse, etc.) beyond his capacity or strength; to weary or exhaust with work. Also *transf.* and *fig.* [over- 27, 21.]

1530 Palsgr. 650/1 Whan I overworke myselfe I am the werier two dayes after. **1574** Hellowes *Gueuara's Fam. Ep.* (1577) 143 Seeing my maister so continually to chide me,.. so to ouerworke me, and so cruelly to deale with me. **1666** Pepys *Diary* 13 Dec., I perceive my overworking my eyes by candlelight do hurt them. **1725** De Foe *Voy. round World* (1840) 103 To keep our men fully employed..and yet not to overwork them. **1870** *Daily News* 8 Dec., To overwork and starve the horses confided to them. *c* **1878** G. M. Hopkins *Loss of Eurydice* in *Poems* (1967) 72 No Atlantic squall overwrought her. **1922** *Times Lit. Suppl.* 12 Oct. 642/2 Gobineau has carefully avoided any such threadbare device as that of the missing heir so overworked by Scott. **1951** T. Sterling *House without Door* iii. 35 Wall Street—you know that phrase is overworked. **1963** P. Phillips in Sissons & French *Age of Austerity* vi. 148 There was a New Look in daffodils..in housing..in furniture... The phrase was disastrously over-worked. **1977** *Times* 7 Apr. 20/4 The episode is characteristic (the one word he overworks in this book).

b. To fill too full with work.

1876 Longf. *Terrace of Aigalades* iii, My days with toil are overwrought. **1880** McCarthy *Own Times* IV. lxii. 374 His life had been overwrought in every way.

c. *intr.* To work to excess, work too much.

1894 O. W. Holmes in *Daily News* 10 Oct. 6/4 For a man who has all his life been overworking, I can at eighty-five but be sincerely thankful for my many mercies.

4. To work too much upon, spend too much work on (a book, speech, etc.); to elaborate to excess. (Only in *pa. pple.*) [over- 27.]

1638 Rouse *Heav. Univ.* (1702) Pref., That such Christians may abound, is the end of this Work; which for ought I know hath not been over-wrought. **1683** Soame & Dryden tr. *Boileau's Art Poetry* i. 4 Sometimes an Author, fond of his own Thought, Pursues his Object till it's over-wrought. **1884** *Daily News* 1 Apr. 4/7 Mr. Gladstone's speech was..not overwrought, it was not a sentence too long.

5. *transf.* and *fig.* To work into a state of excitement or confusion, to stir up or excite excessively.

1645 Milton *Colast.* Wks. (1851) 368 By overworking the settl'd mudd of his fancy, to make him drunk, and disgorge his vileness the more openly. **1816** Byron *Ch. Har.* iii. vii, Till my brain became, In its own eddy boiling and o'erwrought, A whirling gulf of phantasy and flame. **1855** Tennyson *Maud* ii. i. viii, Strange, that the mind, when fraught With a passion so intense..should, by being so overwrought, Suddenly strike on a sharper sense For a shell, or a flower, little things Which else would have been past by.

Hence **overworked** (-ˈwɜːkt) *ppl. a.*, worked too hard or to excess, worked beyond one's strength; also *transf.* and *fig.*; **over'working** *vbl. sb.*, working or being worked too hard; **over'working** *ppl. a.*

1833 J. Macl. Campbell in *Mem.* (1877) I. iv. 107 As to the overworking of mind..I have been myself sensible of it. *Ibid.*, The demand which dear Mr. Erskine's overworking mind makes on others. **1849** H. Crawford *Time's Peerless Gem* 36 The triumph of the over-working system. **1854** C. M. Yonge *Heartsease* II. iii. xiii. 292 Violet..weak, anxious, and overworked. **1859** Longf. in *Life* (1891) II. 384 Agassiz has got run down with overworking. **1864** *Social Sci. Rev.* 4 Time was when the very phrase overworked men would have been considered foolish and out of the question. **1865** *Public Opinion* 4 Feb. 112 The overworking of the service we believe to be the chief cause of the late accidents. **1959** M. Summerton *Small Wilderness* i. 5 That over-worked truism about the wife being the last to know. **1978** *Times* 14 Jan. 14/1 The phrase 'low profile'..an over-worked image almost evacuated of meaning.

'over-'working, *sb.* [f. over- 19 + working *vbl. sb.*] Working beyond or in excess of a specified amount; *pl.* in *Coal-trade*: see quots.

1851 Greenwell *Coal-trade Terms Northumb. & Durh.* 62 Colliery rent consists of a fixed or certain rent, in consideration of which a certain quantity of coals is allowed to be annually worked and vended... Excess above the certain quantity is called 'over-workings'. **1894** *Northumbld. Gloss., Overworkings*, the excess beyond the quantity of coal fixed as the standard to be annually worked from a royalty.

'overworld. [over- 1 d.] **1.** The celestial or immaterial world.

1858 Sears *Athanasia* iii. ix. 325 They [primitive men] believed there was an overworld where God resided in space, and an underworld where all departed spirits were gathered together. **1905** V. McNabb *Oxf. Conf. on Faith* 33 We would then represent our agnostic as saying..'We are quite certain that there are natural forces and a great world of nature, of which we are a part. But we cannot get beyond this world. There may be an overworld, or an immanent world.' **1966** *Punch* 1 June 803/1 Since West Indies cricket was baptised..in 1928, it has produced players fit..to play in some overworld a representative company of cricket immortals. **1973** *Times Lit. Suppl.* 2 Mar. 249/2 Krishnamurti at thirteen found himself translated..into the theosophical over-world or under-world inhabited by the Lords Maitreya and Koot Hoomi on the astral..plane.

2. The terrestrial world, the earth, land, viewed from beneath water.

1911 Beerbohm *Zuleika D.* xix. 290 He floated up. There was air in that over-world. **1958** L. Durrell *Mountolive* i. 15 Water-tortoises and frogs and sliding fish—a whole population disturbed by this intrusion from the overworld.

3. The community of conventional, law-abiding citizens, as opposed to the 'underworld'.

1938 F. D. Sharpe *Sharpe of Flying Squad* i. 13 The difference between the Underworld and the Overworld folk is that one lot works for a living; the other 'acquires' wealth and regards toil as sin. **1950** [see *Mr. Fix* s.v. Mr. 2 e]. **1959** *Encounter* May 29/2 The counter-society or underworld is, like the society or overworld which has expressed it from its own body, class-ridden.

overworn (əʊvəwɔːn, *shifting stress*), *ppl. a.* [f. over- 21, 17 + worn *ppl. a.*; or pa. pple. of overwear *v.*]

1. Much worn, the worse for wear; that has lost its original freshness; shabby, threadbare; faded.

1565 *Wills & Inv. N.C.* (Surtees 1835) 221 One overworne fether bed wt a good boster xs. **1594** Shaks. *Rich. III*, i. i. 81 The iealous ore-worne Widdow, and her selfe,.. Are mighty Gossips in our Monarchy. **1609** Holland *Amm. Marcell.* 400 Come there once over their head a coat of some over-worne colour, it never goes off nor is changed. **1631** Weever *Anc. Fun. Mon.* 49 A beaten-out pulpit cushion, an ore-worne Communion-cloth. **1657** W. Coles *Adam in Eden* cxxviii, The first of the Vipers grasses hath long broad leaves..of an overworn green colour. **1817** Coleridge *Biog. Lit.* 157 Alas! even our prose writings.. trick themselves out in the soiled and over-worn finery of the meretricious muse. *a* **1825** Forby *Voc. E. Anglia* s.v., Apparel worn as long as is thought fit, thrown aside, and given to servants, or the poor, is called 'overworn clothes'.

†**b.** *fig.* Spoilt by too much use; stale. *Obs.*

1579 Lyly *Euphues* (Arb.) 44 You shal assoone catch a Hare with a taber as you shal perswade youth with your aged and ouerworn eloquence. **1601** Shaks. *Twel. N.* iii. i. 66 Who you are, and what you would are out of my welkin, I might say Element, but the word is ouer-worne.

†**2.** Grown out of use or currency, obsolete. *Obs.*

1581 Savile *Tacitus Hist.* i. ix. (1622) 32 They sware, To the Senate and people of Rome, a stile long ago ouerworne. **1603** Knolles *Hist. Turks* (1638) 123 To defend the ouer-worne right that his father and grandfather had vnto that lost kingdome. **1610** Holland *Camden's Brit.* i. 314 Rude verses in an old and ouerworne character.

3. Worn out, exhausted, spent (with age, toil, etc.).

1592 Greene *Upst. Courtier* in *Harl. Misc.* (Malh.) II. 247, I espied, a far off, a certaine kind of an ouerworne gentleman, attired in veluet and sattyn. **1592** Shaks. *Ven. & Ad.* 135 O'erworn, despised, rheumatic and cold. **1611** Speed *Theat. Gt. Brit.* xxii. (1614) 43/1 The Romans.. whose over-worne empire ending in Britaine, the Saxons by strong hand attained this province. **1650** Earl Monm. tr. *Senault's Man bec. Guilty* 390 This overworn mother shall be freed from her care of nourishing man.

4. Spent in time; passed away.

1592 Shaks. *Ven. & Ad.* 866 Musing the morning is so much o'erworn, And yet she hears no tidings of her love. **1850** Tennyson *In Mem.* i, Behold the man that loved and lost, But all he was is overworn.

over-worry to **overwound** (-ˈwuːnd): see over-.

overwound (-ˈwaʊnd), pa. t. and pa. pple. of overwind *v.*

over-wove, -en, pa. t. and pa. pple. of overweave *v.*

overwrap (əʊvəˈræp), *v.* [over- 8.] *trans.* To wrap over or round; to fold over, bind up, envelop. Also *fig.* Hence **over'wrapping** *vbl. sb.*

1816 Kirby & Sp. *Entomol.* (1843) I. 393 Overwrapping each other like the tiles of a house. **1880** L. Wallace *Ben-Hur* viii. ix. 530 Priests..in their plain white garments overwrapped by abnets of many folds. **1887** Browning *Parleyings, F. Furini* ix, Ignorance overwraps his moral sense. **1959** *Times* 12 Aug. 15/6 Rigidity is essential for a material intended for overwrapping. **1967** C. R. Oswin in F. A. Paine *Packaging Materials* xix. 262 This is particularly helpful when bulk overwrapping blocks of small packets. **1972** *Daily Tel.* (Colour Suppl.) 12 May 13/2 Overwrap anything large like poultry with mutton cloth for extra protection [in the freezer]. **1972** Briston & Neill *Packaging Managem.* ix. 180 Regenerated cellulose film, commonly known as 'Cellophane'..is the traditional material used for the overwrapping of products such as biscuits, cigarettes and chocolate.

overwrap (ˈəʊvəræp), *sb.* [over- 8 c.] A flexible wrapping fitted over packaged goods.

1956 *Visible Packaging of Flour Confectionery* (British Cellophane Ltd.) 3 Pastries should not be included in packs which have an overwrap of fully-moistureproof film. **1969** L. S. Mounts in W. R. R. Park *Plastics Film Technol.* v. 122 The greater stiffness [of medium density polyethylene films] improves the machinability for overwrap applications.

over-wrestle: see over-.

overwrite (əʊvəˈraɪt, ˈəʊvə-), *v.* [over- 8, 1, 27, 23, 20.]

I. 1. a. *trans.* To write (something) over other writing, as a palimpsest. **b.** To write over (a surface), to cover *with* writing.

1699 Lister *Journ. Paris* 108 This [MS. of St. Matthew] was cut to pieces..and another Book overwritten in a small Modern Greek Hand, about 150 years ago. **1820** Byron *To Murray* 23 Apr., They have overwritten all the city walls with 'Up with the republic!' **1856** Mrs. Browning *Aur. Leigh* v. 1219 The Elzevirs Have fly-leaves overwritten by his hand.

c. *Computers.* To place new data in a section of memory and destroy what is already there: used with the old data or the location as obj.

1959 [implied in overwriting *vbl. sb.* below]. **1962** *Gloss. Terms Automatic Data Processing* (*B.S.I.*) 25 The previous data is said to be overwritten in this process. **1970** [see overlay *sb.* 6]. **1972** *Computer Jrnl.* XV. 200/2 Only one field, which contains an entry stating who is allowed to overwrite the file, may be altered by the programmer. **1973** C. W. Gear *Introd. Computer Sci.* vi. 245 Storing into a data area will overwrite another piece of data.

†**2.** To write over or above; to superscribe, entitle. *Obs.*

1761 Sterne *Tr. Shandy* IV. i, This [tale]..is overwritten 'The Intricacies of Diego and Julia'.

3. To write over again, re-write.

1874 Nicholson in *New Shaks. Soc. Trans.* 123 When overwriting plays, he left or worked in words and phrases that he found in the original. **1933** W. E. Orchard *From Faith to Faith* v. 67 It did not seem to me to matter much whether the Book of Isaiah had one or more authors, or the Pentateuch had been overwritten by different hands much later than Moses.

II. 4. a. *intr.* To write too much; **b.** *refl.* To injure or exhaust oneself by excessive writing; **c.** *trans.* To write too much about (a subject).

1815 Jane Austen *Let.* 31 Dec. (1952) 449 It encourages me..to believe that I have not yet..overwritten myself. **1837** *Edin. Rev.* LXIV. 312 Paul de Kock never over-writes. **1883** *Pall Mall G.* 8 Nov., It is a pity that the publishers induce so many young authors of promise to over-write themselves. *a* **1889** Browning *Let.* in F. L. Lucas *Tennyson* (1957) iii. 21, I have written too much, my dear Mr. Gosse; I have over-written; I have written myself out. **1895** *Athenæum* 3 Aug. 160/3 Golf is over-written as well as over-played now.

d. *trans.* (freq. in *ppl. adj.* and *vbl. sb.*). To write too elaborately or ornately; to write in a high-coloured, over-rich style.

1923 F. M. Ford *Let.* 15 Oct. (1965) 155, I have by me a story of his that I don't like *much.* I *might* print it—but it is extremely over-written and..the extravagance I least like is over-writing. **1931** *Daily Express* 31 Jan. 8/2 A fortnight ago an over-written but under-nourished play called 'Colonel Satan' broke the Haymarket record for brevity of life. **1937** C. S. Lewis *Let.* 8 Mar. (1966) 158 Have you read F. L. Lucas' *Decline and Fall of the Romantic Ideal?* Hideously over-written in parts, but well worth reading. **1947** —— in *Ess. presented to Charles Williams* p. vii, In the earlier stories ..there was a good deal of over-writing, of excess in the descriptions and, in dialogue, of a false brilliance. **1968** [see Nabokovian *a.*]. **1977** *Times* 28 Apr. 22/3 This book..is.. so over-written at times it irritated me.

Hence **over'writing** *vbl. sb.*; **over'written** *ppl. a.*

1850 J. Miley *Hist. Papal States* I. 8 This palimpsest, or multifariously over-written document, which we have thus discovered the superficies of the Papal territory to be. **1939** H. J. Massingham *Eng. Countryside* iv. 73 These are the legitimate South Downs, the over-written and exploited range. **1949** W. G. Hoskins *Midland England* i. 3 Stone that gives to not a few Midland towns and villages a beauty unsurpassed by the most over-written Cotswold places. **1956** N. R. Ker *Pastoral Care* 23 Besides additions, the text contains erasures, some with and many without overwriting. .. Overwriting where it occurs is mostly in the main hand. **1959** M. H. Wrubel *Primer of Programming* v. 113 A common error made by beginners is to erase program steps by storing data in the same location. An error of this kind, called 'overwriting', is easily detected.

over-wroth: see over-.

overwrought (ˈəʊvəˈrɔːt), *ppl. a.* [pa. pple. of OVERWORK *v.*: = OVERWORKED.]

1. a. Worked to excess, exhausted by overwork. **b.** Worked up to too high a pitch; over-excited.

1670 G. H. *Hist. Cardinals* I. II. 51 This poor overwrought creature comes in. **1825** LYTTON *Falkland* 12 Even the most overwrought excitation can bring neither novelty nor zest. **1886** HALL CAINE *Son of Hagar* II. xiii, Not one moan of an overwrought heart escaped him.

2. Elaborated to excess; over-laboured.

1839 I. TAYLOR *Anc. Chr.* I. iv. 404 One cannot read these overwrought passages.

overˈwroughtness. *rare.* [-NESS.] An overwrought condition.

1923 W. DEEPING *Secret Sanct.* xxii. 229 He..poured out a glass of white wine for Stretton, sensing the man's overwroughtness, and noticing the tense mouth and the troubled eyes.

†**overˈwry,** *v. Obs.* [OE. *oferwréon* (:—*-wrīhan*): see OVER- 8 and WRY *v.*] *trans.* To cover over; to overspread, conceal, clothe.

c **825** *Vesp. Psalter* xxxi[i]. 5 Unrehtwisnisse mine ic ne oferwrah [L. *operui*]. *Ibid.* ciii[i]. 9 Ne bioð forcerde oferwrean eorðan. *c* **1000** *Ags. Gosp.* Matt. vi. 29 Furðon salomon on eallum hys wuldre næs ofer-wrigen swa swa an of ðyson. *c* **1320** *Cast. Love* 716 Þe þridde heuȝ an ouemast Ouer-wriȝeþ al. *c* **1420** *Pallad. on Husb.* IV. 260 And smale yf seedis be, sprynge hem in lond, And ouerwrie hem after with a rake.

overye, obs. form of OVERHIE.

†**over-ˈyear,** *v. Obs.* [OVER- 34.] *trans.* To keep over the year or over years; to load with years, superannuate, make old. Hence **overˈyeared** *ppl. a. dial.*, kept over the year, or from the preceding year.

1574 HELLOWES *Gueuara's Fam. Ep.* (1577) 52 The letters that you haue to sende, and the daughters that you haue to marrie, care ye not to leaue them farre ouer yeared: for in our countrie they do not ouer yeare other things than their bacon, which they will eate, and their store wine which they will drinke. **1600** FAIRFAX *Tasso* II. xiv, Among them dwelt ..A maide, whose fruit was ripe, not oueryeared. **1615** TOMKIS *Albumazar* IV. xiii. in Hazl. *Dodsley* XI. 401 O, what a business These hands must have when you have married me, To pick out sentences that over-year you! **1883** *Cheltenham Exam.* 19 Sept. Suppl. 1/3, 200 over-yeared ewes 60s. a head.

†**overyear,** *a.*[1] *Obs.* [OVER- 32.] That has lasted over some years; superannuated, antiquated.

1585 JAMES I *Ess. Poesie* (Arb.) 37 No more into those oweryere lies delyte, My freinds, cast of that insolent archer quyte.

over-year, *adv.* (*a.*[2]) *dial.* [OVER- 31, 32.] **a.** *adv. phr.* Over the year, till next year. **b.** *adj.* Kept over the year or till next year.

1790 GROSE *Provinc. Gloss.* (ed. 2) Suppl. s.v., Bullocks.. kept..to be fatted the next winter, are said to be kept over-year, and are termed over-year bullocks. **1813** BATCHELOR *Agric.* 507 (E.D.D.) Those who choose to give it [dung] repeated turnings, and keep what is called over year muck. **1877** *Holderness Gloss.*, *Ower-year*,..till next year or season; i.e. over the current year. 'Ah'll keep that pig ower-year'.

overyede, -yode, obs. pa. t. of OVERGO.

†**overˈyoke,** *v. Obs.* In 6 -yock. [OVER- 1.] *trans.* To put a yoke upon, to subjugate.

1545 BRINKLOW *Compl.* 4 Whan so euer any persons be greuyd, oppressyd, or ouer yockyd. *Ibid.* 62 The comynaltye is so oppressed and oueryocked..by wicked lawes, cruel tyrannes.

over-young: see OVER- 28.

over-zeal (ˈəʊvəˈziːl). [OVER- 29 d.] Too great zeal; excess of zeal.

1747 *Mem. Nutrebian Crt.* I. 92 An over-zeal to serve his friend. **1840** CARLYLE *Heroes* i. (1872) 36 King Olaf has been harshly blamed for his over-zeal in introducing Christianity. **1886** P. ROBINSON *Valley Teet. Trees* 143 He..has never been accused of any excessive over-zeal for work.

So †**ˈover-ˈzealed** *a. Obs.* [OVER- 28], too much influenced by zeal, 'ruled by too much zeal' (T.).

1639 FULLER *Holy War* IV. xxvi. (1647) 214 Thus was this good Kings judgement over-zealed.

over-zealous (ˈəʊvəˈzɛləs), *a.* [OVER- 28.] Too zealous; actuated by too much zeal.

a **1635** NAUNTON *Fragm. Reg.* (Arb.) 25 They two were ever of the Kings Religion, and over-zealous professors. *a* **1703** BURKITT *On N.T.* John xviii. 28 When persons are over-zealous for ceremonial observations, they are oftentimes too remiss with reference to moral duties. **1860** FROUDE *Hist. Eng.* V. xxiv. 33 The overzealous curates were committed to the Tower.

So **ˈover-ˈzealously** *adv.*; **ˈoverˈzealousness.**

1667 *Lond. Gaz.* No. 129/3 The Bishop is remembered.. to have over-zealously pursued the French interest. **1849** H. MAYO *Truths in Pop. Superstit.* ii. 41 Cases..in which the anxiety of friends or the overzealousness of a coroner is liable to lead to premature anatomization.

ovese, obs. form of EAVES.

†**ovet.** *Obs.* exc. *dial.* (ovest). [OE. *obet*, *ofet*, a Com. WGer. word: = OHG. *obaz* (MHG. *obez*, Ger. *obst*), OLG., MLG. *ovet* (MDu., Du. *ooft*); ulterior relations uncertain.] Fruit; in *mod. dial.* 'the mast and acorns of the oak' (E.D.D.).

a **700** *Epinal Gloss.* (O.E.T.) 421 *Fraga*, obet [*MS.* obtt, *Erf.* obea]. *c* **725** *Corpus Gl.* 919 *Fraga*, obet. *a* **1000** *Cædmon's Gen.* 655 Adam frea min, þis ofet is swa swete. *a* **1000** *O.E. Glosses* in Wr.-Wülcker 244/8 *Fruges, frumenta*, ofet, wæstm. *c* **1000** *Ælfric's Voc.* ibid. 148/34 *Legumen*, ofet. **1340** *Ayenb.* 262 Y-blissed þou ine wymmen, and y-blissed þet ouet of þine wombe. **1866** BLACKMORE *Cradock Nowell* xxxi. (1883) 176 The hogs skittered home from the ovest.

ovi-[1], combining form of L. *ōvum* egg.

ovi-[2], combining form of L. *ovis* sheep.

†**ˈoviary.** *Obs. rare*—[0]. [ad. L. *oviāria* flock of sheep, f. *ovis* sheep.] A flock of sheep.

1623 COCKERAM, *Ouiarie*, a flock of sheep. **1656** in BLOUNT.

ovibos (ˈəʊvɪbɒs). [mod.L. (H. de Blainville 1816, in *Bull. Sci. Soc. Philomatique Paris* 76), f. L. *ovis* sheep + *bōs* ox, as the animal was considered to represent a type intermediate between the sheep and the ox.] A small, stocky ruminant of the monotypic genus so called, bearing long, shaggy, dark brown fur, and native to Arctic regions of North America and Greenland; = MUSK-OX.

1903 R. LYDEKKER *Mostly Mammals* 287 No objection can be taken to the prefix 'musk'..yet the English title 'ox' is in the highest degree misleading, while the technical 'Ovibos', which suggests characters intermediate between the oxen and the sheep, is equally unsatisfactory. **1921** V. STEFÁNSSON *Friendly Arctic* 342 We found the ancient and far-decayed skull of a female ovibos. *Ibid.* 582, I shot two ovibos as all we needed out of the fifteen or twenty seen. **1925** *Chambers's Jrnl.* 14 Feb. 167/1 Here..will roam large herds of the domesticated musk-ox or ovibos. **1929** *Encycl. Brit.* II. 306/1 With the ovibos domesticated, the potentialities of the Arctic will be greater. *Ibid.* Ovibos beef is indistinguishable from ordinary domestic beef.

ovibovine (əʊvɪˈbəʊvaɪn), *a.* and *sb. Zool.* [ad. mod.L. *Ovibovinæ* fem. pl., f. *Ovibōs* the musk-ox (the typical and only extant genus), f. *ovis* sheep + *bōs* ox.] **a.** *adj.* Belonging to the subfamily *Ovibovinæ* of the family *Bovidæ*, having characters intermediate between those of sheep and oxen. **b.** *sb.* An animal of this subfamily; a musk-ox.

ovicapsule (əʊvɪˈkæpsjuːl). *Anat.* and *Zool.* [f. OVI-[1] + CAPSULE: so in mod.F.] A capsule or sac containing an ovum (*e.g.* a Graafian follicle) or a number of ova (*e.g.* the egg-case of various fishes); an egg-case, an ovisac. Hence **oviˈcapsular** *a.*, pertaining to an ovicapsule.

1853 in DUNGLISON *Med. Lex.* **1859** TODD *Cycl. Anat.* V. 106*/1 Those ova which have left the ovicapsule. **1877** HUXLEY *Anat. Inv. Anim.* vii. 442 But in the larger ova which succeed these, the cells of the ovicapsule rapidly enlarge. *Ibid.*, The indifferent tissue..gives rise not only to ova and ovicapsular epithelium, but to large vitelligenous cells.

ovicell (ˈəʊvɪsɛl). *Biol.* [f. OVI-[1] + CELL, or ad. mod.L. *ovicella*.]

1. A receptacle for the ova in certain Polyzoa; also called *oocyst* or *oœcium*.

1870 ROLLESTON *Anim. Life* 71 Broad-leafed Hornwrack. .. The ovicell, a sort of marsupial pouch,..is inconspicuous in this species. **1877** HUXLEY *Anat. Inv. Anim.* viii. 458 They sometimes..undergo the first stages of their development in dilatations of the wall of the body, termed ovicells.

2. A cell which when impregnated develops into a new individual; an egg-cell; a germ-cell; an ovum or ovule.

1875 HUXLEY & MARTIN *Elem. Biol.* (1877) 47 The first product of the germination of the impregnated ovicell is a hypha-like body, from which the young *Chara* is developed. **1892** *Syd. S.L.*, *Ovicell*, the one-celled Mammalian ovum.

Hence **oviˈcellular** *a.*, pertaining to an ovicell.

1890 in *Cent. Dict.*

ovicide[1] (ˈəʊvɪsaɪd). *humorous.* [f. OVI-[2] + -CIDE 2.] The killing of a sheep; sheep-slaughter. So **ˈovicidal** *a.*, sheep-killing.

a **1845** BARHAM *Ingol. Leg.*, *Jerry Jarvis* (1882) 409 There it [the wig] lay—the little sinister-looking tail impudently perked up... Larceny and Ovicide shone in every hair of it! **1847-9** SIR J. STEPHEN *Eccl. Biog.* (1850) I. 144 An ovicidal wolf..rebuked by this ecclesiastical Orpheus for his carnivorous deeds. **1880** *Daily News* 15 Nov. 5/5 The mutton-bones which tell of unauthorised ovicide. **1883** STEWART *Nether Lochaber* xlv. 285 His ovicidal tendencies.

ovicide[2]. [f. OVI-[1] + -CIDE.] An agent that kills eggs, esp. those of insects. Hence **oviˈcidal** *a.*[2]

1930 *Jrnl. South-Eastern Agric. College, Wye* XXVII. 147 Ovicides, contact insecticides and grease-banding..having been tried. **1932** *Ibid.* XXX. 63 (*heading*) Studies on the ovicidal action of winter washes. **1961** *Lancet* 12 Aug. 371/1 AzUR given orally is an effective ovicide in the mouse, terminating early pregnancy at dosage levels which produce no detectable toxic effect in the mother. *Ibid.*, Different batches vary somewhat in activity, and their ovicidal activity and their toxicity are not necessarily related. **1967** *New Scientist* 20 Apr. 154/2 The experiments dramatically illustrate the effectiveness of juvenile hormone as an ovicide, as well as an insecticide.

oˈvicular, *a. rare.* [f. med. or mod.L. *ōvicul-um* (dim. of *ōvum* egg) + -AR.] Of the shape or nature of an egg.

1774 J. BRYANT *Mythol.* II. 352, I invoke Protogonos, who wandered..inclosed in an ovicular machine. **1816** G. S. FABER *Orig. Pagan Idol.* II. 252 The tempest-tossed egg or ovicular arkite machine.

oˈviculated, *a. Arch.* [f. med. or mod.L. *ōviculum* (see prec.), in Arch. sometimes = OVOLO.] Adorned with egg-shaped ornaments.

1789 SMYTH *Aldrich's Archit.* (1818) 90 It is termed oviculated, because artists imagine the sculpture to represent eggs.

ovicyst (ˈəʊvɪsɪst). *Zool.* [irreg. f. OVI-[1] + CYST; cf. OOCYST.] A receptacle in which the ova are hatched in some ascidians. Hence **oviˈcystic** *a.*, pertaining to an ovicyst.

1877 HUXLEY *Anat. Inv. Anim.* x. 622 The incubatory pouch may be termed the ovicyst. **1890** *Cent. Dict.*, *Ovicystic*.

Ovidian (əʊˈvɪdɪən), *a.* [See -IAN.] Belonging to or characteristic of the Latin poet Ovid (Publius Ovidius Naso, B.C. 43–A.D. 17), or his poetry.

1617 MORYSON *Itin.* I. 113 It hath no light,..but like twilight, or the Ouidian light which is in thicke woods. **1713** ADDISON *Guardian* No. 122 ¶4 They had no relish for any composition..not..in the Ovidian manner. **1809** MALKIN *Gil Blas* IV. vii. ¶10, I carried an Ovidian letter from my master to Euphrasia. **1876** GLADSTONE in *Contemp. Rev.* June 1 It..recalls the Ovidian account of chaos.

oviducal (ˈəʊvɪdjuːkəl), *a. Anat.* and *Zool.* [irreg. f. OVI-[1] + L. *dūcĕre* to lead: after *oviduct*.] Serving to convey the ova or eggs from the ovary; of the nature of an oviduct.

1839-47 TODD *Cycl. Anat.* III. 1010/1 The lining membrane of the oviducal canal. **1877** HUXLEY *Anat. Inv. Anim.* x. 622 A single uterine sac, the outer or oviducal half of which applies itself to the wall of the ovicyst.

So **oviducent** (ˈəʊvɪdjuːsənt), *a.* [L. *dūcent-em*, pr. pple. of *dūcĕre* to lead.] = prec.

1890 in *Cent. Dict.*

oviduct (ˈəʊvɪdʌkt). *Anat.* and *Zool.* [ad. med. or mod. anat. L. *ōviductus* = *ōvī ductus*, DUCT *sb.* or channel of the egg.] The duct or canal forming a passage for the ova or eggs from the ovary, esp. in oviparous animals, as birds; less commonly used of the corresponding structure in mammals (Fallopian tube, uterus, and vagina), or of its upper portion (Fallopian tube) alone.

[**1672** *Phil. Trans.* VII. 4052 The extremity of the Oviductus or Egg-channel ends in a membranous expansion in Birds. **1706** PHILLIPS, *Oviductus* (in Anat.), the Egg-passages, the same as *Tubæ Fallopianæ*.] **1757** T. BIRCH *Hist. Roy. Soc.* III. 498 Its [the torpedo's] ovarium is near the liver and double oviduct and womb, wherein the young ones swim free. **1788** JENNER in *Phil. Trans.* LXXVIII. 232 The membranes which had discharged yolks into the oviduct. **1851-6** WOODWARD *Mollusca* 49 Viviparous reproduction happens in a few..gastropods, through the retention of the eggs in the oviduct.

Hence **oviˈductal** *a.*, pertaining to or of the nature of an oviduct, oviducal.

1860 *N. Syd. Soc. Year-Bk. Med.* 117 On the Aquiferous and Oviductal Systems in the Lamellibranchiate Molluscs.

oviferous (əʊˈvɪfərəs), *a. Anat.* and *Zool.* [f. OVI-[1] + -FEROUS.] Producing, carrying, or conveying ova or eggs; egg-bearing; applied *esp.* to special receptacles in which the ova of some crustaceans are carried.

1828 STARK *Elem. Nat. Hist.* II. 189 Anthosoma,.. extremity of the abdomen with two oviferous cylindrical and elongated tubes. **1836-9** TODD *Cycl. Anat.* II. 408/2 In the oviferous classes. **1844** GOODSIR in *Proc. Berw. Nat. Club* II. 114 The oviferous legs are very strong. **1880** GÜNTHER *Fishes* 159 In Rhodeus the oviduct is periodically prolonged into a long oviferous tube, by means of which the female deposits her ova.

oviform (ˈəʊvɪfɔːm), *a.*[1] [f. OVI-[1] + -FORM: cf. mod.L. *ōviform-is*, F. *oviforme* (Littré).] Having the form of an egg; egg-shaped.

1684 T. BURNET *Th. Earth* I. v. 65 This notion of the Mundane Egg, or that the World was Oviform, hath been the sence and Language of all Antiquity. **1769** W. HEWSON in *Phil. Trans.* LIX. 212 That in the human subject each lacteal forms an ampullula or oviform vesicle. **1816** G. S. FABER *Orig. Pagan Idol.* III. 186 A large orbicular or oviform stone. **1879** J. J. YOUNG *Ceram. Art* 179 A set of three small oviform vases.

†**b.** Consisting of small particles like eggs or the roe of fishes, as ***oviform limestone*** = OOLITE.

1799 KIRWAN *Geol. Ess.* ii. 234 Oviform Limestone. This is not common; the balls or globules have for the most part a grain of sand in the middle. **1816** W. SMITH *Strata Ident.* 29 Freestone, calcareous, soft, oviform.

ˈoviform, *a.*[2] *rare.* [f. OVI-[2] + -FORM.] Of the form of a sheep, or (quot. 1900) of that proper to the sheep.

1890 in *Cent. Dict.* **1900** *Proc. Zool. Soc.* 155 Its [*lobus spigelii*] form in the same species may be either 'rusiform' or 'oviform'.

ovigenetic (ˌəʊvɪdʒɪˈnɛtɪk), *a.* [f. OVI-[1] + -GENETIC.] = OVOGENETIC *a.*
1908 *Lancet* 23 May 1495/2 The spermatogenic and ovigenetic cells of the sexual glands in higher animals.

ovigenous (əʊˈvɪdʒɪnəs), *a. Anat.* [f. OVI-[1] + *-genous* taken in sense 'producing': cf. -GEN 1.] Producing ova or eggs.
1892 *Syd. Soc. Lex.*, *Ovigenous layer*, the peripheral portion of the ovary in which the ova are produced.

ovigerm (ˈəʊvɪdʒɜːm). *Biol.* [f. OVI-[1] + GERM.] A female germ; an (unfertilized) ovum.
1851 DARWIN *Monogr. Cirripedia* I. 58 These..closely resembled, in general appearance and size, the ovigerms, with their germinal vesicles and spots. **1881** MIVART *Cat* 251 The incipient ovum—or ovigerm.

ovigerous (əʊˈvɪdʒərəs), *a. Anat.* and *Zool.* [f. OVI-[1] + -GEROUS.] Bearing or carrying eggs. ***ovigerous frænum***: see quot. 1859.
1835–6 TODD *Cycl. Anat.* I. 36/2 A long filamentary organ, vigerous, rises from the root of the central mass. **1852** DANA *Crust.* II. 809 The ovigerous females are readily distinguished. **1859** DARWIN *Orig. Spec.* vi. (1872) 148 Pedunculated cirripedes have two minute folds of skin, called by me the ovigerous frena, which serve, through the means of a sticky secretion, to retain the eggs until they are hatched.

† **ˈovil.** *Obs. rare*[−0]. [ad. L. *ovīle.*]
1674 BLOUNT *Glossogr.*, *Ovil*, a sheep-coat, or sheep-fold.

oviˈnation. *Med. rare.* [f. L. *ovīn-us* (see next) after *vaccination.*] 'Inoculation with the lymph of sheep-pox' (*Syd. Soc. Lex.*).
1888 W. WILLIAMS *Princ. & Pract. Vet. Med.* (ed. 5) 222 Inoculation or ovination is recommended by very high authorities.

ovine (ˈəʊvaɪn), *a.* and *sb.* [ad. L. *ovīn-us*, f. *ovis* sheep: see -INE[1]: cf. F. *ovine.*]
A. *adj.* **1.** Of, pertaining to, of the nature of, or characteristic of, sheep or a sheep; in *Zool.* belonging to the *Ovinæ*, a subfamily of Ruminants, comprising the various kinds of sheep.
1828 WEBSTER, *Ovine*, pertaining to sheep; consisting of sheep. **1865** *Sat. Rev.* 7 Oct. 455/1 The ovine small-pox of last season. **1874** HELPS *Soc. Press.* xxiv. 375 That most notable instinct of the ovine race to follow thoughtlessly.
2. *fig.* Resembling a sheep; sheeplike, sheepish.
1832 CARLYLE *Misc.* (1857) III. 68 Ponder well these ovine proceedings. **1887** *Daily Tel.* 2 May 3/1 Scarcely, we think, should this amorous and ovine youth be Strephon.
B. *sb.* A member of the *Ovinæ*; a sheep.
1890 in *Cent. Dict.*

† **oˈviparal,** *a. Obs.* [f. as OVIPAROUS + -AL[1].] = OVIPAROUS.
1660 R. COKE *Justice Vind.* 39 All oviparal creatures more wisely distribute to their young ones, then the wisest Man can to his Children.

oviparity (əʊvɪˈpærɪtɪ). *Zool.* [f. L. *ovipar-us* (see next) + -ITY.] The condition or character of being oviparous; in quot. 1858 *loosely*, Reproduction by ova.
1858 LEWES *Sea-side Stud.* 293 The production of Medusæ..being sometimes a process of budding, and sometimes a process of oviparity. **1884** *Athenæum* 25 Oct. 533 The discovery by Mr. Caldwell of the oviparity of the Monotremata..was considered sufficiently important to be telegraphed from Australia to the British Association in Canada.

oviparous (əʊˈvɪpərəs), *a. Zool.* [f. L. *ovipar-us* egg-laying (f. OVI-[1] + *-parus* producing, laying, f. *parĕre* to bring forth) + -OUS. Cf. F. *ovipare* (1712 in Hatz.-Darm.).] Producing ova or eggs; applied to animals that produce young by means of eggs which are 'laid' or expelled from the body of the parent and subsequently hatched. (Opp. to VIVIPAROUS; see also OVO-VIVIPAROUS.)
1646 SIR T. BROWNE *Pseud. Ep.* 297 In creatures oviparous, as birds and fishes. **1684** T. BURNET *Th. Earth* I. 187 All sorts of creatures, whether oviparous or viviparous. **1796** MORSE *Amer. Geog.* I. 217 The alligator is an oviparous animal... They lay from one to two hundred eggs in a nest. **1858** LEWES *Sea-side Stud.* 285 The Aphis produces each year ten larviparous broods, and one which is oviparous.
Hence **oˈviparously** *adv.*, **oˈviparousness.**
1822–34 *Good's Study Med.* (ed. 4) IV. 3 In the warmer summer months the young [of the *daphnia pulex*] are produced viviparously, and in the cooler autumnal months oviparously. **1853** DUNGLISON *Med. Lex.*, Oviparousness.

oviposit (əʊvɪˈpɒzɪt), *v. Zool.* [f. OVI-[1] + L. *posit-*, ppl. stem of *pōnĕre* to place: cf. *deposit.*] *intr.* To deposit or lay an egg or eggs; esp. by means of a special organ (*ovipositor*), as an insect.
1816 KIRBY & SP. *Entomol.* iv. (1828) I. 89 An insect which he informs us gets into the feet of people as they walk ..oviposits in them and so occasions very dangerous ulcers. (*Note.* It is to be hoped this new word may be admitted; as the laying of eggs cannot otherwise be expressed without a periphrasis. For the same reason its substantive *oviposition* will be employed.) *Ibid.* xix. (1818) II. 147 After her great laying of male eggs in.. May she [queen bee] oviposits in the royal cells..which the workers have in the mean time constructed. **1851–6** WOODWARD *Mollusca* 67 The females oviposit on sea-weeds, or in the cavities of empty shells.
b. *trans.* To deposit or lay (an egg).
1847 in WEBSTER. **1871** T. R. JONES *Anim. Kingd.* §879. 363 The ova are developed, impregnated, and oviposited.
Hence **oviˈpositing** *vbl. sb.* and *ppl. a.*
1833 LYELL *Princ. Geol.* III. 317 The shores of those islands may have been frequented, during the ovipositing season, by the turtles and crocodiles. **1887** *Athenæum* 7 May 612/1 In the beehive all the eggs were usually laid by the queen, and in her absence no ovipositing occurs. **1890** *Cent. Dict.* s.v. *Ovipositor*, The ovipositing organ with which many..insects are provided.

oviposition (əʊvɪpəˈzɪʃən). *Zool.* [f. OVI-[1] + L. *positiōn-em* placing: see OVIPOSIT.] The action of depositing or laying an egg or eggs, esp. with an ovipositor. So **ovipoˈsitional** *a.*, of or pertaining to oviposition.
1816 [see OVIPOSIT]. **1816** KIRBY & SP. *Entomol.* xvii. (1818) II. 36 When the business of oviposition commences. **1862** *Zoologist* Ser. I. XX. 8194 On the Oviposition of the Cuckoo. **1931** *Jrnl. Morphol.* LI. 22 The females [of Orthoptera] usually abandon them [*sc.* the eggs] as soon as oviposition is complete. **1965** LEE & KNOWLES *Animal Hormones* ii. 28 There is evidence that LTH is important for oviposition in some of the fishes. **1971** *Nature* 13 Aug. 484/1 Work is in progress..making use of the parasites' ovipositional response as a bioassay for the kairomone. **1973** *Ibid.* 30 Nov. 270/1 After oviposition these juveniles [of the nematode, *Deladenus siricidicola*] escape from the egg and enter a free living phase.

ovipositor (əʊvɪˈpɒzɪtə(r)). *Entom.* [f. OVI-[1] + L. *positor*, agent-n. from *pōnĕre* to place.] A pointed tubular organ at the end of the abdomen of the female in many insects, by means of which the eggs are deposited, and (in many cases) a hole bored to receive them.
1816 KIRBY & SP. *Entomol.* (1843) I. 226 By means of her long ovipositor [the Ichneumon] reaches the..grub..and deposits in it an egg. **1828** STARK *Elem. Nat. Hist.* II. 334 Abdomen..of the females provided with a borer or ovipositor. **1877** HUXLEY *Anat. Inv. Anim.* vii. 431 The saws of the Saw-flies and the stings of other Hymenoptera are to be regarded as specially modified ovipositors.

ovisac (ˈəʊvɪsæk). *Anat.* and *Zool.* [f. OVI-[1] + SAC. So in mod.F. (Littré).] A sac, cell, or pouch containing an ovum (as a Graafian follicle), or a number of ova (as the investing membrane of the roe in some fishes); an egg-case.
1835–6 TODD *Cycl. Anat.* I. 559/1 The ovisacs [in the Octopods] are..connected in bunches. **1872** PEASLEE *Ovar. Tumours* 7 Each mature ovisac contains a mature ovum. **1877** HUXLEY *Anat. Inv. Anim.* vi. 271 The eggs are carried about in the ovisacs until they are hatched.

oviscapt (ˈəʊvɪskæpt). *Entom.* [ad. F. *oviscapte* (De Serres), hybrid f. OVI-[1] + Gr. σκάπτ-ειν to dig (Littré).] = OVIPOSITOR.
1870 ROLLESTON *Anim. Life* 88 Common Cockroach... The [oviducal] infundibula of the two sides..pass beneath the terminal nerve structures and the 'oviscapt' to form a common vagina.

ovism (ˈəʊvɪz(ə)m). *Biol.* [f. L. *ov-um* egg + -ISM: in mod.F. *ovisme* (Littré).] The old theory that the ovum or female reproductive cell contains the whole of the future organism in an undeveloped state, and that the male cell or spermatozoon merely acts as a stimulant to its development: opposed to *spermism* or *animalculism.* (Also OVARISM.)
1892 in *Syd. Soc. Lex.*

ovispermary (əʊvɪˈspɜːmərɪ), *sb.* and *a. Zool.* [f. OVI-[1] + SPERM + -ARY.] **a.** *sb.* An organ which produces both ova and spermatozoa: = OVOTESTIS. **b.** *adj.* Pertaining to such an organ. So **oviˈspermiduct**, a duct which conveys both ova and spermatozoa.
1888 ROLLESTON & JACKSON *Anim. Life* 117 The ovi-spermiduct [in Pulmonate Molluscs] is lined by a ciliated epithelium. **1890** *Cent. Dict.*, Ovispermary.

ovist (ˈəʊvɪst). *Biol.* [f. as OV-ISM + -IST: in mod.F. *oviste* (Littré).] One who holds the theory of OVISM: opp. to *spermist* or *animalculist.* (Also OVARIST, OVULIST.) So **oˈvistic** *a.*
1836–9 TODD *Cycl. Anat.* II. 427/1 According to..the Ovists, the female parent is held to afford all the materials necessary for the formation of the offspring. **1889** GEDDES & THOMSON *Evol. Sex* vii. 84 A..controversy..between two schools, who called each other 'ovists' and 'animalculists'. The former maintained that the female germ element was the more important, and only required to be as it were awakened by the male element to begin the process of unfolding. **1893** VIRCHOW in *Westm. Gaz.* 17 Mar. 7/1 The great gap was closed which Harvey's ovistic theory had left in the history of new growth.

ovi-viviparous: see OVO-VIVIPAROUS.

ovivorous (əʊˈvɪvərəs), *a.*[1] [f. OVI-[1] + L. *-vorus* devouring + -OUS. In mod.F. *ovivore* (Littré).] Egg-devouring, egg-eating.
1812 SOUTHEY *Omniana* II. 321 He was a great eater of eggs; one of his rhyming friends..expresses his astonishment at the Friar's ovivorous propensities. **1896** *Brit. Birds Nests & Eggs* I. 20 Some individuals of the species have ovivorous tendencies.

oˈvivorous, *a.*[2] *rare.* [f. OVI-[2]: cf. prec.] Sheep-devouring, sheep-eating.
1865 *Sat. Rev.* 12 Aug. 203/2 The present dearth [of meat] is supposed..to be partly due to an increased development of the bovivorous and ovivorous quality in our countrymen.

ovo- (əʊvəʊ), used in some words as comb. form of L. *ovum* egg; see most of these in their alphabetical places. Sometimes used with adjectives of form to denote an approach to an oval shape, as in **ovo-eˈlliptic, ovo-ˈpyriform, ovo-rhomˈboidal.**
1861 HULME tr. *Moquin-Tandon* II. vi. i. 292 The head [of the Head Louse] is ovo-rhomboidal. **1885** BEDDOE *Races Brit.* 236 Elliptic and ovo-elliptic forms prevail in the east; pyriform and ovo-pyriform ones in the west.

ovo-alˈbumin. *Chem.* = OVALBUMEN.
1873 RALFE *Phys. Chem.* 28 Ovo-Albumin is coagulated by ether; sero-albumin is not.

ovocyte (ˈəʊvəʊsaɪt). *Biol.* [a. G. *ovocyte*: see OOCYTE.] = OOCYTE.
1905 *Jrnl. Acad. Nat. Sci. Philadelphia* XIII. 9 In a young [ascidian] ovocyte..there is no trace of yolk. **1941** J. F. NONIDEZ *Histol. & Embryol.* 83 After synapsis the female germ cells are known as primary ovocytes. **1967** *Nature* 30 Dec. 1315/2 *Xenopus* ovocytes have hundreds of nucleoli and *Asterias* ovocytes only one.

ovoflavin (əʊvəʊˈfleɪvɪn). *Biochem.* [a. G. *ovoflavin* (R. Kuhn et al. 1933, in *Ber. d. Deut. Chem. Ges.* LXVI. 318): see OVO- and FLAVIN 2.] Riboflavin found in egg-white.
1933 *Chem. Abstr.* XXVII. 3480 The ovoflavin crystallizes from $2N$ AcOH in brown-orange needles. **1943** [see *hepatoflavin* s.v. HEPATO-].

ovogenesis (əʊvəʊˈdʒɛnɪsɪs). *Biol.* [mod.L. (Weismann), f. OVO- + -GENESIS; the etymological form is OOGENESIS.] The production or formation of an ovum. So **ovogeˈnetic, oˈvogenous** *adjs.*, contributing to the formation or growth of the ovum.
1886 A. THOMSON in *Q. Jrnl. Micros. Sc.* June 598 According to Weismann, the parallel would be between the surplus 'ovogenetic' polar vesicles and the surplus spermatogenetic basal protoplasm and nucleus. **1887** *Amer. Nat.* XXI. 947 The interest which attaches to the development of the spermatozoon..is not less than that which attaches to the development of the ovum (ovogenesis). **1889** GEDDES & THOMSON *Evol. Sex* viii. 107 [Weismann] distinguishes in the nucleus of the ovum two kinds of plasma,—(1) the ovogenetic or histogenetic substance, which enables the ovum to accumulate yolk, [etc.]..and (2) the germ-plasma, which enables the ovum to develop into an embryo. **1890** WEISMANN in *Nature* 6 Feb. 322/1, I have interpreted the first polar body of the Metazoan ovum as a carrier of ovogenous plasm, which has to be removed from the ovum in order that the germ-plasm may attain the predominance.

ovoglobulin (əʊvəʊˈglɒbjʊlɪn). *Biochem.* Also †**ovi-.** [ad. F. *ovoglobuline* (Corin & Berard 1889, in *Arch. de Biol.* IX. 12): see OVO- and GLOBULIN.] A globulin present in egg-white.
1889 *Jrnl. Chem. Soc.* LVI. 1075 Their coagulation temperatures are:—oviglobulin α at 57·5°; oviglobulin β at 67°. **1905** [see OVALBUMEN, -IN]. **1959** *New Biol.* XXX. 16 Although the white of the egg contains both albumin and globulin these are chemically different from the blood proteins of the same name and they are usually distinguished by means of a prefix: ovalbumin and ovoglobulin.

ovoid (ˈəʊvɔɪd), *a.* and *sb.* Chiefly *Nat. Hist.* [ad. mod.L. *ōvoīdēs*, in F. *ovoïde*, f. L. *ōv-um* egg: see -OID.]
A. *adj.* **1.** Resembling an egg, egg-shaped; oval with one end more pointed than the other. **a.** Of a solid body. (The regular use.)
1828 STARK *Elem. Nat. Hist.* II. 274 *Dacne*... Antennæ short, terminating abruptly in a perfoliated ovoid club. **1834** MCMURTRIE *Cuvier's Anim. Kingd.* 362 The female.. constructs an ovoid cocoon. **1880** BASTIAN *Brain* ii. 28 The term ganglion is..commonly applied to any round or ovoid nodule containing nerve cells.
b. Of superficial figure.
1828 STARK *Elem. Nat. Hist.* I. 210 Nostrils basal, ovoid, lateral. **1880** H. A. A. NICHOLLS in *Nature* 19 Feb. 373/1 The crater is ovoid, with its long axis running in a direction from west-south-west to east-north-east.
2. *Comb.*: esp. with another adj., denoting modification of the form expressed by the latter, as ***ovoid-oblong.***
1870 HOOKER *Stud. Flora* 337 *Salix Capræa*..catkins silky, male ovoid-oblong. **1892** *Daily News* 14 Sept. 3/2 Among the curiosities in this department are bugles of paper and gutta-percha,.. Hatsany's ovoid-shaped trumpet.
B. *sb.* A body or figure of ovoid form.
1831 R. KNOX *Cloquet's Anat.* 413 The circumference of the cerebellum presents a distinct lobule, resembling a cuneiform segment of an ovoid. **1897** *Allbutt's Syst. Med.* IV. 300 Oxalates are deposited in the urine in the form of oxalate of lime, which tends to crystallise either in octohedra or as dumb-bells or ovoids.

ovoidal (əʊˈvɔɪdəl), *a.* [f. as prec. + -AL[1].] = prec. A. 1 a. † ***ovoidal limestone***, oolite (*obs.*): cf. OVIFORM *a.*[1] b.
1799 KIRWAN *Geol. Ess.* i. 217 Shistose mica, with compressed ovoidal limestone. **1831** R. KNOX *Cloquet's Anat.* 525 This ganglion..is ovoidal or fusiform, broader at

the middle than at the extremities. **1874** Coues *Birds N.W.* 373 The greater number [of eggs] are truly ovoidal..one extremity is narrower and more pointed than the other.

ovolo (ˈəʊvələʊ). *Arch.* Pl. ovoli (-liː). [ad. It. †*ovolo*, now *uovolo*, dim. of †*ovo*, *uovo*:—L. *ovum* egg.] A convex moulding of which the section is a quarter-circle or (approximately) a quarter-ellipse, receding from the vertical downwards; also called *quarter-round* or *echinus*.

1663 Gerbier *Counsel* 32 The List, the Ovolo, the Cimatium. **1688** R. Holme *Armoury* III. 112/2 *Ovolo* is a quarter round under a projecting square. **1847** Smeaton *Builder's Man.* 216 There are eight mouldings introduced in the orders: the ovolo, the talon, the cyma, the cavetto, the torus, the astragal, the scotia, and the fillet. **1862** Rickman *Goth. Archit.* 9 The enriched ovolo of the Ionic capital.

b. *attrib.*

1832 J. L. Loudon *Encycl. Cottage Archit.* Gloss. (1836) 1129 Ovolo moulding..generally applied to Doric columns. **1858** *Skyring's Builders' Prices* (ed. 48) 30, 1½ inch deal ovolo sashes. **1875** Knight *Dict. Mech.*, *Ovolo-plane*, a joiner's plane for working ovolo mouldings on sash, or elsewhere.

ovology (əʊˈvɒlədʒɪ). [f. ovo- + -logy. (The etymologically regular oology is app. not used in this sense.)] That part of biology or embryology which treats of the formation and structure of the ova of animals. So **ovoˈlogical** *a.*, pertaining to ovology; **oˈvologist**, one versed in ovology.

1842 Dunglison *Med. Lex.*, Ovology, *Oologia*. **1857** Bullock *Cazeaux' Midwif.* 198 Investigations..in reference to this interesting point of ovology. *Ibid.* 243 In the present state of ovological knowledge. **1859** Todd *Cycl. Anat.* V. 216/2 The researches of modern ovologists..enable us to assert..the..similarity of structure in the ova of animals.

ovomucin (əʊvəʊˈmjuːsɪn). *Biochem.* [f. ovo- + mucin.] A water-insoluble mucoprotein in egg-white. Cf. ovomucoid.

1898 A. Eichholz in *Jrnl. Physiol.* XXIII. 163 A new constituent of egg-white—ovomucin. I have to call attention to another constituent which has so far not been definitely described as a constituent of white of egg. This substance possesses all the properties assigned generally to mucin, and differs from the mucoids in being insoluble in distilled water. **1936** *Poultry Sci.* XV. 350/2 This change, which involves a decrease in the water insoluble fraction (ovomucin)..accompanies the loss of viscosity in the egg white. **1972** *Agric. & Biol. Chem.* XXXVI. 947 The carbohydrate content of ovomucin gel (B) obtained from the eggs stored in an atmosphere of carbon dioxide was higher than that of ovomucin gel (B) obtained from the eggs stored in air.

ovomucoid (əʊvəʊˈmjuːkɔɪd). *Biochem.* [ad. G. *ovomukoïd* (C. Th. Mörner 1894, in *Zeitschr. f. physiol. Chem.* XVIII. 526): see ovo- and mucoid *a.*] A water-soluble mucoprotein in egg-white (also called *ovomucoid* α); also (*ovomucoid* β) = ovomucin.

1894 *Jrnl. Chem. Soc.* LXVI. I. 264 Ovomucoid... This is the name given to a proteïd-like substance which can be obtained from white of egg, after boiling, acidifying, and filtering to separate albumin and globulin. **1938** K. Meyer in *Cold Spring Harbor Symp. Quant. Biol.* VI. 91 A logical classification of the hexosamine-containing compounds should be based on the nature of the carbohydrate radical... Table I shows the classification which we propose... A. Mucopolysaccharides... B. Glycoproteins, containing neutral mucopolysaccharides of unknown composition. a. ovomucoid-α (formerly called ovomucoid). b. ovomucoid-β (formerly called ovomucin). c. serum mucoid, serum glycoid. d. globulins... e. pregnancy urine hormone. *Ibid.* 100 A very viscous fraction precipitating out by dilution of egg white with water has been called 'ovomucin'. In order to avoid the term 'mucin' we propose the name ovomucoid-β. **1954** A. White et al. *Princ. Biochem.* viii. 142 Well-defined soluble mucoproteins have been obtained from egg white (ovomucoid α), from serum.., and from human pregnancy urine. *Ibid.* 143 Insoluble mucoids have been obtained from egg white (ovomucoid β), chalazae, submaxillary glands, and vitreous humor. **1972** *Jrnl. Biol. Chem.* CCXLVII. 6450/2 The four proteins studied in this paper, ovalbumin, conalbumin, ovomucoid, and lysozyme, ..together account for 85 to 90% of the egg white proteins.

ovon, obs. form of oven.

ovonic (əʊˈvɒnɪk), *a. Electronics.* Also Ovonic. [f. *ov-* (in the name of Stanford R. *Ov*shinsky (b. 1922), the U.S. physicist and industrialist who discovered the property) + *-onic* (in *electronic*).] Pertaining to, involving, or utilizing the property of certain amorphous semi-conductors of making a rapid, reversible transition from a non-conducting to a conducting state on the application of an electric field stronger than some minimum value.

1966 *Electronics* 19 Sept. 191/2 This month, Ovshinsky..was able to let the cat out of the bag. His company..calls the device by its trade name, Ovonic. **1968** S. R. Ovshinsky in *Proc. Electronic Components Conf.* (Washington) 313 The Ovonic Threshold Switch (OTS) and the Ovonic Memory Switch (OMS) are described. **1968** *Daily Tel.* 12 Nov. 22/6 A company founded by Mr. Ovshinsky to develop glass semi-conductors is producing 150,000 'ovonic' devices a day. These are in the form of glass film a twentieth of the thickness of a human hair. **1968** *Economist* 30 Nov. 45/1 The big electronics research laboratories have been sceptical and even a bit cross that Mr Ovshinsky has put his name on to the 'ovonic devices' and the 'Ovshinsky effect'. Bell Telephone Laboratories declared that one of its scientists presented the first paper describing glass semi-conductors six years ago. **1970** S. R. Ovshinsky in *McGraw-Hill Yearbk. Sci. & Technol.* 359/1 Since ovonic switches have a number of unique characteristics, they are applicable to a wide range of uses. **1971** R. G. Neale et al. in W. B. Riley *Electronic Computer Memory Technol.* vii. 192/2 Each cell in the memory consists of an Ovonic amorphous semiconductor device and an isolating diode in series on a silicon substrate. **1973** *IEEE Trans. Electron Devices* XX. 190/1 A very high-speed electrically alterable read-only memory using Ovonic memory cells..has been designed and tested for use in the terminal multiplexor.

Hence **oˈvonics** *sb. pl.* (const. as *sing.*) [-ic 2], the study and application of ovonic effects and devices.

1968 *Economist* 30 Nov. 45/2 There are problems on the ovonics side too. The reliability of the glass semi-conductors is still suspect. **1969** *Sci. Jrnl.* Aug. 78/3 Other fields of application for Ovonics lie in a.c. control where the bidirectionality of Ovonic switches will be of prime importance.

ovoplasm (ˈəʊvəʊplæz(ə)m). *Biol.* [ad. mod.L. *ovoplasma* (Haeckel), f. ovo- + Gr. πλάσμα anything formed or moulded; after *protoplasm*. (The etymologically regular form would be *oöplasm*.)] The protoplasm of the unfertilized ovum. Hence **ovoˈplasmic** *a.*, pertaining to ovoplasm.

1890 in *Cent. Dict.*

ovo-pyriform, ovo-rhomboidal: see ovo-.

‖**ˌovo-ˈtestis.** *Zool.* [mod.L., f. ovo- + testis.] A reproductive organ in certain invertebrates combining the functions of ovary and testis, i.e. producing both ova and spermatozoa; a hermaphrodite gland.

1877 Huxley *Anat. Inv. Anim.* viii. 496 The duct of the ovo-testis may remain single to its termination. **1888** Rolleston & Jackson *Anim. Life* 113 The hermaphrodite gland or ovo-testis [in the Edible Snail].

ovovitellin (əʊvəʊvɪˈtɛlɪn). *Biochem.* Also -ine. [f. ovo- + vitellin.] The vitellin of egg-yolk.

1906 *Westm. Gaz.* 29 Aug. 2/2 The hæmoglobin of the blood of the chick is formed by certain cyanic ferruginous compounds which are found associated with ovovitelline. **1950** Sumner & Myrbäck *Enzymes* I. i. 20 It is likely that such food proteins as casein and ovovitellin are elaborated to serve as sources of amino acids for the suckling mammal or for the incubating embryo.

ovo-viviparous (ˌəʊvəʊvɪˈvɪpərəs), *a. Zool.* Also ovi-viviparous. [f. ovo- + viviparous. (The form in *ovi-* is much less frequent.) In F. *ovo-vivipare* (Duméril 1818).] Combining oviparous and viviparous characters; producing eggs which are hatched within the body of the parent, the young being thus born alive, but not developed in direct (placental) connexion with the parental body as in viviparous animals proper. Such are some reptiles and fishes, and many invertebrates.

1801 Home in *Phil. Trans.* XCII. 82 Lizards which form an egg that is afterwards deposited in a cavity corresponding to the uterus of other animals, where it is hatched; which lizards may therefore be called ovi-viviparous. **1826** Kirby & Sp. *Entomol.* III. 63 The ovo-viviparous tribes at present known are scorpions; the flesh fly and several other flies [etc.]. **1835-6** Todd *Cycl. Anat.* I. 106/1 The viper..is ovo-viviparous. **1883** F. Day *Indian Fish* 37 (Fish. Exhib. Publ.) None of these fish are ovi-viviparous.

Hence **ˌovo-viˈviparism**, **ˌovo-viviˈparity**, the condition or character of being ovo-viviparous.

1865 *Nat. Hist. Rev.* Index, Ovoviviparism in Tinea, 268. **1890** *Cent. Dict.*, *Ovoviviparity*. **1931** H. R. Hagan in *Jrnl. Morphol.* LI. 18 Ovoviviparity. That type of viviparity in which the egg contains sufficient yolk to nourish the embryo until hatching. **1965** Lee & Knowles *Animal Hormones* iii. 62 The term ovoviviparity, in preference to viviparity, is sometimes applied to the birth of live young in reptiles, as it is claimed that the nutrition of the foetus in this class depends on the egg-yolk and not on the placenta. **1973** *Nature* 27 Apr. 617/1 Morphological adaptations to ovoviviparity would..include some means of internal fertilization.

Ovshinsky (ɒvˈʃɪnskɪ). *Electronics.* The name of S. R. *Ovshinsky* (see ovonic *a.*), used *attrib.* in the sense 'ovonic'.

1966 *Electronics* 19 Sept. 192/3 The potential versatility of the 'Ovshinsky effect' was his reason for secrecy. **1968** *Daily Tel.* 12 Nov. 22/6 Mr. Stanford Ovshinsky, 45, a scientist, from Troy, Michigan, explains in the journal the theory behind his discovery of 'The Ovshinsky Effect', which is that amorphous glasses have qualities similar to those of semi-conductors. **1971** *New Scientist* 1 Apr. 29/2 Amorphous semiconductors—the well-known 'Ovshinsky devices'—are being produced and used in the United States ..in a 256-bit 'read-mostly' computer memory.

ovular (ˈəʊvjuːlə(r)), *a. Biol.* [ad. mod.L. *ōvulāris*, f. *ōvul-um* ovule: see -ar.] Of, pertaining to, or of the nature of an ovule.

1855 Ramsbotham *Obstetr. Med.* 68 The foetal surface has..a smooth, glistening appearance, which it obtains from the two ovular membranes. **1857** Mayne *Exp. Lex.*, *Ovularis*,..applied by Turpin to a leaf which..constitutes the ovule of plants: ovular. **1879** *Syd. Soc. Lex.*, *Abortion, ovular*, abortion occurring before the twentieth day of pregnancy.

ovularian (əʊvjuːˈlɛərɪən), *a.* and *sb. Zool.* [f. mod.L. *Ovulāria* neut. pl. (Haeckel) + -an.]

a. *adj.* Belonging to the *Ovularia*, a group of Protozoa in Haeckel's classification, which remain throughout life in the condition of a single cell, thus resembling the ovules or ova of higher animals. **b.** *sb.* An ovularian Protozoon.

1890 in *Cent. Dict.*

ovulary (ˈəʊvjuːlərɪ), *a.* [f. mod.L. *ōvulum* ovule + -ary.] = ovular.

1864 in Webster. **1892** *Syd. Soc. Lex.*, *Ovulary*, same as *Ovular. O. spore*, same as *Megaspore*.

ovulate (ˈəʊvjuːlət), *a.* [f. mod.L. *ōvul-um* ovule + -ate[2].] Having or containing an ovule or ovules. (Chiefly in comb. with an element indicating the number of ovules in the ovary of a plant.)

1861 Bentley *Man. Bot.* 329 They [ovules] may be very numerous, when it [the ovary] is said to be multi-ovulate or indefinite. *Ibid.* 330 When the ovary..has two ovules (biovulate). **1892** in *Syd. Soc. Lex.*

ovulate (ˈəʊvjuːleɪt, ˈɒv-), *v.* [f. as prec. + -ate[3].]

a. *intr.* To produce ovules or ova; to discharge ova from the ovary. Said of an organism and of a Graafian follicle. Hence of an ovum: to be discharged.

1888 H. N. Martin in B. C. Hirst *Syst. Obstetr.* I. 92 Women who have never menstruated have borne children: they must have ovulated without menstruating. **1890** in *Cent. Dict.* **1928** *Q. Jrnl. Exper. Physiol.* XVIII. 197 The group of follicles which will ovulate at an œstrus period undergo nearly their whole maturation growth after the time when the œstrus stimulus becomes operative. **1959** *New Biol.* XXX. 21 The ovary at the time of ovulation looks like a bunch of grapes, but with the difference that all the grapes, or follicles, are of different size. The largest will ovulate first. **1968** D. W. Wood *Animal Physiol.* xiii. 303 Many [mammals] ovulate spontaneously as part of the oestrus cycle, but others require the stimulus of copulation before they will ovulate. Such induced ovulators include the ferret, the cat and the rabbit. **1974** *Biol. of Reproduction* X. 199/1 Amphibia are good subjects for *in vitro* studies of ovulation, for mature ovaries can be maintained in simple salt solutions at room temperature and can be induced to ovulate by the addition of crude extracts of..pituitary glands.

b. *trans.* To discharge (an ovum).

1924 *Amer. Jrnl. Physiol.* LXIX. 587 The periodic formation of new ova in the adult ovary makes it unnecessary to consider that ova in the immature ovary lie dormant until they either degenerate or are ovulated. **1934** *Science* 16 Nov. 462/1 Our observations would indicate that it is not necessary for the egg to be ovulated directly into the infundibulum. **1973** *Nature* 13 July 72/1 One species, the plains viscacha (*Lagostomus maximus*), has a bizarre reproductive habit in that it ovulates between 200 and 800 eggs from ovaries that look more like those of a fish than a mammal.

Hence **ˈovulated** *ppl. a.*, **ˈovulating** *vbl. sb.*

1910 F. H. A. Marshall *Physiol. Reproduction* iv. 133 The second spindle is formed at about the ovulating stage, and the second polar body is discharged into the interior of the Fallopian tube. **1940** *Record of Proc. Amer. Soc. Animal Production* 302 (*heading*) Potential fertility of artificially matured and ovulated ova in cattle. **1959** *New Biol.* XXX. 21 The ovulating hormone..causes the follicle to split along the line of the stigma, thus releasing the mature yolk from the ovary. **1970** *Sci. Jrnl.* June 94/1 This can be righted by supplying the hormone artificially and the ovulated eggs can then be fertilized. **1972** *Amer. Jrnl. Veterinary Res.* XXXIII. 1589, 25 ewes were given estradiol to induce release of endogenous ovulating hormone.

ovulation (əʊvjuːˈleɪʃən, ɒv-). *Physiol.* and *Zool.* [f. ovule or mod.L. *ōvul-um* + -ation: so in mod.Fr.] The formation or development of ovules or ova, and (*esp.*) their discharge from the ovary, as occurring in female mammals; *rarely*, the development and laying of eggs by oviparous animals.

1848 C. D. Meigs *Females & their Diseases* xxxi. 403 The ovulation is marked by a natural return of the mensual hemorrhage. **1853** Dunglison *Med. Lex.*, *Ovulation*... The formation of ova in the ovary, and the discharge of the same. **1872** Peaslee *Ovar. Tumours* 5 The ovary assumes a cicatricial appearance in consequence of repeated ovulations. **1887** F. H. H. Guillemard *Cruise Marchesa* II. 197 The instincts of the bird have been made to suit its unusual ovulation.

ovulator (ˈəʊvjuːleɪtə(r), ˈɒv-). *Physiol.* [f. ovulat(e *v.* + -or.] An animal that ovulates (in a specified way).

1961 *Recent Progress Hormone Res.* XVII. 120 Both the cat and the rabbit are induced ovulators. **1968** [see ovulate *v.* a]. **1971** J. Z. Young *Introd. Study Man* xv. 194 In the doe rabbit and domestic cat ovulation occurs only after copulation... Such animals are..said to be reflex ovulators. It has recently been shown that the rat, long considered to be a spontaneous ovulator, can be stimulated by coitus..to ovulate earlier than it would do otherwise.

ovulatory (əʊvjuːˈleɪtərɪ, ˈɒv-), *a.* [f. as prec. + -ory[2].] Of or pertaining to ovulation.

1931 *Jrnl. Mammalogy* XII. 139 The sterility of the animals is due to the absence of an ovulatory cycle. **1972** *Endocrinology* XCI. 1253/1 The administration of various drugs on the afternoon of proestrus blocks the ovulatory surge of pituitary ovulating hormone. **1977** *Daily Mirror* 15 Mar. 7/4 In some cases when women come off the Pill, we can stimulate the return of periods with an ovulatory drug.

ovule ('əʊvjuːl). [a. F. *ovule* (Mirbel 1808), ad. mod.L. *ōvulum*, dim. of *ōvum* egg.]

1. *Bot.* The rudimentary seed in a phanerogamous plant; the body which contains the female germ-cell, and after fertilization becomes a *seed*; usually formed as a rounded or oval outgrowth of a carpel, and in angiosperms inclosed (one or more) in an *ovary*.

1830 LINDLEY *Nat. Syst. Bot.* 75 Its ovarium contains, instead of three ovules adhering to a central placenta, one only, which is pendulous. **1842** GRAY *Struct. Bot.* vi. §1 (1880) 166 The Ovary..contains the Ovules, or bodies destined to become seeds. **1854** S. THOMSON *Wild Fl.* I. (ed. 4) 72 The young seeds, or ovules, as they are named before they have been subjected to the fertilizing influence of the pollen.

2. *Zool.* and *Physiol.* **a.** The ovum or female germ-cell of an animal, esp. when very small as in mammals; *spec.* the unfertilized ovum.

1857 BULLOCK *Cazeaux' Midwif.* 71 The ovule is completely formed in the ovary during the earlier years of life. **1871** T. R. JONES *Anim. Kingd.* (ed. 4) 131 The ovules have been seen to escape by the mouth; and this..appears to be the general mode of parturition in all the Actinoid polyps.

b. ***ovules of Naboth***: dilated mucous follicles in the neck of the uterus, supposed by the Saxon physician Martin Naboth (1675–1721) to be ova.

[**1831**: see OVULUM 2.] **1892** in *Syd. Soc. Lex.*

ovuliferous (əʊvjuː'lɪfərəs), *a.* [f. mod.L. *ōvulum*, *ōvuli-* + -FEROUS.] Bearing or producing ovules.

1864 in WEBSTER. **1878** MASTERS *Henfrey's Bot.* 211 Four carpels, two of which are ovuliferous. **1880** GRAY *Struct. Bot.* vii. §1. 288 The normal dehiscence of a carpel is by its inner, ventral, or ovuliferous suture.

ovuligerous (-'ɪdʒərəs), *a.* [f. as prec. + -GEROUS.] = prec.; also *Path.* 'applied to cysts containing hordeiform bodies' (*Syd. Soc. Lex.* 1892).

ovuline ('əʊvjuːlaɪn), *a. Zool.* [f. OVULUM 3 + -INE[1].] Belonging to the family *Ovulinæ* of gastropod molluscs, of which the typical genus is *Ovulum* (see OVULUM 3).

1890 in *Cent. Dict.*

ovulist ('əʊvjuːlɪst). *Biol.* [f. mod.L. *ōvul-um* + -IST.] = OVIST.

1879 tr. *Haeckel's Evol. Man* I. 37 The Ovulists (Ovists) or Believers in Eggs..maintained that the egg was the real animal germ, and that the seminal animalcules..only gave the impulse which caused the unfolding of the egg in which all generations were encased one in the other.

ovulite ('əʊvjuːlaɪt). *Palæont.* [f. as prec. + -ITE[1].] A fossil egg of a bird or a reptile.

1848 in CRAIG. **1859–64** PAGE *Hand-bk. Geol. Terms* s.v., Ovulites have been found in the stratified rocks from the Oolite upwards.

‖**ovulum** ('əʊvjuːləm). Pl. ovula. [mod.L. dim. of *ōvum* egg.]

†**1.** *Bot.* = OVULE 1. *Obs.*

1830 LINDLEY *Nat. Syst. Bot.* 174 Ovarium..containing a single erect ovulum.

2. *Zool.* and *Physiol.* = OVULE 2, 2 b. ? *Obs.*

1822–34 *Good's Study Med.* (ed. 4) I. 263 The myriads of invisible ovula with which the atmosphere swarms. *Ibid.* IV. 16 The ovulum is seldom found, even in the fallopian tube, till some time afterwards [i.e. after copulation]. **1831** R. KNOX *Cloquet's Anat.* 826 Frequently..these crypts..assume the form of small semitransparent vesicles projecting into the interior of the uterus. An old author, Naboth, took them for ova, and for this reason these small bodies are sometimes designated by the name of Ovula of Naboth. **1855** RAMSBOTHAM *Obstetr. Med.* 44 A minute body of spheroidal shape,—the ovulum.

3. *Zool.* A genus of gastropod molluscs, including the Egg-shell (*O. ovum*) with an egg-shaped shell.

1837 *Penny Cycl.* VIII. 259/1 Lamarck enumerates eighteen fossil species of Cypræa, and two of Ovulum. **1851–6** WOODWARD *Mollusca* 34 A posterior siphon, generally less developed, but very long in *Ovulum volva.*

‖**ovum** ('əʊvəm). Pl. **ova** (erron. 8 **ovas**, 8–9 **ovæ**). [L. *ōvum* egg.]

1. *Biol.* **a.** *Zool.* The female germ or reproductive cell in animals, produced (usually) by an ovary, and capable when fertilized or impregnated by the male sperm (and in some cases without such fertilization) of developing into a new individual; an egg in the widest sense, including the eggs of birds (the largest of all animal cells), but more commonly applied to the extremely small germs of female mammals, or to the eggs of oviparous animals when of small size, as in fishes, insects, etc.

1706 PHILLIPS, *Ovum*, an Egg; also the Spawn of Fish. **1722** DE FOE *Plague* (1884) 102 Poisonous Ovæ, or Eggs, which mingle themselves with the Blood. **1784** TWAMLEY *Dairying* 129 By burning the Moss, you destroy at the same time, the Ovas or Eggs, the Chrysalis and grubs. **1797** M. BAILLIE *Morb. Anat.* (1807) 403 This arises from the ovum being stopped in its progress from the ovarium to the uterus. **1861** J. R. GREENE *Man. Anim. Kingd., Cœlent.* 14 True reproduction, by contact of ova and spermatozoa. **1879** *Cassell's Techn. Educ.* IV. 154/1 The number of germs or ova brought forth by a single mature oyster exceeds one million. **1889** GEDDES & THOMSON *Evol. Sex* xiii. 169 What we now mean by parthenogenesis, or the development of ova without union with sperms.

†**b.** *Bot.* The ovule or seed of a plant. *rare.*

1760 J. LEE *Introd. Bot.* II. xx. (1765) 119 When the Ova are hatched, the Cotyledons preserve the Form of the halved Seed. **1866** *Treas. Bot., Ovule, Ovum*, the young seed.

2. *Arch.* An egg-shaped ornament or carving.

1727–41 CHAMBERS *Cycl., Ova*, in architecture, are ornaments in form of eggs, carved on the contour of the ovolo, or quarter-round; and separated from each other by anchors, or arrows heads. **1823** P. NICHOLSON *Pract. Build.* Gloss. 589/1 *Ova*, an ornament in form of an egg. **1851** E. J. MILLINGTON tr. *Didron's Chr. Iconogr.* 316 Immediately below the ovæ of the cornice.

3. *attrib.* and *Comb.*, as ***ovum-cycle***, ***-product***; often with the pl., as ***ova-bearing***, ***-containing*** adjs., †***-duct*** (= OVIDUCT), ***-hatching***.

1781 SMEATHMAN in *Phil. Trans.* LXXI. 172 *note*, Two ovaria, in each of which are many hundred ova-ducts. **1846** DANA *Zooph.* v. §85 (1848) 87 The distinction in plants of budding and ova-bearing individuals. **1883** P. GEDDES in *Encycl. Brit.* XVI. 843/2 The genealogical individual of Gallesio and Huxley..may be designated with Haeckel the ovum-product or ovum-cycle. **1898** P. MANSON *Trop. Diseases* 414 Because leprosy is common in the descendants and blood collaterals of lepers, this is no proof of ovum infection.

DOMI MINA
NVS TIO
ILLV MEA